ENGLISH THESAURUS

ENGLISH THESAURUS

Colour Library Direct

CLD 21288. This edition published in 1999 for Colour Library Direct, Godalming Business Centre, Woolsack Way, Godalming, Surrey, GU7 1XW

First published 1997
Reprinted 1999

ISBN 1 84100 043 4

Printed and bound in Indonesia

Contents

A

aback *adv* back, backward, rearward, regressively.
abaft *prep* (*naut*) aft, astern, back of, behind.
abandon *vb* abdicate, abjure, desert, drop, evacuate, forsake, forswear, leave, quit, relinquish, yield; cede, forgo, give up, let go, renounce, resign, surrender, vacate, waive. * *n* careless freedom, dash, impetuosity, impulse, wildness.
abandoned *adj* depraved, derelict, deserted, discarded, dropped, forsaken, left, outcast, rejected, relinquished; corrupt, demoralized, depraved, dissolute, graceless, impenitent, irreclaimable, lost, obdurate, profligate, reprobate, shameless, sinful, unprincipled, vicious, wicked.
abandonment *n* desertion, dereliction, giving up, leaving, relinquishment, renunciation, surrender.
abase *vb* depress, drop, lower, reduce, sink; debase, degrade, disgrace, humble, humiliate.
abasement *n* abjection, debasement, degradation, disgrace, humbleness, humiliation, shame.
abash *vb* affront, bewilder, confound, confuse, dash, discompose, disconcert, embarrass, humiliate, humble, shame, snub.
abashment *n* confusion, embarrassment, humiliation, mortification, shame.
abate *vb* diminish, decrease, lessen, lower, moderate, reduce, relax, remove, slacken; allow, bate, deduct, mitigate, rebate, remit; allay, alleviate, appease, assuage, blunt, calm, compose, dull, mitigate, moderate, mollify, pacify, qualify, quiet, quell, soften, soothe, tranquillize.
abatement *n* alleviation, assuagement, decrement, decrease, extenuation, mitigation, moderation, remission; cessation, decline, diminution, ebb, fading, lowering, sinking, settlement; allowance, deduction, rebate, reduction.
abbey *n* convent, monastery, priory.
abbreviate *vb* abridge, compress, condense, contract, cut, curtail, epitomize, reduce, retrench, shorten.
abbreviation *n* abridgment, compression, condensation, contraction, curtailment, cutting, reduction, shortening.
abdicate *vb* abandon, cede, forgo, forsake, give up, quit, relinquish, renounce, resign, retire, surrender.
abdication *n* abandonment, abdicating, relinquishment, renunciation, resignation, surrender.
abdomen *n* belly, gut, paunch, stomach.
abduct *vb* carry off, kidnap, spirit away, take away.
abduction *n* carrying off, kidnapping, removal, seizure, withdrawal.
aberrant *adj* deviating, devious, divergent, diverging, erratic, rambling, wandering; abnormal, anomalistic, anomalous, disconnected, eccentric, erratic, exceptional, inconsequent, peculiar, irregular, preternatural, singular, strange, unnatural, unusual.
aberration *n* departure, deviation, divergence, rambling, wandering; abnormality, anomaly, eccentricity, irregularity, peculiarity, singularity, unconformity; delusion, disorder, hallucination, illusion, instability.
abet *vb* aid, assist, back, help, support, sustain, uphold; advocate, condone, countenance, encourage, favour, incite, sanction.
abettor *n* ally, assistant; adviser, advocate, promoter; accessory, accomplice, associate, confederate.
abeyance *n* anticipation, calculation, expectancy, waiting; dormancy, inactivity, intermission, quiescence, remission, reservation, suppression, suspension.
abhor *vb* abominate, detest, dislike intensely, execrate, hate, loathe, nauseate, view with horror.
abhorrence *n* abomination, antipathy, aversion, detestation, disgust, hatred, horror, loathing.
abhorrent *adj* abominating, detesting, hating, loathing; hateful, horrifying, horrible, loathsome, nauseating, odious, offensive, repellent, repugnant, repulsive, revolting, shocking.
abide *vb* lodge, rest, sojourn, stay, wait; dwell, inhabit, live, reside; bear, continue, persevere, persist, remain; endure, last, suffer, tolerate; (*with* **by**) act up to, conform to, discharge, fulfil, keep, persist in.
abiding *adj* changeless, constant, continuing, durable, enduring, immutable, lasting, permanent, stable, unchangeable.
ability *n* ableness, adroitness, aptitude, aptness, cleverness, dexterity, efficacy, efficiency, facility, might, ingenuity, knack, power, readiness, skill, strength, talent, vigour; competency, qualification; calibre, capability, capacity, expertness, faculty, gift, parts.
abject *adj* base, beggarly, contemptible, cringing, degraded, despicable, dirty, grovelling, ignoble, low, mean, menial, miserable, paltry, pitiful, poor, servile, sneaking, slavish, vile, worthless, wretched.

abjectness *n* abasement, abjection, baseness, contemptibleness, meanness, pitifulness, servility, vileness.

abjuration *n* abandonment, abnegation, discarding, disowning, rejection, relinquishment, renunciation, repudiation; disavowal, disclaimer, disclaiming, recall, recantation, repeal, retraction, reversal, revocation.

abjure *vb* abandon, discard, disclaim, disown, forgo, forswear, give up, reject, relinquish, renounce, repudiate; disavow, disclaim, recall, recant, renounce, repeal, retract, revoke, withdraw.

able *adj* accomplished, adroit, apt, clever, expert, ingenious, practical, proficient, qualified, quick, skilful, talented, versed; competent, effective, efficient, fitted, quick; capable, gifted, mighty, powerful, talented; athletic, brawny, muscular, robust, stalwart, strong, vigorous.

ablution *n* baptism, bathing, cleansing, lavation, purification, washing.

abnegation *n* abandonment, denial, renunciation, surrender.

abnormal *adj* aberrant, anomalous, divergent, eccentric, exceptional, peculiar, odd, singular, strange, uncomfortable, unnatural, unusual, weird.

abnormality *n* abnormity, anomaly, deformity, idiosyncrasy, irregularity, monstrosity, peculiarity, oddity, singularity, unconformity.

aboard *adv* inside, within, on.

abode *n* domicile, dwelling, habitation, home, house, lodging, quarters, residence, residency, seat.

abolish *vb* abrogate, annul, cancel, eliminate, invalidate, nullify, quash, repeal, rescind, revoke; annihilate, destroy, end, eradicate, extirpate, extinguish, obliterate, overthrow, suppress, terminate.

abolition *n* abrogation, annulling, annulment, cancellation, cancelling, nullification, repeal, rescinding, rescission, revocation; annihilation, destruction, eradication, extinction, extinguishment, extirpation, obliteration, overthrow, subversion, suppression.

abominable *adj* accursed, contemptible, cursed, damnable, detestable, execrable, hellish, horrid, nefarious, odious; abhorrent, detestable, disgusting, foul, hateful, loathsome, nauseous, obnoxious, shocking, revolting, repugnant, repulsive; shabby, vile, wretched.

abominate *vb* abhor, detest, execrate, hate, loathe, recoil from, revolt at, shrink from, shudder at.

abomination *n* abhorrence, antipathy, aversion, detestation, disgust, execration, hatred, loathing, nauseation; contamination, corruption, corruptness, defilement, foulness, impurity, loathsomeness, odiousness, pollution, taint, uncleanness; annoyance, curse, evil, infliction, nuisance, plague, torment.

aboriginal *adj* autochthonal, autochthonous, first, indigenous, native, original, primary, prime, primeval, primitive, pristine.

abortion *n* miscarriage, premature labour; disappointment, failure.

abortive *adj* immature, incomplete, rudimental, rudimentary, stunted, untimely; futile, fruitless, idle, ineffectual, inoperative, nugatory, profitless, unavailing, unsuccessful, useless, vain.

abound *vb* flow, flourish, increase, swarm, swell; exuberate, luxuriate, overflow, proliferate, swarm, teem.

about *prep* around, encircling, surrounding, round; near; concerning, referring to, regarding, relating to, relative to, respecting, touching, with regard to, with respect to; all over, over, through. * *adv* around, before; approximately, near, nearly.

above *adj* above-mentioned, aforementioned, aforesaid, foregoing, preceding, previous, prior. * *adv* aloft, overhead; before, previously; of a higher rank. * *prep* higher than, on top of; exceeding, greater than, more than, over; beyond, superior to.

above-board *adj* candid, frank, honest, open, straightforward, truthful, upright. * *adv* candidly, fairly, openly, sincerely.

abrade *vb* erase, erode, rub off, scrape out, wear away.

abrasion *n* attrition, disintegration, friction, wearing down; scrape, scratch.

abreast *adv* aligned, alongside.

abridge *vb* abbreviate, condense, compress, shorten, summarize; contract, diminish, lessen, reduce.

abridgment *n* compression, condensation, contraction, curtailment, diminution, epitomizing, reduction, shortening; abstract, brief, compendium, digest, epitome, outline, précis, summary, syllabus, synopsis; deprivation, limitation, restriction.

abroad *adv* expansively, unrestrainedly, ubiquitously, widely; forth, out of doors; overseas; extensively, publicly.

abrogate *vb* abolish, annul, cancel, invalidate, nullify, overrule, quash, repeal, rescind, revoke, set aside, vacate, void.

abrogation *n* abolition, annulling, annulment, cancellation, cancelling, repeal rescinding, rescission, revocation, voidance, voiding.

abrupt *adj* broken, craggy, jagged, rough, rugged; acclivous, acclivitous, precipitous, steep; hasty, ill-timed, precipitate, sudden, unanticipated, unexpected; blunt, brusque, curt, discourteous; cramped, harsh, jerky, stiff.

abscess *n* boil, fester, pustule, sore, ulcer.

abscond *vb* bolt, decamp, elope, escape, flee, fly, retreat, run off, sneak away, steal away, withdraw.

absence *n* nonappearance, nonattendance; abstraction, distraction, inattention, musing, preoccupation, reverie; default, defect, deficiency, lack, privation.

absent *adj* abroad, away, elsewhere, gone, not present, otherwhere; abstracted, dreaming, inattentive, lost, musing, napping, preoccupied.

absolute *adj* complete, ideal, independent, perfect, supreme, unconditional, unconditioned, unlimited, unqualified, unrestricted; arbitrary, authoritative, autocratic, despotic, dictatorial, imperious, irresponsible, tyrannical, tyrannous; actual, categorical, certain, decided, determinate, genuine, positive, real, unequivocal, unquestionable, veritable.

absolutely *adv* completely, definitely, unconditionally; actually, downright, indeed, indubitably, infallibly, positively, really, truly, unquestionably.

absoluteness *n* actuality, completeness, ideality, perfection, positiveness, reality, supremeness; absolutism, arbitrariness, despotism, tyranny.

absolution *n* acquittal, clearance, deliverance, discharge, forgiveness, liberation, pardon, release, remission, shrift, shriving.

absolutism *n* absoluteness, arbitrariness, autocracy, despotism, tyranny.

absolve *vb* acquit, clear, deliver, discharge, exculpate, excuse, exonerate, forgive, free, liberate, loose, pardon, release, set free, shrive.

absorb *vb* appropriate, assimilate, drink in, imbibe, soak up; consume, destroy, devour, engorge, engulf, exhaust, swallow up, take up; arrest, engage, engross, fix, immerse, occupy, rivet.

absorbent *adj* absorbing, imbibing, penetrable, porous, receptive.

absorption *adj* appropriation, assimilation, imbibing, osmosis, soaking up; consumption, destroying, devouring, engorgement, engulfing, exhaustion, swallowing up; concentration, engagement, engrossment, immersion, occupation, preoccupation.

abstain *vb* avoid, cease, deny oneself, desist, forbear, refrain, refuse, stop, withhold.

abstemious *adj* abstinent, frugal, moderate, self-denying, sober, temperate.

abstinence *n* abstemiousness, avoidance, forbearance, moderation, self-restraint, soberness, sobriety, teetotalism, temperance.

abstinent *adj* abstaining, fasting; abstemious, restraining, self-denying, self-restraining, sober, temperate.

abstract *vb* detach, disengage, disjoin, dissociate, disunite, isolate, separate; appropriate, purloin, seize, steal, take; abbreviate, abridge, epitomize. * *adj* isolated, separate, simple, unrelated; abstracted, occult, recondite, refined, subtle, vague; nonobjective, nonrepresentational. * *n* abridgment, condensation, digest, excerpt, extract, précis, selection, summary, synopsis.

abstracted *adj* absent, absent-minded, dreaming, inattentive, lost, musing, preoccupied; abstruse, refined, subtle.

abstraction *n* absence, absent-mindedness, brown study, inattention, muse, musing, preoccupation, reverie; disconnection, disjunction, isolation, separation; abduction, appropriation, pilfering, purloining, seizure, stealing, taking.

abstruse *adj* abstract, attenuated, dark, difficult, enigmatic, hidden, indefinite, mysterious, mystic, mystical, obscure, occult, profound, recondite, remote, subtle, transcendental, vague.

absurd *adj* egregious, fantastic, foolish, incongruous, ill-advised, ill-judged, irrational, ludicrous, nonsensical, nugatory, preposterous, ridiculous, self-annulling, senseless, silly, stupid, unreasonable.

absurdity *n* drivel, extravagance, fatuity, folly, foolery, foolishness, idiocy, nonsense.

abundance *n* affluence, amplitude, ampleness, copiousness, exuberance, fertility, flow, flood, largeness, luxuriance, opulence, overflow, plenitude, profusion, richness, store, wealth.

abundant *adj* abounding, ample, bountiful, copious, exuberant, flowing, full, good, large, lavish, rich, liberal, much, overflowing, plentiful, plenteous, replete, teeming, thick.

abuse *vb* betray, cajole, deceive, desecrate, dishonour, misapply, misemploy, misuse, pervert, pollute, profane, prostitute, violate, wrong; harm, hurt, ill-use, ill-treat, injure, maltreat, mishandle; asperse, berate, blacken, calumniate, defame, disparage, lampoon, lash, malign, revile, reproach, satirize, slander, traduce, upbraid, vilify. * *n* desecration, dishonour, ill-use, misuse, perversion, pollution, profanation; ill-treatment, maltreatment, outrage; malfeasance, malversation; aspersion, defamation, disparagement, insult, invective, obloquy, opprobrium, railing, rating, reviling, ribaldry, rudeness, scurrility, upbraiding, vilification, vituperation.

abusive *adj* calumnious, carping, condemnatory, contumelious, damnatory, denunciatory, injurious, insolent, insulting, offensive, opprobrious, reproachful, reviling, ribald, rude, scurrilous, vilificatory, vituperative.

abut *vb* adjoin, border, impinge, meet, project.

abutment *n* bank, bulwark, buttress, embankment, fortification; abutting, abuttal, adjacency, contiguity, juxtaposition.

abuttal *n* adjacency, boundary, contiguity, juxtaposition, nearness, next, terminus.

abyss *n* abysm, chasm, gorge, gulf, pit.

academic *adj* collegiate, lettered, scholastic. * *n* academician, classicist, doctor, fellow, pundit, savant, scholar, student, teacher.

academy *n* college, high school, institute, school.

accede *vb* accept, acquiesce, agree, assent to, comply with, concur, consent, yield.

accelerate *vb* dispatch, expedite, forward, hasten, hurry, precipitate, press on, quicken, speed, urge on.

acceleration *n* expedition, hastening, hurrying, quickening, pickup, precipitation, speeding up, stepping up.

accent *vb* accentuate, emphasize, stress. * *n* cadence, inflection, intonation, tone; beat, emphasis, ictus.

accentuate *vb* accent, emphasize, mark, point up, punctuate, stress; highlight, overemphasize, overstress, underline, underscore.

accept *vb* acquire, derive, get, gain, obtain, receive, take; accede to, acknowledge, acquiesce in, admit, agree to, approve, assent to, avow, embrace; estimate, construe, interpret, regard, value.

acceptable *adj* agreeable, gratifying, pleasant, pleasing, pleasurable, welcome.

acceptance *n* accepting, acknowledgment, receipt, reception, taking; approbation, approval, gratification, satisfaction.

acceptation *n* construction, import, interpretation, meaning, sense, significance, signification, understanding; adoption, approval, currency, vogue.

access *vb* broach, enter, open, open up. * *n* approach, avenue, entrance, entry, passage, way; admission, admittance, audience, interview; addition, accession, aggrandizement, enlargement, gain, increase, increment; (*med*) attack, fit, onset, recurrence.

accession *n* addition, augmentation, enlargement, extension, increase; succession.

accessory *adj* abetting, additional, additive, adjunct, aiding, ancillary, assisting, contributory, helping, subsidiary, subordinate, supplemental. * *n* abettor, accomplice, assistant, associate, confederate, helper; accompaniment, attendant, concomitant, detail, subsidiary.

accident *n* calamity, casualty, condition, contingency, disaster, fortuity, incident, misadventure, miscarriage, mischance, misfortune, mishap; affection, alteration, chance, contingency, mode, modification, property, quality, state.

accidental *adj* casual, chance, contingent, fortuitous, undesigned, unintended; adventitious, dispensable, immaterial, incidental, nonessential.

acclamation *n* acclaim, applause, cheer, cry, plaudit, outcry, salutation, shouting.

acclimatization, acclimation *n* adaptation, adjustment, conditioning, familiarization, habituation, inurement, naturalization.

acclimatize, acclimate *vb* accustom, adapt, adjust, condition, familiarize, habituate, inure, naturalize, season.

acclivity *n* ascent, height, hill, rising ground, steep, upward slope.

accommodate *vb* contain, furnish, hold, oblige, serve, supply; adapt, fit, suit; adjust, compose, harmonize, reconcile, settle.

accommodation *n* advantage, convenience, privilege; adaptation, agreement, conformity, fitness, suitableness; adjustment, harmonization, harmony, pacification, reconciliation, settlement.

accompaniment *n* adjunct, appendage, attachment, attendant, concomitant.

accompany *vb* attend, chaperon, convoy, escort, follow, go with.

accomplice *n* abettor, accessory, ally, assistant, associate, confederate, partner.

accomplish *vb* achieve, bring about, carry, carry through, complete, compass, consummate, do, effect, execute, perform, perfect; conclude, end, finish, terminate.

accomplished *adj* achieved, completed, done, effected, executed, finished, fulfilled, realized; able, adroit, apt, consummate, educated, experienced, expert, finished, instructed, practised, proficient, qualified, ripe, skilful, versed; elegant, fashionable, fine, polished, polite, refined.

accomplishment *n* achievement, acquirement, attainment, qualification; completion, fulfilment.

accord *vb* admit, allow, concede, deign, give, grant, vouchsafe, yield; agree, assent, concur, correspond, harmonize, quadrate, tally. * *n* accordance, agreement, concord, concurrence, conformity, consensus, harmony, unanimity, unison.

accordant *adj* agreeable, agreeing, congruous, consonant, harmonious, suitable, symphonious.

accordingly *adv* agreeably, conformably, consistently, suitably; consequently, hence, so, thence, therefore, thus, whence, wherefore.

accost *vb* address, confront, greet, hail, salute, speak to, stop.

account *vb* assess, appraise, estimate, evaluate, judge, rate; (*with* **for**) assign, attribute, explain, expound, justify, rationalize, vindicate. * *n* inventory, record, register, score; bill, book, charge; calculation, computation, count, reckoning, score, tale, tally; chronicle, detail, description, narration, narrative, portrayal, recital, rehearsal, relation, report, statement, tidings, word; elucidation, explanation, exposition; consideration, ground, motive, reason, regard, sake; consequence, consideration, dignity, distinction, importance, note, repute, reputation, worth.

accountable *adj* amenable, answerable, duty-bound, liable, responsible.

accoutre *vb* arm, dress, equip, fit out, furnish.

accredit *vb* authorize, depute, empower, entrust.

accrue *vb* arise, come, follow, flow, inure, issue, proceed, result.

accumulate *vb* agglomerate, aggregate, amass, bring together, collect, gather, grow, hoard, increase, pile, store.

accumulation *n* agglomeration, aggregation, collection, heap, hoard, mass, pile, store.

accuracy *n* carefulness, correctness, exactness, fidelity, precision, strictness.

accurate *adj* close, correct, exact, faithful, nice, precise, regular, strict, true, truthful.

accusation *n* arraignment, charge, incrimination, impeachment, indictment.

accuse *vb* arraign, charge, censure, impeach, indict, tax.

accustom *vb* discipline, drill, familiarize, habituate, harden, inure, train, use.

ace *n* (*cards, dice*) one spot, single pip, single point; atom, bit, grain, iota, jot, particle, single, unit, whit; expert, master, virtuoso. * *adj* best, expert, fine, outstanding, superb.

acerbity *n* acidity, acridity, acridness, astringency, bitterness, roughness, sourness, tartness; acrimony, bitterness, harshness, severity, venom.

achieve *vb* accomplish, attain, complete, do, effect,

execute, finish, fulfil, perform, realize; acquire, gain, get, obtain, win.

achievement *n* accomplishment, acquirement, attainment, completion, consummation, performance, realization; deed, exploit, feat, work.

acid *adj* pungent, sharp, sour, stinging, tart, vinegary.

acknowledge *vb* recognize; accept, admit, accept, allow, concede, grant; avow, confess, own, profess.

acme *n* apex, climax, height, peak, pinnacle, summit, top, vertex, zenith.

acquaint *vb* familiarize; announce, apprise, communicate, enlighten, disclose, inform, make aware, make known, notify, tell.

acquaintance *n* companionship, familiarity, fellowship, intimacy, knowledge; associate, companion, comrade, friend.

acquiesce *vb* bow, comply, consent, give way, rest, submit, yield; agree, assent, concur, consent.

acquire *vb* achieve, attain, earn, gain, get, have, obtain, procure, realize, secure, win; learn thoroughly, master.

acquirement *n* acquiring, gaining, gathering, mastery; acquisition, accomplishment, attainment.

acquit *vb* absolve, clear, discharge, exculpate, excuse, exonerate, forgive, liberate, pardon, pay, quit, release, set free, settle.

acquittal *n* absolution, acquittance, clearance, deliverance, discharge, exoneration, liberation, release.

acquittance *n* discharge; quittance, receipt.

acrid *adj* biting, bitter, caustic, pungent, sharp.

acrimonious *adj* acrid, bitter, caustic, censorious, crabbed, harsh, malignant, petulant, sarcastic, severe, testy, virulent.

acrimony *n* causticity, causticness, corrosiveness, sharpness; abusiveness, acridity, asperity, bitterness, churlishness, harshness, rancour, severity, spite, venom.

act *vb* do, execute, function, make, operate, work; enact, feign, perform, play. * *n* achievement, deed, exploit, feat, performance, proceeding, turn; bill, decree, enactment, law, ordinance, statute; actuality, existence, fact, reality.

acting *adj* interim, provisional, substitute, temporary. * *n* enacting, impersonation, performance, portrayal, theatre; counterfeiting, dissimulation, imitation, pretence.

action *n* achievement, activity, agency, deed, exertion, exploit, feat; battle, combat, conflict, contest, encounter, engagement, operation; lawsuit, prosecution.

active *adj* effective, efficient, influential, living, operative; assiduous, bustling, busy, diligent, industrious, restless; agile, alert, brisk, energetic, lively, nimble, prompt, quick, smart, spirited, sprightly, supple; animated, ebullient, fervent, vigorous.

actual *adj* certain, decided, genuine, objective, real, substantial, tangible, true, veritable; perceptible, present, sensible, tangible; absolute, categorical, positive.

actuate *vb* impel, incite, induce, instigate, move, persuade, prompt.

acumen *n* acuteness, astuteness, discernment, ingenuity, keenness, penetration, sagacity, sharpness, shrewdness.

acute *adj* pointed, sharp; astute, bright, discerning, ingenious, intelligent, keen, quick, penetrating, piercing, sagacious, sage, sharp, shrewd, smart, subtle; distressing, fierce, intense, piercing, pungent, poignant, severe, violent; high, high-toned, sharp, shrill; (*med*) sudden, temporary, violent.

adage *n* aphorism, dictum, maxim, proverb, saw, saying.

adapt *vb* accommodate, adjust, conform, coordinate, fit, qualify, proportion, suit, temper.

add *vb* adjoin, affix, annex, append, attach, join, tag; sum; sum up, total.

addict *vb* accustom, apply, dedicate, devote, habituate. * *n* devotee, enthusiast, fan; head, junkie, user.

addicted *adj* attached, devoted, given up to, inclined, prone, wedded.

addition *n* augmentation, accession, enlargement, extension, increase, supplement; adjunct, appendage, appendix, extra.

address *vb* accost, apply to, court, direct. * *n* appeal, application, entreaty, invocation, memorial, petition, request, solicitation, suit; discourse, oration, lecture, sermon, speech; ability, adroitness, art, dexterity, expertness, skill; courtesy, deportment, demeanour, tact.

adduce *vb* advance, allege, assign, offer, present; cite, mention, name.

adept *adj* accomplished, experienced, practised, proficient, skilled. * *n* expert, master, virtuoso.

adequate *adj* able, adapted, capable, competent, equal, fit, requisite, satisfactory, sufficient, suitable.

adhere *vb* cling, cleave, cohere, hold, stick; appertain, belong, pertain.

adherent *adj* adhering, clinging, sticking. * *n* acolyte, dependant, disciple, follower, partisan, supporter, vassal.

adhesion *n* adherence, attachment, clinging, coherence, sticking.

adhesive *adj* clinging, sticking; glutinous, gummy, sticky, tenacious, viscous. * *n* binder, cement, glue, paste.

adieu *n* farewell, goodbye, parting, valediction.

adipose *adj* fat, fatty, greasy, oily, oleaginous, sebaceous.

adjacent *adj* adjoining, bordering, conterminous, contiguous, near, near to, neighbouring, touching.

adjoin *vb* abut, add, annex, append, border, combine, neighbour, unite, verge.

adjourn *vb* defer, delay, postpone, procrastinate; close, dissolve, end, interrupt, prorogue, suspend.

adjudge *vb* allot, assign, award; decide, decree, determine, settle.
adjunct *n* addition, advantage, appendage, appurtenance, attachment, attribute, auxiliary, dependency, help.
adjure *vb* beg, beseech, entreat, pray, supplicate.
adjust *vb* adapt, arrange, dispose, rectify; regulate, set right, settle, suit; compose, harmonize, pacify, reconcile, settle; accommodate, adapt, fit, suit.
administer *vb* contribute, deal out, dispense, supply; conduct, control, direct, govern, manage, oversee, superintend; conduce, contribute.
admirable *adj* astonishing, striking, surprising, wonderful; excellent, fine, rare, superb.
admiration *n* affection, approbation, approval, astonishment, delight, esteem, pleasure, regard.
admirer *n* beau, gallant, suitor, sweetheart; fan, follower, supporter.
admissible *adj* allowable, lawful, permissible, possible.
admission *n* access, admittance, entrance, introduction; acceptance, acknowledgement, allowance, assent, avowal, concession.
admit *vb* give access to, let in, receive; agree to, accept, acknowledge, concede, confess; allow, bear, permit, suffer, tolerate.
admonish *vb* censure, rebuke, reprove; advise caution, counsel, enjoin, forewarn, warn; acquaint, apprise, inform, instruct, notify, remind.
admonition *n* censure, rebuke, remonstrance; advice, caution, chiding, counsel, instruction, monition.
adolescence *n* minority, nonage, teens, youth.
adolescent *adj* juvenile, young, youthful. * *n* minor, teenager, youth.
adopt *vb* appropriate, assume; accept, approve, avow, espouse, maintain, support; affiliate, father, foster.
adore *vb* worship; esteem, honour, idolize, love, revere, venerate.
adorn *vb* beautify, decorate, embellish, enrich, garnish, gild, grace, ornament.
adroit *adj* apt, dextrous, expert, handy, ingenious, ready, skilful.
adulation *n* blandishment, cajolery, fawning, flattery, flummery, praise, sycophancy.
adult *adj* grown-up, mature, ripe, ripened. * *n* grown-up person.
adulterate *vb* alloy, contaminate, corrupt, debase, deteriorate, vitiate.
advance *adj* beforehand, forward, leading. * *vb* propel, push, send forward; aggrandize, dignify, elevate, exalt, promote; benefit, forward, further, improve, promote; adduce, allege, assign, offer, propose, propound; augment, increase; proceed, progress; grow, improve, prosper, thrive. * *n* march, progress; advancement, enhancement, growth, promotion, rise; offer, overture, proffering, proposal, proposition, tender; appreciation, rise.
advancement *n* advance, benefit, gain, growth, improvement, profit.
advantage *n* ascendancy, precedence, pre-eminence, superiority, upper-hand; benefit, blessing, emolument, gain, profit, return; account, behalf, interest; accommodation, convenience, prerogative, privilege.
advantageous *adj* beneficial, favourable, profitable.
advent *n* accession, approach, arrival, coming, visitation.
adventitious *adj* accidental, extraneous, extrinsic, foreign, fortuitous, nonessential.
adventure *vb* dare, hazard, imperil, peril, risk, venture. * *n* chance, contingency, experiment, fortuity, hazard, risk, venture; crisis, contingency, event, incident, occurrence, transaction.
adventurous *adj* bold, chivalrous, courageous, daring, doughty; foolhardy, headlong, precipitate, rash, reckless; dangerous, hazardous, perilous.
adversary *n* antagonist, enemy, foe, opponent.
adverse *adj* conflicting, contrary, opposing; antagonistic, harmful, hostile, hurtful, inimical, unfavourable, unpropitious; calamitous, disastrous, unfortunate, unlucky, untoward.
adversity *n* affliction, calamity, disaster, distress, misery, misfortune, sorrow, suffering, woe.
advertise *vb* advise, announce, declare, inform, placard, proclaim, publish.
advertisement *n* announcement, information, notice, proclamation.
advice *n* admonition, caution, counsel, exhortation, persuasion, suggestion, recommendation; information, intelligence, notice, notification; care, counsel, deliberation, forethought.
advisable *adj* advantageous, desirable, expedient, prudent.
advise *vb* admonish, counsel, commend, recommend, suggest, urge; acquaint, apprise, inform, notify; confer, consult, deliberate.
adviser *n* counsellor, director, guide, instructor.
advocate *vb* countenance, defend, favour, justify, maintain, support, uphold, vindicate. * *n* apologist, counsellor, defender, maintainer, patron, pleader, supporter; attorney, barrister, counsel, lawyer, solicitor.
aegis *n* defence, protection, safeguard, shelter.
aesthetic *adj* appropriate, beautiful, tasteful.
affable *adj* accessible, approachable, communicative, conversable, cordial, easy, familiar, frank, free, sociable, social; complaisant, courteous, civil, obliging, polite, urbane.
affair *n* business, circumstance, concern, matter, office, question; event, incident, occurrence, performance, proceeding, transaction; battle, combat, conflict, encounter, engagement, skirmish.
affairs *npl* administration, relations; business, estate, finances, property.
affect *vb* act upon, alter, change, influence, modify, transform; concern, interest, regard, relate; improve, melt, move, overcome, subdue, touch;

aim at, aspire to, crave, yearn for; adopt, assume, feign.

affectation *n* affectedness, airs, artificiality, foppery, pretension, simulation.

affected *adj* artificial, assumed, feigned, insincere, theatrical; assuming, conceited, foppish, vain.

affection *n* bent, bias, feeling, inclination, passion, proclivity, propensity; accident, attribute, character, mark, modification, mode, note, property; attachment, endearment, fondness, goodwill, kindness, partiality, love.

affectionate *adj* attached, devoted, fond, kind, loving, sympathetic, tender.

affiliate *vb* ally, annex, associate, connect, incorporate, join, unite. * *n* ally, associate, confederate.

affinity *n* connection, propinquity, relationship; analogy, attraction, correspondence, likeness, relation, resemblance, similarity, sympathy.

affirm *vb* allege, assert, asseverate, aver, declare, state; approve, confirm, establish, ratify.

affix *vb* annex, attach, connect, fasten, join, subjoin, tack.

afflict *vb* agonize, distress, grieve, pain, persecute, plague, torment, trouble, try, wound.

affliction *n* adversity, calamity, disaster, misfortune, stroke, visitation; bitterness, depression, distress, grief, misery, plague, scourge, sorrow, trial, tribulation, wretchedness, woe.

affluent *adj* abounding, abundant, bounteous, plenteous; moneyed, opulent, rich, wealthy.

afford *vb* furnish, produce, supply, yield; bestow, communicate, confer, give, grant, impart, offer; bear, endure, support.

affray *n* brawl, conflict, disturbance, feud, fight, quarrel, scuffle, struggle.

affright *vb* affray, alarm, appal, confound, dismay, shock, startle. * *n* alarm, consternation, fear, fright, panic, terror.

affront *vb* abuse, insult, outrage; annoy, chafe, displease, fret, irritate, offend, pique, provoke, vex. * *n* abuse, contumely, insult, outrage, vexation, wrong.

afraid *adj* aghast, alarmed, anxious, apprehensive, frightened, scared, timid.

after *prep* later than, subsequent to; behind, following; about, according to; because of, in imitation of. * *adj* behind, consecutive, ensuing, following, later, succeeding, successive, subsequent; aft, back, hind, rear, rearmost, tail.* *adv* afterwards, later, next, since, subsequently, then, thereafter.

again *adv* afresh, anew, another time, once more; besides, further, in addition, moreover.

against *prep* adverse to, contrary to, in opposition to, resisting; abutting, close up to, facing, fronting, off, opposite to, over; in anticipation of, for, in expectation of; in compensation for, to counterbalance, to match.

age *vb* decline, grow old, mature. * *n* aeon, date, epoch, period, time; decline, old age, senility; antiquity, oldness.

agency *n* action, force, intervention, means, mediation, operation, procurement; charge, direction, management, superintendence, supervision.

agent *n* actor, doer, executor, operator, performer; active element, cause, force; attorney, broker, commissioner, deputy, factor, intermediary, manager, middleman.

agglomeration *n* accumulation, aggregation, conglomeration, heap, lump, pile.

agglutinate *vb* cement, fasten, glue, unite.

aggrandize *vb* advance, dignify, elevate, enrich, exalt, promote.

aggravate *vb* heighten, increase, worsen; colour, exaggerate, magnify, overstate; enrage, irritate, provoke, tease.

aggravation *n* exaggeration, heightening, irritation.

aggregate *vb* accumulate, amass, collect, heap, pile. * *adj* collected, total. * *n* amount, gross, total, whole.

aggressive *adj* assailing, assailant, assaulting, attacking, invading, offensive; pushing, self-assertive.

aggressor *n* assailant, assaulter, attacker, invader.

aggrieve *vb* afflict, grieve, pain; abuse, ill-treat, impose, injure, oppress, wrong.

aghast *adj* appalled, dismayed, frightened, horrified, horror-struck, panic-stricken, terrified; amazed, astonished, startled, thunderstruck.

agile *adj* active, alert, brisk, lively, nimble, prompt, smart, ready.

agitate *vb* disturb, jar, rock, shake, trouble; disquiet, excite, ferment, rouse, trouble; confuse, discontent, flurry, fluster, flutter; canvass, debate, discuss, dispute, investigate.

agitation *n* concussion, shake, shaking; commotion, convulsion, disturbance, ferment, jarring, storm, tumult, turmoil; discomposure, distraction, emotion, excitement, flutter, perturbation, ruffle, tremor, trepidation; controversy, debate, discussion.

agnostic *n* doubter, empiricist, sceptic.

agonize *vb* distress, excruciate, rack, torment, torture.

agony *n* anguish, distress, pangs.

agree *vb* accord, concur, harmonize, unite; accede, acquiesce, assent, comply, concur, subscribe; bargain, contract, covenant, engage, promise, undertake; compound, compromise; chime, cohere, conform, correspond, match, suit, tally.

agreeable *adj* charming, pleasant, pleasing.

agreement *n* accordance, compliance, concord, harmony, union; bargain, compact, contract, pact, treaty.

agriculture *n* cultivation, culture, farming, geoponics, husbandry, tillage.

aid *vb* assist, help, serve, support; relieve, succour; advance, facilitate, further, promote. * *n* assistance, cooperation, help, patronage; alms, subsidy, succour, relief.

ailment *n* disease, illness, sickness.

aim *vb* direct, level, point, train; design, intend,

mean, purpose, seek. * *n* bearing, course, direction, tendency; design, object, view, reason.
air *vb* expose, display, ventilate. * *n* atmosphere, breeze; appearance, aspect, manner; melody, tune.
aisle *n* passage, walk.
akin *adj* allied, kin, related; analogous, cognate, congenial, connected.
alacrity *n* agility, alertness, activity, eagerness, promptitude; cheerfulness, gaiety, hilarity, liveliness, vivacity.
alarm *vb* daunt, frighten, scare, startle, terrify. * *n* alarm-bell, tocsin, warning; apprehension, fear, fright, terror.
alert *adj* awake, circumspect, vigilant, watchful, wary; active, brisk, lively, nimble, quick, prompt, ready, sprightly. * *vb* alarm, arouse, caution, forewarn, signal, warn. * *n* alarm, signal, warning.
alertness *n* circumspection, vigilance, watchfulness, wariness; activity, briskness, nimbleness, promptness, readiness, spryness.
alien *adj* foreign, not native; differing, estranged, inappropriate, remote, unallied, separated. * *n* foreigner, stranger.
alienate *vb* (*legal*) assign, demise, transfer; disaffect, estrange, wean, withdraw.
alienation *n* (*legal*) assignment, conveyance, transfer; breach, disaffection, division, estrangement, rupture; (*med*) aberration, delusion, derangement, hallucination, insanity, madness.
alike *adj* akin, analogous, duplicate, identical, resembling, similar. * *adv* equally.
aliment *n* diet, fare, meat, nutriment, provision, rations, sustenance.
alive *adj* animate, breathing, live; aware, responsive, sensitive, susceptible; brisk, cheerful, lively, sprightly.
allay *vb* appease, calm, check, compose; alleviate, assuage, lessen, moderate, solace, temper.
allege *vb* affirm, assert, declare, maintain, say; adduce, advance, assign, cite, plead, produce, quote.
allegiance *n* duty, homage, fealty, fidelity, loyalty, obligation.
allegory *n* apologue, fable, myth, parable, story, tale.
alleviate *vb* assuage, lighten, mitigate, mollify, moderate, quell, quiet, quieten, soften, soothe.
alliance *n* affinity, intermarriage, relation; coalition, combination, confederacy, league, treaty, union; affiliation, connection, relationship, similarity.
allot *vb* divide, dispense, distribute; assign, fix, prescribe, specify.
allow *vb* acknowledge, admit, concede, confess, grant, own; authorize, grant, let, permit; bear, endure, suffer, tolerate; grant, yield, relinquish, spare; approve, justify, sanction; abate, bate, deduct, remit.
allude *vb* glance, hint, mention, imply, insinuate, intimate, refer, suggest, touch.
allure *vb* attract, beguile, cajole, coax, entice, lure, persuade, seduce, tempt. * *n* appeal, attraction, lure, temptation.
allusion *n* hint, implication, intimation, insinuation, mention, reference, suggestion.
ally *vb* combine, connect, join, league, marry, unite. * *n* aider, assistant, associate, coadjutor, colleague, friend, partner.
almighty *adj* all-powerful, omnipotent.
alms *npl* benefaction, bounty, charity, dole, gift, gratuity.
alone *adj* companionless, deserted, forsaken, isolated, lonely, only, single, sole, solitary.
along *adv* lengthways, lengthwise; forward, onward; beside, together, simultaneously.
aloud *adv* audibly, loudly, sonorously, vociferously.
alter *vb* change, conform, modify, shift, turn, transform, transmit, vary.
altercation *n* bickering, contention, controversy, dispute, dissension, strife, wrangling.
alternating *adj* intermittent, interrupted.
alternative *adj* another, different, second, substitute. * *n* choice, option, preference.
although *conj* albeit, even if, for all that, notwithstanding, though.
altitude *n* elevation, height, loftiness.
altogether *adv* completely, entirely, totally, utterly.
always *adv* continually, eternally, ever, evermore, perpetually, unceasingly.
amalgamate *vb* blend, combine, commingle, compound, incorporate, mix.
amass *vb* accumulate, aggregate, collect, gather, heap, scrape together.
amateur *n* dilettante, nonprofessional.
amaze *vb* astonish, astound, bewilder, confound, confuse, dumbfound, perplex, stagger, stupefy.
amazement *n* astonishment, bewilderment, confusion, marvel, surprise, wonder.
ambassador *n* deputy, envoy, legate, minister, plenipotentiary.
ambiguous *adj* dubious, doubtful, enigmatic, equivocal, uncertain, indefinite, indistinct, obscure, vague.
ambition *n* aspiration, emulation, longing, yearning.
ambitious *adj* aspiring, avid, eager, intent.
ameliorate *vb* amend, benefit, better, elevate, improve, mend.
amenability *n* amenableness, responsiveness; accountability, liability, responsibility.
amenable *adj* acquiescent, agreeable, persuadable, responsive, susceptible; accountable, liable, responsible.
amend *vb* better, correct, improve, mend, redress, reform.
amends *npl* atonement, compensation, expiation, indemnification, recompense, reparation, restitution.
amenity *n* agreeableness, mildness, pleasantness, softness; affability, civility, courtesy, geniality, graciousness, urbanity.
amiable *adj* attractive, benign, charming, genial,

good-natured, harmonious, kind, lovable, lovely, pleasant, pleasing, sweet, winning, winsome.

amicable *adj* amiable, cordial, friendly, harmonious, kind, kindly, peaceable.

amiss *adj* erroneous, inaccurate, incorrect, faulty, improper, wrong. * *adv* erroneously, inaccurately, incorrectly, wrongly.

amnesty *n* absolution, condonation, dispensation, forgiveness, oblivion.

amorous *adj* ardent, enamoured, fond, longing, loving, passionate, tender; erotic, impassioned.

amorphous *adj* formless, irregular, shapeless, unshapen; noncrystalline, structureless; chaotic, characterless, clumsy, disorganized, misshapen, unorganized, vague.

amount *n* aggregate, sum, total.

ample *adj* broad, capacious, extended, extensive, great, large, roomy, spacious; abounding, abundant, copious, generous, liberal, plentiful; diffusive, unrestricted.

amputate *vb* clip, curtail, prune, lop, remove, separate, sever.

amuse *vb* charm, cheer, divert, enliven, entertain, gladden, relax, solace; beguile, cheat, deceive, delude, mislead.

amusement *n* diversion, entertainment, frolic, fun, merriment, pleasure.

analeptic *adj* comforting, invigorating, restorative.

analogy *n* correspondence, likeness, parallelism, parity, resemblance, similarity.

analysis *n* decomposition, dissection, resolution, separation.

anarchy *n* chaos, confusion, disorder, misrule, lawlessness, riot.

anathema *n* ban, curse, denunciation, excommunication, execration, malediction, proscription.

anatomy *n* dissection; form, skeleton, structure.

ancestor *n* father, forebear, forefather, progenitor.

ancestry *n* family, house, line, lineage; descent, genealogy, parentage, pedigree, stock.

anchor *vb* fasten, fix, secure; cast anchor, take firm hold. * *n* (*naut*) ground tackle; defence, hold, security, stay.

ancient *adj* old, primitive, pristine; antiquated, antique, archaic, obsolete.

ancillary *adj* accessory, auxiliary, contributory, helpful, instrumental.

angelic *adj* adorable, celestial, cherubic, heavenly, saintly, seraphic; entrancing, enrapturing, rapturous, ravishing.

anger *vb* chafe, displease, enrage, gall, infuriate, irritate, madden. * *n* choler, exasperation, fury, gall, indignation, ire, passion, rage, resentment, spleen, wrath.

angle *vb* fish. * *n* divergence, flare, opening; bend, corner, crotch, cusp, point; fish-hook, hook.

angry *adj* chafed, exasperated, furious, galled, incensed, irritated, nettled, piqued, provoked, resentful.

anguish *n* agony, distress, grief, pang, rack, torment, torture.

anile *adj* aged, decrepit, doting, imbecile, senile.

animadversion *n* comment, notice, observation, remark; blame, censure, condemnation, reproof, stricture.

animate *vb* inform, quicken, vitalize, vivify; fortify, invigorate, revive; activate, enliven, excite, heat, impel, kindle, rouse, stimulate, stir, waken; elate, embolden, encourage, exhilarate, gladden, hearten. * *adj* alive, breathing, live, living, organic, quick.

animosity *n* bitterness, enmity, grudge, hatred, hostility, rancour, rankling, spleen, virulence.

annals *npl* archives, chronicles, records, registers, rolls.

annex *vb* affix, append, attach, subjoin, tag, tack; connect, join, unite.

annihilate *vb* abolish, annul, destroy, dissolve, exterminate, extinguish, kill, obliterate, raze, ruin.

annotation *n* comment, explanation, illustration, note, observation, remark.

announce *vb* advertise, communicate, declare, disclose, proclaim, promulgate, publish, report, reveal, trumpet.

announcement *n* advertisement, annunciation, bulletin, declaration, manifesto, notice, notification, proclamation.

annoy *vb* badger, chafe, disquiet, disturb, fret, hector, irk, irritate, molest, pain, pester, plague, trouble, vex, worry, wound.

annul *vb* abolish, abrogate, cancel, countermand, nullify, overrule, quash, repeal, recall, reverse, revoke.

anoint *vb* consecrate, oil, sanctify, smear.

anonymous *adj* nameless, unacknowledged, unsigned.

answer *vb* fulfil, rejoin, reply, respond, satisfy. * *n* rejoinder, reply, response, retort; confutation, rebuttal, refutation.

answerable *adj* accountable, amenable, correspondent, liable, responsible, suited.

antagonism *n* contradiction, discordance, disharmony, dissonant, incompatibility, opposition.

antecedent *adj* anterior, foregoing, forerunning, precedent, preceding, previous. * *n* forerunner, precursor.

anterior *adj* antecedent, foregoing, preceding, previous, prior; fore, front.

anticipate *vb* antedate, forestall, foretaste, prevent; count upon, expect, forecast, foresee.

anticipation *n* apprehension, contemplation, expectation, hope, prospect, trust; expectancy, forecast, foresight, foretaste, preconception, presentiment.

antidote *n* corrective, counteractive, counter-poison; cure, remedy, restorative, specific.

antipathy *n* abhorrence, aversion, disgust, detestation, hate, hatred, horror, loathing, repugnance.

antique *adj* ancient, archaic, bygone, old, old-fashioned.

anxiety *n* apprehension, care, concern, disquiet, fear, foreboding, misgiving, perplexity, trouble, uneasiness, vexation, worry.

anxious *adj* apprehensive, restless, solicitous, uneasy, unquiet, worried.
apart *adv* aloof, aside, separately; asunder.
apathetic *adj* cold, dull, impassive, inert, listless, obtuse, passionless, sluggish, torpid, unfeeling.
ape *vb* counterfeit, imitate, mimic; affect. * *n* simian, troglodyte; imitator, mimic; image, imitation, likeness, type.
aperture *n* chasm, cleft, eye, gap, opening, hole, orifice, passage.
aphorism *n* adage, apothegm, byword, maxim, proverb, saw, saying.
apish *adj* imitative, mimicking; affected, foppish, trifling.
aplomb *n* composure, confidence, equanimity, self-confidence.
apocryphal *adj* doubtful, fabulous, false, legendary, spurious, uncanonical.
apologetic *adj* exculpatory, excusatory; defensive, vindictive.
apology *n* defence, justification, vindication; acknowledgement, excuse, explanation, plea, reparation.
apostate *adj* backsliding, disloyal, faithless, false, perfidious, recreant, traitorous, untrue. * *n* backslider, deserter, pervert, renegade, turncoat.
apostle *n* angel, herald, messenger, missionary, preacher; advocate, follower, supporter.
apothegm *n* aphorism, byword, dictum, maxim, proverb, saw, saying.
appal *vb* affright, alarm, daunt, dismay, frighten, horrify, scare, shock.
apparel *n* attire, array, clothes, clothing, dress, garments, habit, raiment, robes, suit, trappings, vestments.
apparent *adj* discernible, perceptible, visible; conspicuous, evident, legible, manifest, obvious, open, patent, plain, unmistakable; external, ostensible, seeming, superficial.
apparition *n* appearance, appearing, epiphany, manifestation; being, form; ghost, phantom, spectre, spirit, vision.
appeal *vb* address, entreat, implore, invoke, refer, request, solicit. * *n* application, entreaty, invocation, solicitation, suit.
appear *vb* emerge, loom; break, open; arise, occur, offer; look, seem, show.
appearance *n* advent, arrival, apparition, coming; form, shape; colour, face, fashion, feature, guise, pretence, pretext; air, aspect, complexion, demeanour, manner, mien.
appease *vb* abate, allay, assuage, calm, ease, lessen, mitigate, pacify, placate, quell, soothe, temper, tranquillize.
appellation *n* address, cognomen, denomination, epithet, style, title.
append *vb* attach, fasten, hang; add, annex, subjoin, tack, tag.
appendix *n* addition, adjunct, appurtenance, codicil; excursus, supplement.
appetite *n* craving, desire, longing, lust, passion; gusto, relish, stomach, zest; hunger.
applaud *vb* acclaim, cheer, clap, compliment, encourage, extol, magnify.
applause *n* acclamation, approval, cheers, commendation, plaudit.
applicable *adj* adapted, appropriate, apt, befitting, fitting, germane, pertinent, proper, relevant.
application *n* emollient, lotion, ointment, poultice, wash; appliance, exercise, practice, use; appeal, petition, request, solicitation, suit; assiduity, constancy, diligence, effort, industry.
apply *vb* bestow, lay upon; appropriate, convert, employ, exercise, use; addict, address, dedicate, devote, direct, engage.
appoint *vb* determine, establish, fix, prescribe; bid, command, decree, direct, order, require; allot, assign, delegate, depute, detail, destine, settle; constitute, create, name, nominate; equip, furnish, supply.
apportion *vb* allocate, allot, allow, assign, deal, dispense, divide, share.
apposite *adj* apt, fit, germane, pertinent, relevant, suitable, pertinent.
appraise *vb* appreciate, estimate, prize, rate, value.
appreciate *vb* appreciate, esteem, estimate, rate, realize, value.
apprehend *vb* arrest, catch, detain, seize, take; conceive, imagine, regard, view; appreciate, perceive, realize, see, take in; fear, forebode; conceive, fancy, hold, imagine, presume, understand.
apprehension *n* arrest, capture, seizure; intellect, intelligence, mind, reason; discernment, intellect, knowledge, perception, sense; belief, fancy, idea, notion, sentiment, view; alarm, care, dread, distrust, fear, misgiving, suspicion.
apprise *vb* acquaint, inform, notify, tell.
approach *vb* advance, approximate, come close; broach; resemble. * *n* advance, advent; approximation, convergence, nearing, tendency; entrance, path, way.
approbation *n* approval, commendation, liking, praise; assent, concurrence, consent, endorsement, ratification, sanction.
appropriate *vb* adopt, arrogate, assume, set apart; allot, apportion, assign, devote; apply, convert, employ, use. * *adj* adapted, apt, befitting, fit, opportune, seemly, suitable.
approve *vb* appreciate, commend, like, praise, recommend, value; confirm, countenance, justify, ratify, sustain, uphold.
approximate *vb* approach, resemble. * *adj* approaching, proximate; almost exact, inexact, rough.
apt *adj* applicable, apposite, appropriate, befitting, fit, felicitous, germane; disposed, inclined, liable, prone, subject; able, adroit, clever, dextrous, expert, handy, happy, prompt, ready, skilful.
aptitude *n* applicability, appropriateness, felicity, fitness, pertinence, suitability; inclination, tendency, turn; ability, address, adroitness, quickness, readiness, tact.

arbitrary *adj* absolute, autocratic, despotic, domineering, imperious, overbearing, unlimited; capricious, discretionary, fanciful, voluntary, whimsical.
arcade *n* colonnade, loggia.
arch[1] *adj* cunning, knowing, frolicsome, merry, mirthful, playful, roguish, shrewd, sly; consummate, chief, leading, pre-eminent, prime, primary, principal.
arch[2] *vb* span, vault; bend, curve. * *n* archway, span, vault.
archaic *adj* ancient, antiquated, antique, bygone, obsolete, old.
archives *npl* documents, muniments, records, registers, rolls.
ardent *adj* burning, fiery, hot; eager, earnest, fervent, impassioned, keen, passionate, warm, zealous.
ardour *n* glow, heat, warmth; eagerness, enthusiasm, fervour, heat, passion, soul, spirit, warmth, zeal.
arduous *adj* high, lofty, steep, uphill; difficult, fatiguing, hard, laborious, onerous, tiresome, toilsome, wearisome.
area *n* circle, circuit, district, domain, field, range, realm, region, tract.
argue *vb* plead, reason upon; debate, dispute; denote, evince, imply, indicate, mean, prove; contest, debate, discuss, sift.
arid *adj* barren, dry, parched, sterile, unfertile; dry, dull, jejune, pointless, uninteresting.
aright *adv* correctly, justly, rightly, truly.
arise *vb* ascend, mount, soar, tower; appear, emerge, rise, spring; begin, originate; rebel, revolt, rise; accrue, come, emanate, ensue, flow, issue, originate, proceed, result.
aristocracy *n* gentry, nobility, noblesse, peerage.
arm[1] *n* bough, branch, limb, protection; cove, creek, estuary, firth, fjord, frith, inlet.
arm[2] *vb* array, equip, furnish; clothe, cover, fortify, guard, protect, strengthen.
arms *npl* accoutrements, armour, array, harness, mail, panoply, weapons; crest, escutcheon.
army *n* battalions, force, host, legions, troops; host, multitude, throng, vast assemblage.
around *prep* about, encircling, encompassing, round, surrounding. * *adv* about, approximately, generally, near, nearly, practically, round, thereabouts.
arouse *vb* animate, awaken, excite, incite, kindle, provoke, rouse, stimulate, warm, whet.
arraign *vb* accuse, censure, charge, denounce, impeach, indict, prosecute, tax.
arrange *vb* array, class, classify, dispose, distribute, group, range, rank; adjust, determine, fix upon, settle; concoct, construct, devise, plan, prepare, project.
arrant *adj* bad, consummate, downright, gross, notorious, rank, utter.
array *vb* arrange, dispose, place, range, rank; accoutre, adorn, attire, decorate, dress, enrobe, embellish, equip, garnish, habit, invest. * *n* arrangement, collection, disposition, marshalling, order; apparel, attire, clothes, dress, garments; army, battalions, soldiery, troops.
arrest *vb* check, delay, detain, hinder, hold, interrupt, obstruct, restrain, stay, stop, withhold; apprehend, capture, catch, seize, take; catch, engage, engross, fix, occupy, secure, rivet. * *n* check, checking, detention, hindrance, interruption, obstruction, restraining, stay, staying, stopping; apprehension, capture, detention, seizure.
arrive *vb* attain, come, get to, reach.
arrogance *n* assumption, assurance, disdain, effrontery, haughtiness, loftiness, lordliness, presumption, pride, scornfulness, superciliousness.
arrogate *vb* assume, claim unduly, demand, usurp.
arrow *n* bolt, dart, reed, shaft.
art *n* business, craft, employment, trade; address, adroitness, aptitude, dexterity, ingenuity, knack, readiness, sagacity, skill; artfulness, artifice, astuteness, craft, deceit, duplicity, finesse, subtlety.
artful *adj* crafty, cunning, disingenuous, insincere, sly, tricky, wily.
article *n* branch, clause, division, head, item, member, paragraph, part, point, portion; essay, paper, piece; commodity, substance, thing.
artifice *n* art, chicanery, contrivance, cunning, deception, deceit, duplicity, effort, finesse, fraud, imposture, invention, stratagem, subterfuge, trick, trickery.
artificial *adj* counterfeit, sham, spurious; assumed, affected, constrained, fictitious, forced, laboured, strained.
artless *adj* ignorant, rude, unskilful, untaught; natural, plain, simple; candid, fair, frank, guileless, honest, plain, unaffected, simple, sincere, truthful, unsuspicious.
ascend *vb* arise, aspire, climb, mount, soar, tower.
ascendancy, ascendency *n* authority, control, domination, mastery, power, predominance, sovereignty, superiority, sway.
ascertain *vb* certify, define, determine, establish, fix, settle, verify; discover, find out, get at.
ashamed *adj* abashed, confused.
ask *vb* interrogate, inquire, question; adjure, beg, conjure, crave, desire, dun, entreat, implore, invite, inquire, petition, request, solicit, supplicate, seek, sue.
aspect *n* air, bearing, countenance, expression, feature, look, mien, visage; appearance, attitude, condition, light, phase, position, posture, situation, state, view; angle, direction, outlook, prospect.
asperity *n* ruggedness, roughness, unevenness; acrimony, causticity, corrosiveness, sharpness, sourness, tartness; acerbity, bitterness, churlishness, harshness, sternness, sullenness, severity, virulence.
aspersion *n* abuse, backbiting, calumny, censure, defamation, detraction, slander, vituperation, reflection, reproach.

aspiration *n* aim, ambition, craving, hankering, hope, longing.
aspire *vb* desire, hope, long, yearn; ascend, mount, rise, soar, tower.
assail *vb* assault, attack, invade, oppugn; impugn, malign, maltreat; ply, storm.
assassinate *vb* dispatch, kill, murder, slay.
assault *vb* assail, attack, charge, invade. * *n* aggression, attack, charge, incursion, invasion, onset, onslaught; storm.
assemble *vb* call, collect, congregate, convene, convoke, gather, levy, muster; converge, forgather.
assembly *n* company, collection, concourse, congregation, gathering, meeting, rout, throng; caucus, congress, conclave, convention, convocation, diet, legislature, meeting, parliament, synod.
assent *vb* accede, acquiesce, agree, concur, subscribe, yield. * *n* accord, acquiescence, allowance, approval, approbation, consent.
assert *vb* affirm, allege, aver, asseverate, declare, express, maintain, predicate, pronounce, protest; claim, defend, emphasize, maintain, press, uphold, vindicate.
assertion *n* affirmation, allegation, asseveration, averment, declaration, position, predication, remark, statement, word; defence, emphasis, maintenance, pressing, support, vindication.
assess *vb* appraise, compute, estimate, rate, value; assign, determine, fix, impose, levy.
asseverate *vb* affirm, aver, avow, declare, maintain, protest.
assiduous *adj* active, busy, careful, constant, diligent, devoted, indefatigable, industrious, sedulous, unremitting, untiring.
assign *vb* allot, appoint, apportion, appropriate; fix, designate, determine, specify; adduce, advance, allege, give, grant, offer, present, show.
assist *vb* abet, aid, befriend, further, help, patronize, promote, second, speed, support, sustain; aid, relieve, succour; alternate with, relieve, spell.
associate *vb* affiliate, combine, conjoin, couple, join, link, relate, yoke; consort, fraternize, mingle, sort. * *n* chum, companion, comrade, familiar, follower, mate; ally, confederate, friend, partner, fellow.
association *n* combination, company, confederation, connection, partnership, society.
assort *vb* arrange, class, classify, distribute, group, rank, sort; agree, be adapted, consort, suit.
assuage *vb* allay, alleviate, appease, calm, ease, lessen, mitigate, moderate, mollify, pacify, quell, relieve, soothe, tranquillize.
assume *vb* take, undertake; affect, counterfeit, feign, pretend, sham; arrogate, usurp; beg, hypothesize, imply, postulate, posit, presuppose, suppose, simulate.
assurance *n* assuredness, certainty, conviction, persuasion, pledge, security, surety, warrant; engagement, pledge, promise; averment, assertion, protestation; audacity, confidence, courage, firmness, intrepidity; arrogance, brass, boldness, effrontery, face, front, impudence.
assure *vb* encourage, embolden, hearten; certify, insure, secure against loss, vouch for.
astonish *vb* amaze, astound, confound, daze, dumbfound, overwhelm, startle, stun, stupefy, surprise.
astute *adj* acute, cunning, deep, discerning, ingenious, intelligent, penetrating, perspicacious, quick, sagacious, sharp, shrewd.
asylum *n* refuge, retreat, sanctuary, shelter.
athletic *adj* brawny, lusty, muscular, powerful, robust, sinewy, stalwart, stout, strapping, strong, sturdy.
athletics *npl* aerobics, eurythmics, exercise, exercising, gymnastics, sports, track and field, workout.
atom *n* bit, molecule, monad, particle, scintilla.
atone *vb* answer, compensate, expiate, satisfy.
atonement *n* amends, expiation, propitiation, reparation, satisfaction.
atrocity *n* depravity, enormity, flagrancy, ferocity, savagery, villainy.
attach *vb* affix, annex, connect, fasten, join, hitch, tie; charm, captivate, enamour, endear, engage, win; (*legal*) distress, distrain, seize, take.
attack *vb* assail, assault, charge, encounter, invade, set upon, storm, tackle; censure, criticise, impugn. * *n* aggression, assault, charge, offence, onset, onslaught, raid, thrust.
attain *vb* accomplish, achieve, acquire, get, obtain, secure; arrive at, come to, reach.
attempt *vb* assail, assault, attack; aim, endeavour, seek, strive, try. * *n* effort, endeavour, enterprise, experiment, undertaking, venture; assault, attack, onset.
attend *vb* accompany, escort, follow; guard, protect, watch; minister to, serve, wait on; give heed, hear, harken, listen; be attendant, serve, tend, wait.
attention *n* care, circumspection, heed, mindfulness, observation, regard, watch, watchfulness; application, reflection, study; civility, courtesy, deference, politeness, regard, respect; addresses, courtship, devotion, suit, wooing.
attentive *adj* alive, awake, careful, civil, considerate, courteous, heedful, mindful, observant, watchful.
attenuate *vb* contract, dilute, diminish, elongate, lengthen, lessen, rarefy, reduce, slim, thin, weaken.
attest *vb* authenticate, certify, corroborate, confirm, ratify, seal, vouch; adjure, call to witness, invoke; confess, display, exhibit, manifest, prove, show, witness.
attic *n* garret, loft, upper storey.
Attic *adj* delicate, subtle, penetrating, pointed, pungent; chaste, classic, correct, elegant, polished, pure.

attire *vb* accoutre, apparel, array, clothe, dress, enrobe, equip, rig, robe. * *n* clothes, clothing, costume, dress, garb, gear, habiliment, outfit, toilet, trapping, vestment, vesture, wardrobe.
attitude *n* pose, position, posture; aspect, conjuncture, condition, phase, prediction, situation, standing, state.
attract *vb* draw, pull; allure, captivate, charm, decoy, enamour, endear, entice, engage, fascinate, invite, win.
attraction *n* affinity, drawing, pull; allurement, charm, enticement, fascination, magnetism, lure, seduction, witchery.
attribute *vb* ascribe, assign, impute, refer. * *n* characteristic, mark, note, peculiarity, predicate, property, quality.
attrition *n* abrasion, friction, rubbing.
attune *vb* accord, harmonize, modulate, tune; accommodate, adapt, adjust, attempt.
audacity *n* boldness, courage, daring, fearlessness, intrepidity; assurance, brass, effrontery, face, front, impudence, insolence, presumption, sauciness.
audience *n* assemblage, congregation; hearing, interview, reception.
augment *vb* add to, enhance, enlarge, increase, magnify, multiply, swell.
augmentation *n* accession, addition, enlargement, extension, increase.
augury *n* prediction, prognostication, prophecy, soothsaying; auspice, forerunner, harbinger, herald, omen, precursor, portent, sign.
august *adj* awe-inspiring, awful, dignified, grand, imposing, kingly, majestic, noble, princely, regal, solemn, stately, venerable.
auspicious *adj* fortunate, happy, lucky, prosperous, successful; bright, favourable, golden, opportune, promising, prosperous.
austere *adj* ascetic, difficult, formal, hard, harsh, morose, relentless, rigid, rigorous, severe, stern, stiff, strict, uncompromising, unrelenting.
authentic *adj* genuine, pure, real, true, unadulterated, uncorrupted, veritable; accurate, authoritative, reliable, true, trustworthy.
authority *n* dominion, empire, government, jurisdiction, power, sovereignty; ascendency, control, influence, rule, supremacy, sway; authorization, liberty, order, permit, precept, sanction, warranty; testimony, witness; connoisseur, expert, master.
authorize *vb* empower, enable, entitle; allow, approve, confirm, countenance, permit, ratify, sanction.
auxiliary *adj* aiding, ancillary, assisting, helpful, subsidiary. * *n* ally, assistant, confederate, help.
avail *vb* assist, benefit, help, profit, use, service.
available *adj* accessible, advantageous, applicable, beneficial, profitable, serviceable, useful.
avarice *n* acquisitiveness, covetousness, greediness, penuriousness, rapacity.
avaricious *adj* grasping, miserly, niggardly, parsimonious.
avenge *vb* punish, retaliate, revenge, vindicate.
avenue *n* access, entrance, entry, passage; alley, path, road, street, walk; channel, pass, route, way.
aver *vb* allege, assert, asseverate, avouch, declare, pronounce, protest, say.
averse *adj* adverse, backward, disinclined, indisposed, opposed, unwilling.
aversion *n* abhorrence, antipathy, disgust, dislike, hate, hatred, loathing, reluctance, repugnance.
avid *adj* eager, greedy, voracious.
avocation *n* business, calling, employment, occupation, trade, vocation; distraction, hindrance, interruption.
avoid *vb* dodge, elude, escape, eschew, shun; forebear, refrain from.
avouch *vb* allege, assert, declare, maintain, say.
avow *vb* admit, acknowledge, confess, own.
awaken *vb* arouse, excite, incite, kindle, provoke, spur, stimulate; wake, waken; begin, be excited.
award *vb* adjudge, allot, assign, bestow, decree, grant. * *n* adjudication, allotment, assignment, decision, decree, determination, gift, judgement.
aware *adj* acquainted, apprised, conscious, conversant, informed, knowing, mindful, sensible.
away *adv* absent, not present. * *adj* at a distance; elsewhere; out of the way.
awe *vb* cow, daunt, intimidate, overawe. * *n* abashment, fear, reverence; dread, fear, fearfulness, terror.
awful *adj* august, awesome, dread, grand, inspired; abashed, alarming, appalled, dire, frightful, portentous, tremendous.
awkward *adj* bungling, clumsy, inept, maladroit, unskilful; lumbering, unfit, ungainly, unmanageable; boorish; inconvenient, unsuitable.
axiom *n* adage, aphorism, apothegm, maxim, postulation, truism.
axis *n* axle, shaft, spindle.
azure *adj* blue, cerulean, sky-coloured.

B

babble *vb* blather, chatter, gibber, jabber, prate, prattle. * *n* chat, gossip, palaver, prate, tattle.
babel *n* clamour, confusion, din, discord, disorder, hubbub, jargon, pother.
baby *vb* coddle, cosset, indulge, mollycoddle, pamper, spoil. * *adj* babyish, childish, infantile, puerile; diminutive, doll-like, miniature, pocket, pocket-sized, small-scale. * *n* babe, brat, child, infant, suckling, nursling; chicken, coward, milksop, namby-pamby, sad sack, weakling; miniature; innocent.
bacchanal *n* carouse, debauchery, drunkenness, revelry, roisterousness.
back *vb* abet, aid, countenance, favour, second, support, sustain; go back, move back, retreat, withdraw. * *adj* hindmost. * *adv* in return, in consideration; ago, gone, since; aside, away, behind, by; abaft, astern, backwards, hindwards, rearwards. * *n* end, hind part, posterior, rear.
backbite *vb* abuse, asperse, blacken, defame, libel, malign, revile, scandalize, slander, traduce, vilify.
backbone *n* chine, spine; constancy, courage, decision, firmness, nerve, pluck, resolution, steadfastness.
backslider *n* apostate, deserter, renegade.
backward *adj* disinclined, hesitating, indisposed, loath, reluctant, unwilling, wavering; dull, slow, sluggish, stolid, stupid. * *adv* aback, behind, rearward.
bad *adj* baleful, baneful, detrimental, evil, harmful, hurtful, injurious, noxious, pernicious, unwholesome, vicious; abandoned, corrupt, depraved, immoral, sinful, unfair, unprincipled, wicked; unfortunate, unhappy, unlucky, miserable; disappointing, discouraging, distressing, sad, unwelcoming; abominable, mean, shabby, scurvy, vile, wretched; defective, inferior, imperfect, incompetent, poor, unsuitable; hard, heavy, serious, severe.
badge *n* brand, emblem, mark, sign, symbol, token.
badger *vb* annoy, bait, bother, hector, harry, pester, persecute, tease, torment, trouble, vex, worry.
baffle *vb* balk, block, check, circumvent, defeat, foil, frustrate, mar, thwart, undermine, upset; bewilder, confound, disconcert, perplex.
bait *vb* harry, tease, worry. * *n* allurement, decoy, enticement, lure, temptation.
balance *vb* equilibrate, pose, (*naut*) trim; compare, weigh; compensate, counteract, estimate; adjust, clear, equalize, square. * *n* equilibrium, liberation; excess, remainder, residue, surplus.
bald *adj* bare, naked, uncovered, treeless; dull, inelegant, meagre, prosaic, tame, unadorned, vapid.
baleful *adj* baneful, deadly, calamitous, hurtful, injurious, mischievous, noxious, pernicious, ruinous.
balk *vb* baffle, defeat, disappoint, disconcert, foil, frustrate, thwart.
ball *n* drop, globe, orb, pellet, marble, sphere; bullet, missile, projectile, shot; assembly, dance.
balmy *adj* aromatic, fragrant, healing, odorous, perfumed.
ban *vb* anathematize, curse, execrate; interdict, outlaw. * *n* edict, proclamation; anathema, curse, denunciation, execration; interdiction, outlawry, penalty, prohibition
band[1] *vb* belt, bind, cinch, encircle, gird, girdle; ally, associate, combine, connect, join, league; bar, marble, streak, stripe, striate, vein. * *n* crew, gang, horde, society, troop; ensemble, group, orchestra.
band[2] *n* ligament, ligature, tie; bond, chain, cord, fetter, manacle, shackle, trammel; bandage, belt, binding, cincture, girth, tourniquet.
bandit *n* brigand, freebooter, footpad, gangster, highwayman, outlaw, robber.
baneful *adj* poisonous, venomous; deadly, destructive, hurtful, mischievous, noxious, pernicious.
bang *vb* beat, knock, maul, pommel, pound, strike, thrash, thump; slam; clatter, rattle, resound, ring. * *n* clang, clangour, whang; blow, knock, lick, thump, thwack, whack.
banish *vb* exile, expatriate, ostracize; dismiss, exclude, expel.
bank[1] *vb* incline, slope, tilt; embank. * *n* dike, embankment, escarpment, heap, knoll, mound; border, bound, brim, brink, margin, rim, strand; course, row, tier.
bank[2] *vb* deposit, keep, save. * *n* depository, fund, reserve, savings, stockpile.
banner *n* colours, ensign, flag, standard, pennon, standard, streamer.
banter *vb* chaff, deride, jeer, joke, mock, quiz, rally, ridicule. * *n* badinage, chaff, derision, jesting, joking, mockery, quizzing, raillery, ridicule.
bar *vb* exclude, hinder, obstruct, prevent, prohibit, restrain, stop. * *n* grating, pole, rail, rod; barri-

cade, hindrance, impediment, obstacle, obstruction, stop; bank, sand bar, shallow, shoal, spit; (*legal*) barristers, counsel, court, judgement, tribunal.

barbarian *adj* brutal, cruel, ferocious, fierce, fell, inhuman, ruthless, savage, truculent, unfeeling. * *n* brute, ruffian, savage.

barbaric *adj* barbarous, rude, savage, uncivilized, untamed; capricious, coarse, gaudy, riotous, showy, outlandish, uncouth, untamed, wild.

bare *vb* denude, depilate, divest, strip, unsheathe; disclose, manifest, open, reveal, show. * *adj* denuded, exposed, naked, nude, stripped, unclothed, uncovered, undressed, unsheltered; alone, mere, sheer, simple; bald, meagre, plain, unadorned, uncovered, unfurnished; empty, destitute, indigent, poor.

bargain *vb* agree, contract, covenant, stipulate; convey, sell, transfer. * *n* agreement, compact, contract, covenant, convention, indenture, transaction, stipulation, treaty; proceeds, purchase, result.

barren *adj* childless, infecund, sterile; (*bot*) acarpous, sterile; bare, infertile, poor, sterile, unproductive; ineffectual, unfruitful, uninstructive.

barricade *vb* block up, fortify, protect, obstruct. * *n* barrier, obstruction, palisade, stockade.

barrier *n* bar, barricade, hindrance, impediment, obstacle, obstruction, stop.

barter *vb* bargain, exchange, sell, trade, traffic.

base[1] *adj* cheap, inferior, worthless; counterfeit, debased, false, spurious; baseborn, humble, lowly, mean, nameless, plebeian, unknown, untitled, vulgar; abject, beggarly, contemptible, degraded, despicable, low, menial, pitiful, servile, sordid, sorry, worthless.

base[2] *vb* establish, found, ground. * *n* foundation, fundament, substructure, underpinning; pedestal, plinth, stand; centre, headquarters, HQ, seat; starting point; basis, cause, grounds, reason, standpoint; bottom, foot, foundation, ground.

bashful *adj* coy, diffident, shy, timid.

basis n base, bottom, foundation, fundament, ground, groundwork.

bastard *adj* adulterated, baseborn, counterfeit, false, illegitimate, sham. * *n* love child.

batch *vb* assemble, bunch, bundle, collect, gather, group. * *n* amount, collection, crowd, lot, quantity.

bathe *vb* immerse, lave, wash; cover, enfold, enwrap, drench, flood, infold, suffuse. * *n* bath, shower, swim.

batter[1] *vb* beat, pelt, smite; break, bruise, demolish, destroy, shatter, shiver, smash; abrade, deface, disfigure, indent, mar; incline, recede, retreat, slope. * *n* batsman, striker.

batter[2] *n* dough, goo, goop, gunk, paste, pulp.

battle *vb* contend, contest, engage, fight, strive, struggle. * *n* action, affair, brush, combat, conflict, contest, engagement, fight, fray.

bauble *n* gewgaw, gimcrack, knick-knack, plaything, toy, trifle, trinket.

bawdy *adj* obscene, filthy, impure, indecent, lascivious, lewd, smutty, unchaste.

bawl *vb* clamour, cry, hoot, howl, roar, shout, squall, vociferate, yell.

bay[1] *vb* bark, howl, wail, yell, yelp.

bay[2] *n* alcove, compartment, niche, nook, opening, recess.

bay[3] *n* bight, cove, gulf, inlet.

bays *npl* applause, chaplet, fame, garland, glory, honour, plaudits, praise, renown.

beach *vb* ground, maroon, strand. * *n* coast, margin, rim, sands, seashore, seaside, shore, shoreline, strand, waterfront.

beacon *vb* brighten, flame, shine, signal; enlighten, illuminate, illumine, guide, light, signal. * *n* lighthouse, pharos, watchtower; sign, signal.

beadle *n* apparitor, church officer, crier, servitor, summoner.

beak *n* bill, mandible, (*sl*) nose; (*naut*) bow, prow, stem.

beam *vb* beacon, gleam, glisten, glitter, shine. * *n* balk, girder, joist, scantling, stud; gleam, pencil, ray, streak.

bear *vb* support, sustain, uphold; carry, convey, deport, transport, waft; abide, brook, endure, stand, suffer, tolerate, undergo; carry on, keep up, maintain; cherish, entertain, harbour; produce; cast, drop, sustain; endure, submit, suffer; act, operate, work. * *n* growler, grumbler, moaner, snarler; speculator.

bearable *adj* endurable, sufferable, supportable, tolerable.

bearing *n* air, behaviour, demeanour, deportment, conduct, carriage, conduct, mien, port; connection, dependency, relation; endurance, patience, suffering; aim, course, direction; bringing forth, producing; bed, receptacle, socket.

beastly *adj* abominable, brutish, ignoble, low, sensual, vile.

beat *vb* bang, baste, belabour, buffet, cane, cudgel, drub, hammer, hit, knock, maul, pound, pummel, punch, strike, thrash, thump, thwack, whack, whip; bray, bruise, pound, pulverize; batter, pelt; conquer, defeat, overcome, rout, subdue, surpass, vanquish; pulsate, throb; dash, strike. * *adj* baffled, bamboozled, confounded, mystified, nonplused, perplexed, puzzled, stumped; done, dog-tired, exhausted, tired out, worn out; beaten, defeated, licked, worsted. * *n* blow, striking, stroke; beating, pulsation, throb; accent, metre, rhythm; circuit, course, round.

beatific *adj* ecstatic, enchanting, enraptured, ravishing, rapt.

beatitude *n* blessing, ecstasy, felicity, happiness.

beau *n* coxcomb, dandy, exquisite, fop, popinjay; admirer, lover, suitor, sweetheart.

beautiful *adj* charming, comely, fair, fine, exquisite, handsome, lovely, pretty.

beautify *vb* adorn, array, bedeck, deck, decorate, embellish, emblazon, garnish, gild, grace, ornament, set.

beauty *n* elegance, grace, symmetry; attractiveness, comeliness, fairness, loveliness, seemliness; belle.

become *vb* change to, get, go, wax; adorn, befit, set off, suit.

becoming *adj* appropriate, apt, congruous, decent, decorous, due, fit, proper, right, seemly, suitable; comely, graceful, neat, pretty.

bed *vb* embed, establish, imbed, implant, infix, inset, plant; harbour, house, lodge. * *n* berth, bunk, cot, couch; channel, depression, hollow; base, foundation, receptacle, support, underlay; accumulation, layer, seam, stratum, vein.

bedim *vb* cloud, darken, dim, obscure.

befall *vb* betide, overtake; chance, happen,occur, supervene.

befitting *adj* appropriate, apt, becoming, decorous, fit, proper, right, suitable, seemly.

befool *vb* bamboozle, beguile, cheat, circumvent, delude, deceive, dupe, fool, hoax, hoodwink, infatuate, stupefy, trick.

befriend *vb* aid, benefit, countenance, encourage, favour, help, patronize.

beg *vb* adjure, ask, beseech, conjure, crave, entreat, implore, importune, petition, pray, request, solicit, supplicate.

beggarly *adj* destitute, needy, poor; abject, base, despicable, grovelling, low, mean, miserable, miserly, paltry, pitiful, scant, servile, shabby, sorry, stingy, vile, wretched.

begin *vb* arise, commence, enter, open; inaugurate, institute, originate, start.

beginning *n* arising, commencement, dawn, emergence, inauguration, inception, initiation, opening, outset, start, rise; origin, source.

beguile *vb* cheat, deceive, delude; amuse, cheer, divert, entertain, solace.

behaviour *n* air, bearing, carriage, comportment, conduct, demeanour, deportment, manner, manners, mien.

behest *n* bidding, charge, command, commandment, direction, hest, injunction, mandate, order, precept.

behind *prep* abaft, after, following. * *adv* abaft, aft, astern, rearward. * *adj* arrested, backward, checked, detained, retarded; after, behind. * *n* afterpart, rear, stern, tail; back, back side, reverse; bottom, buttocks, posterior, rump.

behold *vb* consider, contemplate, eye, observe, regard, see, survey, view.

behoove *vb* become, befit, suit; be binding, be obligatory.

being *n* actuality, existence, reality, subsistence; core, essence, heart, root.

beleaguer *vb* besiege, blockade, invest; beset, block, encumber, encompass, encounter, obstruct, surround.

belief *n* assurance, confidence, conviction, persuasion, trust; acceptance, assent, credence, credit, currency; creed, doctrine, dogma, faith, opinion, tenet.

bellow *vb* bawl, clamour, cry, howl, vociferate, yell.

belt *n* band, cincture, girdle, girth, zone; region, stretch, strip.

bemoan *vb* bewail, deplore, lament, mourn.

bemused *adj* bewildered, confused, fuddled, muddled, muzzy, stupefied, tipsy.

bend *vb* bow, crook, curve, deflect, draw; direct, incline, turn; bend, dispose, influence, mould, persuade, subdue; (*naut*) fasten, make fast; crook, deflect, deviate, diverge, swerve; bow, lower, stoop; condescend, deign. * *n* angle, arc, arcuation, crook, curvature, curve, elbow, flexure, turn.

beneath *prep* below, under, underneath; unbecoming, unbefitting, unworthy. * *adv* below, underneath.

benediction *n* beatitude, benefit, benison, blessing, boon, grace, favour.

benefaction *n* alms, boon, charity, contribution, donation, favour, gift, grant, gratuity, offering, present.

beneficent *adj* benevolent, bounteous, bountiful, charitable, generous, kind, liberal.

beneficial *adj* advantageous, favourable, helpful, profitable, salutary, serviceable, useful, wholesome.

benefit *vb* befriend, help, serve; advantage, avail, profit. * *n* favour, good turn, kindness, service; account, advantage, behalf, gain, good, interest, profit, utility.

benevolence *n* beneficence, benignity, generosity, goodwill, humanity, kindliness, kindness.

benevolent *adj* altruistic, benign, charitable, generous, humane, kind, kind-hearted, liberal, obliging, philanthropic, tender, unselfish.

benign *adj* amiable, amicable, beneficent, benevolent, complaisant, friendly, gentle, good, gracious, humane, kind, kindly, obliging.

bent *adj* angled, angular, bowed, crooked, curved, deflected, embowed, flexed, hooked, twisted; disposed, inclined, prone, minded; (*with* **on**) determined, fixed on, resolved, set on. * *n* bias, inclination, leaning, partiality, penchant, predilection, prepossession, proclivity, propensity

bequeath *vb* devise, give, grant, leave, will; impart, transmit.

berate *vb* chide, rate, reprimand, reprove, scold.

bereave *vb* afflict, deprive of, despoil, dispossess, divest, rob, spoil, strip.

beseech *vb* beg, conjure, entreat, implore, importune, petition, supplicate; ask, beg, crave, solicit.

beset *vb* besiege, encompass, enclose, environ, encircle, hem in, surround; decorate, embarrass, embellish, entangle, garnish, ornament, perplex, set.

beside[1] *prep* at the side of, by the side of, close to, near; aside from, not according to, out of the course of, out of the way of; not in possession of, out of.

besides[1] *prep* barring, distinct from, excluding, except, excepting, in addition to, other than, over and above, save.

beside[2], **besides**[2] *adv* additionally, also, further, furthermore, in addition, more, moreover, over and above, too, yet.

besiege *vb* beset, blockade, encircle, encompass, environ, invest, surround.

besot *vb* drench, intoxicate, soak, steep; befool, delude, infatuate, stultify, stupefy.

bespatter *vb* bedaub, befoul, besmirch, smear, spatter.

bespeak *vb* accost, address, declare, evince, forestall, imply, indicate, prearrange, predict, proclaim, solicit.

best *vb* better, exceed, excel, predominate, rival, surpass; beat, defeat, outdo, worst. * *adj* chief, first, foremost, highest, leading, utmost. * *adv* advantageously, excellently; extremely, greatly. * *n* choice, cream, flower, pick.

bestial *adj* beast-like, beastly, brutal, degraded, depraved, irrational, low, vile; sensual.

bestow *vb* deposit, dispose, put, place, store, stow; accord, give, grant, impart.

bet *vb* gamble, hazard, lay, pledge, stake, wage, wager. * *n* gamble, hazard, stake, wager.

bethink *vb* cogitate, consider, ponder, recall, recollect, reflect, remember.

betide *vb* befall, happen, occur, overtake.

betimes *adv* beforehand, early, forward, soon.

betoken *vb* argue, betray, denote, evince, imply, indicate, prove, represent, show, signify, typify.

betray *vb* be false to, break, violate; blab, discover, divulge, expose, reveal, show, tell; argue, betoken, display, evince, expose, exhibit, imply, indicate, manifest, reveal; beguile, delude, ensnare, lure, mislead; corrupt, ruin, seduce, undo.

betroth *vb* affiance, engage to marry, pledge in marriage, plight.

better *vb* advance, amend, correct, exceed, improve, promote, rectify, reform. * *adj* bigger, fitter, greater, larger, less ill, preferable. * *n* advantage, superiority, upper hand, victory; improvement, greater good.

between *prep* amidst, among, betwixt.

bewail *vb* bemoan, deplore, express, lament, mourn over, rue, sorrow.

beware *vb* avoid, heed, look out, mind.

bewilder *vb* confound, confuse, daze, distract, embarrass, entangle, muddle, mystify, nonplus, perplex, pose, puzzle, stagger.

bewitch *vb* captivate, charm, enchant, enrapture, entrance, fascinate, spellbind, transport.

beyond *prep* above, before, farther, over, past, remote, yonder.

bias *vb* bend, dispose, incline, influence, predispose, prejudice. * *n* bent, inclination, leaning, partiality, penchant, predilection, prepossession, proclivity, propensity, slant, tendency, turn.

bicker *vb* argue, dispute, jangle, quarrel, spar, spat, squabble, wrangle.

bid *vb* charge, command, direct, enjoin, order, require, summon; ask, call, invite, pray, request, solicit; offer, propose, proffer, tender. * *n* bidding, offer, proposal.

big *adj* bumper, bulking, bulky, great, huge, large, massive, monstrous; important, imposing; distended, inflated, full, swollen, tumid; fecund, fruitful, productive, teeming.

bigoted *adj* dogmatic, hidebound, intolerant, obstinate, narrow-minded, opinionated, prejudiced.

bill[1] *vb* charge, dun, invoice; programme, schedule; advertise, boost, plug, promote, publicize. * *n* account, charges, reckoning, score; advertisement, banner, hoarding, placard, poster; playbill, programme, schedule; bill of exchange, certificate, money; account, reckoning, statement.

bill[2] *n* beak, mandible, (*sl*) nose; billhook, brushcutter, hedge-bill, hedging knife; caress, fondle, kiss, toy.

billet *vb* allot, apportion, assign, distribute, quarter, station. * *n* accommodation, lodgings, quarters.

billow *vb* surge, wave; heave, roll; bag, baloon, bulge, dilate, swell. * *n* roller, surge, swell, wave.

bin *n* box, bunker, crib, frame, receptacle.

bind *vb* confine, enchain, fetter, restrain, restrict; bandage, tie up, wrap; fasten, lash, pinion, secure, tie, truss; engage, hold, oblige, obligate, pledge; contract, harden, shrink, stiffen.

birth *n* ancestry, blood, descent, extraction, lineage, race; being, creation, creature, offspring, production, progeny.

bit *n* crumb, fragment, morsel, mouthful, piece, scrap; atom, grain, jot, mite, particle, tittle, whit; instant, minute, moment, second.

bite *vb* champ, chew, crunch, gnaw; burn, make smart, sting; catch, clutch, grapple, grasp, grip; bamboozle, cheat, cozen, deceive, defraud, dupe, gull, mislead, outwit, overreach, trick. * *n* grasp, hold; punch, relish, spice, pungency, tang, zest; lick, morsel, sip, taste; crick, nip, pain, pang, prick, sting.

bitter *adj* acrid; dire, fell, merciless, relentless, ruthless; harsh, severe, stern; afflictive, calamitous, distressing, galling, grievous, painful, poignant, sore, sorrowful.

black *adj* dark, ebony, inky, jet, sable, swarthy; dingy, dusky, lowering, murky, pitchy; calamitous, dark, depressing, disastrous, dismal, doleful, forbidding, gloomy, melancholy, mournful, sombre, sullen.

blacken *vb* darken; deface, defile, soil, stain, sully; asperse, besmirch, calumniate, defame, malign, revile, slander, traduce, vilify.

blamable *adj* blameable, blameworthy, censurable, culpable, delinquent. faulty, remiss, reprehensible.

blame *vb* accuse, censure, condemn, disapprove, reflect upon, reprehend, reproach, reprove, upbraid. * *n* animadversion, censure, condemnation, disapproval, dispraise, disapprobation, reprehension, reproach, reproof; defect, demerit, fault, guilt, misdeed, shortcoming, sin, wrong.

blameless *adj* faultless, guiltless, inculpable, innocent, irreproachable, unblemished, undefiled, unimpeachable, unspotted, unsullied, spotless, stainless.
blanch *vb* bleach, fade, etiolate, whiten.
bland *adj* balmy, demulcent, gentle, mild, soothing, soft; affable, amiable, complaisant, kindly, mild, suave.
blandishment *n* cajolery, coaxing, compliment, fascination, fawning, flattery, wheedling
blank *adj* bare, empty, vacuous, void; amazed, astonished, confounded, confused, dumbfounded, nonplussed; absolute, complete, entire, mere, perfect, pure, simple, unabated, unadulterated, unmitigated, unmixed, utter, perfect.
blare *vb* blazon, blow, peal, proclaim, trumpet. * *n* blast, clang, clangour, peal.
blasphemy *n* impiousness, sacrilege; cursing, profanity, swearing.
blast *vb* annihilate, blight, destroy, kill, ruin, shrivel, wither; burst, explode, kill. * *n* blow, gust, squall; blare, clang, peal; burst, discharge, explosion.
blaze *vb* blazon, proclaim, publish; burn, flame, glow. * *n* flame, flare, flash, glow, light.
bleach *vb* blanch, etiolate, render white, whiten.
bleak *adj* bare, exposed, unprotected, unsheltered, storm-beaten, windswept; biting, chill, cold, piercing, raw; cheerless, comfortless, desolate, dreary, uncongenial,
blemish *vb* blur, injure, mar, spot, stain, sully, taint, tarnish; asperse, calumniate, defame, malign, revile, slander, traduce, vilify. * *n* blot, blur, defect, disfigurement, fault, flaw, imperfection, soil, speck, spot, stain, tarnish; disgrace, dishonour, reproach, stain, taint.
blend *vb* amalgamate, coalesce, combine, commingle, fuse, mingle, mix, unite. * *n* amalgamation, combination, compound, fusion, mix, mixture, union.
bless *vb* beatify, delight, gladden; adore, celebrate, exalt, extol, glorify, magnify, praise.
blessedness *n* beatitude, bliss, blissfulness, felicity, happiness, joy.
blight *vb* blast, destroy, kill, ruin, shrivel, wither; annihilate, annul, crush, disappoint, frustrate. * *n* blast, mildew, pestilence.
blind *vb* blear, darken, deprive of sight; blindfold, hoodwink. * *adj* eyeless, sightless, stone-blind, unseeing; benighted, ignorant, injudicious, purblind, undiscerning, unenlightened; concealed, confused, dark, dim, hidden, intricate, involved, labyrinthine, obscure, private, remote; careless, headlong, heedless, inconsiderate, indiscriminate, thoughtless; blank, closed, shut. * *n* cover, curtain, screen, shade, shutter; blinker; concealment, disguise, feint, pretence, pretext, ruse, stratagem, subterfuge.
blink *vb* nictate, nictitate, wink; flicker, flutter, gleam, glitter, intermit, twinkle; avoid, disregard, evade, gloss over, ignore, overlook, pass over. * *n* glance, glimpse, sight, view, wink; gleam, glimmer, sheen, shimmer, twinkle.
bliss *n* beatification, beatitude, blessedness, blissfulness, ecstasy, felicity, happiness, heaven, joy, rapture, transport.
blithe *adj* airy, animated, blithesome, buoyant, cheerful, debonair, elated, happy, jocund, joyful, joyous, lively, mirthful, sprightly, vivacious.
bloat *vb* dilate, distend, inflate, swell.
block *vb* arrest, bar, blockade, check, choke, close, hinder, impede, jam, obstruct, stop; form, mould, shape; brace, stiffen. * *n* lump, mass; blockhead, dunce, fool, simpleton; pulley, tackle; execution, scaffold; jam, obstruction, pack, stoppage.
blood *n* children, descendants, offspring, posterity, progeny; family, house, kin, kindred, line, relations; consanguinity, descent, kinship, lineage, relationship; courage, disposition, feelings, mettle, passion, spirit, temper.
bloom *vb* blossom, blow, flower; thrive, prosper. * *n* blossom, blossoming, blow, efflorescence, florescence, flowering; delicacy, delicateness, flush, freshness, heyday, prime, vigour; flush, glow, rose.
blossom *vb* bloom, blow, flower. * *n* bloom, blow, efflorescence, flower.
blot *vb* cancel, efface, erase, expunge, obliterate, rub out; blur, deface, disfigure, obscure, spot, stain, sully; disgrace, dishonour, tarnish. * *n* blemish, blur, erasure, spot, obliteration, stain; disgrace, dishonour, stigma.
blow[1] *n* bang, beat, buffet, dab, impact, knock, pat, punch, rap, slam, stroke, thump, wallop, buffet, impact; affliction, calamity, disaster, misfortune, setback.
blow[2] *vb* breathe, gasp, pant, puff; flow, move, scud, stream, waft. * *n* blast, gale, gust, squall, storm, wind.
blue *adj* azure, cerulean, cobalt, indigo, sapphire, ultramarine; ghastly, livid, pallid; dejected, depressed, dispirited, downcast, gloomy, glum, mopey, melancholic, melancholy, sad.
bluff[1] *adj* abrupt, blunt, blustering, coarse, frank, good-natured, open, outspoken; abrupt, precipitous, sheer, steep. * *n* cliff, headland, height.
bluff[2] *vb* deceive, defraud, lie, mislead. * *n* deceit, deception, feint, fraud, lie.
blunder *vb* err, flounder, mistake: stumble. * *n* error, fault, howler, mistake, solecism.
blunt *adj* dull, edgeless, obtuse, pointless, unsharpened; insensible, stolid, thick-witted; abrupt, bluff, downright, plain-spoken, outspoken, unceremonious, uncourtly. * *vb* deaden, dull, numb, weaken.
blur *vb* bedim, darken, dim, obscure; blemish, blot, spot, stain, sully, tarnish. * *n* blemish, blot, soil, spot, stain, tarnish; disgrace, smear.
blush *vb* colour, flush, glow, redden. * *n* bloom, flush, glow, colour, reddening, suffusion.
bluster *vb* boast, brag, bully, domineer, roar, swag-

ger, swell, vaunt. * *n* boisterousness, noise, tumult, turbulence; braggadocio, bravado, boasting, gasconade, swaggering.

board *n* deal, panel, plank; diet, entertainment, fare, food, meals, provision, victuals; cabinet, conclave, committee, council; directorate; panel.

boast *vb* bluster, brag, crack, flourish, crow, vaunt. * *n* blustering, boasting, bombast, brag, braggadocio, bravado, bombast, swaggering, vaunt.

bode *vb* augur, betoken, forebode, foreshadow, foretell, portend, predict, prefigure, presage, prophesy.

bodily *adj* carnal, corporeal, fleshly, physical. * *adv* altogether, completely, entirely, wholly.

body *n* carcass, corpse, remains; stem, torso, trunk; aggregate, bulk, corpus, mass; being, individual, mortal creature, person; assemblage, association, band, company, corporation, corps, coterie, force, party, society, troop; consistency, substance, thickness.

boggle *vb* demur, falter, hang fire, hesitate, shrink, vacillate, waver.

boil[1] *vb* agitate, bubble, foam, froth, rage, seethe, simmer. * *n* ebullience, ebullition.

boil[2] (*med*) gathering, pimple, pustule, swelling, tumour.

boisterous *adj* loud, roaring, stormy; clamouring, loud, noisy, obstreperous, tumultuous, turbulent.

bold *adj* adventurous, audacious, courageous; brave, daring, dauntless, doughty, fearless, gallant, hardy, heroic, intrepid, mettlesome, manful, manly, spirited, stouthearted, undaunted, valiant, valorous; assured, confident, self-reliant; assuming, forward, impertinent, impudent, insolent, push, rude, saucy; conspicuous, projecting, prominent, striking; abrupt, precipitous, prominent, steep.

bolster *vb* aid, assist, defend, help, maintain, prop, stay, support. * *n* cushion, pillow; prop, support.

bolt *vb* abscond, flee, fly. * *n* arrow, dart, missile, shaft; thunderbolt.

bombast *n* bluster, brag, braggadocio, fustian, gasconade, mouthing, pomposity, rant.

bond *vb* bind, connect, fuse, glue, join. * *adj* captive, enslaved, enthralled, subjugated. * *n* band, cord, fastening, ligament, ligature, link, nexus; bondage, captivity, chains, constraint, fetters, prison, shackle; attachment, attraction, connection, coupling, link, tie, union; compact, obligation, pledge, promise.

bondage *n* captivity, confinement, enslavement, enthralment, peonage, serfdom, servitude, slavery, thraldom, vassalage.

bonny *adj* beautiful, handsome, fair, fine, pretty; airy, blithe, buoyant, buxom, cheerful, jolly, joyous, merry. playful, sporty, sprightly, winsome.

bonus *n* gift, honorarium, premium, reward, subsidy.

booby *n* blockhead, dunce, fool, idiot, simpleton.

book *vb* bespeak, engage, reserve; programme, schedule; list, log, record, register. * *n* booklet, brochure, compendium, handbook, manual, monograph, pamphlet, textbook, tract, treatise, volume, work.

bookish *adj* erudite, learned, literary, scholarly, studious.

boon *adj* convivial, jolly, jovial, hearty; close, intimate. * *n* benefaction, favour, grant, gift, present; advantage, benefit, blessing, good, privilege.

boor *n* bumpkin, clodhopper, clown, lout, lubber, peasant, rustic, swain.

boorish *adj* awkward, bearish, clownish, course, gruff, ill-bred, loutish, lubberly, rude, rustic, uncivilized, uncouth, uneducated.

bootless *adj* abortive, fruitless, futile, profitless, vain, worthless, useless.

booty *n* loot, pillage, plunder, spoil.

border *vb* bound, edge, fringe, line, march, rim, skirt, verge; abut, adjoin, butt, conjoin, connect, neighbour. * *n* brim, brink, edge, fringe, hem, margin, rim, skirt, verge; boundary, confine, frontier, limit, march, outskirts.

bore[1] *vb* annoy, fatigue, plague, tire, trouble, vex, weary, worry. * *n* bother, nuisance, pest, worry.

bore[2] *vb* drill, perforate, pierce, sink, tunnel. * *n* calibre, hole, shaft, tunnel.

borrow *vb* take and return, use temporarily; adopt, appropriate, imitate; dissemble, feign, simulate.

boss[1] *vb* emboss, stud; * *n* knob, protuberance, stud.

boss[2] *vb* command, direct, employ, run. * *n* employer, foreman, master, overseer, superintendent.

botch *vb* blunder, bungle, cobble, mar, mend, mess, patch, spoil. * *n* blotch, pustule, sore; failure, miscarriage.

bother *vb* annoy, disturb, harass, molest, perplex, pester, plague, tease, trouble, vex, worry. * *n* annoyance, perplexity, plague, trouble, vexation.

bottom *vb* build, establish, found. * *adj* base, basic, ground, lowermost, lowest, nethermost, undermost. * *n* base, basis, foot, foundation, groundwork; dale, meadow, valley; buttocks, fundament, seat; dregs, grounds, lees, sediment.

bounce *vb* bound, jump, leap, rebound, recoil, spring. * *n* knock, thump; bound, jump, leap, spring, vault.

bound[1] *adj* assured, certain, decided, determined, resolute, resolved; confined, hampered, restricted, restrained; committed, contracted, engaged, pledged, promised; beholden, duty-bound, obligated, obliged.

bound[2] *vb* border, delimit, circumscribe, confine, demarcate, limit, restrict, terminate. * *n* boundary, confine, edge, limit, march, margin, periphery, term, verge.

bound[3] *vb* jump, leap, spring. * *n* bounce, jump, leap, spring, vault.

boundary *n* border, bourn, circuit, circumference, confine, limit, march, periphery, term, verge.

boundless *adj* endless, immeasurable, infinite, limitless, unbounded, unconfined, undefined, unlimited, vast.

bountiful *adj* beneficent, bounteous, generous, liberal, munificent, princely.

bounty *n* beneficence, benevolence, charity, donation, generosity, gift, kindness, premium, present, reward.

bourn *n* border, boundary, confine, limit; brook, burn, rill, rivulet, stream, torrent.

bow[1] *n* (*naut*) beak, prow, stem.

bow[2] *vb* arc, bend, buckle, crook, curve, droop, flex, yield; crush, depress, subdue; curtsy, genuflect, kowtow, submit. * *n* arc, bend, bilge, bulge, convex, curve, flexion; bob, curtsy, genuflection, greeting, homage, obeisance; coming out, debut, introduction; curtain call, encore.

bowels *npl* entrails, guts, insides, viscera; compassion, mercy, pity, sympathy, tenderness.

box[1] *vb* fight, hit, mill, spar. * *n* blow, buffet, fight, hit, spar.

box[2] *vb* barrel, crate, pack, parcel. * *n* case, chest, container, crate, portmanteau, trunk.

boy *n* lad, stripling, youth.

brace *vb* make tight, tighten; buttress, fortify, reinforce, shore, strengthen, support, truss. * *n* couple, pair; clamp, girder, prop, shore, stay, support, tie, truss.

brag *vb* bluster, boast, flourish, gasconade, vaunt.

branch *vb* diverge, fork, bifurcate, ramify, spread. * *n* bough, offset, limb, shoot, sprig, twig; arm, fork, ramification, spur; article, department, member, part, portion, section, subdivision.

brand *vb* denounce, stigmatize, mark. * *n* firebrand, torch; bolt, lightning flash; cachet, mark, stamp, tally; blot, reproach, stain, stigma.

brave *vb* dare, defy. * *adj* bold, courageous, fearless, heroic, intrepid, stalwart.

bravery *n* courage, daring, fearlessness, gallantry, valour.

brawl *vb* bicker, dispute, jangle, quarrel, squabble. * *n* broil, dispute, feud, fracas, fray, jangle, quarrel, row, scuffle, squabble, uproar, wrangle.

brawny *adj* athletic, lusty, muscular, powerful, robust, sinewy, stalwart, strapping, strong, sturdy.

bray *vb* clamour, hoot, roar, trumpet, vociferate. * *n* blare, crash, roar, shout.

breach *n* break, chasm, crack, disruption, fissure, flaw, fracture, opening, rent, rift, rupture; alienation, difference, disaffection, disagreement, split.

bread *n* aliment, diet, fare, food, nourishment, nutriment, provisions, regimen, victuals.

break *vb* crack, disrupt, fracture, part, rend, rive, sever; batter, burst, crush, shatter, smash, splinter; cashier, degrade, discard, discharge, dismiss; disobey, infringe, transgress, violate; intermit, interrupt, stop; disclose, open, unfold. * *n* aperture, breach, chasm, fissure, gap, rent, rip, rupture; break-up, crash, debacle.

breast *vb* face, oppose, resist, stem, withstand. * *n* bosom, chest, thorax; affections, conscience, heart; mammary gland, mammary organ, pap, udder.

breath *n* exhaling, inhaling, pant, sigh, respiration, whiff; animation, existence, life; pause, respite, rest; breathing space, instant, moment.

breathe *vb* live, exist; emit, exhale, give out; diffuse, express, indicate, manifest, show.

breed *vb* bear, beget, engender, hatch, produce; bring up, foster, nourish, nurture, raise, rear; discipline, educate, instruct, nurture, rear, school, teach, train; generate, originate. * *n* extraction, family, lineage, pedigree, progeny, race, strain.

brevity *n* briefness, compression, conciseness, curtness, pithiness, shortness, terseness, transiency.

brew *vb* concoct, contrive, devise, excite, foment, instigate, plot. * *n* beverage, concoction, drink, liquor, mixture, potation.

bribe *vb* buy, corrupt, influence, pay off, suborn. * *n* allurement, corruption, enticement, graft, pay-off, subornation.

bridle *vb* check, curb, control, govern, restrain. * *n* check, control, curb.

brief *vb* direct, give directions, instruct; capsulate, summarize, delineate, describe, draft, outline, sketch; (*law*) retain. * *adj* concise, curt, inconsiderable, laconic, pithy, short, succinct, terse; fleeting, momentary, short, temporary, transient. * *n* abstract, breviary, briefing, epitome, compendium, summary, syllabus; (*law*) precept, writ.

brigand *n* bandit, footpad, freebooter, gangster, highwayman, marauder, outlaw, robber, thug.

bright *adj* blazing, brilliant, dazzling, gleaming, glowing, light, luminous, radiant, shining, sparkling, sunny; clear, cloudless, lambent, lucid, transparent; famous, glorious, illustrious; acute, discerning, ingenious, intelligent, keen; auspicious, cheering, encouraging, exhilarating, favourable, inspiring, promising, propitious; cheerful, genial, happy, lively, merry, pleasant, smiling, vivacious.

brilliant *adj* beaming, bright, effulgent, gleaming, glistening, glittering, lustrous, radiant, resplendent, shining, sparkling splendid; admirable, celebrated, distinguished, famous, glorious, illustrious, renowned; dazzling, decided, prominent, signal, striking, unusual.

brim *n* border, brink, edge, rim, margin, skirt, verge; bank, border, coast, margin, shore.

bring *vb* bear, convey, fetch; accompany, attend, conduct, convey, convoy, guide, lead; gain, get, obtain, procure, produce.

brisk *adj* active, alert, agile, lively, nimble, perky, quick, smart, spirited, spry.

brittle *adj* brash, breakable, crisp, crumbling, fragile, frangible, frail, shivery.

broach *vb* open, pierce, set; approach, break, hint, suggest; proclaim, publish, utter.

broad *adj* ample, expansive, extensive, large, spacious, sweeping, vast, wide; enlarged, hospitable, liberal, tolerant; diffused, open, spread;

coarse, gross, indecent, indelicate, unrefined, vulgar.
broaden *vb* augment, enlarge, expand, extend, increase, spread, stretch, widen.
broken *adj* fractured, rent, ruptured, separated, severed, shattered, shivered, torn; exhausted, feeble, impaired, shaken, shattered, spent, wasted; defective, halting, hesitating, imperfect, stammering, stumbling; contrite, humble, lowly, penitent; abrupt, craggy, precipitous, rough.
broker *n* agent, factor, go-between, middleman.
brood *vb* incubate, sit. * *n* issue, offspring, progeny; breed, kind, line, lineage, sort, strain.
brook *vb* abide, bear, endure, suffer, tolerate. * *n* burn, beck, creek, rill, rivulet, run, streamlet.
brotherhood *n* association, clan, clique, coterie, fraternity, junta, society.
brotherly *adj* affectionate, amicable, cordial, friendly, kind.
browbeat *vb* bully, intimidate, overawe, overbear.
bruise *vb* contuse, crunch, squeeze; batter, break, maul, pound, pulverize; batter, deface, indent. * *n* blemish, contusion, swelling.
brush[1] *n* brushwood, bush, scrub, scrubwood, shrubs, thicket, wilderness.
brush[2] *vb* buff, clean, polish, swab, sweep, wipe; curry, groom, rub down; caress, flick, glance, graze, scrape, skim, touch. * *n* besom, broom; action, affair, collision, contest, conflict, encounter, engagement, fight, skirmish.
brutal *adj* barbaric, barbarous, brutish, cruel, ferocious, inhuman, ruthless, savage; bearish, brusque, churlish, gruff, impolite, harsh, rude, rough, truculent, uncivil.
brute *n* barbarian, beast, monster, ogre, savage; animal, beast, creature. * *adj* carnal, mindless, physical; bestial, coarse, gross.
bubble *vb* boil, effervesce, foam. * *n* bead, blob, fluid, globule; bagatelle, trifle; cheat, delusion, hoax.
buccaneer *n* corsair, freebooter, pirate.
buck *vb* jump, leap. * *n* beau, blade, blood, dandy, fop, gallant, spark; male.
bud *vb* burgeon, germinate, push, shoot, sprout, vegetate. * *n* burgeon, gem, germ, gemmule, shoot, sprout.
budget *vb* allocate, cost, estimate. * *n* account, estimate, financial statement; assets, finances, funds, means, resources; bag, bundle, pack, packet, parcel, roll; assortment, batch, collection, lot, set, store.
buffet[1] *vb* beat, box, cuff, slap, smite, strike; resist, struggle against, * *n* blow, box, cuff, slap, strike;
buffet[2] *n* cupboard, sideboard; refreshment counter.
buffoon *n* antic, clown, droll, fool, harlequin, jester, mountebank.
build *vb* construct, erect, establish, fabricate, fashion, model, raise, rear. * *n* body, figure, form, frame, physique; construction, shape, structure.
building *n* construction, erection, fabrication; edifice, fabric, house, pile, substructure, structure,
bulk *n* dimension, magnitude, mass, size, volume; amplitude, bulkiness, massiveness; body, majority, mass.
bully *vb* browbeat, bulldoze, domineer, haze, hector, intimidate, overbear. * *n* blusterer, browbeater, bulldozer, hector, swaggerer, roisterer, tyrant.
bulwark *n* barrier, fortification, parapet, rampart, wall; palladium, safeguard, security.
bump *vb* collide, knock, strike, thump. * *n* blow, jar, jolt, knock, shock, thump; lump, protuberance, swelling.
bunch *vb* assemble, collect, crowd, group, herd, pack. * *n* bulge, bump, bundle, hump, knob, lump, protuberance; cluster, hand, fascicle; assortment, batch, collection, group, lot, parcel, set; knot, tuft.
bundle *vb* bale, pack, package, parcel, truss, wrap. * *n* bale, batch, bunch, collection, heap, pack, package, packet, parcel, pile, roll, truss.
bungler *n* botcher, duffer, fumbler, lout, lubber, mis-manager, muddler.
burden *vb* encumber, grieve, load, oppress, overlay, overload, saddle, surcharge, try. * *n* capacity, cargo, freight, lading, load, tonnage, weight; affliction, charge, clog, encumbrance, impediment, grievance, sorrow, trial, trouble; drift, point, substance, tenor, surcharge.
bureau *n* chest of drawers, dresser; counting room, office.
burial *n* burying, entombment, inhumation, interment, sepulture.
burlesque *vb* ape, imitate, lampoon, mock, ridicule, satirize. * *n* caricature, extravaganza, parody, send-up, take-off, travesty.
burn[1] *n* beck, brook, gill, rill, rivulet, runnel, runlet, stream. water
burn[2] *vb* blaze, conflagrate, enflame, fire, flame, ignite, kindle, light, smoulder; cremate, incinerate; scald, scorch, singe; boil, broil, cook, roast, seethe, simmer, stew, swelter, toast; bronze, brown, sunburn, suntan, tan; bake, desiccate, dry, parch, sear, shrivel, wither; glow, incandesce, tingle, warm. * *n* scald, scorch, singe; sunburn.
burning *adj* aflame, fiery, hot, scorching; ardent, earnest, fervent, fervid, impassioned, intense.
burnish *vb* brighten, buff, furbish, polish, shine. * *n* glaze, gloss, patina, polish, shine.
burst *vb* break open, be rent, explode, shatter, split open. * *adj* broken, kaput, punctured, ruptured, shattered, split. * *n* break, breakage, breach, fracture, rupture; blast, blowout, blowup, discharge, detonation, explosion; spurt; blaze, flare, flash; cloudburst, downpour; bang, crack, crash, report, sound; fusillade, salvo, spray, volley, outburst, outbreak flare-up, blaze, eruption.
bury *vb* entomb, inearth, inhume, inter; conceal, hide, secrete, shroud.
business *n* calling, employment, occupation, pro-

fession, pursuit, vocation; commerce, dealing, trade, traffic; affair, concern, engagement, matter, transaction, undertaking; duty, function, office, task, work.

bustle *vb* fuss, hurry, scurry. * *n* ado, commotion, flurry, fuss, hurry, hustle, pother, stir, tumult.

busy *vb* devote, employ, engage, occupy, spend, work. * *adj* employed, engaged, occupied; active, assiduous, diligent, engrossed, industrious, sedulous, working; agile, brisk, nimble, spry, stirring; meddling, officious.

but *conj* except, excepting, further, howbeit, moreover, still, unless, yet. * *adv* all the same, even, notwithstanding, still, yet.

butchery *n* massacre, murder, slaughter.

butt[1] *vb* bunt, push, shove, shunt, strike; encroach, impose, interfere, intrude, invade, obtrude. * *n* buck, bunt, push, shove, shunt, thrust.

butt[2] *n* barrel, cask.

butt[3] *n* aim, goal, mark, object, point, target; dupe, gull, victim.

butt[4] *vb* abut, adjoin, conjoin, connect, neighbour. * *n* end, piece, remainder, stub, stump; buttocks, posterior, rump.

buttonhole *vb* bore, catch, detain in conversation, importune.

buttress *vb* brace, prop, shore, stay, support. * *n* brace, bulwark, prop, stay, support.

buxom *adj* comely, fresh, healthy, hearty, plump, rosy, ruddy, vigorous.

byword *n* adage, aphorism, apothegm, dictum, maxim, proverb, saying, saw.

C

cabal *vb* conspire, intrigue, machinate, plot. * *n* clique, combination, confederacy, coterie, faction, gang, junta, league, party, set; conspiracy, intrigue, machination, plot.

cabbalistic, cabalistic *adj* dark, fanciful, mysterious, mystic, occult, secret.

cabaret *n* tavern, inn, public house, wine shop.

cabin *n* berth, bunk, cot, cottage, crib, dwelling, hovel, hut, shack, shanty, shed.

cabinet *n* apartment, boudoir, chamber, closet; case, davenport, desk, escritoire; council, ministry.

cachinnation *n* guffaw, laugh, laughter.

cackle *vb* giggle, laugh, snicker, titter; babble, chatter, gabble, palaver, prate, prattle, titter. * *n* babble, chatter, giggle, prate, prattle, snigger, titter.

cacophonous *adj* discordant, grating, harsh, inharmonious, jarring, raucous.

cadaverous *adj* bloodless, deathlike, ghastly, pale, pallid, wan.

cage *vb* confine, immure, imprison, incarcerate. * *n* coop, pen, pound.

caitiff *adj* base, craven, pusillanimous, rascally, recreant. * *n* coward, knave, miscreant, rascal, rogue, scoundrel, sneak, traitor, vagabond, villain, wretch.

cajole *vb* blandish, coax, flatter, jolly, wheedle; beguile, deceive, delude, entrap, inveigle, tempt.

calamity *n* adversity, affliction, blow, casualty, cataclysm, catastrophe, disaster, distress, downfall, evil, hardship, mischance, misery, misfortune, mishap, reverse, ruin, stroke, trial, visitation.

calculate *vb* cast, compute, count, estimate, figure, rate, reckon, weigh; tell.

calculating *adj* crafty, designing, scheming, selfish; careful, cautious, circumspect, far-sighted, politic, sagacious, wary.

calefaction *n* heating, warming; hotness, incandescence, warmth.

calendar *n* almanac, ephemeris, register; catalogue, list, schedule.

calibre *n* bore, capacity, diameter, gauge; ability, capacity, endowment, faculty, gifts, parts, scope, talent.

call *vb* christen, denominate, designate, dub, entitle, name, phrase, style, term; bid, invite, summons; assemble, convene, convoke, muster; cry, exclaim; arouse, awaken, proclaim, rouse, shout, waken; appoint, elect, ordain. * *n* cry, outcry, voice; appeal, invitation, summons; claim, demand, summons; appointment, election, invitation.

calling *n* business, craft, employment, occupation, profession, pursuit, trade.

callous *adj* hard, hardened, indurated; apathetic, dull, indifferent, insensible, inured, obdurate, obtuse, sluggish, torpid, unfeeling, unsusceptible.

callow *adj* naked, unfeathered, unfledged; green, immature, inexperienced, sappy, silly, soft, unfledged, unsophisticated.

calm *vb* allay, becalm, compose, hush, lull, smooth, still, tranquillize; alleviate, appease, assuage, moderate, mollify, pacify, quiet, soften, soothe, tranquillize. * *adj* halcyon, mild, peaceful, placid, quiet, reposeful, serene, smooth, still, tranquil, unruffled; collected, cool, composed, controlled, impassive, imperturbable, sedate, self-possessed, undisturbed, unperturbed, unruffled, untroubled. * *n* lull; equanimity, peace, placidity, quiet, repose, serenity, stillness, tranquillity.

calorific *adj* heat, heat-producing.

calumniate *vb* abuse, asperse, backbite, blacken, blemish, defame, discredit, disparage, lampoon, libel, malign, revile, slander, traduce, vilify.

calumny *n* abuses, aspersion, backbiting, defamation, detraction, evil-speaking, insult, libel, lying, obloquy, slander, vilification, vituperation.

camarilla *n* cabal, clique, junta, ring.

camber *vb* arch, bend, curve. * *n* arch, arching, convexity.

camp[1] *vb* bivouac, encamp, lodge, pitch, tent. * *n* bivouac, cantonment, encampment, laager; cabal, circle, clique, coterie, faction, group, junta, party, ring, set.

camp[2] *adj* affected, artificial, effeminate, exaggerated, mannered, theatrical.

canaille *n* mob, populace, proletariat, rabble, ragbag, riffraff, scum.

canal *n* channel, duct, pipe, tube.

cancel *vb* blot, efface, erase, expunge, obliterate; abrogate, annul, countermand, nullify, quash, repeal, rescind, revoke.

candelabrum *n* candlestick, chandelier, lustre.

candid *adj* fair, impartial, just, unbiased, unprejudiced; artless, frank, free, guileless, honest, honourable, ingenuous, naive, open, plain, sincere, straightforward.

candidate *n* applicant, aspirant, claimant, competitor, probationer.

candour *n* fairness, impartiality, justice; artlessness, frankness, guilelessness, honesty, ingenuousness, openness, simplicity, sincerity, straightforwardness, truthfulness.

canker *vb* corrode, erode, rot, rust, waste; blight, consume, corrupt, embitter, envenom, infect, poison, sour. * *n* gangrene, rot; bale, bane, blight, corruption, infection, irritation.

canon *n* catalogue, criterion, formula, formulary, law, regulation, rule, standard, statute.

canorous *adj* musical, tuneful.

cant[1] *vb* whine. * *adj* current, partisan, popular, rote, routine, set; argotic, slangy. * *n* hypocrisy; argot, jargon, lingo, slang.

cant[2] *vb* bevel, incline, list, slant, tilt, turn. * *n* bevel, inclination, leaning, list, pitch, slant, tilt, turn.

cantankerous *adj* contumacious, crabbed, cross-grained, dogged, headstrong, heady, intractable, obdurate, obstinate, perverse, refractory, stiff, stubborn, wilful, unyielding.

canting *adj* affected, pious, sanctimonious, whining.

canvas *n* burlap, scrim, tarpaulin.

canvass *vb* discuss, dispute; analyze, consider, examine, investigate, review, scrutinize, sift, study; campaign, electioneer, solicit votes. * *n* debate, discussion, dispute; examination, scrutiny, sifting.

canyon *n* gorge, gulch, ravine.

cap *vb* cover, surmount; complete, crown, finish; exceed, overtop, surpass, transcend; match, parallel, pattern. * *n* beret, head-cover, head-dress; acme, chief, crown, head, peak, perfection, pitch, summit, top.

capability *n* ability, brains, calibre, capableness, capacity, competency, efficiency, faculty, force, power, scope, skill.

capable *adj* adapted, fitted, qualified, suited; able, accomplished, clever, competent, efficient, gifted, ingenious, intelligent, sagacious, skilful.

capacious *adj* ample, broad, comprehensive, expanded, extensive, large, roomy, spacious, wide.

capacitate *vb* enable, qualify.

capacity *n* amplitude, dimensions, magnitude, volume; aptitude, aptness, brains, calibre, discernment, faculty, forte, genius, gift, parts, power, talent, turn, wit; ability, capability, calibre, cleverness, competency, efficiency, skill; character, charge, function, office, position, post, province, service, sphere.

caparison *vb* accoutre, costume, equip, outfit, rig out. * *n* accoutrements, armour, get-up, harness, housing, livery, outfit, panoply, tack, tackle, trappings, turnout .

caper *vb* bound, caracole, frisk, gambol, hop, leap, prank, romp, skip, spring. * *n* bound, dance, gambol, frisk, hop, jump, leap, prance, romp, skip.

capillary *adj* delicate, fine, minute, slender.

capital *adj* cardinal, chief, essential, important, leading, main, major, pre-eminent, principal, prominent; fatal; excellent, first-class, first-rate, good, prime, splendid. * *n* chief city, metropolis, seat; money, estate, investments, shares, stock.

caprice *n* crotchet, fancy, fickleness, freak, humour, inconstancy, maggot, phantasy, quirk, vagary, whim, whimsy.

capricious *adj* changeable, crotchety, fanciful, fantastical, fickle, fitful, freakish, humoursome, odd, puckish, queer, uncertain, variable, wayward, whimsical.

capsize *vb* overturn, upset.

capsule *n* case, covering, envelope, sheath, shell, wrapper: pericarp, pod, seed-vessel.

captain *vb* command, direct, head, lead, manage, officer, preside. * *n* chief, chieftain, commander, leader, master, officer, soldier, warrior.

captious *adj* carping, caviling, censorious, critical, fault-finding, hypercritical; acrimonious, cantankerous, contentious, crabbed, cross, snappish, snarling, splenetic, testy, touchy, waspish; ensnaring, insidious.

captivate *vb* allure, attract, bewitch, catch, capture, charm, enamour, enchant, enthral, fascinate, gain, hypnotize, infatuate, win.

captivity *n* confinement, durance, duress, imprisonment; bondage, enthralment, servitude, slavery, subjection, thraldom, vassalage.

capture *vb* apprehend, arrest, catch, seize. * *n* apprehension, arrest, catch, catching, imprisonment, seizure; bag, prize.

carcass *n* body, cadaver, corpse, corse, remains.

cardinal *adj* capital, central, chief, essential, first, important, leading, main, pre-eminent, primary, principal, vital.

care *n* anxiety, concern, perplexity, trouble, solicitude, worry; attention, carefulness, caution, circumspection, heed, regard, vigilance, wariness, watchfulness; charge, custody, guardianship, keep, oversight, superintendence, ward; burden, charge, concern, responsibility.

careful *adj* anxious, solicitous, concerned, troubled, uneasy; attentive, heedful, mindful, regardful, thoughtful; cautious, canny, circumspect, discreet, leery, vigilant, watchful.

careless *adj* carefree, nonchalant, unapprehensive, undisturbed, unperplexed, unsolicitous, untroubled; disregardful, heedless, inattentive, incautious, inconsiderate, neglectful, negligent, regardless, remiss, thoughtless, unobservant, unconcerned, unconsidered, unmindful, unthinking.

carelessness *n* heedlessness, inadvertence, inattention, inconsiderateness, neglect, negligence, remissness, slackness, thoughtlessness, unconcern.

caress *vb* coddle, cuddle, cosset, embrace, fondle, hug, kiss, pet. * *n* cuddle, embrace, fondling, hug, kiss.

caressing *n* blandishment, dalliance, endearment, fondling.

cargo *n* freight, lading. load.

caricature *vb* burlesque, parody, send-up, take-off, travesty. * *n* burlesque, farce, ludicrous, parody, representation, take-off, travesty.

carious *adj* decayed, mortified, putrid, rotten, ulcerated.
cark *vb* annoy, fret, grieve, harass, perplex, worry.
carnage *n* bloodshed, butchery, havoc, massacre, murder, slaughter.
carnal *adj* animal, concupiscent, fleshly, lascivious, lecherous, lewd, libidinous, lubricous, lustful, salacious, sensual, voluptuous; bodily, earthy, mundane. natural, secular, temporal, unregenerate, unspiritual.
carol *vb* chant, hum, sing, warble. * *n* canticle, chorus, ditty, hymn, lay, song, warble.
carousal *n* banquet, entertainment, feast, festival, merry-making, regale; bacchanal, carouse, debauch, jamboree, jollification, orgy, revel, revelling, revelry, saturnalia, spree, wassail.
carp *vb* cavil, censure, criticize, fault.
carping *adj* captious, cavilling, censorious, hypercritical. * *n* cavil, censure, fault-finding, hypercriticism.
carriage *n* conveyance, vehicle; air, bearing, behaviour, conduct, demeanour, deportment, front, mien, port.
carry *vb* bear, convey, transfer, transmit, transport; impel, push forward, urge; accomplish, compass, effect, gain, secure; bear up, support, sustain; infer, involve, imply, import, signify.
cart *n* conveyance, tumbril, van, vehicle, wagon.
carte-blanche *n* authority, power.
carve *vb* chisel, cut, divide, engrave, grave, hack, hew, indent, incise, sculpt, sculpture; fashion, form, mould, shape.
cascade *vb* cataract, descend, drop, engulf, fall, inundate, overflow, plunge, tumble. * *n* cataract, fall, falls, force, linn, waterfall.
case[1] *vb* cover, encase, enclose, envelop, protect, wrap; box, pack. * *n* capsule, covering, sheathe; box, cabinet, container, holder, receptacle.
case[2] *n* condition, plight, predicament, situation, state; example, instance, occurrence; circumstance, condition, contingency, event; action, argument, cause, lawsuit, process, suit, trial.
case-hardened *adj* hardened, indurated, steeled; brazen, brazen-faced, obdurate, reprobate.
cash *n* banknotes, bullion, coin, currency, money, payment, specie.
cashier *vb* break, discard, discharge, dismiss.
cast *vb* fling, hurl, pitch, send, shy, sling, throw, toss; drive, force, impel, thrust; lay aside, put off, shed; calculate, compute, reckon; communicate, diffuse, impart, shed, throw. * *n* fling, throw, toss; shade, tinge, tint, touch; air, character, look, manner, mien, style, tone, turn; form, mould.
castaway *adj* abandoned, cast-off, discarded, rejected. * *n* derelict, outcast, reprobate, vagabond.
caste *n* class, grade, lineage, order, race, rank, species, status.
castigate *vb* beat, chastise, flog, lambaste, lash, thrash, whip; chaste, correct, discipline, punish; criticize, flagellate, upbraid.
castle *n* citadel, fortress, stronghold.
castrate *vb* caponize, emasculate, geld; mortify, subdue, suppress, weaken.
casual *adj* accidental, contingent, fortuitous, incidental, irregular, occasional, random, uncertain, unforeseen, unintentional, unpremeditated; informal, relaxed.
casualty *n* chance, contingency, fortuity, mishap; accident, catastrophe, disaster, mischance, misfortune.
cat *n* grimalkin, kitten, puss, tabby, tomcat.
cataclysm *n* deluge, flood, inundation; disaster, upheaval.
catacomb *n* crypt, tomb, vault.
catalogue *vb* alphabetize, categorize, chronicle, class, classify, codify, file, index, list, record, tabulate. * *n* enumeration, index, inventory, invoice, list, record, register, roll, schedule.
cataract *n* cascade, fall, waterfall.
catastrophe *n* conclusion, consummation, denouement, end, finale, issue, termination, upshot; adversity, blow, calamity, cataclysm, debacle, disaster, ill, misfortune, mischance, mishap, trial, trouble.
catch *vb* clutch, grasp, gripe, nab, seize, snatch; apprehend, arrest, capture; overtake; enmesh, ensnare, entangle, entrap, lime, net; bewitch, captivate, charm, enchant, fascinate, win; surprise, take unawares. * *n* arrest, capture, seizure; bag, find, haul, plum, prize; drawback, fault, hitch, obstacle, rub, snag; captive, conquest.
catching *adj* communicable, contagious, infectious, pestiferous, pestilential; attractive, captivating, charming, enchanting, fascinating, taking, winning, winsome.
catechize *adj* examine, interrogate, question, quiz.
catechumen *n* convert, disciple, learner, neophyte, novice, proselyte, pupil, tyro.
categorical *adj* absolute, direct, downright, emphatic, explicit, express, positive, unconditional, unqualified, unreserved, utter.
category *n* class, division, head, heading, list, order, rank, sort.
catenation *n* conjunction, connection, union.
cater *vb* feed, provide, purvey.
cathartic *adj* abstergent, aperient, cleansing, evacuant, laxative, purgative. * *n* aperient, laxative, physic, purgative, purge.
catholic *adj* general, universal, world-wide; charitable, liberal, tolerant, unbigoted, unexclusive, unsectarian.
cause *vb* breed, create, originate, produce; effect, effectuate, occasion, produce. * *n* agent, creator, mainspring, origin, original, producer, source, spring; account, agency, consideration, ground, incentive, incitement, inducement, motive, reason; aim, end, object, purpose; action, case, suit, trial.
caustic *adj* acrid, cathartic, consuming, corroding, corrosive, eating, erosive, mordant, virulent; biting, bitter, burning, cutting, sarcastic, satirical, scalding, scathing, severe, sharp, stinging.

caution *vb* admonish, forewarn, warn. * *n* care, carefulness, circumspection, discretion, forethought, heed, heedfulness, providence, prudence, wariness, vigilance, watchfulness; admonition, advice, counsel,injunction, warning.
cautious *adj* careful, chary, circumspect, discreet, heedful, prudent, wary, vigilant, wary, watchful.
cavalier *adj* arrogant, curt, disdainful, haughty, insolent, scornful, supercilious; debonair, gallant, gay. * *n* chevalier, equestrian, horseman, horse-soldier, knight.
cave *n* cavern, cavity, den, grot, grotto.
cavil *vb* carp, censure, hypercriticize, object.
cavilling *adj* captious, carping, censorious, critical, hypercritical.
cavity *n* hollow, pocket, vacuole, void.
cease *vb* desist, intermit, pause, refrain, stay, stop; fail; discontinue, end, quit, terminate.
ceaseless *adj* continual, continuous, incessant, unceasing, unintermitting, uninterrupted, unremitting; endless, eternal, everlasting, perpetual.
cede *vb* abandon, abdicate, relinquish, resign, surrender, transfer, yield; convey, grant.
celebrate *vb* applaud, bless, commend, emblazon, extol, glorify, laud, magnify, praise, trumpet; commemorate, honour, keep, observe; solemnize.
celebrated *adj* distinguished, eminent, famed, famous, glorious, illustrious, notable, renowned.
celebrity *n* credit, distinction, eminence, fame, glory, honour, renown, reputation, repute; lion, notable, star.
celerity *n* fleetness, haste, quickness, rapidity, speed, swiftness, velocity.
celestial *adj* empyreal, empyrean; angelic, divine, god-like, heavenly, seraphic, supernal, supernatural.
celibate *adj* single, unmarried. * *n* bachelor, single, virgin.
cellular *adj* alveolate, honeycombed.
cement *vb* attach, bind, join, combine, connect, solder, unite, weld; cohere, stick. * *n* glue, paste, mortar, solder.
cemetery *n* burial-ground, burying-ground, churchyard, god's acre, graveyard, necropolis.
censor *vb* blue-pencil, bowdlerize, cut, edit, expurgate; classify, kill, quash, squash, suppress. * *n* caviller, censurer, faultfinder.
censorious *adj* captious, carping, caviling, condemnatory, faultfinding, hypercritical, severe.
censure *vb* abuse, blame, chide, condemn, rebuke, reprehend, reprimand, reproach, reprobate, reprove, scold, upbraid. **n* animadversion, blame, condemnation, criticism, disapprobation, disapproval, rebuke, remonstrance, reprehension, reproach, reproof, stricture.
ceremonious *adj* civil, courtly, lofty, stately; formal, studied; exact, formal, punctilious, precise, starched, stiff.
ceremony *n* ceremonial, etiquette, form, formality, observance, solemnity, rite; parade, pomp, show, stateliness.
certain *adj* absolute, incontestable, incontrovertible, indisputable, indubitable, positive, undeniable, undisputed, unquestionable, unquestioned; assured, confident, sure, undoubting; infallible, never-failing, unfailing; actual, existing, real; constant, determinate, fixed, settled, stated.
certainty *n* indubitability, indubitableness, inevitableness, inevitability, surety, unquestionability, unquestionableness; assurance, assuredness, certitude, confidence, conviction, surety.
certify *vb* attest, notify, testify, vouch; ascertain, determine, verify, show.
cerulean *adj* azure, blue, sky-blue.
cessation *n* ceasing, discontinuance, intermission, pause, remission, respite, rest, stop, stoppage, suspension.
cession *n* abandonment, capitulation, ceding, concession, conveyance, grant, relinquishement, renunciation, surrender, yielding.
chafe *vb* rub; anger, annoy, chagrin, enrage, exasperate, fret, gall, incense, irritate, nettle, offend, provoke, ruffle, tease, vex; fret, fume, rage.
chaff *vb* banter, deride, jeer, mock, rally, ridicule. scoff. * *n* glumes, hulls, husks; refuse, rubbish, trash, waste.
chaffer *n* bargain, haggle, higgle, negotiate.
chagrin *vb* annoy, chafe, displease, irritate, mortify, provoke, vex. * *n* annoyance, displeasure, disquiet, dissatisfaction, fretfulness, humiliation, ill-humour, irritation, mortification, spleen, vexation.
chain *vb* bind, confine, fetter, manacle, restrain, shackle, trammel; enslave. * *n* bond, fetter, manacle, shackle, union.
chalice *n* bowl, cup, goblet.
challenge *vb* brave, call out, dare, defy, dispute; demand, require. * *n* defiance, interrogation, question; exception, objection.
chamber *n* apartment, hall, room; cavity, hollow.
champion *vb* advocate, defend, uphold. * *n* defender, promoter, protector, vindicator; belt-holder, hero, victor, warrior, winner.
chance *vb* befall, betide, happen, occur. * *adj* accidental, adventitious, casual, fortuitous, incidental, unexpected, unforeseen. * *n* accident, cast, fortuity, fortune, hap, luck; contingency, possibility; occasion, opening, opportunity; contingency, fortuity, gamble, peradventure, uncertainty; hazard, jeopardy, peril, risk.
change *vb* alter, fluctuate, modify, vary; displace, remove, replace, shift, substitute; barter, commute, exchange. * *n* alteration, mutation, revolution, transition, transmutation, turning, variance, variation; innovation, novelty, variety, vicissitude.
changeable *adj* alterable, inconstant, modifiable, mutable, uncertain, unsettled, unstable, unsteadfast, unsteady, variable, variant; capricious, fickle, fitful, flighty, giddy, mercurial, vacillating, volatile, wavering.
changeless *adj* abiding, consistent, constant, fixed,

immutable, permanent, regular, reliable, resolute, settled, stationary, unalterable, unchanging.
channel *vb* chamfer, cut, flute, groove. * *n* canal, conduit, duct, passage; aqueduct, canal, chute, drain, flume, furrow; chamfer, groove, fluting, furrow, gutter.
chant *vb* carol, sing, warble; intone, recite; canticle, song.
chaos *n* anarchy, confusion, disorder.
chapfallen *adj* blue, crest-fallen, dejected, depressed, despondent, discouraged, disheartened, dispirited, downcast, downhearted, low-spirited, melancholy, sad.
chaplet *n* coronal, garland, wreath.
char *vb* burn, scorch.
character *n* emblem, figure, hieroglyph, ideograph, letter, mark, sign, symbol; bent, constitution, cast, disposition, nature, quality; individual, original, person, personage; reputation, repute; nature, traits; eccentric, trait.
characteristic *adj* distinctive, peculiar, singular, special, specific, typical. * *n* attribute, feature, idiosyncrasy, lineament, mark, peculiarity, quality, trait.
charge *vb* burden, encumber, freight, lade, load; entrust; ascribe, impute, lay; accuse, arraign, blame, criminate, impeach, inculpate, indict, involve; bid, command, exhort, enjoin, order, require, tax; assault, attack bear down. * *n* burden, cargo, freight, lading, load; care, custody, keeping, management, ward; commission, duty, employment, office, trust; responsibility, trust; command, direction, injunction, mandate, order, precept; exhortation, instruction; cost, debit, expense, expenditure, outlay; price, sum; assault, attack, encounter, onset, onslaught.
charger *n* dish, platter; mount, steed, war-horse.
charily *adv* carefully, cautiously, distrustfully, prudently, sparingly, suspiciously, warily.
charitable *adj* beneficial, beneficent, benignant, bountiful, generous, kind, liberal, open-handed; candid, considerate, lenient, mild.
charity *n* benevolence, benignity, fellow-feeling, good-nature, goodwill, kind-heartedness, kindness, tenderheartedness; beneficence, bounty, generosity, humanity, philanthropy. liberality.
charlatan *n* cheat, empiric, impostor, mountebank, pretender, quack.
charm *vb* allure, attract, becharm, bewitch, captivate, catch, delight, enamour, enchain, enchant, enrapture, enravish, fascinate, transport, win. * *n* enchantment, incantation, magic, necromancy, sorcery, spell, witchery; amulet, talisman; allurement, attraction, attractiveness, fascination.
charming *adj* bewitching, captivating, delightful, enchanting, enrapturing, fascinating, lovely.
charter *vb* incorporate; hire, let. * *n* franchise, immunity, liberty, prerogation, privilege, right; bond, deed, indenture, instrument, prerogative.
chary *adj* careful, cautious, circumspect, shy, wary; abstemious, careful, choice, economical, frugal, provident, saving, sparing, temperate, thrifty, unwasteful.
chase *vb* follow, hunt, pursue, track; emboss. * *n* course, field-sport, hunt, hunting.
chasm *n* cavity, cleft, fissure, gap, hollow, hiatus, opening.
chaste *adj* clean, continent, innocent, modest, pure, pure-minded, undefiled, virtuous; chastened, pure, simple, unaffected, uncorrupt.
chasten *vb* correct, humble; purify, refine, render, subdue.
chastening *n* chastisement, correction, discipline, humbling.
chastise *vb* castigate, correct, flog, lash, punish, whip; chasten, correct, discipline, humble, punish, subdue.
chastity *n* abstinence, celibacy, continence, innocence, modesty, pure-mindedness, purity, virtue; cleanness, decency; chasteness, refinement, restrainedness, simplicity, sobriety, unaffectedness.
chat *vb* babble, chatter, confabulate, gossip, prate, prattle. * *n* chit-chat, confabulation, conversation, gossip, prattle.
chatter *vb* babble, chat, confabulate, gossip, prate, prattle. * *n* babble, chat, gabble, jabber, patter, prattle.
cheap *adj* inexpensive, low-priced; common, indifferent, inferior, mean, meretricious, paltry, poor.
cheapen *vb* belittle, depreciate.
cheat *vb* cozen, deceive, dissemble, juggle, shuffle; bamboozle, befool, beguile, cajole, circumvent, deceive, defraud, chouse, delude, dupe, ensnare, entrap, fool, gammon, gull, hoax, hoodwink, inveigle, jockey, mislead, outwit, overreach, trick. * *n* artifice, beguilement, blind, catch, chouse, deceit, deception, fraud, imposition, imposture, juggle, pitfall, snare, stratagem, swindle, trap, trick, wile; counterfeit, deception, delusion, illusion, mockery, paste, sham, tinsel; beguiler, charlatan, cheater, cozener, impostor, jockey, knave, mountebank, trickster, rogue, render, sharper, seizer, shuffler, swindler, taker, tearer.
check *vb* block, bridle, control, counteract, curb, hinder, obstruct, repress, restrain; chide, rebuke, reprimand, reprove. * *n* bar, barrier, block, brake, bridle, clog, control, curb, damper, hindrance, impediment, interference, obstacle, obstruction, rebuff, repression, restraint, stop, stopper.
cheep *vb* chirp, creak, peep, pipe, squeak.
cheer *vb* animate, encourage, enliven, exhilarate, gladden, incite, inspirit; comfort, console, solace; applaud, clap. * *n* cheerfulness, gaiety, gladness, glee, hilarity, jollity, joy, merriment, mirth; entertainment, food, provision, repast, viands, victuals; acclamation, hurrah, huzza.
cheerful *adj* animated, airy, blithe, buoyant, cheery, gay, glad, gleeful, happy, joyful, jocund, jolly, joyous, light-hearted, lightsome, lively, merry, mirthful, sprightly, sunny; animating,

cheering, cheery, encouraging, enlivening, glad, gladdening, gladsome, grateful, inspiriting, jocund, pleasant.
cheerless *adj* dark, dejected, desolate, despondent, disconsolate, discouraged, dismal, doleful, dreary, forlorn, gloomy, joyless, low-spirited, lugubrious, melancholy, mournful, rueful, sad, sombre, spiritless, woe-begone.
cherish *vb* comfort, foster, nourish, nurse, nurture, support, sustain; treasure; encourage, entertain, indulge, harbour.
chest *n* box, case, coffer; breast, thorax, trunk.
chew *vb* crunch, manducate, masticate, munch; bite, champ, gnaw; meditate, ruminate.
chicanery *n* chicane, deception, duplicity, intrigue, intriguing, sophistication, sophistry, stratagems, tergiversation, trickery, wiles, wire-pulling.
chide *vb* admonish, blame, censure, rebuke, reprimand, reprove, scold, upbraid; chafe, clamour, fret, fume, scold.
chief *adj* first, foremost, headmost, leading, master, supereminent, supreme, top; capital, cardinal, especial, essential, grand, great, main, master, paramount, prime, principal, supreme, vital. * *n* chieftain, commander; head, leader.
chiffonier *n* cabinet, sideboard.
child *n* babe, baby, bairn, bantling, brat, chit, infant, nursling, suckling, wean; issue, offspring, progeny.
childbirth *n* child-bearing, delivery, labour, parturition, travail.
childish *adj* infantile, juvenile, puerile, tender, young; foolish, frivolous, silly, trifling, weak.
childlike *adj* docile, dutiful, gentle, meek, obedient, submissive; confiding, guileless, ingenuous, innocent, simple, trustful, uncrafty.
chill *vb* dampen, depress, deject, discourage, dishearten. * *adj* bleak, chilly, cold, frigid, gelid. * *n* chilliness, cold, coldness, frigidity; ague, rigour, shiver; damp, depression.
chime *vb* accord, harmonize. * *n* accord, consonance.
chimera *n* crochet, delusion, dream, fantasy, hallucination, illusion, phantom.
chimerical *adj* delusive, fanciful, fantastic, illusory, imaginary, quixotic, shadowy, unfounded, visionary, wild.
chink[1] *vb* cleave, crack, fissure, crevasse, incise, split, slit. * *n* aperture, cleft, crack, cranny, crevice, fissure, gap, opening, slit.
chink[2] *vb, n* jingle, clink, ring, ting, tink, tinkle.
chip *vb* flake, fragment, hew, pare, scrape. * *n* flake, fragment, paring, scrap.
chirp *vb* cheep, chirrup, peep, twitter.
chirrup *vb* animate, cheer, encourage, inspirit.
chisel *vb* carve, cut, gouge, sculpt, sculpture.
chivalrous *adj* adventurous, bold, brave, chivalric, gallant, knightly, valiant, warlike; gallant, generous, high-minded, magnanimous.
chivalry *n* knighthood, knight-errantry; courtesy, gallantry, politeness; courage, valour.
choice *adj* excellent, exquisite, precious, rare, select, superior, uncommon, unusual, valuable; careful, chary, frugal, sparing. * *n* alternative, election, option, selection; favourite, pick, preference.
choke *vb* gag, smother, stifle, strangle, suffocate, throttle; overcome, overpower, smother, suppress; bar, block, close, obstruct, stop.
choleric *adj* angry, fiery, hasty, hot, fiery, irascible, irritable, passionate, petulant, testy, touchy, waspish.
choose *vb* adopt, co-opt, cull, designate, elect, pick, predestine, prefer, select.
chop *vb* cut, hack, hew; mince; shift, veer. * *n* slice; brand, quality; chap, jaw.
chouse *vb* bamboozle, beguile, cheat, circumvent, cozen, deceive, defraud, delude, dupe, gull, hoodwink, overreach, swindle, trick, victimize. * *n* cully, dupe, gull, simpleton, tool; artifice, cheat, circumvention, deceit, deception, delusion, double-dealing, fraud, imposition, imposture, ruse, stratagem, trick, wile.
christen *vb* baptize; call, dub, denominate, designate, entitle, name, style, term, title.
chronic *adj* confirmed, continuing, deep-seated, inveterate, rooted.
chronicle *vb* narrate, record, register. * *n* diary, journal, register; account, annals, history, narration, recital, record.
chuckle *vb* crow, exult, giggle, laugh, snigger, titter. * *n* giggle, laughter, snigger, titter.
chum *n* buddy, companion, comrade, crony, friend, mate, pal.
churl *n* boor, bumpkin, clodhopper, clown, countryman, lout, peasant, ploughman, rustic; curmudgeon, hunks, miser, niggard, scrimp, skinflint.
churlish *adj* brusque, brutish, cynical, harsh, impolite, rough, rude, snappish, snarling, surly, uncivil, waspish; crabbed, ill-tempered, morose, sullen; close, close-fisted, illiberal, mean, miserly, niggardly, penurious, stingy.
churn *vb* agitate, jostle.
cicatrice *n* cicatrix, mark, scar, seam.
cicesbeo *n* beau, escort, gallant, gigolo.
cincture *n* band, belt, cestos, cestus, girdle.
cipher *n* naught, nothing, zero; character, device, monogram, symbol; nobody, nonentity.
circle *vb* compass, encircle, encompass, gird, girdle, ring; gyrate, revolve, rotate, round, turn. * *n* circlet, corona, gyre, hoop, ring, rondure; circumference, cordon, periphery; ball, globe, orb, sphere; compass, enclosure; class, clique, company, coterie, fraternity, set, society; bounds, circuit, compass, field, province, range, region, sphere.
circuit *n* ambit, circumambience, circumambiency, cycle, revolution, turn; bounds, district, field, province, range, region, space, sphere, tract; boundary, compass; course, detour, perambulation, round, tour.

circuitous *adj* ambiguous, devious, indirect, roundabout, tortuous, turning, winding.
circulate *vb* diffuse, disseminate, promulgate, propagate, publish, spread.
circumference *n* bound, boundary, circuit, girth, outline, perimeter, periphery.
circumlocution *n* circuitousness, obliqueness, periphrase, periphrasis, verbosity, wordiness.
circumscribe *vb* bound, define, encircle, enclose, encompass, limit, surround; confine, restrict.
circumspect *adj* attentive, careful, cautious, considerate, discreet, heedful, judicious, observant, prudent, vigilant, wary, watchful.
circumstance *n* accident, incident; condition, detail, event, fact, happening, occurrence, position, situation.
circumstantial *adj* detailed, particular; indirect, inferential, presumptive.
circumvent *vb* check, checkmate, outgeneral, thwart; bamboozle, beguile, cheat, chouse, cozen, deceive, defraud, delude, dupe, gull, hoodwink, inveigle, mislead, outwit, overreach, trick.
circumvention *n* cheat, cheating, chicanery, deceit, deception, duplicity, fraud, guile, imposition, imposture, indirection, trickery, wiles.
cistern *n* basin, pond, reservoir, tank.
citation *n* excerpt, extract, quotation; enumeration, mention, quotation, quoting.
cite *vb* adduce, enumerate, extract, mention, name, quote; call, summon.
citizen *n* burgess, burgher, denizen, dweller, freeman, inhabitant, resident, subject, townsman.
civil *adj* civic, municipal, political; domestic; accommodating, affable, civilized, complaisant, courteous, courtly, debonair, easy, gracious, obliging, polished, polite, refined, suave, urbane, well-bred, well-mannered.
civility *n* affability, amiability, complaisance, courteousness, courtesy, good-breeding, politeness, suavity, urbanity.
civilize *vb* cultivate, educate, enlighten, humanize, improve, polish, refine.
claim *vb* ask, assert, challenge, demand, exact, require. * *n* call, demand, lien, requisition; pretension, privilege, right, title.
clammy *adj* adhesive, dauby, glutinous, gummy, ropy, smeary, sticky, viscid, viscous; close, damp, dank, moist, sticky, sweaty.
clamour *vb* shout, vociferate. * *n* blare, din, exclamation, hullabaloo, noise, outcry, uproar, vociferation.
clan *n* family, phratry, race, sect, tribe; band, brotherhood, clique, coterie, fraternity, gang, set, society, sodality.
clandestine *adj* concealed, covert, fraudulent, furtive, hidden, private, secret, sly, stealthy, surreptitious, underhand.
clap *vb* pat, slap, strike; force, slam; applaud, cheer. * *n* blow, knock, slap; bang, burst, explosion, peal, slam.
clarify *vb* cleanse, clear, depurate, purify, strain.
clash *vb* collide, crash, strike; clang, clank, clatter, crash, rattle; contend, disagree, interfere. * *n* collision; clang, clangour, clank, clashing, clatter, crash, rattle; contradiction, disagreement, interference, jar, jarring, opposition.
clasp *vb* clutch, entwine, grasp, grapple, grip, seize; embrace, enfold, fold, hug. * *n* buckle, catch, hasp, hook; embrace, hug.
class *vb* arrange, classify, dispose, distribute, range, rank. * *n* form, grade, order, rank, status; group, seminar; breed, kind, sort; category, collection, denomination, division, group, head.
classical *adj* first-rate, master, masterly, model, standard; Greek, Latin, Roman; Attic, chaste, elegant, polished, pure, refined.
classify *vb* arrange, assort, categorize, class, dispose, distribute, group, pigeonhole, rank, systematize, tabulate.
clatter *vb* clash, rattle; babble, clack, gabble, jabber, prate, prattle. * *n* clattering, clutter, rattling.
clause *n* article, condition, provision, stipulation.
claw *vb* lacerate, scratch, tear. * *n* talon, ungula.
clean *vb* cleanse, clear, purge, purify, rinse, scour, scrub, wash, wipe. * *adj* immaculate, spotless, unsmirched, unsoiled, unspotted, unstained, unsullied, white; clarified, pure, purified, unadulterated, unmixed; adroit, delicate, dextrous, graceful, light, neat, shapely; complete, entire, flawless, faultless, perfect, unabated, unblemished, unimpaired, whole; chaste, innocent, moral, pure, undefiled. * *adv* altogether, completely, entirely, perfectly, quite, thoroughly, wholly.
cleanse *vb* clean, clear, elutriate, purge, purify, rinse, scour, scrub, wash, wipe.
clear *vb* clarify, cleanse, purify, refine; emancipate, disenthral, free, liberate, loose; absolve, acquit, discharge, exonerate, justify, vindicate; disembarrass, disengage, disentangle, extricate, loosen, rid; clean up, scour, sweep; balance; emancipate, free, liberate. * *adj* bright, crystalline, light, limpid, luminous, pellucid, transparent; pure, unadulterated, unmixed; free, open, unencumbered, unobstructed; cloudless, fair, serene, sunny, unclouded, undimmed, unobscured; net; distinct, intelligible, lucid, luminous, perspicuous; apparent, conspicuous, distinct, evident, indisputable, manifest, obvious, palpable, unambiguous, undeniable, unequivocal, unmistakable, unquestionable, visible; clean, guiltless, immaculate, innocent, irreproachable, sinless, spotless, unblemished, undefiled, unspotted, unsullied; unhampered, unimpeded, unobstructed; euphonious, fluty, liquid, mellifluous, musical, silvery, sonorous.
cleave[1] *vb* crack, divide, open, part, rend, rive, sever, split, sunder.
cleave[2] *vb* adhere, cling, cohere, hold, stick.
cleft *adj* bifurcated, cloven, forked. * *n* breach, break, chasm, chink, cranny, crevice, fissure, fracture, gap, interstice, opening, rent, rift.

clemency *n* mildness, softness; compassion, fellow-feeling, forgivingness, gentleness, kindness, lenience, leniency, lenity, mercifulness, mercy, mildness, tenderness.
clement *adj* compassionate, forgiving, gentle, humane, indulgent, kind, kind-hearted, lenient, merciful, mild, tender, tender-hearted.
clench *vb* close tightly, grip; fasten, fix, rivet, secure.
clergy *n* clergymen, the cloth, ministers.
clever *adj* able, apt, gifted, talented; adroit, capable, dextrous, discerning, expert, handy, ingenious, knowing, quick, ready, skilful, smart, talented.
click *vb* beat, clack, clink, tick. * *n* beat, clack, clink, tick; catch, detent, pawl, ratchet.
cliff *n* crag, palisade, precipice, scar, steep.
climate *n* clime, temperature, weather; country, region.
climax *vb* consummate, crown, culminate, peak. * *n* acme, consummation, crown, culmination, head, peak, summit, top, zenith.
clinch *vb* clasp, clench, clutch, grapple, grasp, grip; fasten, secure; confirm, establish, fix. * *n* catch, clutch, grasp, grip; clincher, clamp, cramp, holdfast.
cling *vb* adhere, clear, stick; clasp, embrace, entwine.
clink *vb, n* chink, jingle, ring, tinkle; chime, rhyme.
clip *vb* cut, shear, snip; curtail, cut, dock, pare, prune, trim. * *n* cutting, shearing; blow, knock, lick, rap, thump, thwack, thump.
clique *n* association, brotherhood, cabal, camarilla, clan, club, coterie, gang, junta, party, ring, set, sodality.
cloak *vb* conceal, cover, dissemble, hide, mask, veil. * *n* mantle, surcoat; blind, cover, mask, pretext, veil.
clock *vb* mark time, measure, stopwatch; clock up, record, register. * *n* chronometer, horologue, timekeeper, timepiece, timer, watch.
clog *vb* fetter, hamper, shackle, trammel; choke, obstruct; burden, cumber, embarrass, encumber, hamper, hinder, impede, load, restrain, trammel. * *n* dead-weight, drag-weight, fetter, shackle, trammel; check, drawback, encumbrance, hindrance, impediment, obstacle, obstruction.
cloister *n* abbey, convent, monastery, nunnery, priory; arcade, colonnade, piazza.
close[1] *adj* closed, confined, snug, tight; hidden, private, secret; incommunicative, reserved, reticent, secretive, taciturn; concealed, retired, secluded, withdrawn; confined, motionless, stagnant; airless, oppressive, stale, stifling, stuffy, sultry; compact, compressed, dense, form, solid, thick; adjacent, adjoining, approaching, immediately, near, nearly, neighbouring; attached, dear, confidential, devoted, intimate; assiduous, earnest, fixed, intense, intent, unremitting; accurate, exact, faithful, nice, precise, strict; churlish, close-fisted, curmudgeonly, mean, illiberal, miserly, niggardly, parsimonious, penurious, stingy, ungenerous. * *n* courtyard, enclosure, grounds, precinct, yard.
close[2] *vb* occlude, seal, shut; choke, clog, estop, obstruct, stop; cease, complete, concede, end, finish, terminate; coalesce, unite; cease, conclude, finish, terminate; clinch, grapple; agree. * *n* cessation, conclusion, end, finish, termination.
closet *n* cabinet, retiring-room; press, store-room.
clot *vb* coagulate, concrete. * *n* coagulation, concretion, lump.
clothe *vb* array, attire, deck, dress, rig; cover,endow, envelop, enwrap, invest with, swathe.
clothes *n* apparel, array, attire, clothing, costume, dress, garb, garments, gear, habiliments, habits, raiment, rig, vestments, vesture.
cloud *vb* becloud, obnubilate, overcast, overspread; befog, darken, dim, obscure, shade, shadow. * *n* cirrus, cumulus, fog, haze, mist, nebulosity, scud, stratus, vapour; army, crowd, horde, host, multitude, swarm, throng; darkness, eclipse, gloom, obscuration, obscurity.
cloudy *adj* clouded, filmy, foggy, hazy, lowering, lurid, murky, overcast; confused, dark, dim, obscure; depressing, dismal, gloomy, sullen; clouded, mottled; blurred, dimmed, lustreless, muddy.
clown *n* churl, clod-breaker, clodhopper, hind, husbandman, lubber; boor, bumpkin, churl, fellow, lout; blockhead, dolt, clodpoll, dunce, dunderhead, numbskull, simpleton, thickhead; buffoon, droll, farceur, fool, harlequin, jack-a-dandy, jack-pudding, jester, merry-andrew, mime, pantaloon, pickle-herring, punch, scaramouch, zany.
clownish *adj* awkward, boorish, clumsy, coarse, loutish, ungainly, rough, rustic; churlish, ill-bred, ill-mannered, impolite, rude, uncivil.
cloy *vb* glut, pall, sate, satiate, surfeit.
club *vb* combine, unite; beat, bludgeon, cudgel. * *n* bat, bludgeon, cosh, cudgel, hickory, shillelagh, stick, truncheon; association, company, coterie, fraternity, set, society, sodality.
clump *vb* assemble, batch, bunch, cluster, group, lump; lumber, stamp, stomp, stump, trudge. * *n* assemblage, bunch, cluster, collection, group, patch, tuft.
clumsy *adj* botched, cumbrous, heavy, ill-made, ill-shaped, lumbering, ponderous, unwieldy; awkward, blundering, bungling, elephantine, heavy-handed, inapt, mal adroit, unhandy, unskilled.
cluster *vb* assemble, batch, bunch, clump, collect, gather, group, lump, throng. * *n* agglomeration, assemblage, batch, bunch, clump, collection, gathering, group, throng.
clutch[1] *vb* catch, clasp, clench, clinch, grab, grapple, grasp, grip, hold, seize, snatch, squeeze. * *n* clasp, clench, clinch, grasp, grip, hold, seizure, squeeze.
clutch[2] *n* aerie, brood, hatching, nest.

clutches *npl* claws, paws, talons; hands, power.
clutter *vb* confuse, disarrange, disarray, disorder, jumble, litter, mess, muss; clatter. * *n* bustle, clatter, clattering, racket; confusion, disarray, disorder, jumble, litter, mess, muss.
coadjutor *n* abettor, accomplice, aider, ally, assistant, associate, auxiliary, collaborator, colleague, cooperator, fellow-helper, helper, helpmate, partner.
coagulate *vb* clot, congeal, concrete, curdle, thicken.
coalesce *vb* amalgamate, blend, cohere, combine, commix, incorporate, mix, unite; concur, fraternize.
coalition *n* alliance, association, combination, compact, confederacy, confederation, conjunction, conspiracy, co-partnership, federation, league, union.
coarse *adj* crude, impure, rough, unpurified; broad, gross, indecent, indelicate, ribald, vulgar; bearish, bluff, boorish, brutish, churlish, clownish, gruff, impolite, loutish, rude, unpolished; crass, inelegant.
coast *vb* flow, glide, roll, skim, sail, slide, sweep. * *n* littoral, seaboard, sea-coast, seaside; shore, strand; border.
coat *vb* cover, spread. * *n* cut-away, frock, jacket; coating, cover, covering; layer.
coax *vb* allure, beguile, cajole, cog, entice, flatter, persuade, soothe, wheedle.
cobble *vb* botch, bungle; mend, patch, repair, tinker.
cobweb *adj* flimsy, gauzy, slight, thin, worthless. * *n* entanglement, meshes, snare, toils.
cochleate *adj* cochlear, cochleary, cochleous, cochleated, spiral, spiry.
cockle *vb* corrugate, pucker, wrinkle.
coddle *vb* caress, cocker, fondle, humour, indulge, nurse, pamper, pet.
codger *n* churl, curmudgeon, hunks, lick-penny, miser, niggard, screw, scrimp, skinflint.
codify *vb* condense, digest, summarize, systematize, tabulate.
coerce *vb* check, curb, repress, restrain, subdue; compel, constrain, drive, force, urge.
coercion *n* check, curb, repression, restraint; compulsion, constraint, force.
coeval *adj* coetaneous, coexistent, contemporaneous, contemporary, synchronous.
coexistent *adj* coetaneous, coeval, simultaneous, synchronous.
coffer *n* box, casket, chest, trunk; money-chest, safe, strongbox; caisson.
cogent *adj* compelling, conclusive, convincing, effective, forcible, influential, irresistible, persuasive, potent, powerful, resistless, strong, trenchant, urgent.
cogitate *vb* consider, deliberate, meditate, ponder, reflect, ruminate, muse, think, weigh.
cognate *adj* affiliated, affined, akin, allied, alike, analogous, connected, kindred, related, similar.
cognizance *n* cognition, knowing, knowledge, notice, observation.
cohere *vb* agree, coincide, conform, fit, square, suit.
coherence *n* coalition, cohesion, connection, dependence, union; agreement, congruity, consistency, correspondence, harmony, intelligibility, intelligible, meaning, rationality, unity.
coherent *adj* adherent, connected, united; congruous, consistent, intelligible, logical.
cohort *n* band, battalion, line, squadron.
coil *vb* curl, twine, twirl, twist, wind. * *n* convolution, curlicue, helix, knot, roll, spiral, tendril, twirl, volute, whorl; bustle, care, clamour, confusion, entanglements, perplexities, tumult, turmoil, uproar.
coin *vb* counterfeit, create, devise, fabricate, forge, form, invent, mint, originate, mould, stamp. * *n* coign, corner, quoin; key, plug, prop, wedge; cash, money, specie.
coincide *vb* cohere, correspond, square, tally; acquiesce, agree, harmonize, concur.
coincidence *n* corresponding, squaring, tallying; agreeing, concurrent, concurring.
cold *adj* arctic, biting, bleak, boreal, chill, chilly, cutting, frosty, gelid, glacial, icy, nipping, polar, raw, wintry; frost-bitten, shivering; apathetic, cold-blooded, dead, freezing, frigid, indifferent, lukewarm, passionless, phlegmatic, sluggish, stoical, stony, torpid, unconcerned, unfeeling, unimpressible, unresponsive, unsusceptible, unsympathetic; dead, dull, spiritless, unaffecting, uninspiring, uninteresting. * *n* chill, chilliness, coldness.
collapse *vb* break down, fail, fall. * *n* depression, exhaustion, failure, faint, prostration, sinking, subsidence.
collar *vb* apprehend, arrest, capture, grab, nab, seize. * *n* collarette, gorget, neckband, ruff, torque; band, belt, fillet, guard, ring, yoke.
collate *vb* adduce, collect, compare, compose.
collateral *adj* contingent, indirect, secondary, subordinate; concurrent, parallel; confirmatory, corroborative; accessory, accompanying, additional, ancillary, auxiliary, concomitant, contributory, simultaneous, supernumerary; consanguineous, related. * *n* guarantee, guaranty, security, surety, warranty; accessory, extra, nonessential, unessential; consanguinean, relative.
collation *n* luncheon, repast, meal.
colleague *n* aider, ally, assistant, associate, auxiliary, coadjutor, collaborator, companion, confederate, confrere, cooperator, helper, partner.
collect *vb* assemble, compile, gather, muster; accumulate, aggregate, amass, garner.
collected *adj* calm, composed, cool, placid, self-possessed, serene, unperturbed.
collection *n* aggregation, assemblage, cluster, crowd, drove, gathering, group, pack; accumulation, congeries, conglomeration, heap, hoard, lot, mass, pile, store; alms, contribution, offering, offertory.

colligate *vb* bind, combine, fasten, unite.
collision *n* clash, concussion, crash, encounter, impact, impingement, shock; conflict, crashing, interference, opposition.
collocate *vb* arrange, dispose, place, set.
colloquy *n* conference, conversation, dialogue, discourse, talk.
collude *vb* concert, connive, conspire.
collusion *n* connivance, conspiracy, coven, craft, deceit.
collusive *adj* conniving, conspiratorial, , dishonest, deceitful, deceptive, fraudulent.
colossal *adj* Cyclopean, enormous, gigantic, Herculean, huge, immense, monstrous, prodigious, vast.
colour *vb* discolour, dye, paint, stain, tinge, tint; disguise, varnish; disguise, distort, garble, misrepresent, pervert; blush, flush, redden, show. * *n* hue, shade, tinge, tint, tone; paint, pigment, stain; redness, rosiness, ruddiness; complexion; appearance, disguise, excuse, guise, plea, pretence, pretext, semblance.
colourless *adj* achromatic, uncoloured, untinged; blanched, hueless, livid, pale, pallid; blank, characterless, dull, expressionless, inexpressive, monotonous.
colours *n* banner, ensign, flag, standard.
column *n* pillar, pilaster; file, line, row.
coma *n* drowsiness, lethargy, somnolence, stupor, torpor; bunch, clump, cluster, tuft.
comatose *adj* drowsy, lethargic, sleepy, somnolent, stupefied.
comb *vb* card, curry, dress, groom, rake, unknot, untangle; rake, ransack, rummage, scour, search. * *n* card, hatchel, ripple; harrow, rake.
combat *vb* contend, contest, fight, struggle, war; battle, oppose, resist, struggle, withstand. * *n* action, affair, battle, brush, conflict, contest, encounter, fight, skirmish.
combative *adj* belligerent, contentious, militant, pugnacious, quarrelsome.
combination *n* association, conjunction, connection, union; alliance, cartel, coalition, confederacy, consolidation, league, merger, syndicate; cabal, clique, conspiracy, faction, junta, ring; amalgamation, compound, mixture.
combine *vb* cooperate, merge, pool, unite; amalgamate, blend, incorporate, mix.
combustible *adj* consumable, inflammable.
come *vb* advance, approach; arise, ensue, flow, follow, issue, originate, proceed, result; befall, betide, happen, occur.
comely *adj* becoming, decent, decorous, fitting, seemly, suitable; beautiful, fair, graceful, handsome, personable, pretty, symmetrical.
comfort *vb* alleviate, animate, cheer, console, encourage, enliven, gladden, inspirit, invigorate, refresh, revive, solace, soothe, strengthen. * *n* aid, assistance, countenance, help, support, succour; consolation, solace, encouragement, relief; ease, enjoyment, peace, satisfaction.
comfortable *adj* acceptable, agreeable, delightful, enjoyable, grateful, gratifying, happy, pleasant, pleasurable, welcome; commodious, convenient, easeful, snug; painless.
comfortless *adj* bleak, cheerless, desolate, drear, dreary, forlorn, miserable, wretched; broken-hearted, desolate, disconsolate, forlorn, heartbroken, inconsolable, miserable, woe-begone, wretched.
comical *adj* amusing, burlesque, comic, diverting, droll, farcical, funny, humorous, laughable, ludicrous, sportive, whimsical.
coming *adj* approaching, arising, arriving, ensuing, eventual, expected, forthcoming, future, imminent, issuing, looming, nearing, prospective, ultimate; emergent, emerging, successful; due, owed, owing. * *n* advent, approach, arrival; imminence, imminency, nearness; apparition, appearance, disclosure, emergence, manifestation, materialization, occurrence, presentation, revelation, rising.
comity *n* affability, amenity, civility, courtesy, politeness, suavity, urbanity.
command *vb* bid, charge, direct, enjoin, order, require; control, dominate, govern, lead, rule, sway; claim, challenge, compel, demand, exact. * *n* behest, bidding, charge, commandment, direction, hest, injunction, mandate, order, requirement, requisition; ascendency, authority, dominion, control, government, power, rule, sway, supremacy.
commander *n* captain, chief, chieftain, commandment, head, leader.
commemorate *vb* celebrate, keep, observe, solemnize.
commence *vb* begin, inaugurate, initiate, institute, open, originate, start.
commend *vb* assign, bespeak, confide, recommend, remit; commit, entrust, yield; applaud, approve, eulogize, extol, laud, praise.
commendation *n* approbation, approval, good opinion, recommendation; praise, encomium, eulogy, panegyric.
commensurate *adj* commeasurable, commensurable; co-extensive, conterminous, equal; adequate, appropriate, corresponding, due, proportionate, proportioned, sufficient.
comment *vb* animadvert, annotate, criticize, explain, interpret, note, remark. * *n* annotation, elucidation, explanation, exposition, illustration, commentary, note, gloss; animadversion, observation, remark.
commentator *n* annotator, commentator, critic, expositor, expounder, interpreter.
commerce *n* business, exchange, dealing, trade, traffic; communication, communion, intercourse.
commercial *adj* mercantile, trading.
commination *n* denunciation, menace, threat, threatening.
commingle *vb* amalgamate, blend, combine,

commix, intermingle, intermix, join, mingle, mix, unite.
comminute *vb* bray, bruise, grind, levigate, powder, pulverize, triturate.
commiserate *vb* compassionate, condole, pity, sympathize.
commiseration *n* compassion, pitying; condolence, pity, sympathy.
commission *vb* authorize, empower; delegate, depute. * *n* doing, perpetration; care, charge, duty, employment, errand, office, task, trust; allowance, compensation, fee, rake-off.
commissioner *n* agent, delegate, deputy.
commit *vb* confide, consign, delegate, entrust, remand; consign, deposit, lay, place, put, relegate, resign; do, enact, perform, perpetrate; imprison; engage, implicate, pledge.
commix *vb* amalgamate, blend, combine, commingle, compound, intermingle, mingle, mix, unite.
commodious *adj* advantageous, ample, comfortable, convenient, fit, proper, roomy, spacious, suitable, useful.
commodity *n* goods, merchandise, produce, wares.
common *adj* collective, public; general, useful; common-place, customary, everyday, familiar, frequent, habitual, usual; banal, hackneyed, stale, threadbare, trite; indifferent, inferior, low, ordinary, plebeian, popular, undistinguished, vulgar.
commonplace *adj* common, hackneyed, ordinary, stale, threadbare, trite. * *n* banality, cliché, platitude; jotting, memoir, memorandum, note, reminder.
common-sense, common-sensical *adj* practical, sagacious, sensible, sober.
commotion *n* agitation, disturbance, ferment, perturbation, welter; ado, bustle, disorder, disturbance, hurly-burly, pother, tumult, turbulence, turmoil.
communicate *vb* bestow, confer, convey, give, impart, transmit; acquaint, announce, declare, disclose, divulge, publish, reveal, unfold; commune, converse, correspond.
communication *n* conveyance, disclosure, giving, imparting, transmittal; commence, conference, conversation, converse, correspondence, intercourse; announcement, dispatch, information, message, news.
communicative *adj* affable, chatty, conversable, free, open, sociable, unreserved.
communion *n* converse, fellowship, intercourse, participation; Eucharist, holy communion, Lord's Supper, sacrament.
community *n* commonwealth, people, public, society; association, brotherhood, college, society; likeness, participancy, sameness, similarity.
compact[1] *n* agreement, arrangement, bargain, concordant, contract, covenant, convention, pact, stipulation, treaty.
compact[2] *vb* compress, condense, pack, press; bind, consolidate, unite. * *adj* close, compressed, condensed, dense, firm, solid; brief, compendious, concise, laconic, pithy, pointed, sententious, short, succinct, terse.
companion *n* accomplice, ally, associate, comrade, compeer, confederate, consort, crony, friend, fellow, mate; partaker, participant, participator, partner, sharer.
companionable *adj* affable, conversable, familiar, friendly, genial, neighbourly, sociable.
companionship *n* association, fellowship, friendship, intercourse, society.
company *n* assemblage, assembly, band, bevy, body, circle, collection, communication, concourse, congregation, coterie, crew, crowd, flock, gang, gathering, group, herd, rout, set, syndicate, troop; party; companionship, fellowship, guests, society, visitor, visitors; association, copartnership, corporation, firm, house, partnership.
compare *vb* assimilate, balance, collate, parallel; liken, resemble.
comparison *n* collation, compare, estimate; simile, similitude.
compartment *n* bay, cell, division, pigeonhole, section.
compass *vb* embrace, encompass, enclose, encircle, environ, surround; beleaguer, beset, besiege, block, blockade, invest; accomplish, achieve, attain, carry, consummate, effect, obtain, perform, procure, realize; contrive, devise, intend, meditate, plot, purpose. * *n* bound, boundary, extent, gamut, limit, range, reach, register, scope, stretch; circuit, round.
compassion *n* clemency, commiseration, condolence, fellow-feeling, heart, humanity, kind-heartedness, kindness, kindliness, mercy, pity, rue, ruth, sorrow, sympathy, tenderheartedness, tenderness.
compassionate *adj* benignant, clement, commiserative, gracious, kind, merciful, pitying, ruthful, sympathetic, tender.
compatible *adj* accordant, agreeable to, congruous, consistent, consonant, reconcilable, suitable.
compeer *n* associate, comrade, companion, equal, fellow, mate, peer.
compel *vb* constrain, force, coerce, drive, necessitate, oblige; bend, bow, subdue, subject.
compend *n* abbreviation, abridgement, abstract, breviary, brief, compendium, conspectus, digest, epitome, précis, summary, syllabus, synopsis.
compendious *adj* abbreviated, abridged, brief, comprehensive, concise, short, succinct, summary.
compensate *vb* counterbalance, counterpoise, countervail; guerdon, recompense, reimburse, remunerate, reward; indemnify, reimburse, repay, requite; atone.
compensation *n* pay, payment, recompense, remuneration, reward, salary; amends, atonement, indemnification, indemnity, reparation, requital,

satisfaction; balance, counterpoise, equalization, offset.
compete *vb* contend, contest, cope, emulate, rival, strive, struggle, vie.
competence *n* ability, capability, capacity, fitness, qualification, suitableness; adequacy, adequateness, enough, sufficiency.
competent *adj* able, capable, clever, equal, endowed, qualified; adapted, adequate, convenient, fit, sufficient, suitable.
competition *n* contest, emulation, rivalry, rivals.
competitor *n* adversary, antagonist, contestant, emulator, opponent.
compile *vb* compose, prepare, write; arrange, collect, select.
complacency *n* content, contentment, gratification, pleasure, satisfaction; affability, civility, complaisance, courtesy, politeness.
complacent *adj* contented, gratified, pleased, satisfied; affable, civil, complaisant, courteous, easy, gracious, grateful, obliging, polite, urbane.
complain *vb* bemoan, bewail, deplore, grieve, groan, grouch, grumble, lament, moan, murmur, repine, whine.
complainant *n* accuser, plaintiff.
complaining *adj* fault-finding, murmuring, querulous.
complaint *n* grievance, gripe, grumble, lament, lamentation, plaint, murmur, wail; ail, ailment, annoyance, disease, disorder, illness, indisposition, malady, sickness; accusation, charge, information.
complete *vb* accomplish, achieve, conclude, consummate, do, effect, effectuate, end, execute, finish, fulfil, perfect, perform, realize, terminate. * *adj* clean, consummate, faultless, full, perfect, perform, thorough; all, entire, integral, total, unbroken, undiminished, undivided, unimpaired, whole; accomplished, achieved, completed, concluded, consummated, ended, finished.
completion *n* accomplishing, accomplishment, achieving, conclusion, consummation, effecting, effectuation, ending, execution, finishing, perfecting, performance, termination.
complex *adj* composite, compound, compounded, manifold, mingled, mixed; complicate, complicated, entangled, intricate, involved, knotty, mazy, tangled. * *n* complexus, complication, involute, skein, tangle; entirety, integration, network, totality, whole; compulsion, fixation, obsession, preoccupation, prepossession; prejudice.
complexion *n* colour, hue, tint.
complexity *n* complication, entanglement, intricacy, involution.
compliance *n* concession, obedience, submission; acquiescence, agreement, assent, concurrence, consent; compliancy, yieldingness.
complicate *vb* confuse, entangle, interweave, involve.
complication *n* complexity, confusion, entanglement, intricacy; combination, complexus, mixture.
compliment *vb* commend, congratulate, eulogize, extol, flatter, laud, praise. * *n* admiration, commendation, courtesy, encomium, eulogy, favour, flattery, honour, laudation, praise, tribute.
complimentary *adj* commendatory, congratulatory, encomiastic, eulogistic, flattering, laudatory, panegyrical.
comply *vb* adhere to, complete, discharge, fulfil, meet, observe, perform, satisfy; accede, accord, acquiesce, agree to, assent, consent to, yield.
component *adj* composing, constituent, constituting. * *n* constituent, element, ingredient, part.
comport *vb* accord, agree, coincide, correspond, fit, harmonize, square, suit, tally.
compose *vb* build, compact, compound, constitute, form, make, synthesize; contrive, create, frame, imagine, indite, invent, write; adjust, arrange, regulate, settle; appease, assuage, calm, pacify, quell, quiet, soothe, still, tranquillize.
composed *adj* calm, collected, cool, imperturbable, placid, quiet, sedate, self-possessed, tranquil, undisturbed, unmoved, unruffled.
composite *adj* amalgamated, combined, complex, compounded, mixed; integrated, unitary. * *n* admixture, amalgam, blend, combination, composition, compound, mixture, unification.
composition *n* constitution, construction, formation, framing, making; compound, mixture; arrangement, combination, conjunction, make-up, synthesize, union; invention, opus, piece, production, writing; agreement, arrangement, compromise.
compost *n* fertilizer, fertilizing, manure, mixture.
composure *n* calmness, coolness, equanimity, placidity, sedateness, quiet, self-possession, serenity, tranquillity.
compotation *n* conviviality, frolicking, jollification, revelling, revelry, rousing, wassailling; bacchanal, carousal, carouse, debauch, orgy, revel, saturnalia, wassail.
compound[1] *vb* amalgamate, blend, combine, intermingle, intermix, mingle, mix, unite; adjust, arrange, compose, compromise, settle. * *adj* complex, composite. * *n* combination, composition, mixture; farrago, hodgepodge, jumble, medley, mess, olio.
compound[2] *n* enclosure, garden, yard.
comprehend *vb* comprise, contain, embrace, embody, enclose, include, involve; apprehend, conceive, discern, grasp, know, imagine, master, perceive, see, understand.
comprehension *n* comprising, embracing, inclusion; compass, domain, embrace, field, limits, province, range, reach, scope, sphere, sweep; connotation, depth, force, intention; conception, grasp, intelligence, understanding; intellect, intelligence, mind, reason, understanding.
comprehensive *adj* all-embracing, ample, broad, capacious, compendious, extensive, full, inclusive, large, sweeping, wide.
compress *vb* abbreviate, condense, constrict, con-

tract, crowd, press, shorten, squeeze, summarize.
compression *n* condensation, confining, pinching, pressing, squeezing; brevity, pithiness, succinctness, terseness.
comprise *vb* comprehend, contain, embody, embrace, enclose, include, involve.
compromise *vb* adjust, arbitrate, arrange, compose, compound, settle; imperil, jeopardize, prejudice; commit, engage, implicate, pledge; agree, compound. * *n* adjustment, agreement, composition, settlement.
compulsion *n* coercion, constraint, force, forcing, pressure, urgency.
compulsory *adj* coercive, compelling, constraining; binding, enforced, imperative, necessary, obligatory, unavoidable.
compunction *n* contrition, misgiving, penitence, qualm, regret, reluctance, remorse, repentance, sorrow.
computable *adj* calculable, numerable, reckonable.
computation *n* account, calculation, estimate, reckoning, score, tally.
compute *vb* calculate, count, enumerate, estimate, figure, measure, number, rate, reckon, sum.
comrade *n* accomplice, ally, associate, chum, companion, compatriot, compeer, crony, fellow, mate, pal.
concatenate *vb* connect, join, link, unite.
concatenation *n* connection; chain, congeries, linking, series, sequence, succession.
concave *adj* depressed, excavated, hollow, hollowed, scooped.
conceal *vb* bury, cover, screen, secrete; disguise, dissemble, mask.
concede *vb* grant, surrender, yield; acknowledge, admit, allow, confess, grant.
conceit *n* belief, conception, fancy, idea, image, imagination, notion, thought; caprice, illusion, vagary, whim; estimate, estimation, impression, judgement, opinion; conceitedness, egoism, self-complacency, priggishness, priggery, self-conceit, self-esteem, self-sufficiency, vanity; crotchet, point, quip, quirk.
conceited *adj* egotistical, opinionated, opinionative, overweening, self-conceited, vain.
conceivable *adj* imaginable, picturable; cogitable, comprehensible, intelligible, rational, thinkable.
conceive *vb* create, contrive, devise, form, plan, purpose; fancy, imagine; comprehend, fathom, think, understand; assume, imagine, suppose; bear, become pregnant.
concern *vb* affect, belong to, interest, pertain to, regard, relate to, touch; disquiet, disturb, trouble. * *n* affair, business, matter, transaction; concernment, consequence, importance, interest, moment, weight; anxiety, care, carefulness, solicitude, worry; business, company, establishment, firm, house.
concert *vb* combine, concoct, contrive, design, devise, invent, plan, plot, project. * *n* agreement, concord, concordance, cooperation, harmony, union, unison.
concession *n* acquiescence, assent, cessation, compliance, surrender, yielding; acknowledgement, allowance, boon, confession, grant, privilege.
conciliate *vb* appease, pacify, placate, propitiate, reconcile; engage, gain, secure, win, win over.
concise *adj* brief, compact, compendious, comprehensive, compressed, condensed, crisp, laconic, pithy, pointed, pregnant, sententious, short, succinct, summary, terse.
conclave *n* assembly, cabinet, council.
conclude *vb* close, end, finish, terminate; deduce, gather, infer, judge; decide, determine, judge; arrange, complete, settle; bar, hinder, restrain, stop; decide, determine, resolve.
conclusion *n* deduction, inference; decision, determination, judgement; close, completion, end, event, finale, issue, termination, upshot; arrangement, closing, effecting, establishing, settlement.
conclusive *adj* clinching, convincing, decisive, irrefutable, unanswerable; final, ultimate.
concoct *vb* brew, contrive, design, devise, frame, hatch, invent, mature, plan, plot, prepare, project.
concomitant *adj* accessory, accompanying, attendant, attending, coincident, concurrent, conjoined. * *n* accessory, accompaniment, attendant.
concord *n* agreement, amity, friendship, harmony, peace, unanimity, union, unison, unity; accord, adaptation, concordance, consonance, harmony.
concordant *adj* accordant, agreeable, agreeing, harmonious.
concordat *n* agreement, bargain, compact, convention, covenant, stipulation, treaty.
concourse *n* confluence, conflux, congress; assemblage, assembly, collection, crowd, gathering, meeting, multitude, throng.
concrete *vb* cake, congeal, coagulate, harden, solidify, thicken. * *adj* compact, consolidated, firm, solid, solidified; agglomerated, complex, conglomerated, compound, concreted; completely, entire, individualized, total. * *n* compound, concretion, mixture; cement.
concubine *n* hetaera, hetaira, mistress, paramour.
concupiscence *n* lasciviousness, lechery, lewdness, lust, pruriency.
concupiscent *adj* carnal, lascivious, lecherous, lewd, libidinous, lustful, prurient, rampant, salacious, sensual.
concur *vb* accede, acquiesce, agree, approve, assent, coincide, consent, harmonize; combine, conspire, cooperate, help.
concurrent *adj* agreeing, coincident, harmonizing, meeting, uniting; associate, associated, attendant, concomitant, conjoined, united.
concussion *n* agitation, shaking; clash, crash, shock.
condemn *vb* adjudge, convict, doom, sentence; disapprove, proscribe, reprobate; blame, censure,

damn, deprecate, disapprove, reprehend, reprove, upbraid.
condemnation *n* conviction, doom, judgement, penalty, sentence; banning, disapproval, proscription; guilt, sin, wrong; blame, censure, disapprobation, disapproval, reprobation, reproof.
condemnatory *adj* blaming, censuring, damnatory, deprecatory, disapproving, reproachful.
condense *vb* compress, concentrate, consolidate, densify, thicken; abbreviate, abridge, contract, curtail, diminish, epitomize, reduce, shorten, summarize; liquefy.
condescend *vb* deign, vouchsafe; descend, stoop, submit.
condescension *n* affability, civility, courtesy, deference, favour, graciousness, obeisance.
condign *adj* adequate, deserved, just, merited, suitable.
condiment *n* appetizer, relish, sauce, seasoning.
condition *vb* postulate, specify, stipulate; groom, prepare, qualify, ready, train; acclimatize, accustom, adapt, adjust, familiarize, habituate, naturalize; attune, commission, fix, overhaul, prepare, recondition, repair, service, tune. * *n* case, circumstances, plight, predicament, situation, state; class, estate, grade, rank, station; arrangement, consideration, provision, proviso, stipulation; attendant, necessity, postulate, precondition, prerequisite.
condole *vb* commiserate, compassionate, console, sympathize.
condonation *n* forgiveness, overlooking, pardon.
condone *vb* excuse, forgive, pardon.
conduce *vb* contribute, lead, tend; advance, aid.
conducive *adj* conducting, contributing, instrumental, promotive, subservient, subsidiary.
conduct *vb* convoy, direct, escort, lead; administer, command, govern, lead, preside, superintend; manage, operate, regulate; direct, lead. * *n* administration, direction, guidance, leadership, management; convoy, escort, guard; actions, bearing, behaviour, career, carriage, demeanour, deportment, manners.
conductor *n* guide, lead; director, leader, manager; propagator, transmitter.
conduit *n* canal, channel, duct, passage, pipe, tube.
confederacy *n* alliance, coalition, compact, confederation, covenant, federation, league, union.
confer *vb* advise, consult, converse, deliberate, discourse, parley, talk; bestow, give, grant, vouchsafe.
confess *vb* acknowledge, admit, avow, own; admit, concede, grant, recognize; attest, exhibit, manifest, prove, show; shrive.
confession *n* acknowledgement, admission, avowal.
confide *vb* commit, consign, entrust, trust.
confidence *n* belief, certitude, dependence, faith, reliance, trust; aplomb, assurance, boldness, cocksureness, courage, firmness, intrepidity, self-reliance; secrecy.
confident *adj* assured, certain, cocksure, positive, sure: bold, presumptuous. sanguine, undaunted.
confidential *adj* intimate, private, secret; faithful, trustworthy.
configuration *n* conformation, contour, figure, form, gestalt, outline, shape.
confine *vb* restrain, shut in, shut up; immure, imprison, incarcerate, impound, jail, mew; bound, circumscribe, limit, restrict. * *n* border, boundary, frontier, limit.
confinement *n* restraint; captivity, duress, durance, immurement, imprisonment, incarceration; childbed, childbirth, delivery, lying-in, parturition.
confines *npl* borders, boundaries, edges, frontiers, limits, marches, precincts.
confirm *vb* assure, establish, fix, settle; strengthen; authenticate, avouch, corroborate, countersign, endorse, substantiate, verify; bind, ratify, sanction.
confirmation *n* establishment, settlement; corroboration, proof, substantiation, verification.
confiscate *vb* appropriate, forfeit, seize.
conflict *vb* clash, combat, contend, contest, disagree, fight, interfere, strive, struggle. * *n* battle, collision, combat, contention, contest, encounter, fight, struggle; antagonism, clashing, disagreement, discord, disharmony, inconsistency, interference, opposition.
confluence *n* conflux, junction, meeting, union; army, assemblage, assembly, concourse, crowd, collection, horde, host, multitude, swarm.
confluent *adj* blending, concurring, flowing, joining, meeting, merging, uniting.
conform *vb* accommodate, adapt, adjust; agree, comport, correspond, harmonize, square, tally.
conformation *n* accordance, agreement, compliance, conformity; configuration, figure, form, manner, shape, structure.
confound *vb* confuse; baffle, bewilder, embarrass, flurry, mystify, nonplus, perplex, pose; amaze, astonish, astound, bewilder, dumfound, paralyse, petrify, startle, stun, stupefy, surprise; annihilate, demolish, destroy, overthrow, overwhelm, ruin; abash, confuse, discompose, disconcert, mortify, shame.
confront *vb* face; challenge, contrapose, encounter, oppose, threaten.
confuse *vb* blend, confound, intermingle, mingle, mix; derange, disarrange, disorder, jumble, mess, muddle; darken, obscure, perplex; befuddle, bewilder, embarrass, flabbergast, flurry, fluster, mystify, nonplus, pose; abash, confound, discompose, disconcert, mortify, shame.
confusion *n* anarchy, chaos, clutter, confusedness, derangement, disarrangement, disarray, disorder, jumble, muddle; agitation, commotion, ferment, stir, tumult, turmoil; astonishment, bewilderment, distraction, embarrassment, fluster, fuddle, perplexity; abashment, discomfiture, mortification, shame; annihilation, defeat, demolition, destruction, overthrow, ruin.
confute *vb* disprove, oppugn, overthrow, refute, silence.
congeal *vb* benumb, condense, curdle, freeze, stiffen, thicken.

congenial *adj* kindred, similar, sympathetic; adapted, agreeable, natural, suitable, suited; agreeable, favourable, genial.
congenital *adj* connate, connatural, inborn.
congeries *n* accumulation, agglomeration, aggregate, aggregation, collection, conglomeration, crowd, cluster, heap, mass.
congratulate *vb* compliment, felicitate, gratulate, greet, hail, salute.
congregate *vb* assemble, collect, convene, convoke, gather, muster; gather, meet, swarm, throng.
congregation *n* assemblage, assembly, collection, gathering, meeting.
congress *n* assembly, conclave, conference, convention, convocation, council, diet, meeting.
congruity *n* agreement, conformity, consistency, fitness, suitableness.
congruous *adj* accordant, agreeing, compatible, consistent, consonant, suitable; appropriate, befitting, fit, meet, proper, seemly.
conjecture *vb* assume, guess, hypothesize, imagine, suppose. surmise, suspect; dare say, fancy, presume. * *n* assumption, guess, hypothesis, supposition, surmise, theory.
conjoin *vb* associate, combine, connect, join, unite.
conjugal *adj* bridal, connubial, hymeneal, matrimonial, nuptial.
conjuncture *n* combination, concurrence, connection; crisis, emergency, exigency, juncture.
conjure *vb* adjure, beg, beseech, crave, entreat, implore, invoke, pray, supplicate; bewitch, charm, enchant, fascinate; juggle.
connect *vb* associate, conjoin, combine, couple, hyphenate, interlink, join, link, unite; cohere, interlock.
connected *adj* associated, coupled, joined, united; akin, allied, related; communicating.
connection *n* alliance, association, dependence, junction, union; commerce, communication, intercourse; affinity, relationship; kindred, kinsman, relation, relative.
connive *vb* collude, conspire, plot, scheme.
connoisseur *n* critic, expert, virtuoso.
connotation *n* comprehension, depth, force, intent, intention, meaning.
connubial *adj* bridal, conjugal, hymeneal, matrimonial, nuptial.
conquer *vb* beat, checkmate, crush, defeat, discomfit, humble, master, overcome, overpower, overthrow, prevail, quell, reduce, rout, subdue, subjugate, vanquish; overcome, surmount.
conqueror *n* humbler, subduer, subjugator, vanquisher; superior, victor, winner.
conquest *n* defeat, discomfiture, mastery, overthrow, reduction, subjection, subjugation; triumph, victor; winning.
consanguinity *n* affinity, kinship, blood-relationship, kin, kindred, relationship.
conscientious *adj* careful, exact, fair, faithful, high-principled, honest, honourable, incorruptible, just, scrupulous, straightforward, uncorrupt, upright.
conscious *adj* intelligent, knowing, percipient, sentient; intellectual, rational, reasoning, reflecting, self-conscious, thinking; apprised, awake, aware, cognizant, percipient, sensible; self-admitted, self-accusing.
consecrate *vb* dedicate, devote, ordain; hallow, sanctify, venerate.
consecutive *adj* following, succeeding.
consent *vb* agree, allow, assent, concur, permit, yield; accede, acquiesce, comply. * *n* approval, assent, concurrence, permission; accord, agreement, consensus, concord, cooperation, harmony, unison; acquiescence, compliance.
consequence *n* effect, end, event, issue, result; conclusion, deduction, inference; concatenation, connection, consecution; concern, distinction, importance, influence, interest, moment, standing, weight.
consequential *adj* consequent, following, resulting, sequential; arrogant, conceited, inflated, pompous, pretentious, self-important, self-sufficient, vainglorious.
conservation *n* guardianship, maintenance, preservation, protection.
conservative *adj* conservatory, moderate, moderationist; preservative; reactionary, unprogressive. * *n* die-hard, reactionary, redneck, rightist, right-winger; moderate; preservative.
conserve *vb* keep, maintain, preserve, protect, save, sustain, uphold. * *n* confit, confection, jam, preserve, sweetmeat.
consider *vb* attend, brood, contemplate, examine, heed, mark, mind, ponder, reflect, revolve, study, weigh; care for, consult, envisage, regard, respect; cogitate, deliberate, mediate, muse, ponder, reflect, ruminate, think; account, believe, deem, hold, judge, opine.
considerate *adj* circumspect, deliberate, discrete, judicious, provident, prudent, serious, sober, staid, thoughtful; charitable, forbearing, patient.
consideration *n* attention, cogitation, contemplation, deliberation, notice, heed, meditation, pondering, reflection, regard; consequence, importance, important, moment, significant, weight; account, cause, ground, motive, reason, sake, score.
consign *vb* deliver, hand over, remand, resign, transfer, transmit; commit, entrust; ship.
consignor *n* sender, shipper, transmitter.
consistency *n* compactness, consistence, density, thickness; agreement, compatibility, conformableness, congruity, consonance, correspondence, harmony.
consistent *adj* accordant, agreeing, comfortable, compatible, congruous, consonant, correspondent, harmonious, logical.
consolation *n* alleviation, comfort, condolence, encouragement, relief, solace.
console *vb* assuage, calm, cheer, comfort, encourage, solace, relieve, soothe.

consolidate *vb* cement, compact, compress, condense, conduce, harden, solidify, thicken; combine, conjoin, fuse, unite.
consolidation *n* solidification; combination, union.
consonance *n* accord, concord, conformity, harmony; accord, accordance, agreement, congruence, congruity, consistency, unison.
consonant *adj* accordant, according, harmonious; compatible, congruous, consistent. * *n* articulation, letter-sound.
consort *vb* associate, fraternize. * *n* associate, companion, fellow, husband, spouse, partner.
conspectus *n* abstract, brief, breviary, compend, compendium, digest, epitome, outline, precis, summary, syllabus, synopsis.
conspicuous *adj* apparent, clear, discernible, glaring, manifest, noticeable, perceptible, plain, striking, visible; celebrated, distinguished, eminent, famed, famous, illustrious, marked, noted, outstanding. pre-eminent, prominent, remarkable, signal.
conspiracy *n* cabal, collusion, confederation, intrigue, league, machination, plot, scheme.
conspire *vb* concur, conduce, cooperate; combine, compass, contrive, devise, project; confederate, contrive, hatch, plot, scheme.
constancy *n* immutability, permanence, stability, unchangeableness; regularity, unchangeableness; decision, determination, firmness, inflexibility, resolution, steadfastness, steadiness; devotion, faithfulness, fidelity, loyalty, trustiness, truth.
constant *adj* abiding, enduring, fixed, immutable, invariable, invariant, permanent, perpetual, stable, unalterable, unchanging, unvaried; certain, regular, stated, uniform; determined, firm, resolute, stanch, steadfast, steady, unanswering, undeviating, unmoved, unshaken, unwavering; assiduous, diligent, persevering, sedulous, tenacious, unremitting; continual, continuous, incessant, perpetual, sustained, unbroken, uninterrupted; devoted, faithful, loyal, true, trusty.
consternation *n* alarm, amazement, awe, bewilderment, dread, fear, fright, horror, panic, terror.
constituent *adj* component, composing, constituting, forming; appointing, electoral. * *n* component, element, ingredient, principal; elector, voter.
constitute *vb* compose, form, make; appoint, delegate, depute, empower; enact, establish, fix, set up.
constitution *n* establishment, formation, make-up, organization, structure; character, characteristic, disposition, form, habit, humour, peculiarity, physique, quality, spirit, temper, temperament.
constitutional *adj* congenital, connate, inborn, inbred, inherent, innate, natural, organic; lawful, legal, legitimate. * *n* airing, exercise, promenade, stretch, walk.
constrain *vb* coerce, compel, drive, force; chain, confine, curb, enthral, hold, restrain; draw, impel, urge.
constriction *n* compression, constraint, contraction.
construct *vb* build, fabricate, erect, raise, set up; arrange, establish, form, found, frame, institute, invent, make, organize, originate.
construction *n* building, erection, fabrication; configuration, conformation, figure, form, formation, made, shape, structure; explanation, interpretation, rendering, version.
construe *vb* analyse, explain, expound, interpret, parse, render, translate.
consult *vb* advise, ask, confer, counsel, deliberate, interrogate, question; consider, regard.
consume *vb* absorb, decay, destroy, devour, dissipate, exhaust, expend, lavish, lessen, spend, squander, vanish, waste.
consummate[1] *vb* accomplish, achieve, compass, complete, conclude, crown, effect, effectuate, end, execute, finish, perfect, perform.
consummate[2] *adj* complete, done, effected, finished, fulfilled, perfect, supreme.
consumption *n* decay, decline, decrease, destruction, diminution, expenditure, use, waste; atrophy, emaciation.
contact *vb* hit, impinge, touch; approach, be heard, communicate with, reach. * *n* approximation, contiguity, junction, juxtaposition, taction, tangency, touch.
contagion *n* infection; contamination, corruption, infection, taint.
contagious *adj* catching, epidemic, infectious; deadly, pestiferous, pestilential, poisonous.
contain *vb* accommodate, comprehend, comprise, embody, embrace, enclose, include; check, restrain.
contaminate *vb* corrupt, defile, deprave, infect, poison, pollute, soil, stain, sully, taint, tarnish, vitiate.
contamination *n* contaminating, defilement, defiling, polluting, pollution; abomination, defilement, impurity, foulness, infection, pollution, stain, taint, uncleanness.
contemn *vb* despise, disdain, disregard, neglect, scorn, scout, slight, spurn.
contemplate *vb* behold, gaze upon, observe, survey; consider, dwell on, meditate on, muse on, ponder, reflect upon, study, survey, think about; design, intend, mean, plan, purpose.
contemplation *n* cogitation, deliberation, meditation, pondering, reflection, speculation, study, thought; prospect, prospective, view; expectation.
contemporaneous *adj* coetaneous, coeval, coexistent, coexisting, coincident, concomitant, contemporary, simultaneous, synchronous.
contemporary *adj* coetaneous, coeval, coexistent, coexisting, coincident, concomitant, concurrent, contemporaneous, current, present, simultaneous, synchronous; advanced, modern, modernistic, progressive, up-to-date. * *n* coeval, coexistent, compeer, fellow.

contempt *n* contumely, derision, despite, disdain, disregard, misprision, mockery, scorn, slight.
contemptible *adj* abject, base, despicable, haughty, insolent, insulting, low, mean, paltry, pitiful, scurvy, sorry, supercilious, vile, worthless.
contemptuous *adj* arrogant, contumelious, disdainful, haughty, insolent, insulting, scornful, sneering, supercilious.
contend *vb* battle, combat, compete, contest, fight, strive, struggle, vie; argue, debate, dispute, litigate; affirm, assert, contest, maintain.
content[1] *n* essence, gist, meaning, meat, stuff, substance; capacity, measure, space, volume.
content[2] *vb* appease, delight, gladden, gratify, humour, indulge, please, satisfy, suffice. * *adj* agreeable, contented, happy, pleased, satisfied. * *n* contentment, ease, peace, satisfaction.
contention *n* discord, dissension, feud, squabble, strife, quarrel, rapture, wrangle, wrangling; altercation, bickering, contest, controversy, debate, dispute, litigation, logomachy.
contentious *adj* belligerent, cross, litigious, peevish, perverse, petulant, pugnacious, quarrelsome, wrangling; captious, caviling, disputatious.
conterminous *adj* adjacent, adjoining, contiguous; co-extensive, coincident, commensurate.
contest *vb* argue, contend, controvert, debate, dispute, litigate, question; strive, struggle; compete, cope, fight, vie. * *n* altercation, contention, controversy, difference, dispute, debate, quarrel; affray, battle, bout, combat, conflict, encounter, fight, match, scrimmage, struggle, tussle; competition, contention, rivalry.
contexture *n* composition, constitution, framework, structure, texture.
contiguous *adj* abutting, adjacent, adjoining, beside, bordering, conterminous, meeting, near, neighbouring, touching.
continent[1] *n* mainland, mass, tract.
continent[2] *adj* abstemious, abstinent, chaste, restrained, self-commanding, self-controlled, moderate, sober, temperate.
contingency *n* accidentalness, chance, fortuity, uncertainty; accident, casualty, event, incident, occurrence.
contingent *adj* accidental, adventitious, casual, fortuitous, incidental; conditional, dependent, uncertain. * *n* proportion, quota, share.
continual *adj* constant, constant, perpetual, unceasing, uninterrupted, unremitting; endless, eternal, everlasting, interminable, perennial, permanent, perpetual, unending; constant, oft-repeated.
continuance *n* abiding, continuation, duration, endurance, lasting, persistence, stay; continuation, extension, perpetuation, prolongation, protraction; concatenation, connection, sequence, succession; constancy, endurance, perseverance, persistence.
continue *vb* endure, last, remain; abide, linger, remain, stay, tarry; endure, persevere, persist, stick; extend, prolong, perpetuate, protract.
continuous *adj* connected, continued, extended, prolonged, unbroken, unintermitted, uninterrupted.
contour *n* outline, profile.
contraband *adj* banned, forbidden, illegal, illicit, interdicted, prohibited, smuggled, unlawful.
contract *vb* abbreviate, abridge, condense, confine, curtail, diminish, epitomize, lessen, narrow, reduce, shorten; absorb, catch, incur, get, make, take; constrict, shrink, shrivel, wrinkle; agree, bargain, covenant, engage, pledge, stipulate. * *n* agreement, arrangement, bargain, bond, compact, concordat, covenant, convention, engagement, pact, stipulation, treaty.
contradict *vb* assail, challenge, controvert, deny, dispute, gainsay, impugn, traverse; abrogate, annul, belie, counter, disallow, negative, contravene, counteract, oppose, thwart.
contradiction *n* controversion, denial, gainsaying; antinomy, clashing, contrariety, incongruity, opposition.
contradictory *adj* antagonistic, contrary, incompatible, inconsistent, negating, opposed, opposite, repugnant.
contrariety *n* antagonism, clashing, contradiction, contrast, opposition, repugnance.
contrary *adj* adverse, counter, discordant, opposed, opposing, opposite; antagonistic, conflicting, contradictory, repugnant, retroactive; forward, headstrong, obstinate, refractory, stubborn, unruly, wayward, perverse. * *n* antithesis, converse, obverse, opposite, reverse.
contrast *vb* compare, differentiate, distinguish, oppose. * *n* contrariety, difference, opposition; comparison, distinction.
contravene *vb* abrogate, annul, contradict, counteract, countervail, cross, go against, hinder, interfere, nullify, oppose, set aside, thwart.
contravention *n* abrogation, contradiction, interference, opposition, transgression, traversal, violation.
contretemps *n* accident, mischance, mishap.
contribute *vb* bestow, donate, give, grant, subscribe; afford, aid, furnish, supply; concur, conduce, conspire, cooperate, minister, serve, tend.
contribution *n* bestowal, bestowment, grant; donation, gift, offering, subscription.
contrite *adj* humble, penitent, repentant, sorrowful.
contrition *n* compunction, humiliation, penitence, regret, remorse, repentance, self-condemnation, self-reproach, sorrow.
contrivance *n* design, inventive, inventiveness; contraption, device, gadget, invention, machine; artifice, device, fabrication, machination, plan, plot, scheme, shift, stratagem.
contrive *vb* arrange, brew, concoct, design, devise, effect, form, frame, hatch, invent, plan, project; consider, plan, plot, scheme; manage, make out.

control *vb* command, direct, dominate, govern, manage, oversee, sway, regulate, rule, superintend; bridle, check, counteract, curb, check, hinder, repress, restrain. * *n* ascendency, command, direction, disposition, dominion, government, guidance, mastery, oversight, regiment, regulation, rule, superintendence, supremacy, sway.

controversy *n* altercation, argument, contention, debate, discussion, disputation, dispute, logomachy, polemics, quarrel, strife; lawsuit.

contumacious *adj* disobedient, cross-grained, disrespectful, haughty, headstrong, intractable, obdurate, obstinate, pertinacious, perverse, rebellious, refractory, stiff-necked, stubborn.

contumacy *n* doggedness, haughtiness, headiness, obduracy, obstinacy, pertinacity, perverseness, stubbornness; contempt, disobedience, disrespect, insolence, insubordination, rebelliousness.

contumelious *adj* abusive, arrogant, calumnious, contemptuous, disdainful, insolent, insulting, opprobrious, overbearing, rude, scornful, supercilious.

contumely *n* abuse, affront, arrogance, contempt, contemptuousness, disdain, indignity, insolence, insult, obloquy, opprobrium, reproach, rudeness, scorn, superciliousness.

contuse *vb* bruise, crush, injure, knock, squeeze, wound.

contusion *n* bruise, crush, injury, knock, squeeze, wound.

convalescence *n* recovery, recuperation.

convene *vb* assemble, congregate, gather, meet, muster; assemble, call, collect, convoke, muster, summon.

convenience *n* fitness, propriety, suitableness; accessibility, accommodation, comfort, commodiousness, ease, handiness, satisfaction, serviceability, serviceableness.

convenient *adj* adapted, appropriate, fit, fitted, proper, suitable, suited; advantageous, beneficial, comfortable, commodious, favourable, handy, helpful, serviceable, timely, useful.

convent *n* abbey, cloister, monastery, priory.

convention *n* assembly, congress, convocation, meeting; agreement, bargain, compact, contract, pact, stipulation, treaty; custom, formality, usage.

conventional *adj* agreed on, bargained for, stipulated; accustomed, approved, common, customary, everyday, habitual, ordinary, orthodox, regular, standard, traditional, usual, wonted.

conversable *adj* affable, communicative, free, open, sociable, social, unreversed.

conversation *n* chat, colloquy, communion, confabulation, conference, converse, dialogue, discourse, intercourse, interlocution, parley, talk.

converse[1] *vb* commune; chat, confabulate, discourse, gossip, parley, talk. * *n* commerce, communication, intercourse; colloquy, conversation, talk.

converse[2] *adj* adverse, contradictory, contrary, counter, opposed, opposing, opposite; *n* antithesis, contrary, opposite, reverse.

conversion *n* change, reduction, resolution, transformation, transmutation; interchange, reversal, transposition.

convert *vb* alter, change, transform, transmute; interchange, reverse, transpose; apply, appropriate, convince. * *n* catechumen, disciple, neophyte, proselyte.

convey *vb* bear, bring, carry, fetch, transmit, transport, waft; abalienate, alienate, cede, consign, deliver, demise, devise, devolve, grant, sell, transfer.

conveyance *n* alienation, cession, transfer, transference, transmission; carriage, carrying, conveying, transfer, transmission.

convict *vb* condemn, confute, convince, imprison, sentence. * *n* criminal, culprit, felon, malefactor, prisoner.

convivial *adj* festal, festive, gay, jolly, jovial, merry, mirthful, social.

convocation *n* assembling, convening, convoking, gathering, summoning; assembly, congress, convention, council, diet, meeting, synod.

convoke *vb* assemble, convene, muster, summon.

convoy *vb* accompany, attend, escort, guard, protect. * *n* attendance, attendant, escort, guard, protection.

convulse *vb* agitate, derange, disorder, disturb, shake, shatter.

convulsion *n* cramp, fit, spasm; agitation, commotion, disturbance, shaking, tumult.

cook *vb* bake, boil, broil, fry, grill, microwave, roast, spit-roast, steam, stir-fry; falsify, garble.

cool *vb* chill, ice, refrigerate; abate, allay, calm, damp, moderate, quiet, temper. * *adj* calm, collected, composed, dispassionate, placid, sedate, self-possessed, quiet, staid, unexcited, unimpassioned, undisturbed, unruffled; cold-blooded, indifferent, lukewarm, unconcerned; apathetic, chilling, freezing, frigid, repellent; bold, impertinent, impudent, self-possessed, shameless. * *n* chill, chilliness, coolness; calmness, composure, coolheadedness, countenance, equanimity, poise, self-possession, self-restraint.

coop *vb* cage, confine, encage, immure, imprison. * *n* barrel, box, cage, pen.

cooperate *vb* abet, aid, assist, co-act, collaborate, combine, concur, conduce, conspire, contribute, help, unite.

cooperation *n* aid, assistance, co-action, concert, concurrence, collaboration, synergy.

coordinate *vb* accord, agree, arrange, equalize, harmonize, integrate, methodize, organize, regulate, synchronize, systematize. * *adj* coequal, equal, equivalent, tantamount; coincident, synchronous. * *n* complement, counterpart, like, pendant; companion, fellow, match, mate.

copartnership *n* association, fraternity, partnership; company, concern, establishment, firm, house.

cope *vb* combat, compete, contend, encounter, engage, strive, struggle, vie.
copious *adj* abundant, ample, exuberant, full, overflowing, plenteous, plentiful, profuse, rich.
copiousness *n* abundance, exuberance, fullness, plenty, profusion, richness.
copse *n* coppice, grove, thicket.
copulation *n* coition, congress, coupling.
copy *vb* duplicate, reproduce, trace, transcribe; follow, imitate, pattern. * *n* counterscript, duplicate, facsimile, off-print, replica, reproduction, transcript; archetype, model, original, pattern; manuscript, typescript.
cord *n* braid, gimp, line, string.
cordate *adj* cordiform, heart-shaped.
cordial *adj* affectionate, ardent, earnest, heartfelt, hearty, sincere, warm, warm-hearted; grateful, invigorating, restorative, pleasant, refreshing. * *n* balm, balsam, elixir, tisane, tonic; liqueur.
core *n* centre, essence, heart, kernel.
corner *vb* confound, confuse, nonplus, perplex, pose, puzzle. * *n* angle, bend, crutch, cusp, elbow, joint, knee; niche, nook, recess, retreat.
corollary *n* conclusion, consequence, deduction, induction, inference.
coronal *n* bays, chaplet, crown, garland, laurel, wreath.
corporal *adj* bodily; corporeal, material, physical.
corporeal *adj* bodily, fleshly, substantial; corporal, material, nonspiritual, physical.
corps *n* band, body, company, contingent, division, platoon, regiment, squad, squadron, troop.
corpse *n* body, carcass, corse, remains; ashes, dust.
corpulent *adj* big, burly, fat, fleshy, large, lusty, obese, plump, portly, pursy, rotund, stout.
corpuscle *n* atom, bit, grain, iota, jot, mite, molecule, monad, particle, scintilla, scrap, whit.
correct *vb* adjust, amend, cure, improve, mend, reclaim, rectify, redress, reform, regulate, remedy; chasten, discipline, punish. * *adj* accurate, equitable, exact, faultless, just, precise, proper, regular, right, true, upright.
correction *n* amendment, improvement, redress; chastening, discipline, punishment.
corrective *adj* alternative, correctory, counteractive, emendatory, improving, modifying, rectifying, reformative, reformatory.
correctness *n* accuracy, exactness, faultlessness, nicety, precision, propriety, rectitude, regularity, rightness, truth.
correlate *n* complement, correlative, counterpart.
correspond *vb* accord, agree, answer, comport, conform, fit, harmonize, match, square, suit, tally; answer, belong, correlate; communicate.
correspondence *n* accord, agreement, coincidence, concurrence, conformity, congruity, fitness, harmony, match; correlation, counterposition; communication, letters, writing.
corroborate *vb* confirm, establish, ratify, substantiate, support, sustain, strengthen.
corrode *vb* canker, erode, gnaw; consume, deteriorate, rust, waste; blight, embitter, envenom, poison.
corrosive *adj* acrid, biting, consuming, cathartic, caustic, corroding, eroding, erosive, violent; consuming, corroding, gnawing, mordant, wasting, wearing; blighting, cankerous, carking, embittering, envenoming, poisoning.
corrugate *vb* cockle, crease, furrow, groove, pucker, rumple, wrinkle.
corrupt *vb* putrefy, putrid, render; contaminate, defile, infect, pollute, spoil, taint, vitiate; degrade, demoralize, deprave, pervert; adulterate, debase, falsify, sophisticate; bribe, entice. * *adj* contaminated, corrupted, impure, infected, putrid, rotten, spoiled, tainted, unsound; abandoned, debauched, depraved, dissolute, profligate, reprobate, vicious, wicked; bribable, buyable.
corruption *n* putrefaction, putrescence, rottenness; adulteration, contamination, debasement, defilement, infection, perversion, pollution, vitiation; demoralization, depravation, depravity, immorality, laxity, sinfulness, wickedness; bribery, dishonesty.
corsair *n* buccaneer, picaroon, pirate, rover, sea-robber, sea-rover.
corset *n* bodice, girdle, stays.
cosmonaut *n* astronaut, spaceman.
cosmos *n* creation, macrocosm, universe, world; harmony, order, structure.
cost *vb* absorb, consume, require. * *n* amount, charge, expenditure, expense, outlay, price; costliness, preciousness, richness, splendour, sumptuousness; damage, detriment, loss, pain, sacrifice, suffering.
costly *adj* dear, expensive, high-priced; gorgeous, luxurious, precious, rich, splendid, sumptuous, valuable.
costume *n* apparel, attire, dress, robes, uniform.
cosy, cozy *adj* comfortable, easy, snug; chatty, conversable, social, talkative.
coterie *n* association, brotherhood, circle, club, set, society, sodality.
cottage *n* cabin, chalet, cot, hut, lodge, shack, shanty.
couch *vb* lie, recline; crouch, squat; bend down, stoop; conceal, cover up, hide; lay, level. * *n* bed, davenport, divan, lounge, seat, settee, settle, sofa.
council *n* advisers, cabinet, ministry; assembly, congress, conclave, convention, convocation, diet, husting, meeting, parliament, synod.
counsel *vb* admonish, advise, caution, recommend, warm. * *n* admonition, advice, caution, instruction, opinion, recommendation, suggestion; deliberation, forethought; advocate, barrister, counsellor, lawyer.
count *vb* enumerate, number, score; calculate, cast, compute, estimate, reckon; account, consider, deem, esteem, hold, judge, regard, think; tell. * *n* reckoning, tally.

countenance *vb* abet, aid, approve, assist, befriend, encourage, favour, patronize, sanction, support. * *n* aspect, look, men; aid, approbation, approval, assistance, encouragement, favour, patronage, sanction, support.

counter[1] *n* abacus, calculator, computer, meter, reckoner, tabulator, totalizator; bar, buffet, shopboard, table; (*naut*) end, poop, stern, tail; chip, token.

counter[2] *vb* contradict, contravene, counteract, oppose, retaliate. * *adj* adverse, against, contrary, opposed, opposite. * *adv* contrariwise, contrary. * *n* antithesis, contrary, converse, opposite, reverse; counterblast, counterblow, retaliation.

counteract *vb* check, contrapose, contravene, cross, counter, counterpose, defeat, foil, frustrate, hinder, oppose, resist, thwart, traverse; annul, countervail, counterbalance, destroy, neutralize, offset.

counteractive *adj* antidote, corrective, counteragent, medicine, remedy, restorative.

counterbalance *vb* balance, counterpoise; compensate, countervail.

counterfeit *vb* forge, imitate; fake, feign, pretend, sham, simulate; copy, imitate. * *adj* fake, forged, fraudulent, spurious, supposititious; false, feigned, hypocritical, mock, sham, simulated, spurious; copied, imitated, resembling. * *n* copy, fake, forgery, sham.

countermand *vb* abrogate, annul, cancel, recall, repeal, rescind, revoke.

counterpane *n* coverlet, duvet, quilt.

counterpart *n* copy, duplicate; complement, correlate, correlative, reverse, supplement; fellow, mate, match, tally, twin.

counterpoise *vb* balance, counteract, countervail, counterbalance, equilibrate, offset. * *n* balance, counterweight.

countersign *n* password, watchword.

countervail *vb* balance, compensate, counterbalance.

country *n* land, region; countryside; fatherland, home, kingdom, state, territory; nation, people, population. * *adj* rural, rustic; countrified, rough, rude, uncultivated, unpolished, unrefined.

countryman *n* compatriot, fellow-citizen; boor, clown, farmer, hind, husbandman, peasant, rustic, swain.

couple *vb* pair, unite; copulate, embrace; buckle, clasp, conjoin, connect, join, link, pair, yoke. * *n* brace, pair, twain, two; bond, coupling, lea, link, tie.

courage *n* audaciousness, audacity, boldness, bravery, daring, derring-do, dauntlessness, fearlessness, firmness, fortitude, gallantry, hardihood, heroism, intrepidity, manhood, mettle, nerve, pluck, prowess, resolution, spirit, spunk, valorousness, valour.

courageous *adj* audacious, brave, bold, chivalrous, daring, dauntless, fearless, gallant, hardy, heroic, intrepid, lion-hearted, mettlesome, plucky, resolute, reliant, staunch, stout, undismayed, valiant, valorous.

course *vb* chase, follow, hunt, pursue, race, run. * *n* career, circuit, race, run; road, route, track, way; bearing, direction, path, tremor, track; ambit, beat, orbit, round; process, progress, sequence; order, regularity, succession, turn; behaviour, conduct, deportment; arrangement, series, system.

court *vb* coddle, fawn, flatter, ingratiate; address, woo; seek; invite, solicit. * *n* area, courtyard, patio, quadrangle; addresses, civilities, homage, respects, solicitations; retinue, palace, tribunal.

courteous *adj* affable, attentive, ceremonious, civil, complaisant, courtly, debonair, elegant, gracious, obliging, polished, polite, refined, respected, urbane, well-bred, well-mannered.

courtesan *n* harlot, prostitute, strumpet, vamp, wanton, wench, whore.

courtesy *n* affability, civility, complaisance, courteousness, elegance, good-breeding, graciousness, polish, politeness, refine, urbanity.

courtly *adj* affable, ceremonious, civil, elegant, flattering, lordly, obliging, polished, polite, refined, urbane.

courtyard *n* area, court, patio, quadrangle, yard.

cove[1] *n* anchorage, bay, bight, creek, firth, fjord, inlet.

cove[2] *n* bloke, chap, character, customer, fellow, type.

covenant *vb* agree, bargain, contract, stipulate. * *n* bond, deed; arrangement, bargain, compact, concordat, contract, convention, pact, stipulation, treaty.

cover *vb* overlay, overspread; cloak, conceal, curtain, disguise, hide, mask, screen, secrete, shroud, veil; defend, guard, protect, shelter, shield; case, clothe, envelop, invest, jacket, sheathe; comprehend, comprise, contain, embody, embrace, include. * *n* capsule, case, covering, integument, tegument, top; cloak, disguise, screen, veil; guard, defence, protection, safeguard, shelter, shield; shrubbery, thicket, underbrush, undergrowth, underwood, woods.

covert *adj* clandestine, concealed, disguised, hidden, insidious, private, secret, sly, stealthy, underhand. * *n* coppice, shade, shrubbery, thicket, underwood; asylum; defence, harbour, hiding-place, refuge, retreat, sanctuary, shelter.

covet *vb* aim after, desire, long for, yearn for; hanker after, lust after.

covetous *adj* acquisitive, avaricious, close-fisted, grasping, greedy, miserly, niggardly, parsimonious, penurious, rapacious.

cow[1] *n* bovine, heifer.

cow[2] *vb* abash, break, daunt, discourage, dishearten, frighten, intimidate, overawe, subdue.

coward *adj* cowardly, timid. * *n* caitiff, craven, dastard, milksop, poltroon, recreant, skulker, sneak, wheyface.

cowardly *adj* base, chicken-hearted, coward, craven, dastardly, faint-hearted, fearful, lily-livered, mean, pusillanimous, timid, timorous, white-livered, yellow.

cower *vb* bend, cringe, crouch, fawn, shrink, squat, stoop.

coxcomb *n* beau, dandy, dude, exquisite, fop, jackanapes, popinjay, prig.

coy *adj* backward, bashful, demure, diffident, distant, modest, reserved, retiring, self-effacing, shrinking, shy, timid.

coyness *n* affectation, archness, backwardness, bashfulness, coquettishness, demureness, diffidence, evasiveness, modesty, primness, reserve, shrinking, shyness, timidity.

cozen *vb* beguile, cheat, chouse, circumvent, deceive, defraud, diddle, dupe, gull, overreach, swindle, trick, victimize.

cozy *see* **cosy**.

crabbed *adj* acrid, rough, sore, tart; acrimonious, cantankerous, captious, caustic, censorious, churlish, cross, growling, harsh, ill-tempered, morose, peevish, petulant, snappish, snarling, splenetic, surly, testy, touchy, waspish; difficult, intractable, perplexing, tough, trying, unmanageable.

crabbedness *n* acridity, acridness, roughness, sourness, tartness; acerbity, acrimonious, asperity, churlishness, harshness, ill-tempered, moodiness, moroseness, sullenness; difficulty, intractability, perplexity.

crack *vb* break; chop, cleave, split; snap; craze, madden; boast, brag, bluster, crow, gasconade, vapour, vaunt. * *adj* capital, excellent, first-class, first-rate, tip-top. * *n* breach, break, chink, cleft, cranny, crevice, fissure, fracture, opening, rent, rift, split; burst, clap, explosion, pop, report; snap.

cracked *adj* broken, crackled, split; crack-brained, crazed, crazy, demented, deranged, flighty, insane.

crackle *vb* crepitate, decrepitate, snap.

craft *n* ability, aptitude, cleverness, dexterity, expertness, power, readiness, skill, tact, talent; artifice, artfulness, cunning, craftiness, deceitfulness, deception, guile, shrewdness, subtlety; art, avocation, business, calling, employment, handicraft, trade, vocation; vessel.

crafty *adj* arch, artful, astute, cunning, crooked, deceitful, designing, fraudulent, guileful, insidious, intriguing, scheming, shrewd, sly, subtle, tricky, wily.

crag *n* rock; neck, throat.

craggy *adj* broken, cragged, jagged, rough, rugged, scraggy, uneven.

cram *vb* fill, glut, gorge, satiate, stuff; compress, crowd, overcrowd, press, squeeze; coach, grind.

cramp *vb* convulse; check, clog, confine, hamper, hinder, impede, obstruct, restrain, restrict. * *n* convulsion, crick, spasm; check, restraint, restriction, obstruction.

crank *vb* bend, crankle, crinkle, turn, twist, wind. * *n* bend, quirk, turn, twist, winding.

cranny *n* breach, break, chink, cleft, crack, crevice, fissure, gap, hole, interstice, nook, opening, rift.

crapulous *adj* crapulent, drunk, drunken, inebriated, intoxicated, tipsy.

crash *vb* break, shatter, shiver, smash, splinter. * *adj* emergency, fast, intensive, rushed, speeded-up. * *n* clang, clash, collision concussion, jar.

crass *adj* coarse, gross, raw, thick, unabated, unrefined.

cravat *n* neckcloth, neckerchief, necktie.

crave *vb* ask, beg, beseech, entreat, implore, petition, solicit, supplicate; desire, hanker after, long for, need, want, yearn for.

craven *n* coward, dastard, milk-sop, poltroon, recreant. **adj* cowardly, chicken-hearted, lily-livered, pusillanimous, yellow.

craving *n* hankering, hungering, longing, yearning.

craw *n* crop, gullet, stomach, throat.

craze *vb* bewilder, confuse, dement, derange, madden; disorder, impair, weaken. * *n* fashion, mania, mode, novelty.

crazy *adj* broken, crank, rickety, shaky, shattered, tottering; crack-brained, delirious, demented, deranged, distracted, idiotic, insane, lunatic, mad, silly.

create *vb* originate, procreate; cause, design, fashion, form, invent, occasion, produce; appoint, constitute, make.

creation *n* formation, invention, origination, production; cosmos, universe; appointment, constitution, establishment, nomination.

creator *n* author, designer, inventor, fashioner, maker, originator; god.

creature *n* animal, beast, being, body, brute, man, person; dependant, hanger-on, minion, parasite, retainer, vassal; miscreant, wretch.

credence *n* acceptance, belief, confidence, credit, faith, reliance, trust.

credentials *npl* certificate, diploma, missive, passport, recommendation, testament, testimonial, title, voucher, warrant.

credibility *n* believability, plausibility, tenability, , trustworthiness.

credit *vb* accept, believe, trust; loan, trust. * *n* belief, confidence, credence, faith, reliance, trust; esteem, regard, reputableness, reputation; influence, power; honour, merit; loan, trust.

creditable *adj* estimable, honourable, meritorious, praiseworthy, reputable, respectable.

credulity *n* credulousness, gullibility, silliness, simplicity, stupidity.

credulous *adj* dupable, green, gullible, naive, over-trusting, trustful, uncritical, unsuspecting, unsuspicious.

creed *n* belief, confession, doctrine, dogma, opinion, profession, tenet.

creek *n* bay, bight, cove, fjord, inlet; rivulet, streamlet.

creep *vb* crawl; steal upon; cringe, fawn, grovel, insinuate. * *n* crawl, scrabble, scramble; fawner, groveller, sycophant, toady.

crenate *adj* indented, notched, scalloped.
crepitate *vb* crack, crackle, decrepitate, snap.
crest *n* comb, plume, topknot, tuft; apex, crown, head, ridge, summit, top; arms, badge, bearings.
crestfallen *adj* chap-fallen, dejected, depressed, despondent, discouraged, disheartened, dispirited, downcast, down-hearted, low-spirited, melancholy, sad.
crevice *n* chink, cleft, crack, cranny, fissure, fracture, gap, hole, interstice, opening, rent, rift.
crew *n* company, complement, hands; company, corps, gang, horde, mob, party, posse, set, squad, team, throng.
crib *vb* cage, confine, encage, enclose, imprison; pilfer, purloin. * *n* manger, rack; bin, bunker; plagiarism, plunder, theft.
crick *vb* jar, rick, wrench, wrick. * *n* convulsion, cramp, jarring, spasm, rick, wrench, wrick.
crime *n* felony, misdeed, misdemeanour, offence, violation; delinquency, fault, guilt, iniquity, sin, transgression, unrighteousness, wickedness, wrong.
criminal *adj* culpable, felonious, flagitious, guilty, illegal, immoral, iniquitous, nefarious, unlawful, vicious, wicked, wrong. * *n* convict, culprit, delinquent, felon, malefactor, offender, sinner, transgressor.
criminate *vb* accuse, arraign, charge, convict, impeach, indict; implicate, involve.
crimp *vb* crisp, curl.
cringe *vb* bend, bow, cower, crouch, fawn, grovel, kneel, sneak, stoop, truckle.
cripple *vb* cramp, destroy, disable, enfeeble, impair, lame, maim, mutilate, paralyse, ruin, weaken.
crisis *n* acme, climax, height; conjuncture, emergency, exigency, juncture, pass, pinch, push, rub, strait, urgency.
crisp *adj* brittle, curled, friable, frizzled.
criterion *n* canon, gauge, measure, principle, proof, rule, standard, test, touchstone.
critic *n* arbiter, caviller, censor, connoisseur, judge, nit-picker, reviewer.
critical *adj* accurate, exact, nice; captious, carping, caviling, censorious, exacting; crucial, decisive, determining, important, turning: dangerous, dubious, exigent, hazardous, imminent, momentous, precarious, ticklish.
criticism *n* analysis, animadversion, appreciation, comment, critique, evaluation, judgement, review, strictures.
criticize *vb* appraise, evaluate, examine, judge.
croak *vb* complain, groan, grumble, moan, mumble, repine; die.
crone *n* hag, witch.
crony *n* ally, associate, chum, friend, mate, mucker, pal.
crook *vb* bend, bow, curve, incurvate, turn, wind. * *n* bend, curvature, flexion, turn; artifice, machination, trick; criminal, thief, villain
crooked *adj* angular, bent, bowed, curved, winding, zigzag; askew, aslant, awry, deformed, disfigured, distorted, twisted, wry; crafty, deceitful, devious, dishonest, dishonourable, fraudulent, insidious, intriguing, knavish, tricky, underhanded, unfair, unscrupulous.
crop *vb* gather, mow, pick, pluck, reap; browse, nibble; clip, curtail, lop, reduce, shorten. * *n* harvest, produce, yield.
cross *vb* intersect, pass over, traverse; hinder, interfere, obstruct, thwart; interbred, intermix. * *adj* transverse; cantankerous, captious, crabbed, churlish, crusty, cynical, fractious, fretful, grouchy, ill-natured, ill-tempered, irascible, irritable, morose, peevish, pettish, petulant, snappish, snarling, sour, spleeny, splenetic, sulky, sullen, surly, testy, touchy, waspish. * *n* crucifix, gibbet, rood; affliction, misfortune, trial, trouble, vexation; cross-breeding, hybrid, intermixture.
cross-grained *adj* cantankerous, headstrong, obdurate, peevish, perverse, refractory, stubborn, untractable, wayward.
crossing *n* intersection, overpass, traversing, under-pass.
crossways, crosswise *adv* across, over, transversely.
crotchet *n* caprice, fad, fancy, freak, quirk, vagary, whim, whimsy.
crouch *vb* cower, cringe, fawn, truckle; crouch, kneel, stoop, squat; bow, curtsy, genuflect.
croup *n* buttocks, crupper, rump.
crow *vb* bluster, boast, brag, chuckle, exult, flourish, gasconade, swagger, triumph, vapour, vaunt.
crowd *vb* compress, cram, jam, pack, press; collect, congregate, flock, herd, huddle, swarm. * *n* assembly, company, concourse, flock, herd, horde, host, jam, multitude, press, throng; mob, pack, populace, rabble, rout.
crown *vb* adorn, dignify, honour; recompense, requite, reward; cap, complete, consummate, finish, perfect. * *n* bays, chaplet, coronal, coronet, garland, diadem, laurel, wreath; monarchy, royalty, sovereignty; diadem; dignity, honour, recompense, reward; apex, crest, summit, top.
crowning *adj* completing, consummating, dignifying, finishing, perfecting.
crucial *adj* intersecting, transverse; critical, decisive, searching, severe, testing, trying.
crude *adj* raw, uncooked, undressed, unworked; harsh, immature, rough, unripe; crass, coarse, unrefined; awkward, immature, indigestible, rude, uncouth, unpolished, unpremeditated.
cruel *adj* barbarous, blood-thirsty, dire, fell, ferocious, inexorable, hard-hearted, inhuman, merciless, pitiless, relentless, ruthless, sanguinary, savage, truculent, uncompassionate, unfeeling, unmerciful, unrelenting; bitter, cold, hard, severe, sharp, unfeeling.
crumble *vb* bruise, crush, decay, disintegrate, perish, pound, pulverize, triturate.
crumple *vb* rumple, wrinkle.

crush *vb* bruise, compress, contuse, squash, squeeze; bray, comminute, crumble, disintegrate, mash; demolish, raze, shatter; conquer, overcome, overpower, overwhelm, quell, subdue.

crust *n* coat, coating, incrustation, outside, shell, surface.

crusty *adj* churlish, crabbed, cross, cynical, fretful, forward, morose, peevish, pettish, petulant, snappish, snarling, surly, testy, touchy, waspish; friable, hard, short.

cry *vb* call, clamour, exclaim; blubber, snivel, sob, wail, weep, whimper; bawl, bellow, hoot, roar, shout, vociferate, scream, screech, squawk, squall, squeal, yell; announce, blazon, proclaim, publish. * *n* acclamation, clamour, ejaculation, exclamation, outcry; crying, lament, lamentation, plaint, weeping; bawl, bellow, howl, roar, scream, screech, shriek, yell; announcement, proclamation, publication.

crypt *n* catacomb, tomb, vault.

cuddle *vb* cosset, nestle, snuggle, squat; caress, embrace, fondle, hug, pet. * *n* caress, embrace, hug.

cudgel *vb* bang, baste, batter, beat, cane, drub, thrash, thump. * *n* bastinado, baton, bludgeon, club, shillelagh, stick, truncheon.

cue *vb* intimate, prompt, remind, sign, signal. * *n* catchword, hint, intimation, nod, prompting, sign, signal, suggestion.

cuff *vb* beat, box, buffet, knock, pummel, punch, slap, smack, strike, thump. * *n* blow, box, punch, slap, smack, strike, thump.

cul-de-sac *n* alley, dead end, impasse, pocket.

cull *vb* choose, elect, pick, select; collect, gather, glean, pluck.

culmination *n* acme, apex, climax, completion, consummation, crown, summit, top, zenith.

culpability *n* blame, blameworthiness, criminality, culpableness, guilt, remissness, sinfulness.

culpable *adj* blameable, blameworthy, censurable, faulty, guilty, reprehensible, sinful, transgressive, wrong.

culprit *n* delinquent, criminal, evil-doer, felon, malefactor, offender.

cultivate *vb* farm, fertilize, till, work; civilize, develop, discipline, elevate, improve, meliorate, refine, train; investigate, prosecute, pursue, search, study; cherish, foster, nourish, patronize, promote.

culture *n* agriculture, cultivation, farming, husbandry, tillage; cultivation, elevation, improvement, refinement.

cumber *vb* burden, clog, encumber, hamper, impede, obstruct, oppress, overload; annoy, distract, embarrass, harass, perplex, plague, torment, trouble, worry.

cumbersome *adj* burdensome, clumsy, cumbrous, embarrassing, heavy, inconvenient, oppressive, troublesome, unmanageable, unwieldy, vexatious.

cuneiform *adj* cuneate, wedge-shaped.

cunning *adj* artful, astute, crafty, crooked, deceitful, designing, diplomatic, foxy, guileful, intriguing, machiavellian, sharp, shrewd, sly, subtle, tricky, wily; curious, ingenious. * *n* art, artfulness, artifice, astuteness, craft, shrewdness, subtlety; craftiness, chicane, chicanery, deceit, deception, intrigue, slyness.

cup *n* beaker, bowl, chalice, goblet, mug; cupful, draught, potion.

cupboard *n* buffet, cabinet, closet.

cupidity *n* avidity, greed, hankering, longing, lust; acquisitiveness, avarice, covetousness, greediness, stinginess.

curative *adj* healing, medicinal, remedial, restorative.

curator *n* custodian, guardian, keeper, superintendent.

curb *vb* bridle, check, control, hinder, moderate, repress, restrain. * *n* bridle, check, control, hindrance, rein, restraint.

cure *vb* alleviate, correct, heal, mend, remedy, restore; kipper, pickle, preserve. * *n* antidote, corrective, help, remedy, reparative, restorative, specific; alleviation, healing, restorative.

curiosity *n* interest, inquiringness, inquisitiveness; celebrity, curio, marvel, novelty, oddity, phenomenon, rarity, sight, spectacle, wonder.

curious *adj* interested, inquiring, inquisitive, meddling, peering, prying, scrutinizing; extraordinary, marvellous, novel, queer, rare, singular, strange, unique, unusual; cunning, elegant, fine, finished, neat, skilful, well-wrought.

curl *vb* coil, twist, wind, writhe; bend, buckle, ripple, wave. * *n* curlicue, lovelock, ringlet; flexure, sinuosity, undulation, wave, waving, winding.

curmudgeon *n* churl, lick-penny, miser, niggard, screw, scrimp, skinflint.

currency *n* publicity; acceptance, circulation, transmission; bills, coins, money, notes.

current *adj* common, general, popular, rife; circulating, passing; existing, instant, present, prevalent, widespread. * *n* course, progression, river, stream, tide, undertow. * *adv* commonly, generally, popularly, publicly.

curry *vb* comb, dress; beat, cudgel, drub, thrash.

curse *vb* anathematize, damn, denounce, execrate, imprecate, invoke, maledict; blast, blight, destroy, doom; afflict, annoy, harass, injure, plague, scourge, torment, vex; blaspheme, swear. * *n* anathema, ban, denunciation, execration, fulmination, imprecation, malediction, malison; affliction, annoyance, plague, scourge, torment, trouble, vexation; ban, condemnation, penalty, sentence.

cursed *adj* accursed, banned, blighted, curse-laden, unholy; abominable, detestable, execrable, hateful, villainous; annoying, confounded, plaguing, scourging, tormenting, troublesome, vexatious.

cursory *adj* brief, careless, desultory, hasty, passing, rapid, slight, summary, superficial, transient, transitory.

curt *adj* brief, concise, laconic, short, terse; crusty, rude, snappish, tart.
curtail *vb* abridge, dock, lop, retrench, shorten; abbreviate, contract, decrease, diminish, lessen.
curtain *vb* cloak, cover, drape, mantle, screen, shade, shield, veil. * *n* arras, drape, drop, portière, screen, shade.
curvature *n* arcuation, bend, bending, camber, crook, curve, flexure, incurvation.
curve *vb* bend, crook, inflect, turn, twist, wind. * *n* arcuation, bend, bending, camber, crook, flexure, incurvation.
curvet *vb* bound, leap, vault; caper, frisk.
cushion *vb* absorb, damp, dampen, deaden, dull, muffle, mute, soften, subdue, suppress; cradle, pillow, support. * *n* bolster, hassock, pad, pillow, woolsack.
cusp *n* angle, horn, point.
custodian *n* curator, guardian, keeper, sacristan, superintendent, warden.
custody *n* care, charge, guardianship, keeping, safe-keeping, protection, watch, ward; confinement, durance, duress, imprisonment, prison.
custom *n* consuetude, convention, fashion, habit, manner, mode, practice, rule, usage, use, way; form, formality, observation; patronage; duty, impost, tax, toll, tribute.
customary *adj* accustomed, common, consuetudinary, conventional, familiar, fashionable, general, habitual, gnomic, prescriptive, regular, usual, wonted.
cut *vb* chop, cleave, divide, gash, incise, lance, sever, slice, slit, wound; carve, chisel, sculpture; hurt, move, pierce, touch; ignore, slight; abbreviate, abridge, curtail, shorten. * *n* gash, groove, incision, nick, slash, slice, slit; channel, passage; piece, slice; fling, sarcasm, taunt; fashion, form, mode, shape, style.
cutthroat *adj* barbarous, cruel, ferocious, murderous; competitive, exacting, exorbitant, extortionate, rivalling, ruthless, usurious, vying.* *n* assassin, murderer, ruffian.
cutting *adj* keen, sharp; acid, biting, bitter, caustic, piercing, sarcastic, sardonic, satirical, severe, trenchant, wounding.
cycle *n* age, circle, era, period, revolution, round.
Cyclopean *adj* colossal, enormous, gigantic, Herculean, immense, vast.
cynical *adj* captious, carping, censorious, churlish, crabbed, cross, crusty, fretful, ill-natured, ill-tempered, morose, peevish, pettish, petulant, sarcastic, satirical, snappish, snarling, surly, testy, touchy, waspish; contemptuous, derisive, misanthropic, pessimistic, scornful.
cynosure *n* attraction, centre.
cyst *n* pouch, sac.

D

dab *vb* box, rap, slap, strike, tap touch; coat, daub, smear. * *adj* adept, expert, proficient; pat. * *n* lump, mass, pat.
dabble *vb* dip, moisten, soak, spatter, splash, sprinkle, wet; meddle, tamper, trifle.
daft *adj* absurd, delirious, foolish, giddy, idiotic, insane, silly, simple, stupid, witless; frolicsome, merry, mirthful, playful, sportive.
dagger *n* bayonet, dirk, poniard, stiletto.
dainty *adj* delicate, delicious, luscious, nice, palatable, savoury, tender, toothsome; beautiful, charming, choice, delicate, elegant, exquisite, fine, neat; fastidious, finical, finicky, over-nice, particular, scrupulous, squeamish. * *n* delicacy, titbit, treat.
dale *n* bottom, dell, dingle, glen, vale, valley.
dalliance *n* caressing, endearments, flirtation, fondling.
dally *vb* dawdle, fritter, idle, trifle, waste time; flirt, fondle, toy.
damage *vb* harm, hurt, impair, injure, mar. * *n* detriment, harm, hurt, injury, loss, mischief.
damages *npl* compensation, fine, forfeiture, indemnity, reparation, satisfaction.
dame *n* babe, baby, broad, doll, girl; lady, madam, matron, mistress.
damn *vb* condemn, doom, kill, ruin. * *n* bean, curse, fig, hoot, rap, sou, straw, whit.
damnable *adj* abominable, accursed, atrocious, cursed, detestable, hateful, execrable, odious, outrageous.
damp *vb* dampen, moisten; allay, abate, check, discourage, moderate, repress, restrain; chill, cool, deaden, deject, depress, dispirit. * *adj* dank, humid, moist, wet. * *n* dampness, dank, fog, mist, moisture, vapour; chill, dejection, depression.
damper *n* check, hindrance, impediment, obstacle; damp, depression, discouragement, wet blanket.
dandle *vb* amuse, caress, fondle, pet, toss; dance.
danger *n* jeopardy, insecurity, hazard, peril, risk, venture.
dangerous *adj* critical, hazardous, insecure, perilous, risky, ticklish, unsafe.
dangle *vb* drape, hang, pend, sway, swing; fawn.
dank *adj* damp, humid, moist, wet.
dapper *adj* active, agile, alert, brisk, lively, nimble, quick, ready, smart, spry; neat, nice, pretty, spruce, trim.
dapple *vb* diversify, spot, variegate. * *adj* dappled, spotted, variegated.
dare *vb* challenge, defy, endanger, hazard, provoke, risk. * *n* challenge, defiance, gage.
daring *adj* adventurous, bold, brave, chivalrous, courageous, dauntless, doughty, fearless, gallant, heroic, intrepid, valiant, valorous. * *n* adventurousness, boldness, bravery, courage, dauntlessness, doughtiness, fearlessness, intrepidity, undauntedness, valour.
dark *adj* black, cloudy, darksome, dusky, ebon, inky, lightless, lurid, moonless, murky, opaque, overcast, pitchy, rayless, shady, shadowy, starless, sunless, swart, tenebrous, umbrageous, unenlightened, unilluminated; abstruse, cabbalistic, enigmatical, incomprehensible, mysterious, mystic, mystical, obscure, occult, opaque, recondite, transcendental, unillumined, unintelligible; cheerless, discouraging, dismal, disheartening, funereal, gloomy; benighted, darkened, ignorant, rude, unlettered, untaught; atrocious, damnable, infamous, flagitious, foul, horrible, infernal, nefarious, vile, wicked. * *n* darkness, dusk, murkiness, obscurity; concealment, privacy, secrecy; blindness, ignorance.
darken *vb* cloud, dim, eclipse, obscure, shade, shadow; chill, damp, depress, gloom, sadden; benight, stultify, stupefy; obscure, perplex; defile, dim, dull, stain, sully.
darkness *n* blackness, dimness, gloom, obscurity; blindness, ignorance; cheerlessness, despondency, gloom, joylessness; privacy, secrecy.
darling *adj* beloved, cherished, dear, loved, precious, treasured. * *n* dear, favourite, idol, love, sweetheart.
dart *vb* ejaculate, hurl, launch, propel, sling, throw; emit, shoot; dash, rush, scoot, spring.
dash *vb* break, destroy, disappoint, frustrate, ruin, shatter, spoil, thwart; abash, confound, disappoint, surprise; bolt, dart, fly, run, speed, rush. * *n* blow, stroke; advance, onset, rush; infusion, smack, spice, sprinkling, tincture, tinge, touch; flourish, show.
dashing *adj* headlong, impetuous, precipitate, rushing; brilliant, gay, showy, spirited.
dastardly *adj* base, cowardly, coward, cowering, craven, pusillanimous, recreant. * *n* coward, craven, milksop, poltroon, recreant.
data *npl* conditions, facts, information, premises.
date *n* age, cycle, day, generation, time; epoch, era, period; appointment, arrangement, assignation, engagement, interview, rendezvous, tryst; catch, steady, sweetheart.

daub *vb* bedaub, begrime, besmear, blur, cover, deface, defile, grime, plaster, smear, smudge, soil, sully. * *n* smear, smirch, smudge.
daunt *vb* alarm, appal, check, cow, deter, discourage, frighten, intimate, scare, subdue, tame, terrify, thwart.
dauntless *adj* bold, brave, chivalrous, courageous, daring, doughty, gallant, heroic, indomitable, intrepid, unaffrighted, unconquerable, undaunted, undismayed, valiant, valorous.
dawdle *vb* dally, delay, fiddle, idle, lag, loiter, potter, trifle.
dawn *vb* appear, begin, break, gleam, glimmer, open, rise. * *n* daybreak, dawning, cockcrow, sunrise, sun-up.
day *n* daylight, sunlight, sunshine; age, epoch, generation, lifetime, time.
daze *vb* blind, dazzle; bewilder, confound, confuse, perplex, stun, stupefy. * *n* bewilderment, confusion, discomposure, perturbation, pother; coma, stupor, swoon, trance.
dazzle *vb* blind, daze; astonish, confound, overpower, surprise. * *n* brightness, brilliance, splendour.
dead *adj* breathless, deceased, defunct, departed, gone, inanimate, lifeless; apathetic, callous, cold, dull, frigid, indifferent, inert, lukewarm, numb, obtuse, spiritless, torpid, unfeeling; flat, insipid, stagnant, tasteless, vapid; barren, inactive, sterile, unemployed, unprofitable, useless. * *adv* absolutely, completely, downright, fundamentally, quite; direct, directly, due, exactly, just, right, squarely, straight. * *n* depth, midst; hush, peace, quietude, silence, stillness.
deaden *vb* abate, damp, dampen, dull, impair, muffle, mute, restrain, retard, smother, weaken; benumb, blunt, hebetate, obtund, paralyse.
deadly *adj* deleterious, destructive, fatal, lethal, malignant, mortal, murderous, noxious, pernicious, poisonous, venomous; implacable, mortal, rancorous, sanguinary.
deal *vb* allot, apportion, assign, bestow, dispense, distribute, divide, give, reward, share; bargain, trade, traffic, treat with. * *n* amount, degree, distribution, extent, lot, portion, quantity, share; bargain, transaction.
dear *adj* costly, expensive, high-priced; beloved, cherished, darling, esteemed, precious, treasured. * *n* beloved, darling, deary, honey, love, precious, sweet, sweetie, sweetheart.
dearth *n* deficiency, insufficiency, scarcity; famine, lack, need, shortage, want.
death *n* cessation, decease, demise, departure, destruction, dissolution, dying, end, exit, mortality, passing.
deathless *adj* eternal, everlasting, immortal, imperishable, undying; boring, dull, turgid.
debacle *n* breakdown, cataclysm, collapse; rout, stampede.
debar *vb* blackball, deny, exclude, hinder, prevent, prohibit, restrain, shut out, stop, withhold.
debase *vb* adulterate, alloy, depress, deteriorate, impair, injure, lower, pervert, reduce, vitiate; abase, degrade, disgrace, dishonour, humble, humiliate, mortify, shame; befoul, contaminate, corrupt, defile, foul, pollute, soil, taint.
debate *vb* argue, canvass, contest, discuss, dispute; contend, deliberate, wrangle. * *n* controversy, discussion, disputation; altercation, contention, contest, dispute, logomachy.
debauch *vb* corrupt, deprave, pollute, vitiate; deflower, ravish, seduce, violate. * *n* carousal, orgy, revel, saturnalia.
debauchery *n* dissipation, dissoluteness, excesses, intemperance; debauch, excess, intemperance, lewdness, licentiousness, lust; bacchanal, carousal, compotation, indulgence, orgies, potation, revelry, revels, saturnalia, spree.
debilitate *vb* enervate, enfeeble, exhaust, prostrate, relax, weaken.
debility *n* enervation, exhaustion, faintness, feebleness, frailty, imbecility, infirmity, languor, prostration, weakness.
debonair *adj* affable, civil, complaisant, courteous, easy, gracious, kind, obliging, polite, refined, urbane, well-bred.
debris *n* detritus, fragments, remains, rubbish, rubble, ruins, wreck, wreckage.
debt *n* arrears, debit, due, liability, obligation; fault, misdoing, offence, shortcoming, sin, transgression, trespass.
decadence *n* caducity, decay, declension, decline, degeneracy, degeneration, deterioration, fall, retrogression.
decamp *vb* abscond, bolt, escape, flee, fly.
decapitate *vb* behead, decollate, guillotine.
decay *vb* decline, deteriorate, disintegrate, fail, perish, wane, waste, wither; decompose, putrefy, rot. * *n* caducity, decadence, declension, decline, decomposition, decrepitude, degeneracy, degeneration, deterioration, dilapidation, disintegration, fading, failing, perishing, putrefaction, ruin, wasting, withering.
deceased *adj* dead, defunct, departed, gone, late, lost.
deceit *n* artifice, cheating, chicanery, cozenage, craftiness, deceitfulness, deception, double-dealing, duplicity, finesse, fraud, guile, hypocrisy, imposition, imposture, pretence, sham, treachery, tricky, underhandedness, wile.
deceitful *adj* counterfeit, deceptive, delusive, fallacious, hollow, illusive, illusory, insidious, misleading; circumventive, cunning, designing, dissembling, dodgy, double-dealing, evasive, false, fraudulent, guileful, hypocritical, insincere, tricky, underhanded, wily.
deceive *vb* befool, beguile, betray, cheat, chouse, circumvent, cozen, defraud, delude, disappoint, double-cross, dupe, ensnare, entrap, fool, gull, hoax, hoodwink, humbug, mislead, outwit, overreach, trick.
deceiver *n* charlatan, cheat, humbug, hypocrite,

knave, impostor, pretender, rogue, sharper, trickster.

decent *adj* appropriate, becoming, befitting, comely, seemly, decorous, fit, proper, seemly; chaste, delicate, modest, pure; moderate, passable, respectable, tolerable.

deception *n* artifice, cheating, chicanery, cozenage, craftiness, deceitfulness, deception, double-dealing, duplicity, finesse, fraud, guile, hoax, hypocrisy, imposition, imposture, pretence, sham, treachery, trick, underhandedness, wile; cheat, chouse, ruse, stratagem, wile.

deceptive *adj* deceitful, deceiving, delusive, disingenuous, fallacious, false, illusive, illusory, misleading.

decide *vb* close, conclude, determine, end, settle, terminate; resolve; adjudge, adjudicate, award.

decided *adj* determined, firm, resolute, unhesitating, unwavering; absolute, categorical, positive, unequivocal; certain, clear, indisputable, undeniable, unmistakable, unquestionable.

deciduous *adj* caducous, nonperennial, temporary.

decipher *vb* explain, expound, interpret, reveal, solve, unfold, unravel; read.

decision *n* conclusion, determination, judgement, settlement; adjudication, award, decree, pronouncement, sentence; firmness, resolution.

decisive *adj* conclusive, determinative, final.

deck *vb* adorn, array, beautify, decorate, embellish, grace, ornament; apparel, attire, bedeck, clothe, dress, robe.

declaim *vb* harangue, mouth, rant, speak, spout.

declamation *n* declaiming, haranguing, mouthing, ranting, spouting.

declamatory *adj* bombastic, discursive, fustian, grandiloquent, high-flown, high-sounding, incoherent, inflated, pompous, pretentious, rhetorical, swelling, turgid.

declaration *n* affirmation, assertion, asseveration, averment, avowal, protestation, statement; announcement, proclamation, publication.

declaratory *adj* affirmative, annunciatory, assertive, declarative, definite, enunciative, enunciatory, expressive; explanatory, expository.

declare *vb* advertise, affirm, announce, assert, asseverate, aver, blazon, bruit, proclaim, promulgate, pronounce, publish, state, utter.

declension *n* decadence, decay, decline, degeneracy, deterioration, diminution; inflection, variation; declination, nonacceptance, refusal.

declination *n* bending, descent, inclination; decadence, decay, decline, degeneracy, degeneration, degradation, deterioration, diminution; aberration, departure, deviation, digression, divagation, divergence; declinature, nonacceptance, refusal.

decline *vb* incline, lean, slope; decay, droop, fail, flag, languish, pine, sink; degenerate, depreciate, deteriorate; decrease, diminish, dwindle, fade, ebb, lapse, lessen, wane; avoid, refuse, reject; inflect, vary. * *n* decadence, decay, declension, declination, degeneracy, deterioration, diminution, wane; atrophy, consumption, marasmus, phthisis; declivity, hill, incline, slope.

declivity *n* declination, descent, incline, slope.

decompose *vb* analyse, disintegrate, dissolve, distil, resolve, separate; corrupt, decay, putrefy, rot.

decomposition *n* analysis, break-up, disintegration, resolution; caries, corruption, crumbling, decay, disintegration, dissolution, putrescence, rotting.

decorate *vb* adorn, beautify, bedeck, deck, embellish, enrich, garnish, grace, ornament.

decoration *n* adorning, beautifying, bedecking, decking, enriching, garnishing, ornamentation, ornamenting; adornment, enrichment, embellishment, ornament.

decorous *adj* appropriate, becoming, befitting, comely, decent, fit, suitable, proper, sedate, seemly, staid.

decorum *n* appropriate behaviour, courtliness, decency, deportment, dignity, gravity, politeness, propriety, sedateness, seemliness.

decoy *vb* allure, deceive, ensnare, entice, entrap, inveigle, lure, seduce, tempt. * *n* allurement, lure, enticement.

decrease *vb* abate, contract, decline, diminish, dwindle, ebb, lessen, subside, wane; curtail, diminish, lessen, lower, reduce, retrench. * *n* abatement, contraction, declension, decline, decrement, diminishing, diminution, ebb, ebbing, lessening, reduction, subsidence, waning.

decree *vb* adjudge, appoint, command, decide, determine, enact, enjoin, order, ordain. * *n* act, command, edict, enactment, fiat, law, mandate, order, ordinance, precept, regulation, statute.

decrement *n* decrease, diminution, lessening, loss, waste.

decrepit *adj* feeble, effete, shattered, wasted, weak; aged, crippled, superannuated.

decry *vb* abuse, belittle, blame, condemn, denounce, depreciate, detract, discredit, disparage, run down, traduce, underrate, undervalue.

dedicate *vb* consecrate, devote, hallow, sanctify; address, inscribe.

deduce *vb* conclude, derive, draw, gather, infer.

deducible *adj* derivable, inferable.

deduct *vb* remove, subtract, withdraw; abate, detract.

deduction *n* removal, subtraction, withdrawal; abatement, allowance, defalcation, discount, rebate, reduction, reprise; conclusion, consequence, corollary, inference.

deed *n* achievement, act, action, derring-do, exploit, feat, performance; fact, truth, reality; charter, contract, document, indenture, instrument, transfer.

deem *vb* account, believe, conceive, consider, count, estimate, hold, imagine, judge, regard, suppose, think; fancy, opine.

deep *adj* abysmal, extensive, great, profound; abstruse, difficult, hard, intricate, knotty, mysterious, recondite, unfathomable; astute, cunning, designing, discerning, intelligent, insidious, penetrating, sagacious, shrewd; absorbed, engrossed; bass, grave, low; entire, great, heartfelt, thorough. * *n* main, ocean, water, sea; abyss, depth, profundity; enigma, mystery, riddle; silence, stillness.

deeply *adv* profoundly; completely, entirely, extensively, greatly, thoroughly; affectingly, distressingly, feelingly, mournfully, sadly.

deface *vb* blotch, deform, disfigure, injure, mar, mutilate, obliterate, soil, spoil, sully, tarnish.

de facto *adj* actual, real. * *adv* actually, in effect, in fact, really, truly.

defalcate *vb* abate, curtail, retrench, lop.

defalcation *n* abatement, deduction, diminution, discount, reduction; default, deficiency, deficit, shortage, shortcoming; embezzlement, fraud.

defamation *n* abuse, aspersion, back-biting, calumny, detraction, disparagement, libel, obloquy, opprobrium, scandal, slander.

defamatory *adj* abusive, calumnious, libellous, slanderous.

defame *vb* abuse, asperse, blacken, belie, besmirch, blemish, calumniate, detract, disgrace, dishonour, libel, malign, revile, slander, smirch, traduce, vilify.

default *vb* defalcate, dishonour, fail, repudiate, welsh. * *n* defalcation, failure, lapse, neglect, offence, omission, oversight, shortcoming ; defect, deficiency, deficit, delinquency, destitution, fault, lack, want.

defaulter *n* delinquent, embezzler, offender, peculator.

defeat *vb* beat, checkmate, conquer, discomfit, overcome, overpower, overthrow, repulse, rout, ruin, vanquish; baffle, balk, block, disappoint, disconcert, foil, frustrate, thwart. * *n* discomfiture, downfall, overthrow, repulse, rout, vanquishment; bafflement, checkmate, frustration.

defect *vb* abandon, desert, rebel, revolt. * *n* default, deficiency, destitution, lack, shortcoming, spot, taint, want; blemish, blotch, error, flaw, imperfection, mistake; failing, fault, foible.

defection *n* abandonment, desertion, rebellion, revolt; apostasy, backsliding, dereliction.

defective *adj* deficient, inadequate, incomplete, insufficient, scant, short; faulty, imperfect, marred.

defence *n* defending, guarding, holding, maintaining, maintenance, protection; buckler, bulwark, fortification, guard, protection, rampart, resistance, shield; apology, excuse, justification, plea, vindication.

defenceless *adj* exposed, helpless, unarmed, unprotected, unguarded, unshielded, weak.

defend *vb* cover, fortify, guard, preserve, protect, safeguard, screen, secure, shelter, shield; assert, espouse, justify, maintain, plead, uphold, vindicate.

defender *n* asserter, maintainer, pleader, upholder; champion, protector, vindicator.

defer[1] *vb* adjourn, delay, pigeonhole, procrastinate, postpone, prorogue, protract, shelve, table.

defer[2] *vb* abide by, acknowledge, bow to, give way, submit, yield; admire, esteem, honour, regard, respect.

deference *n* esteem, homage, honour, obeisance, regard, respect, reverence, veneration; complaisance, consideration; obedience, submission.

deferential *adj* respectful, reverential.

defiance *n* challenge, daring; contempt, despite, disobedience, disregard, opposition, spite.

defiant *adj* contumacious, recalcitrant, resistant; bold, courageous, resistant.

deficiency *n* dearth, default, deficit, insufficiency, lack, meagreness, scantiness, scarcity, shortage, shortness, want; defect, error, failing, falling, fault, foible, frailty, imperfection, infirmity, weakness.

deficient *adj* defective, faulty, imperfect, inadequate, incomplete, insufficient, lacking, scant, scanty, scarce, short, unsatisfactory, wanting.

deficit *n* deficiency, lack, scarcity, shortage, shortness.

defile[1] *vb* dirty, foul, soil, stain, tarnish; contaminate, debase, poison, pollute, sully, taint, vitiate; corrupt, debauch, deflower, ravish, seduce, violate.

defile[2] *vb* file, march, parade, promenade. * *n* col, gorge, pass, passage, ravine, strait.

define *vb* bound, circumscribe, designate, delimit, demarcate, determine, explain, limit, specify.

definite *adj* defined, determinate, determined, fixed, restricted; assured, certain, clear, exact, explicit, positive, precise, specific, unequivocal.

definitive *adj* categorical, determinate, explicit, express, positive, unconditional; conclusive, decisive, final.

deflect *vb* bend, deviate, diverge, swerve, turn, twist, waver, wind.

deflower *vb* corrupt, debauch, defile, seduce.

deform *vb* deface, disfigure, distort, injure, mar, misshape, ruin, spoil.

deformity *n* abnormality, crookedness, defect, disfigurement, distortion, inelegance, irregularity, malformation, misproportion, misshapenness, monstrosity, ugliness.

defraud *vb* beguile, cheat, chouse, circumvent, cozen, deceive, delude, diddle, dupe, embezzle, gull, overreach, outwit, pilfer, rob, swindle, trick.

defray *vb* bear, discharge, liquidate, meet, pay, settle.

deft *adj* adroit, apt, clever, dab, dextrous, expert, handy, ready, skilful.

defunct *adj* dead, deceased, departed, extinct, gone; abrogated, annulled, cancelled, inoperative.

defy *vb* challenge, dare; brave, contemn, despise, disregard, face, flout, provoke, scorn, slight, spurn.

degeneracy *n* abasement, caducity, corruption, debasement, decadence, decay, declension, decline, decrease, degenerateness, degeneration, degradation, depravation, deterioration; inferiority, meanness, poorness.

degenerate *vb* decay, decline, decrease, deteriorate, retrograde, sink. * *adj* base, corrupt, decayed, degenerated, deteriorated, fallen, inferior, low, mean, perverted.

degeneration *n* debasement, decline, degeneracy, deterioration.

degradation *n* deposition, disgrace, dishonour, humiliation, ignominy; abasement, caducity, corruption, debasement, decadence, decline, degeneracy, degeneration, deterioration, perversion, vitiation.

degrade *vb* abase, alloy, break, cashier, corrupt, debase, demote, discredit, disgrace, dishonour, disparage, downgrade, humiliate, humble, lower, pervert, vitiate; deteriorate, impair, lower, sink.

degree *n* stage, step; class, grade, order, quality, rank, standing, station; extent, measure; division, interval, space.

deify *vb* apotheosize, idolize, glorify, revere; elevate, ennoble, exalt.

deign *vb* accord, condescend, grant, vouchsafe.

deject *vb* depress, discourage, dishearten, dispirit, sadden.

dejected *adj* blue, chapfallen, crestfallen, depressed, despondent, disheartened, dispirited, doleful, downcast, down-hearted, gloomy, low-spirited, miserable, sad, wretched.

delay *vb* defer, postpone, procrastinate; arrest, detain, check, hinder, impede, retard, stay, stop; prolong, protract; dawdle, linger, loiter, tarry. * *n* deferment, postponement, procrastination; check, detention, hindrance, impediment, retardation, stoppage; prolonging, protraction; dallying, dawdling, lingering, tarrying, stay, stop.

delectable *adj* agreeable, charming, delightful, enjoyable, gratifying, pleasant, pleasing.

delectation *n* delight, ecstasy, gladness, joy, rapture, ravishment, transport.

delegate *vb* appoint, authorize, mission, depute, deputize, transfer; commit, entrust. * *n* ambassador, commissioner, delegate, deputy, envoy, representative.

delete *vb* cancel, efface, erase, expunge, obliterate, remove.

deleterious *adj* deadly, destructive, lethal, noxious, poisonous; harmful, hurtful, injurious, pernicious, unwholesome.

deliberate *vb* cogitate, consider, consult, meditate, muse, ponder, reflect, ruminate, think, weigh. * *adj* careful, cautious, circumspect, considerate, heedful, purposeful, methodical, thoughtful, wary; well-advised, well-considered; aforethought, intentional, premeditated, purposed, studied.

deliberation *n* caution, circumspection, cogitation, consideration, coolness, meditation, prudence, reflection, thought, thoughtfulness, wariness; purpose.

delicacy *n* agreeableness, daintiness, deliciousness, pleasantness, relish, savouriness; bonne bouche, dainty, tidbit; elegance, fitness, lightness, niceness, nicety, smoothness, softness, tenderness; fragility, frailty, slenderness, slightness, tenderness, weakness; carefulness, discrimination, fastidiousness, finesse, nicety, scrupulousness, sensitivity, subtlety, tact; purity, refinement, sensibility.

delicate *adj* agreeable, delicious, pleasant, pleasing, palatable, savoury; elegant, exquisite, fine, nice; careful, dainty, discriminating, fastidious, scrupulous; fragile, frail, slender, slight, tender, delicate; pure, refined.

delicious *adj* dainty, delicate, luscious, nice, palatable, savory; agreeable, charming, choice, delightful, exquisite, grateful, pleasant.

delight *vb* charm, enchant, enrapture, gratify, please, ravish, rejoice, satisfy, transport. * *n* charm, delectation, ecstasy, enjoyment, gladness, gratification, happiness, joy, pleasure, rapture, ravishment, satisfaction, transport.

delightful *adj* agreeable, captivating, charming, delectable, enchanting, enjoyable, enrapturing, rapturous, ravishing, transporting.

delineate *vb* design, draw, figure, paint, sketch, trace; depict, describe, picture, portray.

delineation *n* design, draught, drawing, figure, outline, sketch; account, description, picture, portrayal.

delinquency *n* crime, fault, misdeed, misdemeanour, offence, wrong-doing.

delinquent *adj* negligent, offending. * *n* criminal, culprit, defaulter, malefactor, miscreant, misdoer, offender, transgressor, wrong-doer.

delirious *adj* crazy, demented, deranged, frantic, frenzied, light-headed, mad, insane, raving, wandering.

delirium *n* aberration, derangement, frenzy, hallucination, incoherence, insanity, lunacy, madness, raving, wandering.

deliver *vb* emancipate, free, liberate, release; extricate, redeem, rescue, save; commit, give, impart, transfer; cede, grant, relinquish, resign, yield; declare, emit, promulgate, pronounce, speak, utter; deal, discharge.

deliverance *n* emancipation, escape, liberation, redemption, release.

delivery *n* conveyance, surrender; commitment, giving, rendering, transference, transferral, transmission; elocution, enunciation, pronunciation, speech, utterance; childbirth, confinement, labour, parturition, travail.

dell *n* dale, dingle, glen, valley, ravine.

delude *vb* beguile, cheat, chouse, circumvent, cozen, deceive, dupe, gull, misguide, mislead, overreach, trick.

deluge *vb* drown, inundate, overflow, overwhelm, submerge. * *n* cataclysm, downpour, flood, inundation, overflow, rush.

delusion *n* artifice, cheat, clap-trap, deceit, dodge,

fetch, fraud, imposition, imposture, ruse, snare, trick, wile; deception, error, fallacy, fancy, hallucination, illusion, mistake, mockery, phantasm.

delusive *adj* deceitful, deceiving, deceptive, fallacious, illusional, illusionary, illusive.

demand *vb* challenge, exact, require; claim, necessitate, require; ask, inquire. * *n* claim, draft, exaction, requirement, requisition; call, want; inquiry, interrogation, question.

demarcation *n* bound, boundary, confine, distinction, division, enclosure, limit, separation.

demeanour *n* air, bearing, behaviour, carriage, deportment, manner, mien.

demented *adj* crack-brained, crazed, crazy, daft, deranged, dotty, foolish, idiotic, infatuated, insane, lunatic.

dementia *n* idiocy, insanity, lunacy.

demerit *n* delinquency, fault, ill-desert.

demise *vb* alienate, consign, convey, devolve, grant, transfer; bequeath, devise, leave, will. * *n* alienation, conveyance, transfer, transference, transmission; death, decease.

demolish *vb* annihilate, destroy, dismantle, level, over-throw, overturn, pulverize, raze, ruin.

demon *n* devil, fiend, kelpie, goblin, troll.

demoniac, demoniacal *adj* demonic, demonical, devilish, diabolic, diabolical, fiendish, hellish, infernal, Mephistophelean, Mephistophelian, satanic; delirious, distracted, frantic, frenzied, feverish, hysterical, mad, overwrought, rabid.

demonstrate *vb* establish, exhibit, illustrate, indicate, manifest, prove, show.

demonstration *n* display, exhibition, manifestation, show.

demonstrative *adj* affectionate, communicative, effusive, emotional, expansive, expressive, extroverted, open, outgoing, passionate, sentimental, suggestive, talkative, unreserved; absolute, apodictic, certain, conclusive, probative; exemplificative, illustrative.

demoralize *vb* corrupt, debase, debauch, deprave, vitiate; depress, discourage, dishearten, weaken.

demulcent *adj* emollient, lenitive, mild, mollifying, sedative, soothing.

demur *vb* halt, hesitate, pause, stop, waver; doubt, object, scruple. * *n* demurral, hesitance, hesitancy, hesitation, objection, pause, qualm, scruple.

demure *adj* prudish; coy, decorous, grave, modest, priggish, prudish, sedate, sober, staid.

den *n* cavern, cave; haunt, lair, resort, retreat.

denial *n* contradiction, controverting, negation; abjuration, disavowal, disclaimer, disowning; disallowance, refusal, rejection.

denizen *n* citizen, dweller, inhabitant, resident.

denominate *vb* call, christen, designate, dub, entitle, name, phrase, style, term.

denomination *n* appellation, designation, name, style, term, title; class, kind, sort; body, persuasion, school, sect.

denote *vb* betoken, connote, designate, imply, indicate, mark, mean, note, show, signify, typify.

dénouement *n* catastrophe, unravelling; consummation, issue, finale, upshot, conclusion, termination.

denounce *vb* menace, threaten; arraign, attack, brand, censure, condemn, proscribe, stigmatize, upbraid; accuse, inform, denunciate.

dense *adj* close, compact, compressed, condensed, thick; dull, slow, stupid.

dent *vb* depress, dint, indent, pit. * *n* depression, dint, indentation, nick, notch.

dentate *adj* notched, serrate, toothed.

denude *vb* bare, divest, strip.

denunciation *n* menace, threat; arraignment, censure, fulmination, invective; exposure.

deny *vb* contradict, gainsay, oppose, refute, traverse; abjure, abnegate, disavow, disclaim, disown, renounce; disallow, refuse, reject, withhold.

depart *vb* absent, disappear, vanish; abandon, decamp, go, leave, migrate, quit, remove, withdraw; decease, die; deviate, diverge, vary.

department *n* district, division, part, portion, province; bureau, function, office, province, sphere, station; branch, division, subdivision.

departure *n* exit, leaving, parting, removal, recession, removal, retirement, withdrawal; abandonment, forsaking; death, decease, demise, deviation, exit.

depend *vb* hang, hinge, turn.

dependant *n* client, hanger-on, henchman, minion, retainer, subordinate, vassal; attendant, circumstance, concomitant, consequence, corollary.

dependence *n* concatenation, connection, interdependence; confidence, reliance, trust; buttress, prop, staff, stay, support, supporter; contingency, need, subjection, subordination.

dependency *n* adjunct, appurtenance; colony, province.

dependent *adj* hanging, pendant; conditioned, contingent, relying, subject, subordinate.

depict *vb* delineate, limn, outline, paint, pencil, portray, sketch; describe, render, represent.

deplete *vb* drain, empty, evacuate, exhaust, reduce.

deplorable *adj* calamitous, distressful, distressing, grievous, lamentable, melancholy, miserable, mournful, pitiable, regrettable, sad, wretched.

deplore *vb* bemoan, bewail, grieve for, lament, mourn, regret.

deploy *vb* display, expand, extend, open, unfold.

deportment *n* air, bearing, behaviour, breeding, carriage, comportment, conduct, demeanour, manner, mien, port.

depose *vb* break, cashier, degrade, dethrone, dismiss, displace, oust, reduce; avouch, declare, depone, testify.

deposit *vb* drop, dump, precipitate; lay, put; bank, hoard, lodge, put, save, store; commit, entrust. * *n* diluvium, dregs, lees, precipitate, precipitation, sediment, settlement, settlings, silt; money, pawn, pledge, security, stake.

depositary *n* fiduciary, guardian, trustee.

deposition *n* affidavit, evidence, testimony; deposit, precipitation, settlement; dethroning, displacement, removal.
depository *n* deposit, depot, storehouse, warehouse.
depot *n* depository, magazine, storehouse, warehouse.
depravation *n* abasement, corruption, deterioration, impairing, injury, vitiation; debasement, degeneracy, degeneration, depravity, impairment.
depraved *adj* abandoned, corrupt, corrupted, debased, debauched, degenerate, dissolute, evil, graceless, hardened, immoral, lascivious, lewd, licentious, lost, perverted, profligate, reprobate, shameless, sinful, vicious, wicked.
depravity *n* corruption, degeneracy, depravedness; baseness, contamination, corruption, corruptness, criminality, demoralization, immorality, iniquity, license, perversion, vice, viciousness, wickedness.
depreciate *vb* underestimate, undervalue, underrate; belittle, censure, decry, degrade, disparage, malign, traduce.
depreciation *n* belittling, censure, derogation, detraction, disparagement, maligning, traducing.
depredation *n* despoiling, devastation, pilfering, pillage, plunder, rapine, robbery, spoliation, theft.
depress *vb* bow, detrude, drop, lower, reduce, sink; abase, abash, degrade, debase, disgrace, humble, humiliate; chill, damp, dampen, deject, discourage, dishearten, dispirit, sadden; deaden, lower.
depression *n* cavity, concavity, dent, dimple, dint, excavation, hollow, hollowness, indentation, pit; blues, cheerlessness, dejection, dejectedness, despondency, disconsolateness, disheartenment, dispiritedness, dole, dolefulness, downheartedness, dumps, gloom, gloominess, hypochondria, melancholy, sadness, vapours; inactivity, lowness, stagnation; abasement, debasement, degradation, humiliation.
deprivation *n* bereavement, dispossession, loss, privation, spoliation, stripping.
deprive *vb* bereave, denude, despoil, dispossess, divest, rob, strip.
depth *n* abyss, deepness, drop, profundity; extent, measure; middle, midst, stillness; astuteness, discernment, penetration, perspicacity, profoundness, profundity, sagacity, shrewdness.
deputation *n* commission, delegation; commissioners, deputies, delegates, delegation, embassies, envoys, legation.
depute *vb* accredit, appoint, authorize, charge, commission, delegate, empower, entrust.
deputy *adj* acting, assistant, vice, subordinate. * *n* agent, commissioner, delegate, envoy, factor, legate, lieutenant, proxy, representative, substitute, viceregent.
derange *vb* confound, confuse, disarrange, disconcert, disorder, displace, madden, perturb, unsettle; discompose, disconcert, disturb, perturb, ruffle, upset; craze, madden, unbalance, unhinge.
derangement *n* confusion, disarrangement, disorder, irregularity; discomposure, disturbance, perturbation; aberration, alienation, delirium, dementia, hallucination, insanity, lunacy, madness, mania.
derelict *adj* abandoned, forsaken, left, relinquished; delinquent, faithless, guilty, neglectful, negligent, unfaithful. * *n* castaway, castoff, outcast, tramp, vagrant, wreck, wretch.
dereliction *n* abandonment, desertion, relinquishement, renunciation; delinquency, failure, faithlessness, fault, neglect, negligence.
deride *vb* chaff, flout, gibe, insult, jeer, lampoon, mock, ridicule, satirize, scoff, scorn, sneer, taunt.
derision *n* contempt, disrespect, insult, laughter, mockery, ridicule, scorn.
derisive *adj* contemptuous, contumelious, mocking, ridiculing, scoffing, scornful.
derivation *n* descent, extraction, genealogy; etymology; deducing, deriving, drawing, getting, obtaining; beginning, foundation, origination, source.
derive *vb* draw, get, obtain, receive; deduce, follow, infer, trace.
derogate *vb* compromise, depreciate, detract, diminish, disparage, lessen.
derogatory *adj* belittling, depreciative, deprecatory, detracting, dishonouring, disparaging, injurious.
descant *vb* amplify, animadvert, dilate, discourse, discuss, enlarge, expatiate. * *n* melody, soprano, treble; animadversion, commentary, remarks; discourse, discussion.
descend *vb* drop, fall, pitch, plunge, sink, swoop; alight, dismount; go, pass, proceed, devolve; derive, issue, originate.
descendants *npl* offspring, issue, posterity, progeny.
descent *n* downrush, drop, fall; descending; decline, declivity, dip, pitch, slope; ancestry, derivation, extraction, genealogy, lineage, parentage, pedigree; assault, attack, foray, incursion, invasion, raid.
describe *vb* define, delineate, draw, illustrate, limn, sketch, specify, trace; detail; depict, explain, narrate, portray, recount, relate, represent; characterize.
description *n* delineation, tracing; account, depiction, explanation, narration, narrative, portrayal, recital, relation, report, representation; class, kind, sort, species.
descry *vb* behold, discover, discern, distinguish, espy, observe, perceive, see; detect, recognize.
desecrate *vb* abuse, pervert, defile, pollute, profane, violate.
desert[1] *n* due, excellence, merit, worth; punishment, reward.
desert[2] *vb* abandon, abscond, forsake, leave, quit, relinquish, renounce, resign, quit, vacate.

desert[3] *adj* barren, desolate, forsaken, lonely, solitary, uncultivated, uninhabited, unproductive, untilled, waste, wild.
deserted *adj* abandoned, forsaken, relinquished.
deserter *n* abandoner, forsaker, quitter, runaway; apostate, backslider, fugitive, recreant, renegade, revolter, traitor, turncoat.
desertion *n* abandonment, dereliction, recreancy, relinquishment.
deserve *vb* earn, gain, merit, procure, win.
desiderate *vb* desire, lack, miss, need, want.
design *vb* brew, concoct, contrive, devise, intend, invent, mean, plan, project, scheme; intend, mean, purpose; delineate, describe, draw, outline, sketch, trace. * *n* aim, device, drift, intent, intention, mark, meaning, object, plan, proposal, project, purport, purpose, scheme, scope; delineation, draught, drawing, outline, plan, sketch; adaptation, artifice, contrivance, invention, inventiveness.
designate *vb* denote, distinguish, indicate, particularize, select, show, specify, stipulate; characterize, define, describe; call, christen, denominate, dub, entitle, name, style; allot, appoint, christen.
designation *n* indication, particularization, selection, specification; class, description, kind; appellation, denomination, name, style, title.
designing *adj* artful, astute, crafty, crooked, cunning, deceitful, insidious, intriguing, Machiavellian, scheming, sly, subtle, treacherous, trickish, tricky, unscrupulous, wily.
desirable *adj* agreeable, beneficial, covètable, eligible, enviable, good, pleasing, preferable.
desire *vb* covet, crave, desiderate, fancy, hanker after, long for, lust after, want, wish, yearn for; ask, entreat, request, solicit. * *n* eroticism, lasciviousness, libidinousness, libido, lust, lustfulness, passion; eagerness, fancy, hope, inclination, mind, partiality, penchant, pleasure, volition, want, wish.
desirous *adj* avid, eager, desiring, longing, solicitous, wishful.
desist *vb* cease, discontinue, forbear, pause, stay, stop.
desolate *vb* depopulate, despoil, destroy, devastate, pillage, plunder, ravage, ruin, sack. * *adj* bare, barren, bleak, desert, forsaken, lonely, solitary, unfrequented, uninhabited, waste, wild; companionable, lonely, lonesome, solitary; desolated, destroyed, devastated, ravaged, ruined; cheerless, comfortless, companionless, disconsolate, dreary, forlorn, forsaken, miserable, wretched.
desolation *n* destruction, devastation, havoc, ravage, ruin; barrenness, bleakness, desolateness, dreariness, loneliness, solitariness, solitude, wildness; gloom, gloominess, misery, sadness, unhappiness, wretchedness.
despair *vb* despond, give up, lose hope. * *n* dejection, desperation, despondency, disheartenment, hopelessness.
despatch *see* **dispatch**.
desperado *n* daredevil, gangster, marauder, ruffian, thug, tough.
desperate *adj* despairing, despondent, desponding, hopeless; forlorn, irretrievable; extreme; audacious, daring, foolhardy, frantic, furious, headstrong, precipitate, rash, reckless, violent, wild, wretched; extreme, great, monstrous, prodigious, supreme.
desperation *n* despair, hopelessness; fury, rage.
despicable *adj* abject, base, contemptible, degrading, low, mean, paltry, pitiful, shameful, sordid, vile, worthless.
despise *vb* contemn, disdain, disregard, neglect, scorn, slight, spurn, undervalue.
despite *n* malevolence, malice, malignity, spite; contempt, contumacy, defiance. * *prep* notwithstanding.
despoil *vb* bereave, denude, deprive, dispossess, divest, strip; devastate, fleece, pillage, plunder, ravage, rifle, rob.
despond *vb* despair, give up, lose hope, mourn, sorrow.
despondency *n* blues, dejection, depression, discouragement, gloom, hopelessness, melancholy, sadness.
despondent *adj* dejected, depressed, discouraged, disheartened, dispirited, low-spirited, melancholy.
despot *n* autocrat, dictator; oppressor, tyrant.
despotic *adj* absolute, arrogant, autocratic, dictatorial, imperious; arbitrary, oppressive, tyrannical, tyrannous.
despotism *n* absolutism, autocracy, dictatorship; oppression, tyranny.
destination *n* appointment, decree, destiny, doom, fate, foreordainment, foreordination, fortune, lot, ordination, star; aim, design, drift, end, intention, object, purpose, scope; bourne, goal, harbour, haven, journey's end, resting-place, terminus.
destine *vb* allot, appoint, assign, consecrate, devote, ordain; design, intend, predetermine; decree, doom, foreordain, predestine.
destitute *adj* distressed, indigent, moneyless, necessitous, needy, penniless, penurious, pinched, poor, reduced, wanting.
destitution *n* indigence, need, penury, poverty, privation, want.
destroy *vb* demolish, overthrow, overturn, subvert, raze, ruin; annihilate, dissolve, efface, quench; desolate, devastate, devour, ravage, waste; eradicate, extinguish, extirpate, kill, uproot, slay.
destruction *n* demolition, havoc, overthrow, ruin, subversion; desolation, devastation, holocaust, ravage; annihilation, eradication, extinction, extirpation; death, massacre, murder, slaughter.
destructive *adj* baleful, baneful, deadly, deleterious, detrimental, fatal, hurtful, injurious, lethal, mischievous, noxious, pernicious, ruinous; annihilatory, eradicative, exterminative, extirpative.

desultory *adj* capricious, cursory, discursive, erratic, fitful, inconstant, inexact, irregular, loose, rambling, roving, slight, spasmodic, unconnected, unmethodical, unsettled, unsystematic, vague, wandering.
detach *vb* disengage, disconnect, disjoin, dissever, disunite, divide, part, separate, sever, unfix; appoint, detail, send.
detail *vb* delineate, depict, describe, enumerate, narrate, particularize, portray, recount, rehearse, relate, specify; appoint, detach, send. * *n* account, narration, narrative, recital, relation; appointment, detachment; item, part.
details *npl* facts, minutiae, particulars, parts.
detain *vb* arrest, check, delay, hinder, hold, keep, restrain, retain, stay, stop; confine.
detect *vb* ascertain, catch, descry, disclose, discover, expose, reveal, unmask.
detention *n* confinement, delay, hindrance, restraint, withholding.
deter *vb* debar, discourage, frighten, hinder, prevent, restrain, stop, withhold.
deteriorate *vb* corrupt, debase, degrade, deprave, disgrace, impair, spoil, vitiate; decline, degenerate, depreciate, worsen.
deterioration *n* corruption, debasement, degradation, depravation, vitiation, perversion; caducity, decadence, decay, decline, degeneracy, degeneration, impairment.
determinate *adj* absolute, certain, definite, determined, established, explicit, express, fixed, limited, positive, settled; conclusive, decided, decisive, definitive.
determination *n* ascertainment, decision, deciding, determining, fixing, settlement, settling; conclusion, judgment, purpose, resolution, resolve, result; direction, leaning, tendency; firmness, constancy, effort, endeavour, exertion, grit, persistence, stamina, resoluteness; definition, limitation, qualification.
determine *vb* adjust, conclude, decide, end, establish, fix, resolve, settle; ascertain, certify, check, verify; impel, incline, induce, influence, lead, turn; decide, resolve; condition, define, limit; compel, necessitate.
detest *vb* abhor, abominate, despise, execrate, hate, loathe, nauseate, recoil from.
detestable *adj* abhorred, abominable, accursed, cursed, damnable, execrable, hateful, odious; disgusting, loathsome, nauseating, offensive, repulsive, sickening, vile.
dethrone *vb* depose, uncrown.
detract *vb* abuse, asperse, belittle, calumniate, debase, decry, defame, depreciate, derogate, disparage, slander, traduce, vilify; deprecate, deteriorate, diminish, lessen.
detraction *n* abuse, aspersion, calumny, censure, defamation, depreciation, derogation, disparagement, slander.
detriment *n* cost, damage, disadvantage, evil, harm, hurt, injury, loss, mischief, prejudice.
detrimental *adj* baleful, deleterious, destructive, harmful, hurtful, injurious, mischievous, pernicious, prejudicial.
devastate *vb* desolate, despoil, destroy, lay waste, harry, pillage, plunder, ravage, sack, spoil, strip, waste.
devastation *n* despoiling, destroying, harrying, pillaging, plundering, ravaging, sacking, spoiling, stripping, wasting; desolation, destruction, havoc, pillage, rapine, ravage, ruin, waste.
develop *vb* disentangle, disclose, evolve, exhibit, explicate, uncover, unfold, unravel; cultivate, grow, mature, open, progress.
development *n* disclosure, disentanglement, exhibition, unfolding, unravelling; growth, increase, maturation, maturing; evolution, growth, progression; elaboration, expansion, explication.
deviate *vb* alter, deflect, digress, diverge, sheer off, slew, tack, turn aside, wheel, wheel about; err, go astray, stray, swerve, wander; differ, vary.
deviation *n* aberration, departure, depression, divarication, divergence, turning; alteration, change, difference, variance, variation.
device *n* contraption, contrivance, gadget, invention; design, expedient, plan, project, resort, resource, scheme, shift; artifice, evasion, fraud, manoeuvre, ruse, stratagem, trick, wile; blazon, emblazonment, emblem, sign, symbol, type.
devil *n* archfiend, demon, fiend, goblin; Apollyon, Belial, Deuce, Evil One, Lucifer, Old Harry, Old Nick, Old Serpent, Prince of Darkness, Satan.
devilish *adj* demon, demonic, demonical, demoniac, demoniacal, diabolic, diabolical, fiendish, hellish, infernal, Mephistophelean, Mephistophelian, satanic; atrocious, barbarous, cruel, malevolent, malicious, malign, malignant, wicked.
devilry *n* devilment, diablerie, mischief; devilishness, fiendishness, wickedness.
devious *adj* deviating, erratic, roundabout, wandering; circuitous, confusing, crooked, labyrinthine, mazy, obscure; crooked, disingenuous, misleading, treacherous.
devise *vb* brew, compass, concert, concoct, contrive, dream up, excogitate, imagine, invent, plan, project, scheme; bequeath, demise, leave, will.
devoid *adj* bare, destitute, empty, vacant, void.
devolve *vb* alienate, consign, convey, deliver over, demise, fall, hand over, make over, pass, transfer.
devote *vb* appropriate, consecrate, dedicate, destine; set apart; addict, apply, give up, resign; consign, doom, give over.
devoted *adj* affectionate, attached, loving; ardent, assiduous, earnest, zealous.
devotee *n* bigot, enthusiast, fan, fanatic, zealot.
devotion *n* consecration, dedication, duty; devotedness, devoutness, fidelity, godliness, holiness, piety, religion, religiousness, saintliness, sanctity; adoration, prayer, worship; affection, attachment, love; ardour, devotedness, eagerness, earnestness, fervour, passion, spirit, zeal.

devotional *adj* devout, godly, pious, religious, saintly.

devour *vb* engorge, gorge, gulp down, raven, swallow eagerly, wolf; annihilate, consume, destroy, expend, spend, swallow up, waste.

devout *adj* devotional, godly, holy, pious, religious, saint-like, saintly; earnest, grave, serious, sincere, solemn.

dexterity *n* ability, address, adroitness, aptitude, aptness, art, cleverness, expertness, facility, knack, quickness, readiness, skilfulness, skill, tact.

dexterous, dextrous *adj* able, adept, adroit, apt, deft, clever, expert, facile, handy, nimble-fingered, quick, ready, skilful.

diabolic, diabolical *adj* atrocious, barbarous, cruel, devilish, fiendish, hellish, impious, infernal, malevolent, malign, malignant, satanic, wicked.

diagram *n* chart, delineation, figure, graph, map, outline, plan, sketch.

dialect *n* idiom, localism, provincialism; jargon, lingo, patois, patter; language, parlance, phraseology, speech, tongue.

dialectal *adj* idiomatic, local, provincial.

dialectic, dialectical *adj* analytical, critical, logical, rational, rationalistic.

dialogue *n* colloquy, communication, conference, conversation, converse, intercourse, interlocution; playbook, script, speech, text, words.

diaphanous *adj* clear, filmy, gossamer, pellucid, sheer, translucent, transparent.

diarrhoea *n* (*med*) flux, looseness, purging, relaxation.

diary *n* chronicle, daybook, journal, register.

diatribe *n* disputation, disquisition, dissertation; abuse, harangue, invective, philippic, reviling, tirade.

dictate *vb* bid, direct, command, decree, enjoin, ordain, order, prescribe, require. * *n* bidding, command, decree, injunction, order; maxim, precept, rule.

dictation *n* direction, order, prescription.

dictator *n* autocrat, despot, tyrant.

dictatorial *adj* absolute, unlimited, unrestricted; authoritative, despotic, dictatory, domineering, imperious, overbearing, peremptory, tyrannical.

dictatorship *n* absolutism, authoritarianism, autocracy, despotism, iron rule, totalitarianism, tyranny.

diction *n* expression, language, phraseology, style, vocabulary, wording.

dictionary *n* glossary, lexicon, thesaurus, vocabulary, wordbook; cyclopedia, encyclopedia.

dictum *n* affirmation, assertion, saying; (*law*) award, arbitrament, decision, opinion.

didactic, didactical *adj* educational, instructive, pedagogic, preceptive.

die *vb* decease, demise, depart, expire, pass on; decay, decline, fade, fade out, perish, wither; cease, disappear, vanish; faint, fall, sink.

diet[1] *vb* eat, feed, nourish; abstain, fast, regulate, slim. * *n* aliment, fare, food, nourishment, nutriment, provision, rations, regimen, subsistence, viands, victuals.

diet[2] *n* assembly, congress, convention, convocation, council, parliament.

differ *vb* deviate, diverge, vary; disagree, dissent; bicker, contend, dispute, quarrel, wrangle.

difference *n* contrariety, contrast, departure, deviation, disagreement, disparity, dissimilarity, dissimilitude, divergence, diversity, heterogeneity, inconformity, nuance, opposition, unlikeness, variation; alienation, altercation, bickering, breach, contention, contest, controversy, debate, disaccord, disagreement, disharmony, dispute, dissension, embroilment, falling out, irreconcilability, jarring, misunderstanding, quarrel, rupture, schism, strife, variance, wrangle; discrimination, distinction.

different *adj* distinct, nonidentical, separate, unlike; contradistinct, contrary, contrasted, deviating, disagreeing, discrepant, dissimilar, divergent, diverse, incompatible, incongruous, unlike, variant, various; divers, heterogeneous, manifold, many, sundry.

difficult *adj* arduous, exacting, hard, Herculean, stiff, tough, uphill; abstruse, complex, intricate, knotty, obscure, perplexing; austere, rigid, unaccommodating, uncompliant, unyielding; dainty, fastidious, squeamish.

difficulty *n* arduousness, laboriousness; bar, barrier, crux, deadlock, dilemma, embarrassment, emergency, exigency, fix, hindrance, impediment, knot, obstacle, obstruction, perplexity, pickle, pinch, predicament, stand, standstill, thwart, trial, trouble; cavil, objection; complication, controversy, difference, embarrassment, embroilment, imbroglio, misunderstanding.

diffidence *n* distrust, doubt, hesitance, hesitancy, hesitation, reluctance; bashfulness, modesty, sheepishness, shyness, timidity.

diffident *adj* distrustful, doubtful, hesitant, hesitating, reluctant; bashful, modest, over-modest, sheepish, shy, timid.

diffuse[1] *vb* circulate, disperse, disseminate, distribute, intermingle, propagate, scatter, spread, strew.

diffuse[2] *adj* broadcast, dispersed, scattered, sparse, sporadic, widespread; broad, extensive, liberal, profuse, wide; copious, loose, prolix, rambling, verbose, wordy.

diffusion *n* circulation, dispersion, dissemination, distribution, extension, propagation, spread, strewing.

diffusive *adj* expansive, permeating, wide-reaching; spreading, dispersive, disseminative, distributive, distributory.

dig *vb* channel, delve, excavate, grub, hollow out, quarry, scoop, tunnel. * *n* poke, punch, thrust.

digest[1] *vb* arrange, classify, codify, dispose, methodize, systemize, tabulate; concoct; assimilate, consider, contemplate, meditate, ponder, reflect upon, study; master; macerate, soak, steep.

digest[2] *n* code, system; abridgement, abstract, brief, breviary, compend, compendium, conspectus, epitome, summary, synopsis.
dignified *adj* august, courtly, decorous, grave, imposing, majestic, noble, stately.
dignify *vb* advance, aggrandize, elevate, ennoble, exalt, promote; adorn, grace, honour.
dignity *n* elevation, eminence, exaltation, excellence, glory, greatness, honour, place, rank, respectability, standing, station; decorum, grandeur, majesty, nobleness, stateliness; preferment; dignitary, magistrate; elevation, height.
digress *vb* depart, deviate, diverge, expatiate, wander.
digression *n* departure, deviation, divergence; episode, excursus.
dilapidate *vb* demolish, destroy, disintegrate, ruin, waste.
dilapidated *adj* decayed, ruined, run down, wasted.
dilapidation *n* decay, demolition, destruction, disintegration, disrepair, dissolution, downfall, ruin, waste.
dilate *vb* distend, enlarge, expand, extend, inflate, swell, tend, widen; amplify, descant, dwell, enlarge, expatiate.
dilation *n* amplification, bloating, distension, enlargement, expanding, expansion, spreading, swelling.
dilatory *adj* backward, behind-hand, delaying, laggard, lagging, lingering, loitering, off-putting, procrastinating, slack, slow, sluggish, tardy.
dilemma *n* difficulty, fix, plight, predicament, problem, quandary, strait.
diligence *n* activity, application, assiduity, assiduousness, attention, care, constancy, earnestness, heedfulness, industry, laboriousness, perseverance, sedulousness.
diligent *adj* active, assiduous, attentive, busy, careful, constant, earnest, hard-working, indefatigable, industrious, laborious, notable, painstaking, persevering, persistent, sedulous, tireless.
dilly-dally *vb* dally, dawdle. delay, lag, linger, loiter, saunter, trifle.
dilute *vb* attenuate, reduce, thin, weaken. * *adj* attenuated, diluted, thin, weak, wishy-washy.
dim *vb* blur, cloud, darken, dull, obscure, sully, tarnish. * *adj* cloudy, dark, dusky, faint, ill-defined, indefinite, indistinct, mysterious, obscure, shadowy; dull, obtuse; clouded, confused, darkened, faint, obscured; blurred, dulled, sullied, tarnished.
dimension *n* extension, extent, measure.
dimensions *npl* amplitude, bigness, bulk, capacity, greatness, largeness, magnitude, mass, massiveness, size, volume; measurements.
diminish *vb* abate, belittle, contract, decrease, lessen, reduce; curtail, cut, dwindle, melt, narrow, shrink, shrivel, subside, taper off, weaken.
diminution *n* abatement, abridgement, attenuation, contraction, curtailment, decrescendo, cut, decay, decrease, deduction, lessening, reduction, retrenchment, weakening.
diminutive *adj* contracted, dwarfish, little, minute, puny, pygmy, small, tiny.
din *vb* beat, boom, clamour, drum, hammer, pound, repeat, ring, thunder. * *n* bruit, clamour, clash, clatter, crash, crashing, hubbub, hullabaloo, hurly-burly, noise, outcry, racket, row, shout, uproar.
dingle *n* dale, dell, glen, vale, valley.
dingy *adj* brown, dun, dusky; bedimmed, colourless, dimmed, dulled, faded, obscure, smirched, soiled, sullied.
dint *n* blow, stroke; dent, indentation, nick, notch; force, power.
diocese *n* bishopric, charge, episcopate, jurisdiction, see.
dip *vb* douse, duck, immerse, plunge, souse; bail, ladle; dive, pitch; bend, incline, slope. * *n* decline, declivity, descent, drop, fall; concavity, depression, hole, hollow, pit, sink; bathe, dipping, ducking, sousing, swim.
diplomat *n* diplomatist, envoy, legate, minister, negotiator.
dire *adj* alarming, awful, calamitous, cruel, destructive, disastrous, dismal, dreadful, fearful, gloomy, horrible, horrid, implacable, inexorable, portentous, shocking, terrible, terrific, tremendous, woeful.
direct *vb* aim. cast, level, point, turn; advise, conduct, control, dispose, guide, govern, manage, regulate, rule; command, bid, enjoin, instruct, order; lead, show; address, superscribe. * *adj* immediate, straight, undeviating; absolute, categorical, express, plain, unambiguous; downright, earnest, frank, ingenuous, open, outspoken, sincere, straightforward, unequivocal.
direction *n* aim; tendency; bearing, course; administration, conduct, control, government, management, oversight, superintendence; guidance, lead; command, order, prescription; address, superscription.
directly *adv* absolutely, expressly, openly, unambiguously; forthwith, immediately, instantly, quickly, presently, promptly, soon, speedily.
director *n* boss, manager, superintendent; adviser, counsellor, guide, instructor, mentor, monitor.
direful *adj* awful, calamitous, dire, dreadful, fearful, gloomy, horrible, shocking, terrible, terrific, tremendous.
dirge *n* coronach, elegy, lament, monody, requiem, threnody.
dirty *vb* befoul, defile, draggle, foul, pollute, soil, sully. * *adj* begrimed. defiled, filthy, foul, mucky, nasty, soiled, unclean; clouded, cloudy, dark, dull, muddy, sullied; base, beggarly, contemptible, despicable, grovelling, low, mean, paltry, pitiful, scurvy, shabby, sneaking, squalid; disagreeable, rainy, sloppy, uncomfortable.
disability *n* disablement, disqualification, impotence, impotency, inability, incapacity, incompetence, incompetency, unfitness, weakness.

disable *vb* cripple, enfeeble, hamstring, impair, paralyse, unman, weaken; disenable, disqualify, incapacitate, unfit.
disabuse *vb* correct, undeceive.
disadvantage *n* disadvantageousness, inconvenience, unfavourableness; damage, detriment, disservice, drawback, harm, hindrance, hurt, injury, loss, prejudice.
disadvantageous *adj* inconvenient, inexpedient, unfavourable; deleterious, detrimental, harmful, hurtful, injurious, prejudicial.
disaffect *vb* alienate, disdain, dislike, disorder, estrange.
disaffected *adj* alienated, disloyal, dissatisfied, estranged.
disaffection *n* alienation, breach, disagreement, dislike, disloyalty, dissatisfaction, estrangement, repugnance, ill will, unfriendliness.
disagree *vb* deviate, differ, diverge, vary; dissent; argue, bicker, clash, debate, dispute, quarrel, wrangle.
disagreeable *adj* contrary, displeasing, distasteful, nasty, offensive, unpleasant, unpleasing, unsuitable.
disagreement *n* deviation, difference, discrepancy, dissimilarity, dissimilitude, divergence, diversity, incongruity, unlikeness; disaccord, dissent; argument, bickering, clashing, conflict, contention, dispute, dissension, disunion, disunity, jarring, misunderstanding, quarrel, strife, variance, wrangle.
disallow *vb* forbid, prohibit; disapprove, reject; deny, disavow, disclaim, dismiss, disown, repudiate.
disappear *vb* depart, fade, vanish; cease, dissolve.
disappoint *vb* baffle, balk, deceive, defeat, delude, disconcert, foil, frustrate, mortify, tantalize, thwart, vex.
disappointment *n* baffling, balk, failure, foiling, frustration, miscarriage, mortification, unfulfilment.
disapprobation *n* blame, censure, condemnation, disapproval, dislike, displeasure, reproof.
disapprove *vb* blame, censure, condemn, deprecate, dislike; disallow, reject.
disarrange *vb* agitate, confuse, derange, disallow, dishevel, dislike, dislocate, disorder, disorganize, disturb, jumble, reject, rumple, tumble, unsettle.
disarray *n* confusion, disorder; dishabille.
disaster *n* accident, adversity, blow, calamity, casualty, catastrophe, misadventure, mischance, misfortune, mishap, reverse, ruin, stroke.
disastrous *adj* adverse, calamitous, catastrophic, destructive, hapless, ill-fated, ill-starred, ruinous, unfortunate, unlucky, unpropitious, unprosperous, untoward.
disavow *vb* deny, disallow, disclaim, disown.
disband *vb* break up, disperse, scatter, separate.
disbelief *n* agnosticism, doubt, nonconviction, rejection, unbelief.
disburden *vb* alleviate, diminish, disburden, discharge, disencumber, ease, free, relieve, rid.
disbursement *n* expenditure, spending.
discard *vb* abandon, cast off, lay aside, reject; banish, break, cashier, discharge, dismiss, remove, repudiate.
discern *vb* differentiate, discriminate, distinguish, judge; behold, descry, discover, espy, notice, observe, perceive, recognize, see.
discernible *adj* detectable, discoverable, perceptible.
discerning *adj* acute, astute, clear-sighted, discriminating, discriminative, eagle-eyed, ingenious, intelligent, judicious, knowing, perspicacious, piercing, sagacious, sharp, shrewd.
discernment *n* acumen, acuteness, astuteness, brightness, cleverness, discrimination, ingenuity, insight, intelligence, judgement, penetration, perspicacity, sagacity, sharpness, shrewdness; beholding, descrying, discerning, discovery, espial, notice, perception.
discharge *vb* disburden, unburden, unload; eject, emit, excrete, expel, void; cash, liquidate, pay; absolve, acquit, clear, exonerate, free, release, relieve; cashier, discard, dismiss, sack; destroy, remove; execute, perform, fulfil, observe; annul, cancel, invalidate, nullify, rescind. * *n* disburdening, unloading; acquittal, dismissal, displacement, ejection, emission, evacuation, excretion, expulsion, vent, voiding; blast, burst, detonation, explosion, firing; execution, fulfilment, observance; annulment, clearance, liquidation, payment, satisfaction, settlement; exemption, liberation, release; flow, flux, execration.
disciple *n* catechumen, learner, pupil, scholar, student; adherent, follower, partisan, supporter.
discipline *vb* breed, drill, educate, exercise, form, instruct, teach, train; control, govern, regulate, school; chasten, chastise, punish. * *n* culture, drill, drilling, education, exercise, instruction, training; control, government, regulation, subjection; chastisement, correction, punishment.
disclaim *vb* abandon, disallow, disown, disavow; reject, renounce, repudiate.
disclose *vb* discover, exhibit, expose, manifest, uncover; bare, betray, blab, communicate, divulge, impart, publish, reveal, show, tell, unfold, unveil, utter.
disclosure *n* betrayal, discovery, exposé, exposure, revelation, uncovering. discolour vb stain, tarnish, tinge.
discomfit *vb* beat, checkmate, conquer, defeat, overcome, overpower, overthrow, rout, subdue, vanquish, worst; abash, baffle, balk, confound, disconcert, foil, frustrate, perplex, upset.
discomfiture *n* confusion, defeat, frustration, overthrow, rout, vexation.
discomfort *n* annoyance, disquiet, distress, inquietude, malaise, trouble, uneasiness, unpleasantness, vexation.

discommode *vb* annoy, disquiet, disturb, harass, incommode, inconvenience, molest, trouble.
discompose *vb* confuse, derange, disarrange, disorder, disturb, embroil, jumble, unsettle; agitate, annoy, chafe, displease, disquiet, fret, harass, irritate, nettle, plague, provoke, ruffle, trouble, upset, vex, worry; abash, bewilder, disconcert, embarrass, fluster, perplex.
disconcert *vb* baffle, balk, contravene, defeat, disarrange, frustrate, interrupt, thwart, undo, upset; abash, agitate, bewilder, confuse, demoralize, discompose, disturb, embarrass, faze, perplex, perturb, unbalance, worry.
disconnect *vb* detach, disengage, disjoin, dissociate, disunite, separate, sever, uncouple, unlink.
disconsolate *adj* broken-hearted, cheerless, comfortless, dejected, desolate, forlorn, gloomy, heartbroken, inconsolable, melancholy, miserable, sad, sorrowful, unhappy, woeful, wretched.
discontent *n* discontentment, displeasure, dissatisfaction, inquietude, restlessness, uneasiness.
discontinuance *n* cessation, discontinuation, disjunction, disruption, intermission, interruption, separation, stop, stoppage, stopping, suspension.
discontinue *vb* cease, intermit, interrupt, quit, stop.
discord *n* contention, difference, disagreement, dissension, opposition, quarrelling, rupture, strife, variance, wrangling; cacophony, discordance, dissonance, harshness, jangle, jarring.
discordance *n* conflict, disagreement, incongruity, inconsistency, opposition, repugnance; discord, dissonance.
discordant *adj* contradictory, contrary, disagreeing, incongruous, inconsistent, opposite, repugnant; cacophonous, dissonant, harsh, inharmonious, jangling, jarring.
discount *vb* allow for, deduct, lower, rebate, reduce, subtract; disregard, ignore, overlook. * *n* abatement, drawback; allowance, deduction, rebate, reduction.
discourage *vb* abase, awe, damp, daunt, deject, depress, deject, dismay, dishearten, dispirit, frighten, intimidate; deter, dissuade, hinder; disfavour, discountenance.
discouragement *n* disheartening; dissuasion; damper, deterrent, embarrassment, hindrance, impediment, obstacle, wet blanket.
discourse *vb* expiate, hold forth, lucubrate, sermonize, speak; advise, confer, converse, parley, talk; emit, utter. * *n* address, disquisition, dissertation, homily, lecture, preachment, sermon, speech, treatise; colloquy, conversation, converse, talk.
discourteous *adj* abrupt, brusque, curt, disrespectful, ill-bred, ill-mannered, impolite, inurbane, rude, uncivil, uncourtly, ungentlemanly, unmannerly.
discourtesy *n* abruptness, brusqueness, ill-breeding, impoliteness, incivility, rudeness.
discover *vb* communicate, disclose, exhibit, impart, manifest, show, reveal, tell; ascertain, behold, discern, espy, see; descry, detect, determine, discern; contrive, invent, originate.
discredit *vb* disbelieve, doubt, question; depreciate, disgrace, dishonour, disparage, reproach. * *n* disbelief, distrust; disgrace, dishonour, disrepute, ignominy, notoriety, obloquy, odium, opprobrium, reproach, scandal.
discreditable *adj* derogatory, disgraceful, disreputable, dishonourable, ignominious, infamous, inglorious, scandalous, unworthy.
discreet *adj* careful, cautious, circumspect, considerate, discerning, heedful, judicious, prudent, sagacious, wary, wise.
discrepancy *n* contrariety, difference, disagreement, discordance, dissonance, divergence, incongruity, inconsistency, variance, variation.
discrete *adj* discontinuous, disjunct, distinct, separate; disjunctive.
discretion *n* care, carefulness, caution, circumspection, considerateness, consideration, heedfulness, judgement, judicious, prudence, wariness; discrimination, maturity, responsibility; choice, option, pleasure, will.
discrimination *n* difference, distinction; acumen, acuteness, discernment, in-sight, judgement, penetration, sagacity.
discriminatory *adj* characteristic, characterizing, discriminating, discriminative, distinctive, distinguishing.
discursive *adj* argumentative, reasoning; casual, cursory, desultory, digressive, erratic, excursive, loose, rambling, roving, wandering, wave.
discus *n* disk, quoit.
discuss *vb* agitate, argue, canvass, consider, debate, deliberate, examine, sift, ventilate.
disdain *vb* contemn, deride, despise, disregard, reject, scorn, slight, scout, spurn. * *n* arrogance, contempt, contumely, haughtiness, hauteur, scorn, sneer, superciliousness.
disdainful *adj* cavalier, contemptuous, contumelious, haughty, scornful, supercilious.
disease *n* affection, affliction, ail, ailment, complaint, disorder, distemper, illness, indisposition, infirmity, malady, sickness.
disembarrass *vb* clear, disburden, disencumber, disengage, disentangle, extricate, ease, free, release, rid.
disembodied *adj* bodiless, disincarnate, immaterial, incorporeal, spiritual, unbodied.
disembowel *vb* degut, embowel, eviscerate.
disengage *vb* clear, deliver, discharge, disembarrass, disembroil, disencumber, disentangle, extricate, liberate, release; detach, disjoin, dissociate, disunite, divide, separate; wean, withdraw.
disentangle *vb* loosen, separate, unfold, unravel, untwist; clear, detach, disconnect, disembroil, disengage, extricate, liberate, loose, unloose.
disfavour *n* disapproval, disesteem, dislike, disrespect; discredit, disregard, disrepute, unacceptableness;

disservice, unkindness. * *vb* disapprove, dislike, object, oppose.

disfigure *vb* blemish, deface, deform, injure, mar, spoil.

disfigurement *n* blemishing, defacement, deforming, disfiguration, injury, marring, spoiling; blemish, defect, deformity, scar, spot, stain.

disgorge *vb* belch, cast up, spew, throw up, vomit; discharge, eject; give up, relinquish, surrender, yield.

disgrace *vb* degrade, humble, humiliate; abase, debase, defame, discredit, disfavour, dishonour, disparage, reproach, stain, sully, taint, tarnish. * *n* abomination, disrepute, humiliation, ignominy, infamy, mortification, shame, scandal.

disgraceful *adj* discreditable, dishonourable, disreputable, ignominious, infamous, opprobrious, scandalous, shameful.

disguise *vb* cloak, conceal, cover, dissemble, hide, mask, muffle, screen, secrete, shroud, veil. * *n* concealment, cover, mask, veil; blind, cloak, masquerade, pretence, pretext, veneer.

disguised *adj* cloaked, masked, veiled.

disgust *vb* nauseate, sicken; abominate, detest, displease, offend, repel, repulse, revolt. * *n* disrelish, distaste, loathing, nausea; abhorrence, abomination, antipathy, aversion, detestation, dislike, repugnance, revulsion.

dish *vb* deal out, give, ladle, serve; blight, dash, frustrate, mar, ruin, spoil. * *n* bowl, plate, saucer, vessel.

dishearten *vb* cast down, damp, dampen, daunt, deject, depress, deter, discourage, dispirit.

dished *adj* baffled, balked, disappointed, disconcerted, foiled, frustrated, upset.

dishevelled *adj* disarranged, disordered, messed, tousled, tumbled, unkempt, untidy, untrimmed.

dishonest *adj* cheating, corrupt, crafty, crooked, deceitful, deceiving, deceptive, designing, faithless, false, falsehearted, fraudulent, guileful, knavish, perfidious, slippery, treacherous, unfair, unscrupulous.

dishonesty *n* deceitfulness, faithlessness, falsehood, fraud, fraudulence, fraudulency, improbity, knavery, perfidious, treachery, trickery.

dishonour *vb* abase, defame, degrade, discredit, disfavour, dishonour, disgrace, disparage, reproach, shame, taint. * *n* abasement, basement, contempt, degradation, discredit, disesteem, disfavour, disgrace, dishonour, disparagement, disrepute, ignominy, infamy, obloquy, odium, opprobrium, reproach, scandal, shame.

dishonourable *adj* discreditable, disgraceful, disreputable, ignominious, infamous, scandalous, shameful; base, false, falsehearted, shameless.

disinclination *n* alienation, antipathy, aversion, dislike, indisposition, reluctance, repugnance, unwillingness.

disinfect *vb* cleanse, deodorize, fumigate, purify, sterilize.

disingenuous *adj* artful, deceitful, dishonest, hollow, insidious, insincere, uncandid, unfair, wily.

disintegrate *vb* crumble, decompose, dissolve, disunite, pulverize, separate.

disinter *vb* dig up, disentomb, disinhume, exhume, unbury.

disinterested *adj* candid, fair, high-minded, impartial, indifferent, unbiased, unselfish, unprejudiced; generous, liberal, magnanimous.

disjoin *vb* detach, disconnect, dissever, dissociate, disunite, divide, part, separate, sever, sunder.

disjointed *adj* desultory, disconnected, incoherent, loose.

disjunction *n* disassociation, disconnection, disunion, isolation, parting, separation, severance.

dislike *vb* abominate, detest, disapprove, disrelish, hate, loathe. * *n* antagonism, antipathy, aversion, disapproval, disfavour, disgust, disinclination, displeasure, disrelish, distaste, loathing, repugnance.

dislocate *vb* disarrange, displace, disturb; disarticulate, disjoint, luxate, slip.

dislodge *vb* dismount, dispel, displace, eject, expel, oust, remove.

disloyal *adj* disaffected, faithless, false, perfidious, traitorous, treacherous, treasonable, undutiful, unfaithful, unpatriotic, untrue.

disloyalty *n* faithlessness, perfidy, treachery, treason, undutifulness, unfaithfulness.

dismal *adj* cheerless, dark, dreary, dull, gloomy, lonesome; blue, calamitous, doleful, dolorous, funereal, lugubrious, melancholy, mournful, sad, sombre, sorrowful.

dismantle *vb* divest, strip, unrig.

dismay *vb* affright, alarm, appal, daunt, discourage, dishearten, frighten, horrify, intimidate, paralyse, scare, terrify. * *n* affright, alarm, consternation, fear, fright, horror, terror.

dismember *vb* disjoint, dislimb, dislocate, mutilate; divide, separate, rend, sever.

dismiss *vb* banish, cashier, discard, discharge, disperse, reject, release, remove.

dismount *vb* alight, descend, dismantle, unhorse; dislodge, displace.

disobedient *adj* froward, noncompliant, noncomplying, obstinate, rebellious, refractory, uncomplying, undutiful, unruly, unsubmissive.

disobey *vb* infringe, transgress, violate.

disobliging *adj* ill-natured, unaccommodating, unamiable, unfriendly, unkind.

disorder *vb* confound, confuse, derange, disarrange, discompose, disorganize, disturb, unsettle, upset. * *n* confusion, derangement, disarrangement, disarray, disorganization, irregularity, jumble, litter, mess, topsy-turvy; brawl, commotion, disturbance, fight, quarrel, riot, tumult; riotousness, tumultuousness, turbulence; ail, ailment, complaint, distemper, illness, indisposition, malady, sickness.

disorderly *adj* chaotic, confused, intemperate, irregular, unmethodical, unsystematic, untidy; lawless, rebellious, riotous, tumultuous, turbulent, ungovernable, unmanageable, unruly.

disorganization *n* chaos, confusion, demoralization, derangement, disorder.
disorganize *vb* confuse, demoralize, derange, disarrange, discompose, disorder, disturb, unsettle, upset.
disown *vb* disavow, disclaim, reject, renounce, repudiate; abnegate, deny, disallow.
disparage *vb* belittle, decry, depreciate, derogate from, detract from, doubt, question, run down, underestimate, underpraise, underrate, undervalue; asperse, defame, inveigh against, reflect on, reproach, slur, speak ill of, traduce, vilify.
disparagement *n* belittlement, depreciation, derogation, detraction, underrating, undervaluing; derogation, detraction, diminution, harm, impairment, injury, lessening, prejudice, worsening; aspersion, calumny, defamation, reflection, reproach, traduction, vilification; blackening, disgrace, dispraise, indignity, reproach.
disparity *n* difference, disproportion, inequality; dissimilarity, dissimilitude, unlikeness.
dispassionate *adj* calm, collected, composed, cool, imperturbable, inexcitable, moderate, quiet, serene, sober, staid, temperate, undisturbed, unexcitable, unexcited, unimpassioned, unruffled; candid, disinterested, fair, impartial, neutral, unbiased.
dispatch, despatch *vb* assassinate, kill, murder, slaughter, slay; accelerate, conclude, dismiss, expedite, finish, forward, hasten, hurry, quicken, speed. * *n* dispatching, sending; diligence, expedition, haste, rapidity, speed; completion, conduct, doing, transaction; communication, document, instruction, letter, message, missive, report.
dispel *vb* banish, disperse, dissipate, scatter.
dispensation *n* allotment, apportioning, apportionment, dispensing, distributing, distribution; administration, stewardship; economy, plan, scheme, system; exemption, immunity, indulgence, licence, privilege.
dispense *vb* allot, apportion, assign, distribute; administer, apply, execute; absolve, excuse, exempt, exonerate, release, relieve.
disperse *vb* dispel, dissipate, dissolve, scatter, separate; diffuse, disseminate, spread; disappear, vanish.
dispirit *vb* damp, dampen, depress, deject, discourage, dishearten.
dispirited *adj* chapfallen, dejected, depressed, discouraged, disheartened, down-cast, downhearted.
displace *vb* dislocate, mislay, misplace, move; dislodge, remove; cashier, depose, discard, discharge, dismiss, oust, replace, unseat.
display *vb* expand, extend, open, spread, unfold; exhibit, show; flaunt, parade. * *n* exhibition, manifestation, show; flourish, ostentation, pageant, parade, pomp.
displease *vb* disgruntle, disgust, disoblige, dissatisfy, offend; affront, aggravate, anger, annoy, chafe, chagrin, fret, irritate, nettle, pique, provoke, vex.
displeasure *n* disaffection, disapprobation, disapproval, dislike, dissatisfaction, distaste; anger, annoyance, indignation, irritation, pique, resentment, vexation, wrath; injury, offence.
disport *vb* caper, frisk, frolic, gambol, play, sport, wanton; amuse, beguile, cheer, divert, entertain, relax, solace.
disposal *n* arrangement, disposition; conduct, control, direction, disposure, government, management, ordering, regulation; bestowment, dispensation, distribution.
dispose *vb* arrange, distribute, marshal, group, place, range, rank, set; adjust, determine, regulate, settle; bias, incline, induce, lead, move, predispose; control, decide, regulate, rule, settle; arrange, bargain, compound; alienate, convey, demise, sell, transfer.
disposed *adj* apt, inclined, prone, ready, tending.
disposition *n* arrangement, arranging, classification, disposing, grouping, location, placing; adjustment, control, direction, disposure, disposal, management, ordering, regulation; aptitude, bent, bias, inclination, nature, predisposition, proclivity, proneness, propensity, tendency; character, constitution, humour, native, nature, temper, temperament, turn; inclination, willingness; bestowal, bestowment, dispensation, distribution.
dispossess *vb* deprive, divest, expropriate, strip; dislodge, eject, oust; disseise, disseize, evict, oust.
dispraise *n* blame, censure; discredit, disgrace, dishonour, disparagement, opprobrium, reproach, shame.
disproof *n* confutation, rebuttal, refutation.
disproportion *n* disparity, inadequacy, inequality, insufficiency, unsuitableness; incommensurateness.
disprove *vb* confute, rebel, rebut.
disputable *adj* controvertible, debatable, doubtful, questionable.
disputation *n* argumentation, controversy, debate, dispute.
disputatious *adj* argumentative, bickering, captious, caviling, contentious, dissentious, litigious, polemical, pugnacious, quarrelsome.
dispute *vb* altercate, argue, debate, litigate, question; bicker, brawl, jangle, quarrel, spar, spat, squabble, tiff, wrangle; agitate, argue, debate, ventilate; challenge, contradict, controvert, deny, impugn; contest, struggle for. * *n* controversy, debate, discussion, disputation; altercation, argument, bickering, brawl, disagreement, dissension, spat, squabble, tiff, wrangle.
disqualification *n* disability, incapitation.
disqualify *vb* disable, incapacitate, unfit; disenable, preclude, prohibit.
disquiet *vb* agitate, annoy, bother, discompose, disturb, excite, fret, harass, incommode, molest, plague, pester, trouble, vex, worry. * *n* anxiety,

discomposure, disquietude, disturbance, restlessness, solicitude, trouble, uneasiness, unrest, vexation, worry.
disquisition *n* dissertation, discourse, essay, paper, thesis, treatise.
disregard *vb* contemn, despise, disdain, disobey, disparage, ignore, neglect, overlook, slight. * *n* contempt, ignoring, inattention, neglect, pretermit, oversight, slight; disesteem, disfavour, indifference.
disrelish *vb* dislike, loathe. * *n* dislike, distaste; flatness, insipidity, insipidness, nauseousness; antipathy, aversion, repugnance.
disreputable *adj* derogatory, discreditable, dishonourable, disgraceful, infamous, opprobrious, scandalous, shameful; base, contemptible, low, mean, vicious, vile, vulgar.
disrepute *n* abasement, degradation, derogation, discredit, disgrace, dishonour, ill-repute, odium.
disrespect *n* disesteem, disregard, irreverence, neglect, slight.
disrespectful *adj* discourteous, impertinent, impolite, rude, uncivil, uncourteous.
dissatisfaction *n* discontent, disquiet, inquietude, uneasiness; disapprobation, disapproval, dislike, displeasure.
dissect *vb* analyze, examine, explore, investigate, scrutinize, sift; cut apart.
dissemble *vb* cloak, conceal, cover, disguise, hide; counterfeit, dissimulate, feign, pretend.
dissembler *n* dissimulator, feigner, hypocrite, pretender, sham.
disseminate *vb* circulate, diffuse, disperse, proclaim, promulgate, propagate, publish, scatter, spread.
dissension *n* contention, difference, disagreement, discord, quarrel, strife, variance.
dissent *vb* decline, differ, disagree, refuse. * *n* difference, disagreement, nonconformity, opposition, recusancy, refusal.
dissentient *adj* disagreeing, dissenting, dissident, factious.
dissertation *n* discourse, disquisition, essay, thesis, treatise.
disservice *n* disadvantage, disfavour, harm, hurt, ill-turn, injury, mischief.
dissidence *n* disagreement, dissent, nonconformity, sectarianism.
dissimilar *adj* different, divergent, diverse, heterogeneous, unlike, various.
dissimilarity *n* dissimilitude, disparity, divergent, diversity, unlikeness, variation.
dissimulation *n* concealment, deceit, dissembling, double-dealing, duplicity, feigning, hypocrisy, pretence.
dissipate *vb* dispel, disperse, scatter; consume, expend, lavish, spend, squander, waste; disappear, vanish.
dissipation *n* dispersion, dissemination, scattering, vanishing; squandering, waste; crapulence, debauchery, dissoluteness, drunkenness, excess, profligacy.
dissociate *vb* disjoin, dissever, disunite, divide, separate, sever, sunder.
dissolute *adj* abandoned, corrupt, debauched, depraved, disorderly, dissipated, graceless, lax, lewd, licentious, loose, profligate, rakish, reprobate, shameless, vicious, wanton, wild.
dissolution *n* liquefaction, melting, solution; decomposition, putrefaction; death, disease; destruction, overthrow, ruin; termination.
dissolve *vb* liquefy, melt; disorganize, disunite, divide, loose, separate, sever; destroy, ruin; disappear, fade, scatter, vanish; crumble, decompose, disintegrate, perish.
dissonance *n* cacophony, discord, discordance, harshness, jarring; disagreement, discrepancy, incongruity, inconsistency.
dissonant *adj* discordant, grating, harsh, jangling, jarring, unharmonious; contradictory, disagreeing, discrepant, incongruous, inconsistent.
distance *vb* excel, outdo, outstrip, surpass. * *n* farness, remoteness; aloofness, coldness, frigidity, reserve, stiffness, offishness; absence, separation, space.
distant *adj* far, far-away, remote; aloof, ceremonious, cold, cool, frigid, haughty, reserved, stiff, uncordial; faint, indirect, obscure, slight.
distaste *n* disgust, disrelish; antipathy, aversion, disinclination, dislike, displeasure, dissatisfaction, repugnance.
distasteful *adj* disgusting, loathsome, nauseating, nauseous, unpalatable, unsavoury; disagreeable, displeasing, offensive, repugnant, repulsive, unpleasant.
distemper *n* ail, ailment, complaint, disease, disorder, illness, indisposition, malady, sickness.
distempered *adj* diseased, disordered; immoderate, inordinate, intemperate, unregulated.
distend *vb* bloat, dilate, enlarge, expand, increase, inflate, puff, stretch, swell, widen.
distil *vb* dribble, drip, drop; extract, separate.
distinct *adj* definite, different, discrete, disjunct, individual, separate, unconnected; clear, defined, manifest, obvious, plain, unconfused, unmistakable, well-defined.
distinction *n* discernment, discrimination, distinguishing; difference; account, celebrity, credit, eminence, fame, name, note, rank, renown, reputation, repute, respectability, superiority.
distinctive *adj* characteristic, differentiating, discriminating, distinguishing.
distinctness *n* difference, separateness; clearness, explicitness, lucidity, lucidness, perspicuity, precision.
distinguish *vb* characterize, mark; differentiate, discern, discriminate, perceive, recognize, see, single out, tell; demarcate, divide, separate; celebrate, honour, signalize.
distinguished *adj* celebrated, eminent, famous, illustrious, noted; conspicuous, extraordinary, laureate, marked, shining, superior, transcendent.

distort *vb* contort, deform, gnarl, screw, twist, warp, wrest; falsify, misrepresent, pervert.

distortion *n* contortion, deformation, deformity, twist, wryness; falsification, misrepresentation, perversion, wresting.

distract *vb* divert, draw away; bewilder, confound, confuse, derange, discompose, disconcert, disturb, embarrass, harass, madden, mystify, perplex, puzzle.

distracted *adj* crazed, crazy, deranged, frantic, furious, insane, mad, raving, wild.

distraction *n* abstraction, bewilderment, confusion, mystification, embarrassment, perplexity; agitation, commotion, discord, disorder, disturbance, division, perturbation, tumult, turmoil; aberration, alienation, delirium, derangement, frenzy, hallucination, incoherence, insanity, lunacy, madness, mania, raving, wandering.

distress *vb* afflict, annoy, grieve, harry, pain, perplex, rack, trouble; distrain, seize, take. * *n* affliction, calamity, disaster, misery, misfortune, adversity, hardship, perplexity, trial, tribulation; agony, anguish, dolour, grief, sorrow, suffering; gnawing, gripe, griping, pain, torment, torture; destitution, indigence, poverty, privation, straits, want.

distribute *vb* allocate, allot, apportion, assign, deal, dispense, divide, dole out, give, mete, partition, prorate, share; administer, arrange, assort, class, classify, dispose.

distribution *n* allocation, allotment, apportionment, assignment, assortment, dispensation, dispensing; arrangement, disposal, disposition, classification, division, dole, grouping, partition, sharing.

district *n* circuit, department, neighbourhood, province, quarter, region, section, territory, tract, ward.

distrust *vb* disbelieve, discredit, doubt, misbelieve, mistrust, question, suspect. * *n* doubt, misgiving, mistrust, question, suspicion.

distrustful *adj* doubting, dubious, suspicious.

disturb *vb* agitate, shake, stir; confuse, derange, disarrange, disorder, unsettle, upset; annoy, discompose, disconcert, disquiet, distract, fuss, incommode, molest, perturb, plague, trouble, ruffle, vex, worry; impede, interrupt, hinder.

disturbance *n* agitation, commotion, confusion, convulsion, derangement, disorder, perturbation, unsettlement; annoyance, discomposure, distraction, excitement, fuss; hindrance, interruption, molestation; brawl, commotion, disorder, excitement, fracas, hubbub, riot, rising, tumult, turmoil, uproar.

disunion *n* disconnection, disjunction, division, separation, severance; breach, feud, rupture, schism.

disunite *vb* detach, disconnect, disjoin, dissever, dissociate, divide, part, rend, separate, segregate, sever, sunder; alienate, estrange.

disuse *n* desuetude, discontinuance, disusage, neglect, nonobservance.

ditch *vb* canalize, dig, excavate, furrow, gouge, trench; abandon, discard, dump, jettison, scrap. * *n* channel, drain, fosse, moat, trench.

divagation *n* deviation, digression, rambling, roaming, straying, wandering.

divan *n* bed, chesterfield, couch, settee, sofa.

divaricate *vb* diverge, fork, part.

dive *vb* explore, fathom, penetrate, plunge, sound. * *n* drop, fall, header, plunge; bar, den, dump, joint, saloon.

diverge *vb* divide, radiate, separate; divaricate, separate; deviate, differ, disagree, vary.

divers *adj* different, manifold, many, numerous, several, sundry, various.

diverse *adj* different, differing, disagreeing, dissimilar, divergent, heterogeneous, multifarious, multiform, separate, unlike, variant, various, varying.

diversion *n* deflection, diverting; amusement, delight, distraction, enjoyment, entertainment, game, gratification, pastime, play, pleasure, recreation, sport; detour, digression.

diversity *n* difference, dissimilarity, dissimilitude, divergence, unlikeness, variation; heterogeneity, manifoldness, multifariousness, multiformity, variety.

divert *vb* deflect, distract, disturb; amuse, beguile, delight, entertain, exhilarate, give pleasure, gratify, recreate, refresh, solace.

divest *vb* denude, disrobe, strip, unclothe, undress; deprive, dispossess, strip.

divide *vb* bisect, cleave, cut, dismember, dissever, disunite, open, part, rend, segregate, separate, sever, shear, split, sunder; allocate, allot, apportion, assign, dispense, distribute, dole, mete, portion, share; compartmentalize, demarcate, partition; alienate, disunite, estrange.

divination *n* augury, divining, foretelling, incantation, magic, sooth-saying, sorcery; prediction, presage, prophecy.

divine *vb* foretell, predict, presage, prognosticate, vaticinate, prophesy; believe, conjecture, fancy, guess, suppose, surmise, suspect, think. * *adj* deiform, godlike, superhuman, supernatural; angelic, celestial, heavenly, holy, sacred, seraphic, spiritual; exalted, exalting, rapturous, supreme, transcendent. * *n* churchman, clergyman, ecclesiastic, minister, parson, pastor, priest.

division *n* compartmentalization, disconnection, disjunction, dismemberment, segmentation, separation, severance; category, class, compartment, head, parcel, portion, section, segment; demarcation, partition; alienation, allotment, apportionment, distribution; breach, difference, disagreement, discord, disunion, estrangement, feud, rupture, variance.

divorce *vb* disconnect, dissolve, disunite, part, put away, separate, sever, split up, sunder, unmarry. * *n* disjunction, dissolution, disunion, division, divorcement, parting, separation, severance.

divulge *vb* communicate, declare, disclose, discover, exhibit, expose, impart, proclaim, promulgate, publish, reveal, tell, uncover.

dizzy *adj* giddy, vertiginous; careless, heedless, thoughtless.

do *vb* accomplish, achieve, act, commit, effect, execute, perform; complete, conclude, end, finish, settle, terminate; conduct, transact; observe, perform, practice; translate, render; cook, prepare; cheat, chouse, cozen, hoax, swindle; serve, suffice. * *n* act, action, adventure, deed, doing, exploit, feat, thing; banquet, event, feast, function, party.

docile *adj* amenable, obedient, pliant, teachable, tractable, yielding.

dock[1] *vb* clip, curtail, cut, deduct, truncate; lessen, shorten.

dock[2] *vb* anchor, moor; join, meet. * *n* anchorage, basin, berth, dockage, dockyard, dry dock, harbour, haven, marina, pier, shipyard, wharf.

doctor *vb* adulterate, alter, cook, falsify, manipulate, tamper with; attend, minister to, cure, heal, remedy, treat; fix, mend, overhaul, repair, service. * *n* general practitioner, GP, healer, leech, medic, physician; adept, savant.

doctrinaire *adj* impractical, theoretical. * *n* ideologist, theorist, thinker.

doctrine *n* article, belief, creed, dogma, opinion, precept, principle, teaching, tenet.

dodge *vb* equivocate, evade, prevaricate, quibble, shuffle. * *n* artifice, cavil, evasion, quibble, subterfuge, trick.

dogged *adj* cantankerous, headstrong, inflexible, intractable, mulish, obstinate, pertinacious, perverse, resolute, stubborn, tenacious, unyielding, wilful; churlish, morose, sour, sullen, surly.

dogma *n* article, belief, creed, doctrine, opinion, precept, principle, tenet.

dogmatic *adj* authoritative, categorical, formal, settled; arrogant, confident, dictatorial, imperious, magisterial, opinionated, oracular, overbearing, peremptory, positive; doctrinal.

dole *vb* allocate, allot, apportion, assign, deal, distribute, divide, share. * *n* allocation, allotment, apportionment, distribution; part, portion, share; alms, donation, gift, gratuity, pittance; affliction, distress, grief, sorrow, woe.

doleful *adj* lugubrious, melancholy, piteous, rueful, sad, sombre, sorrowful, woebegone, woeful; cheerless, dark, dismal, dolorous, dreary, gloomy.

dolorous *adj* cheerless, dark, dismal, gloomy; doleful, lugubrious, mournful, piteous, rueful, sad, sorrowful, woeful.

dolt *n* blockhead, booby, dullard, dunce, fool, ignoramus, simpleton.

domain *n* authority, dominion, jurisdiction, province, sway; empire, realm, territory; lands, estate; branch, department, region.

domestic *n* charwoman, help, home help, maid, servant. * *adj* domiciliary, family, home, household, private; domesticated; internal, intestine.

domesticate *vb* tame; adopt, assimilate, familiarize, naturalize.

domicile *vb* domiciliate, dwell, inhabit, live, remain, reside. * *n* abode, dwelling, habitation, harbour, home, house, residence.

dominant *adj* ascendant, ascending, chief, controlling, governing, influential, outstanding, paramount, predominant, pre-eminent, preponderant, presiding, prevailing, ruling.

dominate *vb* control, rule, sway; command, overlook, overtop, surmount.

domineer *vb* rule, tyrannize; bluster, bully, hector, menace, swagger, swell, threaten.

dominion *n* ascendancy, authority, command, control, domain, domination, government, jurisdiction, mastery, rule, sovereign, sovereignty, supremacy, sway; country, kingdom, realm, region, territory.

donation *n* alms, benefaction, boon, contribution, dole, donative, gift, grant, gratuity, largesse, offering, present, subscription.

done *adj* accomplished, achieved, effected, executed, performed; completed, concluded, ended, finished, terminated; carried on, transacted; rendered, translated; cooked, prepared; cheated, cozened, hoaxed, swindled; (*with* **for**) damned, dished, *hors de combat*, ruined, shelved, spoiled, wound up.

donkey *n* ass, mule; dunce, fool, simpleton.

donor *n* benefactor, bestower, giver; donator.

double *vb* fold, plait; duplicate, geminate, increase, multiply, repeat; return. * *adj* binary, coupled, geminate, paired; dual, twice, twofold; deceitful, dishonest, double-dealing, false, hollow, insincere, knavish, perfidious, treacherous, two-faced. * *adv* doubly, twice, twofold. * *n* doubling, fold, plait; artifice, manoeuvre, ruse, shift, stratagem, trick, wile; copy, counterpart, twin.

doublet *n* jacket, jerkin.

doubt *vb* demur, fluctuate, hesitate, vacillate, waver; distrust, mistrust, query, question, suspect. * *n* dubiety, dubiousness, dubitation, hesitance, hesitancy, hesitation, incertitude, indecision, irresolution, question, suspense, uncertainty, vacillation; distrust, misgiving, mistrust, scepticism, suspicion.

doubtful *adj* dubious, hesitating, sceptical, undecided, undetermined, wavering; ambiguous, dubious, enigmatical, equivocal, hazardous, obscure, problematical, unsure; indeterminate, questionable, undecided, unquestioned.

doubtless *adv* certainly, unquestionably; clearly, indisputably, precisely.

doughty *adj* adventurous, bold, brave, chivalrous, courageous, daring, dauntless, fearless, gallant, heroic, intrepid, redoubtable, valiant, valorous.

douse *see* **dowse**.

dowdy *adj* awkward, dingy, ill-dressed, shabby, slatternly, slovenly; old-fashioned, unfashionable.

dowel *n* peg, pin, pinion, tenon.

dower *n* endowment, gift; dowry; portion, share.
downcast *adj* chapfallen, crestfallen, dejected, depressed, despondent, discouraged, disheartened, dispirited, downhearted, low-spirited, sad, unhappy.
downfall *n* descent, destruction, fall, ruin.
downhearted *adj* chapfallen, crestfallen, dejected, depressed, despondent, discouraged, disheartened, dispirited, downcast, low-spirited, sad, unhappy.
downright *adj* absolute, categorical, clear, explicit, plain, positive, sheer, simple, undisguised, unequivocal, utter; above-board, artless, blunt, direct, frank, honest, ingenuous, open, sincere, straightforward, unceremonious.
downy *adj* lanate, lanated, lanose.
dowse, douse *vb* dip, immerse, plunge, souse, submerge.
doxy *n* mistress, paramour; courtesan, drab, harlot, prostitute, strumpet, streetwalker, whore.
doze *vb* drowse, nap, sleep, slumber. * *n* drowse, forty-winks, nap.
dozy *adj* drowsy, heavy, sleepy, sluggish.
draft *vb* detach, select; commandeer, conscript, impress; delineate, draw, outline, sketch. * *n* conscription, drawing, selection; delineation, outline, sketch; bill, cheque, order.
drag *vb* draw, haul, pull, tow, tug; trail; linger, loiter. * *n* favour, influence, pull; brake, check, curb, lag, resistance, retardation, scotch, skid, slackening, slack-off, slowing.
draggle *vb* befoul, bemire, besmirch, dangle, drabble, trail.
dragoon *vb* compel, drive, force, harass, harry, persecute. * *n* cavalier, equestrian, horse-soldier.
drain *vb* milk, sluice, tap; empty, evacuate, exhaust; dry. * *n* channel, culvert, ditch, sewer, sluice, trench, watercourse; exhaustion, withdrawal.
draught *n* current, drawing, pulling, traction; cup, dose, drench, drink, potion; delineation, design, draft, outline, sketch.
draw *vb* drag, haul, tow, tug, pull; attract; drain, suck, syphon; extract, extort; breathe in, inhale, inspire; allure, engage, entice, induce, influence, lead, move, persuade; extend, protract, stretch; delineate, depict, sketch; deduce, derive, infer; compose, draft, formulate, frame, prepare; blister, vesicate, write.
drawback *n* defect, deficiency, detriment, disadvantage, fault, flaw, imperfection, injury; abatement, allowance, deduction, discount, rebate, reduction.
drawing *n* attracting, draining, inhaling, pulling, traction; delineation, draught, outline, picture, plan, sketch.
dread *vb* apprehend, fear. * *adj* dreadful, frightful, horrible, terrible; awful, venerable. * *n* affright, alarm, apprehension, fear, terror; awe, veneration.
dreadful *adj* alarming, appalling, awesome, dire, direful, fearful, formidable, frightful, horrible, horrid, terrible, terrific, tremendous; awful, venerable.
dream *vb* fancy, imagine, think. * *n* conceit, daydream, delusion, fancy, fantasy, hallucination, illusion, imagination, reverie, vagary, vision.
dreamer *n* enthusiast, visionary.
dreamy *adj* absent, abstracted, fanciful, ideal, misty, shadowy, speculative, unreal, visionary.
dreary *adj* cheerless, chilling, comfortless, dark, depressing, dismal, drear, gloomy, lonely, lonesome, sad, solitary, sorrowful; boring, dull, monotonous, tedious, tiresome, uninteresting, wearisome.
dregs *npl* feculence, grounds, lees, off-scourings, residuum, scourings, sediment, waste; draff, dross, refuse, scum, trash.
drench *vb* dowse, drown, imbrue, saturate, soak, souse, steep, wet; physic, purge.
dress *vb* align, straighten; adjust, arrange, dispose; fit, prepare; accoutre, apparel, array, attire, clothe, robe, rig; adorn, bedeck, deck, decorate, drape, embellish, trim. * *n* apparel, attire, clothes, clothing, costume, garb, guise, garments, habiliment, habit, raiment, suit, toilet, vesture; bedizenment, bravery; frock, gown, rob.
dressing *n* compost, fertilizer, manure; forcemeat, stuffing.
dressy *adj* flashy, gaudy, showy.
driblet *n* bit, drop, fragment, morsel, piece, scrap.
drift *vb* accumulate, drive, float, wander. * *n* bearing, course, direction; aim, design, intent, intention, mark, object, proposal, purpose, scope, tendency; detritus, deposit, diluvium; gallery, passage, tunnel; current, rush, sweep; heap, pile.
drill[1] *vb* bore, perforate, pierce; discipline, exercise, instruct, teach, train. * *n* borer; discipline, exercise, training.
drill[2] *n* channel, furrow, trench.
drink *vb* imbibe, sip, swill; carouse, indulge, revel, tipple, tope; swallow, quaff; absorb. * *n* beverage, draught, liquid, potation, potion; dram, nip, sip, snifter, refreshment.
drip *vb* dribble, drop, leak, trickle; distil, filter, percolate; ooze, reek, seep, weep. * *n* dribble, drippings, drop, leak, leakage, leaking, trickle, tricklet; bore, nuisance, wet blanket.
drive *vb* hurl, impel, propel, send, shoot, thrust; actuate, incite, press, urge; coerce, compel, constrain, force, harass, oblige, overburden, press, rush; go, guide, ride, travel; aim, intend. * *n* effort, energy, pressure; airing, ride; road.
drivel *vb* babble, blether, dote, drool, slaver, slobber. * *n* balderdash, drivelling, fatuity, nonsense, prating, rubbish, slaver, stuff, twaddle.
drizzle *vb* mizzle, rain, shower, sprinkle. * *n* haar, mist, mizzle, rain, sprinkling.
droll *adj* comic, comical, farcical, funny, jocular, ludicrous, laughable, ridiculous; amusing, diverting, facetious, odd, quaint, queer, waggish. * *n* buffoon, clown, comedian, fool, harlequin, jester, punch, Punchinello, scaramouch, wag, zany.

drollery *n* archness, buffoonery, fun, humour, jocularity, pleasantry, waggishness, whimsicality.

drone *vb* dawdle, drawl, idle, loaf, lounge; hum. * *n* idler, loafer, lounger, sluggard.

drool *vb* drivel, slaver.

droop *vb* fade, wilt, wither; decline, fail, faint, flag, languish, sink, weaken; bend, hang.

drop *vb* distil, drip, shed; decline, depress, descend, dump, lower, sink; abandon, desert, forsake, forswear, leave, omit, relinquish, quit; cease, discontinue, intermit, remit; fall, precipitate. * *n* bead, droplet, globule; earring, pendant.

dross *n* cinder, lees, recrement, scoria, scum, slag; refuse, waste.

drought *n* aridity, drouth, dryness, thirstiness.

drove *n* flock, herd; collection, company, crowd.

drown *vb* deluge, engulf, flood, immerse, inundate, overflow, sink, submerge, swamp; overcome, overpower, overwhelm.

drowse *vb* doze, nap, sleep, slumber, snooze. * *n* doze, forty winks, nap, siesta, sleep, snooze.

drowsy *adj* dozy, sleepy; comatose, lethargic, stupid; lulling, soporific.

drub *vb* bang, beat, cane, cudgel, flog, hit, knock, pommel, pound, strike, thrash, thump, whack.

drubbing *n* beating, caning, cudgelling, flagellation, flogging, pommelling, pounding, thrashing, thumping, whacking.

drudge *vb* grub, grind, plod, slave, toil, work. * *n* grind, hack, hard worker, menial, plodder, scullion, servant, slave, toiler, worker.

drug *vb* dose, medicate; disgust, surfeit. * *n* medicine, physic, remedy; poison.

drunk *adj* boozed, drunken, inebriated, intoxicated, maudlin, soaked, tipsy; ablaze, aflame, delirious, fervent, suffused. * *n* alcoholic, boozer, dipsomaniac, drunkard, inebriate, lush, soak; bacchanal, bender, binge.

drunkard *n* alcoholic, boozer, carouser, dipsomaniac, drinker, drunk, inebriate, reveller, sot, tippler, toper.

dry *vb* dehydrate, desiccate, drain, exsiccate, parch. * *adj* desiccated, dried, juiceless, sapless, unmoistened; arid, droughty, parched; drouthy, thirsty; barren, dull, insipid, jejune, plain, pointless, tame, tedious, tiresome, unembellished, uninteresting, vapid; cutting, keen, sarcastic, severe, sharp, sly.

dub *vb* call, christen, denominate, designate, entitle, name, style, term.

dubious *adj* doubtful, fluctuating, hesitant, irresolute, skeptical, uncertain, undecided, unsettled, wavering; ambiguous, doubtful, equivocal, improbable, questionable, uncertain.

duck *vb* dip, dive, immerse, plunge, submerge, souse; bend, bow, dodge, stoop.

duct *n* canal, channel, conduit, pipe, tube; blood-vessel.

ductile *adj* compliant, docile, facile, tractable, yielding; flexible, malleable, pliant; extensible, tensile.

dudgeon *n* anger, indignation, ill will, ire, malice, resentment, umbrage, wrath.

due *adj* owed, owing; appropriate, becoming, befitting, bounden, fit, proper, suitable, right. * *adv* dead, direct, directly, exactly, just, right, squarely, straight. * *n* claim, debt, desert, right.

dulcet *adj* delicious, honeyed, luscious, sweet; harmonious, melodious; agreeable, charming, delightful, pleasant, pleasing.

dull *vb* blunt; benumb, besot, deaden, hebetate, obtund, paralyse, stupefy; dampen, deject, depress, discourage, dishearten, dispirit; allay, alleviate, assuage, mitigate, moderate, quiet, soften; deaden, dim, sully, tarnish. * *adj* blockish, brutish, doltish, obtuse, stolid, stupid, unintelligent; apathetic, callous, dead, insensible, passionless, phlegmatic, unfeeling, unimpassioned, unresponsive; heavy, inactive, inanimate, inert, languish, lifeless, slow, sluggish, torpid; blunt, dulled, hebetate, obtuse; cheerless, dismal, dreary, gloomy, sad, sombre; dim, lack-lustre, lustreless, matt, obscure, opaque, tarnished; dry, flat, insipid, irksome, jejune, prosy, tedious, tiresome, uninteresting, wearisome.

duly *adv* befittingly, decorously, fitly, properly, rightly; regularly.

dumb *adj* inarticulate, mute, silent, soundless, speechless, voiceless.

dumbfound, dumfound *vb* amaze, astonish, astound, bewilder, confound, confuse, nonplus, pose.

dumps *npl* blues, dejection, depression, despondency, gloom, gloominess, melancholy, sadness.

dun[1] *adj* greyish-brown, brown, drab.

dun[2] *vb* beset, importune, press, urge.

dunce *n* ass, block, blockhead, clodpole, dolt, donkey, dullard, dunderhead, fool, goose, halfwit, ignoramus, jackass, lackwit, loon, nincompoop, numskull, oaf, simpleton, thickhead, witling.

dupe *vb* beguile, cheat, chouse, circumvent, cozen, deceive, delude, gull, hoodwink, outwit, overreach, swindle, trick. * *n* gull, simpleton.

duplicate *vb* copy, double, repeat, replicate, reproduce. * *adj* doubled, twofold. * *n* copy, counterpart, facsimile, replica, transcript.

duplicity *n* artifice, chicanery, circumvention, deceit, deception, dishonesty, dissimulation, double-dealing, falseness, fraud, guile, hypocrisy, perfidy.

durable *adj* abiding, constant, continuing, enduring, firm, lasting, permanent, persistent, stable.

duration *n* continuance, continuation, permanency, perpetuation, prolongation; period, time.

duress *n* captivity, confinement, constraint, durance, hardship, imprisonment, restraint; compulsion.

dusky *adj* cloudy, darkish, dim, murky, obscure, overcast, shady, shadowy; dark, swarthy, tawny.

dutiful *adj* duteous, obedient, submissive; deferential, respectful, reverential.

duty *n* allegiance, devoirs, obligation, responsibility, reverence; business, engagement, function, office, service; custom, excise, impost, tariff, tax, toll.

dwarf *vb* lower, stunt. * *n* bantam, homunculus, manikin, midget, pygmy.
dwarfish *adj* diminutive, dwarfed, little, low, pygmy, small, stunted, tiny, undersized.
dwell *vb* abide, inhabit, live, lodge, remain, reside, rest, sojourn, stay, stop, tarry, tenant.
dwelling *n* abode, cot, domicile, dugout, establishment, habitation, home, house, hutch, lodging, mansion, quarters, residence.
dwindle *vb* decrease, diminish, lessen, shrink; decay, decline, deteriorate, pine, sink, waste away.
dye *vb* colour, stain, tinge. * *n* cast, colour, hue, shade, stain, tinge, tint.
dying *adj* expiring; mortal, perishable. * *n* death, decease, demise, departure, dissolution, exit.
dynasty *n* dominion, empire, government, rule, sovereignty.
dyspepsia *n* indigestion.

E

eager *adj* agog, avid, anxious, desirous, fain, greedy, impatient, keen, longing, yearning; animated, ardent, earnest, enthusiastic, fervent, fervid, forward, glowing, hot, impetuous, sanguine, vehement, zealous.

eagerness *n* ardour, avidity, earnestness, enthusiasm, fervour, greediness, heartiness, hunger, impatience, impetuosity, intentness, keenness, longing, thirst, vehemence, yearning, zeal.

eagle-eyed *adj* discerning, hawk-eyed, sharp-sighted.

ear[1] *n* attention, hearing, heed, regard.

ear[2] *n* head, spike.

early *adj* opportune, seasonable, timely; forward, premature; dawning, matutinal. * *adv* anon, beforehand, betimes, ere, seasonably, shortly, soon.

earn *vb* acquire, gain, get, obtain, procure, realize, reap, win; deserve, merit.

earnest *adj* animated, ardent, eager, cordial, fervent, fervid, glowing, hearty, impassioned, importune, warm, zealous; fixed, intent, steady; sincere, true, truthful; important, momentous, serious, weighty. * *n* reality, seriousness, truth; foretaste, pledge, promise; handsel, payment.

earnings *npl* allowance, emoluments, gains, income, pay, proceeds, profits, remuneration, reward, salary, stipend.

earth *n* globe, orb, planet, world; clay, clod, dirt, glebe, ground, humus, land, loam, sod, soil, turf; mankind, world.

earthborn *adj* abject, base, earthly, grovelling, low, mean, unspiritual.

earthly *adj* terrestrial; base, carnal, earthborn, low, gross, grovelling, sensual, sordid, unspiritual, worldly; bodily, material, mundane, natural, secular, temporal.

earthy *adj* clayey, earth-like, terrene; earthly, terrestrial; coarse, gross, material, unrefined.

ease *vb* disburden, disencumber, pacify, quiet, relieve, still; abate, allay, alleviate, appease, assuage, diminish, mitigate, soothe; loosen, release; facilitate, favour. * *n* leisure, quiescence, repose, rest; calmness, content, contentment, enjoyment, happiness, peace, quiet, quietness, quietude, relief, repose, satisfaction, serenity, tranquillity; easiness, facility, readiness; flexibility, freedom, liberty, lightness, naturalness, unconcern, unconstraint; comfort, elbowroom.

easy *adj* light; careless, comfortable, contented, effortless, painless, quiet, satisfied, tranquil, untroubled; accommodating, complaisant, compliant, complying, facile, indolent, manageable, pliant, submissive, tractable, yielding; graceful, informal, natural, unconstrained; flowing, ready, smooth, unaffected; gentle, lenient, mild, moderate; affluent, loose, unconcerned, unembarrassed.

eat *vb* chew, consume, devour, engorge, ingest, ravage, swallow; corrode, demolish, erode; breakfast, dine, feed, lunch, sup.

eatable *adj* edible, esculent, harmless, wholesome.

ebb *vb* abate, recede, retire, subside; decay, decline, decrease, degenerate, deteriorate, sink, wane. * *n* refluence, reflux, regress, regression, retrocedence, retrocession, retrogression, return; caducity, decay, decline, degeneration, deterioration, wane, waning; abatement, decrease, decrement, diminution.

ebullience *n* ebullition, effervescence; burst, bursting, overenthusiasm, overflow, rush, vigour.

ebullition *n* boiling, bubbling; effervescence, fermentation; burst, fit, outbreak, outburst, paroxysm.

eccentric *adj* decentred, parabolic; aberrant, abnormal, anomalous, cranky, erratic, fantastic, irregular, odd, outlandish, peculiar, singular, strange, uncommon, unnatural, wayward, whimsical. * *n* crank, curiosity, original.

eccentricity *n* ellipticity, flattening, flatness, oblateness; aberration, irregularity, oddity, oddness, peculiarity, singularity, strangeness, waywardness.

ecclesiastic[1], **ecclesiastical** *adj* churchish, churchly, clerical, ministerial, nonsecular, pastoral, priestly, religious, sacerdotal.

ecclesiastic[2] *n* chaplain, churchman, clergyman, cleric, clerk, divine, minister, parson, pastor, priest, reverend, shepherd.

echo *vb* reply, resound, reverberate, ring; re-echo, repeat. * *n* answer, repetition, reverberation; imitation.

éclat *n* acclamation, applause, brilliancy, effect, glory, lustre, pomp, renown, show, splendour.

eclipse *vb* cloud, darken, dim, obscure, overshadow, veil; annihilate, annul, blot out, extinguish. * *n* clouding, concealment, darkening, dimming, disappearance, hiding, obscuration, occultation, shrouding, vanishing, veiling; annihilation, blotting out, destruction, extinction, extinguishment, obliteration.

eclogue *n* bucolic, idyl, pastoral.
economize *vb* husband, manage, save; retrench.
economy *n* frugality, husbandry, parsimony, providence, retrenchment, saving, skimping, stinginess, thrift, thriftiness; administration, arrangement, management, method, order, plan, regulation, system; dispensation.
ecstasy *n* frenzy, madness, paroxysm, trance; delight, gladness, joy, rhapsody, rapture, ravishment, transport.
eddy *vb* gurgle, surge, spin, swirl, whirl. * *n* countercurrent; swirl, vortex, whirlpool.
edge *vb* sharpen; border, fringe, rim. * *n* border, brim, brink, bound, crest, fringe, hem, lip, margin, rim, verge; animation, intensity, interest, keenness, sharpness, zest; acrimony, bitterness, gall, sharpness, sting.
edging *n* border, frill, fringe, trimming.
edible *adj* eatable, esculent, harmless, wholesome.
edict *n* act, command, constitution, decision, decree, law, mandate, manifesto, notice, order, ordinance, proclamation, regulation, rescript, statute.
edifice *n* building, fabric, habitation, house, structure.
edify *vb* educate, elevate, enlightenment, improve, inform, instruct, nurture, teach, upbuild.
edition *n* impression, issue, number.
educate *vb* breed, cultivate, develop, discipline, drill, edify, exercise, indoctrinate, inform, instruct, mature, nurture, rear, school, teach, train.
educated *adj* cultured, lettered, literate.
education *n* breeding, cultivation, culture, development, discipline, drilling, indoctrination, instruction, nurture, pedagogics, schooling, teaching, training, tuition.
educe *vb* bring out, draw out, elicit, evolve, extract.
eerie *adj* awesome, fearful, frightening, strange, uncanny, weird.
efface *vb* blot, blot out, cancel, delete, destroy, erase, expunge, obliterate, remove, sponge.
effect *vb* cause, create, effectuate, produce; accomplish, achieve, carry, compass, complete, conclude, consummate, contrive, do, execute, force, negotiate, perform, realize, work. * *n* consequence, event, fruit, issue, outcome, result; efficiency, fact, force, power, reality; validity, weight; drift, import, intent, meaning, purport, significance, tenor.
effective *adj* able, active, adequate, competent, convincing, effectual, sufficient; cogent, efficacious, energetic, forcible, potent, powerful.
effects *npl* chattels, furniture, goods, movables, property.
effectual *adj* operative, successful; active, effective, efficacious, efficient.
effectuate *vb* accomplish, achieve, complete, do, effect, execute, fulfil, perform, secure.
effeminate *adj* delicate, feminine, soft, tender, timorous, unmanly, womanish, womanlike, womanly; camp.
effervesce *vb* bubble, ferment, foam, froth.
effete *adj* addle, barren, fruitless, sterile, unfruitful, unproductive, unprolific; decayed, exhausted, spent, wasted.
efficacious *adj* active, adequate, competent, effective, effectual, efficient, energetic, operative, powerful.
efficacy *n* ability, competency, effectiveness, efficiency, energy, force, potency, power, strength, vigour, virtue.
efficient *adj* active, capable, competent, effective, effectual, efficacious, operative, potent; able, energetic, ready, skilful.
effigy *n* figure, image, likeness, portrait, representation, statue.
effloresce *vb* bloom, flower.
efflorescence *n* blooming, blossoming, flowering.
effluence *n* discharge, efflux, effluvium, emanation, emission, flow, outflow, outpouring.
effort *n* application, attempt, endeavour, essay, exertion, pains, spurt, strain, strife, stretch, struggle, trial, trouble.
effrontery *n* assurance, audacity, boldness, brass, disrespect, hardihood, impudence, incivility, insolence, presumption, rudeness, sauciness, shamelessness.
effulgent *adj* burning, beaming, blazing, bright, brilliant, dazzling, flaming, glowing, lustrous, radiant, refulgent, resplendent, shining, splendid.
effusion *n* discharge, efflux, emission, gush, outpouring; shedding, spilling, waste; address, speech, talk, utterance.
egg *vb* (*with* **on**) encourage, incite, instigate, push, stimulate, urge; harass, harry, provoke.
ego *n* id, self, me, subject, superego.
egotism *n* self-admiration, self-assertion, self-commendation, self-conceit, self-esteem, self-importance, self-praise; egoism, selfishness.
egotistic, egotistical *adj* bumptious, conceited, egoistical, opinionated, self-asserting, self-admiring, self-centred, self-conceited, self-important, self-loving, vain.
egregious *adj* conspicuous, enormous, extraordinary, flagrant, great, gross, huge, monstrous, outrageous, prodigious, remarkable, tremendous.
egress *n* departure, emergence, exit, outlet, way out.
eject *vb* belch, discharge, disgorge, emit, evacuate, puke, spew, spit, spout, spurt, void, vomit; bounce, cashier, discharge, dismiss, disposes, eliminate, evict, expel, fire, oust; banish, reject, throw out.
elaborate *vb* develop, improve, mature, produce, refine, ripen. * *adj* complicated, decorated, detailed, dressy, laboured, laborious, ornate, perfected, studied.
elapse *vb* go, lapse, pass.
elastic *adj* rebounding, recoiling, resilient, springy; buoyant, recuperative.

elated *adj* animated, cheered, elate, elevated, excited, exhilarated, exultant, flushed, puffed up, roused.
elbow *vb* crowd, force, hustle, jostle, nudge, push, shoulder. * *n* angle, bend, corner, flexure, joining, turn.
elder *adj* older, senior; ranking; ancient, earlier, older. * *n* ancestor, senior; presbyter, prior, senator.
elect *vb* appoint, choose, cull, designate, pick, prefer, select. * *adj* choice, chosen, picked, selected; appointed, elected; predestinated, redeemed.
election *n* appointment, choice, preference, selection; alternative, freedom, freewill, liberty; predestination.
elector *n* chooser, constituent, selector, voter.
electrify *vb* charge, galvanize; astonish, enchant, excite, rouse, startle, stir, thrill.
elegance, elegancy *n* beauty, grace, propriety, symmetry; courtliness, daintiness, gentility, nicety, polish, politeness, refinement, taste.
elegant *adj* beautiful, chaste, classical, dainty, graceful, fine, handsome, neat, symmetrical, tasteful, trim, well-made, well-proportioned; accomplished, courtly, cultivated, fashionable, genteel, polished, polite, refined.
elegiac *adj* dirgeful, mournful, plaintive, sorrowful.
elegy *n* dirge, epicedium, lament, ode, threnody.
element *n* basis, component, constituent, factor, germ, ingredient, part, principle, rudiment, unit; environment, milieu, sphere.
elementary *adj* primordial, simple, uncombined, uncomplicated, uncompounded; basic, component, fundamental, initial, primary, rudimental, rudimentary.
elevate *vb* erect, hoist, lift, raise; advance, aggrandize, exalt, promote; dignify, ennoble, exalt, greaten, improve, refine; animate, cheer, elate, excite, exhilarate, rouse.
elfin *adj* elflike, elvish, mischievous, weird.
elicit *vb* draw out, educe, evoke, extort, fetch, obtain, pump, wrest, wring; deduce, educe.
eligible *adj* desirable, preferable; qualified, suitable, worthy.
eliminate *vb* disengage, eradicate, exclude, expel, remove, separate; ignore, omit, reject.
ellipsis *n* gap, hiatus, lacuna, omission.
elliptical *adj* oval; defective, incomplete.
elocution *n* declamation, delivery, oratory, rhetoric, speech, utterance.
elongate *vb* draw, draw out, extend, lengthen, protract, stretch.
elope *vb* abscond, bolt, decamp, disappear, leave.
eloquence *n* fluency, oratory, rhetoric.
else *adv* besides, differently, otherwise.
elucidate *vb* clarify, demonstrate, explain, expound, illuminate, illustrate, interpret, unfold.
elucidation *n* annotation, clarification, comment, commentary, elucidating, explaining, explanation, exposition, gloss, scholium.
elude *vb* avoid, escape, evade, shun, slip; baffle, balk, disappoint, disconcert, escape, foil, frustrate, thwart.
elusive *adj* deceptive, deceitful, delusive, evasive, fallacious, fraudulent, illusory; equivocatory, equivocating, shuffling.
Elysian *adj* blissful, celestial, delightful, enchanting, heavenly, ravishing, seraphic.
emaciation *n* attenuation, lankness, leanness, meagreness, tabes, tabescence, thinness.
emanate *vb* arise, come, emerge, flow, issue, originate, proceed, spring.
emancipate *vb* deliver, discharge, disenthral, enfranchise, free, liberate, manumit, release, unchain, unfetter, unshackle.
emancipation *n* deliverance, enfranchisement, deliverance, freedom, liberation, manumission, release.
emasculate *vb* castrate, geld; debilitate, effeminize, enervate, unman, weaken.
embalm *vb* cherish, consecrate, conserve, enshrine, preserve, store, treasure; perfume, scent.
embargo *vb* ban, bar, blockade, debar, exclude, prohibit, proscribe, restrict, stop, withhold. * *n* ban, bar, blockade, exclusion, hindrance, impediment, prohibition, prohibitory, proscription, restraint, restriction, stoppage.
embark *vb* engage, enlist.
embarrass *vb* beset, entangle, perplex; annoy, clog, bother, distress, hamper, harass, involve, plague, trouble, vex; abash, confound, confuse, discomfit, disconcert, dumbfound, mortify, nonplus, pose, shame.
embellish *vb* adorn, beautify, bedeck, deck, decorate, emblazon, enhance, enrich, garnish, grace, ornament.
embellishment *n* adornment, decoration, enrichment, ornament, ornamentation.
embezzle *vb* appropriate, defalcate, filch, misappropriate, peculate, pilfer, purloin, steal.
embitter *vb* aggravate, envenom, exacerbate; anger, enrage, exasperate, madden.
emblem *n* badge, cognizance, device, mark, representation, sign, symbol, token, type.
embody *vb* combine, compact, concentrate, incorporate; comprehend, comprise, contain, embrace, include; codify, methodize, systematize.
embolden *vb* animate, cheer, elate, encourage, gladden, hearten, inspirit, nerve, reassure.
embosom *vb* bury, cherish, clasp, conceal, enfold, envelop, enwrap, foster, hide, nurse, surround.
embrace *vb* clasp; accept, seize, welcome; comprehend, comprise, contain, cover, embody, encircle, enclose, encompass, enfold, hold, include. * *n* clasp, fold, hug.
embroil *vb* commingle, encumber, ensnarl, entangle, implicate, involve; confuse, discompose, disorder, distract, disturb, perplex, trouble.
embryo *n* beginning, germ, nucleus, root, rudiment.
embryonic *adj* incipient, rudimentary, undeveloped.

emendation *n* amendment, correction, improvement, rectification.
emerge *vb* rise; emanate, escape, issue; appear, arise, outcrop.
emergency *n* crisis, difficulty, dilemma, exigency, extremity, necessity, pass, pinch, push, strait, urgency; conjuncture, crisis, juncture, pass.
emigration *n* departure, exodus, migration, removal.
eminence *n* elevation, hill, projection, prominence, protuberance; celebrity, conspicuousness, distinction, exaltation, fame, loftiness, note, preferment, reputation, repute, renown.
eminent *adj* elevated, high, lofty; celebrated, conspicuous, distinguished, exalted, famous, illustrious, notable, prominent, remarkable, renowned.
emissary *n* messenger, scout, secret agent, spy.
emit *vb* breathe out, dart, discharge, eject, emanate, exhale, gust, hurl, jet, outpour, shed, shoot, spurt, squirt.
emollient *adj* relaxing, softening. soothing. * *n* softener.
emolument *n* compensation, gain, hire, income, lucre, pay, pecuniary, profits, salary, stipend, wages; advantage, benefit, profit, perquisites.
emotion *n* agitation, excitement, feeling, passion, perturbation, sentiment, sympathy, trepidation.
emphasis *n* accent, stress; force, importance, impressiveness, moment, significance, weight.
emphatic *adj* decided, distinct, earnest, energetic, expressive, forcible, impressive, intensive, positive, significant, strong, unequivocal.
empire *n* domain, dominion, sovereignty, supremacy; authority, command, control, government, rule, sway.
empirical, empiric *adj* experimental, experiential; hypothetical, provisional, tentative; charlatanic, quackish.
employ *vb* busy, devote, engage, engross, enlist, exercise, occupy, retain; apply, commission, use. * *n* employment, service.
employee *n* agent, clerk, employee, hand, servant, workman.
employment *n* avocation, business, calling, craft, employ, engagement, occupation, profession, pursuit, trade, vocation, work.
emporium *n* market, mart, shop, store.
empower *vb* authorize, commission, permit, qualify, sanction, warrant; enable.
empty *vb* deplete, drain, evacuate, exhaust; discharge, disembogue; flow, embogue. * *adj* blank, hollow, unoccupied, vacant, vacuous, void; deplete, destitute, devoid, hungry; unfilled, unfurnished, unsupplied; unsatisfactory, unsatisfying, unsubstantial, useless, vain; clear, deserted, desolate, exhausted, free, unburdened, unloaded, waste; foolish, frivolous, inane, senseless, silly, stupid, trivial, weak.
empyrean, empyreal *adj* aerial, airy, ethereal, heavenly, refined, sublimated, sublimed.
emulation *n* competition, rivalry, strife, vying; contention, envy, jealousy.
enable *vb* authorize, capacitate, commission, empower, fit, permit, prepare, qualify, sanction, warrant.
enact *vb* authorize, command, decree, establish, legislate, ordain, order, sanction; act, perform, personate, play, represent.
enactment *n* act, decree, law, edict, ordinance.
enamour *vb* bewitch, captivate, charm, enchant, endear, fascinate.
enchain *vb* bind, confine, enslave, fetter, hold, manacle, restrain, shackle.
enchant *vb* beguile, bewitch, charm, delude, fascinate; captivate, catch, enamour, win; beatify, delight, enrapture, rapture, ravish, transport.
enchanting *adj* bewitching, blissful, captivating, charming, delightful, enrapturing, fascinating, rapturous, ravishing.
enchantment *n* charm, conjuration, incantation, magic, necromancy, sorcery, spell, witchery; bliss, delight, fascination, rapture, ravishment, transport.
encase *vb* encircle, enclose, incase, infix, set; chase, emboss, engrave, inlay, ornament.
encage *vb* confine, coop up, impound, imprison, shut up.
encircle *vb* belt, circumscribe, encompass, enclose, engird, enring, environ, gird, ring, span, surround, twine; clasp, embrace, enfold, fold.
enclose, inclose *vb* circumscribe, corral, coop, embosom, encircle, encompass, environ, fence in, hedge, include, pen, shut in, surround; box, cover, encase, envelop, wrap.
encomium *n* applause, commendation, eulogy, laudation, panegyric, praise.
encompass *vb* belt, compass, encircle, enclose, engird, environ, gird, surround; beset, besiege, hem in, include, invest, surround.
encounter *vb* confront, face, meet; attack, combat, contend, engage, strive, struggle. * *n* assault, attack, clash, collision, meeting, onset; action, affair, battle, brush, combat, conflict, contest, dispute, engagement, skirmish.
encourage *vb* animate, assure, cheer, comfort, console, embolden, enhearten, fortify, hearten, incite, inspirit, instigate, reassure, stimulate, strengthen; abet, aid, advance, approve, countenance, favour, foster, further, help, patronize, promote, support.
encroach *vb* infringe, invade, intrude, tench, trespass, usurp.
encumber *vb* burden, clog, hamper, hinder, impede, load, obstruct, overload, oppress, retard; complicate, embarrass, entangle, involve, perplex.
encumbrance *n* burden, clog, deadweight, drag, embarrassment, hampering, hindrance, impediment, incubus, load; claim, debt, liability, lien.
end *vb* abolish, close, conclude, discontinue, dissolve, drop, finish, stop, terminate; annihilate,

destroy, kill; cease, terminate. * *n* extremity, tip; cessation, close, denouement, ending, expiration, finale, finis, finish, last, period, stoppage, wind-up; completion, conclusion, consummation; annihilation, catastrophe, destruction, dissolution; bound, limit, termination, terminus; consequence, event, issue, result, settlement, sequel, upshot; fragment, remnant, scrap, stub, tag, tail; aim, design, goal, intent, intention, object, objective, purpose.

endanger *vb* compromise, hazard, imperil, jeopardize, peril, risk.

endear *vb* attach, bind, captivate, charm, win.

endearment *n* attachment, fondness, love, tenderness; caress, blandishment, fondling.

endeavour *vb* aim, attempt, essay, labour, seek, strive, struggle, study, try. * *n* aim, attempt, conatus, effort, essay, exertion, trial, struggle, trial.

endless *adj* boundless, illimitable, immeasurable, indeterminable, infinite, interminable, limitless, unlimited; dateless, eternal, everlasting, never-ending, perpetual, unending; deathless, ever-enduring, ever-living, immortal, imperishable, undying.

endorse, indorse *vb* approve, back, confirm, guarantee, ratify, sanction, superscribe, support, visé, vouch for, warrant; superscribe.

endow *vb* bequeath, clothe, confer, dower, endue, enrich, gift, indue, invest, supply.

endowment *n* bequest, boon, bounty, gift, grant, largesse, present; foundation, fund, property, revenue; ability, aptitude, capability, capacity, faculty, genius, gift, parts, power, qualification, quality, talent.

endurance *n* abiding, bearing, sufferance, suffering, tolerance, toleration; backbone, bottom, forbearance, fortitude, guts, patience, resignation.

endure *vb* bear, support, sustain; experience, suffer, undergo, weather; abide, brook, permit, pocket, swallow, tolerate, stomach, submit, withstand; continue, last, persist, remain, wear.

enemy *n* adversary, foe; antagonist, foeman, opponent, rival.

energetic *adj* active, effective, efficacious, emphatic, enterprising, forceful, forcible, hearty, mettlesome, potent, powerful, strenuous, strong, vigorous.

energy *n* activity, dash, drive, efficacy, efficiency, force, go, impetus, intensity, mettle, might, potency, power, strength, verve, vim; animation, life, manliness, spirit, spiritedness, stamina, vigour, zeal.

enervate *vb* break, debilitate, devitalize, emasculate, enfeeble, exhaust, paralyse, relax, soften, unhinge, unnerve, weaken.

enfeeble *vb* debilitate, devitalize, enervate, exhaust, relax, unhinge, unnerve, weaken.

enfold, infold *vb* enclose, envelop, fold, enwrap, wrap; clasp, embrace.

enforce *vb* compel, constrain, exact, force, oblige, require, urge.

enfranchise *vb* emancipate, free, liberate, manumit, release.

engage *vb* bind, commit, obligate, pledge, promise; affiance, betroth, plight; book, brief, employ, enlist, hire, retain; arrest, allure, attach, draw, entertain, fix, gain, win; busy, commission, contract, engross, occupy; attack, encounter; combat, contend, contest, fight, interlock, struggle; embark, enlist; agree, promise, stipulate, undertake, warrant.

engagement *n* appointment, assurance, contract, obligation, pledge, promise, stipulation; affiancing, betrothment, betrothal, plighting; avocation, business, calling, employment, enterprise, occupation; action, battle, combat, encounter, fight.

engender *vb* bear, beget, breed, create, generate, procreate, propagate; cause, excite, incite, occasion, produce.

engine *n* invention, machine; agency, agent, device, implement, instrument, means, method, tool, weapon.

engorge *vb* bolt, devour, eat, gobble, gorge, gulp, swallow; glut, obstruct, stuff.

engrave *vb* carve, chisel, cut, etch, grave, hatch, incise, sculpt; grave, impress, imprint, infix.

engross *vb* absorb, engage, occupy, take up; buy up, forestall, monopolize.

engrossment *n* absorption, forestalling, monopoly.

engulf, ingulf *vb* absorb, overwhelm, plunge, swallow up.

enhance *vb* advance, aggravate, augment, elevate, heighten, increase, intensify, raise, swell.

enhearten *vb* animate, assure, cheer, comfort, console, embolden, encourage, hearten, incite, inspirit, reassure, stimulate.

enigma *n* conundrum, mystery, problem, puzzle, riddle.

enigmatic, enigmatical *adj* ambiguous, dark, doubtful, equivocal, hidden, incomprehensible, mysterious, mystic, obscure, occult, perplexing, puzzling, recondite, uncertain, unintelligible.

enjoin *vb* admonish, advise, urge; bid, command, direct, order, prescribe, require; prohibit, restrain.

enjoy *vb* like, possess, relish.

enjoyment *n* delight, delectation, gratification, happiness, indulgence, pleasure, satisfaction; possession.

enkindle *vb* inflame, ignite, kindle; excite, incite, instigate, provoke, rouse, stimulate.

enlarge *vb* amplify, augment, broaden, develop, dilate, distend, expand, extend, grow, increase, magnify, widen; aggrandize, engreaten, ennoble, expand, exaggerate, greaten; swell.

enlighten *vb* illume, illuminate, illumine; counsel, educate, civilize, inform, instruct, teach.

enlist *vb* enrol, levy, recruit, register; enrol, list; embark, engage.

enliven *vb* animate, invigorate, quicken, reanimate, rouse, wake; exhilarate, cheer, brighten,

delight, elate, gladden, inspire, inspirit, rouse.
enmity *n* animosity, aversion, bitterness, hate, hatred, hostility, ill-will, malevolence, malignity, rancour.
ennoble *vb* aggrandize, dignify, elevate, engreaten, enlarge, exalt, glorify, greaten, raise.
ennui *n* boredom, irksomeness, languor, lassitude, listlessness, tedium, tiresomeness, weariness.
enormity *n* atrociousness, atrocity, depravity, flagitiousness, heinousness, nefariousness, outrageousness, villainy, wickedness.
enormous *adj* abnormal. exceptional, inordinate, irregular; colossal, Cyclopean, elephantine, Herculean, huge, immense, monstrous, vast, gigantic, prodigious, titanic, tremendous.
enough *adj* abundant, adequate, ample, plenty, sufficient. * *adv* satisfactorily, sufficiently. * *n* abundance, plenty, sufficiency.
enquire *see* **inquire**.
enrage *vb* anger, chafe, exasperate, incense, inflame, infuriate, irritate, madden, provoke.
enrapture *vb* beatify, bewitch, delight, enchant, enravish, entrance, surpassingly, transport.
enrich *vb* endow; adorn, deck, decorate, embellish, grace, ornament.
enrobe *vb* clothe, dress, apparel, array, attire, invest, robe.
enrol *vb* catalogue, engage, engross, enlist, list, register; chronicle, record.
ensconce *vb* conceal, cover, harbour, hide, protect, screen, secure, settle, shelter, shield, snugly.
enshrine *vb* embalm, enclose, entomb; cherish, treasure.
ensign *n* banner, colours, eagle, flag, gonfalcon, pennon, standard, streamer; sign, signal, symbol; badge, hatchment.
enslave *vb* captivate, dominate, master, overmaster, overpower, subjugate.
ensnare *vb* catch, entrap; allure, inveigle, seduce; bewilder, confound, embarrass, encumber, entangle, perplex.
ensue *vb* follow, succeed; arise, come, flow, issue, proceed, result, spring.
entangle *vb* catch, ensnare, entrap; confuse, enmesh, intertwine, intertwist, interweave, knot, mat, ravel, tangle; bewilder, embarrass, en--cumber, ensnare, involve, nonplus, perplex, puzzle.
enterprise *n* adventure, attempt, cause, effort, endeavour, essay, project, undertaking, scheme, venture; activity, adventurousness, daring, dash, energy, initiative, readiness, push.
enterprising *adj* adventurous, audacious, bold, daring, dashing, venturesome, venturous; active, adventurous, alert, efficient, energetic, prompt, resourceful, smart, spirited, stirring, strenuous, zealous.
entertain *vb* fete, receive, regale, treat; cherish, foster, harbour, hold, lodge, shelter; admit, consider; amuse, cheer, divert, please, recreate.
entertainment *n* hospitality; banquet, collation, feast, festival, reception, treat; amusement, diversion, pastime, recreation, sport.
enthusiasm *n* ecstasy, exaltation, fanaticism; ardour, earnestness, devotion, eagerness, fervour, passion, warmth, zeal.
enthusiast *n* bigot, devotee, fan, fanatic, freak, zealot; castle-builder, dreamer, visionary.
entice *vb* allure, attract, bait, cajole, coax, decoy, inveigle, lure, persuade, prevail on, seduce, tempt, wheedle, wile.
enticement *n* allurement, attraction, bait, blandishment, inducement, inveiglement, lure, persuasion, seduction.
entire *adj* complete, integrated, perfect, unbroken, undiminished, undivided, unimpaired, whole; complete, full, plenary, thorough; mere, pure, sheer, unalloyed, unmingled, unmitigated, unmixed.
entitle *vb* call, characterize, christen, denominate, designate, dub, name, style; empower, enable, fit for, qualify for.
entomb *vb* bury, inhume, inter.
entrails *npl* bowels, guts, intestines, inwards, offal, viscera.
entrance[1] *n* access, approach, avenue, incoming, ingress; adit, avenue, aperture, door, doorway, entry, gate, hallway, inlet, lobby, mouth, passage, portal, stile, vestibule; beginning, commencement, debut, initiation, introduction; admission, entrée.
entrance[2] *vb* bewitch, captivate, charm, delight, enchant, enrapture, fascinate, ravish, transport.
entrap *vb* catch, ensnare; allure, entice, inveigle, seduce; embarrass, entangle, involve, nonplus, perplex, pose, stagger.
entreat *vb* adjure, beg, beseech, crave, enjoin, implore, importune, petition, pray, solicit, supplicate.
entreaty *n* adjuration, appeal, importunity, petition, prayer, request, solicitation, suit, supplication.
entrée *n* access, admission, admittance.
entrench, intrench *vb* furrow; circumvallate, fortify; encroach, infringe, invade, trench, trespass.
entrenchment, intrenchment *n* entrenching; earthwork, fortification; defence, protection, shelter; encroachment, inroad, invasion.
entrust *vb* commit, confide, consign.
entwine *vb* entwist, interlace, intertwine, interweave, inweave, twine, twist, weave; embrace, encircle, encumber, interlace, surround.
enumerate *vb* calculate, cite, compute, count, detail, mention, number, numerate, reckon, recount, specify, tell.
enunciate *vb* articulate, declare, proclaim, promulgate, pronounce, propound, publish, say, speak, utter.
envelop *vb* encase, enfold, enwrap, fold, pack, wrap; cover, encircle, encompass, enshroud, hide, involve, surround.
envelope *n* capsule, case, covering, integument,

shroud, skin, wrapper, veil, vesture, wrap.
envenom *vb* poison, taint; embitter, malign; aggravate, enrage, exasperate, incense, inflame, irritate, madden, provoke.
environ *n* begird, belt, embrace, encircle, encompass, enclose, engrid, envelop, gird, hedge, hem, surround; beset, besiege, encompass, invest.
environs *npl* neighbourhood, vicinage, vicinity.
envoy *n* ambassador, legate, minister, plenipotentiary; courier, messenger.
envy *vb* hate; begrudge, grudge; covet, emulate, desire. * *n* enviousness, hate, hatred, ill-will, jealousy, malice, spite; grudge, grudging.
enwrap *vb* absorb, cover, encase, engross, envelop, infold, involve, wrap, wrap up.
ephemeral *adj* brief, diurnal, evanescent, fleeting, flitting, fugacious, fugitive, momentary, occasional, short-lived, transient, transitory.
epic *adj* Homeric, heroic, narrative.
epicure *n* gastronome, glutton, gourmand, gourmet; epicurean, sensualist, Sybarite, voluptuary.
epidemic *adj* general, pandemic, prevailing, prevalent. * *n* outbreak, pandemia, pestilence, plague, spread, wave.
epidermis *n* cuticle, scarf-skin.
epigrammatic *adj* antithetic, concise, laconic, piquant, poignant, pointed, pungent, sharp, terse.
episcopal *adj* Episcopalian, pontifical, prelatic.
epistle *n* communication, letter, missive, note.
epithet *n* appellation, description, designation, name, predicate, title.
epitome *n* abbreviation, abridgement, abstract, breviary, brief, comment, compendium, condensation, conspectus, digest, summary, syllabus, synopsis.
epitomize *vb* abbreviate, abridge, abstract, condense, contract, curtail, cut, reduce, shorten, summarize.
epoch *n* age, date, era, period, time.
equable *adj* calm, equal, even, even-tempered, regular, steady, uniform, serene, tranquil, unruffled.
equal *vb* equalize, even, match. * *adj* alike, coordinate, equivalent, like, tantamount; even, level, equable, regular, uniform; equitable, even-handed, fair, impartial, just, unbiased; co-extensive, commensurate, corresponding, parallel, proportionate; adequate, competent, fit, sufficient. * *n* compeer, fellow, match, peer; rival.
equanimity *n* calmness, composure, coolness, peace, regularity, self-possession, serenity, steadiness.
equestrian *adj* equine, horse-like, horsy. * *n* horseman, rider; cavalier, cavalryman, chevalier, horse soldier, knight.
equilibrist *n* acrobat, balancer, funambulist, ropewalker.
equip *vb* appoint, arm, furnish, provide, rig, supply; accoutre, array, dress.
equipage *n* accoutrements, apparatus, baggage, effects, equipment, furniture; carriage, turnout, vehicle; attendance, procession, retinue, suite, train.
equipment *n* accoutrement, apparatus, baggage, equipage, furniture, gear, outfit, rigging.
equipoise *n* balance, equilibrium.
equitable *adj* even-handed, candid, honest, impartial, just, unbiased, unprejudiced, upright; adequate, fair, proper, reasonable, right.
equity *n* just, right; fair play, fairness, impartiality, justice, rectitude, reasonableness, righteousness, uprightness.
equivalent *adj* commensurate, equal, equipollent, tantamount; interchangeable, synonymous. * *n* complement, coordinate, counterpart, double, equal, fellow, like, match, parallel, pendant, quid pro quo.
equivocal *adj* ambiguous; doubtful, dubious, enigmatic, indeterminate, problematical, puzzling, uncertain.
equivocate *vb* dodge, evade, fence, palter, prevaricate, shuffle, quibble.
equivocation *n* evasion, paltering, prevarication, quibbling, shuffling; double entendre, double meaning, quibble.
era *n* age, date, epoch, period, time.
eradicate *vb* extirpate, root, uproot; abolish, annihilate, destroy, obliterate.
erase *vb* blot, cancel, delete, efface, expunge, obliterate, scrape out.
erasure *n* cancellation, cancelling, effacing, expunging, obliteration.
erect *vb* build, construct, raise, rear; create, establish, form, found, institute, plant. * *adj* standing, unrecumbent, uplifted, upright; elevated, vertical, perpendicular, straight; bold, firm, undaunted, undismayed, unshaken, unterrified.
erelong *adv* early, quickly, shortly, soon, speedily.
eremite *n* anchoret, anchorite, hermit, recluse, solitary.
ergo *adv* consequently, hence, therefore.
erode *vb* canker, consume, corrode, destroy, eat away, fret, rub.
erosive *adj* acrid, cathartic, caustic, corroding, corrosive, eating, virulent.
erotic *adj* amorous, amatory, arousing, seductive, stimulating, titillating.
err *vb* deviate, ramble, rove, stray, wander; blunder, misjudge, mistake; fall, lapse, nod, offend, sin, stumble, trespass, trip.
errand *n* charge, commission, mandate, message, mission, purpose.
errant *adj* adventurous, rambling, roving, stray, wandering.
erratic *adj* nomadic, rambling, roving, wandering; moving, planetary; abnormal, capricious, deviating, eccentric, irregular, odd, queer, strange.
erratum *n* correction, corrigendum, error, misprint, mistake.
erroneous *adj* false, incorrect, inaccurate, inexact, mistaken untrue, wrong.
error *n* blunder, fallacy, inaccuracy, misapprehen-

sion, mistake, oversight; delinquency, fault, iniquity, misdeed, misdoing, misstep, obliquity, offence, shortcoming, sin, transgression, trespass, wrongdoing.

erudition *n* knowledge, learning, lore, scholarship.

eruption *n* explosion, outbreak, outburst; sally; rash.

escape *vb* avoid, elude, evade, flee from, shun; abscond, bolt, decamp, flee, fly; slip. * *n* flight; release; passage, passing; leakage.

eschew *vb* abstain, avoid, elude, flee from, shun.

escort *vb* convey, guard, protect; accompany, attend, conduct. * *n* attendant, bodyguard, cavalier, companion, convoy, gallant, guard, squire; protection, safe conduct, safeguard; attendance, company.

esculent *adj* eatable, edible, wholesome.

esoteric *adj* hidden, inmost, inner, mysterious, private, recondite, secret.

especial *adj* absolute, chief, distinct, distinguished, marked, particular, peculiar, principal, singular, special, specific, uncommon, unusual; detailed, minute, noteworthy.

espousal *n* affiancing, betrothing, espousing, plighting; adoption, defence, maintenance, support.

espouse *vb* betroth, plight, promise; marry, wed; adopt, champion, defend, embrace, maintain, support.

espy *vb* descry, detect, discern, discover, observe, perceive, spy, watch.

esquire *n* armiger, attendant, escort, gentleman, squire.

essay[1] *vb* attempt, endeavour, try. * *n* aim, attempt, effort, endeavour, exertion, struggle, trial.

essay[2] *n* article, composition, disquisition, dissertation, paper, thesis.

essence *n* nature, quintessence, substance; extract, part; odour, perfume, scent; being, entity, existence, nature.

essential *adj* fundamental, indispensable, important, inward, intrinsic, necessary, requisite, vital; diffusible, pure, rectified, volatile.

establish *vb* fix, secure, set, settle; decree, enact, ordain; build, constitute, erect, form, found, institute, organize, originate, pitch, plant, raise; ensconce, ground, install, place, plant, root, secure; approve, confirm, ratify, sanction; prove, substantiate, verify.

estate *n* condition, state; position, rank, standing; division, order; effects, fortune, possessions, property; interest.

esteem *vb* appreciate, estimate, rate, reckon, value; admire, honour, like, prize, respect, revere, reverence, value, venerate, worship; account, believe, consider, deem, fancy, hold, imagine, suppose, regard, think. * *n* account, appreciation, consideration, estimate, estimation, judgement, opinion, reckoning, valuation; credit, honour, regard, respect, reverence.

estimable *adj* appreciable, calculable, computable; admirable, credible, deserving, excellent, good, meritorious, precious, respectful, valuable, worthy.

estimate *vb* appraise, appreciate, esteem, prise, rate, value; assess, calculate, compute, count, gauge, judge, reckon. * *n* estimation, judgement, valuation; calculation, computation.

estimation *n* appreciation, estimate, valuation; esteem, estimate, judgement, opinion; honour, reckoning, regard, respect, reverence.

estop *vb* bar, impede, preclude, stop.

estrange *vb* withdraw, withhold; alienate, divert; disaffect, destroy.

estuary *n* creek, inlet, fiord, firth, frith, mouth.

etch *vb* corrode, engrave.

eternal *adj* absolute, inevitable, necessary, self-active, self-existent, self-originated; abiding, ceaseless, endless, ever-enduring, everlasting, incessant, interminable, never-ending, perennial, permanent, perpetual, sempiternal, unceasing, unending; deathless, immortal, imperishable, incorruptible, indestructible, never-dying, undying; immutable, unchangeable; constant, continual, continuous, incessant, persistent, unbroken, uninterrupted.

ethereal *adj* aerial, airy, celestial, empyreal, heavenly, unworldly; attenuated, light, subtle, tenuous, volatile; delicate, fairy, flimsy, fragile, rare, refined, subtle.

eulogize *vb* applaud, commend, extol, laud, magnify, praise.

eulogy *n* discourse, eulogium, panegyric, speech; applause, encomium, commendation, laudation, praise.

euphonious *adj* clear, euphonic, harmonious, mellifluous, mellow, melodious, musical, silvery, smooth, sweet-toned.

evacuant *adj* abstergent, cathartic, cleansing, emetic, purgative. * *n* cathartic, purgative.

evacuate *vb* empty; discharge, clean out, clear out, eject, excrete, expel, purge, void; abandon, desert, forsake, leave, quit, relinquish, withdraw.

evade *vb* elude, escape; avoid, decline, dodge, funk, shun; baffle, elude, foil; dodge, equivocate, fence, palter, prevaricate, quibble, shuffle.

evanescence *n* disappearance, evanishing, evanishment, vanishing; transience, transientness, transitoriness.

evanescent *adj* ephemeral, fleeting, flitting, fugitive, passing, short-lived, transient, transitory, vanishing.

evaporate *vb* distil, volatilize; dehydrate, dry, vaporize; disperse, dissolve, fade, vanish.

evaporation *n* distillation, volatilization; dehydration, drying, vaporization; disappearance, dispersal, dissolution.

evasion *n* artifice, avoidance, bluffing, deceit, dodge, equivocation, escape, excuse, funking, prevarication, quibble, shift, subterfuge, shuffling, sophistical, tergiversation.

evasive *adj* elusive, elusory, equivocating, prevari-

cating, shuffling, slippery, sophistical.
even *vb* balance, equalize, harmonize, symmetrize; align, flatten, flush, level, smooth, square. * *adj* flat, horizontal, level, plane, smooth; calm, composed, equable, equal, peaceful, placid, regular, steady, uniform, unruffled; direct, equitable, fair, impartial, just, straightforward. * *adv* exactly, just, verily; likewise. * *n* eve, evening, eventide, vesper.
evening *n* dusk, eve, even, eventide, nightfall, sunset, twilight.
event *n* circumstance, episode, fact, happening, incident, occurrence; conclusion, consequence, end, issue, outcome, result, sequel, termination; adventure, affair.
eventful *adj* critical, important, memorable, momentous, remarkable, signal, stirring.
eventual *adj* final, last, ultimate; conditional, contingent, possible. * *adv* always, aye, constantly, continually, eternally, ever evermore, forever, incessantly, perpetually, unceasingly.
everlasting *adj* ceaseless, constant, continual, endless, eternal, ever-during, incessant, interminable, never-ceasing, never-ending, perpetual, unceasing, unending, unintermitting, uninterrupted; deathless, ever-living, immortal, imperishable, never-dying, undying.
evermore *adv* always, constantly, continually, eternally, ever, forever, perpetually.
everyday *adj* accustomed, common, commonplace, customary, habitual, routine, usual, wonted.
evict *vb* dispossess, eject, thrust out.
evidence *vb* evince, make clear, manifest, prove, show, testify, vouch. * *n* affirmation, attestation, averment, confirmation, corroboration, deposition, grounds, indication, proof, testimony, token, trace, voucher, witness.
evident *adj* apparent, bald, clear, conspicuous, distinct, downright, incontestable, indisputable, manifest, obvious, open, overt, palpable, patent, plain, unmistakable.
evil *adj* bad, ill; base, corrupt, malicious, malevolent, malign, nefarious, perverse, sinful, vicious, vile, wicked, wrong; bad, deleterious, baleful, baneful, destructive, harmful, hurtful, injurious, mischievous, noxious, pernicious, profane; adverse, calamitous, diabolic, disastrous, unfortunate, unhappy, unpropitious, woeful. * *n* calamity, disaster, ill, misery, misfortune, pain, reverse, sorrow, suffering, woe; badness, baseness, corruption, depravity, malignity, sin, viciousness, wickedness; bale, bane, blast, canker, curse, harm, injury, mischief, wrong.
evince *vb* establish, evidence, manifest, prove, show; disclose, display, exhibit, indicate, reveal.
eviscerate *vb* disembowel, embowel, gut.
evoke *vb* arouse, elicit, excite, provoke, rouse.
evolve *vb* develop, educe, exhibit, expand, open, unfold, unroll.
exacerbate *vb* aggravate, embitter, enrage, exasperate, excite, inflame, infuriate, irritate, provoke, vex.
exact *vb* elicit, extort, mulch, require, squeeze; ask, claim, compel, demand, enforce, requisition, take. * *adj* rigid, rigorous, scrupulous, severe, strict; diametric, express, faultless, precise, true; accurate, close, correct, definite, faithful, literal, undeviating; accurate, critical, delicate, fine, nice, sensitive; careful, methodical, punctilious, orderly, punctual, regular.
exacting *adj* critical, difficult, exactive, rigid, extortionary.
exaction *n* contribution, extortion, oppression, rapacity, tribute.
exactness *n* accuracy, correctness, exactitude, faithfulness, faultlessness, fidelity, nicety, precision, rigour; carefulness, method, precision, regularity, rigidness, scrupulousity, scrupulousness, strictness.
exaggerate *vb* enlarge, magnify, overcharge, overcolour, overstate, romance, strain, stretch.
exalt *vb* elevate, erect, heighten, lift up, raise; aggrandize, dignify, elevate, ennoble; bless, extol, glorify, magnify, praise.
exalted *adj* elated, elevated, high, highflown, lofty, lordly, magnificent.
examination *n* inspection, observation; exploration, inquiry, inquisition, investigation, perusal, research, search, scrutiny, survey; catechism, probation, review, test, trial.
examine *vb* inspect, observe; canvass, consider, explore, inquire, investigate, scrutinize, study, test; catechize, interrogate.
example *n* archetype, copy, model, pattern, piece, prototype, representative, sample, sampler, specimen, standard; exemplification, illustration, instance, precedent, warning.
exanimate *adj* dead, defunct, inanimate, lifeless; inanimate, inert, sluggish, spiritless, torpid.
exasperate *vb* affront, anger, chafe, enrage, incense, irritate, nettle, offend, provoke, vex; aggravate, exacerbate, inflame, rouse.
exasperation *n* annoyance, exacerbation, irritation, pro- vocation; anger, fury, ire, passion, rage, wrath; aggravation, heightening, increase, worsening.
excavate *vb* burrow, cut, delve, dig, hollow, hollow out, scoop, trench.
exceed *vb* cap, overstep, surpass, transcend; excel, outdo, outstrip, outvie, pass.
excel *vb* beat, eclipse, outdo, outrival, outstrip, outvie, surpass; cap, exceed, transcend.
excellence *n* distinction, eminence, pre-eminence, superiority, transcendence; fineness, fitness, goodness, perfection, purity, quality, superiority; advantage; goodness, probity, uprightness, virtue, worth.
excellent *adj* admirable, choice, crack, eminent, first-rate, prime, sterling, superior, tiptop, transcendent; deserving, estimable, praiseworthy, virtuous, worthy.
except *vb* exclude, leave out, omit, reject. * *conj* unless. * *prep* bar, but, excepting, excluding, save.

exceptional *adj* aberrant, abnormal, anomalous, exceptive, irregular, peculiar, rare, special, strange, superior, uncommon, unnatural, unusual.

excerpt *vb* cite, cull, extract, quote, select, take. * *n* citation, extract, quotation, selection.

excess *adj* excessive, unnecessary, redundant, spare, superfluous, surplus. * *n* disproportion, fulsomeness, glut, oversupply, plethora, redundance, redundancy, surfeit, superabundance, superfluity; overplus, remainder, surplus; debauchery, dissipation, dissoluteness, intemperance, immoderation, overindulgence, unrestraint; extravagance, immoderation, overdoing.

excessive *adj* disproportionate, exuberant, superabundant, superfluous, undue; extravagant, enormous, inordinate, outrageous, unreasonable; extreme, immoderate, intemperate; vehement, violent.

exchange *vb* barter, change, commute, shuffle, substitute, swap, trade, truck; bandy, interchange. * *n* barter, change, commutation, dealing, shuffle, substitution, trade, traffic; interchange, reciprocity; bazaar, bourse, fair, market.

excise[1] *n* capitation, customs, dues, duty, tariff, tax, taxes, toll.

excise[2] *vb* cancel, cut, delete, edit, efface, eradicate, erase, expunge, extirpate, remove, strike out.

excision *n* destruction, eradication, extermination, extirpation.

excitable *adj* impressible, nervous, sensitive, susceptible; choleric, hasty, hot-headed, hot-tempered, irascible, irritable, passionate, quick-tempered.

excite *vb* animate, arouse, awaken, brew, evoke, impel, incite, inflame, instigate, kindle, move, prompt, provoke, rouse, spur, stimulate; create, elicit, evoke, raise; agitate, discompose, disturb, irritate.

excitement *n* excitation, exciting; incitement, motive, stimulus; activity, agitation, bustle, commotion, disturbance, ferment, flutter, perturbation, sensation, stir, tension; choler, heat, irritation, passion, violence, warmth.

exclaim *vb* call, cry, declare, ejaculate, shout, utter, vociferate.

exclude *vb* ban, bar, blackball, debar, ostracize, preclude, reject; hinder, prevent, prohibit, restrain, withhold; except, omit; eject, eliminate, expel, extrude.

exclusive *adj* debarring, excluding; illiberal, narrow, narrow-minded, selfish, uncharitable; aristocratic, choice, clannish, cliquish, fastidious, fashionable, select, snobbish; only, sole, special.

excommunicate *vb* anathematize, ban, curse, denounce, dismiss, eject, exclude, expel, exscind, proscribe, unchurch.

excoriate *vb* abrade, flay, gall, scar, scarify, score, skin, strip.

excrement *n* dejections, dung, faeces, excreta, excretion, ordure, stool.

excrescence *n* fungus, growth, knob, lump, outgrowth, protuberance, tumour, wart.

excrete *vb* discharge, eject, eliminate, separate.

excruciate *vb* agonize, rack, torment, torture.

exculpate *vb* absolve, acquit, clear, discharge, exonerate, free, justify, release, set right, vindicate.

excursion *n* drive, expedition, jaunt, journey, ramble, ride, sally, tour, trip, voyage, walk; digression, episode.

excursive *adj* devious, diffuse, digressive, discursive, erratic, rambling, roaming, roving, wandering.

excusable *adj* allowable, defensible, forgivable, justifiable, pardonable, venial, warrantable.

excursus *n* discussion, disquisition, dissertation.

excuse *vb* absolve, acquit, exculpate, exonerate, forgive, pardon, remit; extenuate, justify; exempt, free, release; overlook. * *n* absolution, apology, defence, extenuation, justification, plea; colour, disguise, evasion, guise, pretence, pretext, makeshift, semblance, subterfuge.

execrable *adj* abhorrent, abominable, accursed, cursed, damnable, detestable, hateful, odious; disgusting, loathsome, nauseating, nauseous, obnoxious, offensive, repulsive, revolting, sickening, vile.

execrate *vb* curse, damn, imprecate; abhor, abominate, detest, hate, loathe.

execute *vb* accomplish, achieve, carry out, complete. consummate, do, effect, effectuate, finish, perform, perpetrate; administer, enforce, seal, sign; behead, electrocute, guillotine, hang.

execution *n* accomplishment, achievement, completion, consummation, operation, performance; warrant, writ; beheading, electrocution, hanging.

executive *adj* administrative, commanding, controlling, directing, managing, ministerial, officiating, presiding, ruling. * *n* administrator, director, manager.

exegetic, exegetical *adj* explanatory, explicative, explicatory, expository, hermeneutic, interpretative.

exemplary *adj* assiduous, close, exact, faithful, punctual, punctilious, rigid, rigorous, scrupulous; commendable, correct, good, estimable, excellent, praiseworthy, virtuous; admonitory, condign, monitory, warning.

exemplify *vb* evidence, exhibit, illustrate, manifest, show.

exempt *vb* absolve, except, excuse, exonerate, free, release, relieve. * *adj* absolved, excepted, excused, exempted, free, immune, liberated, privileged, released.

exemption *n* absolution, dispensation, exception, immunity, privilege, release.

exercise *vb* apply, busy, employ, exert, praxis, use; effect, exert, produce, wield; break in, discipline, drill, habituate, school, train; practise, prosecute, pursue; task, test, try; afflict, agitate, annoy, burden, pain, trouble. * *n* appliance, application, custom, employment, operation, performance, play, plying, practice, usage, use, working; action, activity, effort, exertion, labour, toil, work; discipline, drill, drilling, schooling, training; lesson, praxis, study, task, test, theme.

exert *vb* employ, endeavour, exercise, labour, strain, strive, struggle, toil, use, work.

exertion *n* action, exercise, exerting, use; attempt, effort, endeavour, labour, strain, stretch, struggle, toil, trial.

exhalation *n* emission, evaporation; damp, effluvium, fog, fume, mist, reek, smoke, steam, vapour.

exhale *vb* breathe, discharge, elect, emanate, emit, evaporate, reek; blow, expire, puff.

exhaust *vb* drain, draw, empty; consume, destroy, dissipate, expend, impoverish, lavish, spend, squander, waste; cripple, debilitate, deplete, disable, enfeeble, enervate, overtire, prostrate, weaken.

exhaustion *n* debilitation, enervation, fatigue, lassitude, weariness.

exhibit *vb* demonstrate, disclose, display, evince, expose, express, indicate, manifest, offer, present, reveal, show; offer, present, propose.

exhibition *n* demonstration, display, exposition, manifestation, representation, spectacle, show; allowance, benefaction, grant, pension, scholarship.

exhilarate *vb* animate, cheer, elate, enliven, gladden, inspire, inspirit, rejoice, stimulate.

exhilaration *n* animating, cheering, elating, enlivening, gladdening, rejoicing, stimulating; animation, cheer, cheerfulness, gaiety, gladness, glee, good spirits, hilarity, joyousness.

exhort *vb* advise, caution, encourage, incite, persuade, stimulate, urge, warm; preach.

exhume *vb* disentomb, disinhume, disinter, unbury, unearth.

exigency, exigence *n* demand, necessity, need, requirement, urgency, want; conjuncture, crisis, difficulty, distress, emergency, extremity, juncture, nonplus, quandary, pass, pinch, pressure, strait.

exiguous *adj* attenuated, diminutive, fine, small, scanty, slender, tiny.

exile *vb* banish, expatriate, expel, ostracize, proscribe. * *n* banishment, expatriation, expulsion, ostracism, proscription, separation; outcast, refugee.

exist *vb* be, breathe, live; abide, continue, endure, last, remain.

existence *n* being, subsisting, subsistence; being, creature, entity, essence, thing; animation, continuation, life, living, vitality, vivacity.

exit *vb* depart, egress, go, leave. * *n* departure, withdrawal; death, decrease, demise, end; egress, outlet.

exonerate *vb* absolve, acquit, clear, exculpate, justify, vindicate; absolve, discharge, except, exempt, free, release.

exorbitant *adj* enormous, excessive, extravagant, inordinate, unreasonable.

exorcise *vb* cast out, drive away, expel; deliver, purify; address, conjure.

exordium *n* introduction, opening, preamble, preface, prelude, proem, prologue.

exotic *adj* extraneous, foreign; extravagant.

expand *vb* develop, open, spread, unfold, unfurl; diffuse, enlarge, extend, increase, stretch; dilate, distend, enlarge.

expanse *n* area, expansion, extent, field, stretch.

expansion *n* expansion, opening, spreading; diastole, dilation, distension, swelling; development, diffusion, enlargement, increase; expanse, extent, stretch.

ex parte *adj* biased, one-sided, partisan.

expatiate *vb* amplify, decant, dilate, enlarge, range, rove.

expatriate *vb* banish, exile, expel, ostracize, proscribe. * *adj* banished, exiled, refugee. * *n* displaced person, emigrant, exile.

expect *vb* anticipate, await, calculate, contemplate, forecast, foresee, hope, reckon, rely.

expectancy *n* expectance, expectation; abeyance, prospect.

expectation *n* anticipation, expectance, expectancy, hope, prospect; assurance, confidence, presumption, reliance, trust.

expedient *adj* advisable, appropriate, convenient, desirable, fit, proper, politic, suitable; advantageous, profitable, useful. * *n* contrivance, device, means, method, resort, resource, scheme, shift, stopgap, substitute.

expedite *vb* accelerate, advance, dispatch, facilitate, forward, hasten, hurry, precipitate, press, quicken, urge.

expedition *n* alacrity, alertness, celerity, dispatch, haste, promptness, quickness, speed; enterprise, undertaking; campaign, excursion, journey, march, quest, voyage.

expeditious *adj* quick, speedy, swift, rapid; active, alert, diligent, nimble, prompt, punctual, swift.

expel *vb* dislodge, egest, eject, eliminate, excrete; discharge, eject, evacuate, void; bounce, discharge, exclude, exscind, fire, oust, relegate, remove; banish, disown, excommunicate, exile, expatriate, ostracize, proscribe, unchurch.

expend *vb* disburse, spend; consume, employ, exert, use; dissipate, exhaust, scatter, waste.

expenditure *n* disbursement, outlay, outlaying, spending; charge, cost, expenditure, outlay.

expensive *adj* costly, dear, high-priced; extravagant, lavish, wasteful.

experience *vb* endure, suffer; feel, know; encounter, suffer, undergo. * *n* endurance, practice, trial; evidence, knowledge, proof, test, testimony.

experienced *adj* able, accomplished, expert, instructed, knowing, old, practised, qualified, skilful, trained, thoroughbred, versed, veteran, wise.

experiment *vb* examine, investigate, test, try. * *n* assay, examination, investigation, ordeal, practice, proof, test, testimony, touchstone, trial.
expert *adj* able, adroit, apt, clever, dextrous, proficient, prompt, quick, ready, skilful. * *n* adept, authority, connoisseur, crack, master, specialist.
expertise *n* adroitness, aptness, dexterity, facility, promptness, skilfulness, skill.
expiate *vb* atone, redeem, satisfy.
expiration n death, decease, demise, departure, exit; cessation, close, conclusion, end, termination.
expire *vb* cease, close, conclude, end, stop, terminate; emit, exhale; decease, depart, die, perish.
explain *vb* demonstrate, elucidate, expound, illustrate, interpret, resolve, solve, unfold, unravel; account for, justify, warrant.
explanation *n* clarification, description, elucidation, exegesis, explication, exposition, illustration, interpretation; account, answer, deduction, justification, key, meaning, secret, solution, warrant.
explicit *adj* absolute, categorical, clear, definite, determinate, exact, express, plain, positive, precise, unambiguous, unequivocal, unreserved.
explode *vb* burst, detonate, discharge, displode, shatter, shiver; contemn, discard, repudiate, scorn, scout.
exploit *vb* befool, milk, use, utilize. * *n* achievement, act, deed, feat.
explore *vb* examine, fathom, inquire, inspect, investigate, prospect, scrutinize, seek.
explosion *n* blast, burst, bursting, clap, crack, detonation, discharge, displosion, fulmination, pop.
exponent *n* example, illustration, index, indication, specimen, symbol, type; commentator, demonstrator, elucidator, expounder, illustrator, interpreter.
expose *vb* bare, display, uncover; descry, detect, disclose, unearth; denounce, mask; subject; endanger, jeopardize, risk, venture.
exposé *n* exhibit, exposition, manifesto; denouncement, divulgement, exposure, revelation.
exposition *n* disclosure, interpretation; commentary, critique, elucidation, exegesis, explanation, explication, interpretation; display, show.
expound *vb* develop, present, rehearse, reproduce, unfold; clear, elucidate, explain, interpret.
express *vb* air, assert, asseverate, declare, emit, enunciate, manifest, utter, vent, signify, speak, state, voice; betoken, denote, equal, exhibit, indicate, intimate, present, represent, show, symbolize. * *adj* categorical, clear, definite, determinate, explicit, outspoken, plain, positive, unambiguous; accurate, close, exact, faithful, precise, true; particular, special; fast, nonstop, quick, rapid, speedy, swift. * *n* dispatch, message.
expression *n* assertion, asseveration, communication, declaration, emission, statement, utterance, voicing; language, locution, phrase, remark, saying, term, word; air, aspect, look, mien.
expressive *adj* indicative, meaningful, significant; demonstrative, eloquent, emphatic, energetic, forcible, lively, strong, vivid; appropriate, sympathetic, well-modulated.
expulsion *n* discharge, eviction, expelling, ousting; elimination, evacuation, excretion; ejection, excision, excommunication, extrusion, ostracism, separation.
expunge *vb* annihilate, annul, cancel, delete, destroy, efface, erase, obliterate, wipe out.
expurgate *vb* clean, cleanse, purge, purify; bowdlerize, emasculate.
exquisite *adj* accurate, delicate, discriminating, exact, fastidious, nice, refined; choice, elect, excellent, precious, rare, valuable; complete, consummate, matchless, perfect; acute, keen, intense, poignant. * *n* beau, coxcomb, dandy, fop, popinjay.
extant *adj* existent, existing, present, surviving, undestroyed, visible.
extempore *adj* extemporaneous, extemporary, impromptu, improvised. * *adv* offhand, suddenly, unpremeditatedly, unpreparedly.
extend *vb* reach, stretch; continue, elongate, lengthen, prolong, protract, widen; augment, broaden, dilate, distend, enlarge, expand, increase; diffuse, spread; give, impart, offer, yield; lie, range.
extensible *adj* ductile, elastic, extendible, extensile, protractible, protractile.
extension *n* augmentation, continuation, delay, dilatation, dilation, distension, enlargement, expansion, increase, prolongation, protraction.
extensive *adj* broad, capacious, comprehensive, expanded, extended, far-reaching, large, wide, widespread.
extent *n* amplitude, expanse, expansion; amount, bulk, content, degree, magnitude, size, volume; compass, measure, length, proportions, reach, stretch; area, field, latitude, range, scope; breadth, depth, height, width.
extenuate *vb* diminish, lessen, reduce, soften, weaken; excuse, mitigate, palliate, qualify.
exterior *adj* external, outer, outlying, outside, outward, superficial, surface; extrinsic, foreign. * *n* outside, surface; appearance.
exterminate *vb* abolish, annihilate, destroy, eliminate, eradicate, extirpate, uproot.
external *adj* exterior, outer, outside, outward, superficial; extrinsic, foreign; apparent, visible.
extinct *adj* extinguished, quenched; closed, dead, ended, lapsed, terminated, vanished.
extinction *n* death, extinguishment; abolishment, abolition, annihilation, destruction, excision, extermination, extirpation.
extinguish *vb* choke, douse, put out, quell, smother, stifle, suffocate, suppress; destroy, nullify, subdue; eclipse, obscure.
extirpate *vb* abolish, annihilate, deracinate, destroy, eradicate, exterminate, uproot, weed.
extol *vb* celebrate, exalt, glorify, laud, magnify,

praise; applaud, commend, eulogize, panegyrize.

extort *vb* elicit, exact, extract, force, squeeze, wrench, wrest, wring.

extortion *n* blackmail, compulsion, demand, exaction, oppression, overcharge, rapacity, tribute; exorbitance.

extortionate *adj* bloodsucking, exacting, hard, harsh, oppressive, rapacious, rigorous, severe; exorbitant, unreasonable.

extra *adj* accessory, additional, auxiliary, collateral; another, farther, fresh, further, more, new, other, plus, ulterior; side, spare, supernumerary, supplemental, supplementary, surplus; extraordinary, extreme, unusual. * *adv* additionally, also, beyond, farthermore, furthermore, more, moreover, plus. * *n* accessory, appendage, collateral, nonessential, special, supernumerary, supplement; bonus, premium; balance, leftover, remainder, spare, surplus.

extract *vb* extort, pull out, remove, withdraw; derive, distil, draw, express, squeeze; cite, determine, derive, quote, select. * *n* citation, excerpt, passage, quotation, selection; decoction, distillation, essence, infusion, juice.

extraction *n* drawing out, derivation, distillation, elicitation, essence, pulling out; birth, descent, genealogy, lineage, origin, parentage.

extraneous *adj* external, extrinsic, foreign; additional, adventitious, external, superfluous, supplementary, unessential.

extraordinary *adj* abnormal, amazing, distinguished, egregious, exceptional, marvellous, monstrous, particular, peculiar, phenomenal, prodigious, rare, remarkable, signal, singular, special, strange, uncommon, unprecedented, unusual, unwonted, wonderful.

extravagance *n* excess, enormity, exorbitance, preposterousness, unreasonableness; absurdity, excess, folly, irregularity, wildness; lavishness, prodigality, profuseness, profusion, superabundance; waste.

extravagant *adj* excessive, exorbitant, inordinate, preposterous, unreasonable; absurd, foolish, irregular, wild; lavish, prodigal, profuse, spendthrift.

extreme *adj* farthest, outermost, remotest, utmost, uttermost; greatest, highest; final, last, ultimate; drastic, egregious, excessive, extravagant, immoderate, intense, outrageous, radical, unreasonable. * *n* end, extremity, limit; acme, climax, degree, height, pink; danger, distress.

extremity *n* border, edge, end, extreme, limb, termination, verge.

extricate *vb* clear, deliver, disembarrass, disengage, disentangle, liberate, release, relieve.

extrinsic *adj* external, extraneous, foreign, outside, outward, superabundance, superfluity.

exuberance *n* abundance, copiousness, flood, luxuriance, plenitude; excess, lavishness, overabundance, overflow, overgrowth, over-luxuriance, profusion, rankness, redundancy, superabundance, superfluity.

exuberant *adj* abounding, abundant, copious, fertile, flowing, luxuriant, prolific, rich; excessive, lavish, overabundant, overflowing, over-luxuriant, profuse, rank, redundant, superabounding, superabundant, wanton.

exude *vb* discharge, excrete, secrete, sweat; infiltrate, ooze, percolate.

exult *vb* gloat, glory, jubilate, rejoice, transport, triumph, taunt, vault.

exultation *n* delight, elation, joy, jubilation, transport, triumph.

eye *vb* contemplate, inspect, ogle, scrutinize, survey, view, watch. * *n* estimate, judgement, look, sight, vision, view; inspection, notice, observation, scrutiny, sight, vigilance, watch; aperture, eyelet, peephole, perforation; bud, sho0t.

F

fable *n* allegory, legend, myth, parable, story, tale; fabrication, falsehood, fiction, figment, forgery, untruth.

fabric *n* building, edifice, pile, structure; conformation, make, texture, workmanship; cloth, material, stuff, textile, tissue, web.

fabricate *vb* build, construct, erect, frame; compose, devise, fashion, make, manufacture; coin, fake, feign, forge, invent.

fabrication *n* building, construction, erection; manufacture; fable, fake, falsehood, fiction, figment, forgery, invention, lie.

fabulous *adj* amazing, apocryphal, coined, fabricated, feigned, fictitious, forged, imaginary, invented, legendary, marvellous, mythical, romancing, unbelievable, unreal.

façade *n* elevation, face, front.

face *vb* confront; beard, buck, brave, dare, defy, front, oppose; dress, level, polish, smooth; cover, incrust, veneer. * *n* cover, facet, surface; breast, escarpment, front; countenance, features, grimace, physiognomy, visage; appearance, expression, look, semblance; assurance, audacity, boldness, brass, confidence, effrontery, impudence.

facet *n* cut, face, lozenge, surface.

facetious *adj* amusing, comical, droll, funny, humorous, jocose, jocular, pleasant, waggish, witty; entertaining, gay, lively, merry, sportive, sprightly.

facile *adj* easy; affable, approachable, complaisant, conversable, courteous, mild; compliant, ductile, flexible, fluent, manageable, pliable, pliant, tractable, yielding; dextrous, ready, skilful.

facilitate *vb* expedite, help.

facility *n* ease, easiness; ability, dexterity, expertness, knack, quickness, readiness; ductility, flexibility, pliancy; advantage, appliance, convenience, means, resource; affability, civility, complaisance, politeness.

facsimile *n* copy, duplicate, fax, reproduction.

fact *n* act, circumstance, deed, event, incident, occurrence, performance; actuality, certainty, existence, reality, truth.

faction *n* cabal, clique, combination, division, junta, party, side; disagreement, discord, disorder, dissension, recalcitrance, recalcitrancy, refractoriness, sedition, seditiousness, tumult, turbulence, turbulency.

factious *adj* litigious, malcontent, rebellious, recalcitrant, refractory, seditious. turbulent.

factitious *adj* artful, artificial, conventional, false, unnatural, unreal.

factor *n* agent, bailiff, broker, consignee, go-between, steward, component, element, ingredient; influence, reason.

factory *n* manufactory, mill, work, workshop.

faculty *n* ability, capability, capacity, endowment, power, property, quality; ableness, address, adroitness, aptitude, aptness, clearness, competency, dexterity, efficiency, expertness, facility, forte, ingenuity, knack, qualification, quickness, readiness, skill, skilfulness, talent, turn; body, department, profession; authority, prerogative, license, privilege, right.

fade *vb* disappear, die, evanesce, fall, faint, perish, vanish; decay, decline, droop, fall, languish, wither; bleach, blanch, pale; disperse, dissolve.

faeces *npl* dregs, lees, sediment, settlings; dung, excrement, ordure, settlings.

fag *vb* droop, flag, sink; drudge, toil; fatigue, jade, tire, weary. * *n* drudgery, fatigue, work; drudge, grub, hack; cigarette, smoke.

fail *vb* break, collapse, decay, decline, fade, sicken, sink, wane; cease, disappear; fall, miscarry, miss; neglect, omit; bankrupt, break.

failing *adj* deficient, lacking, needing, wanting; declining, deteriorating, fading, flagging, languishing, sinking, waning, wilting; unsuccessful. * *prep* lacking, needing, wanting. * *n* decay, decline; failure, miscarriage; defect, deficiency, fault, foible, frailty, imperfection, infirmity, shortcoming, vice, weakness; error, lapse, slip; bankruptcy, insolvency.

failure *n* defectiveness, deficiency, delinquency, shortcoming; fail, miscarriage, negligence, neglect, nonobservance, nonperformance, omission, slip; abortion, botch, breakdown, collapse, fiasco, fizzle; bankruptcy, crash, downfall, insolvency, ruin; decay, declension, decline, loss.

fain *adj* anxious, glad, inclined, pleased, rejoiced, well-pleased. * *adv* cheerfully, eagerly, gladly, joyfully, willingly.

faint *vb* swoon; decline, fade, fail, languish, weaken. * *adj* swooning; drooping, exhausted, feeble, languid, listless, sickly, weak; gentle, inconsiderable, little, slight, small, soft, thin; dim, dull, indistinct, perceptible, scarce, slight; cowardly, dastardly, faint-hearted, fearful, timid, timorous; dejected, depressed, discouraged, disheartened, dispirited. * *n* blackout, swoon.

faint-hearted *adj* cowardly, dastardly, faint, fearful, timid, timorous.
fair[1] *adj* spotless, unblemished, unspotted, unstained, untarnished; blond, light, white; beautiful, comely, handsome, shapely; clear, cloudless, pleasant, unclouded; favourable, prosperous; hopeful, promising, propitious; clear, distinct, open, plain, unencumbered, unobstructed; candid, frank, honest, honourable, impartial, ingenuous, just, unbiased, upright; equitable, proper; average, decent, indifferent, mediocre, moderate, ordinary, passable, reasonable, respectful, tolerable.
fair[2] *n* bazaar, carnival, exposition, festival, fete, funfair, gala, kermess.
fairy *n* brownie, elf, demon, fay, sprite.
faith *n* assurance, belief, confidence, credence, credit, dependence, reliance, trust; creed, doctrine, dogma, persuasion, religion, tenet; constancy, faithfulness, fidelity, loyalty, truth, truthfulness.
faithful *adj* constant, devoted, loyal, staunch, steadfast, true; honest, upright, reliable, trustworthy, trusty; reliable, truthful; accurate, close, conscientiousness, exact, nice, strict.
faithless *adj* unbelieving; dishonest, disloyal, false, fickle, fluctuating, inconstant, mercurial, mutable, perfidious, shifting, treacherous, truthless, unsteady, untruthful, vacillating, variable, wavering.
fall *vb* collapse, depend, descend, drop, sink, topple, tumble; abate, decline, decrease, depreciate, ebb, subside; err, lapse, sin, stumble, transgress, trespass, trip; die, perish; befall, chance, come, happen, occur, pass; become, get; come, pass. * *n* collapse, comedown, descent, downcome, dropping, falling, flop, plop, tumble; cascade, cataract, waterfall; death, destruction, downfall, overthrow, ruin, surrender; comeuppance, degradation; apostasy, declension, failure, lapse, slip; decline, decrease, depreciation, diminution, ebb, sinking, subsidence; cadence, close; declivity, inclination, slope.
fallacious *adj* absurd, deceptive, deceiving, delusive, disappointing, erroneous, false, illusive, illusory, misleading; paralogistic, sophistical, worthless.
fallacy *n* aberration, deceit, deception, delusion, error, falsehood, illusion, misapprehension, misconception, mistake, untruth; non sequitur, paralogism, sophism, sophistry.
fallibility *n* frailty, imperfection, uncertainty.
fallible *adj* erring, frail, ignorant, imperfect, uncertain, weak.
fallow *adj* left, neglected, uncultivated, unsowed, untilled; dormant, inactive, inert.
false *adj* lying, mendacious, truthless, untrue, unveracious; dishonest, dishonourable, disingenuous, disloyal, double-faced, double-tongued, faithless, false-hearted, perfidious, treacherous, unfaithful; fictitious, forged, made-up, unreliable, untrustworthy; artificial, bastard, bogus, counterfeit, factitious, feigned, forged, hollow, hypocritical, make-believe, pretended, pseudo, sham, spurious, suppositious; erroneous, improper, incorrect, unfounded, wrong; deceitful, deceiving, deceptive, disappointing, fallacious, misleading.
false-hearted *adj* dishonourable, disloyal, double, double-tongued, faithless, false, perfidious, treacherous.
falsehood *n* falsity; fabrication, fib, fiction, lie, untruth; cheat, counterfeit, imposture, mendacity, treachery.
falsify *vb* alter, adulterate, belie, cook, counterfeit, doctor, fake, falsely, garble, misrepresent, misstate, represent; disprove; violate.
falsity *n* falsehood, untruth, untruthfulness.
falter *vb* halt, hesitate, lisp, quaver, stammer, stutter; fail, stagger, stumble, totter, tremble, waver; dodder.
fame *n* bruit, hearsay, report, rumour; celebrity, credit, eminence, glory, greatness, honour, illustriousness, kudos, lustre, notoriety, renown, reputation, repute.
familiar *adj* acquainted, aware, conversant, well-versed; amicable, close, cordial, domestic, fraternal, friendly, homely, intimate, near; affable, accessible, companionable, conversable, courteous, civil, friendly, kindly, sociable, social; easy, free and easy, unceremonious, unconstrained; common, frequent, well-known. * *n* acquaintance, associate, companion, friend, intimate.
familiarity *n* acquaintance, knowledge, understanding; fellowship, friendship, intimacy; closeness, friendliness, sociability; freedom, informality, liberty; disrespect, overfreedom, presumption; intercourse.
familiarize *vb* accustom, habituate, inure, train, use.
family *n* brood, household, people; ancestors, blood, breed, clan, dynasty, kindred, house, lineage, race, stock, strain, tribe; class, genus, group, kind, subdivision.
famine *n* dearth, destitution, hunger, scarcity, starvation.
famish *vb* distress, exhaust, pinch, starve.
famous *adj* celebrated, conspicuous, distinguished, eminent, excellent, fabled, famed, far-famed, great, glorious, heroic, honoured, illustrious, immortal, notable, noted, notorious, remarkable, renowned, signal.
fan[1] *vb* agitate, beat, move, winnow; blow, cool, refresh, ventilate; excite, fire, increase, rouse, stimulate. * *n* blower, cooler, punkah, ventilator.
fan[2] *n* admirer, buff, devotee, enthusiast, fancier, follower, pursuer, supporter.
fanatic *n* bigot, devotee, enthusiast, visionary, zealot.
fanatical *adj* bigoted, enthusiastic, frenzied, mad, rabid, visionary, wild, zealous.
fanciful *adj* capricious, crotchety, imaginary,

visionary, whimsical; chimerical, fantastical, ideal, imaginary, wild.
fancy *vb* apprehend, believe, conjecture, imagine, suppose, think; conceive, imagine. * *adj* elegant, fine, nice, ornamented; extravagant, fanciful, whimsical. * *n* imagination; apprehension, conceit, conception, impression, idea, image, notion, thought; approval, fondness, inclination, judgement, liking, penchant, taste; caprice, crotchet, fantasy, freak, humour, maggot, quirk, vagary, whim, whimsy; apparition, chimera, daydream, delusion, hallucination, megrim, phantasm, reverie, vision.
fanfaron *n* blatherskite, blusterer, braggadocio, bully, hector, swaggerer, vapourer.
fang *n* claw, nail, talon, tooth; tusk.
fantastic *adj* chimerical, fanciful, imaginary, romantic, unreal, visionary; bizarre, capricious, grotesque, odd, quaint, queer, strange, whimsical, wild.
far *adj* distant, long, protracted, remote; farther, remoter; alienated, estranged, hostile. * *adv* considerably, extremely, greatly, very much; afar, distantly, far away, remotely.
farce *n* burlesque, caricature, parody, travesty; forcemeat, stuffing.
farcical *adj* absurd, comic, droll, funny, laughable, ludicrous, ridiculous.
fardel *n* bundle, burden, load, pack; annoyance, burden, ill, trouble.
fare *vb* go, journey, pass, travel; happen, prosper, prove; feed, live, manage, subsist. * *n* charge, price, ticket money; passenger, traveller; board, commons, food, table, victuals, provisions; condition, experience, fortune, luck, outcome.
farewell *n* adieu, leave-taking, valediction; departure, leave, parting, valedictory.
far-fetched *adj* abstruse, catachrestic, forced, recondite, strained.
farrago *n* gallimaufry, hodgepodge, hotchpotch, jumble, medley, miscellany, mixture, potpourri, salmagundi.
farther *adj* additional; further, remoter, ulterior. * *adv* beyond, further; besides, furthermore, moreover.
farthingale *n* crinoline, hoop, hoop skirt.
fascinate *vb* affect, bewitch, overpower, spellbind, stupefy, transfix; absorb, captivate, catch, charm, delight, enamour, enchant, enrapture, entrance.
fascination *n* absorption, charm, enchantment, magic, sorcery, spell, witchcraft, witchery.
fash *vb* harass, perplex, plague, torment, trouble, vex, worry. * *n* anxiety, care, trouble, vexation.
fashion *vb* contrive, create, design, forge, form, make, mould, pattern, shape; accommodate, adapt, adjust, fit, suit. * *n* appearance, cast, configuration, conformation, cut, figure, form, make, model, mould, pattern, shape, stamp; manner, method, sort, wake; conventionalism, conventionality, custom, fad, mode, style, usage, vogue; breeding, gentility; quality.
fashionable *adj* modish, stylish; current, modern, prevailing, up-to-date; customary, usual; genteel, well-bred.
fast[1] *adj* close, fastened, firm, fixed, immovable, tenacious, tight; constant, faithful, permanent, resolute, staunch, steadfast, unswerving, unwavering; fortified, impregnable, strong; deep, profound, sound; fleet, quick, rapid, swift; dissipated, dissolute, extravagant, giddy, reckless, thoughtless, thriftless, wild. * *adv* firmly, immovably, tightly; quickly, rapidly, swiftly; extravagantly, prodigally, reckless, wildly.
fast[2] *vb* abstain, go hungry, starve. * *n* abstention, abstinence, diet, fasting, starvation.
fasten *vb* attach, bind, bolt, catch, chain, cleat, fix, gird, lace, lock, pin, secure, strap, tether, tie; belay, bend; connect, hold, join, unite.
fastidious *adj* critical, dainty, delicate, difficult, exquisite, finical, hypercritical, meticulous, overdelicate, overnice, particular, precise, precious, punctilious, queasy, squeamish.
fat *adj* adipose, fatty, greasy, oily, oleaginous, unctuous; corpulent, fleshy, gross, obese, paunchy, portly, plump, pudgy, pursy; coarse, dull, heavy, sluggish, stupid; lucrative, profitable, rich; fertile, fruitful, productive, rich. * *n* adipose tissue, ester, grease, oil; best part, cream, flower; corpulence, fatness, fleshiness, obesity, plumpness, stoutness.
fatal *adj* deadly, lethal, mortal; baleful, baneful, calamitous, catastrophic, destructive, mischievous, pernicious, ruinous; destined, doomed, foreordained, inevitable, predestined.
fatality *n* destiny, fate; mortality; calamity, disaster.
fate *n* destination, destiny, fate; cup, die, doom, experience, lot, fortune, portion, weird; death, destruction, ruin.
fated *adj* appointed, destined, doomed, foredoomed, predetermined, predestinated, predestined, preordained.
fatherly *adj* benign, kind, paternal, protecting, tender.
fathom *vb* comprehend, divine, penetrate, reach, understand; estimate, gauge, measure, plumb, probe, sound.
fathomless *adj* abysmal, bottomless, deep, immeasurable, profound; impenetrable, incomprehensible, obscure.
fatigue *vb* exhaust, fag, jade, tire, weaken, weary. * *n* exhaustion, lassitude, tiredness, weariness; hardship, labour, toil.
fatuity *n* foolishness, idiocy, imbecility, stupidity; absurdity, folly, inanity, infatuation, madness.
fatuous *adj* dense, drivelling, dull, foolish, idiotic, stupid, witless; infatuated, mad, senseless, silly, weak.
fault *n* blemish, defect, flaw, foible, frailty, imperfection, infirmity, negligence, obliquity, offence, shortcoming, spot, weakness; delinquency, error, indiscretion, lapse, misdeed, misdemeanour,

offence, peccadillo, slip, transgression, trespass, vice, wrong; blame, culpability.

faultless *adj* blameless, guiltless, immaculate, innocent, sinless, spotless, stainless; accurate, correct, perfect, unblemished.

faulty *adj* bad, defective, imperfect, incorrect; blameable, blameworthy, censurable, culpable, reprehensible.

faux pas *n* blunder, indiscretion, mistake.

favour *vb* befriend, countenance, encourage, patronize; approve; ease, facilitate; aid, assist, help, oblige, support; extenuate, humour, indulge, palliate, spare. * *n* approval, benignity, countenance, esteem, friendless, goodwill, grace, kindness; benefaction, benefit, boon, dispensation, kindness; championship, patronage, popularity, support; gift, present, token; badge, decoration, knot, rosette; leave, pardon, permission; advantage, cover, indulgence, protection; bias, partiality, prejudice.

favourable *adj* auspicious, friendly, kind, propitious, well-disposed, willing; conductive, contributing, propitious; adapted, advantage, beneficial, benign, convenient, fair, fit, good, helpful, suitable.

favourite *adj* beloved, darling, dear; choice, fancied, esteemed, pet, preferred.

fawn *vb* bootlick, bow, creep, cringe, crouch, dangle, kneel, stoop, toady, truckle.

fealty *n* allegiance, homage, loyalty, obeisance, submission; devotion, faithfulness, fidelity, honour, loyalty.

fear *vb* apprehend, dread; revere, reverence, venerate. * *n* affright, alarm, apprehension, consternation, dismay, dread, fright, horror, panic, phobia, scare, terror; disquietude, flutter, perturbation, palpitation, quaking, quivering, trembling, tremor, trepidation; anxiety, apprehension, concern, misdoubt, misgiving, qualm, solicitude; awe, dread, reverence, veneration.

fearful *adj* afraid, apprehensive, haunted; chicken-hearted, chicken-livered, cowardly, faint-hearted, lily-livered, nervous, pusillanimous, timid, timorous; dire, direful, dreadful, frightful, ghastly, horrible, shocking, terrible.

fearless *adj* bold, brave, courageous, daring, dauntless, doughty, gallant, heroic, intrepid, unterrified, valiant, valorous.

feasible *adj* achievable, attainable, possible, practicable, suitable.

feast *vb* delight, gladden, gratify, rejoice. * *n* banquet, carousal, entertainment, regale, repast, revels, symposium, treat; celebration, festival, fete, holiday; delight, enjoyment, pleasure.

feat *n* accomplishment, achievement, act, deed, exploit, performance, stunt, trick.

feather *n* plume; kind, nature, species.

featly *adv* adroitly, dextrously, nimbly, skilfully.

feature *vb* envisage, envision, picture, visualize; imagine; specialize; appear in, headline, star. * *n* appearance, aspect, component; conformation, fashion, make; characteristic, item, mark, particularity, peculiarity, property, point, trait; leader, lead item, special; favour, expression, lineament; article, film, motion picture, movie, story; highlight, high spot.

fecund *adj* fruitful, impregnated, productive, prolific, rich.

fecundity *n* fertility, fruitfulness, productiveness.

federation *n* alliance, allying, confederation, federating, federation, leaguing, union, uniting; affiliation, coalition, combination, compact, confederacy, entente, federacy, league, copartnership.

fee *vb* pay, recompense, reward. * *n* account, bill, charge, compensation, honorarium, remuneration, reward, tip; benefice, fief, feud.

feeble *adj* anaemic, debilitated, declining, drooping, enervated, exhausted, frail, infirm, languid, languishing, sickly; dim, faint, imperfect, indistinct.

feed *vb* contribute, provide, supply; cherish, eat, nourish, subsist, sustain. * *n* fodder, food, foodstuff, forage, provender.

feel *vb* apprehend, intuit, perceive, sense; examine, handle, probe, touch; enjoy, experience, suffer; prove, sound, test, try; appear, look, seem; believe, conceive, deem, fancy, infer, opine, suppose, think. * *n* atmosphere, feeling, quality; finish, surface, texture.

feeling *n* consciousness, impression, notion, perception, sensation; atmosphere, sense, sentience, touch; affecting, emotion, heartstrings, impression, passion, soul, sympathy; sensibility, sentiment, susceptibility, tenderness; attitude, impression, opinion.

feign *vb* devise, fabricate, forge, imagine, invent; affect, assume, counterfeit, imitate, pretend, sham, simulate.

feint *n* artifice, blind, expedient, make-believe, pretence, stratagem, trick.

felicitate *vb* complicate, congratulate; beatify, bless, delight.

felicitous *adj* appropriate, apt, fit, happy, ingenious, inspired, opportune, pertinent, seasonable, skilful, well-timed; auspicious, fortunate, prosperous, propitious, successful.

felicity *n* blessedness, bliss, blissfulness, gladness, happiness, joy; appropriateness, aptitude, aptness, felicitousness, fitness, grace, propriety, readiness, suitableness; fortune, luck, success.

fell[1] *vb* beat, knock down, level, prostrate; cut, demolish, hew.

fell[2] *adj* barbarous, bloodthirsty, bloody, cruel, ferocious, fierce, implacable, inhuman, malicious, malign, malignant, pitiless, relentless, ruthless, sanguinary, savage, unrelenting, vandalistic; deadly, destructive.

fellow *adj* affiliated, associated, joint, like, mutual, similar, twin. * *n* associate, companion, comrade; compeer, equal, peer; counterpart, mate, match, partner; member; boy, character, individual, man, person.

fellowship *n* brotherhood, companionship, comradeship, familiarity, intimacy; participation; partnership; communion, converse, intercourse; affability, kindliness, sociability, sociableness.
felon *n* convict, criminal, culprit, delinquent, malefactor, outlaw; inflammation, whitlow.
felonious *adj* atrocious, cruel, felon, heinous, infamous, malicious, malign, malignant, nefarious, perfidious, vicious, villainous.
female *adj* delicate, gentle, ladylike, soft; fertile, pistil-bearing, pistillate.
feminine *adj* affectionate, delicate, gentle, graceful, modest, soft, tender; female, ladylike, maidenly, womanish, womanly; effeminateness, effeminacy, softness, unmanliness, weakness, womanliness.
fen *n* bog, marsh, moor, morass, quagmire, slough, swamp.
fence *vb* defend, enclose, fortify, guard, protect, surround; circumscribe, evade, equivocate, hedge, prevaricate; guard, parry. * *n* barrier, hedge, hoarding, palings, palisade, stockade, wall; defence, protection, guard, security, shield; fencing, swordplay, swordsmanship; receiver.
fenny *adj* boggy, fennish, swampy, marshy.
feral, ferine *adj* ferocious, fierce, rapacious, ravenous, savage, untamed, wild.
ferment *vb* agitate, excite, heat; boil, brew, bubble, concoct, heat, seethe. * *n* barm, leaven, yeast; agitation, commotion, fever, glow, heat, tumult.
ferocious *adj* feral, fierce, rapacious, ravenous, savage, untamed, wild; barbarous, bloody, bloodthirsty, brutal, cruel, fell, inhuman, merciless, murderous, pitiless, remorseless, ruthless, sanguinary, truculent, vandalistic, violent.
ferocity *n* ferociousness, ferocity, fierceness, rapacity, savageness, wildness; barbarity, cruelty, inhumanity.
fertile *adj* bearing, breeding, fecund, prolific; exuberant, fruitful, luxuriant, plenteous, productive, rich, teeming; female, fruit-bearing, pistillate.
fertility *n* fertileness, fertility; abundance, exuberant, fruitfulness, luxuriance, plenteousness, productiveness, richness.
fervent *adj* burning, hot, glowing, melting, seething; animated, ardent, earnest, enthusiastic, fervid, fierce, fiery, glowing, impassioned, intense, passionate, vehement, warm, zealous.
fervour *n* heat, warmth; animation, ardour, eagerness, earnestness, excitement, fervency, intensity, vehemence, zeal.
fester *vb* corrupt, rankle, suppurate, ulcerate; putrefy, rot. * *n* abscess, canker, gathering, pustule, sore, suppination; festering, rankling.
festival *n* anniversary, carnival, feast, fete, gala, holiday, jubilee; banquet, carousal, celebration, entertainment, treat.
festive *adj* carnival, convivial, festal, festival, gay, jolly, jovial, joyful, merry, mirthful, uproarious.
festivity *n* conviviality, festival, gaiety, jollity, joviality, joyfulness, joyousness, merrymaking, mirth.
festoon *vb* adorn, decorate, embellish, garland, hoop, ornament. * *n* decoration, embellishment, garland, hoop, ornament, ornamentation.
fetch *vb* bring, elicit, get; accomplish, achieve, effect, perform; attain, reach. * *n* artifice, dodge, ruse, stratagem, trick.
fetid *adj* foul, malodorous, mephitic, noisome, offensive, rancid, rank, rank-smelling, stinking, strong-smelling.
fetish *n* charm, medicine, talisman.
fetter *vb* clog, hamper, shackle, trammel; bind, chain, confine, encumber, hamper, restrain, tie, trammel. * *n* bond, chain, clog, hamper, shackle.
feud *vb* argue, bicker, clash, contend, dispute, quarrel. * *n* affray, argument, bickering, broil, clashing, contention, contest, discord, dissension, enmity, fray, grudge, hostility, jarring, quarrel, rupture, strife, vendetta.
fever *n* agitation, excitement, ferment, fire, flush, heat, passion.
fey *adj* clairvoyant, ethereal, strange, unusual, whimsical; death-smitten, doomed.
fiasco *n* failure, fizzle.
fiat *n* command, decree, order, ordinance.
fibre *n* filament, pile, staple, strand, texture, thread; stamina, strength, toughness.
fickle *adj* capricious, changeable, faithless, fitful, inconstant, irresolute, mercurial, mutable, shifting, unsettled, unstable, unsteady, vacillating, variable, veering, violate, volatile, wavering.
fiction *n* fancy, fantasy, imagination, invention; novel, romance; fable, fabrication, falsehood, figment, forgery, invention, lie.
fictitious *adj* assumed, fabulous, fanciful, feigned, imaginary, invented, mythical, unreal; artificial, counterfeit, dummy, false, spurious, supposititious.
fiddle *vb* dawdle, fidget, interfere, tinker, trifle; cheat, swindle, tamper. * *n* fraud, swindle; fiddler, violin, violinist.
fiddle-de-dee *interj* fudge, moonshine, nonsense, stuff.
fiddle-faddle *n* frivolity, gabble, gibberish, nonsense, prate, stuff, trifling, trivia, twaddle.
fidelity *n* constancy, devotedness, devotion, dutifulness, faithfulness, fealty, loyalty, trueheartedness, truth; accuracy, closeness, exactness, faithfulness, precision.
fidget *vb* chafe, fret, hitch, twitch, worry. * *n* fidgetiness, impatience, restlessness, uneasiness.
fiduciary *adj* confident, fiducial, firm, steadfast, trustful, undoubting, unwavering; reliable, trustworthy. * *n* depositary, trustee.
field *n* clearing, glebe, meadow; expanse, extent, opportunity, range, room, scope, surface; department, domain, province, realm, region.
fiendish *adj* atrocious, cruel, demoniac, devilish, diabolical, hellish, implacable, infernal, malevolent, malicious, malign, malignant.
fierce *adj* barbarous, brutal, cruel, fell, ferocious,

furious, infuriate, ravenous, savage; fiery, impetuous, murderous, passionate, tearing, tigerish, truculent, turbulent, uncurbed, untamed, vehement, violent.

fiery *adj* fervent, fervid, flaming, heated, hot, glowing, lurid; ardent, fierce, impassioned, impetuous, inflamed, passionate, vehement.

fight *vb* battle, combat, war; contend, contest, dispute, feud, oppose, strive, struggle, wrestle; encounter, engage; handle, manage, manoeuvre. * *n* affair, affray, action, battle, brush, combat, conflict, confrontation, contest, duel, encounter, engagement, melée, quarrel, struggle, war; brawl, broil, riot, row, skirmish; fighting, pluck, pugnacity, resistance, spirit, temper.

figment *n* fable, fabrication, falsehood, fiction, invention.

figurative *adj* emblematical, representative, symbolic, representative, typical; metaphorical, tropical; florid, flowery, ornate, poetical.

figure *vb* adorn, diversify, ornament, variegate; delineate, depict, represent, signify, symbolize, typify; conceive, image, imagine, picture; calculate, cipher, compute; act, appear, perform. * *n* configuration, conformation, form, outline, shape; effigy, image, likeness, representative; design, diagram, drawing, pattern; image, metaphor, trope; emblem, symbol, type; character, digit, number, numeral.

filament *n* cirrus, fibre, fibril, gossamer, hair, strand, tendril, thread.

filch *vb* crib, nick, pilfer, purloin, rob, snitch, seal, thieve.

file[1] *vb* order, pigeonhole, record, tidy. * *n* data, dossier, folder, portfolio; column, line, list, range, rank, row, series, tier.

file[2] *vb* burnish, furbish, polish, rasp, refine, smooth.

filibuster *vb* delay, frustrate, obstruct, play for time, stall, temporize. * *n* frustrater, obstructionist, thwarter; adventurer, buccaneer, corsair, freebooter, pirate.

fill *vb* occupy, pervade; dilate, distend, expand, stretch, trim; furnish, replenish, stock, store, supply; cloy, congest, content, cram, glut, gorge, line, pack, pall, sate, satiate, satisfy, saturate, stuff, suffuse, swell; engage, fulfil, hold, occupy, officiate, perform.

film *vb* becloud, cloud, coat, cover, darken, fog, mist, obfuscate, obscure, veil; photograph, shoot, take. * *n* cloud, coating, gauze, membrane, nebula, pellicle, scum, skin, veil; thread.

filter *vb* filtrate, strain; exude, ooze, percolate, transude. * *n* diffuser, colander, riddle, sieve, sifter, strainer.

filth *n* dirt, nastiness, ordure; corruption, defilement, foulness, grossness, impurity, obscenity, pollution, squalor, uncleanness, vileness.

filthy *adj* defiled, dirty, foul, licentious, nasty, obscene, pornographic, squalid, unclean; corrupt, gross, impure, unclean; miry, mucky, muddy.

final *adj* eventual, extreme, last, latest, terminal, ultimate; conclusive, decisive, definitive, irrevocable.

finale *n* conclusion, end, termination.

finances *npl* funds, resources, revenues, treasury; income, property.

find *vb* discover, fall upon; gain, get, obtain, procure; ascertain, notice, observe, perceive, remark; catch, detect; contribute, furnish, provide, supply. * *n* acquisition, catch, discovery, finding, plum, prize, strike.

fine[1] *vb* filter, purify, refine. * *adj* comminuted, little, minute, small; capillary, delicate, small; choice, light; exact, keen, sharp; attenuated, subtle, tenuous, thin; exquisite, fastidious, nice, refined, sensitive, subtle; dandy, excellent, superb, superior; beautiful, elegant, handsome, magnificent, splendid; clean, pure, unadulterated.

fine[2] *vb* amerce, mulct, penalize, punish. * *n* amercement, forfeit, forfeiture, mulct, penalty, punishment.

finery *n* decorations, frippery, gewgaws, ornaments, splendour, showiness, trappings, trimmings, trinkets.

finesse *vb* manipulate, manoeuvre. * *n* artifice, contrivance, cunning, craft, manipulation, manoeuvre, manoeuvring, ruses, stratagems, strategy, wiles.

finger *vb* handle, manipulate, play, purloin.

finical *adj* critical, dainty, dapper, fastidious, foppish, jaunty, overnice, overparticular, scrupulous, spruce, squeamish, trim.

finish *vb* accomplish, achieve, complete, consummate, execute, fulfil, perform; elaborate, perfect, polish; close, conclude, end, terminate. * *n* elaboration, elegance, perfection, polish; close, end, death, termination, wind-up.

finite *adj* bounded, circumscribed, conditioned, contracted, definable, limited, restricted, terminable.

fire *vb* ignite, kindle, light; animate, enliven, excite, inflame, inspirit, invigorate, rouse, stir up; discharge, eject, expel, hurl. * *n* combustion; blaze, conflagration; discharge, firing; animation, ardour, enthusiasm, fervour, fervency, fever, force, heat, impetuosity, inflammation, intensity, passion, spirit, vigour, violence; light, lustre, radiance, splendour; imagination, imaginativeness, inspiration, vivacity; affliction, persecution, torture, trouble.

firm[1] *adj* established, coherent, confirmed, consistent, fast, fixed, immovable, inflexible, rooted, secure, settled, stable; compact, compressed, dense, hard, solid; constant, determined, resolute, staunch, steadfast, steady, unshaken; loyal, robust, sinewy, stanch, stout, sturdy, strong.

firm[2] *n* association, business, company, concern, corporation, house, partnership.

firmament *n* heavens, sky, vault, welkin.

firmness *n* compactness, fixedness, hardness, solidity; stability, strength; constancy, soundness, steadfastness, steadiness.

first *adj* capital, chief, foremost, highest, leading, prime, principal; earliest, eldest, original; maiden; elementary, primary, rudimentary; aboriginal, primal, primeval, primitive, pristine. * *adv* chiefly, firstly, initially, mainly, primarily, principally; before, foremost, headmost; before, rather, rather than, sooner, sooner than. * *n* alpha, initial, prime.

first-rate *adj* excellent, prime, superior.

fissure *n* breach, break, chasm, chink, cleft, crack, cranny, crevice, fracture, gap, hole, interstice, opening, rent, rift.

fit[1] *vb* adapt, adjust, suit; become, conform; accommodate, equip, prepare, provide, qualify. * *adj* capacitated, competent, fitted; adequate, appropriate, apt, becoming, befitting, consonant, convenient, fitting, good, meet, pertinent, proper, seemly, suitable.

fit[2] *n* convulsion, fit, paroxysm, qualm, seizure, spasm, spell; fancy, humour, whim; mood, pet, tantrum; interval, period, spell, turn.

fitful *adj* capricious, changeable, convulsive, fanciful, fantastic, fickle, humoursome, impulsive, intermittent, irregular, odd, spasmodic, unstable, variable, whimsical; checkered, eventful.

fitness *n* adaptation, appropriateness, aptitude, aptness, pertinence, propriety, suitableness; preparation, qualification.

fix *vb* establish, fasten, place, plant, set; adjust, correct, mend, repair; attach, bind, clinch, connect, fasten, lock, rivet, stay, tie; appoint, decide, define, determine, limit, seal, settle; consolidate, harden, solidify; abide, remain, rest; congeal, stiffen. * *n* difficulty, dilemma, quandary, pickle, plight, predicament.

flabbergast *vb* abash, amaze, astonish, astound, confound, confuse, disconcert, dumbfound, nonplus.

flabby *adj* feeble, flaccid, inelastic, limp, soft, week, yielding.

flaccid *adj* baggy, drooping, flabby, inelastic, lax, limber, limp, loose, pendulous, relaxed, soft, weak, yielding.

flag[1] *vb* droop, hang, loose; decline, droop, fail, faint, lag, languish, pine, sink, succumb, weaken, weary; stale, pall.

flag[2] *vb* indicate, mark, semaphore, sign, signal. * *n* banner, colours, ensign, gonfalon, pennant, pennon, standard, streamer.

flagellate *vb* beat, castigate, chastise, cudgel, drub, flog, scourge, thrash, whip.

flagitious *adj* abandoned, atrocious, corrupt, flagrant, heinous, infamous, monstrous, nefarious, profligate, scandalous, villainous, wicked.

flagrant *adj* burning, flaming, glowing, raging; crying, enormous, flagitious, glaring, monstrous, nefarious, notorious, outrageous, shameful, wanton, wicked.

flake *vb* desquamate, scale. * *n* lamina, layer, scale.

flamboyant *adj* bright, gorgeous, ornate, rococo.

flame *vb* blaze, shine; burn, flash, glow, warm. * *n* blaze, brightness, fire, flare, vapour; affection, ardour, enthusiasm, fervency, fervour, keenness, warmth.

flaming *adj* blazing; burning, bursting, exciting, glowing, intense, lambent, vehement, violent.

flap *vb* beat, flutter, shake, vibrate, wave. * *n* apron, fly, lap, lappet, tab; beating, flapping, flop, flutter, slap, shaking, swinging, waving.

flare *vb* blaze, flicker, flutter, waver; dazzle, flame, glare; splay, spread, widen. * *n* blaze, dazzle, flame, glare.

flash *vb* blaze, glance, glare, glisten, light, shimmer, scintillate, sparkle, twinkle. * *n* instant, moment, twinkling.

flashy *adj* flaunting, gaudy, gay, loud, ostentatious, pretentious, showy, tawdry, tinsel.

flat *adj* champaign, horizontal, level; even, plane, smooth, unbroken; low, prostrate, overthrow; dull, frigid, jejune, lifeless, monotonous, pointless, prosaic, spiritless, tame, unanimated, uniform, uninteresting; dead, flashy, insipid, mawkish, stale, tasteless, vapid; absolute, clear, direct, downright, peremptory, positive. * *adv* flatly, flush, horizontally, level. * *n* bar, sandbank, shallow, shoal, strand; champaign, lowland, plain; apartment, floor, lodging, storey.

flatter *vb* compliment, gratify, praise; blandish, blarney, butter up, cajole, coax, coddle, court, entice, fawn, humour, inveigle, wheedle.

flattery *n* adulation, blandishment, blarney, cajolery, fawning, obsequiousness, servility, sycophancy, toadyism.

flaunt *vb* boast, display, disport, flourish, parade, sport, vaunt; brandish.

flaunting *adj* flashy, garish, gaudy, ostentatious, showy, tawdry.

flavour *n* gust, gusto, relish, savour, seasoning, smack, taste, zest; admixture, lacing, seasoning; aroma, essence, soul, spirit.

flaw *n* break, breach, cleft, crack, fissure, fracture, gap, rent, rift; blemish, defect, fault, fleck, imperfection, speck, spot.

flay *vb* excoriate, flay; criticize.

fleck *vb* dapple, mottle, speckle, spot, streak, variegate. * *n* speckle, spot, streak.

flecked *adj* dappled, mottled, piebald, spotted, straked, striped, variegated.

flee *vb* abscond, avoid, decamp, depart, escape, fly, leave, run, skedaddle.

fleece *vb* clip, shear; cheat, despoil, pluck, plunder, rifle, rob, steal, strip.

fleer *vb* mock, jeer, gibe, scoff, sneer.

fleet[1] *n* armada, escadrille, flotilla, navy, squadron; company, group.

fleet[2] *adj* fast, nimble, quick, rapid, speedy, swift.

fleeting *adj* brief, caducous, ephemeral, evanescent, flitting, flying, fugitive, passing, short-lived, temporary, transient, transitory.

fleetness *n* celerity, nimbleness, quickness, rapidity, speed, swiftness, velocity.

flesh *n* food, meat; carnality, desires; kindred, race, stock; man, mankind, world.
fleshly *adj* animal, bodily, carnal, lascivious, lustful, lecherous, sensual.
fleshy *adj* corpulent, fat, obese, plump, stout.
flexibility *n* flexibleness, limbersome, lithesome, pliability, pliancy, suppleness; affability, complaisance, compliance, disposition, ductility, pliancy, tractableness, tractability, yielding.
flexible *adj* flexible, limber, lithe, pliable, pliant, supple, willowy; affable, complaisant, ductile, docile, gentle, tractable, tractile, yielding.
flexose, flexuous *adj* bending, crooked, serpentine, sinuate, sinuous, tortuous, waxy, winding.
flibbertigibbet *n* demon, imp, sprite.
flight[1] *n* flying, mounting, soaring, volition; shower, flight; steps, stairs.
flight[2] *n* departure, fleeing, flying, retreat, rout, stampede; exodus, hegira.
flighty *adj* capricious, deranged, fickle, frivolous, giddy, light-headed, mercurial, unbalanced, volatile, wild, whimsical.
flimsy *adj* slight, thin, unsubstantial; feeble, foolish, frivolous, light, puerile, shallow, superficial, trashy, trifling, trivial, weak; insubstantial, sleazy.
flinch *vb* blench, flee, recoil, retreat, shirk, shrink, swerve, wince, withdraw.
fling *vb* cast, chuck, dart, emit, heave, hurl, pitch, shy, throw, toss; flounce, wince. * *n* cast, throw, toss.
flippancy *n* volubility; assuredness, glibness, pertness.
flippant *adj* fluent, glib, talkative, voluble; bold, forward, frivolous, glib, impertinent, inconsiderate, irreverent, malapert, pert, saucy, trifling.
flirt *vb* chuck, fling, hurl, pitch, shy, throw, toss; flutter, twirl, whirl, whisk; coquet, dally, philander. * *n* coquette, jilt, philanderer; jerk.
flirtation *n* coquetry, dalliance, philandering.
flit *vb* flicker, flutter, hover; depart, hasten, pass.
flitting *adj* brief, ephemeral, evanescent, fleeting, fugitive, passing, short, transient, transitory.
float *vb* drift, glide, hang, ride, sail, soar, swim, waft; launch, support.
flock *vb* collect, congregate, gather, group, herd, swarm, throng. * *n* collection, group, multitude; bevy, company, convoy, drove, flight, gaggle, herd, pack, swarm, team, troupe; congregation.
flog *vb* beat, castigate, chastise, drub, flagellate, lash, scourge, thrash, whip.
flood *vb* deluge, inundate, overflow, submerge, swamp. * *n* deluge, freshet, inundation, overflow, tide; bore, downpour, eagre, flow, outburst, spate, rush; abundance, excess.
floor *vb* deck, pave; beat, confound, conquer, overthrow, prevail, prostrate, puzzle; disconcert, nonplus. * *n* storey; bottom, deck, flooring, pavement, stage.
florid *adj* bright-coloured, flushed, red-faced, rubicund; embellished, figurative, luxuriant, ornate, rhetorical, rococo.
flounce[1] *vb* fling, jerk, spring, throw, toss, wince. * *n* jerk, spring.
flounce[2] *n* frill, furbelow, ruffle.
flounder *vb* blunder, flop, flounce, plunge, struggle, toss, tumble, wallow.
flourish *vb* grow, thrive; boast, bluster, brag, gasconade, show off, vaunt, vapour; brandish, flaunt, swing, wave. * *n* dash, display, ostentation, parade, show; bombast, fustian, grandiloquence; brandishing, shake, waving; blast, fanfare, tantivy.
flout *vb* chaff, deride, fleer, gibe, insult, jeer, mock, ridicule, scoff, sneer, taunt. * *n* gibe, fling, insult, jeer, mock, mockery, mocking, scoff, scoffing, taunt.
flow *vb* pour, run, stream; deliquesce, liquefy, melt; arise, come, emanate, follow, grow, issue, proceed, result, spring; glide; float, undulate, wave, waver; abound, run. * *n* current, discharge, flood, flux, gush, rush, stream, trickle; abundance, copiousness.
flower *vb* bloom, blossom, effloresce; develop. * *n* bloom, blossom; best, cream, elite, essence, pick; freshness, prime, vigour.
flowery *adj* bloomy, florid; embellished, figurative, florid, ornate, overwrought.
flowing *adj* abundant, copious, fluent, smooth.
fluctuate *vb* oscillate, swing, undulate, vibrate, wave; change, vary; vacillate, waver.
flue *n* chimney, duct; flew, fluff, nap, floss, fur.
fluency *n* liquidness, smoothness; affluence, copiousness; ease, facility, readiness.
fluent *adj* current, flowing, gliding, liquid; smooth; affluent, copious, easy, facile, glib, ready, talkative, voluble.
fluff *vb* blunder, bungle, forget, fumble, mess up, miscue, misremember, muddle, muff. * *n* down, flew, floss, flue, fur, lint, nap; cobweb, feather, gossamer, thistledown; blunder, bungle, fumble, muff.
flume *n* channel, chute, mill race, race.
flummery *n* chaff, frivolity, froth, moonshine, nonsense, trash, trifling; adulation, blandishment, blarney, flattery; brose, porridge, sowens.
flunky, flunkey *n* footman, lackey, livery servant, manservant, valet; snob, toady.
flurry *vb* agitate, confuse, disconcert, disturb, excite, fluster, hurry, perturb. * *n* gust, flaw, squall; agitation, bustle, commotion, confusion, disturbance, excitement, flutter, haste, hurry, hurry-scurry, perturbation, ruffle, scurry.
flush[1] *vb* flow, rush, start; glow, mantle, redden; animate, elate, elevate, erect, excite; cleanse, drench. * *adj* bright, fresh, glowing, vigorous; abundant, affluent, exuberant, fecund, fertile, generous, lavish, liberal, prodigal, prolific, rich, wealthy, well-supplied; even, flat, level, plane. * *adv* evenly, flat, level; full, point-blank, right, square, squarely, straight. * *n* bloom, blush, glow, redness, rosiness, ruddiness; impulse, shock, thrill.

flush[2] *vb* disturb, rouse, start, uncover.
fluster *vb* excite, flush, heat; agitate, disturb, flurry, hurry, perturb, ruffle; confound, confuse, discompose, disconcert. * *n* glow, heat; agitation, flurry, flutter, hurry, hurry-scurry, perturbation, ruffle.
fluted *adj* channelled, corrugated, grooved.
flutter *vb* flap, hover; flirt, flit; beat, palpitate, quiver, tremble; fluctuate, oscillate, vacillate, waver. * *n* agitation, tremor; hurry, commotion, confusion, excitement, flurry, fluster, hurry-scurry, perturbation, quivering, tremble, tumult, twitter.
flux *n* flow, flowing; change, mutation, shifting, transition; diarrhoea, dysentery, looseness; fusing, melting, menstruum, solvent.
fly[1] *vb* aviate, hover, mount, soar; flap, float, flutter, play, sail, soar, undulate, vibrate, wave; burst, explode; abscond, decamp, depart, flee, vanish; elapse, flit, glide, pass, slip.
fly[2] *adj* alert, bright, sharp, smart, wide-awake; astute, cunning, knowing, sly; agile, fleet, nimble, quick, spry.
foal *n* colt, filly.
foam *vb* cream, froth, lather, spume; boil, churn, ferment, fume, seethe, simmer, stew. * *n* bubbles, cream, froth, scum, spray, spume, suds.
fodder *n* feed, food, forage, provender, rations.
foe *n* adversary, antagonist, enemy, foeman, opponent.
fog *vb* bedim, bemist, blear, blur, cloud, dim, enmist, mist; addle, befuddle, confuse, fuddle, muddle. * *n* blear, blur, dimness, film, fogginess, haze, haziness, mist, smog, vapour; befuddlement, confusion, fuddle, maze, muddle.
foggy *adj* blurred, cloudy, dim, dimmed, hazy, indistinct, misty, obscure; befuddled, bewildered, confused, dazed, muddled, muddy, stupid.
foible *n* defect, failing, fault, frailty, imperfection, infirmity, penchant, weakness.
foil[1] *vb* baffle, balk, check, checkmate, circumvent, defeat, disappoint, frustrate, thwart.
foil[2] *n* film, flake, lamina; background, contrast.
foist *vb* impose, insert, interpolate, introduce, palm off, thrust.
fold[1] *vb* bend, cover, double, envelop, wrap; clasp, embrace, enfold, enwrap, gather, infold, interlace; collapse, fail. * *n* double, doubling, gather, plait, plicature.
fold[2] *n* cot, enclosure, pen.
foliaceous *adj* foliate, leafy; flaky, foliated, lamellar, lamellate, lamellated, laminated, scaly, schistose.
folk *n* kindred, nation, people.
follow *vb* ensue, succeed; chase, dog, hound, pursue, run after, trail; accompany, attend; conform, heed, obey, observe; cherish, cultivate, seek; practise, pursue; adopt, copy, imitate; arise, come, flow, issue, proceed, result, spring.
follower *n* acolyte, attendant, associate, companion, dependant, retainer, supporter; adherent, admirer, disciple, partisan, pupil; copier, imitator.
folly *n* doltishness, dullness, imbecility, levity, shallowness; absurdity, extravagance, fatuity, foolishness, imprudence, inanity, indiscretion, ineptitude, nonsense, senselessness; blunder, faux pas, indiscretion, unwisdom.
foment *vb* bathe, embrocate, stupe; abet, brew, encourage, excite, foster, instigate, promote, stimulate.
fond *adj* absurd, baseless, empty, foolish, senseless, silly, vain, weak; affectionate, amorous, doting, loving, overaffectionate, tender.
fondle *vb* blandish, caress, coddle, cosset, dandle, pet.
fondness *n* absurdity, delusion, folly, silliness, weakness; liking, partiality, predilection, preference, propensity; appetite, relish, taste.
food *n* aliment, board, bread, cheer, commons, diet, fare, meat, nourishment, nutriment, nutrition, pabulum, provisions, rations, regimen, subsistence, sustenance, viands, victuals; feed, fodder, forage, provender.
fool *vb* jest, play, toy, trifle; beguile, cheat, circumvent, cozen, deceive, delude, dupe, gull, hoodwink, overreach, trick. * *n* blockhead, dolt, driveller, idiot, imbecile, nincompoop, ninny, nitwit, simpleton; antic, buffoon, clown, droll, harlequin, jester, merry-andrew, punch, scaramouch, zany; butt, dupe.
foolery *n* absurdity, folly, foolishness, nonsense; buffoonery, mummery, tomfoolery.
foolhardy *adj* adventurous, bold, desperate, harebrained, headlong, hot-headed, incautious, precipitate, rash, reckless, venturesome, venturous.
foolish *adj* brainless, daft, fatuous, idiotic, inane, inept, insensate, irrational, senseless, shallow, silly, simple, thick-skulled, vain, weak, witless; absurd, ill-judged, imprudent, indiscreet, nonsensical, preposterous, ridiculous, unreasonable, unwise; childish, contemptible, idle, puerile, trifling, trivial, vain.
foolishness *n* doltishness, dullness, fatuity, folly, imbecility, shallowness, silliness, stupidity; absurdity, extravagance, imprudence, indiscretion, nonsense; childishness, puerility, triviality.
footing *n* foothold, purchase; basis, foundation, groundwork, installation; condition, grade, rank, standing, state, status; settlement, establishment.
footman *n* footboy, menial, lackey, runner, servant.
footpad *n* bandit, brigand, freebooter, highwayman, robber.
footpath *n* footway, path, trail.
footprint *n* footfall, footmark, footstep, trace, track.
footstep *n* footmark, footprint, trace, track; footfall, step, tread; mark, sign, token, trace, vestige.
fop *n* beau, coxcomb, dandy, dude, exquisite, macaroni, popinjay, prig, swell.

foppish *adj* coxcombical, dandified, dandyish, dressy, finical, spruce, vain.
forage *vb* feed, graze, provender, provision, victual; hunt for, range, rummage, search, seek; maraud, plunder, raid. * *n* feed, fodder, food, pasturage, provender; hunt, rummage, search.
foray *n* descent, incursion, invasion, inroad, irruption, raid.
forbear *vb* cease, desist, hold, pause, stop, stay; abstain, refrain; endure, tolerate; avoid, decline, shun; abstain, omit, withhold.
forbearance *n* abstinence, avoidance, forbearing, self-restraint, shunning, refraining; indulgence, leniency, long-suffering, mildness, moderation, patience.
forbid *vb* ban, debar, disallow, embargo, enjoin, hinder, inhibit, interdict, prohibit, proscribe, taboo, veto.
forbidding *adj* abhorrent, disagreeable, displeasing, odious, offensive, repellant, repulsive, threatening, unpleasant.
force *vb* coerce, compel, constrain, necessitate, oblige; drive, impel, overcome, press, urge; ravish, violate. * *n* emphasis, energy, head, might, pith, power, strength, stress, vigour, vim; agency, efficacy, efficiency, cogency, potency, validity, virtue; coercion, compulsion, constraint, enforcement, vehemence, violence; army, array, battalion, host, legion, phalanx, posse, soldiery, squadron, troop.
forcible *adj* all-powerful, cogent, impressive, irresistible, mighty, potent, powerful, strong, weighty; impetuous, vehement, violent, unrestrained; coerced, coercive, compulsory; convincing, energetic, effective, efficacious, telling, vigorous.
forcibly *adv* mightily, powerfully; coercively, compulsorily, perforce, violently; effectively, energetically, vigorously.
ford *n* current, flood, stream; crossing, wading place.
fore *adj* anterior, antecedent, first, foregoing, former, forward, preceding, previous, prior; advanced, foremost, head, leading.
forebode *vb* augur, betoken, foreshow, foretell, indicate, portend, predict, prefigure, presage, prognosticate, promise, signify.
foreboding *n* augury, omen, prediction, premonition, presage, presentiment, prognostication.
forecast *vb* anticipate, foresee, predict; calculate, contrive, devise, plan, project, scheme. * *n* anticipation, foresight, forethought, planning, prevision, prophecy, provident.
foreclose *vb* debar, hinder, preclude, prevent, stop.
foredoom *vb* foreordain, predestine, preordain.
forego *see* **forgo**.
foregoing *adj* antecedent, anterior, fore, former, preceding, previous, prior.
foregone *adj* bygone, former, past, previous.
foreign *adj* alien, distant, exotic, exterior, external, outward, outlandish, remote, strange, unnative; adventitious, exterior, extraneous, extrinsic, inappropriate, irrelevant, outside, unnatural, unrelated.
foreknowledge *n* foresight, prescience, prognostication.
foremost *adj* first, front, highest, leading, main, principal.
foreordain *vb* appoint, foredoom, predestinate, predetermine, preordain.
forerunner *n* avant-courier, foregoer, harbinger, herald, precursor, predecessor; omen, precursor, prelude, premonition, prognosticate, sign.
foresee *vb* anticipate, forebode, forecast, foreknow, foretell, prognosticate, prophesy.
foreshadow *vb* forebode, predict, prefigure, presage, presignify, prognosticate, prophesy.
foresight *n* foreknowledge, prescience, prevision; anticipation, care, caution, forecast, forethought, precaution, providence, prudence.
forest *n* wood, woods, woodland.
forestall *vb* hinder, frustrate, intercept, preclude, prevent, thwart; antedate, anticipate, foretaste; engross, monopolize, regrate.
foretaste *n* anticipation, forestalling, prelibation.
foretell *vb* predict, prophesy; augur, betoken, forebode, forecast, foreshadow, foreshow, portend, presage, presignify, prognosticate, prophesy.
forethought *n* anticipation, forecast, foresight, precaution, providence, prudence.
forever *adv* always, constantly, continually, endlessly, eternally, ever, evermore, everlastingly, perpetually, unceasingly.
forewarn *vb* admonish, advise, caution, dissuade.
forfeit *vb* alienate, lose. * *n* amercement, damages, fine, forfeiture, mulct, penalty.
forfend *vb* avert, forbid, hinder, prevent, protect.
forge *vb* beat, fabricate, form, frame, hammer; coin, devise, frame, invent; counterfeit, falsify, feign. * *n* furnace, ironworks, smithy.
forgery *n* counterfeit, fake, falsification, imitation.
forgetful *adj* careless, heedless, inattentive, mindless, neglectful, negligent, oblivious, unmindful.
forgive *vb* absolve, acquit, condone, excuse, exonerate, pardon, remit.
forgiveness *n* absolution, acquittal, amnesty, condoning. exoneration, pardon, remission, reprieve.
forgiving *adj* absolutory, absolvatory, acquitting, clearing, excusing, pardoning, placable, releasing.
forgo *vb* abandon, cede, relinquish, renounce, resign, surrender, yield.
fork *vb* bifurcate, branch, divaricate, divide. * *n* bifurcation, branch, branching, crotch, divarication, division.
forked *adj* bifurcated, branching, divaricated, furcate, furcated.
forlorn *adj* abandoned, deserted, forsaken, friendless, helpless, lost, solitary; abject, comfortless, dejected, desolate, destitute, disconsolate, helpless, hopeless, lamentable, pitiable, miserable,

woebegone, wretched.

form *vb* fashion model, mould, shape; build, conceive, construct, create, fabricate, make, produce; contrive, devise, frame, invent; compose, constitute, develop, organize; discipline, educate, teach, train. * *n* body, build, cast, configuration, conformation, contour, cut, fashion, figure, format, mould, outline, pattern, shape; formula, formulary, method, mode, practice, ritual; class, kind, manner, model, order, sort, system, type; arrangement, order, regularity, shapeliness; ceremonial, ceremony, conventionality, etiquette, formality, observance, ordinance, punctilio, rite, ritual; bench, seat; class, rank; arrangement, combination, organization.

formal *adj* explicit, express, official, positive, strict; fixed, methodical, regular, rigid, set, stiff; affected, ceremonious, exact, precise, prim, punctilious, starchy. starched; constitutive, essential; external, outward, perfunctory; formative, innate, organic, primordial.

formality *n* ceremonial, ceremony, conventionality, etiquette, punctilio, rite, ritual.

formation *n* creation, genesis, production; composition, constitution; arrangement, combination, disposal, disposition.

formative *adj* creative, determinative, plastic, shaping; derivative, inflectional, nonradical.

former *adj* antecedent, anterior, earlier, foregoing, preceding, previous, prior; late, old-time, quondam; by, bygone, foregone, gone, past.

formidable *adj* appalling, dangerous, difficult, dreadful, fearful, frightful, horrible, menacing, redoubtable, shocking, terrible, terrific, threatening, tremendous.

forsake *vb* abandon, desert, leave, quit; drop, forgo, forswear, relinquish, renounce, surrender, yield.

forsooth *adv* certainly, indeed, really, surely, truly.

forswear *vb* abandon, desert, drop, forsake, leave, quit, reject, renounce; abjure, deny, eschew, perjure, recant, repudiate, retract.

fort *n* bulwark, castle, citadel, defence, fastness, fortification, fortress, stronghold.

forthwith *adv* directly, immediately, instantly, quickly, straightaway.

fortification *n* breastwork, bulwark, castle, citadel, defence, earthwork, fastness, fort, keep, rampart, redoubt, stronghold, tower.

fortify *vb* brace, encourage, entrench, garrison, protect, reinforce, stiffen, strengthen; confirm, corroborate.

fortitude *n* braveness, bravery, courage, determination, endurance, firmness, hardiness, patience, pluck, resolution, strength, valour.

fortuitous *adj* accidental, casual, chance, contingent, incidental.

fortunate *adj* favoured, happy, lucky, prosperous, providential, successful; advantageous, auspicious, favourable, happy, lucky, propitious, timely.

fortune *n* accident, casualty, chance, contingency, fortuity, hap, luck; estate, possessions, property, substance; affluence, felicity, opulence, prosperity, riches, wealth; destination, destiny, doom, fate, lot, star; event, issue, result; favour, success.

forward *vb* advance, aid, encourage, favour, foster, further, help, promote, support; accelerate, dispatch, expedite, hasten, hurry, quicken, speed; dispatch, post, send, ship, transmit. * *adj* ahead, advanced, onward; anterior, front, fore, head; prompt, eager, earnest, hasty, impulsive, quick, ready, willing, zealous; assuming, bold, brazen, brazen-faced, confident, flippant, impertinent, pert, presumptuous, presuming; advanced, early, premature. * *adv* ahead, onward.

foster *vb* cosset, feed, nurse, nourish, support, sustain; advance, aid, breed, cherish, cultivate, encourage, favour, foment, forward, further, harbour, patronize, promote, rear, stimulate.

foul *vb* besmirch, defile, dirty, pollute, soil, stain, sully; clog, collide, entangle, jam. * *adj* dirty, fetid, filthy, impure, nasty, polluted, putrid, soiled, stained, squalid, sullied, rank, tarnished, unclean; disgusting, hateful, loathsome, noisome, odious, offensive; dishonourable, underhand, unfair, sinister; abominable, base, dark, detestable, disgraceful, infamous, scandalous, scurvy, shameful, wile, wicked; coarse, low, obscene, vulgar; abusive, foul-mouthed, foul-spoken, insulting, scurrilous; cloudy, rainy, rough, stormy, wet; feculent, muddy, thick, turbid; entangled, tangled.

foul-mouthed *adj* abusive, blackguardy, blasphemous, filthy, foul, indecent, insolent, insulting, obscene, scurrilous.

found *vb* base, fix, ground, place, rest, set; build, construct, erect, raise; colonize, establish, institute, originate, plant; cast, mould.

foundation *n* base, basis, bed, bottom, footing, ground, groundwork, substructure, support; endowment, establishment, settlement.

founder[1] *n* author, builder, establisher, father, institutor, originator, organizer, planter.

founder[2] *n* caster, moulder.

founder[3] *vb* sink, swamp, welter; collapse, fail, miscarry; fall, stumble, trip.

fountain *n* fount, reservoir, spring, well; jet, upswelling; cause, fountainhead, origin, original, source.

foxy *adj* artful, crafty, cunning, sly, subtle, wily.

fracas *n* affray, brawl, disturbance, outbreak, quarrel, riot, row, uproar, tumult,

fractious *adj* captious, cross, fretful, irritable, peevish, pettish, perverse, petulant, querulous, snappish, splenetic, touchy, testy, waspish.

fracture *vb* break, crack, split. * *n* breaking, rupture; breach, break, cleft, crack, fissure, flaw, opening, rift, rent.

fragile *adj* breakable, brittle, delicate, frangible; feeble, frail, infirm, weak.

fragility *n* breakability, breakableness, brittleness,

frangibility, frangibleness; feebleness, frailty, infirmity, weakness.

fragment *vb* atomize, break, fracture, pulverize, splinter. * *n* bit, chip, fraction, fracture, morsel, part, piece, remnant, scrap.

fragrance *n* aroma, balminess, bouquet, odour, perfume, redolence, scent, smell.

fragrant *adj* ambrosial, aromatic, balmy, odoriferous, odorous, perfumed, redolent, spicy, sweet, sweet-scented, sweet-smelling.

frail *adj* breakable, brittle, delicate, fragile, frangible, slight; feeble, infirm, weak.

frailty *n* feebleness, frailness, infirmity, weakness; blemish, defect, failing, fault, foible, imperfection, peccability, shortcoming.

frame *vb* build, compose, constitute, construct, erect, form, make, mould, plan, shape; contrive, devise, fabricate, fashion, forge, invest, plan. * *n* body, carcass, framework, framing, shell, skeleton; constitution, fabric, form, structure, scheme, system; condition, humour, mood, state, temper.

franchise *n* privilege, right; suffrage, vote; exemption, immunity.

frangible *adj* breakable, brittle, fragile.

frank *adj* artless, candid, direct, downright, frank-hearted, free, genuine, guileless, ingenuous, naive, open, outspoken, outright, plain, plain-spoken, point-blank, sincere, straightforward, truthful, unequivocal, unreserved, unrestricted.

frankness *n* candour, ingenuousness, openness, outspokenness, plain speaking, truth, straightforwardness.

frantic *adj* crazy, distracted, distraught, frenzied, furious, infuriate, mad. outrageous, phrenetic, rabid, raging, raving, transported, wild.

fraternity *n* association, brotherhood, circle, clan, club, company, fellowship, league, set, society, sodality; brotherliness.

fraternize *vb* associate, coalesce, concur, consort, cooperate, harmonize, sympathize, unite.

fraud *n* artifice, cheat, craft, deception, deceit, duplicity, guile, hoax, humbug, imposition, imposture, sham, stratagem, treachery, trick, trickery, wile.

fraudulent *adj* crafty, deceitful, deceptive, dishonest, false, knavish, treacherous, trickish, tricky, wily.

fraught *adj* abounding, big, burdened, charged, filled, freighted, laden, pregnant, stored, weighted.

fray[1] *n* affray, battle, brawl, broil, combat, fight, quarrel, riot.

fray[2] *vb* chafe, fret, rub, wear; ravel, shred.

freak *adj* bizarre, freakish, grotesque, monstrous, odd, unexpected, unforeseen. * *n* caprice, crotchet, fancy, humour, maggot, quirk, vagary, whim, whimsey; antic, caper, gambol; abnormality, abortion, monstrosity.

freakish *adj* capricious, changeable, eccentric, erratic, fanciful, humoursome, odd, queer, whimsical.

free *vb* deliver, discharge, disenthral, emancipate, enfranchise, enlarge, liberate, manumit, ransom, release, redeem, rescue, save; clear, disencumber, disengage, extricate, rid, unbind, unchain, unfetter, unlock; exempt, immunize, privilege. * *adj* bondless, independent, loose, unattached, unconfined, unentangled, unimpeded, unrestrained, untrammelled; autonomous, delivered, emancipated, freeborn, liberated, manumitted, ransomed, released, self-governing; clear, exempt, immune, privileged; allowed, permitted; devoid, empty, open, unimpeded, unobstructed, unrestricted; affable, artless, candid, frank, ingenuous, sincere, unreserved; bountiful, charitable, free-hearted, generous, hospitable, liberal, munificent, openhanded; immoderate, lavish, prodigal; eager, prompt, ready, willing; available, gratuitous, spontaneous; careless, lax, loose; bold, easy, familiar, informal, overfamiliar, unconstrained. * *adv* openly, outright, unreservedly, unrestrainedly, unstintingly; freely, gratis, gratuitously.

freebooter *n* bandit, brigand, despoiler, footpad, gangster, highwayman, marauder, pillager, plunderer, robber; buccaneer, pirate, rover.

freedom *n* emancipation, independence, liberation, liberty, release; elbowroom, margin, play, range, scope, swing; franchise, immunity, privilege; familiarity, laxity, license, looseness.

freethinker *n* agnostic, deist, doubter, infidel, sceptic, unbeliever.

freeze *vb* congeal, glaciate, harden, stiffen; benumb, chill.

freight *vb* burden, charge, lade, load. * *n* burden, cargo, lading, load.

frenzy *n* aberration, delirium, derangement, distraction, fury, insanity, lunacy, madness, mania, paroxysm, rage, raving, transport.

frequent *vb* attend, haunt, resort, visit. * *adj* iterating, oft-repeated; common, customary, everyday, familiar, habitual, persistent, usual; constant, continual, incessant.

fresh *adj* new, novel, recent; renewed, revived; blooming, flourishing, green, undecayed, unimpaired, unfaded, unobliterated, unwilted, unwithered, well-preserved; sweet; delicate, fair, fresh-coloured, ruddy, rosy; florid, hardy, healthy, vigorous, strong; active, energetic, unexhausted, unfatigued, unwearied, vigorous; keen, lively, unabated, undecayed, unimpaired, vivid; additional, further; uncured, undried, unsalted, unsmoked; bracing, health-giving, invigorating, refreshing, sweet; brink, stiff, strong; inexperienced, raw, uncultivated, unpracticed, unskilled, untrained, unused.

freshen *vb* quicken, receive, refresh, revive.

fret[1] *vb* abrade, chafe, fray, gall, rub, wear; affront, agitate, annoy, gall, harass, irritate, nettle, provoke, ruffle, tease, vex, wear, worry; ripple, roughen; corrode; fume, peeve, rage, stew. * *n* agitation, fretfulness, fretting, irritation, peevishness, vexation.

fret[2] *vb* diversify, interlace, ornament, variegate. * *n* fretwork, interlacing, ornament; ridge, wale, whelk.

fretful *adj* captious, cross, fractious, ill-humoured, ill-tempered, irritable, peevish, pettish, petulant, querulous, short-tempered, snappish, spleeny, splenetic, testy, touchy, uneasy, waspish.

friable *adj* brittle, crisp, crumbling, powdery, pulverable.

friction *n* abrasion, attrition, grating, rubbing; bickering, disagreement, dissension, wrangling.

friend *adj* benefactor, chum, companion, comrade, crony, confidant, intimate; adherent, ally, associate, confrere, partisan; advocate, defender, encourager, favourer, patron, supporter, well-wisher.

friendly *adj* affectionate, amiable, benevolent, favourable, kind, kind-hearted, kindly, well-disposed; amicable, cordial, fraternal, neighbourly; conciliatory, peaceable, unhostile.

friendship *n* affection, attachment, benevolence, fondness, goodness, love, regard; fellowship, intimacy; amicability, amicableness, amity, cordiality, familiarity, fraternization, friendliness, harmony.

fright *n* affright, alarm, consternation, dismay, funk, horror, panic, scare, terror.

frighten *vb* affright, alarm, appal, daunt, dismay, intimidate, scare, stampede, terrify.

frightful *adj* alarming, awful, dire, direful, dread, dreadful, fearful, horrible, horrid, shocking, terrible, terrific; ghastly, grim, grisly, gruesome, hideous.

frigid *adj* cold, cool, gelid; dull, lifeless, spiritless, tame, unanimated, uninterested, uninteresting; chilling, distant, forbidding, formal, freezing, prim, repellent, repelling, repulsive, rigid, stiff.

frill *n* edging, frilling, furbelow, gathering, ruche, ruching, ruffle; affectation, mannerism.

fringe *vb* border, bound, edge, hem, march, rim, skirt, verge. * *n* border, edge, edging, tassel, trimming. * *adj* edging, extra, unofficial.

frisk *vb* caper, dance, frolic, gambol, hop, jump, play, leap, romp, skip, sport, wanton.

frisky *adj* frolicsome, coltish, gay, lively, playful, sportive.

frivolity *n* flummery, folly, fribbling, frippery, frivolousness, levity, puerility, trifling, triviality.

frivolous *adj* childish, empty, flighty, flimsy, flippant, foolish, giddy, idle, light, paltry. petty, puerile, silly, trashy, trifling, trivial, unimportant, vain, worthless.

frolic *vb* caper, frisk, gambol, lark, play, romp, sport. * *n* escapade, gambol, lark, romp, skylark, spree, trick; drollery, fun, play, pleasantry, sport.

frolicsome *adj* coltish, fresh, frolic, gamesome, gay, lively, playful, sportive.

front *vb* confront, encounter, face, oppose. * *adj* anterior, forward; foremost, frontal, headmost. * *n* brow, face, forehead; assurance, boldness, brass, effrontery, impudence; breast, head, van, vanguard; anterior, face, forepart, obverse; facade, frontage.

frontier *n* border, boundary, coast, confine, limits, marches.

frosty *adj* chill, chilly, cold, icy, stinging, wintry; cold, cold-hearted, frigid, indifferent, unaffectionate, uncordial, unimpassioned, unloving; dull-hearted, lifeless, spiritless, unanimated; frosted, grey-hearted, hoary, white.

froth *vb* bubble, cream, foam, lather, spume. * *n* bubbles, foam, lather, spume; balderdash, flummery, nonsense, trash, triviality.

frothy *adj* foamy, spumy; empty, frivolous, light, trifling, trivial, unsubstantial, vain.

froward *adj* captious, contrary, contumacious, cross, defiant, disobedient, fractious, impudent, intractable, obstinate, peevish, perverse, petulant, refractory, stubborn, ungovernable, untoward, unyielding, wayward, wilful.

frown *vb* glower, lower, scowl.

frowzy, frowsy *adj* fetid, musty, noisome, rancid, rank, stale; disordered, disorderly, dowdy, slatternly, slovenly.

frugal *adj* abstemious, careful, chary, choice, economical, provident, saving, sparing, temperate, thrifty, unwasteful.

fruit *n* crop, harvest, produce, production; advantage, consequence, effect, good, outcome, product, profit, result; issue, offspring, young.

fruitful *adj* abounding, productive; fecund, fertile, prolific; abundant, exuberant, plenteous, plentiful, rich, teeming.

fruition *n* completion, fulfilment, perfection; enjoyment.

fruitless *adj* acarpous, barren, sterile, infecund, unfertile, unfruitful, unproductive, unprolific; abortive, bootless, futile, idle, ineffectual, profitless, unavailing, unprofitable, useless, vain.

frumpish, frumpy *adj* cross, cross-grained, cross-tempered, dowdy, grumpy, irritable, shabby, slatternly, snappish.

frustrate *vb* baffle, balk, check, circumvent, defeat, disappoint, disconcert, foil, thwart; cross, hinder, outwit.

frustrated *adj* balked, blighted, dashed, defeated, foiled, thwarted; ineffectual, null, useless, vain.

fuddled *adj* befuddled, boozy, corned, crapulous, drunk, groggy, high, inebriated, intoxicated, muddled, slewed, tight, tipsy.

fugacious *adj* evanescent, fleeting, fugitive, transient, transitory.

fugitive *adj* escaping, fleeing, flying; brief, ephemeral, evanescent, fleeting, flitting, fugacious, momentary, short, short-lived, temporal, temporary, transient, transitory, uncertain, unstable, volatile. * *n* émigré, escapee, evacuee, fleer, outlaw, refugee, runaway.

fulfil *vb* accomplish, complete, consummate, effect, effectuate, execute, realize; adhere, discharge, do, keep, obey, observe, perform; answer, fill, meet, satisfy.

full *adj* brimful, filled, flush, replete; abounding, replete, well-stocked; bagging, flowing, loose, voluminous; chock-full, cloyed, crammed, glutted, gorged, overflowing, packed, sated, satiated, saturated, soaked, stuffed, swollen; adequate, complete, entire, mature, perfect; abundant, ample, copious, plenteous, plentiful, sufficient; clear, deep, distinct, loud, rounded, strong; broad, large, capacious, comprehensive, extensive, plump; circumstantial, detailed, exhaustive. * *adv* completely, fully; directly, exactly, precisely.

fullness *n* abundance, affluence, copiousness, plenitude, plenty, profusion; glut, satiety, sating, repletion; completeness, completion, entireness, perfection; clearness, loudness, resonance, strength; dilation, distension, enlargement, plumpness, rotundity, roundness, swelling.

fully *adv* abundantly, amply, completely, copiously, entirely, largely, plentifully, sufficiently.

fulminate *vb* detonate, explode; curse, denounce, hurl, menace, threaten, thunder.

fulsome *adj* excessive, extravagant, fawning; disgusting, nauseous, nauseating, offensive, repulsive; coarse, gross, lustful, questionable.

fumble *vb* bungle, grope, mismanage, stumble; mumble, stammer, stutter.

fume *vb* reek, smoke, vaporize. * *n* effluvium exhalation, reek, smell, smoke, steam, vapour; agitation, fret, fry, fury, passion, pet, rage, storm.

fun *adj* amusing, diverting, droll, entertaining. * *n* amusement, diversion, drollery, frolic, gaiety, humour, jesting, jocularity, jollity, joy, merriment, mirth, play, pranks, sport, pleasantry, waggishness.

function *vb* act, discharge, go, operate, officiate, perform, run, serve, work. * *n* discharge, execution, exercise, operation, performance, purpose, use; activity, business, capacity, duty, employment, occupation, office, part, province, role; ceremony, rite; dependant, derivative.

fund *vb* afford, endow, finance, invest, provide, subsidise, support; garner, hoard, stock, store. * *n* accumulation, capital, endowment, reserve, stock; store, supply; foundation.

fundament *n* bottom, buttocks, seat.

fundamental *adj* basal, basic, bottom, cardinal, constitutional, elementary, essential, indispensable; organic, principal, primary, radical. * *n* essential, principal, rule.

funeral *n* burial, cremation, exequies, internment, obsequies.

funereal *adj* dark, dismal, gloomy, lugubrious, melancholy, mournful, sad, sepulchral, sombre, woeful.

funk *vb* blanch, shrink, quail. * *n* stench, stink; fear, fright, panic.

funny *adj* amusing, comic, comical, diverting, droll, facetious, farcical, humorous, jocose, jocular, laughable, ludicrous, sportive, witty; curious, odd, queer, strange. * *n* jest, joke; cartoon, comic.

furbish *vb* burnish, brighten, polish, renew, renovate, rub, shine.

furious *adj* angry, fierce, frantic, frenzied, fuming, infuriated, mad, raging, violent, wild; boisterous, fierce, impetuous, stormy, tempestuous, tumultuous, turbulent, vehement.

furnish *vb* appoint, endow, provide, supply; decorate, equip, fit; afford, bestow, contribute, give, offer, present, produce, yield.

furniture *n* chattels, effects, household goods, movables; apparatus, appendages, appliances, equipment, fittings, furnishings; decorations, embellishments, ornaments.

furore *n* commotion, craze, enthusiasm, excitement, fad, fury, madness, mania, rage, vogue.

furrow *vb* chamfer, channel, cleave, corrugate, cut, flute, groove, hollow; pucker, seam, wrinkle. * *n* chamfer, channel, cut, depression, fluting, groove, hollow, line, seam, track, trench, rot, wrinkle.

further *vb* advance, aid, assist, encourage, help, forward, promote, succour, strengthen. * *adj* additional. * *adv* also, besides, farther, furthermore, moreover.

furtive *adj* clandestine, hidden, secret, sly, skulking, sneaking, sneaky, stealthy, stolen, surreptitious.

fury *n* anger, frenzy, fit, furore, ire, madness, passion, rage; fierceness, impetuosity, turbulence, turbulency, vehemence; bacchant, bacchante, bedlam, hag, shrew, termagant, virago, vixen.

fuse *vb* dissolve, melt, liquefy, smelt; amalgamate, blend, coalesce, combine, commingle, intermingle, intermix, merge, unite. * *n* match.

fusion *n* liquefaction, melting; amalgamation, blending, commingling, commixture, intermingling, intermixture, union; coalition, merging.

fuss *vb* bustle, fidget; fret, fume, worry. * *n* ado, agitation, bother, bustle, commotion, disturbance, excitement, fidget, flurry, fluster, fret, hurry, pother, stir, worry.

fustian *n* bombast, claptrap, rant, rodomontade; balderdash, inanity, nonsense, stuff, trash, twaddle.

fusty *adj* ill-smelling, malodorous, mildewed, mouldy, musty, rank.

futile *adj* frivolous, trifling, trivial; bootless, fruitless, idle, ineffectual, profitless, unavailing, unprofitable, useless, vain, valueless, worthless.

futility *n* frivolousness, triviality; bootlessness, fruitlessness, uselessness, vanity, worthlessness.

future *adj* coming, eventual, forthcoming, hereafter, prospective, subsequent. * *n* hereafter, outlook, prospect.

G

gabble *vb* babble, chatter, clack, gibber, gossip, prate, prattle. * *n* babble, chatter, clack, gap, gossip, jabber, palaver, prate, prattle, twaddle.
gadabout *n* idler, loafer, rambler, rover, vagrant; gossip, talebearer, vagrant.
gaffer *n* boss, foreman, overseer, supervisor.
gag[1] *n* jape, jest, joke, stunt, wisecrack.
gag[2] *vb* muffle, muzzle, shackle, silence, stifle, throttle; regurgitate, retch, throw up, vomit; choke, gasp, pant. * *n* muzzle.
gage *n* pawn, pledge, security, surety; challenge, defiance, gauntlet, glove.
gaiety *n* animation, blithesomeness, cheerfulness, glee, hilarity, jollity, joviality, merriment, mirth, vivacity.
gain *vb* achieve, acquire, earn, get, obtain, procure, reap, secure; conciliate, enlist, persuade, prevail, win; arrive, attain, reach; clear, net, profit. * *n* accretion, addition, gainings, profits, winnings; acquisition, earnings, emolument, lucre; advantage, benefit, blessing, good, profit.
gainful *adj* advantageous, beneficial, profitable; lucrative, paying, productive, remunerative.
gainsay *vb* contradict, controvert, deny, dispute, forbid.
gait *n* carriage, pace, step, stride, walk.
galaxy *n* assemblage, assembly, cluster, collection, constellation, group.
gale *n* blast, hurricane, squall, storm, tempest, tornado, typhoon.
gall[1] *n* effrontery, impudence; bile; acerbity, bitterness, malice, maliciousness, malignity, rancour, spite.
gall[2] *vb* chafe, excoriate, fret, hurt; affront, annoy, exasperate, harass, incense, irritate, plague, provoke, sting, tease, vex.
gallant *adj* fine, magnificent, showy, splendid, well-dressed; bold, brave, chivalrous, courageous, daring, fearless, heroic, high-spirited, intrepid, valiant, valorous; chivalrous, fine, honourable, high-minded, lofty, magnanimous, noble. * *n* beau, blade, spark; lover, suitor, wooer.
gallantry *n* boldness, bravery, chivalry, courage, courageousness, fearlessness, heroism, intrepidity, prowess, valour; courtesy, courteousness, elegance, politeness.
galling *adj* chafing, irritating, vexing.
gallop *vb* fly, hurry, run, rush, scamper, speed.
gamble *vb* bet, dice, game, hazard, plunge, speculate, wager. * *n* chance, risk, speculation; bet, punt, wager.
gambol *vb* caper, cut, frisk, frolic, hop, jump, leap, romp, skip. * *n* frolic, hop, jump, skip.
game[1] *vb* gamble, sport, stake. * *n* amusement, contest, diversion, pastime, play, sport; adventure, enterprise, measure, plan, project, scheme, stratagem, undertaking; prey, quarry, victim.
game[2] *adj* brave, courageous, dauntless, fearless, gallant, heroic, intrepid, plucky, unflinching, valorous; enduring, persevering, resolute, undaunted; ready, eager, willing.
game[3] *adj* crippled, disabled, halt, injured, lame.
gameness *n* bravery, courage, grit, heart, mettle, nerve, pith, pluck, pluckiness, spirit, stamina.
gamesome *adj* frisky, frolicsome, lively, merry, playful, sportive, sprightly, vivacious.
gammon *vb* bamboozle, beguile, cheat, circumvent, deceive, delude, dupe, gull, hoax, humbug, inveigle, mislead, overreach, outwit. * *n* bosh, hoax, humbug, imposition, nonsense.
gang *n* band, cabal, clique, company, coterie, crew, horde, party, set, troop.
gaol *see* **jail**.
gap *n* breach, break, cavity, chasm, chink, cleft, crack, cranny, crevice, hiatus, hollow, interval, interstice, lacuna, opening, pass, ravine, rift, space, vacancy.
gape *vb* burst open, dehisce, open, stare, yawn.
garb *vb* attire, clothe, dress. * *n* apparel, attire, clothes, costume, dress, garments, habiliment, habit, raiment, robes, uniform, vestment.
garbage *n* filth, offal, refuse, remains, rubbish, trash, waste.
garble *vb* corrupt, distort, falsify, misquote, misrepresent, mutilate, pervert.
gargantuan *adj* big, Brobdingnagian, colossal, enormous, gigantic, huge, prodigious, tremendous.
garish *adj* bright, dazzling, flashy, flaunting, gaudy, glaring, loud, showy, staring, tawdry.
garland *vb* adorn, festoon, wreathe. * *n* chaplet, coronal, crown, festoon, wreath.
garment *n* clothes, clothing, dress, habit, vestment.
garner *vb* accumulate, collect, deposit, gather, hoard, husband, reserve, save, store, treasure.
garnish *vb* adorn, beautify, bedeck, decorate, deck, embellish, grace, ornament, prank, trim. * *n* decoration, enhancement, ornament, trimming.
garrulous *adj* babbling, loquacious, prating, prattling, talkative.

gasconade *n* bluster, boast, brag, bravado, swagger, vaunt, vapouring.
gasp *vb* blow, choke, pant, puff. * *n* blow, exclamation, gulp, puff.
gather *vb* assemble, cluster, collect, convene, group, muster, rally; accumulate, amass, garner, hoard, huddle, lump; bunch, crop, cull, glean, pick, pluck, rake, reap, shock, stack; acquire, gain, get, win; conclude, deduce, derive, infer; fold, plait, pucker, shirr, tuck; condense, grow, increase, thicken.
gathering *n* acquisition, collecting, earning, gain, heap, pile, procuring; assemblage, assembly, collection, company, concourse, congregation, meeting, muster; abscess, boil, fester, pimple, pustule, sore, suppuration, tumour, ulcer.
gauche *adj* awkward, blundering, bungling, clumsy, inept, tactless, uncouth.
gaudy *adj* bespangled, brilliant, brummagem, cheap, flashy, flaunting, garish, gimcrack, glittering, loud, ostentatious, overdecorated, sham, showy, spurious, tawdry, tinsel.
gauge *vb* calculate, check, determine, weigh; assess, estimate, guess, reckon. * *n* criterion, example, indicator, measure, meter, touchstone, yardstick; bore, depth, height, magnitude, size, thickness, width.
gaunt *adj* angular, attenuated, emaciated, haggard, lank, lean, meagre, scraggy, skinny, slender, spare, thin.
gawky *adj* awkward, boorish, clownish, clumsy, green, loutish, raw, rustic, uncouth, ungainly.
gay *adj* bright, brilliant, dashing, fine, showy; flashy, flaunting, garish, gaudy, glittering, loud, tawdry, tinsel; airy, blithe, blithesome, cheerful, festive, frivolous, frolicsome, gladsome, gleeful, hilarious, jaunty, jolly, jovial, light-hearted, lively, merry, mirthful, sportive, sprightly, vivacious.
gear *vb* adapt, equip, fit, suit, tailor. * *n* apparel, array, clothes, clothing, dress, garb; accoutrements, appliances, appointments, appurtenances, array, harness, goods, movables, subsidiaries; harness, rigging, tackle, trappings; apparatus, machinery, mechanics.
gelid *adj* chill, chilly, cold, freezing, frigid, icy.
gem *n* jewel, stone, treasure.
genealogy *n* ancestry, descent, lineage, pedigree, stock.
general *adj* broad, collective, generic, popular, universal, widespread; catholic, ecumenical; common, current, ordinary, usual; inaccurate, indefinite, inexact, vague.
generally *adv* commonly, extensively, universally, usually.
generate *vb* beget, breed, engender, procreate, propagate, reproduce, spawn; cause, form, make, produce.
generation *n* creation, engendering, formation, procreation, production; age, epoch, era, period, time; breed, children, family, kind, offspring, progeny, race, stock.
generosity *n* disinterestedness, high-mindedness, magnanimity, nobleness; bounteousness, bountifulness, bounty, charity, liberality, openhandedness.
generous *adj* high-minded, honourable, magnanimous, noble; beneficent, bountiful, charitable, free, hospitable, liberal, munificent, openhanded; abundant, ample, copious, plentiful, rich.
genial *adj* cheering, encouraging, enlivening, fostering, inspiring, mild, warm; agreeable, cheerful, cordial, friendly, hearty, jovial, kindly, merry, mirthful, pleasant.
genius *n* aptitude, aptness, bent, capacity, endowment, faculty, flair, gift, talent, turn; brains, creative power, ingenuity, inspiration, intellect, invention, parts, sagacity, wit; adeptness, master, master hand, proficiency; character, disposition, naturalness, nature; deity, demon, spirit.
genteel *adj* aristocratic, courteous, gentlemanly, lady-like, polished, polite, refined, well-bred; elegant, fashionable, graceful, stylish.
gentility *n* civility, courtesy, good breeding, politeness, refinement, urbanity.
gentle *adj* amiable, bland, clement, compassionate, humane, indulgent, kind, kindly, lenient, meek, merciful, mild, moderate, soft, tender, tenderhearted; docile, pacific, peaceable, placid, quiet, tame, temperate, tractable; bland, easy, gradual, light, slight; soft; high-born, noble, well-born; chivalrous, courteous, cultivated, knightly, polished, refined, well-bred.
gentlemanly *adj* civil, complaisant, courteous, cultivated, delicate, genteel, honourable, polite, refined, urbane, well-bred.
genuine *adj* authentic, honest, proper, pure, real, right, true, unadulterated, unalloyed, uncorrupted, veritable; frank, native, sincere, unaffected.
genus *n* class, group, kind, order, race, sort, type.
germ *n* embryo, nucleus, ovule, ovum, seed, seed-bud; bacterium, microbe, microorganism; beginning, cause, origin, rudiment, source.
germane *adj* akin, allied, cognate, related; apposite, appropriate, fitting, pertinent, relevant, suitable.
germinate *vb* bud, burgeon, develop, generate, grow, pollinate, push, shoot, sprout, vegetate.
gesture *vb* indicate, motion, signal, wave. * *n* action, attitude, gesticulation, gesturing, posture, sign, signal.
get *vb* achieve, acquire, attain, earn, gain, obtain, procure, receive, relieve, secure, win; finish, master, prepare; beget, breed, engender, generate, procreate.
gewgaw *n* bauble, gimcrack, gaud, kickshaw, knick-knack, plaything, trifle, toy, trinket.
ghastly *adj* cadaverous, corpse-like, death-like, deathly, ghostly, lurid, pale, pallid, wan; dismal, dreadful, fearful, frightful, grim, grisly, grue-

some, hideous, horrible, shocking, terrible.

ghost *n* soul, spirit; apparition, phantom, revenant, shade, spectre, spook, sprite, wraith.

giant *adj* colossal, enormous, Herculean, huge, large, monstrous, prodigious, vast. * *n* colossus, cyclops, Hercules, monster.

gibberish *n* babble, balderdash, drivel, gabble, gobbledygook, jabber, nonsense, prate, prating.

gibe, jibe *vb* deride, fleer, flout, jeer, mock, ridicule, scoff, sneer, taunt. * *n* ridicule, sneer, taunt.

giddiness *n* dizziness, head-spinning, vertigo.

giddy *adj* dizzy, head-spinning, vertiginous; careless, changeable, fickle, flighty, frivolous, harebrained, headlong, heedless, inconstant, irresolute, light-headed, thoughtless, unsteady, vacillating, wild.

gift *n* alms, allowance, benefaction, bequest, bonus, boon, bounty, contribution, donation, dowry, endowment, favour, grant, gratuity, honorarium, largesse, legacy, offering, premium, present, prize, subscription, subsidy, tip; faculty, talent.

gifted *adj* able, capable, clever, ingenious, intelligent, inventive, sagacious, talented.

gigantic *adj* colossal, Cyclopean, enormous, giant, herculean, huge, immense, prodigious, titanic, tremendous, vast.

giggle *vb, n* cackle, grin, laugh, snigger, snicker, titter.

gild *vb* adorn, beautify, bedeck, brighten, decorate, embellish, grace, illuminate.

gimcrack *adj* flimsy, frail, puny; base, cheap, paltry, poor. * *n* bauble, knick-knack, toy, trifle.

gird *vb* belt, girdle; begird, encircle, enclose, encompass, engird, environ, surround; brace, support. * *n* band, belt, cincture, girdle, girth, sash, waistband.

gist *n* basis, core, essence, force, ground, marrow, meaning, pith, point, substance.

give *vb* accord, bequeath, bestow, confer, devise, entrust, present; afford, contribute, donate, furnish, grant, proffer, spare, supply; communicate, impart; deliver, exchange, pay, requite; allow, permit, vouchsafe; emit, pronounce, render, utter; produce, yield; cause, occasion; apply, devote, surrender; bend, sink, recede, retire, retreat, yield.

glad *adj* delighted, gratified, happy, pleased, rejoicing, well-contented; animated, blithe, cheerful, cheery, elated, gladsome, jocund, joyful, joyous, light, light-hearted, merry, playful, radiant; animating, bright, cheering, exhilarating, gladdening, gratifying, pleasing.

gladden *vb* bless, cheer, delight, elate, enliven, exhilarate, gratify, please, rejoice.

gladiator *n* prize-fighter, sword-player, swordsman.

gladness *n* animation, cheerfulness, delight, gratification, happiness, joy, joyfulness, joyousness, pleasure.

gladsome *adj* airy, blithe, blithesome, cheerful, delighted, frolicsome, glad, gleeful, jocund, jolly, jovial, joyful, joyous, light-hearted, lively, merry, pleased, sportive, sprightly, vivacious.

glamour *n* bewitchment, charm, enchantment, fascination, spell, witchery.

glance *vb* coruscate, gleam, glisten, glister, glitter, scintillate, shine; dart, flit; gaze, glimpse, look, view. * *n* gleam, glitter; gleam, look, view.

glare *vb* dazzle, flame, flare, gleam, glisten, glitter, sparkle; frown, gaze, glower. * *n* flare, glitter.

glaring *adj* dazzling, gleaming, glistening, glittering; barefaced, conspicuous, extreme, manifest, notorious, open.

glassy *adj* brilliant, crystal, crystalline, gleaming, lucent, shining, transparent.

glaze *vb* burnish, calender, furbish, gloss, polish. * *n* coat, enamel, finish, glazing, polish, varnish.

gleam *vb* beam, coruscate, flash, glance, glimmer, glitter, shine, sparkle. * *n* beam, flash, glance, glimmer, glimmering, glow, ray; brightness, coruscation, flashing, gleaming, glitter, glittering, lustre, splendour.

glean *vb* collect, cull, gather, get, harvest, pick, select.

glee *n* exhilaration, fun, gaiety, hilarity, jocularity, jollity, joviality, joy, liveliness, merriment, mirth, sportiveness, verve.

glib *adj* slippery, smooth; artful, facile, flippant, fluent, ready, talkative, voluble.

glide *vb* float, glissade, roll on, skate, skim, slide, slip; flow, lapse, run, roll. * *n* gliding, lapse, sliding, slip.

glimmer *vb* flash, flicker, gleam, glitter, shine, twinkle. * *n* beam, gleam, glimmering, ray; glance, glimpse.

glimpse *vb* espy, look, spot, view. * *n* flash, glance, glimmering, glint, look, sight.

glitter *vb* coruscate, flare, flash, glance, glare, gleam, glisten, glister, scintillate, shine, sparkle. * *n* beam, beaming, brightness, brilliancy, coruscation, gleam, glister, lustre, radiance, scintillation, shine, sparkle, splendour.

gloaming *n* dusk, eventide, nightfall, twilight.

gloat *vb* exult, gaze, rejoice, stare, triumph.

globe *n* ball, earth, orb, sphere.

globular *adj* globate, globated, globe-shaped, globose, globous, round, spheral, spheric, spherical.

globule *n* bead, drop, particle, spherule.

gloom *n* cloud, darkness, dimness, gloominess, obscurity, shade, shadow; cheerlessness, dejection, depression, despondency, downheartedness, dullness, melancholy, sadness.

gloomy *adj* dark, dim, dusky, obscure; cheerless, dismal, lowering, lurid; crestfallen, dejected, depressed, despondent, disheartened, dispirited, downcast, downhearted, glum, melancholy, morose, sad, sullen; depressing, disheartening, dispiriting, heavy, saddening.

glorify *vb* adore, bless, celebrate, exalt, extol, honour, laud, magnify, worship; adorn, brighten, elevate, ennoble, make bright.

glorious *adj* celebrated, conspicuous, distinguished, eminent, excellent, famed, famous, illustrious, pre-eminent, renowned; brilliant, bright, grand, magnificent, radiant, resplendent, splendid; consummate, exalted, high, lofty, noble, supreme.
glory *vb* boast, exult, vaunt. * *n* celebrity, distinction, eminence, fame, honour, illustriousness, praise, renown; brightness, brilliancy, effulgence, lustre, pride, resplendence, splendour; exaltation, exceeding, gloriousness, greatness, grandeur, nobleness; bliss, happiness.
gloss[1] *vb* coat, colour, disguise, extenuate, glaze, palliate, varnish, veneer, veil. * *n* coating, lustre, polish, sheen, varnish, veneer; pretence, pretext.
gloss[2] *vb* annotate, comment, elucidate, explain, interpret. * *n* annotation, comment, commentary, elucidation, explanation, interpretation, note.
glove *n* gantlet, gauntlet, handwear, mitt, mitten; challenge.
glow *vb* incandesce, radiate, shine; blush, burn, flush, redden. * *n* blaze, brightness, brilliance, burning, incandescence, luminosity, reddening; ardour, bloom, enthusiasm, fervency, fervour, flush, impetuosity, vehemence, warmth.
glower *vb* frown, glare, lower, scowl, stare. * *n* frown, glare, scowl.
glum *adj* churlish, crabbed, crestfallen, cross-grained, crusty, depressed, frowning, gloomy, glowering, moody, morose, sour, spleenish, spleeny, sulky, sullen, surly.
glut *vb* block up, cloy, cram, gorge, satiate, stuff. * *n* excess, saturation, surfeit, surplus.
glutinous *adj* adhesive, clammy, cohesive, gluey, gummy, sticky, tenacious, viscid, viscous.
glutton *n* gobbler, gorger, gourmand, gormandizer, greedy-guts, lurcher, pig.
gnarled *adj* contorted, cross-grained, gnarly, knotted, knotty, snaggy, twisted.
go *vb* advance, move, pass, proceed, progress repair; act, operate; be about, extravagate, fare, journey, roam, rove, travel, walk, wend; depart, disappear, cease; elapse, extend, lead, reach, run; avail, concur, contribute, tend, serve; eventuate, fare, turn out; afford, bet, risk, wager. * *n* action, business, case, chance, circumstance, doings, turn; custom, fad, fashion, mode, vogue; energy, endurance, power, stamina, verve, vivacity.
goad *vb* annoy, badger, harass, irritate, sting, worry; arouse, impel, incite, instigate, prod, spur, stimulate, urge. * *n* incentive, incitement, pressure, stimulation.
goal *n* bound, home, limit, mark, mete, post; end, object; aim, design, destination.
gobble *vb* bolt, devour, gorge, gulp, swallow.
goblin *n* apparition, elf, bogey, demon, gnome, hobgoblin, phantom, spectre, sprite.
god *n* almighty, creator, deity, divinity, idol, Jehovah, omnipotence, providence.
godless *adj* atheistic, impious, irreligious, profane, ungodly, wicked.
godlike *adj* celestial, divine, heavenly, supernal.
godly *adj* devout, holy, pious, religious, righteous, saint-like, saintly.
godsend *n* fortune, gift, luck, present, windfall.
golden *adj* aureate, brilliant, bright, gilded, resplendent, shining, splendid; excellent, precious; auspicious, favourable, opportune, propitious; blessed, delightful, glorious, halcyon, happy.
good *adj* advantageous, beneficial, favourable, profitable, serviceable, useful; adequate, appropriate, becoming, convenient, fit, proper, satisfactory, suitable, well-adapted; decorous, dutiful, honest, just, pious, reliable, religious, righteous, true, upright, virtuous, well-behaved, worthy; admirable, capable, excellent, genuine, healthy, precious, sincere, sound, sterling, valid, valuable; benevolent, favourable, friendly, gracious, humane, kind, merciful, obliging, well-disposed; fair, honourable, immaculate, unblemished, unimpeachable, unimpeached, unsullied, untarnished; cheerful, companionable, lively, genial, social; able, competent, dextrous, expert, qualified, ready, skilful, thorough, well-qualified; credit-worthy; agreeable, cheering, gratifying, pleasant. * *n* advantage, benefit, boon, favour, gain, profit, utility; interest, prosperity, welfare, weal; excellence, righteousness, virtue, worth.
good breeding *n* affability, civility, courtesy, good manners, polish, politeness, urbanity.
goodbye *n* adieu, farewell, parting.
goodly *adj* beautiful, comely, good-looking, graceful; agreeable, considerate, desirable, happy, pleasant.
good-natured *adj* amiable, benevolent, friendly, kind, kind-hearted, kindly.
goodness *n* excellence, quality, value, worth; honesty, integrity, morality, principle, probity, righteousness, uprightness, virtue; benevolence, beneficence, benignity, good-will, humaneness, humanity, kindness.
goods *npl* belongings, chattels, effects, furniture, movables; commodities, merchandise, stock, wares.
goodwill *n* benevolence, kindness, good nature; ardour, earnestness, heartiness, willingness, zeal; custom, patronage.
gore *vb* horn, pierce, stab, wound.
gorge[1] *vb* bolt, devour, eat, feed, swallow; cram, fill, glut, gormandize, sate, satiate, stuff, surfeit. * *n* craw, crop, gullet, throat.
gorge[2] *n* canyon, defile, fissure, notch, ravine.
gorgeous *adj* bright, brilliant, dazzling, fine, glittering, grand, magnificent, resplendent, rich, shining, showy, splendid, superb.
Gorgon *n* bugaboo, fright, hobgoblin, hydra, ogre, spectre.
gory *adj* bloody, ensanguined, sanguinary.
gospel *n* creed, doctrine, message, news, revelation, tidings.

gossip *vb* chat, cackle, clack, gabble, prate, prattle, tattle. * *n* babbler, busybody, chatterer, gossipmonger, newsmonger, quidnunc, tale-bearer, tattler, tell-tale; cackle, chat, chit-chat, prate, prattle, tattle.

gourmet *n* connoisseur, epicure, epicurean.

govern *vb* administer, conduct, direct, manage, regulate, reign, rule, superintend, supervise; guide, pilot, steer; bridle, check, command, control, curb, restrain, rule, sway.

government *n* autonomy, command, conduct, control, direction, discipline, dominion, guidance, management, regulation, restraint, rule, rulership, sway; administration, cabinet, commonwealth, polity, sovereignty, state.

governor *n* commander, comptroller, director, head, headmaster, manager, overseer, ruler, superintendent, supervisor; chief magistrate, executive; guardian, instructor, tutor.

grab *vb* capture, clutch, seize, snatch.

grace *vb* adorn, beautify, deck, decorate, embellish; dignify, honour. * *n* benignity, condescension, favour, good-will, kindness, love; devotion, efficacy, holiness, love, piety, religion, sanctity, virtue; forgiveness, mercy, pardon, reprieve; accomplishment, attractiveness, charm, elegance, polish, propriety, refinement; beauty, comeliness, ease, gracefulness, symmetry; blessing, petition, thanks.

graceful *adj* beautiful, becoming, comely, easy, elegant; flowing, natural, rounded, unlaboured; appropriate; felicitous, happy, tactful.

graceless *adj* abandoned, corrupt, depraved, dissolute, hardened, incorrigible, irreclaimable, lost, obdurate, profligate, reprobate, repugnant, shameless,

gracious *adj* beneficent, benevolent, benign, benignant, compassionate, condescending, favourable, friendly, gentle, good-natured, kind, kindly, lenient, merciful, mild, tender; affable, civil, courteous, easy, familiar, polite.

grade *vb* arrange, classify, group, order, rank, sort. * *n* brand, degree, intensity, stage, step, rank; gradient, incline, slope.

gradual *adj* approximate, continuous, gentle, progressive, regular, slow, successive.

graduate *vb* adapt, adjust, proportion, regulate. * *n* alumna, alumnus, laureate, postgraduate.

graft *vb* ingraft, inoculate, insert, transplant. * *n* bud, scion, shoot, slip, sprout; corruption, favouritism, influence, nepotism.

grain *n* kernel, ovule, seed; cereals, corn, grist; atom, bit, glimmer, jot, particle, scintilla, scrap, shadow, spark, tittle, trace, whit; disposition, fibre, humour, temper, texture; colour, dye, hue, shade, stain, texture, tincture, tinge.

granary *n* corn-house, garner, grange, store-house.

grand *adj* august, dignified, elevated, eminent, exalted, great, illustrious, lordly, majestic, princely, stately, sublime; fine, glorious, gorgeous, magnificent, pompous, lofty, noble, splendid, superb; chief, leading, main, pre-eminent, principal, superior.

grandee *n* lord, noble, nobleman.

grandeur *n* elevation, greatness, immensity, impressiveness, loftiness, vastness; augustness, dignity, eminence, glory, magnificence, majesty, nobility, pomp, splendour, state, stateliness.

grandiloquent *adj* bombastic, declamatory, high-minded, high-sounding, inflated, pompous, rhetorical, stilted, swelling, tumid, turgid.

grant *vb* accord, admit, allow, sanction; cede, concede, give, impart, indulge; bestow, confer, deign, invest, vouchsafe; convey, transfer, yield. * *n* admission, allowance, benefaction, bestowal, boon, bounty, concession, donation, endowment, gift, indulgence, largesse, present; conveyance, cession.

graphic *adj* descriptive, diagrammatic, figural, figurative, forcible, lively, pictorial, picturesque, striking, telling, vivid, well-delineated, well-drawn.

grapple *vb* catch, clutch, grasp, grip, hold, hug, seize, tackle, wrestle.

grasp *vb* catch, clasp, clinch, clutch, grapple, grip, seize; comprehend, understand. * *n* clasp, grip, hold; comprehension, power, reach, scope, understanding.

grasping *adj* acquisitive, avaricious, covetous, exacting, greedy, rapacious, sordid, tight-fisted.

grate *vb* abrade, rub, scrape, triturate; comminute, rasp; creak, fret, grind, jar, vex. * *n* bars, grating, latticework, screen; basket, fire bed.

grateful *adj* appreciative, beholden, indebted, obliged, sensible, thankful; pleasant, welcome.

gratification *n* gratifying, indulgence, indulging, pleasing, satisfaction, satisfying; delight, enjoyment, fruition, pleasure, reward.

gratify *vb* delight, gladden, please; humour, fulfil, grant, indulge, requite, satisfy.

gratifying *adj* agreeable, delightful, grateful, pleasing, welcome.

grating *adj* disagreeable, displeasing, harsh, irritating, offensive. * *n* grate, partition.

gratis *adv* freely, gratuitously.

gratitude *n* goodwill, gratitude, indebtedness, thankfulness.

gratuitous *adj* free, spontaneous, unrewarded, voluntary; assumed, baseless, groundless, unfounded, unwarranted, wanton.

gratuity *n* benefaction, bounty, charity, donation, endowment, gift, grant, largesse, present.

grave[1] *n* crypt, mausoleum, ossuary, pit, sepulchre, sepulture, tomb, vault.

grave[2] *adj* cogent, heavy, important, momentous, ponderous, pressing, serious, weighty; dignified, sage, sedate, serious, slow, solemn, staid, thoughtful; dull, grim, plain, quiet, sober, sombre, subdued; cruel, hard, harsh, severe; despicable, dire, dismal, gross, heinous, infamous, outrageous, scandalous, shameful, shocking; heavy, hollow, low, low-pitched, sepulchral.

grave³ *vb* engrave, impress, imprint, infix; carve, chisel, cut, sculpt.

gravel *vb* bewilder, embarrass, nonplus, perplex, pose, puzzle, stagger. * *n* ballast, grit, sand, shingle.

graveyard *n* burial ground, cemetery, churchyard, god's acre, mortuary, necropolis.

gravity *n* heaviness, weight; demureness, sedateness, seriousness, sobriety, thoughtfulness; importance, moment, momentousness, weightiness.

graze *vb* brush, glance, scrape, scratch; abrade, shave, skim; browse, crop, feed, pasture. * *n* abrasion, bruise, scrape, scratch.

great *adj* ample, big, bulky, Cyclopean, enormous, gigantic, Herculean, huge, immense, large, pregnant, vast; decided, excessive, high, much, pronounced; countless, numerous; chief, considerable, grand, important, leading, main, pre-eminent, principal, superior, weighty; celebrated, distinguished, eminent, exalted, excellent, famed, famous, far-famed, illustrious, noted, prominent, renowned; august, dignified, elevated, grand, lofty, majestic, noble, sublime; chivalrous, generous, high-minded, magnanimous; fine, magnificent, rich, sumptuous.

greatness *n* bulk, dimensions, largeness, magnitude, size; distinction, elevation, eminence, fame, importance, renown; augustness, dignity, grandeur, majesty, loftiness, nobility, nobleness, sublimity; chivalry, generosity, magnanimity, spirit.

greed, greediness *n* gluttony, hunger, omnivorousness, ravenousness, voracity; avidity, covetousness, desire, eagerness, longing; avarice, cupidity, graspingness, grasping, rapacity, selfishness.

greedy *adj* devouring, edacious, gluttonous, insatiable, insatiate, rapacious, ravenous, voracious; desirous, eager; avaricious, grasping, selfish.

green *adj* aquamarine, emerald, olive, verdant, verdure, viridescent, viridian; blooming, flourishing, fresh, undecayed; fresh, new, recent; immature, unfledged, unripe; callow, crude, inexpert, ignorant, inexperienced, raw, unskilful, untrained, verdant, young; unseasoned; conservationist, ecological, environmentalist. * *n* common, grass plot, lawn, sward, turf, verdure.

greenhorn *n* beginner, novice, tyro.

greet *vb* accost, address, complement, hail, receive, salute, welcome.

greeting *n* compliment, salutation, salute, welcome.

grief *n* affliction, agony, anguish, bitterness, distress, dole, heartbreak, misery, regret, sadness, sorrow, suffering, tribulation, mourning, woe; grievance, trial; disaster, failure, mishap.

grievance *n* burden, complaint, hardship, injury, oppression, wrong; affliction, distress, grief, sorrow, trial, woe.

grieve *vb* afflict, aggrieve, agonize, discomfort, distress, hurt, oppress, pain, sadden, wound; bewail, deplore, mourn, lament, regret, sorrow, suffer.

grievous *adj* afflicting, afflictive, burdensome, deplorable, distressing, heavy, lamentable, oppressive, painful, sad, sorrowful; baleful, baneful, calamitous, destructive, detrimental, hurtful, injurious, mischievous, noxious, troublesome; aggravated, atrocious, dreadful, flagitious, flagrant, gross, heinous, iniquitous, intense, intolerable, severe, outrageous, wicked.

grill *vb* broil, griddle, roast, toast; sweat; cross-examine, interrogate, question; torment, torture. * *n* grating, gridiron; cross-examination, cross-questioning.

grim *adj* cruel, ferocious, fierce, harsh, relentless, ruthless, savage, stern, unyielding; appalling, dire, dreadful, fearful, frightful, grisly, hideous, horrid, horrible, terrific.

grimace *vb, n* frown, scowl, smirk, sneer.

grime *n* dirt, filth, foulness, smut.

grimy *adj* begrimed, defiled, dirty, filthy, foul, soiled, sullied, unclean.

grind *vb* bruise, crunch, crush, grate, grit, pulverize, rub, triturate; sharpen, whet; afflict, harass, oppress, persecute, plague, trouble. * *n* chore, drudgery, labour, toil.

grip *vb* clasp, clutch, grasp, hold, seize. * *n* clasp, clutch, control, domination, grasp, hold.

grisly *adj* appalling, frightful, dreadful, ghastly, grim, grey, hideous, horrible, horrid, terrible, terrific.

grit *vb* clench, grate, grind. * *n* bran, gravel, pebbles, sand; courage, decision, determination, firmness, perseverance, pluck, resolution, spirit.

groan *vb* complain, lament, moan, whine; creak. * *n* cry, moan, whine; complaint; grouse, grumble.

groom *vb* clean, dress, tidy; brush, tend; coach, educate, nurture, train. * *n* equerry, hostler, manservant, ostler, servant, stable-hand, valet, waiter.

groove *n* channel, cut, furrow, rabbet, rebate, recess, rut, scoring; routine.

gross *vb* accumulate, earn, make. * *adj* big, bulky, burly, fat, great, large; dense, dull, stupid, thick; beastly, broad, carnal, coarse, crass, earthy, impure, indelicate, licentious, low, obscene, unbecoming, unrefined, unseemly, vulgar, rough, sensual; aggravated, brutal, enormous, flagrant, glaring, grievous, manifest, obvious, palpable, plain, outrageous, shameful; aggregate, entire, total, whole. * *n* aggregate, bulk, total, whole.

grossness *n* bigness, bulkiness, greatness; density, thickness; coarseness, ill-breeding, rudeness, vulgarity; bestiality, brutality, carnality, coarseness, impurity, indelicacy, licentiousness, sensuality.

grotesque *adj* bizarre, extravagant, fanciful, fantastic, incongruous, odd, strange, unnatural, whimsical, wild; absurd, antic, burlesque, ludicrous, ridiculous.

ground *vb* fell, place; base, establish, fix, found, set; instruct, train. * *n* area, clod, distance, earth, loam, mould, sod, soil, turf; country, domain, land, region, territory; acres, estate, field, property; base, basis, foundation, groundwork, support; account, consideration, excuse, gist, motive, opinion, reason.

groundless *adj* baseless, causeless, false, gratuitous, idle, unauthorized, unfounded, unjustifiable, unsolicited, unsought, unwarranted.

grounds *npl* deposit, dregs, grouts, lees, precipitate, sediment, settlings; accounts, arguments, considerations, reasons, support; campus, gardens, lawns, premises, yard.

group *vb* arrange, assemble, dispose, order. * *n* aggregation, assemblage, assembly, body, combination, class, clump, cluster, collection, order.

grove *n* copse, glade, spinney, thicket, wood, woodland.

grovel *vb* cower, crawl, creep, cringe, fawn, flatter, sneak.

grovelling *adj* creeping, crouching, squat; abject, base, beggarly, cringing, fawning, low, mean, servile, slavish, sneaking, undignified, unworthy, vile.

grow *vb* enlarge, expand, extend, increase, swell; arise, burgeon, develop, germinate, shoot, sprout, vegetate; advance, extend, improve, progress, thrive, wax; cultivate, produce, raise.

growl *vb* complain, croak, find fault, gnarl, groan, grumble, lament, murmur, snarl. * *n* croak, grown, snarl; complaint.

growth *n* augmentation, development, expansion, extension, growing, increase; burgeoning, excrescence, formation, germination, pollution, shooting, sprouting, vegetation; cultivation, produce, product, production; advance, advancement, development, improvement, progress; adulthood, maturity.

grub *vb* clear, dig, eradicate, root. * *n* caterpillar, larvae, maggot; drudge, plodder.

grudge *vb* begrudge, envy, repine; complain, grieve, murmur. * *n* aversion, dislike, enmity, grievance, hate, hatred, ill-will, malevolence, malice, pique, rancour, resentment, spite, venom.

gruff *adj* bluff, blunt, brusque, churlish, discourteous, grumpy, harsh, impolite, rough, rude, rugged, surly, uncivil, ungracious.

grumble *vb* croak, complain, murmur, repine; gnarl, growl, snarl; roar, rumble. * *n* growl, murmur, complaint, roar, rumble.

grumpy *adj* crabbed, cross, glum, moody, morose, sour, sullen, surly.

guarantee *vb* assure, insure, pledge, secure, warrant. * *n* assurance, pledge, security, surety, warrant, warranty.

guard *vb* defend, keep, patrol, protect, safeguard, save, secure, shelter, shield, watch. * *n* aegis, bulwark, custody, defence, palladium, protection, rampart, safeguard, security, shield; keeper, guardian, patrol, sentinel, sentry, warden, watch, watchman; conduct, convoy, escort; attention, care, caution, circumspection, heed, watchfulness.

guarded *adj* careful, cautious, circumspect, reserved, reticent, wary, watchful.

guardian *n* custodian, defender, guard, keeper, preserver, protector, trustee, warden.

guerdon *n* recompense, remuneration, requital, reward.

guess *vb* conjecture, divine, mistrust, surmise, suspect; fathom, find out, penetrate, solve; believe, fancy, hazard, imagine, reckon, suppose, think. * *n* conjecture, divination, notion, supposition, surmise.

guest *n* caller, company, visitant.

guidance *n* conduct, control, direction, escort, government, lead, leadership, pilotage, steering.

guide *vb* conduct, escort, lead, pilot; control, direct, govern, manage, preside, regulate, rule, steer, superintend, supervise. * *n* cicerone, conductor, director, monitor, pilot; adviser, counsellor, instructor, mentor; clew, directory, index, key, thread; guidebook, itinerary, landmark.

guild *n* association, brotherhood, company, corporation, fellowship, fraternity, society, union.

guile *n* art, artfulness, artifice, craft, cunning, deceit, deception, duplicity, fraud, knavery, ruse, subtlety, treachery, trickery, wiles, wiliness.

guileless *adj* artless, candid, frank, honest, ingenuous, innocent, open, pure, simple-minded, sincere, straightforward, truthful, undesigning, unsophisticated.

guilt *n* blame, criminality, culpability, guiltless; ill-desert, iniquity, offensiveness, wickedness, wrong; crime, offence, sin.

guiltless *adj* blameless, immaculate, innocent, pure, sinless, spotless, unpolluted, unspotted, unsullied, untarnished.

guilty *adj* criminal, culpable, evil, sinful, wicked, wrong.

guise *n* appearance, aspect, costume, dress, fashion, figure, form, garb, manner, mode, shape; air, behaviour, demeanour, mien; cover, custom, disguise, habit, pretence, pretext, practice.

gulf *n* abyss, chasm, opening; bay, inlet; whirlpool.

gull *vb* beguile, cheat, circumvent, cozen, deceive, dupe, hoax, overreach, swindle, trick. * *n* cheat, deception, hoax, imposition, fraud, trick; cat's paw, dupe.

gullibility *n* credulity, naiveness, naivety, overtrustfulness, simplicity, unsophistication.

gullible *adj* confiding, credulous, naive, overtrustful, simple, unsophisticated, unsuspicious.

gumption *n* ability, astuteness, cleverness, capacity, common sense, discernment, penetration, power, sagacity, shrewdness, skill; courage, guts, spirit.

gun *n* blunderbuss, cannon, carbine, firearm, musket, pistol, revolver, rifle, shotgun.

gurgle *vb* babble, bubble, murmur, purl, ripple. * *n*

babbling, murmur, ripple.
gush *vb* burst, flood, flow, pour, rush, spout, stream; emotionalize, sentimentalize. * *n* flow, jet, onrush, rush, spurt, surge; effusion, effusiveness, loquacity, loquaciousness, talkativeness.
gushing *adj* flowing, issuing, rushing; demonstrative, effusive, sentimental.
gust *vb* blast, blow, puff. * *n* blast, blow, squall; burst, fit, outburst, paroxysm.
gusto *n* enjoyment, gust, liking, pleasure, relish, zest.
gusty *adj* blustering, blustery, puffy, squally, stormy, tempestuous, unsteady, windy.
gut *vb* destroy, disembowel, embowel, eviscerate, paunch. * *n* bowels, entrails, intestines, inwards, viscera.
gutter *n* channel, conduit, kennel, pipe, tube.
guttural *adj* deep, gruff, hoarse, thick, throaty.
guy *vb* caricature, mimic, ridicule. * *n* boy, man, person; dowdy, eccentric, fright, scarecrow.
guzzle *vb* carouse, drink, gorge, gormandize, quaff, swill, tipple, tope.
gyrate *vb* revolve, rotate, spin, whirl.

H

habiliment *n* apparel, attire, clothes, costume, dress, garb, garment, habit, raiment, robes, uniform, vesture, vestment.
habit *vb* accoutre, array, attire, clothe, dress, equip, robe. * *n* condition, constitution, temperament; addiction, custom, habitude, manner, practice, rule, usage, way, wont; apparel, costume, dress, garb, habiliment.
habitation *n* abode, domicile, dwelling, headquarters, home, house, lodging, quarters, residence.
habitual *adj* accustomed, common, confirmed, customary, everyday, familiar, inveterate, ordinary, regular, routine, settled, usual, wonted.
habituate *vb* accustom, familiarize, harden, inure, train, use.
habitude *n* custom, practice, usage, wont.
hack[1] *vb* chop, cut, hew, mangle, mutilate, notch; cough, rasp. * *n* cut, cleft, incision, notch; cough, rasp.
hack[2] *vb* ride. * *adj* hired, mercenary; banal, hackneyed, pedestrian, uninspired, unoriginal. * *n* horse, nag, pony; hireling, mercenary; journalist, scribbler, writer.
hackneyed *adj* banal, common, commonplace, overworked, pedestrian, stale, threadbare, trite.
hag *n* beldame, crone, fury, harridan, jezebel, she-monster, shrew, termagant, virago, vixen, witch.
haggard *adj* intractable, refractory, unruly, untamed, wild, wayward; careworn, emaciated, gaunt, ghastly, lank, lean, meagre, raw, spare, thin, wasted, worn.
haggle *vb* argue, bargain, cavil, chaffer, dispute, higgle, stickle; annoy, badger, bait, fret, harass, tease, worry.
hail[1] *vb* acclaim, greet, salute, welcome; accost, address, call, hallo, signal. * *n* greeting, salute.
hail[2] *vb* assail, bombard, rain, shower, storm, volley. * *n* bombardment, rain, shower, storm, volley.
halcyon *adj* calm, golden, happy, palmy, placid, peaceful, quiet, serene, still, tranquil, unruffled, undisturbed.
hale *adj* hardy, healthy, hearty, robust, sound, strong, vigorous, well.
halfwit *n* blockhead, dunce, moron, simpleton.
halfwitted *adj* doltish, dull, dull-witted, feeble-minded, foolish, sappy, shallow, silly, simple, soft, stolid, stupid, thick.
hall *n* chamber, corridor, entrance, entry, hallway, lobby, passage, vestibule; manor, manor-house; auditorium, lecture-room.
halloo *vb* call, cry, shout. * *n* call, cry, hallo, holla, hollo, shout.
hallow *vb* consecrate, dedicate, devote, revere, sanctify, solemnize; enshrine, honour, respect, reverence, venerate.
hallowed *adj* blessed, holy, honoured, revered, sacred.
hallucination *n* blunder, error, fallacy, mistake; aberration, delusion, illusion, phantasm, phantasy, self-deception, vision.
halo *n* aura, aureole, glory, nimbus.
halt[1] *vb* cease, desist, hold, rest, stand, stop. * *n* end, impasse, pause, standstill, stop.
halt[2] *vb* hesitate, pause, stammer, waver; falter, hobble, limp. * *adj* crippled, disabled, lame. * *n* hobble, limp.
hammer *vb* beat, forge, form, shape; excogitate, contrive, invent.
hammer and tongs *adv* earnestly, energetically, resolutely, strenuously, vigorously, zealously.
hamper *vb* bind, clog, confine, curb, embarrass, encumber, entangle, fetter, hinder, impede, obstruct, prevent, restrain, restrict, shackle, trammel. * *n* basket, box, crate, picnic basket; embarrassment, encumbrance, fetter, handicap, impediment, obstruction, restraint, trammel.
hand *vb* deliver, give, present, transmit; conduct, guide, lead. * *n* direction, part, side; ability, dexterity, faculty, skill, talent; course, inning, management, turn; agency, intervention, participation, share; control, possession, power; artificer, artisan, craftsman, employee, labourer, operative, workman; index, indicator, pointer; chirography, handwriting.
handbook *n* guidebook, manual.
handcuff *vb* bind, fetter, manacle, shackle. * *n* fetter, manacle, shackle.
handful *n* fistful, maniple, smattering.
handicap *vb* encumber, hamper, hinder, restrict. * *n* disadvantage, encumbrance, hampering, hindrance, restriction.
handicraft *n* hand manufacture, handwork, workmanship.
handle *vb* feel, finger, manhandle, paw, touch; direct, manage, manipulate, use, wield; discourse, discuss, treat. * *n* haft, helve, hilt, stock.
handsome *adj* admirable, comely, fine-looking, stately, well-formed, well-proportioned; appropriate, suitable, becoming, easy, graceful; gener-

ous, gracious, liberal, magnanimous, noble; ample, large, plentiful, sufficient.

handy *adj* adroit, clever, dextrous, expert, ready, skilful, skilled; close, convenient, near.

hang *vb* attach, swing; execute, truss; decline, drop, droop, incline; adorn, drape; dangle, depend, impend, suspend; rely; cling, loiter, rest, stick; float, hover, pay.

hangdog *adj* ashamed, base, blackguard, low, villainous, scurvy, sneaking.

hanger-on *n* dependant, minion, parasite, vassal.

hanker *vb* covet, crave, desire, hunger, long, lust, want, yearn.

hap *n* accident, chance, fate, fortune, lot.

haphazard *adj* aimless, chance, random.

hapless *adj* ill-fated, ill-starred, luckless, miserable, unfortunate, unhappy, unlucky, wretched.

happen *vb* befall, betide, chance, come, occur.

happily *adv* fortunately, luckily; agreeably, delightfully, prosperously, successfully.

happiness *n* brightness, cheerfulness, delight, gaiety, joy, light-heartedness, merriment, pleasure; beatitude, blessedness, bliss, felicity, enjoyment, welfare, well-being.

happy *adj* blessed, blest, blissful, cheerful, contented, joyful, joyous, light-hearted, merry; charmed, delighted, glad, gladdened, gratified, pleased; fortunate, lucky, prosperous, successful; able, adroit, apt, dextrous, expert, ready, skilful; befitting, felicitous, opportune, pertinent, seasonable, well-timed; auspicious, bright, favourable, propitious.

harangue *vb* address, declaim, spout. * *n* address, bombast, declamation, oration, rant, screed, speech, tirade.

harass *vb* exhaust, fag, fatigue, jade, tire, weary; annoy, badger, distress, gall, heckle, disturb, harry, molest, pester, plague, tantalize, tease, torment, trouble, vex, worry.

harbour *vb* protect, lodge, shelter; cherish, entertain, foster, indulge. * *n* asylum, cover, refuge, resting place, retreat, sanctuary, shelter; anchorage, destination, haven, port.

hard *adj* adamantine, compact, firm, flinty, impenetrable, marble, rigid, solid, resistant, stony, stubborn, unyielding; difficult, intricate, knotty, perplexing, puzzling; arduous, exacting, fatiguing, laborious, toilsome, wearying; austere, callous, cruel, exacting, hard-hearted, incorrigible, inflexible, insensible, insensitive, obdurate, oppressive, reprobate, rigorous, severe, unfeeling, unkind, unsusceptible, unsympathetic, unyielding, untender; calamitous, disagreeable, distressing, grievous, painful, unpleasant; acid, alcoholic, harsh, rough, sour; excessive, intemperate. * *adv* close, near; diligently, earnestly, energetically, incessantly, laboriously; distressfully, painfully, rigorously, severely; forcibly, vehemently, violently.

harden *vb* accustom, discipline, form, habituate, inure, season, train; brace, fortify, indurate, nerve, steel, stiffen, strengthen.

hardened *adj* annealed, case-hardened, tempered, indurated; abandoned, accustomed, benumbed, callous, confirmed, deadened, depraved, habituated, impenitent, incorrigible, inured, insensible, irreclaimable, lost, obdurate, reprobate, seared, seasoned, steeled, trained, unfeeling.

hard-headed *adj* astute, collected, cool, intelligent, sagacious, shrewd, well-balanced, wise.

hardhearted *adj* cruel, fell, implacable, inexorable, merciless, pitiless, relentless, ruthless, unfeeling, uncompassionate, unmerciful, unpitying, unrelenting.

hardihood *n* audacity, boldness, bravery, courage, decision, firmness, fortitude, intrepidity, manhood, mettle, pluck, resolution, stoutness; assurance, audacity, brass, effrontery, impudence.

hardly *adv* barely, scarcely; cruelly, harshly, rigorously, roughly, severely, unkindly.

hardship *n* fatigue, toil, weariness; affliction, burden, calamity, grievance, hardness, injury, misfortune, privation, suffering, trial, trouble.

hardy *adj* enduring, firm, hale, healthy, hearty, inured, lusty, rigorous, robust, rugged, sound, stout, strong, sturdy, tough; bold, brave, courageous, daring, heroic, intrepid, manly, resolute, stout-hearted, valiant.

harebrained *adj* careless, changeable, flighty, giddy, harum-scarum, headlong, heedless, rash, reckless, unsteady, volatile, wild.

hark *interj* attend, hear, hearken, listen.

harlequin *n* antic, buffoon, clown, droll, fool, jester, punch, fool.

harm *vb* damage, hurt, injure, scathe; abuse, desecrate, ill-use, ill-treat, maltreat, molest. * *n* damage, detriment, disadvantage, hurt, injury, mischief, misfortune, prejudice, wrong.

harmful *adj* baneful, detrimental, disadvantageous, hurtful, injurious, mischievous, noxious, pernicious, prejudicial.

harmless *adj* innocent, innocuous, innoxious; inoffensive, safe, unoffending.

harmonious *adj* concordant, consonant, harmonic; dulcet, euphonious, mellifluous, melodious, musical, smooth, tuneful; comfortable, congruent, consistent, correspondent, orderly, symmetrical; agreeable, amicable, brotherly, cordial, fraternal, friendly, neighbourly.

harmonize *vb* adapt, attune, reconcile, unite; accord, agree, blend, chime, comport, conform, correspond, square, sympathize, tally, tune.

harmony *n* euphony, melodiousness, melody; accord, accordance, agreement, chime, concord, concordance, consonance, order, unison; adaptation, congruence, congruity, consistency, correspondence, fairness, smoothness, suitableness; amity, friendship, peace.

harness *vb* hitch, tackle. * *n* equipment, gear, tackle, tackling; accoutrements, armour, array, mail, mounting.

harp *vb* dwell, iterate, reiterate, renew, repeat.

harping *n* dwelling, iteration, reiteration, repetition.

harrow *vb* harass, lacerate, rend, tear, torment, torture, wound.

harry *vb* devastate, pillage, plunder, raid, ravage, rob; annoy, chafe, disturb, fret, gall, harass, harrow, incommode, pester, plague, molest, tease, torment, trouble, vex, worry.

harsh *adj* acid, acrid, astringent, biting, caustic, corrosive, crabbed, rough, sharp, sour, tart; cacophonous, discordant, grating, jarring, metallic, raucous, strident, unmelodious; abusive, austere, crabbed, crabby, cruel, disagreeable, hard, ill-natured, ill-tempered, morose, rigorous, severe, stern, unfeeling; bearish, bluff, blunt, brutal, gruff, rude, uncivil, ungracious.

harshness *n* roughness; acerbity, asperity, austerity, churlishness, crabbedness, hardness, ill-nature, ill-temper, moroseness, rigour, severity, sternness, unkindness; bluffness, bluntness, churlishness, gruffness, incivility, ungraciousness, rudeness.

harum-scarum *adj* hare-brained, precipitate, rash, reckless, volatile, wild.

harvest *vb* gather, glean, reap. * *n* crops, produce, yield; consequence, effect, issue, outcome, produce, result.

haste *n* alacrity, celerity, dispatch, expedition, nimbleness, promptitude, quickness, rapidity, speed, urgency, velocity; flurry, hurry, hustle, impetuosity, precipitateness, precipitation, press, rashness, rush, vehemence.

hasten *vb* haste, hurry; accelerate, dispatch, expedite, precipitate, press, push, quicken, speed, urge.

hasty *adj* brisk, fast, fleet, quick, rapid, speedy, swift; cursory, hurried, passing, slight, superficial; ill-advised, rash, reckless; headlong, helter-skelter, pell-mell, precipitate; abrupt, choleric, excitable, fiery, fretful, hot-headed, irascible, irritable, passionate, peevish, peppery, pettish, petulant, testy, touchy, waspish.

hatch *vb* brew, concoct, contrive, excogitate, design, devise, plan, plot, project, scheme; breed, incubate.

hate *vb* abhor, abominate, detest, dislike, execrate, loathe, nauseate. * *n* abomination, animosity, antipathy, detestation, dislike, enmity, execration, hatred, hostility, loathing.

hateful *adj* malevolent, malicious, malign, malignant, rancorous, spiteful; abhorrent, abominable, accursed, damnable, detestable, execrable, horrid, odious, shocking; disgusting, foul, loathsome, nauseous, obnoxious, offensive, repellent, repugnant, repulsive, revolting, vile.

hatred *n* animosity, enmity, hate, hostility, ill-will, malevolence, malice, malignity, odium, rancour; abhorrence, abomination, antipathy, aversion, detestation, disgust, execration, horror, loathing, repugnance, revulsion.

haughtiness *n* arrogance, contempt, contemptuousness, disdain, hauteur, insolence, loftiness, pride, self-importance, snobbishness, stateliness, superciliousness.

haughty *adj* arrogant, assuming, contemptuous, disdainful, imperious, insolent, lofty, lordly, overbearing, overweening, proud, scornful, snobbish, supercilious.

haul *vb* drag, draw, lug, pull, tow, trail, tug. * *n* heaving, pull, tug; booty, harvest, takings, yield.

haunt *vb* frequent, resort; follow, importune; hover, inhabit, obsess. * *n* den, resort, retreat.

hauteur *n* arrogance, contempt, contemptuousness, disdain, haughtiness, insolence, loftiness, pride, self-importance, stateliness, superciliousness.

have *vb* cherish, exercise, experience, keep, hold, occupy, own, possess; acquire, gain, get, obtain, receive; accept, take.

haven *n* asylum, refuge, retreat, shelter; anchorage, harbour, port.

havoc *n* carnage, damage, desolation, destruction, devastation, ravage, ruin, slaughter, waste, wreck.

hawk-eyed *adj* eagle-eyed, sharp-sighted.

hazard *vb* adventure, risk, venture; endanger, imperil, jeopardize. * *n* accident, casualty, chance, contingency, event, fortuity, stake; danger, jeopardy, peril, risk, venture.

hazardous *adj* dangerous, insecure, perilous, precarious, risky, uncertain, unsafe.

haze *n* fog, har, mist, smog; cloud, dimness, fume, miasma, obscurity, pall.

hazy *adj* foggy, misty; cloudy, dim, nebulous, obscure; confused, indefinite, indistinct, uncertain, vague.

head *vb* command, control, direct, govern, guide, lead, rule; aim, point, tend; beat, excel, outdo, precede, surpass. * *adj* chief, first, grand, highest, leading, main, principal; adverse, contrary. * *n* acme, summit, top; beginning, commencement, origin, rise, source; chief, chieftain, commander, director, leader, master, principal, superintendent, superior; intellect, mind, thought, understanding; branch, category, class, department, division, section, subject, topic; brain, crown, headpiece, intellect, mind, thought, understanding; cape, headland, point, promontory.

headiness *n* hurry, precipitation, rashness; obstinacy, stubbornness.

headless *adj* acephalous, beheaded; leaderless, undirected; headstrong, heady, imprudent, obstinate, rash, senseless, stubborn.

headlong *adj* dangerous, hasty, heady, impulsive, inconsiderate, perilous, precipitate, rash, reckless, ruinous, thoughtless; perpendicular, precipitous, sheer, steep. * *adv* hastily, headfirst, helter-skelter, hurriedly, precipitately, rashly, thoughtlessly.

headstone *n* cornerstone, gravestone.

headstrong *adj* cantankerous, cross-grained, dogged, forward, headless, heady, intractable, obstinate, self-willed, stubborn, ungovernable, unruly, violent, wayward.

heady *adj* hasty, headlong, impetuous, impulsive, inconsiderate, precipitate, rash, reckless, rushing, stubborn, thoughtless; exciting, inebriating, inflaming, intoxicating, spirituous, strong.

heal *vb* amend, cure, remedy, repair, restore; compose, harmonize, reconcile, settle, soothe.

healing *adj* curative, palliative, remedial, restoring, restorative; assuaging, assuasive, comforting, composing, gentle, lenitive, mild, soothing.

health *n* healthfulness, robustness, salubrity, sanity, soundness, strength, tone, vigour.

healthy *adj* active, hale, hearty, lusty, sound, vigorous, well; bracing, healthful, health-giving, hygienic, invigorating, nourishing, salubrious, salutary, wholesome.

heap *vb* accumulate, augment, amass, collect, overfill, pile up, store. * *n* accumulation, collection, cumulus, huddle, lot, mass, mound, pile, stack.

hear *vb* eavesdrop, hearken, heed, listen, overhear; ascertain, discover, gather, learn, understand; examine, judge.

heart *n* bosom, breast; centre, core, essence, interior, kernel, marrow, meaning, pith; affection, benevolence, character, disposition, feeling, inclination, love, mind, passion, purpose, will; affections, ardour, emotion, feeling, love; boldness, courage, fortitude, resolution, spirit.

heartache *n* affliction, anguish, bitterness, distress, dole, grief, heartbreak, sorrow, woe.

heartbroken *adj* broken-hearted, cheerless, comfortless, desolate, disconsolate, forlorn, inconsolable, miserable, woebegone, wretched.

hearten *vb* animate, assure, cheer, comfort, console, embolden, encourage, enhearten, incite, inspire, inspirit, reassure, stimulate.

heartfelt *adj* cordial, deep, deep-felt, hearty, profound, sincere, warm.

hearth *n* fireplace, fireside, forge, hearthstone.

heartily *adv* abundantly, completely, cordially, earnestly, freely, largely, sincerely, vigorously.

heartless *adj* brutal, cold, cruel, hard, harsh, merciless, pitiless, unfeeling, unsympathetic; spiritless, timid, timorous, uncourageous.

heart-rending *adj* affecting, afflicting, anguishing, crushing, distressing.

hearty *adj* cordial, deep, earnest, fervent, heartfelt, profound, sincere, true, unfeigned, warm; active, animated, energetic, fit, vigorous, zealous; convivial, hale, healthy, robust, sound, strong, warm; abundant, full, heavy; nourishing, nutritious, rich.

heat *vb* excite, flush, inflame; animate, rouse, stimulate, stir. * *n* calorie, caloricity, torridity, warmth; excitement, fever, flush, impetuosity, passion, vehemence, violence; ardour, earnestness, fervency, fervour, glow, intensity, zeal; exasperation, fierceness, frenzy, rage.

heath *n* field, moor, wasteland, plain.

heathen *adj* animist, animistic; pagan, paganical, paganish, paganistic, unconverted; agnostic, atheist, atheistic, gentile, idolatrous, infidel, irreligious; barbarous, cruel, inhuman, savage. * *n* atheist, gentile, idolater, idolatress, infidel, pagan, unbeliever; barbarian, philistine, savage.

heave *vb* elevate, hoist, lift, raise; breathe, exhale; cast, fling, hurl, send, throw, toss; dilate, expand, pant, rise, swell; retch, throw up; strive, struggle.

heaven *n* empyrean, firmament, sky, welkin; bliss, ecstasy, elysium, felicity, happiness, paradise, rapture, transport.

heavenly *adj* celestial, empyreal, ethereal; angelic, beatific, beatified, cherubic, divine, elysian, glorious, god-like, sainted, saintly, seraphic; blissful, delightful, divine, ecstatic, enrapturing, enravishing, exquisite, golden, rapturous, ravishing, exquisite, transporting.

heaviness *n* gravity, heft, ponderousness, weight; grievousness, oppressiveness, severity; dullness, languor, lassitude, sluggishness, stupidity; dejection, depression, despondency, gloom, melancholy, sadness, seriousness.

heavy *adj* grave, hard, onerous, ponderous, weighty; afflictive, burdensome, crushing, cumbersome, grievous, oppressive, severe, serious; dilatory, dull, inactive, inanimate, indolent, inert, lifeless, listless, sleepy, slow, sluggish, stupid, torpid; chapfallen, crestfallen, crushed, depressed, dejected, despondent, disconsolate, downhearted, gloomy, low-spirited, melancholy, sad, sobered, sorrowful; difficult, laborious; tedious, tiresome, wearisome, weary; burdened, encumbered, loaded; clammy, clayey, cloggy, ill-raised, miry, muddy, soggy; boisterous, deep, energetic, loud, roaring, severe, stormy, strong, tempestuous, violent; cloudy, dark, dense, gloomy, lowering, overcast.

hebetate *adj* blunt; dull, obtuse, sluggish, stupid, stupefied.

hectic *adj* animated, excited, fevered, feverish, flushed, heated, hot.

hector *vb* bluster, boast, bully, menace, threaten; annoy, fret, harass, harry, irritate, provoke, tease, vex, worry. * *n* blusterer, bully, swaggerer.

hedge *vb* block, encumber, hinder, obstruct, surround; enclose, fence, fortify, guard, protect; disappear, dodge, evade, hide, skulk, temporize. * *n* barrier, hedgerow, fence, limit.

heed *vb* attend, consider, mark, mind, note, notice, observe, regard. * *n* attention, care, carefulness, caution, circumspection, consideration, heedfulness, mindfulness, notice, observation, regard, wariness, vigilance, watchfulness.

heedful *adj* attentive, careful, cautious, circumspect, mindful, observant, observing, provident, regardful, watchful, wary.

heedless *adj* careless, inattentive, neglectful, negligent, precipitate, rash, reckless, thoughtless, unmindful, unminding, unobserving, unobservant.

heft *n* handle, haft, helve; bulk, weight.

hegemony *n* ascendancy, authority, headship, leadership, predominance, preponderance, rule.

height *n* altitude, elevation, tallness; acme, apex, climax, eminence, head, meridian, pinnacle, summit, top, vertex, zenith; eminence, hill, mountain; dignity, exaltation, grandeur, loftiness, perfection.

heighten *vb* elevate, raise; ennoble, exalt, magnify, make greater; augment, enhance, improve, increase, strengthen; aggravate, intensify.

heinous *adj* aggravated, atrocious, crying, enormous, excessive, flagitious, flagrant, hateful, infamous, monstrous, nefarious, odious, villainous.

heir *n* child, inheritor, offspring, product.

helical *adj* screw-shaped, spiral, winding.

hellish *adj* abominable, accursed, atrocious, curst, damnable, damned, demoniacal, detestable, devilish, diabolical, execrable, fiendish, infernal, monstrous, nefarious, satanic.

helm *n* rudder, steering-gear, tiller, wheel; command, control, direction, rein, rule.

help *vb* relieve, save, succour; abet, aid, assist, back, cooperate, second, serve, support, sustain, wait; alleviate, ameliorate, better, cure, heal, improve, remedy, restore; control, hinder, prevent, repress, resist, withstand; avoid, forbear, control. * *n* aid, assistance, succour, support; relief, remedy; assistant, helper, servant.

helper *adj* aider, abettor, ally, assistant, auxiliary, coadjutor, colleague, helpmate, partner, supporter.

helpful *adj* advantageous, assistant, auxiliary, beneficial, contributory, convenient, favourable, kind, profitable, serviceable, useful.

helpless *adj* disabled, feeble, imbecile, impotent, infirm, powerless, prostrate, resourceless, weak; abandoned, defenceless, exposed, unprotected; desperate, irremediable, remediless.

helpmate *n* companion, consort, husband, partner, wife; aider, assistant, associate, helper.

helter-skelter *adj* disorderly, headlong, irregular, pell-mell, precipitate. * *adv* confusedly, hastily, headlong, higgledy-piggledy, pell-mell, precipitately, wildly.

hem *vb* border, edge, skirt; beset, confine, enclose, environ, surround, sew; hesitate. * *n* border, edge, trim.

henchman *n* attendant, follower, retainer, servant, supporter.

herald *vb* announce, proclaim, publish. * *n* announcer, crier, publisher; harbinger, precursor, proclaimer.

heraldry *n* blazonry, emblazonry.

herbage *n* greenery, herb, pasture, plants, vegetation.

herculean *adj* able-bodied, athletic, brawny, mighty, muscular, powerful, puissant, sinewy, stalwart, strong, sturdy, vigorous; dangerous, difficult, hard, laborious, perilous, toilsome, troublesome; colossal, Cyclopean, gigantic, great, large, strapping.

herd *vb* drive, gather, lead, tend; assemble, associate, flock. * *n* drover, herder, herdsman, shepherd; crowd, multitude, populace, rabble; assemblage, assembly, collection, drove, flock, pack.

hereditary *adj* ancestral, inheritable, inherited, patrimonial, transmitted.

heresy *n* dissent, error, heterodoxy, impiety, recusancy, unorthodoxy.

heretic *n* dissenter, dissident, nonconformist, recusant, schismatic, sectarian, sectary, separatist, unbeliever.

heretical *adj* heterodox, impious, schismatic, schismatical, sectarian, unorthodox.

heritage *n* estate, inheritance, legacy, patrimony, portion.

hermetic *adj* airtight, impervious; cabbalistic, emblematic, emblematical, magical, mysterious, mystic, mystical, occult, secret, symbolic, symbolical.

hermit *n* anchoress, anchoret, anchorite, ascetic, eremite, monk, recluse, solitaire, solitary.

heroic *adj* bold, brave, courageous, daring, dauntless, fearless, gallant, illustrious, intrepid, magnanimous, noble, valiant; desperate, extravagant, extreme, violent.

heroism *n* boldness, bravery, courage, daring, endurance, fearlessness, fortitude, gallantry, intrepidity, prowess, valour.

hesitate *vb* boggle, delay, demur, doubt, pause, scruple, shilly-shally, stickle, vacillate, waver; falter, stammer, stutter.

hesitation *n* halting, misgiving, reluctance; delay, doubt, indecision, suspense, uncertainty, vacillation; faltering, stammering, stuttering.

heterodox *adj* heretical, recusant, schismatic, unorthodox, unsound; apocryphal, uncanonical.

heterogeneous *adj* contrasted, contrary, different, dissimilar, diverse, incongruous, indiscriminate, miscellaneous, mixed, opposed, unhomogeneous, unlike.

hew *vb* chop, cut, fell, hack; fashion, form, shape, smooth.

hiatus *n* blank, break, chasm, gap, interval, lacuna, opening, rift.

hidden *adj* blind, clandestine, cloaked, close, concealed, covered, covert, enshrouded, latent, masked, occult, private, secluded, secret, suppressed, undiscovered, veiled; abstruse, cabbalistic, cryptic, dark, esoteric, hermetic, inward, mysterious, mystic, mystical, obscure, oracular, recondite.

hide *vb* bury, conceal, cover, secrete, suppress, withhold; cloak, disguise, eclipse, hoard, mask, screen, shelter, veil.

hideous *adj* abominable, appalling, awful, dreadful, frightful, ghastly, ghoulish, grim, grisly, horrible, horrid, repulsive, revolting, shocking, terrible, terrifying.

hie *vb* hasten, speed.

hieratic *adj* consecrated, devoted, priestly, sacred, sacerdotal.
hieroglyph *n* picture-writing, rebus, sign, symbol.
hieroglyphic *adj* emblematic, emblematical, figurative, obscure, symbolic, symbolical.
higgle *vb* hawk, peddle; bargain, chaffer, haggle, negotiate.
higgledy-piggledy *adj* chaotic, confused, disorderly, jumbled. * *adv* confusedly, in disorder, helter-skelter, pell-mell.
high *adj* elevated, high-reaching, lofty, soaring, tall, towering; distinguished, eminent, pre-eminent, prominent, superior; admirable, dignified, exalted, great, noble; arrogant, haughty, lordly, proud, supercilious; boisterous, strong, tumultuous, turbulent, violent; costly, dear, pricey; acute, high-pitched, high-toned, piercing, sharp, shrill; tainted, malodorous. * *adv* powerfully, profoundly; eminently, loftily; luxuriously, richly.
high-flown *adj* elevated, presumptuous, proud, lofty, swollen; extravagant, high-coloured, lofty, overdrawn, overstrained; bombastic, inflated, pompous, pretentious, strained, swollen, turgid.
high-handed *adj* arbitrary, despotic, dictatorial, domineering, oppressive, overbearing, self-willed, violent, wilful.
highly strung *adj* ardent, excitable, irascible, nervous, quick, tense; high-spirited, sensitive.
high-minded *adj* arrogant, haughty, lofty, proud; elevated, high-toned; generous honourable, magnanimous, noble, spiritual.
highwayman *n* bandit, brigand, footpad, freebooter, marauder, outlaw, robber.
hilarious *adj* boisterous, cheerful, comical, convivial, riotous, uproarious, jovial, joyful, merry, mirthful, noisy.
hilarity *n* cheerfulness, conviviality, exhilarated, gaiety, glee, jollity, joviality, joyousness, merriment, mirth.
hill *n* ascent, ben, elevation, eminence, hillock, knoll, mount, mountain, rise, tor.
hind *adj* back, hinder, hindmost, posterior, rear, rearward.
hinder *vb* bar, check, clog, delay, embarrass, encumber, impede, interrupt, obstruct, oppose, prevent, restrain, retard, stop, thwart.
hindrance *n* check, deterrent, encumbrance, hitch, impediment, interruption, obstacle, obstruction, restraint, stop, stoppage.
hinge *vb* depend, hang, rest, turn.
hint *vb* allude, glance, imply, insinuate, intimate, mention, refer, suggest. * *n* allusion, clue, implication, indication, innuendo, insinuation, intimation, mention, reminder, suggestion, taste, trace.
hire *vb* buy, rent, secure; charter, employ, engage, lease, let. * *n* allowance, bribe, compensation, pay, remuneration, rent, reward, salary, stipend, wages.
hireling *n* employee, mercenary, myrmidon.
hirsute *adj* bristled, bristly, hairy, shaggy; boorish, course, ill-bred, loutish, rough, rude, rustic, uncouth, unmannerly.
hiss *vb* shrill, sibilate, whistle, whir, whiz; condemn, damn, ridicule. * *n* fizzle, hissing, sibilant, sibilation, sizzle.
historian *n* annalist, autobiographer, biographer, chronicler, narrator, recorder.
history *n* account, autobiography, annals, biography, chronicle, genealogy, memoirs, narration, narrative, recital, record, relation, story.
hit *vb* discomfit, hurt, knock, strike; accomplish, achieve, attain, gain, reach, secure, succeed, win; accord, fit, suit; beat, clash, collide, contact, smite. * *n* blow, collision, strike, stroke; chance, fortune, hazard, success, venture.
hitch *vb* catch, impede, stick, stop; attach, connect, fasten, harness, join, tether, tie, unite, yoke. * *n* catch, check, hindrance, impediment, interruption, obstacle; knot, noose.
hoar *adj* ancient, grey, hoary, old, white.
hoard *vb* accumulate, amass, collect, deposit, garner, hive, husband, save, store, treasure. * *n* accumulation, collection, deposit, fund, mass, reserve, savings, stockpile, store.
hoarse *adj* discordant, grating, gruff, guttural, harsh, husky, low, raucous, rough.
hoary *adj* grey, hoar, silvery, white; ancient, old, venerable.
hoax *vb* deceive, dupe, fool, gammon, gull, hoodwink, swindle, trick. * *n* canard, cheat, deception, fraud, humbug, imposition, imposture, joke, trick, swindle.
hobble *vb* falter, halt, hop, limp; fasten, fetter, hopple, shackle, tie. * *n* halt, limp; clog, fetter, shackle; embarrassment, difficulty, perplexity, pickle, strait.
hobgoblin *n* apparition, bogey, bugbear, goblin, imp, spectre, spirit, sprite.
hobnail *n* bumpkin, churl, clodhopper, clown, lout, rustic.
hocus-pocus *n* cheater, impostor, juggler, sharper, swindler, trickster; artifice, cheat, deceit, deception, delusion, hoax, imposition, juggle, trick.
hodgepodge *n* farrago, hash, hotchpotch, jumble, medley, miscellany, mixture, ragout, stew.
hog *n* beast, glutton, pig; grunter, porker, swine.
hoggish *adj* brutish, filthy, gluttonish, piggish, swinish; grasping, greedy, mean, selfish, sordid.
hoist *vb* elevate, heave, lift, raise, rear. * *n* elevator, lift.
hold *vb* clasp, clinch, clutch, grasp, grip, seize; have, keep, occupy, possess, retain; bind, confine, control, detain, imprison, restrain, restrict; connect, fasten, fix, lock; arrest, check, stay, stop, suspend, withhold; continue, keep up, maintain, manage, prosecute, support, sustain; cherish, embrace, entertain; account, believe, consider, count, deem, entertain, esteem, judge, reckon, regard, think; accommodate, admit, carry, contain, receive, stow; assemble, conduct, convene; endure, last, persist, remain; adhere, cleave, cling, cohere, stick. * *n* anchor, bite, clasp, control,

embrace, foothold, grasp, grip, possession, retention, seizure; prop, stay, support; claim, footing, vantage point; castle, fort, fortification, fortress, stronghold, tower; locker, storage, storehouse.

hole *n* aperture, opening, perforation; abyss, bore, cave, cavern, cavity, chasm, depression, excavation, eye, hollow, pit, pore, void; burrow, cover, lair, retreat; den, hovel, kennel.

holiday *n* anniversary, celebration, feast, festival, festivity, fete, gala, recess, vacation.

holiness *n* blessedness, consecration, devotion, devoutness, godliness, piety, purity, religiousness, righteousness, sacredness, saintliness, sanctity, sinlessness.

hollow *vb* dig, excavate, groove, scoop. * *adj* cavernous, concave, depressed, empty, sunken, vacant, void; deceitful, faithless, false, false-hearted, hollow-hearted, hypocritical, insincere, pharisaical, treacherous, unfeeling; deep, low, muffled, reverberating, rumbling, sepulchral. * *n* basin, bowl, depression; cave, cavern, cavity, concavity, dent, dimple, dint, depression, excavation, hole, pit; canal, channel, cup, dimple, dig, groove, pocket, sag.

holocaust *n* carnage, destruction, devastation, genocide, massacre.

holy *adj* blessed, consecrated, dedicated, devoted, hallowed, sacred, sanctified; devout, godly, pious, pure, religious, righteous, saintlike, saintly, sinless, spiritual.

homage *n* allegiance, devotion, fealty, fidelity, loyalty; court, deference, duty, honour, obeisance, respect, reverence, service; adoration, devotion, worship.

home *adj* domestic, family; close, direct, effective, penetrating, pointed. * *n* abode, dwelling, seat, quarters, residence.

homely *adj* domestic, familiar, house-like; coarse, commonplace, homespun, inelegant, plain, simple, unattractive, uncomely, unpolished, unpretentious.

homespun *adj* coarse, homely, inelegant, plain, rude, rustic, unpolished.

homicide *n* manslaughter, murder.

homily *n* address, discourse, lecture, sermon.

homogeneous *adj* akin, alike, cognate, kindred, similar, uniform.

honest *adj* equitable, fair, faithful, honourable, open, straight, straightforward; conscientious, equitable, reliable, sound, square, true, trustworthy, trusty, uncorrupted, upright, virtuous; above-board, faithful, genuine, thorough, unadulterated; creditable, decent, proper, reputable, respectable, suitable; chaste, decent; candid, direct, frank, ingenuous, sincere, unreserved.

honesty *n* equity, fairness, faithfulness, fidelity, honour, integrity, justice, probity, trustiness, trustworthiness, uprightness; truth, truthfulness, veracity; genuineness, thoroughness; candour, frankness, ingenuousness, openness, sincerity, straightforwardness, unreserve.

honorary *adj* formal, nominal, titular, unofficial, unpaid.

honour *vb* dignify, exalt, glorify, grace; respect, revere, reverence, venerate; adore, hallow, worship; celebrate, commemorate, keep, observe. * *n* civility, deference, esteem, homage, respect, reverence, veneration; dignity, distinction, elevation, nobleness; consideration, credit, fame, glory, reputation; high-mindedness, honesty, integrity, magnanimity, probity, uprightness; chastity, purity, virtue; boast, credit, ornament, pride.

honourable *adj* elevated, famous, great, illustrious, noble; admirable, conscientious, fair, honest, just, magnanimous, true, trustworthy, upright, virtuous, worshipful; creditable, esteemed, estimable, equitable, proper, respected, reputable, right.

honours *npl* dignities, distinctions, privilege, titles; adornments, beauties, decorations, glories; civilities.

hood *n* capuche, coif, cover, cowl, head.

hoodwink *vb* blind, blindfold; cloak, conceal, cover, hide; cheat, circumvent, cozen, deceive, delete, dupe, fool, gull, impose, overreach, trick.

hook *vb* catch, ensnare, entrap, hasp, snare; bend, curve. * *n* catch, clasp, fastener, hasp; snare, trap; cutter, grass-hook, reaper, reaping-hook, sickle.

hooked *adj* aquiline, bent, crooked, curved, hamate, unciform.

hoop *vb* clasp, encircle, enclose, surround. * *n* band, circlet, girdle, ring; crinoline, farthingale.

hoot *vb* boo, cry, jeer, shout, yell; condemn, decry, denounce, execrate, hiss. * *n* boo, cry, jeer, shout, yell.

hop *vb* bound, caper, frisk, jump, leap, skip, spring; dance, trip; halt, hobble, limp. * *n* bound, caper, dance, jump, leap, skip, spring.

hope *vb* anticipate, await, desire, expect, long; believe, rely, trust. * *n* confidence, belief, faith, reliance, sanguineness, sanguinity, trust; anticipation, desire, expectancy, expectation.

hopeful *adj* anticipatory, confident, expectant, fond, optimistic, sanguine; cheerful, encouraging, promising.

hopeless *adj* abject, crushed, depressed, despondent, despairing, desperate, disconsolate, downcast, forlorn, pessimistic, woebegone; abandoned, helpless, incurable, irremediable, remediless; impossible, impracticable, unachievable, unattainable.

horde *n* clan, crew, gang, troop; crowd, multitude, pack, throng.

horn *vb* gore, pierce. * *n* trumpet, wind instrument; beaker, drinking cup, cornucopia; spike, spur; cusp, prong, wing.

horrid *adj* alarming, awful, bristling, dire, dreadful, fearful, frightful, harrowing, hideous, horrible, horrific, horrifying, rough, terrible, terrific; abominable, disagreeable, disgusting, odious, offensive, repulsive, revolting, shocking, unpleasant, vile.

horrify *vb* affright, alarm, frighten, shock, terrify, terrorise.

horror *n* alarm, awe, consternation, dismay, dread, fear, fright, panic; abhorrence, abomination, antipathy, aversion, detestation, disgust, hatred, loathing, repugnance, revulsion; shuddering.

horse *n* charger, cob, colt, courser, filly, gelding, mare, nag, pad, palfrey, pony, stallion, steed; cavalry, horseman; buck, clotheshorse, frame, sawhorse, stand, support.

horseman *n* cavalier, equestrian, rider; cavalryman, chasseur, dragoon, horse-soldier.

hospitable *adj* attentive, bountiful, kind; bountiful, cordial, generous, liberal, open, receptive, sociable, unconstrained, unreserved.

host[1] *n* entertainer, innkeeper, landlord, master of ceremonies, presenter, proprietor, owner, receptionist.

host[2] *n* array, army, legion; assemblage, assembly, horde, multitude, throng.

host[3] *n* altar bread, bread, consecrated bread, loaf, wafer.

hostile *adj* inimical, unfriendly, warlike; adverse, antagonistic, contrary, opposed, opposite, repugnant.

hostilities *npl* conflict, fighting, war, warfare.

hostility *n* animosity, antagonism, enmity, hatred, ill-will, unfriendliness; contrariness, opposition, repugnance, variance.

hot *adj* burning, fiery, scalding; boiling, flaming, heated, incandescent, parching, roasting, torrid; heated, oppressive, sweltering, warm; angry, choleric, excitable, furious, hasty, impatient, impetuous, irascible, lustful, passionate, touchy, urgent, violent; animated, ardent, eager, fervent, fervid, glowing, passionate, vehement; acrid, biting, highly flavoured, highly seasoned, peppery, piquant, pungent, sharp, stinging.

hotchpotch *n* farrago, jumble, hodgepodge, medley, miscellany, stew.

hotel *n* inn, public house, tavern.

hot-headed *adj* furious, headlong, headstrong, hot-brained, impetuous, inconsiderate, passionate, precipitate, rash, reckless, vehement, violent.

hound *vb* drive, incite, spur, urge; bate, chase, goad, harass, harry, hunt, pursue.

house *vb* harbour, lodge, protect, shelter. * *n* abode, domicile, dwelling, habitation, home, mansion, residence; building, edifice; family, household; kindred, race, lineage, tribe; company, concern, firm, partnership; hotel, inn, public house, tavern.

housing *n* accommodation, dwellings, houses; casing, container, covering, protection, shelter.

hovel *n* cabin, cot, den, hole, hut, shed.

hover *vb* flutter; hang; vacillate, waver.

however *adv* but, however, nevertheless, notwithstanding, still, though, yet.

howl *vb* bawl, cry, lament, ululate, weep, yell, yowl. * *n* cry, yell, ululation.

hoyden *n* romp, tomboy.

hoydenish *adj* bad-mannered, boisterous, bold, ill-behaved, ill-taught, inelegant, romping, rough, rude, rustic, tomboyish, uncouth, ungenteel, unladylike, unruly.

hubbub *n* clamour, confusion, din, disorder, disturbance, hullabaloo, racket, riot, outcry, tumult, uproar.

huckster *n* hawker, peddler, retailer.

huddle *vb* cluster, crowd, gather; crouch, curl up, nestle, snuggle. * *n* confusion, crowd, disorder, disturbance, jumble, tumult.

hue *n* cast, colour, complexion, dye, shade, tinge, tint, tone.

huff *vb* blow, breathe, exhale, pant, puff. * *n* anger, fume, miff, passion, pet, quarrel, rage, temper, tiff.

hug *vb* clasp, cling, cuddle, embrace, grasp, grip, squeeze; cherish, nurse, retain. * *n* clasp, cuddle, embrace, grasp, squeeze.

huge *adj* bulky, colossal, Cyclopean, elephantine, enormous, gigantic, herculean, immense, stupendous, vast,

huggermugger *adj* clandestine, secret, sly; base, contemptible, mean, unfair; confused, disorderly, slovenly.

hull *vb* husk, peel, shell. * *n* covering, husk, rind, shell.

hullabaloo *n* clamour, confusion, din, disturbance, hubbub, outcry, racket, vociferation, uproar.

hum *vb* buzz, drone, murmur; croon, sing.

humane *adj* accommodating, benevolent, benign, charitable, clement, compassionate, gentle, good-hearted, kind, kind-hearted, lenient, merciful, obliging, tender, sympathetic; cultivating, elevating, humanizing, refining, rational, spiritual.

humanity *n* benevolence, benignity, charity, fellow-feeling, humaneness, kind-heartedness, kindness, philanthropy, sympathy, tenderness; humankind, mankind, mortality.

humanize *vb* civilize, cultivate, educate, enlighten, improve, polish, reclaim, refine, soften.

humble *vb* abase, abash, break, crush, debase, degrade, disgrace, humiliate, lower, mortify, reduce, sink, subdue. * *adj* meek, modest, lowly, simple, submissive, unambitious, unassuming, unobtrusive, unostentatious, unpretending; low, obscure, mean, plain, poor, small, undistinguished, unpretentious.

humbug *vb* cheat, cozen, deceive, hoax, swindle, trick. * *n* cheat, dodge, gammon, hoax, imposition, imposture, deception, fraud, trick; cant, charlatanism, charlatanry, hypocrisy, mummery, quackery; charlatan, impostor, fake, quack.

humdrum *adj* boring, dronish, dreary, dry, dull, monotonous, prosy, stupid, tedious, tiresome, wearisome.

humid *adj* damp, dank, moist, wet.

humiliate *vb* abase, abash, debase, degrade, depress, humble, mortify, shame.

humiliation *n* abasement, affront, condescension,

crushing, degradation, disgrace, dishonouring, humbling, indignity, mortification, self-abasement, submissiveness, resignation.
humility *n* diffidence, humbleness, lowliness, meekness, modesty, self-abasement, submissiveness.
humorist *n* comic, comedian, droll, jester, joker, wag, wit.
humorous *adj* comic, comical, droll, facetious, funny, humorous, jocose, jocular, laughable, ludicrous, merry, playful, pleasant, sportive, whimsical, witty.
humour *vb* favour, gratify, indulge. * *n* bent, bias, disposition, predilection, prosperity, temper, vein; mood, state; caprice, crotchet, fancy, freak, vagary, whim, whimsy, wrinkle; drollery, facetiousness, fun, jocoseness, jocularity, pleasantry, wit; fluid, moisture, vapour.
hunch *vb* arch, jostle, nudge, punch, push, shove. * *n* bunch, hump, knob, protuberance; nudge, punch, push, shove; feeling, idea, intuition, premonition.
hungry *adj* covetous, craving, desirous, greedy; famished, starved, starving; barren, poor, unfertile, unproductive.
hunk *n* chunk, hunch, lump, slice.
hunt *vb* chase, drive, follow, hound, pursue, stalk, trap, trail; poach, shoot; search, seek. * *n* chase, field-sport, hunting, pursuit.
hurl *vb* cast, dart, fling, pitch, project, send, sling, throw, toss.
hurly-burly *n* bustle, commotion, confusion, disturbance, hurl, hurly, uproar, tumult, turmoil.
hurricane *n* cyclone, gale, storm, tempest, tornado, typhoon.
hurried *adj* cursory, hasty, slight, superficial.
hurry *vb* drive, precipitate; dispatch, expedite, hasten, quicken, speed; haste, scurry. * *n* agitation, bustle, confusion, flurry, flutter, perturbation, precipitation; celerity, haste, dispatch, expedition, promptitude, promptness, quickness.
hurt *vb* damage, disable, disadvantage, harm, impair, injure, mar; bruise, pain, wound; afflict, grieve, offend; ache, smart, throb. * *n* damage, detriment, disadvantage, harm, injury, mischief; ache, bruise, pain, suffering, wound.
hurtful *adj* baleful, baneful, deleterious, destructive, detrimental, disadvantageous, harmful, injurious, mischievous, noxious, pernicious, prejudicial, unwholesome.
husband *vb* economize, hoard, save, store.
husbandry *n* agriculture, cultivation, farming, geoponics, tillage; economy, frugality, thrift.
hush *vb* quiet, repress, silence, still, suppress; appease, assuage, calm, console, quiet, still. * *n* quiet, quietness, silence, stillness.
hypocrite *n* deceiver, dissembler, impostor, pretender.
hypocritical *adj* deceiving, dissembling, false, insincere, spurious, two-faced.
hypothesis *n* assumption, proposition, supposition, theory.
hypothetical *adj* assumed, imaginary, supposed, theoretical.
hysterical *adj* frantic, frenzied, overwrought, uncontrollable; comical, uproarious.

I

ice *vb* chill, congeal, freeze. * *n* crystal; frosting, sugar.

icy *adj* glacial; chilling, cold, frosty; cold-hearted, distant, frigid, indifferent, unemotional.

idea *n* archetype, essence, exemplar, ideal, model, pattern, plan, model; fantasy, fiction, image, imagination; apprehension, conceit, conception, fancy, illusion, impression, thought; belief, judgement, notion, opinion, sentiment, supposition.

ideal *adj* intellectual, mental; chimerical, fancied, fanciful, fantastic, illusory, imaginary, unreal, visionary, shadowy; complete, consummate, excellent, perfect; impractical, unattainable, utopian. * *n* criterion, example, model, standard.

identical *adj* equivalent, same, selfsame, tantamount.

identity *n* existence, individuality, personality, sameness.

ideology *n* belief, creed, dogma, philosophy, principle.

idiocy *n* fatuity, feebleness, foolishness, imbecility, insanity.

idiosyncrasy *n* caprice, eccentricity, fad, peculiarity, singularity.

idiot *n* blockhead, booby, dunce, fool, ignoramus, imbecile, simpleton.

idiotic *adj* fatuous, foolish, imbecile, irrational, senseless, sottish, stupid.

idle *adj* inactive, unemployed, unoccupied, vacant; indolent, inert, lazy, slothful, sluggish; abortive, bootless, fruitless, futile, groundless, ineffectual, unavailing, useless, vain; foolish, frivolous, trashy, trifling, trivial, unimportant, unprofitable. * *vb* dally, dawdle, laze, loiter, potter, waste; drift, shirk, slack.

idler *n* dawdler, doodle, drone, laggard, lazybones, loafer, lounger, slacker, slowcoach, sluggard, trifler.

idol *n* deity, god, icon, image, pagan, simulacrum, symbol; delusion, falsity, pretender, sham; beloved, darling, favourite, pet.

idolater *n* heathen, pagan; admirer, adorer, worshipper.

idolize *vb* canonize, deify; adore, honour, love, reverence, venerate.

idyll *n* eclogue, pastoral.

if *conj* admitting, allowing, granting, provided, supposing, though, whether. * *n* condition, hesitation, uncertainty.

igneous *adj* combustible, combustive, conflagrative, fiery, molten.

ignite *vb* burn, inflame, kindle, light, torch.

ignoble *adj* base-born, low, low-born, mean, peasant, plebeian, rustic, vulgar; contemptible, degraded, insignificant, mean, worthless; disgraceful, dishonourable, infamous, low, unworthy.

ignominious *adj* discreditable, disgraceful, dishonourable, disreputable, infamous, opprobrious, scandalous, shameful; base, contemptible, despicable.

ignominy *n* abasement, contempt, discredit, disgrace, dishonour disrepute, infamy, obloquy, odium, opprobrium, scandal, shame.

ignoramus *n* blockhead, duffer, dunce, fool, greenhorn, novice, numskull, simpleton.

ignorance *n* benightedness, darkness, illiteracy, nescience, rusticity; blindness, unawareness.

ignorant *adj* blind, illiterate, nescient, unaware, unconversant, uneducated, unenlightened, uninformed, uninstructed, unlearned, unread, untaught, untutored, unwitting.

ignore *vb* disregard, neglect, overlook, reject, skip.

ill *adj* bad, evil, faulty, harmful, iniquitous, naughty, unfavourable, unfortunate, unjust, wicked; ailing, diseased, disordered, indisposed, sick, unwell, wrong; crabbed, cross, hateful, malicious, malevolent, peevish, surly, unkind, ill-bred; ill-favoured, ugly, unprepossessing. * *adv* badly, poorly, unfortunately. * *n* badness, depravity, evil, mischief, misfortune, wickedness; affliction, ailment, calamity, harm, misery, pain, trouble.

ill-advised *adj* foolish, ill-judged, imprudent, injudicious, unwise.

ill-bred *adj* discourteous, ill-behaved, ill-mannered, impolite, rude, uncivil, uncourteous, uncourtly, uncouth.

illegal *adj* contraband, forbidden, illegitimate, illicit, prohibited, unauthorized, unlawful, unlicensed.

illegible *adj* indecipherable, obscure, undecipherable, unreadable.

illegitimate *adj* bastard, misbegotten, natural.

ill-fated *adj* ill-starred, luckless, unfortunate, unlucky.

ill-favoured *adj* homely, ugly, offensive, plain, unpleasant.

ill humour *n* fretfulness, ill-temper, peevishness, petulance, testiness.

illiberal *adj* close, close-fisted, covetous, mean, miserly, narrow, niggardly, parsimonious, penurious, selfish, sordid, stingy, ungenerous; bigoted, narrow-minded, uncharitable, ungentlemanly, vulgar.
illicit *adj* illegal, illegitimate, unauthorized, unlawful, unlegalized, unlicensed; criminal, guilty, forbidden, improper, wrong.
illimitable *adj* boundless, endless, immeasurable, immense, infinite, unbounded, unlimited, vast.
illiterate *adj* ignorant, uneducated, uninstructed, unlearned, unlettered, untaught, untutored.
ill-judged *adj* foolish, ill-advised, imprudent, injudicious, unwise.
ill-mannered *adj* discourteous, ill-behaved, ill-bred, impolite, rude, uncivil, uncourteous, uncourtly, uncouth, unpolished.
ill-natured *adj* disobliging, hateful, malevolent, unamiable, unfriendly, unkind; acrimonious, bitter, churlish, crabbed, cross, cross-grained, crusty, ill-tempered, morose, perverse, petulant, sour, spiteful, sulky, sullen, wayward.
illness *n* ailing, ailment, complaint, disease, disorder, distemper, indisposition, malady, sickness.
illogical *adj* absurd, fallacious, inconsistent, inconclusive, inconsequent, incorrect, invalid, unreasonable, unsound.
ill-proportioned *adj* awkward, ill-made, ill-shaped, misshapen, misproportioned, shapeless.
ill-starred *adj* ill-fated, luckless, unfortunate, unhappy, unlucky.
ill temper *n* bad temper, crabbedness, crossness, grouchiness, ill nature, moroseness, sulkiness, sullenness.
ill-tempered *adj* acrimonious, bad-tempered, crabbed, cross, grouchy, ill-natured, morose, sour, sulky, surly.
ill-timed *adj* inapposite, inopportune, irrelevant, unseasonable, untimely.
ill-treat *vb* abuse, ill-use, injure, maltreat, mishandle, misuse.
illude *vb* cheat, deceive, delude, disappoint, mock, swindle, trick.
illuminate *vb* illume, illumine, light; adorn, brighten, decorate, depict, edify, enlighten, inform, inspire, instruct, make wise.
illusion *n* chimera, deception, delusion, error, fallacy, false appearance, fantasy, hallucination, mockery, phantasm.
illusive, illusory *adj* barmecide, deceitful, deceptive, delusive, fallacious, imaginary, make-believe, mock, sham, unsatisfying, unreal, unsubstantial, visionary, tantalizing.
illustrate *vb* clarify, demonstrate, elucidate, enlighten, exemplify, explain; adorn, depict, draw.
illustration *n* demonstration, elucidation, enlightenment, exemplification, explanation, interpretation; adornment, decoration, picture.
illustrative *adj* elucidative, elucidatory, exemplifying.
illustrious *adj* bright, brilliant, glorious, radiant, splendid; celebrated, conspicuous, distinguished, eminent, famed, famous, noble, noted, remarkable, renowned, signal.
ill will *n* animosity, dislike, enmity, envy, grudge, hate, hatred, hostility, ill nature, malevolence, malice, malignity, rancour, spleen, spite, uncharitableness, unkindness, venom.
image *n* idol, statue; copy, effigy, figure, form, imago, likeness, picture, resemblance, representation, shape, similitude, simulacrum, statue, symbol; conception, counterpart, embodiment, idea, reflection.
imagery *n* dream, phantasm, phantom, vision.
imaginable *adj* assumable, cogitable, conceivable, conjecturable, plausible, possible, supposable, thinkable.
imaginary *adj* chimerical, dreamy, fancied, fanciful, fantastic, fictitious, ideal, illusive, illusory, invented, quixotic, shadowy, unreal, utopian, visionary, wild; assumed, conceivable, hypothetical, supposed.
imagination *n* chimera, conception, fancy, fantasy, invention, unreality; position; contrivance, device, plot, scheme.
imaginative *adj* creative, dreamy, fanciful, inventive, poetical, plastic, visionary.
imagine *vb* conceive, dream, fancy, imagine, picture, pretend; contrive, create, devise, frame, invent, mould, project; assume, suppose, hypothesize; apprehend, assume, believe, deem, guess, opine, suppose, think.
imbecile *adj* cretinous, drivelling, fatuous, feeble, feeble-minded, foolish, helpless, idiotic, imbecilic, inane, infirm, witless. * *n* dotard, driveller.
imbecility *n* debility, feebleness, helplessness, infirmity, weakness; foolishness, idiocy, silliness, stupidity, weak-mindedness.
imbibe *vb* absorb, assimilate, drink, suck, swallow; acquire, gain, gather, get, receive.
imbroglio *n* complexity, complication, embarrassment, entanglement, misunderstanding.
imbrue *vb* drench, embrue, gain, moisten, soak, stain, steep, wet.
imbue *vb* colour, dye, stain, tincture, tinge, tint; bathe, impregnate, infuse, inoculate, permeate, pervade, provide, saturate, steep.
imitate *vb* copy, counterfeit, duplicate, echo, emulate, follow, forge, mirror, reproduce, simulate; ape, impersonate, mimic, mock, personate; burlesque, parody, travesty.
imitation *adj* artificial, fake, man-made, mock, reproduction, synthetic. * *n* aping, copying, imitation, mimicking, parroting; copy, duplicate, likeness, resemblance; mimicry, mocking; burlesque, parody, travesty.
imitative *adj* copying, emulative, imitating, mimetic, simulative; apeish, aping, mimicking.
imitator *n* copier, copycat, copyist, echo, impersonator, mimic, mimicker, parrot.
immaculate *adj* clean, pure, spotless, stainless, unblemished, uncontaminated, undefiled, unpol-

luted, unspotted, unsullied, untainted, untarnished; faultless, guiltless, holy, innocent, pure, saintly, sinless, stainless.

immanent *adj* congenital, inborn, indwelling, inherent, innate, internal, intrinsic, subjective.

immaterial *adj* bodiless, ethereal, extramundane, impalpable, incorporeal, mental, metaphysical, spiritual, unbodied, unfleshly, unsubstantial; inconsequential, insignificant, nonessential, unessential, unimportant.

immature *adj* crude, green, imperfect, raw, rudimental, rudimentary, unfinished, unformed, unprepared, unripe, unripened, youthful; hasty, premature, unseasonable, untimely.

immaturity *n* crudeness, crudity, greenness, imperfection, rawness, unpreparedness, unripeness.

immeasurable *adj* bottomless, boundless, illimitable, immense, infinite, limitless, measureless, unbounded, vast.

immediate *adj* close, contiguous, near, next, proximate; intuitive, primary, unmeditated; direct, instant, instantaneous, present, pressing, prompt.

immediately *adv* closely, proximately; directly, forthwith, instantly, presently, presto, pronto.

immemorial *adj* ancient, hoary, olden.

immense *adj* boundless, illimitable, infinite, interminable, measureless, unbounded, unlimited; colossal, elephantine, enormous, gigantic, huge, large, monstrous, mountainous, prodigious, stupendous, titanic, tremendous, vast.

immensity *n* boundlessness, endlessness, limitlessness, infiniteness, infinitude, infinity; amplitude, enormity, greatness, hugeness, magnitude, vastness.

immerse *vb* baptize, bathe, dip, douse, duck, overwhelm, plunge, sink, souse, submerge; absorb, engage, engross, involve.

immersion *n* dipping, immersing, plunging; absorption, engagement; disappearance; baptism.

imminent *adj* close, impending, near, overhanging, threatening; alarming, dangerous, perilous.

immobile *adj* fixed, immovable, inflexible, motionless, quiescent, stable, static, stationary, steadfast; dull, expressionless, impassive, rigid, stiff, stolid.

immobility *n* fixedness, fixity, immovability, immovableness, motionlessness, stability, steadfastness, unmovableness; dullness, expressionlessness, inflexibility, rigidity, stiffness, stolidity.

immoderate *adj* excessive, exorbitant, extravagant, extreme, inordinate, intemperate, unreasonable.

immodest *adj* coarse, gross, indecorous, indelicate, lewd, shameless; bold, brazen, forward, impudent, indecent; broad, filthy, impure, indecent, obscene, smutty, unchaste.

immodesty *n* coarseness, grossness, indecorum, indelicacy, shamelessness; impurity, lewdness, obscenity, smuttiness, unchastity; boldness, brass, forwardness, impatience.

immolate *vb* kill, sacrifice.

immoral *adj* antisocial, corrupt, loose, sinful, unethical, vicious, wicked, wrong; bad, depraved, dissolute, profligate, unprincipled; abandoned, indecent, licentious.

immorality *n* corruption, corruptness, criminality, demoralization, depravity, impurity, profligacy, sin, sinfulness, vice, wickedness; wrong.

immortal *adj* deathless, ever-living, imperishable, incorruptible, indestructible, indissoluble, never-dying, undying, unfading; ceaseless, continuing, eternal, endless, everlasting, never-ending, perpetual, sempiternal; abiding, enduring, lasting, permanent. * *n* god, goddess; genius, hero.

immortality *n* deathlessness, incorruptibility, incorruptibleness, indestructibility; perpetuity.

immortalize *vb* apotheosize, enshrine, glorify, perpetuate.

immovable *adj* firm, fixed, immobile, stable, stationary; impassive, steadfast, unalterable, unchangeable, unshaken, unyielding.

immunity *n* exemption, exoneration, freedom, release; charter, franchise, liberty, license, prerogative, privilege, right.

immure *vb* confine, entomb, imprison, incarcerate.

immutability *n* constancy, inflexibility, invariability, invariableness, permanence, stability, unalterableness, unchangeableness.

immutable *adj* constant, fixed, inflexible, invariable, permanent, stable, unalterable, unchangeable, undeviating.

imp *n* demon, devil, elf, flibbertigibbet, hobgoblin, scamp, sprite; graft, scion, shoot.

impact *vb* collide, crash, strike. * *n* brunt, impression, impulse, shock, stroke, touch; collision, contact, impinging, striking.

impair *vb* blemish, damage, deface, deteriorate, injure, mar, ruin, spoil, vitiate; decrease, diminish, lessen, reduce; enervate, enfeeble, weaken.

impale *vb* hole, pierce, puncture, spear, spike, stab, transfix.

impalpable *adj* attenuated, delicate, fine, intangible; imperceptible, inapprehensible, incorporeal, indistinct, shadowy, unsubstantial.

impart *vb* bestow, confer, give, grant; communicate, disclose, discover, divulge, relate, reveal, share, tell.

impartial *adj* candid, disinterested, dispassionate, equal, equitable, even-handed, fair, honourable, just, unbiased, unprejudiced, unwarped.

impassable *adj* blocked, closed, impenetrable, impermeable, impervious, inaccessible, pathless, unattainable, unnavigable, unreachable.

impassioned *adj* animated, ardent, burning, excited, fervent, fervid, fiery, glowing, impetuous, intense, passionate, vehement, warm, zealous.

impassive *adj* calm, passionless; apathetic, callous, indifferent, insensible, insusceptible, unfeeling, unimpressible, unsusceptible.

impassivity *n* calmness, composure, indifference,

insensibility, insusceptibility, passionlessness, stolidity.
impatience *n* disquietude, restlessness, uneasiness; eagerness, haste, impetuosity, precipitation, vehemence; heat, irritableness, irritability, violence.
impatient *adj* restless, uneasy, unquiet; eager, hasty, impetuous, precipitate, vehement; abrupt, brusque, choleric, fretful, hot, intolerant, irritable, peevish, sudden, testy, violent.
impeach *vb* accuse, arraign, charge, indict; asperse, censure, denounce, disparage, discredit, impair, impute, incriminate, lessen.
impeachment *n* accusation, arraignment, indictment; aspersion, censure, disparagement, imputation, incrimination, reproach.
impeccable *adj* faultless, immaculate, incorrupt, innocent, perfect, pure, sinless, stainless, uncorrupt.
impede *vb* bar, block, check, clog, curb, delay, encumber, hinder, interrupt, obstruct, restrain, retard, stop, thwart.
impediment *n* bar, barrier, block, check, curb, difficulty, encumbrance, hindrance, obstacle, obstruction, stumbling block.
impel *vb* drive, push, send, urge; actuate, animate, compel, constrain, embolden, incite, induce, influence, instigate, move, persuade, stimulate.
impend *vb* approach, menace, near, threaten.
impending *adj* approaching, imminent, menacing, near, threatening.
impenetrable *adj* impermeable, impervious, inaccessible; cold, dull, impassive, indifferent, obtuse, senseless, stolid, unsympathetic; dense, proof.
impenitence *n* hardheartedness, impenitency, impenitentness, obduracy, stubbornness.
impenitent *adj* hardened, hard-hearted, incorrigible, irreclaimable, obdurate, recusant, relentless, seared, stubborn, uncontrite, unconverted, unrepentant.
imperative *adj* authoritative, commanding, despotic, domineering, imperious, overbearing, peremptory, urgent; binding, obligatory.
imperceptible *adj* inaudible, indiscernible, indistinguishable, invisible; fine, impalpable, inappreciable, gradual, minute.
imperfect *adj* abortive, crude, deficient, garbled, incomplete, poor; defective, faulty, impaired.
imperfection *n* defectiveness, deficiency, faultiness, incompleteness; blemish, defect, fault, flaw, lack, stain, taint; failing, foible, frailty, limitation, vice, weakness.
imperial *adj* kingly, regal, royal, sovereign; august, consummate, exalted, grand, great, kingly, magnificent, majestic, noble, regal, royal, queenly, supreme, sovereign, supreme, consummate.
imperil *vb* endanger, expose, hazard, jeopardize, risk.
imperious *adj* arrogant, authoritative, commanding, compelling, despotic, dictatorial, domineering, haughty, imperative, lordly, magisterial, overbearing, tyrannical, urgent, compelling.
imperishable *adj* eternal, everlasting, immortal, incorruptible, indestructible, never-ending, perennial, unfading.
impermeable *adj* impenetrable, impervious.
impermissible *adj* deniable, insufferable, objectionable, unallowable, unallowed, unlawful.
impersonate *vb* act, ape, enact, imitate, mimic, mock, personate; embody, incarnate, personify, typify.
impersonation *n* incarnation, manifestation, personification; enacting, imitation, impersonating, mimicking, personating, representation.
impertinence *n* irrelevance, irrelevancy, unfitness, impropriety; assurance, boldness, brass, brazenness, effrontery, face, forwardness, impudence, incivility, insolence, intrusiveness, presumption, rudeness, sauciness, pertness.
impertinent *adj* inapplicable, inapposite, irrelevant; bold, forward, impudent, insolent, intrusive, malapert, meddling, officious, pert, rude, saucy, unmannerly.
imperturbability *n* calmness, collectedness, composure, dispassion, placidity, placidness, sedateness, serenity, steadiness, tranquility.
imperturbable *adj* calm, collected, composed, cool, placid, sedate, serene, tranquil, unmoved, undisturbed, unexcitable, unmoved, unruffled.
impervious *adj* impassable, impenetrable, impermeable.
impetuosity *n* force, fury, haste, precipitancy, vehemence, violence.
impetuous *adj* ardent, boisterous, brash, breakneck, fierce, fiery, furious, hasty, headlong, hot, hot-headed, impulsive, overzealous, passionate, precipitate, vehement, violent.
impetus *n* energy, force, momentum, propulsion.
impiety *n* irreverence, profanity, ungodliness; iniquity, sacreligiousness, sin, sinfulness, ungodliness, unholiness, unrighteousness, wickedness.
impinge *vb* clash, dash, encroach, hit, infringe, strike, touch.
impious *adj* blasphemous, godless, iniquitous, irreligious, irreverent, profane, sinful, ungodly, unholy, unrighteous, wicked.
implacable *adj* deadly, inexorable, merciless, pitiless, rancorous, relentless, unappeasable, unforgiving, unpropitiating, unrelenting.
implant *vb* ingraft, infix, insert, introduce, place.
implement *vb* effect, execute, fulfil. * *n* appliance, instrument, tool, utensil.
implicate *vb* entangle, enfold; compromise, concern, entangle, include, involve.
implication *n* entanglement, involvement, involution; connotation, hint, inference, innuendo, intimation; conclusion, meaning, significance.
implicit *adj* implied, inferred, understood; absolute, constant, firm, steadfast, unhesitating, unquestioning, unreserved, unshaken.
implicitly *adv* by implication, silently, tacitly,

unspokenly, virtually, wordlessly.

implore *vb* adjure, ask, beg, beseech, entreat, petition, pray, solicit, supplicate.

imply *vb* betoken, connote, denote, import, include, infer, insinuate, involve, mean, presuppose, signify.

impolicy *n* folly, imprudence, ill-judgement, indiscretion, inexpediency.

impolite *adj* bearish, boorish, discourteous, disrespectful, ill-bred, insolent, rough, rude, uncivil, uncourteous, ungentle, ungentlemanly, ungracious, unmannerly, unpolished, unrefined.

impoliteness *n* boorishness, discourteousness, discourtesy, disrespect, ill-breeding, incivility, insolence, rudeness, unmannerliness.

impolitic *adj* ill-advised, imprudent, indiscreet, inexpedient, injudicious, unwise.

import *vb* bring in, introduce, transport; betoken, denote, imply, mean, purport, signify. * *n* goods, importation, merchandise; bearing, drift, gist, intention, interpretation, matter, meaning, purpose, sense, signification, spirit, tenor; consequence, importance, significance, weight.

importance *n* concern, consequence, gravity, import, moment, momentousness, significance, weight, weightiness; consequence, pomposity, self-importance.

important *adj* considerable, grave, material, momentous, notable, pompous, ponderous, serious, significant, urgent, valuable, weighty; esteemed, influential, prominent, substantial; consequential, pompous, self-important.

importunate *adj* busy, earnest, persistent, pertinacious, pressing, teasing, troublesome, urgent.

importune *vb* ask, beset, dun, ply, press, solicit, urge.

importunity *n* appeal, beseechment, entreaty, petition, plying, prayer, pressing, suit, supplication, urging; contention, insistence; urgency.

impose *vb* lay, place, put, set; appoint, charge, dictate, enjoin, force, inflict, obtrude, prescribe, tax; (*with* **on, upon**) abuse, cheat, circumvent, deceive, delude, dupe, exploit, hoax, trick, victimize.

imposing *adj* august, commanding, dignified, exalted, grand, grandiose, impressive, lofty, magnificent, majestic, noble, stately, striking.

imposition *n* imposing, laying, placing, putting; burden, charge, constraint, injunction, levy, oppression, tax; artifice, cheating, deception, dupery, fraud, imposture, trickery.

impossibility *n* hopelessness, impracticability, inability, infeasibility, unattainability; inconceivability.

impossible *adj* hopeless, impracticable, infeasible, unachievable, unattainable; inconceivable, self-contradictory, unthinkable.

impost *n* custom, duty, excise, rate, tax, toil, tribute.

impostor *n* charlatan, cheat, counterfeiter, deceiver, double-dealer, humbug, hypocrite, knave, mountebank, pretender, quack, rogue, trickster.

imposture *n* artifice, cheat, deceit, deception, delusion, dodge, fraud, hoax, imposition, ruse, stratagem, trick, wile.

impotence *n* disability, feebleness, frailty, helplessness, inability, incapability, incapacity, incompetence, inefficaciousness, inefficacy, inefficiency, infirmity, powerlessness, weakness.

impotent *adj* disabled, enfeebled, feeble, frail, helpless, incapable, incapacitated, incompetent, inefficient, infirm, nerveless, powerless, unable, weak; barren, sterile.

impound *vb* confine, coop, engage, imprison.

impoverish *vb* beggar, pauperize; deplete, exhaust, ruin.

impracticability *n* impossibility, impracticableness, impracticality, infeasibility, unpracticability.

impracticable *adj* impossible, infeasible; intractable, obstinate, recalcitrant, stubborn, thorny, unmanageable; impassable, insurmountable.

impracticality *n* impossibility, impracticableness, impractibility, infeasibility, unpracticability; irrationality, unpracticalness, unrealism, unreality, unreasonableness.

imprecate *vb* anathematize, curse, execrate, invoke, maledict.

imprecation *n* anathema, curse, denunciation, execration, invocation, malediction.

imprecatory *adj* appealing, beseeching, entreating, imploratory, imploring, imprecatory, pleading; cursing, damnatory, execrating, maledictory.

impregnable *adj* immovable, impenetrable, indestructible, invincible, inviolable, invulnerable, irrefrangible, secure, unconquerable, unassailable, unyielding.

impregnate *vb* fecundate, fertilize, fructify; dye, fill, imbrue, imbue, infuse, permeate, pervade, saturate, soak, tincture, tinge.

impress *vb* engrave, imprint, print, stamp; affect, move, strike; fix, inculcate; draft, enlist, levy, press, requisition. * *n* impression, imprint, mark, print, seal, stamp; cognizance, device, emblem, motto, symbol.

impressibility *n* affectibility, impressionability, pliancy, receptiveness, responsiveness, sensibility, sensitiveness, susceptibility.

impressible *adj* affectible, excitable, impressionable, pliant, receptive, responsive, sensitive, soft, susceptible, tender.

impression *n* edition, imprinting, printing, stamping; brand, dent, impress, mark, stamp; effect, influence, sensation; fancy, idea, instinct, notion, opinion, recollection.

impressive *adj* affecting, effective, emphatic, exciting, forcible, moving, overpowering, powerful, solemn, speaking, splendid, stirring, striking, telling, touching.

imprint *vb* engrave, mark, print, stamp; impress, inculcate. * *n* impression, mark, print, sign, stamp.

imprison *vb* confine, jail, immure, incarcerate, shut up.

imprisonment *n* captivity, commitment, confinement, constraint, durance, duress, incarceration, restraint.

improbability *n* doubt, uncertainty, unlikelihood.

improbable *adj* doubtful, uncertain, unlikely, unplausible.

improbity *n* dishonesty, faithlessness, fraud, fraudulence, knavery, unfairness.

impromptu *adj* extempore, improvised, offhand, spontaneous, unpremeditated, unprepared, unrehearsed. * *adv* extemporaneously, extemporarily, extempore, offhand, ad-lib.

improper *adj* immodest, inapposite, inappropriate, irregular, unadapted, unapt, unfit, unsuitable, unsuited; indecent, indecorous, indelicate, unbecoming, unseemly; erroneous, inaccurate, incorrect, wrong.

impropriety *n* inappropriateness, unfitness, unsuitability, unsuitableness; indecorousness, indecorum, unseemliness.

improve *vb* ameliorate, amend, better, correct, edify, meliorate, mend, rectify, reform; cultivate; gain, mend, progress; enhance, increase, rise.

improvement *n* ameliorating, amelioration, amendment, bettering, improving, meliorating, melioration; advancement, proficiency, progress.

improvidence *n* imprudence, thriftlessness, unthriftiness.

improvident *adj* careless, heedless, imprudent, incautious, inconsiderate, negligent, prodigal, rash, reckless, shiftless, thoughtless, thriftless, unthrifty, wasteful.

improvisation *n* ad-libbing, contrivance, extemporaneousness, extemporariness, extemporization, fabrication, invention; (*mus*) extempore, impromptu.

improvise *vb* ad-lib, contrive, extemporize, fabricate, imagine, invent.

imprudence *n* carelessness, heedlessness, improvidence, incautiousness, inconsideration, indiscretion, rashness.

imprudent *adj* careless, heedless, ill-advised, ill-judged, improvident, incautious, inconsiderate, indiscreet, rash, unadvised, unwise.

impudence *n* assurance, audacity, boldness, brashness, brass, bumptiousness, cheek, cheekiness, effrontery, face, flippancy, forwardness, front, gall, impertinence, insolence, jaw, lip, nerve, pertness, presumption, rudeness, sauciness, shamelessness.

impudent *adj* bold, bold-faced, brazen, brazen-faced, cool, flippant, forward, immodest, impertinent, insolent, insulting, pert, presumptuous, rude, saucy, shameless.

impugn *vb* assail, attack, challenge, contradict, dispute, gainsay, oppose, question, resist.

impulse *n* force, impetus, impelling, momentum, push, thrust; appetite, inclination, instinct, passion, proclivity; incentive, incitement, influence, instigation, motive, instigation.

impulsive *adj* impelling, moving, propulsive; emotional, hasty, heedless, hot, impetuous, mad-cap, passionate, quick, rash, vehement, violent.

impunity *n* exemption, immunity, liberty, licence, permission, security.

impure *adj* defiled, dirty, feculent, filthy, foul, polluted, unclean; bawdy, coarse, immodest, gross, immoral, indelicate, indecent, lewd, licentious, loose, obscene, ribald, smutty, unchaste; adulterated, corrupt, mixed.

impurity *n* defilement, feculence, filth, foulness, pollution, uncleanness; admixture, coarseness, grossness, immodesty, indecency, indelicacy, lewdness, licentiousness, looseness, obscenity, ribaldry, smut, smuttiness, unchastity, vulgarity.

imputable *adj* ascribable, attributable, chargeable, owing, referable, traceable, owing.

imputation *n* attributing, charging, imputing; accusation, blame, censure, charge, reproach.

impute *vb* ascribe, attribute, charge, consider, imply, insinuate, refer.

inability *n* impotence, incapacity, incapability, incompetence, incompetency, inefficiency; disability, disqualification.

inaccessible *adj* unapproachable, unattainable.

inaccuracy *n* erroneousness, impropriety, incorrectness, inexactness; blunder, defect, error, fault, mistake.

inaccurate *adj* defective, erroneous, faulty, incorrect, inexact, mistaken, wrong.

inaccurately *adv* carelessly, cursorily, imprecisely, incorrectly, inexactly, mistakenly, unprecisely, wrongly.

inactive *adj* inactive; dormant, inert, inoperative, peaceful, quiet, quiescent; dilatory, drowsy, dull, idle, inanimate, indolent, inert, lazy, lifeless, lumpish, passive, slothful, sleepy, stagnant, supine.

inactivity *n* dilatoriness, idleness, inaction, indolence, inertness, laziness, sloth, sluggishness, supineness, torpidity, torpor.

inadequacy *n* inadequateness, insufficiency; defectiveness, imperfection, incompetence, incompetency, incompleteness, insufficiency, unfitness, unsuitableness.

inadequate *adj* disproportionate, incapable, insufficient, unequal; defective, imperfect, inapt, incompetent, incomplete.

inadmissible *adj* improper, incompetent, unacceptable, unallowable, unqualified, unreasonable.

inadvertence, inadvertency *n* carelessness, heedlessness, inattention, inconsiderateness, negligence, thoughtlessness; blunder, error, oversight, slip.

inadvertent *adj* careless, heedless, inattentive, inconsiderate, negligent, thoughtless, unobservant.

inadvertently *adv* accidently, carelessly, heedlessly, inconsiderately, negligently, thoughtlessly, unintentionally.

inalienable *adj* undeprivable, unforfeitable, untransferable.
inane *adj* empty, fatuous, vacuous, void; foolish, frivolous, idiotic, puerile, senseless, silly, stupid, trifling, vain, worthless.
inanimate *adj* breathless, dead, extinct; dead, dull, inert, lifeless, soulless, spiritless.
inanition *n* emptiness, inanity, vacuity; exhaustion, hunger, malnutrition, starvation, want.
inanity *n* emptiness, foolishness, inanition, vacuity; folly, frivolousness, puerility, vanity, worthlessness.
inapplicable *adj* inapposite, inappropriate, inapt, irrelevant, unfit, unsuitable, unsuited.
inapposite *adj* impertinent, inapplicable, irrelevant, nonpertinent; inappropriate, unfit, unsuitable.
inappreciable *adj* impalpable, imperceptible, inconsiderable, inconspicuous, indiscernible, infinitesimal, insignificant, negligible, undiscernible, unnoticed.
inappropriate *adj* inapposite, unadapted, unbecoming, unfit, unsuitable, unsullied.
inapt *adj* inapposite, unapt, unfit, unsuitable; awkward, clumsy, dull, slow, stolid, stupid.
inaptitude *n* awkwardness, inapplicability, inappropriateness, inaptness, unfitness, unsuitableness.
inarticulate *adj* blurred, indistinct, thick; dumb, mute.
inartificial *adj* artless, direct, guileless, ingenuous, naive, simple, simple-minded, sincere, single-minded.
inasmuch as *conj* considering that, seeing that, since.
inattention *n* absent-mindedness, carelessness, disregard, heedlessness, inadvertence, inapplication, inconsiderateness, neglect, remissness, slip, thoughtlessness, unmindfulness, unobservance
inattentive *adj* absent-minded, careless, disregarding, heedless, inadvertent, inconsiderate, neglectful, remiss, thoughtless, unmindful, unobservant.
inaudible *adj* faint, indistinct, muffled; mute, noiseless, silent, still.
inaugurate *vb* induct, install, introduce, invest; begin, commence, initiate, institute, originate.
inauguration *n* beginning, commencement, initiation, institution, investiture, installation, opening, origination.
inauspicious *adj* bad, discouraging, ill-omened, ill-starred, ominous, unfavourable, unfortunate, unlucky, unpromising, unpropitious, untoward.
inborn *adj* congenital, inbred, ingrained, inherent, innate, instinctive, native, natural.
incalculable *adj* countless, enormous, immense, incalculable, inestimable, innumerable, sumless, unknown, untold.
incandescence *n* candescence, glow, gleam, luminousness, luminosity.
incandescent *adj* aglow, candent, candescent, gleaming, glowing, luminous, luminant, radiant.
incantation *n* charm, conjuration, enchantment, magic, necromancy, sorcery, spell, witchcraft, witchery.
incapability *n* disability, inability, incapacity, incompetence.
incapable *adj* feeble, impotent, incompetent, insufficient, unable, unfit, unfitted, unqualified, weak.
incapacious *adj* cramped, deficient, incommodious, narrow, scant.
incapacitate *vb* cripple, disable; disqualify, make unfit.
incapacity *n* disability, inability, incapability, incompetence; disqualification, unfitness.
incarcerate *vb* commit, confine, immure, imprison, jail, restrain, restrict.
incarnate *vb* body, embody, incorporate, personify. * *adj* bodied, embodied, incorporated, personified.
incarnation *n* embodiment, exemplification, impersonation, manifestation, personification.
incautious *adj* impolitic, imprudent, indiscreet, uncircumspect, unwary; careless, headlong, heedless, inconsiderate, negligent, rash, reckless, thoughtless.
incendiary *adj* dissentious, factious, inflammatory, seditious. * *n* agitator, firebrand, fire-raiser.
incense[1] *vb* anger, chafe, enkindle, enrage, exasperate, excite, heat, inflame, irritate, madden, provoke.
incense[2] *n* aroma, fragrance, perfume, scent; admiration, adulation, applause, laudation.
incentive *n* cause, encouragement, goad, impulse, incitement, inducement, instigation, mainspring, motive, provocation, spur, stimulus.
inception *n* beginning, commencement, inauguration, initiation, origin, rise, start.
incertitude *n* ambiguity, doubt, doubtfulness, indecision, uncertainty.
incessant *adj* ceaseless, constant, continual, continuous, eternal, everlasting, never-ending, perpetual, unceasing, unending, uninterrupted, unremitting.
inchoate *adj* beginning, commencing, inceptive, incipient, initial.
incident *n* circumstance, episode, event, fact, happening, occurrence. * *adj* happening; belonging, pertaining, appertaining, accessory, relating, natural; falling, impinging.
incidental *adj* accidental, casual, chance, concomitant, contingent, fortuitous, subordinate; adventitious, extraneous, nonessential, occasional.
incinerate *vb* burn, char, conflagrate, cremate, incremate.
incipient *adj* beginning, commencing, inchoate, inceptive, originating, starting.
incised *adj* carved, cut, engraved, gashed, graved, graven.
incision *n* cut, gash, notch, opening, penetration.

incisive *adj* cutting; acute, biting, sarcastic, satirical, sharp; acute, clear, distinct, penetrating, sharp-cut, trenchant.
incite *vb* actuate, animate, arouse, drive, encourage, excite, foment, goad, hound, impel, instigate, prod, prompt, provoke, push, rouse, spur, stimulate, urge.
incitement *n* encouragement, goad, impulse, incentive, inducement, motive, provocative, spur, stimulus.
incivility *n* discourteousness, discourtesy, disrespect, ill-breeding, ill-manners, impoliteness, impudence, inurbanity, rudeness, uncourtliness, unmannerliness.
inclemency *n* boisterousness, cruelty, harshness, rigour, roughness, severity, storminess, tempestuousness, tyranny.
inclement *adj* boisterous, harsh, rigorous, rough, severe, stormy; cruel, unmerciful.
inclination *n* inclining, leaning, slant, slope; trending, verging; aptitude, bent, bias, disposition, penchant, predilection, predisposition, proclivity, proneness, propensity, tendency, turn, twist; desire, fondness, liking, taste, partiality, predilection, wish; bow, nod, obeisance.
incline *vb* lean, slant, slope; bend, nod, verge; tend; bias, dispose, predispose, turn; bow. * *n* ascent, descent, grade, gradient, rise, slope.
inclose *see* **enclose**.
include *vb* contain, hold; comprehend, comprise, contain, cover, embody, embrace, incorporate, involve, take in.
inclusive *adj* comprehending, embracing, encircling, enclosing, including, taking in.
incognito, incognita *adj* camouflaged, concealed, disguised, unknown. * *n* camouflage, concealment, disguise.
incoherent *adj* detached, loose, nonadhesive, noncohesive; disconnected, incongruous, inconsequential, inconsistent, uncoordinated; confused, illogical, irrational, rambling, unintelligible, wild.
income *n* earnings, emolument, gains, interest, pay, perquisite, proceeds, profits, receipts, rents, return, revenue, salary, wages.
incommensurate *adj* disproportionate, inadequate, insufficient, unequal.
incommode *vb* annoy, discommode, disquiet, disturb, embarrass, hinder, inconvenience, molest, plague, trouble, upset, vex.
incommodious *adj* awkward, cumbersome, cumbrous, inconvenient, unhandy, unmanageable, unsuitable, unwieldy; annoying, disadvantageous, harassing, irritating, vexatious.
incommunicative *adj* exclusive, unsociable, unsocial, reserved.
incomparable *adj* matchless, inimitable, peerless, surpassing, transcendent, unequalled, unparalleled, unrivalled.
incompatibility *n* contrariety, contradictoriness, discrepancy, incongruity, inconsistency, irreconcilability, unsuitability, unsuitableness
incompatible *adj* contradictory, incongruous, inconsistent, inharmonious, irreconcilable, unadapted, unsuitable.
incompetence *n* inability, incapability, incapacity, incompetency; inadequacy, insufficiency; disqualification, unfitness.
incompetent *adj* incapable, unable; inadequate, insufficient; disqualified, incapacitated, unconstitutional, unfit, unfitted.
incomplete *adj* defective, deficient, imperfect, partial; inexhaustive, unaccompanied, uncompleted, unexecuted, unfinished.
incomprehensible *adj* inconceivable, inexhaustible, unfathomable, unimaginable; inconceivable, unintelligible, unthinkable.
incomputable *adj* enormous, immense, incalculable, innumerable, prodigious.
inconceivable *adj* incomprehensible, incredible, unbelievable, unimaginable, unthinkable.
inconclusive *adj* inconsequent, inconsequential, indecisive, unconvincing. illogical, unproved, unproven.
incongruity *n* absurdity, contradiction, contradictoriness, contrariety, discordance, discordancy, discrepancy, impropriety, inappropriateness, incoherence, incompatibility, inconsistency, unfitness, unsuitableness.
incongruous *adj* absurd, contradictory, contrary, disagreeing, discrepant, inappropriate, incoherent, incompatible, inconsistent, inharmonious, unfit, unsuitable.
inconsequent *adj* desultory, disconnected, fragmentary, illogical, inconclusive, inconsistent, irrelevant, loose.
inconsiderable *adj* immaterial, insignificant, petty, slight, small, trifling, trivial, unimportant.
inconsiderate *adj* intolerant, uncharitable, unthoughtful; careless, heedless, giddy, harebrained, hasty, headlong, imprudent, inadvertent, inattentive, indifferent, indiscreet, lightheaded, negligent, rash, thoughtless.
inconsistency *n* incoherence, incompatibility, incongruity, unsuitableness; contradiction, contrariety; changeableness, inconstancy, instability, vacillation, unsteadiness.
inconsistent *adj* different, discrepant, illogical, incoherent, incompatible, incongruous, inconsequent, inconsonant, irreconcilable, unsuitable; contradictory, contrary; changeable, fickle, inconstant, unstable, unsteady, vacillating, variable.
inconsolable *adj* comfortless, crushed, disconsolate, forlorn, heartbroken, hopeless, woebegone.
inconstancy *n* changeableness, mutability, variability, variation, fluctuation, faithlessness, fickleness, capriciousness, vacillation, uncertainty, unsteadiness, volatility.
inconstant *adj* capricious, changeable, faithless, fickle, fluctuating, mercurial, mutable, unsettled, unsteady, vacillating, variable, varying, volatile,

wavering; mutable, uncertain, unstable.
incontestable *adj* certain, incontrovertible, indisputable, indubitable, irrefrangible, sure, undeniable, unquestionable.
incontinence *n* excess, extravagance, indulgence, intemperance, irrepressibility, lasciviousness, lewdness, licentiousness, prodigality, profligacy, riotousness, unrestraint, wantonness, wildness.
incontinent *adj* debauched, lascivious, lewd, licentious, lustful, prodigal, unchaste, uncontrolled, unrestrained.
incontrovertible *adj* certain, incontestable, indisputable, indubitable, irrefutable, sure, undeniable, unquestionable.
inconvenience *vb* discommode; annoy, disturb, molest, trouble, vex. * *n* annoyance, disadvantage, disturbance, molestation, trouble, vexation; awkwardness, cumbersomeness, incommodiousness, unwieldiness; unfitness, unseasonableness, unsuitableness.
inconvenient *adj* annoying, awkward, cumbersome, cumbrous, disadvantageous, incommodious, inopportune, troublesome, uncomfortable, unfit, unhandy, unmanageable, unseasonable, unsuitable, untimely, unwieldy, vexatious.
incorporate *vb* affiliate, amalgamate, associate, blend, combine, consolidate, include, merge, mix, unite; embody, incarnate. * *adj* incorporeal, immaterial, spiritual, supernatural; blended, consolidated, merged, united.
incorporation *n* affiliation, alignment, amalgamation, association, blend, blending, combination, consolidation, fusion, inclusion, merger, mixture, unification, union, embodiment, incarnation, personification.
incorporeal *adj* bodiless, immaterial, impalpable, incorporate, spiritual, supernatural, unsubstantial.
incorrect *adj* erroneous, false, inaccurate, inexact, untrue, wrong; faulty, improper, mistaken, ungrammatical, unbecoming, unsound.
incorrectness *n* error, inaccuracy, inexactness, mistake.
incorrigible *adj* abandoned, graceless, hardened, irreclaimable, lost, obdurate, recreant, reprobate, shameless; helpless, hopeless, irremediable, irrecoverable, irreparable, irretrievable, irreversible, remediless.
incorruptibility *n* unpurchasableness; deathlessness, immortality, imperishableness, incorruptibleness, incorruption, indestructibility.
incorruptible *adj* honest, unbribable; imperishable, indestructible, immortal, undying, deathless, everlasting.
increase *vb* accrue, advance, augment, enlarge, extend, grow, intensify, mount, wax; multiply; enhance, greaten, heighten, raise, reinforce; aggravate, prolong. * *n* accession, accretion, accumulation, addition, augmentation, crescendo, development, enlargement, expansion, extension, growth, heightening, increment, intensification, multiplication, swelling; gain, produce, product, profit; descendants, issue, offspring, progeny.
incredible *adj* absurd, inadmissible, nonsensical, unbelievable.
incredulity *n* distrust, doubt, incredulousness, scepticism, unbelief.
incredulous *adj* distrustful, doubtful, dubious, sceptical, unbelieving.
increment *n* addition, augmentation, enlargement, increase.
incriminate *vb* accuse, blame, charge, criminate, impeach.
incubate *vb* brood, develop, hatch, sit.
inculcate *vb* enforce, implant, impress, infix, infuse, ingraft, inspire, instil.
inculpable *adj* blameless, faultless, innocent, irreprehensible, irreproachable, irreprovable, sinless, unblamable, unblameable.
inculpate *vb* accuse, blame, censure, charge, incriminate, impeach, incriminate.
inculpatory *adj* criminatory, incriminating.
incumbent *adj* binding, devolved, devolving, laid, obligatory; leaning, prone, reclining, resting. * *n* holder, occupant.
incur *vb* acquire, bring, contract.
incurable *adj* cureless, hopeless, irrecoverable, remediless; helpless, incorrigible, irremediable, irreparable, irretrievable, remediless.
incurious *adj* careless, heedless, inattentive, indifferent, uninquisitive, unobservant, uninterested.
incursion *n* descent, foray, raid, inroad, irruption.
incursive *adj* aggressive, hostile, invasive, predatory, raiding.
incurvate *vb* bend, bow, crook, curve. * *adj* (*bot*) aduncous, arcuate, bowed, crooked, curved, hooked.
indebted *adj* beholden, obliged, owing.
indecency *n* impropriety, indecorum, offensiveness, outrageousness, unseemliness; coarseness, filthiness, foulness, grossness, immodesty, impurity, obscenity, vileness.
indecent *adj* bold, improper, indecorous, offensive, outrageous, unbecoming, unseemly; coarse, dirty, filthy, gross, immodest, impure, indelicate, lewd, nasty, obscene, pornographic, salacious, shameless, smutty, unchaste.
indecipherable *adj* illegible, undecipherable, undiscoverable, inexplicable, obscure, unintelligible, unreadable.
indecision *n* changeableness, fickleness, hesitation, inconstancy, irresolution, unsteadiness, vacillation.
indecisive *adj* dubious, hesitating, inconclusive, irresolute, undecided, unsettled, vacillating, wavering.
indecorous *adj* coarse, gross, ill-bred, impolite, improper, indecent, rude, unbecoming, uncivil, unseemly.
indecorum *n* grossness, ill-breeding, ill manners, impoliteness, impropriety, incivility, indecency, indecorousness.

indeed *adv* absolutely, actually, certainly, in fact, in truth, in reality, positively, really, strictly, truly, verily, veritably. * *interj* really! you don't say so! is it possible!
indefatigable *adj* assiduous, never-tiring, persevering, persistent, sedulous, tireless, unflagging, unremitting, untiring, unwearied.
indefeasible *adj* immutable, inalienable, irreversible, irrevocable, unalterable.
indefensible *adj* censurable, defenceless, faulty, unpardonable, untenable; inexcusable, insupportable, unjustifiable, unwarrantable, wrong.
indefinite *adj* confused, doubtful, equivocal, general, imprecise, indefinable, indecisive, indeterminate, indistinct, inexact, inexplicit, lax, loose, nondescript, obscure, uncertain, undefined, undetermined, unfixed, unsettled, vague.
indelible *adj* fast, fixed, ineffaceable, ingrained, permanent.
indelicacy *n* coarseness, grossness, indecorousness, indecorum, impropriety, offensiveness, unseemliness, vulgarity; immodesty, indecency, lewdness, unchastity; foulness, obscenity.
indelicate *adj* broad, coarse, gross, indecorous, intrusive, rude, unbecoming, unseemly; foul, immodest, indecent, lewd, obscene, unchaste, vulgar.
indemnification *n* compensation, reimbursement, remuneration, security.
indemnify *vb* compensate, reimburse, remunerate, requite, secure.
indent *vb* bruise, jag, notch, pink, scallop, serrate; bind, indenture.
indentation *n* bruise, dent, depression, jag, notch.
indenture *vb* bind, indent. * *n* contract, instrument; indentation.
independence *n* freedom, liberty, self-direction; distinctness, nondependence, separation; competence, ease.
independent *adj* absolute, autonomous, free, self-directing, uncoerced, unrestrained, unrestricted, voluntary; (*person*) self-reliant, unconstrained, unconventional.
indescribable *adj* ineffable, inexpressible, nameless, unutterable.
indestructible *adj* abiding, endless, enduring, everlasting, fadeless, imperishable, incorruptible, undecaying.
indeterminate *adj* indefinite, uncertain, undetermined, unfixed.
index *vb* alphabetize, catalogue, codify, earmark, file, list, mark, tabulate. * *n* catalogue, list, register, tally; indicator, lead, mark, pointer, sign, signal, token; contents, table of contents; forefinger; exponent.
indicate *vb* betoken, denote, designate, evince, exhibit, foreshadow, manifest, mark, point out, prefigure, presage, register, show, signify, specify, tell; hint, imply, intimate, sketch, suggest.
indication *n* hint, index, manifestation, mark, note, sign, suggestion, symptom, token.
indicative *adj* significant, suggestive, symptomatic; (*gram*) affirmative, declarative.
indict *vb* (*law*) accuse, charge, present.
indictment *n* (*law*) indicting, presentment; accusation, arraignment, charge, crimination, impeachment.
indifference *n* apathy, carelessness, coldness, coolness, heedlessness, inattention, insignificance, negligence, unconcern, unconcernedness, uninterestedness; disinterestedness, impartiality, neutrality.
indifferent *adj* apathetic, cold, cool, dead, distant, dull, easy-going, frigid, heedless, inattentive, incurious, insensible, insouciant, listless, lukewarm, nonchalant, perfunctory, regardless, stoical, unconcerned, uninterested, unmindful, unmoved; equal; fair, medium, middling, moderate, ordinary, passable, tolerable; mediocre, so-so; immaterial, unimportant; disinterested, impartial, neutral, unbiased.
indigence *n* destitution, distress, necessity, need, neediness, pauperism, penury, poverty, privation, want.
indigenous *adj* aboriginal, home-grown, inborn, inherent, native.
indigent *adj* destitute, distressed, insolvent, moneyless, necessitous, needy, penniless, pinched, poor, reduced.
indigested *adj* unconcocted, undigested; crude, ill-advised, ill-considered, ill-judged; confused, disorderly, ill-arranged, unmethodical.
indigestion *n* dyspepsia, dyspepsy.
indignant *adj* angry, exasperated, incensed, irate, ireful, provoked, roused, wrathful, wroth.
indignation *n* anger, choler, displeasure, exasperation, fury, ire, rage, resentment, wrath.
indignity *n* abuse, affront, contumely, dishonour, disrespect, ignominy, insult, obloquy, opprobrium, outrage, reproach, slight.
indirect *adj* circuitous, circumlocutory, collateral, devious, oblique, roundabout, sidelong, tortuous; deceitful, dishonest, dishonorable, unfair; mediate, remote, secondary, subordinate.
indiscernible *adj* imperceptible, indistinguishable, invisible, undiscernible, undiscoverable.
indiscipline *n* laxity, insubordination.
indiscreet *adj* foolish, hasty, headlong, heedless, imprudent, incautious, inconsiderate, injudicious, rash, reckless, unwise.
indiscretion *n* folly, imprudence, inconsiderateness, rashness; blunder, faux pas, lapse, mistake, misstep.
indiscriminate *adj* confused, heterogeneous, indistinct, mingled, miscellaneous, mixed, promiscuous, undiscriminating, undistinguishable, undistinguishing.
indispensable *adj* essential, expedient, necessary, needed, needful, requisite.
indisputable *adj* certain, incontestable, indubitable, infallible, sure, undeniable, undoubted,

unmistakable, unquestionable.

indisposed *adj* ailing, ill, sick, unwell; averse, backward, disinclined, loath, reluctant, unfriendly, unwilling.

indisposition *n* ailment, illness, sickness; aversion, backwardness, dislike, disinclination, reluctance, unwillingness.

indisputable *adj* certain, incontestable, indutitable, infallible, sure, undeniable, undoubted, unmistakable, unquestionable.

indissoluble *adj* abiding, enduring, firm, imperishable, incorruptible, indestructible, lasting, stable, unbreakable.

indistinct *adj* ambiguous, doubtful, uncertain; blurred, dim, dull, faint, hazy, misty, nebulous, obscure, shadowy, vague; confused, inarticulate, indefinite, indistinguishable, undefined, undistinguishable.

indistinguishable *adj* imperceptible, indiscernible, unnoticeable, unobservable; chaotic, confused, dim, indistinct, obscure, vague.

indite *vb* compose, pen, write.

individual *adj* characteristic, distinct, identical, idiosyncratic, marked, one, particular, personal, respective, separate, single, singular, special, unique; peculiar, proper; decided, definite, independent, positive, self-guided, unconventional. * *n* being, character, party, person, personage, somebody, someone; type, unit.

individuality *n* definiteness, indentity, personality; originality, self-direction, self-determination, singularity, uniqueness.

individualize *vb* individuate, particularize, singularize, specify.

indivisible *adj* incommensurable, indissoluble, inseparable, unbreakable, unpartiable.

indocile *adj* cantankerous, contumacious, dogged, froward, inapt, headstrong, intractable, mulish, obstinate, perverse, refractory, stubborn, ungovernable, unmanageable, unruly, unteachable.

indoctrinate *vb* brainwash, imbue, initiate, instruct, rehabilitate, teach.

indoctrination *n* grounding, initiation, instruction, rehabilitation.

indolence *n* idleness, inactivity, inertia, inertness, laziness, listlessness, sloth, slothfulness, sluggishness.

indolent *adj* easy, easy-going, inactive, inert, lazy, listless, lumpish, otiose, slothful, sluggish, supine.

indomitable *adj* invincible, unconquerable, unyielding.

indorse *see* **endorse**.

indubitable *adj* certain, evident, incontestable, incontrovertible, indisputable, sure, undeniable, unquestionable.

induce *vb* actuate, allure, bring, draw, drive, entice, impel, incite, influence, instigate, move, persuade, prevail, prompt, spur, urge; bring on, cause, effect, motivate, lead, occasion, produce.

inducement *n* allurement, draw, enticement, instigation, persuasion; cause, consideration, impulse, incentive, incitement, influence, motive, reason, spur, stimulus.

induct *vb* inaugurate, initiate, install, institute, introduce, invest.

induction *n* inauguration, initiation, institution, installation, introduction; conclusion, generalization, inference.

indue *vb* assume, endow, clothe, endue, invest, supply.

indulge *vb* gratify, license, revel, satisfy, wallow, yield to; coddle, cosset, favour, humour, pamper, pet, spoil; allow, cherish, foster, harbour, permit, suffer.

indulgence *n* gratification, humouring, pampering; favour, kindness, lenience, lenity, liberality, tenderness; (*theol*) absolution, remission.

indulgent *adj* clement, easy, favouring, forbearing, gentle, humouring, kind, lenient, mild, pampering, tender, tolerant.

indurate *vb* harden, inure, sear, strengthen.

induration *n* hardening, obduracy.

industrious *adj* assiduous, diligent, hard-working, laborious, notable, operose, sedulous; brisk, busy, persevering, persistent.

industry *n* activity, application, assiduousness, assiduity, diligence; perseverance, persistence, sedulousness, vigour; effort, labour, toil.

inebriated *adj* drunk, intoxicated, stupefied.

ineffable *adj* indescribable, inexpressible, unspeakable, unutterable.

ineffaceable *adj* indelible, indestructible, inerasable, inexpungeable, ingrained.

ineffectual *adj* abortive, bootless, fruitless, futile, inadequate, inefficacious, ineffective, inoperative, useless, unavailing, vain; feeble, inefficient, powerless, impotent, weak.

inefficacy *n* ineffectualness, inefficiency.

inefficient *adj* feeble, incapable, ineffectual, ineffective, inefficacious, weak.

inelastic *adj* flabby, flaccid, inductile, inflexible, irresilient.

inelegant *adj* abrupt, awkward, clumsy, coarse, constrained, cramped, crude, graceless, harsh, homely, homespun, rough, rude, stiff, tasteless, uncourtly, uncouth, ungainly, ungraceful, unpolished, unrefined.

ineligible *adj* disqualified, unqualified; inexpedient, objectionable, unadvisable, undesirable.

inept *adj* awkward, improper, inapposite, inappropriate, unapt, unfit, unsuitable; null, useless, void, worthless; foolish, nonsensical, pointless, senseless, silly, stupid.

ineptitude *n* inappositeness, inappropriateness, inaptitude, unfitness, unsuitability, unsuitableness; emptiness, nullity, uselessness, worthlessness; folly, foolishness, nonsense, pointlessness, senselessness, silliness, stupidity.

inequality *n* disproportion, inequitableness, injustice, unfairness; difference, disparity, dissimilarity, diversity, imparity, irregularity, roughness, unevenness; inadequacy, incompetency, insufficiency.

inequitable *adj* unfair, unjust.

inert *adj* comatose, dead, inactive, lifeless, motionless, quiescent, passive; apathetic, dronish, dull, idle, indolent, lazy, lethargic, lumpish, phlegmatic, slothful, sluggish, supine, torpid.

inertia *n* apathy, inertness, lethargy, passiveness, passivity, slothfulness, sluggishness.

inestimable *adj* incalculable, invaluable, precious, priceless, valuable.

inevitable *adj* certain, necessary, unavoidable, undoubted.

inexact *adj* imprecise, inaccurate, incorrect; careless, crude, loose.

inexcusable *adj* indefensible, irremissible, unallowable, unjustifiable, unpardonable.

inexhaustible *adj* boundless, exhaustless, indefatigable, unfailing, unlimited.

inexorable *adj* cruel, firm, hard, immovable, implacable, inflexible, merciless, pitiless, relentless, severe, steadfast, unbending, uncompassionate, unmerciful, unrelenting, unyielding.

inexpedient *adj* disadvantageous, ill-judged, impolitic, imprudent, indiscreet, injudicious, inopportune, unadvisable, unprofitable, unwise.

inexperience *n* greenness, ignorance, rawness.

inexperienced *adj* callow, green, raw, strange, unacquainted, unconversant, undisciplined, uninitiated, unpractised, unschooled, unskilled, untrained, untried, unversed, young.

inexpert *adj* awkward, bungling, clumsy, inapt, maladroit, unhandy, unskilful, unskilled.

inexpiable *adj* implacable, inexorable, irreconcilable, unappeasable; irremissible, unatonable, unpardonable.

inexplicable *adj* enigmatic, enigmatical, incomprehensible, inscrutable, mysterious, strange, unaccountable, unintelligible.

inexpressible *adj* indescribable, ineffable, unspeakable, unutterable; boundless, infinite, surpassing.

inexpressive *adj* blank, characterless, dull, unexpressive.

inextinguishable *adj* unquenchable.

in extremis *adv* moribund.

inextricable *adj* entangled, intricate, perplexed, unsolvable.

infallibility *n* certainty, infallibleness, perfection.

infallible *adj* certain, indubitable, oracular, sure, unerring, unfailing.

infamous *adj* abominable, atrocious, base, damnable, dark, detestable, discreditable, disgraceful, dishonorable, disreputable, heinous, ignominious, nefarious, odious, opprobrious, outrageous, scandalous, shameful, shameless, vile, villainous, wicked.

infamy *n* abasement, discredit, disgrace, dishonour, disrepute, ignominy, obloquy, odium, opprobrium, scandal, shame; atrocity, detestableness, disgracefulness, dishonorableness, odiousness, scandalousness, shamefulness, villainy, wickedness.

infancy *n* beginning, commencement; babyhood, childhood, minority, nonage, pupillage.

infant *n* babe, baby, bairn, bantling, brat, chit, minor, nursling, papoose, suckling, tot.

infantile *adj* childish, infantine, newborn, tender, young; babyish, childish, weak; babylike, childlike.

infatuate *vb* befool, besot, captivate, delude, prepossess, stultify.

infatuation *n* absorption, besottedness, folly, foolishness, prepossession, stupefaction.

infeasible *adj* impractical, unfeasible.

infect *vb* affect, contaminate, corrupt, defile, poison, pollute, taint, vitiate.

infection *n* affection, bane, contagion, contamination, corruption, defilement, pest, poison, pollution, taint, virus, vitiation.

infectious *adj* catching, communicable, contagious, contaminating, corrupting, defiling, demoralizing, pestiferous, pestilential, poisoning, polluting, sympathetic, vitiating.

infecund *adj* barren, infertile, sterile, unfruitful, unproductive, unprolific.

infecundity *n* unfruitfulness.

infelicitous *adj* calamitous, miserable, unfortunate, unhappy, wretched; inauspicious, unfavourable, unpropitious; ill-chosen, inappropriate, unfitting.

infer *vb* collect, conclude, deduce, derive, draw, gather, glean, guess, presume, reason.

inference *n* conclusion, consequence, corollary, deduction, generalization, guess, illation, implication, induction, presumption.

inferior *adj* lower, nether; junior, minor, secondary, subordinate; bad, base, deficient, humble, imperfect, indifferent, mean, mediocre, paltry, poor, second-rate, shabby.

inferiority *n* juniority, subjection, subordination, mediocrity; deficiency, imperfection, inadequacy, shortcoming.

infernal *adj* abominable, accursed, atrocious, damnable, dark, demoniacal, devilish, diabolical, fiendish, fiendlike, hellish, malicious, nefarious, satanic, Stygian.

infertility *n* barrenness, infecundity, sterility, unfruitfulness, unproductivity.

infest *vb* annoy, disturb, harass, haunt, molest, plague, tease, torment, trouble, vex, worry; beset, overrun, possess, swarm, throng.

infidel *n* agnostic, atheist, disbeliever, heathen, heretic, sceptic, unbeliever.

infidelity *n* adultery, disloyality, faithlessness, treachery, unfaithfulness; disbelief, scepticism, unbelief.

infiltrate *vb* absorb, pervade, soak.

infinite *adj* boundless, endless, illimitable, immeasurable, inexhaustible, interminable, limitless, measureless, perfect, unbounded, unlimited; enormous, immense, stupendous, vast;

absolue, eternal, self-determined, self-existent, unconditioned.

infinitesimal *adj* infinitely small; microscopic, miniscule.

infinity *n* absoluteness, boundlessness, endlessness, eternity, immensity, infiniteness, infinitude, interminateness, self-determination, self-existence, vastness.

infirm *adj* ailing, debilitated, enfeebled, feeble, frail, weak, weakened; faltering, irresolute, vacillating, wavering; insecure, precarious, unsound, unstable.

infirmity *n* ailment, debility, feebleness, frailness, frailty, weakness; defect, failing, fault, foible, weakness.

infix *vb* fasten, fix, plant, set; implant, inculcate, infuse, ingraft, instil.

inflame *vb* animate, arouse, excite, enkindle, fire, heat, incite, inspirit, intensify, rouse, stimulate; aggravate, anger, chafe, embitter, enrage, exasperate, incense, infuriate, irritate, madden, nettle, provoke.

inflammability *n* combustibility, combustibleness, inflammableness.

inflammable *adj* combustible, ignitible; excitable.

inflammation *n* burning, conflagration; anger, animosity, excitement, heat, rage, turbulence, violence.

inflammatory *adj* fiery, inflaming; dissentious, incendiary, seditious.

inflate *vb* bloat, blow up, distend, expand, swell, sufflate; elate, puff up; enlarge, increase.

inflated *adj* bloated, distended, puffed-up, swollen; bombastic, declamatory, grandiloquent, high-flown, magniloquent, overblown, pompous, rhetorical, stilted, tumid, turgid.

inflation *n* enlargement, increase, overenlargement, overissue; bloatedness, distension, expansion, sufflation; bombast, conceit, conceitedness, self-conceit, self-complacency, self-importance, self-sufficiency, vaingloriousness, vainglory.

inflect *vb* bend, bow, curve, turn; (*gram*) conjugate, decline, vary.

inflection *n* bend, bending, crook, curvature, curvity, flexure; (*gram*) accidence, conjugation, declension, variation; (*mus*) modulation.

inflexibility *n* inflexibleness, rigidity, stiffness; doggedness, obstinacy, perinacity, stubbornness; firmness, perseverance, resolution, tenacity.

inflexible *adj* rigid, rigorous, stiff, unbending; cantankerous, cross-grained, dogged, headstrong, heady, inexorable, intractable, obdurate, obstinant, pertinacious, refractory, stubborn, unyielding, wilful; firm, immovable, persevering, resolute, steadfast, unbending.

inflict *vb* bring, impose, lay on.

infliction *n* imposition, inflicting; judgment, punishment.

inflorescence *n* blooming, blossoming, flowering.

influence *vb* affect, bias, control, direct, lead, modify, prejudice, prepossess, sway; actuate, arouse, impel, incite, induce, instigate, move, persuade, prevail upon, rouse. * *n* ascendancy, authority, control, mastery, potency, predominance, pull, rule, sway; credit, reputation, weight; inflow, inflowing, influx; magnetism, power, spell.

influential *adj* controlling, effective, effectual, potent, powerful, strong; authoritative, momentous, substantial, weighty.

influx *n* flowing in, introduction.

infold *see* **enfold**.

inform *vb* animate, inspire, quicken; acquaint, advise, apprise, enlighten, instruct, notify, teach, tell, tip, warn.

informal *adj* unceremonious, unconventional, unofficial; easy, familiar, natural, simple; irregular, nonconformist, unusual.

informality *n* unceremoniousness; unconventionality; ease, familiarity, naturalness, simplicity; noncomformity, irregularity, unusualness.

informant *n* advertiser, adviser, informer, intelligencer, newsmonger, notifier, relator; accuser, complainant, informer.

information *n* advice, data, intelligence, knowledge, notice; advertisement, enlightenment, instruction, message, tip, word, warning; accusation, complaint, denunciation.

informer *n* accuser, complainant, informant, snitch.

infraction *n* breach, breaking, disobedience, encroachment, infringement, nonobservance, transgression, violation.

infrangible *adj* inseparable, inviolable, unbreakable.

infrequency *n* rareness, rarity, uncommonness, unusualness.

infrequent *adj* rare, uncommon, unfrequent, unusual; occasional, scant, scarce, sporadic.

infringe *vb* break, contravene, disobey, intrude, invade, transgress, violate.

infringement *n* breach, breaking, disobedience, infraction, nonobservance, transgression, violation.

infuriated *adj* angry, enraged, furious, incensed, maddened, raging, wild.

infuse *vb* breathe into, implant, inculcate, ingraft, insinuate, inspire, instil, introduce; macerate, steep.

infusion *n* inculcation, instillation, introduction; infusing, macerating, steeping.

ingathering *n* harvest.

ingenious *adj* able, adroit, artful, bright, clever, fertile, gifted, inventive, ready, sagacious, shrewd, witty.

ingenuity *n* ability, acuteness, aptitude, aptness, capacity, capableness, cleverness, faculty, genius, gift, ingeniousness, inventiveness, knack, readiness, skill, turn.

ingenuous *adj* artless, candid, childlike, downright, frank, generous, guileless, honest, innocent, naive, open, open-hearted, plain, simple-minded, sincere, single-minded, straightforward, transparent, truthful, unreserved.

ingenuousness *n* artlessness, candour, childlikeness, frankness, guilelessness, honesty, naivety, open-heartedness, openness, sincerity, single-mindedness, truthfulness.

inglorious *adj* humble, lowly, mean, nameless, obscure, undistinguished, unhonoured, unknown, unmarked, unnoted; discreditable, disgraceful, humiliating, ignominous, scandalous, shameful.

ingloriousness *n* humbleness, lowliness, meanness, namelessness, obscurity; abasement, discredit, disgrace, dishonour, disrepute, humiliation, infamy, ignominousness, ignominy, obloquy, odium, opprobrium, shame.

ingraft *vb* graft, implant, inculcate, infix, infuse, instil.

ingrain *vb* dye, imbue, impregnate.

ingratiate *vb* insinuate.

ingratitude *n* thanklessness, ungratefulness, unthankfulness.

ingredient *n* component, constituent, element.

ingress *n* entrance, entré, entry, introgression.

ingulf *see* **engulf**.

inhabit *vb* abide, dwell, live, occupy, people, reside, sojourn.

inhabitable *adj* habitable, livable.

inhabitant *n* citizen, denizen, dweller, inhabiter, resident.

inhalation *n* breath, inhaling, inspiration; sniff, snuff.

inhale *vb* breathe in, draw in, inbreathe, inspire.

inharmonious *adj* discordant, inharmonic, out of tune, unharmonious, unmusical.

inhere *vb* cleave to, stick, stick fast; abide, belong, exist, lie, pertain, reside.

inherent *adj* essential, immanent, inborn, inbred, indwelling, ingrained, innate, inseparable, intrinsic, native, natural, proper; adhering, sticking.

inherit *vb* get, receive.

inheritance *n* heritage, legacy, patrimony; inheriting.

inheritor *n* heir, (*law*) parcener.

inhibit *vb* bar, check, debar, hinder, obstruct, prevent, repress, restrain, stop; forbid, interdict, prohibit.

inhibition *n* check, hindrance, impediment, obstacle, obstruction, restraint; disallowance, embargo, interdict, interdiction, prevention, prohibition.

inhospitable *adj* cool, forbidding, unfriendly, unkind; bigoted, illiberal, intolerant, narrow, prejudiced, ungenerous, unreceptive; barren, wild.

inhospitality *n* inhospitableness, unkindness; illiberality, narrowness.

inhuman *adj* barbarous, brutal, cruel, fell, ferocious, merciless, pitiless, remorseless, ruthless, savage, unfeeling; nonhuman.

inhumanity *n* barbarity, brutality, cruelty, ferocity, savageness; hard-heartedness, unkindness.

inhume *vb* bury, entomb, inter.

inimical *adj* antagonistic, hostile, unfriendly; adverse, contrary, harmful, hurtful, noxious, opposed, pernicious, repugnant, unfavourable.

inimitable *adj* incomparable, matchless, peerless, unequalled, unexampled, unmatched, unparagoned, unparalleled, unrivalled, unsurpassed.

iniquitous *adj* atrocious, criminal, flagitious, heinous, inequitable, nefarious, sinful, wicked, wrong, unfair, unjust, unrighteous.

iniquity *n* injustice, sin, sinfulness, unrighteousness, wickedness, wrong; crime, misdeed, offence.

initial *adj* first; beginning, commencing, incipient, initiatory, introductory, opening, original; elementary, inchoate, rudimentary.

initiate *vb* begin, commence, enter upon, inaugurate, introduce, open; ground, indoctrinate, instruct, prime, teach.

initiation *n* beginning, commencement, inauguration, opening; admission, entrance, introduction; indoctrinate, instruction.

initiative *n* beginning; energy, enterprise.

initiatory *adj* inceptive, initiative.

inject *vb* force in, interject, insert, introduce, intromit.

injudicious *adj* foolish, hasty, ill-advised, ill-judged, imprudent, incautious, inconsiderate, indiscreet, rash, unwise.

injunction *n* admonition, bidding, command, mandate, order, precept.

injure *vb* damage, disfigure, harm, hurt, impair, mar, spoil, sully, wound; abuse, aggrieve, wrong; affront, dishonour, insult.

injurious *adj* baneful, damaging, deadly, deleterious, destructive, detrimental, disadvantageous, evil, fatal, hurtful, mischievous, noxious, pernicious, prejudicial, ruinous; inequitable, iniquitous, unjust, wrongful; contumelious, detractory, libellous, slanderous.

injury *n* evil, ill, injustice, wrong; damage, detriment, harm, hurt, impairment, loss, mischief, prejudice.

injustice *n* inequity, unfairness; grievance, iniquity, injury, wrong.

inkhorn *n* inkbottle, inkstand.

inkling *n* hint, intimation, suggestion, whisper.

inky *adj* atramentous, black, murky.

inland *adj* domestic, hinterland, home, upcountry; interior, internal.

inlet *n* arm, bay, bight, cove, creek; entrance, ingress, passage.

inmate *n* denizen, dweller, guest, intern, occupant.

inmost *adj* deepest, innermost.

inn *n* hostel, hostelry, hotel, pub, public house, tavern.

innate *adj* congenital, constitutional, inborn, inbred, indigenous, inherent, inherited, instinctive, native, natural, organic.

inner *adj* interior, internal.
innermost *adj* deepest, inmost.
innkeeper *n* host, innholder, landlady, landlord, tavernkeeper.
innocence *n* blamelessness, chastity, guilelessness, guiltlessness, purity, simplicity, sinlessness, stainlessness; harmlessness, innocuousness, innoxiousness, inoffensiveness.
innocent *adj* blameless, clean, clear, faultless, guiltless, immaculate, pure, sinless, spotless, unfallen, upright; harmless, innocuous, innoxious, inoffensive; lawful, legitimate, permitted; artless, guileless, ignorant, ingenuous, simple. * *n* babe, child, ingénue, naif, naive, unsophisticate.
innocuous *adj* harmless, innocent, inoffensive, safe.
innovate *vb* change, introduce.
innovation *n* change, introduction; departure, novelty.
innuendo *n* allusion, hint, insinuation, intimation, suggestion.
innumerable *adj* countless, numberless.
inoculate *vb* infect, vaccinate.
inoffensive *adj* harmless, innocent, innocuous, innoxious, unobjectionable, unoffending.
inoperative *adj* inactive, ineffectual, inefficacious, not in force.
inopportune *adj* ill-timed, inexpedient, infelicitous, mistimed, unfortunate, unhappy, unseasonable, untimely.
inordinate *adj* excessive, extravagant, immoderate, intemperate, irregular.
inorganic *adj* inanimate, unorganized; mineral.
inquest *n* inquiry, inquisition, investigation, quest, search.
inquietude *n* anxiety, disquiet, disquietude, disturbance, restlessness, uneasiness.
inquire, enquire *vb* ask, catechize, interpellate, interrogate, investigate, query, question, quiz.
inquiry, enquiry *n* examination, exploration, investigation, research, scrutiny, study; interrogation, query, question, quiz.
inquisition *n* examination, inquest, inquiry, investigation, search.
inquisitive *adj* curious, inquiring, scrutinizing; curious, meddlesome, peeping, peering, prying.
inroad *n* encroachment, foray, incursion, invasion, irruption, raid.
insalubrious *adj* noxious, unhealthful, unhealthy, unwholesome.
insane *adj* abnormal, crazed, crazy, delirious, demented, deranged, distracted, lunatic, mad, maniacal, unhealthy, unsound.
insanity *n* craziness, delirium, dementia, derangement, lunacy, madness, mania, mental aberration, mental alienation.
insatiable *adj* greedy, rapacious, voracious; insatiate, unappeasable.
inscribe *vb* emblaze, endorse, engrave, enroll, impress, imprint, letter, mark, write; address, dedicate.
inscrutable *adj* hidden, impenetrable, incomprehensible, inexplicable, mysterious, undiscoverable, unfathomable, unsearchable.
inscrutableness *n* impenetrability, incomprehensibility, incomprehensibleness, inexplicability, inscrutability, mysteriousness, mystery, unfathomableness, unsearchableness.
insecure *adj* risky, uncertain, unconfident, unsure; exposed, ill-protected, unprotected, unsafe; dangerous, hazardous, perilous; infirm, shaking, shaky, tottering, unstable, weak, wobbly.
insecurity *n* riskiness, uncertainty; danger, hazardousness, peril; instability, shakiness, weakness, wobbliness.
insensate *adj* dull, indifferent, insensible, torpid; brutal, foolish, senseless, unwise; inanimate, insensible, insentient, nonpercipient, unconscious, unperceiving.
insensibility *n* dullness, insentience, lethargy, torpor; apathy, indifference, insusceptibility, unfeelingness, dullness, stupidity; anaesthesia, coma, stupor, unconsciousness.
insensible *adj* imperceivable, imperceptible, undiscoverable; blunted, brutish, deaf, dull, insensate, numb, obtuse, senseless, sluggish, stolid, stupid, torpid, unconscious; apathetic, callous, phlegmatic, impassive, indifferent, insensitive, insentient, unfeeling, unimpressible, unsusceptible.
insensibly *adv* imperceptibly.
insentient *adj* inert, nonsentient, senseless; inanimate, insensible, insensate, nonpercipient, unconscious, unperceiving.
inseparable *adj* close, friendly, intimate, together; indissoluble, indivisible, inseverable.
insert *vb* infix, inject, intercalate, interpolate, introduce, inweave, parenthesize, place, put, set.
inside *adj* inner, interior, internal; confidential, exclusive, internal, private, secret. * *adv* indoors, within. * *n* inner part, interior; nature.
insidious *adj* creeping, deceptive, gradual, secretive; arch, artful, crafty, crooked, cunning, deceitful, designing, diplomatic, foxy, guileful, intriguing, Machiavellian, sly, sneaky, subtle, treacherous, trickish, tricky, wily.
insight *n* discernment, intuition, penetration, perception, perspicuity, understanding.
insignia *npl* badges, marks.
insignificance *n* emptiness, nothingenss, paltriness, triviality, unimportance.
insignificant *adj* contemptible, empty, immaterial, inconsequential, inconsiderable, inferior, meaningless, paltry, petty, small, sorry, trifling, trivial, unessential, unimportant.
insincere *adj* deceitful, dishonest, disingenuous, dissembling, dissimulating, double-faced, double-tongued, duplicitous, empty, faithless, false, hollow, hypocritical, pharisaical, truthless, uncandid, untrue.
insincerity *n* bad faith, deceitfulness, dishonesty, disingenuousness, dissimulation, duplicity, falseness, faithlessness, hypocrisy.

insinuate *vb* hint, inculcate, infuse, ingratiate, instil, intimate, introduce, suggest.
insipid *adj* dead, dull, flat, heavy, inanimate, jejune, lifeless, monotonous, pointless, prosaic, prosy, spiritless, stupid, tame, unentertaining, uninteresting; mawkish, savourless, stale, tasteless, vapid, zestless.
insipidity, insipidness *n* dullness, heaviness, lifelessness, prosiness, stupidity, tameness; flatness, mawkishness, staleness, tastlessness, unsavouriness, vapidness, zestlessness.
insist *vb* demand, maintain, urge.
insistence *n* importunity, solicitousness, urging, urgency.
insnare *see* **ensnare**.
insolence *n* impertinence, impudence, malapertness, pertness, rudeness, sauciness; contempt, contumacy, contumely, disrespect, frowardness, insubordination.
insolent *adj* abusive, contemptuous, contumelious, disrespectful, domineering, insulting, offensive, overbearing, rude, supercilious; cheeky, impertinent, impudent, malapert, pert, saucy; contumacious, disobedient, froward, insubordinate.
insoluble *adj* indissoluble, indissolvable, irreducible; inexplicable, insolvable.
insolvable *adj* inexplicable.
insolvent *adj* bankrupt, broken, failed, ruined.
insomnia *n* sleeplessness, wakefulness.
inspect *vb* examine, investigate, look into, pry into, scrutinize; oversee, superintend, supervise.
inspection *n* examination, investigation, scrutiny; oversight, superintendence, supervision.
inspector *n* censor, critic, examiner, visitor; boss, overseer, superintendent, supervisor.
inspiration *n* breathing, inhalation; afflatus, fire, inflatus; elevation, exaltation; enthusiasm.
inspire *vb* breathe, inhale; infuse, instil; animate, cheer, enliven, inspirit; elevate, exalt, stimulate; fill, imbue, impart, inform, quicken.
inspirit *vb* animate, arouse, cheer, comfort, embolden, encourage, enhearten, enliven, fire, hearten, incite, invigorate, quicken, rouse, stimulate.
instable *see* **unstable**.
instability *n* changeableness, fickleness, inconstancy, insecurity, mutability.
install, instal *vb* inaugurate, induct, introduce; establish, place, set up.
installation *n* inauguration, induction, instalment, investiture.
instalment *n* earnest, payment, portion.
instance *vb* adduce, cite, mention, specify. * *n* case, example, exemplification, illustration, occasion; impulse, incitement, instigation, motive, prompting, request, solicitation.
instant *adj* direct, immediate, instantaneous, prompt, quick; current, present; earnest, fast, imperative, importunate, pressing, urgent; ready cooked. * n flash, jiffy, moment, second, trice, twinkling; hour, time.
instantaneous *adj* abrupt, immediate, instant, quick, sudden.
instantaneously *adv* forthwith, immediately, presto, quickly, right away.
instauration *n* reconstitution, reconstruction, redintegration, re-establishment, rehabilitation, reinstatement, renewal, renovation, restoration.
instead *adv* in lieu, in place, rather.
instigate *vb* actuate, agitate, encourage, impel, incite, influence, initiate, move, persuade, prevail upon, prompt, provoke, rouse, set on, spur on, stimulate, stir up, tempt, urge.
instigation *n* encouragement, incitement, influence, instance, prompting, solicitation, urgency.
instil, instill *vb* enforce, implant, impress, inculcate, ingraft; impart, infuse, insinuate.
instillation *n* infusion, insinuation, introduction.
instinct *n* natural impulse.
instinctive *adj* automatic, inherent, innate, intuitive, involuntary, natural, spontaneous; impulsive, unreflecting.
institute[1] *n* academy, college, foundation, guild, institution, school; custom, doctrine, dogma, law, maxim, precedent, principle, rule, tenet.
institute[2] *vb* begin, commence, constitute, establish, found, initial, install, introduce, organize, originate, start.
institution *n* enactment, establishment, foundation, institute, society; investiture; custom, law, practice.
instruct *vb* discipline, educate, enlighten, exercise, guide, indoctrinate, inform, initiate, school, teach, train; apprise, bid, command, direct, enjoin, order, prescribe to.
instruction *n* breeding, discipline, education, indoctrination, information, nurture, schooling, teaching, training, tuition; advice, counsel, precept; command, direction, mandate, order.
instructor *n* educator, master, preceptor, schoolteacher, teacher, tutor.
instrument *n* appliance, apparatus, contrivance, device, implement, musical instrument, tool, utensil; agent, means, medium; charter, deed, document, indenture, writing.
instrumental *adj* ancillary, assisting, auxiliary, conducive, contributory, helpful, helping, ministerial, ministrant, serviceable, subservient, subsidiary.
instrumentality *n* agency, intermediary; intervention, means, mediation.
insubordinate *adj* disobedient, disorderly, mutinous, refractory, riotous, seditious, turbulent, ungovernable, unruly.
insubordination *n* disobedience, insurrection, mutiny, revolt, riotousness, sedition; indiscipline, laxity.
insufferable *adj* intolerable, unbearable, unendurable, insupportable; abominable, detestable, disgusting, execrable, outrageous.
insufficiency *n* dearth, defectiveness, deficiency, lack, inadequacy, inadequateness, incapability,

incompetence, paucity, shortage.

insufficient *adj* deficient, inadequate, incommensurate, incompetent, scanty; incapable, incompetent, unfitted, unqualified, unsuited, unsatisfactory.

insular *adj* contracted, illiberal, limited, narrow, petty, prejudiced, restricted; isolated, remote.

insulate *vb* detach, disconnect, disengage, disunite, isolate, separate.

insulation *n* disconnection, disengagement, isolation, separation.

insult *vb* abuse, affront, injure, offend, outrage, slander, slight. * *n* abuse, affront, cheek, contumely, indignity, insolence, offence, outrage, sauce, slight.

insulting *adj* abusive, arrogant, contumelious, impertinent, impolite, insolent, rude, vituperative.

insuperable *adj* impassable, insurmountable.

insupportable *adj* insufferable, intolerable, unbearable, unendurable.

insuppressible *adj* irrepressible, uncontrollable.

insurance *n* assurance, security.

insure *vb* assure, guarantee, indemnify, secure, underwrite.

insurgent *adj* disobedient, insubordinate, mutinous, rebellious, revolting, revolutionary, seditious. * *n* mutineer, rebel, revolter, revolutionary.

insurmountable *adj* impassable, insuperable.

insurrection *n* insurgence, mutiny, rebellion, revolt, revolution, rising, sedition, uprising.

intact *adj* scathless, unharmed, unhurt, unimpaired, uninjured, untouched; complete, entire, integral, sound, unbroken, undiminished, whole.

intangible *adj* dim, impalpable, imperceptible, indefinite, insubstantial, intactile, shadowy, vague; aerial, phantom, spiritous.

intangibility *n* imperceptibility, insubstantiality, intangibleness, shadowiness, vagueness.

integral *adj* complete, component, entire, integrant, total, whole.

integrity *n* goodness, honesty, principle, probity, purity, rectitude, soundness, uprightness, virtue; completeness, entireness, entirety, wholeness.

integument *n* coat, covering, envelope, skin, tegument.

intellect *n* brains, cognitive faculty, intelligence, mind, rational faculty, reason, reasoning, faculty, sense, thought, understanding, wit.

intellectual *adj* cerebral, intelligent, mental, scholarly, thoughtful. * *n* academic, highbrow, pundit, savant, scholar.

intelligence *n* acumen, apprehension, brightness, discernment, imagination, insight, penetration, quickness, sagacity, shrewdness, understanding, wits; information, knowledge; advice, instruction, news, notice, notification, tidings; brains, intellect, mentality, sense, spirit.

intelligent *adj* acute, alert, apt, astute, brainy, bright, clear-headed, clear-sighted, clever, discerning, keen-eyed, keen-sighted, knowing, long-headed, quick, quick-sighted, sagacious, sensible, sharp-sighted, sharp-witted, shrewd, understanding.

intelligibility *n* clarity, comprehensibility, intelligibleness, perspicuity.

intelligible *adj* clear, comprehensible, distinct, evident, lucid, manifest, obvious, patent, perspicuous, plain, transparent, understandable.

intemperate *adj* drunken; excessive, extravagant, extreme, immoderate, inordinate, unbridled, uncontrolled, unrestrained; self-indulgent.

intend *vb* aim at, contemplate, design, determine, drive at, mean, meditate, propose, purpose, think of.

intendant *n* inspector, overseer, superintendent, supervisor.

intense *adj* ardent, earnest, fervid, passionate, vehement; close, intent, severe, strained, stretched, strict; energetic, forcible, keen, potent, powerful, sharp, strong, vigorous, violent; acute, deep, extreme, exquisite, grievous, poignant.

intensify *vb* aggravate, concentrate, deepen, enhance, heighten, quicken, strengthen, whet.

intensity *n* closeness, intenseness, severity, strictness; excess, extremity, violence; activity, energy, force, power, strength, vigour; ardour, earnestness, vehemence.

intensive *adj* emphatic, intensifying.

intent *adj* absorbed, attentive, close, eager, earnest, engrossed, occupied, pre-occupied, zealous; bent, determined, decided, resolved, set. * *n* aim, design, drift, end, import, intention, mark, meaning, object, plan, purport, purpose, purview, scope, view.

intention *n* aim, design, drift, end, import, intent, mark, meaning, object, plan, purport, purpose, purview, scope, view.

intentional *adj* contemplated, deliberate, designed, intended, preconcerted, predetermined, premeditated, purposed, studied, voluntary, wilful.

inter *vb* bury, commit to the earth, entomb, inhume, inurn.

intercalate *vb* insert, interpolate.

intercede *vb* arbitrate, interpose, mediate; entreat, plead, supplicate.

intercept *vb* cut off, interrupt, obstruct, seize.

intercession *n* interposition, intervention, mediation; entreaty, pleading, prayer, supplication.

intercessor *n* interceder, mediator.

interchange *vb* alternate, change, exchange, vary. * *n* alternation.

interchangeableness *n* interchangeability.

interchangeably *adv* alternately.

intercourse *n* commerce, communication, communion, connection, converse, correspondence, dealings, fellowship, truck; acquaintance, intimacy.

interdict *vb* debar, forbid, inhibit, prohibit, prescribe, proscribe, restrain from. * *n* ban, decree, interdiction, prohibition.

interest *vb* affect, concern, touch; absorb, attract, engage, enlist, excite, grip, hold, occupy. * *n* advantage, benefit, good, profit, weal; attention, concern, regard, sympathy; part, participation, portion, share, stake; discount, premium, profit.
interested *adj* attentive, concerned, involved, occupied; biassed, patial, prejudiced; selfish, self-seeking.
interesting *adj* attractive, engaging, entertaining, pleasing.
interfere *vb* intermeddle, interpose, meddle; clash, collide, conflict.
interference *n* intermeddling, interposition; clashing, collision, interfering, opposition.
interim *n* intermediate time, interval, meantime.
interior *adj* inmost, inner, internal, inward; inland, remote; domestic, home. * *n* inner part, inland, inside.
interjacent *adj* intermediate, interposed, intervening, parenthetical.
interject *vb* comment, inject, insert, interpose.
interjection *n* exclamation.
interlace *vb* bind, complicate, entwine, intersperse, intertwine, interweave, inweave, knit, mix, plait, twine, twist, unite.
interlard *vb* difersify, interminate, intersperse, intertwine, mix, vary.
interline *vb* insert, write between.
interlineal *adj* interlinear, interlined.
interlink, interlock *vb* connect, interchain, interrelate, join.
interlocution *n* colloquy, conference, dialogue, interchange.
interlocutor *n* respondent, speaker.
interloper *n* intruder, meddler.
intermeddle *vb* interfere, interpose, meddle.
intermediary *n* go-between, mediator.
intermediate *adj* interjacent, interposed, intervening, mean, median, middle, transitional.
interment *n* burial, entombment, inhumation, sepulture.
interminable *adj* boundless, endless, illimitable, immeasurable, infinite, limitless, unbounded, unlimited; long-drawn-out, tedious, wearisome.
intermingle *vb* blend, commingle, commix, intermix, mingle, mix.
intermission *n* cessation, interruption, interval, lull, pause, remission, respite, rest, stop, stoppage, suspension.
intermit *vb* interrupt, intervene, stop, suspend; discontinue, give over, leave off; abate, subside.
intermittent *adj* broken, capricious, discontinuous, fitful, flickering, intermitting, periodic, recurrent, remittent, spasmodic.
intermix *vb* blend, commingle, commix, intermingle, mingle, mix.
internal *adj* inner, inside, interior, inward; incorporeal, mental, spiritual; deeper, emblematic, hidden, higher, metaphorical, secret, symbolical, under; genuine, inherent, intrinsic, real, true; domestic, home, inland, inside.
international *adj* cosmopolitan, universal.
internecine *adj* deadly, destructive, exterminating, exterminatory, interneciary, internecinal, internecive, mortal.
interpellate *vb* interrogate, question.
interpellation *n* interruption; intercession, interposition; interrogation, questioning.
interplay *n* interaction.
interpolate *vb* add, foist, insert, interpose; (*math*) intercalate, introduce.
interpose *vb* arbitrate, intercede, intervene, mediate; interfere, intermeddle, interrupt, meddle, tamper; insert, interject, put in, remark, sandwich, set between; intrude, thurst in.
interposition *n* intercession, interpellation, intervention, mediation.
interpret *vb* decipher, decode, define, elucidate, explain, expound, solve, unfold, unravel; construe, render, translate.
interpretation *n* meaning, sense, signification; elucidation, explanation, explication, exposition; construction, rendering, rendition, translation, version.
interpreter *n* expositor, expounder, translator.
interrogate *vb* ask, catechize, examine, inquire of, interpellate, question.
interrogation *n* catechizing, examination, examining, interpellation, interrogating, questioning; inquiry, query, question.
interrogative *adj* interrogatory, questioning.
interrupt *vb* break, check, disturb, hinder, intercept, interfere with, obstruct, pretermit, stop; break, cut, disconnect, disjoin, dissever, dissolve, disunite, divide, separate, sever, sunder; break off, cease, discontinue, intermit, leave off, suspend.
interruption *n* hindrance, impediment, obstacle, obstruction, stop, stoppage; cessation, discontinuance, intermission, pause, suspension; break, breaking, disconnecting, disconnection, disjunction, dissolution, disunion, disuniting, division, separation, severing, sundering.
intersect *vb* cross, cut, decussate, divide, interrupt.
intersection *n* crossing.
interspace *n* interlude, interstice, interval.
intersperse *vb* intermingle, scatter, sprinkle; diversify, interlard, mix.
interstice *n* interspace, interval, space; chink, crevice.
interstitial *adj* intermediate, intervening.
intertwine *vb* interlace, intertwine, interweave, inweave, twine.
interval *n* interim, interlude, interregnum, pause, period, recess, season, space, spell, term; interstice, skip.
intervene *vb* come between, interfere, mediate; befall, happen, occur.
intervening *adj* interjacent, intermediate; interstitial.
intervention *n* interference, interposition; agency, mediation.

interview *n* conference, consultation, parley; meeting.
interweave *vb* interlace, intertwine, inweave, weave; intermingle, intermix, mingle, mix.
intestinal *adj* domestic, interior, internal.
intestines *npl* bowels, entrails, guts, insides, inwards, viscera.
intimacy *n* close acquaintance, familiarity, fellowship, friendship; closeness, nearness.
intimate[1] *adj* close, near; familiar, friendly; bosom, chummy, close, dear, homelike, special; confidential, personal, private, secret; detailed, exhaustive, first-hand, immediate, penetrating, profound; cosy, warm. * *n* chum, confidant, companion, crony, friend.
intimate[2] *vb* allude to, express, hint, impart, indicate, insinuate, signify, suggest, tell.
intimately *adv* closely, confidentially, familiarly, nearly, thoroughly.
intimation *n* allusion, hint, innuendo, insinuation, suggestion.
intimidate *vb* abash, affright, alarm, appal, browbeat, bully, cow, daunt, dishearten, dismay, frighten, overawe, scare, subdue, terrify, terrorize.
intimidation *n* fear, intimidating, terror, terrorism.
intolerable *adj* insufferable, insupportable, unbearable, unendurable.
intolerance *n* bigotry, narrowness; impatience, rejection.
intolerant *adj* bigoted, narrow, proscriptive; dictatorial, impatient, imperious, overbearing, supercilious.
intonation *n* cadence, modulation, tone; musical recitation.
in toto *adv* entirely, wholly.
intoxicate *vb* fuddle, inebriate, muddle.
intoxicated *adj* boozy, drunk, drunken, fuddled, inebriated, maudlin, mellow, muddled, stewed, tight, tipsy.
intoxication *n* drunkenness, ebriety, inebriation, inebriety; excitement, exhilaration, infatuation.
intractability *n* cantankerousness, contrariety, inflexibility, intractableness, obduracy, obstinacy, perverseness, perversity, pig-headedness, stubbornness, wilfulness.
intractable *adj* cantankerous, contrary, contumacious, cross-grained, dogged, froward, headstrong, indocile, inflexible, mulish, obdurate, obstinate, perverse, pig-headed, refractory, restive, stubborn, tough, uncontrollable, ungovernable, unmanageable, unruly, unyielding, wilful.
intrench *see* **entrench**.
intrenchment *see* **entrenchment**.
intrepid *adj* bold, brave, chivalrous, courageous, daring, dauntless, doughty, fearless, gallant, heroic, unappalled, unawed, undaunted, undismayed, unterrified, valiant, valorous.
intrepidity *n* boldness, bravery, courage, daring, dauntlessness, fearlessness, gallantry, heroism, intrepidness, prowess, spirit, valour.
intricacy *n* complexity, complication, difficulty, entanglement, intricateness, involution, obscurity, perplexity.
intricate *adj* complicated, difficult, entangled, involved, mazy, obscure, perplexed.
intrigue *vb* connive, conspire, machinate, plot, scheme; beguile, bewitch, captivate, charm, fascinate. * *n* artifice, cabal, conspiracy, deception, finesse, Machiavelianism, machination, manoeuvre, plot, ruse, scheme, stratagem, wile; amour, liaison, love affair.
intriguing *adj* arch, artful, crafty, crooked, cunning, deceitful, designing, diplomatic, foxy, Machiavelian, insidious, politic, sly, sneaky, subtle, tortuous, trickish, tricky, wily.
intrinsic *adj* essential, genuine, real, sterling, true; inborn, inbred, ingrained, inherent, internal, inward, native, natural.
intrinsically *adv* essentially, really, truly; inherently, naturally.
introduce *vb* bring in, conduct, import, induct, inject, insert, lead in, usher in; present; begin, broach, commence, inaugurate, initiate, institute, start.
introduction *n* exordium, preface, prelude, proem; introducing, ushering in; presentation.
introductory *adj* precursory, prefatory, preliminary, proemial.
introspection *n* introversion, self-contemplation.
intrude *vb* encroach, impose, infringe, interfere, interlope, obtrude, trespass.
intruder *n* interloper, intermeddler, meddler, stranger.
intrusion *n* encroachment, infringement, intruding, obtrusion.
intrusive *adj* obtrusive, trespassing.
intuition *n* apprehension, cognition, insight, instinct; clairvoyance, divination, presentiment.
intuitive *adj* instinctive, intuitional, natural; clear, distinct, full, immediate.
intumesce *vb* bubble up, dilate, expand, swell.
intumescence *n* inturgescence, swelling, tumefaction, turgescence.
inundate *vb* deluge, drown, flood, glut, overflow, overwhelm, submerge.
inundation *n* cataclysm, deluge, flood, glut, overflow, superfluity.
inure *vb* accustom, discipline, familiarize, habituate, harden, toughen, train, use.
inutile *adj* bootless, ineffectual, inoperative, unavailing, unprofitable, useless.
invade *vb* encroach upon, infringe, violate; attack, enter in, march into.
invalid[1] *adj* baseless, fallacious, false, inoperative, nugatory, unfounded, unsound, untrue, worthless; (*law*) null, void.
invalid[2] *adj* ailing, bedridden, feeble, frail, ill, infirm, sick, sickly, valetudinary, weak, weakly. * *n* convalescent, patient, valetudinarian.
invalidate *vb* abrogate, annul, cancel, nullify, overthrow, quash, repeal, reverse, undo, unmake, vitiate.

invalidity *n* baselessness, fallaciousness, fallacy, falsity, unsoundness.
invaluable *adj* inestimable, priceless.
invariable *adj* changeless, constant, unchanging, uniform, unvarying; changeless, immutable, unalterable, unchangeable.
invariableness *n* changelessness, constancy, uniformity, unvaryingness; changelessness, immutability, unchangeableness, invariability.
invasion *n* encroachment, incursion, infringement, inroad; aggression, assault, attack, foray, raid.
invective *n* abuse, censure, contumely, denunciation, diatribe, railing, reproach, sarcasm, satire, vituperation.
inveigh *vb* blame, censure, condemn, declaim against, denounce, exclaim against, rail at, reproach, vituperate.
inveigle *vb* contrive, devise; concoct, conceive, create, design, excogitate, frame, imagine, originate; coin, fabricate, forge, spin.
invent *vb* concoct, contrive, design, devise, discover, fabricate, find out, frame, originate.
invention *n* creation, discovery, ingenuity, inventing, origination; contrivance, design, device; coinage, fabrication, fiction, forgery.
inventive *adj* creative, fertile, ingenious.
inventor *n* author, contriver, creator, originator.
inventory *n* account, catalogue, list, record, roll, register, schedule.
inverse *adj* indirect, inverted, opposite, reversed.
inversion *n* inverting, reversing, transposal, transposition.
invert *vb* capsize, overturn; reverse, transpose.
invertebrate *adj* invertebral; spineless.
invest *vb* put money into; confer, endow, endue; (*mil*) beset, besiege, enclose, surround; array, clothe, dress.
investigate *vb* canvass, consider, dissect, examine, explore, follow up, inquire into, look into, overhaul, probe, question, research, scrutinize, search into, search out, sift, study.
investigation *n* examination, exploration, inquiry, inquisition, overhauling, research, scrutiny, search, sifting, study.
investiture *n* habilitation, induction, installation, ordination.
investment *n* money invested; endowment; (*mil*) beleaguerment, siege; clothes, dress, garments, habiliments, robe, vestment.
inveteracy *n* inveterateness, obstinacy.
inveterate *adj* accustomed, besetting, chronic, confirmed, deep-seated, habitual, habituated, hardened, ingrained, long-established, obstinate.
invidious *adj* disagreeable, envious, hateful, odious, offensive, unfair.
invigorate *vb* animate, brace, energize, fortify, harden, nerve, quicken, refresh, stimulate, strengthen, vivify.
invincible *adj* impregnable, indomitable, ineradicable, insuperable, insurmountable, irrepressible, unconquerable, unsubduable, unyielding.
inviolable *adj* hallowed, holy, inviolate, sacramental, sacred, sacrosanct, stainless.
inviolate *adj* unbroken, unviolated; pure, stainless, unblemished, undefiled, unhurt, uninjured, unpolluted, unprofaned, unstained; inviolable, sacred.
invisibility *n* imperceptibility, indistinctness, invisibleness, obscurity.
invisible *adj* impalpable, imperceptible, indistinguishable, intangible, unapparent, undiscernable, unperceivable, unseen.
invitation *n* bidding, call, challenge, solicitation, summons.
invite *vb* ask, bid, call, challenge, request, solicit, summon; allure, attract, draw on, entice, lead, persuade, prevail upon.
inviting *adj* alluring, attractive, bewitching, captivating, engaging, fascinating, pleasing, winning; prepossessing, promising.
invocation *n* conjuration, orison, petition, prayer, summoning, supplication.
invoice *vb* bill, list. * *n* bill, inventory, list, schedule.
invoke *vb* adjure, appeal to, beseech, beg, call upon, conjure, entreat, implore, importune, pray, pray to, solicit, summon, supplicate.
involuntary *adj* automatic, blind, instinctive, mechanical, reflex, spontaneous, unintentional; compulsory, reluctant, unwilling.
involve *vb* comprise, contain, embrace, imply, include, lead to; complicate, compromise, embarrass, entangle, implicate, incriminate, inculpate; cover, envelop, enwrap, surround, wrap; blend, conjoin, connect, join, mingle; entwine, interlace, intertwine, interweave, inweave.
invulnerability *n* invincibility, invulnerableness.
invulnerable *adj* incontrovertible, invincible, unassailable, irrefragable.
inward[1] *adj* incoming, inner, interior, internal; essential, hidden, mental, spiritual; private, secret.
inward[2], **inwards** *adv* inwardly, towards the inside, within.
inweave *vb* entwine, interlace, intertwine, interweave, weave together.
iota *n* atom, bit, glimmer, grain, jot, mite, particle, scintilla, scrap, shadow, spark, tittle, trace, whit.
irascibility *n* hastiness, hot-headedness, impatience, irascibleness, irritability, peevishness, petulance, quickness, spleen, testiness, touchiness.
irascible *adj* choleric, cranky, hasty, hot, hotheaded, impatient, irritable, nettlesome, peevish, peppery, pettish, petulant, quick, splenetic, snappish, testy, touchy, waspish.
irate *adj* angry, incensed, ireful, irritated, piqued.
ire *n* anger, choler, exasperation, fury, indignation, passion, rage, resentment, wrath.
ireful *adj* angry, furious, incensed, irate, raging, passionate.
iridescent *adj* irisated, nacreous, opalescent, pavonine, prismatic, rainbow-like.

iris *n* rainbow; (*bot*) fleur-de-lis, flower-de-luce; diaphragm of the eye.
irksome *adj* annoying, burdensome, humdrum, monotonous, tedious, tiresome, wearisome, weary, wearying.
iron *adj* ferric, ferrous.
ironic, ironical *adj* mocking, sarcastic.
irons *npl* chains, fetters, gyves, hampers, manacles, shackles.
irony *n* mockery, raillery, ridicule, sarcasm, satire.
irradiate *vb* brighten, illume, illuminate, illumine, light up, shine upon.
irrational *adj* absurd, extravagant, foolish, injudicious, preposterous, ridiculous, silly, unwise; unreasonable, unreasoning, unthinking; brute, brutish; aberrant, alienated, brainless, crazy, demented, fantastic, idiotic, imbecilic, insane, lunatic.
irrationality *n* absurdity, folly, foolishness, unreasonableness; brutishness.
irreclaimable *adj* hopeless, incurable, irrecoverable, irreparable, irretrievable, irreversible, remediless; abandoned, graceless, hardened, impenitent, incorrigible, lost, obdurate, profligate, recreant, reprobate, shameless, unrepentant.
irreconcilable *adj* implacable, inexorable, inexpiable, unappeasable; incompatible, incongruous, inconsistent.
irrecoverable *adj* hopeless, incurable, irremediable, irreparable, irretrievable, remediless.
irrefragable *adj* impregnable, incontestable, incontrovertible, indisputable, invincible, irrefutable, irresistible, unanswerable, unassailable, undeniable.
irrefutable *adj* impregnable, incontestable, incontrovertible, indisputable, invincible, irrefragable, irresistible, unanswerable, unassailable, undeniable.
irregular *adj* aberrant, abnormal, anomalistic, anomalous, crooked, devious, eccentric, erratic, exceptional, heteromorphous, raged, tortuous, unconformable, unusual; capricious, changeable, desultory, fitful, spasmodic, uncertain, unpunctual, unsettled, variable; disordered, disorderly, improper, uncanonical, unparliamentary, unsystematic; asymmetric, uneven, unsymmetrical; disorderly, dissolute, immoral, loose, wild. * *n* casual, freelance, hireling, mercenary.
irregularity *n* aberration, abnormality, anomaly, anomalousness, singularity; capriciousness, changeableness, uncertainty, variableness; asymmetry; disorderliness, dissoluteness, immorality, laxity, looseness, wildness.
irrelevance, irrelevancy *n* impertinency, inapplicability, nonpertinency.
irrelevant *adj* extraneous, foreign, illogical, impertinent, inapplicable, inapposite, inappropriate, inconsequent, unessential, unrelated.
irreligion *n* atheism, godlessness, impiety, ungodliness.
irreligious *adj* godless, ungodly, undevout; blasphemous, disrespectful, impious, irreverent, profane, ribald, wicked.
irremediable *adj* hopeless, incurable, immedicable, irrecoverable, irreparable, remediless.
irremissible *adj* binding, inexpiable, obligatory, unatonable, unpardonable.
irreparable *adj* irrecoverable, irremediable, irretrievable, remediless.
irreprehensible *adj* blameless, faultless, inculpable, innocent, irreproachable, irreprovable, unblamable.
irrepressible *adj* insuppressible, uncontrollable, unquenchable, unsmotherable.
irreproachable *adj* blameless, faultless, inculpable, innocent, irreprehensible, irreprovable, unblamable.
irresistible *adj* irrefragable, irrepressible, overpowering, overwhelming, resistless.
irresolute *adj* changeable, faltering, fickle, hesitant, hesitating, inconstant, mutable, spineless, uncertain, undecided, undetermined, unsettled, unstable, unsteady, vacillating, wavering.
irrespective *adj* independent, regardless.
irresponsible *adj* unaccountable; untrustworthy.
irretrievable *adj* incurable, irrecoverable, irremediable, irreparable, remediless.
irreverence *n* blasphemy, impiety, profaneness, profanity; disesteem, disrespect.
irreverent *adj* blasphemous, impious, irreligious, profane; disrespectful, slighting.
irreversible *adj* irrepealable, irrevocable, unalterable, unchangeable; changeless, immutable, invariable.
irrevocable *adj* irrepealable, irreversible, unalterable, unchangeable.
irrigate *vb* moisten, wash, water, wet.
irrigation *n* watering.
irritability *n* excitability, fretfulness, irascibility, peevishness, petulance, snappishness, susceptibility, testiness.
irritable *adj* captious, choleric, excitable, fiery, fretful, hasty, hot, irascible, passionate, peppery, peevish, pettish, petulant, snappish, splenetic, susceptible, testy, touchy, waspish.
irritate *vb* anger, annoy, chafe, enrage, exacerbate, exasperate, fret, incense, jar, nag, nettle, offend, provoke, rasp, rile, ruffle, vex; gall, tease; (*med*) excite, inflame, stimulate.
irritation *n* irritating; anger, exacerbation, exasperation, excitement, indignation, ire, passion, provocation, resentment, wrath; (*med*) excitation, inflammation, stimulation; burn, itch.
irruption *n* breaking in, bursting in; foray, incursion, inroad, invasion, raid.
island *n* atoll, isle, islet, reef.
isochronal *adj* isochronous, uniform.
isolate *vb* detach, dissociate, insulate, quarantine, segregate, separate, set apart.
isolated *adj* detached, separate, single, solitary.

isolation *n* detachment, disconnection, insulation, quarantine, segregation, separation; loneliness, solitariness, solitude.

issue *vb* come out, flow out, flow forth, gush, run, rush out, spout, spring, spurt, well; arise, come, emanate, ensue, flow, follow, originate, proceed, spring; end, eventuate, result, terminate; appear, come out, deliver, depart, debouch, discharge, emerge, emit, put forth, send out; distribute, give out; publish, utter. * *n* conclusion, consequence, consummation, denouement, end, effect, event, finale, outcome, result, termination, upshot; antagonism, contest, controversy; debouchment, delivering, delivery, discharge, emergence, emigration, emission, issuance; flux, outflow, outpouring, stream; copy, edition, number; egress, exit, outlet, passage out, vent, way out; escape, sally, sortie; children, offspring, posterity, progeny.

itch *vb* tingle. * *n* itching; burning, coveting, importunate craving, teasing desire, uneasy hankering.

itching *n* itch; craving, longing, importunate craving, desire, appetite, hankering.

item *adv* also, in like manner. * *n* article, detail, entry, particular, point.

iterate *vb* reiterate, repeat.

itinerant *adj* nomadic, peripatetic, roaming, roving, travelling, unsettled, wandering.

itinerary *n* guide, guidebook; circuit, route.

J

jabber *vb* chatter, gabble, prate, prattle.
jacket *n* casing, cover, sheath; anorak, blazer coat, doublet, jerkin.
jaded *adj* dull, exhausted, fatigued, satiated, tired, weary.
jagged *adj* cleft, divided, indented, notched, serrated, ragged, uneven.
jail, gaol *n* bridewell, (*sl*) clink, dungeon, lockup, (*sl*) nick, penitentiary, prison.
jam *vb* block, crowd, crush, press. * *n* block, crowd, crush, mass, pack, press.
jangle *vb* bicker, chatter, dispute, gossip, jar, quarrel, spar, spat, squabble, tiff, wrangle. * *n* clang, clangour, clash, din, dissonance.
jar[1] *vb* clash, grate, interfere, shake; bicker, contend, jangle, quarrel, spar, spat, squabble, tiff, wrangle; agitate, jolt, jounce, shake. * *n* clash, conflict, disaccord, discord, jangle, dissonance; agitation, jolt, jostle, shake, shaking, shock, start.
jar[2] *n* can, crock, cruse, ewer, flagon.
jarring *adj* conflicting, discordant, inconsistent, inconsonant, wrangling.
jargon *n* gabble, gibberish, nonsense, rigmarole: argot, cant, lingo, slang; chaos, confusion, disarray, disorder, jumble.
jaundiced *adj* biased, envious, prejudiced.
jaunt *n* excursion, ramble, tour, trip.
jaunty *adj* airy, cheery, garish, gay, fine, fluttering, showy, sprightly, unconcerned.
jealous *adj* distrustful, envious, suspicious; anxious, apprehensive, intolerant, solicitous, zealous.
jealousy *n* envy, suspicion, watchfulness.
jeer *vb* deride, despise, flout, gibe, jape, jest, mock, scoff, sneer, spurn, rail, ridicule, taunt. * *n* abuse, derision, mockery, sneer, ridicule, taunt.
jeopardize *vb* endanger, hazard, imperil, risk, venture.
jeopardy *n* danger, hazard, peril, risk, venture.
jerk *vb, n* flip, hitch, pluck, tweak, twitch, yank.
jest *vb* banter, joke, quiz. * *n* fun, joke, pleasantry, raillery, sport.
jester *n* humorist, joker, wag; buffoon, clown, droll, fool, harlequin, punch.
jibe *see* **gibe**.
jiffy *n* instant, moment, second, twinkling, trice.
jilt *vb* break with, deceive, disappoint, discard. * *n* coquette, flirt, light-o'-love.
jingle *vb* chink, clink, jangle, rattle, tinkle. * *n* chink, clink, jangle, rattle, tinkle; chorus, ditty, melody, song.
jocose *adj* comical, droll, facetious, funny, humorous, jesting, jocular, merry, sportive, waggish, witty.
jocund *adj* airy, blithe, cheerful, debonair, frolicsome, jolly, joyful, joyous, lively, merry, playful.
jog *vb* jostle, notify, nudge, push, remind, warn; canter, run, trot. * *n* push, reminder.
join *vb* add, annex, append, attach; cement, combine, conjoin, connect, couple, dovetail, link, unite, yoke; amalgamate, assemble, associate, confederate, consolidate.
joint *vb* fit, join, unite. * *adj* combined, concerted, concurrent, conjoint. * *n* connection, junction, juncture, hinge, splice.
joke *vb* banter, jest, frolic, rally. * *n* crank, jest, quip, quirk, witticism.
jolly *adj* airy, blithe, cheerful, frolicsome, gamesome, facetious, funny, gay, jovial, joyous, merry, mirthful, jocular, jocund, playful, sportive, sprightly, waggish; bouncing, chubby, lusty, plump, portly, stout.
jolt *vb* jar, shake, shock. * *n* jar, jolting, jounce, shaking.
jostle *vb* collide, elbow, hustle, joggle, shake, shoulder, shove.
jot *n* ace, atom, bit, corpuscle, iota, grain, mite, particle, scrap, whit.
journal *n* daybook, diary, log; gazette, magazine, newspapers, periodical.
journey *vb* ramble, roam, rove, travel: fare, go, proceed. * *n* excursion, expedition, jaunt, passage, pilgrimage, tour, travel, trip, voyage.
jovial *adj* airy, convivial, festive, jolly, joyous, merry, mirthful.
joy *n* beatification, beatitude, delight, ecstasy, exultation, gladness, glee, mirth, pleasure, rapture, ravishment, transport; bliss, felicity, happiness.
joyful *adj* blithe, blithesome, buoyant, delighted, elate, elated, exultant, glad, happy, jocund, jolly, joyous, merry, rejoicing.
jubilant *adj* exultant, exulting, rejoicing, triumphant.
judge *vb* conclude, decide, decree, determine, pronounce; adjudicate, arbitrate, condemn, doom, sentence, try, umpire; account, apprehend, believe, consider, deem, esteem, guess, hold, imagine, measure, reckon, regard, suppose, think; appreciate, estimate. * *n* adjudicator, arbiter, arbitrator, bencher, justice, magistrate, moderator, referee, umpire, connoisseur, critic.

judgment, judgement *n* brains, ballast, circumspection, depth, discernment, discretion, discrimination, intelligence, judiciousness, penetration, prudence, sagacity, sense, sensibility, taste, understanding, wisdom, wit; conclusion, consideration, decision, determination, estimation, notion, opinion, thought; adjudication, arbitration, award, censure, condemnation, decree, doom, sentence.

judicious *adj* cautious, considerate, cool, critical, discriminating, discreet, enlightened, provident, politic, prudent, rational, reasonable, sagacious, sensible, sober, solid, sound, staid, wise.

jug *n* cruse, ewer, flagon, pitcher, vessel.

juicy *adj* lush, moist, sappy, succulent, watery; entertaining, exciting, interesting, lively, racy, spicy.

jumble *vb* confound, confuse, disarrange, disorder, mix, muddle. * *n* confusion, disarrangement, disorder, medley, mess, mixture, muddle.

jump *vb* bound, caper, clear, hop, leap, skip, spring, vault. * *n* bound, caper, hop, leak, skip, spring, vault; fence, hurdle, obstacle; break, gap, interruption, space; advance, boost, increase, rise; jar, jolt, shock, start, twitch.

junction *n* combination, connection, coupling, hook-up, joining, linking, seam, union; conjunction, joint, juncture.

junta *n* cabal, clique, combination, confederacy, coterie, faction, gang, league, party, set.

just *adj* equitable, lawful, legitimate, reasonable, right, rightful; candid, even-handed, fair, fair-minded, impartial; blameless, conscientious, good, honest, honourable, pure, square, straightforward, virtuous; accurate, correct, exact, normal, proper, regular, true; condign, deserved, due, merited, suitable.

justice *n* accuracy, equitableness, equity, fairness, honesty, impartiality, justness, right; judge, justiciary.

justifiable *adj* defensible, fit, proper, right, vindicable, warrantable.

justification *n* defence, exculpation, excuse, exoneration, reason, vindication, warrant.

justify *vb* approve, defend, exculpate, excuse, exonerate, maintain, vindicate, support, warrant.

justness *n* accuracy, correctness, fitness, justice, precision, propriety.

juvenile *adj* childish, immature, puerile, young, youthful. * *n* boy, child, girl, youth.

juxtaposition *n* adjacency, contiguity, contact, proximity.

K

keen[1] *adj* ardent, eager, earnest, fervid, intense, vehement, vivid; acute, sharp; cutting; acrimonious, biting, bitter, caustic, poignant, pungent, sarcastic, severe; astute, discerning, intelligent, quick, sagacious, sharp-sighted, shrewd.

keen[2] *vb* bemoan, bewail, deplore, grieve, lament, mourn, sorrow, weep. * *n* coronach, dirge, elegy, lament, lamentation, monody, plaint, requiem, threnody.

keenness *n* ardour, eagerness, fervour, vehemence, zest; acuteness, sharpness; rigour, severity, sternness; acrimony, asperity, bitterness, causticity, causticness, pungency; astuteness, sagacity, shrewdness.

keep *vb* detain, hold, retain; continue, preserve; confine, detain, reserve, restrain, withhold; attend, guard, preserve, protect; adhere to, fulfil; celebrate, commemorate, honour, observe, perform, solemnize; maintain, support, sustain; husband, save, store; abide, dwell, lodge, stay, remain; endure, last. * *n* board, maintenance, subsistence, support; donjon, dungeon, stronghold, tower.

keeper *n* caretaker, conservator, curator, custodian, defender, gaoler, governor, guardian, jailer, superintendent, warden, warder, watchman.

keeping *n* care, charge, custody, guard, possession; feed, maintenance, support; agreement, conformity, congruity, consistency, harmony.

keepsake *n* memento, souvenir, token.

ken *n* cognizance, sight, view.

key *adj* basic, crucial, essential, important, major, principal. * *n* lock-opener, opener; clue, elucidation, explanation, guide, solution, translation; (*mus*) keynote, tonic; clamp, lever, wedge.

kick *vb* boot, punt; oppose, rebel, resist, spurn. * *n* force, intensity, power, punch, vitality; excitement, pleasure, thrill.

kidnap *vb* abduct, capture, carry off, remove, steal away.

kill *vb* assassinate, butcher, dispatch, destroy, massacre, murder, slaughter, slay.

kin *adj* akin, allied, cognate, kindred, related. * *n* affinity, consanguinity, relationship; connections, family, kindred, kinsfolk, relations, relatives, siblings.

kind[1] *adj* accommodating, amiable, beneficent, benevolent, benign, bland, bounteous, brotherly, charitable, clement, compassionate, complaisant, gentle, good, good-natured, forbearing, friendly, generous, gracious, humane, indulgent, lenient, mild, obliging, sympathetic, tender, tender-hearted.

kind[2] *n* breed, class, family, genus, race, set, species, type; brand, character, colour, denomination, description, form, make, manner, nature, persuasion, sort, stamp, strain, style,

kindle *vb* fire, ignite, inflame, light; animate, awaken, bestir, exasperate, excite, foment, incite, provoke, rouse, stimulate, stir, thrill, warm.

kindliness *n* amiability, benevolence, benignity, charity, compassion, friendliness, humanity, kindness, sympathy; gentleness, mildness, softness.

kindly *adj* appropriate, congenial, kindred, natural, proper; benevolent, considerate, friendly, gracious, humane, sympathetic, well-disposed. * *adv* agreeably, graciously, humanely, politely, thoughtfully.

kindness *n* benefaction, charity, favour; amiability, beneficence, benevolence, benignity, clemency, generosity, goodness, grace, humanity, kindliness, mildness, philanthropy, sympathy, tenderness.

kindred *adj* akin, allied, congenial, connected, related, sympathetic. * *n* affinity, consanguinity, flesh, relationship; folks, kin, kinsfolk, kinsmen, relations, relatives.

king *n* majesty, monarch, sovereign.

kingdom *n* dominion, empire, monarchy, rule, sovereignty, supremacy; region, tract; division, department, domain, province, realm.

kingly *adj* imperial, kinglike, monarchical, regal, royal, sovereign; august, glorious, grand, imperial, imposing, magnificent, majestic, noble, splendid.

kink *n* cramp, crick, curl, entanglement, knot, loop, twist; crochet, whim, wrinkle.

kinsfolk *n* kin, kindred, kinsmen, relations, relatives.

kit *n* equipment, implements, outfit, set, working.

knack *n* ability, address, adroitness, aptitude, aptness, dexterity, dextrousness, expertness, facility, quickness, readiness, skill.

knave *n* caitiff, cheat, miscreant, rascal, rogue, scamp, scapegrace, scoundrel, sharper, swindler, trickster, villain.

knavery *n* criminality, dishonesty, fraud, knavishness, rascality, scoundrelism, trickery, villainy.

knavish *adj* dishonest, fraudulent, rascally, scoundrelly, unprincipled, roguish, trickish, tricky, villainous.

knell *vb* announce, peal, ring, toll. * *n* chime, peal, ring, toll.

knife *vb* cut, slash, stab. * *n* blade, jackknife, lance.

knit *vb* connect, interlace, join, unite, weave.

knob *n* boss, bunch, hunch, lump, protuberance, stud.

knock *vb* clap, cuff, hit, rap, rattle, slap, strike, thump; beat, blow, box. * *n* blow, slap, smack, thump; blame, criticism, rejection, setback.

knoll *n* hill, hillock, mound.

knot *vb* complicate, entangle, gnarl, kink, tie, weave. * *n* complication, entanglement; connection, tie; joint, node, knag; bunch, rosette, tuft; band, cluster, clique, crew, gang, group, pack, set, squad.

knotty *adj* gnarled, hard, knaggy, knurled, knotted, rough, rugged; complex, difficult, harassing, intricate, involved, perplexing, troublesome.

know *vb* apprehend, comprehend, cognize, discern, perceive, recognize, see, understand; discriminate, distinguish.

knowing *adj* accomplished, competent, experienced, intelligent, proficient, qualified, skilful, well-informed; aware, conscious, percipient, sensible, thinking; cunning, expressive, significant.

knowingly *adv* consciously, intentionally, purposely, wittingly.

knowledge *n* apprehension, command, comprehension, discernment, judgment, perception, understanding, wit; acquaintance, acquirement, attainments, enlightenment, erudition, information, learning, lore, mastery, scholarship, science; cognition, cognizance, consciousness, ken, notice, prescience, recognition.

knowledgeable *adj* aware, conscious, experienced, well-informed; educated, intelligent, learned, scholarly.

knuckle *vb* cringe, crouch, stoop, submit, yield.

L

laborious *adj* assiduous, diligent, hardworking, indefatigable, industrious, painstaking, sedulous, toiling; arduous, difficult, fatiguing, hard, Herculean, irksome, onerous, tiresome, toilsome, wearisome.

labour *vb* drudge, endeavour, exert, strive, toil, travail, work. * *n* drudgery, effort, exertion, industry, pains, toil, work; childbirth, delivery, parturition.

labyrinth *n* entanglement, intricacy, maze, perplexity, windings.

labyrinthine *adj* confused, convoluted, intricate, involved, labyrinthian, labyrinthic, perplexing, winding.

lace *vb* attach, bind, fasten, intertwine, tie, twine. * *n* filigree, lattice, mesh, net, netting, network, openwork, web.

lacerate *vb* claw, cut, lancinate, mangle, rend, rip, sever, slash, tear, wound; afflict, harrow, rend, torture, wound.

lack *vb* need, want. * *n* dearth, default, defectiveness, deficiency, deficit, destitution, insufficiency, need, scantiness, scarcity, shortcoming, shortness, want.

lackadaisical *adj* languishing, sentimental, pensive.

laconic *adj* brief, compact, concise, pithy, sententious, short, succinct, terse.

lad *n* boy, schoolboy, stripling, yoüngster, youth.

lading *n* burden, cargo, freight, load.

ladylike *adj* courtly, genteel, refined, well-bred.

lag *vb* dawdle, delay, idle, linger, loiter, saunter, tarry.

laggard *n* idler, lingerer, loiterer, lounger, saunterer, sluggard.

lair *n* burrow, couch, den, form, resting place.

lambent *adj* flickering, gliding, gleaming, licking, touching, twinkling.

lame *vb* cripple, disable, hobble. * *adj* crippled, defective, disabled, halt, hobbling, limping; feeble, insufficient, poor, unsatisfactory, weak.

lament *vb* complain, grieve, keen, moan, mourn, sorrow, wail, weep; bemoan, bewail, deplore, regret. * *n* complaint, lamentation, moan, moaning, plaint, wailing; coronach, dirge, elegy, keen, monody, requiem, threnody.

lamentable *adj* deplorable, doleful, grievous, lamented, melancholy, woeful; contemptible, miserable, pitiful, poor, wretched.

lamentation *n* dirge, grief, lament, moan, moaning, mourning, plaint, ululation, sorrow, wailing.

lampoon *vb* calumniate, defame, lash, libel, parody, ridicule, satirize, slander. * *n* calumny, defamation, libel, parody, pasquinade, parody, satire, slander.

land *vb* arrive, debark, disembark. * *n* earth, ground, soil; country, district, province, region, reservation, territory, tract, weald.

landlord *n* owner, proprietor; host, hotelier, innkeeper.

landscape *n* prospect, scene, view.

language *n* dialect, speech, tongue, vernacular; conversation; expression, idiom, jargon, parlance, phraseology, slang, style, terminology; utterance, voice.

languid *adj* drooping, exhausted, faint, feeble, flagging, languishing, pining, weak; dull, heartless, heavy, inactive, listless, lukewarm, slow, sluggish, spiritless, torpid.

languish *vb* decline, droop, fade, fail, faint, pine, sicken, sink, wither.

languor *n* debility, faintness, feebleness, languidness, languishment, weakness; apathy, ennui, heartlessness, heaviness, lethargy, listlessness, torpidness, torpor, weariness.

lank *adj* attenuated, emaciated, gaunt, lean, meagre, scraggy, slender, skinny, slim, starveling, thin.

lap[1] *vb* drink, lick, mouth, tongue; plash, ripple, splash, wash; quaff, sip, sup, swizzle, tipple. * *n* draught, dram, drench, drink, gulp, lick, swig, swill, quaff, sip, sup, suck; plash, splash, wash.

lap[2] *vb* cover, enfold, fold, turn, twist, swaddle, wrap; distance, pass, outdistance, overlap. * *n* fold, flap, lappet, lapel, ply, plait; ambit, beat, circle, circuit, cycle, loop, orbit, revolution, round, tour, turn, walk.

lapse *vb* glide, sink, slide, slip; err, fail, fall. * *n* course, flow, gliding; declension, decline, fall; error, fault, indiscretion, misstep, shortcoming, slip.

larceny *n* pilfering, robbery, stealing, theft, thievery.

large *adj* big, broad, bulky, colossal, elephantine, enormous, heroic, great, huge, immense, vast; broad, expanded, extensive, spacious, wide; abundant, ample, copious, full, liberal, plentiful; capacious, comprehensive.

lascivious *adj* concupiscent, immodest, incontinent,

goatish, lecherous, lewd, libidinous, loose, lubricious, lustful, prurient, salacious, sensual, unchaste, voluptuous, wanton.

lash[1] *vb* belay, bind, strap, tie; fasten, join, moor, pinion, secure.

lash[2] *vb* beat, castigate, chastise, flagellate, flail, flay, flog, goad, scourge, swinge, thrash, whip; assail, censure, excoriate, lampoon, satirize, trounce. * *n* scourge, strap, thong, whip; cut, slap, smack, stroke, stripe.

lass *n* damsel, girl, lassie, maiden, miss.

lassitude *n* dullness, exhaustion, fatigue, languor, languidness, prostration, tiredness, weariness.

last[1] *vb* abide, carry on, continue, dwell, endure, extend, maintain, persist, prevail, remain, stand, stay, survive.

last[2] *adj* hindermost, hindmost, latest; conclusive, final, terminal, ultimate; eventual, endmost, extreme, farthest, ultimate; greatest, highest, maximal, maximum, most, supreme, superlative, utmost; latest, newest; aforegoing, foregoing, latter, preceding; departing, farewell, final, leaving, parting, valedictory. * *n* conclusion, consummation, culmination, end, ending, finale, finis, finish, termination.

last[3] *n* cast, form, matrix, mould, shape, template.

lasting *adj* abiding, durable, enduring, fixed, perennial, permanent, perpetual, stable.

lastly *adv* conclusively, eventually, finally, ultimately.

late *adj* behindhand, delayed, overdue, slow, tardy; deceased, former; recent. * *adv* lately, recently, sometime; tardily.

latent *adj* abeyant, concealed, hidden, invisible, occult, secret, unseen, veiled.

latitude *n* amplitude, breadth, compass, extent, range, room, scope; freedom, indulgence, liberty; laxity.

latter *adj* last, latest, modern, recent.

lattice *n* espalier, grating, latticework, trellis.

laud *vb* approve, celebrate, extol, glorify, magnify, praise.

laudable *adj* commendable, meritorious, praiseworthy.

laugh *vb* cackle, chortle, chuckle, giggle, guffaw, snicker, snigger, titter. * *n* chortle, chuckle, giggle, guffaw, laughter, titter.

laughable *adj* amusing, comical, diverting, droll, farcical, funny, ludicrous, mirthful, ridiculous.

laughter *n* cackle, chortle, chuckle, glee, giggle, guffaw, laugh, laughing.

launch *vb* cast, dart, dispatch, hurl, lance, project, throw; descant, dilate, enlarge, expiate; begin, commence, inaugurate, open, start.

lavish *vb* dissipate, expend, spend, squander, waste. * *adj* excessive, extravagant, generous, immoderate, overliberal, prodigal, profuse, thriftless, unrestrained, unstinted, unthrifty, wasteful.

law *n* act, code, canon, command, commandment, covenant, decree, edict, enactment, order, precept, principle, statute, regulation, rule; jurisprudence; litigation, process, suit.

lawful *adj* constitutional, constituted, legal, legalized, legitimate; allowable, authorized, permissible, warrantable; equitable, rightful, just, proper, valid.

lawless *adj* anarchic, anarchical, chaotic, disorderly, insubordinate, rebellious, reckless, riotous, seditious, wild.

lawyer *n* advocate, attorney, barrister, counsel, counsellor, pettifogger, solicitor.

lax *adj* loose, relaxed, slow; drooping, flabby, soft; neglectful, negligent, remiss; dissolute, immoral, licentious, seditious, wild.

lay[1] *vb* deposit, establish, leave, place, plant, posit, put, set, settle, spread; arrange, dispose, locate, organize, position; bear, produce; advance, lodge, offer, submit; allocate, allot, ascribe, assign, attribute, charge, impute; concoct, contrive, design, plan, plot, prepare; apply, burden, encumber, impose, saddle, tax; bet, gamble, hazard, risk, stake, wager; allay, alleviate, appease, assuage, calm, relieve, soothe, still, suppress; disclose, divulge, explain, reveal, show, unveil; acquire, grab, grasp, seize; assault, attack, beat up; discover, find, unearth; bless, confirm, consecrate, ordain. * *n* arrangement, array, form, formation; attitude, aspect, bearing, demeanour, direction, lie, pose, position, posture, set.

lay[2] *adj* amateur, inexpert, nonprofessional; civil, laic, laical, nonclerical, nonecclesiastical, nonreligious, secular, temporal, unclerical.

lay[3] *n* ballad, carol, ditty, lied, lyric, ode, poem, rhyme, round, song, verse.

layer *n* bed, course, lay, seam, stratum.

laziness *n* idleness, inactivity, indolence, slackness, sloth, fulness, sluggishness, tardiness.

lazy *adj* idle, inactive, indolent, inert, slack, slothful, slow, sluggish, supine, torpid.

lead *vb* conduct, deliver, direct, draw, escort, guide; front, head, precede; advance, excel, outstrip, pass; allure, entice, induce, persuade, prevail; conduce, contribute, serve, tend. * *adj* chief, first, foremost, main, primary, prime, principal. * *n* direction, guidance, leadership; advance; precedence, priority.

leader *n* conductor, director, guide; captain, chief, chieftain, commander, head; superior, dominator, victor.

leading *adj* governing, ruling; capital, chief, first, foremost, highest, principal, superior.

league *vb* ally, associate, band, combine, confederate, unite. * *n* alliance, association, coalition, combination, combine, confederacy, confederation, consortium, union.

leak *vb* drip, escape, exude, ooze, pass, percolate, spill. * *n* chink, crack, crevice, hole, fissure, oozing, opening; drip, leakage, leaking, percolation.

lean[1] *adj* bony, emaciated, gaunt, lank, meagre, poor, skinny, thin; dull, barren, jejune, meagre, tame; inadequate, pitiful, scanty, slender; bare, barren, infertile, unproductive.

lean[2] *vb* incline, slope; bear, recline, repose, rest; confide, depend, rely, trust.
leaning *n* aptitude, bent, bias, disposition, inclination, liking, predilection, proneness, propensity, tendency.
leap *vb* bound, clear, jump, spring, vault; caper, frisk, gambol, hop, skip. * *n* bound, jump, spring, vault; caper, frisk, gambol, hop, skip.
learn *vb* acquire, ascertain, attain, collect, gain, gather, hear, memorize.
learned *adj* erudite, lettered, literate, scholarly, well-read; expert, experienced, knowing, skilled, versed, well-informed.
learner *n* beginner, novice, pupil, student, tyro.
learning *n* acquirements, attainments, culture, education, information, knowledge, lore, scholarship, tuition.
least *adj* meanest, minutest, smallest, tiniest.
leave[1] *vb* abandon, decamp, go, quit, vacate, withdraw; desert, forsake, relinquish, renounce; commit, consign, refer; cease, desist from, discontinue, refrain, stop; allow, let, let alone, permit; bequeath, demise, desist, will.
leave[2] *n* allowance, liberty, permission, licence, sufferance; departure, retirement, withdrawal; adieu, farewell, goodbye.
leaven *vb* ferment, lighten, raise; colour, elevate, imbue, inspire, lift, permeate, tinge; infect, vitiate. * *n* barm, ferment, yeast; influence, inspiration.
leavings *npl* bits, dregs, fragments, leftovers, pieces, relics, remains, remnants, scraps.
lecherous *adj* carnal, concupiscent, incontinent, lascivious, lewd, libidinous, lubricious, lustful, wanton, salacious, unchaste.
lechery *n* concupiscence, lasciviousness, lewdness, lubriciousness, lubricity, lust, salaciousness, salacity.
lecture *vb* censure, chide, reprimand, reprove, scold, sermonize; address, harangue, teach. * *n* censure, lecturing, lesson, reprimand, reproof, scolding; address, discourse, prelection.
ledge *n* projection, ridge, shelf.
lees *npl* dregs, precipitate, refuse, sediment, settlings.
leg *n* limb, prop.
legacy *n* bequest, gift, heirloom; heritage, inheritance, tradition.
legal *adj* allowable, authorized, constitutional, lawful, legalized, legitimate, proper, sanctioned.
legalize *vb* authorize, legitimate, legitimatize, legitimize, permit, sanction.
legend *n* fable, fiction, myth, narrative, romance, story, tale.
legendary *adj* fabulous, fictitious, mythical, romantic.
legible *adj* clear, decipherable, fair, distinct, plain, readable; apparent, discoverable, recognizable, manifest.
legion *n* army, body, cohort, column, corps, detachment, detail, division, force, maniple, phalanx, platoon; squad; army, horde, host, multitude, number, swarm, throng. * *adj* many, multitudinous, myriad, numerous.
legislate *vb* enact, ordain.
legitimacy *n* lawfulness, legality; genuineness.
legitimate *adj* authorized, lawful, legal, sanctioned; genuine, valid; correct, justifiable, logical, reasonable, warrantable, warranted.
leisure *n* convenience, ease, freedom, liberty, opportunity, recreation, retirement, vacation.
lend *vb* advance, afford, bestow, confer, furnish, give, grant, impart, loan, supply.
lengthen *vb* elongate, extend, produce, prolong, stretch; continue, protract.
lengthy *adj* diffuse, lengthened, long, long-drawn-out, prolix, prolonged, protracted.
lenience, leniency *n* clemency, compassion, forbearance, gentleness, lenity, mercy, mildness, tenderness.
lenient *adj* assuasive, lenitive, mitigating, mitigative, softening, soothing; clement, easy, forbearing, gentle, humouring, indulgent, long-suffering, merciful, mild, tender, tolerant.
lesion *n* derangement, disorder, hurt, injury.
less *adj* baser, inferior, lower, smaller; decreased, fewer, lesser, reduced, smaller, shorter; * *adv* barely, below, least, under; decreasingly. * *prep* excepting, lacking, minus, sans, short of, without.
lessen *vb* abate, abridge, contract, curtail, decrease, diminish, narrow, reduce, shrink; degrade, lower; dwindle, weaken.
lesson *n* exercise, task; instruction, precept; censure, chiding, lecture, lecturing, rebuke, reproof, scolding.
let[1] *vb* admit, allow, authorize, permit, suffer; charter, hire, lease, rent.
let[2] *vb* hinder, impede, instruct, prevent. * *n* hindrance, impediment, interference, obstacle, obstruction, restriction.
lethal *adj* deadly, destructive, fatal, mortal, murderous.
lethargic *adj* apathetic, comatose, drowsy, dull, heavy, inactive, inert, sleepy, stupid, stupefied, torpid.
lethargy *n* apathy, coma, drowsiness, dullness, hypnotism, inactiveness, inactivity, inertia, sleepiness, sluggishness, stupefaction, stupidity, stupor, torpor.
letter *n* epistle, missive, note.
lettered *adj* bookish, educated, erudite, learned, literary, versed, well-read.
levee *n* ceremony, entertainment, reception, party, soiree; embankment.
level *vb* equalize, flatten, horizontalize, smooth; demolish, destroy, raze; aim, direct, point. * *adj* equal, even, flat, flush, horizontal, plain, plane, smooth. * *n* altitude, degree, equality, evenness, plain, plane, smoothness; deck, floor, layer, stage, storey, tier.
levity *n* buoyancy, facetiousness, fickleness,

flightiness, flippancy, frivolity, giddiness, inconstancy, levity, volatility.

levy *vb* collect, exact, gather, tax; call, muster, raise, summon. * *n* duty, tax.

lewd *adj* despicable, impure, lascivious, libidinous, licentious, loose, lustful, profligate, unchaste, vile, wanton, wicked.

liability *n* accountableness, accountability, duty, obligation, responsibility, tendency; exposedness; debt, indebtedness, obligation.

liable *adj* accountable, amenable, answerable, bound, responsible; exposed, likely, obnoxious, subject.

liaison *n* amour, intimacy, intrigue; connection, relation, union.

libel *vb* calumniate, defame, lampoon, satirize, slander, vilify. * *n* calumny, defamation, lampoon, satire, slander, vilification, vituperation.

liberal *adj* beneficent, bountiful, charitable, disinterested, free, generous, munificent, openhearted, princely, unselfish; broad-minded, catholic, chivalrous, enlarged, high-minded, honourable, magnanimous, tolerant, unbiased, unbigoted; abundant, ample, bounteous, full, large, plentiful, unstinted; humanizing, liberalizing, refined, refining.

liberality *n* beneficence, bountifulness, bounty, charity, disinterestedness, generosity, kindness, munificence; benefaction, donation, gift, gratuity, present; broad-mindedness, catholicity, candour, impartiality, large-mindedness, magnanimity, toleration.

liberate *vb* deliver, discharge, disenthral, emancipate, free, manumit, ransom, release.

libertine *adj* corrupt, depraved, dissolute, licentious, profligate, rakish. * *n* debauchee, lecher, profligate, rake, roue, voluptuary.

liberty *n* emancipation, freedom, independence, liberation, self-direction, self-government; franchise, immunity, privilege; leave, licence, permission.

libidinous *adj* carnal, concupiscent, debauched, impure, incontinent, lascivious, lecherous, lewd, loose, lubricious, lustful, salacious, sensual, unchaste, wanton, wicked.

licence *n* authorization, leave, permission, privilege, right; certificate, charter, dispensation, imprimatur, permit, warrant; anarchy, disorder, freedom, lawlessness, laxity, liberty.

license *vb* allow, authorize, grant, permit, warrant; suffer, tolerate.

licentious *adj* disorderly, riotous, uncontrolled, uncurbed, ungovernable, unrestrained, unruly, wanton; debauched, dissolute, lax, libertine, loose, profligate, rakish; immoral, impure, lascivious, lecherous, lewd, libertine, libidinous, lustful, sensual, unchaste, wicked.

lick *vb* beat, flog, spank, thrash; lap, taste. * *n* blow, slap, stroke; salt-spring.

lie[1] *vb* couch, recline, remain, repose, rest; consist, pertain.

lie[2] *vb* equivocate, falsify, fib, prevaricate, romance. * *n* equivocation, falsehood, falsification, fib, misrepresentation, prevarication, untruth; delusion, illusion.

lief *adv* freely, gladly, willingly.

life *n* activity, alertness, animation, briskness, energy, sparkle, spirit, sprightliness, verve, vigour, vivacity; behaviour, conduct, deportment; being, duration, existence, lifetime; autobiography, biography, curriculum vitae, memoirs, story.

lifeless *adj* dead, deceased, defunct, extinct, inanimate; cold, dull, flat, frigid, inert, lethargic, passive, pulseless, slow, sluggish, tame, torpid.

lift *vb* elevate, exalt, hoist, raise, uplift. * *n* aid, assistance, help; elevator.

light[1] *vb* alight, land, perch, settle. * *adj* porous, sandy, spongy, well-leavened; loose, sandy; free, portable, unburdened, unencumbered; inconsiderable, moderate, negligible, slight, small, trifling, trivial, unimportant; ethereal, feathery, flimsy, gossamer, insubstantial, weightless; easy, effortless, facile; fickle, frivolous, unsettled, unsteady, volatile; airy, buoyant, carefree, lighthearted, lightsome; unaccented, unstressed, weak.

light[2] *vb* conflagrate, fire, ignite, inflame, kindle; brighten, illume, illuminate, illumine, luminate, irradiate, lighten. * *adj* bright, clear, fair, lightsome, luminous, pale, pearly, whitish. * *n* dawn, day, daybreak, sunrise; blaze, brightness, effulgence, gleam, illumination, luminosity, phosphorescence, radiance, ray; candle, lamp, lantern, lighthouse, taper, torch; comprehension, enlightenment, information, insight, instruction, knowledge; elucidation, explanation, illustration; attitude, construction, interpretation, observation, reference, regard, respect, view.

lighten[1] *vb* allay, alleviate, ease, mitigate, palliate; disburden, disencumber, relieve, unburden, unload.

lighten[2] *vb* brighten, gleam, shine; light, illume, illuminate, illumine, irradiate; enlighten, inform; emit, flash.

light-headed *adj* dizzy, giddy, vertiginous; confused, delirious, wandering; addle-pated, frivolous, giddy, heedless, indiscreet, light, rattlebrained, thoughtless, volatile.

light-hearted *adj* blithe, blithesome, carefree, cheerful, frolicsome, gay, glad, gladsome, gleeful, happy, jocund, jovial, joyful, lightsome, merry.

lightness *n* flightiness, frivolity, giddiness, levity, volatility; agility, buoyancy, facility.

like[1] *vb* approve, please; cherish, enjoy, love, relish; esteem, fancy, regard; choose, desire, elect, list, prefer, select, wish. * *n* liking, partiality, preference.

like[2] *adj* alike, allied, analogous, cognate, corresponding, parallel, resembling, similar; equal, same; likely, probable. * *adv* likely, probably. * *n* counterpart, equal, match, peer, twin.

likelihood *n* probability, verisimilitude.

likely *adj* credible, liable, possible, probable; agreeable, appropriate, convenient, likable, pleasing, suitable, well-adapted, well-suited. * *adv* doubtlessly, presumably, probably.

likeness *n* appearance, form, parallel, resemblance, semblance, similarity, similitude; copy, counterpart, effigy, facsimile, image, picture, portrait, representation.

liking *n* desire, fondness, partiality, wish; appearance, bent, bias, disposition, inclination, leaning, penchant, predisposition, proneness, propensity, tendency, turn.

limb *n* arm, extremity, leg, member; bough, branch, offshoot.

limit *vb* bound, circumscribe, define; check, condition, hinder, restrain, restrict. * *n* bound, boundary, bourn, confine, frontier, march, precinct, term, termination, terminus; check, hindrance, obstruction, restraint, restriction.

limitation *n* check, constraint, restraint, restriction.

limitless *adj* boundless, endless, eternal, illimitable, immeasurable, infinite, never-ending, unbounded, undefined, unending, unlimited.

limp[1] *vb* halt, hitch, hobble, totter. * *n* hitch, hobble, shamble, shuffle, totter.

limp[2] *adj* drooping, droopy, floppy, sagging, weak; flabby, flaccid, flexible, limber, pliable, relaxed, slack, soft.

limpid *adj* bright, clear, crystal, crystalline, lucid, pellucid, pure, translucent, transparent.

line *vb* align, line up, range, rank, regiment; border, bound, edge, fringe, hem, interline, march, rim, verge; seam, stripe, streak, striate, trace; carve, chisel, crease, cut, crosshatch; define, delineate, describe. * n mark, streak, stripe; cable, cord, rope, string, thread; rank, row; ancestry, family, lineage, race, succession; course, method; business, calling, employment, job, occupation, post, pursuit.

lineage *n* ancestry, birth, breed, descendants, descent, extraction, family, forebears, forefathers, genealogy, house, line, offspring, progeny, race.

lineament *n* feature, line, outline, trait.

linen *n* cloth, fabric, flax, lingerie.

linger *vb* dally, dawdle, delay, idle, lag, loiter, remain, saunter, stay, tarry, wait.

link *vb* bind, conjoin, connect, fasten, join, tie, unite. * *n* bond, connection, connective, copula, coupler, joint, juncture; division, member, part, piece.

liquefy *vb* dissolve, fuse, melt, thaw.

liquid *adj* fluid; clear, dulcet, flowing, mellifluous, mellifluent, melting, soft. * *n* fluid, liquor.

list[1] *vb* alphabetize, catalogue, chronicle, codify, docket, enumerate, file, index, inventory, record, register, tabulate, tally; enlist, enroll; choose, desire, elect, like, please, prefer, wish. * *n* catalogue, enumeration, index, inventory, invoice, register, roll, schedule, scroll, series, table, tally; border, bound, limit; border, edge, selvedge, strip, stripe; fillet, listel.

list[2] *vb* cant, heel, incline, keel, lean, pitch, tilt, tip. * *n* cant, inclination, incline, leaning, pitch, slope, tilt, tip.

listen *vb* attend, eavesdrop, hark, hear, hearken, heed, obey, observe.

listless *adj* apathetic, careless, heedless, impassive, inattentive, indifferent, indolent, languid, torpid, vacant, supine, thoughtless, vacant.

listlessness *n* apathy, carelessness, heedlessness, impassivity, inattention, indifference, indolence, languidness, languor, supineness, thoughtlessness, torpor, torpidity, vacancy.

literally *adv* actually, really; exactly, precisely, rigorously, strictly.

literary *adj* bookish, book-learned, erudite, instructed, learned, lettered, literate, scholarly, well-read.

literature *n* erudition, learning, letters, lore, writings.

lithe *adj* flexible, flexile, limber, pliable, pliant, supple.

litigation *n* contending, contest, disputing, lawsuit.

litigious *adj* contentious, disputatious, quarrelsome; controvertible, disputable.

litter *vb* derange, disarrange, disorder, scatter, strew; bear. * *n* bedding, couch, palanquin, sedan, stretcher; confusion, disarray, disorder, mess, untidiness; fragments, rubbish, shreds, trash.

little *adj* diminutive, infinitesimal, minute, small, tiny, wee; brief, short, small; feeble, inconsiderable, insignificant, moderate, petty, scanty, slender, slight, trivial, unimportant, weak; contemptible, illiberal, mean, narrow, niggardly, paltry, selfish, stingy. * *n* handful, jot, modicum, pinch, pittance, trifle, whit.

live[1] *vb* be, exist; continue, endure, last, remain, survive; abide, dwell, reside; fare, feed, nourish, subsist, support; continue, lead, pass.

live[2] *adj* alive, animate, living, quick; burning, hot, ignited; bright, brilliant, glowing, lively, vivid; active, animated, earnest, glowing, wide-awake.

livelihood *n* living, maintenance, subsistence, support, sustenance.

liveliness *n* activity, animation, briskness, gaiety, spirit, sprightliness, vivacity.

lively *adj* active, agile, alert, brisk, energetic, nimble, quick, smart, stirring, supple, vigorous, vivacious; airy, animated, blithe, blithesome, buoyant, frolicsome, gleeful, jocund, jolly, merry, spirited, sportive, sprightly, spry; bright, brilliant, clear, fresh, glowing, strong, vivid; dynamic, forcible, glowing, impassioned, intense, keen, nervous, piquant, racy, sparkling, strenuous, vigorous.

living *adj* alive, breathing, existing, live, organic, quick; active, lively, quickening. * *n* livelihood, maintenance, subsistence, support; estate, keeping; benefice.

load *vb* freight, lade; burden, cumber, encumber, oppress, weigh. * *n* burden, freightage, pack, weight; cargo, freight, lading; clog, deadweight, encumbrance, incubus, oppression, pressure.
loafer *n* (*sl*) bum, idler, lounger, vagabond, vagrant.
loath *adj* averse, backward, disinclined, indisposed, reluctant, unwilling.
loathe *vb* abhor, abominate, detest, dislike, hate, recoil.
loathing *n* abhorrence, abomination, antipathy, aversion, detestation, disgust, hatred, horror, repugnance, revulsion.
loathsome *adj* disgusting, nauseating, nauseous, offensive, palling, repulsive, revolting, sickening; abominable, abhorrent, detestable, execrable, hateful, odious, shocking.
local *adj* limited, neighbouring, provincial, regional, restricted, sectional, territorial, topical.
locality *n* location, neighbourhood, place, position, site, situation, spot.
locate *vb* determine, establish, fix, place, set, settle.
lock[1] *vb* bolt, fasten, padlock, seal; confine; clog, impede, restrain, stop; clasp, embrace, encircle, enclose, grapple, hug, join, press. * *n* bolt, fastening, padlock; embrace, grapple, hug.
lock[2] *n* curl, ringlet, tress, tuft.
lodge *vb* deposit, fix, settle; fix, place, plant; accommodate, cover, entertain, harbour, quarter, shelter; abide, dwell, inhabit, live, reside, rest; remain, rest, sojourn, stay, stop. * *n* cabin, cot, cottage, hovel, hut, shed; cave, den, haunt, lair; assemblage, assembly, association club, group, society.
lodging *n* abode, apartment, dwelling, habitation, quarters, residence; cover, harbour, protection, refuge, shelter.
loftiness *n* altitude, elevation, height; arrogance, haughtiness, pride, vanity; dignity, grandeur, sublimity.
lofty *adj* elevated, high, tall, towering; arrogant, haughty, proud; eminent, exalted, sublime; dignified, imposing, majestic, stately.
logical *adj* close, coherent, consistent, dialectical, sound, valid; discriminating, rational, reasoned.
loiter *vb* dally, dawdle, delay, dilly-dally, idle, lag, linger, saunter, stroll, tarry.
loneliness *n* isolation, retirement, seclusion, solitariness, solitude; desolation, dreariness, forlornness.
lonely *adj* apart, dreary, isolated, lonesome, remote, retired, secluded, separate, sequestrated, solitary; alone, lone, companionless, friendless, unaccompanied; deserted, desolate, forlorn, forsaken, withdrawn.
lonesome *adj* cheerless, deserted, desolate, dreary, gloomy, lone, lonely.
long[1] *vb* anticipate, await, expect; aspire, covet, crave, desire, hanker, lust, pine, wish, yearn.
long[2] *adj* drawn-out, extended, extensive, far-reaching, lengthy, prolonged, protracted, stretched; diffuse, long-winded, prolix, tedious, wearisome; backward, behindhand, dilatory, lingering, slack, slow, tardy.
longing *n* aspiration, coveting, craving, desire, hankering, hunger, pining, yearning.
long-suffering *adj* enduring, forbearing, patient. * *n* clemency, endurance, forbearing.
look *vb* behold, examine, notice, see, search; consider, inspect, investigate, observe, study, contemplate, gaze, regard, scan, survey, view; anticipate, await, expect; heed, mind, watch; face, front; appear, seem. * *n* examination, gaze, glance, peep, peer, search; appearance, aspect, complexion; air, aspect, manner, mien.
loophole *n* aperture, crenellation, loop, opening; excuse, plea, pretence, pretext, subterfuge.
loose *vb* free, liberate, release, unbind, undo, unfasten, unlash, unlock, untie; ease, loosen, relax, slacken; detach, disconnect, disengage. * *adj* unbound, unconfined, unfastened, unsewn, untied; disengaged, free, unattached; relaxed; diffuse, diffusive, prolix, rambling, unconnected; ill-defined, indefinite, indeterminate, indistinct, vague; careless, heedless, negligent, lax, slack; debauched, dissolute, immoral, licentious, unchaste, wanton.
loosen *vb* liberate, relax, release, separate, slacken, unbind, unloose, untie.
looseness *n* easiness, slackness; laxity, levity; lewdness, unchastity, wantonness, wickedness; diarrhoea, flux.
loot *vb* pillage, plunder, ransack, rifle, rob, sack. * *n* booty, plunder, spoil.
lop *vb* cut, truncate; crop, curtail, dock, prune; detach, dissever, sever.
loquacious *adj* garrulous, talkative, voluble, wordy; noisy, speaking, talking; babbling, blabbing, tattling, tell-tale.
loquacity *n* babbling, chattering, gabbling, garrulity, loquaciousness, talkativeness, volubility.
lord *n* earl, noble, nobleman, peer, viscount; governor, king, liege, master, monarch, prince, ruler, seigneur, seignior, sovereign, superior; husband, spouse.
lordly *adj* aristocratic, dignified, exalted, grand, lofty, majestic, noble; arrogant, despotic, domineering, haughty, imperious, insolent, masterful, overbearing, proud, tyrannical; large, liberal.
lordship *n* authority, command, control, direction, domination, dominion, empire, government, rule, sovereignty, sway; manor, domain, seigneury, seigniory.
lore *n* erudition, knowledge, learning, letters, scholarship; admonition, advice, counsel, doctrine, instruction, lesson, teaching, wisdom.
lose *vb* deprive, dispossess, forfeit, miss; dislodge, displace, mislay, misspend, squander, waste; decline, fall, succumb, yield.
loss *n* deprivation, failure, forfeiture, privation; casualty, damage, defeat, destruction, detriment, disadvantage, injury, overthrow, ruin; squandering, waste.

lost *adj* astray, missing; forfeited, missed, unredeemed; dissipated, misspent, squandered, wasted; bewildered, confused, distracted, perplexed, puzzled; absent, absent-minded, abstracted, dreamy, napping, preoccupied; abandoned, corrupt, debauched, depraved, dissolute, graceless, hardened, incorrigible, irreclaimable, licentious, profligate, reprobate, shameless, unchaste, wanton; destroyed, ruined.

lot *n* allotment, apportionment, destiny, doom, fate; accident, chance, fate, fortune, hap, haphazard, hazard; division, parcel, part, portion.

loth *adj* averse, disinclined, disliking, reluctant, unwilling

loud *adj* high-sounding, noisy, resounding, sonorous; deafening, stentorian, strong, stunning; boisterous, clamorous, noisy, obstreperous, tumultuous, turbulent, uproarious, vociferous; emphatic, impressive, positive, vehement; flashy, gaudy, glaring, loud, ostentatious, showy, vulgar.

lounge *vb* loll, recline, sprawl; dawdle, idle, loaf, loiter.

love *vb* adore, like, worship. * *n* accord, affection, amity, courtship, delight, fondness, friendship, kindness, regard, tenderness, warmth; adoration, amour, ardour, attachment, passion; devotion, inclination, liking; benevolence, charity, goodwill.

lovely *adj* beautiful, charming, delectable, delightful, enchanting, exquisite, graceful, pleasing, sweet, winning; admirable, adorable, amiable.

loving *adj* affectionate, dear, fond, kind, tender.

low[1] *vb* bellow, moo.

low[2] *adj* basal, depressed, profound; gentle, grave, soft, subdued; cheap, humble, mean, plebeian, vulgar; abject, base, base-minded, degraded, dirty, grovelling, ignoble, low-minded, menial, scurvy, servile, shabby, slavish, vile; derogatory, disgraceful, dishonourable, disreputable, unbecoming, undignified, ungentlemanly, unhandsome, unmanly; exhausted, feeble, reduced, weak; frugal, plain, poor, simple, spare; lowly, reverent, submissive; dejected, depressed, dispirited.

lower[1] *vb* depress, drop, sink, subside; debase, degrade, disgrace, humble, humiliate, reduce; abate, decrease, diminish, lessen. * *adj* baser, inferior, less, lesser, shorter, smaller; subjacent, under.

lower[2] *vb* blacken, darken, frown, glower, threaten.

lowering *adj* dark, clouded, cloudy, lurid, murky, overcast, threatening.

lowliness *n* humbleness, humility, meekness, self-abasement, submissiveness.

lowly *adj* gentle, humble, meek, mild, modest, plain, poor, simple, unassuming, unpretending, unpretentious; low-born, mean, servile.

loyal *adj* constant, devoted, faithful, patriotic, true.

loyalty *n* allegiance, constancy, devotion, faithfulness, fealty, fidelity, patriotism.

lubricious *adj* slippery, smooth; uncertain, unstable, wavering; impure, incontinent, lascivious, lecherous, lewd, libidinous, licentious, lustful, salacious, unchaste, wanton.

lucid *adj* beaming, bright, brilliant, luminous, radiant, resplendent, shining, clear, crystalline, diaphanous, limpid, lucent, pellucid, pure, transparent; clear, distinct, evident, intelligible, obvious, perspicuous, plain; reasonable, sane, sober, sound.

luck *n* accident, casualty, chance, fate, fortune, hap, haphazard, hazard, serendipity, success.

luckless *adj* ill-fated, ill-starred, unfortunate, unhappy, unlucky, unpropitious, unprosperous, unsuccessful.

lucky *adj* blessed, favoured, fortunate, happy, successful; auspicious, favourable, propitious, prosperous.

lucrative *adj* advantageous, gainful, paying, profitable, remunerative.

ludicrous *adj* absurd, burlesque, comic, comical, droll, farcical, funny, laughable, odd, ridiculous, sportive.

lugubrious *adj* complaining, doleful, gloomy, melancholy, mournful, sad, serious, sombre, sorrowful.

lukewarm *adj* blood-warm, tepid, thermal; apathetic, cold, dull, indifferent, listless, unconcerned, torpid.

lull *vb* calm, compose, hush, quiet, still, tranquillize; abate, cease, decrease, diminish, subside. * *n* calm, calmness, cessation.

lumber[1] *vb* rumble, shamble, trudge.

lumber[2] *n* refuse, rubbish, trash, trumpery; wood.

luminous *adj* effulgent, incandescent, radiant, refulgent, resplendent, shining; bright, brilliant, clear; clear, lucid, lucent, perspicuous, plain.

lunacy *n* aberration, craziness, dementia, derangement, insanity, madness, mania.

lunatic *adj* crazy, demented, deranged, insane, mad, psychopathic. * *n* madman, maniac, psychopath.

lurch *vb* appropriate, filch, pilfer, purloin, steal; deceive, defeat, disappoint, evade; ambush, lurk, skulk; contrive, dodge, shift, trick; pitch, sway.

lure *vb* allure, attract, decoy, entice, inveigle, seduce, tempt. * *n* allurement, attraction, bait, decoy, enticement, temptation.

lurid *adj* dismal, ghastly, gloomy, lowering, murky, pale, wan; glaring, sensational, startling, unrestrained.

lurk *vb* hide, prowl, skulk, slink, sneak, snoop.

luscious *adj* delicious, delightful, grateful, palatable, pleasing, savoury, sweet.

lush *adj* fresh, juicy, luxuriant, moist, sappy, succulent, watery.

lust *vb* covet, crave, desire, hanker, need, want, yearn. * *n* cupidity, desire, longing; carnality, concupiscence, lasciviousness, lechery, lewdness, lubricity, salaciousness, salacity, wantonness.

lustful *adj* carnal, concupiscent, hankering, lascivious, lecherous, licentious, libidinous, lubricious, salacious.
lustily *adv* strongly, vigorously.
lustiness *n* hardihood, power, robustness, stoutness, strength, sturdiness, vigour.
lustre *n* brightness, brilliance, brilliancy, splendour.
lusty *adj* healthful, lively, robust, stout, strong, sturdy, vigorous; bulky, burly, corpulent, fat, large, stout.
luxuriance *n* exuberance, profusion, superabundance.
luxuriant *adj* exuberant, plenteous, plentiful, profuse, superabundant.
luxuriate *vb* abound, delight, enjoy, flourish, indulge, revel.
luxurious *adj* epicurean, opulent, pampered, self-indulgent, sensual, sybaritic, voluptuous.
luxury *n* epicureanism, epicurism, luxuriousness, opulence, sensuality, voluptuousness; delight, enjoyment, gratification, indulgence, pleasure; dainty, delicacy, treat.
lying *adj* equivocating, false, mendacious, untruthful, untrue.
lyric *adj* dulcet, euphonious, lyrical, mellifluous, mellifluent, melodic, melodious, musical, poetic, silvery, tuneful.
lyrical *adj* ecstatic, enthusiastic, expressive, impassion; dulcet, lyric, mellifluous, mellifluent, melodic, melodious, musical, poetic.

M

macabre *adj* cadaverous, deathlike, deathly, dreadful, eerie, frightening, frightful, ghoulish, grim, grisly, gruesome, hideous, horrid, morbid, unearthly, weird.

mace *n* baton, staff, truncheon.

macerate *vb* harass, mortify, torture; digest, soak, soften, steep.

Machiavellian *adj* arch, artful, astute, crafty, crooked, cunning, deceitful, designing, diplomatic, insidious, intriguing, shrewd, sly, subtle, tricky, wily.

machination *n* artifice, cabal, conspiracy, contrivance, design, intrigue, plot, scheme, stratagem, trick.

machine *n* instrument, puppet, tool; machinery, organization, system; engine.

mad *adj* crazed, crazy, delirious, demented, deranged, distracted, insane, irrational, lunatic, maniac, maniacal; enraged, furious, rabid, raging, violent; angry, enraged, exasperated, furious, incensed, provoked, wrathful; distracted, infatuated, wild; frantic, frenzied, raving.

madden *vb* annoy, craze, enrage, exasperate, inflame, infuriate, irritate, provoke.

madness *n* aberration, craziness, dementia, derangement, insanity, lunacy, mania; delirium, frenzy, fury, rage.

magazine *n* depository, depot, entrepot, receptacle, repository, storehouse, warehouse; pamphlet, paper, periodical.

magic *adj* bewitching, charming, enchanting, fascinating, magical, miraculous, spellbinding. * *n* conjuring, enchantment, necromancy, sorcery, thaumaturgy, voodoo, witchcraft; char, fascination, witchery.

magician *n* conjurer, enchanter, juggler, magus, necromancer, shaman, sorcerer, wizard.

magisterial *adj* august, dignified, majestic, pompous; authoritative, despotic, domineering, imperious, dictatorial.

magnanimity *n* chivalry, disinterestedness, forbearance, high-mindedness, generosity, nobility.

magnificence *n* brilliance, éclat, grandeur, luxuriousness, luxury, majesty, pomp, splendour.

magnificent *adj* elegant, grand, majestic, noble, splendid, superb; brilliant, gorgeous, imposing, lavish, luxurious, pompous, showy, stately.

magnify *vb* amplify, augment, enlarge; bless, celebrate, elevate, exalt, extol, glorify, laud, praise; exaggerate.

magnitude *n* bulk, dimension, extent, mass, size, volume; consequence, greatness, importance; grandeur, loftiness, sublimity.

maid *n* damsel, girl, lass, lassie, maiden, virgin; maidservant, servant.

maiden *adj* chaste, pure, undefiled, virgin; fresh, new, unused. * *n* girl, maid, virgin.

maidenly *adj* demure, gentle, modest, maidenlike, reserved.

maim *vb* cripple, disable, disfigure, mangle, mar, mutilate. * *n* crippling, disfigurement, mutilation; harm, hurt, injury, mischief.

main[1] *adj* capital, cardinal, chief, leading, principal; essential, important, indispensable, necessary, requisite, vital; enormous, huge, mighty, vast; pure, sheer; absolute, direct, entire, mere. * *n* channel, pipe; force, might, power, strength, violence.

main[2] *n* high seas, ocean; continent, mainland.

maintain *vb* keep, preserve, support, sustain, uphold; hold, possess; defend, vindicate, justify; carry on, continue, keep up; feed, provide, supply; allege, assert, declare; affirm, aver, contend, hold, say.

maintenance *n* defence, justification, preservation, support, sustenance, vindication; bread, food, livelihood, provisions, subsistence, sustenance, victuals.

majestic *adj* august, dignified, imperial, imposing, lofty, noble, pompous, princely, stately, regal, royal; grand, magnificent, splendid, sublime.

majesty *n* augustness, dignity, elevation, grandeur, loftiness, stateliness.

majority *n* bulk, greater, mass, more, most, plurality, preponderance, superiority; adulthood, manhood.

make *vb* create; fashion, figure, form, frame, mould, shape; cause, construct, effect, establish, fabricate, produce; do, execute, perform, practice; acquire, gain, get, raise, secure; cause, compel, constrain, force, occasion; compose, constitute; go, journey, move, proceed, tend, travel; conduce, contribute, effect, favour, operate; estimate, judge, reckon, suppose, think. * *n* brand, build, constitution, construction, form, shape, structure.

maker *n* creator, god; builder, constructor, fabricator, framer, manufacturer; author, composer, poet, writer.

maladministration *n* malversation, misgovernment, misrule.

maladroit *adj* awkward, bungling, clumsy, inept, inexpert, unhandy, unskilful, unskilled.
malady *n* affliction, ailment, complaint, disease, disorder, illness, indisposition, sickness.
malcontent *adj* discontented, dissatisfied, insurgent, rebellious, resentful, uneasy, unsatisfied. * *n* agitator, complainer, fault-finder, grumbler, spoilsport.
malediction *n* anathema, ban, curse, cursing, denunciation, execration, imprecation, malison.
malefactor *n* convict, criminal, culprit, delinquent, evildoer, felon, offender, outlaw.
malevolence *n* hate, hatred, ill-will, malice, malignity, rancour, spite, spitefulness, vindictiveness.
malevolent *adj* evil-minded, hateful, hostile, ill-natured, malicious, malignant, mischievous, rancorous, spiteful, venomous. vindictive.
malice *n* animosity, bitterness, enmity, grudge, hate, ill-will, malevolence, maliciousness, malignity, pique, rancour, spite, spitefulness, venom, vindictiveness.
malicious *adj* bitter, envious, evil-minded, ill-disposed, ill-natured, invidious, malevolent, malignant, mischievous, rancorous, resentful, spiteful, vicious.
malign *vb* abuse, asperse, blacken, calumniate, defame, disparage, revile, scandalize, slander, traduce, vilify. * *adj* malevolent, malicious, malignant, ill-disposed; baneful, injurious, pernicious, unfavourable, unpropitious.
malignant *adj* bitter, envious, hostile, inimical, malevolent, malicious, malign, spiteful, rancorous, resentful, virulent; heinous, pernicious; ill-boding, unfavourable, unpropitious; dangerous, fatal.
malignity *n* animosity, hatred, ill-will, malice, malevolence, maliciousness, rancour, spite; deadliness, destructiveness, fatality, harmfulness, malignancy, perniciousness, virulence; enormity, evilness, heinousness.
malpractice *n* dereliction, malversation, misbehaviour, misconduct, misdeed, misdoing, sin, transgression.
maltreat *vb* abuse, harm, hurt, ill-treat, ill-use, injure.
mammoth *adj* colossal, enormous, gigantic, huge, immense, vast.
man *vb* crew, garrison, furnish; fortify, reinforce, strengthen. * *n* adult, being, body, human, individual, one, person, personage, somebody, soul; humanity, humankind, mankind; attendant, butler, dependant, liege, servant, subject, valet, vassal; employee, workman.
manacle *vb* bind, chain, fetter, handcuff, restrain, shackle, tie. * *n* bond, chain, handcuff, gyve, hand-fetter, shackle.
manage *vb* administer, conduct, direct, guide, handle, operate, order, regulate, superintend, supervise, transact, treat; control, govern, rule; handle, manipulate, train, wield; contrive, economize, husband, save.
manageable *adj* controllable, docile, easy, governable, tamable, tractable.
management *n* administration, care, charge, conduct, control, direction, disposal, economy, government, guidance, superintendence, supervision, surveillance, treatment.
manager *n* comptroller, conductor, director, executive, governor, impresario, overseer, superintendent, supervisor.
mandate *n* charge, command, commission, edict, injunction, order, precept, requirement.
manful *adj* bold, brave, courageous, daring, heroic, honourable, intrepid, noble, stout, strong, undaunted, vigorous.
mangily *adv* basely, foully, meanly, scabbily, scurvily, vilely.
mangle[1] *vb* hack, lacerate, mutilate, rend, tear; cripple, crush, destroy, maim, mar, spoil.
mangle[2] *vb* calender, polish, press, smooth.
manhood *n* virility; bravery, courage, firmness, fortitude, hardihood, manfulness, manliness, resolution; human nature, humanity; adulthood, maturity.
mania *n* aberration, craziness, delirium, dementia, derangement, frenzy, insanity, lunacy, madness; craze, desire, enthusiasm, fad, fanaticism.
manifest *vb* declare, demonstrate, disclose, discover, display, evidence, evince, exhibit, express, reveal, show. * *adj* apparent, clear, conspicuous, distinct, evident, glaring, indubitable, obvious, open, palpable, patent, plain, unmistakable, visible.
manifestation *n* disclosure, display, exhibition, exposure, expression, revelation.
manifold *adj* complex, diverse, many, multifarious, multiplied, multitudinous, numerous, several, sundry, varied, various.
manipulate *vb* handle, operate, work.
manliness *n* boldness, bravery, courage, dignity, fearlessness, firmness, heroism, intrepidity, nobleness, resolution, valour.
manly *adj* bold, brave, courageous, daring, dignified, firm, heroic, intrepid, manful, noble, stout, strong, undaunted, vigorous; male, masculine, virile.
manner *n* fashion, form, method, mode, style, way; custom, habit, practice; degree, extent, measure; kind, kinds, sort, sorts; air, appearance, aspect, behaviour, carriage, demeanour, deportment, look, mien; mannerism, peculiarity; behaviour, conduct, habits, morals; civility, deportment.
mannerly *adj* ceremonious, civil, complaisant, courteous, polite, refined, respectful, urbane, well-behaved, well-bred.
manners *npl* conduct, habits, morals; air, bearing, behaviour, breeding, carriage, comportment, deportment, etiquette.
manoeuvre *vb* contrive, finesse, intrigue, manage, plan, plot, scheme. * *n* evolution, exercise, movement, operation; artifice, finesse, intrigue, plan, plot, ruse, scheme, stratagem, trick.

mansion *n* abode, dwelling, dwelling house, habitation, hall, residence, seat.
mantle *vb* cloak, cover, discover, obscure; expand, spread; bubble, cream, effervesce, foam, froth, sparkle. * *n* chasuble, cloak, toga; cover, covering, hood.
manufacture *vb* build, compose, construct, create, fabricate, forge, form, make, mould, produce, shape. * *n* constructing, fabrication, making, production.
manumission *n* deliverance, emancipation, enfranchisement, freedom, liberation, release.
manumit *vb* deliver, emancipate, enfranchise, free, liberate, release.
manure *vb* enrich, fertilize. * *n* compost, dressing, fertilizer, guano, muck.
many *adj* abundant, diverse, frequent, innumerable, manifold, multifarious, multifold, multiplied, multitudinous, numerous, sundry, varied, various. * *n* crowd, multitude, people.
map *vb* chart, draw up, plan, plot, set out, sketch. * *n* chart, diagram, outline, plot, sketch.
mar *vb* blot, damage, harm, hurt, impair, injure, ruin, spoil, stain; deface, deform, disfigure, maim, mutilate.
marauder *n* bandit, brigand, desperado, filibuster, freebooter, outlaw, pillager, plunderer, ravager, robber, rover.
march *vb* go, pace, parade, step, tramp, walk. * *n* hike, tramp, walk; parade, procession; gait, step, stride; advance, evolution, progress.
marches *npl* borders, boundaries, confines, frontiers, limits, precincts.
margin *n* border, brim, brink, confine, edge, limit, rim, skirt, verge; latitude, room, space, surplus.
marine *adj* oceanic, pelagic, saltwater, sea; maritime, naval, nautical. * *n* navy, shipping; sea-dog, sea soldier, soldier; sea piece, seascape.
mariner *n* navigator, sailor, salt, seafarer, seaman, tar.
marital *adj* connubial, conjugal, matrimonial.
maritime *adj* marine, naval, nautical, oceanic, sea, seafaring, seagoing; coastal, seaside.
mark *vb* distinguish, earmark, label; betoken, brand, characterize, denote, designate, engrave, impress, imprint, indicate, print, stamp; evince, heed, note, notice, observe, regard, remark, show, spot. * *n* brand, character, characteristic, impression, impress, line, note, print, sign, stamp, symbol, token, race; evidence, indication, proof, symptom, trace, track, vestige; badge; footprint; bull's-eye, butt, object, target; consequence, distinction, eminence, fame, importance, notability, position, preeminence, reputation, significance.
marked *adj* conspicuous, distinguished, eminent, notable, noted, outstanding, prominent, remarkable.
marriage *n* espousals, nuptials, spousals, wedding; matrimony, wedlock; union; alliance, association, confederation.
marrow *n* medulla, pith; cream, essence, quintessence, substance.
marsh *n* bog, fen, mire, morass, quagmire, slough, swamp.
marshal *vb* arrange, array, dispose, gather, muster, range, order, rank; guide, herald, lead. * *n* conductor, director, master of ceremonies, regulator; harbinger, herald, pursuivant.
marshy *adj* boggy, miry, mossy, swampy, wet.
martial *adj* brave, heroic, military, soldier-like, warlike.
marvel *vb* gape, gaze, goggle, wonder. * *n* miracle, prodigy, wonder; admiration, amazement, astonishment, surprise.
marvellous *adj* amazing, astonishing, extraordinary, miraculous, prodigious, strange, stupendous, wonderful, wondrous; improbable, incredible, surprising, unbelievable.
masculine *adj* bold, hardy, manful, manlike, manly, mannish, virile; potent, powerful, robust, strong, vigorous; bold, coarse, forward.
mask *vb* cloak, conceal, cover, disguise, hide, screen, shroud, veil. * *n* blind, cloak, disguise, screen, veil; evasion, pretence, plea, pretext, ruse, shift, subterfuge, trick; masquerade; bustle, mummery.
masquerade *vb* cover, disguise, hide, mask, revel, veil. * *n* mask, mummery, revel, revelry.
Mass *n* communion, Eucharist.
mass *vb* accumulate, amass, assemble, collect, gather, rally, throng. * *adj* extensive, general, large-scale, widespread. * *n* cake, clot, lump; assemblage, collection, combination, congeries, heap; bulk, dimension, magnitude, size; accumulation, aggregate, body, sum, total, totality, whole.
massacre *vb* annihilate, butcher, exterminate, kill, murder, slaughter, slay. * *n* annihilation, butchery, carnage, extermination, killing, murder, pogrom, slaughter.
massive *adj* big, bulky, colossal, enormous, heavy, huge, immense, ponderous, solid, substantial, vast, weighty.
master *vb* conquer, defeat, direct, govern, overcome, overpower, rule, subdue, subjugate, vanquish; acquire, learn. * *adj* cardinal, chief, especial, grand, great, main, leading, prime, principal; adept, expert, proficient. * *n* director, governor, lord, manager, overseer, superintendent, ruler; captain, commander; instructor, pedagogue, preceptor, schoolteacher, teacher, tutor; holder, owner, possessor, proprietor; chief, head, leader, principal.
masterly *adj* adroit, clever, dextrous, excellent, expert, finished, skilful, skilled; arbitrary, despotic, despotical, domineering, imperious.
mastery *n* command, dominion, mastership, power, rule, supremacy, sway; ascendancy, conquest, leadership, preeminence, superiority, upper-hand, victory; acquisition, acquirement, attainment; ability, cleverness, dexterity, proficiency, skill.

masticate *vb* chew, eat, munch.

match *vb* equal, rival; adapt, fit, harmonize, proportion, suit; marry, mate; combine, couple, join, sort; oppose, pit; correspond, suit, tally. * *n* companion, equal, mate, tally; competition, contest, game, trial; marriage, union.

matchless *adj* consummate, excellent, exquisite, incomparable, inimitable, peerless, perfect, surpassing, unequalled, unmatched, unparalleled, unrivalled.

mate *vb* marry, match, wed; compete, equal, vie; appal, confound, crush, enervate, subdue, stupefy. * *n* associate, companion, compeer, consort, crony, friend, fellow, intimate; companion, equal, match; assistant, subordinate; husband, spouse, wife.

material *adj* bodily, corporeal, nonspiritual, physical, temporal; essential, important, momentous, relevant, vital, weighty. * *n* body, element, stuff, substance.

maternal *adj* motherlike, motherly.

matrimonial *adj* conjugal, connubial, espousal, hymeneal, marital, nuptial, spousal.

matrimony *n* marriage, wedlock.

matter *vb* import, signify, weigh. * *n* body, content, sense, substance; difficulty, distress, trouble; material, stuff; question, subject, subject matter, topic; affair, business, concern, event; consequence, import, importance, moment, significance; discharge, purulence, pus.

mature *vb* develop, perfect, ripen. * *adj* complete, fit, full-grown, perfect, ripe; completed, prepared, ready, well-considered, well-digested.

maturity *n* completeness, completion, matureness, perfection, ripeness.

mawkish *adj* disgusting, flat, insipid, nauseous, sickly, stale, tasteless, vapid; emotional, feeble, maudlin, sentimental.

maxim *n* adage, aphorism, apothegm, axiom, byword, dictum, proverb, saw, saying, truism.

maze *vb* amaze, bewilder, confound, confuse, perplex. * *n* intricacy, labyrinth, meander; bewilderment, embarrassment, intricacy, perplexity, puzzle, uncertainty.

mazy *adj* confused, confusing, intricate, labyrinthian, labyrinthic, labyrinthine, perplexing, winding.

meagre *adj* emaciated, gaunt, lank, lean, poor, skinny, starved, spare, thin; barren, poor, sterile, unproductive; bald, barren, dry, dull, mean, poor, prosy, feeble, insignificant, jejune, scanty, small, tame, uninteresting, vapid.

mean[1] *vb* contemplate, design, intend, purpose; connote, denote, express, imply, import, indicate, purport, signify, symbolize.

mean[2] *adj* average, medium, middle; intermediate, intervening. * *n* measure, mediocrity, medium, moderation; average; agency, instrument, instrumentality, means, measure, method, mode, way.

mean[3] *adj* coarse, common, humble, ignoble, low, ordinary, plebeian, vulgar; abject, base, base-minded, beggarly, contemptible, degraded, dirty, dishonourable, disingenuous, grovelling, low-minded, pitiful, rascally, scurvy, servile, shabby, sneaking, sorry, spiritless, unfair, vile; illiberal, mercenary, miserly, narrow, narrow-minded, niggardly, parsimonious, penurious, selfish, sordid, stingy, ungenerous, unhandsome; contemptible, despicable, diminutive, insignificant, paltry, petty, poor, small, wretched.

meaning *n* acceptation, drift, import, intention, purport, purpose, sense, signification.

means *npl* instrument, method, mode, way; appliance, expedient, measure, resource, shift, step; estate, income, property, resources, revenue, substance, wealth, wherewithal.

measure *vb* mete; adjust, gauge, proportion; appraise, appreciate, estimate, gauge, value. * *n* gauge, meter, rule, standard; degree, extent, length, limit; allotment, share, proportion; means, step; foot, metre, rhythm, tune, verse.

measureless *adj* boundless, endless, immeasurable, immense, limitless, unbounded, unlimited, vast.

meat *n* aliment, cheer, diet, fare, feed, flesh, food, nourishment, nutriment, provision, rations, regimen, subsistence, sustenance, viands, victuals.

mechanic *n* artificer, artisan, craftsman, hand, handicraftsman, machinist, operative, workman.

meddle *vb* interfere, intermeddle, interpose, intrude.

meddlesome *adj* interfering, intermeddling, intrusive, officious, prying.

mediate *vb* arbitrate, intercede, interpose, intervene, settle. * *adj* interposed, intervening, middle.

mediation *n* arbitration, intercession, interposition, intervention.

mediator *n* advocate, arbitrator, interceder, intercessor, propitiator, umpire.

medicine *n* drug, medicament, medication, physic; therapy.

mediocre *adj* average, commonplace, indifferent, mean, medium, middling, ordinary.

meditate *vb* concoct, contrive, design, devise, intend, plan, purpose, scheme; chew, contemplate, ruminate, study; cogitate, muse, ponder, think.

meditation *n* cogitation, contemplation, musing, pondering, reflection, ruminating, study, thought.

meditative *adj* contemplative, pensive, reflective, studious, thoughtful.

medium *adj* average, mean, mediocre, middle. * *n* agency, channel, intermediary, instrument, instrumentality, means, organ; conditions, environment, influences; average, means.

medley *n* confusion, farrago, hodgepodge, hotchpotch, jumble, mass, melange, miscellany, mishmash, mixture.

meed *n* award, guerdon, premium, prize, recompense, remuneration, reward.

meek *adj* gentle, humble, lowly, mild, modest, pacific, soft, submissive, unassuming, yielding.

meekness *n* gentleness, humbleness, humility, lowliness, mildness, modesty, submission, submissiveness.

meet *vb* cross, intersect, transact; confront, encounter, engage; answer, comply, fulfil, gratify, satisfy; converge, join, unite; assemble, collect, convene, congregate, forgather, muster, rally. * *adj* adapted, appropriate, befitting, convenient, fit, fitting, proper, qualified, suitable, suited.

meeting *n* encounter, interview; assemblage, assembly, audience, company, concourse, conference, congregation, convention, gathering; assignation, encounter, introduction, rendezvous; confluence, conflux, intersection, joining, junction, union; collision.

melancholy *adj* blue, dejected, depressed, despondent, desponding, disconsolate, dismal, dispirited, doleful, down, downcast, downhearted, gloomy, glum, hypochondriac, low-spirited, lugubrious, moody, mopish, sad, sombre, sorrowful, unhappy; afflictive, calamitous, unfortunate, unlucky; dark, gloomy, grave, quiet. * *n* blues, dejection, depression, despondency, dismals, dumps, gloom, gloominess, hypochondria, sadness, vapours.

melee *n* affray, brawl, broil, contest, fight, fray, scuffle.

mellifluous, mellifluent *adj* dulcet, euphonic, euphonical, euphonious, mellow, silver-toned, silvery, smooth, soft, sweet.

mellow *vb* mature, ripen; improve, smooth, soften, tone; pulverize; perfect. * *adj* mature, ripe; dulcet, mellifluous, mellifluent, rich, silver-toned, silvery, smooth, soft; delicate; genial, good-humoured, jolly, jovial, matured, softened; mellowy, loamy, unctuous; perfected, well-prepared; disguised, fuddled, intoxicated, tipsy.

melodious *adj* arioso, concordant, dulcet, euphonious, harmonious, mellifluous, mellifluent, musical, silvery, sweet, tuneful.

melody *n* air, descant, music, plainsong, song, theme, tune.

melt *vb* dissolve, fuse, liquefy, thaw; mollify, relax, soften, subdue; dissipate, waste; blend, pass, shade.

member *n* arm, leg, limb, organ; component, constituent, element, part, portion; branch, clause, division, head.

memento *n* memorial, remembrance, reminder, souvenir.

memoir *n* account, autobiography, biography, journal, narrative, record, register.

memorable *adj* celebrated, distinguished, extraordinary, famous, great, illustrious, important, notable, noteworthy, remarkable, signal, significant.

memorandum *n* minute, note, record.

memorial *adj* commemorative, monumental. * *n* cairn, commemoration, memento, monument, plaque, record, souvenir; memorandum, remembrance.

memory *n* recollection, remembrance, reminiscence; celebrity, fame, renown, reputation; commemoration, memorial.

menace *vb* alarm, frighten, intimidate, threaten. * *n* danger, hazard, peril, threat, warning; nuisance, pest, troublemaker.

menage *n* household, housekeeping, management.

mend *vb* darn, patch, rectify, refit, repair, restore, retouch; ameliorate, amend, better, correct, emend, improve, meliorate, reconcile, rectify, reform; advance, help; augment, increase.

mendacious *adj* deceitful, deceptive, fallacious, false, lying, untrue, untruthful.

mendacity *n* deceit, deceitfulness, deception, duplicity, falsehood, lie, untruth.

mendicant *n* beggar, pauper, tramp.

menial *adj* base, low, mean, servile, vile. * *n* attendant, bondsman, domestic, flunkey, footman, lackey, serf, servant, slave, underling, valet, waiter.

mensuration *n* measurement, measuring; survey, surveying.

mental *adj* ideal, immaterial, intellectual, psychiatric, subjective.

mention *vb* acquaint, allude, cite, communicate, declare, disclose, divulge, impart, inform, name, report, reveal, state, tell. * *n* allusion, citation, designation, notice, noting, reference.

mentor *n* adviser, counsellor, guide, instructor, monitor.

mephitic *adj* baleful, baneful, fetid, foul, mephitical, noisome, noxious, poisonous, pestilential.

mercantile *adj* commercial, marketable, trading.

mercenary *adj* hired, paid, purchased, venal; avaricious, covetous, grasping, mean, niggardly, parsimonious, penurious, sordid, stingy. * *n* hireling, soldier.

merchandise *n* commodities, goods, wares.

merchant *n* dealer, retailer, shopkeeper, trader, tradesman.

merciful *adj* clement, compassionate, forgiving, gracious, lenient, pitiful; benignant, forbearing, gentle, humane, kind, mild, tender, tender-hearted.

merciless *adj* barbarous, callous, cruel, fell, hard-hearted, inexorable, pitiless, relentless, remorseless, ruthless, savage, severe, uncompassionate, unfeeling, unmerciful, unrelenting, unrepenting, unsparing.

mercurial *adj* active, lively, nimble, prompt, quick, sprightly; cheerful, light-hearted; changeable, fickle, flighty, inconstant, mobile, volatile.

mercy *n* benevolence, clemency, compassion, gentleness, kindness, lenience, leniency, lenity, mildness, pity, tenderness; blessing, favour, grace; discretion, disposal; forgiveness, pardon.

mere *adj* bald, bare, naked, plain, sole, simple; absolute, entire, pure, sheer, unmixed. * *n* lake, pond, pool.

meretricious *adj* deceitful, brummagem, false,

gaudy, make-believe, sham, showy, spurious, tawdry.

merge *vb* bury, dip, immerse, involve, lose, plunge, sink, submerge.

meridian *n* acme, apex, climax, culmination, summit, zenith; midday, noon, noontide.

merit *vb* deserve, earn, incur; acquire, gain, profit, value. * *n* claim, right; credit, desert, excellence, goodness, worth, worthiness.

meritorious *adj* commendable, deserving, excellent, good, worthy.

merriment *n* amusement, frolic, gaiety, hilarity, jocularity, jollity, joviality, laughter, liveliness, mirth, sport, sportiveness.

merry *adj* agreeable, brisk, delightful, exhilarating, lively, pleasant, stirring; airy, blithe, blithesome, buxom, cheerful, comical, droll, facetious, frolicsome, gladsome, gleeful, hilarious, jocund, jolly, jovial, joyous, light-hearted, lively, mirthful, sportive, sprightly, vivacious.

mess *n* company, set; farrago, hodgepodge, hotchpotch, jumble, medley, mass, melange, miscellany, mishmash, mixture; confusion, muddle, perplexity, pickle, plight, predicament.

message *n* communication, dispatch, intimation, letter, missive, notice, telegram, wire, word.

messenger *n* carrier, courier, emissary, envoy, express, mercury, nuncio; forerunner, harbinger, herald, precursor.

metamorphic *adj* changeable, mutable, variable.

metamorphose *vb* change, mutate, transfigure, transform, transmute.

metamorphosis *n* change, mutation, transfiguration, transformation, transmutation.

metaphorical *adj* allegorical, figurative, symbolic, symbolical.

metaphysical *adj* abstract, allegorical, figurative, general, intellectual, parabolic, subjective, unreal.

mete *vb* dispense, distribute, divide, measure, ration, share. * *n* bound, boundary, butt, limit, measure, term, terminus.

meteor *n* aerolite, falling star, shooting star.

method *n* course, manner, means, mode, procedure, process, rule, way; arrangement, classification, disposition, order, plan, regularity, scheme, system.

methodical *adj* exact, orderly, regular, systematic, systematical.

metropolis *n* capital, city, conurbation.

mettle *n* constitution, element, material, stuff; character, disposition, spirit, temper; ardour, courage, fire, hardihood, life, nerve, pluck, sprightliness, vigour.

mettlesome *adj* ardent, brisk, courageous, fiery, frisky, high-spirited, lively, spirited, sprightly.

mew *vb* confine, coop, encase, enclose, imprison; cast, change, mould, shed.

microscopic *adj* infinitesimal, minute, tiny.

middle *adj* central, halfway, mean, medial, mid; intermediate, intervening. * *n* centre, halfway, mean, midst.

middleman *n* agent, broker, factor, go-between, intermediary.

mien *n* air, appearance, aspect, bearing, behaviour, carriage, countenance, demeanour, deportment, look, manner.

might *n* ability, capacity, efficacy, efficiency, force, main, power, prowess, puissance, strength.

mighty *adj* able, bold, courageous, potent, powerful, puissant, robust, strong, sturdy, valiant, valorous, vigorous; bulky, enormous, huge, immense, monstrous, stupendous, vast.

migratory *adj* nomadic, roving, shifting, strolling, unsettled, wandering, vagrant.

mild *adj* amiable, clement, compassionate, gentle, good-natured, indulgent, kind, lenient, meek, merciful, pacific, tender; bland, pleasant, soft, suave; calm, kind, placid, temperate, tranquil; assuasive, compliant, demulcent, emollient, lenitive, mollifying, soothing.

mildness *n* amiability, clemency, gentleness, indulgence, kindness, meekness, moderation, softness, tenderness, warmth.

mildew *n* blight, blast, mould, must, mustiness, smut, rust.

milieu *n* background, environment, sphere, surroundings.

militant *adj* belligerent, combative, contending, fighting.

military *adj* martial, soldier, soldierly, warlike. * *n* army, militia, soldiers.

mill *vb* comminute, crush, grate, grind, levigate, powder, pulverize. * *n* factory, manufactory; grinder; crowd, throng.

mimic *vb* ape, counterfeit, imitate, impersonate, mime, mock, parody. * *adj* imitative, mock, simulated. * *n* imitator, impersonator, mime, mocker, parodist, parrot.

mince[1] *vb* chop, cut, hash, shatter. * *n* forcemeat, hash, mash, mincemeat.

mince[2] *vb* attenuate, diminish, extenuate, mitigate, palliate, soften; pose, sashay, simper, smirk.

mind[1] *vb* attend, heed, mark, note, notice, regard, tend, watch; obey, observe, submit; design, incline, intend, mean; recall, recollect, remember, remind; beware, look out, watch out. * *n* soul, spirit; brains, common sense, intellect, reason, sense, understanding; belief, consideration, contemplation, judgement, opinion, reflection, sentiment, thought; memory, recollection, remembrance; bent, desire, disposition, inclination, intention, leaning, purpose, tendency, will.

mind[2] *vb* balk, begrudge, grudge, object, resent.

mindful *adj* attentive, careful, heedful, observant, regardful, thoughtful.

mindless *adj* dull, heavy, insensible, senseless, sluggish, stupid, unthinking; careless, forgetful, heedless, neglectful, negligent, regardless.

mine *vb* dig, excavate, quarry, unearth; sap, undermine, weaken; destroy, ruin. * *n* colliery, deposit, lode, pit, shaft.

mingle *vb* blend, combine, commingle, compound, intermingle, intermix, join, mix, unite.

miniature *adj* bantam, diminutive, little, small, tiny.
minion *n* creature, dependant, favourite, hanger-on, parasite, sycophant; darling, favourite, flatterer, pet.
minister *vb* administer, afford, furnish, give, supply; aid, assist, contribute, help, succour. * *n* agent, assistant, servant, subordinate, underling; administrator, executive; ambassador, delegate, envoy, plenipotentiary; chaplain, churchman, clergyman, cleric, curate, divine, ecclesiastic, parson, pastor, preacher, priest, rector, vicar.
ministry *n* agency, aid, help, instrumentality, interposition, intervention, ministration, service, support; administration, cabinet, council, government.
minor *adj* less, smaller; inferior, junior, secondary, subordinate, younger; inconsiderable, petty, unimportant, small.
minstrel *n* bard, musician, singer, troubadour.
mint *vb* coin, stamp; fabricate, fashion, forge, invent, make, produce. * *adj* fresh, new, perfect, undamaged. * *n* die, punch, seal, stamp; fortune, (*inf*) heap, million, pile, wad.
minute[1] *adj* diminutive, fine, little, microscopic, miniature, slender, slight, small, tiny; circumstantial, critical, detailed, exact, fussy, meticulous, nice, particular, precise.
minute[2] *n* account, entry, item, memorandum, note, proceedings, record; instant, moment, second, trice, twinkling.
miracle *n* marvel, prodigy, wonder.
miraculous *adj* supernatural, thaumaturgic, thaumaturgical; amazing, extraordinary, incredible, marvellous, unaccountable, unbelievable, wondrous.
mirror *vb* copy, echo, emulate, reflect, show. * *n* looking-glass, reflector, speculum; archetype, exemplar, example, model, paragon, pattern, prototype.
mirth *n* cheerfulness, festivity, frolic, fun, gaiety, gladness, glee, hilarity, festivity, jollity, joviality, joyousness, laughter, merriment, merry-making, rejoicing, sport.
mirthful *adj* cheery, cheery, festive, frolicsome, hilarious, jocund, jolly, merry, jovial, joyous, lively, playful, sportive, vivacious; comic, droll, humorous, facetious, funny, jocose, jocular, ludicrous, merry, waggish, witty.
misadventure *n* accident, calamity, catastrophe, cross, disaster, failure, ill-luck, infelicity, mischance, misfortune, mishap, reverse.
misanthrope *n* cynic, egoist, egotist, man-hater, misanthropist.
misapply *vb* abuse, misuse, pervert.
misapprehend *vb* misconceive, mistake, misunderstand.
misbehaviour *n* ill-behaviour, ill-conduct, incivility, miscarriage, misconduct, misdemeanour, naughtiness, rudeness.
miscarriage *n* calamity, defeat, disaster, failure, mischance, mishap; misbehaviour, misconduct, ill-behaviour.
miscellaneous *adj* confused, diverse, diversified, heterogeneous, indiscriminate, jumbled, many, mingled, mixed, promiscuous, stromatic, stromatous, various.
miscellany *n* collection, diversity, farrago, gallimaufry, hodgepodge, hotchpotch, jumble, medley, mishmash, melange, miscellaneous, mixture, variety.
mischance *n* accident, calamity, disaster, ill-fortune, ill-luck, infelicity, misadventure, misfortune, mishap.
mischief *n* damage, detriment, disadvantage, evil, harm, hurt, ill, injury, prejudice; ill-consequence, misfortune, trouble; devilry, wrong-doing.
mischievous *adj* destructive, detrimental, harmful, hurtful, injurious, noxious, pernicious; malicious, sinful, vicious, wicked; annoying, impish, naughty, troublesome, vexatious.
misconceive *vb* misapprehend, misjudge, mistake, misunderstand.
misconduct *vb* botch, bungle, misdirect, mismanage. * *n* bad conduct, ill-conduct, misbehaviour, misdemeanour, rudeness, transgression; ill-management, mismanagement.
misconstrue *vb* misread, mistranslate; misapprehend, misinterpret, mistake, misunderstand.
miscreant *adj* corrupt, criminal, evil, rascally, unprincipled, vicious, villainous, wicked. * *n* caitiff, knave, ragamuffin, rascal, rogue, ruffian, scamp, scoundrel, vagabond, villain.
misdemeanour *n* fault, ill-behaviour, misbehaviour, misconduct, misdeed, offence, transgression, trespass.
miser *n* churl, curmudgeon, lickpenny, money-grabber, niggard, penny-pincher, pinch-fist, screw, scrimp, skinflint.
miserable *adj* afflicted, broken-hearted, comfortless, disconsolate, distressed, forlorn, heartbroken, unhappy, wretched; calamitous, hapless, ill-starred, pitiable, unfortunate, unlucky; poor, valueless, worthless; abject, contemptible, despicable, low, mean, worthless.
miserly *adj* avaricious, beggarly, close, close-fisted, covetous, grasping, mean, niggardly, parsimonious, penurious, sordid, stingy, tight-fisted.
misery *n* affliction, agony, anguish, calamity, desolation, distress, grief, heartache, heavy-heartedness, misfortune, sorrow, suffering, torment, torture, tribulation, unhappiness, woe, wretchedness.
misfortune *n* adversity, affliction, bad luck, blow, calamity, casualty, catastrophe, disaster, distress, hardship, harm, ill, infliction, misadventure, mischance, mishap, reverse, scourge, stroke, trial, trouble, visitation.
misgiving *n* apprehension, distrust, doubt, hesitation, suspicion, uncertainty.
mishap *n* accident, calamity, disaster, ill luck, misadventure, mischance, misfortune.

misinterpret *vb* distort, falsify, misapprehend, misconceive, misconstrue, misjudge.
mislead *vb* beguile, deceive, delude, misdirect, misguide.
mismanage *vb* botch, fumble, misconduct, mishandle, misrule.
misprize *vb* slight, underestimate, underrate, undervalue.
misrepresent *vb* belie, caricature, distort, falsify, misinterpret, misstate, pervert.
misrule *n* anarchy, confusion, disorder, maladministration, misgovernment, mismanagement.
miss[1] *vb* blunder, err, fail, fall short, forgo, lack, lose, miscarry, mistake, omit, overlook, trip; avoid, escape, evade, skip, slip; feel the loss of, need, want, wish. * *n* blunder, error, failure, fault, mistake, omission, oversight, slip, trip; loss, want.
miss[2] *n* damsel, girl, lass, maid, maiden.
misshapen *adj* deformed, ill-formed, ill-shaped, ill-proportioned, misformed, ugly, ungainly.
missile *n* projectile, weapon.
mission *n* commission, legation; business, charge, duty, errand, office, trust; delegation, deputation, embassy.
missive *n* communication, epistle, letter, message, note.
mist *vb* cloud, drizzle, mizzle, smog. * *n* cloud, fog, haze; bewilderment, obscurity, perplexity.
mistake *vb* misapprehend, miscalculate, misconceive, misjudge, misunderstand; confound, take; blunder, err. * *n* misapprehension, miscalculation, misconception, mistaking, misunderstanding; blunder, error, fault, inaccuracy, oversight, slip, trip.
mistaken *adj* erroneous, inaccurate, incorrect, misinformed, wrong.
mistrust *vb* distrust, doubt, suspect; apprehend, fear, surmise, suspect. * *n* doubt, distrust, misgiving, suspicion.
misty *adj* cloudy, clouded, dark, dim, foggy, obscure, overcast.
misunderstand *vb* misapprehend, misconceive, misconstrue, mistake.
misunderstanding *n* error, misapprehension, misconception, mistake; difference, difficulty, disagreement, discord, dissension, quarrel.
misuse *vb* desecrate, misapply, misemploy, pervert, profane; abuse, ill-treat, maltreat, ill-use; fritter, squander, waste. * *n* abuse, perversion, profanation, prostitution; ill-treatment, ill-use, ill-usage, misusage; misapplication, solecism.
mitigate *vb* abate, alleviate, assuage, diminish, extenuate, lessen, moderate, palliate, relieve; allay, appease, calm, mollify, pacify, quell, quiet, reduce, soften, soothe; moderate, temper.
mitigation *n* abatement, allaying, alleviation, assuagement, diminution, moderation, palliation, relief.
mix *vb* alloy, amalgamate, blend, commingle, combine, compound, incorporate, interfuse, interlard, mingle, unite; associate, join. * *n* alloy, amalgam, blend, combination, compound, mixture.
mixture *n* admixture, association, intermixture, union; compound, farrago, hash, hodgepodge, hotchpotch, jumble, medley, melange, mishmash; diversity, miscellany, variety.
moan *vb* bemoan, bewail, deplore, grieve, groan, lament, mourn, sigh, weep. * *n* groan, lament, lamentation, sigh, wail.
mob *vb* crowd, jostle, surround, swarm, pack, throng. * *n* assemblage, crowd, rabble, multitude, throng, tumult; dregs, canaille, populace, rabble, riffraff, scum.
mobile *adj* changeable, fickle, expressive, inconstant, sensitive, variable, volatile.
mock *vb* ape, counterfeit, imitate, mimic, take off; deride, flout, gibe, insult, jeer, ridicule, taunt; balk, cheat, deceive, defeat, disappoint, dupe, elude, illude, mislead. * *adj* assumed, clap-trap, counterfeit, fake, false, feigned, make-believe, pretended, spurious. * *n* fake, imitation, phoney, sham; gibe, insult, jeer, scoff, taunt.
mockery *n* contumely, counterfeit, deception, derision, imitation, jeering, mimicry, ridicule, scoffing, scorn, sham, travesty.
mode *n* fashion, manner, method, style, way; accident, affection, degree, graduation, modification, quality, variety.
model *vb* design, fashion, form, mould, plan, shape. * *adj* admirable, archetypal, estimable, exemplary, ideal, meritorious, paradigmatic, perfect, praiseworthy, worthy. * *n* archetype, design, mould, original, pattern, protoplast, prototype, type; dummy, example, form; copy, facsimile, image, imitation, representation.
moderate *vb* abate, allay, appease, assuage, blunt, dull, lessen, soothe, mitigate, mollify, pacify, quell, quiet, reduce, repress, soften, still, subdue; diminish, qualify, slacken, temper; control, govern, regulate. * *adj* abstinent, frugal, sparing, temperate; limited, mediocre; abstemious, sober; calm, cool, judicious, reasonable, steady; gentle, mild, temperate, tolerable.
moderation *n* abstemiousness, forbearance, frugality, restraint, sobriety, temperance; calmness, composure, coolness, deliberateness, equanimity, mildness, sedateness.
modern *adj* fresh, late, latest, new, novel, present, recent, up-to-date.
modest *adj* bashful, coy, diffident, humble, meek, reserved, retiring, shy, unassuming, unobtrusive, unostentatious, unpretending, unpretentious; chaste, proper, pure, virtuous; becoming, decent, moderate.
modesty *n* bashfulness, coyness, diffidence, humility, meekness, propriety, prudishness, reserve, shyness, unobtrusiveness; chastity, purity, virtue; decency, moderation.
modification *n* alteration, change, qualification,

reformation, variation; form, manner, mode, state.
modify *vb* alter, change, qualify, reform, shape, vary; lower, moderate, qualify, soften.
modish *adj* fashionable, stylish; ceremonious, conventional, courtly, genteel.
modulate *vb* attune, harmonize, tune; inflict, vary; adapt, adjust, proportion.
moiety *n* half; part, portion, share.
moil *vb* drudge, labour, toil; bespatter, daub, defile, soil, splash, spot, stain; fatigue, weary, tire.
moist *adj* damp, dank, humid, marshy, muggy, swampy, wet.
moisture *n* dampness, dankness, humidity, wetness.
mole *n* breakwater, dike, dyke, jetty, mound, pier, quay.
molecule *n* atom, monad, particle.
molest *vb* annoy, badger, bore, bother, chafe, discommode, disquiet, disturb, harass, harry, fret, gull, hector, incommode, inconvenience, irritate, oppress, pester, plague, tease, torment, trouble, vex, worry.
mollify *vb* soften; appease, calm, compose, pacify, quiet, soothe, tranquillize; abate, allay, assuage, blunt, dull, ease, lessen, mitigate, moderate, relieve, temper; qualify, tone down.
moment *n* flash, instant, jiffy, second, trice, twinkling, wink; avail, consequence, consideration, force, gravity, importance, significance, signification, value, weight; drive, force, impetus, momentum.
momentous *adj* grave, important, serious, significant, vital, weighty.
momentum *n* impetus, moment.
monarch *n* autocrat, despot; chief, dictator, emperor, king, potentate, prince, queen, ruler, sovereign.
monastery *n* abbey, cloister, convent, lamasery, nunnery, priory.
monastic *adj* coenobitic, coenobitical, conventual, monkish, secluded.
money *n* banknotes, cash, coin, currency, riches, specie, wealth.
moneyed, monied *adj* affluent, opulent, rich, well-off, well-to-do.
monitor *vb* check, observe, oversee, supervise, watch. * *n* admonisher, admonitor, adviser, counsellor, instructor, mentor, overseer.
monomania *n* delusion, hallucination, illusion, insanity, self-deception.
monopolize *vb* control, dominate, engross, forestall.
monotonous *adj* boring, dull, tedious, tiresome, undiversified, uniform, unvaried, unvarying, wearisome.
monotony *n* boredom, dullness, sameness, tedium, tiresomeness, uniformity, wearisomeness.
monster *adj* enormous, gigantic, huge, immense, mammoth, monstrous. * *n* enormity, marvel, prodigy, wonder; brute, demon, fiend, miscreant, ruffian, villain, wretch.
monstrous *adj* abnormal, preternatural, prodigious, unnatural; colossal, enormous, extraordinary, huge, immense, stupendous, vast; marvellous, strange, wonderful; bad, base, dreadful, flagrant, frightful, hateful, hideous, horrible, shocking, terrible.
monument *n* memorial, record, remembrance, testimonial; cairn, cenotaph, gravestone, mausoleum, memorial, pillar, tomb, tombstone.
mood *n* disposition, humour, temper, vein.
moody *adj* capricious, humoursome, variable; angry, crabbed, crusty, fretful, ill-tempered, irascible, irritable, passionate, pettish, peevish, petulant, snappish, snarling, sour, testy; cross-grained, dogged, frowning, glowering, glum, intractable, morose, perverse, spleeny, stubborn, sulky, sullen, wayward; abstracted, gloomy, melancholy, pensive, sad, saturnine.
moonshine *n* balderdash, fiction, flummery, fudge, fustian, nonsense, pretence, stuff, trash, twaddle, vanity.
moor[1] *vb* anchor, berth, fasten, fix, secure, tie.
moor[2] *n* bog, common, heath, moorland, morass, moss, wasteland.
moot *vb* agitate, argue, debate, discuss, dispute. * *adj* arguable, debatable, doubtful, unsettled.
mopish *adj* dejected, depressed, desponding, downcast, down-hearted, gloomy, glum, sad.
moral *adj* ethical, good, honest, honourable, just, upright, virtuous; abstract, ideal, intellectual, mental. * *n* intent, meaning, significance.
morals *npl* ethics, morality; behaviour, conduct, habits, manners.
morass *n* bog, fen, marsh, quagmire, slough, swamp.
morbid *adj* ailing, corrupted, diseased, sick, sickly, tainted, unhealthy, unsound, vitiated; depressed, downcast, gloomy, pessimistic, sensitive.
mordacious *adj* acrid, biting, cutting, mordant, pungent, sharp, stinging; caustic, poignant, satirical, sarcastic, scathing, severe.
mordant *adj* biting, caustic, keen, mordacious, nipping, sarcastic.
moreover *adv, conj* also, besides, further, furthermore, likewise, too.
morning *n* aurora, daybreak, dawn, morn, morningtide, sunrise.
morose *adj* austere, churlish, crabbed, crusty, dejected, desponding, downcast, downhearted, gloomy, glum, melancholy, moody, sad, severe, sour, sullen, surly.
morsel *n* bite, mouthful, titbit; bit, fragment, part, piece, scrap.
mortal *adj* deadly, destructive, fatal, final, human, lethal, perishable, vital. * *n* being, earthling, human, man, person, woman.
mortality *n* corruption, death, destruction, fatality.
mortification *n* chagrin, disappointment, discontent, dissatisfaction, displeasure, humiliation, trouble, shame, vexation; humility, penance, self-abasement, self-denial; gangrene, necrosis.

mortify *vb* annoy, chagrin, depress, disappoint, displease, disquiet, dissatisfy, harass, humble, plague, vex, worry; abase, abash, confound, humiliate, restrain, shame, subdue; corrupt, fester, gangrene, putrefy.

mortuary *n* burial place, cemetery, churchyard, graveyard, necropolis; charnel house, morgue.

mostly *adv* chiefly, customarily, especially, generally, mainly, particularly, principally.

mote *n* atom, corpuscle, flaw, mite, particle, speck, spot.

motherly *adj* affectionate, kind, maternal, paternal, tender.

motion *vb* beckon, direct, gesture, signal. * *n* action, change, drift, flux, movement, passage, stir, transit; air, gait, port; gesture, impulse, prompting, suggestion; proposal, proposition.

motionless *adj* fixed, immobile, quiescent, stable, stagnant, standing, stationary, still, torpid, unmoved.

motive *adj* activating, driving, moving, operative. * *n* cause, consideration, ground, impulse, incentive, incitement, inducement, influence, occasion, prompting, purpose, reason, spur, stimulus.

motley *adj* coloured, dappled, mottled, speckled, spotted, variegated; composite, diversified, heterogeneous, mingled, mixed.

mottled *adj* dappled, motley, piebald, speckled, spotted, variegated.

mould[1] *vb* carve, cast, fashion, form, make, model, shape. * *n* cast, character, fashion, form, matrix, pattern, shape; material, matter, substance.

mould[2] *n* blight, mildew, mouldiness, must, mustiness, rot; fungus, lichen, mushroom, puffball, rust, smut, toadstool; earth, loam, soil.

moulder *vb* crumble, decay, perish, waste.

mouldy *adj* decaying, fusty, mildewed, musty.

mound *n* bank, barrow, hill, hillock, knoll, tumulus; bulwark, defence, rampart.

mount[1] *n* hill, mountain, peak.

mount[2] *vb* arise, ascend, climb, rise, soar, tower; escalate, scale; embellish, ornament; bestride, get upon. * *n* charger, horse, ride, steed.

mountain *n* alp, height, hill, mount, peak; abundance, heap, mound, stack.

mountebank *n* charlatan, cheat, impostor, pretender, quack.

mourn *vb* bemoan, bewail, deplore, grieve, lament, sorrow, wail.

mournful *adj* afflicting, afflictive, calamitous, deplorable, distressed, grievous, lamentable, sad, woeful; doleful, heavy, heavy-hearted, lugubrious, melancholy, sorrowful, tearful.

mouth *vb* clamour, declaim, rant, roar, vociferate. * *n* chaps, jaws; aperture, opening, orifice; entrance, inlet; oracle, mouthpiece, speaker, spokesman.

movables *npl* chattels, effects, furniture, goods, property, wares.

move *vb* dislodge, drive, impel, propel, push, shift, start, stir; actuate, incite, instigate, rouse; determine, incline, induce, influence, persuade, prompt; affect, impress, touch, trouble; agitate, awaken, excite, incense, irritate; propose, recommend, suggest; go, march, proceed, walk; act, live; flit, remove. * *n* action, motion, movement.

movement *n* change, move, motion, passage; emotion; crusade, drive.

moving *adj* impelling, influencing, instigating, persuading, persuasive; affecting, impressive, pathetic, touching.

mucous *adj* glutinous, gummy, mucilaginous, ropy, slimy, viscid.

mud *n* dirt, mire, muck, slime.

muddle *vb* confuse, disarrange, disorder; fuddle, inebriate, stupefy; muff, mull, spoil. * *n* confusion, disorder, mess, plight, predicament.

muddy *vb* dirty, foul, smear, soil; confuse, obscure. * *adj* dirty, foul, impure, slimy, soiled, turbid; bothered, confused, dull, heavy, stupid; incoherent, obscure, vague.

muffle *vb* cover, envelop, shroud, wrap; conceal, disguise, involve; deaden, soften, stifle, suppress.

mulish *adj* cross-grained, headstrong, intractable, obstinate, stubborn.

multifarious *adj* different, divers, diverse, diversified, manifold, multiform, multitudinous, various.

multiloquence *n* garrulity, loquacity, loquaciousness, talkativeness.

multiply *vb* augment, extend, increase, spread.

multitude *n* numerousness; host, legion; army, assemblage, assembly, collection, concourse, congregation, crowd, horde, mob, swarm, throng; commonality, herd, mass, mob, pack, populace, rabble.

mundane *adj* earthly, secular, sublunary, temporal, terrene, terrestrial, worldly.

munificence *n* benefice, bounteousness, bountifulness, bounty, generosity, liberality.

munificent *adj* beneficent, bounteous, bountiful, free, generous, liberal, princely.

murder *vb* assassinate, butcher, destroy, dispatch, kill, massacre, slaughter, slay; abuse, mar, spoil. * *n* assassination, butchery, destruction, homicide, killing, manslaughter, massacre.

murderer *n* assassin, butcher, cut-throat, killer, manslaughterer, slaughterer, slayer.

murderous *adj* barbarous, bloodthirsty, bloody, cruel, fell, sanguinary, savage.

murky *adj* cheerless, cloudy, dark, dim, dusky, gloomy, hazy, lowering, lurid, obscure, overcast.

murmur *vb* croak, grumble, mumble, mutter; hum, whisper. * *n* complaint, grumble, mutter, plaint, whimper; hum, undertone, whisper.

muscular *adj* sinewy; athletic, brawny, powerful, lusty, stalwart, stout, strong, sturdy, vigorous.

muse *vb* brood, cogitate, consider, contemplate, deliberate, dream, meditate, ponder, reflect, ruminate, speculate, think. * *n* abstraction, musing, reverie.

music *n* harmony, melody, symphony.
musical *adj* dulcet, harmonious, melodious, sweet, sweet-sounding, symphonious, tuneful.
musing *adj* absent-minded, meditative, preoccupied. * *n* absent-mindedness, abstraction, contemplation, daydreaming, meditation, muse, reflection, reverie, rumination.
muster *vb* assemble, collect, congregate, convene, convoke, gather, marshal, meet, rally, summon. * *n* assemblage, assembly, collection, congregation, convention, convocation, gathering, meeting, rally.
musty *adj* fetid, foul, fusty, mouldy, rank, sour, spoiled; hackneyed, old, stale, threadbare, trite; ill-favoured, insipid, vapid; dull, heavy, rusty, spiritless.
mutable *adj* alterable, changeable; changeful, fickle, inconstant, irresolute, mutational, unsettled, unstable, unsteady, vacillating, variable, wavering.
mutation *n* alteration, change, variation.
mute *vb* dampen, lower, moderate, muffle, soften. * *adj* dumb, voiceless; silent, speechless, still, taciturn.
mutilate *vb* cripple, damage, disable, disfigure, hamstring, injure, maim, mangle, mar.
mutinous *adj* contumacious, insubordinate, rebellious, refractory, riotous, tumultuous, turbulent, unruly; insurgent, seditious.
mutiny *vb* rebel, revolt, rise, resist. * *n* insubordination, insurrection, rebellion, revolt, revolution, riot, rising, sedition, uprising.
mutter *vb* grumble, muffle, mumble, murmur.
mutual *adj* alternate, common, correlative, interchangeable, interchanged, reciprocal, requited.
myopic *adj* near-sighted, purblind, short-sighted.
myriad *adj* innumerable, manifold, multitudinous, uncounted. * *n* host, million(s), multitude, score(s), sea, swarm, thousand(s).
mysterious *adj* abstruse, cabbalistic, concealed, cryptic, dark, dim, enigmatic, enigmatical, hidden, incomprehensible, inexplicable, inscrutable, mystic, mystical, obscure, occult, puzzling, recondite, secret, sphinx-like, unaccountable, unfathomable, unintelligible, unknown.
mystery *n* enigma, puzzle, riddle, secret; art, business, calling, trade.
mystical *adj* abstruse, cabbalistic, dark, enigmatical, esoteric, hidden, inscrutable, mysterious, obscure, occult, recondite, transcendental; allegorical, emblematic, emblematical, symbolic, symbolical.
mystify *vb* befog, bewilder, confound, confuse, dumbfound, embarrass, obfuscate, perplex, pose, puzzle.
myth *n* fable, legend, tradition; allegory, fiction, invention, parable, story; falsehood, fancy, figment, lie, untruth.
mythical *adj* allegorical, fabled, fabulous, fanciful, fictitious, imaginary, legendary, mythological.

N

nab *vb* catch, clutch, grasp, seize.
nag[1] *vb* carp, fuss, hector, henpeck, pester, torment, worry. * *n* nagger, scold, shrew, tartar.
nag[2] *n* bronco, crock, hack, horse, pony, scrag.
naive *adj* artless, candid, ingenuous, natural, plain, simple, unaffected, unsophisticated.
naked *adj* bare, nude, uncovered; denuded, unclad, unclothed, undressed; defenceless, exposed, open, unarmed, unguarded, unprotected; evident, manifest, plain, stark, unconcealed, undisguised; mere, sheer, simple; bare, destitute, rough, rude, unfurnished, unprovided; uncoloured, unexaggerated, unvarnished.
name *vb* call, christen, denounce, dub, entitle, phrase, style, term; mention; denominate, designate, indicate, nominate, specify. * *n* appellation, cognomen, denomination, designation, epithet, nickname, surname, sobriquet, title; character, credit, reputation, repute; celebrity, distinction, eminence, fame, honour, note, praise, renown.
narcotic *adj* stupefacient, stupefactive, stupefying. * *n* anaesthetic, anodyne, dope, opiate, sedative, stupefacient, tranquillizer.
narrate *vb* chronicle, describe, detail, enumerate, recite, recount, rehearse, relate, tell.
narration *n* account, description, chronicle, history, narrative, recital, rehearsal, relation, story, tale.
narrow *vb* confine, contract, cramp, limit, restrict, straiten. * *adj* circumscribed, confined, contracted, cramped, incapacious, limited, pinched, scanty, straitened; bigoted, hidebound, illiberal, ungenerous; close, near.
nastiness *n* defilement, dirtiness, filth, filthiness, foulness, impurity, pollution, squalor, uncleanness; indecency, grossness, obscenity, pornography, ribaldry, smut, smuttiness.
nasty *adj* defiled, dirty, filthy, foul, impure, loathsome, polluted, squalid, unclean; gross, indecent, indelicate, lewd, loose, obscene, smutty, vile; disagreeable, disgusting, nauseous, odious, offensive, repulsive, sickening; aggravating, annoying, pesky, pestering, troublesome.
nation *n* commonwealth, realm, state; community, people, population, race, stock, tribe.
native *adj* aboriginal, autochthonal, autochthonous, domestic, home, indigenous, vernacular; genuine, intrinsic, natural, original, real; congenital, inborn, inbred, inherent, innate, natal. * *n* aborigine, autochthon, inhabitant, national, resident.
natty *adj* dandyish, fine, foppish, jaunty, neat, nice, spruce, tidy.
natural *adj* indigenous, innate, native, original; characteristic, essential; legitimate, normal, regular; artless, authentic, genuine, ingenious, unreal, simple, spontaneous, unaffected; bastard, illegitimate.
nature *n* universe, world; character, constitution, essence; kind, quality, species, sort; disposition, grain, humour, mood, temper; being, intellect, intelligence, mind.
naughty *adj* bad, corrupt, mischievous, perverse, worthless.
nausea *n* queasiness, seasickness; loathing, qualm; aversion, disgust, repugnance.
nauseous *adj* abhorrent, disgusting, distasteful, loathsome, offensive, repulsive, revolting, sickening.
naval *adj* marine, maritime, nautical.
navigate *vb* cruise, direct, guide, pilot, plan, sail, steer.
navy *n* fleet, shipping, vessels.
near *vb* approach, draw close. * *adj* adjacent, approximate, close, contiguous, neighbouring, nigh; approaching, forthcoming, imminent, impending; dear, familiar, friendly, intimate; direct, immediate, short, straight; accurate, literal; narrow, parsimonious.
nearly *adv* almost, approximately, well-nigh; closely, intimately, pressingly; meanly, parsimoniously, penuriously, stingily.
neat *adj* clean, cleanly, orderly, tidy, trim, unsoiled; nice, smart, spruce; chaste, pure, simple; excellent, pure, unadulterated; adroit, clever, exact, finished; dainty, nice.
nebulous *adj* cloudy, hazy, misty.
necessary *adj* inevitable, unavoidable; essential, expedient, indispensable, needful, requisite; compelling, compulsory, involuntary. * *n* essential, necessity, requirement, requisite.
necessitate *vb* compel, constrain, demand, force, impel, oblige.
necessitous *adj* destitute, distressed, indigent, moneyless, needy, penniless, pinched, poor, poverty-stricken; narrow, pinching.
necessity *n* inevitability, inevitableness, unavoidability, unavoidableness; compulsion, destiny, fatality, fate; emergency, urgency; exigency, indigence, indispensability, indispensableness, need, needfulness, poverty, want; essentiality, essentialness, requirement, requisite.

necromancy *n* conjuration, divination, enchantment, magic, sorcery, witchcraft, wizardry.
necropolis *n* burial ground, cemetery, churchyard, crematorium, graveyard, mortuary.
need *vb* demand, lack, require, want. * *n* emergency, exigency, extremity, necessity, strait, urgency, want; destitution, distress, indigence, neediness, penury, poverty, privation.
needful *adj* distressful, necessitous, necessary; essential, indispensable, requisite.
needless *adj* superfluous, unnecessary, useless.
needy *adj* destitute, indigent, necessitous, poor.
nefarious *adj* abominable, atrocious, detestable, dreadful, execrable, flagitious, heinous, horrible, infamous, iniquitous, scandalous, vile, wicked.
negation *n* denial, disavowal, disclaimer, rejection, renunciation.
neglect *vb* condemn, despise, disregard, forget, ignore, omit, overlook, slight. * *n* carelessness, default, failure, heedlessness, inattention, omission, remissness; disregard, disrespect, slight; indifference, negligence.
negligence *n* carelessness, disregard, heedlessness, inadvertency, inattention, indifference, neglect, remissness, slackness, thoughtlessness; defect, fault, inadvertence, omission, shortcoming.
negligent *adj* careless, heedless, inattentive, indifferent, neglectful, regardless, thoughtless.
negotiate *vb* arrange, bargain, deal, debate, sell, settle, transact, treat.
neighbourhood *n* district, environs, locality, vicinage, vicinity; adjacency, nearness, propinquity, proximity.
neighbourly *adj* attentive, civil, friendly, kind, obliging, social.
neophyte *n* beginner, catechumen, convert, novice, pupil, tyro.
nerve *vb* brace, energize, fortify, invigorate, strengthen. * *n* force, might, power, strength, vigour; coolness, courage, endurance, firmness, fortitude, hardihood, manhood, pluck, resolution, self-command, steadiness.
nervous *adj* forcible, powerful, robust, strong, vigorous; irritable, fearful, shaky, timid, timorous, weak, weakly.
nestle *vb* cuddle, harbour, lodge, nuzzle, snug, snuggle.
nettle *vb* chafe, exasperate, fret, harass, incense, irritate, provoke, ruffle, sting, tease, vex.
neutral *adj* impartial, indifferent; colourless, mediocre.
neutralize *vb* cancel, counterbalance, counterpoise, invalidate, offset.
nevertheless *adv* however, nonetheless, notwithstanding, yet.
new *adj* fresh, latest, modern, novel, recent, unused; additional, another, further; reinvigorated, renovated, repaired.
news *n* advice, information, intelligence, report, tidings, word.
nice *adj* accurate, correct, critical, definite, delicate, exact, exquisite, precise, rigorous, strict; dainty, difficult, exacting, fastidious, finical, punctilious, squeamish; discerning, discriminating, particular, precise, scrupulous; neat, tidy, trim; fine, minute, refined, subtle; delicate, delicious, luscious, palatable, savoury, soft, tender; agreeable, delightful, good, pleasant.
nicety *n* accuracy, exactness, niceness, precision, truth, daintiness, fastidiousness, squeamishness; discrimination, subtlety.
niggard *n* churl, curmudgeon, miser, screw, scrimp, skinflint.
niggardly *adj* avaricious, close, close-fisted, illiberal, mean, mercenary, miserly, parsimonious, penurious, skinflint, sordid, stingy.
nigh *adj* adjacent, adjoining, contiguous, near; present, proximate. * *adv* almost, near, nearly.
nimble *adj* active, agile, alert, brisk, lively, prompt, quick, speedy, sprightly, spry, swift, tripping.
nobility *n* aristocracy, dignity, elevation, eminence, grandeur, greatness, loftiness, magnanimity, nobleness, peerage, superiority, worthiness.
noble *adj* dignified, elevated, eminent, exalted, generous, great, honourable, illustrious, magnanimous, superior, worthy; choice, excellent; aristocratic, gentle, high-born, patrician; grand, lofty, lordly, magnificent, splendid, stately. * *n* aristocrat, grandee, lord, nobleman, peer.
noctambulist *n* sleepwalker, somnambulist.
noise *vb* bruit, gossip, repeat, report, rumour. * *n* ado, blare, clamour, clatter, cry, din, fuss, hubbub, hullabaloo, outcry, pandemonium, racket, row, sound, tumult, uproar, vociferation.
noiseless *adj* inaudible, quiet, silent, soundless.
noisome *adj* bad, baneful, deleterious, disgusting, fetid, foul, hurtful, injurious, mischievous, nocuous, noxious, offensive, pernicious, pestiferous, pestilential, poisonous, unhealthy, unwholesome.
noisy *adj* blatant, blustering, boisterous, brawling, clamorous, loud, uproarious, riotous, tumultuous, vociferous.
nomadic *adj* migratory, pastoral, vagrant, wandering.
nominal *adj* formal, inconsiderable, minimal, ostensible, pretended, professed, so-called, titular.
nominate *vb* appoint, choose, designate, name, present, propose.
nonchalant *adj* apathetic, careless, cool, indifferent, unconcerned.
nondescript *adj* amorphous, characterless, commonplace, dull, indescribable, odd, ordinary, unclassifiable, uninteresting, unremarkable.
nonentity *n* cipher, futility, inexistence, inexistency, insignificance, nobody, nonexistence, nothingness.
nonplus *vb* astonish, bewilder, confound, confuse, discomfit, disconcert, embarrass, floor, gravel, perplex, pose, puzzle.
nonsensical *adj* absurd, foolish, irrational, senseless, silly, stupid.

norm *n* model, pattern, rule, standard.
normal *adj* analogical, legitimate, natural, ordinary, regular, usual; erect, perpendicular, vertical.
notable *adj* distinguished, extraordinary, memorable, noted, remarkable, signal; conspicuous, evident, noticeable, observable, plain, prominent, striking; notorious, rare, well-known. * *n* celebrity, dignitary, notability, worthy.
note *vb* heed, mark, notice, observe, regard, remark; record, register; denote, designate. * *n* memorandum, minute, record; annotation, comment, remark, scholium; indication, mark, sign, symbol, token; account, bill, catalogue, reckoning; billet, epistle, letter; consideration, heed, notice, observation; celebrity, consequence, credit, distinction, eminence, fame, notability, notedness, renown, reputation, respectability; banknote, bill, promissory note; song, strain, tune, voice.
noted *adj* celebrated, conspicuous, distinguished, eminent, famed, famous, illustrious, notable, notorious, remarkable, renowned, well-known.
nothing *n* inexistence, nonentity, nonexistence, nothingness, nullity; bagatelle, trifle.
notice *vb* mark, note, observe, perceive, regard, see; comment on, mention, remark; attend to, heed. * *n* cognizance, heed, note, observation, regard; advice, announcement, information, intelligence, mention, news, notification; communication, intimation, premonition, warning; attention, civility, consideration, respect; comments, remarks.
notify *vb* advertise, announce, declare, publish, promulgate; acquaint, apprise, inform.
notion *n* concept, conception, idea; apprehension, belief, conceit, conviction, expectation, estimation, impression, judgement, opinion, sentiment, view.
notoriety *n* celebrity, fame, figure, name, note, publicity, reputation, repute, vogue.
notorious *adj* apparent, egregious, evident, notable, obvious, open, overt, manifest, patent, well-known; celebrated, conspicuous, distinguished, famed, famous, flagrant, infamous, noted, remarkable, renowned.
notwithstanding *conj* despite, however, nevertheless, yet. * *prep* despite.
nourish *vb* feed, nurse, nurture; maintain, supply, support; breed, educate, instruct, train; cherish, encourage, foment, foster, promote, succour.
nourishment *n* aliment, diet, food, nutriment, nutrition, sustenance.
novel *adj* fresh, modern, new, rare, recent, strange, uncommon, unusual. * *n* fiction, romance, story, tale.
novice *n* convert, proselyte; initiate, neophyte, novitiate, probationer; apprentice, beginner, learner, tyro.
noxious *adj* baneful, deadly, deleterious, destructive, detrimental, hurtful, injurious, insalubrious, mischievous, noisome, pernicious, pestilent, poisonous, unfavourable, unwholesome.
nude *adj* bare, denuded, exposed, naked, uncovered, unclothed, undressed.
nugatory *adj* frivolous, insignificant, trifling, trivial, vain, worthless; bootless, ineffectual, inefficacious, inoperative, null, unavailing, useless.
nuisance *n* annoyance, bore, bother, infliction, offence, pest, plague, trouble.
null *adj* ineffectual, invalid, nugatory, useless, void; characterless, colourless.
nullify *vb* abolish, abrogate, annul, cancel, invalidate, negate, quash, repeal, revoke.
numb *vb* benumb, deaden, stupefy. * *adj* benumbed, deadened, dulled, insensible, paralysed.
number *vb* calculate, compute, count, enumerate, numerate, reckon, tell; account, reckon. * *n* digit, figure, numeral; horde, multitude, numerousness, throng; aggregate, collection, sum, total.
numerous *adj* abundant, many, numberless.
nuncio *n* ambassador, legate, messenger.
nunnery *n* abbey, cloister, convent, monastery.
nuptial *adj* bridal, conjugal, connubial, hymeneal, matrimonial.
nuptials *npl* espousal, marriage, wedding.
nurse *vb* nourish, nurture; rear, suckle; cherish, encourage, feed, foment, foster, pamper, promote, succour; economize, manage; caress, dandle, fondle. * *n* auxiliary, orderly, sister; amah, *au pair*, babysitter, nanny, nursemaid, nurserymaid,
nurture *vb* feed, nourish, nurse, tend; breed, discipline, educate, instruct, rear, school, train. * *n* diet, food, nourishment; breeding, discipline, education, instruction, schooling, training, tuition; attention, nourishing, nursing.
nutriment *n* aliment, food, nourishment, nutrition, pabulum, subsistence, sustenance.
nutrition *n* diet, food, nourishment, nutriment.
nutritious *adj* invigorating, nourishing, strengthening, supporting, sustaining.
nymph *n* damsel, dryad, lass, girl, maid, maiden, naiad.

O

oaf *n* blockhead, dolt, dunce, fool, idiot, simpleton.
oath *n* blasphemy, curse, expletive, imprecation, malediction; affirmation, pledge, promise, vow.
obduracy *n* contumacy, doggedness, obstinacy, stubbornness, tenacity; depravity, impenitence.
obdurate *adj* hard, harsh, rough, rugged; callous, cantankerous, dogged, firm, hardened, inflexible, insensible, obstinate, pigheaded, unfeeling, stubborn, unbending, unyielding; depraved, graceless, lost, reprobate, shameless, impenitent, incorrigible, irreclaimable.
obedience *n* acquiescence, agreement, compliance, duty, respect, reverence, submission, submissiveness, subservience.
obedient *adj* acquiescent, compliant, deferential, duteous, dutiful, observant, regardful, respectful, submissive, subservient, yielding.
obeisance *n* bow, courtesy, curtsy, homage, reverence, salutation.
obelisk *n* column, pillar.
obese *adj* corpulent, fat, fleshy, gross, plump, podgy, portly, stout.
obesity *n* corpulence, corpulency, embonpoint, fatness, fleshiness, obeseness, plumpness.
obey *vb* comply, conform, heed, keep, mind, observe, submit, yield.
obfuscate *vb* cloud, darken, obscure; bewilder, confuse, muddle.
object[1] *vb* cavil, contravene, demur, deprecate, disapprove of, except to, impeach, oppose, protest, refuse.
object[2] *n* particular, phenomenon, precept, reality, thing; aim, butt, destination, end, mark, recipient, target; design, drift, goal, intention, motive, purpose, use, view.
objection *n* censure, difficulty, doubt, exception, protest, remonstrance, scruple.
objurgate *vb* chide, reprehend, reprove.
oblation *n* gift, offering, sacrifice.
obligation *n* accountability, accountableness, responsibility; agreement, bond, contract, covenant, engagement, stipulation; debt, indebtedness, liability.
obligatory *adj* binding, coercive, compulsory, enforced, necessary, unavoidable.
oblige *vb* bind, coerce, compel, constrain, force, necessitate, require; accommodate, benefit, convenience, favour, gratify, please; obligate, bind.
obliging *adj* accommodating, civil, complaisant, considerate, kind, friendly, polite.
oblique *adj* aslant, inclined, sidelong, slanting; indirect, obscure.
obliterate *vb* cancel, delete, destroy, efface, eradicate, erase, expunge.
oblivious *adj* careless, forgetful, heedless, inattentive, mindless, negligent, neglectful.
obloquy *n* aspersion, backbiting, blame, calumny, censure, contumely, defamation, detraction, disgrace, odium, reproach, reviling, slander, traducing.
obnoxious *adj* blameworthy, censurable, faulty, reprehensible; hateful, objectionable, obscene, odious, offensive, repellent, repugnant, repulsive, unpleasant, unpleasing.
obscene *adj* broad, coarse, filthy, gross, immodest, impure, indecent, indelicate, ribald, unchaste, lewd, licentious, loose, offensive, pornographic, shameless, smutty; disgusting, dirty, foul.
obscure *vb* becloud, befog, blur, cloud, darken, eclipse, dim, obfuscate, obnubilate, shade; conceal, cover, equivocate, hide. * *adj* dark, darksome, dim, dusky, gloomy, lurid, murky, rayless, shadowy, sombre, unenlightened, unilluminated; abstruse, blind, cabbalistic, difficult, doubtful, enigmatic, high, incomprehensible, indefinite, indistinct, intricate, involved, mysterious, mystic, recondite, undefined, unintelligible, vague; remote, secluded; humble, inglorious, nameless, renownless, undistinguished, unhonoured, unknown, unnoted, unnoticed.
obsequious *adj* cringing, deferential, fawning, flattering, servile, slavish, supple, subservient, sycophantic, truckling.
observant *adj* attentive, heedful, mindful, perceptive, quick, regardful, vigilant, watchful.
observation *n* attention, cognition, notice, observance; annotation, note, remark; experience, knowledge.
observe *vb* eye, mark, note, notice, remark, watch; behold, detect, discover, perceive, see; express, mention, remark, say, utter; comply, conform, follow, fulfil, obey; celebrate, keep, regard, solemnize.
obsolete *adj* ancient, antiquated, antique, archaic, disused, neglected, old, old-fashioned, obsolescent, out-of-date, past, passé, unfashionable.
obstacle *n* barrier, check, difficulty, hindrance, impediment, interference, interruption, obstruction, snag, stumbling block.

obstinacy *n* contumacy, doggedness, headiness, firmness, inflexibility, intractability, obduracy, persistence, perseverance, perversity, resoluteness, stubbornness, tenacity, wilfulness.

obstinate *adj* cross-grained, contumacious, dogged, firm, headstrong, inflexible, immovable, intractable, mulish, obdurate, opinionated, persistent, pertinacious, perverse, resolute, self-willed, stubborn, tenacious, unyielding, wilful.

obstreperous *adj* boisterous, clamorous, loud, noisy, riotous, tumultuous, turbulent, unruly, uproarious, vociferous.

obstruct *vb* bar, barricade, block, blockade, block up, choke, clog, close, glut, jam, obturate, stop; hinder, impede, oppose, prevent; arrest, check, curb, delay, embrace, interrupt, retard, slow.

obstruction *n* bar, barrier, block, blocking, check, difficulty, hindrance, impediment, obstacle, stoppage; check, clog, embarrassment, interruption, obturation.

obtain *vb* achieve, acquire, attain, bring, contrive, earn, elicit, gain, get, induce, procure, secure; hold, prevail, stand, subsist.

obtrude *vb* encroach, infringe, interfere, intrude, trespass.

obtrusive *adj* forward, interfering, intrusive, meddling, officious.

obtuse *adj* blunt; blockish, doltish, dull, dull-witted, heavy, stockish, stolid, stupid, slow, unintellectual, unintelligent.

obviate *vb* anticipate, avert, counteract, preclude, prevent, remove.

obvious *adj* exposed, liable, open, subject; apparent, clear, distinct, evident, manifest, palatable, patent, perceptible, plain, self-evident, unmistakable, visible.

occasion *vb* breed, cause, create, originate, produce; induce, influence, move, persuade. * *n* casualty, event, incident, occurrence; conjuncture, convenience, juncture, opening, opportunity; condition, necessity, need, exigency, requirement, want; cause, ground, reason; inducement, influence; circumstance, exigency.

occasional *adj* accidental, casual, incidental, infrequent, irregular, uncommon; causative, causing.

occasionally *adv* casually, sometimes.

occult *adj* abstruse, cabbalistic, hidden, latent, secret, invisible, mysterious, mystic, mystical, recondite, shrouded, undetected, undiscovered, unknown, unrevealed, veiled. * *n* magic, sorcery, witchcraft.

occupation *n* holding, occupancy, possession, tenure, use; avocation, business, calling, craft, employment, engagement, job, post, profession, trade, vocation.

occupy *vb* capture, hold, keep, possess; cover, fill, garrison, inhabit, take up, tenant; engage, employ, use.

occur *vb* appear, arise, offer; befall, chance, eventuate, happen, result, supervene.

occurrence *n* accident, adventure, affair, casualty, event, happening, incident, proceeding, transaction.

odd *adj* additional, redundant, remaining; casual, incidental; inappropriate, queer, unsuitable; comical, droll, erratic, extravagant, extraordinary, fantastic, grotesque, irregular, peculiar, quaint, singular, strange, uncommon, uncouth, unique, unusual, whimsical.

odds *npl* difference, disparity, inequality; advantage, superiority, supremacy.

odious *adj* abominable, detestable, execrable, hateful, shocking; hated, obnoxious, unpopular; disagreeable, forbidding, loathsome, offensive.

odium *n* abhorrence, detestation, dislike, enmity, hate, hatred; odiousness, repulsiveness; obloquy, opprobrium, reproach, shame.

odorous *adj* aromatic, balmy, fragrant, perfumed, redolent, scented, sweet-scented, sweet-smelling.

odour *n* aroma, fragrance, perfume, redolence, scent, smell.

offal *n* carrion, dregs, garbage, refuse, rubbish, waste.

offence *n* aggression, attack, assault; anger, displeasure, indignation, pique, resentment, umbrage, wrath; affront, harm, injury, injustice, insult, outrage, wrong; crime, delinquency, fault, misdeed, misdemeanour, sin, transgression, trespass.

offend *vb* affront, annoy, chafe, displease, fret, gall, irritate, mortify, nettle, provoke, vex; molest, pain, shock, wound; fall, sin, stumble, transgress.

offender *n* convict, criminal, culprit, delinquent, felon, malefactor, sinner, transgressor, trespasser.

offensive *adj* aggressive, attacking, invading; disgusting, loathsome, nauseating, nauseous, repulsive, sickening; abominable, detestable, disagreeable, displeasing, execrable, hateful, obnoxious, repugnant, revolting, shocking, unpalatable, unpleasant; abusive, disagreeable, impertinent, insolent, insulting, irritating, opprobrious, rude, saucy, unpleasant. * *n* attack, onslaught.

offer *vb* present, proffer, tender; exhibit; furnish, propose, propound, show; volunteer; dare, essay, endeavour, venture. * *n* overture, proffering, proposal, proposition, tender, overture; attempt, bid, endeavour, essay.

offhand *adj* abrupt, brusque, casual, curt, extempore, impromptu, informal, unpremeditated, unstudied. * *adv* carelessly, casually, clumsily, haphazardly, informally, slapdash; ad-lib, extemporaneously, extemporarily, extempore, impromptu.

office *n* duty, function, service, work; berth, place, position, post, situation; business, capacity, charge, employment, trust; bureau, room.

officiate *vb* act, perform, preside, serve.

officious *adj* busy, dictatorial, forward, impertinent, interfering, intermeddling, meddlesome, meddling, obtrusive, pushing, pushy.

offset *vb* balance, counteract, counterbalance, counterpoise. * *n* branch, offshoot, scion, shoot, slip, sprout, twig; counterbalance, counterpoise, set-off, equivalent.
offspring *n* brood, children, descendants, issue, litter, posterity, progeny; cadet, child, scion.
often *adv* frequently, generally, oftentimes, repeatedly.
ogre *n* bugbear, demon, devil, goblin, hobgoblin, monster, spectre.
old *adj* aged, ancient, antiquated, antique, archaic, elderly, obsolete, olden, old-fashioned, superannuated; decayed, done, senile, worn-out; original, primitive, pristine; former, preceding, preexisting.
oleaginous *adj* adipose, fat, fatty, greasy, oily, sebaceous, unctuous.
omen *n* augury, auspice, foreboding, portent, presage, prognosis, sign, warning.
ominous *adj* inauspicious, monitory, portentous, premonitory, threatening, unpropitious.
omission *n* default, failure, forgetfulness, neglect, oversight.
omit *vb* disregard, drop, eliminate, exclude, miss, neglect, overlook, skip.
omnipotent *adj* almighty, all-powerful.
omniscient *adj* all-knowing, all-seeing, all-wise.
oneness *n* individuality, singleness, unity.
onerous *adj* burdensome, difficult, hard, heavy, laborious, oppressive, responsible, weighty.
one-sided *adj* partial, prejudiced, unfair, unilateral, unjust.
only *adj* alone, single, sole, solitary. * *adv* barely, merely, simply.
onset *n* assault, attack, charge, onslaught, storm, storming.
onus *n* burden, liability, load, responsibility.
ooze *vb* distil, drip, drop, shed; drain, exude, filter, leak, percolate, stain, transude. * *n* mire, mud, slime.
opaque *adj* dark, dim, hazy, muddy; abstruse, cryptic, enigmatic, enigmatical, obscure, unclear.
open *vb* expand, spread; begin, commence, initiate; disclose, exhibit, reveal, show; unbar, unclose, uncover, unlock, unseal, untie. * *adj* expanded, extended, unclosed, spread wide; aboveboard, artless, candid, cordial, fair, frank, guileless, hearty, honest, sincere, openhearted, single-minded, undesigning, undisguised, undissembling, unreserved; bounteous, bountiful, free, generous, liberal, munificent; ajar, uncovered; exposed, undefended, unprotected; clear, unobstructed; accessible, public, unenclosed, unrestricted; mild, moderate; apparent, debatable, evident, obvious, patent, plain, undetermined.
opening *adj* commencing, first, inaugural, initiatory, introductory. * *n* aperture, breach, chasm, cleft, fissure, flaw, gap, gulf, hole, interspace, loophole, orifice, perforation, rent, rift; beginning, commencement, dawn; chance, opportunity, vacancy.
openly *adv* candidly, frankly, honestly, plainly, publicly.
openness *n* candour, frankness, honesty, ingenuousness, plainness, unreservedness.
operate *vb* act, function, work; cause, effect, occasion, produce; manipulate, use, run.
operation *n* manipulation, performance, procedure, proceeding, process; action, affair, manoeuvre, motion, movement.
operative *adj* active, effective, effectual, efficient, serviceable, vigorous; important, indicative, influential, significant. * *n* artisan, employee, labourer, mechanic, worker, workman.
opiate *adj* narcotic, sedative, soporiferous, soporific. * *n* anodyne, drug, narcotic, sedative, tranquillizer.
opine *vb* apprehend, believe, conceive, fancy, judge, suppose, presume, surmise, think.
opinion *n* conception, idea, impression, judgment, notion, sentiment, view; belief, persuasion, tenet; esteem, estimation, judgment.
opinionated *adj* biased, bigoted, cocksure, conceited, dictatorial, dogmatic, opinionative, prejudiced, stubborn.
opponent *adj* adverse, antagonistic, contrary, opposing, opposite, repugnant. * *n* adversary, antagonist, competitor, contestant, counteragent, enemy, foe, opposite, opposer, party, rival.
opportune *adj* appropriate, auspicious, convenient, favourable, felicitous, fit, fitting, fortunate, lucky, propitious, seasonable, suitable, timely, well-timed.
opportunity *n* chance, convenience, moment, occasion.
oppose *vb* combat, contravene, counteract, dispute, obstruct, oppugn, resist, thwart, withstand; check, prevent; confront, counterpoise.
opposite *adj* facing, fronting; conflicting, contradictory, contrary, different, diverse, incompatible, inconsistent, irreconcilable; adverse, antagonistic, hostile, inimical, opposed, opposing, repugnant. * *n* contradiction, contrary, converse, reverse.
opposition *n* antagonism, antinomy, contrariety, inconsistency, repugnance; counteraction, counterinfluence, hostility, resistance; hindrance, obstacle, obstruction, oppression, prevention.
oppress *vb* burden, crush, depress, harass, load, maltreat, overburden, overpower, overwhelm, persecute, subdue, suppress, tyrannize, wrong.
oppression *n* abuse, calamity, cruelty, hardship, injury, injustice, misery, persecution, severity, suffering, tyranny; depression, dullness, heaviness, lassitude.
oppressive *adj* close, muggy, stifling, suffocating, sultry.
opprobrious *adj* abusive, condemnatory, contemptuous, damnatory, insolent, insulting, offensive, reproachable, scandalous, scurrilous, vituperative; despised, dishonourable, disreputable, hateful, infamous, shameful.

opprobrium *n* contumely, scurrility; calumny, disgrace, ignominy, infamy, obloquy, odium, reproach.

oppugn *vb* assail, argue, attack, combat, contravene, oppose, resist, thwart, withstand.

option *n* choice, discretion, election, preference, selection.

optional *adj* discretionary, elective, nonobligatory, voluntary.

opulence *n* affluence, fortune, independence, luxury, riches, wealth.

opulent *adj* affluent, flush, luxurious, moneyed, plentiful, rich, sumptuous, wealthy.

oracular *adj* ominous, portentous, prophetic; authoritative, dogmatic, magisterial, positive; aged, grave, wise; ambiguous, blind, dark, equivocal, obscure.

oral *adj* nuncupative, spoken, verbal, vocal.

oration *n* address, declamation, discourse, harangue, speech.

orb *n* ball, globe, sphere; circle, circuit, orbit, ring; disk, wheel.

orbit *vb* circle, encircle, revolve around. * *n* course, path, revolution, track.

ordain *vb* appoint, call, consecrate, elect, experiment, constitute, establish, institute, regulate; decree, enjoin, enact, order, prescribe.

order *vb* adjust, arrange, methodize, regulate, systematize; carry on, conduct, manage; bid, command, direct, instruct, require. * *n* arrangement, disposition, method, regularity, symmetry, system; law, regulation, rule; discipline, peace, quiet; command, commission, direction, injunction, instruction, mandate, prescription; class, degree, grade, kind, rank; family, tribe; brotherhood, community, fraternity, society; sequence, succession.

orderly *adj* methodical, regular, systematic; peaceable, quiet, well-behaved; neat, shipshape, tidy.

ordinance *n* appointment, command, decree, edict, enactment, law, order, prescript, regulation, rule, statute; ceremony, observance, sacrament, rite, ritual.

ordinary *adj* accustomed, customary, established, everyday, normal, regular, settled, wonted, everyday, regular; common, frequent, habitual, usual; average, commonplace, indifferent, inferior, mean, mediocre, second-rate, undistinguished; homely, plain.

organization *n* business, construction, constitution, organism, structure, system.

organize *vb* adjust, constitute, construct, form, make, shape; arrange, coordinate, correlate, establish, systematize.

orgy *n* carousal, debauch, debauchery, revel, saturnalia.

orifice *n* aperture, hole, mouth, perforation, pore, vent.

origin *n* beginning, birth, commencement, cradle, derivation, foundation, fountain, fountainhead, original, rise, root, source, spring, starting point; cause, occasion; heritage, lineage, parentage.

original *adj* aboriginal, first, primary, primeval, primitive, primordial, pristine; fresh, inventive, novel; eccentric, odd, peculiar. * *n* cause, commencement, origin, source, spring; archetype, exemplar, model, pattern, prototype, protoplast, type.

originate *vb* arise, begin, emanate, flow, proceed, rise, spring; create, discover, form, invent, produce.

originator *n* author, creator, former, inventor, maker, parent.

orison *n* petition, prayer, solicitation, supplication.

ornament *vb* adorn, beautify, bedeck, bedizen, decorate, deck, emblazon, garnish, grace. * *n* adornment, bedizenment, decoration, design, embellishment, garnish, ornamentation.

ornate *adj* beautiful, bedecked, decorated, elaborate, elegant, embellished, florid, flowery, ornamental, ornamented.

orthodox *adj* conventional, correct, sound, true.

oscillate *vb* fluctuate, sway, swing, vacillate, vary, vibrate.

ostensible *adj* apparent, assigned, avowed, declared, exhibited, manifest, presented, visible; plausible, professed, specious.

ostentation *n* dash, display, flourish, pageantry, parade, pomp, pomposity, pompousness, show, vaunting; appearance, semblance, showiness.

ostentatious *adj* boastful, dashing, flaunting, pompous, pretentious, showy, vain, vainglorious; gaudy.

ostracize *vb* banish, boycott, exclude, excommunicate, exile, expatriate, expel, evict.

oust *vb* dislodge, dispossess, eject, evict, expel.

outbreak *n* ebullition, eruption, explosion, outburst; affray, broil, conflict, commotion, fray, riot, row; flare-up, manifestation.

outcast *n* exile, expatriate; castaway, pariah, reprobate, vagabond.

outcome *n* conclusion, consequence, event, issue, result, upshot.

outcry *n* cry, scream, screech, yell; bruit, clamour, noise, tumult, vociferation.

outdo *vb* beat, exceed, excel, outgo, outstrip, outvie, surpass.

outlandish *adj* alien, exotic, foreign, strange; barbarous, bizarre, uncouth.

outlaw *vb* ban, banish, condemn, exclude, forbid, make illegal, prohibit. * *n* bandit, brigand, crook, freebooter, highwayman, lawbreaker, marauder, robber, thief.

outlay *n* disbursement, expenditure, outgoings.

outline *vb* delineate, draft, draw, plan, silhouette, sketch. * *n* contour, profile; delineation, draft, drawing, plan, rough draft, silhouette, sketch.

outlive *vb* last, live longer, survive.

outlook *n* future, prospect, sight, view; lookout, watch-tower.

outrage *vb* abuse, injure, insult, maltreat, offend, shock, injure. * *n* abuse, affront, indignity, insult, offence.

outrageous *adj* abusive, frantic, furious, frenzied, mad, raging, turbulent, violent, wild; atrocious, enormous, flagrant, heinous, monstrous, nefarious, villainous; enormous, excessive, extravagant, unwarrantable.
outré *adj* excessive, exorbitant, extravagant, immoderate, inordinate, overstrained, unconventional.
outrun *vb* beat, exceed, outdistance, outgo, outstrip, outspeed, surpass.
outset *n* beginning, commencement, entrance, opening, start, starting point.
outshine *vb* eclipse, outstrip, overshadow, surpass.
outspoken *adj* abrupt, blunt, candid, frank, plain, plainspoken, unceremonious, unreserved.
outstanding *adj* due, owing, uncollected, ungathered, unpaid, unsettled; conspicuous, eminent, prominent, striking.
outward *adj* exterior, external, outer, outside.
outwit *vb* cheat, circumvent, deceive, defraud, diddle, dupe, gull, outmanoeuvre, overreach, swindle, victimize.
overawe *vb* affright, awe, browbeat, cow, daunt, frighten, intimidate, scare, terrify.
overbalance *vb* capsize, overset, overturn, tumble, upset; outweigh, preponderate.
overbearing *adj* oppressive, overpowering; arrogant, dictatorial, dogmatic, domineering, haughty, imperious, overweening, proud, supercilious.
overcast *vb* cloud, darken, overcloud, overshadow, shade, shadow. * *adj* cloudy, darkened, hazy, murky, obscure.
overcharge *vb* burden, oppress, overburden, overload, surcharge; crowd, overfill; exaggerate, overstate, overstrain.
overcome *vb* beat, choke, conquer, crush, defeat, discomfit, overbear, overmaster, overpower, overthrow, overturn, overwhelm, prevail, rout, subdue, subjugate, surmount, vanquish.
overflow *vb* brim over, fall over, pour over, pour out, shower, spill; deluge, inundate, submerge. * *n* deluge, inundation, profusion, superabundance.
overhaul *vb* overtake; check, examine, inspect, repair, survey. * *n* check, examination, inspection.
overlay *vb* cover, spread over; overlie, overpress, smother; crush, overpower, overwhelm; cloud, hide, obscure, overcast. * *n* appliqué, covering, decoration, veneer.
overlook *vb* inspect, oversee, superintend, supervise; disregard, miss, neglect, slight; condone, excuse, forgive, pardon, pass over.
overpower *vb* beat, conquer, crush, defeat, discomfit, overbear, overcome, overmaster, overturn, overwhelm, subdue, subjugate, vanquish.
overreach *vb* exceed, outstrip, overshoot, pass, surpass; cheat, circumvent, deceive, defraud.
override *vb* outride, outweigh, pass, quash, supersede, surpass.
overrule *vb* control, govern, sway; annul, cancel, nullify, recall, reject, repeal, repudiate, rescind, revoke, reject, set aside, supersede, suppress.
oversight *n* care, charge, control, direction, inspection, management, superintendence, supervision, surveillance; blunder, error, fault, inadvertence, inattention, lapse, miss, mistake, neglect, omission, slip, trip.
overt *adj* apparent, glaring, open, manifest, notorious, patent, public, unconcealed.
overthrow *vb* overturn, upset, subvert; demolish, destroy, level; beat, conquer, crush, defeat, discomfit, foil, master, overcome, overpower, overwhelm, rout, subjugate, vanquish, worst. * *n* downfall, fall, prostration, subversion; destruction, demolition, ruin; defeat, discomfiture, dispersion, rout.
overturn *vb* invert, overthrow, reverse, subvert, upset.
overture *n* invitation, offer, proposal, proposition.
overweening *adj* arrogant, conceited, consequential, egotistical, haughty, opinionated, proud, supercilious, vain, vainglorious.
overwhelm *vb* drown, engulf, inundate, overflow, submerge, swallow up, swamp; conquer, crush, defeat, overbear, overcome, overpower, subdue, vanquish.
overwrought *adj* overdone, overelaborate; agitated, excited, overexcited, overworked, stirred.
own[1] *vb* have, hold, possess; avow, confess; acknowledge, admit, allow, concede.
own[2] *adj* particular, personal, private.
owner *n* freeholder, holder, landlord, possessor, proprietor.

P

pace *vb* go, hasten, hurry, move, step, walk. * *n* amble, gait, step, walk.
pacific *adj* appeasing, conciliatory, ironic, mollifying, placating, peacemaking, propitiatory; calm, gentle, peaceable, peaceful, quiet, smooth, tranquil, unruffled.
pacify *vb* appease, conciliate, harmonize, tranquillize; allay, appease, assuage, calm, compose, hush, lay, lull, moderate, mollify, placate, propitiate, quell, quiet, smooth, soften, soothe, still.
pack *vb* compact, compress, crowd, fill; bundle, burden, load, stow. * *n* bale, budget, bundle, package, packet, parcel; burden, load; assemblage, assembly, assortment, collection, set; band, bevy, clan, company, crew, gang, knot, lot, party, squad.
pact *n* agreement, alliance, bargain, bond, compact, concordat, contract, convention, covenant, league, stipulation.
pagan *adj* heathen, heathenish, idolatrous, irreligious, paganist, paganistic. * *n* gentile, heathen, idolater.
pageantry *n* display, flourish, magnificence, parade, pomp, show, splendour, state.
pain *vb* agonize, bite, distress, hurt, rack, sting, torment, torture; afflict, aggrieve, annoy, bore, chafe, displease, disquiet, fret, grieve, harass, incommode, plague, tease, trouble, vex, worry; rankle, smart, shoot, sting, twinge. * *n* ache, agony, anguish, discomfort, distress, gripe, hurt, pang, smart, soreness, sting, suffering, throe, torment, torture, twinge; affliction, anguish, anxiety, bitterness, care, chagrin, disquiet, dolour, grief, heartache, misery, punishment, solicitude, sorrow, trouble, uneasiness, unhappiness, vexation, woe, wretchedness.
painful *adj* agonizing, distressful, excruciating, racking, sharp, tormenting, torturing; afflicting, afflictive, annoying, baleful, disagreeable, displeasing, disquieting, distressing, dolorous, grievous, provoking, troublesome, unpleasant, vexatious; arduous, careful, difficult, hard, severe, sore, toilsome.
pains *npl* care, effort, labour, task, toilsomeness, trouble; childbirth, labour, travail.
painstaking *adj* assiduous, careful, conscientious, diligent, hardworking, industrious, laborious, persevering, plodding, sedulous, strenuous.
paint *vb* delineate, depict, describe, draw, figure, pencil, portray, represent, sketch; adorn, beautify, deck, embellish, ornament. * *n* colouring, dye, pigment, stain; cosmetics, greasepaint, make-up.
pair *vb* couple, marry, mate, match. * *n* brace, couple, double, duo, match, twosome.
pal *n* buddy, chum, companion, comrade, crony, friend, mate, mucker.
palatable *adj* acceptable, agreeable, appetizing, delicate, delicious, enjoyable, flavourful, flavoursome, gustative, gustatory, luscious, nice, pleasant, pleasing, savoury, relishable, tasteful, tasty, toothsome.
palaver *vb* chat, chatter, converse, patter, prattle, say, speak, talk; confer, parley; blandish, cajole, flatter, wheedle. * *n* chat, chatter, conversation, discussion, language, prattle, speech, talk; confab, confabulation, conference, conclave, parley, powwow; balderdash, cajolery, flummery, gibberish.
pale *vb* blanch, lose colour, whiten. * *adj* ashen, ashy, blanched, bloodless, pallid, sickly, wan, white; blank, dim, obscure, spectral. * *n* picket, stake; circuit, enclosure; district, region, territory; boundary, confine, fence, limit.
pall[1] *n* cloak, cover, curtain, mantle, pallium, shield, shroud, veil.
pall[2] *vb* cloy, glut, gorge, satiate, surfeit; deject, depress, discourage, dishearten, dispirit; cloak, cover, drape, invest, overspread, shroud.
palliate *vb* cloak, conceal, cover, excuse, extenuate, hide, gloss, lessen; abate, allay, alleviate, assuage, blunt, diminish, dull, ease, mitigate, moderate, mollify, quell, quiet, relieve, soften, soothe, still.
pallid *adj* ashen, ashy, cadaverous, colourless, pale, sallow, wan, whitish.
palm[1] *vb* foist, impose, obtrude, pass off; handle, touch.
palm[2] *n* bays, crown, laurels, prize, trophy, victory.
palmy *adj* flourishing, fortunate, glorious, golden, halcyon, happy, joyous, prosperous, thriving, victorious.
palpable *adj* corporeal, material, tactile, tangible; evident, glaring, gross, intelligible, manifest, obvious, patent, plain, unmistakable.
palpitate *vb* flutter, pulsate, throb; quiver, shiver, tremble.
palter *vb* dodge, equivocate, evade, haggle, prevaricate, quibble, shift, shuffle, trifle.
paltry *adj* diminutive, feeble, inconsiderable, insig-

nificant, little, miserable, petty, slender, slight, small, sorry, trifling, trivial, unimportant, wretched.
pamper *vb* baby, coddle, fondle, gratify, humour, spoil.
panacea *n* catholicon, cure-all, medicine, remedy.
panegyric *adj* commendatory, encomiastic, encomiastical, eulogistic, eulogistical, laudatory, panegyrical. * *n* eulogy, laudation, praise, paean, tribute.
pang *n* agony, anguish, distress, gripe, pain, throe, twinge.
panic *vb* affright, alarm, scare, startle, terrify; become terrified, overreact. * *n* alarm, consternation, fear, fright, jitters, terror.
pant *vb* blow, gasp, puff; heave, palpitate, pulsate, throb; languish; desire, hunger, long, sigh, thirst, yearn. * *n* blow, gasp, puff.
parable *n* allegory, fable, story.
paraclete *n* advocate, comforter, consoler, intercessor, mediator.
parade *vb* display, flaunt, show, vaunt. * *n* ceremony, display, flaunting, ostentation, pomp, show; array, pageant, review, spectacle; mall, promenade.
paradox *n* absurdity, contradiction, mystery.
paragon *n* flower, ideal, masterpiece, model, nonpareil, pattern, standard.
paragraph *n* clause, item, notice, passage, section, sentence, subdivision.
parallel *vb* be alike, compare, conform, correlate, match. * *adj* abreast, concurrent; allied, analogous, correspondent, equal, like, resembling, similar. * *n* conformity, likeness, resemblance, similarity; analogue, correlative, counterpart.
paramount *adj* chief, dominant, eminent, pre-eminent, principal, superior, supreme.
paraphernalia *n* accoutrements, appendages, appurtenances, baggage, belongings, effects, equipage, equipment, ornaments, trappings.
parasite *n* bloodsucker, fawner, flatterer, flunky, hanger-on, leech, spaniel, sycophant, toady, wheedler.
parcel *vb* allot, apportion, dispense, distribute, divide. * *n* budget, bundle, package; batch, collection, group, lot, set; division, part, patch, pierce, plot, portion, tract.
parched *adj* arid, dry, scorched, shrivelled, thirsty.
pardon *vb* condone, forgive, overlook, remit; absolve, acquit, clear, discharge, excuse, release. * *n* absolution, amnesty, condonation, discharge, excuse, forgiveness, grace, mercy, overlook, release.
parentage *n* ancestry, birth, descent, extraction, family, lineage, origin, parenthood, pedigree, stock.
pariah *n* outcast, wretch.
parish *n* community, congregation, parishioners; district, subdivision.
parity *n* analogy, correspondence, equality, equivalence, likeness, sameness, similarity.
parody *vb* burlesque, caricature, imitate, lampoon, mock, ridicule, satirize, travesty. * *n* burlesque, caricature, imitation, ridicule, satire, travesty.
paroxysm *n* attack, convulsion, exacerbation, fit, outburst, seizure, spasm, throe.
parsimonious *adj* avaricious, close, close-fisted, covetous, frugal, grasping, grudging, illiberal, mean, mercenary, miserly, near, niggardly, penurious, shabby, sordid, sparing, stingy, tightfisted.
parson *n* churchman, clergyman, divine, ecclesiastic, incumbent, minister, pastor, priest, rector.
part *vb* break, dismember, dissever, divide, sever, subdivide, sunder; detach, disconnect, disjoin, dissociate, disunite, separate; allot, apportion, distribute, divide, mete, share; secrete. * *n* crumb, division, fraction, fragment, moiety, parcel, piece, portion, remnant, scrap, section, segment, subdivision; component, constituent, element, ingredient, member, organ; lot, share; concern, interest, participation; allotment, apportionment, dividend; business, charge, duty, function, office, work; faction, party, side; character, cue, lines, role; clause, paragraph, passage.
partake *vb* engage, participate, share; consume, eat, take;evince, evoke, show, suggest.
partial *adj* component, fractional, imperfect, incomplete, limited; biased, influential, interested, one-sided, prejudiced, prepossessed, unfair, unjust, warped; fond, indulgent.
participate *vb* engage in, partake, perform, share.
particle *n* atom, bit, corpuscle, crumb, drop, glimmer, grain, granule, iota, jot, mite, molecule, morsel, mote, scrap, shred, snip, spark, speck, whit.
particular *adj* especial, special, specific; distinct, individual, respective, separate, single; characteristic, distinctive, peculiar; individual, intimate, own, personal, private; notable, noteworthy; circumstantial, definite, detailed, exact, minute, narrow, precise; careful, close, conscientious, critical, fastidious, nice, scrupulous, strict; marked, odd, singular, strange, uncommon. * *n* case, circumstance, count, detail, feature, instance, item, particularity, point, regard, respect.
parting *adj* breaking, dividing, separating; final, last, valedictory; declining, departing. * *n* breaking, disruption, rupture, severing; detachment, division, separation; death, departure, farewell, leave-taking.
partisan *adj* biased, factional, interested, partial, prejudiced. * *n* adherent, backer, champion, disciple, follower, supporter, votary; baton, halberd, pike, quarterstaff, truncheon, staff.
partition *vb* apportion, distribute, divide, portion, separate, share. * *n* division, separation; barrier, division, screen, wall; allotment, apportionment, distribution.
partner *n* associate, colleague, copartner, partaker, participant, participator; accomplice, ally, coadjutor, confederate; companion, consort, spouse.
partnership *n* association, company, copartner-

ship, firm, house, society; connection, interest, participation, union.
parts *npl* abilities, accomplishments, endowments, faculties, genius, gifts, intellect, intelligence, mind, qualities, powers, talents; districts, regions.
party *n* alliance, association, cabal, circle, clique, combination, confederacy, coterie, faction, group, junta, league, ring, set; body, company, detachment, squad, troop; assembly, gathering; partaker, participant, participator, sharer; defendant, litigant, plaintiff; individual, one, person, somebody; cause, division, interest, side.
pass[1] *vb* devolve, fall, go, move, proceed; change, elapse, flit, glide, lapse, slip; cease, die, fade, expire, vanish; happen, occur; convey, deliver, send, transmit, transfer; disregard, ignore, neglect; exceed, excel, surpass; approve, ratify, sanction; answer, do, succeed, suffice, suit; express, pronounce, utter; beguile, wile.
pass[2] *n* avenue, ford, road, route, way; defile, gorge, passage, ravine; authorization, licence, passport, permission, ticket; condition, conjecture, plight, situation, state; lunge, push, thrust, tilt; transfer, trick.
passable *adj* admissible, allowable, mediocre, middling, moderate, ordinary, so-so, tolerable; acceptable, current, receivable; navigable, traversable.
passage *n* going, passing, progress, transit; evacuation, journey, migration, transit, voyage; avenue, channel, course, pass, path, road, route, thoroughfare, vennel, way; access, currency, entry, reception; act, deed, event, feat, incidence, occurrence, passion; corridor, gallery, gate, hall; clause, paragraph, sentence, text; course, death, decease, departure, expiration, lapse; affair, brush, change, collision, combat, conflict, contest, encounter, exchange, joust, skirmish, tilt.
passenger *n* fare, itinerant, tourist, traveller, voyager, wayfarer.
passionate *adj* animated, ardent, burning, earnest, enthusiastic, excited, fervent, fiery, furious, glowing, hot-blooded, impassioned, impetuous, impulsive, intense, vehement, warm, zealous; hot-headed, irascible, quick-tempered, tempestuous, violent.
passive *adj* inactive, inert, quiescent, receptive; apathetic, enduring, long-suffering, nonresistant, patient, stoical, submissive, suffering, unresisting.
past *adj* accomplished, elapsed, ended, gone, spent; ancient, bygone, former, obsolete, outworn. * *adv* above, extra, beyond, over. * *prep* above, after, beyond, exceeding. * *n* antiquity, heretofore, history, olden times, yesterday.
pastime *n* amusement, diversion, entertainment, hobby, play, recreation, sport.
pastor *n* clergyman, churchman, divine, ecclesiastic, minister, parson, priest, vicar.
pat[1] *vb* dab, hit, rap, tap; caress, chuck, fondle, pet. * *n* dab, hit, pad, rap, tap; caress.
pat[2] *adj* appropriate, apt, fit, pertinent, suitable. * *adv* aptly, conveniently, fitly, opportunely, seasonably.
patch *vb* mend, repair. * *n* repair; parcel, plot, tract.
patent *adj* expanded, open, spreading; apparent, clear, conspicuous, evident, glaring, indisputable, manifest, notorious, obvious, public, open, palpable, plain, unconcealed, unmistakable. * *n* copyright, privilege, right.
paternity *n* derivation, descent, fatherhood, origin.
path *n* access, avenue, course, footway, passage, pathway, road, route, track, trail, way.
pathetic *adj* affecting, melting, moving, pitiable, plaintive, sad, tender, touching.
patience *n* endurance, fortitude, long-sufferance, resignation, submission, sufferance; calmness, composure, quietness; forbearance, indulgence, leniency; assiduity, constancy, diligence, indefatigability, indefatigableness, perseverance, persistence.
patient *adj* meek, passive, resigned, submissive, uncomplaining, unrepining; calm, composed, contented, quiet; indulgent, lenient, long-suffering; assiduous, constant, diligent, indefatigable, persevering, persistent. * *n* case, invalid, subject, sufferer.
patrician *adj* aristocratic, blue-blooded, highborn, noble, senatorial, well-born. * *n* aristocrat, blue blood, nobleman.
patron *n* advocate, defender, favourer, guardian, helper, protector, supporter.
patronize *vb* aid, assist, befriend, countenance, defend, favour, maintain, support; condescend, disparage, scorn.
pattern *vb* copy, follow, imitate. * *n* archetype, exemplar, last, model, original, paradigm, plan, prototype; example, guide, sample, specimen; mirror, paragon; design, figure, shape, style, type.
paucity *n* deficiency, exiguity, insufficiency, lack, poverty, rarity, shortage.
paunch *n* abdomen, belly, gut, stomach.
pauperism *n* beggary, destitution, indigence, mendicancy, mendicity, need, poverty, penury, want.
pause *vb* breathe, cease, delay, desist, rest, stay, stop, wait; delay, forbear, intermit, stay, stop, tarry, wait; deliberate, demur, hesitate, waver. * *n* break, caesura, cessation, halt, intermission, interruption, interval, remission, rest, stop, stoppage, stopping, suspension; hesitation, suspense, uncertainty; paragraph.
pawn[1] *n* cat's-paw, dupe, plaything, puppet, stooge, tool, toy.
pawn[2] *vb* bet, gage, hazard, lay, pledge, risk, stake, wager. * *n* assurance, bond, guarantee, pledge, security.
pay *vb* defray, discharge, discount, foot, honour, liquidate, meet, quit, settle; compensate, recompense, reimburse, requite, reward; punish, revenge; give, offer, render. * *n* allowance, commission, compensation, emolument, hire, recom-

pense, reimbursement, remuneration, requital, reward, salary, wages.

peace *n* calm, calmness, quiet, quietness, repose, stillness; accord, amity, friendliness, harmony; composure, equanimity, imperturbability, placidity, quietude, tranquillity; agreement, armistice.

peaceable *adj* pacific, peaceful; amiable, amicable, friendly, gentle, inoffensive, mild; placid, quiet, serene, still, tranquil, undisturbed, unmoved.

peaceful *adj* quiet, undisturbed; amicable, concordant, friendly, gentle, harmonious, mild, pacific, peaceable; calm, composed, placid, serene, still.

peak *vb* climax, culminate, top; dwindle, thin. * *n* acme, apex, crest, crown, pinnacle, summit, top, zenith.

peaked *adj* piked, pointed, thin.

peasant *n* boor, countryman, clown, hind, labourer, rustic, swain.

peculate *vb* appropriate, defraud, embezzle, misappropriate, pilfer, purloin, rob, steal.

peculiar *adj* appropriate, idiosyncratic, individual, proper; characteristic, eccentric, exceptional, extraordinary, odd, queer, rare, singular, strange, striking, uncommon, unusual; individual, especial, particular, select, special, specific.

peculiarity *n* appropriateness, distinctiveness, individuality, speciality; characteristic, idiosyncrasy, oddity, peculiarity, singularity.

pedantic *adj* conceited, fussy, officious, ostentatious, over-learned, particular, pedagogical, pompous, pragmatical, precise, pretentious, priggish, stilted.

pedlar *n* chapman, costermonger, hawker, packman, vendor.

pedigree *adj* purebred, thoroughbred. * *n* ancestry, breed, descent, extraction, family, genealogy, house, line, lineage, race, stock, strain.

peer[1] *vb* gaze, look, peek, peep, pry, squinny, squint; appear, emerge.

peer[2] *n* associate, co-equal, companion, compeer, equal, equivalent, fellow, like, mate, match; aristocrat, baron, count, duke, earl, grandee, lord, marquis, noble, nobleman, viscount.

peerless *adj* excellent, incomparable, matchless, outstanding, superlative, unequalled, unique, unmatched, unsurpassed.

peevish *adj* acrimonious, captious, churlish, complaining, crabbed, cross, crusty, discontented, fretful, ill-natured, ill-tempered, irascible, irritable, pettish, petulant, querulous, snappish, snarling, splenetic, spleeny, testy, waspish; forward, headstrong, obstinate, self-willed, stubborn; childish, silly, thoughtless, trifling.

pellucid *adj* bright, clear, crystalline, diaphanous, limpid, lucid, transparent.

pelt[1] *vb* assail, batter, beat, belabour, bombard, pepper, stone, strike; cast, hurl, throw; hurry, rush, speed, tear.

pelt[2] *n* coat, hide, skin.

pen[1] *vb* compose, draft, indite, inscribe, write.

pen[2] *vb* confine, coop, encage, enclose, impound, imprison, incarcerate. * *n* cage, coop, corral, crib, hutch, enclosure, paddock, pound, stall, sty.

penalty *n* chastisement, fine, forfeiture, mulct, punishment, retribution.

penance *n* humiliation, maceration, mortification, penalty, punishment.

penchant *n* bent, bias, disposition, fondness, inclination, leaning, liking, predilection, predisposition, proclivity, proneness, propensity, taste, tendency, turn.

penetrate *vb* bore, burrow, cut, enter, invade, penetrate, percolate, perforate, pervade, pierce, soak, stab; affect, sensitize, touch; comprehend, discern, perceive, understand.

penetrating *adj* penetrative, permeating, piercing, sharp, subtle; acute, clear-sighted, discerning, intelligent, keen, quick, sagacious, sharp-witted, shrewd.

penetration *n* acuteness, discernment, insight, sagacity.

penitence *n* compunction, contrition, qualms, regret, remorse, repentance, sorrow.

penitent *adj* compunctious, conscience-stricken, contrite, regretful, remorseful, repentant, sorrowing, sorrowful. * *n* penance-doer, penitentiary, repentant.

penniless *adj* destitute, distressed, impecunious, indigent, moneyless, pinched, poor, necessitous, needy, pensive, poverty-stricken, reduced.

pensive *adj* contemplative, dreamy, meditative, reflective, sober, thoughtful; grave, melancholic, melancholy, mournful, sad, serious, solemn.

penurious *adj* inadequate, ill-provided, insufficient, meagre, niggardly, poor, scanty, stinted; avaricious, close, close-fisted, covetous, illiberal, grasping, grudging, mean, mercenary, miserly, near, niggardly, parsimonious, sordid, stingy, tightfisted.

penury *n* beggary, destitution, indigence, need, poverty, privation, want.

people *vb* colonize, inhabit, populate. * *n* clan, country, family, nation, race, state, tribe; folk, humankind, persons, population, public; commons, community, democracy, populace, proletariat; mob, multitude, rabble.

perceive *vb* behold, descry, detect, discern, discover, discriminate, distinguish, note, notice, observe, recognize, remark, see, spot; appreciate, comprehend, know, understand.

perceptible *adj* apparent, appreciable, cognizable, discernible, noticeable, perceivable, understandable, visible.

perception *n* apprehension, cognition, discernment, perceiving, recognition, seeing; comprehension, conception, consciousness, perceptiveness, perceptivity, understanding, feeling.

perchance *adv* haply, maybe, mayhap, peradventure, perhaps, possibly, probably.

percolate *vb* drain, drip, exude, filter, filtrate, ooze, penetrate, stain, transude.

percussion *n* collision, clash, concussion, crash, encounter, shock.
perdition *n* damnation, demolition, destruction, downfall, hell, overthrow, ruin, wreck.
peremptory *adj* absolute, authoritative, categorical, commanding, decisive, express, imperative, imperious, positive; determined, resolute, resolved; arbitrary, dogmatic, incontrovertible.
perennial *adj* ceaseless, constant, continual, deathless, enduring, immortal, imperishable, lasting, never-failing, permanent, perpetual, unceasing, undying, unfailing, uninterrupted.
perfect *vb* accomplish, complete, consummate, elaborate, finish. * *adj* completed, finished; complete, entire, full, unqualified, utter, whole; capital, consummate, excellent, exquisite, faultless, ideal; accomplished, disciplined, expert, skilled; blameless, faultless, holy, immaculate, pure, spotless, unblemished.
perfection *n* completeness, completion, consummation, correctness, excellence, faultlessness, finish, maturity, perfection, perfectness, wholeness; beauty, quality.
perfidious *adj* deceitful, dishonest, disloyal, double-faced, faithless, false, false-hearted, traitorous, treacherous, unfaithful, untrustworthy, venal.
perfidy *n* defection, disloyalty, faithlessness, infidelity, perfidiousness, traitorousness, treachery, treason.
perforate *vb* bore, drill, penetrate, pierce, pink, prick, punch, riddle, trepan.
perform *vb* accomplish, achieve, compass, consummate, do, effect, transact; complete, discharge, execute, fulfil, meet, observe, satisfy; act, play, represent.
performance *n* accomplishment, achievement, completion, consummation, discharge, doing, execution, fulfilment; act, action, deed, exploit, feat, work; composition, production; acting, entertainment, exhibition, play, representation, hold; execution, playing.
perfume *n* aroma, balminess, bouquet, fragrance, incense, odour, redolence, scent, smell, sweetness.
perfunctory *adj* careless, formal, heedless, indifferent, mechanical, negligent, reckless, slight, slovenly, thoughtless, unmindful.
perhaps *adv* haply, peradventure, perchance, possibly.
peril *vb* endanger, imperil, jeopardize, risk. * *n* danger, hazard, insecurity, jeopardy, pitfall, risk, snare, uncertainty.
perilous *adj* dangerous, hazardous, risky, unsafe.
period *n* aeon, age, cycle, date, eon, epoch, season, span, spell, stage, term, time; continuance, duration; bound, conclusion, determination, end, limit, term, termination; clause, phrase, proposition, sentence.
periodical *adj* cyclical, incidental, intermittent, recurrent, recurring, regular, seasonal, systematic. * *n* magazine, paper, review, serial, weekly.
periphery *n* boundary, circumference, outside, perimeter, superficies, surface.
perish *vb* decay, moulder, shrivel, waste, wither; decease, die, expire, vanish.
perishable *adj* decaying, decomposable, destructible; dying, frail, mortal, temporary.
perjured *adj* false, forsworn, perfidious, traitorous, treacherous, untrue.
permanent *adj* abiding, constant, continuing, durable, enduring, fixed, immutable, invariable, lasting, perpetual, persistent, stable, standing, steadfast, unchangeable, unchanging, unfading, unmovable.
permissible *adj* admissible, allowable, free, lawful, legal, legitimate, proper, sufferable, unprohibited.
permission *n* allowance, authorization, consent, dispensation, leave, liberty, licence, permit, sufferance, toleration, warrant.
permit *vb* agree, allow, endure, let, suffer, tolerate; admit, authorize, consent, empower, license, warrant. * *n* leave, liberty, licence, passport, permission, sanction, warrant.
pernicious *adj* baleful, baneful, damaging, deadly, deleterious, destructive, detrimental, disadvantageous, fatal, harmful, hurtful, injurious, malign, mischievous, noisome, noxious, prejudicial, ruinous; evil-hearted, malevolent, malicious, malignant, mischief-making, wicked.
perpetrate *vb* commit, do, execute, perform.
perpetual *adj* ceaseless, continual, constant, endless, enduring, eternal, ever-enduring, everlasting, incessant, interminable, never-ceasing, never-ending, perennial, permanent, sempiternal, unceasing, unending, unfailing, uninterrupted.
perplex *vb* complicate, encumber, entangle, involve, snarl, tangle; beset, bewilder, confound, confuse, corner, distract, embarrass, fog, mystify, nonplus, pother, puzzle, set; annoy, bother, disturb, harass, molest, pester, plague, tease, trouble, vex, worry.
persecute *vb* afflict, distress, harass, molest, oppress, worry; annoy, beset, importune, pester, solicit, tease.
perseverance *n* constancy, continuance, doggedness, indefatigableness, persistence, persistency, pertinacity, resolution, steadfastness, steadiness, tenacity.
persevere *vb* continue, determine, endure, maintain, persist, remain, resolve, stick.
persist *vb* continue, endure, last, remain; insist, persevere.
persistent *adj* constant, continuing, enduring, fixed, immovable, persevering, persisting, steady, tenacious; contumacious, dogged, indefatigable, obdurate, obstinate, pertinacious, perverse, pigheaded, stubborn.
personable *adj* comely, good-looking, graceful, seemly, well-turned-out.
personal *adj* individual, peculiar, private, special; bodily, corporal, corporeal, exterior, material, physical.

personate *vb* act, impersonate, personify, play, represent; disguise, mast; counterfeit, feign, simulate.
perspective *n* panorama, prospect, view, vista; proportion, relation.
perspicacious *adj* keen-sighted, quick-sighted, sharp-sighted; acute, clever, discerning, keen, penetrating, sagacious, sharp-witted, shrewd.
perspicacity *n* acumen, acuteness, astuteness, discernment, insight, penetration, perspicaciousness, sagacity, sharpness, shrewdness.
perspicuity *n* clearness, distinctness, explicitness, intelligibility, lucidity, lucidness, perspicuousness, plainness, transparency.
perspicuous *adj* clear, distinct, explicit, intelligible, lucid, obvious, plain, transparent, unequivocal.
perspire *vb* exhale, glow, sweat, swelter.
persuade *vb* allure, actuate, entice, impel, incite, induce, influence, lead, move, prevail upon, urge; advise, counsel; convince, satisfy; inculcate, teach.
persuasion *n* exhortation, incitement, inducement, influence; belief, conviction, opinion; creed, doctrine, dogma, tenet; kind, sort, variety.
persuasive *adj* cogent, convincing, inducing, inducible, logical, persuading, plausible, sound, valid, weighty.
pert *adj* brisk, dapper, lively, nimble, smart, sprightly, perky; bold, flippant, forward, free, impertinent, impudent, malapert, presuming, smart, saucy.
pertain *vb* appertain, befit, behove, belong, concern, refer, regard, relate.
pertinacious *adj* constant, determined, firm, obdurate, persevering, resolute, staunch, steadfast, steady; dogged, headstrong, inflexible, mulish, intractable, obstinate, perverse, stubborn, unyielding, wayward, wilful.
pertinent *adj* adapted, applicable, apposite, appropriate, apropos, apt, fit, germane, pat, proper, relevant, suitable; appurtenant, belonging, concerning, pertaining, regarding.
perturb *vb* agitate, disquiet, distress, disturb, excite, trouble, unsettle, upset, vex, worry; confuse.
pervade *vb* affect, animate, diffuse, extend, fill, imbue, impregnate, infiltrate, penetrate, permeate.
perverse *adj* bad, disturbed, oblique, perverted; contrary, dogged, headstrong, mulish, obstinate, pertinacious, perversive, stubborn, ungovernable, intractable, unyielding, wayward, wilful; cantankerous, churlish, crabbed, cross, cross-grained, crusty, cussed, morose, peevish, petulant, snappish, snarling, spiteful, spleeny, surly, testy, touchy, wicked, wrong-headed; inconvenient, troublesome, untoward, vexatious.
perversion *n* abasement, corruption, debasement, impairment, injury, prostitution, vitiation.
perverted *adj* corrupt, debased, distorted, evil, impaired, misguiding, vitiated, wicked.
pessimistic *adj* cynical, dark, dejected, depressed, despondent, downhearted, gloomy, glum, melancholy, melancholic, morose, sad.
pest *n* disease, epidemic, infection, pestilence, plague; annoyance, bane, curse, infliction, nuisance, scourge, trouble.
pestilent *adj* contagious, infectious, malignant, pestilential; deadly, evil, injurious, malign, mischievous, noxious, poisonous; annoying, corrupt, pernicious, troublesome, vexatious.
petition *vb* ask, beg, crave, entreat, pray, solicit, sue, supplicate. * *n* address, appeal, application, entreaty, prayer, request, solicitation, supplication, suit.
petrify *vb* calcify, fossilize, lapidify; benumb, deaden; amaze, appal, astonish, astound, confound, dumbfound, paralyse, stun, stupefy.
petty *adj* diminutive, frivolous, inconsiderable, inferior, insignificant, little, mean, slight, small, trifling, trivial, unimportant.
petulant *adj* acrimonious, captious, cavilling, censorious, choleric, crabbed, cross, crusty, forward, fretful, hasty, ill-humoured, ill-tempered, irascible, irritable, peevish, perverse, pettish, querulous, snappish, snarling, testy, touchy, waspish.
phantom *n* apparition, ghost, illusion, phantasm, spectre, vision, wraith.
pharisaism *n* cant, formalism, hypocrisy, phariseeism, piety, sanctimoniousness, self-righteousness.
phenomenal *adj* marvellous, miraculous, prodigious, wondrous.
philanthropy *n* alms-giving, altruism, benevolence, charity, grace, humanitarianism, humanity, kindness.
philosophical, philosophic *adj* rational, reasonable, sound, wise; calm, collected, composed, cool, imperturbable, sedate, serene, stoical, tranquil, unruffled.
phlegmatic *adj* apathetic, calm, cold, cold-blooded, dull, frigid, heavy, impassive, indifferent, inert, sluggish, stoical, tame, unfeeling.
phobia *n* aversion, detestation, dislike, distaste, dread, fear, hatred.
phrase *vb* call, christen, denominate, designate, describe, dub, entitle, name, style. * *n* diction, expression, phraseology, style.
phraseology *n* diction, expression, language, phrasing, style.
physical *adj* material, natural; bodily, corporeal, external, substantial, tangible, sensible.
physiognomy *n* configuration, countenance, face, look, visage.
picaroon *n* adventurer, cheat, rogue; buccaneer, corsair, freebooter, marauder, pirate, plunderer, sea-rover.
pick *vb* peck, pierce, strike; cut, detach, gather, pluck; choose, cull, select; acquire, collect, get; pilfer, steal. * *n* pickaxe, pike, spike, toothpick.
picture *vb* delineate, draw, imagine, paint, represent. * *n* drawing, engraving, painting, print; copy, counterpart, delineation, embodiment, illustration, image, likeness, portraiture, portrayal, semblance, representation, resemblance, similitude; description.

picturesque *adj* beautiful, charming, colourful, graphic, scenic, striking, vivid.
piece *vb* mend, patch, repair; augment, complete, enlarge, increase; cement, join, unite. * *n* amount, bit, chunk, cut, fragment, hunk, part, quantity, scrap, shred, slice; portion; article, item, object; composition, lucubration, work, writing.
pied *adj* irregular, motley, mottled, particoloured, piebald, spotted, variegated.
pierce *vb* gore, impale, pink, prick, stab, transfix; bore, drill, excite, penetrate, perforate, puncture; affect, move, rouse, strike, thrill, touch.
piety *n* devotion, devoutness, holiness, godliness, grace, religion, sanctity.
pile[1] *vb* accumulate, amass; collect, gather, heap, load. * *n* accumulation, collection, heap, mass, stack; fortune, wad; building, edifice, erection, fabric, pyramid, skyscraper, structure, tower; reactor, nuclear reactor.
pile[2] *n* beam, column, pier, pillar, pole, post.
pile[3] *n* down, feel, finish, fur, fluff, fuzz, grain, nap, pappus, shag, surface, texture.
pilfer *vb* filch, purloin, rob, steal, thieve.
pilgrim *n* journeyer, sojourner, traveller, wanderer, wayfarer; crusader, devotee, palmer.
pilgrimage *n* crusade, excursion, expedition, journey, tour, trip.
pillage *vb* despoil, loot, plunder, rifle, sack, spoil, strip. * *n* depredation, destruction, devastation, plundering, rapine, spoliation; despoliation, plunder, rifling, sack, spoils.
pillar *n* column, pier, pilaster, post, shaft, stanchion; maintainer, prop, support, supporter, upholder.
pilot *vb* conduct, control, direct, guide, navigate, steer. * *adj* experimental, model, trial. * *n* helmsman, navigator, steersman; airman, aviator, conductor, director, flier, guide.
pinch *vb* compress, contract, cramp, gripe, nip, squeeze; afflict, distress, famish, oppress, straiten, stint; frost, nip; apprehend, arrest; economize, spare, stint. * *n* gripe, nip; pang, throe; crisis, difficulty, emergency, exigency, oppression, pressure, push, strait, stress.
pine *vb* decay, decline, droop, fade, flag, languish, waste, wilt, wither; desire, long, yearn.
pinion *vb* bind, chain, fasten, fetter, maim, restrain, shackle. * *n* pennon, wing; feather, quill, pen, plume, wing; fetter.
pinnacle *n* minaret, turret; acme, apex, height, peak, summit, top, zenith.
pious *adj* filial; devout, godly, holy, religious, reverential, righteous, saintly.
piquant *adj* biting, highly flavoured, piercing, prickling, pungent, sharp, stinging; interesting, lively, racy, sparkling, stimulating; cutting, keen, pointed, severe, strong, tart.
pique *vb* goad, incite, instigate, spur, stimulate, urge; affront, chafe, displease, fret, incense, irritate, nettle, offend, provoke, sting, vex, wound. * *n* annoyance, displeasure, irritation, offence, resentment, vexation.
pirate *vb* copy, crib, plagiarize, reproduce, steal. * *n* buccaneer, corsair, freebooter, marauder, picaroon, privateer, seadog, sea-robber, sea-rover, sea wolf.
pit *vb* match, oppose; dent, gouge, hole, mark, nick, notch, scar. * *n* cavity, hole, hollow; crater, dent, depression, dint, excavation, well; abyss, chasm, gulf; pitfall, snare, trap: auditorium, orchestra.
pitch *vb* fall, lurch, plunge, reel; light, settle, rest; cast, dart, fling, heave, hurl, lance, launch, send, toss, throw; erect, establish, fix, locate, place, plant, set, settle, station. * *n* degree, extent, height, intensity, measure, modulation, rage, rate; declivity, descent, inclination, slope; cast, jerk, plunge, throw, toss; place, position, spot; field, ground; line, patter.
piteous *adj* affecting, distressing, doleful, grievous, mournful, pathetic, rueful, sorrowful, woeful; deplorable, lamentable, miserable, pitiable, wretched; compassionate, tender.
pith *n* chief, core, essence, heart, gist, kernel, marrow, part, quintessence, soul, substance; importance, moment, weight; cogency, force, energy, strength, vigour.
pithy *adj* cogent, energetic, forcible, powerful; compact, concise, brief, laconic, meaty, pointed, short, sententious, substantial, terse; corky, porous.
pitiable *adj* deplorable, lamentable, miserable, pathetic, piteous, pitiable, woeful, wretched; abject, base, contemptible, despicable, disreputable, insignificant, low, paltry, mean, rascally, sorry, vile, worthless.
pitiably *adv* deplorably, distressingly, grievously, lamentably, miserably, pathetically, piteously, woefully, wretchedly.
pitiful *adj* compassionate, kind, lenient, merciful, mild, sympathetic, tender, tenderhearted; deplorable, lamentable, miserable, pathetic, piteous, pitiable, wretched; abject, base, contemptible, despicable, disreputable, insignificant, mean, paltry, rascally, sorry, vile, worthless.
pitiless *adj* cruel, hardhearted, implacable, inexorable, merciless, unmerciful, relentless, remorseless, unfeeling, unpitying, unrelenting, unsympathetic.
pittance *n* allowance, allotment, alms, charity, dole, gift; driblet, drop, insufficiency, mite, modicum, trifle.
pity *vb* commiserate, condole, sympathize. * *n* clemency, commiseration, compassion, condolence, fellow-feeling, grace, humanity, leniency, mercy, quarter, sympathy, tenderheartedness.
pivot *vb* depend, hinge, turn. * *n* axis, axle, centre, focus, hinge, joint.
place *vb* arrange, bestow, commit, deposit, dispose, fix, install, lay, locate, lodge, orient, orientate, pitch, plant, pose, put, seat, set, settle, situate, stand, station, rest; allocate, arrange, class, classify, identify, order, organize, recognize; ap-

point, assign, commission, establish, induct, nominate. * *n* area, courtyard, square; bounds, district, division, locale, locality, location, part, position, premises, quarter, region, scene, site, situation, spot, station, tract, whereabouts; calling, charge, employment, function, occupation, office, pitch, post; calling, condition, grade, precedence, rank, sphere, stakes, standing; abode, building, dwelling, habitation, mansion, residence, seat; city, town, village; fort, fortress, stronghold; paragraph, part, passage, portion; ground, occasion, opportunity, reason, room; lieu, stead.

placid *adj* calm, collected, composed, cool, equable, gentle, peaceful, quiet, serene, tranquil, undisturbed, unexcitable, unmoved, unruffled; halcyon, mild, serene.

plague *vb* afflict, annoy, badger, bore, bother, pester, chafe, disquiet, distress, disturb, embarrass, harass, fret, gall, harry, hector, incommode, irritate, molest, perplex, tantalize, tease, torment, trouble, vex, worry. * *n* disease, pestilence, pest; affliction, annoyance, curse, molestation, nuisance, thorn, torment, trouble, vexation, worry.

plain *adj* dull, even, flat, level, plane, smooth, uniform; clear, open, unencumbered, uninterrupted; apparent, certain, conspicuous, evident, distinct, glaring, manifest, notable, notorious, obvious, overt, palpable, patent, prominent, pronounced, staring, transparent, unmistakable, visible; explicit, intelligible, perspicuous, unambiguous, unequivocal; homely, ugly; aboveboard, blunt, crude, candid, direct, downright, frank, honest, ingenuous, open, openhearted, sincere, single-minded, straightforward, undesigning, unreserved, unsophisticated: artless, common, natural, simple, unaffected, unlearned; absolute, mere, unmistakable; clear, direct, easy; audible, articulate, definite; frugal, homely; unadorned, unfigured, unornamented, unvariegated. * *n* expanse, flats, grassland, pampas, plateau, prairie, steppe, stretch.

plaint *n* complaint, cry, lament, lamentation, moan, wail.

plaintiff *n* accuser, prosecutor.

plaintive *adj* dirge-like, doleful, grievous, melancholy, mournful, piteous, rueful, sad, sorrowful, woeful.

plan *vb* arrange, calculate, concert, delineate, devise, diagram, figure, premeditate, project, represent, study; concoct, conspire, contrive, design, digest, hatch, invent, manoeuvre, machinate, plot, prepare, scheme. * *n* chart, delineation, diagram, draught, drawing, layout, map, plot, sketch; arrangement, conception, contrivance, design, device, idea, method, programme, project, proposal, proposition, scheme, system; cabal, conspiracy, intrigue, machination; custom, process, way.

plane *vb* even, flatten, level, smooth; float, fly, glide, skate, skim, soar. * *adj* even, flat, horizontal, level, smooth. * *n* degree, evenness, level, levelness, smoothness; aeroplane, aircraft; groover, jointer, rabbet, rebate, scraper.

plant *vb* bed, sow; breed, engender; direct, point, set; colonize, furnish, inhabit, settle; establish, introduce; deposit, establish, fix, found, hide. * *n* herb, organism, vegetable; establishment, equipment, factory, works.

plaster *vb* bedaub, coat, cover, smear, spread. * *n* cement, gypsum, mortar, stucco.

plastic *adj* ductile, flexible, formative, mouldable, pliable, pliant, soft.

platitude *n* dullness, flatness, insipidity, mawkishness; banality, commonplace, truism; balderdash, chatter, flummery, fudge, jargon, moonshine, nonsense, palaver, stuff, trash, twaddle, verbiage.

plaudit *n* acclaim, acclamation, applause, approbation, clapping, commendation, encomium, praise.

plausible *adj* believable, credible, probable, reasonable; bland, fair-spoken, glib, smooth, suave.

play *vb* caper, disport, frisk, frolic, gambol, revel, romp, skip, sport; dally, flirt, idle, toy, trifle, wanton; flutter, hover, wave; act, impersonate, perform, personate, represent; bet, gamble, stake, wager. * *n* amusement, exercise, frolic, gambols, game, jest, pastime, prank, romp, sport; gambling, gaming; act, comedy, drama, farce, performance, tragedy; action, motion, movement; elbowroom, freedom, latitude, movement, opportunity, range, scope, sweep, swing, use.

playful *adj* frisky, frolicsome, gamesome, jolly, kittenish, merry, mirthful, rollicking, sportive; amusing, arch, humorous, lively, mischievous, roguish, skittish, sprightly, vivacious.

plead *vb* answer, appeal, argue, reason; argue, defend, discuss, reason, rejoin; beg, beseech, entreat, implore, petition, sue, supplicate.

pleasant *adj* acceptable, agreeable, delectable, delightful, enjoyable, grateful, gratifying, nice, pleasing, pleasurable, prepossessing, seemly, welcome; cheerful, enlivening, good-humoured, gracious, likable, lively, merry, sportive, sprightly, vivacious; amusing, facetious, humorous, jocose, jocular, sportive, witty.

please *vb* charm, delight, elate, gladden, gratify, pleasure, rejoice; content, oblige, satisfy; choose, like, prefer.

pleasure *n* cheer, comfort, delight, delectation, elation, enjoyment, exhilaration, joy, gladness, gratifying, gusto, relish, satisfaction, solace; amusement, diversion, entertainment, indulgence, refreshment, treat; gratification, luxury, sensuality, voluptuousness; choice, desire, preference, purpose, will, wish; favour, kindness.

plebeian *adj* base, common, ignoble, low, lowborn, mean, obscure, popular, vulgar. * *n* commoner, peasant, proletarian.

pledge *vb* hypothecate, mortgage, pawn, plight;

affiance, bind, contract, engage, plight, promise. * *n* collateral, deposit, gage, pawn; earnest, guarantee, security; hostage, security.

plenipotentiary *n* ambassador, envoy, legate, minister.

plenitude *n* abundance, completeness, fullness, plenteousness, plentifulness, plenty, plethora, profusion, repletion.

plentiful *adj* abundant, ample, copious, full, enough, exuberant, fruitful, luxuriant, plenteous, productive, sufficient.

plenty *n* abundance, adequacy, affluence, amplitude, copiousness, enough, exuberance, fertility, fruitfulness, fullness, overflow, plenteousness, plentifulness, plethora, profusion, sufficiency, supply.

pleonastic *adj* circumlocutory, diffuse, redundant, superfluous, tautological, verbose, wordy.

plethora *n* fullness, plenitude, repletion; excess, redundance, redundancy, superabundance, superfluity, surfeit.

pliable *adj* flexible, limber, lithe, lithesome, pliable, pliant, supple; adaptable, compliant, docile, ductile, facile, manageable, obsequious, tractable, yielding.

plight[1] *n* case, category, complication, condition, dilemma, imbroglio, mess, muddle, pass, predicament, scrape, situation, state, strait.

plight[2] *vb* avow, contract, covenant, engage, honour, pledge, promise, propose, swear, vow. * *n* avowal, contract, covenant, oath, pledge, promise, troth, vow, word; affiancing, betrothal, engagement.

plod *vb* drudge, lumber, moil, persevere, persist, toil, trudge.

plot[1] *vb* connive, conspire, intrigue, machinate, scheme; brew, concoct, contrive, devise, frame, hatch, compass, plan, project; chart, map. * *n* blueprint, chart, diagram, draft, outline, plan, scenario, skeleton; cabal, combination, complicity, connivance, conspiracy, intrigue, plan, project, scheme, stratagem; script, story, subject, theme, thread, topic.

plot[2] *n* field, lot, parcel, patch, piece, plat, section, tract.

pluck[1] *vb* cull, gather, pick; jerk, pull, snatch, tear, tug, twitch.

pluck[2] *n* backbone, bravery, courage, daring, determination, energy, force, grit, hardihood, heroism, indomitability, indomitableness, manhood, mettle, nerve, resolution, spirit, valour.

plump[1] *adj* bonny, bouncing, buxom, chubby, corpulent, fat, fleshy, full-figured, obese, portly, rotund, round, sleek, stout, well-rounded; distended, full, swollen, tumid.

plump[2] *vb* dive, drop, plank, plop, plunge, plunk, put; choose, favour, support * *adj* blunt, complete, direct, downright, full, unqualified, unreserved.

plunder *vb* desolate, despoil, devastate, fleece, forage, harry, loot, maraud, pillage, raid, ransack, ravage, rifle, rob, sack, spoil, spoliate, plunge. * *n* freebooting, devastation, harrying, marauding, rapine, robbery, sack; booty, pillage, prey, spoil.

ply[1] *vb* apply, employ, exert, manipulate, wield; exercise, practise; assail, belabour, beset, press; importune, solicit, urge; offer, present.

ply[2] *n* fold, layer, plait, twist; bent, bias, direction, turn.

pocket *vb* appropriate, steal; bear, endure, suffer, tolerate. * *n* cavity, cul-de-sac, hollow, pouch, receptacle.

poignant *adj* bitter, intense, penetrating, pierce, severe, sharp; acrid, biting, mordacious, piquant, prickling, pungent, sharp, stinging; caustic, irritating, keen, mordant, pointed, satirical, severe.

point *vb* acuminate, sharpen; aim, direct, level; designate indicate, show; punctuate. * *n* apex, needle, nib, pin, prong, spike, stylus, tip; cape, headland, projection, promontory; eve, instant, moment, period, verge; place, site, spot, stage, station; condition, degree, grade, state; aim, design, end, intent, limit, object, purpose; nicety, pique, punctilio, trifle; position, proposition, question, text, theme, thesis; aspect, matter, respect; characteristic, peculiarity, trait; character, mark, stop; dot, jot, speck; epigram, quip, quirk, sally, witticism; poignancy, sting.

point-blank *adj* categorical, direct, downright, explicit, express, plain, straight. * *adv* categorically, directly, flush, full, plainly, right, straight.

pointless *adj* blunt, obtuse; aimless, dull, flat, fruitless, futile, meaningless, vague, vapid, stupid.

poise *vb* balance, float, hang, hover, support, suspend. * *n* aplomb, balance, composure, dignity, equanimity, equilibrium, equipoise, serenity.

poison *vb* adulterate, contaminate, corrupt, defile, embitter, envenom, impair, infect, intoxicate, pollute, taint, vitiate. * *adj* deadly, lethal, poisonous, toxic. * *n* bane, canker, contagion, pest, taint, toxin, venom, virulence, virus.

poisonous *adj* baneful, corruptive, deadly, fatal, noxious, pestiferous, pestilential, toxic, venomous.

poke *vb* jab, jog, punch, push, shove, thrust; interfere, meddle, pry, snoop. * *n* jab, jog, punch, push, shove, thrust; bag, pocket, pouch, sack.

pole[1] *n* caber, mast, post, rod, spar, staff, stick; bar, beam, pile, shaft; oar, paddle, scull.

pole[2] *n* axis, axle, hub, pivot, spindle.

poles *npl* antipodes, antipoles, counterpoles, opposites.

policy *n* administration, government, management, rule; plan, plank, platform, role; art, address, cunning, discretion, prudence, shrewdness, skill, stratagem, strategy, tactics; acumen, astuteness, wisdom, wit.

polish *vb* brighten, buff, burnish, furbish, glaze, gloss, scour, shine, smooth; civilize, refine. * *n* brightness, brilliance, brilliancy, lustre, splendour; accomplishment, elegance, finish, grace, refinement.

polished *adj* bright, burnished, glossed, glossy, lustrous, shining, smooth; accomplished, cultivated, elegant, finished, graceful, polite, refined.

polite *adj* attentive, accomplished, affable, chivalrous, civil, complaisant, courtly, courteous, cultivated, elegant, gallant, genteel, gentle, gentlemanly, gracious, mannerly, obliging, polished, refined, suave, urbane, well, well-bred, well-mannered.

politic *adj* civic, civil, political; astute, discreet, judicious, long-headed, noncommittal, provident, prudent, prudential, sagacious, wary, wise; artful, crafty, cunning, diplomatic, expedient, foxy, ingenious, intriguing, Machiavellian, shrewd, skilful, sly, subtle, strategic, timeserving, unscrupulous, wily; well-adapted, well-devised.

political *adj* civic, civil, national, politic, public.

pollute *vb* defile, foul, soil, taint; contaminate, corrupt, debase, demoralize, deprave, impair, infect, pervert, poison, stain, tarnish, vitiate; desecrate, profane; abuse, debauch, defile, deflower, dishonour, ravish, violate.

pollution *n* abomination, contamination, corruption, defilement, foulness, impurity, pollutedness, taint, uncleanness, vitiation.

poltroon *n* coward, crave, dastard, milksop, recreant, skulk, sneak.

pomp *n* display, flourish, grandeur, magnificence, ostentation, pageant, pageantry, parade, pompousness, pride, show, splendour, state, style.

pompous *adj* august, boastful, bombastic, dignified, gorgeous, grand, inflated, lofty, magisterial, ostentatious, pretentious, showy, splendid, stately, sumptuous, superb, vainglorious.

ponder *vb* cogitate, consider, contemplate, deliberate, examine, meditate, muse, reflect, study, weigh.

ponderous *adj* bulky, heavy, massive, weighty; dull, laboured, slow-moving; important, momentous; forcible, mighty.

poniard *n* dagger, dirk, stiletto.

poor *adj* indigent, necessitous, needy, pinched, straitened; destitute, distressed, embarrassed, impecunious, impoverished, insolvent, moneyless, penniless, poverty-stricken, reduced, seedy, unprosperous; emaciated, gaunt, spare, lank, lean, shrunk, skinny, spare, thin; barren, fruitless, sterile, unfertile, unfruitful, unproductive, unprolific; flimsy, inadequate, insignificant, insufficient, paltry, slender, slight, small, trifling, trivial, unimportant, valueless, worthless; decrepit, delicate, feeble, frail, infirm, unsound, weak; inferior, shabby, valueless, worthless; bad, beggarly, contemptible, despicable, humble, inferior, low, mean, pitiful, sorry; bald, cold, dry, dull, feeble, frigid, jejune, languid, meagre, prosaic, prosing, spiritless, tame, vapid, weak; ill-fated, ill-starred, inauspicious, indifferent, luckless, miserable, pitiable, unfavourable, unfortunate, unhappy, unlucky, wretched; deficient, imperfect, inadequate, insufficient, mediocre, scant, scanty; faulty, unsatisfactory; feeble.

populace *n* citizens, crowd, inhabitants, masses, people, public, throng.

popular *adj* lay, plebeian, public; comprehensible, easy, familiar, plain; acceptable, accepted, accredited, admired, approved, favoured, liked, pleasing, praised, received; common, current, prevailing, prevalent; cheap, inexpensive.

pore[1] *n* hole, opening, orifice, spiracle.

pore[2] *vb* brood, consider, dwell, examine, gaze, read, study.

porous *adj* honeycombed, light, loose, open, penetrable, perforated, permeable, pervious, sandy.

porridge *n* broth, gruel, mush, pap, pottage, soup.

port[1] *n* anchorage, harbour, haven, shelter; door, entrance, gate, passageway; embrasure, porthole.

port[2] *n* air, appearance, bearing, behaviour, carriage, demeanour, deportment, mien, presence.

portable *adj* convenient, handy, light, manageable, movable, portative, transmissible.

portend *vb* augur, betoken, bode, forebode, foreshadow, foretoken, indicate, presage, procrastinate, signify, threaten.

portent *n* augury, omen, presage, prognosis, sign, warning; marvel, phenomenon, wonder.

portion *vb* allot, distribute, divide, parcel; endow, supply. * *n* bit, fragment, morsel, part, piece, scrap, section; allotment, contingent, dividend, division, lot, measure, quantity, quota, ration, share; inheritance.

portly *adj* dignified, grand, imposing, magisterial, majestic, stately; bulky, burly, corpulent, fleshy, large, plump, round, stout.

portray *vb* act, draw, depict, delineate, describe, paint, picture, represent, pose, position, sketch.

pose *vb* arrange, place, set; bewilder, confound, dumbfound, embarrass, mystify, nonplus, perplex, place, puzzle, set, stagger; affect, attitudinize. * *n* attitude, posture; affectation, air, facade, mannerism, pretence, role.

position *vb* arrange, array, fix, locate, place, put, set, site, stand. * *n* locality, place, post, site, situation, spot, station; relation; attitude, bearing, posture; affirmation, assertion, doctrine, predication, principle, proposition, thesis; caste, dignity, honour, rank, standing, status; circumstance, condition, phase, place, state; berth, billet, incumbency, place, post, situation.

positive *adj* categorical, clear, defined, definite, direct, determinate, explicit, express, expressed, precise, unequivocal, unmistakable, unqualified; absolute, actual, real, substantial, true, veritable; assured, certain, confident, convinced, sure; decisive, incontrovertible, indisputable, indubitable, inescapable; imperative, unconditional, undeniable; decided, dogmatic, emphatic, obstinate, overbearing, overconfident, peremptory, stubborn, tenacious.

possess *vb* control, have, hold, keep, obsess, obtain, occupy, own, seize.

possession *n* monopoly, ownership, proprietorship; control, occupation, occupancy, retention, tenancy, tenure; bedevilment, lunacy, madness, obsession; (*pl*) assets, effects, estate, property, wealth.

possessor *n* owner, proprietor.

possible *adj* conceivable, contingent, imaginable, potential; accessible, feasible, likely, practical, practicable, workable.

possibly *adv* haply, maybe, mayhap, peradventure, perchance, perhaps.

post[1] *vb* advertise, announce, inform, placard, publish; brand, defame, disgrace, vilify; enter, slate, record, register. * *n* column, picket, pier, pillar, stake, support.

post[2] *vb* establish, fix, place, put, set, station. * *n* billet, employment, office, place, position, quarter, seat, situation, station.

post[3] *vb* drop, dispatch, mail. * *n* carrier, courier, express, mercury, messenger, postman; dispatch, haste, hurry, speed.

posterior *adj* after, ensuing, following, later, latter, postprandial, subsequent. * *n* back, buttocks, hind, hinder, rump.

posterity *n* descendants, offspring, progeny, seed; breed, brood, children, family, heirs, issue.

postpone *vb* adjourn, defer, delay, procrastinate, prorogue, retard.

postscript *n* addition, afterthought, appendix, supplement.

postulate *vb* assume, presuppose; beseech, entreat, solicit, supplicate. * *n* assumption, axiom, conjecture, hypothesis, proposition, speculation, supposition, theory.

posture *vb* attitudinize, pose. * *n* attitude, pose, position; condition, disposition, mood, phase, state.

pot *n* kettle, pan, saucepan, skillet; can, cup, mug, tankard; crock, jar, jug.

potency *n* efficacy, energy, force, intensity, might, power, strength, vigour; authority, control, influence, sway.

potent *adj* efficacious, forceful, forcible, intense, powerful, strong, virile; able, authoritative, capable, efficient, mighty, puissant, strong; cogent, influential.

potentate *n* emperor, king, monarch, prince, sovereign, ruler.

potential *adj* able, capable, inherent, latent, possible. * *n* ability, capability, dynamic, possibility, potentiality, power.

pother *vb* beset, bewilder, confound, confuse, embarrass, harass, perplex, pose, puzzle, tease. * *n* bustle, commotion, confusion, disturbance, flutter, fuss, huddle, hurly-burly, rumpus, tumult, turbulence, turmoil.

pound[1] *vb* beat, strike, thump; bray, bruise, comminute, crush, levigate, pulverize, triturate; confound, coop, enclose, impound.

pound[2] *n* enclosure, fold, pen.

pour *vb* cascade, emerge, flood, flow, gush, issue, rain, shower, stream.

pouting *adj* bad-tempered, cross, ill-humoured, moody, morose, sulky, sullen.

poverty *n* destitution, difficulties, distress, impecuniosity, impecuniousness, indigence, necessity, need, neediness, penury, privation, straits, want; beggary, mendicancy, pauperism, pennilessness; dearth, jejuneness, lack, scantiness, sparingness, meagreness; exiguity, paucity, poorness, smallness; humbleness, inferiority, lowliness; barrenness, sterility, unfruitfulness, unproductiveness.

power *n* ability, ableness, capability, cogency, competency, efficacy, faculty, might, potency, validity, talent; energy, force, strength, virtue; capacity, susceptibility; endowment, faculty, gift, talent; ascendancy, authoritativeness, authority, carte blanche, command, control, domination, dominion, government, influence, omnipotence, predominance, prerogative, pressure, proxy, puissance, rule, sovereignty, sway, warrant; governor, monarch, potentate, ruler, sovereign; army, host, troop.

powerful *adj* mighty, potent, puissant; able-bodied, herculean, muscular, nervous, robust, sinewy, strong, sturdy, vigorous, vivid; able, commanding, dominating, forceful, forcible, overpowering; cogent, effective, effectual, efficacious, efficient, energetic, influential, operative, valid.

practicable *adj* achievable, attainable, bearable, feasible, performable, possible, workable; operative, passable, penetrable.

practical *adj* hardheaded, matter-of-fact, pragmatic, pragmatical; able, experienced, practised, proficient, qualified, trained, skilled, thoroughbred, versed; effective, useful, virtual, workable.

practice *n* custom, habit, manner, method, repetition; procedure, usage, use; application, drill, exercise, pursuit; action, acts, behaviour, conduct, dealing, proceeding.

practise *vb* apply, do, exercise, follow, observe, perform, perpetrate, pursue.

practised *adj* able, accomplished, experienced, instructed, practical, proficient, qualified, skilled, thoroughbred, trained, versed.

pragmatic *adj* impertinent, intermeddling, interfering, intrusive, meddlesome, meddling, obtrusive, officious, over-busy; earthy, hard-headed, matter-of-fact, practical, pragmatical, realistic, sensible, stolid.

praise *vb* approbate, acclaim, applaud, approve, commend; celebrate, compliment, eulogize, extol, flatter, laud; adore, bless, exalt, glorify, magnify, worship. * *n* acclaim, approbation, approval, commendation; encomium, eulogy, glorification, laud, laudation, panegyric; exaltation, extolling, glorification, homage, tribute, worship; celebrity, distinction, fame, glory, honour, renown; desert, merit, praiseworthiness.

praiseworthy *adj* commendable, creditable, good, laudable, meritorious.

prank *n* antic, caper, escapade, frolic, gambol, trick.
prate *vb* babble, chatter, gabble, jabber, palaver, prattle, tattle. * *n* chatter, gabble, nonsense, palaver, prattle, twaddle.
pray *vb* ask, beg, beseech, conjure, entreat, implore, importune, invoke, petition, request, solicit, supplicate.
prayer *n* beseeching, entreaty, imploration, petition, request, solicitation, suit, supplication; adoration, devotion(s), litany, invocation, orison, praise, suffrage.
preach *vb* declare, deliver, proclaim, pronounce, publish; inculcate, press, teach, urge; exhort, lecture, moralize, sermonize.
preamble *n* foreword, introduction, preface, prelude, prologue.
precarious *adj* critical, doubtful, dubious, equivocal, hazardous, insecure, perilous, unassured, riskful, risky, uncertain, unsettled, unstable, unsteady.
precaution *n* care, caution, circumspection, foresight, forethought, providence, prudence, safeguard, wariness; anticipation, premonition, provision.
precautionary *adj* preservative, preventative, provident.
precede *vb* antedate, forerun, head, herald, introduce, lead, utter.
precedence *n* advantage, antecedence, lead, pre-eminence, preference, priority, superiority, supremacy.
precedent *n* antecedent, authority, custom, example, instance, model, pattern, procedure, standard, usage.
precept *n* behest, bidding, canon, charge, command, commandment, decree, dictate, edict, injunction, instruction, law, mandate, ordinance, ordination, order, regulation; direction, doctrine, maxim, principle, teaching, rubric, rule.
preceptor *n* instructor, lecturer, master, pedagogue, professor, schoolteacher, teacher, tutor.
precinct *n* border, bound, boundary, confine, environs, frontier, enclosure, limit, list, march, neighbourhood, purlieus, term, terminus; area, district.
precious *adj* costly, inestimable, invaluable, priceless, prized, valuable; adored, beloved, cherished, darling, dear, idolized, treasured; fastidious, overnice, over-refined, precise.
precipice *n* bluff, cliff, crag, steep.
precipitate *vb* advance, accelerate, dispatch, expedite, forward, further, hasten, hurry, plunge, press, quicken, speed. * *adj* hasty, hurried, headlong, impetuous, indiscreet, overhasty, rash, reckless; abrupt, sudden, violent.
precipitous *adj* abrupt, cliffy, craggy, perpendicular, uphill, sheer, steep.
precise *adj* accurate, correct, definite, distinct, exact, explicit, express, nice, pointed, severe, strict, unequivocal, well-defined; careful, scrupulous; ceremonious, finical, formal, prim, punctilious, rigid, starched, stiff.
precision *n* accuracy, correctness, definiteness, distinctness, exactitude, exactness, nicety, preciseness.
preclude *vb* bar, check, debar, hinder, inhibit, obviate, prevent, prohibit, restrain, stop.
precocious *adj* advanced, forward, overforward, premature.
preconcert *vb* concoct, prearrange, predetermine, premeditate, prepare.
precursor *n* antecedent, cause, forerunner, predecessor; harbinger, herald, messenger, pioneer; omen, presage, sign.
precursory *adj* antecedent, anterior, forerunning, precedent, preceding, previous, prior; initiatory, introductory, precursive, prefatory, preliminary, prelusive, prelusory, premonitory, preparatory, prognosticative.
predatory *adj* greedy, pillaging, plundering, predacious, rapacious, ravaging, ravenous, voracious.
predestination *n* doom, fate, foredoom, foreordainment, foreordination, necessity, predetermination, preordination.
predicament *n* attitude, case, condition, plight, position, posture, situation, state; corner, dilemma, emergency, exigency, fix, hole, impasse, mess, pass, pinch, push, quandary, scrape.
predict *vb* augur, betoken, bode, divine, forebode, forecast, foredoom, foresee, forespeak, foretell, foretoken, forewarn, portend, prognosticate, prophesy, read, signify, soothsay.
predilection *n* bent, bias, desire, fondness, inclination, leaning, liking, love, partiality, predisposition, preference, prejudice, prepossession.
predisposition *n* aptitude, bent, bias, disposition, inclination, leaning, proclivity, proneness, propensity, willingness.
predominant *adj* ascendant, controlling, dominant, overruling, prevailing, prevalent, reigning, ruling, sovereign, supreme.
predominate *vb* dominate, preponderate, prevail, rule.
pre-eminent *adj* chief, conspicuous, consummate, controlling, distinguished, excellent, excelling, paramount, peerless, predominant, renowned, superior, supreme, surpassing, transcendent, unequalled.
preface *vb* begin, introduce, induct, launch, open, precede. * *n* exordium, foreword, induction, introduction, preamble, preliminary, prelude, prelusion, premise, proem, prologue, prolusion.
prefatory *adj* antecedent, initiative, introductory, precursive, precursory, preliminary, prelusive, prelusory, preparatory, proemial.
prefer *vb* address, offer, present, proffer, tender; advance, elevate, promote, raise; adopt, choose, elect, fancy, pick, select, wish.
preference *n* advancement, choice, election, estimation, precedence, priority, selection.
preferment *n* advancement, benefice, dignity, elevation, exaltation, promotion.

pregnant *adj* big, enceinte, parturient; fraught, full, important, replete, significant, weighty; fecund, fertile, fruitful, generative, potential, procreant, procreative, productive, prolific.

prejudice *vb* bias, incline, influence, turn, warp; damage, diminish, hurt, impair, injure. * *n* bias, intolerance, partiality, preconception, predilection, prejudgement, prepossession, unfairness; damage, detriment, disadvantage, harm, hurt, impairment, injury, loss, mischief.

prejudiced *adj* biased, bigoted, influenced, one-sided, partial, partisan, unfair.

preliminary *adj* antecedent, initiatory, introductory, precedent, precursive, precursory, prefatory, prelusive, prelusory, preparatory, previous, prior, proemial. * *n* beginning, initiation, introduction, opening, preamble, preface, prelude, start.

prelude *n* introduction, opening, overture, prelusion, preparation, voluntary; exordium, preamble, preface, preliminary, proem.

premature *adj* hasty, ill-considered, precipitate, unmatured, unprepared, unripe, unseasonable, untimely.

premeditation *n* deliberation, design, forethought, intention, prearrangement, predetermination, purpose.

premise *vb* introduce, preamble, preface, prefix. * *n* affirmation, antecedent, argument, assertion, assumption, basis, foundation, ground, hypothesis, position, premiss, presupposition, proposition, support, thesis, theorem.

premium *n* bonus, bounty, encouragement, fee, gift, guerdon, meed, payment, prize, recompense, remuneration, reward; appreciation, enhancement.

premonition *n* caution, foreboding, foreshadowing, forewarning, indication, omen, portent, presage, presentiment, sign, warning.

preoccupied *adj* absent, absentminded, abstracted, dreaming, engrossed, inadvertent, inattentive, lost, musing, unobservant.

prepare *vb* adapt, adjust, fit, qualify; arrange, concoct, fabricate, make, order, plan, procure, provide.

preponderant *adj* outweighing, overbalancing, preponderating.

prepossessing *adj* alluring, amiable, attractive, bewitching, captivating, charming, engaging, fascinating, inviting, taking, winning.

preposterous *adj* absurd, excessive, exorbitant, extravagant, foolish, improper, irrational, monstrous, nonsensical, perverted, ridiculous, unfit, unreasonable, wrong.

prerogative *n* advantage, birthright, claim, franchise, immunity, liberty, privilege, right.

presage *vb* divine, forebode; augur, betoken, bode, foreshadow, foretell, foretoken, indicate, portend, predict, prognosticate, prophesy, signify, soothsay. * *n* augury, auspice, boding, foreboding, foreshowing, indication, omen, portent, prognostication, sign, token; foreknowledge, precognition, prediction, premonition, presentiment, prophecy.

prescribe *vb* advocate, appoint, command, decree, dictate, direct, enjoin, establish, institute, ordain, order.

presence *n* attendance, company, inhabitance, inhabitancy, nearness, neighbourhood, occupancy, propinquity, proximity, residence, ubiquity, vicinity; air, appearance, carriage, demeanour, mien, personality.

present[1] *adj* near; actual, current, existing, happening, immediate, instant, living; available, quick, ready; attentive, favourable. * *n* now, time being, today.

present[2] *n* benefaction, boon, donation, favour, gift, grant, gratuity, largesse, offering.

present[3] *vb* introduce, nominate; exhibit, offer; bestow, confer, give, grant; deliver, hand; advance, express, prefer, proffer, tender.

presentiment *n* anticipation, apprehension, foreboding, forecast, foretaste, forethought, prescience.

presently *adv* anon, directly, forthwith, immediately, shortly, soon.

preservation *n* cherishing, conservation, curing, maintenance, protection, support; safety, salvation, security; integrity, keeping, soundness.

preserve *vb* defend, guard, keep, protect, rescue, save, secure, shield; maintain, uphold, sustain, support; conserve, economize, husband, retain. * *n* comfit, compote, confection, confiture, conserve, jam, jelly, marmalade, sweetmeat; enclosure, warren.

preside *vb* control, direct, govern, manage, officiate.

press *vb* compress, crowd, crush, squeeze; flatten, iron, smooth; clasp, embrace, hug; force, compel, constrain; emphasize, enforce, enjoin, inculcate, stress, urge; hasten, hurry, push, rush; crowd, throng; entreat, importune, solicit. * *n* crowd, crush, multitude, throng; hurry, pressure, urgency; case, closet, cupboard, repository.

pressing *adj* constraining, critical, distressing, imperative, importunate, persistent, serious, urgent, vital.

pressure *n* compressing, crushing, squeezing; influence, force; compulsion, exigency, hurry, persuasion, press, stress, urgency; affliction, calamity, difficulty, distress, embarrassment, grievance, oppression, straits; impression, stamp.

prestidigitation *n* conjuring, juggling, legerdemain, sleight-of-hand.

prestige *n* credit, distinction, importance, influence, reputation, weight.

presume *vb* anticipate, apprehend, assume, believe, conjecture, deduce, expect, infer, surmise, suppose, think; consider, presuppose; dare, undertake, venture.

presumption *n* anticipation, assumption, belief, concession, conclusion, condition, conjecture, deduction, guess, hypothesis, inference, opinion, supposition, understanding; arrogance, assurance, audacity, boldness, brass, effrontery, forwardness, haughtiness, presumptuousness; probability.

presumptuous *adj* arrogant, assuming, audacious, bold, brash, forward, irreverent, insolent, intrusive, presuming; foolhardy, overconfident, rash.

pretence *n* affectation, cloak, colour, disguise, mask, semblance, show, simulation, veil, window-dressing; excuse, evasion, fabrication, feigning, makeshift, pretext, sham, subterfuge; claim, pretension.

pretend *vb* affect, counterfeit, deem, dissemble, fake, falsify, feign, sham, simulate; act, imagine, lie, profess; aspire, claim.

pretension *n* assertion, assumption, claim, demand, pretence; affectation, airs, conceit, ostentation, pertness, pretentiousness, priggishness, vanity.

pretentious *adj* affected, assuming, conceited, conspicuous, ostentatious, presuming, priggish, showy, tawdry, unnatural, vain.

preternatural *adj* abnormal, anomalous, extraordinary, inexplicable, irregular, miraculous, mysterious, odd, peculiar, strange, unnatural.

pretext *n* affectation, appearance, blind, cloak, colour, guise, mask, pretence, semblance, show, simulation, veil; excuse, justification, plea, vindication.

pretty *adj* attractive, beautiful, bonny, comely, elegant, fair, handsome, neat, pleasing, trim; affected, foppish. * *adv* fairly, moderately, quite, rather, somewhat.

prevail *vb* overcome, succeed, triumph, win; obtain, predominate, preponderate, reign, rule.

prevailing *adj* controlling, dominant, effectual, efficacious, general, influential, operative, overruling, persuading, predominant, preponderant, prevalent, ruling, successful.

prevalent *adj* ascendant, compelling, efficacious, governing, predominant, prevailing, successful, superior; extensive, general, rife, widespread.

prevaricate *vb* cavil, deviate, dodge, equivocate, evade, palter, pettifog, quibble, shift, shuffle, tergiversate.

prevent *vb* bar, check, debar, deter, forestall, help, hinder, impede, inhibit, intercept, interrupt, obstruct, obviate, preclude, prohibit, restrain, save, stop, thwart.

prevention *n* anticipation, determent, deterrence, deterrent, frustration, hindrance, interception, interruption, obstruction, preclusion, prohibition, restriction, stoppage.

previous *adj* antecedent, anterior, earlier, foregoing, foregone, former, precedent, preceding, prior.

prey *vb* devour, eat, feed on, live off; exploit, intimidate, terrorize; burden, distress, haunt, oppress, trouble, worry. * *n* booty, loot, pillage, plunder, prize, rapine, spoil; food, game, kill, quarry, victim; depredation, ravage.

price *vb* assess, estimate, evaluate, rate, value. * *n* amount, cost, expense, outlay, value; appraisal, charge, estimation, excellence, figure, rate, quotation, valuation, value, worth; compensation, guerdon, recompense, return, reward.

priceless *adj* dear, expensive, precious, inestimable, invaluable, valuable; amusing, comic, droll, funny, humorous, killing, rich.

prick *vb* perforate, pierce, puncture, stick; drive, goad, impel, incite, spur, urge; cut, hurt, mark, pain, sting, wound; hasten, post, ride. * *n* mark, perforation, point, puncture; prickle, sting, wound.

pride *vb* boast, brag, crow, preen, revel in. * *n* conceit, egotism, self-complacency, self-esteem, self-exaltation, self-importance, self-sufficiency, vanity; arrogance, assumption, disdain, haughtiness, hauteur, insolence, loftiness, lordliness, pomposity, presumption, superciliousness, vainglory; decorum, dignity, elevation, self-respect; decoration, glory, ornament, show, splendour.

priest *n* churchman, clergyman, divine, ecclesiastic, minister, pastor, presbyter.

prim *adj* demure, formal, nice, precise, prudish, starch, starched, stiff, strait-laced.

primary *adj* aboriginal, earliest, first, initial, original, prime, primitive, primeval, primordial, pristine; chief, main, principal; basic, elementary, fundamental, preparatory: radical.

prime[1] *adj* aboriginal, basic, first, initial, original, primal, primary, primeval, primitive, primordial, pristine; chief, foremost, highest, leading, main, paramount, principal; blooming, early; capital, cardinal, dominant, predominant; excellent, first-class, first-rate, optimal, optimum, quintessential, superlative; beginning, opening. * *n* beginning, dawn, morning, opening; spring, springtime, youth; bloom, cream, flower, height, heyday, optimum, perfection, quintessence, zenith.

prime[2] *vb* charge, load, prepare, undercoat; coach, groom, train, tutor.

primeval *adj* original, primitive, primordial, pristine.

primitive *adj* aboriginal, first, fundamental, original, primal, primary, prime, primitive, primordial, pristine; ancient, antiquated, crude, old-fashioned, quaint, simple, uncivilized, unsophisticated.

prince *n* monarch, potentate, ruler, sovereign; dauphin, heir apparent, infant; chief, leader, potentate.

princely *adj* imperial, regal, royal; august, generous, grand, liberal, magnanimous, magnificent, majestic, munificent, noble, pompous, splendid, superb, titled; dignified, elevated, high-minded, lofty, noble, stately.

principal *adj* capital, cardinal, chief, essential, first, foremost, highest, leading, main, pre-eminent, prime. * *n* chief, head, leader; head teacher, master.

principally *adv* chiefly, essentially, especially, mainly, particularly.
principle *n* cause, fountain, fountainhead, groundwork, mainspring, nature, origin, source, spring; basis, constituent, element, essence, substratum; assumption, axiom, law, maxim, postulation; doctrine, dogma, impulse, maxim, opinion, precept, rule, tenet, theory; conviction, ground, motive, reason; equity, goodness, honesty, honour, incorruptibility, integrity, justice, probity, rectitude, righteousness, trustiness, truth, uprightness, virtue, worth; faculty, power.
prink *vb* adorn, deck, decorate; preen, primp, spruce.
print *vb* engrave, impress, imprint, mark, stamp; issue, publish. * *n* book, periodical, publication; copy, engraving, photograph, picture; characters, font, fount, lettering, type, typeface.
prior *adj* antecedent, anterior, earlier, foregoing, precedent, preceding, precursory, previous, superior.
priority *n* antecedence, anteriority, precedence, pre-eminence, pre-existence, superiority.
priory *n* abbey, cloister, convent, monastery, nunnery.
prison *n* confinement, dungeon, gaol, jail, keep, lockup, penitentiary, reformatory; can, clink, cooler, jug.
pristine *adj* ancient, earliest, first, former, old, original, primary, primeval, primitive, primordial.
privacy *n* concealment, secrecy; retirement, retreat, seclusion, solitude.
private *adj* retired, secluded, sequestrated, solitary; individual, own, particular, peculiar, personal, special, unofficial; confidential, privy; clandestine, concealed, hidden, secret. * *n* GI, soldier, tommy.
privation *n* bereavement, deprivation, dispossession, loss; destitution, distress, indigence, necessity, need, want; absence, negation; degradation.
privilege *n* advantage, charter, claim, exemption, favour, franchise, immunity, leave, liberty, licence, permission, prerogative, right.
privy *adj* individual, particular, peculiar, personal, private, special; clandestine, secret; retired, sequestrated.
prize[1] *vb* appreciate, cherish, esteem, treasure, value.
prize[2] *adj* best, champion, first-rate, outstanding, winning. * *n* guerdon, honours, meed, premium, reward; cup, decoration, medal, laurels, palm, trophy; booty, capture, lot, plunder, spoil; advantage, gain, privilege.
probability *n* chance, prospect, likelihood, presumption; appearance, credibility, credibleness, likeliness, verisimilitude.
probable *adj* apparent, credible, likely, presumable, reasonable.
probably *adv* apparently, likely, maybe, perchance, perhaps, presumably, possibly, seemingly.
probation *n* essay, examination, ordeal, proof, test, trial; novitiate.
probe *vb* examine, explore, fathom, investigate, measure, prove, scrutinize, search, sift, sound, test, verify. * *n* examination, exploration, inquiry, investigation, scrutiny, study.
probity *n* candour, conscientiousness, equity, fairness, faith, goodness, honesty, honour, incorruptibility, integrity, justice, loyalty, morality, principle, rectitude, righteousness, sincerity, soundness, trustworthiness, truth, truthfulness, uprightness, veracity, virtue, worth.
problem *adj* difficult, intractable, uncontrollable, unruly. * *n* dilemma, dispute, doubt, enigma, exercise, proposition, puzzle, riddle, theorem.
problematic *adj* debatable, disputable, doubtful, dubious, enigmatic, problematical, puzzling, questionable, suspicious, uncertain, unsettled.
procedure *n* conduct, course, custom, management, method, operation, policy, practice, process; act, action, deed, measure, performance, proceeding, step, transaction.
proceed *vb* advance, continue, go, pass, progress; accrue, arise, come, emanate, ensue, flow, follow, issue, originate, result, spring.
proceeds *npl* balance, earnings, effects, gain, income, net, produce, products, profits, receipts, returns, yield.
process *vb* advance, deal with, fulfil, handle, progress; alter, convert, refine, transform. * *n* advance, course, progress, train; action, conduct, management, measure, mode, operation, performance, practice, procedure, proceeding, step, transaction, way; action, case, suit, trial; outgrowth, projection, protuberance.
procession *n* cavalcade, cortege, file, march, parade, retinue, train.
proclaim *vb* advertise, announce, blazon, broach, broadcast, circulate, cry, declare, herald, promulgate, publish, trumpet; ban, outlaw, proscribe.
proclamation *n* advertisement, announcement, blazon, declaration, promulgation, publication; ban, decree, edict, manifesto, ordinance.
proclivity *n* bearing, bent, bias, determination, direction, disposition, drift, inclination, leaning, predisposition, proneness, propensity, tendency, turn; aptitude, facility, readiness.
procrastinate *vb* adjourn, defer, delay, postpone, prolong, protract, retard; neglect, omit; lag, loiter.
procrastination *n* delay, dilatoriness, postponement, protraction, slowness, tardiness.
procreate *vb* beget, breed, engender, generate, produce, propagate.
procurable *adj* acquirable, compassable, obtainable.
procurator *n* agent, attorney, deputy, proctor, proxy, representative, solicitor.
procure *vb* acquire, gain, get, obtain; cause, compass, contrive, effect.
procurer *n* bawd, pander, pimp.

prodigal *adj* abundant, dissipated, excessive, extravagant, generous, improvident, lavish, profuse, reckless, squandering, thriftless, unthrifty, wasteful. * *n* spendthrift, squanderer, waster, wastrel.
prodigality *n* excess, extravagance, lavishness, profusion, squandering, unthriftiness, waste, wastefulness.
prodigious *adj* amazing, astonishing, astounding, extraordinary, marvellous, miraculous, portentous, remarkable, startling, strange, surprising, uncommon, wonderful, wondrous; enormous, huge, immense, monstrous, vast.
prodigy *n* marvel, miracle, phenomenon, portent, sign, wonder; curiosity, monster, monstrosity.
produce *vb* exhibit, show; bear, beget, breed, conceive, engender, furnish, generate, hatch, procreate, yield; accomplish, achieve, cause, create, effect, make, occasion, originate; accrue, afford, give, impart, make, render; extend, lengthen, prolong, protract; fabricate, fashion, manufacture. * *n* crop, fruit, greengrocery, harvest, product, vegetables, yield.
producer *n* creator, inventor, maker, originator; agriculturalist, farmer, greengrocer, husbandman, raiser.
product *n* crops, fruits, harvest, outcome, proceeds, produce, production, returns, yield; consequence, effect, fruit, issue, performance, production, result, work.
production *n* fruit, produce, product; construction, creation, erection, fabrication, making, performance; completion, fruition; birth, breeding, development, growth, propagation; opus, publication, work; continuation, extension, lengthening, prolongation.
productive *adj* copious, fertile, fruitful, luxuriant, plenteous, prolific, teeming; causative, constructive, creative, efficient, life-giving, producing.
proem *n* exordium, foreword, introduction, preface, prelims, prelude, prolegomena.
profane *vb* defile, desecrate, pollute, violate; abuse, debase. * *adj* blasphemous, godless, heathen, idolatrous, impious, impure, pagan, secular, temporal, unconsecrated, unhallowed, unholy, unsanctified, worldly, unspiritual; impure, polluted, unholy.
profanity *n* blasphemy, impiety, irreverence, profaneness, sacrilege.
profess *vb* acknowledge, affirm, allege, aver, avouch, avow, confess, declare, own, proclaim, state; affect, feign, pretend.
profession *n* acknowledgement, assertion, avowal, claim, declaration; avocation, evasion, pretence, pretension, protestation, representation; business, calling, employment, engagement, occupation, office, trade, vocation.
proffer *vb* offer, propose, propound, suggest, tender, volunteer. * *n* offer, proposal, suggestion, tender.
proficiency *n* advancement, forwardness, improvement; accomplishment, aptitude, competency, dexterity, mastery, skill.
proficient *adj* able, accomplished, adept, competent, conversant, dextrous, expert, finished, masterly, practised, skilled, skilful, thoroughbred, trained, qualified, well-versed. * *n* adept, expert, master, master-hand.
profit *vb* advance, benefit, gain, improve. * *n* aid, clearance, earnings, emolument, fruit, gain, lucre, produce, return; advancement, advantage, benefit, interest, perquisite, service, use, utility, weal.
profitable *adj* advantageous, beneficial, desirable, gainful, productive, useful; lucrative, remunerative.
profitless *adj* bootless, fruitless, unprofitable, useless, valueless, worthless.
profligate *adj* abandoned, corrupt, corrupted, degenerate, depraved, dissipated, dissolute, graceless, immoral, shameless, vicious, vitiated, wicked. * *n* debauchee, libertine, rake, reprobate, roué.
profound *adj* abysmal, deep, fathomless; heavy, undisturbed; erudite, learned, penetrating, sagacious, skilled; deeply felt, far-reaching, heartfelt, intense, lively, strong, touching, vivid; low, submissive; abstruse, mysterious, obscure, occult, subtle, recondite; complete, thorough.
profundity *n* deepness, depth, profoundness.
profuse *adj* abundant, bountiful, copious, excessive, extravagant, exuberant, generous, improvident, lavish, overabundant, plentiful, prodigal, wasteful.
profusion *n* abundance, bounty, copiousness, excess, exuberance, extravagance, lavishness, prodigality, profuseness, superabundance, waste.
progenitor *n* ancestor, forebear, forefather.
progeny *n* breed, children, descendants, family, issue, lineage, offshoot, offspring, posterity, race, scion, stock, young.
prognostic *adj* foreshadowing, foreshowing, foretokening. * *n* augury, foreboding, indication, omen, presage, prognostication, sign, symptom, token; foretelling, prediction, prophecy.
prognosticate *vb* foretell, predict, prophesy; augur, betoken, forebode, foreshadow, foreshow, foretoken, indicate, portend, presage.
prognostication *n* foreknowledge, foreshowing, foretelling, prediction, presage; augury, foreboding, foretoken, indication, portent, prophecy.
progress *vb* advance, continue, proceed; better, gain, improve, increase. * *n* advance, advancement, progression; course, headway, ongoing, passage; betterment, development, growth, improvement, increase, reform; circuit, procession.
prohibit *vb* debar, hamper, hinder, preclude, prevent; ban, disallow, forbid, inhibit, interdict.
prohibition *n* ban, bar, disallowance, embargo, forbiddance, inhibition, interdict, interdiction, obstruction, prevention, proscription, taboo, veto.

prohibitive *adj* forbidding, prohibiting, refraining, restrictive.
project *vb* cast, eject, fling, hurl, propel, shoot, throw; brew, concoct, contrive, design, devise, intend, plan, plot, purpose, scheme; delineate, draw, exhibit; bulge, extend, jut, protrude. * *n* contrivance, design, device, intention, plan, proposal, purpose, scheme.
projectile *n* bullet, missile, shell.
projection *n* delivery, ejection, emission, propulsion, throwing; contriving, designing, planning, scheming; bulge, extension, outshoot, process, prominence, protuberance, salience, saliency, salient, spur; delineation, map, plan.
proletarian *adj* mean, plebeian, vile, vulgar. * *n* commoner, plebeian.
proletariat *n* commonality, hoi polloi, masses, mob, plebs, working class.
prolific *adj* abundant, fertile, fruitful, generative, productive, teeming.
prolix *adj* boring, circumlocutory, discursive, diffuse, lengthy, long, long-winded, loose, prolonged, protracted, prosaic, rambling, tedious, tiresome, verbose, wordy.
prologue *n* foreword, introduction, preamble, preface, preliminary, prelude, proem.
prolong *vb* continue, extend, lengthen, protract, sustain; defer, postpone.
promenade *vb* saunter, walk. * *n* dance, stroll, walk; boulevard, esplanade, parade, walkway.
prominent *adj* convex, embossed, jutting, projecting, protuberant, raised, relieved; celebrated, conspicuous, distinguished, eminent, famous, foremost, influential, leading, main, noticeable, outstanding; conspicuous, distinctive, important, manifest, marked, principal, salient.
promiscuous *adj* confused, heterogeneous, indiscriminate, intermingled, mingled, miscellaneous, mixed; abandoned, dissipated, dissolute, immoral, licentious, loose, unchaste, wanton.
promise *vb* covenant, engage, pledge, subscribe, swear, underwrite, vow; assure, attest, guarantee, warrant; agree, bargain, engage, stipulate, undertake. * *n* agreement, assurance, contract, engagement, oath, parole, pledge, profession, undertaking, vow, word.
promising *adj* auspicious, encouraging, hopeful, likely, propitious.
promote *vb* advance, aid, assist, cultivate, encourage, further, help, promote; dignify, elevate, exalt, graduate, honour, pass, prefer, raise.
promotion *n* advancement, encouragement, furtherance; elevation, exaltation, preferment.
prompt *vb* actuate, dispose, impel, incite, incline, induce, instigate, stimulate, urge; remind; dictate, hint, influence, suggest. * *adj* active, alert, apt, quick, ready; forward, hasty; disposed, inclined, prone; early, exact, immediate, instant, precise, punctual, seasonable, timely. * *adv* apace, directly, forthwith, immediately, promptly. * *n* cue, hint, prompter, reminder, stimulus.
promptly *adv* apace, directly, expeditiously, forthwith, immediately, instantly, pronto, punctually, quickly, speedily, straightway, straightaway, summarily, swiftly.
promptness *n* activity, alertness, alacrity, promptitude, readiness, quickness.
promulgate *vb* advertise, announce, broadcast, bruit, circulate, declare, notify, proclaim, publish, spread, trumpet.
prone *adj* flat, horizontal, prostrate, recumbent; declivitous, inclined, inclining, sloping; apt, bent, disposed, inclined, predisposed, tending; eager, prompt, ready.
pronounce *vb* articulate, enunciate, frame, say, speak, utter; affirm, announce, assert, declare, deliver, state.
proof *adj* firm, fixed, impenetrable, stable, steadfast. * *n* essay, examination, ordeal, test, trial; attestation, certification, conclusion, conclusiveness, confirmation, corroboration, demonstration, evidence, ratification, substantiation, testimony, verification.
prop *vb* bolster, brace, buttress, maintain, shore, stay, support, sustain, truss, uphold. * *n* support, stay; buttress, fulcrum, pin, shore, strut.
propaganda *n* inculcation, indoctrination, promotion.
propagate *vb* continue, increase, multiply; circulate, diffuse, disseminate, extend, promote, promulgate, publish, spread, transmit; beget, breed, engender, generate, originate, procreate.
propel *vb* drive, force, impel, push, urge; cast, fling, hurl, project, throw.
propensity *n* aptitude, bent, bias, disposition, inclination, ply, proclivity, proneness, tendency.
proper *adj* individual, inherent, natural, original, particular, peculiar, special, specific; adapted, appropriate, becoming, befitting, convenient, decent, decorous, demure, fit, fitting, legitimate, meet, pertinent, respectable, right, seemly, suitable; accurate, correct, exact, fair, fastidious, formal, just, precise; actual, real.
property *n* attribute, characteristic, disposition, mark, peculiarity, quality, trait, virtue; appurtenance, assets, belongings, chattels, circumstances, effects, estate, goods, possessions, resources, wealth; ownership, possession, proprietorship, tenure; claim, copyright, interest, participation, right, title.
prophecy *n* augury, divination, forecast, foretelling, portent, prediction, premonition, presage, prognostication; exhortation, instruction, preaching.
prophesy *vb* augur, divine, foretell, predict, prognosticate.
propinquity *n* adjacency, contiguity, nearness, neighbourhood, proximity, vicinity; affinity, connection, consanguinity, kindred, relationship.
propitiate *vb* appease, atone, conciliate, intercede, mediate, pacify, reconcile, satisfy.
propitious *adj* benevolent, benign, friendly, gracious, kind, merciful; auspicious, encouraging,

favourable, fortunate, happy, lucky, opportune, promising, prosperous, thriving, timely, well-disposed.

proportion *vb* adjust, graduate, regulate; form, shape. * *n* arrangement, relation; adjustment, commensuration, dimension, distribution, symmetry; extent, lot, part, portion, quota, ratio, share.

proposal *n* design, motion, offer, overture, proffer, proposition, recommendation, scheme, statement, suggestion, tender.

propose *vb* move, offer, pose, present, propound, proffer, put, recommend, state, submit, suggest, tender; design, intend, mean, purpose.

proposition *vb* accost, proffer, solicit. * *n* offer, overture, project, proposal, suggestion, tender, undertaking; affirmation, assertion, axiom, declaration, dictum, doctrine, position, postulation, predication, statement, theorem, thesis.

proprietor *n* lord, master, owner, possessor, proprietary.

propriety *n* accuracy, adaptation, appropriation, aptness, becomingness, consonance, correctness, fitness, justness, reasonableness, rightness, seemliness, suitableness; conventionality, decency, decorum, demureness, fastidiousness, formality, modesty, properness, respectability.

prorogation *n* adjournment, continuance, postponement.

prosaic *adj* commonplace, dull, flat, humdrum, matter-of-fact, pedestrian, plain, prolix, prosing, sober, stupid, tame, tedious, tiresome, unentertaining, unimaginative, uninspired, uninteresting, unromantic, vapid.

proscribe *vb* banish, doom, exile, expel, ostracize, outlaw; exclude, forbid, interdict, prohibit; censure, condemn, curse, denounce, reject.

prosecute *vb* conduct, continue, exercise, follow, persist, pursue; arraign, indict, sue, summon.

prospect *vb* explore, search, seek, survey. * *n* display, field, landscape, outlook, perspective, scene, show, sight, spectacle, survey, view, vision, vista; picture, scenery; anticipation, calculation, contemplation, expectance, expectancy, expectation, foreseeing, foresight, hope, presumption, promise, trust; likelihood, probability.

prospectus *n* announcement, conspectus, description, design, outline, plan, programme, sketch, syllabus.

prosper *vb* aid, favour, forward, help; advance, flourish, grow rich, thrive, succeed; batten, increase.

prosperity *n* affluence, blessings, happiness, felicity, good luck, success, thrift, weal, welfare, well-being; boom, heyday.

prosperous *adj* blooming, flourishing, fortunate, golden, halcyon, rich, successful, thriving; auspicious, booming, bright, favourable, good, golden, lucky, promising, propitious, providential, rosy.

prostrate *vb* demolish, destroy, fell, level, overthrow, overturn, ruin; depress, exhaust, overcome, reduce. * *adj* fallen, prostrated, prone, recumbent, supine; helpless, powerless.

prostration *n* demolition, destruction, overthrow; dejection, depression, exhaustion.

prosy *adj* prosaic, unpoetic, unpoetical; dull, flat, jejune, stupid, tedious, tiresome, unentertaining, unimaginative, uninteresting.

protect *vb* cover, defend, guard, shield; fortify, harbour, house, preserve, save, screen, secure, shelter; champion, countenance, foster, patronize.

protector *n* champion, custodian, defender, guardian, patron, warden.

protest *vb* affirm, assert, asseverate, attest, aver, avow, declare, profess, testify; demur, expostulate, object, remonstrate, repudiate. * *n* complaint, declaration, disapproval, objection, protestation.

prototype *n* archetype, copy, exemplar, example, ideal, model, original, paradigm, precedent, protoplast, type.

protract *vb* continue, extend, lengthen, prolong; defer, delay, postpone.

protrude *vb* beetle, bulge, extend, jut, project.

protuberance *n* bulge, bump, elevation, excrescence, hump, lump, process, projection, prominence, roundness, swelling, tumour.

proud *adj* assuming, conceited, contended, egotistical, overweening, self-conscious, self-satisfied, vain; arrogant, boastful, haughty, high-spirited, highly strung, imperious, lofty, lordly, presumptuous, supercilious, uppish, vainglorious.

prove *vb* ascertain, conform, demonstrate, establish, evidence, evince, justify, manifest, show, substantiate, sustain, verify; assay, check, examine, experiment, test, try.

proverb *n* adage, aphorism, apothegm, byword, dictum, maxim, precept, saw, saying.

proverbial *adj* acknowledged, current, notorious, unquestioned.

provide *vb* arrange, collect, plan, prepare, procure; gather, keep, store; afford, contribute, feed, furnish, produce, stock, supply, yield; cater, purvey; agree, bargain, condition, contract, covenant, engage, stipulate.

provided, providing *conj* granted, if, supposing.

provident *adj* careful, cautious, considerate, discreet, farseeing, forecasting, forehanded, foreseeing, prudent; economical, frugal, thrifty.

province *n* district, domain, region, section, territory, tract; colony, dependency; business, calling, capacity, charge, department, duty, employment, function, office, part, post, sphere; department, division, jurisdiction.

provincial *adj* annexed, appendant, outlying; bucolic, countrified, rude, rural, rustic, unpolished, unrefined; insular, local, narrow. * *n* peasant, rustic, yokel.

provision *n* anticipation, providing; arrangement, care, preparation, readiness; equipment, fund, grist, hoard, reserve, resources, stock, store, supplies, supply; clause, condition, prerequisite, proviso, reservation, stipulation.

provisions *npl* eatables, fare, food, provender, supplies, viands, victuals.

proviso *n* clause, condition, provision, stipulation.

provocation *n* incentive, incitement, provocativeness, stimulant, stimulus; affront, indignity, insult, offence; angering, vexation.

provoke *vb* animate, arouse, awaken, excite, impel, incite, induce, inflame, instigate, kindle, move, rouse, stimulate; affront, aggravate, anger, annoy, chafe, enrage, exacerbate, exasperate, incense, infuriate, irritate, nettle, offend, pique, vex; cause, elicit, evoke, instigate, occasion, produce, promote.

provoking *adj* aggravating, annoying, exasperating, irritating, offensive, tormenting, vexatious, vexing.

prowess *n* bravery, courage, daring, fearlessness, gallantry, heroism, intrepidity, valour; aptitude, dexterity, expertness, facility.

proximity *n* adjacency, contiguity, nearness, neighbourhood, propinquity, vicinage, vicinity.

proxy *n* agent, attorney, commissioner, delegate, deputy, lieutenant, representative, substitute.

prudence *n* carefulness, caution, circumspection, common sense, considerateness, discretion, forecast, foresight, judgment, judiciousness, policy, providence, sense, tact, wariness, wisdom.

prudent *adj* cautious, careful, circumspect, considerate, discreet, foreseeing, heedful, judicious, politic, provident, prudential, wary, wise.

prudish *adj* coy, demure, modest, precise, prim, reserved, strait-laced.

prune *vb* abbreviate, clip, cut, dock, lop, thin, trim; dress, preen.

prurient *adj* covetous, craving, desiring, hankering, itching, lascivious, libidinous, longing, lustful.

pry *vb* examine, ferret, inspect, investigate, peep, peer, question, scrutinize, search; force, lever, prise.

public *adj* civil, common, countrywide, general, national, political, state; known, notorious, open, popular, published, well-known. * *n* citizens, community, country, everyone, general public, masses, nation, people, population; audience, buyers, following, supporters.

publication *n* advertisement, announcement, disclosure, divulgement, divulgence, proclamation, promulgation, report; edition, issue, issuance, printing.

publicity *n* daylight, currency, limelight, notoriety, spotlight; outlet, vent.

publish *vb* advertise, air, bruit, announce, blaze, blazon, broach, communicate, declare, diffuse, disclose, disseminate, impart, placard, post, proclaim, promulgate, reveal, tell, utter, vent, ventilate.

pucker *vb* cockle, contract, corrugate, crease, crinkle, furrow, gather, pinch, purse, shirr, wrinkle. * *n* crease, crinkle, fold, furrow, wrinkle.

puerile *adj* boyish, childish, infantile, juvenile, youthful; foolish, frivolous, idle, nonsensical, petty, senseless, silly, simple, trifling, trivial, weak.

puffy *adj* distended, swelled, swollen, tumid, turgid; bombastic, extravagant, inflated, pompous.

pugnacious *adj* belligerent, bellicose, contentious, fighting, irascible, irritable, petulant, quarrelsome.

puissant *adj* forcible, mighty, potent, powerful, strong.

pull *vb* drag, draw, haul, row, tow, tug; cull, extract, gather, pick, pluck; detach, rend, tear, wrest. * *n* pluck, shake, tug, twitch, wrench; contest, struggle; attraction, gravity, magnetism; graft, influence, power.

pulsate *vb* beat, palpitate, pant, throb, thump, vibrate.

pulverize *vb* bruise, comminute, grind, levigate, triturate.

pun *vb* assonate, alliterate, play on words. * *n* assonance, alliteration, clinch, conceit, double-meaning, paranomasia, play on words, quip, rhyme, witticism, wordplay.

punctilious *adj* careful, ceremonious, conscientious, exact, formal, nice, particular, precise, punctual, scrupulous, strict.

punctual *adj* exact, nice, precise, punctilious; early, prompt, ready, regular, seasonable, timely.

puncture *vb* bore, penetrate, perforate, pierce, prick. * *n* bite, hole, sting, wound.

pungent *adj* acid, acrid, biting, burning, caustic, hot, mordant, penetrating, peppery, piercing, piquant, prickling, racy, salty, seasoned, sharp, smart, sour, spicy, stimulating, stinging; acute, acrimonious, cutting, distressing, irritating, keen, painful, peevish, poignant, pointed, satirical, severe, tart, trenchant, waspish.

punish *vb* beat, castigate, chasten, chastise, correct, discipline, flog, lash, scourge, torture, whip.

punishment *n* castigation, chastening, chastisement, correction, discipline, infliction, retribution, scourging, trial; judgment, nemesis, penalty.

puny *adj* feeble, inferior, weak; dwarf, dwarfish, insignificant, diminutive, little, petty, pygmy, small, stunted, tiny, underdeveloped, undersized.

pupil *n* beginner, catechumen, disciple, learner, neophyte, novice, scholar, student, tyro.

pupillage *n* minority, nonage, tutelage, wardship.

puppet *n* doll, image, manikin, marionette; cat's-paw, pawn, tool.

purchase *vb* buy, gain, get, obtain, pay for, procure; achieve, attain, earn, win. * *n* acquisition, buy, gain, possession, property; advantage, foothold, grasp, hold, influence, support.

pure *adj* clean, clear, fair, immaculate, spotless, stainless, unadulterated, unalloyed, unblemished, uncorrupted, undefiled, unpolluted, unspotted, unstained, unsullied, untainted, untarnished; chaste, continent, guileless, guiltless, holy, honest, incorrupt, innocent, modest, sincere, true, uncorrupt, upright, virgin, virtuous; genuine, perfect, real, simple, true, unadorned; absolute, essential, mere, sheer, thorough; classic, classical.

purge *vb* cleanse, clear, purify; clarify, defecate, evacuate; deterge, scour; absolve, pardon, shrive. * *n* elimination, eradication, expulsion, removal, suppression; cathartic, emetic, enema, laxative, physic.

purify *vb* clean, cleanse, clear, depurate, expurgate, purge, refine, wash; clarify, fine.

puritanical *adj* ascetic, narrow-minded, overscrupulous, prim, prudish, rigid, severe, strait-laced, strict.

purity *n* clearness, fineness; cleanness, correctness, faultlessness, immaculacy, immaculateness; guilelessness, guiltlessness, holiness, honesty, innocence, integrity, piety, simplicity, truth, uprightness, virtue; excellence, genuineness; homogeneity, simpleness; chasteness, chastity, continence, modesty, pudency, virginity.

purlieus *npl* borders, bounds, confines, environs, limits, neighbourhood, outskirts, precincts, suburbs, vicinage, vicinity.

purloin *vb* abstract, crib, filch, pilfer, rob, steal, thieve.

purport *vb* allege, assert, claim, maintain, pretend, profess; denote, express, imply, indicate, mean, signify, suggest. * *n* bearing, current, design, drift, gist, import, intent, meaning, scope, sense, significance, signification, spirit, tendency, tenor.

purpose *vb* contemplate, design, intend, mean, meditate; determine, resolve. * *n* aim, design, drift, end, intent, intention, object, resolution, resolve, view; plan, project; meaning, purport, sense; consequence, effect.

pursue *vb* chase, dog, follow, hound, hunt, shadow, track; conduct, continue, cultivate, maintain, practise, prosecute; seek, strive; accompany, attend.

pursuit *n* chase, hunt, race; conduct, cultivation, practice, prosecution, pursuance; avocation, calling, business, employment, fad, hobby, occupation, vocation.

pursy *adj* corpulent, fat, fleshy, plump, podgy, pudgy, short, thick; short-breathed, short-winded; opulent, rich.

purview *n* body, compass, extent, limit, reach, scope, sphere, view.

push *vb* elbow, crowd, hustle, impel, jostle, shoulder, shove, thrust; advance, drive, hurry, propel, urge; importune, persuade, tease. * *n* pressure, thrust; determination, perseverance; emergency, exigency, extremity, pinch, strait, test, trial; assault, attack, charge, endeavour, onset.

pusillanimous *adj* chicken, chicken-hearted, cowardly, dastardly, faint-hearted, feeble, lily-livered, mean-spirited, spiritless, timid, recreant, timorous, weak.

pustule *n* abscess, blain, blister, blotch, boil, fester, gathering, pimple, sore, ulcer.

put *vb* bring, collocate, deposit, impose, lay, locate, place, set; enjoin, impose, inflict, levy; offer, present, propose, state; compel, constrain, force, oblige; entice, incite, induce, urge; express, utter.

putative *adj* deemed, reckoned, reported, reputed, supposed.

putrefy *vb* corrupt, decay, decompose, fester, rot, stink.

putrid *adj* corrupt, decayed, decomposed, fetid, rank, rotten, stinking.

puzzle *vb* bewilder, confound, confuse, embarrass, gravel, mystify, nonplus, perplex, pose, stagger; complicate, entangle.* *n* conundrum, enigma, labyrinth, maze, paradox, poser, problem, riddle; bewilderment, complication, confusion, difficulty, dilemma, embarrassment, mystification, perplexity, point, quandary, question.

pygmy *adj* diminutive, dwarf, dwarfish, Lilliputian, little, midget, stunted, tiny. * *n* dwarf, Lilliputian, midget.

Q

quack[1] *vb, n* cackle, cry, squeak.
quack[2] *adj* fake, false, sham. * *n* charlatan, empiric, humbug, impostor, mountebank, pretender.
quadruple *adj* fourfold, quadruplicate.
quagmire *n* bog, fen, marsh, morass, slough, swamp; difficulty, impasse, muddle, predicament.
quail *vb* blench, cower, droop, faint, flinch, shrink, tremble.
quaint *adj* antiquated, antique, archaic, curious, droll, extraordinary, fanciful, odd, old-fashioned, queer, singular, uncommon, unique, unusual; affected, fantastic, far-fetched, whimsical; artful, ingenious.
quake *vb* quiver, shake, shiver, shudder; move, vibrate. * *n* earthquake, shake, shudder.
qualification *n* ability, accomplishment, capability, competency, eligibility, fitness, suitability; condition, exception, limitation, modification, proviso, restriction, stipulation; abatement, allowance, diminution, mitigation.
qualified *adj* accomplished, certificated, certified, competent, fitted, equipped, licensed, trained; adapted, circumscribed, conditional, limited, modified, restricted.
qualify *vb* adapt, capacitate, empower, entitle, equip, fit; limit, modify, narrow, restrain, restrict; abate, assuage, ease, mitigate, moderate, reduce, soften; diminish, modulate, temper, regulate, vary.
quality *n* affection, attribute, characteristic, colour, distinction, feature, flavour, mark, nature, peculiarity, property, singularity, timbre, tinge, trait; character, condition, disposition, humour, mood, temper; brand, calibre, capacity, class, description, excellence, grade, kind, rank, sort, stamp, standing, station, status, virtue; aristocracy, gentility, gentry, noblesse, nobility.
qualm *n* agony, pang, throe; nausea, queasiness, sickness; compunction, remorse, uneasiness, twinge.
quandary *n* bewilderment, difficulty, dilemma, doubt, embarrassment, perplexity, pickle, plight, predicament, problem, puzzle, strait, uncertainty.
quantity *n* content, extent, greatness, measure, number, portion, share, size; aggregate, batch, amount, bulk, lot, mass, quantum, store, sum, volume; duration, length.
quarrel *vb* altercate, bicker, brawl, carp, cavil, clash, contend, differ, dispute, fight, jangle, jar, scold, scuffle, spar, spat, squabble, strive, wrangle. * *n* altercation, affray, bickering, brawl, breach, breeze, broil, clash, contention, contest, controversy, difference, disagreement, discord, dispute, dissension, disturbance, feud, fight, fray, imbroglio, jar, miff, misunderstanding, quarrelling, row, rupture, spat, squabble, strife, tiff, tumult, variance, wrangle.
quarrelsome *adj* argumentative, choleric, combative, contentious, cross, discordant, disputatious, dissentious, fiery, irascible, irritable, petulant, pugnacious, ugly, wranglesome.
quarter *vb* billet, lodge, post, station; allot, furnish, share. * *n* abode, billet, dwelling, habitation, lodgings, posts, quarters, stations; direction, district, locality, location, lodge, position, region, territory; clemency, mercy, mildness.
quash *vb* abate, abolish, annul, cancel, invalidate, nullify, overthrow; crush, extinguish, repress, stop, subdue, suppress.
queasy *adj* nauseated, pukish, seasick, sick, squeamish.
queer *vb* botch, harm, impair, mar, spoil. * *adj* curious, droll, extraordinary, fantastic, odd, peculiar, quaint, singular, strange, uncommon, unusual, whimsical; gay, homosexual.
quell *vb* conquer, crush, overcome, overpower, subdue; bridle, check, curb, extinguish, lay, quench, rein in, repress, restrain, stifle; allay, calm, compose, hush, lull, pacify, quiet, quieten, still, tranquillize; alleviate, appease, blunt, deaden, dull, mitigate, mollify, soften, soothe.
quench *vb* extinguish, put out; check, destroy, repress, satiate, stifle, still, suppress; allay, cool, dampen, extinguish, slake.
querulous *adj* bewailing, complaining, cross, discontented, dissatisfied, fretful, fretting, irritable, mourning, murmuring, peevish, petulant, plaintive, touchy, whining.
query *vb* ask, enquire, inquire, question; dispute, doubt. * *n* enquiry, inquiry, interrogatory, issue, problem, question.
quest *n* expedition, journey, search, voyage; pursuit, suit; examination, enquiry, inquiry; demand, desire, invitation, prayer, request, solicitation.
question *vb* ask, catechize, enquire, examine, inquire, interrogate, quiz, sound out; doubt, query; challenge, dispute. * *n* examination, enquiry,

inquiry, interpellation, interrogation; enquiry, inquiry, interrogatory, query; debate, discussion, disquisition, examination, investigation, issue, trial; controversy, dispute, doubt; motion, mystery, point, poser, problem, proposition, puzzle, topic.

questionable *adj* ambiguous, controversial, controvertible, debatable, doubtful, disputable, equivocal, problematic, problematical, suspicious, uncertain, undecided.

quibble *vb* cavil, equivocate, evade, prevaricate, shuffle. * *n* equivocation, evasion, pretence, prevarication, quirk, shift, shuffle, sophism, subtlety, subterfuge.

quick *adj* active, agile, alert, animated, brisk, lively, nimble, prompt, ready, smart, sprightly; expeditious, fast, fleet, flying, hurried, rapid, speedy, swift; adroit, apt, clever, dextrous, expert, skilful; choleric, hasty, impetuous, irascible, irritable, passionate, peppery, petulant, precipitate, sharp, unceremonious, testy, touchy, waspish; alive, animate, live, living.

quicken *vb* animate, energize, resuscitate, revivify, vivify; cheer, enliven, invigorate, reinvigorate, revive, whet; accelerate, dispatch, expedite, hasten, hurry, speed; actuate, excite, incite, kindle, refresh, sharpen, stimulate; accelerate, live, take effect.

quickly *adv* apace, fast, immediately, nimbly, quick, rapidly, readily, soon, speedily, swiftly.

quickness *n* celerity, dispatch, expedition, haste, rapidity, speed, swiftness, velocity; agility, alertness, activity, briskness, liveliness, nimbleness, promptness, readiness, smartness; adroitness, aptitude, aptness, dexterity, facility, knack; acumen, acuteness, keenness, penetration, perspicacity, sagacity, sharpness, shrewdness.

quiescent *adj* at rest, hushed, motionless, quiet, resting, still; calm, mute, placid, quiet, serene, still, tranquil, unagitated, undisturbed, unruffled.

quiet *adj* hushed, motionless, quiescent, still, unmoved; calm, contented, gentle, mild, meek, modest, peaceable, peaceful, placid, silent, smooth, tranquil, undemonstrative, unobtrusive, unruffled; patient; retired, secluded. * *n* calmness, peace, repose, rest, silence, stillness.

quieten *vb* arrest, discontinue, intermit, interrupt, still, stop, suspend; allay, appease, calm, compose, lull, pacify, sober, soothe, tranquillize; hush, silence; alleviate, assuage, blunt, dull, mitigate, moderate, mollify, soften.

quip *n* crank, flout, gibe, jeer, mock, quirk, repartee, retort, sarcasm, sally, scoff, sneer, taunt, witticism.

quit *vb* absolve, acquit, deliver, free, release; clear, deliver, discharge from, free, liberate, relieve; acquit, behave, conduct; carry through, perform; discharge, pay, repay, requite; relinquish, renounce, resign, stop, surrender; depart from, leave, withdraw from; abandon, desert, forsake, forswear. * *adj* absolved, acquitted, clear, discharged, free, released.

quite *adv* completely, entirely, exactly, perfectly, positively, precisely, totally, wholly.

quiver *vb* flicker, flutter, oscillate, palpitate, quake, play, shake, shiver, shudder, tremble, twitch, vibrate. * *n* shake, shiver, shudder, trembling.

quixotic *adj* absurd, chimerical, fanciful, fantastic, fantastical, freakish, imaginary, mad, romantic, utopian, visionary, wild.

quiz *vb* examine, question, test; peer at; banter, hoax, puzzle, ridicule. * *n* enigma, hoax, jest, joke, puzzle; jester, joker, hoax.

quota *n* allocation, allotment, apportionment, contingent, portion, proportion, quantity, share.

quotation *n* citation, clipping, cutting, extract, excerpt, reference, selection; estimate, rate, tender.

quote *vb* adduce, cite, excerpt, extract, illustrate, instance, name, repeat, take; estimate, tender.

R

rabble *n* commonality, horde, mob, populace, riffraff, rout, scum, trash.
rabid *adj* frantic, furious, mad, raging, wild; bigoted, fanatical, intolerant, irrational, narrow-minded, rampant.
race[1] *n* ancestry, breed, family, generation, house, kindred, line, lineage, pedigree, stock, strain; clan, folk, nation, people, tribe; breed, children, descendants, issue, offspring, progeny, stock.
race[2] *vb* career, compete, contest, course, hasten, hurry, run, speed. * *n* career, chase, competition, contest, course, dash, heat, match, pursuit, run, sprint; flavour, quality, smack, strength, taste.
rack *vb* agonize, distress, excruciate, rend, torment, torture, wring; exhaust, force, harass, oppress, strain, stretch, wrest. * *n* agony, anguish, pang, torment, torture; crib, manger; neck, crag; dampness, mist, moisture, vapour.
racket *n* clamour, clatter, din, dissipation, disturbance, fracas, frolic, hubbub, noise, outcry, tumult, uproar; game, graft, scheme, understanding.
racy *adj* flavoursome, palatable, piquant, pungent, rich, spicy, strong; forcible, lively, pungent, smart, spirited, stimulating, vigorous, vivacious.
radiance *n* brightness, brilliance, brilliancy, effluence, efflux, emission, glare, glitter, light, lustre, refulgence, resplendence, shine, splendour.
radiant *adj* beaming, brilliant, effulgent, glittering, glorious, luminous, lustrous, resplendent, shining, sparkling, splendid; ecstatic, happy, pleased.
radiate *vb* beam, gleam, glitter, shine; emanate, emit; diffuse, spread.
radical *adj* constitutional, deep-seated, essential, fundamental, ingrained, inherent, innate, native, natural, organic, original, uncompromising; original, primitive, simple, uncompounded, underived; complete, entire, extreme, fanatic, insurgent, perfect, rebellious, thorough, total. * *n* etymon, radix, root; fanatic, revolutionary.
rage *vb* bluster, boil, chafe, foam, fret, fume, ravage, rave. * *n* excitement, frenzy, fury, madness, passion, rampage, raving, vehemence, wrath; craze, fashion, mania, mode, style, vogue.
ragged *adj* rent, tattered, torn; contemptible, mean, poor, shabby; jagged, rough, rugged, shaggy, uneven; discordant, dissonant, inharmonious, unmusical.
raid *vb* assault, forage, invade, pillage, plunder. * *n* attack, foray, invasion, inroad, plunder.
rail *vb* abuse, censure, inveigh, scoff, scold, sneer, upbraid.
raillery *n* banter, chaff, irony, joke, pleasantry, ridicule, satire.
raiment *n* array, apparel, attire, clothes, clothing, costume, dress, garb, garments, habiliment, habit, vestments, vesture.
rain *vb* drizzle, drop, fall, pour, shower, sprinkle, teem; bestow, lavish. * *n* cloudburst, downpour, drizzle, mist, shower, sprinkling.
raise *vb* boost, construct, erect, heave, hoist, lift, uplift, upraise, rear; advance, elevate, ennoble, exalt, promote; aggravate, amplify, augment, enhance, heighten, increase, invigorate; arouse, awake, cause, effect, excite, originate, produce, rouse, stir up, occasion, start; assemble, collect, get, levy, obtain; breed, cultivate, grow, propagate, rear; ferment, leaven, work.
rake[1] *vb* collect, comb, gather, scratch; ransack, scour.
rake[2] *n* debauchee, libertine, profligate, roué.
rakish *adj* debauched, dissipated, dissolute, lewd, licentious; cavalier, jaunty.
ramble *vb* digress, maunder, range, roam, rove, saunter, straggle, stray, stroll, wander. * *n* excursion, rambling, roving, tour, trip, stroll, wandering.
rambling *adj* discursive, irregular; straggling, strolling, wandering.
ramification *n* arborescence, branching, divarication, forking, radiation; branch, division, offshoot, subdivision; consequence, upshot.
ramify *vb* branch, divaricate, extend, separate.
rampant *adj* excessive, exuberant, luxuriant, rank, wanton; boisterous, dominant, headstrong, impetuous, predominant, raging, uncontrollable, unbridled, ungovernable, vehement, violent.
rampart *n* bulwark, circumvallation, defence, fence, fortification, guard, security, wall.
rancid *adj* bad, fetid, foul, fusty, musty, offensive, rank, sour, stinking, tainted.
rancorous *adj* bitter, implacable, malevolent, malicious, malign, malignant, resentful, spiteful, vindictive, virulent.
rancour *n* animosity, antipathy, bitterness, enmity, gall, grudge, hate, hatred, ill-will, malevolence, malice, malignity, spite, venom, vindictiveness.
random *adj* accidental, casual, chance, fortuitous,

haphazard, irregular, stray, wandering.
range *vb* course, cruise, extend, ramble, roam, rove, straggle, stray, stroll, wander; bend, lie, run; arrange, class, dispose, rank. * *n* file, line, row, rank, tier; class, kind, order, sort; excursion, expedition, ramble, roving, wandering; amplitude, bound, command, compass, distance, extent, latitude, reach, scope, sweep, view; register.
rank[1] *vb* arrange, class, classify, range. * *n* file, line, order, range, row, tier; class, division, group, order, series; birth, blood, caste, degree, estate, grade, position, quality, sphere, stakes, standing; dignity, distinction, eminence, nobility.
rank[2] *adj* dense, exuberant, luxuriant, overabundant, overgrown, vigorous, wild; excessive, extreme, extravagant, flagrant, gross, rampant, sheer, unmitigated, utter, violent; fetid, foul, fusty, musty, offensive, rancid; fertile, productive, rich; coarse, disgusting.
ransack *vb* pillage, plunder, ravage, rifle, sack, strip; explore, overhaul, rummage, search thoroughly.
ransom *vb* deliver, emancipate, free, liberate, redeem, rescue, unfetter. * *n* money, payment payoff, price; deliverance, liberation, redemption, release.
rant *vb* declaim, mouth, spout, vociferate. * *n* bombast, cant, exaggeration, fustian.
rapacious *adj* predacious, preying, raptorial; avaricious, grasping, greedy, ravenous, voracious.
rapid *adj* fast, fleet, quick, swift; brisk, expeditious, hasty, hurried, quick, speedy.
rapine *n* depredation, pillage, plunder, robbery, spoliation.
rapt *adj* absorbed, charmed, delighted, ecstatic, engrossed, enraptured, entranced, fascinated, inspired, spellbound.
rapture *vb* enrapture, ravish, transport. * *n* delight, exultation, enthusiasm, rhapsody; beatification, beatitude, bliss, ecstasy, felicity, happiness, joy, spell, transport.
rare[1] *adj* sparse, subtle, thin; extraordinary, infrequent, scarce, singular, strange, uncommon, unique, unusual; choice, excellent, exquisite, fine, incomparable, inimitable.
rare[2] *adj* bloody, underdone.
rarity *n* attenuation, ethereality, etherealness, rarefaction, rareness, tenuity, tenuousness, thinness; infrequency, scarcity, singularity, sparseness, uncommonness, unwontedness.
rascal *n* blackguard, caitiff, knave, miscreant, rogue, reprobate, scallywag, scapegrace, scamp, scoundrel, vagabond, villain.
rash[1] *adj* adventurous, audacious, careless, foolhardy, hasty, headlong, headstrong, heedless, incautious, inconsiderate, indiscreet, injudicious, impetuous, impulsive, incautious, precipitate, quick, rapid, reckless, temerarious, thoughtless, unguarded, unwary, venturesome.
rash[2] *n* breaking-out, efflorescence, eruption; epidemic, flood, outbreak, plague, spate.
rashness *n* carelessness, foolhardiness, hastiness, heedlessness, inconsideration, indiscretion, precipitation, recklessness, temerity, venturesomeness.
rate[1] *vb* appraise, compute, estimate, value. * *n* cost, price; class, degree, estimate, rank, value, valuation, worth; proportion, ration; assessment, charge, impost, tax.
rate[2] *vb* abuse, berate, censure, chide, criticize, find fault, reprimand, reprove, scold.
ratify *vb* confirm, corroborate, endorse, establish, seal, settle, substantiate; approve, bind, consent, sanction.
ration *vb* apportion, deal, distribute, dole, restrict. * *n* allowance, portion, quota, share.
rational *adj* intellectual, reasoning; equitable, fair, fit, just, moderate, natural, normal, proper, reasonable, right; discreet, enlightened, intelligent, judicious, sagacious, sensible, sound, wise.
raucous *adj* harsh, hoarse, husky, rough.
ravage *vb* consume, desolate, despoil, destroy, devastate, harry, overrun, pillage, plunder, ransack, ruin, sack, spoil, strip, waste. * *n* desolation, despoilment, destruction, devastation, havoc, pillage, plunder, rapine, ruin, spoil, waste.
ravenous *adj* devouring, ferocious, gluttonous, greedy, insatiable, omnivorous, ravening, rapacious, voracious.
ravine *n* canyon, cleft, defile, gap, gorge, gulch, gully, pass.
raving *adj* delirious, deranged, distracted, frantic, frenzied, furious, infuriated, mad, phrenetic, raging. * *n* delirium, frenzy, fury, madness, rage.
ravish *vb* abuse, debauch, defile, deflower, force, outrage, violate; captivate, charm, delight, enchant, enrapture, entrance, overjoy, transport; abduct, kidnap, seize, snatch, strip.
raw *adj* fresh, inexperienced, unpractised, unprepared, unseasoned, untried, unskilled; crude, green, immature, unfinished, unripe; bare, chafed, excoriated, galled, sensitive, sore; bleak, chilly, cold, cutting, damp, piercing, windswept; uncooked.
ray *n* beam, emanation, gleam, moonbeam, radiance, shaft, streak, sunbeam.
raze *vb* demolish, destroy, dismantle, extirpate, fell, level, overthrow, ruin, subvert; efface, erase, obliterate.
reach *vb* extend, stretch; grasp, hit, strike, touch; arrive at, attain, gain, get, obtain, win. * *n* capability, capacity, grasp.
readily *adv* easily, promptly, quickly; cheerfully, willingly.
readiness *n* alacrity, alertness, expedition, quickness, promptitude, promptness; aptitude, aptness, dexterity, easiness, expertness, facility, quickness, skill; preparation, preparedness, ripeness; cheerfulness, disposition, eagerness, ease, willingness.
ready *vb* arrange, equip, organize, prepare. * *adj* alert, expeditious, prompt, quick, punctual,

speedy; adroit, apt, clever, dextrous, expert, facile, handy, keen, nimble, prepared, prompt, ripe, quick, sharp, skilful, smart; cheerful, disposed, eager, free, inclined, willing; accommodating, available, convenient, near, handy; easy, facile, fluent, offhand, opportune, short, spontaneous.

real *adj* absolute, actual, certain, literal, positive, practical, substantial, substantive, veritable; authentic, genuine, true; essential, internal, intrinsic.

realize *vb* accomplish, achieve, discharge, effect, effectuate, perfect, perform; apprehend, comprehend, experience, recognize, understand; externalize, substantiate; acquire, earn, gain, get, net, obtain, produce, sell.

reality *n* actuality, certainty, fact, truth, verity.

really *adv* absolutely, actually, certainly, indeed, positively, truly, verily, veritably.

reap *vb* acquire, crop, gain, gather, get, harvest, obtain, receive.

rear[1] *adj* aft, back, following, hind, last. * *n* background, reverse, setting; heel, posterior, rear end, rump, stern, tail; path, trail, train, wake.

rear[2] *vb* construct, elevate, erect, hoist, lift, raise; cherish, educate, foster, instruct, nourish, nurse, nurture, train; breed, grow; rouse, stir up.

reason *vb* argue, conclude, debate, deduce, draw from, infer, intellectualize, syllogize, think, trace. * *n* faculty, intellect, intelligence, judgement, mind, principle, sanity, sense, thinking, understanding; account, argument, basis, cause, consideration, excuse, explanation, gist, ground, motive, occasion, pretence, proof; aim, design, end, object, purpose; argument, reasoning; common sense, reasonableness, wisdom; equity, fairness, justice, right; exposition, rationale, theory.

reasonable *adj* equitable, fair, fit, honest, just, proper, rational, right, suitable; enlightened, intelligent, judicious, sagacious, sensible, wise; considerable, fair, moderate, tolerable; credible, intellectual, plausible, well-founded; sane, sober, sound; cheap, inexpensive, low-priced.

rebate *vb* abate, bate, blunt, deduct, diminish, lessen, reduce; cut, pare, rabbet. * *n* decrease, decrement, diminution, lessening; allowance, deduction, discount, reduction.

rebel *vb* mutiny, resist, revolt, strike. * *adj* insubordinate, insurgent, mutinous, rebellious. * *n* insurgent, mutineer, traitor.

rebellion *n* anarchy, insubordination, insurrection, mutiny, resistance, revolt, revolution, uprising.

rebellious *adj* contumacious, defiant, disloyal, disobedient, insubordinate, intractable, obstinate, mutinous, rebel, refractory, seditious.

rebuff *vb* check, chide, oppose, refuse, reject, repel, reprimand, resist, snub. * *n* check, defeat, discouragement, opposition, rejection, resistance, snub.

rebuke *vb* blame, censure, chide, lecture, upbraid, reprehend, reprimand, reprove, scold, silence. * *n* blame, censure, chiding, expostulation, remonstrance, reprimand, reprehension, reproach, reproof, reproval; affliction, chastisement, punishment.

recall *vb* abjure, abnegate, annul, cancel, countermand, deny, nullify, overrule, recant, repeal, repudiate, rescind, retract, revoke, swallow, withdraw; commemorate, recollect, remember, retrace, review, revive. * *n* abjuration, abnegation, annulment, cancellation, nullification, recantation, repeal, repudiation, rescindment, retraction, revocation, withdrawal; memory, recollection, remembrance, reminiscence.

recant *vb* abjure, annul, disavow, disown, recall, renounce, repudiate, retract, revoke, unsay.

recapitulate *vb* epitomize, recite, rehearse, reiterate, repeat, restate, review, summarize.

recede *vb* desist, ebb, retire, regress, retreat, retrograde, return, withdraw.

receive *vb* accept, acquire, derive, gain, get, obtain, take; admit, shelter, take in; entertain, greet, welcome; allow, permit, tolerate; adopt, approve, believe, credit, embrace, follow, learn, understand; accommodate, carry, contain, hold, include, retain; bear, encounter, endure, experience, meet, suffer, sustain.

recent *adj* fresh, new, novel; latter, modern, young; deceased, foregoing, late, preceding, retiring.

reception *n* acceptance, receipt, receiving; entertainment, greeting, welcome; levee, soiree, party; admission, credence; belief, credence, recognition.

recess *n* alcove, corner, depth, hollow, niche, nook, privacy, retreat, seclusion; break, holiday, intermission, interval, respite, vacation; recession, retirement, retreat, withdrawal.

reciprocal *adj* alternate, commutable, complementary, correlative, correspondent, mutual.

recital *n* rehearsal, repetition, recitation; account, description, detail, explanation, narration, relation, statement, telling.

recite *vb* declaim, deliver, rehearse, repeat; describe, mention, narrate, recount, relate, tell; count, detail, enumerate, number, recapitulate.

reckless *adj* breakneck, careless, desperate, devil-may-care, flighty, foolhardy, giddy, harebrained, headlong, heedless, inattentive, improvident, imprudent, inconsiderate, indifferent, indiscreet, mindless, negligent, rash, regardless, remiss, thoughtless, temerarious, uncircumspect, unconcerned, unsteady, volatile, wild.

reckon *vb* calculate, cast, compute, consider, count, enumerate, guess, number; account, class, esteem, estimate, regard, repute, value.

reckoning *n* calculation, computation, consideration, counting; account, bill, charge, estimate, register, score; arrangement, settlement.

reclaim *vb* amend, correct, reform; recover, redeem, regenerate, regain, reinstate, restore; civilize, tame.

recline *vb* couch, lean, lie, lounge, repose, rest.

recluse *adj* anchoritic, anchoritical, cloistered,

eremitic, eremitical, hermitic, hermitical, reclusive, solitary. * *n* anchorite, ascetic, eremite, hermit, monk, solitary.

reclusive *adj* recluse, retired, secluded, sequestered, sequestrated, solitary.

recognition *n* identification, memory, recollection, remembrance; acknowledgement, appreciation, avowal, comprehension, confession, notice; allowance, concession.

recognize *vb* apprehend, identify, perceive, remember; acknowledge, admit, avow, confess, own; allow, concede, grant; greet, salute.

recoil *vb* react, rebound, reverberate; retire, retreat, withdraw; blench, fail, falter, quail, shrink. * *n* backstroke, boomerang, elasticity, kick, reaction, rebound, repercussion, resilience, revulsion, ricochet, shrinking.

recollect *vb* recall, remember, reminisce.

recollection *n* memory, remembrance, reminiscence.

recommend *vb* approve, commend, endorse, praise, sanction; commit; advise, counsel, prescribe, suggest.

recommendation *n* advocacy, approbation, approval, commendation, counsel, credential, praise, testimonial.

recompense *vb* compensate, remunerate, repay, requite, reward, satisfy; indemnify, redress, reimburse. * *n* amends, compensation, indemnification, indemnity, remuneration, repayment, reward, satisfaction; requital, retribution.

reconcilable *adj* appeasable, forgiving, placable; companionable, congruous, consistent.

reconcile *vb* appease, conciliate, pacify, placate, propitiate, reunite; content, harmonize, regulate; adjust, compose, heal, settle.

recondite *adj* concealed, dark, hidden, mystic, mystical, obscure, occult, secret, transcendental.

record *vb* chronicle, enter, note, register. * *n* account, annals, archive, chronicle, diary, docket, enrolment, entry, file, list, minute, memoir, memorandum, memorial, note, proceedings, register, registry, report, roll, score; mark, memorial, relic, trace, track, trail, vestige; memory, remembrance; achievement, career, history.

recount *vb* describe, detail, enumerate, mention, narrate, particularize, portray, recite, relate, rehearse, report, tell.

recover *vb* recapture, reclaim, regain; rally, recruit, repair, retrieve; cure, heal, restore, revive; redeem, rescue, salvage, save; convalesce, recuperate.

recreant *adj* base, cowardly, craven, dastardly, faint-hearted, mean-spirited, pusillanimous, yielding; apostate, backsliding, faithless, false, perfidious, treacherous, unfaithful, untrue. * *n* coward, dastard; apostate, backslider, renegade.

recreation *n* amusement, cheer, diversion, entertainment, fun, game, leisure, pastime, play, relaxation, sport.

recreational *adj* amusing, diverting, entertaining, refreshing, relaxing, relieving.

recruit *vb* repair, replenish; recover, refresh, regain, reinvigorate, renew, renovate, restore, retrieve, revive, strengthen, supply. * *n* auxiliary, beginner, helper, learner, novice, tyro.

rectify *vb* adjust, amend, better, correct, emend, improve, mend, redress, reform, regulate, straighten.

rectitude *n* conscientiousness, equity, goodness, honesty, integrity, justice, principle, probity, right, righteousness, straightforwardness, uprightness, virtue.

recumbent *adj* leaning, lying, prone, prostrate, reclining; idle, inactive, listless, reposing.

recur *vb* reappear, resort, return, revert.

recusancy *n* dissent, heresy, heterodoxy, nonconformity.

redeem *vb* reform, regain, repurchase, retrieve; free, liberate, ransom, rescue, save; deliver, reclaim, recover, reinstate; atone, compensate for, recompense; discharge, fulfil, keep, perform, satisfy.

redemption *n* buying, compensation, recovery, repurchase, retrieval; deliverance, liberation, ransom, release, rescue, salvation; discharge, fulfilment, performance.

redolent *adj* aromatic, balmy, fragrant, odoriferous, odorous, scented, sweet, sweet-smelling.

redoubtable *adj* awful, doughty, dreadful, formidable, terrible, valiant.

redound *vb* accrue, conduce, contribute, result, tend.

redress *vb* amend, correct, order, rectify, remedy, repair; compensate, ease, relieve. * *n* abatement, amends, atonement, compensation, correction, cure, indemnification, rectification, repair, righting, remedy, relief, reparation, satisfaction.

reduce *vb* bring; form, make, model, mould, remodel, render, resolve, shape; abate, abbreviate, abridge, attenuate, contract, curtail, decimate, decrease, diminish, lessen, minimize, shorten, thin; abase, debase, degrade, depress, dwarf, impair, lower, weaken; capture, conquer, master, overpower, overthrow, subject, subdue, subjugate, vanquish; impoverish, ruin; resolve, solve.

redundant *adj* copious, excessive, exuberant, fulsome, inordinate, lavish, needless, overflowing, overmuch, plentiful, prodigal, superabundant, replete, superfluous, unnecessary, useless; diffuse, periphrastic, pleonastic, tautological, verbose, wordy.

reel[1] *n* capstan, winch, windlass; bobbin, spool.

reel[2] *vb* falter, flounder, heave, lurch, pitch, plunge, rear, rock, roll, stagger, sway, toss, totter, tumble, wallow, welter, vacillate; spin, swing, turn, twirl, wheel, whirl. * *n* gyre, pirouette, spin, turn, twirl, wheel, whirl.

re-establish *vb* re-found, rehabilitate, reinstall, reinstate, renew, renovate, replace, restore.

refer *vb* commit, consign, direct, leave, relegate, send, submit; ascribe, assign, attribute, impute;

appertain, belong, concern, pertain, point, relate, respect, touch; appeal, apply, consult; advert, allude, cite, quote.
referee *vb* arbitrate, judge, umpire. * *n* arbiter, arbitrator, judge, umpire.
reference *n* concern, connection, regard, respect; allusion, ascription, citation, hint, intimation, mark, reference, relegation.
refine *vb* clarify, cleanse, defecate, fine, purify; cultivate, humanize, improve, polish, rarefy, spiritualize.
refined *adj* courtly, cultured, genteel, polished, polite; discerning, discriminating, fastidious, sensitive; filtered, processed, purified.
refinement *n* clarification, filtration, purification, sublimation; betterment, improvement; delicacy, cultivation, culture, elegance, elevation, finish, gentility, good breeding, polish, politeness, purity, spirituality, style.
reflect *vb* copy, imitate, mirror, reproduce; cogitate, consider, contemplate, deliberate, meditate, muse, ponder, ruminate, study, think.
reflection *n* echo, shadow; cogitation, consideration, contemplation, deliberation, idea, meditation, musing, opinion, remark, rumination, thinking, thought; aspersion, blame, censure, criticism, disparagement, reproach, slur.
reflective *adj* reflecting, reflexive; cogitating, deliberating, musing, pondering, reasoning, thoughtful.
reform *vb* amend, ameliorate, better, correct, improve, mend, meliorate, rectify, reclaim, redeem, regenerate, repair, restore; reconstruct, remodel, reshape. * *n* amendment, correction, progress, reconstruction, rectification, reformation.
reformation *n* amendment, emendation, improvement, reform; adoption, conversion, redemption; refashioning, regeneration, reproduction, reconstruction.
refractory *adj* cantankerous, contumacious, crossgrained, disobedient, dogged, headstrong, heady, incoercible, intractable, mulish, obstinate, perverse, recalcitrant, self-willed, stiff, stubborn, sullen, ungovernable, unmanageable, unruly, unyielding.
refrain[1] *vb* abstain, cease, desist, forbear, stop, withhold.
refrain[2] *n* chorus, song, undersong.
refresh *vb* air, brace, cheer, cool, enliven, exhilarate, freshen, invigorate, reanimate, recreate, recruit, reinvigorate, revive, regale, slake.
refreshing *adj* comfortable, cooling, grateful, invigorating, pleasant, reanimating, restful, reviving.
refuge *n* asylum, covert, harbour, haven, protection, retreat, safety, sanction, security, shelter.
refulgent *adj* bright, brilliant, effulgent, lustrous, radiant, resplendent, shining.
refund *vb* reimburse, repay, restore, return. * *n* reimbursement, repayment.
refuse[1] *n* chaff, discard, draff, dross, dregs, garbage, junk, leavings, lees, litter, lumber, offal, recrement, remains, rubbish, scoria, scum, sediment, slag, sweepings, trash, waste.
refuse[2] *vb* decline, deny, withhold; disallow, disavow, exclude, rebuff, reject, renege, renounce, repel, repudiate, repulse, revoke, veto.
refute *vb* confute, defeat, disprove, overcome, overthrow, rebut, repel, silence.
regain *vb* recapture, recover, re-obtain, repossess, retrieve.
regal *adj* imposing, imperial, kingly, noble, royal, sovereign.
regale *vb* delight, entertain, gratify, refresh; banquet, feast.
regard *vb* behold, gaze, look, notice, mark, observe, remark, see, view, watch; attend to, consider, heed, mind, respect; esteem, honour, revere, reverence, value; account, believe, estimate, deem, hold, imagine, reckon, suppose, think, treat, use. * *n* aspect, gaze, look, view; attention, attentiveness, care, concern, consideration, heed, notice, observance; account, reference, relation, respect; admiration, affection, attachment, deference, esteem, estimation, favour, honour, interest, liking, love, respect, reverence, sympathy, value; account, eminence, note, reputation, repute; condition, matter, point.
regardful *adj* attentive, careful, considerate, deferential, heedful, mindful, observing, thoughtful, watchful.
regarding *prep* concerning, respecting, touching.
regardless *adj* careless, disregarding, heedless, inattentive, indifferent, mindless, neglectful, negligent, unconcerned, unmindful, unobservant. * *adv* however, irrespectively, nevertheless, nonetheless, notwithstanding.
regenerate *vb* reproduce; renovate, revive; change, convert, renew, sanctify. * *adj* born-again, converted, reformed, regenerated.
regime *n* administration, government, rule.
region *n* climate, clime, country, district, division, latitude, locale, locality, province, quarter, scene, territory, tract; area, neighbourhood, part, place, portion, spot, space, sphere, terrain, vicinity.
register *vb* delineate, portray, record, show. * *n* annals, archive, catalogue, chronicle, list, record, roll, schedule; clerk, registrar, registry; compass, range.
regret *vb* bewail, deplore, grieve, lament, repine, sorrow; bemoan, repent, mourn, rue. * *n* concern, disappointment, grief, lamentation, rue, sorrow, trouble; compunction, contrition, penitence, remorse, repentance, repining, self-condemnation, self-reproach.
regular *adj* conventional, natural, normal, ordinary, typical; correct, customary, cyclic, established, fixed, habitual, periodic, periodical, recurring, reasonable, rhythmic, seasonal, stated, usual; steady, constant, uniform, even; just, methodical, orderly, punctual, systematic, unvarying; complete, genuine, indubitable, out-and-

out, perfect, thorough; balanced, consistent, symmetrical.
regulate *vb* adjust, arrange, dispose, methodize, order, organize, settle, standardize, time, systematize; conduct, control, direct, govern, guide, manage, rule.
regulation *adj* customary, mandatory, official, required, standard. * *n* adjustment, arrangement, control, disposal, disposition, law, management, order, ordering, precept, rule, settlement.
rehabilitate *vb* reinstate, re-establish, restore; reconstruct, reconstitute, reintegrate, reinvigorate, renew, renovate.
rehearsal *n* drill, practice, recital, recitation, repetition; account, history, mention, narration, narrative, recounting, relation, statement, story, telling.
rehearse *vb* recite, repeat; delineate, depict, describe, detail, enumerate, narrate, portray, recapitulate, recount, relate, tell.
reign *vb* administer, command, govern, influence, predominate, prevail, rule. * *n* control, dominion, empire, influence, power, royalty, sovereignty, power, rule, sway.
reimburse *vb* refund, repay, restore; compensate, indemnify, requite, satisfy.
rein *vb* bridle, check, control, curb, guide, harness, hold, restrain, restrict. * *n* bridle, check, curb, harness, restraint, restriction.
reinforce *vb* augment, fortify, strengthen.
reinstate *vb* re-establish, rehabilitate, reinstall, replace, restore.
reject *vb* cashier, discard, dismiss, eject, exclude, pluck; decline, deny, disallow, despise, disapprove, disbelieve, rebuff, refuse, renounce, repel, repudiate, scout, slight, spurn, veto. * *n* cast-off, discard, failure, refusal, repudiation.
rejoice *vb* cheer, delight, enliven, enrapture, exhilarate, gladden, gratify, please, transport; crow, exult, delight, gloat, glory, jubilate, triumph, vaunt.
rejoin *vb* answer, rebut, respond, retort.
relate *vb* describe, detail, mention, narrate, recite, recount, rehearse, report, tell; apply, connect, correlate.
relation *n* account, chronicle, description, detail, explanation, history, mention, narration, narrative, recital, rehearsal, report, statement, story, tale; affinity, application, bearing, connection, correlation, dependency, pertinence, relationship; concern, reference, regard, respect; alliance, nearness, propinquity, rapport; blood, consanguinity, cousinship, kin, kindred, kinship, relationship; kinsman, kinswoman, relative.
relax *vb* loose, loosen, slacken, unbrace, unstrain; debilitate, enervate, enfeeble, prostrate, unbrace, unstring, weaken; abate, diminish, lessen, mitigate, reduce, remit; amuse, divert, ease, éntertain, recreate, unbend.
release *vb* deliver, discharge, disengage, exempt, extricate, free, liberate, loose, unloose; acquit, discharge, quit, relinquish, remit. * *n* deliverance, discharge, freedom, liberation; absolution, dispensation, excuse, exemption, exoneration; acquaintance, clearance.
relentless *adj* cruel, hard, impenitent, implacable, inexorable, merciless, obdurate, pitiless, rancorous, remorseless, ruthless, unappeasable, uncompassionate, unfeeling, unforgiving, unmerciful, unpitying, unrelenting, unyielding, vindictive.
relevant *adj* applicable, appropriate, apposite, apt, apropos, fit, germane, pertinent, proper, relative, suitable.
reliable *adj* authentic, certain, constant, dependable, sure, trustworthy, trusty, unfailing.
reliance *n* assurance, confidence, credence, dependence, hope, trust.
relic *n* keepsake, memento, memorial, remembrance, souvenir, token, trophy; trace, vestige.
relics *npl* fragments, leavings, remainder, remains, remnants, ruins, scraps; body, cadaver, corpse, remains.
relict *n* dowager, widow.
relief *n* aid, alleviation, amelioration, assistance, assuagement, comfort, deliverance, ease, easement, help, mitigation, reinforcement, respite, rest, succour, softening, support; indemnification, redress, remedy; embossment, projection, prominence, protrusion; clearness, distinction, perspective, vividness.
relieve *vb* aid, comfort, help, spell, succour, support, sustain; abate, allay, alleviate, assuage, cure, diminish, ease, lessen, lighten, mitigate, remedy, remove, soothe; indemnify, redress, right, repair; disengage, free, release, remedy, rescue.
religious *adj* devotional, devout, god-fearing, godly, holy, pious, prayerful, spiritual; conscientious, exact, rigid, scrupulous, strict; canonical, divine, theological.
relinquish *vb* abandon, desert, forsake, forswear, leave, quit, renounce, resign, vacate; abdicate, cede, forbear, forgo, give up, surrender, yield.
relish *vb* appreciate, enjoy, like, prefer; season, flavour, taste. * *n* appetite, appreciation, enjoyment, fondness, gratification, gusto, inclination, liking, partiality, predilection, taste, zest; cast, flavour, manner, quality, savour, seasoning, sort, tang, tinge, touch; appetizer, condiment.
reluctance *n* aversion, backwardness, disinclination, dislike, loathing, repugnance, unwillingness.
reluctant *adj* averse, backward, disinclined, hesitant, indisposed, loath, unwilling.
rely *vb* confide, count, depend, hope, lean, reckon, repose, trust.
remain *vb* abide, continue, endure, last; exceed, persist, survive; abide, continue, dwell, halt, inhabit, rest, sojourn, stay, stop, tarry, wait.
remainder *n* balance, excess, leavings, remains, remnant, residue, rest, surplus.

remark *vb* heed, notice, observe, regard; comment, express, mention, observe, say, state, utter. * *n* consideration, heed, notice, observation, regard; annotation, comment, gloss, note, stricture; assertion, averment, comment, declaration, saying, statement, utterance.

remarkable *adj* conspicuous, distinguished, eminent, extraordinary, famous, notable, noteworthy, noticeable, pre-eminent, rare, singular, strange, striking, uncommon, unusual, wonderful.

remedy *vb* cure, heal, help, palliate, relieve; amend, correct, rectify, redress, repair, restore, retrieve. * *n* antidote, antitoxin, corrective, counteractive, cure, help, medicine, nostrum, panacea, restorative, specific; redress, reparation, restitution, restoration; aid, assistance, relief.

remembrance *n* recollection, reminiscence, retrospection; keepsake, memento, memorial, memory, reminder, souvenir, token; consideration, regard, thought.

reminiscence *n* memory, recollection, remembrance, retrospective.

remiss *adj* backward, behindhand, dilatory, indolent, languid, lax, lazy, slack, slow, tardy; careless, dilatory, heedless, idle, inattentive, neglectful, negligent, shiftless, slothful, thoughtless.

remission *n* abatement, decrease, diminution, lessening, mitigation, moderation, reduction, relaxation; cancellation, discharge, release, relinquishment; intermission, interruption, pause, rest, stop, stoppage, suspense, suspension; absolution, acquittal, excuse, exoneration, forgiveness, indulgence, pardon.

remit *vb* replace, restore, return; abate, bate, diminish, relax; release; absolve, condone, excuse, forgive, overlook, pardon; relinquish, resign, surrender; consign, forward, refer, send, transmit. * *n* authorization, brief, instructions, orders.

remnant *n* remainder, remains, residue, rest, trace; fragment, piece, scrap.

remorse *n* compunction, contrition, penitence, qualm, regret, repentance, reproach, self-reproach, sorrow.

remorseless *adj* cruel, barbarous, hard, harsh, implacable, inexorable, merciless, pitiless, relentless, ruthless, savage, uncompassionate, unmerciful, unrelenting.

remote *adj* distant, far, out-of-the-way; alien, far-fetched, foreign, inappropriate, unconnected, unrelated; abstracted, separated; inconsiderable, slight; isolated, removed, secluded, sequestrated.

removal *n* abstraction, departure, dislodgement, displacement, relegation, remove, shift, transference; elimination, extraction, withdrawal; abatement, destruction; discharge, dismissal, ejection, expulsion.

remove *vb* carry, dislodge, displace, shift, transfer, transport; abstract, extract, withdraw; abate, banish, destroy, suppress; cashier, depose, discharge, dismiss, eject, expel, oust, retire; depart, move.

remunerate *vb* compensate, indemnify, pay, recompense, reimburse, repay, requite, reward, satisfy.

remuneration *n* compensation, earnings, indemnity, pay, payment, recompense, reimbursement, reparation, repayment, reward, salary, wages.

remunerative *adj* gainful, lucrative, paying, profitable; compensatory, recompensing, remuneratory, reparative, requiting, rewarding.

rend *vb* break, burst, cleave, crack, destroy, dismember, dissever, disrupt, divide, fracture, lacerate, rive, rupture, sever, shiver, snap, split, sunder, tear.

render *vb* restore, return, surrender; assign, deliver, give, present; afford, contribute, furnish, supply, yield; construe, interpret, translate.

rendition *n* restitution, return, surrender; delineation, exhibition, interpretation, rendering, representation, reproduction; translation, version.

renegade *adj* apostate, backsliding, disloyal, false, outlawed, rebellious, recreant, unfaithful. * *n* apostate, backslider, recreant, turncoat; deserter, outlaw, rebel, revolter, traitor; vagabond, wretch.

renew *vb* rebuild, recreate, re-establish, refit, refresh, rejuvenate, renovate, repair, replenish, restore, resuscitate, revive; continue, recommence, repeat; iterate, reiterate; regenerate, transform.

renounce *vb* abjure, abnegate, decline, deny, disclaim, disown, forswear, neglect, recant, repudiate, reject, slight; abandon, abdicate, drop, forgo, forsake, desert, leave, quit, relinquish, resign.

renovate *vb* reconstitute, re-establish, refresh, refurbish, renew, restore, revamp; reanimate, recreate, regenerate, reproduce, resuscitate, revive, revivify.

renown *n* celebrity, distinction, eminence, fame, figure, glory, honour, greatness, name, note, notability, notoriety, reputation, repute.

renowned *adj* celebrated, distinguished, eminent, famed, famous, honoured, illustrious, remarkable, wonderful.

rent[1] *n* breach, break, crack, cleft, crevice, fissure, flaw, fracture, gap, laceration, opening, rift, rupture, separation, split, tear; schism.

rent[2] *vb* hire, lease, let. * *n* income, rental, revenue.

repair[1] *vb* mend, patch, piece, refit, retouch, tinker, vamp; correct, recruit, restore, retrieve. * *n* mending, refitting, renewal, reparation, restoration.

repair[2] *vb* betake oneself, go, move, resort, turn.

repairable *adj* curable, recoverable, reparable, restorable, retrievable.

reparable *adj* curable, recoverable, repairable, restorable, retrievable.

reparation *n* renewal, repair, restoration; amends, atonement, compensation, correction, indemnification, recompense, redress, requital, restitution, satisfaction.

repay *vb* refund, reimburse, restore, return; compensate, recompense, remunerate, reward, satisfy; avenge, retaliate, revenge.

repeal *vb* abolish, annul, cancel, recall, rescind, reverse, revoke. * *n* abolition, abrogation, annulment, cancellation, rescission, reversal, revocation.

repeat *vb* double, duplicate, iterate; cite, narrate, quote, recapitulate, recite, rehearse; echo, renew, reproduce. * *n* duplicate, duplication, echo, iteration, recapitulation, reiteration, repetition.

repel *vb* beat, disperse, repulse, scatter; check, confront, oppose, parry, rebuff, resist, withstand; decline, refuse, reject; disgust, revolt, sicken.

repellent *adj* abhorrent, disgusting, forbidding, repelling, repugnant, repulsive, revolting, uninviting.

repent *vb* atone, regret, relent, rue, sorrow.

repentance *n* compunction, contriteness, contrition, penitence, regret, remorse, self-accusation, self-condemnation, self-reproach.

repentant *adj* contrite, penitent, regretful, remorseful, rueful, sorrowful, sorry.

repercussion *n* rebound, recoil, reverberation; backlash, consequence, result.

repetition *n* harping, iteration, recapitulation, reiteration; diffuseness, redundancy, tautology, verbosity; narration, recital, rehearsal, relation, retailing; recurrence, renewal.

repine *vb* croak, complain, fret, grumble, long, mope, murmur.

replace *vb* re-establish, reinstate, reset; refund, repay, restore; succeed, supersede, supplant.

replenish *vb* fill, refill, renew, re-supply; enrich, furnish, provide, store, supply.

replete *adj* abounding, charged, exuberant, fraught, full, glutted, gorged, satiated, well-stocked.

repletion *n* abundance, exuberance, fullness, glut, profusion, satiation, satiety, surfeit.

replica *n* autograph, copy, duplicate, facsimile, reproduction.

reply *vb* answer, echo, rejoin, respond. * *n* acknowledgement, answer, rejoinder, repartee, replication, response, retort.

report *vb* announce, annunciate, communicate, declare; advertise, broadcast, bruit, describe, detail, herald, mention, narrate, noise, promulgate, publish, recite, relate, rumour, state, tell; minute, record. * *n* account, announcement, communication, declaration, statement; advice, description, detail, narration, narrative, news, recital, story, tale, talk, tidings; gossip, hearsay, rumour; clap, detonation, discharge, explosion, noise, repercussion, sound; fame, reputation, repute; account, bulletin, minute, note, record, statement.

repose[1] *vb* compose, recline, rest, settle; couch, lie, recline, sleep, slumber; confide, lean. * *n* quiet, recumbence, recumbency, rest, sleep, slumber; breathing time, inactivity, leisure, respite, relaxation; calm, ease, peace, peacefulness, quietness, quietude, stillness, tranquillity.

repose[2] *vb* place, put, stake; deposit, lodge, reposit, store.

repository *n* conservatory, depository, depot, magazine, museum, receptacle, repertory, storehouse, storeroom, thesaurus, treasury, vault.

reprehend *vb* accuse, blame, censure, chide, rebuke, reprimand, reproach, reprove, upbraid.

reprehensible *adj* blameable, blameworthy, censurable, condemnable, culpable, reprovable.

reprehension *n* admonition, blame, censure, condemnation, rebuke, reprimand, reproof.

represent *vb* exhibit, express, show; delineate, depict, describe, draw, portray, sketch; act, impersonate, mimic, personate, personify; exemplify, illustrate, image, reproduce, symbolize, typify.

representation *n* delineation, exhibition, show; impersonation, personation, simulation; account, description, narration, narrative, relation, statement; image, likeness, model, portraiture, resemblance, semblance; sight, spectacle; expostulation, remonstrance.

representative *adj* figurative, illustrative, symbolic, typical; delegated, deputed, representing. * *n* agent, commissioner, delegate, deputy, emissary, envoy, legate, lieutenant, messenger, proxy, substitute.

repress *vb* choke, crush, dull, overcome, overpower, silence, smother, subdue, suppress, quell; bridle, chasten, chastise, check, control, curb, restrain; appease, calm, quiet.

reprimand *vb* admonish, blame, censure, chide, rebuke, reprehend, reproach, reprove, upbraid. * *n* admonition, blame, censure, rebuke, reprehension, reproach, reprobation, reproof, reproval.

reprint *vb* republish. * *n* reimpression, republication; copy.

reproach *vb* blame, censure, rebuke, reprehend, reprimand, reprove, upbraid; abuse, accuse, asperse, condemn, defame, discredit, disparage, revile, traduce, vilify. * *n* abuse, blame, censure, condemnation, contempt, contumely, disapprobation, disapproval, expostulation, insolence, invective, railing, rebuke, remonstrance, reprobation, reproof, reviling, scorn, scurrility, upbraiding, vilification; abasement, discredit, disgrace, dishonour, disrepute, indignity, ignominy, infamy, insult, obloquy, odium, offence, opprobrium, scandal, shame, slur, stigma.

reproachful *adj* abusive, censorious, condemnatory, contemptuous, contumelious, damnatory, insolent, insulting, offensive, opprobrious, railing, reproving, sacrifice, scolding, scornful, scurrilous, upbraiding, vituperative; base, discreditable, disgraceful, dishonourable, disreputable, infamous, scandalous, shameful, vile.

reprobate *vb* censure, condemn, disapprove, discard, reject, reprehend; disallow; abandon, disown. * *adj* abandoned, base, castaway, corrupt, depraved, graceless, hardened, irredeemable, lost, profligate, shameless, vile, vitiated, wicked.

* *n* caitiff, castaway, miscreant, outcast, rascal, scamp, scoundrel, sinner, villain.

reproduce *vb* copy, duplicate, emulate, imitate, print, repeat, represent; breed, generate, procreate, propagate.

reproof *n* admonition, animadversion, blame, castigation, censure, chiding, condemnation, correction, criticism, lecture, monition, objurgation, rating, rebuke, reprehension, reprimand, reproach, reproval, upbraiding.

reprove *vb* admonish, blame, castigate, censure, chide, condemn, correct, criticize, inculpate, lecture, objurgate, rate, rebuke, reprimand, reproach, scold, upbraid.

reptilian *adj* abject, crawling, creeping, grovelling, low, mean, treacherous, vile, vulgar.

repudiate *vb* abjure, deny, disavow, discard, disclaim, disown, nullify, reject, renounce.

repugnance *n* contrariety, contrariness, incompatibility, inconsistency, irreconcilability, irreconcilableness, unsuitability, unsuitableness; contest, opposition, resistance, struggle; antipathy, aversion, detestation, dislike, hatred, hostility, reluctance, repulsion, unwillingness.

repugnant *adj* incompatible, inconsistent, irreconcilable; adverse, antagonistic, contrary, hostile, inimical, opposed, opposing, unfavourable; detestable, distasteful, offensive, repellent, repulsive.

repulse *vb* check, defeat, refuse, reject, repel. * *n* repelling, repulsion; denial, refusal; disappointment, failure.

repulsion *n* abhorrence, antagonism, anticipation, aversion, discard, disgust, dislike, hatred, hostility, loathing, rebuff, rejection, repugnance, repulse, spurning.

repulsive *adj* abhorrent, cold, disagreeable, disgusting, forbidding, frigid, harsh, hateful, loathsome, nauseating, nauseous, odious, offensive, repellent, repugnant, reserved, revolting, sickening, ugly, unpleasant.

reputable *adj* creditable, estimable, excellent, good, honourable, respectable, worthy.

reputation *n* account, character, fame, mark, name, repute; celebrity, credit, distinction, eclat, esteem, estimation, glory, honour, prestige, regard, renown, report, respect; notoriety.

repute *vb* account, consider, deem, esteem, estimate, hold, judge, reckon, regard, think.

request *vb* ask, beg, beseech, call, claim, demand, desire, entreat, pray, solicit, supplicate. * *n* asking, entreaty, importunity, invitation, petition, prayer, requisition, solicitation, suit, supplication.

require *vb* beg, beseech, bid, claim, crave, demand, dun, importune, invite, pray, requisition, request, sue, summon; need, want; direct, enjoin, exact, order, prescribe.

requirement *n* claim, demand, exigency, market, need, needfulness, requisite, requisition, request, urgency, want; behest, bidding, charge, command, decree, exaction, injunction, mandate, order, precept.

requisite *adj* essential, imperative, indispensable, necessary, needful, needed, required. * *n* essential, necessity, need, requirement.

requite *vb* compensate, pay, remunerate, reciprocate, recompense, repay, reward, satisfy; avenge, punish, retaliate, satisfy.

rescind *vb* abolish, abrogate, annul, cancel, countermand, quash, recall, repeal, reverse, revoke, vacate, void.

rescue *vb* deliver, extricate, free, liberate, preserve, ransom, recapture, recover, redeem, release, retake, save. * *n* deliverance, extrication, liberation, redemption, release, salvation.

research *vb* analyse, examine, explore, inquire, investigate, probe, study. * *n* analysis, examination, exploration, inquiry, investigation, scrutiny, study.

resemblance *n* affinity, agreement, analogy, likeness, semblance, similarity, similitude; counterpart, facsimile, image, representation.

resemble *vb* compare, liken; copy, counterfeit, imitate.

resentful *adj* angry, bitter, choleric, huffy, hurt, irascible, irritable, malignant, revengeful, sore, touchy.

resentment *n* acrimony, anger, annoyance, bitterness, choler, displeasure, dudgeon, fury, gall, grudge, heartburning, huff, indignation, ire, irritation, pique, rage, soreness, spleen, sulks, umbrage, vexation, wrath.

reservation *n* reserve, suppression; appropriation, booking, exception, restriction, saving; proviso, salvo; custody, park, reserve, sanctuary.

reserve *vb* hold, husband, keep, retain, store. * *adj* alternate, auxiliary, spare, substitute. * *n* reservation; aloofness, backwardness, closeness, coldness, concealment, constraint, suppression, reservedness, retention, restraint, reticence, uncommunicativeness, unresponsiveness; coyness, demureness, modesty, shyness, taciturnity; park, reservation, sanctuary.

reserved *adj* coy, demure, modest, shy, taciturn; aloof, backward, cautious, cold, distant, incommunicative, restrained, reticent, self-controlled, unsociable, unsocial; bespoken, booked, excepted, held, kept, retained, set apart, taken, withheld.

reside *vb* abide, domicile, domiciliate, dwell, inhabit, live, lodge, remain, room, sojourn, stay.

residence *n* inhabitance, inhabitancy, sojourn, stay, stop, tarrying; abode, domicile, dwelling, habitation, home, house, lodging, mansion.

residue *n* leavings, remainder, remains, remnant, residuum, rest; excess, overplus, surplus.

resign *vb* abandon, abdicate, abjure, cede, commit, disclaim, forego, forsake, leave, quit, relinquish, renounce, surrender, yield.

resignation *n* abandonment, abdication, relinquishment, renunciation, retirement, surrender;

acquiescence, compliance, endurance, forbearance, fortitude, long-sufferance, patience, submission, sufferance.

resist *vb* assail, attack, baffle, block, check, confront, counteract, disappoint, frustrate, hinder, impede, impugn, neutralize, obstruct, oppose, rebel, rebuff, stand against, stem, stop, strive, thwart, withstand.

resolute *adj* bold, constant, decided, determined, earnest, firm, fixed, game, hardy, inflexible, persevering, pertinacious, relentless, resolved, staunch, steadfast, steady, stout, stouthearted, sturdy, tenacious, unalterable, unbending, undaunted, unflinching, unshaken, unwavering, unyielding.

resolution *n* boldness, disentanglement, explication, unravelling; backbone, constancy, courage, decision, determination, earnestness, energy, firmness, fortitude, grit, hardihood, inflexibility, intention, manliness, pluck, perseverance, purpose, relentlessness, resolve, resoluteness, stamina, steadfastness, steadiness, tenacity.

resolve *vb* analyse, disperse, scatter, separate, reduce; change, dissolve, liquefy, melt, reduce, transform; decipher, disentangle, elucidate, explain, interpret, unfold, solve, unravel; conclude, decide, determine, fix, intend, purpose, will. * *n* conclusion, decision, determination, intention, will; declaration, resolution.

resonant *adj* booming, clangorous, resounding, reverberating, ringing, roaring, sonorous, thundering, vibrant.

resort *vb* frequent, haunt; assemble, congregate, convene, go, repair. * *n* application, expedient, recourse; haunt, refuge, rendezvous, retreat, spa; assembling, confluence, concourse, meeting; recourse, reference.

resound *vb* echo, re-echo, reverberate, ring; celebrate, extol, praise, sound.

resource *n* dependence, resort; appliance, contrivance, device, expedient, instrumentality, means, resort.

resources *npl* capital, funds, income, money, property, reserve, supplies, wealth.

respect *vb* admire, esteem, honour, prize, regard, revere, reverence, spare, value, venerate; consider, heed, notice, observe. * *n* attention, civility, courtesy, consideration, deference, estimation, homage, honour, notice, politeness, recognition, regard, reverence, veneration; consideration, favour, goodwill, kind; aspect, bearing, connection, feature, matter, particular, point, reference, regard, relation.

respects *npl* compliments, greetings, regards.

respectable *adj* considerable, estimable, honourable, presentable, proper, upright, worthy; adequate, moderate; tolerable.

respectful *adj* ceremonious, civil, complaisant, courteous, decorous, deferential, dutiful, formal, polite.

respire *vb* breathe, exhale, live.

respite *vb* delay, relieve, reprieve. * *n* break, cessation, delay, intermission, interval, pause, recess, rest, stay, stop; forbearance, postponement, reprieve.

resplendent *adj* beaming, bright, brilliant, effulgent, lucid, glittering, glorious, gorgeous, luminous, lustrous, radiant, shining, splendid.

respond *vb* answer, reply, rejoin; accord, correspond, suit.

response *n* answer, replication, rejoinder, reply, retort.

responsible *adj* accountable, amenable, answerable, liable, trustworthy.

rest[1] *vb* cease, desist, halt, hold, pause, repose, stop; breathe, relax, unbend; repose, sleep, slumber; lean, lie, lounge, perch, recline, ride; acquiesce, confide, trust; confide, rely, trust; calm, comfort, ease. * *n* fixity, immobility, inactivity, motionlessness, quiescence, quiet, repose; hush, peace, peacefulness, quietness, relief, security, stillness, tranquillity; cessation, intermission, interval, lull, pause, relaxation, respite, stop, stay; siesta, sleep, slumber; death; brace, stay, support; axis, fulcrum, pivot.

rest[2] *vb* be left, remain. * *n* balance, remainder, remnant, residuum; overplus, surplus.

restaurant *n* bistro, café, cafeteria, chophouse, eatery, eating house, pizzeria, trattoria.

restitution *n* restoration, return; amends, compensation, indemnification, recompense, rehabilitation, remuneration, reparation, repayment, requital, satisfaction.

restive *adj* mulish, obstinate, stopping, stubborn, unwilling; impatient, recalcitrant, restless, uneasy, unquiet.

restless *adj* disquieted, disturbed, restive, sleepless, uneasy, unquiet, unresting; changeable, inconstant, irresolute, unsteady, vacillating; active, astatic, roving, transient, unsettled, unstable, wandering; agitated, fidgety, fretful, turbulent.

restoration *n* recall, recovery, re-establishment, reinstatement, reparation, replacement, restitution, return; reconsideration, redemption, reintegration, renewal, renovation, repair, resuscitation, revival; convalescence, cure, recruitment, recuperation.

restorative *adj* curative, invigorating, recuperative, remedial, restoring, stimulating. * *n* corrective, curative, cure, healing, medicine, remedy, reparative, stimulant.

restore *vb* refund, repay, return; caulk, cobble, emend, heal, mend, patch, reintegrate, re-establish, rehabilitate, reinstate, renew, repair, replace, retrieve; cure, heal, recover, revive; resuscitate.

restrain *vb* bridle, check, coerce, confine, constrain, curb, debar, govern, hamper, hinder, hold, keep, muzzle, picket, prevent, repress, restrict, rule, subdue, tie, withhold; abridge, circumscribe, narrow.

restraint *n* bridle, check, coercion, control, compulsion, constraint, curb, discipline, repression, suppression; arrest, deterrence, hindrance, inhibition, limitation, prevention, prohibition, restriction, stay, stop; confinement, detention, imprisonment, shackles; constraint, stiffness, reserve, unnaturalness.

restrict *vb* bound, circumscribe, confine, limit, qualify, restrain, straiten.

restriction *n* confinement, limitation; constraint, restraint; reservation, reserve.

result *vb* accrue, arise, come, ensue, flow, follow, issue, originate, proceed, spring, rise; end, eventuate, terminate. * *n* conclusion, consequence, deduction, inference, outcome; corollary, effect, end, event, eventuality, fruit, harvest, issue, product, sequel, termination; decision, determination, finding, resolution, resolve, solution, verdict.

resume *vb* continue, recommence, renew, restart, summarize.

résumé *n* abstract, curriculum vitae, epitome, recapitulation, summary, synopsis.

resuscitate *vb* quicken, reanimate, renew, resurrect, restore, revive, revivify.

retain *vb* detain, hold, husband, keep, preserve, recall, recollect, remember, reserve, save, withhold; engage, maintain.

retainer *n* adherent, attendant, dependant, follower, hanger-on, servant.

retaliate *vb* avenge, match, repay, requite, retort, return, turn.

retaliation *n* boomerang, counterstroke, punishment, repayment, requital, retribution, revenge.

retard *vb* check, clog, hinder, impede, obstruct, slacken; adjourn, defer, delay, postpone, procrastinate.

reticent *adj* close, reserved, secretive, silent, taciturn, uncommunicative.

retinue *n* bodyguard, cortege, entourage, escort, followers, household, ménage, suite, tail, train.

retire *vb* discharge, shelve, superannuate, withdraw; depart, leave, resign, retreat.

retired *adj* abstracted, removed, withdrawn; apart, private, secret, sequestrated, solitary.

retirement *n* isolation, loneliness, privacy, retreat, seclusion, solitude, withdrawal.

retiring *adj* coy, demure, diffident, modest, reserved, retreating, shy, withdrawing.

retort *vb* answer, rejoin, reply, respond. * *n* answer, rejoinder, repartee, reply, response; crucible, jar, vessel, vial.

retract *vb* reverse, withdraw; abjure, cancel, disavow, recall, recant, revoke, unsay.

retreat *vb* recoil, retire, withdraw; recede. * *n* departure, recession, recoil, retirement, withdrawal; privacy, seclusion, solitude; asylum, cove, den, habitat, haunt, niche, recess, refuge, resort, shelter.

retrench *vb* clip, curtail, cut, delete, dock, lop, mutilate, pare, prune; abridge, decrease, diminish, lessen; confine, limit; economize, encroach.

retribution *n* compensation, desert, judgement, nemesis, penalty, recompense, repayment, requital, retaliation, return, revenge, reward, vengeance.

retrieve *vb* recall, recover, recoup, recruit, re-establish, regain, repair, restore.

retrograde *vb* decline, degenerate, recede, retire, retrocede. * *adj* backward, inverse, retrogressive, unprogressive.

retrospect *n* recollection, re-examination, reminiscence, re-survey, review, survey.

return *vb* reappear, recoil, recur, revert; answer, reply, respond; recriminate, retort; convey, give, communicate, reciprocate, recompense, refund, remit, repay, report, requite, send, tell, transmit; elect. * *n* payment, reimbursement, remittance, repayment; recompense, recovery, recurrence, renewal, repayment, requital, restitution, restoration, reward; advantage, benefit, interest, profit, rent, yield.

reunion *n* assemblage, assembly, gathering, meeting, re-assembly; rapprochement, reconciliation.

reveal *vb* announce, communicate, confess, declare, disclose, discover, display, divulge, expose, impart, open, publish, tell, uncover, unmask, unseal, unveil.

revel *vb* carouse, disport, riot, roister, tipple; delight, indulge, luxuriate, wanton. * *n* carousal, feast, festival, saturnalia, spree.

revelry *n* bacchanal, carousal, carouse, debauch, festivity, jollification, jollity, orgy, revel, riot, rout, saturnalia, wassail.

revenge *vb* avenge, repay, requite, retaliate, vindicate. * *n* malevolence, rancour, reprisal, requital, retaliation, retribution, vengeance, vindictiveness.

revengeful *adj* implacable, malevolent, malicious, malignant, resentful, rancorous, spiteful, vengeful, vindictive.

revenue *n* fruits, income, produce, proceeds, receipts, return, reward, wealth.

reverberate *vb* echo, re-echo, resound, return.

revere *vb* adore, esteem, hallow, honour, reverence, venerate, worship.

reverence *vb* adore, esteem, hallow, honour, revere, venerate, worship. * *n* adoration, awe, deference, homage, honour, respect, veneration, worship.

reverential *adj* deferential, humble, respectful, reverent, submissive.

reverse *vb* invert, transpose; overset, overthrow, overturn, quash, subvert, undo, unmake; annul, countermand, repeal, rescind, retract, revoke; back, back up, retreat. * *adj* back, converse, contrary, opposite, verso. * *n* back, calamity, check, comedown, contrary, counterpart, defeat, opposite, tail; change, vicissitude; adversity, affliction, hardship, misadventure, mischance, misfortune, mishap, trial.

revert *vb* repel, reverse; backslide, lapse, recur, relapse, return.

review *vb* inspect, overlook, reconsider, re-examine, retrace, revise, survey; analyse, criticize, discuss, edit, judge, scrutinize, study. * *n* reconsideration, re-examination, re-survey, retrospect, survey; analysis, digest, synopsis; commentary, critique, criticism, notice, review, scrutiny, study.

revile *vb* abuse, asperse, backbite, calumniate, defame, execrate, malign, reproach, slander, traduce, upbraid, vilify.

revise *vb* reconsider, re-examine, review; alter, amend, correct, edit, overhaul, polish.

revive *vb* reanimate, reinspire, reinspirit, reinvigorate, resuscitate, revitalize, revivify; animate, cheer, comfort, invigorate, quicken, reawaken, recover, refresh, renew, renovate, rouse, strengthen; reawake, recall.

revocation *n* abjuration, recall, recantation, repeal, retraction, reversal.

revoke *vb* abolish, abrogate, annul, cancel, countermand, invalidate, quash, recall, recant, repeal, repudiate, rescind, retract.

revolt *vb* desert, mutiny, rebel, rise; disgust, nauseate, repel, sicken. * *n* defection, desertion, faithlessness, inconstancy; disobedience, insurrection, mutiny, outbreak, rebellion, sedition, strike, uprising.

revolting *adj* abhorrent, abominable, disgusting, hateful, monstrous, nauseating, nauseous, objectionable, obnoxious, offensive, repulsive, shocking, sickening; insurgent, mutinous, rebellious.

revolution *n* coup, disobedience, insurrection, mutiny, outbreak, rebellion, sedition, strike, uprising; change, innovation, reformation, transformation, upheaval; circle, circuit, cycle, lap, orbit, rotation, spin, turn..

revolve *vb* circle, circulate, rotate, swing, turn, wheel; devolve, return; consider, mediate, ponder, ruminate, study.

revulsion *n* abstraction, shrinking, withdrawal; change, reaction, reversal, transition; abhorrence, disgust, loathing, repugnance.

reward *vb* compensate, gratify, indemnify, pay, punish, recompense, remember, remunerate, requite. * *n* compensation, gratification, guerdon, indemnification, pay, recompense, remuneration, requital; bounty, bonus, fee, gratuity, honorarium, meed, perquisite, premium, remembrance, tip; punishment, retribution.

rhythm *n* cadence, lilt, pulsation, swing; measure, metre, number.

ribald *adj* base, blue, coarse, filthy, gross, indecent, lewd, loose, low, mean, obscene, vile.

rich *adj* affluent, flush, moneyed, opulent, prosperous, wealthy; costly, estimable, gorgeous, luxurious, precious, splendid, sumptuous, superb, valuable; delicious, luscious, savoury; abundant, ample, copious, enough, full, plentiful, plenteous, sufficient; fertile, fruitful, luxuriant, productive, prolific; bright, dark, deep, exuberant, vivid; harmonious, mellow, melodious, soft, sweet; comical, funny, humorous, laughable.

riches *npl* abundance, affluence, fortune, money, opulence, plenty, richness, wealth, wealthiness.

rickety *adj* broken, imperfect, shaky, shattered, tottering, tumbledown, unsteady, weak.

rid *vb* deliver, free, release; clear, disburden, disencumber, scour, sweep; disinherit, dispatch, dissolve, divorce, finish, sever.

riddance *n* deliverance, disencumberment, extrication, escape, freedom, release, relief.

riddle[1] *vb* explain, solve, unriddle. * *n* conundrum, enigma, mystery, puzzle, rebus.

riddle[2] *vb* sieve, sift, perforate, permeate, spread. * *n* colander, sieve, strainer.

ridge *n* chine, hogback, ledge, saddle, spine, rib, watershed, weal, wrinkle.

ridicule *vb* banter, burlesque, chaff, deride, disparage, jeer, mock, lampoon, rally, satirize, scout, taunt. * *n* badinage, banter, burlesque, chaff, derision, game, gibe, irony, jeer, mockery, persiflage, quip, raillery, sarcasm, satire, sneer, squib, wit.

ridiculous *adj* absurd, amusing, comical, droll, eccentric, fantastic, farcical, funny, laughable, ludicrous, nonsensical, odd, outlandish, preposterous, queer, risible, waggish.

rife *adj* abundant, common, current, general, numerous, plentiful, prevailing, prevalent, replete.

riffraff *n* horde, mob, populace, rabble, scum, trash.

rifle *vb* despoil, fleece, pillage, plunder, ransack, rob, strip.

rift *vb* cleave, rive, split. * *n* breach, break, chink, cleft, crack, cranny, crevice, fissure, fracture, gap, opening, reft, rent.

rig *vb* accoutre, clothe, dress. * *n* costume, dress, garb; equipment, team.

right *vb* adjust, correct, regulate, settle, straighten, vindicate. * *adj* direct, rectilinear, straight; erect, perpendicular, plumb, upright; equitable, even-handed, fair, just, justifiable, honest, lawful, legal, legitimate, rightful, square, unswerving; appropriate, becoming, correct, conventional, fit, fitting, meet, orderly, proper, reasonable, seemly, suitable, well-done; actual, genuine, real, true, unquestionable; dexter, dextral, right-handed. * *adv* equitably, fairly, justly, lawfully, rightfully, rightly; correctly, fitly, properly, suitably, truly; actually, exactly, just, really, truly, well. * *n* authority, claim, liberty, permission, power, privilege, title; equity, good, honour, justice, lawfulness, legality, propriety, reason, righteousness, truth.

righteous *adj* devout, godly, good, holy, honest, incorrupt, just, pious, religious, saintly, uncorrupt, upright, virtuous; equitable, fair, right, rightful.

righteousness *n* equity, faithfulness, godliness, goodness, holiness, honesty, integrity, justice, piety, purity, right, rightfulness, sanctity, uprightness, virtue.

rightful *adj* lawful, legitimate, true; appropriate, correct, deserved, due, equitable, fair, fitting, honest, just, legal, merited, proper, reasonable, suitable.

rigid *adj* firm, hard, inflexible, permanent, stiff, stiffened, unbending, unpliant, unyielding; bristling, erect, precipitous, steep; austere, conventional, correct, exact, formal, harsh, meticulous, precise, rigorous, severe, sharp, stern, strict, unmitigated; cruel.

rigmarole *n* balderdash, flummery, gibberish, gobbledegook, jargon, nonsense, palaver, trash, twaddle, verbiage.

rigour *n* hardness, inflexibility, rigidity, rigidness, stiffness; asperity, austerity, harshness, severity, sternness; evenness, strictness; inclemency.

rile *vb* anger, annoy, irritate, upset, vex.

rim *n* brim, brink, border, confine, curb, edge, flange, girdle, margin, ring, skirt.

ring[1] *vb* circle, encircle, enclose, girdle, surround. * *n* circle, circlet, girdle, hoop, round, whorl; cabal, clique, combination, confederacy, coterie, gang, junta, league, set.

ring[2] *vb* chime, clang, jingle, knell, peal, resound, reverberate, sound, tingle, toll; call, phone, telephone. * *n* chime, knell, peal, tinkle, toll; call, phone call, telephone call.

riot *vb* carouse, luxuriate, revel. * *n* affray, altercation, brawl, broil, commotion, disturbance, fray, outbreak, pandemonium, quarrel, squabble, tumult, uproar; dissipation, excess, luxury, merrymaking, revelry.

riotous *adj* boisterous, luxurious, merry, revelling, unrestrained, wanton; disorderly, insubordinate, lawless, mutinous, rebellious, refractory, seditious, tumultuous, turbulent, ungovernable, unruly, violent.

ripe *adj* advanced, grown, mature, mellow, seasoned, soft; fit, prepared, ready; accomplished, complete, consummate, finished, perfect, perfected.

ripen *vb* burgeon, develop, mature, prepare.

rise *vb* arise, ascend, clamber, climb, levitate, mount; excel, succeed; enlarge, heighten, increase, swell, thrive; revive; grow, kindle, wax; begin, flow, head, originate, proceed, spring, start; mutiny, rebel, revolt; happen, occur. * *n* ascension, ascent, rising; elevation, grade, hill, slope; beginning, emergence, flow, origin, source, spring; advance, augmentation, expansion, increase.

risible *adj* amusing, comical, droll, farcical, funny, laughable, ludicrous, ridiculous.

risk *vb* bet, endanger, hazard, jeopardize, peril, speculate, stake, venture, wager. * *n* chance, danger, hazard, jeopardy, peril, venture.

rite *n* ceremonial, ceremony, form, formulary, ministration, observance, ordinance, ritual, rubric, sacrament, solemnity.

ritual *adj* ceremonial, conventional, formal, habitual, routine, stereotyped. * *n* ceremonial, ceremony, liturgy, observance, rite, sacrament, service; convention, form, formality, habit, practice, protocol.

rival *vb* emulate, match, oppose. * *adj* competing, contending, emulating, emulous, opposing. * *n* antagonist, competitor, emulator, opponent.

rive *vb* cleave, rend, split.

river *n* affluent, current, reach, stream, tributary.

road *n* course, highway, lane, passage, path, pathway, roadway, route, street, thoroughfare, track, trail, turnpike, way.

roam *vb* jaunt, prowl, ramble, range, rove, straggle, stray, stroll, wander.

roar *vb* bawl, bellow, cry, howl, vociferate, yell; boom, peal, rattle, resound, thunder. * *n* bellow, roaring; rage, resonance, storm, thunder; cry, outcry, shout; laugh, laughter, shout.

rob *vb* despoil, fleece, pilfer, pillage, plunder, rook, strip; appropriate, deprive, embezzle, plagiarize.

robber *n* bandit, brigand, desperado, depredator, despoiler, footpad, freebooter, highwayman, marauder, pillager, pirate, plunderer, rifler, thief.

robbery *n* depredation, despoliation, embezzlement, freebooting, larceny, peculation, piracy, plagiarism, plundering, spoliation, theft.

robe *vb* array, clothe, dress, invest. * *n* attire, costume, dress, garment, gown, habit, vestment; bathrobe, dressing gown, housecoat.

robust *adj* able-bodied, athletic, brawny, energetic, firm, forceful, hale, hardy, hearty, iron, lusty, muscular, powerful, seasoned, self-assertive, sinewy, sound, stalwart, stout, strong, sturdy, vigorous.

rock[1] *n* boulder, cliff, crag, reef, stone; asylum, defence, foundation, protection, refuge, strength, support; gneiss, granite, marble, slate, etc.

rock[2] *vb* calm, cradle, lull, quiet, soothe, still, tranquillize; reel, shake, sway, teeter, totter, wobble.

rogue *n* beggar, vagabond, vagrant; caitiff, cheat, knave, rascal, scamp, scapegrace, scoundrel, sharper, swindler, trickster, villain.

roguish *adj* dishonest, fraudulent, knavish, rascally, scoundrelly, trickish, tricky; arch, sportive, mischievous, puckish, waggish, wanton.

role *n* character, function, impersonation, part, task.

roll *vb* gyrate, revolve, rotate, turn, wheel; curl, muffle, swathe, wind; bind, involve, enfold, envelop; flatten, level, smooth, spread; bowl, drive; trundle, wheel; gybe, lean, lurch, stagger, sway, yaw; billow, swell, undulate; wallow, welter; flow, glide, run. * *n* document, scroll, volume; annals, chronicle, history, record, rota; catalogue, inventory, list, register, schedule; booming, resonance, reverberation, thunder; cylinder, roller.

rollicking *adj* frisky, frolicking, frolicsome, jolly, jovial, lively, swaggering.

romance *vb* exaggerate, fantasize. * *n* fantasy, fiction, legend, novel, story, tale; exaggeration, falsehood, lie; ballad, idyll, song.

romantic *adj* extravagant, fanciful, fantastic, ideal, imaginative, sentimental, wild; chimerical, fabulous, fantastic, fictitious, imaginary, improbable, legendary, picturesque, quixotic, sentimental. * *n* dreamer, idealist, sentimentalist, visionary.

romp *vb* caper, gambol, frisk, sport. * *n* caper, frolic, gambol.

room *n* accommodation, capacity, compass, elbowroom, expanse, extent, field, latitude, leeway, play, scope, space, swing; place, stead; apartment, chamber, lodging; chance, occasion, opportunity.

roomy *adj* ample, broad, capacious, comfortable, commodious, expansive, extensive, large, spacious, wide.

root[1] *vb* anchor, embed, fasten, implant, place, settle; confirm, establish. * *n* base, bottom, foundation; cause, occasion, motive, origin, reason, source; etymon, radical, radix, stem.

root[2] *vb* destroy, eradicate, extirpate, exterminate, remove, unearth, uproot; burrow, dig, forage, grub, rummage; applaud, cheer, encourage.

rooted *adj* chronic, confirmed, deep, established, fixed, radical.

roseate *adj* blooming, blushing, rose-coloured, rosy, rubicund; hopeful.

rostrum *n* platform, stage, stand, tribune.

rosy *adj* auspicious, blooming, blushing, favourable, flushed, hopeful, roseate, ruddy, sanguine.

rot *vb* corrupt, decay, decompose, degenerate, putrefy, spoil, taint. * *n* corruption, decay, decomposition, putrefaction.

rotary *adj* circular, rotating, revolving, rotatory, turning, whirling.

rotten *adj* carious, corrupt, decomposed, fetid, putrefied, putrescent, putrid, rank, stinking; defective, unsound; corrupt, deceitful, immoral, treacherous, unsound, untrustworthy.

rotund *adj* buxom, chubby, full, globular, obese, plump, round, stout; fluent, grandiloquent.

roué *n* debauchee, libertine, profligate, rake.

rough *vb* coarsen, roughen; manhandle, mishandle, molest. * *adj* bumpy, craggy, irregular, jagged, rugged, scabrous, scraggy, scratchy, stubby, uneven; approximate, cross-grained, crude, formless, incomplete, knotty, rough-hewn, shapeless, sketchy, uncut, unfashioned, unfinished, unhewn, unpolished, unwrought, vague; bristly, bushy, coarse, disordered, hairy, hirsute, ragged, shaggy, unkempt; austere, bearish, bluff, blunt, brusque, burly, churlish, discourteous, gruff, harsh, impolite, indelicate, rude, surly, uncivil, uncourteous, ungracious, unpolished, unrefined; harsh, severe, sharp, violent; astringent, crabbed, hard, sour, tart; discordant, grating, inharmonious, jarring, raucous, scabrous, unmusical; boisterous, foul, inclement, severe, stormy, tempestuous, tumultuous, turbulent, untamed, violent, wild; acrimonious, brutal, cruel, disorderly, riotous, rowdy, severe, uncivil, unfeeling, ungentle. * *n* bully, rowdy, roughneck, ruffian; draft, outline, sketch, suggestion; unevenness.

round *vb* curve; circuit, encircle, encompass, surround. * *adj* bulbous, circular, cylindrical, globular, orbed, orbicular, rotund, spherical; complete, considerable, entire, full, great, large, unbroken, whole; chubby, corpulent, plump, stout, swelling; continuous, flowing, harmonious, smooth; brisk, quick; blunt, candid, fair, frank, honest, open, plain, upright. * *adv* around, circularly, circuitously. * *prep* about, around. * *n* bout, cycle, game, lap, revolution, rotation, succession, turn; canon, catch, dance; ball, circle, circumference, cylinder, globe, sphere; circuit, compass, perambulation, routine, tour, watch.

roundabout *adj* circuitous, circumlocutory, indirect, tortuous; ample, broad, extensive; encircling, encompassing.

rouse *vb* arouse, awaken, raise, shake, wake, waken; animate, bestir, brace, enkindle, excite, inspire, kindle, rally, stimulate, stir, whet; startle, surprise.

rout *vb* beat, conquer, defeat, discomfit, overcome, overpower, overthrow, vanquish; chase away, dispel, disperse, scatter. * *n* defeat, discomfiture, flight, ruin; concourse, multitude, rabble; brawl, disturbance, noise, roar, uproar.

route *vb* direct, forward, send, steer. * *n* course, circuit, direction, itinerary, journey, march, road, passage, path, way.

routine *adj* conventional, familiar, habitual, ordinary, standard, typical, usual; boring, dull, humdrum, predictable, tiresome. * *n* beat, custom, groove, method, order, path, practice, procedure, round, rut.

rove *vb* prowl, ramble, range, roam, stray, struggle, stroll, wander.

row[1] *n* file, line, queue, range, rank, series, string, tier; alley, street, terrace.

row[2] *vb* argue, dispute, fight, quarrel, squabble. * *n* affray, altercation, brawl, broil, commotion, dispute, disturbance, noise, outbreak, quarrel, riot, squabble, tumult, uproar.

royal *adj* august, courtly, dignified, generous, grand, imperial, kingly, kinglike, magnanimous, magnificent, majestic, monarchical, noble, princely, regal, sovereign, splendid, superb.

rub *vb* abrade, chafe, grate, graze, scrape; burnish, clean, massage, polish, scour, wipe; apply, put, smear, spread. * *n* caress, massage, polish, scouring, shine, wipe; catch, difficulty, drawback, impediment, obstacle, problem.

rubbish *n* debris, detritus, fragments, refuse, ruins, waste; dregs, dross, garbage, litter, lumber, scoria, scum, sweepings, trash, trumpery.

rubicund *adj* blushing, erubescent, florid, flushed, red, reddish, ruddy.

rude *adj* coarse, crude, ill-formed, rough, rugged, shapeless, uneven, unfashioned, unformed, unwrought; artless, barbarous, boorish, clownish, ignorant, illiterate, loutish, raw, savage, uncivilized, uncouth, uncultivated, undisciplined, unpolished, ungraceful, unskilful, unskilled, untaught, untrained, untutored, vulgar; awkward, barbarous, bluff, blunt, boorish, brusque, brutal, churlish, gruff, ill-bred, impertinent, impolite, impudent, insolent, insulting, ribald, saucy, uncivil, uncourteous, unrefined; boisterous, fierce, harsh, severe, tumultuous, turbulent, violent; artless, inelegant, rustic, unpolished; hearty, robust.

rudimentary *adj* elementary, embryonic, fundamental, initial, primary, rudimental, undeveloped.

rue *vb* deplore, grieve, lament, regret, repent.

rueful *adj* dismal, doleful, lamentable, lugubrious, melancholic, melancholy, mournful, penitent, regretful, sad, sorrowful, woeful.

ruffian *n* bully, caitiff, cutthroat, hoodlum, miscreant, monster, murderer, rascal, robber, roisterer, rowdy, scoundrel, villain, wretch.

ruffle *vb* damage, derange, disarrange, dishevel, disorder, ripple, roughen, rumple; agitate, confuse, discompose, disquiet, disturb, excite, harass, irritate, molest, plague, perturb, torment, trouble, vex, worry; cockle, flounce, pucker, wrinkle. * *n* edging, frill, ruff; agitation, bustle, commotion, confusion, contention, disturbance, excitement, fight, fluster, flutter, flurry, perturbation, tumult.

rugged *adj* austere, bristly, coarse, crabbed, cragged, craggy, hard, hardy, irregular, ragged, robust, rough, rude, scraggy, severe, seamed, shaggy, uneven, unkempt, wrinkled; boisterous, inclement, stormy, tempestuous, tumultuous, turbulent, violent; grating, harsh, inharmonious, unmusical, scabrous.

ruin *vb* crush, damn, defeat, demolish, desolate, destroy, devastate, overthrow, overturn, overwhelm, seduce, shatter, smash, subvert, wreck; beggar, impoverish. * *n* damnation, decay, defeat, demolition, desolation, destruction, devastation, discomfiture, downfall, fall, loss, perdition, prostration, rack, ruination, shipwreck, subversion, undoing, wrack, wreck; bane, mischief, pest.

ruination *n* demolition, destruction, overthrow, ruin, subversion.

ruinous *adj* decayed, demolished, dilapidated; baneful, calamitous, damnatory, destructive, disastrous, mischievous, noisome, noxious, pernicious, subversive, wasteful.

rule *vb* bridle, command, conduct, control, direct, domineer, govern, judge, lead, manage, reign, restrain; advise, guide, persuade; adjudicate, decide, determine, establish, settle; obtain, prevail, predominate. * *n* authority, command, control, direction, domination, dominion, empire, government, jurisdiction, lordship, mastery, mastership, regency, reign, sway; behaviour, conduct; habit, method, order, regularity, routine, system; aphorism, canon, convention, criterion, formula, guide, law, maxim, model, precedent, precept, standard, system, test, touchstone; decision, order, prescription, regulation, ruling.

ruler *n* chief, governor, king, lord, master, monarch, potentate, regent, sovereign; director, head, manager, president; controller, guide, rule; straight-edge.

ruminate *vb* brood, chew, cogitate, consider, contemplate, meditate, muse, ponder, reflect, think.

rumour *vb* bruit, circulate, report, tell. * *n* bruit, gossip, hearsay, report, talk; news, report, story, tidings; celebrity, fame, reputation, repute.

rumple *vb* crease, crush, corrugate, crumple, disarrange, dishevel, pucker, ruffle, wrinkle. * *n* crease, corrugation, crumple, fold, pucker, wrinkle.

run *vb* bolt, career, course, gallop, haste, hasten, hie, hurry, lope, post, race, scamper, scour, scud, scuttle, speed, trip; flow, glide, go, move, proceed, stream; fuse, liquefy, melt; advance, pass, proceed, vanish; extend, lie, spread, stretch; circulate, pass, press; average, incline, tend; flee; pierce, stab; drive, force, propel, push, thrust, turn; cast, form, mould, shape; follow, perform, pursue, take; discharge, emit; direct, maintain, manage. * *n* race, running; course, current, flow, motion, passage, progress, way, wont; continuance, currency, popularity; excursion, gallop, journey, trip, trot; demand, pressure; brook, burn, flow, rill, rivulet, runlet, runnel, streamlet.

rupture *vb* break, burst, fracture, sever, split. * *n* breach, break, burst, disruption, fracture, split; contention, faction, feud, hostility, quarrel, schism.

rural *adj* agrarian, bucolic, country, pastoral, rustic, sylvan.

ruse *n* artifice, deception, deceit, fraud, hoax, imposture, manoeuvre, sham, stratagem, trick, wile.

rush *vb* attack, career, charge, dash, drive, gush, hurtle, precipitate, surge, sweep, tear. * *n* dash, onrush, onset, plunge, precipitance, precipitancy, rout, stampede, tear.

rust *vb* corrode, decay, degenerate. * *n* blight, corrosion, crust, mildew, must, mould, mustiness.

rustic *adj* country, rural; awkward, boorish, clownish, countrified, loutish, outlandish, rough, rude, uncouth, unpolished, untaught; coarse, countrified, homely, plain, simple, unadorned; artless, honest, unsophisticated. * *n* boor, bumpkin, clown, countryman, peasant, swain, yokel.

ruthless *adj* barbarous, cruel, fell, ferocious, hardhearted, inexorable, inhuman, merciless, pitiless, relentless, remorseless, savage, truculent, uncompassionate, unmerciful, unpitying, unrelenting, unsparing.

S

sable *adj* black, dark, dusky, ebony, sombre.
sabulous *adj* gritty, sabulose, sandy.
sack[1] *n* bag, pouch.
sack[2] *vb* despoil, devastate, pillage, plunder, ravage, spoil. * *n* desolation, despoliation, destruction, devastation, havoc, ravage, sacking, spoliation, waste; booty, plunder, spoil.
sacred *adj* consecrated, dedicated, devoted, divine, hallowed, holy; inviolable, inviolate; sainted, venerable.
sacrifice *vb* forgo, immolate, surrender. * *n* immolation, oblation, offering; destruction, devotion, loss, surrender.
sacrilege *n* desecration, profanation, violation.
sacrilegious *adj* desecrating, impious, irreverent, profane.
sad *adj* grave, pensive, sedate, serious, sober, sombre, staid.
saddle *vb* burden, charge, clog, encumber, load.
sadly *adv* grievously, miserable, mournfully, sorrowfully; afflictively, badly, calamitously; darkly; gravely, seriously, soberly.
sadness *n* dejection, depression, despondency, melancholy, mournful, sorrow, sorrowfulness; dolefulness, gloominess, grief, mournfulness, sorrow; gravity, sedateness, seriousness.
safe *adj* undamaged, unharmed, unhurt, unscathed; guarded, protected, secure, snug, unexposed; certain, dependable, reliable, sure, trustworthy; good, harmless, sound, whole. * *n* chest, coffer, strongbox.
safeguard *vb* guard, protect. * *n* defence, protection, security; convoy, escort, guard, safe-conduct; pass, passport.
sagacious *adj* acute, apt, astute, clear-sighted, discerning, intelligent, judicious, keen, penetrating, perspicacious, rational, sage, sharp-witted, wise, shrewd.
sagacity *n* acuteness, astuteness, discernment, ingenuity, insight, penetration, perspicacity, quickness, readiness, sense, sharpness, shrewdness, wisdom.
sage *adj* acute, discerning, intelligent, prudent, sagacious, sapient, sensible, shrewd, wise; judicious, well-judged; grave, serious, solemn. * *n* philosopher, pundit, savant.
sailor *n* mariner, navigator, salt, seafarer, seaman, tar.
saintly *adj* devout, godly, holy, pious, religious.
sake *n* end, cause, purpose, reason; account, consideration, interest, regard, respect, score.
saleable *adj* marketable, merchantable, vendible.
salacious *adj* carnal, concupiscent, incontinent, lascivious, lecherous, lewd, libidinous, loose, lustful, prurient, unchaste, wanton.
salary *n* allowance, hire, pay, stipend, wages.
salient *adj* bounding, jumping, leaping; beating, springing, throbbing; jutting, projecting, prominent; conspicuous, remarkable, striking.
saline *adj* briny, salty.
sally *vb* issue, rush. * *n* digression, excursion, sortie, run, trip; escapade, frolic; crank, fancy, jest, joke, quip, quirk, sprightly, witticism.
salt *adj* saline, salted, salty; bitter, pungent, sharp. * *n* flavour, savour, seasoning, smack, relish, taste; humour, piquancy, poignancy, sarcasm, smartness, wit, zest; mariner, sailor, seaman, tar.
salubrious *adj* beneficial, benign, healthful, healthy, salutary, sanitary, wholesome.
salutary *adj* healthy, healthful, helpful, safe, salubrious, wholesome; advantageous, beneficial, good, profitable, serviceable, useful.
salute *vb* accost, address, congratulate, greet, hail, welcome. * *n* address, greeting, salutation.
salvation *n* deliverance, escape, preservation, redemption, rescue, saving.
same *adj* ditto, identical, selfsame; corresponding, like, similar.
sample *vb* savour, sip, smack, sup, taste; test, try; demonstrate, exemplify, illustrate, instance. * *adj* exemplary, illustrative, representative. * *n* demonstration, exemplification, illustration, instance, piece, specimen; example, model, pattern.
sanctify *vb* consecrate, hallow, purify; justify, ratify, sanction.
sanctimonious *adj* affected, devout, holy, hypocritical, pharisaical, pious, self-righteous.
sanction *vb* authorize, countenance, encourage, support; confirm, ratify. * *n* approval, authority, authorization, confirmation, countenance, endorsement, ratification, support, warranty; ban, boycott, embargo, penalty.
sanctity *n* devotion, godliness, goodness, grace, holiness, piety, purity, religiousness, saintliness.
sanctuary *n* altar, church, shrine, temple; asylum, protection, refuge, retreat, shelter.
sane *adj* healthy, lucid, rational, reasonable, sober, sound.
sang-froid *n* calmness, composure, coolness,

imperturbability, indifference, nonchalance, phlegm, unconcern.

sanguinary *adj* bloody, gory, murderous; barbarous, bloodthirsty, cruel, fell, pitiless, savage, ruthless.

sanguine *adj* crimson, florid, red; animated, ardent, cheerful, lively, warm; buoyant, confident, enthusiastic, hopeful, optimistic; full-blooded.

sanitary *adj* clean, curative, healing, healthy, hygienic, remedial, therapeutic, wholesome.

sanity *n* normality, rationality, reason, saneness, soundness.

sapient *adj* acute, discerning, intelligent, knowing, sagacious, sage, sensible, shrewd, wise.

sarcastic *adj* acrimonious, biting, cutting, mordacious, mordant, sardonic, satirical, sharp, severe, sneering, taunting.

sardonic *adj* bitter, derisive, ironical, malevolent, malicious, malignant, sarcastic.

satanic *adj* devilish, diabolical, evil, false, fiendish, hellish, infernal, malicious.

satellite *adj* dependent, subordinate, tributary, vassal. * *n* attendant, dependant, follower, hanger-on, retainer, vassal.

satiate *vb* fill, sate, satisfy, suffice; cloy, glut, gorge, overfeed, overfill, pall, surfeit.

satire *n* burlesque, diatribe, invective, fling, irony, lampoon, pasquinade, philippic, ridicule, sarcasm, skit, squib.

satirical *adj* abusive, biting, bitter, censorious, cutting, invective, ironical, keen, mordacious, poignant, reproachful, sarcastic, severe, sharp, taunting.

satirize *vb* abuse, censure, lampoon, ridicule.

satisfaction *n* comfort, complacency, contentment, ease, enjoyment, gratification, pleasure, satiety; amends, appeasement, atonement, compensation, indemnification, recompense, redress, remuneration, reparation, requital, reward.

satisfactory *adj* adequate, conclusive, convincing, decisive, sufficient; gratifying, pleasing.

satisfy *vb* appease, content, fill, gratify, please, sate, satiate, suffice; indemnify, compensate, liquidate, pay, recompense, remunerate, requite; discharge, settle; assure, convince, persuade; answer, fulfil, meet.

saturate *vb* drench, fill, fit, imbue, soak, steep, wet.

saturnine *adj* dark, dull, gloomy, grave, heavy, leaden, morose, phlegmatic, sad, sedate, sombre; melancholic, mournful, serious, unhappy; mischievous, naughty, troublesome, vexatious, wicked.

sauce *n* cheekiness, impudence, insolence; appetizer, compound, condiment, relish, seasoning.

saucy *adj* bold, cavalier, disrespectful, flippant, forward, immodest, impertinent, impudent, insolent, pert, rude.

saunter *vb* amble, dawdle, delay, dilly-dally, lag, linger, loiter, lounge, stroll, tarry. * *n* amble, stroll, walk.

savage *vb* attack, lacerate, mangle, maul. * *adj* rough, uncultivated, wild; rude, uncivilized, unpolished, untaught; bloodthirsty, feral, ferine, ferocious, fierce, rapacious, untamed, vicious; beastly, bestial, brutal, brutish, inhuman; atrocious, barbarous, barbaric, bloody, brutal, cruel, fell, fiendish, hardhearted, heathenish, merciless, murderous, pitiless, relentless, ruthless, sanguinary, truculent; native, rough, rugged. * *n* barbarian, brute, heathen, vandal.

save *vb* keep, liberate, preserve, rescue; salvage, recover, redeem; economize, gather, hoard, husband, reserve, store; hinder, obviate, prevent, spare. * *prep* but, deducting, except.

saviour *n* defender, deliverer, guardian, protector, preserver, rescuer, saver.

savour *vb* affect, appreciate, enjoy, like, partake, relish; flavour, season. * *n* flavour, gusto, relish, smack, taste; fragrance, odour, smell, scent.

savoury *adj* agreeable, delicious, flavourful, luscious, nice, palatable, piquant, relishing.

saw *n* adage, aphorism, apothegm, axiom, byword, dictum, maxim, precept, proverb, sententious saying.

say *vb* declare, express, pronounce, speak, tell, utter; affirm, allege, argue; recite, rehearse, repeat; assume, presume, suppose. * *n* affirmation, declaration, speech, statement; decision, voice, vote.

saying *n* declaration, expression, observation, remark, speech, statement; adage, aphorism, byword, dictum, maxim, proverb, saw.

scale[1] *n* basin, dish, pan; balance.

scale[2] *n* flake, lamina, lamella, layer, plate.

scale[3] *vb* ascend, climb, escalate, mount. * *n* graduation.

scamp *n* cheat, knave, rascal, rogue, scapegrace, scoundrel, swindler, trickster, villain.

scamper *vb* haste, hasten, hie, run, scud, speed, trip.

scan *vb* examine, investigate, scrutinize, search, sift.

scandal *vb* asperse, defame, libel, traduce. * *n* aspersion, calumny, defamation, obloquy, reproach; discredit, disgrace, dishonour, disrepute, ignominy, infamy, odium, opprobrium, offence, shame.

scandalize *vb* offend; asperse, backbite, calumniate, decry, defame, disgust, lampoon, libel, reproach, revile, satirize, slander, traduce, vilify.

scandalous *adj* defamatory, libellous, opprobrious, slanderous; atrocious, disgraceful, disreputable, infamous, inglorious, ignominious, odious, shameful.

scanty *adj* insufficient, meagre, narrow, scant, small; hardly, scarce, short, slender; niggardly, parsimonious, penurious, scrimpy, skimpy, sparing.

scar[1] *vb* hurt, mark, wound. * *n* cicatrice, cicatrix, seam; blemish, defect, disfigurement, flaw, injury, mark.

scar[2] *n* bluff, cliff, crag, precipice.

scarce *adj* deficient, wanting; infrequent, rare,

uncommon. * *adv* barely, hardly, scantily.

scarcely *adv* barely, hardly, scantily.

scarcity *n* dearth, deficiency, insufficiency, lack, want; infrequency, rareness, rarity, uncommonness.

scare *vb* affright, alarm, appal, daunt, fright, frighten, intimidate, shock, startle, terrify. * *n* alarm, fright, panic, shock, terror.

scathe *vb* blast, damage, destroy, injure, harm, haste. * *n* damage, harm, injury, mischief, waste.

scatter *vb* broadcast, sprinkle, strew; diffuse, disperse, disseminate, dissipate, distribute, separate, spread; disappoint, dispel, frustrate, overthrow.

scene *n* display, exhibition, pageant, representation, show, sight, spectacle, view; place, situation, spot; arena, stage.

scent *vb* breathe in, inhale, nose, smell, sniff; detect, smell out, sniff out; aromatize, perfume. * *n* aroma, balminess, fragrance, odour, perfume, smell, redolence.

sceptic *n* doubter, freethinker, questioner, unbeliever.

sceptical *adj* doubtful, doubting, dubious, hesitating, incredulous, questioning, unbelieving.

scepticism *n* doubt, dubiety, freethinking, incredulity, unbelief.

schedule *vb* line up, list, plan, programme, tabulate. * *n* document, scroll; catalogue, inventory, list, plan, record, register, roll, table, timetable.

scheme *vb* contrive, design, frame, imagine, plan, plot, project. * *n* plan, system, theory; cabal, conspiracy, contrivance, design, device, intrigue, machination, plan, plot, project, stratagem; arrangement, draught, diagram, outline.

schism *n* division, separation, split; discord, disunion, division, faction, separation.

scholar *n* disciple, learner, pupil, student; don, fellow, intellectual, pedant, savant.

scholarship *n* accomplishments, acquirements, attainments, erudition, knowledge, learning; bursary, exhibition, foundation, grant, maintenance.

scholastic *adj* academic, bookish, lettered, literary; formal, pedantic.

school *vb* drill, educate, exercise, indoctrinate, instruct, teach, train; admonish, control, chide, discipline, govern, reprove, tutor. * *adj* academic, collegiate, institutional, scholastic, schoolish. * *n* academy, college, gymnasium, institute, institution, kindergarten, lyceum, manège, polytechnic, seminary, university; adherents, camarilla, circle, clique, coterie, disciples, followers; body, order, organization, party, sect.

schooling *n* discipline, education, instruction, nurture, teaching, training, tuition.

scintillate *vb* coruscate, flash, gleam, glisten, glitter, sparkle, twinkle.

scoff *vb* deride, flout, jeer, mock, ridicule, taunt; gibe, sneer. * *n* flout, gibe, jeer, sneer, mockery, taunt; derision, ridicule.

scold *vb* berate, blame, censure, chide, rate, reprimand, reprove; brawl, rail, rate, reprimand, upbraid, vituperate. * *n* shrew, termagant, virago, vixen.

scope *n* aim, design, drift, end, intent, intention, mark, object, purpose, tendency, view; amplitude, field, latitude, liberty, margin, opportunity, purview, range, room, space, sphere, vent; extent, length, span, stretch, sweep.

scorch *vb* blister, burn, char, parch, roast, sear, shrivel, singe.

score *vb* cut, furrow, mark, notch, scratch; charge, note, record; impute, note; enter, register. * *n* incision, mark, notch; account, bill, charge, debt, reckoning; consideration, ground, motive, reason.

scorn *vb* condemn, despise, disregard, disdain, scout, slight, spurn. * *n* contempt, derision, disdain, mockery, slight, sneer; scoff.

scornful *adj* contemptuous, defiant, disdainful, contemptuous, regardless.

scot-free *adj* untaxed; clear, unhurt, uninjured, safe.

scoundrel *n* cheat, knave, miscreant, rascal, reprobate, rogue, scamp, swindler, trickster, villain.

scour[1] *vb* brighten, buff, burnish, clean, cleanse, polish, purge, scrape, scrub, rub, wash, whiten; rake; efface, obliterate, overrun.

scour[2] *vb* career, course, range, scamper, scud, scuttle; comb, hunt, rake, ransack, rifle, rummage, search.

scourge *vb* lash, whip; afflict, chasten, chastise, correct, punish; harass, torment. * *n* cord, cowhide, lash, strap, thong, whip; affliction, bane, curse, infliction, nuisance, pest, plague, punishment.

scout *vb* contemn, deride, disdain, despise, ridicule, scoff, scorn, sneer, spurn; investigate, probe, search. * *n* escort, lookout, precursor, vanguard.

scowl *vb* frown, glower, lower. * *n* frown, glower, lower.

scraggy *adj* broken, craggy, rough, rugged, scabrous, scragged, uneven; attenuated, bony, emaciated, gaunt, lank, lean, meagre, scrawny, skinny, thin.

scrap[1] *vb* discard, junk, trash. * *n* bit, fragment, modicum, particle, piece, snippet; bite, crumb, morsel, mouthful; debris, junk, litter, rubbish, rubble, trash, waste.

scrap[2] *vb* altercate, bicker, dispute, clash, fight, hassle, quarrel, row, spat, squabble, tiff, tussle, wrangle. * *n* affray, altercation, bickering, clash, dispute, fight, fray, hassle, melee, quarrel, row, run-in, set-to, spat, squabble, tiff, tussle, wrangle.

scrape *vb* bark, grind, rasp, scuff; accumulate, acquire, collect, gather, save; erase, remove. * *n* difficulty, distress, embarrassment, perplexity, predicament.

scream *vb* screech, shriek, squall, ululate. * *n* cry, outcry, screech, shriek, shrill, ululation.

screen *vb* cloak, conceal, cover, defend, fence, hide,

mask, protect, shelter, shroud. * *n* blind, curtain, lattice, partition; defence, guard, protection, shield; cloak, cover, veil, disguise; riddle, sieve.

screw *vb* force, press, pressurize, squeeze, tighten, twist, wrench; oppress, rack; distort. * *n* extortioner, extortionist, miser, scrimp, skinflint; prison guard; sexual intercourse.

scrimmage *n* brawl, melee, riot, scuffle, skirmish.

scrimp *vb* contract, curtail, limit, pinch, reduce, scant, shorten, straiten.

scrimpy *adj* contracted, deficient, narrow, scanty.

scroll *n* inventory, list, parchment, roll, schedule.

scrub[1] *adj* contemptible, inferior, mean, niggardly, scrubby, shabby, small, stunted. * *n* brushwood, underbrush, underwood.

scrub[2] *vb* clean, cleanse, rub, scour, scrape, wash.

scruple *vb* boggle, demur, falter, hesitate, object, pause, stickle, waver. * *n* delicacy, hesitancy, hesitation, nicety, perplexity, qualm.

scrupulous *adj* conscientious, fastidious, nice, precise, punctilious, rigorous, strict; careful, cautious, circumspect, exact, vigilant.

scrutinize *vb* canvass, dissect, examine, explore, investigate, overhaul, probe, search, sift, study.

scrutiny *n* examination, exploration, inquisition, inspection, investigation, search, searching, sifting.

scud *vb* flee, fly, haste, hasten, hie, post, run, scamper, speed, trip.

scuffle *vb* contend, fight, strive, struggle. * *n* altercation, brawl, broil, contest, encounter, fight, fray, quarrel, squabble, struggle, wrangle.

sculpt vb carve, chisel, cut, sculpture; engrave, grave.

scurrilous *adj* abusive, blackguardly, contumelious, foul, foul-mouthed, indecent, infamous, insolent, insulting, offensive, opprobrious, reproachful, ribald, vituperative; coarse, gross, low, mean, obscene, vile, vulgar.

scurry *vb* bustle, dash, hasten, hurry, scamper, scud, scutter. * *n* burst, bustle, dash, flurry, haste, hurry, scamper, scud, spurt.

scurvy *adj* scabbed, scabby, scurfy; abject, bad, base, contemptible, despicable, low, mean, pitiful, sorry, vile, vulgar, worthless; malicious, mischievous, offensive.

scuttle[1] *vb* hurry, hustle, run, rush, scamper, scramble, scud, scurry. * *n* dash, drive, flurry, haste, hurry, hustle, race, rush, scamper, scramble, scud, scurry.

scuttle[2] *vb* capsize, founder, go down, sink, overturn, upset. * *n* hatch, hatchway.

seal *vb* close, fasten, secure; attest, authenticate, confirm, establish, ratify, sanction; confine, enclose, imprison. * *n* fastening, stamp, wafer, wax; assurance, attestation, authentication, confirmation, pledge, ratification.

seamy *adj* disreputable, nasty, seedy, sordid, unpleasant.

sear *vb* blight, brand, cauterize, dry, scorch, wither. * *adj* dried up, dry, sere, withered.

search *vb* examine, explore, ferret, inspect, investigate, overhaul, probe, ransack, scrutinize, sift; delve, hunt, forage, inquire, look, rummage. * *n* examination, exploration, hunt, inquiry, inspection, investigation, pursuit, quest, research, seeking, scrutiny.

searching *adj* close, keen, penetrating, trying; examining, exploring, inquiring, investigating, probing, seeking.

seared *adj* callous, graceless, hardened, impenitent, incorrigible, obdurate, shameless, unrepentant.

season *vb* acclimatize, accustom, form, habituate, harden, inure, mature, qualify, temper, train; flavour, spice. * *n* interval, period, spell, term, time, while.

seasonable *adj* appropriate, convenient, fit, opportune, suitable, timely.

seasoning *n* condiment, flavouring, relish, salt, sauce.

seat *vb* establish, fix, locate, place, set, station. * *n* place, site, situation, station; abode, capital, dwelling, house, mansion, residence; bottom, fundament; bench, chair, pew, settle, stall, stool.

secede *vb* apostatize, resign, retire, withdraw.

secluded *adj* close, covert, embowered, isolated, private, removed, retired, screened, sequestrated, withdrawn.

seclusion *n* obscurity, privacy, retirement, secrecy, separation, solitude, withdrawal.

second[1] *n* instant, jiffy, minute, moment, trice.

second[2] *vb* abet, advance, aid, assist, back, encourage, forward, further, help, promote, support, sustain; approve, favour. * *adj* inferior, second-rate, secondary; following, next, subsequent; additional, extra, other; double, duplicate. * *n* another, other; assistant, backer, supporter.

secondary *adj* collateral, inferior, minor, subsidiary, subordinate. * *n* delegate, deputy, proxy.

secrecy *n* clandestineness, concealment, furtiveness, stealth, surreptitiousness.

secret *adj* close, concealed, covered, covert, cryptic, hid, hidden, mysterious, privy, shrouded, veiled, unknown, unrevealed, unseen; cabbalistic, clandestine, furtive, privy, sly, stealthy, surreptitious, underhand; confidential, private, retired, secluded, unseen; abstruse, latent, mysterious, obscure, occult, recondite, unknown. * *n* confidence, enigma, key, mystery.

secretary *n* clerk, scribe, writer; escritoire, writing-desk.

secrete[1] *vb* bury, cache, conceal, disguise, hide, shroud, stash; screen, separate.

secrete[2] *vb* discharge, emit, excrete, exude, release, secern.

secretive *adj* cautious, close, reserved, reticent, taciturn, uncommunicative, wary.

sect *n* denomination, faction, schism, school.

section *n* cutting, division, fraction, part, piece, portion, segment, slice.

secular *adj* civil, laic, laical, lay, profane, temporal, worldly.

secure *vb* guard, protect, safeguard; assure, ensure, guarantee, insure; fasten; acquire, gain, get, obtain, procure. * *adj* assured, certain, confident, sure; insured, protected, safe; fast, firm, fixed, immovable, stable; careless, easy, undisturbed, unsuspecting; heedless, inattentive, incautious, negligent, overconfident.
security *n* bulwark, defence, guard, palladium, protection, safeguard, safety, shelter; bond, collateral, deposit, guarantee, pawn, pledge, stake, surety, warranty; carelessness, heedlessness, overconfidence, negligence; assurance, assuredness, certainty, confidence, ease.
sedate *adj* calm, collected, composed, contemplative, cool, demure, grave, placid, philosophical, quiet, serene, serious, sober, still, thoughtful, tranquil, undisturbed, unemotional, unruffled.
sedative *adj* allaying, anodyne, assuasive, balmy, calming, composing, demulcent, lenient, lenitive, soothing, tranquillizing. * *n* anaesthetic, anodyne, hypnotic, narcotic, opiate.
sedentary *adj* inactive, motionless, sluggish, torpid.
sediment *n* dregs, grounds, lees, precipitate, residue, residuum, settlings.
sedition *n* insurgence, insurrection, mutiny, rebellion, revolt, riot, rising, treason, tumult, uprising, uproar.
seditious *adj* factious, incendiary, insurgent, mutinous, rebellious, refractory, riotous, tumultuous, turbulent.
seduce *vb* allure, attract, betray, corrupt, debauch, deceive, decoy, deprave, ensnare, entice, inveigle, lead, mislead.
seductive *adj* alluring, attractive, enticing, tempting.
sedulous *adj* active, assiduous, busy, diligent, industrious, laborious, notable, painstaking, persevering, unremitting, untiring.
see *vb* behold, contemplate, descry, glimpse, sight, spot, survey; comprehend, conceive, distinguish, espy, know, notice, observe, perceive, recognize, remark, understand; beware, consider, envisage, regard, visualize; experience, feel, suffer; examine, inspire, notice, observe; discern, look; call on, visit.
seed *n* semen, sperm; embryo, grain, kernel, matured ovule; germ, original; children, descendants, offspring, progeny; birth, generation, race.
seedy *adj* faded, old, shabby, worn; destitute, distressed, indigent, needy, penniless, pinched, poor.
seek *vb* hunt, look, search; court, follow, prosecute, pursue, solicit; attempt, endeavour, strive, try.
seem *vb* appear, assume, look, pretend.
seeming *adj* apparent, appearing, ostensible, specious. * *n* appearance, colour, guise, look, semblance.
seemly *adj* appropriate, becoming, befitting, congruous, convenient, decent, decorous, expedient, fit, fitting, meet, proper, right, suitable; beautiful, comely, fair, good-looking, graceful, handsome, pretty, well-favoured.
seer *n* augur, diviner, foreteller, predictor, prophet, soothsayer.
segment *n* bit, division, part, piece, portion, section, sector.
segregate *vb* detach, disconnect, disperse, insulate, part, separate.
segregation *n* apartheid, discrimination, insulation, separation.
seize *vb* capture, catch, clutch, grab, grapple, grasp, grip, snatch; confiscate, impress, impound; apprehend, comprehend; arrest, take.
seldom *adv* infrequently, occasionally, rarely.
select *vb* choose, cull, pick, prefer. * *adj* choice, chosen, excellent, exquisite, good, picked, rare, selected.
selection *n* choice, election, pick, preference.
self-conscious *adj* awkward, diffident, embarrassed, insecure, nervous.
self-control *n* restraint, willpower.
self-important *adj* assuming, consequential, proud, haughty, lordly, overbearing, overweening.
selfish *adj* egoistic, egotistical, greedy, illiberal, mean, narrow, self-seeking, ungenerous.
self-possessed *adj* calm, collected, composed, cool, placid, sedate, undisturbed, unexcited, unruffled.
self-willed *adj* contumacious, dogged, headstrong, obstinate, pig-headed, stubborn, uncompliant, wilful.
sell *vb* barter, exchange, hawk, market, peddle, trade, vend.
semblance *n* likeness, resemblance, similarity; air, appearance, aspect, bearing, exterior, figure, form, mien, seeming, show; image, representation, similitude.
seminal *adj* important, original; germinal, radical, rudimental, rudimentary, unformed.
seminary *n* academy, college, gymnasium, high school, institute, school, university.
send *vb* cast, drive, emit, fling, hurl, impel, lance, launch, project, propel, throw, toss; delegate, depute, dispatch; forward, transmit; bestow, confer, give, grant.
senile *adj* aged, doddering, superannuated; doting, imbecile.
senior *adj* elder, older; higher.
seniority *n* eldership, precedence, priority, superiority.
sensation *n* feeling, sense, perception; excitement, impression, thrill.
sensational *adj* exciting, melodramatic, startling, thrilling.
sense *vb* appraise, appreciate, estimate, notice, observe, perceive, suspect, understand. * *n* brains, intellect, intelligence, mind, reason, understanding; appreciation, apprehension, discernment, feeling, perception, recognition, tact; connotation, idea, implication, judgment, notion,

opinion, sentiment, view; import, interpretation, meaning, purport, significance; sagacity, soundness, substance, wisdom.

senseless *adj* apathetic, inert, insensate, unfeeling; absurd, foolish, ill-judged, nonsensical, silly, unmeaning, unreasonable, unwise; doltish, foolish, simple, stupid, witless, weak-minded.

sensible *adj* apprehensible, perceptible; aware, cognizant, conscious, convinced, persuaded, satisfied; discreet, intelligent, judicious, rational, reasonable, sagacious, sage, sober, sound, wise; observant, understanding; impressionable, sensitive.

sensitive *adj* perceptive, sentient; affected, impressible, impressionable, responsive, susceptible; delicate, tender, touchy.

sensual *adj* animal, bodily, carnal, voluptuous; gross, lascivious, lewd, licentious, unchaste.

sentence *vb* condemn, doom, judge. * *n* decision, determination, judgment, opinion, verdict; doctrine, dogma, opinion, tenet; condemnation, conviction, doom; period, proposition.

sententious *adj* compendious, compact, concise, didactic, laconic, pithy, pointed, succinct, terse.

sentiment *n* judgment, notion, opinion; maxim, saying; emotion, tenderness; disposition, feeling, thought.

sentimental *adj* impressible, impressionable, overemotional, romantic, tender.

sentinel *n* guard, guardsman, patrol, picket, sentry, watchman.

separate *vb* detach, disconnect, disjoin, disunite, dissever, divide, divorce, part, sever, sunder; eliminate, remove, withdraw; cleave, open. * *adj* detached, disconnected, disjoined, disjointed, dissociated, disunited, divided, parted, severed; discrete, distinct, divorced, unconnected; alone, segregated, withdrawn.

separation *n* disjunction, disjuncture, dissociation; disconnection, disseverance, disseveration, disunion, division, divorce; analysis, decomposition.

sepulchral *adj* deep, dismal, funereal, gloomy, grave, hollow, lugubrious, melancholy, mournful, sad, sombre, woeful.

sepulchre *n* burial place, charnel house, grave, ossuary, sepulture, tomb.

sequel *n* close, conclusion, denouement, end, termination; consequence, event, issue, result, upshot.

sequence *n* following, graduation, progression, succession; arrangement, series, train.

sequestrated *adj* hidden, private, retired, secluded, unfrequented, withdrawn; seized.

seraphic *adj* angelic, celestial, heavenly, sublime; holy, pure, refined.

serene *adj* calm, collected, placid, peaceful, quiet, tranquil, sedate, undisturbed, unperturbed, unruffled; bright, calm, clear, fair, unclouded.

serenity *n* calm, calmness, collectedness, composure, coolness, imperturbability, peace, peacefulness, quiescence, sedateness, tranquillity; brightness, calmness, clearness, fairness, peace, quietness, stillness.

serf *n* bondman, servant, slave, thrall, villein.

serfdom *n* bondage, enslavement, enthralment, servitude, slavery, subjection, thraldom.

series *n* chain, concatenation, course, line, order, progression, sequence, succession, train.

serious *adj* earnest, grave, demure, pious, resolute, sedate, sober, solemn, staid, thoughtful; dangerous, great, important, momentous, weighty.

sermon *n* discourse, exhortation, homily, lecture.

serpentine *adj* anfractuous, convoluted, crooked, meandering, sinuous, spiral, tortuous, twisted, undulating, winding.

servant *n* attendant, dependant, factotum, helper, henchman, retainer, servitor, subaltern, subordinate, underling; domestic, drudge, flunky, lackey, menial, scullion, slave.

serve *vb* aid, assist, attend, help, minister, oblige, succour; advance, benefit, forward, promote; content, satisfy, supply; handle, officiate, manage, manipulate, work.

service *vb* check, maintain, overhaul, repair. * *n* labour, ministration, work; attendance, business, duty, employ, employment, office; advantage, benefit, good, gain, profit; avail, purpose, use, utility; ceremony, function, observance, rite, worship.

serviceable *adj* advantageous, available, beneficial, convenient, functional, handy, helpful, operative, profitable, useful.

servile *adj* dependent, menial; abject, base, beggarly, cringing, fawning, grovelling, low, mean, obsequious, slavish, sneaking, sycophantic, truckling.

servility *n* bondage, dependence, slavery; abjection, abjectness, baseness, fawning, meanness, obsequiousness, slavishness, sycophancy.

servitor *n* attendant, dependant, footman, lackey, retainer, servant, squire, valet, waiter.

servitude *n* bondage, enslavement, enthralment, serfdom, service, slavery, thraldom.

set[1] *vb* lay, locate, mount, place, put, stand, station; appoint, determine, establish, fix, settle; risk, stake, wager; adapt, adjust, regulate; adorn, stud, variegate; arrange, dispose, pose, post; appoint, assign, predetermine, prescribe; estimate, prize, rate, value; embarrass, perplex, pose; contrive, produce; decline, sink; congeal, concern, consolidate, harden, solidify; flow, incline, run, tend; (*with* **about**) begin, commence; (*with* **apart**) appropriate, consecrate, dedicate, devote, reserve, set aside; (*with* **aside**) abrogate, annul, omit, reject; reserve, set apart; (*with* **before**) display, exhibit; (*with* **down**) chronicle, jot down, record, register, state, write down; (*with* **forth**) display, exhibit, explain, expound, manifest, promulgate, publish, put forward, represent, show; (*with* **forward**) advance, further, promote; (*with* **free**) acquit, clear, emancipate, liberate, release; (*with* **off**) adorn, decorate, embellish; define, portion off; (*with* **on**) actuate, encourage, impel, influence, incite, instigate, prompt, spur, urge; attack, assault, set upon; (*with* **out**) display, issue, publish, proclaim, prove, recommend, show; (*with* **right**) correct, put in order; (*with* **to rights**) adjust, regulate; (*with* **up**) elevate, erect, exalt, raise; establish, found, institute; (*with* **upon**) assail, assault, attack, fly at, rush upon. * *adj* appointed, established, formal, ordained, prescribed, regular, settled; determined, fixed, firm, obstinate, positive, stiff, unyielding; immovable, predetermined; located, placed, put. * *n* attitude, position, posture; scene, scenery, setting.

set[2] *n* assortment, collection, suit; class, circle, clique, cluster, company, coterie, division, gang, group, knot, party, school, sect.

setback *n* blow, hitch, hold-up, rebuff; defeat, disappointment, reverse.

set-off *n* adornment, decoration, embellishment, ornament; counterbalance, counterclaim, equivalent.

settle *vb* adjust, arrange, compose, regulate; account, balance, close up, conclude, discharge, liquidate, pay, pay up, reckon, satisfy, square; allay, calm, compose, pacify, quiet, repose, rest, still, tranquillize; confirm, decide, determine, make clear; establish, fix, set; fall, gravitate, sink, subside; abide, colonize, domicile, dwell, establish, inhabit, people, place, plant, reside; (*with* **on**) determine on, fix on, fix upon; establish. * *n* bench, seat, stool.

settled *adj* established, fixed, stable; decided, deep-rooted, steady, unchanging; adjusted, arranged; methodical, orderly, quiet; common, customary, everyday, ordinary, usual, wonted.

set-to *n* combat, conflict, contest, fight.

sever *vb* divide, part, rend, separate, sunder; detach, disconnect, disjoin, disunite.

several *adj* individual, single, particular; distinct, exclusive, independent, separate; different, divers, diverse, manifold, many, sundry, various.

severance *n* partition, separation.

severe *adj* austere, bitter, dour, hard, harsh, inexorable, morose, painful, relentless, rigid, rigorous, rough, sharp, stern, stiff, strait-laced, unmitigated, unrelenting, unsparing; accurate, exact, methodical, strict; chaste, plain, restrained, simple, unadorned; biting, caustic, cruel, cutting, harsh, keen, sarcastic, satirical, trenchant; acute, afflictive, distressing, excruciating, extreme, intense, stringent, violent; critical, exact.

severity *n* austerity, gravity, harshness, rigour, seriousness, sternness, strictness; accuracy, exactness, niceness; chasteness, plainness, simplicity; acrimony, causticity, keenness, sharpness; afflictiveness, extremity, keenness, stringency, violence; cruelty.

sew *vb* baste, bind, hem, stitch, tack.

sex *n* gender, femininity, masculinity, sexuality; coitus, copulation, fornication, love-making.

shabby *adj* faded, mean, poor, ragged, seedy, threadbare, worn, worn-out; beggarly, mean, paltry, penurious, stingy, ungentlemanly, unhandsome.

shackle *vb* chain, fetter, gyve, hamper, manacle; bind, clog, confine, cumber, embarrass, encumber, impede, obstruct, restrict, trammel. * *n* chain, fetter, gyve, hamper, manacle.

shade *vb* cloud, darken, dim, eclipse, obfuscate, obscure; cover, ensconce, hide, protect, screen, shelter. * *n* darkness, dusk, duskiness, gloom, obscurity, shadow; cover, protection, shelter; awning, blind, curtain, screen, shutter, veil; degree, difference, kind, variety; cast, colour, complexion, dye, hue, tinge, tint, tone; apparition, ghost, manes, phantom, shadow, spectre, spirit.

shadow *vb* becloud, cloud, darken, obscure, shade; adumbrate, foreshadow, symbolize, typify; conceal, cover, hide, protect, screen, shroud. * *n* penumbra, shade, umbra, umbrage; darkness, gloom, obscurity; cover, protection, security, shelter; adumbration, foreshadowing, image, prefiguration, representation; apparition, ghost, phantom, shade, spirit; image, portrait, reflection, silhouette.

shadowy *adj* shady, umbrageous; dark, dim, gloomy, murky, obscure; ghostly, imaginary, impalpable, insubstantial, intangible, spectral, unreal, unsubstantial, visionary.

shady *adj* shadowy, umbrageous; crooked.

shaft *n* arrow, missile, weapon; handle, helve; pole, tongue; axis, spindle; pinnacle, spire; stalk, stem, trunk.

shaggy *adj* rough, rugged.

shake *vb* quake, quaver, quiver, shiver, shudder, totter, tremble; agitate, convulse, jar, jolt, stagger; daunt, frighten, intimidate; endanger, move, weaken; oscillate, vibrate, wave; move, put away, remove, throw off. * *n* agitation, concussion, flutter, jar, jolt, quaking, shaking, shivering, shock, trembling, tremor.

shaky *adj* jiggly, quaky, shaking, tottering, trembling.

shallow *adj* flimsy, foolish, frivolous, puerile, trashy, trifling, trivial; empty, ignorant, silly, slight, simple, superficial, unintelligent.

sham *vb* ape, feign, imitate, pretend; cheat, deceive, delude, dupe, impose, trick. * *adj* assumed, counterfeit, false, feigned, mock, make-believe, pretended, spurious. * *n* delusion, feint, fraud, humbug, imposition, imposture, pretence, trick.

shamble *vb* hobble, shuffle.

shambles *npl* abattoir, slaughterhouse; confusion, disorder, mess.

shame *vb* debase, degrade, discredit, disgrace, dishonour, stain, sully, taint, tarnish; abash, confound, confuse, discompose, disconcert, humble, humiliate; deride, flout, jeer, mock, ridicule, sneer. * *n* contempt, degradation, derision, discredit, disgrace, dishonour, disrepute, ignominy, infamy, obloquy, odium, opprobrium; abashment, chagrin, confusion, embarrassment, humiliation, mortification; reproach, scandal; decency, decorousness, decorum, modesty, propriety, seemliness.

shamefaced *adj* bashful, diffident, overmodest.

shameful *adj* atrocious, base, disgraceful, dishonourable, disreputable, heinous, ignominous, infamous, nefarious, opprobrious, outrageous, scandalous, vile, villainous, wicked; degrading, indecent, unbecoming.

shameless *adj* assuming, audacious, bold-faced, brazen, brazen-faced, cool, immodest, impudent, indecent, indelicate, insolent, unabashed, unblushing; abandoned, corrupt, depraved, dissolute, graceless, hardened, incorrigible, irreclaimable, lost, obdurate, profligate, reprobate, sinful, unprincipled, vicious.

shape *vb* create, form, make, produce; fashion, model, mould; adjust, direct, frame, regulate; conceive, conjure up, figure, image, imagine. * *n* appearance, aspect, fashion, figure, form, guise, make; build, cast, cut, model, mould, pattern; apparition, image.

shapeless *adj* amorphous, formless; grotesque, irregular, rude, uncouth, unsymmetrical.

shapely *adj* comely, symmetrical, trim, well-formed.

share *vb* apportion, distribute, divide, parcel out, portion, split; partake, participate; experience, receive. * *n* part, portion, quantum; allotment, allowance, contingent, deal, dividend, division, interest, lot, proportion, quantity, quota.

sharer *n* communicant, partaker, participator.

sharp *adj* acute, cutting, keen, keen-edged, knife-edged, razor-edged, trenchant; acuminate, needle-shaped, peaked, pointed, ridged; apt, astute, canny, clear-sighted, clever, cunning, discerning, discriminating, ingenious, inventive, keen-witted, penetrating, perspicacious, quick, ready, sagacious, sharp-witted, shrewd, smart, subtle, witty; acid, acrid, biting, bitter, burning, high-flavoured, high-seasoned, hot, mordacious, piquant, poignant, pungent, sour, stinging; acrimonious, biting, caustic, cutting, harsh, mordant, sarcastic, severe, tart, trenchant; cruel, hard, rigid; afflicting, distressing, excruciating, intense, painful, piercing, shooting, sore, violent; nipping, pinching; ardent, eager, fervid, fierce, fiery, impetuous, strong; high, screeching, shrill; attentive, vigilant; severe; close, exacting, shrewd, cold, crisp, freezing, icy wintry. * *adv* abruptly, sharply, suddenly; exactly, precisely, punctually.

sharp-cut *adj* clear, distinct, well-defined.

sharpen *vb* edge, intensify, point.

sharper *n* cheat, deceiver, defrauder, knave, rogue, shark, swindler, trickster.

sharply *adv* rigorously, roughly, severely; acutely, keenly; vehemently, violently; accurately, exactly, minutely, trenchantly, wittily; abruptly, steeply.

sharpness *n* acuteness, keenness, trenchancy; acuity, spinosity; acumen, cleverness, discernment, ingenuity, quickness, sagacity, shrewdness, smartness, wit; acidity, acridity, piquancy, pungency, sting, tartness; causticness, incisiveness, pungency, sarcasm, satire, severity; afflictiveness, intensity, painfulness, poignancy; ardour, fierceness, violence; discordance, dissonance, highness, screechiness, squeakiness, shrillness.

sharp-sighted *adj* clear-sighted, keen, keen-eyed, keen-sighted.

sharp-witted *adj* acute, clear-sighted, cunning, discerning, ingenious, intelligent, keen, keen-sighted, long-headed, quick, sagacious, sharp, shrewd.

shatter *vb* break, burst, crack, rend, shiver, smash, splinter, split; break up, derange, disorder, overthrow.

shave *vb* crop, cut off, mow, pare; slice; graze, skim, touch.

shaver *n* boy, child, youngster; bargainer, extortioner, sharper.

shear *vb* clip, cut, fleece, strip; divest; break off.

sheath *n* case, casing, covering, envelope, scabbard, sheathing.

sheathe *vb* case, cover, encase, enclose.

shed[1] *n* cabin, cot, hovel, hut, outhouse, shack, shelter.

shed[2] *vb* effuse, let fall, pour out, spill; diffuse, emit, give out, scatter, spread; cast, let fall, put off, slough, throw off.

sheen *n* brightness, gloss, glossiness, shine, spendour.

sheep *n* ewe, lamb, ram.

sheepish *adj* bashful, diffident, overmodest, shamefaced, timid, timorous.

sheer[1] *adj* perpendicular, precipitous, steep, vertical; clear, downright, mere, pure, simple, unadulterated, unmingled, unmixed, unqualified, utter; clear; fine, transparent. * *adv* outright; perpendicularly, steeply.

sheer[2] *vb* decline, deviate, move aside, swerve. * *n* bow, curve.

shelf *n* bracket, console, ledge, mantelpiece.

shell *vb* exfoliate, fall off, peel off; bombard. * *n* carapace, case, covering, shard; bomb, grenade, sharpnel; framework.

shelter *vb* cover, defend, ensconce, harbour, hide, house, protect, screen, shield, shroud. * *n* asylum, cover, covert, harbour, haven, hideaway, refuge, retreat, sanctuary; defence, protection, safety, screen, security, shield; guardian, protector.

shelve *vb* dismiss, put aside; incline, slope.

shepherd *vb* escort, guide, marshal, usher; direct, drive, drove, herd, lead; guard, tend, watch over. * *n* drover, grazier, herder, herdsman; chaplain, churchman, clergyman, cleric, divine, ecclesiastic, minister, padre, parson, pastor; chaperon, duenna, escort, guide, squire, usher.

shield *vb* cover, defend, guard, protect, shelter; repel, ward off; avert, forbid, forfend. * *n* aegis, buckler, escutcheon, scutcheon, targe; bulwark, cover, defence, guard, palladium, protection, rampart, safeguard, security, shelter.

shift *vb* alter, change, fluctuate, move, vary; chop, dodge, swerve, veer; contrive, devise, manage, plan, scheme, shuffle. * *n* change, substitution, turn; contrivance, expedient, means, resort, resource; artifice, craft, device, dodge, evasion, fraud, mask, ruse, stratagem, subterfuge, trick, wile; chemise, smock.

shiftless *adj* improvident, imprudent, negligent, slack, thriftless, unresourceful.

shifty *adj* tricky, undependable, wily.

shillyshally *vb* hesitate, waver. * *n* hesitation, irresolute, wavering.

shimmer *vb* flash, glimmer, glisten, shine. * *n* blink, glimmer, glitter, twinkle.

shin *vb* climb, swarm. * *n* shinbone, tibia.

shindy *n* disturbance, riot, roughhouse, row, spree, uproar.

shine *vb* beam, blaze, coruscate, flare, give light, glare, gleam, glimmer, glisten, glitter, glow, lighten, radiate, sparkle; excel. * *n* brightness, brilliancy, glaze, gloss, polish, sheen.

shining *adj* beaming, bright, brilliant, effulgent, gleaming, glowing, glistening, glittering, luminous, lustrous, radiant, resplendent, splendid; conspicuous, distinguished, illustrious.

shiny *adj* bright, clear, luminous, sunshiny, unclouded; brilliant, burnished, glassy, glossy, polished.

ship *n* boat, craft, steamer, vessel.

shipshape *adj* neat, orderly, tidy, trim, well-arranged.

shipwreck *vb* cast away, maroon, strand, wreck. * *n* demolition, destruction, miscarriage, overthrow, perdition, ruin, subversion, wreck.

shirk *vb* avoid, dodge, evade, malinger, quit, slack; cheat, shark, trick.

shiver[1] *vb* break, shatter, splinter. * *n* bit, fragment, piece, slice, sliver, splinter.

shiver[2] *vb* quake, quiver, shake, shudder, tremble. * *n* shaking, shivering, shuddering, tremor.

shivery[1] *adj* brittle, crumbly, frangible, friable, shatterable, splintery.

shivery[2] *adj* quaking, quavering, quivering, shaky, trembly, tremulous; chilly, shivering.

shoal[1] *vb* crowd, throng. * *n* crowd, horde, multitude, swarm, throng.

shoal[2] *n* sandbank, shallows; danger.

shock *vb* appall, horrify; disgust, disquiet, disturb, nauseate, offend, outrage, revolt, scandalize, sicken; astound, stagger, stun; collide with, jar, jolt, shake, strike against; encounter, meet. * *n* agitation, blow, offence, stroke, trauma; assault, brunt, conflict; clash, collision, concussion, impact, percussion.

shocking *adj* abominable, detestable, disgraceful, disgusting, execrable, foul, hateful, loathsome, obnoxious, odious, offensive, repugnant, repulsive, revolting; appalling, awful, dire, dreadful, fearful, frightful, ghastly, hideous, horrible, horrid, horrific, monstrous, terrible.

shoot *vb* catapult, expel, hurl, let fly, propel; discharge, fire, let off; dart, fly, pass, pelt; extend, jut, project, protrude, protuberate, push, put forth, send forth, stretch; bud, germinate, sprout; (*with* **up**) grow increase, spring up, run up, start up. * *n* branch, offshoot, scion, sprout, twig.

shop *n* emporium, market, mart, store; workshop.

shore[1] *n* beach, brim, coast, seabord, seaside, strand, waterside.

shore[2] *vb* brace, buttress, prop, stay, support. * *n* beam, brace, buttress, prop, stay, support.

shorn *adj* cut-off; deprived.

short *adj* brief, curtailed; direct, near, straight; compendious, concise, condensed, laconic, pithy, terse, sententious, succinct, summary; abrupt, curt, petulant, pointed, sharp, snappish, uncivil; defective, deficient, inadequate, insufficient, niggardly, scanty, scrimpy; contracted, desitute, lacking, limited, minus, wanting; dwarfish, squat, undersized; brittle, crisp, crumbling, friable. * *adv* abruptly, at once, forthwith, suddenly.

shortcoming *n* defect, deficiency, delinquency, error, failing, failure, fault, imperfection, inadequacy, remissness, slip, weakness.

shorten *vb* abbreviate, abridge, curtail, cut short; abridge, contract, diminish, lessen, retrench, reduce; cut off, dock, lop, trim; confine, hinder, restrain, restrict.

shortening *n* abbreviation, abridgment, contraction, curtailment, diminution, retrenchment, reduction.

shorthand *n* brachygraphy, stenography, tachygraphy.

short-lived *adj* emphemeral, transient, transitory.

shortly *adv* quickly, soon; briefly, concisely, succinctly, tersely.

short-sighted *adj* myopic, nearsighted, purblind; imprudent, indiscreet.

shot[1] *n* discharge; ball, bullet, missile, projectile; marksman, shooter.

shot[2] *adj* chatoyant, iridescent, irisated, moiré, watered; intermingled, interspersed, interwoven.

shoulder *vb* bear, bolster, carry, hump, maintain, pack, support, sustain, tote; crowd, elbow, jostle, press forward, push, thrust. * *n* projection, protuberance.

shoulder blade *n* blade bone, omoplate, scapula, shoulder bone.

shout *vb* bawl, cheer, clamour, exclaim, halloo, roar, vociferate, whoop, yell. * *n* cheer, clamour, exclamation, halloo, hoot, huzza, outcry, roar, vociferation, whoop, yell.

shove *vb* jostle, press against, propel, push, push aside; (*with* **off**) push away, thrust away.

show *vb* blazon, display, exhibit, flaunt, parade, present; indicate, mark, point out; disclose, discover, divulge, explain, make clear, make known, proclaim, publish, reveal, unfold; demonstrate, evidence, manifest, prove, verify; conduct, guide, usher; direct, inform, instruct, teach; expound, elucidate, interpret; (*with* **off**) display, exhibit, make a show, set off; (*with* **up**) expose. * *n* array, exhibition, representation, sight, spectacle; blazonry, bravery, ceremony, dash, demonstration, display, flourish, ostentation, pageant, pageantry, parade, pomp, splendour, splurge; likeness, resemblance, semblance; affectation, appearance, colour, illusion, mask, plausibility, pose, pretence, pretext, simulation, speciousness; entertainment, production.

showy *adj* bedizened, dressy, fine, flashy, flaunting, garish, gaudy, glaring, gorgeous, loud, ornate, smart, swanky, splendid; grand, magnificent, ostentatious, pompous, pretentious, stately, sumptuous.

shred *vb* tear. * *n* bit, fragment, piece, rag, scrap, strip, tatter.

shrew *n* brawler, fury, scold, spitfire, termagant, virago, vixen.

shrewd *adj* arch, artful, astute, crafty, cunning, Machiavellian, sly, subtle, wily; acute, astute, canny, discerning, discriminating, ingenious, keen, knowing, penetrating, sagacious, sharp, sharp-sighted.

shrewdness *n* address, archness, art, artfulness, astuteness, craft, cunning, policy, skill, slyness, subtlety; acumen, acuteness, discernment, ingenuity, keenness, penetration, perspicacity, sagacity, sharpness, wit.

shrewish *adj* brawling, clamorous, froward, peevish, petulant, scolding, vixenish.

shriek *vb* scream, screech, squeal, yell, yelp. * *n* cry, scream, screech, yell.

shrill *adj* acute, high, high-toned, high-pitched, piercing, piping, sharp.

shrine *n* reliquary, sacred tomb; altar, hallowed place, sacred place.

shrink *vb* contract, decrease, dwindle, shrivel, wither; balk, blench, draw back, flinch, give way, quail, recoil, retire, swerve, wince, withdraw.

shrivel *vb* dry, dry up, parch; contract, decrease, dwindle, shrink, wither, wrinkle.

shroud *vb* bury, cloak, conceal, cover, hide, mask, muffle, protect, screen, shelter, veil. * *n* covering, garment; grave clothes, winding sheet.

shrub *n* bush, dwarf tree, low tree.

shrubby *adj* bushy.

shudder *vb* quake, quiver, shake, shiver, tremble. * *n* shaking, shuddering, trembling, tremor.

shuffle *vb* confuse, disorder, intermix, jumble, mix, shift; cavil, dodge, equivocate, evade, prevaricate, quibble, vacillate; struggle. * *n* artifice, cavil, evasion, fraud, pretence, pretext, prevarication, quibble, ruse, shuffling, sophism, subterfuge, trick.

shun *vb* avoid, elude, eschew, escape, evade, get clear of.

shut *vb* close, close up, stop; confine, coop up, enclose, imprison, lock up, shut up; (*with* **in**) confine, enclose; (*with* **off**) bar, exclude, intercept; (*with* **up**) close up, shut; confine, enclose, fasten in, imprison, lock in, lock up.

shy *vb* cast, chuck, fling, hurl, jerk, pitch, sling, throw, toss; boggle, sheer, start aside. * *adj* bashful, coy, diffident, reserved, retiring, sheepish, shrinking, timid; cautious, chary, distrustful, heedful, wary. * *n* start; fling, throw.

sibilant *adj* buzzing, hissing, sibilous.

sick *adj* ailing, ill, indisposed, laid-up, unwell, weak; nauseated, queasy; disgusted, revolted, tired, weary; diseased, distempered, disordered, feeble, morbid, unhealthy, unsound, weak; languishing, longing, pining.

sicken *vb* ail, disease, fall sick, make sick; nauseate; disgust, weary; decay, droop, languish, pine.

sickening *adj* nauseating, nauseous, palling, sickish; disgusting, distasteful, loathsome, offensive, repulsive, revolting.

sickly *adj* ailing, diseased, faint, feeble, infirm, languid, languishing, morbid, unhealthy, valetudinary, weak, weakly.

sickness *n* ail, ailment, complaint, disease, disorder, distemper, illness, indisposition, invalidism, malady, morbidity; nausea, qualmishness, queasiness.

side *vb* border, bound, edge, flank, frontier, march, rim, skirt, verge; avert, turn aside; (*with* **with**) befriend, favour, flock to, join with, second, support. * *adj* flanking, later, skirting; indirect, oblique; extra, odd, off, spare. * *n* border, edge, flank, margin, verge; cause, faction, interest, party, sect.

sideboard *n* buffet, dresser.

side by side abreast, alongside, by the side.

sidelong *adj* lateral, oblique. * *adv* laterally, obliquely; on the side.

sidewalk *n* footpath, footway, pavement.

sideways, sidewise *adv* laterally. * *adv* athwart, crossways, crosswise, laterally, obliquely, sidelong, sidewards.

siesta *n* doze, nap.

sift *vb* part, separate; bolt, screen, winnow; analyse, canvass, discuss, examine, fathom, follow up, inquire into, investigate, probe, scrutinze, sound, try.

sigh *vb* complain, grieve, lament, mourn. * *n* long breath, sough, suspiration.

sight *vb* get sight of, perceive, see. * *n* cognizance, ken, perception, view; beholding, eyesight, seeing, vision; exhibition, prospect, representation, scene, show, spectacle, wonder; consideration, estimation, knowledge; examination, inspection.

sightless *adj* blind, eyeless, unseeing.

sightly *adj* beautiful, comely, handsome.

sign *vb* indicate, signal, signify; countersign, endorse, subscribe. * *n* emblem, index, indication, manifestation, mark, note, proof, signal, signification, symbol, symptom, token; beacon; augury, auspice, foreboding, miracle, omen, portent, presage, prodigy, prognostic, wonder; type; countersign, password.

signal *vb* flag, glance, hail, nod, nudge, salute, sign, signalize, sound, speak, touch, wave, wink. * *adj* conspicuous, eminent, extraordinary, memorable, notable, noteworthy, remarkable. * *n* cue, indication, mark, sign, token.

signalize *vb* celebrate, distinguish, make memorable.

signature *n* mark, sign, stamp; autograph, hand.

significance *n* implication, import, meaning, purport, sense; consequence, importance, moment, portent, weight; emphasis, energy, expressiveness, force, impressiveness.

significant *adj* betokening, expressive, indicative, significative, signifying; important, material, momentous, portentous, weighty; forcible, emphatic, expressive, telling.

signification *n* expression; acceptation, import, meaning, purport, sense.

signify *vb* betoken, communication, express, indicate, intimate; denote, imply, import, mean, purport, suggest; announce, declare, give notice of, impart, make known, manifest, proclaim, utter; augur, foreshadow, indicate, portend, represent; matter, weigh.

silence *vb* hush, muzzle, still; allay, calm, quiet. * *interj* be silent, be still, hush, soft, tush, tut, whist. * *n* calm, hush, lull, noiselessness, peace, quiet, quietude, soundlessness, stillness; dumbness, mumness, muteness, reticence, speechlessness, taciturnity.

silent *adj* calm, hushed, noiseless, quiet, soundless, still; dumb, inarticulate, mum, mute, nonvocal, speechless, tacit; reticent, taciturn, uncommunicative.

silken *adj* flossy, silky, soft.

silkiness *n* smoothness, softness.

silly *adj* brainless, childish, foolish, inept, senseless, shallow, simple, stupid, weak-minded, witless; absurd, extravagant, frivolous, imprudent, indiscreet, nonsensical, preposterous, trifling, unwise. * *n* ass, duffer, goose, idiot, simpleton.

silt *n* alluvium, deposit, deposition, residue, settlement, settlings, sediment.

silver *adj* argent, silvery; bright, silvery, white; clear, mellifluous, soft.

similar *adj* analogous, duplicate, like, resembling, twin; homogeneous, uniform.

similarity *n* agreement, analogy, correspondence, likeness, parallelism, parity, resemblance, sameness, semblance, similitude.

simile *n* comparison, metaphor, similitude.

similitude *n* image, likeness, resemblance; comparison, metaphor, simile.

simmer *vb* boil, bubble, seethe, stew.

simper *vb* smile, smirk.

simple *adj* bare, elementary, homogeneous, incomplex, mere, single, unalloyed, unblended, uncombined, uncompounded, unmingled, unmixed; chaste, plain, homespun, inornate, natural, neat, unadorned, unaffected, unembellished, unpretentious, unstudied, unvarnished; artless, downright, frank, guileless, inartificial, ingenuous, naive, open, simple-hearted, simple-minded, sincere, single-minded, straightforward, true, unconstrained, undesigning, unsophisticated; credulous, fatuous, foolish, shallow, silly, unwise, weak; clear, intelligible, understandable, uninvolved, unmistakable.

simple-hearted *adj* artless, frank, ingenuous, open, simple, single-hearted.

simpleton *n* fool, greenhorn, nincompoop, ninny.

simplicity *n* chasteness, homeliness, naturalness, neatness, plainness; artlessness, frankness, naivety, openness, simplesse, sincerity; clearness; gullibility, folly, silliness, weakness.

simply *adv* artlessly, plainly, sincerely, unaffectedly; barely, merely, of itself, solely; absolutely, alone.

simulate *vb* act, affect, ape, assume, counterfeit, dissemble, feign, mimic, pretend, sham.

simulation *n* counterfeiting, feigning, personation, pretence.

simultaneous *adj* coeval, coincident, concomitant, concurrent, contemporaneous, synchronous.

sin *vb* do wrong, err, transgress, trespass. * *n* delinquency, depravity, guilt, iniquity, misdeed, offence, transgression, unrighteousness, wickedness, wrong.

since *conj* as, because, considering, seeing that. * *adv* ago, before this; from that time. * *prep* after, from the time of, subsequently to.

sincere *adj* pure, unmixed; genuine, honest, inartificial, real, true, unaffected, unfeigned, unvarnished; artless, candid, direct, frank, guileless, hearty, honest, ingenuous, open, plain, single, straightforward, truthful, undissembling, upright, whole-hearted.

sincerity *n* artlessness, candour, earnestness, frankness, genuineness, guilelessness, honesty, ingenuousness, probity, truth, truthfulness, unaffectedness, veracity.

sinew *n* ligament, tendon; brawn, muscle, nerve, strength.

sinewy *adj* able-bodied, brawny, firm, Herculean, muscular, nervous, powerful, robust, stalwart, strapping, strong, sturdy, vigorous, wiry.

sinful *adj* bad, criminal, depraved, immoral, iniquitous, mischievous, peccant, transgressive, unholy, unrighteous, wicked, wrong.

sinfulness *n* corruption, criminality, depravity, iniquity, irreligion, ungodliness, unholiness, unrighteousness, wickedness.

sing *vb* cantillate, carol, chant, hum, hymn, intone, lilt, troll, warble, yodel.

singe *vb* burn, scorch, sear.

singer *n* cantor, caroler, chanter, gleeman, prima donna, minstrel, psalmodist, songster, vocalist.

single *vb* (*with* **out**) choose, pick, select, single. * *adj* alone, isolated, one only, sole, solitary; individual, particular, separate; celibate, unmarried,

unwedded; pure, simple, uncompounded, unmixed; honest, ingenuous, sincere, unbiased, uncorrupt, upright.
single-handed *adj* alone, by one's self, unaided, unassisted.
single-minded *adj* artless, candid, guileless, ingenuous, sincere.
singleness *n* individuality, unity; purity, simplicity; ingenuousness, integrity, sincerity, uprightness.
singular *adj* eminent, exceptional, extraordinary, rare, remarkable, strange, uncommon, unusual, unwonted; particular, unexampled, unparalleled, unprecedented; unaccountable; bizarre, curious, eccentric, fantastic, odd, peculiar, queer; individual, single; not complex, single, uncompounded, unique.
singularity *n* aberration, abnormality, irregularity, oddness, rareness, rarity, strangeness, uncommonness; characteristic, idiosyncrasy, individuality, particularity, peculiarity; eccentricity, oddity.
sinister *adj* baleful, injurious, untoward; boding ill, inauspicious, ominous, unlucky; left, on the left hand.
sink *vb* droop, drop, fall, founder, go down, submerge, subside; enter, penetrate; collapse, fail; decay, decline, decrease, dwindle, give way, languish, lose strength; engulf, immerse, merge, submerge, submerse; dig, excavate, scoop out; abase, bring down, crush, debase, degrade, depress, diminish, lessen, lower, overbear; destroy, overthrow, overwhelm, reduce, ruin, swamp, waste. * *n* basin, cloaca, drain.
sinless *adj* faultless, guiltless, immaculate, impeccable, innocent, spotless, unblemished, undefiled, unspotted, unsullied, untarnished.
sinner *n* criminal, delinquent, evildoer, offender, reprobate, wrongdoer.
sinuosity *n* crook, curvature, flexure, sinus, tortuosity, winding.
sinuous *adj* bending, crooked, curved, curvilinear, flexuous, serpentine, sinuate, sinuated, tortuous, undulating, wavy, winding.
sip *vb* drink, suck up, sup; absorb, drink in. * *n* small draught, taste.
sire *vb* father, reproduce; author, breed, conceive, create, generate, originate, produce, propagate. * *n* father, male parent, progenitor; man, male person; sir, sirrah; author, begetter, creator, father, generator, originator.
siren *adj* alluring, bewitching, fascinating, seducing, tempting. * *n* mermaid; charmer, Circe, seducer, seductress, tempter, temptress.
sit *vb* be, remain, repose, rest, stay; bear on, lie, rest; abide, dwell, settle; perch; brood, incubate; become, be suited, fit.
site *vb* locate, place, position, situate, station. * *n* ground, locality, location, place, position, seat, situation, spot, station, whereabouts.
sitting *n* meeting, session.
situation *n* ground, locality, location, place, position, seat, site, spot, whereabouts; case, category, circumstances, condition, juncture, plight, predicament, state; employment, office, place, post, station.
size *n* amplitude, bigness, bulk, dimensions, expanse, greatness, largeness, magnitude, mass, volume.
skeleton *n* framework; draft, outline, sketch.
sketch *vb* design, draft, draw out; delineate, depict, paint, portray, represent. * *n* delineation, design, draft, drawing, outline, plan, skeleton.
sketchy *adj* crude, incomplete, unfinished.
skilful *adj* able, accomplished, adept, adroit, apt, clever, competent, conversant, cunning, deft, dexterous, dextrous, expert, handy, ingenious, masterly, practised, proficient, qualified, quick, ready, skilled, trained, versed, well-versed.
skill *n* ability, address, adroitness, aptitude, aptness, art, cleverness, deftness, dexterity, expertise, expertness, facility, ingenuity, knack, quickness, readiness, skilfulness; discernment, discrimination, knowledge, understanding, wit.
skim *vb* brush, glance, graze, kiss, scrape, scratch, sweep, touch lightly; coast, flow, fly, glide, sail, scud, whisk; dip into, glance at, scan, skip, thumb over, touch upon.
skin *vb* pare, peel; decorticate, excoriate, flay. * *n* cuticle, cutis, derm, epidermis, hide, integument, pellicle, pelt; hull, husk, peel, rind.
skinflint *n* churl, curmudgeon, lickpenny, miser, niggard, scrimp.
skinny *adj* emaciated, lank, lean, poor, shrivelled, shrunk, thin.
skip *vb* bound, caper, frisk, gambol, hop, jump, leap, spring; disregard, intermit, miss, neglect, omit, pass over, skim. * *n* bound, caper, frisk, gambol, hop, jump, leap, spring.
skirmish *vb* battle, brush, collide, combat, contest, fight, scuffle, tussle. * *n* affair, affray, battle, brush, collision, combat, conflict, contest, encounter, fight, scuffle, tussle.
skirt *vb* border, bound, edge, fringe, hem, march, rim; circumnavigate, circumvent, flank, go along. * *n* border, boundary, edge, margin, rim, verge; flap, kilt, overskirt, petticoat.
skittish *adj* changeable, fickle, inconstant; hasty, volatile, wanton; shy, timid, timorous.
skulk *vb* hide, lurk, slink, sneak.
skulker *n* lurker, sneak; shirk, slacker, malingerer.
skull *n* brain pan, cranium.
sky *n* empyrean, firmament, heaven, heavens, welkin.
sky-blue *adj* azure, cerulean, sapphire, sky-coloured.
skylarking *n* carousing, frolicking, sporting.
slab *adj* slimy, thick, viscous. * *n* beam, board, layer, panel, plank, slat, table, tablet; mire, mud, puddle, slime.
slabber *vb* drivel, slaver, slobber; drop, let fall, shed, spill.
slack *vb* ease off, let up; abate, ease up, relax,

slacken; malinger, shirk; choke, damp, extinguish, smother, stifle. * *adj* backward, careless, inattentive, lax, negligent, remiss; abated, dilatory, diminished, lingering, slow, tardy; loose, relaxed; dull, idle, inactive, quiet, sluggish. * *n* excess, leeway, looseness, play; coal dust, culm, residue.

slacken *vb* abate, diminish, lessen, lower, mitigate, moderate, neglect, remit, relieve, retard, slack; loosen, relax; flag, slow down; bridle, check, control, curb, repress, restrain.

slackness *n* looseness; inattention, negligence, remissness; slowness, tardiness.

slander *vb* asperse, backbite, belie, brand, calumniate, decry, defame, libel, malign, reproach, scandalize, traduce, vilify; detract from, disparage. * *n* aspersion, backbiting, calumny, defamation, detraction, libel, obloquy, scandal, vilification.

slanderous *adj* calumnious, defamatory, false, libellous, malicious, maligning.

slang *n* argo, cant, jargon, lingo.

slant *vb* incline, lean, lie obliquely, list, slope. * *n* inclination, slope, steep, tilt.

slap *vb* dab, clap, pat, smack, spank, strike. * *adv* instantly, quickly, plumply. * *n* blow, clap.

slapdash *adv* haphazardly, hurriedly, precipitately.

slash *vb* cut, gash, slit. * *n* cut, gash, slit.

slashed *adj* cut, slit; (*bot*) jagged, laciniate, multifid.

slattern *adj* slatternly, slovenly, sluttish. * *n* drab, slut, sloven, trollop.

slatternly *adj* dirty, slattern, slovenly, sluttish, unclean, untidy. * *adv* carelessly, negligently, sluttishly.

slaughter *vb* butcher, kill, massacre, murder, slay. * *n* bloodshed, butchery, carnage, havoc, killing, massacre, murder, slaying.

slaughterer *n* assassin, butcher, cutthroat, destroyer, killer, murderer, slayer.

slave *vb* drudge, moil, toil. * *n* bondmaid, bondservant, bondslave, bondman, captive, dependant, henchman, helot, peon, serf, thrall, vassal, villein; drudge, menial.

slavery *n* bondage, bond-service, captivity, enslavement, enthralment, serfdom, servitude, thraldom, vassalage, villeinage; drudgery, mean labour.

slavish *adj* abject, beggarly, base, cringing, fawning, grovelling, low, mean, obsequious, servile, sycophantic; drudging, laborious, menial, servile.

slay *vb* assassinate, butcher, dispatch, kill, massacre, murder, slaughter; destroy, ruin.

slayer *n* assassin, destroyer, killer, murderer, slaughterer.

sledge *n* drag, sled; cutter, pung, sleigh.

sleek *adj* glossy, satin, silken, silky, smooth.

sleekly *adv* evenly, glossily, nicely, smoothly.

sleep *vb* catnap, doze, drowse, nap, slumber. * *n* dormancy, hypnosis, lethargy, repose, rest, slumber.

sleeping *adj* dormant, inactive, quiescent.

sleepwalker *n* night-walker, noctambulist, somnambulist.

sleepwalking *n* somnambulism.

sleepy *adj* comatose, dozy, drowsy, heavy, lethargic, nodding, somnolent; narcotic, opiate, slumberous, somniferous, somnific, soporiferous, soporific; dull, heavy, inactive, lazy, slow, sluggish, torpid.

sleight *n* adroitness, dexterity, manoeuvring.

sleight of hand *n* conjuring, hocus-pocus, jugglery, legerdemain, prestdigitation.

slender *adj* lank, lithe, narrow, skinny, slim, spindly, thin; feeble, fine, flimsy, fragile, slight, tenuous, weak; inconsiderable, moderate, small, trivial; exiguous, inadequate, insufficient, lean, meagre, pitiful, scanty; abstemious, light, simple, spare, sparing.

slice *vb* cut, divide, part, section; cut off, sever. * *n* chop, collop, piece.

slick *adj* glassy, glossy, polished, sleek, smooth; alert, clever, cunning, shrewd, slippery, unctuous. *vb* burnish, gloss, lacquer, polish, shine, sleek, varnish; grease, lubricate, oil.

slide *vb* glide, move smoothly, slip. * *n* glide, glissade, skid, slip.

sliding *adj* gliding, slippery, uncertain. * *n* backsliding, falling, fault, lapse, transgression.

slight *vb* cold-shoulder, disdain, disregard, neglect, snub; overlook; scamp, skimp, slur. * *adj* inconsiderable, insignificant, little, paltry, petty, small, trifling, trivial, unimportant, unsubstantial; delicate, feeble, frail, gentle, weak; careless, cursory, desultory, hasty, hurried, negligent, scanty, superficial; flimsy, perishable; slender, slim. * *n* discourtesy, disregard, disrespect, inattention, indignity, neglect.

slightingly *adv* contemptuously, disrespectfully, scornfully, slightly.

slightly *adv* inconsiderably, little, somewhat; feebly, slenderly, weakly; cursorily, hastily, negligently, superficially.

slim *vb* bant, diet, lose weight, reduce, slenderize. * *adj* gaunt, lank, lithe, narrow, skinny, slender, spare; inconsiderable, paltry, poor, slight, trifling, trivial, unsubstantial, weak; insufficient, meagre.

slime *n* mire, mud, ooze, sludge.

slimy *adj* miry, muddy, oozy; clammy, gelatinous, glutinous, gummy, lubricious, mucilaginous, mucous, ropy, slabby, viscid, viscous.

sling *vb* cast, fling, hurl, throw; hang up, suspend.

slink *vb* skulk, slip away, sneak, steal away.

slip *vb* glide, slide; err, mistake, trip; lose, omit; disengage, throw off; escape, let go, loose, loosen, release, . * *n* glide, slide, slipping; blunder, lapse, misstep, mistake, oversight, peccadillo, trip; backsliding, error, fault, impropriety, indiscretion, transgression; desertion, escape; cord, leash, strap, string; case, covering, wrapper.

slippery *adj* glib, slithery, smooth; changeable,

insecure, mutable, perilous, shaky, uncertain, unsafe, unstable, unsteady; cunning, dishonest elusive, faithless, false, knavish, perfidious, shifty, treacherous.

slipshod *adj* careless, shuffling, slovenly, untidy.

slit *vb* cut; divide, rend, slash, split, sunder. * *n* cut, gash.

slobber *vb* drivel, drool, slabber, slaver; daub, obscure, smear, stain.

slobbery *adj* dank, floody, moist, muddy, sloppy, wet.

slope *vb* incline, slant, tilt. * *n* acclivity, cant, declivity, glacis, grade, gradient, incline, inclination, obliquity, pitch, ramp.

sloping *adj* aslant, bevelled, declivitous, inclining, oblique, shelving, slanting.

sloppy *adj* muddy, plashy, slabby, slobbery, splashy, wet.

sloth *n* dilatoriness, slowness, tardiness; idleness, inaction, inactivity, indolence, inertness, laziness, lumpishness, slothfulness, sluggishness, supineness, torpor.

slothful *adj* dronish, idle, inactive, indolent, inert, lazy, lumpish, slack, sluggish, supine, torpid.

slouch *vb* droop, loll, slump; shamble, shuffle. * *n* malingerer, shirker, slacker; shamble, shuffle, stoop.

slouching *adj* awkward, clownish, loutish, lubberly, uncouth, ungainly.

slough[1] *n* bog, fen, marsh, morass, quagmire; dejection, depression, despondence, despondency.

slough[2] *vb* cast, desquamate, excuviate, moult, shed, throw off; cast off, discard, divest, jettison, reject. * *n* cast, desquamation.

sloven *n* slattern, slob, slouch, slut.

slovenly *adj* unclean, untidy; blowsy, disorderly, dowdy, frowsy, loose, slatternly, tacky, unkempt, untidy; careless, heedless, lazy, negligent, perfunctory.

slow *vb* abate, brake, check, decelerate, diminish, lessen, mitigate, moderate, modulate, reduce, weaken; delay,detain, retard; ease, ease up, relax, slack, slacken, slack off. * *adj* deliberate, gradual; dead, dull, heavy, inactive, inert, sluggish, stupid; behindhand, late, tardy, unready; delaying, dilatory, lingering, slack.

sludge *n* mire, mud; slosh, slush.

sluggard *n* dawdler, drone, idler, laggard, lounger, slug.

sluggish *adj* dronish, drowsy, idle, inactive, indolent, inert, languid, lazy, listless, lumpish, phlegmatic, slothful, torpid; slow; dull, stupid, supine, tame.

sluice *vb* drain, drench, flood, flush, irrigate. * *n* floodgate, opening, vent.

slumber *vb* catnap, doze, nap, repose, rest, sleep. * *n* catnap, doze, nap, repose, rest, siesta, sleep.

slumberous *adj* drowsy, sleepy, somniferous, somnific, soporific.

slump *vb* droop, drop, fall, flop, founder, sag, sink, sink down; decline, depreciate, deteriorate, ebb, fail, fall away, lose ground, recede, slide, slip, subside, wane. * *n* droop, drop, fall, flop, lowering, sag, sinkage; decline, depreciation, deterioration, downturn, downtrend, subsidence, ebb, falling off, wane; crash, recession, smash.

slur *vb* asperse, calumniate, disparage, depreciate, reproach, traduce; conceal, disregard, gloss over, obscure, pass over, slight. * *n* mark, stain; brand, disgrace, reproach, stain, stigma; innuendo.

slush *n* slosh, sludge.

slushy *vb* plashy, sloppy, sloshy, sludgy.

slut *n* drab, slattern, sloven, trollop.

sluttish *adj* careless, dirty, disorderly, unclean, untidy.

sly *adj* artful, crafty, cunning, insidious, subtle, wily; astute, cautious, shrewd; arch, knowing, clandestine, secret, stealthy, underhand.

smack[1] *vb* smell, taste. * *n* flavour, savour, tang, taste, tincture; dash, infusion, little, space, soupçon, sprinkling, tinge, touch; smattering.

smack[2] *vb* slap, strike; crack, slash, snap; buss, kiss. * *n* crack, slap, slash, snap; buss, kiss.

small *adj* diminutive, Lilliputian, little, miniature, petite, pygmy, tiny, wee; infinitesimal, microscopic, minute; inappreciable, inconsiderable, insignificant, petty, trifling, trivial, unimportant; moderate, paltry, scanty, slender; faint, feeble, puny, slight, weak; illiberal, mean, narrow, narrow-minded, paltry, selfish, sorded, ungenerous, unworthy.

small talk *n* chat, conversation, gossip.

smart[1] *vb* hurt, pain, sting; suffer. * *adj* keen, painful, poignant, pricking, pungent, severe, sharp, stinging.

smart[2] *adj* active, agile, brisk, fresh, lively, nimble, quick, spirited, sprightly, spry; effective, efficient, energetic, forcible, vigorous; adroit, alert, clever, dexterous, dextrous, expert, intelligent, stirring; acute, apt, pertinent, ready, witty; chic, dapper, fine, natty, showy, spruce, trim.

smartness *n* acuteness, keenness, poignancy, pungency, severity, sharpness; efficiency, energy, force, vigour; activity, agility, briskness, liveliness, nimbleness, sprightliness, spryness, vivacity; alertness, cleverness, dexterity, expertise, expertness, intelligence, quickness; acuteness, aptness, pertinency, wit, wittiness; chic, nattiness, spruceness, trimness.

smash *vb* break, crush, dash, mash, shatter. * *n* crash, debacle, destruction, ruin; bankruptcy, failure.

smattering *n* dabbling, smatter, sprinkling.

smear *vb* bedaub, begrime, besmear, daub, plaster, smudge; contaminate, pollute, smirch, smut, soil, stain, sully, tarnish. * *n* blot, blotch, daub, patch, smirch, smudge, spot, stain; calumny, defamation, libel, slander.

smell *vb* scent, sniff, stench, stink. * *n* aroma, bouquet, fragrance, fume, odour, perfume, redolence, scent, stench, stink; sniff, snuff.

smelt *vb* fuse, melt.

smile *vb* grin, laugh, simper, smirk. * *n* grin, simper, smirk.

smite *vb* beat, box, collide, cuff, knock, strike, wallop, whack; destroy, kill, slay; afflict, chasten, punish; blast, destroy.

smitten *adj* attracted, captivated, charmed, enamoured, fascinated, taken; destroyed, killed, slain; smit, struck; afflicted, chastened, punished.

smock *n* chemise, shift, slip; blouse, gaberdine.

smoke *vb* emit, exhale, reek, steam; fumigate, smudge; discover, find out, smell out. * *n* effluvium, exhalation, fume, mist, reek, smother, steam, vapour; fumigation, smudge.

smoky *adj* fuliginous, fumid, fumy, smudgy; begrimed, blackened, dark, reeky, sooty, tanned.

smooth *vb* flatten, level, plane; ease, lubricate; extenuate, palliate, soften; allay, alleviate, assuage, calm, mitigate, mollify. * *adj* even, flat, level, plane, polished, unruffled, unwrinkled; glabrous, glossy, satiny, silky, sleek, soft, velvet; euphonious, flowing, liquid, mellifluent; fluent, glib, voluble; bland, flattering, ingratiating, insinuating, mild, oily, smooth-tongued, soothing, suave, unctuous.

smoothly *adv* evenly; easily, readily, unobstructedly; blandly, flatteringly, gently, mildly, pleasantly, softly, soothingly.

smooth-tongued *adj* adulatory, cozening, flattering, plausible, smooth, smooth-spoken.

smother *vb* choke, stifle, suffocate; conceal, deaden, extinguish, hide, keep down, repress, suppress; smoke, smoulder.

smudge *vb* besmear, blacken, blur, smear, smut, smutch, soil, spot, stain. * *n* blur, blot, smear, smut, spot, stain.

smug *adj* complacent, self-satisfied; neat, nice, spruce, trim.

smuggler *n* contrabandist, runner.

smut *vb* blacken, smouch, smudge, soil, stain, sully, taint, tarnish. * *n* dirt, smudge, smutch, soot; nastiness, obscenity, ribaldry, smuttiness; pornography.

smutty *adj* coarse, gross, immodest, impure, indecent, indelicate, loose, nasty; dirty, foul, nasty, soiled, stained.

snack *n* bite, light meal, nibble.

snag *vb* catch, enmesh, entangle, hook, snare, sniggle, tangle. * *n* knarl, knob, knot, projection, protuberance, snub; catch, difficulty, drawback, hitch, rub, shortcoming, weakness; obstacle.

snaky *adj* serpentine, snaking, winding; artful, cunning, deceitful, insinuating, sly, subtle.

snap *vb* break, fracture; bite, catch at, seize, snatch at, snip; crack; crackle, crepitate, decrepitate, pop. * *adj* casual, cursory, hasty, offhand, sudden, superficial. * *n* bite, catch, nip, seizure; catch, clasp, fastening, lock; crack, fillip, flick, flip, smack; briskness, energy, verve, vim.

snappish *adj* acrimonious, captious, churlish, crabbed, cross, crusty, froward, irascible, ill-tempered, peevish, perverse, pettish, petulant, snarling, splenetic, surly, tart, testy, touchy, waspish.

snare *vb* catch, ensnare, entangle, entrap. * *n* catch, gin, net, noose, springe, toil, trap, wile.

snarl[1] *vb* girn, gnarl, growl, grumble, murmur. * *n* growl, grumble.

snarl[2] *vb* complicate, disorder, entangle, knot; confuse, embarrass, ensnare. * *n* complication, disorder, entanglement, tangle; difficulty, embarrassment, intricacy.

snatch *vb* catch, clutch, grasp, grip, pluck, pull, seize, snip, twich, wrest, wring, * *n* bit, fragment, part, portion; catch, effort.

sneak *vb* lurk, skulk, slink, steal; crouch, truckle. * *adj* clandestine, concealed, covert, hidden, secret, sly, underhand. * *n* informer, telltale; lurker, shirk.

sneaky *adj* furtive, skulking, slinking; abject, crouching, grovelling, mean; clandestine, concealed, covert, hidden, secret, sly, underhand.

sneer *vb* flout, gibe, jeer, mock, rail, scoff; (*with* **at**) deride, despise, disdain, laugh at, mock, rail at, scoff, spurn. * *n* flouting, gibe, jeer, scoff.

snicker *vb* giggle, laugh, snigger, titter.

sniff *vb* breathe, inhale, snuff; scent, smell.

snip *vb* clip, cut, nip; snap, snatch. * *n* bit, fragment, particle, piece, shred; share, snack.

snivel *vb* blubber, cry, fret, sniffle, snuffle, weep, whimper, whine.

snivelly *adj* snotty; pitiful, whining.

snob *n* climber, toady.

snooze *vb* catnap, doze, drowse, nap, sleep, slumber. * *n* catnap, nap, sleep, slumber.

snout *n* muzzle, nose; nozzle.

snowy *adj* immaculate, pure, spotless, unblemished, unstained, unsullied, white.

snub[1] *vb* abash, cold-shoulder, cut, discomfit, humble, humiliate, mortify, slight, take down. * *n* check, rebuke, slight.

snub[2] *vb* check, clip, cut short, dock, nip, prune, stunt. * *adj* pug, retroussé, snubbed, squashed, squat, stubby, turned-up.

snuff[1] *vb* breathe, inhale, sniff; scent, smell; snort.

snuff[2] *vb* (*with* **out**) annihilate, destroy, efface, extinguish, obliterate.

snuffle *vb* sniffle; snort, snuff.

snug *adj* close, concealed; comfortable, compact, convenient, neat, trim.

snuggle *vb* cuddle, nestle, nuzzle.

so *adv* thus, with equal reason; in such a manner; in this way, likewise; as it is, as it was, such; for this reason, therefore; be it so, thus be it. * *conj* in case that, on condition that, provided that.

soak *vb* drench, moisten, permeate, saturate, wet; absorb, imbibe; imbue, macerate, steep.

soar *vb* ascend, fly aloft, glide, mount, rise, tower.

sob *vb* cry, sigh convulsively, weep.

sober *vb* (*with* **up**) calm down, collect oneself, compose oneself, control oneself, cool off, master, moderate, simmer down. * *adj* abstemious, abstinent, temperate, unintoxicated; rational, reasonable, sane, sound; calm, collected, composed, cool, dispassionate, moderate, rational, reasonabler, regular, restrained, steady, temperate, unimpassioned, unruffled, well-regulated; demure, grave, quiet, sedate, serious, solemn, sombre, staid; dark, drab, dull-looking, quiet, sad, subdued.

sobriety *n* abstemiousness, abstinence, soberness, temperance; calmness, coolness, gravity, sedateness, sober-mindedness, staidness, thoughtfulness; gravity, seriousness, solemnity.

sobriquet *n* appellation, nickname, nom de plume, pseudonym.

sociability *n* companionableness, comradeship, good fellowship, sociality.

sociable *adj* accessible, affable, communicative, companionable, conversable, friendly, genial, neighbourly, social.

social *adj* civic, civil; accessible, affable, communicative, companionable, familiar, friendly, hospitable, neighbourly, sociable; convivial, festive, gregarious. * *n* conversazione, gathering, get-together, party, reception, soiree.

society *n* association, companionship, company, converse, fellowship; the community, populace, the public, the world; élite, *monde*; body, brotherhood, copartnership, corporation, club, fraternity, partnersnip, sodality, union.

sodden *adj* drenched, saturated, soaked, steeped, wet; boiled, decocted, seethed, stewed.

sofa *n* couch, davenport, divan, ottoman, settee.

soft *adj* impressible, malleable, plastic, pliable, yielding; downy, fleecy, velvety, mushy, pulpy, squashy; compliant, facile, irresolute, submissive, undecided, weak; bland, mild, gentle, kind, lenient, soft-hearted, tender; delicate; easy, even, quiet, smooth-going, steady; effeminate, luxurious, unmanly; dulcet, fluty, mellifluous, melodious, smooth. * *interj* hold, stop.

soften *vb* intenerate, mellow, melt, tenderize; abate, allay, alleviate, appease, assuage, attemper, balm, blunt, calm, dull, ease, lessen, make easy, mitigate, moderate, mollify, milden, qualify, quell, quiet, relent, relieve, soothe, still, temper; extenuate, modify, palliate, qualify; enervate, weaken.

soil[1] *n* earth, ground loam, mould; country, land.

soil[2] *vb* bedaub, begrime, bemire, besmear, bespatter, contaminate, daub, defile, dirty, foul, pollute, smirch, stain, sully, taint, tarnish. * *n* blemish, defilement, dirt, filth, foulness; blot, spot, stain, taint, tarnish.

sojourn *vb* abide, dwell, live, lodge, remain, reside, rest, stay, stop, tarry, visit. * *n* residence, stay.

solace *vb* cheer, comfort, console, soothe; allay, assuage, mitigate, relieve, soften. * *n* alleviation, cheer, comfort, consolation, relief.

soldier *n* fighting man, man-at-arms, warrior; GI, private.

soldierly *adj* martial, military, warlike; brave, courageous, gallant, heroic, honourable, intrepid, valiant.

sole *adj* alone, individual, one, only, single, solitary, unique.

solecism *n* barbarism, blunder, error, faux pas, impropriety, incongruity, mistake, slip.

solemn *adj* ceremonial, formal, ritual; devotional, devout, religious, reverential, sacred; earnest, grave, serious, sober; august, awe-inspiring, awful, grand, imposing, impressive, majestic, stately, venerable.

solemnity *n* celebration, ceremony, observance, office, rite; awfulness, sacredness, sanctity; gravity, impressiveness, seriousness.

solemnize *vb* celebrate, commemorate, honour, keep, observe.

solicit *vb* appeal to, ask, beg, beseech, conjure, crave, entreat, implore, importune, petition, pray, press, request, supplicate, urge; arouse, awaken, entice, excite, invite, summon; canvass, seek.

solicitation *n* address, appeal, asking, entreaty, imploration, importunity, insistence, petition, request, suit, supplication, urgency; bidding, call, invitation, summons.

solicitor *n* attorney, law agent, lawyer; asker, canvasser, drummer, petitioner, solicitant.

solicitous *adj* anxious, apprehensive, careful, concerned, disturbed, eager, troubled, uneasy.

solicitude *n* anxiety, care, carefulness, concern, perplexity, trouble.

solid *adj* congealed, firm, hard, impenetrable, rock-like; compact, dense, impermeable, massed; cubic; sound, stable, stout, strong, substantial; just, real, true, valid, weighty; dependable, faithful, reliable, safe, staunch, steadfast, trustworthy, well established.

solidarity *n* communion of interests, community, consolidation, fellowship, joint interest, mutual responsibility.

solidify *vb* compact, congeal, consolidate, harden, petrify.

solidity *n* compactness, consistency, density, firmness, hardness, solidness; fullness; massiveness, stability, strength; dependability, gravity, justice, reliability, soundness, steadiness, validity, weight; cubic content, volume.

soliloquy *n* monologue.

solitariness *n* isolation, privacy, reclusion, retirement, seclusion; loneliness, solitude.

solitary *adj* alone, companionless, lone, lonely, only, separate, unaccompanied; individual, single, sole; desert, deserted, desolate, isolated, lonely, remote, retired, secluded, unfrequented.

solitude *n* isolation, loneliness, privacy, recluseness, retiredness, retirement, seclusion, solitariness; desert, waste, wilderness.

solution *n* answer, clue, disentanglement, elucidation, explication, explanation, key, resolution, unravelling, unriddling; disintegration, dissolution, liquefaction, melting, resolution, separation; breach, disconnection, discontinuance, disjunction, disruption.

solve *vb* clear, clear up, disentangle, elucidate, explain, expound, interpret, make plain, resolve, unfold.
solvent *n* diluent, dissolvent, menstruum.
somatic *adj* bodily, corporeal.
sombre *adj* cloudy, dark, dismal, dull, dusky, gloomy, murky, overcast, rayless, shady, sombrous, sunless; doleful, funereal, grave, lugubrious, melancholy, mournful, sad, sober.
some *adj* a, an, any, one; about, near; certain, little, moderate, part, several.
somebody *n* one, someone, something; celebrity, VIP.
somehow *adv* in some way.
something *n* part, portion, thing; somebody; affair, event, matter.
sometime *adj* former, late. * *adv* formerly, once; now and then, at one time or other, sometimes.
sometimes *adv* at intervals, at times, now and then, occasionally; at a past period, formerly, once.
somewhat *adv* in some degree, more or less, rather, something. * *n* something, a little, more or less, part.
somewhere *adv* here and there, in one place or another, in some place.
somnambulism *n* sleepwalking, somnambulation.
somnambulist *n* night-walker, noctambulist, sleepwalker, somnambulator, somnambule.
somniferous *adj* narcotic, opiate, slumberous, somnific, soporific, soporiferous.
somnolence *n* doziness, drowsiness, sleepiness, somnolency.
somnolent *adj* dozy, drowsy, sleepy.
son *n* cadet, heir, junior, scion.
song *n* aria, ballad, canticle, canzonet, carol, ditty, glee, lay, lullaby, snatch; descant, melody; anthem, hymn, poem, psalm, strain; poesy, poetry, verse.
sonorous *adj* full-toned, resonant, resounding, ringing, sounding; high-sounding, loud.
soon *adv* anon, before long, by and by, in a short time, presently, shortly; betimes, early, forthwith, promptly, quick; gladly, lief, readily, willingly.
soot *n* carbon, crock, dust.
soothe *vb* cajole, flatter, humour; appease, assuage, balm, calm, compose, lull, mollify, pacify, quiet, soften, still, tranquillize; allay, alleviate, blunt, check, deaden, dull, ease, lessen, mitigate, moderate, palliate, qualify, relieve, repress, soften, subdue, temper.
soothsayer *n* augur, diviner, foreteller, necromancer, predictor, prophet, seer, sorcerer, vaticinator.
sooty *adj* black, dark, dusky, fuliginous, murky, sable.
sophism *n* casuistry, fallacy, paralogism, paralogy, quibble, specious argument.
sophist *n* quibbler.
sophistical *adj* casuistical, fallacious, illogical, quibbling, subtle, unsound.
soporific *adj* dormitive, hypnotic, narcotic, opiate, sleepy, slumberous, somnific, somniferous, soporiferous, soporous.
soppy *adj* drenched, saturated, soaked, sopped; emotional, mawkish, sentimental.
soprano *n* (*mus*) descant, discant, treble.
sorcerer *n* charmer, conjurer, diviner, enchanter, juggler, magician, necromancers, seer, shaman, soothsayer, thaumaturgist, wizard.
sorcery *n* black art, charm, divination, enchantment, necromancy, occultism, shamanism, spell, thaumaturgy, voodoo, witchcraft.
sordid *adj* base, degraded, low, mean, vile; avaricious, close-fisted, covetous, illiberal, miserly, niggardly, penurious, stingy, ungenerous.
sore *adj* irritated, painful, raw, tender, ulcerated; aggrieved, galled, grieved, hurt, irritable, vexed; afflictive, distressing, severe, sharp, violent. * *n* abscess, boil, fester, gathering, imposthume, pustule, ulcer; affliction, grief, pain, sorrow, trouble.
sorely *adv* greatly, grievously, severely, violently.
sorrily *adv* despicably, meanly, pitiably, poorly, wretchedly.
sorrow *vb* bemoan, bewail, grieve, lament, mourn, weep. * *n* affliction, dolour, grief, heartache, mourning, sadness, trouble, woe.
sorrowful *adj* afflicted, dejected, depressed, grieved, grieving, heartsore, sad; baleful, distressing, grievous, lamentable, melancholy, mournful, painful; disconsolate, dismal, doleful, dolorous, drear, dreary, lugubrious, melancholy, piteous, rueful, woebegone, woeful.
sorry *adj* afflicted, dejected, grieved, pained, poor, sorrowful; distressing, pitiful; chagrined, mortified, pained, regretful, remorseful, sad, vexed; abject, base, beggarly, contemptible, despicable, low, mean, paltry, insignificant, miserable, shabby, worthless, wretched.
sort *vb* arrange, assort, class, classify, distribute, order; conjoin, join, put together; choose, elect, pick out, select; associate, consort, fraternize; accord, agree with, fit, suit. * *n* character, class, denomination, description, kind, nature, order, race, rank, species, type; manner, way.
sortie *n* attack, foray, raid, sally.
so-so *adj* indifferent, mediocre, middling, ordinary, passable, tolerable.
sot *n* blockhead, dolt, dullard, dunce, fool, simpleton; drunkard, tippler, toper.
sottish *adj* doltish, dull, foolish, senseless, simple, stupid; befuddled, besotted, drunken, insensate, senseless, tipsy.
sotto voce *adv* in a low voice, in an undertone, softly.
sough *n* murmur, sigh; breath, breeze, waft.
soul *n* mind, psyche, spirit; being, person; embodiment, essence, personification, spirit, vital principle; ardour, energy, fervour, inspiration, vitality.
soulless *adj* dead, expressionless, lifeless, unfeeling.
sound[1] *adj* entire, intact, unbroken, unhurt,

unimpaired, uninjured, unmutilated, whole; hale, hardy, healthy, hearty, vigorous; good, perfect, undecayed; sane, well-balanced; correct, orthodox, right, solid, valid, well-founded; legal; deep, fast, profound, unbroken, undisturbed; forcible, lusty, severe, stout.

sound[2] *n* channel, narrows, strait.

sound[3] *vb* resound; appear, seem; play on; express, pronounce, utter; announce, celebrate, proclaim, publish, spread. * *n* noise, note, tone, voice, whisper.

sound[4] *vb* fathom, gauge, measure, test; examine, probe, search, test, try.

sounding *adj* audible, resonant, resounding, ringing, sonorous; imposing, significant.

soundless *adj* dumb, noiseless, silent; abysmal, bottomless, deep, profound, unfathomable, unsounded.

soundly *adv* satisfactorily, thoroughly, well; healthily, heartily; forcibly, lustily, severely, smartly, stoutly; correctly, rightly, truly; firmly, strongly; deeply, fast, profoundly.

soundness *n* entireness, entirety, integrity, wholeness; healithness, vigour, saneness, sanity; correctness, orthodoxy, rectitude, reliability, truth, validity; firmness, solidity, strength, validity.

soup *n* broth, consommé, purée.

sour *vb* acidulate; embitter, envenom. * *adj* acetose, acetous, acid, astringent, pricked, sharp, tart, vinegary; acrimonious, crabbed, cross, crusty, fretful, glum, ill-humoured, ill-natured, ill-tempered, peevish, pettish, petulant, snarling, surly; bitter, disagreeable, unpleasant; austere, dismal, gloomy, morose, sad, sullen; bad, coagulated, curdled, musty, rancid, turned.

source *n* beginning, fountain, fountainhead, head, origin, rise, root, spring, well; cause, original.

sourness *n* acidity, sharpness, tartness; acrimony, asperity, churlishness, crabbedness, crossness, discontent, harshness, moroseness, peevishness.

souse *vb* pickle; dip, douse, immerse, plunge, submerge.

souvenir *n* keepsake, memento, remembrance, reminder.

sovereign *adj* imperial, monarchical, princely, regal, royal, supreme; chief, commanding, excellent, highest, paramount, predominant, principal, supreme, utmost; efficacious, effectual. * *n* autocrat, monarch, suzerain; emperor, empress, king, lord, potentate, prince, princess, queen, ruler.

sovereignty *n* authority, dominion, empire, power, rule, supremacy, sway.

sow *vb* scatter, spread, strew; disperse, disseminate, propagate, spread abroad; plant; besprinkle, scatter.

space *n* expanse, expansion, extension, extent, proportions, spread; accommodation, capacity, room, place; distance, interspace, interval.

spacious *adj* extended, extensive, vast, wide; ample, broad, capacious, commodious, large, roomy, wide.

span *vb* compass, cross, encompass, measure, overlay. * *n* brief period, spell; pair, team, yoke.

spank *vb* slap, strike.

spar[1] *n* beam, boom, pole, sprit, yard.

spar[2] *vb* box, fight; argue, bicker, contend, dispute, quarrel, spat, squabble, wrangle.

spare *vb* lay aside, lay by, reserve, save, set apart, set aside; dispense with, do without, part with; forbear, omit, refrain, withhold; exempt, forgive, keep from; afford, allow, give, grant; save; economize, pinch. * *adj* frugal, scanty, sparing, stinted; chary, parsimonious; emaciated, gaunt, lank, lean, meagre, poor, thin, scraggy, skinny, raw-boned; additional, extra, supernumerary.

sparing *adj* little, scanty, scarce; abstemious, meagre, spare; chary, economical, frugal, parsimonious, saving; compassionate, forgiving, lenient, merciful.

spark *vb* scintillate, sparkle; begin, fire, incite, instigate, kindle, light, set off, start, touch off, trigger. * *n* scintilla, scintillation, sparkle; beginning, element, germ, seed.

sparkle *vb* coruscate, flash, gleam, glisten, glister, glitter, radiate, scintillate, shine, twinkle; bubble, effervesce, foam, froth. * *n* glint, scintillation, spark; luminosity, lustre.

sparkling *adj* brilliant, flashing, glistening, glittering, glittery, twinkling; bubbling, effervescing, eloquent, foaming, frothing, mantling; brilliant, glowing, lively, nervous, piquant, racy, spirited, sprightly, witty.

sparse *adj* dispersed, infrequent, scanty, scattered, sporadic, thin.

spartan *adj* bold, brave, chivalric, courageous, daring, dauntless, doughty, fearless, hardy, heroic, intrepid, lion-hearted, undaunted, valiant, valorous; austere, exacting, hard, severe, tough, unsparing; enduring, long-suffering, self-controlled, stoic.

spasm *n* contraction, cramp, crick, twitch; fit, paroxysm, seizure, throe.

spasmodic *adj* erratic, fitful, intermittent, irregular, sporadic; convulsive, paroxysmal, spasmodical, violent.

spat *vb* argue, bicker, dispute, jangle, quarrel, spar, squabble, wrangle.

spatter *vb* bespatter, besprinkle, plash, splash, sprinkle; spit, sputter.

spawn *vb* bring forth, generate, produce. * *n* eggs, roe; fruit, offspring, product.

speak *vb* articulate, deliver, enunciate, express, pronounce, utter; announce, confer, declare, disclose, mention, say, tell; celebrate, make known, proclaim, speak abroad; accost, address, greet, hail; exhibit; argue, converse, dispute, talk; declaim, discourse, hold forth, harangue, orate, plead, spout, treat.

speaker *n* discourse, elocutionist, orator, prolocutor, spokesman; chairman, presiding officer.

speaking *adj* rhetorical, talking; eloquent, expressive; lifelike. * *n* discourse, talk, utterance; declamation, elocution, oratory.

spear *n* dart, gaff, harpoon, javelin, lance, pike; shoot, spire.

special *adj* specific, specifical; especial, individual, particular, peculiar, unique; exceptional, extraordinary, marked, particular, uncommon; appropriate, express.

speciality, specialty *n* particularity; feature, forte, pet subject.

species *n* assemblage, class, collection, group; description, kind, sort, variety; (*law*) fashion, figure, form, shape.

specific *adj* characteristic, especial, particular, peculiar; definite, limited, precise, specified.

specification *n* characterization, designation; details, particularization.

specify *vb* define, designate, detail, indicate, individualize, name, show, particularize.

specimen *n* copy, example, model, pattern, sample.

specious *adj* manifest, obvious, open, showy; flimsy, illusory, ostensible, plausible, sophistical.

speck *n* blemish, blot, flaw, speckle, spot, stain; atom, bit, corpuscle, mite, mote, particle, scintilla.

spectacle *n* display, exhibition, pageant, parade, representation, review, scene, show, sight; curiosity, marvel, phenomenon, wonder.

spectacles *npl* glasses, goggles, shades.

spectator *n* beholder, bystander, observer, onlooker, witness.

spectral *adj* eerie, ghostlike, ghostly, phantomlike, shadowy, spooky, weird, wraithlike.

spectre, specter *n* apparition, banshee, ghost, goblin, hobgoblin, phantom, shade, shadow, spirit, sprite, wraith.

spectrum *n* appearance, image, representation.

speculate *vb* cogitate, conjecture, contemplate, imagine, meditate, muse, ponder, reflect, ruminate, theorize, think; bet, gamble, hazard, risk, trade, venture.

speculation *n* contemplation, intellectualization; conjecture, hypothesis, scheme, supposition, reasoning, reflection, theory, view.

speculative *adj* contemplative, philosophical, speculatory, unpractical; ideal, imaginary, theoretical; hazardous, risky, unsecured.

speculator *n* speculatist, theorist, theorizer; adventurer, dealer, gambler, trader.

speech *n* articulation, language, words; dialect, idiom, locution, tongue; conversation, oral communication, parlance, talk, verbal intercourse; mention, observation, remark, saying; address, declaration, discourse, harangue, oration, palaver.

speechless *adj* dumb, gagged, inarticulate, mute, silent; dazed, dumbfounded, flabbergasted, shocked.

speed *vb* hasten, hurry, rush, scurry; flourish, prosper, succeed, thrive; accelerate, expedite, hasten, hurry, quicken, press forward, urge on; carry through, dispatch, execute; advance, aid, assist, help; favour. * *n* acceleration, celerity, dispatch, expedition, fleetness, haste, hurry, quickness, rapidity, swiftness, velocity; good fortune, good luck, prosperity, success; impetuosity.

speedy *adj* fast, fleet, flying, hasty, hurried, hurrying, nimble, quick, rapid, swift; expeditious, prompt, quick; approaching, early, near.

spell[1] *n* charm, exorcism, hoodoo, incantation, jinx, witchery; allure, bewitchment, captivation, enchantment, entrancement, fascination.

spell[2] *vb* decipher, interpret, read, unfold, unravel, unriddle.

spell[3] *n* fit, interval, period, round, season, stint, term, turn.

spellbound *adj* bewitched, charmed, enchanted, entranced, enthralled, fascinated.

spend *vb* disburse, dispose of, expend, lay out, part with; consume, dissipate, exhaust, lavish, squander, use up, wear, waste; apply, bestow, devote, employ, pass.

spendthrift *n* prodigal, spender, squanderer, waster.

spent *adj* exhausted, fatigued, played out, used up, wearied, worn out.

spew *vb* cast up, puke, throw up, vomit; cast forth, eject.

spheral *adj* complete, perfect, symmetrical.

sphere *n* ball, globe, orb, spheroid; ambit, beat, bound, circle, circuit, compass, department, function, office, orbit, province, range, walk; order, rank, standing; country, domain, quarter, realm, region.

spherical *adj* bulbous, globated, globous, globular, orbicular, rotund, round, spheroid; planetary.

spice *n* flavour, flavouring, relish, savour, taste; admixture, dash, grain, infusion, particle, smack, soupçon, sprinkling, tincture.

spicily *adv* pungently, wittily.

spicy *adj* aromatic, balmy, fragrant; keen, piquant, pointed, pungent, sharp; indelicate, off-colour, racy, risqué, sensational, suggestive.

spill *vb* effuse, pour out, shed. * *n* accident, fall, tumble.

spin *vb* twist; draw out, extend; lengthen, prolong, protract, spend; pirouette, turn, twirl, whirl. * *n* drive, joyride, ride; autorotation, gyration, loop, revolution, rotation, turning, wheeling; pirouette, reel, turn, wheel, whirl.

spindle *n* axis, shaft.

spine *n* barb, prickle, thorn; backbone; ridge.

spinose *adj* briery, spinous, spiny, thorny.

spiny *adj* briery, prickly, spinose, spinous, thorny; difficult, perplexed, troublesome.

spiracle *n* aperture, blowhole, orifice, pore, vent.

spiral *adj* cochlear, cochleated, curled, helical, screw-shaped, spiry, winding. * *n* helix, winding, worm.

spire *n* curl, spiral, twist, wreath; steeple; blade, shoot, spear, stalk; apex, summit.

spirit *vb* animate, encourage, excite, inspirit; carry

off, kidnap. * *n* immaterial substance, life, vital essence; person, soul; angel, apparition, demon, elf, fairy, genius, ghost, phantom, shade, spectre, sprite; disposition, frame of mind, humour, mood, temper; spirits; ardour, cheerfulness, courage, earnestness, energy, enterprise, enthusiasm, fire, force, mettle, resolution, vigour, vim, vivacity, zeal; animation, cheerfulness, enterprise, esprit, glow, liveliness, piquancy, spice, spunk, vivacity, warmth; drift, gist, intent, meaning, purport, sense, significance, tenor; character, characteristic, complexion, essence, nature, quality, quintessence; alcohol, liquor; (*with* **the**) Comforter, Holy Ghost, Paraclete.

spirited *adj* active, alert, animated, ardent, bold, brisk, courageous, earnest, frisky, high-mettled, high-spirited, high-strung, lively, mettlesome, sprightly, vivacious.

spiritless *adj* breathless, dead, extinct, lifeless; dejected, depressed, discouraged, dispirited, low-spirited; apathetic, cold, dull, feeble, languid, phlegmatic, sluggish, soulless, torpid, unenterprising; dull, frigid, heavy, insipid, prosaic, prosy, stupid, tame, uninteresting.

spiritual *adj* ethereal, ghostly, immaterial incorporeal, psychical, supersensible; ideal, moral, unwordly; divine, holy, pure, sacred; ecclesiastical.

spiritualize *vb* elevate, etherealize, purify, refine.

spirituous *adj* alcoholic, ardent, spiritous.

spit[1] *vb* impale, thrust through, transfix.

spit[2] *vb* eject, throw out; drivel, drool, expectorate, salivate, slobber, spawl, splutter. * *n* saliva, spawl, spittle, sputum.

spite *vb* injure, mortify, thwart; annoy, offend, vex. * *n* grudge, hate, hatred, ill-nature, ill-will, malevolence, malice, maliciousness, malignity, pique, rancour, spleen, venom, vindictiveness.

spiteful *adj* evil-minded, hateful, ill-disposed, ill-natured, malevolent, malicious, malign, malignant, rancorous.

spittoon *n* cuspidor.

splash *vb* dabble, dash, plash, spatter, splurge, swash, swish. * *n* blot, daub, spot.

splay *adj* broad, spreading out, turned out, wide.

spleen *n* anger, animosity, chagrin, gall, grudge, hatred, ill-humour, irascibility, malevolence, malice, malignity, peevishness, pique, rancour, spite.

spleeny *adj* angry, fretful, ill-tempered, irritable, peevish, spleenish, splenetic.

splendid *adj* beaming, bright, brilliant, effulgent, glowing, lustrous, radiant, refulgent, resplendent, shining; dazzling, gorgeous, imposing, kingly, magnificent, pompous, showy, sumptuous, superb; celebrated, conspicuous, distinguished, eminent, excellent, famous, glorious, illustrious, noble, pre-eminent, remarkable, signal; grand, heroic, lofty, noble, sublime.

splendour *n* brightness, brilliance, brilliancy, lustre, radiance, refulgence; display, éclat, gorgeousness, grandeur, magnificence, parade, pomp, show, showiness, stateliness; celebrity, eminence, fame, glory, grandeur, renown; grandeur, loftiness, nobleness, sublimity.

splenetic *adj* choleric, cross, fretful, irascible, irritable, peevish, pettish, petulant, snappish, testy, touchy, waspish; churlish, crabbed, morose, sour, sulky, sullen; gloomy, jaundiced.

splice *vb* braid, connect, join, knit, mortise.

splinter *vb* rend, shiver, sliver, split. * *n* fragment, piece.

split *vb* cleave, rive; break, burst, rend, splinter; divide, part, separate, sunder. * *n* crack, fissure, rent; breach, division, separation.

splotch *n* blot, daub, smear, spot, stain.

splutter *vb* sputter, stammer, stutter.

spoil *vb* despoil, fleece, loot, pilfer, plunder, ravage, rob, steal, strip, waste; corrupt, damage, destroy, disfigure, harm, impair, injure, mar, ruin, vitiate; decay, decompose. * *n* booty, loot, pillage, plunder, prey; rapine, robbery, spoliation, waste.

spoiler *n* pillager, plunderer, robber; corrupter, destroyer.

spokesman *n* mouthpiece, prolocutor, speaker.

spoliate *vb* despoil, destroy, loot, pillage, plunder, rob, spoil.

spoliation *n* depradation, deprivation, despoliation, destruction, robbery; destruction, devastation, pillage, plundering, rapine, ravagement.

sponge *vb* cleanse, wipe; efface, expunge, obliterate, rub out, wipe out.

sponger *n* hanger-on, parasite.

spongy *adj* absorbent, porous, spongeous; rainy, showery, wet; drenched, marshy, saturated, soaked, wet.

sponsor *vb* back, capitalize, endorse, finance, guarantee, patronize, promote, support, stake, subsidize, take up, underwrite. * *n* angel, backer, guarantor, patron, promoter, supporter, surety, underwriter; godfather, godmother, godparent.

spontaneity *n* improvisation, impulsiveness, spontaneousness.

spontaneous *adj* free, gratuitous, impulsive, improvised, instinctive, self-acting, self-moving, unbidden, uncompelled, unconstrained, voluntary, willing.

sporadic *adj* dispersed, infrequent, isolated, rare, scattered, separate, spasmodic.

sport *vb* caper, disport, frolic, gambol, have fun, make merry, play, romp, skip; trifle; display, exhibit. * *n* amusement, diversion, entertainment, frolic, fun, gambol, game, jollity, joviality, merriment, merry-making, mirth, pastime, pleasantry, prank, recreation; jest, joke; derision, jeer, mockery, ridicule; monstrosity.

sportive *adj* frisky, frolicsome, gamesome, hilarious, lively, merry, playful, prankish, rollicking, sprightly, tricksy; comic, facetious, funny, humorous, jocose, jocular, lively, ludicrous, mirthful, vivacious, waggish.

spot *vb* besprinkle, dapple, dot, speck, stud,

variegate; blemish, disgrace, soil, splotch, stain, sully, tarnish; detect, discern, espy, make out, observe, see, sight. * *n* blot, dapple, fleck, freckle, maculation, mark, mottle, patch, pip, speck, speckle; blemish, blotch, flaw, pock, splotch, stain, taint; locality, place, site.

spotless *adj* perfect, undefaced, unspotted; blameless, immaculate, innocent, irreproachable, pure, stainless, unblemished, unstained, untainted, untarnished.

spotted *adj* bespeckled, bespotted, dotted, flecked, freckled, maculated, ocellated, speckled, spotty.

spousal *adj* bridal, conjugal, connubial, hymeneal, marital, matrimonial, nuptial, wedded.

spouse *n* companion, consort, husband, mate, partner, wife.

spout *vb* gush, jet, pour out, spirit, spurt, squirt; declaim, mouth, speak, utter. * *n* conduit, tube; beak, nose, nozzle, waterspout.

sprain *vb* overstrain, rick, strain, twist, wrench, wrick.

spray[1] *vb* atomize, besprinkle, douche, gush, jet, shower, splash, splatter, spout, sprinkle, squirt. * *n* aerosol, atomizer, douche, foam, froth, shower, sprinkler, spume.

spray[2] *n* bough, branch, shoot, sprig, twig.

spread *vb* dilate, expand, extend, mantle, stretch; diffuse, disperse, distribute, radiate, scatter, sprinkle, strew; broadcast, circulate, disseminate, divulge, make known, make public, promulgate, propagate, publish; open, unfold, unfurl; cover, extend over, overspread. * *n* compass, extent, range, reach, scope, stretch; expansion, extension; circulation, dissemination, propagation; cloth, cover; banquet, feast, meal.

spree *n* bacchanal, carousal, debauch, frolic, jollification, orgy, revel, revelry, saturnalia.

sprig *n* shoot, spray, twig; lad, youth.

sprightliness *n* animation, activity, briskness, cheerfulness, frolicsomeness, gaiety, life, liveliness, nimbleness, vigour, vivacity.

sprightly *adj* airy, animated, blithe, blithesome, brisk, buoyant, cheerful, debonair, frolicsome, joyous, lively, mercurial, vigorous, vivacious.

spring *vb* bound, hop, jump, leap, prance, vault; arise, emerge, grow, issue, proceed, put forth, shoot forth, stem; derive, descend, emanate, flow, originate, rise, start; fly back, rebound, recoil; bend, warp; grow, thrive, wax. * *adj* hopping, jumping, resilient, springy. * *n* bound, hop, jump, leap, vault; elasticity, flexibility, resilience, resiliency, springiness; fount, fountain, fountainhead, geyser, springhead, well; cause, origin, original, principle, source; seed time, springtime.

springe *n* gin, net, noose, snare, trap.

springiness *n* elasticity, resilience, spring; sponginess, wetness.

springy *adj* bouncing, bounding, elastic, rebounding, recoiling, resilient.

sprinkle *vb* scatter, strew; bedew, besprinkle, dust, powder, sand, spatter; wash, cleanse, purify, shower.

sprinkling *n* affusion, baptism, bedewing, spattering, splattering, spraying, wetting; dash, scattering, seasoning, smack, soupçon, suggestion, tinge, touch, trace, vestige.

sprite *n* apparition, elf, fairy, ghost, goblin, hobgoblin, phantom, pixie, shade, spectre, spirit.

sprout *vb* burgeon, burst forth, germinate, grow, pullulate, push, put forth, ramify, shoot, shoot forth. * *n* shoot, sprig.

spruce *vb* preen, prink; adorn, deck, dress, smarten, trim. * *adj* dandyish, dapper, fine, foppish, jaunty, natty, neat, nice, smart, tidy, trig, trim.

spry *adj* active, agile, alert, brisk, lively, nimble, prompt, quick, ready, smart, sprightly, stirring, supple.

spume *n* foam, froth, scum, spray.

spumy *adj* foamy, frothy, spumous.

spur *vb* gallop, hasten, press on, prick; animate, arouse, drive, goad, impel, incite, induce, instigate, rouse, stimulate, urge forward. * *n* goad, point, prick, rowel; fillip, impulse, incentive, incitement, inducement, instigation, motive, provocation, stimulus, whip; gnarl, knob, knot, point, projection, snag.

spurious *adj* bogus, counterfeit, deceitful, false, feigned, fictitious, make-believe, meretricious, mock, pretended, sham, supposititious, unauthentic.

spurn *vb* drive away, kick; contemn, despise, disregard, flout, scorn, slight; disdain, reject, repudiate.

spurt *vb* gush, jet, spirt, spout, spring out, stream out, well. * *n* gush, jet, spout, squirt; burst, dash, rush.

sputter *vb* spawl, spit, splutter, stammer.

spy *vb* behold, discern, espy, see; detect, discover, search out; explore, inspect, scrutinize, search; shadow, trail, watch. * *n* agent, detective, double agent, mole, scout, undercover agent.

squabble *vb* brawl, fight, quarrel, scuffle, struggle, wrangle; altercate, bicker, contend, dispute, jangle. * *n* brawl, dispute, fight, quarrel, rumpus, scrimmage.

squad *n* band, bevy, crew, gang, knot, lot, relay, set.

squalid *adj* dirty, filthy, foul, mucky, slovenly, unclean, unkempt.

squalidness *n* filthiness, foulness, squalidity, squalor.

squall *vb* bawl, cry, cry out, scream, yell. * *n* bawl, cry, outcry, scream, yell; blast, flurry, gale, gust, hurricane, storm, tempest.

squally *adj* blustering, blustery, gusty, stormy, tempestuous, windy.

squander *vb* dissipate, expend, lavish, lose, misuse, scatter, spend, throw away, waste.

squanderer *n* lavisher, prodigal, spendthrift, waster.

square *vb* make square, quadrate; accommodate,

adapt, fit, mould, regulate, shape, suit; adjust, balance, close, make even, settle; accord, chime in, cohere, comport, fall in, fit, harmonize, quadrate, suit. * *adj* four-square, quadrilateral, quadrate; equal, equitable, exact, fair, honest, just, upright; adjusted, balanced, even, settled; true, suitable. * *n* four-sided figure, quadrate, rectangle, tetragon; open area, parade, piazza, plaza.

squash *vb* crush, mash.

squashy *adj* pulpy, soft.

squat *vb* cower, crouch; occupy, plant, settle. * *adj* cowering, crouching; dumpy, pudgy, short, stocky, stubby, thickset.

squeal *vb* creak, cry, howl, scream, screech, shriek, squawk, yell; betray, inform on. * *n* creak, cry, howl, scream, screech, shriek, squawk, yell.

squeamish *adj* nauseated, qualmish, queasy, sickish; dainty, delicate, fastidious, finical, hypercritical, nice, over-nice, particular, priggish.

squeeze *vb* clutch, compress, constrict, grip, nip, pinch, press; drive, force; crush, harass, oppress; crowd, force through; press; (*with* **out**) extract. * *n* congestion, crowd, crush, throng; compression.

squelch *vb* crush, quash, quell, silence, squash, suppress.

squib *n* firework, fuse; lampoon, pasquinade, satire.

squint *vb* look askance, look obliquely, peer. * *adj* askew, aslant, crooked, oblique, skew, skewed, twisted.

squire *vb* accompany, attend, escort, wait on.

squirm *vb* twist, wriggle, writhe.

squirt *vb* eject, jet, splash, spurt.

stab *vb* broach, gore, jab, pierce, pink, spear, stick, transfix, transpierce; wound. * *n* cut, jab, prick, thrust; blow, dagger-stroke, injury, wound.

stability *n* durability, firmness, fixedness, immovability, permanence, stableness, steadiness; constancy, firmness, reliability.

stable *adj* established, fixed, immovable, immutable, invariable, permanent, unalterable, unchangeable; constant, firm, staunch, steadfast, steady, unwavering; abiding, durable, enduring, fast, lasting, permanent, perpetual, secure, sure.

staff *n* baton, cane, pole, rod, stick, wand; bat, bludgeon, club, cudgel, mace; prop, stay, support; employees, personnel, team, workers, work force.

stage *vb* dramatize, perform, present, produce, put on. * *n* dais, platform, rostrum, scaffold, staging, stand; arena, field; boards, playhouse, theatre; degree, point, step; diligence, omnibus, stagecoach.

stagey *adj* bombastic, declamatory, dramatic, melodramatic, ranting, theatrical.

stagger *vb* reel, sway, totter; alternate, fluctuate, overlap, vacillate, vary; falter, hesitate, waver; amaze, astonish, astound, confound, dumbfound, nonplus, pose, shock, surprise.

stagnant *adj* close, motionless, quiet, standing; dormant, dull, heavy, inactive, inert, sluggish, torpid.

stagnate *vb* decay, deteriorate, languish, rot, stand still, vegetate.

staid *adj* calm, composed, demure, grave, sedate, serious, settled, sober, solemn, steady, unadventurous.

stain *vb* blemish, blot, blotch, discolour, maculate, smirch, soil, splotch, spot, sully, tarnish; colour, dye, tinge; contaminate, corrupt, debase, defile, deprave, disgrace, dishonour, pollute, taint. * n blemish, blot, defect, discoloration, flaw, imperfection, spot, tarnish; contamination, disgrace, dishonour, infamy, pollution, reproach, shame, taint, tarnish.

stainless *adj* spotless, unspotted, untarnished; blameless, faultless, innocent, guiltless, pure, spotless, uncorrupted, unsullied.

stairs *npl* flight of steps, staircase, stairway.

stake[1] *vb* brace, mark, prop, secure, support. * *n* pale, palisade, peg, picket, post, stick.

stake[2] *vb* finance, pledge, wager; hazard, imperil, jeopardize, peril, risk, venture. * *n* bet, pledge, wager; adventure, hazard, risk, venture.

stale *adj* flat, fusty, insipid, mawkish, mouldy, musty, sour, tasteless, vapid; decayed, effete, faded, old, time-worn, worn-out; common, commonplace, hackneyed, stereotyped, threadbare, trite.

stalk[1] *n* culm, pedicel, peduncle, petiole, shaft, spire, stem, stock.

stalk[2] *vb* march, pace, stride, strut, swagger; follow, hunt, shadow, track, walk stealthily.

stall[1] *n* stable; cell, compartment, recess; booth, kiosk, shop, stand.

stall[2] *vb* block, delay, equivocate, filibuster, hinder, postpone, procrastinate, temporize; arrest, check, conk out, die, fail, halt, stick, stop.

stalwart *adj* able-bodied, athletic, brawny, lusty, muscular, powerful, robust, sinewy, stout, strapping, strong, sturdy, vigorous; bold, brave, daring, gallant, indomitable, intrepid, redoubtable, resolute, valiant, valorous. * *n* backer, member, partisan, supporter.

stamina *n* energy, force, lustiness, power, stoutness, strength, sturdiness, vigour.

stammer *vb* falter, hesitate, stutter. * *n* faltering, hesitation, stutter.

stamp *vb* brand, impress, imprint, mark, print. * *n* brand, impress, impression, print; cast, character, complexion, cut, description, fashion, form, kind, make, mould, sort, type.

stampede *vb* charge, flee, panic. * *n* charge, flight, rout, running away, rush.

stanch *see* **staunch**[1].

stanchion *n* prop, shore, stay, support.

stand *vb* be erect, remain upright; abide, be fixed, continue, endure, hold good, remain; halt, pause, stop; be firm, be resolute, stand ground, stay; be valid, have force; depend, have support, rest; bear, brook, endure, suffer, sustain, weather; abide, admit, await, submit, tolerate, yield; fix, place, put, set upright; (*with* **against**) oppose, resist, withstand; (*with* **by**) be near, be present; aid, assist, defend, help, side with, support; defend, make good, justify, maintain, support, vindicate; (*naut*) attend, be ready; (*with* **fast**) be fixed, be immovable; (*with* **for**) mean, represent, signify; aid, defend, help, maintain, side with, support; (*with* **off**) keep aloof, keep off; not to comply; (*with* **out**) be prominent, jut, project, protrude; not comply, not yield, persist; (*with* **up for**) defend, justify, support, sustain, uphold; (*with* **with**) agree. * *n* place, position, post, standing place, station; halt, stay, stop; dais, platform, rostrum; booth, stall; opposition, resistance.

standard[1] *n* banner, colours, ensign, flag, gonfalon, pennon, streamer.

standard[2] *adj* average, conventional, customary, normal, ordinary, regular, usual; accepted, approved, authoritative, orthodox, received; formulary, prescriptive, regulation. * *n* canon, criterion, model, norm, rule, test, type; gauge, measure, model, scale; support, upright.

standing *adj* established, fixed, immovable, settled; durable, lasting, permanent; motionless, stagnant. * *n* position, stand, station; continuance, duration, existence; footing, ground, hold; condition, estimation, rank, reputation, status.

standpoint *n* point of view, viewpoint.

standstill *n* cessation, interruption, stand, stop; deadlock.

stanza *n* measure, staff, stave, strophe, verse.

staple *adj* basic, chief, essential, fundamental, main, primary, principal. * *n* fibre, filament, pile, thread; body, bulk, mass, substance.

star *vb* act, appear, feature, headline, lead, perform, play; emphasize, highlight, stress, underline. * *adj* leading, main, paramount, principal; celebrated, illustrious, well-known. * *n* heavenly body, luminary; asterisk, pentacle, pentagram; destiny, doom, fate, fortune, lot; diva, headliner, hero, heroine, lead, leading lady, leading man, prima ballerina, prima donna, principal, protagonist.

starchy *adj* ceremonious, exact, formal, precise, prim, punctilious, rigid, starched, stiff.

stare *vb* gape, gaze, look intently, watch.

stark *adj* rigid, stiff; absolute, bare, downright, entire, gross, mere, pure, sheer, simple. * *adv* absolutely, completely, entirely, fully, wholly.

starry *adj* astral, sidereal, star-spangled, stellar; bright, brilliant, lustrous, shining, sparkling, twinkling.

start *vb* begin, commence, inaugurate, initiate, institute; discover, invent; flinch, jump, shrink, startle, wince; alarm, disturb, fright, rouse, scare; depart, set off, take off; arise, call forth, evoke, raise; dislocate, move suddenly, spring. * *n* beginning, commencement, inauguration, outset; fit, jump, spasm, twitch; impulse, sally.

startle *vb* flinch, shrink, start, wince; affright, alarm, fright, frighten, scare, shock; amaze, astonish, astound.

startling *adj* abrupt, alarming, astonishing, shocking, sudden, surprising, unexpected, unforeseen, unheard of.

starvation *n* famine, famishment.

starve *vb* famish, perish; be in need, lack, want; kill, subdue.

starveling *adj* attenuated, emaciated, gaunt, hungry, lank, lean, meagre, scraggy, skinny, thin. * *n* beggar, mendicant, pauper.

state *vb* affirm, assert, aver, declare, explain, expound, express, narrate, propound, recite, say, set forth, specify, voice. * *adj* civic, national, public. * *n* case, circumstances, condition, pass, phase, plight, position, posture, predicament, situation, status; condition, guise, mode, quality, rank; dignity, glory, grandeur, magnificence, pageantry, parade, pomp, spendour; body politic, civil community, commonwealth, nation, realm.

statecraft *n* diplomacy, political subtlety, state management, statesmanship.

stated *adj* established, fixed, regular, settled; detailed, set forth, specified.

stately *adj* august, dignified, elevated, grand, imperial, imposing, lofty, magnificent, majestic, noble, princely, royal; ceremonious, formal, magisterial, pompous, solemn.

statement *n* account, allegation, announcement, communiqué, declaration, description, exposition, mention, narration, narrative, recital, relation, report, specification; assertion, predication, proposition, pronouncement, thesis.

statesman *n* politician.

station *vb* establish, fix, locate, place, post, set. * *n* location, place, position, lost, seat, situation; business, employment, function, occupation, office; character, condition, degree, dignity, footing, rank, standing, state, status; depot, stop, terminal.

stationary *adj* fixed, motionless, permanent, quiescent, stable, standing, still.

statuary *n* carving, sculpture, statues.

statue *n* figurine, image, statuette.

stature *n* height, physique, size, tallness; altitude, consequence, elevation, eminence, prominence.

status *n* caste, condition, footing, position, rank, standing, station.

statute *n* act, decree, edict, enactment, law, ordinance, regulation.

staunch[1], **stanch** *vb* arrest, block, check, dam, plug, stem, stop.

staunch[2] *adj* firm, sound, stout, strong; constant, faithful, firm, hearty, loyal, resolute, stable, steadfast, steady, strong, trustworthy, trusty, unwavering, zealous.

stave *vb* break, burst; (*with* **off**) adjourn, defer, delay, postpone, procrastinate, put off, waive.

stay *vb* abide, dwell, lodge, rest, sojourn, tarry;

continue, halt, remain, stand still, stop; attend, delay, linger, wait; arrest, check, curb, hold, keep in, prevent, rein in, restrain, withhold; delay, detain, hinder, obstruct; hold up, prop, shore up, support, sustain, uphold. * *n* delay, repose, rest, sojourn; halt, stand, stop; bar, check, curb, hindrance, impediment, interruption, obstacle, obstruction, restraint, stumbling block; buttress, dependence, prop, staff, support, supporter.

stead *n* place, room.

steadfast *adj* established, fast, firm, fixed, stable; constant, faithful, implicit, persevering, pertinacious, resolute, resolved, staunch, steady, unhesitating, unreserved, unshaken, unwavering, wholehearted.

steadiness *n* constancy, firmness, perseverance, persistence, resolution, steadfastness; fixedness, stability.

steady *vb* balance, counterbalance, secure, stabilize, support. * *adj* firm, fixed, stable; constant, equable, regular, undeviating, uniform, unremitting; persevering, resolute, staunch, steadfast, unchangeable, unwavering.

steal *vb* burglarize, burgle, crib, embezzle, filch, peculate, pilfer, plagiarize, poach, purloin, shoplift, thieve; creep, sneak, pass stealthily.

stealing *n* burglary, larceny, peculation, shoplifting, robbery, theft, thievery.

stealth *n* secrecy, slyness, stealthiness.

stealthy *adj* clandestine, furtive, private, secret, skulking, sly, sneaking, surreptitious, underhand.

steam *vb* emit vapour, fume; evaporate, vaporize; coddle, cook, poach; navigate, sail; be hot, sweat. * *n* vapour; effluvium, exhalation, fume, mist, reek, smoke.

steamboat *n* steamer, steamship.

steamy *adj* misty, moist, vaporous; erotic, voluptuous.

steed *n* charger, horse, mount.

steel *vb* case-harden, edge; brace, fortify, harden, make firm, nerve, strengthen.

steep[1] *adj* abrupt, declivitous, precipitous, sheer, sloping, sudden. * *n* declivity, precipice.

steep[2] *vb* digest, drench, imbrue, imbue, macerate, saturate, soak.

steeple *n* belfry, spire, tower, turret.

steer *vb* direct, conduct, govern, guide, pilot, point.

steersman *n* conductor, guide, helmsman, pilot.

stellar *adj* astral, starry, star-spangled, stellary.

stem[1] *vb* (*with* **from**) bud, descend, generate, originate, spring, sprout. * *n* axis, stipe, trunk; pedicel, peduncle, petiole, stalk; branch, descendant, offspring, progeny, scion, shoot; ancestry, descent, family, generation, line, lineage, pedigree, race, stock; (*naut*) beak, bow, cutwater, forepart, prow; helm, lookout; etymon, radical, radix, origin, root.

stem[2] *vb* breast, oppose, resist, withstand; check, dam, oppose, staunch, stay, stop.

stench *n* bad smell, fetor, offensive odour, stink.

stenography *n* brachygraphy, shorthand, tachygraphy.

stentorian *adj* loud-voiced, powerful, sonorous, thundering, trumpet-like.

step *vb* pace, stride, tramp, tread, walk. * *n* footstep, pace, stride; stair, tread; degree, gradation, grade, interval; advance, advancement, progression; act, action, deed, procedure, proceeding; footprint, trace, track, vestige; footfall, gait, pace, walk; expedient, means, measure, method; round, rundle, rung.

steppe *n* pampa, prairie, savannah.

sterile *adj* barren, infecund, unfruitful, unproductive, unprolific; bare, dry, empty, poor; (*bot*) acarpous, male, staminate.

sterility *n* barrenness, fruitlessness, infecundity, unfruitfulness, unproductiveness.

sterling *adj* genuine, positive, pure, real, sound, standard, substantial, true.

stern[1] *adj* austere, dour, forbidding, grim, severe; bitter, cruel, hard, harsh, inflexible, relentless, rigid, rigorous, severe, strict, unrelenting; immovable, incorruptible, steadfast, uncompromising.

stern[2] *n* behind, breach, hind part, posterior, rear, tail; (*naut*) counter, poop, rudderpost, tailpost; butt, buttocks, fundament, rump.

sternness *n* austerity, rigidity, severity; asperity, cruelty, harshness, inflexibility, relentlessness, rigour.

sternum *n* (*anat*) breastbone, sternon.

stertorous *adj* hoarsely breathing, snoring.

stew *vb* boil, seethe, simmer, stive. * *n* ragout; confusion, difficculty, mess, scrape.

steward *n* chamberlain, majordomo, seneschal; manciple, purveyor.

stick[1] *vb* gore, penetrate, pierce, puncture, spear, stab, transfix; infix, insert, thrust; attach, cement, glue, paste; fix in, set; adhere, cleave, cling, hold; abide, persist, remain, stay, stop; doubt, hesitate, scruple, stickle, waver; (*with* **by**) adhere to, be faithful, support. * *n* prick, stab, thrust.

stick[2] *n* birch, rod, switch; bat, bludgeon, club, cudgel, shillelah; cane, staff, walking stick; cue, pole, spar, stake.

stickiness *n* adhesiveness, glutinousness, tenacity, viscosity, viscousness.

stickle *vb* altercate, contend, contest, struggle; doubt, hesitate, scruple, stick, waver.

sticky *adj* adhesive, clinging, gluey, glutinous, gummy, mucilaginous, tenacious, viscid, viscous.

stiff *adj* inflexible, rigid, stark, unbending, unyielding; firm, tenacious, thick; obstinate, pertinacious, strong, stubborn; absolute, austere, dogmatic, inexorable, peremptory, positive, rigorous, severe, straitlaced, strict, stringent, uncompromising; ceremonious, chilling, constrained, formal, frigid, prim, punctilious, stately, starchy, stilted; abrupt, cramped, crude, graceless, harsh, inelegant.

stiff-necked *adj* contumacious, cross-grained, dogged, headstrong, intractable, mulish, obdurate, obstinate, stubborn, unruly.

stiffness *n* hardness, inflexibility, rigidity, rigidness, rigour, starkness; compactness, consistence, denseness, density, thickness; contumaciousness, inflexibility, obstinacy, pertinacity, stubbornness; austerity, harshness, rigorousness, severity, sternness, strictness; constraint, formality, frigidity, precision, primness, tenseness.

stifle *vb* choke, smother, suffocate; check, deaden, destroy, extinguish, quench, repress, stop, suppress; conceal, gag, hush, muffle, muzzle, silence, smother, still.

stigma *n* blot, blur, brand, disgrace, dishonour, reproach, shame, spot, stain, taint, tarnish.

stigmatize *vb* brand, defame, discredit, disgrace, dishonour, post, reproach, slur, villify.

stiletto *n* dagger, dirk, poniard, stylet; bodkin, piercer.

still[1] *vb* hush, muffle, silence, stifle; allay, appease, calm, compose, lull, pacify, quiet, smooth, tranquillize; calm, check, immobilize, restrain, stop, subdue, suppress. * *adj* hushed, mum, mute, noiseless, silent; calm, placid, quiet, serene, stilly, tranquil, unruffled; inert, motionless, quiescent, stagnant, stationary. * *n* hush, lull, peace, quiet, quietness, quietude, silence, stillness, tranquillity; picture, photograph, shot.

still[2] *n* distillery, still-house; distillatory, retort, stillatory.

still[3] *adv, conj* till now, to this time, yet; however, nevertheless, notwithstanding; always, continually, ever, habitually, uniformly; after that, again, in continuance.

stilted *adj* bombastic, fustian, grandiloquent, grandiose, high-flown, high-sounding, inflated, magniloquent, pompous, pretentious, stilty, swelling, tumid, turgid.

stimulant *adj* exciting, stimulating, stimulative. * *n* bracer, cordial, pick-me-up, tonic; fillip, incentive, provocative, spur, stimulus.

stimulate *vb* animate, arouse, awaken, brace, encourage, energize, excite, fire, foment, goad, impel, incite, inflame, inspirit, instigate, kindle, prick, prompt, provoke, rally, rouse, set on, spur, stir up, urge, whet, work up.

stimulus *n* encouragement, fillip, goad, incentive, incitement, motivation, motive, provocation, spur, stimulant.

sting *vb* hurt, nettle, prick, wound; afflict, cut, pain.

stinging *adj* acute, painful, piercing; biting, nipping, pungent, tingling.

stingy *adj* avaricious, close, close-fisted, covetous, grudging, mean, miserly, narrow-hearted, niggardly, parsimonious, penurious.

stink *vb* emit a stench, reek, smell bad. * *n* bad smell, fetor, offensive odour, stench.

stint *vb* bound, confine, limit, restrain; begrudge, pinch, scrimp, skimp, straiten; cease, desist, stop. * *n* bound, limit, restraint; lot, period, project, quota, share, shift, stretch, task, time, turn.

stipend *n* allowance, compensation, emolument, fee, hire, honorarium, pay, remuneration, salary, wages.

stipulate *vb* agree, bargain, condition, contract, covenant, engage, provide, settle terms.

stipulation *n* agreement, bargain, concordat, condition, contract, convention, covenant, engagement, indenture, obligation, pact.

stir *vb* budge, change place, go, move; agitate, bestir, disturb, prod; argue, discuss, moot, raise, start; animate, arouse, awaken, excite, goad, incite, instigate, prompt, provoke, quicken, rouse, spur, stimulate; appear, happen, turn up; get up, rise; (*with* **up**) animate, awaken, incite, instigate, move, provoke, quicken, rouse, stimulate. * *n* activity, ado, agitation, bustle, confusion, excitement, fidget, flurry, fuss, hurry, movement; commotion, disorder, disturbance, tumult, uproar.

stirring *adj* active, brisk, diligent, industrious, lively, smart; animating, arousing, awakening, exciting, quickening, stimulating.

stitch *vb* backstitch, baste, bind, embroider, fell, hem, seam, sew, tack, whip.

stive *vb* stow, stuff; boil, seethe, stew; make close, hot or sultry.

stock *vb* fill, furnish, store, supply; accumulate, garner, hoard, lay in, reposit, reserve, save, treasure up. * *adj* permanent, standard, standing. * *n* assets, capital, commodities, fund, principal, shares; accumulation, hoard, inventory, merchandise, provision, range, reserve, store, supply; ancestry, breed, descent, family, house, line, lineage, parentage, pedigree, race; cravat, neckcloth; butt, haft, hand; block, log, pillar, post, stake; stalk, stem, trunk.

stockholder *n* shareholder.

stocking *n* hose, sock.

stock market *n* stock exchange; cattle market.

stocks *npl* funds, public funds, public securities; shares.

stockstill *adj* dead-still, immobile, motionless, stationary, still, unmoving.

stocky *adj* chubby, chunky, dumpy, plump, short, stout, stubby, thickset.

stoic, stoical *adj* apathetic, cold-blooded, impassive, imperturbable, passionless, patient, philosophic, philosophical, phlegmatic, unimpassioned.

stoicism *n* apathy, coldness, coolness, impassivity, indifference, insensibility, nonchalance, phlegm.

stolen *adj* filched, pilfered, purloined; clandestine, furtive, secret, sly, stealthy, surreptitious.

stolid *adj* blockish, doltish, dull, foolish, heavy, obtuse, slow, stockish, stupid.

stolidity *n* doltishness, dullness, foolishness, obtuseness, stolidness, stupidity.

stomach *vb* abide, bear, brook, endure, put up with, stand, submit to, suffer, swallow, tolerate.

* *n* abdomen, belly, gut, paunch, pot, tummy; appetite, desire, inclination, keenness, liking, relish, taste.

stone *vb* cover, face, slate, tile; lapidate, pelt. * *n* boulder, cobble, gravel, pebble, rock; gem, jewel, precious stone; cenotaph, gravestone, monument, tombstone; nut, pit; adamant, agate, flint, gneiss, granite, marble, slate, etc.

stony *adj* gritty, hard, lapidose, lithic, petrous, rocky; adamantine, flinty, hard, inflexible, obdurate; cruel, hard-hearted, inexorable, pitiless, stony-hearted, unfeeling, unrelenting.

stoop *vb* bend forward, bend down, bow, lean, sag, slouch, slump; abase, cower, cringe, give in, submit, succumb, surrender; condescend, deign, descend, vouchsafe; fall, sink. * *n* bend, inclination, sag, slouch, slump; descent, swoop.

stop *vb* block, blockade, close, close up, obstruct, occlude; arrest, check, halt, hold, pause, stall, stay; bar, delay, embargo, hinder, impede, intercept, interrupt, obstruct, preclude, prevent, repress, restrain, staunch, suppress, thwart; break off, cease, desist, discontinue, forbear, give over, leave off, refrain from; intermit, quiet, quieten, terminate; lodge, tarry. * *n* halt, intermission, pause, respite, rest, stoppage, suspension, truce; block, cessation, check, hindrance, interruption, obstruction, repression; bar, impediment, obstacle; full stop, point.

stopcock *n* cock, faucet, tap.

stoppage *n* arrest, block, check, closure, hindrance, interruption, obstruction, prevention.

stopper *n* cork, plug, stopple.

store *vb* accumulate, amass, cache, deposit, garner, hoard, husband, lay by, lay in, lay up, put by, reserve, save, store up, stow away, treasure up; furnish, provide, replenish, stock, supply. * *n* accumulation, cache, deposit, fund, hoard, provision, reserve, stock, supply, treasure, treasury; abundance, plenty; storehouse; emporium, market, shop.

storehouse *n* depository, depot, godown, magazine, repository, store, warehouse.

storm *vb* assail, assault, attack; blow violently; fume, rage, rampage, rant, rave, tear. * *n* blizzard, gale, hurricane, squall, tempest, tornado, typhoon, whirlwind; agitation, clamour, commotion, disturbance, insurrection, outbreak, sedition, tumult, turmoil; adversity, affliction, calamity, distress; assault, attack, brunt, onset, onslaught; violence.

storminess *n* inclemency, roughness, tempestuousness.

stormy *adj* blustering, boisterous, gusty, squally, tempestuous, windy; passionate, riotous, rough, turbulent, violent, wild; agitated, furious.

story *n* annals, chronicle, history, record; account, narration, narrative, recital, record, rehearsal, relation, report, statement, tale; fable, fiction, novel, romance; anecdote, incident, legend, tale; canard, fabrication, falsehood, fib, figure, invention, lie, untruth.

storyteller *n* bard, chronicler, narrator, raconteur.

stout *adj* able-bodied, athletic, brawny, lusty, robust, sinewy, stalwart, strong, sturdy, vigorous; courageous, hardy, indomitable, stouthearted; contumacious, obstinate, proud, resolute, stubborn; compact, firm, solid, staunch; bouncing, bulky, burly, chubby, corpulent, fat, heavy, jolly, large, obese, plump, portly, stocky, strapping, thickset.

stouthearted *adj* fearless, heroic, redoubtable; bold, brave, courageous, dauntless, doughty, firm, gallant, hardy, indomitable, intrepid, resolute, valiant, valorous.

stow *vb* load, pack, put away, store, stuff.

straddle *vb* bestride.

straggle *vb* rove, wander; deviate, digress, ramble, range, roam, stray, stroll.

straggling *adj* rambling, roving, straying, strolling, wandering; scattered.

straight *adj* direct, near, rectilinear, right, short, undeviating, unswerving; erect, perpendicular, plumb, right, upright, vertical; equitable, fair, honest, honourable, just, square, straightforward. * *adv* at once, directly, forthwith, immediately, straightaway, straightway, without delay.

straightaway, straightway *adv* at once, directly, forthwith, immediately, speedily, straight, suddenly, without delay.

straighten *vb* arrange, make straight, neaten, order, tidy.

straight-laced *see* **strait-laced**.

strain[1] *vb* draw tightly, make tense, stretch, tighten; injure, sprain, wrench; exert, overexert, overtax, rack; embrace, fold, hug, press, squeeze; compel, constrain, force; dilute, distill, drain, filter, filtrate, ooze, percolate, purify, separate; fatigue, overtask, overwork, task, tax, tire. * *n* stress, tenseness, tension, tensity; effort, exertion, force, overexertion; burden, task, tax; sprain, wrech; lay, melody, movement, snatch, song, stave, tune.

strain[2] *n* manner, style, tone, vein; disposition, tendency, trait, turn; descent, extraction, family, lineage, pedigree, race, stock.

strait *adj* close, confined, constrained, constricted, contracted, narrow; rigid, rigorous, severe, strict; difficult, distressful, grievous, straitened. * *n* channel, narrows, pass, sound.

straits *npl* crisis, difficulty, dilemma, distress, embarrassment, emergency, exigency, extremity, hardship, pass, perplexity, pinch, plight, predicament.

straiten *vb* confine, constrain, constrict, contract, limit; narrow; intensify, stretch; distress, embarrass, perplex, pinch, press.

straitened *adj* distressed, embarrassed limited, perplexed, pinched.

strait-laced, straight-laced *adj* austere, formal, prim, rigid, rigorous, stern, stiff, strict, uncompromising.

straitness *n* narrowness, rigour, severity, strictness;

difficulty, distress, trouble; insufficiency, narrowness, scarcity, want.

strand[1] *vb* abandon, beach, be wrecked, cast away, go aground, ground, maroon, run aground, wreck. * *n* beach, coast, shore.

strand[2] *n* braid, cord, fibre, filament, line, rope, string, tress.

stranded *adj* aground, ashore, cast away, lost, shipwrecked, wrecked.

strange *adj* alien, exotic, far-fetched, foreign, outlandish, remote; new, novel; curious, exceptional, extraordinary, irregular, odd, particular, peculiar, rare, singular, surprising, uncommon, unusual; abnormal, anomalous, extraordinary, inconceivable, incredible, inexplicable, marvellous, mysterious, preternatural, unaccountable, unbelievable, unheard of, unique, unnatural, wonderful; bizarre, droll, grotesque, quaint, queer; inexperienced, unacquainted, unfamiliar, unknown; bashful, distant, distrustful, reserved, shy, uncommunicative.

strangeness *n* foreignness; bashfulness, coldness, distance, reserve, shyness, uncommunicativeness; eccentricity, grotesqueness, oddness, singularity, uncommonness, uncouthness.

stranger *n* alien, foreigner, newcomer, immigrant, outsider; guest, visitor.

strangle *vb* choke, contract, smother, squeeze, stifle, suffocate, throttle, tighten; keep back, quiet, repress, still, suppress.

strap *vb* beat, thrash, whip; bind, fasten, sharpen, strop. * *n* thong; band, ligature, strip, tie; razorstrap, strop.

strapping *adj* big, burly, large, lusty, stalwart, stout, strong, tall.

stratagem *n* artifice, cunning, device, dodge, finesse, intrigue, machination, manoeuvre, plan, plot, ruse, scheme, trick, wile.

strategic, strategical *adj* calculated, deliberate, diplomatic, manoeuvering, planned, politic, tactical; critical, decisive, key, vital.

strategy *n* generalship, manoeuvering, plan, policy, stratagem, strategetics, tactics.

stratum *n* band, bed, layer.

straw *n* culm, stalk, stem; button, farthing, fig, penny, pin, rush, snap.

stray *vb* deviate, digress, err, meander, ramble, range, roam, rove, straggle, stroll, swerve, transgress, wander. * *adj* abandoned, lost, strayed, wandering; accidental, erratic, random, scattered.

streak *vb* band, bar, striate, stripe, vein; dart, dash, flash, hurtle, run, speed, sprint, stream, tear. * *n* band, bar, belt, layer, line, strip, stripe, thread, trace, vein; cast, grain, tone, touch, vein; beam, bolt, dart, dash, flare, flash, ray, stream.

streaky *adj* streaked, striped, veined.

stream *vb* course, flow, glide, pour, run, spout; emit, pour out, shed; emanate, go forth, issue, radiate; extend, float, stretch out, wave. * *n* brook, burn, race, rill, rivulet, run, runlet, runnel, trickle; course, current, flow, flux, race, rush, tide, torrent, wake, wash; beam, gleam, patch, radiation, ray, streak.

streamer *n* banner, colours, ensign, flag, pennon, standard.

street *n* avenue, highway, road, way.

strength *n* force, might, main, nerve, potency, power, vigour; hardness, solidity, toughness; impregnability, proof; brawn, grit, healthy, lustiness, muscle, robustness, sinew, stamina, thews, vigorousness; animation, courage, determination, firmness, fortitude, resolution, spirit; cogency, efficacy, soundness, validity; emphasis, energy; security, stay, support; brightness, brilliance, clearness, intensity, vitality, vividness; body, excellence, virtue; impetuosity, vehemence, violence; boldness.

strengthen *vb* buttress, recruit, reinforce; fortify; brace, energize, harden, nerve, steel, stimulate; freshen, invigorate, vitalize; animate, encourage; clench, clinch, confirm, corroborate, establish, fix, justify, sustain, support.

strenuous *adj* active, ardent, eager, earnest, energetic, resolute, vigorous, zealous; bold, determined, doughty, intrepid, resolute, spirited, strong, valiant.

stress *vb* accent, accentuate, emphasize, highlight, point up, underline, underscore; bear, bear upon, press, pressurize; pull, rack, strain, stretch, tense, tug. * *n* accent, accentuation, emphasis; effort, force, pull, strain, tension, tug; boisterousness, severity, violence; pressure, urgency.

stretch *vb* brace, screw, strain, tense, tighten; elongate, extend, lengthen, protract, pull; display, distend, expand, spread, unfold, widen; sprain, strain; distort, exaggerate, misrepresent. * *n* compass, extension, extent, range, reach, scope; effort, exertion, strain, struggle; course, direction.

strict *adj* close, strained, tense, tight; accurate, careful, close, exact, literal, particular, precise, scrupulous; austere, inflexible, harsh, orthodox, puritanical, rigid, rigorous, severe, stern, straitlaced, stringent, uncompromising, unyielding.

stricture *n* animadversion, censure, denunciation, criticism, compression, constriction, contraction.

strife *n* battle, combat, conflict, contention, contest, discord, quarrel, struggle, warfare.

strike *vb* bang, beat, belabour, box, buffet, cudgel, cuff, hit, knock, lash, pound, punch, rap, slap, slug, smite, thump, whip; impress, imprint, stamp; afflict, chastise, deal, give, inflict, punish; affect, astonish, electrify, stun; clash, collide, dash, touch; surrender, yield; mutiny, rebel, rise.

stringent *adj* binding, contracting, rigid, rigorous, severe, strict.

strip[1] *n* piece, ribbon, shred, slip.

strip[2] *vb* denude, hull, skin, uncover; bereave, deprive, deforest, desolate, despoil, devastate, disarm, dismantle, disrobe, divest, expose, fleece, loot, shave; plunder, pillage, ransack, rob, sack, spoil; disrobe, uncover, undress.

strive *vb* aim, attempt, endeavour, exert, labour, strain, struggle, toil; contend, contest, fight, tussle, wrestle; compete, cope.

stroke[1] *n* blow, glance, hit, impact, knock, lash, pat, percussion, rap, shot, switch, thump; attack, paralysis, stroke; affliction, damage, hardship, hurt, injury, misfortune, reverse, visitation; dash, feat, masterstroke, touch.

stroke[2] *vb* caress, feel, palpate, pet, knead, massage, nuzzle, rub, touch.

stroll *vb* loiter, lounge, ramble, range, rove, saunter, straggle, stray, wander. * *n* excursion, promenade, ramble, rambling, roving, tour, trip, walk, wandering.

strong *adj* energetic, forcible, powerful, robust, sturdy; able, enduring; cogent, firm, valid.

structure *vb* arrange, constitute, construct, make, organize. * *n* arrangement, conformation, configuration, constitution, construction, form, formation, make, organization; anatomy, composition, texture; building, edifice, fabric, framework, pile.

struggle *vb* aim, endeavour, exert, labour, strive, toil, try; battle, contend, contest, fight, wrestle; agonize, flounder, writhe. * n effort, endeavour, exertion, labour, pains; battle, conflict, contention, contest, fight, strife; agony, contortions, distress.

stubborn *adj* contumacious, dogged, headstrong, heady, inflexible, intractable, mulish, obdurate, obstinate, perverse, positive, refractory, ungovernable, unmanageable, unruly, unyielding, willful; constant, enduring, firm, hardy, persevering, persistent, steady, stoical, uncomplaining, unremitting; firm, hard, inflexible, stiff, strong, tough, unpliant, studied.

studious *adj* contemplative, meditative, reflective, thoughtful; assiduous, attentive, desirous, diligent, eager, lettered, scholarly, zealous.

study *vb* cogitate, lucubrate, meditate, muse, ponder, reflect, think; analyze, contemplate, examine, investigate, ponder, probe, scrutinize, search, sift, weigh. * *n* exercise, inquiry, investigation, reading, research, stumble; cogitation, consideration, contemplation, examination, meditation, reflection, thought; stun; model, object, representation, sketch; den, library, office, studio.

stunning *adj* deafening, stentorian; dumbfounding, stupefying.

stunted *adj* checked, diminutive, dwarfed, dwarfish, lilliputian, little, nipped, small, undersized.

stupendous *adj* amazing, astonishing, astounding, marvellous, overwhelming, surprising, wonderful; enormous, huge, immense, monstrous, prodigious, towering, tremendous, vast.

stupid *adj* brainless, crass, doltish, dull, foolish, idiotic, inane, inept, obtuse, pointless, prosaic, senseless, simple, slow, sluggish, stolid, tedious, tiresome, witless.

stupor *n* coma, confusion, daze, lethargy, narcosis, numbness, stupefaction, torpor.

sturdy *adj* bold, determined, dogged, firm, hardy, obstinate, persevering, pertinacious, resolute, stiff, stubborn, sturdy; athletic, brawny, forcible, lusty, muscular, powerful, robust, stalwart, stout, strong, thickset, vigorous, well-set.

style *vb* address, call, characterize, denominate, designate, dub, entitle, name, term. * *n* dedication, expression, phraseology, turn; cast, character, fashion, form, genre, make, manner, method, mode, model, shape, vogue, way; appellation, denomination, designation, name, title; chic, elegance, smartness; pen, pin, point, stylus.

stylish *adj* chic, courtly, elegant, fashionable, genteel, modish, polished, smart.

suave *adj* affable, agreeable, amiable, bland, courteous, debonair, delightful, glib, gracious, mild, pleasant, smooth, sweet, oily, unctuous, urbane.

subdue *vb* beat, bend, break, bow, conquer, control, crush, defeat, discomfit, foil, master, overbear, overcome, overpower, overwhelm, quell, rout, subject, subjugate, surmount, vanquish, worst; allay, choke, curb, mellow, moderate, mollify, reduce, repress, restrain, soften, suppress, temper.

subject *vb* control, master, overcome, reduce, subdue, subjugate, tame; enslave, enthral; abandon, refer, submit, surrender. * *adj* beneath, subjacent, underneath; dependent, enslaved, inferior, servile, subjected, subordinate, subservient; conditional, obedient, submissive; disposed, exposed to, liable, obnoxious, prone. * *n* dependent, henchman, liegeman, slave, subordinate; matter, point, subject matter, theme, thesis, topic; nominative, premise; case, object, patient, recipient; ego, mind, self, thinking.

subjoin *vb* add, affix, annex, append, join, suffix.

subjugate *vb* conquer, enslave, enthral, master, overcome, overpower, overthrow, subdue, subject, vanquish.

sublimate *vb* alter, change, repress.

sublime *adj aloft, elevated, high,* sacred; eminent, exalted, grand, great, lofty, mighty; august, glorious, magnificent, majestic, noble, stately, solemn, sublunary; elated, elevated, eloquent, exhilarated, raised.

submission *n* capitulation, cession, relinquishment, surrender, yielding; acquiescence, compliance, obedience, resignation; deference, homage, humility, lowliness, obeisance, passiveness, prostration, self-abasement, submissiveness.

submissive *adj* amenable, compliant, docile, pliant, tame, tractable, yielding; acquiescent, long-suffering, obedient, passive, patient, resigned, unassertive, uncomplaining, unrepining; deferential, humble, lowly, meek, obsequious, prostrate, self-abasing.

submit *vb* cede, defer, endure, resign, subject, surrender, yield; commit, propose, refer; offer;

acquiesce, bend, capitulate, comply, stoop, succumb.

subordinate *adj* ancillary, dependent, inferior, junior, minor, secondary, subject, subservient, subsidiary. * *n* assistant, dependant, inferior, subject, underling.

subscribe *vb* accede, approve, agree, assent, consent, yield; contribute, donate, give, offer, promise.

subscription *n* aid, assistance, contribution, donation, gift, offering.

subsequent *adj* after, attendant, ensuing, later, latter, following, posterior, sequent, succeeding.

subservient *adj* inferior, obsequious, servile, subject, subordinate; accessory, aiding, auxiliary, conducive, contributory, helpful, instrumental, serviceable, useful.

subside *vb* settle, sink; abate, decline, decrease, diminish, drop, ebb, fall, intermit, lapse, lessen, lower, lull, wane.

subsidence *n* settling, sinking; abatement, decline, decrease, descent, ebb, diminution, lessening.

subsidiary *adj* adjutant, aiding, assistant, auxiliary, cooperative, corroborative, helping, subordinate, subservient.

subsidize *vb* aid, finance, fund, sponsor, support, underwrite.

subsidy *n* aid, bounty, grant, subvention, support, underwriting.

subsist *vb* be, breathe, consist, exist, inhere, live, prevail; abide, continue, endure, persist, remain; feed, maintain, ration, support.

subsistence *n* aliment, food, livelihood, living, maintenance, meat, nourishment, nutriment, provision, rations, support, sustenance, victuals.

substance *n* actuality, element, groundwork, hypostasis, reality, substratum; burden, content, core, drift, essence, gist, heart, import, meaning, pith, sense, significance, solidity, soul, sum, weight; estate, income, means, property, resources, wealth.

substantial *adj* actual, considerable, essential, existent, hypostatic, pithy, potential, real, subsistent, virtual; concrete, durable, positive, solid, tangible, true; corporeal, bodily, material; bulky, firm, goodly, heavy, large, massive, notable, significant, sizable, solid, sound, stable, stout, strong, well-made; cogent, just, efficient, influential, valid, weighty.

substantially *adv* adequately, essentially, firmly, materially, positively, really, truly.

substantiate *vb* actualize, confirm, corroborate, establish, prove, ratify, verify.

subterfuge *n* artifice, evasion, excuse, expedient, mask, pretence, pretext, quirk, shift, shuffle, sophistry, trick.

subtle *adj* arch, artful, astute, crafty, crooked, cunning, designing, diplomatic, intriguing, insinuating, sly, tricky, wily; clever, ingenious; acute, deep, discerning, discriminating, keen, profound, sagacious, shrewd; airy, delicate, ethereal, light, nice, rare, refined, slender, subtle, thin, volatile.

subtlety *n* artfulness, artifice, astuteness, craft, craftiness, cunning, guile, subtleness; acumen, acuteness, cleverness, discernment, intelligence, keenness, sagacity, sharpness, shrewdness; attenuation, delicacy, fitness, nicety, rareness, refinement.

subtract *vb* deduct, detract, diminish, remove, take, withdraw.

suburbs *npl* environs, confines, neighbourhood, outskirts, precincts, purlieus, vicinage.

subversive *adj* destructive, overthrowing, pervasive, ruining, upsetting. * *n* collaborator, dissident, insurrectionist, saboteur, terrorist, traitor.

subvert *vb* invert, overset, overthrow, overturn, reverse, upset; demolish, destroy, extinguish, raze, ruin; confound, corrupt, injure, pervert.

succeed *vb* ensue, follow, inherit, replace; flourish, gain, hit, prevail, prosper, thrive, win.

success *n* attainment, issue, result; fortune, happiness, hit, luck, prosperity, triumph.

successful *adj* auspicious, booming, felicitous, fortunate, happy, lucky, prosperous, victorious, winning.

succession *n* chain, concatenation, cycle, consecution, following, procession, progression, rotation, round, sequence, series, suite; descent, entail, inheritance, lineage, race, reversion.

succinct *adj* brief, compact, compendious, concise, condensed, curt, laconic, pithy, short, summary, terse.

succour *vb* aid, assist, help, relieve; cherish, comfort, encourage, foster, nurse. * *n* aid, assistance, help, relief, support.

succulent *adj* juicy, luscious, lush, nutritive, sappy.

succumb *vb* capitulate, die, submit, surrender, yield.

sudden *adj* abrupt, hasty, hurried, immediate, instantaneous, rash, unanticipated, unexpected, unforeseen, unusual; brief, momentary, quick, rapid.

sue *vb* charge, court, indict, prosecute, solicit, summon, woo; appeal, beg, demand, entreat, implore, petition, plead, pray, supplicate.

suffer *vb* feel, undergo; bear, endure, sustain, tolerate; admit, allow, indulge, let, permit.

sufferable *adj* allowable, bearable, endurable, permissible, tolerable.

sufferance *n* endurance, inconvenience, misery, pain, suffering; long-suffering, moderation, patience, submission; allowance, permission, toleration.

suffice *vb* avail, content, satisfy, serve.

sufficient *adj* adequate, ample, commensurate, competent, enough, full, plenteous, satisfactory; able, equal, fit, qualified, responsible.

suffocate *vb* asphyxiate, choke, smother, stifle, strangle.

suffrage *n* ballot, franchise, voice, vote; approval, attestation, consent, testimonial, witness.

suggest *vb* advise, allude, hint, indicate, insinuate, intimate, move, present, prompt, propose, propound, recommend.
suggestion *n* allusion, hint, indication, insinuation, intimation, presentation, prompting, proposal, recommendation, reminder.
suit *vb* accommodate, adapt, adjust, fashion, fit, level, match; accord, become, befit, gratify, harmonize, please, satisfy, tally. * *n* appeal, entreaty, invocation, petition, prayer, request, solicitation, supplication; courtship, wooing; action, case, cause, process, prosecution, trial; clothing, costume, habit.
suitable *adj* adapted, accordant, agreeable, answerable, apposite, applicable, appropriate, apt, becoming, befitting, conformable, congruous, convenient, consonant, correspondent, decent, due, eligible, expedient, fit, fitting, just, meet, pertinent, proper, relevant, seemly, worthy.
suite *n* attendants, bodyguard, convoy, cortege, court, escort, followers, staff, retainers, retinue, train; collection, series, set, suit; apartment, rooms.
sulky *adj* aloof, churlish, cross, cross-grained, dogged, grouchy, ill-humoured, ill-tempered, moody, morose, perverse, sour, spleenish, spleeny, splenetic, sullen, surly, vexatious, wayward.
sullen *adj* cross, crusty, glum, grumpy, ill-tempered, moody, morose, sore, sour, sulky; cheerless, cloudy, dark, depressing, dismal, foreboding, funereal, gloomy, lowering, melancholy, mournful, sombre; dull, heavy, slow, sluggish; intractable, obstinate, perverse, refractory, stubborn, vexatious; baleful, evil, inauspicious, malign, malignant, sinister, unlucky, unpropitious.
sully *vb* blemish, blot, contaminate, deface, defame, dirty, disgrace, dishonour, foul, smirch, soil, slur, spot, stain, tarnish.
sultry *adj* close, damp, hot, humid, muggy, oppressive, stifling, stuffy, sweltering.
sum *vb* add, calculate, compute, reckon; collect, comprehend, condense, epitomize, summarize. * *n* aggregate, amount, total, totality, whole; compendium, substance, summary; acme, completion, height, summit.
summary *adj* brief, compendious, concise, curt, laconic, pithy, short, succinct, terse; brief, quick, rapid. * *n* abridgement, abstract, brief, compendium, digest, epitome, precis, résumé, syllabus, synopsis.
summit *n* acme, apex, cap, climax, crest, crown, pinnacle, top, vertex, zenith.
summon *vb* arouse, bid, call, cite, invite, invoke, rouse; convene, convoke; charge, indict, prosecute, subpoena, sue.
sumptuous *adj* costly, dear, expensive, gorgeous, grand, lavish, luxurious, magnificent, munificent, pompous, prodigal, rich, showy, splendid, stately, superb.
sunburnt *adj* bronzed, brown, ruddy, tanned.
sunder *vb* break, disconnect, disjoin, dissociate, dissever, disunited, divide, part, separate, sever.
sundry *adj* different, divers, several, some, various.
sunny *adj* bright, brilliant, clear, fine, luminous, radiant, shining, unclouded, warm; cheerful, genial, happy, joyful, mild, optimistic, pleasant, smiling.
superannuated *adj* aged, anile, antiquated, decrepit, disqualified, doting, effete, imbecile, passé, retired, rusty, time-worn, unfit.
superb *adj* august, beautiful, elegant, exquisite, grand, gorgeous, imposing, magnificent, majestic, noble, pompous, rich, showy, splendid, stately, sumptuous.
supercilious *adj* arrogant, condescending, contemptuous, dictatorial, domineering, haughty, high, imperious, insolent, intolerant, lofty, lordly, magisterial, overbearing, overweening, proud, scornful, vainglorious.
superficial *adj* external, flimsy, shallow, untrustworthy.
superfluity *n* excess, exuberance, redundancy, superabundance, surfeit.
superfluous *adj* excessive, redundant, unnecessary.
superintend *vb* administer, conduct, control, direct, inspect, manage, overlook, oversee, supervise.
superintendence *n* care, charge, control, direction, guidance, government, inspection, management, oversight, supervision, surveillance.
superior *adj* better, greater, high, higher, finer, paramount, supreme, ultra, upper; chief, foremost, principal; distinguished, matchless, noble, pre-eminent, preferable, sovereign, surpassing, unrivalled, unsurpassed; predominant, prevalent. * *n* boss, chief, director, head, higher-up, leader, manager, principal, senior, supervisor.
superiority *n* advantage, ascendency, lead, odds, predominance, pre-eminence, prevalence, transcendence; excellence, nobility, worthiness.
superlative *adj* consummate, greatest, incomparable, peerless, pre-eminent, supreme, surpassing, transcendent.
supernatural *adj* abnormal, marvellous, metaphysical, miraculous, otherworldly, preternatural, unearthly.
supernumerary *adj* excessive, odd, redundant, superfluous.
supersede *vb* annul, neutralize, obviate, overrule, suspend; displace, remove, replace, succeed, supplant.
supervise *vb* administer, conduct, control, direct, inspect, manage, overlook, oversee, superintend.
supine *adj* apathetic, careless, drowsy, dull, idle, indifferent, indolent, inert, languid, lethargic, listless, lumpish, lazy, negligent, otiose, prostrate, recumbent, sleepy, slothful, sluggish, spineless, torpid.
supplant *vb* overpower, overthrow, undermine;

displace, remove, replace, supersede.
supple *adj* elastic, flexible, limber, lithe, pliable, pliant; compliant, humble, submissive, yielding; adulatory, cringing, fawning, flattering, grovelling, obsequious, oily, parasitical, servile, slavish, sycophantic.
supplement *vb* add, augment, extend, reinforce, supply. * *n* addendum, addition, appendix, codicil, complement, continuation, postscript.
suppliant *adj* begging, beseeching, entreating, imploring, precative, precatory, praying, suing, supplicating. * *n* applicant, petitioner, solicitor, suitor, supplicant.
supplicate *vb* beg, beseech, crave, entreat, implore, importune, petition, pray, solicit.
supplication *n* invocation, orison, petition, prayer; entreaty, petition, prayer, request, solicitation.
supply *vb* endue, equip, furnish, minister, outfit, provide, replenish, stock, store; afford, accommodate, contribute, furnish, give, grant, yield. * *n* hoard, provision, reserve, stock, store.
support *vb* brace, cradle, pillow, prop, sustain, uphold; bear, endure, undergo, suffer, tolerate; cherish, keep, maintain, nourish, nurture; act, assume, carry, perform, play, represent; accredit, confirm, corroborate, substantiate, verify; abet, advocate, aid, approve, assist, back, befriend, champion, countenance, encourage, favour, float, hold, patronize, relieve, reinforce, succour, vindicate. * *n* bolster, brace, buttress, foothold, guy, hold, prop, purchase, shore, stay, substructure, supporter, underpinning; groundwork, mainstay, staff; base, basis, bed, foundation; keeping, living, livelihood, maintenance, subsistence, sustenance; confirmation, evidence; aid, assistance, backing, behalf, championship, comfort, countenance, encouragement, favour, help, patronage, succour.
suppose *vb* apprehend, believe, conceive, conclude, consider, conjecture, deem, imagine, judge, presume, presuppose, think; assume, hypothesize; imply, posit, predicate, think; fancy, opine, speculate, surmise, suspect, theorize, wean.
supposition *n* conjecture, guess, guesswork, presumption, surmise; assumption, hypothesis, postulation, theory, thesis; doubt, uncertainty.
suppress *vb* choke, crush, destroy, overwhelm, overpower, overthrow, quash, quell, quench, smother, stifle, subdue, withhold; arrest, inhibit, obstruct, repress, restrain, stop; conceal, extinguish, keep, retain, secret, silence, stifle, strangle.
supremacy *n* ascendancy, domination, headship, lordship, mastery, predominance, pre-eminence, primacy, sovereignty.
supreme *adj* chief, dominant, first, greatest, highest, leading, paramount, predominant, pre-eminent, principal, sovereign.
sure *adj* assured, certain, confident, positive; accurate, dependable, effective, honest, infallible, precise, reliable, trustworthy, undeniable, undoubted, unmistakable, well-proven; guaranteed, inevitable, irrevocable; fast, firm, safe, secure, stable, steady.
surely *adv* assuredly, certainly, infallibly, sure, undoubtedly; firmly, safely, securely, steadily.
surety *n* bail, bond, certainty, guarantee, pledge, safety, security.
surfeit *vb* cram, gorge, overfeed, sate, satiate; cloy, nauseate, pall. * *n* excess, fullness, glut, oppression, plethora, satiation, satiety, superabundance, superfluity.
surge *vb* billow, rise, rush, sweep, swell, swirl, tower. * *n* billow, breaker, roller, wave, white horse.
surly *adj* churlish, crabbed, cross, crusty, discourteous, fretful, gruff, grumpy, harsh, ill-natured, ill-tempered, morose, peevish, perverse, pettish, petulant, rough, rude, snappish, snarling, sour, sullen, testy, touchy, uncivil, ungracious, waspish; dark, tempestuous.
surmise *vb* believe, conclude, conjecture, consider, divine, fancy, guess, imagine, presume, suppose, think, suspect. * *n* conclusion, conjecture, doubt, guess, notion, possibility, supposition, suspicion, thought.
surmount *vb* clear, climb, crown, overtop, scale, top, vault; conquer, master, overcome, overpower, subdue, vanquish; exceed, overpass, pass, surpass, transcend.
surpass *vb* beat, cap, eclipse, exceed, excel, outdo, outmatch, outnumber, outrun, outstrip, override, overshadow, overtop, outshine, surmount, transcend.
surplus *adj* additional, leftover, remaining, spare, superfluous, supernumerary, supplementary. * *n* balance, excess, overplus, remainder, residue, superabundance, surfeit.
surprise *vb* amaze, astonish, astound, bewilder, confuse, disconcert, dumbfound, startle, stun. * *n* amazement, astonishment, blow, shock, wonder.
surprising *adj* amazing, astonishing, astounding, extraordinary, marvellous, unexpected, remarkable, startling, strange, unexpected, wonderful.
surrender *vb* cede, sacrifice, yield; abdicate, abandon, forgo, relinquish, renounce, resign, waive; capitulate, comply, succumb. * *n* abandonment, capitulation, cession, delivery, relinquishment, renunciation, resignation, yielding.
surreptitious *adj* clandestine, fraudulent, furtive, secret, sly, stealthy, unauthorized, underhand.
surround *vb* beset, circumscribe, compass, embrace, encircle, encompass, environ, girdle, hem, invest, loop.
surveillance *n* care, charge, control, direction, inspection, management, oversight, superintendence, supervision, surveyorship, vigilance, watch.
survey *vb* contemplate, observe, overlook, reconnoitre, review, scan, scout, view; examine, inspect, scrutinize; oversee, supervise; estimate,

measure, plan, plot, prospect. * *n* prospect, retrospect, sight, view; examination, inspection, reconnaissance, review; estimating, measuring, planning, plotting, prospecting, work-study.

survive *vb* endure, last, outlast, outlive.

susceptible *adj* capable, excitable, impressible, impressionable, inclined, predisposed, receptive, sensitive.

suspect *vb* believe, conclude, conjecture, fancy, guess, imagine, judge, suppose, surmise, think; distrust, doubt, mistrust. * *adj* doubtful, dubious, suspicious.

suspend *vb* append, hang, sling, swing; adjourn, arrest, defer, delay, discontinue, hinder, intermit, interrupt, postpone, stay, withhold; debar, dismiss, rusticate.

suspicion *n* assumption, conjecture, dash, guess, hint, inkling, suggestion, supposition, surmise, trace; apprehension, distrust, doubt, fear, jealousy, misgiving, mistrust.

suspicious *adj* distrustful, jealous, mistrustful, suspect, suspecting; doubtful, questionable.

sustain *vb* bear, bolster, fortify, prop, strengthen, support, uphold; maintain, nourish, perpetuate, preserve; aid, assist, comfort, relieve; brave, endure, suffer, undergo; approve, confirm, ratify, sanction, validate; confirm, establish, justify, prove.

sustenance *n* maintenance, subsistence, support; aliment, bread, food, nourishment, nutriment, nutrition, provisions, supplies, victuals.

swagger *vb* bluster, boast, brag, bully, flourish, hector, ruffle, strut, swell, vapour. * *n* airs, arrogance, bluster, boastfulness, braggadocio, ruffling, strut.

swain *n* clown, countryman, hind, peasant, rustic; adorer, gallant, inamorata, lover, suitor, wooer.

swallow *vb* bolt, devour, drink, eat, englut, engorge, gobble, gorge, gulp, imbibe, ingurgitate, swamp; absorb, appropriate, arrogate, devour, engulf, submerge; consume, employ, occupy; brook, digest, endure, pocket, stomach; recant, renounce, retract. * *n* gullet, oesophagus, throat; inclination, liking, palate, relish, taste; deglutition, draught, gulp, ingurgitation, mouthful, taste.

swamp *vb* engulf, overwhelm, sink; capsize, embarrass, overset, ruin, upset, wreck. * *n* bog, fen, marsh, morass, quagmire, slough.

sward *n* grass, lawn, sod, turf.

swarm *vb* abound, crowd, teem, throng. * *n* cloud, concourse, crowd, drove, flock, hive, horde, host, mass, multitude, press, shoal, throng.

swarthy *adj* black, brown, dark, dark-skinned, dusky, tawny.

sway *vb* balance, brandish, move, poise, rock, roll, swing, wave, wield; bend, bias, influence, persuade, turn, urge; control, dominate, direct, govern, guide, manage, rule; hoist, raise; incline, lean, lurch, yaw. * *n* ascendency, authority, command, control, domination, dominion, empire, government, mastership, mastery, omnipotence, predominance, power, rule, sovereignty; bias, direction, influence, weight; preponderance, preponderation; oscillation, sweep, swing, wag, wave.

swear *vb* affirm, attest, avow, declare, depose, promise, say, state, testify, vow; blaspheme, curse.

sweep *vb* clean, brush; graze, touch; rake, scour, traverse. * *n* amplitude, compass, drive, movement, range, reach, scope; destruction, devastation, havoc, ravage; curvature, curve.

sweeping *adj* broad, comprehensive, exaggerated, extensive, extravagant, general, unqualified, wholesale.

sweet *adj* candied, cloying, honeyed, luscious, nectareous, nectarous, sugary, saccharine; balmy, fragrant, odorous, redolent, spicy; harmonious, dulcet, mellifluous, mellow, melodious, musical, pleasant, soft, tuneful, silver-toned, silvery; beautiful, fair, lovely; agreeable, charming, delightful, grateful, gratifying; affectionate, amiable, attractive, engaging, gentle, mild, lovable, winning; benignant, serene; clean, fresh, pure, sound. * *n* fragrance, perfume, redolence; blessing, delight, enjoyment, gratification, joy, pleasure; candy, treat.

swell *vb* belly, bloat, bulge, dilate, distend, expand, inflate, intumesce, puff, swell, tumefy; augment, enlarge, increase; heave, rise, surge; strut, swagger. * *n* swelling; augmentation, excrescence, protuberance; ascent, elevation, hill, rise; force, intensity, power; billows, surge, undulation, waves; beau, blade, buck, coxcomb, dandy, exquisite, fop, popinjay.

swerve *vb* deflect, depart, deviate, stray, turn, wander; bend, incline, yield; climb, swarm, wind.

swift *adj* expeditious, fast, fleet, flying, quick, rapid, speedy; alert, eager, forward, prompt, ready, zealous; instant, sudden.

swiftness *n* celerity, expedition, fleetness, quickness, rapidity, speed, velocity.

swindle *vb* cheat, con, cozen, deceive, defraud, diddle, dupe, embezzle, forge, gull, hoax, overreach, steal, trick, victimize. * *n* cheat, con, deceit, deception, fraud, hoax, imposition, knavery, roguery, trickery.

swindler *n* blackleg, cheat, defaulter, embezzler, faker, fraud, impostor, jockey, knave, peculator, rogue, sharper, trickster.

swing *vb* oscillate, sway, vibrate, wave; dangle, depend, hang; brandish, flourish, whirl; administer, manage. * *n* fluctuation, oscillation, sway, undulation, vibration; elbow-room, freedom, margin, play, range, scope, sweep; bias, tendency.

swoop *vb* descend, pounce, rush, seize, stoop, sweep. * *n* clutch, pounce, seizure; stoop, descent.

sword *n* brand, broadsword, claymore, cutlass, epee, falchion, foil, hanger, rapier, sabre, scimitar.

sybarite *n* epicure, voluptuary.
sycophancy *n* adulation, cringing, fawning, flattery, grovelling, obsequiousness, servility.
sycophant *n* cringer, fawner, flunky, hanger-on, lickspittle, parasite, spaniel, toady, wheedler.
syllabus *n* abridgement, abstract, breviary, brief, compendium, digest, epitome, outline, summary, synopsis.
symbol *n* badge, emblem, exponent, figure, mark, picture, representation, representative, sign, token, type.
symbolic, symbolical *adj* emblematic, figurative, hieroglyphic, representative, significant, typical.
symmetry *n* balance, congruity, evenness, harmony, order, parallelism, proportion, regularity, shapeliness.
sympathetic *adj* affectionate, commiserating, compassionate, condoling, kind, pitiful, tender.
sympathy *n* accord, affinity, agreement, communion, concert, concord, congeniality, correlation, correspondence, harmony, reciprocity, union; commiseration, compassion, condolence, fellow-feeling, kindliness, pity, tenderness, thoughtfulness.
symptom *n* diagnostic, indication, mark, note, prognostic, sign, token.
symptomatic *adj* characteristic, indicative, symbolic, suggestive.
synonymous *adj* equipollent, equivalent, identical, interchangeable, similar, tantamount.
synopsis *n* abridgement, abstract, compendium, digest, epitome, outline, precis, résumé, summary, syllabus.
system *n* method, order, plan.
systematic *adj* methodic, methodical, orderly, regular.

T

tabernacle *n* pavilion, tent; cathedral, chapel, church, minster, synagogue, temple.

table *vb* enter, move, propose, submit, suggest. * *n* plate, slab, tablet; board, counter, desk, stand; catalogue, chart, compendium, index, list, schedule, syllabus, synopsis, tabulation; diet, fare, food, victuals.

tableau *n* picture, scene, representation.

taboo *vb* forbid, interdict, prohibit, proscribe. * *adj* banned, forbidden, inviolable, outlawed, prohibited, proscribed. * *n* ban, interdict, prohibition, proscription.

tacit *adj* implicit, implied, inferred, silent, understood, unexpressed, unspoken.

taciturn *adj* close, dumb, laconic, mum, reserved, reticent, silent, tight-lipped, uncommunicative.

tack *vb* add, affix, append, attach, fasten, tag; gybe, yaw, zigzag. * *n* nail, pin, staple; bearing, course, direction, heading, path, plan, procedure.

tackle *vb* attach, grapple, seize; attempt, try, undertake. * *n* apparatus, cordage, equipment, furniture, gear, harness, implements, rigging, tackling, tools, weapons.

tact *n* address, adroitness, cleverness, dexterity, diplomacy, discernment, finesse, insight, knack, perception, skill, understanding.

tail *vb* dog, follow, shadow, stalk, track. * *adj* abridged, curtailed, limited, reduced. * *n* appendage, conclusion, end, extremity, stub; flap, skirt; queue, retinue, train.

taint *vb* imbue, impregnate; contaminate, corrupt, defile, inflect, mildew, pollute, poison, spoil, touch; blot, stain, sully, tarnish. * *n* stain, tincture, tinge, touch; contamination, corruption, defilement, depravation, infection, pollution; blemish, defect, fault, flaw, spot.

take *vb* accept, obtain, procure, receive; clasp, clutch, grasp, grip, gripe, seize, snatch; filch, misappropriate, pilfer, purloin, steal; abstract, apprehend, appropriate, arrest, bag, capture, ensnare, entrap; attack, befall, smite; capture, carry off, conquer, gain, win; allure, attract, bewitch, captivate, charm, delight, enchant, engage, fascinate, interest, please; consider, hold, interrupt, suppose, regard, understand; choose, elect, espouse, select; employ, expend, use; claim, demand, necessitate, require; bear, endure, experience, feel, perceive, tolerate; deduce, derive, detect, discover, draw; carry, conduct, convey, lead, transfer; clear, surmount; drink, eat, imbibe, inhale, swallow. * *n* proceeds, profits, return, revenue, takings, yield.

tale *n* account, fable, legend, narration, novel, parable, recital, rehearsal, relation, romance, story, yarn; catalogue, count, enumeration, numbering, reckoning, tally.

talent *n* ableness, ability, aptitude, capacity, cleverness, endowment, faculty, forte, genius, gift, knack, parts, power, turn.

talk *vb* chatter, communicate, confer, confess, converse, declaim, discuss, gossip, pontificate, speak. * *n* chatter, communication, conversation, diction, gossip, jargon, language, rumour, speech, utterance.

talkative *adj* chatty, communicative, garrulous, loquacious, voluble.

tally *vb* accord, agree, conform, coincide, correspond, harmonize, match, square, suit. * *n* match, mate; check, counterpart, muster, roll call; account, reckoning.

tame *vb* domesticate, reclaim, train; conquer, master, overcome, repress, subdue, subjugate. * *adj* docile, domestic, domesticated, gentle, mild, reclaimed; broken, crushed, meek, subdued, unresisting, submissive; barren, commonplace, dull, feeble, flat, insipid, jejune, languid, lean, poor, prosaic, prosy, spiritless, tedious, uninteresting, vapid.

tamper *vb* alter, conquer, dabble, damage, interfere, meddle; intrigue, seduce, suborn.

tang *n* aftertaste, flavour, relish, savour, smack, taste; keenness, nip, sting.

tangible *adj* corporeal, material, palpable, tactile, touchable; actual, certain, embodied, evident, obvious, open, perceptible, plain, positive, real, sensible, solid, stable, substantial.

tangle *vb* complicate, entangle, intertwine, interweave, mat, perplex, snarl; catch, ensnare, entrap, involve, catch; embarrass, embroil, perplex. * *n* complication, disorder, intricacy, jumble, perplexity, snarl; dilemma, embarrassment, quandary, perplexity.

tantalize *vb* balk, disappoint, frustrate, irritate, provoke, tease, torment, vex.

tantamount *adj* equal, equivalent, synonymous.

tantrum *n* fit, ill-humour, outburst, paroxysm, temper, whim.

tap[1] *vb* knock, pat, rap, strike, tip, touch. * *n* pat, tip, rap, touch.

tap[2] *vb* broach, draw off, extract, pierce; draw on,

exploit, mine, use, utilize; bug, eavesdrop, listen in. * *n* faucet, plug, spigot, spout, stopcock, valve; bug, listening device, transmitter.

tardiness *n* delay, dilatoriness, lateness, procrastination, slackness, slowness.

tardy *adj* slow, sluggish, snail-like; backward, behindhand, dilatory, late, loitering, overdue, slack.

tarn *n* bog, fen, marsh, morass, swamp.

tarnish *vb* blemish, deface, defame, dim, discolour, dull, slur, smear, soil, stain, sully. * *n* blemish, blot, soiling, spot, stain.

tarry *vb* delay, dally, linger, loiter, remain, stay, stop, wait; defer; abide, lodge, rest, sojourn.

tart *adj* acid, acidulous, acrid, astringent, piquant, pungent, sharp, sour; acrimonious, caustic, crabbed, curt, harsh, ill-humoured, ill-tempered, keen, petulant, sarcastic, severe, snappish, testy.

task *vb* burden, overwork, strain, tax. * *n* drudgery, labour, toil, work; business, charge, chore, duty, employment, enterprise, job, mission, stint, undertaking; assignment, exercise, lesson.

taste *vb* experience, feel, perceive, undergo; relish, savour, sip. * *n* flavour, gusto, relish, savour, smack, piquancy; admixture, bit, dash, fragment, hint, infusion, morsel, mouthful, sample, shade, sprinkling, suggestion, tincture; appetite, desire, fondness, liking, partiality, predilection; acumen, cultivation, culture, delicacy, discernment, discrimination, elegance, fine-feeling, grace, judgement, polish, refinement; manner, style.

tasteful *adj* appetizing, delicious, flavoursome, palatable, savoury, tasty, toothsome; aesthetic, artistic, attractive, elegant.

tasteless *adj* flat, insipid, savourless, stale, watery; dull, mawkish, uninteresting, vapid.

tattle *vb* babble, chat, chatter, jabber, prate, prattle; blab, gossip, inform. * *n* gabble, gossip, prate, prattle, tittle-tattle, twaddle.

taunt *vb* censure, chaff, deride, flout, jeer, mock, scoff, sneer, revile, reproach, ridicule, twit, upbraid. * *n* censure, derision, gibe, insult, jeer, quip, quirk, reproach, ridicule, scoff.

taut *adj* strained, stretched, tense, tight.

tautology *n* iteration, pleonasm, redundancy, reiteration, repetition, verbosity, wordiness.

tavern *n* bar, chophouse, hostelry, inn, pub, public house.

tawdry *adj* flashy, gaudy, garish, glittering, loud, meretricious, ostentatious, showy.

tax *vb* burden, demand, exact, load, overtax, require, strain, task; accuse, charge. * *n* assessment, custom, duty, excise, impost, levy, rate, taxation, toll, tribute; burden, charge, demand, requisition, strain; accusation, censure.

teach *vb* catechize, coach, discipline, drill, edify, educate, enlighten, inform, indoctrinate, initiate, instruct, ground, prime, school, train, tutor; communicate, disseminate, explain, expound, impart, implant, inculcate, infuse, instil, interpret, preach, propagate; admonish, advise, counsel, direct, guide, signify, show.

teacher *n* coach, educator, inculcator, informant, instructor, master, pedagogue, preceptor, schoolteacher, trainer, tutor; adviser, counsellor, guide, mentor; pastor, preacher.

tear *vb* burst, slit, rive, rend, rip; claw, lacerate, mangle, shatter, rend, wound; sever, sunder; fume, rage, rant, rave. * *n* fissure, laceration, rent, rip, wrench.

tease *vb* annoy, badger, beg, bother, chafe, chagrin, disturb, harass, harry, hector, importune, irritate, molest, pester, plague, provoke, tantalize, torment, trouble, vex, worry.

tedious *adj* dull, fatiguing, irksome, monotonous, tiresome, trying, uninteresting, wearisome; dilatory, slow, sluggish, tardy.

teem *vb* abound, bear, produce, swarm; discharge, empty, overflow.

teeming *adj* abounding, fraught, full, overflowing, pregnant, prolific, replete, swarming.

tell *vb* compute, count, enumerate, number, reckon; describe, narrate, recount, rehearse, relate, report; acknowledge, announce, betray, confess, declare, disclose, divulge, inform, own, reveal; acquaint, communicate, instruct, teach; discern, discover, distinguish; express, mention, publish, speak, state, utter.

temper *vb* modify, qualify; appease, assuage, calm, mitigate, mollify, moderate, pacify, restrain, soften, soothe; accommodate, adapt, adjust, fit, suit. * *n* character, constitution, nature, organization, quality, structure, temperament, type; disposition, frame, grain, humour, mood, spirits, tone, vein; calmness, composure, equanimity, moderation, tranquillity; anger, ill-temper, irritation, spleen, passion.

temperament *n* character, constitution, disposition, habit, idiosyncrasy, nature, organization, temper.

temperate *adj* abstemious, ascetic, austere, chaste, continent, frugal, moderate, self-controlled, self-denying, sparing; calm, cool, dispassionate, mild, sober, sedate.

tempest *n* cyclone, gale, hurricane, squall, storm, tornado; commotion, disturbance, excitement, perturbation, tumult, turmoil.

temporal *adj* civil, lay, mundane, political, profane, secular, terrestrial, worldly; brief, ephemeral, evanescent, fleeting, momentary, short-lived, temporal, transient, transitory.

temporary *adj* brief, ephemeral, evanescent, fleeting, impermanent, momentary, short-lived, transient, transitory.

tempt *vb* prove, test, try; allure, decoy, entice, induce, inveigle, persuade, seduce; dispose, incite, incline, instigate, lead, prompt, provoke.

tempting *adj* alluring, attractive, enticing, inviting, seductive.

tenable *adj* defensible, maintainable, rational, reasonable, sound.

tenacious *adj* retentive, unforgetful; adhesive, clinging, cohesive, firm, glutinous, gummy, resisting, retentive, sticky, strong, tough, unyielding, viscous; dogged, fast, obstinate, opinionated, opinionative, pertinacious, persistent, resolute, stubborn, unwavering.
tenacity *n* retentiveness, tenaciousness; adhesiveness, cohesiveness, glutinosity, glutinousness, gumminess, toughness, stickiness, strength, viscidity; doggedness, firmness, obstinacy, perseverance, persistency, pertinacity, resolution, stubbornness.
tend[1] *vb* accompany, attend, graze, guard, keep, protect, shepherd, watch.
tend[2] *vb* aim, exert, gravitate, head, incline, influence, lead, lean, point, trend, verge; conduce, contribute.
tendency *n* aim, aptitude, bearing, bent, bias, course, determination, disposition, direction, drift, gravitation, inclination, leaning, liability, predisposition, proclivity, proneness, propensity, scope, set, susceptibility, turn, twist, warp.
tender[1] *vb* bid, offer, present, proffer, propose, suggest, volunteer. * *n* bid, offer, proffer, proposal; currency, money.
tender[2] *adj* callow, delicate, effeminate, feeble, feminine, fragile, immature, infantile, soft, weak, young; affectionate, compassionate, gentle, humane, kind, lenient, loving, merciful, mild, pitiful, sensitive, sympathetic, tender-hearted; affecting, disagreeable, painful, pathetic, touching, unpleasant.
tenebrous *adj* cloudy, dark, darksome, dusky, gloomy, murky, obscure, shadowy, shady, sombre, tenebrious.
tenement *n* abode, apartment, domicile, dwelling, flat, house.
tenet *n* belief, creed, position, dogma, doctrine, notion, opinion, position, principle, view.
tenor *n* cast, character, cut, fashion, form, manner, mood, nature, stamp, tendency, trend, tone; drift, gist, import, intent, meaning, purport, sense, significance, spirit.
tense *vb* flex, strain, tauten, tighten. * *adj* rigid, stiff, strained, stretched, taut, tight; excited, highly strung, intent, nervous, rapt.
tentative *adj* essaying, experimental, provisional, testing, toying.
tenure *n* holding, occupancy, occupation, possession, tenancy, tenement, use.
term *vb* call, christen, denominate, designate, dub, entitle, name, phrase, style. * *n* bound, boundary, bourn, confine, limit, mete, terminus; duration, period, season, semester, span, spell, termination, time; denomination, expression, locution, name, phrase, word.
termagant *n* beldam, hag, scold, shrew, spitfire, virago, vixen.
terminal *adj* bounding, limiting; final, terminating, ultimate. * *n* end, extremity, termination; bound, limit; airport, depot, station, terminus.
terminate *vb* bound, limit; end, finish, close, complete, conclude; eventuate, issue, prove.
termination *n* ending, suffix; bound, extend, limit; end, completion, conclusion, consequence, effect, issue, outcome, result.
terms *npl* conditions, provisions, stipulations.
terrestrial *adj* earthly, mundane, subastral, subcelestial, sublunar, sublunary, tellurian, worldly. * *n* earthling, human.
terrible *adj* appalling, dire, dreadful, fearful, formidable, frightful, gruesome, hideous, horrible, horrid, shocking, terrific, tremendous; alarming, awe-inspiring, awful, dread; great, excessive, extreme, severe.
terrific *adj* marvellous, sensational, superb; immense, intense; alarming, dreadful, formidable, frightful, terrible, tremendous.
terrify *vb* affright, alarm, appal, daunt, dismay, fright, frighten, horrify, scare, shock, startle, terrorize.
territory *n* country, district, domain, dominion, division, land, place, province, quarter, region, section, tract.
terror *n* affright, alarm, anxiety, awe, consternation, dismay, dread, fear, fright, horror, intimidation, panic, terrorism.
terse *adj* brief, compact, concise, laconic, neat, pithy, polished, sententious, short, smooth, succinct.
test *vb* assay; examine, prove, try. * *n* attempt, essay, examination, experiment, ordeal, proof, trial; criterion, standard, touchstone; example, exhibition; discrimination, distinction, judgment.
testify *vb* affirm, assert, asseverate, attest, avow, certify, corroborate, declare, depose, evidence, state, swear.
testimonial *n* certificate, credential, recommendation, voucher; monument, record.
testimony *n* affirmation, attestation, confession, confirmation, corroboration, declaration, deposition, profession; evidence, proof, witness.
testy *adj* captious, choleric, cross, fretful, hasty, irascible, irritable, quick, peevish, peppery, pettish, petulant, snappish, splenetic, touchy, waspish.
tetchy *adj* crabbed, cross, fretful, irritable, peevish, sullen, touchy.
tether *vb* chain, fasten, picket, stake, tie. * *n* chain, fastening, rope.
text *n* copy, subject, theme, thesis, topic, treatise.
texture *n* fabric, web, weft; character, coarseness, composition, constitution, fibre, fineness, grain, make-up, nap, organization, structure, tissue.
thankful *adj* appreciative, beholden, grateful, indebted, obliged.
thankfulness *n* appreciation, gratefulness, gratitude.
thankless *adj* profitless, ungracious, ungrateful, unthankful.
thaw *vb* dissolve, liquefy, melt, soften, unbend.

theatre *n* opera house, playhouse; arena, scene, seat, stage.

theatrical *adj* dramatic, dramaturgic, dramaturgical, histrionic, scenic, spectacular; affected, ceremonious, meretricious, ostentatious, pompous, showy, stagy, stilted, unnatural.

theft *n* depredation, embezzlement, fraud, larceny, peculation, pilfering, purloining, robbery, spoliation, stealing, swindling, thieving.

theme *n* composition, essay, motif, subject, text, thesis, topic, treatise.

theoretical *adj* abstract, conjectural, doctrinaire, ideal, hypothetical, pure, speculative, unapplied.

theory *n* assumption, conjecture, hypothesis, idea, plan, postulation, principle, scheme, speculation, surmise, system; doctrine, philosophy, science; explanation, exposition, philosophy, rationale.

therefore *adv* accordingly, afterward, consequently, hence, so, subsequently, then, thence, whence.

thesaurus *n* dictionary, encyclopedia, repository, storehouse, treasure.

thick *adj* bulky, chunky, dumpy, plump, solid, squab, squat, stubby, thickset; clotted, coagulated, crass, dense, dull, gross, heavy, viscous; blurred, cloudy, dirty, foggy, hazy, indistinguishable, misty, obscure, vaporous; muddy, roiled, turbid; abundant, frequent, multitudinous, numerous; close, compact, crowded, set, thickset; confused, guttural, hoarse, inarticulate, indistinct; dim, dull, weak; familiar, friendly, intimate, neighbourly, well-acquainted. * *adv* fast, frequently, quick; closely, densely, thickly. * *n* centre, middle, midst.

thicket *n* clump, coppice, copse, covert, forest, grove, jungle, shrubbery, underbrush, undergrowth, wood, woodland.

thief *n* depredator, filcher, pilferer, lifter, marauder, purloiner, robber, shark, stealer; burglar, corsair, defaulter, defrauder, embezzler, footpad, highwayman, housebreaker, kidnapper, pickpocket, pirate, poacher, privateer, sharper, swindler, peculator.

thieve *vb* cheat, embezzle, peculate, pilfer, plunder, purloin, rob, steal, swindle.

thin *vb* attenuate, dilute, diminish, prune, reduce, refine, weaken. * *adj* attenuated, bony, emaciated, fine, fleshless, flimsy, gaunt, haggard, lank, lanky, lean, meagre, peaked, pinched, poor, scanty, scraggy, scrawny, slender, slight, slim, small, sparse, spindly.

thing *n* being, body, contrivance, creature, entity, object, something, substance; act, action, affair, arrangement, circumstance, concern, deed, event, matter, occurrence, transaction.

think *vb* cogitate, contemplate, dream, meditate, muse, ponder, reflect, ruminate, speculate; consider, deliberate, reason, undertake; apprehend, believe, conceive, conclude, deem, determine, fancy, hold, imagine, judge, opine, presume, reckon, suppose, surmise; design, intend, mean, purpose; account, count, deem, esteem, hold, regard; compass, design, plan, plot. * *n* assessment, contemplation, deliberation, meditation, opinion, reasoning, reflection.

thirst *n* appetite, craving, desire, hunger, longing, yearning; aridity, drought, dryness.

thirsty *adj* arid, dry, parched; eager, greedy, hungry, longing, yearning.

thorn *n* prickle, spine; annoyance, bane, care, evil, infliction, nettle, nuisance, plague, torment, trouble, scourge.

thorny *adj* briary, briery, prickly, spinose, spinous, spiny; acuminate, barbed, pointed, prickling, sharp, spiky; annoying, difficult, harassing, perplexing, rugged, troublesome, trying, vexatious.

thorough, thoroughgoing *adj* absolute, arrant, complete, downright, entire, exhaustive, finished, perfect, radical, sweeping, total unmitigated, utter; accurate, correct, reliable, trustworthy.

though *conj* admitting, allowing, although, granted, granting, if, notwithstanding, still. * *adv* however, nevertheless, still, yet.

thought *n* absorption, cogitation, engrossment, meditation, musing, reflection, reverie, rumination; contemplation, intellect, ratiocination, thinking, thoughtfulness; application, conception, consideration, deliberation, idea, pondering, speculation, study; consciousness, imagination, intellect, perception, understanding; conceit, fancy, notion; conclusion, judgment, motion, opinion, sentiment, supposition, view; anxiety, attention, care, concern, provision, regard, solicitude, thoughtfulness; design, expectation, intention, purpose.

thoughtful *adj* absorbed, contemplative, deliberative, dreamy, engrossed, introspective, pensive, philosophic, reflecting, reflective, sedate, speculative; attentive, careful, cautious, circumspect, considerate, discreet, heedful, friendly, kindhearted, kindly, mindful, neighbourly, provident, prudent, regardful, watchful, wary; quiet, serious, sober, studious.

thoughtless *adj* careless, casual, flighty, heedless, improvident, inattentive, inconsiderate, neglectful, negligent, precipitate, rash, reckless, regardless, remiss, trifling, unmindful, unthinking; blank, blockish, dull, insensate, stupid, vacant, vacuous.

thraldom *n* bondage, enslavement, enthralment, serfdom, servitude, slavery, subjection, thrall, vassalage.

thrash *vb* beat, bruise, conquer, defeat, drub, flog, lash, maul, pommel, punish, thwack, trounce, wallop, whip.

thread *vb* course, direction, drift, tenor; reeve, trace. * *n* cord, fibre, filament, hair, line, twist; pile, staple.

threadbare *adj* napless, old, seedy, worn; common,

commonplace, hackneyed, stale, trite, worn-out.
threat *n* commination, defiance, denunciation, fulmination, intimidation, menace, thunder, thunderbolt.
threaten *vb* denounce, endanger, fulminate, intimidate, menace, thunder; augur, forebode, foreshadow, indicate, portend, presage, prognosticate, warn.
threshold *n* doorsill, sill; door, entrance, gate; beginning, commencement, opening, outset, start.
thrift *n* economy, frugality, parsimony, saving, thriftiness; gain, luck, profit, prosperity, success.
thriftless *adj* extravagant, improvident, lavish, profuse, prodigal, shiftless, unthrifty, wasteful.
thrifty *adj* careful, economical, frugal, provident, saving, sparing; flourishing, prosperous, thriving, vigorous.
thrill *vb* affect, agitate, electrify, inspire, move, penetrate, pierce, rouse, stir, touch. * *n* excitement, sensation, shock, tingling, tremor.
thrilling *adj* affecting, exciting, gripping, moving, sensational, touching.
thrive *vb* advance, batten, bloom, boom, flourish, prosper, succeed.
throng *vb* congregate, crowd, fill, flock, pack, press, swarm. * *n* assemblage, concourse, congregation, crowd, horde, host, mob, multitude, swarm.
throttle *vb* choke, silence, strangle, suffocate.
throw *vb* cast, chuck, dart, fling, hurl, lance, launch, overturn, pitch, pitchfork, send, sling, toss, whirl. * *n* cast, fling, hurl, launch, pitch, sling, toss, whirl; chance, gamble, try, venture.
thrust *vb* clap, dig, drive, force, impel, jam, plunge, poke, propel, push, ram, run, shove, stick. * *n* dig, jab, lunge, pass, plunge, poke, propulsion, push, shove, stab, tilt.
thump *vb* bang, batter, beat, belabour, knock, punch, strike, thrash, thwack, whack. * *n* blow, knock, punch, strike, stroke.
thwart *vb* baffle, balk, contravene, counteract, cross, defeat, disconcert, frustrate, hinder, impede, oppose, obstruct, oppugn; cross, intersect, traverse.
tickle *vb* amuse, delight, divert, enliven, gladden, gratify, please, rejoice, titillate.
ticklish *adj* dangerous, precarious, risky, tottering, uncertain, unstable, unsteady; critical, delicate, difficult, nice.
tide *n* course, current, ebb, flow, stream.
tidings *npl* advice, greetings, information, intelligence, news, report, word.
tidy *vb* clean, neaten, order, straighten. * *adj* clean, neat, orderly, shipshape, spruce, trig, trim.
tie *vb* bind, confine, fasten, knot, lock, manacle, secure, shackle, fetter, yoke; complicate, entangle, interlace, knit; connect, hold, join, link, unite; constrain, oblige, restrain, restrict. * *n* band, fastening, knot, ligament, ligature; allegiance, bond, obligation; bow, cravat, necktie.
tier *n* line, rank, row, series.
tiff *n* fit, fume, passion, pet, miff, rage.
tight *adj* close, compact, fast, firm; taut, tense, stretched; impassable, narrow, strait.
till *vb* cultivate, plough, harrow.
tillage *n* agriculture, cultivation, culture, farming, geoponics, husbandry.
tilt *vb* cant, incline, slant, slope, tip; forge, hammer; point, thrust; joust, rush. * *n* awning, canopy, tent; lunge, pass, thrust; cant, inclination, slant, slope, tip.
time *vb* clock, control, count, measure, regulate, schedule. * *n* duration, interim, interval, season, span, spell, tenure, term, while; aeon, age, date, epoch, eon, era; term; cycle, dynasty, reign; confinement, delivery, parturition; measure, rhythm.
timely *adj* acceptable, appropriate, apropos, early, opportune, prompt, punctual, seasonable, well-timed.
timid *adj* afraid, cowardly, faint-hearted, fearful, irresolute, meticulous, nervous, pusillanimous, skittish, timorous, unadventurous; bashful, coy, diffident, modest, shame-faced, shrinking.
tincture *vb* colour, dye, shade, stain, tinge, tint; flavour, season; imbue, impregnate, impress, infuse. * *n* grain, hue, shade, stain, tinge, tint, tone; flavour, smack, spice, taste; admixture, dash, infusion, seasoning, sprinkling, touch.
tinge *vb* colour, dye, stain, tincture, tint; imbue, impregnate, impress, infuse. * *n* cast, colour, dye, hue, shade, stain, tincture, tint; flavour, smack, spice, quality, taste.
tint *n* cast, colour, complexion, dye, hue, shade, tinge, tone.
tiny *adj* diminutive, dwarfish, Lilliputian, little, microscopic, miniature, minute, puny, pygmy, small, wee.
tip[1] *n* apex, cap, end, extremity, peak, pinnacle, point, top, vertex.
tip[2] *vb* incline, overturn, tilt; dispose of, dump. * *n* donation, fee, gift, gratuity, perquisite, reward; inclination, slant; hint, pointer, suggestion; strike, tap.
tirade *n* abuse, denunciation, diatribe, harangue, outburst.
tire *vb* exhaust, fag, fatigue, harass, jade, weary; bore, bother, irk.
tiresome *adj* annoying, arduous, boring, dull, exhausting, fatiguing, fagging, humdrum, irksome, laborious, monotonous, tedious, wearisome, vexatious.
tissue *n* cloth, fabric; membrane, network, structure, texture, web; accumulation, chain, collection, combination, conglomeration, mass, series, set.
titanic *adj* colossal, Cyclopean, enormous, gigantic, herculean, huge, immense, mighty, monstrous, prodigious, stupendous, vast.
title *vb* call, designate, name, style, term. * *n* caption, legend, head, heading; appellation, application, cognomen, completion, denomination, des-

ignation, epithet, name; claim, due, ownership, part, possession, prerogative, privilege, right.
tittle *n* atom, bit, grain, iota, jot, mite, particle, scrap, speck, whit.
tittle-tattle *vb, n* babble, cackle, chatter, discourse, gabble, gossip, prattle.
toast *vb* brown, dry, heat; honour, pledge, propose, salute. * *n* compliment, drink, pledge, salutation, salute; favourite, pet.
toil *vb* drudge, labour, strive, work. * *n* drudgery, effort, exertion, exhaustion, grinding, labour, pains, travail, work; gin, net, noose, snare, spring, trap.
toilsome *adj* arduous, difficult, fatiguing, hard, laborious, onerous, painful, severe, tedious, wearisome.
token *adj* nominal, superficial, symbolic. * *n* badge, evidence, index, indication, manifestation, mark, note, sign, symbol, trace, trait; keepsake, memento, memorial, reminder, souvenir.
tolerable *adj* bearable, endurable, sufferable, supportable; fair, indifferent, middling, ordinary, passable, so-so.
tolerance *n* endurance, receptivity, sufferance, toleration.
tolerate *vb* admit, allow, indulge, let, permit, receive; abide, brook, endure, suffer.
toll[1] *n* assessment, charge, customs, demand, dues, duty, fee, impost, levy, rate, tax, tribute; cost, damage, loss.
toll[2] *vb* chime, knell, peal, ring, sound. * *n* chime, knell, peal, ring, ringing, tolling.
tomb *n* catacomb, charnel house, crypt, grave, mausoleum, sepulchre, vault.
tone *vb* blend, harmonize, match, suit. * *n* note, sound; accent, cadence, emphasis, inflection, intonation, modulation; key, mood, strain, temper; elasticity, energy, force, health, strength, tension, vigour; cast, colour, manner, hue, shade, style, tint; drift, tenor.
tongue *n* accent, dialect, language, utterance, vernacular; discourse, parlance, speech, talk; nation, race.
too *adv* additionally, also, further, likewise, moreover, overmuch.
toothsome *adj* agreeable, dainty, delicious, luscious, nice, palatable, savoury.
top *vb* cap, head, tip; ride, surmount; outgo, surpass. * *adj* apical, best, chief, culminating, finest, first, foremost, highest, leading, prime, principal, topmost, uppermost. * *n* acme, apex, crest, crown, head, meridian, pinnacle, summit, surface, vertex, zenith.
topic *n* business, question, subject, text, theme, thesis; division, head, subdivision; commonplace, dictum, maxim, precept, proposition, principle, rule; arrangement, scheme.
topple *vb* fall, overturn, tumble, upset.
torment *vb* annoy, agonize, distress, excruciate, pain, rack, torture; badger, fret, harass, harry, irritate, nettle, plague, provoke, tantalize, tease, trouble, vex, worry. * *n* agony, anguish, pang, rack, torture.
tornado *n* blizzard, cyclone, gale, hurricane, storm, tempest, typhoon, whirlwind.
torpid *adj* benumbed, lethargic, motionless, numb; apathetic, dormant, dull, inactive, indolent, inert, listless, sleepy, slothful, sluggish, stupid.
torpor *n* coma, insensibility, lethargy, numbness, torpidity; inaction, inactivity, inertness, sluggishness, stupidity.
torrid *adj* arid, burnt, dried, parched; burning, fiery, hot, parching, scorching, sultry, tropical, violent.
tortuous *adj* crooked, curved, curvilineal, curvilinear, serpentine, sinuate, sinuated, sinuous, twisted, winding; ambiguous, circuitous, crooked, deceitful, indirect, perverse, roundabout.
torture *vb* agonize, distress, excruciate, pain, rack, torment.* *n* agony, anguish, distress, pain, pang, rack, torment.
toss *vb* cast, fling, hurl, pitch, throw; agitate, rock, shake; disquiet, harass, try; roll, writhe. * *n* cast, fling, pitch, throw.
total *vb* add, amount to, reach, reckon. * *adj* complete, entire, full, whole; integral, undivided. * *n* aggregate, all, gross, lump, mass, sum, totality, whole.
totter *vb* falter, reel, stagger, vacillate; lean, oscillate, reel, rock, shake, sway, tremble, waver; fail, fall, flag.
touch *vb* feel, graze, handle, hit, pat, strike, tap; concern, interest, regard; affect, impress, move, stir; grasp, reach, stretch; melt, mollify, soften; afflict, distress, hurt, injure, molest, sting, wound. * *n* hint, smack, suggestion, suspicion, taste, trace; blow, contract, hit, pat, tap.
touchiness *n* fretfulness, irritability, irascibility, peevishness, pettishness, petulance, snappishness, spleen, testiness.
touching *adj* affecting, heart-rending, impressive, melting, moving, pathetic, pitiable, tender; abutting, adjacent, bordering, tangent.
touchy *adj* choleric, cross, fretful, hot-tempered, irascible, irritable, peevish, petulant, quick-tempered, snappish, splenetic, tetchy, testy, waspish.
tough *adj* adhesive, cohesive, flexible, tenacious; coriaceous, leathery; clammy, ropy, sticky, viscous; inflexible, intractable, rigid, stiff; callous, hard, obdurate, stubborn; difficult, formidable, hard, troublesome. * *n* brute, bully, hooligan, ruffian, thug.
tour *vb* journey, perambulate, travel, visit. * *n* circuit, course, excursion, expedition, journey, perambulation, pilgrimage, round.
tow *vb* drag, draw, haul, pull, tug. * *n* drag, lift, pull.
tower *vb* mount, rise, soar, transcend. * *n* belfry, bell tower, column, minaret, spire, steeple, turret; castle, citadel, fortress, stronghold; pillar, refuge, rock, support.

towering *adj* elevated, lofty; excessive, extreme, prodigious, violent.

toy *vb* dally, play, sport, trifle, wanton. * *n* bauble, doll, gewgaw, gimmick, knick-knack, plaything, puppet, trinket; bagatelle, bubble, trifle; play, sport.

trace *vb* follow, track, train; copy, deduce, delineate, derive, describe, draw, sketch. * *n* evidence, footmark, footprint, footstep, impression, mark, remains, sign, token, track, trail, vestige, wake; memorial, record; bit, dash, flavour, hint, suspicion, streak, tinge.

track *vb* chase, draw, follow, pursue, scent, track, trail. * *n* footmark, footprint, footstep, spoor, trace, vestige; course, pathway, rails, road, runway, trace, trail, wake, way.

trackless *adj* pathless, solitary, unfrequented, unused.

tract[1] *n* area, district, quarter, region, territory; parcel, patch, part, piece, plot, portion.

tract[2] *n* disquisition, dissertation, essay, homily, pamphlet, sermon, thesis, tractate, treatise.

tractable *adj* amenable, docile, governable, manageable, submissive, willing, yielding; adaptable, ductile, malleable, plastic, tractile.

trade *vb* bargain, barter, chaffer, deal, exchange, interchange, sell, traffic. * *n* bargaining, barter, business, commerce, dealing, traffic; avocation, calling, craft, employment, occupation, office, profession, pursuit, vocation.

traditional *adj* accustomed, apocryphal, customary, established, historic, legendary, old, oral, transmitted, uncertain, unverified, unwritten.

traduce *vb* abuse, asperse, blemish, brand, calumniate, decry, defame, depreciate, disparage, revile, malign, slander, vilify.

traducer *n* calumniator, defamer, detractor, slanderer, vilifier.

traffic *vb* bargain, barter, chaffer, deal, exchange, trade. * *n* barter, business, chaffer, commerce, exchange, intercourse, trade, transportation, truck.

tragedy *n* drama, play; adversity, calamity, catastrophe, disaster, misfortune.

tragic *adj* dramatic; calamitous, catastrophic, disastrous, dreadful, fatal, grievous, heart-breaking, mournful, sad, shocking, sorrowful.

trail *vb* follow, hunt, trace, track; drag, draw, float, flow, haul, pull. * *n* footmark, footprint, footstep, mark, trace, track.

train *vb* drag, draw, haul, trail, tug; allure, entice; discipline, drill, educate, exercise, instruct, school, teach; accustom, break in, familiarize, habituate, inure, prepare, rehearse, use. * *n* trail, wake; entourage, cortege, followers, retinue, staff, suite; chain, consecution, sequel, series, set, succession; course, method, order, process; allure, artifice, device, enticement, lure, persuasion, stratagem, trap.

trait *n* line, mark, stroke, touch; characteristic, feature, lineage,particularity, peculiarity, quality.

traitor *n* apostate, betrayer, deceiver, Judas, miscreant, quisling, renegade, turncoat; conspirator, deserter, insurgent, mutineer, rebel, revolutionary.

traitorous *adj* faithless, false, perfidious, recreant, treacherous; insidious, treasonable.

trammel *vb* clog, confine, cramp, cumber, hamper, hinder, fetter, restrain, restrict, shackle, tie. * *n* bond, chain, fetter, hindrance, impediment, net, restraint, shackle.

tramp *vb* hike, march, plod, trudge, walk. * *n* excursion, journey, march, walk; landloper, loafer, stroller, tramper, vagabond, vagrant.

trample *vb* crush, tread; scorn, spurn.

trance *n* dream, ecstasy, hypnosis, rapture; catalepsy, coma.

tranquil *adj* calm, hushed, peaceful, placid, quiet, serene, still, undisturbed, unmoved, unperturbed, unruffled, untroubled.

tranquillity *n* calmness, peace, peacefulness, placidity, placidness, quiet, quietness, serenity, stillness, tranquilness.

tranquillize *vb* allay, appease, assuage, calm, compose, hush, lay, lull, moderate, pacify, quell, quiet, silence, soothe, still.

transact *vb* conduct, dispatch, enact, execute, do, manage, negotiate, perform, treat.

transaction *n* act, action, conduct, doing, management, negotiation, performance; affair, business, deal, dealing, incident, event, job, matter, occurrence, procedure, proceeding.

transcend *vb* exceed, overlap, overstep, pass, transgress; excel, outstrip, outrival, outvie, overtop, surmount, surpass.

transcendent *adj* consummate, inimitable, peerless, pre-eminent, supereminent, surpassing, unequalled, unparalleled, unrivalled, unsurpassed; metempiric, metempirical, noumenal, supersensible.

transcript *n* duplicate, engrossment, rescript.

transfer *vb* convey, dispatch, move, remove, send, translate, transmit, transplant, transport; abalienate, alienate, assign, cede, confer, convey, consign, deed, devise, displace, forward, grant, pass, relegate. * *n* abalienation, alienation, assignment, bequest, carriage, cession, change, conveyance, copy, demise, devisal, gift, grant, move, relegation, removal, shift, shipment, transference, transferring, transit, transmission, transportation.

transfigure *vb* change, convert, dignify, idealize, metamorphose, transform.

transform *vb* alter, change, metamorphose, transfigure; convert, resolve, translate, transmogrify, transmute.

transgress *vb* exceed, transcend, overpass, overstep; break, contravene, disobey, infringe, violate; err, intrude, offend, sin, slip, trespass.

transgression *n* breach, disobedience, encroachment, infraction, infringement, transgression, violation; crime, delinquency, error, fault, iniquity, misdeed, misdemeanour, misdoing, offence, sin, slip, trespass, wrongdoing.

transient *adj* diurnal, ephemeral, evanescent, fleeting, fugitive, impertinent, meteoric, mortal, passing, perishable, short-lived, temporary, transitory, volatile; hasty, imperfect, momentary, short.

transitory *adj* brief, ephemeral, evanescent, fleeting, flitting, fugacious, momentary, passing, short, temporary, transient.

translate *vb* remove, transfer, transport; construe, decipher, decode, interpret, render, turn.

translucent *adj* diaphanous, hyaline, pellucid, semi-opaque, semi-transparent.

transmit *vb* forward, remit, send; communicate, conduct, radiate; bear, carry, convey.

transparent *adj* bright, clear, diaphanous, limpid, lucid; crystalline, hyaline, pellucid, serene, translucent, transpicuous, unclouded; open, porous, transpicuous; evident, obvious, manifest, patent.

transpire *vb* befall, chance, happen, occur; evaporate, exhale.

transport *vb* bear, carry, cart, conduct, convey, fetch, remove, ship, take, transfer, truck; banish, expel; beatify, delight, enrapture, enravish, entrance, ravish. * *n* carriage, conveyance, movement, transportation, transporting; beatification, beatitude, bliss, ecstasy, felicity, happiness, rapture, ravishment; frenzy, passion, vehemence, warmth.

transude *vb* exude, filter, ooze, percolate, strain.

trap *vb* catch, ensnare, entrap, noose, snare, springe; ambush, deceive, dupe, trick; enmesh, tangle, trepan. * *n* gin, snare, springe, toil; ambush, artifice, pitfall, stratagem, trepan.

trappings *npl* adornments, decorations, dress, embellishments, frippery, gear, livery, ornaments, paraphernalia, rigging; accoutrements, caparisons, equipment, gear.

trash *n* dregs, dross, garbage, refuse, rubbish, trumpery, waste; balderdash, nonsense, twaddle.

travel *vb* journey, peregrinate, ramble, roam, rove, tour, voyage, walk, wander; go, move, pass. * *n* excursion, expedition, journey, peregrination, ramble, tour, trip, voyage, walk.

traveller *n* excursionist, explorer, globe-trotter, itinerant, passenger, pilgrim, rover, sightseer, tourist, trekker, tripper, voyager, wanderer, wayfarer.

traverse *vb* contravene, counteract, defeat, frustrate, obstruct, oppose, thwart; ford, pass, play, range.

travesty *vb* imitate, parody, take off. * *n* burlesque, caricature, imitation, parody, take-off.

treacherous *adj* deceitful, disloyal, faithless, false, false-hearted, insidious, perfidious, recreant, sly, traitorous, treasonable, unfaithful, unreliable, unsafe, untrustworthy.

treachery *n* betrayal, deceitfulness, disloyalty, double-dealing, faithlessness, foul play, infidelity, insidiousness, perfidiousness, treason, perfidy.

treason *n* betrayal, disloyalty, lèse-majesté, lese-majesty, perfidy, sedition, traitorousness, treachery.

treasonable *adj* disloyal, traitorous, treacherous.

treasure *vb* accumulate, collect, garner, hoard, husband, save, store; cherish, idolize, prize, value, worship. * *n* cash, funds, jewels, money, riches, savings, valuables, wealth; abundance, reserve, stock, store.

treasurer *n* banker, bursar, purser, receiver, trustee.

treat *vb* entertain, feast, gratify, refresh; attend, doctor, dose, handle, manage, serve; bargain, covenant, negotiate, parley. * *n* banquet, entertainment, feast; delight, enjoyment, entertainment, gratification, luxury, pleasure, refreshment.

treatise *n* commentary, discourse, dissertation, disquisition, monograph, tractate.

treatment *n* usage, use; dealing, handling, management, manipulation; doctoring, therapy.

treaty *n* agreement, alliance, bargain, compact, concordat, convention, covenant, entente, league, pact.

tremble *vb* quake, quaver, quiver, shake, shiver, shudder, vibrate, wobble. * *n* quake, quiver, shake, shiver, shudder, tremor, vibration, wobble.

tremendous *adj* colossal, enormous, huge, immense; excellent, marvellous, wonderful; alarming, appalling, awful, dreadful, fearful, frightful, horrid, horrible, terrible.

tremor *n* agitation, quaking, quivering, shaking, trembling, trepidation, tremulousness, vibration.

tremulous *adj* afraid, fearful, quavering, quivering, shaking, shaky, shivering, timid, trembling, vibrating.

trench *vb* carve, cut; ditch, channel, entrench, furrow. * *n* channel, ditch, drain, furrow, gutter, moat, pit, sewer, trough; dugout, entrenchment, fortification.

trenchant *adj* cutting, keen, sharp; acute, biting, caustic, crisp, incisive, pointed, piquant, pungent, sarcastic, sententious, severe, unsparing, vigorous.

trend *vb* drift, gravitate, incline, lean, run, stretch, sweep, tend, turn. * *n* bent, course, direction, drift, inclination, set, leaning, tendency, trending.

trepidation *n* agitation, quaking, quivering, shaking, trembling, tremor; dismay, excitement, fear, perturbation, tremulousness.

trespass *vb* encroach, infringe, intrude, trench; offend, sin, transgress. * *n* encroachment, infringement, injury, intrusion, invasion; crime, delinquency, error, fault, sin, misdeed, misdemeanour, offence, transgression; trespasser.

trial *adj* experimental, exploratory, testing. * *n* examination, experiment, test; experience, knowledge; aim, attempt, effort, endeavour, essay, exertion, struggle; assay, criterion, ordeal, prohibition, proof, test, touchstone; affliction, burden, chagrin, dolour, distress, grief, hardship, heartache, inclination, misery, mortification, pain, sorrow, suffering, tribulation, trouble, unhappiness, vexation, woe, wretchedness; action, case, cause, hearing, suit.

tribe *n* clan, family, lineage, race, sept, stock; class, distinction, division, order.

tribulation *n* adversity, affliction, distress, grief, misery, pain, sorrow, suffering, trial, trouble, unhappiness, woe, wretchedness.

tribunal *n* bench, judgement seat; assizes, bar, court, judicature, session.

tribute *n* subsidy, tax; custom, duty, excise, impost, tax, toll; contribution, grant, offering.

trice *n* flash, instant, jiffy, moment, second, twinkling.

trick *vb* cheat, circumvent, cozen, deceive, defraud, delude, diddle, dupe, fob, gull, hoax, overreach. * *n* artifice, blind, deceit, deception, dodge, fake, feint, fraud, game, hoax, imposture, manoeuvre, shift, ruse, swindle, stratagem, wile; antic, caper, craft, deftness, gambol, sleight; habit, mannerism, peculiarity, practice.

trickle *vb* distil, dribble, drip, drop, ooze, percolate, seep. * *n* dribble, drip, percolation, seepage.

tricky *adj* artful, cunning, deceitful, deceptive, subtle, trickish.

trifle *vb* dally, dawdle, fool, fribble, palter, play, potter, toy. * *n* bagatelle, bauble, bean, fig, nothing, triviality; iota, jot, modicum, particle, trace.

trifling *adj* empty, frippery, frivolous, inconsiderable, insignificant, nugatory, petty, piddling, shallow, slight, small, trivial, unimportant, worthless.

trill *vb* shake, quaver, warble. * *n* quaver, shake, tremolo, warbling.

trim *vb* adjust, arrange, prepare; balance, equalize, fill; adorn, array, bedeck, decorate, dress, embellish, garnish, ornament; clip, curtail, cut, lop, mow, poll, prune, shave, shear; berate, chastise, chide, rebuke, reprimand, reprove, trounce; fluctuate, hedge, shift, shuffle, vacillate. * *adj* compact, neat, nice, shapely, snug, tidy, well-adjusted, well-ordered; chic, elegant, finical, smart, spruce. * *n* dress, embellishment, gear, ornaments, trappings, trimmings; case, condition, order, plight, state.

trinket *n* bagatelle, bauble, bijoux, gewgaw, gimcrack, knick-knack, toy, trifle.

trinkets *npl* bijouterie, jewellery, jewels, ornaments.

trip *vb* caper, dance, frisk, hop, skip; misstep, stumble; bungle, blunder, err, fail, mistake; overthrow, supplant, upset; catch, convict, detect. * *n* hop, skip; lurch, misstep, stumble; blunder, bungle, error, failure, fault, lapse, miss, mistake, oversight, slip; circuit, excursion, expedition, jaunt, journey, ramble, route, stroll, tour.

trite *adj* banal, beaten, common, commonplace, hackneyed, old, ordinary, stale, stereotyped, threadbare, usual, worn.

triturate *vb* beat, bray, bruise, grind, pound, rub, thrash; comminute, levigate, pulverize.

triumph *vb* exult, rejoice; prevail, succeed, win; flourish, prosper, thrive; boast, brag, crow, gloat, swagger, vaunt. * *n* celebration, exultation, joy, jubilation, jubilee, ovation; accomplishment, achievement, conquest, success, victory.

triumphant *adj* boastful, conquering, elated, exultant, exulting, jubilant, rejoicing, successful, victorious.

trivial *adj* frivolous, gimcrack, immaterial, inconsiderable, insignificant, light, little, nugatory, paltry, petty, small, slight, slim, trifling, trumpery, unimportant.

trollop *n* prostitute, slattern, slut, whore.

troop *vb* crowd, flock, muster, throng. * *n* company, crowd, flock, herd, multitude, number, throng; band, body, party, squad, troupe.

trophy *n* laurels, medal, palm, prize.

troth *n* candour, sincerity, truth, veracity, verity; allegiance, belief, faith, fidelity, word; betrothal.

trouble *vb* agitate, confuse, derange, disarrange, disorder, disturb; afflict, ail, annoy, badger, concern, disquiet, distress, fret, grieve, harass, molest, perplex, perturb, pester, plague, torment, vex, worry. * *n* adversity, affliction, calamity, distress, dolour, grief, hardship, misfortune, misery, pain, sorrow, suffering, tribulation, woe; ado, annoyance, anxiety, bother, care, discomfort, embarrassment, fuss, inconvenience, irritation, pains, perplexity, plague, torment, vexation, worry; commotion, disturbance, row; bewilderment, disquietude, embarrassment, perplexity, uneasiness.

troublesome *adj* annoying, distressing, disturbing, galling, grievous, harassing, painful, perplexing, vexatious, worrisome; burdensome, irksome, tiresome, wearisome; importunate, intrusive, teasing; arduous, difficult, hard, inconvenient, trying, unwieldy.

troublous *adj* agitated, disquieted, disturbed, perturbed, tumultuous, turbulent.

trough *n* hutch, manger; channel, depression, hollow, furrow.

truant *vb* be absent, desert, dodge, malinger, shirk, skive. * *n* absentee, deserter, idler, laggard, loiterer, lounger, malingerer, quitter, runaway, shirker, vagabond.

truce *n* armistice, breathing space, cessation, delay, intermission, lull, pause, recess, reprieve, respite, rest.

truck *vb* barter, deal, exchange, trade, traffic. * *n* lorry, van, wagon.

truckle *vb* roll, trundle; cringe, crouch, fawn, knuckle, stoop, submit, yield.

truculent *adj* barbarous, bloodthirsty, ferocious, fierce, savage; cruel, malevolent, relentless; destructive, deadly, fatal, ruthless.

true *adj* actual, unaffected, authentic, genuine, legitimate, pure, real, rightful, sincere, sound, truthful, veritable; substantial, veracious; constant, faithful, loyal, staunch, steady; equitable, honest, honourable, just, upright, trusty, trustworthy, virtuous; accurate, correct, even, exact, right, straight, undeviating. * *adv* good, well.

truism *n* axiom, commonplace, platitude.

trumpery *adj* pinchbeck, rubbishy, trashy, trifling, worthless. * *n* deceit, deception, falsehood, humbug, imposture; frippery, rubbish, stuff, trash, trifles.

truncheon *n* club, cudgel, nightstick, partisan, staff; baton, wand.

trunk *n* body, bole, butt, shaft, stalk, stem, stock, torso; box, chest, coffer.

trundle *vb* bowl, revolve, roll, spin, truckle, wheel.

truss *vb* bind, bundle, close, cram, hang, pack. * *n* bundle, package, packet; apparatus, bandage, support.

trust *vb* confide, depend, expect, hope, rely; believe, credit; commit, entrust. * *n* belief, confidence, credence, faith; credit, tick; charge, deposit; commission, duty, errand; assurance, conviction, expectation, hope, reliance, secutrity.

trustful *adj* confiding, trusting, unquestioning, unsuspecting; faithful, trustworthy, trusty.

trustworthy *adj* confidential, constant, credible, dependable, faithful, firm, honest, incorrupt, upright, reliable, responsible, straightforward, staunch, true, trusty, uncorrupt, upright.

truth *n* fact, reality, veracity; actuality, authenticity, realism; canon, law, oracle, principle; right, truthfulness, veracity; candour, fidelity, frankness, honesty, honour, ingenuousness, integrity, probity, sincerity, virtue; constancy, devotion, faith, fealty, loyalty, steadfastness; accuracy, correctness, exactitude, exactness, nicety, precision, regularity, trueness.

truthful *adj* correct, reliable, true, trustworthy, veracious; artless, candid, frank, guileless, honest, ingenuous, open, sincere, straightforward, trusty.

truthless *adj* canting, disingenuous, dishonest, false, faithless, hollow, hypocritical, insincere, pharisaical, treacherous, unfair, untrustworthy.

try *vb* examine, prove, test; attempt, essay; adjudicate, adjudge, examine, hear; purify, refine; sample, sift, smell, taste; aim, attempt, endeavour, seek, strain, strive. * *n* attempt, effort, endeavour, experiment, trial.

trying *adj* difficult, fatiguing, hard, irksome, tiresome, wearisome; afflicting, afflictive, calamitous, deplorable, dire, distressing, grievous, hard, painful, sad, severe.

tryst *n* appointment, assignation, rendezvous.

tube *n* bore, bronchus, cylinder, duct, hollow, hose, pipe, pipette, worm.

tuft *n* brush, bunch, crest, feather, knot, plume, topknot, tussock; clump, cluster, group.

tug *vb* drag, draw, haul, pull, tow, wrench; labour, strive, struggle. * *n* drag, haul, pull, tow, wrench.

tuition *n* education, instruction, schooling, teaching, training.

tumble *vb* heave, pitch, roll, toss, wallow; fall, sprawl, stumble, topple, trip; derange, disarrange, dishevel, disorder, disturb, rumple, tousle. * *n* collapse, drop, fall, plunge, spill, stumble, trip.

tumbler *n* acrobat, juggler; glass.

tumid *adj* bloated, distended, enlarged, puffed-up, swelled, swollen, turgid; bombastic, declamatory, fustian, grandiloquent, grandiose, high-flown, inflated, pompous, puffy, rhetorical, stilted, swelling.

tumour *n* boil, carbuncle, swelling, tumefaction.

tumult *n* ado, affray, agitation, altercation, bluster, brawl, disturbance, ferment, flurry, feud, fracas, fray, fuss, hubbub, huddle, hurly-burly, melee, noise, perturbation, pother, quarrel, racket, riot, row, squabble, stir, turbulence, turmoil, uproar.

tumultuous *adj* blustery, breezy, bustling, confused, disorderly, disturbed, riotous, turbulent, unruly.

tune *vb* accord, attune, harmonize, modulate; adapt, adjust, attune. * *n* air, aria, melody, strain, tone; agreement, concord, harmony; accord, order.

tuneful *adj* dulcet, harmonious, melodious, musical.

turbid *adj* foul, impure, muddy, thick, unsettled.

turbulence *n* agitation, commotion, confusion, disorder, disturbance, excitement, tumult, tumultuousness, turmoil, unruliness, uproar; insubordination, insurrection, mutiny, rebellion, riot, sedition.

turbulent *adj* agitated, disturbed, restless, tumultuous, wild; blatant, blustering, boisterous, brawling, disorderly, obstreperous, tumultuous, uproarious, vociferous; factious, insubordinate, insurgent, mutinous, raging, rebellious, refractory, revolutionary, riotous, seditious, stormy, violent.

turf *n* grass, greensward, sod, sward; horse racing, racecourse, race-ground.

turgid *adj* bloated, distended, protuberant, puffed-up, swelled, swollen, tumid; bombastic, declamatory, diffuse, digressive, fustian, high-flown, inflated, grandiloquent, grandiose, ostentatious, pompous, puffy, rhetorical, stilted.

turmoil *n* activity, agitation, bustle, commotion, confusion, disorder, disturbance, ferment, flurry, huddle, hubbub, hurly-burly, noise, trouble, tumult, turbulence, uproar.

turn *vb* revolve, rotate; bend, cast, defect, inflict, round, spin, sway, swivel, twirl, twist, wheel; crank, grind, wind; deflect, divert, transfer, warp; form, mould, shape; adapt, fit, manoeuvre, suit; alter, change, conform, metamorphose, transform, transmute, vary; convert, persuade, prejudice; construe, render, translate; depend, hang, hinge, pivot; eventuate, issue, result, terminate; acidify, curdle, ferment. * *n* cycle, gyration, revolution, rotation, round; bending, deflection, deviation, diversion, doubling, flection, flexion, flexure, reel, retroversion, slew, spin, sweep, swing, swirl, swivel, turning, twist, twirl, whirl, winding; alteration, change, variation, vicissitude; bend, circuit, drive, ramble, run, round, stroll; bout, hand, innings, opportunity, shift, spell; act, action, deed, office; convenience, occasion, purpose; cast, fashion, form, guise, manner, mould, phase, shape; aptitude, bent, bias, disposition, faculty, genius, gift, inclination, leaning, proclivity, proneness, propensity, talent, tendency.

turncoat *n* apostate, backslider, deserter, recreant, renegade, traitor, wretch.

turpitude *n* baseness, degradation, depravity, vileness, wickedness.

turret *n* cupola, minaret, pinnacle.

tussle *vb* conflict, contend, contest, scuffle, struggle, wrestle. * *n* conflict, contest, fight, scuffle, struggle.

tutelage *n* care, charge, dependence, guardianship, protection, teaching, tutorage, tutorship, wardship.

tutor *vb* coach, educate, instruct, teach; discipline, train. * *n* coach, governess, governor, instructor, master, preceptor, schoolteacher, teacher.

twaddle *vb* chatter, gabble, maunder, prate, prattle. * *n* balderdash, chatter, flummery, gabble, gibberish, gobbledegook, gossip, jargon, moonshine, nonsense, platitude, prate, prattle, rigmarole, stuff, tattle.

tweak *vb, n* jerk, pinch, pull, twinge, twitch.

twig[1] *n* bough, branch, offshoot, shoot, slip, spray, sprig, stick, switch.

twig[2] *vb* catch on, comprehend, discover, grasp, realize, recognize, see, understand.

twin *vb* couple, link, match, pair. * *adj* double, doubled, duplicate, geminate, identical, matched, matching, second, twain. * *n* corollary, double, duplicate, fellow, likeness, match.

twine *vb* embrace, encircle, entwine, interlace, surround, wreathe; bend, meander, wind; coil, twist. * *n* convolution, coil, twist; embrace, twining, winding; cord, string.

twinge *vb* pinch, tweak, twitch. * *n* pinch, tweak, twitch; gripe, pang, spasm.

twinkle *vb* blink, twink, wink; flash, glimmer, scintillate, sparkle. * *n* blink, flash, gleam, glimmer, scintillation, sparkle; flash, instant, jiffy, moment, second, tick, trice, twinkling.

twinkling *n* flashing, sparkling, twinkle; flash, instant, jiffy, moment, second, tick, trice.

twirl *vb* revolve, rotate, spin, turn, twist, twirl. * *n* convolution, revolution, turn, twist, whirling.

twist *vb* purl, rotate, spin, twine; complicate, contort, convolute, distort, pervert, screw, wring; coil, writhe; encircle, wind, wreathe. * *n* coil, curl, spin, twine; braid, roll; change, complication, development, variation; bend, convolution, turn; defect, distortion, flaw, imperfection; jerk, pull, sprain, wrench; aberration, characteristic, eccentricity, oddity, peculiarity, quirk.

twit[1] *vb* banter, blame, censure, reproach, taunt, tease, upbraid.

twit[2] *n* blockhead, fool, idiot, nincompoop, nitwit.

twitch *vb* jerk, pluck, pull, snatch. * *n* jerk, pull; contraction, pull, quiver, spasm, twitching.

type *n* emblem, mark, stamp; adumbration, image, representation, representative, shadow, sign, symbol, token; archetype, exemplar, model, original, pattern, prototype, protoplast, standard; character, form, kind, nature, sort; figure, letter, text, typography.

typical *adj* emblematic, exemplary, figurative, ideal, indicative, model, representative, symbolic, true.

typify *vb* betoken, denote, embody, exemplify, figure, image, indicate, represent, signify.

tyrannical *adj* absolute, arbitrary, autocratic, cruel, despotic, dictatorial, domineering, high, imperious, irresponsible, severe, tyrannical, unjust; galling, grinding, inhuman, oppressive, overbearing, severe.

tyranny *n* absolutism, autocracy, despotism, dictatorship, harshness, oppression.

tyrant *n* autocrat, despot, dictator, oppressor.

tyro *n* beginner, learner, neophyte, novice; dabbler, smatterer.

U

ubiquitous *adj* omnipresent, present, universal.
udder *n* nipple, pap, teat.
ugly *adj* crooked, homely, ill-favoured, plain, ordinary, unlovely, unprepossessing, unshapely, unsightly; forbidding, frightful, gruesome, hideous, horrible, horrid, loathsome, monstrous, shocking, terrible, repellent, repulsive; bad-tempered, cantankerous, churlish, cross, quarrelsome, spiteful, surly, spiteful, vicious.
ulcer *n* boil, fester, gathering, pustule, sore.
ulterior *adj* beyond, distant, farther; hidden, personal, secret, selfish, undisclosed.
ultimate *adj* conclusive, decisive, eventual, extreme, farthest, final, last. * *n* acme, consummation, culmination, height, peak, pink, quintessence, summit.
ultra *adj* advanced, beyond, extreme, radical.
umbrage *n* shadow, shade; anger, displeasure, dissatisfaction, dudgeon, injury, offence, pique, resentment.
umpire *vb* adjudicate, arbitrate, judge, referee. * *n* adjudicator, arbiter, arbitrator, judge, referee.
unabashed *adj* bold, brazen, confident, unblushing, undaunted, undismayed.
unable *adj* impotent, incapable, incompetent, powerless, weak.
unacceptable *adj* disagreeable, distasteful, offensive, unpleasant, unsatisfactory, unwelcome.
unaccommodating *adj* disobliging, noncompliant, uncivil, ungracious.
unaccomplished *adj* incomplete, unachieved, undone, unperformed, unexecuted, unfinished; ill-educated, uncultivated, unpolished.
unaccountable *adj* inexplicable, incomprehensible, inscrutable, mysterious, unintelligible; irresponsible, unanswerable.
unaccustomed *adj* uninitiated, unskilled, unused; foreign, new, strange, unfamiliar, unusual.
unaffected *adj* artless, honest, naive, natural, plain, simple, sincere, real, unfeigned; chaste, pure, unadorned; insensible, unchanged, unimpressed, unmoved, unstirred, untouched.
unanimity *n* accord, agreement, concert, concord, harmony, union, unity.
unanimous *adj* agreeing, concordant, harmonious, like-minded, solid, united.
unassuming *adj* humble, modest, reserved, unobtrusive, unpretending, unpretentious.
unattainable *adj* inaccessible, unobtainable.
unavailing *adj* abortive, fruitless, futile, ineffectual, ineffective, inept, nugatory, unsuccessful, useless, vain.
unbalanced *adj* unsound, unsteady; unadjusted, unsettled.
unbearable *adj* insufferable, insupportable, unendurable.
unbecoming *adj* inappropriate, indecent, indecorous, improper, unbefitting, unbeseeming, unseemly, unsuitable.
unbelief *n* disbelief, dissent, distrust, incredulity, incredulousness, miscreance, miscreancy, nonconformity; doubt, freethinking, infidelity, scepticism.
unbeliever *n* agnostic, deist, disbeliever, doubter, heathen, infidel, sceptic.
unbending *adj* inflexible, rigid, stiff, unpliant, unyielding; firm, obstinate, resolute, stubborn.
unbiased *adj* disinterested, impartial, indifferent, neutral, uninfluenced, unprejudiced, unwarped.
unbind *vb* loose, undo, unfasten, unloose, untie; free, unchain, unfetter.
unblemished *adj* faultless, guiltless, immaculate, impeccable, innocent, intact, perfect, pure, sinless, spotless, stainless, undefiled, unspotted, unsullied, untarnished.
unblushing *adj* boldfaced, impudent, shameless.
unbounded *adj* absolute, boundless, endless, immeasurable, immense, infinite, interminable, measureless, unlimited, vast; immoderate, uncontrolled, unrestrained, unrestricted.
unbridled *adj* dissolute, intractable, lax, licensed, licentious, loose, uncontrolled, ungovernable, unrestrained, violent, wanton.
unbroken *adj* complete, entire, even, full, intact, unimpaired; constant, continuous, fast, profound, sound, successive, undisturbed; inviolate, unbetrayed, unviolated.
unbuckle *vb* loose, unfasten, unloose.
uncanny *adj* inopportune, unsafe; eerie, eery, ghostly, unearthly, unnatural, weird.
unceremonious *adj* abrupt, bluff, blunt, brusque, course, curt, gruff, plain, rough, rude, ungracious; casual, familiar, informal, offhand, unconstrained.
uncertain *adj* ambiguous, doubtful, dubious, equivocal, indefinite, indeterminate, indistinct, questionable, unsettled; insecure, precarious, problematical; capricious, changeable, desultory, fitful, fluctuating, irregular, mutable, shaky, slippery, unreliable, variable.

unchaste *adj* dissolute, incontinent, indecent, immoral, lascivious, lecherous, libidinous, lewd, loose, obscene, wanton.

unchecked *adj* uncurbed, unhampered, unhindered, unobstructed, unrestrained, untrammelled.

uncivil *adj* bearish, blunt, boorish, brusque, discourteous, disobliging, disrespectful, gruff, ill-bred, ill-mannered, impolite, irreverent, rough, rude, uncomplaisant, uncourteous, uncouth, ungentle, ungracious, unmannered, unseemly.

unclean *adj* abominable, beastly, dirty, filthy, foul, grimy, grubby, miry, muddy, nasty, offensive, purulent, repulsive, soiled, sullied; improper, indecent, indecorous, obscene, polluted, risqué, sinful, smutty, unholy, uncleanly.

uncomfortable *adj* disagreeable, displeasing, disquieted, distressing, disturbed, uneasy, unpleasant, restless; cheerless, close, oppressive; dismal, miserable, unhappy.

uncommon *adj* choice, exceptional, extraordinary, infrequent, noteworthy, odd, original, queer, rare, remarkable, scarce, singular, strange, unexampled, unfamiliar, unusual, unwonted.

uncommunicative *adj* close, inconversable, reserved, reticent, taciturn, unsociable, unsocial.

uncomplaining *adj* long-suffering, meek, patient, resigned, tolerant.

uncompromising *adj* inflexible, narrow, obstinate, orthodox, rigid, stiff, strict, unyielding.

unconcerned *adj* apathetic, careless, indifferent.

unconditional *adj* absolute, categorical, complete, entire, free, full, positive, unlimited, unqualified, unreserved, unrestricted.

uncongenial *adj* antagonistic, discordant, displeasing, ill-assorted, incompatible, inharmonious, mismatched, unsuited, unsympathetic.

uncouth *adj* awkward, boorish, clownish, clumsy, gawky, inelegant, loutish, lubberly, rough, rude, rustic, uncourtly, ungainly, unpolished, unrefined, unseemly; odd, outlandish, strange, unfamiliar, unusual.

uncover *vb* denude, divest, lay bare, strip; disclose, discover, expose, reveal, unmask, unveil; bare, doff; open, unclose, unseal.

unctuous *adj* adipose, greasy, oily, fat, fatty, oleaginous, pinguid, sebaceous; bland, lubricious, smooth, slippery; bland, fawning, glib, obsequious, plausible, servile, suave, sycophantic; fervid, gushing.

uncultivated *adj* fallow, uncultured, unreclaimed, untilled; homely, ignorant, illiterate, rude, uncivilized, uncultured, uneducated, unfit, unlettered, unpolished, unread, unready, unrefined, untaught; rough, savage, sylvan, uncouth, wild.

undaunted *adj* bold, brave, courageous, dauntless, fearless, intrepid, plucky, resolute, undismayed.

undefiled *adj* clean, immaculate, pure, spotless, stainless, unblemished, unspotted, unsullied, untarnished; honest, innocent, inviolate, pure, uncorrupted, unpolluted, unstained.

undemonstrative *adj* calm, composed, demure, impassive, modest, placid, quiet, reserved, sedate, sober, staid, tranquil.

undeniable *adj* certain, conclusive, evident, incontestable, incontrovertible, indisputable, indubitable, obvious, unquestionable.

under *prep* below, beneath, inferior to, lower than, subordinate to, underneath. * *adv* below, beneath, down, lower.

underestimate *vb* belittle, underrate, undervalue.

undergo *vb* bear, endure, experience, suffer, sustain.

underhand *adj* clandestine, deceitful, disingenuous, fraudulent, hidden, secret, sly, stealthy, underhanded, unfair. * *adv* clandestinely, privately, secretly, slyly, stealthily, surreptitiously; fraudulently, unfairly.

underling *n* agent, inferior, servant, subordinate.

undermine *vb* excavate, mine, sap; demoralize, foil, frustrate, thwart, weaken.

understand *vb* apprehend, catch, comprehend, conceive, discern, grasp, know, penetrate, perceive, see, seize, twig; assume, interpret, take; imply, mean.

understanding *adj* compassionate, considerate, forgiving, kind, kindly, patient, sympathetic, tolerant. * *n* brains, comprehension, discernment, faculty, intellect, intelligence, judgement, knowledge, mind, reason, sense.

undertake *vb* assume, attempt, begin, embark on, engage in, enter upon, take in hand; agree, bargain, contract, covenant, engage, guarantee, promise, stipulate.

undertaking *n* adventure, affair, attempt, business, effort, endeavour, engagement, enterprise, essay, move, project, task, venture.

undesigned *adj* spontaneous, unintended, unintentional, unplanned, unpremeditated.

undigested *adj* crude, ill-advised, ill-considered, ill-judged; confused, disorderly, ill-arranged, unmethodical.

undivided *adj* complete, entire, whole; one, united.

undo *vb* annul, cancel, frustrate, invalidate, neutralize, nullify, offset, reverse; disengage, loose, unfasten, unmake, unravel, untie; crush, destroy, overturn, ruin.

undoubted *adj* incontrovertible, indisputable, indubitable, undisputed, unquestionable, unquestioned.

undress *vb* denude, dismantle, disrobe, unclothe, unrobe, peel, strip. * *n* disarray, nakedness, nudity; mufti, negligee.

undue *adj* illegal, illegitimate, improper, unlawful, excessive, disproportionate, disproportioned, immoderate, unsuitable; unfit.

undulation *n* billowing, fluctuation, pulsation, ripple, wave.

undying *adj* deathless, endless, immortal, imperishable.

unearthly *adj* preternatural, supernatural, uncanny, weird.

uneasy *adj* disquieted, disturbed, fidgety, impatient, perturbed, restless, restive, unquiet, worried; awkward, stiff, ungainly, ungraceful; constraining, cramping, disagreeable, uncomfortable.
unending *adj* endless, eternal, everlasting, interminable, never-ending, perpetual, unceasing.
unequal *adj* disproportionate, disproportioned, ill-matched, inferior, irregular, insufficient, not alike, uneven.
unequalled *adj* exceeding, incomparable, inimitable, matchless, new, nonpareil, novel, paramount, peerless, pre-eminent, superlative, surpassing, transcendent, unheard of, unique, unparalleled, unrivalled.
unequivocal *adj* absolute, certain, clear, evident, incontestable, indubitable, positive; explicit, unambiguous, unmistakable.
uneven *adj* hilly, jagged, lumpy, ragged, rough, rugged, stony; motley, unequal, variable, variegated.
uneventful *adj* commonplace, dull, eventless, humdrum, quiet, monotonous, smooth, uninteresting.
unexceptionable *adj* excellent, faultless, good, irreproachable.
unexpected *adj* abrupt, sudden, unforeseen.
unfair *adj* dishonest, dishonourable, faithless, false, hypocritical, inequitable, insincere, oblique, one-sided, partial, unequal, unjust, wrongful.
unfaithful *adj* adulterous, derelict, deceitful, dishonest, disloyal, false, faithless, fickle, perfidious, treacherous, unreliable; negligent; changeable, inconstant, untrue.
unfamiliar *adj* bizarre, foreign, new, novel, outlandish, queer, singular, strange, uncommon, unusual.
unfashionable *adj* antiquated, destitute, disused, obsolete, old-fashioned, unconventional.
unfavourable *adj* adverse, contrary, disadvantageous, discouraging, ill, inauspicious, inimical, inopportune, indisposed, malign, sinister, unfriendly, unlucky, unpropitious, untimely; foul, inclement.
unfeeling *adj* apathetic, callous, heartless, insensible, numb, obdurate, torpid, unconscious, unimpressionable; adamantine, cold-blooded, cruel, hard, merciless, pitiless, stony, unkind, unsympathetic.
unfit *vb* disable, disqualify, incapacitate. * *adj* improper, inappropriate, incompetent, inconsistent, unsuitable; ill-equipped, inadequate, incapable, unqualified, useless; debilitated, feeble, flabby, unhealthy, unsound.
unflagging *adj* constant, indefatigable, never-ending, persevering, steady, unfaltering, unremitting, untiring, unwearied.
unflinching *adj* firm, resolute, steady, unshrinking.
unfold *vb* display, expand, open, separate, unfurl, unroll; declare, disclose, reveal, tell; decipher, develop, disentangle, evolve, explain, illustrate, interpret, resolve, unravel.
unfortunate *adj* hapless, ill-fated, ill-starred, infelicitous, luckless, unhappy, unlucky, unprosperous, unsuccessful, wretched; calamitous, deplorable, disastrous; inappropriate, inexpedient.
unfrequented *adj* abandoned, deserted, forsaken, lone, solitary, uninhabited, unoccupied.
unfruitful *adj* barren, fruitless, sterile; infecund, unprolific; unprofitable, unproductive.
ungainly *adj* awkward, boorish, clownish, clumsy, gawky, inelegant, loutish, lubberly, lumbering, slouching, stiff, uncourtly, uncouth, ungraceful.
ungentlemanly *adj* ill-bred, impolite, rude, uncivil, ungentle, ungracious, unmannerly.
unhappy *adj* afflicted, disastrous, dismal, distressed, drear, evil, inauspicious, miserable, painful, unfortunate, wretched.
unhealthy *adj* ailing, diseased, feeble, indisposed, infirm, poorly, sickly, toxic, unsanitary, unsound, toxic, venomous.
uniform *adj* alike, constant, even, equable, equal, smooth, steady, regular, unbroken, unchanged, undeviating, unvaried, unvarying. * *n* costume, dress, livery, outfit, regalia, suit.
uniformity *n* constancy, continuity, permanence, regularity, sameness, stability; accordance, agreement, conformity, consistency, unanimity.
unimportant *adj* immaterial, inappreciable, inconsequent, inconsequential, inconsiderable, indifferent, insignificant, mediocre, minor, paltry, petty, small, slight, trifling, trivial.
unintentional *adj* accidental, casual, fortuitous, inadvertent, involuntary, spontaneous, undesigned, unmeant, unplanned, unpremeditated, unthinking.
uninterrupted *adj* continuous, endless, incessant, perpetual, unceasing.
union *n* coalescence, coalition, combination, conjunction, coupling, fusion, incorporation, joining, junction, unification, uniting; agreement, concert, concord, concurrence, harmony, unanimity, unity; alliance, association, club, confederacy, federation, guild, league.
unique *adj* choice, exceptional, matchless, only, peculiar, rare, single, sole, singular, uncommon, unexampled, unmatched.
unison *n* accord, accordance, agreement, concord, harmony.
unite *vb* amalgamate, attach, blend, centralize, coalesce, confederate, consolidate, embody, fuse, incorporate, merge, weld; associate, conjoin, connect, couple, link, marry; combine, join; harmonize, reconcile; agree, concert, concur, cooperate, fraternize.
universal *adj* all-reaching, catholic, cosmic, encyclopedic, general, ubiquitous, unlimited; all, complete, entire, total, whole.
unjust *adj* inequitable, injurious, partial, unequal,

unfair, unwarranted, wrong, wrongful; flagitious, heinous, influenced, iniquitous, nefarious, unrighteous, wicked; biased, prejudiced, uncandid.

unjustifiable *adj* indefensible, unjust, unreasonable, unwarrantable; inexcusable, unpardonable.

unknown *adj* unappreciated, unascertained; undiscovered, unexplored, uninvestigated; concealed, dark, enigmatic, hidden, mysterious, mystic; anonymous, incognito, inglorious, nameless, obscure, renownless, undistinguished, unheralded, unnoted.

unladylike *adj* ill-bred, impolite, rude, uncivil, ungentle, ungracious, unmannerly.

unlamented *adj* unmourned, unregretted.

unlimited *adj* boundless, infinite, interminable, limitless, measureless, unbounded; absolute, full, unconfined, unconstrained, unrestricted; indefinite, undefined.

unlucky *adj* baleful, disastrous, ill-fated, ill-starred, luckless, unfortunate, unprosperous, unsuccessful; ill-omened, inauspicious; miserable, unhappy.

unmanageable *adj* awkward, cumbersome, inconvenient, unwieldy; intractable, unruly, unworkable, vicious; difficult, impractical.

unmatched *adj* matchless, unequalled, unparalleled, unrivalled.

unmitigated *adj* absolute, complete, consummate, perfect, sheer, stark, thorough, unqualified, utter.

unnatural *adj* aberrant, abnormal, anomalous, foreign, irregular, prodigious, uncommon; brutal, cold, heartless, inhuman, unfeeling, unusual; affected, artificial, constrained, forced, insincere, self-conscious, stilted, strained; factitious.

unpleasant *adj* disagreeable, displeasing, distasteful, obnoxious, offensive, repulsive, unlovely, ungrateful, unacceptable, unpalatable, unwelcome.

unpremeditated *adj* extempore, impromptu, offhand, spontaneous, undesigned, unintentional, unstudied.

unprincipled *adj* bad, crooked, dishonest, fraudulent, immoral, iniquitous, knavish, lawless, profligate, rascally, roguish, thievish, trickish, tricky, unscrupulous, vicious, villainous, wicked.

unqualified *adj* disqualified, incompetent, ineligible, unadapted, unfit; absolute, certain, consummate, decided, direct, downright, full, outright, unconditional, unmeasured, unrestricted, unmitigated; exaggerated, sweeping.

unreal *adj* chimerical, dreamlike, fanciful, flimsy, ghostly, illusory, insubstantial, nebulous, shadowy, spectral, visionary, unsubstantial.

unreasonable *adj* absurd, excessive, exorbitant, foolish, ill-judged, illogical, immoderate, impractical, injudicious, irrational, nonsensical, preposterous, senseless, silly, stupid, unfair, unreasoning, unwarrantable, unwise.

unreliable *adj* fallible, fickle, irresponsible, treacherous, uncertain, undependable, unstable, unsure, untrustworthy.

unremitting *adj* assiduous, constant, continual, diligent, incessant, indefatigable, persevering, sedulous, unabating, unceasing.

unrepentant *adj* abandoned, callous, graceless, hardened, impenitent, incorrigible, irreclaimable, lost, obdurate, profligate, recreant, seared, shameless.

unrequited *adj* unanswered, unreturned, unrewarded.

unreserved *adj* absolute, entire, full, unlimited; above-board, artless, candid, communicative, fair, frank, guileless, honest, ingenuous, open, sincere, single-minded, undesigning, undissembling; demonstrative, emotional, openhearted.

unresisting *adj* compliant, long-suffering, non-resistant, obedient, passive, patient, submissive, yielding.

unresponsive *adj* irresponsive, unsympathetic.

unrestrained *adj* unbridled, unchecked, uncurbed, unfettered, unhindered, unobstructed, unreserved; broad, dissolute, incontinent, inordinate, lax, lewd, licentious, loose, wanton; lawless, wild.

unrestricted *adj* free, unbridled, unconditional, unconfined, uncurbed, unfettered, unlimited, unqualified, unrestrained; clear, open, public, unobstructed.

unrevealed *adj* hidden, occult, secret, undiscovered, unknown.

unrewarded *adj* unpaid, unrecompensed.

unriddle *vb* explain, expound, solve, unfold, unravel.

unrighteous *adj* evil, sinful, ungodly, unholy, vicious, wicked, wrong; heinous, inequitable, iniquitous, nefarious, unfair, unjust.

unripe *adj* crude, green, hard, immature, premature, sour; incomplete, unfinished.

unrivalled *adj* incomparable, inimitable, matchless, peerless, unequalled, unexampled, unique, unparalleled.

unrobe *vb* disrobe, undress.

unroll *vb* develop, discover, evolve, open, unfold; display, lay open.

unromantic *adj* literal, matter-of-fact, prosaic.

unroot *vb* eradicate, extirpate, root out, uproot.

unruffled *adj* calm, peaceful, placid, quiet, serene, smooth, still, tranquil; collected, composed, cool, imperturbable, peaceful, philosophical, placid, tranquil, undisturbed, unexcited, unmoved.

unruly *adj* disobedient, disorderly, fractious, headstrong, insubordinate, intractable, mutinous, obstreperous, rebellious, refractory, riotous, seditious, turbulent, ungovernable, unmanageable, wanton, wild; lawless, obstinate, rebellious, stubborn, vicious.

unsafe *adj* dangerous, hazardous, insecure, perilous, precarious, risky, treacherous, uncertain, unprotected.

unsaid *adj* tacit, unmentioned, unspoken, unuttered.
unsanctified *adj* profane, unhallowed, unholy.
unsatisfactory *adj* insufficient; disappointing; faulty, feeble, imperfect, poor, weak.
unsatisfied *adj* insatiate, unsated, unsatiated, unstaunched; discontented, displeased, dissatisfied, malcontent; undischarged, unpaid, unperformed, unrendered.
unsavoury *adj* flat, insipid, mawkish, savourless, tasteless, unflavoured, unpalatable, vapid; disagreeable, disgusting, distasteful, nasty, nauseating, nauseous, offensive, rank, revolting, sickening, uninviting, unpleasing.
unsay *vb* recall, recant, retract, take back.
unscathed *adj* unharmed, uninjured.
unschooled *adj* ignorant, uneducated, uninstructed; undisciplined, untrained.
unscrupulous *adj* dishonest, reckless, ruthless, unconscientious, unprincipled, unrestrained.
unsealed *adj* open, unclosed.
unsearchable *adj* hidden, incomprehensible, inscrutable, mysterious.
unseasonable *adj* ill-timed, inappropriate, infelicitous, inopportune, untimely; late, too late; inexpedient, undesireable, unfit, ungrateful, unsuitable, unwelcome; premature, too early.
unseasonably *adv* malapropos, unsuitably, untimely.
unseasoned *adj* inexperienced, unaccustomed, unqualified, untrained; immoderate, inordinate, irregular; green; fresh, unsalted.
unseeing *adj* blind, sightless.
unseemly *adj* improper, indecent, inappropriate, indecorous, unbecoming, uncomely, unfit, unmeet, unsuitable.
unseen *adj* undiscerned, undiscovered, unobserved, unperceived; imperceptible, indiscoverable, invisible, latent.
unselfish *adj* altruistic, devoted, disinterested, generous, high-minded, impersonal, liberal, magnanimous, self-denying, self-forgetful, selfless, self-sacrificing.
unserviceable *adj* ill-conditioned, unsound, useless; profitless, unprofitable.
unsettle *vb* confuse, derange, disarrange, disconcert, disorder, disturb, trouble, unbalance, unfix, unhinge, upset.
unsettled *adj* changeable, fickle, inconstant, restless, transient, unstable, unsteady, vacillating, wavering; inequable, unequal; feculent, muddy, roiled, roily, turbid; adrift, afloat, homeless, unestablished, uninhabited; open, tentative, unadjusted, undecided, undetermined; due, outstanding, owing, unpaid; perturbed, troubled, unnerved.
unshackle *vb* emancipate, liberate, loose, release, set free, unbind, unchain, unfetter.
unshaken *adj* constant, firm, resolute, steadfast, steady, unmoved.
unshapen *adj* deformed, grotesque, ill-formed, ill-made, ill-shaped, misshapen, shapeless, ugly, uncouth.
unsheltered *adj* exposed, unprotected.
unshrinking *adj* firm, determined, persisting, resolute, unblenching, unflinching.
unshroud *vb* discover, expose, reveal, uncover.
unsightly *adj* deformed, disagreeable, hideous, repellent, repulsive, ugly.
unskilful, unskillful *adj* awkward, bungling, clumsy, inapt, inexpert, maladroit, rough, rude, unhandy, unskilled, unversed.
unskilled *adj* inexperienced, raw, undisciplined, undrilled, uneducated, unexercised, unpractised, unprepared, unschooled; unskilful.
unslaked *adj* unquenched, unslacked.
unsleeping *adj* unslumbering, vigilant, wakeful, watchful.
unsmirched *adj* undefiled, unpolluted, unspotted.
unsociable *adj* distant, reserved, retiring, segregative, shy, solitary, standoffish, taciturn, uncommunicative, uncompanionable, ungenial, unsocial; inhospitable, misanthropic, morose.
unsoiled *adj* clean, spotless, unspotted, unstained, unsullied, untarnished.
unsophisticated *adj* genuine, pure, unadulterated; good, guileless, innocent, undepraved, unpolluted, invitiated; artless, honest, ingenuous, naive, natural, simple, sincere, straightforward, unaffected, undesigning, unstudied.
unsound *adj* decayed, defective, impaired, imperfect, rotten, thin, wasted, weak; broken, disturbed, light, restless; diseased, feeble, infirm, morbid, poorly, sickly, unhealthy, weak; deceitful, erroneous, fallacious, false, faulty, hollow, illogical, incorrect, invalid, ill-advised, irrational, questionable, sophistical, unreasonable, unsubstantial, untenable, wrong; dishonest, false, insincere, unfaithful, untrustworthy, untrue; insubstantial, unreal; heretical, heterodox, unorthodox.
unsparing *adj* bountiful, generous, lavish, liberal, profuse, ungrudging; harsh, inexorable, relentless, rigorous, ruthless, severe, uncompromising, unforgiving.
unspeakable *adj* indescribable, ineffable, inexpressible, unutterable.
unspiritual *adj* bodily, carnal, fleshly, sensual.
unspotted *adj* clean, spotless, unsoiled, unstained, unsullied, untarnished; faultless, immaculate, innocent, pure, stainless, unblemished, uncorrupted, undefiled, untainted.
unstable *adj* infirm, insecure, precarious, top-heavy, tottering, unbalanced, unballasted, unreliable, unsafe, unsettled, unsteady; changeable, erratic, fickle, inconstant, irresolute, mercurial, mutable, vacillating, variable, wavering, weak, volatile.—*also* **instable**.
unstained *adj* colourless, uncoloured, undyed, untinged; clean, spotless, unspotted.
unsteady *adj* fluctuating, oscillating, unsettled; insecure, precarious, unstable; changeable, desul-

tory, ever-changing, fickle, inconstant, irresolute, mutable, unreliable, variable, wavering; drunken, jumpy, tottering, vacillating, wobbly, tipsy.

unstinted *adj* abundant, ample, bountiful, full, large, lavish, plentiful, prodigal, profuse.

unstrung *adj* overcome, shaken, unnerved, weak.

unstudied *adj* extempore, extemporaneous, impromptu, offhand, spontaneous, unpremeditated; inexpert, unskilled, unversed.

unsubdued *adj* unbowed, unbroken, unconquered, untamed.

unsubmissive *adj* disobedient, contumacious, indocile, insubordinate, obstinate, perverse, refractory, uncomplying, ungovernable, unmanageable, unruly, unyielding.

unsubstantial *adj* airy, flimsy, gaseous, gossamery, light, slight, tenuous, thin, vaporous; apparitional, bodiless, chimerical, cloudbuilt, dreamlike, empty, fantastical, ideal, illusory, imaginary, imponderable, moonshiny, spectral, unreal, vague, visionary; erroneous, fallacious, flimsy, groundless, illogical, unfounded, ungrounded, unsolid, unsound, untenable, weak.

unsuccessful *adj* abortive, bootless, fruitless, futile, ineffectual, profitless, unavailing, vain; ill-fated, ill-starred, luckless, unfortunate, unhappy, unlucky, unprosperous.

unsuitable *adj* ill-adapted, inappropriate, malapropos, unfit, unsatisfactory, unsuited; improper, inapplicable, inapt, incongruous, inexpedient, infelicitous, unbecoming, unbeseeming, unfitting.

unsuited *adj* unadapted, unfitted, unqualified.

unsullied *adj* chaste, clean, spotless, unsoiled, unspotted, unstained, untarnished; immaculate, pure, stainless, unblemished, uncorrupted, undefiled, untainted, untouched, virginal.

unsupplied *adj* destitute, unfurnished, unprovided.

unsupported *adj* unaided, unassisted; unbacked, unseconded, unsustained, unupheld.

unsurpassed *adj* matchless, peerless, unequalled, unexampled, unexcelled, unmatched, unparagoned, unparalleled, unrivalled.

unsusceptible *adj* apathetic, cold, impassive, insusceptible, phlegmatic, stoical, unimpressible, unimpressionable.

unsuspecting *adj* confiding, credulous, trusting, unsuspicious.

unsuspicious *adj* confiding, credulous, gullible, simple, trustful, unsuspecting.

unsustainable *adj* insupportable, intolerable; controvertible, erroneous, unmaintainable, untenable.

unswerving *adj* direct, straight, undeviating; constant, determined, firm, resolute, staunch, steadfast, steady, stable, unwavering.

unsymmetrical *adj* amorphous, asymmetric, disproportionate, formless, irregular, unbalanced.

unsystematic, unsystematical *adj* casual, disorderly, haphazard, irregular, planless, unmethodical.

untainted *adj* chaste, clean, faultless, fresh, healthy, pure, sweet, wholesome; spotless, unsoiled, unstained, unsullied, untarnished; immaculate, stainless, unblemished, uncorrupted, undefiled, unspotted.

untamable *adj* unconquerable.

untamed *adj* fierce, unbroken, wild.

untangle *vb* disentangle, explain, explicate.

untarnished *adj* chaste, clean, spotless, unsoiled, unspotted, unstained, unsullied; immaculate, pure, spotless, stainless, unblemished, uncorrupted, undefiled, unspotted, unsullied, untainted, virginal, virtuous.

untaught *adj* illiterate, unenlightened, uninformed, unlettered; ignorant, inexperienced, undisciplined, undrilled, uneducated, uninitiated, uninstructed, untutored.

untenable *adj* indefensible, unmaintainable, unsound; fallacious, hollow, illogical, indefensible, insupportable, unjustifiable, weak.

untenanted *adj* deserted, empty, tenantless, uninhabited, unoccupied.

unterrified *adj* fearless, unappalled, unawed, undismayed, undaunted, unscared.

unthankful *adj* thankless, ungrateful.

unthinking *adj* careless, heedless, inconsiderate, thoughtless, unreasoning, unreflecting; automatic, mechanical.

unthoughtful *adj* careless, heedless, inconsiderable, thoughtless.

unthrifty *adj* extravagant, improvident, lavish, prodigal, profuse, thriftless, wasteful.

untidy *adj* careless, disorderly, dowdy, frumpy, mussy, slatternly, slovenly, unkempt, unneat.

untie *vb* free, loose, loosen, unbind, unfasten, unknot, unloose; clear, resolve, solve, unfold.

until *adv, conj* till, to the time when; to the place, point, state or degree that; * *prep* till, to.

untimely *adj* ill-timed, immature, inconvenient, inopportune, mistimed, premature, unseasonable, unsuitable; ill-considered, inauspicious, uncalled for, unfortunate. * *adv* unseasonably, unsuitably.

untinged *adj* achromatic, colourless, hueless, uncoloured, undyed, unstained.

untiring *adj* persevering, incessant, indefatigable, patient, tireless, unceasing, unfatiguable, unflagging, unremitting, unwearied, unwearying.

untold *adj* countless, incalculable, innumerable, uncounted, unnumbered; unrelated, unrevealed.

untouched *adj* intact, scatheless, unharmed, unhurt, uninjured, unscathed; insensible, unaffected, unmoved, unstirred.

untoward *adj* adverse, froward, intractable, perverse, refractory, stubborn, unfortunate; annoying, ill-timed, inconvenient, unmanageable, vexatious; awkward, uncouth, ungainly, ungraceful.

untrained *adj* green, ignorant, inexperienced, raw, unbroken, undisciplined, undrilled, uneducated, uninstructed, unpractised, unskilled, untaught, untutored.
untrammelled *adj* free, unhampered.
untried *adj* fresh, inexperienced, maiden, new, unassayed, unattempted, unattested, virgin; undecided.
untrodden *adj* pathless, trackless, unbeaten.
untroubled *adj* calm, careless, composed, peaceful, serene, smooth, tranquil, undisturbed, unvexed.
untrue *adj* contrary, false, inaccurate, wrong; disloyal, faithless, perfidious, recreant, treacherous, unfaithful.
untrustworthy *adj* deceitful, dishonest, inaccurate, rotten, slippery, treacherous, undependable, unreliable; disloyal, false; deceptive, fallible, illusive, questionable.
untruth *n* error, faithlessness, falsehood, falsity, incorrectness, inveracity, treachery; deceit, deception, fabrication, fib, fiction, forgery, imposture, invention, lie, misrepresentation, misstatement, story.
untutored *adj* ignorant, inexperienced, undisciplined, undrilled, uneducated, uninitiated, uninstructed, untaught; artless, natural, simple, unsophisticated.
untwist *vb* disentangle, disentwine, ravel, unravel, unwreathe.
unused *adj* idle, unemployed, untried; new, unaccustomed, unfamiliar.
unusual *adj* abnormal, curious, exceptional, extraordinary, odd, peculiar, queer, rare, recherché, remarkable, singular, strange, unaccustomed, uncommon, unwonted.
unutterable *adj* incommunicable, indescribable, ineffable, inexpressible, unspeakable.
unvarnished *adj* unpolished; candid, plain, simple, true, unadorned, unembellished.
unvarying *adj* constant, invariable, unchanging.
unveil *vb* disclose, expose, reveal, show, uncover, unmask.
unveracious *adj* false, lying, mendacious, untruthful.
unversed *adj* inexperienced, raw, undisciplined, undrilled, uneducated, unexercised, unpractised, unprepared, unschooled; unskilful.
unviolated *adj* inviolate, unbetrayed, unbroken.
unwarlike *adj* pacific, peaceful.
unwarped *adj* impartial, unbiased, undistorted, unprejudiced.
unwarrantable *adj* improper, indefensible, unjustifiable.
unwary *adj* careless, hasty, heedless, imprudent, incautious, indiscreet, precipitate, rash, reckless, remiss, uncircumspect, unguarded.
unwavering *adj* constant, determined, firm, fixed, resolute, settled, staunch, steadfast, steady, unhesitating.
unwearied *adj* unfatigued; constant, continual, incessant, indefatigable, persevering, persistent, unceasing, unremitting, untiring.
unwelcome *adj* disagreeable, unacceptable, ungrateful, unpleasant, unpleasing.
unwell *adj* ailing, delicate, diseased, ill, indisposed, sick.
unwept *adj* unlamented, unmourned, unregretted.
unwholesome *adj* baneful, deleterious, injurious, insalubrious, noisome, noxious, poisonous, unhealthful, unhealthy; injudicious, pernicious, unsound; corrupt, tainted.
unwieldy *adj* bulky, clumsy, cumbersome, cumbrous, elephantine, heavy, hulking, large, massy, ponderous, unmanageable, weighty.
unwilling *adj* averse, backward, disinclined, indisposed, laggard, loath, opposed, recalcitrant, reluctant; forced, grudging.
unwind *vb* unravel, unreel, untwine, wind off; disentangle.
unwise *adj* brainless, foolish, ill-advised, ill-judged, impolitic, imprudent, indiscreet, injudicious, inexpedient, senseless, silly, stupid, unwary, weak.
unwitnessed *adj* unknown, unseen, unspied.
unwittingly *adv* ignorantly, inadvertently, unconsciously, undesignedly, unintentionally, unknowingly.
unwonted *adj* infrequent, rare, uncommon, unusual; unaccustomed, unused.
unworthy *adj* undeserving; bad, base, blameworthy, worthless; shameful, unbecoming, vile; contemptible, derogatory, despicable, discreditable, mean, paltry, reprehensible, shabby.
unwrap *vb* open, unfold.
unwrinkled *adj* smooth, unforrowed.
unwritten *adj* oral, traditional, unrecorded; conventional, customary.
unwrought *adj* crude, rough, rude, unfashioned, unformed.
unyielding *adj* constant, determined, indomitable, inflexible, pertinacious, resolute, staunch, steadfast, steady, tenacious, uncompromising, unwavering; headstrong, intractable, obstinate, perverse, self-willed, stiff, stubborn, wayward, wilful; adamantine, firm, grim, hard, immovable, implastic, inexorable, relentless, rigid, unbending.
unyoke *vb* disconnect, disjoin, part, separate.
unyoked *adj* disconnected, separated; licentious, loose, unrestrained.
upbraid *vb* accuse, blame, chide, condemn, criticize, denounce, fault, reproach, reprove, revile, scold, taunt, twit.
upheaval *n* elevation, upthrow; cataclysm, convulsion, disorder, eruption, explosion, outburst, overthrow.
uphill *adj* ascending, upward; arduous, difficult, hard, laborious, strenuous, toilsome, wearisome.
uphold *vb* elevate, raise; bear up, hold up, support, sustain; advocate, aid, champion, countenance, defend, justify, maintain, vindicate.
upland *n* down, fell, ridge, plateau.

uplift *vb* raise, upraise; animate, elevate, inspire, lift, refine. * *n* ascent, climb, elevation, lift, rise, upthrust; exaltation, inspiration, uplifting; improvement, refinement.
upon *prep* on, on top of, over; about, concerning, on the subject of, relating to; immediately after, with.
upper hand *n* advantage, ascendancy, control, dominion, mastership, mastery, pre-eminence, rule, superiority, supremacy, whip hand.
uppermost *adj* foremost, highest, loftiest, supreme, topmost, upmost.
uppish *adj* arrogant, assuming, haughty, perky, proud, smart.
upright *adj* erect, perpendicular, vertical; conscientious, equitable, fair, faithful, good, honest, honourable, incorruptible, just, pure, righteous, straightforward, true, trustworthy, upstanding, virtuous.
uprightness *n* erectness, perpendicularity, verticality; equity, fairness, goodness, honesty, honour, incorruptibility, integrity, justice, probity, rectitude, righteousness, straightforwardness, trustiness, trustworthiness, virtue, worth.
uproar *n* clamour, commotion, confusion, din, disturbance, fracas, hubbub, hurly-burly, noise, pandemonium, racket, riot, tumult, turmoil, vociferation.
uproarious *adj* boisterous, clamorous, loud, noisy, obstreperous, riotous, tumultuous.
uproot *vb* eradicate, extirpate, root out.
upset *vb* capsize, invert, overthrow, overtumble, overturn, spill, tip over, topple, turn turtle; agitate, confound, confuse, discompose, disconcert, distress, disturb, embarrass, excite, fluster, muddle, overwhelm, perturb, shock, startle, trouble, unnerve, unsettle; checkmate, defeat, overthrow, revolutionize, subvert; foil, frustrate, nonplus, thwart. * *adj* disproved, exposed, overthrown; bothered, confused, disconcerted, flustered, mixed-up, perturbed; shocked, startled, unsettled; beaten, defeated, overcome, overpowered, overthrown; discomfited, distressed, discomposed, overexcited, overwrought, shaken, troubled, unnerved. * *n* confutation, refutation; foiling, frustration, overthrow, revolution, revulsion, ruin, subversdion, thwarting.
upshot *n* conclusion, consummation, effect, end, event, issue, outcome, result, termination.
upside down *adj* bottom side up, bottom up, confused, head over heels, inverted, topsy-turvy.
upstart *n* adventurer, arriviste, parvenu, snob, social cimber, yuppie.
upturned *adj* raised, uplifted; retroussé.
upward *adj* ascending, climbing, mounting, rising, uphill. * *adv* above, aloft, overhead, up; heavenwards, skywards.
urbane *adj* civil, complaisant, courteous, courtly, elegant, mannerly, polished, polite, refined, smooth, suave, well-mannered.
urbanity *n* amenity, civility, complaisance, courtesy, politeness, smoothness, suavity.
urchin *n* brat, child, kid, ragamuffin, rascal, scrap, squirt, tad.
urge *vb* crowd, drive, force on, impel, press, press on, push, push on; beg, beseech, conjure, entreat, exhort, implore, importune, ply, solicit, tease; animate, egg on, encourage, goad, hurry, incite, instigate, quicken, spur, stimulate. * *n* compulsion, desire, drive, impulse, longing, pressure, wish, yearning.
urgency *n* drive, emergency, exigency, haste, necessity, press, pressure, push, stress; clamorousness, entreaty, insistence, importunity, instance, solicitation; goad, incitement, spur, stimulus.
urgent *adj* cogent, critical, crucial, crying, exigent, immediate, imperative, important, importunate, insistent, instant, pertinacious, pressing, serious.
urinal *n* chamber, chamber pot, lavatory, pot, potty, jordan, toilet.
urinate *vb* make water, pee, pee-pee, piddle, piss, stale, wee.
usage *n* treatment; consuetude, custom, fashion, habit, method, mode, practice, prescription, tradition, use.
use *vb* administer, apply, avail oneself of, drive, employ, handle, improve, make use of, manipulate, occupy, operate, ply, put into action, take advantage of, turn to account, wield, work; exercise, exert, exploit, practice, profit by, utilize; absorb, consume, exhaust, expend, swallow up, waste, wear out; accustom, familiarize, habituate, harden, inure, train; act toward, behave toward, deal with, manage, treat; be accustomed, be wont. * *n* appliance, application, consumption, conversion, disposal, exercise, employ, employment, practice, utilization; adaptability, advantage, avail, benefit, convenience, profit, service, usefulness, utility, wear; exigency, necessity, indispensability, need, occasion, requisiteness; custom, habit, handling, method, treatment, usage, way.
useful *adj* active, advantageous, available, availing, beneficial, commodious, conducive, contributory, convenient, effective, good, helpful, instrumental, operative, practical, profitable, remunerative, salutary, suitable, serviceable, utilitarian; available, helpful, serviceable, valuable.
usefulness *n* advantage, profit, serviceableness, utility, value.
useless *adj* abortive, bootless, fruitless, futile, helpless, idle, incapable, incompetent, ineffective, ineffectual, inutile, nugatory, null, profitless, unavailing, unprofitable, unproductive, unserviceable, valueless, worthless; good for nothing, waste.
usher *vb* announce, forerun, herald, induct, introduce, precede; conduct, direct, escort, shepherd, show. * *n* attendant, conductor, escort, shepherd, squire.
usual *adj* accustomed, common, customary, every-

day, familiar, frequent, general, habitual, normal, ordinary, prevailing, prevalent, regular, wonted.
usurp *vb* appropriate, arrogate, assume, seize.
usurpation *n* assumption, dispossession, infringement, seizure.
usury *n* interest; exploitation, extortion, profiteering.
utensil *n* device, implement, instrument, tool.
utility *n* advantageousness, avail, benefit, profit, service, use, usefulness; happiness, welfare.
utilize *vb* employ, exploit, make use of, put to use, turn to account, use.
utmost *adj* extreme, farthest, highest, last, main, most distant, remotest; greatest, uttermost. * *n* best, extreme, maximum, most.
Utopian *adj* air-built, air-drawn, chimerical, fanciful, ideal, imaginary, visionary, unreal.
utricle *n* bladder, cyst, sac, vesicle.
utter[1] *adj* complete, entire, perfect, total; absolute, blank, diametric, downright, final, peremptory, sheer, stark, thorough, thoroughgoing, unconditional, unqualified, total.
utter[2] *vb* articulate, breathe, deliver, disclose, divulge, emit, enunciate, express, give forth, pronounce, reveal, speak, talk, tell, voice; announce, circulate, declare, issue, publish.
utterance *n* articulation, delivery, disclosure, emission, expression, pronouncement, pronunciation, publication, speech.
utterly *adv* absolutely, altogether, completely, downright, entirely, quite, totally, unconditionally, wholly.
uttermost *adj* extreme, farthest; greatest, utmost.

V

vacant *adj* blank, empty, unfilled, void; disengaged, free, unemployed, unoccupied, unencumbered; thoughtless, unmeaning, unthinking, unreflective; uninhabited, untenanted.
vacate *vb* abandon, evacuate, relinquish, surrender; abolish, abrogate, annul, cancel, disannul, invalidate, nullify, overrule, quash, rescind.
vacillate *vb* dither, fluctuate, hesitate, oscillate, rock, sway, waver.
vacillation *n* faltering, fluctuation, hesitation, inconstancy, indecision, irresolution, reeling, rocking, staggering, swaying, unsteadiness, wavering.
vacuity *n* emptiness, inanition, vacancy; emptiness, vacancy, vacuum, void; expressionlessness, inanity, nihility.
vacuous *adj* empty, empty-headed, unfilled, vacant, void; inane, unintelligent.
vacuum *n* emptiness, vacuity, void.
vagabond *adj* footloose, idle, meandering, rambling, roving, roaming, strolling, vagrant, wandering. * *n* beggar, castaway, landloper, loafer, lounger, nomad, outcast, tramp, vagrant, wanderer.
vagary *n* caprice, crotchet, fancy, freak, humour, whim.
vagrant *adj* erratic, itinerant, roaming, roving, nomadic, strolling, unsettled, wandering. * *n* beggar, castaway, landloper, loafer, lounger, nomad, outcast, tramp, vagabond, wanderer.
vague *adj* ambiguous, confused, dim, doubtful, indefinite, ill-defined, indistinct, lax, loose, obscure, uncertain, undetermined, unfixed, unsettled.
vain *adj* baseless, delusive, dreamy, empty, false, imaginary, shadowy, suppositional, unsubstantial, unreal, void; abortive, bootless, fruitless, futile, ineffectual, nugatory, profitless, unavailing, unprofitable; trivial, unessential, unimportant, unsatisfactory, unsatisfying, useless, vapid, worthless; arrogant, conceited, egotistical, flushed, high, inflated, opinionated, ostentatious, overweening, proud, self-confident, self-opinionated, vainglorious; gaudy, glittering, gorgeous, showy.
valediction *n* adieu, farewell, goodbye, leave-taking.
valet *n* attendant, flunky, groom, lackey, servant.
valetudinarian *adj* delicate, feeble, frail, infirm, sickly.
valiant *adj* bold, brave, chivalrous, courageous, daring, dauntless, doughty, fearless, gallant, heroic, intrepid, lion-hearted, redoubtable, Spartan, valorous, undaunted.
valid *adj* binding, cogent, conclusive, efficacious, efficient, good, grave, important, just, logical, powerful, solid, sound, strong, substantial, sufficient, weighty.
valley *n* basin, bottom, canyon, dale, dell, dingle, glen, hollow, ravine, strath, vale.
valorous *adj* bold, brave, courageous, dauntless, doughty, intrepid, stout.
valour *n* boldness, bravery, courage, daring, gallantry, heroism, prowess, spirit.
valuable *adj* advantageous, precious, profitable, useful; costly, expensive, rich; admirable, estimable, worthy. * *n* heirloom, treasure.
value *vb* account, appraise, assess, estimate, price, rate, reckon; appreciate, esteem, prize, regard, treasure. * *n* avail, importance, usefulness, utility, worth; cost, equivalent, price, rate; estimation, excellence, importance, merit, valuation.
valueless *adj* miserable, useless, worthless.
vandal *n* barbarian, destroyer, savage.
vandalism *n* barbarism, barbarity, savagery.
vanish *vb* disappear, dissolve, fade, melt.
vanity *n* emptiness, falsity, foolishness, futility, hollowness, insanity, triviality, unreality, worthlessness; arrogance, conceit, egotism, ostentation, self-conceit.
vanquish *vb* conquer, defeat, outwit, overcome, overpower, overthrow, subdue, subjugate; crush, discomfit, foil, master, quell, rout, worst.
vapid *adj* dead, flat, insipid, lifeless, savourless, spiritless, stale, tasteless; dull, feeble, jejune, languid, meagre, prosaic, prosy, tame.
vapour *n* cloud, exhalation, fog, fume, mist, rack, reek, smoke, steam; daydream, dream, fantasy, phantom, vagary, vision, whim, whimsy.
variable *adj* changeable, mutable, shifting; aberrant, alterable, capricious, fickle, fitful, floating, fluctuating, inconstant, mobile, mutable, protean, restless, shifting, unsteady, vacillating, wavering.
variance *n* disagreement, difference, discord, dissension, incompatibility, jarring, strife.
variation *n* alteration, change, modification; departure, deviation, difference, discrepancy, innovation; contrariety, discordance.
variegated *adj* chequered, dappled, diversified,

flecked, kaleidoscopic, mottled, multicoloured, pied, spotted, striped.
variety *n* difference, dissimilarity, diversity, diversification, medley, miscellany, mixture, multiplicity, variation; kind, sort.
various *adj* different, diverse, manifold, many, numerous, several, sundry.
varnish *vb* enamel, glaze, japan, lacquer; adorn, decorate, embellish, garnish, gild, polish; disguise, excuse, extenuate, gloss over, palliate. * *n* enamel, lacquer, stain; cover, extenuation, gloss.
vary *vb* alter, metamorphose, transform; alternate, exchange, rotate; diversify, modify, variegate; depart, deviate, swerve.
vassal *n* bondman, liegeman, retainer, serf, slave, subject, thrall.
vassalage *n* bondage, dependence, serfdom, servitude, slavery, subjection.
vast *adj* boundless, infinite, measureless, spacious, wide; colossal, enormous, gigantic, huge, immense, mighty, monstrous, prodigious, tremendous; extraordinary, remarkable.
vaticination *n* augury, divination, prediction, prognostication, prophecy.
vault[1] *vb* arch, bend, curve, span. * *n* cupola, curve, dome; catacomb, cell, cellar, crypt, dungeon, tomb; depository, strongroom.
vault[2] *vb* bound, jump, leap, spring; tumble, turn. * *n* bound, leap, jump, spring.
vaunt *vb* advertise, boast, brag, display, exult, flaunt, flourish, parade.
veer *vb* change, shift, turn.
vegetate *vb* blossom, develop, flourish, flower, germinate, grow, shoot, sprout, swell; bask, hibernate, idle, stagnate.
vehemence *n* impetuosity, violence; ardour, eagerness, earnestness, enthusiasm, fervency, fervour, heat, keenness, passion, warmth, zeal; force, intensity.
vehement *adj* furious, high, hot, impetuous, passionate, rampant, violent; ardent, burning, eager, earnest, enthusiastic, fervid, fiery, keen, passionate, sanguine, zealous; forcible, mighty, powerful, strong.
veil *vb* cloak, conceal, cover, curtain, envelop, hide, invest, mask, screen, shroud. * *n* cover, curtain, film, shade, screen; blind, cloak, disguise, mask, muffler, visor.
vein *n* course, current, lode, seam, streak, stripe, thread, wave; bent, character, faculty, humour, mood, talent, turn.
velocity *n* acceleration, celerity, expedition, fleetness, haste, quickness, rapidity, speed, swiftness.
velvety *adj* delicate, downy, smooth, soft.
venal *adj* corrupt, mean, purchasable, sordid.
vend *vb* dispose, flog, hawk, retail, sell.
venerable *adj* grave, respected, revered, sage, wise; awful, dread, dreadful; aged, old, patriarchal.
venerate *vb* adore, esteem, honour, respect, revere.
veneration *n* adoration, devotion, esteem, respect, reverence, worship.
vengeance *n* retaliation, retribution, revenge.
venial *adj* allowed, excusable, pardonable, permitted, trivial.
venom *n* poison, virus; acerbity, acrimony, bitterness, gall, hate, ill-will, malevolence, malice, maliciousness, malignity, rancour, spite, virulence.
venomous *adj* deadly, poisonous, septic, toxic, virulent; caustic, malicious, malignant, mischievous, noxious, spiteful.
vent *vb* emit, express, release, utter. * *n* air hole, hole, mouth, opening, orifice; air pipe, air tube, aperture, blowhole, bunghole, hydrant, plug, spiracle, spout, tap, orifice; effusion, emission, escape, outlet, passage; discharge, expression, utterance.
ventilate *vb* aerate, air, freshen, oxygenate, purify; fan, winnow; canvass, comment, discuss, examine, publish, review, scrutinize.
venture *vb* adventure, dare, hazard, imperil, jeopardize, presume, risk, speculate, test, try, undertake. * *n* adventure, chance, hazard, jeopardy, peril, risk, speculation, stake.
venturesome *adj* adventurous, bold, courageous, daring, doughty, enterprising, fearless, foolhardy, intrepid, presumptuous, rash, venturous.
veracious *adj* reliable, straightforward, true, trustworthy, truthful; credible, genuine, honest, unfeigned.
veracity *n* accuracy, candour, correctness, credibility, exactness, fidelity, frankness, honesty, ingenuousness, probity, sincerity, trueness, truth, truthfulness.
verbal *adj* nuncupative, oral, spoken, unwritten.
verbose *adj* diffusive, long-winded, loquacious, talkative, wordy.
verdant *adj* fresh, green, verdure, verdurous; green, inexperienced, raw, unsophisticated.
verdict *n* answer, decision, finding, judgement, opinion, sentence.
verge *vb* bear, incline, lean, slope, tend; approach, border, skirt. * *n* mace, rod, staff; border, boundary, brink, confine, edge, extreme, limit, margin; edge, eve, point.
verification *n* authentication, attestation, confirmation, corroboration.
verify *vb* attest, authenticate, confirm, corroborate, prove, substantiate.
verily *adv* absolutely, actually, confidently, indeed, positively, really, truly.
verity *n* certainty, reality, truth, truthfulness.
vermicular *adj* convoluted, flexuose, flexuous, meandering, serpentine, sinuous, tortuous, twisting, undulating, waving, winding, wormish, wormlike.
vernacular *adj* common, indigenous, local, mother, native, vulgar. * *n* cant, dialect, jargon, patois, speech.
versatile *adj* capricious, changeable, erratic, mobile, variable; fickle, inconstant, mercurial, unsteady; adaptable, protean, plastic, varied.
versed *adj* able, accomplished, acquainted, clever,

conversant, practised, proficient, qualified, skilful, skilled, trained.
version *n* interpretation, reading, rendering, translation.
vertex *n* apex, crown, height, summit, top, zenith.
vertical *adj* erect, perpendicular, plumb, steep, upright.
vertiginous *adj* rotatory, rotary, whirling; dizzy, giddy.
vertigo *n* dizziness, giddiness.
verve *n* animation, ardour, energy, enthusiasm, force, rapture, spirit.
very *adv* absolutely, enormously, excessively, hugely, remarkably, surpassingly. * *adj* actual, exact, identical, precise, same; bare, mere, plain, pure, simple.
vesicle *n* bladder, blister, cell, cyst, follicle.
vest *vb* clothe, cover, dress, envelop; endow, furnish, invest. * *n* dress, garment, robe, vestment, vesture, waistcoat.
vestibule *n* anteroom, entrance hall, lobby, porch.
vestige *n* evidence, footprint, footstep, mark, record, relic, sign, token.
veteran *adj* adept, aged, experienced, disciplined, seasoned, old. * *n* campaigner, old soldier; master, past master, old-timer, old-stager.
veto *vb* ban, embargo, forbid, interdict, negate, prohibit. * *n* ban, embargo, interdict, prohibition, refusal.
vex *vb* annoy, badger, bother, chafe, cross, distress, gall, harass, harry, hector, molest, perplex, pester, plague, tease, torment, trouble, roil, spite, worry; affront, displease, fret, irk, irritate, nettle, offend, provoke; agitate, disquiet, disturb.
vexation *n* affliction, agitation, chagrin, discomfort, displeasure, disquiet, distress, grief, irritation, pique, sorrow, trouble; annoyance, curse, nuisance, plague, torment; damage, troubling, vexing.
vexed *adj* afflicted, agitated, annoyed, bothered, disquieted, harassed, irritated, perplexed, plagued, provoked, troubled, worried.
vibrate *vb* oscillate, sway, swing, undulate, wave; impinge, quiver, sound, thrill; fluctuate, hesitate, vacillate, waver.
vibration *n* nutation, oscillation, vibration.
vicarious *adj* commissioned, delegated, indirect, second-hand, substituted.
vice *n* blemish, defect, failing, fault, imperfection, infirmity; badness, corruption, depravation, depravity, error, evil, immorality, iniquity, laxity, obliquity, sin, viciousness, vileness, wickedness.
vicinity *n* nearness, proximity; locality, neighbourhood, vicinage.
vicious *adj* abandoned, atrocious, bad, corrupt, degenerate, demoralized, depraved, devilish, diabolical, evil, flagrant, hellish, immoral, iniquitous, mischievous, profligate, shameless, sinful, unprincipled, wicked; malicious, spiteful, venomous; foul, impure; debased, faulty; contrary, refractory.
viciousness *n* badness, corruption, depravity, immorality, profligacy.
vicissitude *n* alteration, interchange; change, fluctuation, mutation, revolution, variation.
victim *n* martyr, sacrifice, sufferer; prey; cat's-paw, cull, cully, dupe, gull, gudgeon, puppet.
victimize *vb* bamboozle, befool, beguile, cheat, circumvent, cozen, deceive, defraud, diddle, dupe, fool, gull, hoax, hoodwink, overreach, swindle, trick.
victor *n* champion, conqueror, vanquisher, winner.
victorious *adj* conquering, successful, triumphant, winning.
victory *n* achievement, conquest, mastery, triumph.
victuals *npl* comestibles, eatables, fare, food, meat, provisions, repast, sustenance, viands.
vie *vb* compete, contend, emulate, rival, strive.
view *vb* behold, contemplate, eye, inspect, scan, survey; consider, inspect, regard, study. * *n* inspection, observation, regard, sight; outlook, panorama, perspective, prospect, range, scene, survey, vista; aim, intent, intention, design, drift, object, purpose, scope; belief, conception, impression, idea, judgement, notion, opinion, sentiment, theory; appearance, aspect, show.
vigilance *n* alertness, attentiveness, carefulness, caution, circumspection, observance, watchfulness.
vigilant *adj* alert, attentive, careless, cautious, circumspect, unsleeping, wakeful, watchful.
vigorous *adj* lusty, powerful, strong; active, alert, cordial, energetic, forcible, strenuous, vehement, vivid, virile; brisk, hale, hardy, robust, sound, sturdy, healthy; fresh, flourishing; bold, emphatic, impassioned, lively, nervous, piquant, pointed, severe, sparkling, spirited, trenchant.
vigour *n* activity, efficacy, energy, force, might, potency, power, spirit, strength; bloom, elasticity, haleness, health, heartiness, pep, punch, robustness, soundness, thriftiness, tone, vim, vitality; enthusiasm, freshness, fire, intensity, liveliness, piquancy, strenuousness, vehemence, verve, raciness.
vile *adj* abject, base, beastly, beggarly, brutish, contemptible, despicable, disgusting, grovelling, ignoble, low, odious, paltry, pitiful, repulsive, scurvy, shabby, slavish, sorry, ugly; bad, evil, foul, gross, impure, iniquitous, lewd, obscene, sinful, vicious, wicked; cheap, mean, miserable, valueless, worthless.
vilify *vb* abuse, asperse, backbite, berate, blacken, blemish, brand, calumniate, decry, defame, disparage, lampoon, libel, malign, revile, scandalize, slander, slur, traduce, vituperate.
villain *n* blackguard, knave, miscreant, rascal, reprobate, rogue, ruffian, scamp, scapegrace, scoundrel.
villainous *adj* base, mean, vile; corrupt, depraved, knavish, unprincipled, wicked; atrocious, heinous, outrageous, sinful; mischievous, sorry.

vindicate *vb* defend, justify, uphold; advocate, avenge, assert, maintain, right, support.
vindication *n* apology, excuse, defence, justification.
vindictive *adj* avenging, grudgeful, implacable, malevolent, malicious, malignant, retaliative, revengeful, spiteful, unforgiving, unrelenting, vengeful.
violate *vb* hurt, injure; break, disobey, infringe, invade; desecrate, pollute, profane; abuse, debauch, defile, deflower, outrage, ravish, transgress.
violent *adj* boisterous, demented, forceful, forcible, frenzied, furious, high, hot, impetuous, insane, intense, stormy, tumultuous, turbulent, vehement, wild; fierce, fiery, fuming, heady, heavy, infuriate, passionate, obstreperous, strong, raging, rampant, rank, rapid, raving, refractory, roaring, rough, tearing, towering, ungovernable; accidental, unnatural; desperate, extreme, outrageous, unjust; acute, exquisite, poignant, sharp.
virago *n* amazon, brawler, fury, shrew, tartar, vixen.
virgin *adj* chaste, maidenly, modest, pure, undefiled, stainless, unpolluted, vestal, virginal; fresh, maiden, untouched, unused. * *n* celibate, damsel, girl, lass, maid, maiden.
virile *adj* forceful, manly, masculine, robust, vigorous.
virtual *adj* constructive, equivalent, essential, implicit, implied, indirect, practical, substantial.
virtue *n* chastity, goodness, grace, morality, purity; efficacy, excellence, honesty, integrity, justice, probity, quality, rectitude, worth.
virtuous *adj* blameless, equitable, exemplary, excellent, good, honest, moral, noble, righteous, upright, worthy; chaste, continent, immaculate, innocent, modest, pure, undefiled; efficacious, powerful.
virulent *adj* deadly, malignant, poisonous, toxic, venomous; acrid, acrimonious, bitter, caustic.
visage *n* aspect, countenance, face, guise, physiognomy, semblance.
viscera *n* bowels, entrails, guts, intestines.
viscous *adj* adhesive, clammy, glutinous, ropy, slimy, sticky, tenacious.
visible *adj* observable, perceivable, perceptible, seeable, visual; apparent, clear, conspicuous, discoverable, distinct, evident, manifest, noticeable, obvious, open, palpable, patent, plain, revealed, unhidden, unmistakable.
vision *n* eyesight, seeing, sight; eyeshot, ken; apparition, chimera, dream, ghost, hallucination, illusion, phantom, spectre.
visionary *adj* imaginative, impractical, quixotic, romantic; chimerical, dreamy, fancied, fanciful, fantastic, ideal, illusory, imaginary, romantic, shadowy, unsubstantial, utopian, wild. * *n* dreamer, enthusiast, fanatic, idealist, optimist, theorist, zealot.
vital *adj* basic, cardinal, essential, indispensable, necessary, needful; animate, alive, existing, life-giving, living; paramount.
vitality *n* animation, life, strength, vigour, virility.
vitiate *vb* adulterate, contaminate, corrupt, debase, defile, degrade, deprave, deteriorate, impair, infect, injure, invalidate, poison, pollute, spoil.
vitiation *n* adulteration, corruption, degeneracy, degeneration, degradation, depravation, deterioration, impairment, injury, invalidation, perversion, pollution, prostitution.
vituperate *vb* abuse, berate, blame, censure, denounce, overwhelm, rate, revile, scold, upbraid, vilify.
vituperation *n* abuse, blame, censure, invective, reproach, railing, reviling, scolding, upbraiding.
vivacious *adj* active, animated, breezy, brisk, buxom, cheerful, frolicsome, gay, jocund, light-hearted, lively, merry, mirthful, spirited, sportive, sprightly.
vivacity *n* animation, cheer, cheerfulness, gaiety, liveliness, sprightliness.
vivid *adj* active, animated, bright, brilliant, clear, intense, fresh, lively, living, lucid, quick, sprightly, strong; expressive, graphic, striking, telling.
vivify *vb* animate, arouse, awake, quicken, vitalize.
vixen *n* brawler, scold, shrew, spitfire, tartar, virago.
vocabulary *n* dictionary, glossary, lexicon, word-book; language, terms, words.
vocation *n* call, citation, injunction, summons; business, calling, employment, occupation, profession, pursuit, trade.
vociferate *vb* bawl, bellow, clamour, cry, exclaim, rant, shout, yell.
vociferous *adj* blatant, clamorous, loud, noisy, obstreperous, ranting, stunning, uproarious.
vogue *adj* fashionable, modish, stylish, trendy. * *n* custom, fashion, favour, mode, practice, repute, style, usage, way.
voice *vb* declare, express, say, utter. * *n* speech, tongue, utterance; noise, notes, sound; opinion, option, preference, suffrage, vote; accent, articulation, enunciation, inflection, intonation, modulation, pronunciation, tone; expression, language, words.
void *vb* clear, eject, emit, empty, evacuate. * *adj* blank, empty, hollow, vacant; clear, destitute, devoid, free, lacking, wanting, without; inept, ineffectual, invalid, nugatory, null; imaginary, unreal, vain. * *n* abyss, blank, chasm, emptiness, hole, vacuum.
volatile *adj* gaseous, incoercible; airy, buoyant, frivolous, gay, jolly, lively, sprightly, vivacious; capricious, changeable, fickle, flighty, flyaway, giddy, harebrained, inconstant, light-headed, mercurial, reckless, unsteady, whimsical, wild.
volition *n* choice, determination, discretion, option, preference, will.
volley *n* fusillade, round, salvo; blast, burst, discharge, emission, explosion, outbreak, report, shower, storm.

voluble *adj* fluent, garrulous, glib, loquacious, talkative.
volume *n* book, tome; amplitude, body, bulk, compass, dimension, size, substance, vastness; fullness, power, quantity.
voluminous *adj* ample, big, bulky, full, great, large; copious, diffuse, discursive, flowing.
voluntary *adj* free, spontaneous, unasked, unbidden, unforced; deliberate, designed, intended, purposed; discretionary, optional, willing.
volunteer *vb* offer, present, proffer, propose, tender.
voluptuary *n* epicure, hedonist, sensualist.
voluptuous *adj* carnal, effeminate, epicurean, fleshy, licentious, luxurious, sensual, sybaritic.
vomit *vb* discharge, eject, emit, puke, regurgitate, spew, throw up.
voracious *adj* devouring, edacious, greedy, hungry, rapacious, ravenous.
vortex *n* eddy, maelstrom, whirl, whirlpool.
votary *adj* devoted, promised. * *n* adherent, devotee, enthusiast, follower, supporter, votarist, zealot.
vote *vb* ballot, elect, opt, return; judge, pronounce, propose, suggest. * *n* ballot, franchise, poll, referendum, suffrage, voice.
vouch *vb* affirm, asseverate, attest, aver, declare, guarantee, support, uphold, verify, warrant.
vouchsafe *vb* accord, cede, deign, grant, stoop, yield.
vow *vb* consecrate, dedicate, devote; asseverate. * *n* oath, pledge, promise.
voyage *vb* cruise, journey, navigate, ply, sail. * *n* crossing, cruise, excursion, journey, passage, sail, trip.
vulgar *adj* base-born, common, ignoble, lowly, plebeian; boorish, cheap, coarse, discourteous, flashy, homespun, garish, gaudy, ill-bred, inelegant, loud, rustic, showy, tawdry, uncultivated, unrefined; general, ordinary, popular, public; base, broad, loose, low, gross, mean, ribald, vile; inelegant, unauthorized.
vulgarity *n* baseness, coarseness, grossness, meanness, rudeness.
vulnerable *adj* accessible, assailable, defenceless, exposed, weak.

W

waddle *vb* toddle, toggle, waggle, wiggle, wobble.
waft *vb* bear, carry, convey, float, transmit, transport. * *n* breath, breeze, draught, puff.
wag[1] *vb* shake, sway, waggle; oscillate, vibrate, waver; advance, move, progress, stir. * *n* flutter, nod, oscillation, vibration.
wag[2] *n* humorist, jester, joker, wit.
wage *vb* bet, hazard, lay, stake, wager; conduct, undertake.
wager *vb* back, bet, gamble, lay, pledge, risk, stake. * *n* bet, gamble, pledge, risk, stake.
wages *npl* allowance, compensation, earnings, emolument, hire, pay, payment, remuneration, salary, stipend.
waggish *adj* frolicsome, gamesome, mischievous, roguish, tricksy; comical, droll, facetious, funny, humorous, jocular, jocose, merry, sportive.
wagon *n* cart, lorry, truck, van, waggon, wain.
wail *vb* bemoan, deplore, lament, mourn; cry, howl, weep. * *n* complaint, cry, lamentation, moan, wailing.
waist *n* bodice, corsage, waistline.
wait *vb* delay, linger, pause, remain, rest, stay, tarry; attend, minister, serve; abide, await, expect, look for. * *n* delay, halt, holdup, pause, respite, rest, stay, stop.
waiter, waitress *n* attendant, lackey, servant, servitor, steward, valet.
waive *vb* defer, forgo, surrender, relinquish, remit, renounce; desert, reject.
wake[1] *vb* arise, awake, awaken; activate, animate, arouse, awaken, excite, kindle, provoke, stimulate. * *n* vigil, watch, watching.
wake[2] *n* course, path, rear, track, trail, wash.
wakeful *adj* awake, sleepless, restless; alert, observant, vigilant, wary, watchful.
wale *n* ridge, streak, stripe, welt, whelk.
walk *vb* advance, depart, go, march, move, pace, saunter, step, stride, stroll, tramp. * *n* amble, carriage, gait, step; beat, career, course, department, field, province; conduct, procedure; alley, avenue, cloister, esplanade, footpath, path, pathway, pavement, promenade, range, sidewalk, way; constitutional, excursion, hike, ramble, saunter, stroll, tramp, turn.
wall *n* escarp, parapet, plane, upright.
wallet *n* bag, knapsack, pocketbook, purse, sack.
wan *adj* ashen, bloodless, cadaverous, colourless, haggard, pale, pallid.
wand *n* baton, mace, truncheon, sceptre.
wander *vb* forage, prowl, ramble, range, roam, rove, stroll; deviate, digress, straggle, stray; moon, rave. * *n* amble, cruise, excursion, ramble, stroll.
wane *vb* abate, decrease, ebb, subside; decline, fail, sink. * *n* decrease, diminution, lessening; decay, declension, decline, failure.
want *vb* crave, desire, need, require, wish; fail, lack, neglect, omit. * *n* absence, defect, default, deficiency, lack; defectiveness, failure, inadequacy, insufficiency, meagreness, paucity, poverty, scantiness, scarcity, shortness; requirement; craving, desire, longing, wish; destitution, distress, indigence, necessity, need, penury, poverty, privation, straits.
wanton *vb* caper, disport, frisk, frolic, play, revel, romp, sport; dally, flirt, toy, trifle. * *adj* free, loose, unchecked, unrestrained, wandering; abounding, exuberant, luxuriant, overgrown, rampant; airy, capricious, coltish, frisky, playful, skittish, sportive; dissolute, irregular, licentious, loose; carnal, immoral, incontinent, lascivious, lecherous, lewd, libidinous, light, lustful, prurient, salacious, unchaste; careless, gratuitous, groundless, heedless, inconsiderate, needless, perverse, reckless, wayward, wilful. * *n* baggage, flirt, harlot, light-o'-love, prostitute, rake, roué, slut, whore.
war *vb* battle, campaign, combat, contend, crusade, engage, fight, strive. * *n* contention, enmity, hostility, strife, warfare.
warble *vb* sing, trill, yodel. * *n* carol, chant, hymn, hum.
ward *vb* guard, watch; defend, fend, parry, protect, repel. * *n* care, charge, guard, guardianship, watch; defender, guardian, keeper, protector, warden; custody; defence, garrison, protection; minor, pupil; district, division, precinct, quarter; apartment, cubicle.
warehouse *n* depot, magazine, repository, store, storehouse.
wares *npl* commodities, goods, merchandise, movables.
warfare *n* battle, conflict, contest, discord, engagement, fray, hostilities, strife, struggle, war.
warily *adv* carefully, cautiously, charily, circumspectly, heedfully, watchfully, vigilantly.
wariness *n* care, caution, circumspection, foresight, thought, vigilance.
warlike *adj* bellicose, belligerent, combative,

hostile, inimical, martial, military, soldierly, watchful.

warm *vb* heat, roast, toast; animate, chafe, excite, rouse. * *adj* lukewarm, tepid; genial, mild, pleasant, sunny; close, muggy, oppressive; affectionate, ardent, cordial, eager, earnest, enthusiastic, fervent, fervid, glowing, hearty, hot, zealous; excited, fiery, flushed, furious, hasty, keen, lively, passionate, quick, vehement, violent.

warmth *n* glow, tepidity; ardour, fervency, fervour, zeal; animation, cordiality, eagerness, earnestness, enthusiasm, excitement, fervency, fever, fire, flush, heat, intensity, passion, spirit, vehemence.

warn *vb* caution, forewarn; admonish, advise; apprise, inform, notify; bid, call, summon.

warning *adj* admonitory, cautionary, cautioning, monitory. * *n* admonition, advice, caveat, caution, monition; information, notice; augury, indication, intimation, omen, portent, presage, prognostic, sign, symptom; call, summons; example, lesson, sample.

warp *vb* bend, bias, contort, deviate, distort, pervert, swerve, turn, twist. * *n* bent, bias, cast, crook, distortion, inclination, leaning, quirk, sheer, skew, slant, slew, swerve, twist, turn.

warrant *vb* answer for, certify, guarantee, secure; affirm, assure, attest, avouch, declare, justify, state; authorize, justify, license, maintain, sanction, support, sustain, uphold. * *n* guarantee, pledge, security, surety, warranty; authentication, authority, commission, verification; order, pass, permit, summons, subpoena, voucher, writ.

warrantable *adj* admissible, allowable, defensible, justifiable, lawful, permissible, proper, right, vindicable.

warrior *n* champion, captain, fighter, hero, soldier.

wary *adj* careful, cautious, chary, circumspect, discreet, guarded, heedful, prudent, scrupulous, vigilant, watchful.

wash *vb* purify, purge; moisten, wet; bathe, clean, flush, irrigate, lap, lave, rinse, sluice; colour, stain, tint. * *n* ablution, bathing, cleansing, lavation, washing; bog, fen, marsh, swamp, quagmire; bath, embrocation, lotion; laundry, washing.

washy *adj* damp, diluted, moist, oozy, sloppy, thin, watery, weak; feeble, jejune, pointless, poor, spiritless, trashy, trumpery, unmeaning, vapid, worthless.

waspish *adj* choleric, fretful, irascible, irritable, peevish, petulant, snappish, testy, touchy; slender, slim, small-waisted.

waste *vb* consume, corrode, decrease, diminish, emaciate, wear; absorb, deplete, devour, dissipate, drain, empty, exhaust, expend, lavish, lose, misspend, misuse, scatter, spend, squander; demolish, desolate, destroy, devastate, devour, dilapidate, harry, pillage, plunder, ravage, ruin, scour, strip; damage, impair, injure; decay, dwindle, perish, wither. * *adj* bare, desolated, destroyed, devastated, empty, ravaged, ruined, spoiled, stripped, void; dismal, dreary, forlorn; abandoned, bare, barren, uncultivated, unimproved, uninhabited, untilled, wild; useless, valueless, worthless; exuberant, superfluous. * *n* consumption, decrement, diminution, dissipation, exhaustion, expenditure, loss, wasting; destruction, dispersion, extravagance, loss, squandering, wanton; decay, desolation, destruction, devastation, havoc, pillage, ravage, ruin; chaff, debris, detritus, dross, excrement, husks, junk, matter, offal, refuse, rubbish, trash, wastrel, worthlessness; barrenness, desert, expanse, solitude, wild, wilderness.

wasteful *adj* destructive, ruinous; extravagant, improvident, lavish, prodigal, profuse, squandering, thriftless, unthrifty.

watch *vb* attend, guard, keep, oversee, protect, superintend, tend; eye, mark, observe. * *n* espial, guard, outlook, wakefulness, watchfulness, watching, vigil, ward; alertness, attention, inspection, observation, surveillance; guard, picket, sentinel, sentry, watchman; pocket watch, ticker, timepiece, wristwatch.

watchful *adj* alert, attentive, awake, careful, circumspect, guarded, heedful, observant, vigilant, wakeful, wary.

watchword *n* catchword, cry, motto, password, shibboleth, word.

waterfall *n* cascade, cataract, fall, linn.

watery *adj* diluted, thin, waterish, weak; insipid, spiritless, tasteful, vapid; moist, wet.

wave *vb* float, flutter, heave, shake, sway, undulate, wallow; brandish, flaunt, flourish, swing; beckon, signal. * *n* billow, bore, breaker, flood, flush, ripple, roll, surge, swell, tide, undulation; flourish, gesture, sway; convolution, curl, roll, unevenness.

waver *vb* flicker, float, undulate, wave; reel, totter; falter, fluctuate, flutter, hesitate, oscillate, quiver, vacillate.

wax *vb* become, grow, increase, mount, rise.

way *n* advance, journey, march, progression, transit, trend; access, alley, artery, avenue, beat, channel, course, highroad, highway, passage, path, road, route, street, track, trail; fashion, manner, means, method, mode, system; distance, interval, space, stretch; behaviour, custom, form, guise, habit, habitude, practice, process, style, usage; device, plan, scheme.

wayfarer *n* itinerant, nomad, passenger, pilgrim, rambler, traveller, walker, wanderer.

wayward *adj* capricious, captious, contrary, forward, headstrong, intractable, obstinate, perverse, refractory, stubborn, unruly, wilful.

weak *adj* debilitated, delicate, enfeebled, enervated, exhausted, faint, feeble, fragile, frail, infirm, invalid, languid, languishing, shaky, sickly, spent, strengthless, tender, unhealthy, unsound, wasted, weakly; accessible, defenceless, unprotected, vulnerable; light, soft, unstressed; boneless, cowardly, infirm; compliant, irresolute, pliable, pliant, undecided, undetermined, unsettled, unstable, unsteady, vacillating, wavering, yielding; childish, foolish, imbecile, senseless, shallow, silly, simple, stupid, weak-minded, witless; erring, foolish, indiscreet, injudicious, unwise; gentle, indistinct, low, small; adulterated, attenuated, diluted, insipid, tasteless, thin, watery; flimsy, frivolous, poor, sleazy, slight, trifling; futile, illogical, inconclusive, ineffective, ineffectual, inefficient, lame, unconvincing, unsatisfactory, unsupported, unsustained, vague, vain; unsafe, unsound, unsubstantial, untrustworthy; helpless, impotent, powerless; breakable, brittle, delicate, frangible; inconsiderable, puny, slender, slight, small.

weaken *vb* cramp, cripple, debilitate, devitalize, enervate, enfeeble, invalidate, relax, sap, shake, stagger, undermine, unman, unnerve, unstring; adulterate, attenuate, debase, depress, dilute, exhaust, impair, impoverish, lessen, lower, reduce.

weakness *n* debility, feebleness, fragility, frailty, infirmity, languor, softness; defect, failing, fault, flaw; fondness, inclination, liking.

weal *n* advantage, good, happiness, interest, profit, utility, prosperity, welfare; ridge, streak, stripe.

wealth *n* assets, capital, cash, fortune, funds, goods, money, possessions, property, riches, treasure; abundance, affluence, opulence, plenty, profusion.

wean *vb* alienate, detach, disengage, withdraw.

wear *vb* bear, carry, don; endure, last; consume, impair, rub, use, waste. * *n* corrosion, deterioration, disintegration, erosion, wear and tear; consumption, use; apparel, array, attire, clothes, clothing, dress, garb, gear.

wearied *adj* apathetic, bored, exhausted, fagged, fatigued, jaded, tired, weary, worn.

weariness *n* apathy, boredom, ennui, exhaustion, fatigue, languor, lassitude, monotony, prostration, sameness, tedium.

wearisome *adj* annoying, boring, dull, exhausting, fatiguing, humdrum, irksome, monotonous, prolix, prosaic, slow, tedious, tiresome, troublesome, trying, uninteresting, vexatious.

weary *vb* debilitate, exhaust, fag, fatigue, harass, jade, tire. * *adj* apathetic, bored, drowsy, exhausted, jaded, spent, tired, worn; irksome, tiresome, wearisome.

weave *vb* braid, entwine, interlace, lace, mat, plait, pleat, twine; compose, construct, fabricate, make.

wed *vb* contract, couple, espouse, marry, unite.

wedding *n* bridal, espousal, marriage, nuptials.

wedlock *n* marriage, matrimony.

ween *vb* fancy, imagine, suppose, think.

weep *vb* bemoan, bewail, complain, cry, lament, sob.

weigh *vb* balance, counterbalance, lift, raise; consider, deliberate, esteem, examine, study.

weight *vb* ballast, burden, fill, freight, load; weigh. * *n* gravity, heaviness, heft, tonnage; burden, load, pressure; consequence, efficacy, emphasis, importance, impressiveness, influence, moment, pith, power, significance, value.

weighty *adj* heavy, massive, onerous, ponderous, unwieldy; considerable, efficacious, forcible, grave, important, influential, serious, significant.

weird *adj* eerie, ghostly, strange, supernatural, uncanny, unearthly, witching.

welcome *vb* embrace, greet, hail, receive. * *adj* acceptable, agreeable, grateful, gratifying, pleasant, pleasing, satisfying. * *n* greeting, reception, salutation.

welfare *n* advantage, affluence, benefit, happiness, profit, prosperity, success, thrift, weal, wellbeing.

well[1] *vb* flow, gush, issue, jet, pour, spring. * *n* fount, fountain, reservoir, spring, wellhead, wellspring; origin, source; hole, pit, shaft.

well[2] *adj* hale, healthy, hearty, sound; fortunate, good, happy, profitable, satisfactory, useful. * *adv* accurately, adequately, correctly, efficiently, properly, suitably; abundantly, considerably, fully, thoroughly; agreeably, commendably, favourably, worthily.

wellbeing *n* comfort, good, happiness, health, prosperity, welfare.

welter *vb* flounder, roll, toss, wallow. * *n* confusion, jumble, mess.

wet *vb* dabble, damp, dampen, dip, drench, moisten, saturate, soak, sprinkle, water. * *adj* clammy, damp, dank, dewy, dripping, humid, moist; rainy, showery, sprinkly. * *n* dampness, humidity, moisture, wetness.

whack *vb, n* bang, beat, rap, strike, thrash, thump, thwack.

wharf *n* dock, pier, quay.

wheedle *vb* cajole, coax, flatter, inveigle, lure.

wheel *vb* gyrate, revolve, roll, rotate, spin, swing, turn, twist, whirl, wind. * *n* circle, revolution, roll, rotation, spin, turn, twirl.

whet *vb* grind, sharpen; arouse, awaken, excite, provoke, rouse, stimulate; animate, inspire, kindle, quicken, warm.

whiff *vb, n* blast, gust, puff.

whim *n* caprice, crotchet, fancy, freak, frolic, humour, notion, quirk, sport, vagary, whimsy, wish.

whimsical *adj* capricious, crotchety, eccentric, erratic, fanciful, frolicsome, odd, peculiar, quaint, singular.

whine *vb* cry, grumble, mewl, moan, snivel, wail, whimper. * *n* complaint, cry, grumble, moan, sob, wail, whimper.

whip *vb* beat, lash, strike; flagellate, flog, goad, horsewhip, scourge, slash; hurt, sting; jerk, snap, snatch, whisk. * *n* bullwhip, cane, crop, horsewhip, knout, lash, scourge, switch, thong.

whipping *n* beating, castigation, dusting, flagellation, flogging, thrashing.
whirl *vb* gyrate, pirouette, roll, revolve, rotate, turn, twirl, twist, wheel. * *n* eddy, flurry, flutter, gyration, rotation, spin, swirl, twirl, vortex.
whit *n* atom, bit, grain, iota, jot, mite, particle, scrap, speck, tittle.
white *adj* argent, canescent, chalky, frosty, hoary, ivory, milky, silver, snowy; grey, pale, pallid, wan; candid, clean, chaste, immaculate, innocent, pure, spotless, unblemished.
whole *adj* all, complete, entire, intact, integral, total, undivided; faultless, firm, good, perfect, strong, unbroken, undivided, uninjured; healthy, sound, well. * *adv* entire, in one. * *n* aggregate, all, amount, ensemble, entirety, gross, sum, total, totality.
wholesome *adj* healthy, healthful, invigorating, nourishing, nutritious, salubrious, salutary; beneficial, good, helpful, improving, salutary; fresh, sound, sweet.
wholly *adv* altogether, completely, entirely, fully, totally, utterly.
whoop *vb* halloo, hoot, roar, shout, yell. * *n* bellow, hoot, roar, shout, yell.
whore *n* bawd, courtesan, drab, harlot, prostitute, streetwalker, strumpet.
wicked *adj* abandoned, abominable, depraved, devilish, godless, graceless, immoral, impious, infamous, irreligious, irreverent, profane, sinful, ungodly, unholy, unprincipled, unrighteous, vicious, vile, worthless; atrocious, bad, black, criminal, dark, evil, heinous, ill, iniquitous, monstrous, nefarious, unjust, villainous.
wide *adj* ample, broad, capacious, comprehensive, distended, expanded, large, spacious, vast; distant, remote; prevalent, rife, widespread. * *adv* completely, farthest, fully.
wield *vb* brandish, flourish, handle, manipulate, ply, work; control, manage, sway, use.
wild *adj* feral, undomesticated, untamed; desert, desolate, native, rough, rude, uncultivated; barbarous, ferocious, fierce, savage, uncivilized; dense, luxuriant, rank; disorderly, distracted, frantic, frenzied, furious, impetuous, irregular, mad, outrageous, raving, turbulent, ungoverned, uncontrolled, violent; dissipated, fast, flighty, foolish, giddy, harebrained, heedless, ill-advised, inconsiderate, reckless, thoughtless, unwise; boisterous, rough, stormy; crazy, extravagant, fanciful, grotesque, imaginary, strange. * *n* desert, waste, wilderness.
wilderness *n* desert, waste, wild.
wilful *adj* cantankerous, contumacious, dogged, headstrong, heady, inflexible, intractable, mulish, obdurate, obstinate, perverse, pig-headed, refractory, self-willed, stubborn, unruly, unyielding; arbitrary, capricious; deliberate, intended, intentional, planned, premeditated.
will *vb* bid, command, decree, direct, enjoin, ordain; choose, desire, elect, wish; bequeath, convey, demise, devise, leave. * *n* decision, determination, resoluteness, resolution, self-reliance; desire, disposition, inclination, intent, pleasure, purpose, volition, wish; behest, command, decree, demand, direction, order, request, requirement.
willing *adj* adaptable, amenable, compliant, desirous, disposed, inclined, minded; deliberate, free, intentional, spontaneous, unasked, unbidden, voluntary; cordial, eager, forward, prompt, ready.
willingly *adv* cheerfully, gladly, readily, spontaneously, voluntarily.
wily *adj* arch, artful, crafty, crooked, cunning, deceitful, designing, diplomatic, foxy, insidious, intriguing, politic, sly, subtle, treacherous, tricky.
win *vb* accomplish, achieve, acquire, catch, earn, effect, gain, gather, get, make, obtain, procure, reach, realize, reclaim, recover; gain, succeed, surpass, triumph; arrive; allure, attract, convince, influence, persuade. * *n* conquest, success, triumph, victory.
wind[1] *n* air, blast, breeze, draught, gust, hurricane, whiff, zephyr; breath, breathing, expiration, inspiration, respiration; flatulence, gas, windiness.
wind[2] *vb* coil, crank, encircle, involve, reel, roll, turn, twine, twist; bend, curve, meander, zigzag. * *n* bend, curve, meander, twist, zigzag.
winding *adj* circuitous, devious, flexuose, flexuous, meandering, serpentine, tortuous, turning, twisting. * *n* bend, curve, meander, turn, twist.
windy *adj* breezy, blowy, blustering, boisterous, draughty, gusty, squally, stormy, tempestuous; airy, empty, hollow, inflated. **winning** *adj* alluring, attractive, bewitching, brilliant, captivating, charming, dazzling, delightful, enchanting, engaging, fascinating, lovely, persuasive, pleasing, prepossessing; conquering, triumphant, victorious.
winnow *vb* cull, glean, divide, fan, part, select, separate, sift.
winsome *adj* blithe, blithesome, bonny, buoyant, charming, cheerful, debonair, jocund, lighthearted, lively, lovable, merry, pleasant, sportive, winning.
wintry *adj* arctic, boreal, brumal, cold, frosty, icy, snowy.
wipe *vb* clean, dry, mop, rub. * *n* mop, rub, blow, hit, strike; gibe, jeer, sarcasm, sneer, taunt.
wisdom *n* depth, discernment, far-sightedness, foresight, insight, judgement, judiciousness, prescience, profundity, prudence, sagacity, sapience, sense, solidity, understanding, wiseness; attainment, edification, enlightenment, erudition, information, knowledge, learning, lore, scholarship; reason.
wise *adj* deep, discerning, enlightened, intelligent, judicious, penetrating, philosophical, profound, rational, seasonable, sensible, sage, sapient, solid, sound; erudite, informed, knowing,

learned, scholarly; crafty, cunning, designing, foxy, politic, sly, subtle, wary, wily.

wish *vb* covet, desire, hanker, list, long; bid, command, desire, direct, intend, mean, order, want. * *n* behest, desire, intention, mind, pleasure, want, will; craving, desire, hankering, inclination, liking, longing, want, yearning.

wistful *adj* contemplative, engrossed, meditative, musing, pensive, reflective, thoughtful; desirous, eager, earnest, longing.

wit *n* genius, intellect, intelligence, reason, sense, understanding; brightness, banter, cleverness, drollery, facetiousness, fun, humour, jocularity, piquancy, point, raillery, satire, sparkle, whim; conceit, epigram, jest, joke, pleasantry, quip, quirk, repartee, sally, witticism; humorist, joker, wag.

witch *n* charmer, enchantress, fascinator, sorceress; crone, hag, sibyl.

witchcraft *n* conjuration, enchantment, magic, necromancy, sorcery, spell.

withdraw *vb* abstract, deduct, remove, retire, separate, sequester, sequestrate, subduct, subtract; disengage, wean; abjure, recall, recant, relinquish, resign, retract, revoke; abdicate, decamp, depart, dissociate, retire, shrink, vacate.

wither *vb* contract, droop, dry, sear, shrivel, wilt, wizen; decay, decline, languish, pine, waste.

withhold *vb* check, detain, hinder, repress, restrain, retain, suppress.

withstand *vb* confront, defy, face, oppose, resist.

witless *adj* daft, dull, foolish, halfwitted, obtuse, senseless, shallow, silly, stupid, unintelligent.

witness *vb* corroborate, mark, note, notice, observe, see. * *n* attestation, conformation, corroboration, evidence, proof, testimony; beholder, bystander, corroborator, deponent, eyewitness, onlooker, spectator, testifier.

witty *adj* bright, clever, droll, facetious, funny, humorous, jocose, jocular, pleasant, waggish; alert, penetrating, quick, sparkling, sprightly.

wizard *n* charmer, diviner, conjurer, enchanter, magician, necromancer, seer, soothsayer, sorcerer.

woe *n* affliction, agony, anguish, bitterness, depression, distress, dole, grief, heartache, melancholy, misery, sorrow, torture, tribulation, trouble, unhappiness, wretchedness.

woeful *adj* afflicted, agonized, anguished, burdened, disconsolate, distressed, melancholy, miserable, mournful, piteous, sad, sorrowful, troubled, unhappy, wretched; afflicting, afflictive, calamitous, deplorable, depressing, disastrous, distressing, dreadful, tragic, tragical, grievous, lamentable, pitiable, saddening.

wonder *vb* admire, gape, marvel; conjecture, ponder, query, question, speculate. * *n* amazement, astonishment, awe, bewilderment, curiosity, marvel, miracle, prodigy, surprise, stupefaction, wonderment.

wonderful *adj* amazing, astonishing, astounding, awe-inspiring, awesome, awful, extraordinary, marvellous, miraculous, portentous, prodigious, startling, stupendous, surprising.

wont *adj* accustomed, customary, familiar, habitual, ordinary, usual. * *n* custom, habit, practice, rule, usage.

wonted *adj* accustomed, common, conventional, customary, everyday, familiar, frequent, habitual, ordinary, regular, usual.

wood *n* coppice, copse, covert, forest, greenwood, grove, spinney, thicket, woodland.

word *vb* express, phrase, put, say, state, term, utter. * *n* expression, name, phrase, term, utterance; account, advice, information, intelligence, message, news, report, tidings; affirmation, assertion, averment, avowal, declaration, statement; conversation, speech; agreement, assurance, engagement, parole, pledge, plight, promise; behest, bidding, command, direction, order, precept; countersign, password, signal, watchword.

wordy *adj* circumlocutory, diffuse, garrulous, inflated, lengthened, long-winded, loquacious, periphrastic, rambling, talkative, tedious, verbose, windy.

work *vb* act, operate; drudge, fag, grind, grub, labour, slave, sweat, toil; move, perform, succeed; aim, attempt, strive, try; effervesce, ferment, leaven, rise; accomplish, beget, cause, effect, engender, manage, originate, produce; exert, strain; embroider, stitch. * *n* exertion, drudgery, grind, labour, pain, toil; business, employment, function, occupation, task; action, accomplishment, achievement, composition, deed, feat, fruit, handiwork, opus, performance, product, production; fabric, manufacture; ferment, leaven; management, treatment.

workman *n* journeyman, employee, labourer, operative, worker, wright; artisan, craftsman, mechanic.

world *n* cosmos, creation, earth, globe, nature, planet, sphere, universe.

worldly *adj* common, earthly, human, mundane, sublunary, terrestrial; carnal, fleshly, profane, secular, temporal; ambitious, grovelling, irreligious, selfish, proud, sordid, unsanctified, unspiritual; sophisticated, worldly-wise.

worry *vb* annoy, badger, bait, beset, bore, bother, chafe, disquiet, disturb, fret, gall, harass, harry, hector, infest, irritate, molest, persecute, pester, plague, tease, torment, trouble, vex. * *n* annoyance, anxiety, apprehensiveness, care, concern, disquiet, fear, misgiving, perplexity, solicitude, trouble, uneasiness, vexation.

worship *vb* adore, esteem, honour, revere, venerate; deify, idolize; aspire, pray. * *n* adoration, devotion, esteem, homage, idolatry, idolizing, respect, reverence; aspiration, exultation, invocation, laud, praise, prayer, supplication.

worst *vb* beat, choke, conquer, crush, defeat, discomfit, foil, master, overpower, overthrow, quell, rout, subdue, subjugate, vanquish.

worth *n* account, character, credit, desert, excellence, importance, integrity, merit, nobleness, worthiness, virtue; cost, estimation, price, value.

worthless *adj* futile, meritless, miserable, nugatory, paltry, poor, trifling, unproductive, unsalable, unserviceable, useless, valueless, wretched; abject, base, corrupt, degraded, ignoble, low, mean, vile.

worthy *adj* deserving, fit, suitable; estimable, excellent, exemplary, good, honest, honourable, reputable, righteous, upright, virtuous. * *n* celebrity, dignitary, luminary, notability, personage, somebody, VIP.

wound *vb* damage, harm, hurt, injure; cut, gall, harrow, irritate, lacerate, pain, prick, stab; annoy, mortify, offend. * *n* blow, hurt, injury; damage, detriment; anguish, grief, pain, pang, torture.

wraith *n* apparition, ghost, phantom, spectre, vision.

wrangle *vb* argue, bicker, brawl, cavil, dispute, jangle, jar, quarrel, squabble, spar, spat. * *n* altercation, argument, bickering, brawl, contest, controversy, jar, quarrel, squabble.

wrap *vb* cloak, cover, encase, envelop, muffle, swathe, wind. * *n* blanket, cape, cloak, cover, overcoat, shawl.

wrath *n* anger, choler, exasperation, fury, heat, resentment, indignation, ire, irritation, offence, passion, rage.

wrathful *adj* angry, enraged, exasperated, furious, hot, indignant, infuriated, irate, mad, passionate, provoked, rageful.

wreak *vb* execute, exercise, indulge, inflict, work.

wreath *n* chaplet, curl, festoon, garland, ring, twine.

wreathe *vb* encircle, festoon, garland, intertwine, surround, twine, twist.

wreck *vb* founder, shipwreck, strand; blast, blight, break, devastate, ruin, spoil. * *n* crash, desolation, destruction, perdition, prostration, ruin, shipwreck, smash, undoing.

wrench *vb* distort, pervert, twist, wrest, wring; sprain, strain; extort, extract. * *n* twist, wring; sprain, strain; monkey wrench, spanner.

wrest *vb* force, pull, strain, twist, wrench, wring.

wrestle *vb* contend, contest, grapple, strive, struggle.

wretch *n* outcast, pariah, pilgarlic, troglodyte, vagabond, victim, sufferer; beggar, criminal, hound, knave, miscreant, rascal, ruffian, rogue, scoundrel, villain.

wretched *adj* afflicted, comfortless, distressed, forlorn, sad, unfortunate, unhappy, woebegone; afflicting, calamitous, deplorable, depressing, pitiable, sad, saddening, shocking, sorrowful; bad, beggarly, contemptible, mean, paltry, pitiful, poor, shabby, sorry, vile, worthless.

wring *vb* contort, twist, wrench; extort, force, wrest; anguish, distress, harass, pain, rack, torture.

wrinkle[1] *vb* cockle, corrugate, crease, gather, pucker, rumple. * *n* cockle, corrugation, crease, crimp, crinkle, crumple, fold, furrow, gather, plait, ridge, rumple.

wrinkle[2] *n* caprice, fancy, notion, quirk, whim; device, tip, trick.

writ *n* decree, order, subpoena, summons.

write *vb* compose, copy, indite, inscribe, pen, scrawl, scribble, transcribe.

writer *n* amanuensis, author, clerk, penman, scribe, secretary.

writhe *vb* contort, distort, squirm, twist, wriggle.

written *adj* composed, indited, inscribed, penned, transcribed.

wrong *vb* abuse, encroach, injure, maltreat, oppress. * *adj* inequitable, unfair, unjust, wrongful; bad, criminal, evil, guilty, immoral, improper, iniquitous, reprehensible, sinful, vicious, wicked; amiss, improper, inappropriate, unfit, unsuitable; erroneous, false, faulty, inaccurate, incorrect, mistaken, untrue. * *adv* amiss, erroneously, falsely, faultily, improperly, inaccurately, incorrectly, wrongly. * *n* foul, grievance, inequity, injury, injustice, trespass, unfairness; blame, crime, dishonesty, evil, guilt, immorality, iniquity, misdeed, misdoing, sin, transgression, unrighteousness, vice, wickedness, wrongdoing; error, falsity.

wroth *adj* angry, enraged, exasperated, furious, incensed, indignant, irate, passionate, provoked, resentful.

wrought *adj* done, effected, performed, worked.

wry *adj* askew, awry, contorted, crooked, distorted, twisted.

XYZ

xanthous *adj* blonde, fair, light-complexioned, xanthic, yellow.
xiphoid *adj* ensiform, gladiate, sword-like, sword-shaped.
Xmas *n* Christmas, Christmastide, Noel, Yule, Yuletide.
X-ray *n* roentgen ray, röntgen ray.
xylograph *n* cut, woodcut, wood engraving.
xylographer *n* wood engraver.
xylophagous *adj* wood-eating, wood-nourished.

yap *vb* bark, cry, yelp. * *n* bark, cry, yelp.
yard *n* close, compound, court, courtyard, enclosure, garden.
yarn *n* anecdote, boasting, fabrication, narrative, story, tale, untruth.
yawn *vb* dehisce, gape, open wide. * *n* gap, gape, gulf.
yearn *vb* crave, desire, hanker after, long for.
yell *vb* bawl, bellow, cry out, howl, roar, scream, screech, shriek, squeal.* *n* cry, howl, roar, scream, screech, shriek.
yellow *adj* aureate, gilded, gilt, gold, golden, lemon, primrose, saffron, xanthic, xanthous.
yelp *vb* bark, howl, yap; complain, bitch, grouse. * *n* bark, sharp cry, howl.
yet *adv* at last, besides, further, however, over and above, so far, still, thus far, ultimately.* *conj* moreover, nevertheless, notwithstanding, now.
yield *vb* afford, bear, bestow, communicate, confer, fetch, furnish, impart, produce, render, supply; accede, accord, acknowledge, acquiesce, allow, assent, comply, concede, give, grant, permit; abandon, abdicate, cede, forgo, give up, let go, quit, relax, relinquish, resign, submit, succumb, surrender, waive. * *n* earnings, income, output, produce, profit, return, revenue.
yielding *adj* accommodating, acquiescent, affable, compliant, complaisant, easy, manageable, obedient, passive, submissive, unresisting; bending, flexible, flexile, plastic, pliant, soft, supple, tractable; fertile, productive.
yoke *vb* associate, bracket, connect, couple, harness, interlink, join, link, unite. * *n* bond, chain, ligature, link, tie, union; bondage, dependence, enslavement, service, servitude, subjection, vassalage; couple, pair.
yokel *n* boor, bumpkin, countryman, peasant, rustic.
yore *adj* ancient, antique, old, olden. * *n* long ago, long since, olden times.
young *adj* green, ignorant, inexperienced, juvenile, new, recent, youthful. * *n* young people, youth; babies, issue, brood, offspring, progeny, spawn.
youngster *n* adolescent, boy, girl, lad, lass, stripling, youth.
youth *n* adolescence, childhood, immaturity, juvenile, juvenility, minority, nonage, pupillage, wardship; boy, girl, lad, lass, schoolboy, schoolgirl, slip, sprig, stripling, youngster.
youthful *adj* boyish, childish, girlish, immature, juvenile, puerile, young.

zany adj comic, comical, crazy, droll, eccentric, funny, imaginative, scatterbrained; clownish, foolish, ludicrous, silly. * *n* buffoon, clown, droll, fool, harlequin, jester, punch.
zeal *n* alacrity, ardour, cordiality, devotedness, devotion, earnestness, eagerness, energy, enthusiasm, fervour, glow, heartiness, intensity, jealousness, passion, soul, spirit, warmth.
zealot *n* bigot, devotee, fanatic, freak, partisan.
zealous *adj* ardent, burning, devoted, eager, earnest, enthusiastic, fervent, fiery, forward, glowing, jealous, keen, passionate, prompt, ready, swift, warm.
zenith *n* acme, apex, climax, culmination, heyday, pinnacle, prime, summit, top, utmost, height.
zero *n* cipher, naught, nadir, nil, nothing, nought.
zest *n* appetite, enjoyment, exhilaration, gusto, liking, piquancy, relish, thrill; edge, flavour, salt, savour, tang, taste; appetizer, sauce.
zone *n* band, belt, cincture, girdle, girth; circuit, clime, region.
zymotic *adj* bacterial, fermentative, germinating.

Phrasefinder

A

A

—**A1** first class, of the highest quality: *The produce must be A1. The firm has an A1 staff.* <A1 is the highest rating given to the condition of ships for Lloyd's Register, Lloyds of London being a major insurance company>.

—**ABC** basic knowledge: *The book sets out the ABC of carpentry.*

—**as easy as ABC** very simple: *Getting them to agree was as easy as ABC.*

—**from A to Z** thoroughly, comprehensively: *They have studied the facts from A to Z.*

aback

—**taken aback** surprised, disconcerted: *She was taken aback when she discovered that he was her cousin.* <A sailing ship was said to be taken aback when the sails were blown against the mast causing the ship to stop suddenly>.

above

—**above board** open, honest and without trickery: *His negotiations to get planning permission were all above board.* <Card cheats tend to keep their cards under the table, or board>.

—**above (someone's) head** too difficult to understand: *Computers are away above his head.*

—**above suspicion** too much respected or thought to be too honourable to be suspected of doing wrong: *The police must be above suspicion.*

—**get a bit above oneself** to become very vain or conceited: *Since his promotion he has got a bit above himself.*

accident

—**accidents will happen** things go wrong at some time in everyone's life: *It's a pity the child broke the vase, but accidents will happen*

—**a chapter of accidents** a series of misfortunes: *Their holiday seems to have been a chapter of accidents.*

accord

—**according to one's lights** in keeping with one's beliefs or attitudes: *I disapprove of his actions, but he acted according to his lights.*

—**of one's own accord** of one's own free will, without being forced: *He left his job of his own accord.*

—**with one accord** together, in unison: *With one accord the audience left.*

account

—**by all accounts** in the opinion of most people: *By all accounts he is not very honest.*

—**give a good account of oneself** to do well: *They didn't win the match, but they gave a good account of themselves.*

—**on my** *or* **your** *or* **his** *or* **her, etc, account** because of me, etc, for my, etc, sake: *Don't leave early on my account.*

—**on no account** not for any reason whatsoever: *On no account accept a lift from a stranger.*

ace

—**an ace in the hole** something kept in reserve for emergencies: *The hostages were regarded by the terrorists as their ace in the hole.* <From the game of stud poker>.

—**within an ace of** very close to: *He came within an ace of winning the match.* <From the game of dice, ace being the term for the side of a dice with one spot>.

Achilles

—**Achilles' heel** the one weak spot in a person. *The boy is a good student, but maths is his Achilles' heel.* <Achilles, the legendary Greek hero, is said to have been dipped in the River Styx by his mother at birth to make him invulnerable but his heel, by which she was holding him, remained unprotected and he was killed by an arrow through his heel>.

acid

—**acid test** a test that will prove or disprove something conclusively: *He claims to be a good golfer but playing against the professional will be the acid test.* <From the use of nitric acid to ascertain whether a metal was gold or not. If it was not gold the acid decomposed it>.

acquire

—**acquired taste** something that one comes to like gradually, often after an original dislike: *To some people very dry wine is an acquired taste.*

across

—**across the board** applying to everyone or to all cases: *The pay increase was across the board.*

—**put one across on (someone)** to deceive or

trick (someone): *I really thought he was penniless. He certainly put one across on me.*

act

—**act of faith** an action that demonstrates one's trust in someone or something: *Lending the young man such a large sum of money was a real act of faith.*

—**act of God** a happening, usually sudden and unexpected, for which no human can be held responsible: *It is difficult to obtain insurance coverage against acts of God such as earthquakes and floods.*

—**act of war** an act of violence or other hostile act for which only war is thought to be a suitable response: *Invading Belgium was an act of war.*

—**act up** to behave badly, to act badly or wrongly: *The child acts up when her father is here. The car is acting up again.*

—**catch (someone) in the act** *see* **catch**.

—**get in on the act** to become involved in some profitable or advantageous activity, especially an activity related to someone else's success: *Now that her fashion business is making a profit her sister wants to get in on the act and become a partner.*

—**get one's act together** to get organized: *If you are hoping to pass the exams you had better get your act together and allow some time for study.*

action

—**action stations** a state of preparedness for some activity: *Action stations! The guests are arriving.* <From positions taken up by soldiers in readiness for battle>.

—**get a piece** *or* **slice of the action** to be involved in something, get a share of something: *He's setting up a new company. If you want a piece of the action you had better go and see him.*

actress

—**as the actress said to the bishop** an expression added to a seemingly ordinary statement to draw attention to its possible sexual double meaning: *You can't have it both ways at once, as the actress said to the bishop.*

ad

—**ad hoc** for a particular (usually exclusive) purpose: *This is an ad hoc bonus. It will not be an annual occurrence.* <Latin, to this>.

—**ad infinitum** without limit or end: *This road seems to go on ad infinitum.* <Latin>.

—**ad-lib** to speak without preparation, to improvise: *I have forgotten my notes. I shall have to ad-lib.* <Latin *ad libitum*, according to pleasure>.

—**ad nauseam** to an excessive degree, seemingly endlessly: *He talks about his work ad nauseam.* <Latin, literally to sickness>.

Adam <refers to the biblical Adam>

—**Adam's ale** water: *We have no beer or wine. It will have to be Adam's ale.*

—**not to know (someone) from Adam** not to recognize (someone): *He said he was my neighbour's son, but I didn't know him from Adam.*

—**the old Adam in us** the sin or evil that is in everyone: *I was surprised that he had an affair, but I suppose it was just the old Adam in him.*

add

—**add fuel to the fire** to make a difficult situation worse: *Making excuses for being late will just add fuel to the fire.*

—**add insult to injury** to make matters worse: *Having given his first play a bad review, the critic added insult to injury by ignoring his next one.*

—**add up** to seem logical: *No one understands why he left so suddenly. It just doesn't add up.*

Adonis

—**an Adonis** a very attractive young man: *The advert for suntan lotion showed a bronzed Adonis.* <In Greek legend Adonis was a beautiful young man who was loved by Aphrodite, the goddess of love, and who was killed by a boar while hunting>.

advantage

—**have the advantage of (someone)** to recognize (someone) without oneself being recognized by that person: *She looked in puzzlement at the woman who spoke to her and said, "I am afraid that you have the advantage of me."*

—**take advantage of (someone)** to exploit or make use of (someone) for one's own ends: *The young mother takes advantage of her neighbour by asking her to babysit practically every evening.*

—**take advantage of (something)** to make use of (something), to put (something) to good use: *You should take advantage of that holiday offer.*

—**to advantage** favourably, so that the good points are emphasized: *She rarely wears dresses that show her figure to advantage.*

aegis

—**under the aegis of (someone)** with the support or backing of (someone): *The project is under the aegis of the local council.* <In Greek legend *aegis* was the shield of the god Zeus>.

after

—**after a fashion** in a manner that is barely adequate: *She cleaned the silver after a fashion, but it was not very shiny.*

—**aftermath** something that happens after, or as a result of, an important, often a disastrous, event: *Housing was scarce in the aftermath of the flood.* <A 'math' was a crop of grass and an 'aftermath' was a second crop of grass mowed in the same season>.

—**after (someone's) own heart** to one's liking; liked or admired by (someone): *His son-in-law is a man after his own heart. They are both avid football fans.*

—**after the fact** after something, especially a crime, has taken place: *His wife was an accessory after the fact.*

against

—**against the clock** in a hurry to get something done before a certain time: *The staff are working against the clock to finish the order on time.*

—**be up against it** to be in a difficult or dangerous situation: *The family have really been up against it since the father lost his job.*

age

—**a golden age** a time of great achievement: *The reign of Elizabeth Tudor is often regarded as having been a golden age.*

—**a ripe old age** a very old age: *Despite her injury she lived to a ripe old age.*

—**of a certain age** no longer young: *Women of a certain age sometimes feel jealous of younger women.*

—**come of age** to reach the age when one is legally considered an adult (in Britain 18): *The boy will receive his inheritance when he comes of age.*

—**the age of consent** the age someone must be before he or she can legally have sexual intercourse: *She looks quite old but she is below the age of consent. The boy in the homosexual relationship was below the age of consent.*

—**under age** under the legal age for something, too young: *The teenagers won't be served at the bar. They're under age.*

agony

—**agony aunt** *or* **uncle** a woman or man who gives advice on personal problems either in a newspaper or magazine column, or on television or radio: *The battered wife wrote to the agony aunt of her local paper for advice.*

—**agony column** a newspaper or magazine column in which readers write in with their problems, which are answered by the agony aunt or uncle. <Originally a newspaper column containing advertisements for missing relatives and friends>.

ahead

—**ahead of the game** in an advantageous position; in front of one's rivals: *Their firm always seems to be ahead of the game. They keep getting most of the orders.*

—**ahead of time** early, before the appointed time: *It's as well to get to the theatre ahead of time to get a good seat.*

—**streets ahead of (someone** *or* **something)** much better than (someone or something): *The local firm's furniture is streets ahead of the chain store's.*

aid

—**aid and abet (someone)** to help and encourage (someone), especially in something wrong or illegal: *He was the thief but he was aided and abetted by his sister.* <A legal term>.

—**what is (something) in aid of?** what is (something) for? why has (something) been done?: *What are those labels in aid of? What's all this formality in aid of?*

air

—**air** *or* **wash one's dirty linen in public** to discuss private or personal matters in public: *When they were quarrelling they really aired their dirty linen in public by making all those comments about their marriage.*

—**air one's grievances** to make public one's complaints: *After suffering in silence she aired her grievances about her neighbours.*

—**clear the air** to make a situation less tense: *If you discuss your disagreement you will at least clear the air.*

—**hot air** boasting; empty or meaningless words: *He says he's going to climb Everest but it's just hot air.*

—**in the air** current; around; in circulation: *There's hostility in the air.*

—**into thin air** seemingly into nowhere: *One minute she was there, the next she had disappeared into thin air.*

—**on the air** on radio or television.

—**put on airs** to behave as though one were superior to others, to act in a conceited way: *She's really put on airs since she got promotion.*

—**take the air** go for a walk or a drive: *It's such a nice evening. Let's take some air.*

—**up in the air** uncertain, undecided: *Her career plans are still up in the air.*

—**walk on air** to be very happy: *They've been walking on air since they got engaged.*

Aladdin

—**Aladdin's cave** a place full of valuable or desirable objects: *The local toyshop is an Aladdin's cave to the children.* <From the tale of Aladdin in the Arabian Nights who gained access to such a cave with the help of the genie from his magic lamp>.

alarm

—**a false alarm** a warning about some danger or difficulty which does not happen: *Someone told him that he might lose his job but it proved to have been a false alarm.*

—**alarms** *or* **alarums and excursions** confused and noisy activity: *There were alarums and excursions when we thought we heard a burglar.* <In Shakespeare's history plays, the expression 'alarms and excursions' was used as a stage direction calling for activity typical of the scene at the edge of a battle>.

alive

—**alive and kicking** in a good or healthy condition: *His old mother is still alive and kicking. Some ancient New Year customs are alive and kicking.*

—**alive with** full of, covered in: *The place was alive with tourists.*

all

—**all and sundry** everybody, one and all: *They invited all and sundry from the village to the party.*

—**all chiefs and no Indians** a surplus of people wishing to give orders or to administrate and a deficiency of people willing to carry orders out or to do the work: *The firm failed largely because it was a case of all chiefs and no Indians to do the actual work.*

—**all ears** listening intently: *Tell me all the details. I'm all ears.*

—**all for (someone** *or* **something)** completely in favour of (someone or something): *We're all for having an extra holiday.*

—**all hours** for long periods of time, from early in the morning until late at night: *The shop is open all hours.*

—**all in** exhausted: *The marathon runners are all in.*

—**all in a day's work** *see* **day**.

—**all in all** taking everything into consideration: *We had some rain but all in all it was a good summer.*

—**all in one piece** safely, undamaged: *I was glad to see the children back all in one piece after their bike ride.*

—**all my eye and Betty Martin** *see* **eye**.

—**all out** with as much effort as possible: *He's going all out to win the race.*

—**all over** at an end: *Their romance is all over.*

—**all over bar the shouting** at an end to all intents and purposes: *The other competitors can't overtake him now. It's all over bar the shouting.*

—**all set** ready to go, prepared: *We're all set for the journey.*

—**all systems go** *see* **system**.

—**all the best** best wishes, good luck: *All the best with the exams.*

—**all the rage** *see* **rage**.

—**all there** having all one's faculties, alert and intelligent: *She is not academically clever, but she's all there when it comes to dealing with money.*

—**all told** altogether, including everything or everyone: *There were 20 cars and 60 people all told.*

—**be all things to all men** to try constantly to agree with or fit in with whomever one is with at the time: *The young man seems to have no opinions of his own but is trying to be all things to all men.*

—**it is all up with (someone)** there is no hope left for (someone): *It is all up with the accused. He has been identified by an eye witness.*

—**on all fours** on one's hands and knees: *He got down on all fours to look for the contact lens.*

alley

—**alley cat** a wild or promiscuous person: *The woman he married is respectable now but she used to be a real alley cat.*

—**blind alley** an action or situation that cannot be advantageous: *His present job is just a blind alley. There's no hope of advancement.*

allowance

—**make allowances for (someone)** to expect a less high standard from (someone) because of particular circumstances: *The teacher should make allowances for the pupil as he has been ill.*

alma mater

—one's old university, college or school: *They are going to a reunion at their alma mater.* <Latin, 'bountiful mother'>.

alpha

—**alpha and omega** the beginning and the end: *We have witnessed the alpha and omega of the relationship.* <The first and last letters of the Greek alphabet>.

also

—**also-ran** an unsuccessful person: *He will never get promotion. He's an also-ran.* <A horse-racing term for a horse that is not one of the first three horses in a race>.

alter ego

—a person who is very close or dear to someone: *The girl next door is our daughter's alter ego. They're never apart.* <Latin, "other self">.

alternative

—**alternative medicine** the treatment of diseases or disorders that uses techniques other than those of conventional medicine, including homoeopathy, osteopathy, acupuncture, aroma-therapy, etc: *She is reluctant to take drugs and so she is turning to alternative medicine for herbal remedies.*

—**have no alternative** to be forced to take a certain course of action because it is the only possible one: *He does not wish to resign, but after his quarrel with management he has no alternative.*

altogether

—**in the altogether** in the nude: *You can't answer the door—you're in the altogether.*

Amazon

—a very strong or well-built woman: *He expected the women's rugby team to be Amazons* .<In Greek legend the Amazons were a race of female warriors who had their right breasts removed in order to draw their bows better>.

amiss

—**take (something) amiss** to take offence or be upset at (something): *They took it amiss that they were not invited to the wedding although they could not have gone to it.*

angel

—**an angel of mercy** a person who gives help and comfort, especially one who appears unexpectedly: *When he collapsed in the street an unknown angel of mercy took him to hospital.*

—**angels' visits** visits that are rare and short but very pleasant: *Her son lives far away but pays his mother a series of angels' visits.*

—**entertain an angel unawares** to meet and talk to someone whose worth or fame one is unaware of: *The winner of the literary prize was at the party but we were entertaining an angel unawares. No one told us who he was.*

—**on the side of the angels** supporting or agreeing with what is regarded as being the good or the right side: *The teacher has to pretend to be on the side of the angels and support his colleagues although he has some sympathy with the pupils.*

—**fools rush in where angels fear to tread** *see* **fool**.

—**write like an angel** to write well and movingly: *I cannot wait for her next novel. She writes like an angel.* <Originally the term referred to handwriting rather than to style of writing, being derived from the name of Angelo Vergece, who was a famous 16th-century calligrapher at the court of Francis I of France>.

anger

—**more in sorrow than in anger** *see* **sorrow**.

angry

—**angry young man** a person who expresses angry dissatisfaction with established social, political and intellectual values. <A term applied to British dramatist, John Osborne, author of the play *Look Back in Anger*>.

answer

—**know all the answers** to have all the information that is required to deal successfully with a situation, especially when one is conceited about this: *She won't listen to any advice. She acts as if she knows all the answers.*

—**not to take no for an answer** to urge very strongly that one's request, invitation or suggestion is accepted: *Of course you must stay and have dinner. I won't take no for an answer.*

—**the answer to a maiden's prayer** exactly what one desires and is looking for: *She's found the perfect job—the answer to a maiden's prayer.* <The answer to a maiden's prayer was thought to be an eligible bachelor>.

ant

—**have ants in one's pants** to be restless or agitated: *She's got ants in her pants waiting to hear the results of the exams.*

ante

—**up** *or* **raise the ante** to increase the amount of money required or offered for something: *If you want to buy that house you'll have to up the ante.* <Refers to increasing the money one bets in a game of cards, the other player having to match this amount in order to stay in the game>.

any

—**anybody's guess** something which no one can be certain about: *How they make their money is anybody's guess.*

—**any day** whatever the circumstances: *I would rather read a book than watch television any day.*

—**any old how** in an untidy and careless way: *The books in the bookcase were arranged any old how.*

—**anything but** not at all: *He doesn't dislike her—anything but.*

—**anything goes** any kind of behaviour, dress, etc, is acceptable: *It's not a formal party—anything goes.*

—**like anything** very much, hard, fast, energetically, etc: *He tried like anything to get a job.*

apart

—**be poles** *or* **worlds apart** to be completely different: *Husband and wife are poles apart in their attitudes to bringing up children.*

—**take (someone) apart** to scold or criticize (someone) severely: *Your mother will take you apart if you break the window.*

apology

—**an apology for (something)** a very poor example of (something): *The cafe served us up an apology for a meal.*

appearance

—**from** *or* **to all appearances** judging only from what can be seen: *Apparently they are going to divorce but to all appearances they made the perfect couple.*

—**keep up appearances** to behave in public in such a way as to hide what is going on in private: *He has lost his job but he keeps up appearances by leaving the house at his usual time every morning.*

—**put in an appearance at (something)** to attend a meeting, function, etc, especially for a short time or because it is one's duty to do so: *All the teachers are expected to put in an appearance at the school's annual concert.*

apple

—**apple of discord** a cause of quarrelling: *The leather coat in the sale was a real apple of discord. Several women were fighting over it.* <From the golden apple in Greek legend inscribed "for the fairest", which Eris, the goddess of discord, threw and which three other goddesses, Aphrodite, Pallas Athene and Hera, quarrelled over>.

—**apple-pie bed** a bed made up, as a practical joke, in such a way that it is impossible to get into: *She was so tired that she didn't notice that the children had made her an apple-pie bed.*

—**in apple-pie order** with everything tidy and correctly arranged: *She always leaves the office files in apple-pie order.* <From the French *nappe pliée*, "folded linen," linen neatly laid out>.

—**rotten apple** a person who is bad or unsatisfactory and will have a bad influence on others: *The class is mostly well-behaved, but there are one or two rotten apples who cause trouble.*

—**the apple of (someone's) eye** a favourite, a person who is greatly loved by (someone): *There are five girls in the family but the only boy is the apple of his father's eye.* <Apple refers to the pupil of the eye>.

—**upset the apple-cart** to spoil plans or arrangements: *The teenagers were going to have a party but their parents upset the apple-cart by coming home early.* <From the practice of selling fruit from carts in street markets>.

apron

—**tied to (someone's) apron-strings** completely dependent on a woman, especially one's mother or wife: *He's so tied to his mother's apron-strings that I cannot see him getting married.*

ark

—**like something out of the ark** very old-fashioned looking: *She wears clothes that are like something out of the ark.* <From Noah's ark in the Bible>.

arm

—**armed to the hilt** *or* **teeth** provided with all the equipment that one could possibly need: *The enemy soldiers were armed to the hilt. The tourists were armed to the teeth with guide books and cameras.*

—**a shot in the arm** *see* **shot**.

—**be up in arms** to protest angrily: *The residents are up in arms about the proposed shopping centre.*

—**chance one's arm** to take a risk: *You're really chancing your arm by asking for more time off. We're so understaffed.*

—**cost an arm and a leg** to cost a great deal of money: *His new car must have cost him an arm and a leg.*

—**give one's right arm for (something)** to be willing to go to any lengths to get something: *He'd give his right arm to get a job as a pilot.*

—**keep (someone) at arm's length** to avoid becoming too close to or too friendly with someone: *As the boss he has to keep everyone at arm's length or he gets accused of favouritism.*

—**lay down one's arms** to stop fighting or opposing: *We lost our appeal against the new road. Now we will just have to lay down our arms.* <A military reference to soldiers laying down their arms when they surrender>.

—**the long arm of the law** the power or authority of the police: *The crook thought he had got away with the bank robbery, but the long arm of the law caught up with him as he was leaving the country.*

—**right arm** chief source of help and support: *His secretary is his right arm, and he can't cope without her.*

—**take up arms** to become actively involved in a quarrel or dispute: *The whole village took up arms when the post office was threatened with closure.* <A military reference to soldiers taking up arms to go into battle>.

—**twist (someone's) arm** to force (someone) to do (something), to persuade (someone) to do (something): *If you want to get him to cut the grass you'll have to twist his arm—he hates doing it. I don't really want another drink but you could twist my arm.*

—**with one arm tied behind one's back** very easily: *She could beat him at tennis with one arm tied behind her back.*

—**with open arms** welcomingly: *They will receive your offer of help with open arms.*

armour

—**chink in (someone's) armour** a weak or vulnerable spot in someone who is otherwise very strong and difficult to get through to or attack: *The old man is very stern but his granddaughter has found the chink in his armour. The Opposition are always trying to find a chink in the Government's armour.* <A knight in armour could be injured only through a flaw or opening in his protective armour>.

—**knight in shining armour** a person who it is hoped will save a situation or come to one's aid: *A knight in shining armour helped her to change the wheel of her car.* <From medieval legends in which knights in armour came to the aid of damsels in distress>.

around

—**have been around** (1) to have had a lot of experience of life: *She's not as innocent as she looks. She's been around a bit.* (2) to have been alive. *He said that he had been around so long he could remember Queen Victoria.*

ashes

—**rake over the ashes** to discuss things that are passed, especially things that are best forgotten: *There's no point in raking over the ashes of their relationship. They're divorced, and that's that.*

—**rise from the ashes** to develop and flourish out of ruin and destruction: *The firm had to close last year but a new one has risen from the ashes.* <In Greek legend the phoenix, a mythical bird, who after a certain number of years of life set fire to itself and was then reborn from the ashes>.

—**sackcloth and ashes** *see* **sack**.

—**the Ashes** the trophy, originally mythical, contended for in the cricket test matches between Britain and Australia: *The winner of the Ashes will be decided by the third test match.* <When England was beaten by Australia in 1882 the *Sporting Times* published a humorous epitaph on English cricket saying, "The body will be cremated and the ashes taken back to Australia">.

ask

—**ask for the moon** *see* **moon**.

—**be asking for it** to behave in such a way as to invite something unpleasant, such as a beating: *You shouldn't have hit that young man even if he was asking for it by making nasty comments about you.*

—**be (someone's) for the asking** for something to be available to someone who wishes it without payment: *I don't want any money for the books. They're yours for the asking.*

attendance

—**dance attendance on (someone)** to stay close to (someone) in order to carry out all his or her wishes and so gain favour: *The new girl in the office has all the men dancing attendance on her.*

auld lang syne

—times that are past, especially times remembered with fondness: *The two men who had been at school together had a drink together for auld lang syne.* <A Scots phrase meaning 'old long since'>.

aunt

—**Aunt Sally** a person or thing that is being subjected to general abuse, mockery and criticism: *Whenever people are angry about the high cost of living they treat the government like an Aunt Sally.* <An Aunt Sally at a fair was a wooden model of a woman's head, mounted on a pole, at which people threw sticks or balls in order to win a prize>.

avail

—**of no avail** of no use, without effect: *All our efforts to revive him were of no avail.*

—**to no avail** without success: *We tried to dissuade her from leaving but to no avail.*

away

—**do away with (someone** *or* **something)** to get rid of something, to abolish something: *They've done away with all the old customs.*

—**get away from it all** to escape from the problems of daily life, usually by taking a holiday: *He's going to a small island in Scotland to get away from it all.*

—**get away with you!** I don't believe you!: *Get away with you! You can't have seen a ghost.*

—**the one that got away** a chance of success which one either did not or could not take of advantage at the time but which one always remembers: *He talks frequently of his first girlfriend, the one that got away.* <Refers to a supposedly large fish which an angler fails to catch but about which he tells many stories>.

axe

—**get the axe** to be dismissed: *With so few orders some of the workers are bound to get the axe.*

—**have an axe to grind** to have a personal, often selfish, reason for being involved in something: *She has an axe to grind by being so kind to her old uncle. She hopes he will leave her some money in his will.* <From a story told by Benjamin Franklin, the American politician, about how a man had once asked him in his boyhood to demonstrate the working of his father's grindstone and had sharpened his own axe on it while it was working>.

B

babe

—**babe in arms** an inexperienced or naive person: *He'll never succeed in business. He's just a babe in arms.*

baby

—**be left holding the baby** to be left to cope with a difficult situation that has been abandoned by the person who is really responsible for it: *They were meant to be organizing the birthday party but I was left holding the baby.*

—**throw out the baby with the bathwater** accidentally to get rid of something desirable or essential when trying to get rid of undesirable or unnecessary things: *We must try to salvage some of the best of the old methods when we reorganize. Let's not throw out the baby with the bathwater.*

—**wet the baby's head** to drink the health of a new-born baby: *The father got drunk wetting the baby's head.*

back

—**at the back of (something)** responsible for something, usually something bad: *You should have guessed that he was at the back of the smear campaign.*

—**backhanded compliment** a supposed compliment that sounds more like criticism: *It's a backhanded compliment for him to tell the girl that she is as attractive as her mother. He thoroughly dislikes her mother.*

—**back number** a person or thing that is no longer of importance or of use: *He used to be a famous comedian but he is a back number now.* <Refers to an out-of-date or back copy of a newspaper or magazine>.

—**backscratching** doing favours for someone so that he or she will in turn do favours for one: *There's a lot of backscratching goes on in the financial world.*

—**backseat driver** (1) a passenger in a car who gives unasked-for and unwanted advice: *His mother doesn't drive but she's a real backseat driver who's always shouting out directions when she's in the car.* (2) a person who is not directly involved in some activity but who offers unwanted advice: *It's his wife who's our accountant but he's a backseat driver who tells us what to do about our tax problems.*

—**back to the drawing board** it will be necessary to start again on a project or activity: *Our holiday tour's been cancelled, so it's back to the drawing board.* <Refers to the board on which plans of buildings, etc, are drawn before being built>.

—**back to the grindstone** back to work: *We've had lunch and so it's back to the grindstone.*

—**backwater** an isolated place unaffected by what is happening in the world outside: *How can he bear to live in such a backwater where nothing ever happens?*

—**behind someone's back** without the knowledge or permission of the person concerned: *She married him behind her father's back.*

—**bend over backwards** to go to great trouble: *We bent over backwards to be nice to the shy new girl.*

—**break one's back** to put in a great deal of effort: *The salesman really broke his back to get that order.*

—**break the back of (something)** to complete the largest or most difficult part: *He hasn't finished the essay but at least he's broken the back of it.*

—**flat on one's back** ill in bed: *He's been flat on his back since the accident.*

—**get off (someone's) back** to stop harassing or bothering (someone): *The teacher should get off Tom's back or he'll leave school.*

—**get one's own back** to take one's revenge: *He is determined to get his own back on the person who damaged his car.*

—**give one's back** *or* **eye teeth** *see* **teeth**.

—**have (someone** *or* **something) at one's back** have (someone or something) as a help or support: *She is a single parent but she has her parents at her back.*

—**have one's back to the wall**: to be in a very difficult or desperate situation: *They had their backs to the wall so they had no choice but to accept his offer.* <Someone being pursued has to face his or her pursuers or be captured when a wall prevents retreat>.

—**know (something) backwards** *or* **like the back of one's hand** to know all there is to know about (something): *The professor knows his subject backwards.*

—**know (someone** *or* **something) like the back of one's hand** to know (someone or something) very well indeed: *She can always tell when her husband is lying. She knows him like the back of her hand.*

—**put one's back into (something)** to put the greatest possible effort into (something): *They're really putting their backs into their new business.*

—**put (someone's) back up:** to annoy (someone): *My friend always puts my back up when she's late.* <A cat's back arches up when it is angry>.

—**see the back of (someone** *or* **something)** to get rid of (someone or something), not to see (someone or something) again: *He'll be glad to see the back of his lodger.*

—**take a back seat** to take an unimportant or minor role: *The older children have taken a back seat with the arrival of the new baby.*

—**talk through the back of one's head** to talk nonsense: *If she said that he's married she's talking through the back of her head.*

—**the back of beyond** a very remote place: *We hardly ever visit them because they live in the back of beyond.*

—**when (someone's) back is turned** when (someone) is either not present or is not noticing what is happening: *The children steal money from their mother's purse when her back is turned.*

bacon

—**bring home the bacon** (1) to earn money to support one's family: *She regards her husband just as someone who brings home the bacon.* (2) to succeed in doing (something): *Mending the table's a difficult task but that carpenter will bring home the bacon.* <Perhaps from the winning of a greased pig as a prize at a country fair>.

—**save (someone's) bacon** to save someone from a danger or difficulty: *If you hadn't saved my bacon by giving me a lift I would have been late.*

bad

—**bad egg** a worthless or law-breaking person: *Her husband was a bad egg who ended up in prison.*

—**badly off** without much money: *They're too badly off to go on holiday.*

—**go to the bad** to become immoral or criminal: *Her parents are afraid of her coming to the city in case she goes to the bad.*

—**hit a bad patch** to encounter difficulties or a difficult period: *You've hit a bad patch but things will improve.*

—**in bad odour** in disfavour: *He's been in bad odour with her parents since he brought her home late.*

—**in (someone's) bad** *or* **black books** out of favour with (someone): *They're in the teacher's bad books for being late.* <Refers to an account book where bad debts are noted>.

—**not half bad** quite good, very good: *This cake's not half bad.*

—**too bad** unfortunate: *It's too bad you have to leave early.*

—**with a bad grace** in an unwilling and bad-tempered way: *They eventually came with us but with a bad grace.*

bag

—**bag and baggage** all one's belongings, or equipment: *They had to get out of the house bag and baggage when the new tenant came.*

—**bag lady** a homeless woman who carries all her belongings with her in bags: *During the recession more and more bag ladies appeared on the streets.*

—**bag of bones** a person who is extremely thin: *The student had so little money to spend on food that he was a bag of bones.*

—**bag of nerves** a very nervous or anxious person: *She worries about everything. She's just a bag of nerves.*

—**bag of tricks** the equipment necessary to do something: *The joiner arrived with his bag of tricks to mend the floor.*

—**cannot punch one's way out of a paper bag** to be totally lacking in ability or power: *He won't succeed in business. He couldn't punch his way out of a paper bag.*

—**in the bag** certain to be obtained: *He think's the job's in the bag but I think he's wrong.* <From the bag used in hunting to carry what one has shot or caught>.

—**let the cat out of the bag** *see* **cat**.

—**mixed bag** a very varied mixture: *This new set of pupils is a mixed bag.*

bait

—**rise to the bait** to do what someone has been trying to get one to do: *She knew that he was trying to get her to lose her temper but she refused to rise to the bait.* <Refers to fish rising to the

surface to reach the bait on an angler's line>.

—**swallow the bait** to accept completely an offer, proposal, etc, that has been made purely to tempt one: *They swallowed the bait and took the money from the company without realizing that they had actually sold their houses to them.* <As above>.

baker

—**baker's dozen** thirteen. <From the former custom of bakers adding an extra bun or loaf to a dozen in order to be sure of not giving short weight>.

balance

—**in the balance** undecided, uncertain: *The fate of the old building is in the balance although we have worked hard to preserve it.* <A balance is a pair of hanging scales>.

—**on balance** considering everything: *There are good points on each side but on balance I think the older man is the better candidate.*

—**strike a balance** to reach an acceptable compromise: *Try to strike a balance between going out every night and never going out at all.*

—**throw (someone) off balance** to cause (someone) to be disconcerted or confused: *The lecturer was thrown off balance by some of the questions from the audience.*

—**tip the balance** to exert an influence which, although slight, is enough to alter the outcome of something: *There was very little to choose between the candidates but one of them lived locally, which tipped the balance.*

bald

—**bald as a coot** extremely bald. <A coot is a bird with a spot of white feathers on its head>.

ball[1]

—**have a ball** to have a very enjoyable time: *The children had a ball at the birthday party.*

ball[2]

—**have the ball at one's feet** to be in a position to be successful: *The young graduate thought he had the ball at his feet when he got his degree.* <From football>.

—**on the ball** alert, quick-witted, attentive to what is going on around one: *If he had been on the ball he would have sold his shares earlier.* <Referring to a football player who watches the ball carefully in order to be prepared if it comes to him>.

—**play ball** to act in accordance with someone else's wishes: *We had hoped that he would play ball and leave quietly.*

—**play ball with (someone)** to cooperate with (someone): *He's decided to play ball with the police and tell them all he knows.*

—**set** *or* **start the ball rolling** to start off an activity of some kind, often a discussion: *Now that we are all present for the staff meeting perhaps someone will set the ball rolling.*

balloon

—**when the balloon goes up** when something serious, usually something that is expected and feared, happens: *The real trouble-makers had run away before the balloon went up and the headmaster discovered the broken windows.* <From balloons sent up to undertake military observation in World War I, signifying that action was about to start>.

banana

—**go bananas** to go mad, to get extremely angry: *Her mother will go bananas if she comes home late.*

—**slip on a banana skin** to do something that causes one humiliation or public embarrassment: *The politician thought that her speech was going very well until she slipped on a banana skin and got the name of the town wrong.* <Cartoons often show people literally slipping on banana skins>.

band

—**jump on the bandwagon** to show an interest in, or become involved in, something simply because it is fashionable or financially advantageous: *When blue denim became popular a lot of manufacturers jumped on the bandwagon.* <Refers to a brightly coloured wagon for carrying the band at the head of a procession>.

—**looking as though one has stepped out of a bandbox** looking very neat and elegant: *Even after the long journey she still looked as though she had stepped out of a bandbox.* <Refers to a lightweight box formerly used for holding small articles of clothing such as hats>.

—**to beat the band** *see* **beat**.

bang

—**bang goes (something)** that puts a sudden end to (something): *I have extra work to do, so bang goes my holiday.*

—**bang one's head against a brick wall** to do (something) in vain: *You're banging your head against a brick wall if you try to get him to change his mind.*

—**bang on** exactly, precisely: *He was bang on time.*

—**go with a bang** to be very successful: *The jum-*

ble sale went with a bang—we made a lot of money.

bank

—**break the bank** to leave (onself or someone) without any money: *If he buys a cup of coffee it won't exactly break the bank.* <In gambling terms, to win all the money that a casino is prepared to pay out in one night>.

baptism

—**baptism of fire** a first, usually difficult or unpleasant, experience of something: *She had a real baptism of fire when she had to represent her new company at an international conference.* <From Christian baptism>.

bar

—**behind bars** in prison: *The victim's family want to see the accused behind bars.*

bare

—**bare one's soul** to tell (someone) one's private feelings or thoughts: *She bared her soul to her best friend after the break-up of the marriage.*

—**the bare bones of (something)** the essential and basic details of (something): *Tell me the bare bones of the project.*

—**with one's bare hands** using one's hands rather than tools or weapons: *He tried to dig the dog's grave with his own hands.*

bargain

—**into the bargain** in addition, as well: *We bought their house and their car into the bargain.*

—**drive a hard bargain** to try to get a deal that is very favourable to oneself: *We're going to refuse his offer to buy the firm because he's trying to drive too hard a bargain.*

—**strike a bargain** to reach a settlement or agreement: *They struck a bargain that one firm would do the production work and the other the marketing.*

barge

—**wouldn't touch (someone** *or* **something) with a bargepole**: to wish to have absolutely no contact with (someone or something): *I'm not considering him for the job—I wouldn't touch him with a bargepole.*

bark

—**bark up the wrong tree** to have the wrong idea or impression about (something), to approach (something) in the wrong way: *You are barking up the wrong tree if you ask him for help because he is incredibly mean.* <From raccoon-hunting, in which dogs were used to locate trees that had raccoons in them>.

—**(someone's) bark is worse than his** *or* **her bite** a person is not as dangerous or as harmful as he or she appears to be: *His father shouts a lot but his bark is worse than his bite. He never hits his son.* <Refers to a barking dog that is often quite friendly>.

barrel

—**have (someone) over a barrel** to get (someone) into such a position that one can get him or her to do anything that one wants: *Since she owes the landlord a lot of money he has her over a barrel.* <From holding someone over a barrel of boiling oil, etc, where the alternatives for the victim are to agree to demands or be dropped in the barrel>.

—**scrape the (bottom of the) barrel** to have to use someone or something of poor or inferior quality because that is all that is available: *They are really scraping the bottom of the barrel if they have appointed him to the job since he has absolutely no experience.* <Referring to the fact that people will only scrape out the bottom of an empty barrel if they have no more full ones left>.

base

—**get to** *or* **make** *or* **reach first base** to complete the important first stage of a process: *He has some good ideas but none of his projects ever gets to first base.* <From baseball, to complete the first section of a run>.

bat[1]

—**not to bat an eyelid** *see* **eye**.

—**off one's own bat** by oneself, without the help or permission of any one else: *Her mother didn't tell her to write to you. She did it off her own bat.* <From the game of cricket>.

bat[2]

—**blind as a bat** having very poor eyesight: *Her aunt can't look up the number in the telephone directory since she's blind as a bat.* <Referring to the fact that bats live their lives in darkness>.

—**like a bat out of hell** very quickly: *When he saw the police he ran away like a bat out of hell.*

bate

—**with bated breath** anxiously: *They waited with bated breath for the results of the tests.*

bay

—**keep (someone** *or* **something) at bay** to to keep (someone or something) from coming too close: *She tries to keep her inquisitive neighbours at bay.*

be

—**the be-all and end-all** the most important aim or purpose: *Making a lot of money is the be-*

all and end-all of her existence. <From Shakespeare's *Macbeth*, Act 1, scene vii.

beam

—**broad in the beam** wide in the hips or buttocks: *She really is too broad in the beam to wear those trousers.* <Used of a ship to mean wide according to its length>.

—**off beam** (1) on the wrong course: *The police are looking for the criminal in the wrong place—they are away off beam.* (2) inaccurate: *The results of your calculations are completely off beam.* <From the radio beam that is used to bring aircraft to land in poor visibility>.

—**on one's beam ends** very short of money: *Neither of them can get a job and they're now on their beam ends.* <Originally a nautical term used to describe a ship lying on its side and in danger of capsizing completely>.

bean

—**full of beans** very lively, in good spirits: *She was ill and depressed but she's full of beans after her holiday.* <Originally referring to a horse fed on beans, a high energy food>.

—**know how many beans make five** to be experienced in the ways of the world: *The new barmaid will be able to cope with the difficult customers. She knows how many beans make five.*

—**not have a bean** to have no money whatsoever: *The rent is due and they haven't a bean.*

—**not know beans about (something)** to know nothing whatsoever about (something): *He's bought a pub but he does not know beans about running a business.*

—**spill the beans** to reveal a secret or confidential information: *His mother asked him not to tell anyone her age, but he spilled the beans to his friends.*

bear[1]

—**bear down on (someone)** to come towards (someone) in a determined and often threatening way: *The child saw his angry mother bearing down on him waving the letter from the school.*

—**bear fruit** to produce results: *Our fashion ideas are beginning to bear fruit—we've made a profit this year.*

—**bear fruit** a disorderly gathering: *Parliament sometimes resembles a bear garden.*

—**bear in mind** to remember: *Bear in mind that Monday is a public holiday.*

—**bear (something) out** to confirm (something): *The evidence at the scene of the crime bore out the witnesses' account of the attack.*

—**bear up** to keep cheerful or strong under strain or stress: *I know you've a lot to put up with but you must try to bear up.*

—**grin and bear it** *see* **grin**.

—**have a cross to bear** *see* **cross**.

bear[2]

—**bear garden** a noisy, rowdy place: *With all those kids around, their house is a bear garden.* <Originally referred to a public place used for bear-baiting, in which dogs were made to attack bears and get them angry, for public amusement>.

—**like a bear with a sore head** extremely bad-tempered: *When the boss has a hangover he's like a bear with a sore head.*

beard

—**beard the lion in its den** to confront or face (someone) openly and boldly: *If you want to get a rise you'll have to go the boss's office and beard the lion in his den.*

beat

—**beat about the bush** to approach (something) in an indirect way: *If you want her to leave, tell her frankly. Don't beat about the bush.* <In game-bird hunting, bushes are beaten to make the birds appear>.

—**beat a (hasty) retreat** to run away: *The boys beat a hasty retreat when they saw the police.* <Military orders used to be conveyed by a series of different drum signals>.

—**beat (someone) hollow** to defeat (someone) soundly: *He beat his father hollow at chess.*

—**beat it** to run away: *When the old man saw the children stealing apples in his garden he told them to beat it.*

—**beat the drum** to try to attract public attention: *They're beating the drum for their new perfume at the exhibition.* <The noise of a drum makes people stop and listen>.

—**beat (someone) to it** to succeed in doing something before someone else can: *He was going to pay the restaurant bill but his partner beat him to it.*

—**if you can't beat them** *or* **'em, join them** *or* **'em** if you cannot persuade other people to think and act like you, the most sensible course of action is for you to begin to think and act like them: *Go on, take the money from the gamblers. After all, if you can't beat 'em, join 'em.*

—**off the beaten track** in an isolated position, away from towns or cities: *She likes to live somewhere quiet that is off the beaten track.*

—**take some** *or* **a lot of beating** to be of such high quality that it is difficult to improve on: *His performance will take some beating. The food at that restaurant takes a lot of beating.*

—**to beat the band** with great force or vigour: *The child is yelling to beat the band.* <Refers to a sound that is louder than that produced by a band>.

beauty

—**beauty is in the eye of the beholder** different people have different ideas of what is beautiful: *Beauty is certainly in the eye of the beholder. He said his new wife is wildly attractive, but to me she's plain.*

—**beauty is only skin deep** people have more important qualities than how they look: *Beauty is only skin deep. His sister may be very pretty but she is also very spiteful.*

beaver

—**eager beaver** a very enthusiastic and hard-working person: *The new employee is a real eager beaver who works late every night.*

—**work like a beaver** to work very industriously and enthusiastically: *They're working like beavers to decorate the house.* <Beavers are small animals that build dams, etc, with great speed and skill>.

beck

—**at (someone's) beck and call** having to be always available to carry out (someone's) orders or wishes: *She isn't as much of an invalid as she makes out—she likes having everyone at her beck and call.* <Beck is a form of "beckon">.

bed

—**bed of nails** *or* **thorns** a very unpleasant or difficult situation: *His early life in the slums was an absolute bed of thorns.*

—**bed of roses** an easy, comfortable or happy situation: *He says that being a travel writer is not a bed of roses.*

—**get out of bed on the wrong side** to start the day in a very bad-tempered mood: *The boss is criticizing everybody. He must have got out of bed on the wrong side today.*

bee

—**have a bee in one's bonnet** to have an idea that one cannot stop thinking or talking about, to have an obsession: *The old lady has got a bee in her bonnet about going on a cruise but she is not fit to go.* <A bee trapped under one's hat cannot escape>.

—**busy bee** a person who is very active and industrious: *Her mother's such a busy bee that she never seems to rest.* <Bees are reputed to be very hard-working creatures>.

—**make a beeline for (someone** *or* **something)** to go directly and quickly to (someone or something): *The children made a beeline for the table where the food was.* <Bees are reputed to fly back to their hives in straight lines>.

—**the birds and the bees** *see* **bird**.

—**think one** *or* **someone is the bee's knees** to consider oneself or someone else to very special and important: *She think she's the bees knees and won't speak to any of the other workers.*

beer

—**not all beer and skittles** not consisting just of pleasant or enjoyable things: *He's discovered that being a travel courier is definitely not all beer and skittles.*

—**small beer** something unimportant: *His present job is very small beer compared with his last one.*

beetroot

—**go beetroot** to blush deeply: *The girl went beetroot when he paid her a compliment.*

before

—**before one can say Jack Robinson** very rapidly, in an instant: *The waiter brought the food before we could say Jack Robinson.*

—**before one knows where one is** very quickly, before one can grasp the situation: *Before we knew where we were he had booked the tickets for the holiday.*

—**before the flood** a very long time ago: *They've known each other since before the flood.* <Referring to the Flood described in the Bible in Genesis 7:9>.

beg

—**beggar description** to be such that words cannot describe it: *The richness of the furnishings beggars description.* <From Shakespeare's *Antony and Cleopatra*, Act 2, scene ii>.

—**beg the question** in an argument, to take for granted the very point that requires to be proved; to fail to deal effectively with the point being discussed: *Politicians are noted for their ability to beg the question.*

—**going a-begging** unclaimed or unsold: *At the end of the sale several articles were going a-begging.*

bell

—**bell the cat** to be the person in a group who undertakes something dangerous for the good of the group: *Someone has to bell the cat and tell the boss that we want more money.* <Re-

ferring to a story about some mice who wanted to put a bell on the neck of the cat so that they would hear it coming and who needed a volunteer to do it>.

—**ring a bell** to bring back vague memories: *His name rings a bell but I can't think where I've heard it.*

—**saved by the bell** rescued from an unpleasant situation by something suddenly bringing that situation to an end: *The teacher asked him for his homewor, which he hadn't done. He was saved by the bell by a parent arriving to see her.* <From the bell that marks the end of a round in boxing>.

belt

—**below the belt** unfair: *To refer in public to his father being in prison was below the belt.* <In boxing, a blow below the belt is against the rules>.

—**tighten one's belt** to reduce one's expenditure: *In the recession most firms had to tighten their belts.* <Belts have to be tightened if one loses weight—in this case from spending less on food>.

—**under one's belt** achieved or accomplished: *We've got 200 miles under our belts.*

bend

—**bend over backwards** *see* **back**.

—**on bended knee** very humbly or earnestly: *On bended knee I ask you not to sack them.*

—**round the bend** mad: *The children are driving their father round the bed with their noise.*

berth

—**give (someone) a wide berth** to keep well away from (someone): *Give that man a wide berth. He looks violent.* <Refers to a ship that keeps a good distance away from others>.

beside

—**be beside oneself** to be in a state of great emotion: *The child was beside himself with joy at receiving the prize.*

—**beside the point** not directly concerned with the issue being discussed: *She has to stay here. Whether she wants to go abroad is beside the point.*

best

—**do one's level best** to try as hard as one can: *We'll do our level best to get there on time.*

—**have the best of both worlds** to benefit from the advantages of two sets of circumstances: *She thinks she has the best of both worlds by working at home. She earns some money but can look after the children herself.*

—**put one's best foot forward** to make the best attempt possible: *If you want to pass the exam you had better put your best foot forward.*

—**the best part of (something)** most of (something), nearly all of (something): *They spent the best part of £3000 on plane fares.*

—**with the best of them** as well as other people who are more experienced, better qualified, etc: *She started to learn to skate only this year but already she can skate with the best of them*

—**with the best will in the world** no matter how much one wants to do something: *With the best will in the world I couldn't get there in time.*

bet

—**hedge one's bets** to try to protect oneself from possible loss, failure, disappointment, etc: *We decided to hedge our bets and book seats for both performances in case we missed the first one.* <From betting the same amount on each side to make sure of not losing>.

better

—**better off** (1) happier: *She says that she's better off without her husband.* (2) richer: *His family is much better off than hers.*

—**go one better than (someone)** to improve on something that someone has done: *She won three prizes but her sister went one better and won five.*

—**get the better of (someone)** to overcome or defeat (someone): *His son always gets the better of him at chess.*

—**have seen better days:** to be no longer new or fresh: *This coat has seen better days. I need a new one.*

—**the better part of (something)** a large part of (something), most of (something): *They stayed for the better part of four hours.*

—**think better of (something)** to reconsider (something), to change one's mind about (something): *They should think better of buying such an expensive house when money is tight.*

beyond

—**beyond compare** unrivalled, without equal: *The queen's beauty was beyond compare.*

—**beyond one's ken** *see* **ken**.

—**beyond the pale** beyond normal or acceptable limits: *When he drinks too much his behaviour is completely beyond the pale.* <The pale was an area of English government in Ireland in the 16th century>.

bide

—**bide one's time** to wait for a suitable opportunity: *They haven't given up the plan to climb the mountain. They're biding their time until the weather improves.*

big

—**a big fish in a small pond** a person who seems better, more important, etc, than he or she is because he or she operates in a small, limited area: *He did well in the village school where he was a big fish in a small pond, but when he went to a large city school he was just average.*

—**be big of (someone)** to be generous of (someone): *It was big of them to give us a day's holiday.*

—**Big Brother** *see* **brother**.

—**big guns** the most important people in an organization: *The big guns are having a board meeting.*

—**the Big Apple** New York: *He's excited about flying to the Big Apple.*

—**the Big Smoke** London: *They would hate to live in the Big Smoke.*

bill

—**a clean bill of health** verification that someone is well and fit: *The footballer has been given a clean bill of health after treatment for his injury.* <Ships were given clean bills of health and allowed to sail when it was certified that no one aboard had an infectious disease>.

—**fill the bill** to be exactly what is required: *They're seeking peace and quiet. At last they've found a cottage that fits the bill.* <Refers originally to a handbill or public notice>.

—**foot the bill** to pay for something, usually something expensive: *He had to foot the bill for the repairs to his own car and the other one.*

—**top the bill** to be the most important performer in a show: *A world-famous pianist topped the bill.* <On theatrical advertising bills or posters the star performer's name is at the top>.

bird

—**a bird in the hand is worth two in the bush** something that one already has is much more valuable than things that one might or might not acquire. *Hang on to that old car. A bird in the hand is worth two in the bush.* <A bird in the bush might fly away>.

—**a little bird told me** I found out by a means which I do not wish to reveal: *A little bird told me that she is having a baby.*

—**birds of a feather flock together** people who share the same interests, ideas, etc, usually form friendships. *The football fans are like birds of a feather, they flock together.*

—**give (someone) the bird** of an audience, to express its disapproval of a performer by hissing or booing so that he or she leaves the stage: *The comic was so bad that the gave him the bird after five minutes.* <From the resemblance of the noise of the audience to the hissing of geese>.

—**go like a bird** to go very well or very easily: *The car goes like a bird with the new engine.*

—**kill two birds with one stone** to fulfil two purposes with one action: *By spending the weekend there we were able to kill two birds with one stone. We did some business and we were able to visit my parents.*

—**strictly for the birds** acceptable only to people who are not very clever, fashionable, etc. *You can't tell me the moon is made of green cheese. That's strictly for the birds.*

—**the birds and the bees** the basic facts of human sexual behaviour and reproduction: *The mother explained to her young daughter about the birds and the bees.*

—**the early bird catches the worm** a person who arrives early or acts promptly is in a position to gain advantage over others.

biscuit

—**take the biscuit** to be much worse than anything that has happened so far: *He is always rude but his latest insults take the biscuit.*

bit

—**champing at the bit** very impatient: *The children are champing at the bit to open their presents.*<A horse chews at its bit when it is impatient>.

—**take the bit between one's teeth** to act on one's own and cease to follow other people's instructions or advice: *He dismissed his advisers, took the bit between his teeth and ruled the country on his own.* <Refers to a horse escaping from the control of its rider>.

bite

—**bite off more than one can chew** to try to do more than one can without too much difficulty: *When she took over the running of both firms she was biting off more than she can chew.*

—**bite the bullet** to do something unpleasant but unavoidable with courage: *He can't afford to take a reduction in salary but he's just going to have to bite the bullet and agree to it.*

—**bite the dust** to die or cease to operate or function: *The society bit the dust for lack of membership.*

—**bite the hand that feeds one** to treat badly

someone who has helped one: *He got the girl her first job but she won't even speak to him now—a real case of biting the hand that feeds you.*

—**have more than one bite at the cherry** to have more than one opportunity to succeed at something: *You can always take the exam again. You have more than one bite at the cherry.*

bitter

—**a bitter pill to swallow** something unpleasant or difficult that one has to accept: *When he got engaged to someone else it was a bitter pill for her to swallow.*

—**to the bitter end** right to the very end, however unpleasant that is: *We had to stay at the boring concert to the bitter end.* <A bitt is a post on a ship's deck for tying cable or rope to and the part of the cable fastened round it is the bitter end. When the cable is let out to the bitter end, no further adjustment is possible>.

black

—**as black as one is painted** as bad as everyone says one is: *She can be very helpful, not nearly as black as she is painted.*

—**black sheep** a member of a family or group who is not up to the standard of the rest of the group. *They never talk about the youngest son. He was the black sheep of the family.*

—**in black and white** in writing or in print: *We must have the details of the agreement in black and white.*

—**in (someone's) black books** *same as* **in (someone's) bad books**—*see* **bad**.

—**in the black** showing a profit, not in debt: *His bank account is rarely in the black.* <From the use of black ink to make entries on the credit side of a ledger>.

—**the pot calling the kettle black** *see* **pot**.

blank

—**blank cheque** permission to do exactly what one wants: *The manager has been given a blank cheque in the reorganization of the firm.* <Refers to a cheque made out to someone with the amount left blank>.

—**draw a blank** to fail to find out anything after much searching or research.

blanket

—**on the wrong side of the blanket** illegitimate: *The prince fathered many children who were born on the wrong side of the blanket.*

—**wet blanket** a dull person who makes other people feel depressed: *We were all enjoying the party until the host's girlfriend started asking everyone to leave. She's such a wet blanket.*

blessing

—**a blessing in disguise** something that turns out to advantage after at first seeming unfortunate: *Getting the sack was a blessing in disguise. He got a much better job after that.*

—**a mixed blessing** something that has disadvantages as well as advantages: *Having a lodger was a mixed blessing. The extra income was useful but he interfered with their privacy.*

blind

—**blind alley** *see* **alley**.

—**blind as a bat** *see* **bat**.

—**the blind leading the blind** referring to a situation in which the person who is in charge of others knows as little as they do: *He's supposed to be a skiing instructor but he's only a beginner himself. It's an obvious case of the blind leading the blind.*

blood

—**bad blood** hostile feelings: *There has been bad blood between the two sisters.*

—**in cold blood** deliberately and calmly: *She killed her husband in cold blood. She wasn't hysterical at the time.*

—**like getting blood out of a stone** very difficult, almost impossible: *Getting him to say anything is like getting blood out of a stone.*

—**new blood** new members of an organization: *Most of the members of the club are old and it desperately needs some new blood.*

—**sweat blood** to put a very deal of effort into something: *She sweated blood to save the money.*

blow

—**blow hot and cold** to keep changing one's mind or attitude: *Sometimes he's friendly, sometimes he's nasty. He keeps blowing hot and cold.*

—**blow over** to cease and be forgotten: *Their disagreement soon blew over.*

—**blow one's own trumpet** to boast about one's achievements: *We're tired of her blowing her own trumpet since she won the contest.*

—**blow the gaff** to tell something secret, often something illegal, to someone, often the police: *He blew the gaff on his fellow burglar.* <Perhaps from gaff, meaning mouth>.

—**blow the whistle on (someone)** to reveal or report someone's wrongdoing so that it will be stopped: *He blew the whistle on the smugglers.* <From the practice of blowing a whistle to indicate a foul in some ball games>.

—**see which way the wind blows** to wait and find out how a situation is developing before making a decision: *He's going to wait and see* *which way the wind blows before asking for promotion.* <From sailing>.

blue

—**blue-eyed boy** a person who is someone's favourite: *The young clerk will soon be promoted. He's the manager's blue-eyed boy.*

—**bluestocking** an educated, intellectual woman: *He calls any intelligent woman a bluestocking.* <From a group of women in the 18th century who met in London to discuss intellectual and philosophical issues and some of whom wore blue worsted stockings>.

—**once in a blue moon** hardly ever: *Once in a blue moon he sends her flowers.*

—**out of the blue** without warning: *The news of his death came out of the blue.*

bluff

—**call (someone's) bluff** to make (someone) prove that what he or she says is true is really genuine: *He kept telling his colleagues that he wanted to leave until the boss called his bluff and asked him if it was indeed the case.* <Refers to poker, the card game>.

board

—**above board** *see* **above**.

—**across the board** *see* **across**.

—**go by the board** to be abandoned: *His dreams of going to university have gone by the board with the death of his father.* <The board here is a ship's board or side, and to go by the board literally was to vanish overboard>.

—**sweep the board** to win all the prizes: *The young tennis player has swept the board at all the local contests.* <The board referred to is the surface on which card games are played and on which the bets are placed>.

boat

—**burn one's boats** to do something that makes it impossible to go back to one's previous position: *You've given up your job, you'll have to go now—you've burned your boats.*

—**in the same boat** in the same situation: *Both of them are in the same boat—they're both single mothers.*

—**miss the boat** to fail to take advantage of a opportunity: *The application forms had to be in yesterday —so you've missed the boat.*

—**rock the boat** to do something to endanger or spoil a comfortable or happy situation: *You have a good job here—so don't rock the boat by calling a strike.*

bolt

—**a bolt from the blue** something very sudden and unexpected: *His transfer to another branch was a bolt from the blue.*

—**shoot one's bolt** to make one's final effort, have no other possible course of action: *When he reported the teacher to the headteacher he shot his bolt because the head rejected the complaint.*

bone

—**a bone of contention** a cause of dispute: *The state of her bedroom is a bone of contention between her and her mother.* <Dogs fight over bones>.

—**have a bone to pick with (someone)** to have a matter to disagree about with (someone): *He said to the other man that he had a bone to pick with him for going out with his girlfriend.* <From dogs fighting over a bone>.

—**make no bones about (something)** to have no hesitation or restraint about (saying or doing something openly): *She made no bones about the fact that she disliked him.* <Originally a reference to finding no bones in one's soup, which was therefore easier to eat>.

—**near the bone** (1) referring too closely to something that should not be mentioned; tactless: *Some of the guests remarks about adultery were a bit near the bone. The host's having an affair.* (2) slightly indecent or crude: *Some of the comedian's jokes were a bit near the bone.*

—**the bare bones (of something)** *see* **bare**.

boo

—**would not say boo to a goose** to be extremely timid: *She's very aggressive but her husband wouldn't say boo to a goose.*

book

—**a closed book** something about which one knows nothing, something that one does not understand: *The new technology is a closed book to older members of staff.*

—**an open book** something that is easily understood: *His motives were an open book to all of us.*

—**bring (someone) to book** to make (someone) explain or be punished for his or her actions: *They thought they could cause the damage and walk away but they were soon brought to book.* <Perhaps referring to a book where a police officer keeps a note of crimes>.

—**by the book** strictly according to the rules: *The headteacher won't give us a day off. He does everything by the book.*

—**cook the books** illegally to alter accounts or financial records: *He had been cooking the books, so they did not know money had gone missing.*

—**in someone's black books** *see* **bad**.

—**read (someone) like a book** to understand (someone) completely, not to be deceived by someone: *I know that he's planning something nasty. I can read him like a book.*

—**suit (someone's) book** to be advantageous to (someone): *It doesn't suit her book for him to leave.* <Perhaps referring to a bookmaker who accepts bets only if he thinks he will not lose too much money on them, in other words if the bets suit his book>.

—**take a leaf out of (someone's) book** *see* **leaf**.

—**throw the book at (someone)** to criticize or punish (someone) severely, to charge (someone) with several crimes at once: *The judge threw the book at him. He's got a ten-year sentence.* <Literally, to charge someone with every crime listed in a book>.

boot

—**get the boot** to be dismissed or discharged from one's job: *The woman got the boot for stealing.*

—**give (someone) the boot** to dismiss or discharge (someone): *They're giving all the older workers the boot.*

—**hang up one's boots** to retire from work, to cease doing an activity: *The elderly man has played bowls for years but he is hanging up his boots now.* <From hanging up football boots after a game>.

—**lick (someone's) boots** to flatter (someone) and do everything he or she wants: *The new boy is licking the boss's boots to get promotion.*

—**pull oneself up by one's bootstraps** to become successful through one's own efforts: *He owns several stores but he started as an errand boy and pulled himself up by his bootstraps.*

—**put the boot in (someone)** (1) to kick (someone) when he or she is already lying on the ground injured: *The bullies put the boot in and kicked their victim to death.* (2) to treat (someone) cruelly or harshly after he or she has suffered already: *He lost his job and his wife put the boot in and left him.*

—**the boot is on the other foot** the situation has been completely turned round: *She begged him to stay but now the boot is on the other foot and he is pleading to be allowed back.*

—**too big for one's boots** too conceited: *Since she won the beauty contest she has been too big for her boots.*

bottle

—**crack a bottle** to open a bottle: *Let's crack a bottle of wine to celebrate.*

—**hit the bottle** to drink a great deal of alcohol: *Since his wife died he's been hitting the bottle.*

—**on the bottle** drinking a great deal of alcohol regularly: *He's been on the bottle since he lost his job.*

bottom

—**at the bottom of (something)** the cause of (something): *I might have known that he was at the bottom of the rumours that were going around about his wife.*

—**bottom drawer** a collection of articles for the home, which a young woman gathered together before her marriage: *She's keen to get married so she's already started collecting linen and cutlery for her bottom drawer.*

—**get to the bottom of (something)** to find out the exact cause of (something) or the true nature of (something): *The doctors cannot get to the bottom of her chest complaint.*

—**hit rock bottom** to reach the lowest possible level: *Share prices hit rock bottom last week. Her spirits have hit rock bottom since her friend left.*

—**scrape the (bottom of the) barrel** *see* **barrel**.

bow[1]

—**bow and scrape** to behave in a very humble and respectful way: *They expect the staff to bow and scrape to the rich guests.*

—**bow out** to leave or cease to take part in a project, organization, etc: *She's been secretary for three years but she's bowing out now.* <From performers bowing to the audience at the end of a show>.

—**take a bow** to accept acknowledgement of one's achievements: *Everyone thinks you've done a good job, so take a bow.* <As above>.

bow[2]

—**draw the long bow** to exaggerate: *He said that she was absolutely penniless but he was drawing the long bow.* <An archer carries a spare bow in case one breaks>.

—**have another** *or* **more than one string to one's bow** to have another possibility, plan, etc, available to one: *He's applied for other jobs as well as that one because it's as well to have more than one string to your bow.*

brain

—**cudgel** *or* **rack one's brains** to think very hard: *I racked my brains to remember the first name of her husband.*

—**have (something) on the** *or* **one's brain** to think or worry about (something) continuously: *She's got marriage on the brain.*

—**pick (someone's) brains** to find out (someone's) ideas and knowledge about a subject so that one can put them to one's own use: *Stop picking my brains and use an encyclopedia.*

brass

—**get down to brass tacks** to consider the basic facts or issues of something: *We must get down to brass tacks and discuss how much rent we can afford.*

—**the top brass** the most important people in an organization, especially originally in the army: *The top brass have individual offices but the staff all work in one room.* <From the metal decoration on military uniforms>.

bread

—**bread and butter** one's basic living: *How does he earn his bread and butter?*

—**know which side one's bread is buttered** to know the course of action that is to one's greatest advantage: *He certainly won't leave his wife. He knows which side his bread is buttered.*

—**on the breadline** with scarcely enough money to live on: *Since the father lost his job the family has been on the breadline.*

—**the greatest thing since sliced bread** a person or thing that is greatly admired and appreciated: *He is a careless worker but he thinks he is the greatest thing since sliced bread.*

break

—**break even** to have one's losses balanced by one's gains, to make neither a loss nor a profit: *I didn't make any money on my investment but at least I broke even.*

—**break of day** dawn: *The first train to town leaves at break of day.*

—**break the bank** *see* **bank**.

—**break the ice** *see* **ice**.

—**break the news** *see* **news**.

—**make a break for it** to attempt to escape: *The prisoner made a break for it when he was being led into court.*

breath

—**catch one's breath** (1) to breathe in sharply in fear, surprise or pain: *She caught her breath when she saw the huge dark shape.* (2) to rest for a short time: *I'll have to catch my breath after climbing the hill.*

—**hold one's breath** to wait anxiously for something: *We held our breath as the child walked along the roof edge.*

—**save one's breath** to stop talking since one's words are having no effect: *Save your breath. He'll leave school if he wants to.*

—**take (someone's) breath away** to surprise (someone) greatly: *They took her parents' breath away when they announced that they were married.*

—**under one's breath** very quietly, in a whisper: *He asked what time it was under his breath.*

—**waste one's breath** to say something that is not taken heed of: *I tried to persuade them to stay but I was wasting my breath.*

breathe

—**be able to breathe again** to be able to relax after a period of anxiety, etc: *You can breathe again! The police have gone.*

—**breathe down (someone's) neck** (1) to be very close behind (someone): *He was in the lead but there were several runners breathing down his neck.* (2) to be waiting impatiently for something from (someone): *The boss is breathing down her neck for those letters.*

—**breathe one's last** to die: *He breathed his last just before midnight.*

brick

—**bang one's head against a brick wall** *see* **bang**.

—**drop a brick** to say something tactless or undiplomatic: *She dropped a brick when she introduced the boss's wife as the cleaner.*

—**like a cat on hot bricks** very nervous or restless: *He is like a cat on hot bricks when he is waiting for a phone call from her.*

—**like a ton of bricks** to treat or punish (someone) severely: *The headmaster came down on the boys like a ton of bricks for playing truant.*

—**try to make bricks without straw** to try to do something without the necessary materials or equipment: *She has so few supplies in her kitchen that trying to make a meal there is like trying to make bricks without straw.* <A biblical reference, from Pharaoh's command concerning the Israelites in Exodus 5:7>.

bridge

—**burn one's bridges** *same as* **burn one's boats** —*see* **boat**.

—**cross a bridge when one comes to it** to worry about or deal with a problem only when it actually arises: *She keeps worrying about what might happen in the future. She must learn to cross a bridge only when she comes to it.*

—**try to build bridges** to try to put right a disagreement or a quarrel: *The feud's still on. I tried to build bridges but without success.*

—**water under the bridge** *see* **water**.

brief

—**hold no brief for (someone** *or* **something)**

not to support or defend (someone or something): *I hold no brief for these new methods.*

bright

—**bright-eyed and bushy-tailed** very cheerful and lively: *They were both bright-eyed and bushy-tailed when they came back from holiday.*

—**look on the bright side** to be optimistic, to see the advantages of one's situation: *You might not like your present job but look on the bright side—it's well paid.*

bring

—**bring down to earth** *see* **earth**.

—**bring home the bacon** *see* **bacon**.

—**bring home to** *see* **home**.

—**bring (someone) round** (1) to bring (someone) back from unconsciousness: *The doctor brought him round with the kiss of life.* (2) to persuade (someone) to do something: *He was reluctant to participate but we brought him round eventually.*

—**bring to a head** *see* **head**.

broad

—**broad in the beam** *see* **beam**.

—**have broad shoulders** to be able to accept a great deal of responsibility, criticism, etc: *I don't mind them blaming me. I've got broad shoulders.*

—**in broad daylight** during the day: *The child was attacked in broad daylight.*

broken

—**broken reed** *see* **reed**.

brother

—**am I my brother's keeper?** the actions or affairs of other people are not my responsibility: *So my colleague was rude to you. Am I my brother's keeper?* <From the biblical story of Cain and Abel, Genesis 4:9>.

—**Big Brother** a powerful person or organization thought to be constantly monitoring and controlling people's actions: *I prefer to work for a small company. In a big organization I get a feeling that Big Brother is watching me.* <From the dictator in George Orwell's novel *1984*>.

brown

—**in a brown study** deep in thought: *She won't hear you. She's in a brown study.*

brush

—**brush up on (something)** to refresh one's knowledge of (something): *You should brush up on your French before you go on holiday.*

—**get the brush-off** to be rejected or refused abruptly: *He asked her to the cinema but he got the brush-off when she said "no."*

bucket

—**a drop in the bucket** a very small part of what is needed: *Our contribution to the famine fund is only a drop in the bucket.*

—**come down in buckets** to rain heavily: *As usual in August, it's coming down in buckets.*

—**kick the bucket** to die: *They were just waiting for the old man to kick the bucket.* <"Bucket" here is perhaps a beam from which pigs were hung after being killed>.

—**weep buckets** to cry a great deal: *She wept buckets at the sad film.*

Buggins

—**Buggins' turn** one's turn to be promoted, according to some automatic or routine system, not according to merit. *He got the job because it's Buggins' turn, not because he's good.*

bull

—**hit the bull's eye** to do or say something that is very appropriate or relevant: *You hit the bull's eye when you said you thought she was pregnant.* <The exact centre of a dart board>.

—**like a bull in a china shop** in a very clumsy way: *She went charging off like a bull in a china shop and knocked my papers to the floor.*

—**like a red rag to a bull** *see* **red**.

—**take the bull by the horns** to tackle (something) boldly: *If you want them to stop the noise you'll have to take the bull by the horns and complain.*

bullet

—**bite the bullet** *see* **bite**.

—**get the bullet** to be dismissed or discharged: *Half the firm have got the bullet.*

—**give (someone) the bullet** to dismiss or discharge (someone): *The boss will give you the bullet if you don't turn up.*

burden

—**the burden of proof** the responsibility for proving something: *The burden of proof lies with the accuser.* <A legal term>.

burn

—**burn one's boats** *or* **bridges** *see* **boat**.

—**burn one's fingers** *see* **finger**.

—**burn the candle at both ends** *see* **candle**.

—**burn the midnight oil** *see* **midnight**.

—**the burning question** a question of great interest to many people: *The burning question is who is our new owner?*

Burton

—**gone for a Burton** dead, ruined, broken, etc: *The old car's gone for a Burton.* <Originally a military term from Burton, a kind of ale>.

bus

—**busman's holiday** a holiday spent doing much the same as one does when one is at work: *The house-painter's wife expects him to take a busman's holiday and redecorate their house.* <Refers to a bus driver who drives a bus on holiday>.

bush

—**beat about the bush** *see* **beat**.

—**bush telegraph** the fast spreading of information by word of mouth: *I heard on the bush telegraph that he had resigned.* <A reference to the Australian bush>.

bushel

—**hide one's light under a bushel** *see* **light**.

business

—**mean business** to be determined (to do something), to be serious: *He was not joking about the redundancies. He means business.*

—**mind one's own business** to concern oneself with one's own affairs and not interfere in those of other people: *When he tried to give advice to the girl she asked him to mind his own business.*

bust

—**bust a gut** *see* **gut**.

—**go bust** to fail, to be financially ruined: *During the recession many firms went bust.*

butter

—**butterfingers** a person who often drops things: *She's such a butterfingers. She dropped the tray full of dishes.*

—**butter (someone) up** to flatter (someone) a great deal, usually in order to get him or her to do something for one. *He doesn't really like the boss, but he's buttering him up to get a pay rise.*

—**know which side of one's bread is buttered** *see* **bread**.

—**look as though butter would not melt in one's mouth** to appear very innocent, respectable, etc: *The girl looks as though butter wouldn't melt in her mouth but she actually behaves very wildly.*

butterfly

—**have butterflies in one's stomach** to have a fluttering sensation in one's stomach as a sign of nervousness. *Every night she has butterflies in her stomach before she goes on stage.*

button

—**buttonhole (someone)** to catch (someone's) attention and engage him or her in conversation: *The minister buttonholed me as I came out of the church.* <Originally "button hold", to hold by the button>.

C

cabbage

—**not as green as one is cabbage-looking** not as foolish or inexperienced as one appears to be: *He won't accept a reduction in salary. He's not as green as he is cabbage-looking.*

cahoots

—**in cahoots with (someone)** forming a secret partnership with (someone), especially to do something dishonest or illegal: *The police think that the bank clerk was in cahoots with the robbers.* <Cahoot, a partnership, perhaps from *cahute*, French, a cabin>.

Cain

—**raise Cain** to make a great deal of noise or fuss: *He will raise Cain when he sees the damage to his car.* <Refers to Cain in the Bible who killed his brother Abel, Genesis 4>.

cake

—**a piece of cake** something easy to do: *Winning the race was a piece of cake.*

—**a slice** *or* **share of the cake** a share of something desirable or valuable: *You should invest some money in the firm and get a slice of the cake.*

—**cakes and ale** pleasant or enjoyable activity: *A student's life is not all cakes and ale. You have to do some work.* <From Shakespeare's *Twelfth Night*, Act 2, scene iii>.

—**have one's cake and eat it** *or* **eat one's cake and have it** to have the advantages of two things or situations when doing, possessing, etc, one of them would normally make the other one impossible: *He's engaged to one of the sisters but he would like to have his cake and eat it and go out with the other one.*

—**icing on the cake** *see* **ice**.

—**sell** *or* **go like hot cakes** to sell very quickly: *That computer game is selling like hot cakes since it was advertised on TV.*

—**take the cake** *same as* **take the biscuit**—*see* **biscuit**.

calf

—**calf love** love felt by a very young, inexperienced person: *He is unhappy that she has gone away but calf love soon passes.*

—**kill the fatted calf** to provide a lavish meal, especially to mark a celebration of someone's arrival or return: *Our daughter's coming home from Canada, so we're killing the fatted calf.* <From the parable of the prodigal son in the Bible, Luke 15:23>.

call

—**a close call** *same as* **a close shave**—*see* **close**[2].

—**answer** *or* **obey the call of nature** to go to the toilet: *Where is the nearest public toilet? I need to answer the call of nature.*

—**call a spade** *see* **spade**.

—**call it a day** *see* **day**.

—**call it quits** *see* **quit**.

—**call the shots** *see* **shot**.

—**pay a call** to go to the toilet: *Excuse me, I have to pay a call.*

camel

—**the straw that breaks the camel's back** *see* **straw**.

—**swallow a camel** to regard something as being acceptable, true, fair, etc, when it is quite clearly not so: *How can they swallow the camel of their colleague's unfair dismissal?*

camp

—**have a foot in both camps** to have associations with two groups who have opposing and conflicting views and attitudes: *He is a member of staff but he has shares in the company, so he has a foot in both camps.*

can

—**carry the can** to accept blame or responsibility, usually for something that someone else has done: *Several of the pupils set fire to the school but the one who was caught carried the can.*

—**in the can** certain, agreed or decided upon: *He had a good interview so the job's in the can.* <Refers to a completed cinema film that is stored in large metal containers or cans>.

candle

—**burn the candle at both ends** to work and/or to play during too many hours of the day: *He has a full-time job and studies at night. He is certainly burning the candle at both ends.*

—**cannot hold a candle to (someone)** to be not nearly as good or as talented as (someone): *The rest of the football team cannot hold a candle to the new player.* <Literally, someone who is

not good enough even to hold a light while someone else does the work>.

—**the game is not worth the candle** something that is not worth the effort that has to be spent on it: *She's well paid but she works such long hours that she has decided that the game is not worth the candle.* <From the translation of the French phrase *le jeu n'en vaut la chandelle,* referring to a gambling session in which the amount of money at stake was not enough to pay for the candles required to give light at the game>.

canoe

—**paddle one's own canoe** to control one's own affairs without help from anyone else: *Now her father's dead she'll have to paddle her own canoe.*

cap

—**a feather in one's cap** *see* **feather**.

—**cap in hand** humbly: *He has gone back cap in hand to ask for his job back.* <Removing one's cap in someone's presence is a sign of respect>.

—**if the cap fits, wear it** if what has been said applies to you, then you should take note of it: *I simply said that honesty was not common these days, but if the cap fits, wear it.*

—**put one's thinking cap on** to think very carefully about a problem: *If we put our thinking caps on I am sure we can find our way out of the difficulty.*

—**set one's cap at (someone)** to try to attract (someone of the opposite sex): *She was so anxious to get married that she set her cap at every man in sight.* <Perhaps a mistranslation of French *metter le cap,* to head towards>.

—**to cap it all** on top of everything else, finally: *I was late for work and then to cap it all I missed the bus.*

capital

—**make capital out of (something)** to make use of (something) for one's own advantage: *The counsel for the defence made capital out of the witness's nervousness.*

—**with a capital A, B, C, etc** used to emphasize that the person or thing described is an extreme example of his, her or its kind: *They are certainly villains with a capital V.*

card

—**get one's cards** to be dismissed or discharged: *The clerk got his cards for stealing money.*

—**have a card up one's sleeve** to have an idea, plan of action, etc, in reserve to be used if necessary: *They think that they have won but their opponent has a card up his sleeve.* <From cheating at cards>.

—**on the cards** likely: *Their dismissal is very much on the cards.* <From reading the cards in fortune-telling>.

—**play one's cards close to one's chest** to be secretive or non-communicative about one's plans or intentions: *I think that they are moving overseas but they are playing their cards very close to their chest.* <From holding one's cards close to one in card-playing so that one's opponents will not see them>.

—**play one's cards right** to act in such a way as to take advantage of a situation: *If she plays her cards right he will marry her.*

—**put one's cards on the table** to make known one's plans or intentions: *If you want us to help you'll have to put your cards on the table.* <In card-playing, to show one's opponent one's cards>.

—**stack the cards against (someone)** to make it very difficult for (someone) to succeed: *The cards are stacked against him finding a job because he has no qualifications.*

carpet

—**on the carpet** about to be rebuked or punished by someone in authority: *She will be on the carpet when the boss discovers that she is late.* <Refers to the piece of carpet in front of a desk, where someone might stand to be rebuked>.

—**sweep (something) under the carpet** to try to hide or forget about (something unpleasant): *They try to sweep under the carpet the fact that their son's in prison.*

—**the red carpet** special, respectful treatment: *They're rolling out the red carpet. They've invited the boss and his wife to dinner.* <Refers to the red carpet put down for a royal person to walk on during official visits>.

carrot

—**carrot and stick** reward and punishment as a method of persuasion: *The headmaster uses a policy of carrot and stick with the pupils. He praises them a lot but he punishes them a lot also.* <See below>.

—**hold out a carrot to (someone)** to promise (someone) a reward in order to get him or her to do something: *If you want them to work late you'll have to hold out the carrot of extra money.* <From urging a donkey forward by holding a carrot in front of it>.

carry

—**carry a torch for (someone)** to be in love with someone, especially with someone who does not return it: *She's carried the torch for the boss for years but he doesn't even notice her.* <A torch or a flame was regarded as symbolic of love>.

—**carry coals to Newcastle** *see* **coal**.

—**carry the can** *see* **can**.

—**carry the day** *see* **day**.

cart

—**put the cart before the horse** to do or say things in the wrong order: *He painted the walls before the ceiling. He certainly put the cart before the horse.*

carte

—**be given carte blanche** to be given complete freedom to act as one wishes: *The owner has given him carte blanche to furnish her house.* <Literally, a blank card>.

Casanova

—**Casanova** a man who has relationships with many women: *He's a real Casanova. He's been out with most of the girls in the office.* <From Giacomo Casanova, a famous 18th-century Italian lover and adventurer>.

Cassandra

—**Cassandra** a person who makes predictions about unpleasant future events but who is never believed: *She's a real Cassandra, she's always seeing gloom ahead.* <In Greek legend, Cassandra, who was the daughter of Priam, king of Troy, had the gift of prophecy but was destined never to be believed. She predicted the fall of Troy>.

cast

—**cast pearls before swine** to offer something valuable or desirable to someone who does not appreciate it: *Taking her to the opera was a case of casting pearls before swine.* <A biblical reference to Matthew 7:6>.

—**cast the first stone** to be the first person to blame or criticize someone: *Eventually everyone blamed him but it was his sister who cast the first stone.* <A biblical reference to John 8:7, about a woman who was to be punished by being stoned to death>.

—**the die is cast** *see* **die**[2].

castle

—**castles in the air** *or* **castles in Spain** dreams or hopes that are unlikely ever to be realized: *She builds castles in the air about being a princess.*

cat

—**a cat may look at a king** there is nothing to prevent an ordinary person from looking at someone important: *She asked me why I was looking at her but I just said, "A cat can look at a king".*

—**bell the cat** *see* **bell**.

—**curiosity killed the cat** said as a warning not to pry into other people's affairs: *One day someone is going to hit him for asking personal questions, and he'll find out that curiosity killed the cat.*

—**has the cat got your tongue?** said to someone who does not say anything out of timidity, etc, to encourage him or her to speak: *What have you got to say in your defence? Has the cat got your tongue?*

—**let the cat out of a bag** to reveal something secret or confidential, especially accidentally or at an inappropriate time. *They didn't want anyone to know that they had been married that day but their friend let the cat out of the bag.* <Supposedly referring to a fairground trick in which a customer was offered a cat in a bag when he or she thought it was a piglet in the bag>.

—**like a cat on hot bricks** *see* **brick**.

—**like a scalded cat** in a rapid, excited way: *She's rushing around like a scalded cat to get the meal ready for the guests.*

—**like something the cat brought** *or* **dragged in** very untidy or bedraggled: *After the football match the boys looked like something the cat brought in.*

—**not to be enough room to swing a cat** for there to be very little space: *She can't stay at her daughter's house. There's not enough room there to swing a cat.*

—**not to have a cat's chance in hell** *or* **a cat's chance in hell** to have no chance at all: *They don't have a cat's chance in hell of winning.*

—**play cat and mouse with (someone)** to treat (someone) in such a way that he or she does not know what is going to happen to them at any time: *The terrorists were playing cat and mouse with the hostages. One minute they thought that they were going to be released, the next they thought that they were going to be killed.* <A cat often plays with its prey, a mouse, before killing it>.

—**put** *or* **set the cat among the pigeons** to cause a disturbance, especially a sudden or unexpected one: *Her neighbour certainly put the cat among the pigeons when he accidentally mentioned her husband's affair.*

—**rain cats and dogs** to rain very heavily: *The picnic's cancelled—it's raining cats and dogs.*

—**see which way the cat jumps** to wait and see what other people are going to do and how the situation is developing before deciding on one's course of action: *I'm not going to rush into putting in an offer for the house. I'm going to wait and see how the cat jumps.*

—**the cat's pyjamas** *or* **whiskers** a person who is very highly regarded: *He thinks he's the cat's pyjamas in his new sports car.*

—**there's more than one way to kill** *or* **skin a cat** there's more than one way method of doing things: *He left, not because he disliked the work, but because his colleagues were so unpleasant to him. There's more than one way to kill a cat*

—**when the cat's away, the mice will play** when the person in charge or in control is not present the people whom he or she is in charge of will work less hard, misbehave, etc. *When the boss is away, they take very long lunch breaks. When the cat's away, the mice will play.*

catch

—**catch (someone) in the act** to catch (someone) actually doing something wrong or bad: *He hoped to steal the money and run but he was caught in the act by the police.*

—**catch it** to be scolded or punished: *He'll catch it when his father sees what he's done to the car.*

—**catch one's breath** *see* **breath**.

—**catch one's death (of cold)** *see* **death**.

—**catch (someone) napping** to surprise (someone) when he or she is unprepared or inattentive: *The early winter caught them napping. They had no fuel for the fire.*

—**catch (someone) on the hop** *see* **hop**.

—**catch (someone) red-handed** *see* **red**.

—**catch the sun** to become sunburnt or suntanned: *The child's caught the sun although she was outside for only a short time.*

—**Catch 22** a situation in which one can never win or from which one can never escape, being constantly hindered by a rule or restriction that itself changes to block any change in one's plans; a difficulty that prevents one from escaping from an unpleasant or dangerous situation. *If you need an emergency loan you can apply to the Social Fund, but it is a loan for credit-worthy people so you won't get it. It's Catch 22.* <From the title of a novel by Joseph Heller>.

—**catch (someone) with his** *or* **her pants** *or* **trousers down** to surprise (someone) when he or she is unprepared or doing something wrong, especially when this causes embarrassment: *The boss found his assistant manager chatting to his secretary instead of writing the monthly report. He certainly regretted being caught with his pants down.* <Refers to walking in on someone partially dressed>.

caviar

—**caviar to the general** something considered to be too sophisticated to be appreciated by ordinary people: *Only intellectuals read his books. They're caviar to the general.* <From Shakespeare's *Hamlet*, Act 2, scene ii>.

ceiling

—**go through the ceiling** to rise very high, to soar: *House prices went through the ceiling.*

—**hit the ceiling** *or* **roof** to lose one's temper completely: *She hit the ceiling when he cancelled the appointment.*

ceremony

—**stand on ceremony** to behave in a formal manner: *You can take your jacket off. You don't have to stand on ceremony.*

certain

—**in a certain condition** pregnant: *She has been sick because she is in a certain condition.*

—**of a certain age** *see* **age**.

chalk

—**as different as chalk and cheese** completely different: *They're sisters but they are as different as chalk and cheese.*

—**chalk it up to experience** accept the inevitability of something: *You won't get your money back from the con-man. You might as well chalk it up to the experience*

—**not by a long chalk** not by a long way, by no means: *They haven't given up yet, not by a long chalk.* <From the vertical chalk lines drawn to mark scores in a game, the longer lines representing the greater number of points>.

champ

—**champing at the bit** *see* **bit**.

chance

—**chance it** to take a risk: *I won't take an umbrella. I think I'll chance it.*

—**chance one's arm** *see* **arm**.

—**fancy one's chances** to think that one is highly likely to succeed: *Even with so many top-class competitors he still fancies his chances.*

—**have a fighting chance** to have a possibility of success if a great effort is made: *The team still have a fighting chance of winning the tournament but they face tough opposition.*

—**have an eye to the main chance** to watch carefully for what will be advantageous or profitable to oneself: *He's learning to play golf because the boss plays it and he always has an eye to the main chance.*

—**have a sporting chance** to have a reasonable chance of success: *Many experienced people have applied for the job but with his qualifications he has at least a sporting chance.*

—**not to have a cat's chance in hell** *see* **cat**.

—**not to have the ghost of a chance** not to have the slightest possibility of success: *He hopes to win the race but he really doesn't have the ghost of a chance.*

—**on the off-chance (of** *or* **that)** in the hope (of or that), assuming there is the possibility (of or that): *We went to the theatre on the off-chance of getting seats.You should go early in the off-chance that you get in.*

—**take one's chance** *or* **chances** to take a risk or take advantage of an opportunity on the understanding that one accepts whatever happens: *You'll just have to take your chance and apply for the job. If your present employer finds out it's too bad.*

change

—**change hands** to pass into different ownership: *Houses in that street change hands extremely quickly.*

—**change horses in mid-stream** to change one's opinions, plans, sides, etc, in the middle of something: *At the beginning of the election campaign he was going to vote Conservative but he changed horses in mid-stream.*

—**change one's mind** to alter one's decision or intention: *They were going to go to Greece but they have changed their mind.*

—**change one's tune** to change one's attitude or opinion: *He disagreed with me yesterday but he changed his tune when he heard the facts.*

—**chop and change** *see* **chop**.

—**have a change of heart** to alter one's opinion or decision, usually to a better or kinder one: *The headmaster was going to expel the girl but he had a change of heart when he saw how sorry she was.*

—**ring the changes** to add variety by doing or arranging things in different ways: *She cannot afford new furniture but she rings the changes by shifting the furniture around from room to room.*

chapter

—**a chapter of accidents** *see* **accident**.

—**chapter and verse** detailed sources for a piece of information: *Don' t just make vague references in your essay to other writers. You must give chapter and verse.* <From the method of referring to biblical texts>.

charity

—**charity begins at home** one must take care of oneself and one's family before concerning oneself with others: *She would like to be able to contribute to the welfare of children overseas but her own children need new clothes and charity begins at home.*

—**cold as charity** extremely cold: *When the central heating went off in the huge house it was as cold as charity.* <Charity is referred to as cold since it tends to be given to the poor and disadvantaged by organizations rather than by individual people and so lacks human feeling or warmth>.

charm

—**lead a charmed life** regularly to have good fortune and avoid misfortune, harm or danger: *The racing driver seems to lead a charmed life. He has never been involved in an accident.*

—**work like a charm** to be very effective, to work very well: *His efforts to persuade her to go out with him worked like a charm.*

chase

—**chase after rainbows** to spend time and effort in thinking about, or in trying to obtain, things that it is impossible for one to achieve: *He should concentrate on doing his job and stop applying for ones he won't get. He spends most of his time chasing rainbows.*

cheek

—**cheek by jowl** side by side, very close together: *Workers and management work cheek by jowl in the same large office.*

—**turn the other cheek** to take no action against someone who has harmed one, thereby giving him or her the opportunity to harm one again: *I know he insulted you but it will cause less trouble for everyone if you turn the other cheek rather than take your revenge on him.* <A biblical reference to Matthew 5:39, "Whosoever shall smite thee on thy right cheek, turn to him the left one also">.

cheese

—**as different as chalk and cheese** *see* **chalk**.

—**cheesed off** bored, weary or dissatisfied: *He's really cheesed off with his present job.*

—**hard cheese** bad luck, a sentiment usually expressed by someone who does not care about another's misfortune: *It's hard cheese for him if* *he has to work late but the rest of us can leave early.*

—**say "cheese"** to smile when one has one's photograph taken: *Don't look so glum, say "cheese".* <When one says "cheese" one's mouth forms a smile>.

cherry

—**have more than one bite at the cherry** *see* **bite**.

cheque

—**blank cheque** *see* **blank**.

Cheshire

—**grin like a Cheshire cat** to smile broadly so as to show one's teeth: *She was grinning like a Cheshire cat as they handed her the prize.* <Refers to *Alice's Adventures in Wonderland* by Lewis Carroll, in which the Cheshire cat gradually disappears except for its smile>.

chest

—**get (something) off one's chest** to tell (someone) about something that is upsetting, worrying or annoying one: *If you know something about the accident you had better get it off your chest and tell the police.*

—**play one's cards close to one's chest** *see* **card**.

chestnut

—**old chestnut** an old joke, usually one no longer funny: *The comedian wasn't amusing. His jokes were old chestnuts I had heard before.*

—**pull (someone's) chestnuts out of the fire** to rescue (someone) from a difficult or dangerous situation, often by putting oneself in difficulty or danger: *He is continually getting himself into financial trouble and he always expects his brother to pull his chestnuts out of the fire and lend him money.* <From a story by the 17th-century French writer La Fontaine, in which a monkey use a cat's paw to get hot nuts from a fire>.

chew

—**bite off more than one can chew** *see* **bite**.

—**chew the cud** to think deeply about something: *I'll have to chew the cud a lot before deciding whether or not to move house.*

—**chew the fat** to have a discussion or conversation: *Let's not rush out anywhere. I think we should chew the fat first.*

chicken

—**chicken-feed** something of very little value or importance; an insignificant amount of money: *They paid her chicken-feed for that valuable desk.*

—**chickens come home to roost** misdeeds, mistakes, etc, that come back with an unpleasant effect on the person who performed the misdeed, especially after a considerable time: *He told everyone that he had never been married, but his chickens came home to roost when his ex-wife turned up.*

—**count one's chickens before they are hatched** to make plans which depend on something that is still uncertain: *Don't give up this job before you are officially offered the other. It's unwise to count your chickens before they're hatched.*

child

—**child's play** something that is very easy to do: *you will find the work child's play.*

—**second childhood** a time when an adult person, often an old person, behaves like a child: *The little boy's father seems to be in his second childhood and keeps playing with the train set. The old man seems to have entered a second childhood—he won't let anyone touch his belongings.*

—**the child is father of the man** the character of an adult is formed from childhood influences: *He's been in and out of prison but his father and uncle were both burglars. The child is father of the man.*

chin

—**keep one's chin up** not to show feelings of depression, worry or fear: *I know it's difficult to find a job but you should keep your chin up and go on trying.*

—**stick one's chin out** to show determination in opposing someone or something: *Her parents tried to stop her going to university but she stuck her chin out and went ahead against their wishes.*

—**take it on the chin** to accept or to suffer (something) with courage: *He was upset when she broke their engagement but he took it on the chin and went out with other girls.*

chink

—**chink in (someone's) armour** *see* **armour**.

chip

—**a chip off the old block** a person who is very like one of his or her parents: *That boy's a real chip off the old block. He's already as good a salesman as his father.*

—**cash in one's chips** to die: *I hear that the old man cashed in his chips on the way to the hospital.* <Refers to a gambler cashing in his or her chips or tokens in exchange for money at the end of a session>.

—**have a chip on one's shoulder** to have an aggressive attitude and act as if everyone is going to insult or ill-treat one, often because one feels inferior: *He has a chip on his shoulder about his lack of education and is always belligerent towards academics.* <Refers to a former American custom by which a young man who wished to provoke a fight would place a piece of wood on his shoulder and dare someone to knock it off>.

—**have had one's chips** to have had, and failed at, all the chances of success one is likely to get: *If he fails the exam this time he's had his chips because he's not allowed to resit it.* <Refers to gambling tokens>.

—**when the chips are down** when a situation has reached a critical stage: *He thought he had many friends but when the chips were down and he was unemployed he found he had only one.* <A gambling terms indicating that the bets have been placed>.

choice

—**Hobson's choice** no choice at all; a choice between accepting what is offered or having nothing at all: *We've only got one empty room for tonight. It's Hobson's choice, I'm afraid.* <Refers to the practice of Tobias Hobson, an English stable-owner in the 17th century, of offering customers only the horse nearest the stable door>.

chop

—**chop and change** to keep altering (something),to keep changing (something): *He's furious at them for chopping and changing their holiday arrangements.*

—**get the chop** (1) to be dismissed or discontinued: *Both he and his research project got the chop.* (2) to be killed: *The gang made sure that their enemy got the chop.*

chord

—**strike a chord** to be familiar in some way: *Something about his voice struck a chord.*

—**touch a chord** to arouse emotion or sympathy: *He is usually very hard-hearted but the little girl's tears touched a chord.*

circle

—**come full circle** to return to the position or situation from which one started: *Diet advice has come full circle. Dieters used to be told to avoid bread but now they are told to eat it.*

—**go round in circles** to keep going over the same ideas without reaching a satisfactory decision or answer: *I think we should postpone this discussion until we have more information. We're just going round in circles.*

—**run round in circles** to dash about and appear to be very busy without accomplishing anything: *She's been running round in circles preparing for the guests—none of the rooms is ready yet.*

—**vicious circle** an unfortunate or bad situation, the result of which produces the original cause of the situation or something similar: *They're stuck in a vicious circle—his wife nags him for going out, and he has to go out to get away from her nagging.* <In logic, the term for the fallacy of proving one statement by the evidence of another which is itself only valid if the first statement is valid>.

clanger

—**drop a clanger** *same as* **drop a brick**—*see* **brick.**

clapper

—**like the clappers** extremely rapidly: *You'll have to go like the clappers to get there on time.*

class

—**in a class by oneself** *or* **itself,** *or* **in a class of its, etc, own** far better than other people or things of the same type, without equal: *The ice cream in that shop is in a class by itself. As an actress, she's in a class of her own.*

clay

—**have feet of clay** *see* **feet.**

clean

—**a clean bill of health** *see* **bill.**

—**a clean slate** a record free of any discredit; an opportunity to make a fresh start: *He has paid the penalty for his wrongdoing and now starts the new job with a clean slate.* <Slates were formerly used for writing on in schools>.

—**clean as a whistle** (1) extremely clean: *The kitchen surfaces were clean as a whistle.* (2) completely without guilt, blameless: *They thought that he was selling drugs but he was found to be clean as a whistle.*

—**cleanliness is next to godliness** it is almost as important to be clean as it is to be religious and virtuous: *The teacher was always trying to get the children to wash their hands by telling them that cleanliness is next to godliness.*

—**come clean** to tell the truth about something, especially after lying about it: *He finally decided to come clean and tell the police about his part in the crime.*

—**(my** *or* **his** *or* **her) hands are clean** I am or he or she is, etc, not guilty or responsible: *The police can question him if they like but his hands are clean.*

—**keep one's nose clean** to keep out of trouble,

to behave well or legally: *If you keep your nose clean for the rest of the term I think the teacher will forget about what you did.*

—**make a clean breast of (something)** to admit to (something), especially after having denied it: *At first they said that they hadn't been involved but then they made a clean breast of it.*

—**make a clean sweep** to get rid of everything which is unnecessary or unwanted: *If you have doubts about most of the existing staff you should make a clean sweep and dismiss them all.*

—**Mr Clean** a person who is highly trusted or respected: *Some of the members of the government are under suspicion but he's Mr Clean.*

—**pick (something) clean** to take or steal everything that can be removed from (something or somewhere): *The burglars picked his house clean.*

—**show a clean pair of heels** to run away very quickly: *When the burglar saw the police he instantly showed a clean pair of heels.*

—**squeaky clean** free of all guilt or blame: *The police investigated him but he's squeaky clean.* <Clean surfaces tend to squeak when wiped>.

—**take (someone) to the cleaners** to cause (someone) to spend or lose a great deal of money: *The firm was really taken to the cleaners by the suppliers who provided the goods in a hurry.*

clear

—**clear as a bell** very easy to hear: *The international telephone call was clear as a bell.* <Bells, such as church bells, are very audible>.

—**clear as crystal** very easy to understand or grasp: *It's clear as crystal that he's in love with her.*

—**clear as mud** not at all easy to understand or grasp: *He tried to explain but his explanation was clear as mud.*

—**clear the air** *see* **air**.

—**clear the decks** to tidy up, especially as a preparation for some activity or project: *I'll have to clear the decks and put all this shopping away before I start cooking lunch.* <Refers to getting a ship ready for battle>.

—**in the clear** free from suspicion: *the police suspected him but he has an alibi so he's in the clear.*

—**steer clear of (someone** *or* **something)** to keep away from or avoid (someone or something): *You should steer clear of badly lit streets.*

—**the coast is clear** the danger or difficulty is now past: *She doesn't want to go into the house when her father's there,so tell her when he's gone out and the coast is clear.* <Probably a military term indicating that there were no enemy forces near the coast and so an invasion was possible>.

cleft

—**in a cleft stick** unable to decide between two equally important or difficult courses of action: *He's in a cleft stick. He's promised to take his wife out to celebrate their wedding anniversary but his boss is insisting on him working late.*

clip

—**clip (someone's) wings** to limit the freedom, power or influence of (someone): *She used to go out every night but her wings have been clipped since she had a baby.* <From the practice of clipping the wings of a bird to prevent it flying away>.

cloak

—**cloak-and-dagger** involving or relating to a great deal of plotting and scheming: *He's resigned from the board of directors because of all the cloak-and dagger business surrounding the sacking of the chairman.* <The combination of a cloak and a dagger suggests conspiracy>.

clock

—**against the clock** *see* **against**.

—**as regular as clockwork** perfectly regularly: *His visits to his mother were as regular as clockwork.*

—**like clockwork** very smoothly, without problems: *The escape plan worked like clockwork.*

—**put back the clock** *or* **turn the clock back** to return to the conditions or situation of a former time: *Some employers would like to put back the clock sixty years and pay their employers practically nothing. He wishes he could turn the clock back and be at home again with his family.*

—**round the clock** all the time; for twenty-four hours a day: *The rescue services are working round the clock searching for survivors.*

close[1]

—**a closed book** *see* **book**.

—**behind closed doors** in secret: *The committee is meeting behind closed doors.*

—**close one's eyes to (something)** *see* **eye**.

—**close ranks** *see* **rank**.

close[2]

—**a close shave** something that was only just avoided, especially an escape from danger, failure, etc: *He had a close shave when his car skidded out of control and ran into a wall.*

—**at close quarters** very close, from a position

nearby: *I thought she was young but when you see her at close quarters she looks quite old.*

—**close to home** referring to something about which someone is very sensitive or which relates very closely to someone: *Talking about law and order in front of her was a bit close to home since her husband's in prison.*

—**sail close to the wind** *see* **sail**.

—**too close for comfort** so near that one feels uncomfortable, worried, etc: *The meeting is a bit close for comfort as I haven't prepared for it.*

cloud

—**cast a cloud over (something)** to spoil (something), to introduce something unpleasant or sad into a pleasant or happy situation: *Her mother's illness cast a cloud over their holiday.*

—**cloud cuckoo land** an imaginary place, where everything is perfect; an unreal world: *They're living in cloud cuckoo land if they think they can afford that house.*

—**every cloud has a silver lining** something good happens for every bad or unpleasant thing: *He has no job, but every cloud has a silver lining as he is able to spend time with his children.*

—**have one's head in the clouds** to be daydreaming and not paying attention to what is going on around one: *She has her head in the clouds thinking about her wedding.*

—**on cloud nine** extremely happy: *She's been on cloud nine since she met her new boyfriend.*

—**under a cloud** under suspicion, in trouble: *He left his previous job under a cloud.*

clover

—**in clover** in great comfort: *They're living in clover since he won the pools.* <Refers to farm animals which have rich food>.

club

—**in the club** pregnant: *His girlfriend just told him that she's in the club.*

—**join the club** you are in the same unfortunate situation that I am or we are: *If you haven't done any work for the exams join the club. Neither have we.*

clue

—**be clued up on (something)** to be very well-informed about (something): *You'll have to be clued up on computers to get that job.*

—**not to have a clue about (something)** to have no knowledge of (something), to be badly-informed about (something): *She set off without having a clue about how to get to her destination.*

clutch

—**clutch at straws** *see* **straw**.

coach

—**drive a coach and horses through (something)** to destroy (an argument etc) completely by detecting and making use of the weak points in it: *The defence lawyer drove a coach and horses through the prosecution's case against his client.* <Refers to the fact that the defects (or holes) in the argument are so large as to let a coach and horses through them>.

coal

—**carry** *or* **take coals to Newcastle** to do something that is completely unnecessary, especially to take something to a place where there is already a great deal of it: *Taking a cake to her would be like carrying coals to Newcastle. She spends most of her time baking.* <Refers to Newcastle in England, which was a large coal-mining centre>.

—**haul (someone) over the coals** to scold (someone) very severely: *The assistant was hauled over the coals for being rude to a customer.*

—**heap coals of fire on** *or* **upon (someone's) head** to do good or be kind to (someone) who has done one harm so that he or she feels sorry or ashamed: *When the boy tried to steal her purse she heaped coals of fire on his head by offering him money to buy food.* <A biblical reference to Proverbs 25:21-22>.

—**rake over the coals** *same as* **rake over the ashes**—*see* **ashes**.

coast

—**the coast is clear** *see* **clear**.

coat

—**cut one's coat according to one's cloth** to organize one's ideas and aims, particularly one's financial aims, so that they are within the limits of what one has or possesses: *We'd like to buy a big house but we'll have to cut our coat according to our cloth and buy a smaller one. Our income is not large.*

—**turn one's coat** to change sides: *He supported the king at first but he turned his coat and joined the enemy army.* <Refers to a soldier's coat whose colour and markings showed which army he belonged to. If he turned it inside out the colour was hidden>.

cock

—**a cock-and-bull story** an absurd story that is unlikely to be believed: *She told me some cock-and-bull story about finding the money in a waste-paper basket.*

—**cock a snook at (someone)** to express one's defiance or contempt of (someone): *Now that* *he has another job he can cock a snook at his previous employer.* <Originally referring to a rude gesture of contempt made by putting the end of one's thumb on the end of one's nose and spreading out and moving one's fingers>.

—**cock of the walk** the person who is the most important or influential member in a group and who is very proud of this fact: *The boy was cock of the walk at school until a new boy beat him in a fight.* <The pen in which fighting cocks were kept and bred was called a walk>.

—**go off at half cock** to be unsuccessful because of lack of preparation or because of a premature start: *The government scheme went off at half cock because of lack of preliminary research.* <Refers to a gun that fires too soon>.

coffin

—**a nail in (someone's) coffin** *see* **nail**.

cog

—**a cog in the wheel** a person who plays a small or unimportant part in a large organization: *He boasts about his job in the international company but he's really just a cog in the wheel.*

coin

—**coin it in** to make a great deal of money: *Local shopkeepers have been coining it in since the oil business came to the area.*

—**pay (someone) back in his** *or* **her own coin** to get one's revenge on someone who has done harm to one by treating him or her in the same way. *Now he's in charge he's paying his former boss back in his own coin by not promoting him.*

—**the other side of the coin** the opposite argument, point of view, etc: *She has a really successful career and a family, but the other side of the coin is that she can spend hardly any time with her children.*

cold

—**as cold as charity** *see* **charity**.

—**cold comfort** no consolation at all: *When one suffers a misfortune it is cold comfort to be told that there are other people who are much worse off.*

—**come in from the cold** to be allowed to take part in some activity that one was excluded from before: *After months of not being selected, he's come in from the cold and been offered a game with the team this week.*

—**get cold feet** to become nervous and change one's mind about being involved in (something): *He was going to row the Atlantic but got cold feet at the last minute.*

—**give (someone) the cold shoulder** to act in an unfriendly way to (someone) by ignoring him or her: *She has tried to be friendly to her parents-in-law but they keep giving her the cold shoulder.*

—**in a cold sweat** in a state of great fear or anxiety: *He was in a cold sweat when the police were searching his flat.* <From the fact that the skin tends to become cold and damp when one is very frightened>.

—**in cold blood** *see* **blood**.

—**leave (someone) cold** to fail to impress or excite (someone): *The new dance group left the audience cold.*

—**make (someone's) blood run cold** to cause terror or great distress in (someone): *The ghostly figure made my blood run cold.*

—**out in the cold** not taking part, not included: *Only her richer friends were asked to her party—the rest of us were out in the cold.*

—**pour** *or* **throw cold water on (something)** to discourage enthusiasm for (something): *We were all looking forward to the dance but the organizer poured cold water on the idea by saying it would run at a loss.*

—**stone cold** extremely cold: *This soup's supposed to be hot but it's stone cold.*

colour[1]

—**a horse of a different colour** someone or something that is completely different from someone or something else: *The previous headmaster was very kind to the pupils but the new one is a horse of a different colour.*

colour[2]

—**change colour** to become either very pale or else very red in the face through fear, distress, embarrassment, anger, guilt, etc: *She changed colour when she was caught with the money in her hands.*

—**nail one's colours to the mast** to commit oneself to a point of view or course of action in a very obvious and final way: *Most people are undecided about who to vote for in the election but the young people have nailed their colours to the mast by putting up posters for the Green Party candidate.* <Refers to a ship's colours or flag. If this was nailed to the mast it could not be lowered, lowering the flag being a sign of surrender>.

—**off-colour** unwell: *Travelling always makes her feel off-colour.* <People tend to turn pale when they are unwell>.

—**show oneself in one's true colours** to reveal what one is really like after pretending to be otherwise: *She pretended to be his friend but she* *showed herself in her true colours by reporting him to the boss.* <Refers to a ship raising its colours or flag to indicate which country or side it was supporting>.

—**with flying colours** with great success: *They both passed the exam with flying colours.* <Refers to a ship leaving a battle with its colours or flag still flying as opposed to lowering them in surrender>.

come

—**come a cropper** to suffer misfortune, to fail: *He came a cropper when he bought a hotel without knowing anything about the business.* <Originally a hunting phrase meanint to take a serious fall>.

—**come clean** *see* **clean**.

—**come down on (someone) like a ton of bricks** *see* **brick**.

—**come in for (something)** to be the receiver or target of (something): *The organizers came in for a great deal of criticism when the fete was cancelled.*

—**come in from the cold** *see* **cold**.

—**come into one's own** *see* **own**.

—**come of age** *see* **age**.

—**come off it** don't be ridiculous, don't try to deceive me: *Come off it! You couldn't possibly have been at work and be back so early.*

—**come to grief** *see* **grief**.

—**come to grips with (something)** *see* **grip**.

—**come to light** *see* **light**.

—**come to nothing** *see* **nothing**.

—**come to one's senses** *see* **sense**.

—**come to that** taking into consideration other facts: *She's not qualified for the job, but come to that he's not qualified for it either.*

—**come unstuck** to fail, to suffer a major setback: *Our holiday plans have come unstuck. I have to work that week.*

—**have it coming to one** to deserve the punishment, misfortune, etc, that one is going to get: *I'm not sorry that he's been dismissed. He's had it coming for years.*

common

—**common-or-garden** completely ordinary: *I'm not going to wear anything special: I'll wear a common-or-garden skirt and top.*

—**the common touch** the ability to get on well with ordinary people: *He is a prince but most of his friends are just ordinary students. He has the common touch.*

compare

—**beyond compare** *see* **beyond**.

confidence

—**a vote of confidence** *see* **vote**.

—**confidence trick** the act of a swindler who gains the trust of someone and then persuades him or her to hand over money: *The old lady thought she was giving money to charity but the collector played a confidence trick on her and kept the money for himself.*

conjure

—**a name to conjure with** the name of someone very important, influential or well-known: *Now that's a name to conjure with. He was one of our really great players.* <The suggestion is that such people have magical powers>.

conscience

—**in all conscience** being completely fair and honest: *In all conscience we cannot appoint him if he is not qualified for the job.*

contention

—**a bone of contention** *see* **bone**.

contradiction

—**a contradiction in terms** a statement, idea, etc, that contains a contradiction: *He is a cynic and thinks that a happy husband is a contradiction in terms.*

convert

—**preach to the converted** to speak enthusiatically in favour of something to people who already admire it or are in favour of it: *You are preaching to the converted by praising the candidate to us. We already voted for him.*

cook

—**cook (someone's) goose** *see* **goose**.

—**cook the books** *see* **book**.

—**too many cooks spoil the broth** if there are a great many people involved in a project they are more likely to hinder it than help it: *Let's appoint a very small organizing committee. Too many cooks spoil the broth.*

—**what's cooking?** what is happening?, what is going on?: *What's cooking? Everyone seems very busy.*

cookie

—**that's the way the cookie crumbles** that is the situation and one must just accept it: *He doesn't like working at weekends but that's the way the cookie crumbles.* <Cookie is American English for biscuit>.

cool

—**cool as a cucumber** very calm and unexcited: *She hit the burglar over the head, cool as a cucumber.*

—**cool, calm and collected** completely calm, in

full control of one's emotions: *She was cool, calm and collected when she told him to get out.*

—**cool** *or* **kick one's heels** to be kept waiting: *My meeting has not finished yet. You'll just have to cool your heels.*

—**keep one's cool** to remain calm: *She always keeps her cool in a crisis.*

—**lose one's cool** to become angry, excited etc: *It's easy to lose one's cool when the children are naughty.*

coot

—**bald as a coot** *see* **bald**.

cop

—**cop it** (1) to be scolded or punished: *You'll cop it from your father if you go home late.* (2) to die: *Three terrorists copped it in the attack.*

—**not much cop** not very good, desirable, useful, etc: *The new teacher isn't much cop.*

copy

—**blot one's copybook** to spoil a previously good record of behaviour, achievement, etc, by doing something wrong: *He was thought certain to get the manager's job but he blotted his copybook by losing a large export order.*

—**carbon copy** a person or thing that is very like someone or something else: *His new girlfriend's a carbon copy of his previous one.*

corn

—**tread on (someone's) corns** to offend (someone): *You fairly trod on her corns by criticizing the new secretary—that's her daughter.*

corner

—**cut corners** to use less money, materials, effort, time, etc, than is usually required or than is required to give a good result: *The production department is going to have to have a tighter budget and cut a few corners.*

—**drive (someone) into a corner** to force (someone) into a difficult or dangerous situation: *The firm are trying to drive their competitors into a corner by charging low prices.*

—**from all (four) corners of the earth** from every part of the world, from everywhere: *The conference was attended by people from all corners of the earth.*

—**in a tight corner** in an awkward, difficult or dangerous situation: *They were in a tight corner with their escape route cut off by the enemy.*

—**turn the corner** to begin to get better or improve: *The accident victim was very ill but he has turned the corner at last.*

cost

—**at all cost** *or* **costs** no matter what must be done, given, suffered etc, whatever happens: *We must stop the enemy advancing at all costs.*

—**cost a bomb** *or* **a packet** to cost a very great deal of money: *His new car cost him a bomb.*

—**cost an arm and a leg** to cost an excessive amount of money: *Those houses cost an arm and a leg.*

—**cost the earth** to cost a very great deal of money: *That holiday cost them the earth.*

—**count the cost** to consider the risks, difficulties and possible losses involved in doing something: *He didn't stop to count the cost before he had an affair, and his wife left him.*

—**to one's cost** to one's disadvantage or loss: *It will be to your cost if you offend the office manager. She's the chairman's wife.*

count

—**count one's chickens before they are hatched** *see* **chicken**.

—**count the cost** *see* **cost**.

—**out for the count** unconscious or deeply asleep: *The children are out for the count after their long walk.* <Refers to boxing where a boxer who has been knocked down by his opponent has to get up again before the referee counts to ten in order to stay in the match>.

—**stand up and be counted** *see* **stand**.

counter

—**under the counter** secretly or illegally: *When meat was rationed he used to supply his richer customers under the counter.*

country

—**country cousin** a person from the country, considered unsophisticated by a town or city dweller: *His country cousin has never been to a pop concert.*

—**go to the country** to hold a general election: *When the government was defeated on the employment bill the prime minister decided to go to the country.*

courage

—**Dutch courage** *see* **Dutch**.

—**have the courage of one's convictions** to be brave enough to do what one thinks one should: *If you are sure that your colleague stole the money you should have the courage of your convictions and report him.*

—**pluck up** *or* **screw up courage** to force oneself to be brave: *Finally he plucked up courage and asked her to marry him.*

course

—**horses for courses** *see* **horse**.

—**par for the course** *see* **par**.

—**run its course** *see* **run**.
—**stay the course** *see* **stay**.

court

—**laugh (someone** *or* **something) out of court** not to give serious consideration to (someone or something): *Management laughed our request for a salary increase out of court.* <Refers to a trivial legal case>.
—**pay court to (someone)** to try to gain the love of (someone): *The prince is paying court to a foreign princess.*
—**the ball is in (someone's) court** it is (someone's) turn to take action: *I've done all I can. The ball's in your court now.*
—**rule (something) out of court** to prevent (something) from being considered for (something): *His prospects of marrying her have been ruled out of court by her father because he cannot afford to support a wife.* <Refers to a court of law where evidence, etc, ruled out of court has no effect on the case>.

Coventry

—**send (someone) to Coventry** collectively to refuse to associate with (someone): *His colleagues sent him to Coventry for working during the strike.* <Perhaps from an incident in the English Civil War when Royalists captured in Birmingham were sent to the stronghold of Coventry>.

cow

—**a sacred cow** something that is regarded with too much respect for people to be allowed to criticize it freely: *You musn't say the old town hall is ugly—it's one of the village's sacred cows.* <The cow is considered sacred by Hindus>.
—**till** *or* **until the cows come home** for an extremely long time: *I could listen to her music until the cows come home.* <Cows walk very slowly from the field to the milking sheds unless someone hurries them along>.

crack

—**a fair crack of the whip** a fair share, a fair chance of doing (something): *The children were supposed to take turns at playing on the swing but the little ones did not get a fair crack of the whip.*
—**a hard nut to crack** *see* **nut**.
—**at (the) crack of dawn** very early in the morning: *We must leave for the airport at crack of dawn.*
—**crack a bottle** *see* **bottle**.
—**crack the whip** to treat sternly or severely those under one's control or charge: *If you want the workers to finish the orders on time you'll have to start cracking the whip. They take too much time off.* <From the use of a whip to punish people>.
—**get cracking** to start moving, working, etc, quickly: *You had better get cracking or you'll miss the train.*
—**have a crack at (something)** to have a try at (something): *Why not have a crack at the competition?*
—**not all it's cracked up to be** not to be as good as it is said to be: *The holiday resort is not all it's cracked up to be.*
—**paper over the cracks** *see* **paper**.
—**take a sledgehammer to crack a nut** to spend a great deal of effort on a small task or problem: *We don't need a whole team of workmen to mend one small hole in the roof. That really is taking a sledgehammer to crack a nut.*

creature

—**creature comforts** things that contribute to one's physical well-being: *Her adult son still lives at home because he likes his creature comforts.*

creek

—**up the creek** in trouble, in serious difficulties: *We'll be up the creek if the car breaks down here. It's miles to the nearest garage.*

creep

—**give (someone) the creeps** to arouse dislike, disgust or fear in (someone): *I don't like the new boss. He gives me the creeps.*
—**make (someone's) flesh creep** to arouse fear or horror in (someone): *The eerie howling made my flesh creep.*

cricket

—**lively as a cricket** very lively: *The old lady's as lively as a cricket.* <A reference to the insect>.
—**not cricket** not fair or honourable, unsportsmanlike: *It's not cricket to ask him to pay the bill for all of us.* <The game of cricket is regarded as being played in a gentlemanly way>.

crocodile

—**crocodile tears** a pretended show of grief or sorrow: *She wept at her uncle's funeral, but they were crocodile tears as she really disliked him.* <Refers to an old belief that crocodiles weep while eating their prey>.

cross

—**cross a bridge when one comes to it** *see* **bridge**.
—**cross one's fingers** *see* **finger**.
—**cross one's heart** *see* **heart**.
—**cross one's mind** *see* **mind**.

—**cross swords with (someone)** *see* **sword**.

—**cross the Rubicon** to do something that commits one completely to a course of action that cannot be undone: *He has crossed the Rubicon. He has sent in his letter of resignation.* <Julius Caesar's crossing of the River Rubicon in 49BC committed him to war with the Senate>.

—**dot the i's and cross the t's** *see* **dot**.

—**have a cross to bear** to have to suffer or tolerate a responsibility, inconvenience or source of distress: He *certainly has a cross to bear. He has to look after both his elderly parents and go to work.* <Refers to the fact that in the days of crucifixions, those being crucified had to carry their own crosses>.

—**talk at cross purposes** to be involved in a misunderstanding because of talking or thinking about different things without realizing it: *We've been talking at cross purposes. I was referring to a different Mr Smith.*

crow

—**as the crow flies** measured in a straight line: *As the crow flies the town is five miles away but by road it is ten.*

—**eat crow** to have to admit or accept that one was wrong: *He had to eat crow when he got the capital of Australia wrong.*

crunch

—**when it comes to the crunch** when a time of testing comes, when a decision has to be made: *When it came to the crunch I decided not to leave.*

cry

—**a crying shame** a great shame, a disgrace: *It's a crying shame that those children are dressed in rags.*

—**a far cry from (something)** a long way from (something), very different from (something): *His present lifestyle is a far cry from that of his parents.*

—**a shoulder to cry on** *see* **shoulder**.

—**cry for the moon** *same as* **ask for the moon**—*see* **moon**.

—**crying out for (something)** to be badly in need of something or something to be done: *The old house is in a bad state. It's crying out for a new coat of paint.*

—**cry one's eyes out** *see* **eye**.

—**cry over spilt milk** to waste time regretting a misfortune or accident that cannot be undone: *I know you're sorry that you didn't get the job but there's no use crying over spilt milk.*

—**cry wolf** *see* **wolf**.

—**for crying out loud** a phrase used to express annoyance, impatience, irritation, etc: *For crying out loud! Their phone's been engaged for hours.*

—**in full cry** enthusiastically and excitedly pursuing something: *The crowd were in full cry after the thief.* <Refers to the cry made by hunting dogs>.

cuckoo

—**cloud cuckoo land** *see* **cloud**.

cucumber

—**cool as a cucumber** *see* **cool**.

cud

—**chew the cud** *see* **chew**.

cudgel

—**cudgel one's brains** *see* **brain**.

—**take up the cudgels on behalf of (someone** *or* **something)** to fight strongly on behalf of (someone or something), to support (someone or something) vigorously: *She's taken up the cudgels on behalf of children's rights.*

cue

—**take one's cue from (someone)** to use the actions or reactions of (someone) as a guide to one's own, to copy (someone's) actions: *The children took their cue from their mother and remained silent.* <A theatrical term, literally meaning to use the words of another actor as a signal for one to speak or move>.

cuff

—**off the cuff** without preparation: *The speaker gave a clever talk, completely off the cuff.* <Refers to the habit of some after-dinner speakers of making brief headings on the celluloid cuffs of their evening shirts as a reminder of what he or she wanted to say rather than preparing a formal speech>.

cup

—**not be one's cup of tea** not to be something which one likes or appreciates: *Seaside holidays are not really our cup of tea.*

—**in one's cups** under the influence of alcohol: *He starts singing when he's in his cups.*

—**there's many a slip 'twixt cup and lip** *see* **slip**.

cupboard

—**cupboard love** pretended affection shown for a person because of the things he or she gives one: *The child always kisses her aunt but that's because she knows she will bring her a present. It's just cupboard love.* <From people and animals liking those who feed them, food being kept in cupboards>.

—**have a skeleton in the cupboard** *see* **skeleton**.

curiosity

—**curiosity killed the cat** *see* **cat**.

curry

—**curry favour with (someone)** to try to gain the approval or favour of (someone) by insincere flattery or by being extremely nice to him or her all the time: *The girl thinks that she will pass the test if she curries favour with the teacher.* <Originally curry favel, from Old French *estriller fauvel, fauvel* being a chestnut horse>.

curtain

—**be curtains for (someone** *or* **something)** to be the end of (someone or something): *The change of ownership means curtains for the present manager.* <Refers to curtains falling at the end of a stage performance>.

—**curtain lecture** a private scolding, especially one given by a wife to a husband: *I bet he got a curtain lecture when he got home for flirting at the party.* <From the curtains that formerly were hung round a bed>.

—**curtain raiser** something that begins or acts as an introduction to something: *Her appearance on the school stage was a curtain raiser for a long and successful career as an actress.*

—**ring down the curtain on (something)** to cause (something) to come to an end: *The government are ringing down the curtain on that scheme.* <See above>.

cut

—**a cut above (someone** *or* **something)** rather better than (someone or something): *The office workers think they are a cut above the factory workers.*

—**cut a long story short** to give a brief account of something quite complicated or lengthy: *I could go into a great deal of detail but, to cut a long story short, they've gone.*

—**cut and dried** settled and definite: *We cannot change our plans. They're cut and dried.* <Refers to wood that has been cut and dried and made ready for use>.

—**cut and thrust** methods and techniques of rivalry, argument or debate: *The politician is skilled in the cut and thrust of parliamentary debate.* <Refers to sword fighting>.

—**cut both ways** to have an equal or the same effect on both parts of a question or on both people involved in something: *We can impose sanctions on the enemy country but sanctions can cut both ways.*

—**cut corners** *see* **corner**.

—**cut (someone) dead** *see* **dead**.

—**cut (someone) down to size** *see* **size**.

—**cut it fine** to allow hardly enough time to do or get something: *You're cutting it a bit fine. You might miss the bus.*

—**cut it out** to stop doing (something): *The children were teasing the cat but I told them to cut it out.*

—**cut no ice** *see* **ice**.

—**cut off one's nose to spite one's face** *see* **nose**.

—**cut one's coat according to one's cloth** *see* **coat**.

—**cut one's teeth on (something)** *see* **teeth**.

—**cut one's own (own) throat** *see* **throat**.

—**cut the Gordian knot** *see* **Gordian**.

—**cut (someone) to the quick** *see* **quick**.

—**cut up** upset: *She is cut up about the death of her dog.*

—**cut up rough** *see* **rough**.

—**not cut out for (something)** not naturally suited to: *He wants to be a doctor, but he's not cut out for medicine.*

cylinder

—**firing on all cylinders** working or operating at full strength: *The factory hasn't been firing on all cylinders for some time.* <Literally used of an internal combustion engine>.

D

dab

—**a dab hand at (something)** an expert at (something): *He's a dab hand at carpentry.*

daddy

—**the daddy of them all** the most extreme example of (something), the finest or the worst example, often the worst: *He has made many mistakes so far but his latest one is the daddy of them all.*

dagger

—**at daggers drawn** feeling or showing great hostility towards each other: *They're been at daggers drawn ever since the breakup of their marriage.*

—**cloak-and-dagger** *see* **cloak**.

—**look daggers at (someone)** to look with great dislike or hostility at (someone): *When she won the prize her fellow contestants looked daggers at her.*

daily

—**daily bread** basic living costs: *They have to struggle to earn the daily bread for their family.*

—**daily dozen** a series of physical exercises done every day, usually every morning: *He always does his daily dozen before breakfast.*

—**the daily round** the usual routine of daily life: *He's tired of the daily round and he's given up his job to travel round the world.*

daisy

—**be pushing up the daisies** to be dead: *I saw his obituary today but I thought he'd been pushing up the daisies for years.*

—**fresh as a daisy** not at all tired, lively: *The old lady was fresh as a daisy after her long journey.*

damage

—**what's the damage?** what does it cost?, what's the total cost?: *"What's the damage?" the diners asked the waiter.*

Damocles

—**the sword of Damocles** *see* **sword**.

Damon

—**Damon and Pythias** sworn friends: *His political opinions would have estranged Damon and Pythias.* <Refers to a Classical legend.>

damp

—**a damp squib** something that is expected to be exciting, effective, etc, but fails to live up to its expectations: *Everyone looked forward to the Christmas party but it turned out to be a damp squib.* <Refers to a wet firework that fails to go off>.

—**put a damper on (something)** to reduce the enjoyment, optimism, happiness of (something): *Her parents arrived home early and instantly put a damper on the party.*

dance

—**dance attendance on (someone)** *see* **attendance**.

—**dance to a different tune** to act or think in a completely different way, especially when forced to do so: *At first she refused to leave but she danced to a different tune when the police arrived.*

—**lead (someone) a (merry) dance** to cause (someone) a series of great, usually unnecessary, problems or irritations: *Their daughter led them a merry dance by going to stay with an old school friend without telling them. They spent ages looking for her.*

dander

—**get one's dander up** to become very angry: *The headmaster's really got his dander up about people who play truant.* <Originally Northern English dialect>.

dandy

—**fine and dandy** quite all right: *We had problems with the holiday bookings but everything's fine and dandy now.*

Darby

—**Darby and Joan** a devoted elderly couple: *So many people get divorced nowadays that it is a refreshing change to meet a Darby and Joan.* <From the names of such a couple in an 18th-century English ballad>.

dark

—**a leap in the dark** an action or decision, the result of which is unknown or unpredictable: *Her new job is a bit of a leap in the dark but there are no other possibilities at the moment.*

—**a shot in the dark** an attempt or guess based on very little information: *We don't know his exact address, but it's worth taking a shot in the* *dark and looking up his name in the telephone directory.*

—**dark horse** a person or thing whose abilities, worth, etc, is unknown: *He thinks that he is certain to win but there is at least one dark horse in the race.*

—**in the dark** lacking knowledge or awareness: *Everyone else seems to know all about the plans but I am still in the dark.*

—**keep it** *or* **something dark** to keep it or something secret: *We know all about his prison record but we must keep it dark from other people in the firm.*

—**not darken (someone's) door** not to dare to visit (someone): *When his daughter stole his money he told her not to darken his door again.*

dash

—**cut a dash** to wear very smart or unusual clothes and so impress others: *He cut quite a dash in his scarlet suit.*

daunt

—**nothing daunted** not discouraged in any way: *She had a bad start to the race but nothing daunted she went on to win.*

Davy Jones

—**Davy Jones's locker** the bottom of the sea: *The ship and all the sailors on board went to Davy Jones's locker.* <Davy Jones was a name given in the 18th century to the ruler of the evil spirits of the sea>.

dawn

—**at (the) crack of dawn** *see* **crack**.

day

—**all in a day's work** all part of one's normal routine, not requiring extra or unusual effort: *Of course the hotel receptionist will get the theatre tickets for you. It's all in a day's work.*

—**any day of the week** whatever the circumstances: *His horse can race faster than yours any day of the week.*

—**at the end of the day** when everything has been taken into consideration: *At the end of the day we must find someone to do the job.*

—**call it a day** to put an end to (something); to stop doing (something), especially to stop working: *It's too dark to see to work. Let's call it a day.*

—**carry** *or* **win the day** to be successful, to gain a victory: *The lawyer's argument carried the day.* <Originally a military term meaning to win a battle>.

—**day in, day out** every day without exception: *It's rained day in, day out for a month.*

—**daylight robbery** the charging of prices that are far too high: *Taxi prices in that city are daylight robbery.*

—**(your, etc) days are numbered** you are about to be dismissed, be killed, etc: *When the boss finds out about that mistake your days are numbered.*

—**every dog has his day** everyone will get an opportunity at some time: *Every dog has his day. Your turn will come.*

—**happy as the day is long** very happy: *The children are happy as the day is long playing on the beach.*

—**have a field day** *see* **field**.

—**have had one's** *or* **its day** to be past the most successful part of one's or its life: *I thought the cinema had had its day but it has been revived.*

—**have seen better days** *see* **better**.

—**live from day to day** to think only about the present without making any plans for the future: *With so little money it is difficult to do anything other than live from day to day.*

—**make (someone's) day** to make (someone) very pleased or happy: *He really made his mother's day by sending her flowers.*

—**name the day** to announce the date of one's wedding: *At last the engaged couple have named the day.*

—**not to be one's day** to be a day when nothing seems to go right for one: *I couldn't find a place to park, I got a parking ticket and then I ran out of petrol. It just hasn't been my day.*

—**one of these days** at some time in the future: *One of these days you'll have a home of your own.*

—**one of those days** a day when nothing seems to go right: *I'll be glad to go to bed. It's been one of those days.*

—**save the day** to prevent something from going wrong or from being a failure: *When it rained we had no place to hold the fete but the headmaster saved the day by lending us the school hall.*

—**see daylight** to be coming to the end of a long task: *I've been working for weeks on the research project but at last I'm beginning to see daylight.*

—**that will be the day** that is extremely unlikely to happen: *"Perhaps your boss will offer you a salary increase." " That'll be the day."*

—**the order of the day** *see* **order**.

—**the other day** one day recently: *I saw him just the other day.*

—**those were the days** the times in the past about which we are talking were good times:

Do you remember our schooldays? Those were the days!

dead

—**a dead duck** a person or thing that is very unlikely to survive or continue: *The proposed new traffic scheme is a dead duck. Most of the committee are going to vote against it.*

—**a dead end** a situation from which it is impossible to progress: *That factory job's a dead end. You have no prospects.*

—**a dead loss** a person or thing that is completely useless or unprofitable: *He's a dead loss as a teacher as he can't maintain discipline.*

—**a dead ringer** *see* **ring**.

—**at dead of night** in the middle of the night when people are usually asleep: *The burglars broke in at dead of night.*

—**cut (someone) dead** to ignore (someone) completely: *My neighbour's been cutting me dead since our children quarrelled.*

—**dead and buried** completely dead or extinct with no chance of being revived: *The issue of the proposed new motorway is dead and buried.*

—**dead as a dodo** completely dead or out of fashion: *They're trying to revive village traditions that have been dead as a dodo for years.* <Refers to a flightless bird that has been extinct since 1700>.

—**dead beat** exhausted: *I'm dead beat after walking up that hill.*

—**dead from the neck up** extremely stupid: *Don't take his advice. He's dead from the neck up.*

—**Dead Sea fruit** a thing that appears to be, or is expected to be, of great value but proves to be valueless: *Her job abroad sounded very glamorous but it turned out to be a case of Dead Sea fruit.* <Refers to a fruit, the apple of Sodom, that was thought to grow on trees beside the shores of the Dead Sea. It was beautiful to look at but fell to ashes when touched or tasted>.

—**dead set on (something)** determined to have or to do (something): *His son is dead set on going to university.*

—**dead to the world** in a very deep sleep: *I didn't hear the phone. I was dead to the world.*

—**dead wood** a person or thing that is no longer necessary or useful: *The new management say that they are going to get rid of all the dead wood.*

—**enough to waken the dead** extremely loud: *The children's rowdy game was enough to waken the dead.*

—**flog a dead horse** *see* **horse**.

—**let the dead bury their dead** past problems, quarrels, etc, are best forgotten: *You must stop thinking about your divorce. It was a long time ago and you should let the dead bury their dead.* <A biblical reference to Matthew 8:22, in which Jesus said, "Follow me and let the dead bury their dead">.

—**over my dead body** in the face of my fierce opposition: *The council will pull my house down over my dead body.*

—**step into** *or* **fill dead men's shoes** to take over the position of someone who has died or left under unfortunate circumstances: *If you want promotion in that firm you'll have to step into dead men's shoes. No one ever leaves to go elsewhere.*

—**would not be seen dead in** *or* **with, etc**, extremely unlikely to be seen wearing something, accompanying someone, etc, because of an extreme dislike or aversion: *He wouldn't be seen dead in flared trousers. She wouldn't be seen dead in public with him.*

deaf

—**deaf as a post** completely deaf: *There's no point in shouting. The old man is deaf as a post.*

—**fall on deaf ears** not to be listened to, to go unnoticed or disregarded: *There's no point in giving her advice. It will just fall on deaf ears.*

—**stone deaf** completely deaf: *The old man is stone deaf but he refuses to wear a hearing aid.*

—**turn a deaf ear to (something)** to refuse to listen to (something), to take no notice of (something): *He turned a deaf ear to her appeals for help.*

deal

—**a raw deal** unfair treatment: *The younger son got a raw deal when his father's estate was divided.*

—**a square deal** fair or honest treatment: *I don't feel that I got a square deal when I bought that car.*

—**wheeling and dealing** *see* **wheel**.

death

—**at death's door** extremely ill, dying: *He seemed to be at death's door yesterday but he shows signs of recovery today.*

—**be in at the death** to be present at the end or final stages of something: *The factory closed today. It was sad to be in at the death.* <Refers originally to being present at the death of the prey in a hunt>.

—**catch one's death (of cold)** to become infected with a very bad cold: *You'll catch your death of cold in those wet clothes.*

—**death trap** a building that is in a dangerous state: *That high building with no fire escape is a death trap.*

—**dice with death** to do something extremely risky and dangerous: *She's dicing with death driving a car with faulty brakes.*

—**die the death** to be badly received: *His proposals have died the death. They were rejected by the committee.* <Refers originally to an actor or performer getting a poor reception from the audience>.

—**flog (something) to death** to discuss or deal with (something) to such an extent that it is no longer interesting: *The newspapers have really flogged the story about the politician and the model to death.*

—**hang on** *or* **hold on like grim death** *see* **grim**.

—**kiss of death** *see* **kiss**.

—**look** *or* **feel like death warmed up** to look or feel very unwell or very tired: *You've looked like death warmed up ever since you had the flu.*

—**put the fear of death** *or* **God into (someone)** *see* **fear**.

—**sick** *or* **tired to death of (someone** *or* **something)** extremely weary or bored with (someone or something): *I'm sick to death of that piece of music.*

—**sign one's own death warrant** to bring about one's own downfall, ruin, etc: *He signed his own death warrant when he criticized the firm's product to a competitor.*

—**will be the death of (someone)** (1) to cause the death of (someone): *That son of hers worries his mother so much that he'll be the death of her.* (2) to make (someone) laugh a great deal: *"That comedian will be the death of me," gasped my father.*

deck

—**clear the decks** *see* **clear**.

deep

—**beauty is only skin deep** *see* **beauty**.

—**be thrown in at the deep end** to be put suddenly into a difficult situation of which one has no experience: *The trainee journalist was thrown in at the deep end and sent out on a story on his first morning in the office.* <Refers to the deep end of a swimming pool>.

—**go off at the deep end** to lose one's temper: *His father went off at the deep end when he saw his wrecked car.* (See above).

—**in deep water** in great difficulties or trouble: *Financially they've been in deep water since he lost his job.*

—**still waters run deep** *see* **still**.

degree

—**give (someone) the third degree** to subject (someone) to intense questioning, especially by using severe methods: *The officer gave the captured enemy soldiers the third degree.*

—**one degree under** slightly unwell: *She's not at work—she's feeling one degree under.*

—**to the nth degree** to the greatest possible degree, extent or amount: *They will back you to the nth degree.* <Refers to the use of n as a symbol to represent a number, especially a large number>.

delicate

—**in a delicate condition** pregnant: *She announced to the group that her daughter was in a delicate condition.*

dent

—**make a dent in (something)** to reduce (something) by a considerable amount: *My holiday abroad has made a dent in my savings.*

depth

—**in depth** thoroughly: *You must study the problem in depth before making a recommendation.*

—**out of one's depth** in a situation which one cannot cope with: *The child is out of his depth in that class. The work is too hard for him.* <Refers literally to being in water deeper than one can stand up in>.

—**plumb the depths of (something)** to reach the lowest level of unhappiness, misfortune, etc: *He really plumbed the depths of misery when his wife died.*

deserts

—**get one's just deserts** to be treated as one deserves, especially to receive deserved punishment: *The burglar got his just deserts when he was sent to prison.*

design

—**have designs upon (someone** *or* **something)** to wish to possess (someone or something), usually belonging to someone else: *Look out. I think he has designs on your job.*

device

—**leave (someone) to his** *or* **her own devices** to leave (someone) to look after himself or herself, often after having tried unsuccessfully to help him or her: *You've done all you can. Now you must leave him to his own devices.*

devil

—**be the very devil** to be very difficult or troublesome: *Getting to that town by public transport is the very devil.*

—**better the devil you know** it is preferable to have someone or something that one knows to be bad than take a chance with someone or something that might turn out even worse: *I think we should keep our present suppliers. At least we can cope with their faults, and it's a case of better the devil you know.*

—**between the devil and the deep blue sea** faced with two possible courses of action each of which is as unacceptable as the other: *He's between the devil and the deep sea. If he takes promotion he has to move to another part of the country. If he stays where he is he will be downgraded.*

—**devil take the hindmost** the person who is last must accept the worst fate or the least acceptable conditions, so everyone should take care to avoid this position: *There are so few jobs and so many young people looking for them nowadays that it is devil take the hindmost.*

—**give the devil his due** to be fair to someone, even although one dislikes him or her: *I cannot stand him but give the devil his due he's an excellent worker.*

—**needs must when the devil drives** if it is absolutely necessary that something must be done then one must do it: *I would like to take some time off, but this work is needed for next week and needs must when the devil drives.*

—**play the devil's advocate** to put forward objections to a plan, idea, etc, simply in order to test the strength of the arguments in its favour: *It's really important that there are no flaws in our proposal for change. That's why I'm playing devil's advocate.*

—**speak of the devil** here is the very person whom we have just been referring to: *Speak of the devil. There's the man we've been discussing.* <Short for "speak of the devil and he will appear", which refers to a superstition by which it was thought that talking about evil gave it the power to appear>.

—**there will be the devil to pay** there will be serious trouble: *There'll be the devil to pay when the boss finds out we all left early.* <From legendary bargains struck with the devil by which one could have immediate worldly success, happiness and riches, if one gave him one's soul at a later date.>

diamond

—**rough diamond** a person who behaves in a rough manner but who has good or valuable qualities: *He's extremely good at his job but he'll hate the formal reception. He's a real rough diamond.*

dice

—**dice with death** *see* **death**.

—**load the dice against (someone)** to arrange things so that (someone) has no chance of success: *Since he has no qualifications the dice are loaded against him in his job hunt.* <Refers to a method of cheating in gambling by putting lead or similar heavy material into a dice so that only certain numbers will come up>.

die[1]

—**be dying for (something)** to be longing for (something): *He's dying for a cigarette.*

—**die hard** to take a long time to disappear or become extinct: *He can't get used to new methods of production—old habits die hard.*

—**die laughing** to be extremely amused: *We nearly died at the clown's antics.*

—**die the death** *see* **death**.

—**die with one's boots on** to die while still working: *He refused to retire but died with his boots on.* <Refers to soldiers dying in active service>.

—**do or die** *see* **do**.

—**never say die** never give up hope: *You may have lost your girlfriend but never say die. You'll find someone else.*

die[2]

—**the die is cast** a step has been taken that makes the course of future events inevitable: *The die is cast—he has asked her to marry him.* <A translation of the Latin *iacta alea est*, supposedly said by Julius Caesar when he crossed the Rubicon in 49 BC and so committed himself to a war with the Senate>.

differ

—**a different kettle of fish** *see* **kettle**.

—**agree to differ** to agree not to argue about something any more since neither party is likely to change his or her opinion: *We are reasonably friendly now since we agreed to differ about politics. We used to quarrel all the time.*

—**as different as chalk and cheese** *see* **chalk**.

—**sink one's differences** to forget about past disagreements: *The two members of the board will never agree about company policy but in the interests of the firm they have agreed to sink their differences.*

—**split the difference** to agree on an amount of money halfway between two amounts, especially between the amount that one person is charging for something and the amount that someone else is willing to pay for it: *He's asking £200 for the bike and you only want to pay £100. Why don't you split the difference and offer him £150?*

dig

—**dig one's heels in** to show great determination, especially in order to get one's own wishes carried out: *You won't persuade him to attend the meeting. He's digging his heels in and refusing to go.*

—**dig one's own grave** to be the cause of one's own misfortune: *I feel sorry for the young man who lost his job but he dug his own grave when he kept taking days off.*

dilemma

—**on the horns of a dilemma** in a position where it is necessary to choose between two courses of action: *The old lady's on the horns of a dilemma. She can't decide which of her grandchildren's invitations to accept.* <In medieval rhetoric a dilemma was likened to a two-horned animal on one of whose horns the person making the decision had to throw himself or herself>.

dim

—**take a dim view of (something)** to look with disapproval on (something) *The boss takes a dim view of his employee's inability to get to work on time.*

dine

—**dine out on (something)** to be given social invitations because of information, gossip, etc, one can pass on: *Ever since he got back to America he's been dining out on having met the queen.*

dinner

—**like a dog's dinner** an untidy mess: *The pupil's written work is like a dog's dinner.*

—**more of (something) than you have had hot dinners** a very great deal of (something): *He's been in jail for burglary more times than I've had hot dinners.*

dirt

—**dirty old man** an elderly man who shows a sexual interest in young girls or young boys: *The police are keeping an eye on the dirty old man in the park.*

—**do (someone's) dirty work** to do something wrong or unpleasant on behalf of (someone else): *The manager has asked his deputy to do his dirty work and sack half the workforce.*

—**do the dirty on (someone)** to treat (someone) in an unfair, dishonest or disloyal way: *He did the dirty on his friend and told the police about her part in the crime.*

—**(someone's) name is dirt** *or* **mud** (someone) is in great disfavour: *When he was company secretary he embezzled money, so now his name is dirt around here.*

—**treat (someone) like dirt** to treat (someone) with contempt: *The new head of the household treats the staff like dirt.*

—**wash one's dirty linen in public** *same as* **air one's dirty linen**—*see* **air**.

discord

—**apple of discord** *see* **apple**.

discretion

—**discretion is the better part of valour** it is wise not to take any unnecessary risks: *I thought of betting all my winnings on the next race but I decided that discretion was the better part of valour.* <Refers to Shakespeare's *Henry IV Part 1*, Act 5,.scene iv.>.

distance

—**go the distance** to complete something successfully, to last until the end of something: *I didn't think that he would go the distance but he finished the marathon race easily.*

—**keep one's distance** not to come too close, not to be too friendly: *It is important for teachers to keep their distance from their pupils.*

—**within striking distance** reasonably close: *He was within striking distance of the town when he collapsed.*

do

—**do (someone) a good turn** *see* **turn**.

—**do away with (someone** *or* **something)** *see* **away**.

—**do one's bit** to do one's share of the work, etc: *If we all do our bit to collect donations we should reach our target amount.*

—**do (someone) down** (1) to do (someone) harm, to cheat (someone): *The businessman made his fortune from doing other people down.* (2) to speak unfavourably of or criticize (someone): *Salesmen usually do down the products of their competitors.*

—**do (someone) in** to kill (someone): *The police are looking for the person who did her in.*

—**do (someone** *or* **something) justice** *see* **justice**.

—**do one's level best** *see* **best**.

—**done for** without any hope of rescue, help or recovery: *We're done for. Our enemies are gaining on us.*

—**done to a turn** *see* **turn**.

—**do one's nut** *see* **nut**.
—**do one's own thing** *see* **thing**.
—**do or die** to make the greatest effort possible at the risk of killing, injuring, ruining, etc, oneself: *The soldiers were told that if the battle was to be won their next attack on the enemy would be a case of do or die.*
—**do (someone) out of (something)** to prevent (someone) from getting (something), usually by dishonest or deceitful means: *The other brothers did the youngest brother out of his inheritance by telling their father that he was dead.*
—**do (someone) proud** *see* **proud**.
—**do the honours** to act as host, to serve food or drink to one's guests: *His wife did the honours and poured the cocktails.*
—**do the trick** *see* **trick**.
—**do time** to serve a prison sentence: *I'm sure he'll do time for shooting the policeman.*
—**do (something) up** to renovate or redecorate (something): *We're doing up an old coach house.*
—**fair do's** (1) fair treatment: *Everybody in the group is entitled to fair do's.* (2) be fair! *Fair do's! It's my turn to have the car.*
—**make do with (something)** to make use of (something) as a substitute for something better: *They would really like to buy a house but they will have to make do meanwhile with rented accommodation.*
—**not the done thing** not acceptable behaviour: *It's not the done thing to smoke at the table.*
—**nothing doing** certainly not: *"Would you lend me £10?" "Nothing doing!"*
—**take some doing** to take a great deal of effort: *We might just get there on time but it'll take some doing.*
—**the do's and don'ts** what one should or should not do in a particular situation: *It's difficult to know the do's and don'ts when you go to a new school.*

doctor
—**just what the doctor ordered** exactly what is required: *A cool drink is just what the doctor ordered in this heat.*

dodo
—**dead as a dodo** *see* **dead**.

dog
—**a dog in the manger** a person who stops someone else from doing or having something which he or she does not want: *The child's a real dog in the manger. He doesn't want to play with his model cars but he won't lend them to his friends.* <From one of Aesop's fables in which a dog prevents the horses from eating the hay in the feeding rack although he himself did not want to eat the hay>.
—**a dog's life** a miserable life: *He leads a dog's life with his nagging wife.*
—**a hair of the dog (that bit one)** *see* **hair**.
—**dog eat dog** a ruthless struggle against one's rivals to survive or be successful: *It's dog eat dog in the business world during a recession.*
—**dogsbody** someone who is given all the odd jobs, particularly unpleasant ones, to do: *The boss treats her like the office dogsbody and gets her to run errands and make the coffee.*
—**every dog has his day** *see* **day**.
—**go to the dogs** to be no longer good, moral, successful, etc: *He used to be such a hard-working young man but since his mother died he's gone to the dogs.*
—**give a dog a bad name** if bad things are said about a person's character they will stay with him or her for the rest of his or her life: *He's actually a very good worker, but he's got a reputation for laziness, and you know what they say about giving a dog a bad name.*
—**in the doghouse** in disfavour: *He's in the doghouse for being late for dinner.*
—**keep a dog and bark oneself** to employ someone to do a job and then do it oneself: *She has a secretary and yet she does all her own typing. Talk about keeping a dog and barking oneself.*
—**let sleeping dogs lie** do not look for trouble; if there is no trouble, do not cause any: *I think that she's forgotten about my mistake, so don't remind her. Just let sleeping dogs lie.*
—**let the dog see the rabbit** let me, etc, come near, get a view, etc: *Could you all get away from the television screen and let the dog see the rabbit. I want to watch something.*
—**like a dog's dinner** *see* **dinner**.
—**rain cats and dogs** *see* **cat**.
—**shaggy dog story** a very long joke with a pointless or a ridiculous ending: *His uncle's shaggy dog stories go on for ages.*
—**throw (someone) to the dogs** deliberately to cause (someone) to suffer an unpleasant fate, especially when this is done for selfish or dishonest reasons: *It was he who made the mistake but he threw his assistant to the dogs and had him sacked for it.*
—**top dog** the person who is in charge: *Now that the manager has left, several of the workers are fighting to be top dog.*

—**you can't teach an old dog new tricks** the older you get the more difficult it is to learn new skills or accept ideas or new fashions: *The old man resigned from his caretaker's job when they called for new security methods. "You can't teach a dog new tricks," he said.*

doggo

—**lie doggo** to remain in hiding, not to do anything that will draw attention to oneself: *Lie doggo. The police are looking for you.*

done *see* **do**.

donkey

—**donkey's ages** *or* **years** a very long time: *He's been with that firm for donkey's ages.* <Perhaps from a pun on donkey's ears, which are very long>.

—**donkey work** the hard, often tiring or physical, part of any job: *They're doing all the painting of the house themselves but they're hiring someone to the donkey work.*

—**talk the hind legs off a donkey** to talk too much or to talk for a very long time: *I try to avoid my neighbour if I'm in a hurry. She can talk the hind legs off a donkey.*

door

—**at death's door** *see* **death**.

—**darken (someone's) door** to come or go into (someone's) house: *He told his son never to darken his door again.*

—**behind closed doors** in private, secretly: *Something's wrong. The boss is talking to them behind closed doors.*

—**have a** *or* **one foot in the door** to start to gain entrance to somewhere or something when entrance is difficult: *He hasn't been invited to join the golf club but he's been asked to play there. That's one foot in the door.* <Refers to someone putting a foot in a door to wedge it open in order to gain entrance>.

—**keep the wolf from the door** *see* **wolf**.

—**lay (something) at (someone's) door** to blame (someone) for (something): *The police are trying to lay the crime at his door just because he's an ex-convict.*

—**on (someone's) doorstep** very close to where (someone) lives: *Understandably they don't want a motorway on their doorstep.*

—**open doors** to give someone an opportunity to improve his or her position, to improve someone's chances of success: *Having his father in the same profession will open doors for him when he applies for a job.*

—**show (someone) the door** to make (someone) leave: *If those people are disturbing the other customers show them the door.*

dose

—**a dose** *or* **taste of one's own medicine** something unpleasant done to a person who is in the habit of doing similar things to other people: *He's always bullying the younger boys but he got a dose of his own medicine when one of their brothers beat him up.*

—**like a dose of salts** very quickly or very efficiently: *She got through the typing like a dose of salts.* <Refers to Epsom salts which is used as a purgative>.

dot

—**dot the i's and cross the t's** to attend to details: *She's good at general planning but you'll need someone to dot the i's and cross the t's.*

—**on the dot** (1) exactly on time: *They arrived on the dot for the meeting.* (2) exactly at the time stated: *You must be there at six o'clock on the dot.* <Refers to the dots on the face of a clock>.

double

—**at the double** very quickly: *You had better get your homework handed in—on the double.* <A military term, literally at twice the normal marching speed>.

—**do a double take** to look at or think about (someone or something) a second time because one has not taken it in or understood it the first time: *I did a double take when I saw my old friend. I hadn't seen him for thirty years.*

—**double back** to turn round and go back the way one has come: *The fox doubled back and avoided the hounds.*

—**double Dutch** unintelligible words or language: *I couldn't understand what the lecturer was talking about—it was double Dutch to me.* <Refers to the fact that Dutch sounds a very difficult language to those who are not native speakers of it>.

—**see double** to see two images of everything instead of one: *I thought I was seeing double when the twins walked into the room.*

doubt

—**a doubting Thomas** a person who will not believe something without strong proof: *He won't believe that you're back until he sees you. You know what a doubting Thomas he is.* <Refers to the biblical story Thomas, the disciple who doubted Christ, John 21:24-29>.

down

—**down-and-out** (a person who is) without money or a means of support, homeless: *The*

down-and-outs are sleeping under the bridge.
—**down-at-heel** untidy, uncared-for, poorly dressed: *She's a bit down-at-heel but she can't afford to buy new clothes.*
—**down in the dumps** *or* **down in the mouth** depressed, in low spirits: *He's always down in the dumps in the winter.*
—**down on one's luck** *see* **luck**.
—**down the drain** completely wasted: *Something went wrong with the computer and I lost all my material when it crashed. That was a day's work down the drain.*
—**down-to-earth** very practical: *He does not wish to be involved with the theory of the project. He is a very down-to earth person.*
—**down under** Australia: *He has many relatives down under.*
—**get down to (something)** to begin to work at (something) in earnest: *The exams are next week. You'll have to get down to some revising.*
—**go down big** to be a great success: *The conjuror went down big with the children.*
—**go downhill** to get worse and worse, to deteriorate: *The old lady's gone downhill mentally since I last saw her.*
—**have a down on (someone** *or* **something)** to be very hostile or opposed to (someone or something): *The teacher seems to have a down on the new boy for some reason.*
—**let the side down** *see* **side**.
—**play (something) down** *see* **play**.
—**sell (someone) down the river** *see* **river**.
—**suit (someone) down to the ground** *see* **ground**.
—**talk down to (someone)** *see* **talk**.

dozen
—**baker's dozen** *see* **baker**.
—**daily dozen** *see* **daily**.
—**talk nineteen to the dozen** *see* **talk**.

draw
—**back to the drawing board** *see* **back**.
—**draw a blank** *see* **blank**.
—**draw a veil over (something)** *see* **veil**.
—**draw in one's horns** *see* **horn**.
—**draw on** to approach (of time): *And so the time of depature drew on.*
—**draw rein** to stop, to check one's course: *The rider drew rein at the door.*
—**draw the line** *see* **line**.
—**draw the long bow** *see* **bow**.
—**draw the teeth of (someone** *or* **something)** *see* **teeth**.
—**long drawn out** going on for a long time, especially unnecessarily: *The reception was a long-drawn-out affair.*
—**bottom drawer** *see* **bottom**.
—**out of the top drawer** from the upper classes or aristocracy: *They are out of the top drawer although they are absolutely penniless.*

dress
—**dressed to kill** *or* **dressed to the nines** dressed in one's smartest clothes so as to attract attention: *She was dressed to kill for their first date.*

drift
—**get the drift** to understand the general meaning of something: *I got the drift of the lecturer's talk although I didn't understand all the details.*

drink
—**drink like a fish** to drink a great deal of alcoholic drinks. *He has a terrible complexion as he drinks like a fish.*
—**drink to (someone** *or* **something)** to toast (someone's) health: *Let's drink to the new baby.*

drive
—**be driving at** to be suggesting or trying to say: *I wasn't sure what he was driving at but I thought that he was implying I was lying.*
—**drive a coach and horses through (something)** *see* **coach**.
—**drive a hard bargain** *see* **bargain**.
—**drive (something) home to (someone)** *see* **home**.

drop
—**a drop in the bucket** *see* **bucket**.
—**at the drop of a hat** immediately, requiring only the slightest excuse: *He will start singing at the drop of a hat.*
—**drop a brick** *see* **brick**.
—**drop in** to pay a casual visit: *Do drop in if you are passing.*
—**drop into (someone's) lap** to happen to (someone) without any effort: *The job abroad just dropped into his lap. He didn't even apply for it.*
—**drop off** to fall asleep: *My father dropped off during the sermon.*
—**drop out** to withdraw from school, university, etc, or from society: *After his first year at college he dropped out. He hated his parent's lifestyle so much that he decided to drop out and live rough.*
—**let (something) drop** to let (something) be known accidentally: *She let it drop that he was married.*
—**the penny drops** *see* **penny**.
—**you could have heard a pin drop** *see* **pin**.

drown
—**drown one's sorrows** to take alcoholic drink in order to forget one's unhappiness. *The day he was made redundant he drowned his sorrows in the pub.*

drum
—**beat the drum** *see* **beat**.
—**drum (someone) out** to send (someone) away, to ask (someone) to leave: *They've drummed him out of the club for starting a fight.* <Refers to the use of drums when an officer was being publicly dismissed from his regiment>.

dry
—**a dry run** a practice attempt, a rehearsal: *The headmaster wants a dry run of tomorrow's speech day.*
—**dry as a bone** extremely dry: *The grass is dry as a bone.*
—**dry as dust** extremely dull or boring: *Some of the texts we have to read this year are dry as dust.*
—**dry up** to forget what one was going to say: *It was embarrassing for everyone when the speaker dried up.*
—**home and dry** *see* **home**.
—**keep one's powder dry** to remain calm and prepared for immediate action: *Don't do anything just now. Keep your powder dry and wait to see what the opposition do.* <Refers to the fact that gunpowder must be kept dry to be effective>.
—**leave (someone) high and dry** *see* **high**.

duck
—**a dead duck** *see* **dead**.
—**a lame duck** a weak or inefficient person or organization: *You shouldn't keep helping him. He's just a lame duck who's relying on you too much.*
—**a sitting duck** a person or thing that is very easy to attack: *Their firm was a sitting duck for take-over bids as it was obviously in financial trouble.* <Refers to the fact that a sitting duck is easier to shoot at than one flying in the air>.
—**be water off a duck's back** be totally ineffective: *Don't bother offering him advice—it's water off a duck's back.* <Refers to the fact that water runs straight off the oily feathers on a duck's back>.
—**break one's duck** to have one's first success: *We were worried about the trainee salesman but he's broken his duck. He's made his first sale.* <A cricketing term—no score in cricket is known as a duck>.
—**take to (something) like a duck to water**: to be able to do (something) right from the beginning naturally and without difficulty. *The child took to skiing like a duck to water.*
—**ugly duckling** an unattractive or uninteresting person or thing that develops in time into someone or something very attractive, interesting or successful: *She is now an international model but as a child she was a real ugly duckling.* <Refers to the story by Hans Andersen about a baby swan that is brought up by ducks who consider it ugly by their standards until it grows into a beautiful swan>.

dust
—**bite the dust** *see* **bite**.
—**be like gold dust** *see* **gold**.
—**dry as dust** *see* **dry**.
—**shake the dust from one's feet** to leave somewhere, usually gladly: *I've been in this town long enough. It's time to shake the dust from my feet.*
—**throw dust in (someone's eyes)** to attempt to confuse or deceive (someone): *They threw dust in the policeman's eyes by saying that they had seen an intruder but this was just to give the real burglar time to get away.* <Dust temporarily blinds people if it gets into their eyes>.
—**not see (someone) for dust** not to see (someone) again because he has run away: *When he discovers that he's the father of her child you won't see him for dust.* <Refers to clouds of dust left behind by horses or vehicles when they are moving fast>.

Dutch
—**double Dutch** *see* **double**.
—**Dutch auction** an auction in which the auctioneer starts with a high price and reduces it until someone puts in a bid: *I got the table quite cheaply in a Dutch auction.*
—**Dutch courage** courage that is not real courage but induced by drinking alcohol: *He needed some Dutch courage before asking for a salary increase.* <Perhaps from a Dutch military custom of drinking alcohol before going into battle, perhaps from the fact that gin was introduced into England by the Dutch followers of William III>.
—**Dutch treat** a kind of entertainment or celebration where everyone concerned pays for himself or herself: *He's asked us to help him celebrate his promotion but it's to be a Dutch treat.* <From Dutch lunch, to which all of the guests were expected to contribute some of the food>.

—**go Dutch** to share expenses: *I'll accept your dinner invitation if we go Dutch.*

—**I'm a Dutchman** a phrase used to indicate that one does not at all believe what is being said: *If that politician means what he says then I'm a Dutchman.*

—**talk to (someone) like a Dutch uncle** to scold (someone) or talk to (someone) for what is supposedly his or her own good: *He's her younger brother but he talks to her like a Dutch uncle.* <Perhaps from the reputation that the Dutch have for maintaining strict family discipline>.

dye

—**dyed-in-the-wool** thorough, of firmly fixed opinions: *He's a dyed-in-the-wool Arsenal supporter.* <Refers to the dyeing of material while it is in its raw state before being spun so that the colour is deeper and lasts longer>.

—**dying** *see* **die**.

E

eager

eager beaver *see* **beaver**.

ear

—**a flea in one's ear** *see* **flea**.

—**all ears** *see* **all**.

—**be out on one's ear** to be suddenly dismissed: *He was out on his ear as soon as the manager discovered that he had taken money from the till.*

—**fall on deaf ears** *see* **deaf**.

—**give one's ears for (something)** *same as* **give one's right arm for (something)** *see* **arm**.

—**go in one ear and out the other** not to make any lasting impression: *I gave my assistant detailed instructions but they went in one ear and out the other.*

—**have (someone's) ear** to have the sympathetic attention of (someone, usually someone influential): *He may well get the manager's job—he has the ear of the directors.*

—**have** *or* **keep one's ear to the ground** to keep oneself informed about what is happening around one: *The caretaker will know if there are any vacant rooms. He keeps his ear to the ground.* <Perhaps from a North American Indian method of tracking prey>.

—**(my, etc) ears are burning** someone somewhere is talking about (me, etc): *My ears should have been burning this morning—I believe the board were discussing my promotion.* <The belief that one's ears grow hot when someone is talking about one is mentioned by Pliny, the Roman writer>.

—**pin back one's ears** to listen attentively: *Pin back your ears if you hear his name mentioned.*

—**play it by ear** to deal with matters as they arise without making plans beforehand: *It's difficult to know how they will react to your suggestion. You will have to play it by ear.* <Refers to playing a piece of music from memory rather than from printed music>.

—**prick up one's ears** to begin to listen attentively: *He was bored by the speech but he pricked up his ears when he heard his name mentioned.* <Refers to animals literally pricking up their ears when they are listening attentively>.

—**turn a deaf ear to (something)** *see* **deaf**.

—**up to one's ears in (something)** deeply involved in (something): *I'm up to my ears in work this week.* <A comparison with someone who is almost submerged by very deep water>.

—**walls have ears** *see* **wall**.

—**wet behind the ears** *see* **wet**.

—**you can't make a silk purse out of a pig's ear** *see* **silk**.

early

—**the early bird catches the worm** *see* **bird**.

earth

—**bring (someone) (back) down to earth** to make (someone) aware of the practicalities of life or of a situation: *She was daydreaming about a career on the stage but was brought down to earth by her boss asking her to do some typing.*

—**cost the earth** *see* **cost**.

—**go to earth** to go into hiding: *The criminals went to earth after the robbery.* <Refers to a fox escaping into its earth or hole during a hunt>.

—**move heaven and earth** *see* **heaven**.

—**not have** *or* **stand an earthly** (1) not to have the slightest chance: *The youngest competitor doesn't stand an earthly in the competition against the experienced players.* (2) to have no knowledge or information: *I haven't an earthly where he lives.* <A shortened form of a religious expression, not to have an earthly hope>.

—**run (someone** *or* **something) to earth** to find (someone or something) after a long search: *I finally ran the book to earth in a second-hand book shop.* <Refers to a hunting term for chasing a fox into its earth or hole>.

—**the salt of the earth** *see* **salt**.

easy

—**easy as falling off a log** *or* **easy as pie** extremely easy: *Passing the exam was easy as falling off a log.*

—**easy meat** someone or something that is easily taken advantage of: *She was so naive that she was easy meat for lecherous men.*

—**easy on the eye** very attractive: *He always employs secretaries who are easy on the eye.*

—**go easy on (someone** *or* **something)** (1) not to

treat (someone) too sternly: *Go easy on the child—she didn't mean to spill the coffee.* (2) not to use very much of (something): *Go easy on the milk—we haven't much left.*

—**take it easy** (1) not to hurry or expend much effort: *Take it easy. We've got plenty of time to catch the bus.* (2) not to get upset or angry: *Take it easy. Losing your temper won't help the situation.*

eat

—**eat crow** *see* **crow**.

—**eat one's heart out** *see* **heart**.

—**eat humble pie** *see* **humble**.

—**eat one's words** *see* **word**.

—**have one's cake and eat it** *see* **cake**.

—**have (someone) eating out of one's hand** to have (someone) doing everything that one wishes, because he or she likes or admires one: *The boss is usually a very stern, unfriendly man but the secretary has him eating out of her hand.* <Refers to an animal that is so tame that it will eat out of someone's hand>.

—**I'll eat my hat** *see* **hat**.

—**what's eating you?** what's annoying or troubling you?: *What's eating you? You've been in a bad mood all morning.*

ebb

—**at a low ebb** in a poor or depressed state: *She has been at a low ebb since the death of her husband.* <Refers to the tide when it has flowed away from the land>.

edge

—**get a word in edgeways** *or* **edgewise** *see* **word**.

—**have the edge on (someone** *or* **something)** to have the advantage of (someone or something): *He should win. With his experience he has the edge on the other competitors.*

—**on edge** nervous: *She was on edge until she heard the results of the tests.*

—**set one's teeth on edge** *see* **teeth**.

—**take the edge off (something)** to reduce (something), to make (something) less sharp, etc: *His smile took the edge of his criticism.*

egg

—**a nest-egg** *see* **nest**.

—**bad egg** *see* **bad**.

—**be left with egg on one's face** to be left looking foolish: *He told everyone that his horse would certainly win but he was left with egg on his face when it came in last.*

—**put all one's eggs in one basket** to rely entirely on the success of one project, etc: *The young graduate has put all her eggs in one basket and only applied for one job.*

—**teach one's grandmother to suck eggs** to try to tell someone how to do something when he or she is much more experienced than oneself at it: *We've been playing chess for years, but the young beginner was giving us hints—certainly a case of teaching one's grandmother to suck eggs.*

eight

—**be** *or* **have one over the eight** to be or to have had too much to drink: *He started a fight when he was one over the eight.* <Refers to a former belief that one could have eight drinks before one is drunk>.

elbow

—**elbow grease** hard physical work: *New polishes are all very well but it will take elbow grease to get a shine on that table.*

—**elbow room** space enough to move or to do something: *I'll need elbow room in the kitchen if I am to get the meal ready.*

—**give (someone) the elbow** to get rid of (someone), to end a relationship with (someone): *She's given her fiance the elbow and is going out with someone else.*

—**more power to (someone's) elbow** *see* **power**.

—**out at elbow** ragged, having holes: *That old sweater is out at elbow. Throw it out.*

—**up to one's elbows** *same as* **up to one's ears** *see* **ear**.

element

—**in one's element** in a situation in which one is happy or at one's best: *He's in his element sailing boats.* <Refers to the four elements of medieval science of fire, earth, air and water>.

elephant

—**a white elephant** something which is useless and troublesome to look after: *The vase my aunt gave me is a real white elephant. It's ugly and impossible to dust.* <White elephants were given by the Kings of Siam by followers who had displeased them since the cost of keeping such an elephant was such that it would ruin the follower>.

—**have a memory like an elephant** never to forget things: *Her mother won't forget that I borrowed her dress. She's got a memory like an elephant.*

—**see pink elephants** to have hallucinations, especially when one has drunk too much alcohol: *The drunk man saw pink elephants at the foot of his bed.*

eleventh

—**at the eleventh hour** at the last possible minute: *She handed in her essay at the eleventh hour.* <A biblical reference to the parable of the labourers in the vineyard in Matthew 20>.

empty

—**empty vessels make most noise** the most foolish or least informed people are most likely to voice their opinions: *She complains all the time about the new scheme but she knows nothing about them. Empty vessels make most noise.*

end

—**a dead end** *see* **dead**.

—**at a loose end** with nothing to do, with no plans: *The young man's been at a loose end since he finished his exams.*

—**at the end of the day** *see* **day**.

—**at the end of one's tether** at the end of one's patience, tolerance, etc: *She's at the end of her tether looking after three small children.* <Refers to a rope that will only extend a certain distance to let the animal attached to it graze>.

—**at one's wits' ends** *see* **wit**.

—**come to a sticky end** *see* **stick**.

—**keep one's end up** to perform as well as other people involved: *I didn't know much about the subject being discussed but I kept my end up.*

—**make ends meet** to live within the limits of one's income: He *earns very little but somehow they make ends meet.* <The ends referred to are the start and finish of one's annual accounts>.

—**the end justifies the means** if the result is good it does not matter how one achieved it: *She cheated in order to pass the exam but she says that the end justifies the means.*

—**the end of the line** *or* **road** the point beyond which survival is impossible: *Their marriage has reached the end of the line.*

—**get hold of the wrong end of the stick** *see* **stick**.

—**the thin end of the wedge** *see* **wedge**.

enfant

—**enfant terrible** a younger person who embarrasses older people with his or her unconventional ideas or behaviour: *The new committee member is an enfant terrible and shocked the older members by suggesting radical changes.*

error

—**trial and error** *see* **trial**.

essence

—**of the essence** of the greatest importance: *Speed is of the essence in this project.*

establishment

—**the Establishment** the group who hold positions of authority in a country, society, etc: *Young people often rebel against the Establishment.*

eternal

—**eternal rest** death: *The old man has gone to his eternal rest.*

—**eternal triangle** a sexual relationship between two men and one woman or between two women and one man: *He is married but he has a mistress—the eternal triangle.*

even

—**break even** *see* **even**.

—**get even with (someone)** to be revenged on (someone): *He vowed to get even with his opponent for committing a foul.*

—**get** *or* **keep on an even keel** to be or keep steady or calm with no sudden changes: *One minute she's up, the next she's down. She must get on an even keel.*

event

—**be wise after the event** to realize how a situation should have been dealt with after it is over: *Her father never knows what to do at the time but he's always wise after the event.*

—**in the event** as it happened: *We thought he would lose but in the event he lost.*

—**in the event of (something)** if (something) happens: *He inherits in the event of his father's death.*

every

—**every inch a** *or* **the** *see* **inch**.

—**every man jack** *see* **jack**.

evidence

—**in evidence** easily seen: *His love for her is much in evidence.*

—**turn Queen's** *or* **King's evidence** to give evidence against a fellow criminal in order to have one's own sentence reduced: *The accused turned Queen's evidence and spilled the beans about his accomplice.*

evil

—**the evil eye** *see* **eye**.

—**put off the evil hour** *or* **day** to keep postponing something unpleasant: *He should go to the dentist but he keeps postponing the evil hour.*

ewe

—**(someone's) ewe lamb** (someone's) favourite: *Her youngest son is her ewe lamb.* <A biblical reference to Samuel 12:3>.

exception

—**the exception that proves the rule** the fact

that an exception has to be made for a particular example of something proves that the general rule is valid: *All the family have black hair. The youngest member who is fair-haired is the exception that proves the rule.*

—**take exception to (something)** to take offence at (something): *I took exception to his overcritical comments about my outfit.*

exhibition

—**make an exhibition of oneself** to behave embarrassingly in public: *She made an exhibition of herself at the office party by getting very drunk.*

expense

—**at the expense of (someone** *or* **something)** causing loss, harm, embarrassment, etc: *He won the race, but at the expense of his health.*

eye

—**all my eye (and Betty Martin)** completely untrue: *He told me he was wealthy, but I knew that it was all my eye.*

—**an eye for an eye (and a tooth for a tooth)** a punishment to match the offence committed: *He killed the son of the man who murdered his daughter.* <A biblical reference to Exodus 21:23>.

—**a sight for sore eyes** a pleasant or welcome sight: *"Well, you're a sight for sore eyes," said the old man to his son who was just back from a long trip abroad.*

—**a smack in the eye for (someone)** an insult or rebuff for (someone): *When she married someone else it was a real smack in the eye for her ex-boyfriend.*

—**beauty is in the eye of the beholder** *see* **beauty**.

—**be one in the eye for (someone)** to be something unpleasant that happens to someone who deserves it: *He tried to get the boss to sack her, but it was one in the eye for him when she was promoted.*

—**can see with half an eye** to see or understand without difficulty: *You can see with half an eye that he is seriously ill.*

—**close one's eyes to (something)** deliberately to ignore (something blameworthy): *The local policeman closed his eyes to the pub being open after closing time.*

—**cry one's eyes out** to weep bitterly: *The little girl cried her eyes out when her rabbit died.*

—**easy on the eye** *see* **easy**.

—**eye-opener** something which reveals an unexpected fact: *When he stood up to the bully it was a real eye-opener to her. She'd thought he was a coward.*

—**eyesore** something extremely ugly: *That new building is an eyesore.*

—**give one's eye teeth** *see* **teeth**.

—**give (someone) the glad eye** *see* **glad**.

—**have an eye for (someone** *or* **something)** to be a good judge of (someone or something), to be able to spot (someone or something) as a good example: *She has an eye for a bargain when it comes to antiques.*

—**have an eye to the main chance** *see* **chance**.

—**in the twinkling of an eye** very rapidly, immediately: *The child disappeared in the twinkling of an eye.*

—**keep a weather eye open** *or* **keep one's eyes peeled** *or* **skinned** to keep a close watch, to be alert: *Keep your eyes peeled in case the police come.* <A nautical term for watching for changes in the weather>.

—**make eyes at (someone)** to look at (someone) with sexual interest: *She was making eyes at the man at the bar.*

—**not to bat an eyelid** not to show any surprise, distress, etc: *He didn't bat an eyelid when the police charged him.*

—**open (someone's) eyes to (something)** to make (someone) aware of (something, usually unpleasant) previously unknown: *They finally opened his eyes to his wife's adultery.*

—**pull the wool over (someone's) eyes** *see* **wool**.

—**see eye to eye with (someone)** to be in agreement with (someone): *The couple rarely see eye to eye about how to bring up their children.*

—**the apple of (someone's) eye** *see* **apple**.

—**the evil eye** the supposed power of causing harm by a look: *I think he's put the evil eye on me. I always play chess badly when I'm playing against him.*

—**there's more to (someone** *or* **something) than meets the eye** the true worth or state of (someone or something) is not immediately obvious: *I think that there's more to his illness than meets the eye.*

—**turn a blind eye to (something)** *same as* **close one's eyes to (something)** *see above.*

—**up to one's eyes** *same as* **up to one's ears (in something)** *see* **ear**.

—**with one's eyes open** fully aware of one's actions: *She married him with her eyes open. She knew he was violent.*

F

face

—**a slap in the face** *see* **slap**.

—**cut off one's nose to spite one's face** *see* **nose**.

—**face the music** to face and deal with a situation caused by one's actions: *At first he ran away after the crime but he returned to face the music.* <Perhaps from a performer facing the musicians below the front of the stage as he or she makes an entrance on stage>.

—**fly in the face of (something)** to oppose or defy (something): *She takes pleasure in flying in the face of convention.* <Refers to a dog attacking>.

—**give (something) a face-lift** to make (something) look better, to renovate (something): *They've given the old house a complete face-lift.* <Refers to a cosmetic operation to raise the skin of the lower face to improve the appearance>.

—**have a long face** to look unhappy. *Judging from his long face I assume that he didn't get the job.*

—**have a face like thunder** to be very angry-looking: *She had a face like thunder when he was late for dinner.*

—**in the face of (something)** while having to cope with (something unpleasant): *She succeeded in the face of great hardship.*

—**laugh on the other side of one's face** *see* **laugh**.

—**lose face** to suffer a loss of respect or reputation: *She refused to apologize to her employee because she thought she would lose face by doing so.*

—**make** *or* **pull a face** to twist one's face into a strange or funny expression: *She made a face behind her father's back.*

—**put a brave face on it** to try to appear brave when one is feeling afraid, distressed, etc: *I'm nervous about the interview but I'm putting a brave face on it.*

—**save (someone's) face** to prevent (someone) from appearing stupid or wrong: *It was her mistake but her secretary saved her face by taking responsibility for it.*

—**set one's face against (someone** *or* **something)** to oppose (someone or something) with great determination: *The chairman has set his face against the proposal and that's the end of it.*

—**show one's face** to put in an appearance, especially when one will not be welcome or when one will be embarrassed: *I'm surprised that she showed her face at the party after she got so drunk at the last one.*

—**take (someone** *or* **something) at face value** to judge (someone or something) on outward appearance: *She takes him at face value, but his sincerity is false.* <Refers to the value of a coin or note printed on it>.

faint

—**faint heart never won fair lady** boldness is necessary to achieve what one desires: *You won't get a job sitting there. Faint heart never won fair lady.*

—**not to have the faintest** not to have the slightest idea: *I haven't the faintest who he is.*

fair

—**a fair crack of the whip** *see* **crack**.

—**by fair means or foul** by any method whatsoever: *He's determined to get that job by fair means or foul.*

—**fair and square** (1) honestly, in a fair way: *He won the contest fair and square, not because he was the umpire's son.* (2) straight, directly: *He hit him fair and square on the nose.*

—**fair do's** *see* **do**.

—**fair game** a person or thing that it is considered quite reasonable to attack, make fun of, etc: *Politicians are fair game to the press.*

—**fair play** fairness and justice: *The children are organizing the sports themselves but there will have to be some teachers there to see fair play.*

—**fairweather friends** people who are friendly towards one only when one is not in trouble: *All his fairweather friends deserted him when he lost his job.*

—**in a fair way to** very likely to: *He's in a fair way to becoming a director.*

faith

—**in (all) good faith** with honest and sincere intentions: *I recommended the job to him in all good faith.*

fall

—**fall about** to be extremely amused: *The children fell about at the clown's antics.*

—**fall back on (someone** *or* **something)** to rely on (someone or something) if all else fails: *When her husband left her she knew that she could fall back on her parents.*

—**fall between two stools** *see* **stool**.

—**fall by the wayside** *see* **wayside**.

—**fall down on (something)** to do badly at (something): *Since he was ill he has been falling down on his job.*

—**fall flat** to fail, to have no effect: *The comedian's jokes fell completely flat.*

—**fall for (someone** *or* **something)** (1) to be deceived by (something): *She fell for his charm but he was a rogue.* (2) to be attracted to or fall in love with (someone or something): *He fell for his best friend's girlfriend.*

—**fall foul of (something** *or* **something)** to do something that arouses someone's anger or hostility: *He fell foul of the law at an early age.*

—**fall from grace** to lose (someone's) favour: *She used to be her father's favourite but she fell from grace when she married without his permission.*

—**fall into place** *see* **place**.

—**fall on deaf ears** *see* **deaf**.

—**fall** *or* **land on one's feet** *see* **feet**.

—**fall out** to quarrel: *He fell out with his neighbour over the repair of their communal wall.*

—**fall over oneself to** to set about doing something with great willingness and eagerness: *She fell over herself to make her rich guest welcome.*

false

—**a false alarm** *see* **alarm**.

—**a false start** *see* **start**.

—**under false pretences** by using deceit: *They got into the house under false pretences by saying they were workmen.*

familiarity

—**familiarity breeds contempt** people cease to appreciate people or things they know well: *He doesn't realize what a marvellous wife he has because familiarity has bred contempt.*

family

—**in the family way** pregnant: *Her son's scarcely a year old, but she's in the family way again.*

—**run in the family** to be a characteristic found in many members of the same family: *Violence runs in that family. At least three of them are in prison.*

fancy

—**(footloose and) fancy free** not in love with anyone, not romantically attached: *He used to be married but he's fancy free now.*

—**fancy one's chances** *see* **chance**.

—**take** *or* **tickle one's fancy** to attract one, to arouse a liking in one: *She has seen a dress that took her fancy.*

far

—**a far cry from (something)** *see* **cry**.

—**far and away** by a very great amount: *He's far and away the best salesman.*

—**far be it from (someone) to** (someone) has no right to do something: *Far be it from me to presume to advise you, but are you doing the right thing?*

—**go far** to be very successful: *The boy is not academic but I think he will go far.*

—**go too far** to do or say something that is beyond the limits of what is acceptable: *The young employee went too far when he hit the supervisor.*

—**so far, so good** up until now the project, etc, has been successful: *So far so good, but we don't know what will happen in the future.*

fashion

—**after a fashion** *see* **after**.

fast

—**hard-and-fast** *see* **hard**.

—**play fast and loose with (something)** to act irresponsibly with (something): *He had no intentions of marrying her. He was just playing fast and loose with her affections.*

—**pull a fast one on (someone)** to deceive (someone): *He pulled a fast one on me by selling me a stolen car.* <Refers to bowling a fast ball in cricket>.

fat

—**chew the fat** *see* **chew**.

—**kill the fatted calf** *see* **calf**.

—**live off the fat of the land** to live in a luxurious fashion: *While he was successful they lived off the fat of the land.*

—**the fat is in the fire** trouble has been started and it cannot be stopped: *The fat was in the fire when his parents discovered he had been out all night.* <Fat causes a fire to flare up>.

fate

—**a fate worse than death** something terrible that happens to one, often rape: *The village girls suffered a fate worse than death at the hands of the invaders.*

—**seal (someone's) fate** to ensure that something, usually unpleasant, happens to (someone): *The workers' fate was sealed when the firm was bought over. They lost their jobs.*

—**tempt fate** to act in a way that is likely to bring one ill luck or misfortune: *You're tempting fate by having a party outside. It's bound to rain now.*

father

—**the child is father of the man** *see* **child**.

—**the father and mother of (something)** an extreme example of (something, usually something bad): *The couple had the father and mother of a row last night.*

fault

—**to a fault** to too great an extent: *He embarrasses her by his lavish gifts. He's generous to a fault.*

favour

—**curry favour with (someone)** *see* **curry**.

fear

—**put the fear of death** *or* **God into (someone)** to terrify (someone): *Hearing the eerie shrieks in the graveyard put the fear of God into him.*

—**there is no fear of (something)** it is not likely that (something) will happen: *There's no fear of our getting an extra holiday.*

—**without fear or favour** with complete fairness: *You must conduct the investigation into the frauds without fear or favour.*

feather

—**a feather in one's cap** something of which one can be proud: *Winning the tournament was a real feather in the young player's cap.*

—**birds of a feather flock together** *see* **bird**.

—**feather one's (own) nest** to make a profit for oneself, often at the expense of someone else: *All the years that he was storekeeper with the firm he was feathering his nest.*

—**make the feathers** *or* **fur fly** to cause trouble or a quarrel: *The politician made the feathers fly when he announced the privatization of the industry.* <Refers to birds or animals fighting>.

—**show the white feather** to show signs of cowardice: *His colleagues accused him of showing the white feather when he refused to ask for a salary increase.* <A white feather in the tail of a fighting cock was a sign of inferior breeding>.

feel

—**feel at home** *see* **home**.

—**feel free** to do what you wish: *Feel free to borrow the car.*

—**feel in one's bones** to know (something) by instinct: *I felt in my bones that he was lying.*

—**feel one's feet** to be becoming used to a situation: *He's not very good at the job yet but he's just feeling his feet.*

—**feel the pinch** *see* **pinch**.

feet

—**at (someone's) feet** easily within (someone's) reach or power: (1) *With his qualifications the world is at his feet.* 2 greatly admiring of (someone): *All the young men were at the feet of the beautiful woman.*

—**fall** *or* **land on one's feet** to be fortunate or successful, especially after a period of uncertainty or misfortune: *After being unemployed he landed on his feet with a job in management.*

—**find one's feet** to become capable of coping with a situation: *She felt overwhelmed by motherhood at first but she's finding her feet now.*

—**get cold feet** *see* **cold**.

—**have feet of clay** to have a surprising weakness, despite having been thought to be perfect: *He thought his wife was an angel, but he discovered that she had feet of clay when she was rude to the workman.* <A biblical reference to Daniel 2:31-34>.

—**have both feet on the ground** or have one's feet on the ground to be practical and sensible: *Her husband is a dreamer but she has her feet on the ground.*

—**have the ball at one's feet** *see* **ball**.

—**have two left feet** *see* **left**.

—**get under (someone's) feet** to hinder or get in (someone's) way: *The children get under her feet when she's doing the housework.*

—**put one's feet up** to take a rest: *He's been working hard all his life and it's time for him to put his feet up.*

—**shake the dust from one's feet** *see* **dust**.

—**sit at (someone's) feet** receive tuition from (someone) and be influenced by (him or her): *He sat at Picasso's feet as a student.*

—**stand on one's own feet** to be independent: *Your children will have to learn to stand on their own feet some day.*

—**sweep (someone) off his** *or* **her feet** to affect (someone) with great enthusiasm or emotion; to influence (someone) to do as one wishes: *She should never have married her but he swept her off his feet.*

fence

—**mend fences** to put things right after a quarrel, etc: *Your quarrel with your father was a long time ago. You should try to mend fences now.*

—**rush one's fences** to act too hurriedly or

rashly: *I know you're attracted to her, but don't rush your fences by asking her to marry you until you get to know her properly.* <A horse-riding term>.

—**sit on the fence** to refuse to take sides in a dispute, etc: *My mother and my sister have quarrelled but I find it's wiser to sit on the fence.*

fiddle

—**fiddle while Rome burns** *see* **Rome**.

—**fit as a fiddle** extremely fit: *His father has been ill but he's fit as a fiddle now.*

—**play second fiddle to (someone)** to be in a subordinate or inferior position to (someone): *She always plays second fiddle to her glamorous sister at parties.*

field

—**fresh fields and pastures new** new areas of activity, new places: *I'm tired of working here. I'm looking for fresh fields and pastures new.* <From Lycidas, a poem by John Milton>.

—**have a field day** to have a very busy, successful or enjoyable day: *The journalists had a field day when the prime minister resigned.*

—**play the field** to take advantage of many chances offered to one, especially to go out with several members of the opposite sex: *He's played the field for years but she wants to get married now.*

fight

—**fighting fit** extremely healthy and in good condition: *The player was injured but he's fighting fit now.*

—**fight like Kilkenny cats** to fight fiercely: *The two boys fought like Kilkenny cats.* <Refers to a story of two cats in the town of Kilkenny who were tied together by their tails and fought until only the tails were left>.

—**fight shy of (something)** to avoid (something): *He's been fighting shy of telling her he's leaving.*

—**have a fighting chance** *see* **chance**.

fill

—**fill a dead man's shoes** *same as* **step into a dead man's shoes**—*see* **dead**.

—**fill out** to get plumper: *She was very thin but she's beginning to fill out.*

—**fill the bill** *see* **bill**.

—**have had one's fill** to have had enough, to be unable to tolerate any more: *He says he's had his fill of his boring job.*

find

—**find one's feet** *see* **feet**.

—**find one's** *or* **its own level** *see* **level**.

—**find out the hard way** to find out (something) by one's own experience rather than from others: *He found out the hard way that it's difficult to get into acting.*

fine

—**cut it fine** *see* **cut**.

—**get (something) down to a fine art** to have learned to do (something) extremely well: *She's got getting out quickly in the morning down to a fine art.*

—**go through (something) with a fine-tooth comb**: to search (something) very carefully: *You must go through the written contract with a fine-tooth comb.* <A fine-tooth comb is used to remove lice from hair>.

finger

—**be all fingers and thumbs** to be clumsy or awkward when using one's hands: *I'm so nervous. I'm all fingers and thumbs.*

—**burn one's fingers** *or* **get one's fingers burnt** to suffer because of something that one has been involved in: *He hoped to make money by investing in the firm but he got his fingers burnt when it went bankrupt*

—**cross one's fingers** to hope for good fortune: *Cross your fingers that it doesn't rain tomorrow.*

—**get** *or* **pull one's finger out** to stop wasting time and get on with something: *If that job is to be finished on time you'll have to get your finger out.*

—**have a finger in every pie** to be involved in a large number of projects, organizations, etc: *I'm not sure what business he's in—he has a finger in every pie.*

—**have a finger in the pie** to be involved in something: *I wondered who had caused the trouble. I might have known that he would have a finger in the pie.*

—**have (something) at one's fingertips** to know all the information about (something): *She has the history of the village at her fingertips.*

—**have green fingers** *see* **green**.

—**keep one's finger on the pulse** *see* **pulse**.

—**let (something) slip through one's fingers** to lose (an advantage, opportunity, etc), often by one's inaction: *He let the job slip through his fingers by not applying in time.*

—**point the finger at (someone)** to indicate who is to blame: *She would point the finger at anyone to save her son who has been accused.*

—**put one's finger on (something)** to identify (something) exactly: *I could not put my finger on why I disliked him.*

—**twist** *or* **wrap (someone) round one's little finger** to be able to get (someone) to do exactly as one wishes: *Her father will lend her the money. She can twist him round her little finger.*

fire

—**add fuel to the fire** *see* **add**.

—**baptism of fire** *see* **baptism**.

—**firing on all cylinders** *see* **cylinder**.

—**get on like a house on fire** to get on very well: *I didn't think my two friends would like each other but they get on like a house on fire.*

—**hang fire** to wait or be delayed: *His holiday plans are hanging fire until his health improves.* <Refers to a gun in which there is a delay between the trigger being pulled and the gun being fired>.

—**have many** *or* **several irons in the fire** *see* **iron**.

—**out of the frying pan into the fire** *see* **fry**.

—**play with fire** to take tasks, to do something dangerous: *The child is playing with fire by teasing that dog. It will bite him.*

—**pull (someone's) chestnuts out of the fire** *see* **chestnut**.

—**set the Thames** *or* **world on fire** to do something remarkable: *He'll never set the Thames on fire but he'll do quite well at his job.* <Refers to the River Thames, which it would be impossible to set alight>.

—**the fat is in the fire** *see* **fat**.

—**there's no smoke without fire** *see* **smoke**.

—**under fire** being attacked: *The new traffic plans have come under fire from several organizations.* <Refers literally to being shot at>.

first

—**at first hand** directly: *I got my information about the council meeting at first hand from my cousin who attended it.*

—**first thing** early in the morning or in the working day: *The boss wants to see you first thing.*

—**get to** *or* **make** *or* **reach first base** *see* **base**.

—**in the first flush of (something)** in the early and vigorous stages of (something): *He offered to work overtime in the first flush of enthusiasm for the job.*

—**in the first place** *see* **place**.

—**not to know the first thing about (something)** to know nothing about (something): *He doesn't know the first thing about computers.*

—**of the first water** of the highest quality, of the most extreme type: *She is a doctor of the first water.* <Refers to a top-quality diamond, diamonds being graded into three "waters" according to clarity>.

fish

—**a big fish in a small pond** *see* **big**.

—**a pretty kettle of fish** *see* **kettle**.

—**a queer fish** a person who is considered strange or eccentric: *He's a queer fish who seems to have no friends.*

—**drink like a fish** *see* **drink**.

—**fish in muddy** *or* **troubled waters** to concern oneself with matters that are unpleasant or confused: *You'll really be fishing in troubled waters if you investigate the employment practices in that firm.*

—**have other fish to fry** to have something else to do, especially something that is more important or more profitable: *We asked him to join us but he had other fish to fry. He has a new girlfriend.*

—**like a fish out of water** ill at ease and unaccustomed to a situation: *Having come from a small office she felt like a fish out of water in the huge firm.*

—**there's plenty more fish in the sea** many more opportunities will arise; many more members of the opposite sex are around: *I know your girlfriend has left you but there are plenty more fish in the sea.*

fit

—**by fits and starts** irregularly, often stopping and starting: *He tends to work by fits and starts, rather than continuously.*

—**fit as a fiddle** *see* **fiddle**.

—**fit like a glove** *see* **glove**.

—**if the cap fits, wear it** *see* **cap**.

five

—**a bunch of fives** a clenched fist, a blow with one's fist: *The bully said he'd give him a bunch of fives if he didn't give him money.*

—**know how many beans make five** *see* **bean**.

fix

—**in a fix** in an awkward or difficult situation: *I'm in a fix now that I've lost my wallet.*

flag

—**hang** *or* **put the flags out** to celebrate something (a rare event): *The day she smiles at a customer I'll hang the flags out.*

—**show the flag** to attend an event only so that one can say that one has been present, or in order to make sure that one's firm, organization, etc, is represented: *I really don't want to go to the bank's party but as no one else from the company is going. I'll have to show the flag.*

flame

—**an old flame** a former boyfriend or girlfriend: *His wife objected to him seeing an old flame who was in town.*

—**fan the flames** to make a difficult situation worse: *She quarrelled with him, and her friend fanned the flames by telling her what he had said about her in anger.*

—**shoot (someone) down in flames** *see* **shoot**.

flash

—**a flash in the pan** a sudden, brief success: *He did well in the first match but it was just a flash in the pan. He lost the rest.* <Refers to a flintlock gun in which the spark from the flint ignited the gunpowder in the priming pan, the flash then travelling to the main barrel. If this failed to go off there was only a flash>.

flat

—**fall flat** *see* **fall**.

—**flat on one's back** *see* **back**.

—**in a flat spin** in a state of confused excitement: *She was in a flat spin when she heard her fiancé was coming home from the war.*

flea

—**a flea in one's ear** a sharp scolding: *He got a flea in his ear from the teacher for being late.*

—**flea-market** a market where second-hand or cheap clothes and goods are sold: *She got a lovely skirt at a stall in the flea-market.* <From the *Marché aux Puces* in Paris>.

flesh

—**a thorn in (someone's) flesh** a permanent source of annoyance or irritation: *Her younger son is a thorn in her flesh. He's always getting into trouble.* <A biblical reference to II Corinthians 12:7>.

—**flesh and blood** (1) family, relations: *Surely they'll take her in. She's their own flesh and blood.* (2) human beings in general: *Resisting the delicious-looking cake was more than flesh and blood could stand.*

—**get** *or* **have one's pound of flesh** to obtain everything that one is entitled to, especially if this causes difficulties or suffering to those who have to give it: *The factory owner gets his pound of flesh from his workers. They work long hours at boring work.* <Refers to Shakespeare's play *The Merchant of Venice*, in which Shylock tries to enforce an agreement by which he can cut a pound of flesh from Antonio>.

—**in the flesh** in real life, not in a photograph: *She never dreamt that she'd see her favourite filmstar in the flesh.*

—**make (someone's) flesh creep** *see* **creep**.

—**the flesh-pots** luxurious living: *She's enjoying the flesh-pots of the Bahamas.* <A biblical reference to Exodus 16:3>.

—**the spirit is willing (but the flesh is weak)** *see* **spirit**.

flog

—**flog a dead horse** *see* **horse**.

flood

—**before the flood** a very long time ago: *The clothes she wears were in fashion before the flood.* <Refers to the Great Flood in the Bible in Genesis 7:9>.

floor

—**get in on the ground floor** *see* **ground**.

—**take the floor** (1) to rise to make a public speech: *The chairman took the floor to introduce the speakers.* (2) to begin to dance: *The couple took the floor to do the tango.*

—**wipe the floor with (someone)** to defeat (someone) thoroughly: *The experienced player wiped the floor with the young player.*

flush

—**in the first flush of (something)** *see* **first**.

fly[1]

—**a fly in the ointment** something that spoils something: *The holiday was enjoyable—the only fly in the ointment was that I lost my wallet.*

—**there are no flies on (someone)** there is no possibility of deceiving (someone), there is no lack of sense in (someone): *She won't buy his old car—there are no flies on her.*

—**would like to be a fly on the wall** would like to be present and able to hear what is going on without being seen: *I would like to have been a fly on the wall when she told him what she thought of him.*

fly[2]

—**as the crow flies** *see* **crow**.

—**be flying high** to be very successful, to be in a position of power: *He's flying high nowadays as chairman of the company, but he started off as the errand boy.*

—**fly a kite** see **kite**.

—**fly in the face of (something)** *see* **face**.

—**fly off the handle** *see* **handle**.

—**get off to a flying start** to have a very successful beginning: *Our appeal got off to a flying start with a donation of £1000.*

—**pigs might fly** *see* **pig**.

—**with flying colours** *see* **colour**.

foam

—**foam at the mouth** to be very angry: *He was*

foaming at the mouth when he got a parking ticket. <Mad dogs foam at the mouth>.

fog

—**not to have the foggiest** not to have the slightest idea: *I haven't the foggiest where she's gone.*

follow

—**follow in (someone's) footsteps** *see* **foot**.

—**follow one's nose** *see* **nose**.

—**follow suit** to do just as someone else has done: *He got up to leave and everyone followed suit.* <A reference to card-playing when a player plays the same suit as the previous player>.

food

—**food for thought** something to make one think carefully: *The managing director's talk about the state of the firm gave us food for thought.*

fool

—**a fool's paradise** a state of happiness that is based on something that is not true or realistic: *She lived in a fool's paradise thinking that he was going to marry her.*

—**be nobody's fool** to have a good deal of common sense: *She's nobody's fool. She knows the salary they offered her is too low.*

—**fools rush in (where angels fear to tread)** an ignorant person can sometimes achieve what a warier person cannot: *Fools rush in—he went straight to the top person and got our complaint settled.* <From Alexander Pope's *An Essay on Criticism*>.

—**make a fool of oneself** to make oneself appear ridiculous or stupid: *He thought that he would make a fool of himself if he sang in public.*

—**make a fool of (someone)** to make (someone) appear ridiculous or stupid: *She made a fool of him by imitating his accent.*

—**not to suffer fools gladly** not to have any patience with foolish or stupid people: *Clever children get on with that teacher but she doesn't suffer fools gladly.*

foot

—**follow in (someone's) footsteps** to do the same as someone else, particularly a relative, has done before: *He's following in his father's footsteps and studying medicine.*

—**footloose and fancy free** *see* **fancy**.

—**get off on the wrong foot** to get off to a bad or unfortunate start: *He got off on the wrong foot with her parents by arriving late.*

—**have a** *or* **one foot in the door** *see* **door**.

—**have one foot in the grave** to be very old: *Young people tend to think that anyone over 50 has one foot in the grave!*

—**the boot is on the other foot** *see* **boot**.

—**put one's best foot forward** *see* **best**.

—**put one's foot down** to be firm about something, to forbid someone to do something: *She wanted to hitch-hike but her mother put her foot down and she's going by bus.*

—**put one's foot in it** to do or say something tactless: *You put your foot in it when you mentioned her husband. He's just left her.*

fork

—**speak with a forked tongue** to tell lies: *He was speaking with a forked tongue when he said he loved her.* <Supposedly a phrase used by North American Indians>.

form

—**be good** *or* **bad form** be in or not in accordance with social conventions or customs: *It is bad form to smoke between courses at the dinner table.*

—**on form** in good condition, fit and in a good humour: *He's been ill but he's back on form again.* <Form refers to the condition of a horse>.

—**true to form** in accordance with someone's usual pattern of behaviour: *True to form, he arrived about an hour early.*

fort

—**hold the fort** to take temporary charge of something: *The owner of the shop is in hospital and I'm holding the fort.*

forty

—**forty winks** a short nap: *I'll just have forty winks before I go out.*

foul

—**by fair means or foul** *see* **fair**

—**fall foul of (someone** *or* **something)** *see* **fall**.

—**foul play** a criminal act, especially one involving murder: *The police have found a body and they're suspecting foul play.* <A legal term>.

four

—**on all fours** *see* **all**.

free

—**(footloose and) fancy free** *see* **fancy**.

—**feel free** *see* **feel**.

—**free and easy** informal, casual: *He's the boss but he's always very free and easy with his employees.*

—**free-for-all** an argument or fight in which everyone joins in an uncontrolled way: *It started off as a quarrel between husband and wife* *but it ended up as a free-for-all with all the neighbours involved.*

—**give (someone) a free hand** give (someone) permission to do as he or she wishes: *They gave the interior decorator a free hand with the renovation of their house.*

—**scot-free** unhurt or unpunished: *He was charged with the crime but he got away scot-free for lack of evidence.*

French

—**take French leave** to stay away from work, etc, without permission: *He might well be dismissed for taking French leave.* <Refers to an 18th-century French custom of leaving a party without saying goodbye to one's host>.

fresh

—**fresh as a daisy** *see* **daisy**.

—**fresh fields and pastures new** *see* **field**.

Freudian

—**a Freudian slip** the use of a wrong word while speaking that is supposed to indicate an unconscious thought: *The policeman made a Freudian slip when he said the accused was being persecuted for hitting another policeman. He meant to say prosecuted.* <Refers to the theories of the psychologist Sigmund Freud>.

Friday

—**man** *or* **girl Friday** an invaluable assistant: *The boss cannot find anything in the office when his man Friday is away.* <Refers to Friday, a character in *Robinson Crusoe* by Daniel Defoe.

friend

—**a friend in need is a friend indeed** a friend who helps when one is in trouble is truly a friend: *She visited him regularly in prison. A friend in need is a friend indeed.*

—**fairweather friends** *see* **fair**.

—**have a friend at court** *or* **have a friend in high places** to have a friend in an influential position who will be able to help one: *They say she got a the job because she has a friend at court. Her cousin is on the board.*

frog

—**have a frog in one's throat** to to be hoarse: *We couldn't hear what she was saying as she had a frog in her throat.*

fruit

—**bear fruit** *see* **bear**.

—**Dead Sea fruit** *see* **dead**.

—**forbidden fruit** something desirable that is made even more so because one is forbidden for some reason to obtain it: *He is in love with her but she is forbidden fruit, being his brother's wife.* <Refers to the biblical tree in the Garden of Eden whose fruit Adam was forbidden by God to eat in Genesis 3>.

fry

—**have other fish to fry** *see* **fish**.

—**out of the frying pan into the fire** free of a difficult or dangerous situation only to get into a worse one: *He was in debt to the bank and now he is in debt to a money-lender—he's definitely out of the frying pan and into the fire.*

fuel

—**add fuel to the fire** *see* **add**.

full

—**be full of oneself** to be very conceited: *She's so full of herself since she married a rich man.*

—**come full circle** *see* **circle**.

—**full of beans** *see* **bean**.

—**in full** completely, with nothing left out: *You must complete the form in full.*

—**in full cry** *see* **cry**.

—**in full swing** *see* **swing**.

—**in the fullness of time** when the proper time has arrived, eventually: *In the fullness of time her baby was born.*

fun

—**fun and games** a lively time, an amusing time: *We had fun and games when the grandchildren came to stay.*

—**make fun of (someone)** *or* **poke fun at (someone)** to laugh at (someone), to make mocking remarks about (someone): *Her classmates made fun of her for wearing old-fashioned clothes.*

funeral

—**that's my, etc, funeral** that's my, etc, problem and I must deal with it: *He's spent all his money but that's his funeral.*

funny

—**funny business** unfair activities, deception: *There's some funny business going on in that firm because they keep losing staff.*

fur

—**make the fur fly** *same as* **make the feathers fly** *see* **feather**.

furrow

—**plough a lonely furrow** to work or make one's way alone without help: *Single parents often have to plough a lonely furrow.*

fuss

—**make a fuss** to complain vigorously: *She got her money back from the shop when she made a fuss.*

—**make a fuss of (someone)** to pay a lot of attention to (someone), to show (someone) a lot of affection: *She always makes a fuss of her niece.*

G

gab
—**the gift of the gab** the ability to talk readily and easily: *He loves public speaking. He has the gift of the gab.*
gaff
—**blow the gaff** *see* **blow**.
gain
—**gain ground** to make progress, to become more generally acceptable or popular: *The campaign against the nuclear base is gaining ground.*
—**gain time** to arrange things so that one has more time to do something: *The student should have handed in his essay yesterday but he pretended to be ill to gain time.*
—**nothing ventured, nothing gained** *see* **nothing**.
gallery
—**play to the gallery** to act in an amusing or showy way to the ordinary people in an organization, etc, in order to gain popularity or their support: *The politician was playing to the gallery at the party conference.*
game
—**beat (someone) at his** *or* **her own game** to do better than (someone) at his or her activity, especially a cunning or dishonest one: *In previous years he won the cross-country race by taking a short cut but this year another competitor beat him at his own game.*
—**fair game** *see* **fair**.
—**give the game away** to reveal a secret plan, trick, etc, usually accidentally: *We planned a surprise party for her birthday but her mother gave the game away.*
—**play the game** to behave fairly and honourably: *Play the game. You shouldn't accuse him in his absence.*
—**the game is not worth the candle** *see* **candle**.
—**the game is up** the plan, trick, crime, etc, has been discovered and so has failed: *The game is up. Our parents have found out about our plan to hold a party when they are away.*
—**the name of the game** *see* **name**.
garden
—**bear garden** *see* **bear**.
—**everything in the garden is lovely** everything is fine: *She was unhappy in that job but she says everything in the garden's lovely now that she's used to it.*
—**lead (someone) up the garden path** to mislead or deceive (someone): *She thought he was going to marry her but he was just leading her up the garden path.*
gasp
—**at one's last gasp** just about to collapse, be ruined, die, etc: *We were at our last gasp when we reached the top of the mountain.*
gauntlet
—**run the gauntlet** to be exposed or subjected to blame, criticism or risk: *Before he married her he had to run the gauntlet of her family's disapproving comments.* <"Gauntlet" is a mistaken form of Swedish *gatlopp*. "Running the gatlopp" was a military punishment in which the culprit had to run between two lines of men with whips who struck him as he passed>.
—**throw down the gauntlet** to issue a challenge: *The work force threw down the gauntlet to management by saying they would go on strike unless their pay was increased.* <Throwing down a gauntlet, a protective glove, was the traditional method of challenging someone to a fight in medieval times>.
get
—**be getting on for (something)** to be close to (a particular age, time, etc): *It's getting on for midnight. Despite his young appearance he's getting on for fifty.*
—**get a bit above oneself** *see* **above**.
—**get away from it all** *see* **away**.
—**get even with (someone)** *see* **even**.
—**get nowhere** to make no progress: *We've been looking for the lost dog for hours and we're getting nowhere.*
—**get** *or* **pull one's finger out** *see* **finger**.
—**play hard to get** *see* **play**.
—**tell (someone) where to get off** to tell (someone) that one will not tolerate him or her or his or her behaviour anymore: *He kept borrowing things from me until I finally told him where to get off.*

ghost

—**give up the ghost** to die, stop working, etc: *My old washing machine finally gave up the ghost.* <Ghost refers to a person's spirit—a biblical reference to Job 14:10>.

—**not to have the ghost of a chance** *see* **chance**.

gift

—**Greek gift** *see* **Greek**.

—**look a gift horse in the mouth** to criticize something that has been given to one: *Don't look for flaws in that table. It was a gift and you mustn't look a gift horse in the mouth.* <Looking at a horse's teeth is a way of telling its age and so estimating its value>.

—**the gift of the gab** *see* **gab**.

—**think one is God's gift (to someone)** *see* **God**.

gild

—**gild the lily** to add unnecessary decoration or detail: *She looks at her best without make-up but she gilds the lily by wearing a lot of cosmetics.* <An adaptation of a speech from Shakespeare's *King John*, Act 4, scene ii>.

gilt

—**take the gilt off the gingerbread** to take away what makes something attractive: *She loved the job when she travelled a lot but the gilt was taken off the gingerbread when her boss asked her to stay in the office all day.* <Gingerbread used to be sold in fancy shapes and decorated with gold leaf>.

gird

—**gird up one's loins** to prepare oneself for action: *I'll be late for work. I had better gird up my loins.* <A biblical phrase from the fact that robes had to be tied up with a girdle before men began work, Acts 12:8>.

give

—**give a dog a bad name** *see* **dog**.

—**give a good account of oneself** *see* **account**.

—**give and take** willingness to compromise: *There has to be some give and take in marriage. You can't get your own way all the time.*

—**give as good as one gets** *see* **good**.

—**give (something) away** to let (some information, etc) be revealed accidentally: *I meant to keep our destination a secret but my father gave it away.*

—**give (someone) his** *or* **her head** *see* **head**.

—**give (someone) the glad eye** *see* **glad**.

—**give the game away** *see* **game**.

—**give up the ghost** *see* **ghost**.

glad

—**glad rags** best clothes worn for special occasions: *They got into their glad rags and went out for dinner.*

—**give (someone) the glad eye** to look at (someone) in a way that shows that one is romantically or sexually interested in him or her: *He was giving the glad eye to all the girls at the party.*

glass

—**people who live in glass houses should not throw stones** people with faults themselves should not criticize faults in others: *He criticized his wife for arriving late, but he himself is hardly ever on time. Someone should tell him that people in glass houses shouldn't throw stones.*

glove

—**be hand in glove (with someone)** *see* **hand**.

—**fit like a glove** to fit perfectly: *That new dress fits her like a glove.*

—**handle (someone** *or* **something) with kid gloves** *see* **kid**.

—**take the gloves off** to begin to fight, argue, etc, in earnest: *So far our discussions about the disputed will have been gentlemanly but now the gloves are off.* <Refers to boxers who wear protective gloves to soften their blows>.

gnat

—**strain at a gnat (and swallow a camel)** to trouble oneself over a matter of no importance, something only slightly wrong, etc, (but be unconcerned about a matter of great importance, something very wrong, etc): *The headmaster was really straining at a gnat when he expelled four boys for smoking.* <A biblical reference to Matthew 23:23-24>.

go

—**from the word go** right from the very start: *Their marriage went wrong right from the word go.*

—**give (someone** *or* **something) the go-by** to ignore or disregard (someone or something): *He asked her out but she gave him the go-by.*

—**go against the grain** *see* **grain**.

—**go bust** *see* **bust**.

—**go downhill** *see* **downhill**.

—**go far** *see* **far**.

—**go for (someone** *or* **something)** (1) to attack (someone or something) either physically or verbally: *The press really went for the government about the unemployment figures.* (2) be attracted by: *He always goes for older women.*

—**go great guns** *see* **gun**.

—**go halves with (someone)** *see* **half**.

—**go places** *see* **place**.

—**go steady** *see* **steady**.

—**go the whole hog** *see* **hog**.
—**go to (someone's) head** *see* **head**.
—**go to town** *see* **town**.
—**go to the wall** *see* **wall**.
—**go with a bang** *see* **bang**.
—**go with a swing** *see* **swing**.
—**have a go** (1) to make an attempt: *I'm no cook, but I'll have a go at baking a cake.* (2) to try to stop a criminal escaping from the scene of a crime: *The old man got badly injured when he had a go at the armed bank-robber.*
—**it's touch and go** *see* **go**.
—**make a go of it** *or* **something** to make a success of something: *I hope he makes a go of it in his new job. Perhaps they will make a go of their new project.*
—**no go** impossible, not given approval: *We asked if we could leave early but it was no go.*
—**on the go** continually active, busy: *She's quite elderly but she's always on the go.*

goat
—**act the goat** to behave in an intentionally silly way: *He was acting the goat to amuse the children.*
—**get (someone's) goat** to irritate (someone): *Her high-pitched laugh really gets my goat.*
—**separate the sheep from the goats** *see* **sheep**.

God, god
—**act of God** *see* **act**.
—**a little tin god** a person who thinks that he or she is more important than he or she is and tries to order others around: *The workers are tired of the little tin god that is the deputy manager.*
—**in the lap of the gods** uncertain, left to chance or fate: *It's in the lap of the gods whether we get there on time or not.*
—**put the fear of God into (someone)** *see* **fear**.
—**there but for the grace of God go I** if I had not been fortunate that could easily have happened to me: *My colleague is now unemployed, and there but for the grace of God go I. There were many redundancies in the firm.*
—**think one is God's gift to (someone)** to have a very conceited opinion of oneself: *He thinks he's God's gift to women.*

gold
—**a golden age** *see* **age**.
—**a gold mine** a source of wealth or profit: *The health food shop turned out to be a real gold mine.*
—**be like gold dust** be very scarce: *Food is like gold dust in some areas of the world.*
—**golden boy** a young man who is popular or successful: *He was the golden boy in our year at school winning all the academic and all the sports prizes.*
—**golden handshake** a large amount of money given to someone who is leaving a job, usually because he or she has been declared redundant: *He has started his own business with his golden handshake.*
—**good as gold** very well-behaved: *The children were good as gold when their grandmother was looking after them.*
—**kill the goose that lays the golden egg** *see* **goose**.
—**the crock** *or* **pot of gold at the end of the rainbow** wealth or good fortune that one will never achieve: *He's always looking for a well-paid job, but with his lack of qualifications it's as much use as looking for the crock of gold at the end of the rainbow.*
—**silence is golden** *see* **silence**.
—**the golden rule** a principle or practice that it is vital to remember: *The golden rule when making a sponge cake is never to open the oven door while it is cooking.* <Originally the golden rule was that one should do to others as one would wish them to do to oneself>.
—**worth its** *or* **one's weight in gold** extremely valuable or useful: *Their baby-sitter is worth her weight in gold.*

gone
—**gone on (someone)** very much attracted to (someone): *He's gone on my sister.*

good
—**a good job** a satisfactory or fortunate state of affairs: *It was a good job that I took an umbrella. It was pouring.*
—**all to the good** to one's benefit or advantage: *He arrived late but that was all to the good as we were not quite ready.*
—**be as good as one's word** to do what one has promised do: *He said he would lend her the money and he was as good as his word.*
—**be on to a good thing** *or* **have a good thing going** to be in a desirable or profitable situation: *He lives there rent free. He's certainly on to a good thing.*
—**be up to no good** to be planning something wrong or illegal: *His wife knew before the robbery that he was up to no good.*
—**for good (and all)** for ever, permanently: *They're leaving town for good and all.*
—**for good measure** *see* **measure**.
—**give as good as one gets** to be as successful as

one's opponent in an argument, contest, fight, etc: *He was shouting at his wife but she gave as good as she got by yelling back.*

—**good as gold** *see* **gold**.

—**good for nothing** worthless: *She's a hard worker but she married a man who's good for nothing.*

—**have a good mind to (do something)** *see* **mind**.

—**in (someone's) good books** in favour with (someone): *She's in her mother's good books for cleaning the house.*

—**in good hands** *see* **hand**.

—**in good time** *see* **time**.

—**in (someone's) own good time** *see* **time**.

—**make good** to be successful in one's career or business: *He was penniless when he arrived, but he soon made good.*

—**make good time** *see* **time**.

—**put in a good word for (someone)** *see* **word**.

—**take (something) in good part** to accept (something) without being offended or angry: *We thought she would be furious at the practical joke but she took it in good part.*

—**to good purpose** with useful or successful results: *She used her qualifications to good purpose.*

—**to the good** richer: *After the fete the charity was £500 to the good.*

—**with a bad** *or* **good grace** *see* **grace**.

goods

—**deliver the goods** to do what one is required or expected to do: *Don't promise to help if you can't deliver the goods.*

—**goods and chattels** movable property: *He was asked to leave taking all his goods and chattels.* <An old legal term>.

goose

—**a wild-goose chase** *see* **wild**.

—**cook (someone's) goose** to ruin (someone's) chances of success: *She had a good job but she cooked her goose by arriving late every morning and so she was sacked.*

—**kill the goose that lays the golden egg** to destroy something that is a source of profit or advantage to oneself: *Her mother used to babysit for them regularly but she stopped after they left the children with her for three weeks. They certainly killed the goose that laid the golden egg.* <Refers to one of Aesop's fables in which the owner of a goose that laid golden eggs killed it and opened it up, thinking to get all the golden eggs at once, only to discover that there were none>.

—**what's sauce for the goose is sauce for the gander** what applies to one person should apply to another, usually to a member of the opposite sex: *If women have to work and look after the house so should men. After all, what's sauce for the goose is sauce for the gander.*

—**would not say boo to a goose** *see* **boo**.

gooseberry

—**play gooseberry** to be the third person present with a couple who wish to be alone: *When they go to the cinema her young sister always plays gooseberry.*

Gordian

—**cut the Gordian knot** to solve a problem or end a great difficulty by a vigorous or drastic method: *He was going to give the lazy worker a warning, but he decided to cut the Gordian knot and sack her right away.* <Refers to a legend in which whoever could untie a knot in a rope belonging to King Gordius, king of Phrygia, would be made ruler of all Asia. Alexander the Great severed the knot by cutting through it with a sword>.

gospel

—**take (something) as gospel** to accept (something) as absolutely true: *She takes everything her husband says as gospel, although everyone else knows that he is a liar.* <The gospel refers to the books of the Bible dealing with the life and teachings of Christ>.

grab

—**how does that grap you?** what do you think of that?: *I thought we might go out for a meal. How does that grab you?*

—**up for grabs** ready to be taken, bought, etc: *There's a job up for grabs at the factory.*

grace

—**fall from grace** *see* **fall**.

—**(someone's** *or* **something's) saving grace** a good quality that prevents someone or something from being completely bad, worthless, etc: *She is rather a horrible person. Her saving grace is that she is a good mother.*

—**there but for the grace of God go I** *see* **God**.

—**with a bad** *or* **good grace** in an unpleasant or pleasant and unwilling or willing way: *He acknowledged his opponent the winner with a good grace.*

grain

—**go against the grain** to be against someone's inclinations, feelings or wishes: *It goes against the grain for her to be pleasant to him. She loathes him.* <Refers to the direction of the grain in

wood, it being easier to cut or smooth wood with the grain rather than across or against it>.

—**take (something) with a grain** *or* **pinch of salt** *see* **salt**.

grape

—**sour grapes** saying that something that one cannot have is not worth having: *He said that it was a very boring job but that was just sour grapes because he wasn't offered it.* <Refers to one of Aesop's fables in which a fox that failed to reach a bunch of grapes growing above his head said that they were sour anyhow>.

—**the grapevine** an informal and unofficial way of passing news and information from person to person, gossip: *I heard on the grapevine that they had got married.*

grasp

—**grasp the nettle** *see* **nettle**.

grass

—**a snake in the grass** *see* **snake**.

—**grass widow** a woman whose husband is away from home for a short time for reasons of business or sport: *She's a grass widow while her husband is abroad on business.* <Originally the term referred to an unmarried woman who had sexual relations with a man or men, the origin being that such relations usually took place out of doors>.

—**let the grass grow under one's feet** to delay or waste time: *If you want that contract you had better apply for it now. Don't let the grass grow under your feet.*

—**put** *or* **turn (someone) out to grass** to cause (someone) to retire: *The company have decided to put the caretaker out to grass although he's not retirement age yet.* <Refers to turning out a horse into a field after its working life>.

—**the grass is always greener on the other side of the fence** another set of circumstances or lifestyle always seems preferable to one's own: *She has just started a new job but she's already envying her sister's. The grass is always greener on the other side of the fence.* <Refers to the habit of grazing animals of grazing through the fence separating them from the next field>.

—**the grass roots** the ordinary people in an organization, etc: *The politician ignored the grass roots opinion in his constituency.*

grasshopper

—**knee-high to a grasshopper** extremely small: *Our family have known her since she was knee-high to a grasshopper.*

grave

—**dig one's own grave** *see* **dig**.

—**have one foot in the grave** *see* **foot**.

—**(someone) would turn in his** *or* **her grave** (someone) would be very annoyed or upset: *Her father would turn in his grave if he could see her in prison.*

gravy

—**the gravy train** an easy method of getting a great deal of money or other advantages: *His present job allows him such a generous expenses budget that he is on a real gravy train.* <Gravy is a slang term for a gain or profit made easily>.

great

—**go great guns** *see* **gun**.

—**great minds think alike** *see* **mind**.

Greek

—**be all Greek to me, etc,** I, etc, don't understand any of it: *They demonstrated the machine, but it was all Greek to me.* <Refers to the fact that ancient Greek was considered a difficult language to learn>.

—**Greek gift** a gift that is dangerous or disadvantageous to the person given it: *The loan of his cottage turned out to be a Greek gift. The roof fell in and injured us.* <Refers to the gift of a wooden horse to the Trojans from the Greeks which contained Greek soldiers who attacked the Trojans and led to the fall of Troy>.

—**the Greek calends** never: *They will get married on the Greek calends.* <It was the Roman calendar, not the Greek, that had calends, the first day of the month>.

green

—**give the green light to (something)** give one's permission for (something): *The new road has been given the green light by the council.*

—**green about the gills** looking as though one were going to be sick: *They were decidedly green about the gills during the sea crossing.*

—**have green fingers** to be good at growing plants: *He grows a whole range of vegetables. He really has green fingers.*

—**not as green one is cabbage-looking** *see* **cabbage**.

—**the green-eyed monster** jealousy: *She is suffering from the green-eyed monster over her sister's new car.*

grey

—**a grey area** a part of a subject, etc, where it is difficult to distinguish between one category and another, an area of confusion: *The question of school security is a grey area. The teachers are responsible for some aspects and the caretaker for others.*

—**grey matter** brain, powers of reasoning: *You'll just have to use your grey matter to work out how to get there.*

grief

—**come to grief** to suffer misfortune or failure: *Our plans have come to grief. The council have turned them down.*

grim

—**hang on** *or* **hold on like grim death** to take a firm, determined hold of something in difficult or dangerous circumstances: *The boy held on like grim death to the high branch of the tree until help arrived.*

grin

—**grin like a Cheshire cat** *see* **Cheshire**.

—**grin and bear it** to tolerate something without complaining: *It's a boring job but you'll just have to grin and bear it. Jobs are so scarce.*

grind

—**grind to a halt** slowly begin to stop or cease working: *Without more money the work of the charity will grind to a halt.*

—**back to the grindstone** *see* **back**.

—**keep (one's** *or* **someone's) nose to the grindstone** *see* **nose**.

—**have an axe to grind** *see* **axe**.

grip

—**get a grip (of** *or* **on something** *or* **oneself)** to take firm control (of something or oneself): *He must get a grip on his drinking or he will lose his job.*

—**get** *or* **come to grips with (something)** to begin to deal with (something): *You cannot ignore the naughtiness of the children. You must come to grips with the problem.*

—**in the grip of (someone** *or* **something)** in the control or power of (someone or something): *The country is in the grip of a cruel tyrant.*

grist

—**it's all grist to the** *or* **someone's mill** all this experience, information will prove useful in some way: *His job as a paper boy pays very little but all is grist to the mill. He's saving to go on holiday.* <Grist means corn for grinding>.

grit

—**grit one's teeth** to make every effort not to show one's feelings of pain, disappointment, etc: *He gritted his teeth as the nurse cleaned his wound.*

ground

—**break new** *or* **fresh ground** to deal with a subject, etc, for the first time: *She's breaking new ground by writing fiction. She usually writes biographies.*

—**cut the ground from under (someone's) feet** to cause (someone's) actions, arguments, etc, to be ineffective, often by acting before he or she does: *When the boss sacked him he cut the ground from under his feet by telling him he had already posted his letter of resignation.*

—**gain ground** *see* **gain**.

—**get in on the ground floor** to be in at the very start of a project, business, etc: *You might get in on the ground floor of the company. They're looking for investors.*

—**get (something) off the ground** to get (a project) started: *I don't think his research scheme will ever get off the ground.* <Refers literally to a plane>.

—**have both feet on the ground** *or* **have one's feet on the ground** *see* **feet**.

—**have** *or* **keep one's ear to the ground** *see* **ear**.

—**ground rules** basic rules which must be obeyed or applied: *If we're going to share a house we must have a few ground rules.*

—**lose ground** *see* **lose**.

—**on one's own ground** dealing with a subject, situation, etc, with which one is familiar: *He's usually shy but he's on his own ground when it comes to discussing golf.*

—**run (someone** *or* **something) to ground** *same as* **run (someone** *or* **something) to earth** *see* **earth**.

—**shift one's ground** to change one's opinions, attitude, etc: *He was wildly opposed to the scheme but he's shifted his ground.*

—**stand one's ground** to remain firm, not to yield: *Everyone tried to get him to change his mind but he stood his ground.*

—**suit (someone) down to the ground** to suit someone perfectly: *The cottage suits them down to the ground. It's in the country but near town.*

—**thin** *or* **thick on the ground** scarce or plentiful: *Tourists are thick on the ground in summer but thin on the ground in winter.*

Grundy

—**Mrs Grundy** a narrow-minded person who is censorious of other people's behaviour: *The old woman's a Mrs Grundy who objected to the young couple kissing in the park.* <Refers to a character in *Speed the Plough* by Thomas Morton>.

guard

—**on** *or* **off one's guard** prepared or unprepared for any situation, especially a dangerous or difficult one: *The examiner caught him off guard by asking him about a subject which he hadn't revised.* <Refers to fencing>.

—**the old guard** *see* **old**.

guess

—**anybody's guess** *see* **anybody**.

—**your guess is as good as mine** I have no idea: *Your guess is as good as mine as to how we'll get home.*

guinea

—**guinea pig** a person who is the subject of an experiment: *The patient felt that the doctor had used him as a guinea pig with the new treatment.* <Refers to the use of guinea pigs in medical experiments>.

gullet

—**stick in one's gullet** *same as* **stick in one's throat**—*see* **throat**.

gum

—**gum up the works** to cause a machine, system, etc, to break down: *When the computer broke down it gummed up the entire works.*

—**up a gum tree** in a very difficult or hopeless situation: *He's up a gum tree if he can't get his car to start.* <Refers to an opossum climbing such a tree when being hunted>.

gun

—**be gunning for (someone)** to plan to harm (someone): *Her head of department is gunning for her, and she's scared of losing her job.*

—**big guns** *see* **big**.

—**go great guns** to be going or performing very well: *The firm's going great guns with a full order book.*

—**jump the gun** to start before the proper time: *You jumped the gun by applying for the job. It's not been advertised yet.* <Refers to athletes starting a race before the starting gun goes>.

—**spike (someone's) guns** to cause (someone's) plans or actions to be ineffective: *He was planning to come to our party uninvited but we spiked his guns by changing the date.* <Refers historically to driving a metal spike into the touch-hole of a captured enemy gun in order to render it useless>.

—**stick to one's guns** to remain firm in one's opinions, etc: *They tried to get him to say he was mistaken about the time of the offence was committed but he stuck to his guns.* <Refers to a soldier who keeps shooting at the enemy and does not run away>.

gut

—**bust a gut** to make a tremendous effort to do something: *We'll have to bust a gut to finish this project in time.*

H

hackles

—**make (someone's) hackles rise** to make (someone) angry: *The shop assistant's rudeness made my mother's hackles rise.* <Hackles are the feathers on the necks of male birds which rise when the bird is angry>.

hair

—**a hair of the dog (that bit one)** an alcoholic drink taken as a supposed cure for having consumed too much alcohol the night before: *He took a hair of the dog the morning after the party.* <From an old belief that if you were bitten by a mad dog and got rabies you could be cured by having hairs of the dog laid on the wound>.

—**get in (someone's) hair** to irritate (someone): *She's not in a good mood—the children are getting in her hair.*

—**keep one's hair on** to remain calm and not get angry: *Keep your hair on. He didn't mean to bump your car.*

—**let one's hair down** to behave in an informal, relaxed manner: *She fairly let her hair down at the party and danced on the table.*

—**make (someone's) hair stand on end** to terrify or horrify (someone): *Some of the policeman's accounts of murders he had investigated made her hair stand on end.*

—**not to turn a hair** not to show any sign of fear, distress, etc: *He didn't turn a hair when the bully threatened him.*

—**split hairs** to argue about small unimportant details, to quibble: *He's a crook. There's no point in splitting hairs over whether he's a burglar or a robber.*

—**tear one's hair (out)** to show frustration or irritation: *The shop assistant was tearing her hair out over the indecision of her customer.*

half

—**(someone's) better half** (someone's) wife or husband: *Where's your better half this evening?*

—**can see with half an eye** *see* **eye**.

—**do things by half**: to do things in an incomplete, careless way: *He will have attended to every detail. He never does things by halves.*

—**go halves with (someone)** to share costs with (someone): *The rent won't be all that expensive if we go halves.*

—**go off at half cock** *see* **cock**.

—**half a loaf is better than no bread** a little of something desirable is better than nothing: *We would have liked a bigger garden but half a loaf is better than no bread.*

—**meet (someone) halfway** to reach a compromise agreement with (someone): *Neither of us got all our demands. We met each other halfway.*

—**not half** very much so: *"Is he a good player?" "Not half, he's brilliant".*

—**the half of it** only part of the problem, situation, etc: *I had heard he was violent towards her but I didn't know the half of it.*

hammer

—**come under the hammer** to be for sale at an auction: *The paintings came under the hammer as one lot.* <Refers to the hammer that an auctioneer bangs on the table to indicate that a sale has been made>.

—**go at it hammer and tongs** to fight or quarrel loudly and fiercely: *The two neighbours were going at it hammer and tongs over repairs to the garden fence.* <Refers to a blacksmith holding a piece of heated iron in his tongs and striking it loudly with his hammer>.

hand

—**a dab hand at (something)** *see* **dab**.

—**an old hand** *see* **old**.

—**at first hand** *see* **first**.

—**at** *or* **on hand** available, ready for use, ready to help: *The invalid needs to keep his painkillers at hand. The nurse is on hand if you need her.*

—**be hand in glove with (someone)** to be closely associated with (someone) for a bad or illegal purpose: *One of the assistants in the jewellery shop was hand in glove with the jewel thieves.*

—**bite the hand that feeds one** *see* **bite**.

—**cap in hand** *see* **cap**.

—**change hands** *see* **change**.

—**close at hand** very near: *Her mother lives close at hand.*

—**force (someone's) hand** to force (someone) to do something that he or she may not want to do or be ready to do: *He didn't want to move to a new house yet but his wife forced his hand.*

—**give (someone) a free hand** *see* **free**.

—**give** *or* **lend (someone) a (helping) hand** to help (someone): *She gave her mother a hand with the housework.*

—**go hand in hand** to be closely connected: *Poverty and crime often go hand in hand.*

—**hand (something) down** to pass (something) from one generation to another: *Some of the village traditions have been handed down from Tudor times.*

—**hand over fist** in large amounts, very rapidly: *The owners of the new restaurant are making money hand over fist.* <Originally a nautical term meaning rapid progress such as can be made by hauling on a rope putting one hand after the other>.

—**have a hand in (something)** to be involved in (something), to have contributed to the cause of (something): *The police are sure that he had a hand in the robbery.*

—**have (someone) eating out of one's hand** *see* **eat**.

—**have (something) handed to one on a plate** *see* **plate**.

—**have one's hands full** to be very busy: *She has her hands full.*

—**have** *or* **get the upper hand (of** *or* **over someone)** *see* **upper**.

—**have the whip hand over (someone)** *see* **whip**.

—**in good hands** well looked after: *The patient is in good hands. He's an excellent doctor.*

—**in hand** (1) remaining, not used, etc: *After we have paid all the bills we will have £30 in hand.* (2) being dealt with: *The matter of your complaint is in hand.*

—**keep one's hand in** to retain one's skill at something by doing it occasionally: *The ex-champion doesn't play tennis very often but he plays enough to keep his hand in.*

—**know (someone** *or* **something) backwards** *or* **like the back of one's hand** *see* **back**.

—**lend (someone) a hand** to help (someone): *Could you lend me a hand to change the wheel? I have a flat tyre.*

—**live from hand to mouth** to have enough money only to pay for one's present needs without having any to save: *They earn so little that all they can do is to live from hand to mouth.* <Whatever money comes into one's hand is used to put food in one's mouth>.

—**many hands make light work** a job is easier to do if there are several people doing it: *If we all help we'll soon get the house painted. Many hands make light work.*

—**my, etc, hands are tied** something prevents me from acting as I, etc, might wish to: *I would like to refund your money but my hands are tied. There is a shop rule against this.*

—**not to do a hand's turn** to do nothing: *I've been cleaning the house all morning but she's not done a hand's turn.*

—**off hand** (1) without further consideration or research: *I can't say off hand what the population of the town is.* (2) abrupt, curt: *The customers complained about her being so off hand.*

—**out of hand** (1) out of control: *The protest march was getting out of hand.* (2) without consideration of the matter: *She dismissed my suggestion out of hand.*

—**play into (someone's) hands** to do exactly what someone wants one to do because it is to his or her advantage: *You shouldn't have got angry. You played right into his hands because he had just told the boss that you are bad-tempered with the staff.* <Refers to playing one's hand at cards so as to benefit another player>.

—**put one's hand in one's pocket** to spend or give money: *All of you will have to put your hands in your pockets to pay for the damage.*

—**show one's hand** to reveal to others one's plans or intentions, previously kept secret: *She really showed her hand when she told his wife about their affair. She wanted to marry him.* <Refers to showing one's hand to other players in a card game>.

—**take (someone) in hand** to train or discipline (someone): *It's time (someone) took that boy in hand. He's out of control.*

—**take one's life in one's hands** *see* **life**.

—**take the law into one's hands** *see* **law**.

—**throw in one's hand** to give up, to abandon a course of action, etc: *He tried to persuade her to marry him but finally threw in his hand.* <Refers to a card player throwing his cards on the table to indicate that he is out of the game>.

—**turn one's hand to (something)** to do, to be able to do: *He is a philosopher but he can turn his hand to carpentry and plumbing.*

—**wait on (someone) hand and foot** to look after (someone) to such an extent that he or she does not have to do anything for himself or herself: *The mother waits on her sons hand and foot.*

—**wash one's hands of (someone** *or* **something)** to refuse to be involved any longer in (something) or to be responsible for (someone or something): *His father said he would wash his hands of him if he got into trouble with the police again.* <A biblical reference to the action of Pontius Plate after the crucifixion of Jesus in Matthew 27:24>.

—**with one hand tied behind one's back** very easily: *He could have won the fight with one hand tied behind his back.*

handle

—**fly off the handle** to lose one's temper: *She flies off the handle whenever anyone disagrees with her.* <Refers to an axehead which flies off the handle when it is being used>.

hang

—**a hanging matter** a very serious subject or deed: *I was surprised that he was dismissed. I wouldn't have thought what he did was a hanging matter.* <Literally, a crime punishable by death or by hanging>.

—**get the hang of (something)** to learn how to do (something) or begin to understand (something): *I think she's finally got the hang of changing gears.*

—**hang by a thread** *see* **thread**.

—**hang fire** *see* **fire**.

—**hang one's head** to look ashamed or embarrassed: *The little girl hung her head when her mother scolded her.*

—**hang on** *or* **hold on like grim death** *see* **grim**.

—**hang on (someone's) words** *see* **word**.

—**hang the flags out** *see* **flag**.

—**hang up one's hat** *see* **hat**.

—**hung up on (someone** *or* **something)** obsessed with (someone or something): *He's completely hung up on horror movies.*

—**(someone) might as well be hanged for a sheep as a lamb** *see* **sheep**.

—**thereby hangs a tale** *see* **tale**.

happy

—**go to the happy hunting ground** to die: *I didn't realize the old man had gone to the happy hunting ground.* <Originally an American Indian phrase>.

—**happy as a lark** *or* **sand-boy** extremely happy: *The child was happy as a sand-boy playing with her new doll.*

—**happy event** the birth of a baby: *When is the happy event?*

—**happy hunting ground** a place where someone finds what he or she desires or where he or she is successful: *That shop is a happy hunting ground for her. She buys most of her clothes there.*

—**the** *or* **a happy medium** a sensible middle course between two extremes: *She's spends her time either over-eating or fasting. She should find a happy medium.*

hard

—**a hard nut to crack** *see* **nut**.

—**be hard put to it (to do something)** to have great difficulty (in doing something): *You would be hard put to it to find a better teacher.*

—**give (someone) a hard time** to act in an unpleasant, unsympathetic or tough way towards (someone): *They wanted him to leave and gave him a hard time until he did.*

—**hard-and-fast** not to be changed or ignored: *There is a hard-and-fast office rule that no one takes time off without prior permission.* <Refers to a ship that is stuck fast from having run aground>.

—**hard as nails** lacking in pity, sympathy, softer feelings, etc: *She wasn't moved by that child's tears but then she's hard as nails.*

—**hard-bitten** tough, toughened by experience of life: *She was very gentle when she was young but years in business have made her hard-bitten.*

—**hard-boiled** not influenced by emotion: *Even the hard-boiled politician shed a tear at the sight of the starving children.* <Refers to hard-boiled eggs>.

—**hard cash** coins and bank-notes as opposed to cheques, etc: *The workman wanted to be paid in hard cash and refused a cheque.*

—**hard done by** unfairly treated: *She felt hard done by because her father gave her less money than he gave her brother.*

—**hard facts** facts that cannot be disputed: *The hard facts are that we are losing money.*

—**hard-headed** practical and not influenced by emotion: *She's too hard-headed a business woman to give you a job because she's sorry for you.*

—**hard lines** bad luck: *It was hard lines that the champion didn't win.* <Perhaps a reference to a ship's ropes being made hard by ice>.

—**hard-luck story** a story of misfortune told to gain sympathy: *He got money from all of us by telling us all the same hard-luck story.*

—**hard of hearing** rather deaf: *The old lady's hard of hearing but she won't wear a hearing-aid.*

—**hard-pressed** in difficulties, in trouble: *They will be hard-pressed this month to pay the rent.*

—**hard up** not having much money: *They're too hard up to go on holiday.*
—**take a hard line** to take strong, stern or unyielding action or have strong opinions about something: *The headmaster took a hard line with pupils who played truant.*
—**the hard stuff** strong alcoholic drink, spirits: *He drinks wine but not the hard stuff.*

hare
—**mad as a March hare** *see* **mad**.
—**run with the hare and hunt with the hounds** to try to give one's support to two opposing sides at once: *You're going to have to vote for one of the candidates. You can't go on running with the hare and hunting with the hounds.*
—**start a hare** to raise a subject in the course of a discussion, often to divert attention from what was the main subject of it: *During the discussion about increasing salaries the manager started a hare about people smoking in the office.* <Refers to causing a hare to leave its hiding place to distract the hounds taking part in a fox hunt>.

hark
—**hark back to (something)** to refer to (something that has been said or has happened early): *She kept harking back to how things used to be done.* <Refers to a hunting term which is a command to the hounds and their handlers to double back and try to pick up a lost scent>.

harp
—**harp on (something)** to keep on talking about (something): *She kept harping on about how badly paid she was.* <Refers to playing the harp with one string only>.

hash
—**make a hash of (something)** to ruin or spoil (something), to do (something) badly: *He made a real hash of putting up those shelves.* <Refers to a dish made from chopped up pieces of meat mixed together, which looks rather messy>.
—**settle (someone's) hash** to deal with (someone) in such a way that he or she causes no more trouble or is prevented from doing what was intended: *He refused to give up the key to her flat but sh settled his hash by changing the locks.*

haste
—**more haste less speed** if one attempts to do something in too much of a hurry one makes careless mistakes and ends up taking longer to do it: *If you try to hurry the typist she makes mistakes. You know what they say about more haste less speed.*

hat
—**at the drop of a hat** *see* **drop**.
—**hang up one's hat** to move into a house, job, etc, with the intention of staying a long time: *She thought her father-in-law was just staying for the weekend but he's really hung up his hat.* <Refers to hanging up one's hat in someone's hat stand>.
—**hats off to (someone)** (someone) should be praised and congratulated: *Hats off to the new girl for slapping the office womanizer on the face.*
—**hat trick** any action done three times in a row: *We sold three houses this morning—a hat trick.* <Refers originally to a cricketer receiving a hat from his club for putting out three batsmen with three balls in a row>.
—**I'll eat my hat** an expression used to express total disbelief in a fact, statement, etc: *I'll eat my hat if he isn't guilty.*
—**keep (something) under one's hat** to keep (something) secret: *He was told to keep his salary increase under his hat.*
—**knock (someone** *or* **something) into a cocked hat** to defeat or surpass (someone or something) completely: *Her dress knocked all the others into a cocked hat.* <A cocked hat was a three-cornered hat in the 18th-century made by folding the edges of a round hat into corners>.
—**old hat** *see* **old**.
—**pass the hat round** to ask for contributions of money: *We passed the hat round the office for her leaving present.*
—**take one's hat off to (someone)** to express or show one's admiration for someone): *You must take your hat off to her for supporting the family all these years.*
—**talk through one's hat** to talk about something without any knowledge about it, to talk nonsense: *Pay no attention to his advice on investments. He knows nothing whatsoever about finance and is talking through his hat.*
—**throw one's hat in the ring** to declare oneself a contender or candidate for something: *He's decided to throw his hat in the ring and apply for the post of managing director.* <Refers to a method of making a challenge in prize boxing matches at fairgrounds, etc>.
—**wear a different** *or* **another hat** to speak as the holder of a different position: *She was*

speaking as a teacher but now she's wearing a different hat and speaking as a parent.

hatch

—**batten down the hatches** to prepare for trouble: *In the recession a lot of firms had to batten down the hatches and think of ways of saving money.* <Refers to preparations for a storm on a ship at sea>.

—**hatches, matches and despatches** the announcement of births, marriages and deaths in a newspaper.

hatchet

—**bury the hatchet** to agree to be friends again after a quarrel: *The two families have been hostile to each other for years but they've finally decided to bury the hatchet.* <Refers to an American Indian custom of burying tomahawks when peace was made>.

hatter

—**mad as a hatter** *see* **mad**.

haul

—**haul (someone) over the coals** *see* **coal**.

have

—**have had it** to have no hope of survival, success, etc: *The little corner shop will have had it when the supermarket opens.*

—**have it coming to one** *see* **come**.

—**have it in for (someone)** to try to cause trouble for (someone): *The manager has had it in for her since she refused to go out with him.*

—**have it in one** to have the ability, courage, etc, to do something: *I didn't think he had it in him to argue with the boss.*

—**have it out with (someone)** to discuss areas of disagreement or discontent with someone in order to settle it: *Don't go around complaining about her treatment of you. Have it out with her.*

—**have (someone) on** to try to deceive (someone), often for a joke: *The police aren't looking for you. Your friends are having you on.*

—**let (someone) have it** suddenly to attack (someone) either physically or verbally: *She was tired of never arriving on time and finally let him have it.*

havoc

—**play havoc with (something)** to cause serious damage to (something): *His stressful job played havoc with his health.*

hawk

—**watch (someone) like a hawk** to watch (someone) very carefully: *They are watching her like a hawk because they suspect her of stealing money.*

hay

—**go haywire** to go completely wrong, to go out of control: *The organization of the office went haywire when she was away.* <Refers to wire that was used to bind hay. It very easily became twisted and therefore came to symbolize confusion>.

—**hit the hay** *or* **sack** to go to bed: *He was so tired that he hit the hay immediately after dinner.* <Beds were formerly filled with hay or made from the same material as sacks>.

—**like looking for a needle in a haystack** *see* **needle**.

—**make hay (while the sun shines)** to profit or take advantage of an opportunity while one has the chance: *He's been offered a lot of overtime and he needs the money. He might as well make hay while the sun shines.* <Haymaking is only possible in fine weather>.

head

—**above (someone's) head** *see* **above**.

—**bang one's head against a brick wall** *see* **bang**.

—**bite** *or* **eat** *or* **snap (someone's) head off** to speak very sharply and angrily to (someone): *What's wrong with her? She's been biting everyone's head off all morning.*

—**bring (something) to a head** to bring something to a state where something must be done about it: *There has been hostility between them for some time but his public criticism of her brought matters to a head.* <Refers to bringing a boil, etc, to a head>.

—**bury one's head in the sand** to deliberately ignore a situation so that one does not have to deal with it: *He says his job is safe but he is burying his head in the sand. The factory is closing down.* <Refers to the old belief that ostriches hide their heads in the sand when they are in danger because they think that then they cannot be seen>.

—**cannot make head nor tail of (something)** cannot understand (something) at all: *I can't make head nor tail of these instructions.*

—**get one's head down** (1) to start working hard: *The exams are next week. I had better get my head down.* (2) to have a sleep or a nap: *If I just get my head down for an hour I'll be all right.*

—**give (someone) his** *or* **her head** to allow (someone) to do as he or she wishes: *The owner gives the manager his head in the running of the firm.* <Refers literally to slackening one's hold on the reins of a horse>.

—**go to (someone's) head** (1) to make (someone) arrogant or conceited: *Winning the prize went to his head and he goes around boasting.* (2) to make (someone) slightly drunk: *One glass of wine seems to go to her head.*

—**hang one's head** *see* **hang**.

—**have a head for (something)** to have an ability or aptitude for (something): *He can't climb the ladder. He has no head for heights.*

—**have a (good) head on one's shoulders** to be clever or sensible: *The boy should go to college. He has a good head on his shoulders.*

—**have one's head screwed on the right way** to to be sensible: *He won't give up his job. He's got his head screwed on the right way.*

—**head over heels** completely: *They're head over heels in love.*

—**heads will roll** someone is going to get into serious trouble: *Heads will roll when mother sees the mess the house is in.* <Refers to the use of the guillotine to execute criminals>.

—**hit the headlines** to attract a great deal of media attention: *He hit the headlines last year when he married a film-star.*

—**hold a pistol to (someone's) head** *see* **pistol**.

—**hold one's head up (high)** not to feel ashamed or guilty, to remain dignified: *After her crime she'll never hold her head up in the village again.*

—**keep a level head** *or* **keep one's head** to remain calm and sensible, especially in a difficult situation: *When he discovered the fire he kept a level head and phoned for the fire brigade.*

—**keep one's head above water** to have enough money to keep out of debt: *With so many children they have great difficulty in keeping their heads above water.*

—**knock (something) on the head** to put an end to (something): *Our plans for a picnic were knocked on the head by the rain.*

—**laugh one's head off** to laugh very loudly: *They laughed their heads off when he slipped on a banana skin.*

—**like a bear with a sore head** *see* **bear**.

—**lose one's head** to cease to remain calm, to act foolishly: *She lost her head during her driving test and made a lot of mistakes.*

—**make headway** to make progress: *They don't seem to be making much headway with their research project.* <Refers originally to ships>.

—**need one's head examined** to be foolish or insane: *If you believe his story you need your head examined.*

—**not to know whether one is on one's head** *or* **one's feet** *or* **heels** to be totally confused: *I served so many customers that I didn't know whether I was on my head or my feet.*

—**off one's head** insane, not rational: *The old man was off his head to give his daughters his house.*

—**off the top of one's head** *see* **top**.

—**on (someone's) (own) head be it** (someone) must take responsibility or blame: *On your head be it if mother is annoyed. You made us late.*

—**over (someone's) head** (1) too difficult for (someone) to understand: *The explanation of the scientific experiment was right over my head.* (2) when (someone) seems to have a better right: *They promoted him over her head although she was better qualified.* (3) beyond (someone) to a person of higher rank: *He went over the departmental manager's head and reported the matter to the managing director.*

—**put** *or* **lay one's head on the block** to leave oneself open to blame, punishment, danger, etc: *He laid his head on the block by letting his assistants have the afternoon off.* <Refers to laying one's head on the block before being beheaded>.

—**put our, etc, heads together** to discuss something together, to share thoughts on something: *If we put our heads together we'll come up with a plan.*

—**rear its ugly head** to appear or happen: *They were happy at first but jealousy reared its ugly head.*

—**scratch one's head** to be puzzled: *The police are scratching their heads over the motive for the crime.*

—**soft** *or* **weak in the head** not very intelligent, mentally retarded: *He must be soft in the head to trust her again.*

—**talk one's head off** to talk a great deal: *We hadn't seen each other for a long time and so we talked our heads off.*

—**talk through the back of one's head** *see* **back**.

—**turn (someone's) head** to make (someone) conceited: *Her head was turned by his extravagant compliments.*

heart

—**after (someone's) own heart** *see* **after**.

—**a heart-to-heart** a private talk where one tells one's thoughts, troubles, etc, openly: *She had a heart-to-heart with her mother about her health fears.*

—**at heart** basically, really: *He seems unfriendly at*

first but at heart he's very kind and sympathetic.

—**break (someone's) heart** to make (someone) very sad: *He broke her heart when he left town without telling her.*

—**cross one's heart** said to emphasize the truth of what one is saying: *I'll be there on time. Cross my heart.*

—**do (someone's) heart good** to give (someone) pleasure: *It did my heart good to see the children playing.*

—**eat one's heart out** to be distressed because one cannot have someone or something which one is longing for: *She is eating her heart out for her ex-fiancé.*

—**faint heart never won fair lady** *see* **faint**.

—**from the bottom of one's heart** most sincerely, very much: *I apologize from the bottom of my heart for the mistake.*

—**have a change of heart** *see* **change**.

—**have (something) at heart** to be deeply interested or concerned about (something): *Your father may seem discouraging about the job but he has your interests at heart.*

—**have one's heart in one's mouth** to feel afraid or anxious: *She had her heart in her mouth as she watched the young man standing on the edge of the roof.*

—**heart and soul** completely, with all one's energy: *She pledged herself heart and soul to look after the children.*

—**(someone's) heart goes out to (someone)** (someone) feels sympathy or pity for (someone): *Our hearts went out to the orphaned children.*

—**(someone's) heart is in the right place** (someone) is basically kind, sympathetic, etc, although not appearing to be so: *Our neighbour seems very stern, but her heart's in the right place.*

—**(someone's) heart is not in it** (someone) is not enthusiastic about something: *He's given up teaching because his heart wasn't in it.*

—**(someone's) heart sinks** (someone) feels depressed, disappointed, etc: *Her heart sank as she saw the policeman standing on her doorstep.*

—**in good heart** cheerful and confident: *The soldiers were in good heart before the battle.*

—**in (someone's) heart of hearts** in the deepest part of one's mind or feelings: *In her heart of hearts she knew her mother was right.*

—**learn something by heart** to memorize (something) thoroughly: *The teacher told the pupils to learn the poem by heart.*

—**lose heart** to grow discouraged: *She was very enthusiastic about her plan but she lost heart when no one seemed interested.*

—**not to have the heart (to do something)** not to be unkind, unsympathetic, etc, enough (to do something): *I didn't have the heart to tell her that her husband was a rogue.*

—**put new heart into (someone)** to make (someone) feel encouraged and more hopeful: *Scoring a goal put new heart into the team.*

—**set one's heart on** *or* **have one's heart set on (something)** to desire (something) very much: *He's set his heart on buying a motor bike.*

—**take heart** to become encouraged: *The travellers took heart when they saw the town ahead.*

—**take (something) to heart** (1) to be upset by (something): *He was only teasing but she took his remarks to heart.* (2) to be influenced by and take notice of (something): *She took the doctor's advice to heart.*

—**warm the cockles of the heart** to make one feel happy and contented: *Watching her with the baby would warm the cockles of the heart.*

—**wear one's heart on one's sleeve** to let one's feelings be obvious: *She was badly hurt by him although she's not one to wear her heart on her sleeve.*

—**with a heavy heart** *see* **heavy**.

—**with all one's heart** most sincerely: *I hope with all my heart that you will be happy.*

heat

—**in the heat of the moment** while influenced by the excitement or emotion of the occasion: *They were having a quarrel and in the heat of the moment she threatened to kill him.*

—**take the heat out of (something)** to make (a situation) less emotional, tense, etc: *They were just about to fight each other when their friend took the heat out of the situation by suggesting they sit down and talk.*

heave

—**give (someone) the (old) heave-ho** to get rid of (someone), to dismiss (someone): *He's been given the old heave-ho from the firm for embezzlement.*

heaven

—**in seventh heaven** extremely happy: *She was in seventh heaven when her son was born.* <In Jewish literature the seventh heaven is the highest of all heavens and the one where God lives>.

—**manna from heaven** something advantageous which happens unexpectedly, especially in a time of trouble: *My parents' offer of a* *loan was manna from heaven. We were practically penniless.* <A biblical reference to Exodus 16:15>.

—**move heaven and earth** to make every effort possible: *The doctor moved heaven and earth to save the patient's life.*

—**pennies from heaven** a sudden and unexpected sum of money: *They were very poor, so the prize money from the competition was pennies from heaven.*

—**smell** *or* **stink to high heaven** to have a strong and nasty smell: *The drains stink to high heaven.*

heavy

—**heavy-going** difficult to make progress with or cope with: *I found the climb heavy going.* <Refers originally to the surface of a horse-race track>.

—**make heavy weather of (something)** to make more effort to do something than should be required: *The pupils made heavy weather of the exam paper although it was quite easy.* <Refers originally to a ship which does not handle well in difficult conditions>.

—**with a heavy heart** with great sadness or despondency: *It was with a heavy heart that she left her family home.*

hedge

—**hedge one's bets** *see* **bet**.

—**look as though one has been dragged through a hedge backwards** to look very untidy: *The little boy always looks as though he has been dragged through a hedge backwards when he comes home from school.*

heel

—**Achilles' heel** *see* **Achilles**.

—**bring (someone) to heel** to bring (someone) under one's control: *The new teacher soon brought the unruly class to heel.* <Refers to making a dog walk to heel>.

—**cool** *or* **kick one's heels** *see* **heel**.

—**dig one's heels in** *see* **dig**.

—**down-at-heel** *see* **down**.

—**head over heels** *see* **head**.

—**show a clean pair of heels** *see* **clean**.

—**take to one's heels** to run away: *She took to her heels when she saw the bull in the field.*

—**turn on one's heel** to turn and walk away in the opposite direction: *When he was rude she turned on her heel and left.*

helm

—**at the helm** in charge: *With a new person at the helm in the company there are bound to be changes.* <Refers to the helm of a ship>.

help

—**give** *or* **lend (someone) a (helping) hand** *see* **hand**.

hen

—**like a hen on a hot girdle** very nervous and restless: *She was like a hen on a hot girdle waiting for the telephone to ring.*

here

—**neither here nor there** of no importance: *It's neither here nor there whether he comes or not.*

—**the hereafter** life after death: *He does not believe in the hereafter.*

herring

—**a red herring** a piece of information which misleads (someone) or draws (someone's) attention away from the truth, often introduced deliberately: *She told the police that she had seen a man at the door of the burgled house but it proved to be a red herring.* <A red herring is a strong-smelling fish whose scent could mislead hunting dogs if it were dragged across the path they were pursuing>.

—**neither fish nor fowl nor good red herring** neither one thing nor the other: *He has lived in so many parts of the country that his accent is neither fish nor fowl, nor good red herring.*

—**packed like herring in a barrel**: very tightly packed: *The audience were packed like herring in a barrel at the pop concert.*

hide

—**hide one's light under a bushel** *see* **light**.

—**neither hide nor hair of (someone** *or* **something)** no trace at all of (someone or something): *The police searched for the missing prisoner but they could find nether hide nor hair of him.*

—**on a hiding to nothing** in a situation where one cannot possibly win: *She wants to be a vet but she's on a hiding to nothing because she hasn't the academic ability.* <Perhaps a reference to boxing>.

—**tan (someone's) hide** to beat or thrash (someone): *The boy's father threatened to tan his hide if he got into trouble at school again.* <Refers to leather-making>.

high

—**a high flier** a person who is bound to be very successful or who has achieved great success: *She was one of the high fliers in our year at university.*

—**be for the high jump** to be about to be punished or scolded: *You're for the high jump when your mother sees that torn jacket.*

—**be high time** to be time something was done without delay: *It is high time you cut the grass.*

—**be** *or* **get on one's high horse** to be or become offended in a haughty manner: *She gets on her high horse if you ask her to do some typing. She says she is a personal assistant.*

—**high and mighty** arrogant: *Since he became rich he's so high and mighty he won't speak to his former neighbours.*

—**high spot** an exceptionally good part of something: *One of the high spots of their holiday was their visit to Rome.*

—**hunt** *or* **search high and low for (someone** *or* **something)** to search absolutely everywhere for (someone or something): *I've hunted high and low for my address book but in vain.*

—**leave (someone) high and dry** to leave (someone) in a difficult or helpless state: *His secretary walked out and left him and dry in middle of the busiest time of year.*

—**riding high** very successful: The firm was riding high until the recession began. <Used literally of the moon being high in the sky>.

—**run high** of feelings, tempers, etc, to be extremely angry, agitated, etc: *Feelings ran high among the crowd when the police arrested the young boy.* <Refers to the sea when there is a strong current and high waves>.

hill

—**old as the hills** *see* **old**.

—**over the hill** past one's youth or one's best: *In that firm you're over the hill at 35.*

hilt

—**armed to the hilt** *see* **armed**.

—**back (someone) to the hilt** to support (someone) totally: *Her parents backed her to the hilt when she decided to have the baby.* <Refers to the hilt of a sword>.

hind

—**devil take the hindmost** *see* **devil**.

history

—**be history** to be past, to be no longer relevant or important: *I know he has a police record but that's history. It happened when he was a youth.*

—**make history** to do something remarkable that will be remembered in the future: *He made medical history by performing the first heart transplant.*

hit

—**a smash hit** *see* **smash**.

—**be a hit with (someone)** to be popular with (someone): *The magician was a real hit with the children at the party.*

—**hit a bad patch** *see* **bad**.

—**hit a man when he's down** to attack someone who is already suffering from some misfortune: *His wife left him just after he lost his job. She really knows how to hit a man when he's down.*

—**hit-and-run accident** an accident involving a vehicle where the driver who caused it does not stop or report the accident: *The little girl was killed in a hit-and-run accident.*

—**hit it off** to get on well, to become friendly: *I knew they would hit it off. They have so much in common.*

—**hit the ceiling** *or* **roof** *see* **ceiling**.

—**hit the hay** *or* **sack** *see* **hay**.

—**hit the headlines** *see* **head**.

—**hit the jackpot** *see* **jackpot**.

—**hit the mark** *see* **mark**.

—**hit the nail on the head** *see* **nail**.

—**hit the road** *see* **road**.

Hobson

—**Hobson's choice** *see* **choice**.

hog

—**go the whole hog** to do something completely and thoroughly: *We decorated one room and then decided to go the whole hog and do the whole house.* <Perhaps referring to buying a whole pig for meat rather than just parts of it>.

hoist

—**hoist with one's own petard** *see* **petard**.

hold

—**hang on** *or* **hold on like grim death** *see* **grim**.

—**have a hold over (someone)** to have power or influence over (someone): *I think the old man has some kind of hold over him. He always does what he says.*

—**hold (something) against (someone)** to dislike (someone) because of (something) he or she has done: *He always held it against her that she had her child adopted.*

—**hold a pistol to (someone's) head** *see* **pistol**.

—**hold forth** to talk for a long time forcefully or pompously: *The lecturer held forth on his views on the political situation.*

—**hold good** to be valid or applicable: *The rules that applied last year hold good this year.*

—**hold one's breath** *see* **breath**.

—**hold one's head up (high)** *see* **head**.

—**hold one's horses** *see* **horse**.

—**hold one's own** *see* **own**.

—**hold one's tongue** *see* **tongue**.

—**hold out on (someone)** not to tell (someone):

He's been holding out on us. He's engaged to be married.

—**hold the fort** *see* **fort**.

—**no holds barred** no restrictions on what is permitted: *It was a case of no holds barred in the election campaign. All the candidates criticized their opponents savagely.*

hole

—**hole-and-corner** secret and often dishonourable: *Their romance is a hole-and-corner affair because she is married.*

—**in a hole** in an awkward or difficult situation: *They're in a real hole. They've lost their return plane tickets.*

—**make a hole in (something)** to use a large part of (something): *Holding the party left a huge hole in our supply of wine.*

—**need (something) like (someone) needs a hole in the head** to regard (something) as being completely unwelcome or undesirable: *The firm needs a strike at the moment like they need a hole in the head.*

—**pick holes in (something)** to find faults in (a theory, plan, etc): *He had no suggestions of his own but he picked holes in mine.*

—**talk through a hole in one's head** *same as* **talk through the back of one's head** *see* **back**.

holy

—**holier-than-thou** acting as though one is more moral, more pious, etc, than other people: *She is so holier-than-thou that you wouldn't believe that she once spent a night in the police cells.* <A biblical reference to Isaiah 65.5>.

—**the holy of holies** a private or special place inside a building: *That's her father's study. It's the holy of holies in their house.* <A literal translation of the the Hebrew name of the inner sanctuary in the Jewish Temple where the Ark of the Covenant was kept>.

home

—**a home from home** a place where one feels comfortable and relaxed: *Our holiday accommodation was a home from home.*

—**bring** *or* **drive (something) home to (someone)** to cause someone fully to understand or believe (something): *Their mother's illness really brought home to them how much they relied on her.*

—**do one's homework** to prepare thoroughly for a meeting, etc, by getting all the necessary information: *You will have to do your homework if you are going to win that export order.*

—**feel at home** to feel comfortable and relaxed: *She's from Italy originally but she feels completely at home here now.*

—**home and dry** having successfully completed an objective: *I didn't think we'd get the contract but it's just been signed so we're home and dry.*

—**home truth** a plain, direct statement of something that is true but unpleasant or difficult for someone to accept: *I told her a few home truths about how his behaviour was affecting the family.*

—**make oneself at home** to make oneself comfortable and relaxed: *Make yourself at home while I prepare the meal.*

—**nothing to write home about** not very special, not remarkable: *The food in the hotel was all right but nothing to write home about.*

—**romp home** to win easily: *Our candidate romped home to win the election by a huge majority.* <Refers to horse-racing>.

—**till** *or* **until the cows come home** *see* **cow**.

honour

—**do the honours** *see* **do**.

hook

—**by hook or by crook** by any means possible: *She's says she'll get to the party by hook or by crook although she has no transport.*

—**off the hook** free from some difficulty, problem, etc, or something one does not want to do: *I didn't want to go to the party and my friend let me off the hook by asking me to baby-sit.* <A reference to angling>.

—**sling one's hook** to go away: *Why don't you sling your hook and leave us alone?*

—**swallow (something) hook, line and sinker** to believe (something) completely: *His story was obviously untrue but she swallowed it hook, line and sinker.* <Refers to a fish that swallows not only the hook but the whole of the end section of the fishing line>.

hoop

—put (someone) through the hoop to cause (someone) to experience something unpleasant or difficult: *The interviewers certainly put the candidates through the hoop by asking searching questions.* <Refers to circus performers who jump through hoops set on fire>.

hop

—**catch (someone) on the hop** to find (someone) unprepared: *My guests arrived early and caught me on the hop without the meal ready.*

—**hopping mad** extremely angry: *He was hopping mad when his new car broke down.*

—**keep (someone) on the hop** to keep (someone) busy or active: *Her grandchildren keep her on the hop.*

hope

—**great white hope** someone or something that is expected to bring victory, fame, glory, etc, to a group: *We have won nothing so far but the youngest member of the team is our great white hope in the 100 metres race.* <Refers originally to a white boxer attempting to defeat a black boxer, black boxers often being the champions>.

—**have high hopes of (something)** to be extremely hopeful of success in (something): *He has high hopes of getting into university.*

—**hope against hope** to continue to hope although there is little reason to be hopeful: *She is seriously ill but they are hoping against hope that she will recover completely.*

—**hope springs eternal (in the human breast)** it is of the nature of human beings to hope: *So far he doesn't have a job but hope springs eternal (in the human breast).* <Refers to a quotation from Alexander Pope's poem *An Essay on Criticism*>.

—**pin one's hopes on (someone** *or* **something)** to rely on (someone or something) helping one in some way: *They have no money and they're pinning their hopes on the horse they backed winning.*

horn

—**draw in one's horns** to restrain one's actions, particularly the spending of money: *Now that they have a child they will have to draw in their horns.* <Refers to a snail drawing in its horns if it is in danger>.

—**horn in on (something)** to join in on (something) uninvited and unwanted: *She's trying to horn in on the organization of the party.*

—**lock horns** to argue or fight: *It wasn't long before the new boss and the union leader locked horns*: <Refers to horned male animals who sometimes get their horns caught together when fighting>.

—**on the horns of a dilemma** *see* **dilemma**.

hornet

—**stir up a hornet's nest** to cause a great deal of trouble: *The headmaster stirred up a hornet's nest when he suggested changing the school uniform.*

horse

—**a horse of a different colour** *see* **colour**[1].

—**back the wrong horse** to show support for the person, side, plan, etc, that turns out to be the loser in some way: *You backed the wrong horse when you appointed him treasurer. He's hopeless with money.*

—**be** *or* **get on one's high horse** *see* **high**.

—**change horses in mid-stream** *see* **change**.

—**dark horse** *see* **dark**.

—**eat like a horse** to eat a great deal: *Like most teenage boys he eats like a horse.*

—**flog a dead horse** to continue to try to arouse interest, enthusiasm, etc, in something which is obviously not, or no longer, of interest: *He's trying to sell life insurance to his neighbours but he's flogging a dead horse. An agent from another firm has already been round the area.*

—**hold one's horses** not to move so fast: *Hold your horses! I haven't agreed to your plan yet.*

—**horse sense** common sense, practicability: *She has no specialist knowledge of the business but she has horse sense.*

—**horses for courses** certain people are better suited to certain tasks or situations: *He's good at planning things and she is good at putting plans into action. It's a case of horses for courses.* <Some horses run better on certain types of ground>.

—**lock the stable door after the horse has bolted** *see* **stable**.

—**look a gift horse in the mouth** *see* **gift**.

—**put the cart before the horse** *see* **cart**.

—**straight from the horse's mouth** from someone closely connected with a situation and therefore knowledgeable about it: *I got it straight from the horse's mouth. She told me herself she was leaving.* <As though a horse is giving a tip about a race in which it is running>.

—**wild horses would not drag (someone) to something** *or* **somewhere** nothing would persuade (someone) to attend something or go somewhere: *Wild horses wouldn't drag me to his party. I loathe him.*

—**willing horse** someone who is keen to work or help: *She is chairman of the organizing committee but it's the willing horses who do all the work.*

—**you can take a horse to the water but you cannot make it drink** you can encourage someone to do something but you cannot force him or her to do it: *You can get the university prospectuses for your son, but after that it's for him to decide. You can take a horse to water but you can't make it drink.*

hot

—**blow hot and cold** *see* **blow**.

—**hot air** *see* **air**.

—**hot line** a direct telephone line for use in emergencies: *The two leaders have spoken on the hot line.*

—**hot on (someone's) heels** close behind (someone): *She arrived and then hot on her heels he rushed in.*

—**hot potato** something which it is difficult or dangerous to deal with: *The complaint about faulty goods is a hot potato. Pass it to the manager.*

—**hot under the collar** angry or agitated: *He got very hot under the collar when she refused to believe him.*

—**in hot water** in trouble: *The boy will be in hot water when his father sees the damage he caused.*

—**in the hot seat** in a position where one has responsibility for important and difficult issues: *The acting manager director is in the hot seat now.*

—**like a cat on hot bricks** *see* **cat**.

—**make it** *or* **things hot for (someone)** to make a situation unpleasant or impossible for (someone): *You might as well leave. He'll just make things hot for you if you stay.*

—**piping hot** very hot: *I like soup to be piping hot.*

—**sell** *or* **go like hot cakes** *see* **cake**.

hour

—**after hours** during the period when a shop, etc, would be normally be shut for business: *The pub owner has been selling alcohol after hours.*

—**all hours** *see* **all**.

—**at the eleventh hour** *see* **eleven**.

—**put off the evil hour** *see* **evil**.

—**the (wee) small hours** the hours immediately following midnight (1 a.m, 2 a.m, etc): *They danced until the wee small hours.*

—**the witching hour** midnight: *It's time we went home. It's the witching hour.* <Witches traditionally are supposed to be active at midnight>.

house

—**bring the house down** to cause great amusement or applause: *The comedian's jokes brought the house down.*

—**eat (someone) out of house and home**: to eat a great deal and so be expensive to feed: *When all the grandchildren stayed with their grandparents they ate them out of house and home.*

—**get on like a house on fire** *see* **fire**.

—**keep open house** always to be ready and willing to welcome guests: *Why don't you pay them a visit. They keep open house.*

—**on the house** paid by the owner of shop, pub, etc: *The drinks are on the house to celebrate the birth of the baby.*

—**put one's house in order** to make sure that one's affairs are well arranged and organized: *His will is perfectly legal. He put his house in order before his death.*

—**safe as houses** completely safe: *The children will be safe as houses with their grandmother.*

hue

—**a hue and cry** a loud protest: *There was a hue and cry about the council's proposal to close the local school.* <An old legal term meaning a summons for people to join in a hunt for a criminal>.

humble

—**eat humble pie** to have to admit that one has been wrong: *He had to eat humble pie when his wife passed her driving test. He said she wasn't good enough.* <Refers originally to a dish made from the umble or offal of a deer eaten by the lower classes>.

hunt

—**hunt high and low for (someone** *or* **something)** *see* **high**.

—**run with the hare and hunt with the hounds** *see* **hare**.

I

i

—**dot the i's and cross the t's** *see* **dot**.

ice

—**break the ice** to ease the shyness or formality of a social occasion: *The baby's laughter broke the ice at the lunch party.*

—**cut no ice** to have no effect: *His charm cut no ice with her mother.*

—**icing on the cake** a desirable but unnecessary addition: *The garden's the icing on the cake. It's the size of the house that matters.*

—**on ice** put aside for future use or attention: *Our expansion plans will have to be put on ice.*

—**(skate) on thin ice** (to be) in a risky or dangerous position: *You're skating on thin ice by criticizing his sister.*

—**the tip of the iceberg** a small sign of a much larger problem: *Painting the new house will cost about £1000 and that's the tip of the iceberg—we need new carpets and curtains.* <Refers to the fact that the bulk of an iceberg is hidden underwater>.

ill

—**ill-gotten gains** possessions acquired dishonestly: *He got her jewels from her by blackmail and then sold his ill-gotten gains* .

—**it's an ill wind** (that blows nobody any good) in almost every misfortune there is something of benefit to someone: *There was an accident on the road and we might have been involved in it if the car hadn't broken down. It's an ill wind.*

—**take (something) ill out** to be offended or annoyed at (something): *She took it ill out that we hadn't invited her.*

image

—**be the spitting image of** *or* **the spit and image of (someone** *or* **something)** *see* **spit**.

imagination

—**a figment of one's imagination** something which has no reality: *His cottage in the country is a figment of his imagination.*

immemorial

—**from time immemorial** from a time beyond anyone's memory, written records, etc; for an extremely long time: *The family has lived in the village from time immemorial.* <In legal phraseology the expression means "before the beginning of legal memory">.

in

—**be in for (something)** to be likely to experience (something, often something unpleasant): *The sky looks as if we're in for a storm.*

—**be in on (something)** to be involved in (something), to know about (something): *Not many were in on the secret.*

—**be in with (someone)** to be friendly with or in favour with (someone): *She's in with the boss.*

—**have it in for (someone)** *see* **have**.

—**the ins and outs of (something)** the details of (something): *I don't know the ins and outs of their disagreement.*

inch

—**be** *or* **come within an inch of (something)** to be or come very close to: *He came within an inch of being killed by the falling chimney.*

—**every inch a** *or* **the (something)** exactly the type of (something): *The old man is every inch a gentleman.*

—**give (someone) an inch (and he** *or* **she will take a mile** *or* **an ell)** if someone yields in any way to (someone) he or she will make even greater demands: *If you give him an extra day to write his essay he will expect an extra week next time. Give him an inch and he'll take a mile.* <An ell is an old form of measurement>.

Indian

—**an Indian summer** a time of fine, warm weather in autumn: *I've put away all my light clothes but we are having an Indian summer.* <Perhaps from a feature of the climate of North America whose original inhabitants were Indians>.

innings

—**have a good innings** to enjoy a considerable period of life, success etc: *To die at 90 is to have had a good innings.* <Refers to the batting turn of a player or team in cricket>.

insult

—**add insult to injury** *see* **add**.

interest

—**a vested interest in (something)** a personal and biased interest in (something): *She has a* *vested interest in campaigning against the proposed new pub. It would be competition for hers.*

—**in an interesting condition** pregnant: *She's not drinking alcohol because she's in an interesting condition.*

—**with interest** to an even greater extent than something has been done, etc, to someone: *He returned his insults with interest.*

iron

—**have many** *or* **several irons in the fire** to be involved in several projects, etc, at the same time: *One of his firms has gone bankrupt but he has several irons in the fire.* < Refers to a blacksmith who heats pieces of iron before shaping them>.

—**rule (someone** *or* **something) with a rod of iron** to rule with the sternness or ruthlessness. *All the children are scared of the head teacher. She rules them with a rod of iron.*

—**strike while the iron is hot** to act at a point at which things are favourable to one: *Your father is in a good mood. Why don't you strike while the iron is hot and ask him for a loan now.* <Refers to a blacksmith's work>.

—**the iron hand in the velvet glove** sternness or ruthlessness hidden under an appearance of gentleness: *Her father looks very kindly but he frequently beats his children. It's a case of the iron hand in the velvet glove.*

—**the iron horse** railway engines or trains: *Travel was much more difficult before the invention of the iron horse.*

itch

—**be itching to (do something)** to want very much to (do something): *He was itching to slap the naughty little boy.*

—**have an itching palm** to be greedy for money: *The shopkeeper always overcharges—she's got an itching palm.*

ivory

—**live in an ivory tower** to have a way of life protected from difficulty or unpleasantness: *The writer lives in an ivory tower. He doesn't realize how badly off his family are.* <*La toure d'ivoire*, French for "ivory tower", was coined by the poet Charles Augustin Saint-Beuve in 1837>.

—**tickle the ivories** to play the piano: *There's a man in the pub who likes to tickle the ivories.* <The keys of a piano are made of ivory>.

J

jack, Jack

—**a jack of all trades (and master of none)** someone who can do several different kinds of job (but does not do any of them very well): *He's their gardener as well as their plumber. He's a jack of all trades.*

—**a jack in office** a pompous, dictatorial official: *That jack in office says that we will have to fill in all the forms again.*

—**all work and no play makes Jack a dull boy** *see* **work**.

—**before you can say Jack Robinson** extremely rapidly: *Your mother will be home before you can say Jack Robinson.*

—**every man jack** absolutely everyone: *Every man jack of you must attend tomorrow.* <Perhaps from the fact that Jack is a very common first name>.

—**I'm all right, Jack** my situation is satisfactory, the implication being that it does not matter about anyone else: *The manager has got a pay increase and it's a case of I'm all right Jack. He's not bothered about the workers' pay.*

jackpot

—**hit the jackpot** to have a great success, often involving a large sum of money: *He hit the jackpot when he married the boss's daughter.* <Refers to the pool of money in poker>.

jam

—**jam tomorrow** the promise of better things in the future: *Governments often promise jam tomorrow but many people would prefer some improvements now.* <From a statement by the Red Queen in *Alice Through the Looking-Glass* by Lewis Carroll>.

—**money for jam** *or* **old rope** *see* **money**.

—**want jam on it** to want an even better situation, etc, than one has already: *She should be glad that she has a well-paid job but she wants jam on it. She wants longer holidays.* <Refers to asking for jam on bread when bread is quite sufficient>.

Jekyll

—**a Jekyll and Hyde** someone with two completely different sides to his or her personality: *One day he is charming, the next he is very rude. He's a real Jekyll and Hyde.* <Refers to the character in *The Strange Case of Dr Jekyll and Mr Hyde,* a novel by Robert Louis Stevenson>.

Jeremiah

—**a Jeremiah** a pessimist: *My neighbour's a Jeremiah who says that the economic situation is going to get even worse.* <A biblical reference to the Lamentations of Jeremiah>.

jet

—**the jet set** wealthy people who can afford to travel a great deal. <Refers to jet planes>.

job

—**a good job** *see* **good**.

—**a job lot** a mixed collection: *The furniture in the flat is a real job lot.* <Refers to auctioneering>.

—**a put-up job** *see* **put**.

—**give (something) up as a bad job** to stop doing (something) because one has little hope of success: *I tried to persuade her to stay but I eventually gave it up as a bad job.*

—**have a job** to have difficulty: *If you're trying to get a contribution from her you'll have a job. She's incredibly mean.*

—**just the job** exactly what is required: *This cold drink is just the job in this heat.*

—**jobs for the boys** employment given to friends or supporters: *As soon as he got elected he gave appointments to most of his campaign committee—a clear case of jobs for the boys.*

—**make the best of a bad job** to obtain the best results possible from something unsatisfactory: *The house is in a terrible state of disrepair but we'll just have to make the best of a bad job and paint it.*

Job

—**a Job's comforter** someone who brings no comfort at all but makes one feel worse: *She supposedly came to cheer me up but she was a real Job's comforter and told me how ill I looked.* <A biblical reference to the friends of Job>.

—**enough to try the patience of Job** so irritating as to make the most patient of people angry: *Their deliberate lack of cooperation was enough to try the patience of Job.* <A biblical reference to

Job who had to suffer many misfortunes patiently>.

jockey

—**jockey for position** to try to manoeuvre oneself into a favourable or advantageous position: *Very few people will be promoted and ambitious members of staff are jockeying for position.*

Joe

—**Joe Bloggs** *or* **Public** *or* **Soap** the ordinary, average person: *Some politicians only bother about what Joe Bloggs thinks at election times.*

join

—**if you can't beat them** *or* **'em join them** *or* **'em** *see* **beat**.

—**join the club** *see* **club**.

joint

—**case the joint** to inspect premises carefully, especially with a view to later burglary: *They weren't window-cleaners at all. They were burglars casing the joint.*

—**put (someone's) nose out of joint** *see* **nose**.

joke

—be no joke to be a serious matter: *It was no joke when we missed the last bus.*

—**beyond a joke** no longer amusing, rather serious or annoying: *His remarks about women drivers are beyond a joke.*

—**crack a joke** to make a funny remark, to tell a funny story: *The comedian cracked a series of bad jokes.*

Jonah

—a Jonah someone who brings bad luck: *His workmates regard him as a Jonah. Things always go wrong when he's around.* <a biblical reference to the book of Jonah, Jonah 1:4-7>.

Jones

—**keep up with the Joneses** to make an effort to remain on the same social level as one's neighbours by buying what they have, etc: *Their neighbours are going to Florida, so they'll be going next year. They spend their time keeping up with the Joneses.*

jowl

—**cheek by jowl** *see* **cheek**.

joy

—**full of the joys of spring** very happy and cheerful: *She was full of the joys of spring when she was planning her holiday.*

—**no joy** no success, no luck: *We looked for the missing glove but no joy.*

—**wish (someone) joy of (something)** *see* **wish**.

juice

—**stew in one's juice** to suffer because of one's own foolish actions: *She'll just have to stew in her own juice. She shouldn't have left her husband.*

jump

—**a jumping-off point** a place from which to begin: *We have to start the investigation somewhere. This is as good a jumping-off point as any.*

—**be for the high jump** *see* **high**.

—**be** *or* **stay one jump ahead** to be or keep slightly ahead of someone or something in some way: *Both of them are looking for clues but the policeman is one jump ahead of the private investigator.*

—**jump down (someone's) throat** *see* **throat**.

—**jump on the bandwagon** *see* **band**.

—**jump out of one's skin** *see* **skin**.

—**jump the gun** *see* **gun**.

—**jump the queue** *see* **queue**.

—**jump to it** hurry up: *Jump to it! You're going to be late.*

jungle

—**the law of the jungle** *see* **law**.

just

—**get one's just deserts** *see* **desert**.

—**just so** very neatly arranged: *She likes everything in her kitchen to be just so.*

—**just the job** *see* **job**.

justice

—**do (someone** *or* **something) justice** (1) to show the true value of (someone or something): *The photograph doesn't do justice to her beauty.* (2) to eat (a meal, etc) with a good appetite: *I really couldn't do justice to the dessert. I had eaten too much meat.*

—**do justice to oneself** to behave in a way that is worthy of one's ability: *The pupil didn't do justice to himself in the exam.*

—**poetic justice** *see* **poetic**.

K

keel
—**get** *or* **keep on an even keel** *see* **even**.
keen
—**keen as mustard** *see* **mustard**.
keep
—**bear** *or* **keep (something) in mind** *see* **bear**.
—**for keeps** permanently: *She's gone abroad for keeps.*
—**keep a level head** *or* **keep one's head** *see* **head**.
—**keep an open mind** *see* **open**.
—**keep (someone) at arm's length** *see* **arm**.
—**keep in with (someone)** to remain friendly with (someone) or in (someone's) favour: *She keeps in with her aunt because the old lady is wealthy.*
—**keep it up** to carry on doing something as well as one is doing it: *There's been an improvement in your work—keep it up.* <Perhaps from the game of shuttlecock the aim of which was to keep the shuttlecock in the air>.
—**keep on at (someone)** to urge (someone) constantly to do something, to nag (someone): *She kept on at him to get a new car.*
—**keep one's chin up** *see* **chin**.
—**keep one's cool** *see* **cool**.
—**keep one's distance** *see* **distance**.
—**keep one's end up** *see* **end**.
—**keep one's hair on** *see* **hair**.
—**keep one's hand in** *see* **hand**.
—**keep one's head above water** *see* **head**.
—**keep one's nose clean** *see* **clean**.
—**keep one's own counsel** to keep one's opinions, problems, etc, secret: *I thought of telling him about my health fears but decided to keep my own counsel.*
—**keep oneself to oneself** not to seek the company of others much, to tell others very little about oneself: *Our new neighbours keep themselves very much to themselves.*
—**keep one's shirt on** *see* **shirt**.
—**keep one's word** *see* **word**.
—**keep pace with (someone** *or* **something)** *see* **pace**.
—**keep (someone) posted** *see* **post**[2].
—**keep tabs on (someone** *or* **something)** *see* **tab**.
—**keep the peace** *see* **peace**.
—**keep the wolf from the door** *see* **wolf**.
—**keep time** *see* **time**.
—**keep (something) to oneself** to keep (something) secret: *The child kept her worries about school to herself.*
—**keep** *or* **lose track of (something)** *see* **track**.
—**keep (something) under one's hat** *see* **hat**.
—**keep (something) under wraps** *see* **wrap**.
—**keep up appearances** *see* **appear**.
—**keep up with the Joneses** *see* **Jones**.
ken
—**beyond one's ken** outside the range of one's knowledge or understanding: *Why he did it is beyond my ken.* <Literally, ken used to mean range of vision>.
kettle
—**a different kettle of fish** a completely different set of circumstances: *Your previous suggestion was turned down, but your latest one is a completely different kettle of fish.*
—**a pretty kettle of fish** an awkward or difficult situation: *We're lost without a map. This is a pretty kettle of fish.*
—**the pot calling the kettle black** *see* **pot**.
kibosh
—**put the kibosh on (something)** to spoil or ruin (something's) chances of success: *My broken arm put the kibosh on my holiday plans last year.*
kick
—**alive and kicking** *see* **alive**.
—**for kicks** for thrills or fun: *The children broke the windows for kicks.*
—**kick oneself** to be annoyed with oneself: *I could have kicked myself when I realized my mistake.*
—**kick one's heels** *same as* **cool one's heels**—*see* **cool**.
—**kick (someone) in the teeth** *see* **teeth**.
—**kick over the traces** to defy rules that control one's behaviour: *Her parents were very strict but she kicked over the traces and eloped.* <Refers to a horse drawing a cart which gets out of control of the driver>.
—**kick the bucket** *see* **bucket**.

kid
—**handle (someone** *or* **something) with kid gloves** to deal with (someone or something) very tactfully or delicately: *The boss is furious. You'll have to handle him with kid gloves today.*
Kilkenny
—**fight like Kilkenny cats** *see* **fight**.
kill
—**curiosity killed the cat** *see* **cat**.
—**kill the fatted calf** *see* **calf**.
—**kill the goose that lays the golden egg** *see* **goose**.
—**kill time** *see* **time**.
—**kill two birds with one stone** *see* **bird**.
—**kill (someone) with kindness** to spoil (someone) to the extent that it is a disadvantage to him or her: *The old lady is killing her dog with kindness by over-feeding it.*
—**make a killing** to make a large profit: *He made a killing when he sold his shop.*
kind1
—**of a kind** of poor quality: *They provided a meal of a kind.*
—**two of a kind** *see* **two**.
kind2
—**kill (someone) with kindness** *see* **kill**.
—**the milk of human kindness** *see* **milk**.
king
—**a cat may look at a king** *see* **cat**.
—**a king's ransom** a vast sum of money: *They paid a king's ransom for that house.*
kingdom
—**till kingdom come** for a very long time: *Those two will gossip until kingdom come.* <Refers to the Lord's Prayer>.
—**to kingdom come** to death: *That bomb would blow us to kingdom come.* <See above>.
kiss
—**kiss of death** something which causes the end, ruin or death of something: *His appointment as managing director was the kiss of death to the firm.* <A biblical reference to the kiss by which Judas betrayed Jesus>.
kite
—**fly a kite** to start a rumour about a new project to see how people would react if the project were put into operation: *I think the rumour going around about moving to a new building is a kite flown by management.* <Refers to the use of kites to discover the direction and strength of the wind>.
kitten
—**have kittens** to get very agitated or angry: *She'll have kittens when she sees the mess in the kitchen.*
knee
—**bring (someone) to his** *or* **her knees** to humble or ruin (someone): *The workers went on strike but they were brought to their knees by lack of money.* <Refers to going on one's knees to beg for something>.
—**knee-high to a grasshopper** *see* **grasshopper**.
knickers
—**get one's knickers in a twist** to become agitated: *Don't get your knickers in a twist. They'll be here soon.*
knife
—**have one's knife in (someone)** to wish to harm (someone): *He's got his knife in her because she got the job his sister wanted.*
—**on a knife edge** in a very uncertain or risky state: *The financial state of the company is on a knife edge.*
—**the night of the long knives** a time when an act of great disloyalty is carried out, usually by the sudden removal of several people from power or employment: *She went in one morning to discover that she and her team had been sacked. It had been the night of the long knives.* <Refers to 19 June 1934, when the German leader Adolf Hitler had a number of his Nazi colleagues imprisoned or killed>.
knock
—**beat** *or* **knock the living daylights out of (someone)** *see* **live**.
—**knock (someone) for six** *see* **six**.
—**knock (something) into a cocked hat** *see* **hat**.
—**knock (someone** *or* **something) into shape** *see* **shape**.
—**knock (something) on the head** *see* **head**.
—**knock spots off (someone)** *see* **spot**.
—**knock the stuffing out of (someone)** *see* **stuff**.
knot
—**at a rate of knots** extremely rapidly: *She's getting through the work at a rate of knots.* <Refers to a method of measuring the speed of ships>.
—**cut the Gordian knot** *see* **Gordian**.
—**tie (oneself** *or* **someone) in knots** to get (oneself or someone) in a confused state: *The defence lawyer is tying the witness in knots.*
know
—**in the know** knowing facts, etc, that are known only to a small group of people: *Someone in the know told me that he has won.*
—**know all the answers** *see* **answer**.

—**know a thing or two** *see* **thing**.
—**know (something) backwards** *or* **like the back of one's hand** *see* **back**.
—**know (someone) by sight** *see* **sight**.
—**know one's onions** *see* **onion**.
—**know one's place** *see* **place**.
—**know the ropes** *see* **rope**.
—**know the score** *see* **score**.
—**know which side one's bread is buttered** *see* **bread**.
—**know what's what** *see* **what**.
—**know where one stands** *see* **stand**.
—**not to know one is born** to lead a trouble-free, protected life: *She doesn't know she's born. She has a well-paid job and works very few hours.*

knuckle
—**near the knuckle** *or* **bone** *see* **bone**.
—**rap (someone) over the knuckles** to scold or criticize (someone): *They were rapped over the knuckles for being rude to customers.*

L

labour

—**a labour of love** a long or difficult job done for one's own satisfaction or from affection for someone rather than for reward: *Ironing all her husband's shirts is a real labour of love.*

la-di-dah

—**la-di-dah** upper-class: *The children laugh at the teacher's la-di-da accent.* <From the supposed sound of upper-class speech>.

lady

—**ladies' man** a man who likes the company of women and tries to charm them: *He rarely goes out with male friends. He's a real ladies' man.*

—**lady bountiful** a rich, generous, and often patronizing woman: *She likes playing lady bountiful to her badly off relatives.* <Refers to a character in George Farquhar's play, *The Beaux' Stratagem*>.

—**lady-killer** a man who likes going out with women: *He still goes out with other women even now that they are married. He always was a lady-killer.*

lamb

—**(someone's) ewe lamb** *see* **ewe**.

—**in two shakes of a lamb's tail** *see* **shake**.

—**like a lamb to the slaughter** meekly, without arguing or resisting, often because unaware of danger or difficulty: *Young soldiers went to fight in World War I like lambs to the slaughter.* <A biblical reference to Isaiah 53:7>.

—**(someone) might as well be hanged for a sheep as a lamb** *see* **sheep**.

—**mutton dressed as lamb** *see* **mutton**.

lame

—**a lame duck** *see* **duck**.

—**help a lame dog over a stile** to give help to someone in difficulties: *The old lady has very little money but she's always helping lame dogs over stiles.*

lamp

—**smell of the lamp** of a piece of writing, to show signs of research and revision rather than originality: *He doesn't show much creativity in his essays. They smell of the lamp.*

land

—**a land of milk and honey** a place where life is pleasant, with plenty of food and possibilities of success: *The refugees saw their new country as a land of milk and honey.* <A biblical reference to the Promised Land of the Israelites described in Exodus 3:8>.

—**cloud cuckoo land** *see* **cloud**.

—**fall** *or* **land on one's feet** *see* **feet**.

—**live off the fat of the land** *see* **fat**.

—**see how the land lies** to look carefully at a situation before taking any action or decision: *I don't know how long I'll stay with my friends. I'll see how the land lies.* <Refers literally to sailors looking at the shore before landing>.

—**the land of Nod** *see* **nod**.

lane

—**it's a long lane that has no turning** every period of misfortune, unhappiness, etc, comes to an end or changes to happier circumstances eventually: *He'll find happiness one day. It's a long lane that has no turning.*

language

—**speak the same language** to have similar tastes and views: *It's good to meet someone who speaks the same language.*

lap

—**drop into (someone's) lap** *see* **drop**.

—**in the lap of luxury** in luxurious conditions: *Film-stars usually live in the lap of luxury.*

—**in the lap of the gods** *see* **god**.

large

—**large as life** in person, actually present: *We had just been asking where he was when he came in large as life.* <From works of art, particularly sculptural, which are life-size>.

—**larger than life** extraordinary, behaving, etc, in an extravagant way: *He is very quiet and shy but his wife is larger than life.*

lark

—**get up** *or* **rise with the lark** to rise very early in the morning: *We got up with the lark to catch the train.*

—**happy as a lark** *see* **happy**.

last[1]

—**as a** *or* **in the last resort** when all other methods have failed: *In the last resort you can sell your house to pay your debts.*

—**at one's last gasp** *see* **gasp**.
—**breathe one's last** *see* **breathe**.
—**have the last laugh** *see* **laugh**.
—**have the last word** to make the last or decisive statement in an argument, etc: *His wife always has to have the last word.*
—**on one's** *or* **its last legs** near to collapse: *The factory is on its last legs after losing a major order.*
—**the last straw** *same as* **the straw that breaks the camel's back**—*see* **straw**.
—**the last word** the most fashionable or up-to-date example of something: *He has the last word in recording equipment.*

last[2]

—**stick to one's last** to continue to do the job that one is experienced in: *He's a computer specialist and he should stick to his last rather than try to become a journalist.* <From the sayin, "The cobbler should stick to his last", literally, a shoemaker should concern himself only with making or mending shoes>.

late

—**better late than never** better for something to arrive, happen, etc, late than never to do so at all: *He arrived at midnight but that was better late than never.*
—**late in the day** when a project, activity, etc, is well advanced: *It's a bit late in the day to propose changes to the scheme.*

laugh

—**have the last laugh** to be victorious or proved right in the end, especially after being scorned, criticized, etc: *His neighbours teased him for entering the garden competition, but he had the last laugh when he won it.* <From the saying that he who laughs last laughs longest>.
—**laugh and the world laughs with you (weep and you weep alone)** when someone is cheerful or happy, other people share in his or her joy (but when he or she is sad or miserable, people tend to avoid him or her): *His friends all went to see him when he won the prize, but the year when he came last in the compeition, no one went near him. Laught and the world laughs with you, weep and you weep alone.*
—**laugh like a drain** *or* **laugh one's head off** to laugh very loudly: *They laughed like a drain when the bully tripped and fell.*
—**laugh on the other side of one's face** to suffer disappointment or misfortune after seeming to be successful or happy: *They were sure his side had won but they laughed on the other side of their faces when the opposing side scored a late goal.*
—**laugh (someone** *or* **something) out of court** *see* **court**.
—**laugh up one's sleeve** to be secretly amused: *She thought she was impressing them but they were laughing up their sleeves at her.*
—**no laughing matter** a very serious matter: *His playing truant is no laughing matter.*

laurel

—**look to one's laurels** to be careful not to lose one's position or reputation because of better performances by one's rivals: *The champion had better look to her laurels. The new young tennis player is very good.* <A reference to to the laurel wreath with which the ancient Greeks crowned their poets and victors>.
—**rest on one's laurels** to be content with past successes without trying for any more: *The firm used to have a good reputation but it has been resting on its laurels for too long.* <Another reference to the Greek laurel wreath>.

law

—**be a law unto oneself** to behave as one wishes rather than obeying the usual rules and conventions: *He was the only one not wearing evening dress but then he's always a law unto himself.*
—**lay down the law** to state one's opinions with great force, to give orders dictatorially: *Her father lays the law down about which friends she should see.*
—**take the law into one's own hands** to take action against a crime or injustice witnout involving the police or courts: *The villagers took the law into their own hands and nearly killed the child's murderer.*
—**the law of the jungle** the unofficial rules for survival or success in a dangerous or difficult situation where civilized laws are not effective: *He's beating him up because he raped his sister. The law of the jungle applies in these parts.*
—**the letter of the law** *see* **letter**.
—**the long arm of the law** *see* **arm**.

lay

—**lay (something) at (someone's) door** *see* **door**.
—**lay down one's arms** *see* **arm**.
—**lay it on the line** *see* **line**.
—**lay it on thick** *or* **lay it on with a trowel** to exaggerate greatly in one's praise, compliments, etc, to someone: *He was laying it on with a trowel when he was telling her how beautiful she was.*

—**lay (someone) low** to make (someone) ill: *He's been laid low by a stomach bug.*

—**lay odds** *see* **odd**.

—**lay** *or* **put (something) on the line** *see* **line**.

—**lay waste** *see* **waste**.

—**lay oneself (wide) open to (something)** *see* **open**.

lead[1]

—**a leading question** a question asked in such a way as to suggest the answer the questioner wants to hear: *The defence counsel asked his witness a series of leading questions.*

—**lead (someone) by the nose** *see* **nose**.

—**leading light** an important person in a certain group, field, etc: *She's one of the leading lights of the local dramatic society.*

—**lead the way** *see* **way**.

—**lead (someone) up the garden path** *see* **garden**.

lead[2]

—**swing the lead** to avoid doing one's work, usually by inventing deceitful excuses: *He said the soil was too dry to dig but he knew he was swinging the lead.* <Originally an expression from naval slang>.

leaf

—**take a leaf out of (someone's) book** to use (someone) as an example: *You should take a leaf out of your sister's book and start doing some work.*

—**turn over a new leaf** to change one's behaviour, etc, for the better: *He was wild as a teenager but he's turned over a new leaf now.*

league

—**be in league with (someone)** to have joined together with (someone), usually for a bad purpose: *He was in league with the men who broke into the shop.*

—**not be in the same league as (someone)** not to be as able as (someone): *The new teacher's not in the same league as our previous one.* <Refers to the grouping of clubs in soccer, etc, according to ability>.

lean

—**lean on (someone)** to use force on (someone) to persuade him or her to do something: *They must have leant on him to get him to give them an alibi.*

—**lean over backwards** *same as* **bend over backwards**—*see* **back**.

leap

—**a leap in the dark** an action or decision the results of which cannot be foreseen: *It's foolish to take a leap in the dark and emigrate to a new country without a job.*

—**by leaps and bounds** very quickly or successfully: *The children are progressing by leaps and bounds in their new school.*

—**look before you leap** *see* **look**.

lease

—**give (someone** *or* **something) a new lease of life** to cause (someone) to have a longer period of active life or usefulness or to have a happier or more interesting life: *Her hip operation has given the old lady a new lease of life.*

leash

—**strain at the leash** to be impatient or very eager to do something: *The children were straining at the leash to get out to play.* <Refers to a dog on a leash straining to get its freedom>.

least

—**least said soonest mended** the less one says in a difficult situation the less harm will be done: *I was so angry that I wanted to tell her what I thought of her but least said soonest mended.*

leave

—**leave (someone) in the lurch** to leave (someone) in a difficult or dangerous situation without any help: *She walked out and left her husband in the lurch with three young children.* <A lurch refers to a position at the end of certain games, such as cribbage, in which the loser has either lost by a huge margin or scored no points at all>.

—**leave** *or* **let well alone** to make no change to something that is already reasonably satisfactory: *You've just made the television picture worse by trying to fix it. You should have left well alone.*

—**take French leave** *see* **French**.

—**take it or leave it** *see* **take**.

—**take leave of one's senses** *see* **sense**.

leech

—**stick to (someone) like a leech** to be constantly with (someone) or constantly to follow (someone): *His new girlfriend sticks to him like a leech. His friends never see him alone.* <Formerly leeches were used in medicine and were stuck firmly to patients to suck blood>.

leeway

—**make up leeway** to take action to recover from a setback or loss of advantage: *After his illness he had a lot of schoolwork to do in order to catch up on his classmates but he soon made up leeway.* <Leeway refers to the distance a sail-

ing ship is blown sideways off its course by the wind>.

left

—**have two left feet** to be clumsy or awkward with one's feet, e.g. when dancing: *I tried to waltz with him but he has two left feet.*

—**left, right and centre** everywhere, to an extreme degree: *He gives a bad impression of the firm left, right and centre.*

—**(someone's) left hand does not know what his** *or* **her right hand is doing** (someone's) affairs are extremely complicated: *He has so many different business interests that his left hand doesn't know what his right hand is doing.*

leg

—**cost an arm and a leg** *see* **arm**.

—**give (someone) a leg up** to give (someone) some assistance to achieve advancement: *The manager would still be working on the factory floor if the previous manager hadn't given him a leg up.*

—**not to have a leg to stand on** to have no defence or justification for one's actions: *He was drunk when he ran over the old man and he does not have a leg to stand on.*

—**on one's** *or* **its last legs** *see* **last**.

—**pull (someone's) leg** to try as a joke to make (someone) believe something that is not true: *There's not really an escaped lion in the street. He's pulling your leg.*

—**stretch one's legs** to go for a walk: *I'm stiff from sitting in the car for so long. I must stretch my legs.*

legion

—**their name is legion** there are a great many of them: *It's difficult to estimate how many people have applied. Their name is legion.* <A biblical reference to Mark 5:9>.

length

—**go to great lengths** to take absolutely any action in order to achieve what one wants: *He'll go to any lengths to get that job, including bribery.*

leopard

—**the leopard never changes its spots** a person's basic character does not change. *I don't believe that he was acting out of kindness. The leopard never changes his spots.*

let

—**let alone (someone** *or* **something)** not taking into consideration (someone or something): *We haven't really enough room for her, let alone the three children.*

—**let oneself go** (1) to enjoy oneself without restraint: *He seems very formal but he really lets himself go at parties.* (2) to stop taking trouble over one's appearance: *She used to be elegantly dressed but since her husband's death she's let herself go.*

—**let (someone) have it** *see* **have**.

—**let (someone) in on something** to share something secret with (someone): *They let him in on their plans to escape.*

—**let off steam** *see* **steam**.

—**let (something) slip** *see* **slip**.

—**let the grass grow under one's feet** *see* **grass**.

—**let well alone** *same as* **leave well alone**—*see* **leave**.

letter

—**a red-letter day** *see* **red**.

—**the letter of the law** the exact wording of a law, rule, agreement clause: *According to the letter of the law, you are responsible for half the costs of the repairs, but in your financial circumstances, it would be unreasonable of him to expect you to pay it.* <A biblical reference to II Corinthians 3:6>.

—**to the letter** in every detail: *You must follow the instructions to the letter.*

level

—**do one's level best** *see* **best**.

—**find one's** *or* **its (own) level** to find out what situation, position, etc, one is naturally suited to: *There's no point in expecting all the pupils to go to university. Each has to find his or her own level.*

—**on the level** honest, trustworthy: *His father's a crook but he's on the level.*

liberty

—**Liberty Hall** a place where one can do as one pleases: *It's Liberty Hall in their house at the moment. Their parents are abroad for a year.*

—**take liberties with (something)** to treat (something) with too much freedom or with not enough respect: *The writer of the book thought that the makers of the film had taken liberties with her text and had changed the plot totally.*

—**take the liberty of (doing something)** to dare to do (something) without prior permission or without being asked to: *I took the liberty of borrowing a pen from your desk. I hope you don't mind.*

licence

—**poetic licence** *see* **poetic**.

lick

—**a lick and a promise** a quick, not thorough,

wash or clean: *She's given the kitchen floor a lick and a promise.*

—**lick (someone** *or* **something) into shape** to improve (someone or something) greatly to bring up to standard: *The report he wrote was inadequate, but I helped him lick it into shape.* <Refers to an old belief that bear cubs are born shapeless and have to be licked into shape by their mothers>.

—**lick one's lips** *see* **lip**.

lid

—**blow** *or* **take the lid off (something)** to reveal the truth about (something): *The sacked worker blew the lid off the company's tax evasion.*

—**put the (tin) lid on (something)** to finish (something) off usually in an unpleasant way: *The recession put the tin lid on his already failing business.*

lie[1]

—**give the lie to (something)** to show that (something) is untrue: *The letters the police found gave the lie to his denial of the crime.*

—**lie in** *or* **through one's teeth** to tell lies obviously and unashamedly: *He was lying through his teeth when he told the police that he hadn't been near the scene of the crime.*

—**live a lie** to live a way of life about which there is something dishonest: *His wife didn't know that he had committed bigamy and was living a lie.*

—**white lie** *see* **white**.

lie[2]

—**lie heavy on (someone)** to be a burden or source of anxiety to (someone): *The guilt of his crime lay heavy on him.*

—**lie in wait for (someone)** *see* **wait**.

—**lie low** *see* **low**.

—**see how the land lies** *see* **land**.

—**take (something) lying down** to accept an unpleasant situation without protesting or taking action against it: *The workers have been dismissed unfairly but they're not taking it lying down. They're taking it to a tribunal.*

—**the lie of the land** the nature and details of a situation: *Find out the lie of the land before applying for a job with that organization.* <Refers to sailors studying the nature of the coastline>.

life

—**a dog's life** *see* **dog**.

—**a matter of life and death** *see* **matter**.

—**breathe new life into (something)** to make (something) more lively, active or successful: *The club needs new members to breathe new life into it.*

—**come to life** to become active or lively: *The restaurants there don't come to life until late in the evening.*

—**large as life** *see* **large**.

—**for dear life** *or* **for dear life's sake** to a very great extent, very rapidly, hard, etc: *We had to run for dear life to catch the bus.*

—**for the life of me** if my life depended on it: *I can't for the life of me remember his name.*

—**give (someone** *or* **something) a new lease of life** *see* **lease**.

—**have the time of one's life** *see* **time**.

—**lead a charmed life** *see* **charm**.

—**lead a double life** to follow two completely different ways of life, one of which is usually secret and deceitful: *The salesman was leading a double life. He had one wife in London and one in Leeds.*

—**lead** *or* **live the life of Riley** to lead a comfortable and trouble-free life: *She married a rich old man and led the life of Riley.*

—**not on your life** certainly not: *"Are you going to accept that?" "Not on your life."*

—**risk life and limb** to risk death or physical injury, to take extreme risks: *Soldiers know they must risk life and limb in the course of their jobs.*

—**see life** to have wide experience, especially of varying conditions of life: *She certainly sees life as a social worker.*

—**take one's life in one's hands** to take the risk of being killed, injured or harmed: *You take your life in your hands when you cross that road.*

—**the facts of life** the facts about sex or reproduction: *The child is too young to understand the facts of life.*

—**the life and soul of the party** someone who is very lively and amusing on social occasions: *Although she is quite an elderly person, she was the life and soul of the party.*

—**(someone) to the life** exactly like (someone): *The old man's Churchill to the life.*

—**while** *or* **where there's life there's hope** one should not despair of a situation while there is still a possibility of improvement: *The firm is in a pretty bad state financially but while there's life there's hope.*

light[1]

—**according to one's lights** *see* **accord**.

—**bring (something) to light** to reveal or uncover (something): *The police investigation has brought new facts to light.*

—**come to light** to be revealed or uncovered: *New evidence has come to light.*
—**give the green light to (something)** *see* **green**.
—**hide one's light under a bushel** to be modest or silent about one's abilities or talents: *We discovered accidentally that she's a marvellous piano player. She's certainly been hiding her light under a bushel.* <A biblical reference to Matthew 5:15, quoting Christ>.
—**in the cold light of day** when one looks at something practically and calmly: *At the party we planned a world trip but in the cold light of day we realized that we couldn't afford it.*
—**leading light** *see* **lead**.
—**light at the end of the tunnel** possibility of success, happiness, etc, after a long period of suffering, misery etc: *He's been depressed about being unemployed. Now he's been promised a job there is light at the end of the tunnel.*
—**see the light** (1) to understand something after not doing so: *She was having trouble with the maths problem but she suddenly saw the light.* (2) to agree with someone's opinions or beliefs after not doing so: *She laughed at vegetarianism but then she suddenly saw the light.* (3) (*also* **see the light of day**) to come into existence: *I don't think the book he's supposed to be writing will ever see the light.*
—**shed** *or* **throw light on (something)** to make (something) clearer, e.g. by providing more information about it: *Can his parents shed any light on why he ran away?*
—**the light of (someone's) life** the most important person or thing in (someone's) life: *Her dogs are the light of her life.*

light[2]
—**be light-fingered** to be likely to steal: *Lock your money and jewels away. I think she is light-fingered.*
—**make light of (something)** to treat (something) as unimportant: *He made light of his injury and worked on.*
—**many hands make light work** *see* **hand**.

lightning
—**lightning never strikes twice (in the same place)** the same misfortune is unlikely to occur more than once: *Having been burgled once we're hoping lightning doesn't strike twice.*
—**quick as lightning** *or* **like greased lightning** extremely rapidly: *Quick as lightning he snatched my purse from my hand.*

lily
—**be lily-livered** to be cowardly: *He's lily-livered. He won't accept a challenge to fight.* <Refers to an old belief that the liver had no blood in it>.
—**gild the lily** *see* **gild**.

limb
—**out on a limb** in a risky and often lonely position; having ideas, opinions, etc, different from other people: *He went out on a limb and disagreed publicly with the scientific research of his professor.* <Refers to being stuck in an isolated position on the branch of a tree>.
—**risk life and limb** *see* **life**.

limbo
—**in limbo** in a forgotten or neglected position: *He's in limbo in a small department far from the head office.*

limelight
—**in the limelight** in a situation where one attracts a great deal of public attention: *Leading politicians must get used to being in the limelight.*

limit
—**be the limit** to be as much as, or more than, one can tolerate: *That postman's the limit. He gets later and later.*
—**off limits** beyond what is allowed: *They told him not to go out with their sister but he can't resist someone that's off limits.*
—**the sky's the limit** *see* **sky**.

line
—**all along the line** at every point in an action, process, etc: *All along the line it was obvious that their marriage was in difficulties.*
—**along** *or* **on the lines of (something)** similar to (something): *Our pay scale should be along the lines of that of the other parts of the firm.*
—**be in line for (something)** to be likely to get (something): *He's in line for promotion.*
—**bring (something) into line with (something)** to make (something) the same as or comparable with (something else): *The aim is to bring the agricultural policies of all the countries into line.*
—**draw the line** to fix a limit: *We can't invite everyone. We must draw the line somewhere.*
—**hard lines** *see* **hard**.
—**hot line** *see* **hot**.
—**lay it on the line** to make (something) absolutely clear to someone: *If you want him to understand the seriousness of the position you will have to lay it on the line to him.*
—**lay** *or* **put (something) on the line** to risk losing (something): *He laid his job on the line by supporting the strikers.*

—**line one's pocket** *see* **pocket**.

—**read between the lines** to understand or deduce something from a statement, situation, etc, although this has not actually been stated: *Her family says that she is well but, reading between the lines, I think that she is unlikely to recover.* <Refers to a method of writing secret messages by writing in invisible ink between the lines of other messages>.

—**shoot a line** to to exaggerate or boast about one's abilities, achievements, etc: *Beware of candidates who shoot a line at their interviews.*

—**step out of line** to behave differently from what is usually acceptable or expected: *There's no point in deliberately stepping out of line and wearing jeans to the formal party.* <Refers to a line of soldiers on parade>.

—**take a hard line** *see* **hard**.

—**the line of least resistance** the course of action that will cause one least effort or trouble: *She won't disagree with the rest of the committee. She always takes the line of least resistance.*

—**toe the line** to obey the rules or orders: *The new teacher will soon get the children to toe the line.* <Refers to competitors having to stand with their toes to a line when starting a race, etc>.

linen

—**air** *or* **wash one's dirty linen in public** *see* **air**.

lion

—**beard the lion in its den** *see* **beard**.

—**lion-hunter** a person who tries very hard to become friendly with famous people: *When the actor became famous he tried to avoid lion-hunters.* <Refers to people formerly going to see the lions at the Tower of London as part of the sight-seeing tour of London>.

—**put one's head in the lion's mouth** to put oneself in a very dangerous or difficult position: *She put her head in the lion's mouth by asking her boss for a rise when he had just paid all the bills.*

—**the lion's share** a much larger share than anyone else: *His eldest son got the lion's share of the old man's estate.* <Refers to one of Aesop's fables in which the lion, being a very fierce animal, claimed three quarters of the food which he and other animals had hunted for>.

—**throw (someone) to the lions** deliberately to put (someone) in a in a dangerous or difficult position, often to protect oneself: *They were both responsible for the mistakes, but he threw his colleague to the lions by telling the manager it was her fault alone.* <Refers to a form of entertainment in ancient Rome in which prisoners were thrown to wild animals to be attacked and killed>.

lip

—**keep a stiff upper lip** to show no emotion, such as fear or disappointment when danger, trouble, etc, arises: *The boy was sad not to receive a present but his father had taught him to keep a stiff upper lip.*

—**lick one's lips** to look forward to something with pleasure: *He was licking his lips at the thought of his holiday cruise.* <A reference to licking one's lips at the thought of appetizing food>.

—**(someone's) lips are sealed** (someone) will not reveal something secret: *I know what he has got you for your birthday but my lips are sealed.*

—**pay lip-service to (something)** to say that one believes in or agrees with (something) without really doing so and without acting as if one did: *She pays lip-service to feminism but she pays her female workers a lot less than her male ones.*

—**there's many a skip 'twixt cup and lip** *see* **slip**.

list

—**enter the lists** to join in a contest or argument: *My father and brother are arguing about holidays and my sister has now entered the lists.*

live[1]

—**beat** *or* **knock the living daylights out of (someone)** to give (someone) a severe beating: *He'll knock the living daylights out of you if he finds out you lost him his job.*

—**live and let live** to get on with one's own life and let other people get on with theirs without one interfering: *I wouldn't complain about my neighbours. I believe in live and let live.*

—**live by one's wits** *see* **wit**.

—**live from hand to mouth** *see* **hand**.

—**live in sin** *see* **sin**.

—**live it up** to have an enjoyable and expensive time: *He was living it up on his trips at the firm's expense.*

—**live like a lord** *see* **lord**.

—**live up to one's reputation** *see* **reputation**.

live[2]

—**a live wire** an energetic, enthusiastic person: *She's a live wire who'll introduce new ideas.* <Refers to a live electrical wire>.

load

—**a loaded question** a question intended to lead

someone into admitting to or agreeing with something when he or she does not wish to do so: *The accused was tricked into admitting his presence at the crime by a loaded question from the prosecuting barrister.* <Refers to a dice loaded or weighted so that it tends always to show the same score>.

loaf

—**half a loaf is better than no bread** *see* **half**.

—**use one's loaf** to use one's brains, to think clearly: *He'll have to use his loaf if he is to do the navigating on our car journey.*

lock

—**lock horns** *see* **lock**.

—**lock, stock and barrel** completely, with everything included: *They are moving overseas lock, stock and barrel.* <Refers to the main components of a gun>.

—**lock the stable door after the horse has bolted** *see* **stable**.

—**under lock and key** in a place which is locked for security: *She keeps her jewels under lock and key.*

log

—**easy as falling off a log** *see* **easy**.

—**sleep like a log** to sleep very soundly: *We slept like logs after our long journey.*

loin

—**gird up one's loins** *see* **gird**.

lone

—**a lone wolf** someone who prefers to be alone: *We asked him to join us on holiday but he went off somewhere by himself. He's a real lone wolf.*

long

—**a long shot** *see* **shot**.

—**be** *or* **get long in the tooth** *see* **tooth**.

—**draw the long bow** *see* **bow**[2].

—**have a long face** *see* **face**.

—**in the long run** in the end, after everything has been considered: *In the long run you would be better to buy a house than rent one.*

—**it's a long lane that has no turning** *see* **lane**.

—**the long and the short of it** the only thing that need be said, to sum the story up in a few words: *The long and the short of it is that she left him.*

—**the long arm of the law** *see* **arm**.

look

—**look askance at (someone** *or* **something)** to regard with disapproval or distrust: *He always looked askance at the neighbour's offers of help.*

—**look before you leap** give careful consideration before you act: *Don't rush into changing jobs. Look before you leap.*

—**look daggers at (someone)** *see* **dagger**.

—**look down one's nose at (someone** *or* **something)** *see* **nose**.

—**look down on (someone)** to regard and treat (someone) as being inferior: *She looks down on people who work in factories.*

—**look in on (someone)** to pay (someone) a brief visit, usually without prior notice or invitation: *I'll look in on the old lady on my way past.*

—**look sharp** *see* **sharp**.

—**look the other way** *see* **other**.

—**look the part** *see* **part**.

—**look to one's laurels** *see* **laurel**.

—**look up** (1) to improve: *Things are looking up. He's found a job.* (2) to pay (someone) a visit: *We decided to look you up as we were passing through your village.*

—**look (someone) up and down** to look at someone carefully and critically: *She looked him up and down and then said he wasn't suitable for the job.*

—**look up to (someone)** to regard (someone) with great respect or admiration: *He always looked up his elder brother.*

—**make (someone) look small** *see* **small**.

—**not to get a look-in** not to have a chance of winning, succeeding, being noticed, etc: *He entered the race but he didn't get a look-in.*

loose

—**at a loose end** *see* **end**.

—**have a screw loose** *see* **screw**.

—**on the loose** enjoying freedom and pleasure: *The girls from the boarding school were on the loose in the town at the weekend.* <Refers originally to prisoners escaped from jail>.

lord

—**drunk as a lord** extremely drunk: *He staggered home drunk as a lord.*

—**live like a lord** to live in rich and luxurious way: *He lives like a lord in big house while his mother lives in a rented room.*

—**lord it over (someone)** to act in a proud and commanding manner to (someone): *He lords it over the poorer children in the class.*

lose

—**lose face** *see* **face**.

—**lose ground** to lose one's advantage or strong position: *The political party is losing ground to its nearest rival.*

—**lose heart** *see* **heart**.

—**lose one's cool** *see* **cool**.
—**lose one's grip** to lose control: *They sacked the manager because he was losing his grip.*
—**lose one's head** *see* **head**.
—**lose one's nerve** *see* **nerve**.
—**lose one's rag** *see* **rag**.
—**lose one's touch** *see* **touch**.
—**lose one's way** *see* **way**.
—**lose out** to suffer loss or disadvantage: *New workers lost out on the bonus payments.*
—**lose sleep over (something)** *see* **sleep**.
—**lose the thread** *see* **thread**.
—**lose track of (someone** *or* **something)** *see* **track**.
—**lost cause** an aim, ideal, etc, that cannot be achieved: *They are hopeful that the campaign to save the whale will not be yet another lost cause.*
—**lost on (someone)** not appreciated by, or having no effect on, (someone): *The humour of the situation was lost on her.*
—**play a losing game** to go on with something that is obviously going to be unsuccessful: *The campaigners are still trying to stop the building of the new airport but they're playing a losing game.*

loss
—**cut one's losses** not to spend any more time, money or effort on something on which one has already spent a lot to little benefit: *You've tried to help her and she's rejected you. It's time to cut your losses.*

love
—**a labour of love** *see* **labour**.
—**not for love nor money** not in any way at all: *We couldn't get a taxi for love nor money on Saturday night.*
—**there's no love lost between them** they are hostile to each other: *They are brothers-in-law but there's no love lost between them.*

low
—**hunt** *or* **search high and low for (someone** *or* **something)** *see* **high**.
—**keep a low profile** not to draw attention to oneself or one's actions or opinions: *She kept a low profile after the boss gave her a warning.*
—**lay (someone) low** *see* **lay**.
—**lie low** to stay quiet or hidden: *The criminals are lying low until the police hunt is called off.*
—**the low-down** information, especially of a secret or damaging nature: *The press have got hold of the low-down on the politician's affair.*

luck
—**down on one's luck** experiencing misfortune: *He's helping a friend who's down on his luck.*
—**hard-luck story** *see* **hard**.
—**push one's luck** to risk failure by trying to gain too much: *He's pushing his luck by asking for yet more time off.*
—**strike it lucky** to have good fortune: *The actor struck it lucky when he met a film director at a party.*
—**take pot-luck** *see* **pot**.
—**thank one's lucky stars** to be grateful for one's good fortune: *You should thank your lucky stars that you have a job.*
—**worse luck** unfortunately: *We have to stay and work, worse luck.*

lull
—**lull (someone) into a false sense of security** to lead (someone) into thinking that all is well in order to attack when he or she is not prepared: *The workers were lulled into a false sense of security by the management's statement and then received their redundancy notices the following week.*

lumber
—**get lumbered with (something)** to be given an unwanted task or responsibility: *She's got lumbered with looking after the children all day.*

lump
—**lump it** to put up with (something) whether one likes it or not: *I don't like the new arrangement but I can't change it and so I'll just have to lump it.*

lurch
—**leave (someone) in the lurch** *see* **leave**.

lute
—**a rift in the lute** *see* **rift**.

luxury
—**in the lap of luxury** *see* **lap**.

M

mackerel

—**a sprat to catch a mackerel** *see* **sprat**.

mad

—**go** *or* **run mad after (something)** to develop a violent passion for (something): *As Dryden wrote, "The world is running mad after farce".*

—**hopping mad** *see* **hop**.

—**in** *or* **for the main** for the most part: *New ideas on education have, for the main, been current for about a year.*

—**like mad** in an excited fashion, hurriedly: *No one would have recognized the head teacher in the figure that came flying across the meadow, his hat dangling and leapng like mad behind him.*

—**mad as a hatter** utterly insane, extremely foolish or eccentric: *The villagers thought the inventor of strange gadgets was mad as a hatter.* <Hat-making used to involve the use of nitrate of mercury, exposure to which could cause a nervous illness which people thought was a symptom of insanity>.

—**mad as a March hare** insane, silly, extremely eccentric: *His neighbours regard him as being mad as a March hare because of the peculiar clothes he wears.* <Hares tend to leap around wildly in the fields during March, which is their breeding season>.

—**midsummer madness** *see* **midsummer**.

maiden

—**maiden speech** the first speech made as a member of the British House of Commons: *The press were heavily critical of the politician's maiden speech.*

—**maiden voyage** the first voyage undertaken by a ship: *The ship ran aground on its maiden voyage.*

main

—**have an eye to the main chance** *see* **chance**.

—**splice the mainbrace** *see* **splice**.

—**with might and main** *see* **might**.

make

—**be the making of (someone)** to cause the improvement or successful development of (someone): *People said that being in the army would be the making of him.*

—**have the makings of (something)** to have the abilities or qualities necessary to become (something): *That young man has the makings of an excellent teacher.*

—**in the making** being formed or developed: *Some of the members of the school debating society may be politicians in the making.*

—**make a day** *or* **night of it** to spend a whole day or night enjoying oneself in some way: *After dinner we decided to make a night of it and go to a nightclub.*

—**make** *or* **pull a face** *see* **face**.

—**make a fool of (someone)** *see* **fool**.

—**make a go of (something)** *see* **go**.

—**make a meal of (something)** *see* **meal**.

—**make a name for oneself** *see* **name**.

—**make a pass at (someone)** *see* **pass**.

—**make a play for (someone** *or* **something)** *see* **play**.

—**make a point of (doing something)** *see* **point**.

—**make as if to (do something)** to act as if one were about to (do something). *He made as if to hit her.*

—**make a stand against (something)** *see* **stand**.

—**make believe** to pretend or imagine: *The children made believe that they were soldiers.*

—**make bricks without straw** to work without having the necessary materials supplied: *To expect him to write an autobiography when he is only twenty-five is like making bricks without straw.* <A biblical reference to Exodus 5:7>.

—**make do with (something)** to use (something) as a poor or temporary substitute for something: *The poor family had no carpet but had to make do with a piece of sacking on the floor.*

—**make eyes at (someone)** *see* **eye**.

—**make free with (something)** to use without permission or ceremony: In his review the literary critic made free with the greatest names.

—**make good** *see* **good**.

—**make hay (while the sun shines)** *see* **hay**.

—**make headway against (something)** to progress, to overcome some obstacle: *With the new evidence, his defence lawyer hopes to make headway against the prosecution's case.* <Originally a nautical term>.

—**make heavy weather of (something)** *see* **heavy**.
—**make it** (1) to be successful: *He was determined to make it before he was 30.* (2) to arrive somewhere: *I will be at the meeting if I can make it in time.*
—**make it up** to become friendly again after a quarrel: *The feuding families have made it up.*
—**make light of (something)** *see* **light**.
—**make one's mark** *see* **mark**.
—**make merry** *see* **merry**.
—**make much of (someone** *or* **something)** *see* **much**.
—**make off with (something)** to run away: The burglar made off with his loot.
—**make-or-break** bringing either success or failure: *This is a make or-break year for the team.*
—**make one's peace with (someone)** *see* **peace**.
—**make one's point** *see* **point**.
—**make the best of a bad job** *see* **job**.
—**make the grade** to do as well as necessary for something, to reach the required standard: *She didn't become an opera singer. She didn't make the grade.* <Originally referred to a train that succeeded in climbing a steep section of track>.
—**make the most of (something)** *see* **most**.
—**make tracks (for)** *see* **track**.
—**make up one's mind** *see* **mind**.
—**make up to (someone)** to flatter or try to please (someone) in order to gain favour.
—**make one's way** *see* **way**.
—**make way (for someone** *or* **something)** *see* **way**.
—**on the make** trying to make a profit for oneself: *Don't buy a car from him. He's always on the make.*

man
—**a man of his word** someone who always does as he promises: *He'll be there if he said he would be. He's a man of his word.*
—**be a marked man** *see* **mark**.
—**be one's own man** to be independent in one's actions, opinions, etc: *He's not his own man since he married. He simply agrees with what his wife says.*
—**every man jack** *see* **jack**.
—**hit a man when he's down** *see* **hit**.
—**man-about-town** a sophisticated, fashionable man: *He likes football and beer but his brother's a man-about-town.*
—**man Friday** *see* **Friday**.
—**man of straw** a man who is considered to be of not much worth or substance: *He won't oppose the powerful members of the board. He is a man of straw.*
—**man to man** frankly: *They need to talk man to man about their disagreement.*
—**odd man out** *see* **odd**.
—**right-hand man** *or* **woman** *see* **right**.
—**the man in the street** *or* **in the Clapham omnibus** the ordinary, average person: *Politicians should pay more attention to the man in the street.*
—**the man of the moment** the person who is currently dealing with a situation: *The defence secretary is the man of the moment. He is taking part in talks to try to end the war.*
—**to a man** everyone without exception: *The workers voted to a man to return to work.*

manger
—a dog in the manger *see* **dog**.

manna
—**manna from heaven** *see* **heaven**.

manner
—**in a manner of speaking** in a way, in a sense: *I suppose you could call him her guardian in a manner of speaking.*
—**to the manner born** as if accustomed since birth to a particular way of behaviour etc: *She comes from a poor family but she acts like an aristocrat to the manner born.* <Refers to a quotation from Shakespeare's *Hamlet*, act 1, scene iv>.

many
—**many hands make light work** *see* **hand**.

map
—**put (somewhere) on the map** to cause (somewhere) to become well-known or important: *Finding gold there certainly put the town on the map.*

marble
—**have marbles in one's mouth** to speak with an upper-class accent: *Since she went to that school she sounds as though she has marbles in her mouth.*
—**lose one's marbles** to become insane or senile: *The poor old man is losing his marbles.*

march
—**get one's marching orders** to be told to leave, to be dismissed: *She was given her marching orders for persistent late arrival.* <Refers to a military term>.
—**steal a march on (someone)** to gain an advantage over (someone) by doing something earlier than expected: *We stole a march on them by*

launching our new product before they could launch a similar one. <Refers literally to moving an army unexpectedly while the enemy is resting>.

mare

—**a mare's nest** a supposed discovery of something, which turns out to be imaginary or completely different from what was expected: *The publicized new cure for cancer turned out to be a mare's nest.*

marine

—**tell that to the marines** I do not believe you: *You're working hard when you have time to gossip? Tell that to the marines.* <Refers to the fact that sailors used to consider marines to be ignorant about the sea>.

mark

—**be a marked man** *or* **woman** to be in danger or trouble because people are trying to harm one: *He's marked man. His wife's brother has just found out he's having an affair.* <In this case, "marked" means watched>.

—**beside** *or* **wide of the mark** off the target or subject: *His guess was wide of the mark.* <Refers to hitting the target in archery>.

—**be up to the mark** to reach the required or normal standard: *His work just isn't up to the mark.*

—**get off one's mark** to get started quickly on an undertaking: *If you want to buy his car you better get off your mark. Someone else is interested.* <Refers to track events in athletics>.

—**hit the mark** to be correct or accurate: *You certainly hit the mark when you said the house would be expensive.* <Refers to the target in archery>.

—**make one's mark** to make oneself well-known, to make a lasting impression: *He wants to make his mark in the world of theatre.*

—**mark time** *see* **time**.

—**quick off the mark** quick to act: *You'll have to be quick off the mark if you want to get to the shop before it closes.* <Refers literally to a runner starting quickly in a race>.

marrow

—**chilled** *or* **frozen to the marrow** extremely cold: *We got chilled to the marrow waiting for the bus.*

mass

—**the masses** the ordinary people, taken as a whole: *He wants to provide entertainment for the masses.*

mast

—**sail** *or* **serve before the mast** to be an ordinary sailor: *He had spent his career sailing before the mast.* <In sailing ships, the sailors' quarters, or forecastle, are in the bow of the vessel.

master

—**old master** *see* **old**.

—**past master** *see* **past**.

match

—**meet one's match** to find oneself against someone who has the ability to defeat one in a contest, argument or activity: *She has been winning the annual tennis match for years but she has met her match in that young player.*

matter

—**a matter of life or death** something of great urgency, something that might involve loss of life: *Tell the doctor that it is a matter of life and death.*

—**as a matter of course** as part of a routine: *That garage is very good. They'll clean your car as a matter of course.*

—**be the matter** be the problem, be what is wrong: *There is something the matter with this car.*

meal

—**make a meal of (something)** to treat (something) as it it is more complicated or time-consuming than it is: *He's really making a meal of painting that door.*

—**square meal** *see* **square**.

means

—**ways and means** *see* **way**.

measure

—**for good measure** as something in addition to what is necessary: *He locked the door and for good measure put the chain on.*

—**have (someone's) measure** to have formed an impression or judgement of (someone): *You had his measure when you said he was not to be trusted.*

meat

—**be meat and drink to (someone)** be very important to (someone): *Reading is meat and drink to the old lady.*

—**one man's meat is another man's poison** people have different tastes: *I liked the film but you may not. After all, one man's meat is another man's poison.*

Mecca

—**a Mecca** a place that is important to a certain group of people and is visited by them: *Liverpool was a Mecca for fans of the Beatles.* <Refers to the birthplace of Mohammed to which Muslims make pilgrimages>.

medicine

—**a dose** *or* **taste of one's own medicine** *see* **dose**.

medium

—**the** *or* **a happy medium** *see* **happy**.

meet

—**meet (someone) halfway** *see* **half**.

—**meet one's match** *see* **match**.

—**meet one's Waterloo** to be finally defeated: *The tennis champion met his Waterloo when he played the younger player.* <Napoleon was defeated for the last time at the Battle of Waterloo by Wellington in 1815>.

melt

—**be in the melting-pot** to be in the process of changing: *The government's education policy is in the melting-pot again.* <Refers to melting down and reshaping metal>.

mend

—**be on the mend** to be getting better: *He nearly died, but now he's on the mend.*

—**least said, soonest mended** *see* **least**.

—**mend one's ways** *see* **way**.

mercy

—**an angel of mercy** *see* **angel**.

—**at the mercy of (someone** *or* **something)** wholly in the power or control of (someone or something): *The villagers are at the mercy of the cruel tyrant.*

—**be thankful for small mercies** to be grateful for minor benefits or advantages in an otherwise difficult situation: *We have no meat or vegetables but we do have some bread. Let's be thankful for small mercies.*

merry

—**make merry** to have an enjoyable, entertaining time, to have a party: *The students are making merry after their exams.*

—**the more the merrier** *see* **more**.

message

—**get the message** to understand: *When he made cocoa his guests got the message. He wanted them to go.*

method

—**there is method in one's madness** someone has a good, logical reason for acting as he or she does, although his or her actions may appear to be strange or unreasonable: *We thought he was a fool to resign but he got his redundancy money and the firm went bankrupt two months later. There was method in his madness.* <A reference to Shakespeare's *Hamlet* Act 2, scene ii>.

mettle

—**on one's mettle** prepared to make a great effort: *You'd better be on your mettle. The owner of the firm is making a tour of inspection today.*

mickey, micky

—**Mickey Finn** a drink that has been drugged: *They gave him a Mickey Finn and kidnapped him.*

—**take the mickey** *or* **micky out of (someone)** to make fun of or ridicule (someone): *The other pupils take the mickey out of her because of her accent.*

Midas

—**the Midas touch** the ability to make money or be successful easily: *All his firms are extremely profitable. He has the Midas touch.* <Refers to a Greek legend about a king of Phrygia whose touch turned everything to gold>.

middle

—**middle-of-the-road** moderate, midway between extremes: *His political views are middle-of-the-road.*

midnight

—**burn the midnight oil** to work or study until late at night: *The student had to burn the midnight oil to finish his essay.*

midsummer

—**midsummer madness** utter lunacy: To expect him to win the election is midsummer madness.

might

—**high and mighty** *see* **high**.

—**with might and main** with maximum strength and power: *He rowed with might and main in the stormy sea.*

mile

—**a miss is as good as a mile** *see* **miss**.

—**give (someone) an inch** *or* **ell and he** *or* **she will take a mile** *see* **inch**.

—**milestone** a very important event: *The discovery of anaesthetics was a milestone in medical history.* <Refers literally to a stone set at the edge of a road to indicate the number of miles to the next town, etc>.

—**stand** *or* **stick out a mile** to be extremely obvious: *It stuck out a mile that he was jealous.*

milk

—**a land of milk and honey** *see* **land**.

—**cry over spilt milk** *see* **cry**.

—**the milk of human kindness** natural kindness and sympathy towards others: *He won't give anything to charity. He's completely lacking in the milk of human kindness.* <A quotation from Shakespeare's *Macbeth*, Act 1, scene v>.

mill

—**a millstone round one's neck** a heavy burden or responsibility: *Our high mortgage is a millstone round our necks.*

—**calm as a millpond** extremely calm: *The sea was calm as a millpond.*

—**it's all grist to the** *or* **someone's mill** *see* **grist**.

—**go through the mill** to experience a series of difficult or troublesome events, periods or tests: *She's really been through the mill recently. She's had one illness after another.* <From the grinding of corn in a mill>.

—**run-of-the-mill** usual, not special: *They're wealthy but they live in a run-of-the mill kind of house.*

—**the mills of God grind slowly (but they grind exceedingly small)** the proper punishment or reward for someone's actions may be slow in coming but it will certainly come: *His second wife has left him in the same way as he left his first wife. The mills of God grind slowly.*

million

—**one in a million** someone or something that is exceptionally good or special in some way: *The teacher is one in a million. She has helped many parents as well as the children.*

mince

—**make mincemeat of (someone** *or* **something)** to defeat (someone) soundly, to destroy (something): *The defence barrister made mincemeat of the prosecution's allegations against his client.*

—**not to mince matters** to speak completely frankly without trying to be too kind, etc: *Her tutor didn't mince matters when he told the student her essay was very poor.*

mind

—**a gold mine** *see* **gold**.

—**a mine of information** a rich or productive source of information: *The old man's a mine of information on local history.*

—**be** *or* **go out of one's mind** to be or become insane: *She must be out of her mind to go to live in that remote place.*

—**bear** *or* **keep (something) in mind** *see* **bear**.

—**blow (someone's) mind** to amaze (someone), to excite (someone) greatly: *The singer's excellent performance really blew our minds.*

—**cross one's mind** to enter one's mind briefly: *It crossed my mind that I hadn't seen him for a while.*

—**give (someone) a piece of one's mind** to scold or criticize (someone) angrily: *She gave the bus driver a piece of her mind for not stopping at the bus stop.*

—**great minds think alike** clever people tend to have the same ideas and opinions: *I see we both bought him the same book. Great minds think alike!*

—**have a good mind to (do something)** to feel inclined to (do something): *I have a good mind to take the day off.*

—**have a mind of one's own** to form one's own opinions, to be independent: *She won't vote for the party her husband tells her to. She has a mind of her own.*

—**have a one-track mind** *see* **one**.

—**have half a mind to (do something)** to feel slightly inclined to (do something): *I have half a mind to go and live in the country.*

—**in one's right mind** sane, rational: *Her family say that she cannot have been in her right mind when she signed the will.*

—**in two minds** undecided: *They're in two minds about moving house.*

—**keep an open mind** *see* **open**.

—**make up one's mind** to reach a decision: *I can't make up my mind where to go on holiday.*

—**mind one's own business** *see* **business**.

—**mind one's p's and q's** *see* **p**.

—**not to know one's own mind** not to know what one really wants to do: *She doesn't know her own mind. She can't decide whether to live in the town or the country.*

—**out of sight, out of mind** *see* **sight**.

—**presence of mind** *see* **presence**.

—**put (someone) in mind of (someone** *or* **something)** to remind (someone) of (someone or something): *She puts me in mind of her mother when she was that age.*

—**put** *or* **set (someone's) mind at rest** to free (someone) from anxiety and worry: *Telephone and tell your mother that you're all right. It'll put her mind at rest.*

—**slip one's mind** to be temporarily forgotten: *I meant to telephone you but it slipped my mind.*

—**to my mind** in my opinion: *To my mind she would be better staying here.*

mint

—**a mint of money** a large fortune: *She shopped as if she had a mint of money instead of a small bequest.*

—**in mint condition** used but in extremely good condition: *He'll buy your books only if they're in mint condition.* <Literally the unused condition of a newly minted coin>.

minute
—**up to the minute** modern or fashionable: *He's up to the minute on information about computers. She wears up-to-the-minute clothes.*

miscarriage
—**a miscarriage of justice** a mistaken verdict or decision in a court of law, etc: *The accused was released from jail after a year. The appeal court found that there had been a miscarriage of justice.*

mischief
—**do (oneself** *or* **someone) a mischief** to hurt or harm (oneself or someone): *The child might do herself a mischief if she plays on that fence.*
—**make mischief** to cause trouble: *Her mother tried to make mischief between husband and wife.*

misery
—**put (someone) out of his** *or* **her misery** to end a time of worry, anxiety or suspense for (someone): *Put the students out of their misery and tell them which of them passed.* <Originally a term for putting to death a wounded and suffering animal>.

miss
—**a miss is as good as a mile** if one fails at something it does not matter how close he or she came to succeeding: *He failed the exam by two marks but a miss is as good as a mile.*
—**a near miss** *see* **near**.
—**give (something) a miss** not to go to or attend (something): *I think I'll give the party a miss.*
—**miss the boat** *see* **boat**.

mistake
—**and no mistake** without any doubt: *I was terrified and no mistake.*

mix
—**a mixed blessing** *see* **bless**.
—**mixed bag** *see* **bag**.

moment
—**have one's moments** to have times of success, happiness: *She may live a boring life now but she's had her moments.*
—**in a weak moment** *see* **weak**.
—**not for a moment** not at all: *I didn't for one moment believe him.*
—**on the spur of the moment** *see* **spur**.
—**the man of the moment** *see* **man**.
—**the moment of truth** a crucial time, a time when one has to make an important decision, face a crisis, etc: *It was the moment of truth for her. She had to decide whether to marry him or not.*

money
—**a run for (someone's) money** *see* **run**.
—**be in the money** to be well off, sometimes temporarily: *Let him pay for dinner. He's in the money for once.*
—**for my money** in my opinion, as my choice: *For my money I'd rather live in the city than the country.* <Literally what one would spend one's money on>.
—**have money to burn** to have enough money to be able to spend it in ways considered foolish: *She must have money to burn if she can afford clothes like that.*
—**money for jam** *or* **old rope** money obtained in exchange for very little work, effort, etc: *She gets paid very highly for writing two reports a week. It's money for jam.* <Originally army slang>.
—**money** *or* **distance, etc, is no object** *see* **object**.
—**money talks** rich people have influence simply because they have money: *The local council should not alter their plans because of the local landowners but money talks.*
—**not for love nor money** *see* **love**.
—**put one's money where one's mouth is** to give money for a cause or purpose which one claims to support: *She is in favour of a new library being built but she won't put her money where her mouth is and contribute to the building fund.*
—**ready money** *see* **ready**.
—**spend money like water** to spend money very freely: *When he received his redundancy pay the family spent money like water.*
—**throw good money after bad** to spend money in an unsuccessful attempt to retrieve money which one has already lost: *Borrowing thousands of pounds from the bank to try to make that firm profitable is simply throwing good money after bad.*

monkey
—**monkey business** action likely to cause trouble, illegal or unfair activities: *There seems to have been some monkey business in the accounts department.*
—**not to give a monkey's** not to care at all: *He says he doesn't give a monkey's whether he gets the sack or not.*

month
—**a month of Sundays** an extremely long time: *You'll never finish that piece of work in a month of Sundays.*

moon
—**ask** *or* **cry for the moon** to ask for something that it is impossible to get: *The young woman is*

looking for a well-paid and undemanding job without any qualifications. She is crying for the moon.

—**do a moonlight (flit)** to move away suddenly: *They did a moonlight to avoid paying the rent.*

—**over the moon** extremely happy: *They were over the moon to hear that they had passed their exams.*

moral

—**moral support** encouragement but not actual physical, financial, etc, help: *Her parents could not afford to give her money to help with her college studies but they gave her their moral support.*

more

—**the more the merrier** the more people that are involved the better: *Come and join our outing to the cinema. It'll be fun—the more the merrier.*

morning

—**the morning after the night before** a morning when one is suffering from a hangover caused by drinking too much alcohol the night before: *He looked absolutely terrible at this morning's meeting. It was obviously a case of the morning after the night before.*

most

—**make the most of (something)** to take maximum advantage of (an opportunity, occasion, etc): *Make the most of your last university vacation. You probably won't get such a long holiday again.*

mother

—**a mother's** *or* **mummy's boy** a boy or man who depends too much on his mother; a weak, effeminate boy or man: *He's such a mother's boy that he probably won't marry till his mother dies.*

—**mother's milk** something that one needs or enjoys very much: *Modern novels are mother's milk to him.*

—**the father and mother of** *see* **father**.

motion

—**go through the motions** to make a show of doing something, to pretend to do something: *I'm bored stiff but I'll have to go through the motions of enjoying myself.*

—**set the wheels in motion** *see* **wheel**.

mould

—**cast in the same mould (as someone)** very similar (to someone): *She's cast in the same mould as her cousin. They're both hot-tempered.* <Refers to iron-working>.

mountain

—**make a mountain out of a molehill** greatly to exaggerate the extent of a problem, etc: *It's not a very complicated journey. She's just making a mountain out of a molehill.*

mouth

—**down in the dumps** *or* **down in the mouth** *see* **down**.

—**foam at the mouth** *see* **foam**.

—**have a big mouth** to talk a lot, especially about things, such as secrets, that one should not: *She told him where we're going. She's got a big mouth.*

—**put one's money where one's mouth is** *see* **money**.

—**shoot one's mouth off** to talk in a loud and often boastful or threatening manner: *He was shooting his mouth off about what he would do if he didn't get a pay increase.*

move

—**get a move on** to hurry: *We had better get a move on or we'll miss the bus.*

—**move heaven and earth** *see* **heaven**.

much

—**make much of (someone** *or* **something)** to pay (someone or something) a great deal of attention: *Their grandmother always makes much of the children.*

—**make much of (something)** to treat (something) as being of great importance: *They made much of the fact that I was late although it was only by a few minutes.*

—**much ado about nothing** a great fuss about something very minor: *The boy only broke a very small window but the owner sent for the police. It was a case of much ado about nothing.* <From Shakespeare's play of the same name>.

—**much of a muchness** very similar: *The houses we looked at were much of a muchness. We're still looking.*

—**not much of a (something)** not a very good (something): *She's not much of a cook.*

—**not to think much of (someone** *or* **something)** *see* **think**.

—**not up to much** not very good: *The holiday hotel was not up to much.*

—**without so much as** without even: *They left suddenly without so much as saying goodbye.*

muck

—**muck in** to join in a task, etc: *If we all muck in we should finish by this evening.* <Originally army slang>.

—**muck-raking** searching for scandalous information, usually with the intention of publishing it: *The Sunday newspaper was accused of muck-raking to discredit the new president.*

—**where there's muck there's brass** where there is dirt and ugliness in a place there is often industry and so wealth: *The son objected to the ugly factory chimneys but his wealthy grandfather said, "Where there's muck there's brass".*

mud

—**clear as mud** *see* **clear**.

—**(someone's) name is mud** (someone) is in disfavour or is being criticized: *Your name will be mud if you don't go to her party.*

—**sling** *or* **throw mud at (someone** *or* **something)** to say bad or insulting things about (someone or something): *The candidates in the election kept slinging mud at each other.*

—**stick-in-the mud** *see* **stick**.

mug

—**a mug's game** something that only foolish people would involve themselves in: *He has decided that marriage is a mug's game.*

mule

—**stubborn as a mule** extremely stubborn: *The old lady is stubborn as a mule and will not accept help with her housework.*

multitude

—**cover a multitude of sins** to be able to apply or refer to a large number of different things: *In an office the term personal assistant can cover a multitude of sins.* <A misquotation from the Bible, I Peter 4:8—"Charity shall cover the multitude of sins">.

mum

—**keep mum** to stay silent: *He was told to keep mum if anyone questioned him about the accident.*

—**mum's the word** do not say anything: *We're planning a surprise party for her and so mum's the word.*

mummy

—**mummy's boy** *same as* **mother's boy** *see* **mother**.

murder

—**get away with murder** to do something bad, irresponsible, etc, without suffering punishment: *When their mother's away their father lets the children away with murder.*

mustard

—**keen as mustard** very eager and enthusiastic: *The trainee chef is keen as mustard.*

mutton

—**mutton dressed as lamb** an older person, usually a woman, dressed in clothes suitable for young people: *She thinks she looks very smart but she's mutton dressed as lamb.*

N

n

—**to the nth degree** *see* **degree**.

nail

—**a nail in (someone's) coffin** something which helps to bring about (someone's) downfall or destruction: *The customer's complaint about him was yet another nail in his coffin.*

—**hard as nails** *see* **hard**.

—**hit the nail on the head** to be extremely accurate in one's description, judgement, etc, of someone or something: *She certainly hit the nail on the head when she said he was work-shy.*

—**nail one's colours to the mast** *see* **colour**.

—**pay (something) on the nail** to pay (something) immediately: *He always pays his account on the nail.*

name

—**a name to conjure with** *see* **conjure**.

—**call (someone) names** to apply insulting or rude names to (someone): *The other children called him names because he wore second-hand clothes.*

—**clear (someone's) name** to prove that (someone) was not involved in a crime or misdeed of which he or she was accused: *He finally cleared his name by finding out the real culprit.*

—**give (someone** *or* **something) a bad name** to damage the reputation of (someone or something): *All these complaints about late deliveries are giving the firm a bad name.*

—**in name only** not in practice: *They're man and wife in name only. They don't live together.*

—**make a name for oneself** to become famous or well-known: *She's already made a name for herself as a dancer.*

—**name-dropping** the habit of mentioning the names of famous or important people as though they were friends: *She was trying to impress us by name-dropping but it was just embarrassing.*

—**(someone's) name is mud** *see* **mud**.

—**name names** to give the names of people, especially people who are guilty or accused of wrong-doing: *The children are being bullied but they are afraid of naming names.*

—**name the day** *see* **day**.

—**no names, no pack-drill** no names will be mentioned and so no one will get into trouble: *If you repair the damage you have done, there will be no names, no pack-drill.* <"Pack-drill" refers to a form of army punishment in which the soldiers being punished were forced to march up and down carrying all their equipment>.

—**the name of the game** the important or central thing: *Persistence—that's the name of the game in job-hunting.*

—**take (someone's) name in vain** *see* **vain**.

—**their name is legion** *see* **legion**.

—**to one's name** in one's possession or ownership: *He has scarcely a penny to his name.*

—**worthy of the name** deserving to be so called: *Any teacher worthy of the name would punish the pupil.*

nap

—**catch (someone) napping** *see* **catch**.

narrow

—**a narrow squeak** *see* **squeak**.

—**the straight and narrow (path)** *see* **straight**.

nasty

—**a nasty piece of work** someone who is very unpleasant or behaves very unpleasantly: *Try not to argue with him. He's a really nasty piece of work.*

native

—**go native** to live according to the customs, fashions, etc, of the foreign country in which one is living: *Although she has only been in India a short time she's gone native and wears a sari.*

nature

—**answer** *or* **obey the call of nature** *see* **call**.

—**in a state of nature** naked: *The man was found in the cave in a state of nature and raving mad.*

—**second nature** *see* **second**.

near

—**a near miss** something unpleasant that very nearly happened, often the near collision of two planes in the sky: *The chimney fell to the ground just beside me. It was a near miss.*

—**a near thing** the act of just avoiding an accident, misfortune, etc: *We arrived at the station on time but it was a near thing.*

—**one's nearest and dearest** one's close family: *Even her nearest and dearest criticize her.*

neat

—**neat as a pin** very neat and tidy: Everything was as neat as a pin in the house.

neck

—**a millstone round one's neck** *see* **mill**.

—**a pain in the neck** *see* **pain**.

—**be in (something) up to one's neck** to be very much involved in something bad or illegal: *The police were convinced that he was up to his neck in drug-smuggling.*

—**be neck or nothing** to be a braving of all dangers, the risking of everything: *It's neck or nothing for the party if it wants to win the election.*

—**breathe down (someone's) neck** *see* **breathe**.

—**get it in the neck** to be severely scolded or punished: *You'll get it in the neck if you're not home by midnight.*

—**have the brass neck to (do something)** to have the impertinence or brazenness to (do something): *She had the brass neck to expect us to pay for her cinema ticket.*

—**neck and neck** exactly equal: *The two football teams were neck and neck at the end of the season.*

—**risk one's neck** to put one's life, job, etc, in danger: *Firemen risk their necks to save other people.*

—**stick one's neck out** to take a risk, to or do something that may cause trouble: *I know I'm sticking my neck out but hasn't your husband had too much to drink?*

—**this** *or* **that, etc, neck of the woods** this or that, etc, part of the country: *Why did you come to this neck of the woods?* <Originally a term for a remote community in the woods of the early 19th-century American frontier>.

need

—**needs must when the devil drives** *see* **devil**.

—**the needful** money: *We don't have the needful to pay the rent.*

needle

—**like looking for a needle in a haystack** an impossible search: *Looking for a contact lens on this carpet is like looking like for a needle in a haystack.*

—**on pins and needles** *see* **pin**.

nerve

—**bag of nerves** *see* **bag**.

—**get on (someone's) nerves** to irritate (someone): *His constant whistling gets on my nerves.*

—**have a nerve** to be impertinent or brazen: *They had the nerve to ask us for another loan when they still owed us money.*

—**lose one's nerve** to become scared, and so be unable to continue with an activity or course of action: *The diver lost his nerve on the high diving-board.*

nest

—**a mare's nest** *see* **mare**.

—**a nest-egg** savings for the future: *She had to spend her nest-egg to pay her son's fine.*

—**feather one's nest** *see* **feather**.

nettle

—**grasp the nettle** to set about an unpleasant or difficult task in a firm and determined manner: *You must grasp the nettle and tell her that her work is not up to standard.*

never

—**never-never land** an imaginary land where conditions are ideal: *They live in a never-never land and don't seem to realize how bad their financial situation is.* <Refers to the idealized land in J. M. Barrie's play *Peter Pan*>.

—**never say die** don't despair, persevere: *You'll pass your exams if you study properly—never say die.*

—**on the never-never** by hire purchase: *They're buying the furniture for their new house on the never-never.*

new

—**new blood** *see* **blood**.

—**new broom** someone who has just been appointed to a post and who is eager to be efficient, make changes, etc: *Our office system works very well but the new manager is a new broom who wants to revolutionize the whole thing.* <From the saying a new broom sweeps clean, a new broom being more effective than the old one>.

—**put new heart into (someone)** *see* **heart**.

—**turn over a new leaf** *see* **leaf**.

news

—**break the news to (someone)** to tell (someone) about something, usually something unpleasant or sad, that has happened: *The policewoman had to break the news of her son's fatal road accident to her.*

—**no news is good news** if one has not received any information about someone or something then all is likely to be well since if something bad, such as an accident, had happened one would have heard: *Our son is very late but no news is good news. He's probably just been delayed on the journey.*

next

—**next door to (something)** very nearly (something): *Her recent actions have been next door to insanity.*

—**next one's heart** very dear to one: *Football is a subject that is next his heart.*

—**next to nothing** almost nothing, very little: *The second-hand furniture cost next to nothing.*

nick

—**in good** *or* **poor nick** in good or poor condition: *The car is in good nick for its age.*

—**in the nick of time** just in time, at the last possible time: *We arrived in the nick of time to save him from drowning.*

night

—**a one-night stand** *see* **one**.

—**night-owl** someone who is in the habit of staying up very late at night: *She never goes to bed before 2 a.m. She's a real night-owl.*

nine

—**a nine days' wonder** something that arouses surprise and interest for a short time only: *His marriage to a much younger girl was a nine days' wonder.* <Refers to a saying quoted by Chaucer—"where is no wonder so great that it lasts more than nine days">.

—**a stitch in time saves nine** *see* **stitch**.

—**dressed to the nines** *see* **dress**.

nineteen

—**talk nineteen to the dozen** *see* **talk**.

nip

—**nip (something) in the bud** to put a stop or end to (something) as soon as it develops: *Her father tried to nip the romance in the bud by sending her to college in France.*

nit

—**get down to the nitty-gritty** to begin to deal with the basic practical details, problems, etc: *It's time to get down to the nitty-gritty and discuss the funding of the project.*

—**nit-picking** the act of finding very minor faults in something, quibbling: *He ignores all the major issues and spends his time nit-picking.* <Refers to picking nits out of hair>.

no

—**be no joke** *see* **joke**.

—**no end of (something)** a great deal of (something): *There will be no end of trouble if the boss finds out.*

—**no go** unsuccessful, in vain: *We applied for planning permission but it was no go.*

—**no holds barred** *see* **hold**.

—**no time at all** *see* **time**.

—**no way** under no circumstances: *There's no way that we'll get there in time.*

noble

—**noble savage** a primitive person brought up in primitive surroundings, thought of as being less corrupt, more worthy, more innocent, etc, than people brought up in a more civilized environment: *The explorer was a great believer in the concept of the noble savage and eventually went to live in the jungle.* <From a quotation by John Dryden, the English dramatist, and a theory developed by Jean Jacques Rousseau, the French philosopher>.

nobody

—**be nobody's fool** *see* **fool**.

—**like nobody's business** very rapidly, energetically, etc: *We worked liked nobody's business to finish the job in time.*

nod

—**a nod is as good as a wink (to a blind horse)** there is no use repeating a sign to those who cannot or do not choose to see: *Management won't improve conditions unless the workers take action—a nod is as good as a wink.*

—**have a nodding acquaintance with (someone** *or* **something)** to know (someone or something) slightly: *I have a nodding acquaintance with the history of the period.* <Refers to knowing someone well enough to nod in greeting to him or her>.

—**nod off** to fall asleep, sometimes accidentally: *His lecture was so boring that the students nodded off.*

—**the land of Nod** sleep: *It's time the children were in the land of Nod.* <Refers to a place mentioned in the Bible in Genesis 4:16 and the fact that nodding is associated with falling asleep>.

noise

—**big noise** an important person: *The big noises on the board are looking round the factory today.*

—**empty vessels make most noise** *see* **empty**.

none

—**none the wiser** *see* **wise**.

—**none too** not very: *He looks none too happy.*

nook

—**every nook and cranny** absolutely everywhere: *We searched in every nook and cranny of the house for the last earring.* <Literally, in all the corners and cracks>.

nose

—**cut off one's nose to spite one's face** to do something that harms oneself, usually in order to harm someone else: *Refusing to work overtime because you quarrelled with your boss is cutting off your nose to spite your face. You need the extra money.*

—**follow one's nose** to go straight forward: *You'll reach the village if you follow your nose all the way from here.*

—**keep one's nose clean** *see* **clean**.

—**keep (one's** *or* **someone's) nose to the grindstone** to keep (someone) working hard without stopping: *I'll have to keep my nose to the grindstone to finish this in time.*

—**lead (someone) by the nose** to get (someone) to do whatever one wants: *He leads the other children in the class by the nose.* <Refers to the ring on a bull's nose>.

—**look down one's nose at (someone** *or* **something)** to regard or treat (someone or something) with disdain or contempt: *She looks down her nose at people from the council housing estate.*

—**nosey parker** someone who is too inquisitive about other people's affairs: *I'm tired of that nosey parker asking where I'm going.*

—**no skin off my, etc, nose** *see* **skin**.

—**pay through the nose** to pay a great deal of money for something: *You'll pay through the nose for a house in that area.*

—**poke one's nose into (something)** to pry into or interfere in other people's affairs: *I wish she'd stop poking her nose into my mother's business.* <Refers literally to a dog>.

—**put (someone's) nose out of joint** to make (someone) jealous or offended by taking a place usually held by him or her e.g. in the affections of a person whom he or she loves: *The teenager's nose has been put out of joint by the new baby in the house.* <Refers to a person whose nose has been broken by being hit in the face>.

—**rub (someone's) nose in it** to keep on reminding (someone) about something he or she has done wrong: *I know I shouldn't have lent him money but there's no need to rub my nose in it.* <Refers literally to rubbing a dog's nose in its faeces when house-training it>.

—**see further than the end of one's nose** to be concerned with more than just what is happening in the immediate present and in the immediate vicinity: *He can't see further than the end of his nose, so he doesn't give any thought to what his children will do if he and his wife emigrate.*

—**thumb one's nose at (someone** *or* **something)** *see* **thumb**.

—**turn up one's nose at (something)** to treat (something) with dislike or disgust: *The child was used to sophisticated food and turned up his nose at fish fingers.*

—**under (someone's) (very) nose** (1) right in front of (someone) and so easily seen: *The book which I couldn't find had been right under my nose all the time.* (2) while (someone) is actually present: *She stole my suitcase from under my very nose.*

note

—**of note** famous or important: *They want someone of note to open the new store.*

—**strike the right note** to say or do something suitable for the occasion: *The clothes which the princess wore struck just the right note at the children's sports day.* <Refers to playing a musical instrument>.

nothing

—**come to nothing** to fail: *His plans to start his own business came to nothing.*

—**go for nothing** to be wasted or unsuccessful: *All our efforts to save the old building went for nothing.*

—**have nothing on (someone)** (1) not to be nearly as good, skilful, bad, etc, as (someone else): *She may have a quick temper but I bet she has nothing on my mother.* (2) to have no proof or evidence of (someone's) wrong doing: *The police have nothing on the burglar. They can't arrest him.*

—**have nothing to do with (someone** *or* **something)** to avoid contact with (someone or something): *They have had nothing to do with each other since their divorce.*

—**next to nothing** *see* **next**.

—**nothing to write home about** *see* **home**.

—**nothing ventured, nothing gained** one cannot achieve anything if one does not make an attempt or take a risk: *It's not a good time to open a small business but there again nothing ventured nothing gained.*

—**stop at nothing** *see* **stop**.

—**sweet nothings** *see* **sweet**.

—**there is nothing to choose between (two people** *or* **things)** there is hardly any difference in quality, ability, etc, between (two people or things): *Either of the candidates will do for the job. There's nothing to choose between them in qualifications or experience.*

—**there's nothing to it** it is very easy: *I'm sure*

that you can assemble the furniture yourself. There's nothing to it.

—**think nothing of (something)** not to regard (something) as out of the ordinary, difficult, etc: *She thinks nothing of driving hundreds of miles every weekend to see her boyfriend.*

—**think nothing of it** do not worry about it. It does not matter: *"I'm sorry that I took your coat by mistake." "Think nothing of it."*

nowhere

—**get** *or* **be nowhere** to make no progress, to have no success: *I tried to explain my difficulty to the passport office but I got absolutely nowhere.*

—**nowhere near** not nearly: *They've nowhere near enough money to put a deposit on a house.*

number

—**back number** *see* **back**.

—**(your, etc) days are numbered** *see* **day**.

—**get** *or* **have (someone's) number** to find out or know what kind of person (someone) is and what he or she is likely to do: *I've got his number. He's a con-man who's trying to get money out of my aunt.*

—**in penny numbers** *see* **penny**.

—**(someone's) number is up** (someone) is about to suffer something unpleasant, such as dying, failing, being punished, being caught, etc: *He has been stealing from the firm for years but his number is up. The manager is conducting an investigation.*

—**number one** oneself: *For once I must think of number one.*

—**(someone's) opposite number** *see* **opposite**.

—**there's safety in numbers** *see* **safe**.

nut

—**a hard nut to crack** a difficult problem or person to deal with: *I don't know how we'll get there by public transport. That's a hard nut to crack.*

—**be nuts about (someone** *or* **something)** to like (someone or something) a very great deal, to be wildly enthusiastic about (someone or something): *He's nuts about jazz.*

—**do one's nut** to get very angry: *The teacher will do her nut if you're late again.*

—**in a nutshell** briefly, to sum up: *The trial went on for days but in a nutshell he was acquitted.*

—**the nuts and bolts of (something)** the basic details or practicalities of (something): *He wants to buy a pub but he knows nothing whatsoever about the nuts and bolts of running a business.*

O

oar

—**put** *or* **stick one's oar in** to interfere in another's affairs, conversation, e.g. by offering unwanted opinions: *They would have settled their argument if she had not stuck her oar in.* <Perhaps refers to someone who is being rowed in a boat by others and who suddenly decides to take part in the rowing unasked>.

—**rest on one's oars** to take a rest after working very hard: *The students are resting on their oars after their exams before looking for holiday jobs.* <Refers literally to rowing>.

oat

—**off one's oats** not feeling well and so not eating much: *I've been off my oats ever since I had flu last week.* <Literally used of horses>.

—**sow one's wild oats** *see* **wild**.

oath

—**take one's oath** to swear that something one has said is true: *I will take my oath that I saw him enter my office.*

object

—**money, distance, etc, is no object** it does not matter how much money, distance, etc, is involved in the particular situation: *The delivery service says that distance is no object in their business.* <Originally "money is no object" meant money or profits were not the main aim but it came to be misapplied>.

occasion

—**rise to the occasion** to be able to carry out whatever action is required in an important or urgent situation: *He had never played the piano in public before but he rose to the occasion.*

ocean

—**a drop in the ocean** *same as* **a drop in the bucket** *see* **bucket**.

odd

—**against all the odds** in spite of major difficulties: *Traffic conditions were terrible but against all the odds we arrived in time.*

—**be at odds with (someone** *or* **something)** to be in disagreement with (someone or something), not to be in accordance with (something): *His work performance is at odds with his brilliant reference.*

—**lay odds** to bet: *I'll lay odds that he won't turn up.* <Refers to betting on horses>.

—**make no odds** to be of no importance, to make no difference: *It makes no odds whether it rains or not. The party is indoors.*

—**odd man out** someone or something that is different from others: *He's the odd man out in the family. He doesn't have black hair.* <Refers literally to someone left out of a game when the teams have been chosen>.

—**odds and ends** small objects of different kinds: *All our holiday packing is done apart from odds and ends such as suntan oil.*

—**odds and sods** a mixed selection of people or things not considered important: *I knew most of the people at the party but there were a few odds and sods that I didn't recognize.*

—**over the odds** more than one would usually expect to pay: *The restaurant charges over the odds in the tourist season.* <Refers originally to a horse-racing term>.

odour

—**an odour of sanctity** an air of excessive piety or virtue: *There's such an odour of sanctity about her that he's afraid to ask her out.*

—**in bad odour** in disfavour: *He's in bad odour with management for supporting the strikers.* <From a French term for the sweet smell reputed to be given off by the corpses of saints>.

off

—**badly** *or* **well off** *see* **bad** *or* **well**.

—**get off (something)** to be given a lesser punishment than expected: *She got off with a fine instead of imprisonment.*

—**go off** to begin to dislike (someone or something previously liked): *She went off cheese when she was pregnant.*

—**know (something) off by heart** to have committed to memory: *He was so fond of the poem he knew it off by heart.*

—**off and on** *or* **on and off** occasionally: *We've met for lunch off and on over the years.*

—**off-colour** *see* **colour**.

—**off one's head** *see* **head**.

—**off the cuff** *see* **cuff**.

—**off the hook** *see* **hook**.
—**off the peg** *see* **peg**.
—**off the rails** *see* **rail**.
—**off the record** *see* **record**.
—**off the top of one's head** *see* **top**.
—**on the off-chance (of** *or* **that)** *see* **chance**.
—**put (someone) off his** *or* **her stroke** *see* **stroke**.

office
—**seek office** to wish or apply for a position: *The minister is retiring shortly and has told his colleagues he will not be seeking office.*
—**the usual offices** a lavatory: *The estate agent assured the client that the building had the usual offices.*

offing
—**in the offing** about to or likely to happen, appear, etc: *He doesn't have a job yet but there are one or two in the offing.* <A nautical term—refers to the whole area of sea that can be seen from a particular point on shore>.

oil
—**burn the midnight oil** *see* **midnight**.
—**oil the wheels** to make something easier to do or obtain: *She got a visa quite quickly. Knowing someone at the embassy oiled the wheels.* <Wheels turn more easily if oil is applied to them>.
—**pour oil on troubled waters** to to attempt to bring a state of calm and peace to a situation of disagreement or dispute: *When the children quarrel their mother always tries to pour oil on troubled waters.* <Since oil floats on water it has the effect of making waves flat>.
—**strike oil** to obtain exactly what one wants, to be successful: *We've never found a comfortable holiday house but this year we struck oil.*

ointment
—**a fly in the ointment** *see* **fly**[1].

old
—**an old hand** someone who is very experienced (at doing something): *She's an old hand at serving in a bar.*
—**any old how** *see* **any**.
—**a ripe old age** *see* **age**.
—**money for old rope** *see* **money**.
—**old as the hills** extremely old: *Some of the village traditions are old as the hills.*
—**old hat** old-fashioned, no longer popular: *His ideas are considered old hat nowadays.*
—**old master** (a work by) any great painter before the 19th century, especially of the 15th and 16th centuries: *The art gallery has had several old masters stolen.*
—**the old-boy network** a system in which jobs and other advantages are obtained on the basis of knowing the right people rather than on ability or worth: *His father got him a job in a bank although he's hopeless with figures. It was obviously a case of the old-boy network.* <The basic connection with such people is often that one was at school with them>.
—**the old country** the country from which an immigrant or his or her parents or grandparents originally came: *The Swedish farmer enjoyed his new life in the USA, but his wife would often think about the old country.*
—**the old guard** the older members of a group who are old-fashioned in their opinions and tastes: *The old guard in the club voted against having women members.* <The translation of the name applied to the most experienced section of Napoleon's army>.

olive
—**olive branch** a sign of a wish for peace: *He had a bitter quarrel with his wife then sent her a huge bouquet of flowers as an olive branch.* <The olive branch was an ancient symbol of peace>.

on
—**be on to (someone)** having discovered some previously secret or unknown information about (someone) or his or her activities: *The police are on to his drug-dealing.*
—**be on for (something)** to be ready to take part in (something): *Are you on for a row on the river?*
—**on and off** *see* **off**.

once
—**give (someone) the once-over** to look at or study (someone or something) quickly: *I know that you're in a hurry but would you give this report the once-over?*
—**once and for all** *or* **once for all** now and for the last time, finally: *Once and for all I am telling you to go.*
—**once and again** repeatedly, often: *I have told you once and again that you must not smoke in this room.*
—**once in a blue moon** *see* **blue**.
—**you're only young once** *see* **young**.

one
—**a one-horse race** a competition, contest, etc, in which one person or side is certain to win: *There was no point in advertising the manager's job. It's a one-horse race because his assistant is bound to get it.*
—**a one-night stand** a relationship, arrange-

ment, etc, that lasts for one evening or night only: *She should be careful. One-night stands can be dangerous.* <Literally a single performance in one place given by a pop group, etc, on tour>.

—**a quick one** *see* **quick**.

—**be at one with (someone)** to be in agreement with (someone): *I am at one with her on the subject of childcare.*

—**be one in the eye for (someone)** *see* **eye**.

—**be one too many for (someone)** to be more powerful or cunning than (someone): *The interviewer and the opposition politician were one too many for the minister.*

—**be one up on (someone)** to have an advantage over (someone): *They've both applied for the post but with his qualifications he's one up on his rival.*

—**have a one-track mind** to think only of one subject all the time: *She has a one-track mind. She can't stop thinking about getting married.*

—**just one of those things** *see* **thing**.

—**not be oneself** to be feeling slightly unwell, to be more depressed, etc, than usual: *She's not been herself since the death of her husband.*

—**number one** *see* **number**.

—**one for the road** *see* **road**.

—**one in a million** *see* **million**.

—**one of these days** soon, shortly: *There will be a general election one of these days.*

—**one way and another** *see* **way**.

—**the one that got away** *see* **away**.

onion

—**know one's onions** to know a subject, one's job, etc: *He'll be able to fix the computer. He really knows his onions.*

open

—**an open book** *see* **book**.

—**an open-and-shut case** free from uncertainty, having an obvious outcome: *The trial will not take long. It's an open-and-shut case.*

—**an open secret** a supposed secret that is known to many people: *It's an open secret that he's having an affair with his friend's wife while the friend is working abroad.*

—**be open as the day** to be utterly without deception or hypocrisy: *Open as the day, he made no secret of the fact that he was alone in the world.*

—**keep an open mind** to be willing to listen to other people's suggestions, ideas, etc, instead of just concentrating on one's own point of view: *The members of the jury should keep an open mind until all the evidence has been heard.*

—**keep open house** *see* **house**.

—**keep one's options open** *see* **option**.

—**lay oneself (wide) open to (something)** to put oneself in a position in which one is liable to be in receipt of (blame, criticism, accusations, attack, etc): *If you go out to dinner with one of the job applicants you'll be laying yourself open to charges of bribery.*

—**with one's eyes open** *see* **eye**.

—**with open arms** *see* **arm**.

opposite

—**(someone's) opposite number** the person in another company, country, etc, whose job or role corresponds to someone's: *The Chancellor of the Exchequer met with his opposite numbers in the EEC countries.*

option

—**keep one's options open** to delay making a definite decision so that all choices are available as long as possible: *Try to avoid replying to the job offer until you hear about the others. It is as well to keep your options open.*

—**soft option** *see* **soft**.

oracle

—**work the oracle** to produce the desired result, to obtain what one wants, especially by using cunning, influence or bribery: *We couldn't get tickets but her uncle's the theatre manager so she phoned him and that worked the oracle.* <Refers to the oracle at Delphi that foretold the future in Greek legend>.

order

—**a tall order** *see* **tall**.

—**call (someone or something) to order**: to restore calm to: *He kept on interrupting the meeting so the chairman had to call him to order.*

—**get one's marching orders** *see* **march**.

—**in apple-pie order** *see* **apple**.

—**just what the doctor ordered** *see* **doctor**.

—**out of order** (1) not working properly: *The coffee machine is out of order.* (2) not according to the conventions or rules of meetings, etc: *The chairman should have ruled his interruption out of order.*

—**take orders** to become a member of the clergy: *Although he never could be persuaded to take orders, theology was his favourite subject.*

—**the order of the day** something that should be done, worn, etc, because conventional, common, fashionable, etc: *Hats will be the order of the day at the royal garden party.*

—**the orders of the day** the list of business to be conducted on a particular day by an organization, especially Parliament: *The Speaker announced the orders of the day.*

other

—**look the other way** to ignore or disregard something wrong, illegal, etc: *The local policeman would look the other way when the village pub was open after hours.*

—**or other** not known or decided: *Someone or other will have to go.*

—**pass by on the other side** *see* **pass**.

out

—**be** *or* **go out of one's mind** *see* **mind**.

—**be well out of (something)** *see* **well**.

—**be out of place** to be unsuitable or improper: *Smoking in church is out of place.*

—**come out** to make public the fact that one is a homosexual: *He came out when they began living together.*

—**have it out with (someone)** *see* **have**.

—**out and about** going around outside, e.g. after an illness: *He was confined to bed for weeks but he's out and about now.*

—**out-and-out** thoroughgoing, complete: *It's an out-and-out scandal—he's left his wife for another woman.*

—**out at elbow** *see* **elbow**.

—**out for (something)** wanting and trying to get (something): *She's only out for a good time.*

—**out of hand** *see* **hand**.

—**out of order** *see* **order**.

—**out of pocket** *see* **pocket**.

—**out of sight, out of mind** *see* **sight**.

—**out of sorts** *see* **sort**.

—**out of turn** *see* **turn**.

—**out on a limb** *see* **limb**.

—**out to (do something)** determined to (do something): *She's out to cause trouble.*

—**take it out on (someone)** *see* **take**.

outside

—**at the outsid**e at the most: *The drive will take an hour at the outside.*

over

—**be all over (someone)** to be extremely friendly and attentive to (someone): *She was all over him as soon as she discovered he had money.*

—**over and above** in addition, besides, extra: *He earns a commission over and above his salary.*

—**over and done with** completely finished, at an end: *They once went out with each other but that's over and done with.*

—**over my dead body** *see* **dead**.

—**over the hill** *see* **hill**.

—**over the odds** *see* **odd**.

—**over the top** *see* **top**.

overboard

—**go overboard (about** *or* **for someone** *or* **something)** to be extremely enthusiastic about (someone or something): *All the men have gone overboard for the new girl in the office.*

own

—**be one's own man** *see* **man**.

—**come into one's own** to have the opportunity to show one's good qualities, talent, skill, etc: *She is a marvellous hostess and really comes into her own at dinner parties.*

—**do one's (own) thing** *see* **thing**.

—**get one's own back** *see* **back**.

—**hold one's own** (1) to perform as well as one's opponents in a contest, an argument, etc: *The younger team held their own against the much more experienced side.* (2) to be surviving, to be holding on to life: *The accident is very bad but he is holding his own.*

—**in one's own right** *see* **right**.

P

p

—**mind one's p's and q's** to be very careful, to be polite and well-behaved: *You'll have to mind your p's and q's when you meet your girlfriend's mother for the first time.* <Perhaps refers to a warning to a printer to be careful of the letters p and q so as not to confuse them>.

pace

—**keep pace with (someone** *or* **something)** to progress or develop at the same rate as (a person, subject or situation) with regard to social or financial standing, knowledge, etc: *Their salaries have not kept pace with those of workers in comparable industries.* <Literally refers to going as fast as someone else in a race>.

—**put (someone** *or* **something) through its** *or* **his** *or* **her paces** to test the ability of (someone or something) by getting them to demonstrate what it, he or she is capable of: *He wants to see the car put through his paces before he buys it.* <Refers originally to assessing how a horse walks, ambles, trots, canters and gallops>.

—**set the pace for** to establish the rate at which, or the manner in which, an activity is carried out: *Their research team has made such rapid progress with cancer drugs that they have set the pace for the other teams.* <Refers originally to horse-racing>.

—**show one's paces** to demonstrate one's abilities: *The sales manager went round with all the salesmen to watch them show their paces with the customers.*

—**stay the pace** to maintain progress in an activity at the same rate as others: *Small electronic firms find it difficult to stay the pace in these days of rapid technological change.*

pack

—**no names, no pack-drill** *see* **name**.

—**packed like herring in a barrel** *see* **herring**.

—**packed like sardines** *see* **sardine**.

—**pack it in** to stop doing something, e.g. working at something: *I've nearly finished this project so I think I'll pack it in for tonight.*

—**send (someone) packing** to send (someone) away firmly and frankly: *She always sends door-to-door salesmen packing immediately.*

paddle

—**paddle one's own canoe** *see* **canoe**.

pain

—**a pain in the neck** someone or something that constantly irritates one: *I work with a real pain in the neck who's always complaining.*

—**be at** *or* **take pains** to take trouble, to be careful: *He is at at pains to be on good terms with his mother-in-law.*

—**for one's pains** as reward for one's trouble and effort: *She nursed the old man for years and got nothing for her pains when he died.*

—**on pain of (something)** at the risk of (some kind of punishment, etc): *The workers were told on pain of instant dismissal not to talk to the rival company about the new product.*

paint

—**paint the town red** to go out and celebrate in a lively, noisy manner: *As soon as they finished their exams the students went out to paint the town red.*

pair

—**pair** *or* **pair off** (1) of a member of Parliament, to abstain from voting having made an arrangement with a member of the opposite side that he or she will also abstain: *The members for Kensington and Cardiff have paired for the vote.* (2) to take as a partner: *He paired off for the dance with the most attractive girl in the room.*

pale

—**beyond the pale** *see* **beyond**.

palm[1]

—**grease (someone's) palm** to give (someone) money, to bribe (someone): *We had to grease the hotel owner's palm to get our passports back.*

—**have an itching palm** *see* **itch**.

—**have (someone) in the palm of one's hand** to have (someone) in one's power and ready to do as one wishes: *The landowner has the local officials in the palm of his hand.*

palm[2]

—**bear the palm** to be pre-eminent: *The promising young athlete bore the palm at the Olympic Games when he won the 100 metres.* <Like the laurel, the leaves of the palm tree were used

as symbols of victory, and a palm leaf or branch was carried before a conqueror>.

—**give the palm to (someone)** to acknowledge (someone) as superior: *The retiring footballer gave the palm to the young player.*

pan

—**a flash in the pan** *see* **flash**.

—**out of the frying pan into the fire** *see* **fry**.

Pandora

—**Pandora's box** a collection of evils: *Pandora's box was opened for him, and all the pains and griefs his imagination had ever figured were abroad.* <Refers to the Greek legend of Prometheus in which Pandora, the all-gifted goddess, is said to have brought from heaven a box containing all human ills, which, the lid having been opened, escaped and spread over the world>.

pants

—**catch (someone) with his** *or* **her pants** *or* **trousers down** *see* **catch**.

paper

—**paper over the cracks** to try to hide faults, mistakes, difficulties, etc, in a hasty or careless way in order to pretend that there were no faults, mistakes, etc: *The couple tried to paper over the cracks in their marriage and always appeared very loving in public but they divorced soon after.*

—**paper tiger** someone or something that has the outward appearance of being powerful and threatening but is in fact ineffective: *The president of the country used to be feared by everyone but ever since the attempted coup he's been a paper tiger.*

—**paper war** a dispute carried on in writing: *The two columnists carried on a paper war in their respective newspapers.*

par

—**below** *or* **not up to par** (1) not up to the usual or required standard: *Her work has been below par recently.* (2) not completely well: *He's been feeling below par since he had the flu.*

—**on a par with (something)** of the same standard as (something), as good as (something): *His painting is not on a par with that of his contemporaries.*

—**par for the course** what might be expected, what usually happens: *He came late to the party but that's par for the course.* <Originally a golfing term meaning the number of strokes that would be made in a perfect round on the course>.

paradise

—**a fool's paradise** *see* **fool**.

parrot

—**parrot-fashion** repeating words or ideas without understanding what they mean: *The student learns her notes parrot-fashion but can't apply them when writing essays.*

—**sick as a parrot** *see* **sick**.

part

—**for my, etc, part** as far as I, etc, am concerned: *For my part I prefer autumn to spring.*

—**look the part** to have the appropriate appearance of a particular kind of person: *If she wants to be a top executive, she must look the part.*

—**(someone) of parts** an able person: *The position as head of the arts organization requires and man or woman of parts and experience.*

—**part and parcel (of something)** something that is naturally or basically part (of something): *Stress is part and parcel of a senior job.*

—**take (something) in good part** to accept (something) without being angry or offended: *She took the other children's teasing in good part.*

—**take (someone's) part** to support (someone) in an argument, etc: *She always takes her brother's part when he quarrels with their sister.*

—**the parting of the ways** the point at which people must go different ways, take different courses of action, make different decisions, etc: *The sale of their company was the parting of the ways for the two business partners.* <A biblical reference to Ezekiel 21:21>.

party

—**(someone's) party piece** an act, joke, speech that someone frequently performs in public: *The managing director always gives the same welcoming speech to new employees. It's his party piece.*

—**the life and soul of the party** *see* **life**.

—**the party line** the official opinions, ideas, attitudes, etc, as set down by the leaders of a particular group: *The politician refused to follow the party line.*

—**the party's over** a pleasant or happy time has come to an end: *This used to be a pleasant department but the party's over now. The new manager is very strict and gloomy.*

pass

—**come to a pretty pass** *see* **pretty**.

—**let (something) pass** to choose to disregard (something): *He was very rude to me but I let it pass. I could see he was upset.*

—**make a pass at (someone)** to try to start a romantic or sexual relationship with (someone): *He made a pass at the girl at the next table.* <Originally a fencing term, meaning to thrust with a foil>.

—**pass away** to die: *The old lady passed away in the night.*

—**pass by on the other side** to ignore someone in trouble and not help him or her: *When he was made homeless he did not expect his friends to pass by on the other side.* <A biblical reference to the parable of the Samaritan—Luke 10>.

—**pass for (someone** *or* **something)** to be mistaken for (someone or something): *She could easily pass for her sister.*

—**pass out** to faint: *She passed out in the extreme heat.*

—**pass the hat round** *see* **hat**.

—**pass (something) up** not to accept (something): *I'm going to have to pass up her invitation. I have another engagement.*

—**ships that pass in the night** *see* **ship**.

passage

—**passage of arms** a dispute, a quarrel, real or playful: *It seemed as if the two women could not meet without a passage of arms.*

—**rite of passage** *see* **rite**.

passing

—**passing rich** very wealthy: *As Alexander Pope wrote, "A man he was to all the country dear / And passing rich on forty pounds a year."* <Passing is frequently used as an intensifier by Shakespeare>.

past

—**I, etc, would not put it past (someone) to (do something)** I, etc, think (someone) is quite capable of (doing something bad): *I wouldn't put it past him to steal money from an old woman.*

—**past one's** *or* **its best** *or* **past it** less good, etc, than when one or it was not so old: *The runner is still fast but he's past his best.*

—**past master** someone extremely talented or skilful: *He is a past master at the art of charming women.*

pat

—**a pat on the back** an indication of praise or approval: *She got a pat on the back for her handling of the difficult customer.*

patch

—**hit a bad patch** *see* **bad**.

—**not to be a patch on (someone** *or* **something)** not to be nearly as good as (someone or something): *Her cooking isn't a patch on his.*

—**patch it** *or* **things up** to become friends again after a quarrel: *The two sisters haven't spoken to each other for years but we're trying to get them to patch things up.*

path

—**beat a path to (someone's) door** to visit (someone) very frequently or in large numbers: *The world's press beat a path to the door of the new tennis champion.*

patience

—**enough to try the patience of Job** *see* **Job**.

pave

—**pave the way for (something)** to make it possible or easier for (something to happen): *The student's research paved the way for the development of the new drug.*

pay

—**pay (someone) back in his** *or* **her own coin** *see* **coin**.

—**pay court to (someone)** *see* **court**.

—**pay lip-service to (something)** *see* **lip**.

—**pay one's way** to pay one's own expenses without going into debt, to meet one's obligations, to live free of debt: *He did not have a credit card as he wanted to be able to pay his way.*

—**pay the piper** *see* **piper**.

—**pay through the nose** *see* **nose**.

—**put paid to (something)** to prevent (an action, plan, etc) from being carried out: *She was planning to come uninvited to our party but we put paid to that by changing the date.*

—**rob Peter to pay Paul** *see* **rob**.

—**there will be the devil to pay** *see* **devil**.

pea

—**like as two peas in a pod** exactly or extremely alike: *The twins are like as two peas in a pod.*

peace

—**keep the peace** to prevent disturbances, fighting, quarrelling, etc: *The police were on duty at the football match to keep the peace.*

—**make one's peace with (someone)** to become, or try to become, friendly with (someone) again after a period of disagreement: *She made peace with her family before she died.*

peacock

—**proud as a peacock** extremely proud: *He's proud as a peacock of his baby son.*

pearl

—**cast pearls before swine** *see* **cast**.

peck

—**keep one's pecker up** to remain in good spirits: *Keep your pecker up. You'll get a job soon.* <Pecker means beak or nose>.

pedestal
—**put (someone) on a pedestal** to treat (someone) with great respect and admiration: *She put her music teacher on a pedestal.* <Refers to the practice of putting statues of famous people on pedestals>.

peep
—**a peeping Tom** *see* **Tom**.

peg
—**bring (someone) down a peg or two** to make (someone) more humble: *He was boasting about his wealth but she took him down a peg or two by reminding of his poverty-stricken youth.* <Refers to the tuning of musical instruments by adjusting pegs>.
—**off the peg** of clothes, ready to wear, not made for one specially: *He's so tall it is difficult for him to buy clothes off the peg.*

penny
—**a penny for them** *or* **your thoughts** what are you thinking of?: *You were lost in thought. A penny for them.*
—**cost a pretty penny** *see* **pretty**.
—**in for a penny, in for a pound** if one is going to do something one might as well do it boldly and thoroughly: *We've very little money but if we're going on holiday we might as well go somewhere exciting. In for a penny, in for a pound.*
—**in penny numbers** a very few, a very little at a time: *They came to the jumble sale in penny numbers.* <Refers to a method of selling encyclopedias, etc, in parts, originally at a penny per part>.
—**not to have a penny to one's name** to have no money at all: *When he died he didn't have a penny to his name.*
—**penny wise and pound foolish** being careful with small items of expenditure and extravagant with large ones: *She always buys the cheapest food and then goes on world cruises. She really is penny wise and pound foolish.*
—**spend a penny** to urinate: *Their little girl wants to spend a penny.* <From the former price of admission to the cubicle of a public toilet>.
—**the penny drops** I, etc, suddenly understand: *At first she didn't know what he was talking about but then the penny dropped.* <Refers to a coin in a slot machine>.
—**turn up like a bad penny** to reappear or keep reappearing although not wanted or welcome: *Her son turned up like a bad penny to borrow money from her.*
—**two a penny** of little value because very common: *China bowls like that are two a penny. There's no point in selling it.*

perfect
—**the pink of perfection** *see* **pink**.

period
—**period piece** something or someone that is exceptionally typical of the time when he or she was born or it was made: *She has a houseful of Victorian furniture—all period pieces.*

person
—**in person** not through a deputy, with bodily presence: *Her curt reply on the phone brought him in person to her apartment.*

petard
—**hoist with one's own petard** to be the victim of one's own action which was intended to harm someone else: *My neighbour was hoist with his own petard. He put broken glass on the top of his wall to prevent trespassers and then cut his hand on it.* <Refers to Shakespeare's *Hamlet*, Act 3, scene iv. A petard was a kind of bomb used by military engineers>.

petrel
—**a stormy petrel** *see* **storm**.

petticoat
—**in petticoats** still a child, still in the nursery: *I was earning my own living while you were still in petticoats.*
—**petticoat government** the rule of women: *The friendship of Queen Anne and the Duchess of Marlborough constituted a kind of petticoat government.*

philistine
—someone who is not interested in artistic or intellectual pursuits: *Don't ask her to go to the opera. She's a real Philistine.* <The Philistines were a fierce race of people who fought against the Israelites in biblical times. The present meaning was influenced by German>.

phoenix
—**rise like a phoenix from the ashes** *same as* **rise from the ashes**—*see* **ashes**.

pick
—**have a bone to pick with (someone)** *see* **bone**.
—**pick and choose** to choose very carefully from a range of things: *Surely there are enough dresses here for you to pick and choose from.*
—**pick (someone's) brains** *see* **brain**.
—**pick holes in (something)** *see* **hole**.
—**pick up the tab (for something)** *see* **tab**.

picture
—**put (someone) in the picture** to give (some-

one) all the information and detail about a situation: *Could you put me in the picture about what happened while I was on holiday.*

pie

—**have a finger in every pie** *see* **finger**.

—**have a finger in the pie** *see* **finger**.

—**pie in the sky** something good expected or promised in the future which is unlikely to come about: *He is planning a trip round the world but it's pie in the sky. He'll never save that much money.* <Refers to a quotation from a poem by the American poet Joe Hill>.

piece

—**a nasty piece of work** *see* **nasty**.

—**a piece of cake** *see* **cake**.

—**give (someone) a piece of one's mind** *see* **mind**.

—**go to pieces** to be unable to continue coping with a situation, life, etc: *She goes to pieces in an emergency.*

—**nasty piece of work** *see* **nasty**.

pig

—**buy a pig in a poke** to buy (something) without examining it carefully or without knowing its worth: *The second-hand washing machine she bought doesn't work. She bought a pig in a poke.* <Supposedly referring to a fairground trick in which a prospective customer was sold a cat in a bag thinking that it was a piglet>.

—**make a pig of oneself** to eat greedily, to eat a great deal. *The food was so good that we all made pigs of ourselves.*

—**make a pig's ear of (something)** to make a mess of (something) to do (something) very badly or clumsily: *She made a real pig's ear of knitting a sweater.*

—**pigs might fly** it is extremely unlikely that that will happen: *You think he'll marry her? Pigs might fly.*

pigeon

—**put** *or* **set the cat among the pigeons** *see* **cat**.

—**that's not my pigeon** that is not my responsibility or area of interest: *The accounts are not in order but that's not my pigeon. We have an accountant.* <Originally "not my pidgin" with its origins in pidgin English>.

pikestaff

—**plain as a pikestaff** very obvious: *The motive for his crime is plain as pikestaff.* <Pikestaff was originally packstaff, a staff for holding a traveller's pack and lacking any ornamentation. This sense of plain has been confused with that of plain meaning clear>.

pill

—**sugar the pill** *see* **sugar**.

pillar

—**from pillar to post** from one place to another, often repeatedly: *The authorities sent us from pillar to post in search of a visa.* <Refers originally to the game of real tennis>.

pin

—**for two pins** given the least encouragement or reason: *For two pins I'd take the day off.*

—**on pins and needles** in a state of anxiety or suspense: *We're on pins and needles waiting to find out who's won.*

—**pin back one's ears** *see* **ear**.

—**pin one's hopes on (someone** *or* **something)** *see* **hope**.

—**you could have heard a pin drop** there was silence: *You could have heard a pin drop after she made the accusation.*

pinch

—**at a pinch** if it is absolutely necessary: *At a pinch we could accommodate three of you.*

—**feel the pinch** to have financial problems: *We were all right last year but the firm is feeling the pinch this year.*

—**take (something) with a grain** *or* **pinch of salt** *see* **salt**..

pink

—**be tickled pink** *see* **tickle**.

—**in the pink** in good health: *The family have all been ill but we're in the pink now.* <Refers to the pink complexion of some healthy people>.

—**the pink of perfection** absolute perfection: *If her cakes are not in the pink of perfection she throws them out.* <Refers to a quotation from Oliver Goldsmith's play, *She Stoops to Conquer*>.

pip

—**pipped at the post** beaten at the last minute: *I thought we would get the house for the price we offered but we were pipped at the post by someone who suddenly offered more.* <Refers originally to horse-racing. A horse is pipped at the post if another horse passes it at the end of the race>.

pipe

—**put that in your pipe and smoke it!** listen to that remark and think it over: *Always allow time for traffic delays if you want to arrive in time—put that in your pipe and smoke it!* <Generally accompanies a rebuke>.

—**pipe dream** a wish or idea that can never be

realized: *She talks of buying a cottage in the country but it's a pipe dream. She has very little money.* <Refers to visions experienced by opium smokers>.

pipeline

—**in the pipeline** in preparation, happening soon: *There are some new jobs in the pipeline but appointments will not be made until next year.* <Refers to crude oil being piped from the well to the refineries>.

piper

—**pay the piper** to provide the money for something and therefore be entitled to have a say in the organization of it: *Father should be allowed a say in where we go on holiday. After all he's paying the piper.* <Refers to the saying "He who pays the piper calls the tune">.

—**piping hot** *see* **hot**.

—**put that in your pipe and smoke it!** See how you like that!: *I know you think you're better at French than I am, but I've just heard that I passed the exam and you failed. Put that in your pipe and smoke it!*

pistol

—**hold a pistol to (someone's) head** to use force or threats to get (someone) to do as one wishes: *He had to sell the firm to get some money. The bank was holding a pistol to his head.*

pitch

—**black as pitch** extremely black: *The night was black as pitch.*

—**queer (someone's) pitch** *see* **queer**.

place

—**fall into place** to become understood when seen in terms of its relationship to other things: *The reason for her fear of men fell into place when we realized that she had been abused by her father as a child.*

—**go places** to be successful in one's career: *That young research worker is going places.*

—**in the first place** (1) in the beginning, to start with: *I regret going. I didn't want to go in the first place.* (2) as the first point in an argument, etc: *We can't cope with so many people. In the first place we have not got enough food.*

—**know one's place** to accept the lowliness of one's position and act accordingly: *It was made clear to the trainee teacher that she should know her place in the staff-room.*

—**out of place** *see* **out**.

—**pride of place** *see* **pride**.

—**put oneself in (someone's) place** to imagine what it would be like to be in (someone else's) circumstances: *I know you don't approve of strikes but put yourself in the workers' place. What else could they do?*

—**put (someone) in his** *or* **her place** to remind (someone) angrily of the lowliness of his or her position or of his or her lack of experience, knowledge, etc: *He tried to take over the running of the meeting but the chairman soon put him in his place.*

plain

—**plain as a pikestaff** *see* **pikestaff**.

—**plain sailing** easy progress: *Making alterations to the building will be plain sailing if we get planning permission.* <Perhaps confused with plane sailing, a method of making navigational calculations at sea in which the earth's surface is treated as though it were flat>.

plate

—**have (something) handed to one on a plate** to get (something) without having to put any effort into it: *Her schoolfriend works at weekends to buy clothes but she has a clothes allowance from her father. She has everything handed to her on a plate.*

play

—**all work and no play makes Jack a dull boy** *see* **work**.

—**bring into play** to begin to use or employ: *He had to bring all his powers of persuasion into play to get her to go.*

—**child's play** *see* **child**.

—**fair play** *see* **fair**.

—**make a play for (someone** *or* **something)** to try to obtain (someone or something): *He's making a play for his friend's job.*

—**play a losing game** *see* **lose**.

—**play (something) down** to try to make (something) appear less important, grave, etc: *Management are trying to play down the seriousness of the firm's financial position.*

—**played out** (1) exhausted: *The children are played out after the part.* (2) no longer having any interest, influence, usefulness, etc: *His ideas on education are played out.*

—**play fast and loose with (something)** *see* **fast**.

—**play for time** *see* **time**.

—**play gooseberry** *see* **gooseberry**.

—**play hard to get** to make it difficult for someone to get to know one in order to make him or her more keen to do so: *She regretted playing hard to get when he started going out with another girl.*

—**play havoc with (something)** *see* **havoc**.
—**play it by ear** *see* **ear**.
—**play (someone) off against (someone else)** to use two people for one's own purposes, to make two people act upon each other so as to bring about a desired result: *The spoiled child played his father off against his mother so that he was always getting treats.*
—**play possum** *see* **possum**.
—**play second fiddle (to someone)** *see* **fiddle**.
—**play the devil's advocate** *see* **devil**.
—**play the field** *see* **field**.
—**play the game** *see* **game**.
—**play one's trump card** *see* **trump**.
—**play (someone) up** to cause trouble to or annoy (someone): *The children always play their father up when he's looking after them.*
—**play up to (someone)** to flatter (someone) and pay (someone) a great deal of attention for one's own advantage: *She's playing up to her father because she wants him to buy her a new dress.*
—**play with fire** *see* **fire**.

please
—**pleased as Punch** *see* **Punch**.

plot
—**the plot thickens** the situation is getting more complicated and more interesting: *He is having an affair with his secretary and it turns out that his wife is having an affair with her boss. The plot thickens.* <Refers to a quotation from George Villiers' play *The Rehearsal*>.

plough
—**put one's hand to the plough** to begin serious work, to undertake important duties: *The students must put their hands to the plough and begin studying for the examination.*

pocket
—**in (someone's) pocket** under the control or influence of (someone): *The board will vote with the managing director. He has them all in his pocket.*
—**line one's pocket** to make money for oneself dishonestly: *The boss found out that he had been lining his pocket by taking bribes from suppliers.*
—**out of pocket** having made a loss: *Not only did the dance not make a profit but the organizing committee were all out of pocket.*

poetic
—**poetic justice** deserved but accidental punishment or reward: *The burglar left his bag of stolen jewellery on the train. That was poetic justice.*
—**poetic licence** the disregarding of established rules of form, grammar, fact, etc, by writers to achieve a desired effect: *The poet uses no capital letters or punctuation and includes other forms of poetic licence in his works.*

point
—**a sore point** *see* **sore**.
—**beside the point** *see* **beside**.
—**come** *or* **get to the point** to reach the most important part of a discussion, etc: *I wish the lecturer would stop rambling on and get to the point.*
—**make a point of (doing something)** to be exceptionally careful about (doing something): *She makes a point of visiting her elderly parents at least once a week.*
—**make one's point** to state one's opinion clearly: *Now you've made your point please give others the chance to speak.*
—**point the finger at (someone** *or* **something)** *see* **finger**.
—**stretch a point** *see* **stretch**.
—**the point of no return** the stage in a process, etc. when it becomes impossible either to stop or change one's mind: *The divorce papers have been signed. They've reached the point of no return.* <Originally referred to the point in the flight of an aircraft after which it did not have enough fuel to return to its place of departure>.
—**up to a point** to some extent but not completely: *I agree with your views up to a point but I do have reservations.*

poison
—**poison-pen letter** an anonymous letter saying bad things about someone: *She received a poison-pen letter saying her husband was an adulterer.*

pole
—**be poles apart** *see* **apart**.

pony
—**on shanks's pony** *see* **shanks**.

pop
—**pop the question** *see* **question**.

port
—**any port in a storm** any solution to a problem or difficulty will suffice. *I don't like asking my parents for a loan but my rent is overdue. It's a case of any port in a storm.*

possum
—**play possum** to pretend to be asleep, unconscious or dead: *He played possum when the children crept into his bedroom. He was too tired to play with them.* <The possum pretends to be

dead when it is under threat of attack from another animal>.

post[1]

—**deaf as a post** *see* **deaf**.

—**from pillar to post** from one place to another, often repeatedly: *The authorities chased us from pillar to post trying to get a visa.*

—**pipped at the post** *see* **pip**.

post[2]

—**keep (someone) posted** to keep (someone) informed about developments in a situation: *The boss wants to be kept posted about the export deal although he's on holiday.*

pot

—**go to pot** to get into a bad or worse state: *The firm went to pot when the old man died.* <Refers to meat being cut up and stewed in a pot).

—**take pot-luck** to have a meal at someone's house, etc, without having anything specially prepared for one: *You're welcome to stay to dinner but you'll have to take pot-luck.* <Literally to take whatever happens to be in the cooking-pot at the time>.

—**the pot calling the kettle black** someone criticizing (someone) for doing (something) that he or she does himself or herself: *His father scolded him for being untidy although he himself leaves things lying around—a case of the pot calling the kettle black.*

—**the** *or* **a watched pot never boils** when one is waiting for something to happen, etc, the time taken seems longer if one is constantly thinking about it. *Stop thinking about the letter with the exam results. It won't make the postman arrive any sooner. A watched pot never boils.*

potato

—**hot potato** *see* **hot**.

pound

—**get** *or* **have one's pound of flesh** *see* **flesh**.

pour

—**it never rains but it pours** when something goes wrong it goes wrong very badly or other things go wrong too: *I forgot where I parked the car and then I got a parking ticket. It never rains but it pours.*

—**pour oil on troubled waters** *see* **oil**.

power

—**more power to (someone's) elbow** may (someone) be successful: *I hear that he's started a charity for handicapped children. More power to his elbow.*

—**the power behind the throne** the person who is really in charge of or in control of an organization, etc, while giving the impression that it is someone else: *He is the chairman of the company, but his wife is the power behind the throne.*

—**the powers that be** the people in charge, the authorities: *The powers that be have decided that the shop assistants should wear a uniform.*

practice

—**practice makes perfect** if one practises doing something one will eventually be good at it: *They say that practice makes perfect, but I'll never be good at sewing.*

—**sharp practice** *see* **sharp**.

practise

—**practise what one preaches** to act in the way that one recommends to others: *He tells the children to come home on time but he's always late himself. He should practise what he preaches.*

praise

—**praise (someone** *or* **something) to the skies** *see* **sky**.

—**sing (someone's** *or* **something's) praises** to praise (someone or something) with great enthusiasm: *She keeps singing the praises of her new washing machine.*

preach

—**preach to the converted** *see* **convert**.

—**practise what he preaches** *see* **practise**.

premium

—**be at a premium** to be much in demand and, therefore, difficult to obtain: *Tickets for the pop concert are at a premium. The group is very popular.* <A financial term meaning literally "sold at more than the nominal value">.

presence

—**presence of mind** the ability to keep calm and think and act sensibly whatever the situation: *She had the presence of mind to throw a wet cloth over the pan when it caught fire.*

present

—**there's no time like the present** *see* **time**.

press

—**be pressed for (something)** to be short of (something, such as time or money): *I'm really pressed for time.*

—**press-gang (someone) into (doing something)** to force (someone) or persuade (someone) against his or her will to (do something): *She's pressganged us into being in charge of a stall at the fête.* <The press gang was a group of sailors in the 18th century who seized men and forced them to join the navy>.

—**press (someone** *or* **something) into service** to

make use of (someone or something), especially in an emergency or on a special occasion: *My vacuum cleaner has broken down and so I'll have to press the old one into service.*

pressure

—**pressure group** a group of people who try to bring the attention of the authorities, etc, to certain issues, usually with a view to influencing them into making some changes: *She's part of a pressure group that is campaigning for more state nursery schools.*

pretence

—**under false pretences** *see* **false**.

pretty

—**a pretty kettle of fish** *see* **kettle**.

—**come to a pretty pass** to get into a bad state: *Things have come to a pretty pass if the firm is making people redundant.*

—**cost a pretty penny** to cost a large amount of money: *His new car must have cost a pretty penny.*

—**sitting pretty** in a very comfortable or advantageous position: *She's the boss's daughter. She's sitting pretty while the rest of us are worried about our jobs.*

prey

—**be a prey to (something)** regularly to suffer from (something): *She has been a prey to headaches all her life.*

—**prey on (someone's) mind** to cause constant worry or anxiety to (someone): *The accident in which he knocked over a child preyed on his mind all his life.*

price

—**at a price** at a very high price: *You can get a drink in the hotel—at a price!*

—**a price on (someone's) head** a reward offered for the capture or killing of (someone): *The escaped convict was never found even though there was a price on his head.*

—**what price (something)?** what do you think of (something)?, what is the value of (something)?: *He's been charged with drink driving. What price his lectures on the dangers of alcohol abuse now?*

prick

—**kick against the pricks** to show opposition to those in control or power: *The ordinary people will start kicking against the pricks if the government raise interest rates again.* <From cattle kicking against being driven forward by a sharp stick>.

—**prick up one's ears** *see* **ear**.

pride

—**pride goes before a fall** being too conceited often leads to misfortune: *The player who was boasting about how good she was got beaten. It just proves that pride goes before a fall.*

—**pride of place** the most important or privileged position: *Her son's photograph has pride of place on her mantelpiece.*

—**swallow one's pride** to behave in a more humble way than one usually does or than one would wish to do: *She had no money for food and so she swallowed her pride and asked her father for some.*

prime

—**be cut off in one's prime** to die or be killed in one's youth or at the most successful period in one's life: *They mourned for the soldiers cut off in their prime.*

—**prime mover** someone or something that gets something started: *She was the prime mover in the campaign against the new motorway.*

print

—**the small print** *see* **small**.

private

—**private eye** a private detective: *He hired a private eye to discover the identity of his wife's lover.*

pro

—**the pros and cons** the arguments for and against: *The council will consider the pros and cons of the new road tomorrow.* <Latin *pro*, for, and *contra*, against>.

profile

—**keep a low profile** *see* **low**.

proof

—**the proof of the pudding is in the eating** the real worth of something is found only when it has been into practice or use: *The government's theories on education are all very well, but the proof of the pudding will be in the eating.*

proportion

—**sense of proportion** the ability to decide what is important, etc, and what is not: *She has no sense of proportion. She went into hysterics just because she got a small stain on her dress.*

proud

—**do (someone) proud** to treat (someone) exceptionally well or lavishly: *I must say they did the old age pensioners proud at their Christmas party.*

public

—**public spirit** a wish to do things for the good of the community as a whole: *He's full of public spirit. He even picks up the litter in the park.*

pull

—**pull a face** *see* **face**.

—**pull a fast one on (someone)** *see* **fast**.

—**pull (something) off** to be successful in (something): *We were all surprised when he pulled off a victory against the golf champion.*

—**pull one's punches** *see* **punch**.

—**pull one's socks up** *see* **sock**.

—**pull one's weight** *see* **weight**.

—**pull out all the stops** *see* **stop**.

—**pull strings** *see* **string**.

—**pull through** to survive, to get better: *We thought that he was going to die after the operation but he pulled through.*

pulse

—**keep one's finger on the pulse** to keep oneself informed about recent developments in a situation, organization, etc, or in the world: *The old man has retired but still keeps his finger on the pulse by reading all the company reports.* <Refers to a doctor checking the rate of someone's pulse for health reasons>.

Punch

—**pleased as Punch** extremely pleased or happy: *The little girl was pleased as Punch with her new dress.* <Refers to the puppet show character who is usually portrayed smiling gleefully>.

punch

—**pull one's punches** to be less forceful or harsh in one's attack or criticism than one is capable of: *The manager rarely pulls his punches when he is criticizing someone's work.* <Refers to striking blows in boxing without using one's full strength>.

pup

—**sell (someone) a pup** to deceive (someone), often to sell or recommend something that turns out not to be as good as he or she thought: *That computer keeps breaking down. I think we've been sold a pup.*

pure

—**pure as the driven snow** exceptionally virtuous or moral: *She was pure as the driven snow but her sister was wild.* <Refers to snow that has been blown into heaps by the wind and has not yet become dirty>.

purpose

—**at cross purposes** involved in a misunderstanding because of talking or thinking about different things without realizing it: *No wonder I couldn't understand what she was talking about. We were talking at cross purposes.*

—**serve a** *or* **the purpose** to be useful in a particular situation, to fulfil a need: *I really need a lever for this but a knife will serve the purpose.*

purse

—**you can't make a silk purse out of a sow's ear** *see* **silk**.

push

—**push one's luck** *see* **luck**.

—**push off** to go away: *It's getting late. I'd better push off.*

put

—**be put upon** to be made use of for someone else's benefit, to be taken advantage of: *Her mother's really put upon by her daughter. She expects her to baby-sit every night.*

—**put a brave face on it** *see* **face**.

—**put (someone) in mind of (someone** *or* **something)** *see* **mind**.

—**put (someone) in his** *or* **her place** *see* **place**.

—**put (someone) in the picture** *see* **picture**.

—**put it on** to feign, to pretend: *She said that she had sprained her ankle but she was putting it on.*

—**put (someone's) nose out of joint** *see* **nose**.

—**put one across (someone)** *see* **across**.

—**put one's finger on (something)** *see* **finger**.

—**put the cat among the pigeons** *see* **cat**.

—**put-up job** something done to deceive or trick (someone): *The police pretended to believe him but it was a put-up job. They were trying to get him to confess.*

pyjamas

—**the cat's pyjamas** *see* **cat**.

putty

—**putty in (someone's) hands** easily influenced or manipulated by (someone): *She'll do whatever he wants. She's putty in his hands.* <Putty is a malleable substance>.

Pyrrhic

—**Pyrrhic victory** a a success of some kind in which what it takes to achieve is not worth it: *She was eventually awarded compensation for unfair dismissal but the money all went in legal costs. It was indeed a Pyrrhic victory.* <From the costly victory of Pyrrhus, king of Epirus, over the Romans at Heraclea in 280 BC>.

Q

q

—**mind one's p's and q's** *see* **p**.

quantity

—**an unknown quantity** someone or something of which very little is known: *One of the players in the tournament is an unknown quantity.* <Refers literally to a mathematical term>.

quarter

—**at close quarters** nearby, at or from a short distance away: *At close quarters she looks older.*

—**give** *or* **show quarter** to act with clemency, to be merciful, to be lenient: *The general ordered that no quarter should be given and that all prisoners should be killed.*

queer

—**a queer fish** *see* **fish**.

—**in Queer Street** in financial difficulties: *If we both lose our jobs we'll be in Queer Street.* <Perhaps changed from Carey Street in London where the bankruptcy courts were>.

—**queer (someone's) pitch** to upset (someone's) plans or arrangements: *He was going to ask her out but his best friend queered his pitch by asking her first.* <Pitch here refers to the site of a market stall. Originally to queer someone's pitch was to set up a stall beside it selling the same kind of goods>.

question

—**a loaded question** *see* **load**.

—**a vexed question** *see* **vex**.

—**beg the question** *see* **beg**.

—**call (something) in question** to express doubts regarding (something), to find fault with (something): *After the bad traffic jam, the police were called in question for their handling of it.*

—**out of the question** not possible: *Further salary increases are out of question.*

—**pop the question** to ask (someone) to marry one: *He popped the question on her birthday.*

—**rhetorical question** *see* **rhetorical**.

—**the burning question** *see* **burn**.

—**the sixty-four (thousand) dollar question** *see* **sixty**.

queue

—**jump the queue** to go ahead of others in a queue without waiting for one's proper turn: *She jumped the queue and went straight up to the shop counter.*

qui

—**on the qui vive** very alert: *The child was on the qui vive and heard her father's car.* <From the challenge of a French sentry *Qui vive?*—"Long live who, whose side are you on?">.

quick

—**a quick one** a quick drink: *The pubs will be closing soon but there's time for a quick one.*

—**cut (someone) to the quick** to hurt (someone's) feelings very badly: *She cut him to the quick when she rejected his present.* <The quick is the sensitive skin under the nail>.

—**quick as lightning** *see* **lightning**.

—**quick on the uptake** *see* **uptake**.

quid

—**quids in** a fortunate position: *If you get a job with that firm you'll be quids in.*

quit

—**call it quits** to agree that neither person owes the other one anything and that neither one has any kind of advantage over the other: *You paid for lunch and I paid for dinner. Let's call it quits.*

quite

—**quite something** something special or remarkable: *Her new hat is quite something.*

R

R

—**the three R's** reading, writing and arithmetic, thought of as the essential basics of education: *The teacher spends much time on the three R's.* <From reading, writing and arithmetic>.

race

—**one-horse race** *see* **one**.

—**the rat race** *see* **rat**.

rack[1]

—**go to rack and ruin** to fall into a state of disrepair or into a worthless condition: *The estate has gone to rack and ruin because the duke has no money.* <"Rack" means destruction>.

rack[2]

—**on the rack** in distress, under strain: *He's on the rack worrying about losing his job.* <The rack was an instrument of torture on which a person's body was stretched in both directions at once>.

—**rack one's brains** *see* **brain**.

racket

—**be on the racket** to spend one's time in idleness and dissipation: *He had been off on the racket for perhaps a week at a time.*

rag

—**like a red rag to a bull** *see* **red**.

—**lose one's rag** to lose one's temper: *The teacher completely lost her rag and shouted at the children.*

—**the ragtag and bobtail** the common people: *The decent citizens did not attend the meeting; only the ragtag and bobtail were present, and their views carry no weight.*

rage

—**all the rage** very fashionable or popular: *Mini skirts were all the rage then.*

rail

—**off the rails** not sensible, disorganized, deranged: *He used to be one of our best workers but he seems to have gone a bit off the rails.* <Refers to a train leaving the track>.

rain

—**it never rains but it pours** a rapid succession of events: *He not only received a legacy from his uncle but also one from his friend—it never rains but it pours.*

—**keep** *or* **put away** *or* **save (something) for a rainy day** to keep (something, especially money) until one really needs it: *The old lady does not have enough food but she insists on keeping a large sum of money for a rainy day.* <Formerly most jobs, such as farm jobs, were dependent on the weather. Since they could not be carried out in rainy weather no money was earned then>.

—**right as rain** perfectly all right, completely well: *She's had flu but she's right as rain now.*

—**rain or shine** whatever the weather: *He plays golf rain or shine.*

—**rain like cats and dogs** *see* **cat**.

raise

—**raise Cain** *see* **Cain**.

—**raise one's back** to grow obstinate, to rebel: *The clergyman raised his back against orders emanating from the bishop's palace.*

—**raise the wind** *see* **wind**.

rake

—**thin as a rake** extremely thin: *She eats huge amounts but stays thin as a rake.*

ram

—**ram (something) down (someone's) throat** *see* **throat**.

rampage

—**be** *or* **go on the rampage** to rush about wildly or violently: *The crowd went on the rampage and some people were trampled to death.*

rank

—**close ranks** to act together and support each other as a defensive measure: *The dead patient's husband tried to enquire into the cause of her death but the doctors closed ranks and would tell him nothing.*

—**the rank and file** the ordinary people or the ordinary members of an organization, etc: *The union leaders should pay attention to the views of the rank and file.* <Literally ranks and files were the horizontal and vertical lines in which battalions of soldiers were drawn up on parade>.

ransom

—**a king's ransom** *see* **king**.

—**hold (someone) to ransom** to demand something (from someone) by threatening to take harmful action if it is not given: *The newspaper said that the firemen were holding the government to ransom by threatening to go on strike.* <Literally to hold someone as a hostage until a sum of money is paid for his or her release>.

rant

—**rant and rave** to shout angrily: *Her father's ranting and raving about how late she came home.*

rap

—**not care a rap** not to care at all about what anybody says: *I shall do as I like—I don't care a rap.*

—**rap over the knuckles** to administer a sharp reproof, to censure sharply: *The children were rapped over the knuckles by the policeman for running out onto the road without looking.*

—**take the rap for (something)** to take the blame or punishment for (something): *He committed the crime but his friend took the rap for it and went to prison.*

rarin'

—**rarin' to go** extremely eager to begin or set off: *I promised to take the children on a picnic and they're rarin' to go.* <Dialect for "rearing">.

rat

—**like a drowned rat** soaking wet: *They came in from the storm like drowned rats.*

—**rat on (someone)** to report or betray (someone): *The head knew that they had played truant because another pupil had ratted on them.*

—**smell a rat** to have a suspicion that something is wrong or that one is being deceived: *I smelt a rat when he did not invite me into the house.* <Refers to a terrier hunting>.

—**the rat race** the fierce competitive struggle for success in business, etc: *He's given up the rat race and gone to live on an island.* <A nautical phrase for a fierce tidal current>.

rate

—**at a rate of knots** *see* **knot**.

raw

—**a raw deal** *see* **deal**.

—**in the raw** in the natural state without civilization, comfort, etc: *He chose life in the raw rather than city life and lives in a hut in the country.*

—**touch (someone) on the raw** to hurt or anger (someone): *You touched him on the raw when you mentioned his children. He's lost contact with them.*

razor

—**sharp as a razor** quick-witted and very intelligent: *The child's sharp as a razor. Watch what you say in front of him.*

read

—**take (something) as read** to assume (something): *You can take it as read that all the candidates are suitably qualified.*

ready

—**ready money** money that can be immediately made use of, money in one's hands, cash: *He couldn't pay the window cleaner as he had no ready money.*

real

—**the real McCoy** something genuine and very good as opposed to others like it which are not: *This lasagne is the real McCoy, not something out of a freezer.* <Perhaps from Kid McCoy, an American boxer who was called The Real McCoy to distinguish him from other boxers of the same name>.

reason

—**it stands to reason that** it is logical, or obvious that: *It stands to reason that she would be in pain. Her leg is broken.*

—**ours, etc, not to reason why** it is not for us, etc, to question orders: *If the boss says to come in half-an-hour early tomorrow we had better do it. Ours not to reason why.*

—**see reason** to be persuaded by someone's advice, etc, to act or think sensibly.

—**within reason** within sensible limits: *You can choose your birthday present—within reason.*

—**without rhyme or reason** *see* **rhyme**.

rebound

—**on the rebound** while suffering from the disappointment of the end of a relationship: *She married him on the rebound from a broken engagement.*

rebuff

—**meet with a rebuff** to encounter opposition: *The poor man met with a rebuff when he asked the millionaire for his daughter's hand. He was refused absolutely.*

reckon

—**reckon on** *or* **upon** to expect: *You reckon on losing your friends' kindness if you impose too much.*

—**reckon without one's host** to calculate blindly, to enter rashly on any undertaking: *We thought our troubles would end after the election but we reckoned without our host.*

record

—**break the record** to do something better, faster, etc, than it has been done before: *The sprinter has broken the world record.*

—**for the record** so that it will be noted: *For the record I do not agree with the committee's decision.*

—**off the record** not to be made public: *Don't say anything off the record to a journalist. He'll just publish it anyhow.*

—**on record** noted officially: *The politician is on record as saying that he won't resign.*

—**set the record straight** to put right a mistake or misunderstanding: *He thought that I had voted against him but I was able to set the record straight.*

—**(someone's) track record** *see* **track**.

red

—**a red herring** *see* **herring**.

—**a red-letter day** a day remembered because something particularly pleasant or important happened or happens on it: *It will be a red-letter day for her when her husband comes home from the war.* <From the fact that important dates in the year are sometimes shown in red on calendars>.

—**catch (someone) red-handed** to find (someone) in the act of doing something wrong or unlawful: *We caught the thief red-handed with the stolen necklace in his hand.* <Refers to finding a murderer with the blood of a victim on his or her hands>.

—**in the red** in debt, overdrawn: *My bank account is in the red but it's nearly pay-day.* <From the use of red ink to make entries on the debit side of an account>.

—**like a red rag to a bull** certain to make (someone) angry: *Any criticism of the government is like a red rag to a bull to the old man.* <From the widespread belief that bulls are angered by the sight of the colour red although they are in fact colour-blind>.

—**on red alert** ready for an an immediate danger: *The area was put on red alert because of the forest fire.* <Originally a military term for mobilizing civilians during an air-raid>.

—**paint the town red** *see* **paint**.

—**red-hot** very enthusiastic or dedicated: *She's a red-hot fan of the group.*

—**red tape** the rules and regulations official papers, etc, that are thought to characterize government departments: *With all the red tape it could take quite a long time to get a visa.* <From the reddish tape used by government offices to tie bundles of papers>.

—**see red** to get very angry: *She saw red when she witnessed him kick the dog.*

—**the red carpet** *see* **carpet**.

reed

—**a broken reed** someone who is too weak or unreliable to be depended upon: *She has to work to support her five children because her husband is a broken reed.*

region

—**in the region of (something)** about, approximately: *The price will be in the region of £60,000.*

rein

—**give free rein to (something)** to allow complete freedom to (one's imagination, emotions, etc) : *She gave free rein to her creative powers in her recent writings.* <Refers to a horse that is allowed to go as fast as it likes>.

—**keep a tight rein on (someone** *or* **something)** to keep strict control over (someone or something): *We must keep a tight rein on our expenditure this year.* <Refers to a horse strictly controlled by the rider>.

reputation

—**live up to one's reputation** to behave in the way that one is reputed or expected to behave: *He lived up to his reputation as as womanizer by making a pass at our hostess.*

resort

—**as a** *or* **in the last resort** *see* **last**.

resistance

—**the line of least resistance** *see* **line**.

resource

—**leave (someone) to his** *or* **her own resources** to let (someone) find his or her own way of solving a problem, entertaining himself or herself, etc: *You can't be responsible for her all the time. You'll have to leave her to her own resources some time.*

respect

—**be no respecter of persons** not to be influenced by the standing, importance, money, etc, of people: *Illness is no respecter of persons.*

rest

—**come to rest** to stop: *The child's train came to rest just in front of me.*

—**lay (someone) to rest** to bury (someone): *We laid the old man to rest yesterday.*

—**rest assured** you can be quite certain: *Rest assured we will do a good job.*

—**rest on one's laurels** *see* **laurel**.

—**rest on one's oars** *see* **oar**.

retreat

—**beat a (hasty) retreat** *see* **beat**.

return

—**return to the fold** to come or back to one's

family, an organization, a set of principles or beliefs, etc, which one has previously left: *He left the firm to work overseas but he has now returned to the fold.* <Refers to a sheep returning to the sheep-pen>.

—**the point of no return** *see* **point**.

rhetorical

—**rhetorical question** a question which does not require an answer: *What happened to the summers of our youth?*

rhyme

—**without rhyme or reason** without any logical or sensible reason or explanation: *His attitude to his children is without rhyme or reason.*

rich

—**rich as Croesus** extremely rich: *He can well afford to pay for the party. He's rich as Croesus.* <Croesus was a ruler of the kingdom of Lydia who was very wealthy>.

—**strike it rich** to obtain wealth, often suddenly or unexpectedly: *He struck it rich when he went to work for the old lady. She left him all her money.*

Richmond

—**another Richmond in the field** another unexpected adversary: *When a rival suitor appeared, his temper rose when he saw another Richmond in the field.* <From Shakespeare's Richard III, act V, scene iv, when at the Battle of Bosworth King Richard replies to his attendant Catesby, who urges him to flee, "I think there be six Richmonds in the field. Five I have slain today instead of him.">

riddance

—**good riddance to (someone** *or* **something)** I am glad to have got rid of (someone or something): *Good riddance to him. He was just a troublemaker.*

ride

—**be riding for a fall** to be on a course of action that is likely to lead to unpleasant results or disaster for oneself: *Just because she's a friend of the manager she thinks she can come to work as late as she likes. She's riding for a fall.* <Refers originally to hunting>.

—**have a rough ride** to receive harsh treatment or suffer an unpleasant experience: *I hear he had rather a rough ride at his interview.*

—**ride out (something)** to survive until (something difficult) is over: *Many small companies did not ride out the recession.* <Used literally of a ship keeping afloat during a storm>.

—**ride roughshod over (someone)** *see* **rough**.

—**riding high** *see* **high**.

—**take (someone) for a ride** to deceive or trick (someone): *He was taking her for a ride pretending to be wealthy. He's actually penniless.* <Originally American gangsters' slang for killing someone, from the practice of killing someone in a moving vehicle so as not to attract attention>.

rift

—**a rift in the lute** a slight disagreement or difficulty that might develop into a major one and ruin a project or relationship: *They've only been divorced for a short time but I noticed a rift in the lute right at the beginning of their marriage.* <Refers to a quotation from Tennyson's *Idylls*>.

rig

—**rig the market** to buy shares of a stock in which one is interested in order to force up the price so that a profit is made on reselling: *The financier was not interested in the company—he was rigging the market.*

right

—**by rights** rightly, justly: *By rights he should not be in a senior position.*

—**get** *or* **keep on the right side of (someone)** to act in such a way that (someone) feels or continues to feel friendly and well disposed towards one: *It is important to keep on the right side of your girlfriend's mother.*

—**give one's right arm for (something)** *see* **arm**.

—**have one's heart in the right place** *see* **heart**.

—**in one's own right** independently, because of one's own social position, ability, work, etc: *She is a princess in her own right, not because her husband is a prince.*

—**in one's right mind** *see* **mind**.

—**(someone's) left hand does not know what his** *or* **her right one is doing** *see* **left**.

—**left, right and centre** *see* **left**.

—**Mr** *or* **Miss Right** the perfect man or woman for one to marry: *She's turned down several proposals of marriage. She says she's waiting for Mr Right.*

—**not right in the head** deranged, insane, mentally handicapped: *The young man who attacked her is not right in the head.*

—**on the right track** *see* **track**.

—**put (something) right** to repair, to make all right, to rectify: *The machine has been put right. The misunderstanding between them has been put right.*

—**put (someone) right** to cause (someone) to realize his mistake, incorrect beliefs, etc: *He* *thought they were still married but I was able to put him right.*

—**right arm** *see* **arm**.

—**right as a trivet** safe and sound, in a thoroughly satisfactory condition: *Once he had won the lottery his financial affairs were right as a trivet.*

—**right as rain** *see* **rain**.

—**right-hand man** *or* **woman** someone's most valuable and helpful assistant: *The chief mechanic is the garage owner's right-hand man.*

—**right off** immediately: *They told me the name of the nearest supplier right off.*

—**serve (someone) right** to be something unpleasant that (someone) deserves: *It serves her right that he has left her. She was having an affair with his best friend.*

—**set (something) to rights** to bring (something) into a correct, organized, desired, etc, state: *The filing system is chaotic but we'll soon set it to rights.*

—**strike the right note** *see* **note**.

ring

—**a dead ringer** someone who looks extremely like someone else: *He's a dead ringer for my younger brother.* <Perhaps from the use of the phrase to mean a horse, similar to the original, illegally substituted in a race>.

—**have a ringside seat** to be in a position to observe clearly what is happening: *His mother's had a ringside seat at their marital quarrels for years.* <Originally refers to boxing>.

—**ring a bell** *see* **bell**.

—**ring down the curtain (on something)** *see* **curtain**.

—**ring the changes** *see* **change**.

—**ring true** to sound true, to be convincing: *Something about his account of the accident did not hold true.*

riot

—**read the riot act to (someone)** to scold (someone) severely and warn him or her to behave better: *Their mother read the riot act to the children about the state of their rooms.* <The Riot Act of 1715 was read to unlawful gatherings of people to break the gathering up. If the people refused to disperse action could be taken against them>.

—**riotous living** extravagant, energetic living: *After the riotous living of Christmas I'm glad to take things quietly.*

—**run riot** to get out of control: *The children run riot in her class. Wild roses run riot in her garden.*

ripe

—**a ripe old age** *see* **age**.

rise

—**get up with** *or* **rise with the lark** *see* **lark**.

—**rise and shine** to get out of bed and be lively and cheerful: *It's time to rise and shine.*

—**rise from the ashes** *see* **ashes**.

—**rise to the bait** *see* **bait**.

—**rise to the occasion** *see* **occasion**.

—**take a rise out of (someone)** to tease or make fun of (someone) so that he or she gets annoyed: *You should try to ignore it when he takes a rise out of you.*

risk

—**risk life and limb** *see* **life**.

—**risk one's neck** *see* **neck**.

—**run the risk of (something** *or* **doing something)** to do (something) that involves a risk of (something or doing something): *He runs the risk of killing himself when he drives so fast.*

—**rite of passage** a ceremony or event marking the transition from one period or status in life to the next: The

river

—**sell (someone) down the river** to betray or be disloyal to (someone): *He sold his friend down the river by telling the police that she had been present at the crime.* <Refers historically to selling slaves from the upper Mississippi states to buyers in Louisiana where working and living conditions were much harsher>.

road

—**all roads lead to Rome** *see* **Rome**.

—**a royal road** a road without difficulties: There is no royal road to learning.

—**get the show on the road** *see* **show**.

—**hit the road** start out on a journey: *If we're to get there by nightfall we'll have to hit the road now.*

—**one for the road** one last drink before leaving: *Don't go yet. Let's have one for the road.*

roaring

—**do a roaring trade in (something)** to be selling a lot of (something): *We're doing a roaring trade in ice-cream in this hot weather.*

—**roaring drunk** extremely, and often noisily, drunk: *They all got roaring drunk after their team won.*

rob

—**daylight robbery** *see* **day**.

—**rob Peter to pay Paul** to pay (someone) with the money that should go to pay a debt owed to (someone else): *He paid the gas bill with the* *rent money, which was just robbing Peter to pay Paul.* <Refers to Saints Peter and Paul who share the same feast day, 29 July>.

rock

—**on the rocks** (1) in difficulties, in danger of being destroyed or ruined: *Their marriage is on the rocks.* (2) of a drink, served with ice cubes: *The customer in the bar asked for a whisky on the rocks.*

—**steady as a rock** extremely steady, motionless: *The surgeon's hand was steady as a rock.*

rod

—**make a rod for one's own back** to do something that is going to cause harm or problems for oneself in the future: *If you charge too little for your work now you will be making a rod for one's own back. Your employers will not want to raise the rate.*

—**rule (someone** *or* **something) with a rod of iron** *see* **iron**.

—**spare the rod and spoil the child** if a child is not punished for being naughty it will have a bad effect on his or her character: *She lets that child do what he likes and she will regret it. It will be a case of spare the rod and spoil the child.*

rogue

—**a rogue's gallery** a police collection of photographs of known criminals: *When she was attacked the police asked her if she recognized anybody in their rogue's gallery.*

roll

—**a rolling stone (gathers no moss)** a person who does not stay very long in one place (does not acquire very much in the way of possessions or responsibilities): *He has no furniture to put in an unfurnished flat. He's a rolling stone.*

—**be rolling in it** *or* **in money** to have a great deal of money: *He lives in a very small flat although he's rolling in it.*

—**be rolling in the aisles** to be laughing very heartily: *The comedian had the audience rolling in the aisles.*

—**heads will roll** *see* **head**.

—**roll on** may (a particular time) come soon: *Roll on the return to school! The children are driving me mad.*

Rome

—**all roads lead to Rome** all ways of fulfilling an aim or intention end in the same result and so it does not does not matter which way one uses: *You might not like my method of fund-raising but all roads lead to Rome.*

—**fiddle while Rome burns** to do nothing while something important is being ruined or destroyed: *By doing nothing about the rate of unemployment the government is being accused of fiddling while Rome burns.* <The Emperor Nero was said to have played on a lyre while Rome was burning>.

—**Rome was not built in a day** a difficult task cannot be completed satisfactorily quickly: *The new company has very few orders yet, but Rome was not built in a day.*

—**when in Rome do as the Romans do** one should follow the customs, behaviour, etc, of the people one is visiting or living with: *He should try to eat some Spanish food instead of looking for somewhere that sells English food. When in Rome do as the Romans do.* <A saying of St Ambrose>.

romp

—**romp home** *see* **home**.

roof

—**have a roof over one's head** to have somewhere to live: *It's just a small room in a flat but at least it's a roof over your head.*

—**hit the roof** *same as* **hit the ceiling**—*see* **ceiling**.

room

—**not to be enough room to swing a cat** *see* **cat**.

roost

—**chickens come home to roost** *see* **chicken**.

—**rule the roost** to be the person in charge whose wishes or orders are obeyed: *The son rules the roost in that household. The father hardly ever speaks.*

root

—**root and branch** thoroughly and completely: *The government should get rid of that out-dated law root and branch.*

—**rooted to the spot** *see* **spot**.

—**root (something) out** to destroy or get rid of something completely: *The new regime was determined to root out any opposition.*

—**the grass roots** *see* **grass**.

rope

—**give (someone) enough rope (and he will hang himself)** let (someone foolish) act as he or she pleases and he or she will bring about his or her own ruin, downfall, misfortune, etc: *I know he's running the department badly but don't interfere. Give him enough rope and he will hang himself.*

—**know the ropes** to know the details and methods associated with a business, procedure, activity, etc: *This is his first day as manager. He'll soon to get to know the ropes.*

—**money for old rope** *see* **money**.

—**rope (someone) in** to include (someone), to ask (someone) to join in, often against his or her will: *I've been roped in to help with the running of the school dance.* <Refers to lassoing cattle in the American West>.

—**show (someone) the ropes** to teach (someone) the details and methods involved (in something): *You'll soon know your way around the school. Your sister will show you the ropes.*

rose

—**bed of roses** *see* **bed**.

—**everything's coming up roses** everything is turning out to be successful or happy: *The business was doing badly last year but now everything's coming up roses.*

—**look at (someone** *or* **something) through rose-coloured** *or* **rose-tinted spectacles** *or* **glasses** to view (someone or something) in an extremely optimistic light: *She doesn't see his faults. She looks at him through rose-coloured spectacles.*

rough

—**cut up rough** to get very nasty: *He always seemed so pleasant but he cut up rough when he didn't get his own way.*

—**give (someone) the rough edge of one's tongue** to scold or criticize (someone) severely: *I'll give that child the rough edge of my tongue for letting the dog out.*

—**live rough** to live without proper housing, often outside all the time, and without the usual amenities: *The escaped prisoner lived rough before he was caught.*

—**ride roughshod over (someone)** to treat (someone) without any respect and without any regard for his or her views or feelings: *He never listens to anything anyone else suggests. He just rides roughshod over them and carries out his own ideas.* <Horses are roughshod to give a better grip on icy, etc, roads>.

—**rough and ready** (1) not polished or carefully done or made, but good enough: *His cooking is a bit rough and ready but the food tastes all right.* (2) not having polished manners: *The villagers made us welcome but they were a bit rough and ready.*

—**rough and tumble** disorderly struggle: *He was too timid for the rough and tumble of the business world.* <Originally boxing slang for a fight in which the usual rules do not apply>.

—**rough diamond** *see* **diamond**.

—**take the rough with the smooth** to accept the disadvantages as well as the advantages and benefits of a situation: *The baby cries all night but she's adorable and you have to take the rough with the smooth.*

round

—**get round to (something)** to find time and opportunity to do (something), to do something when one can: *I never seem to get round to writing letters.*

—**go the rounds** to be passed from person to person : *I believe there's flu going the rounds.*

—**in round figures** *or* **numbers** to the nearest whole number, especially one that can be divided by ten: *He would prefer the quote in round figures, i.e. £500.*

—**round the twist** *see* **twist**.

—**round trip** the journey to somewhere plus the journey back: *The round trip to my parents' home will take about five hours.*

royal

—**royal road** *see* **road**.

rub

—**rub (something) in** to keep reminding someone about (something which he or she would rather forget): *I know I shouldn't have offended her, but there's no need to rub it in.*

—**rub (someone's) nose in it** *see* **nose**.

—**rub off on (to) (someone)** to be passed to (someone), to affect (someone): *Some of his rudeness seems to have rubbed off onto his friends.*

—**rub salt in the wound** *see* **salt**.

—**rub shoulders with (someone)** *see* **shoulder**.

—**rub (someone) up the wrong way** to irritate (someone): *He always seems to rub people up the wrong way.* <Refers to rubbing an animal's coat up the wrong way>.

—**there's the rub** that's the problem: *We need an assistant but we need to find the money to pay one. There's the rub.* <Refers to a quotation from Shakespeare's *Hamlet*, Act 3, scene i, "To sleep, perchance to dream. Ay, there's the rub.">.

Rubicon

—**cross the Rubicon** *see* **cross**.

rug

—**pull the rug (out) from under (someone)** suddenly to stop giving important help or support to (someone), to leave (someone) in a weak position: *The landlord pulled the rug from under her by asking her to leave when the baby was born.*

ruin

—**go to rack and ruin** *see* **rack.**

rule

—**ground rules** *see* **ground.**

—**rule of thumb** a rough or inexact guide used for calculations of some kind: *I just measured the windows by rule of thumb.*

—**rule (someone** *or* **something) with a rod of iron** *see* **iron.**

—**rule the roost** *see* **roost.**

—**the exception proves the rule** *see* **exception.**

—**the golden rule** *see* **gold.**

run

—**a dry run** *see* **dry.**

—**a run for (someone's) money** a creditable or worthy performance or opposition: *They thought they would defeat us easily but we gave them a run for their money and nearly won.* <A racing term indicating that the horse one has backed has actually raced although it has not won>.

—**(someone's) cup runneth over** someone feels very happy: *Her cup runneth over. Her son has returned from the war.* <A biblical reference to Psalm 23:5>.

—**in the long run** *see* **long.**

—**in the running** with a chance of success: *We don't know if he'll get the job but he's certainly in the running for it.*

—**make the running** to be the leader, to set the pace, fashion or standard: *The large firms make the running in the technological industry.*

—**on the run** running away: *There are two prisoners on the run.*

—**run across (someone** *or* **something)** to meet or find (someone or something) by chance: *I ran across an old friend yesterday.*

—**run a tight ship** *see* **tight.**

—**run high** *see* **high.**

—**run in the family** *see* **family.**

—**run its course** to continue to its natural end, to develop naturally: *Your child will be all right. Just let the infection run its course.*

—**runner-up** the person, animal or thing that comes second in a competition, race, etc. : *The runner-up got a silver medal.*

—**run-of-the-mill** *see* **mill.**

—**run out of steam** *see* **steam.**

—**run out on (someone** *or* **something)** to abandon (someone or something): *She ran out on her husband and children.*

—**run riot** *see* **riot.**

—**run the gauntlet** *see* **gauntlet.**

—**run (someone** *or* **something) to earth** *see* **earth.**

—**run wild** *see* **wild.**

—**take a running jump** to go away: *He asked her out but she told him to take a running jump.*

rush

—**be rushed off one's feet** to be very busy: *We were rushed off our feet in the shop today.*

—**rush one's fences** *see* **fence.**

—**the rush hour** a period when there is a lot of traffic on the roads, usually when people are going to, or leaving, work: *I avoid the rush hour by going to work early.*

rut

—**in a rut** in a routine, monotonous way of life: *He's leaving his job because he feels he's in a rut.* <Refers to the rut made by a cartwheel, etc>.

S

sabre

—**rattle one's sabre** to put on a show of anger or fierceness without resorting to physical force in order to frighten someone: *It is unlikely the dictator will invade the neighbouring country. He's only rattling his sabre.*

sack

—**get the sack** to be dismissed from one's job: *If he's late for work once more he'll get the sack.* <From the sack in which workman carried their tools and belongings>.

—**sackcloth and ashes** sorrow or apology for what one has done or failed to do: *He apologized profusely to her for being so late. It was a case of sackcloth and ashes.* <People in mourning used to wear sackcloth and throw ashes over their heads. The phrase has several biblical references, e.g. Matthew 11:21>.

sacred

—**a sacred cow** *see* **cow**.

safe

—**be on the safe side** not to take any risks: *I don't think it will rain but I'll take my umbrella to be on the same side.*

—**safe and sound** totally unharmed: *The missing children were found safe and sound at a friend's house.*

—**safe as houses** *see* **house**.

—**there's safety in numbers** it is safer to undertake a risky venture if there are several people involved: *He wouldn't go on strike on his own but his colleagues are joining him and there's safety in numbers.*

sail

—**plain sailing** *see* **plain**.

—**sail before the mast** *see* **mast**.

—**sail close to the wind** to come close to breaking the law or a rule: *The second-hand car dealer is not a convicted criminal but he sails very close to the wind.*

—**sail under false colours** to pretend to be different in character, beliefs, status, work, etc, than is really the case: *He said that he is a qualified teacher but he is sailing under false colours.* <Refers to a ship flying a flag other than its own, as pirate ships sometimes did>.

—**take the wind out of (someone's) sails** *see* **wind**.

salad

—**(someone's) salad days** (someone's) carefree and inexperienced youth: *In our salad days we didn't mind the discomfort of camping.*

salt

—**below the salt** in a humble, lowly or despised position: *Now that she is in an executive position she regards all her former colleagues as being below the salt.* <Formerly the salt container marked the division at a dinner table between the rich and important people and the more lowly people, the important people being near the top and so above the salt>.

—**like a dose of salts** *see* **dose**.

—**rub salt in the wound** to make someone feel worse: *He left her and rubbed salt in the wound by laughing about it with his friends.* <Salt used to be used as an antiseptic but it was painful on raw wounds>.

—**take (something) with a grain** *or* **pinch of salt** to treat (something) with some disbelief: *He says that he is an experienced sailor but I'd take that with a pinch of salt.*

—**the salt of the earth** someone very worthy or good: *Her mother would help anyone in trouble. She's the salt of the earth.* <A biblical reference to Matthew 5:13>.

—**worth one's salt** worth the money one is paid, of any worth: *If she can't take telephone messages properly she's not worth her salt.* <Salt was once a valuable commodity and the reference is to that given to servants or workers>.

Samaritan

—**a good Samaritan** someone who helps people when they are in need : *A good Samaritan gave me a lift to the garage when I ran out of petrol.* <A biblical reference to the parable in Luke 10>.

same

—**be all the same to (someone)** to be a matter of no importance to (someone): *It's all the same to me if he goes or stays.*

—**not be in the same league as (someone)** *see* **league**.

—**the same old story** *see* **story**.

sand

—**build (something) on sand** to establish (something) without having enough support, money, likelihood of survival, etc, to make it secure or practicable: *The new business is built on sand. The market for its products is too small.* <A biblical reference to Matthew 7:26>.

—**happy as a sandboy** *see* **happy**.

sardine

—**packed like sardines** crowded very close together: *So many people turned up to the protest meeting that we were packed like sardines.* <Sardines are sold tightly packed in tins>.

savage

—**noble savage** *see* **noble**.

save

—**keep** *or* **put away** *or* **save (something) for a rainy day** *see* **rain**.

—**saved by the bell** *see* **bell**.

—**save one's skin** *see* **skin**.

—**save the day** *see* **day**.

sauce

—**what's sauce for the goose is sauce for the gander** *see* **goose**.

say

—**say the word** *see* **word**.

—**say** *or* **have one's say** to tell one's own story in one's own way: *He was an enlightened employer and let his employees say their say.*

—**there's no saying** it is impossible to know or guess, there is no way of knowing or guessing: *There's no saying how long the meeting will last.*

—**you can say that again!** you're absolutely right!: *"I think that shop is very expensive." "You can say that again!"*

scales

—**tip the scales** to be the factor that decides some issue, or causes events to happen in a certain way: *We couldn't decide between a holiday in Greece or one in Italy but the cheaper flight tipped the scales in favour of Italy.*

scarce

—**make oneself scarce** to withdraw, to go off: *When he hears his parents arguing he makes himself scarce.*

scarlet

—**scarlet woman** an immoral or promiscuous woman: *His mother treats her like a scarlet woman because she is divorced.* <A biblical reference to the woman in scarlet in Revelation 17>.

scene

—**behind the scenes** out of sight of the public, etc: *Our hostess took all the credit for the successful dinner party but she had a team of caterers working behind the scenes.* <Refers literally to people in a theatrical production who work behind the scenery offstage>.

—**come on the scene** to arrive or appear: *They were happily married until that young woman came on the scene.*

—**not (someone's) scene** not the kind of thing that (someone) likes: *Opera is not his scene; he prefers pop.*

—**set the scene for (something)** to prepare the way for (something), to be the forerunner of (something): *His disagreement with his assistant on his first day in the job set the scene for their working relationship all the time he was with the firm.* <Refers originally to the preparation of the stage for theatrical action>.

scent

—**throw (someone) off the scent** to distract (someone) from a search for someone or something, e.g. by giving him or her wrong information: *The police were put off the scent of the real killer by someone making a false confession.* <Refers literally to dogs>.

scheme

—**the best-laid schemes of mice and men (gang aft agley)** the most carefully arranged plans (often go wrong): *We had checked our holiday itinerary to the last detail but you know what they say about the best laid plans of mice and men.* <Refers to a quotation from Robert Burns's poem, "To a Mouse">.

school

—**of the old school** believing in or practising customs, codes of behaviour, ideas, etc, no longer popular: *She's of the old school. She always wears a hat and gloves when going out.*

—**the schoolmaster is abroad** good education is spreading everywhere: *The improvement in the area's examination results means the schoolmaster has been abroad.* <Often wrongly used in the opposite sense to imply that the schoolmaster is absent and is much needed>.

score

—**know the score** to know exactly what is involved, to know all the facts of a situation : *They knew the score. They were aware that he had a police record before they employed him.* <Literally to know from the score in a game who is likely to win or lose>.

—**settle old scores** to get revenge for wrongs

committed in the past: *I know he went off with your wife years ago but there's no point in settling old scores.*

scot

—**scot-free** without being punished or hurt: *The police knew he was guilty but he got off scot-free because she gave him a false alibi.* <Originally referred to not having to pay a form of tax>.

scrape

—**scrape the (bottom of the) barrel** *see* **barrel**.

scratch

—**backscratching** *see* **back**.

—**scratch the surface (of something)** *see* **surface**.

—**start from scratch** to start from the very beginning, without any advantages: *There were no furniture and fittings at all in the new house. We had to start from scratch and buy it.* <Refers to the starting line (formerly scratched on the ground), from which runners start unless their handicap allows them to start further down the track>.

—**up to scratch** up to the required standard: *The pupil will have to repeat the year if his work is not up to scratch.* <Refers originally to a scratch in the centre of a boxing ring to which boxers had to make their way unaided after being knocked down to prove that they were fit to continue>.

screw

—**have a screw loose** to be deranged, to be very foolish: *She must have a screw loose to marry such a violent man.* <Refers literally to malfunctioning machinery>.

—**put the screws on (someone)** to exert pressure or force to get (someone) to do something: *He didn't want to give them a room but they really put the screws on him.* <Refers to thumbscrews, an instrument of torture>.

—**screw up one's courage** *see* **courage**.

Scrooge

—**Scrooge** an extremely mean person: *He didn't give them a wedding present. He's an old Scrooge.* <Refers to a character in Charles Dickens's *A Christmas Carol*>.

sea

—**all at sea** puzzled, bewildered: *She was all at sea trying to cope with the rows of figures.*

seal

—**(someone's) lips are sealed** *see* **lip**.

—**seal (someone's) fate** *see* **fate**.

—**set one's** *or* **the seal (of approval) on (something)** to give one's agreement or approval to (something): *The council have set their seal on our proposal for a new nursery school.* <Literally to sign (something) by attaching a wax seal to it>.

seam

—**come** *or* **fall apart at the seams** to be in a state of collapse or ruin: *The educational system there is in danger of falling apart at the seams.* <From clothes coming to pieces>.

—**the seamy side (of life)** the rough, nasty, low aspect (of life): *She saw the seamy side of life when she was homeless.* <Refers to the seamed or wrong side of a garment in Shakespeare's *Othello*, Act 4, scene ii.>.

search

—**search high and low for (someone or something)** *same as* **hunt high and low**—*see* **high**.

season

—**the silly season** *see* **silly**.

seat

—**have a ringside seat** *see* **ring**.

—**in the hot seat** *see* **hot**.

second

—**at second hand** not directly, from someone else: *I didn't hear about his injury from him. I heard it at second hand.*

—**come off second best** to be defeated: *In the fight the younger boxer came off second best.*

—**play second fiddle to (someone)** *see* **fiddle**.

—**second childhood** *see* **child**.

—**second nature** a firmly established habit: *It is second nature to her to work night shift.*

—**second-rate** not of the highest quality, inferior: *Their team last year was very good but this year's one is second-rate.*

—**second sight** the supposed power of seeing into the future: *She said that she had second sight and knew that she would die young.*

—**second thoughts** a change of opinion, decision, etc: *They've had second thoughts about emigrating.*

secret

—**an open secret** *see* **open**.

see

—**have seen better days** of people, to have been in a higher social position; of things, to have been in a better condition: *His clothes were threadbare and had obviously seen better days.*

—**see daylight** *see* **day**.

—**see double** *see* **double**.

—**see eye to eye with (someone)** *see* **eye**.

—**see further than the end of one's nose** *see* **nose**.

—**see how the land lies** *see* **land**.
—**see life** *see* **life**.
—**see red** *see* **red**.
—**see stars** *see* **star**.
—**see things** *see* **thing**.
—**see through (someone** *or* **something)** not to be deceived by (someone or something): *We saw through his trick to get us out of the house.*
—**see which way the wind blows** *see* **blow**.

seed
—**go to seed** to become shabby and uncared-for: *This area of town has gone to seed.* <Refers literally to plants seeding after flowering and being no longer attractive or useful>.

sell
—**sell (someone) a pup** *see* **pup**.
—**sell (someone) down the river** *see* **river**.

send
—**send (someone) packing** *see* **pack**.
—**send (someone) to Coventry** *see* **Coventry**.
—**send (something) up** to ridicule or make fun of (something), especially through parody or satire: *In the playwright's latest comedy he sends up the medical profession.*

sense
—**a sixth sense** *see* **six**.
—**come to one's senses** to begin to behave or think sensibly: *He was going to leave his job but he came to his senses when he looked around for another.*
—**horse sense** *see* **horse**.
—**sense of proportion** *see* **proportion**.
—**take leave of one's senses** to become deranged or very foolish: *I think she's taken leave of her senses. She's going to marry that womanizer from the office.*

separate
—**separate the sheep from the goats** *see* **sheep**.

sepulchre
—**whited sepulchre** *see* **white**.

serve
—**serve a** *or* **the purpose** *see* **purpose**.
—**serve (someone) right** *see* **right**.

service
—**at (someone's) service** ready to be of assistance to (someone): *His chauffeur is at our service for the day.*
—**have seen good service** to have been well used and reliable.
—**press (someone** *or* **something) into service** *see* **press**.

set
—**set about (someone** *or* **something)** (1) to begin (something or doing something): *How will you set about finding someone for the job?* (2) to attack (someone): *The thug set about the old man with an iron bar.*
—**set one's cap at (someone)** *see* **cap**.
—**set one's face against (someone** *or* **something)** *see* **face**.
—**set one's heart on (something)** *see* **heart**.
—**set one's** *or* **the seal (of approval) on (something)** *see* **seal**.
—**set one's sights on (something)** *see* **sight**.
—**set one's teeth on edge** *see* **teeth**.
—**set the cat among the pigeons** *see* **cat**.
—**set the pace for** *see* **pace**.
—**set the Thames** *or* **world on fire** to be conspicuously able or important: *I don't expect he'll set the Thames on fire, but I hope his mother will be proud of him.*
—**set the wheels in motion** *see* **wheel**.
—**set (something) to rights** *see* **right**.

settle
—**settle old scores** *see* **score**.
—**settle up (with someone)** to pay what one owes (someone): *If you pay the bill now we'll settle up with you later.*

seven
—**at sixes and seven** *see* **six**.
—**in seventh heaven** *see* **heaven**.

sewn
—**(all) sewn up** completely settled or arranged: *If we get the finance, our expansion plans are all sewn up.*

shade
—**put (someone** *or* **something) in the shade** to be much better, etc, than (someone or something): *Her dancing puts that of her fellow pupils totally in the shade.* <Refers to making someone seem dark by being so much brighter oneself>.
—**shades of (someone** *or* **something)** that reminds me of (someone or something): *Shades of school! The food served at this conference is exactly like school dinners.* <It is as though the shade or ghost of someone or something were present>.

shadow
—**worn to a shadow** made exhausted and thin by over-working: *She's worn to a shadow because of all the overtime she has had to do.*

shaggy
—**a shaggy dog story** *see* **dog**.

shakes
—**in two shakes of a lamb's tail** in a very short

time: *I'll get it for you in two shakes of a lamb's tail.*
—**no great shakes** not very good or important: *She's no great shakes as tennis player.*

shame
—**a crying shame** *see* **cry**.

shank
—**on shanks's pony** on foot: *There's no proper road. You'll have to go on shanks's pony.* <Refers to shank meaning leg>.

shape
—**knock (someone** *or* **something) into shape** to get (something) into the desired or good condition: *The office system is chaotic but we'll soon knock it into shape.*
—**lick (someone** *or* **something) into shape** *see* **lick**.
—**shape up** to be developing into the desired state or form: *The new player wasn't very good to start with but he's shaping up.*

sharp
—**look sharp** be quick: *Look sharp. The bus is coming.*
—**sharp as a razor** *see* **razor**.
—**sharp practice** dishonest dealing: *Their accounts department has been found guilty of sharp practice.*

sheep
—**a wolf in sheep's clothing** *see* **wolf**.
—**black sheep** *see* **black**.
—**(someone) might as well be hanged for a sheep as a lamb** if (someone) is going to do something slightly wrong and have to pay a penalty one might as well do something really wrong and get more benefit: *Your wife is going to be angry at you being late home, anyhow. Have another drink and be hanged for a sheep as a lamb.* <Refers to the fact that stealing a lamb or a sheep used to be punishable by death>.
—**separate the sheep from the goats** to distinguish in some way the good, useful, talented, etc, people from the bad, useless or stupid, etc, ones: *The teacher said that the exam would separate the sheep from the goats.* <A biblical reference to Matthew 25:32>.

sheet
—**white as a sheet** extremely pale: *She went white as a sheet when she heard the news.*

shelf
—**on the shelf** unmarried and unlikely to get married because of being unattractive, old, etc: *She thinks she's on the shelf at 23!* <Refers to goods that are not sold>.

shell
—**come out of one's shell** to become less shy: *The child has come out of her shell since she went to school.* <Refers to a tortoise or crab, etc>.

shine
—**take a shine to (someone)** to become fond of (someone): *He's taken a real shine to the girl in the office.*

ship
—**run a tight ship** *see* **tight**.
—**shipshape and Bristol fashion** neat, in good order: *She likes everything shipshape and Bristol fashion.* <Originally applied to ships. Bristol was formerly the largest port in Britain>.
—**ships that pass in the night** people who meet by chance and only on one occasion: *I met her at a conference but she was just a ship that passed in the night.* <Refers to a quotation from "Tales of a Wayside Inn" poem by Henry Wadsworth Longfellow>.
—**spoil the ship for a ha'porth of tar** to spoil something of value by not buying or doing something which would improve it but not cost very much: *She spent a fortune on an evening dress but refused to buy an evening bag—she carries her old handbag. Trust her to spoil a ship for a ha'porth of tar.* <Ship is dialect here for sheep—tar used to be used to prevent infections in sheep or to treat wounds>.
—**when (someone's) ship comes in** when (someone) becomes rich or successful: *We'll buy a new car when my ship comes in.* <Refers to merchants waiting for their ships to return with goods to sell>.

shirt
—**a stuffed shirt** *see* **stuff**.
—**keep one's shirt on** not to become angry: *Keep your shirt on. She didn't mean to bump your car.*
—**put one's shirt on (someone** *or* **something)** to bet everything on (someone or something): *I would have put my shirt on her winning the match.*

shoe
—**in (someone's) shoes** in (someone else's) place: *I wouldn't want to be in your shoes when he sees the damage.*
—**on a shoestring** using very little money: *We organized our holiday on a shoestring.*
—**step into dead men's shoes** *see* **dead**.

shoot
—**shoot a line** *see* **line**.
—**shoot (something) down in flames** to destroy: *Recent research will shoot his theory down*

in flames. <Refers literally to destroying aircraft by shooting at them>.

—**shoot one's mouth off** *see* **mouth**.

—**the whole (bang) shoot** *or* **the whole shooting match** absolutely the whole lot: *He wants to sell the whole bang shoot before he goes abroad.*

shop

—**all over the shop** all over the place: *In her office there are books all over the shop.*

—**shut up shop** to stop working: *It's 5 o'clock—time to shut up shop.*

—**talk shop** to talk about one's work: *I try to avoid my colleagues socially. They keep talking shop.*

short

—**by a short head** by a very small amount: *She got there before me by a short head.* <Refers to horse-racing>.

—**caught** *or* **taken short** having a sudden, urgent need to go to the toilet: *He was caught short and looked for a public toilet.*

—**cut a long story short** *see* **cut**.

—**give (someone** *or* **something) short shrift** to spend very little time or thought on (someone or something): *He gave her short shrift when she asked for her job back.* <Short shrift was the short time given to a criminal for confession before execution>.

—**go short** not to have or take enough of something that one needs: *She goes short of food herself to feed the children.*

—**make short work of (something)** to deal with or get rid of (something) very quickly: *We'll make short work of washing these dishes.*

—**run short of (something)** to begin not to have enough of (something): *We're running short of milk.*

—**sell (someone** *or* **something) short** not to do justice to, to belittle (someone or something): *He always sells his wife short but she's very pleasant and efficient.* <Literally to give a customer less than the correct amount of something>.

—**short and sweet** short and to the point: *His goodbye was short and sweet.*

—**stop short of (something)** *see* **stop**.

shot

—**a long shot** a guess or attempt unlikely to be accurate or successful, but worth trying: *It's a long shot but you might get his name from the local shop.*

—**a shot across the bows** something given as a warning: *The lawyer's letter was just a shot across the bows.* <From naval warfare>.

—**a shot in the arm** something that helps to revive (something): *He should look for more investors. The business needs a shot in the arm.* <Literally, an injection in the arm>.

—**a shot in the dark** *see* **dark**.

—**big shot** an important person: *The big shots on the board are having a meeting.*

—**call the shots** to be in charge of events or a situation: *The old man's retired and it's his son who's calling the shots in the firm now.*

—**like a shot** very quickly or willingly: *If they invite me to visit them I'll go like a shot.*

—**shotgun wedding** a forced wedding, usually because the bride is pregnant: *He was forced into a shotgun wedding by her father.* <From the idea that the groom was forced into the wedding by shotgun>.

shoulder

—**a shoulder to cry on** a sympathetic listener: *She doesn't need someone to scold her. She needs a shoulder to cry on.*

—**give (someone) the cold shoulder** *see* **cold**.

—**have a chip on one's shoulder** *see* **chip**.

—**have a (good) head on one's shoulders** *see* **head**.

—**have broad shoulders** *see* **broad**.

—**put one's shoulder to the wheel** to begin to work hard: *If this project is going to be finished on time, we'll have to put our shoulders to the wheel.* <Refers to putting one's shoulder to the wheel of a cart, etc, to push it out of muddy ground, etc>.

—**rub shoulders with (someone)** to associate closely with (someone): *She rubbed shoulders with all kinds of people in her job.*

—**shoulder to shoulder** side by side: *The two men fought shoulder to shoulder in the last war.*

show

—**a show of hands** a vote expressed by people raising their hands: *The decision to strike was taken by a show of hands.*

—**for show** for appearance, in order to impress people: *The country's annual military procession is just for show.*

—**get the show on the road** to get something started or put into operation: *Get everybody out of bed! It's time we got this show on the road.* <Used originally of a theatre company going on tour>.

—**run the show** to be in charge of an organisation, etc: *I don't know what will happen to our jobs. There's a new man running the show now.* <Refers literally to the theatre>.

—**show one's face** *see* **face**.
—**show one's hand** *see* **hand**.
—**show oneself in one's true colours** *see* **colour**.
—**show off** to behave in such a way as to impress others with one's possessions, ability, etc: *The child has just learnt to dance and is showing off.*
—**show one's paces** *see* **pace**.
—**show one's teeth** *see* **teeth**.
—**show the flag** *see* **flag**.
—**show the white feather** *see* **feather**.
—**show (someone) up** to reveal to the world a person's real character: *His reaction to the beggar showed him up as a miser.*
—**steal the show** to attract the most attention at an event: *The little flower girl stole the show at her sister's wedding.* <Refers to someone getting most of the applause at a theatrical performance>.

shrift
—**give (someone** *or* **something) short shrift** *see* **short**.

shy
—**fight shy of (something)** *see* **fight**.

sick
—**sick and tired of something** weary of or bored of something: *I'm sick of the sight of this old coat. I wish I had a new one.*
—**sick as a parrot** very disappointed: *He's sick as a parrot he didn't get the job.*
—**sick at heart** very sad: *She is sick at heart because her husband is seriously ill.*

side
—**get** *or* **keep on the right side of (someone)** *see* **right**.
—**get on the wrong side of (someone)** *see* **wrong**.
—**let the side down** to hinder one's colleagues by not performing, etc, as well as they have: *His team-mates all won their matches but he let the side down by being beaten very badly.*
—**on the side** in a way other than by means of one's ordinary occupation: *He has a full-time job as a teacher but he earns a lot on the side as a barman.*
—**on the side of the angels** *see* **angel**.
—**pass by on the other side** *see* **other**.
—**side by side** beside one another: *They climbed the hill side by side.*
—**take sides** to support a particular person, group, etc, against another: *Two of the women in the office quarrelled and everyone else took sides.*

sieve
—**have a memory like a sieve** to be extremely forgetful: *Don't expect him to remember the date of the party. He's got a memory like a sieve.*

sight
—**a sight for sore eyes** *see* **eye**.
—**have** *or* **set one's sights on (something)** to try to obtain (something): *She set her sights on the big house at the edge of the village.* <Refers to the sights of a gun>.
—**know (someone) by sight** to be able to recognise (someone) without ever having spoken to them: *I know some of the other parents by sight.*
—**not be able to stand the sight of (someone)** to dislike (someone) very much: *The two women are friendly but their husbands can't stand the sight of each other.*
—**out of sight** beyond comparison, incomparably: *The new automobile is out of sight the best car on the market.*
—**out of sight, out of mind** one ceases to think about someone who has gone away or about something which is no longer in front of one: *He rarely mentions his girlfriend, who is overseas. It seems to be a case of out of sight, out of mind.*
—**second sight** *see* **second**.

silence
—**silence is golden** it is better to say nothing in a particular situation: *In order to keep the children quiet the teacher told them that silence is golden.*

silent
—**silent as the grave** wholly silent, saying nothing, making no noise: *The children promised to be silent as the grave in the theatre.*
—**the silent majority** the people who make up most of the population but who rarely make their views known although these are thought to be moderate and reasonable: *The politician said it was time the silent majority had an influence on the country.*

silk
—**take silk** to be made a Queen's or King's Counsel at the bar and be entitled to wear a silk robe: *The law student eventually became a distinguished barrister and in due course took silk.*
—**you can't make a silk purse out of a sow's ear** one cannot make something good or special out of poor materials: *She is not really a poor teacher. The pupils aren't very bright and you can't make a silk purse out of a sow's ear.*

silly

—**the silly season** a period of the year, usually late summer, when the newspapers have a lot of unimportant stories in the absence of important news: *There's a story in this about a funny-shaped potato. It must be the silly season.*

silver

—**born with a silver spoon in one's mouth** to be born into an aristocratic or wealthy family: *She's never worked in her life. She was born with a silver spoon in her mouth.* <Perhaps from the custom of giving a christening present of a silver teaspoon>.

—**every cloud has a silver lining** *see* **cloud**.

sin

—**cover a multitude of sins** *see* **multitude**.

—**live in sin** to live together without being married: *Her parents regard their living together as living in sin.*

—**ugly as sin** extremely ugly: *He said the girl we invited as his partner was ugly as sin.*

sink

—**leave (someone) to sink or swim** to let (someone) succeed or fail without helping: *When he came out of prison his parents left him to sink or swim.*

sing

—**sing (someone's** *or* **something's) praises** *see* **praise**.

sit

—**a sitting duck** *see* **duck**.

—**sit at (someone's) feet** *see* **feet**.

—**sit on the fence** *see* **fence**.

—**sit (something) out** to do nothing and simply wait for the end of (something) unpleasant: *Small firms should try to sit out the recession.*

—**sit tight** *see* **tight**.

—**sitting pretty** *see* **pretty**.

six

—**a sixth sense** intuition, an ability to feel or realize something not perceived by the five senses: *A sixth sense told him he was not alone.*

—**at sixes and sevens** in a state of confusion and chaos: *With so many visitors staying the house was at sixes and sevens.*

—**knock (someone) for six** to take (someone) completely by surprise: *The news of his promotion knocked him for six.* <Refers to cricket—literally to score six runs off a bowl>.

—**six of one and half a dozen of another** so similar as to make no difference: *We can either go by train or car. It is six of one and half a dozen of another.* <Half a dozen is six>.

sixty

—**the sixty-four (thousand) dollar question** the most important and/or difficult question: *Only one of us will be promoted. The sixty-four thousand dollar question is who it will be.* <From an American quiz game in which the contestant won one dollar for the first question, two for the second, four for the third, up to the last when he or she won sixty-four dollars or lost it all.>

size

—**cut (someone) down to size** to humble (someone), to reduce (someone's) sense of his or her own importance: *He threatened to cut his assistant down to size for being impertinent.*

—**size up (someone** *or* **something)** to consider carefully and form an opinion of the worth, nature, etc, of (someone or something): *You should size up the employment situation before leaving your job.*

skate

—**get one's skates on** to hurry up: *Get your skates on. We'll miss the train.*

—**skate on thin ice** *see* **ice**.

skeleton

—**have a skeleton in the cupboard** to have a closely kept secret about some cause of shame: *We didn't know that they had a skeleton in the cupboard until a family friend told us that their grandfather had murdered their grandmother.*

skin

—**by the skin of one's teeth** only just, very narrowly: *He passed the exam by the skin of his teeth.*

—**jump out of one's skin** to get a very great fright or shock: *I jumped out of my skin when the door creaked.*

—**no skin off my, etc, nose** no difference to me, etc, of no concern to me, etc: *It's no skin off my nose whether he comes to the party or not.*

—**save one's skin** to save one's life or one's career: *He didn't bother about his wounded friend. He just wanted to save his own skin.*

—**skin and bone** extremely thin: *That pony is just skin and bone.*

sky

—**go sky-high** to go very high: *The price of petrol has gone sky-high.*

—**pie in the sky** *see* **pie**.

—**praise (someone** *or* **something) to the skies** to praise (someone) extremely highly: *He praises his new assistant to the skies.*

—**the sky's the limit** there is no upper limit: *He*

doesn't think about money when he buys her presents. The sky's the limit.

slap

—**a slap in the face** a rebuff: *Her refusal to come to dinner was a slap in the face to her mother.*

—**a slap on the wrist** a reprimand: *She'll get a slap on the wrist for forgetting to give the boss that message.*

—**slap and tickle** playful lovemaking: *They were having a bit of slap and tickle on the park bench.*

sleep

—**let sleeping dogs lie** *see* **dog**.

—**lose sleep (over something)** to worry or be anxious about (something): *She's left him but he won't lose any sleep over that.*

—**put (something) to sleep** to kill (an animal) painlessly because it is incurably ill, etc: *The vet put the dog to sleep when it lost the use of its limbs.*

—**sleep around** to be promiscuous: *She seems very respectable now but she slept around in her youth.*

—**sleep like a log** *see* **log**.

—**sleep like a top** *see* **top**.

—**sleep with (someone)** to have sexual intercourse with (someone): *His wife doesn't know that he is sleeping with another woman.*

sleeve

—**have** *or* **keep (something) up one's sleeve** to keep (a plan, etc) in reserve or secret for possible use at a later time: *We're not beaten yet. I have a scheme up my sleeve.* <Refers to cheating at cards by having a card up one's sleeve>.

—**laugh up one's sleeve at (someone** *or* **something)** *see* **laugh**.

—**wear one's heart on one's sleeve** *see* **heart**.

slice

—**a slice of the cake** *see* **cake**.

slip

—**a Freudian slip** *see* **Freudian**.

—**a slip of the tongue** a word or phrase said in mistake for another: *He called her Mary but it was just a slip of the tongue.*

—**give (someone) the slip** to succeed in escaping from or evading (someone): *The escaped prisoner gave the police the slip.*

—**let (something) slip** to say or reveal (something) accidentally: *I'm sorry I let slip that you are leaving.*

—**slip one's mind** *see* **mind**.

—**there's many a slip 'twixt cup and lip** something can easily go wrong with a project, etc, before it is completed: *We hope we'll get the house but the contract isn't signed yet and there's many a slip 'twixt cup and lip.*

slow

—**go slow** deliberately to work less quickly than usual as a form of protest: *The voters voted not to strike but to go slow.*

—**slow on the uptake** *see* **uptake**.

small

—**it's a small world** an expression used when one meets someone one knows somewhere unexpected: *We went to India on holiday and met our next-door neighbours. It's a small world!*

—**make (someone) look small** to make (someone) seem foolish or insignificant: *He made her look small by criticizing her work in front of all of us.*

—**small talk** light conversation about trivial matters: *He always talks about his work. He has no small talk.*

—**small wonder** it is not at all surprising: *Small wonder she's got no money. She spends it all on clothes.*

—**the small print** the parts of a document where important information is given without being easily noticed: *Read all those legal clauses very carefully. If you ignore the small print you could be signing anything.*

—**the (wee) small hours** *see* **hour**.

smart

—**a smart Alec** someone who thinks he or she is very clever: *He's such a smart Alec that he tries to teach us our jobs.*

—**look smart** to be quick: *If you look smart you'll catch the last bus.*

smash

—**a smash-and-grab** a robbery in which a shop window is smashed and goods grabbed from behind it.

—**a smash hit** a great success: *The magician was a smash hit at the children's party.* <Originally referred to a very successful popular song>.

smear

—**smear campaign** an attempt to blacken or damage someone's reputation by making accusations or spreading rumours about him or her: *He started a smear campaign against the opposing candidate.*

smell

—**smell a rat** *see* **rat**.

—**smell of the lamp** *see* **lamp**.

smoke

—**go up in smoke** to end in nothing: *He had a great many plans but they all went up in smoke.*

—**put that in your pipe and smoke it!** *see* **pipe**.
—**there's no smoke without fire** there is always some kind of basis to a rumour, however untrue it appears to be: *He denies that he ever fathered a son but there's no smoke without fire.*

snail
—**at a snail's pace** extremely slowly: *The children wandered along at a snail's pace.*

snake
—**a snake in the grass** a treacherous person: *Be careful of him. He appears to be very friendly and helpful but he's a real snake in the grass.* <From Virgil's *Aeneid*>.

sneeze
—**not to be sneezed at** not to be ignored or disregarded: *It's not a large salary but on the other hand it's not to be sneezed at.*

snook
—**cock a snook at (someone)** *see* **cock**.

snow
—**pure as the driven snow** *see* **pure**.
—**snowed under** overwhelmed: *We're snowed under with work just now.*

soap
—**soap opera** a radio or television serial broadcast regularly and dealing with the daily lives, problems, etc, of the characters: *Life in their house is like a soap opera. They've had to cope with all kinds of problems.* <Refers to the fact that such series were often sponsored by soap manufacturers in America where they were first made>.

sock
—**pull one's socks up** to make an effort to improve: *You had better pull your socks up or you won't pass your exams.*
—**put a sock in it** to be quiet: *I wish you'd put a sock in it. I want to listen to the music.*
—**sock it to (someone)** to put as much effort and energy as possible into (something): *The singer really socked it to the audience.*

soft[1]
—**have a soft spot for (someone)** to have a weakness, affection or exceptional liking for (someone): *The old man has soft spot for his youngest granddaughter.*
—**soft in the head** *see* **head**.

soft[2]
—**a soft touch** *or* **mark** someone who is easily taken advantage of, deceived etc: *He would lend money to anyone. He's a soft touch.*
—**soft option** a choice or alternative which is easier or more pleasant than the others: *At school camp there was a choice of climbing the mountain or walking along the river bank and most of the children chose the soft option.*

sold
—**be sold on (something)** to be keen on (something): *They're sold on the idea of going to Turkey on holiday.*

song
—**for a song** for very little money: *They bought that house for a song.*
—**make a song and dance about (something)** to cause an unnecessary fuss about (something): *She really made a song and dance about losing her glove.*
—**(someone's) swan song** *see* **swan**.

soon
—**no sooner said than done** a request will be fulfilled as soon as it is made: *You asked for a pizza? No sooner said than done.*
—**speak too soon** to say something that takes for granted something not yet accomplished: *We started to congratulate him on his horse winning but we spoke too soon. It was disqualified.*

sore
—**a sight for sore eyes** *see* **eye**.
—**a sore point** a subject which annoys or offends someone: *Don't mention cars—they're a sore point with him. He's just had his stolen.*
—**stick out like a sore thumb** to be very noticeable: *The fact that they had been quarrelling stuck out like a sore thumb.*

sorrow
—**drown one's sorrows** *see* **drown**.
—**more in sorrow than in anger** more disappointed than angry at someone's behaviour: *The headmaster said that it was more in sorrow than in anger that he was expelling the boys.*

sort
—**it takes all sorts (to make a world)** one should be tolerant of everyone whatever they are like: *Don't be so critical of your fellow workers. It takes all sorts.*
—**not a bad sort** quite a nice person: *He's not a bad sort when you get to know him.*
—**out of sorts** not feeling quite well, rather bad-tempered: *He's been out of sorts ever since he had flu.*

soul
—**not to be able to call one's soul one's own** to be under the constant control of someone else: *Since he married he's not been able to call his soul his own. His wife orders him around.*
—**the soul of (something)** a perfect example of

(something): *She's the soul of tact. She won't say anything indiscreet.*

soup

—**in the soup** in serious trouble: *We'll be in the soup if we're caught in the school after hours.*

sour

—**sour grapes** *see* **grape**.

sow[1]

—**sow one's wild oats** *see* **wild**.

sow[2]

—**you can't make a silk purse out of a sow's ear** *see* **silk**.

spade

—**call a spade a spade** to speak bluntly and forthrightly: *Stop trying to break the news to me gently. I'd rather you called a spade a spade.*

—**do the spadework** to do the hard preparatory work at the beginning of a project: *There's a lot of spadework to be done before we open for business.* <Digging is the first stage of building houses, etc>.

spanner

—**throw a spanner in the works** to hinder or spoil (a project, plan, etc): *We were going on holiday but my boss threw a spanner in the works by asking me to do some urgent work.*

spar

—**sparring partner** someone with whom one often enjoys a lively argument: *I missed my brother when he left home. He was a good sparring partner.* <Literally refers to someone with whom a boxer practises>.

spare

—**go spare** to become very angry or distressed: *You're so late that your wife will be going spare.*

—**spare tyre** a roll of fat round the middle of the body: *She's trying to get rid of her spare tyre before the start of her holiday.* <From its supposed resemblance to a spare car tyre>.

speak

—**be on speaking terms** to be friendly towards someone and communicate with him or her: *He is not on speaking terms with her since she crashed his car.*

—**in a manner of speaking** *see* **manner**.

—**speak for itself** to need no explanation: *The evidence speaks for itself. They're obviously guilty.*

—**speak the same language** *see* **language**.

—**speak too soon** *see* **soon**.

—**speak volumes** *see* **volume**.

—**speak with a forked tongue** *see* **fork**.

—**to speak of** worth mentioning: *He has no money to speak of.*

spectacles

—**look at (someone** *or* **something) through rose-coloured** *or* **rose-tinted spectacles** *or* **glasses** *see* **rose**.

spell

—**spell (something) out** to explain (something) plainly and in detail: *Let me spell out what will happen if you get into trouble with the police again.*

spend

—**spend a penny** *see* **penny**.

—**spend money like water** *see* **money**.

spice

—**variety is the spice of life** *see* **variety**.

spick

—**spick and span** clean and tidy: *The old lad's house was spick and span.*

spike

—**spike (someone's) guns** *see* **gun**.

spill

—**cry over spilt milk** *see* **cry**.

—**spill the beans** *see* **bean**.

spin

—**in a flat spin** *see* **flat**.

—**spin a yarn** *see* **yarn**.

spirit

—**public spirit** *see* **public**.

—**spirit (someone** *or* **something) away** to carry away (someone or something) secretly and suddenly: *They spirited the princess away before the press could interview her.*

—**the spirit is willing (but the flesh is weak)** one is not always physically able to do the things that one wishes do: *They've asked him to join their climbing expedition but he says he won't—the spirit is willing but the flesh is weak.* <A biblical quotation—Matthew 26:40–41>.

spit

—**be the spitting image** *or* **the spit and image** *or* **the dead spit of (someone** *or* **something)** to be extremely like (someone or something): *The child is the spitting image of his grandfather.*

—**spit and polish** cleaning: *The house could be doing with a bit of spit and polish.* <Refers to the habit of using spit as well as polish to clean boots>.

splash

—**splash out on (something)** to spend a great deal of money on (something): *Let's splash out on some champagne.*

spleen

—**vent one's spleen** to express one's anger and frustration: *He had a row with his wife and* *vented his spleen by shouting at the children.* <The spleen was thought to be the source of spite and melancholy>.

splice

—**splice the mainbrace** to serve alcoholic drinks. *It's six o'clock. It's time to splice the mainbrace.* <Naval slang>.

splinter

—**splinter group** a group that is formed by breaking away from a larger one: *we formed a splinter group because we didn't agree with all the views of the parent group.*

split

—**a split second** a fraction of a second: *For a split second she thought she was going to be killed.*

—**split hairs** *see* **hair**.

spoil

—**be spoiling for (something)** to be eager for (a fight, etc): *He was drunk and spoiling for a fight.*

—**spoil the ship for a ha'porth of tar** *see* **ship**.

—**too many cooks spoil the broth** *see* **cook**.

spoke

—**put a spoke in (someone's) wheel** to hinder (someone's) activity: *They had a monopoly of the market in electrical goods and charged a lot in the area but a local firm has put a spoke in their wheel.* <Spoke is from Dutch spoak, a bar formerly jammed under a cartwheel to act as a brake when going downhill>.

sponge

—**throw up the sponge** to give up a contest, struggle, argument, etc: *He was getting beaten badly at chess and so he threw up the sponge.* <Refers originally to a method of conceding defeat in boxing>.

spoon

—**born with a silver spoon in one's mouth** *see* **silver**.

sport

—**have a sporting chance** *see* **chance**.

spot

—**have a soft spot for (someone)** *see* **soft**.

—**in a spot** in trouble, in difficulties: *He's in a spot. His car is beyond repair, and he lives in a remote cottage.*

—**knock spots off (someone)** to beat or surpass (someone) thoroughly: *The youngest Scrabble player knocked spots off the rest of the family.*

—**put (someone) on the spot** to place (someone) in a difficult or awkward situation: *Having boasted about his ability at chess for a long time, he was put on the spot when he was challenged to a match.*

—**rooted to the spot** unable to move from fear, horror, etc: *She stood rooted to the spot as the bull charged.*

—**spot on** absolutely accurate: *His answer was spot on.*

sprat

—**a sprat to catch a mackerel** something minor or trivial given or conceded in order to obtain some major gain or advantage: *Our chairman asked the owner of that small local firm to a supposedly informal friendly lunch but it was a sprat to catch a mackerel. He wants to buy his firm.*

spread

—**spread like wildfire** *see* **wild**.

—**spread one's wings** *see* **wing**.

spur

—**on the spur of the moment** suddenly, without previous planning: *They decided to go on holiday on the spur of the moment.*

square

—**a square deal** *see* **deal**.

—**back to square one** back at the beginning: *I thought I'd found a job but it's back to square one. I'm back job hunting again.* <Refers to an instruction in board games>.

—**fair and square** *see* **fair**.

—**square meal** a nourishing and filling meal: *He's been living on snacks. He hasn't had a square meal in ages.*

—**square up with (someone)** to settle a bill with (someone): *You paid my train fare. I had better square up with you.*

—**square up to (someone** *or* **something)** to face and tackle (someone or something) boldly: *She is going to have to square up to her financial problems.*

squeak

—**a narrow squeak** a narrow escape: *That was a narrow squeak. That car nearly ran me over.*

squib

—**a damp squib** *see* **damp**.

stab

—**have a stab at (something)** to have a try at (something): *I've never papered a room but I'll have a stab at it.*

—**stab (someone) in the back** to behave treacherously towards (someone), to betray (someone): *He stabbed his best friend in the back by going off with his wife when he was in hospital.*

stable

—**lock the stable door after the horse has bolted** to take precautions against something happening after it has already happened:

Now that they have been burgled they have installed a burglar alarm. It is a case of locking the stable door after the horse has bolted.

stack

—**stack the cards against (someone)** *see* **card**.

stage

—**a stage whisper** a loud whisper that is intended to be heard by people other than the person to whom it is directed: *She said to me in a stage whisper that she would like to meet the man by the bar.* <From the fact that whispers on stage have to be audible to the audience>.

—**stage fright** the nervousness, sometimes leading to him or her forgetting words, felt by an actor when in front of an audience; often extended to that felt by anyone making a public appearance: *She suddenly got stage fright when she saw the size of the gathering that she was to address.*

—**stage-manage (something)** to be in overall charge of (something): *She stage-managed the business conference.* <Literally to be in charge of the scenery and equipment for a play>.

stake

—**be at stake** to be in peril or at risk: *If the publishing company does not get the book out on time, its future is at stake.*

—**go to the stake** to suffer severe punishment or retribution: *The women won't mind going to the stake if they can stop the nuclear waste dump being sited here.* <From people being burned while tied to a stake, often because of their religious beliefs>.

—**have a stake in (something)** to have an interest or investment in (something): *We all have a stake in the family business.*

—**stake a claim in (something)** to assert or establish one's right to or ownership of (something): *The youngest sister got a lawyer to stake her claim to a share in the family home.* <Refers originally to gold-mining>.

stamp

—**(someone's) stamping ground** a place where (someone) goes regularly: *The pub in the village is his stamping ground.* <Refers literally to animals>.

stand

—**a standing joke** *see* **joke**.

—**it stands to reason that** *see* **reason**.

—**know where one stands** to know the exact nature of one's position or situation: *With so much talk of redundancy the workers must know where they stand.*

—**make a stand against (something)** to oppose or resist (something one believes to be wrong etc): *We should all make a stand against racism.*

—**not to stand an earthly** *same as* **not to have an earthly**—*see* **earthly**.

—**stand at ease** to take the position of rest allowed to soldiers in the intervals of drill: *The sergeant major told the company to stand at ease while the orders of the day were read.*

—**stand by** (1) to provide help and support for (someone): *Her parents stood by her when she had the baby.* (2) to be ready to take action: *The emergency services are standing by. There has been an accident at the mine.*

—**stand corrected** to accept that one has been wrong: *I thought they lived in Leeds but he tells me it's Liverpool. I stand corrected.*

—**stand one's ground** *see* **ground**.

—**stand in for (someone)** to act as a substitute for (someone): *She is just standing in for his usual nurse who is on holiday.*

—**stand (someone) in good stead** *see* **stead**.

—**stand on ceremony** to be very formal: *Take your jacket off if you like. There is no need to stand on ceremony.*

—**stand on end** of the hairs on the head of a frightened person, to stand erect: *The thought of a ghost in the house makes my hair stand on end.*

—**stand out for (something)** to go on protesting or resisting until one gets (something): *The unions are standing out for more money.*

—**stand to reason** to be logially certain, to be an undoubted fact: *It stands to reason that I must either be driven along with the crowd or else be left behind.*

—**stand (someone) up** not to keep a promise to meet (someone): *We were supposed to be going to the cinema together but he stood me up.*

—**stand up and be counted** to declare one's opinions publicly: *She says she's in favour of equal rights for women but she won't stand up and be counted by coming with us to ask the boss for fairer wages.*

—**stand up for (someone)** to support or defend (someone): *His brother stood up for him when he was being bullied.*

—**stand up to (someone)** to face (someone) boldly, to show resistance to (someone): *She should stand up to her husband and refuse to be bullied.*

star

—**see stars** to see flashes of light as a result of a

bang on the head: *I saw stars when the branch fell on my head.*

start

—**a false start** an unsuccessful beginning, resulting in one in having to start again: *He's had one false start with his first restaurant and he's now bought another.* <From a start in a race which has to be repeated, e.g. because a runner has left the starting line before the signal has been given>.

—**for starters** to begin with: *For starters we need more money.* <Starter refers literally to the first course of a meal>.

—**start from scratch** *see* **scratch**.

statistics

—**vital statistics** *see* **vital**.

status

—**status quo** the situation as it is, or was, before a change: *The experiment has obviously failed and we should return to the status quo.* <Latin, literally "the state in which">.

—**status symbol** a possession that supposedly demonstrates someone's elevated social position: *He bought his Rolls Royce as a status symbol.*

stay

—**stay the course** to continue to the end or completion of (something): *She's gone on a diet but she'll never stay the course.*

—**stay the pace** *see* **pace**.

stead

—**stand (someone) in good stead** to be useful or advantageous in the future: *The job may not be interesting but the experience of it will stand you in good stead when you look for another.*

steady

—**steady as a rock** *see* **rock**.

—**go steady** to go out together regularly, to have a romantic attachment to each other: *The young people are not engaged but they're going steady.*

steal

—**steal a march on (someone)** *see* **march**.

—**steal the show** *see* **show**.

—**steal (someone's) thunder** *see* **thunder**.

steam

—**get all steamed up** to get angry or agitated: *There's no point in getting all steamed up about the ugly new building . There's nothing you can do about it.*

—**get up steam** to gather energy and impetus to do (something): *I should finish this work today but I can't seem to get up steam.* <Literally used of increasing the pressure of steam in an engine before it goes into operation>.

—**let off steam** to give free expression to one's feelings or energies: *He wrote the letter to the council to let off steam about his objections to the new road. The children need to let off steam after they've been sitting in school all day.* <Literally to release steam from a steam engine to in order to reduce pressure>.

—**run out of steam** to become exhausted, to lose enthusiasm: *I think our campaign is running out of steam. Hardly anyone turns up to our public meetings.* <Refers literally to the steam engine>.

—**under one's own steam** entirely through one's own efforts: *He got the job under his own steam even although his father's in the same business.*

step

—**step by step** gradually: *You won't get better right away. You must take it step by step.*

—**step in** to intervene: *The two children are quarrelling but the parents shouldn't step in.*

—**step on it** to hurry: *Step on it. We're going to be late.* <Refers to putting one's foot down hard on the accelerator of a car>.

—**step out of line** *see* **line**.

—**step (something) up** to increase (something): *The police are going to step up their investigation.*

—**take steps** to take action of some kind: *The government must take steps to improve the economy.*

stick

—**be on a sticky wicket** to be in a difficult or awkward situation that is difficult to defend: *He's on a sticky wicket if he sold goods that he knew had been stolen.* <Refers to cricket when the state of the ground or the weather makes it difficult for the batsman or woman to hit the ball>.

—**come to a sticky end** to meet some misfortune or an unpleasant death: *He was murdered by a gang. People weren't surprised that he came to a sticky end after the life of violence he had led.*

—**get hold of the wrong end of the stick** to misunderstand a situation or something said or done: *I didn't tell her she could go. She must have got hold of the wrong end of the stick.*

—**give (someone) stick** to scold or criticize (someone): *His father will give him stick when he hears his exam results.* <Refers literally to beating someone with a stick>.

—**in a cleft stick** *see* **cleft**.

—**stick by (someone)** to support and defend (someone), especially when he or she is in trouble: *His wife stuck by him when he was in prison.*

—**stick-in-the-mud** someone who is unwilling to try anything new or exciting: *She certainly won't go trekking in the Himalayas. She's a real stick-in-the-mud.*

—**stick one's neck out** *see* **neck**.

—**stick one's oar in** *see* **oar**.

—**stick out a mile** *see* **mile**.

—**stick out like a sore thumb** *see* **sore**.

—**stick to one's guns** *see* **gun**.

—**stick to one's last** *see* **last**[2].

—**stick up for (someone)**: *When all the other children were blaming him she stuck up for him.*

stiff

—**bore (someone) stiff** to bore (someone) a great deal: *The audience were bored stiff by the play.*

—**keep a stiff upper lip** *see* **lip**.

still

—**still waters run deep** quiet people often think very deeply or have strong emotions: *He hardly said a word during the discussion, but that doesn't mean he doesn't feel strongly about it. Still waters run deep.*

stitch

—**a stitch in time saves nine** prompt action at the first sign of trouble saves a lot of time and effort later: *You should repair that broken roof tile or your ceiling may get damaged. A stitch in time saves nine.*

—**have (someone) in stitches** to make (someone) laugh a great deal: *The comedian had the audience in stitches.*

—**without a stitch on** completely naked: *He stood at the window without a stitch on.*

stock

—**on the stocks** in preparation, in the process of being made or arranged: *We have a new product on the stocks but it won't be on the market until next year.* <Refers to the fact that a ship is supported on stocks, a wooden frame, while being built>.

—**take stock (of something)** to assess (a situation): I *took stock of my life and decided I need a change.*

stomach

—**have no stomach for (something)** not to have the inclination, toughness, etc, for (something): *They are a peace-loving people. They have no stomach for a war.* <Refers to a medieval belief that the stomach was the seat of physical courage>.

—**turn (someone's) stomach** to make (someone) feel sick, to disgust (someone): *The sight of blood turns his stomach.*

stone

—**a stone's throw** a very short distance: *Their house is a stone's throw away from here.*

—**leave no stone unturned** to try every means possible: *The police left no stone unturned in their search for clues.*

stool

—**fall between two stools** to try to gain two aims and fail with regard to both of them, usually because of indecision: *The student's essay falls between two stools. In part of it he is trying to be funny and in the other he is trying to be very serious and the two styles don't marry.*

stop

—**pull out all the stops** to put as much effort and energy into something as possible: *If you're going to win that race you'll have to pull out all the stops.* <Refers to pulling out the stops of an organ so that it plays at full volume>.

—**stop at nothing** to be willing to do absolutely anything, however wrong, etc: *He will stop at nothing to get those jewels.*

—**stop dead** to stop suddenly and abruptly: *He stopped dead when saw his ex-wife.*

—**stop over** to stay overnight somewhere while on a journey: *He stopped over at Amsterdam.*

—**stop short of (something** *or* **doing something)** not to go as far as (something or doing something): *I hope he would stop short of murder.*

store

—**in cold storage** in reserve: *Our plans for expansion are in cold storage until the recession is over.*

—**in store** in the future, coming to one: *There's trouble in store for you if you go home late again.*

—**set great store by (something)** to consider (something) to be of great importance or value: *My neighbour sets great store by a tidy house.*

storm

—**any port in a storm** *see* **port**.

—**a storm in a teacup** a great fuss made over a trivial matter: *She kept going on about her ruined dress but it was a storm in a teacup. You could hardly see the stain.* <Refers to the title of a farce written by William Bernard in 1854>.

—**stormy petrel** someone whose presence indicates that there is likely to be some kind of trouble in the near future: *She's a stormy petrel in a bar. Men always end up fighting over her.* <Refers to a small bird that lives in areas where storms are common>.

—**take (someone** *or* **something) by storm** to make a very great and immediate impression (on someone or something): *The young opera singer took London by storm.* <Literally to capture a fort, etc, by a sudden violent military attack>.

—**weather the storm** to survive a difficult or troublesome situation or period of time: *The company found it difficult to weather the storm during the recession.* <Refers originally to ships>.

story

—**a tall story** *see* **tall**.

—**cut a long story short** *see* **cut**.

—**the same old story** a situation, etc, that occurs frequently: *It was the same old story. As soon as he got out of prison he committed another crime.*

—**the story goes (that)** people say that, rumours suggest (that): *The story goes that they are not married.*

straight

—**go straight** to start leading an honest life: *He has been in prison twice but he's going straight now.*

—**get (something) straight** to get all the facts and details of a situation so as to understand it fully: *Let's get this straight. You say that you have never met the man who claims to be your husband.*

—**set the record straight** *see* **record**.

—**straight as a die** completely honest and fair. *You can trust that estate agent. He's straight as a die.*

—**straight from the horse's mouth** *see* **horse**.

—**straight talking** a frank and honest statement or conversation: *You've tried to tell her tactfully she has to leave. Now it's time for some straight talking.*

—**the straight and narrow (path)** a good, virtuous way of life: *He left the straight and narrow when he left home.* <A variation on a biblical reference—"Straight is the gate and narrow is the way which leadeth unto life", Matthew 7:4>.

stranger

—**be a stranger to (something)** to have no experience of (something): *He is a stranger to poverty.*

straw

—**a straw in the wind** a small or minor incident, etc, that indicates what may happen in the future: *The bye-election result might be interpreted as a straw in the wind for the general election.*

—**clutch at straws** to hope that something may happen to get one out of a difficulty or danger when this is extremely unlikely: *He is hoping that his wife will live but he's clutching at straws. She's terminally ill with cancer.* <From the saying "A drowning man will clutch at a straw">.

—**man of straw** *see* **man**.

—**straw poll** an unofficial poll to get some idea of general opinion: *The union took a straw poll on the possibility of a strike.* <Refers to drawing straws>.

—**the last straw** *or* **the straw that breaks the camel's back** an event, etc, which, added to everything that has already happened, makes a situation impossible: *Her boss's criticism was the last straw and she walked out.* <From the saying that it is the last straw added to its burden that breaks the camel's back>.

—**try to make bricks without straw** *see* **brick**.

street

—**be on the streets** to be homeless: *They'll be on the streets soon if they can't pay the rent.*

—**be right up (someone's) street** to be exactly what what one likes or what is suitable for one: *That job abroad is right up her street.*

—**go on the streets** to become a prostitute: *She went on the streets to support herself and the children.*

—**in Queer Street** *see* **queer**.

—**streets ahead of (someone** *or* **something)** *see* **ahead**.

—**the man in the street** *see* **man**.

strength

—**a tower of strength** *see* **tower**.

—**from strength to strength** to progress successfully from one achievement to another: *The firm's going from strength to strength since it expanded.*

—**on the strength of (something)** relying on (something): *We're going on a cruise on the strength of our pools win.*

stretch

—**at full stretch** using all one's energy, abilities, powers, etc, as much as possible: *We're working at full stretch these days.*

—**stretch a point** to go further than the rules or regulations allow in giving permission, etc, for something: *I shouldn't really let you take this book out but I suppose I could stretch a point.*

—**stretch one's legs** *see* **leg**.

stride

—**get into one's stride** to become accustomed to doing something and so do it well and effectively: *He was slow at the job at first but he soon got into his stride.* <A reference to the pace one is comfortable with when running>.

—**make great strides** to make very good progress: *Her son is making great strides with his studies in senior school.*

—**take (something) in one's stride** to cope with (something) without worrying about it: *She failed the exam but she took it in her stride.* <Refers to a horse jumping an obstacle without altering its stride>.

strike

—**strike a balance** *see* **balance**.

—**strike a bargain** *see* **bargain**.

—**strike a chord** *see* **chord**.

—**strike it lucky** *see* **luck**.

—**strike it rich** *see* **rich**.

—**strike (someone) off (something)** to remove (something—especially a doctor's name) from a professional register, etc, e.g. for misconduct: *I won't go to that doctor. From the rumours I hear he'll soon be struck off.*

—**strike the right note** *see* **note**.

—**strike while the iron is hot** *see* **iron**.

string

— **have another** *or* **more than one string to one's bow** *see* **bow**.

—**have (someone) on a string** to have (someone) in one's control: *He has her on a string—she owes him money.* <Refers to someone manipulating a puppet>.

—**pull strings** to use influence to gain an advantage or benefit of some kind: *He may have to pull a few strings to get a visa for her.* <As above>.

—**tied to (someone's) apron-strings** *see* **apron**.

—**with no strings attached** without any conditions or provisos: *Father will lend us the money with no strings attached.*

stroke

—**at a stroke** with a single effort or attempt: *That loan would solve all our financial problems at a stroke.*

—**put (someone) off his** *or* **her stroke** to hinder or prevent (someone) from proceeding smoothly with an activity: *By laughing at him while he was playing bowls they put him off his stroke.* <Refers to upsetting the rhythm of someone's rowing>.

strong

—**be (someone's) strong suit** be something at which (someone) is very good: *Organization is not his strong suit.* <Refers to card-playing>.

stubborn

—**stubborn as a mule** *see* **mule**.

stuck

—**stuck for (something)** in need of (something), unable to go on without (something): *I can't finish the decorating. I'm stuck for wallpaper.*

—**stuck on (someone** *or* **something)** very fond of (someone or something): *He's stuck on her younger sister.*

—**stuck with (someone** *or* **something)** burdened with (something): *She's got stuck with the club bore.*

stuff

—**a stuffed shirt** a pompous, over-formal person: *He never seems to enjoy himself. He's a real stuffed shirt.* <Refers to a shop dummy>.

—**do one's stuff** to do something that is necessary and that one either specializes in or does skilfully: *Here's the equipment. Go and do your stuff.*

—**get stuffed** an angry expression used in refusing someone's request, opinion, etc: *You want me to go and get your slippers? Get stuffed!*

—**knock the stuffing out of (someone)** (1) to beat (someone) severely: *The older boy knocked the stuffing out of the bully.* (2) to discourage (someone) completely, to deprive (someone) of vitality: *It knocked the stuffing out of him when he was declared redundant.* <Refers to stuffed animals>.

—**know one's stuff** to be knowledgeable about one's subject, job, etc: *Our neighbour works in computers and he really knows his stuff.*

stumbling

—**a stumbling block** something that hinders or prevents progress: *The cost of the venture is the main stumbling block.* <A biblical reference to Romans 14:13>.

stump

—**stir one's stumps** to hurry up: *You better stir your stumps. Our guests will soon be here.* <Stumps here means legs>.

style

—**cramp (someone's) style** to hinder (someone) from acting in the way that he or she would like or is accustomed to: *His style has been cramped by a wife and two children.*

—**in style** elegantly, luxuriously: *She arrived in style in a chauffeur-driven limousine.*

such

—**such as it is** although it hardly deserves the name: *You are welcome to borrow our wheelbarrow, such as it is.*

suffer

—**not to suffer fools gladly** *see* **fool**.

sugar

—**sugar daddy** an elderly man who has a young girlfriend or mistress to whom he gives expensive presents: *She looks like a Christmas tree wearing all the jewellery her sugar daddy has given her.*

—**sugar the pill** to make something unpleasant more pleasant: *She was told she was losing her job but the boss sugared the pill by offering her some part-time work occasionally.*

suit

—**be (someone's) strong suit** *see* **strong**.

—**one's birthday suit** nakedness: *He ran along the corridor to the bathroom in his birthday suit.*

—**follow suit** *see* **follow**.

—**suit (someone) down to the ground** *see* **ground**.

—**suit oneself** to do as one wishes: *We're all going but you can suit yourself.*

summer

—**an Indian summer** *see* **Indian**.

—**one swallow does not make a summer** *see* **swallow**[1].

sun

—**catch the sun** *see* **catch**.

—**under the sun** in the whole world: *He would like to visit every country under the sun.*

Sunday

—**a month of Sundays** *see* **month**.

—**(someone's) Sunday best** (someone's) smartest, formal clothes, of the kind worn to church on Sundays: *He's wearing his Sunday best because he's going for a job interview.*

sundry

—**all and sundry** *see* **all**.

sure

—**be** *or* **feel sure of oneself** to be confident, to have self-confidence: *He's not very good at his job but he's very sure of himself.*

—**sure enough** as was expected: *I said the parcel would arrive today, and sure enough it came before lunch.*

—**to be sure** certainly: *To be sure, he seems to be very pleasant but I do not trust him.*

surface

—**scratch the surface of (something)** to deal with only a very small part of (something): *In one term you will only scratch the surface of the history of the period.*

suspicion

—**above suspicion** *see* **above**.

swallow[1]

—**one swallow does not make a summer** a single success, etc, does not mean that a generally successful, etc, time is about to come: *He sold his first car on the first morning in the garage and thinks he's going to be a top-class salesman. We couldn't resist telling him that one swallow does not make a summer.* <Refers to the fact that swallows begin to come to Britain at the start of summer>.

swallow[2]

—**swallow one's pride** *see* **pride**.

swan

—**swan around** to wander about in a leisurely way: *We were all working hard and she was swanning about giving orders.*

—**(someone's) swan song** the last work or performance by a musician, poet, playwright, actor, etc, before his or her death or retirement; by extension also applied to anyone who does anything for the last time: *The theatre was full because everyone wanted to be present at the great actress's swan song. He was not to know that that conference speech was his swan song. He died the next week.* <Refers to an ancient legend that the swan sings as it is dying although it is otherwise silent>.

swear

—**swear by (someone** *or* **something)** to have complete trust and faith in (someone or something), to recommend (someone or something) very highly: *He swears by that make of car.*

—**swear like a trooper** *see* **trooper**.

sweat

—**in a cold sweat** *see* **cold**.

—**no sweat!** no trouble, no problem: *No sweat! I'll get your package there on time.*

—**sweat blood** *see* **blood**.

—**the sweat of one's brow** one's hard work: *She spends all the money that he earns by the sweat of his brow.*

sweep

—**make a clean sweep** *see* **clean**.

—**sweep (someone) off his** *or* **her feet** *see* **feet**.

—**sweep (something) under the carpet** *see* **carpet**.

sweet

—**be all sweetness and light** to seem to be

pleasant and good-tempered: *She's all sweetness and light when she gets what she wants.*

—**be sweet on (someone)** to be fond of (someone): *I think he's sweet on my daughter.*

—**have a sweet tooth** to like sweets, cakes and deserts: *She has a real sweet tooth. She always has a bar of chocolate in her bag.*

—**sweet nothings** affectionate things said to someone with whom one is in love, endearments: *We were embarrassed when he sat and whispered sweet nothings in her ear in our kitchen.*

swim

—**be in the swim** be actively involved in social or business activities: *She was in mourning for a long time but she's back in the social swim now.*

—**leave (someone) to sink or swim** *see* **sink**.

swing

—**get into the swing of things** to become accustomed to (something) and begin to understand and enjoy it: *I hated the job at first but now I'm into the swing of things I'm quite happy.* <Refers to the swing of a pendulum>.

—**go with a swing** to be very successful: The opening of the exhibition went with a swing.

—**in full swing** at the most lively or busy part of something: *He came into the hall when the meeting was in full swing.*

—**not to be enough room to swing a cat** *see* **cat**.

—**swing the lead** *see* **lead**[2].

—**what you lose on the swings you gain on the roundabouts** disadvantages in one area of life are usually cancelled out by advantages in another: *I got a parking ticket today but I won a prize in a raffle. What you lose on the swings you gain on the roundabouts.*

swoop

—**at** *or* **in one fell swoop** in one single action or attempt, at the same time: *I threw out all my old clothes in one fell swoop.* <Refers to a quotation from Shakespeare's *Macbeth*, Act 4, scene iii, the reference being to a hawk swooping on poultry>.

sword

—**cross swords with (someone)** to enter into a dispute with (someone): *Those two always cross swords at committee meetings. They never agree.*

—**the sword of Damocles** a threat of something bad that is likely to happen at any time: *Possible redundancy is hanging over her like the sword of Damocles.* <Refers to a legend in which Damocles was forced by Dionysius of Syria to sit through a banquet with a sword hanging by a single hair over his head>.

system

—**all systems go** everything is functioning and active: *It's all systems go here today. We have so much work to get through.* <The phrase is used by the controllers of a space flight to indicate that everything is ready for the spaceship to be launched>.

T

T

—**to a T** exactly, very well: *That portrait of my aunt is her to a T.* <Perhaps T stands for tittle, a small dot or point>.

tab

—**keep tabs on (someone** *or* **something)** to keep a check on (someone or something): *He keeps tabs on his wife's spending as she's extravagant.*

—**pick up the tab for (something)** to pay for (something): *He picked up the tab for the whole party of us.* <Tab is an American term for bill>.

table

—**turn the tables on (someone)** to change a situation so that one gains the advantage (over someone) after having been at a disadvantage: *At first they were winning but we soon turned the tables on them.* <From the medieval game of tables, of which backgammon is a form, in which turning the board round would exactly reverse the position of the players>.

tail

—**with one's tail between one's legs** in an ashamed, miserable or defeated state: *The children went home with their tails between their legs after the farmer scolded them for stealing apples.* <From the behaviour of an unhappy dog>.

take

—**be taken with (someone** *or* **something)** to find (someone or something) attractive: *She was quite taken with the little dog.*

—**take after (someone)** to resemble: *She takes after her father.*

—**take (something) as gospel** *see* **gospel**.

—**take (something) as read** *see* **read**.

—**take one's cue from (someone)** *see* **cue**.

—**take (someone) for a ride** *see* **ride**.

—**take heart** *see* **heart**.

—**take (someone) in** to deceive (someone): *She really took the old lady in by pretending to be a social worker.*

—**take it easy** *see* **easy**.

—**take it from me (that)** you can believe me when I say (that): *You can take it from me that he won't come back.*

—**take it or leave it** either to accept (something) or refuse (something) as one wishes but it will not be alter: *That is my final price. Take it or leave it.*

—**take it out on (someone)** to treat (someone) in an angry or nasty way because one is disappointed, angry, etc, about something: *She turned down his proposal and he took it out on the dog.*

—**take off** suddenly to become successful: *His business has really taken off.* <Refers to the launching of a rocket>.

—**take (someone) off** to mimic (someone): *She was taking off her friend's father when he entered the room.*

—**take sides** *see* **side**.

—**take steps** *see* **step**.

—**take the floor** *see* **floor**.

—**take one's time** *see* **time**.

—**take up arms** *see* **arm**.

—**take (someone) up on (something)** to accept (someone's offer, etc): *I'll take you up on your invitation to dinner.*

—**take up the cudgels** *see* **cudgel**.

—**take (something) up with (someone)** to raise (a matter) with (someone): *You should take your complaint up with the manager.*

tale

—**tell its, etc, own tale** to indicate clearly what took place: *The charred remains told their own tale.*

—**tell tales** to report someone's wrong-doing: *Don't let her see you smoking. She'll tell tales to the teacher.*

—**thereby hangs a tale** there is a story associated with that: *He recognized the woman who came into the room and thereby hangs a tale.* <A pun on tail, used by Shakespeare>.

talk

—**money talks** *see* **money**.

—**straight talking** *see* **straight**.

—**talk about (something)!** that is a good example of (something): *Talk about conceit! He looks at himself in every shop window.*

—**talk down to (someone)** to speak to (someone) in a condescending way as if he or she were inferior: *Adults often talk down to teenagers.*

—**talk one's head off** *see* **head**.

—**talk nineteen to the dozen** to talk a great deal and usually very rapidly: *She and her friend talk nineteen to the dozen when they get together.*

—**talk shop** *see* **shop**.

—**talk through one's hat** *see* **hat**.

—**talk through the back of one's head** *see* **back**.

—**talk turkey** *see* **turkey**.

—**the talk of the town** someone or something that is the subject of general conversation or gossip: *Their sordid affair is the talk of the town.*

tall

—**a tall order** a difficult task: *It's a tall order to get the book for you by tomorrow.*

—**a tall story** a story that is extremely unlikely: *His latest tall story is that he has seen a Martian.*

tan

—**tan (someone's) hide** *see* **hide**.

tangent

—**go** *or* **fly off at a tangent** suddenly to leave the subject being discussed or the task being undertaken and move to a completely different subject or task: *It is difficult to follow the speaker's line of thought. She keeps going off at tangents.*

tap

—**on tap** available, ready for use: *There was coffee on tap all day.*

tape

—**have** *or* **get (someone** *or* **something) taped** to have a full knowledge or understanding of (someone or something): *She thought she could deceive me but I have her taped.* <As if measured with a tape>.

—**red tape** *see* **red**.

tar

—**be tarred with the same brush** to have the same faults: *He and his father are tarred with the same brush. They're both crooks.*

—**spoil the ship for a ha'porth of tar** *see* **ship**.

task

—**take (someone) to task** to reprimand or criticize (someone): *The teacher took the pupil to task for being impertinent.*

taste

—**a taste of one's own medicine** *same as* **a dose of one's own medicine**—*see* **dose**.

tea

—**a storm in a teacup** *see* **storm**.

—**not be one's cup of tea** *see* **cup**.

—**not for all the tea in China** not for anything at all, certainly not: *I wouldn't work there for all the tea in China.* <For a long time, China was the source of the world's tea>.

teach

—**teach one's grandmother to suck eggs** *see* **egg**.

tear[1]

—**tear a strip off (someone)** to scold (someone) severely: *The boss tore a strip off them for their carelessness.*

—**tear one's hair out** *see* **hair**.

tear[2]

—**crocodile tears** *see* **crocodile**.

teeth

—**armed to the teeth** *see* **arm**.

—**by the skin of one's teeth** *see* **skin**.

—**cut one's teeth on (something)** to practise on or get early experience from (something): *The Everest climber had cut his teeth on the hill behind his home.* <Refers to children being given something to chew on to help their teeth come through>.

—**draw the teeth of (someone** *or* **something)** to make (someone or something) no longer dangerous: *He drew the teeth of the blackmailer by threatening to go the police.* <Refers to pulling out an animal's teeth.>

—**get one's teeth into (something)** to tackle (something) vigorously: *He likes a problem that he can get his teeth into.*

—**give one's eye** *or* **back teeth** to be willing to do anything in order to obtain something: *They'd give their eye teeth to go to Australia.*

—**gnash one's teeth** to be angry and disappointed: *We gnashed our teeth as the bus drove away before we reached it.* <A biblical reference to Matthew 8:12>.

—**grit one's teeth** *see* **grit**.

—**in the teeth of (something)** against (something): *They married in the teeth of much opposition.*

—**lie in** *or* **through one's teeth** *see* **lie**[1].

—**kick (someone) in the teeth** to refuse to help or support (someone) when he or she is in need of it: *She had helped him in the past, but when she was in trouble he kicked her in the teeth.*

—**set one's teeth on edge** to irritate one: *His constant whistling sets my teeth on edge.*

—**show one's teeth** to demonstrate one's fierceness, to show that one can be aggressive: *They withdrew their opposition to our scheme when we showed our teeth.* <Refers to a dog, etc, showing its teeth in anger>.

—**teething troubles** problems occurring at the very beginning of a new project, etc: *Our new factory has recovered from its teething troubles.* <From the pain experienced by babies when teeth are just coming through>.

tell

—**I told you so** I warned you and I was right to do so: *"I've discovered he's a real rogue." "I told you so but you wouldn't listen."*

—**tell its own tale** *see* **tale**.

—**tell tales** *see* **tale**.

—**tell (someone) where to get off** *see* **get**.

—**there's no telling** it is impossible to know: *There's no telling how many people will come.*

—**you never can tell** it is possible: *We might get a heat wave. You never can tell.*

—**you're telling me!** that is definitely the case: *You're telling me he's bad -tempered!*

tender

—**leave (someone** *or* **something) to (someone's) tender mercies** to leave (someone or something) in the care of (someone inefficient, etc): *My mother-in-law is so vague that I didn't want to leave the children to her tender mercies.*

tenterhooks

—**be on tenterhooks** be very anxious or agitated waiting for something to happen: *We were on tenterhooks waiting for the exam results to be delivered.* <Tenterhooks were hooks for stretching newly woven cloth>.

term

—**be on speaking terms** *see* **speak**.

—**come to terms with (something)** to accept (something) as unavoidable and try to deal with it as best one can: *She will have to come to terms with her widowhood.*

tether

—**at the end of one's tether** *see* **end**.

thank

—**be thankful for small mercies** *see* **mercy**.

—**have only oneself to thank for (something)** to be the cause of (one's own misfortune): *You've only yourself to thank for the children being cheeky. You spoil them.*

that

—**just like that** immediately, without further consideration, discussion, etc: *When she asked for more money he sacked her— just like that.*

—**that's that** there is no more to be said or done: *He's gone and that's that.*

thick

—**a bit thick** more than can be tolerated: *It was a bit thick for her to invite herself round.*

—**give (someone) a thick ear** to slap (someone) across the ear, to box (someone's) ears: *My big brother will give you a thick ear if you hit me.*

—**lay it on thick** *see* **lay**.

—**the plot thickens** *see* **plot**.

—**thick and fast** in great quantities and at a fast rate: *The replies are coming in thick and fast.*

—**thick as thieves** extremely friendly: *The little girls quarrelled but they're thick as thieves now.*

—**thick as two short planks** extremely stupid: *Don't ask him to be in your quiz team. He's as thick as two short planks.*

—**through thick and thin** whatever difficulties arise: *He will support his leader through thick and thin.*

thief

—**set a thief to catch a thief** the best way to catch or outwit a dishonest or deceitful person is to use the help of another who is dishonest as he or she knows the technique: *The ex-convict has become a police informer and they have made many arrests thanks to him. It's true what they say about setting a thief to catch a thief.*

—**thick as thieves** *see* **thick**.

thin

—**be thin on top** to be balding: *He wears a hat to hide the fact he's thin on top.*

—**have a thin time of it** to have an unpleasant or difficult time, especially because of money difficulties: *They're having a thin time of it since she stopped work to have the baby.*

—**into thin air** *see* **air**.

—**(skate) on thin ice** *see* **ice**.

—**the thin end of the wedge** *see* **wedge**.

—**thin as a rake** extremely thin: *She insists on dieting although she's thin as a rake.*

—**thin on the ground** *see* **ground**.

thing

—**a near thing** *see* **near**.

—**be all things to all men** *see* **all**.

—**do one's (own) thing** to do what one likes to do or what one is good at doing: *At the recreation club we all do our own thing.*

—**first things first** *see* **first**.

—**have a thing about (someone** *or* **something)** (1) to be very fond of or be particularly attracted to (someone or something): *He has a thing about small blonde women.* (2) to be scared of, to have a phobia about (someone or something): *She has a thing about spiders.*

—**just one of those things** something that must be accepted: *Our flight has been delayed but that's just one of those things.*

—**know a thing or two** to be astute and sensible : *He wouldn't drink and drive. He knows a thing or two.*
—**make (quite) a thing of (something)** to treat (something) as very important, to make a fuss about (something): *She's making quite a thing of her birthday.*
—**no such thing** something quite different: *He says he's a qualified teacher but he's no such thing.*
—**not to know the first thing about (something)** *see* **first**.
—**see things** to see someone or something that is not there: *She must be seeing things. She said she thought saw a large snake in the bedroom.*
—**the thing is** the most important point or question is: *The thing is how will we get the money.*
—**the very thing** *see* **very**.

think
—**have another think coming** to be quite mistaken: *If you think they'll sleep here you have another think coming. The room is damp.*
—**not to think much of (someone** *or* **something)** to have a low opinion of (someone or something): *I didn't think much of the play.*
—**put one's thinking cap on** *see* **cap**.
—**think better of (something)** *see* **better**.
—**think nothing of (something)** *see* **nothing**.
—**think nothing of it** *see* **nothing**.
—**think (something) up** to invent (something): *He's thought up a good plot for a play.*
—**think the world of (someone)** *see* **world**.
—**think twice** *see* **twice**.

third
—**give (someone) the third degree** *see* **degree**.

Thomas
—**a doubting Thomas** *see* **doubt**.

thorn
—**a thorn in (someone's) flesh** *see* **flesh**.

thought
—**food for thought** *see* **food**.
—**second thoughts** *see* **thought**.

thread
—**hang by a thread** to be in a very precarious or uncertain state: *Our chances victory are hanging by a thread. We are waiting to hear if two players will be fit.* <Probably a reference to the sword of Damocles (*see*)>.
—**lose the thread** to cease to follow the course or development of an argument, conversation, etc: *The lecturer rambled on and I lost the thread.*

three
—**the three R's** *see* **R**.

throat
—**at each other's throats** quarrelling fiercely: *They're at each other's throats over custody of their child.*
—**cut one's own throat** to cause damage or harm to oneself by one's own action: *The firm says that if the workers insist on having a pay rise they will be cutting their own throats because some of them will have to be declared redundant.*
—**have a frog in one's throat** *see* **frog**.
—**jump down (someone's) throat** to attack (someone) verbally or in an angry or violent manner: *She jumped down my throat when I tried to explain my absence.*
—**ram (something) down (someone's) throat** to try forcefully to make (someone) accept ideas, opinions, etc: *He's always ramming his political views down our throats.*
—**stick in one's throat** *or* **gullet** to be difficult for one to accept or tolerate: *It sticks in my throat the way he treats her.*

throne
—**the power behind the throne** *see* **power**.

throw
—**throw in one's hand** *see* **hand**.
—**throw in the towel** *see* **towel**.
—**throw (someone) over** to leave or abandon (a girlfriend or boyfriend): *She threw him over to go out with someone else.*
—**throw (someone) to the lions** *see* **lion**.
—**throw up** to vomit: *The child threw up in the car.*
—**throw up the sponge** *see* **sponge**.
—**throw one's weight about** *see* **weight**.

thumb
—**rule of thumb** *see* **rule**.
—**stick out like a sore thumb** *see* **sore**.
—**thumb a lift** to ask for (and get) a lift in someone's vehicle by signalling with one's thumb: *Two hikers were standing at the roadside thumbing a lift.*
—**thumb one's nose at (someone or something)** to express defiance or contempt at (someone or something), originally by making the rude gesture of putting one's thumb to one's nose: *The new pupil thought it was clver to thumb her nose at the teachers.*
—**thumbs down** rejection or disapproval: *The proposal got the thumbs down from the council.* <From the method employed by the crowds in ancient Rome to indicate whether they thought the defeated gladiator should live or die after a fight between two gladiators. If the crowds turned their thumbs down the gladia-

tor died. If they turned them up the gladiator lived.>

—**thumbs up** acceptance or approval: *Our dress designs have been given the thumbs up from the manufacturers.* <See above>.

—**twiddle one's thumbs** to do nothing, to be idle: *Friday was so quiet in the office everyone was sitting twiddling their thumbs.* <Literally to rotate one's thumbs round each other, indicating a state of boredom>.

—**under (someone's) thumb** under one's control or domination: *The whole family is under the father's thumb.*

thunder

—**steal (someone's) thunder** to spoil (someone's) attempt at impressing people by doing what he or she intended to do before him or her: *She knew her sister was going to announce her engagement on Christmas Day and she deliberately announced hers on Christmas Eve to steal her thunder.* <John Dennis, a 17th/18th century playwright, invented a machine for simulating thunder in plays. When someone else used a similar device in a rival play Dennis said that he had stolen his thunder>.

tick

—**give (someone) a ticking-off** to scold (someone) sharply: *The teacher gave the boy a ticking-off for bullying.*

—**tick over** to run quietly and smoothly. *Sales aren't brilliant but they're ticking over.* <Used literally of a car engine>.

ticket

—**just the ticket** exactly what is required: *A plate of hot soup is just the ticket on a cold winter's day.*

—**meal ticket** someone who can be relied upon to support one, providing food and so on: *She regards her husband purely as a meal ticket.*

tickle

—**be tickled pink** to be delighted: *She was tickled pink with her birthday present.*

—**tickle one's fancy** *see* **fancy**.

tie

—**be tied up** to be busy or engaged: *I'm afraid you can't see the manager. He's tied up in a meeting.*

—**tie (someone) down** to limit (someone's) freedom: *She feels that children would tie her down.*

—**tie (oneself** *or* **someone) in knots** *see* **knot**.

tight

—**in a tight corner** *or* **spot** in a difficult or dangerous situation: *We were in a tight corner practically surrounded by the enemy.*

—**keep a tight rein on (something)** *see* **rein**.

—**run a tight ship** to run an efficient, well-organized firm etc: *During a recession it is exceptionally important to run a tight ship.*

—**sit tight** to be unwilling to move or take action: *Now is not the time to change jobs. Sit tight for a while.*

—**tighten one's belt** *see* **belt**.

tile

—**a night on the tiles** a celebratory evening spent in a wild and unrestrained manner: *They had a night on the tiles after the exams.* <Refers to roof tiles and to cats sitting on them at night>.

tilt

—**at full tilt** at maximum speed: *The boy ran down the street at full tilt to catch the bus.* <Refers to knights tilting or jousting>.

—**tilt at windmills** *see* **windmill**.

time

—**ahead of one's time** with ideas in advance of one's contemporaries, often not understood: *The philosopher was not highly rated as he was ahead of his time.*

—**all in good time** soon, when it is the right time: *The guests will arrive all in good time.*

—**a stitch in time saves nine** *see* **stitch**.

—**at one time** at a time in the past: *At one time he was quite famous.*

—**be high time** *see* **high**.

—**behind the times** not up-to-date, old-fashioned: *His ideas are behind the times.*

—**bide one's time** *see* **bide**.

—**do time** to be in prison: *He's doing time for murder.*

—**from time immemorial** *see* **immemorial**.

—**gain time** *see* **gain**.

—**half the time** for a good part of the time, frequently: *Half the time she doesn't know where her husband is.*

—**have a thin time of it** *see* **thin**.

—**have a time of it** to have a difficult time: *The family have had a time of it since the father lost his job.*

—**have no time for (someone** *or* **something)** to have a very low opinion of (someone or something) and to wish not to associate with him or her or it: *I have no time for people who are rude to old people.*

—**have the time of one's life** to have a very enjoyable time: *The children had the time of their lives at the fair.*

—**have time on one's hands** to have more free

time than one can usefully fill with work, etc: *I could help you in the shop. I have some time on my hands just now.*

—**in good time** early enough, with time to spare: *You should get to your interview in good time.*

—**in (someone's) own good time** when it is convenient for (someone), at whatever time or speed he or she chooses: *There's no point in rushing him. He'll get there in his own good time.*

—**in the fullness of time** *see* **full**.

—**in the nick of time** *see* **nick**.

—**in time** early enough: *If we hurry we'll still get there in time.*

—**keep time** (1) of a clock to show the time accurately: *The grandfather clock keeps excellent time.* (2) to perform an action in the same rhythm as someone else: *She kept time with the musicians by clapping her hands.*

—**kill time** to find something to do to pass some idle time, especially time spent waiting for someone or something: *I'm waiting to see the boss. I'm just killing time by reading a magazine.*

—**make good time** to have as rapid, or more rapid, a journey as one expected: *We made good time on the motorway, but the country roads slowed us up.*

—**mark time** to remain in one's present position without progressing or taking any action: *He's not applying for other jobs which come up. He's marking time until something just right comes up.* <Refers to soldiers moving their feet as if marching but not actually moving forwards>.

—**not before time** not too soon, rather late: *You've arrived? Not before time.*

—**no time at all** a very short time: *It will be no time at all before your mother comes back.*

—**on time** at the right time: *You'll be sent away if you don't get there on time.*

—**pass the time of day with (someone)** to greet (someone) and have a brief conversation, e.g. about the weather: *Whenever I meet the postman in the street, I pass the time of day with him.*

—**play for time** to act so as to delay an action, event, etc, until the time that conditions are better for oneself: *He played for time by saying that he would have to discuss the situation with his wife before reaching a decision.* <In games such as cricket it means to play in such a way as to avoid defeat by playing defensively until the close of the game>.

—**take one's time** not to hurry, to take as much time as wishes to do something: *Take your time. The bus isn't due for ten minutes.*

—**take time by the forelock** to act quickly and without delay: *If you want to travel the world take time by the forelock and go now.* <Refers to the fact that time was often represented by an old man with no hair except for a forelock, a length of hair over his forehead>.

—**take time off** to take a break from work: *He has taken time off to look after his sick wife.*

—**there's no time like the present** if one has decided on a course of action one should get started on it right away: *If you're going to take up running there's no time like the present.*

—**time and tide wait for no man** time moves on without regard for human beings and therefore opportunities should be grasped as they arise as they may not be there for very long: *If you want to marry her you should ask her now. Time and tide wait for no man.*

—**time and time again** repeatedly: *I've told the child time and time again not to go out of the garden gate.*

—**time flies** time passes very quickly: *Is it that time already? Doesn't time fly?*

—**time is getting on** time is passing, it is growing late: *We had better get home. Time is getting on.*

—**time out of mind** *same as* **time immemorial**—*see* **immemorial**.

—**time was** there was a time when: *Time was when he could have climbed that hill but he's old and stiff now.*

tin

—**a little tin god** *see* **god**.

—**put the tin lid on (something)** *see* **lid**.

tip

—**be on the tip of one's tongue** to be about to be said: *It was on the tip of my tongue to tell him to leave immediately.*

—**the tip of the iceberg** *see* **ice**.

—**tip (someone) off** to give (someone) some private or secret information: *She was leaving without saying goodbye but he tipped me off.*

—**tip the scales** *see* **scale**.

—**tip (someone) the wink** *see* **wink**.

tit

—**tit for tat** repayment of injury or harm for injury or harm: *Your child hit mine and he hit yours. That was simply tit for tat.* <Perhaps a variation on tip for tap, blow for blow>.

to

—**toing and froing** repeatedly going backwards

and forwards: *There's been a lot of toing and froing between the two board rooms. We think a merger is planned.*

toast

—**warm as toast** very warm and cosy: *The child was warm as toast under her quilt.*

tod

—**on one's tod** alone: *He prefers to go on holiday on his tod.* <From Cockney rhyming slang "on one's Tod Sloan", meaning "on one's own", Tod Sloan having been a famous American jockey>.

toe

—**be on one's toes** to be alert and prepared for action: *You had better all be on your toes today. The school inspector is coming.*

—**toe the line** *see* **line**.

—**tread on (someone's) toes** to offend (someone) by doing or saying (something) that is against his or her beliefs or opinions: *I obviously trod on his toes by criticizing the government.*

toffee

—**not for toffee** not at all: *She can't sing for toffee.*

token

—**by the same token** in addition: *If the firm expands we'll need more staff and by the same token more facilities for them.*

told see **tell**.

Tom

—**a peeping Tom** a man who gets sexual enjoyment from secretly watching women undress or women who are naked, especially by looking through the windows of their houses: *The police have arrested the peeping Tom who has been creeping around our gardens.* <From the story of Lady Godiva who is said to have ridden naked through the streets of Coventry as part of a bargain made with her husband, Leofric, Earl of Mercia, to persuade him to lift a tax he had placed on his tenants. Everyone was to stay indoors so as not to see her but a character, later called Peeping Tom, looked out to see her and was struck blind>.

—**every** *or* **any Tom, Dick and Harry** absolutely everyone or anyone, every ordinary person: *The club does not admit every Tom, Dick and Harry.* <From the fact that all three are common English Christian names>.

tongs

—**go at it hammer and tongs** *see* **hammer**.

tongue

—**a slip of the tongue** *see* **slip**.

—**be on the tip of one's tongue** *see* **tip**.

—**have one's tongue in one's cheek** to say something that one does not mean seriously or literally, sometimes to say the opposite of what one means for a joke: *He said that he worked for a very generous company but I could tell that he had his tongue in his cheek.*

—**hold one's tongue** to remain silent or to stop talking: *I wanted to tell him what I thought of his actions but I decided to hold my tongue.*

tooth

—**be** *or* **get long in the tooth** to be or become old: *That actor's getting a bit long in the tooth for that part.*

—**fight tooth and nail** to fight, struggle or argue fiercely and determinedly: *She fought tooth and nail to get her children back.*

—**have a sweet tooth** *see* **sweet**.

top[1]

—**be thin on top** *see* **thin**.

—**blow one's top** to lose one's temper: *She blew her top when he came home drunk.*

—**off the top of one's head** without much thought, without research or preparation: *I don't know exactly how far it is, but off the top of my head I'd say 500 miles.*

—**on top of the world** *see* **world**.

—**out of the top drawer** *see* **drawer**.

—**over the top** too much, to too great an extent: *He went completely over the top with his criticism of the play.*

—**top the bill** *see* **bill**.

—**the top brass** *see* **brass**.

—**the top of the ladder** *or* **tree** the highest point in a profession, etc: *The young doctor got to the top of the surgical ladder.*

top[2]

—**sleep like a top** to sleep very soundly: *We slept like tops after our long walk.* <A pun on the fact that sleep used of a top means "to spin steadily without wobbling">.

torch

—**carry a torch for (someone)** *see* **carry**.

toss

—**argue the toss** to dispute a decision: *There's no point in arguing the toss. The judge's decision is final.* <Refers to arguing about the result of tossing a coin>.

touch

—**a soft touch** *see* **soft**[2].

—**in touch with (someone)** in communication with (someone): *I tried to get in touch with an old friend.*

—**it's touch and go** it's very uncertain or precarious: *It's touch and go with the invalid's condition.* <Perhaps refers to a ship that touches rocks or the ground but goes on past the danger without being damaged>.

—**lose one's touch** to lose one's usual skill or knack: *He used to be good at getting the children to sleep but he's lost his touch.* <Probably refers to someone's touch on piano keys>.

—**out of touch with (someone)** (1) no longer in contact or communication with (someone): *The two friends have been out of touch for years.* (2) not understanding or sympathetic towards: *She's out of touch with the people in her old neighbourhood.*

—**the common touch** the ability to understand and get on with ordinary people: *The prince has the common touch.*

—**the finishing touches** the final details which complete something: *I'm just putting the finishing touches to my report.*

—**the Midas touch** *see* **Midas**.

—**touch a chord** *see* **chord**.

—**touch (something) off** to cause (something), to give rise to (something): *His remarks sparked off a rebellion.*

—**touch wood** *see* **wood**.

tow

—**have (someone) in tow** to have someone following closely behind one: *She had her three children in tow.*

towel

—**throw in the towel** to give up, to admit defeat: *The student can't cope with his studies and he is throwing in the towel.* <From a method of conceding defeat in boxing>.

tower

—**a tower of strength** someone who is very helpful and supportive: *He was a real tower of strength when her husband died.*

—**live in an ivory tower** *see* **ivory**.

town

—**go out on the town** to go out for a night's entertainment: *We're going out on the town to celebrate their engagement.*

—**go to town** to act or behave without restraint, with great enthusiasm or with great expense: *They've fairly gone to town on decorating the new house.*

—**paint the town red** *see* **paint**.

—**the talk of the town** *see* **talk**.

track

—**cover one's tracks** to hide one's activities or movements: *The bank raiders tried to cover their tracks by changing cars.*

—**keep** *or* **lose track of (someone** *or* **something)** to keep or fail to keep oneself informed about the whereabouts or progress of (someone or something): *He must find it difficult to keep track of all his business interests. I lost track of my university friends years ago.*

—**have a one-track mind** *see* **one**.

—**make tracks (for)** to leave or set out (for): *It's late. We must be making tracks (for home).*

—**off the beaten track** *see* **beat**.

—**on the right** *or* **wrong track** on the right or wrong course to get the correct answer or desired result: *The police think they're on the right track to find the killer.*

—**(someone's) track record** the extent of a person's success or failure in his or her profession or trade: *The salesman has an excellent track record.*

trail

—**blaze a trail** to show or lead the way in some new activity or area of knowledge: *His research blazed a trail in cancer treatment.* <Refers to explorers going along a path and marking the way for those coming after them by stripping sections of bark from trees (blazing)>.

tread

—**tread on (someone's) corns** *see* **corn**.

—**tread on (someone's) toes** *see* **toe**.

—**tread water** *see* **water**.

tree

—**bark up the wrong tree** *see* **bark**.

—**not to be able to see the wood for the trees** *see* **wood**.

—**the top of the tree** *see* **top**.

—**up a gum tree** *see* **gum**.

tremble

—**to be** *or* **go in fear and trembling of (someone** *or* **something)** to be extremely afraid: *The children go in fear and trembling of the school bully.* <A biblical reference to Philippians 2:12>.

trial

—**trial and error** the trying out of various approaches or methods of doing something until one finds the right one: *They found a cure for the skin rash by trial and error.*

—**trials and tribulations** difficulties and hardships: *She was complaining about the trials and tribulations of being a mother.*

triangle

—**the eternal triangle** *see* **eternal**.

trick
—**bag of tricks** *see* **bag**.
—**confidence trick** *see* **confidence**.
—**do the trick** to have the desired effect, to achieve the desired result: *It's proved difficult to cure her cough but the doctor said that this would do the trick.*
—**never to miss a trick** never to fail to take advantage of a favourable situation or opportunity to bring advantage to oneself: *He was selling insurance to people in his holiday hotel. He never misses a trick.*
—**up to one's (old) tricks** acting in one's usual (wrong, dishonest or deceitful) way: *The police suspect that the local villain is up to his old tricks.*
trooper
—**swear like a trooper** to swear very frequently or very strongly: *He was shocked to hear the young woman swearing like a trooper.* <A trooper was an ordinary cavalry soldier>.
trot
—**on the trot** (1) one after the other: *He won three years on the trot.* (2) very active and busy: *With three children she's on the trot from morning till night.*
trouble
—**fish in troubled waters** *see* **fish**.
—**pour oil on troubled waters** *see* **oil**.
trousers
—**catch (someone) with his** *or* **her trousers down** *see* **catch**.
—**wear the trousers** to make all the important decisions in a household: *There's no point in asking him if they need any gardening work done. His wife wears the trousers.*
trowel
—**lay it on with a trowel** *see* **lay**.
truck
—**have no truck with (someone** *or* **something)** to have no contact or dealings with (someone or something): *I wouldn't have any truck with them. They're always in trouble with the police.*
true
—**ring true** *see* **true**.
—**true to form** *see* **form**.
trump
—**play one's trump card** to use something very advantageous to oneself that one has had in reserve for use when really necessary: *The shop manager refused to exchange the faulty stereo system until he played his trump card and said he wrote about consumers' rights.* <In card games a trump is the a card of whichever suit has been declared to be higher-ranking than the others>.
—**turn up trumps** to do the right or required thing in a difficult situation, especially unexpectedly: *I didn't think our team member would beat the champion but he turned up trumps.* <See above—refers to drawing a card from the trump suit>.
truth
—**home truth** *see* **home**.
—**truth will out** the true facts of a situation will not remain hidden or secret forever: *He thought that no one would find out that he had committed bigamy, but his neighbour did. Truth will out.*
try
—**try it on** to act in a bold way in order to find out to what extent it will be tolerated: *He didn't expect to be allowed to go to the all-night party. He was just trying it on.*
tug
—**tug of love** a struggle involving the custody of a child: *No-one has asked the child's opinion in the tug of love.*
tune
—**call the tune** to be the person in control who gives the orders: *It's his deputy who's calling the tune since he's been ill.*<Refers to the saying "He who pays the piper calls the tune">.
—**change one's tune** *see* **change**.
—**in tune with (something)** in agreement with (something), compatible with (something): *Our ideas on the environment are very much in tune.*
—**to the tune of (something)** to the stated sum of money, usually high or higher than is expected or is reasonable: *Instead of hundreds he had to pay to the tune of thousands for that antique.*
tunnel
—**light at the end of the tunnel** *see* **light**.
turkey
—**cold turkey** a form of treatment for drug or alcohol abuse involving sudden and complete withdrawal as opposed to gradual withdrawal: *He's having a hard time trying to get off drugs cold turkey.*
—**talk turkey** to talk plainly and honestly: *If you're interested in this business deal let's talk turkey.*
turn
—**a turn-up for the books** something favour-

able which happens unexpectedly: *He discovered there was a later bus after all. That was a turn-up for the books.* <Referred originally to a horse that unexpectedly won a race, the book meaning the total number of bets on a race>.

—**do (someone) a good turn** to help (someone) in some way: *The boy did the old man a good turn and cut his lawn for him.*

—**do a U-turn** *see* **U**.

—**done to a turn** cooked exactly right, cooked to perfection: *The roast beef was done to a turn.*

—**even the worm turns** *see* **worm**.

—**give (someone) quite a turn** to give (someone) a sudden shock or surprise: *You gave me quite a turn coming up behind me so quietly.*

—**not to turn a hair** *see* **hair**.

—**out of turn** (1) out of the correct order, not at the correct time: *You played out of turn. It was my turn.* (2) at the wrong time, without consideration for the circumstances of the situation, someone's feelings, etc: *I hope I'm not talking out of turn but I think you're doing the wrong thing.*

—**the turn of the year** *or* **century** the end of one year or century and the beginning of the next: *He's changing jobs at the turn of the year.*

—**turn a blind eye to (something)** *see* **eye**.

—**turn (someone's) head** *see* **head**.

—**turn of phrase** a way of expressing something: *The novelist has a fine turn of phrase.*

—**turn (someone) off** to arouse feelings of dislike, disgust, etc in (someone): *The sight of the greasy food turned me right off.*

—**turn one's coat** *see* **coat**.

—**turn one's hand to (something)** *see* **hand**.

—**turn (someone) on** to arouse feelings of excitement, interest or lust in (somone): *Jazz really turns him on.*

—**turn on one's heel** *see* **heel**.

—**turn over a new leaf** *see* **leaf**.

—**turn the corner** *see* **corner**.

—**turn the other cheek** *see* **cheek**.

—**turn the tables on (someone)** *see* **table**.

—**turn turtle** to turn upside down, to capsize: *We were afraid that the boat would turn turtle in the rough seas.* <A turtle is helpless and easy to kill if it is turned over on its back>.

—**turn up one's nose at (something)** *see* **nose**.

—**turn up trumps** *see* **trump**.

turtle

—**turn turtle** *see* **turn**.

twice

—**think twice** to give careful consideration: *She wouldn't think twice about leaving him if someone richer came along.*

twiddle

—**twiddle one's thumbs** *see* **thumb**.

twinkle

—**in the twinkling of an eye** *see* **eye**.

—**when (someone) was just a twinkle in his** *or* **her daddy's eye** before (someone) was born, a long time ago: *You were just a twinkle in your daddy's eye when I first met them.*

twist

—**get one's knickers in a twist** *see* **knickers**.

—**round the twist** insane, very foolish: *She's round the twist to buy the house. It's falling to bits.*

—**twist (someone's) arm** *see* **arm**.

—**twist (someone) round one's little finger** *see* **finger**.

two

—**a bird in the hand is worth two in the bush** *see* **bird**.

—**for two pins** *see* **pin**.

—**in two minds** *see* **mind**.

—**in two shakes of a lamb's tail** *see* **shake**.

—**in two ticks** in a very short time indeed: *I'll attend to it in two ticks.* <Refers to the ticking of a clock>.

—**like as two peas in a pod** *see* **pea**.

—**put two and two together** to come to a (correct) conclusion from what one sees and hears: *Eventually I put two and two together and realized he had been in prison.*

—**there are no two ways about it** *see* **way**.

—**two a penny** *see* **penny**.

—**two of a kind** two people of a very similar type or character: *Don't worry about her treating him badly. They're two of a kind.*

—**two's company, (three's a crowd)** a third person who is with a couple is often unwanted as they want to be alone: *Her mother wouldn't let her go on holiday with her boyfriend unless her sister went too but it was very much a question of two's company.*

—**two wrongs do not make a right** a second wrong action does not lead to good and does not improve a situation: *Don't take revenge by damaging his car because he damaged yours: two wrongs don't make a right.*

tyre

—**spare tyre** *see* **spare**.

U

ugly

—**ugly as sin** *see* **sin**.

—**ugly duckling** *see* **duck**.

umbrage

—**take umbrage** to show that one is offended: *She took umbrage at not being asked to join our trip to the beach.* <Originally meant to feel overshadowed—from Latin *umbra*, shade>.

uncle

—**Bob's your uncle** everything is or will be all right: *Just apologize to him and Bob's your uncle.*

—**talk to (someone) like a Dutch uncle** *see* **Dutch**.

—**Uncle Sam** the United States of America: *Uncle Sam is supplying some of the aid.* <Probably from the Initials "U.S." which were stamped on government supplies, possibly because someone called Uncle Sam was employed in handling such supplies>.

Uriah

—**Uriah Heep** a sycophant, someone who always fawns over and toadies to others: *He's volunteered to go and get the boss's car. He's a real Uriah Heep.* <Refers to a character in Charles Dickens's novel *David Copperfield*>.

under

—**come under the hammer** *see* **hammer**.

—**take (someone) under one's wing** *see* **wing**.

—**under (someone's) (very) nose** *see* **nose**.

—**under one's own steam** *see* **steam**.

—**under the influence** under the influence of alcohol, drunk: *He was caught driving under the influence.*

—**under the weather** *see* **weather**.

—**under (someone's) thumb** *see* **thumb**.

—**under way** *see* **way**.

unknown

—**an unknown quantity** *see* **quantity**.

unsound

—**of unsound mind** insane, deranged: *He murdered his wife while of unsound mind.*

unstuck

—**come unstuck** *see* **come**.

up

—**be in (something) up to one's neck** *see* **neck**.

—**be one up on (someone)** *see* **one**.

—**be on the up-and-up** to be making successful progress: *The firm was doing badly but it's on the up-and up now.*

—**be right up (someone's) street** *see* **street**.

—**be up against it** *see* **against**.

—**be (well) up in** *or* **on (something)** to have an extensive knowledge of (something): *He's well up in modern medical techniques.*

—**be up in arms** *see* **arm**.

—**be up to (someone)** it is (someone's) responsibility or duty: *It's up to him whether he joins or not.*

—**be up to (something)** (1) to be occupied with or in (something, often something dishonest, etc): *What's that crook up to now?* (2) to be good enough, strong enough, etc, to do (something): *She's obviously not up to the job.*

—**be up to no good** *see* **good**.

—**be up to the mark** *see* **mark**.

—**be up with (someone)** to be wrong with (someone): *What's up with him?*

—**it is all up with (someone)** *see* **all**.

—**not up to much** *see* **much**.

—**(someone's) number is up** *see* **number**.

—**up and about** out of bed, after an illness: *He was ill for a time but he's up and about now.*

—**up-and-coming** likely to be successful, rising in popularity or prominence: *She is an up-and-coming young singer.*

—**up and doing** active and busy: *I don't like doing nothing. I like to be up and doing.*

—**up for grabs** *see* **grab**.

—**ups and downs** good fortune and bad fortune, successful periods and unsuccessful periods: *Their relationship has had its ups and downs.*

—**upstage (someone** *or* **something)** to take attention or interest away from (someone or something): *She tried to upstage the other girls at the ball with a very revealing ball gown.*

—**up the wall** *see* **wall**.

—**up to a point** *see* **point**.

—**up to one's ears in (something)** *see* **ear**.

—**up to the minute** *see* **minute**.

upshot

—**the upshot** the result or outcome: *They quar-*

relled and the upshot was that she left. <Literally the last shot in an archery competition>.

upper

—**have** *or* **get the upper hand (of** *or* **over) (someone)** have or get an advantage or control (over someone): *She has the upper hand in the custody dispute as the child lives with her.*

—**keep a stiff upper lip** *see* **lip**.

—**on one's uppers** very poor: *We can't pay the rent. We're on our uppers.* <Literally with no soles on one's shoes>.

—**upper-crust** of the upper class or aristocracy: *She has an upper-crust accent.* <Refers literally to the upper part of the pastry of a pie above the filling>.

upside

—**be** *or* **get upsides with (someone)** to be or become on a level with or equal with (someone): *She's upsides with you now. She has a new car too.*

—**turn (something) upside down** to put (something) into a state of disorder and confusion: *We turned the house upside down looking for the lost document.*

uptake

—**quick** *or* **slow on the uptake** quick or slow to understand: *She's so slow on the uptake that everything has to be explained several times.*

use

—**come in useful** to be useful in the future: *Don't throw out that box. It might come in useful.*

—**have no use for (someone** *or* **something)** to wish not to be associated with (someone or something), to think little of (someone or something): *He has no use for people who lie.*

—**make use of (someone)** to to use (someone) for one's own gain or benefit, to take advantage of (someone): *She just makes use of her mother. She expects her to look after her children every day.*

—**use one's loaf** *see* **loaf**.

U-turn

—**do a U-turn** to change one's opinion, policy, etc, completely: *The government have done a U-turn on their health policy.* <Refers originally to vehicle drivers making a turn in the shape of the letter U to reverse direction>.

V

vain

—**take (someone's) name in vain** to use (someone's) name disrespectfully, especially to swear using God's name: *They were punished for taking the Lord's name in vain.* <A biblical reference to Exodus 20:7>.

value

—**take (someone** *or* **something) at face value** *see* **face**.

variety

—**variety is the spice of life** the opportunity to do different things, experience different situations, etc, is what makes life interesting. *I will go to the pop concert although I'm really a jazz fan as variety is the spice of life.* <A quotation from a poem by William Cowper>.

veil

—**draw a veil over (something)** not to discuss (something), to keep (something) hidden or secret: *If I were him I would draw a veil over his part in the affair.*

velvet

—**the iron hand in the velvet glove** *see* **iron**.

vengeance

—**with a vengeance** very strongly, much, etc: *It's snowing with a vengeance now.*

vent

—**vent one's spleen** *see* **spleen**.

venture

—**nothing ventured, nothing gained** *see* **nothing**.

very

—**the very thing** exactly what is required: *That scarf is the very thing for her birthday present.*

vessel

—**empty vessels make most noise** *see* **empty**.

vested

—**a vested interest in (something)** *see* **interest**.

vex

—**a vexed question** a difficult issue or problem that is much discussed without being resolved: *Then there is the vexed question of who is responsible for paying for the repairs.*

vicious

—**vicious circle** *see* **circle**.

victory

—**landslide victory** a victory in an election by a very large number of votes: *We expected a victory but not a landslide one.*

—**Pyrrhic victory** *see* **Pyrrhic**.

view

—**a bird's-eye view of (something)** (1) a view of (something) seen from high above: *We got a marvellous bird's-eye view of the town from the top of the tower.* (2) a brief description, etc, of (something): *The book gives a bird's-eye view of alternative medicine, but you will require something more detailed.*

—**in view of (something)** considering (something), because of (something): *In view of his behaviour he will have to be punished.*

—**take a dim view of (something)** *see* **dim**.

villain

—**the villain of the piece** the person responsible for an act of evil or wrongdoing: *We wondered who had broken the window—the boy next door turned out to be the villain of the piece.* <Refers originally to the villain in a play>.

vine

—**a clinging vine** a possessive person, someone who likes always to be with someone else: *His wife's a real clinging vine.*

—**wither on the vine** to die to come to an end without being used, finished, etc: *The research department has some good ideas but they wither on the vine because the company does not have the money to put them into practice.* <Literally of grapes withering on the vine instead of being picked and eaten or made into wine>.

violet

—**a shrinking violet** a very timid, shy person: *She won't speak in public. She's very much a shrinking violet.*

viper

—**nurse a viper in one's bosom** to be helpful to or supportive of someone who does one harm: *The boy whom they were fostering attacked their son with a knife. They were nursing a viper in their bosom.* <A viper is a poisonous snake>.

vital

—**vital statistics** one's chest, waist and hip measurements: *The announcer at the beauty* *contest gave everyone's vital statistics.* <Refers originally to statistics dealing with population>.

voice

—**at the top of one's voice** loudly, in a high voice: *The teacher shouted at the children at the top of his voice.*

—**a voice crying in the wilderness** (someone) expressing an opinion or warning that no one takes any notice of: *She told them that the proposed product would not sell but she was a voice crying in the wilderness.* <A biblical reference to John the Baptist in Matthew 3:3>.

—**the still, small voice (of reason)** the expression of a calm, sensible point of view: *The still, small voice of reason told her not to accept a lift from the stranger, but she did.* <A biblical reference to I Kings 19:12>.

volume

—**speak volumes** to express a great deal of meaning without putting it into words: *She made no reply to his insult but her look spoke volumes.*

vote

—**a vote of confidence** a vote taken to establish whether or not the government, a group of people, a person, etc, is still trusted and supported: *The chairman survived the board's vote of confidence.*

—**vote with one's feet** to leave: *The workers had no confidence in the new management and so they voted with their feet by finding other jobs.*

W

wagon

—**hitch one's wagon to a star** to have noble or high ambitions or aims: *He was born into a very poor family but he had hitched his wagon to a star and was determined to go to university.* <Refers to a quotation from *Society at Solitude* by Ralph Waldo Emerson>.

—**on the wagon** not drinking alcohol: *He's on the wagon for health reasons.* <Refers to a water wagon>.

wait

—**lie in wait** to be on the watch (for someone), to ambush (someone). *The rock star tried to leave by the back exit, but his fans were lying in wait for him.*

—**waiting in the wings** *see* **wing**.

wake

—**in the wake of (something)** immediately following, and often caused by (something): *Disease came in the wake of the flood.* <Refers literally to the strip of water left by the passing of a ship>.

walk

—**cock of the walk** *see* **cock**.

—**walk it** to win or succeed easily: *He was nervous about the match but he walked it.*

—**walk of life** occupation or profession, way of earning a living: *People from all walks of life joined the campaign.*

—**walk on air** *see* **air**.

wall

—**go to the wall** to suffer ruin: *Many small firms went to the wall during the recession.* <Origin uncertain>.

—**have one's back to the wall** *see* **back**.

—**the writing on the wall** *see* **write**.

—**up the wall** very annoyed, irritated, harassed, etc: *These children are driving me up the wall with their noise.*

—**walls have ears** someone may be listening (to a secret conversation): *Be careful what you say in the restaurant. It's not busy but walls have ears.*

—**would like to be a fly on the wall** *see* **fly**.

Walter

—**a Walter Mitty** someone who invents stories about himself to make his life seem more exciting: *I was amazed at some of his adventures until I discovered that he was a Walter Mitty.* <Refers to a character in a James Thurber short story>.

war

—**have been in the wars** to have a slight injury: *"You've been in the wars," said the nurse to the little boy who had broken his leg falling off a swing.*

—**on the warpath** very angry: *Look out. Father's discovered the broken window and he's on the warpath.* <An North American Indian expression>.

warm

—**warm as toast** *see* **toast**.

—**warm the cockles of the heart** *see* **heart**.

wart

—**warts and all** including all the faults, disadvantages: *Her husband is a bit irresponsible, but she loves him warts and all.* <Refers to the fact that Oliver Cromwell instructed his portrait painter, Sir Peter Lely, to paint him as he really was, including his warts, rather than try to make him look more handsome>.

wash

—**come out in the wash** to come to a satisfactory end: *Don't worry about making a mistake on your first day. It'll all come out in the wash.* <Used literally of a stain on clothes, etc, that comes out when the article is washed>.

—**wash one's dirty linen in public** *same as* **air one's dirty linen in public**—*see* **air**.

—**washed-out** exhausted: *She felt washed-out after her illness.* <Used literally of garments having lost colour as a result of washing>.

—**washed-up** ruined, finished: *Their relationship is all washed up.* <Refers to a shipwreck>.

—**wash one's hands of (something)** *see* **hand**.

waste

—**lay waste (something)** to destroy or ruin (something) by force: *The invading army laid waste the city.*

—**waste not, want not** if one is careful not to waste anything it is likely that one will never be in want: *Don't throw out that bread. Waste not, want not.*

watch

—**the** *or* **a watched pot never boils** *see* **pot**.

—**watch (someone) like a hawk** *see* **hawk**.

water

—**be water off a duck's back** *see* **duck**.

—**hold water** to be accurate, to be able to be proved true: *Your theory won't hold water.* <From a vessel that is not broken>.

—**in deep water** *see* **deep**.

—**like a fish out of water** *see* **fish**.

—**of the first water** *see* **first**.

—**pour oil on troubled waters** *see* **oil**.

—**pour** *or* **throw cold water on (something)** *see* **cold**.

—**spend money like water** *see* **money**.

—**still waters run deep** *see* **still**.

—**take to (something) like a duck to water** *see* **duck**.

—**tread water** to take very little action: *This is not a time to expand the business. We should tread water for a while.* <Literally to keep oneself afloat in water by moving the legs (and arms) rather than by swimming>.

—**water (something) down** to make (something) less serious, exciting, etc, than it really was: *We had better water down the account of the accident for my mother or she'll worry.* <Literally to dilute with water>.

—**water under the bridge** something that is past and cannot be changed and should be forgotten: *Stop worrying about our quarrel. It's water under the bridge.*

Waterloo

—**meet one's Waterloo** *see* **meet**.

wave

—**on the same wavelength as (someone)** having the same opinions, attitudes, tastes, etc, as (someone): *We'll never be friends. We're just not on the same wavelength.*

way

—**get into the way of (something** *or* **doing something)** to become accustomed to (something or doing something): *She can't get into the way of using the computer.*

—**get** *or* **have one's own way** to do or get what one wants: *We all wanted to go the beach but as usual she got her own way and we went to the cinema.*

—**go out of one's way** to do more than is really necessary, to make a special effort: *She went out of her way to be kind to the new girl.*

—**go the way of all flesh** to die or come to an end: *He must have gone the way of all flesh by now. Otherwise he would be over 100 years old.*

—**have a way with (someone** *or* **something)** to have a special knack with (someone or something), to be good at handling (someone or something): *He has a way with words.*

—**have everything one's own way** to get everything done according to one's wishes: *The boss won't listen to any suggestions. He likes to have everything his own way.*

—**have it both ways** to have the advantages of two sets of situations, each of which usually excludes the possibility of the other: *She wants a full-time job but she wants to look after her children herself. She's not going to be able to have it both ways.*

—**in a bad way** very ill, injured, distressed, etc: *The accident victim is in a bad way.*

—**lead the way** to go first, to be in front: *Which country leads the way in electronics?*

—**look the other way** *see* **other**.

—**lose one's way** to cease to know where one is or which direction one is going in: *We lost our way in the mist.*

—**make one's way** to go, to progress: *Make your way to the first floor.*

—**make way for (someone** *or* **something)** to stand aside to leave room for (someone or something): *Older people must retire and make way for the young.*

—**mend one's ways** to improve one's behaviour: *You'll have to mend your ways if you want to stay with the firm.*

—**no way** *see* **no**.

—**one way and another** in various ways: *He was made to feel very unwelcome in one way and another.*

—**on the way** about to happen or arrive: *The food's on its way.*

—**pave the way for (something)** *see* **pave**.

—**pay one's own way** *see* **pay**.

—**see one's way to (doing something)** to be able and willing to (do something): *Could you see your way to giving me a lift to work?*

—**there are no two ways about it** no other opinion, attitude, etc, is possible: *He's guilty. There are no two ways about it.*

—**under way** in progress: *His plans are well under way.*

—**ways and means** methods, especially unofficial ones: *We don't have the money yet, but there are ways and means of getting it.*

wayside

—**fall by the wayside** to fail to continue to the

end of something; to give up in the course of doing something: *Not all students graduate. Some fall by the wayside.* <A biblical reference to the parable of the sower in Luke 8:5>.

weak

—**in a weak moment** at a time when one is feeling unusually kind, generous, etc: *In a weak moment I agreed to let her stay at my house.*

wear

—**wear one's heart on one's sleeve** *see* **heart**.

weather

—**keep a weather eye open** *see* **eye**.

—**make heavy weather of (something)** *see* **heavy**.

—**under the weather** unwell: *She left work early feeling under the weather.*

—**weather the storm** *see* **storm**.

wedding

—**shotgun wedding** *see* **shot**.

wedge

—**the thin end of the wedge** a minor event or action which could be the first stage of something major and serious or harmful: *Letting her stay for a week is the thin end of the edge. She'll want to stay permanently.*

weep

—**weep buckets** *see* **bucket**.

weight

—**carry weight** to have influence, to be considered important: *Their opinion won't carry any weight.*

—**pull one's weight** to do one's fair share of work, etc: *We'll finish this in time if we all pull our weight.*

—**throw one's weight about** *or* **around** to use one's power and influence in a bullying way: *The deputy manager is throwing his weight around when the manager is away.*

—**weigh (something) up** to assess (something): *It's difficult to weigh up our chances of success.*

—**worth its** *or* **one's weight in gold** *see* **gold**.

well

—**be well out of (something)** to be fortunate in having got out of (something): *You're well out of that relationship. She's not to be trusted.*

—**well off** (1) having plenty of money, rich: *They're very well off althoug they live very simply.* (2) in a fortunate situation: *He's looking for a new job. He doesn't know when he's well off.*

west

—**go west** to be ruined, to be finished: *Our hopes of victory have gone west.* <Airmen's slang from World War 1>.

wet

—**wet behind the ears** to be young, inexperienced and naive: *You can't expect him to deal with that difficult client. He's wet behind the ears.*

—**wet blanket** *see* **blanket**.

—**wet one's whistle** *see* **whistle**.

whale

—**have a whale of a time** to have an extremely enjoyable time: *The children had a whale of a time at the beach.*

what

—**give (someone) what for** to scold or punish (someone): *You'll get what for for borrowing his bike without permission.*

—**know what's what** to know the details of a situation, to know what is going on: *The accountant is the only person who know's what's what in the firm.*

—**what have you** and similar things: *Put your suitcase and what have you over there.*

—**what of it?** what does it matter?: *So I've annoyed him. What of it?*

wheel

—**oil the wheels** *see* **oil**.

—**put a spoke in (someone's) wheel** *see* **spoke**.

—**put one's shoulder to the wheel** *see* **shoulder**.

—**set the wheels in motion** to start a process off: *If you want to get planning permission you'll have to set the wheels in motion right away.*

—**wheeling and dealing** acting in an astute but sometimes dishonest or immoral way, especially in business: *He made a lot of money from wheeling and dealing in the antiques trade.*

while

—**worth (someone's) while** worth (someone's) time and effort: *If you do the work he'll make it worth your while.*

whip

—**a whipping boy** someone who is blamed and punished for someone else's mistakes: *The young clerk is the whipping boy for the whole department.* <Refers literally to a boy who was punished for any misdeeds a royal prince made, since the tutor was not allowed to strike a member of the royal family>.

—**have the whip hand** to have control or an advantage: *He has the whip hand in that relationship. He makes all the decisions.* <Refers to coach-driving>.

whisker

—**win by a whisker** to win by a very short amount: *The government won the election by a whisker.*

—**the cat's whiskers** *same as* **the cat's pyjamas**—*see* **cat**.

whisper

—**in a stage whisper** *see* **stage**.

whistle

—**blow the whistle on (someone)** *see* **blow**.

—**clean as a whistle** *see* **clean**.

—**wet one's whistle** to have a drink: *It's hot. Let's stop and wet our whistles.*

—**whistle for (something)** to ask for (something) with no hope of getting it: *You may need extra money but you can whistle for it.* <Perhaps from an old sailors' superstition that when a ship is becalmed whistling can summon up a wind>.

white

—**a whited sepulchre** someone who pretends to be moral and virtuous but is in fact bad: *He seems to be a whited sepulchre but I've heard that he beats his wife and children.* <A biblical reference to Matthew 23:27>.

—**a white elephant** *see* **elephant**.

—**show the white feather** *see* **feather**.

—**white as a sheet** *see* **sheet**.

—**white lie** a not very serious lie: *I'd rather tell her a white lie than tell her I don't like her dress.*

whole

—**go the whole hog** *see* **hog**.

—**the whole (bang) shoot** *or* **the whole shooting match** *see* **shoot**.

whoop

—**whoop it up** to celebrate in a noisy, extravagant way: *He really whooped it up before his wedding.*

wick

—**get on (someone's) wick** to annoy or irritate (someone) greatly.

wicket

—**be on a sticky wicket** *see* **stick**.

widow

—**grass widow** *see* **grass**.

wild

—**a wild goose chase** a search or hunt that cannot end in success: *I knew it was a wild goose chase to look for an open restaurant at that time in the morning.*

—**run wild** to behave in an uncontrolled, undisciplined way: *The children run wild while their parents are at work.*

—**sow one's wild oats** to enjoy oneself in a wild and sometimes promiscuous way when one is young: *He's sown his wild oats now and he wants to get married and settle down.*

—**spread like wildfire** to spread extremely rapidly: *The disease spread like wildfire through the small community.* <Wildfire was probably a kind of fire started by lightning>.

—**wild horses would not drag (someone) to something** *or* **somewhere** *see* **horse**.

wilderness

—**a voice crying in the wilderness** *see* **voice**.

will

—**willing horse** *see* **horse**.

—**with a will** enthusiastically and energetically: *The children worked with a will weeding the garden.*

—**with the best will in the world** *see* **best**.

win

—**win the day** *same as* **carry the day**—*see* **day**.

wind

—**a straw in the wind** *see* **straw**.

—**get wind of (something)** to receive information about (something) *indirectly or secretly: We got wind of the enemy's plans.* <Referring to the scent of an animal carried by the wind>.

—**in the wind** about to happen, being placed or prepared: *I think major changes are in the wind at work.*

—**get the wind up** to become frightened or nervous: *He got the wind up when he heard the police were after him.*

—**raise the wind** to get enough money to do (something): *They're trying to raise the wind to buy a house.*

—**sail close to the wind** *see* **sail**.

—**see which way the wind blows** *see* **blow**.

—**take the wind out of (someone's) sails** to reduce (someone's) pride in his or her cleverness, abilities, etc: *She was boasting about how many exams she had passed when we took the wind out of her sails by telling her that everyone else had passed more.* <Refers to the fact that a ship takes the wind out of another ship's sails if it passes close to it on the windward side>.

—**throw caution to the (four) winds** to begin to behave recklessly: *She had very little money but she threw caution to the winds and bought a new dress.*

windmill

—**tilt at windmills** to struggle against imaginary opposition: *She thinks everyone in the office is in trying to get rid of her but she is tilting at windmills.* <Refers to an episode in Cervantes's novel *Don Quixote* in which the hero mistakes a row of windmills for giants and attacks them>.

window

—**window-dressing** the presentation of something to show the most favourable parts and hide the rest: *There's a lot of window-dressing in this report. It mentions all the benefits of the scheme but it glosses over the disadvantages.* <Refers literally to the arranging of goods in a shop window to attract customers>.

wing

—**clip (someone's) wings** *see* **clip**.

—**spread one's wings** (1) to leave home: *I like living at home but I think it's time to spread my wings and find a flat.* (2) to try to put into practice one's own ideas, to make use of one's abilities: *So far she has been carrying out the head of department's suggestions but it is time for her to spread her wings.* <Refers to young birds ready to try to fly and leave the nest>.

—**take (someone) under one's wing** to take (someone) under one's protection and guidance: *Someone should take the new girl under her wing. She feels lost in this large firm.* <Refers to the practice of some birds of covering their young with their wings>.

—**waiting in the wings** in a state of readiness to do something, especially to take over someone else's job: *She's afraid to be away from the office for very long because her assistant is just waiting in the wings.* <Literally waiting in the wings of a theatre stage ready to go on>.

wink

—**forty winks** *see* **forty**.

—**tip (someone) the wink** to give (someone) information secretly or privately: *He tipped me the wink that the it was her birthday.*

wipe

—**wipe the floor with (someone)** *see* **floor**.

wire

—**get** *or* **have one's wires crossed** to be involved in a misunderstanding: I *thought it was tomorrow we were meeting. I must have got my wires crossed.* <Refers to telephone wires>.

wise

—**a wise guy** someone who thinks that he is smart, knowledgeable, etc, and acts as if he is: *He's such a wise guy that everybody dislikes him.*

—**be wise after the event** *see* **event**.

—**none the wiser** knowing no more than one did before: *I was none the wiser after his explanation.*

—**put (someone) wise to (something)** to give (someone) information about (something), make (someone) aware of (something): *Her friend put her wise to his police record.*

wish

—**wishful thinking** believing that, or hoping that, something unlikely is true or will happen just because one wishes that it would: *I hoped that we would win but it was just wishful thinking.*

—**wish (someone) joy of (something)** to wish that (something) will be a pleasure or benefit to someone (although one doesn't think it will): *I wish you joy of that car, but I found it unreliable.*

wit

—**at one's wits' end** worried and desperate: *She's at her wits' end about her missing husband.*

—**keep one's wits about one** to be alert and watchful: *Keep your wits about you when doing business with him. People say he is a crook.*

—**live by one's wits** to live by cunning schemes rather than by working: *He hasn't done a day's work in his life. He lives by his wits.*

—**scare (someone) out of his** *or* **her wits** to frighten (someone) very much: *They were scared out of their wits when they saw the man with a gun.*

witch

—**witch-hunt** a search for and persecution of people who are thought to have done something wrong, hold opinions which are thought to be dangerous etc: *The company are conducting a witch-hunt of certain union members.* <Refers historically to organized hunts for people thought to be witches>.

without

—**without rhyme or reason** *see* **rhyme**.

—**without so much as a** *see* **much**.

wolf

—**a lone wolf** *see* **lone**.

—**a wolf in sheep's clothing** someone evil and dangerous who seems to be gentle and harmless: *She trusted him but when he turned nasty she realized that he was a wolf in sheep's clothing.* <A biblical reference to Matthew 7:15>.

—**cry wolf** to give a false warning of danger, to call unnecessarily for help: *She said there was an intruder in the garden but she was only crying wolf.* <Refers to one of Aesop's fables in which a shepherd boy used to amuse himself by calling out that a wolf was coming to attack his sheep and did this so many times when it was not true that no one believed when it was true, and all his sheep were killed>.

—**keep the wolf from the door** to prevent poverty and hunger: *He earns very little but enough to keep the wolf from the door.*

wonder

—**a nine days' wonder** *see* **nine**.

—**no wonder** it is not surprising: *No wonder you're tired. It's very late.*

—**small wonder** *see* **small**.

wood

—**not to be able to see the wood for the trees** not to be able to consider the general nature of a situation, etc, because one is concentrating too much on details: *She's busy worrying about putting the commas in the right place that she doesn't appreciate the quality of the text. She can't see the wood for the trees.*

—**out of the woods** out of danger or difficulties: *The patient is improving but he's not out of the woods yet.*

—**this** *or* **that, etc, neck of the woods** *see* **neck**.

—**touch wood** to touch something made of wood supposedly to keep away bad luck: *None of us is poverty-stricken. Touch wood!* <Refers to a well-known superstition>.

wool

—**pull the wool over (someone's) eyes** to deceive (someone): *He pulled the wool over her eyes by pretending to be in love with her but he was really after her money.*

—**wool-gathering** day-dreaming: *The boss complains about her wool-gathering. She has no concentration.* <Refers to someone wandering around hedges gathering wool left by sheep>.

word

—**a man of his word** *see* **man**.

—**be as good as one's word** *see* **good**.

—**eat one's words** to admit that one was wrong in what one said: *I said he would be last but I was forced to eat my words when he won.*

—**from the word go** *see* **go**.

—**get a word in edgeways** *or* **edgewise** to have difficulty in breaking into a conversation: *The old friends were so busy chatting that their husbands couldn't get a word in edgeways.*

—**hang on (someone's) words** to listen carefully and eagerly to everything that someone says: *The student hangs on the lecturer's words.*

—**have a word in (someone's) ear** to tell (someone) something in private: *She doesn't know he's married. You should have a word in her ear.*

—**have a word with (someone)** to have a short conversation with (someone): *I'd like a word with you before the meeting.*

—**have the last word** *see* **last**.

—**have words** to argue or quarrel: *You can tell from their expressions that they've had words.*

—**in a word** briefly: *In a word I dislike him.*

—**keep one's word** to do as one promised to do: *He said he would be there and he kept his word.*

—**mum's the word** *see* **mum**.

—**put in a good word for (someone)** to say something favourable about (someone), to recommend (someone): *You might get the job if he puts a good word in for you.*

—**say the word** say what you want and your wishes will be carried out: *If you want some food just say the word.*

—**take (someone) at his** *or* **her word** to believe (someone) without question and act accordingly: *He said I could buy goods at a discount, and I took him at his word.*

—**take the words out of (someone's) mouth** to say what (someone) was just about to say: *You took the words right out of my mouth. I was going to suggest a trip to the cinema.*

—**words fail me** I cannot put my feelings into words: *Words fail me when I think of their behaviour.*

work

—**all in a day's work** *see* **day**.

—**all work and no play makes Jack a dull boy** people should take some leisure time and not work all the time: *Take some time off and come swimming. All work and no play makes Jack a dull boy.*

—**a nasty piece of work** *see* **nasty**.

—**give (someone) the works** to give (someone) the complete treatment: *She went to the beauty salon and had the works.* <Originally slang for to kill someone>.

—**gum up the works** *see* **gum**.

—**have one's work cut out** to face a very difficult task: *You'll have your work cut out to get there on time.* <Literally to have a lot of work ready for on>.

—**nasty piece of work** *see* **nasty**.

—**throw a spanner in the works** *see* **spanner**.

—**worked up** agitated, annoyed: *She's all worked up because they're late.*

—**work out** to come to a successful conclusion: *I'm glad things worked out for you.*

world

—**a man of the world** a sophisticated and worldly man: *He won't be shocked by her behaviour. He's a man of the world.*

—**dead to the world** *see* **dead**.

—**for all the world like (someone** *or* **something)** exactly like (someone or something): *She looked for all the world like a witch.*
—**have** *or* **get the best of both worlds** *see* **best**.
—**it's a small world** *see* **small**.
—**it takes all sorts (to make a world)** *see* **sort**.
—**on top of the world** very cheerful and happy: *She's on top of the world with her new baby.*
—**out of this world** remarkably good: *The food was out of this world.*
—**think the world of (someone)** to be extremely fond of (someone): *He thinks the world of his children.*
—**with the best will in the world** *see* **best**.
—**the world is (someone's) oyster** (someone) has a great many possible opportunities or chances: *With those qualifications the world is your oyster.* <Refers to a quotation from Shakespeare's *The Merry Wives of Windsor*, Act 2, scene ii>.

worm
—**(even) the worm turns** even the most humble or meek person will protest if treated badly enough: *He had bullied her for years, so it was no surprise when she eventually left him—even the worm turns.*

worth
—**for all one is worth** using maximum effort: *We ran for all we were worth to catch the last bus.*
—**worth its** *or* **one's weight in gold** *see* **gold**.
—**worth one's salt** *see* **salt**.
—**worth (someone's) while** *see* **while**.

wound
—**rub salt in the wound** *see* **salt**.

wrap
—**keep (something) under wraps** to keep (something) secret or hidden: *We're keeping our new product under wraps until the launch.*
—**wrapped up in (someone** *or* **something)** absorbed in, giving all one's attention to (someone or something): *She's completely wrapped up in her work.*
—**wrap (something) up** to finish (something) completely: *At last the contract is all wrapped up.*

wrist
—**a slap on the wrist** *see* **slap**.

write
—**nothing to write home about** *see* **nothing**.
—**the writing on the wall** something which indicates that something unpleasant, such as failure, unhappiness, disaster, etc, will happen: *She should have seen the writing on the wall when her boss kept complaining about her work.* <A biblical reference to Daniel 5:5-31, in which the coming destruction of the Babylonian empire is made known to Belshazzar at a feast through mysterious writing on a wall>.

wrong
—**be in the wrong** to be blameworthy, to be guilty of error: *You must admit that you were in the wrong.*
—**get hold of the wrong end of the stick** *see* **stick**.
—**get off on the wrong foot** *see* **foot**.
—**get out of bed on the wrong side** *see* **bed**.
—**get on the wrong side of (someone)** to cause (someone) to dislike or be hostile to one: *It's unwise to get on the wrong side of the headmaster.*
—**not to put a foot wrong** not to make a mistake of any kind: *The player didn't put a foot wrong in the whole match.*
—**on the wrong track** *see* **track**.
—**rub (someone) up the wrong way** *see* **rub**.
—**two wrongs do not make a right** *see* **two**.

YZ

yarn

—**spin a yarn** to tell a long story, especially an untrue one that is given as an excuse: *When he was late he spun some yarn about being delayed by a herd of cows.* <Telling a story is compared to spinning a long thread>.

year

—**the year dot** a long time, the beginning of time: *I've known him since the year dot.*

—years of discretion an age when one is able to judge between what is right and what is wrong: She can stay out until

yesterday

—**not born yesterday** experienced and not easily fooled: *You don't expect me to believe that! I wasn't born yesterday!*

young

—**you're only young once** one should take advantage of the opportunities that arise when one is young and has the energy, freedom, etc, to enjoy or exploit them: *You should take the job abroad. After all, you're only young once.*

zero

—**zero hour** the time at which something is due to begin: *The party begins at six and it's only two hours until zero hour.* <Originally a military term>.

Eponyms and Abbreviations

Eponyms

ampere the standard metric unit by which an electric current is measured, called after the French physicist André Marie Ampère, (1775–1836).

atlas a book of maps, called after Atlas, in Greek mythology the leader of the Titans who attempted to storm the heavens and for this supreme treason was condemned by Zeus to hold up the vault of heaven on his head and hands for the rest of his life. The geographer Gerardus Mercator (*see* Mercator projection) used the figure of Atlas bearing the globe as a frontispiece in his 16th-century collection of maps and charts.

aubrietia a trailing purple-flowered perennial plant, called after Claude Aubriet (1665–1742), a French painter of animals and flowers.

Bailey bridge a type of temporary military bridge that can be assembled very quickly, called after Sir Donald Bailey (1901–85), the English engineer who invented it.

baud a unit used in measuring telecommunications transmission speed denoting the number of discrete signal elements that can be transmitted per second, called after the French telecommunications pioneer, Jean M. Baudot (1845–1903).

Beaufort scale a international system of measuring of wind speed, from) (calm) to 12 (hurricane), called after Admiral Sir Francis Beaufort (1774–1857), the British surveyor who devised it.

becquerel the standard metric unit of radioactivity, defined as decay per second, called after the French physicist Antoine-Henri Becquerel (1852–1908), who began the study of radioactivity.

begonia a genus of tropical plants cultivated for their showy petalless flowers and ornamental lopsided succulent leaves, called after Michel Begon (1638–1710), a French patron of botany.

Belisha beacon a post surmounted by a flashing light in an orange globe that marks a road crossing for pedestrians, called after the British politician Leslie Hore-Belisha (1893–1957).

Biro™ a type of ball-point pen, called after its Hungarian-born inventor, Laszlo Jozsef Biro (1900–85).

bloomers a women's underpants with full, loose legs gathered at the knee, called after the American social reformer Amelia Jenks Bloomer (1818–94).

bougainvillea a genus of tropical plants with large rosy or purple bracts, called after the French navigator Louis Antoine de Bougainville (1729–1811).

bowdlerize to remove what are considered to be indelicate or indecent words or passages from a book, called after the British doctor, Thomas Bowdler (1754–1825) who produced an expurgated edition of Shakespeare.

bowie knife a type of hunting knife with a long curving blade, called after the American soldier and adventurer James Bowie (1799–1836) who made it popular

boycott to refuse to deal with or trade with a person, organization, etc, in order to punish or coerce, called after the Irish land agent Captain Charles Cunningham Boycott (1832–97) who was accorded such treatment after refusing to reduce rents.

Boyle's law the scientific principle that a volume of gas varies inversely with the pressure of the gas when the temperature is constant, called after the Irish-born British physicist, Robert Boyle (1627–91), who formulated it.

Braille the system of printing for the blind using a system of raised dots that can be understood by touch, called after the blind French musician, Louis Braille (1809–52), who invented it.

Brownian motion the random movement of minutes particles, which occurs in both gases and liquids, called after the Scottish botanist Robert Brown (1773–1858), who first discovered the phenomenon in 1827.

buddleia a genus of shrubs and trees with lilac or yellowish- white flowers, called after Adam Buddle (d.1715), English clergyman and botanist.

Bunsen burner a burner with an adjustable air inlet that mixes gas and air to produce a smokeless flame of great heat, called after the German scientist, Robert Wilhelm Bunsen (1811–99), who invented it.

camellia a genus of oriental evergreen ornamental shrubs, called after the Moravian Jesuit missionary, George Joseph Kamel (1661–1706), who introduced it into Europe.

cardigan a knitted jacket fastened with buttons, called after James Thomas Brudenell, 7th Earl of Cardigan (1797–1868) who was fond of wearing such a garment and was the British cavalry officer who led the unsuccessful Charge of the Light Brigade during the Crimean War (1854).

Celsius the scale of temperature in which 0° is the freezing point of water and 100° the boiling point, called after Anders Celsius (1701–44), the Swedish astronomer and scientist who invented it.

chauvinism an aggressive patriotism, called after Nicolas Chauvin of Rochefort, 19th-century French soldier in Napoleon's army, and now used to apply to excessive devotion to a belief or case, especially a man's belief in the superiority of men over women.

clerihew a four-line verse consisting of two rhymed couplets of variable length, often encapsulating an unreliable biographical anecdote, called after the English writer, Edmund Clerihew Bentley (1875–1956), who invented it.

coulomb the standard metric unit for measuring electric charge, called after the French physicist, Charles Augustin de Coulomb (1736–1806).

dahlia a genus of half-hardy herbaceous perennial plants of the aster family grown for its colourful blooms, called after the Swedish botanist Anders Dahl (1751–89).

daltonism colour blindness, especially the confusion between green and red, called after the British chemist and physicist, John Dalton (1766–1844), who first described it.

Darwinism the theory of evolution by natural selection, called after the British naturalist Charles Robert Darwin (1809–82), who first described the theory.

Davy lamp a safety lamp used by miners to detect combustible gas, called after the English chemist, Sir Humphry Davy (1778–1829), who invented it.

degauss to neutralize or remove a magnetic field, called after the German mathematician Karl Friedrich Gauss (1777–1855). *See also* GAUSS.

derrick now any crane-like apparatus but formerly a word for a gallows, called after a 17th-century English hangman at Tyburn with the surname of Derrick.

diesel an internal-combustion engine in which ignition is produced by the heat of highly compressed air, called after the German engineer, Rudolf Diesel (1858–1913), who invented it.

Doberman pinscher a breed of dog with a smooth glossy black and tan coat and docked tail, called after the German dog breeder, Ludwig Dobermann (1834–94), who bred it.

Dolby™ an electronic noise-reduction system used in sound recording and playback systems, called after the American engineer, R. Dolby (1933–), who invented it.

Don Quixote a chivalrous or romantic person who tends to be carried away by his ideals and notions, called after Don Quixote, hero of the novel *Don Quixote de la Mancha* by the Spanish novelist Miguel de Cervantes Saavedra (1547–1616). *See also* **quixotic**.

Doppler effect *or* **Doppler shift** a change in the observed frequency of a wave as a result of the relative motion between the wave source and the detector, called after the Austrian physicist, Christian Johann Doppler (1803–53).

draconian an adjective meaning very cruel or severe, called after Draco, the 7th-century BC Athenian statesman who formulated extremely harsh laws.

dunce a person who is stupid or slow to learn, called after the Scottish theologian, John Duns Scotus, Scottish (*c*.1265–1308).

Earl Grey a blend of Chinese teas flavoured with oil of bergamot, called after the British statesman, Charles, 2nd Earl Grey (1764–1845).

Eiffel Tower the tall tower in the centre of Paris, called after the French engineer, Alexandre Gustave Eiffel (1832–1923, who built it.

einsteinium an artificial radioactive chemical element, called after the German-born American physicist, Albert Einstein (1879–1955).

Everest the highest mountain in the world, called after Sir George Everest (1790–1866), who was Surveyor-General of India.

Fallopian tube either of the two tubes through which the egg cells pass from the ovary to the uterus in female mammals, called after the Italian anatomist, Gabriel Fallopius (1523–62), who first described them.

Fahrenheit the scale of temperatures in which 32° is the freezing point of water and 212° the boiling point, called after the German scientist, Gabriel Daniel Fahrenheit (1686–1736), who invented it.

farad the standard metric unit of capacitance, called after the English physicist and chemist, Michael Faraday (1791–1867), who discovered magnetic induction.

fermi a unit of length employed in nuclear physics, called after the Italian-born American physicist, Enrico Fermi (1901–54).

fermium an artificially produced radioactive element, called after the Italian-born American physicist, Enrico Fermi (1901–54).

forsythia a genus of widely cultivated yellow-flowered ornamental shrubs of the olive family, called after the English botanist, William Forsyth (1737–1804).

Fraunhofer lines dark lines that occur in the continuous spectrum of the sun, called after the German physicist and optician, Joseph von Fraunhofer (1787–1826).

freesia a type of sweet-smelling ornamental flower of the iris family, called after the German physician Friedrich Heinrich Theodor Freese (d. 1876).

fuchsia a genus of decorative shrubs of Central and South America, called after the German botanist and physician, Leonhard Fuchs (1501–66).

Gallup poll a sampling of public opinion, especially to help forecast the outcome of an election, called after the American statistician, George Horace Gallup (1901–84), who devised it.

galvanize to coat one type of metal with another, more reactive metal, e.g. iron or steel coated with zinc, to protect the underlying metal; now also meaning to stimulate into action, called after the Italian physician, Luigi Galvani (1737–98).

gardenia a genus of ornamental tropical trees and shrubs with fragrant white or yellow flowers, called after the Scottish-born American botanist, Dr Alexander Garden (1730–91).

garibaldi a type of biscuit with a layer of currants in it, called after Giuseppe Garibaldi (1807–82), the Italian soldier patriot who is said to have enjoyed such biscuits

gauss a standard unit for measuring magnetic flux density, called after the German mathematician, Karl Friedrich Gauss (1777–1855), who developed the theory of numbers and applied mathematics to electricity, magnetism and astronomy. *See also* **degauss**.

Geiger counter an electronic instrument that can detect and measure radiation, called after the German physicist, Hans Geiger (1882–1945), who developed it.

gerrymander to rearrange the boundaries of a voting district to favour a particular party or candidate, called after the American politician, Elbridge Gerry (1744–1814).

Granny Smith a variety of hard green apple, called after the Australian gardener, Maria Ann Smith, known as Granny Smith (d.1870) who first grew the apple in Sydney in the 1860s.

greengage a type of greenish plum, called after Sir William Gage (1777–1864), who introduced it into Britain from France.

guillotine an instrument for beheading people by allowing a heavy blade to descend between grooved posts, called after the French physician, Joseph Ignace Guillotin (1738–1814), who advocated its use in the French Revolution.

Halley's comet a periodic comet that appears about every 76 years, called after the British astronomer, Edmund Halley (1656–1742), who calculated its orbit.

Heath Robinson of or pertaining to an absurdly complicated design for a simple mechanism, called after the English artist, William Heath Robinson (1872–1944).

henry a metric unit of electric inductance, called after the American physicist, Joseph Henry (1797–1878), who discovered the principle of electromagnetic induction.

Herculean of extraordinary strength, size or difficulty, called after Hercules, the Roman name for Heracles, in Greek mythology the son of Zeus and the most celebrated hero or semi-divine personage, best known for completing twelve difficult tasks known as the labours of Hercules.

Hoover™ a kind of vacuum cleaner, called after the American businessman, William Henry Hoover (1849–1932).

Jacuzzi™ a device that swirls water in a bath and massages the body, called after the Italian-born engineer, Candido Jacuzzi (*c*.1903–86).

JCB™ a mechanical earth-mover that has an hydraulically powered shovel and an excavator arm, called after its English manufacturer, Joseph Cyril Bamford (1916–).

joule the metric unit of all energy measurements, called after the British physicist, James Prescott Joule (1818–89) who investigated the relationship between mechanical, electrical and heat energy.

kelvin the metric unit of thermodynamic temperature, called after the Scottish physicist, William Thomson, 1st Baron Kelvin (1824–1907).

Köchel number a number in a catalogue of the works of Mozart, called after the Austrian scientist, Ludwig Alois Friedrich von Köchel (1800–1877), a great admirer of Mozart, who compiled his catalogue in 1862.

leotard a one-piece, close-fitting garment worn by acrobats and dancers, called after the French acrobat, Jules Leotard (1842–70), who introduced the costume as a circus garment.

listeria a bacterium that causes a serious form of food poisoning, listeriosis, called after the British surgeon, Joseph Lister (1827–1912), who pioneered the use of antiseptics.

lobelia a genus of flowers that produce showy blue, red, yellow or white flowers, called after the Flemish botanist, Matthias de Lobel (1538–1616).

loganberry a hybrid plant developed from the blackberry and the red raspberry that produces large sweet purplish-red berries, called after the American lawyer and horticulturist, James Harvey Logan (1841–1928), who first grew it in 1881.

Luddite an opponent of industrial change or innovation, called after Ned Ludd, the 18th-century British labourer who destroyed industrial machinery.

macadam a road surface composed of successive layers of small stones compacted into a solid mass, called after the Scottish engineer, John Loudon McAdam, (1756–1836), who invented it.

Machiavellian cunning, deceitful, double-dealing, using opportunist methods, called after the Florentine statesman and political theorist, Niccolò Machiavelli (1469–1527), author of *The Prince*.

Mach number the ratio of the speed of a body in a particular medium to the speed of sound in the same medium, called after the Austrian physicist and philosopher, Ernst Mach (1838–1916), who devised it.

mackintosh a type of raincoat, especially one made of rubberized cloth, called after the Scottish chemist, Charles Macintosh (1760–1843), who patented it in the early 1820s.

malapropism the unintentional misuse of a word by confusing it with another and so producing a ridiculous effect (e.g. "She is as headstrong as an allegory on the banks of the Nile"), called after Mrs Malaprop, a character in the play *The Rivals* (1775), by the Irish playwright Richard Brinsley Sheridan (1751–1816).

martinet a person who exerts strong discipline, called after Jean Martinet (d.1672), a French army drill master during the reign of Louis XIV.

maverick a stray animal or an independent-minded or unorthodox person, called after the American rancher in Texas, Samuel Augustus Maverick (1803–70), who refused to brand his cattle.

Melba sauce a sauce that is made from raspberries and served with fruit, peach melba, etc, called after the Australian operatic singer Dame Nellie Melba [Helen Porter Mitchell] (1861–1931), for whom it was made. *See also* **Melba toast, peach melba**.

Melba toast bread that is thinly sliced and toasted, called after the Australian operatic singer Dame Nellie Melba [Helen Porter Mitchell] (1861–1931), for whom it was made. *See also* **Melba sauce, peach melba**.

Mercator projection a type of projection for the drawing of maps two-dimensionally, called after the Flemish geographer, Gerardus Mercator [Gerhard Kremer] (1512–94).

mesmerize to hypnotize or to fascinate or spellbind, called after the Austrian physician and pioneer of hypnotism, Franz Anton Mesmer (1734–1815).

Molotov cocktail a kind of crude incendiary weapon made by filling a bottle with petrol and inserting a short short-delay wick or use, called after the Soviet statesman Vyacheslav Mikhailovich Molotov (1890–1986).

Montessori method a system of educating very young children through play, based on free discipline, with each child developing at his or her own pace, called after Maria Montessori (1870–1952), the Italian physicist and educator who developed it.

Moog synthesizer™ a type of synthesizer for producing music electronically, called after Robert Arthur Moog (b. 1934), the American physicist and engineer who developed it.

Morse code a code in which letters are represented by dots and dashes or long and short sounds and are transmitted by visual or audible signals, called after the American artist and inventor, Samuel Finley Breese Morse (1791–1872), who invented it.

narcissism excessive interest in one's own body or self, self-love, called after Narcissus, a handsome young man in Greek mythology who was punished for his coldness of heart in not returning the love of Echo by being made to fall in love with his own reflection in water and who pined away because he was unable to embrace himself.

newton the standard metric unit of force, called after the British physicist and mathematician, Sir Isaac Newton (1642–1727).

Nobel prize an annual international prize given for distinction in one of six areas: physics, chemistry, physiology and medicine, economics, literature, and promoting peace, called after the Swedish chemist and engineer, Alfred Nobel (1833–96), who founded them.

ohm a metric unit of electrical resistance, called after the German physicist, Georg Simon Ohm (1787–1854).

Pareto principle an economic principle that 80 per cent of the sales may come from 20 per cent of the customers, called after the Italian economist and sociologist, Vilfredo Pareto (1848–1923).

Parkinson's disease a progressive nervous disease resulting in tremor, muscular rigidity, partial paralysis and weakness, called after the British surgeon, James Parkinson (1755–1824), who first described it.

Parkinson's law the law that states that work expands to fill the time available for its completion, called after the British historian and author, Cyril Northcote Parkinson (1909–93), who devised it.

pasteurize to sterilize drink or food by heat or radiation in order to destroy bacteria, called after the French chemist and bacteriologist, Louis Pasteur (1822–95).

pavlova a dessert of meringue cake with a topping of cream and fruit, called after the Russian ballerina, Anna Pavlova (1885–1931), for whom it was made.

peach melba a dessert of peaches, ice cream and Melba sauce, called after the Australian operatic soprano singer, Dame Nellie Melba [Helen Porter Mitchell] (1861–1931), for whom it was made. *See also* **Melba sauce, Melba toast**.

Peter principle the principle that in a hierarchy every employee tends to rise to the level of his or her incompetence, called after the Canadian educator, Laurence J. Peter (1919–90), who formulated it.

Peter's projection a form of projection for depicting the countries of the world two-dimensionally, called after the German history, Dr Arno Peters (1916–), who devised it.

platonic of a close relationship between two people, spiritual and free from physical desire, called after the Greek philosopher, Plato (*c*.427–347 BC).

plimsoll a type of light rubber-soled canvas shoe, called after Samuel Plimsoll (see Plimsoll line) because the upper edge of the rubber was thought to resemble the Plimsoll line.

Plimsoll line the set of markings on the side of a ship that indicate the levels to which the ship may be safely be loaded, called after the English shipping reform leader, Samuel Plimsoll (1824–98).

poinsettia a South American evergreen plant, widely cultivated at Christmas for its red bracts, which resemble petals, called after the American diplomat, Joel Roberts Poinsett (1779–1851), who introduced it into the USA.

praline a type of confectionery made from nuts and sugar, called after Count Plessis-Praslin (1598–1675), a French field marshal, whose chef is said to have been the first person to make the sweet

Pulitzer prize one of a series of prizes that are awarded annually for outstanding achievement in American journalism, literature, and music, called after the Hungarian-born US newspaper publisher, Joseph Pulitzer (1847–1911).

Pullman a railway carriage that offers luxury accommodation, called after the American inventor, George Mortimer Pullman (1831–97), who first manufactured them.

quisling a traitor who aids an invading enemy to regularize its conquest of his or her country, called after the Norwegian politician, Vidkun Abraham Quisling (1887–1945), who collaborated with the Nazis.

quixotic, quixotical of a person, chivalrous or romantic to extravagance, unrealistically idealistic, called after Don Quixote, hero of the novel *Don Quixote de la Mancha* by the Spanish novelist Miguel de Cervantes Saavedra (1547–1616).

rafflesia a genus of parasitic Asian leafless plants, called after the British colonial administrator, Sir Thomas Stamford Raffles (1781–1826), who discovered it.

raglan a type of loose sleeve cut in one piece with the shoulder of a garment, called after the British field marshal,, Fitzroy James Henry Somerset, 1st Baron Raglan (1788–1855).

Richter scale a scale ranging from 1 to 10 for measuring the intensity of an earthquake, called after the American seismologist, Charles Richter (1900–85), who devised it.

Romeo a romantic lover, called after Romeo, the hero of Shakespeare's tragedy *Romeo and Juliet*.

Rorschach test a personality test in which the subject has to interpret a series of unstructured ink blots, called after the Swiss psychiatrist, Hermann Rorschach (1884–1922), who devised it.

Rubik cube *or* **Rubik's cube** a puzzle that consists of a cube of six colours with each face divided into nine small squares, eight of which can rotate around a central square, called after the Hungarian designer, Erno Rubik (1944–), who invented it.

rutherford a unit of radioactivity, called after the British physicist, Ernest Rutherford, 1st Baron Rutherford (1871–1937).

sadism sexual pleasure obtained from inflicting cruelty upon another, called after the French soldier and writer, Count Donatien Alphonse François de Sade, known as Marquis de Sade (1740–1814).

salmonella the bacteria that cause some diseases such as food poisoning, called after Daniel Elmer Salmon (1850–1914), the American veterinary surgeon who identified it

sandwich a snack consisting of two pieces of buttered bread with a filling, called after John Montagu, 4th Earl of Sandwich (1718–92), who was such a compulsive gambler that he would not leave the gaming tables to eat but had some cold beef between two slices of bread brought to him

saxophone a type of keyed brass instrument often used in jazz music, called after Adolphe Sax (1814–94), the Belgian instrument-maker who invented it.

sequoia one of two lofty coniferous Californian trees, called after the American Indian leader and scholar, Sequoya (*c*.1770–1843), also known as George Guess.

shrapnel an explosive projectile that contains bullets or fragments of metal and a charge that is exploded before impact, called after the British army officer, Henry Shrapnel (1761–1842), who invented it.

siemens the standard metric unit of electrical conductance, called after the German engineer and inventor, Ernst Werner von Siemens (1816–92).

silhouette the outline of a shape against light or a lighter background, called after the French politician, Etienne de Silhouette (1709–67).

simony the buying or selling of ecclesiastical benefits or offices, called after the sorcerer Simon Magnus, who lived in the 1st century AD.

sousaphone the large tuba that encircles the body of the player and has a forward-facing bell, called after the American bandmaster and composer, John Philip Sousa (1854–1932), who invented it.

spoonerism the accidental transposition of the initial letters or opening syllables of two or more words, often with an amusing effect (e.g. "queer old dean" for "dear old queen"), called after the British scholar and clergyman, William Archibald Spooner (1844–1930).

stetson a type of wide-brimmed, high-crowned felt hat, called after its designer, the American hat-maker John Batterson Stetson (1830–1906)

tantalize to tease or torment by presenting something greatly desired but keeping it inaccessible, called after Tantalus, the mythical Greek king of Phrygia, who was punished in Hades for his misdeeds by being forced to stand in water that receded when he tried to drink and under fruit that moved away as he tried to eat.

tontine a financial arrangement in which a group of subscribers contribute equally to a prize that is eventually awarded to the last survivor, called after the Italian banker, Lorenzo Tonti (1635–90), who devised it.

tradescantia a genus of flowering plants cultivated for their foliage, called after the English botanist, gardener and plant hunter, John Tradescant (*c*.1570–1638).

trilby a type of soft felt hat with an indented crown, called after *Trilby*, the dramatized version of the novel by the English writer George du Maurier. The heroine of the play, Trilby O'Ferral, wore such a hat.

Turing machine a hypothetical universal computing machine, called after the British mathematician, Alan Mathison Turing (1912–54), who conceived it.

Venn diagram a diagram in which overlapping circles are used to show the mathematical and logical relationships between sets, called after the British mathematician and logician, John Venn (1834–1923).

volt the metric unit of measure of the force of an electrical current, called after the Italian physicist, Count Alessandro Volta (1745–1827).

Wankel engine a kind of four-stroke internal-combustion engine with a triangular-shaped rotating piston within an elliptical combustion chamber, called after the German engineer, Felix Wankel (1902–88), who invented it.

watt a metric unit of electrical power, called after the Scottish engineer and inventor, James Watt (1736–1819).

wellington a waterproof rubber boot with no fastenings that extends to the knee, called after Arthur Wellesley, 1st Duke of Wellington (1769–1852), the British soldier who defeated Napoleon at Waterloo (1815).

wisteria *or* **wistaria** a genus of purple-flowered climbing plants, called after the American anatomist, Caspar Wistar (1761–1818).

Zeppelin a rigid cigar-shaped airship, called after the German general and aeronautical pioneer, Count Ferdinand von Zeppelin (1838–1917), who designed and manufactured them.

Abbreviations

A Adult; alcohol; alto; America; American; ampere; angstrom; anode; answer; April; (*math*) area; (*chem*) argon; Associate; atomic weight; IVR Austria.
Å Angstrom unit.
a acre; are (measure).
a. adjective; alto; ampere; *anno* (*Latin* year); anode; answer; *ante* (*Latin* before); *aqua* (*Latin* water); area.
A1 first class.
AA Alcoholics Anonymous; anti-aircraft; Automobile Association.
AAA Amateur Athletic Association; American Automobile Association.
AAC Amateur Athletic Club; *anno ante Christum* (*Latin* in the year before Christ).
AAM air-to-air missile.
A & A additions and amendments.
A & M Hymns Ancient and Modern.
A & N Army and Navy.
A & R Artist and Repertoire.
AAPO African Peoples' Organization.
aar against all risks; average annual rainfall.
AAU Amateur Athletic Union.
AB able-bodied seaman; *Artium Baccalaureus* (*Latin* Bachelor of Arts).
Ab (*chem*) alabamine.
ABA Amateur Boxing Association.
Abb. Abbess; Abbey; Abbot.
abbr., abbrev. abbreviated; abbreviation.
ABC Advance Booking Charter; American Broadcasting Company; Associated British Cinemas; Audit Bureau of Circulations; automatic binary computer.
abd abdicated abridged.
ab init. *ab initio* (*Latin* from the beginning).
abl. ablative.
ABM anti-ballistic missile.
ABMEWS anti-ballistic missile early warning system.
ABP arterial blood pressure.
Abp Archbishop.
abr. abridged; abridgement.
abs. absence; absent; absolute; abstract.
absol. absolute.
abstr. abstract.
abt about.
ABTA Association of British Travel Agents.
abv. above.
AC Air Command; Air Corps; Aircraftman; Alternating Current; analog computer; Annual Conference; *ante Christum* (*Latin* before Christ); Appeal Case; Appeal Court; Army Corps; Arts Council; Assistant Commissioner; Athletic Club.
A/C account; account current.
Ac (*chem*) actinium.
ac. acre.
a.c. *ante cibum* (*Latin* before meals).
acad. academic; academy.
ACAS Advisory, Conciliation and Arbitration Service.
ACC Army Catering Corps.
acc. acceleration; accent; accepted; accompanied; according; account; accusative.
accel. (*mus*) *accelerando* (*Italian* more quickly).
Accred Accredited.
acct account.
accy accountancy.
ACF Army Cadet Force.
ACG automatic control gear.
ACGB Arts Council of Great Britain.
ack. acknowledge(d).
ackt acknowledgment.
ACLS Automatic Carrier Landing System.
ACM Air Chief Marshal.
ACN *ante Christum natum* (*Latin* before the birth of Christ).
ACOP Association of Chief Officers of Police.
ACORN (*comput*) automatic checkout and recording network.
ACP American College of Physicians.
acpt. acceptance.
ACSIR Advisory Council for Scientific and Industrial Research.
Act. Acting.
act. active.
actg acting.
ACTH adrenocorticotrophic hormone, an anti-rheumatic drug.
ACV actual cash value; air cushion vehicle (hovercraft).

ACW Aircraftwoman; alternating continuous waves.
AD (*milit*) active duty; air defence; *anno Domini* (*Latin* in the year of our Lord).
ad. adverb; advertisement.
ADC Aide-de-Camp; (*comput*) analog to digital converter; automatic digital calculator.
add. addendum; addition; additional; address.
ADF automatic direction finder.
ad fin. *ad finem* (*Latin* near the end).
ad inf. *ad infinitum* (*Latin* to infinity).
ad imt. *ad initium* (*Latin* at the beginning).
ad int. *ad interim* (*Latin* in the meantime).
adj, adj. adjacent; adjective; adjoining; adjourned; adjudged; adjunct; adjustment; adjutant.
Adjt Adjutant.
Adjt-Gen. Adjutant-General.
ad lib. *ad libitum* (*Latin* at will).
ad loc. *ad locum* (*Latin* at the place).
adm. administration; administrative; admitted.
admin. administration.
ADN IVR People's Democratic Republic of Yemen.
ADP automatic data processing.
adv. advance; advent; adverb; adverbial; *adversus* (*Latin* against); advertisement; advisory; advocate.
ad val. *ad valorem* (*Latin* according to the value).
advt advertisement.
ADW Air Defence Warning.
AE Atomic Energy.
AEA Atomic Energy Authority.
AE & P Ambassador Extraordinary and Plenipotentiary.
AEF Amalgamated Union of Engineering and Foundry Workers.
AEI Associated Electrical Industries.
AELTC All England Lawn Tennis Club.
aer. aeronautics; aeroplane.
AERE Atomic Energy Research Establishment.
aeron. aeronautical; aeronautics.
AEU Amalgamated Engineering Union (now AUEW).
AEW airborne early warning.
AF Admiral of the Fleet; Air Force; Anglo-French; audio-frequency.
A/F as found.
AFA Amateur Football Association.
AFC Association Football Club; automatic frequency control.
affil. affiliated.
afft affidavit.
AFG IVR Afghanistan.
AFI American Film Institute.
AFM Air Force Medal.
AFN American Forces Network; Armed Forces Network.
Afr. Africa; African.
Afrik. Afrikaans.
AFS Auxiliary Fire Service.
afsd aforesaid.
AFV armoured fighting vehicle.
AG Adjutant General; Attorney General.
Ag (*chem*) silver.
AGC automatic gain control.
AGCA automatic ground controlled approach.
AGCL automatic ground controlled landing.
agcy agency.
AGM air-to-ground missile; Annual General Meeting.
AGR advanced gas-cooled reactor.
agr., agric. agricultural; agriculture.
agst against.
agt agent; agreement.
a.g.w. actual gross weight.
AH *anno Hegirae* (*Latin* in the year of the Hegira).
AI Amnesty International; artificial insemination.
a.i. *ad interim* (*Latin* in the meantime).
AID acute infectious disease; Army Intelligence Department; artificial insemination by donor.
AIH artificial insemination by husband.
AL IVR Albania; Anglo-Latin.
Al (*chem*) aluminium.
al. alcohol; alcoholic.
ALBM air-launched ballistic missile.
Ald. Alderman.
Alg. Algeria; Algerian.
alg, alg. algebra.
ALGOL (*comput*) algorithmic language.
alk. alkali.
alt. alteration; alternate; alternative; altitude; alto.
alter. alteration.
alum. aluminium.
AM Air Marshal; Air Ministry; Albert Medal; amplitude modulation; *anno mundi* (*Latin* in the year of the world); *ante meridiem* (*Latin* before noon); arithmetic mean; *Artium Magister* (*Latin* Master of Arts); Associate Member.
Am (*chem*) americium.
Am. America; American.
a.m. ante meridiem.
amal. amalgamated.

AMDG *ad majorem Dei gloriam* (*Latin* to the greater glory of God).
Amer. America; American.
AMM anti-missile missile.
amn. amunition.
amp. amperage; ampere; amplifier; amplitude.
AMS Ancient Monuments Society.
amt amount.
AMU atomic mass unit.
AN Anglo-Norman.
An (*chem*) actinon.
an. *anno* (*Latin* in the year); anonymous; *ante* (*Latin* before).
anag. anagram.
anal. analogous; analogy; analysis; analytic.
anat. anatomical; anatomist; anatomy.
ANC African National Congress.
anc. ancient; anciently.
AND IVR Andorra.
and. (*mus*) *andante* (*Italian* moderately slow).
Angl. Anglican; Anglicized.
anim. (*mus*) *animato* (*Italian* animated).
ann. annual; annuity.
anniv. anniversary.
annot. annotated; annotation; annotator.
anon. anonymous.
ANS Army Nursing Service.
ans. answer.
ant. antenna; antiquarian; antique; antonym.
anthol. anthology.
anthrop. anthropological; anthropology.
antiq. antiquarian; antiquity.
ANZAC Australian and New Zealand Army Corps.
a/o account of.
AOB any other business.
AOCB any other competent business.
AOC-in-C Air Officer Commander-in-Chief.
AP *ante prandium* (*Latin* before meals); Associated Press; atmospheric pressure.
Ap. Apostle; April.
ap. apothecary.
APC automatic phase control; automatic pitch control.
APEX Advance Purchase Excursion.
aph. aphorism.
apo. apogee.
Apoc. Apocalypse; Apocrypha.
app. apparatus; apparent; appendix; applied; appointed; apprentice; approved; approximate.
appro. approbation; approval.
approx. approximate; approximately.
apptd appointed.
Apr, Apr. April.
APT advanced passenger train.
apt. apartment.
APWU Amalgamated Postal Workers' Union.
aq. *aqua* (*Latin* water).
AR Autonomous Republic.
Ar (*chem*) argon.
Ar. Arabic; Aramaic.
ar. arrival; arrives.
a.r. *anno regni* (*Latin* in the year of the reign).
ARA Associate of the Royal Academy.
Arab Arabian; Arabic.
arb. arbiter; arbitration.
ARC Aeronautical Research Council; American Red Cross; automatic relay calculator.
Arch. Archbishop; Archdcacon; Archduke; Archipelago; Architecture.
arch. archaic; archaism; archery; archipelago; architect; architecture; archive.
archaeol. archaeology.
Archd. Archdeacon; Archduke.
archit. architecture.
ARCS Australian Red Cross Society.
ARD acute respiratory disease.
Arg. Argentina; Argyll (former county).
arg. *argentum* (*Latin* silver).
arith. arithmetic(al).
Ariz. Arizona.
Ark. Arkansas.
ARM anti-radar missile.
ARP air raid precautions.
ARR *anno regni regis* or *regine* (*Latin* in the year of the king's or queen's reign).
arr. arranged; arrangement; arrival.
art. article; artificial; artillery.
ARTC Air Route Traffic Control.
AS Anglo-Saxon; *anno salutis* (*Latin* in the year of salvation); anti-submarine; Assistant Secretary.
As (*chem*) arsenic.
ASA Advertising Standards Authority.
a.s.a.p. as soon as possible.
ASAT Anti-Satellite.
ASCII (*comput*) American Standard Code for Information Interchange.
ASDIC Allied Submarine Detection Investigation Committee.
ASE American Stock Exchange.
a.s.e. air standard efficiency.
ASH Action on Smoking and Health.
ASI air speed indicator.
ASLEF Associated Society of Locomotive Engineers and Firemen.

ASLIB Association of Special Libraries and Information Bureaux.
ASM air-to-surface missile.
ASN Army Service Number.
ASPCA American Society for the Prevention of Cruelty to Animals.
Ass. Assembly.
ass. assistant; association; assorted.
Asscn., Assn. Association.
Assoc. Associate; Association.
asst assistant.
AST Atlantic Standard Time.
ASTMS Association of Scientific, Technical, and Managerial Staffs.
astr. astronomer; astronomical; astro-nomy.
astrol. astrologer; astrological; astrology.
astron. astronomer; astronomical; astro-nomy.
ASW anti-submarine warfare.
AT alternativetechnology; anti-tank.
At (*chem*) astatine.
at. airtight; atmosphere; atomic.
ATA Atlantic Treaty Association.
ATC Air Traffic Control; Air Training Corps.
Atl. Atlantic.
atm. atmosphere; atmospheric.
at. no. atomic number.
ATS (*comput*) Administrative Terminal System; anti-tetanus serum; Auxiliary Territorial Service (now WRAC).
a.t.s. (*law*) at the suit of.
att. attached; attention; attorney.
attn. attention.
attrib. attribute; attributive.
at. vol. atomic volume.
at. wt. atomic weight.
AU Angstrom unit; astronomical unit.
Au (*chem*) gold.
AUBTW Amalgamated Union of Building Trade Workers.
AUEW Amalgamated Union of Engineering Workers.
Aug. August.
AUM air-to-underwater missile.
AUS IVR Australia.
Aust. Australia; Australian.
Austl. Australasia.
AUT Association of University Teachers.
aut. automatic.
auth. author; authority; authorized.
Auth. Ver. Authorized Version.
auto. automatic; automobile; automotive.
aux. auxiliary.
AV audio-visual; Authorized Version.
Av. Avenue.
av. average; avoirdupois.
a.v. *ad valorem* (*Latin* according to the value).
avdp. avoirdupois.
Ave Avenue.
avg. average.
AVM Air Vice-Marshal.
AVR Army Volunteer Reserve.
a.w. atomic weight.
AWOL absent without official leave.
ax. axiom; axis.
az. azimuth.
B Bachelor; bacillus; Baron; base; (*mus*) bass; IVR Belgium; Bible; Blessed; book; born; (*chem*) boron; bowled (in cricket); breadth; British; Brother.
BA *Baccalaureus Artium* (*Latin* Bachelor of Arts); British Academy; British Airways; Buenos Aires.
Ba (*chem*) barium.
BAA British Airports Authority.
BAAB British Amateur Athletic Board.
Bach. Bachelor.
bact. bacteria; bacteriology; bacterium.
bacteriol. bacteriological; bacteriology.
BAFO British Army Forces Overseas.
BAL (*comput*) basic assembly language.
bal. balance.
ball. ballast; ballistics.
BALPA British Air Line Pilots' Association.
B & B bed and breakfast.
b & s brandy and soda.
b & w black and white.
BAOR British Army of the Rhine.
Bap. Baptist.
bap. baptized.
bar. barometer; barometric; barrel; barrister.
barit. baritone.
barr. barrister.
Bart. Baronet.
BASIC (*comput*) Beginners' All-purpose Symbolic Instruction Code.
bat., batt. battalion; battery.
BB Boys' Brigade; double black (pencils).
bb. books.
BBB triple black (pencils).
BBBG British Boxing Board of Control.
BBC British Broadcasting Corporation.
BBFC British Board of Film Censors.
bbl. barrel.
BC before Christ; British Council.
BCC British Council of Churches.
BCD (*comput*) binary coded decimal notation.

BCG Bacillus Calmette-Guerin, antituberculosis vaccine.
BCh *Baccalaureus Chirurgiae* (*Latin* Bachelor of Surgery).
BD Bachelor of Divinity.
B/D bank draft.
bd. board; bond; bound; bundle.
BDA British Dental Association.
bdl. bundle.
BDS Bachelor of Dental Surgery; IVR Barbados.
BDU Bomb Disposal Unit.
BE Bachelor of Education; Bank of England; Bill of Exchange; British Embassy.
Be (*chem*) beryllium.
BEAB British Electrical Approvals Board.
bec. because.
BEd Bachelor of Education.
Beds. Bedfordshire.
BEF British Expeditionary Force.
bef. before.
beg. begin; beginning.
Belg. Belgian; Belgium.
BEM British Empire Medal.
BEng Bachelor of Engineering.
Beng. Bengal, Bengali.
beq. bequeath; bequeathed.
beqt bequest.
Berks. Berkshire.
bet. between.
BeV billion electron-volts.
B/F brought forward.
b.f. bloody fool; (*print*) bold face; *bona fide* (*Latin* genuine, genuinely).
BFBS British Forces Broadcasting Service.
BFI British Film Institute.
BFN British Forces Network.
BG BrigadierGeneral; IVR Bulgaria.
bg bag.
BH IVR British Honduras.
B'ham Birmingham.
BHC British High Commissioner.
b.h.p. brake horsepower.
Bi (*chem*) bismuth.
Bib. Bible; Biblical.
Bibl. Biblical.
bibliog. bibliographer; bibliography.
bicarb. bicarbonate of soda.
b.i.d. *bis in die* (*Latin* twice daily).
BIM British Institute of Management.
biog. biographical; biographer; biography.
biol. biological; biologist; biology.
BIT (*comput*) binary digit.
Bk (*chem*) berkelium.
bk. bank; bark; block; book; break.
bkcy. bankruptcy.
bkg. banking.
bkpt. bankrupt.
bkt. basket; bracket.
BL Bachelor of Laws; Bachelor of Letters; British Legion (now RBL); British Library.
B/L Bill of Lading.
bldlg. building.
BLit Bachelor of Literature.
BLitt *Baccalaureus Litterarum* (*Latin* Bachelor of Letters).
blk black; block; bulk.
B.LL. Bachelor of Laws.
blvd boulevard.
BM Bachelor of Medicine; *Beatae Memoriae* (*Latin* of blessed memory); bench mark; bowel movement; British Museum.
BMA British Medical Association.
BMC British Medical Council.
BMJ British Medical Journal.
BML British Museum Library.
BMR basal metabolic rate.
BMus Bachelor of Music.
BN banknote.
Bn Baron; Battalion.
BO body odour; Box Office; Broker's Order; Buyer's Option.
b/o brought over.
BOA British Olympic Association.
BOD biochemical oxygen demand.
Boh. Bohemia, Bohemian.
Bol. Bolivia, Bolivian.
bor. borough.
BOT Board of Trade.
bot. botanical; botanist; botany; bottle; bought.
boul. boulevard.
BP British Petroleum; British Pharmacopoeia.
b/p bills payable; blueprint.
bp. baptized; birthplace; bishop.
b.p. below proof; bill of parcels; boiling point.
BPh, BPhil Bachelor of Philosolphy.
bpl. birthplace.
BR IVR Brazil; British Rail.
B/R bills receivable.
Br (*chem*) bromine.
Br. Breton; Britain; British; Brother.
br. branch; brand; brig; bronze; brother; brown.
Braz. Brazil, Brazilian.
BRCS British Red Cross Society.
BRDC British Research and Development Corporation.
Brig. Brigade; Brigadier.

Brig. Gen. Brigadier General.
Brit. Britain; Britannia; British; Briton.
BRN IVR Bahrain.
bro. brother.
BRU IVR Brunei.
BS Bachelor of Science; Bachelor of Surgery; IVR Bahamas; Balance Sheet; Bill of Sale; Blessed Sacrament; British Standards.
b.s. balance sheet; bill of sale.
BSc *Baccalaureus Scientiae* (*Latin* Bachelor of Science).
BSG British Standard Gauge.
BSI British Standards Institution; Building Societies' Institute.
bskt basket.
BSS British Standards Specification.
BST British Standard Time; British Summer Time.
Bt. Baronet.
BTA British Travel Association.
BTh Bachelor of Theology.
BThU British thermal unit.
btl. bottle.
BTU Board of Trade Unit.
Btu British thermal unit.
bu. bureau; bushel.
Bucks. Buckinghamshire.
BUP British United Press.
BUPA British United Provident Association.
BUR IVR Burma.
Bur. Burma; Burmese.
bus. business.
BV *beata virgo* (*Latin* Blessed Virgin); *bene vale* (*Latin* farewell).
b/w black and white.
bx. box; boxes.
Bz (*chem*) benzene.
C Canon; (*physics*) capacitance; Cape; Captain; (*chem*) carbon; Catechism; Catholic; Celsius; Celtic; Centigrade; Central; Century; Chancellor; Chancery; Chapter; Chief; Church; Circuit; Collected; Commander; Confessor; Confidential; Congregational; Congress; Conservative; Constable; Consul; Contralto; Contrast; Corps; coulomb; Count; County; Court; IVR Cuba; Cubic; (*physics*) heat capacity; 100 (Roman numeral).
c. candle; canon; carat; case; cathode; cent; centavo; centigram; centimetre; central; centre; century; chapter; charge; *circa* (*Latin* about); city; class; college; (*math*) constant; contralto; copyright; cubic; cup; currency; current; cycle; (*physics*) specific heat capacity.
CA Central America; Chartered Accountant; Civil Aviation; Consumers' Association; Court of Appeal; Crown Agent.
C/A Credit Account; Current Account.
Ca (*chem*) calcium.
ca. *circa* (*Latin* about).
CAA Civil Aviation Authority.
CAB Citizens' Advice Bureau.
CAD (*comput*) computer-aided design.
cad. (*mus*) *cadenza* (*Italian* final flourish).
Caern. Caernarvonshire (former county).
Caith. Caithness (former county).
cal. calendar; calibre; calorie.
Cambs. Cambridgeshire.
Can. Canon; Canto.
can. canal; cancel; cannon; canton.
Canad. Canadian.
canc. cancellation; cancelled.
cand. candidate.
C & W (*mus*) country and western.
Cantab. *Cantabrigiensis* (*Latin* of Cambridge).
CAP Code of Advertising Practice; Common Agricultural Policy (of EC).
cap. capacity; capital; capitalize; captain; *caput* (*Latin* chapter).
caps. capital letters; capsule.
Capt. Captain.
car. carat.
Card. Cardiganshire (former county); Cardinal.
Carms. Carmarthenshire (former county).
carp. carpenter; carpentry.
carr. carriage.
cartog. cartography.
cas. casual; casualty.
CAT College of Advanced Technology.
cat. catalogue; catechism.
Cath. Cathedral; Catholic.
cath. cathode.
caus. causation; causative.
cav. cavalier; cavalry.
CB Cape Breton; Citizens' Band; Companion of the Order of the Bath; (*milit*) confinement to barracks.
Cb (*chem*) columbium.
CBC Canadian Broadcasting Corporation.
c.b.d. cash before delivery.
CBE Commander of the Order of the British Empire.
CBI Central Bureau of Investigation (USA); Confederation of British Industry.
CBS Columbia Broadcasting System.
CBW chemical and biological warfare.
CC carbon copy; Chamber of Commerce; Chief

Clerk; closed circuit; County Council; Cricket Club.
cc cubic centimetre; cubic centimetres.
cc. centuries; chapters; copies.
CCC County Cricket Club.
CCF Combined Cadet Force.
CCP Chinese Communist Party.
CCTV closed circuit television.
c.c.w. counter-clockwise.
CD Civil Defence; contagious disease; Corps Diplomatique; compact disc.
Cd (*chem*) cadmium.
cd candela.
cd. cord; could.
c.d. cash discount.
c/d carried down.
CDC Commonwealth Development Corporation.
CDN IVR Canada.
Cdr Commander; Conductor.
Cdre Commodore.
CDSO Companion of the Distinguished Service Order.
CE Chancellor of the Exchequer; Church of England; Civil Engineer; Council of Europe.
Ce (*chem*) cerium.
Cel. Celsius.
Celt. Celtic.
Cem. Cemetery.
cen. central; centre; century.
cent. centavo; centigrade; centime; centimetre; central; *centum* (*Latin* a hundred; century.
cer. ceramics.
cert. certain; certificate; certification; certified; certify.
CET Central European Time.
CF Chaplain to the Forces.
Cf (*chem*) californium.
cf. *confer* (*Latin* compare).
c/f carried forward.
cfm cubic feet per minute.
cfs cubic feet per second.
cft cubic foot or feet.
CG Coast Guard; Commanding General; Consul General.
cg centigram.
c.g. centre of gravity.
CGI City and Guilds Institute.
CGM Conspicuous Gallantry Medal.
cgm centigram.
cgs centimetre-gram-second.
CH Companion of Honour; IVR Switzerland.
Ch. Chairman; China; Chinese.
ch. chain; champion; chaplain; chapter; check; chemical; chemistry; chief; child; choir; church.
c.h. central heating.
Chal. Chaldaic; Chaldee.
Chanc. Chancellor; Chancery.
Chap. Chapel; Chaplain.
chap. chapter.
char. character.
ChB *Chirurgiae Baccalaureus* (*Latin* Bachelor of Surgery).
chem, chem. chemical; chemist; chemistry.
Ches. Cheshire.
chg. change; charge.
Chin. China; Chinese.
Chm Chairman.
chq. cheque.
Chr. Christ; Christian; Chronicles.
chron. chronicle; chronological.
chs chapters.
CI Channel Islands; Commonwealth Institute; IVR Ivory Coast.
Ci. cirrus; curie.
CIA Central Intelligence Agency (USA).
Cicestr. *Cicestrensis* (*Latin* of Chichester).
CID Criminal Investigation Department.
cif cost, insurance and freight.
C-in-C Commander-in-Chief.
CIS Commonwealth of Independent States.
cit. cited.
ckw clockwise.
CL IVR Sri Lanka.
Cl (*chem*) chlorine.
cl centilitre.
cl. class; classical; classification; clause.
cld. called; cancelled; cleared; coloured; could.
clin. clinical.
Cllr Councillor.
Cm (*chem*) curium.
cm centimetre.
Cmdr Commander.
Cmdre Commodore.
Cmdt Commandant.
CMG Companion of the Order of St Michael and St George.
CMO Chief Medical Officer.
CND Campaign for Nuclear Disarmament.
CNS central nervous system; Chief of Naval Staff.
CO Cash Order; IVR Colombia; Commanding Officer; conscientious objector; Criminal Office; Crown Office.
Co (*chem*) cobalt.
Co. Company; County.

c/o care of; carried over.
COBOL (*comput*) common business oriented language.
COD cash on delivery.
cod. codicil.
coef. coefficient.
C of E Church of England; Council of Europe.
C of I Church of Ireland.
C of S Chief of Staff; Church of Scotland.
c.o.h. cash on hand.
COHSE Confederation of Health Service Employees.
COI Central Office of Information.
COL computer-oriented language.
Col. Colonel; Colorado; (*Scrip*) Colossians; Columbia; Columbian.
col. column.
coll. collateral; colleague; collection; collector; college; collegiate; colloquial.
colloq, colloq. colloquial; colloquialism; colloquially.
comp. companion; comparative; compare; comparison; compensation; competitor; compiled; compilation; complete; composer; composition; compositor; compound; comprehensive; comprising.
compar. comparative; comparison.
compd compound.
compl. complement; complete; compliment; complimentary.
COMSAT Communications Satellite (USA).
con. concentration; concerning; concerto; conclusion; *conjunx* (*Latin* wife); connection; consolidated; *contra* (*Latin* against); convenience.
conc. concentrate; concentrated; concentration; concerning.
conf. *confer* (*Latin* compare); conference.
conj, conj. conjugation; conjunction.
conn. connected; connection; connotation.
Cons. Conservative; Constable.
const. constant.
Cont. Continental.
cont. containing; contents; continent; continental; continued; *contra* (*Latin* against); contract.
contd contained; continued.
contr. contract; contraction; contralto; contrary; contrast; control; controller.
contrib. contribution; contributor.
co-op co-operative.
corr. correct; correction; correspondence; corresponding; corrugated; corruption.
cos (*math*) cosine.
cosec (*math*) cosecant.
cosh (*math*) hyperbolic cosine.
cot, cotan (*math*) cotangent.
Cox. Coxswain.
CP Carriage Paid; Common Prayer; Communist Party.
cp. compare.
CPI consumer price index.
cpi characters per inch.
Cpl. Corporal.
cpm cycles per minute.
CPR Canadian Pacific Railway.
cps characters per second; cycles per second.
CPU (*comput*) central processing unit.
CR IVR Costa Rica.
Cr (*chem*) chromium.
CRE Commission for Racial Equality.
Cres. Crescent.
cres. (*mus*) *crescendo* (*Italian* increasing).
crit. criticism; criticize.
CRO cathode-ray oscillograph; Criminal Records Office.
CRT cathode-ray tube.
cryst. crystalline; crystallized; crystallography.
CS IVR Czechoslovakia.
Cs (*chem*) caesium; (*meteor*) cirrostratus.
csch (*math*) hyperbolic cosecant.
CSE Certificate of Secondary Education.
CSEU Confederation of Shipbuilding and Engineering Unions.
CSM Company Sergeant-Major.
CSU Civil Service Union.
ct. carat; cent; *centum* (*Latin* hundred); certificate; county; court.
Cu (*chem*) copper.
cu. cubic.
Cumb. Cumberland (former county).
CUP Cambridge University Press.
CV Curriculum Vitae.
Cwlth Commonwealth.
c.w.o. cash with order.
cwt. hundredweight.
CY IVR Cyprus.
D Democratic; Department; *Deus* (*Latin* God); (*chem*) deuterium; dimension; Director; *Dominus* (*Latin* Lord); Duchess; Duke; Dutch; IVR Germany; 500 (Roman numeral).
d. date; day; dead; deceased; decree; degree; delete; *denarius* (*Latin* penny); density; departs; deputy; diameter; died.
DA Deposit Account; District Attorney.
Dak. Dakota.
Dan. (*Scrip*) Daniel; Danish.
D & C dilation and curettage.

dat. dative.
dB decibel.
d.b.a. doing business as.
DBE Dame Commander of the Order of the British Empire.
D. Bib. Douay Bible.
dbl. double.
DBST Double British Summer Time.
DC Death Certificate; Depth Charge; Diplomatic Corps; direct current; District of Columbia.
d.c. (*mus*) *da capo* (*Italian* repeat from beginning); direct current.
DCB Dame Commander of the Order of the Bath.
DCM Distinguished Conduct Medal.
DCMG Dame Commander of the Order of St Michael and St George.
dct document.
DCVO Dame Commander of the Royal Victorian Order.
DD direct debit; *Divinitatis Doctor* (*Latin* Doctor of Divinity).
DDC Dewey Decimal Classification.
DDR Deutsche Demokratische Republik (German Democratic Republic).
DDT dichlorodiphenyltrichlorethane, an insecticide.
deb. debenture; debit.
Dec. December.
dec. deceased; decimal; decimetre; declaration; declension; declination; decrease; (*mus*) *decrescendo* (*Italian* becoming softer).
decd deceased.
decl. declaration; declension.
def. defective; defence; defendant; deferred; deficit; definite; definition.
deg. degree.
Del. Delaware.
del. delegate; delegation; delete.
Dem. Democratic.
Den. Denmark.
Denb. Denbighshire (former county).
dep. department; departs; departure; deponent; deposed; deposit; depot; deputy.
dept department.
der., deriv. derivation; derivative; derived.
Derbys. Derbyshire.
DERV diesel engined road vehicle.
DES Department of Education and Science.
Det. Detective.
det. detachment; detail.
Det. Con. Detective Constable.
Det. Insp. Detective Inspector.
Det. Sgt. Detective Sergeant.
Deut. (*Scrip*) Deuteronomy.
dev. development; deviation.
DF *Defensor Fidei* (*Latin* Defender of the Faith).
DFC Distinguished Flying Cross.
DFM Diploma in Forensic Medicine.
DG *Dei gratia* (*Latin* by the grace of God); *Deo gratias* (*Latin* thanks to God).
dia. diagram; dialect; diameter.
diag. diagonal; diagram.
dial. dialect; dialogue.
diam. diameter.
dict. dictionary.
diff. difference; different; differential.
dig. digest; digit; digital.
dim. dimension; diminished; (*mus*) *diminuendo* (*Italian* becoming softer).
dimin. (*mus*) *diminuendo* (*Italian* becoming softer); diminutive.
Dioc. Diocesan; Diocese.
Dip. Diploma.
Dir. Director.
dis. discontinued; discount; distance; distant; distribute.
disc. discount; discovered.
disp. dispensary; dispensation.
dist distant; district.
distr. distribute; distributed; distribution; distributor.
div. dividend; division; divorce.
DIY do-it-yourself.
DJ dinner jacket; disc jockey.
DK IVR Denmark.
dlvy delivery.
dly daily.
DM Deutsche Mark.
dm decimetre.
DMZ demilitarized zone.
DNA (*chem*) deoxyribonucleic acid.
do. *ditto* (*Italian* the same).
DOA dead on arrival.
d.o.b. date of birth.
doc. document.
DOE Department of the Environment.
dol. (*mus*) *dolce* (*Italian* sweet); dollar.
DOM *Deo optimo maximo* (*Latin* to God, the best and greatest); IVR Dominican Republic.
doz. dozen.
DP data processing; displaced person.
DPh, DPhil Doctor of Philosophy.
DPP Director of Public Prosecutions.
dpt department; deponent; deposit; depot.

Dr Doctor.
Dr. Drive.
dram. pers. *dramatis personae* (*Latin* characters present in the drama).
DS (*mus*) *dal segno* (*Italian* from the sign); disseminated sclerosis.
DSC Distinguished Service Cross.
DSM Distinguished Service Medal.
DSO Distinguished Service Order.
d.s.p. *decessit sine prole* (*Latin* died without issue).
DST Daylight Saving Time.
DT data transmission; delirium tremens.
DTI Department of Trade and Industry.
Du. Duchy; Duke; Dutch.
Dumb. Dumbarton.
Dumf. Dumfriesshire (former county).
Dunb. Dunbartonshire (former county).
dup. duplicate.
DV defective vision; *Deo volente* (*Latin* God willing); Douay Version (of the Bible).
DY IVR Dahomey.
Dy (*chem*) dysprosium.
DZ IVR Algeria.
dz. dozen.
E East; Easter; Eastern; England; English; IVR Spain.
e. elder; electric.
ea. each.
EAK IVR Kenya.
E & OE errors and omissions excepted.
EAT IVR Tanzania.
EAU IVR Uganda.
EAZ IVRTanzania.
EC East Central; IVR Ecuador; European Community.
eccles ecclesiastical.
Eccles. (*Scrip*) Ecclesiastes.
ECG electrocardiogram; electrocardiograph.
ecol. ecological; ecology.
econ. economical; ecomics; economy.
ECT electroconvulsive therapy.
ed. edited; edition; editor; education.
EDC (*med*) expected date of confinement.
EDD (*med*) expected date of delivery.
edit. edited; edition; editor.
EDP electronic data processing.
educ. educated; education; educational.
EEC European Economic Community.
EEG electroencephalogram; electroencephalograph.
EEOC Equal Employment Opportunities Commission.
EFL English as a foreign language.
EFT electronic funds transfer.
EFTA European Free Trade Association.
e.g. *exempli gratia* (*Latin* for example).
EHF extremely high frequency.
elect. electric; electrical; electricity.
elem. element; elementary.
elev. elevation.
Eliz. Elizabethan.
ELT English Language Teaching.
EM electromagnetic; electromotive.
EMF, emf electromotive force.
EMI Electrical and Musical Industries.
Emp. Emperor; Empire; Empress.
EMR electronic magnetic resonance.
EMS European Monetary System.
EMU, emu electromagnetic unit; European monetary unit.
enc., encl enclosed; enclosure.
ENE east-northeast.
Eng. England; English.
eng. engine; engineer; engineering; engraved; engraver.
enl. enlarged; enlisted.
Ens. Ensign.
ENSA Entertainments National Services Association.
ENT ear, nose and throat.
entom. entomology.
env. envelope.
EO Executive Officer.
EoC Equal Opportunities Commission.
EP electroplate; extended play (record).
Ep. Epistle.
EPNS electroplated nickel silver.
eq. equal.
ER *Elizabeth Regina* (*Latin* Queen Elizabeth).
Er (*chem*) erbium.
ERNIE Electronic Random Number Indicator Equipment.
Es (*chem*) einsteinium.
ESE east-southeast.
ESL English as a second language.
ESN educationally subnormal.
ESP extrasensory perception.
esp, esp. especially.
Esq. Esquire.
ESRO European Space Research Organization.
Est. Established; Estate.
est. estimated; estuary.
ET IVR Egypt; extra-terrestrial.
ETA estimated time of arrival.
et al. *et alii* (*Latin* and others).

etc, etc. *et cetera* (*Latin* and so on).
ETD estimated time of departure.
ethnol. ethnology.
ETU Electrical Trades Union.
etym. etymological; etymology.
Eu (*chem*) europium.
Eu., Eur. Europe; European.
EV, e.v. electron volt.
ex. examination; excellent; except; exchange; excluding; excursion; executed; executive; exempt; express; export; extra.
exam. examination.
Exe. Excellency.
exch. exchange; exchequer.
excl. exclamation; excluding.
exclam, exclam. exclamation.
exec. executive; executor.
ex lib. *ex libris* (*Latin* from the library of).
ex off. *ex officio* (*Latin* by virtue of office).
ext. extension; exterior; external; extinct; extra; extract; extreme.
F Fahrenheit; farad; Father; fathom; February; Fellow; Finance; (*chem*) fluorine; folio; (*mus*) *forte* (*Italian* loud); IVR France; French; frequency; Friday; function.
f. farad; farthing; fathom; feet; female; feminine; filly; fine; fluid; folio; following; foot; (*mus*) *forte* (*Italian* loud); foul; franc; frequency; from; furlong.
FA Fanny Adams; Football Association.
f.a. free alongside.
Fac. Faculty.
fam. family.
FAO Food and Agriculture Organization.
f.a.s. free alongside ship.
fath. fathom.
FBI Federal Bureau of Investigation (USA).
FC Football Club.
FCI Foreign and Commonwealth Office.
FD *Fidei Defensor* (*Latin* Defender of the Faith).
fd. forward; found; founded.
Fe (*chem*) iron.
Feb, Feb. February.
fec. *fecit* (*Latin* he or she made).
fed. federal; federated; federation.
fem. female; feminine.
ff (*mus*) *fortissimo* (*Italian* very loud).
ff. folios; the following.
fict. fiction; fictitious.
Fid. Def. *Fidei Defensor* (*Latin* Defender of the Faith).
fig. figuratively; figure.
Fin. Finland; Finnish.
fin. final; finance; financial; finish.
Finn. Finnish.
FJI IVR Fiji.
FL Flight Lieutenant; IVR Liechtenstein.
Fl. Flanders; Flemish.
fl. floor; florin; *floruit* (*Latin* flourished); fluid.
Flem. Flemish.
Flor. Florida.
flor. *floruit* (*Latin* flourished).
fl. oz. fluid ounce.
FMD foot and mouth disease.
fn. footnote.
FO Flying Officer; Foreign Office.
fo. folio.
f.o.b. free on board.
FOC (*print*) Father of the Chapel (union official); free of charge.
fol. folio; followed; following.
foll. following.
for. foreign; forestry.
fort, fort. fortification; fortified.
FORTRAN (*comput*) Formula Translation.
FP former pupil; freezing point.
fp (*mus*) *forte piano* (*Italian* loud and then immediately soft).
f.p. freezing point.
FPA Family Planning Association.
f.p.s. feet per second; foot-pound-second; (*photog*) frames per second.
Fr (*chem*) francium.
Fr. Father; France; *frater* (*Latin* brother); French; Friar; Friday.
fr. fragment; franc; frequent; from.
f.r. *folio recto* (*Latin* right-hand page).
FRCP Fellow of the Royal College of Physicians.
FRCS Fellow of the Royal College of Surgeons.
freq. frequent; frequentative; frequently.
Fri. Friday.
front. frontispiece.
FRS Fellow of the Royal Society.
FSH follicle-stimulating hormone.
ft, ft. feet; foot; fort; fortification.
fur. furlong.
fut. future.
f.v. *folio verso* (*Latin* left-hand page).
fwd forward.
f.w.d. four-wheel drive; front-wheel drive.
FYI for your information.
fz (*mus*) *forzando* (*Italian* to be strongly accentuated).
G (*physics*) conductance; gauge; German; giga; grain; gram; grand; (*physics*) gravitational constant; guilder; guinea; gulp; gravity.

g gram, gramme; (*physics*) gravitational acceleration.
g. genitive; guinea.
Ga (*chem*) gallium.
Ga. Georgia.
Gael. Gaelic.
gal., gall. gallon.
galv. galvanic; galvanism.
GATT General Agreement on Tariffs and Trade.
gaz. gazette; gazetteer.
GB IVR Great Britain and Northern Ireland.
GBA IVR Alderney.
GBE Grand Cross of the Order of the British Empire.
GBG IVR Guernsey.
g.b.h. grievous bodily harm.
GBJ IVR Jersey.
GBM IVR Isle of Man.
GBZ IVR Gibraltar.
GC George Cross; Golf Club.
GCA IVR Guatemala.
GCE General Certificate of Education.
GCF greatest common factor.
GCMG Knight *or* Dame Grand Cross of the Order of St Michael and St George.
GCVO Grand Cross of the Royal Victorian Order.
Gd (*chem*) gadolinium.
gd good; guard.
Gdns Gardens.
GDR German Democratic Republic.
gds goods.
Ge (*chem*) germanium.
GEC General Electric Company.
Gen. General; (*Scrip*) Genesis.
gen. gender; general; generally; generator; generic; genetics; genitive; genuine; genus.
gent gentleman.
Geo. Georgia.
geog. geographer; geographic; geographical; geography.
geol. geologic; geological; geologist; geology.
geom. geometric; geometrical; geometrician; geometry.
Ger. German; Germany.
ger. gerund; gerundive.
GeV giga-electronvolts.
GG Girl Guides; Governor General.
GH IVR Ghana.
GHQ General Headquarters.
GI gastrointestinal; general issue; Government Issue.
Gib. Gibraltar.
Gk. Greek.
gl. glass.
g/l grams per litre.
Glam. Glamorganshire (former county).
Glas. Glasgow.
GLC Greater London Council.
Glos. Gloucestershire.
gloss. glossary.
GM Geiger-Müller counter; General Manager; George Medal; Grand Master; Guided Missile.
gm gram.
gm^2 grames per square metre.
GMB Grand Master of the Order of the Bath.
GMBE Grand Master of the Order of the British Empire.
GMC General Medical Council.
Gmc Germanic.
GMT Greenwich Mean Time.
GMWU National Union of General and Municipal Workers.
GNP Gross National Product.
gns. guineas.
GOC General Officer Commanding.
Goth. Gothic.
Gov. Governor.
Govt Government.
GP Gallup Poll; (*med*) general paresis; (*mus*) general pause; General Practitioner; general purpose; *Gloria Patri* (*Latin* Glory to the Father); Grand Prix.
gp group.
Gp Capt. Group Captain.
GPO General Post Office.
GR *Geogius Rex* (*Latin* King George).
Gr. Grecian; Greece; Greek.
gr. grade; grain; grammar; gravity; great; gross; group.
grad. gradient; graduate.
gram. grammar; grammarian; grammatical.
Gr. Br. Great Britain.
gr. wt. gross weight.
GS General Secretary; General Staff; ground speed.
gs. guineas.
gsm grams per square metre.
GT Grand Tourer.
gtd guaranteed.
GTS Greenwich Time Signal.
GU gastriculcer; genitourinary.
guar. guaranteed.
GUY IVR Guyana.
GW gigawatt.
gym. gymnasium; gymnastics.

gyn. gynaecological; gynaecology.
H hard (pencils); hecto-; (*physics*) henry; heroin; hospital; IVR Hungary; hydrant; (*chem*) hydrogen.
h hour.
h. harbour; hard; height; high; hit; horizontal; (*mus*) horn; hour; hundred; husband.
ha hectare.
hab. habitat.
Haw. Hawaii; Hawaiian.
HB hard black (pencils).
HC House of Commons.
HCF highest common factor.
HCJ High Court Judge.
HD heavy duty.
hd hand; head.
hdbk handbook.
hdqrs headquarters.
HE high explosive; His Eminence; His or Her Excellency.
He (*chem*) helium.
Heb. Hebrew.
her., heral. heraldic; heraldry.
Herts. Hertfordshire.
hex. hexagon; hexagonal.
HF high frequency.
Hf (*chem*) hafnium.
hf half.
HG High German; Horse Guards.
Hg (*chem*) mercury.
hgt. height.
HGV heavy goods vehicle.
HH double hard (pencils); His *or* Her Highness; His Holiness; His *or* Her Honour.
Hind. Hindi; Hindu.
hist. histology; historian; historical; history.
HIV human immunodeficiency virus.
HJ *hic jacet* (*Latin* here lies).
HJS *hic jacet sepultus* (*Latin* here lies buried).
HK IVR Hong Kong; House of Keys (Manx Parliament).
HKJ IVR Jordan.
HL Honours List; House of Lords.
hl hectolitre.
HM His *or* Her Majesty.
HMG Higher Middle German; His *or* Her Majesty's Government.
HMI His *or* Her Majesty's Inspector.
HMS His *or* Her Majesty's Service; His *or* Her Majesty's Ship.
HMSO His *or* Her Majesty's Stationery Office.
HMV His Master's Voice.
HNC Higher National Certificate.
HND Higher National Diploma.
HO Home Office.
Ho (*chem*) holmium.
ho. house.
Hon. Honorary; Honourable.
Hons Honours.
Hon. Sec. Honorary Secretary.
hort. horticultural; horticulture.
hosp. hospital.
HP hire purchase; horse power; Houses of Parliament.
HQ Headquarters.
hr hour.
HRH His *or* Her Royal Highness.
HS *hic sepultus* (*Latin* here is buried); High School; Home Secretary.
HT high tension.
ht. heat; height.
Hung. Hungarian; Hungary.
Hunts. Huntingdonshire (former county).
HV high velocity; high voltage.
hwy highway.
hyd. hydraudics; hydrostatics.
Hz hertz.
I (*physics*) current; incisor; Independence; (*physics*) inertia; Institute; Institution; Interest; International; intransitive; (*chem*) iodine; Island; Isle; (*physics*) isospin; IVR Italy; 1 (Roman numeral).
IABA International Amateur Boxing Association.
IAM Institute of Advanced Motorists.
ib. *ibidem* (*Latin* in the same place).
IBA Independent Broadcasting Authority.
ibid. *ibidem* (*Latin* in the same place).
IC integrated circuit.
i/c in charge; internal combustion.
ICA Institute of Contemporary Art.
ICBM intercontinental ballistic missile.
ICI Imperial Chemical Industries.
icon. iconographic; iconography.
ICU intensive care unit.
ID identification.
id. *idem* (*Latin* the same).
IDP integrated data processing.
i.e. *id est* (*Latin* that is).
IL IVR Israel.
ILEA Inner London Education Authority.
Ill. Illinois.
ill., illus. illustrated; illustration.
ILO International Labour Organization.
ILP Independent Labour Party.
ILTF International Lawn Tennis Federation.

IM Isle of Man.
IMF International Monetary Fund.
imit. imitation; imitative.
imp. imperative; imperfect; imperial; impersonal; implemerlt; import; important; importer; *imprimatur* (*Latin* let it be printed); imprint; improper; improved; improvement.
imper. imperative.
imperf. imperfect.
impers. impersonal.
impf. imperfect.
imp. gall. imperial gallon.
In (*chem*) indium.
in. inch.
Inc. Incorporated.
inc. included; including; inclusive; income; incomplete; increase.
incl. including; inclusive.
incog. incognito.
incor. incorporated.
incr. increase; increased; increasing.
IND IVR India.
Ind. Independent; India; Indian; Indies.
ind. independence; independent; index; indicative; indirect; industrial; industry.
indef. indefinite.
indic. indicating; indicative; indicator.
individ. individual.
Inf. Infantry.
inf. inferior; infinitive; influence; information; *infra* (*Latin* below).
infin. infinitive.
init. initial; *initio* (*Latin* in the beginning).
in loc. cit. *in loco citato* (*Latin* in the place cited).
ins. inches; inspector; insulated; insulation; insurance.
Insp. inspected; inspector.
Inst. Institute.
inst. instant; instantaneous; instrumental.
instr. instructor; instrument; instrumental.
int. interest; interim; interior; interjection; internal; international; interpreter; intransitive.
intens. intensified; intensive.
inter. intermediate.
interj. interjection.
INTERPOL International Criminal Police Commission.
interrog. interrogation; interrogative.
intr., intrans. intransitive.
intro. introduction; introductory.
inv. invented; invention; inventor; invoice.
I/O (*comput*) input/output.
Io (*chem*) ionium.
Io. Iowa.
IOC International Olympic Committee.
IOM Isle of Man.
IOU I owe you.
IOW Isle of Wight.
IPA International Phonetic Alphabet or Association.
IPBM interplanetary ballistic missile.
IQ intelligence quotient.
IR infrared; Inland Revenue; IVR Iran.
Ir (*chem*) iridium.
Ir. Ireland; Irish.
IRA Irish Republican Army.
IRBM intermediate range ballistic missile.
IRC International Red Cross.
IRL IVR Republic of Ireland.
IRQ IVR Iraq.
IS IVR Iceland.
Is. (*Scrip*) Isaiah; Island; Isle.
ISBN International Standard Book Number.
isl. island; isle.
isth. isthmus.
It. Italian; Italic; Italy.
ITA Independent Television Authority; Initial Teaching Alphabet.
Ital. Italian; Italic.
ITN Independent Television News.
ITV Independent Television.
IUD intra-uterine device.
i.v. intravenous.
IVR International Vehicle Registration.
IVS International Voluntary Service.
IW Isle of Wight.
J IVR Japan; (*physics*) joule; Journal; Judge; Justice.
JA IVR Jamaica.
Ja. January.
Jan. January.
Jap. Japan; Japanese.
Jas James.
JATO jet-assisted take-off.
JC Jesus Christ; Jockey Club.
JCB (trademark) Joseph Cyril Bamford (manufacturer of an earth-moving vehicle).
jct. junction.
Jl. July.
Jnr Junior.
JP Justice of the Peace.
Jr Junior.
jt joint.
Ju. June.
Jul. July.
Jun. June; Junior.

junc. junction.
Junr Junior.
Jus. Justice.
juv. juvenile.
Jy July.
K (*elect*) capacity; carat; (*math*) constant; (*physics*) kaon; (*physics*) kelvin; IVR Khmer Republic; kilo; King; knight; knit; kopeck; (*chem*) potassium.
K. (*mus*) Köchel (number) (Mozart catalogue).
KB King's Bench; Knight of the Order of the Bath.
KBE Knight of the Order of the British Empire.
KC Kennel Club; King's Counsel; Knight Commander.
kc kilocycle.
KCB Knight Commander of the Order of the Bath.
KCMG Knight Commander of the Order of St Michael and St Gearge.
KCVC Knight Commander of the Royal Victorian Order.
keV kilo-electronvolt.
KG Knight of the Order of the Garter.
kg kilogram.
KGB Komitet Gosudarstvennoi Bezopasnosti (*Russian* Committee of State Security, former USSR).
KGCB Knight of the Grand Cross of the Order of the Bath.
kHz kilohertz.
KIA killed in action.
kilo kilogram.
kJ kilojoule.
KJV King James Version (of the Bible).
KKK Ku Klux Klan.
kl kilolitre.
km kilometre.
km/h kilometres per hour.
kn (*naut*) knot.
KO knock-out.
Kr (*chem*) krypton.
Kt Knight.
kV kilovolt.
kW kilowatt.
kWh kilowatt-hour.
KWT IVR Kuwait.
L (*elect*) inductance; Lake; Latin; learner driver; Liberal; longitude; IVR Luxembourg; 50 (Roman numeral).
l litre.
l. lake; land; latitude; left; length; *liber* (*Latin* book); *libra* (*Latin* pound); line; lire; low.
LA Los Angeles.
La (*chem*) lanthanum.
Lab. Labour; Labrador.
lab. labial; laboratory.
Lancs. Lancashire.
lang. language.
LAO IVR Laos.
LAR IVR Libya.
Lat. Latin.
lat. latitude.
LB IVR Liberia.
lb. pound.
l.b.w. leg before wicket (in cricket).
LC Lance Corporal.
L/C Letter of Credit.
lc, l.c. *loco citato* (*Latin* in the place cited); (*print*) lower case.
LCC London County Council.
LCD lowest common denominator.
LCM lowest common multiple.
L/Cpl Lance Corporal.
Ld. Lord.
Ldg. Leading.
LEA Local Education Authority.
leg. legal; (*mus*) *legato* (*Italian* smooth).
Leics. Leicestershire.
LEM lunar excursion module.
LEV lunar excursion vehicle.
LF low frequency.
LG Low German.
lg. large.
lgth length.
LH luteinizing hormone.
l.h. left hand.
l.h.d. left hand drive.
Li (*chem*) lithium.
Lib. Liberal.
Lieut, Lieut. Lieutenant.
Lincs. Lincolnshire.
ling. linguistics.
lit. literal; literary; literature; litre.
LL Lord Lieutenant.
ll. lines.
LL.B. *Legum Baccalaureus* (*Latin* Bachelor of Laws).
LL.D. *Legum Doctor* (*Latin* Doctor of Laws).
lm (*physics*) lumen.
LMT local mean time.
LNG liquefied natural gas.
LOA leave of absence.
loc. cit. *loco citato* (*Latin* in the place cited).
log. logarithm.
long. longitude.

loq. *loquitur* (*Latin* he or she speaks).
LP long-playing (record); London Philharmonia.
LPG liquefied petroleum gas.
LPO London Philharmonic Orchestra.
L'pool Liverpool.
Lr (*chem*) lawrencium.
LRBM long range ballistic missile.
LRS Lloyd's Register of Shipping.
LS IVR Lesotho.
LSD *librae, solidi, denarii* (*Latin* pounds, shillings, pence); lysergic acid diethylamide.
LSE London School of Economics.
LSO London Symphony Orchestra.
Lt. Lieutenant.
l.t. local time.
LTA Lawn Tennis Association.
Lt. Col. Lieutenant Colonel.
Lt. Comdr Lieutenant Commander.
Ltd Limited.
Lu (*chem*) lutetium.
LV luncheon voucher.
LW long wave.
Lw (*chem*) lawrencium.
LWM low water mark.
lx (*physics*) lux.
M mach (number); Majesty; IVR Malta; Manitoba; Marquis; Master; (*physics*) maxwell; Medieval; Member; (*mus*) *mezzo* (*Italian* half); Middle; Monday; Monsieur; motorway; Mountain; 1000 (Roman numeral).
m (*physics*) mass; metre.
m. male; married; masculine; medium; meridian; mile; million; minim; minute; modulus; month; moon; morning.
MA *Magister Artium* (*Latin* Master of Arts); IVR Morocco.
mach. machine; machinery; machinist.
mag. magazine; magnetic; magnetism; magnesium; magneto; magnitude.
Maj. Major.
MAL IVR Malaysia.
manuf. manufacture.
MAO (*chem*) monoamine oxidase.
Mar. March.
mar. marine; maritime.
March. Marchioness; margin, marginal.
marg. margin; marginal.
Marq. Marquess; Marquis.
masc. masculine.
Mass. Massachusetts.
math. mathematics.
Matt. Matthew.
max. maximum.
MB *Medicinae Baccalaureus* (*Latin* Bachelor of Medicine).
MC Master of Ceremonies; Medical Corps; Military Cross; IVR Monaco.
mc megacycle; millicurie.
MCC Marylebone Cricket Club.
MCP male chauvinist pig.
MCS missile control system.
MD Managing Director; *Medicinae Doctor* (*Latin* Doctor of Medicine); mentally deficient.
Md (*chem*) mendelivium.
Md. Maryland.
Mdm Madam.
ME myalgic encephalomyelitis.
Me (*chem*) methyl.
Me. Maine.
mech. mechanical; mechanics; mechanism.
Med. Mediterranean.
med. medical; medicine; medieval; medium.
Medit. Mediterranean.
mem. member; *memento* (*Latin* remember); memoir; memorandum; memorial.
MEP Member of the European Parliament.
met. metaphor; metaphysics; meteorological; meteorology; metropolitan.
metal. metallurgical; metallurgy.
metaph. metaphor; metaphysics.
meteor. meteorological; meteorology.
MeV mega-electron-volt; million electron-volts.
MEX IVR Mexico.
MF medium frequency.
mf (*mus*) *mezzo forte* (*Italian* moderately loud).
mfd manufactured.
mfr. manufacture; manufacturer.
Mg (*chem*) magnesium; megagram.
mg milligram.
Mgr Manager.
mgt management.
MHF medium high frequency.
MHG Middle High German.
MHz megahertz.
MI MilitaryIntelligence.
mi. mile.
MI5 Military Intelligence, section 5.
MIA missing in action.
MICR (*comput*) magnetic ink character recognition.
Middx Middlesex (former county).
mil millilitre.
mil., milit military.
Min. Ministry.
min. mineralogical; mineralogy; minim; mini-

mum; mining; minister; ministry; minor; minute.
mineral. mineralogical; mineralogy.
MIRAS mortgage interest relief at source.
MIRV multiple independently targetted re-entry vehicle.
misc. miscellaneous; miscellany.
mk mark.
mks metre-kilogram-second.
mkt market.
ml mile; millilitre.
Mlle Mademoiselle.
MLR minimum lending rate.
MM Military Medal.
mm millimetre.
Mme Madame.
MMR measles, mumps and rubella (combined vaccine against these).
Mn (*chem*) manganese.
MO Medical Officer; *modus operandi* (*Latin* mode of operation); Money Order.
Mo (*chem*) molybdenum.
Mo. Monday.
mo. month.
MOD Ministry of Defence.
mod. moderate; modern; modulus.
mod. cons. modern conveniences.
MOH Medical Officer of Health.
mol (*chem*) mole.
mol. molecular; molecule.
mol. wt. molecular weight.
Mon. Monday; Monmouthshire (former county).
Mont. Montgomeryshire (former county).
MOR middle-of-the-road.
MORI Market and Opinion Research Institute.
morph. morphological; morphology.
MOT Ministry of Transport.
MP Member of Parliament; Metropolitan Police; Military Police; Mounted Police.
mp (*mus*) *mezzo piano* (*Italian* moderately soft).
m.p. melting point.
mph miles per hour.
Mr, Mr. Mister.
MRBM medium range ballistic missile.
MRC Medical Research Council.
MRCP Member of the Royal College of Physicians.
MRCS Member of the Royal College of Surgeons.
MRP Manufacturer's Recommended Price.
Ms a title used before a woman's name instead of Miss or Mrs.
MS manuscript; IVR Mauritius; multiple sclerosis.
ms millisecond.
m/s metres per second.
MSC Manpower Services Commission.
MSc Master of Science.
MSG (*chem*) monosodium glutamate.
Msgr. Monseigneur; Monsignor.
msl mean sea level.
MT mean time.
Mt Mount.
mtg. meeting; mortgage.
mth month.
mtn mountain.
Mt. Rev. Most Reverend.
mun. municipal.
mus. museum; music; musical; musician.
mV millivolt.
m.v. (*mus*) *mezzo voce* (*Italian* half the power of voice); motor vessel.
MW IVR Malawi; medium wave; megawatt.
mW milliwatt.
Mx Middlesex (former county).
MY motor yacht.
mycol. mycological; mycology.
myth. mythological; mythology.
N National; Nationalist; Navy; (*physics*) newton; (*chem*) nitrogen; Norse; North; IVR Norway; November.
n. name; *natus* (*Latin* born); navy; nephew; net; neuter; (*physics*) neutron; new; nominative; noon; note; noun; number.
NA IVR Netherlands Antilles; North America.
Na (*chem*) sodium.
n/a no account; not applicable; not available.
NAAFI Navy, Army and Air Force Institutes.
NALGO National and Local Government Officers' Association.
NASA National Aeronautics and Space Administration (USA).
nat. national; native; natural.
NATO North Atlantic Treaty Organization.
NATSOPA National Society of Operative Printers and Assistants.
naut. nautical.
nav. naval; navigable; navigation; navy.
navig. navigation; navigator.
NB *nota bene* (*Latin* note well).
Nb (*chem*) niobium.
NBC National Broadcasting Corporation (USA).
NCB National Coal Board.
NCCL National Council for Civil Liberties.

NCO Noncommissioned Officer.
ncv no commercial value.
Nd (*chem*) neodymium.
NE northeast.
Ne (*chem*) neon.
NEB New English Bible.
NEC National Executive Committee.
NEDC National Economic Development Council.
neg. negative; negatively.
nem. con. *nemine contradicente* (*Latin* no one opposing).
neurol. neurol. neurology.
neut. neuter; neutral.
NF no funds.
NFT National Film Theatre.
NFU National Farmers' Union.
NHS National Health Service.
NI National Insurance; Northern Ireland.
Ni (*chem*) nickel.
NIC IVR Nicaragua.
NIG IVR Niger.
NL IVR Netherlands.
n.l. new line.
NMR nuclear magnetic resonance.
NNE north-northeast.
NNW north-northwest.
No (*chem*) nobelium.
No. Number.
n.o. not out (in cricket).
nol. pros. *nolle prosequi* (*Latin* do not continue).
nom. nominal; nominative.
noncom. noncommissioned.
non seq. *non sequitur* (*Latin* it does not follow logically).
Nor. Norman; North; Norway; Norwegian.
norm. normal.
Northants. Northamptonshire.
Northumb. Northumberland.
nos. numbers.
Notts. Nottinghamshire.
Nov. November.
NP Notary Public.
Np (*chem*) neptunium.
n.p. new paragraph.
NPT normal pressure and temperature.
nr near.
NRC Nuclear Research Council.
ns nanosecond.
n.s. new style.
NSB National Savings Bank.
n.s.f. not sufficient funds.
NSPCC National Society for the Prevention of Cruelty to Children.
NSU (*med*) non-specific urethritis.
NT National Trust; New Testament.
NTS National Trust for Scotland.
NUGMW National Union of General and Municipal Workers.
NUJ National Union of Journalists.
NUM National Union of Mineworkers.
num. number; numeral.
numis. numismatics.
NUPE National Union of Public Employees.
NUR National Union of Railwaymen.
NUS National Union of Seamen; National Union of Students.
NUT National Union of Teachers.
NV New Version (of the Bible).
n.v.d. no value declared.
NVQ National Vocational Qualification.
NW northwest.
NY New York.
NYC New York City.
NZ IVR New Zealand.
O Ocean; octavo; October; Ohio; Old; Ontario; Oregon; (*chem*) oxygen.
O & M Organization and Methods.
OAP Old Age Pensioner; Old Age Pensioner.
OB outside broadcast.
ob. *obiit* (*Latin* he *or* she died).
obb. (*mus*) *obbligato* (*Italian* obligatory).
OBE Officer of the Order of the British Empire.
obj. object; objection; objective.
obl. obligation; oblique; oblong.
obs. obsolete.
obstet. obstetrics.
obv. obverse.
OC Officer Commanding.
OCR (*comput*) Optical Character Reader; Optical Character Recognition.
Oct. October.
oct. octave; octavo.
OD Officer of the Day; overdose; overdraft.
OE Old English.
OECD Organization for Economic Cooperation and Development.
OED Oxford English Dictionary.
OF Old French.
off. offer; office; office; official.
OFT Office of Fair Trading.
OGM Ordinary General Meeting.
OHG Old High German.
OHMS On His *or* Her Majesty's Service.
OM Order of Merit.
o.n.o. or nearest offer.
Ont. Ontario.

o.p. out of print.
op. cit. *opere citato* (*Latin* in the work cited).
OPEC Organization of Petroleum Exporting Countries.
opp. opposed; opposite.
OR Official Receiver; operational research; other ranks.
orch. orchestra; orchestral.
ord. ordained; order; ordinal; ordinance; ordinary; ordnance.
Ore. Oregon.
org. organic; organization.
orig. origin; original; originally.
ornith. ornithology.
orth. orthography; orthopaedic; orthodox.
OS Old Style; Ordinary Seaman; Ordnance Survey; Outsize.
Os (*chem*) osmium.
o.s. out of stock; outsize.
OT Old Testament.
OU Open University.
OXFAM Oxford Committee for Famine Relief.
Oxon. *Oxoniensis* (*Latin* of Oxford).
oz. ounce.
P (*chem*) phosphorus; IVR Portugal; President.
p. page; paragraph; part; participle; past; penny; per; pint; *post* (*Latin* after); power; *pro* (*Latin* in favour of); purl.
PA IVR Panama; Personal Assistant; Press Agent; Press Association; Public Address.
p.a. per annum.
PAK IVR Pakistan.
P & L Profit and Loss.
P & O Peninsular and Oriental (Steamship Company).
p & p postage and packing.
par. paragraph; parallel; parenthesis.
Parl. Parliament(ary).
part. participial; participle; partner.
partn. partnership.
pass. passage; passenger; *passim* (*Latin* here and there); passive.
pat. patent; patented.
path., pathol. pathological; pathology.
Pat. Off. Patent Office.
pat. pend. patent pending.
patt. pattern.
PAYE Pay As You Earn.
Pb (*chem*) lead.
PBS Public Broadcasting System (US).
PBT President of the Board of Trade.
PC personal computer; Police Constable; political correctness; Privy Council.
p.c. per cent; postcard; *post cibum* (*Latin* after meals).
Pd (*chem*) palladium.
pd paid; passed.
pdq (*colloq*) pretty damn quickly.
PDSA People's Dispensary for Sick Animals.
PE IVR Peru; physical education.
PEI Prince Edward Island.
pen. peninsula; penitentiary.
per. period; person.
perf. perfect.
perm. permanent; permutation.
perp. perpendicular.
per pro. *per procurationem* (*Latin* on behalf of).
pers. person; personal.
PFA Professional Footballers' Association.
PG paying guest; Postgraduate.
pg. page.
PGA Professional Golfers' Association.
pharm. pharmacist; pharmacology; pharmacy.
PhD *Philosophiae Doctor* (*Latin* Doctor of Philosophy).
Phil. Philadelphia; Philharmonic.
phil. philology; philosopher; philosophical; philosophy.
philos. philosopher; philosophical; philosophy.
phon. phonetics; phonology.
phot. photograph; photography.
phr. phrase; phraseology.
phys. physical; physician; physics; physiological; physiology.
PI IVR Philippine Islands.
PIN personal identification number.
pizz. (*mus*) *pizzicato* (*Italian* plucking strings with fingers).
pk. pack; park; peak; peck.
pkg. package; packing.
pkt. packet; pocket.
PL Poet Laureate; IVR Poland.
P/L Profit and Loss.
Pl. Place.
pl. place; plate; platoon; plural.
PLA Port of London Authority.
PLC, plc public limited company.
PLO Palestine Liberation Organization.
PLP Parliamentary Labour Party.
PLR Public Lending Right.
plupf. pluperfect.
plur. plural.
PM *post meridiem* (*Latin* after noon); Post Mortem; Prime Minister.
Pm (*chem*) promethium.
p.m. *post meridiem* (*Latin* after noon).

PMT pre-menstrual tension.
PNdb perceived noise decibel.
PO Personnel Officer; Postal Order; Post Office.
Po (*chem*) polonium.
POD pay on delivery.
poet. poetic; poetical; poetry.
pol. political; politics.
pop. popular; popularly; population.
POS point of sale.
pos. position; positive.
poss. possessive; possible; possibly.
pot. potential.
POW prisoner of war.
PP Past President.
pp *per procurationem* (*Latin* on behalf of); (*mus*) *pianissimo* (*Italian* very soft).
pp. pages.
p.p. past participle; *post prandium* (*Latin* after meals).
PPE Philosophy, Politics and Economics.
PPS Parliamentary Private Secretary; *post postscriptum* (*Latin* additional postscript).
PR Proportional Representation; Public Relations.
Pr (*chem*) praseodymium.
pr. pair; paper; power; preferred; present; price; pronoun.
PRC People's Republic of China.
prec. preceding.
pred. predicate.
pref. preface; prefatory; preference; preferred; prefix.
prelim. preliminary.
prep. preparation; preparatory; preposition.
Pres. Presbyterian; President.
pres. present.
pres. part. present participle.
pret. preterit.
prev. previous; previously.
prim. primary; primitive.
prin. principal; principally; principle.
priv. private; privative.
PRO Public Records Office; Public Relations Officer.
pro. professional; prostitute.
proc. proceedings.
prod. product.
Prof. Professor.
prog. programme; progress; progressive.
prom. promenade.
pron. pronoun; pronounced.
prop. proper ; proprietor.
pros. prosody.
Prot. Protectorate; Protestant.
Prov. (*Scrip*) Proverbs; Province.
prov. proverb; proverbial; province; provincial; provisional.
prox. *proximo* (*Latin* next month).
prs. pairs.
PS Parliamentary Secretary; permanent secretary; postscript; Private Secretary.
Ps. (*Scrip*) Psalms.
PSBR public sector borrowing requirement.
pseud. pseudonym.
psi pounds per square inch.
PSV Public Service Vehicle.
psych. psychological; psychology.
PT Pacific Time; physical training.
Pt (*chem*) platinum.
pt. part; patient; payment; pint; point; port; preterit.
p.t. past tense.
PTA Parent-Teacher Association.
ptg printing.
PTO please turn over.
Pty Proprietary.
Pu (*chem*) plutonium.
pub. public; publication; published; publisher; publishing.
PVC polyvinyl chloride.
PVS post-viral symdrome.
Pvt., Pvte Private.
PW Policewoman; prisoner of war.
PY IVR Paraguay.
Q Quebec; Queen.
q. quart; quarter; quarto; quasi; question.
QB Queen 's Bench.
QC Queen's Counsel.
QED *quod erat demonstrandum* (*Latin* that was to be proved).
q.i.d. *quater in die* (*Latin* four times daily).
qlty quality.
QMG Quartermaster General.
qnty quantity.
qt quart.
q.t. quiet.
qto quarto.
qtr. quarter; quarterly.
qty quantity.
quad. quadrangle; quadrant; quadrilateral.
Quango quasi autonomous non-governmental organization.
quot. quotation.
q.v. *quod vide* (*Latin* which see).
R *Regina* (*Latin* Queen); *Rex* (*Latin* King); (*physics*) roentgen, röntgen; IVR Romania.

r. radius; right; river; road.
RA IVR Argentina; Royal Academician.
Ra (*chem*) radium.
RAC Royal Automobile Club.
RADA Royal Academy of Dramatic Art.
RAF Royal Air Force.
rall. (*mus*) *rallentando* (*Italian* gradually decreasing speed).
R & B (*mus*) rhythm and blues.
R & D research and development.
RB IVR Botswana.
Rb (*chem*) rubidium.
RC IVR China; Red Cross; Roman Catholic.
RCA IVR Central African Republic; Royal College of Art.
RCB IVR Congo.
rcd received.
RCH IVR Republic of Chile.
RCM Royal College of Music.
RCMP Royal Canadian Mounted Police.
rcpt receipt.
R/D Refer to Drawer.
Rd Road.
RDC Rural District Council.
RE (*chem*) rare earth elements; Royal Engineers.
Re (*chem*) rhenium.
rec. receipt; recipe; record; recorded; recorder; recording.
recd received.
recit. (*mus*) *recitativo* (*Italian* recitative).
rect. receipt; rectangle.
ref. refer; referee; reference.
refl. reflection; reflective; reflex.
Reg. Regent; Regiment; *Regina* (*Latin* Queen).
reg. regiment; region; register; registrar; registry; regular; regulation.
regd registered.
Regt Regent; Regiment.
rel. relating; relative; relatively.
relig. religion; religious.
REM rapid eye movement.
REME Royal Electrical and Mechanical Engineers.
Renf. Renfrewshire (former county).
Rep. Repertory; Representative; Republic; Republican.
rep. repeat; report; reported; reporter; representative; reprint.
repro. reproduction.
req. request; required; requisition.
res. research; reserve; residence.
resp. respective; respectively.
ret. retain; retired; return; returned.
Rev. (*Scrip*) Revelation; Reverend.
rev. revenue; reverse; revise; revision; revolution.
Revd Reverend.
RF radio frequency.
rgd registered.
Rgt Regiment.
RH IVR Republic of Haiti; Royal Highness.
Rh rhesus; (*chem*) rhodium.
r.h. right hand.
r.h.d. right hand drive.
rhet. rhetoric; rhetorical.
RHF Royal Highland Fusiliers.
RHG Royal Horse Guards.
RHS Royal Horticultural Society.
RI religious instruction; IVR Republic of Indonesia; Rhode Island.
RIBA Royal Institute of British Architects.
RIM IVR Republic of Mauritania.
RIP *requiescat in pace* (*Latin* may he or she rest in peace).
rit. (*mus*) *ritardando* (*Italian* decrease pace).
RL IVR Republic of Lebanon; Rugby League.
rly railway.
RM IVR Malagasy Republic; Royal Mail.
rm ream; room.
RMA Royal Military Academy.
RMM IVR Republic of Mali.
RN Registered Nurse; Royal Navy.
Rn (*chem*) radon.
RNA ribonucleic acid.
RNIB Royal National Institute for the Blind.
RNID Royal National Institute for the Deaf.
RNLI Royal National Lifeboat Institution.
RNR Royal Naval Reserve; IVR Zambia.
RNVR Royal Naval Volunteer Reserve.
ROC Royal Observer Corps.
ROK IVR Republic of Korea.
Rom. Roman; Romania; (*Scrip*) Romans.
rom. roman (type).
RoSPA Royal Society for the Prevention of Accidents.
RP Received Pronunciation.
RPI retail price index.
rpm revolutions per minute.
rps revolutions per second.
rpt. repeat; report.
RRP recommended retail price.
RS Royal Society.
r.s. right side.
RSA Royal Scottish Academy.
RSFSR Russian Soviet Federated Socialist Republic.

RSM Regimental Sergeant-Major; IVR San Marino.
RSPB Royal Society for the Protection of Birds.
RSPCA Royal Society for the Prevention of Cruelty to Animals.
RSPCC Royal Scottish Society for the Prevention of Cruelty to Children.
RSR IVR Rhodesia.
RSV Revised Standard Version (of the Bible).
RSVP *répondez s'il vous plait* (*French* please reply).
rt right.
Rt Hon. Right Honourable.
Rt Rev. Right Reverend.
RU IVR Burundi; Rugby Union.
Ru (*chem*) ruthenium.
RUC Royal Uster Constabulary.
Russ. Russia; Russian.
RV Revised Version (of the Bible).
RWA IVR Rwanda.
S Saint; Saturday; Saxon; School; Senate; September; Society; South; Southern; (*chem*) sulphur; Sunday; IVR Sweden.
S second.
S. section; series; shilling; signed; singular; soprano.
SA Salvation Army; South Africa; South America; South Australia.
Sab. Sabbath.
SAD seasonal affective disorder.
s.a.e. stamped addressed envelope.
SALT Strategic Arms Limitation Talks.
SAM surface-to-air missile.
Sans., Sansk. Sanskrit.
SARAH Search and Rescue and Homing.
Sat. Saturday; Saturn.
Sax. Saxon; Saxony.
sax. saxophone.
SAYE Save As You Earn.
SB Special Branch.
Sb (*chem*) antimony.
sb. substantive.
SBN Standard Book Number.
Sc (*chem*) scandium.
Sc. Scots; Scottish.
sc. scene; science; *sculpsit* (*Latin* he or she engraved it).
s.c. small capitals.
Scand. Scandinavia; Scandinavian.
SCE Scottish Certificate of Education.
SCF Save the Children Fund.
sci. science; scientific.
sci-fi science fiction.
Scot. Scotland; Scottish.
sculp. *sculpsit* (*Latin* he or she engraved it); sculptor; sculpture.
SD IVR Swazilarld.
sd sound.
s.d. *sine die* (*Latin* without date); standard deviation.
SDLP Social and Democratic Labour Party (Northern Ireland).
SDP Social Democratic Party.
SE southeast.
Se (*chem*) selenium.
SEATO Southeast Asia Treaty Organization.
sec. secant; second; secondary; secretary; section; security.
sect. section.
Secy Secretary.
Selk. Selkirkshire (former county).
SEN State Enrolled Nurse.
Sen. Senate; Senator; Senior.
Sep. September; Septuagint.
sep. separate.
Sept. September; Septuagint.
seq. sequel; *sequens* (*Latin* the following).
ser. serial; series; sermon.
Serg. Sergeant.
SF IVR Finland; San Francisco; Science Fiction; Sinn Fein.
sf. (*mus*) *sforzando* (*Italian* with a strong accent on a single note or chord).
SFA Scottish Football Association; (*colloq*) Sweet Fanny Adams, i.e. nothing.
sgd signed.
SGP IVR Singapore.
Sgt Sergeant.
Sgt Maj. Sergeant Major.
Shak. Shakespeare.
SHAPE Supreme Headquarters Allied Powers Europe.
SHO (*med*) senior house officer.
SI *Système Internationale* (*French* international system).
Si (*chem*) silicon.
SIDS sudden infant death syndrome.
sig. signal; signature.
sing. singular.
sinh (*math*) hyperbolic sine.
SLADE Society of Lithographic Artists, Designers, Engravers and Process Workers.
SLP Socialist Labour Party.
SM Sergeant Major.
Sm (*chem*) samarium.
SME IVR Surinam.

SN IVR Senegal.
Sn (*chem*) tin.
SNP Scottish National Party.
Snr Senior.
SOB (*sl*) son of a bitch.
Soc. Socialist; Society.
SOGAT Society of Graphical and Allied Trades.
Som. Somerset.
SONAR Sound Navigation and Ranging.
sop. soprano.
SOR sale or return.
SoS Save our Souls.
SP starting price.
Sp. Spain; Spaniard; Spanish.
sp. special; species; specific; specimen; spelling; spirit; sport.
s.p. *sine prole* (*Latin* without issue).
spec special; specification; speculation.
sp. gr. specific gravity.
SPQR *Senatus Populusque Romanus* (*Latin* the senate and people of Rome).
Sq. Squadron; Square.
sq. sequence; *sequens* (*Latin* the following); squadron; square.
sq. ft square foot.
sq. in. square inch.
SR self-raising.
Sr (*chem*) strontium.
Sr. Senior; Sister.
SRBM short range ballistic missile.
SRC Science Research Council; Student Representative Council.
SRN State Registered Nurse.
SRO standing room only; Statutory Rules and Orders.
SS Secretary of State; Social Security; steamship; *supra scriptum* (*Latin* written above).
SSE south-southeast.
SSM surface-to-surface missile.
SSPCA Scottish Society for the Prevention of Cruelty to Animals.
SSW south-southwest.
St Saint; Strait; Street.
Sta. Station.
Staffs. Staffordshire.
Stir. Stirlingshire (former county).
STOL short take-off and landing.
str. strait.
STUC Scottish Trades Union Congress.
STV Scottish Television.
sub. subaltern; subeditor; subject; submarine; subscription; substitute; suburb; suburban; subway.
subj. subject; subjective; subjectively; subjunctive.
subst. substantive; substitute.
Suff. Suffolk.
suff. suffix.
SUM surface-to-underwater missile.
Sun. Sunday.
supp., suppl. supplement; supplementary.
Supt Superintendent.
surg. surgeon; surgery; surgical.
surv. survey; surveying; surveyor.
SW shortwave; southwest.
Sw. Sweden; Swedish; Swiss.
SWA IVR South West Africa.
SWG standard wire gauge.
Swit., Switz. Switzerland.
SWAPO South West Africa People's Organization.
Sx Sussex.
SY IVR Seychelles.
syll. syllable; syllabus.
sym. symbol; symmetrical; symphony; symptom.
syn. synonym.
SYR IVR Syria.
T temperature; Testament; IVR Thailand; (*chem*) tritium; Tuesday.
t. tense; ton.
TA TerritorialArmy.
Ta (*chem*) tantalum.
tab. table; tablet.
tan (*math*) tangent.
TB tuberculosis.
Tb (*chem*) terbium.
tbs. tablespoon.
TC Tennis Club; Town Councillor.
Tc (*chem*) technetium.
Te (*chem*) tellurium.
tech. technical.
technol. technological; technology.
telecomm. telecommunications.
teleg. telegram; telegraph.
temp. temperate; temperature; temporary; *tempore* (*Latin* in the time of).
ten. (*mus*) *tenuto* (*Italian* sustained).
Terr. Terrace; Territory.
Test. Testament.
TF Task Force.
TG IVR Togo.
TGWU Transport and General Workers' Union.
Th (*chem*) thorium.
Th. Thursday.
theat. theatrical.

theol. theologian; theological; theology.
theor. theorem.
Thos Thomas.
Thurs. Thursday.
Ti (*chem*) titanium.
t.i.d. *tres in die* (*Latin* three times daily).
tkt ticket.
Tl (*chem*) thallium.
TM trademark; transcendental meditation.
Tm (*chem*) thulium.
TN IVR Tunisia.
tn town.
TNT (*chem*) trinitrotoluene, an explosive.
t.o. turn over.
tog. together.
topog. topographical; topography.
TR IVR Turkey.
tr. transitive; transpose.
trad. traditional.
trans. transaction; transferred; transitive; transpose.
transl. translated; translation; translator.
transp. transport.
TRH Their Royal Highnesses.
trig. trigonometrical; trigonometry.
tripl. triplicate.
TRM trademark.
trs. transfer; transpose.
tsp. teaspoon.
TT teetotal; teetotaller; IVR Trinidad and Tobago; tuberculin tested.
TU Trade Union.
Tu. Tuesday.
TUC Trades Union Congress.
Tues. Tuesday.
TV television.
U (*chem*) uranium; IVR Uruguay.
u. unit; upper.
UAE United Arab Emirates.
UAM underwater-to-air missile.
UAR United Arab Republic.
u.c. upper case.
UCCA Universities Central Council on Admissions.
UDC Urban District Council.
UDI Unilateral Declaration of Independence.
UDR Ulster Defence Regiment.
UEFA Union of European Football Associations.
UFO unidentified flying object.
UGC University Grants Committee.
UHF ultrahigh frequency.
UHT ultra-heat treated.
UK United Kingdom.
UKAEA United Kingdom Atomic Energy Authority.
ult. ultimate; *ultimo* (*Latin* last month).
UN United Nations.
UNA United Nations Association.
UNESCO United Nations Educational, Scientific and Cultural Organization.
UNICEF United Nations International Children's Emergency Fund.
univ. university.
UNO United Nations Organization.
US United States.
USA Union of South Africa; IVR United States of America.
USDAW Union of Shop, Distributive and Allied Workers.
USM underwater-to-surface missile.
USSR Union of Soviet Socialist Republics.
usu. usually.
USW ultrashort waves; ultrasonic waves.
UT Universal Time.
UV ultraviolet.
V 5 (Roman numeral); (*chem*) vanadium; IVR Vatican City; (*math*) vector; velocity; volt.
v. verb; verse; *verso* (*Latin* left-hand page); *versus* (*Latin* against); very; *vice* (*Latin* in the place of); *vide* (*Latin* see); voice; volt; voltage.
vac. vacancy; vacant.
val. valuation; value.
var. variant; variety; various.
VAT Value Added Tax.
Vat. Vatican.
vb verb.
VC Victoria Cross; Viet Cong.
VDU (*comput*) visual display unit.
VE Victory in Europe.
veg. vegetable.
vet. veteran.
VF video frequency; voice frequency.
v.g. very good.
VHF very high frequency.
VI Virgin Islands.
v.i. verb intransitive; *vide infra* (*Latin* see below).
Vic. Victoria.
VIP very important person.
Vis. Viscount.
viz. *videlicit* (*Latin* namely).
VJ Victory in Japan.
VLF very low frequency.
VM Victoria Medal.
VN IVR Vietnam.
vo. *verso* (**Latin** left-hand page).
voc. vocative.

vocab. vocabulary.
vol. volume.
vs. *versus* (*Latin* against).
VSO very superior old; Voluntary Service Overseas.
VSOP very superior old pale.
v.t. verb transitive.
VTOL vertical take-off and landing.
VTR videotape recorder.
vulg. vulgar.
Vulg. Vulgate.
v.v. *viva voce* (*Latin* spoken aloud).
W (*chem*) tungsten; Wales; Wednesday; Welsh; west; western; women's.
w. week; weight; width; with; won.
WA West Africa; Western Australia.
WAAA Women's Amateur Athletic Association.
WAAC Women's Auxiliary Army Corps.
WAAF Women's Auxiliary Air Force.
WAG IVR Gambia.
WAL IVR Sierra Leone.
WAN IVR Nigeria.
War. Warwickshire.
WASP White Anglo-Saxon Protestant.
Wb (*physics*) weber.
WBA World Boxing Association.
WBC World Boxing Council.
WC West Central.
w.c. watercloset.
WCC World Council of Churches.
W/Cdr Wing Commander.
WD IVR Dominica.
wd. ward; word; would.
WEA Workers' Educational Association.
Wed. Wednesday.
w.e.f. with effect from.
w.f. (*print*) wrong fount.
WG IVR Grenada.
w.g. wire gauge.
WHO World Health Organization.
WI Women's Institute.
Wilts. Wiltshire.
wk week; work.
WL IVR St Lucia; wavelength.
WNP Welsh Nationalist Party.
WNW west-northwest.
WO War Office; Warrant Officer.
w/o without.
Worcs. Worcestershire (former county).
WPC Woman Police Constable.
wpm words per minute.
WRAC Women's Royal Army Corps.
WRAF Women's Royal Air Force.
WRI Women's Rural Institute.
WRNS Women's Royal Naval Service.
WRVS Women's Royal Voluntary Service.
WS IVR Western Samoa; West Saxon; Writer to the Signet.
WSW west-southwest.
wt weight.
WV IVR St Vincent.
WVS Women's Voluntary Service.
WWI World War I (First World War).
WWII World War II (Second World War).
WX women's extra large size.
WYSIWYG (*comput*) what you see is what you get.
X 10 (Roman numeral).
Xe (*chem*) xenon.
XL extra large.
Xmas Christmas.
x.ref. cross reference.
xs. expenses.
Y (*chem*) yttrium.
y. year.
YB (*chem*) ytterbium.
yd. yard.
YHA Youth Hostels Association.
YMCA Young Men's Christian Association.
Yorks. Yorkshire.
yr. year; younger; your.
yrs. years; yours.
YTS Youth Training Scheme.
YU IVR Yugoslavia.
YV IVR Venezuela.
YWCA Young Women's Christian Association.
Z (*chem*) atomic number; IVR Zambia.
z. zero; zone.
ZA IVR South Africa.
ZANU Zimbabwe African National Union.
ZAIPU Zimbabwe African People's Union.
Zn (*chem*) zinc.
zool. zoological; zoology.
ZPG zero population growth.
ZR IVR Zaire.
Zr (*chem*) zirconium.

Gastrointestinal and Oesophageal Pathology

For Churchill Livingstone

Commissioning Editor: Geoff Nuttall
Project Editor: Lowri Daniels
Copy Editor: Andrew Gardiner
Indexer: Jill Halliday
Design Direction: Sarah Cape
Project Manager: Mark Sanderson
Sales Promotion Executive: Douglas McNaughton

SECOND EDITION

Gastrointestinal and Oesophageal Pathology

EDITED BY

R. Whitehead MD FRCPath FRCPA

Emeritus Professor of Pathology, Flinders University of South Australia;
Consultant to Clinpath Laboratories, Adelaide, South Australia

Churchill Livingstone

EDINBURGH
HONG KONG
LONDON
MADRID
MELBOURNE
AND
NEW YORK
1995

CHURCHILL LIVINGSTONE
Medical Division of Longman Group Limited

Distributed in the United States of America by Churchill Livingstone Inc., 650 Avenue of the Americas, New York. N.Y. 10011, and by associated companies, branches and representatives throughout the world.

First Edition 1989
Second edition 1995

ISBN 0 443 04764 2

British Library Cataloguing in Publication Data
A catalogue record for this book is available from the British Library.

Library of Congress Cataloging in Publication Data
A catalog record for this book is available from the Library of Congress.

The publisher's policy is to use **paper manufactured from sustainable forests**

Printed in Hong Kong
SWT/01

Contents

SECTION 6
Tumours

SECTION 7
Miscellaneous conditions

Contributors

John R. Bennett MD FRCP
Consultant Physician and Gastroenterologist, Hull Royal Infirmary, Hull, UK

Wladimir V. Bogomoletz MD FRCPath
Head of Pathology Laboratory, Institut Jean Godinot, Reims, France

A. J. Bourne MB BS FRCPA
Director of Histopathology, Adelaide Children's Hospital, North Adelaide, Australia

C. H. S. Cameron PhD
Lecturer, Department of Pathology, School of Clinical Medicine, The Queen's University of Belfast, Northern Ireland, UK

Rodney F. Carter MD FRCPath FRCPA
Chief of Service, Laboratory Medicine, Women's and Children's Hospital, Adelaide, South Australia

Pelayo Correa MD
Professor of Pathology, LSU Medical Center, New Orleans, Louisiana, USA

John H. Cummings MA MSc FRCP
Sceintific Staff, Medical Research Council, Dunn Clinical Nutrition Centre, Cambridge; Honorary Consultant Physician, Addenbrooke's Hospital, Cambridge, UK

J. D. Davies MD BS(Lond) FRCPath
Director and Consultant Senior Lecturer in Pathology, Regional Breast Pathology Unit, Southmead Hospital, Bristol, UK

D. W. Day MB BChir FRCPath
Consultant Histopathologist, Torbay Hospital, Torquay, UK

Derek J. deSa MB BS DPhil (Oxon) FRCPath FRCP (C)
Professor of Pathology, McMaster University, Hamilton, Ontario, Canada

Michael F. Dixon MD FRCPath
Reader in Gastrointestinal Pathology, University of Leeds; Consultant Histopathologist, General Infirmary, Leeds, UK

William F. Doe MB BS MSc FRCP FRACP
Professor of Medicine and Clinical Sciences, John Curtin School of Medical Research, Australian National University, Canberra; Director of Gastroenterology, Woden Valley Hospital, Canberra, Australia

Bohumil S. Drasar PhD DSc FRCPath
Professor of Bacteriology, Department of Clinical Sciences, London School of Hygiene and Tropical Medicine, London, UK

Clair du Boulay DM FRCPath
Consultant and Senior Lecturer in Pathology, Southampton University Hospitals Trust, Southampton, UK

Volker F. Eckardt
Associate Professor of Medicine, Johannes Gutenberg Universität, Mainz, Germany

Arzu Ensari MD
Lecturer in Pathology, University of Ankara, Ankara, Turkey; Honorary Research Fellow, University Department of Medicine, Hope Hospital (University of Manchester Graduate School of Medicine), Saiford, UK

Luis F. Fajardo L-G MD
Professor of Pathology, Stanford University School of Medicine, California; Chief, Pathology Service, Veterans' Affairs Medical Center, Palo Alto, California, USA

Sture E. Falkmer MD PhD
Emeritus Professor of Tumour Pathology, Karolinska Institute and Hospital, Stockholm, Sweden

Cecilia Fenoglio-Preiser MD
McKinsey Professor and Director, Department of Pathology and Laboratory Medicine, University of Cincinnati Medical Center, Cincinnati, USA

M. Isabel Filipe MB BS PhD FRCPath
Reader in Gastrointestinal Pathology and Honorary Consultant in Histopathology, United Medical and Dental Schools, Guy's Hospital, London, UK

Giuseppe Franzin MD
Senior Consultant in Endoscopy and Gastrointestinal Pathology, Institute of Anatomical Pathology, University of Verona, Verona, Italy

Bren J. Gannon BSc PhD (Melb)
Reader in Anatomy and Histology, Flinders University of South Australia, Australia

K. Geboes MD PhD AggHO
Professor of Pathology, University Hospital, Catholic University of Leuven, Leuven, Belgium

Glenn R. Gibson BSc PhD
Microbiologist, Medical Research Council, Dunn Clinical Nutrition Centre, Cambridge, UK

Hugh M. Gilmour MB ChB FRCPath
Senior Lecturer, Department of Pathology, University of Edinburgh, UK

Robert A. Goodlad BSc PhD
Chief Research Officer, Histopathology Unit, Imperial Cancer Research Fund and Histopathology Department, Royal Postgraduate Medical School, Hammersmith Hospital, London, UK

Sibrand Gratama MD PhD
Pathologist, Stichting Pathan, Rotterdam, The Netherlands

Stanley R. Hamilton MD
Professor of Pathology and Oncology, The Johns Hopkins University School of Medicine, Baltimore, Maryland, USA

Peter J. Heenan MB BS FRCPath FRCPA
Senior Lecturer, Department of Pathology, The University of Western Australia, Nedlands, Australia

Michael R. Hendrickson MD
Associate Professor and Co-Director, Department of Surgical Pathology, Stanford University Medical Center, Stanford, California, USA

David Hopwood BSc PhD MD FRCPath
Reader in Pathology, Ninewells Hospital, Dundee, UK

P. G. Isaacson DM DSC FRCPath
Professor and Head, Department of Histopathology, University College London Medical School, London, UK

P. D. James MB BS MRCP FRCPath
Consultant Histopathologist, University Hospital, Nottingham, UK

Aage Johansen MD DMSc
Consultant Pathologist and Head, Department of Pathology, Bispebjerg Hospital, Copenhagen, Denmark

Peter F. Jones MChir FRCSEd
Emeritus Clinical Professor of Surgery, University of Aberdeen, Aberdeen, UK

Jean W. Keeling MB FRCPath FRCP (Edin)
Consultant Paediatric Pathologist and Honorary Senior Lecturer, Royal Hospital for Sick Children, Edinburgh, UK

Richard L. Kempson MD
Professor and Co-Director, Department of Surgical Pathology, Stanford University Medical Center, Stanford, California, USA

Brian D. Lake BSc PhD FRCPath
Professor of Histochemistry, Hospitals for Sick Children and Institute of Child Health, London, UK

Frederick D. Lee MD FRCP (Glas) FRCPath
Consultant and Honorary Professor, University Department of Pathology, Glasgow Royal Infirmary, Glasgow, UK

Ling Li MD
Professor of Pathology, Cancer Institute, Chinese Academy of Medical Sciences, Beijing, China

J. Lindeman MD PhD
Head, Department of Pathology, Slotervaar Hospital, Amsterdam, Netherlands

George T. MacFarlane BSc PhD
Senior Microbiologist, Medical Research Council, Dunn Clinical Nutrition Centre, Cambridge, UK

A. M. Mandard MD
Head of Pathology Department, Centre François Baclesse, Caen, France

Michael N. Marsh DSc DM FRCP
Reader in Medicine, University of Manchester; Consultant Physican, Hope Hospital, Salford, UK

Minnie M. Mathan MD PhD
Professor of Pathology and Head, Department of Gastrointestinal Sciences, Christian Medical College and Hospital, Vellore, India

C. J. L. M. Meijer MD PhD
Chairman and Director, Department of Pathology, Free University Hospital, Amsterdam, Netherlands

Amy E. Noffsinger MD
Assistant Professor, Department of Pathology and Laboratory Medicine, University of Cincinnati College of Medicine, Cincinnati, Ohio, USA

Paul Pavli MB BS(Hons) PhD FRACP
Senior Specialist, Gastroenterology Unit, Woden Valley Hospital, Canberra; Visiting Fellow, John Curtin School of Medical Research, Australian National University, Canberra, Australia

Alan D. Phillips BA PhD
Electron Microscopist and Honorary Lecturer in Paediatric Gastroenterology, Queen Elizabeth Hospital for Children, London, UK

Juan Piris LMS DPhil FRCPath
Senior Lecturer and Consultant Pathologist, Department of Pathology, University Medical School, Edinburgh, UK

Sue Ramachandra MB BS MRCPath
Senior Registrar in Histopathology, Department of Histopathology, United Medical and Dental Schools, Guy's Hospital, London, UK

C. A. Rubio MD PhD FIAC
Associate Professor and Chief, Gastrointestinal Pathology Laboratory, Karolinska Institute, Stockholm, Sweden

Aldo Scarpa MD
Associate Professor of Pathology, Institute of Anatomical Pathology, University of Verona, Verona, Italy

Michael D. Schuffler MD
Professor, Department of Medicine, University of Washington School of Medicine; Chief, Division of Gastroenterology, Pacific Medical Center, Seattle, Washington, USA

A. K. M. Shamsuddin MD PhD
Professor of Pathology, The University of Maryland School of Medicine, Baltimore, Maryland, USA

P. Sipponen MD
Head of Department of Pathology, Jorvi Hospital, Espoo, Finland

James M. Sloan MD FRCPath
Consultant Pathologist, Royal Victorial Hospital, Belfast; Reader in Pathology, Queen's University, Belfast, UK

Henry Thompson MD FRCPath
Senior Research Fellow in Pathology, Birmingham University, Birmingham; Formerly Reader in Pathology, University of Birmingham and Honorary Consultant Pathologist, Birmingham Central Health District, Birmingham, UK

P. G. Toner DSc FRCPath FRCP(G)
Musgrave Professor of Pathology, Queen's University, Belfast, UK

Bryan F. Warren MB ChB MRCPath
Lecturer in Pathology, University of Bristol, Bristol, UK

R. Whitehead MD FRCPath FRCPA
Emeritus Professor of Pathology, Flinders University of South Australia; Consultant to Clinpath Laboratories, Adelaide, South Australia

Sven Widgren MD
Reader in Pathology, Consultant Pathologist, Institut de Pathologie Clinique, Hôpital Cantonal Universitaire, Geneva, Switzerland

Erik Wilander MD PhD
Chairman, Department of Clinical Cytology, Institute of Pathology, University Hospital, Uppsala, Sweden

Richard A. Williams MB BS FRCPA FHKAM(Path) MIAC
Director of Pathology, Wangaratta & District Pathology Service; Senior Associate in Pathology, Melbourne University, Melbourne, Victoria, Australia

Dennis H. Wright BSc MD FRCPath
Professor of Pathology, Southampton University Hospitals, Southampton, UK

Nicholas A. Wright MA MD PhD DSc FRCPath
Professor of Histopathology, Royal Postgraduate Medical School, Hammersmith Hospital; Director of Clinical Research, Imperial Cancer Research Fund, London, UK

Guang Yu Yang MD PhD
Associate Professor of Oncology, China Medical University, Shenyang, People's Republic of China

Giuseppe Zamboni MD
Senior Consultant in Pathology, Institute of Anatomical Pathology, University of Verona, Verona, Italy

Preface to the Second Edition

Since the first edition of this book the application of new and more sophisticated techniques for morphological study has resulted in a plethora of publications concerning the gastrointestinal tract and its diseases. Not all of this lends itself to inclusion in this edition which still has as its aim a facilitation of the pathophysiological approach to gastrointestinal disease. Thus whilst there is much that is new in this edition the contributions have been made with this very much in mind. There is still the hope, therefore, that it will continue to be used in the diagnostic process by tissue pathologists, but that it will also aid all those concerned with the investigation and delineation of gastrointestinal disturbances and disorders on a broad front.

Preface to the First Edition

The seemingly simple tubular structure of the gastrointestinal tract belies a complex organ system. It is concerned with the sophisticated yet fundamental process of digestion. In contrast to most other organs it is directly exposed to external environmental influences and it is a cause of wonderment that it has the capacity to remain intact. No less surprising is its ability to withstand the physiological processes that are involved in the breakdown and absorption of complex chemical substances which are so essentially similar to those which go to make up this remarkable organ. There is a highly organised transport system by which foodstuffs delivered at the proximal end are eventually discharged as waste at the distal end. This system needs to be intimately integrated with a multitude of sequenced biochemical events which ensures the optimum digestive process. The whole of the functions of the gastrointestinal tract are carried out in the face of threatened assault by a truly horrendous mixture of potential pathogenic organisms of every shape and size. Indeed it is perhaps the greatest marvel of all that, in view of even the resident microbial population, regardless of those constantly introduced, the gastrointestinal tract for the most part remains intact.

Inevitably, however, its integrity is compromised and gastrointestinal disease results. The challenge that this constitutes for those in medicine with a particular interest in this field is one of both complexity and size.

This is particularly true for the tissue pathologist who is primarily concerned with the characterisation of disease by observation of the gross and microscopic changes which result. In order fully to understand pathological processes, however, it is not sufficient simply to recognise and describe structural changes. It is necessary to elucidate how and why these have come about. So much of traditional tissue pathology has been concerned with the accurate and detailed description of end-stage disease. It is becoming increasingly plain, however, that benefits for mankind will more likely come from study of the earliest manifestations. This is particularly true of malignancy, a field in which the last decade has seen the recognition of its earlier and earlier stages, and made more possible, not only the success of therapy, but the reality of prevention. This book has been compiled in order to facilitate this approach to gastrointestinal pathology and to focus some attention on the pathophysiological basis of gastrointestinal disease. As a consequence Section 1 dwells at length not only on normal structure but also on the kinetics of its maintenance and on function and motility and makes possible a somewhat more basic scientific approach to the delineation of disease. The remainder concerns an in depth consideration of pathological states. These are dealt with under the broad general heading of pathological processes rather than on a regional basis. This facilitates the avoidance of repetition when a disease process affects several regions of the bowel. The hope is that it will not only serve as a text for the diagnostic tissue pathologist, but will also act as a stimulus to investigate those aspects of gastrointestinal disorders which are less well understood. It is thus envisaged that clinicians, radiologists and basic scientists will find it of value in recognising the growing points and new frontiers in gastrointestinal disease.

R. W.
1989

Acknowledgements

Dr W. V. Bogomoletz

The author is indebted to the following pathologist colleagues for providing material for the illustrations of this chapter: Dr T. Takubo, Saitama Cancer Center Research Institute, Japan (Figures 38.42, 38.43 and 38.44), Dr NBN Ibrahim, Frenchway Hospital, Bristol, UK (Figures 38.45 and 38.46), Dr C. E. H. du Boulay, The University of Southampton, UK (Figures 38.47, 38.48 and 38.49) and Prof E. C. Sweeney, St James Hospital, Dublin, Ireland (Fig 38.50).

Dr C. E. H. du Boulay

I am grateful to Andrew Blasczyk for providing much of the specimen material for my chapter and to Mr B. Mepham and his staff for photographic assistance.

Professors S. Falkmer and E. Wilander

This chapter is based upon original work supported by grants from the Swedish Medical Research Council (Project Nos 12x–718 and 12x–6817). The Swedish Diabetes Association, the Cancer Society of Stockholm, the King Gustaf V Jubilee Fund, and the Faculty of Medicine at the Karolinska Institute, Stockholm.

Dr G. Franzin

I am indebted to Professor W. F. Grigioni MD, of the Institute of Pathology, University of Bologna, Italy and Dr S. Coverlizza MD, of the Pathology Service of the Ospedale Maggiore San Giovanni Battista, Torino, Italy for providing Figures 41.16, 41.18, 41.19, 41.21, 41.22 respectively.

Dr B. Gannon

It is a pleasure to thank Professor John Diana, Associate Dean for Research and Basic Medical Sciences, University of Kentucky for the provision of facilities at the Tobacco and Health Research Institute (THRI), to allow the completion of this chapter, while the author was a Visiting Professor in Physiology at the University of Kentucky. The author is grateful to Dr Barney Fleming and Dr Dan Matulionis, of THRI and Flinders University, South Australia for constructive criticism of the manuscript, to Laura McIlwain for assistance with bibliography, to Martha Butts for typing and patience with his poor calligraphy, to Carol Smith for proofreading and to Kerri Hunt and Danny Walls for photographic assistance. Support for the chapter also came from a grant to the author from the National Health and Medical Research Council of Australia.

Professor P. F. Jones

Figures 21.1 to 21.8 appear with the agreement of Blackwell Scientific Publications, Oxford, UK.

Dr A. M. Mandard

The author is grateful to Mrs Blondel for her help in documentation and typewriting the manuscript, Merle Shore for translating it and thanks P. Herlin, M. Michel and J. Marnay for their technical assistance.

Professor A. M. Shamsuddin

The author gratefully acknowledges the contribution of the following individuals in preparation of this manuscript: Diane Dix, Wayne Ivusich, Millie Michalisko, Alaaeldeen M. Elsayed MD, Patricia C. Phelps, Dallas M. Purnell PhD, Kathryn McKenzie and Benjamin F. Trump, MD. This work was supported in part by a grant from the American Cancer Society (ACS–PDT 184) and a contract from the US National Cancer Institute

(NO1–CP–15738). Figures 4.1, 4.2, 4.4, 4.5, 4.6, 4.7 and 4.11 have been reproduced with permission from W.B. Saunders and Company, Philadelphia (reference No 31).

Dr J. M. Sloan

I am most grateful to Miss Kathleen McAteer for secretarial assistance and for typing this manuscript. I am also grateful to Mr Roy Creighton for photographic assistance.

Professor P.G. Toner, Drs P. C. H. Watt and S. M. Boyd

The authors are grateful to Mrs P. Clark and Miss P. Carvill for typographical assistance and to Mr R. Creighton, Dr C. H. S. Cameron, Mr T. McLaughlin and the staff of the EM Unit for photographic and technical support.

Dr R. A. Williams

Permission to use portions of the text, figures and figure captions, and Table 42.1 from Williams and Whitehead (1986) has been obtained from the editors of Pathology. I would like to thank Drs T. C. Schultz and R. M. Mounsey, and Professor H. Attwood for reading through the texts on appendiceal pathology and offering valuable comment and advice.

Professors D. H. Wright and P. G. Isaacson

Figure 37.2 was previously published in *Human Pathology*. Figures 37.3, 37.4, 37.6 and 37.7 were previously published in *The Journal of Pathology*. Figures 37.14 and 37.23 were previously published in *Seminars in Diagnostic Pathology*. Figures 37.19, 37.20, 37.21 and 37.22 were previously published in *Histopathology*. We acknowledge these journals for permission to reproduce these illustrations. We should like to thank Miss Julie Foster for her secretarial assistance.

SECTION

1

The oesophagus and the gastrointestinal tract: normal structure, functional aspects and pathophysiology

CHAPTER

1 The oesophageal lining

D. Hopwood

The oesophagus is a tube connecting the pharynx to the stomach and is 25 cm long, beginning 15 cm from the incisor teeth. It is lined by stratified squamous non-keratinized epithelium and has a submucosa containing the oesophageal glands.

LIGHT MICROSCOPY

The oesophageal epithelium (Fig. 1.1) has an easily recognizable basal cell component composed of basophilic cells, lacking glycogen, which, in the normal individual

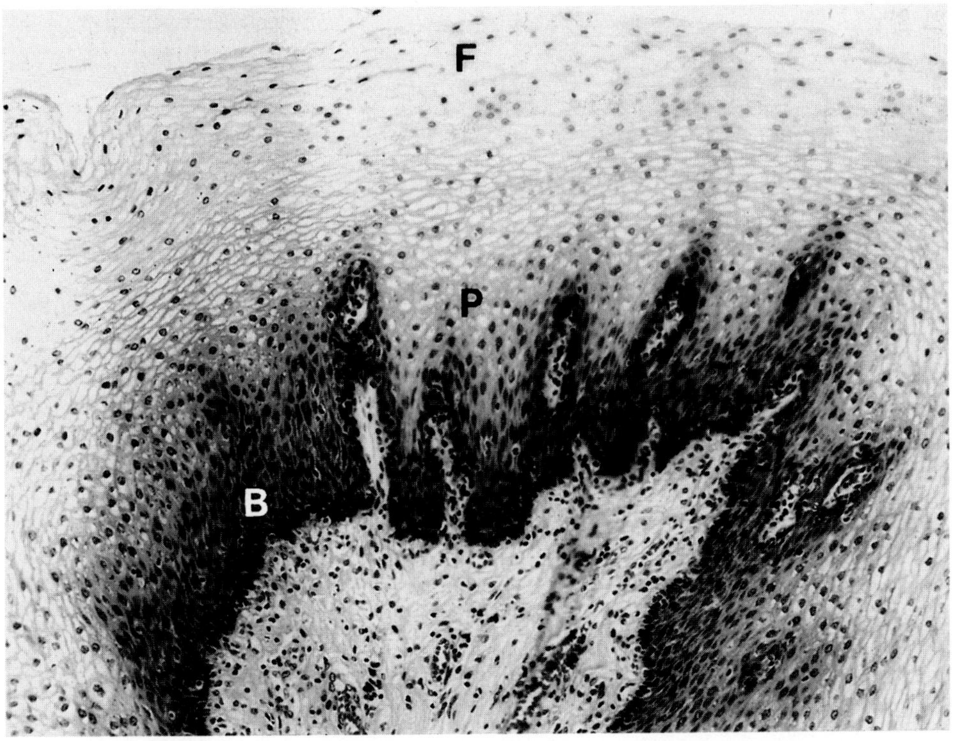

Fig. 1.1 Paraffin section. Oesophageal mucosa showing stratified squamous epithelium from a surgical specimen. Three layers can be seen, basal (B), prickle (P) and functional (F). Papillae extend into the epithelium. (H&E, ×125)

comprises no more than 10–15% of the total thickness of the epithelium. In the distal 2 cm or so of the oesophagus, the basal cell layer is thicker and this probably represents a response to the normal physiological regurgitation of gastric contents.[1] The basal cell layer is concerned with cellular regeneration and scattered mitoses may be found, usually within one or two cells of the basement membrane.

In recent studies proliferation of the basal cells has been investigated using tritiated thymidine and autoradiography compared with proliferating cell nuclear antigen (PCNA). It was found that the papillae were covered with cells with a slower cycle time than the interpapillary basal cells. The papillary basal cells may represent functional stem cells and their daughter cells in the interpapillary regions, the more rapidly dividing transit amplifying cells.[2]

In the basal layer, argyrophil cells may occasionally be seen. The incidence reported from autopsy material varies from 4 to 36% of cases.[3,4] These represent melanoblasts[3] and endocrine cells. No argyrophil cells are seen in relation to oesophageal glands or their ducts. The possibility of racial variation in argyrophil cell number has been raised. A number of papillae with a connective tissue core, carrying blood vessels, project into the lower half or two thirds of the epithelium.

Daughter cells are budded off into the prickle cell layer where maturation occurs. Prickle cells avidly take up the fluid phase marker horseradish peroxidase with transit to the late endosomes in short term culture.[5] There is well developed, functioning Golgi apparatus in the prickle cells which may be manipulated morphologically and functionally by drugs active against microtubules, such as colchicine, or by incubation at lowered temperatures. What role these functions may have in normal oesophageal mucosa remains uncertain.

The prickle cell layers and outermost, the functional layers, are often difficult to distinguish in conventional paraffin sections stained with haematoxylin and eosin (Fig. 1.1). They are more easily differentiated in plastic sections (Fig. 1.2) in which the wide spaces between the prickle cells are clearly apparent. The functional cells lie more superficially and may be divided into two layers (Figs 1.1, 1.2). The most superficial cells stain poorly due to partial loss of cytoplasm and contain basophilic granules which correspond to clumped organelles including RNA. The deeper cells have little space between them and probably represent the barrier between the oesophageal lumen and the internal milieu.

The epithelial cells of the functional and prickle cell layers contain abundant glycogen, but the basal cell layer does not. There is some evidence of a change in sugars in the glycocalyx with maturation of the epithelial cells, with the appearance of acid mucosubstances and fucosyl residues (Fig. 1.3). Cationized ferritin, used in short-term incubation with human oesophageal biopsies, demonstrates the presence of sialyl residues.[6] This can be used to show lateral movement of the cell membrane along with membrane retrieval which may represent a defence mecha-

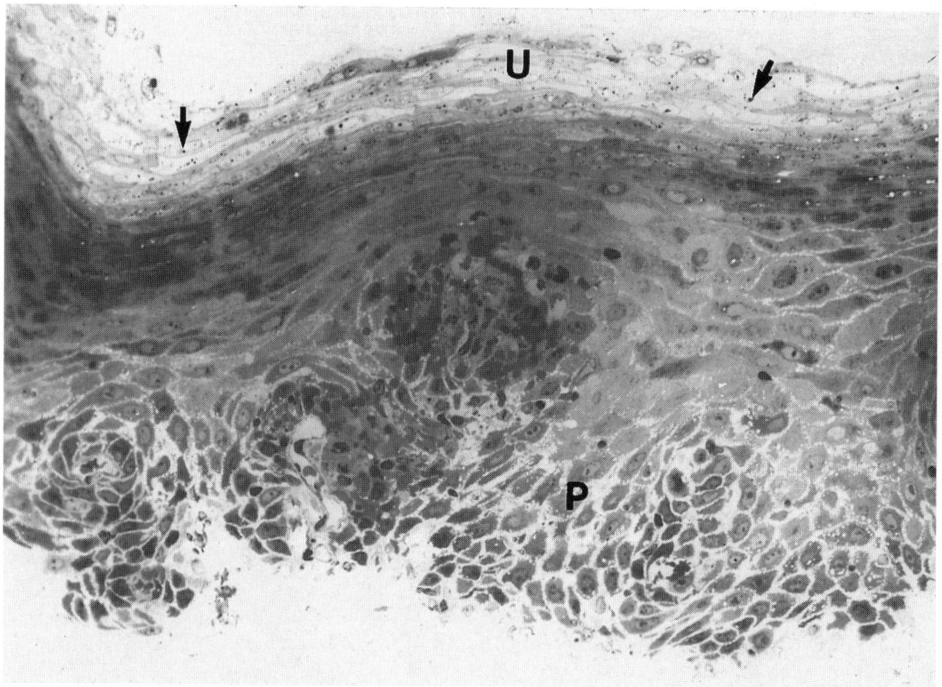

Fig. 1.2 Plastic section of a biopsy specimen. The prickle cells are clearly separated (P). the upper functional layer (U) is less heavily stained, clearly showing the basophilic bodies (arrows). (Toluidine blue, ×275)

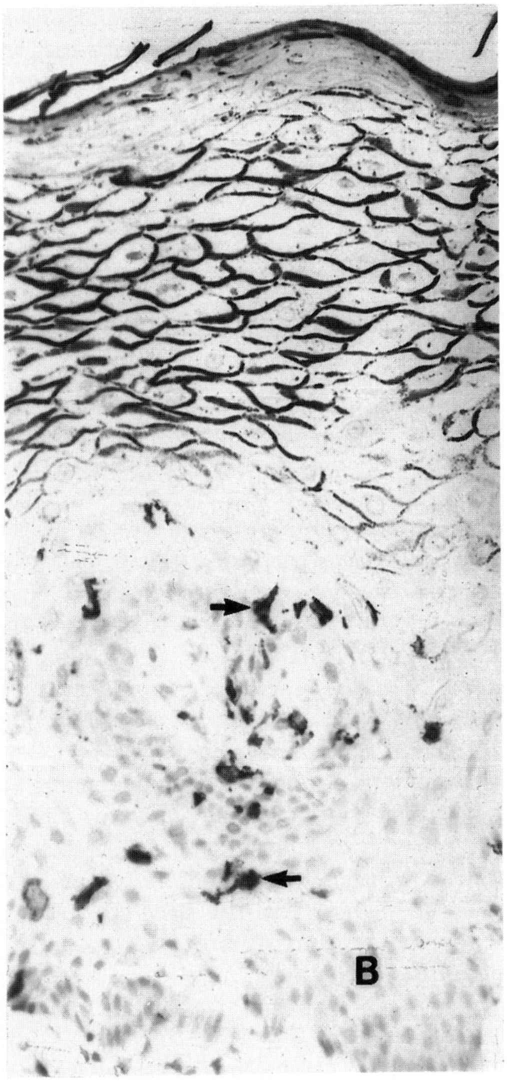

Fig. 1.3 Immunoperoxidase with MC2 after neuraminidase to demonstrate subterminal fucosyl groups. Note the absence of fucosyl groups on the basal cell membranes (B). Langerhan's cells are also shown (arrows). (×275)

nism. Thus by exocytosis the squames are able to insert new cell membrane granules and by endocytosis retrieve any damaged material. Small neutral fat droplets (1–2 μ) are found in layers but are most abundant in the functional layer. Using tritiated palmitate which is taken up readily by oesophageal epithelium in vitro,[7] it appears the accumulation of lipid may be related to changes in metabolism. This is influenced by the distance of the epithelial cells from the capillary and factors such as cell damage due to gastric reflux or mechanical trauma.

The histochemical profile of the oesophageal epithelium has been studied[8] and the findings are summarised in Table 1.1. Indeed, a variety of biochemical estimations can be performed on oesophageal biopsies and can provide evidence of oesophageal reflux.[7] The human oesophagus has also been shown to have a specific pattern of

Table 1.1 Histochemistry of oesophageal stratified squamous epithelium

	Functional		Prickle		Basal	
	CM	Cyto	CM	Cyto	CM	Cyto
PAS	+	+	+	+	+	–
Distase-PAS	+	–	+	–	+	–
Alcian blue	+	–	–	–	–	–
Colloidal iron	+	–	+	–	–	–
Cationized ferritin	+	–	+	–	+	–
Concanavalin A	+	+	+	+	+	+
AcPase	–	+	–	+	–	–
Nonspecific esterase	–	+	–	+	–	+
NADH	–	–	–	+	–	+
Glutathione transferase	–	–	–	–	+	+
Neutral Lipid	–	+	–	–	–	–

CM — cell membrane; Cyto — cytoplasm

keratins which differ from human epidermis and from the oesophagus of other species.[9]

Disaggregated oesophageal pinch biopsies give a 90–95% pure preparation of cells. These can be labelled and analysed by flow cytometry. The distribution of markers for differentiation and maturity — CD15 — and division and immaturity — epidermal growth factor receptor (EGFR) — in biopsies from patients with oesophagitis have been compared with normal controls. This opens a new way for investigating quantitatively the oesophageal mucosa in health and disease. Normal tissue is associated with a higher proportion of CD15 labelling and biopsies from oesophagitis with EGFR (Fig. 1.4).

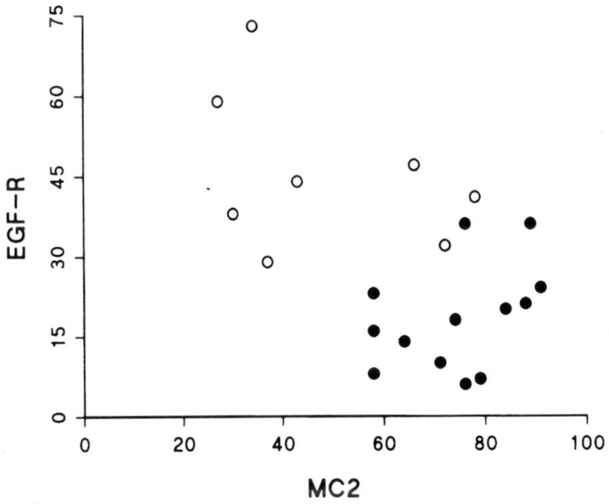

Fig. 1.4 Plot of epidermal growth factor receptor-positive cells against MC2 (CD15) positive cells from aliquots of cells prepared from the same biopsies. Points were plotted according to the percentage of EGFR positive (immature cells) and MC2 positive cells (mature cells). The axes represent the percentage of these cells showing the markers. (●) cells from normal oesophaguses; (○) cells from inflamed oesophaguses (reproduced from the *Journal of Pathology* with permission of the editor).

ELECTRON MICROSCOPY

The fine structural details of the human oesophagus have only been reported in detail relatively recently using either endoscopic biopsies or surgical resection specimens.[10,11] The first short report was by Desmet and Tytgat.[12] Each of the three layers, superficial, prickle and basal, has its own fine structural characteristics and functions.

The true nature of the superficial cells is only seen in biopsies taken as the endoscope is advanced. These cells are otherwise shed during the examination and adhere to the instrument, from which they can be recovered by washing at the end of the instrumentation procedure. In biopsies taken at the end of endoscopy, most superficial cells have a clean luminal surface. In biopsies taken on advancing the endoscope, a different picture is seen. Bacteria and occasional fungi are seen adhering to some surface squames (Fig. 1.5). If the biopsy is taken from the lowest 5 cm of the oesophagus, to which level reflux occurs physiologically,[1] then the superficial cells appear less electron dense, are glycogen depleted and fragments of cells are adherent to the surface with a pattern suggesting damage due to simple acid gastric reflux.[13]

The cells of the superficial or functional zone are flattened with the long axis parallel to the surface. The surface is thrown up into a complex pattern of microplicas and occasional holes can be seen by scanning microscopy (Fig. 1.6). Transmission electron microscopy shows the cells to contain numerous tonofilaments, varying amounts of glycogen, scattered lipid droplets and organelles (Fig. 1.7). Especially if the biopsy is from the lowest 5 cm, the organelles show signs of damage due to swelling and they tend to clump together. These changes correspond to the basophilic, RNA positive granules commonly seen by light microscopy. Occasional cells also contain parakeratotic granules and residual bodies.[14,15]

A few membrane coating granules may be found, less in areas of acid reflux. The cells are connected together by desmosomes. The intercellular space is relatively narrow and may contain some granular debris. Glycogen is relatively abundant, sometimes as intracellular fields.

The prickle cells show less flattening than the superficial squames and the desmosomes are more numerous, often at the end of processes and sometimes forming a labyrinth which may contain non-epithelial cells. Occasional cilia which, of course, are abundant during the later stages of fetal development, project into the intercellular space. The organelles show little evidence of damage, the Golgi apparatus is prominent, membrane coating granules are present, there are numerous tonofilaments and glycogen is relatively abundant.

The basal cells are cuboidal or columnar and attached to the basement membrane by frequent hemidesmosomes (Fig. 1.8). The cell membrane is thrown into a series of processes ending in desmosomes connecting to adjacent cells. A few bundles of tonofilaments run through the cytoplasm between desmosomes and hemidesmosomes. The nuclei are centrally placed and mitoses are occasionally encountered. The cytoplasm is relatively simple, with little endoplasmic reticulum, some free ribosomes and no glycogen rosettes of significance.

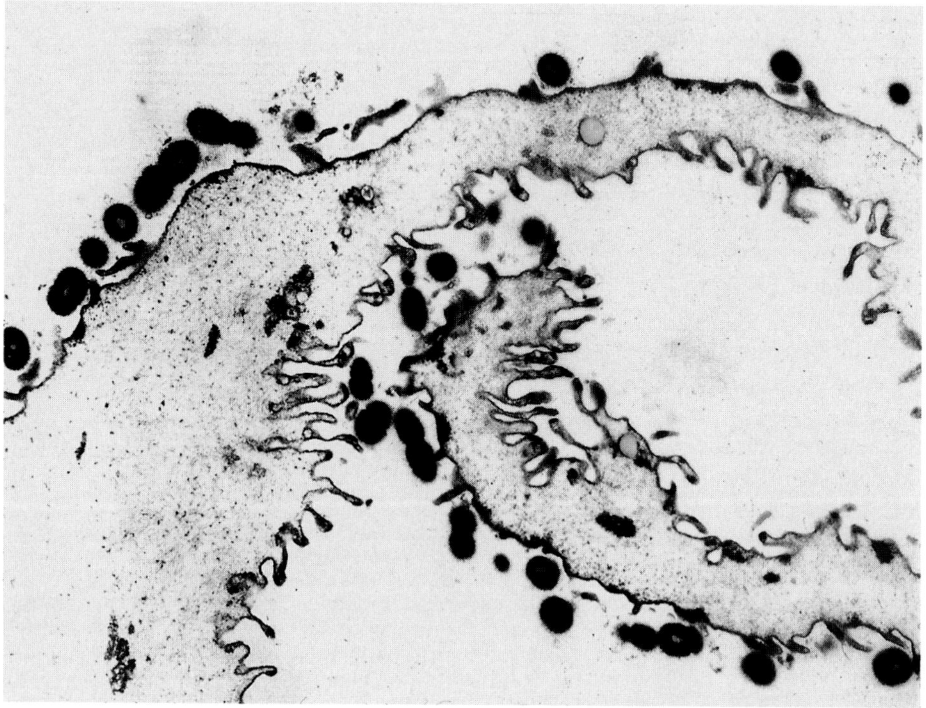

Fig. 1.5 Superficial squame from biopsy obtained on advancing endoscope. Note the associated bacteria and the low electron density of the cytoplasm due to cell leakiness. (×14 025)

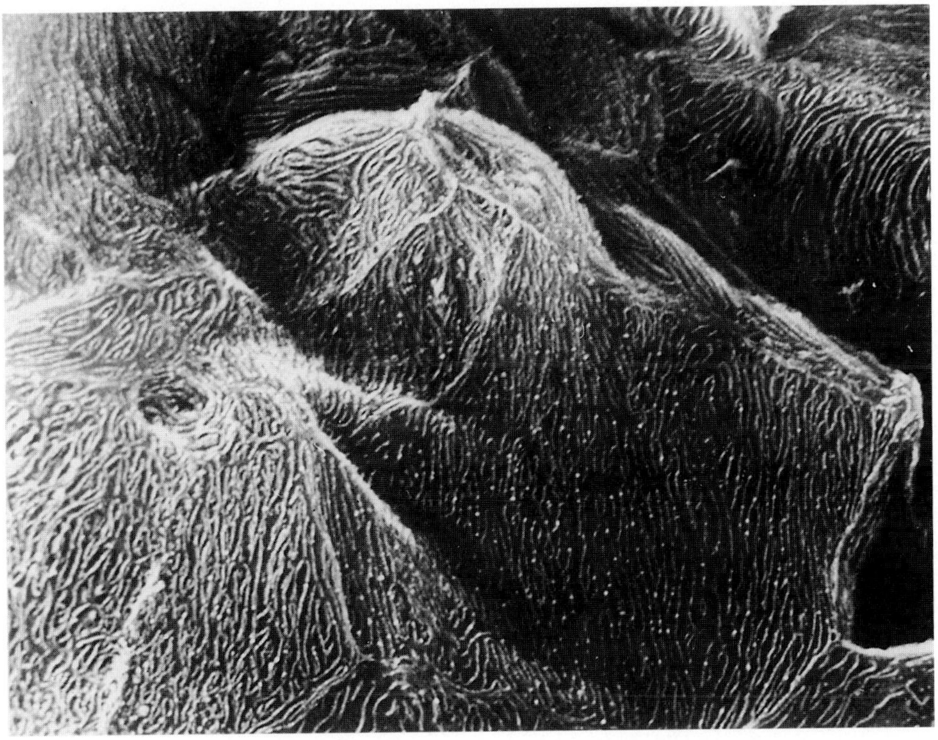

Fig. 1.6 SEM of superficial cells showing microplicae. (×1800)

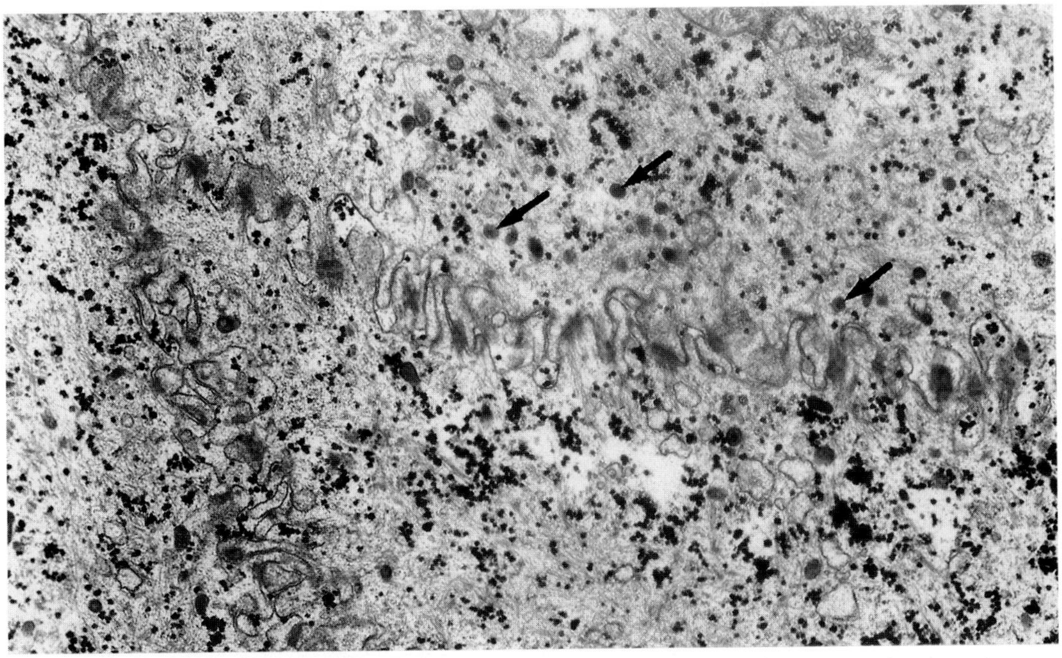

Fig. 1.7 Cells of the lower functional layer with small intercellular spaces and numerous desmosomes. The cytoplasm contains numerous tonofilaments, glycogen and membrane coating granules (arrows). (×5400)

The most abundant cell junction is the desmosome which, with the tonofilaments inserted into it, gives the tissue its mechanical strength. The hemidesmosomes in relation to the basement membrane serve a similar anchoring function. Occasional intracytoplasmic desmosomes have been reported.[10] In the superficial cells these have been related to alkaline reflux.[13] Gap junctions play a role in co-ordinating cell maturation[15,16] and tight junctions are occasionally seen in the inflamed state.

The basement membrane, which is occasionally reduplicated, is in general a simple structure with a lamina rara interna and lamina densa. This is connected to the underlying connective tissue by a number of anchoring fibrils (Fig. 1.8).

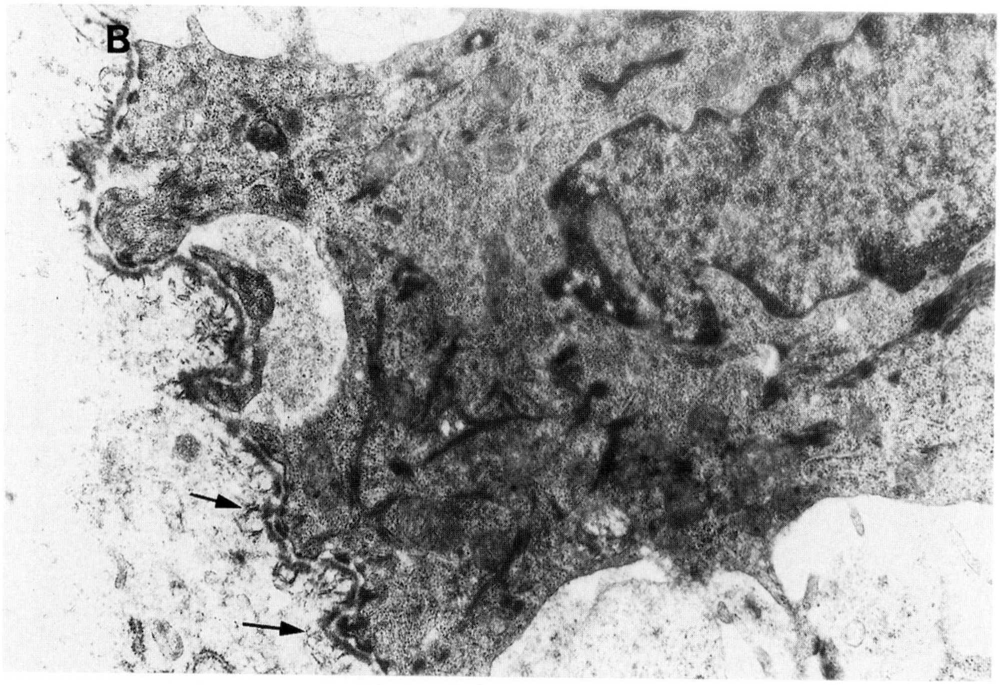

Fig. 1.8 Basal cells are columnar and attached to the basement membrane (B). Note anchoring fibrils (arrows). (×15 300)

MEMBRANE COATING GRANULES

Membrane coating granules were first described in human skin by Selby[17] and since have been reported in all mammalian stratified squamous epithelia, including the nonkeratinized oesophagus.[10,11] Similar structures have been observed in birds and reptiles[18] and the subject has been reviewed.[19,20]

Membrane coating granules vary in diameter from 0.1–0.3 μm and are limited by a single 10 nm membrane. In nonkeratinized epithelia they contain only occasional internal lamellae. In oesophageal epithelium, they are otherwise completely filled with electron dense granular material, whereas those from the buccal mucosa have a clear peripheral halo (Fig. 1.9). Within superficial and intermediate zones of the oesophageal epithelium, they are more numerous near the luminal border of the cells. Morphometric techniques have shown that the volume density of membrane coating granules in buccal mucosa is 0.11% in the stratum spinosum and 0.7% in the surface cells.[21] Although these techniques have not been applied to human oesophagus, the pattern is probably the same.

Oesophageal membrane coating granules contain mucosubstances, probably a glycoprotein. They contain lipids in keratinizing epithelia,[18] but probably only small amounts are present in oesophageal granules.

Acid phosphatase and arylsulphatase have been demonstrated in membrane coating granules in various sites.[20,22] In the oesophagus they also contain acid phosphatase, an enzyme which is also secreted into the intercellular space.[23]

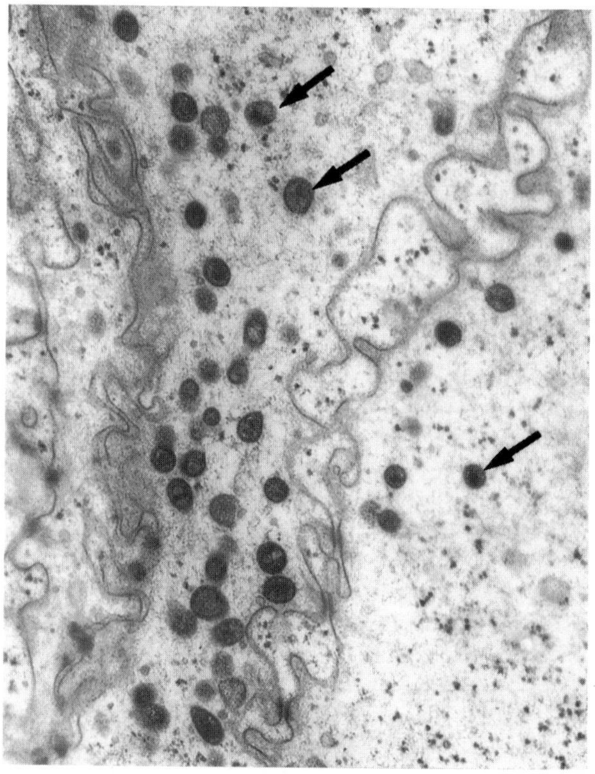

Fig. 1.9 Intermediate cells with numerous membrane coating granules of varying morphologies (arrows). (×20 000)

There is conjecture as to their function,[19,22] but because they contain acid hydrolases, they are believed to be part of the lysosomal system. They may play a role in reducing the number of desmosomes as the squames progress towards the oesophageal lumen. In the skin, membrane coating granules are believed to play an important barrier role in preventing water loss.[24] Their contents are secreted into the intercellular spaces of the stratum corneum, where the lipid laminae may be clearly visualized. A barrier role in the oesophagus is less important as far as water loss is concerned. Indeed, in the buccal mucosa of man, there is continual permeability to water.[25] The barrier may be important, however, in preventing the permeation of gastric juices between the squames, because this has obvious potential for cell damage.

The stimulus causing the secretion of membrane coating granules from the oesophageal epithelium, appears to be a low pH. The evidence for this comes from electron microscopic studies of oesophageal biopsies from patients with reflux oesophagitis[26] and similar studies after incubating oesophageal mucosa with gastrointestinal fluids.[13]

MECHANISMS OF CELL ADHESION AND SHEDDING

Cell adhesion is important in maintaining the normal form of the oesophageal mucosa and its barrier function. Two mechanisms are involved — cell junctions and cell adhesion molecules. In the oesophageal mucosa, desmosomes are the chief cell junction in this respect.[11]

Cell adhesion molecules are described in three families — immunoglobulin super family (CD15), cadherins and integrins. We have previously shown the presence of a CD15 molecule — detected by the monoclonal antibody MC2 — on the suprabasal cells of the oesophageal mucosa.[27] Recently, we have shown the presence of E cadherin and various types of the α and β chains of the integrins. They are distributed uniformly in a chicken wire pattern throughout the epithelium. We have also found the integrin α_6 β_4 as part of the hemidesmosomes. Cadherin function is controlled by catenin molecules which bind to the intracellular moiety. If the catenins are not present due to loss from leaky superficial cells, then cadherins lose their adhesion properties[28] allowing the superficial cells to be shed. Desmosomes show significant changes in diameter and their number/unit length cell membrane (frequency) as the oesophageal squames mature. They are largest between the basal cells and become significantly smaller between the superficial cells. Their frequency increases significantly between prickle and functional layer, but this is associated with change in cell shape from one with numerous processes carrying desmosomes to the much flatter superficial cells. There is evidence that an endogenous serine proteinase is involved with desmosomal breakdown. Removal of calcium ions by EDTA/EGTA produces a preferential loss of mature squames from oesophageal biopsies.

NON-EPITHELIAL ELEMENTS

Intra-epithelial cell types are not easy to see in standard paraffin sections stained with haematoxylin and eosin. Differentiation is, however, possible using plastic sections, electron microscopy or immunoperoxidase preparations.

Lymphocytes

The presence of lymphocytes has been documented using electron microscopy[10,11] and characterization of the subsets achieved using monoclonal antibodies.[29] In normal oesophageal epithelium most lymphocytes are cytotoxic T-cells (T8 positive) whilst those in the lamina propria are largely helper T-cells (Fig. 1.10).

Granulocytes

It appears that very small numbers of granulocytes are found in normal human oesophageal epithelium.[30] Basophils and neutrophils can occasionally be identified even in electron microscopic surveys, but macrophages only occur in relation to oesophagitis, as do eosinophils.[31]

Langerhans' cells

Langerhans' cells in the oesophagus were first demonstrated by electron microscopy[10,11] and occur in the super-

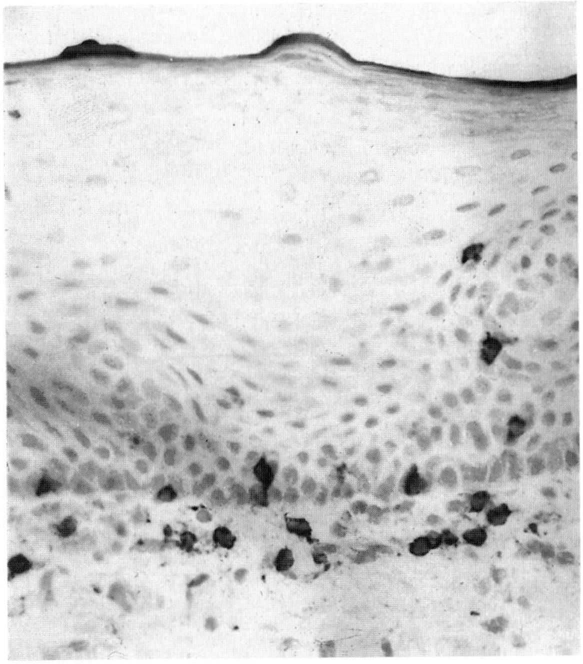

Fig. 1.10 OK T8 positive lymphocytes, submucosal and intra-epithelial. (×325)

ficial and middle layers of the epithelium. They contain typical granules which are up to 460 nm long and have a laminated or periodic internal structure. Occasionally, they are dilated at one end up to 150 nm and assume the shape of a tennis racket. Langerhans' cells bind T6 monoclonal antibodies[29] and in addition to skin and oesophagus, occur in the vaginal and cervical epithelium as well as the buccal mucosa. They contain histochemically demonstrable ATPase and fucosyl groups (Fig. 1.3) and calcitonin gene related peptide.[32]

In the skin and cervix they are thought to be able to take up and process antigens and present them to lymphocytes. They could thus have a pivotal role in a variety of disease processes. The oesophagus has a leaky epithelium, especially in reflux oesophagitis, and the Langerhans' cells have been shown to increase in number in oesophagitis.[29]

Oesophageal glands

The oesophageal submucosal glands are arranged in straight rows from above downwards and occur both in the mucous and submucous connective tissue. They number up to some 700–800 in the adult[33,34] and each gland is connected to the surface by a straight duct. They consist of a number of lobules composed of ductules and acini and are comparable to the labial salivary glands containing both mucus (chief) and serous (subsidiary) secreting cells (Fig. 1.11).[35] Parietal cells have also been described in the oesophageal glands[32], but are regarded as being heterotopic.

The mucous cells have a pyramidal shape and contain numerous large pale secretory granules. The usual array of organelles are to be found, pushed to the periphery by the secretory granules. The luminal cell membrane bears a few short microvilli. The granules of the subsidiary secretory cells are more electron dense than those of the mucous cells and have similarities both to labial glands and gastric mucous cells.[35] They may represent a transition between acinar and duct cells corresponding to the centro-acinar cells of the pancreas.

A third cell type is the myoepithelial cell which is comparable to that of salivary glands. It has abundant contractile microfilaments and attachments both to the secretory cells and the underlying basement membrane.

Finally, oncocytes may also be seen. They are also similar to those in the salivary glands[36] and are found at the junction of the duct and acini. Characteristically, as when occurring in other sites, they contain numerous close-packed mitochondria.

The oesophageal gland ducts are lined by a flattened cuboidal epithelium at the junction with the acini which becomes stratified as it reaches the lumen. The cells exhibit numerous short microvilli at their luminal surface and they contain numerous cytoplasmic microfilaments. These cells do not appear to be involved in fluid or electrolyte transfer.

The histochemistry of the oesophageal submucosal

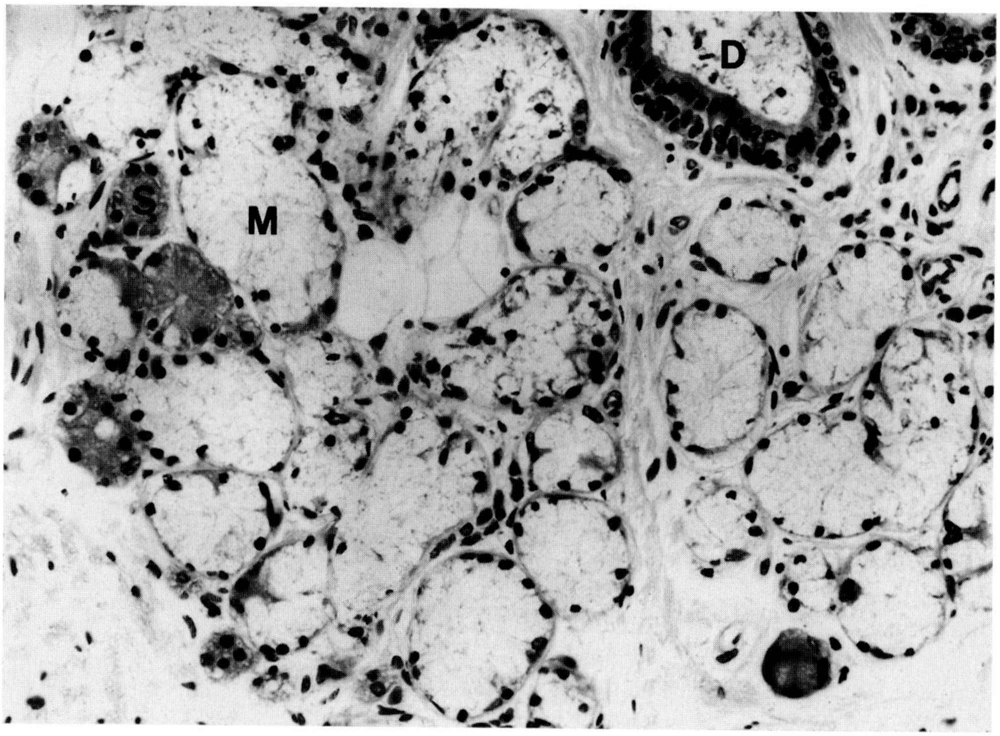

Fig. 1.11 Oesophageal gland. Chief cells (mucus secreting) – M; subsidiary cells – S: duct – D (H&E, ×275)

Table 1.2 Histochemistry of oesophageal submucoal glands[50]

	Chief cell	Subsidiary cell	Duct lumen	cells
PAS	+	a, g	+	a
AB pH 2.5	+	a	+	a
HID	+	–	+	–
MC2	–	–	–	–
Sialidase MC2	–	+	±	–
Cytokeratin	–	–	–	+
Lysozyme	–	+	±	+
CEA-monoclonal	–	a	±	a

a — apical; g — granular
MC2 is an antibody which demonstrates fucosyl groups after neuraminidase digestion.

gland is summarized in Table 1.2. No lipids have been detected and alkaline phosphatase and ATPase have been demonstrated only in the capillary endothelium of vessels in the glands. The duct epithelium shows a little non-specific esterase activity insensitive to the inhibitor E600, which probably reflects lysosomal enzyme activity.

Heterotopias

Islets of heterotopic gastric mucosa, which are described by endoscopists as velvety red patches, occur in the upper oesophagus in approximately 4% of patients.[37] They vary in size from a few millimetres to being circumferential. Biopsy shows gastric body mucosa with chief and parietal cells sometimes with mild chronic inflammatory changes. The larger patches can respond to pentagastrin stimulation which is shown by a local fall in pH, but clinically they are usually asymptomatic. In an autopsy study of 1000 children, aberrant gastric mucosa was detected in 7.8% of blocks taken from random levels.[38] Most islands (51%) were in the upper one-third.

The presence of heterotopic gastric mucosa appears to have an embryological basis and there is probably no relationship between this phenomenon and Barrett's oesophagus. There have been suggestions that the heterotopia may rarely give rise to ulcers, haemorrhage, oesophageal cysts and adenocarcinoma, and intestinal metaplasia has also been described.

There is a single report in the English literature describing a pancreatic heterotopia of the lower oesophagus associated with gastrointestinal haemorrhage.[39]

The presence of sebaceous glands in the oesophagus, often found by chance, is also recorded.[40,41] In a formal necropsy study, however, sebaceous glands were found in four out of 200 patients.[42] It was suggested that they represented metaplasia rather than ectopia.

Embryology

The ontogeny of the human oesophageal epithelium occurs in three phases.[34,43] First, in embryos measuring 30 mm from crown to rump, it is composed of two layers of simple low columnar cells with no cilia. Later, at the 40–130 mm stage, a third layer becomes interposed, the whole epithelium being up to six cells thick. The columnar surface cells contain apical mucous droplets and some are ciliated. Occasional goblet cells may be found. The mucosubstances include sialomucins and sulphomucins, and glycogen is also present. In the later phases of development, from the 130 mm stage to birth, the proportion of cells bearing mucus and cilia decreases, the intermediate cells become more prominent and the surface cells take on a squamous appearance.

The superficial mucous secreting oesophageal glands develop at the upper and lower ends as tubular buds of the columnar epithelial cells and sometimes come to contain parietal cells. The deep submucous glands develop late in gestation, apparently from the squamous cells.

Nerve endings

Using light microscopy, there have been claims for interepithelial nerve fibres in silver or osmium-zinc iodide preparations. However, these have not been confirmed by electron microscopy in man, which is at variance with findings in cats and *Macaca mulatta*.[44]

Unmyelinated nerve fibres are frequently found in the peri-acinar connective tissue of the submucous glands.[36]

Histometry

The basal cell layer is concerned with regeneration of the oesophageal epithelium and in biopsies from asymptomatic and endoscopically normal patients, it comprises up to 15% of the volume of the total epithelium.[7,45–47] In PAS preparations, this basal compartment is easily demonstrated because it contains little or no glycogen.[7]

While one morphometric study combined with oesophageal pH measurements[48] has shown that increased activity causes basal compartment hyperplasia and an increase in length of the papillae, this was not confirmed by others.[30]

A different approach, however, using measurement of nuclear size and density in the basal and intermediate layers of oesophageal epithelium, which is independent of orientation of biopsies, has confirmed that in patients with reflux oesophagitis the changes before and after therapy were consistent with an increased rate of cell turnover in oesophagitis.[49]

Form and function

In general, it is held that stratified squamous epithelia are well able to withstand wear and tear. The large number of tonofilaments inserted into desmosomes are believed to produce this mechanical strength. In the normal oesophagus, the epithelial cells are subject to the mechanical trauma of swallowed food and, in the lowest 5 cm, the regurgitation of gastric contents, especially after a meal. These contents contain proteases and detergents which can disaggregate and damage the epithelium[12] and the normal equilibrium is shifted towards excess loss of cells in reflux oesophagitis.

REFERENCES

1. Kaye MD. Postprandial gastro-oesophageal reflux in healthy people. Gut 1977; 18: 709–712.
2. Jankowski J, Austin W, Howat K, Coghill G, Hopwood D, Dover R, Wormsley KG. Proliferating cell nuclear antigen in oesophageal mucosa: comparison with autoradiography. Eur J Gastroenterol Hepatol 1992; 4: 579–584.
3. De La Pava S, Nigogosyan G, Pickren JW, Cabrera A. Melanosis of the oesophagus. Cancer 1963; 16: 48–50.
4. Tateishi R, Taniguchi K, Horai T et al. Argyrophil cell carcinoma (Apudoma) of the oesophagus. Virchows Arch (A) 1976; 371: 283–294.
5. Hopwood D, Milne G, Jankowski J, Howat K, Wormsley KG. Uptake of horseradish peroxidase by human and oesophageal explants over 24 hours. Histochem J 1991; 23: 409–414.
6. Hopwood D, Curtis M, Nicholson G, Milne G. The distribution and mobility of surface anionic groups of normal human oesophageal epithelium following interaction with cationized ferritin. Virchows Arch (B) 1980; 31: 277–288.
7. Hopwood D, Ross PE, Bouchier IAD. Reflux oesophagitis. Clin Gastroenterol 1981; 10: 505–520.
8. Hopwood D, Logan KR, Coghill G, Bouchier IAD. Histochemical studies of mucosubstances and lipids in normal human oesophageal epithelium. Histochem J 1977; 9: 153–161.
9. Banks-Schlegel SP, Harris CC. Tissue specific expression of keratin proteins in human oesophageal and epidermal epithelium and their cultured keratinocytes. Exp Cell Res 1983; 146: 271–280.
10. Al Yassin TM, Toner PG. Langerhans'cells in the human oesophagus. J Anat 1976; 122: 435–445.
11. Hopwood D, Logan KR, Bouchier IAD. The electron microscopy of normal human oesophageal epithelium. Virchows Arch 1978; B26: 345–358.
12. Desmet JT, Tytgat GN. Histology and electron microscopy of the oesophagus. Ch. 1 In: von Trappen G, Hellemans J. eds, Diseases of the oesophagus, Vol I. Handbuch der inneren Medizin. Berlin: Springer, 1974.
13. Bateson MC, Hopwood D, Milne G, Bouchier IAD. Oesophageal epithelial ultrastructure after incubation with gastrointestinal fluids and their components. J Pathol 1980; 133: 33–51.
14. Ferey L, Herlin P, Marnay J et al. Histology and ultrastructure of the human oesophageal epithelium. I. Normal and parakeratotic epithelium. J Submicrosc Cytol 1985; 17: 651–665.
15. Logan KR, Hopwood D, Milne G. Cellular junctions in human oesophageal epithelium. J Pathol 1978; 126: 157–163.
16. McNutt NS, Hershberg RA, Weinstein RS. Further observations on the occurrences of nexuses in benign and malignant human cervical epithelium. J Cell Biol 1971; 51: 805–825.
17. Selby CC. An electron microscope study of thin sections of human skin. J Invest Dermatol 1957; 29: 131–149.
18. Landmann L. Lamellar granules in mammalian, avian and reptilian epidermis. J Ultrastruct Res 1980; 72: 245–263.
19. Hayward AF. Membrane coating granules. Int Rev Cytol 1979; 89: 97–127.
20. Odland GF, Holbrook K. The lamellar granules of epidermis. Curr Probl Dermatol 1981; 9: 29–49.
21. Landay M, Schroeder HE. Quantitative electron microscopic analysis of the stratified epithelium of normal human buccal mucosa. Cell Tissue Res 1977; 177: 383.
22. Wolff-Schreiner EC. Ultrastructural cytochemistry of the epidermis. Int J Dermatol 1977; 16: 77–102.
23. Hopwood D, Logan KR, Milne G. Light and electron microscopic distribution of acid phosphatase activity in normal human oesophageal epithelium. Histochem J 1978; 10: 159–170.
24. Elias PM, Goerke J, Friend DS. Mammalian epidermal barrier layer lipids: composition and influence on structure. J Invest Dermatol 1979; 69: 535.
25. Kaaber S. Studies on the permeability of human oral mucosa IV. Regional changes in outflow of water hydrated and dehydrating oral mucosa. Acta Odontol Scand 1973; 31: 89–99.
26. Hopwood D, Milne G, Logan KR. Electron microscopic change in human oesophageal epithelium in oesophagitis. J Pathol 1979; 129: 161–167.
27. Sanders DSA, Kerr MA, Hopwood D, Coghill G, Milne G. Expression of the 3-fucosyl N-acetyllactosamine (CD15) antigen in normal metaplastic, dysplastic and neoplastic squamous epithelia. J Pathol 1988; 154: 255–262.
28. Hirano S, Kimoto N, Shimoyama Y, Hirohashi S, Takeishi M. Identification of a neural-catenin as a key regulator of cadherin function and multicellular organisation. Cell 1992; 70: 293–301.
29. Geboes K, De Wolf-Reeters C, Rutgeerts P, Jansens J, van Trappen G, Desmet V. Lymphocytes and Langerhans' cells in the human oesophageal epithelium. Virchows Arch (A) 1983; 401: 45–55.
30. Seefeld U, Krejs GJ, Siebenmann RE, Blum AL. Esophageal histology in gastro-esophageal reflux. Dig Dis Sci 1977; 22: 956–964.
31. Winter HS, Madara J, Stafford RJ, Grand RJ, Quinlan JE, Goldman H. Intraepithelial eosinophils: a new diagnostic criterion for reflux esophagitis. Gastroenterology 1982; 83: 818–823.
32. Singaram C, Sengupta A, Stevens C, Spechler SJ, Goyal RK. Localisation of calcitonin-gene related peptide in human esophageal Langerhans' cells. Gastroenterology 1991; 100: 560–563.
33. Goetsche E. The structure of the mammalian oesophagus. Am J Anat 1910; 10: 1–40.
34. Mottet NK. Mucin biosynthesis by chick and human oesophagus during ontogenetic metaplasia. J Anat 1970; 107: 49–66.
35. Tandler B, Denning CR, Mandel ID, Kutscher AH. Ultrastructure of human labial salivary glands I. Acinar secretory cells. J Morphol 1969; 127: 383–408.
36. Schridde H. Uber Magenschleimhaut-Inseln vom Bau der Cardialdrussenzone und Fundusdrusenregion und der unteren, oesophagealen Cardialdrussen gleidende Drussen in obersten Oesophagusabschnitt. Virchows Arch (A) 1904; 175: 1–15.
37. Jabbari M, Goresky CA, Lough J, Yaffe C, Daly D, Cote C. The inlet patch: Heterotopic gastric mucosa in the upper esophagus. Gastroenterology 1985; 89: 352–356.
38. Rector LE, Connerley ML. Aberrant mucosa in the oesophagus in infants and in children. Arch Pathol 1941; 31: 285–294.
39. Razi M. Ectopic pancreatic tissue of esophagus with massive upper gastrointestinal bleeding. Arch Surg 1966; 92: 101–104.
40. Wormann B, Otenjann ER, Seib HJ. Talgdrussen-Heterotopian in oesophagus. Dtsch Med Wochensch 1984; 109: 1503.
41. Zak FG. Sebaceous gland in the esophagus. Arch Dermatol 1976; 112: 1153–1154.
42. De La Pava S, Pickren JS. Ectopic sebaceous gland in the esophagus. Arch Pathol 1962; 73: 397–399.
43. Johns BAE. Developmental changes in the oesophageal epithelium of man. J Anat 1952; 86: 431–446.
44. Robles-Chillida EM, Rodrigo J, Mayo I, Arnedo A, Gomez A. Ultrastructure of free nerve endings in oesophageal epithelium. J Anat 1981; 133: 227–233.
45. Behar J, Sheahan DG, Biancani P, Spiro HM, Storer EH. Medical and surgical management of reflux esophagitis. N Engl J Med 1975; 293: 263–268.
46. Livingstone EM, Sheahan DG, Behar J. Studies of oesophageal epithelial cell proliferation in patients with reflux oesophagitis. Gastroenterology 1977; 73: 1315–1319.

47. Collins BJ, Elliot H, Sloan JM, McFarland RJ, Lowe AHG. Oesophageal histology in reflux oesophagitis. J Clin Pathol 1985; 38: 1265–1272.
48. Johnson LF, Demeester TR, Hagitt RC. Esophageal epithelial response to gastro-esophageal reflux. A quantitative study. Am J Dig Dis 1978; 23: 498–509.
49. Jarvis LR, Dent J, Whitehead R. Morphometric assessment of reflux oesophagitis in fibreoptic biopsy specimens. J Clin Pathol 1985; 38: 44–48.
50. Hopwood D, Coghill G, Sanders DSA. Human oesophageal submucosal glands: their detection, mucin, enzyme and secretory protein content. Histochemistry 1986; 86: 107–112.

CHAPTER 2

The gastric mucosa

P. G. Toner   C. H. S. Cameron

The stomach lies in the epigastric, umbilical and left hypochondrial regions of the abdominal cavity. It has a volume of about 30 ml at birth and 1000 ml in the adult, with a substantially greater capacity in the obese.[1]

The literature recognizes four anatomical zones. The cardia is the area around the cardiac orifice and is of ill-defined extent. The fundus lies above a horizontal line through the cardia. The body is that part between the fundus and cardia proximally and the antrum distally. The body and antrum are divided by a line from the incisura angularis downwards and to the left towards the greater curve. The antrum occupies the distal third of stomach and narrows down into the pyloric channel, which opens into the duodenum. In North America the body and fundus are often referred to together as the fundus. The different anatomical zones of the stomach correspond roughly but not exactly to the different mucosal types.

Computerized tomography and ultrasound measurements[2,3] have estimated the thickness of the stomach wall in healthy adults to be between 3 and 7 mm. It can be divided histologically into four layers. The mucous membrane or mucosa comprises the luminal surface layer or epithelium, the gastric pits and glands, the lamina propria and the lamina muscularis mucosae. The applied anatomy of the gastric mucosa has been reviewed by Owen (1986).[4]

The surface epithelium is the same in all parts of the stomach. The lamina propria lies between the basement membrane of the surface epithelium and the muscularis mucosae, separating and investing the gastric glands. The muscularis mucosae consists of an inner circular and an outer longitudinal layer of smooth muscle. Some smooth muscle fibres extend up into the lamina propria, especially in pyloric type mucosa.

SURFACE FEATURES

On endoscopy, the mucosa of the fundus and body is glistening and red; when the stomach is empty it is thrown up into coarse irregular longitudinal folds or rugae, most prominent towards the greater curve and least prominent towards the lesser curve. The rugal folds flatten out when the stomach is dilated by insufflation of air. The antral mucosa is paler, flatter and more firmly attached to the underlying submucosa.

Close inspection shows that the surface is divided by intersecting furrows into small bulging 'areae gastricae' each 1–3 mm in diameter.[5] The furrows are formed by the fusion of gastric pits near the surface, producing a cobblestone effect. They are well demonstrated by contrast radiology and can be appreciated histologically in large sections of gastric mucosa as shallow depressions on the surface. The areae gastricae are an intrinsic feature of gastric anatomy and are not dependent on the state of contraction of the stomach.[5] Subtle changes in the patterns of the areae gastricae as demonstrated on contrast radiology may indicate such lesions as early gastric cancer.[6]

The surface of each area gastrica has a honeycomb appearance consisting of closely packed papillae, each with a round central pit. This appearance was described and illustrated as long ago as 1836 by Boyd in his 'Essay on the Structure of the Mucous Membrane of the Stomach'.[7] Salem and Truelove[8] confirmed this appearance in the gastric body by using the dissecting microscope, whereas in the antrum and cardiac regions they found a mosaic or fish-scale pattern, with several papillae in each part of the pattern. Scanning electron microscopy[9,10] reinforces these results and reveals individual cell outlines, surface microvilli and micropits corresponding to granule discharge from surface mucous cells.

The surface area of the stomach is greatly increased by some 3.5 million gastric pits (foveolar crypts) which open onto the mucosal surface as described above. Each pit is about 70 μm wide and 200 μm deep, and drains on average four of the 15 million gastric glands. The three dimensional structure of the gastric pits was investigated by Goldstein et al,[11] who found that in both cats and humans, 2–4 deep pit branches merge to form a roughly cylindrical pit. Adjacent pits may fuse to form more or less complex stellate crevices, the largest of which form the borders of the areae gastricae. This is more often seen in the antrum, whereas in the gastric body most pits open directly onto the surface of the area gastrica.

Surface epithelium

The cells lining the gastric pits and covering the intervening surface mucosa are the same in all regions of the stomach. (Fig. 2.1). They are simple columnar cells, with a basal nucleus and a superficial cup-shaped clear or slightly eosinophilic mucin vacuole. The nuclei are rounded or ovoid, depending on the size of the mucin vacuole, with inconspicuous nucleoli. Unlike the small intestine, the surface epithelium of the stomach does not have a brush border containing alkaline phosphatase or aminopeptidase and the presence of these features in a gastric biopsy indicates intestinal metaplasia. The surface cells contain carbonic anhydrase, which is involved in bicarbonate secretion. They probably also secrete the blood group substances along with their mucus.

The epithelial cells of the pit become longer and contain more mucin towards the surface. This correlates with autoradiographic data showing that active cell division occurs in the neck region from whence cells move upwards and undergo differentiation. Surface mucous cells are completely renewed every one to three days.[12,13]

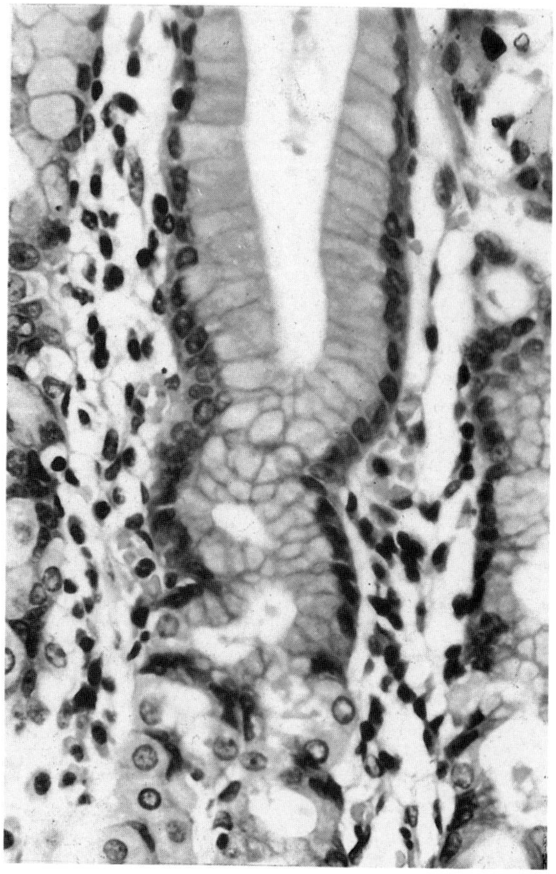

Fig 2.1 Surface epithelium. (H&E, ×400)

The numerous irregular secretory granules are produced in the supranuclear Golgi apparatus and form a compact, closely packed apical mass, the volume of which may vary from cell to cell. Individual granules measure

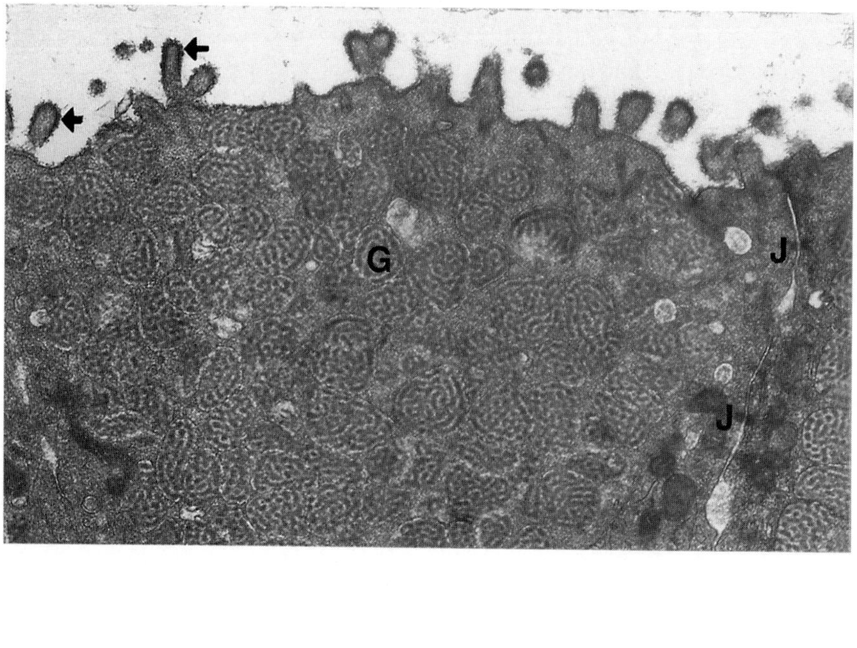

Fig 2.2 Apical cytoplasm of a surface mucous cell containing coarsely stippled granules (G). The apical microvilli have a densely-stained surface coat or glycocalyx (arrows). Adjacent cells are joined by apical junctional complexes (J). Human gastric mucosa. (×16 650)

up to 1 μm in diameter. They have a distinctive stippled appearance. The most superficial granules lie directly under the apical surface and individual granules are discharged by exocytosis, although bulk granule release may also occur. The scattered short stubby microvilli at the cell apex have a visible surface coat or glycocalyx (Fig. 2.2).

The other cytoplasmic organelles are displaced to the sides and base of the cell by the apical mass of secretion. The granular endoplasmic reticulum lies in strands parallel to the long axis of the cell. Mitochondria, lysosomes, lipid droplets, diffuse fibrillar material and glycogen particles may be found in the cytoplasm.

Although firmly attached by apical junctional complexes and scattered desmosomes, the lateral cell surfaces tend to separate, more markedly so towards the base (Fig. 2.3). The intercellular spaces thus formed are bridged by cytoplasmic processes and the interrupted channels which result are probably concerned with fluid and electrolyte transport, perhaps reflecting bicarbonate secretion. Surface mucous cells at the lower levels of the gastric pits are packed more tightly, with numerous cytoplasmic interdigitations and basal infoldings, increasing the metabolic interface with the lamina propria.

The mucus layer

The neutral secretion produced by the surface mucous cells stains PAS. positive but alcian blue negative. The mucin forms a continuous surface layer around 0.5 mm in thickness[14] although this varies considerably in different parts of the stomach.[15] The role of the mucus layer in the protection of the mucosal surface from acid and pepsin is controversial, although recently it has been proposed as the basis of an unstirred layer in which bicarbonate, secreted by both antral and body/fundal mucosa, slowly diffuses outwards towards the lumen and neutralizes gastric

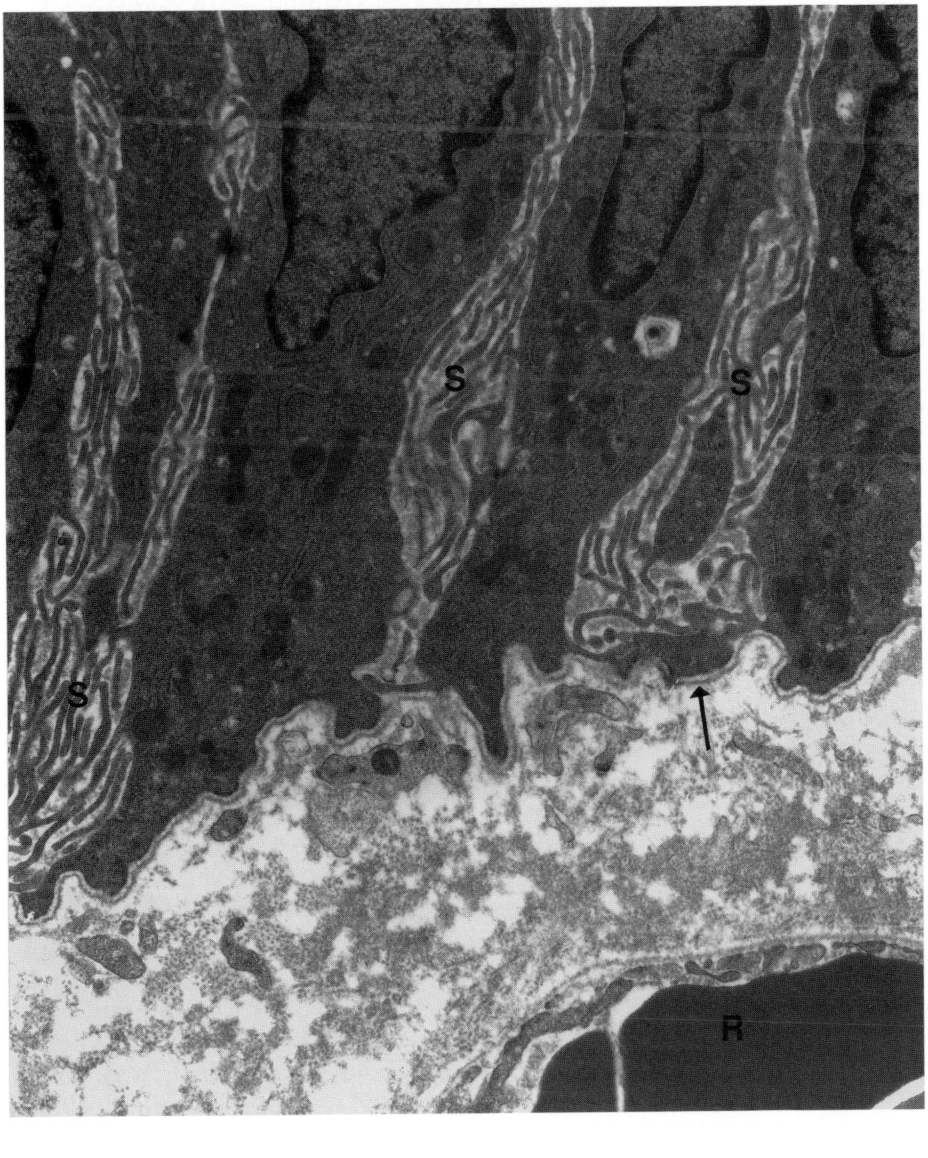

Fig 2.3 Gastric surface epithelium, showing separation of the columnar cells, forming wide intercellular spaces (S) above the basal lamina (arrow). A capillary vessel in the lamina propria contains red blood cells (R). Human gastric mucosa (×12 000)

acid diffusing inwards.[16] In support of this view, pH sensitive micro-electrodes can demonstrate a substantial pH gradient across the gastric mucous layer in humans.[17]

MUCOSAL TYPES

Cardiac mucosa

On endoscopy, cardiac type mucosa starts abruptly at the oesophageal squamo-columnar junction and extends into the stomach for 0.5–4 cm. It therefore straddles the anatomical junction between oesophagus and stomach. Half of the mucosal thickness is occupied by gastric pits and half by cardiac glands, which are loosely packed simple tubular or compound tubulo-racemose glands,[18] often with cystic dilatation. The cardiac glands contain mainly simple mucus secreting cells which have ill-defined borders and a bubbly cytoplasm, unlike the mucus secreting cells of the surface epithelium.[4] Endocrine cells and occasional parietal cells may be seen, although chief cells are rare. The transition zone between cardiac and body mucosa contains glands with features of both mucosal types.[19]

Body/fundal mucosa

The mucosa lining the stomach between the cardiac mucosa proximally and the pyloric mucosa distally is of one type, and is termed fundal or body mucosa. It is 400–1500 µm thick, the luminal quarter being composed of gastric pits with intervening lamina propria and the remaining three quarters containing densely packed glands which extend down to the muscularis mucosae (Figs 2.4, 2.5). They tend to be straight at the top and slightly coiled at the base. Between three to seven glands drain through constricted necks into each gastric pit. Four main cell types are recognized: mucous neck cells, parietal or oxyntic cells, chief or zymogen cells and endocrine cells (Fig. 2.6). The relative proportion of each cell type in body mucosa is given in Table 2.1.[20]

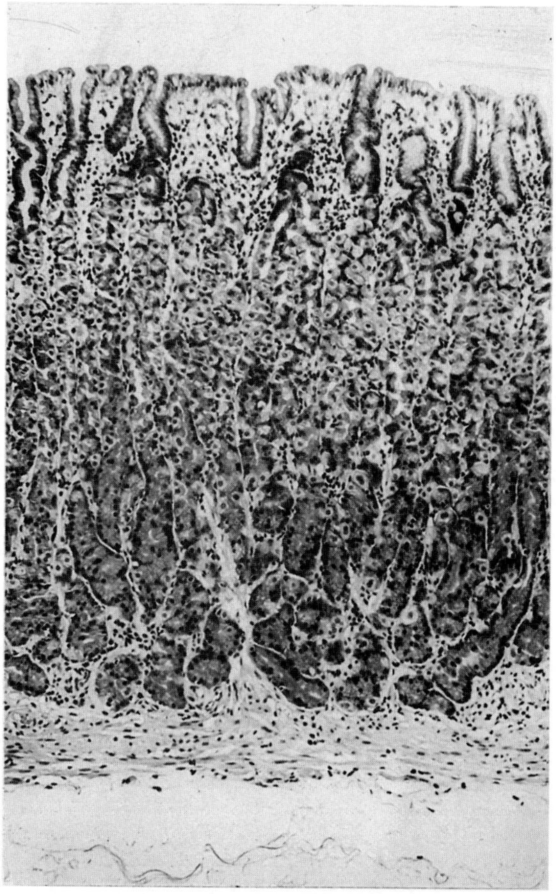

Fig 2.4 Gastric body mucosa. (H&E, ×80)

Pyloric mucosa

The pyloric mucosa varies in thickness from 200–1100 µm. The gastric pits are longer than in body mucosa and constitute 50% of its thickness. The deeper half is composed of tortuous mucin secreting glands, the cells of which are similar to those in cardiac mucosa and resemble mucous neck cells. Tominaga[21] identified parietal cells in the pyloric mucosa in 98.3% of cases and considered them to be a normal finding. Endocrine cells, particularly gastrin producing (G) cells, are frequently identified, although chief cells are unusual.

The area of the stomach lined by pyloric mucosa is variable. The transition from pyloric to body mucosa is gradual, with glands showing features of both mucosal types in the junctional zone. Landboe-Christensen[22] showed that the border between duodenal and pyloric mucosa lies either on the perpendicular duodenal side of the pyloric ring, at the top of the ring, or on the sloping gastric side of the ring. With ageing there is a tendency for the border to shift from the duodenal to the gastric side. Pyloric mucosa extends across 40% of the lesser curve but only about 12% of the greater curve.[23,24] It tends to extend higher up the lesser curve in women than in men and increases in extent relative to body mucosa with increasing age in both sexes.

The antro-duodenal junction was studied in detail by Lawson[25] who identified three normal patterns of duodenal mucosa at this site, which he termed ‘antral type’, ‘transitional type’ and ‘jejunal type’ duodenal mucosa.

EPITHELIAL CELL TYPES

Parietal cells

General features

The human stomach has been estimated to contain a billion parietal cells. They are large, between 20–30 µm

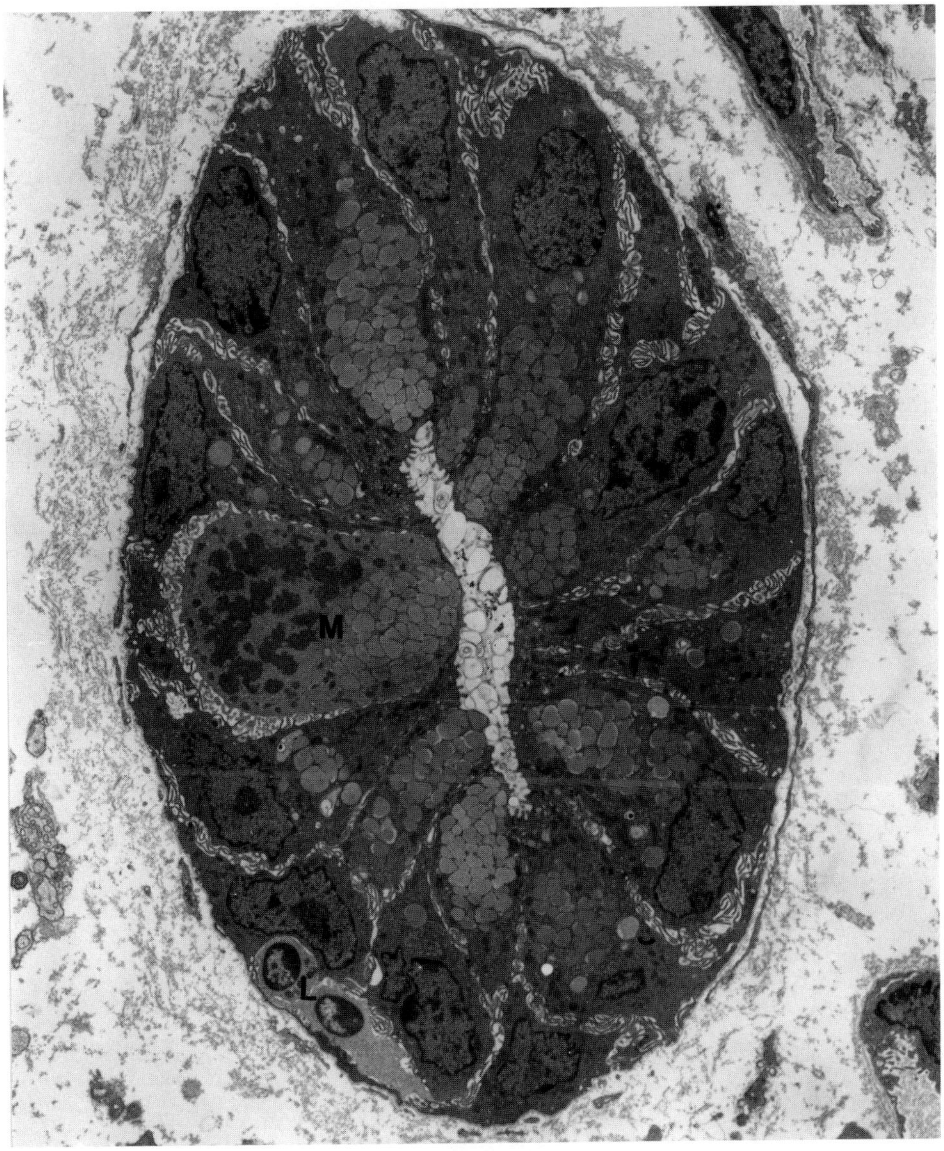

Fig 2.5 Neck region of gastric gland, lined by mucous neck cells, one of which (M) is in mitosis. Two intraepithelial lymphocytes are seen (L). Human gastric mucosa. (×3000).

across, with central nuclei and deep pink cytoplasm on H & E staining. The mean parietal cell volume in man is calculated at 5500 μm.[4,6]

Parietal cells are most numerous in the upper part of the gastric gland where they are interspersed with mucous neck cells. Each cell is roughly triangular with a long basal face closely applied to the basement membrane and an apex wedged between adjacent cells. In the lower part of the gland, the parietal cells are displaced by chief cells towards the basement membrane, although they still maintain a narrow connection with the gland lumen (Fig. 2.7).[20] A technique has been described for the isolation and separation of enriched fractions of viable parietal cells, which can then be used for experimental and ultrastructural studies.[26]

Ultrastructural features. Detailed information on the electron microscopic features of the parietal cell can be found in original papers and reviews of gastric ultrastructure dating back over 25 years.[27–31] Technical imperfections in material published prior to the mid 1960s limit the usefulness of the earlier ultrastructural literature, although it still contains much of interest.

The cytoplasmic eosinophilia is mostly attributable to numerous large mitochondria, which occupy up to 40% of the cell volume. They have oval or circular profiles and their transverse cristae are closely packed, reflecting the high oxidative metabolism associated with gastric acid secretion (Figs 2.7, 2.8).

The two most distinctive ultrastructural features of parietal cells are the intracellular canalicular system and

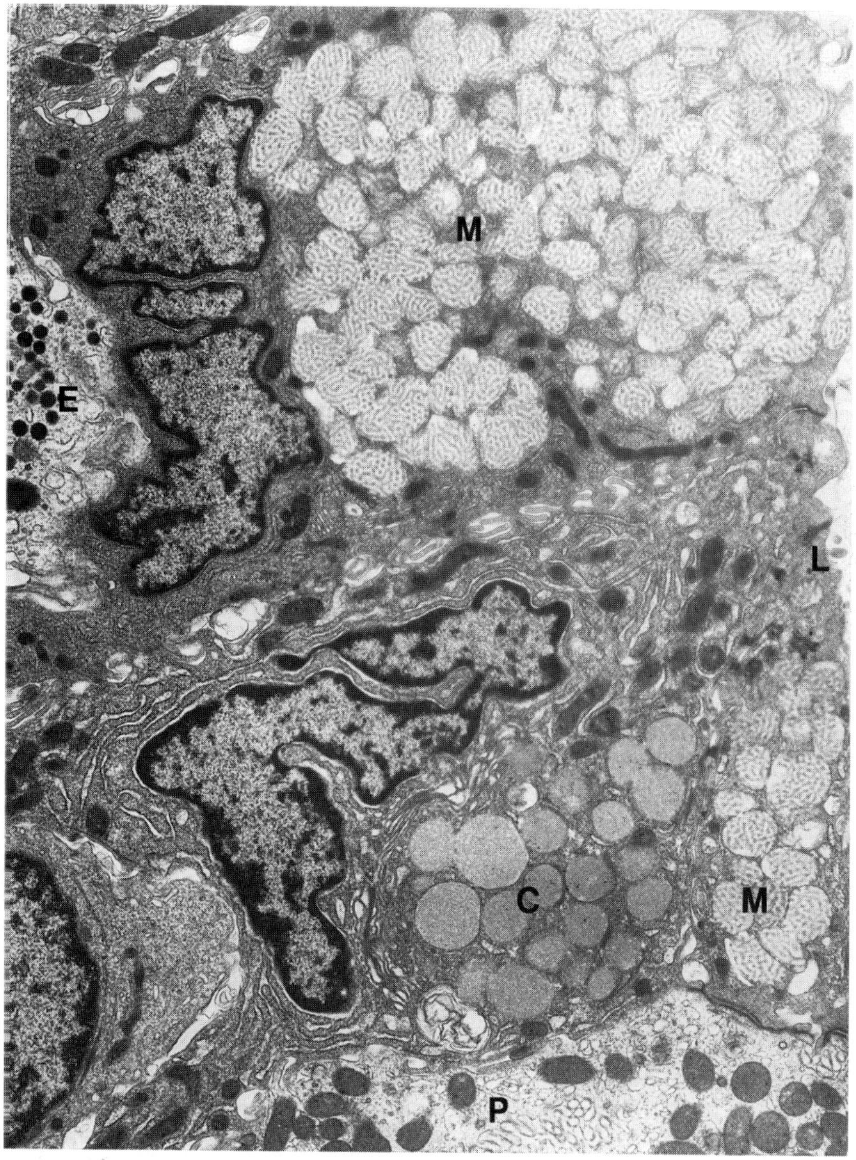

Fig 2.6 Fundal gland in oblique section showing parts of two mucous neck cells (M), a chief cell (C), a parietal cell (P) and an endocrine cell (E). The lumenal surface is identified (L). Human gastric mucosa. (×8625)

Table 2.1 Mean percentage (and range) of gastric body mucosa occupied by the main cell types, using a point counting technique.[20]

	Percentage
Parietal cell	32 (24–38)
Chief cell	26 (20–30)
Mucous surface cell	17 (12–20)
Mucous neck cell	6 (4–9)
Lamina propria	20 (16–26)

the underlying complex of cytoplasmic tubulovesicles. The canalicular system is an elaborate branching tubular invagination of the apical surface (Figs 2.8, 2.9, 2.10). It extends around and below the nucleus, increasing the secretory surface area, which is further augmented by sinuous microvilli with slightly bulbous tips which project into the lumen and extend to the free apical surface. Although electron micrographs show no obvious glycocalyx or cell coat on these microvilli, special techniques including the use of biotinylated lectins permit the demonstration of surface polysaccharides or specific surface sugar residues.[32,33]

The tubulovesicles lie in the cytoplasm adjacent to the canalicular system (Figs 2.8, 2.9, 2.10). These membranes were originally thought to be a form of smooth endoplasmic reticulum but are now seen as a distinctive specialization, perhaps more closely related to the cell membrane. This system is particularly sensitive to artefact[34] but its true physiological state is probably a network of interwoven partially ordered and mostly non-branching tubules, about 1 μm in length and 50–70 nm in diameter, often lying perpendicular to the surface of the canaliculus. In some cells the presence of coated vesicles attached to the ends of tubulovesicles, or to the cell membrane, or

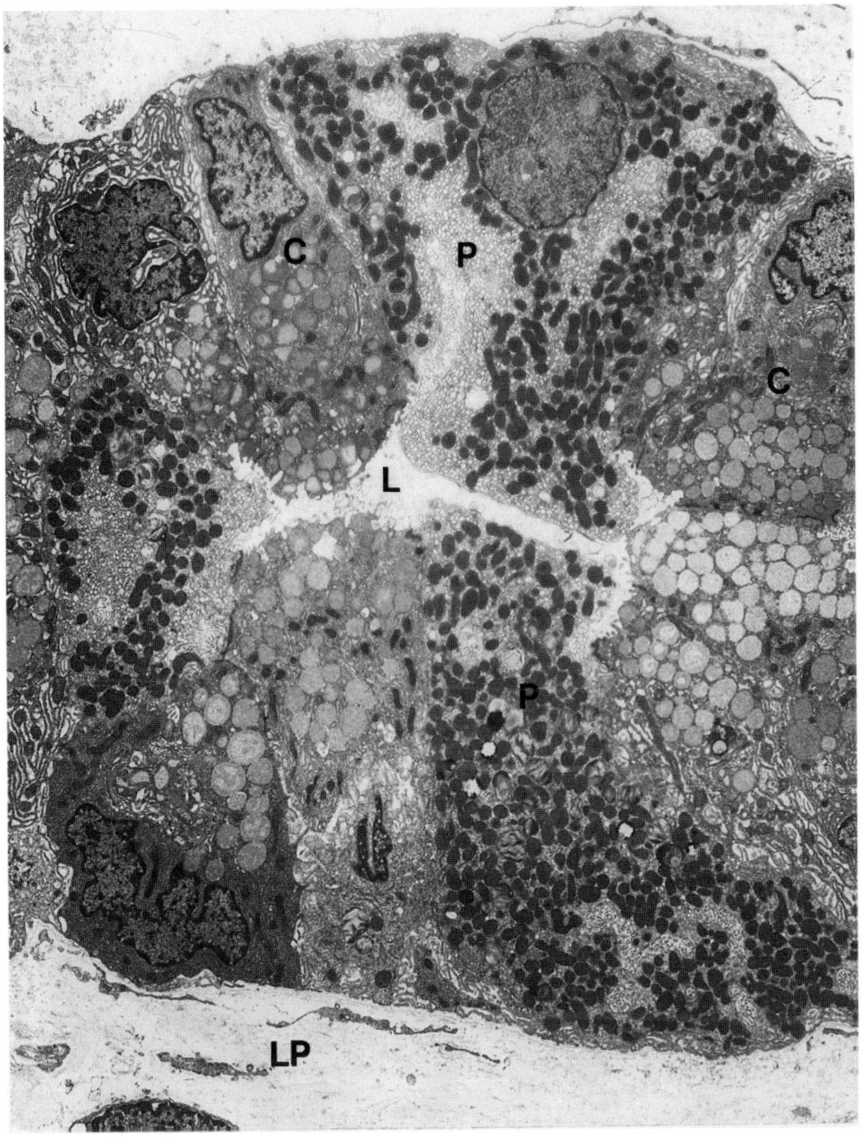

Fig 2.7 Fundal gland showing the central lumen (L) and surrounding lamina propria (LP). In this region the gland is lined entirely by parietal cells (P) and chief cells (C). Human gastric mucosa. (×3150)

lying free in the cytoplasm has suggested a possible shuttle mechanism for the transfer of material from one compartment to the other. This view of the tubulovesicle system is supported by rapid freezing and freeze substitution processing,[35] which reduces artefact to a minimum.

Ultrastructural studies of parietal cells have shed some light on the mechanism of acid secretion, although several questions remain unresolved. Resting or secretion-inhibited cells show numerous tubulovesicles around a collapsed canalicular system. By contrast, during maximal acid secretion the extent of the canalicular system increases, along with its calibre, the numbers of the microvilli projecting into its lumen and consequently its surface area. A six-fold increase has been recorded in stereological studies of histamine stimulation. At the same time, the tubulovesicle system reduces to about half of its original extent. The newly expanded cell surface may be restored to the resting state by endocytosis of areas of the surface membrane or even of whole microvilli, giving rise to the five-layered membrane structures which are sometimes seen in these cells.

These structural and functional changes have suggested that active acid secretion involves the fusion of tubulovesicle membranes with the cell surface and the discharge of tubulovesicle contents into the canalicular lumen. This hypothesis is supported by cytochemical evidence and by the finding of another secretory product, intrinsic factor, in association with the tubulovesicle membranes.[36] It would be tempting to suppose that the accumulated tubulovesicles contain preformed hydrochloric acid but this is probably over-simplistic. Alternatively, the tubulovesicle membranes might contain a ‘proton pump’ mechanism,[37] incorporated in an activated form into the cell surface by the fusion of tubulovesicles with the canalicular system. The consequent increase in the surface area of the cell would account for the proliferation of microvilli.

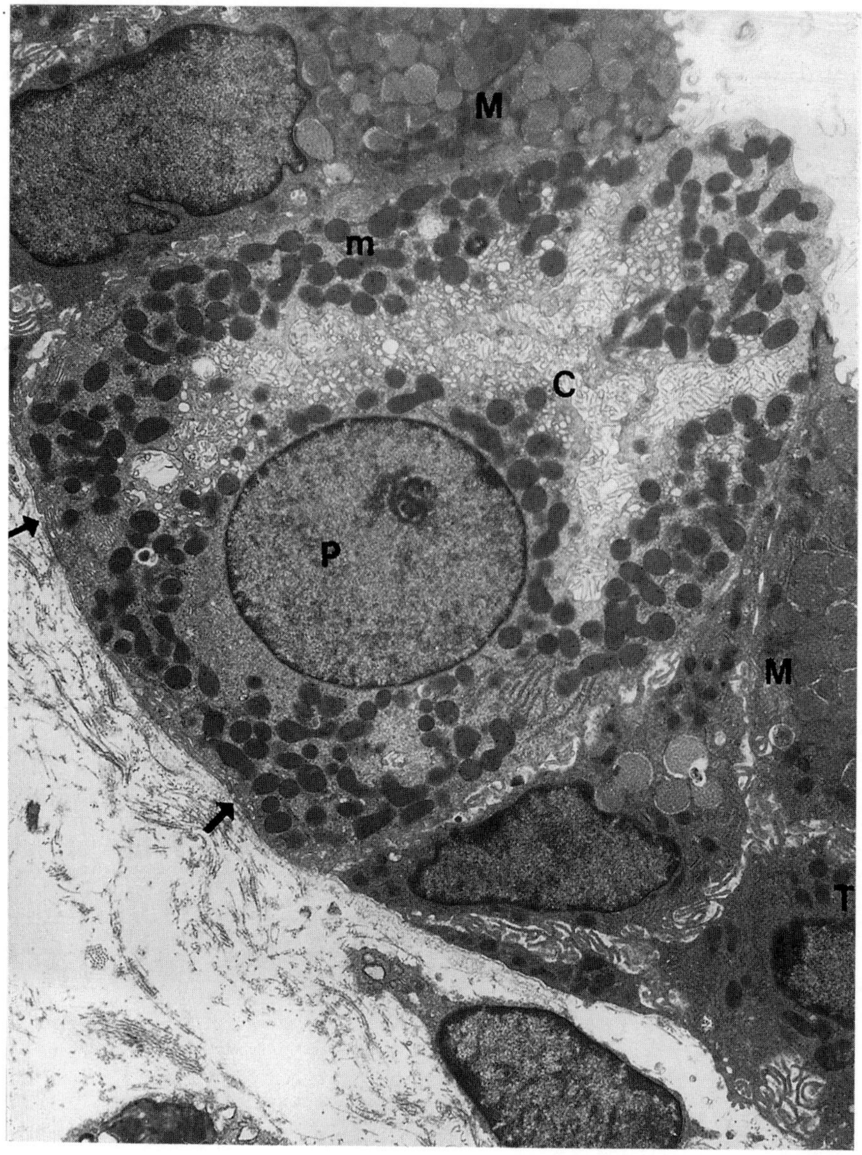

Fig 2.8 Fundal gland showing a parietal cell (P) flanked by mucous neck cells (M). Note the canalicular system ramifying around and above the nucleus. There are numerous dense mitochondria (M). The cell membrane is infolded at the base (arrows). Human gastric mucosa. (×6600)

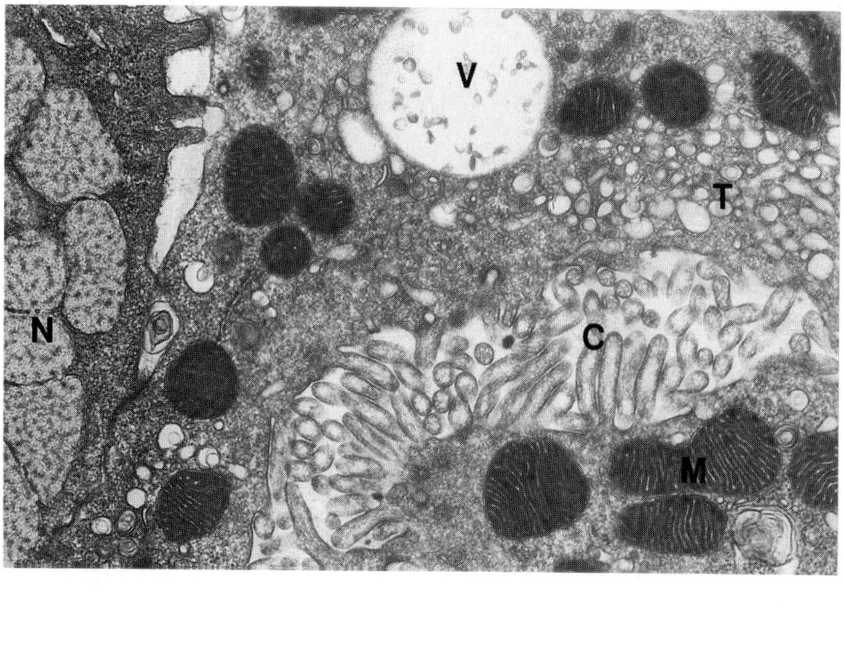

Fig 2.9 A mucous neck cell (N) lies beside a parietal cell. The parietal cell canaliculus (C) is lined by characteristic microvilli. The adjacent cytoplasm contains tubulovesicles (T) mitochondria (M) and a multivesicular body (V). Human gastric mucosa. (×21 225)

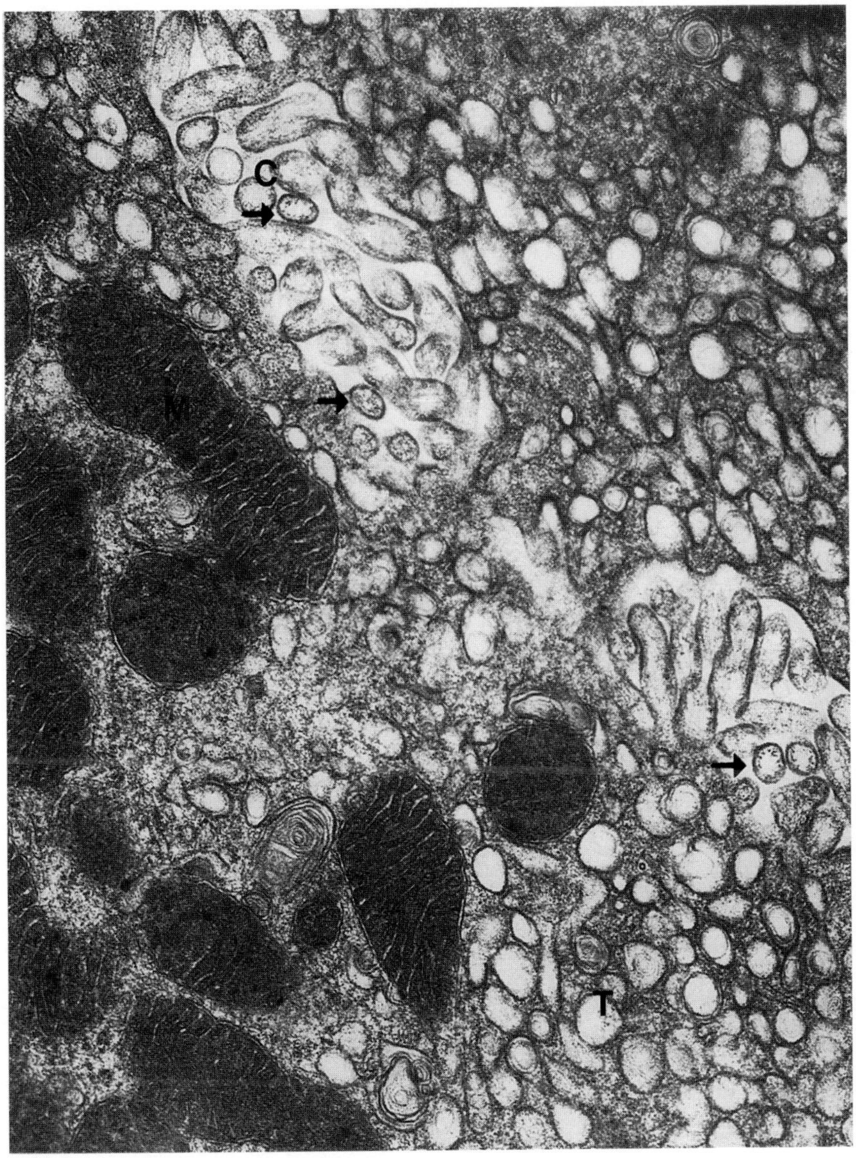

Fig 2.10 Parietal cell cytoplasm showing the canaliculus (C) lined by microvilli. Some of these (arrows) display cross-sectioned microfilaments. The tubulo-vesicles (T) show both tubular and vesicular profiles. The mitochondria (M) have closely-packed cristae. Human gastric mucosa. (×37 050)

Unfortunately, however, direct communications between the tubulovesicles and the surface membranes of the canalicular system have not been identified, although they may be so rapid and transient that they are not visualized by current specimen preparation techniques.

Various other difficulties still remain. The inverse relationship between tubulovesicle membranes and the secretory surface membrane of the parietal cell is not on a direct one to one basis,[38] which implies some more complex mechanism than simple linear fusion. The tubulovesicles may first fuse with each other, forming cytoplasmic clefts, which then help to remodel the canalicular lining.[34] The relationship between these membrane systems remains the central structural enigma of the acid secretory mechanism.

A further specialization of parietal cells is seen at intervals along the basal surface, where the cell membrane is underlain by the basal lamina (Fig. 2.8). Prominent basal infoldings of the cell membrane increase the surface area available for metabolic transport to and from the lamina propria. The complexity of the basal infoldings increases after active secretion, as can be seen in frozen and freeze-fractured tissue specimens.[39] Parietal cells may shrink during secretion and it has been suggested that these basal infoldings act as 'tucks' in the cell surface, providing a reservoir for redundant membrane material.

The other cytoplasmic features of the parietal cell are nonspecific, including a small inconspicuous Golgi apparatus, secondary lysosomes containing osmiophilic material and multivesicular bodies, which are generally regarded as a lysosome variant. Ultrastructural immunolocalization has demonstrated human intrinsic factor in the granular endoplasmic reticulum, Golgi apparatus, multivesicular bodies and tubulovesicles.[36]

Diurnal variations. The terms 'resting' and 'stimulated', when applied to physiological or experimental studies, specify an average state of the gastric mucosa, rather than the precise status of each parietal cell, which in fact varies widely. Circadian ultrastructural changes have been identified in fasting rats, paralleling a known diurnal rhythmicity of acid production.[40,41] Individual cells could be placed in one of four groups in a study by Zaviacic.[41] Averaged over all time points, 38% of parietal cells showed morphological features consistent with active secretion, while 35% were apparently in a resting state. Eighteen per cent of cells appeared to be in transition from the secreting to the resting state, whereas 9% showed features suggestive of a transition from the resting to the early secretory state. The subsequent detailed breakdown of individual time points showed an increase in resting cells in the morning and a decrease in the evening, with converse results for actively secreting cells. No doubt these changes will prove to be linked to neural and hormonal rhythms. Experimental evidence for an effect of sex hormones on parietal cell numbers and on basal acid secretion has been presented by Adeniyi.[42]

Individual cell variations. Distinct differences have been noted between parietal cells located at different levels in the gastric gland, both in fine structure and in response to stimulation.[43–45] 'Neck' parietal cells containing occasional mucus granules have probably only recently differentiated from proliferating precursor cells. Gradients of structural features and enzyme activity have been described between these upper parietal cells and those in the lower regions. The increased prominence of lysosomes in the deeper cells is taken to imply that they are an older and more mature population. However, the more superficial parietal cells have a proportionately larger secretory surface[40] and may actually produce more gastric acid than the deeper cells. Superficial and basal parietal cells differ in the concentration of orthogonal arrays of particles present in their basolateral cell membranes in freeze fractured preparations.[44]

Clinical studies. Most clinical studies have concentrated on parietal cell morphology in peptic ulcer patients or following clinical or experimental vagotomy, and on regenerating gastric mucosa in man or experimental animals.

In a study of patients with recurrent duodenal ulcer, the parietal cells responded more rapidly to tetragastrin stimulation than the cells of normal subjects or of patients without recurrence, suggesting an enhanced sensitivity to stimulation. The early effects of vagotomy include a significant reduction at seven days in the parietal cell volume fraction.[46] Lysosomes are increased, but other cellular features appear unchanged, as is the ultrastructural response to pentagastrin stimulation. Six months after parietal cell vagotomy, the secretory surface of parietal cells is significantly reduced and the area occupied by tubulovesicles is increased.[47] After 2–3 years the cells regain their preoperative structure, although not their secretory capacity.

Cellular aberrations during epithelial repair at the edge of chronic gastric ulcers in the human stomach have been examined by light and electron microscopy.[48] An animal model has more recently been used to study the healing of experimental mucosal wounds.[49,50] This showed that parietal cells are the last of the specialized cell types to reappear in regenerated mucosa.[49,50] They are ultrastructurally immature, but respond normally to stimulation.

The ultrastructural effects of antrectomy, pyloroplasty and vagotomy on parietal cell regeneration in gastric wounds have been investigated.[51] A trophic effect of long-term pentagastrin administration on rat parietal cells[52] is seen as being mediated through the precursor cell population.

Chief cells

These cells, which secrete pepsinogen and other proenzymes, are most numerous in the basal portion of the gland. They are pyramidal to columnar, with a large basal nucleus containing one or more nucleoli. The cytoplasm is a grey blue colour on H & E and in freshly fixed material contains refractile basophilic granules.[18]

The ultrastructural features are similar to those of zymogenic cells elsewhere. Light microscopic basophilia is explained by an extensive granular endoplasmic reticulum and numerous free ribosomes. The cisternae tend to lie parallel to the lateral and basal surfaces of the cell and concentric with the nucleus, but become broken up into short strands in the apical region by the presence of secretory granules.

The zymogen granules are formed in the elaborate supranuclear golgi apparatus (Fig. 2.11), have a mean diameter of around 0.7 μm and occupy 30% of the 'resting' cell volume. They are enclosed by a smooth surfaced membrane and appear homogeneous or finely granular with low to medium electron density. When secretory activity is stimulated by pilocarpine or secretin, they are released at the luminal surface by merocrine discharge. The mitochondria of the chief cell are scanty by comparison with the parietal cell, occupying less than 5% of the cytoplasm. Occasional lysosomes are seen.

Quantitative ultrastructural changes in the chief cell following stimulation[53,54] include a significant increase in the amount of granular endoplasmic reticulum, reflecting an increase in pepsinogen production and a decrease in zymogen granules, parallel with their discharge into the lumen. Following stimulation by secretin, there is no apparent change in overall cell size but the remaining cytoplasmic granules are smaller than in resting cells. After inhibition of secretion by atropine, individual granules increase in both numbers and size. Studies of chief cell

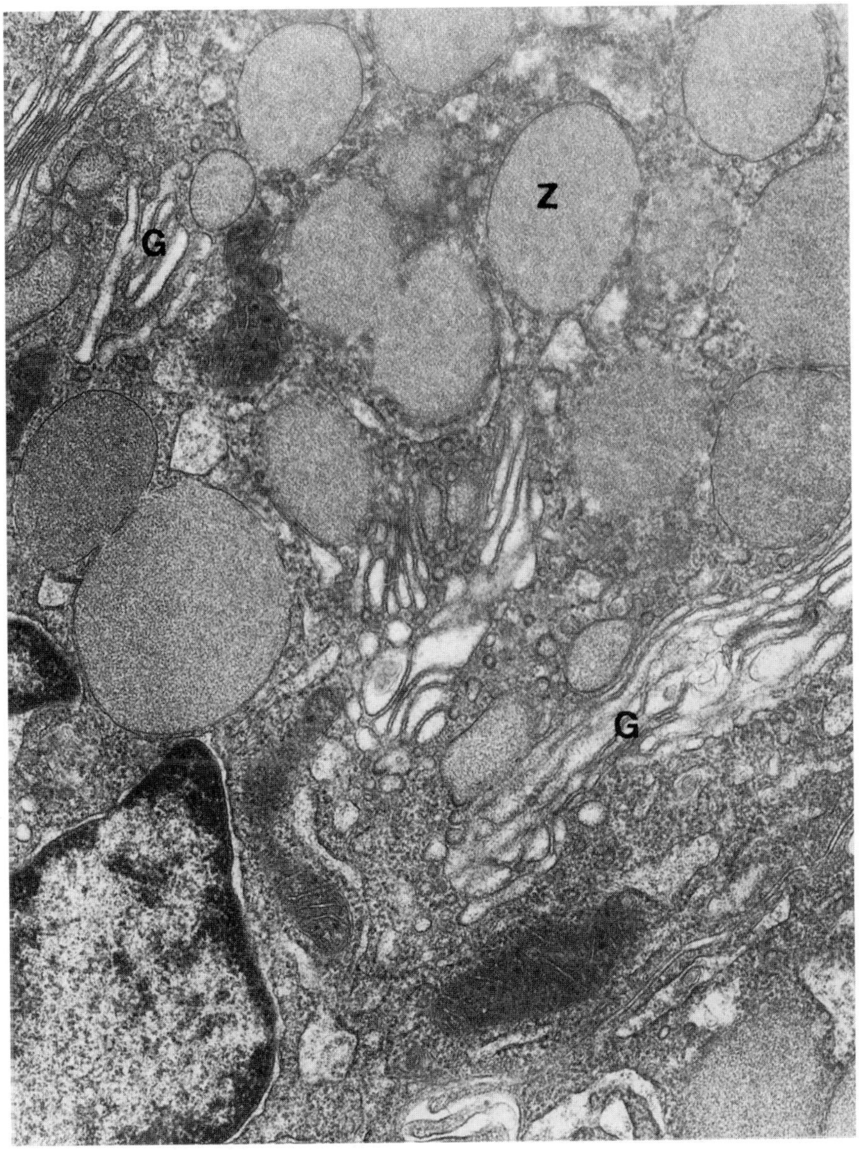

Fig 2.11 Chief cell showing the extensive supranuclear Golgi apparatus (G) and associated zymogen granules (Z). Human gastric mucosa. (×25 875)

secretion have recently been carried out using isolated cell preparations, achieving 90% purity and 99% viability, with good preservation of ultrastructure.[55]

Mucous neck cells

These are situated singly or in small groups between the parietal cells of the neck region and occasionally deeper in the gland (Figs 2.6, 2.8). They are inconspicuous on H & E staining, but more easily identified with PAS. The nucleus is basal and the cytoplasm slightly basophilic and finely granular. Their cytoplasmic mucin is relatively evenly dispersed, unlike the surface epithelial cells, where mucin is confined to the apex. Mucin produced by the neck cells is similar to the mucin of the cardiac and antral glands, but is more acidic and less viscous than that of the surface epithelium.

Apart from their secretory role, the major function of the mucous neck cells is probably proliferation and mucosal regeneration. Mitotic cells in the neck region often contain granules of mucous neck cell type (Fig. 2.5, 2.12). After cell division, daughter cells migrate upwards to form surface epithelial cells or downwards to form gland cells. Intermediate forms between mucous neck cells and the other differentiated cell types have been described. Some investigators, however, believe that there is a separate population of undifferentiated proliferative cells in the neck region.[20] The turnover rate of cells in the gastric glands, about 1–3 years, is much slower than in the surface epithelium.

On electron microscopy, the cytoplasmic granules of mucous neck cells, though fewer than those of the surface cells, are larger and less coarsely stippled (Fig. 2.13). Homogeneous granules are sometimes interspersed with

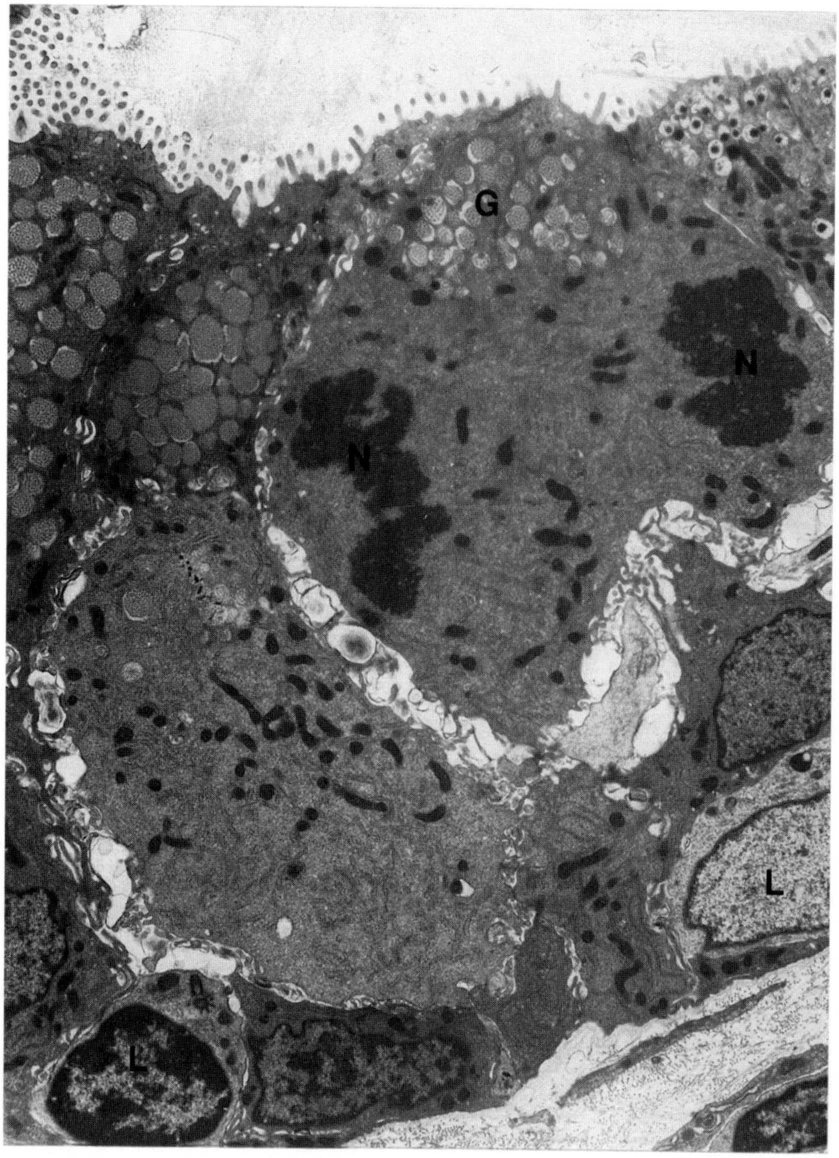

Fig 2.12 Antral gland showing a dividing mucous neck cell with re-forming daughter nuclei (N) and persisting apical mucus granules (G). Apical microvilli project into the lumen. Two lymphocytes (L) are seen between the gland cells at the base of the epithelium. Human gastric mucosa. (×7350)

others showing areas of varying density. An elaborate supranuclear Golgi complex produces the secretory granules.

The mucous neck cells have inconspicuous surface microvilli. Adjacent cells are linked by junctional complexes and desmosomes and their lateral membranes frequently interdigitate. The base of the cell contains strands of granular endoplasmic reticulum, with free ribosomes which gradually decrease in number, as does cytoplasmic basophilia, with increasing distance of the cell from the neck region of the gland. Mitochondria are not prominent. They are often closely associated with the endoplasmic reticulum.

Pyloric gland cells

These line the glands of the pyloric antral region[29] and resemble the mucous neck cells. They have abundant and often heterogeneous supranuclear mucus granules (Fig. 2.14). A second reported type of granule, with a homogeneous appearance, resembles the zymogen granule of the chief cell. This might indicate a different type of mucin, or might represent the formation of pyloric pepsinogen. There is an elaborate supranuclear Golgi complex and granular endoplasmic reticulum fills the lateral and basal cytoplasm. Small microvilli are present at the cell surface. There are apical junctional complexes and lateral desmosomes. Adjacent cells interdigitate along their lateral contact surfaces, particularly towards the basement membrane.

Endocrine cells

The endocrine cells of the gastrointestinal tract are discussed in Chapter 6. They can sometimes be recognized in H & E staining as rounded cells with clear cytoplasm or as basally located pyramidal cells with basal eosinophilic

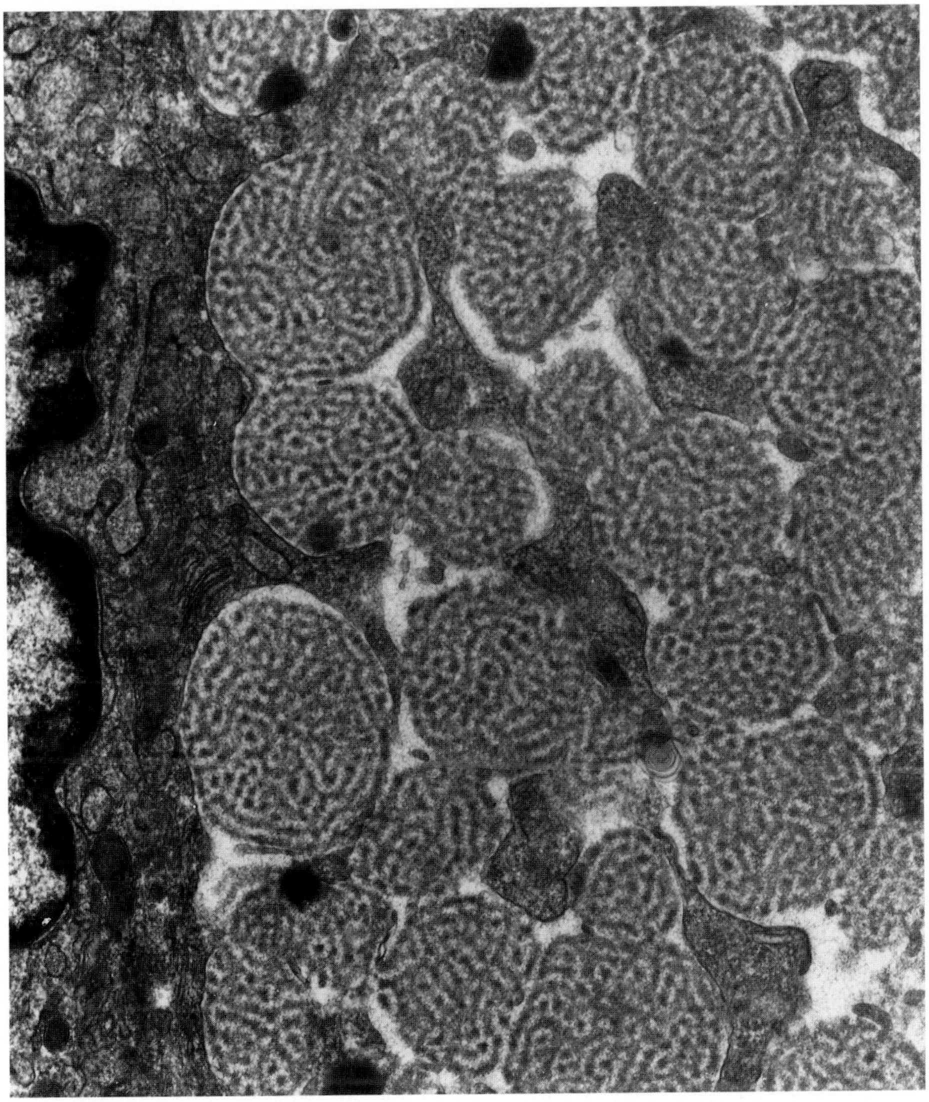

Fig 2.13 Mucous neck cell, showing coalescent, reticulated granules. Human gastric mucosa. (×28 500).

granulation, wedged between the basement membrane and surrounding epithelial cells. In the pyloric mucosa, but not usually elsewhere, the endocrine cells often reach the gland lumen (Fig. 2.14). All endocrine cells have an extensive basal surface, towards which their distinctive secretory granules are preferentially orientated (Fig. 2.15). Wide variations in granule morphology provide the basis for recognition and quantitation of the various endocrine cell types.[56]

Other cell types

The 'tuft' cell, recently characterized by electron microscopy[57–59] has also been called 'fibrillovesicular', 'undifferentiated', and by various other names. An apical tuft of long thick microvilli projects from the cell surface. Their cores of closely packed parallel filaments run into the apical cytoplasm and interweave. Surface membrane invaginations occurring between the microvilli and the apical cytoplasm contain vesicular and tubular profiles between the filament bundles. Lysosomes are usually present.

There are no ultrastructural links with any of the other gastric cell types and in particular, no specific features suggestive of an endocrine function. Similar cells are described throughout the gastrointestinal and biliary tract and elsewhere, in man and various laboratory animals. Their function remains obscure.

Ciliated cells in the human stomach have been reported[60] in demonstrably pathological mucosa showing intestinal metaplasia or polyp formation. This probably represents no more than an extreme manifestation of metaplasia. Mucus-negative ciliated cells have been reported by Torikata et al[61] in the pyloric glands of the stomach in intestinal metaplasia. Such cells may undergo autophagic degenerative changes, causing cytoplasmic vacuolation.

Migratory lymphoid cells passing between epithelial cells are a normal finding, particularly in the surface epi-

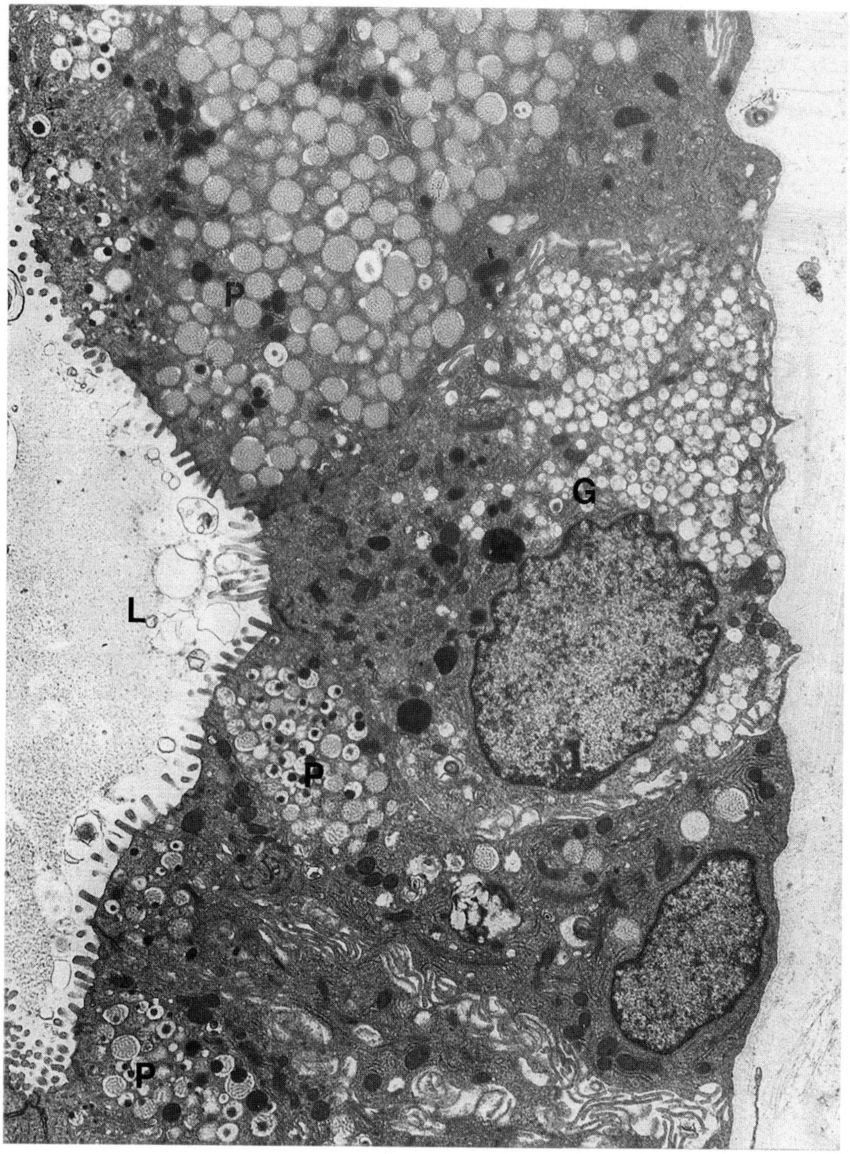

Fig 2.14 Antral gland lined by pyloric gland cells (P) containing apical mucus granules of heterogenous appearance. An endocrine cell of G cell type (G), with basal granules, has a narrow apex which makes contact with the gland lumen (L). Human gastric mucosa. (×6000)

thelium (Fig. 2.16). These have the ultrastructural features of lymphocytes elsewhere, their relatively scanty cytoplasm showing few formed organelles. They are not attached to their epithelial neighbours by desmosomes and are presumably temporary residents, as in the intestinal epithelium. Mast cells are occasionally seen between epithelial cells in the gastric glands (Fig. 2.16).

THE LAMINA PROPRIA

The lamina propria, the connective tissue component of the mucosa, consists of a meshwork of reticulin together with some elastic and collagen fibres. Reticulin staining shows that the basement membrane of the surface epithelium, pits and glands is a single layer of fibres with delicate surrounding strands of supporting connective tissue lying between and around the capillaries.[62]

The lamina propria is most prominent in the superficial part of the gastric mucosa between the gastric pits and forms a rather tight sheath around the neck region. It is scanty in the deep part of the body mucosa but is more visible in pyloric and especially in cardiac mucosa, where the glands are loosely packed. The lamina propria contains the capillaries, arterioles, lymphatics and non-myelinated nerve fibres which supply the mucosa. Cell types include fibroblasts, smooth muscle cells, histiocytes, plasma cells, lymphocytes and occasional polymorphs. Lymphocytes of the lamina propria are predominantly of IgA secreting B cell type, whereas the less frequent intraepithelial lymphocytes are mainly of T cell type. Lymphoid follicles are normally present, especially in the antrum.

It is unclear what constitutes the normal complement of inflammatory cells in the mucous membrane of the

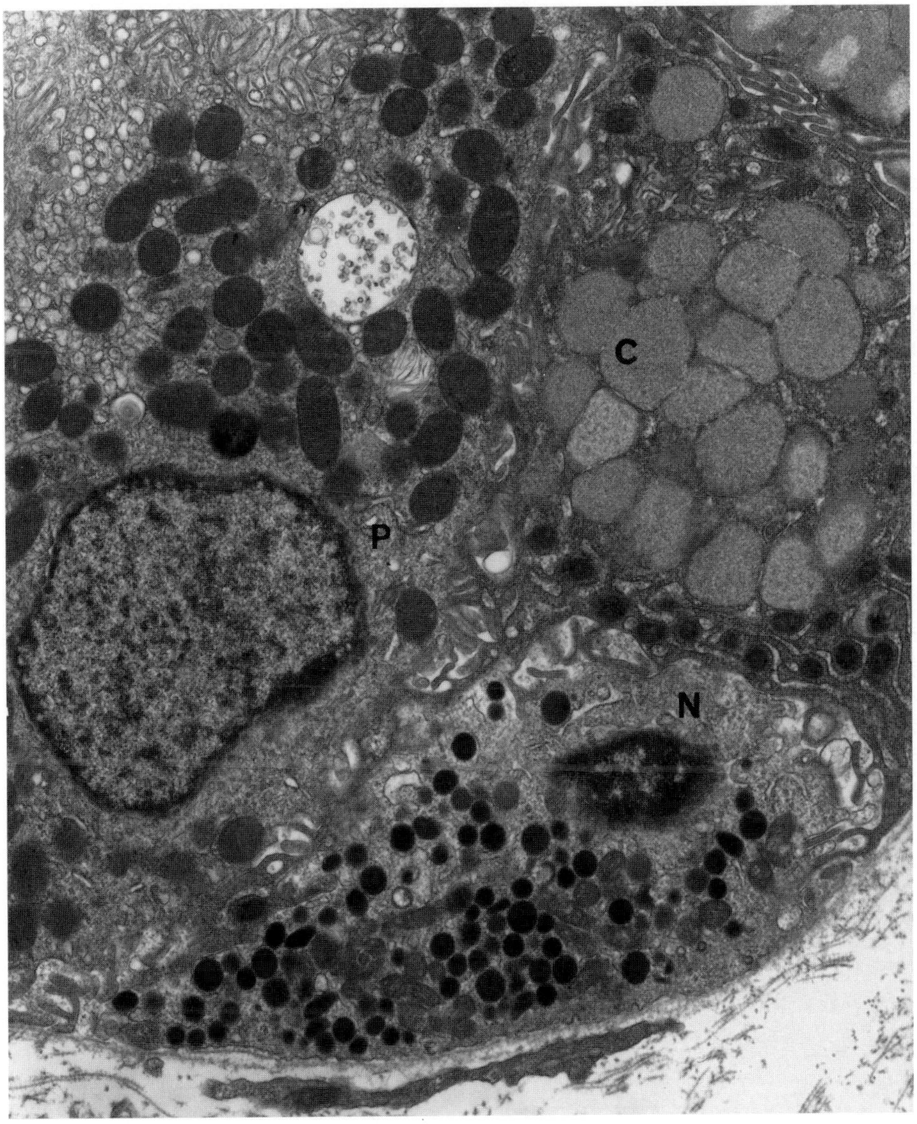

Fig 2.15 Fundic gland showing a parietal cell, (P) a chief cell (C) and a neuroendocrine cell (N) containing large dense granules of enterochromaffin type. Human gastric mucosa. (×11 000).

stomach. Kreuning et al,[63] found histological evidence of gastritis in the antrum and fundus in 18 out of 50 volunteers who had no history of gastrointestinal disease. Myren and Serck-Hanssen[64] diagnosed superficial gastritis in 4 out of 10 healthy medical students aged 22 to 23 years. These studies, however, were based on subjective observation, without a clear definition of normality. Counts of cells present in the lamina propria of body and antral mucosal biopsies from 9 healthy volunteers (age range 25–45) (Table 2.2) show that mononuclear cells are more frequent than polymorphs, but that wide variation exists. This indicates that there is probably at present no satisfactory definition of the normal number of inflammatory cells in the mucosa of the stomach.

THE DEVELOPMENT OF THE STOMACH

This was reviewed extensively by Salenius[65] (1962), with subsequent ultrastructural studies.[66,67] The embryonic stomach is first lined by a simple columnar epithelium, which later becomes stratified. Solitary cilia may be found on the surface cells at this stage. Gastric pits first appear along the lesser curvature between 6 and 9 weeks, and the gastric glands develop progressively from 11 to 13 weeks onwards.

The first endocrine cells are recognizable in the human stomach between 8 and 9 weeks. The period from 11 to 15 weeks sees the morphological differentiation of mucous neck cells, surface mucous cells, parietal cells and chief cells, although parietal cell canaliculi and chief cell zymogen granules do not appear until around the 21st week, and immunostaining for pepsinogen becomes intense only after the 5th month.

By term, the ratio of gastric glands per pit has only reached a figure of 2.4, in comparison with the adult ratio of around 4, but in the immediate post-natal period there

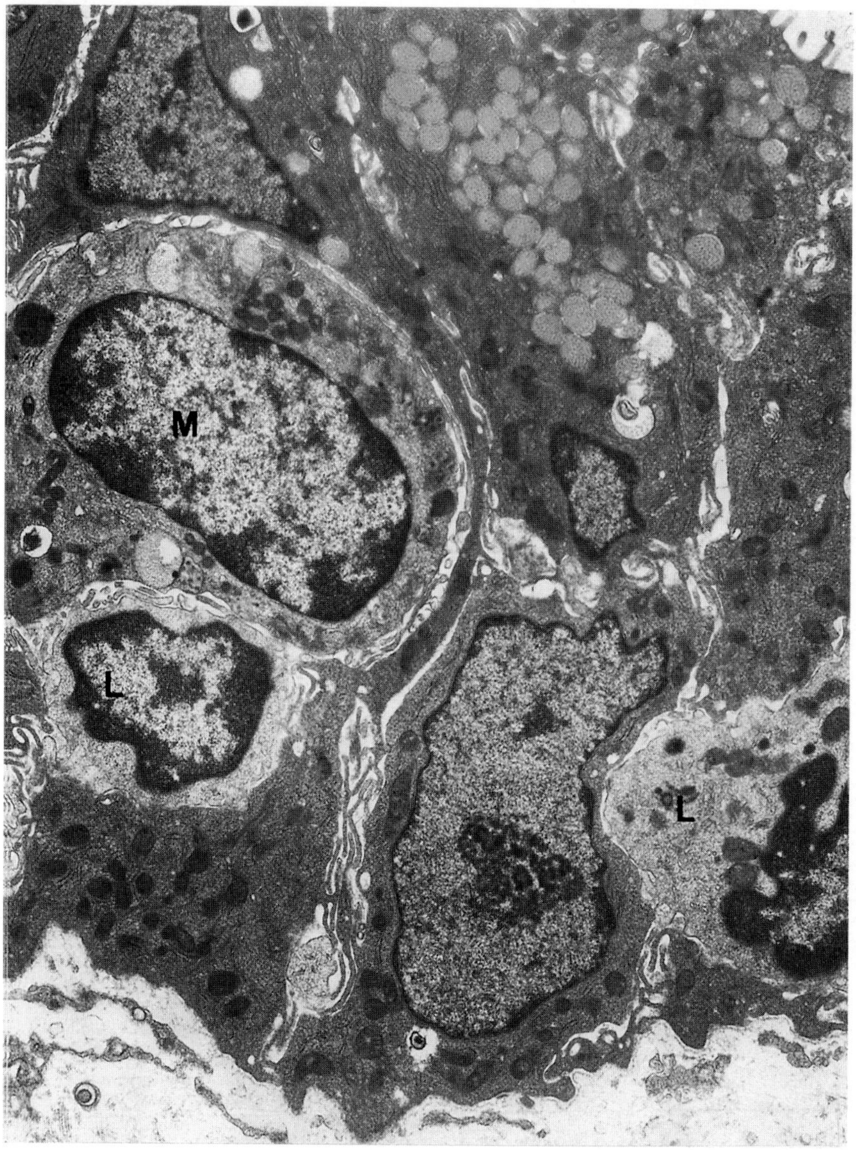

Fig 2.16 Antral gland showing intraepithelial lymphocytes (L) and a mast cell (M) lying between mucous neck cells. Human gastric mucosa. (×7500)

Table 2.2 Mononuclear cells and polymorphs in the stomach of nine healthy volunteers with age range 25–45 and male:female ratio 5:4. The data show means with ranges per mm^2.

	Antrum	Fundus
Mononuclear cells	2210 (210–4766)	2034 (232–3306)
Polymorphs	21 (0–66)	9 (0–28)

is a rapid development of the specific features of parietal cell ultrastructure in parallel with a marked enhancement of acid secretion.[33] In the newborn human infant, the parietal cell mass per unit of mucosa is two to three times the value found in the adult.[68]

REFERENCES

1. Granstrom L, Backman L. Stomach distension in extremely obese and in normal subjects. Acta Chir Scand 1985; 151: 367–370.
2. Karantanas AH, Tsianos EB, Kontogiannis DS, Pappas IJ, Katsios PA. CT demonstration of normal gastric wall thickness: the value of administering gas-producing and paralytic agents. Computerized Medical Imaging and Graphics 1988; 12: 333–337.
3. Rappaccini GL, Pompili AM, Grattagliano A, Anti M, Merlino B, Gambassi G. Gastric wall thickness in normal and neoplastic subjects: a prospective study performed by abdominal ultrasound. Gastrointestinal Radiology 1988; 13: 197–199.
4. Owen DA. Normal histology of the stomach. Am J Surg Pathol 1986; 10: 48–61.
5. Mackintosh CE, Kreel L. Anatomy and radiology of the areae gastricae. Gut 1977; 18: 855–864.
6. Fu-sheng L, Tie-liang Z, Mao-hua H. Areae Gastricae. Comparative pathologic and radiologic study on 50 human stomach specimens. Chin Med J 1984; 97: 885–892.

7. Boyd S. Essay on the structure of the mucous membrane of the stomach. Edinburgh Med J 1836; 46: 382–404.
8. Salem SN, Truelove SC. Dissecting microscope appearances of the gastric mucosa. Br Med J 1964; 2: 1503–1504.
9. Pfeiffer CJ. Surface topology of the stomach in man and the laboratory ferret. J Ultrastruct Res 1970; 33: 252–262.
10. Takagi T, Takebayashi S, Tokuyasu K, Tsuji K. Scanning electron microscopy on the human gastric mucosa: fetal, normal and various pathological conditions. Acta Pathol Jpn 1974; 24: 233–247.
11. Goldstein AMB, Brothers MR, Davis EA. The architecture of the superficial layer of the gastric mucosa. J Anat 1969; 104: 539–551.
12. Baker BL. Cell replacement in the stomach. Gastroenterology 1964; 46: 202–203.
13. Lipkin M, Sherlock P, Bell B. Cell proliferation kinetics in the gastrointestinal tract of man. II. Cell renewal in stomach, ileum, colon and rectum. Gastroenterology 1963; 45: 721–729.
14. Bickel M, Kauffman GL. Gastric gel mucous thickness: effect of distension, 16, 16-Dimethyl prostaglandin e_2 and carbenoxolone. Gastroenterology 1981; 80: 770–775.
15. Kerss S, Allen A, Garner A. A simple method for measuring thickness of the mucus gel layer adherent to rat, frog and human gastric mucosa: Influence of feeding prostaglandin, N acetyl cysteine and other agents. Clin Sci 1982; 63: 187–195.
16. Turnberg LA. The gastric mucosal barrier. In: Jewell DP, Gibson PR (eds) Topics in gastroenterology. Oxford: Blackwell, 1985; 12: 181–191.
17. Bahari HMM, Ross IN, Turnberg LA. Demonstration of a pH gradient across the mucus layer on the surface of human gastric mucosa in vitro. Gut 1982; 23: 513–516.
18. Bensley RR. The cardiac glands of mammals. Am J Anat 1902; 2: 115–156.
19. Kelly DE, Wood RL, Lenders AC. Baileys textbook of microscopic anatomy. Baltimore: Williams-Wilkins, 1984.
20. Hogben AMC, Kent TH, Woodward PA, Sill AJ. Quantitative histology of the gastric mucosa: man, dog, cat, guinea pig and frog. Gastroenterology 1974; 67: 1143–1154.
21. Tominaga K. Distribution of parietal cells in the antral mucosa of human stomach. Gastroenterology 1975; 69: 1201–1207.
22. Landboe-Christensen E. The duodenal glands of Brunner in man, their distribution and quality. Acta Pathol Microbiol Scand 1944; 52 (Suppl.): 11–267.
23. Landboe-Christensen E. Extent of the pylorus zone in the human stomach. Acta Pathol Microbiol Scand 1944; 53(Suppl): 671–691.
24. Schrager J, Spink R, Mitra S. The antrum in patients with duodenal and gastric ulcers. Gut 1967; 8: 497–508.
25. Lawson HH. Definition of gastroduodenal junction in healthy subjects. J Clin Pathol 1988; 41: 393–396.
26. Romrell LJ, Coppe MR, Munro DR, Ito S. Isolation and separation of highly enriched fractions of viable mouse gastric parietal cells by velocity sedimentation. J Cell Biol 1975; 65: 428–438.
27. Lillibridge CB. The fine structure of normal human gastric mucosa. Gastroenterology 1964; 47: 269–289.
28. Rubin W, Ross LL, Sleisenger MH, Jeffries GH. The normal human gastric epithelia: A fine structural study. Lab Invest 1968; 19: 598–625.
29. Krause WJ, Ivey KJ, Baskin WN, MacKercher P. Ultrastructure of the human pyloric glands with emphasis on the mucous cell component. Acta Anat 1977; 99: 1–10.
30. Toner PG, Carr KE, Wyburn GM. The digestive system. An ultrastructural atlas and review. Edinburgh: Churchill Livingstone, 1971.
31. Helander HF. The cells of the gastric mucosa. Int Rev Cytol 1981; 70: 217–289.
32. Sedar AW. Electron microscopic demonstration of polysaccharides associated with acid-secreting cells of the stomach after 'inert dehydration'. J Ultrastruct Res 1969; 28: 112–124.
33. Kessimian N, Langner BJ, McMillan PN, Jauregui H0. Lectin binding to parietal cells of human gastric mucosa. J Histochem Cytochem 1986; 34: 237–243.
34. Vial JD, Garrido J, Gonzalez A. The early changes of parietal cell structure in the course of secretory activity in the rat. Am J Anat 1985; 172: 291–306.
35. Sugai N, Ito S, Ichikawa A, Ichikawa M. The fine structure of the tubulovesicular system in mouse gastric parietal cell processed by cryofixation method. J Electron Microsc 1985; 34: 113–122.
36. Levine JS, Nakane PK, Allen RH. Immunocytochemical localization of human intrinsic factor: The nonstimulated stomach. Gastroenterology 1980; 79: 493–502.
37. Koenig CS. Redistribution of gastric K^+-NPPase in vertebrate oxyntic cells in relation to hydrochloric acid secretion: A cytochemical study. Anat Rec 1984; 215: 28–34.
38. Zalewsky CA, Moody FG. Stereological analysis of the parietal cell during acid secretion and inhibition. Gastroenterology 1977; 73: 66–74.
39. Taira K, Yasuno K, Shibasaki S. A freeze-fracture study on the basolateral plasma membrane of the gastric parietal cells in fasting and refed rats. Arch Histol Jpn 1984; 47: 495–503.
40. Jacobs DM, Sturtevant RP. Circadian ultrastructural changes in rat gastric parietal cells under altered feeding regimens: A morphometric study. Anat Rec 1982; 203: 101–113.
41. Zaviacic M, Borozman M, Jakubovsky J, Mikulecky M, Blazekova J. Circadian ultrastructural changes in rat gastric parietal cells. Exp Pathol 1980; 18: 85–95.
42. Adeniyi KO. Gastric acid secretion and parietal cell mass: effect of sex hormones. Gastroenterology 1991; 101: 66–69.
43. Helander HF, Sundell GW. Ultastructure of inhibited parietal cells in the rat. Gastroenterology 1984; 87: 1064–1071.
44. Bordi C, Amherdt M, Perrelet A. Orthogonal arrays of particles in the gastric parietal cell of the rat: Differences between superficial and basal cells in the gland and after pentagastrin or metiamide treatment. Anat Rec 1986; 215: 28–34.
45. Morozov IA. Topographic peculiarities of the ultra-structure of the parietal cells of the gastric mucosa (morphometric study). Byul Eksp Biol Med 1976; 82: 1390–1394.
46. Aase S, Roland M, Liavag I, Dahl E. Morphometric studies of human parietal cells before and 7 days after proximal gastric vagotomy. Scand J Gastroenterol 1984; 19: 697–706.
47. Romeo G, Sanfilippo G, Basile F et al. Ultrastructural study of parietal cells before and after parietal cell vagotomy in patients with duodenal ulcer. Surg Gynecol Obstet 1981; 153: 61–64.
48. Adair HM. Epithelial repair in chronic gastric ulcers. Br J Exp Pathol 1978; 59: 229–236.
49. Blom H, Helander HF. Quantitative ultrastructural studies on parietal cell regeneration in experimental ulcers in rat gastric mucosa. Gastroenterology 1981; 80: 334–343.
50. Blom H. Light- and electron-microscopy of normal and regenerating gastric mucosa with special reference to the parietal cells. Scand J Gastroenterol 1984; 105(Suppl): 33–45.
51. Blom H, Elstig H, Helander HF. Effects of pyloroplasty, truncal vagotomy and antrectomy on parietal cell regeneration in experimental gastric wounds in the rat. Scand J Gastroenterol 1983; 18: 859–864.
52. Blom H, Erikoinen T. Trophic effect of pentagastrin on normal and regenerating parietal cells: A light and electron microscopic study in rats. Gastroenterology 1984; 87: 537–541.
53. Stachura J, Ivey KJ, Tarnawski A, Krause WJ, Stogsdill P. Fine-morphology of chief cells in human gastric mucosa after secretin. Scand J Gastroenterol 1981; 16: 713–720.
54. Helander HF. Quantitative ultrastructural studies on rat gastric zymogen cells under different physiological and experimental conditions. Cell Tissue Res 1978; 189: 287–303.
55. Raufman J-P, Sutliff VE, Kasbekar DK, Jensen RT, Gardner JD. Pepsinogen secretion from dispersed chief cells from guinea pig stomach. Am J Physiol 1984; 247 (Gastrointest Liver Physiol 10): G95–G104.
56. D'Adda T, Bertele A, Pilato FP, Bordi C. Quantitative electron microscopy of endocrine cells in oxyntic mucosa of normal human stomach. Cell and Tissue Research 1989; 255: 41–48.
57. Isomaki AM. A new cell type (tuft cell) in the gastrointestinal mucosa of the rat. Acta Pathol Microbiol Scand (A) 1973; (Suppl. 240).
58. Nabeyama A, Leblond CP. Caveolated cells characterised by deep

surface invaginations and abundant filaments in mouse gastrointestinal epithelium. Am J Anat 1974; 140: 147–165.
59. Johnson FR, Young BA. Undifferentiated cells in gastric mucosa. J Anat 1968; 102: 541–551.
60. Okuda T, Ogata T. An electron microscopic study of the ciliated cells in the human gastric mucosa. Arch Histol Jpn 1976; 39: 149–156.
61. Torikata C, Mukai M, Kawikata H. Ultrastructure of the mucus-negative vacuolated cells in the metaplastic pyloric gland of the human stomach. Human Pathology 1989; 20: 437–440.
62. Whitehead R. Mucosal biopsy of the gastrointestinal tract. 3rd ed. Philadelphia: Saunders, 1985.
63. Kreuning J, Bosman FT, Kuiper G, Van der Wal AM, Lindeman J. Gastric and duodenal mucosa in 'healthy' individuals. J Clin Pathol 1978; 31: 69–77.
64. Myren J, Serck-Hanssen A. Gastroscopic observations related to bioptical histology in healthy medical students. Scand J Gastroenterol 1975; 10: 353–355.
65. Salenius P. On the ontogenesis of the human gastric epithelial cells. A histologic and histochemical study. Acta Anat 1962; 50(Suppl. 46): 1–76.
66. Grabitz K. Die ultrastruktur des epithels menschlicher corpora ventriculi wahrend der ontogenese. Z Mikrosk Anat Forsch Leipzig 1976; 90: 577–609.
67. De Lemos C. The ultrastructure of endocrine cells in the corpus of the stomach of human fetuses. Am J Anat 1977; 148: 359–384.
68. Polacek MA, Ellison EH. Gastric acid secretion and parietal cell mass in the stomach of a newborn infant. Am J Surg 1966; 111: 777–781.

CHAPTER 3

The small intestinal mucosa

A. D. Phillips

The small intestine, delimited proximally by the pylorus and distally by the ileo-caecal valve, is the longest segment of the gastrointestinal tract. At post mortem it measures 3–4 m in children,[1,2] and around 6 m in adults.[3] However, in vivo it measures only 3 m in adults[4] and this is probably due to longitudinal muscle tone.

It is divided somewhat arbitrarily into the duodenum, jejunum and ileum. In adults the proximal 20 cm is the duodenum and includes the pancreatic and bile duct openings; the jejunum, which begins at the duodeno-jejunal flexure, constitutes 40% of the remaining small intestine and the ileum makes up the remainder. Brunner's glands are found in the duodenum and proximal jejunum.

The mucosa is thrown into folds (folds of Kerckring) which run parallel to the longitudinal axis of the bowel; these are most prominent between the mid duodenum and jejunum and absent in the distal ileum. They increase the surface area and by altering the exposure of the mucosa to luminal contents produce variations in the microenvironment.[2,5]

Normal small intestinal morphology can be defined as 'that which is found in healthy individuals, living under optimal conditions of nutrition and hygiene'.[6]

Post-mortem tissue from all age groups is readily available, but is subject to rapid autolysis which reduces its value.[7] The technique of small intestinal biopsy,[8,9] however, provides mucosal samples suitable for light and electron microscopic analysis and some instruments are capable of taking two[10] or more[11] specimens. Generally these are suction instruments guided radiologically and are used for obtaining samples from the distal duodenal/proximal jejunal area. Fibreoptic endoscopes with biopsy facilities are commonly used to obtain samples from the proximal and second part of the duodenum and from the distal ileum. The use of narrow diameter endoscopes has enabled biopsy samples to be taken from very young, malnourished infants, facilitating diagnosis in cases such as intractable diarrhoea in infancy.

Although volunteer studies in healthy adults have been performed, this is not so for entirely normal children and all control data in this age group emanates from observations on biopsies from children with previous or current gastrointestinal symptoms.

GROSS APPEARANCE

The mucosa has two main components: the epithelium and the underlying connective tissue, or lamina propria. These form the basic structure of villi protruding from a basal region, or crypt zone. On longitudinal section well orientated villi appear tall and of even width. However, in the third dimension the appearance of villi varies according to their location in the small bowel and with age. Accepted terminology of villi as viewed is that they may be finger-like if circular in cross section, leaf-like when breadth is greater than the width but not height, and ridge-like when breadth appears greater than the height. Some workers have also used the term leaf-like to include any villus which does not appear finger-like,[12] and others include the term tongue-like to describe villi which are intermediate in appearance between leaf-like and ridge-like villi and which taper in breadth from base to tip.[2]

In normal adults finger-like villi predominate at all levels of the small intestine,[6] but leaf-like[12,13] and, less frequently, ridge-like[14] villi can also be found proximally with occasional leaf-like villi distally.[13] In the proximal small intestine of young children leaf-like and ridge-like villi predominate and finger-like villi are few (Fig. 3.1a). Some have only ridge-like villi, whereas in older children the adult picture of a mixed appearance of villous types may be present (Fig. 3.1b). In the distal small bowel finger- and leaf-like villi are found.[2] There is a rapid change in gross appearance in the first few months of life because in stillborn foetuses[15,16] and newborn[2] finger-like villi usually predominate. Such changes are also seen in some animal species.[17,18] Villi of variable form are generally of similar height.

Other structures visible on gross examination are lymphoid follicles. These appear as dome-shaped protrusions of varying size and occur singly as isolated lymphoid follicles or in groups as Peyer's patches. Peyer's patches are large and numerous in the ileum, smaller and fewer in the jejunum, and infrequent in the duodenum. They increase in number and size from early foetal life to puberty. Thereafter they undergo a rapid involution which slows down in the mid-twenties, and they never disappear.[19] In children isolated lymphoid follicles are often found on proximal mucosal biopsy (Fig. 3.1a), being most common around 1 to 2 years of age, when one in three biopsies will contain a follicle.[20] Isolated follicles are rarely seen in proximal biopsies in adults.

The use of scanning electron microscopy has provided even greater detail of the characteristics of the surface of the small intestinal mucosa. The villous surface is not flat but shows infoldings and in the upper villus it appears rather uneven (Fig. 3.2a). If the villi are displaced several crypt openings can be seen around each villus.[21] The longer the breadth of the villus the more openings there are in attendance. Epithelial cells in the process of extrusion show obvious surface cytoplasmic blebs and/or very obvious microvilli due to the loss of their surface glycocalyx.[22] Such cells are mostly found near villus tips (Fig. 3.2b) but can also be seen lower down in man[22] and over the whole villus in the mouse.[23] Goblet cells can be recognized by foci of mucus discharge (Fig. 3.2b). In normal mucosa there is no evidence that interepithelial cells migrate into the gut lumen.

When lymphoid follicles from rats and mice are studied, cells with poorly developed microvilli can be easily identified in the overlying epithelium. These cells have been termed follicle associated epithelium[24] or M cells[25] and have been reported in adult Peyer's patches.[25]

MUCOSAL DIMENSIONS

In well orientated sections of proximal mucosal biopsies the parameters most often used to assess normality are villous height and crypt depth. In adults, villus height is approximately three or more times the depth of crypts (Fig. 3.3a), whereas in children a ratio of 2:1 is considered normal (Fig. 3.3b). Quantitative morphometry can also be used in order to establish normal ranges on a more objective basis. Several techniques are available ranging from the use of single eyepiece micrometers[26] to computerized image analysis[27,28] and the systems of measurement are usually accurate and reliable. However, a consistent approach is needed and site of biopsy, tissue processing, sample orientation, and a precise definition of what is to be measured should be standardized. A method using an intersecting line and point-counting principles which give an index of the mucosal surface to volume ratio is also available.[29]

The measurements of villus height and surface area index are, in essence, indirect means of assessing the villus epithelial cell population. Because of the variability in villus shape, measurements in a two-dimensional section have the potential of giving inaccurate results, par-

A B

Fig. 3.1 Dissecting microscopy. **A.** Mainly ridge-like villi from a 14 month old girl. Note presence of mucosal lymphoid follicle (arrow) (×125). **B.** Mixed appearance of finger and leaf-like villi from a 12 year old boy (×125).

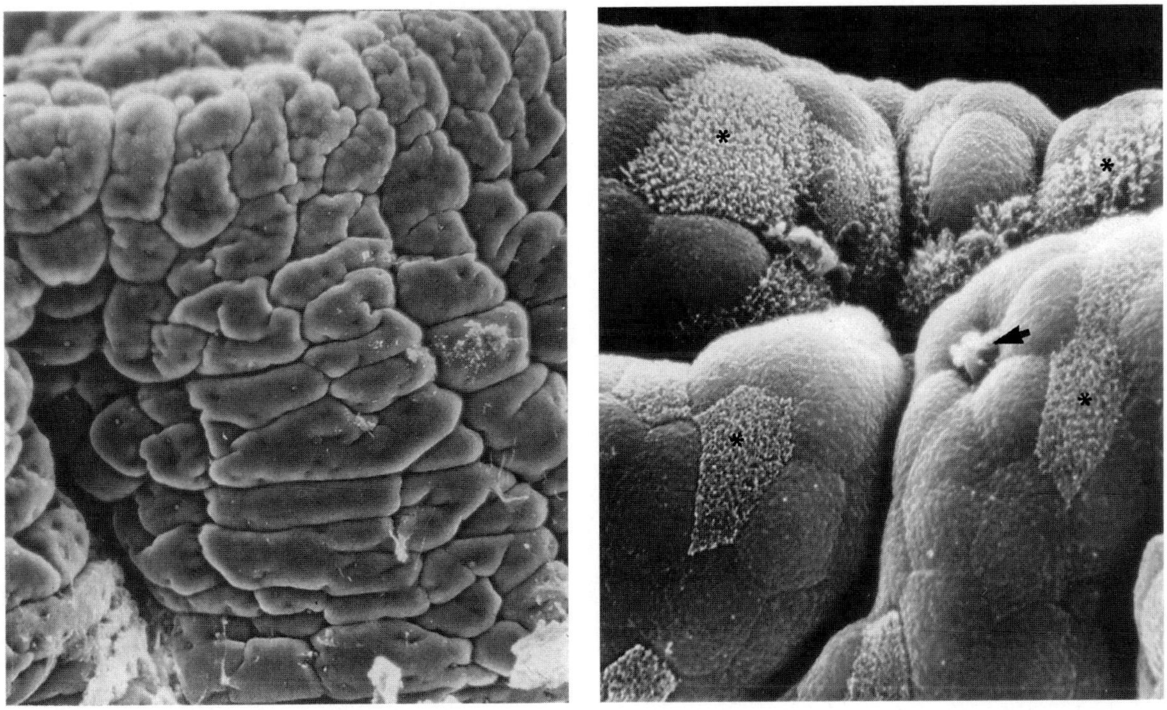

A B

Fig. 3.2 Scanning electron microscopy. **A.** Lateral view of a ridge-like villus. Note infoldings and uneven upper surface (×250). **B**. Detail from **A** showing extrusion zone at villus tip. Note 5- and 6-sided enterocyte outlines, mucus discharge from a goblet cell (arrow), and loss of glycocalyx to expose microvilli of extruding cells (*). Reproduced from Phillips[114] (×2100).

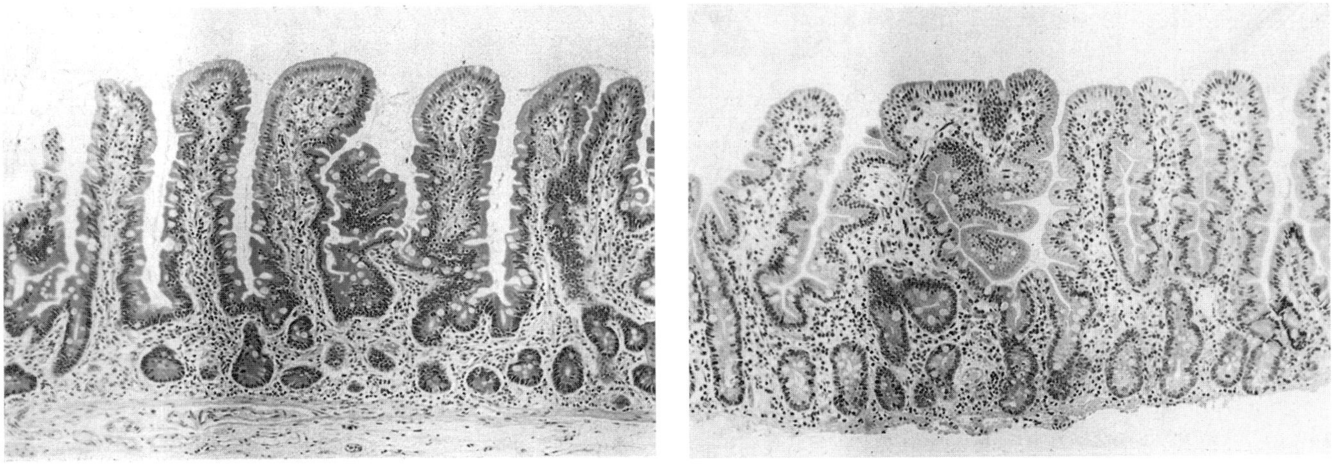

A B

Fig. 3.3 Longitudinal section of normal small intestinal mucosa. Note serrated edge of villi. H&E (×10). **A** Adult mucosa showing villus/crypt ratio of at least 3:1. (Illustration kindly provided by Professor G. Slavin, St Bartholomew's Hospital, London). **B** Childhood mucosa, villus/crypt ratio less than adult, approximately 2:1

ticularly if only a few sections of an abnormal mucosa are examined.[30] An alternative method, although impractical as a routine, involves staining of mucosal samples followed by the micro-dissection and squashing of individual villi and the counting of epithelial nuclei to give an absolute number of cells per villus.[31,32] This avoids the errors inherent in measurements from tissue sections, and can also be applied to crypts. There is, however, a consistent relationship between villus height as measured in sections and the results obtained using 'squashed' villi.[31] Moreover, villus height and total cell population also show good correlation when both are assessed in the squash technique.[32] A recent improvement using confocal microscopy to view intact crypts in order to determine cell numbers and count mitotic figures has demonstrated that crypts are flask-like, rather than simple tubes, with wider dimensions basally.[33]

Although subjectively villi are considered to be shorter in the ileum than in the jejunum,[34] this was not confirmed in a single morphometric study.[13] Ileal villi were taller, and the crypt depth less in the ileum as compared to the jejunum,[13] leaving the matter open to debate. In children jejunal villus height is less and crypt depth is greater than in adults, and may be considered abnormal by comparison (Fig. 3.3).[26] Villus height is also reduced in the elderly, producing a significant reduction in mucosal surface area.[35] Thus the dimensions of the mucosa varies according to its site in the intestine and with age. The structural arrangement of the folds of Kerckring and villi combine to produce an absorptive surface area which is estimated to be 30 times greater than that of a simple cylinder,[36] an obvious aid to digestion and absorption. This is further enhanced by the presence of microvilli on the epithelium as discussed later.

Geographical variation

In the past it was considered that normal mucosal appearance may vary in different ethnic or population groups and that what may pass as normal in a tropical climate would be considered abnormal in a temperate climate.[37] There is no doubt that mucosal abnormalities do occur in apparently healthy individuals in the Indian subcontinent,[38] Africa,[16] and the Caribbean.[39] However, these individuals are actually malabsorbing one or more substances[38,40,41] and when they move to temperate regions there is an improvement in small bowel morphology.[42] This indicates that environmental, rather than genetic factors are responsible and that these individuals have a subclinical enteropathy.

The fact that these changes are common in a population does not warrant the assumption that they are normal for that population.[43] Furthermore, not all individuals show abnormalities and a recent study has demonstrated that in healthy north Indian adults the proximal small intestinal mucosa may be similar to that of an adult Caucasian population.[44]

EPITHELIUM

The epithelium, a single cell thick layer lining the crypts of Lieberkuhn and covering the villi, forms a 20–30 μm barrier between the external environment and the internal milieu of the body. It can be divided into several compartments but in terms of digestive/absorptive function, there is a crypt zone consisting of immature cells and a villous zone consisting of mature cells. There is a gradual change in morphology from the stem cell region to the villus tip.

The detailed kinetics of the epithelium are discussed elsewhere (see Ch. 8), but it is important to remember that the epithelium is in a state of rapid renewal with each cell having a life of approximately five days.[45] The gross appearance of the mucosa is largely considered to be a result of the balance between cell production and cell loss.[37] In childhood the wider range of villus appearances and their relative shortness results in a smaller surface area to volume ratio when compared to adults. Cell production is actually greater in childhood,[46] indicating that cell loss is increased, due either to increased epithelial susceptibility to damage, a more hostile luminal environment or both.

The epithelial cell is polarized, having distinct apical, mid and basal regions. The apical region is characterized by the microvillous brush border, underneath which is a region of lysosomal bodies and smooth endoplasmic reticulum, followed by an area of rough endoplasmic reticulum and mitochondria (Fig. 3.4A). The mid region comprises the Golgi complex and nucleus (Fig. 3.4B) and the basal region, which extends from the nucleus to the basal membrane, contains free and polyribosomes and mitochondria. A characteristic of gut epithelium is the presence of paired centrioles just under the brush border, rather than next to the nucleus (Fig. 3.5).

The microvilli serve to increase the cell surface area by up to 40 times and are the site of ion transport mechanisms and several enzymes which include alkaline phosphatase, glycosidases, peptidases and lipases.[47] Even though microvilli increase surface area for digestion and absorption, substances crossing the membrane must enter the cell through the base of the microvillus, a very small area by comparison.[48] Despite this, monosaccharides released from disaccharide hydrolysis are efficiently captured.[48] Additionally, as indicated by the high turnover of brush border enzymes,[49] traffic in the opposite direction also occurs; disaccharidases, for example, being synthesized in rough endoplasmic reticulum, glycosylated in the golgi complex, and transported to the brush border for insertion.[50] Approximately 5% is thought to be degraded by lysosomes via a crinophagic pathway.[51] Part of the role of the epithelium is to exclude potentially damaging macromolecules,[52] and although proteins enter via pinocytosis[53] the lysosomes under the terminal web are suitably positioned to reduce entry of intact molecules any further.

Each cell is joined to its neighbours along the lateral membrane by an apical tight junction, desmosomes (Fig. 3.5) and by membranous inter-digitations (Fig. 3.4B). There are marked differences between the apical and baso-lateral membranes. For example the baso-lateral membrane is the site of sodium–potassium ATPase activity, secretory component localization for dimeric IgA attachment (prior to transport to the apical membrane), and the transfer of chylomicrons and other foodstuffs into the intercellular space and the lamina propria. The tight

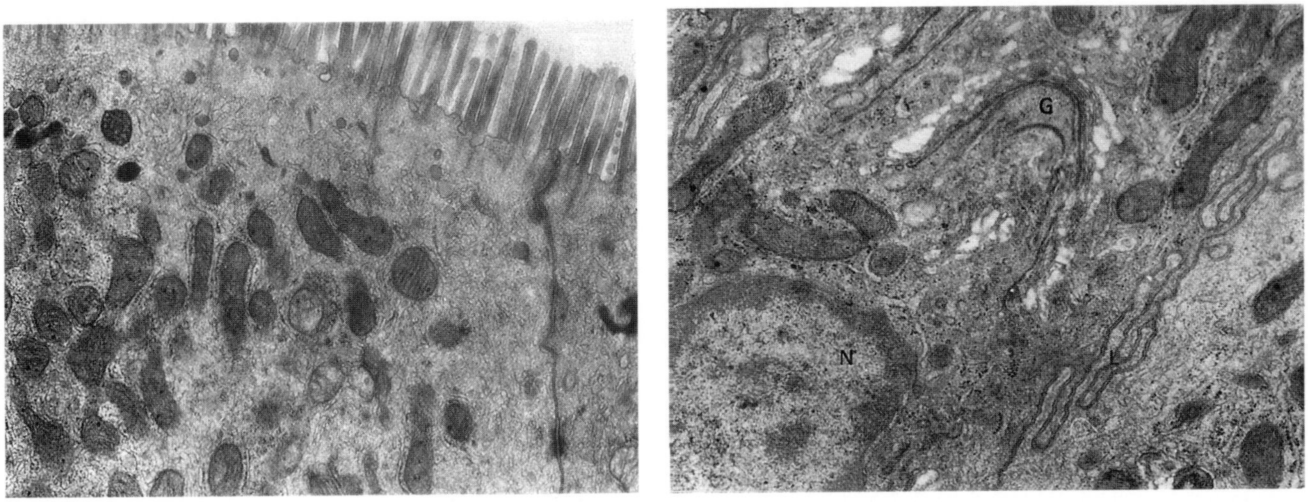

A B

Fig. 3.4 Transmission electron microscopy. Upper villus enterocyte (×16 800). **A** Apical region. Note uneven height of microvilli. **B** Mid region. N = nucleus, G = Golgi complex, L = infoldings of lateral cell membranes.

junction serves to maintain these differences by preventing lateral movement of membrane components.[54] The junctional complex also ensures epithelial integrity and limits molecular entry via the paracellular route. Filaments from the zonula adherens of the tight junction extend into the terminal web to form part of the cytoskeleton. The cytoskeletal framework of the brush border region is a complex arrangement.[55] Actin, with villin, fimbrin, and other proteins, form the core filament bundles of the microvilli which run into, and form part of, the terminal web. The terminal web contains several other proteins including myosin, tropomyosin and vinculin.[56] The complete structure acts as a framework for the microvilli but is also considered to have the potential of producing their controlled movement,[55] and to be involved in the transport of substances in and out of the cell.

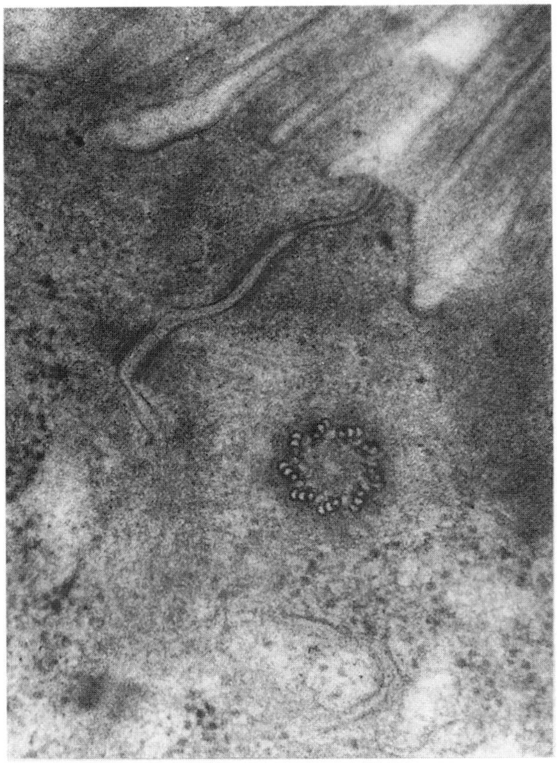

Fig. 3.5 Centriole in the terminal web region (×60 700).

Although epithelial cells are attached laterally the intercellular space is not fixed. In the resting state the spaces between enterocytes are collapsed, whereas during net water absorption they are expanded, particularly towards the basal region, the basal membrane remaining in contact with the basement membrane and with neighbouring cells.[57,58] Thus a two-way polarization of the epithelium exists, ensuring ionic balance, dietary intake and antigen exclusion.

Changes in epithelium along the crypt/villus axis

Morphological studies show that crypt epithelium is basophilic and villous epithelium is acidophilic,[59] reflecting the observation that crypt cells contain more free and polyribosomes and less rough endoplasmic reticulum than villous cells, and demonstrating that a process of cell development takes place along the crypt/villus axis. Mitotic figures are only seen in crypts and thymidine kinase activity is also localized to this region.[60] The crypt–villus junction appears to be a site of change. In addition to the above phenomena glutaminase activity is highest in this area[61] and there is a rapid increase in sodium–glucose linked transporter mRNA levels[62] and in brush border enzymes (see below).

In the low crypt region, microvilli are short and irregular, there are few cytoplasmic organelles, and the basal region is limited in size due to the basal location of the nucleus (Fig. 3.6). Further up the crypt mitotic figures are sometimes seen and it appears that the microvilli remain during cell division and are not dissolved and resynthesized. There is an increase in organelle content and microvilli become taller[63] and more numerous. In the low villus region microvillus density increases and tufting may be seen, in the mid region of the villus microvilli continue to increase in height and number, resulting in a maximal increase in cell surface area here because the microvillus height and number decrease in the upper region,[64,65] along with enterocyte height.[65]

The changes in microvilli in the low to mid villous region are paralleled by rapid increases in what are considered to be biochemical markers of enterocyte maturity, i.e. brush border disaccharidases and alkaline phosphatase.[66] Similarly the reduction in microvillus surface area in the upper villous region occurs along with a reduction in brush border enzymes.[67] Whether the reduction in enzymes implies that cell function is compromised is uncertain as the cell's capacity for digestion may still exceed the load placed upon it. However, the morphological and histochemical findings indicate that the mid villous region is best adapted for digestion and absorption and that an ageing process occurs in the upper villous region. Other organelle changes which also indicate cell ageing are an increase in secondary lysosomes, mitochondrial dissolution, the presence of autophagic vacuoles in cells at the villus tip and extrusion.[22] These changes make it important to determine the site of observation in investigations of disease states.

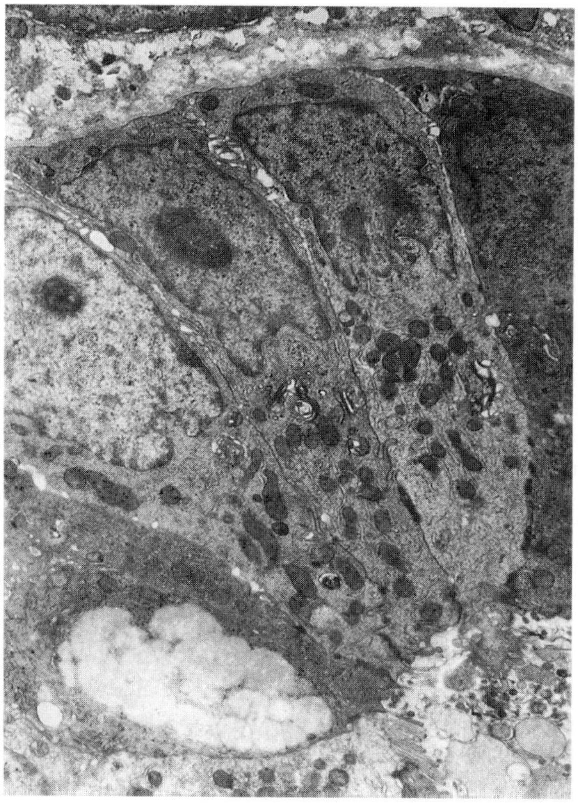

Fig. 3.6 Enteroblasts in low crypt region (×9700).

Epithelial cell types

These epithelial cells are connected to neighbouring cells by tight junctions and desmosomes, but are distinct from the columnar epithelial cells. Although they can be separated into subtypes it is considered that all gut epithelial cells may be derived from the same stem cell.[68]

Goblet cells and endocrine cells

Goblet cells, which increase in number between the duodenum and ileum, and endocrine cells, which are generally confined to the crypt region, are covered in detail in Chapters 4 and 6.

Paneth cells

Paneth cells[69] are found at the base of small intestinal crypts and can be recognized by the presence of large, apically situated, electron dense granules surrounded by rough endoplasmic reticulum (Fig. 3.7). Their presence and number varies in different species, being absent in

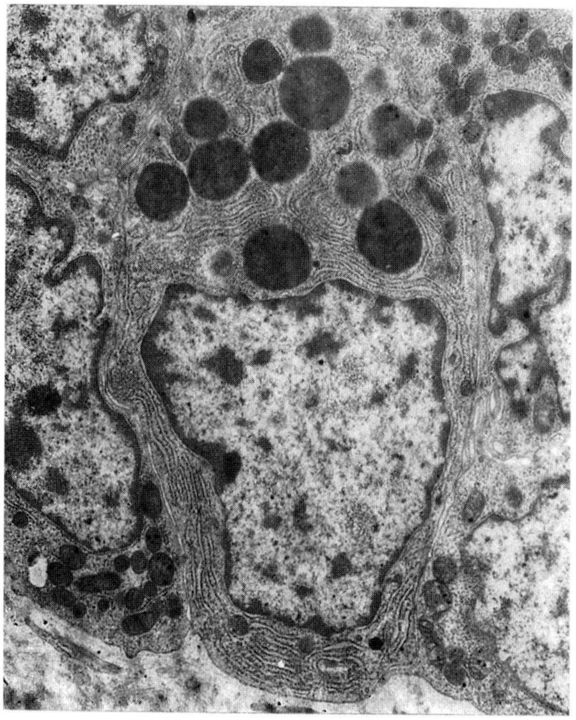

Fig. 3.7 Paneth cell at base of crypt (×8200).

cats[70] and occupying nearly the whole crypt in ant-eating Brazilian bears.[71] Their functions are unknown although a defensive role is indicated by the presence of lysozyme,[72] immunoglobulins A and G,[73] and mRNAs for tumour necrosis factor[74] and alpha-1-antitrypsin.[75]

Tuft cells

These infrequently encountered cells are distinguished from other epithelial cells by an apical tuft of microvilli and deep surface invaginations termed caveolae.[76,77] They are distributed throughout the stomach and intestine, but their function is unknown.

M cells

M cells are readily identified in the epithelium overlying lymphoid follicles in rodents,[78] however they are very infrequently found in isolated lymphoid follicles from proximal and distal small intestinal biopsies in children.[79] For further details see Chapter 11.

Intraepithelial cells

These cells are normally found within the epithelial layer and show no morphological connections with epithelial cells, i.e. desmosomes, tight junctions or membranous interdigitations. They represent migratory populations which are presumably in states of flux.

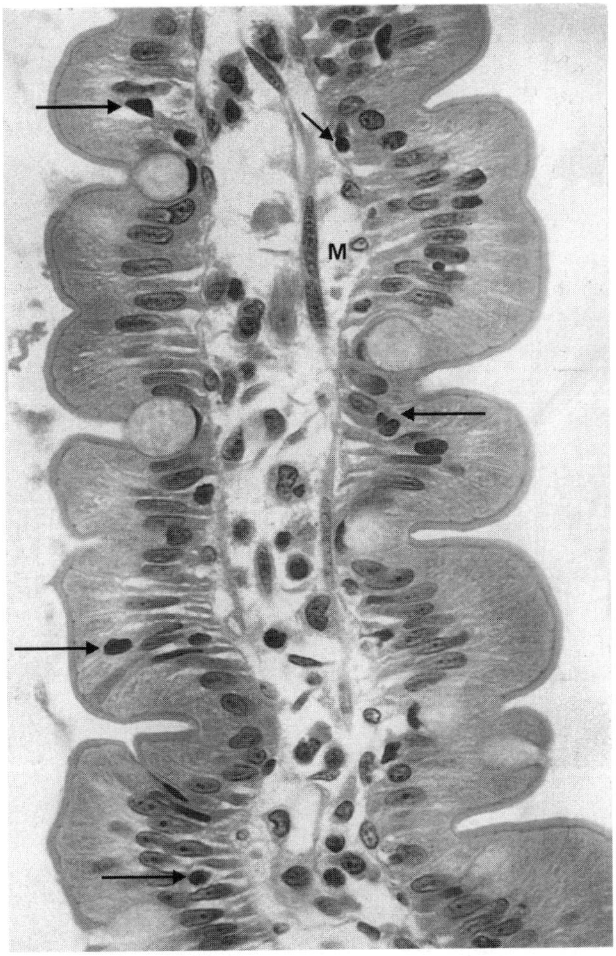

Fig. 3.8 Upper villous region. Intraepithelial lymphocytes are arrowed, M = muscle cell. H&E (×495).

Lymphocytes

Lymphocytes[80] are the predominant 'non-epithelial' intraepithelial cell (Fig. 3.8). They are mainly found in basal positions in the interepithelial cell spaces,[81] but can also be seen lying across the basement membrane, indicating movement between the epithelial and lamina propria compartments. There is no evidence of lymphocytes traversing the tight junction in normal human mucosa.

In the jejunum there are usually between 12 and 35 lymphocytes per 100 villous epithelial cells in both adults[82] and children;[83] fewer are present in the ileum.[80] Intraepithelial lymphocytes (IEL) form a heterogenous population varying in size, organelle content and phenotype.

Diameters of IEL range from 3–11 μm; those having diameters greater than 9 μm (2.5%) are considered to be blast cells.[84] Most IELs have a small cytoplasmic–nuclear ratio, contain few organelles,[85] and possess a variable number of small electron dense granules[84] which are probably lysosomes.[86] Most of the lymphocytes are T cells, of which approximately 85% are of the suppressor/cytotoxic phenotype and 15% are helper/inducer phenotype.[87] This is in contrast to lamina propria lymphocytes which are mainly helper/inducer phenotype,[87] and indicates a preferential lodging of suppressor cells in the epithelium. IEL are also present in fetal human gut and suppressor/cytotoxic cells again predominate.[88] Their exact functions are unknown but their position and phenotype suggest that they are involved in modulating local immune responses. It is also possible that they are involved in antigen handling via epithelial cell presentation.[89,90]

Eosinophils and other cells

Eosinophils are occasionally seen in the epithelium in normal mucosa, and in children the jejunum contains only approximately 3 eosinophils per cm of villous epithelium.[28] Lymphocytes, by comparison, would number nearly 500 cells per cm.

Sub-epithelial macrophages may be seen extending across the basement membrane into the epithelium, and rare examples of intraepithelial mast cells may be found in crypts.[81] Other lamina propria cells have not been described in intraepithelial positions in normal human mucosa.

BASEMENT MEMBRANE

The basement membrane represents the interface between the epithelium and lamina propria and although it has a relatively simple morphological appearance its functions appear complex and, at times, contradictory. It allows for attachment of the epithelium, limits the lamina propria, and is part of the structural framework of the villus, yet it also permits epithelial migration along it, various leucocytes to travel through it, and presumably does not impede the transfer of absorbed foodstuffs or lamina propria products.

The main characteristic of the basement membrane is the presence of a basal lamina which is composed of two parts: a lamina rara and a lamina densa, situated just beneath the epithelial basal membrane. Beneath the basal lamina is a layer of sub-epithelial fibroblasts (Fig. 3.9). This arrangement occurs in continuum under the epithelium, and anything moving between the epithelium and lamina propria must pass through it. Basement membrane structure is similar in different tissue sites and species,[91] and because specific investigations of enterocyte basement membranes are few by comparison, much of its structure and function has been inferred from other studies. The components of the basal lamina are considered to be derived from the overlying epithelium[92] and they self-assemble.[93]

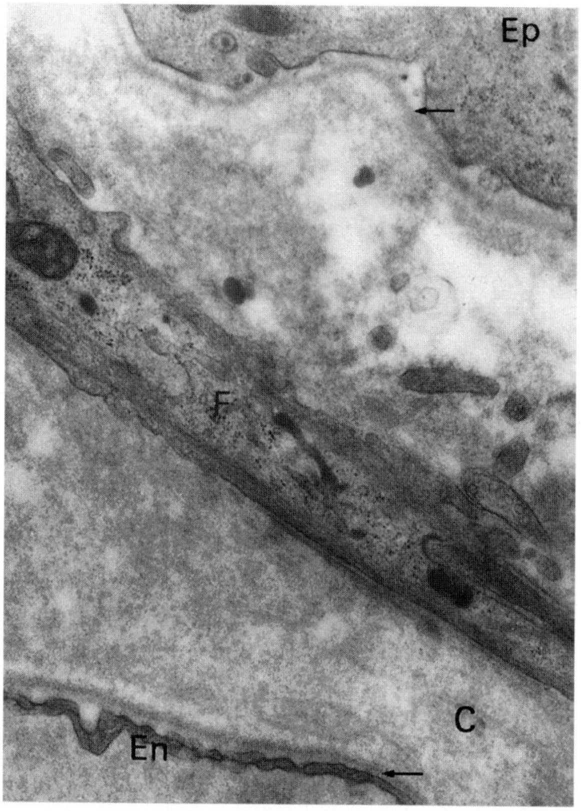

Fig. 3.9 Basement membrane region. Epithelial and endothelial basal laminae are arrowed. Ep = epitheliaum, F = fibroblast, C = collagen, En = fenestrated endothelium (×28 500).

In the rabbit and mouse, changes are apparent in the distribution of sub-epithelial fibroblasts along the crypt–villus axis.[94–96] Around the bases of crypts, overlapping (shingling) of the fibroblasts occurs whilst at higher crypt levels a single layer is apparent, and on the villus fibroblasts are widely separated, although contact with the basal lamina is maintained by cell processes. Animal studies concerning the proliferation of subepithelial fibroblasts have produced conflicting results. Some workers conclude that the fibroblast population migrates with epithelial cells,[94,95] others find no such evidence and suggest that cell division merely represents turnover of a slowly renewing cell population.[97,98]

LAMINA PROPRIA

The lamina propria has not been studied with the same intensity as the epithelium, and only in recent work is the diversity of cells within it being revealed.

Lymphocytes and plasma cells

There are several thousand cells per mm^2 of lamina propria in normal adult jejunum,[99,100] more being present in the crypt region than in the villous region.[99] Most of the cells are plasma cells and lymphocytes. The majority of plasma cells are IgA containing, although IgM, IgG, and IgE cells are also present. Most lymphocytes (60–70%) are of helper/inducer phenotype, 30–40% are suppressor/cytotoxic cells, and there is a scattering of activated T cells.[87] These cells will be considered in more detail elsewhere (Ch. 11).

Polymorphonuclear cells

The only polymorphonuclear leucocyte regularly encountered in normal mucosa is the eosinophil. It is easily distinguished from neutrophils and basophils by its characteristic eosinophilic granules which contain a crystalloid centre. There are 100–200 eosinophils per mm^2 of lamina propria in the jejunum.[28,101] Basophils, with granules of similar appearance to stippled mast cell granules, are rarely seen in the lamina propria. The presence of neutrophils outside capillaries is considered abnormal.

Mast cells

Mast cells[102,103] are present throughout the mucosa but are more often seen in the crypt than the villous region.[104] They can be detected using light microscopy although fixation and staining conditions need to be optimized for their full assessment.[104] Light microscopy of tissue processed for electron microscopy also gives excellent mast cell detail.[105]

In normal adult jejunum there are just under 300 mast cells per mm^2 of mucosa,[104] compared with around 750 mast cells per mm^2 of ileal lamina propria in childhood.[106] Granules have a variable sub-structure ranging from a stippled appearance to whorled and/or scrolled contents. Normally there is a full granule content, a central nucleus, and microvillus-like projections on the external membrane, producing a clear area around the cell (Fig. 3.10). Any evidence of degranulation is an abnormal event and indicates release of histamine, proteoglycans and chemotactic factors. In rodents mucosal mast cells appear to be different to connective tissue mast cells[107] and human mast cells may also form a heterogenous population.[108]

Macrophages and histiocytes

In common with lymphocytes, plasma cells and perhaps mast cells, histiocytes form a heterogenous population varying in morphology, histochemistry and immunocytochemistry. Macrophages expressing class II histocompatability antigens can be divided into two villous populations in normal mucosa. The large round macrophages with strong alkaline phosphatase activity (10–20%) are thought to carry out a scavenging role engulfing particulate antigens, and small stellate macrophages with strong ATPase activity (80–90%) are thought to be involved in ingesting soluble antigens and presenting them to T lymphocytes.[109] On electron microscopy, macrophages are readily seen near the basement membrane, particularly in the upper villus region, where they are presumably well located to perform their antigen-associated functions. The ability to isolate and maintain human intestinal macrophages in culture has recently been reported and describes macrophages as esterase positive and peroxidase negative cells possessing surface receptors for IgG and complement.[110]

Smooth muscle

Smooth muscle cells can be found running down the centre of the villous lamina propria (Fig. 3.9) and within the crypt zone. Contraction of these cells is presumed to shorten the villi and may allow a pumping motion.[111]

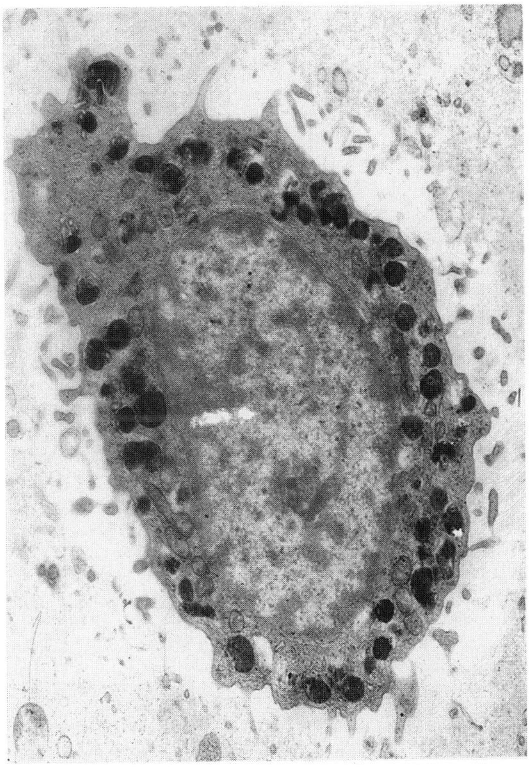

Fig. 3.10 Mast cell (×11 600).

REFERENCES

1. Bryant J. Observations upon the growth and length of the human intestine. Am J Med Sci 1924; 167: 499.
2. Walker-Smith JA. Dissecting microscope appearances of the small intestine in childhood: a post-mortem study. MD Thesis (University of Sydney) 1970.
3. Underhill BML. Intestinal length in man. Br Med J 1955; 2: 1243–1246.
4. Hirsch J, Ahrens EH, Blankenhorn DH. Measurement of the human intestinal length in vivo and some causes of variation. Gastroenterology 1956; 31: 274–284.
5. Creamer B, Lepperd P. Post-mortem examination of a small intestine in the coeliac syndrome. Gut 1965; 6: 466–471.
6. Baker SJ. Geographical variations in the morphology of the small intestinal mucosa in apparently healthy individuals. Path Microbiol 1973; 39: 222–237.
7. Loehry CA, Creamer B. Post-mortem study of small intestinal mucosa. Br Med J 1966; 1: 827–829.
8. Shiner M. Jejunal biopsy tube. Lancet 1956; 1: 85.
9. Crosby WH, Kugler HW. Intraluminal biopsy of the small intestine: the intestinal biopsy capsule. Am J Dig Dis 1957; 2: 236–241.
10. Kilby A. Paediatric small intestinal biopsy capsule with two ports. Gut 1976; 17: 158–159.
11. Baker SJ, Hughes A. Multiple-retrieving small intestinal biopsy tube. Lancet 1960; 2: 686.
12. Holmes R, Hourihane D O'B, Booth CC. Dissecting microscope appearances of jejunal biopsy specimens from patients with idiopathic steatorrhoea. Lancet 1961; 1: 81–83.
13. Stewart JS, Pollock DJ, Hoffbrand AV, Mollin DL, Booth CC. A study of proximal and distal intestinal structure and absorptive function in idiopathic steatorrhoea. Q J Med 1967; 143: 425–444.
14. Cocco AE, Dohrmann MJ, Hendrix TR. Reconstruction of human jejunal biopsies: three dimensional histology. Gastroenterology 1966; 51: 24–31.
15. Chacko CJ, Paulson AK, Mathan VI, Baker SJ. The villus architecture of the small intestine in the tropics: a necropsy study. J Pathol 1969; 98: 146–151.
16. Cook GC, Kajubi SK, Lee FD. Jejunal morphology of the African in Uganda. J Pathol 1969; 98: 157–169.
17. Baker SJ, Mathan VI, Cherian V. The nature of the villi in the small intestine of the rat. Lancet 1963; 1: 860.

18. van Lennep EW. The histology of the mucosa of the small intestine of the long-nosed bandicoot. Acta Anat 1962; 50: 73.
19. Cornes JS. Number, size, and distribution of Peyer's patches in the human small intestine. Gut 1965; 6: 225–233.
20. Jackson D, Walker-Smith JA, Phillips AD. Small intestinal lymphoid follicles in childhood. Pediatr Res 1981; 15: 1196.
21. Marsh MN, Swift JA. A study of the small intestinal mucosa using the scanning electron microscope. Gut 1969; 10: 940–949.
22. Phillips AD, France N, Walker-Smith JA. The structure of the enterocyte in relation to its position on the villus — an electron microscopical study. Histopathology 1979; 3: 117–130.
23. Potten CS, Allen TD. Ultrastructure of cell loss in intestinal mucosa. J Ultrastruct Res 1977; 60: 272–277.
24. Bockman DE, Cooper MD. Pinocytosis by epithelium associated with lymphoid follicles in the bursa of Fabricius, appendix, and Peyer's patches. An electron microscopic study. Am J Anat 1973; 136: 455–478.
25. Owen RL, Jones AL. Epithelial cell specialisation within human Peyer's patches: an ultrastructural study of intestinal lymphoid follicles. Gastroenterology 1974; 66: 189–203.
26. Penna FJ, Hill ID, Kingston D, Robertson K, Slavin G, Shiner M. Jejunal mucosal morphometry in children with and without gut symptoms and in normal adults. J Clin Pathol 1981; 34: 386–392.
27. Slavin G, Sowter C, Robertson K, McDermott S, Paton K. Measurement in jejunal biopsies by computer-aided microscopy. J Clin Pathol 1980; 33: 254–261.
28. Maluenda C, Phillips AD, Briddon A, Walker-Smith JA. Quantitative analysis of small intestinal mucosa in cow's milk sensitive enteropathy. J Pediatr Gastroenterol Nutr 1984; 3: 349–356.
29. Dunnill MS, Whitehead R. A method for the quantitation of small intestinal biopsy specimens. J Clin Pathol 1972; 25: 243–246.
30. Wright NA. The experimental analysis of changes in proliferative and morphological status in studies on the intestine. Scand J Gastroenterol 1982; 17(Suppl 74): 3–10.
31. Ferguson A, Sutherland A, MacDonald TT, Allan F. Technique for microdissection and measuremant in biopsies of human small intestine. J Clin Pathol 1977; 30: 1068–1073.
32. Hasan M, Ferguson A. Measurements of intestinal villi in non-specific and ulcer-associated duodenitis — correlation between area of microdissected villus and villus epithelial cell count. J Clin Pathol 1981; 34: 1181–1186.
33. Savidge TC, Smith MW, Walker-Smith JA, Phillips AD. Measuring intestinal crypt cell proliferation by confocal microscopy. Proc Nutr Soc 1993; in press (Abstract).
34. Whitehead R. Mucosal biopsy of the gastrointestinal tract. 3rd ed. Philadelphia: WB Saunders, 1985.
35. Warren PM, Pepperman MA, Montgomery RD. Age changes in small intestinal mucosa. Lancet 1978; 2: 849–850.
36. Eggermont E. The intestinal brush border. Acta Paediatr Belg 1979; 32: 163–172.
37. Lee FD, Toner PG. Biopsy pathology of the small intestine. London: Chapman and Hall, 1980.
38. Lindenbaum J, Alam AKM, Kent TH. Subclinical small intestinal disease in East Pakistan. Br Med J 1966; 2: 1616–1619.
39. Brunser O, Eidelman S, Klipstein FA. Intestinal morphology of rural Haitians. A comparison between overt tropical sprue and asymptomatic subjects. Gastroenterology 1970; 58: 655–668.
40. Rhodes AR, Shea N, Lindenbaum J. Malabsorption in asymptomatic Liberian children. Am J Clin Nutr 1971; 24: 574–577.
41. Falaiye JM. Present status of subclinical intestinal malabsorption in the tropics. Br Med J 1971; 4: 454–458.
42. Lindenbaum J, Harmon JW, Gerson CD. Subclinical malabsorption in developing countries. Am J Clin Nutr 1972; 25: 1056–1061.
43. Schenk EA, Klipstein FA, Tomasini JT. Morphologic characteristics of jejunal biopsies from asymptomatic Haitians and Puerto Ricans. Am J Clin Nutr 1972; 25: 1080–1083.
44. Bennet MK, Sachdev GK, Jewell DP, Anand BS. Jejunal morphology in healthy north Indian subjects. J Clin Pathol 1985; 38: 368–371.
45. MacDonald WC, Trier JS, Everett NB. Cell proliferation and migration in the stomach, duodenum, and rectum of man: radioautographic studies. Gastroenterology 1964; 45: 405–417.
46. Wright N, Watson A, Morley A, Appleton D, Marks J. Cell kinetics in flat (avillous) mucosa of the human small intestine. Gut 1973; 14: 701–710.
47. Field M. Pathways for ion and water movements across intestine: an overview. In: Turnberg LA ed. Intestinal Secretion. Proceedings of the third BSG.SK&F International Workshop 1982: 1–4.
48. Parsons DS. Introductory remarks on the brush border. In: Brush border membranes. London: Pitman. Ciba Found Symp 1983; 95: 3–11.
49. Alpers DH, Seetharam B. Pathophysiology of diseases involving brush border proteins. N Engl J Med 1977; 296: 1047–1050.
50. Dalqvist A, Semenza G. Disaccharidases of small intestinal mucosa. J Pediatr Gastroenterol Nutr 1985; 4: 857–867.
51. Blok J, Fransen JAM, Ginsel LA. Turnover of brush border glycoproteins in human intestinal absorptive cells: do lysosomes have a regulatory function? Cell Biol Int Rep 1984; 8: 993–1014.
52. Walker WA. Antigen handling by the small intestine. Clin Gastroenterol 1986; 15: 1–20.
53. Jackson D, Walker-Smith JA, Phillips AD. Macromolecular absorption by histologically normal and abnormal small intestinal mucosa in childhood: an in vitro study using organ culture. J Pediatr Gastroenterol Nutr 1983; 2: 235–247.
54. Dragsten PR, Blumenthal R, Handler JS. Membrane asymmetry in epithelia: is the tight junction a barrier to diffusion in the plasma membrane? Nature 1981; 294: 718–722.
55. Mooseker MS, Bonder EM, Oonzelman KA, Fishkind DJ, Howe CL, Keller TCS. Brush border cytoskeleton and integration of cellular functions. J Cell Biol 1984; 99: 104–112.
56. Carruthers L, Phillips AD, Dourmashkin R. Disorders of the cytoskeleton of the enterocyte. Clin Gastroenterol 1986; 15: 105–120.
57. Melligott TF, Beck IT, Dinda PK, Thompson S. Correlation of structural changes at different levels of the jejunal villus with positive net water transport in vivo and in vitro. Can J Physiol Pharmacol 1975; 53: 439–450.
58. Phillips AD, Sandhu BK, Milla P, Harries JT. Effects of loperamide on the morphology of the small intestine: an enigma in answer to a question. Pediatr Res 1983; 17: 428.
59. Padykula HA, Strauss EW, Ladman AJ, Gardner FH. A morphologic and histochemical analysis of the human jejunal epithelium in nontropical sprue. Gastroenterology 1961; 40: 735–765.
60. Fortin-Magana R, Hurwitz R, Herbst JJ, Kretchmer N. Intestinal enzymes: indicators of proliferation and differentiation in the jejunum. Science 1970; 167: 1627–1628.
61. Nagy LE, Pittler A, Kretchmer N. Development of glutaminase along the villus-crypt axis in the jejunum of the rat. J Pediatr Gastroenterol Nutr 1988; 7: 907–913.
62. Smith MW, Turvey A, FreemanTC. Appearance of phloridzin-sensitive glucose transport is not controlled at mRNA level in rabbit jejunal enterocytes. Exp Physiol 1992; 77: 525–528.
63. Iancu T, Elian E. The intestinal microvillus — ultrastructural variability in coeliac disease and cow's milk protein intolerance. Acta Paediatr Scand 1976; 65: 65–73.
64. Phillips AD, France NE, Walker-Smith JA. The structure of the enterocyte in relation to its position on the villus — an electron microscopical study. Histopathology 1979; 3: 117–130.
65. Sinclair TS, Jones DA, Kumar PJ, Phillips AD. The microvillus in adult jejunal mucosa — an electron microscopic study. Histopathology 1984; 8: 739–746.
66. Smith MW, Phillips AD, Walker-Smith JA. Selective inhibition of brush border hydrolase development in coeliac disease and cow's milk protein intolerance. Pediatr Res 1986; (abstract) (in press).
67. Nordstrom C, Dalqvist A. Quantitative distribution of some enzymes along the villi and crypts of human small intestine. Scand J Gastroenterol 1973; 8: 407–416.
68. Cheng H, Leblond CP. Origin, differentiation, and renewal of the four main epithelial cell types in the mouse small intestine. I. Columnar cell. Am J Anat 1974; 141: 537–562.

69. Sandow MJ, Whitehead R. The Paneth cell. Gut 1979; 20: 420–431.
70. Creamer B. Paneth cell function. Lancet 1967; 1: 314–316.
71. Marques de Castro N, da Silva Sasso W, Saad FA. Preliminary observations of Paneth cells of Tamandua Tetradactyla Lin. Acta Anat 1959; 38: 345–352.
72. Erlandsen SL, Rodning CB, Montero C, Parsons JA, Lewis EA, Wilson ID. Ultrastructural immunocytochemical localisation of lysozyme in the Paneth cells of man. J Histochem Cytochem 1974; 22: 401–413.
73. Rodning CB, Wilson ID, Erlandsen SL. Immunoglobulins within human small intestinal Paneth cells. Lancet 1976; 1: 984–987.
74. Keshav S, Lawson I, Chung LP, Stein M, Perry VH. Tumor necrosis factor and mRNA localised to Paneth cells of normal murine intestinal epithelium by in situ hybridization. J Exp Med 1990; 171: 327–332.
75. Koopman P, Povey S, Lovell-Badge RH. Widespread expression of human alpha-1-antitrypsin in transgenic mice revealed by in situ hybridization. Genes Dev 1989; 3: 16–25.
76. Isomaki AM. A new cell type (tuft cell) in the gastrointestinal mucosa of the rat. Acta Pathol Microbiol Scand 1973; 240(Suppl.): 1–67.
77. Nabeyama A, Leblond CP. Caveolated cells characterised by deep surface invaginations and abundant filaments in mouse gastrointestinal epithelia. Am J Anat 1974; 140: 147–165.
78. Bye WA, Allan CH, Trier JS. Structure, distribution, and origin of M cells in Peyer's patches of mouse ileum. Gastroenterology 1984; 86: 789–801.
79. Jackson D, Walker-Smith JA, Phillips AD. M cells in rat and childhood follicles associated epithelium in the small intestine. Gut 1982; 23: A923.
80. Dobbins WO III. Human intestinal intraepithelial lymphocytes. Gut 1986; 27: 972–985.
81. Toner PG, Ferguson A. Intraepithelial cells in the human intestinal mucosa. J Ultrastruct Res 1971; 34: 329–344.
82. Ferguson A, Murray D. Quantitation of intraepithelial lymphocytes in human jejunum. Gut 1971; 12: 988–994.
83. Phillips AD, Rice SJ, France NE, Walker-Smith JA. Small intestinal intraepithelial lymphocyte levels in cow's milk protein intolerance. Gut 1979; 20: 509–512.
84. Marsh MN. Studies of intestinal lymphoid tissue. III. Quantitative analysis of epithelial lymphocytes in the small intestine of human control subjects and of patients with celiac sprue. Gastroenterology 1980; 79: 481–492.
85. Austin LL, Dobbins WO III. Intraepithelial leucocytes of the intestinal mucosa in normal man and in Whipple's disease: a light and electron microscopic study. Dig Dis Sci 1982; 27: 311–320.
86. Parker JW, Wakasa H, Lukes RJ. The morphologic and cytochemical demonstration of lysosomes in lymphocytes incubated with phytohemagglutinin by electron microscopy. Lab Invest 1965; 14: 1736–1743.
87. Selby WS, Janossy G, Bofill M, Jewell DP. Lymphocyte subpopulations in the human small intestine. The findings in normal mucosa and in the mucosa of patients with coeliac disease. Clin Exp Immunol 1983; 52: 219–228.
88. Spencer JM, Dillon SB, Isaacson PG, McDonald TT. T cell subclasses in human fetal ileum. Clin Exp Immunol 1986; 65: 553–558.
89. Cerf-Bensussan N, Quaroni A, Kurnick JT, Bhan AK. Intraepithelial lymphocytes modulate Ia expression by intestinal epithelial cells. J Immunol 1984; 132: 2244–2252.
90. Spencer J, Finn T, Isaacson PG. Expression of HLA-DR antigens on epithelium associated with lymphoid tissue in the human gastrointestinal tract. Gut 1986; 27: 153–157.
91. Madari JA, Pratt BM, Yurchenco PD, Furthmayr H. The ultrastructural organisation and architecture of basement membrane. In: Basement Membranes and Cell Movement. London: Pitman. Ciba Found Symp 1984; 108: 6–18.
92. Bernfield MR, Banerjee SD. The basal lamina in epithelial–mesenchymal morphogenetic interactions. In: Kefalides NA ed. Biology and Chemistry of Basement Membranes. New York: Academic Press, 1978: 137–148.
93. Yurchenco PD, Tsilibary EC, Charonis AS, Furthmayr H. Models for the self-assembly of basement membrane. J Histochem Cytochem 1986; 34: 93–102.
94. Parker FG, Barnes EN, Kaye GI. The pericryptal fibroblast sheath. IV. Replication, migration, and differentiation of the subepithelial fibroblasts of the crypt and villus of the rabbit jejunum. Gastroenterology 1974; 67: 607–621.
95. Marsh MN, Trier JS. Morphology and cell proliferation of subepithelial fibroblasts in adult mouse jejunum. I. Structural features. Gastroenterology 1974; 67: 622–635.
96. Marsh MN, Trier JS. Morphology and cell proliferation of subepithelial fibroblasts in adult mouse jejunum. II. Radioautographic studies. Gastroenterology 1974; 67: 636–645.
97. Maskens AP, Rahier JR, Meersseman FP, Dujardin-Loits R-M, Haot JG. Cell proliferation of pericryptal fibroblasts in the rat colon mucosa. Gut 1979; 20: 775–779.
98. Neal JV, Potten CS. Description and basic cell kinetics of the murine pericryptal fibroblast sheath. Gut 1981; 22: 19–24.
99. Montgomery RD, Shearer ACI. The cell population of the upper jejunal mucosa in tropical sprue and postinfective malabsorption. Gut 1974; 15: 387–391.
100. Ferguson R, Asquith P, Cooke WT. The jejunal infiltrate in coeliac disease complicated by lymphoma. Gut 1974; 15: 458–461.
101. Lancaster-Smith M, Kumar PJ, Dawson AM. The cellular infiltrate of the jejunum in adult coeliac disease and dermatitis herpetiformis following the reintroduction of dietary gluten. Gut 1975; 16: 683–688.
102. Pepys J, Edwards AM (eds). The mast cell, its role in health and disease. London: Pitman, 1979.
103. Lemanske RF, Atkins FM, Metcalfe DD. Gastrointestinal mast cells in health and disease. Part I. J Pediatr 1983; 103: 177–184.
104. Strobel S, Miller HRP, Ferguson A. Human intestinal mast cells: evaluation of fixation and staining techniques. J Clin Pathol 1981; 34: 851–858.
105. Strobel S, Hasan M, Ferguson A. Staining properties of human intestinal mucosal mast cells after glutaraldehyde fixation. J Clin Pathol 1982; 35: 897–899.
106. Sanderson IR, Leung KBP, Pearce FL, Walker-Smith JA. J Clin Pathol 1986; 39: 279–283.
107. Bienenstock J, Befus AD, Pearce F, Denburg J, Goodacre R. Mast cell heterogeneity: derivation and function with emphasis on the intestine. J Allergy Clin Immunol 1982; 70: 407–412.
108. Fox CC, Dvorak AM, Peters SP, Kagey-Sobotka A, Lichtenstein LM. Isolation and characterisation of human intestinal mucosal mast cells. J Immunol 1985; 135: 483–491.
109. Selby WS, Poulter LW, Hobbs S, Jewell DP, Janossy G. Heterogeneity of HLA-DR-positive histiocytes in human intestinal lamina propria: a combined histochemical and immunohistological analysis. J Clin Pathol 1983; 36: 379–384.
110. Winter HS, Cole FS, Huffer LM, Davidson CB, Katz AJ, Edelson PJ. Isolation and characterisation of resident macrophages from guinea pig and human intestine. Gastroenterology 1983; 85: 358–363.
111. Verzar F. Absorption from the intestine. London: Longmans, 1936: 294.

CHAPTER

4

The large intestinal mucosa

A. K. M. Shamsuddin G. Y. Yang

The colon, as described in anatomy texts, includes the caecum, ascending, transverse and descending colon, and not the rectum; the large intestine, however, includes the rectum.[1]

Conventional autopsies performed between 12 and 36 hours after somatic death provide material which is unsuitable for detailed study because of changes occurring after cell death.[2] This leads to the use of the normal mucosa in specimens resected for carcinoma.[3–5] However, it has been shown that apparently normal mucosa in cancer-bearing large bowel is far from being truly normal.[6]

This account of the normal large intestinal mucosa is thus based upon tissues from 'brain dead' patients who were autopsied one to three minutes after cessation of their cardiorespiratory function.[2] These patients were usually in their third decade (mean age of 30 years), their age ranging from 14 to 79 years. They were mostly Caucasians; rarely Negroids and Mongoloids. They were usually victims of severe trauma and free of known neoplastic diseases.

Blood pressure before death was in the normal range, and patients were maintained on artificial respiration: thus, their organs were quite reasonably well-perfused and well-oxygenated.

At autopsy the large intestine was rapidly sampled. Tissues for light microscopy, histochemistry and electron microscopy were taken from the ascending, transverse, descending colon and rectum and appropriately processed.[7–10]

LIGHT MICROSCOPY

The large intestinal epithelium is composed of uniform test-tube shaped crypts, between which is the intervening lamina propria. The lamina propria, situated between the basement membrane of the epithelial crypts and the muscularis mucosa, consists of fibroblasts, capillaries, macrophages, eosinophils, lymphocytes, plasma cells and nerve fibres. Occasionally, lymphocytes or eosinophils are seen between the epithelial cells. They are clearly separated from the adjacent epithelial cells by the plasma membranes. Crypt columnar cells contain a variable number of cytoplasmic mucous granules. Towards the upper portion of the crypts, the population of mucus containing cells decreases and cells with eosinophilic cytoplasm occur; however, mucous cells are still abundant and the granules appear larger, giving the cells a 'wine glass' (goblet) appearance. The surface epithelium is composed of a mixture of eosinophilic columnar cells and fewer mucous cells.

The lower part of the crypts of the ascending colon often contain mucous cells that have a reticulated appearance (Fig. 4.1); such an appearance is uncommon at other sites. Compared to the rest of the large intestine, the rectum appears to have many more mucous cells, both in the crypts as well as in the surface in between the crypts (Fig. 4.2).

The lymphoid cells in the large intestine are often aggregated into lymphoid follicles. These may be seen in the submucosa beneath the muscularis mucosae, or they may be present as confluent masses on both sides of the muscularis mucosae or entirely in the lamina propria. Cells in the basal part of the crypts immediately adjacent to these lymphoid aggregates frequently show decreased amounts of mucus, cytoplasmic basophilia and an increased nucleo-cytoplasmic ratio (Fig. 4.3). Rarely, these crypts may be seen within the lymphoid aggregates. When

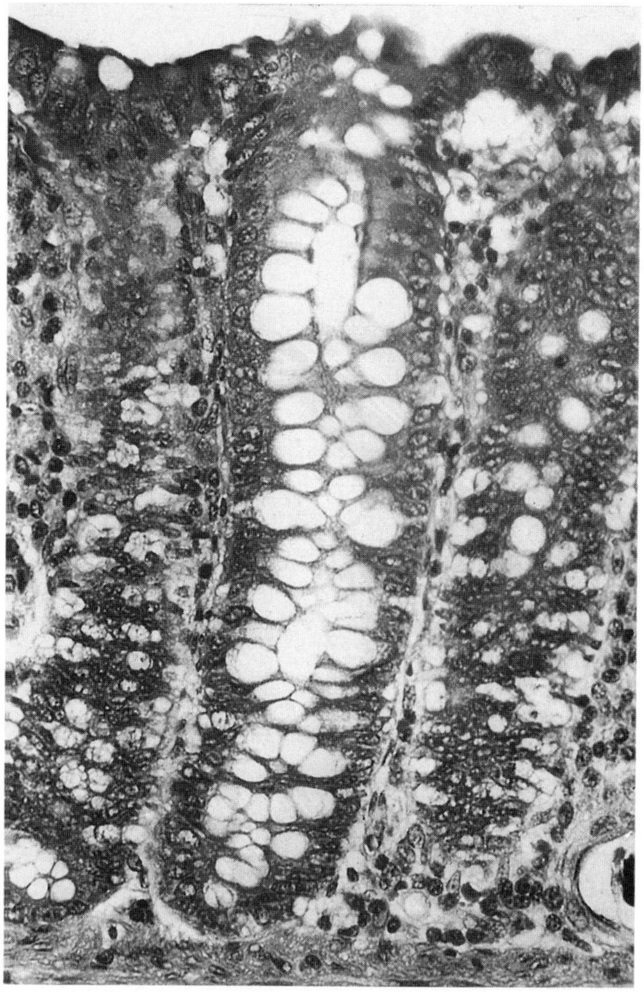

Fig. 4.1 Ascending colon: the crypts are straight and test-tube shaped. MC at the base of the crypts have a reticulated appearance. The granules are small compared to large homogeneous clear granules in the upper crypt. (H&E, ×940)

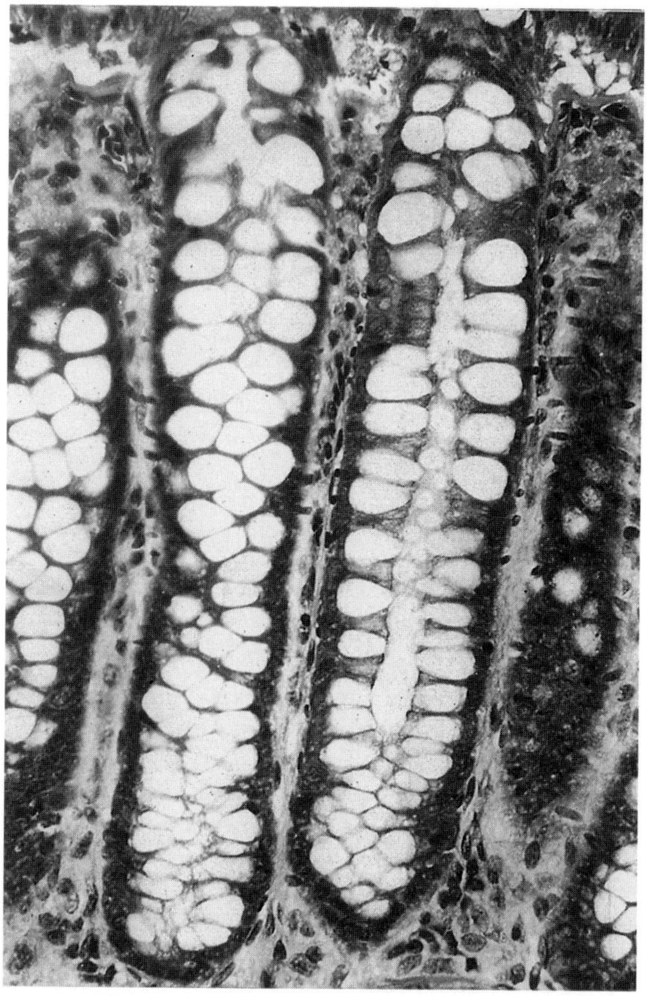

Fig. 4.2 Rectum: note the increased number of MC and their uniform distribution throughout the crypt as compared to the ascending colon. (H&E, ×940)

the lymphoid follicles extend from the mucosa to the submucosa, the crypts also extend into the submucosa, forming so-called lympho-glandular complexes. It has been suggested that they are involved in carcinogenesis[11] and although this is speculative, similar changes are described in rats given suboptimal doses of the carcinogen azoxymethane.[12]

Histochemistry

Alcian blue–periodic acid Schiff preparations of ascending colon reveal purple, magenta and blue cells, indicating the presence of weakly acidic, neutral and strongly acidic mucin, respectively. In the distal colon and rectum there are fewer magenta cells and more blue cells (see Table 4.1). Many mucous cells reveal heterogeneous staining even within the same cell. In sharp contrast to the ascending colon, the rectum usually shows blue staining acidic mucopolysaccharide in all mucous cells.

The columnar cells in the surface that appear eosinophilic in H & E preparations show minute vacuoles of magenta coloured neutral mucin in all the segments of the large intestine, including the rectum. Thus, these cells appear to represent mucous cells with a depleted mucus content. In differentiating between the sialomucin and sulphomucin, the high iron diamine alcian blue method can be used. It demonstrates that the acidic mucin of the epithelium of the large intestine is predominantly sulphomucin. A trace amount of sialomucin may occasionally be seen in the ascending colon and rarely in the transverse colon. However, sialomucin is rarely detected in the descending colon and rectum of normal humans.

Lectin binding properties (see also Ch. 7)

The binding of Ulex europaeus agglutinin (UEA-1), specific for alpha-fucosyl residues, is seen only in the goblet cells of the caecum, ascending and transverse colon and

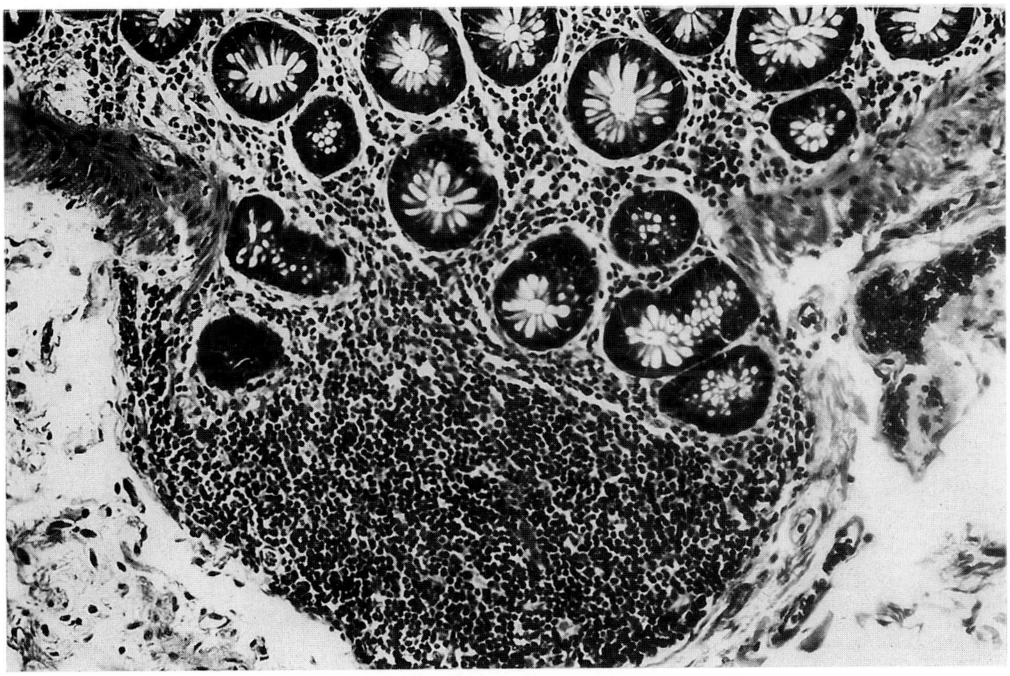

Fig. 4.3 Lymphoid follicle in the mucosa. Note that the cells of the crypt in close contact with the lymphoid aggregate show increased basophilia. (H&E, ×370).

is absent from the distal colon and rectum.[13] Binding of Dolichos biflorus agglutinin (DBA) to galNAc residues in the proximal colon occurs to goblet cells in the upper crypts, and in the descending colon, sigmoid colon and rectum the binding is progressively more uniform throughout the crypt.[14]

Whilst peanut agglutinin (PNA) does not bind with the normal epithelium, a variable binding occurs with malignant and premalignant lesions of the large intestine and to ostensibly normal mucosa in colons resected for carcinoma.[15] This is in support of earlier observations that the epithelium remote from a carcinoma may be abnormal.[6,16] These abnormalities are comparable to those induced in the colon of rats using carcinogenic agents[17,18] and are also in keeping with changes in mucin and the distribution of certain blood group antigens which occur with the malignant process.[19,20]

Carcino-embryonic antigen (CEA)

Contrary to the previously published reports of the presence of CEA in normal epithelium of the human large intestine as well as in cancer,[21–24] the presence of CEA in normal epithelium is an artefact of fixation (personal observation). Formaldehyde or, yet better, 4% formaldehyde + 1% glutaraldehyde fixation eliminates the diffuse CEA immunoreactivity in normal epithelium seen with other fixatives while preserving the immunoreactivity of cells in 36% of adenocarcinomas (personal observation).

Table 4.1 Morphological and histochemical differences between the various segments of the large intestine (adapted from Shamsuddin et al[31]).

	Ascending colon	Transverse colon	Descending colon	Rectum mucin
'Neutral'	++++	+++	++	+/0
Acidic	+/0	++	+++	++++
Sialomucin	+	+/0	+/0	+/0
Sulphomucin	+++	++++	++++	++++
Goblet-type MC	++	+++	+++	++++
Apical vesicles in MC	Markedly electron dense	Moderately electron dense	Electron lucent	Electron lucent
Endocrine	+	+	+	+++

0 — not detected; + — trace amount or few in number; ++++ — large amount or numerous in number.

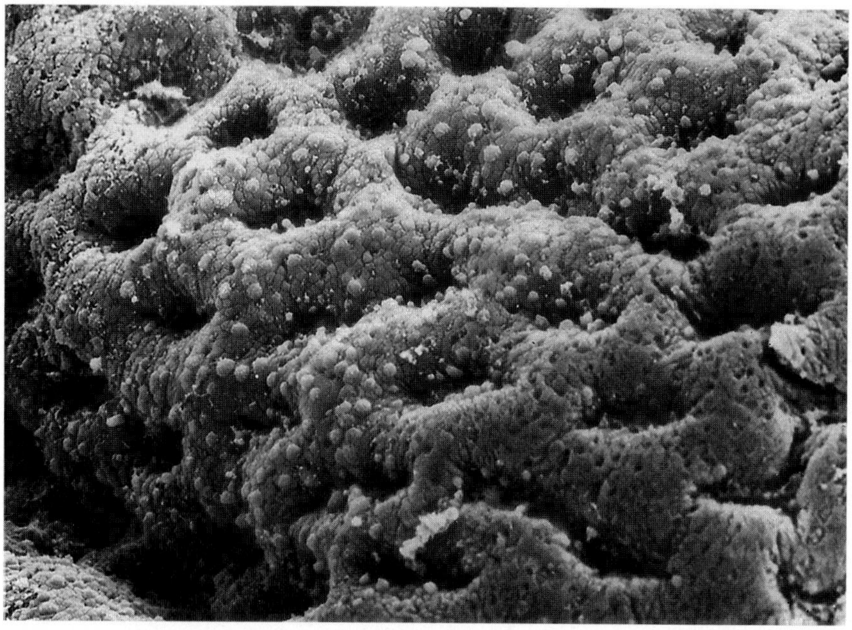

Fig. 4.4 Descending colon: morphology of luminal surface of the large bowel. The pits are the openings of the individual crypts. The epithelial cells in between the crypts appear as ridges. (SEM, ×325)

SCANNING ELECTRON MICROSCOPY

At low magnification, the surface of the large intestinal epithelium shows a fairly regular pattern, with prominent crypt openings giving a honeycomb appearance (Fig. 4.4). In the human, each crypt is estimated to contain approximately 2250 cells and there are approximately 20 crypts per 10 000 μm^2 area. At high magnification, two types of cell surface characteristics are observed. The predominant type is that of the columnar cell with uniform microvilli. The less common type is that of the goblet type of mucous cell (Fig. 4.5). These often intrude into the lumen, and their surface has rounded bleb-like configurations representing the mucous vacuoles. A variable number of microvilli are seen in mucous cells. Transitional forms of cells partly showing the surface characteristics of the columnar cell and partly showing mucous vacuoles can often also be identified (Fig. 4.5). These cells provide further morphological evidence that the mucous and columnar cells are merely two stages of a single type of cell. Occasionally, the surface epithelium shows empty pits which are the site of cell exfoliation (Fig. 4.5). Differences in the surface patterns between various segments of large intestine are

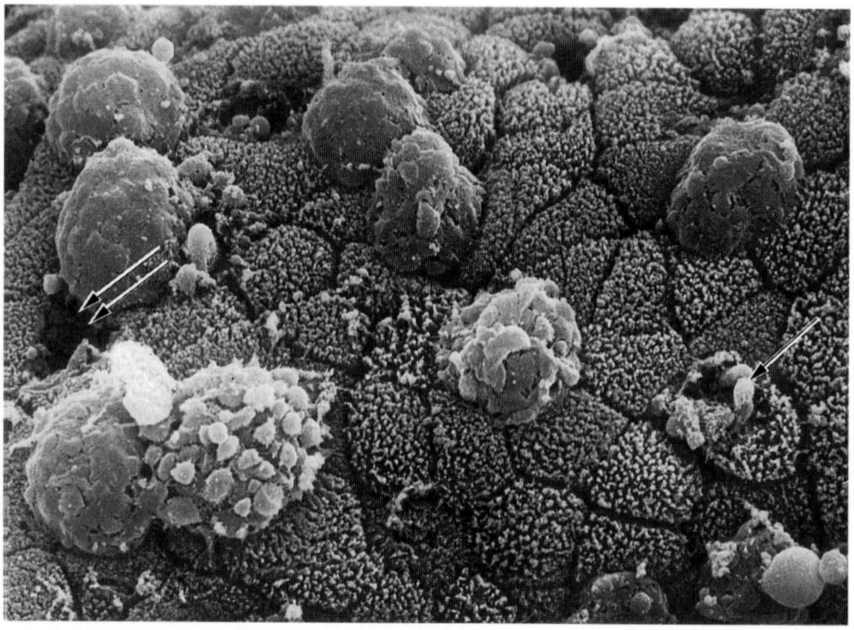

Fig. 4.5 Descending colon: higher magnification view of the surface epithelium. The majority of the cells are CC, being polygonal in shape with uniform fine microvilli. The goblet-type MC are protruding above the surface and the mucous granules appear as blebs. A transitional form of cell showing both uniform microvilli and disrupted mucous vacuoles is seen at the right (arrow). The empty pit at the left (double arrows) is the hallmark of cell exfoliation. (SEM, ×2925)

not observed. However, mucosa sampled from surgical specimens resected for carcinoma occasionally shows an irregular surface morphology distinctly different from the normal honeycomb. It is of some interest that rare instances of non-polypoid carcinoma-in-situ may be visible by surface viewing at endoscopy.[25]

TRANSMISSION ELECTRON MICROSCOPY

The normal large intestinal epithelium contains three basic cell types: undifferentiated cell (UC), mucous cell (MC) and endocrine cell (EC). These same cell types are seen in all the segments, but their proportion, degree of differentiation and cytoplasmic content vary depending on their position in the epithelium.

Crypts: The crypt cells are mostly mucous secreting cells, but a few UC and EC are also seen. The EC are discussed in Chapter 6.

Undifferentiated cell

The UC are located towards the basal aspect of the crypts, and usually lie on the basement membrane, not reaching the crypt lumen. UC have a rounded shape and cytoplasm which is usually electron lucent. The cytoplasm contains only a few polysomes and one or two mitochondria. The nucleus is markedly indented with a convoluted nuclear envelope and prominent nucleoli. The first signs of differentiation to MC or EC are the acquisition of Golgi and RER or dense core secretory granules, respectively.

Mucous cell

The MC population shows marked variations in degree of differentiation. At the very early stage, they contain a few profiles of RER and Golgi, and their cytoplasm becomes progressively electron dense. Mucous granules of various sizes and density are later seen in these cells which appear to undergo cycles of mucus accumulation and discharge. Discharge seems to occur only when the cells become hyperdistended with mucin. During the process of discharge, individual mucous granules coalesce, their partitioning membranes disappear and the mucus assumes a fibrillar appearance. Mucous granules showing widely different densities are commonly seen in the ascending and

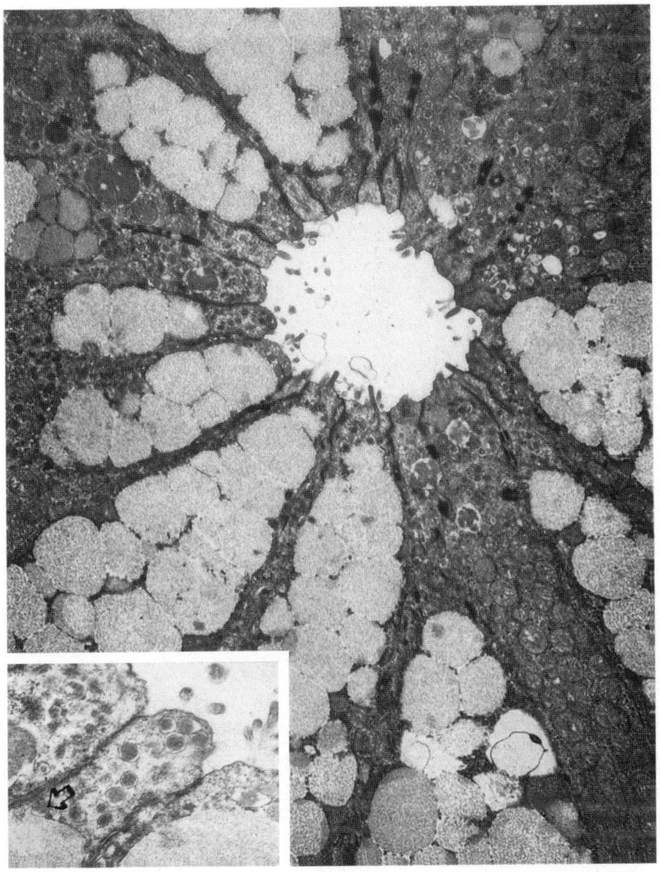

Fig. 4.6 Ascending colon: low magnification picture of cross section of a crypt. Note abundant MC, dense apical granules in MC and heterogeneous mucus. (TEM, ×4300)
Inset: Dense granules in the same cell with mucous granules. A dense granule is seen in the process of fusion with a mucous granule (arrow). (TEM, ×16 250)

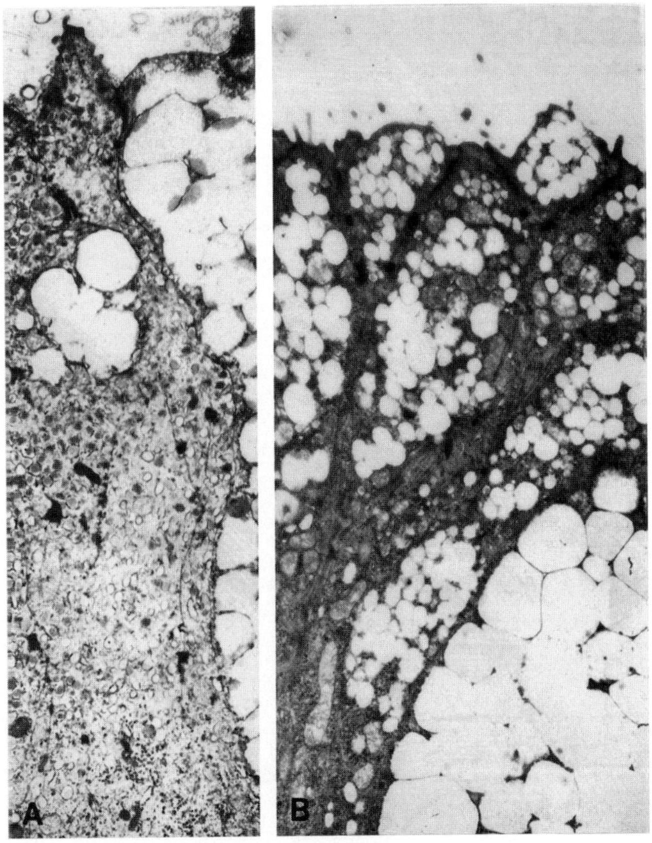

Fig. 4.7 A Transverse colon: electron dense apical granules in mucous cells. (TEM, ×4758) **B** Rectum: clear apical granules in MC of rectum with transitional forms and more dense mucous granules. Compare with the denser granules of the ascending colon (Fig. 4.6). (TEM, ×5260)

transverse colon. A frequent appearance is the presence of aggregates of small granules in the apical cytoplasm. The number of these seems to be inversely proportional to the number of larger more usual mucous granules, i.e. the more of the latter there are, the fewer are the former. These small granules are seen in MC of all segments of the large intestine. They are moderately or markedly electron dense in the ascending colon (Fig. 4.6) and less so in the transverse and descending colon. In striking contrast to the ascending colon, they are electron lucent in the rectum and appear as vesicles (Fig. 4.7). They are surrounded by a trilaminar membrane having the same thickness as the apical plasma membrane and vary in size from 200 to 650 nm in diameter. Occasionally they are seen to coalesce with the larger mucous granules (Fig. 4.6 inset). In resin embedded thin sections using an appropriate method[10] they are shown to contain mucosubstances, as are the larger granules.

The nuclei are usually situated at the basal part of the cell, the lateral plasma membranes interdigitate and the apical plasma membrane shows a variable configuration depending on the amount of mucus present in the cell. When cells are distended with mucus, the apical plasma membrane flattens and exhibits few or no microvilli. On the other hand, when there are only a few mucous granules, the apical plasma membranes form finger-like microvilli, which are often uniform in size and shape.

Figure 4.8 shows mucous cells stained for mucin type in the ascending colon and rectum.

THE SURFACE EPITHELIUM

The surface epithelium which lies between the crypts contains between 5 and 10 cells. In the past the majority of these have been called absorptive cells, but they are probably senescent mucous cells which, because they are

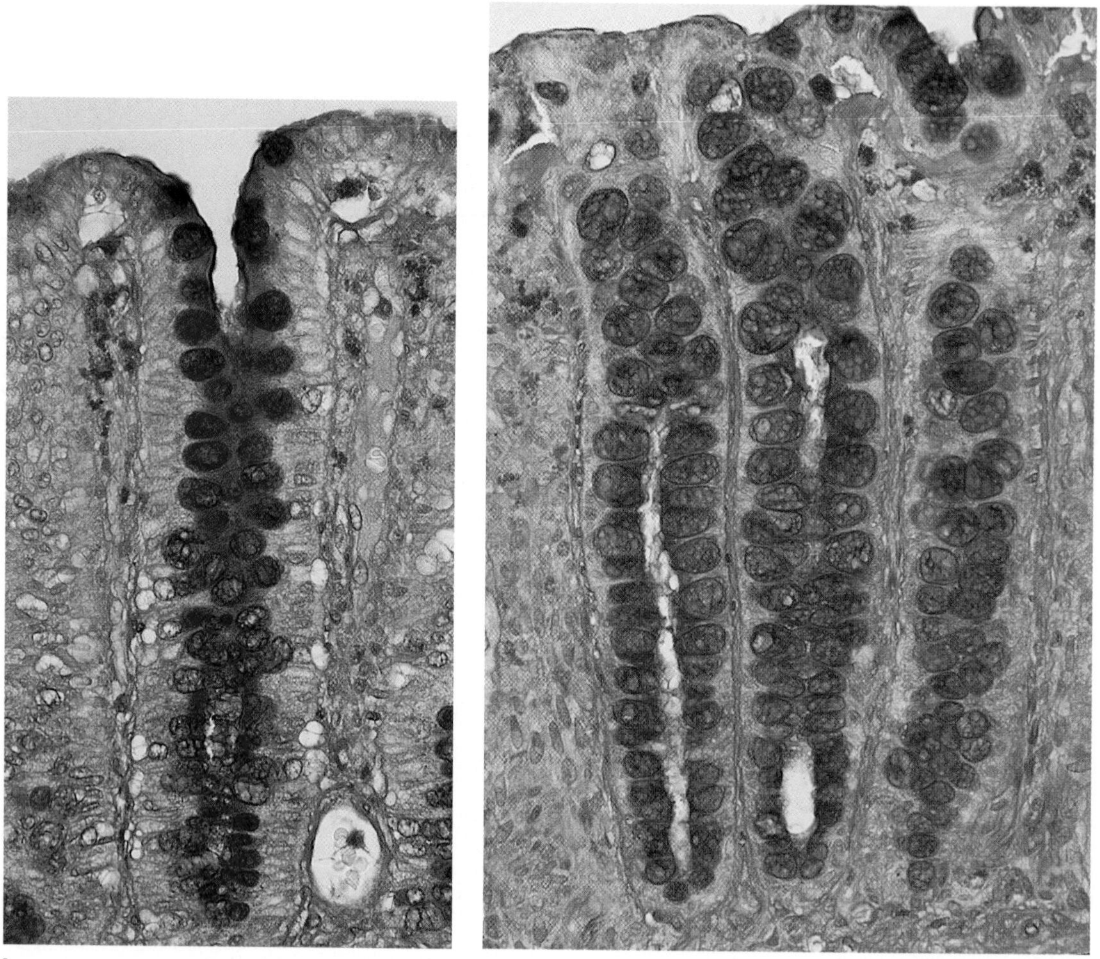

A B

Fig. 4.8 A Ascending colon. The mucous cells contain predominantly magenta neutral mucin with some purple mixed neutral and acid mucin. The surface cells show minute vesicles of magenta neutral mucin. (Alcian blue–PAS stain, ×1094) **B** Rectum. Here the mucous cells contain predominantly blue acidic mucin. Minute amounts of magenta neutral mucin can be seen in the surface cells. (Alcian blue–PAS stain, ×1094) somewhat morphologically different from active mucous cells, are here designated columnar cells (CC).

Columnar cell

The CC have slender elongated cytoplasm with basal rounded nuclei and abundant supranuclear Golgi, mitochondria, some profiles of RER and free polysomes. The apical part of the cytoplasm contains numerous clear secretory granules (200–300 nm), microfilaments (6–8 nm), a well-developed terminal web and microvillous core rootlets. They have the usual organelles for mucus production and indeed, mucus has been demonstrated in them.[26] They are probably senescent MC, which will soon be extruded from the surface. The CC can be divided into two types: electron lucent or light cells and electron dense or dark cells. The dark cells may be the form which immediately follows complete discharge of mucus, the density of the cytoplasm corresponding to that of the fully developed goblet-type MC. The light cells appear to represent a later stage of the dark cell. The number of surface dark cells seems to be highest in the rectum, which correlates with the high number of MC in that region.

The CC are situated on the basal lamina and there are few basal plasma membrane infoldings. This contrasts with the lateral plasma membrane which shows extensive interdigitations and no intercellular spaces. The apical plasma membrane is thrown into regular uniform microvilli that are surrounded by the 'fuzzy coat' or glycocalyx. Small 30–100 nm vesicles are seen at the cell surface closely associated with the microvilli. They are limited by a unit membrane measuring 9 nm in thickness and contain glycocalyx-like material.[4] They are thus called glycocalyceal bodies and probably have a pinocytotic origin. In the rectal mucosa, some of the CC also show membrane bound bodies which were first reported by Biempica et al[27] to be different from secondary lysosomes and multivesicular bodies. These structures are of the same size as mitochondria and are bound by two layers of membrane, an inner and an outer. Within these are elongated rod-shaped structures of the same thickness as the cristae of adjacent mitochondria. In some instances, transitional forms between mitochondria and these structures are observed and they are now regarded as altered mitochondria.

CELL TURNOVER

Cell division in the normal large bowel epithelium is restricted to the lower two-thirds of the crypts where occasional mitotic figures are seen (Fig. 4.9). The cells in mitosis are either undifferentiated or show some apical vesicles and short strands of RER indicative of an early MC. It is the midportion of the surface epithelium farthest

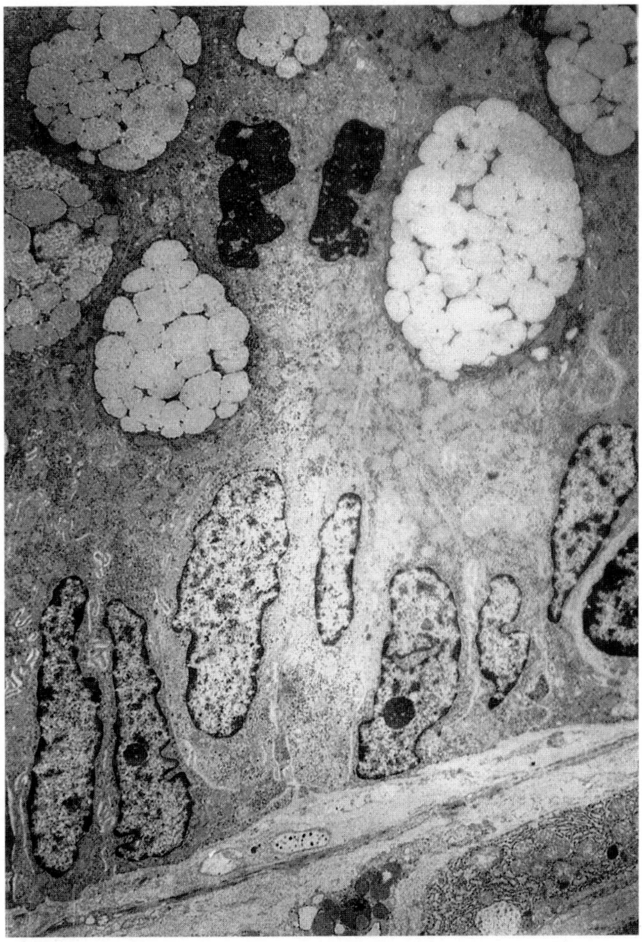

Fig. 4.9 Cell division: a relatively undifferentiated cell is seen in cell division. (TEM, ×4375)

from the crypt openings which is the putative site for the exfoliation of cells. For it is here that the most dedifferentiated forms of MC occur. Occasional cells show a homogeneous appearance of the cytoplasm, widened lateral intercellular spaces, disrupted cell junctions and marked irregularities of the surface plasma membrane. The cytoplasm may be electron lucent or electron dense. Finally, the cell seems to lose all of its attachments with its neighbours, its plasma membranes disintegrate, the cell exfoliates and leaves an empty V-shaped gap or space as seen by TEM (Figs 4.10, 4.11) and an empty pit as seen by SEM (Fig. 4.5). The mitochondria of such a cell show subtle alteration of the matrix density. However, there is no evidence of irreversible cell injury such as high amplitude swelling with flocculent densities. Thus, it appears that the exfoliating cells are morphologically viable during the process of extrusion from the surface.

The process of cell death and disintegration must, therefore, take place after exfoliation. In Fischer 344 rats, however, some of the exfoliating cells show evidence of cell death while the cells are still on the surface epithelium.[28]

The variations in the ultrastructural appearances of the

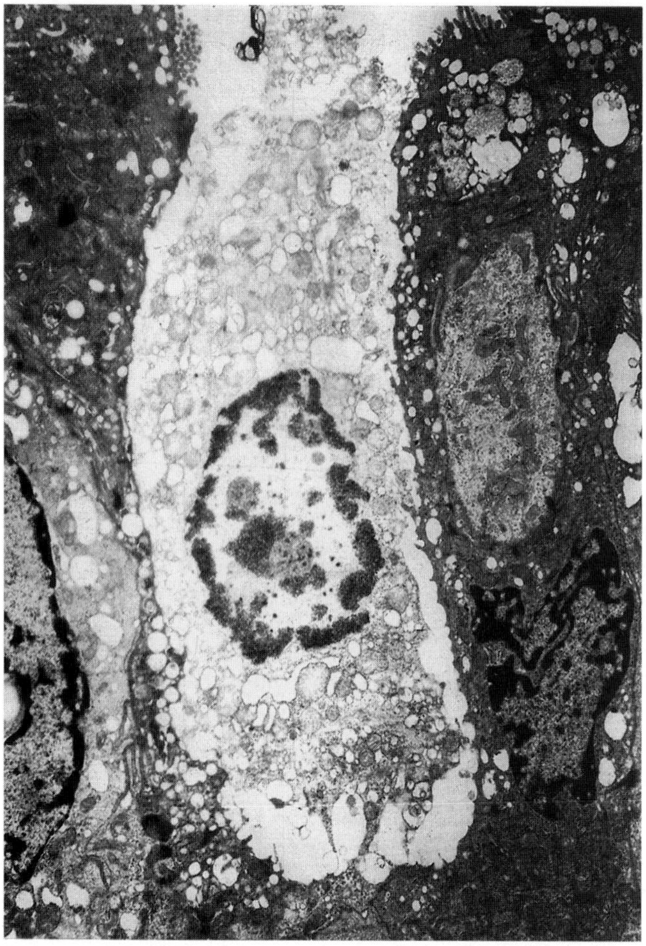

Fig. 4.10 Stages in cell loss: the cell has lost most of its attachments to the adjacent cells. Its membrane is in the process of disintegration. (TEM, ×5530)

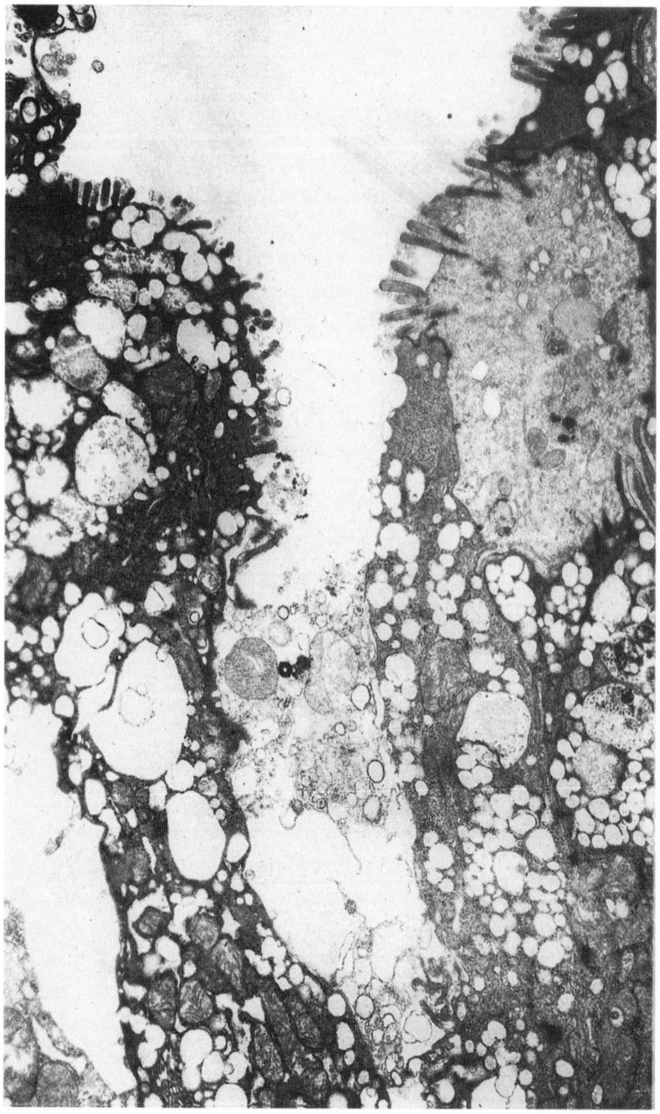

Fig. 4.11 Stages in cell loss: an empty space represents an area of cell exfoliation. A few organelles are all that remain. This space corresponds to the empty pit seen by SEM in Fig. 4.5. (TEM, ×7072)

colonic mucosa dictate that extreme caution be exercised in the interpretation of putative abnormalities. For example, the importance of electron dense bodies in the apical cytoplasm of cells in the mucosa between polyps in polyposis coli patients[29,30] needs to be seen in the light of the variation in the density of such apical granules which occurs in different parts of the normal colon. The same applies to the claim for an increased number of immature cells in the non-polypoid mucosae of these patients.[30] Because of variations in the MC population with site[31] it is crucial that sampling ensures that like is being compared to like.

The appearance of the mucus in MC has also received undue significance because of its wide spectrum. The presence of heterogeneous mucous vacuoles, primarily due to focal increased density, has been associated with neoplastic and preneoplastic conditions such as polyps[32] and the mucosa of familial polyposis.[29,30] However, heterogeneous mucous vacuoles are not uncommon, particularly in ascending and transverse colon, whereas they are rare in the rectal mucosa.[31]

There seems to be little doubt that in the past there was a tendency to subdivide epithelial cells of the large intestine into several different types. Latterly the opposite direction has been taken, but it is pertinent that as long ago as 1960 Florey[33] demonstrated that goblet cells after discharge of their mucus came to resemble so-called absorptive cells. Similarly Chang and Leblond[34] had demonstrated that in the mouse, 'absorptive cells' were derived from mucous cells. Further work on the Fischer rats[28] and two strains of mice[35] supports these observations.

The concept of the absorptive cell possibly arose because of a principal function of the large intestinal mucosa in the absorption of water and electrolytes. However, the task of absorbing 500–600 ml of fluid/day seems at variance with the relatively small number of so-called absorptive cells. Observations of phagocytosis of bacteria by the

MC of mouse colon[35] raise the possibility that the function of 'absorption' may not necessarily be restricted to the so-called absorptive cells. The retention of the term columnar cell serves as a reminder that a definitive functional analysis of these cells is still required. The dark and light CC on the surface, for example, seem to represent two stages of the same cell. The density of the cytoplasm of a dark cell is the same as that of a goblet-type MC. It is at least conceivable that the increased volume of mucus results in extraction of water from the cytosol of goblet cells, causing increased electron density. Subsequent to mucus discharge, these cells may retain their increased electron density only until they absorb sufficient water from the bowel lumen to become electron lucent again. Since the contents of the ascending colon are more fluid, the sparsity of dark cells in this region may denote that once having discharged, the MC is able to absorb water quickly. In the rectum, on the other hand, the need to absorb water is much less and this would be in keeping with the high proportion of MC in the mucosa and an increased number of dark CC in the surface epithelium.

The interrelationship of the various cell types in the large intestinal mucosa is shown in Figure 4.12.

STEM CELLS AND DIFFERENTIATION

Colonic epithelial stem cells (undifferentiated cells) of the basal portions of the crypts comprise the proliferative compartment and a pluripotent capability for differentiation, including pathways toward transporting epithelial cells, goblet cells (both called mucous cells) and neuroendocrine cells. Another potential differentiation pathway is toward Paneth cells, which are poorly understood.[36] Stem cells generally are defined by several features. They have a high capacity for self-renewal and a very low probability for differentiation. They are capable of asymmetric division, yielding one daughter that remains a stem cell (assuring self-maintenance) while the other undergoes an irreversible commitment to enter a differentiation pathway. Finally, they are capable of retaining their position in a particular environment or niche. A stem cell may be multipotent or omnipotent, capable of giving rise to multiple lineages or a single lineage.[37]

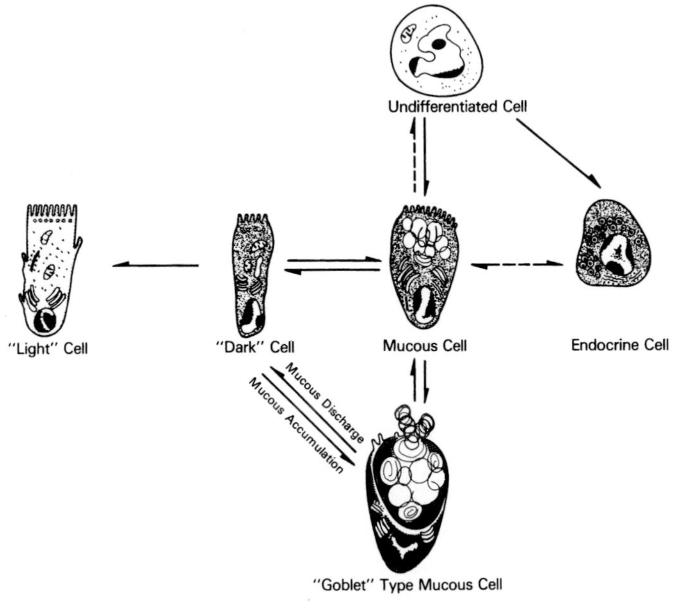

Fig. 4.12 Inter-relationship between large intestinal epithelial cells.

The proliferation and differentiation of stem cells

The proliferative capacity of the adult gut is enormous. Early data have shown that each crypt in the ascending colon of the mouse contains about 100 proliferating cells and produces 6 cells per hour, whereas in the distal colon each crypt contains approximately 200 proliferating cells that yield 21 cells per crypt per hour.[38] Recent work suggests that in the mouse there is a total of between 300–450 cells per crypt depending on the location. The cell cycle of the bulk of the crypt cells appears to be between 24–26 hours, but the stem cells cycle more slowly, probably with a cell cycle time of >36 hours.[39,40]

The number of stem cells per crypt, which will also determine the number of proliferative transit generations, is somewhat uncertain for the human. However, for the mouse colon the number probably lies between one to four per crypt; this would mean that there are between five and nine dividing transit generations (i.e. amplifying divisions).[41] Based on a study of somatic mutation in colonic mucosa, Williams et al proposed a stem cell niche theory which states that crypts are maintained by essentially a single stem cell dividing every 1–3 weeks.[42]

Cell differentiation in the colon is associated with migration. Cells migrate from each colonic crypt (gland) to a hexagonal-shaped area of surface epithelial cells that surround the orifice of each gland, i.e. enterocytes, goblet and enteroendocrine cells differentiate and mature during an orderly migration that take them from the crypt to the orifice of each gland. It is not known whether one or more adjacent colonic crypts supply cells to the same area.[43]

Colon epithelial cell markers

Analysis of cell population in the colonic mucosa remains primarily morphological and is restricted to a limited number of cell types, including the absorptive epithelial cell, the goblet cell and scattered enteroendocrine populations. It would be of enormous value to generate a panel of monoclonal antibodies that recognize intermediate cell populations, thus permitting facile discrimination between, e.g. a stem cell population, a newly derived daughter cell, cells entering quiescence and populations that are fully differentiated. With the availability of such markers, many critical studies could be performed, including elucidation of the differentiation/maturation lineages responsible for generating cell types with distinct end-cell functions and detailed analysis of the cellular composition of colorectal tumors at different stages in their evolution.[44–49]

General organotypic marker

A variety of antibodies have been useful for organotypic characterization of the colon. These include antibodies against mucins, villin, CEA and various glycoproteins, such as detected by monoclonal antibodies GNM or 5E113, etc.[50–52] Many types of glycoproteins are organotypic for the colon. Mucins are very large complex molecules that play a major role in protecting the mucosa. Some aspects of their biochemical properties have been discussed by Byrd et al.[53] Price et al[49] present a monoclonal antibody GL-013 against this mucin, the epitope being specific to goblet cells of the gastrointestinal tract. Antibodies against other specific glycoproteins, such as 6NM or 5E113 antigens, detect colon specific antigens in normal and malignant tissues, as well as cultured cells. Such organotypic antibodies are important in verifying the origin of the cells being cultured in vitro, especially when culture extends over long periods.[46,50–52]

Epithelial cell typic markers

Some antibodies have been shown to be specific for particular epithelial cell types. Villin, which is normally tightly associated with actin, intestinal fibrin and a 110 kDa calmodulin complex, has Mg^{2+}–ATPase activity and is almost exclusively associated with microvilli.[54] It is an excellent marker for absorptive enterocytes, proximal renal tubules, a small number of other transporting cell types and normal or malignant cells of the small intestine and colon. Normal colon and ileal cells preferentially express villin on their luminal, brush border surface, although diffuse cytoplasmic staining is seen in some crypt cells.[55] Sucrase–isomaltose is often used as a marker for differentiated enterocytes, associated with brush borders of absorptive cells.[56]

The most important known function of goblet cells is secretion of mucin, which not only acts as lubricant for the passage of luminal contents, but also provides a physical barrier to bacterial or viral ingress. There are qualitative and quantitative changes in the goblet cell population and mucin production during some colonic diseases such as ulcerative colitis and colon cancer. A variety of monoclonal antibodies against goblet cells have been found which appear to be specific for the mucin antigens of goblet cells.[45,46,49]

Neuroendocrine (NE) cells have distinctive ultrastructural inclusions and synthesize a variety of hormones, but these features are not easily discernible by light microscopy. The numbers and types of NE cells vary significantly at different sites in the gut, and there are greater number of NE cells in the distal colon than in the proximal colon.[36] The usual methods for demonstrating NE cells in the gut are the acidified toluidine blue and that of Grimelius but markers such as chromagranin or neuron-specific enolase, have also proved use-ful in demonstrating the NE cells irrespective of their location.[57]

Models for colon epithelial cell differentiation in vitro

Long-term culture of normal human colonic epithelial cells in vitro

The data on cell proliferation, differentiation and renewal in the human colonic crypts indicate that the vast majority of the crypt cells are terminally differentiated to mucin-producing goblet cells or surface absorptive cells, and they lose their ability to divide; only a few stem cells retain the ability to divide.[31] It has been observed in organ culture models that soon after placement of explants in the culture media, the majority of the terminally differentiated cells exfoliate and die. From the few surviving stem cells, the crypts repopulate and viable epithelial cells are seen in about a week.[58]

At 5 months the epithelial nature of these cells is shown by light and electron microscopic morphology and by keratin immunoreactivity and mucin histochemistry.[59] These successful long-term cultures will contribute to better understanding of the function of normal cells, their nutritional requirements, growth factors, cell metabolism and cell differentiation, as well as pathogenesis of human colon diseases.

Colon organ culture in vitro

In long-term organ culture of the colon in vitro the explants remain viable for up to 9 weeks.[58] Although the colonic crypts appear distorted, preservation of crypt architecture is visible up to 6 weeks. Explants sampled at 9 weeks do not show crypts, but maintain a single layer of columnar cells that prove to be colonic by their ultrastructural morphology, histochemical properties of mucin production and the incorporation of tritiated thymidine and leucine. In general, human colonic explants lose their normal morphological architecture during extended in vitro culture. Valerio et al,[60] Shimosato et al[61] and Sakamoto et al[62] reported that following short-term organ culture, various epithelia, including that from the colon, can be xenotransplanted into athymic nude mice and maintained for a prolonged period. These models may have potential for studies of human large intestinal epithelial cells.

REFERENCES

1. Warwick R, Williams PL. Gray's Anatomy, 35th British Edition. W. B. Saunders, 1973: 1284–1297.
2. Trump BF, Valigorsky JM, Dees JH, et al. Cellular change in human disease. A new method of pathological analysis. Hum Pathol 1973; 4: 89–109.
3. Filipe MI, Branfoot AC. Abnormal patterns of mucus secretion in apparently normal mucosa of large intestine with carcinoma. Cancer 1974; 34: 282–290.
4. Pittman FE, Pittman JC. An electron microscopic study of the epithelium of normal human sigmoid colonic mucosa. Gut 1966; 7: 644–661.
5. Kaye GI, Fenoglio CM, Pascal RR, Lane N. Comparative electron microscopic features of normal, hyperplastic and adenomatous human colonic epithelium. Gastroenterology 1973; 64: 926–945.
6. Shamsuddin AKM, Weiss L, Phelps PC, Trump BF. Colon epithelium. IV. Human colon mucosa adjacent to and remote from carcinoma of the colon. JNCI 1981; 66: 413–419.
7. McDowell EM, Trump BF. Histologic fixative suitable for diagnostic light and electron microscopy. Arch Pathol Lab Med 1976; 100: 405–414.
8. Kuhlmann WD, Peschke P, Wurster K. Lectin-peroxidase conjugates in histopathology of gastrointestinal mucosa. Virchows Archiv (A) 1983; 298: 319–328.
9. Kelley RO, Dekker RAF, Bluemink JG. Ligand-mediated osmium binding: Its application in coating biological specimens for scanning electron microscopy. J Ultrastruct Res 1973; 45: 254–258.
10. Thiery JP. Mise en evidence des polysaccharides sur coupes fines en microscopie electronique. J Microsc 1967; 6: 987–1041.
11. Oohara T, Ogino A, Tohma H. Microscopic adenoma in nonpolyposis coli: Incidence and relation to basal cells and lymphoid follicles. Dis Colon Rectum 1981; 24: 120–126.
12. Shamsuddin AKM, Hogan ML. Large intestinal carcinogenesis. II. Histogenesis and unusual features of low dose azoxymethane induced carcinomas in Fischer 344 rats. JNCI 1984; 73: 1297–1305.
13. Yonezawa S, Nakamura T, Tanaka S, Sato E. Glycoconjugate with Ulex europaeus agglutinin-I-binding sites in normal mucosa, adenoma and carcinoma of the human large bowel. JNCI 1982; 69: 777–785.
14. Bresalier RS, Boland CR, Kim YS. Regional differences in normal and cancer-associated glycoconjugates of the human colon. JNCI 1985; 75: 249–260.
15. Xu H, Sakamoto K, Shamsuddin A M. Detection of the tumour marker D-galactose-β[1-3]-N-acetyl-D-galactosamine in colon cancer and precancer. Arch Path Lab Med 1992; 116: 1234–1238.
16. Lev R, Grover R. Precursors of human colon carcinoma: a serial section study of colectomy specimens. Cancer 1981; 47: 2007–2015.
17. Shamsuddin AKM, Trump BF. Colon epithelium. II. In vivo studies of colon carcinogenesis. Light microscopic, histochemical and ultrastructural studies of histogenesis of azoxymethane-induced colon carcinomas in Fischer 344 rats. JNCI 1981; 66: 389–401.
18. Shamsuddin AKM, Trump BF. Colon epithelium. III. In vitro studies of colon carcinogenesis in Fischer 344 rats. N-methyl-N-nitro-N-nitrosoguanidine induced changes in colon epithelium in explant culture. JNCI 1981; 66: 403–411.
19. Boland CR, Montgomery CK, Kim YS. Alterations in colonic mucin occurring with cellular differentiation and malignant transformation. Proc Natl Acad Sci USA 1982; 79: 2051–2055.
20. Yuan M, Itzkowitz SH, Palekar A et al. Distribution of blood group antigens A, B, H, Lea and Leb in normal, fetal and malignant colonic tissue. Cancer Res 1985; 45: 4499–4551.
21. Huitric E, Laumonier R, Burtin P, et al. An optical and ultrastructural study of the localization of carcinoembryonic antigens (CEA) in normal and cancerous human rectocolonic mucosa. Lab Invest 1976; 34: 97–107.
22. Wagener C, Csaszar H, Totovic V, et al. A highly sensitive method for the demonstration of carcinoembryonic antigen in normal and neoplastic colonic tissue. Histochemistry 1978; 58: 1–11.
23. Fritsche R, Mach JP. Isolation and characterization of carcinoembryonic antigen (CEA) extracted from normal human colon mucosa. Immunochemistry 1977; 14: 119–127.
24. Klein PJ, Osmers R, Vierbuchen M, et al. The importance of lectin binding sites and carcinoembryonic antigen with regard to normal, hyperplastic, adenomatous and carcinomatous colonic mucosa. Recent Results Cancer Res 1981; 79: 1–9.
25. Shamsuddin AKM, Kato Y, Kunishima N, Sugano H, Trump BF. Carcinoma in situ in flat mucosa of large intestine. Report of a case with significance in strategies for early detection. Cancer 1985; 56: 2849–2854.
26. Dawson PA, Filipe MI. An ultrastructural application of silver methenamine to the study of mucin changes in the colonic mucosa adjacent to and remote from carcinoma. Histochem J 1976; 8: 143–158.
27. Biempica L, Sternlieb I, Sohn HB, Ali M. R-bodies of human rectal epithelial cells. Arch Pathol Lab Med 1976; 100: 78–80.
28. Shamsuddin AKM, Trump BF. Colonic epithelium. I. Light microscopic, histochemical and ultrastructural features of normal colon epithelium of male Fischer 344 rats. JNCI 1981; 66: 375–388.
29. Dawson PA, Filipe MI, Bussey HJ. Ultrastructural features of the colonic epithelium in familial polyposis coli. Histopathology 1977; 1: 105–113.
30. Mughal S, Filipe MI. Ultrastructural study of the normal mucosa–adenoma-cancer sequence in the development of familial polyposis coli. JNCI 1978; 60: 753–768.
31. Shamsuddin AKM, Phelps PC, Trump, BF. Human large intestinal epithelium: light microscopy, histochemistry, and ultrastructure. Hum Pathol 1982; 13: 790–803.
32. Spjut HJ, Smith MN. A comparative electron microscopic study of human and rat colonic polyps and carcinomas. Exp Mol Pathol 1967; 6: 11–24.
33. Florey HW. Electron microscopic observations on goblet cells of the rat's colon. Q J Exp Physiol 1960; 45: 329–336.
34. Chang WWL, Leblond PC. Renewal of the epithelium in the descending colon of the mouse. I. Presence of three cell populations, vacuolated-columnar, mucous and argentaffin. Am J Anat 1971; 131: 73–100.
35. Shamsuddin AKM, Elsayed AM. Ultrastructural features of normal mouse colon epithelium: Unique characteristics of a species. J Submicros Cytol 1986; 18: 761–771.
36. Wright, Alison. The Biology of Epithelial Cell Populations. Clarendon, Oxford, 1984.
37. Gordon JI, Gunter H, et al. Studies of intestinal stem cells using normal, chimeric, and transgenic mice. FASEB J 1992; 6: 3039–3050.
38. Sunter JP, Appleton DR, DeRodriguex MSB, et al. A comparison of cell proliferation at different sites within the large bowel of the mouse. J Anat 1979; 129: 833–842.
39. Kellett M, Potten CS, Rew DA. A comparison of in vivo cell proliferation measurements in the intestine of mouse and man: Is the mouse a good model for man? Epithelial Cell Biol 1992; 1: 147–155.
40. Potten CS. Regeneration in epithelial proliferation units as exemplified by small intestine. CIBA Foundation Publ 160. Regeneration of Neuroepithelium. John Wiley, Chichester, pp 54–76.
41. Potten CS, Loeffler M. Stem cells, attributes, cycles, spirals, uncertainties and pitfalls; Lessons for and from the crypt. Development 1990; 110: 1001–1019.
42. Williams GD, Alison P, Lowes D, et al. A stem cell niche theory of intestinal crypt maintenance based on a study of somatic mutation in colonic mucosa. Am J Pathol 1992; 141: 773–776.
43. Schmidt GH et al. Cell migration pathway in the intestinal epithelium: An in situ marker system using mouse aggregation chimeras. Cell 1985; 40: 425–429.
44. Richman PI, Tilley R, Jass JR, et al. Colonic pericrypt sheath cells: Characterization of cell type with new monoclonal antibody. J Clin Pathol 1987; 40: 593–600.
45. Vecchi M, Sikamaki S, Diamond B, et al. Development of a monoclonal antibody specifically reactive to gastrointestinal Goblet cells. Proc Natl Acad Sci USA 1987; 84: 3425–3429.

46. Hughes NR, Walls RS, Newland RC, et al. Antigen expression in normal and neoplastic colonic mucosa; three tissue-specific antigens using monoclonal antibodies to isolate colonic glands. Cancer Res 1986; 46: 2164–2171.
47. Morson BC, Jass JR, Sobin LH. Precancerous lesions of the gastrointestinal tract. A Histological Classification. Bailliere Tindall, Philadelphia, 1985.
48. Yang GY, Price MR. Analysis of monoclonal antibodies for the identification of antigens associated with tumors of the gastrointestinal tract. Anticancer Res 1989; 9: 1707.
49. Price MR, Yang GY, et al. Reactivity of an anti-(human gastric carcinoma) monoclonal antibody with core-related peptides of gastrointestinal mucin. Cancer Immunol Immunother 1991; 33: 80–84.
50. Rutzky LP. The biology of human colon cancer cell lines. Adv Cell Cult 1985; 4: 47–83.
51. Gold DV, Nocera MA, Stephens R, Goldenberg DM, et al. Murine monoclonal antibodies to colon-specific antigen p. Cancer Res 1990; 50: 6405–6409.
52. Gold DV, Ishizaki G, Keller P, Karen LeW, et al. Generation of a monoclonal antibody (Gq) reactive with an organ-specific, tumor–associated epitope of human colon carcinoma. Cancer Res 1989; 49: 6412–6418.
53. Byrd JC, Nardelli J, Siddiqui B, Kim YS. Isolation and characterization of colon cancer mucin from xenografts of LS 174 T cells. Cancer Res 1988; 48: 6678–6685.
54. Conzelman KA, Mooseker MS. The 110-kd protein-calmodulin complex of the intestinal microvillus is an actin-activated Mg ATPase. J Cell Biol 1987; 105:313–324.
55. West AB, Isaac CA, Carboni JM, et al. Localization of villin, a cytoskeletal protein specific to microvilli, in human ileum and colon and in colonic neoplasms. Gastroenterology 1988; 94: 343–352.
56. Hauri HP, Sterchi GG, Bienz D, et al. Expression and intracellular transport of microvillus membrane hydrolases in human intestinal epithelial cells. J Cell Biol 1985; 101: 838–851.
57. Moyer MP, Poste GH. Colon Cancer Cells. 1988, Academic Press, pp 85–136.
58. Shamsuddin AKM. Colon organ culture as a model for carcinogenesis. In: Moyer MP, Poste GH (eds) Colon Cancer Cells, pp 137–153, Academic, San Diego, CA.
59. Baten A, Sakamoto K, Shamsuddin AKM. Long-term culture of normal human colonic epithelia cells in vitro. FASEB J 1992; 6: 2726–2734.
60. Valerio MG, Fineman GL, et al. Long-term survival of normal adult human tissues as xenografts in congenitally athymic nude mice. J Natl Cancer Inst 1981; 66: 849–858.
61. Shimosato Y, Kodama T, et al. Induction of squamous cell carcinoma in human bronchi transplanted into nude mice. Jpn J Cancer Res 1981; 71: 402–407.
62. Sakamoto K, Resau JH, Shamsuddin AKM, et al. Long-term explant culture of human colon and a 3-step transformation model for rat colonic epithelium. Pathobiology 1991; 59: 404–411.

CHAPTER 5

The anal region

F. D. Lee

ANATOMICAL CONSIDERATIONS (See also Chs 17 & 43)

Considerable confusion exists in the literature regarding the definition of the anal canal. Most pathologists, being pragmatists, accept the concept of the 'surgical' canal. By this convention there is broad agreement that the junction between the upper anal canal and rectum is represented by a muscular structure known as the *anorectal ring* which is formed collectively by the proximal edge of the internal anal sphincter, the deep part of the external anal sphincter, and between them the puborectalis portion of the levator ani (Fig. 5.1). Whilst in strict anatomical terms the distal boundary of the anal canal should be located at the level of the groove between the terminal ends of the two sphincters (corresponding to the so-called white line of Hilton), it is usually placed more distally, i.e. at the lower border of the external sphincter (Fig. 5.1).

According to this view the anal canal measures 30–40 mm in length and its boundaries are coterminous with those of the voluntary muscle of the external anal sphincter. It is to be noted that the internal sphincter, consisting of involuntary muscle, represents a distal expansion of the circular component of the muscularis propria of the rectum. The longitudinal component, having fused with fibres of the puborectalis muscle at the anorectal ring, gradually transforms into a fibroelastic septum which passes downwards between the two sphincters and ultimately divides into a series of strands extending towards the mucosal surface beyond the distal edge of the internal sphincter. The most prominent of these strands separates the distal margins of the two sphincters to reach the mucosal surface at the level of the intersphincteric groove (Fig. 5.1). Some of these strands also pass through the internal sphincter more proximally to form a faint muscular band in the submucosa of the distal part of the anal canal.[1]

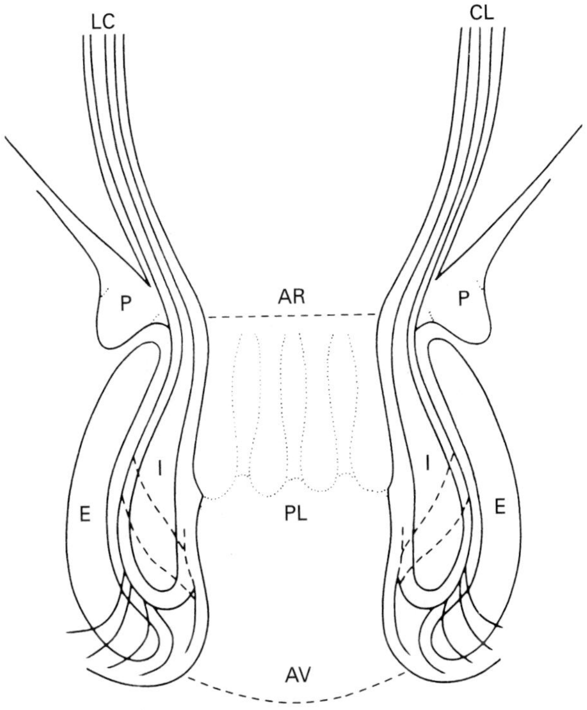

Fig. 5.1 A diagrammatic representation of the anal region in cross section. AR = anorectal ring; PL = pectinate line; AV = anal verge; L = longitudinal muscle of rectum; C = circular muscle of rectum; P = puborectalis muscle; I = internal anal sphincter; E = external anal sphincter.

Acceptance of the above definition also implies that the anal canal has a dual derivation, the upper part being formed from the endoderm of the post-allantoic gut and the lower part from the ectoderm of the anal pit (proctodaeum). There are sound reasons for supposing that the junction between these two parts is a structure usually referred to as the pectinate line.[2] This is also known as the 'dentate line', because it is beset by a series of valve-like structures enclosing small recesses (anal sinuses) and separated by mucosal projections called anal papillae. The valves actually represent the lower edges of depressions between prominent mucosal folds (anal columns) which extend upwards from the pectinate line (Fig. 5.1) and contain radicles of the superior rectal artery and vein which may form arteriovenous complexes, sometimes referred to as 'anal-glomeruli'. These veins, which drain into the portal venous system, also extend distally beyond the pectinate line to anastomose with branches of the systemic venous system at the level of the intersphincteric groove. Abnormal dilatation of venous channels proximal to this level is the cause of internal haemorrhoids. In the normal state they assist in the formation of the so-called anal cushions. These are thought to be of importance in preventing anal incontinence by maintaining effective closure of the anal canal which, in the resting state, is represented by an anteroposterior Y-shaped slit. It is to be noted that the lymphatics draining the anal canal superior to the pectinate line pass mainly to the internal iliac lymph nodes, while lymphatics from the distal anal canal drain into the superficial inguinal nodes.

Histological features

An understanding of the mucosal structure of the anal canal is of particular importance to the histopathologist. Except for a small zone immediately proximal to the pectinate line, the mucosa of the upper part of the anal canal is lined by columnar epithelium similar to that of the rectum. It is, however, notable that in the anal canal, the crypts of Lieberkuhn tend to be somewhat irregular and there is often some fibromuscular thickening of the lamina propria, especially over the anal columns. This is probably due to minor degrees of trauma or prolapse related to the development of internal haemorrhoids (Fig. 5.2). For these reasons, biopsy at this site should be avoided in the investigation of colorectal disease, since it might give a false impression of the overall state of the large intestinal mucosa.

In rare instances the columnar epithelium gives way quite abruptly to nonkeratinizing squamous epithelium a short distance above the pectinate line (PL). More often, however, there is some admixture between the two types of epithelium with tongues of columnar epithelium extending down to the pectinate line; or conversely islands of squamous epithelium being found quite high up on the anal columns. In the great majority of instances, however,

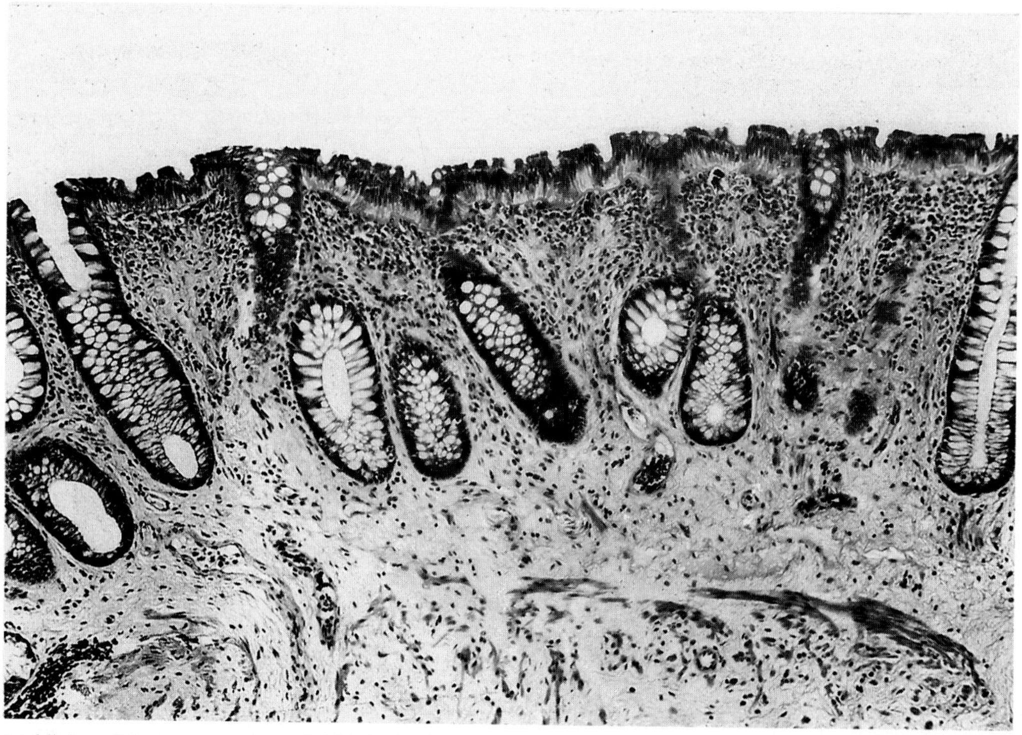

Fig. 5.2 The mucosal lining of the upper anal canal. This is similar to that of the rectum but often shows minor degrees of crypt irregularity and fibromuscular thickening of the lamina propria (×80).

the two main epithelial types are separated by what has been described as the 'anal transitional zone' (ATZ) (Fig. 5.3). This usually starts at the PL and extends proximally for a distance of between 3–20 mm: much less frequently it starts either below or above the PL.[3] The appearance of the epithelium in this zone varies considerably. It is often referred to in its typical form as 'transitional' epithelium which is characterized by a surface layer

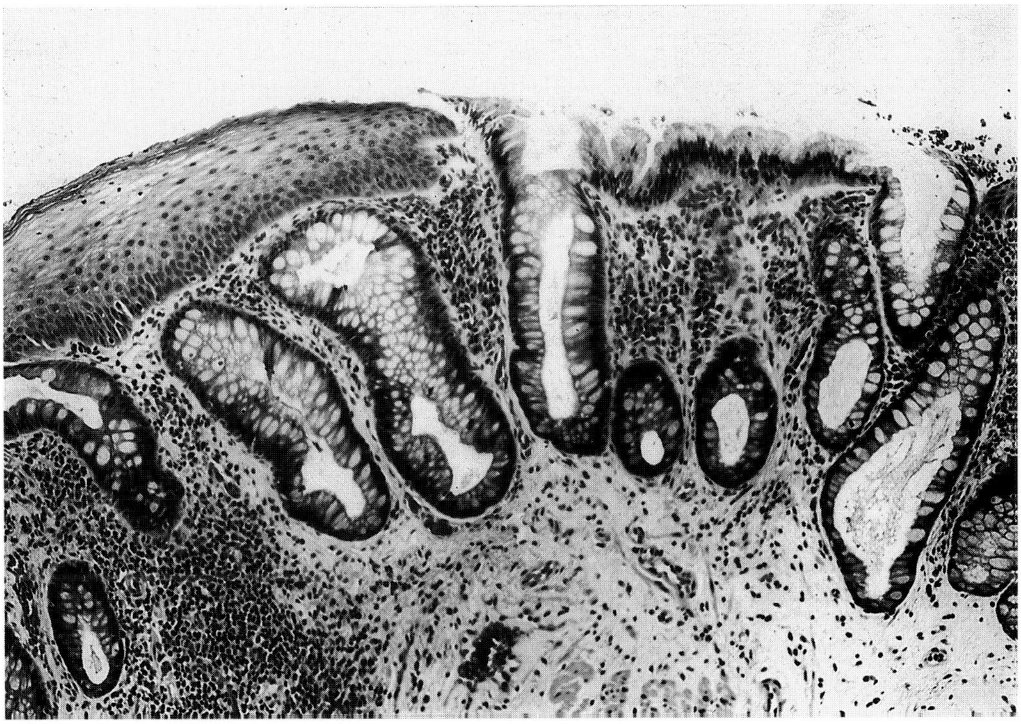

Fig. 5.3 The junction between columnar and squamous epithelium immediately proximal to the pectinate line (×106).

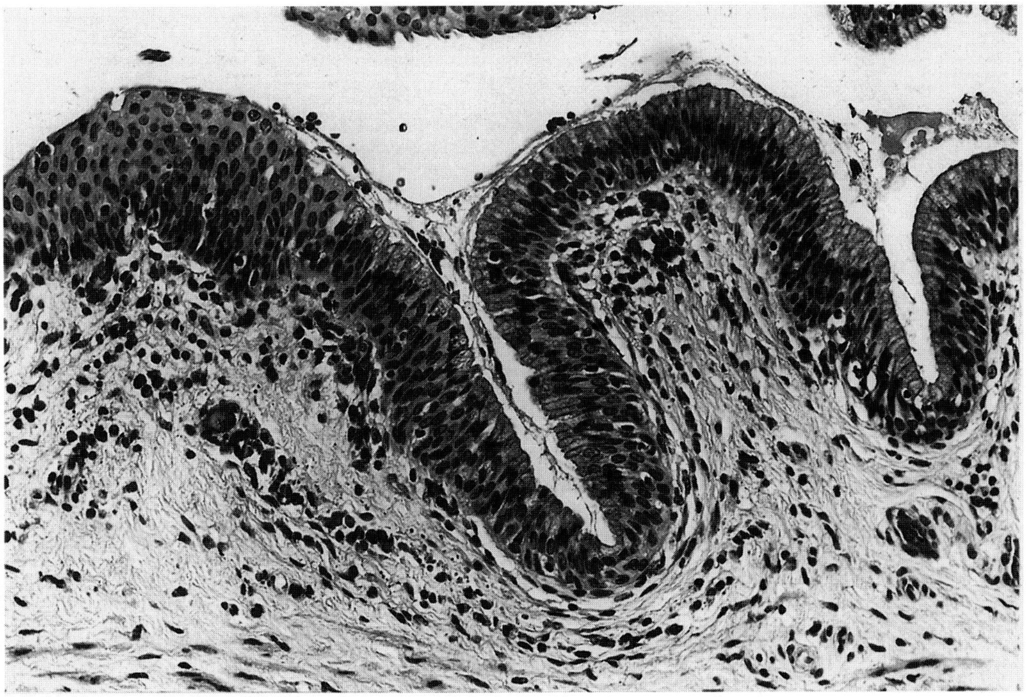

Fig. 5.4 Transitional mucosa. Early stratification of epithelial cells is taking place beneath a layer of columnar epithelium (×200).

of columnar, cuboidal or flattened mucin secreting epithelial cells overlying an accummulation of basal or parabasal cells, such as may be seen in the early stage of squamous metaplasia (Fig. 5.4). For a distance of about 15 mm below the pectinate line, there is a zone (known in the past as the pecten) which is lined by squamous epithelium, for the most part nonkeratinized (Fig. 5.5). This epithelial layer is separated from the underlying muscle of the internal sphincter by dense connective tissue which replaces the lamina propria, lamina muscularis mucosae

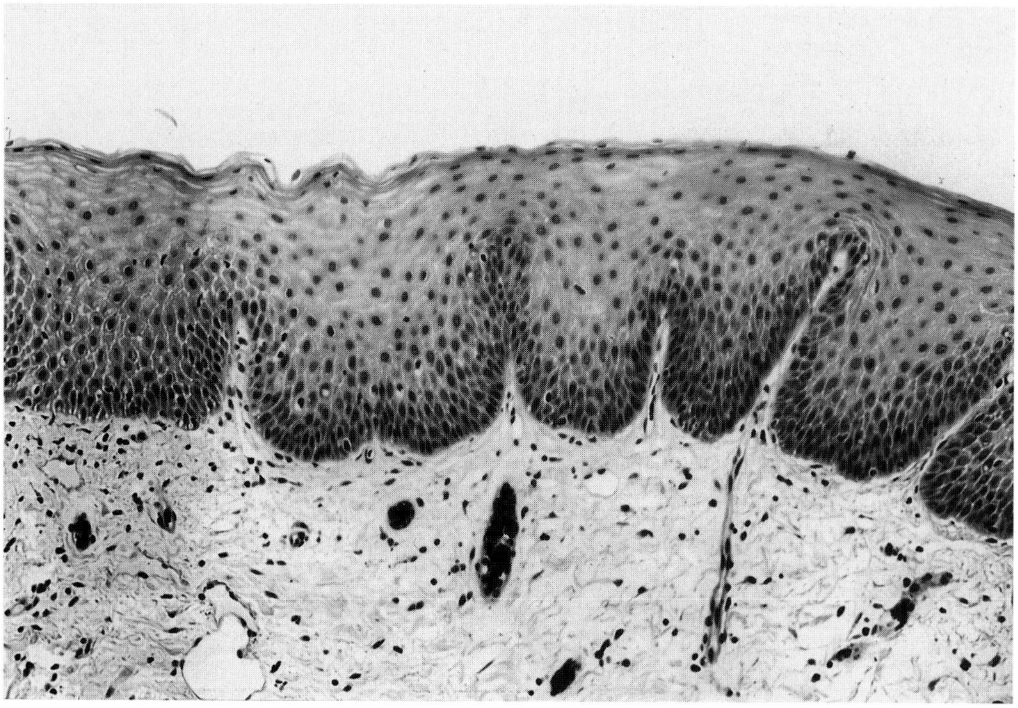

Fig. 5.5 Non-keratinizing squamous epithelium lining the distal anal canal or pecten (×167).

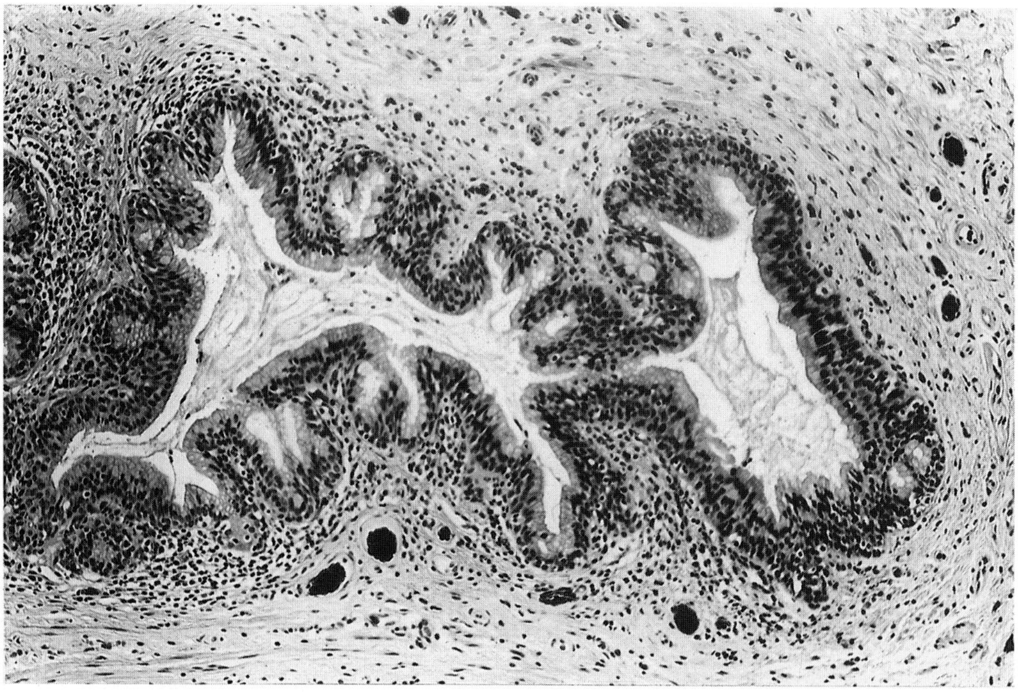

Fig. 5.6 Anal gland. Note the pseudo-stratified epithelial lining and the gland-like structures lined by mucin-secreting epithelium (×120).

and submucosa of the endoderm-derived upper anal canal at the pectinate line; it may, however, contain some muscle strands derived from the intermuscular septum as described above. The squamous epithelium of the distal part of the pecten may become keratinized before giving way to true anal skin complete with appendages such as hair follicle apparatus and sweat glands at the level of the intersphincteric groove. The anal skin is often pigmented; melanocytes may also be present in the pecten but are very rarely found proximal to the pectinate line.

Lastly, mention must be made of the so-called anal glands which are actually out-pouchings (6 to 8 in number) of the anal mucosa extending into the submucosa and even penetrating the internal sphincter. They usually arise within the anal sinuses in the ATZ just proximal to the pectinate line and pursue either a horizontal or downward (never upward) direction. In accordance with their origin, they are either lined by columnar or pseudo-stratified transitional epithelium which may show branching and includes racemose or microcystic gland-like structures lined by mucin-secreting epithelium (Fig. 5.6). Subepithelial lymphoid tissue may also be a feature of these glands and may be so prominent that reference is sometimes made to the existence of an 'anal tonsil'. The anal glands are of importance in that they may provide a potential channel for the deep spread of infection from the anal sinuses and occasionaly are a source of neoplastic change.

REFERENCES

1. Goligher J. Surgery of anus rectum and colon. 5th ed. London: Bailliere Tindall, 1984.
2. Hughes E, Cuthbertson AM, Killingback MK. Colorectal Surgery. Edinburgh: Churchill Livingstone, 1983.
3. Fenger C, Nielsen K. Stereomicroscopic investigation of the anal canal epithelium. Scand J Gastroenterol 1982; 17: 571–575.

CHAPTER 6

The endocrine cell population

S. Falkmer   E. Wilander

The disseminated gastrointestinal mucosal endocrine system is by far the largest in the whole body and it produces the widest range of hormones.[1,2] It was half a century ago that Friedrich Feyrter introduced the idea of a 'diffuse endocrine system' ('das Helle-Zellen-Organ') when he described the presence of numerous 'clear cells' to which he attributed a local endocrine ('paracrine') role.[2] In the last decade or so, with success in the identification of the biogenic amines produced and in the peptide hormones secreted by these endocrine cells, and with the advent of immunohistochemistry, great advances in our understanding of this system have been made. Now, at least a dozen different types of endocrine cell are known to occur in the gastrointestinal mucosa, and the number of peptide hormones they produce is even higher. It is likely that other gastrointestinal endocrine cells are still to be discovered and those that are characterized may prove to produce additional peptide hormones.[3,4]

There are some fairly recent and comprehensive accounts of both the cytological features of endocrine cells of the gastrointestinal mucosa in mammals and of the histopathology of tumours derived from them in man.[5,6]

PHYLOGENETIC BACKGROUND

The gastrointestinal endocrine cells belong, from an evolutionary point of view, to the large neuroendocrine system.[7–9] It consists of three major parts:

(a) neuronal cells in the central and peripheral nervous systems and their nerve fibres ('the peptidergic nervous system')
(b) endocrine cells of open or closed type, widely disseminated in the mucosa not only of the gastrointestinal canal, but also in that of several other hollow organs, e.g. the respiratory and urinary tracts
(c) the classical endocrine glands, such as the adenohypophysis, the islets of Langerhans, the C-cells of the thyroid,the parathyroid glands and the adrenal medulla.

Phylogenetically, it seems as if these three major parts of the neuroendocrine system represent three steps of evolution (Fig. 6.1). In the most 'primitive' invertebrates, all neuro-hormonal peptides appear to be produced by neuronal cells only. Thus cells storing insulin and such classical gastro-intestinal hormones as gastrin and secretin seem to be confined to the nervous system in most of the invertebrates of the protostomian evolution line. It is not until the developmental stage of the protochordates (invertebrates of the Deuterostomian line) that endocrine cells of open type are more regularly found in the gastrointestinal mucosa. There is no endocrine pancreas but the insulin producing cells appear as endocrine cells of open type in the gastrointestinal mucosa.

For most of the major peptide hormones, a so-called brain-gut axis[7] can be shown to occur; an excellent example of this feature can be seen in the tunicates, where such an axis exists for several neurohormonal peptides, including all the four islet hormones[9] and gastrin/CCK ('cionin').

The third component of the neuroendocrine system are the classical endocrine glands, which are confined to the vertebrates.[7] In the most 'primitive' vertebrates, the jawless fish (Agnatha; Cyclostomes), the manner in which the two-hormone islet organ buds out from the endocrine

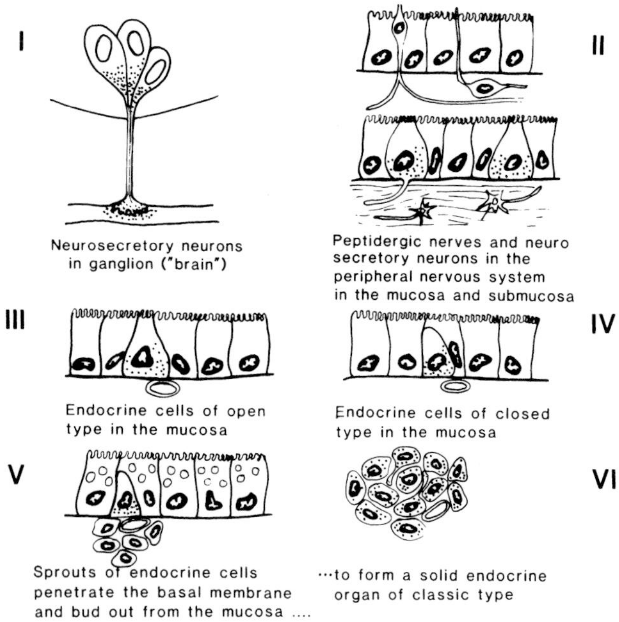

Fig. 6.1 Schematic outline of the three main components of the neuroendocrine system and their possible evolutionary interrelationship. I. The neurosecretory neurons in the brain or cerebral ganglia; II. the peptidergic nerves and neurosecretory neurons in the peripheral nervous system in the submucosa (Fig. 6.6) and mucosa of hollow organs, such as the digestive tract; III, IV. the epithelial endocrine cells of open (III) and closed (IV) type in the mucosa; V, VI. the ultimate development of a solid endocrine gland of classic type (VI) via a budding-out process (V) of epithelial endocrine cells of closed type from the mucosa of a hollow organ, e.g. the formation of the islets of Langerhans from the ductular epithelium in the pancreas in vertebrates.

cells of closed type in the bile duct mucosa (in the hagfish) or from the gut epithelium (in the lamprey) can be visualized.[7] In the mucosal surface of some invertebrates, peptide immunoreactive neuronal cells are found to be intercalated between the epithelial cells. They could be interpreted as open cells of 'endocrine' type and thus evidence of an evolutionary interconnection between the components (a) and (b) of the neuroendocrine system in the gastrointestinal tract of man. There are also 'functional' signs of an evolutionary interconnection between the component (a) and the other two components of the neuro-endocrine system. An example of this is the presence of the neuronal marker enzyme neuron-specific enolase (see below) in the endocrine cells of both the gastrointestinal mucosa and the islet parenchyma (as well as in other endocrine organs).

With this phylogenetic background in mind, it is easy to understand how such 'atavistic' features can occur in neoplasms derived from the endocrine cell population in the gastro-entero-pancreatic organs. The presence of gastrin-immunoreactive cells in islet cell tumours of the pancreas and insulin-immunoreactive cells in carcinoids of the rectum are examples.[10] Other neuronal markers such as synaptophysin and chromogranin A and B, are well known constituents of the secretion granules of the gastrointestinal endocrine cells; they also occur in the carcinoid tumours derived from them.[11,12] Whether or not another neuronal marker, namely synaptophysin, can be found in the gastrointestinal endocrine cells, is currently being investigated.[11] It is known to occur in the carcinoid tumours derived from them.[12]

HISTOLOGICAL TECHNIQUES

Gastrointestinal endocrine cells can be readily recognized at light microscope level by the utilization of formalin-induced fluorescence,[13-16] or a variety of silver stains.[17-20] For more precise identification, electron microscopy (EM) and immunological techniques are needed.

Formalin-induced fluorescence

In freeze-dried tissue, gaseous formaldehyde can be used, but the method can also be applied to unstained tissue sections obtained from formalin-fixed paraffin-embedded material. It is based upon the conversion of catecholamines to tetrahydro-isoquinoline and serotonin to tetrabeta-carboline. When exposed to ultraviolet light, catecholamines thus display green fluorescence whereas the fluorescence from serotonin is yellow. By using different filter combinations, the different monoamines can be identified. This method detects monoamine-containing cells in some of the endocrine cell systems of the digestive tract: mainly serotonin in the enterochromaffin (EC) cells (Figs 6.2 & 6.3).[15-23]

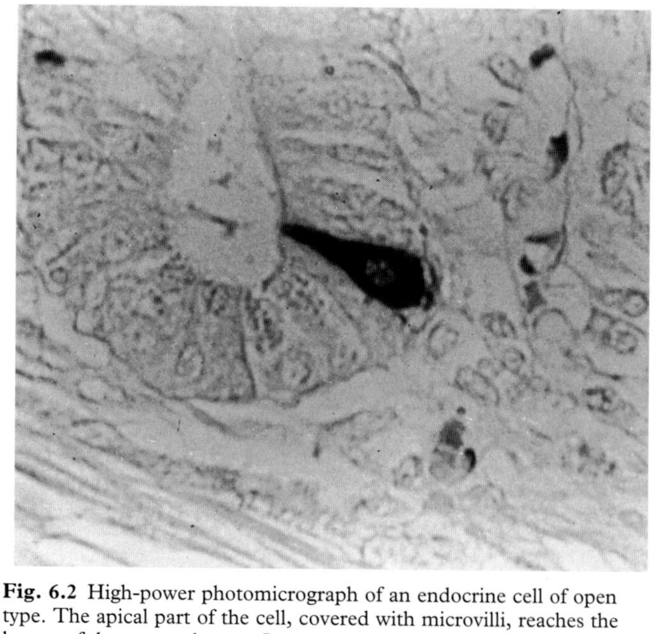

Fig. 6.2 High-power photomicrograph of an endocrine cell of open type. The apical part of the cell, covered with microvilli, reaches the lumen of the mucosal crypt. Immunohistochemical staining with monoclonal serotonin antibodies, (×570)

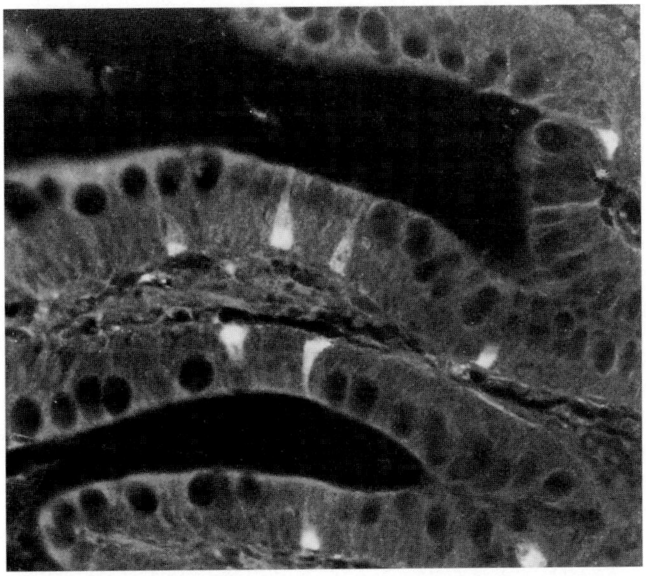

Fig. 6.3 Medium power photomicrograph of serotonin-storing EC cells of the intestinal mucosa, visualized by their fluorescence when exposed to UV light. (×304)

Silver stains

General considerations

Prior to the development of immunohistochemical methods, silver staining was the usual means of identifying and characterizing gastrointestinal endocrine cells.[17–20,24] These silver stains are still in common use, although they were developed empirically, and their precise chemical basis is not always clear. Many of the techniques are simple to perform and give reproducible results that are easily evaluated.

A distinction is made between methods giving argyrophil and argentaffin reactions.[17] Cells displaying an argyrophil reaction retain silver ions from the impregnation solution, but metallic silver only appears after a subsequent reducing process, brought about by an external agent. Cells showing an argentaffin reaction contain one or more chemical substances which both retain silver ions from an ammoniacal silver solution and reduce them to metallic silver.[20]

The argentaffin reaction

Formalin, glutaraldehyde and glutaraldehyde-picric acid mixture are fixatives suitable for the Masson technique. Bouin's fluid gives a relatively weak or inconstant staining. The argentaffin method has been much modified but the best known variants are those described by Hamperl[18] and Singh.[19] Recently, another simple modification has been described,[20] in which the sections are placed in a 5% ammoniacal silver solution at 60°C for 1 h. This modification gives reproducible results and distinct staining of the EC-cells (Fig. 6.4A). In contrast to the argyrophil methods, the chemical basis of the argentaffin reaction is known to be the result of interaction of serotonin with formaldehyde.[21,22] Electron microscopic studies have demonstrated that the reduced silver is formed in the pleomorphic secretory granules of the EC cells.[23]

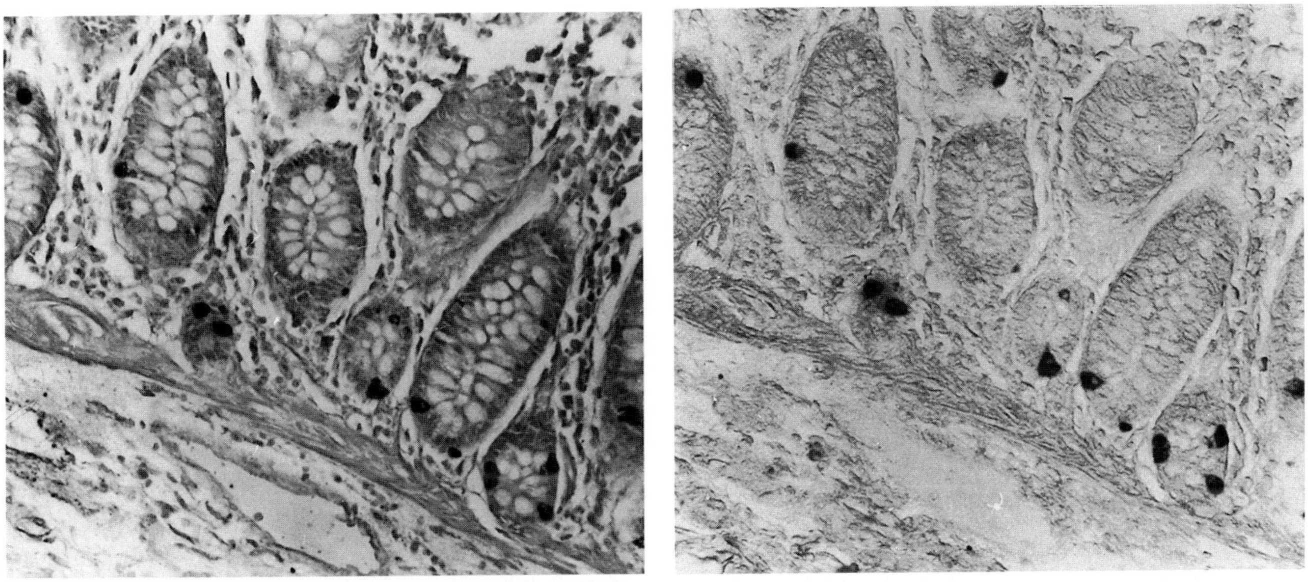

A B

Fig. 6.4 Low power photomicrographs of endocrine cells of the intestinal mucosa, stained with non-discriminatory techniques. **A** shows the argyrophil reaction of Grimelius and **B** shows the immunohistochemical results with PAP technique after exposure to chromogranin antibodies. (Sequential staining of identical section, ×190)

The argyrophil reaction of Grimelius

The best fixatives for this stain are a formalin-glutaraldehyde mixture or Bouin's fluid, and whereas solutions containing ethanol, mercuric chloride, bichromate and osmium are more or less unsatisfactory,[17,24] conventional formalin-fixed tissue give acceptable results.

Frozen sections give poor or negative results and ordinary paraffin sections are preferable. There are two variants of the method, one with impregnation at 37°C for 24 h and other at 60°C for 3 h.[20] The positive argyrophil reaction appears as brown to brownish-black cytoplasmic grains, but it can be intensified by increasing the silver nitrate concentration from 0.03% to 0.07%, and the temperature of the reducing solution to 55°C.[20] A weak reaction can be improved by reimpregnation,[20] by rinsing the silver-stained sections in redistilled water and placing them in another freshly prepared silver solution at room temperature for 15 min and then a reducing solution at 55°C for 1 min. The composition of the silver nitrate and the reducing solution are the same as those used in the primary impregnation and reducing steps.

The argyrophil reaction of Grimelius has the advantage over the previous, rather precarious Bodian technique in that the silver nitrate solution is easily commercially available, chemically exact and stable. In contrast, the silver proteinate used in the Bodian technique was difficult to obtain, unstable and of inconstant composition.

The Grimelius technique identifies endocrine cells in normal tissues irrespective of hormone content and is almost non-discriminating. A positive reaction is obtained in most normal endocrine cell types of the gastrointestinal canal with the exception of cells storing CCK (cholecystokinin), somatostatin and PYY (pancreatic polypeptide YY).[17,20] It is also well-known that insulin containing cells are non-argyrophil unless they are immature or neoplastic, when they too may be argyrophilic.[25–26]

Ultrastructurally, it has been repeatedly shown that the silver reaction is concentrated exclusively in the secretion granules;[23] here, it is based on a reaction with the chromogranins as shown both in vitro and in vivo.[11] Counterstaining can be used in order to increase orientation but is usually not needed.

The argyrophil reaction of Sevier-Munger

As in the Grimelius procedure for gastrointestinal endocrine cells, the best fixatives for the Sevier-Munger technique are formalin and Bouin's fluid. Ordinary formalin-fixed and paraffin-embedded material can thus be used. Rather than follow the original method,[27] collodion coating of the section and immersion in sodium thiosulphate after staining in the ammoniacal silver-formaldehyde solution are best avoided. Counterstaining is usually not indicated, because the yellow to golden-brown appearance of the tissue allows orientation.

Although the Sevier-Munger stain was originally devised for visualizing neural elements,[27] a strong reaction occurs in EC cells, enterochromaffin-like (ECL) cells and gastric-inhibitory peptide (GIP) cells of the gastrointestinal mucosa.[17] The method is especially important for identification of the ECL cells which are argyrophilic but non-argentaffin.

The argyrophil reaction of Davenport

The Davenport silver impregnation procedure was also originally used for staining central nervous tissue. For the visualization of gastro-entero-pancreatic endocrine cells, the modification described in 1960 by Hellerstrom and Hellman is more commonly used.[28] Suitable fixatives are formalin, Bouin's fluid and even Zenker-formol, thus conventional formalin-fixed, paraffin sections can be used.

The silver impregnation solution consists of a 10% silver nitrate solution, dissolved in 85% ethanol with a pH adjusted to 5.2. This adjustment can be difficult and if the pH is incorrect, false negative results may occur. The somatostatin (D) cells of the pancreatic islets and the gastrointestinal mucosa are detected by this technique,[28] and at electron microscopy the silver grains are shown to be concentrated in the secretory granules.[29]

The argyrophil reaction of Churukian-Schenk

The most recent technique for visualizing the endocrine cell population in the human gut mucosa is the argyrophil reaction of Churukian-Schenk.[30] It is actually a modification of Pascual's argyrophil method,[31] and has fixation rquirements which are similar to the other argyrophil techniques. An acid 0.15% silver nitrate solution is used with the same reducing agent as in the Grimelius technique. This is a double impregnation method in that the sections pass through the staining procedure twice. The results with respect to the gastrointestinal endocrine cell population have not yet been fully evaluated.

Light-microscopical immunohistochemistry

The different endocrine cells of the gastrointestinal mucosa are most accurately demonstrated at light microscopy by immunohistochemical techniques, using hormone-specific antisera.[32,33] The most convenient technique is the peroxidase-anti peroxidase (PAP) procedure,[32] which can be used on conventional formalin-fixed, paraffin-embedded tissue. In contrast to the previously commonly used indirect immunofluorescence technique,[32] a fluorescence microscope is not required and the consumption of often expensive antisera is much lower. There are improvements, like the Avidin-Biotin technique, which have a higher sensitivity.[33]

With these methods, all cell types with significant hormone production can be visualized, irrespective of whether they are argyrophil or not. Individual hormonal peptides are generally stored in separate endocrine cell types, but serotonin and a peptide hormone may be costored in the same EC cell. Sometimes two peptide hormones are present in the same secretory granules. Glicentin and PYY, for example, occur in the same endocrine cells in the human rectal mucosa.[3,4]

There are some 'panendocrine' markers of the neuroendocrine cell population of the gastrointestinal tract. The two most commonly demonstrated are neuron-specific enolase and chromogranins; more recently, synaptophysin has been described.

Neuron-specific enolase

Neuron-specific enolase (NSE) is a metabolic enzyme which was first considered to be localized exclusively in neurons and present only in the central nervous system but it has subsequently been found in peripheral endocrine cells.[34–36]

Immunoreactive NSE cells are located in the mucosal crypts and display either a diffuse positivity of the cytoplasm or show a concentrated immunoreaction in the perinuclear space and a nonreactive periphery. Since NSE is a glycolytic enzyme, it is not related to the hormonal secretory granules and its immunoreactivity may be weak. In routinely processed histopathological specimens, the NSE reaction is not always entirely reliable. Nevertheless, almost all the NSE immuno-reactive cells are either argyrophil or argentaffin positive, the exceptions being insulin, somatostatin, and CCK cells.

Chromogranins

The chromogranins are a family of acidic polypeptides of varying molecular size.[37,38] They constitute a major part of the soluble proteins of the secretory granules of several, but not all, polypeptide or biogenic amine-storing endocrine cell types.[37–39] Monoclonal and polyclonal antisera against several chromogranins are becoming more readily available.[40,41] Sequential staining with silver stains, and serotonin and chromogranin antibodies reveal that both intestinal argentaffin and argyrophil endocrine cells display chromogranin immunoreactivity (Fig. 6.4b). Chromogranin antibodies usually give positive staining over most of the cytoplasmic area but it may be accentuated at the basal part of the endocrine cells. The chromogranin reaction is a useful adjunct for the identification of peripheral endocrine cells. Although there is a good correlation between cells showing argyrophilia with the Grimelius method and chromogranin immunoreactivity, this is not always so.[39–41]

Synaptophysin

Originally discovered in nerve cell synapses, synaptophysin has also recently been introduced as a 'pan-neuroendocrine' marker.[42] It is a single-chain peptide, containing amino acid residues. Monoclonal antibodies against synaptophysin have been used to demonstrate synaptophysin in endocrine cells of the gastrointestinal mucosa and their tumours,[12] as well as in the islets of Langerhans.[11]

Ultrastructural immunocytochemistry

Although the PAP procedure also can be used ultrastructurally,[32,33] there are some immunocytochemical techniques that are specially designed for EM analysis of peptide hormones. The best known and most popular are the protein-A-gold method[43] and the immunogold techniques.[44] With both, it is possible to trace the production of one or a few peptide hormones to a particular organelle in the neuroendocrine cell. The localization of two or more hormones to one and the same secretory granule can be demonstrated ultrastructurally by using different antisera[43,44] which are bound to gold particles of different sizes.

THE DIFFERENT ENDOCRINE CELL TYPES

Open and closed endocrine mucosal cells; hormone production

In the gastrointestinal mucosa there are two principal types of endocrine cells, namely open and closed, which are structurally different (Fig. 6.1). The closed cells are mainly localized in the body and fundic area of the stomach, i.e. the oxyntic mucosa. They are not in contact with the luminal aspect of the mucosal glands. The open cell type is found in the rest of the digestive system, i.e. the antrum of the stomach, duodenum, small intestine, appendix, colon and rectum. These cells are flask-shaped, and their apices reach the crypt lumen (Figs 6.2 & 6.3). It is thought that the closed cells respond to distension or to humoral stimulation, whereas the open cells monitor minor changes in the pH or in the composition of the luminal contents of the gut.[45]

The hormonal products of the endocrine cells are stored in membrane-bound secretory granules, predominantly occurring in the basal area of the cells. The structure of the secretory granules seems to vary with their hormone contents, and accordingly, these cells have tentatively been subgrouped on the basis of their ultrastructural features and on their peptide hormone immunoreactivity.[46,47] The main endocrine cell types and their topographical distribution are illustrated in Table 6.1. The different endocrine cell types overlap in their topographical distribution although each cell population usually predominates in a specific region.

On stimulation, the hormonal products of the endocrine cells are released, either locally or into the circulation. Some of the endocrine cell types elaborate

Table 6.1 Classification and distribution of endocrine cell types in the gastrointestinal tract.

Hormone	Ultrastructural *classification*	Stomach *Fundus*	Stomach *Antrum*	Small intestine *Duodenum, jejunum, ileum*	Large intestine *Colon*	Large intestine *Rectum*
Serotonin (substance P)	EC_1			——	——	——
Serotonin (motilin-like)	EC_2			—— — — —		
Serotonin	EC_n	——	——			
Unknown (+ histamine)	ECL	——				
Gastrin (ACTH, metenkephalin)	G		——	— —		
Gastrin	IG			—— — — —		
Tetragastrin	TG			—— — — —		
Cholecystokinin	I			—— — — —		
Secretin	S			—— — — —		
GIP	K			—— — — —		
VIP-like peptide	D_1	——	——			
Enteroglucagon	L			— — — ——	— —	— ——
Pancreatic polypeptide	PP				— —	— ——
PYY	H				— —	— ——
Neurotensin	N			— — — ——		
Motilin	Mo			—— —		
Bombesin-like peptide	P		——	——		
Unknown	X	——				
Somatostatin	D	——	——	——	——	——

neuron-like cytoplasmic extensions from their basal aspect which envelop and terminate around neighbouring exocrine or endocrine cells, whose function they then modulate. These 'paracrine' cells, which release hormonal substances that act on adjacent target cells, were first described by Feyrter.[2]

The EC cells

The EC cell is found in the mucosa of the entire gastrointestinal canal, and constitutes the predominating cell population of the digestive endocrine cell system.[48,49] Although the main secretory product of the EC cells is serotonin (Fig. 6.5), immunoreactions to peptide hormones such as substance P, leu-enkephalin and motilin have been described.[4–6]

Serotonin in EC cells[21,48–50] can be detected by several techniques in routine paraffin sections after conventional formalin fixation, the argentaffin reaction of Masson,[18,19] the formalin-induced fluorescence technique[13] and immunohistochemical methods with polyclonal or monoclonal antibodies against serotonin being the most commonly used.[51–53] Non-immunological procedures all have their limitations. Thus, the argentaffin reaction is of low chemical specificity, and formalin-induced fluorescence might be due to other biogenic amines that can give yellow fluorescence.[13,14,53] The EC cells are also argyrophil positive with the Grimelius procedure, but this technique also stains most of the endocrine cell population of the gastrointestinal tract.[17]

The different techniques used to visualize the EC cells also vary in the intensity of the cytoplasmic staining they produce. The argentaffin and the argyrophil reactions are mostly limited to the basal part of the endocrine cells, leaving the apical area unreactive. With formalin-induced fluorescence, both the apical and basal parts of the cells are fluorescent (Fig. 6.3), but the intensity of the reaction is more pronounced at the basal parts. The application of monoclonal antiserotonin antibodies, however, results in a strong immunostaining of almost equal intensity all over the whole cytoplasm.[51]

Other peptide hormone-producing mucosa cells

In addition to the EC cells, the mucosa of the stomach and intestine is endowed with endocrine cells which

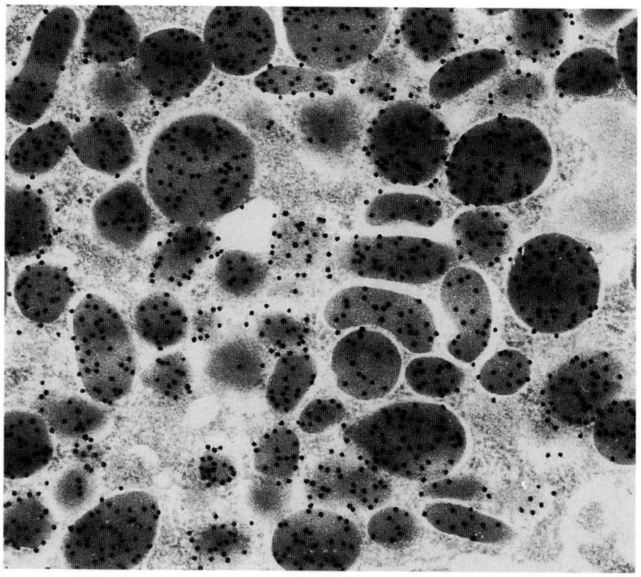

Fig. 6.5 Electron micrograph of pleomorphic secretory granules in an EC cell. The granules store serotonin as revealed after colloid-gold labelling of monoclonal serotonin antibodies. (×33 440)

produce and store a great number of active hormonal peptides, serotonin and histamine[3–6,11,54] (Table 6.1). Of these, the D cell, storing somatostatin, shows the widest distribution. Of greatest current interest is, however, the histamine-producing ECL cell of the fundic mucosa. They are known to undergo a whole spectrum of hyperplastic and even genuinely neoplastic lesions, evoked by sustained hypergastrinaemia, secondary to inhibition of gastric acid secretion.[55,56] In the antral mucosa, the gastrin (G) cells predominate. The duodenal mucosa is rich in G cells, secretin (S) cells and CCK (I) cells. In the rest of the intestinal canal, the peptide hormone-producing endocrine cells occur as minor cell populations in comparison with the EC cells. In the rectum, the number of endocrine cells is high, and, in addition to EC cells, several cells storing pancreatic polypeptide (PP), enteroglucagon and PYY are found.[4–6]

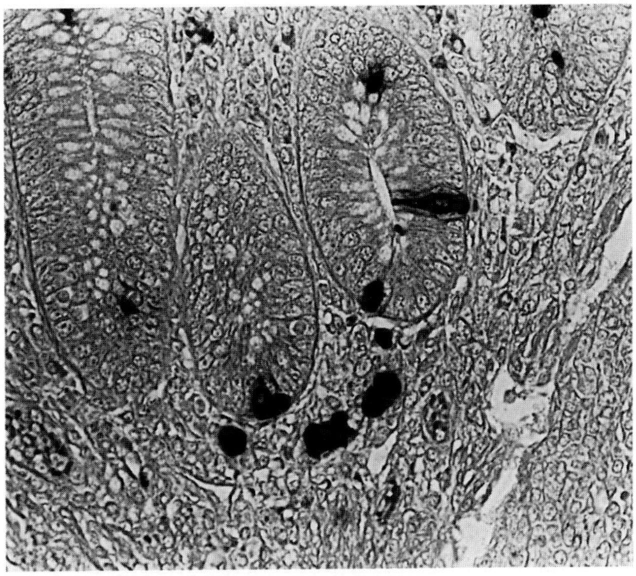

Fig. 6.6 Medium power photomicrograph of an appendix specimen, showing intraepithelial and subepithelial endocrine cells, the latter localized in the lamina propria. Both cell types stain for serotonin. (×304)

Endocrine cells in the subepithelial stroma

Cells with tinctorial and immunocytochemical properties indicative of endocrine differentiation are not exclusively localized in the mucosa of the gastrointestinal canal but are also present in the subepithelial stroma (Fig. 6.1). In 1928, Masson reported the presence of argentaffin cells in the lamina propria of the appendix.[57] He thought these cells were derived from the epithelial argentaffin (Kultchitsky) cells, which, by a budding process, migrated from the crypts of Lieberkuhn to their final location in the lamina propria. The subepithelial endocrine cells of the appendix are relatively frequent and can be identified in most appendiceal specimens. They display, in addition to an argentaffin and an argyrophil reaction, serotonin and NSE immunoreactivity (Fig. 6.6).[58–62] At the EM level, heteromorphous secretory granules are seen similar to those observed in the mucosal EC cells. The subepithelial endocrine cells are single or occur in small clusters in the deeper part of the lamina propria beneath or between the epithelial crypts.

Serotonin-immunoreactive cells can also be found in the submucosa of the appendix, sometimes in close contact with ganglion cells, although they are relatively few. The subepithelial endocrine cells are frequently surrounded by cells with long cytoplasmic processes displaying S-100 protein immunoreactivity. These cells have been regarded as of Schwann cell origin — a proposal which is supported by ultrastructural observation that the subepithelial endocrine cells are in close contact with multiple nerve fibres and nonmyelinated Schwann cells.[60] Although common in the appendix, subepithelial endocrine cells have also been seen in the small intestine, but they are few in number. There has not been a systematic study of subepithelial endocrine cells in other areas of the gastrointestinal tract.

Acknowledgements: This chapter is based upon original work supported by grants from the Swedish Medical Research Council (Projects Nos. 12x-718 and 12x-6817), The Swedish Diabetes Association, the Cancer Society of Stockholm, the Gustaf V Jubilee Fund, and the Faculty of Medicine at the Karolinska Institute, Stockholm.

REFERENCES

1. Pearse AGE. The cytochemistry and ultrastructure of polypeptide hormone-producing cells of the APUD series, and the embryonic, physiologic and pathologic implications of the concept. J Histochem Cytochem 1969; 17: 303–313.
2. Feyrter F. Ober diffuse endokrine epitheliale Organe. Leipzig: Barth 1938; 6–17.
3. Fiocca R, Rindi G, Capella C, et al. Glucagon, glicentin, proglucagon, PYY, PP and pro-PP-icosapeptide immunoreactivities of rectal carcinoid tumors and related non-tumor cells. Regul Pept 1987; 17: 9–29.
4. Ali-Rachedi A, Varndell IM, Adrian TE, et al. Peptide YY (PYY) immunoreactivity is co-stored with glucagon-related immunoreactants in endocrine cells of the gut and pancreas. Histochemistry 1984; 80: 487–491.
5. Solcia E, Capella C, Buffa R, et al. Cytology of tumours in the gastroenteropancreatic and diffuse (neuro)endocrine system. In: Falkmer S, Hakanson R, Sundler F, eds. Evolution and tumour pathology of the neuroendocrine system. Amsterdam: Elsevier, 1984: 453–480.
6. Solcia E, Capella C, Buffa R, et al. The contribution of immunohistochemistry to the diagnosis of neuroendocrine tumors. Seminars Diagn Pathol 1984; 1: 285–296.
7. Falkmer S, El-Salhy M, Titlbach M. Evolution of the neuroendocrine system in vertebrates. A review with particular reference to the phylogeny and postnatal maturation of the islet parenchyma. In: Falkmer S, Hakanson R, Sundler F, eds. Evolution and tumour pathology of the neuroendocrine system. Amsterdam: Elsevier, 1984: 59–87.

8. Falkmer S, Van Noorden S. Ontogeny and phylogeny of the glucagon cell. Handb Exp Pharmacol 1983; 66: 81–119.
9. Thorndyke MC, Falkmer S. Evolution of gastro-entero-pancreatic endocrine systems in lower vertebrates. In: Foreman RE, Gorbman A, Dodds JM, Olsson R, eds. Evolutionary biology of primitive fishes. New York: Plenum Press, 1985: 379–400.
10. Alumets J, Alm P, Falkmer S, et al. Immunohistochemical evidence of peptide hormones in endocrine tumours of the rectum. Cancer 1981; 48: 2409–2415.
11. Larsson L, Alumets J, Eriksson B, Hakanson R, Lundquist G, Oberg K, Sundler F. Antiserum directed against chromogranin A and B (CAB) is a useful marker for peptide-hormone-producing endocrine cells and tumours. Endocr Pathol 1992; 3: 14–22.
12. Wiedenmann B, Franke, WW, Kuhn C, Moll R, Gould VE. Synaptophysin: A marker protein for neuroendocrine cells and neoplasms. Proc Natl Acad Sci (USA) 1986; 83: 3500–3504.
13. Falck B, Hillarp NA, Thieme G, Torp A. Fluorescence of catecholamine and related compounds condensed with formaldehyde. J Histochem Cytochem 1962; 10: 348–354.
14. Bjorklund A, Falck B, Owman C. Fluorescence, microscopic and microspectrofluorometric techniques for the cellular localization and characterization of biogenic amines. Methods Invest Diagn Endocrinol 1972; 7: 318–368.
15. Owman C, Hakanson R, Sundler F. Occurrence and function of amines in endocrine cells producing polypeptide hormones. Fed Proc 1973; 32: 1785–1791.
16. Sundler F, Hakanson R, Loren I, Lundquist I. Amine storage and function in peptide hormone-producing cells. Invest Cell Pathol 1980; 3: 87–103.
17. Grimelius L, Wilander E. Silver stains in the study of endocrine cells of the gut and pancreas. Invest Cell Pathol 1980; 3: 3–12.
18. Hamperl H. Ober die gelben (chromaffinen) Zellen im gesunden und kranken Magendarmschlauch. Virchows Arch (A) 1927; 266: 509–548.
19. Singh I. A modification of the Masson-Hamperl method for staining of argentaffin cells. Anat Anz 1964; 115: 81–82.
20. Portela-Gomes GM. Enterochromaffin cells. A qualitative and quantitative study. Thesis, Uppsala Univ Faculty Med, 1982: 1–44.
21. Barter R, Pearse AGE. Detection of 5-hydroxytryptamine in mammalian enterochromaffin cells. Nature 1953; 171: 810.
22. Barter R, Pearse AGE. Mammalian enterochromaffin cells as the source of serotonin (5-hydroxytryptamine). J Pathol Bacteriol 1955; 69: 25–31.
23. Vasallo G, Capella C, Solcia E. Endocrine cells of the human gastric mucosa. Z Zellforsch 1971; 118: 49–67.
24. Grimelius L. A silver nitrate stain for alpha$_2$ cells of human pancreatic islets. Acta Soc Med Upsal 1968; 73: 243–270.
25. Titlbach M, Falt K, Falkmer S. Postnatal maturation of the islets of Langerhans in sheep. Light microscopic, immunohistochemical, morphometric, and ultrastructural investigations with particular reference to the transient appearance of argyrophil insulin immuno-reactive cells. Diab Res 1985; 2: 5–15.
26. Titlbach M, Falkmer S. Ontogeny of the pancreatic islet parenchymal cells in the rabbit. An immunohistochemical and ultrastructural study with particular regard to the earliest appearance of argyrophil insulin-immunoreactive cells. Diab Res 1987; 5: 105–117.
27. Sevier AC, Munger BL. A silver method for paraffin sections of neural tissue. J Neuropathol Exp Neurol 1965; 24: 130–135.
28. Hellerstrom C, Hellman B. Some aspects of silver impregnation of the islets of Langerhans in the rat. Acta Endocrinol 1960; 35: 518–532.
29. Grimelius L, Strand A. Ultrastructural studies of the argyrophil reaction in A$_1$ cells in human pancreatic islets. Virchows Arch (A) 1974; 364: 129–135.
30. Churukian CJ, Schenk EA. A modification of Pascual's argyrophil method. J Histotechnol 1979; 2: 102–103.
31. Pascual HS. A new method for easy demonstration of argyrophil cells. Stain Technol 1976; 51: 231–235.
32. Sternberger LA. Immunocytochemistry. 2nd ed. New York: Wiley, 1979.
33. Van Noorden S, Polak JM, eds. Immunocytochemistry. Modern methods and applications. 2nd ed. Bristol: Wright, 1986.
34. Facer P, Polak JM, Marangas PJ, Pearse AGE. Immunohistochemical localization of neurone specific enolase (NSE) in the gastrointestinal tract. Proc Microsc Soc (London) 1976; 15: 113–114.
35. Schmechel D, Marangos PJ, Brightman M. Neurone-specific enolase is a molecular marker for peripheral and central neuroendocrine cells. Nature 1978; 276: 834–836.
36. Lundqvist M, Wilander E, Esscher T, Pahlman S. Neuron-specific enolase in mucosal endocrine cells and carcinoid tumours of the small intestine: A comparative study with neuron-specific enolase immunocytochemistry and silver stains. Histochem J 1985; 17: 323–331.
37. Blaschko H, Comline RS, Schneider FH, Silver M, Smith AD. Secretion of a chromaffin granule protein, chromo- granin, from the adrenal gland after splachnic stimulation. Nature 1983; 215: 58–59.
38. O'Connor DT, Frigon FP, Sokoloff RL. Human chromogranin A: Purification and characterization from catecholamine storage vesicles of pheochromocytoma. Hypertension 1983; 6: 2–12.
39. Varndell IM, Lloyd RV, Wilson BS, Polak JM. Ultrastructural localization of chromogranin: A potential marker for the electron microscopic recognition of endocrine secretory granules. Histochem J 1985; 17: 981–992.
40. Wilson BS, Lloyd RV. Detection of chromogranin in neuroendocrine cells with a monoclonal antibody. Am J Pathol 1984; 115: 458–468.
41. Facer P, Bishop AE, Lloyd RV, Wilson BS, Hennessy RJ, Polak JM. Chromogranin: A newly recognised marker for endocrine cells of the human gastrointestinal tract. Gastroenterol 1985; 89: 1366–1373.
42. Wiedenmann B, Franke WW. Identification and localization of synaptophysin, an integral membrane glycoprotein of M_r 38,000 characteristic of presynaptic vesicles. Cell 1985; 41: 1017–1028.
43. Roth J, Kasper M, Heitz PU, Labat F. What's new in light and electron microscopic immunocytochemistry? Application of the protein A-gold technique to routinely processed tissue. Path Res Pract 1985; 180: 711–717.
44. Doerr-Schott J, Lichte CM. A triple ultrastructural immunogold staining method. Application to the simulta- neous demonstration of three hypophyseal hormones. J Histochem Cytochem 1986; 34: 1101–1104.
45. Kobayashi S, Chiba T, eds. Paraneurons. New concepts on neuroendocrine relatives. Arch Histol Japon 1977; 40(suppl): 99–117.
46. Solcia E, Polak JM, Larsson LI, Buchan AMJ, Capella C. Update on Lausanne classification of endocrine cells. In: Bloom SR, Polak JM, eds. Gut hormones. 2nd ed. Edinburgh: Churchill Livingstone, 1981: 96–100.
47. Solcia E, Creutzfeldt W, Falkmer S, et al. Human gastro-enteropancreatic endocrine-paracrine cells: Santa Monica 1980 classification. UCLA Forum Med Sci 1981; 23: 159–165.
48. Erspamer V. Quantitative estimation of 5-hydroxytryptamine in gastrointestinal mucosa, spleen and blood of vertebrates. In: Wolstenholme G, Cameron MN, eds. Ciba Foundation Symposium on Hypertension. London: Churchill-Livingstone, 1954: 78–84.
49. Pentilla A. Histochemical reactions of enterochromaffin cells and the 5-HT content of human duodenum. Acta Physiol Scand 1966; 281(suppl 1): 1–77.
50. Facer P, Polak JM, Jaffe BM, Pearse AGE. Immunocytochemical demonstration of 5-hydroxytryptamine in gastrointestinal endocrine cells. Histochem J 1979; 11: 117–121.
51. Consolazione A, Milstein C, Wright B, Cuello AC. Immunocytochemical detection of serotonin with monoclonal antibodies. J Histochem Cytochem 1981; 29: 1425–1430.
52. Milstein C, Wright B, Cuello AC. The discrepancy between the cross-reactivity of a monoclonal antibody to serotonin and its immunohistochemical specificity. Molec Immunol 1983; 20: 113–123.
53. Lundqvist M, Wilander E. Small intestinal chromaffin cells and carcinoid tumours: A study with silver stains, formalin-induced fluorescence and monoclonal antibodies to serotonin. Histochem J 1984; 16: 1247–1256.

54. Sundler F, Eriksson B, Grimelius L, Hakason R, Lonroth H, Lundell L. Histamine in gastric carcinoid tumours: Immunocytochemical evidence. Endocr Pathol 1992; 3: 23–27.
55. Lee H, Hakanson R, Karlsson A, Mattsson H, Sundler F. Lansoprazole and omeprazole have similar effects on plasma gastrin levels, enterochromaffin-like cells, gastrin cells, and somatostatin cells in the rat stomach. Digestion 1992; 51: 125–132.
56. Solcia E, Bordi C, Creutzfeldt W, Dayal AD, Falkmer S, Grimelius L, Havu N. Histopathological classification of nonantral gastric endocrine growth in man. Digestion 1988; 41: 185–200.
57. Masson P. Carcinoids (argentaffin-cell tumors) and nerve hyperplasia of the appendicular mucosa. Am J Pathol 1928; 4: 181–211.
58. Rode J, Dhillan AP, Papadaki L, Griffiths D. Neuro-secretory cells of the lamina propria of the appendix and their possible relationship to carcinoids. Histopathol 1982; 6: 69–79.
59. Rode J, Dhillan AP, Papadaki L. Serotonin immunoreactive cells in the lamina propria plexus of the appendix. Human Pathol 1983; 145: 464–469.
60. Millikin PD. Extraepithelial enterochromaffin cells and Schwann cells in the human appendix. Arch Pathol Lab Med 1983; 107: 189–194.
61. Lundqvist M, Wilander E. Subepithelial neuroendocrine cells and carcinoid tumours of the human small intestine and appendix. A comparative immunohistochemical study with regard to serotonin, neurone-specific enolase and S-100 protein reactivity. J Pathol 1986; 48: 141–147.
62. Aubock L, Hofler H. Extraepithelial intraneural endocrine cells as starting points for gastro-intestinal carcinoids. Virchows Arch (A) 1983;401: 17–23.

CHAPTER

7 The histochemistry of intestinal mucins; changes in disease

M. I. Filipe   S. Ramachandra

One of the important functions of gastrointestinal epithelium is the secretion of mucus. The major component of mucus is a high molecular weight glycoprotein (mucous glycoprotein or mucin). Apart from lubrication and protection, mucins are frequently altered in cancer, thus potentially useful as tumour markers. Glycoproteins are also an important component of extra cellular matrix (ECM) implicated in cell adhesion, migration, differentiation and malignancy.

STRUCTURE OF INTESTINAL MUCINS

Mucins consist of a central protein core to which numerous carbohydrate chains are attached in 'bottle-brush' fashion forming a protective shell around the polypeptide chain. The carbohydrate side chains contain a relatively low number of sugars (oligosaccharide units) which show marked variations in length, branching and acidity in different gastrointestinal mucins. The most common sugars (monosaccharides) in the oligosaccharide units are fucose, galactose, N-acetylglucosamine, N-acetylgalactosamine and sialic acids. Ester sulphates can also occur, but uronic acid is not present, and mannose — which is a principal sugar in the plasma and membrane glycoproteins — is either absent or found in traces only. The carbohydrate moiety and the polypeptide chain are linked by an O-glycosidic bond between the oxygen atom of serine or threonine residues and N-acetylgalactosamine. The mucin structure consists of heavily glycosylated protein regions interspersed with carbohydrate-free 'naked' stretches of protein, which enable neighbouring chains to be linked together through disulphide bonds of cystine.[1–4]

In the oligosaccharide chain, three areas with distinct structure and antigenic determinants are recognized: core, backbone and peripheral (terminal) (Fig. 7.1). The carbohydrate side chains of mucin glycoproteins may exhibit multiple cancer-associated antigenic epitopes. These include core region carbohydrates such as Tn, sialyl Tn or T-antigens, or peripheral backbone region carbohydrates such as extended and/or polyfucosylated Le^x or Le^y antigens or sialylated Le^x antigens.[5] These can be demonstrated in situ in the tissue by using lectins and monoclonal antibodies.

Most of the gastrointestinal mucins contain sialic acid residues and sulphate groups which confer the polyanionic character of these molecules. Sialic acids and sulphate may be present in the same glycoprotein molecule but in different oligosaccharide units, with sialylated chains generally being shorter than the sulphated ones. Sialic acid in gastrointestinal mucins is frequently found in terminal position linked to galactose though it can occur in internal sites linked to GalNAc, and sometimes in conjunction with blood group antigens. Unlike sialic acids, sulphate groups are located internally linked to GlcNAc or Gal.[1–4]

Sialic acids occur in several forms, differing in the position and number of the substituent groups. This structural variability is a noteworthy cause of considerable problems

Backbone   Core

Gal-beta-(1—>3/4)-GlcNAc-beta-(1—>-- GalNAc-O-Serine/Threonine
Fuc-alpha-(1——>2)
Peripheral

Fig. 7.1 Diagram representing the carbohydrate side chain of blood group H determinant.

in biochemical and histochemical analysis of mucus glycoproteins. Sialic acids are the N- and O-acyl derivatives of a nine-carbon sugar, neuraminic acid, NeuAc, which contains both a carbohydrate and an amino group, with the latter most commonly substituted with an acetyl or a glycolyl group. The most common derivative is N-acetyl neuraminic acid (NANA).[6–8]

Further information pertaining to mucin structure and expression may lead to a better understanding of the pathology of several diseases.

Molecular basis of mucin biology

To date five different genes have been identified which code for mucins or mucin-like proteins. The sequences obtained show that in each case a large domain of the mucin is made up of tandem repeats, with a different sequence for each mucin. They have been identified as separate genes by virtue of the fact that they are located on different human chromosomes and/or show no overlap in nucleotide sequence. The three best known are MUC1, MUC2, MUC3.[9–14]

MUC1 gene was cloned from breast and pancreatic cells, and encodes a transmembrane protein and is located in chromosome 1q21–24. MUC1 has also been designated polymorphic epithelial mucin (PEM), peanut-lectin binding urinary mucin (PUM), episialin or MAM-6, DF3 antigen, H23 antigen, PAS-O, epithelial membrane antigen (EMA) and NCRC11 antigen.[15] MUC2 and MUC3 genes were cloned from human colon cancer cells and small intestinal mucin respectively.

MUC2 gene is located on chromosome 11 p15-5 and MUC3 on chromosome 7. All three genes are polymorphic. There is evidence that more than one gene is expressed in the different mucosae tested but there are differences in their relative expression.

Immunohistochemistry and in situ hybridization are still needed to determine whether the different genes are expressed in different cells or whether more than one mucin is synthesized within the same cell. The extent to which these different gene products differ in their glycosylation is also not known, nor whether the differences in mucin expression detected by histochemical methods in any way correlate with the expression of different genes.[16–18]

At present histochemical and immunohistochemical methods to identify and define mucin changes in tissue are still useful diagnostic tools.

This chapter will include:

(i) Histochemical characterization of mucin in the gastrointestinal tract
(ii) Application of mucin histochemistry to diagnosis in the GI tract, and
(iii) A brief report on the expression of MUCl, MUC2 and MUC3 in the gastrointestinal epithelium and altered patterns in malignancy.

HISTOCHEMICAL CHARACTERIZATION AND NOMENCLATURE

Classical methods

Mucins are classified into neutral and acidic and the latter further separated into sialomucins and sulphomucins. The sialomucins can be further divided into N- and O-acetyl types[19,20] (Tables 7.1, 7.2). The most widely used histochemical stains are the PAS techniques and cationic dyes such as alcian blue (AB) and high iron diamine (HID).

The PAS method is based on a selective oxidation of vicinal glycols to produce aldehydes which combine with a Schiff's leucobase to form a red-colour product. The sugars responsible for a positive PAS reaction in mucins are galactose, fucose (mannose and glucose if present) and, under certain circumstances, N-acetylhexosamines (GlcNAc and Ga1NAc)[1] and non-substituted sialic acids (N-acyl sialic acids).[7,8,21]

Sialic acids can be further characterized by modified PAS techniques involving borohydride blockage and potassium hydroxide saponification (PB/KOH/PAS) and periodate thionin-Schiff/potassium hydroxide/periodic acid-Schiff (PT/KOH/PAS).[22] In the former a positive red PAS reaction may indicate O-acylated sialic acids (N-acyl sialic acids and neutral sugars will not stain) whereas in the second method a blue colour (thionin) indicates non-

Table 7.1 Histochemical techniques to characterize epithelial mucins.

	PAS[20]	ABpH2.5[19]	ABpH2.5/PAS[19]	HID[19,24]	HID/ABpH2.5[19,24]	KOH/ABpH1.0/mPAS[28]*
Mucins:						
Neutral	○	–	○	–	–	–
Acidic	○/–	●	●	Ø/–	Ø/●	○/●
Sialylated	○	●	●	–	●	○
Sulphated	–	●	●	Ø	Ø	●

Colour key: ○ = Red; ● = Blue; Ø = Brown; – = negative (no colour)
Abbreviations: PAS = Periodic acid Schiff; AB = Alcian blue; HID = High-iron diamine; KOH/ABpH1.0/mPAS = Potassium hydroxide (Saponification)/Alcian blue at pH1.0/mild PAS
(*) A version of this technique uses Phenylhydrazine (Ph) to block neutral sugars (KOH/ABpH1.0/PA/Ph/s)[29]

Table 7.2 Histochemical techniques to identify sialic acids.

	Sialic acids				
	N-acylated	O-acylated			Neutral sugars
	Co	C7	C8	C9	
PAS	○	○	–	○	○
D-PAS(*)[20]	○	○	–	○	○
PAPhS[23]	○	○	–	○	–
KOH/PAPhS[23]	○	○	○	○	–
mPAS[7]	○	○	○	○?	–
KOH/mPAS[7]	○	○	○	○	–
mPB/KOH/mPAS[7]	–	○	○	○	–
PB/KOH/PAS[8]	–	○	○	–	–
PAT/KOH/Bh/PAS[22]	●	●	○	●	●
PAPhT/KOH/Bh/PAS[22]	●	●	○	●	–

Colour key: ○ = red; ● = blue; – = negative (no colour); ? = doubtful
Abbreviations: PAS = Periodic acid Schiff; D-PAS = Diastase-PAS; PAPhS = Periodic acid/Phenylhydrazine/Schiff; KOH/PAPhS = Potassium hydroxide (Saponification)/PAPhS; mPAS = mild PAS; mPB/KOH/mPAS = mild Periodic acid/Borohydride/KOH/mPAS; PAT/KOH/Bh/PAS = Periodic acid Thionine Schiff/KOH/Borohydride/PAS; PAPhT/KOH/Bh/PAs = Periodic acid/Phenylhydrazine/Thionine Schiff/KOH/Bh/PAS.
(*) D-PAS: removes glycogen. This step may be important in foetal gut and in tumours which contain significant amounts of glycogen.

substituted sialic acids and neutral sugars and a red colour indicates the O-acylated sialic acids. Other steps and permutations can be used to block periodate reactivity due to neutral sugars (phenylhydrazine),[23] to discriminate between the various O-acylated sialic acids and the specific removal of sialic acids by neuraminidase (Table 7.2).[7,22]

Acid mucins are identified by cationic dyes (basic dyes), the most common of which is alcian blue (AB). The distinction between sialylated and sulphated mucins can be achieved by varying the pH of the alcian blue solution or by the high iron diamine method (HID) which specifically stains sulphomucins (brown) but not sialomucins. In the combined HID/AB stain the sulphated groups react with the diamines and stain brown whilst sialic acids react with alcian blue and stain blue. Ferric chloride added to the solution acts as an oxidant and, by lowering the pH of the solution (pH 1.3), prevents the ionization of carboxyl groups (mainly sialic acids and nucleic acids) which could otherwise react with the positively charged diamine content.[19,24–26]

Combination of stains such as AB/PAS and/or HID/AB enables the simultaneous assessment of the proportions of the various mucin types in the epithelium examined.

The nomenclature proposed is very simple and the following points need to be stressed. Neutral mucins are defined by the failure to demonstrate the presence of acidic groups reacting with cationic dyes (alcian blue or HID). It does not preclude the presence of sialic acid or sulphate in small amounts which may not be detectable by histochemical methods.[23] Conversely, an acidic mucin includes in its structure large numbers of neutral sugars. On HID/AB staining the presence of a blue colour indicative of sialomucins does not preclude the presence of sulphate, nor a brown colour indicate absence of sialic acid, but more often indicates proportions of the different groups. The stain may give different results depending on the concentration of the ferric chloride, the exact formulae of the diamine salts and their known instability.[27] The use of the correct technique is paramount for consistent results.[19] Another factor is the masking effect of the combined stains making it difficult to assess a mixture of acidic glycoproteins.

An alternative technique to HID/AB involves saponification followed by alcian blue pH 1.0, followed by mild PAS (KOH/AB pH 1.O/mPAS).[28] This method is similar to that described by Reid et al[29] which gives vivid and reproducible staining of sulphate groups and sialic acids. However, the method is too laborious to perform and the sharp differences in sialo/sulphomucin content seen in certain conditions using HID/AB, are blurred when KOH/AB pH 1.0/PAS is applied. On the identification of the various types of sialic acids, a positive PAS staining, following blockade and saponification, indicates the presence of O-acylated substitutes, but the same molecule may contain N-acetyl groups and it is therefore more correct to refer to relative proportions of N- and O-acetyl sialic acids rather than use mutually exclusive terminology.

Provided that the techniques are carefully controlled and standardized, the limitations recognized and the right nomenclature used, these methods form a strong basis for the characterization of mucins in individual cells. Details of the methods and their interpretation are given in Tables 7.1 and 7.2.

Lectin binding

Lectins are specific carbohydrate-binding proteins of non-immune origin. They bind non-covalently to exposed terminal sugar residues of mucous glycoproteins and other glycoconjugates. Those more commonly used in the study of gastrointestinal mucins and their sugar specificities are shown in Table 7.3.[30]

The specificity of a lectin is generally described in terms of binding to free monosaccharide but it is important to realize that the patterns of lectin binding are more complex than the quoted monosaccharide specificities would suggest. Thus, the correlation of lectin histochemical findings with specific hexoses must be interpreted with caution until the precise nature of the lectin receptor is known.

Antibodies to carbohydrate-associated antigens

In recent years there has been a great deal of interest in carbohydrate-associated tissue and tumour-specific antigens and their potential role as markers of malignant change, especially in the gastrointestinal tract. Monoclonal antibodies have been extensively used in this work and in general it seems that the altered antigenic expression in tumour cells is related to changes in the carbohydrate end chains.

Many of these monoclonal antibodies recognize carbohydrate structures related to blood group antigens. Some of the cancer associated antigens include the A, B, H blood group substances, Le^a and Le^b, sialylated Le^a, Le^x, sialylated Le^x, I, and T-antigen.

MUCIN IN FETAL GASTROINTESTINAL EPITHELLUM

Stomach

Glycogen is present in vacuoles in the surface epithelium in early fetal life (12 weeks) but not from 24 weeks onwards.[31] At 14 weeks the mucous surface epithelium is well-formed, a few specialized cells appear and incipient mucous gland-like structures can be identified. Throughout fetal life, gastric surface mucous secretion contains a mixture of sialo- and neutral mucins in varying proportions (Fig. 7.2). The high sialo/neutral mucin ratio seen at 18 weeks gradually decreases, and at 23 weeks gestation neutral mucins are predominant, reaching an adult pattern at birth. Sialomucins, however, persist in the neck region, particularly in the body of the stomach. O-acylated

Table 7.3 Lectins used to investigate gastrointestinal mucins and their sugar specificities.

Common abbreviation	Source	Sugar specificity	References
BPA	*Bauhinia purpura*	GalNAc > D-Gal	Colon[34,109,110] Stomach[71] Colon[91]
BSA(I)	*Bandeirea simplicifolia*	Alpha-D-Gal > alpha-D-GalNAc	
BSA(II) or GSA(I) + (II)	*Griffonia simplicifolia*	Beta-D-GlcNAc Beta-D-GlcNAc	
ConA	Jack bean (*Canavalia ensiformis*)	Alpha-D-Man > alpha-D-Glc > alpha-D-GlcNAc	Stomach[43,71] Colon[91]
DBA	Horse gram (*Dolichos biflorus*)	Alpha-D-Gal-NAc >> alpha-D-Gal	Stomach[44,71] Small intestine[78] Colon[34,90,109,110]
HPA	*Helix pomatia* (edible snail)	Alpha-D-GalNAc > alpha-D-GlcNAc > Alpha-DGal	Stomach[43,44]
LCA	Lentil bean (*Lens culinaris*)	Alpha-D-MAn > alpha-D-Glc or Alpha-D-GlcNAc	Colon[91]
LFA	*Limax flavus* (slug)	N-acetylneuraminic acid N-glycolylneuraminic acid	Stomach[43]
PNA	Peanut (*Arachis hypogaea*)	Beta-D-Gal-(1 → 3)-D-GalNAc > D-GalNH$_2$ or Alpha-D-Gal	Stomach[43,44,71] Small intestine[78] Colon[34,91,108–110,135,136]
RCA$_1$	Castor bean (*Ricinus communis*)	Beta-D-Gal > alpha-D-Gal	Stomach[43,71] Small intestine[78] Colon[34,89,109,110]
SBA	Soybean (*Glycine max*)	Alpha-D-GalNAc > beta-D-GalNAc >> alpha-D-Gal	Stomach[44,71] Small intestine[78] Colon[34,110,125]
UEA$_1$	Gorse seed (*Ulex europea*)	Alpha-L-Fuc	Stomach[43,71] Small intestine[78] Colon[88–90]
VVA	*Vicia villosa*	D-GalNAc	Colon[91]
WGA	Wheat germ (*Triticum vulgaris*)	Beta-D-GlcNAcp(1 —> 4)-beta-D-GlcNAcp (1 —> 4)GlcNAc > beta-D-GlcNAcp (1 —> 4)beta-D-GlcNAc	Stomach[43,71] Small intestine[78] Colon[34,91,109,110]

Abbreviations: Fucose = Fuc; Galactose = Gal; Glucose = Glc; N-acetylgalactosamine = GalNAc; N-acetylglucosamine = GlcNAc.

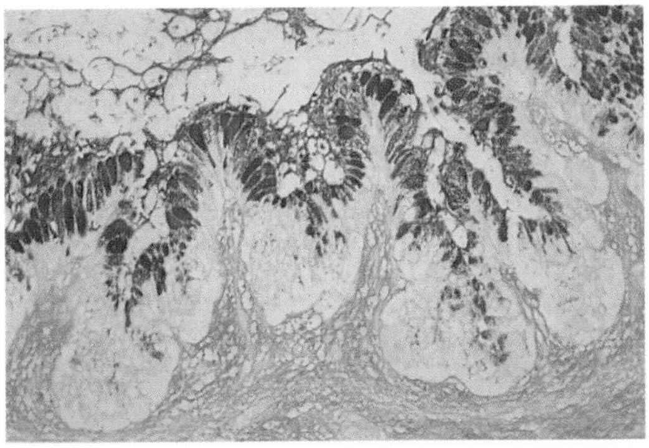

Fig. 7.2 Fetal stomach at 15 weeks' gestation. Columnar cells in the surface and glandular epithelium secrete a mixture of neutral (red) and acid mucins (blue and purple). Some cells have a 'goblet'-like shape. (AB/PAS, ×88)

sialomucins and sulphated material are not normally detected but occasionally a trace of HID positivity is seen in the body neck region.

It is also interesting that 'goblet-like' mucus secreting cells occur in the surface and pit epithelium in 18–23 week fetus (Fig. 7.2), a feature resembling incomplete intestinal metaplasia type II, described below. Rarely a tiny focus of intestinal metaplasia occurs in the newborn.[32]

Throughout fetal life mucous cells in the surface and pit epithelium and in the glands reveal a strong affinity for UEA_1, the lectin which correlates well with the mucin pattern (Fig. 7.3). PNA reactivity is weak and focal in the surface and pit mucous cells at 14–15 weeks, increases in intensity reaching a peak at 23 weeks, but decreases with maturation and is absent or found in traces only in the supranuclear cellular region at birth.[32]

Small intestine

Villi begin to form at 7 weeks' gestation and goblet cells appear at 10–12 weeks. Glycogen is present in the vacuolated cells between goblet cells from 12–16 weeks' gestation but then decreases with age and is undetected after birth.[31]

Between 12–15 weeks, goblet cells on the villi contain mainly neutral mucin with little or no sialomucin. The

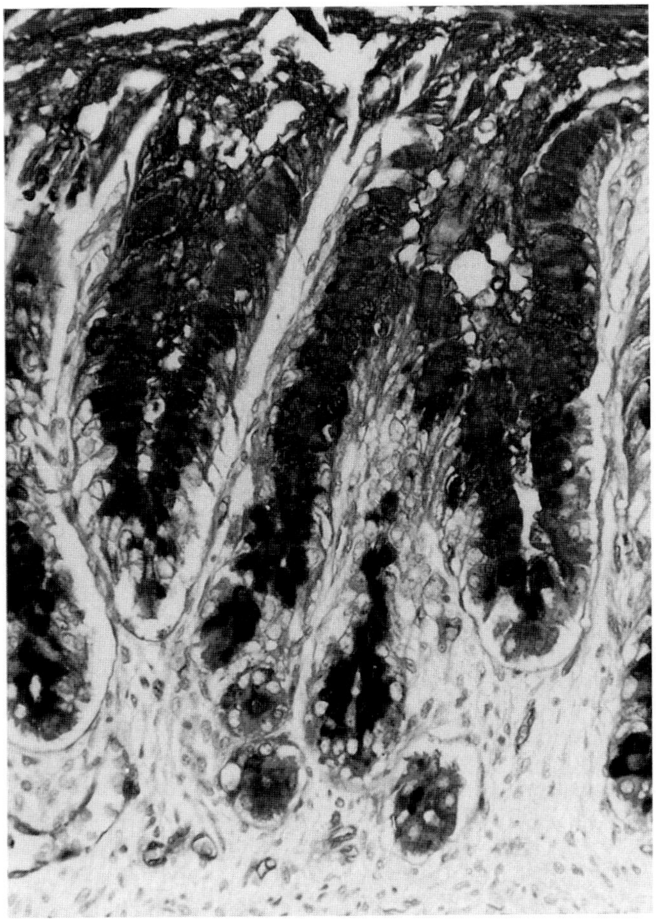

Fig. 7.3 Fetal stomach at 23 weeks' gestation: strong UEA_1 binding to mucous cells in the surface and glandular epithelium. (Direct immunoperoxidase, ×320)

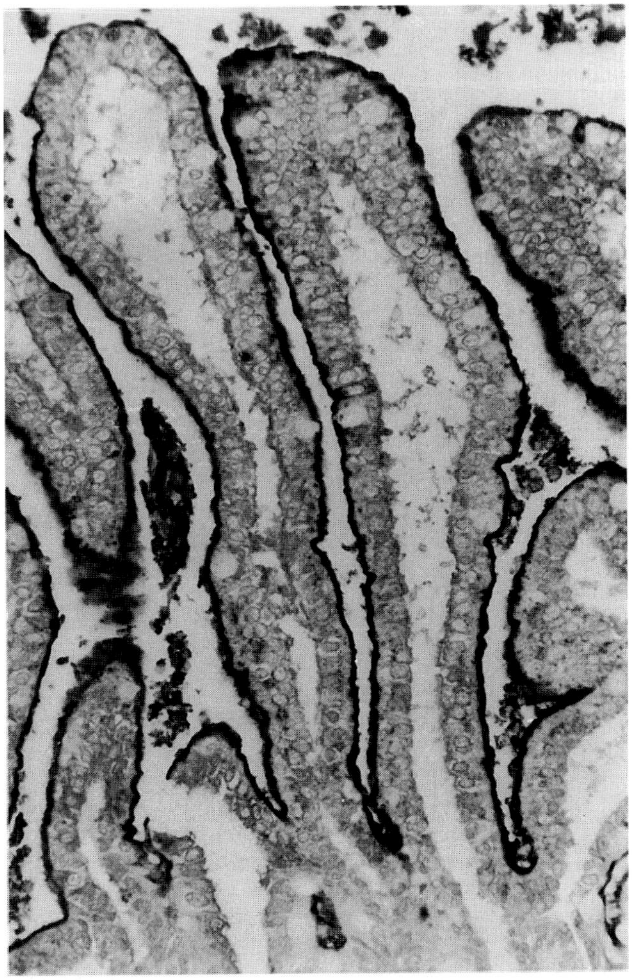

Fig. 7.4 Fetal small intestine at 23 weeks' gestation: PNA binds to the glycocalyx but not to goblet cell mucin. (Direct immunoperoxidase, ×320)

sialomucin content then gradually increases first in the goblet cells of the villi and then later in the crypt cells also. At birth, neutral mucins still persist in the crypt cells but are absent in cells in the villi. Occasionally traces of O-acylated sialic acids are observed, but sulphomucins are not seen.[32,33]

Affinity for UEA_1 is usually absent although occasional goblet cells at 20–30 weeks show positive binding. UEA_1 reactivity, though weak, is more consistently observed focally in the glycocalyx and in the crypt base cells from 14–23 weeks. At birth the glycocalyx displays a more pronounced UEA_1 binding. There is little or no affinity for PNA in either goblet or absorptive cells, though traces can be observed in the supranuclear region, particularly after neuraminidase treatment. The occasional goblet cells show positive PNA staining following neuraminidase digestion whereas the glycocalyx consistently binds PNA throughout development and this is unaffected by neuraminidase (Fig. 7.4).[32]

Colon

In early uterine life the colonic epithelium forms broad and short villi covered by glycogen-rich vacuolated cells.[31] Mucin-secreting goblet cells only appear later at 14–15 weeks and thereafter display a weak PAS reaction and intense staining with alcian blue at pH 2.5. Mucin composition changes from right to left colon and from lower to upper crypt.

Throughout fetal development acid mucins predominate. In the upper half of the crypt sialomucins are the only detectable acidic group up to 18 weeks gestation. Sulphated mucins appear in a few goblet cells at 20 weeks and then increase in amount gradually so that at birth, as in the adult, they predominate. In contrast sulphomucin appears earlier at 14 weeks in the crypt cells and is the main acid mucin at 20 weeks (Fig. 7.5A,B). A higher O/N-acylated sialomucin ratio is revealed at 22–23 weeks and at birth the pattern of staining is similar to the adult.[32]

As in the adult, differences exist between right and left colon. In the right side goblet cells in the lower half of the crypt contain mainly sialomucins whilst sulphomucins predominate in the upper crypt. The converse pattern is seen in the left colon. Furthermore, the right side shows a strong PAS reactivity and a higher proportion of neuraminidase sensitive sialic acids than the left, though the

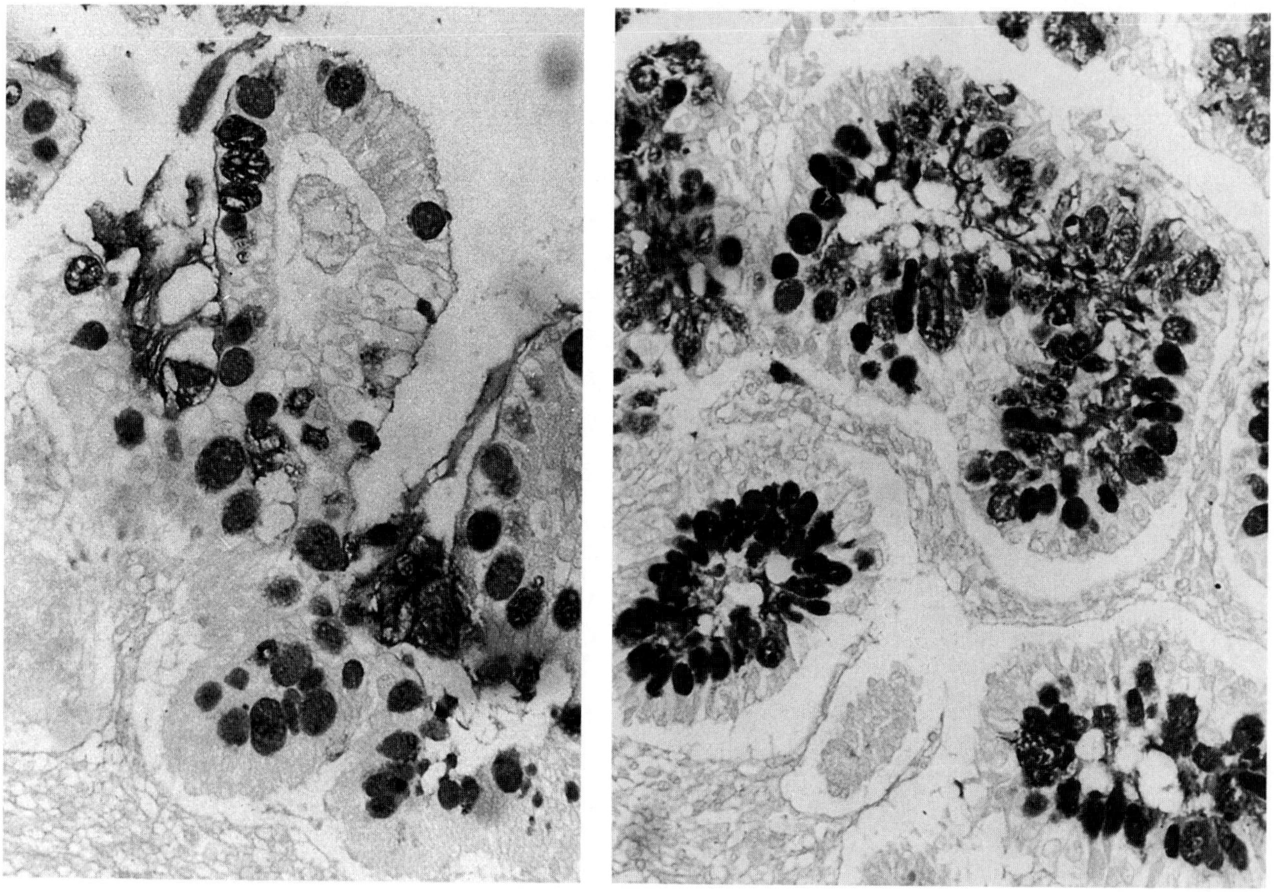

A B

Fig. 7.5 Fetal colon: **A** at 15 weeks goblet cells, both in lower and upper crypt, contain mainly sialomucins (grey); **B** Sulphomucins (black) gradually appear, being predominant at 23 weeks. (HID/AB, ×320)

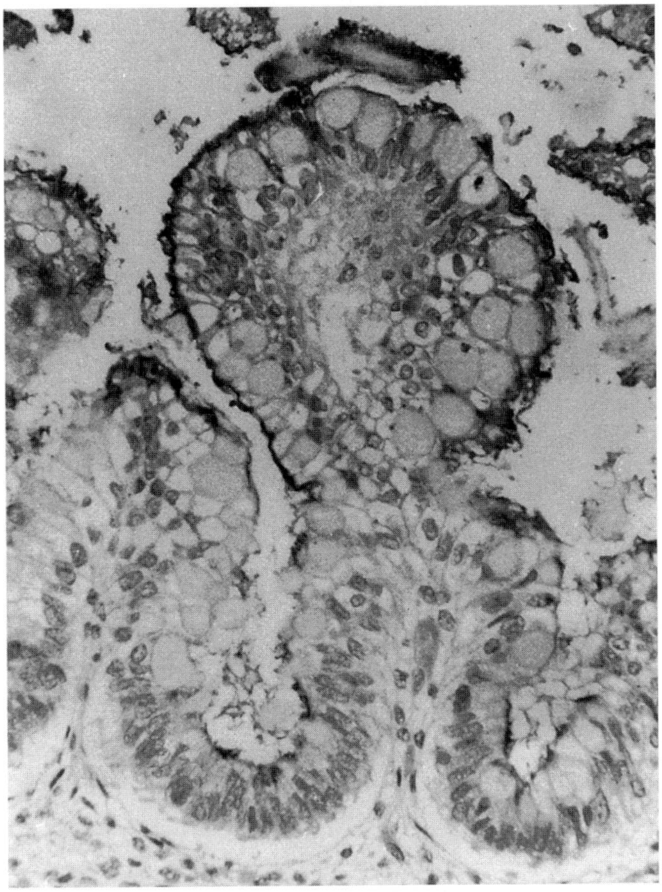

Fig. 7.6 Fetal colon at 15 weeks shows broad villi formation and PNA binding to glycocalyx but not to goblet cell mucin. Traces of positive PNA staining may be found in crypt base cells. (Direct immunoperoxidase, ×340)

neuraminidase effect decreases at the later stages of development.[31,32]

No UEA_1 binding is seen throughout fetal development in the colon, but occasionally at 14 weeks, 20 weeks, and at birth, focal positive staining of the glycocalyx is present. Fetal colon does not show affinity for PNA. Occasional binding is observed in the glycocalyx and in a few cells at the crypt base (Fig. 7.6). DBA affinity is seen in the goblet cells throughout fetal life.[30,32–35]

MUCIN IN OESOPHAGEAL, GASTRIC AND INTESTINAL EPITHELIUM: CHANGES IN DISEASE

Oesophagus

The submucosal glands of the lower oesophagus secrete a mixture of neutral, sialo- and, predominantly, sulphomucins.[36,37]

In Barrett's oesophagus, the squamous epithelium of the lower oesophagus is replaced by a columnar mucus secreting epithelium with histochemical characteristics similar to those observed in the gastric mucosa. This condition predisposes to the development of oesophageal adenocarcinoma and is generally regarded as a premalignant lesion. The columnar epithelium of Barrett's oesophagus is complex and three types are identified: fundic, cardiac and intestinal. Most adenocarcinomas arise from dysplasia in areas of intestinal metaplasia. Intestinal metaplasia shows the same variants as those observed in the gastric epithelium. A high frequency of incomplete sulphomucin secreting type III intestinal metaplasia and loss of O-acylated sialomucins have been described in association with adenocarcinoma though the significance of the altered mucin as a predictor of malignancy is still debatable in the Barrett's epithelium.[38,39]

Stomach

In the normal gastric mucosa, neutral mucins are predominant in the columnar mucous cells of the surface and foveolar epithelium, in the mucous neck cells and in the antral and cardiac glands. Traces of acid mucins, both sialyl and sulphated, are not uncommon in the body region in cells at the base of the pits, in the mucous neck cells and focally at the base of antral glands. Sialomucins, and less frequently sulphomucins, have also been demonstrated in cardiac epithelium and in gastro-oesophageal glands in biopsies from patients with reflux oesophagitis.[39] O-acylated sialomucins are not detected in the normal gastric epithelium.[40–42] Normal gastric mucus secreting cells seem to react with almost all of the commonly investigated lectins (Table 7.3).

The surface and foveolar epithelia show strong affinity for UEA_1, HPA, DBA, BSA, SBA, less for WGA, but not for ConA or LFA.[43] There are conflicting results regarding the presence or absence of PNA.[44] The intense RCA staining of the deep foveolar cells decreases as cells become differentiated towards the surface.[43]

The undifferentiated cells in the isthmus region reveal a distinct PNA binding selective to the Golgi region, a weaker RCA_1, and traces of UEA_1, and HPA binding to the Golgi.[43] Mucous neck cells, antral and cardiac glands show an affinity for all the lectins referred to above except LFA, and in the case of ConA and SBA, the results are conflicting. Parietal cells display strong reaction with HPA, PNA, UEA_1, DBA, and SBA. Chief cells show intense staining with RCA_1, PNA, BSA, and DBA. Neuraminidase digestion does not seem to affect the binding to HPA, DBA, PNA or SBA in normal gastric epithelium.[42–44]

Some of the differences in lectin binding profiles, referred to by various authors, may be related to the effect of the blood group and secretor status of the individual. It has been shown that PNA binding to surface mucous cells occurred in non-secretors, but not in secretors, independent of ABO blood group, whereas binding to DBA and HPA is related to group A secretors, and SBA shows no relationship with either blood group or secretor status. Lectin affinity in other sites, such as mucous neck cells, pyloric glands, parietal and chief cells is not affected by either blood group or secretor status.[44]

Precancerous lesions and carcinoma

Gastric carcinoma frequently develops in the presence of atrophic gastritis and intestinal metaplasia (IM), and there is strong evidence for a sequence of chronic atrophic gastritis, intestinal metaplasia, dysplasia and eventually carcinoma of the intestinal type, a process that may take as long as 20 years.[45]

Intestinal metaplasia (IM)

The heterogeneity of IM has been recognized by ultrastructure, enzymatic profile, mucin secretion and antigenic expression.[46] Based on cell differentiation and mucin secretion three types of IM can be recognized.[46]

Type 1 (complete). This comprises straight crypts with regular architecture, and lined by mature absorptive and goblet cells. Goblet cells secrete sialomucins with a high proportion of N-acylated derivates and occasionally sulphomucins. The absorptive cells are non-secretory. Paneth cells are often present (Fig. 7.7).

Type II (incomplete). There is mild architectural distortion with slightly irregular crypts lined by few or no absorptive cells, goblet cells and columnar mucous cells in various stages of differentiation. These secrete a mixture of neutral and sialomucin. The goblet cells secrete sialo- and occasionally sulphomucins. No O-acylated sialomucins are detected, either in goblet or columnar cells. Paneth cells are less conspicuous. (Figs 7.8, 7.9, 7.10A).

Type III (incomplete). This type shows a variable degree of distorted glandular architecture. Cell atypia and dedifferentiation is more marked than in type II. Columnar cells secrete predominantly sulphomucins, and goblet

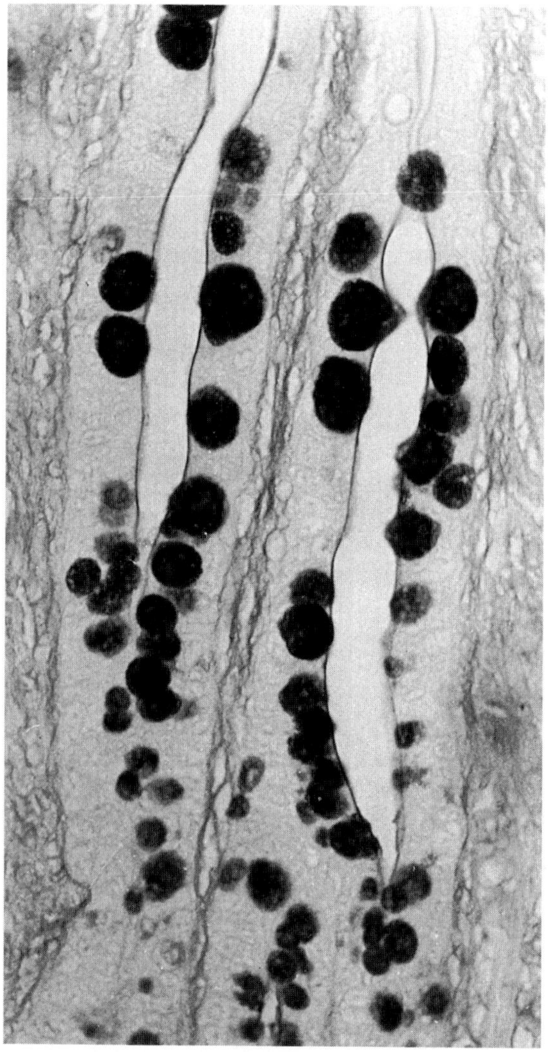

Fig. 7.7 Gastric mucosa: intestinal metaplasia type I. Straight crypts lined by goblet cells secreting acid mucins and mature non-secreting absorptive cells in between. (AB/PAS, ×680)

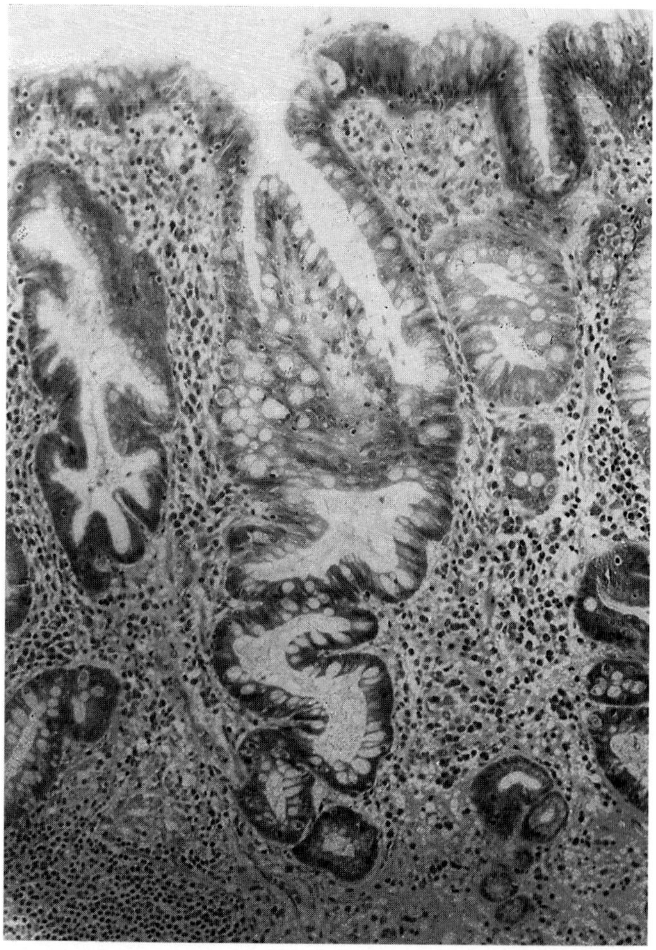

Fig. 7.8 Gastric mucosa: intestinal metaplasia incomplete (types II or III). The crypts are often tortuous and lined by goblet cells with columnar mucus-secreting cells in between. (H & E, ×320) (See Figs 7.9 & 7.10).

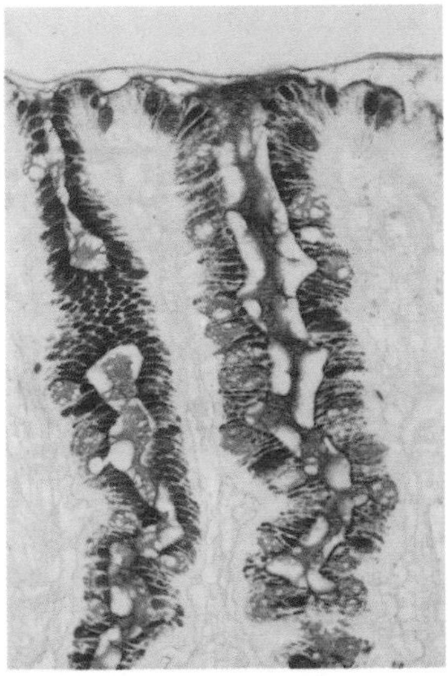

Fig. 7.9 Gastric mucosa. Intestinal metaplasia incomplete (types II or III). The incomplete types II and III show similar features on AB/PAS stain. Goblet cells contain acid mucins and stain blue, whilst columnar mucous cells secrete a mixture of neutral and acid mucins (red, blue, purple). The two types can be distinguished on HID/AB stain shown in Fig. 7.10. (AB/PAS, ×88)

cells contain sialo and/or sulphomucins. Paneth cells are reduced in number. (Plates 7.9, 7.10B).

Sulphomucins may be present in goblet cells regardless of the type of IM and is not a criterion for type III IM.[46,47] Sulphomucins may also be detected in the base of antral and pyloric glands, within cysts and very occasionally in trace amounts in mucous neck cells. It is interesting to note that increased sulphomucin in these non-metaplastic epithelia is not uncommon in gastric biopsies from patients in high risk cancer areas.[48] In addition to these three variants there are transitional forms, which suggest the metaplastic process is a dynamic one in which one form may evolve to another or even regress.[49]

Similar types of metaplasia based on mucin profiles have been referred to as 'small intestinal' and 'colonic' or 'enterocolic' by others[50,51] and roughly they correspond to type I and III as above. Other classifications further subdivide IM into different categories according to the staining patterns of the goblet cells, and the presence or absence of O-acylated sialomucins.[52]

Mucins and mucin — associated antigens in the screening for gastric cancer

Intestinal metaplasia and dysplasia

Retrospective studies in different populations from various centres have indicated a close association between incomplete sulphomucin secreting type 3 IM and gastric carcinoma. Types 1 and 2 non-sulphated are not discriminatory, being prevalent in both benign and malignant conditions.[46,51,53–55]

Of all instances in which IM occurs, type I is the most common. The prevalence of type 3 IM varies in high and low risk cancer areas. In low risk areas, type 3 IM is observed in approximately 10% of biopsies[53,54,56] compared to 24–41% in Slovenia[48] and Venezuela,[57] countries with a high incidence of gastric cancer. A significantly higher risk of developing gastric cancer in patients with type 3 IM has been confirmed in a large cohort study in Slovenia.[58] An increased frequency of detection of early gastric carcinoma has been reported in patients with type 3 IM who were closely followed-up with endoscopy and biopsy.[59]

The presence of type 3 IM in patients with chronic atrophic gastritis is often related to chronicity of disease and can evolve to dysplasia. In gastric ulcer patients type

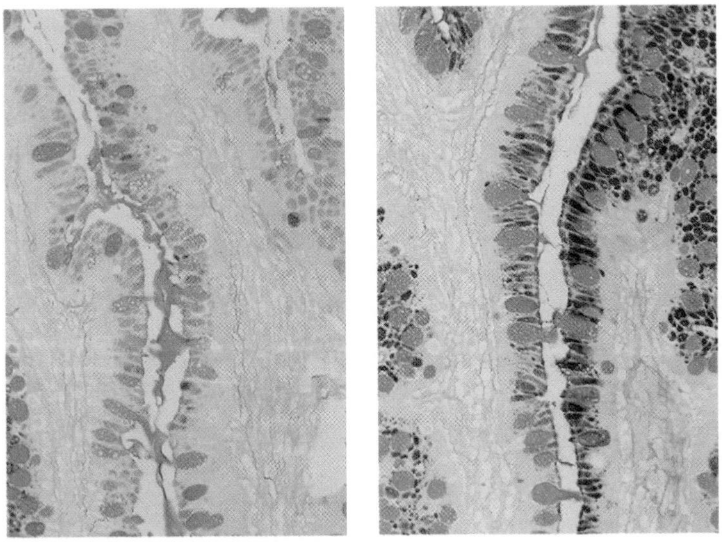

A B

Fig. 7.10 Gastric mucosa. Intestinal metaplasia incomplete: **A** Type II IM on HID/AB stain shows columnar mucous cells and goblet cells secreting sialomucins (blue). Goblet cells may secrete sulphomucins. In this figure tiny specks of sulphomucins are seen in the occasional columnar cell — this is one example of perhaps a transition to **B** a definite type III IM with columnar mucous cells secreting predominantly sulphomucins (brown). (HID/AB, ×88)

3 IM is often associated with delayed healing and recurrency indicating that screening for these patients is important.[49] A higher incidence of sulphomucin secreting intestinal metaplasia has been reported in pernicious anaemia patients and in first degree cancer relatives than in age-matched controls.[51]

Dysplasia in flat mucosa or in adenomatous polyps often shares mucin profiles with incomplete sulphated intestinal metaplasia. Hyperplastic polyps which have low malignant potential secrete only traces of sulphomucins or more frequently none at all.[60] Hyperplastic polyps that occasionally undergo malignant change appear to do so in areas of intestinal metaplasia within the polyps.[61]

Abnormal expression of Le^a antigens in gastric epithelium in patients with Le(a–b+)phenotype, has been detected with increasing frequency in type 3 IM and dysplasia and it appears that the combination of both Le^a antigen expression and sulphomucin staining for IM may prove to be a more sensitive marker for cancer risk in type 3 IM and dysplasia than either marker alone.[62]

These markers are currently being used in the screening for identification of cancer risk in precancer lesions and detection of early stage gastric cancer in various populations. As the lesions are focal and intestinal metaplasia is associated with intestinal rather than diffuse type gastric carcinoma, one should be aware of the limitations and multiple biopsies from different areas need to be taken.

In addition to the blood group antigens described above, other mucin associated antigens have been identified which are expressed in fetal gut and can reappear in the course of malignant transformation.

Fetal sulphoglycoprotein antigen (FSA): This antigen cross-reacts with CEA and is found in fetal stomach, gastric carcinoma and in the adjacent non neoplastic epithelium.[63] It is not clear whether the distribution of FSA correlates with sulphomucin-secreting incomplete IM.

Intestinal mucin antigens (M_3SI, M_3D, and M_3C):[64–66] These antigens, prepared from duodenal and colonic epithelium, are expressed in the goblet cells of normal adult small intestine (M_3SI), duodenal villi (M_3D), and large intestine (M_3C). The small intestinal antigens (M_3SI and M_3D) are all detected in fetal duodenum. M_3C, in association with the other two antigens, is only observed in a few goblet cells in a later stage of fetal development.

Intestinal metaplasia in benign conditions expresses both small intestinal antigens (M_3SI and M_3D). By contrast, IM adjacent to gastric carcinoma, whatever the histological type, produces M_3C (in addition to M_3D and M_3SI antigens) — a pattern similar to that seen in fetal duodenal mucosa. The antigenic phenotype of type 3 IM suggests fetal duodenal features rather than colonic differentiation. Some gastric carcinomas, particularly the intestinal type, produce the same colonic M_3C antigen as the neighbouring IM.[65,66]

M_3SI, M_3C and M_3D antigenic determinants appear to be distinct from other antigens of both normal and malignant gastrointestinal tissues such as colonic specific antigen (CSA),[66] and colonic mucosa antigen (CMA).[67]

Mucin profile in carcinomas

Gastric carcinomas are generally divided into two broad categories according to Lauren and Ming classifications:

(i) Intestinal type (IGCa) often showing an expanding growth pattern and arising in a background of intestinal metaplasia
(ii) Diffuse type (DGCa), with little glandular differentiation and infiltrative growth seem to develop from non-metaplastic epithelium.

These two types of carcinoma differ in their biological behaviour.[68,69]

Marked heterogeneity of mucus secretion is often seen in gastric carcinomas. The majority secrete acid mucins, but whereas acid mucins and particular sulphomucins predominate in the intestinal type, neutral or sialomucins are more abundant in diffuse and mucoid carcinomas. N-acylated sialomucins can be found in either type but O-acylated sialic acids have not been detected in gastric carcinomas.[40–42,70]

The increased presence of sialomucins in the surface of tumour cells may be related to metastatic potential by concealing recognition sites on the tumour cells responsible for specific or non-specific immunological modulation of tumour growth and also affect cell/cell and cell/mesenchymal interactions, as described later in this chapter.

Mucus-associated antigen, M_3C,[64,66] is often expressed in gastric carcinomas, especially the intestinal type. The sialylated Lewis blood group determinant Ca 19-9 is also found in gastrointestinal carcinomas and also frequently expressed in benign gastric epithelium,[71] thus it has little practical value in assessing premalignancy.

The distribution of different lectin binding sites varies considerably within a given tumour and in different tumour types. In general, there is a decrease or loss of lectin binding affinity as compared to the normal gastric epithelium.[43,72] The pattern of staining also varies in relation to blood group and secretor status. The HPA and DBA binding by mucous cells, which is related to blood group A secretor status, is partially retained in carcinoma, whereas PNA binding related to non-secretor status is lost in carcinoma.[44] In general, most IGCa reveal intense PNA affinity which is not influenced by neuraminidase treatment. The binding with other lectins is less intense. In contrast, DGCa shows a higher affinity for HPA, RCA_1,and UEA_1, accompanied by a decrease in PNA which can, however, be detected following neuraminidase digestion. Other studies report extensive masking of lectin binding by sialic acid in carcinomas, particularly with

PNA and to a lesser degree with HPA, SBA and DBA.[44] The differences in lectin binding between IGCa and DGCa seem to correlate with the predominant neutral and sialomucin secretion in DGCa demonstrated by conventional histochemical methods described above.

Small intestine

Normal

Goblet cells in the normal duodenum, jejunum and ileum secrete PAS-positive material which contains both neutral and sialomucins. Sialomucins are predominantly N-acylated, and sulphomucins are either not detected or found in a few goblet cells in areas close to the ileo-caecal valve.[36,73,74]

Brunner's glands mucus gives a strong PAS reaction which is totally abolished by prior saponification, gives a blue-grey colour with the Thionin Schiff-Saponification-PAS sequence and does not stain with HID/AB indicating the presence of neutral mucins.[74]

The proportions of the different types of mucins in the goblet cells vary along the crypts and villi and in the various regions of the small intestine. Goblet cells in the crypts produce mainly neutral mucins, whereas sialomucins predominate in cells on the villi. The proportion of N- and O-acylated sialomucins and neutral mucins, and their distribution in both villus and crypt, becomes particularly noticeable in sections stained with ABpH2.5/PAS following pretreatment with neuraminidase, where a display of red, blue and purple shades of colour reveals the sharp difference in mucin composition between these two sites (Fig. 7.11A,B). In the crypts, goblet cell mucin reveals a negative PAS reaction after saponification (PB/KOH/PAS) indicating the absence of O-acylated derivatives of sialic acid. By contrast, a variable number of goblet cells on the villi still retain some PAS reactivity. In the Thionin Schiff KOH-PAS sequence, goblet cells in the crypts stain blue (N-acylated sialomucin and/or neutral mucin) while those on the villi are coloured blue, purple or red, indicating the presence of a variable proportion of N- and O-acylated sialomucins.[36,74] These differences are considered to be a reflection of cell differentiation and maturation, with neutral mucin produced by immature cells in the crypts and sialomucins synthesized as the cells mature and migrate up the villi. This alteration in glycoprotein synthesis with maturation finds support in parallel changes observed in glycosyl and sialyltransferases[75] and mimics mucin profiles during fetal gut development.

The gradient of change in mucin composition from proximal to distal small intestine is characterized by a decreasing fucose to sialic acid ratio, an increase in O-acylated-neuraminidase resistant sialomucins, and the increasing presence of sulphated groups. It appears as a gradual transition to colonic mucins which contain a larger proportion of O-acylated sialomucins and sulphated groups.[36,73,74,76,77]

Lectin binding by the small intestinal epithelium is seen in Table 7.3. Binding occurs with WGA and UEA_1, by both goblet cell mucin and the columnar cell brush border. The affinity for both lectins is weaker or absent at the crypt base, increasing gradually towards the villus tip. A similar pattern is observed in the brush border. Traces of RCA_1 binding are detected in the goblet cell mucin of the villus, but not in the crypt base. Affinity for PNA, DBA and SBA has not been demonstrated.[78] There is strong PNA binding in goblet cells following neuraminidase digestion in trypsinized sections.

The crypt–villus gradient of lectin binding is consistent with a sequential scheme of glycosylation, with GlcNAc

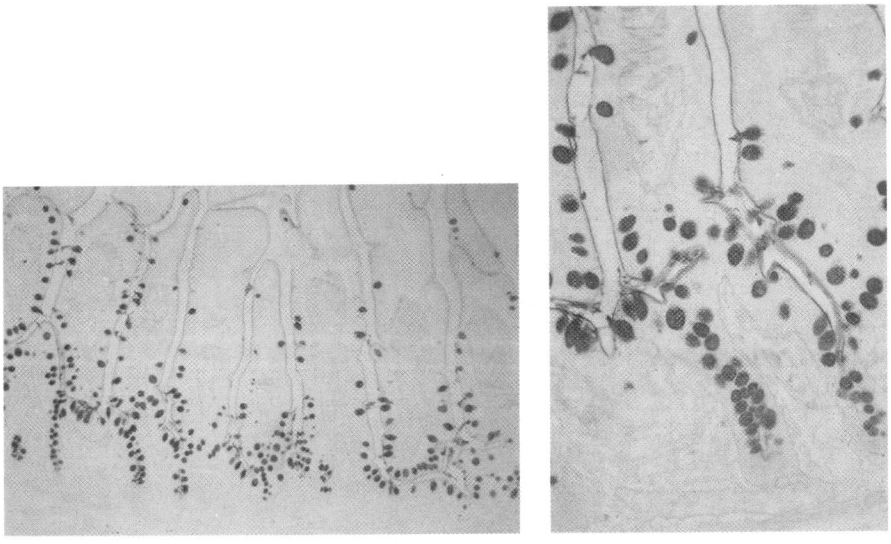

A B

Fig. 7.11 Normal small intestine. **A** On AB/PAS, goblet cells in both villi and crypt stain blue, indicative of acid mucins. (AB/PAS, ×44) **B** Following neuraminidase digestion (on trypsinized sections) a different mucin composition between crypt and villi emerges: the crypt goblet cell mucin has a higher neutral (red)/sialomucin (blue) ratio and the sialic acid content is more labile to neuraminidase than in the villi (Neuraminidase/AB/PAS, ×88) being added at an early stage and detected in the immature cells at the crypt base, followed by the addition of galactose and terminal sugars, such as fucose and sialic acids, as cells migrate and mature on the villus. This correlates well with the mucin patterns observed with the classical mucin stains.

Cystic fibrosis

Changes in the carbohydrate composition of mucus glycoproteins with increased fucose has been detected by biochemical analysis in the meconium and in membrane glycoproteins in fibroblasts. Histochemical studies with a large panel of lectins confirmed intense binding with Lotus Tetragonolobus (LTG) for a-L-fucose, which persist up to term and beyond, in contrast with normal controls, where binding of fucose decreases with fetal maturation and is absent at term and beyond. Abnormal fucosylation is present in cystic fibrosis.[79,80] Other lectins investigated showed no changes compared to matched controls. These alterations in fucosylation and composition of mucins may lead to altered rehological properties of mucus, and enhanced viscosity. Other studies at both histochemical and biochemical level have shown an increase in sulphomucins and a more dense and highly glycosylated mucin containing more sulphate, increased galactose, GlcNAc and a higher fucose–sialylic acid molar ratio than in normal controls but no change in the total sialylic acid. Affinity for various lectins, particularly WGA and UEA_1, did not differ qualitatively from normal.[78,81]

Benign tumours

The few benign tumours reported have grossly followed the pattern of mucin secretion of the normal tissue of origin.[74]

Adenocarcinoma and adjacent mucosa

Carcinomas secrete a variety of mucins which differ from case to case and in different areas within the same tumour. Usually there is a mixture of neutral mucins, both N- and O-acylated sialomucins and sulphomucins which are independent of the site of origin.[74]

Large intestine

Normal

Goblet cells in the normal colorectal epithelium secrete neutral and acid mucins (sulphomucins and sialomucins).[36,82] Sulphomucins are predominant (Fig. 7.12) and both N- and O-acylated sialic substituents are represented (Fig. 7.13), including mono-, di- and tri-O-acyl derivatives.[83] Colonic sialomucins are largely resistant to vibrio cholerae neuraminidase digestion. This may be due to the

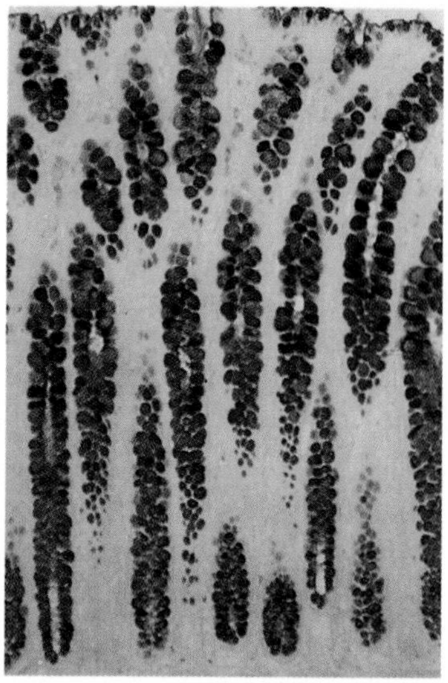

Fig. 7.12 Normal colonic mucosa: goblet cells contain predominantly sulphomucins (brown). (HID/AB, ×44)

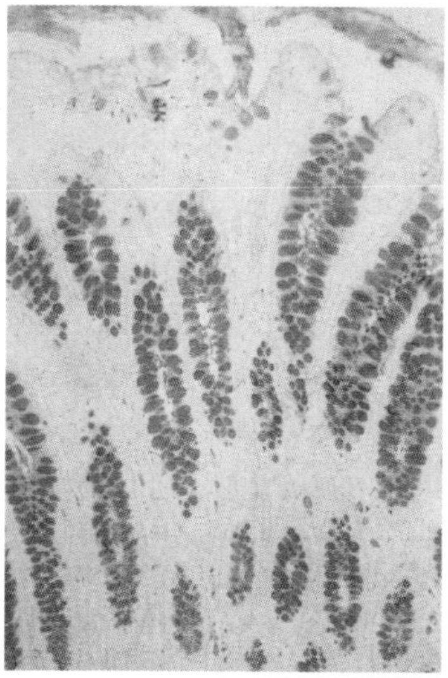

Fig. 7.13 Normal colonic mucosa stained with PATS/KOH/PAS method, to differentiate N- and O-acylated sialomucins, demonstrates the predominance of O-acylated sialic acids (red) in the goblet cell mucin. (×44)

presence of O-acetyl groups in the polyhydroxy side chain or at position C4, or both, or to neuraminidase-resistant glycosidic linkages.[84]

The composition of goblet cell mucin varies with their levels in the crypt and in the different segments of the colon. In the left colon, sulphomucins predominate in the lower half of the crypt, whereas in the upper crypt and surface epithelium, a variable proportion of sulpho- and sialomucins are often demonstrated. The converse is noted in the right colon. From proximal to distal, the ratio of fucose to sialic acid decreases, total sialic acid increases, and there are also differences in the susceptibility of the saponified glycoprotein to neuraminidase digestion. O-acylated sialomucins are predominant in the left colon, but the proportion of N- to O-acylated sialic acids vary in the different parts of the colon.[36,84–86]

Recent studies suggest that O-acetylation of colonic mucins is under the control of a single polymorphic gene.[87] A homozygous acetylator phenotype will show a homogenous negative staining, the homozygous defective phenotype will show a positive uniform staining and scattered positive crypts in the heterozygous phenotype. These phenotypes show a highly significant racial variation in frequency.[87a] Details of the lectin binding by the human colonic mucosa, and the sugar specificities are shown in Tables 7.3 and 7.4.

In the normal colonic epithelium, the lectin binding profiles of the goblet cell mucin vary both within the crypt and in the different regions of the colon, as shown in Table 7.4.[30,88–91]

Transitional mucosa

The term 'Transitional mucosa' (TM) was introduced in 1969[92] to describe 'a zone of transition from frank carcinoma to histochemically normal mucosa and characterized by abnormal mucin secretion'. It was suggested that it might represent an early neoplastic change in colorectal mucosa.[82,92] The concept of TM has since been the source of considerable controversy.[27]

Table 7.4 Lectins profile of goblet cell mucin in the normal colonic epithelium.

Lectins	Right colon		Left colon	References
UEA_1	++	↓↓	+	88–90(a)
RCA_1	+++	↓	++	89
RCA_1			0(b) / +++	
DBA	+		+	89, 90(c)
DBA			+++ / +	34
WGA			+++(d) / +	
WGA			+++	34, 91
BPA			+ / +++	34
SBA			+++ / +	34
PNA			O(e)	34
PNA			O(Sn)(f)	91, 108
VVA			O(Sn)(f)	91
GSA-II			O(Sn)(f)	91
LCA			+++	91
ConA			+++	91

Key: Staining intensity: +++ Strong; ++ Moderate; + Weak; O Negative; ↓↓ Marked decrease; ↓ slight decrease.
(a) Yonezawa et al refer to transitional mucosa not to normal, but the gradient was similar.
(b) Goblet cells in the upper crypt also show binding sites but only after neuraminidase digestion.
(c) Bresalier et al demonstrated DBA staining in the goblet cells in the upper crypt in the right colon whereas in the left side goblet cells all along the crypt are DBA positive.
(d) Also in apical cytoplasm of columnar cells.
(e) With or without neuraminidase.
(f) Some goblet cells after neuraminidase.
Sn = supranuclear binding.

Differences between crypt levels are shown as $\frac{\text{upper crypt}}{\text{lower crypt}}$.

Recently the hypothesis of TM being a paracrine effect of the adjacent tumour has been raised. Nevertheless, TM is an interesting area to explore. Transitional mucosa (TM) is often slightly thicker than normal with elongated and branched glands which are lined by goblet cells showing increased mucus secretion which forms a thick surface coat. Mature absorptive cells are decreased in number and replaced by highly vesiculated mucus secreting 'intermediate' cells. These changes are more conspicuous in the immediate vicinity of the carcinoma, where there is also a concomitant reduction in the number of goblet cells.[82]

Goblet cell mucins contain a higher sialomucin/sulphomucin ration (Fig. 7.14) and a variable reduction of O-acylated sialomucins with an increased proportion of neuraminidase-sensitive sialic acids and altered ratios of the various sugars.[36,82–85,93]

It is postulated that deficiency of O-acetyl transferase activity, determined by homozygosity for a single polymorphic gene, could account for the 9% of subjects secreting N-acetyl as opposed to O-acetyl sialic acids.[87,87a] However, reduced O-acetylation in as much as 34% of TM has been reported.[93] The fact that crypts showing increased N- to O-acylated sialic acid ratios are more frequently seen in colons harbouring carcinoma than in controls, has been interpreted by some as functional metaplasia rather than a sign of early neoplastic change because identical changes are observed in metaplastic polyps of the colorectum.[86,94] However, this does not explain the

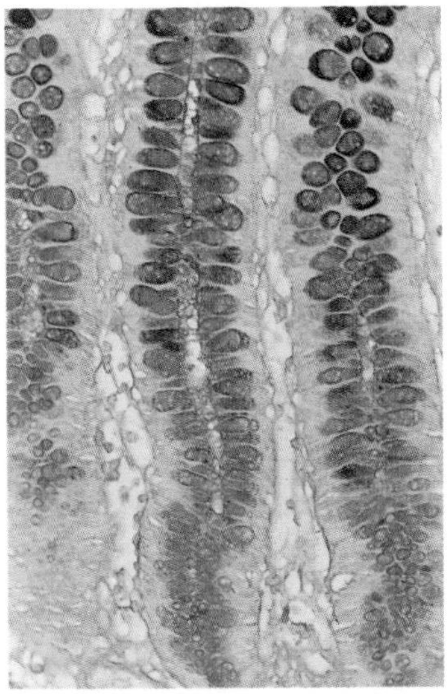

Fig. 7.14 'Transitional' colonic mucosa adjacent to carcinoma. Goblet cells contain predominantly sialomucins (blue). (HID/AB, ×88)

sharp loss of O-acylation in malignant change in adenomas, carcinomas and in dysplasia in ulcerative colitis.[42,84,93,95] The frequency of TM in various conditions is summarised as follows:

1. TM adjacent to 98% of carcinomas, and also found in areas in the colonic mucosa at some distance from the tumour.[42,82,96]
2. TM in the mucosa adjacent to adenomas[95] and in the non-neoplastic mucosa between polyps in familial adenomatous polyposis (FAP).[97,98]
3. TM adjacent to 13% of non-adenocarcinomatous neoplasias of the colorectum,[84,99,100] and similarly adjacent to non-adenomatous polyps, i.e. juvenile, inflammatory and metaplastic.[101,102] The N- to O-acylated sialomucin ratio in TM in these conditions is similar to that of the normal mucosa.[103]
4. TM is absent in colectomy specimens resected for non-neoplastic disorders, though patches of TM have been described in the mucosa from colectomies following traumatic injury,[99] and excess sialomucins have also been reported in a variety of conditions not associated with malignancy such as solitary ulcer syndrome,[104] at the site of colostomy,[100,102] diverticular disease and in cases of Crohn's disease in the absence of dysplasia.[102,105] However, normal mucin profiles are maintained in non-specific proctitis and other miscellaneous conditions of the large bowel, even when inflammation is severe.[104,105]
5. Ulcerative colitis may show an abnormal mucin pattern with excess sialomucins, but the features with few exceptions are not those of TM. 6. TM is identified in certain conditions associated with an increased risk of colorectal cancer such as in uretersigmoidostomy sites[106] and colonic anastomoses following large bowel cancer surgery.[107]

In TM, PNA consistently binds with the Golgi zone and apical cytoplasm of 'intermediate' columnar cells, particularly following neuraminidase digestion and with goblet cell mucin.[30,108,109] No change as compared to normal or only a moderately increased affinity was noted for WGA or ConA, whereas that of DBA, BPA and SBA was markedly decreased. RCA_1 binding is found to be reduced. Whereas UEA_1 binding to TM is seen with carcinomas of the right colon, it is said not to occur in association with carcinoma of the rectum, but this has not been the author's (MIF) experience in which binding has occurred independent of carcinoma site.[34,88]

Staining of TM for mucin associated antigens closely resembles that of the adjacent tumour (see Carcinoma).

Adenomas and carcinoma

Adenomas secrete a mixture of neutral, sialo- and sulphomucins. Although excess sialomucin is more often seen in the larger polyps and in those with severe dysplasia, sulphomucins predominate in villous adenomas, and there is no clear relationship between type of mucin and grade of dysplasia in this group.[36,82,95,97] Mucins seem to have no value in assessing malignant change in adenomas.[95] Similar mixed mucin profiles are common in non-neoplastic polyps.[94,101] In contrast O-acylated mucins, which are present in normal mucosa and in adenomas, are shown to be markedly reduced or absent in areas of high grade dysplasia and villous adenomas.[95] The loss of O-acylation has been noted in a few adenomas with no evidence of high grade dysplasia, but these were either large polyps or synchronous adenomas from colons harbouring carcinoma. This feature is not seen in inflammatory polyps, but metaplastic polyps may reveal reduced O-acylation with increasing size. Loss of O-acylation due to homozygosity cannot be excluded.

In FAP, an increased proportion of sialomucin is noted in the flat mucosa between the polyps.[97,98] These mucin changes are more extensive in the left than in the right colon and, though consistently present bordering any carcinoma present, they are also found in patches of mucosa distant from the tumour. Furthermore, they are more marked in the non-involved mucosa from patients harbouring carcinoma than in those free of malignancy. Muto et al[98] have confirmed the excess of sialomucins in the flat mucosa in FPC patients associated with loss of O-acylation. Whether this change is genetic or acquired is not yet known.

PNA labelling increases with the severity of dysplasia, the size of adenomas, and in villous and synchronous adenomas, as compared to tubular and incidental lesions.[36,91,108,109] PNA staining is seen in the Golgi area of goblet cells and in the goblet mucin. As the degree of dysplasia increases, one observes a shift of PNA binding sites from the goblet mucin to the apical cytoplasm and/or glycocalyx of the non-mucinous columnar cells. This pattern is also observed with VVA and GSA-II[91] There are contradictory reports regarding the effect of neuraminidase on PNA affinity in both normal and adenomatous colonic epithelium.[91,110] ConA, LCA and WGA binding to goblet mucin is gradually reduced concomitant with its increased presence in the glycocalyx and/or apical cytoplasm of columnar cells, in direct relationship with the degree of dysplasia.[91]

Carcinoma

The amount of mucus and mucin composition in colorectal carcinomas varies from case to case and within the tumour. In general, it is a mixture of neutral, sialo- and sulphomucins. Sialomucins are often predominant in mucoid carcinomas, and differ from those in the normal colonic mucosa in the relative proportion of different O-acylated sialic acids and a great susceptibility to neuraminidase digestion.[36,42,84,111]

Mucin stains have limited value in identifying the site of origin of an adenocarcinoma, though the presence of O-acylated sialic acids in colorectal carcinomas, and their absence from carcinomas elsewhere, may help in the identification of the colonic origin of metastatic adenocarcinoma.[41] Conversely, a negative reaction does not exclude a carcinoma from the lower gastrointestinal tract; loss of O-acylation has been described in poorly differentiated colorectal carcinomas and in those arising in the right colon.[36,42]

The pattern of lectin binding in carcinomas is also heterogeneous. The majority of carcinomas show positive PNA, particularly the well differentiated.[34,91] It is interesting to note that UEA_1 is present in the majority of carcinomas regardless of the site of origin in the right or left colon, (Fig. 7.15) which is in contrast with the regional variations observed in the normal epithelium, and in TM adjacent to tumours.[35,88,90]

On the other hand, there is a significant difference in the DBA binding by right-sided carcinomas, and its virtual absence in those from the left, whereas in the normal colon DBA binding is weak and shows no proximal to distal gradient.[89,90] Expression of RCA_1, BPA, WGA and LCA is commonly seen, but affinity for ConA, VVA and GSA-II is variable.[34,91]

Abnormal expression of blood group antigens has been reported in neoplastic and preneoplastic lesions of the colon and a number of monoclonal antibodies have been developed which may be useful in diagnosis. Monoclonal antibodies CC-1 and CC-2 (to extended L^y antigens) and KH-1 to Trifucosyl Le^y show preferential expression for colonic carcinoma (60–80%), particularly to well differentiated types. In adenomas they correlate with size, villous pattern and degree of dysplasia. These antibodies are not expressed in hyperplastic polyps and rarely observed in the normal epithelium. It is interesting to note that those cancer- associated antigens detected by KH-1 and CC-2 have been observed in transitional mucosa in the distal colon, a site normally devoid of these antigens. These monoclonal antibodies may be useful as highly specific markers for malignant and premalignant lesions in the colon.[112–114]

Monoclonal antibodies (FH1, FH4, FH6, 1B9) recognizing long chain polyfucosylated and sialylated Le^x related antigens appear to be useful for detection of colonic carcinoma (70%). Expression of these antigens is heterogenous within the tumour and shows a proximal distal gradient. FH6 is the most specific, being negative in normal colonic epithelium. However, FH6 is not expressed in poorly differentiated carcinomas. In contrast, FH4 expression is not related to differentiation. All these antibodies show positive staining in adenomas but not in hyperplastic polyps. With a few exceptions, transitional mucosa shows the same pattern of expression as in the adjacent tumour. All these antibodies are applied to formalin fixed paraffin embedded tissues.[5,115,116]

Monoclonal antibodies raised to Tn, sialyl-Tn and T antigens also show specificity for colonic carcinoma (75–90%), particularly in poorly differentiated and mucoid tumours. Normal mucosa is negative but transitional mucosa adjacent to carcinoma shows positive staining in some cases.[117,118]

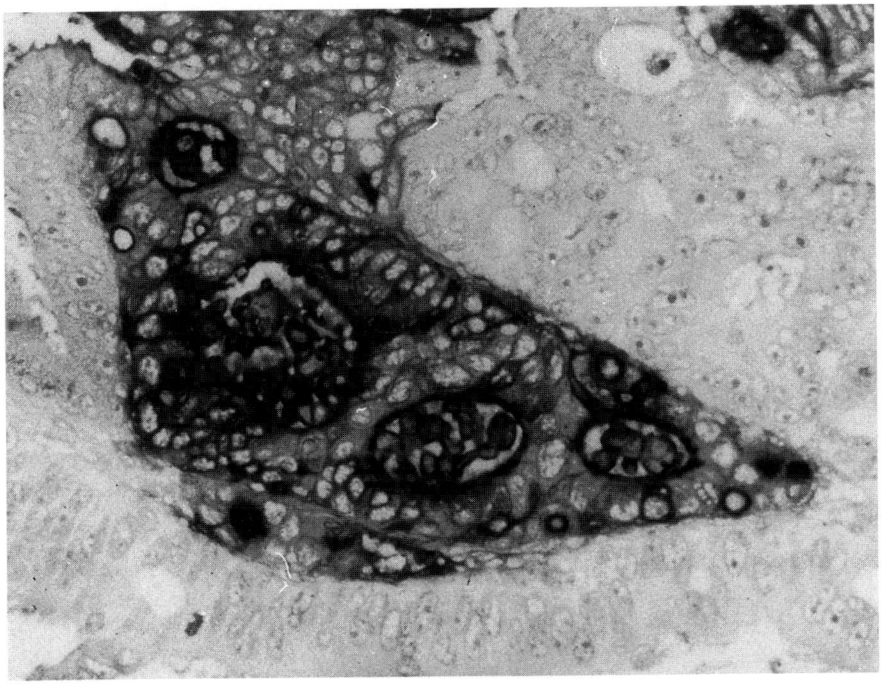

Fig. 7.15 Adenocarcinoma from the left colon showing heterogenous UEA_1 binding. (Direct immunoperoxidase, ×400)

Other monoclonal antibodies raised against mucin antigens which may be used as markers for colonic and other gastrointestinal carcinomas are available, and described below.

AM-3 raised against a mucin extracted from human colorectal carcinoma detects sialomucin. It is not expressed in normal gastrointestinal tract epithelium but it shows positive staining in several other normal and malignant tissues. In colonic adenomas, expression of AM-3 correlates with the degree of dysplasia. AR-3 monoclonal antibody reacts with an epitope (CAR-3) carried on a high molecular weight glycoprotein associated with carcinoma. The CAR-3 epitope is related or in close topographic proximity to Lewis^a and Lewis^b antigens. It appears that the same mucin carrying CAR-3 bears also CA19-9, CA125 and BW494 epitopes. CAR-3 is expressed in high frequency in carcinoma of the pancreas, stomach and colon and can also be detected in other malignancies. In colonic adenomas, CAR-3 expression relates to degree of dysplasia.[119,120]

Colonic mucin antigen (CMA)[67,121] is a high molecular weight glycoprotein isolated from normal adult colonic mucosa. CMA reactivity is limited to the colon but is not detected in other normal adult tissues. It is expressed in normal and diseased large intestine including transitional mucosa, ulcerative colitis and adenomas. The majority of adenocarcinomas (60%) expressed the antigen, particularly the well differentiated tumours but rarely in poor differentiated types. Mucinous ovarian cystadenocarcinoma may be positive. Two types of mucin, A and B, have been identified in CMA and it seems that they are a sialomucin and fucomucin respectively. Mucin B seems to be present in all mucin secreting tissues, in upper and lower gastrointestinal tract epithelial neoplasms, as well as in endometrial and ovarian carcinomas. In contrast, mucin A is found only in normal colonic epithelium and in colonic carcinomas. It could prove useful as an organ specific marker in the diagnosis of metastases of unknown origin. CMA has no use in the detection of premalignant change.

The monoclonal antibody C50 raised against the human colon adenocarcinoma derived cell, Colo 205, has proved useful in the detection of carcinoma-associated antigens in serological and immunohistochemical assays.[122] C50 has been shown to react with the carcinoma associated sialyl-Lewis^a and sialyl-lactotetraose epitopes. Intestinal mucin antigens (M-antigens)[65,123–125] consist of M1 present in the columnar cells of the gastric epithelium, M2 in mucous cells in gastric and Brunner's glands and the M3 antigen in goblet cells of the intestinal mucosa. In colonic carcinomas the three antigens show different patterns of expression. A proportion of colonic tumours (47%) show no M-antigens. All the others express M3 either alone (24%) or associated with either M1 (19%) or both M1, M2 (10%) and there seems to be a relationship between the expression of these antigens and the degree of differentiation of the tumour. Poorly differentiated carcinomas express none, whereas they are present in about 50% of well differentiated adenocarcinomas. Mucoid carcinomas express all three antigens. In transitional mucosa adjacent to carcinoma, M1 antigens (absent in normal) are extensively expressed.

We can conclude that mucins are the main secreted glycoproteins of the colon and altered expression is observed in malignancy. Quantitative and qualitative changes in these high molecular weight O-linked glycoproteins as described above could alter biological behaviour of carcinomas arising in this epithelium. In the majority of colonic carcinomas sialomucins are the predominant component of the mucus. They are more frequent in advanced stage (Dukes' C) and poorly differentiated carcinomas, and, in particular, mucoid and signet ring types are often associated with loss of O-acetylation.[111] These are tumours with very poor prognoses and changes in mucin may be related to the potential for metastasis as observed in experimental animal models.[15,126–130] Furthermore, altered mucin in the cell surface can interfere with cell–cell adhesion and cell/mesenchymal interaction.[126]

Ulcerative colitis and Crohn's disease

Changes in the composition of colonic mucin in inflammatory bowel disease may provide information on the underlying mechanism of disease and in assessing cancer risk in colitis.

As described above, mucus in the normal colon contains a high proportion of sulphomucins and sialomucins with O-acylated groups substituted at position C4, 7, 8 and 9. In ulcerative colitis increased production of sialomucins, decreased sulphomucins and reduction or loss of O-acylation are observed. These changes appear to be related to the degree of inflammation, are particularly marked in dysplastic epithelium in the absence of inflammation and more frequently in colitic patients at increased risk of cancer.[105,131–133] (Fig. 7.16).

The loss of O-acylation in these patients is unlikely to relate to an underlying heterogeneity of the goblet cell mucins within the general population.[86,87,133] It is more likely that this abnormality is related to the profound alteration in glycoprotein associated with the progression of the disease, particularly as these changes are similar to those occurring during the course of neoplastic transformation in adenomas and carcinomas.

Lectins have been useful in detecting subtle changes in the carbohydrate structure of both mucus and mucosal glycoprotein. Changes in PNA (galactose 1-3 N acetylgalactosamine or T antigen) and Ulex Europaeus1 (fucose, blood group H antigen) are seen in ulcerative colitis, Crohn's disease and similarly in colonic adenomas and carcinomas. Though PNA binding is related to dysplasia

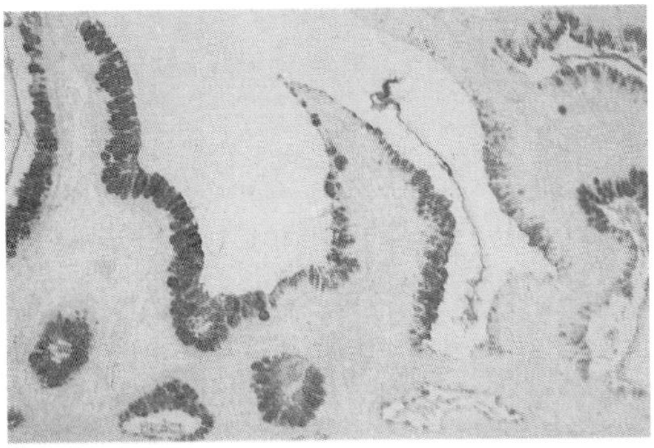

Fig. 7.16 Rectal mucosa in ulcerative colitis with dysplasia stained with PATS/KOH/PAS method to identify N-acylated (blue) and O-acylated (red) sialomucins. Regenerative hyperplastic epithelium (left) shows a predominance of O-acylated sialic acids as in the normal (Fig. 7.13), whilst dysplastic epithelium (right) stains blue-purple, indicative of a higher N-/O-acylated sialic acid ratio. (×44)

in ulcerative colitis, it is also common in active disease in the absence of dysplasia, thus it is of little value in surveillance of patients at risk. The changes are often focal or patchy and the intensity and frequency of the staining increases following neuraminidase digestion, indicating a higher proportion of neuraminidase sensitive sialic acids, probably related to a shift from O- to N-acylated sialic acids as shown in the PATS/PB/KOH/PAS stain (Fig. 7.16). UEA_1 binding in the rectal mucosa of colitics with rectal cancer is more intense and frequent than with PNA, and shows a similar increased gradient of binding sites from apparently 'normal' mucosa to dysplasia (Fig. 7.17). This contrasts with the absence of UEA_1 expression in normal rectal epithelium. These findings support the concept of an aberrant glycoprotein synthesis with the re-appearance of alpha-L-fucosyl residue in the oligosaccharide chain.[134,135]

Biochemical analysis of colonic mucus glycoproteins in ulcerative colitis reveals a significant decrease in both the carbohydrate content and size of the oligosaccharide units, and a specific increase in mannose-containing glycoprotein.[136] Altered affinity for the UEA_1 and DBA has been observed in both Crohn's disease and ulcerative colitis.

Podolsky and Isselbacher[137,138] identified 6 species of human colonic mucin, each showing a distinct hexose, hexosamine, sialic acid and sulphate content as well as blood group activities. A selective reduction of species IV was noted in ulcerative colitis compared with controls and Crohn's disease. This reduction was not related to site or to inflammation. Mucin IV contains substantial amounts of both sulphate and sialic acid and appears to represent the major sulphomucin species present. Whether the decrease in species IV represents a defect in synthesis or abnormal degradation is not known. The significance of these changes in the pathogenesis of the disease needs to be clarified, and indeed these claims have been disputed by others.[139]

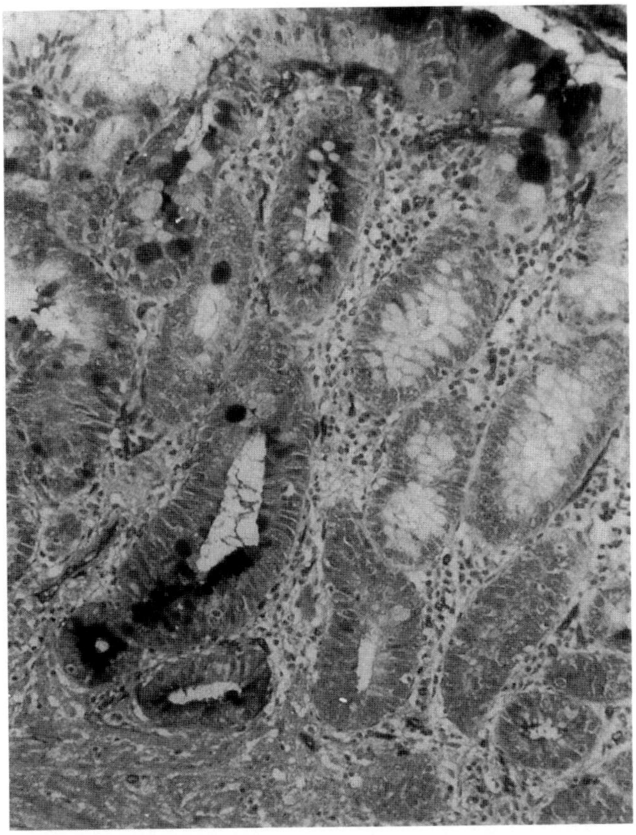

Fig. 7.17 Rectal mucosa in ulcerative colitis with dysplasia showing positive UEA_1 binding in dysplastic epithelium. (Direct immunoperoxidase, ×180)

Colonic mucins have an important role in mucosal protection and lubrication, as well as acting as a defence barrier to the gut microenvironment. Changes in its composition may alter its physical and chemical properties and interfere with its functional capacity. An altered glycoprotein may be more susceptible to enzyme degradation, which could leave the mucosa more vulnerable to its hostile environment.[140–142] Though speculative, it is possible that a genetic defect in mucin glycoprotein production combined with an injury factor (diet, bacteria, altered immunity) will trigger disease activity.[143]

It has been proposed that alterations in sialylation and sulphation of mucins and in the O-acetylation of the mucin sialic acids could have an effect on the resistance of the mucins to bacterial enzymatic attack. In Crohn's disease, however, a relative resistance of rectal mucins to bacterial de-sialation has been reported.[139]

NEW DEVELOPMENTS

Mucin gene expression

MUC-2 gene product is expressed in normal colon, small intestine and gastric and colonic tumours, and possibly other tissues, suggesting that MUC-2 is physiologically important in many organs.[11]

Monoclonal antibodies CCP31, CCP37, CCP58 were produced using MUC-2, MI-29. These antibodies do not react with MUC-1 or MUC-3. These MUC-2 monoclonal antibodies are specific for intestinal tissue and highly expressed in gastric and colonic carcinomas. Using immunoperoxidase staining, CCP58 shows strong expression in gastric cancer but not in normal gastric epithelium (fresh tissue only). It also reacts with colonic carcinoma and normal intestine both in fresh and formalin fixed tissues, but no other formalin fixed tissue is reactive with the antibody. CCP31 and CCP37 react with fresh tissue only. These antibodies show positive staining for normal intestine but not stomach and for both gastric (weak) and colonic (strong) carcinomas. All these antibodies appear to be relatively specific for the intestine and its expression in gastric carcinoma could be a useful diagnostic tool and may be used, in future, in anti-tumour therapy.[144]

MUC-1 gene product (Episialin or PEM) is expressed by many tumours, including those in the colon.[126,145] The sugar side–chains of Episialin carry many sialic acid residues. Episialin is present at the apical surface of most glandular epithelial cells and may have a protective function. Increased expression over the entire cell surface is often seen in carcinoma cells. These changes in the level of expression and distribution appear to affect cellular interactions, further enhanced by the negative charges of a large number of sialic residues on the molecule. These changes in the expression of MUC-1 gene product might increase metastatic potential and invasiveness of tumour cells. Furthermore, cells may also escape immune surveillance.[145]

MUC-3 gene product, as MUC-2, is expressed in colonic tumours.[146,147]

Extracellular–matrix

Epithelial–mesenchymal interactions have been implicated in the morphogenesis and differentiation of many tissues and organs including the gut.[148] It is believed that cell–matrix interactions, mediate through extracellular matrix (ECM) glycoproteins and a variety of cell membrane receptors, and influence cell shape and other features of their differentiated state.[149] These account for, at least in part, the effect of mesenchyme in the regulation of epithelial differentiation and also influence the phenotype of neoplastic epithelium; alterations in these interactions are important events in tumour progression.[150] A number of ECM glycoproteins have been implicated in cell adhesion, migration, differentiation and tissue morphogenesis, including fibronectin (FN), tenascin (TN) and laminin (LN), a major component of basal lamina . The primary cellular receptors for these and other matrix proteins belong to a super family of homologous, transmembrane glycoproteins known as integrins and they also play a major role in cell adhesion and migration as well as differentiation, and may have a role in oncogenesis.[151–157]

In gastric carcinoma a study on ECM glycoproteins, including fibronectin, tenascin and laminin and the integrin receptors alpha$_2$beta$_1$, alpha$_3$beta$_1$ and alpha$_6$beta$_1$, show an up-regulation of two isoforms of fibronectin as well as tenascin in tumour associated matrix compared to normal stroma. Enhanced expression of the alpha integrin chains is reported to be more related to well/moderately differentiated tumours compared to poorly differentiated carcinomas irrespective of tumour type, either diffuse or intestinal. Cell adhesion assays also revealed that the ability of gastric carcinoma cell lines to interact between matrix components was related to their degree of differentiation. In addition, two poorly differentiated cell lines showed a down-regulation in alpha$_2$ and alpha$_6$ expression respectively. This observation suggests the concept that architectural and cytological differentiation in gastric carcinoma relates to altered patterns of expression of matrix glycoproteins and ECM receptors; the traditional Lauren classification seems to reflect these differences in cell–matrix interactions (Fig. 7.18A,B). Differing patterns of expression of those molecules involved in cell–matrix interactions may prove to be a more objective and biologically more relevant means of classifying gastric cancer.[158]

The importance of elucidating the mechanisms controlling tumour differentiation lies in the predictive value of histological architecture as a measure of malignancy and thus prognosis. In the light of considerable evidence for the role of cell matrix interactions in determining patterns of differentiation, it is proposed that the difference between the two biologically distinct forms of gastric carcinoma (intestinal and diffuse) relates to altered patterns of expression of matrix glycoproteins and/or their receptors. Moreover, an understanding of the biological basis of matrix-regulated cell differentiation may enable novel therapeutic measures to be investigated, e.g. the induction of aggressive malignant tumours to the normal differentiated state.[159]

SUMMARY AND CONCLUSIONS

The factors controlling synthesis, intracellular transport and secretion are complex and not yet fully understood. The assembly of the protein backbone in the ribosomes is determined genetically, while that of the carbohydrate moiety is post-ribosomal and not directed by a nuclei acid template. However, it is under indirect genetic control, for this operates through the synthesis of glycosyltransferases. Thus changes in the composition and secretion of glycoproteins may be induced by genetic, physiological and pathological factors, leading to incomplete glycoprotein synthesis or to new glycoproteins.

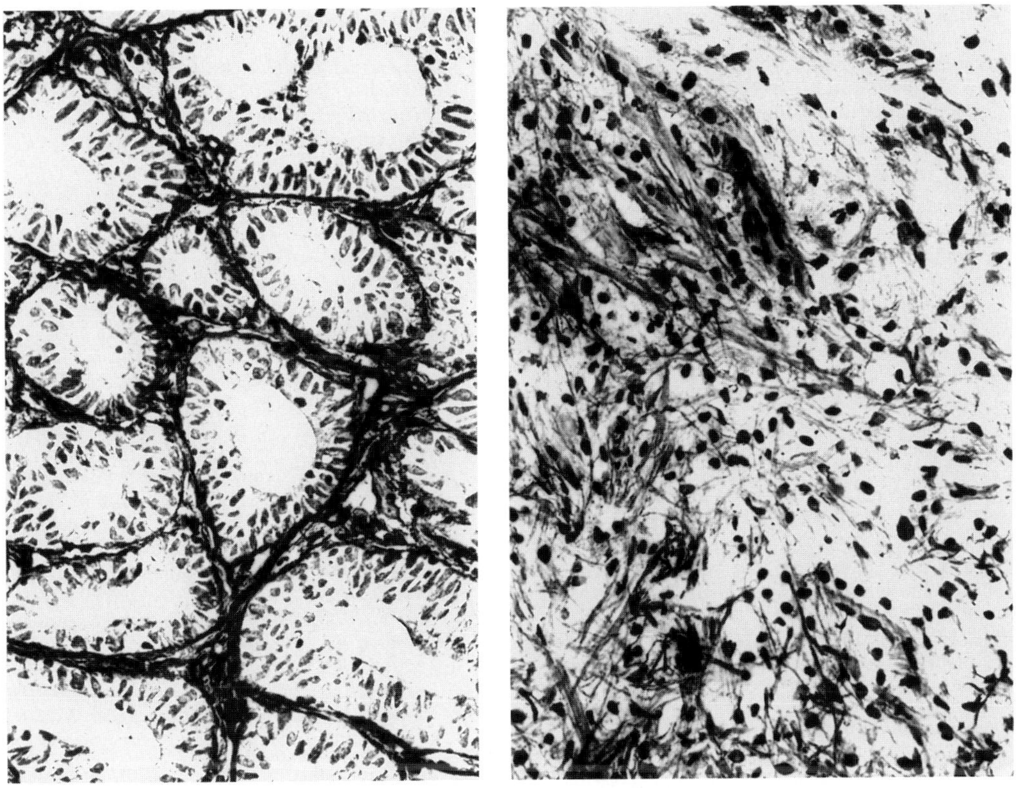

Fig. 7.18 **A** Tenascin expression pattern in well differentiated intestinal type gastric carcinoma. (ABC immmunoperoxidase, ×200). **B** Tenascin expression pattern in poorly differentiated diffuse type gastric carcinoma. (ABC immmunoperoxidase, ×200)

The biological functions of mucus glycoproteins are intimately related to their composition. Apart from a lubricative role, mucus acts as an important mucosal protective barrier by excluding large dissimilar molecules, trapping enzymes, viruses, toxins and bacteria. The non-mucin components enhance the protective role of mucus, as seen in the gastric mucosa where active bicarbonate ion secretion protects the mucosa from acid. The presence of lysozyme, lactoferrin and antibodies (IgA) are further evidence of a role for mucus in defence mechanisms.

Changes in mucus may profoundly alter these properties, rendering the glycoprotein more susceptible to enzyme degradation and leaving the mucosa more exposed to environmental damage.

Carbohydrates are intimately related to cell functions such as cell adhesion and antigenicity, the latter being well illustrated in the blood group antigens profile. The altered carbohydrate metabolism during carcinogenesis may explain differences in behaviour of normal and malignant cells.

In recent times, genes encoding a variety of glycoproteins have been identified; these open new fields for diagnosis and therapeutic intervention, both in non-neoplastic and neoplastic diseases.

REFERENCES

1. Neutra MR, Forstner JF. Gastrointestinal mucus: synthesis, secretion and function. In: Johnson LR ed. Physiology of the Gastrointestinal Tract. New York; Raven Press 1987.
2. Allen A. Structure of gastrointestinal mucin glycoproteins and the viscous and gel forming properties of mucins. Br Med Bull 1978; 31: 28–33.
3. Carlstedt I, Sheehan J, Corfield AP, Gallagher JT. Essays in Biochemistry 1985; 20: 40–46.
4. Feizi T, Gooi HC, Childs RA et al. Tumour-associated and differentiating antigens on the carbohydrate moieties of mucintype glycoproteins. Biochem Soc Trans 1984; 12: 591–596.
5. Yuan M. Itzkowitz SH, Ferrell LD, Fukushi Y, Palekar A, Hakomori S, Kim YS. Expression of Lewis^x and sialylated Lewis^x antigens in human colorectal polyps. J Natl Cancer Institute 1987; 78: 479–488.
6. Corfield AP, Schauer R. Metabolism of sialic acids. In: Schauer R. ed. Sialic acids, Chemistry, Metabolism and Function. Cell Biol Monograph. Berlin: Springer-Verlag, 1982; Vol. 20, pp 195–261.
7. Veh RW, Meesen D, Kuntz HD, May B. Histochemical demonstration of side-chain substituted sialic acids. In: Malt RA, Williamson RCN, eds. Colonic Carcinogenesis. Lancaster: MTP 1982: 355–365.
8. Culling CFA, Reid PE. Specific techniques for the identification

of O-acylated sialic acids in colonic mucins. J Microscopy 1980; 119: 415–425.
9. Gendler SJ, Lancaster CA, Taylor-Papadimitriou J, Duhig T, Peat N, Burchell J, Pemberton L, Lalani EN & Wilson D. Molecular cloning and expression of human tumour-associated polymorphic epithelial mucin. J Biol Chem 1990; 265: 15286–15293.
10. Swallow DM, Gendler S, Griffiths B, Kearney A, Povey S, Sheer D, Palmer RW & Taylor-Papadimitriou J. The hypervariable gene locus PUM, which codes for the tumour associated epithelial mucins, is located on chromosome 1, within the region 1q21–24. Ann Hum Genet 1987; 51: 289–294.
11. Toribara NW, Gum JR, Culhane PJ, Lagace RE, Hicks JW, Petersen GM & Kim YS. MUC-2 Human small intestinal mucin gene structure. Repeated arrays and polymorphism. J Clin Invest 1991; 88: 1005–1013.
12. Griffiths B, Matthews DJ, West L, Attwood J, Povey S, Swallow DM, Gum JR & Kim YS. Assignment of the polymorphic intestinal mucin gene (MUC2) to chromosome 11p15. Ann Hum Genet 1990; 54: 277–285.
13. Kim YS, Gum JR jr., Byrd JC, Toribara NW. The structure of Human Intestinal Apomucins. Am Rev Respir Dis 1991; 144: 510–514.
14. Fox MF, Lahbib F, Pratt W, Attwood J, Gum J, Kim Y & Swallow DM. Regional localization of the intestinal mucin gene MUC3 to chromosome 7_q22. Hum Genet 1992; 56: 281–287.
15. Gendler SJ, Spicer AP, Lahani E-N, Duhig T, Peat N, Burchell J, Pemberton L, Bashall M, Taylor-Papadimitriou J. Structure and biology of a carcinoma-associated mucin, MUC1. Am Rev Respir Dis 1991; 144: 542–547.
16. Swallow DM (personal communication) 2nd Int. Workshop on Carcinoma-Associated mucins; Cambridge: August 1992.
17. Real FX, Carrato C, Gonzalez E, Balague C, Bolos C, Gambus G. Differential expression of apomucins in human tissue analysed with antibodies. 2nd Int. Workshop on Carcinoma-Associated Mucins. Abstract book p.16. Cambridge: August 1992 (unpublished data).
18. Durrant LG, Jacobs E, Robertshaw J, Price MR. Production of monoclonal antibodies recognising the MUC2 intestinal mucin. 2nd Int. Workshop on Carcinoma-Associated Mucins. Abstract book p60. Cambridge: August 1992 (unpublished data).
19. Filipe MI, Lake BD. Histochemistry in Pathology. Edinburgh: Churchill Livingstone, 1983.
20. Pearse AGE. Histochemistry. Theoretical and Applied. 3rd ed. Edinburgh: Churchill Livingstone, 1985.
21. Reid RE, Culling CFA, Dunn WL, Clay MG, Ramey CW. A correlative chemical and histochemical study of the O-acetylated sialic acids of human colonic epithelial glycoproteins in formalin fixed paraffin embedded tissues. J Histochem Cytochem 1978; 26: 1033–1041.
22. Reid PE, Dunn WL, Ramey CW, Coret E, Trueman L, Clay MG. Histochemical identification of side chain substituted O-acylated sialic acids. The PAT-KOH-Bh-PAS and the PAPT-KOH-Bh-PAS procedures. Histochem J 1984; 16: 623–639.
23. Reid PE, Dunn WL, Ramey CW, Coret E, Trueman L, Clay MG. Histochemical studies of the mechanism of the periodic acidphenyl-hydrazine-Schiff (PAPs) procedure. Histochem J 1984; 16: 641–649.
24. Spicer SS. Diamine methods for differentiating mucosubstances histochemically. J Histochem Cytochem 1965; 13: 211–234.
25. Gad A, Sylven B. On the nature of the high-iron diamine method for sulphomucins. J Histochem Cytochem 1969; 17: 156–160.
26. Sorvari TE, Arvilommi HS. Some chemical, physical and histochemical properties of three diamine fractions obtained by gel chromatography from the high-iron diamine staining solution used for localizing sulphated mucosaccharides. Histochem J 1973; 5: 119–130.
27. Williams GT. Transitional mucosa of the large intestine. Commentary. Histopathology 1985; 9: 1237–1243.
28. Buk SJA, Filipe MI. Histochemical staining of sulphated and nonsulphated sialomucin in intestinal epithelium: practical difficulties associated with the KOH-ABph 1.0-PAPs method. Histochem J 1986; 18: 576–578.
29. Reid PE, Owen DA, Ramey CW, Dunn WL, Clay MG, Jones EA. Histochemical procedures for the simultaneous visualization of sialic acid, its side chain O-acyl variants and O-sulphate ester. Histochem J 1985; 17: 113–117.
30. Filipe MI. Gastrointestinal Tract. In: Spicer SS ed. Histochemistry in Pathologic Diagnosis. New York: Marcel Dekker, 1987.
31. Lev R. A histochemical study of glycogen and mucin in developing fetal epithelia. Histochem J 1968; 2: 152–165.
32. Filipe MI, Sandey A, Carapeti EA. Goblet cell mucin in human foetal colon, its composition and susceptibility to enzyme degradation. A histochemical study. In: 'Mucins and Related Topics, p. 248–258. Chandler E & Ratcliffe NA eds. Soc for Experimental Biology. Publ.: London 1989.
33. Lev R, Siegel HI, Bartman J. Histochemical studies of developing human fetal small intestine. Histochemie 1972; 29: 103–119.
34. Boland CR, Kim YS. Lectin markers of differentiation and malignancy. In: Wolman SR. Mastromarino AJ. eds. Markers of Colonic Cell Differentiation. Vol. 29. Progress in Cancer Research and Therapy. New York: Raven, 1984: 253–266.
35. Yuan M, Itzkowitz SH, Palekar A, et al. Distribution of blood group antigens A, B, H, Lewis[a] and Lewis[b] in human normal, fetal and malignant colonic tissue. Cancer Res 1985; 45: 447–452.
36. Filipe MI. Mucins in the human gastrointestinal epithelium. A review. Invest Cell Pathol 1979; 2: 195–216.
37. Jass JR. Mucin histochemistry of the columnar epithelium of the oesophagus: a retrospective study. J Clin Pathol 1981; 34: 866–870.
38. Lapertosa G, Barracchini P, Fulcheri E and the operative group for the study of oesophageal precancer. Mucin histochemical analysis in the interpretation of Barrett's oesophagus: results of a multicenter study. Am J Clin Pathol 1992; 98: 61–66.
39. Peuchmaur M, Potet F, Goldfain D. Mucin histochemistry of the columnar epithelium of the oesophagus (Barrett's oesophagus). A prospective biopsy study. J Clin Pathol 1984; 37: 607–610.
40. Jass JR, Filipe MI. The mucin profile of normal gastric mucosa, intestinal metaplasia and its variants and gastric carcinoma. Histochem J 1981; 13: 931–939.
41. Culling CFA, Reid PE, Burton JD, Dunn WL. A histochemical method of differentiating lower gastrointestinal tract mucin from other mucins in primary or metastatic tumours. J Clin Pathol 1975; 28: 656–658.
42. Montero C, Segura DI. Retrospective histochemical study of mucosubstances in adenocarcinomas of the gastrointestinal tract. Histopathology 1980; 4: 281–291.
43. Fisher J, Klein PJ, Vierbuchen M, Skutta B, Uhlenbruck G, Fisher R. Characterization of glycoconjugates of human gastrointestinal mucosa by lectins. l. Histochemial distribution of lectin binding sites in normal alimentary tract as well as benign and malignant gastric neoplasms. J Histochem Cytochem 1984; 32: 681–689.
44. McCartney JC. Lectin histochemistry of galactose and N-acetyl-galactosamine glycoconjugates in normal gastric mucosa and gastric cancer and the relationship with ABO and secretor status. J Pathol 1986; 150: 135–144.
45. Correa P. A human model of gastric carcinogenesis. Cancer Res 1988; 48: 3554–3560.
46. Filipe MI, Jass JR. Intestinal metaplasia subtypes and cancer risk. In: Filipe MI, Jass JR, eds. Gastric Carcinoma. Edinburgh: Churchill Livingstone, 1986; pp 87–115.
47. Rothery GA, Day DW. Intestinal metaplasia in endoscopic biopsy specimens of gastric mucosa. J Clin Pathol 1985; 38: 613–621.
48. Filipe MI. Unpublished observations.
49. Silva S, Filipe MI, Pinho A. Variants of intestinal metaplasia in the evolution of chronic atrophic gastritis and gastric ulcer. A follow-up study. Gut 1990; 31: 1097–1104.
50. Teglbjaerg PS, Nielsen HO. 'Small intestinal type' and 'Colonic type' intestinal metaplasia of the human stomach. Acta Pathol Microbiol Scand 1978; 86: 351–355.
51. Sipponen P, Seppala K, Varis E et al. Intestinal metaplasia with colonic-type sulphomucins in the gastric mucosa, its association with gastric carcinoma. Acta Pathol Microbiol Scand 1980; 88: 217–224.

52. Segura DI, Montero C. Histochemical characterization of different types of intestinal metaplasia in gastric mucosa. Cancer 1983; 52: 498–503.
53. Filipe MI, Potet F, Bogomoletz WV, et al. Incomplete sulphomucin secreting intestinal metaplasia for gastric cancer. Preliminary data from a prospective study from three centres. Gut 1985; 26: 1319–1326.
54. Silva S, Filipe Ml. Intestinal metaplasia and its variants in the gastric mucosa of Portuguese subjects: a comparative analysis of biopsy and gastrectomy material. Hum Pathol 1986; 17: 988–995.
55. Matsukura N, Zuzuki K, Kawachi T, et al. Distribution of marker enzymes and mucin in intestinal metaplasia in human stomachs and relation of complete and incomplete types of intestinal metaplasia to minute gastric carcinoma. J Natl Cancer Inst 1980; 65: 231–240.
56. Filipe MI. Borderline lesions of the gastric epithelium: new indicators of cancer risk and clinical implications. In: Progress in Surgical Pathology. Vol. XII pp 269–290. Eds. Fenoglio-Preiser et al. Field & Wood Publ. 1992.
57. Filipe MI. Unpublished observations.
58. Filipe MI et al. In preparation.
59. Rokkas T, Filipe MI, Sladen GE. Detection of an increased incidence of early gastric cancer in patients with intestinal metaplasia type III who are closely followed-up. Gut 1991; 32: 1110–1113.
60. Jass JR, Filipe MI. Sulphomucins and precancerous lesions of the human stomach. Histopathology 1980; 4: 271–279.
61. Kozuka S. Gastric Polyps. In: Filipe MI, Jass JR, eds. Gastric Carcinoma. Edinburgh: Churchill Livingstone, 1986; pp 132–151.
62. Torrado J, Correa P, Ruiz B, Bernadi P, Zavala D, Bara J. Lewis antigen alterations in gastric cancer precusors. Gastroenterology 1992; 102: 424–430.
63. Hakkinen IPT, Heinonen R, Inberg MV, Jarvi OH, Vanjalahti P, Viikari S. Clinicopathological study of gastric cancers and precancerous states detected by fetal sulphoglycoprotein antigen screening. Cancer Res 1980; 40: 4308–4312.
64. Nardelli J, Bara J, Rosa B, Burtin P. Intestinal metaplasia and carcinomas of the human stomach: an immunological study. Histochem Cytochem 1983; 31: 366–375.
65. Bara J, Paul-Gardais A, Loisillier F, Burtin P. Isolation of a sulfated glycopeptidic antigen from human gastric tumours: its localization in normal and cancerous gastrointestinal tissues. Int J Cancer l978; 21: 133–139.
66. Bara J, Hamelin L, Martin E, Burtin P. Intestinal M_3 antigen, a marker for the intestinal type differentiation of gastric carcinomas. Int J Cancer 1981; 28: 711–719.
67. Gold DV, Miller F. A mucoprotein with colonic-specific determinants. Tissue Antigens 1978; 11: 362–371.
68. Lauren P. The two histological main types of gastric carcinoma, diffuse and so-called intestinal type carcinoma. An attempt at histoclinical classification. Acta Pathol Microbiol Scand 1965; 64: 31–49.
69. Ming S-C. Classification of gastric carcinoma. In: Filipe MI, Jass JR. eds. Gastric Carcinoma. Edinburgh: Churchill Livingstone, 1986; pp 197–216.
70. Cook HC. Neutral mucin content of gastric carcinomas as a diagnostic aid in the identification of secondary deposits. Histopathology 1982; 6: 591–599.
71. Sipponen P, Lindgren J. Sialylated $Lewis_a$ determinant CA 19-9 in benign and malignant gastric tissue. Acta Pathol Microbiol Immunol Scand (A) 1986; 94: 305–311.
72. Bur M, Franklin WA. Lectin binding to human gastric carcinoma and adjacent tissues. Am J Pathol 1985; 119: 279–287.
73. Culling CFA, Reid PE, Dunn WL, Clay MG. Histochemical comparison of the epithelial mucin in the ileum in Crohn's disease and in normal controls. J Clin Pathol 1977; 30: 1063–1067.
74. Filipe MI, Fenger C. Histochemical characteristics of mucins in the small intestine. A comparative study of normal mucosa, benign epithelial tumours and carcinoma. Histochem J 1979; 11: 277–287.
75. Isselbacher KJ. The intestinal cell surface: some properties of normal, undifferentiated and malignant cells. Ann Intern Med 1974; 81: 681–686.
76. Reid PE, Culling CFA, Dunn WL, Clay MG. Chemical and histochemical studies of normal and diseased human gastrointestinal tract. II. A comparison between histologically normal small intestine and Crohn's disease of the small intestine. Histochem J 1984; 16: 253–264.
77. Wesley AW, Forstner JF, Forstner GG. Structure of intestinal-mucus glycoprotein from human post-mortem or surgical tissue: inferences from correlation analysis of sugar and sulfate composition of individual mucins. Carbohydrate Res 1983; 115: 151–163.
78. Jacobs LR, De Fontes D, Cox KL. Cytochemical localization of small intestinal glycoconjugates by lectin histochemistry in controls and subjects with cystic fibrosis. Dig Dis Sci 1983; 28: 422–428.
79. Thiru S. Devereux G, King A. Abnormal fucosylation of ileal mucus in cystic fibrosis: I. A histochemical study using peroxidase labelled lectins. J Clin Pathol 1990; 43: 1014–1018.
80. King A, McLeish M, Thiru S. Abnormal fucosylation of ileal mucus in cystic fibrosis: II. A histochemical study using monoclonal antibodies to fucosyl oligosaccharides. J Clin Pathol 1990; 43: 1019–1022.
81. Wesley A, Forstner J, Qureshi R, Mantle M, Forstner G. Human intestinal mucin in cystic fibrosis. Paediatr Res 1983; 17: 65–69.
82. Filipe MI, Branfoot AC. Mucin histochemistry of the colon. In: Morson BC, ed. Current Topics in Pathology. Heidelberg: Springer-Verlag, 1976: pp 143–178.
83. Rogers CM, Cooke KB, Filipe MI. The sialic acids of human large bowel mucosa: O-acylated variants in normal and malignant states. Gut 1978; 19: 587–592.
84. Reid PE, Culling CFA, Dunn WL, Ramey CW, Clay MG. Chemical and histochemical studies of normal and diseased human gastro-intestinal tract. I. A comparison between histologically normal colon, colonic tumours, ulcerative colitis and diverticular disease of the colon. Histochem J 1984; 26: 235–252.
85. Dawson PA, Patel J, Filipe MI. Variations in sialomucins in the mucosa of large intestine in malignancy: a quantimet and statistical analysis. Histochem J 1978; 10: 559–572.
86. Sugihara K, Jass JR. Colorectal goblet cell sialomucin heterogeneity: its relation to malignant disease. J Clin Pathol 1986; 39: 1088–1095.
87A. Campbell F, Ng I, Williams GT, Williams ED. Histochemical demonstration of racial variation in a polymorphic gene expressed in human colon. J Path 1992; 167: 95A.
87. Fuller CE, Davies RP, Williams GT, Williams ED. Crypt restricted heterogeneity of goblet cell mucus glycoprotein in histologically normal colonic mucosa — a potential marker of somatic mutation. Brit J Cancer 1990; 61: 382–384.
88. Yonezawa S, Nakamura T, Tanaka S, Sato E. Glycoconjugate with Ulex europaeus agglutinin-l-binding sites in normal mucosa, adenoma and carcinoma of the human large bowel. J Natl Cancer Inst 1982; 69: 777–785.
89. Jacobs LR, Huber PW. Regional distribution and alterations of lectin binding to colorectal mucin in mucosal biopsies from controls and subjects with inflammatory bowel disease. J Clin lnvest 1985; 75: 112–118.
90. Bresalier RS, Boland CR, Kim YS. Regional differences in normal and cancer-associated glycoconjungates of the human colon. J Natl Cancer Inst 1985; 75: 249–260.
91. Kellokumpu I, Karhi K, Anderson LC. Lectin binding sites in normal, hyperplastic, adenomatous and carcinomatous human colorectal mucosa. Acta Pathol Microbiol Immunol Scand (A) 1986; 94: 271–280.
92. Filipe MI. Value of histochemical reactions for mucosubstances in the diagnosis of certain pathological conditions of the colon and rectum. Gut 1969; 10: 577–586.
93. Reid PE, Owen DA, Dunn WL, Ramey CW, Lazosky DA, Clay MG. Chemical and histochemical studies of normal and diseased human gastrointestinal tract. III. Changes in the histochemical and chemical properties of the epithelial glycoproteins in the mucosa close to colonic tumours. Histochem J 1985; 17: 171–181.
94. Jass JR, Filipe MI, Abbas S, Falcon CAJ, Wilson Y, Lovell D. A morphological and histochemical study of metaplastic polyps of the colorectum. Cancer 1984; 53: 510–515.

95. Greaves P, Filipe MI, Abbas S, Ormerod MG. Sialomucins and carcinoembryonic antigen in the evolution of colorectal cancer. Histopathology 1984; 8: 825–834.
96. Greaves P, Filipe MI, Branfoot AC. Transitional mucosa and survival in human colorectal cancer. Cancer 1980; 46: 764–770.
97. Filipe MI, Mughal S, Bussey HJ. Patterns of mucus secretion in the colonic epithelium in familial polyposis. Invest Cell Pathol 1980; 3: 329–343.
98. Muto T, Kamiya J, Sawada T, Agawa S, Morioka Y, Utsunomiya J. Mucin abnormality of colonic mucosa in patients with familial polyposis coli. A new tool for early detection of the carrier? Dis Colon Rectum 1985; 28: 147–148.
99. Listinsky CM, Riddell RH. Patterns of mucin secretion in neoplastic and non-neoplastic disease of the colon. Hum Pathol 1981; 12: 923–929.
100. Isaacson P, Attwood PRA. Failure to demonstrate specificity of the morphological and histochemical changes in mucosa adjacent to colonic carcinoma (transitional mucosa). J Clin Pathol 1979; 32: 214–218.
101. Franzin G, Zamboni G, Dina R, Scarpa A, Fratton A. Juvenile and inflammatory polyps of the colon — a histological and histochemical study. Histopathology 1983; 7: 719–728.
102. Franzin G, Grigioni WF, Dina R, Scarpa A, Zamboni G. Mucin secretion and morphological changes of the mucosa in non-neoplastic diseases of the colon. Histopathology 1983; 7: 707–718.
103. Lapertose G, Fulcheri E, Acquarone M, Filipe MI. Mucin profiles in the mucosa adjacent to large bowel non-adenocarcinoma neoplasia. Histopathology 1984; 8: 805–811.
104. Ehsanullah M, Filipe MI, Gazzard B. Morphological and mucus secretion criteria for differential diagnosis of solitary ulcer syndrome and non-specific proctitis. J Clin Pathol 1982; 35: 26–30.
105. Ehsanullah M, Filipe MI, Gazzard B. Mucin secretion in inflammatory bowel disease: correlation with disease activity and dysplasia. Gut 1982; 23: 485–489.
106. Iannoni C, Marcheggiano A, Pallone F et al. Abnormal patterns of colorectal mucin secretion after urinary diversion of different types. A histochemical and lectin binding study. Hum Pathol 1986; 17: 834–840.
107. Sunter JP, Higgs MJ, Cowan WM. Mucosal abnormalities at the anastomosis site in patients who have had intestinal resection for colonic cancer. J Clin Pathol 1985; 38: 385–389.
108. Cooper HS, Reuter VR. Peanut lectin binding sites in polyps of the colon and rectum. Adenomas, hyperplastic polyps and adenomas with in situ carcinoma. Lab Invest 1983; 49: 655–661.
109. Boland CR, Montgomery CK, Kim YS. Alterations in human colonic mucin occurring with cellular differentiation and malignant transformation. Proc Natl Acad Sci 1982; 79: 2051–2055.
110. Boland CR, Montgomery CK, Kim YS. A cancer associated mucin alteration in benign colonic polyps. Gastroenterology 1982; 82: 664–672.
111. Lapertosa G, Baracchini P, Abbas S, Fulcheri E, Tanzi R, Filipe MI. Tissue evaluation of epithelial and functional markers of cell differentiation and mucins in colonic malignancy: assessment of diagnostic and prognostic value. Pathologica 1988; 80: 145–157.
112. Kim YS, Yuan M. Itzkowitz SH, Sun Q, Kaizu T, Palekar A, Trump BF, Hakomori S. Expression of Le^y and extended Le^y blood group-related antigens in human malignant, premalignant and non malignant colonic tissues. Cancer Research 1986; 46: 5985–5992.
113. Hakomori S, Philip Levine. Award Lecture: Blood group glycolipid antigens and their modifications as human cancer antigens. Am J Clin Pathol 1984; 82: 635–648.
114. Abe K, Hakomori S, Obshiba S. Differential expression of difucosyl type 2 chain (Le^y) defined by monoclonal antibody AH6 in different locations of colonic epithelia, various histological types of colonic polyps, and adeno-carcinomas. Cancer Res 1986; 46: 2639–2644.
115. Itzkowitz SH, Yuan M, Fukushi Y, Palekar A, Phelps PC, Shamsuddin AM, Trump BF, Hakomori S, Kim YS. $Lewis^x$ and sialylated $Lewis^x$-related antigen expression in human malignant and non malignant colonic tissues. Cancer Research 1986; 46: 2627–2632.
116. Fukushi Y, Hakamori S, Nudelman E, Cochran N. Novel fucolipids accumulating in human adenocarcinoma. II. Selective isolation of hybridoma antibodies that differentially recognise mono-, di-, and trifucosylated type 2 chain. J Biol Chem 1984; 259: 4681–4685.
117. Yuan M, Itzkowitz SH, Boland CR, Kim YD, Tomita JT, Palekar A, Bennington JL, Trump BF, Kim YS. Comparison of T-antigen expression in normal, premalignant and malignant human colonic tissue using lectin and antibody immunohistochemistry. Cancer Research 1986; 46: 4841–4847.
118. Itzkowitz SH, Yuan M, Montgomery CK, Kjeldsen T, Takahashi HK, Bigbee WL, Kim YS. Expression of Tn, sialosyl-Tn and T antigens in human colon cancer. Cancer Research 1989; 49: 197–204.
119. Hanski C, Bornhoeft G, Topf N, Hermann U, Stein H, Riecken EO. Detection of a mucin marker for the adenoma-carcinoma sequence in human colonic mucosa by monoclonal antibody AM-3. J Clin Pathol 1990; 43: 579–584.
120. Prat M, Medico E, Rossino P, Garrino C, Comoglio PM. Biochemical and immunological properties of the human carcinoma-associated CAR-3 epitope defined by the monoclonal antibody AR-3. Cancer Research 1989; 49: 1415–1421.
121. Gold DV, Sochat D. Immunological studies on colonic mucins. In: Wolman SR, Mastromarino AJ, eds. Progress in Cancer Research Therapy. New York: Raven, 1984; Vol 29, pp 159–167.
122. Baeckstrom D, Hansson GC, Nilsson O, Johansson C, Gendler SJ, Lindholm L. Purification and characterization of a membrane-bound and a secreted mucin-type glycoprotein carrying the carcinoma-associated sialyl-Le^a epitope on distinct core proteins. J Biol Chem 1991; 266: 21537–21547.
123. Bara J, Andre J, Gautier R, Burtin P. Abnormal pattern of mucus-associated Ml antigens in histologically normal mucosa adjacent to colonic adenocarcinomas. Cancer Res 1984; 44: 4040–4045.
124. Bara J, Loisillier F, Burtin P. Antigens of gastric and intestinal mucous cells in human colonic tumours. Br J Cancer 1980; 41: 209–221.
125. Bara J, Burtin P. Mucus-associated gastrointestinal antigens in transitional mucosa adjacent to human colonic adenocarcinomas: their 'fetal-type' association. Eur J Cancer 1980; 16: 1303–1310.
126. Ligtenberg MJL, Buijs F, Vos HL, Hilkens J. Suppression of cellular aggregation by high levels of episialin. Cancer Res 1992; 52: 2318–2324.
127. Irimura T, Carlson DA, Price J, Yamori T, Giavazzi R, Ota DM, Cleary KR. Differential expression of a sialoglycoprotein with an approximate molecular weight of 900,000 on metastatic human colon carcinoma cells growing in culture and in tumour tissues. Cancer Research 1988; 48: 2353–2360.
128. Yamori T, Kimura H, Stewart K, Ota DM, Cleary KR, Irimura T. Differential production of high molecular weight sulfated glycoproteins in normal colonic mucosa, primary colon carcinoma and metastases. Cancer Research 1987; 47: 2741–2747.
129. Bresalier RS, Rockwell RW, Dahiya R, Dul Q, Kim YS. Surface sialoprotein alterations in metastatic murine colon cancer cell lines selected in an animal model for colon cancer metastasis. Cancer Research 1990; 50: 1299–1307.
130. Bresalier RS, Niv Y, Byrd JC, Duh Q-Y, Toribara NW, Rockwell RW, Dahiya R, Kim YS. Mucin production by human colonic carcinoma cells correlate with their metastatic potential in animal models of colon cancer metastasis. J Clin Invest 1991; 87: 1037–1045.
131. Ehsanullah M, Nauton-Morgan M, Filipe MI, Gazzard B. Sialomucins in the assessment of dysplasia and cancer risk patients with ulcerative colitis treated with colectomy and ileorectal anastomosis. Histopathology 1985; 9: 223–236.
132. Filipe MI, Edwards MR, Ehsanullah M. A prospective study of dysplasia and carcinoma in the rectal biopsies and rectal stump of eight patients following ileorectal anastomosis in ulcerative colitis. Histopathology 1985; 9: 1139–1153.
133. Jass JR, England J, Miller K. Value of mucin histochemistry in follow-up surveillance of patients with longstanding ulcerative colitis. J Clin Pathol 1986; 39: 393–398.

134. Boland CR, Lance P, Levin B, Riddell RH, Kim YS. Abnormal goblet cell glycoconjugates in rectal biopsies associated with an increased risk of neoplasia in patients with ulcerative colitis: early results of a prospective study. Gut 1984; 25: 1364–1371.
135. Pihl E, Peura A, Johnson WR, McDermott FT, Hughes ESR. T-antigen expression by Peanut agglutinin staining relates to mucosal dysplasia in ulcerative colitis. Dis Colon Rectum 1985; 28: 11–17.
136. Clamp JR, Frazer G, Read AE. Study of the carbohydrate content of mucus glycoprotein from normal and diseased colons. Clin Sci 1981; 61: 229–234.
137. Podolsky DK, Isselbacher KJ. Composition of human colonic mucin: selective alteration in inflammatory bowel disease. J Clin Invest 1983; 72: 142–153.
138. Podolsky DK, Isselbacher KJ. Glycoprotein compositon of colonic mucosa. Specific alterations in ulcerative colitis. Gastroenterology 1984; 87: 991–998.
139. Rhodes JM. Colonic mucins and mucosal glycoproteins: key to colitis and cancer? Gut 1989; 30: 1660–1666.
140. Rhodes JM, Gallimore R, Elias E, Allan RN, Kennedy JF. Faecal mucus degrading glycosidases in ulcerative colitis and Crohn's disease. Gut 1985; 26: 761–765.
141. Corfield AP, Williams AJK, Clamp JR, Wagner SA, Mountford RA. Degradation by bacterial enzymes of colonic mucus from normal subjects and patients with inflammatory bowel disease: the role of sialic acid metabolism and the detection of a novel O-acetylsialic acid esterase. Clin Sci 1988; 74: 71–78.
142. Rhodes JM, Black RR, Gallimore R, Savage A. Histochemical demonstration of desialation and desulphation of normal and inflammatory bowel disease rectal mucus by faecal extracts. Gut 1985; 26: 1312–1318.
143. Hoskins LC, Boulding ET. Mucin degradation in human colon ecosystems. Evidence for the existence and role of bacterial subpopulations producing glycosidases as extracellular enzymes. J Clin Invest 1981; 67: 163–172.
144. Xing P-X, Prenzoska J, Layton GT, Devine PL, McKenzie IFC. Second-generation monoclonal antibodies to intestinal MUC2 peptide reactive with colon cancer. J Natl Cancer Inst 1992; 84: 699–703.
145. Lalani E-N, Berdichevsky F, Bosheall M, Shearer M, Wilson D, Stauss H, Gendler SJ, Taylor-Papadimitriou J. Expression of the gene coding for a human mucin in mouse mammary tumour cells can affect their tumorigenicity. J Biol Chem 1991; 266: 15420–15426.
146. Gum JR, Hicks JW, Swallow DN, Lagace RL, Byrd JC, Lamport DTA, Siddiki B, Kim YS. Molecular cloning of CDNAs derived from a novel human intestinal mucin gene. Biochem and Biophys Res Coms 1990; 171: 407–415.
147. Fox MF, Lahbib F, Pratt W, Attwood J, Gum J, Kim Y, Swallow DM. Regional localization of the intestinal mucin gene MUC3 to chromosome 7_q22. Ann Hum Genet 1992; 56: 281–287.
148. Sagagami Y, Inaguma Y, Sakakura T, Nishizuka Y. Intestine-like remodeling of adult mouse glandular stomach by implanting of fetal intestinal mesenchyme. Cancer Research 1984; 44: 5845–5849.
149. Bissell MJ, Hall HG, Parry G. How does the extracellular matrix direct gene expression? Journal of Theoretical Biology 1982; 99: 31–68.
150. Shepherd NA, Hall PA. Epithelial-mesenchymal interactions can influence the phenotype of carcinoma metastases in the mucosa of the intestine. J Pathol 1990; 160: 103–109.
151. Barlow DP, Green NM, Kurkinen M, Hogan BL. Sequencing of laminin B chain cDNAs reveals C-terminal regions of coiled-coil alpha helix. EMBO Journal 1984; 3: 2355–2362.
152. Chiquet-Ehrismann R, Mackie EJ, Pearson CA, Sakakura T. Tenascin: an extracellular matrix protein involved in tissue interactions during fetal development and oncogenesis. Cell 1986; 47: 131–139.
153. Chiquet-Ehrismann R, Kalla P, Pearson CA, Beck K, Chiquet M. Tenascin interfers with fibronectin action. Cell 1988; 53: 383–390.
154. Koukoulis GK, Gould VE, Bhattacharyya A, Gould JE, Howeedy AA, Virtanen I. Tenascin in normal, reactive, hyperplastic and neoplastic tissues: biologic and pathologic implications. Human Pathology 1991; 22: 636–643.
155. Hynes RO. Integrins: versatility, modulation, and signaling in cell adhesion. Cell 1992; 69: 11–25.
156. Pignatelli M, Smith MEF, Bodmer WF. Low expression of collagen receptors in moderate and poorly differentiated colorectal carcinomas. Br J Cancer 1990; 61: 636–638.
157. Fench-Constant C, Hynes RO. Alternative splicing of fibronectin is temporally and spatially regulated in the chick embryo. Development 1989; 106: 375–388.
158. Kamkissoon YD, Wilding JC, Filipe MI, Hall PA. Cell-matrix interactions in gastric carcinoma. J Path 1993; 169: Suppl. 4.
159. Pierce GB, Speers WC. Tumours as caricatures of the process of tissue renewal: prospects for therapy by directing differentiation. Cancer Research 1988; 48: 1996–2004.

CHAPTER 8

Epithelial kinetics; control and consequences of alteration in disease

R. A. Goodlad   N. A. Wright

INTRODUCTION

Mucosal cell proliferation is essential for the maintenance of the integrity of the multilayered defence and absorption system that is the gastrointestinal tract. The gastrointestinal epithelium is second only to the haemopoetic system in turnover time, being renewed by a process of continuous cell division. The study of gastrointestinal epithelial cell proliferation is of great interest in its own right, and also has considerable implications for the study of gastrointestinal carcinogenesis and pathophysiology, especially as enhanced proliferation can act as a promoter of, and can even be considered to be a cause of carcinogenesis.[1] Recent developments in molecular biology have provided several tools that have had, and will have, considerable impact on our understanding of intestinal growth control. The ability to create transgenic animals expressing various growth moderating agents is one example.[2–4] Furthermore, the availability of large quantities of recombinant growth factors has already transformed experimental approaches, and may soon prove to be of great therapeutic use. The first use of recombinant growth factors is likely to be in ameliorating the adverse side effects of cancer therapy. This is of particular significance as the understanding of growth control factors in the haemopoietic system now makes it possible to protect the bone marrow, which was previously the dose-limiting tissue.

Cell division in the gastrointestinal tract is restricted to anatomically discrete and definable zones, which combined with its high proliferative rates makes it in many ways the ideal system for the study of epithelial growth control. Determination of proliferative rates in man is severely limited by ethical constraints, which preclude the use of many of the best proliferative methods, nevertheless, much useful information can be obtained, and several recent advances in technique offer great prospect.

Perturbation of proliferation can either lead to atrophy and hypofunction or hyperplasia and ultimately neoplasia. The elucidation of the stimuli and the mechanisms underlying cell division control is thus a matter of some importance. Most of our knowledge of intestinal epithelial cell renewal and its control is derived from animal studies, thus a proviso about extrapolation between species needs to be made, but once made, it can also be pointed out that the relatively small number of valid human studies support the conclusions reached from animal studies.

This chapter will start with a brief translation of the vocabulary of proliferation and the organization of the gut as a renewal system. The methods employed to determine proliferation will be discussed in some depth, as serious mischief has been done by misapplication or misinterpretation of methods.

THE CELL DIVISION CYCLE

The process of cell division can be divided into four phases known as the cell cycle (Fig. 8.1). The chromosomes can easily be seen separating at mitosis, which is called the M phase of the cell cycle. The daughter cells then enter the first portion of interphase, the postmitotic, presynthetic gap called G_1. Cells can remain in G_1 or they may go on to the next phase of the cell cycle, the S phase, where DNA synthesis occurs to duplicate the genetic material. Before division, cells must ensure that DNA replication and segregation are finished; this involves several

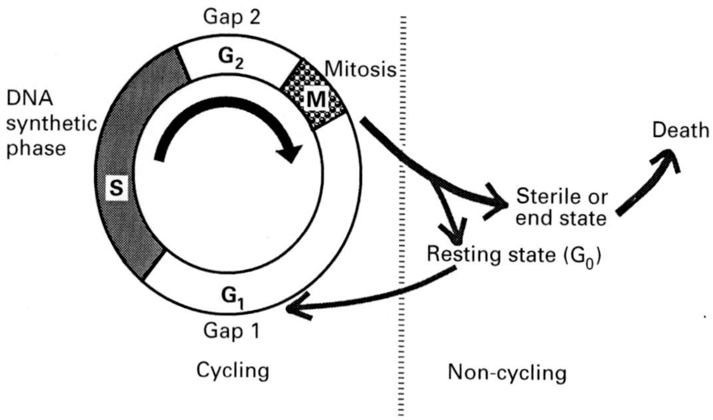

Fig. 8.1 The cell (division) cycle. Cells synthesise DNA in the S phase, enter a short gap (G_2) and divide in mitosis. There is then a longer gap (G_1), from which they may leave the cycle.

feedback controls, failure of which may contribute to the generation of cancer.[5] There is then a short, second, gap phase known as G_2, where the cell prepares for mitosis and assembles the spindle proteins. If differentiation occurs after mitosis the cells eventually pass a critical stage and are incapable of returning to the cell cycle.[6,7]

The duration of the cell cycle is mainly determined by the length of the G_1 phase, the other phases being relatively constant. The variability of G_1 suggests that it contains a control point, so that in late G_1 a genetically controlled event triggers the host of enzymes which are required for DNA synthesis. This may either be signalled or may be regarded as a transition probability event. In the transition probability model, the probability is high in the gut, so that cells cycle rapidly.[8] Cells eventually leave the cell cycle, and may differentiate. In some tissues they may enter a resting phase, known as G_O, although some would argue that this is just a long G_1. There is little evidence for G_O cells in the gut, although it has been suggested that these may occur in the colon.[9] Differentiated cells are generally considered to have lost their proliferative activity, nevertheless, in extreme conditions, they can be persuaded to re-enter the cell cycle.[4]

There are marked circadian rhythms in proliferative activity in the gut, which appear to be entrained to the food intake pattern several hours previously. These may be more pronounced in the colon.[10] Similar rhythms are also seen in the human rectal mucosa.[11]

Stem cells

A small number of cells at the base of the proliferative hierarchy give rise to all the other cells in the epithelium,[12] and can, therefore, be regarded as the functional 'stem' cells.[13] These are likely to be the main target for carcinogenesis inasmuch as they do not migrate, whereas their daughter cells are transitory. A carcinogen would have to make the daughter cells both dedifferentiate and stop migrating.[14] There is a large variation in the estimates of the numbers of stem cells per crypt. Clonogenic assays, which determine the number of cells capable of repopulating a crypt will be an overestimate, as this measures *potential* stem cells rather than *functional* stem cells. Hard evidence concerning the nature of the stem cell is scarce, but several particular attributes have been proposed.[15] Stem cell autoregulation may even be enough to explain adaptive responses after tissue damage.[16] Stem cells are thought to divide slowly and be extremely radiosensitive, leading to the intriguing proposition that they may be preprogrammed to self-destruct if their DNA template is badly damaged. They may also have special abilities to protect the genome by selectively retaining the parent, original copy DNA,[17] although there is little evidence to back this up. Several of the questions regarding the importance of intestinal stem cells might eventually be resolved by studying the rate of stem cell mutation in cogenic mice heterozygous for lectin (*Dolichos biflorus agglutin*) binding.[18] The spontaneous mutation in these mice is 1 per 10^4 villi per month and only those mutations which occur in the stem cell region will become permanent, thus this model has the potential to provide an unique insight into the renewal of these elusive stem cells.[19] The mutation rate can be modified by external agents, such as irradiation,[20] and thus should be subject to the same experimental modifications as can be applied to experimental tumourogenesis.[21]

Cell loss — apoptosis

Tissue mass is the balance between cell production and cell loss. While most cell loss occurs at the various extrusion layers, cell loss in the progenitor zones also occurs. Cell death can either be a passive process, as in cell necrosis, or it can be an active, gene directed, endonuclease activating process known as apoptosis.[22] The cell contents of the dying cells are contained by a membrane and rapidly eliminated by phagocytosis (by neighbouring cells or macrophages). Extrinsic signals can both stimulate and inhibit apoptosis, which can also be activated directly by cell damage. Apoptosis plays a major role in tissue remodelling in the embryo, and in the adult occurs in response to various insults,[23] so that it can be regarded as an altruistic suicide. Rat studies indicate that apoptosis is a rare but constant phenomenon, and as an expression of 'programmed cell death', it is likely to contribute to the normal intestinal epithelial cell turnover.[17] Apoptosis seems to be concentrated in the 'stem cell' zone of the small bowel, but not of the colon, which has been proffered as an explanation of the higher incidence of cancer in the latter.[24] Recent studies have also implicated a role for growth factors and cytokines in the control of apoptosis, as TGF beta[25] and tumour necrosis factor[22] can induce apoptosis in carcinoma cells. A number of genes including c-myc, bcl-2 and p53 are also implicated in the modification of apoptotic rates.[26]

Crypt cycle

The number of crypts in the intestine increases with age especially in the postnatal period,[27] when large numbers of crypts are seen in fission. In the rat the number of crypts feeding an ileal villus increases from 4 to 8 between weeks 3 and 6.[28] Crypt number can also increase after intestinal damage[29] or intestinal resection.[30] Crypts can thus divide in the adult by a process of crypt fission, which can be considered to be a 'crypt cycle', indicating that the adult intestine is not in a steady state.[31] Most fissures are seen in the bottom quarter of the crypt, so that division into two crypts would appear to occur soon after fissure extends beyond this region.[32] Up to 30% of small intestinal crypts may be branched in young mice,[33] and a similar number have been observed in some human neonatal tissue.[34] Just because a crypt is branching does not imply that it must divide, as the adult rat colon has up to 60% of its crypts branching (Goodlad, unpublished). If the crypt cycle hypothesis is correct,[31] there must also be a process of crypt deletion, but there is not as yet any evidence for this. It has been estimated that the rate of crypt fission in the human intestinal mucosa is such that there would be a doubling every 17 years.[35] Perhaps some branching crypts are in fusion not fission.

ORGANIZATION OF GASTROINTESTINAL RENEWAL SYSTEMS

One of the beauties of the gastrointestinal system is that the proliferative organization is so well ordered, and the familiar diagrams of the gastrointestinal units can be redrawn in terms of proliferation, maturation and function, as represented in Figure 8.2.

Small intestine

Proliferation in the small intestine is confined to the crypts of Lieberkuhn. There is little proliferative activity in the basal cell positions, partially due to the non-dividing Paneth cells. Proliferative rates are, however, still low if Paneth cells are excluded from the analysis. The non-Paneth basal cells have a long cell cycle time and constitute the crypt's *functional* stem cell pool.[36] The use of the term functional, while describing their action perfectly, does not imbue them with the dogma sometimes associated with stem cells. These cells are pluripotent and give rise to the columnar, mucous, entero-endocrine and Paneth cells.[12,37]

Almost all daughter cells migrate upwards, undergo two or three subsequent transit divisions and differentiate. All the cells in the bottom two thirds of the crypt are in the cell division cycle. Cells higher up the crypt progressively leave the cell cycle (decycle) so that no labelled or mitotic cells are seen at the top of the crypt which is the nonproliferative maturation compartment.[38,39] The decision to decycle may be preprogrammed, and intestinal cell population dynamics can be adequately modelled on the simple premise that the first generation of cells are initially set for 3–5 divisions.[40] Notwithstanding this, crypt dynamics can also be modelled using an alternative hypothesis, namely, that the cells sense their position and thus their generation age in the crypt.[41]

Crypt cells start to differentiate in the maturation zones, however, enterocytes are not fully functional until they reach the top third of the villus.[42] Cells take about 2–3 days to transit the villus in the rodent and 5–6 days in the human.[43] Mucous cells first appear as immature oligomucous cells and mature mucous cells are seen first in the upper portions of the crypt. Cells leaving the crypt are generally considered to be terminally differentiated, nevertheless, in extreme conditions, they can be persuaded to re-enter the cell cycle. This requires the molecular equivalent of the sledge hammer, the SV40 large T antigen, linked to the intestinal fatty acid binding promoter. Labelled and mitotic cells were then clearly observed in the villus epithelium when the antigen was expressed in the villus compartment.[4]

At first, it appears that there is one crypt per villus, but examination of whole-tissue preparations shows that several crypts, in fact, feed one villus. There is a proximo-distal gradient in this crypt to villus ratio. In the rat there are 27 crypts per villus in the duodenum and 10 in the terminal ileum,[44] whilst the range in the mouse is 14:1–6:1. In man, the duodenal crypt/villus ratio is approximately 7:1. A proximal-distal gradient of villus size also follows the gradient in crypt villus ratio, consequentially, total crypt and villus cell populations are almost equivalent throughout the gut[10] and the cell production rates per crypt also remain relatively constant throughout the gut, despite the reduction in tissue mass. Furthermore, examination of human biopsy tissue has also revealed that whilst the length of the glands and crypts throughout the intestine was approximately the same, the diameter and hence the area, varied considerably, so that there was also a marked proximo-distal gradient in both mitotic activity and area (Fig. 8.3).[45]

The gastric epithelium

The main gastric cell types are the basally located pepsinogen-containing chief cells, the acid producing parietal cells, the mucous and undifferentiated neck cells and the foveolar mucous or surface mucous cells.[46]

Proliferation predominantly occurs in the neck and isthmus region (Fig. 8.4).[47] Mitotic figures are found higher up the gland than labelled cells, again indicating a 'slow cut off' of cell division as the probability of cells dividing decreases and the cells leave the cell cycle. Most cells migrate towards the gastric lumen in an orderly first in, first out, journey to the surface[48] which takes one to two weeks. The downwards migration is far less orderly, migration rates tailing off as cells descend and are lost[49] and this may take over 200 days.[50] Although parietal cells were once thought to be self-renewing, it now seems that like the surface mucous cells, they arise from a common precursor. Some chief and endocrine cells can take up ^{3}H-thymidine after a flash label, nevertheless, they also need an influx from the main progenitor region. The common precursor cell in this region is probably the undifferentiated neck cell, which may in turn be fed from the mucous neck cell.

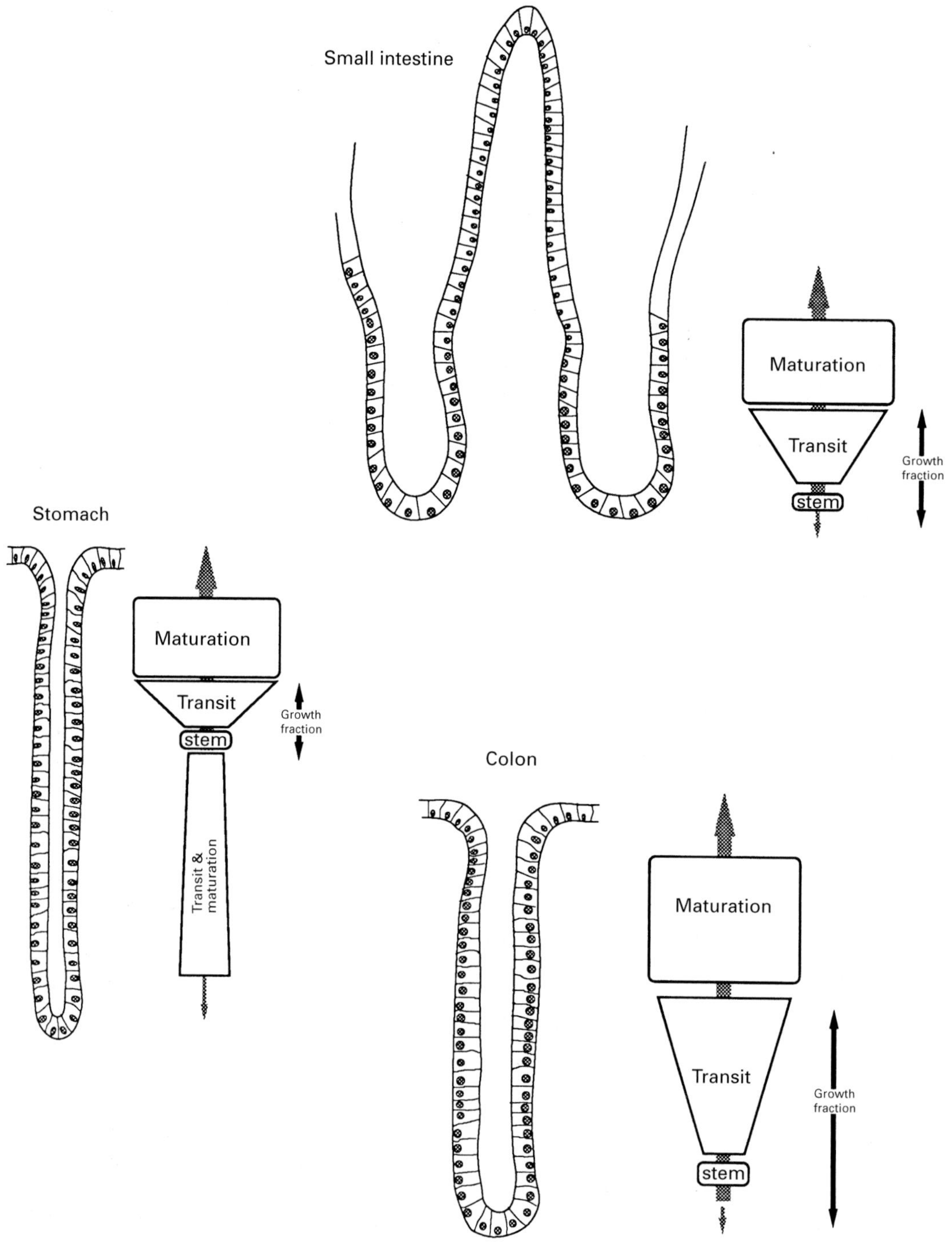

Fig. 8.2 Generalized representation of the proliferative zones of the main regions of the gastrointestinal tract. The pluripotent stem cells feed the transit compartment, with most of the flux going towards the intestinal lumen.

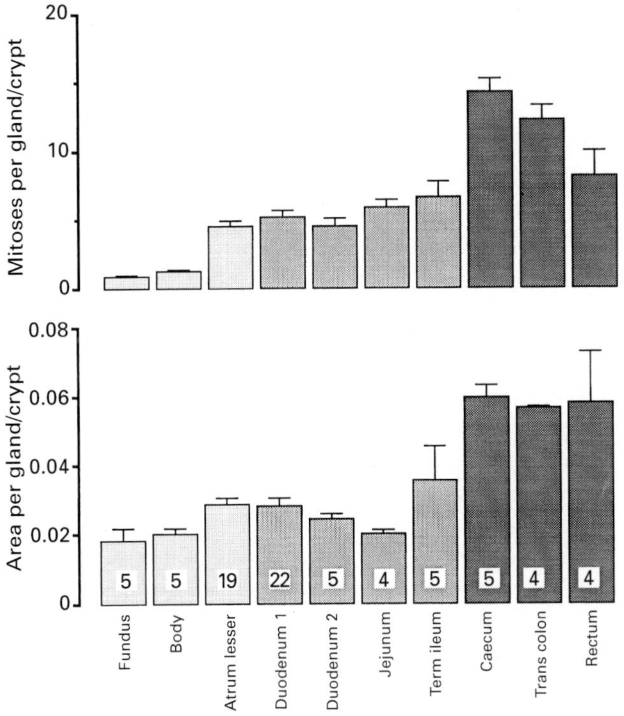

Fig. 8.3 Proliferative activity and gland or crypt area in the human intestine. Mitoses were counted per crypt or per gland and the areas were also measured in these microdissected units. The numbers in the lower histogram refer to the number of patients studied. 15–20 proliferative units were scored per patient. From reference no. 45.

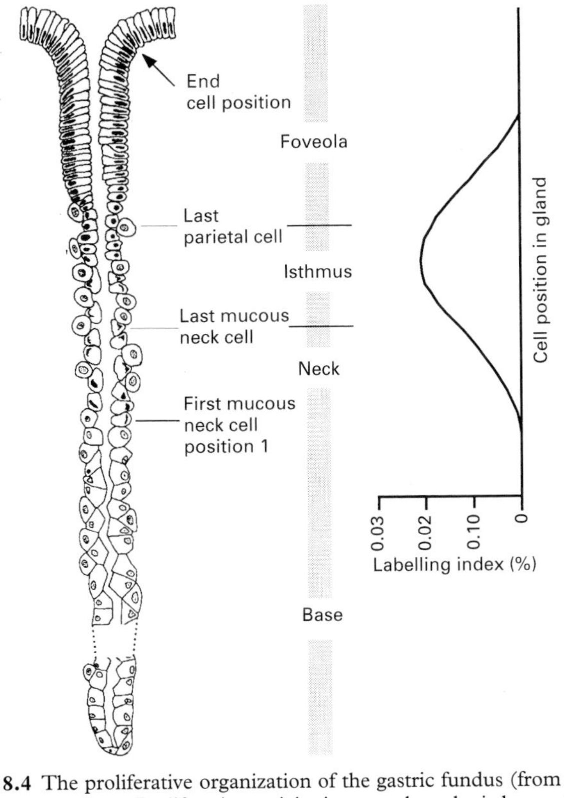

Fig. 8.4 The proliferative organization of the gastric fundus (from reference no. 124). Proliferative activity is centred on the isthmus, but S-phase labelled cells are seen quite high up the foveolus.

The situation in the fundic regions of the stomach may also be similar to that of the small bowel in that several glands may open onto the foveolus or pit.

The colon

At first sight, the general kinetic organization of the colon is broadly similar to that of the small intestine except that the flat surface of the colon necessitates the role of the upper portion of the crypt having to include function as well as maturation. The different cell types (columnar absorptive, mucous and entero-endocrine) probably also originate from a common stem cell in the base of the crypts,[51] undergo transit divisions, decycle and migrate to the lumen and are eventually extruded. There is more variation between the various regions of the colon than in the small intestine, with the smallest and least proliferative crypts found near to the caecum. In the distal colon of the rat, the stem cell zone is in the base of the crypts, as it is in the small bowel. In the proximal rat colon, however, the proliferative zone is located in the middle of the crypt, with a bidirectional flux of daughter cells, as is seen in the stomach.[52] Proliferative parameters also vary between the apex and the base of the mucosal folds.[53] Labelling distribution curves show that although some sites in the colon show a pattern similar to that of the small intestine, others do not,[54,55] indicating that the classical renewal format seen in the small intestine is not necessarily appropriate to the colon. Crypt cell production rates (CCPRs) in the colon are less than half those found in the small intestine[56,57] and the maximum labelling index is far less than that expected if all the cells in the lower two thirds of the crypt were continuously dividing (as in the small intestine). The greater variability seen in the colon may provide some clues regarding the hundred fold greater neoplastic potential of the colon when compared to the small bowel.[58]

METHODS

The study of intestinal adaptation requires careful application of various cell kinetic techniques and many published papers (and their conclusions) are rendered invalid by either the use of inappropriate, or the misuse of appropriate techniques. This is especially the case when bulk uptake of tritiated thymidine has been used as the end point.[59]

While quantification of thymidine-labelled cells (in autoradiographs) can yield very useful data, the quantification of the rate of entry of cells into mitosis using the metaphase arrest agent, vincristine, to determine the crypt cell production rate (CCPR) is far quicker and, in very many ways, is also more robust.[60] One of the advantages of this technique is that it allows one to express results on a per crypt basis and thus avoid the several pitfalls associated with scoring crypt sections. A great advantage of the technique is that it can account for all the factors involved in cell renewal, i.e. phase duration, growth fraction and compartment size. A further bonus is that one does not need to count interphase cells. The basis of the technique is shown in Figure 8.5. The CCPR method does, however, require a reasonable number of animals and if numbers are short a two hour metaphase collection would be better; although this is a less robust measure, it is more precise and enables more complex, multivariate, analysis to be performed.

Much useful information can be, and has been, obtained from the painstaking analysis of sections. The principle of such scoring is shown in Figures 8.6 and 8.7. Crypt cell population can be taken as the product of column length and diameter, which has been shown to be one of the most accurate ways of calculating crypt cell populations in sectioned material. When scoring mitoses, results will be overestimated by 30–40% due to the luminal migration of mitosis. This must be corrected for by measuring Tannock's factor,[61] as shown in Figure 8.8.

The analysis of mitotic distribution in sections can, however, provide much useful information. Variations in crypt size can make the interpretation of distribution curves difficult, and it may be necessary to normalize the crypts.[38,62] As the number of S-phase cells greatly outnumbers that of M-phase cells, information is more readily gleaned from scoring labelled cells. S-phase cells can be visualized by using tritiated thymidine or bromodeoxyuridine.[63] Double labelling with these agents can furthermore allow the determination of the rates of entry and exit form the S-phase.

The use of nucleotides or metaphase agents in man would rarely be considered ethical nowadays, nevertheless there is some very useful baseline data from an early, more heroic era.[64,65] Recent human studies have gone in one of three directions. Several groups have generated data using in vitro incubation techniques to label dividing cells with tritiated thymidine or bromodeoxyuridine. As they are detecting S-phase cells, labelling distribution curves can be generated and the search for the upward expansion of the proliferative zone continued.[66] The reliability of in vitro techniques is, however, still a matter of some concern.[67] Furthermore, these techniques also require the immediate incubation of the biopsy. This prohibits retrospective studies and demands a considerable degree of perseverance. The interest in the development and application of antibodies to 'dividing' cells is thus readily understood, however what most antibodies have detected is sometimes far less so. A classic example of this is the proliferation of papers concerning the so-called proliferating cell nuclear antigen (PCNA).[68] While PCNA, as a cofactor for DNA polymerase-delta, is required for DNA synthesis, and can be used to demonstrate dividing cells, the results generated are highly dependant on the prior treatment of the tissue. Furthermore, the antigen can also be expressed in tissue adjacent to a tumour, or in tissue after growth factor treatment.[69] The antigen Ki67 is more directly associated with proliferating cells and has also generated considerable interest, but its application was seriously hampered by its requirement for frozen tissue. Recent developments have, however, shown that a new antibody raised against the ki67 gene product, MIB1, can be applied to conventional, paraffin embedded tissue, especially if the antigen is 'exposed' by brief microwave irradiation. This antibody has not, as yet, been fully evaluated, but appears to correlate well with semiconservative DNA synthesis[70] and to offer great promise.

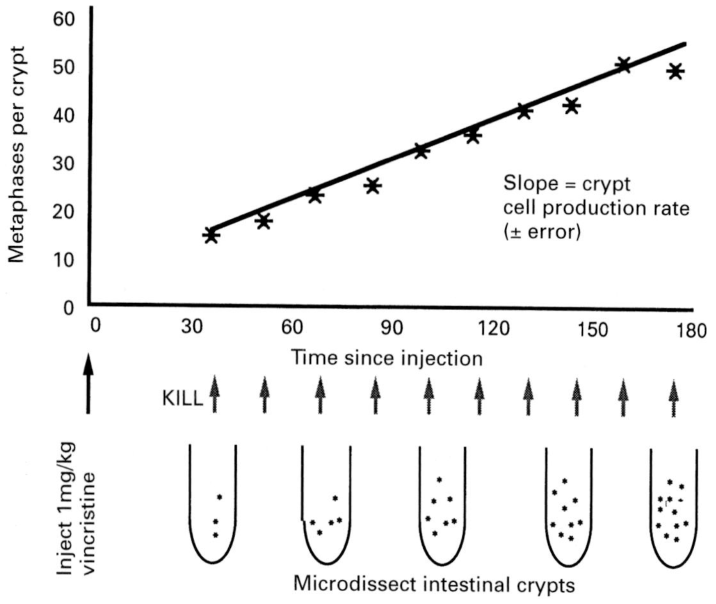

Fig. 8.5 The crypt cell production rate (CCPR) method. Animals are injected with the metaphase arrest agent vincristine at time 0, and then killed at timed intervals between 30 and 180 minutes. The number of arrested metaphases per whole crypt is then scored and regressed against time. The slope of the line (fitted by least squares linear regression) gives the rate of entry of cells into mitosis (CCPR).

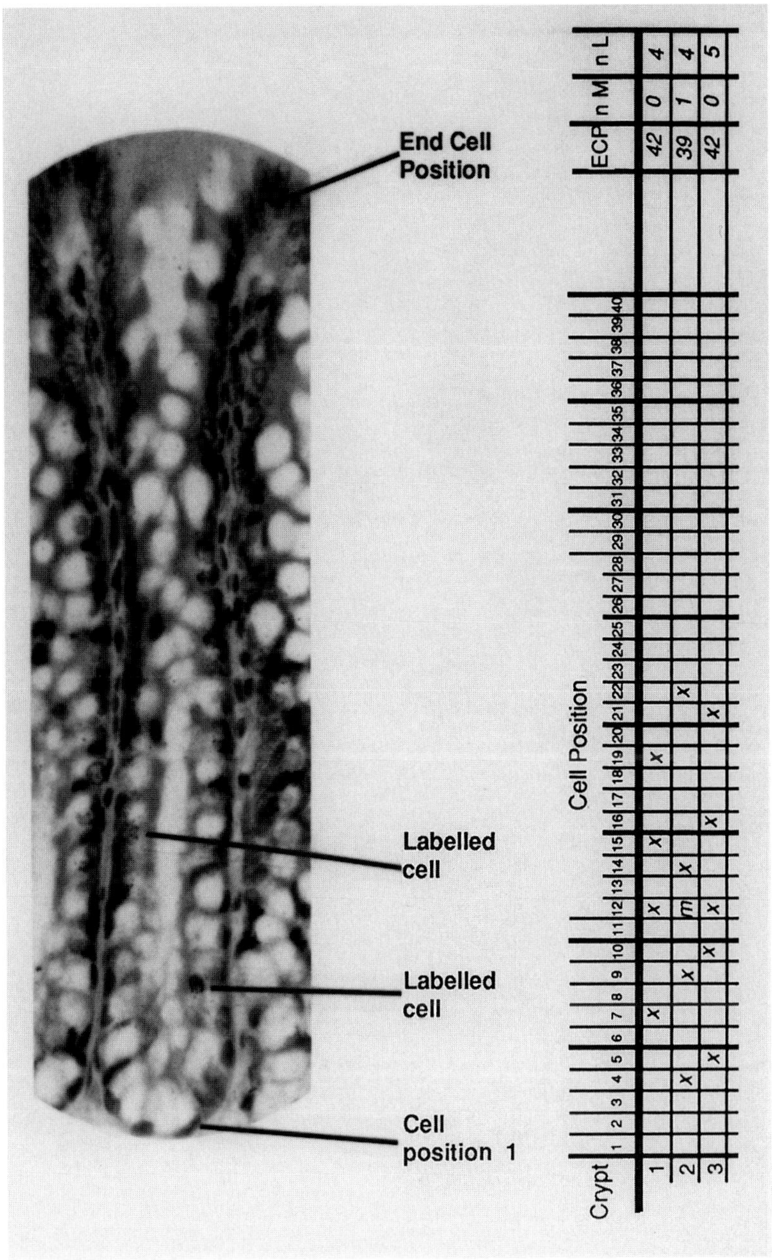

Fig. 8.6 How to score a crypt (from reference no. 63). First, find 30 or more well oriented, axially sectioned crypts, then record the location of labelled and/or mitotic cells. The data can then be analysed vertically to plot distribution curves, or horizontally to derive labelling or mitotic indices, and, perhaps more importantly, mean crypt length.

Nevertheless, all antibody techniques cannot escape from two serious problems. The first is the inherent difficulty in standardizing immunohistochemical techniques and in setting thresholds for scoring a cell as labelled or not, and the second is related to the problems of scoring sections, as results may (and often have been) confounded by concomitant changes in crypt size. This was demonstrated in our studies of the effects of a prostaglandin analogue on the stomach, where there was no significant effect on the labelling index, however this was because both the number of labelled cells and the size of the gastric gland had increased. If results were expressed on a per gland basis, it could be seen that cell production had almost doubled.[71] These problems can be avoided if the whole crypt is quantified by a 'microdissection' based technique. Such a method has recently been validated for quantifying proliferation in human intestinal biopsy samples.[45] The technique was validated by comparing results with data from animals that had been previously quantified using well-established kinetic methods. The microdissection method gave identical results, but in less than one sixth of the time taken to score sections. Typical microdissected crypts are shown in Figure 8.9. Although there are far less M-phase cells than S-phase cells, this is compensated for by being able to see and score every mitosis in the crypts, and on average there were up to 15 times more mitoses in

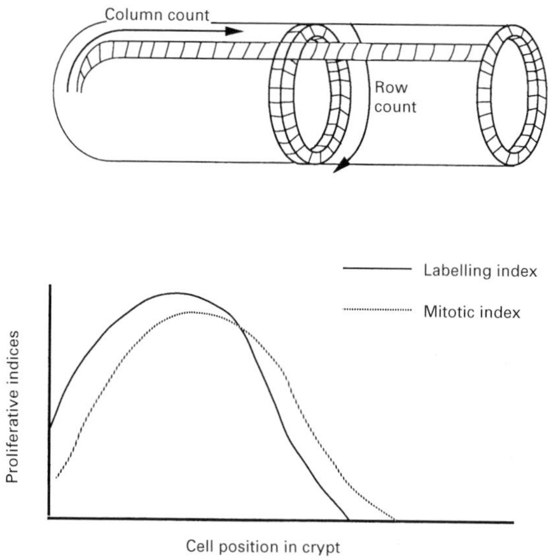

Fig. 8.7 Distribution of labelled and mitotic cells in a crypt. The crypt length or column count multiplied by the row count can be used to define the crypt cell population.

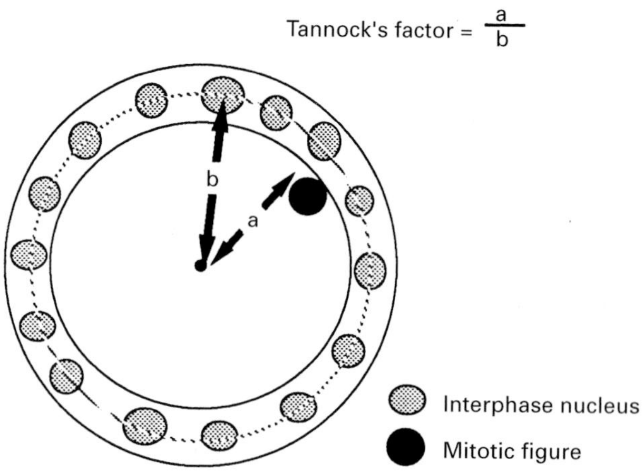

Fig. 8.8 Tannock's factor. As mitoses migrate luminally, scoring axially sectioned crypts will over estimate mitotic indices. This is corrected for by measuring the two diameters, a and b, to derive Tannock's factor.

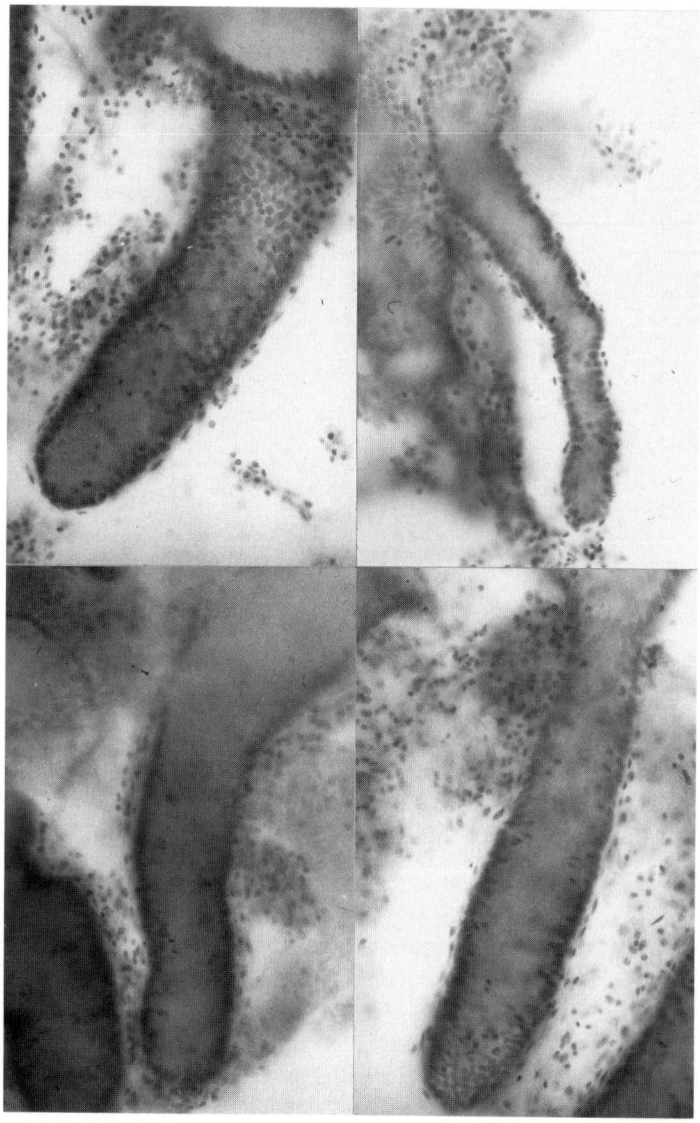

Fig. 8.9 Photo of 'microdissected' human glands and crypts from (top left) the gastric antrum, the ileum, the caecum and the colon (from reference no. 45).

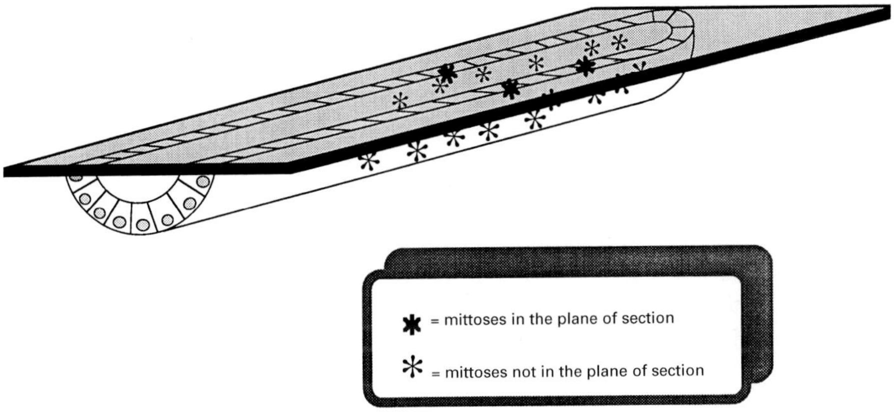

Fig. 8.10 Diagram of a crypt in histological section, showing that there are far fewer mitoses in the plane of section than there are in the whole crypt (from reference no. 45).

whole crypts as were seen in a crypt in section (Fig. 8.10). Biopsies need little special treatment, apart from the use of Carnoy's fluid for fixation. The tissue can then be stored in 70% ethanol almost indefinitely before being stained, gently teased apart (microdissected) and the number of mitoses per crypt determined. Crypt size and crypt area can also be readily determined using a drawing tube. Quantification of the drawings can be performed using a image scanner and image analysis program. The NIH public domain program 'Image' for the Apple Macintosh is a powerful and very cost effective option.

The ease of use, the requirement of less than half a biopsy sample (which can be stored for years) and the ability to score every mitotic figure present, without concern over stereological artefacts, makes this method the method of choice for measuring proliferative changes in the human gut. Furthermore, positional data similar to that obtained from scoring S-phase labelled cells can also be obtained from microdissected tissue.[72] Moreover, if a very detailed, positional analysis is desired, cells can be accurately counted in microdissected crypts optically sectioned using a confocal laser scanning microscope. This enables one to score through what appears to be perfectly oriented, serial, semi-thin sections of the entire crypt.[73]

MECHANISMS OF INTESTINAL ADAPTATION

Cell production in the gut can be increased or decreased to allow the intestine to adapt to a wide variety of circumstances. This may either be in response to physiological stimuli, the main one being related to altered food intake, or in pathological circumstances. A classic example of the latter is the proliferative response seen after gluten-induced cell loss in coeliac disease. There are several ways in which the cell renewal system can be adjusted to increase or decrease cell production (Fig. 8.11). Crypt cell production (crypt efflux) is the product of the growth fraction, cell cycle time and crypt size. Villus influx is the product of crypt cell production and crypt/villus ratio. Although all of these parameters can change, and in some circumstances do, in general adaptive responses only involve moderation of a few of these parameters. Changes in the cell cycle time, usually via altered G1 duration (or transition probability), can occur, as can changes in the duration of the S-phase, but this may be short-lived.[74]

In most hyperplastic models, the growth fraction remains constant, e.g. after continuous irradiation,[75] intestinal resection[76] and lactation.[62] Nevertheless, in some other models, such as starvation, the growth fraction may fall,[77] and the massive hyperproliferative crypts seen in active coeliac disease actually have a decreased growth fraction.[78] In one model, after the administration of androgens, the proliferative response would appear to be entirely the consequence of increased growth fraction.[79] In some conditions the growth fraction is distorted by the changes in crypt size, thus in the extremely hypoplastic crypts of intravenously fed rats, the relative growth fraction is, in fact, increased, and in the large crypts of EGF-infused

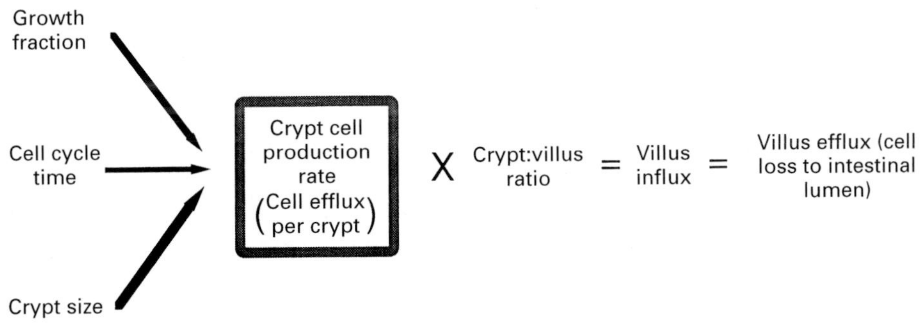

Fig. 8.11 The factors which determine crypt cell production and villus influx.

animals, the growth fraction is reduced.[57] The anomalies can be attributed to expressing the growth fraction as a percentage of crypt length which was markedly altered. The size of the proliferative compartment is usually the most important parameter in most models of intestinal adaptation. Cell cycle time and growth fraction alterations usually make a more minor contribution to proliferative status.[38]

In almost all adaptive responses, the crypt/villus ratio (and the total number of villi) does not appear to alter, but there is a profound alteration in the crypt/villus ratio in the weanling animals.[28] There is a small increase in the total number of crypts with age and a large increase in the postnatal period,[27] when large numbers of crypts are seen in fission.

The ability to switch on different mechanisms in isolation would argue for there being separate control mechanisms for those parameters which determine cell production, namely the growth fraction, compartment size and cell cycle times. The question then arises as to how these changes are effected. It has been suggested that each parameter changes sequentially according to critical levels of cell loss, however, there is little evidence to support this. The second alternative is that all the mechanisms are initiated at the same time, or that modulation is achieved by changing a single parameter, i.e. by modifying the size of the proliferative compartment.[38]

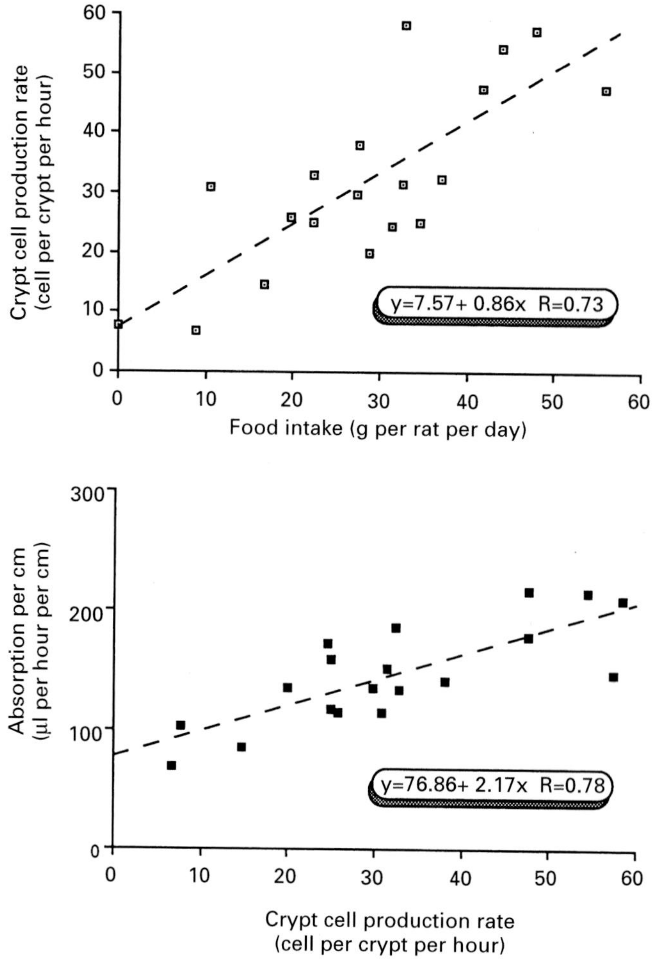

Fig. 8.12 The relationship between crypt cell production rates and food intake, and between absorption and crypt cell production rates, based on data from reference no. 82.

CONTROL OF INTESTINAL CELL PROLIFERATION

The control of gastrointestinal epithelial cell proliferation will undoubtedly prove to be a multifactorial affair. There are generally considered to be three main mechanisms. The first is a local negative feedback from the structural to the reproductive compartments. The second relates to the concept of luminal nutrition, and the third to the effects of systemic factors.[7] Mesochymal, immunological[80] and neural factors may also be involved.

Luminal nutrition, as a proliferative stimulus, can be either direct or indirect, but there is no doubt that the presence of food in the gut is the best predictor of function and proliferation. Intestinal proliferation and absorption correlate well in 'steady-state' systems.[81] Figure 8.12 shows the correlation between absorption, crypt cell production rate and food intake in a range of rat models. The lowest CCPRs were seen in starved rats and hypophysectomized rats, whilst the highest were seen in streptozotocin induced diabetes and in lactation.[82]

The correlation between intestinal proliferation and absorption does not always hold, as there may be a short-term recruitment and migration of immature enterocytes in perturbed systems, so that absorptive capacity can increase before proliferation in a starved and refed rodent.[83,84] This presumably reflects a short-term reserve of cells that should help the animal respond rapidly to an upturn in its fortunes. In addition this also confirms that cell migration is not 'driven by mitotic pressure'. In fact, migration can still occur even in the absence of mitotic activity.[85,86]

Systemic factors

Trophic effects on the gut may be moderated by the local and systemic effects of hormones, peptides and growth factors.[87] Enteroglucagon, or members of the enteroglucagon family, are among the front-runners for this role. The story started with the observation that an enteroglucagon-secreting tumour was associated with villus enlargement.[88] Several studies have provided evidence, albeit circumstantial, that enteroglucagon is involved.[89,90] Pure enteroglucagon is unfortunately not yet available in quantity. Enteroglucagon, a 69 amino acid peptide, is part of a larger preproglucagon, which contains glicentin-related pancreatic polypeptide (GRPP), glucagon, oxyntomodulin and the glucagon-like peptides, GLP1 and GLP2.[91] Reports of a trophic effect of G1-21 on rat intestinal cells in vitro[92] was not supported by more extensive studies, where, in fact, a negative effect was observed, perhaps as a result of decreased endogenous enteroglucagon levels.[93]

Gastrin is also implicated, especially in the stomach. The introduction of the very effective proton pump inhibitors have rekindled interest in the effects and potential risks of elevated gastrin levels on intestinal epithelial cell proliferation. The feedback between acid inhibition and gastrin levels is well known, but even here there can be some surprises.[94,95] While there is little evidence to support a proliferative effect of gastrin throughout the gut, its role in gastric hyperplasia and especially endocrine cell growth is well established,[96] and the general conclusion would appear to be that acid-inhibiting drug-induced hyperplasia is mediated via gastrin.[97] Lifelong gastrin-induced enterochromaffin-like (ECL) cell hyperplasia[98,99] in experimental animals can lead to low malignancy non-metastasizing carcinoid tumours,[100] however, rats may be particularly prone to these[101] and carcinoids are relatively rare, even in patients with the massive hypergastrinaemia associated with the Zollinger-Ellison syndrome and pernicious anaemia.[102]

The original suggestion[103] that gastrin has a general trophic role throughout the gastrointestinal tract, led to a spate of publications refuting this.[7] The refutal was attributed to the application of inappropriate kinetic techniques. Nevertheless, there is still considerable interest in the effects of gastrin on the colon, especially as it is trophic to several colon cell lines and carcinomas,[104] and postprandial gastrin levels are higher in colon cancer patients.[105]

Insulin does not appear to have a role to play in the control of intestinal cell division[106] neither does peptide YY (PYY).[107]

One of the most potent agents for stimulating gastrointestinal epithelial cell renewal is the epidermal growth factor (urogastrone). EGF has considerable growth promoting effects in vitro and in vivo, in addition to inhibiting gastric acid and intrinsic factor secretion.[108] EGF is present in a variety of biological fluids, including milk, and stimulates proliferation and maturation of the pre- and postnatal intestine.[109] EGF is also a very potent stimulator of epithelial cell production in the adult intestine of rats and of humans.[34,110] EGF also has effects on enzyme induction.[111] The proliferative effects in the rat are seen throughout the gastrointestinal tract, but we have found this only when EGF is given systemically.[56] Others have, however, suggested otherwise.[112] Lack of luminal effect could either be because of it being broken down by the digesta[113] or due to its receptors being basolateral.[114] TGF alpha, which binds to the same receptor as EGF,[115] also stimulates gastrointestinal epithelial cell proliferation throughout the gut, but to a lesser extent.[116,117]

A new, fashionable, group of potential growth factors are the trefoil peptides,[118] so called because of their distinctive cysteine-rich three-leafed structure 'trefoil' domains.[119] They have some superficial structural similarity with that of the EGF/TGF alpha, IGF family, indicating that they may be growth factors. Trefoils are a normal secretory product of human gastric mucosa[120] and some have mitogenic actions on colorectal cells.[121] Related trefoils are seen in abundance in regions of the GI tract particularly susceptible to mucosal damage and ulceration. In several conditions where endodermal damage occurs, such as peptic ulceration, ulcerative colitis and Crohn's disease, a newly recognized cell lineage, the ulcer-associated cell lineage (UACL), develops.[122] The phenotype of the cells of this lineage varies dependent upon the cells' positions, expressing the trefoils hSP, pS2 and also EGF. The entire lineage also stains intensely with antibody to TGF alpha. This is of interest because the TGF alpha gene is induced by EGF/URO.[123]

Prostaglandins can increase gastric cell proliferation and cell migration.[71,124] Proliferative effects were also seen in the small bowel,[125] but effects in the colon were far less marked.[126] Large differences in proliferation were also seen between human biopsies taken from the edge of an ulcer and from a non-affected region of the stomach or the duodenum. Non-steroidal anti-inflammatory drugs (NSAIDs) appear to abolish this regenerative difference, but in an interactive manner, and prostaglandins protect the mucosa from this effect.[127,128]

Effects of diet

The importance of 'luminal nutrition' can be seen in the profound atrophy associated with low residue 'elemental diets'[129] and even more so after total parenteral nutrition.[57]

It is a difficult task to dissect out the effects of dietary risk factors (for gastrointestinal cancer) from other concomitant changes,[130] thus, although epidemiological studies can demonstrate increased risks with low fibre diets, these also turn out to be high in animal products and fat. The multifactorial nature of the problem further complicates the issue. High risk may be ameliorated by other factors, e.g. the ingestion of some toxic chemicals which paradoxically may be protective, as some vegetables, especially the brassicas, induce the production of xenobiotic detoxification enzymes.[131]

Fibre-free, elemental diets are associated with enteral atrophy[132] which can be reduced by the addition of dietary fibre, but not inert bulk.[129] The magnitude of the trophic effect depends on the 'fermentability' of the fibre.[133] This is a trophic effect of the short chain fatty acids (SCFA), which are the product of fibre fermentation by the microbiological flora.[134] The response is abolished in the germ-free rat,[135] confirming that it is the products of the microbial fermentation of fibre, not fibre itself, that stimulate gastrointestinal cell proliferation. Direct infusion studies[136] have confirmed this. A second effect of fibre is to stimulate intestinal muscle mass.[129] A third effect of fibre is a different, direct, trophic effect on cell division in the stomach.[137]

Increased proliferation can act as a promoter of carcinogenesis, and some fibres have been shown to do this.[138] Dietary fibre has a multitude of effects on the gut, and proliferation is just one of these: other effects may well outweigh the proliferative risk.

Several other nutritional factors may also influence intestinal epithelial cell proliferation and thus risk of carcinogenesis, and a lot of interest is presently focused on calcium as a protective agent.[139,140] It could be that ω_3 fish oils may also be of benefit, perhaps by modulating prostaglandin synthesis.[141] The modulation of prostaglandin synthesis in the colon may be of importance in carcinogenesis avoidance, and recent studies have suggested a beneficial effect for aspirin in the colon,[142] however others studies have suggested that the NSAIDs may stimulate colonic cell proliferation.[143] The role of vitamins has also recently generated some interest.[144]

Defence and disease

The gastrointestinal tract must protect the organism from a wide range of pathogenic assaults, while at the same time being able to absorb the various products of digestion. In addition, every day we are, on average, exposed to a cocktail of over 2 g of toxic chemicals which are part of the natural defence mechanisms of plants. These include a wide variety of antifungal and bacteriostatic agents, pesticides and antipredator compounds. In comparison we are unlikely to ingest more than 100 µg of man-made pesticides. On average, the proportion of the few 'natural' chemicals which have been tested and found to be carcinogenic is similar to that of the many 'man-made' chemicals now evaluated. Furthermore, the modern, 'western' diet will also contain a large variety of burnt material, replete with carcinogens.[145] It can thus be seen that the intestinal mucosa is part of a multilayered defence system, but when this is breached, the pathologist may become involved.

Mucosal ulceration

Ulceration can be regarded as an imbalance when cell loss or deletion exceeds cell replacement. When one considers ulceration and its repair, it is important to distinguish between the effects of proliferation and of restitution. Cell restitution can occur within a matter of minutes and is attributed to a process of cellular migration and re-epithelialization.[146,147] Acute mucosal lesions induced by local irritants are accompanied by widespread damage of surface epithelium followed by almost immediate repair due to mucosal cell restitution, which is unrelated to cell proliferation, but dependent on the intrinsic property of mucosal cells to cover superficial defects.[148] Rapid epithelial restitution can now be considered as one of the main basic defence mechanisms of the gastrointestinal mucosa and is not necessarily related to the presence of an acidic environment in the stomach or duodenum.[149] Whilst deep injury requires cell division to replace the damaged tissue, superficial injury is initially repaired rapidly as follows: the damaged surface epithelial cells are shed and form a layer that protects the restituting mucosa. Viable epithelial cells then become flattened and rapidly migrate over the denuded basal lamina. The epithelium is re-established when migrating cells touch and form new tight junctions.[150] This process is very dependant on mucosal blood flow.[151]

Gastric and duodenal ulceration reflects a failure in the balance between the many aggressive factors and protective factors and mechanisms.[152] The attacking factors include acid, pepsin, duodenal contents, bile, drugs, alcohol, smoking and microorganisms. While much has been made of the links between *Helicobacter pylori* (HP) and intestinal ulceration, it should not be forgotten that urease producing bacteria adherent to the epithelium are widespread in many species[153,154] and that although *H. pylori* causes gastritis and is found in over 80% of gastric or duodenal ulcer patients, a causal role has not been proved. Intestinal defences start with mucosal bicarbonate secretion and the mucus barrier, and if these are breached cellular migration and cell restitution should occur within a matter of minutes. Mucosal blood flow plays an important role, as do the prostaglandins, which can protect the gastric lining from the effects of many noxious agents, and are also potent inhibitors of gastric acid secretion.[155] Prostaglandins also increase mucosal mass[156] by increasing epithelial cell production,[71] not decreasing cell loss.[124] Damage associated with non-steroidal anti-inflammatory agents (NSAIDs) can thus be accounted for by their blocking the processes of restitution initiated by the prostanoids.[127]

Menetrier's disease

In Menetrier's disease — a protein losing, hypertrophic gastroenteropathy — large increases in labelling index are seen in the gastric antrum.[157,158] Dramatic structural and functional lesions of the glandular stomach, very similar to Menetrier's disease, are seen in transgenic mice overexpressing TGF-alpha in the stomach. Symptoms included severe adenomatous hyperplasia and a striking hypertrophy of the gastric mucosa. Parietal cell function was also greatly impaired, indicating that overproduction of TGF alpha can stimulate cellular proliferation, suppress acid secretion and perturb organogenesis of the stomach of transgenic mice.[159] TGF alpha immunoreactivity is also increased in patients with Menetrier's, as is TGF alpha and EGF-receptor RNA expression.[3] It is of interest that TGF alpha, like EGF can also protect the stomach from various insults.[160]

Chronic atrophic gastritis

Whereas atrophic gastritis is not necessarily associated with intestinal metaplasia,[161] intestinal metaplasia is not seen without atrophic gastritis.[162] Proliferative indices are increased in gastritic patients, indicating rapid epithelial proliferation in the progression from normal to severe atrophic gastritis.[163] Despite the increased proliferation, the replacement time of the tissue is decreased[163] so that the mucosa becomes thinner. Upward expansion of the proliferative zone has also been reported, which parallels the severity of gastritis,[164] so that mitoses are seen on the surface in severe cases.[161,164]

Interest in the association between gastritis and carcinogenesis has been revived by the association of the presence of *Helicobacter pylori* (HP) with increased gastric cancer risk. The involvement of HP in gastrointestinal ulceration, especially duodenal, is now well established,[165] and HP infection is also associated with gastritis. Analysis of banked plasma has linked the development of gastric cancer to the presence of HP antibodies in stored plasma.[166] HP infection is proportional to age and (in the West) inversely proportional to social status.[167] A positive correlation is seen between (PCNA) labelling index and the intensity of both chronic corpus gastritis and active corpus gastritis, suggesting that the inflammatory response to HP in the corpus may influence the corpus mucosal cell proliferation rate, which could thus act as a promoter for gastric carcinogenesis.[168] Notwithstanding this, other studies have not found a link with gastric cancer risk and HP antibodies.[167,169]

Coeliac disease

Analysis of mitotic distribution on a positional basis in active coeliac disease has revealed that the crypt population increases four-fold, the number of proliferating cells three-fold and the crypt cell production rate six-fold.[78,170,171] There is thus a massive increase in cell production, mainly effected by increasing crypt size to attempt to maintain mucosal integrity in the face of the massive gluten-induced, immunologically mediated, villus cell loss. Cell cycle times are also reduced. As the crypts are so much increased in size, the growth fraction (fraction of the crypt involved in proliferation) appears decreased. The villus cell loss is so great (increased six-fold) that, despite the massive increase in crypt efflux, a flat mucosa is seen. These changes would suggest that cell production is determined by the size of the functional compartment.

A convoluted mucosa is seen in the more distal parts of the intestine of patients with coeliac disease, in the early stages of coeliac disease and in patients recovering on a gluten free diet. The convolutions are intertwining flexous ridges, containing at least two curves greater than 180° and represent an intermediate degree of abnormality, correlating with the histological term 'partial villus atrophy'.[172] Increasing numbers of convolutions are associated with increased crypt population size and proliferation, but the growth fraction remains relatively constant. Cell cycle times are reduced. Mucosal labelling indices in coeliac remission may be at the same level as in non-coeliac biopsies.[173] The kinetic parameters form various studies are summarized in Table 8.1.

Ulcerative colitis

The colon differs from the small bowel in that proliferating and non-proliferating cells coexist in the basal two thirds of the crypt,[174] but in active ulcerative colitis there is a hyperproliferative state,[175] and one result of this is that there is insufficient time for the completion of mucous cell differentiation, so that goblet cell depletion occurs.

Risk of colorectal carcinoma is reportedly increased among patients with longstanding ulcerative colitis and Crohn's disease and the risk is related to a long prior history of chronic inflammation and the subsequent development of epithelial dysplasia.[176] Whether there is increased proliferation in non-involved mucosa is a matter of debate, and poses certain ethical problems in its study. Upward extension of the proliferative compartment, but with no correlation between the labelling index and disease, has been reported,[177–179] as has upward migration of the proliferative cells and increased labelling.[180]

The increased growth fraction in colitis may be related to short chain fatty acid deficiency, as butyrate enemas can reduce upper crypt labelling.[181] This would at first conflict with our observations that short chain fatty acids can stimulate cell division, but butyrate has differentiative as well as proliferative actions. Modern treatment regimens appear to restore proliferative parameters to normal,[182] and a recent large scale study concluded that virtually no increased risk of colorectal malignancy occurred with an active approach to medical and surgical treatment.[183]

Animal models for experimental ulcerative colitis show many morphological similarities with human ulcerative colitis and although several of these provided variable results, a reproducible, standardized model has been described.[184] An alternative model is seen in the cotton-tailed tamarin, which spontaneously develop colitis.[185]

Carcinogenesis

The development of cancer is generally considered to be a multistage process involving permanent alterations in

Table. 8.1 Kinetic parameters in groups of patients with control, convoluted and flat coeliac mucosae, and in individuals studied with the metaphase-arrest method.

	Crypt column length (cells)	Column count (cells)	Crypt population (%) (cells)	Mitotic index (%)	Growth fraction	Proliferating population (cells)	Migration rate (cell positions/h)	Crypt cell production rate (cells/ crypt/h)	Mitotic duration (h)	Cell cycle time (h)	Birth rate (%/h)
Groups of patients											
Controls (adult)[a]	32	24	780	2.1	0.72	560	0.7	17	–	–	–
Group 1 convoluted (15 patients)	37	25	950	2.4	0.74	700	0.9	23	–	–	–
Group 2 convoluted (18 patients)	39	27	1060	2.6	0.69	730	1.0	28	–	–	–
Group 3 convoluted (14 patients)	49	31	1510	3.8	0.77	1160	1.9	58	–	–	–
Coeliac disease[b] (adult) flat mucosa (13 patients)	74	41	3050	3.6	0.55	1370	2.6	107	–	–	–
Individual patients											
Adult control[c]	32	22	710	–	0.81	580	0.5	10	1.1	36	1.5
Convoluted mucosa[d]	50	29	1460	–	0.72	1050	1.7	50	1.2	19	2.6
Flat mucosa[e]	67	39	2040	–	0.60	1220	1.7	50	1.3	16	2.7

[a]A series of 75 biopsies of morphologically normal mucosa. [b]A group of 13 biopsies of flat avillous mucosa of adult coeliacdisease.[78,8] [c]A patient with morphologically normal mucosa. [d]A patient with dermatitis herpetiformis and a totally convoluted mucosa, which would place it in Group 3 convoluted.[65,9] [e]A patient with dermatitis herpetiformis and a flat avillous mucosa.
The data for all three of the individuals has been reanalysed so as to give more accurate readings; this includes using theTannock correction factor.

DNA that include base modification, cross-linkage and strand breakage, clonal expansion leading to the development of a malignant phenotype.[186,187] Most animal carcinogenesis experiments use very powerful agents to initiate the process, and may thus concentrate excessively on the end stages of this.

Hyperproliferation is also generally considered to be part of this process. Nuclear DNA is subjected to thousands of 'hits' per nucleus per day.[188] While tumours can be readily induced in the stomach and colon, few tumours are seen in the small intestine of experimental animals and a similar pattern is seen in man. The reason for this can only be speculative, but one possible explanation can be attributed to the difficulty of transformed cells establishing a carcinogenic advantage in this rapidly dividing tissue and then growing downwards against the prevailing current of cell migration.[38] The majority of experimental carcinogens initially inhibit cell division and kill mucosal cells, a compensatory proliferative response is then observed, followed by a return to an apparently normal morphological and kinetic state. Chronic carcinogen treatment leads to a generalized change to a more hyperplastic mucosa, perhaps linked to a failure to repress DNA synthesis. A population of transformed cells will eventually evolve out of this hyperplastic population. The earliest detectable stage of this process may be in the form of 'aberrant crypt foci', which may serve as an intermediate marker.[189]

Although the high rates of cell division usually protect the mucosa by 'washing out' altered cells, proliferation may also act to 'fix' damaged DNA before it can be repaired. Cancer is a multistage process and once an event has become initiated, hyperplasia will encourage tumourogenesis by acting as a promoter. This is demonstrated by the increased risk associated with active ulcerative colitis and by the increased risk of gastric carcinoids with hypergastrinaemia.[190] The consensus of opinion is that most tumours arise from foci of dysplasia and atypia,[191] first manifested by a loss of differentiation and an upwards expansion of the proliferative zone. The crypt is thus repopulated with transformed cells, and while the lesion may regress they may also accumulate in the upper crypt to form a small adenoma.

According to conventional dogma, a few of these adenomas will then progress to carcinomas, although the poorly differentiated carcinomas may arise de novo. There is a progressive upward migration in the size of the proliferative compartment, and the increased proliferation in the top of the lengthened crypts leads to the formation of glandular buds and the typical fungiform adenoma.[192] The significance of the upward migration is less clear, as careful analysis of tumour development indicates that the original lesions arise in the (normal) proliferative zone of the crypt, sprout out of the lamina propria mucosa, and move upward with migration of the epithelial cells of the crypts.[193]

Cell division (or differentiation) may be stimulated by the interaction of cell surface receptors with soluble proteins or growth factors, or through their interaction with the proteins of the extracellular matrix. These signals may be distorted by the genetic changes associated with the transition to a cancerous state, which could explain why many of the oncogenes are altered growth factors or growth factor receptors, and why extracellular matrix receptor expression is often aberrant in tumours. The binding of a growth factor to its receptor triggers growth (or differentiation) by turning on or off specific genes. It is likely that many of the genetic changes involved in tumour initiation and promotion are associated with these intracellular signal cascades.[194]

In adenomatous polyps, labelling is seen throughout the crypts, and abnormal proliferation patterns such as denseness, stratification, expansion and budding of the labelled cells tended to increase in accordance with the degree of the histological atypism. The labelling index of the polyps may increase proportionally to their histological atypism.[180]

CONCLUSION

It is generally accepted that increased cell proliferation predisposes towards the risk of cancer, and may even be considered to be a cause of cancer. Proliferation is a prerequisite for carcinogenesis, as non-dividing cells have little clonogenic potential, and continually renewing cells are at a statistical disadvantage. The general theory is that proliferation usually promotes rather than initiates carcinogenesis, either by fixing mutations before genetic housekeeping in G_O and repair can occur.

Nevertheless, the dearth of tumours in the small bowel, the most proliferative part of the gastrointestinal tract, shows that proliferation is not the only answer.

In most animal studies, increased proliferation increased tumour yield, where several models of altered proliferation were associated with altered tumour yield. However, these models are extreme and it can be argued that they are studying the end stage, or final harvest of what is a very prolonged, multistage process. Many experimental carcinogens severely damage the tissue, causing ulceration, cell loss and then a proliferative response and regeneration. Proliferative rates may then remain elevated. Increased proliferation is also seen near the gut-associated lymphoid tissue and near sites of damage. Increased carcinogenesis is also seen at these sites.

Most 'precancerous' states in the human are generally considered to involve increased intestinal epithelial proliferation, perhaps with accompanying upward migration of the proliferative zone. The upward migration is, however, not always seen, especially in more meticulous studies.[193] Precancerous lesions or risk factors in the gastrointestinal tract are generally considered to include the inflammatory bowel diseases, metaplasia, adenomatous and hyperplastic polyps, familial polyposis coli and gastritis (with or without *Helicobacter pylori*). It has been stated earlier in this chapter that there is debate as to the extent of these risks, and the role of proliferation is not the only factor. For example, in ulcerative colitis, in addition to the proliferative effects in the active phases, tissue damage also occurs, so that the basal cells are exposed directly to the colonic contents. Interest in the role of the proliferation has been stirred up in the recent controversy concerning proton pump inhibitors, hypergastrinaemia and increased proliferation in the stomach and perhaps in the colon.

It also needs to be pointed out that the importance of general increases in proliferation depends on one's view of the role of the elusive stem cell.

The role of food intake may be the main factor in setting proliferative rates in the intestine, as there is little doubt that one of the best ways to prolong the life of rats and reduce the incidence of tumourogenesis is long term calorie restriction, nevertheless, we have problems convincing members of our families or our colleagues to put this into practice.

REFERENCES

1. Preston-Martin S, Pike MC, Ross RK, Jones PA, Henderson BE. Increased cell division as a cause for human cancer. Cancer Research 1990; 50: 7415–7421.
2. Adams JM, Cory S. Transgenic models of tumour development. Science 1991; 254: 1161–1166.
3. Dempsey PJ, Goldenring JR, Soroka CJ, et al. Possible role of transforming growth factor a in the pathogenesis of Menetrier's disease: supportive evidence from humans and transgenic mice. Gastroenterology 1992; 103: 1950–1963.
4. Hauft SM, Kim SH, Schmidt GH, et al. Expression of sv40 t-antigen in the small intestinal epithelium of transgenic mice results in proliferative changes in the crypt and re-entry of villus-associated enterocytes into the cell-cycle but has no apparent effect on cellular-differentiation programs and does not cause neoplastic transformation. J Cell Biol 1992; 117: 825–839.
5. Murray AW. Creative blocks: cell-cycle checkpoints and feedback controls. Nature 1992; 359: 599–604.
6. Aherne WA, Camplejohn RS, Wright NA. An introduction to cell population kinetics. London: Edward Arnold, 1977.
7. Wright NA, Alison MR. The biology of epithelial cell populations. Oxford: Oxford University Press, 1984; vol 1.
8. Smith JA. The cell cycle and related concepts in cell proliferation. J Pathol 1982; 136: 149–166.
9. Sunter JP. Cell proliferation studies on normal, carcinogen-damaged and neoplastic epithelia [MD]. University of Newcastle-upon-Tyne, 1981.
10. Wright NA, Irwin M. The kinetics of villus cell populations in the mouse small intestine. I. Normal villi: the steady state requirement. Cell & Tiss Kinet 1982; 15: 595–609.
11. Buchi KN, Moore JG, Hrushesky WJM, Sothern RB, Rubin NH. Circadian rhythm of cellular proliferation in human rectal mucosa. Gastroenterology 1991; 101: 410–415.
12. Cheng H, Leblond CP. Origin, differentiation and renewal of the four main epithelial cell types of the mouse small intestine. V. Unitarian theory of the origin of the four epithelial cell types. Am J Anat 1974; 144: 537–562.
13. Potten CS, Loeffler M. A comprehensive model of the crypts of the small intestine of the mouse provides insight into the mechanisms of cell migration and the proliferative hierarchy. J Theor Biol 1987; 127: 381–391.
14. Potten CS. Clonogenic, stem and carcinogen-target cells in small intestine. Scand J Gastroenterology 1984; 19(Suppl 104): 3–14.

15. Hall PA, Watt FM. Stem cells: the generation and maintenance of cellular diversity. Development 1989; 106: 619–633.
16. Paulus U, Potten CS, Loeffler M. A model of the control of cellular regeneration in the intestinal crypt after perturbation based solely on local stem-cell regulation. Cell Proliferation 1992; 25: 559–578.
17. Cairns J. Mutation Selection and the natural history of cancer. Nature (Lond) 1975; 225: 197–200.
18. Winton DJ, Bount MA, Ponder BAJ. A clonal marker induced by mutation in mouse intestinal epithelium. Nature (Lond) 1988; 333: 463–466.
19. Winton DJ, Ponder BAJ. Stem cell organisation in mouse intestinal epithelium. Proc R Soc Lond B 1990; 241: 13–18.
20. Winton DJ, Peacock JH, Ponder BAJ. Effect of gamma irradiation at high and low dose rate on a novel in vivo mutation assay in mouse intestine. Mutagenesis 1989; 4: 404–406.
21. Gross L, Dreyfuss Y. Reduction in the incidence of radiation-induced tumours in rats after restriction of food intake. Proc Natl Acad Sci 1984; 81: 7596–7598.
22. Alison MR, Sarraf CE. Apoptosis: a gene-directed programme of cell death. J Royal College of Physicians of London 1992; 26: 25–35.
23. Anilkumar TV, Sarraf CE, Hunt T, Alison MR. The nature of cytotoxic drug-induced cell death in murine intestinal crypts. Br J Cancer 1992; 65: 552–558.
24. Potten CS, Li YQ, Oconnor PJ, Winton DJ. A possible explanation for the differential cancer incidence in the intestine, based on distribution of the cytotoxic effects of carcinogens in the murine large-bowel. Carcinogenesis 1992; 13: 2305–2312.
25. Yanagihara K, Tsumuraya M. Transforming growth factor beta 1 induces apoptotic cell death in cultured human gastric carcinoma cells. Cancer Res 1992; 52: 4042–4045.
26. Oren M. The involvement of oncogenes and tumour suppressor genes in the control of apoptosis. Cancer and Metastatic Review 1992; 11: 141–148.
27. St Clair WH, Osborne JW. Crypt fission and crypt number in the small and large bowel of postnatal rats. Cell Tiss Kinet 1985; 18: 255–262.
28. Goodlad RA, Wright NA. Changes in intestinal cell proliferation, absorptive capacity and structure in young, adult and old rats. J Anat 1990; 173: 109–118.
29. Cairnie AB, Millen BH. Fission of crypts in the small intestine of the irradiated mouse. Cell Tissue Kinetics 1975; 8: 189–196.
30. Cheng H, McCulloch C, Bjerknes M. Effects of 30% intestinal resection on whole population cell kinetics of mouse intestinal epithelium. Anat Record 1986; 215: 35–41.
31. Totafurno J, Bjerknes M, Cheng H. The crypt cycle: Crypt and villus production in adult intestinal epithelium. Biophy J 1987; 52: 279–294.
32. Clarke RM. The effects of growth and fasting on the number of villi and crypts in the small intestine of the albino rat. J Anat 1972; 112: 27–33.
33. Cheng H, Bjerknes M. Whole population cell kinetics and postnatal development of the mouse intestinal epithelium. Anat Record 1985; 211: 420–426.
34. Sullivan PB, Brueton MJ, Tabara Z, Goodlad RA, Lee CY, Wright NA. Epidermal growth factor in necrotising enteritis. Lancet 1991; 338: 53–54.
35. Cheng H, Bjerknes M, Amar J, Gardiner G. Crypt production in normal and diseased human colonic epithelium. Anat Rec 1986; 216: 44–8.
36. Al-Dewachi HS, Appleton DR, Watson AJ, Wright NA. Variations in the cell cycle time in the crypts of Lieberkuhn of the mouse. Virchows Arch (Cell Pathol) 1979; 31: 37–44.
37. Kirkland SC. Clonal origin of columnar, mucous and endocrine cell lineages in human colorectal epithelium. Cancer 1988; 61: 1359–1363.
38. Wright NA, Alison MR. The biology of epithelial cell populations. Oxford: Oxford University Press, 1984; vol 2.
39. Cairnie AB, Lamerton LF, Steel GG. Cell proliferation studies in the epithelium of the rat. II. Theoretical aspects. Expl Cell Res 1965; 39: 539–553.
40. Meinzer HP, Sandblad B. Evidence for cell generation controlled proliferation in the small intestinal crypt. Cell Tiss Kinet 1987; 19: 581–590.
41. Loeffler M, Stein R, Wichman HE, Potten CS, Kaur P, Chwalinski S. Intestinal cell proliferation. I. A comprehensive model of steady-state proliferation in the crypt. Cell Tiss Kinet 1986; 19: 627–645.
42. Levin RJ. Intestinal adaptation to dietary change as exemplified by dietary restriction studies. In: Blatt R, Lawrence TLJ, eds. Function and dysfunction of the small intestine in animals. Liverpool: Liverpool University Press, 1984: 167–198.
43. Eastwood GL. Gastrointestinal epithelial renewal. Gastroenterology 1977; 72: 962–975.
44. Clarke RM. Mucosal architecture and epithelial cell production rate in the small intestine of the albino rat. J Anat 1970; 107: 519–529.
45. Goodlad RA, Levi S, Lee CY, Mandir N, Hodgeson H, Wright NA. Morphometry and cell proliferation in endoscopic biopsies: evaluation of a technique. Gastroenterology 1991; 101: 1235–1241.
46. Hellander HE. The cells of the gastric mucosa. Int Rev Cytol 1981; 70: 217–282.
47. Goodlad RA, Wright NA. The gastric epithelium. GI Futures 1987; 1: 16–19.
48. Lee ER. Dynamic histology of the antral epithelium in the mouse stomach. III. Ultrastructure and renewal of pit cells. Amer J Anat 1985; 172: 225–240.
49. Lee ER, Leblond, CP. Dynamic histology of the antral epithelium in the mouse stomach. III. Ultrastructure and renewal of pit cells. Amer J Anat 1985; 172: 241–259.
50. Hattori T. Tritiated thymidine autoradiographic study on cellular migration in the gastric gland of the golden hamster. Cell Tiss Res 1976; 172: 171–184.
51. Chang WW, Leblond CP. Renewal of the epithelium in the descending colon of the mouse. I. Presence of three cell populations: vacuolated-columnar, mucous and argentaffin. Amer J Anat 1971; 131: 73–100.
52. Sato M, Ahnen DJ. Regional variability of colonocyte growth and differentiation in the rat. Anat Record 1992; 233: 409–414.
53. Sawicki W, Rowinski J. Proliferation kinetics in epithelium of guinea pig colon. I. Variations depending on crypt length and its localisation. Cell Tiss Kinet 1970; 3: 375–383.
54. Sunter JP, Appleton DR, Rodriguez MSB, Wright NA, Watson AJ. A comparison of cell proliferation at different sites in the large bowel of the mouse. J Anat 1979; 129: 833–842.
55. Sunter JP, Watson AJ, Wright NA, Appleton DR. Cell proliferation at different sites in the colon of the male rat. Virchow Arch (Cell Path) 1979; 26: 275–287.
56. Goodlad RA, Wilson TG, Lenton W, Wright NA, Gregory H, McCullagh KG. Intravenous but not intragastric urogastrone-EGF is trophic to the intestinal epithelium of parenterally fed rats. Gut 1987; 28: 573–582.
57. Goodlad RA, Lee CY, Wright NA. Cell proliferation in the small intestine and colon of intravenously fed rats: effect of urogastrone-epidermal growth fraction. Cell Proliferation 1992; 25: 393–404.
58. Bristol JR, Williamson RCN. Large bowel growth. Scand J Gastroenterol 1984; 19(Suppl 93)
59. Maurer HR. Potential pitfalls of 3H-thymidine technique to measure cell proliferation. Cell Tiss Kinet 1981; 14: 111–120.
60. Goodlad RA, Wright NA. Quantitative studies on epithelial replacement in the gut. In: Titchen TA, ed. Techniques in the life sciences: Techniques in digestive physiology. Ireland: Elsevier Biomedical Press, 1982: 212/1–212/21. (vol P2).
61. Tannock IF. A comparison of the relative efficiencies of various metaphase arrest agents. Expl Cell Res 1967; 47: 345–56.
62. Cairnie AB, Bentley J. Cell proliferation studies in the intestinal epithelium of the rat. Hyperplasia during lactation. Expl Cell Res 1967; 46: 428–440.
63. Goodlad RA, Lee CY, Wright NA. Colonic cell proliferation and growth fraction in young, adult and old rats. Virchows Arch (Cell Path) 1992; 61: 415–417.
64. Camplejohn RS, Bone G, Aherne WA. Cell proliferation in rectal carcinoma and rectal mucosa. Eur J Cancer 1973; 9: 577–581.

65. Wright NA, Appleton DR, Marks J, Watson AJ. Cytokinetic studies of crypts in convoluted human small-intestinal mucosa. J Clin Path 1979; 32: 462–470.
66. Gerdes H, Gillin JS, Zimbalist E, Urmacher C, Lipkin M, Winawer SJ. Expansion of the epithelial-cell proliferative compartment and frequency of adenomatous polyps in the colon correlate with the strength of family history of colorectal cancer. Cancer Res 1993; 53: 279–282.
67. Wanders SL, ten Kate J, van der Linden E, Derrhaag LJ, Dinjens WNM, Bosman FT. Does ex vivo labelling of proliferating cells in colonic and vaginal mucosa reflect the S-phase fraction in vivo? Histochemistry 1992; 98: 267–270.
68. Hall PA, Levison DA, Wright NA. Assessment of cellular proliferation in histological material. Berlin: Springer Verlag, 1992.
69. Hall PA, Hart I, Goodlad RA, Coates PJ, Lane DP. Expression of proliferating cell nuclear antigen in non-cycling cells. J Pathol 1992; 168: 97A.
70. McCormick D, Chong H, Hobbs C, Hall PA. Reliable detection of the Ki67 antigen in fixed and wax embedded sections with the novel monoclonal antibody MIB1. J Pathol 1993; 169: 175A.
71. Goodlad RA, Madgwick AJA, Moffatt MR, Levin S, Allen JL, Wright NA. Prostaglandins and the gastric epithelium: Effects of misoprostol on gastric epithelial cell proliferation in the dog. Gut 1989; 30: 316–321.
72. Matthew JA, Pell JD, Prior A, Kennedy H, Gee JM, Johnson IT. Detection of abnormal mucosal cell replication in humans: a new technique. In: Food and Cancer Prevention. Royal Society of Chemistry, 1993.
73. Savidge TC, Smith MW, Walker-Smith JA, Phillips AD. Measuring intestinal crypt cell proliferation by confocal microscopy. Proc Nutr Soc 1993 (in press).
74. Goodlad RA. Some effects of diet on the mitotic index and the cell cycle of ruminal epithelium of sheep. Q J Exp Physiol 1981; 66: 487–499.
75. Rijke RPC, Plaisier H, Hoogeveau AT, Lamerton LF, Galjaard H. The effects of continuous irradiation on cell proliferation and maturation in the small intestinal epithelium. Cell Tiss Kinet 1975; 8: 441–453.
76. Hanson WR. Proliferative and morphological adaptation of the intestine to experimental resection. Scand J Gastroenterol 1982; 17(Suppl 74): 11–20.
77. Al-Dewachi HS, Appleton DR, Watson AJ, Wright NA. The effects of starvation and refeeding on cell population kinetics in the rat small bowel mucosa. J Anat 1975; 119: 105–116.
78. Wright NA, Morley A, Appleton D, Marks J. Cell kinetics in flat avillous mucosa of the human small intestine. Gut 1973; 14: 701–710.
79. Wright NA, Morley AR, Appleton DR. The action of testosterone on cell proliferation and differentiation in the small bowel. J Endocrinology 1972; 52: 161–175.
80. Hammann A, Arveux P, Martin M. Effect of gut-associated lymphoid tissue on cellular proliferation in proximal and distal colon of the rat. Dig Dis Sci 1992; 37: 1099–1104.
81. Clarke RM. Luminal nutrition versus functional workload as controllers of mucosal morphology in epithelial replacement in the rat small intestine. Digestion 1976; 15: 411–429.
82. Goodlad RA, Plumb JA, Wright NA. The relationship between intestinal crypt cell proliferation and water absorption measured in vitro in the rat. Clin Sci 1987; 72: 297–304.
83. Goodlad RA, Wright NA. The effects of starvation and refeeding on intestinal cell proliferation in the mouse. Virchow Arch (Cell Path) 1984; 45: 63–73.
84. Goodlad RA, Plumb JA, Wright NA. Epithelial cell proliferation and intestinal absorptive function during starvation and refeeding in the rat. Clin Sci 1988; 74: 301–306.
85. Altman GG. Influence of starvation and refeeding on mucosal size and epithelial renewal in the rat small intestine. Am J Anat 1972; 133: 391–400.
86. Potten CS, Chwalinski S, Swindell R, Palmer M. The spatial organisation of the hierarchical proliferative cells of the small intestine into clusters of 'synchronised' cells. Cell Tissue Kinetics 1982; 15: 351–370.
87. Goodlad RA, Wright NA. Growth control factors in the gastrointestinal tract. Bailliere's Clinical Gastroenterology 1990; 4: 97–119.
88. Bloom SR. An enteroglucagon tumour in man. Gut 1972; 13: 520–23.
89. Al-Mukhtar MYT, Polak JM, Bloom SR, Wright NA. The role of pancreatico-biliary secretions in intestinal adaptation after resection, and its relationship to plasma enteroglucagon. Br J Surg 1983; 70: 398–400.
90. Goodlad RA, Wright NA. Peptides and epithelial growth regulation. In: Polak J, ed. Regulatory Peptides. Basel: Birkhauser Verlag, 1989: 180–192.
91. Orscov C, Holst JJ, Poulsen SS, Kirkegaard P. Pancreatic and intestinal processing of proglucagon in man. Diabetologia 1987; 30: 874–881.
92. Watanabe N, Matsuyama T, Namba M, et al. Trophic effects of glucagon 1–21 peptide on rat intestine. Biomedical Research 1988; 9(Suppl 1): 74.
93. Goodlad RA, Ghatei MA, Bloom SR, Wright NA. Glucagon1-21 reduced intestinal epithelial cell proliferation in parenterally fed rats. Exp Physiol 1991; 76: 943–949.
94. Calam J, Goodlad RA, Lee CY, et al. Achlorhydria-induced hypergastinaemia: the role of Bacteria. Clin Sci 1991; 80: 281–284.
95. Deprez PH, Ghosh P, Goodlad RA, et al. Hypergastrinaemia: a new mechanism. Lancet 1991; 338: 410–411.
96. Walsh JH. Role of gastrin as a trophic hormone. Digestion 1990; 47: 11–6.
97. Carlsson E, Havu N, Mattsson H, Ekman L. Gastrin and gastric enterochromaffin-like cell carcinoids in the rat. Digestion 1990; 47(Suppl 1): 17–23.
98. Tielemans Y, Hakanson R, Sundler F, Willems G. Proliferation of enterochromaffin-like cells in omeprazole-treated hypergastrinemic rats. Gastroenterology 1989; 96: 723–9.
99. Eissele R, Roskopf B, Koop H, Adler G, Arnold R. Proliferation of endocrine cells in the rat stomach caused by drug-induced achlorhydria. Gastroenterology 1991; 101: 70–76.
100. Havu N. Enterochromaffin-like cell carcinoids of gastric mucosa in rats after life-long inhibition of gastric secretion. Digestion 1986; 35: 42–55.
101. Holt S, Powers RE, Howden CW. Antisecretory therapy and genotoxicity. Dig Dis Sci 1991; 36: 545–547.
102. Berlin RG. Omeprazole — gastrin and gastric endocrine cell data from clinical-studies. Dig Dis Sci 1991; 36: 129–136.
103. Johnson LR. Regulation of gastrointestinal growth. In: Johnson LR, ed. Physiology of the digestive tract. New York: Raven Press, 1981: 169–196.
104. Eggstein S, Imdahl A, Kohler M, Waibel M, Farthmann EH. Influence of gastrin, gastrin receptor blockers, epidermal growth factor, and difluoromethylornithine on the growth and the activity of ornithine decarboxylase of colonic carcinoma cells. J Cancer Res Clin Oncol 1991; 117: 37–42.
105. Wong K, Beardshall K, Waters CM, Calam J, Poston GJ. Postprandial hypergastrinaemia in patients with colorectal cancer. Gut 1991; 32: 1352–1354.
106. Goodlad RA, Lee CY, Gilbey S, Ghatei MA, Bloom SR, Wright NA. Dietary elevation of endogenous insulin does not influence intestinal epithelial cell renewal. J Exp Physiology 1993; 78: 697–709.
107. Goodlad RA, Ghatei MA, Domin J, Bloom SR, Wright NA. Is PYY trophic to the intestinal epithelium of parenterally fed rats? Digestion 1990; 46(Suppl 2): 177–181.
108. Carpenter G. Epidermal growth factor. In: Baserga R, ed. Tissue growth factors. Berlin: Springer-Verlag, 1981: 89–123.
109. Weaver LT, Walker WA. Epidermal growth factor and the developing human gut. Gastroenterology 1988; 94: 845–847.
110. Walker-Smith JA, Phillips AD, Walford N, et al. Intravenous epidermal growth factor/urogastrone increases small intestinal cell proliferation in congenital microvillous atrophy. Lancet 1985; 11: 1239–40.
111. Goodlad RA, Raja KB, Peters TK, Wright NA. The effects of urogastrone-EGF on small intestinal brush boarder enzymes and mitotic activity. Gut 1991; 32: 994–998.

112. Ulshen MH, Lyn-Cook LE, Raasch RH. Effects of intraluminal EGF on mucosal proliferation in the small intestine of adult rats. Gastroenterology 1986; 91: 1134–40.
113. Playford RJ, Woodman AC, Clark P, et al. Preservation of luminal growth factors: a novel mechanism in clinical nutrition. Lancet 1993; 341: 843–848.
114. Scheving LA, Shiurba RA, Nguyen TD, Gray GM. Epidermal growth factor receptor of the intestinal enterocyte. Localisation to laterobasal but not brush border membrane. J Biol Chem 1989; 264: 1735–41.
115. Burgess AW. Epidermal growth factor and transforming growth factor a. British Medical Bulletin 1989; 45: 401–424.
116. Goodlad RA, Lee CY, Wright NA. TGF-a and intestinal epithelial cell proliferation in parenterally fed rats. Gut 1990; 31: A1197.
117. Sandgren EP, Luetteke NC, Paliter RD, Brinster RL, Lee DC. Overexpression of TGFa in transgenic mice: induction of epithelial hyperplasia, pancreatic metaplasia and carcinoma of the breast. Cell 1990; 61: 1121–1135.
118. Wright NA, Poulson R, Stamp G, et al. Trefoil gene expression in gastrointestinal epithelial cells in inflammatory bowel disease. Gastroenterology 1993; 104: 12–20.
119. Poulsom R, Chinery R, Sarraf C, et al. Trefoil peptide gene expression in intestinal adaptation and renewal. Scand J Gastroenterol 1992; 27(Suppl 192): 17–28.
120. Rio M, Bellocq JP, Daniel JY, et al. Breast cancer-associated pS2 protein: synthesis and secretion by normal stomach mucosa. Science 1988; 241(4866): 705–8.
121. Hoosein NM, Thim L, Jorgensen KH, Brattain MG. Growth stimulatory effect of pancreatic spasmolytic polypeptide on cultured colon and breast tumour cells. FEBS Lett 1989; 247: 303–6.
122. Wright NA, Pike C, Elia G. Induction of a novel epidermal growth factor-secreting cell lineage by mucosal ulceration in human gastrointestinal stem cells. Nature 1990; 343: 82–85.
123. Raja RH, Paterson AJ, Shin TH, Kudlow JE. Transcriptional regulation of the human transforming growth factor-a gene. Mol Endocrinol 1991; 5: 514–20.
124. Goodlad RA, Madgwick AJA, Moffatt MR, Levin S, Allen JL, Wright NA. Prostaglandins and the gastric epithelium: Effects of misoprostol on cell migration and transit in the dog stomach. Gastroenterology 1990; 96: 1–6.
125. Goodlad RA, Lee CY, Levin S, Wright NA. The effects of the prostaglandin E1 analogue, misoprostol, on cell proliferation in the canine small intestine. Experimental Physiol 1991; 76: 561–566.
126. Goodlad RA, Mandir N, Levin S, Allen JL, Wright NA. Prostaglandins and the colonic epithelium: Effects of misoprostol on colonic epithelial cell proliferation and migration in the dog. Gastroenterology 1991; 101: 1229–1234.
127. Levi S, Goodlad RA, Lee CY, et al. Inhibitory effect of non-steroidal anti-inflammatory drugs on mucosal cell proliferation associated with gastric ulcer healing. Lancet 1990; 336: 840–843.
128. Levi S, Goodlad RA, Stamp G, et al. Effects of non-steroidal anti-inflammatory drugs and misoprostol on gastric and duodenal epithelial proliferation in patients with arthritis. Gastroenterology 1992; 102: 1605–1611.
129. Goodlad RA, Wright NA. The effects of addition of cellulose or kaolin to an elemental diet on intestinal cell proliferation in the mouse. British Journal of Nutrition 1983; 50: 91–98.
130. Willett W. The search for the causes of breast and colon cancer. Nature (Lond) 1989; 338: 389–394.
131. Hoensch H, Steinhardt HJ, Weiss G, Haug D, Maier A, Malchow H. Effects of semisythetic diets on xenobiotic metabolising enzyme activity and morphology of small intestinal mucosa in humans. Gastroenterology 1984; 86: 1519–1530.
132. Janne P, Carpenter Y, Willems G. Colonic mucosal atrophy induced by a liquid elemental diet in rats. Am J Dig Dis 1977; 22: 808–812.
133. Goodlad RA, Lenton W, Ghatei MA, Adrian TE, Bloom SR, Wright NA. Effects of an elemental diet, inert bulk and different types of dietary fibre on the response of the intestinal epithelium to refeeding in the rat and relationship to plasma gastrin, enteroglucagon, and PYY concentrations. Gut 1987; 28: 171–80.
134. Sakata T, Yajima T. Influence of short chain fatty acids on the epithelial cell division of digestive tracts. Q J Exp Physiol 1984; 69: 639–648.
135. Goodlad RA, Ratcliffe BR, Fordham JP, Wright NA. Does dietary fibre stimulate intestinal epithelial cell proliferation in germ-free rats? Gut 1989; 30: 820–825.
136. Kripke SA, Fox AD, Berman JA, Settle RG, Rombeau JL. Stimulation of intestinal mucosal growth with intracolonic infusion of short chain fatty acids. J Parenteral and Enteral nutrition 1989; 13: 109–116.
137. Goodlad RA, Ratcliffe B, Lee CY, Wright NA. Proliferative effects of dietary fibre on the gastrointestinal epithelium: the stomach has a different response than the small intestine and colon in conventional and germ-free rats. In: Food and Cancer Prevention. Royal Society of Chemistry, 1993.
138. Jacobs LR. Stimulation of rat colonic crypt cell proliferative activity by bran consumption during the stages of 1,2-dimethydrazine administration. Cancer Res 1984; 44: 2458–2463.
139. Beaty MM, Lee EY, Glauert HP. Influence of dietary calcium and vitamin-d on colon epithelial-cell proliferation and 1,2-dimethylhydrazine-induced colon carcinogenesis in rats fed high-fat diets. J Nutr 1993; 123: 144–152.
140. Bostick RM, Potter JD, Fosdick L, et al. Calcium and colorectal epithelial-cell proliferation — a preliminary randomized, double-blind, placebo-controlled clinical trial. J Natl Cancer Inst 1993; 85: 132–141.
141. Wargovich MJ. Fish oils and cancer. Gastroenterology 1992; 103: 1096–1101.
142. Thun MJ, M.M. N, Heath CW. Asprin use and reduced risk of fatal colon cancer. New England Journal of Medicine 1991; 325: 1593–1596.
143. Craven PA, Thornburg K, DeRubertis FR. Sustained increase in the proliferation of rat colonic mucosa during chronic treatment with aspirin. Gastroenterology 1988; 94: 567–7.
144. Newmark HL, Lipkin M. Calcium, vitamin D, and colon cancer. Cancer Res 1992; 52: 2067s–2070s.
145. Ames BN. Mutagenesis and carcinogenesis: endogenous and exogenous factors. Environ Mol Mutagen 1989; 14(Suppl 16): 66–77.
146. Lacy ER, Ito S. Ethanol induced injury to the superficial rat gastric epithelium: a study of damage and rapid repair. In: Allen A, Flemstrom G, Garner A, Silen W, Turnberg LA, eds. Mechanisms of mucosal protection in the upper gastrointestinal tract. New York: Raven Press, 1984:
147. Silen W. Gastroduodenal mucosal integrity, injury and repair. In: Garner A, Whittle BJR, eds. Advances in drug therapy of gastrointestinal ulceration. Chichester: John Wiley & Sons, 1989: 131–138.
148. Konturek SJ. Role of growth factors in gastroduodenal protection and healing of peptic ulcers. Gastroenterol Clin North Am 1990; 19: 41–46.
149. Feil W, Lacy ER, Wong YM, et al. Rapid epithelial restitution of human and rabbit colonic mucosa. Gastroenterology 1989; 97: 685–701.
150. Lacy ER. Epithelial restitution in the gastrointestinal tract. J Clin Gastroenterol 1988; 10(Suppl 1): S72–77.
151. Gronbech JE, Matre K, Stangeland L, Svanes K, Varhaug J. Gastric mucosal repair in the cat: role of the hyperemic response to mucosal damage. Gastroenterology 1988; 95: 311–320.
152. Misiewicz JJ. Aetiology of peptic ulcer. In: Garner A, Whittle BJR, eds. Advances in drug therapy of gastrointestinal ulceration. Chichester: John Wiley & Sons Ltd, 1989: 1–16.
153. Dinsdale D, Cheng KJ, Wallace RJ, Goodlad RA. Digestion of epithelial tissue of the rumen wall by adherent bacteria in infused and conventionally fed sheep. Applied and Environmental Biology 1980; 39: 1059–1066.
154. Cheng KJ, Costerton JW. Adherent rumen bacteria — their role in the digestion of plant material, urea and epithelial cells. In: Ruckebusch Y, Thivend P, eds. Digestive Physiology and Metabolism in Ruminants. Lancaster: MTP Press, 1980: 227–250.
155. Tsai BS, Kessler LK, Butchko GM, Bauer RF. Effects of

misoprostol on histamine-stimulated acid secretion and cyclic AMP formation in isolated canine parietal cells. Dig Dis Sci 1987; 32: 1010–1016.

156. Dembinski A, Konturek SJ. Effects of E, F, and I series prostaglandins and analogues on growth of gastrointestinal mucosa and pancreas. Am J Physiol 1985; 248: G170–G175.
157. Hansen OH, Jensen KB, Larsen JK, Soltoft J. Gastric mucosal cell proliferation and immunoglobulin-containing cells in Menetrier's Disease. Digestion 1977; 16: 293–8.
158. Hansen OH, Johansen AA, Larsen JK, Svendsen LB. Cell proliferation in normal and diseased gastric mucosa. Acta Pathol Microbiol Scand (A) 1979; 87: 217–222.
159. Takagi H, Jhappan C, Sharp R, Merlino G. Hypertrophic gastropathy resembling Menetrier's disease in transgenic mice overexpressing transforming growth factor alpha in the stomach. J Clin Invest 1992; 90: 1161–7.
160. Romano M, Polk WH, Awad JA, et al. Transforming growth factor-alpha protection against drug-induced injury to the rat gastric-mucosa in vivo. J Clin Invest 1992; 90: 2409–2421.
161. Liavag I. Mitotic activity of the gastric mucosa: a study by means of colcemid. Acta Pathol Microbiol Scand 1968; 72: 43–63.
162. Graham RI, Schade ROK. The distribution of intestinal metaplasia in macroscopic specimens demonstrated by a histochemical method. Acta Pathol Microbiol Scand 1965; 65: 53–59.
163. Lehnert T, Deschner EE. Cell kinetics of gastric cancer and precancer. In: Filipe MIJ J.R., eds. Gastric carcinoma. Edinburgh: Churchill Livingstone 1986: 54.
164. Deschner EE, Winawer SJ, Lipkin M. Patterns of nucleic acid and protein synthesis in normal human gastric mucosa and atrophic gastritis. J Nat Cancer Inst 1972; 48: 1567–1574.
165. Ateshkadi A, Lam NP, Johnson CA. Helicobacter pylori and peptic-ulcer disease. Clinical Pharmacy 1993; 12: 34–48.
166. Forman D. Helicobacter pylori infection: a novel risk factor in the aetiology of gastric cancer. Journal of the National Cancer Institute 1991; 83: 1702–1703.
167. Palli D, Decarli A, Cipriani F, et al. Helicobacter pylori antibodies in areas of Italy at varying gastric cancer risk. Cancer Epidemiology Biomarkers & Prevention 1993; 2: 37–40.
168. Buset M, De KE, Deprez C, Nyst JF, Deltenre M, Galand P. Gastric corpus cell proliferation, corpus gastritis and Helicobacter pylori (meeting abstract). Proc Am Assoc Cancer Res 1992; 33: 38.
169. Sierra R, Munoz N, Pena AS, et al. Antibodies to Helicobacter pylori and pepsinogen levels in children from Costa-Rica — comparison of 2 areas with different risks for stomach cancer. Cancer Epidemiology Biomarkers & Prevention 1992; 1: 449–454.
170. Watson AJ, Wright NA. Morphology and cell kinetics of jejunal mucosa in untreated patients. In: Clinics in Gastroenterology. Eastbourne: Saunders, 1974: 11–13, vol 3.
171. Fluge G, Aksnes L. Mitotic rate and mitotic time in coeliac and non-coeliac duodenal biopsies maintained in organ culture. Virchows Arch B (Cell Pathol) 1981; 38: 159–67.
172. Zucoloto S, Bramble MG, Wright NA, Record CO. Acute gluten challenge in treated coeliac disease: a morphometric and enzymatic study. Gut 1985; 26: 169–174.
173. Fluge G, Aksnes L. Labelling indices after 3H-thymidine incorporation during organ culture of duodenal mucosa in coeliac disease. Scand J Gastroenterol 1981; 16: 921–8.
174. Appleton DR, Sunter JP, de Rodriguez MSB, Watson AJ. Cell proliferation in the mouse large bowel, with details of the analysis of experimental data. In: Appleton DR, Sunter JP, eds. Cell proliferation in the gastrointestinal tract. London: Pitman Medical, 1980: 40–53.
175. Bleiberg H, Mainguet P, Galand P, Chretien J, Dupont-Mairesse N. Cell renewal in the human rectum; in-vitro autoradiographic study on active ulcerative colitis. Gastroenterology 1970; 58: 851–855.
176. Levin B. Ulcerative-colitis and colon cancer — biology and surveillance. Journal of Cellular Biochemistry 1992; 1992(16g): 47–50.
177. Lehy T, Mignon M, Abitbol JL. Epithelial cell proliferation in the rectal stump of patients with ileorectal anastomosis for ulcerative colitis. Gut 1983; 24: 1048–56.
178. Deschner EE, Winawer SJ, Katz S, Katzka I, Kahn E. Proliferative defects in ulcerative colitis patients. Cancer Invest 1983; 1: 41–7.
179. Biasco G, Paganelli GM, Miglioli M, et al. Rectal cell proliferation and colon cancer risk in ulcerative colitis. Cancer Res 1990; 50: 1156–9.
180. Kanemitsu T, Koike A, Yamamoto S. Study of the cell proliferation kinetics in ulcerative colitis, adenomatous polyps, and cancer. Cancer 1985; 56: 1094–8.
181. Scheppach W, Sommer H, Kirchner T, et al. Effect of butyrate enemas on the colonic mucosa in distal ulcerative colitis (see comments). Gastroenterology 1992; 103: 51–6.
182. Zaitoun AM, Cobden I, H. a-M, Record CO. Morphometric studies in rectal biopsy specimens from patients with ulcerative colitis: effect of oral 5 amino salicylic acid and rectal prednisolone treatment. Gut 1991; 32: 183–7.
183. Langholz E, Munkholm P, Davidsen M, Binder V. Colorectal cancer risk and mortality in patients with ulcerative colitis. Gastroenterology 1992; 103: 1444–1451.
184. Fabia R. Acetic acid-induced colitis in the rat — a reproducible. European Surgical Research 1992; 24: 211–225.
185. Makwakwa KEB, Warren BF, Watkins PE, Bradfield JWB. Colonic mucins in the cotton top tamarin. Journal of Pathology 1992; 168: 144–144.
186. Fearon ER, Vogelstein B. A genetic model for colorectal tumorigenesis. Cell 1990; 61: 759–767.
187. Solomon E, Borrow J, Goddard AD. Chromosome aberrations and cancer. Science 1991; 254: 1153–1160.
188. Ames BN 1S16-7. Endogenous oxidative DNA damage, ageing, and cancer. Free Radic Res Commun 1989; 7: 121–128.
189. Wargovich MJ, Harris C, Chen CD, Palmer C, Steele VE, Kelloff GJ. Growth-kinetics and chemoprevention of aberrant crypts in the rat colon. Journal of Cellular Biochemistry 1992; 16g: 51–54.
190. Larsson H, Carlsson E, Mattsson H, et al. Plasma gastrin and gastric enterochromaffin-like cell activation and proliferation. Studies with omeprazole and ranitidine in intact and antrectomized rats. Gastroenterology 1986; 90: 391–9.
191. Chang WWL. Pathogenesis and biological behaviour of 1,2-dimethylhydrazine-induced colonic neoplasms in the mouse. In: Appleton DR, Sunter JP, Watson AJ, eds. Cell Proliferation in the Gastrointestinal Tract. London: Pitman Medical Press 1979: 277–297.
192. Weibecke B, Brandts A, Elder M. Epithelial proliferation and morphogenesis of hyperplastic, adenomatous and villus polyps of the human colon. Virch Arch 1974; 364: 35–49.
193. Nakamura S, Kino I. Morphogenesis of minute adenomas in familial popyposis coli. JNCI 1984; 73: 41–49.
194. Alberts B, Bray D, Lewis J, Raff M, Roberts K, Watson JD. Molecular biology of the cell. New York: Garland Publishing, 1989.

CHAPTER 9

Gastrointestinal motility and its contribution to disease

J. R. Bennett

NORMAL GUT MOTILITY

The oesophagus

Neuromusculature of the oesophagus

In humans the densely innervated pharyngeal muscles (predominantly the three constrictors) join the tubular oesophagus at the level of the cricopharyngeus which, aided by the inferior constrictor, forms the upper oesophageal sphincter. Below this the 20–25 cm of oesophagus has two muscle layers, longitudinal and circular. It used to be said that the upper third was striated muscle, the distal third smooth muscle, and the middle third mixed, but more recent autopsy studies[1] suggest that only 4.2% (circular) and 5.7% (longitudinal) is striated. At least the lower half is pure smooth muscle (62% circular, 54% longitudinal), and the mixed or transitional zone makes up 35% of circular and 41% of longitudinal muscle.

The upper (cricopharyngeal) sphincter is an anatomically distinct ring of striated muscle (derived from cricopharyngeus, lower constrictor and upper oesophagus) under voluntary control. The lower (gastro-oesophageal, cardiac) sphincter is usually considered to be an anatomically undetectable but functionally specialized segment of smooth muscle (though Liebermann-Meffert has demonstrated a perceptible thickening in the area[2]).

The extrinsic innervation of the oesophagus is by branches of the vagus and sympathetic nerves; intrinsically, there is a clear myenteric plexus between the two muscle layers. Neural control is mainly by cholinergic and nonadrenergic noncholinergic nerves.

Alpha adrenergic neurotransmitters increase the gastro-oesophageal sphincter tone, beta stimulation lowers it, but adrenergic nerves play little part in controlling motility of the body which predominantly receives excitatory vagal innervation. Cholinergic stimulation increases and cholinergic blockade diminish peristaltic pressures in the distal oesophagus. The gastro-oesophageal sphincter is tonically contracted, due to intrinsic muscle control. Relaxation (during swallowing) is vagally mediated by preganglionic cholinergic nerves and postganglionic nonadrenergic noncholinergic nerves. The relevant neurotransmitter remains uncertain; once thought to be predominantly VIP[3], 5 hydroxy tryptamine[4] and nitric oxide[5,6] are now recognized as more important.

Normal oesophageal motility

The gastro-oesophageal sphincter is closed at rest, opening with each swallow, the continuous resting electrical spike activity being transiently arrested and its tone reducing to about that in the gastric fundus. This relaxation is followed by a brief 'after-contraction', and then resumption of resting tone.

Resting tone of the sphincter is modulated by a number of agents[7] including:

—prostaglandins
—nonadrenergic/noncholinergic nerves via VIP, $5HT_3$, nitric oxide
—inhibitory β adrenergic receptors
—dopaminergic and H_2 receptors
—several hormones, including gastrin, motilin, cholecystokinin
—the migrating interdigestive complex.[8]

Voluntary swallowing initiates a sequence of efferent discharges from the swallowing centre in the medulla, programmed to pass progressively to more distal segments of the oesophagus, or penetrating in a sequential manner because of increasing latency, possibly caused by the intracellular potassium gradient or nitric oxide.[9] A wave of excitation passes down the oesophagus as bursts of electrical spike activity. This results in a ring of muscular contraction passing distally at 2–4 cm/sec. The squeeze pressure is highest in the lowest few cm, and equal in the rest except for a trough 4–6 cm below the cricopharyngeal sphincter.

The stomach

The stomach is considered to have two main motor functions: to act as a reservoir and to mix and break down the solid constituents of food.

The reservoir function is predominantly served by the fundus and body. Large volumes can be accommodated with little pressure change because of adaptive relaxation. Inhibitory vagal discharges to the fundal musculature (especially the oblique layer) triggered by the effects of distension (and to a lesser effect by swallowing itself) reduce the sequence of slow, sustained contractions which occur in the fundus. This adaptive relaxation is not complete, and the tonic pressure within the fundus (with the slow pressure waves) seems to control the rate at which liquids initially empty through the pylorus, though other control mechanisms take over later.

The antrum has an important mixing and grinding action employing regular (3/minute) peristaltic waves combined with terminal antral (and pyloric) closure, producing a to-and-fro motion which reduces solids to small particles. Those less than 2 mm in size are emptied more slowly than liquids, but by a similar mechanism — the fundal–duodenal gradient. Larger particles are propelled by a cycle of electromechanical activity known as the migrating motor complex (MMC).

The normal cycle of gastric peristaltic contractions is initiated from a pacemaker on the greater curvature aspect of the upper body of the stomach.[10] Only those pacemaker potentials which have action potentials superimposed cause a peristaltic contraction; their occurrence is related to different phases of the MMC, enhanced by gastrin, motilin and probably other factors. In the body of the stomach propagation of these pacemaker potentials is at about 0.5 cm/sec but may reach 4 cm/sec in the antrum.[11] Coordination of antrum, pylorus and duodenum is important for normal, regulated gastric function.[12]

Gastric emptying

Gastric emptying is a complex function because of the heterogeneity of gastric contents — their physical, chemical and calorific properties, particularly. Tests of gastric emptying need to study liquids and solids of known particle size. The resulting technical problems cause continuing difficulties of interpretation but many principles are agreed.

The main determinant of *liquid* emptying rates is volume; the rate is exponential, so that the volume emptied in unit time is proportional to the volume present. However this simple arrangement is modified by several factors, the rate being significantly slowed by acidity, osmolarity, fat content, amino acid content and energy content. A 'braking' effect seems to be exerted by small bowel receptors acting by neural and/or hormonal pathways.

Emptying of solids (which are first ground to 2 mm particles) is linear in rate, controlled by the MMC.

As the terminal antral contraction occurs (and the pylorus closes), the previously relaxed duodenum contracts, propelling onwards the contents just expelled from the stomach. The emptying rate is slowed by increased viscosity and fibre content. Solid particles greater than 2 mm in size are retained until phase III of the MMC sweeps them out.

The period of frequent action potentials (and therefore regular peristaltic waves) is phase I of the interdigestive myoelectric complex.[13] It lasts about 5 min, and migrates slowly down the duodenum and small intestine. In the stomach, it is usually able to complete emptying of all but large solid particles.

Small intestine

There are cycles of gut motor activity controlled by a complex pattern of electrical excitation. The electrical 'pace-setter' in the upper small intestine — (or distal stomach) generates slow electrical waves at about 11–13/ minute. These are conducted along the longitudinal muscle layer of the intestine slowing to a rate of about 6–8/ minute in the ileum. These electrical 'slow' waves are caused by episodic depolarization of cells; mechanical contraction of muscle only accompanies such a 'slow' wave if the coordinating neural system produces associated 'spike' action potentials in a rapid burst during the slow wave. These action potentials cause rings of contraction in the circular muscle which may be conducted along the length of the gut as a peristaltic wave, or may recur intermittently at the same site as segmenting contractions. The rate of mechanical contraction therefore depends on the proportion of slow waves during which depolarization and spikes occur.

The best recognized pattern of activity is known as the migrating motor complex (MMC) seen in the fasting gut.[13] Although the slow electrical wave pattern continues regularly, the cycle begins with a period of motor quiescence for about 40 minutes (phase I). Phase II consists of irregular contractions for another 40 minutes or so. The end of phase II may be marked, especially in the jejunum, by propagated bursts of spike activity over a few cm recurring at intervals of one-half to two minutes. Eventually phase II merges into a short (5–10 minutes) sequence of regular contractions at the rate of the pacemaker (phase III). This last phase is also known as the activity front. The whole cycle passes slowly down the length of the small intestine in about one and a half hours, and recurs at intervals varying from 15 minutes to 6 hours. They are more frequent at night. It is supposed that the activity front propels small bowel contents along. Food entering the small intestine temporarily abolishes the MMC, which returns about the time that gastric emptying ends.

The digestive pattern of intermittent, apparently random spiking and contractions possibly delays forward progress of chyme and enables mixing to occur. Propagating contractions also occur, propelling contents along varying distances.[14]

Transit

The speed of transit of material through the small intestine depends in part on the motor sequences described above, but little information is available about their relationships. Motor and electrical events are difficult to record in the human, and measurement of transit is not easy. Certainly, most of the more obvious abnormalities of small intestinal transit are the consequence of gastric disorders or of gross effects on all gut motility — as in thyrotoxicosis, autonomic neuropathy or widespread smooth muscle disease — rather than of subtle derangements of motor coordination.

Ileo-caecal valve

The ileum enters the caecum through a 'valve' having upper and lower lips. The muscle of the terminal three cm of the ileum is thickened. This segment is associated with a high resting pressure, suggesting it is a true sphincter. Evidence is also accumulating of specialized motor activity within this area, the distal ileum and proximal colon. Phase II of the MMC in this segment appears to consist of less random contractions with more discrete bursts. Phase III (as noted above) propagates more slowly than in the jejunum, and additionally there are reports of prolonged propagated contractions — a form of peristalsis, occurring 3–4 times an hour, expelling ileal contents into the colon.

These patterns of motility are often propagated into the proximal colon.[15]

Colon

Ninety per cent of whole gut transit time in man is accounted for by the colon, emphasizing its reservoir function. Its motor function is only poorly understood, however. This is mainly due to inadequacies of recording technique, as mechanical events at one site of the colon cannot be entirely insulated from events in neighbouring segments. In circular muscle, electric oscillations occur from 4–60 cpm, and in longitudinal muscle from 20–40 cpm, providing a variable rate of mechanical contraction. With slow wave frequencies over 12 cpm and spiking, contractions may fuse together causing a sustained contraction.[16,17] Action potentials (spike bursts) lasting about 20 s and progressing orally or aborally associated with mechanical contractions have been described,[18,19] as have short spike bursts lasting 1.5–3.5 s. Pressure recordings show periods of quiescence with bursts of activity. Overall low frequency contractions (0–9 cpm) are similar in proximal and distal colon, with higher frequency (9–13) found in the transverse; the frequency appears to diminish from the sigmoid to rectum. However, transit velocity seems similar for all segments of the colon.[20]

The contractions are thought mostly to be segmenting, mixing and delaying contents rather than propelling them. Forward transit is usually gradual (due to systolic propulsion, haustral indentations temporarily disappearing), but also depends on 'mass movements' caused by transient disappearance of the haustra.[21] Under normal circumstances in man these probably occur only once or twice a day.[22] They may be the mechanical result of electrically recorded giant migrating contractions.[23]

Long spike bursts, lasting 10–30 s, occur for 3 hours after feeding associated with muscular contractions. Probably both neural and hormonal factors act as mediators.[24] A second period of activity sometimes occurs after 90 min. The first peak of activity is abolished by anticholinergic drugs but the second is not[25] suggesting a predominantly neural pathway for the first and possibly a hormonal stimulus for the second.

The anus

The internal anal sphincter, 3–3.5 cm long, is a condensation of the circular muscle of the rectum, and is under autonomic nervous control. It is encircled by the external sphincter, composed of skeletal muscle (associated with the levator ani and pubo rectalis) and supplied by the somatic nervous system via the pudendal nerves (S2, S3, S4). Maximum basal (resting) pressure of the sphincter is 60–120 cm water, voluntary contraction of the external sphincter ('squeeze pressure') adding a further 60–80 cm of water. Basal pressure fluctuates (slow waves) 10–20/min.

Rectal distension normally causes a transient relaxation of the internal sphincter accompanied by rectal contractions at 5–10/min. There is an initial *increase* in external sphincter activity, but as rectal distension continues this diminishes and stops.[26]

Continence depends only partly on the sphincters and may be retained even when they are disrupted, provided that the deep portion of the external sphincter (contiguous with the pelvic muscles) is left intact. More important is the anorectal angle (normally about 90°), maintained by the sling formed by the puborectalis.

Gall bladder

In the resting, interdigestive state the gall bladder pressure is 0–16 cm water with occasional rhythmic contractions.[27] The chief motor action of the gall bladder is a slow, tonic contraction occurring soon after a meal, discharging most of the contained bile into the duodenum. Emptying of the gall bladder begins soon after food ingestion, about 15% entering the duodenum before gastric emptying begins, suggesting an early phase of control. Subsequent emptying can be expressed as a double exponential function.[28] The stimulus to this contraction is directly on muscle cells by cholecystokinin (CCK) enhanced by secretin and probably by vagal stimuli. Other peptides including gastrin and motilin may cause contractions, while vasoactive intestinal polypeptide (VIP) and pancreatic polypeptide inhibit contraction.

Less prominent (but possibly physiologically important) contractions occur during phase II of the MMC, causing periodic fluctuations in gall bladder bile concentrations. It is postulated that this aids the process of bile concentration and that subsequent relaxation draws in hepatic bile.[29] It is possible that there is a rapid, alternating pump action (like a bellows) and that filling and emptying are constantly alternating.[30]

Common bile duct

Manometric studies (using catheters inserted through the ampulla at endoscopy) show that the region of Oddi's sphincter has a resting tone of 12–15 cm water (higher than the duodenum) and also phasic contractions lasting 7–8 s, 3–4 times a minute.[31]

The tone is lowered by CCK, but is also influenced by the MMC.[32] Opening of the sphincter and contraction both cause bile flow, contraction squirting bile out, relaxation allowing flow according to the duct–duodenum pressure gradient.

THE CONTRIBUTION OF DISTURBED MOTILITY TO GASTROINTESTINAL DISORDERS

Even in the few 'diseases' in which abnormal motility is the sole problem, the mechanisms are not entirely clear. In the many other conditions in which motility is disturbed it is often impossible to be certain whether the motor problem is causative or secondary to the disease process. In the thumb-nail sketches which follow it should always be remembered that measurement of motor function in humans is difficult and crude, that controls of motor activity are poorly understood, and that we have few means of controlling motility.

Diverticula

Occasional diverticula are found in every segment of the gut. They are often harmless but inevitably excite interest simply by being there and because of the relative ease of demonstrating them. Although most diverticula have been considered at some time to be congenital (due to an embryonic defect), attention has been focussed in recent years on motility abnormalities as their cause. Simple mechanical theory would suggest the possibility that excess intraluminal pressures generated by abnormal physical conditions in the lumen, or by incoordination of normal activity could cause them ('pulsion diverticula'). Despite investigation of these possibilities, little certainty exists.

Pharyngeal (Zenker's) diverticulum

The potentially weak junctional area of the pharyngeal constrictor muscles known as Killian's dehiscence is the site of these diverticula. It has been suggested that high pressure may be generated in the pharynx causing a mucosal protrusion, and several theories exist as to the potential cause of high pressure. Tonic contraction of the cricopharyngeal sphincter, suggested by endoscopic observations, has not been confirmed by manometry. Incoordination (the sphincter failing to relax adequately during pharyngeal contraction, or too early) had some manometric support[33] but other studies[34–36] have failed to confirm this. In fact, pharyngeal pressures tend to be low rather than high.

Mid-oesophageal diverticula

There is good evidence that abnormal motility can be demonstrated in the oesophagus of most subjects who have a mid-oesophageal diverticulum. Usually the manometric abnormality is a disturbance of peristalsis, often with 'spasm'.[37–39]

Epiphrenic diverticula

Abnormal oesophageal motility is more readily demonstrated in patients who have an epiphrenic diverticulum, and often the disturbance is gross, e.g. 'diffuse oesophageal spasm'.[40,41]

Gastric and small intestinal diverticula

No useful information exists about the motor abnormalities which may cause those diverticula in the stomach, duodenum and jejunum which are not produced by inflammatory scarring and traction. Gastric diverticula seem to cause no problem, but duodenal diverticula (which occur in 2–5% of people)[42] are implicated as a contributory factor in common bile duct stone formation,[43] possibly because of bacterial proliferation or interference with normal papillary muscle dysfunction.[44] Jejunal diverticula may be a cause of intestinal malabsorption because of bacterial overgrowth within them leading to bile salt deconjugation.

Colonic diverticula

Some diverticula of the colon may be congenital, or due to a congenital weakness in the wall, but the great majority are acquired. In the condition known as colonic diverticular disease, multiple diverticula are found, most commonly and most numerously in the sigmoid, but sometimes affecting all parts.

Such diverticula could be the result of weak areas in the colonic wall, or to abnormal pressures in the lumen, or to a combination of factors. Weakness of the wall is suggested by the predeliction of diverticula for the areas of colon tunnelled by segmental blood vessels, and the undoubted reductions in tensile strength of muscles with age.[45] Abnormally increased pressure in response to stimuli such as morphine or prostigmine was recorded within the lumen in the original work of Arfwidsson,[46] subsequently confirmed by others.[47,48] Suggestions of delayed transit which might lead to exaggeration of the Type II contraction have not been confirmed.[49]

It seems likely that diminution in muscle and collagen strength with advancing age predispose to the development of diverticula, which may be worsened by excessive pressure response to stimuli, and that symptoms are generally associated with an abnormal pattern of pressure.[50]

Achalasia, diffuse oesophageal spasm and Chagas' disease

These disorders are discussed together because, although characteristic achalasia and typical diffuse spasm can be clearly differentiated, there are many examples of intermediate forms of motility disorder which point to links between them.[51–53] Chagas' disease, which closely resembles achalasia, is the only one with an identified cause.

Normal function of pharynx and cricopharyngeal sphincter is retained, and in some cases, especially of achalasia, the normal sequence of a progressive peristaltic contraction may be retained in the upper few centimetres of oesophagus or may return after treatment.[51,54,55] Distal to this, however, peristalsis disappears. In diffuse spasm and some cases of achalasia (sometimes called vigorous achalasia), high pressure contractions occur both spontaneously and in response to swallows. They are often recorded simultaneously at many points within the oesophagus, but this may simply be the 'common cavity' phenomenon, pressures being equal at every point within the open lumen. The gross appearance of these contractions causes distortion of the oesophagus visible radiologically as irregular contractions of varying depth. In some cases the contractions appear to become 'fixed' and to promote true or pseudo-diverticula.

The gastro-oesophageal sphincter is of great importance and its abnormal behaviour may be fundamental in these disorders. In achalasia, Chagas' disease and some cases of diffuse spasm, the sphincter's resting tone is elevated, and usually relaxes incompletely on swallowing. It is this abnormal sphincteric behaviour which causes the patients' dysphagia,[56,57] and quite possibly the disorganization of motility in the oesophageal body may in part be secondary to the sphincter abnormality, as structural stenosis of the lower oesophagus in man can lead to similar but reversible changes.[58]

Gross structural changes may be limited to dilatation of the oesophageal body, but in some cases of diffuse spasm marked muscular thickening of the oesophageal body is evident. The sphincter region is often grossly normal, or only slightly thickened. Microscopically the most striking and characteristic change is loss of ganglion cells from the myenteric plexus in the sphincteric region in achalasia and Chagas' disease[59,60] — data on diffuse oesophageal spasm are few. There may also be degeneration of the vagal nerve trunk and loss of ganglion cells from the dorsal vagal nuclei.[61] In Chagas' disease it is presumed that the neural destruction is caused by the trypanosomal infection, but no aetiological factor has been determined in achalasia. The cholinergic innervation appears to be intact,[62] but the concentration of VIP is decreased.[63]

Immunohistochemical methods have demonstrated excess eosinophil cationic protein (ECP), whose cytotoxic activity may contribute to destruction of peptidergic cells.[64]

A rare but well described phenomenon is simulation of achalasia by malignancies in or near the gastro-oesophageal junction, sometimes called 'pseudo-achalasia'.[65] In the few cases with clear histology the myenteric plexus has been infiltrated by tumour.

Reflux oesophagitis

Causes of gastro-oesophageal reflux

The fundamental abnormality in reflux oesophagitis is incompetence of the gastro-oesophageal barrier. All normal humans demonstrate episodes of gastro-oesophageal reflux several times each day. It seems that oesophagitis results when the frequency of reflux episodes, or the duration of contact of refluxed material with the oesophagus, increases beyond certain limits. It is likely that the reason for increased reflux varies from patient to patient.

Identified potential causes are listed in Table 9.1 — it is likely that more than one of these applies in any particular case. A detailed discussion of these is beyond the scope of this chapter, but it will be clear that the multiplicity of potential structural and functional abnormalities make it difficult to design therapy (medical or surgical) appropriate to every case.

Oesophageal defences

Although the main defence of the oesophageal mucosa to erosion by acid-peptic digestive juice may be a function of the mucosa itself,[70] mechanical activity of the oesophagus is also important.

Secondary peristalsis. Distension of the oesophagus initiates a peristaltic contraction without a voluntary swallow. This wave begins below the cricopharyngeal sphincter and is thereafter identical to a primary peristaltic wave induced by a swallow. It empties the oesophagus of most material within the lumen.

'Oesophageal clearing'. If a bolus of acid at pH1 is placed in the lower oesophagus, the pH rises to 6 or 7 after a few swallows in normal subjects, but often takes many more swallows in subjects with reflux oesophagitis. This was thought at first to be due to failure of some mechanical 'clearing' function,[71,72] but later it was shown that the rise in pH is in part due to neutralization by alkaline saliva.[73] Salivation may itself be defective in patients with reflux oesophagitis.[74]

Gastric emptying

In some patients with reflux oesophagitis it can be demonstrated that gastric emptying is slower than normal.[75–77] The proportion of subjects in whom this is found varies between series. It is not known whether this is a causative abnormality, in some way secondary to the oesophagitis, or caused by a common motor failure (e.g. partial vagal denervation).

Table 9.1 Potential causes of gastro-oesophageal reflux.

Failure of extrinsic mechanisms[66]	
Diaphragmatic pinch-cock	or congenital/acquired
Right diaphragmatic sling	or congenital/acquired
Oesophago-gastric angle	or congenital/acquired
Gastric sling	or congenital/acquired
Gastro-oesophageal sphincter	
Low resting tone	—intrinsic
	—acquired from smoking, drugs, hormones (sometimes transient)
Inadequate response to abdominal compression[67]	
Inappropriate relaxation[68]	
Vagal denervation[69]	

Disordered gastric emptying and duodeno-gastric reflux

The normal pattern of gastro-duodenal motility is now well established. It is also recognized that it may become abnormal under various circumstances, though the nature of the abnormality and its cause are often unclear.[11,78] The motor abnormalities which have been identified will first be briefly described, and then clinical syndromes which may result.

Identifiable abnormalities of gastro-duodenal motility

Loss of receptive relaxation. Vagotomy severs the reflex arc responsible for fundal relaxation. The consequence is decreased accommodation of liquids and more rapid liquid emptying.

Antral hypomotility. Where motility of the antrum is reduced, there is differentially slower emptying of solids than liquids. This phenomenon is seen in a variety of disorders, including systemic sclerosis, idiopathic gastroparesis and in eating disorders. This is also seen after vagotomy and slows the emptying of solids because the strength and frequency of antral contractions is reduced.

Gastroparesis. Under some circumstances it seems that all gastric motor activity disappears. This may occur postoperatively, but has been seen after acute viral infections.[79] Loss of phase III activity limited to the stomach has been observed in diabetic gastroparesis.

Failure of antro-duodenal coordination. As indicated above, during phase III activity emptying of gastric contents occurs as powerful antral contractions coincide with proximal duodenal relaxation, followed by an appropriate duodenal contraction which propels the contents onwards. This 'linkage' can be measured.[80] It has been shown that the frequency of synchronization is increased by the drug metoclopramide and the lack of coordination has been suggested as the cause of gall stone associated dyspepsia.[81]

Gastric arrhythmias. There are a few reports of abnormally frequent pacemaker potentials — 5 or more a minute — resulting in delayed gastric emptying with associated symptoms.[82,83] This has been termed tachygastria. In experimental animals the spread of the arrythmia may be retrograde.[84]

Clinical syndromes

Measurements of gastric emptying rates have shown delay in some patients with all these conditions. There may be associated symptoms — fullness, nausea, vomiting, easy satiety, but the actual motor defect has been identified uncommonly. It is often not known whether the abnormal gastric emptying is a cause or a consequence of the disease. However, the association between results of gastric emptying tests and symptoms is poor, as is the effect of drugs known to accelerate emptying.[85]

Flatulent or functional dyspepsia is a syndrome in which the symptoms listed above occur in the absence of identifiable structural changes in stomach or duodenum. In a few cases failure of antro-duodenal coordination has been demonstrated, in others tachygastria has been found. In many patients disordered mood or other psychological factors are recognizable.

Duodeno-gastric reflux

Reflux of material from duodenum to stomach is normal, but variable in frequency and amount. It occurs mainly during phase II (the period of irregular, mainly non-propulsive) activity of the interdigestive motor complex.[86] It is increased by smoking.[87]

Identification of abnormal duodeno-gastric reflux is usually achieved by measuring the amount of duodenal contents in the stomach — usually bile, or a chemical marker introduced into the duodenum through tubes, or by excretion into the duodenum with bile, e.g. HIDA. (Tube aspiration may give rise to experimental artefact).[88]

Some bile reflux occurs at some time in most normal people, but attention has been directed to certain disorders in which the frequency or quantity of bile reflux is abnormally high.

Gastric ulcer

Increased concentrations of bile acid conjugates are found in the stomachs of patients with gastric ulcers[89] whether fasting or after meals.[90] Duodeno-gastric reflux demonstrable radiologically is also commoner in gastric ulcer patients.[91] It is postulated that bile salts reduce mucosal resistance and allow access of H^+ and pepsin to the mucosa with resultant damage,[92] though Fimmel and Blum[93] rightly question whether their role is primary, or is an aggravating factor to another causative mechanism.

Gastritis and flatulent dyspepsia

The syndrome of flatulent dyspepsia referred to above may be associated with abnormalities of gastro-duodenal motor coordination or changes in antral contraction rates.[81] In similar patients increased duodeno-gastric reflux has been seen.[94,95]

Postoperative gastritis

When a gastro-duodenostomy or a pyloroplasty is created, the normal mechanics of gastro-duodenal coordination are of no avail in preventing bile from entering the stomach. Of the various uncomfortable syndromes recognized as possible consequences of such gastric surgery some (such as dumping and nutritional deficiencies) have other causes. The main syndrome attributable to postoperative bile reflux is epigastric discomfort, bilious vomiting and weight loss. Gastritis may be visible at endoscopy.[96]

Abnormal small intestinal motility

Although the normal pattern of small bowel contractions and their electrical control are well described, few studies of this type have been performed in disease states, mainly because of the mechanical difficulties. Transit rates through the small gut may be readily measured, so presumptions of disordered motility are usually based on abnormal transit times, though this may also be affected by secretory and absorptive abnormalities.

Accelerated transit

Rapid small bowel transit has been observed in the syndromes listed in Table 9.2, but the motor mechanisms underlying it are uncertain.[97]

Delayed transit

Chronic intestinal pseudo-obstruction. Occasional cases are reported in which there are symptoms and signs of bowel obstruction without any occluding lesion. The syndrome has been reported in association with a variety of other diseases including collagen, neurological and endocrine disorders, but most often there is no predisposing cause apparent. A few have been familial (autosomal dominant). Physiological studies in a few patients suggest that the neural plexuses are intact anatomically and functionally, but that the electrical control activity is at fault. The MMC is not normally propagated.[100]

The symptoms are usually of intermittent episodes of apparent intestinal obstruction, and the duodenum may be markedly dilated. No specific therapy is available.[101] In diabetic autonomic neuropathy and other dysautonomias small bowel transit may be abnormal.

Myopathic disorders of small intestine. Abnormalities of smooth muscle contractility may affect any part of the

Table 9.2 Syndrome associated with rapid small bowel transit.

Syndrome	Comment
Hypersecretion in gastrinoma	Volume overload
Infective diarrhoea	Volume overload
Carcinoid syndrome	Excess hydroxy-tryptamine increases motor activity
Diabetic diarrhoea	?Autonomic neuropathy
Thyrotoxicosis	Thyroid hormone affects muscular contractility?[98]
Irritable bowel	Psychological stress[99]
Partial gastrectomy	
Vagotomy	

gut, most commonly the oesophagus, with loss of peristalsis and weakening of the gastro-oesophageal sphincter. This occurs in systemic sclerosis, amyloidosis and some disorders of generalized somatic muscle disease.[102]

Small bowel abnormalities are seen in about 40% of cases. Motility recordings[103] show that in some patients the normal cycles of activity are absent, and in others the motor activity per cycle is reduced. The effect of this diminished motility is to cause dilation and slow transit, and sometimes pseudo-diverticula. Abnormal bacterial proliferation tends to occur and may lead to malabsorption by causing bile salt deconjugation.

Irritable bowel syndrome. In some patients with abdominal pain and distension without evidence of structural disease, delayed small bowel transit has been observed.[104] The symptoms of bloating may be specifically related to slow transit from ileum to caecum.[105] The frequency of MMCs may be reduced[106] or (in patients with diarrhoea) increased.[107]

Colon motor abnormalities

Diverticular disease is discussed above.

Hirschprung's disease

A congenital absence of ganglia probably combined with adrenergic denervation leads to spasm in a segment of the colon. It becomes narrow and inert, failing to transmit intestinal contents and thus leading to partial obstruction with dilatation of the proximal colon. Sometimes mass contractions affect the abnormal segment. The normal rhythmical contractions in the distal rectum and anal canal are enhanced.

The irritable bowel syndrome

A syndrome of altered bowel habit, abdominal pain, distension, often with other gastrointestinal complaints but without evidence of any organic disease, is well recognized by clinicians as a common problem — and under other titles has been known for at least a century. The nature of the symptoms lead to the obvious presumption that they arise from altered gut motility combined with a heightened perception of discomfort from areas of distension or contraction. Thus distension of a segment of gut may cause pain similar to the patient's spontaneous symptoms, and such distension is tolerated less well than by normal subjects. Abnormalities of colorectal motility and transit have been described but they are not uniformly demonstrable. However, in patients with the syndrome, changes in motor function may often be found elsewhere in the gut — oesophageal, gastric and small bowel motility have been shown as abnormal at different times.

The origin of the abnormalities is unknown, and as similar symptoms have been discovered in many members of the population who consider themselves normal and have not sought medical advice it is possible that it is the patient's reaction to somatic sensations which is at fault rather than the motility itself being abnormal. The fact that there is a high incidence of neurotic and other psychiatric disorders in the patients could explain either theory.[108] Nevertheless, abnormally high pressure contractions have been recorded from various parts of the gut during painful episodes.[109]

Ulcerative colitis

Motility abnormalities do contribute to the symptoms and complications of ulcerative colitis, and it has been suggested (though not generally accepted) that they may be causative.[110]

The inflamed mucosa leads to increased volume of colonic exudate, though the volume of diarrhoea, especially in limited proctitis, may not be high. The rectum's capacity to retain a fluid load is reduced. The frequency of segmenting contractions in the colon is reduced (as it is in other forms of diarrhoea).

Acute 'toxic' dilatation of the colon is one of the most dangerous complications of colitis. There is extensive inflammation throughout the depth of the muscle and it is presumed that the normal neuromuscular control of tone in the muscular wall is impaired.

Anorectal disorders

A general and imprecise recognition that there is a relationship between disturbed bowel function, haemorrhoids, rectal prolapse and other anorectal disorders has existed for many years, but efforts to delineate the precise type of physiological defect are only now bearing fruit.

Constipation

Most constipation is a consequence of faulty diet, poor habits, drugs or minor behavioural abnormalities. Metabolic disorders or neurological disease are uncommon causes. There is a significant group of patients with habitual constipation which does not readily respond to dietary measures or simple laxative administration. Their stasis is predominantly in the right colon.[111] The main abnormalities of function recognizable in them are:

—a more capacious colon
—slower colonic transit
—diminished pelvic floor relaxation
—diminished rectal sensation.

Some of these abnormalities could be secondary to the longstanding constipation, but it seems likely that there are fundamental defects of colonic motility or of anorectal coordination which are responsible.[112]

Descending perineum

In some patients who have for years had constipation and the need to strain at stool, a syndrome occurs in which the perineum descends further than normal during such straining (normally the perineum lies 2.5 cm above the ischial tuberosities and descends by about 1.6 cm).[113] When perineal descent occurs, patients are troubled by rectal bleeding, pruritus or even overt rectal prolapse. Defaecation may be so obstructed that patients have to force a finger into the anus to push aside the prolapsing mucosa.

In some of these patients a solitary rectal ulcer is seen. This appears to arise as a consequence of frequent prolapse of the anterior rectal mucosa.[114]

Colonic pseudo-obstruction

Colonic pseudo-obstruction may be secondary to a variety of systemic disorders[115] or primary. In the primary form there may be muscular hypertrophy, taenia fibrosis or normal appearances.

Rectal prolapse

Rectal prolapse may occur at any age, but mainly in the very young and the aged. There may be congenital anatomical predispositions, but there is increasing evidence of weakness of the internal anal sphincter and also external sphincter and puborectalis. Some histological studies have suggested that there is a defect of pudendal nerve function with consequent alteration of the anorectal angle.[116,117]

Haemorrhoids

Haemorrhoids are not the varicose veins they were once considered to be, but swollen, engorged versions of the vascular cushions which normally surround the anus and assist in maintaining continence. It is thought that the anal mucosa can slide up and down. There may be abnormally high anal sphincter pressures and ultraslow waves.[118] Straining with defaecation increases the degree of sliding and of congestion, and ultimately venous drainage is impeded.[119]

Biliary motility abnormalities

Gall stones

For cholesterol gall stones to be formed it seems essential that the liver secretes 'lithogenic' bile in which the proportion of cholesterol to bile salts and phospholipids is greater than normal. Gall stones may result from this alteration of bile composition alone, but defective gall bladder emptying increases the likelihood of stone formation.[120,121] This probably accounts for their increased frequency after vagotomy, in pregnancy and after total parenteral nutrition. It has been noted that gall stones occur in up to 50% of people treated with octreotide (somatostatin analogue) and complicate spontaneously occurring somatostatinomas. The likely cause is gall bladder inertia, though alterations of bile constitution have not been ruled out.[122]

Lithogenic bile itself appears to diminish gall bladder contractility and slows flow through the cystic duct.[123] Where gall bladder contractility is diminished, (in total parenteral nutrition, or after vagotomy), gall stone formation is more likely. Interestingly, during gall stone dissolution therapy gall bladder emptying may be further delayed.[124]

Biliary dyskinesia

Some patients experience pain characteristic of biliary colic but without evidence of gall stones. Although some may be accounted for by pain arising from other organs, it is thought that motor dysfunction of the sphincter of Oddi or of the gall bladder may sometimes cause the symptoms.[125]

When the gall bladder has been removed, the likely culprit is the pancreatic–biliary sphincter ('papillary stenosis').[126] Fibrous stenosis may occur,[127,128] but in other patients abnormalities of motor pattern within the sphincter have been described both with operative measurements and cannulation via an endoscope.[129,130] Some workers have described good results from operative or endoscopic sphincterotomy.[131]

With the gall bladder in situ (but apparently structurally normal) diagnosis is less certain, but abnormal emptying of the gall bladder (when stimulated by cholecystokinin) may be observed.

REFERENCES

1. Meyer GW, Castell DO. Anatomy and physiology of the esophageal body. In Esophageal Function in Health and Disease. Ed. Castell DO, Johnson LF. Elsevier, New York, 1983.
2. Liebermann-Meffert D, Allgower M, Schmid P, Blum A. Muscular equivalent of the lower esophageal sphincter. Gastroenterology 1979; 76: 31–38.
3. Goyal RK, Rattan S, Said SI. VIP as a possible neurotransmitter of non-cholinergic non-adrenenergic inhibitory neurones. Nature 1980; 288: 378.
4. Rattan S, Goyal RK. Evidence of 5 HT participation of vagal inhibitory pathway to opossum CES. Am J Physiol 1978; 234: E273–276.
5. Tottrup A, Svane D, Forman A. Nitric oxide mediating NANC inhibition in opossum lower esophageal sphincter. Am J Physiol 1991; 260: G385–G389.
6. Yamato S, Saha JK, Goyal RK. Role of nitric oxide in lower esophageal sphincter relaxation to swallowing. Life Sci 1992; 50: 1263–1272.

7. Diamant NE. Physiology of the esophagus. Gastrointestinal Disease — Pathophysiology, Diagnosis, Management, 4th Ed., pp. 548–559. Ed. MH Sleisenger, JS Fordtran, Saunders, Philadelphia 1989.
8. Dent J, Dodds, Sekigucki T, Hogan WJ, Arndorfer RC. Interdigestive phasic contractions of the human lower esophageal sphincter. Gastroenterology 1983; 84: 453–460.
9. Yamato S, Spechler SJ, Goyal RK. Role of nitric oxide in esophageal peristalsis in the opossum. Gastroenterology 1992; 103: 197–2041.
10. Hinder RA, Kelly KA. Human gastric pace setter potential: site of organ, spread and response to gastric transection and proximal gastric vagotomy. Amer J Surg 1977; 139: 29–33.
11. Minamini H, McCallum RW. The physiology and pathophysiology of gastric emptying in humans. Gastroenterology 1984; 86: 1592–1610.
12. Houghton LA, Read NW, Heddle R, Maddern GJ, Downton J, Toouli J, Dent J. Motor activity of the gastric antrum, pylorus and duodenum under fasted conditions and after a liquid meal. Gastroenterology 1988; 94: 1276–1284.
13. Szurszewski JH. A migrating electric complex of the canine small intestine. Am J Physiol 1969; 217: 1757–1763.
14. Ehrlein HJ, Schemann M, Siegel ML. 1985. Motor patterns in the canine small intestine. Dig Dis Sci 1985; 30: 767.
15. Quigley EMM, Phillips SF, Dent J. Distinctive patterns of interdigestive motility at the canine ileo- colonic junction. Gastroenterology 1984; 87: 836–844.
16. Huizinga JD. Electrophysiology of human colonic motility in health and disease. In: Clinics in Gastroenterology: Pathophysiology of non-neoplastic colonic disorders. Ed. AI Mendeloff, pp. 874–901, 1986. London, WB Saunders.
17. Gill RC, Cote KR, Bowes KL, Kinsma TJ. Human colonic smooth muscle: electrical and contractile activity in vitro. Gut 1986; 27: 292–299.
18. Bueno L, Fioramanti J, Ruckebusch Y, Frexinos J, Coulon P. Evaluation of colonic myoelectrical activity in health and functional disorders. Gut 1980; 21: 480–485.
19. Sarna CK, Condon RE, Cowles V. Colonic migrating and non-migrating motor complexes in dogs. Amer J Physiol 1984; 246: G355–G360.
20. Metcalf AM, Phillips SF, Zinsheister AR, MacCarty RL, Beart RW, Wolff BG. Simplified assessment of segmental colonic transit. Gastroenterology 1987; 92: 40–47.
21. Holdstock DJ, Misiewicz JJ, Smith T, Rowlands EN. Propulsion (mass movements) in the human colon and its relationship to meals and somatic activity. Gut 1970; 11: 91–99.
22. Narducci F, Bassatti G, Gaburri M, Morelle A. Circadian rhythms of human colonic motility. Dig Dis Sci 1985; 30: 784.
23. Karaus M, Sarna SK. Giant migrating contractions during defecation in the dog colon. Gastroenterology 1987; 92: 925–933.
24. Frexinos J, Bueno L, Fioramanti J. Diurnal changes in myoelectric spiking activity of the human colon. Gastroenterology 1985; 88: 1104–1110.
25. Snape WJ, Wright SH, Battle WM, Cohen S. The gastrocolic response: evidence for a neural mechanism. Gastroenterology 1979; 77: 1235–1240.
26. Ihre T. Studies in anal function in continent and incontinent patients. Scand J Gastroenterology 1974; 9: Suppl. 2J.
27. Torsoli A. Sul meccanismo fisiologico di svuotamento della cistifellea. Radiol med 1961; 45: 57.
28. Baxter JN, Grime JS, Critchley M, Shields R. Relationship between gastric emptying of solids and gall bladder emptying in normal subjects. Gut 1985; 26: 342–351.
29. Itoh Z, Takatoshi I et al. Interdigestive gall bladder bile concentrations in relation to periodic contraction of the gall bladder in the dog. Gastroenterology 1982; 83: 645–651.
30. Lanzini A, Jazravi RJ, Northfield TC. Does the gall bladder function as a pump or as a bellows? Gut 1983; 24: A475.
31. Geenen JE, Hogan WJ, Dodds WJ, Stewart ET. Intraluminal pressure recording from the human sphincter of Oddi. Gastroenterology 1980; 78: 317–324.
32. Torsoli A, Corazziari E, Habib FI, de Masi E, Biliotti D, Mazzarella R, Giubilei D, Fegiz G. Frequencies and cyclical pattern of the human sphincter of Oddi phasic activity. Gut 1986; 27: 363–369.
33. Ellis FH, Schlegel JF, Lynch VP, Payne WS. Cricopharyngeal myotomy for pharyngo-esophageal diverticulum. Annals of Surgery 1969; 170: 340–350.
34. Kodicek J, Creamer BA study of pharyngeal pouches. J Laryng. Otol 1961; 75: 406–411.
35. Pedersen SA, Hansen JB, Alstrup P. Pharyngo-oesophageal diverticula. Scand J Thoracic Cardiovasc Surg 1973; 7: 87–90.
36. Knuff TE, Benjamin SB, Castell DO. Pharyngeosophageal diverticulum: a re-appraisal. Gastroenterology 1982; 82: 734–736.
37. Kaye M, Esophageal motor dysfunction in patients with diverticula of the mid-thoracic esophagus. Thorax 1974; 29: 666.
38. Dodds WJ, Steff JJ, Hogan WJ et al. Radial distribution of esophageal peristaltic pressure in normal subjects and in patients with esophageal diverticulum. Gastroenterology 1975; 69: 584.
39. Borrie J, Wilson RJ. Esophageal diverticula. Principles of management and appraisal of classification. Thorax 1980; 35: 759.
40. Harrington SW. Surgical treatment of pulsion diverticula of the thoracic esophagus. Ann Surg 1949; 129: 606.
41. Debas HT, Payne WS, Cameron AJ et al. Pathophysiology of lower esophageal diverticulum and its implications for treatment. Surg Gynec Obstet 1980; 151: 593–601.
42. Afridi SA. Fichtenbaum CJ, Taubin H. Review of duodenal diverticula. Amer J Gastroenterology 1991; 86: 935–938.
43. Eggert A, Teichmann G, Wiltman DH. The pathological implications of duodenal diverticula. Surg Gynec Obstet 1982; 154: 62–64.
44. Kubota K, Ituh T, Shibayama K, Shimada K, Nomura Y, Idezuki Y. Papillary function of patients with juxta papillary duodenal diverticula. Consideration of pathogenesis of common bile duct stones. Seard J Gastroenterology 1989; 24: 140–144.
45. Yamada H. Strength of Biological materials. Baltimore, 1970, Williams & Wilkins.
46. Arfwidsson S. Pathogenesis of multiple diverticula of the sigmoid colon in diverticular disease. Acta Chir Scand 1964; Suppl. 342.
47. Painter NS, Truelove SC. The intra luminal pressure patterns in diverticulosis of the colon. Gut 1964; 5: 201–213.
48. Trotman IF, Misiewicz JJ. Sigmoid motility in diverticular disease and the irritable bowel syndrome. Gut 1988; 29: 218–222.
49. Kirwan WO, Smith AN. Colonic propulsion in diverticular disease, idiopathic constipation and the irritable bowel syndrome. Scan J Gastroenterology 1977; 12: 331–335.
50. Eastwood MA, Walters DAK, Smith AN. Diverticular disease — is it a motility disorder? Clinics in Gastroenterology 1982; 11: 545–561.
51. Vantrappen G, Janssens J, Hellemans J, Coremans G. Achalasia, diffuse esophageal spasm and related motility disorders. Gastroenterology 1979; 76: 450–457.
52. Benjamin SB, Castell DO. Chest pain of esophageal origin. Arch Intern Med 1983; 772–776.
53. Blackwell JN, Castell DO. Oesophageal motility: recent advances and implications. Clin Science 1984; 67: 145–151.
54. Mellow MH. Return of esophageal peristalsis in idiopathic achalasia. Gastroenterology 1976; 70: 1148–1151.
55. Bianco A, Cagassi M, Scrimeri D, Greco AV. Appearance of esophageal peristalsis in treated idiopathic achalasia. Dig Dis Sci 1986; 31: 40–48.
56. Cohen S, Lipshutz W. Lower esophageal sphincter dysfunction in achalasia. Gastroenterology 1971; 60: 769–772.
57. Katz PO, Richter JE, Cowan R, Castell DO. Apparent complete lower esophageal sphincter relaxation in achalasia. Gastroenterology 1986; 90: 976–987.
58. Kelley ML. Intra luminal manometry in the evaluation of malignant disease of the esophagus. Cancer 1968; 21: 1011–1018.
59. Trounce JR, Deuchar DC, Kauntze R, Thomas GA. Studies in achalasia of the cardia. Quart J Med 1957; 28: 433–434.
60. Misiewicz JJ, Waller SL, Anthony PP, Gummer JWP. Pharmacology and histopathology of isolated cardiac muscle from patients with and without achalasia. Quart J Med 1969; 38: 17–30.

61. Cassella R, Ellis FH, Brown AL. Fine structure changes in achalasia of the esophagus. Amer J Pathology 1965; 46: 279–288.
62. Holloway RH, Dodds WJ, Helm JF et al. Integrity of cholinergic innervation to the lower esophageal sphincter in achalasia. Gastroenterology 1986; 90: 924–929.
63. Aggestrup S, Uddman R, Sundler F. Lack of vasoactive intestinal polypeptide nerves in esophageal achalasia. Gastroenterology 1983; 84: 924–927.
64. Tottrup A, Fredens K, Funch-Jensen P, Aggestrup S, Dahl R. Eosinophil infiltration in primary esophageal achalasia: a possible pathogenic role. Dig Dis Sci 1989; 34: 1894–1899.
65. Bennett JR. Not . . . achalasia. Brit Med J 1984; 288: 93–94.
66. Skinner DB. Pathophysiology of gastroesophageal reflux. Annals of Surgery 1985; 202: 546–556.
67. Wankling WJ, Warrian WG, Lind JF. The gastro oesophageal sphincter in hiatus hernia. Canad J Surg 1965; 8: 61–67.
68. Dent J, Dodds WJ, Friedman RH et al. Mechanism of gastroesophageal reflux in recumbent asymptomatic human subjects. J Clin Invest 1980; 65: 256–258.
69. Ogilvie AJ, James PD, Atkinson M. Impairment of vagal function in reflux oesophagitis. Quart J Med 1985; 54: 61–73.
70. Orlando RC. Esophageal epithelial resistance. J Clin Gastroenterology 1986; 8 (Suppl. 1): 12–16.
71. Booth DJ, Kemmerer WT, Skinner DB. Acid clearing from the distal esophagus. Arch Surg 1968; 96: 731–734.
72. Stanciu C, Bennett JR. Oesophageal acid clearing: one factor in the production of reflux oesophagitis. Gut 1974; 15: 852–857.
73. Helm JF, Dodds WJ, Riedel DR et al. Determinants of esophageal acid clearance in normal subjects. Gastroenterology 1983; 85: 607–612.
74. Sonnenberg A, Steinkamp U, Weiss A, et al. Salivary secretion in reflux esophagitis. Gastroenterology 1982; 83: 889–895.
75. McCallum RW, Berkowitz DM, Lerner E. Gastric emptying in patients with gastroesophageal reflux. Gastroenterology 1981; 80: 285–291.
76. Little AG, De Meester TR et al. Pathogenesis of esophagitis in patients with gastroesophageal reflux. Surgery 1980; 88: 101–107.
77. Maddern GU, Chatterton BE et al. Solid and liquid gastric emptying in patients with gastric oesophageal reflux. Brit J Surg 1985; 72: 344–347.
78. Heading RC. Gastric emptying: a clinical perspective. Clin Sci 1982; 63: 231–235.
79. Horowitz M, Dent J. Disordered gastric emptying: mechanical basis, assessment and treatment. Bailliere's Clinical Gastroenterology 1991; 5: 371–407.
80. Read NW, Houghton LA. Physiology of gastric emptying and pathophysiology of gastric paresis. Gastroenterology Clinics of North America 1989; 18: 359–373.
81. Johnson AG. Flatulent dyspepsia. Postgrad Med J 1973; 49: 104–106.
82. Malagelada JR, Stanghellini V. Manometric evaluation of functional upper gut symptoms. Gastroenterology 1985; 88: 1223–1231.
83. Bortolotti M, Sarti P, Barbara L, Brunelli F. Gastric myoelectrical activity in patients with chronic idiopathic gastroparesis. J Gastrointestinal Motility 1990; 2: 104–108.
84. Kim CH, Azpiroz F, Malagelada JR. Characteristics of spontaneous and drug-induced gastric dysrhythmias in a chronic canine model. Gastroenterology 1986; 90: 421–427.
85. Talley NJ, Shuter B, McCrudden S, Jones M, Hoschl R, Piper DW. Lack of association between gastric emptying of solids and symptoms in non-ulcer dyspepsia. J Clin Gastroenterology 1989; 11: 625–630.
86. Keane FB, Dimagno ED, Malagelada JR. Duodeno gastric reflux in humans: its relationship to fasting antro deuodenal motility and gastric, pancreatic and biliary secretion. Gastroenterology 1981; 81: 726–731.
87. Valenzuela J, Defilippi C, Csendes A. Manometric studies on the human pyloric sphincter. Gastroenterology 1976; 70: 481–493.
88. Muller-Lissner S, Froass C. Measurements of bile salt reflux are influenced by the method of collecting gastric juice. Gastroenterology 1985; 89: 1338–1341.
89. Du Plessis DJ. Pathogenesis of gastric ulceration. Lancet 1965; 1: 974–979.
90. Rhodes J, Barnardo DE, Phillips SF, Rovelstad RA, Hofmann AF. Increased reflux of bile into the stomach in patients with gastric ulcer. Gastroenterology 1969; 57: 241–245.
91. Capper WM, Airth GR, Kilby JO. A test of pyloric regurgitation. Lancet 1966; 2: 621–623.
92. Rees W, Rhodes J. Bile reflux in gastro-oesophageal disease. Clinics in Gastroenterology 1977; 6: 179–200.
93. Fimmel CJ, Blum AL. 'Bile in the stomach in 'Bile Acids in Gastroenterology'. Ed. Barbara L, Dowling RH, Hoffman AF, Roda E. MTP Press Ltd, Lancaster 1983.
94. Johnson AG. Cholecystectomy and gallstone dyspepsia. Clinical and physiological study of a symptom complex. Ann Roy Coll Surg 1975; 56: 69–80.
95. Capper WM, Butler TJ, Kilby JO, Gibson MJ. Gall-stones, gastric secretion, and flatulent dyspepsia. Lancet 1967; 1: 413–415.
96. Meyer JH. Reflections on reflux gastritis. Gastroenterology 1979; 77: 1143–1145.
97. Read NW. Diarrhee notrice. Clinics in Gastroenterology 1986; 15: 657–686.
98. Evans DF, Ballantyne KC, Pegg CA, Hardcastle JD. Abnormal motility patterns in thyrotoxicosis. Dig Dis Sci 1985; 30: 768.
99. Cann PA, Read NW, Cannock I et al. Physiological stress and the passage of a standard meal through the stomach and small intestine of man. Gut 1983; 24: 236–240.
100. Stanghellini V, Camilleri M, Malagelada TR. Chronic intestinal pseudo obstruction: clinical and manometric findings. A Gut 1987; 28: 5–12.
101. Schuffler MD, Rohmann CA et al. Chronic intestinal pseudo-obstruction: a report of 27 cases and review of the literature. Medicine 1981; 60: 173–195.
102. Camilleri M, Vassallo M. Small intestinal motility and transit in disease. Bailliere's Clinical Gastroenterology 1991; 5: 431–451.
103. Rees WDW, Leigh RJ, Christofides ND, Bloom SR, Turnberg LA. Interdigestive motor activity in patients with systemic sclerosis. Gastroenterology 1982; 83: 575–580.
104. Cann PA, Read NW, Brown C, Hobson N, Holdsworth CA. Irritable bowel syndrome: relationship of disorders in the transit of a single solid meal to symptom patterns. Gut 1983; 24: 405–411.
105. Trotman IF, Price CC. Bloated irritable bowel syndrome defined by dynamic 99uTC bran scan. Lancet 1986; 364–366.
106. Kumar D, Wingate DL. The irritable bowel syndrome: a paroxysmal motor disorder. Lancet 1985; 2: 973–977.
107. Kellow JE, Phillips SF. Altered small bowel motility in irritable bowel syndrome is correlated with symptoms. Gastroenterology 1987; 92: 1885–1893.
108. Read NW (Ed.). Irritable Bowel Syndrome. Grune and Stratton, London, 1985.
109. Harvey RF. Colonic motility in proctalgia fugax. Lancet 1979; 2: 713–714.
110. Hiatt RR. Abnormal intestinal motility as an etiological factor in inflammatory bowel disease. J Clin Gastroenterology 1984; 6: 201–203.
111. Chaussade S, Khyari A, Roche H. Determination of total and segmental colonic transit time in constipated patients. Dig Dis Sci 1989; 34: 1168–1172.
112. Preston DM, Lennard-Jones JE. Severe chronic constipation of young women: 'idiopathic slow transit constipation'. Gut 1986; 27: 41–48.
113. Henry MM, Parks AG, Luash M. The pelvic floor musculature in the descending perineum syndrome. Brit J Surg 1982; 69: 470–472.
114. Rutter KRP, Riddell RH. The solitary ulcer syndrome of the rectum. Clinics in Gastroenterology 1975; 4: 505–530.
115. Anuras S, Baker CRF. The colon in the pseudo obstructive syndrome. Clinics in Gastroenterology 1986; 15: 745–762.
116. Beersiek F, Parks AG, Surash N. Pathogenesis of ano-rectal incontinence: a histometric study of the anal sphincter musculature. J Neurological Sciences 1979; 42: 111–127.
117. Parks AG, Surash M, Urich H. Sphincter denervation in

anorectal incontinence and rectal prolapse. Gut 1977; 18: 656–665.
118. Sun WM, Read NW, Shorthouse AJ. Hypertensive anal cushions as a cause of the high anal pressure in patients with haemorrhoids. Brit J Surg 1990; 77: 458–462.
119. Thomson WHF. The nature of haemorrhoids. Brit J Surg 1975; 62: 542–552.
120. Spellman SJ, Straffen EA, Rosenthall L. Gallbladder emptying in response to cholecystokinin. Gastroenterology 1939; 77: 115–120.
121. Pomeranz IS, Shaffer EA. Abnormal gall bladder emptying in a subgroup of patients with gallstones.
122. Dowling RH, Hussaini SH, Murphy GM, Besser GM, Wass JAH. Gallstones during octreotide therapy. Metabolism 1992; 41: 22–33.
123. Doty JE, Pitt HA, Kuchenbeker SL. Den Besten L. Impaired gallbladder emptying before gallstone formation in the prairie dog. Gastroenterology 1983; 85: 168–174.
124. Forgacs IC, Massey MN, Murphy GM, Dowling RH. Influence of gallstones and ursodeoxycholic acid therapy on gallbladder emptying. Gastroenterology 1984; 87: 299–307.
125. Toouli J. Biliary tract motor dysfunction. Bailliere's Clinical Gastroenterology 1991; 5: 409, 430.
126. Sivak MV. Papillary stenosis. In 'Therapeutic endoscopy and radiology of the gut'. Eds JR Bennett, RH Hunt, 1990; pp. 267–282. Chapman and Hall, London.
127. Goldstein F, Grant R, Margulies M. Cholecystokinin-cholecystography in the differential diagnosis of acalculous gallbladder disease. Digestive Disease 1974; 19: 835–849.
128. Nardi GL, Acosta JM. Papillitis as a cause of pancreatitis and abdominal pain. Role of evocative tests, operative pancreatography and histological evaluation. Annals of Surgery 1966; 164: 611–621.
129. Bar-Meir, Geenen JE, Hogan WJ et al. Biliary and pancreatic duct pressures measured by ERCP manometry in patients with suspected papillary stenosis. Digestive Disease & Sciences 1979; 24: 209–213.
130. Carr-Locke DL, Gregg JA. Endoscopic manometry of biliary and pancreatic sphincters. Findings in biliary and pancreatic disease and after sphincter surgery. Amer J Gastroenterology 1979; 72: 333.
131. Geenen JE, Hogan WJ, Dodds WJ, Stewart ET, Arndorfer RC. The efficiency of endoscopic sphincteotomy in post-cholecystectomy patients with sphincter of oddi dysfunction. Gastroenterology 1989; 98: 317–324.

CHAPTER 10

The vasculature and lymphatic drainage

B. Gannon

The alimentary tract is constructed of a variety of tissue types, which are each highly ordered in space to subserve the particular functions of the tract's various component segments.

Each tissue type receives its nutrients, eliminates its wastes and is in contact with circulating humoral agents via the microvascular and lymphatic systems; in addition, the luminal epithelial cell layer passes on digested food components using these systems. Each portion of this vasculature must be adapted in its spatial organization, volume density, vessel spatial frequency, vessel wall structure, capillary-to-cell diffusion distances and vascular physiology to subserve the needs of the particular tissue(s) supplied by and dependent on it.

Perhaps the major structural feature of the alimentary tract, which distinguishes it from other organs in a functional sense, is its mucosal lining. This tissue, except in the oesophagus, is specialized for secretion and absorption of large volumes of fluid; the human alimentary tract lumen receives approximately 10 l of fluid per day, and all but approximately 1% is normally absorbed.[1] The microvasculature is the ultimate source of all secreted fluid, and the microvasculature plus lymphatics are the final sink for all absorbed fluid. However, since alimentary tract lymph volume flows (approximately 0.5–1.0 l/d) are small compared to total fluid absorption (approximately 10 l/d), and minute compared to vascular flows (approximately 0.1% thereof), absorbed fluid leaves the gut primarily via the microvasculature. The capillaries are also chiefly responsible for removal of digested nutrients from their absorption site at the gut mucosal surface. Only absorbed triglycerides, together with any lipid soluble substances dissolved in them, plus a small volume of macromolecule-rich serous fluid, are principally carried away from the gut wall by the lymphatics.

Because of this specialization of the gut mucosa for comparatively large fluid fluxes and nutrient absorption, and the role of the microvasculature in these fluxes, it should come as no surprise that the microvessels of the gut mucosa appear to reflect this specialization in their

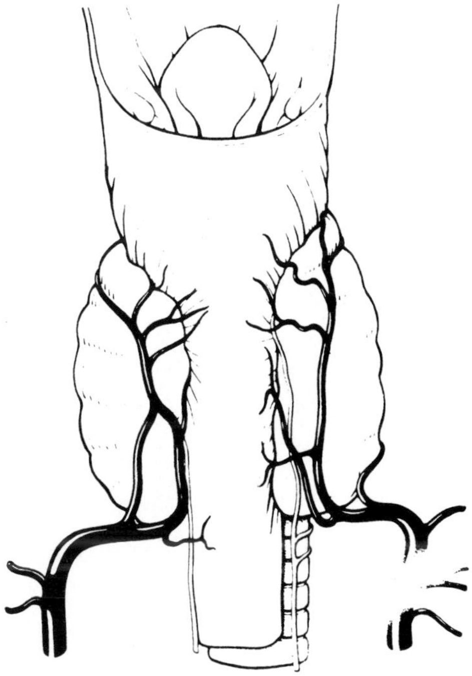

Fig. 10.1 Schematic diagram of the arterial supply of the cervical oesophagus by branches from the inferior thyroid arteries; posterior view. *Reproduced from reference no. 12 by permission of AG Karger)

location, organization, spatial density and ultrastructure. The vascular beds of the other tissues of the gut serve typical nutritive roles and do not display marked differences from those of similar tissues in most other organs.

THE OESOPHAGUS

Extrinsic arterial supply

The oesophagus traverses three body regions, and its arterial supply reflects its cervical, thoracic and abdominal segments. The first accounts of its vasculature were given by Versalius[2] and Bartholin,[3] and the essential details of the arterial supply of the oesophagus[4–11] were well established by about 1950.[6]

The cervical oesophagus usually receives branches from the left and right inferior thyroid arteries, typically from the terminal branches, and less often from the ascending portion (Fig. 10.1).[12] The most superior vessels from the inferior thyroid-derived supply may send branches to both the posterior wall of the trachea and to the anterior wall of the oesophagus; surgical separation of the upper cervical oesophagus from the trachea may compromise the arterial supply of the upper oesophagus.[12] In a few cases, additional branches, originating directly from the subclavian, common carotid or vertebral artery(ies), occur.[12]

The thoracic oesophagus lies in the superior and then the posterior mediastinum, and may be considered as having two parts: the upper pars bifurcalis adjacent to the tracheal bifurcation and the aortic arch, and the lower pars thoracicalis extending below the aortic arch to the diaphragm (Fig. 10.2).[10]

The arterial supply to the pars bifurcalis is facilitated by several branches to its posterolateral margin(s) from the left or, less usually, from left and right, or right only, bronchial arteries; these branches may anastomose posterior to the oesophagus across the midline, and may also give descending branches. Additional supply vessels here include the often present (anterior) oesophagotracheal

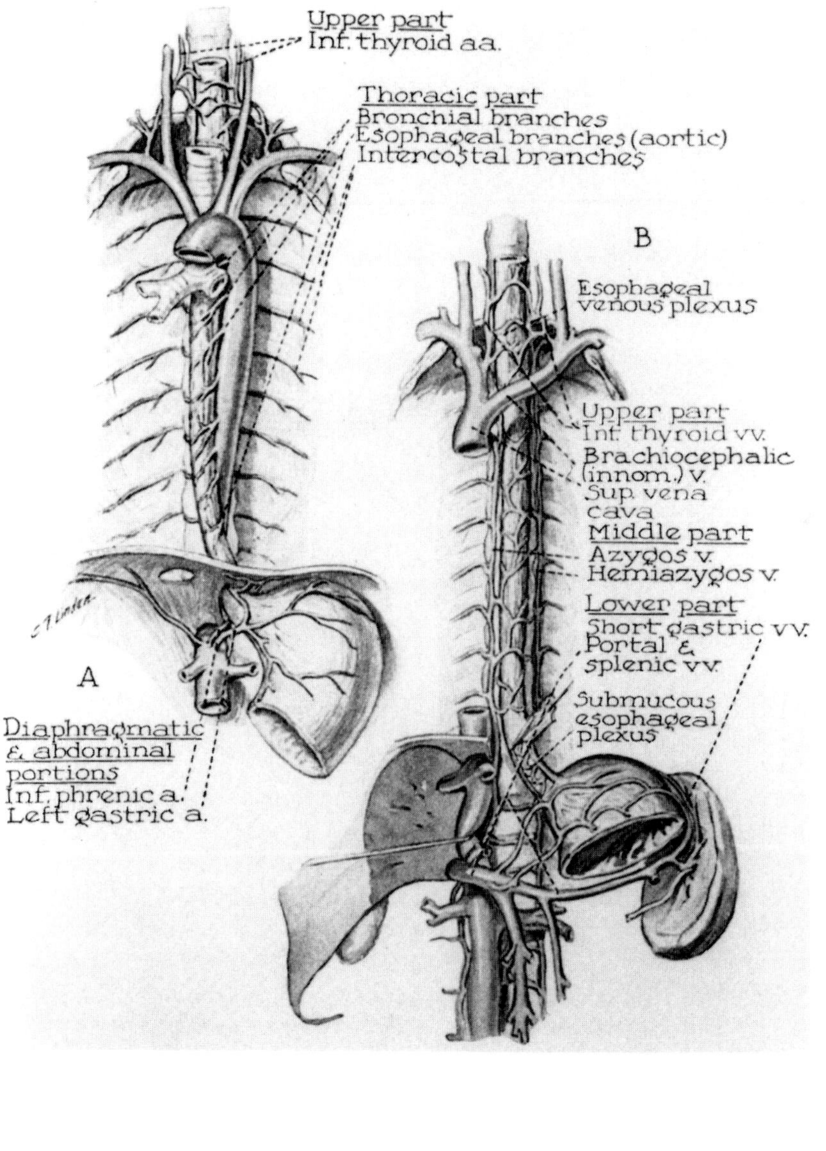

Fig. 10.2 Diagrams of arterial supply (**A**) and venous drainage (**B**) of the human oesophagus. (Reproduced from reference no. 50 by permission of Springer Verlag)

artery of Demel,[7] arising directly from the right side of the aortic arch.[13]

The pars thoracicalis receives:

(i) descending branches from the bronchial arteries described above
(ii) 1–3 oesophageal arteries arising directly from the aorta: a constant inferior oesophageal (great oesophageal) vessel arising from the anterior surface of the aorta between intercostals 7 and 8; a small oesophageal artery, usually present, arising below the 6th intercostal; and an occasional oesophagopericardial artery, sometimes arising from the aorta between intercostals 4 and 6. These arteries decrease in size and constancy from distal to proximal vessel[10,13]
(iii) a series of small arterial twigs from the right posterior intercostal arteries,[10,11] as these pass from the aorta anterior to the vertebral bodies; these branches are likely to be of minimal importance.[13]

The abdominal oesophagus typically receives on its right side several arterial twigs from the left gastric branch of the coeliac artery, and receives others from an inferior phrenic artery, usually on the left. The vessels to the abdominal oesophagus anastomose with the arterial plexus in the outermost layer (fibrosa) of the lower thoracic oesophagus through the diaphragmatic opening (Fig. 10.2).

Hypovascularized oesophageal regions

A 2–3 cm segment between the lower ramifications of the bronchial or intercostal vessels and the aortic oesophageal branches, and also the supradiaphragmatic zone, are considered to have the poorest blood supply[11,13] and, due to this, are the regions of the organ reportedly most susceptible to failure of surgical anastomoses.[14] This conclusion is, however, disputed by Potter and Holyoake,[9] who found extensive intramural longitudinal arterial anastomoses in the submucosal arterial plexus at dissection of post-mortem human specimens and by Williams and Payne,[15] who have mobilized the entire human oesophagus on its pharyngo-oesophageal vessels; they consider that the intramural longitudinal vascular anastomoses can supply the entire length from its proximal vascular connections, and suggest that anastomotic failures are more likely due to vascular inadequacy of the gut segment being anastomosed with the oesophagus. These findings contradict the assertions of Sweet,[14] who had previously claimed, essentially on anatomical grounds, that intramural longitudinal arterial blood flow could not compensate for extensive interruption of the extrinsic vessels at all levels of the oesophagus.

Intramural arterial distribution

Study of the intramural vasculature of the oesophagus has principally concentrated on the veins, especially in relation to varices, with less attention being directed to the arteries. The extrinsic arteries form a minor plexus in the external fibrosa layer of the oesophagus,[10,11] with main supply arteries (longitudinally oriented extensions of the extrinsic arteries) in the fibrosa giving rise to circumferential branches at right angles approximately every 250 μm, to pass around the organ. From these circumferential fibrosal arteries arise penetrating branches,[16] which pass at right angles through the muscle layers to reach a submucous arterial plexus; muscular branches[9] (and possibly branches to Auerbach's plexus), are given off en-route (Fig. 10.3). The submucous arterial plexus is well developed, with 9–12 predominantly longitudinally oriented arteries found at all levels in cross-sections of the organ. There are also lateral (i.e. circumferential) anastomoses around the mucosa in this submucous arterial plexus.[9]

Oesophageal microvasculature

Reasonably detailed studies of the microvessels of the muscularis externa and mucosa of the oesophagus for guinea-pig,[17,18] rabbit and human infant[16,18] have been reported recently.

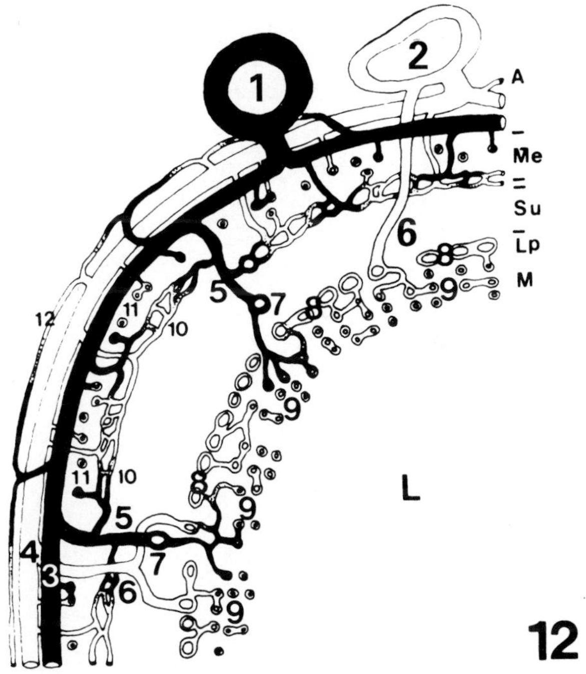

Fig. 10.3 Schema of oesophageal vasculature, as seen in transverse section. Black vessels = arteries and arterioles; white vessels = veins, venules and capillaries. **1** = main supply artery in fibrosa; **2** = main draining vein in fibrosa; **3** = circumferential arteriole in fibrosa; **4**= circumferential venule in fibrosa; **5** = perforating arteriole; **6** = perforating venule; **7** = longitudinally oriented continuation of perforating arteriole; **8** = longitudinally oriented venules of the lamina propria; **9** = mucosal capillaries; **10** = vessels of the internal layer of the tunica muscularis running circularly; **11** = vessels of the external layer of the tunica muscularis running longitudinally; **12** = vessels of the adventitia (serosa); L = lumen. (Reproduced from reference no. 17 by permission of AMF O'Hare)

Muscularis

The microvasculature of the outer longitudinal layer of the external muscle coats (muscularis propria) of the oesophagus contains relatively large diameter (10 μm) short capillaries with a cork-screw course[18] oriented parallel to the longitudinal muscle bundles.[17] The inner circular muscle (in guinea-pigs) is relatively richly supplied with fine capillaries (5 μm diameter) paralleling the muscle fibre axis, but with the undulating course typical of skeletal muscle microvessels; these are here presumed to be continuous capillaries, similar to those in the muscularis propria of the rat forestomach.[20]

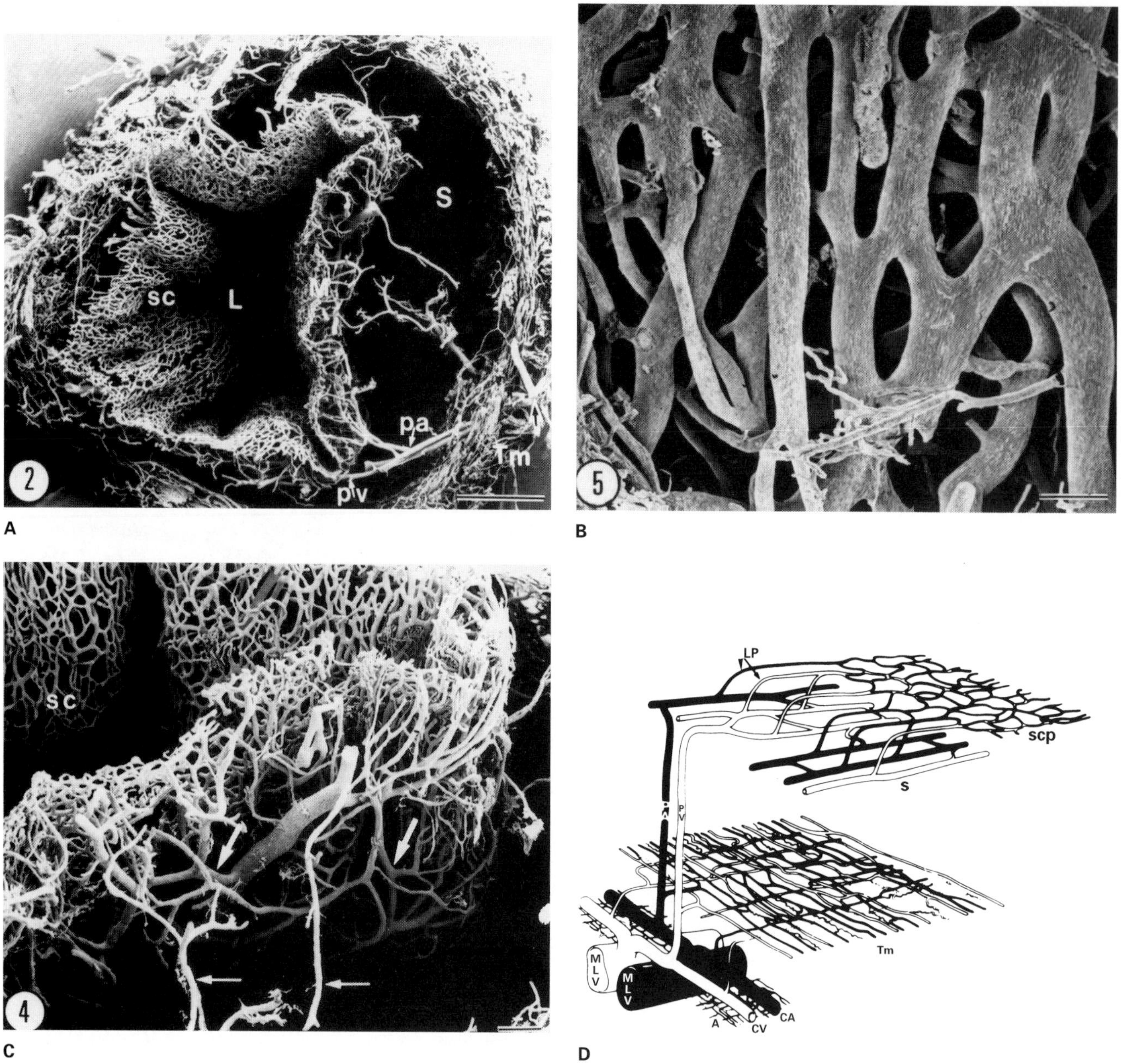

Fig. 10.4 **A** Cross-sectioned corrosion cast of human neonatal oesophagus, mid-oesophageal segment. L = Lumen; M = mucosa; S = submucosa; Tm = tunica muscularis; pv, pa = perforating vein and artery; sc = subepithelial capillaries. Small arrow marks a main artery. Bar = 1 mm **B** Pharyngo-esophageal transition zone in human oesophagus. Luminal aspect of the submucosal venous plexus after removing the lamina proprial vessels. Note the absence of venous valve imprints. Bar = 250 μ **C** Venous plexuses of human oesophagus draining the subepithelial capillary network, mid-oesophageal segment. Supplying arteries are marked by small arrows, anastomosing mucosal and submucosal veins by large arrows; sc = subepithelial capillaries. Bar = 200μm **D** Schematic diagram of the vasculature of human infant oesophagus. MLA, MLV = main longitudinal artery and vein; CA, CV = circumferential artery and vein; PA, PV = perforating artery and vein; SCP = subepithelial capillary plexus; A = adventitia; Tm = tunica muscularis (muscularis propria); S = submucosa; Lp = lamina propria. Note the architecture of subepithelial capillaries without any recognizable arrangement and the relatively few veins in the submucosa. (Reproduced from reference no. 16)

Submucosa

The arterial vessels here are derived from the perforating arteries which arise from the fibrosal circumferential arteries. The initial course of the submucosal arteries is circumferential (transverse), but these branch give rise to longitudinally oriented submucosal arterioles, and also centripetally directed branches to the lamina propria.[16]

Mucosa

The muscularis mucosa has a sparse net of principally longitudinally oriented capillaries derived from longitudinal mucosal arterioles in the base of the lamina propria (Fig. 10.4A,B). The multilayered epithelium (20–50 squamous cell layers) is underlain by a planar mesh of 2–3 capillaries deep, which shows no preferential orientation in the human infant.[16] These capillaries are presumably non-fenestrated continuous capillaries (as in rat forestomach — Fig. 10.5A,B), which are located at least 2 μm from the epithelial basal lamina.[21] This subepithelial capillary net is drained to a prominent intramucosal (i.e. subepithelial or lamina proprial) venous plexus by centrifugally oriented vessels (Figs 10.3, 10.4B,D; see below).

Epithelium

The epithelium of the oesophagus, as is typical of epithelia elsewhere and might be expected (except within the lower oesophageal sphincter see below), is devoid of capillaries.

The microvasculature of the oesophageal mucosa, except at the upper and lower oesophageal sphincters (UOS and LOS), is similarly organized throughout the length of the organ; there is, however, a decreasing lamina proprial microvessel density from UOS to LOS in humans.[16] This gradient correlates with the endoscopic appearance, with the upper oesophagus reportedly pink, while the lower oesophagus appears grey.[22] Such a gradient is not found in laboratory animals, including the rabbit, which has been proposed as a model of human oesophageal vasculature; it may be that the upright human posture and greater length of the human organ is significant in this regard. Specific microvascular networks are to be expected around the relatively infrequent oesophageal glands and their ducts, but have not yet been reported; a separate circulation of Auerbach's and Meissner's enteric nerve plexuses may also be expected in the oesophagus, as has been reported in the intestines (see below).

Intramural veins of the oesophagus

The veins of the human oesophagus are arranged in three main venous plexuses (Fig. 10.4D):

(i) a subepithelial plexus in the lamina propria, close to the muscularis mucosa
(ii) a submucous plexus which lies in the outer aspect of the muscularis mucosa, and
(iii) a superficial or perioesophageal plexus, which lies in the fibrosa, external to the musularis propria.[23]

The subepithelial or lamina proprial venous plexus extends for the whole length of the oesophagus in the lamina propria; it is comprised of a coarse meshwork of veins, which are usually 30–40 μm in diameter, but with some vessels reaching 170 μm in diameter in adults. This venous mesh drains the subepithelial capillary plexus, and is similar throughout the oesophagus, except near its upper and lower ends[23,24] (see below).

The oesophageal subepithelial venous plexus is drained by many short centrifugally directed branches, which perforate the muscularis mucosae to reach the submucous

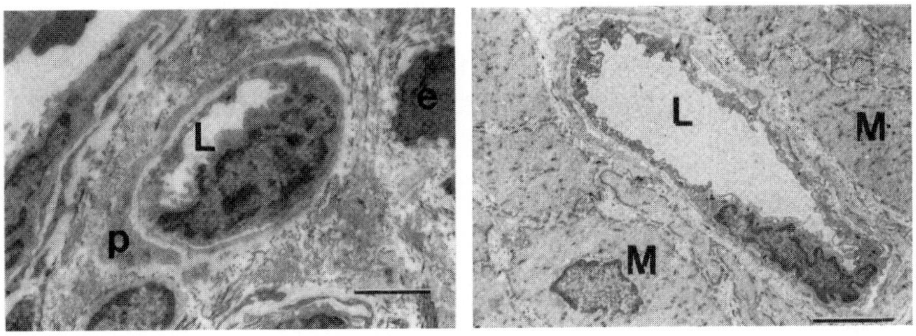

A B

Fig. 10.5 Transmission electron micrographs of capillaries of rat stomach. **A** TEM of capillary (L = lumen) of the subepithelial plexus which underlies a basal epithelial cell (e) of the stratified squamous epithelium of the forestomach. Capillary endothelium is continuous, with endothelial vesicles, and is largely surrounded by pericyte processes (p). Bar = 2.5 μm **B** TEM of capillary (L = lumen) from the muscularis externa of rat gastric corpus. The endothelium is continuous, with frequent endothelial vesicles and is largely surrounded by pericyte processes; M = smooth muscle cells. Bar = 2.5 μm (Reprinted from reference no. 20 by permission of the International Journal of Microcirculation: Clinical and Experimental) venous plexus. This latter plexus, the main intramural venous plexus of the organ, lies about midway between the muscularis mucosae and the circular muscle coat of the muscularis externa. The submucosal venous plexus is comprised of 10–15 veins of up to 1 mm in diameter, which are principally oriented along the long axis of the oesophagus, but which have frequent cross-anastomoses. Centrifugal branches from the submucosal venous plexus perforate out through the muscularis propria (usually as venae comitantes in pairs adjacent to perforating arteries), receiving venous tributaries from the muscle layers en route to the fibrosal plexus of veins. There is little difference in the submucosal plexus along the length of the oesophagus, except at the levels of the upper and lower oesophageal sphincters.[23] In the wall of the proximal oesophagus, at the level of the lower border of the cricoid cartilage (the anatomical pharyngo-oesophageal junction), the muscularis mucosae thins out and disappears, and the sub-epithelial venous plexus merges with that of the submucosa.[23] The fibrosal venous plexus drains to the heart through the extrinsic veins of the organ via either the systemic or the portal venous system (see below).

The perioesophageal plexus drains the submucous plexus of the majority of the oesophagus via a series of perforating veins, which pierce the muscle coat to reach the perioesophageal venous plexus.[6,23,31] This plexus is formed by the coalescence of several adjacent perforating veins within the fibrosa, and consists of a series of short veins which are drained by frequent extrinsic veins to nearby large veins (see below). The series of essentially separate local groupings of perforating and perioesophageal veins are interconnected by the venae comitantes of the right and left vagi and venae comitantes of the recurrent laryngeal nerves,[23] which run in the oesophageal fibrosa (Fig. 10.6).

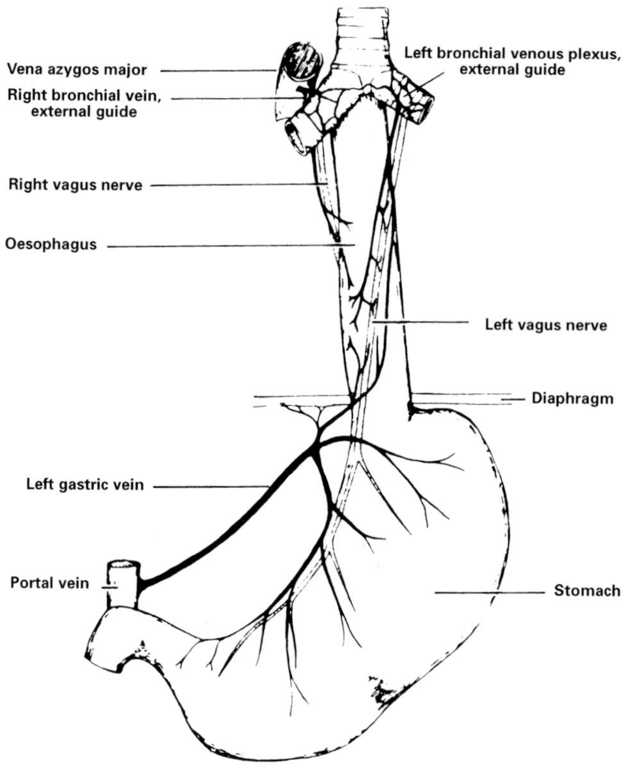

Fig. 10.6 Diagram of the venae comitantes of the vagus nerves connecting the left gastric vein to the azygous and bronchial veins. (Reprinted from reference no. 23 by permission of Thorax)

Regional specializations of oesophageal veins

There are two regions of the oesophagus where the intramural veins exhibit marked anatomical differences to the remainder of the organ: at its exit and entry sphincter regions, i.e. at the LOS and UOS.

Venous specialization at the LOS. In the region from the distal oesophagus, about 3–5 cm above the oesophagogastric epithelial transition, through into the proximal cardia of the stomach, the intramural veins are organized differently from the remainder of these organs. Vianna[25] recognized four distinct zones in the lower abdominal oesophagus/proximal stomach (Fig. 10.7):

(a) *Gastric zone*, in the proximal gastric cardia, characterized by a longitudinal venous distribution in the submucosa, as distinct from a more polygonal arrangement elsewhere in the stomach (Fig. 10.7B).

(b) *Palisade zone*, composed of parallel veins arranged in groups, lying mainly in the lamina propria; this zone extends from the oesophagogastric junction up the lower oesophagus for 3–5 cm (Fig. 10.7B, C).

(c) *Perforating zone*, a short zone above the palisade zone characterized by the presence of 'treble clef' shaped perforating veins which collect blood from the intrinsic veins of the regions above and below, and connect to the extrinsic veins; this region also has a fine polygonal subepithelial venous network similar to that present throughout the more proximal region of the organ (Fig. 10.7B, C, D).

(d) *Truncal zone*, 8–10 cm long, immediately proximal to the perforating zone; here there are 4–5 deep-lying submucosal veins located mainly within the mucosal folds. Proximally, the veins are frequent but small, but these fuse distally into fewer larger trunks which drain to the 'treble clef' perforating veins of the perforating zone below (Fig. 10.7B).

In the palisade zone, the subepithelial veins are principally longitudinally oriented (Fig. 10.7A); they are of larger size and frequency here,[26] so that they occupy almost 20% of the lamina propria at the level of the LOS,[27] as opposed to less than 3% more proximally (Table 10.1). This zone of the subepithelial venous plexus at the LOS has been termed a venous 'rete mirabile' (Fig. 10.8);[26] some consider that, when engaged, it may

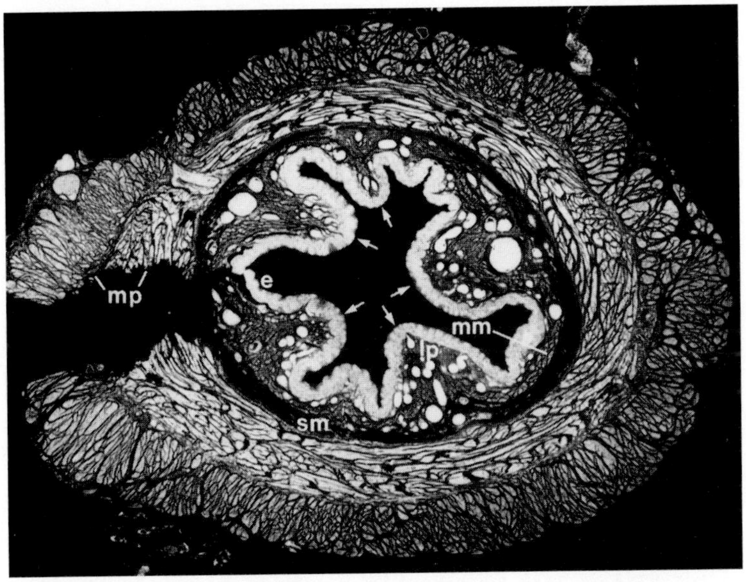

A

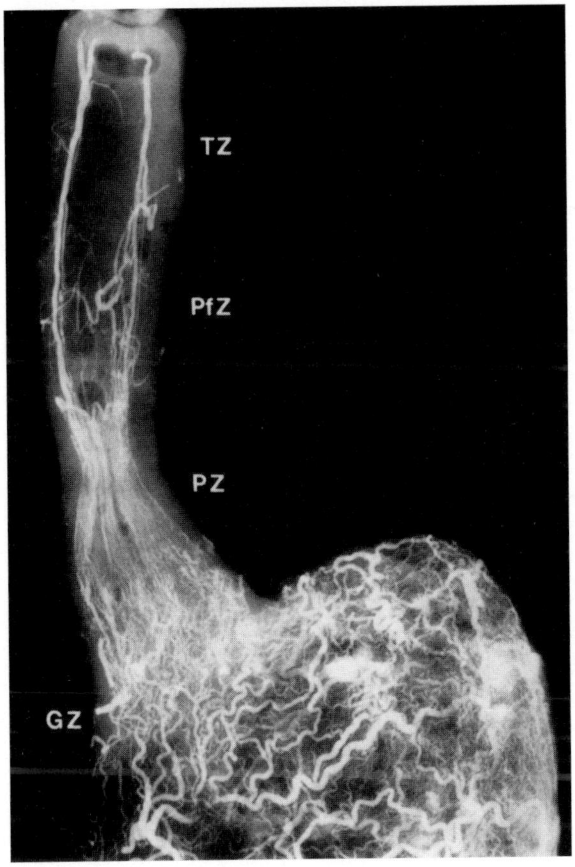

B

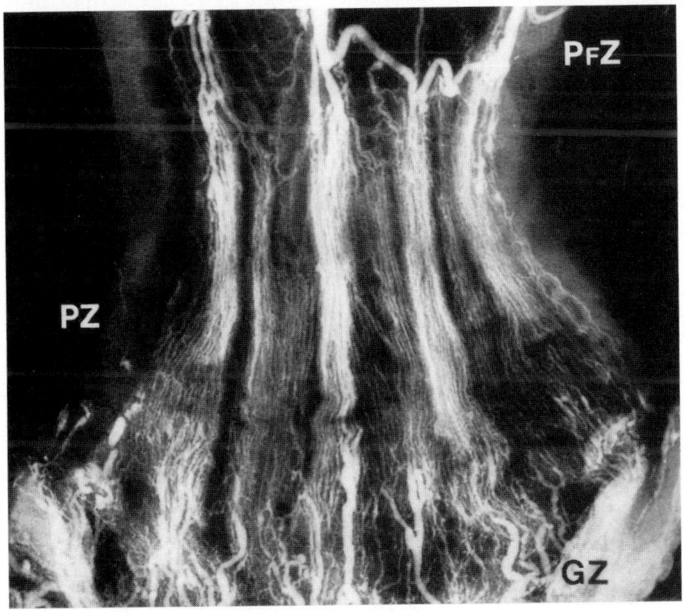

C

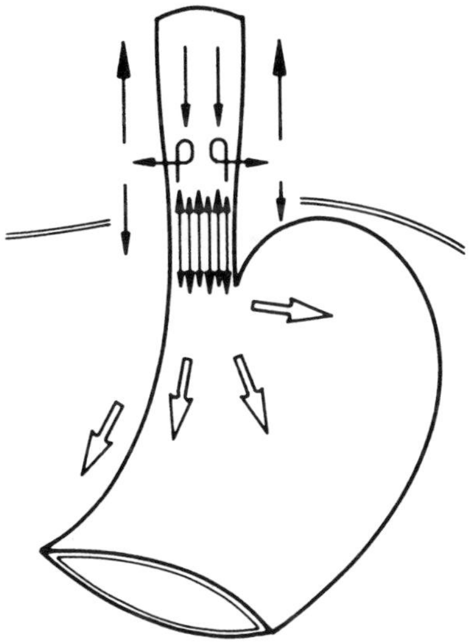

D

Fig. 10.7 Transverse oesophageal section of a human oesophagus injected intra-arterially with barium-gelatine. **A** Transverse section 3 cm above oesophagogastric junction, showing the venous circulation distributed predominantly within the longitudinal mucosal folds (arrows). lp = lamina propria; sm = submucosa; mm = muscularis mucosae; e = epithelium; mp = muscularis propria. **B** A–P radiograph of human oesophagus and stomach. TZ = truncal zone; PfZ = perforating zone; PZ = palisade zone; GZ = gastric zone. Note the large number of small longitudinal (subepithelial) veins in the palisade zone. **C** Radiograph of a specimen opened along the left border and greater curvature of the stomach, to demonstrate the palisade zone (PZ). Note the longitudinal veins in this area anastomosing with venous trunks at the proximal perforating zone (PfZ) and the distal gastric zone (GZ). Magnification × 2.1 **D** Diagrammatic representation of the pattern of normal venous drainage of the lower oesophagus, as postulated by Vianna (ref. 13a). Note the bidirectional venous flow pattern in the palisade zone, and the 'treble clef' veins of the perforating zone. (Reprinted from reference no. 25)

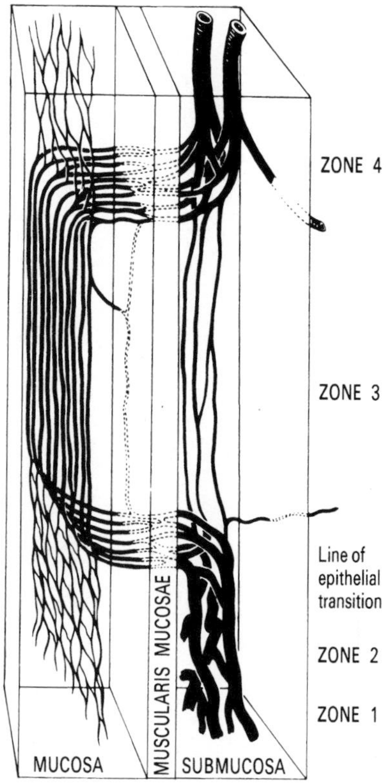

Fig. 10.8 Schematic diagram of the venous drainage of mucosa and submucosa of the lower oesophagus and cardia, according to de Carvallho.[26] Zone 1 = cardia of stomach; zone 2 = cardia immediately distal to the level of the oesophagogastric epithelial transition; zone 3 = region extending proximally from the oesophagogastric epithelial transition approximately for the extent of the lower oesophageal sphincter (LOS); zone 4 = lower oesophagus above LOS. Note large numbers of subepithelial veins in zone 3. (Reproduced from reference no. 26 by permission of Acta Anatomica.)

contribute to the complete occlusion of the lower oesophageal opening.[26,28] It should be noted in this context that intraluminal LOS pressures are 15–35 mmHg, while portal pressures in small veins, at least in the intestine, are around 10–15 mmHg[29] (see also footnote* (p. 138)).

At the LOS level, in contrast to the subepithelial veins, the submucosal veins become smaller in size and fewer in number.[26,27] The venous volume density falls from around 20% in midoesophageal submucosa to less than 7% at the LOS, as measured morphometrically in routine histological section of postmortem material (Table 10.1).[27]

Table 10.1 Percentage relative area occupied by veins in lamina propria and submucosa of the oesophagus in normal patients and patients with oesophageal varices (mean + s.e.m.). Data from Spence[27]

	Normal (n = 20)		Varices (n = 7)	
Zone	Lamina propria	Submucosa	Lamina propria	Submucosa
1	2.61 (0.21)	19.25 (1.49)	3.69 (0.38)	30.59 (4.54)
2	19.83 (1.25)	6.85 (0.65)	32.76 (3.92)	11.07 (1.60)
3	4.91 (0.34)	20.45 (1.51)	6.15 (0.53)	35.67 (2.47)

Zone 1 = proximal stomach (cardia), 1–3 cm below the oesophagogastric junction; Zone 2 = distal oesophagus (lower oesophageal sphincter location), 0–5 cm above the oesophagogastric junction (i.e. palisade zone of Vianna[25]; Zone 3 = mid-oesophagus, 11–16 cm above the oesophagogastric junction (i.e. the truncal zone of Vianna).

In cases of oesophageal varices, the size and the volume occupied by the subepithelial veins at the LOS is substantially higher (Table 10.1).[27] The subepithelial venous plexus is continuous with the subepithelial veins of the gastric mucosa beyond the squamous to gastric epithelial transition, forming a large number of small portosystemic venous connections.

The major clinical significance of the veins of this region is the development of oesophageal varices (see below and also Ch. 30).

Venous specialization at the UOS

The second area of specialization in the submucosal venous plexus is at the functional upper oesophageal sphincter, at the level of the cricoid cartilage. This site is technically situated outside the oesophagus, which is defined anatomically as commencing at the lower border of the cricoid cartilage; however Butler[23] argues that the oesophagus begins functionally at the upper margin of the functional upper oesophageal sphincter, i.e. at the upper margin of the cricoid, and that this region (the region of the laryngopharynx or hypopharynx) lying posterior to the cricoid cartilage should be regarded as the most proximal part of the oesophagus, since this is the region closed functionally by the UOS. A prominent subepithelial venous plexus in this region is variously termed the 'pharyngolaryngeal plexus', the 'hypopharyngeal plexus' or the 'rete mirabile of the mouth of the oesophagus'.[23]

This plexus, not mentioned in current anatomy texts, is comprised of two portions: a smaller, paired ventral plexus lying in the submucosa of the oesophagus immediately posterior to the cricoid cartilage, and a larger dorsal plexus. The ventral portion of the hypopharyngeal plexus is comprised of two parts, each about 2 cm wide, and extends to the height of the cricoid cartilage. The parts lie to either side of the midline, and are separated by a gap of about 5 mm. Each is comprised of many large, tortuous interconnecting veins up to 4 mm in diameter. The larger dorsal portion is triangular in shape (approximately 2 cm across the base, by 1.5–2.5 cm high), with the apex pointed down the oesophagus (Fig. 10.9);[24] it lies in the lamina propria of the posterior wall of the laryngopharynx immediately posterior to the cricoid cartilage and the paired ventral portions of the plexus (see also Fig. 10.4C).

The precise role of these venous plexuses, which are similarly sized in both sexes and are well developed at birth, is unknown. Last century von Luschka[28] believed that there was no muscular sphincter at the upper oesophageal opening and that it was closed by engorgement and distension of these veins. Subsequent electrophysio-

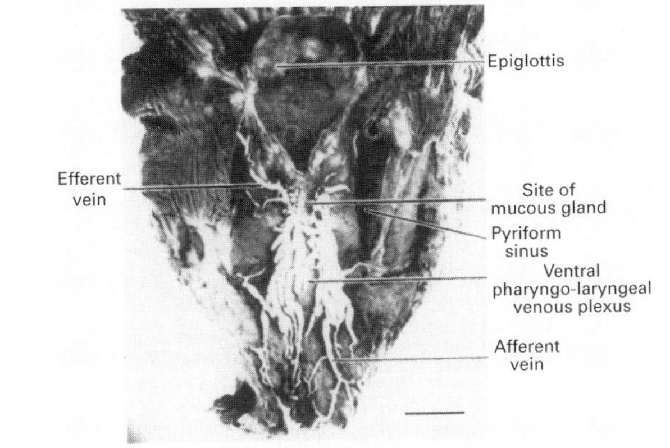

A

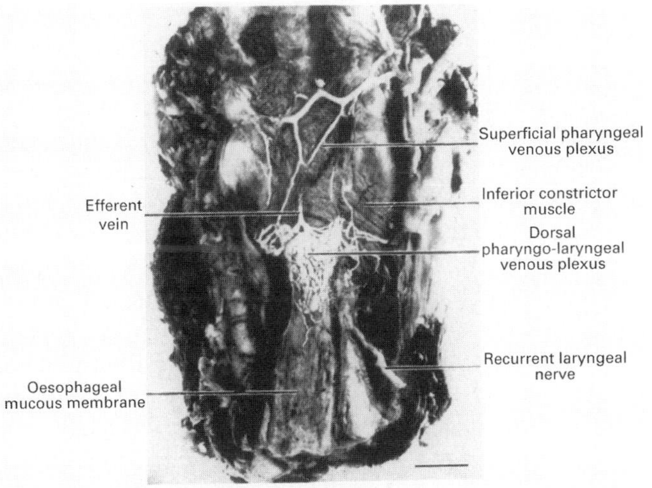

B

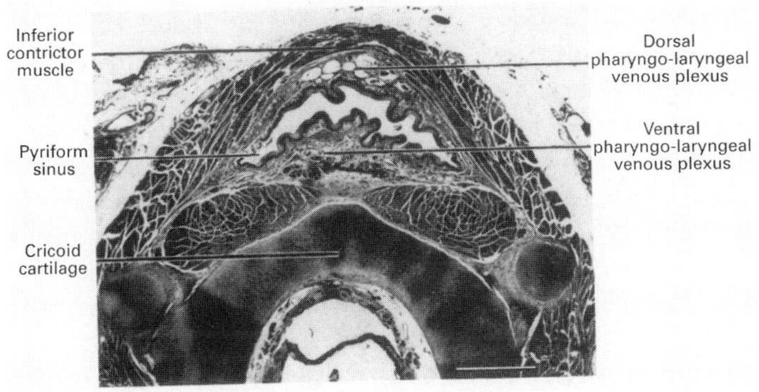

C

Fig. 10.9 Illustrations of the pharyngolaryngeal venous plexus; human latex injection preparations (**A**,**B**) and tissue section (**C**). **A** Ventral portion of adult plexus, viewed from its dorsal aspect; note the paired ventral plexus extending to the height of the cricoid cartilage. **B** Dorsal portion of adult plexus, viewed from its ventral aspect. Note the large size of the individual veins of the plexus. **C** Superior view of transverse section of the upper oesophagus at the level of the pharyngolaryngeal plexus in a human neonate. Calibration bars = 1.0 cm (**A**,**B**) and 1.0 mm (**C**) (Reproduced from reference no. 23 by permission by permission of Thorax)

logical studies of the constrictor muscles have clearly shown that this concept is not correct; furthermore, the high intraluminal pressures measured at the UOS are well above pressures in similar sized systemic or portal veins,[1] and thus engorgement of these vessels is generally considered as being not sufficient to account for (or presumably to contribute to) UOS closure.*

An alternative explanation offered for the role of these plexuses is in swallowing. During the swallowing of liquid, bolus division occurs at the epiglottis, and is maintained down the pyriform fossae, so that two streams pass to either side of the laryngeal inlet. Approximation of the mid-anterior and mid-posterior epithelial surfaces of the upper oesophagus could result from engorgement of the underlying venous plexuses and this would maintain the separation and lateral displacement of the two liquid streams to well below the midline tracheal inlet,[23,30] ensuring that aspiration would be avoided. In accord with this explanation is the prominent development of this hypopharyngeal venous plexus in neonates, and their ability to breathe while suckling a liquid diet.[23]

The venous drainage of the paired ventral hypopharyngeal venous plexus is principally via the superior laryngeal veins, with a minor component of the drainage passing to the lingual veins on the dorsum of the tongue. The dorsal plexus drains via major branches to the superficial pharyngeal plexus, or to the superficial venous plexus of the upper pole of the thyroid gland;[6,23] venous valves ensure a cephalad drainage direction, rather than one down the oesophagus.

*The argument that venous pressures (systemic or portal) are insufficient to account for venous engorgement of these vessels to sphincter pressures is apparently correct based upon the obvious requirement of need for rapidly changing sphincter function, but, at the same time, it is inappropriate. A similar absurd proposition would be that the venous sinusoids in the corpora cavernosa of the penis cannot be responsible for penile erection. It would appear likely that venous pressures within veins luminal to the muscularis propria at both the UOS and the LOS must be at least equal to, or perhaps are greater than, intraoesophageal luminal pressures at each of these locations, at least in order to maintain venous luminal patency; a further function of raised mucosal/submucosal venous pressures may be a topological one to functionally increase the local tissue volume inside the constricted sphincter muscle ring, thereby to expand the mucosal ridges, fill-in the mucosal folds and thus ensure that the mucosal surface completely seals the oesophageal lumen at the UOS (and similarly at the LOS). For this venous engorgement at elevated pressure to occur, there must be either functional or structural 'sphincters' or chokes between the veins within the sphincter zones and the general systemic or portal veins, there must be sphincters between the intrasphincter veins and the submucosal/mucosal veins both cephalad and caudad to them, as well as between the veins within the sphincter zone and the perioesophageal (fibrosal) venous plexus outside the constricted sphincter muscle of the muscularis propria. Such chokes on intrasphincter venous drainage would allow engorgement of these veins to pressures exceeding typical venous pressures, and could even permit pressures in these veins to approach arterial pressure. Such venous 'chokes' have not been identified to date; however, the 'treble clef' perforating veins reported by Vianna et al[25] would appear to be likely sites for such structural aids to the sphincter at the upper extremity of the LOS.

Extrinsic venous drainage of the oesophagus

The venous drainage of the oesophagus is complex.[6,23,31] The upper portion of the cervical oesophagus drains via lingual, superior laryngeal and thyroid veins and the superficial pharyngeal venous plexus (Fig. 10.1). The remainder of the cervical oesophagus drains via tributaries to the inferior thyroid and vertebral veins.

The dual drainage pattern of its lower third into both thoracic systemic veins and abdominal portal veins was first recognized by Dionis[4] and Portal.[5] The thoracic oesophagus drains via a series of veins which are not strictly segmental; there is usually one drainage vessel to the first intercostal vein, 8–10 vessels to the azygous vein and 5–8 vessels to the hemiazygous vein, plus branches to right and left bronchial veins or to bronchial venous plexuses. There are a few small venous branches passing to the inferior phrenic (systemic) veins, mainly on the left,[23,31] as the oesophagus passes the diaphragm. In the abdomen, three or four oesophageal veins join the left gastric vein (which drains via the portal system) as it enters the lesser omentum. These veins drain the lower part of the thoracic oesophagus and also connect with the venae comitantes of the vagus nerves (which also connect higher in the thorax to the azygous venous system); these connections form a potential portal to systemic venous connection external to the oesophageal/gastric muscularis propria.

Intramural lymphatics and lymph drainage of the oesophagus

Intramural lymphatics

There are no recent systematic studies of the oesophageal lymphatics, most descriptions[6,32,33] being based on the studies of Sakata[34] in 1903, as confirmed by Rouviere[35,36] in 1932. Previously, identification of lymphatics required either expert interpretation of the results of direct intramural injection, or ultrastructural identification (Table 10.2); however, recent developments in histochemical techniques now allow the demonstration of lymphatic endothelial cells in cryostat sections distinct from capillary profiles (in oesophagus and elsewhere)[37] due to the high activity of the enzyme 5-nucleotidase in the former cells. Future studies of intramural lymphatics in the oesophagus will be possible on small specimens and will not be restricted to injection methods on large specimens commonly used previously.

There is a rich pattern of primary lymph capillaries in the deeper layer of the lamina propria, but not in the superficial layer, with a secondary lymph plexus in the submucosa just external to the muscularis mucosae. There are so many anastomoses between these two levels that they form essentially one continuous mucosal/submucosal lymphatic plexus, whose arrangement is reportedly quite independent of the mucosal and submucosal vascular plexuses. The submucosal lymph vessels are denser at the upper and lower ends of the oesophagus than in the remainder. Near the cardia, they are continuous with the lymphatics of the stomach, without any apparent barrier to flow in either direction. There is a sparser lymph drainage of the muscular layers than of the mucosa, and there appears to be no connection between the intramuscular lymphatics and the mucosal/submucosal plexus, except in so far as they drain to common trunks outside the organ in the fibrosa. This separate nature of mucosal and muscular lymphatic networks, but with a common drainage pattern, is similar to that reported recently for small intestine (see below). Of particular importance appears to be the preferentially longitudinal orientation of the submucous lymphatics and/or interstitial tissue channels, and the apparent lack of lymphatic valves; dye injected into the deep mucosal interstitium typically spreads in superio-inferior directions to about six times the distance it spreads circumferentially around the oesophagus.[34] The upper half of the submucosal oesophageal lymph plexus normally drains upwards and the lower half downwards toward the cardia in submucous lymphatics. These extend from mid-thoracic region to cervical or cardia levels before connecting to branches penetrating the muscle layers and passing to adjacent nodes, via the perioesophageal lymphatics. Lymph drainage from the oesophageal muscularis, in contrast, travels a far shorter course of several centimetres only, before passing to the perioesophageal lymph plexus via perforating vessels.

Table 10.2 Some ultrastructural characteristics of lymph and blood capillaries in gastric mucosa

Type of vessel	Lymph	Blood
Diameter of vessel	>10 µm	<7 µm
Substance in lumen	Lighter	Darker
Shape of vessel	Irregular	Round
Endothelial lumen surface	Very irregular; (lamelliform) projections	Varied, less irregular; microvillous in places
Fenestrations	Absent	Present in large numbers
Endothelial vesicles	Present	Present
Caviolae	Present	Present
Intercell junctions	Gaps or overlapping of adjacent cells	Tight junctions
Basal lamina	Incomplete	Complete
Collagen anchoring filaments	Attached to basal lamina	Absent

Oesophageal lymphatic drainage pathways

The lymph trunks of the fibrosa drain chiefly to three sets of nodes:

1. lymph from the upper oesophagus passes to paratracheal, jugular, supraclavicular and inferior deep cervical nodes

2. lymph from the mid-oesophagus passes to paraoesophageal, mediastinal and bronchial nodes
3. lymph from the lower oesophagus passes to mediastinal, coeliac and suprapancreatic nodes, or to the nodes of the cardia (see 2).

There is one report of direct lymphatic drainage from the oesophagus to the thoracic duct.[38]

Because of the long submucosal lymphatic pathways and their proximity to the epithelial layer, this system must be considered important in the distant metastatic spread of carcinoma. Metastases from an oesophageal primary tumour may be anticipated as far as jugular or coeliac nodes, as well as producing regional mediastinal node involvement.[39] In addition distant spread from a gastric primary tumour may occur, e.g. as far as the deep cervical nodes, via the oesophageal lymphatics, because of extensive intramural lymphatic connections across the oesophagogastric and pharyngo-oesophageal junctions. Lymph drainage pathways can now be reliably imaged clinically by SPECT following intramucosal injection of radiolabelled colloid, which demonstrates that the lymph flow from the upper third of the oesophagus tends to move mainly upwards to cervical and mediastinal nodes, while that of the lower third moves mainly downwards to mediastinal and abdominal nodes.[51]

Oesophageal microvascular alterations in gastric reflux, portal hypertension and oesophageal varices

Experimental irrigation of healthy mammalian lower oesophageal lumen with 20–100 mmol/l HCl produces a series of microvascular and epithelial changes which include early increases in transendothelial permeability to plasma albumin, opening of interendothelial cell junctions to large tracer molecules, oedema and inflammatory cell infiltrate of the lamina propria, substantial loss of plasma albumin into the oesophageal lumen, a subsequent fall in transepithelial potential difference, and, at the higher acid levels, sloughing of epithelial layers.[40] Other experimental animal studies suggest that arachadonic acid metabolites may be responsible for the microvascular changes induced by intraoesophageal acid,[41] and that drugs which block parts of this pathway may be useful in treatment of reflux oesophagitis.[42]

Microvascular alterations in patients with portal hypertension occur principally in the lower oesophagus. Intramural venous dilatation is observed as varices in both the proximal cardia of the stomach and the distal few centimetres of the oesophagus. In the cardia, approximately 2 cm from the oesophagogastric epithelial transition, adjacent to the connection of extrinsic left gastric vein branches to the submucous venous plexus, the deep submucosal and intramucosal veins can be markedly dilated into prominent varices; these gastric deep submucosal veins connect to oesophageal deep submucosal veins across the oesophagogastric junction.[43] In the lower oesophagus, approximately 1.5–3 cm above the epithelial transition, one to four giant oesophageal varices of one of two types occur (Fig. 10.10):

- Type I: Palisading type, in which well developed intraepithelial channels (see below), subepithelial superficial and collateral (deep lamina proprial) veins and deep submucosal veins are all substantially dilated; these vessels extend in a longitudinal direction. Some 40% of patients with palisade-type oesophageal varices have a history of variceal bleeding, but patients with this type of oesophageal varices do not have gastric varices (this type of varix may be thought of as principally a dilatation of the 'Palisade zone' of the normal oesophagus described by de Carvalho;[26] (see Fig. 10.7D).
- Type II: Bar type, in which intraepithelial channels and small collateral veins are not well developed. These varices are either closely subjacent to the epithelium or else erode into it; some oral ends of the superficial veins cover the lower portion of the giant varices before connecting into them. The reported 'varices on varices' or 'cherry-red' spots and 'red wale' markings seen at endoscopy, and considered predictors of impending variceal rupture,[44] may be these superficial vessels seen through the (? thinned) epithelium.[43] The number of dilated veins in this type is less than in the palisading type, but these varices are greater than three times the diameter of type I; 75% of patients with this type had experienced variceal bleeds.[43]

The extent of venous dilation in the lower oesophagus in patients with varices is substantial: in the region of the oesophagus immediately above the transition, total venous cross-sectional area increased by a factor of three in the lamina propria and by two in the submucosa[27] (see also Table 10.1). Studies of blood flow direction in varices indicates that this is usually in a cephalad direction, but that the direction can be reversed towards the stomach during the respiratory cycle in quietly breathing, lightly anaesthetized recumbent patients.[49]

Of particular interest is the reported occurrence of intraepithelial veins or vascular channels between the squamous epithelial cells, in patients undergoing treatment for oesophageal varices and also, albeit at lower frequency, in normal human oesophagus;[45] these 'vessels' appear to be carrying blood, rather than being blood-filled blisters (Fig. 10.11A,B), but are lined with flattened epithelial cells at electron microscopy, which nevertheless exhibit factor VIII antigen, as might be expected of vascular endothelial cells (Fig. 10.11C).[46]

Given the effects of luminal acid on the microvasculature of the lower oesophagus (see above) and the superficial nature and substantial size of sub-and perhaps intraepithelial vascular channels in the varix-prone region of the lower oesophagus, the suggestion that reflux oesophagitis and acid erosion are the precipitating causes of variceal bleeds seems logical;[47] however, subsequent studies do not show lamina propria inflammatory changes in patients who have experienced an oesophageal bleed, except in those treated subsequently with intra-oesophageal balloon tube tamponade to control variceal bleeding.[46,48] Thus, the consensus of evidence currently is against gastric reflux precipitating variceal bleeds.

THE STOMACH

The human stomach is a C-shaped abdominal structure, with an entry at the cardia, where the oesophagus joins it, and an exit at the pylorus, where it joins the duodenum. The stomach is maintained in situ partly by those attachments, and partly by its suspension within the abdominal cavity by the lesser omentum, the gastrosplenic ligament and, to some extent, by the root of the greater omentum and the transverse mesocolon, to which the latter is fused. These sheets of visceral peritoneum not only anchor the stomach in position, but also contain its extrinsic blood and lymph vessels.

Extrinsic arterial supply

There are several current detailed accounts of the extrinsic arterial supply, and of the venous and lymphatic drainage of the stomach.[23,50,53–56]

In brief, the stomach receives its blood supply from the coeliac artery, which arises from the aorta just below the

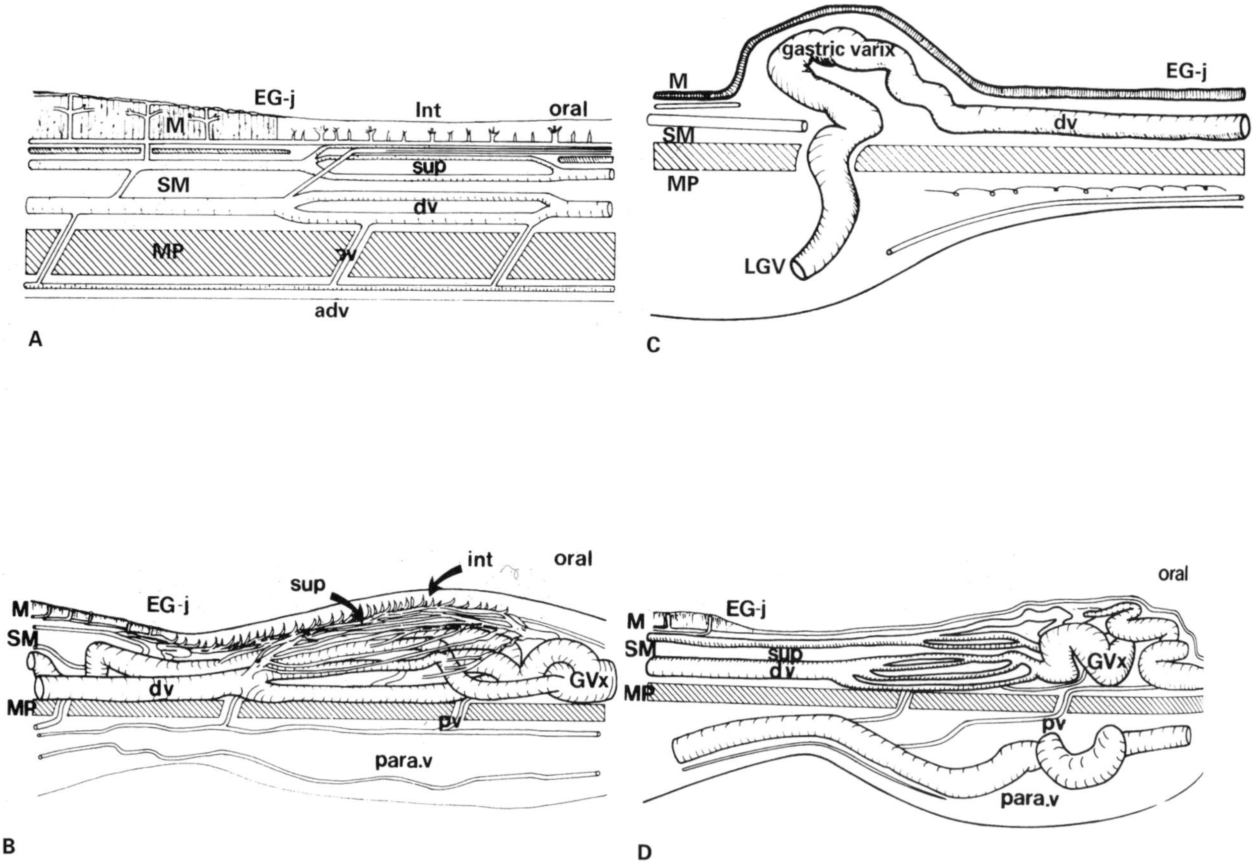

Fig. 10.10 Schematics of the vascular structure of the lower oesophagus/proximal stomach. **A** Normal arrangement: EGj = oesophagogastric junction; M = mucosa; SM = submucosa; MP = muscularis propria; int = intra-epithelial channels; sup = subepithelial superficial vein; dv = deep submucosal vein; pv = perforating vein; adv = adventitial vein. **B** Palisading type of oesophageal varices in portal hypertensive patients: numerous dilated intra-epithelial channels (int), subepithelial superficial (sup) and small collateral veins are well developed and extended in a longitudinal orientation. **C** Giant gastric varix formed in the submucosa where one of the branches of the left gastric vein (LGV) perpendicularly penetrates the gastric wall: schema from an elastomer injected specimen. M = mucosa; SM = submucosa; MP = muscularis propria; EG-j = oesophagogastric junction; dv = deep submucosal vein. **D** Bar type of oesophageal varices: the number of subepithelial superficial veins is small, but the superficial veins are markedly dilated, as are the deep submucosal veins (dv). Giant oesophageal varices (GVx) form 2–3 cm above the oeosophagogastric junction (EGj) by collection of those branches of the lower oesophageal varices. The paraoesophageal veins (para. v) extending from the branches of the left gastric vein connected with the lower oesophageal varices via a perforating vein (pv). M = mucosa; SM = submucosa; MP = muscularis propria. (Reproduced from reference no. 43 by permission of The American Association for the study of Liver Diseases)

diaphragm. After a course of approximately 1 cm, it gives rise to the splenic, common hepatic and left gastric arteries, each of which contributes to the gastric blood supply.

The stomach is supplied principally from two extrinsic arcading anastomotic arterial loops. The superior loop lies in the lesser omentum close to the lesser curve of the stomach. At the left extremity, this loop is supplied by the left gastric artery, and at its right by the right gastric artery, a branch of the hepatic artery, itself arising from the common hepatic artery. The inferior arterial loop lies in the greater omentum close to the greater curve of the stomach; its left-hand origin is the left gastroepiploic artery, which is a branch of the splenic artery, while its right-hand origin is the right gastroepiploic artery, a branch of the gastroduodenal artery (Fig. 10.12A).

The superior arterial loop in the lesser omentum gives off a series of alternating short branches to the anterior and posterior gastric walls along the lesser curvature. A similar arrangement to supply the greater curvature is found from the lower arterial loop in the greater omentum. Arterial supply to the fundus and left margin of the greater curve is provided by a series of about five short gastric arteries, which are derived from branches of the splenic artery at the splenic hilum. These arteries pass to the stomach in the gastrosplenic ligament (Fig. 10.12B). There are many anatomical variants, including absence of particular vessels, and the presence of aberrant additional

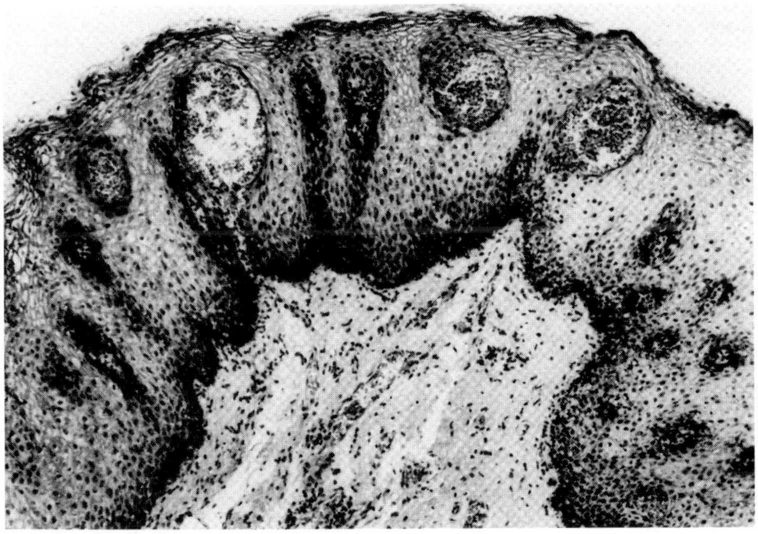

A

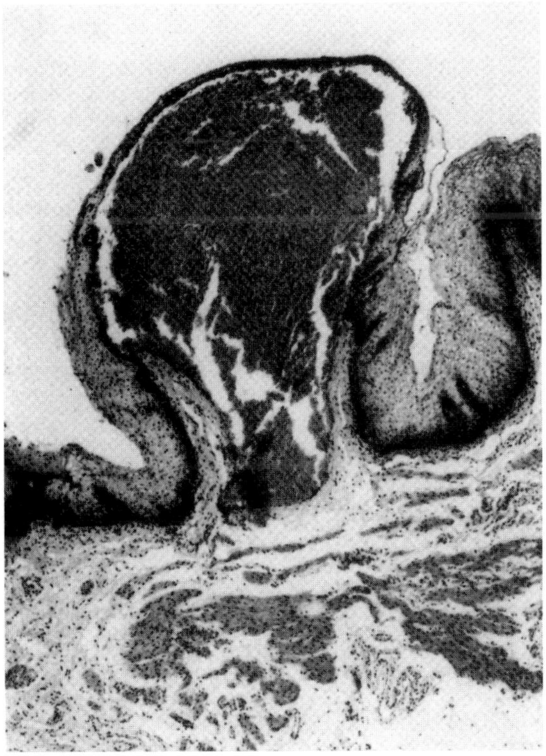

B

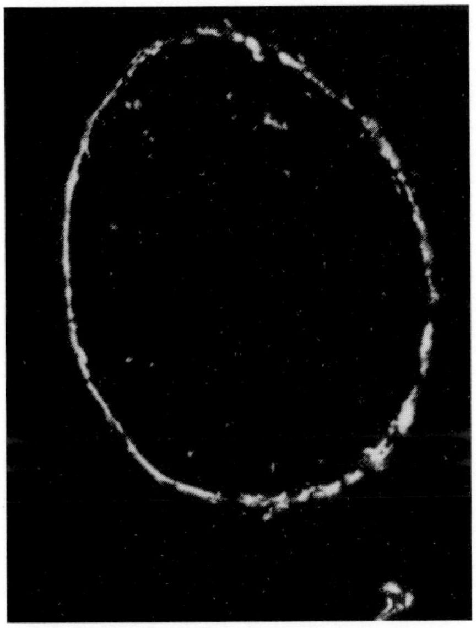

C

Fig. 10.11 **A** Histological cross-section of oesophageal mucosa illustrating dilated blood-filled, epithelially-lined channels within the squamous epithelium of the oesophagus in a patient with varices. A connection between one of the channels and a papillary capillary is seen at left centre. (H&E, ×54) **B** A large subepithelial channel. Blood is separated from oesophageal lumen only by a thin layer of squamous cells. (H&E, ×27) **C** Distribution of factor VIII-related antigen around the periphery of an intraepithelial channel. Antigen is also seen within endothelial cells of nearby intact intraepithelial capillary. (Indirect immunofluorescence, ×67) (Reproduced from reference no. 45) vessels.[23,50] One additional gastric artery reportedly commonly present, with likely surgical significance, is the posterior gastric artery, a branch derived from the splenic artery, usually from its middle third; it passes anteriorly to the stomach behind the posterior peritoneum, to supply both anterior and posterior gastric walls (Fig. 10.12C) (accounts give varying incidences from 37–84%; the higher incidence seems probable).[52]

Intramural gastric arterial distribution

The anterior and posterior branches from the superior arcade between left and right gastric arteries pass to the stomach between the layers of the lesser omentum; they run under the serosal covering of the stomach and perpendicularly away from the line of the lesser curve for distances of ~5 cm on the anterior and posterior walls of

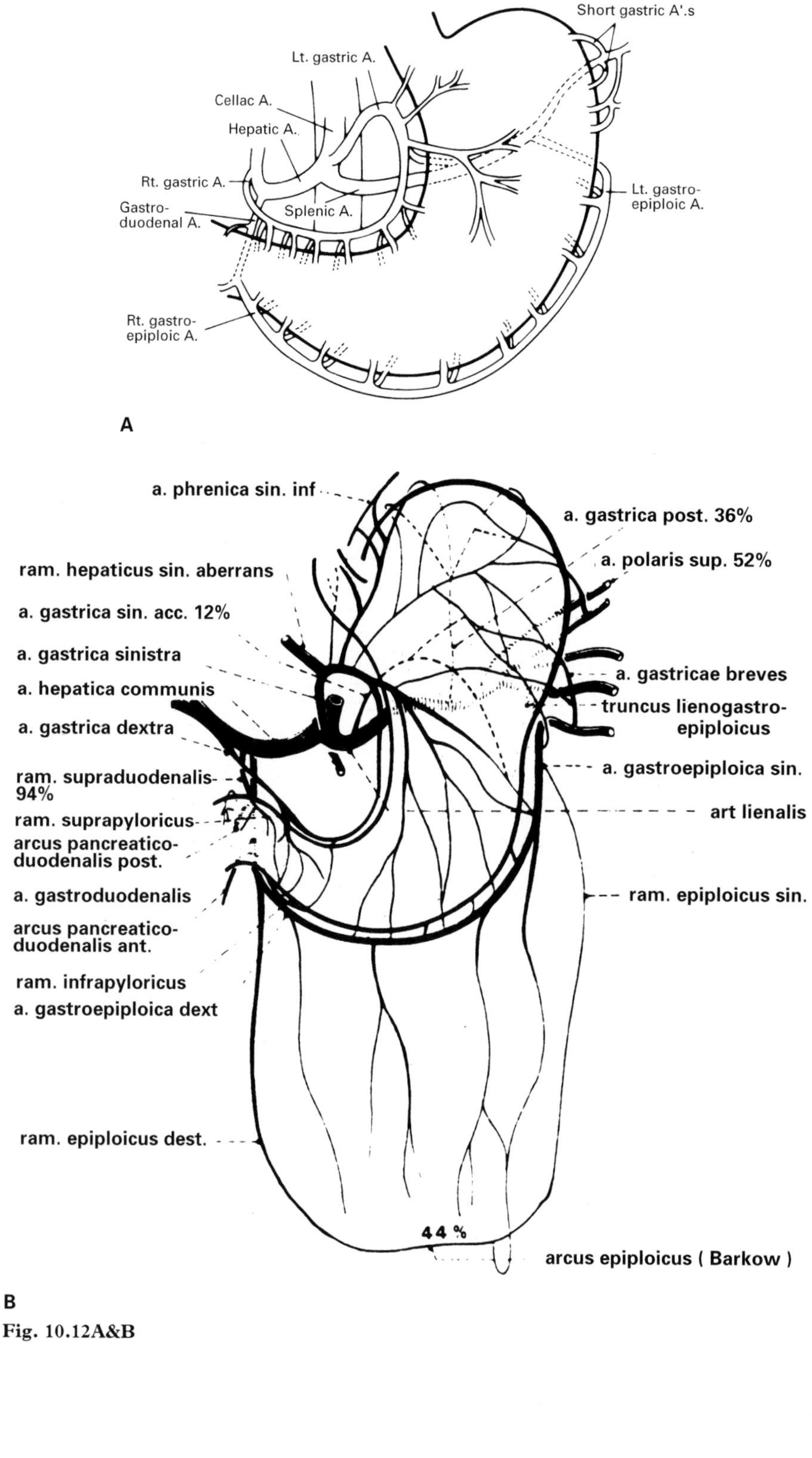

Fig. 10.12A&B

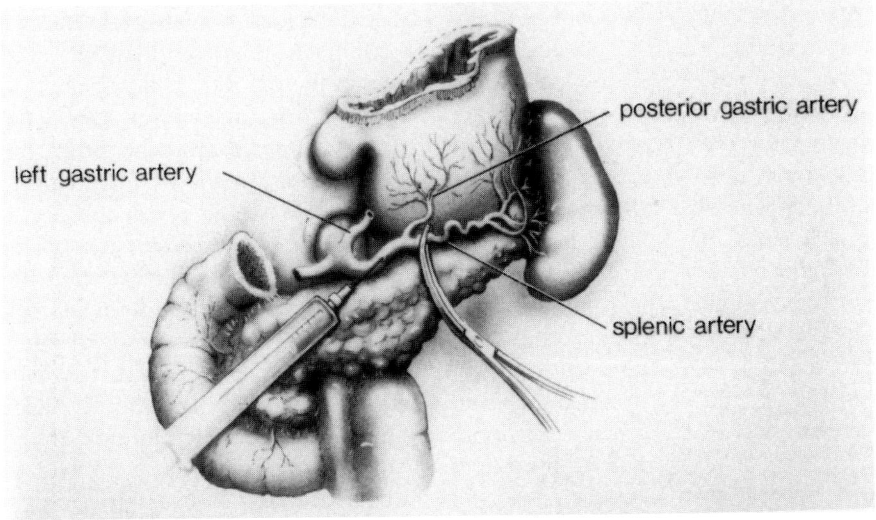

C

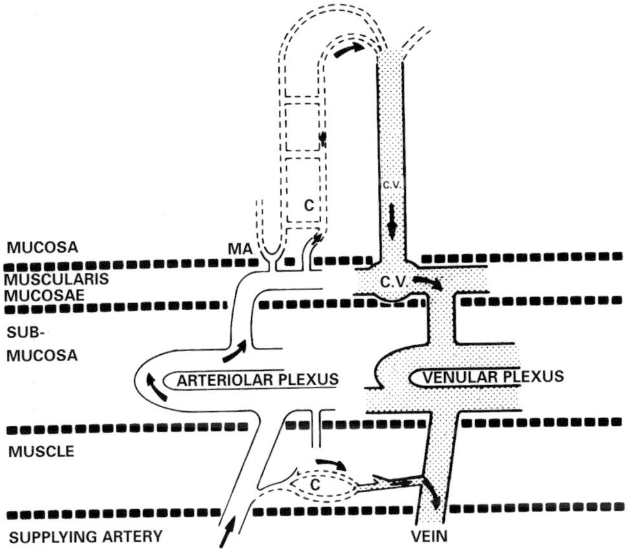

D

Fig. 10.12 Schematic illustrations of gastric vasculature. **A** Arterial supply of the stomach. **B** Arterial supply to the stomach and omentum. **C** Illustration of the origin of the posterior gastric artery; both the posterior and anterior walls of the stomach are stained when 0.5 ml of 1% methylene blue solution is injected into this vessel. **D** Gastric microcirculation. MA = mucosal arteriole; C = capillary; CV = collecting vein. Microvasculature of muscle layer is in parallel with that of mucosa, while microvasculature of submucosa is in series with that of mucosa. There are no arteriovenous anastomoses. (Fig. 10.12A reprinted from reference no. 55 by permission of Raven Press; Fig. 10.12B reprinted from reference no. 54; Fig. 10.12C reprinted from reference no 52; Fig. 10.12D reprinted from reference no. 56)

the stomach, each giving off several subserosal branches. Similarly, subserosal gastric branches from the inferior arterial arcade arriving via the greater omentum are distributed on anterior and posterior aspects of the stomach for several centimetres from the greater curvature. This plexus of arteries shows little cross-anastomosis along the greater or lesser curves, and no anastomosis of subserosal arteries of the greater with those of the lesser curve. These vessels quickly become smaller and appear to peter out as they pass from the greater or lesser curves, resulting in an area several centimetres wide in the mid-anterior and mid-posterior walls which is devoid of obvious subserosal arterial or venous vessels.[23,57]

From this subserosal distribution of arteries, perforating branches are given off, which pass through the external muscle layers to reach the richly anastomotic submucosal arterial plexus. Small side-branches are given off to the external muscle layers and to Auerbach's plexus en route, although the majority of arterioles to the external muscle coats are given off from the submucous arterial plexus (Fig. 10.12D). The anastomotic submucous arterial network extends between the greater and lesser curves, in contrast to the subserosal arterial net, which does not.[57–59] Thus there is anastomosis between the vessels derived from the lesser curve and those derived from the greater curve only at the submucosal level.

Gastric microvascular organization

Muscularis

There has been little detailed study of the microvascular

supply to the external muscle coats of the stomach, or of that supplying the myenteric plexus. The arterial supply is partly derived from the perforating arteries as they pass from subserosal arteries to the submucosa; this occurs adjacent to the greater and lesser curves and near the short gastric arteries. Elsewhere, the principal arterial supply to the muscularis is by branches arising directly from the submucous arterial plexus.[60–62] The muscle itself is supplied by continuous capillaries which are non-fenestrated, and surrounded by a well developed basal lamina (see Fig. 10.5B).[20] These capillaries run parallel to the adjacent smooth muscle cells. Diffusion distances are of the order of several micrometres between capillaries and muscle cells. There are no morphometric studies of capillary densities in this tissue.

There are no investigations as to whether a separate microvascular plexus supplying the myenteric neural plexus exists, but one might be expected because of the presence of a specialized lymphatic drainage of this area (see below).[63] A similar specialized lymphatic drainage of the myenteric neural plexus is reported in the small intestine, where there is a separate capillary network supplying the myenteric plexus.[64]

Mucosa

There are three distinct types of mucosa in the human stomach: that of the cardia near the gastric inlet, that of the fundus and body of the stomach and that of the gastric antrum adjacent to the gastric outlet at the pylorus. Studies of surgical specimens to determine human gastric mucosal microvascular organization[65,67] have resulted in conflicting accounts of the microvascular architecture of the gastric body (corpus) (see also below).

Studies of the microvascular organization of the gastric mucosa in a number of laboratory animal species[66,69] has revealed both regional differences in microvascular architecture within the gastric mucosa of the same species, and interspecies differences in the microvascular architecture of the largest region of the stomach, the gastric body plus fundus. A comparison of the accounts of the mucosal microvascular architecture of the different species studied also suggests a resolution of the conflicting accounts regarding the microvasculature of human gastric corpus, points to the likely microvascular organization in human gastric antrum and suggests appropriate model species for further experimental study of the role of mucosal microvessels in gastric mucosal injury and disease.

Mucosa of the gastric body (corpus) and fundus

The microvascular organization of the mucosa of the gastric corpus has been investigated recently in humans[65,67,68] and several other mammalian species.[60,62,66,69–74] The findings have been essentially similar, except for the account of Raschke et al[67] for the human stomach, and the report on rabbit stomach microvasculature[66] (see discussion under Mucosa of the gastric antrum, below).

Mucosal arterial supply is from a series of small (approximately 12 μm luminal diameter) branches from the submucosal arterial plexus, which pass perpendicularly through the muscularis mucosae to gain the deepest level of the lamina propria (Fig. 10.13A); these mucosal arterioles do not penetrate into the mucosa further than the base of the gastric glands. Prominent endothelial cell intra-arterial cushions, containing accumulations of autonomically innervated smooth muscle cells with frequent myoendothelial cell contacts, protrude into the arteriolar lumen at its branching here, immediately abluminal to the muscularis mucosa,[75] and may play a role in control of mucosal perfusion and/or local blood haematocrit perfusing the mucosa. These arterioles branch into 7–10 capillaries, each of 6–7 μm diameter, which then run towards the luminal surface in the lamina propria between the gastric glands and largely parallel to them. There are frequent approximately horizontal cross-anastomoses between adjacent capillaries (Fig. 10.13B); nevertheless, despite these cross-anastomoses, the individual mucosal arterioles appear to function as end arteries, as experimental ligation of a single mucosal arteriole in guinea-pigs results in full thickness necrosis of the mucosa (Fig. 10.14).[75] Capillary red blood cell velocities are of the order of 0.15 mm/s in resting gastric mucosa.[76]

At the most luminal level of the lamina propria, just subjacent to the epithelial surface mucous cells, the capillaries join a planar polygonal network of capillaries and small subepithelial postcapillary venules which surround the necks of the gastric pits (Fig. 10.13C). Within this subepithelial planar network, blood drains to infrequently occurring mucosal venules, of 15–20 μm luminal diameter, which are oriented perpendicular to the mucosal surface and are spaced within the mucosa at intervals of 350–500 μm separation (Figs 10.13D, 10.15). In rats, each mucosal venule drains the blood from the interstitium surrounding approximately 60 gastric pits, and red cell velocities are of the order of 0.5 mm/s in these venules in resting mucosa.[76] In their passage perpendicular to the plane of the mucosa to reach the submucous venous plexus, these mucosal venules receive all their direct capillary tributaries, and usually all their small subepithelial venular tributaries also, at the most luminal level of the lamina propria. In some instances, additional venular tributaries, which have arisen subepithelially, pass to the mucosal venules deeper in the lamina propria. Nevertheless, there are no direct capillary tributaries to the mucosal venules within the lamina propria, except at their most distal (i.e. luminal) end. Thus there is no possible intramucosal short circuit or shunt between arteriole and venule which might by-pass the most luminal level of the lamina propria (Fig. 10.16).

The microvascular architecture of the gastric fundus in humans, and presumably in the dog and cat, is essentially the same as that of the gastric body in these species. This is in contrast to the stomachs of rats and hamsters (at least), species which have a nonglandular squamous epithelium-lined forestomach mucosa in the anatomical location of the fundus. The forestomach mucosal epithelium is underlain by a relatively sparse planar capillary network similar to that which underlies the oesophageal epithelium; the forestomach can be considered as a dilated lower oesophagus, and hence is *not* a model for the human gastric fundus.

Mucosa of the gastric (pyloric) antrum

In the mucosa of the canine antrum, there are two distinct capillary beds (Fig. 10.17A,B):

(i) a basal capillary bed of small tortuous capillaries (7.3 µm diameter) which arise from arterioles which branch terminally at the level of the muscularis mucosa; these capillaries are more sparsely distributed than those of the gastric corpus and are located at some distance from the surrounding gastric glands. These capillaries drain into the larger diameter superficial capillary bed lying luminal to them.

(ii) a superficial bed of larger (10.8 µm diameter) parallel capillaries, which commence at midmucosal level, at about the transition from the antral gastric gland necks to the bases of the superficial gastric pits; these superficial capillaries are supplied by a set of ascending intramucosal arterioles which course through approximately the basal half of the lamina propria and the basal capillary network without connecting to it, before branching terminally to form the superficial capillaries. The small tortuous basal capillaries drain into the proximal portions of these larger superficial capillaries. These superficial capillaries proceed luminally in the lamina propria surrounding the gastric pits and are sparser in spatial density than the capillaries of the lamina propria of the gastric corpus.

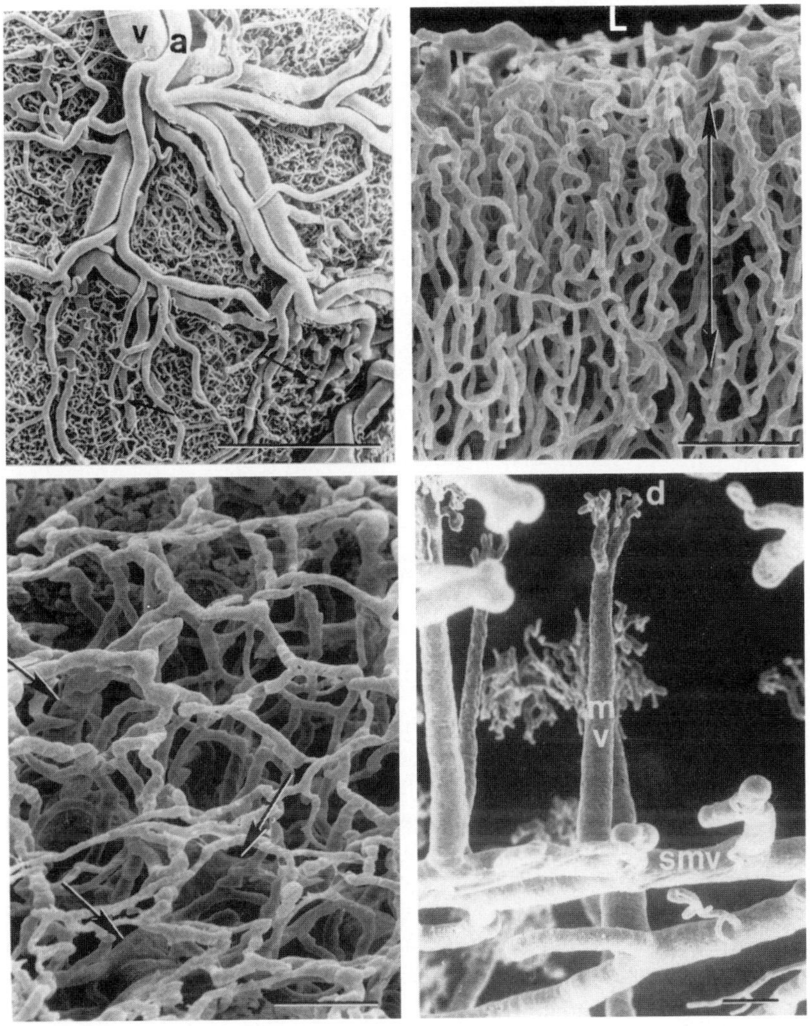

A B C D

Fig. 10.13 Scanning electron micrographs of microvascular corrosion casts of gastric tissue of rat and human. **A** View of the submucosal aspect of a cast of rat gastric corpus mucosa plus submucosa; note parallel branching pattern of submucosal arterioles (a) and venules (v). The fine meshwork seen between these is the commencement of the mucosal capillary network. Note also occasional fine vessels running in the plane of the submucosa (arrows). Bar = 1.0 mm **B** View of the fractured edge of a mucosal cast of rat gastric corpus showing capillaries are orientated principally perpendicular (arrows) to the plane of the gastric luminal surface (L); note, however, frequent cross-connections, which may be important in healing of ulcerated gastric mucosa. Bar = 100 µm **C** View of luminal aspect of cast of mucosal microvasculature of human gastric body. Note the polygonal array of the most luminal capillaries, which define the openings of the gastric pits. Some larger mucosal venule tributaries (arrows) can be seen just below the most superficial capillaries. Bar = 100 µm **D** View of the fractured edge of a partial vascular cast of rat gastric corpus, in which only the venules and venous ends of the capillaries were filled (by retrograde injection of plastic). A mucosal venule (mv) proceeds from its drainage of subsurface capillaries (d) to the submucous venous plexus (smv) without additional capillary tributaries. Note also infrequency of mucosal venules. Bar = 100 µm (Fig. 10.13A,B,D reprinted from reference no. 60 by permission of the Journal of Anatomy; Fig. 10.13C reprinted from reference no. 65 by permission of Gastroenterology)

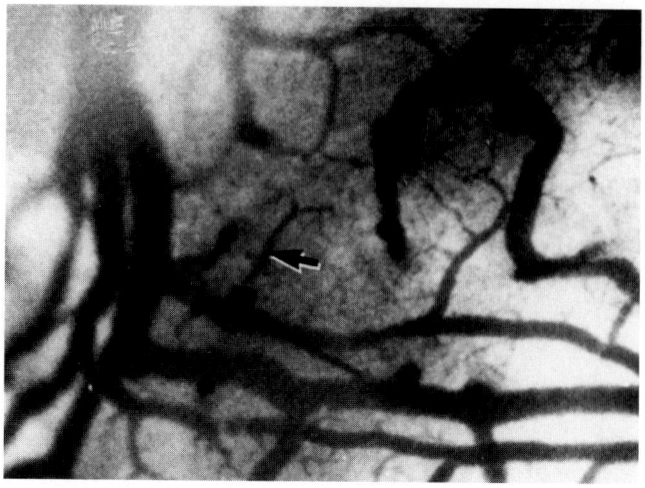

A

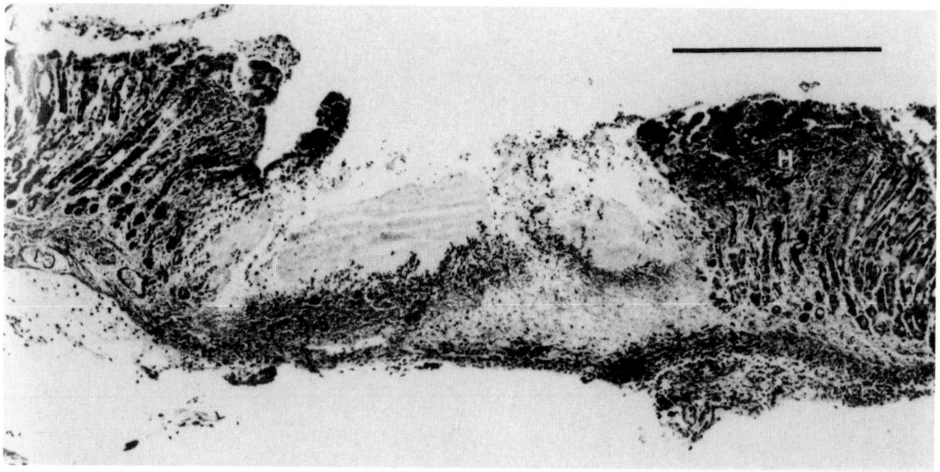

B

Fig. 10.14 Ulceration of gastric mucosa from ligation of a single mucosal arteriole. **A** Macroscopic view of transilluminated gastric submucosa and mucosa in vivo. Submucous plexus arteries and veins, and mucosal arteries (small black arrow) and veins are shown, with a single mucosal artery ligated (arrow) with a microsuture. **B** Full-thickness mucosal necrosis, one day after ligating a single mucosal arteriole. In the centre is a necrotic mass, at the left and right edges there is relatively normal mucosa. Between the mucosa at the edges and the central mass there is an area of haemorrhage and disruption best seen to the right of the necrotic mass. H = haemorrhage. H&E. Bar = 0.5 mm (Reproduced from reference no. 75)

In the rabbit,[66] there are two distinct arteriolar supplies throughout the gastric corpus: short arterioles arise from the submucosal arterial plexus and break up into a capillary network with numerous cross-anastomoses that surrounds the gastric glands; long arterioles also arise from the submucosal arterioles, to course through most of the thickness of the lamina propria, before terminating in a dense capillary immediately beneath the surface epithelium in the inter-pit regions. Connections were noted between the two capillary networks at the level of the gastric gland necks. This arrangement in the rabbit gastric corpus of two arteriolar supplies and two interconnected capillary beds is reminiscent of that found in dog gastric antrum.[69]

Raschke's report of a dual arteriolar supply to human gastric corpus[67] similar to rabbit[66] is at variance with the other reports of this bed in humans.[19,65] The specimens taken in Raschke's study[67] apparently came from the gastric corpus adjacent to the antrum (personal communication 1987). Given the consensus of other workers about a single arteriolar supply to human gastric corpus mucosa, the report of a dual arteriolar supply to canine antral mucosa[69] and the fact that India-ink injected specimens of human gastric antral mucosa[74] appear identical to similarly prepared specimens from dogs,[69] it seems likely that the pattern observed by Raschke et al[67] was, in fact, of human antral mucosa, which therefore apparently has a dual arteriolar supply to two interconnected capillary beds, as in the dog[69] (Fig. 10.17B).

Mucosa of the cardia

Reports of mucosal microvascular organization of the cardia are incidental to studies of the oesophagogastric junction. The microvascular architecture is apparently the same as in the fundus and body, with the exception that the submucosal venous plexus is comprised of a series of parallel veins oriented towards the oesophagogastric junction.[25] These vessels, and the intramucosal venules draining to them, may become enlarged and distorted in portal hypertension to form gastric varices[27,43] (see above).

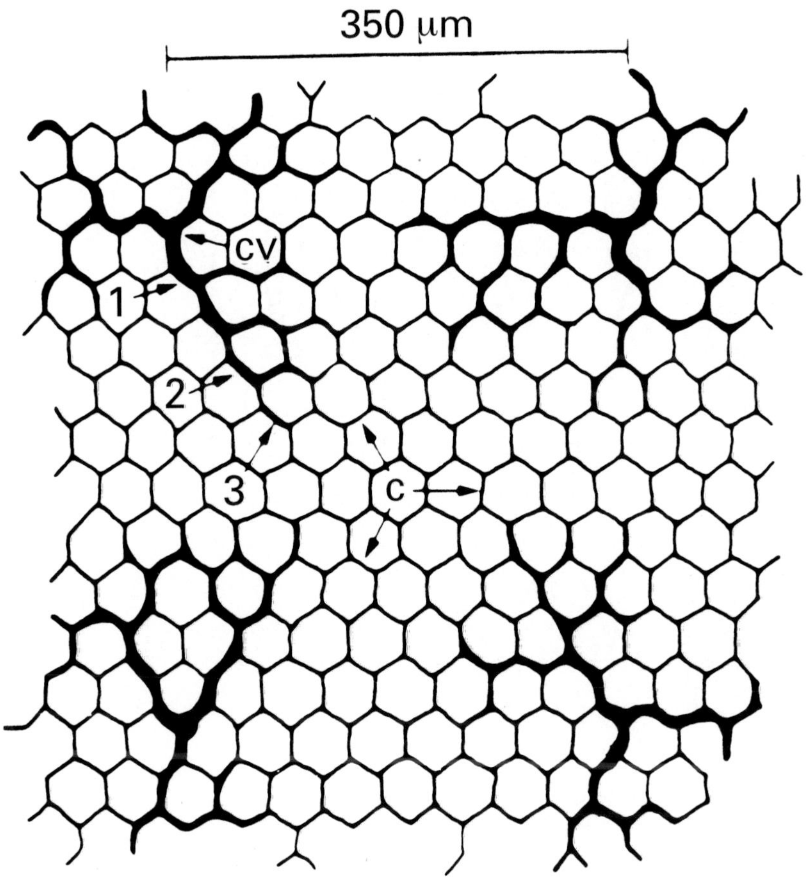

Fig. 10.15 Diagrammatic representation of the rat gastric corpus mucosal microvasculature, gastric luminal aspect. Capillary loops (C) surrounding the necks of gastric pits coalesce to form third, second and first order (3, 2, 1) subepithelial postcapillary venules. These vessels converge on infrequent mucosal venules (CV) which drain directly away from the mucosal surface towards the submucosa (i.e. into the page in this diagram). Each mucosal venule drains flow from capillary rings around approximately 60 gastric pits, and is separated from its nearest neighbour by about 350 μm. (Reproduced from reference no. 60 by permission of the American Journal of Physiology)

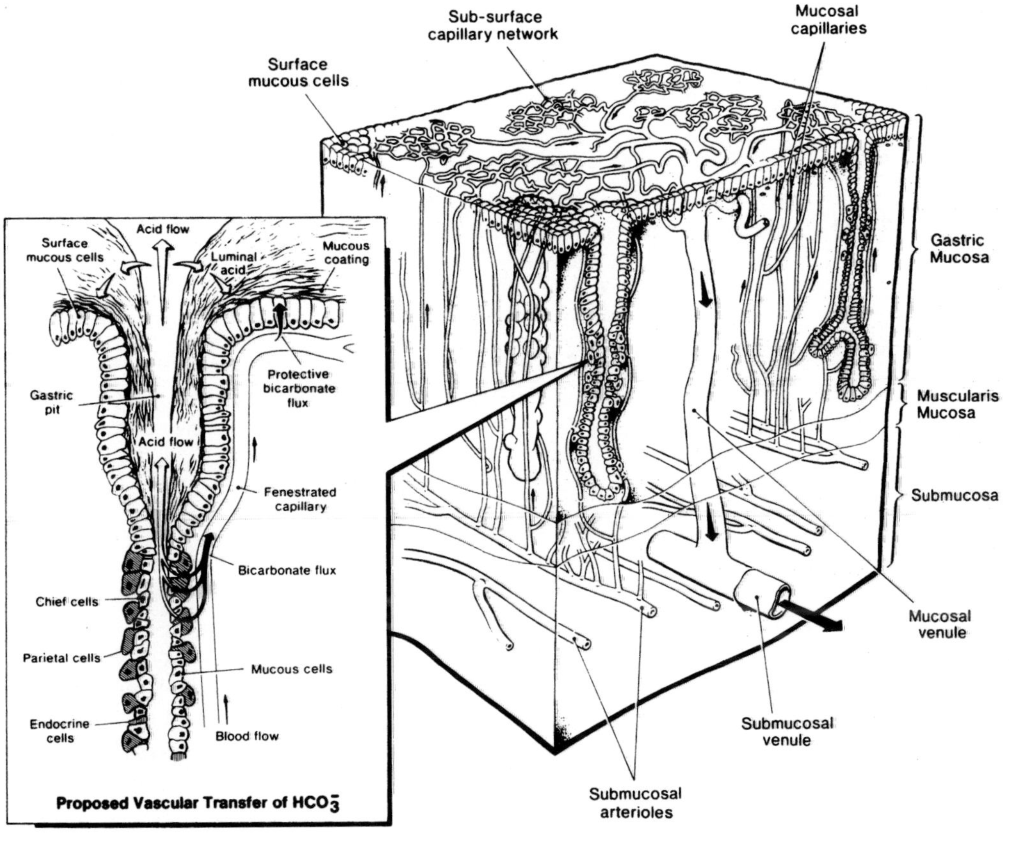

Fig. 10.16 Schematic diagram of the microvascular organization of oxyntic mucosa of the stomach, and the proposed pathway of intramucosal microvascular transport of HCO_3^-, produced by parietal cells, towards the surface mucous cells in a 'local portal' pattern (inset left). (Reproduced from reference no. 65 by permission of Gastroenterology)

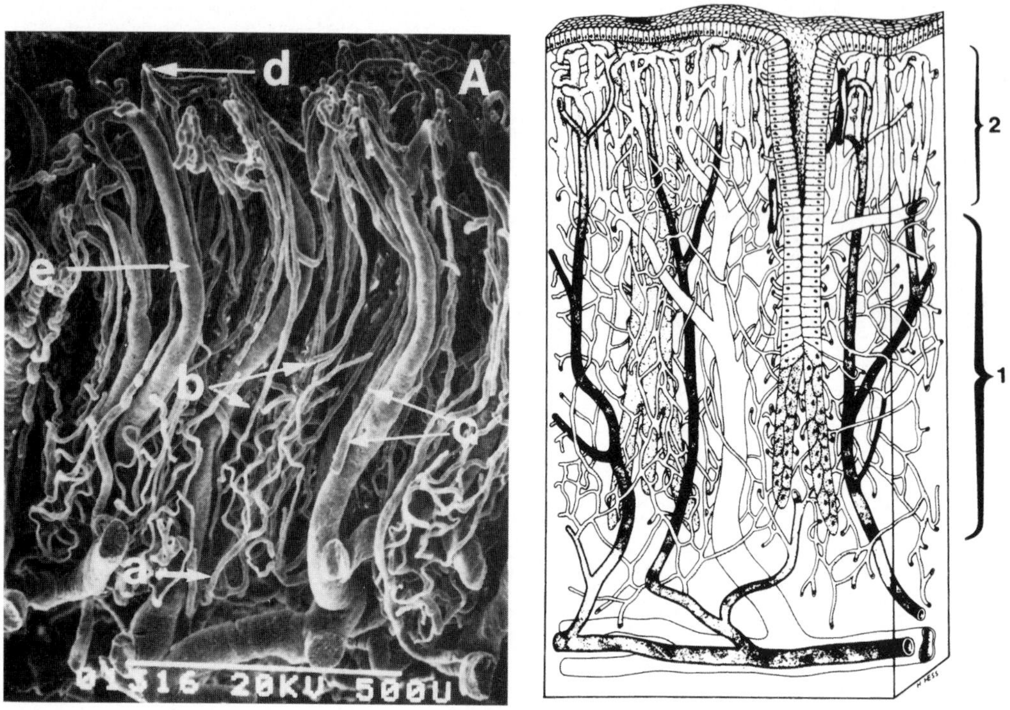

A B

Fig. 10.17 Gastric Antral microvasculature. **A** Corrosion vascular cast of canine antral mucosa, lateral aspect of fractured cast; scanning electron micrograph. Arrow a = small arterioles feeding basal capillary network; arrow b = connections between basal and superficial capillaries; arrow c = arterioles passing through but not connecting to the basal capillary network, but directly connecting to superficial capillaries; arrow d = superficial capillaries draining into central vein; arrow e = central vein. Note that there is no connection between basal small tortuous capillaries and the central vein. Bar = 500 µm **B** Scheme of proposed microangio-architecture of human antral mucosa, similar to the dog (arterioles = dark-coloured; venules = light-coloured). Short arterioles branch into a basal capillary network (1) reaching from the base to the isthmus of the gastric glands. Long arterioles ascend into the mucosa and branch into a layer of wide, apical capillaries (2). This schema almost certainly represents the arrangement in human antral mucosa, as also found in dogs,[69] although originally proposed by Raschke et al as the pattern in human fundic mucosa;[67] see text for discussion. (Fig. 10.17A reproduced from reference no. 69; Fig. 10.17B reproduced from reference no. 67 by permission of AG Karger)

Absence of arteriovenous anastomoses (AVAs) in the gastric mucosa

As indicated above, there are no capillary short circuits within the gastric mucosa which bypass the subsurface drainage pathway to postcapillary venules and the gastric luminal end of mucosal venules. In addition, due to improvements in techniques for discerning microvessel connectivity in three dimensions, it is now reasonably certain that there are also no direct arteriovenous anastomoses (AVAs) either in the mucosa or in any other layer of the wall of normal stomachs,[65,69,75] despite earlier reports of their presence and frequency.[77,78] Two types of AVAs have been described in the past:

(a) glomus-like structures resembling the AVAs of the skin, in which the distal segment contains large epithelioid cells in the vessel wall;[79] such structures were reported in human gastric mucosa and submucosa

(b) direct arteriolar to venular connections by capillaries of normal wall structure, but of wider than usual luminal diameter; such structures were reported in human gastric mucosa[77,78,80] and in rat gastric mucosa and submucosa.[79,81]

Recent studies using a variety of approaches including theoretical analysis of the results of microsphere injections,[82] intravital microscopy,[83] and detailed microvascular cast analysis[60,62,65] have failed to demonstrate glomus-type AVA structures in normal stomachs.

There is a report of a few intramucosal structures possibly interpretable as AVAs found in patients with cirrhosis,[84] however the entire gastric mucosal and submucosal microvascular networks are also dilated and gastric microvessel diameters are twice the normal in these patients. Glomeruloid or glomus-like microvascular structures have also been reported in differentiated (intestinal type) gastric carcinomas, and appear similar to the microvasculature in inflammatory granulation tissue.[85–87] Capillaries of larger than usual gastric capillary diameter (10.8 μm compared to 7–8 μm) were demonstrated convincingly in the superficial capillary layer of dog gastric antral mucosa[69] and seem likely to represent the 'shunt' pathway taken by the 63% of 9 μm microspheres which traverse this microvascular bed, but which are 100% entrapped elsewhere in the microvessel beds of the gastric wall.

Direct arteriolar to venular connections have been reported to appear in the submucous plexus in stressed rats after burn or restraint/water immersion,[88] however such structures have yet to be convincingly illustrated.

Gastric venous drainage

Mucosal venules drain into the submucous venous plexus, which is richly anastomotic throughout the stomach. This plexus is also continuous with the submucous venules of the oesophagus and the duodenum by many small venular connections. Drainage of the muscle layers also occurs to the submucous venous plexus, although there are additional direct venular tributaries from the muscle capillaries to the perforating veins, as they pass to the subserosal veins. These latter vessels largely parallel the subserosal arteries along the greater and lesser curves of the stomach, and drain to arcading veins in the greater and lesser omenta and others in the gastrosplenic ligament. All these veins drain to the portal venous system, and any compromise of portal flow may cause marked distension of gastric intramural microvessels.[84] There is a potentially significant portosystemic venous connection between the left gastric vein and the azygous vein via the external veins of the oesophagus through the venae comitantes of the vagus nerves,[23] as well as via the submucosal and, especially, the subepithelial venous plexuses, which continue across the oesophagogastric junction (see above and also Ch. 30).

Gastric microvessel ultrastructure

Gastric mucosal capillaries are continuous vessels, of relatively regular cross-sectional profile, and with luminal diameters of 5–7 μm (see table 10.2). Their walls are composed of an attenuated endothelial cell layer and a prominent basal lamina, approximately 50–100 nm thick, which is not associated with collagenous anchoring filaments (Fig. 10.18A,B).[60,65,89–92] Pericytes are frequently associated with the capillaries, and, where these are located, the basal lamina of the capillary splits to enclose the pericyte also. A prominent feature of the mucosal endothelial cells is the presence of large numbers of fenestrae where the capillary wall is devoid of cytoplasm. The fenestrae are approximately 60 nm in diameter, are usually covered by a diaphragm continuous with the cell membrane and are presumably highly permeable to water and hydrophilic solutes as large as horseradish peroxidase.

Junctions between adjacent mucosal capillary endothelial cells are relatively less frequent than in muscle, lung and other tissues and probably contribute little to overall blood–tissue exchange. There are significant numbers of endothelial vesicles in the gastric mucosal capillaries, but their numbers in fenestrated capillaries, at least in the intestine, are much less than the number found in skeletal muscle. The vesicles may nevertheless be important in macromolecular transport between capillary lumen and interstitium.[93] Some charge selectivity of vesicle macromolecular transport has been reported.[94] Weibel-Palade bodies containing factor VIII/von Willebrand factor are present in mucosal capillary endothelial cells,[95] and increased numbers of these organelles are present in capillaries surrounding cancer cell nests in differentiated gastric carcinoma.[86] In gastric lymphomas, there is evidence of alteration of mucosal venular endothelium to the high endothelium form, as normally found only in lymph nodes,[87] perhaps as a result of locally released cytokines.[316]

In the body of the stomach, the capillaries are found in close contact with the basal membranes of parietal cells. Diffusion distances between parietal cell basal membrane and outer endothelial membrane of less than 0.3 μm are typical (Fig. 10.18B). The mucosal capillaries are found in preferential spatial association with parietal cells, as compared to other cells of the gastric glands.[96] Parietal cells contain the highest number of mitochondria of any normal cell type yet found, and clearly have a high metabolic requirement. The capillaries and subepithelial venules lying immediately subjacent to the surface mucous cells of the gastric lining are also fenestrated and lie within 3 μm of the basal membranes of the overlying surface mucous cell.[59] The mucosal venules consist of a continuous endothelial lining without fenestrae and with few endothelial vesicles; the endothelium is surrounded by a 5–7 μm thick collagenous sheath, which contains several fibroblast laminae.[60]

In portal hypertension, the microvessels of the gastric wall show a vasculopathy, with thickened endothelial cells with numerous cytoplasmic projections into the microvessel lumen, and an increased pinocytotic vesicle number, resulting in compromise of the microvessel lumina, presumably resulting in mucosal hypoperfusion.[97]

Intramucosal local portal transfer of HCO_3^-

It has been recently proposed that the gastric mucosal microvasculature may play a significant role in the intrinsic defence mechanisms of the mucosa against attack by luminal acid.[60,65] Parietal cells pump one HCO_3^- ion across their basal membranes for each H^+ they secrete into their canaliculi (which are continuous with the gastric gland lumen) to maintain charge balance.[98] This interstitially released HCO_3^- must diffuse to, and rapidly be picked up by, the closely adjacent fenestrated mucosal capillaries, to

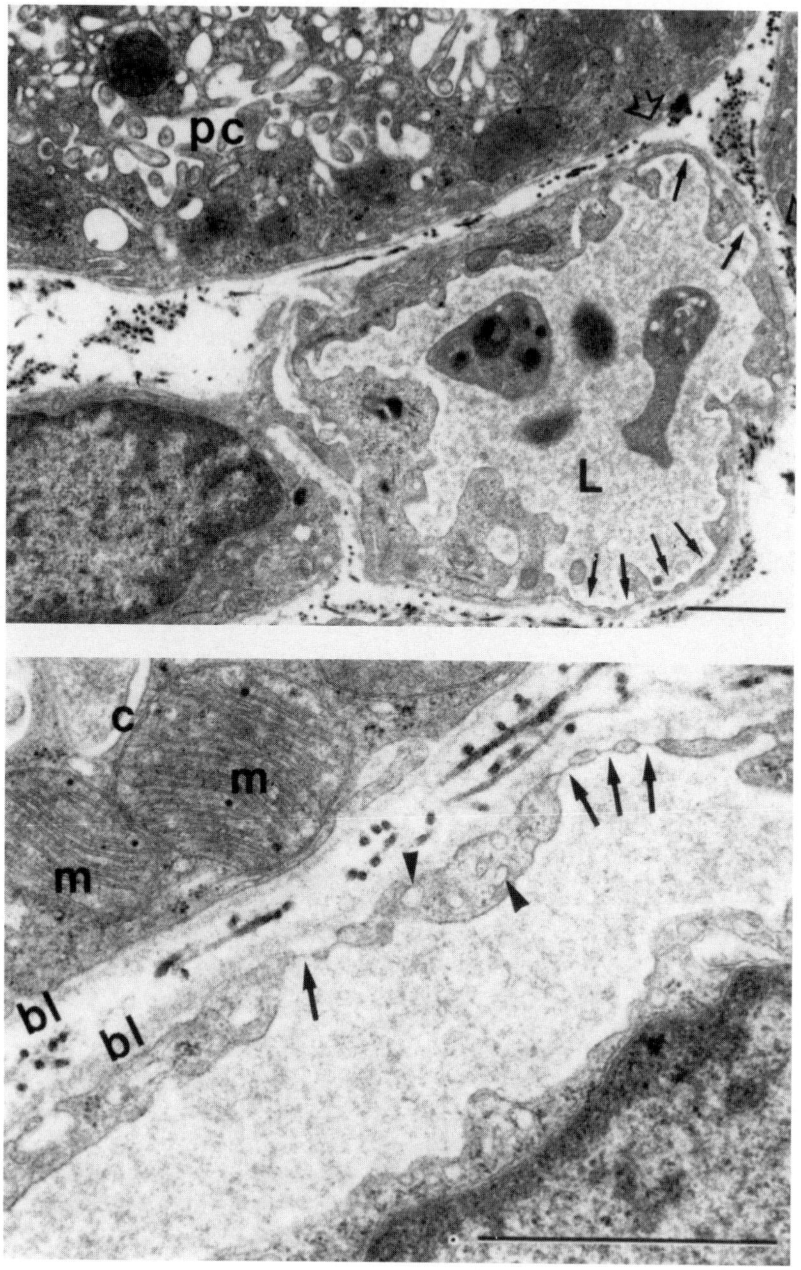

Fig. 10.18 Electron micrographs of rat gastric microvessels. **A** TEM of capillary (L = lumen) adjacent to two parietal cells (pc). Note fenestrations in capillary endothelium (solid arrows) and close proximity of capillary to parietal cells (open arrows). Bar = 1.0 µm **B** TEM, at higher magnification, of capillary close to parietal cells. Note fenestrae with diaphragm (solid arrows) and endothelial vesicles (arrowheads) in endothelium, separate basal laminal (bl) of capillary and parietal cell, and mitochondria (m) and canaliculi (c) of the parietal cell. Bar = 1.0 µm (Reproduced from reference no. 60 by permission of the Journal of Anatomy)

be carried to the basal aspect of the surface mucous cells. These cells are close to subepithelial capillaries, and secrete HCO_3^- into the surface mucous gel, to form a barrier which neutralizes H^+ ions back-diffusing from the gastric lumen, and thereby aids in preventing mucosal ulceration. Thus there appears to be a local portal system for intramucosal transfer of HCO_3^- via capillary blood (Fig. 10.16). The conclusion that HCO_3^- must take the route proposed is inescapable, given the microangio-architecture and the well documented spill-over of HCO_3^- from the gastric mucosa into the general circulation as the postprandial alkaline tide. The presence of the enzyme carbonic anhydrase, which accelerates the interconversion of CO_2 and HCO_3^- in gastric capillary endothelial cells, as well as in parietal cells and gastric surface epithelial cells,[99] lends further support to the HCO_3^- local portal system concept.

It is of interest to note that chronic gastric ulceration most commonly occurs in the gastric antrum[100] where there are many fewer parietal cells, and hence where such a mechanism of local bicarbonate portal transfer would not be possible; nevertheless, the antral mucosa does secrete HCO_3^-.[101] Also relevant is the fact that the antral mucosa is subjected to lower acid concentrations than is the oxyntic mucosa of the gastric body where acid secretion actually occurs; nevertheless, it is the former site that is at greatest risk of chronic gastric ulceration. The different microvascular architecture in antral mucosa as compared to mucosa elsewhere in the stomach (in the canine and probably in the human), as well as possibly different regional mucosal physiology, may account for the differing ulcerative susceptibilities.

Gastric mucosal microvasculature in mucosal injury

The gastric mucosa normally contains and withstands the acutely hostile environment of the gastric lumen. This environment includes a luminal pH of around 1.5–2.0, digestive enzymes and a wide chemical and textural variety of swallowed substances which are ingested over a broad range of temperatures. However, mucosal ability to withstand attack by gastric juice may be compromised in a variety of situations, including stress, hypovolaemic and toxic shock and following alcohol or drug ingestion. Evidence is accumulating that acute compromise of the mucosal microcirculation is an early, if not primary, event in the development of mucosal erosion and gastric ulceration (Fig. 10.19; Table 10.3),[102–104,108] while maintenance of an adequate blood flow may be critical for healing or restitution of the mucosa after injury.[105–107,109]

Administration of nonsteroidal anti-inflammatory drugs, e.g. aspirin, causes mucosal pallor, a reduction in mucosal blood flow and focal ischaemia.[103,111] Focal surface erosions, corresponding to areas of compromised microcirculation, rapidly ensue and large accumulations of neutrophils[112] and platelet thrombi[104] are found at these sites. In hypovolaemic shock, compromise of mucosal blood flow occurs with resulting mucosal erosions in the oxyntic mucosa of the stomach;[113] sloughing of small intestinal and colonic mucosa also occurs in such patients. In studies of the pathogenesis of experimental gastric ulceration caused by intragastric administration of concentrated ethanol,[114] it appears that platelet adhesion to mucosal capillaries[104] and formation of thrombi at the venular ends of mucosal capillaries, or in the subepithelial venules, is one of the earliest detectable events;[115] arrest of the local circulation follows quickly and occurs prior to breach of the surface epithelium.[116] The adhesion of platelets to capillary endothelium may be mediated via the adhesion molecule GMP-140 (P-selectin), which is expressed on both activated platelets and gastric mucosal microvessel endothelium.[117] Subsequently, mucosal capillaries become permeable to albumin and lamina propria oedema occurs (Fig. 10.20); significant interstitial accumulation of red blood cells ensues, following capillary rupture.[118,120]

In these experimental acute ulcerative conditions, it is pertinent to note that ulceration occurs mainly in the

Table 10.3 Time sequence of mucosal changes during formation and development of acetic acid-induced gastric ulcer in the rat; note vascular/microvascular involvement

1 min after insult
Vasodilation of large submucosal veins and arteries and overlying mucosal collecting venules
Focal oedema of submucosa
Mucosal swelling of stromal tissue, but surface epithelial cells (SEC) and glands look normal

15 min after insult (additional changes)
Blood clots in submucosal dilated veins
Marked oedema of submucosa
Delineated areas of mucosal swelling and deterioration of surface integrity in affected area

1 h after insult (additional changes)
Blood clots in submucosal arteries
Clearly disintegrating surface with desquamating SEC
Cellular depletion of the glandular mucosa

3 h after insult (additional changes)
More pronounced disintegration of the mucosa; transition zone between necrotic and normal mucosa involves 2–4 glands
Accumulating of polymorphonuclear cells (PMNs) in submucosal vessels and in the submucosa
Beginning of detachment of larger necrotic masses from the necrotic mucosa

24 h after insult
Generalized tissue necrosis and sloughing from the ulcer crater
Necrosis involves muscularis propria
Prominent inflammatory infiltration of serosa

48 h after insult
Craters free of necrotic tissue
Necrotic and purulent muscularis propria
Purulent serosa

72 h after insult
Granulation tissue covers the ulcer bottom
Some ulcers ruptured through the serosa
'Chronic' appearance of ulcerations
Granulation tissue often penetrates into surroundings, especially the pancreas
Mucosa at the ulcer margin forms a transitional healing zone

120 h after insult
Large amount of granulation tissue in ulcer craters
Increased mitotic activity in transitional zone
Cells in transitional zone poorly differentiated (most likely dedifferentiated)

(Reprinted from reference no. 108 by permission of Raven Press)

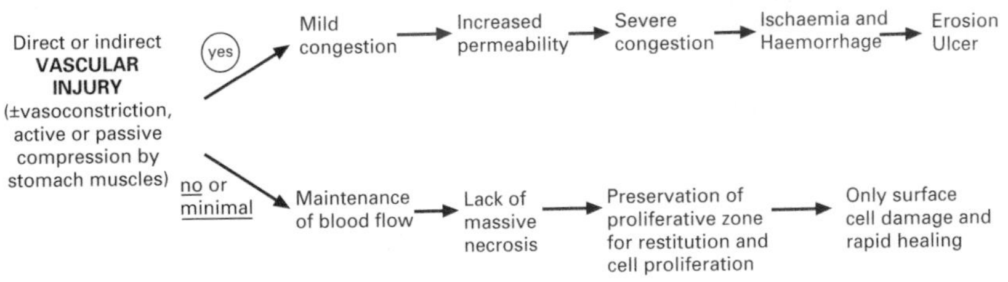

Fig. 10.19 The importance of vascular injury in gastric mucosal injury and protection, as deduced from numerous investigations using damaging and gastroprotective agents. (Reproduced from reference no. 110)

oxyntic mucosa, i.e. that which normally secretes acid, rather than in the antral mucosa, which is the usual site of chronic ulceration.[100] The explanation of this may at least in part be that the oxyntic mucosa is subject to the highest H^+ concentrations at its luminal surface, and that the intramucosal local portal carriage of HCO_3^-, as described above, is interrupted locally, with consequent loss of HCO_3^- supply to the overlying surface mucous cells for the formation of the mucous–HCO_3^- barrier. Clearly, of course, adequate supply of oxygen and other nutrients to the surface epithelial cells will also be important. Experimental ligation of a single mucosal arteriole produces a full thickness gastric ulcer;[75] it has been demonstrated that gastric ulceration can rapidly result from local interruption of the gastric circulation by strong gastric contractions, which stop local mucosal perfusion[121] and result in linear ulcer formation.[122]

The phenomenon of gastric 'cytoprotection' is of relevance here also. Robert et al[114] showed that, in rats treated with low doses of prostaglandins (PG) of the PGE series, acute mucosal insults (hot water, 30–100% ethyl alcohol (ETOH), acetic acid, etc.) which would normally produce acute mucosal erosions (Fig. 10.20B,D) were no longer effective (Fig. 10.20C). This 'cytoprotective' effect was not due to inhibition of acid secretion since it occurred at much lower doses, and was even effective in stomachs stimulated to secrete acid at maximal rates. Subsequent study has shown that effective cytoprotective doses of PGEs, which are too small to inhibit acid secretion, nevertheless stimulate mucosal blood flow, and this may be the major mechanism of their 'cytoprotective' effect;[123,124] sulphydryls are similarly effective.[124] It is clear, however, that the prostaglandins also enhance epithelial cellular resistance to exogenous damaging agents, since they are effective in preventing alcohol damage to non-perfused mucosal sheets in vitro, and also in preventing damage by low level ETOH to isolated gastric surface epithelial and glandular cells.[125]

A B C D

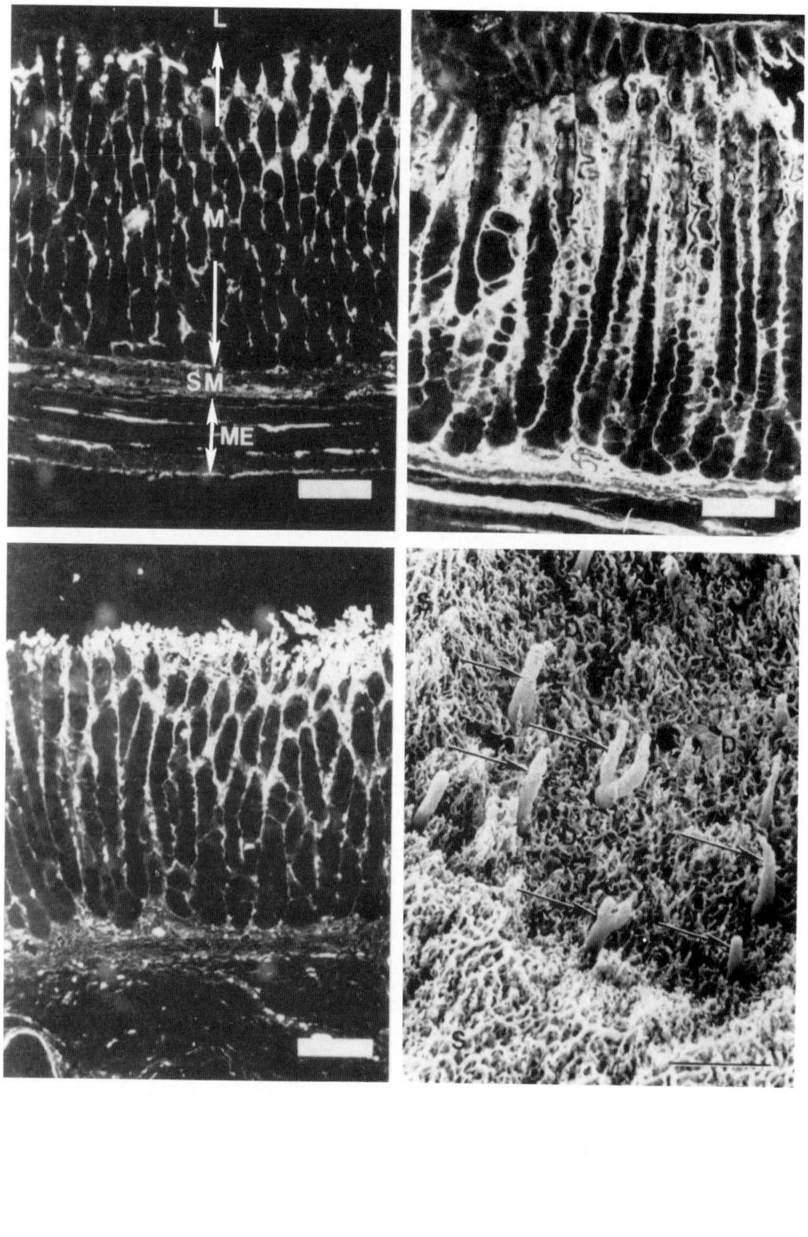

Fig. 10.20 Rat gastric mucosal microvasculature in ethanol-induced gastric mucosal injury.

A Fluorescence micrograph of control stomach after administration of FITC-albumin as a plasma marker; transverse section of gastric wall. L = lumen; M = mucosa; SM = submucosa; ME = muscularis externa (see arrows). Note that the fluorescence is confined to the microvessel lumina and is not seen within the interstitium. Bar = 100 μm

B Micrograph as in **A**, but 15 min after intragastric administration of 1 ml of absolute ethanol. An intact surface epithelium overlies a lamina propria in which there is extensive diffuse fluorescence due to extravasation of FITC-albumin tracer throughout the mucosa, and into the submucosa. Bar = 100 μm

C Micrograph as in **B** in animal pretreated with the synthetic prostaglandin analogue, enprostil. There is damage to superficial microvessels in the mucosa, as evidenced by interstitial leakage of FITC-albumin; however, deeper in the mucosa, the microvessels are able to withhold albumin from the interstitium. Bar = 100 μm

D View of luminal aspect of corrosion microvascular cast of gastric corpus mucosa of rat treated with intragastric 1 ml absolute ethanol 10 min prior to casting. An area of intact subepithelial microvasculature (S) borders an area of deep damage to mucosal microvessels (D). In the damaged area, mucosal venules (arrows) have been filled retrogradely. Compare with Fig. 10.13. Bar = 250 μm (Reproduced from reference no. 118 by permission of the American Journal of Medicine)

Another related phenomenon is that of adaptive cytoprotection. Application of a non-effective low dose of an agent which is injurious at higher dose will induce a resistance in the gastric mucosa to injury by the higher, usually effective dose.[126] Thus pretreatment with 20% ETOH will protect the rat gastric mucosa against damage by 100% ETOH. This 'adaptive cytoprotection' is not agent-specific, and so subthreshold treatment with one damaging agent will protect against potentially damaging doses of other agents.[127] The effect appears to be largely due to the induction of an increase in endogenous PGE production within the gastric mucosa, which promotes mucosal blood flow, and presumably also exerts other cellular effects which stabilize the gastric mucosa in the presence of the applied insult. In this context, the generally claimed digestive benefits of the consumption of wine before and/or with meals could perhaps represent the unwitting initiation of adaptive cytoprotection of the gastric and perhaps duodeno-intestinal mucosa by the mild alcohol dose, to ameliorate possible mucosal injury from mucosal irritants in the food.

While the precise effects of both the direct PGE administration and of stimulation of endogenous PG production in adaptive cytoprotection remain to be elucidated, one consistent observation is that the most luminal lamina propria becomes oedematous (Fig. 10.21).[118,119] However, there is little or no plasma protein in this interstitial fluid; this may indicate that there is a rise in intramucosal venular pressure in response to local PGE, and that a low protein transudate is formed at the venous ends of the mucosal capillaries and at the postcapillary venules by the altered Starling forces there. It is relevant that there are no mucosal lymphatics at this superficial level of the gastric mucosa (see below). The mechanism of cytoprotection may in part involve a dilution of the injurious agent in the interstitium of the lamina propria, after it has crossed the surface epithelial layer, by this accumulated interstitial fluid. Alternatively or additionally, if this interstitial fluid is turning over quickly and percolating through tissue spaces, e.g. to the lymphatics at the muscularis mucosae level, this may flush any injurious agent away from the mucosa, and thereby prevent its accumulation to cytotoxic levels within the mucosa.[119]

The recurrence of 'healed' gastric ulcers at the same site is a well-established phenomonon.[128] The sites of grossly healed previous corpus ulcers remain histologically abnormal, with dilated glands and an abnormally low number of parietal cells;[129] this low parietal cell number would prevent the local intramucosal HCO_3– translocation from occurring at these sites, and may explain the susceptibility of previous ulcer sites to re-ulceration. Thus, gross re-epithelialization is not an adequate endpoint for ulcer healing, and the 'Quality of ulcer healing' may determine the susceptibility of the site to re-ulceration.[130]

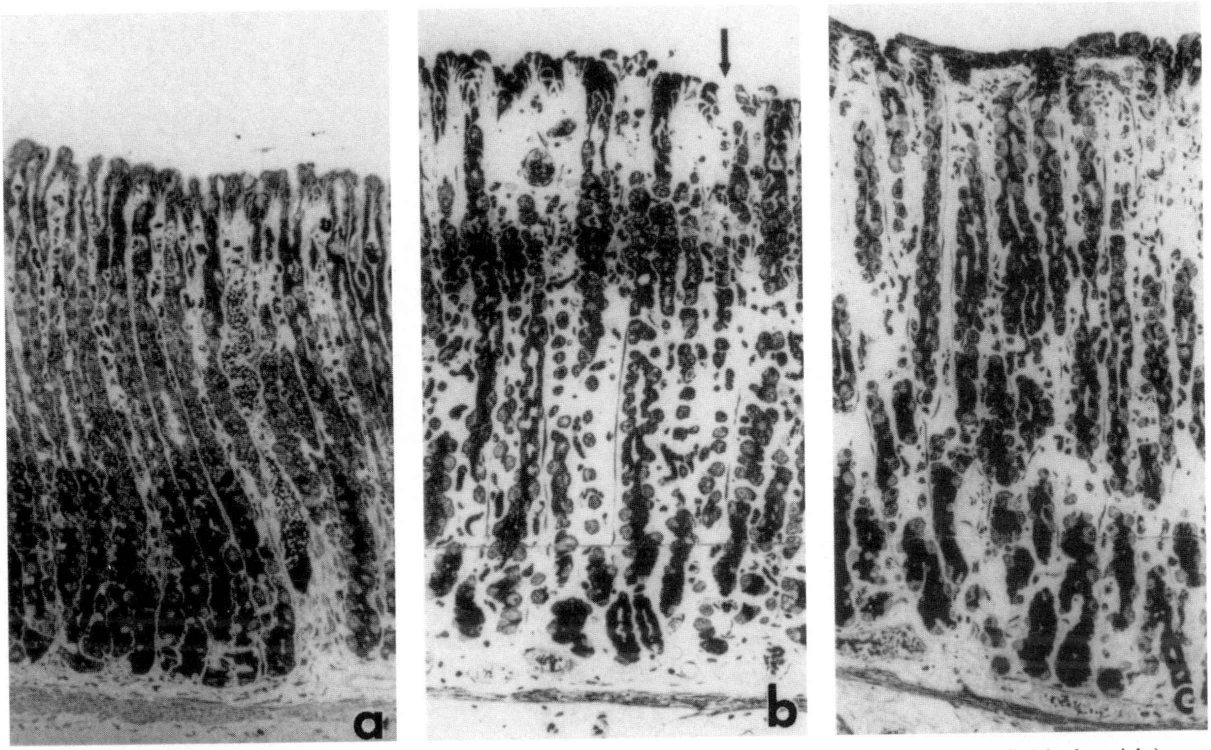

Fig. 10.21 Light micrographs of rat fundic mucosa fixed 30 min after instillation of (**A**) buffer; (**B**) misoprostol (1 mg/kg) body weight); (**C**) cimetidine (1 mg/kg body weight). Control tissue (**A**) had normal appearance. Misoprostol (**B**) caused swelling of the interstitium; surface epithelium has dilated intercellular spaces or frank discontinuities (arrow). Cimetidine (**C**) caused flattening of the surface epithelium but swelling of the interstitium. (×131) (Reproduced from reference no. 119)

Lymphatics of the stomach

Intramural lymphatics

The lymphatics of the mucosal lamina propria begin as blind-ending lymph capillaries called initial lymphatics lying between the bases of the gastric glands, and are found only in the deepest levels of the lamina propria,[63,89,131] throughout the fundus, pylorus and antrum.[132] These initial vessels pass to a polygonal network of lymph channels termed collecting lymphatics, which lie between the muscularis mucosae and the bases of the gastric glands (Fig. 10.22B). In the rat, this network is comprised of a single layer of 15–60 μm diameter vessels; individual vessel lengths between nodes of the plexus are approximately 150 μm. This plexus drains to a larger submucosal lymphatic plexus (Fig. 10.22A,C) via perpendicular or oblique vessels which perforate the muscularis mucosae.

The submucosal lymphatic plexus connects to a subserosal lymph plexus by perforating branches which pass through the muscularis externa (Fig. 10.22D) and which

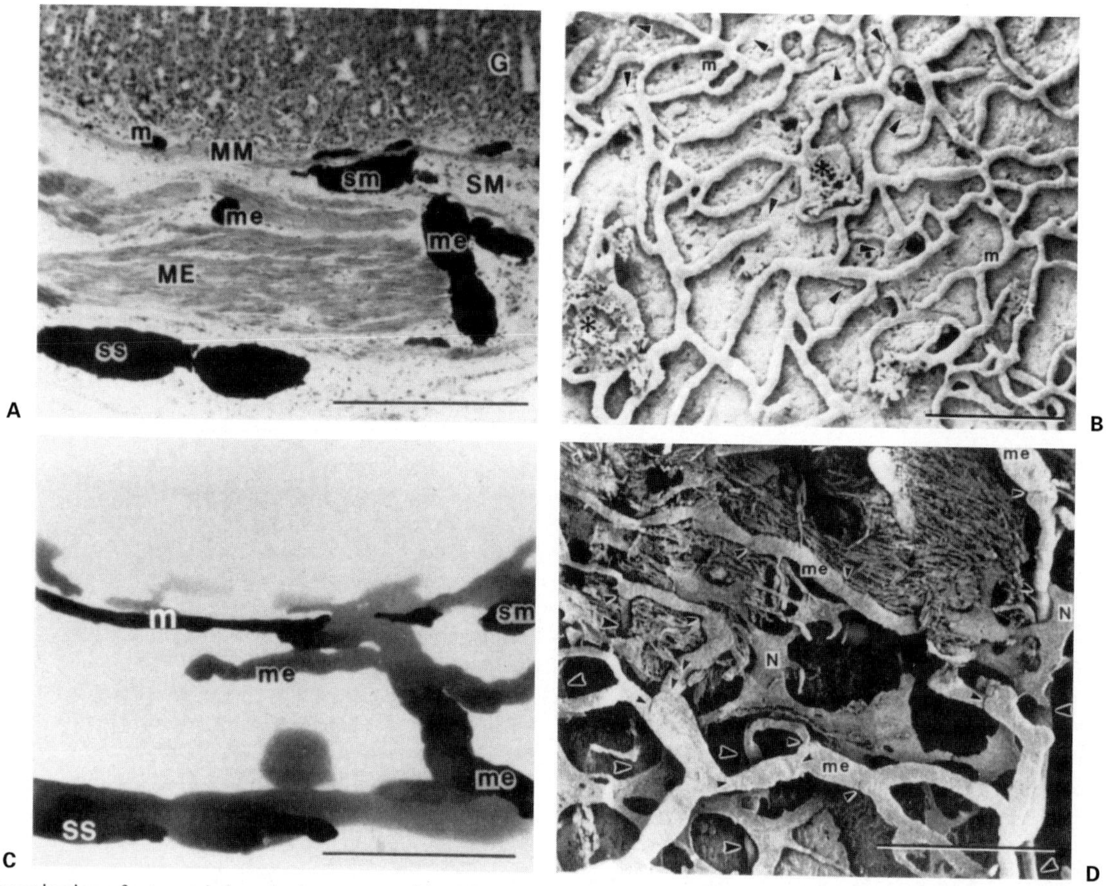

Fig. 10.22 Organization of rat gastric lymphatic system and its relationship to other tissue elements revealed by light and scanning electron microscopy.

A,B A representation of serial sections (H&E stained, the lymphatics being injected with India ink) which are reconstructed in **B**. G = gastric gland; MM = muscularis mucosae; SM = submucosa; ME = muscularis externa;
SS = subserosa; m, sm, me, ss = lymphatics in the mucosa, submucosa, muscularis externa and subserosa respectively. Bar = 250μm

C Scanning electron micrograph of corrosion cast showing a lymphatic network (m) in the base of the gastric mucosa. The network consists of meshes of various sizes, and some blind-ended lymphatics. The network is collected into slightly thicker lymphatics (arrowheads) which pierce the muscularis mucosae to reach the submucosal lymphatics. The cast with scrambled egg-like appearance, which forms the background of this micrograph, replicates the interstitial spaces of the submucosa. * = Cast of the interstitial spaces in the base of the mucosa. Bar = 250μm

D Scanning electron micrograph of corrosion cast of lymphatics (me in the muscularis externa. The lymphatics (large arrowheads) in the inner layer of the muscularis externa lead into those in the superficial layer. Here they form a network which is gradually collected into thicker lymphatics. Note the notches (small arrowheads) indicative of valve locations. In the upper half, the slender tubular structures represent the interstitial spaces of the superficial layer of the muscularis externa, while in the lower half there are scrambled egg-like structures which are replicated interstitial spaces of the submucosa. A network composed of flat tubular casts (N) probably represents the myenteric nervous plexus. Bar = 250 μm (Reproduced from reference no. 63) also collect the lymph drainage of the muscularis externa. Intramuscular lymphatics begin as blind-ending initial lymphatics or lymph capillaries which lie between and parallel to muscle bundles of the muscularis externa (Fig. 10.23). The larger collecting lymphatic vessels in the submucosal and subserosal lymph plexuses are valved, while the smaller intramucosal and intramuscular lymphatics are not.

Newer histochemical[90] and immunohistochemical methods[132] allow distinction between blood and lymphatic capillaries at the light microscopic level in the gastric mucosa in routine histological sections, as well as at electron microscopy.[91,92] Ultrastructurally, the lymphatic capillaries are quite distinctive: their outlines are irregular and the lumen contains a fine granular precipitate, but no red cells. The endothelial cell lining is thin (approximately 0.25 μm) and contains no fenestrae, but does show endothelial vesicles and occasional caveolae (Table 10.3). Lymphatic endothelial cell cytoplasm contains foci of 10 nm vimentin filaments and occasional Weibel-Palade bodies. There is no continuous basal lamina, but only scattered pieces associated with fine collagen anchoring filaments. At boundaries of adjacent lymphatic endothelial cells, there are either small gaps between cell processes (0.25 μm) or else extensive overlapping (~5 μm) of thin processes of adjacent cells, without membrane junctions between the two cells. There are no pericytes associated with the lymph capillaries. The lymph capillaries are not situated near the gastric glands, nor are they associated with the blood capillaries.[89]

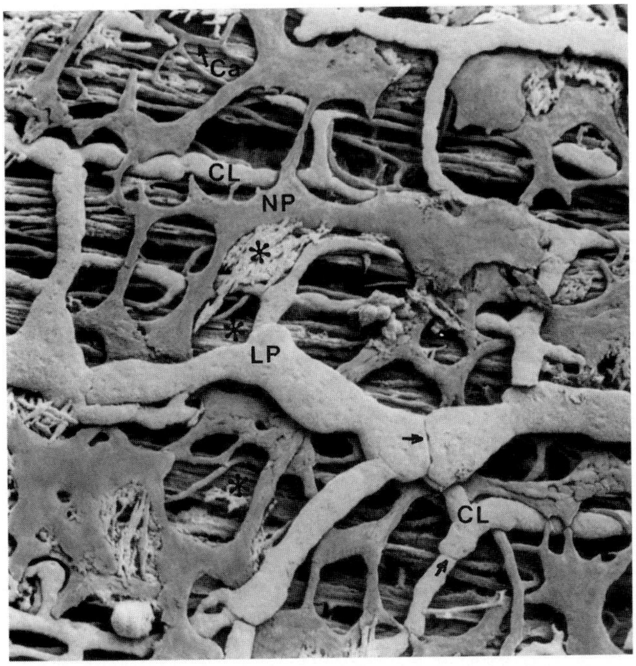

Fig. 10.23 Corrosion lymphatic cast of the intermuscular layer of rat stomach; scanning electron micrograph. Note the cast of the plexus of larger lymphatics (LP) which show valve leaflet (arrows) and endothelial cell impressions; smaller collecting lymphatics (CL) drain initial lymphatics (unlabelled) into the intermuscular lymphatic plexus. The more stellate cast of the network of fluid compartment spaces surrounding the myenteric nerve plexus (NP) underlies the intermuscular lymphatic plexus. Replicated capillaries (Ca) are evident in some places, as are casts of the interstitial space (*). (Reproduced from reference no. 63)

Earlier studies[133] emphasized the extensive nature of the intramucosal lymphatic network, and reported that it extended throughout the lamina propria. However, more recently it has been demonstrated by transmission electron microscopy,[89] scanning electron microscopy,[63] intravital microscopy[131] and histochemical methods[90,91] that lymphatics of the lamina propria do not commence until the most basal level of the gastric glands (Fig. 10.22). While there may be relatively open channels in the interstitium of the more luminal lamina propria to permit drainage of interstitial fluid, it appears that these are not endothelially lined and so could not be termed lymphatics, but might be called tissue channels. Alternatively, it is possible that there is little or no need for lymphatics or tissue channels in the more luminal gastric lamina propria. This may be because of the unique ‘polarization’ of the gastric mucosal microvasculature, so that all the arterial ends of capillaries are at the base of the mucosa, and all venous ends are near the gastric lumen (see Figs 10.16, 10.17B)[28,60] This being the case, transcapillary fluid fluxes out of the gastric microvessels would be restricted to the basal portion of the mucosa, where the arterial ends of the capillaries lie. There may be no need for interstitial drainage in the more luminal mucosa, since Starling forces at the venous ends of the capillaries there would favour fluid absorption back into these capillaries. Nevertheless, it is clear that in atrophic gastritis, in which the overall height of the mucosa is decreased, lymphatic capillaries may be found near the surface epithelium.[132]

The restriction of the lymphatic drainage to the most basal portion of the lamina propria is likely to be of significance in the pattern of spread of gastric carcinoma (Fig. 10.24). An analysis of published work[89] found lymph node metastases reported in almost 17% of more than 1500 patients when the primary gastric tumour had spread as far as the submucosa, but found only 4% in a similar number of patients where the primary tumour was confined to the mucosa itself (Table 10.4). These differences in frequency of metastatic spread were also reflected in differing five-year survival rates between mucosal and submucosal degrees of penetration of the primary tumour (Table 10.5).

An apparently distinct interstitial fluid compartment, which surrounds Auerbach's plexus, is composed of a single layer of cells (Fig. 10.23) which have been variously described as enteroglial, S100 immunopositive or as interstitial cells of Cajal.[63,134,135] The space enclosed by these cells is replicated by interstitial injection of plastic into the muscle layers, and is clearly connected to the muscle

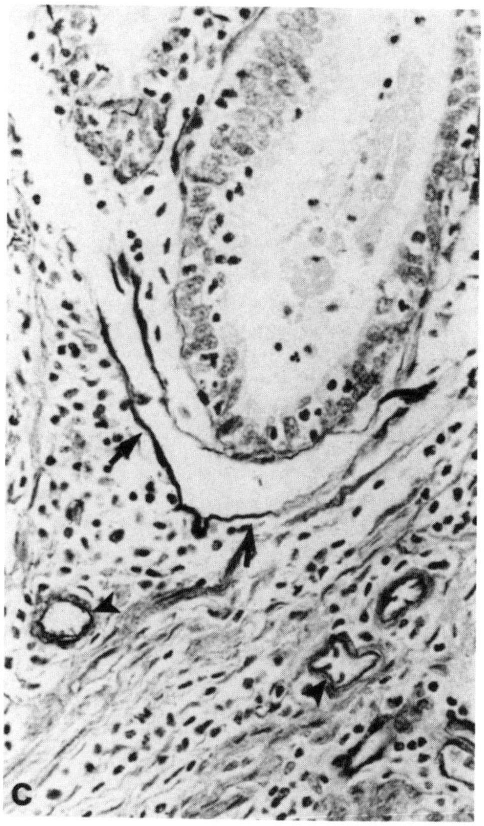

Fig. 10.24 Section of an adenomatous polyp stained with anti-laminin. Base of polyp with open lymphatic vessel (arrow) adjacent to neoplastic gland. Capillaries (arrowheads) have continuous laminin staining. (Methylene blue counterstain, ×27) (Reproduced from reference no. 132)

lymphatics.[63] This separate tissue fluid compartment may control the local neuronal environment, may have a role in local neurotransmitter economy and/or may prevent uncontrolled diffusion of neurally derived substances from the plexus itself to adjacent visceral or vascular smooth muscle cells; the recognition that nitric oxide (NO) is a neurotransmitter in the enteric nervous system, as well as the most significant, if not only, component of endothelially derived relaxing factor (EDRF) derived from vascular and microvascular endothelium, indicates that this compartmentalization of the perineural space from the surrounding interstitial space may be physiologically necessary. Whether this fluid compartment can be appropriately termed lymphatic is doubtful, because the lining cells are clearly different from lymphatic endothelium.

Gastric lymphatic drainage pathways

The lymphatic drainage of the human stomach has been studied by observing the drainage pathway of dyes injected intramurally into the stomachs of cadavers,[134–139] and by intraoperative injection of carbon particle suspensions.[140–142] Apart from separate lymph trunks in the omenta, there are additional networks of lymphatic drainage vessels surrounding the main gastric arterial supply vessels.[52] The stomach wall can be divided into four lymphatic drainage regions.

(a) *Hepatic*. This comprises the antrum and most of the body of the stomach, and drains principally to five small groups of nodes following the gastroduodenal artery (including the right gastroepiploic and pyloric nodes) and

Table 10.4 Depth of invasion and frequency of lymph node metastasis in early gastric cancer, Comparison of a number of published patient series. Data from Lehnert et al[89]

		Depth of tumour infiltration into the gastric wall					
			Mucosa			*Submucosa*	
Author	Year	Patients with metastases	Total no. of patients	Metastatic %	Patients with	Total no. of patients	Metastatic %
Grigoni	1980	0	22	0	4	24	16.7
Steil	1982	0	8	0	1	8	12.5
Sowa	1981	0	88	0	23	174	13.2
Elster	1978	3	199	1.5	4	101	4.0
Meyer	1981	1	51	1.9	10	39	25.6
Georgii	1982	2	108	1.9	14	114	12.3
Abe	1984	1	42	2.4	18	95	19.0
Murakami	1979	2	69	2.9	9	57	15.9
Sakakibara	1976	4	102	3.9	10	104	9.6
Kodama	1981	4	85	4.7	11	80	13.7
Miwa	1972	0	198	5.1	44	196	22.4
Kidokoro	1980	0	184	5.4	34	183	18.6
Sakamoto	1971	2	35	5.7	19	60	31.7
Murakami	1974	3	46	6.5	9	39	24.3
Muhe	1980	3	47	6.5	4	49	8.0
Takagi	1976	11	129	8.5	29	140	20.7
Soga	1979	4	34	11.7	10	46	21.7
Total		60	1447	4.2	253	1509	16.8

Table 10.5 Depth of tumour infiltration into the gastric wall and 5-year survival after early gastric cancer. Comparison of a number of published patient series. Data from Lehnert et al[89]

		Mucosa		*Submucosa*	
Author	Year	No. of patients	5-year survival %	No. of patients	5-year survival %
Kidokoro	1971	173	98	156	93
Takagi	1976	129	94	140	89
Gentsch	1981	54	96	59	79
Fielding	1980	34	71	56	54
Gennari	1981	11	100	23	90
Total		401	91.8	434	81.0

another small group following the right gastric artery (right gastric nodes).

(b) *Splenic*. This includes the fundus of the stomach which drains to pancreaticosplenic nodes along the posterior gastric artery.[52]

(c) *Coronary*. The lesser curve and adjacent mid-anterior and mid-posterior wall region drains to three sets of nodes, a gastropancreatic group, a group on the lesser curvature (left gastric nodes) and a group of parietal and paracardiac nodes. In some cases there are long lymphatic pathways from this region, which reach the liver via the lesser omentum. Other long collecting trunks of the cardiac nodes may turn back from the cardio-oesophageal junction to reach the lymph plexus surrounding the coeliac trunk, and other vessels are directed towards the nodes of the left renal pedicle.[136]

(d) *The common region*. This is drained via several pathways and includes the superior half of the anterior and posterior gastric walls to the right of the incisura, the right two-thirds of the anterior and posterior walls from the incisura to the fundus and a narrow strip of the anterior and posterior gastric walls below the fundus at the level of the cardiac opening, extending from the greater curve towards the cardia for about one-third of the distance from the greater curve.[136]

There is extensive communication between the submucous and subserosal lymphatics of the stomach and those of the oesophagus, and numerous fine connections between the gastric and duodenal lymphatics. Thus nodal metastases from a gastric primary carcinoma might be anticipated as far as deep cervical, bronchial, mediastinal, left renal, coeliac or hepatic nodes, in addition to those draining the stomach itself.[139] However, the main lymphatic drainage of the lower oesophagus passes to both lower mediastinal and upper gastric nodes, while the cardia drains mainly to upper gastric, paracoeliac and para-aortic nodes.[140]

The mechanisms of drainage of interstitial fluid into the gastric initial lymphatics, and the subsequent drainage of the intramural lymphatics into the extramural lymph trunks, probably involves gastric motility and also perhaps arterial pulsation, as in the intestine[180] (see below).

THE SMALL INTESTINE — JEJUNUM AND ILEUM

Extrinsic arterial supply

10–15 jejunal/ileal arterial branches arise from the left side of the superior mesenteric artery, which originates at the abdominal aorta approximately 1–2 cm below the coeliac artery. These arteries branch and anastomose several times en route to the bowel wall, thereby forming arcades. Blood then reaches the intestine by way of short, straight branches — vasa recta. In the upper jejunum there are only one or two arcades and the vasa recta are 3–5 cm long, whereas arcade number increase up to five towards the distal ileum where the vasa recta are short and usually obscured by the fat within the mesentery adjacent to the bowel wall.[146] The final arcade forms a marginal arterial vessel which results in a significant degree of functional anastomosis between duodenum, jejunum, ileum and the adjacent ascending colon (Fig. 10.25).[22,146] Because of the high degree of anastomosis of both arteries and veins, occlusion of one or several is unlikely to compromise functional blood supply to the bowel wall.[143] However, complete experimental obstruction of the cat superior mesenteric artery (SMA) reduces blood flow to the small intestine and the proximal colon by about 60%,[144] and embolization of the SMA in patients usually results in extensive bowel infarction.

Intramural arterial distribution

The vasa recta penetrate the external muscular layers of the bowel wall to reach a profusely anastomotic submucous arterial plexus from which arterioles originate and supply blood to the mucosa, submucosa and muscular layers. The mucosa receives approximately 75% of the flow, with approximately 20% going to the muscularis. Small intestinal blood flow increases by 30–130% after a meal, as does oxygen extraction from the blood; the majority of the increased blood flow goes to the mucosa.

Intestinal microvascular organization

Muscularis

The microvascular supply of the muscularis propria[145] and myenteric plexus is derived from arterial branches from the submucous arterial plexus.[64,145] These vessels branch by four to six orders to supply capillaries lying between, and largely parallel to, smooth muscle cell bundles as in

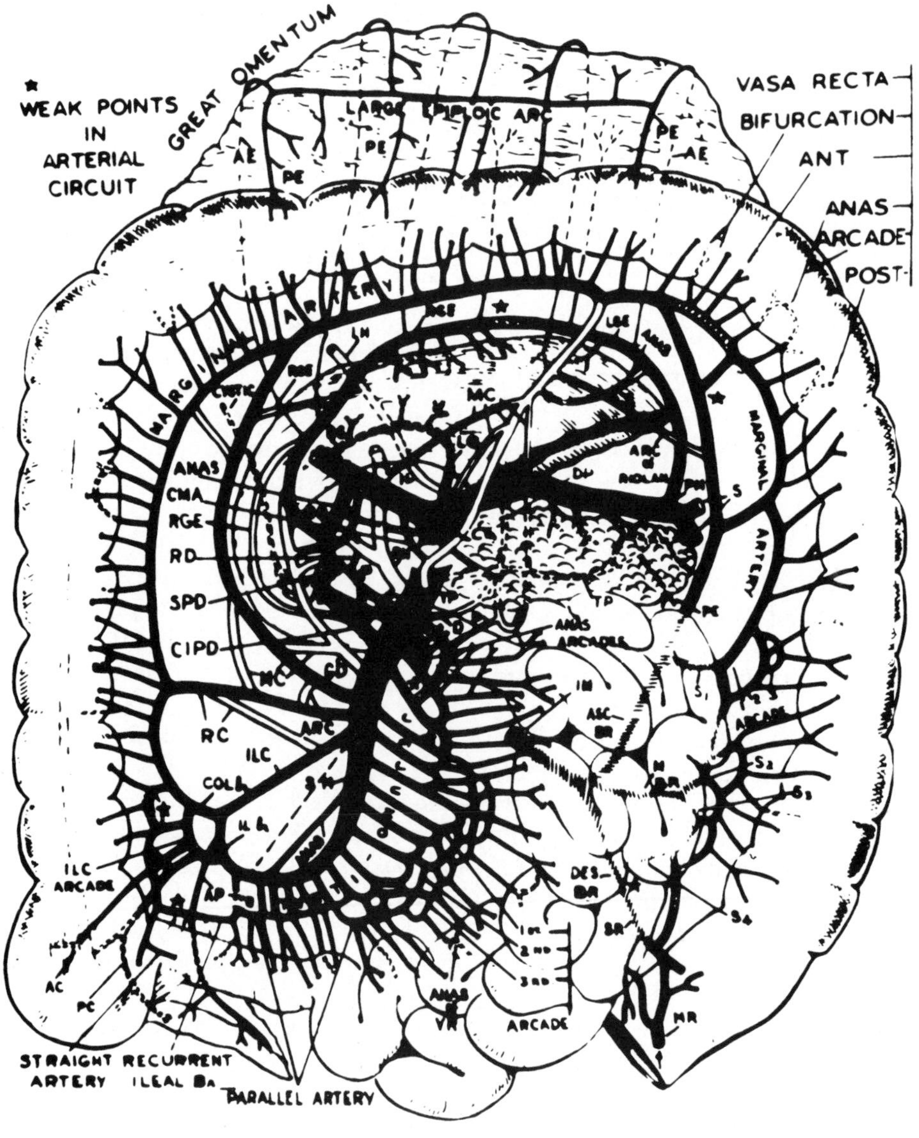

Fig. 10.25 Composite drawing of many possible routes of collateral circulation of the small and large intestines, including critical areas of blood supply and weak points in the arterial circuit. Constant arteries in black, inconstant in white; cross-hatched arteries are critical areas.
Complex of routes involving coeliac and superior mesenteric intercommunications, especially via the gastroduodenal (GD) or right hepatic (RH) artery of superior origin.
Posterior pancreaticoduodenal arcade created by the retroduodenal artery (RD) (i.e., the postero-superior pancreaticoduodenal artery) and its connections with the first and second jejunal arteries.
Relations of superior mesenteric (SM) artery to biliary vascularization, via cystic artery derived from a retroduodenal (RD) artery.
Parallel vessel of Dwight, composed of bases of last jejunal and ileal arcades and continuous from common inferior pancreaticoduodenal artery to marginal artery of Drummond, with which it anastomoses.
Ileocolic arcade, a landmark in 76% of patients.
The marginal artery is continuous from the caecocolic junction to the middle rectal (MR) artery and is sufficient, when not interrupted, to fill all arteries of the descending colon when the inferior mesenteric artery is ligated.
Middle colic (MC) artery, its varied origin from superior mesenteric (SM), coeliac, right hepatic, or gastroduodenal artery of SM origin from the dorsal pancreatic (DP) artery of splenic origin, and from the right and left gastroepiploic arteries.
Epiploic arc, in posterior layer of great omentum, furnishing added blood supply, via posterior epiploics to the transverse colon.
Critical areas (cross-hatched) of tenuous vascularization at the fourth part of the duodenum, via anastomosing arc, at the terminal ileum, via the recurrent ileal branch, at the splenic flexure at Griffith's point in the marginal artery, and at Sudeck's point at the last sigmoid.
Weak points in the arterial circuit are marked by asterisks: 1. between the right gastroepiploic (RGE) and left gastroepiploic (LGE) arteries (10%); 2. between the inferior pancreaticoduodenal (IPD) artery and the first and second jejunal arteries; 3. absence of recurrent ileal artery (61%); 4. absence of caecolic anastomosis (10%); 5. absent (7%) or poor (32%) anastomosis of marginal artery at the splenic flexure; and 6. Sudeck's point between the last sigmoid and the superior rectal. (Reproduced from reference no. 251)

the stomach. Venules of the muscle layers drain to the submucous venous plexus.

There are conflicting accounts as to the presence or absence of a blood/neural plexus barrier in the intestine similar to the blood/brain and blood/nerve barriers. Gershon and Bursztajn[146] reported that macromolecular tracers Evans blue-albumin or horseradish peroxidase (HRP) readily pass from the fenestrated mucosal capillaries to the mucosal and submucosal interstitium. However, neither fluorescent-labelled albumin nor HRP enter the interstitium of the ganglia or the interstitium of the muscle in detectable quantities. In the continuous capillaries of the muscular layers, adjacent endothelial cells are joined by tight junctions, and the small amount of HRP escaping via endothelial vesicles appeared to accumulate in pericytes and tissue macrophages. These findings contrast with those of Jacobs[147] who found no barrier to the passage of intravascular HRP to the interstitium of the muscle layers and the myenteric plexus. Of further interest are the observations in both reports that the intestinal myenteric plexus is devoid of capillaries in mice, guinea-pigs and rats and that the myenteric plexus receives its nutrients from capillaries in the adjacent muscle layers. These findings are, however, at variance with those of Stach and coworkers,[64,148] who found that separate microvascular networks supply the myenteric and submucous neural plexuses in cats; a distinct microcirculatory bed of the myenteric plexus has also been reported in pigeon intestine.[149] It may be that the presence or absence of such a separate capillary supply to the enteric neural plexuses is a function of the size of the ganglia in the plexus, and/or the size of the animal.

Mucosa

Accounts of the microvascular architecture of the mucosa, and especially of the villi, vary considerably,[19,162,163] not only between different species, but for the same species, particularly in the older literature; this probably reflects inadequacies of the techniques previously available. The account below is a synthesis of more recent findings in human and other mammalian small intestine.

The blood supply to the mucosa is by separate arterioles of 12–15 μm luminal diameter which arise from the submucous arterial plexus. A single arteriole will supply either a single villus or a group of crypts of Lieberkuhn.[57,145,150–152] The arterioles to the villi pass without branching in the lamina propria of the villus core

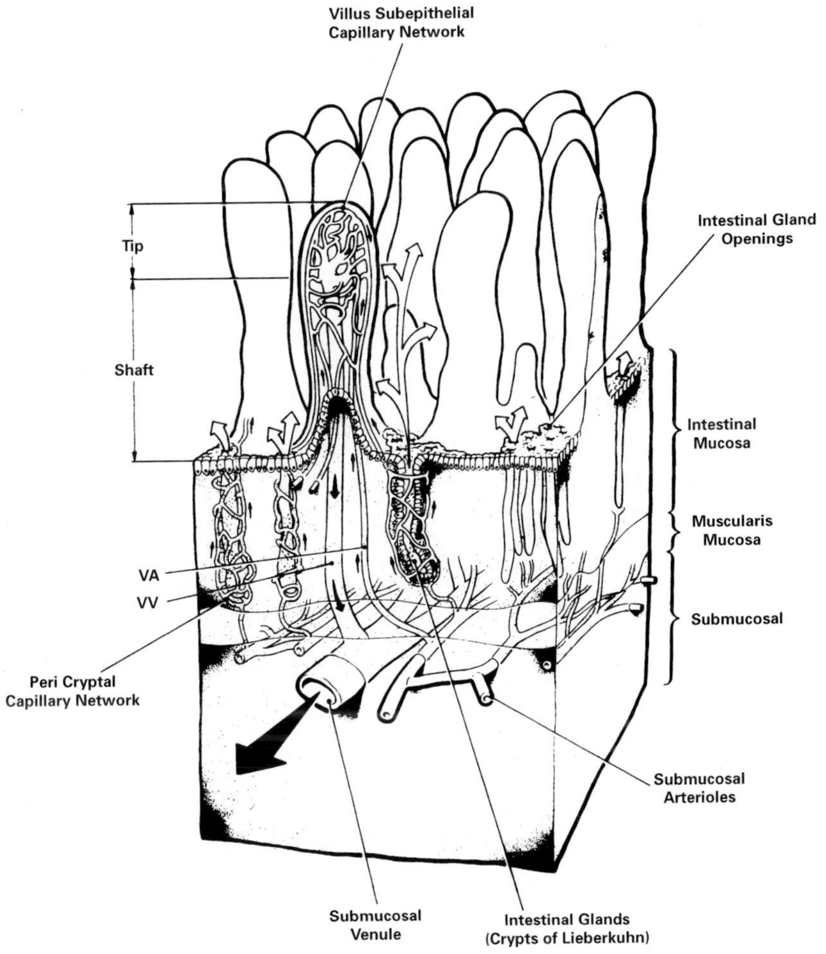

Fig. 10.26 Schematic diagram of the mucosal microcirculation typical of human and rabbit small intestine. VA = villus arteriole; VV = villus venule. Solid arrows indicate direction of blood flow, and open arrows indicate directions of secretion and absorption of intestinal fluid. (Reproduced from reference no. 156 by permission of Raven Press)

to reach the most apical position, usually running to one side of centre. At the villus tip, the arteriole breaks up in a fountain pattern into a leash of capillaries which closely underlie (1–3 μm) the villous epithelial basal lamina. This plexus of capillaries continues down the villus to its base for a distance of approximately 1000 μm and is usually drained by a single venule, which commences high in the villus.[153,155] This venule accepts most of its capillary tributaries at approximately 150 μm after its commencement and virtually no other tributaries in its lower half.[145,156] The subepithelial capillaries of the lower portion of the villus have a lower spatial density than is found at the villus tip region.[157] The capillaries of the lower villus are continuous with the capillary rings surrounding the necks of the intestinal gland. The intestinal glands receive their arterial supply adjacent to the muscularis mucosae and are surrounded by a rich capillary network, which drains to the plexus of capillary rings surrounding their openings between the villi (Fig. 10.26).[145,153] Rabbits (Fig. 10.27A) have a similar mucosal microvascular architecture to humans (Fig. 10.27B); microscopic study of blood flow in vivo in rabbits has shown that blood from the intestinal gland circulation passes to the lower portion of the villus shaft, and then passes up the shaft to drain via the villus venule to the submucous venous plexus.[153] There are no arteriovenous anastomoses in the intestinal mucosa.[154]

In 1941 Florey and coworkers[158] proposed a 'fluid recycling scheme in the intestine, whereby blood effluent from the villi would pass to the pericryptal capillaries, there to supply fluid for secretion of intestinal juice. This secreted fluid would then pass into the small intestinal lumen, wash the partially digested food, and be absorbed at the villous surface, carrying with it any dissolved digestion products by solvent drag (see also reference no. 159). However, recent findings indicate that Florey's 'fluid recycling' model had the direction of blood flow between villus and crypt capillaries erroneously reversed. Nevertheless, the direction of secretory fluid flow and absorption proposed by Florey is entirely compatible with blood supplied first to the crypt capillaries at higher pressure than blood effluent from the pericryptal plexus arriving at the villus shaft, which would also be at an elevated colloid osmotic pressure, i.e. a condition ideally suited for fluid absorption (Fig. 10.26). It is now clearly established that villi are the site of fluid absorption, and crypts the site of fluid secretion.[115,116,160,161]

The pattern of microvessel distribution within the villi, and especially the location of the villus venules, varies markedly in different mammalian species[19,162,163] and may reflect, in part, marked differences in villus shape (Fig. 10.28A,B,C,D). However, the differences may also reflect villus vasculatures adapted for other reasons, e.g. differing diets. It is notable that in the cat villus, the mucosal venules commence at the bases of the villi, and thus there can be no local portal vascular arrangement between the pericryptal plexus and capillaries of the lower villus

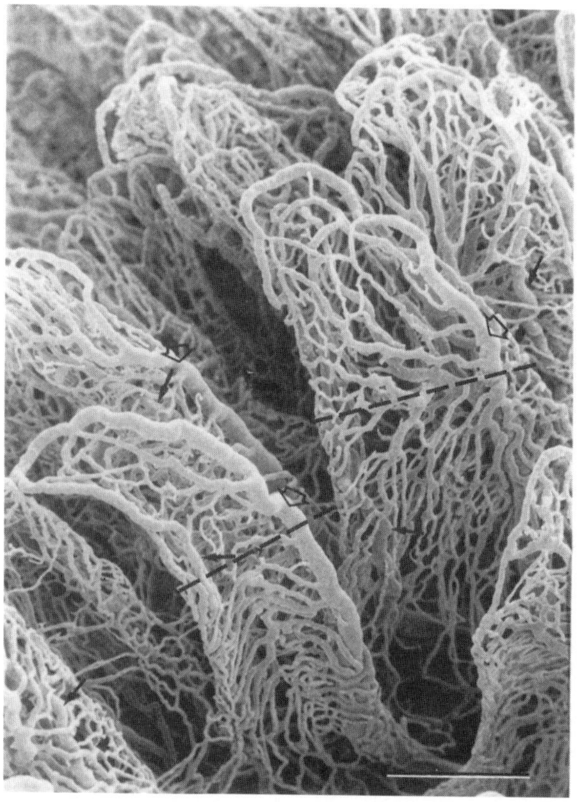
A

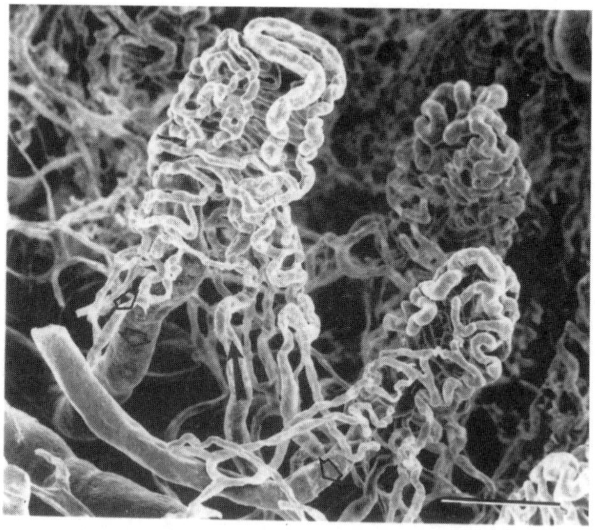
B

Fig. 10.27 Villus microvasculature of rabbit and human small intestine. **A** Corrosion vascular cast of villi of rabbit small intestine. Note arteriole (solid arrow) and laterally-placed venule (open arrow) in each villus. Note also pattern of capillaries converging into the villus venule. Dotted lines indicate presumed boundary between capillaries of 'tip' and 'shaft' region for two villi (see text for significance). Bar = 250 μm **B** Microvascular corrosion casts of human intestinal villi. Note arteriole (solid arrow) and venule (open arrow). Bar = 100 μm (Reproduced from reference no. 156 by permission of Raven Press) shaft in cats, this angio-architecture perhaps reflecting the cat's essentially carnivorous diet. Another unusual feature of the cat villus is the close proximity of the central arteriole and draining capillaries, which are arranged in a countercurrent fashion. This arrangement may result in an impediment to O_2 delivery and both CO_2 and absorbed nutrient clearance at the villus tip in this species, due to passive countercurrent exchange down concentration gradients between afferent arteriolar blood and efferent capillary blood,[164] at least at low flow rates. This countercurrent exchange has been argued as being important in functioning as a countercurrent multiplier to set up a standing solute gradient in the villus to effect water absorption.[165] Given, however, the profound differences in villus size and shape and in mucosal microvascular architecture between cats and humans, it would seem unwise to extrapolate this countercurrent mechanism to human intestine.[166,167]

Nitric oxide synthase (NOS), the enzyme responsible for synthesis of nitric oxide (NO), identified as the major component of endothelially derived (vascular) relaxing factor (EDRF), has been identified at discrete sites in mucosal arteriolar endothelial lining (Fig. 10.29).[168]

Veins of the small intestine

Venous drainage of each of the small intestinal capillary beds passes to the submucous venous plexus, which anastomose both longitudinally and circumferentially in the bowel wall. This plexus is drained by short veins, which penetrate the external muscle layers, chiefly along the mesenteric margin of the intestine, and then pass to branches of the superior mesenteric vein in the mesentery. Within the mesentery, there are extensive anastomoses between adjacent veins, which gradually coalesce to form the superior mesenteric vein. The venous branching pattern largely parallels that of the arterial supply. The superior mesenteric vein receives venous drainage of the distal duodenum, the jejunum, ileum, appendix and caecum, the ascending and transverse colon, and a right gastroepiploic vein draining the stomach, before joining the splenic vein to form the hepatic portal vein. The latter vessel courses to the liver in the free edge of the lesser omentum, and divides within the liver to supply blood to the sinusoids, the principal microvascular bed of the liver.[22,50,53]

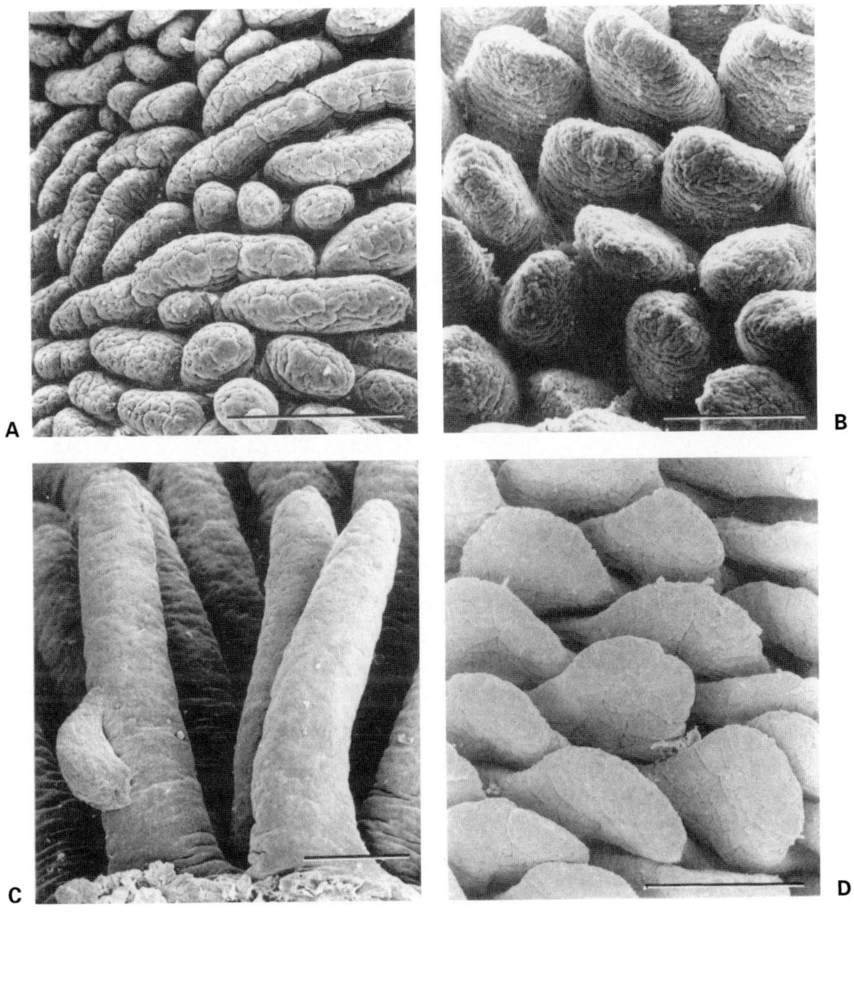

Fig. 10.28 Scanning electron micrographs of villi of critical-point dried small intestine from several species. **A** Human villi. Note variety of villus shapes; luminal view. Bar = 500 µm **B** Dog villi. Note stout cylindrical shape; luminal view. Bar = 250 µm **C** Cat villi. Note slender finger-like shape; lateral view. Bar = 100 µm **D** Rat villi. Note flattened leaf-like shape; oblique view. Bar = 250 µm (Reproduced from reference no. 156 by permission of Raven Press)

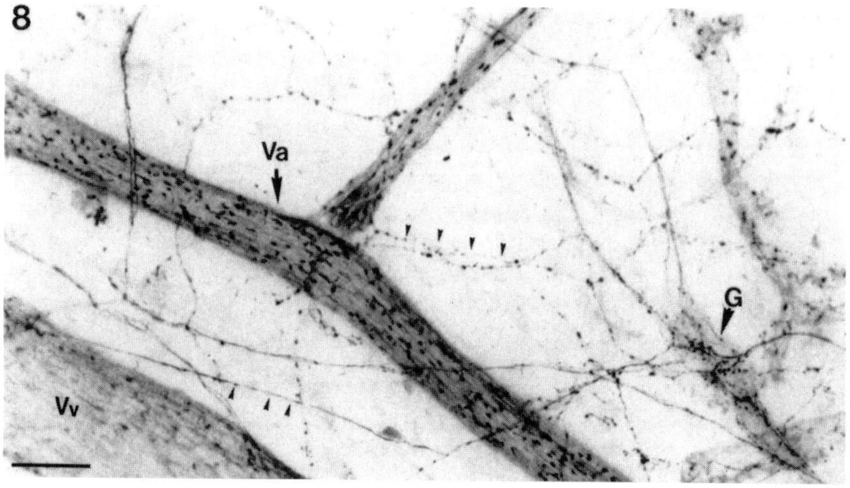

Fig. 10.29 Light microscopic micrograph of submucosa of guinea-pig proximal jejunum treated for histochemical localization of NO synthase-related diaphorase activity. Intensely-stained varicose unmyelinated nerve fibres in nerve bundles of Henle's plexus are seen, including a ganglion (G). Arterioles (Va) but not venules (Vv) of the submucosal vascular plexuses exhibit intensely-stained punctate deposits. Bar = 100 µm (Reproduced from reference no. 168)

Lymphatics of the small intestine

Study of the lymphatic system began with the discovery, by Aselli in 1662,[169] of the chyliferous ducts in the mesentery in the carcass of a recently fed dog. Within each villus of the small intestine lie one or more blind-ending lymphatic channels, approximately 500 µm in length and 60–120 µm in diameter.[150,170–176] Throughout cat and dog intestine (Fig. 10.30C,D), and in the lower rabbit ileum, there is usually only one lacteal per villus (Fig. 10.30B), but higher in the rabbit intestine there may be up to five lacteals in the broader villi[170] and these multiple lacteals join to form a single channel at the villus base. This lymphatic channel has a reduced diameter of 15–30 µm as it passes from the villus base to the submucosal lymph plexus. In rats, there are 1–3 lacteals per villus in the upper jejunum, but up to 5–10 in each of the broader villous ridges of the lower ileum (Figs 10.30A, 10.31A,B,C). Such multiple lacteals are arranged in a palisade pattern with some cross-connection between adjacent lacteals. The lacteals fuse together at the level of the villus base to form a wide, flat sinus.[170,173,174] From the base of this sinus, 2–3 draining lymphatics pass perpendicularly or obliquely though the crypt layer and muscularis mucosae to reach the submucosal lymphatic plexus (Fig. 10.15A,B,C). There is evidence of separate initial lymphatics surrounding the intestinal glands[171] which may drain hormones produced by epithelial cells of the glands. Molecules identified as involved in endothelial–leucocyte attachment and adhesion have been identified expressed on the endothelial cell luminal surface of the normal bowel microvessels;[172] these molecules include ICAM-1, VCAM-1, E-and P-selectins (Table 10.6); expression of these molecules is enhanced in inflammatory bowel lesions (Table 10.6).

The submucous lymphatic plexus is composed of large collecting lymphatic vessels of 150–200 µm diameter, which usually run in pairs over straight courses of 1–2 µmm between nodes. Within the meshes of this plexus of larger lymphatics, there is a fine plexus of lymphatic vessels of approximately 50 µm diameter.[170,173] There is no evidence of valves in the initial lymphatics, since the lacteal(s) of one villus freely interconnect(s) with those of adjacent villi in rats and rabbits.[170–176] There are valves in the submucous collecting lymphatic plexus of rats, rabbits and larger mammals.[170,173,176] Some submucosal lymphatics are spontaneously cyclicly contractile;[176,177] there is recent evidence that the lymphatic endothelium can release nitric oxide on pharmacological stimulation, which can cause dilation of local arterioles.[177]

The larger submucosal lymphatic vessels lie in close proximity to arterioles in rabbits and larger animals, where paired lymphatics share a common connective tissue sheath with the submucosal arteries.[173] Arterial pulsation and/or slow arterial diameter variation (vasomotion) may, by periodic segmental compression of the adjacent conducting lymphatics, aid in propulsion of lymph in these valved lymph vessels (Fig. 10.32). A similar arrangement is found in skeletal muscle, where it is considered important in harnessing arterial pulsation and/or vasomotion in lymph propulsion in conducting lymphatics.[178,179] Submucous lymphatic vessel association with submucosal arteries is normally seen in rabbits[173] whereas these lymphatics are not vessel associated in rats, but are closely associated with the muscularis mucosa.[173,174]

Of course, these mechanisms do not explain how lymph gets from the interstitial compartment into the initial lymphatics in the first place. Contraction of villous lacteals is seldom observed, except in cats and dogs.[176] In skeletal muscle, the initial lymphatics are non-contractile, and so periodic muscle contraction is considered essential to induce tissue fluid flow into these initial lymphatics.[179] Elevations in lymphatic pressure in the submucous lym-

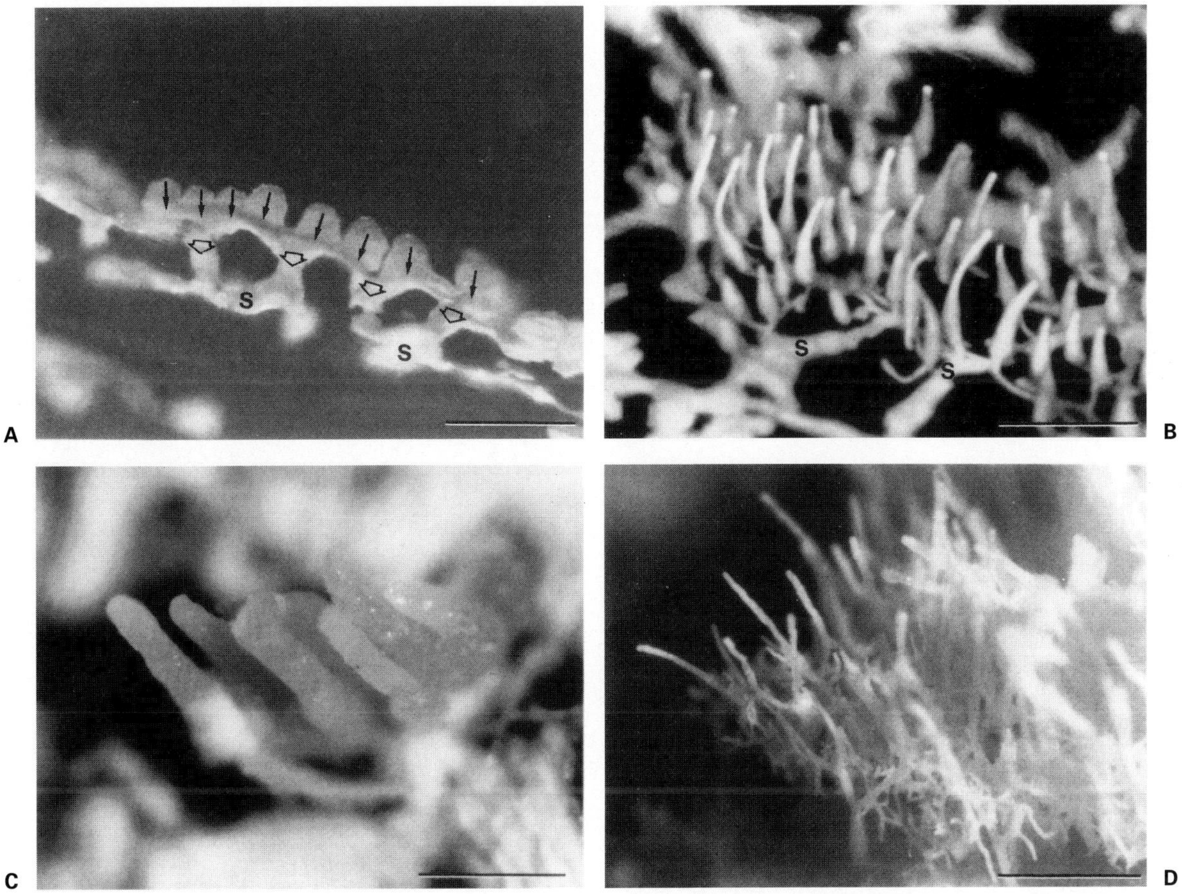

Fig. 10.30 Micrographs of villus lacteals of rat, rabbit, dog and cat small intestine. Casts of rat (**A**) and rabbit (**B**) made by injection of microfil into a single villus lacteal. Casts of dog (**C**) and cat (**D**) lacteals made by injection of Mercox plastic interstitially into the submucosa. **A** Note seven lacteals in two rat villi. The lacteals of each villus are fused together to form a larger lymphatic sinus (solid arrows) at the villus base. Note larger lymphatic drainage vessels (open arrows), connecting villus lymphatic sinuses to submucosal lymphatics (s). **B** Rabbit villi each contain a single cylindrical lacteal which connects to the submucosal lymphatic plexus (s). **C,D** Single lacteals in each villus of dog are cylindrical and stout, whereas in cat (**D**) they are cylindrical and slender. Bars = 500 μm (Reproduced from reference no. 176 by permission of the American Journal of Physiology)

phatic network coincide with local bowel motility[176,181] and intralymphatic pressures reflect bowel lumen distending pressure, which suggests that local bowel muscle motility is a major mechanism of inducing at least clearance of initial lymphatic content centrally (see also reference no. 180). Whether it is contraction of the external muscle coats or of the muscularis mucosa which is effective in filling/clearing intramucosal lymphatics is uncertain; alternatively, contraction of the villus myofibroblast layer which underlies the villus epithelium[204,181] may ensure interstitial fluid mobilization and/or clearance of mucosal lymphatics.

The intestinal submucous lymphatic plexus drains to a subserosal lymphatic plexus via penetrating lymphatics, which do not connect with the intramuscular lymphatic network en route (Fig. 10.33).[176]

The intramuscular network of initial lymphatics is drained by separate channels to the subserosal lymph plexus. The subserosal plexus drains to the large conducting lymphatics within the mesentery, the chyliferous ducts of up to 1 mm in diameter, which converge on lymph nodes at the root of the mesentery. These chyliferous ducts or conducting lymphatics are extensively valved and can be considered to be composed of a series of units termed lymphangions, each comprised of a tubular vessel segment approximately 600–800 μm long by 60–100 μm diameter plus the associated outflow valve pair. Most lymphangions exhibit individual spontaneous contractions at about 10 cycles per minute; individual contractile cycles may propagate to the adjacent lymphangion in about 80% of instances, propagation being retrograde in about half the instances and orthograde in the rest.[180] Additional blind-ending lymph capillaries arise within the mesentery itself, and drain via collecting vessels to the main collecting lymph trunks. Unlike the clear lymph elsewhere, during absorption of fat mesenteric lymph draining from the intestine (but not from the mesentery itself) is milky white, due to suspended chylomicra (typically 0.2–0.3 μm in diameter).[169,182]

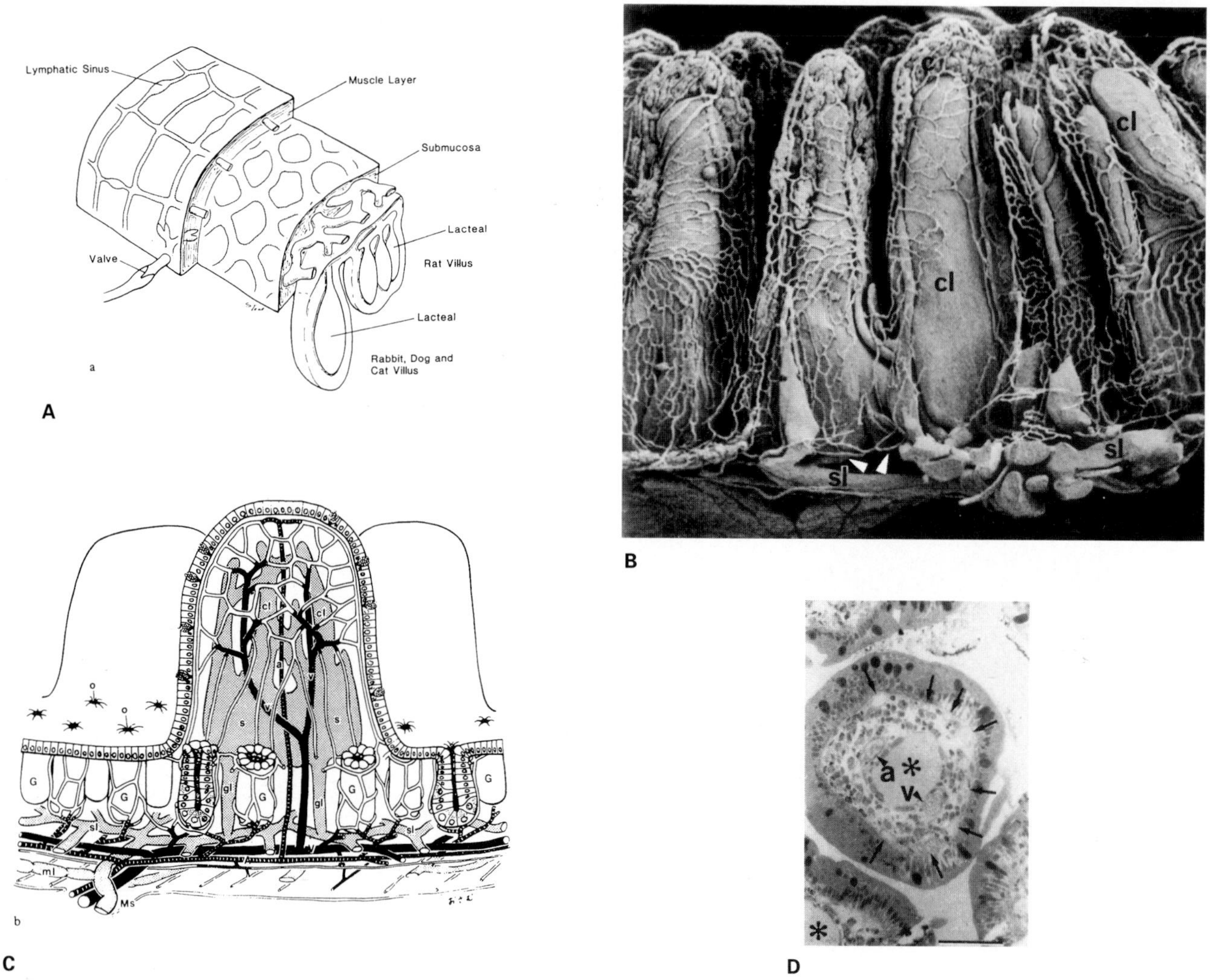

Fig. 10.31 **A** Schematic of basic anatomical features of lymphatics of intestinal mucosa, submucosa and external muscular layers. The villus with a single lacteal is characteristic of dogs, cats and rabbits, and the villus with multiple lacteals is characteristic of rats. Villus lacteals connect with the submucosal lymphatics. Muscle layer lymphatics do not connect directly with submucosal lymphatics, but join with larger collecting lymphatics near the mesenteric border. Muscle layer lymphatics of dogs and cats are much more extensive than is illustrated in this diagram. **B** Scanning electron micrograph of a lymphatic/blood vascular corrosion cast of rabbit jejunum. The villous subepithelial capillary networks (c) each surround 1–3 (interconnected) central lacteals (cl). The central lacteals are connected at their base to thin lymphatics which connect to the submucosal lymphatic plexus (sl). Some leaked resin between the capillaries and the lymphatics has possibly filled tissue channels. (×40) **C** Schematic representation of relationship of lymphatic vessels and blood vessels in rat intestinal mucosa around a single villus. Cl = central lymphatics; S = villus lymphatic sinus; gl = interglandular lymphatics; sl = submucosal lymphatic plexus; ml = muscle layer lymphatics; ms = mesentery; v = villus venule; A = submucosal artery; g = intestinal gland; o = intestinal gland (crypt) opening. **D** Transverse section of a single dog villus at mid-shaft. Note central lacteal (*), arteriole (a), venule (v) and subepithelial capillaries (arrows). Bar = 100 μm (Fig. 10.31A) reproduced from reference no. 176 by permission of the American Journal of Physiology; Fig. 10.31B reproduced from reference no. 170; Fig 10.31C reproduced from reference. 173 by permission of Cell and Tissue Research; Fig. 10.31D reproduced from reference no. 156 by permission of Raven Press)

Table 10.6 Cell adhesion molecule expression in inflammatory bowel disease (IBD)

	Normal mucosa	IBD mucosa (active)	IBD (ulcer base)	Lymph node
ICAM-1	EC (cap)	EC↑, Ly↑, PC↑, Mø↑, IDC	EC↑ (venules), Ly↑, PC↑, Mø↑, IDC	FDC, IDC, HEV
LFA-1	Ly (rare)	Ly↑, PC↑, PMN (rare)	Ly↑, PC↑, PMN (rare)	Ly (germinal centre and T-zone)
VCAM-1	(–)	FDC	FDC, FB	FDC, IDC (rare)
	**	*	EC (venules, rare)	
VLA-4	Ly	Ly↑	Ly↑	Ly (B-zone)
E-selection (ELAM-1)	EC (rare)	EC↑ (venules)	EC↑ (venules)	HEV, FDC (rare)
P-selection (GMP 140)	EC (rare)	EC↑ (venules)	EC↑ (venules)	HEV

Abbreviations: EC = endothelial cell; Ly = lymphocyte; PC = plasma cell; FDC = follicular dendritic cell; IDC = interdigitating cell; M = macrophage; HEV = high endothelial venule; PMN = polymorphonuclear leukocyte; FB = fibroblast; *, ** = EC of venules and arterioles in submucosa were sporadically positive for VCAM-1 both in the normal tissue and IBD; ↑ = the number of positive cells remarkably increased cf. those in the normal tissue. Data from Nakamura et al,[172] and reproduced by permission of The United States and Canadian Academy of Pathologists, Inc.

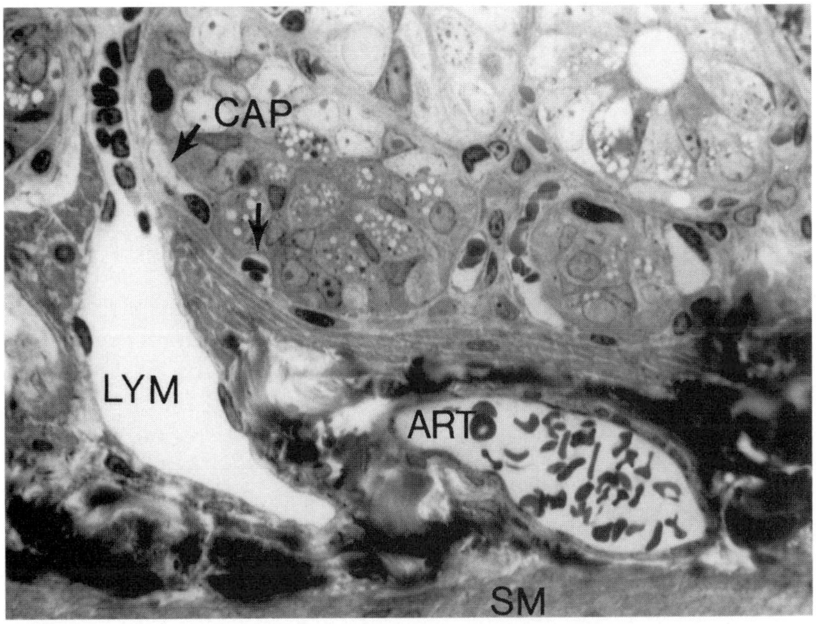

Fig. 10.32 Light micrograph of rat small intestine, fixed uncontracted, illustrating submucosal arteriole (ART) and adjacent lymphatic (LYM) profiles. The arteriole has a single smooth muscle coat, but the lymphatic lacks a muscular coat; note open lymphatic channel. (Reproduced from reference no. 180)

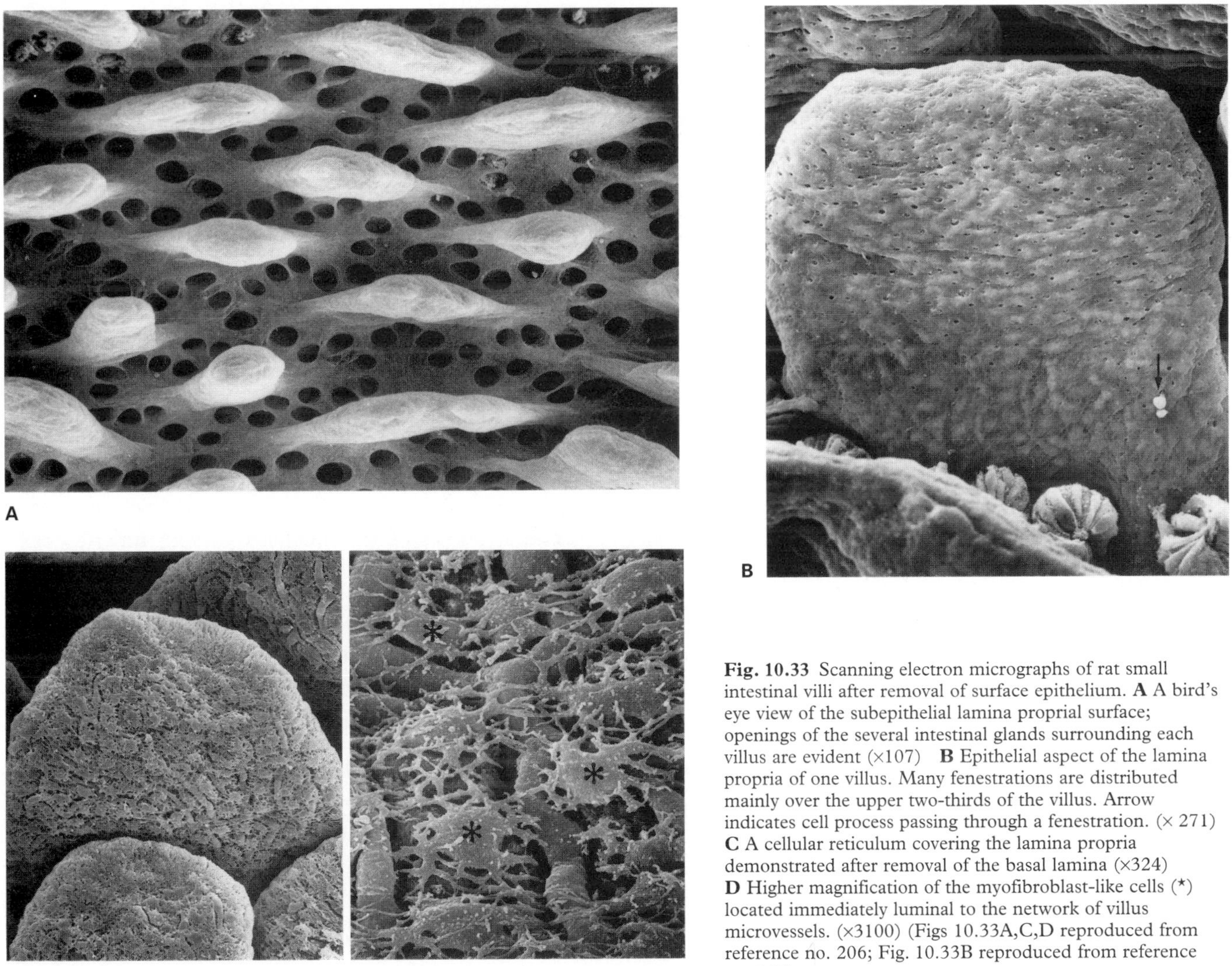

Fig. 10.33 Scanning electron micrographs of rat small intestinal villi after removal of surface epithelium. **A** A bird's eye view of the subepithelial lamina proprial surface; openings of the several intestinal glands surrounding each villus are evident (×107) **B** Epithelial aspect of the lamina propria of one villus. Many fenestrations are distributed mainly over the upper two-thirds of the villus. Arrow indicates cell process passing through a fenestration. (× 271) **C** A cellular reticulum covering the lamina propria demonstrated after removal of the basal lamina (×324) **D** Higher magnification of the myofibroblast-like cells (*) located immediately luminal to the network of villus microvessels. (×3100) (Figs 10.33A,C,D reproduced from reference no. 206; Fig. 10.33B reproduced from reference no. 207)

The lymph trunks of the small intestine converge on a superior mesenteric group of pre-aortic lymph nodes within and at the base of the mesentery. From there, lymph passes to the cisterna chyli, a lymph sac situated retroperitoneally just behind the aorta and immediately below the diaphragm, from which the thoracic duct arises.

Patency of intestinal lymphatics is clearly important for normal intestinal function, and there are generally enough anastomoses to obviate lymphoedema following gut surgery. When there is significant lymphatic obstruction, however, oedema of all gut layers may develop and this can lead to chylous ascites or anastomotic leakage and peritonitis, with a propensity for wound dehiscence.[183] Following mobilization and autologous transplantation of a bowel loop involving severing of lymphatic drainage pathways, lymphatic pathway regeneration and normal lymphatic drainage is not fully re-established until 14 days postoperatively, in rats.[184]

In experimental lymphostasis, after ligation of the mesenteric lymphatics and sclerosing injection mesenteric lymph nodes, severe oedematous swelling occurs in all layers of the intestinal wall.[185,186] There is an albumin transudation and a protein-losing diarrhoea, with mucosal inflammation and ulceration. Oedema of the muscular layers also occurs. Equivalent states occur in patients with a variety of diseases which result in substantial blockage of mesenteric lymphatics. Such conditions include congenital lymphatic malformation, Crohn's disease,[187] malignancy, schistosomiasis and strongyloidiasis. Lymphostasis is a common finding in Whipple's disease, and may be a late complication of radiation enteritis.[185]

Microvessel ultrastructure

The microvessels of the intestine are similar in ultrastructure to those of the stomach (Table 10.2). Capillaries of the external muscular layers are continuous and non-fenestrated. The fenestrae of the mucosal capillaries have a mean radius of 27 nm and their large numbers result in a hydraulic conductivity about 20 times larger than that found in continuous capillaries of skeletal muscle and the muscular layers of the bowel.[165,188]

The spatial frequency of fenestrated mucosal capillaries is highest around the intestinal crypts and at the villus tips, and lowest in the lower portion of the villus shaft. The number of fenestrae of the capillary endothelium is also higher at the villus tip than at the villus base, at least in cats[189] which, given known capillary flow directions in cat villi, means that the fenestral frequency is higher at the arterial end of villous capillaries than at the venous end. This is contrary to conventional opinion since the fenestral frequency, and therefore permeability, is normally considered to be higher at the venous end of a capillary than at its arterial end. The macromolecular permeability of capillary fenestrae of the villus tip, villus shaft and pericryptal regions are equivalent for smaller tracers such as horseradish peroxidase (3.0 nm radius) and haemoglobin (3.2 nm radius). However, there is differential permeability to slightly larger tracers such as catalase (5.2 nm radius) and ferritin (6.1 nm radius), which do not pass through the large number of fenestrae of the villus tip capillaries, but which readily pass the fenestrae of the pericryptal capillaries and also the less frequent fenestrae of the villus shaft capillaries.[157] Intestinal capillaries all have a low permeability to glycogen (15 nm radius). The reason for this differential fenestral macromolecular permeability is presumably structural, but remains unknown.

Ohtani and Ohtsuka[170] observed large interstitial spaces in the lamina propria of the villus tip region, which appeared to extend between the epithelial basal lamina and capillary layer to clefts in the endothelium near the tip of the adjacent villus lacteal. The capillaries of the mucosa contain large numbers of fenestrae and have typical endothelial vesicles. However, the number of vesicles is only 10–20% of the number found in skeletal muscle.[190] Therefore the large numbers of fenestrae in the arterial ends of the capillaries may be important in producing a substantial microvascular transudate and interstitial fluid flux within the villus tip. This flow would wash the contents of the villus tip interstitium to the lacteal, carrying with it salts, nutrients, water and chylomicra, which appear in the interstitium below the epithelial basal lamina as a result of absorptive activity by the enterocytes of the villous surface.[191] It is pertinent that, at low distending pressures of the bowel lumen, absorption is mainly confined to the tip region of the villi, since the sides of the tightly packed villi are not effectively exposed to gut luminal contents.[192] Studies of the separate effects of bowel distension and of stirring of the luminal contents indicate that the principal site of facilitated transport mediated absorption (e.g. of glucose, alanine) is at the villus tip,[192] a conclusion supported by ultrastructural studies; passive absorption (e.g. of water and urea) mainly occurs on the sides of the villi.[192]

The arterioles of rat villi have smooth muscle proximally, but become devoid of smooth muscle within the villus proper.[193] They are surrounded by occasional pericytes and the endothelial cells also show actin microfilaments, which may be responsible for control of the villus arterial supply vessel.[194] In humans, rabbits and dogs, arterial smooth muscle continues up the villus arteriole to its branching at or near the villus tip. The villus venules are lined by continuous endothelium and are surrounded by pericytes distally, which also contain actin. More proximally, smooth muscle surrounds the villus venules.[193] Pericytes are not found around the intramural lymphatic vessels.[174]

In mucosa associated with Peyer's patches (see below), but not elsewhere, high endothelial venules similar to those found in lymph nodes are seen. These are thought to be the site of transendothelial migration of lymphocytes.[195] The route of turnover of the remainder of the lamina propria lymphocytes must be via unspecialized mucosal microvessels and lymphatics.

The lymphatic lacteal is comprised of a thin endothelial lining which contains endothelial vesicles but no fenestrae and is surrounded by a discontinuous basal lamina. There are gaps or overlaps between adjacent lymphatic endothelial cells, and chylomicra are known to be able to pass easily through these intercellular 'junctions'.[197,199] Within the lacteal, there are occasional trabeculae formed by endothelial cell protrusions across the lumen, which may serve to prevent both lacteal collapse and over-distension of the vessel. Lymphocytes are quite often found within the lacteal lumen[170,173, 195] and presumably represent lymphocyte traffic between the circulation and the resident lymphocyte population of the lamina propria. Entry of circulating lymphocytes into the lamina propria is via the venular endothelium at the base of the villi; the venous endothelium at this site has a positive staining for MECA-325, a monoclonal antibody specific for high endothelial venules (HEVs) in lymphoid organs.[198] The endothelium of these venules is normally flat, not high, and lymphocyte transmigration is less efficient at these MECA-325 endothelial cells than at HEVs; this endothelium can be induced to increase in thickness to resemble HEVs by local intestinal inflammation.

A variety of disturbances to villus lacteal ultrastructure are observed in a range of diseases, e.g. in areas of bowel affected by Crohn's disease,[187] in which measles virus particles have been identified in mucosal microvessel endothelium (13 of 15 cases), arguably causing foci of granulomatous vasculitis;[200] villus vasculature and presumably also villus lacteals are also disturbed in diabetes,[201] when the individual villi become substantially enlarged: the villus central arteriolar lumen is increased by approximately 50% and the endothelial cells and their basal laminae are thickened, and there are fewer than normal endothelial fenestrae. In coeliac disease in humans,[202] when the villi become entirely atrophic, their contained microvasculature and lacteal must become markedly compressed and/or distorted. Ligation of small bowel lymphatics in newborn mammals produces intestinal lymphatic engorgement, and, when combined with arterial ligation, produces pneumatosis of the bowel wall similar to necrotizing enterocolitis (NEC).[203]

The villi and crypts each possess a plexus of myofibroblast-like cells, which immediately underlie the epithelial basal lamina.[204–206] These cells (Fig. 10.33C,D; see also Fig. 10.45C,D,E) form close associations with the underlying capillary network and may be involved in local control of capillary blood flow. Additionally, or alternatively, these cells might, on coordinated contraction, cause an increase in lamina propria pressure within one villus, and thereby promote fluid flow from the villus interstitium into the lacteal and then on to the submucous lymphatics. Alternatively, their contraction might simply compress the lacteal and thereby clear it by propelling its contained lymph to the submucosal lymphatic plexus. These myofibroblast cells stain for the S100 protein, and may be related to the sheath of satellite cells surrounding the ganglia of Auerbach's plexus.[135]

Ultrastructural studies of the specialized endothelial cells of the high endothelial venules of Peyer's patches[208,209] indicate that their cell processes interweave to produce a multilayered endothelium (See Fig. 10.54). Adjacent endothelial cells are joined by tight junctions near to the luminal surface. Lymphocyte diapedesis is primarily transcellular, rather than intercellular, at least for the most luminal part of their migration.[208] High endothelial cells express luminal marker molecules recognizable by circulating lymphocytes and responsible for lymphocyte homing.[209]

Intestinal microvasculature in mucosal injury

The microvasculature responds to injury of the intestinal wall, and this response may significantly affect or be the predominate overall response of the bowel. A simple example is the effect of tension on experimental surgical anastomoses. Significant levels of longitudinal tension, or of distending pressure, will reduce local wall blood flow in the region of the anastomosis and, if the reduction is sufficient, will lead to ischaemia sufficient to cause local necrosis and anastomotic dehiscence.[210] Intestinal microvasculature varies regionally in sensitivity to applied tension; in jejunum and ileum relatively high tensile loads (8–10 g/mm^2) are required to produce a 20% reduction in local submucosal flow, whereas a similar load will produce a 50% reduction in blood flow adjacent to a colonic anastomosis. This may account, in part, for the clinical observation that colonic anastomoses are more likely to fail than are anastomoses of the small bowel. A further relevant factor may be the high intraluminal pressures which are developed in the colon during normal bowel movements (> 100 mmHg). These are substantially higher than those developed in the small intestine and may, by causing tissue ischaemia, contribute to anastomosis failure.[210] Indeed, even at normal intestinal suture, avascular (i.e. non-perfused) areas are a usual finding.[210,211]

Damage to vascular endothelium should clearly be considered as one of the possible side-effects in hyperthermia. Burn injury to the skin, if extensive, causes reduced mesenteric blood flow and bowel ischemic damage via a thromboxane A2 effect, which results in a breaching of the bowel mucosal barrier, and systemic uptake of enteric bacteria,[212] possibly leading to systemic infection and multi-organ failure; bacteremia causes hypoperfusion of small intestinal mucosa.[213] Systemic challenge with bacterial lipopolysaccharide toxins may cause intestinal microvascular lesions including arteriolar occlusion due to endothelial cell vacuolization (Fig. 10.34),[214] disturb mucosal blood flow and cause acute diarrhoea,[215] while luminal application of the gut bacteria released peptide, FMLP, causes mucosal inflammation.[216] Mesenteric hypoperfusion is implicated as a causative factor in the development of increased intestinal permeability in endotoxemia.[217] Rotaviris infection in neonates produces a villus microvascular injury thought to lead to persistent diarrhoea.[218] The intestinal microvasculature is severely affected by lower body hyperthermia in mice.[211] Temperatures of 41.5°C for 1 h cause villous vascular endothelial destruction in proximal duodenum, but less severe damage to villous vasculature of jejunum or ileum. Damage to the endothelium of the muscle layers is still less, and it requires temperatures of 42–42.5°C for complete compromise of the muscle microvessels; elevated temperature exacerbates other forms of intestinal injury and hypothermia is generally protective.

The process of intestinal graft rejection following allograft transplantation appears to significantly involve the mucosal microvessels.[219,220] These vessels show a characteristic injury pattern, with endothelial cell swelling, cytoplasmic vacuolization and microvessel occlusion by swollen endothelial cells being observed from day 3 post-transplantation. The damaged endothelial cells are associated with accumulation of large lymphoid cells in the adjacent interstitium. There is also a reduction in enterocyte production, with consequent shortening of the crypts and villi. While these epithelial effects may be a direct part of the rejection process, they might alternatively be interpreted as the result of local tissue ischaemia consequent on the developing microvascular injury.[219,220] Structural integrity and function of the graft can be preserved by cyclosporin treatment, which is effective in suppressing allograft transplant rejection in other organs for up to 75 days in a primate model,[221] and by direct chemical ablation of T lymphocytes in the transplant ex vivo prior to transplantation.[222]

In another model of intestinal allograft transplantation, in which graft-versus-host disease (GVHD) is the predominant response, it could be prevented by in vitro irradiation of cold ischaemic transplants (1000 rad) prior to transplantation.[223] In control transplanted animals, recipient intestine showed marked enteritis, with severe mucosal destruction and splenomegaly. However, with irradiated intestine, there was survival of both transplant and host, with no detectable structural change in transplanted or host bowel wall, or reduction in recipient growth rate; destruction of the lymphocytes in the transplant may be the crucial step in prevention of GVHD in this model, which otherwise appears to produce mucosal inflammation and microvascular damage of the recipient intestine.

Intestinal microvessels are, of course, susceptible to damage by higher doses of ionizing radiation, resulting in a characteristic vasculopathy which is time and dose dependent,[224] and radiation-induced enteritis is a major complication limiting the radiotherapy of tumours located in or adjacent to the gut. Within the first 24 h after a single 1000 rad ^{60}Co exposure, there is an acute inflammatory response, with interstitial oedema, vasodilation and a substantial elevation in mucosal neutrophil numbers.[225] Four days after a 1500 rad X-ray dose, endothelial cells show minor signs of damage, with cytoplasmic vacuolization and swollen mitochondria. With 2000 rad,

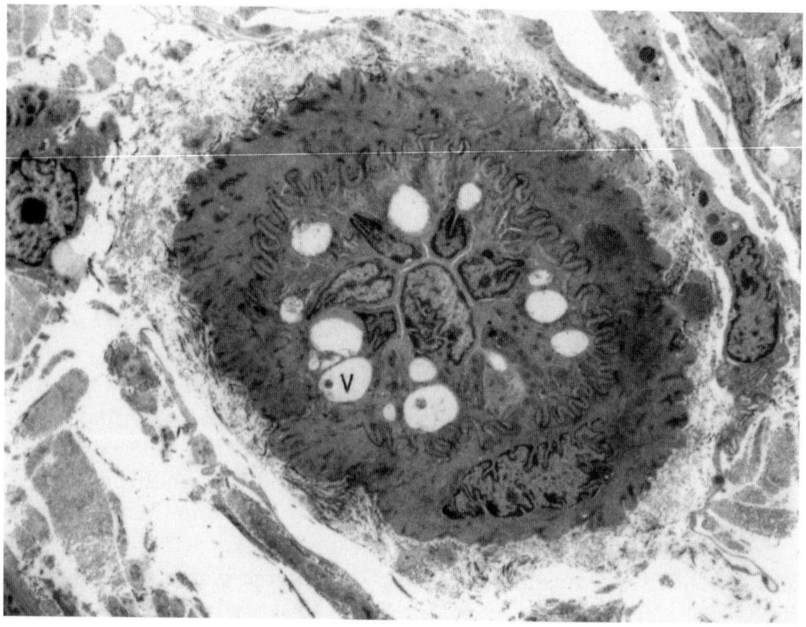

Fig. 10.34 Cross-section of an arteriole from the lower small intestine, 15 min after LPS challenge, shows marked constriction. Numerous subnuclear cytoplasmic vacuoles (V) are present in the endothelial cell. (×2850) (Reproduced from reference no. 214)

endothelial cell rupture and local tissue oedema are observed, while after 2500 rad there are frequent microthrombi in mucosal microvessels. The epithelial cells appear to have a slightly lower radiation threshold than the endothelial cells. Higher doses lead to a shrinking of villous height, which recovers after 1500 rad, but which persists after higher doses. Long-term reduction in both mucosal and muscularis vascularity, with disruption of normal angio-architecture, occurs following doses of 2000 rad or more.[226,227]

A further example of bowel damage following microvascular injury is that seen after bowel ischaemia. It has been long established that either complete blockage or severe impairment of blood flow to a segment of bowel can lead to tissue death and necrosis in the affected bowel wall. However, the effects of transient ischaemia of the bowel had not been studied until the last few years. During bowel hypoperfusion ischaemia, as in hypovolaemic shock, there is a change in ischaemic tissue purine metabolism, which results in an abnormally high metabolism of AMP and adenosine to hypoxanthine, which accumulates during the ischaemic period (Fig. 10.35A).[228,229] In addition, the enzyme xanthine dehydrogenase undergoes minor proteolysis to its oxidase form. Upon re-establishment of perfusion at normal rates and normal oxygen levels, there is rapid metabolism of the accumulated hypoxanthine by the newly modified oxidase form of the xanthine degradative enzyme. This enzyme directly utilizes molecular oxygen, and produces the highly reactive superoxide free radical $O^{2\cdot-}$ as a by-product. Additional oxygen-derived free radical species ($OH\cdot$ and H_2O_2 and lipid- and lipid peroxide-derived free radicals) are produced by subsequent reaction of $O^{2\cdot-}$ in the presence of Fe^{3+} and they also participate in the rapid chemical damage of local tissues (Fig. 10.17B). Pretreatment with the xanthine oxidase enzyme blocking drug allopurinol (Fig. 10.35A), even via the enteral route,[230] protects significantly against mucosal ischaemia–reperfusion injury. Ischaemia–reperfusion injury has been implicated in the development of the potentially fatal disease, necrotizing enterocolitis of the newborn; prenatal transplacental and postnatal breast-fed nutrition of the individual perinate with a high tungsten/molybdenum-free diet, which lowers intestinal xanthine oxidase activity, affords significant protection against intestinal ischaemia–reperfusion in the newborn (Fig. 10.35B,C).[229]

Intestinal ischaemia causes a marked (1800%) increase in neutrophil infiltration into the small bowel.[226] This infiltration can be prevented by drug pretreatments which interfere with the initial metabolic consequences of ischaemia, e.g. by pretreatment with allopurinol, and with the superoxide radical scavenger enzyme, superoxide dismutase. Tissue injury produced in the postischaemic period is due, in large part at least, to the activity of neutrophils recruited into the tissue from the circulation.[231] The initial superoxide radical production by xanthine oxidase appears to be the trigger for neutrophil–endothelial adherence,[232] and recruitment into the mucosa. Free radicals may mediate release of tissue proteases capable of interacting with the complement system to yield chemoattractants such as C5a and/or C3a, or they may interact with lipoproteins to yield other potent chemoattractants.[239] In either case, subsequent tissue damage, initially caused by superoxide from xanthine oxidase, is greatly amplified by the neutrophil-derived cytotoxic oxidants ($O^{2\cdot-}$, $OH\cdot$, H_2O_2, HOCI) and N-chloro amines (Fig. 10.35A). The endothelium of mucosal capillaries synthesizes and expresses the leucocyte adhesion molecule, ELAM-1, on its luminal surface in inflamed but not in normal intestine. In animals which have been rendered leucocytopenic by pretreatment with anti-neutrophil antibodies or in which anti-CD11/CD18 anti-neutrophil antibodies are circulating, there is marked reduction in ischaemia–reperfusion induced gastric or intestinal injury,[240–242] and a marked supression of neutrophil recruitment into the postischaemic bowel mucosa.

One of the most sensitive tissues to ischaemia–reperfusion injury appears to be the fenestrated microvascular endothelium of the intestinal mucosa, which rapidly loses its ability to withhold serum albumin from the interstitium. In consequence, lymph to plasma protein concentration ratios climb rapidly, and mucosal oedema develops. Periods of 60–120 min partial ischaemia (mesenteric arterial pressure < 40 mmHg) result in this type of injury on reperfusion.[229] In the case of complete occlusion of mucosal blood flow followed by reperfusion, ischaemic periods as short as 10 min can result in microvascular injury at 5 min into the reperfusion period in proximal rat small bowel, while longer ischaemic periods (20–30 min) are required to produce a similar degree of injury in distal small bowel (Fig. 10.36);[234] these findings are of obvious importance for arterial clamping during abdominal surgery, e.g. in abdominal aortic grafting. Mesenteric ischaemia is being recognized as the cause of a range of bowel disorders, especially in the elderly,[235] and may also be involved in necrotizing enterocolitis of the newborn.[236] A potentially iatrogenic mucosal ischaemia can be caused by the use of intraluminal water-soluble contrast media, which are markedly hyperosmolar, for the diagnosis of obstructed small bowel; such agents may severely compromise mucosal perfusion, leading to mucosal necrosis (Fig. 10.37).[237,238]

A common factor in intestinal injury due to ischaemia is damage to the endothelium. Control of intestinal submucosal arteriolar tone, and hence of local blood flow, involves release of an endothelially derived vasodilator substance (EDRF) from the venule accompanying each arteriole (Fig. 10.38).[241] This locally released substance diffuses the very short distance to the arteriolar smooth muscle to produce arteriolar vasodilation. Its release can

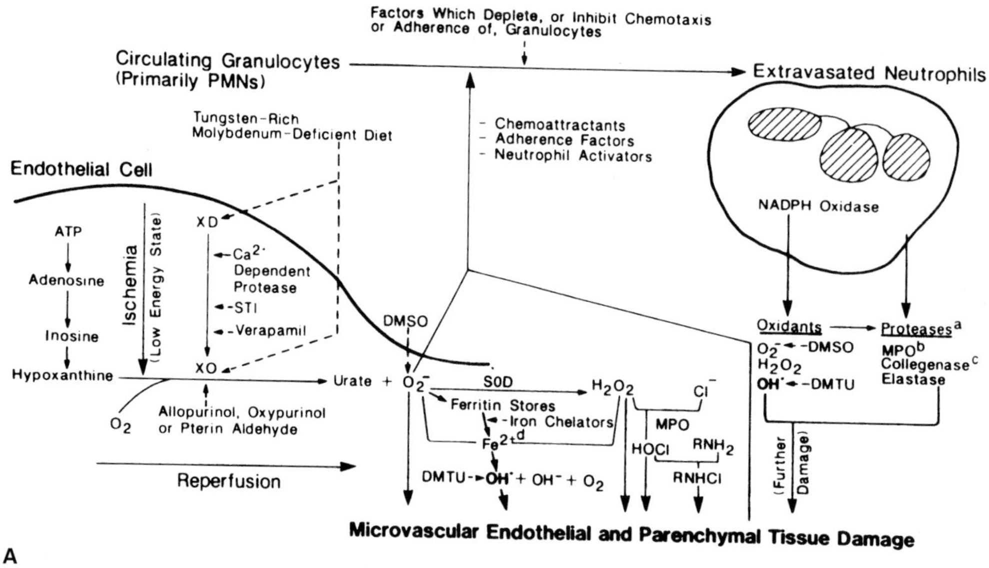

A

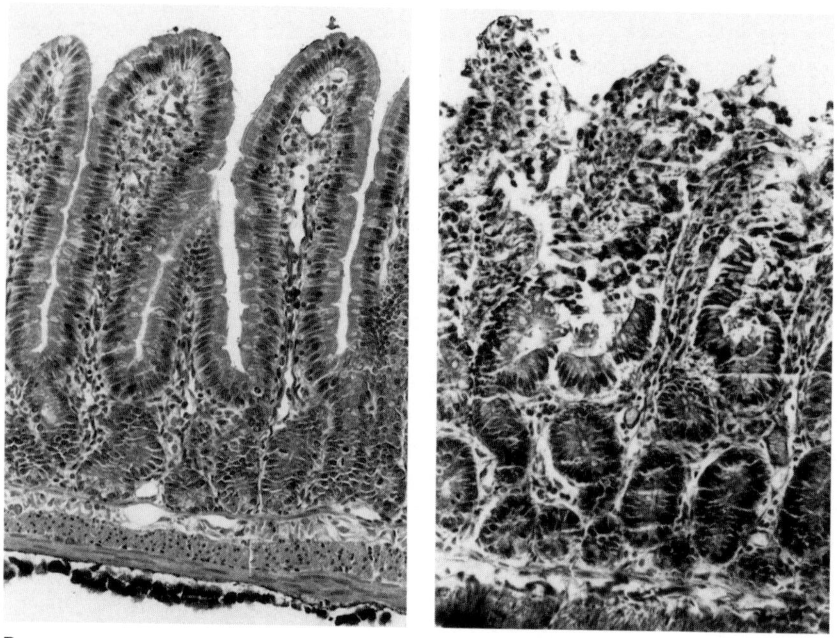

B C

Fig. 10.35 A Proposed scheme of intestinal ischaemia-reperfusion injury involving XO generated superoxide radical ($O^{2\cdot -}$) and granulocyte infiltration. OH· (hydroxyl radical) is thought to be the primary oxidant responsible for injury. (a) Other released products: lactoferrin, cationic proteases and arachidonate metabolites. (b) Myeloperoxidase catalyses HOCI production. (c) Activated by HOCI production. (d) Haber–Weiss reaction. STI = soybean trypsin inhibitor; DMSO = dimethyl sulfoxide; DMTU = dimethylthiourea; dotted lines = inhibitory mechanisms. (See original reference no. 233 for details) **B,C** Sections of pig and pup antimesenteric small intestine 7 days after experimental ischaemia-reperfusion injury. **B** preservation of wall architecture in pigs on tungsten supplemented diet; **C** villus necrosis and severe lamina proprial and submucosal oedema in unsupplemented pups. The Tungsten is thought to prevent conversion of xanthine dehydrogenase to its oxidase form in ischaemia. (H&E, ×75) (Reproduced from reference no. 233)

also be induced by local iontophoretic application of acetylcholine to the venule, and apparently similar arteriolar responses are produced by local hypoxia. Thus local control of tissue perfusion may be effected, in part at least, by mucosal venular endothelium; in addition, the pumping cycle of mucosal lymphatics is augmented (see above). The identity of this venular derived vasodilator substance is currently uncertain; experiments indicate that EDRF includes nitric oxide (NO), although it may contain other compounds as well.

Other studies of the mesenteric arteriolar vasodilator responses to acute transient ischaemia indicate, that they are reduced or abolished in several models of shock.[242] Shock produces large amounts of powerful vasodilator substances (acetylcholine, histamine, kinins, prostanoids, adenine nucleotides, etc.), but they are apparently ineffective in these situations.[243] In studies of large blood vessels, agents which produce vasodilation in intact vessels are transformed into vasoconstrictors in the absence of endothelium. These two lines of investigation thus suggest that the compromise of the gut microcirculatory bed in a variety of ischaemic and shock situations is due, in part at least, to interference in the ability of the venular endothelium to properly respond to tissue vasodilator metabolites and/or hypoxia. Thus the release of adequate endothelial vasodilator substances is impaired and an appropriate

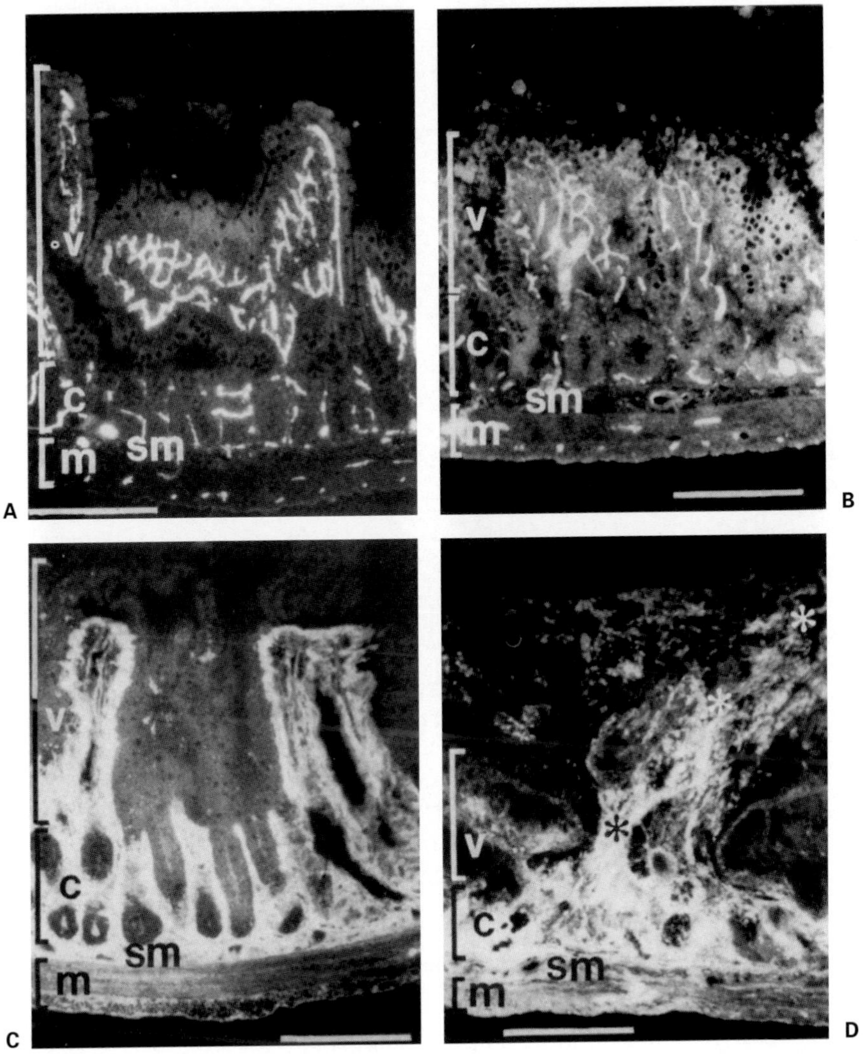

Fig. 10.36 Effects of ischaemia only and of ischaemia-reperfusion injury (IRI) on the distribution of FITC-tagged albumin (250 mg/kg, i.v.) in rat small intestine. Bars = 250 μm
A Control small intestine. Note discrete bright fluorescence of FITC-albumin is confined to the plasma space in capillaries in the lamina propria of villi (v), around crypts (c) and in the muscularis layer (m). No large vessels are evident in the submucosa (sm) in this particular section.
B Small intestine subjected to 15 min total ischaemia, without reperfusion. Note evidence of villus epithelial lifting and less discrete capillaries with some interstitial FITC-albumin fluorescence around capillaries of villi (v) and muscularis (m). This section illustrates the maximum disruption observed from ischaemia alone; most such tissue looked more similar to control **A**. **C** Intestine following 15 min ischaemia and 10 min reperfusion. Note intense interstitial albumin fluorescence of villus (v), pericryptal (c) lamina propria and submucosa (sm) to the extent that the intramural vessels are no longer discernible. Interstitial leakage of a lesser extent is evident in the muscularis (m) and some villus epithelial lifting is also apparent. **D** Intestine subjected to IRI as for **C**. Site for a focal haemorrhage into the gut lumen (*) as evident by the fluorescent albumin. Such sites were occasionally found following this treatment. (Reproduced from reference no. 234)

effect on local arteriolar tone and lymphangion pumping is lost.

THE SMALL INTESTINE — DUODENUM

Extrinsic vasculature

The arterial supply of the duodenum is via a pair of pancreaticoduodenal arterial loops, which lie along the inner curvature of the duodenum.[54] One is anterior and one posterior to the head of the pancreas. They are each connected superiorly to either the anterior or posterio-superior pancreaticoduodenal artery, and inferiorly to the anterior or posterior pancreaticoduodenal arteries, respectively. The superior vessels are derived from the coeliac axis via the gastroduodenal branch of the hepatic artery and the inferior vessels are derived from the superior mesenteric artery. The duodenal wall is supplied by a series of short arteries from these loops, which perforate the duodenal wall to reach the submucosal arterial plexus. This plexus anastomoses along and around the duodenal wall, but to a lesser extent than in more distal small bowel, so that, especially in the proximal duodenum, the tissue is effectively supplied by end-arteries.[59] This vascular arrangement may partly account for the susceptibility of the proximal duodenum to ulceration.[58]

Venous drainage of the duodenum largely parallels the arterial supply, except that in the proximal duodenum there is extensive intramural venous anastomosis, in contrast to the end-artery arrangement. The inferior pancreaticoduodenal veins usually pass to the right gastroepiploic vein, whereas the superior veins directly enter the portal vein. Lymphatic drainage of the duodenum is via anterior and posterior vessels, which run parallel to the arterial supply. The lymph vessels pass to a series of small pyloric nodes superiorly, and to preaortic lumbar nodes inferiorly.[22]

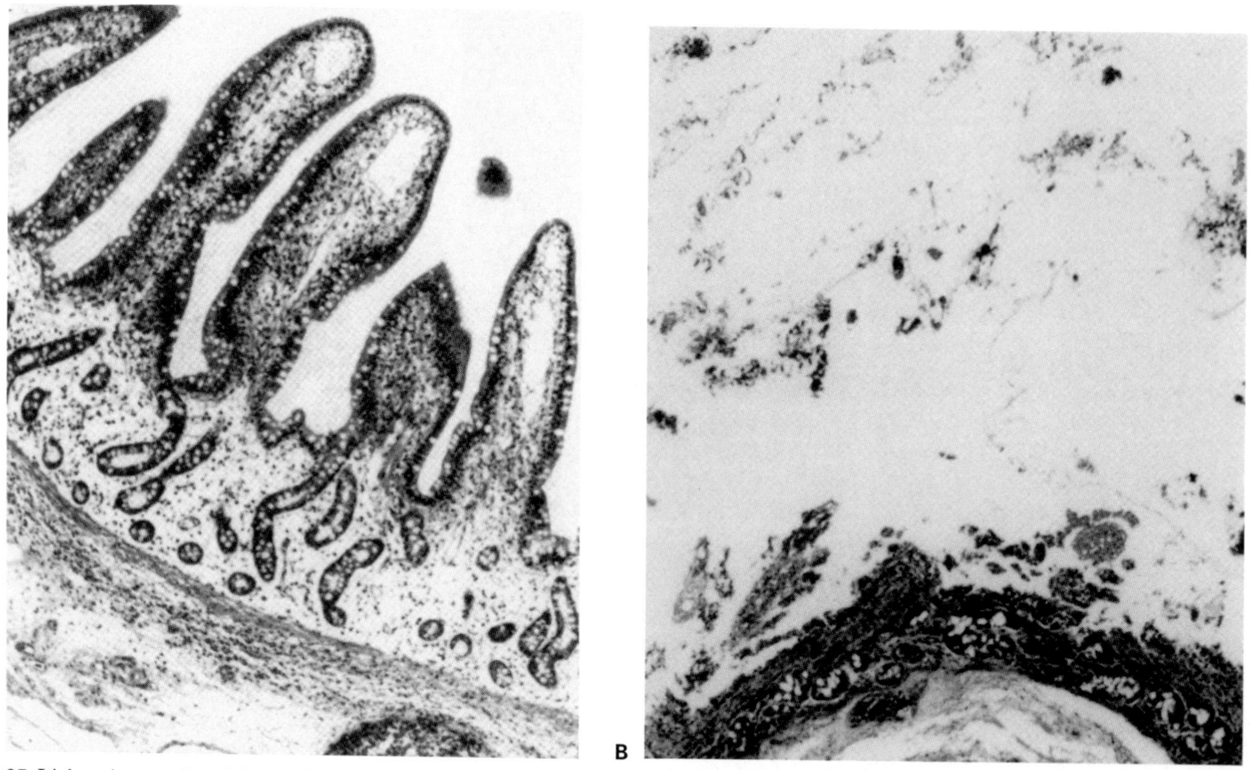

Fig. 10.37 Light micrographs of pig small intestine 8 h after intestinal closed-loop obstruction and instillation of fluid. (H&E, ×42) **A** Instillation of physiological saline; normal appearance. **B** Instillation of sodium diatrizoate. Note marked loss of epithelium and lamina propria; only the bases of the crypts are spared. (Reproduced from reference no. 237)

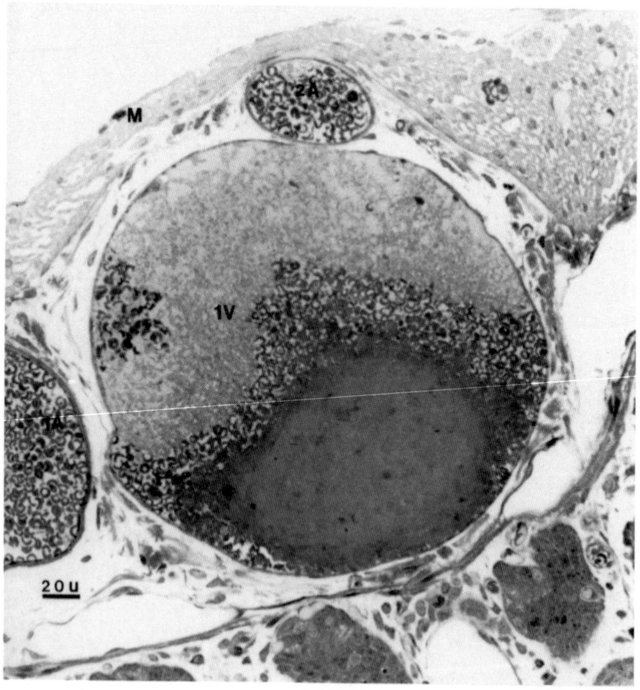

Fig. 10.38 Electron micrograph of a paired large submucosal arteriole (1A, at left) and venule (1V); small arteriole (2A) branched from 1A and crossed over the large venule at minimal separation distance. M = visceral smooth muscle of muscularis mucosa, separated from arterioles and venule by connective tissue. Rat small intestine. (Reproduced from reference no. 241 by permission of The American Physiological Society)

Duodenal microvascular organization

Unlike the more distal intestine, the duodenum contains the submucosal Brunner's gland tissue (Fig. 10.39A,B,C), which secretes a bicarbonate-rich fluid. The glands vary in gross form in different animals;[244] in humans they form a relatively compact mass.[245,246]

The microvascular architecture of Brunner's glands has only been investigated to date in the rat, which may serve as a model for the human. Brunner's gland acini are each surrounded by a basket-like plexus of capillaries. Adjacent capillary nets interconnect, or are shared between adjacent acini, to produce a complex microvascular web of vessels in which there is no clearly discernible repeating microvascular unit.[247] The capillaries are fenestrated[244,250] and the network receives an arteriolar supply and has a venous drainage separate from and parallel to that of the overlying villi.[247] There are some capillary connections between this periacinar plexus and the pericryptal plexus surrounding the crypts. In addition, there are fairly common connections between the pericryptal capillary plexus and the villus venules en route from the villi to the submucous venous plexus. Therefore, the capillaries of the lower portion of the villus shaft may receive blood from the villus tip, and not from the capillaries supplying

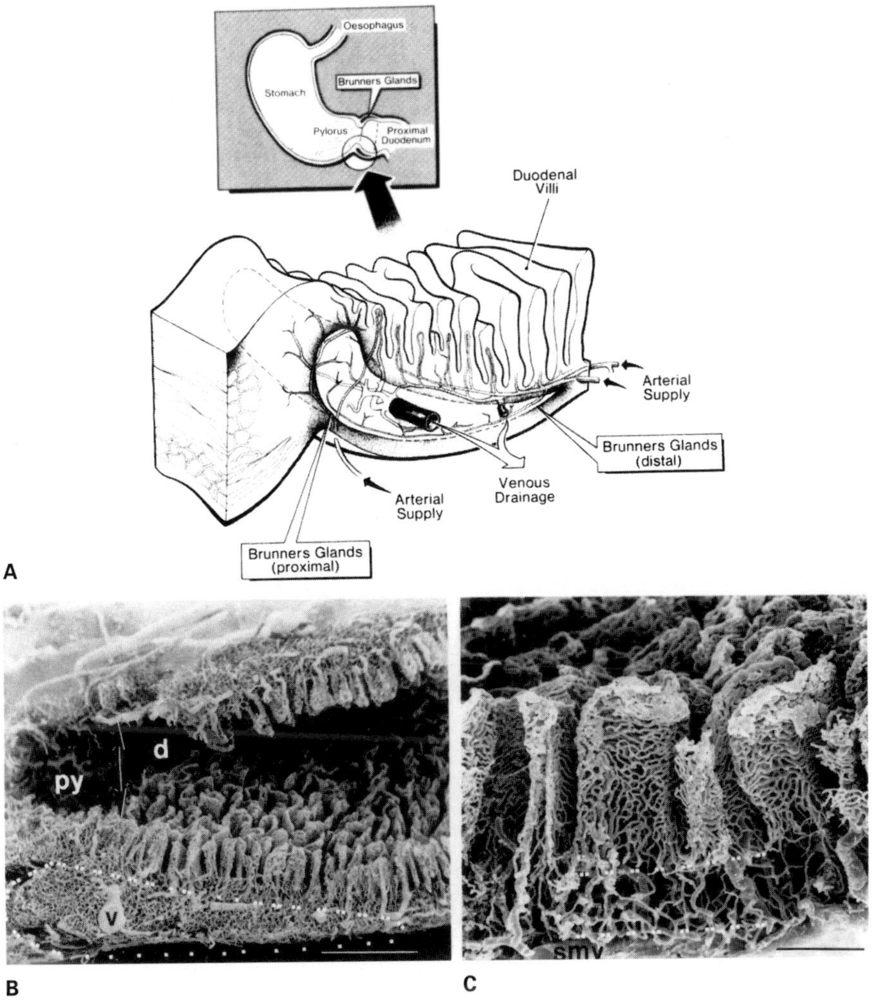

Fig. 10.39 **A** Diagrammatic representation of major vascular supply and drainage routes of Brunner's gland tissue in rat proximal duodenum. Inset: dorsal view of a horizontal schematic section of rat stomach, indicating the location of Brunner's glands. **B** corrosion microvascular cast of rat pyloroduodenal junction and proximal duodenum, showing the area of Brunner's glands (dotted). py = pylorus; d = duodenum; arrows indicate gastric to duodenal mucosal transition. Note the transverse orientation of the flattened villi. Bar = 1.0 mm **C** Rat mid-duodenum beyond the Brunner's gland region. Note pericryptal capillary plexus between the bases of the villi and the submucosal vascular plexus (SMV), i.e. between the dotted lines. Bar = 250 μm (Reproduced from reference no. 247 by courtesy of Biomedical Research)

the crypts as they do in the lower intestine. Alternatively, the flow in this lower shaft region of duodenal villi may be derived from either the pericryptal plexus or the villus tip capillaries, depending on physiological circumstance (Fig. 10.40).

The parallel circulations of Brunner's glands and duodenal villi (Fig. 10.20) may be of functional significance. The acini of Brunner's glands secrete a HCO_3^- rich fluid. This secretion must cause acidification of the local interstitium, which will be reflected in venous effluent. Supply of this acidified blood to the villous epithelial cells of the proximal duodenum (which are potentially subject to high luminal acid loads, and therefore need HCO_3^- for neutralization of any trans-epithelially diffusing H^+ ions) would clearly be physiologically inappropriate.

The luminal surface of the duodenum is covered by villi, each underlain by a capillary plexus similar to the remainder of the small bowel, except at the opening of the common bile duct on the crown of the duodenal papilla; here, the epithelium immediately surrounding the opening is devoid of villi, and the subsurface capillary network is arranged similarly to the luminal aspect of the gastric mucosa.[248]

There are no comprehensive studies of duodenal microvascular ultrastructure or of intramural lymphatics; there is evidence that duodenal villus lymphatics are innervated by nerves immunoreactive for the neuropeptides, substance P and CGRP, which may be afferents for lymphatic pressure, and may also be efferent lymphomodulators.[249]

The mechanisms underlying duodenal ulceration and duodenal mucosal protection are essentially similar to those occurring in the stomach and small intestine.[105,109]

THE LARGE INTESTINE

Extrinsic arterial supply

The arteries supplying the colon are the superior and inferior mesenteric arteries (Fig. 10.25).[251] The ascending colon and some two-thirds of the proximal transverse colon are supplied by the ileocolic, right colic and middle

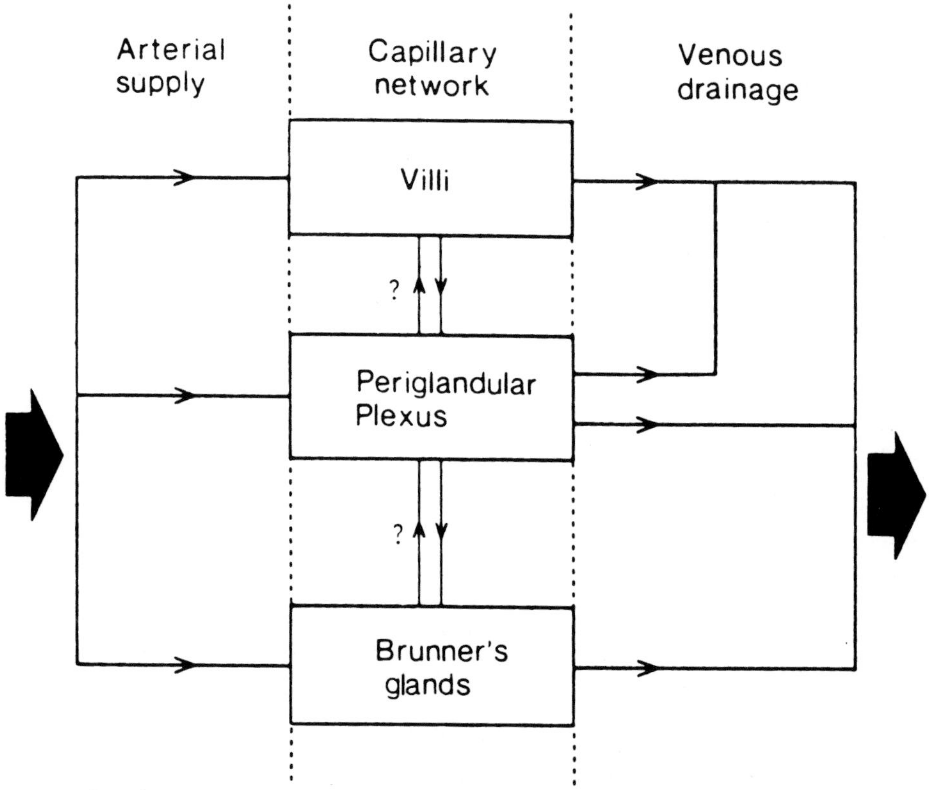

Fig. 10.40 Schematic representation of parallel nature of the separate circulations of Brunner's glands, and of villus tip and shaft in the proximal duodenum. Note that presumably acidified blood (after HCO_3^- secretion in Brunner's glands) is not supplied to the villi, which have to cope with an exogenous H^+ load from the duodenal lumen (ex gastric juice). (Reproduced from reference no. 247 by courtesy of Biomedical Research)

colic arteries which arise from the right side of the superior mesenteric artery. The distal one-third of the transverse colon and the descending colon are supplied by a left colic branch of the inferior mesenteric artery, which passes to the colon at about the midpoint of the descending colon. The sigmoid colon receives 2–3 sigmoid branches of the inferior mesenteric artery, which pass to it via the transverse mesocolon and are also termed inferior left colic arteries.

The vessels to the ascending and descending colon branch in the retroperitoneal fascia, while those to the transverse colon and the sigmoid colon branch in the transverse and sigmoid mesocolons respectively. There is little arcading until the vessels are within 2 cm of the colon wall, where there is a single large vessel anastomosis. This anastomotic or marginal vessel runs retroperitoneally, close to the left side of the ascending colon, extending from the ileocaecal junction to the hepatic flexure, and continues within the transverse mesocolon close to its attachment to the colon wall. This vessel continues retroperitoneally just medial to the descending colon and extends from the splenic flexure down to and into the sigmoid mesocolon close to its attachment to the sigmoid colon. The marginal artery of the colon thus acts as an anastomotic channel between ileocolic, right colic, middle colic, left colic and sigmoid arteries. It continues down to the upper rectum to anastomose with the superior rectal artery (see below). Short (2–3 cm) vasa recta pass from this marginal artery to the colon wall, with few or no anastomoses en route. Upon reaching the colon, the vasa recta divide to provide subserosal branches and others which penetrate the outer muscle coat (see below).

The proximal part of the rectum is supplied by the superior rectal branch of the inferior mesenteric artery. This artery runs in the mesentery of the sigmoid colon to reach the rectum, branching at the level of the third sacral vertebra into a pair of vessels which run down either side of the rectum, until they peter out at about mid-rectal level. These latter vessels give off a series of short arteries which pierce the rectal muscularis coat to reach the anastomotic submucosal arterial plexus. A pair of middle rectal arteries (left and right) pass to the rectum from the internal iliac arteries, and a pair of inferior rectal arteries, derived from the internal pudendal arteries, supply the lower rectum. These vessels send short arteries — vasa recta — to the wall of the rectum (Fig. 10.41).

Intramural arterial and venous distribution

The straight arteries (vasa recta) which pass to the colonic wall from the marginal artery, branch at the bowel wall to provide:

(i) subserosal arteries which pass circumferentially around the bowel wall, and
(ii) penetrating arteries which pass to the subserosal arterial plexus but which give off small branches to the muscle layers en route, and larger branches to the intermuscular arterial plexus, which lies between the longitudinal and circular muscular layers (Fig. 10.42).[252]

There are anastomoses within the subserosal plexus between the subserosal branches of adjacent vasa recta. This plexus also gives off additional perforating branches around the colon wall distant from the 'mesenteric' margin, which penetrate the muscle layers to reach the submucous arterial plexus, giving off branches to the intermuscular arterial plexus and also small feeder arterioles to the muscular layers en route. There are additional direct branches to the intra- and intermuscular arterial plexuses from the submucous arterial plexus. The subserosal arteries also give branches to supply the microvascular beds of the appendices epiploicae, the subserosal fat, and — in the transverse colon — to the fatty tissue of the greater omentum, to which the transverse colon is fused.

The penetrating branches of the vasa recta pass through the muscularis to reach the submucous arterial plexus. There is extensive anastomosis in the submucous plexus, both circumferentially around the rectum and also longitudinally, so that there is anastomosis and functional overlap between the areas of supply from superior, middle and inferior rectal arteries.

The intramural venous drainage network is essentially similar in distribution to the arterial supply vessels, with the vessels usually running as artery–vein pairs, both within the colon wall and in the extrinsic vascular pathways of the colon. In the areas where the large intestine is retroperitoneal (ascending and descending colon, plus upper and mid-rectum) or subperitoneal (lower rectum), there is the potential for the development of many small portosystemic venous anastomoses between the intramural veins of the large bowel, or its extrinsic veins, and the somatic veins of the adjacent body wall, to which the large bowel is adherent.

Microvessels of the large intestine

There has been relatively little study of the microvasculature of the colon. The focus of these few studies has been principally on the mucosa, with little study of the microvasculature of the colonic muscularis. The arrangement and ultrastructure of the microvessels of the colonic muscle coat,[253,254] presumably of the myenteric plexus, as well as the muscle of the caecum, appendix and rectum, are similar to the equivalent layers in small intestine and stomach. Thus, continuous capillaries without fenestrae, with a well developed basal lamina and with frequent endothelial vesicles are to be expected in the muscularis externa. The microvasculature underlying the colonic

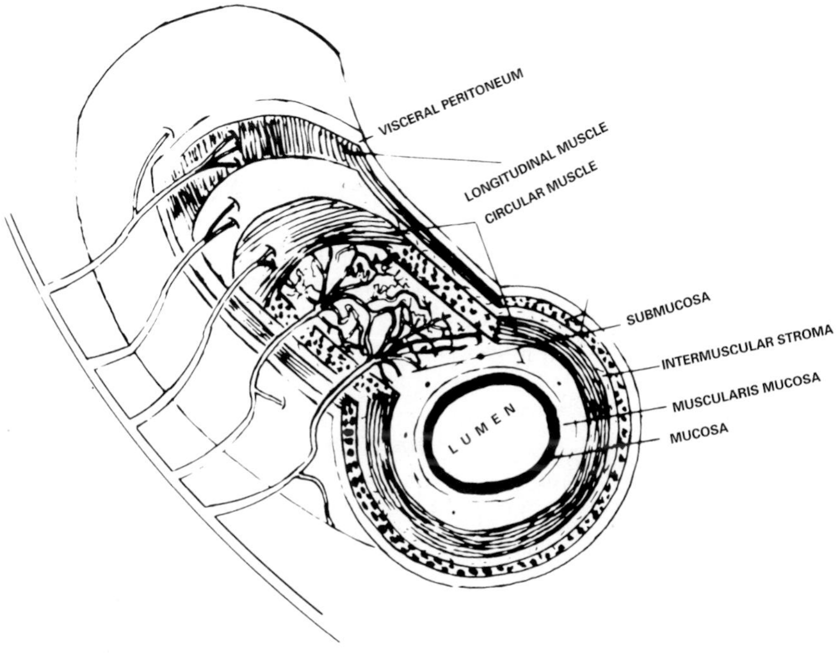

Fig. 10.41 Intramural arterial plexus of the colon in the submucosal plane: the vasa recta pierce the muscular layers and enter the submucous plane to form a continuous plexus. In the cross-section there are arterioles seen at variable intervals around the entire submucosa. (Reproduced from reference no. 251)

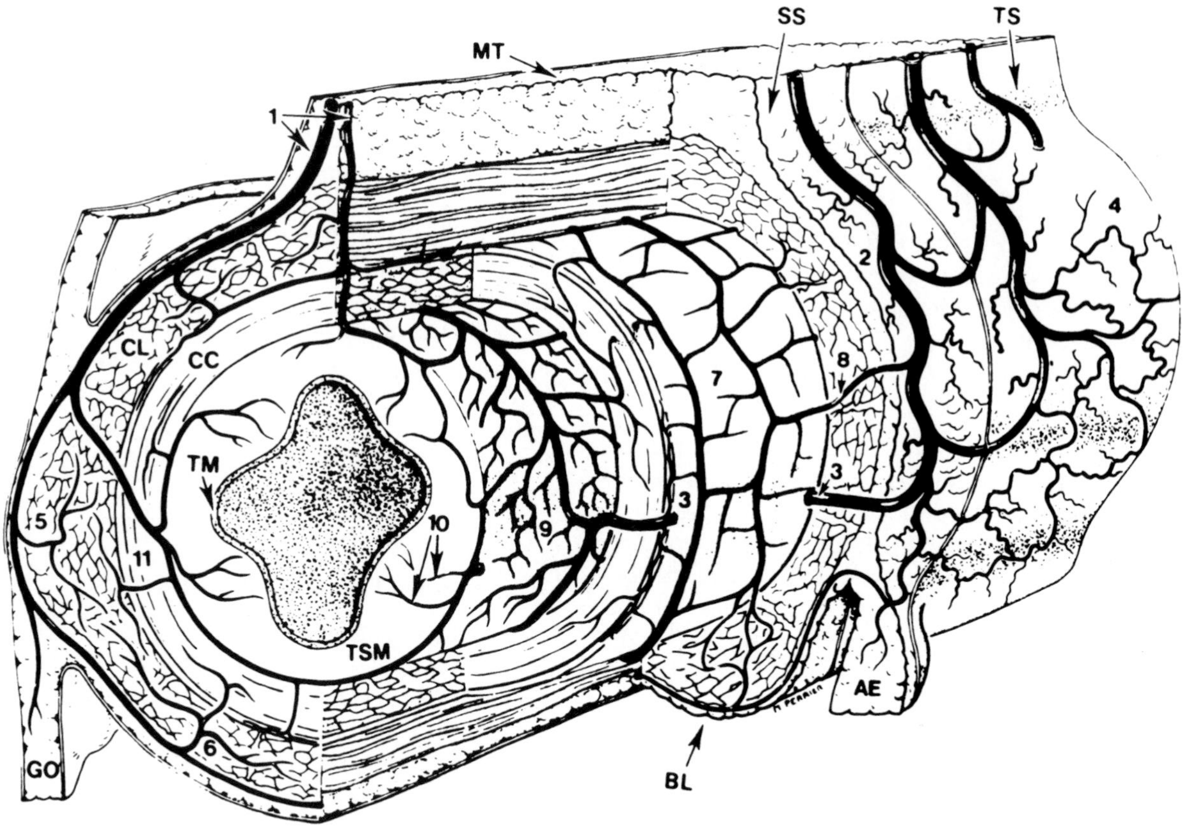

Fig. 10.42 Schematic view of the arterial circulation of the (transverse) colon; dorsolateral view. **1.** Vasa recta and their branches within the transverse mesocolon (MT). **2.** Subserosal artery which anastomoses with adjacent arteries to form a subserosal arterial plexus. **3.** Penetrating artery which traverses the external muscle coats to reach the submucous arterial plexus. **4.** Subserosal arterial plexus which supplies the subserosa and the greater omentum (GO); the appendices epiploicae (AE) may be supplied either from this plexus or from short (**5**) or long (**6**) arteries from the muscle coats. **7.** Plexus of intermuscular arteries between the longitudinal (CL) and circular (CC) external muscle coats, supplied by small branches (**8**) from the subserosal arterial plexus. **9.** Submucosal arterial plexus in the submucosa (TSM), supplied by penetrating branches from longer and shorter subserosal encircling branches of the vasa recta. **10.** Mucosal arteries and also recurrent arteries (**11**) to the muscularis externa (principally to circular muscle) are give off from the submucosal arterial plexus. (Reproduced from reference no. 252 by permission of Acta Anatomica)

serosa, and extending into the appendices epiploicae, has not been examined in any detail but will presumably be similar to the continuous capillaries supplying the equivalent tissues in the mesentery (see below).

The microvascular organization of the colonic mucosa[252,255,256]. is essentially equivalent to that found in the gastric mucosa. Arteriolar branches from the submucous arterial plexus penetrate the muscularis mucosae, and then break up into a leash of capillaries between the bases of the colonic tubular glands. The capillaries pass towards the colonic luminal surface in the lamina propria, with frequent cross-anastomoses. At the most luminal level of the mucosa, they join a polygonal array of capillaries and subepithelial postcapillary venule rings, which lie just beneath the colonic surface epithelial cells and surround the necks of the colonic glands. This subepithelial plexus is drained by occasional mucosal venules, which pass through the lamina propria largely at right angles to the mucosal surface, to reach the submucous venous plexus without receiving further capillary tributaries en route (Fig. 10.43).[255] There are no arteriovenous anastomoses in the mucosa of the colon, or in any other layer of this organ. The angio-architecture of the colonic mucosa is similar in rats,[255] humans and cotton-top marmoset monkeys.[257] The capillaries in the colonic mucosa tend to be closer to the lamina propria membranes of the colonic surface enterocytes (approximately 1.0 μm) than are those of the small intestine (approximately 2.0 μm), at least in dogs (Fig. 10.43C).[254] This small diffusion distance between surface colonocytes and the venous end of mucosal capillaries presumably aids in absorbed fluid clearance from the colonic interstitium, which is thought to be an almost exclusive function of the microvasculature. Lymphatic capillaries are confined to the base of the mucosa in the colon and do not appear to be significantly involved in removal of fluid absorbed from the colonic lumen (Flig. 10.44A).[254] There is a subepithelial layer of myoepithelial cells arranged in a network, between the basal lamina of the colonic enterocytes and the subepithelial capillary plexus, as in the small intestine

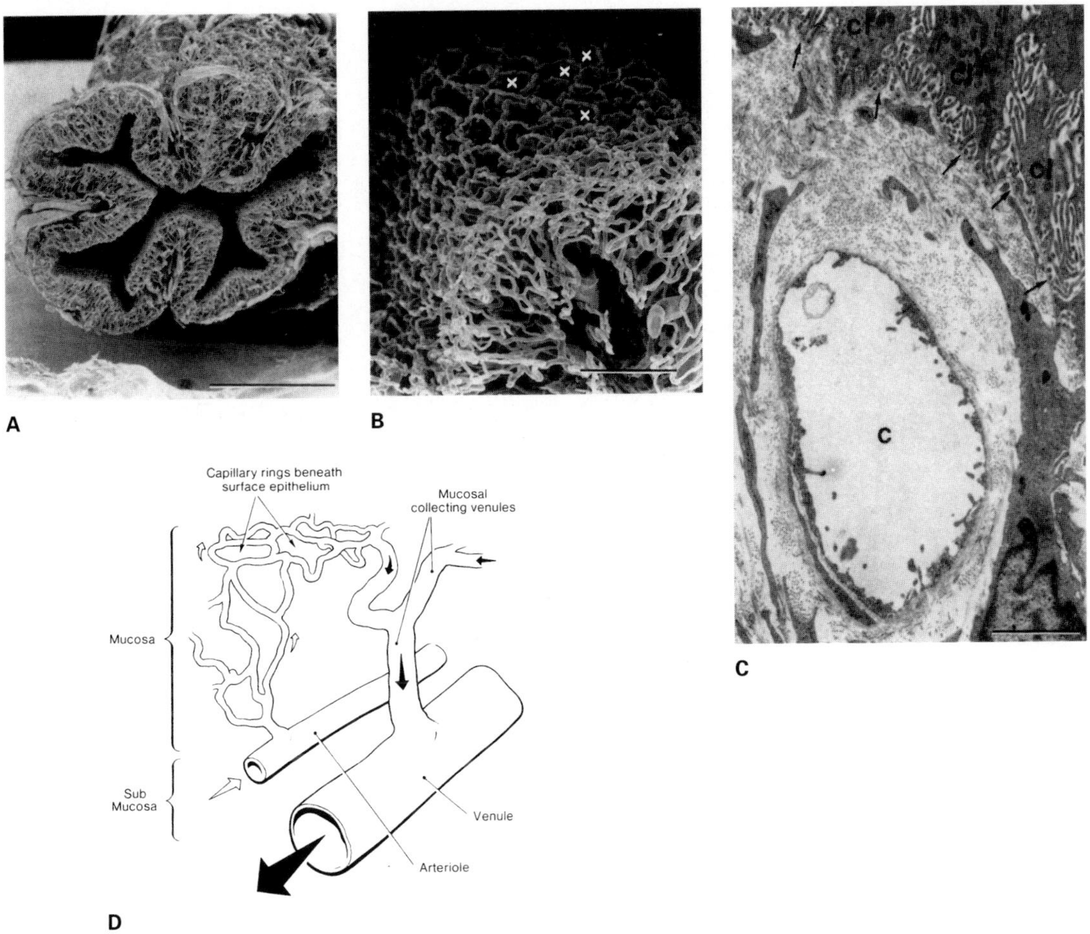

Fig. 10.43 The microvasculature of rat colon; transmission and scanning electron micrographs. **A** Transverse section of cast of rat distal colon. Note-star-shaped lumen and the folding of the submucosal vascular plexus with the mucosa. Bar = 1.0 mm **B** Corrosion vascular cast of rat colonic mucosa — cut edge of a mucosal fold. Note the capillary rings surrounding the necks of the crypts (white crosses). Bar = 50 μm.
C Fenestrated capillary (c) of rat colonic mucosa, situated just beneath colonic epithelial basal lamina and the colonocyte layer (cl). Bar = 2.5 μm.
D Schematic representation of the microvascular flow pattern in the mucosa of rat colon. These flow directions, as deduced from the casts, have been confirmed by intravital microscopy. (Figs 10.43A,B,D reproduced from reference no. 255 by permission of Acta Anatomica)

(Fig. 10.45);[206] the function of this network remains unclear, but could be to pressurize the lamina propria and clear interstitial fluid into the initial lymphatics located at the base of the mucosa.

The mucosal capillaries throughout the large intestine are ultrastructurally similar to those of the small intestine. Thus they are fenestrated with a well developed basal lamina (Fig. 10.44A), with few endothelial vessels (< 20%) compared to non-fenestrated capillaries. The fenestrae are reportedly impervious to ferritin, even in inflamed bowel.[253] Studies of the osmotic reflection coefficient to plasma proteins in dog colonic mucosa indicate that they are slightly more permeable to plasma macromolecules than are small intestinal capillaries.[258] The spatial frequency of colonic mucosal capillaries falls from proximal to distal colon in rats, as does the fenestral frequency per capillary,[257] presumably reflecting the change in role of the colon from proximal absorption to distal faecal storage.

Venous drainage of the large intestine

The venous drainage of the colon largely parallels its arterial supply.[251] Straight veins drain the submucous, intermuscular and subserosal venous plexuses into an anastomosing marginal vein. This latter vessel is drained by a series of vessels which converge as the ileocolic and right colic vein from the ascending colon, and as the middle colic from the transverse colon. These drain to the superior mesenteric vein. Along the descending and sigmoid colon and the upper rectum, a series of branches pass from the marginal veins to the inferior mesenteric vein, which empties into the splenic vein. The superior mesenteric and splenic veins join to form the portal vein,

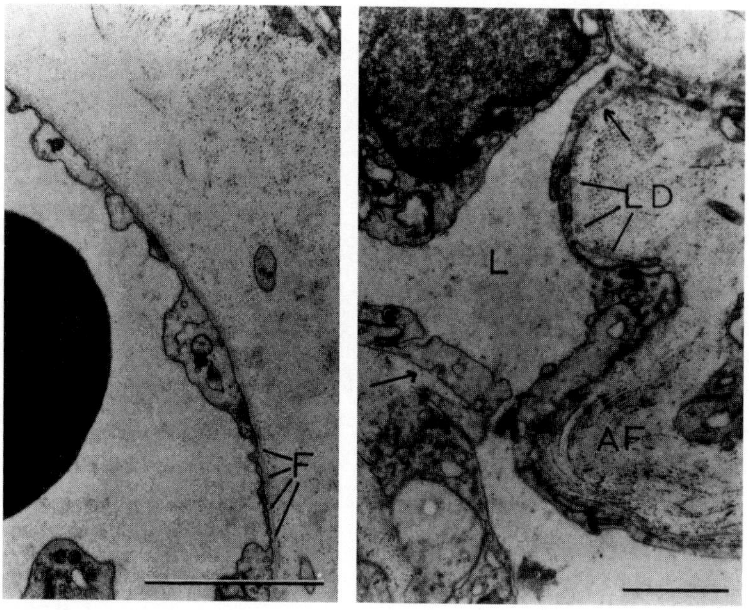

A B

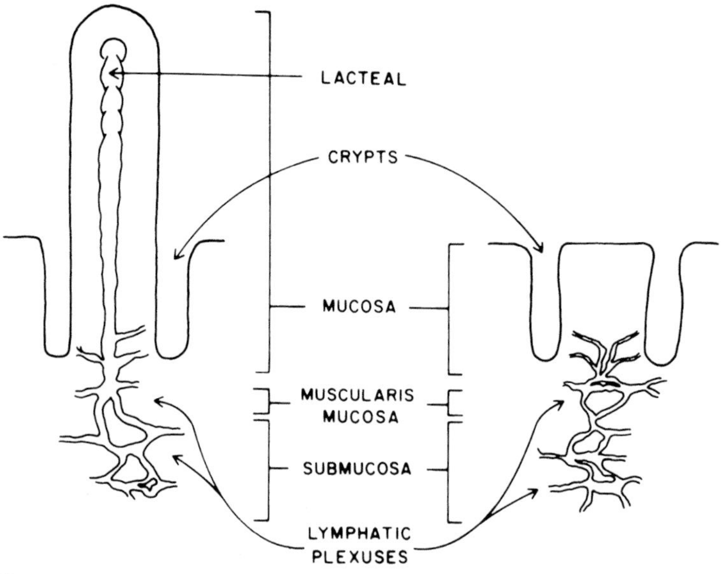

C

Fig. 10.44 A,B Comparison of the ultrastructures of a colonic capillary with an initial lymphatic. Fenestrae (F) are found in the capillary, anchoring filaments (AF) attach to the lamina densa of the lymphatic basal lamina, which is incomplete. Vesicles open on the luminal (L) and abluminal (arrow) surface of the lymphatic endothelium. Bars: A = 2.5 μm, B = 5 μm.
C Comparison of the lymphatics of small intestinal (left) and colonic mucosa (right). The initial lymphatics in the colon do not penetrate much beyond the muscularis mucosae, a situation reminiscent of the stomach. (Fig. 10.44A,B from reference no. 259; Fig. 10.44C reproduced from reference no. 254 by permission of Gastroenterology)

which passes to the liver to supply the sinusoidal microvascular bed. The three venous plexuses of the rectum are an external, a small intramuscular and a major submucosal plexus. These are interconnected by frequent veins, which perforate the muscle layers.[252] The external venous plexus of the lower rectum drains via inferior rectal veins to the internal pudendal veins.

The external venous plexus of the mid-part of the rectum connects to middle rectal branches of the internal iliac veins, whereas the external venous plexus of the upper rectum drains via superior rectal veins to the inferior mesenteric vein. Thus, within the three plexuses of the rectum (submucosal, intermuscular and external), there exists a relatively free communication between the portal and systemic venous systems by many small intramural veins.

Lymphatics of the large intestine

There is general agreement about the location of lymphatics in the colonic mucosa. In humans and a number of other species, it is generally accepted that the lymph capillaries commence in the lamina propria at the level of the bases of the colonic glands (Fig. 10.44B,C).[254,259] An electron microscopic report claiming the presence of very superficial lymphatics, just under the most luminal capillaries, in the lamina propria of dog colon[260] has been subsequently confirmed by injection studies in this species.[261]

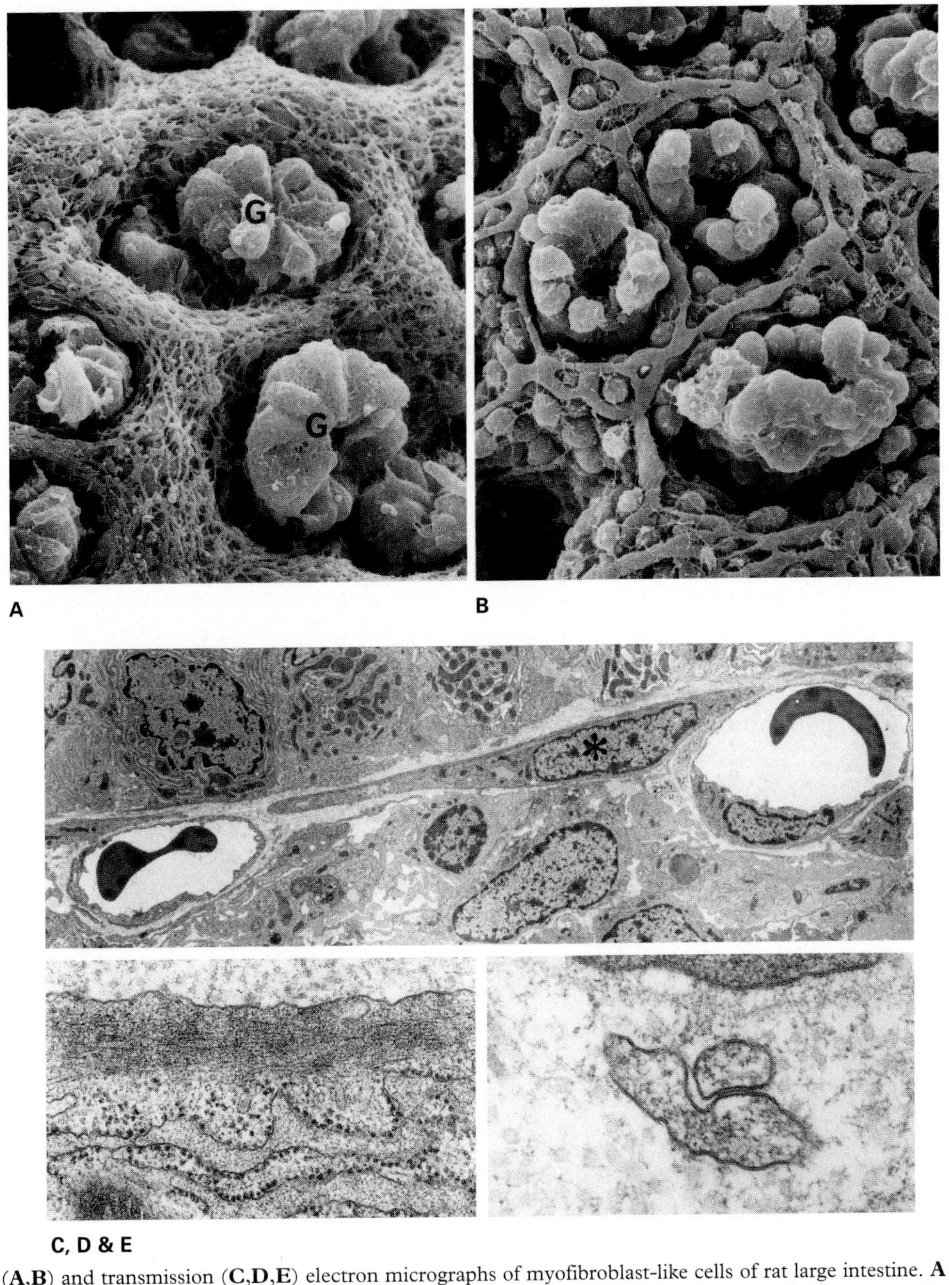

Fig. 10.45 Scanning (**A**,**B**) and transmission (**C**,**D**,**E**) electron micrographs of myofibroblast-like cells of rat large intestine. **A** A cellular reticulum located beneath the epithelium. G = unremoved glandular epithelial cells. (×1050) **B** Microvascular network demonstrated by the removal of the cellular network as seen in A. (×1050) **C** Myofibroblast-like cell (*) located between the blood capillaries, immediately beneath the epithelial basal lamina. (×2400) **D** Part of a myofibroblast-like cell containing a bundle of microfilaments in the cytoplasm facing the epithelium. (×27 000) **E** A gap-junction formed between the thin processes of the myofibroblast-like cells. (×60 000) (Reproduced from reference no. 206)

Whether this represents species differences between dog and human, or whether there is a previously unrecognized superficial lymphatic network in human colon, must await clarification.

There are additional lymph capillaries within the muscularis mucosae, and these are all drained to a valved plexus in the submucosa. There are blind-ending lymph capillaries or initial lymphatics in the external muscle layers of the colon, as in the stomach and intestine. Both submucosal and intramuscular lymphatics are drained to a subserosal lymphatic network, which drains to the mesenteric lymphatics. At sites where the colon is adherent to the posterior body wall, anastomoses between external lymphatics of the colon wall and those of the adjacent fascia and somatic muscle are to be expected, although this has yet to be critically evaluated. Similar lymphatic anastomoses may be expected in the regions of developmental adhesion of the mesenteries of the ascending and descending colon, and the partial adhesion of the sigmoid mesocolon (and of the mesentery of the duodenum).

There are a series of small paracolic lymph nodes along the marginal artery of the colon, with others along the ileocolic, right colic and middle colic vessels. These nodes collect draining lymphatics from adjacent areas of large bowel and drain to superior mesenteric nodes. The little nodes along the left colic, sigmoid and superior rectal vessels drain those areas of large bowel to inferior mesenteric nodes.[262]

The upper rectum drains via a set of pararectal nodes superiorly to the inferior mesenteric group of preaortic nodes. The mid-rectum, the 10 cm above the mucocutaneous line, drains in three different directions. It drains in part superiorly via the pararectal nodes of the upper rectum to the inferior mesenteric nodes, in part laterally along the course of the middle rectal vessels to the internal iliac nodes and in part inferiorly along the course of the inferior rectal vessels to nodes there. The anal canal, distal to the mucocutaneous line, is drained by the most inferior lymphatics, which pass via lymph vessels in adjacent skin and perineal superficial fascia to the superficial inguinal nodes.[272] Lymph drainage of the rectum is important in the pattern of metastatic spread from anorectal cancers.[262–266] In Kaposi's sarcoma in AIDS patients, aberrant peripheral lymphaticovenous connections are established between lymphatics in the submucosa and submucosal venules in GI tract lesions early in the development of the disease (and also in skin, liver, deep fat and lymph nodes).[267,273]

Microvessels in large bowel disease and injury

Specific alterations of the colonic intramural vasculature have been reported in a variety of conditions affecting the colon, including inflammatory bowel disease,[268] radiation bowel disease,[269] following hypotension in haemorrhagic shock and in portal hypertension as a result of mesenteric arteriovenous fistula.[271]

In diffuse Crohn's disease, as in fulminating ulcerative colitis, there is a hypermicrovascularity and severe disorganization of intramural vascular and microvascular architecture in the regions of inflammatory disruption of the mucosa and submucosa. The microvascular pattern remains normal in the external muscle coat in ulcerative colitis, but there are local areas of increased vascularity in the muscle in Crohn's disease at sites of mucosal ulceration and transmural inflammation. In segmental Crohn's disease, there is a local gross thickening of the bowel wall, with a reduction in submucosal vascularity; the submucous vessels become narrower in calibre and have more irregular courses.[268] There are claims based upon immunohistochemical and in situ hybridization studies that Crohn's disease may represent a persistent granulomatous vasculitis secondary to continuing measles virus infection of colonic mucosal microvessel endothelium.[200]

In radiation bowel disease (see Ch. 44) following therapeutic pelvic irradiation for carcinoma of the cervix, bowel stricture, ulceration, ileal and rectosigmoid necrosis with perforation or development of rectovaginal fistula may occur.[269] Quantitative studies of the vascular space within normal and radiation-injured bowel indicate a substantial reduction in bowel wall vascularity following radiation therapy. Adjacent to strictures, the reduction in vascularity occurs in all layers of the bowel wall. Fibrin thrombi occlude capillaries and there is intimal fibrosis of the intramural arterioles. Adjacent to sites of bowel perforation, the microvascular bed of part or all of the bowel wall is totally occluded; fibrinoid necrosis and thrombosis of the intramural vessels are the histological findings in these areas. Submucosal oedema is also seen in these patients, suggesting that compromise of the lymphatic drainage of these areas is another complication of radiation damage to the bowel.

Necrosis of the ascending colon and caecum is a complication of post-traumatic hypotension, which is sometimes found 2–3 days after resuscitation. There may also be perforation which, if it occurs, is usually located at the hepatic flexure. This condition is typically found in patients who were profoundly hypotensive for 30–200 min, and who required large volumes of intravenous fluid.[270] The cause of this colonic necrosis is presumed to be ischaemic, although why the necrosis should be largely restricted to the right colon is not apparent. One possible explanation is that much of the fluid and electrolyte absorption from the lumen normally occurs in the ascending colon. Extended interruption of blood flow may result in the accumulation of trans-epithelially absorbed fluid in the mucosal interstitium during the period of abnormally low mucosal blood flow. On re-establishment of normal vascular pressures, increased interstitial pressure could prevent hyperaemia and clearance of this fluid by capillary blood flow. A gradually worsening positive feedback cycle could ensue, until ischaemia compromised epithelial viability.

An interesting parallel condition is found in some haemodialysis patients, who have had an episode of extreme dehydration due to excessively aggressive dialysis. In those patients, too, necrosis of the right colon, and sometimes also of the transverse colon, occurs.[272] Presumably the bowel infarction is due to hypovolaemia and/or hyperviscosity, with resulting low peripheral blood flow. However, precisely why this condition should preferentially affect the right colon is again not clear. Both conditions may be analogous to the ischaemia–reperfusion injury seen in the small bowel, in which oxygen-derived free radical generation and tissue damage have been implicated (see above).

One perhaps surprising potential cause of bowel mucosal ischaemia is distention of the lower bowel with air to enable colonoscopy, which depresses colonic mucosal perfusion to about half; use of CO_2 instead of air as the insufflation gas increases mucosal perfusion by 70% above baseline,[235] minimizes the probability of mucosal ischaemia and is readily absorbed by the colonic lining, reducing subsequent patient discomfort.

Another condition affecting the intramural vasculature of both the large and small bowel is portal venous hypertension (Fig. 10.46). An illustrative demonstration of the susceptibility of the colonic microvasculature to raised portal venous pressure occurred in a patient with the unusual development of a post-surgical inferior mesenteric arteriovenous fistula.[271] Ascites, colonic mucosal oedema, multiple mucosal ulcerations and severe bloody diarrhoea were observed, and biopsy demonstrated features of acute ischaemic colitis. Haematemesis from bleeding oesophageal varices also occurred; there was fever, liver function was markedly depressed and there was accompanying mental confusion. This constellation of findings suggests significant effects apparently extending throughout the tissues drained by the portal venous system. All symptoms resolved rapidly following intra-arterial embolization of the fistula. It is interesting to speculate whether an increased mucosal capillary pressure due to raised portal venous pressure caused capillary rupture or resulted in a reduced capillary flow. Alternatively, a reduced capillary flow could have resulted from raised interstitial pressure as a result of the mucosal oedema, due to a net fluid transudate from the mucosal capillaries secondary to increased capillary pressure.

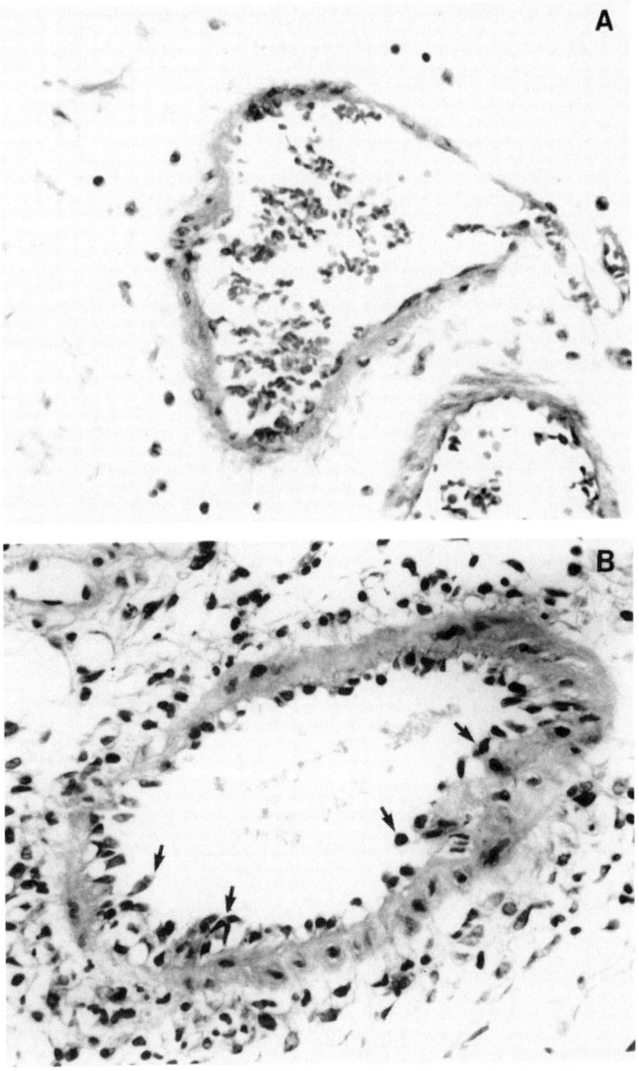

Fig. 10.46 Histological sections of rat submucosal venules. (H&E, ×510) **A** Control; the wall is thin and endothelial cells lining the lumen are flat. **B** In portal hypertension, the vein wall is thickened, and the endothelial cells protrude into the lumen (arrows). (Reproduced from reference no. 43)

Microvessels in tumours of the large bowel

The microvasculature of experimental tumours is a major focus of current investigations of tumour biology. Given the knowledge that vascularization is a critical step permitting rapid growth and tissue invasion in most tumours,[274] it is surprising that studies are so few.

The ultrastructure of human colorectal adenomas and carcinomas[275] indicates that the microvessels in adenomas are minimally changed and appear essentially normal. The perinuclear zone of the capillary endothelial cells frequently appears enlarged, and the cytoplasm contains increased numbers of a variety of organelles. Basal lamina is more prominent and perivascular collagen fibres are more frequent than in normal mucosa.

In carcinomas, the capillaries may be essentially normal, but have a thickened, multilayered basal lamina and fewer than normal numbers of fenestrae. Others have thickened endothelial cells, slit-like lumina and large numbers of cellular organelles with pericytes less closely associated with the outer surface of the endothelium than usual. The pericyte basal lamina may be largely or completely separate from that of the endothelium. Some microvessels have extremely irregular lumina with numerous fenestrae devoid of endothelial basal lamina. Thick-walled microvessels are also seen and have a prominent perivascular layer with both endothelial and perivascular cells rich in lysosomes, phagosomes and frequent myelin figures. Dilated and thin-walled venules which exhibit a discontinuous smooth muscle investment, and several reduplications of basal lamina, are also seen. Some of these electron microscopic changes are more common at the invading margins of the tumour.

In some experimental carcinomas of rat colon,[276] both differentiated and undifferentiated tumours have an equivalent degree of vascularization and are less well vascularized than normal mucosa. Capillary diameters are larger in differentiated tumours than in normal tissue, whereas hypertrophied endothelial cells with abundant rough endoplasmic reticulum positive for von Willebrand factor, and having a narrowed capillary lumen, are found in undifferentiated carcinomas;[277] mean intercapillary distances in both tumour types are longer than normal. Tumour cell proliferation is negligible at distances of greater than 80 μm from capillaries.

Study of experimentally induced rat colonic tumours[278] has shown a three-dimensional pattern of tumour microvessels similar to that of microvessels in human basal cell carcinomas.[279] This would indicate that microvessel endothelium of tumours of widely differing origin may be responding to the presence of the tumour in a quite similar way, both architecturally and cytostructurally.

THE LARGE INTESTINE — VERMIFORM APPENDIX

The appendix is a narrow, blind-ending segment of large bowel continuing inferiorly from the posterio-medial wall of the caecum. This is the point where the three taeniae coli converge to form a complete layer of longitudinal muscle over the appendix, in contrast to the rest of the large bowel. The appendix is suspended from a fold of the mesentery of the terminal ileum — the mesoappendix — which contains, near its free left crescentic margin, the appendicular artery, a branch of the posterior caecal artery which arises from the ileocolic branch of the superior mesenteric. Venous and lymph drainage vessels of the appendix are also contained in the mesoappendix. Apart from the continuous longitudinal muscle layer, its wall structure is essentially that of the large bowel. The luminal epithelial lining contains frequent pits — the crypts of Lieberkuhn — which are essentially similar to those of the remainder of the large bowel. At the level of the muscularis mucosae, however, there is extensive development of lymphoid nodules, each of which usually extends from the submucosa well into the lamina propria.

The lymphoid tissue of the appendix has been extensively used in studies of lymphoid tissue structure and function. There have been surprisingly few studies on the vasculature, microvasculature and lymphatics of this organ,[280–284] despite its frequent surgical removal from humans, either in a diseased or normal state.[285] A recent study[286] demonstrates that the mucosal microvascular architecture is essentially similar to that of the large bowel, except where the mucosa is largely occupied by lymph nodules, where the microvascular architecture resembles that of Peyer's patches (see below).[315]

The lymphatics of the mucosa, and of the intra- and interfollicular tissue of the appendix have been recently investigated (Fig. 10.47A,B,C).[284] The most luminal lymphatics occur just subjacent to the capillary rings surrounding the openings of the crypts.[284] These vessels, 40–80 μm in luminal diameter, form a superficial network of polygonal rings which surround the necks of the crypts. This network connects to finer (25–50 μm) lymph vessels which run down through the lamina propria and connect to large flat sinusoidal spaces that surround the individual lymphoid follicles of the thymus-dependent area of the appendix. Additional blind-ending initial lymphatics commence in the lamina propria between the follicles, and also drain to the perifollicular lymph sinuses. The lymph sinuses are drained by fine lymph vessels to a substantial submucous lymphatic plexus, which is extensively valved in the rabbit.[284]

Within the follicles, the microvessels and the lymphatics are structurally similar to those of other lymph nodules in Peyer's patches and in the mesenteric lymph nodes.[284] Thus, there are prominent high endothelial venules present, and there is structural evidence of lymphocyte diapedesis between the lymphoid nodules and the high endothelial venules and also between the nodules and the lymphatic sinuses. These structural features indicate that the appendix is specialized for a high degree of lymphocyte traffic between blood, appendix lymphoid nodules and lymph vessels efferent from the appendix.

The possible roles of the microvasculature and lymphatics in appendicitis have hardly been investigated.[287,288] Borchard[287] showed that a type of experimental appendicitis could be produced by ligation of the extrinsic lymphatics draining the appendix. In over two-thirds of inflamed appendices, there is faecalith in the lumen.[285] It is possible that this may have precipitated the acute inflammation, perhaps by causing a rise in intraluminal pressure which compromises blood flow within its wall.

Histological findings indicate that a marked infiltration of the mucosa with neutrophils is one of the earliest signs of pathology of the appendix in acute appendicitis.[285] It is tempting to speculate that circulating neutrophils are recruited from the circulation during the reperfusion period following an ischaemic episode of the appendix, as has been shown during experimental ischaemia of the small bowel and stomach.[234,239] These cells might then release oxygen-derived free radicals and/or hypochlorite, etc. which may further damage appendiceal tissues, microvessels and lymphatics. This could greatly increase transcapillary fluid transudation, compromise lymphatic drainage, cause marked tissue oedema, and lead to a progressively worsening cycle of tissue destruction. Additionally/alternatively, the proposed free radical damage could damage venular endothelium, thereby inhibiting the possible local venular control of small arteriolar tone (see above), so promoting hyperaemia and oedema.

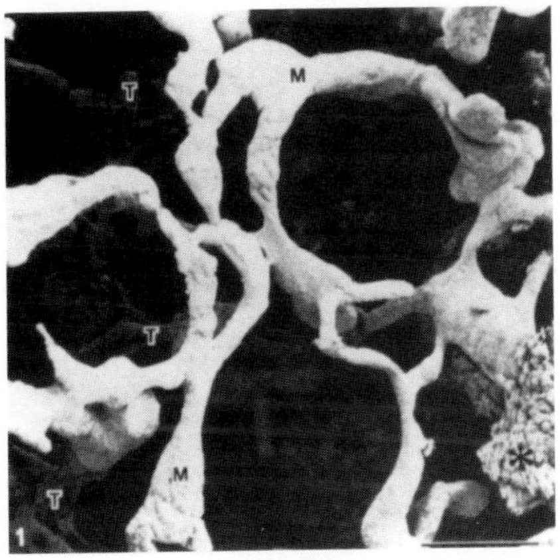

A

Fig. 10.47 Lymphatics of the rabbit appendix. **A** A scanning electron micrograph of a lymphatic corrosion cast (luminal view), showing a network of irregularly-shaped lymphatics (M) in the mucosal layer, connecting with lymphatics (T) in the thymus-dependent lymphatic follicular area. * = leaked resin. Bar = 250 µm **B** A schematic representation of the lymphatic system (shaded area) in the rabbit appendix. The left half of the figure shows the surface of the cross-section and the luminal surface, and the right half shows the lymphatic system revealed by scanning electron microscopy of corrosion casts. D = dome; P = pit resulting from infolding of the mucosal epithelium over the dome of the lymphoid follicle; GC = germinal centre; arrowheads = opening of the gland; G = intestinal glands; TDA = thymus-dependent area; H = high endothelial venules; M = mucosal lymphatic plexus; i = straight lymphatics crossing the isthmus and connecting mucosal lymphatics with the lymphatic plexus (T) of the thymus-dependent area (TDA); S = perifollicular lymphatic sinuses; SM = submucosa. **C** A scanning electron micrograph of a lymphatic corrosion cast (lateral view). The lymphatic network in the mucosa (M) is connected across the isthmus by straight lymphatics (i) continuous with the lymphatic plexus in the TDA (T). The lymphatic plexus in the TDA is continuous with the upper ends of the perifollicular lymphatic sinuses (S). The perifollicular sinuses are not continuous along the entire wall of each follicle, but show some interruptions. Bar = 500 µm (Reproduced from reference no. 284 by permission of Gastroenterology)

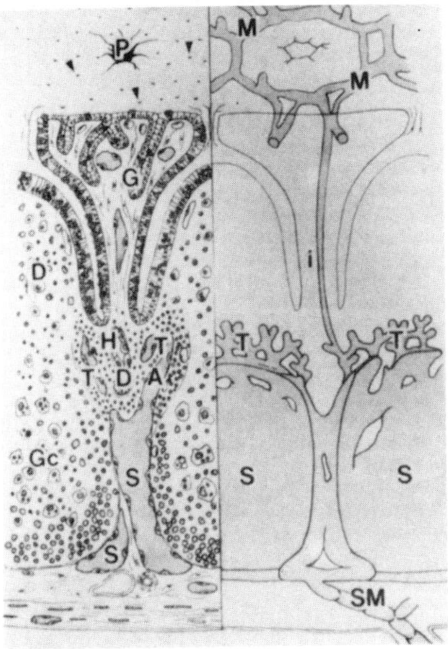

B

C

THE MESENTERIES OF THE GUT AND ASSOCIATED LYMPHATIC TISSUES

The mesenteries of the stomach and intestines form a large surface area for fluid and cellular exchange with the peritoneal space. This is of considerable clinical importance in peritoneal dialysis.[272] While the microvessels of the mesentery have been extensively studied by intravital microscopy,[289–292] there have been fewer studies of the lymphatics of the mesentery[293,294] and of the omental-associated lymphoid tissue[295,296] and fewer still of the microvasculature and lymphatics of the diaphragm[297,298] and the parietal body wall immediately external to the parietal peritoneum.[299]

Large vessels of the mesentery

The large arterial and venous vessels and the lymphatic trunks of the mesentery supply and drain the bowel wall.[22,289] As detailed above, the extrinsic vessels of the duodenum, ascending and descending colon, the medial part of the course of those of the sigmoid colon, and those of the rectum are retroperitoneal in their courses between the major vessels of the abdomen and the gut. Thus there is the possibility of development of venous portosystemic shunting at anastomoses at these sites in situations of raised portal venous pressure. Similar lymphatic anastomoses may develop between the chyliferous ducts of the mesentery and the lymphatics of the adjacent body wall.[299]

The large arterial vessels of the mesentery are under profound sympathetic nervous control and can dilate markedly, e.g. during digestion.[165] It is calculated that these vessels are the predominant site of vascular resistance in the overall blood supply to the intestine. The large arterial and venous vessels in the mesentery run closely opposed and in counter-current directions over substantial distances.[22,289] It therefore seems possible that the mesentery could be the site of counter-current exchange between arterial and portal venous blood or lymph, at least for lipid soluble and/or highly diffusible substances.

In addition to providing large anastomotic branches

which are involved in the anastomotic arcading of vessels en route to/from the bowel, there are also smaller branches of 100–200 μm, which supply and drain the fine microvascular beds which are developed in the polygonal planar spaces between the larger vessels of the mesentery. These microvascular networks supply not only the tissues of the mesentery itself, but also the fat deposits which develop in some parts of the mesentery.[289,290]

Microvasculature and lymphatics of the mesentery

Rabbit mesentery is only approximately 13 μm thick at its thinnest intervascular areas.[293] It is covered by mesothelial cells, which are joined by tight junctions to form a continuous sheet. The peritoneal surface of these cells has moderate numbers of microvilli, large numbers of cytoplasmic vesicles and frequent caveolae in the membrane of both peritoneal and basal lamina aspects, which is suggestive of a high degree of trans-mesothelial vesicular transport. The mesothelium is underlain by a continuous basal lamina, beneath which there are fibroblasts, collagen bundles, capillaries, lymphatics, and, in some regions, adipocytes.[293]

The microvasculature of the mesentery of the small bowel, the mesoappendix and the omentum have all been studied extensively, especially by in vivo microscopy.[289,290] A series of lateral arteriolar branches are given off the mesenteric arteries en route to the small gut. These larger arterioles branch and anastomose with each other, and with branches from adjacent mucosal arteries, to form a planar arcading arterial network. This supplies the smaller arteriolar and capillary networks found there (Fig. 10.48).[289–304] Venular drainage is similarly anastomotic and passes to the jejunal and ileal veins. The capillaries are continuous, with diameters in rat mesentery of 5–22 μm (mean 11 μm), and lengths of 100–1100 μm (mean 350 μm). Capillary exchange surface area is approximately 11% of tissue surface area.[291] The mesenteric veins within the mesentery are affected by reperfusion injury, causing neutrophil adherence and extravasation;[292] careful handling and the avoidance of vascularly occlusive compression or dehydration of the mesentery are obviously indicated in abdominal surgery.

Lymphatic capillaries are approximately 20 μm in diameter and are a common feature in the mesentery, as are larger lymphatic lacunae (approximately 50–70 μm diameter) (Fig. 10.49). These lymphatics are devoid of pericytes and have only an intermittent basal lamina associated with collagen anchoring filaments, as is found elsewhere in the initial lymphatics. The lymphatic endothelial cells contain frequent cytoplasmic vesicles and also caveolae on both luminal and abluminal membranes, suggestive of active transendothelial vesicular transport. Junctions between adjacent lymphatic endothelial cells are frequently lacking, and instead there are either gaps

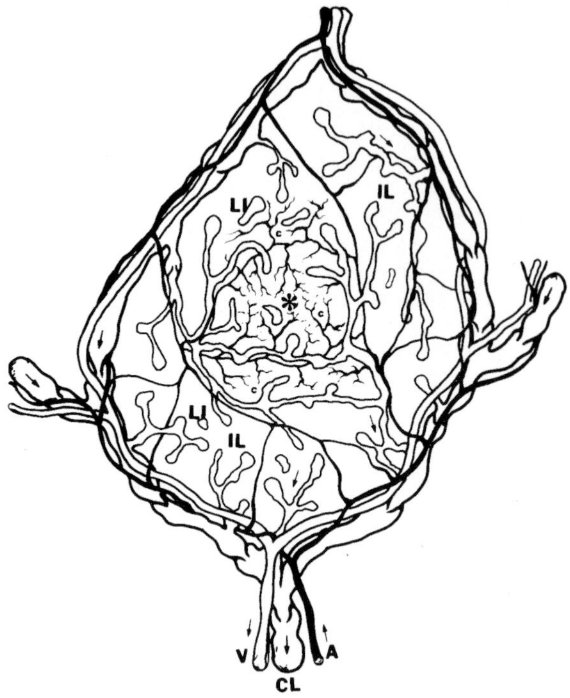

Fig. 10.48 A schematic diagram of the lymphatic system in the monkey mesentery, from enzyme histochemistry. IL = initial lymphatics; LI = lymphatic island; CL = collecting lymphatics; A = artery; V = vein; C = capillaries. The initial lymphatics with knob-like blind endings are distributed in about the centre of the lobular segment (*). (Reproduced from reference no. 294)

or an overlapping of cells without membrane junctions.[293] The thinness of the mesenteric membrane, and the structural and functional evidence of transendothelial and trans-mesothelial vesicular transport, suggests a significant role for this structure in fluid and solute exchange with peritoneal fluid,[299] of obvious significance for peritoneal dialysis patients. Interstitial proteins, including albumin, are rapidly leached from the mesentery by superfusion with protein-free solution;[300] this may account for some of the plasma protein loss in peritoneal dialysis.[301]

Parietal peritoneum in humans is 40–200 μm thick and contains large numbers of lymphatics. The subserosal circulation of the gut wall, and also the vasculature and lymphatics immediately subjacent to the parietal peritoneal layer of the body wall surrounding the peritoneal cavity, are also thought to be significantly involved in turnover of peritoneal fluid. The lymphatics of the diaphragm play a major role in the rapid clearance of macromolecules and larger structures, including peritoneal macrophages and blood cells, from the peritoneal cavity.

There are frequent openings called stomata[302] in the mesothelial covering of the muscular and central tendon parts of the peritoneal (but not the pleural) surface of the diaphragm, of 3–8 μm in diameter, which open directly

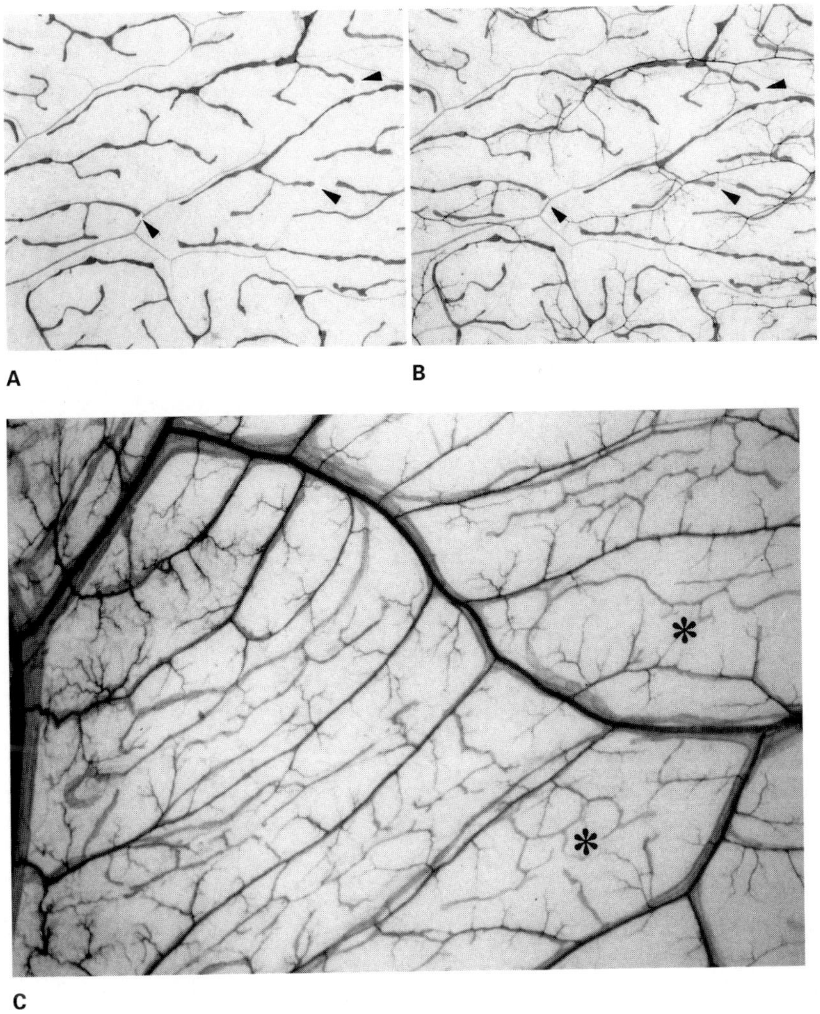

Fig. 10.49 Light micrographs of whole mounts of monkey mesentery of small (**A**,**B**) and large (**C**) intestine, with enzyme-histochemical demonstration of the lymphatics and blood vessels. **A** 5′-Nase activity. Lymphatics are pale-coloured due to positive 5′-Nase activity, whereas blood vessels reveal lower or no activity. **B** 5′-Nase and ALPase activity of the same preparation as in A; the arterioles and capillaries are darkly stained due to ALPase activity. The knob-like portions of initial lymphatics are indicated with arrowheads.(×6.3) **C** Mesocolon shows dense 5′-Nase-positive lymphatic networks located throughout without accompanying blood capillaries at about the centre (*) of lobular segments. Each 5′-Nase-positive initial lymphatic appears tubuloscaccular shaped, branching in an antler-like fashion. (×28) (Reproduced from reference no. 294)

into the rich plexus of lymphatic lacunae within the diaphragm[297,298,303–309] The surface mesothelium is underlain by a fibrous sheet of dense collagenous connective tissue, which exhibits clusters of 20–250 closely adjacent foramina 3–15 μm in diameter, termed macula cribriformis.[298] These maculae are irregularly distributed on the central tendon portion, but are arranged in rows on the muscular portion of the diaphragm, and are entirely absent from the pleural subserosal surface; the number of foramina in the maculae cribriformes exceeds the number of stomata in the overlying mesothelium significantly. Transit of macrophages, erythrocytes and leucocytes across the peritoneal stomata, through the maculae and into the diaphragmatic lymphatics has been confirmed in normal primate tissue (Fig. 10.51);[298] transit of intraperitoneally instilled tumour cells via the diaphragmatic stomata and lymphatics into the thoracic duct has been confirmed in dogs.[298,310] Clearance of particles instilled into peritoneal fluid via the diaphragmatic lymphatic lacunae is rapid (within 30 min) and is presumably enhanced by the rhythmic movements of the diaphragm in breathing. Clearance of peritoneal fluid by this route in portal hypertension is a major mechanism preventing the accumulation of ascites fluid.[293] The mesothelial covering of the inferior surface of the diaphragm is commonly denuded in peritoneal dialysis patients,[311] presumably allowing greater access of peritoneal and dialysis fluid to the diaphragmatic maculae cribriformes and lymphatics than normal, in these patients. Congested mesenteric and peritoneal lymphatics are a common finding in congestive cardiac failure.[312]

Lymphatic drainage of the mesentery is to the lymph nodes of that part of the gut it suspends. Drainage of the greater omentum is to right gastroepiploic and pyloric nodes, and on the right to the pancreaticosplenic nodes.[284,313,314]

Lymphatic tissue microvasculature

Apart from the diffuse lymphocytic seeding of the lamina propria, there are three distinct types of compact lym-

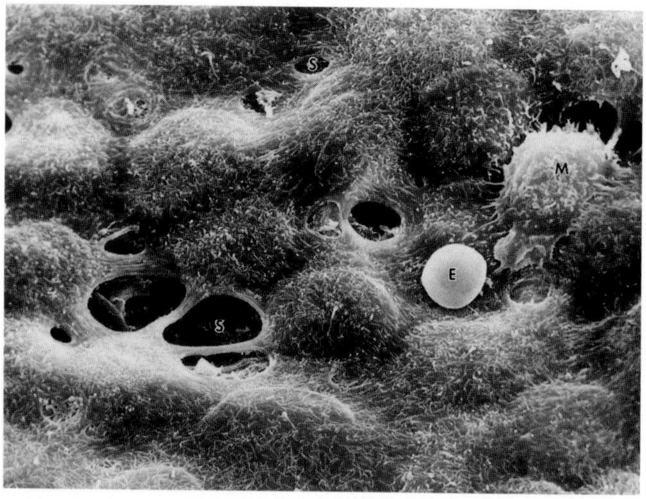

A

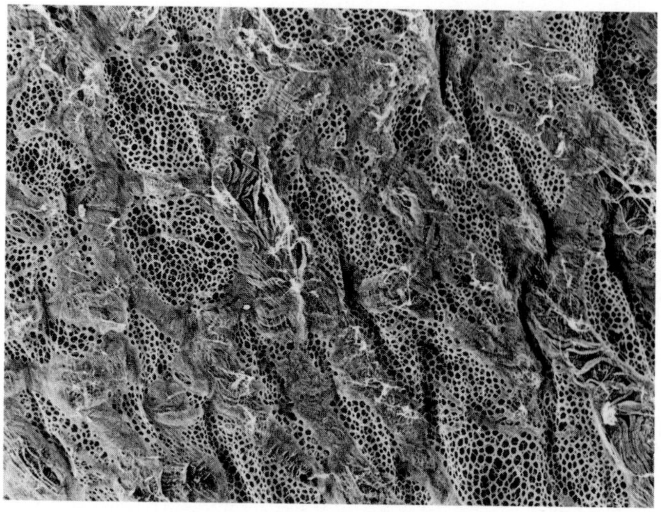

B

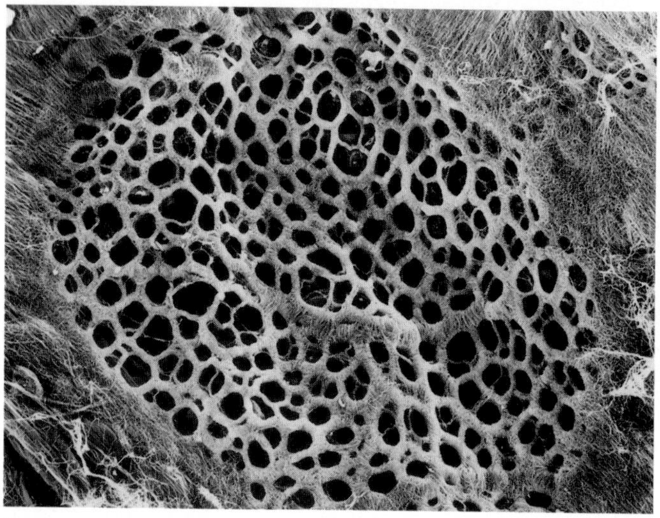

C

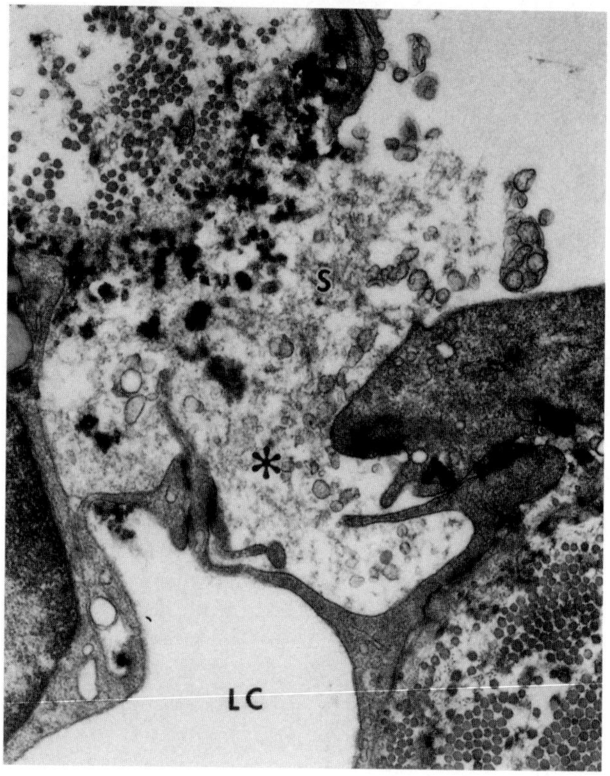

D

Fig. 10.50 Scanning (**A,B,C**) and transmission (**D**) electron micrographs of the peritoneal aspect of monkey diaphragm. **A** Peritoneal mesothelial surface. Round or oval peritoneal stomata (S) interposed between neighbouring cells of the mesothelium vary in size. E = erythrocyte; M = macrophage. (×1980) **B** Tendinous portion of diaphragm treated with 2 N NaOH for 4 days to remove mesothelium; the layer of subperitoneal connective tissue contains clusters of irregularly distributed foraminae. (×108) **C** Higher power view of **B**; a cluster of subperitoneal foraminae shows a cribriform appearance, corresponding to the macula cribriformis of Kihara. (×396) **D** Section of the muscular portion of the diaphragm 30 min after intraperitoneal injection of India ink. Carbon particles are seen passing through a peritoneal stomata (S) and the subperitoneal space (*) into the lumen of a lymphatic capillary (LC). (×11 250) (Reproduced from reference no. 298)

phatic tissue associated with the alimentary tract. These three are the Peyer's patches of the small intestine, the lymph nodes located usually at the base of the mesentery and the 'milky spots' of the omentum,[295,296] the latter considered to be a source of the cells normally present in peritoneal fluid.

Peyer's patches tend to be located towards the antimesenteric border of the intestine.[22,315] Each patch is comprised of a group of lymphoid follicles which are closely packed together to fill the mucosa locally. The patches disturb the normal architecture of the mucosa, so that villi are no longer present. They protrude somewhat into the intestinal lumen as a collection of dome-shaped structures, covered by epithelium. The epithelial basal lamina, where it overlies the patch, contains a very large number of pores up to 10 μm in diameter, and processes of epithe-

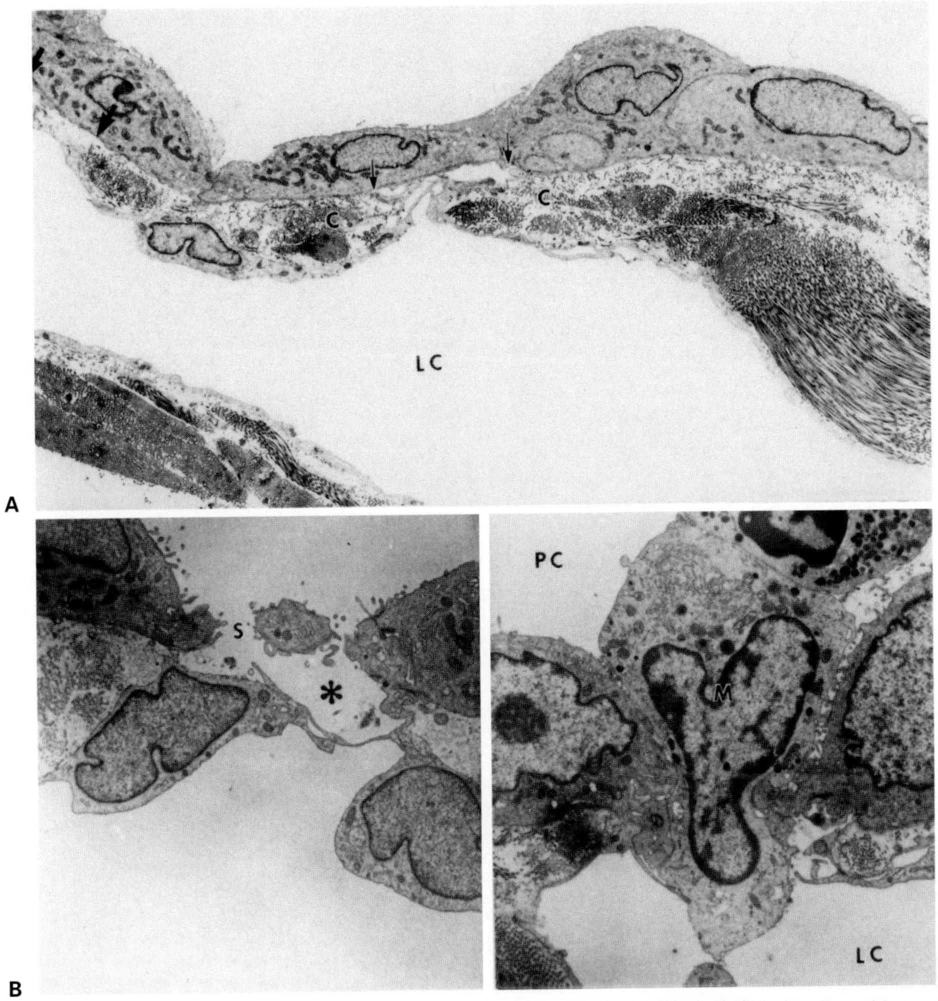

Fig. 10.51 A TEM images of the peritoneal side of the monkey diaphragm. A lymphatic capillary (LC) is distributed beneath the mesothelium. Some areas (between arrows) in the subperitoneal layer have no bundles of collagen fibrils (C). (×3630) **B** A peritoneal stoma (S) seen between neighbouring mesothelial cells. Note that the subperitoneal space (*) lies beneath the stoma. (×4620) **C** A macrophage (M) entering the lumen of a lymphatic capillary (LC). The cell is passing via the peritoneal stoma and the subperitoneal space into the lymphatic capillary. PC = peritoneal cavity. (×5830) (Reproduced from reference no. 298 by permission of the Japanese Society for Histological Documentation)

lial and lamina proprial cells pass through these pores. In the adjacent mucosa, as in the rest of the intestine, there is a virtually complete epithelial basal lamina sheet, with only occasional pores of 1.0 μm or less (Fig. 10.52A,B).[315] The junctions between the epithelial cells overlying the patch dome are not tight, so that intestinal luminal fluid may be in continuity with the interstitial spaces of the nodule,[317] permitting continuous monitoring by the cells in the patch of antigens in the intestinal lumen.

Each nodule in a patch is supplied by 2–4 arterioles which enter near its serosal or lateral aspects. These arterioles break up into a dense capillary network which permeates the compact lymphatic tissue (Fig. 10.53A). The nodule is largely drained by high endothelial venules which predominate on the superficial serosal aspect of the nodule (Fig. 10.53A).[315,318] The luminal surface of the endothelial lining of these vessels has a characteristic cobblestone-like appearance (Fig.10.54A) to which lymphocytes are usually found adherent in large numbers (Fig. 10.54B,C).[318] The location of the high endothelial venules (HEVs) downstream from the capillaries of the nodule has been suggested to indicate that the induction of high endothelium here is a function of nodule cell released cytokines.[316]

Lymphocytes transit the endothelium of the HEVs[315,317] both between endothelial cells and directly through the cytoplasm of the high endothelial cells in large numbers. Attachment of lymphocytes to vascular endothelial cells is controlled by the regulated expression of a series of cell surface molecules on both the lymphocyte and the

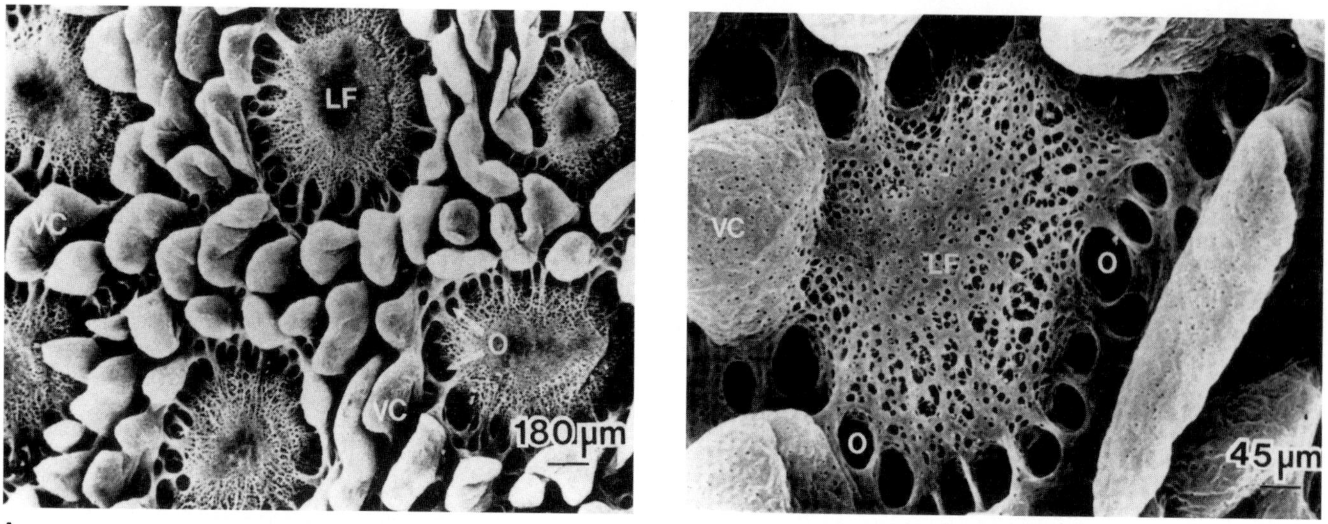

A B

Fig. 10.52 Scanning electron micrographs of the small intestinal epithelial basal lamina of villi and overlying Peyer's patches. **A** Small intestine, rat. Epithelial removal is complete in all figures. Several lymphoid follicles (LF) are located within a Peyer's patch surrounded by villus cores (VC). The porosity of the basement membrane overlying the follicles is greater than that of the villus cores. Ostia (O) of crypts of Lieberkuhn are also evident. Bar = 180 µm **B** Small intestine, rat. An isolated lymphoid follicle (LF) between several villus cores (VC). The porosity of the basement membrane is markedly increased on the lymphoid follicles. Ostia (O) of crypts of Lieberkuhn are also evident. Bar = 45 µm (Reproduced from reference no. 317 by permission of Gastroenterology)

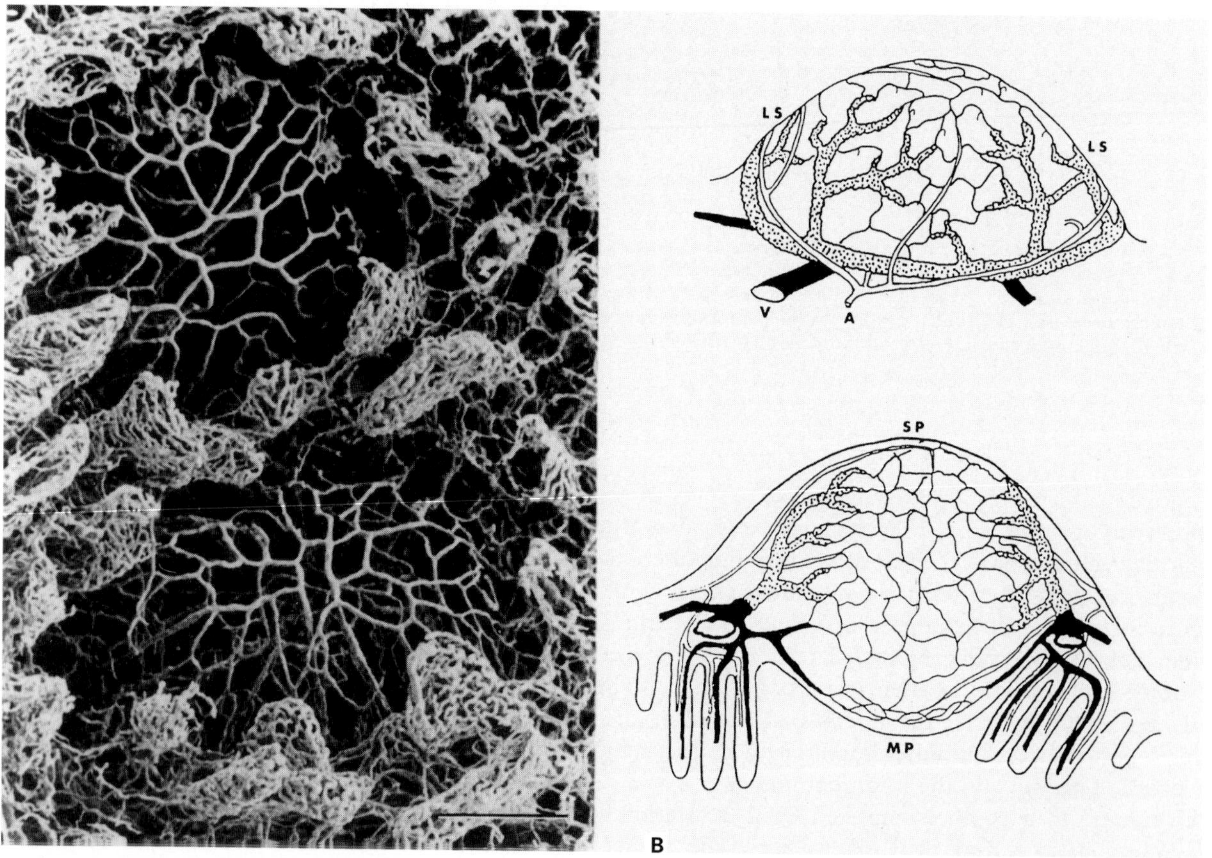

A B

Fig. 10.53 Lymphatics of Peyer's patches. **A** Corrosion microvascular cast of mouse small intestine: luminal view of two nodules of a Peyer's patch, with surrounding villi. Note the flat capillary plexus that covers the dome areas of the nodules. Bar = 250 µm **B** Diagrammatic representation of blood vessels associated with lymphoid nodules of the Peyer's patch as seen from the serosal surface (top) and in cross-section (bottom). Arteries (A) are shown in outline, venules and small veins (V) with attenuated endothelium in solid black. Stippling = high endothelial venules; LS = lateral surface; SP = serosal pole; MR = mucosal pole or dome area. (Reproduced from reference no. 315 by permission of the Anatomical Record)

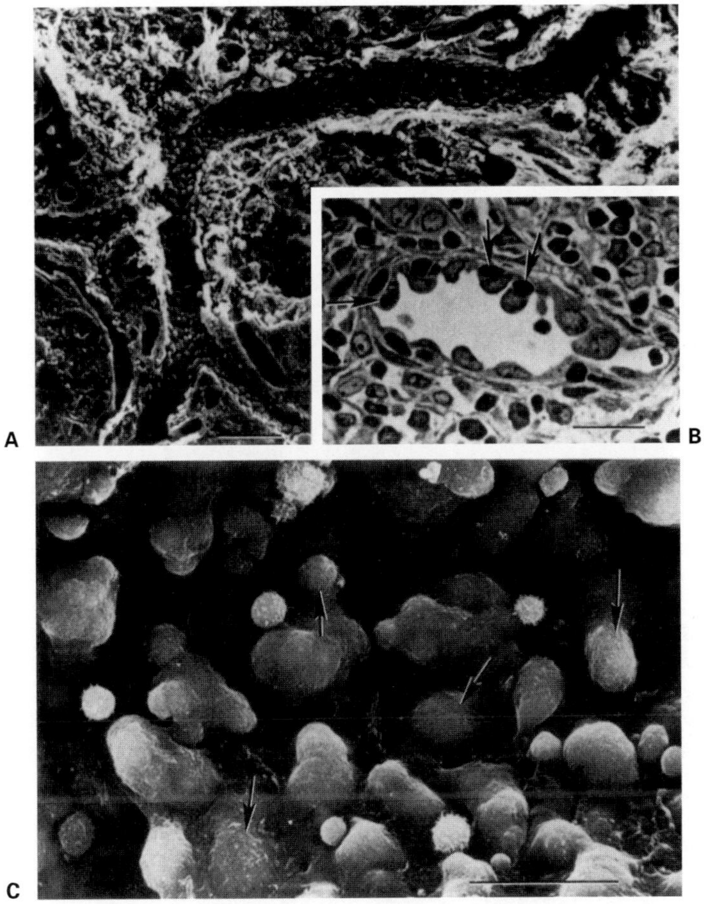

Fig. 10.54 High endothelial venules of Peyer's patches. **A** Low magnification of the lumen of a high endothelial venule from an animal depleted of lymphocytes. There are few lymphocytes adherent to the luminal surface. Bar = 100 µm **B** Transverse section of a high endothelial venule as in A. Some lymphocytes are seen within the vascular wall (arrows), presumably in transit through it. Bar = 25 µm **C** Luminal aspect of a venule 45 min after syngeneic spleen cells had been injected into an animal depleted of lymphocytes. Many lymphocytes are adhering to the surface, and the outline of others can be perceived under the endothelium (arrows). Bar = 25 µm (Reproduced from reference no. 209 by permission of the Anatomical Record)

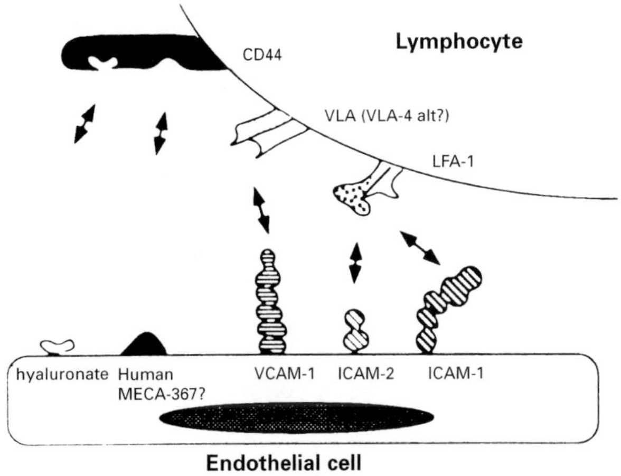

Fig. 10.55 Diagrammatic illustation of some of the molecules involved in lymphocyte binding to the endothelium of vessel walls in mucosa-associated lymphatic tissues. (Reproduced from reference no. 196)

endothelium which together act as 'adressin' molecules, to ensure the appropriate targeting of particular lymphocytes to specific tissue sites (Fig. 10.55).

The HEVs are connected to the arterioles by 'thoroughfare channels' which may be functionally equivalent to arteriovenous anastomoses (AVA), although they lack the specific structure of AVAs found in the skin. In addition to the HEVs, there are conventional venules lined by attenuated continuous endothelium which drain around the mucosal dome aspect of the nodule (Fig. 10.53B).[315]

The mesenteric lymph nodes have a microvascular and lymphatic circulation similar to other lymph nodes (Figs 10.56, 10.57).[319–322] Afferent lymphatic channels from the mesentery connect into the intranodal sinuses, and also have connections to the efferent lymphatics of the node, which permits lymph flow to by-pass the intranodal lymphatic sinuses (Fig. 10.57). This connection may be important in permitting lymph-borne metastatic cells from an alimentary tract tumour to by-pass the mesenteric nodes, and to gain access to the general circulation via the cisterna chyli, the thoracic duct and the left subclavian vein.

The omentum is largely covered with an attenuated mesothelium which exhibits frequent gaps between cell borders in the transparent regions, giving these regions a net-like appearance; these mesothelial cells are underlain by a discontinuous basal lamina, and both fenestrated and continuous capillaries are present within the connective tissue of the transparent regions of the omentum (Fig. 10.58). Within the omentum there are oval opaque areas or 'milky spots,' sometimes termed macrophagal plaques, about 1 mm in length with a frequency ranging from 2 per cm^2 in human adults to 40 per cm^2 in neonates. The mesothelium overlying the milky spots is composed of thicker-domed mesothelial cells; the milky spot is vascularized by a characteristic network of microvessels termed an omental glomerulus, and a specialized lymphatic network drains the spot. Macrophages are the most prevalent parenchymal cell type in milky spots, with T- and B-lymphocytes and mast cells making up the remainder. Macrophages migrate between the mesothelial cells into the peritoneal cavity in normal animals and numbers are greatly increased in peritoneal infection (Fig. 10.59).[295] Normal peritoneal macrophages and monocytes are derived from progenitor cells in the milky spots.

Resident macrophages in milky spots take up particles, e.g. India-ink, injected into the peritoneal cavity within 30 min. Gastrointestinal and ovarian tumours frequently

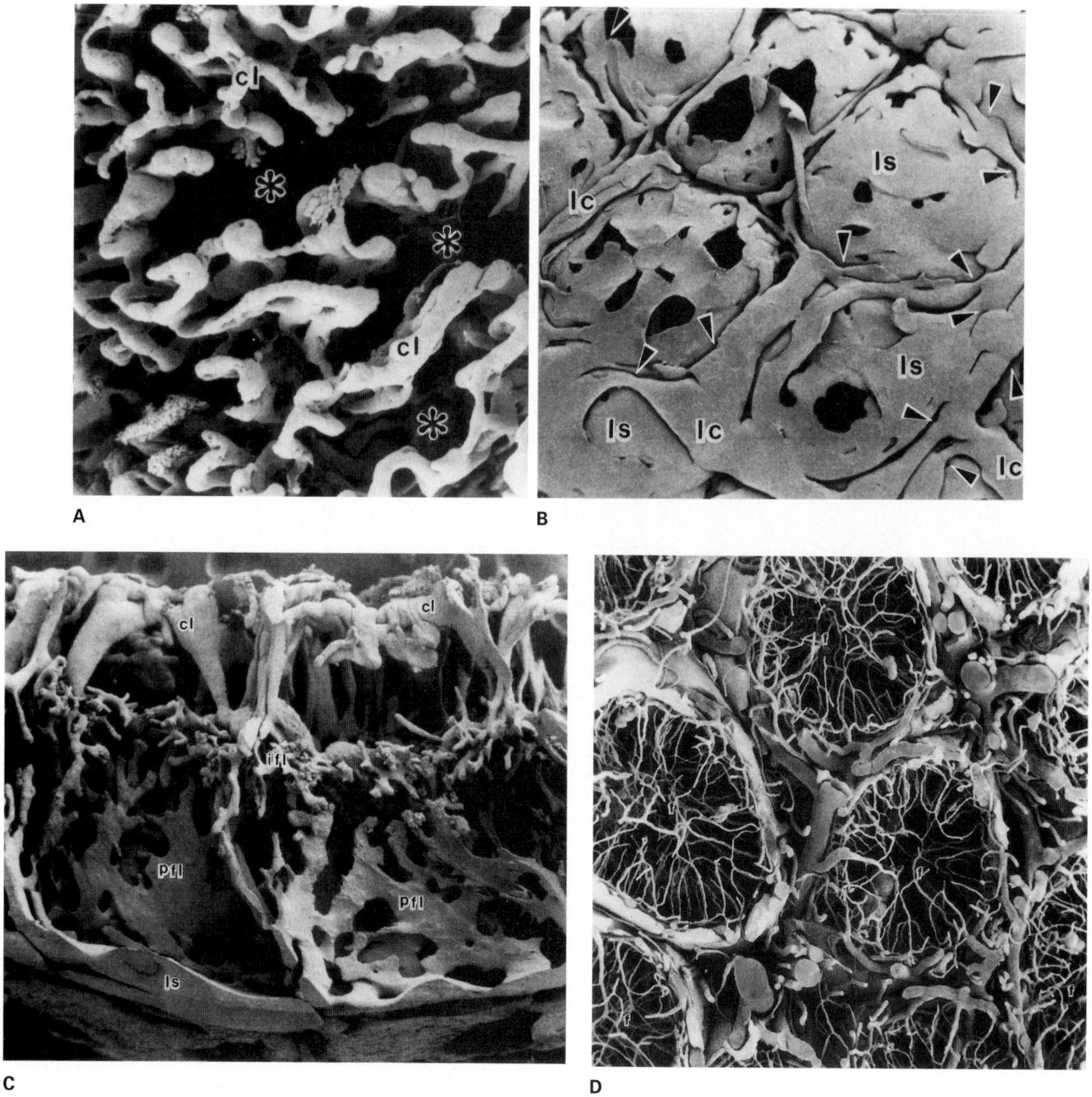

Fig. 10.56 SEM images of lymphatic corrosion casts of the Peyer's patches. **A** A luminal view. Interconnected central lacteals (cl) surround the holes (*) which are occupied by lymphoid follicles in their natural state. (×45) **B** A serosal view. Bottoms of the follicles are widely covered with lymphatic sinuses (ls). The sinuses drain into collecting lymphatic vessels (1c) which show notches (arrowheads) indicative of valve locations. (×36) **C** SEM image of a lymphatic corrosion cast of a Peyer's patch (lateral view). The interconnecting central lacteals (cl) are linked across the interglandular area by straight lymphatic vessels with the lymphatic plexus in the interfollicular area (ifl). The lymphatic plexus gradually converges into the perifollicular lymphatic sinuses (pfl), which incompletely surround the follicle. The bottoms of the follicles are also covered with wide lymphatic sinuses (1s). (×62) **D** SEM view of a lymphatic/blood vascular corrosion cast of the rabbit Peyer's patch (a section parallel to the serosal surface) The capillary networks of the follicles (f) are surrounded by the perifollicular lymphatic sinuses (pale). In the interfollicular area there are only a few capillaries and arteries, but many high endothelial venules (darker) which are closely associated with the perifollicular lymphatic networks. (×47) (Reproduced from reference no. 316 by permission of the Japanese Society for Histological Documentation)

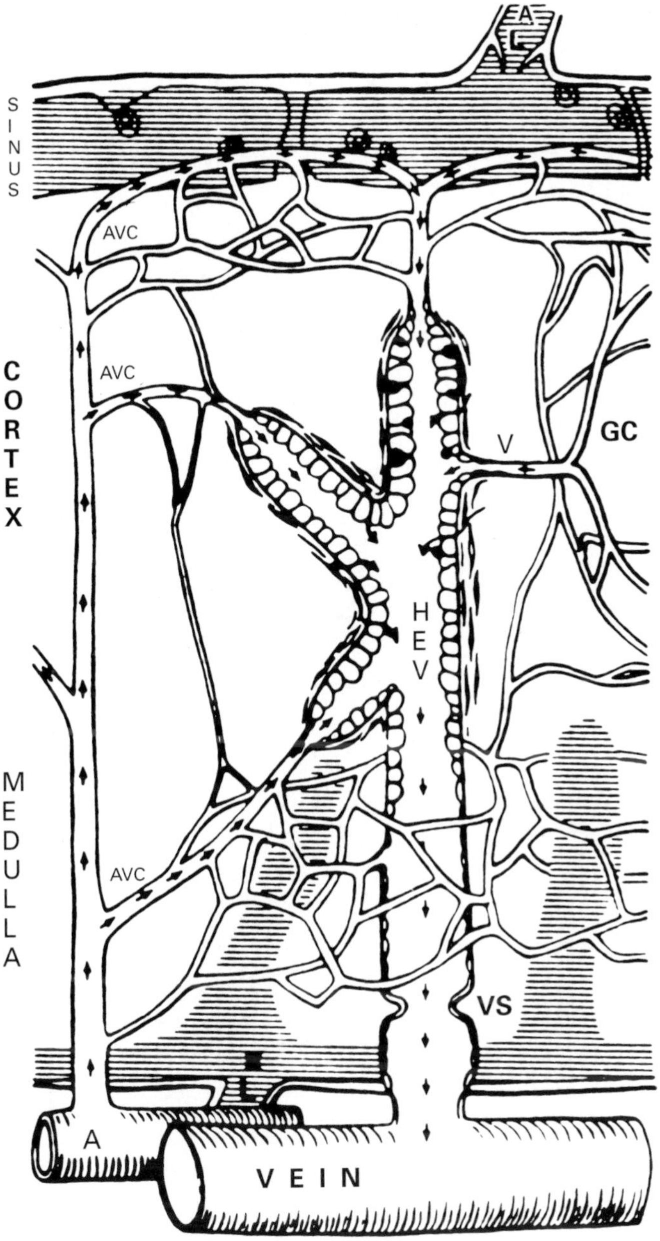

Fig. 10.57 Schematic diagram of the vascular anatomy of rat lymph nodes. The location of high endothelial venules (HEV) between arteriovenous communications (AVC) and venous sphincters (VS) provides a unique system for regulating blood flow in these venules. Cross-hatching indicates the distribution of lymphatic sinuses. Afferent lymphatics (AL), efferent lymphatics (EL) and germinal centres (GC) are also illustrated (Reproduced from reference no. 320 by permission of the American Journal of Pathology)

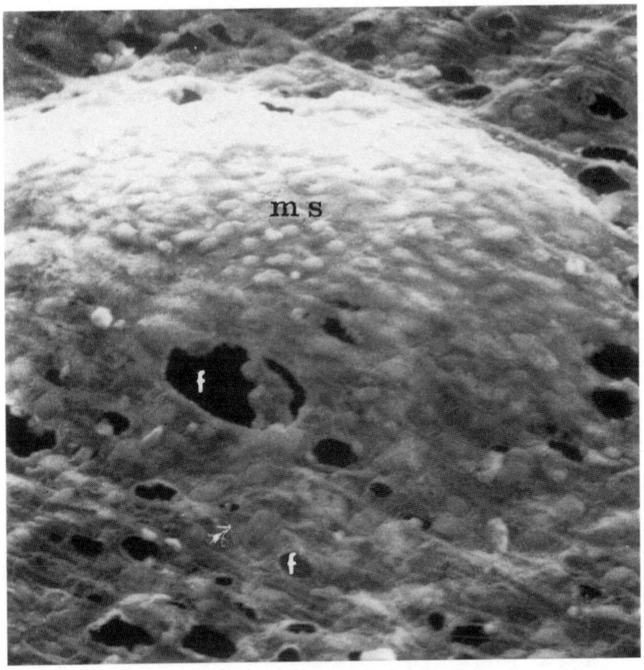

A

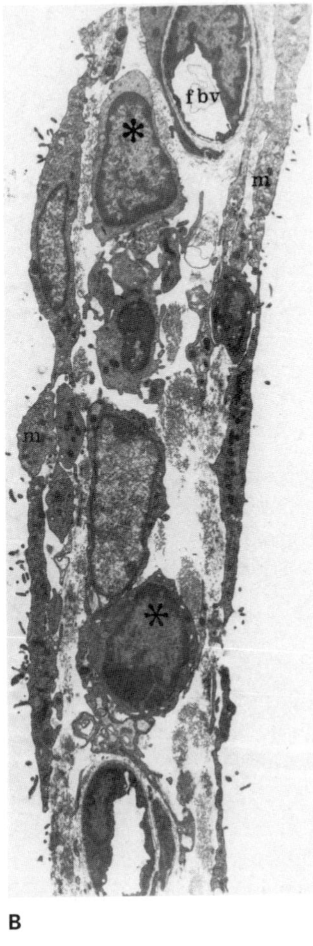

B

Fig. 10.58 A This low-power scanning electron micrograph demonstrates the net-like region (transparent region) of the greater omentum as well as an omental milky spot (ms). Numerous fenestrae (f) are found in the net-like regions, but are absent from the milky spot. (×405) **B** Electron micrograph of the thin region of the greater omentum showing mesothelial (m) layers and fenetrated (fbv) blood vessels. Connective tissue cells (*) are also shown in the connective tissue layer . (× 2205) (Reproduced from reference no. 295 by permission of the Japanese Society for Histological Documentation)

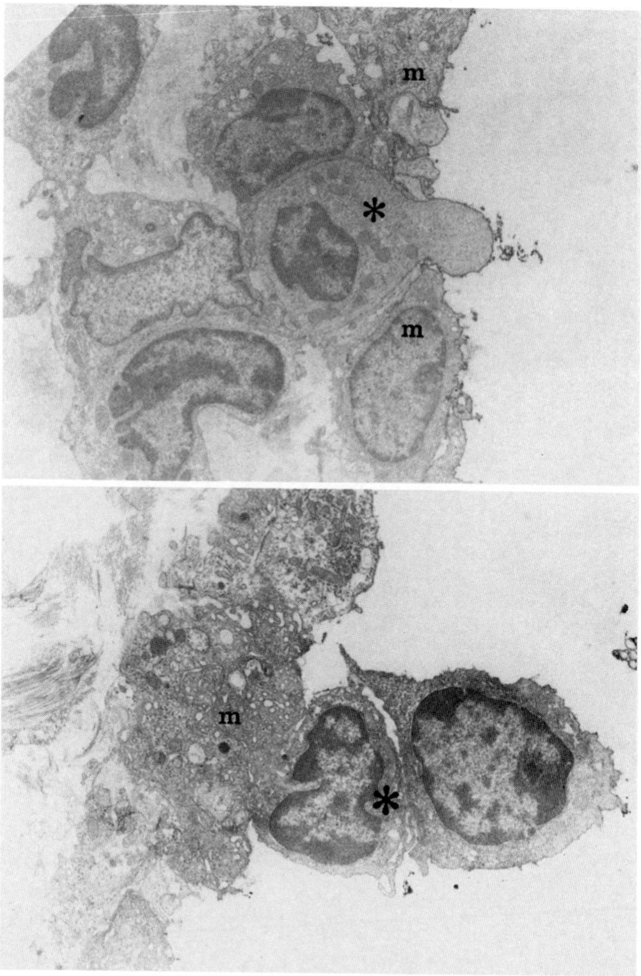

A

B

Fig. 10.59 A Section of mesothelial (m) lining of milky spot showing a cell (*) in the process of migrating across the mesothelial lining into the peritoneal cavity. (×14 560) **B** Electron micrograph showing peritoneal cells (*) attached to mesothelial (m) lining of milky spot. (×14 800) (Reproduced from reference no. 295 by permission of the Japanese Society for Histological Documentation)

metastasize to the greater omentum, and it is presumed that the milky spots are the usual metastatic site via peritoneal fluid;[296] presumably, endometriosis of the omentum also localizes to these sites initially via peritoneal fluid spread after retrograde flow of menstrual products.

CONCLUSION

In the last decade, the many active roles of microvascular endothelial cells in normal tissue function have been identified, including the synthesis and release of the potent vasodilator nitric oxide (EDRF), the powerful vasoconstrictor peptide endothelin, and the regulated expression of a variety of molecules mediating leucocyte rolling, adhesion and transmigratory diapedesis. It is now established that microvascular endothelial cells actively and apparently separately regulate local blood perfusion, tissue leucocyte recruitment and blood–tissue macromolecular permeability. The role of these cells in disease processes poses significant challenges for further research.

REFERENCES

1. Granger DN, Barrowman JA, Kvietys PR. Clinical gastrointestinal physiology. Philadelphia: Saunders, 1985.
2. Versalius A. De humani corporis fabrica, lib 5, figs 15, 16. Basilae, 1543: pp 367–368. (Cited in Butler [12])
3. Bartholin T. Anatome ex omnium veterum recentiorumque observationibus. Lugdunum Batavotum, 1673: p 447. (Cited in Butler [12])
4. Dionis P. The anatomy of humane bodies. London, 1703 p 302. (Cited in Butler [12])
5. Portal A. Cours d'anatomie medicale, Vol 4. Paris, 1803 pp 447, 533, 539. (Cited in: Butler [12])
6. Postlethwait RW. Surgery of the oesophagus. 2nd ed. Norwark: Appleton-Century-Crofts, 1986.
7. Demel R. Die gefassversorgung der speiserohre. Ein betrag zur oesophaguschirurgie. Arch Klin Chir 1924; 128: 453–504.
8. Lendrum FC. Anatomic features of the cardiac orifice of the stomach with special reference to cardiospasm. Arch Intern Med 1937; 59: 474–511.
9. Potter SE, Holyoke EA. Observations on the intrinsic blood supply of the oesophagus. Arch Surg 1950; 61: 944–948.
10. Shapiro AL, Robillard GL. The esophageal arteries: their configurational anatomy and variations in relation to surgery. Ann Surg 1950; 131: 171–185.
11. Swigart LL, Siekert RG, Hambley WC, Anson BJ. The esophageal arteries: an anatomic study of 150 specimens. Surg Gynecol Obstet 1950; 90: 234–243.
12. Burger D, Piehslinger E. Die blutversorgung des zervikalen osophagus. Acta Anat 1991; 142: 204–207.
13. Caix M, Descottes B, Rousseau D, Grousseau D. The arterial vascularisation of the middle and lower oesophagus. Anat Clin 1981; 3: 95–106.
14. Sweet RH. Subtotal esophagectomy with high intrathoracic esophago-gastric anastamosis in the treatment of extensive cicatrical obliteration of the oesophagus. Surg Gynecol Obstet 1946; 83: 417–427.
15. Williams DB, Payne WS. Observations on esophageal blood supply. Mayo Clin Proc 1982; 57: 448–453.
16. Aharinejad S, Bock P, Lametschwandtner A. Scanning electron microscopy of esophageal microvasculature in human infants and rabbits. Anat Embryol 1992; 186: 33–40.
17. Aharinejad S, Franz P, Lametschwandtner A, Firbas W. Esophageal vasculature in guinea pigs. A scanning electron microscope study of vascular corrosion casts. Scanning Microsc 1989; 3: 567–574.
18. Aharinejad S, Franz P, Lametschwandtner A, Firbas W, Fakhari M. The microvasculature of the oesophagus in humans and in other mammals. Anat Anz (Suppl) 1991; 170: 145–146.
19. Aharinejad S, Lametschwandtner A, Franz P, Firbas W. The vascularization of the digestive tract studied by scanning electron microscopy with special emphasis on the teeth, oesophagus, stomach, small and large intestine, pancreas and liver. Scanning Microsc 1991; 5: 811–849.
20. Browning J, Gannon BJ, O'Brien P. The microvasculature and gastric luminal pH of the forestomach of the rat: a comparison with the glandular stomach. Int J Microcirc Clin Exp 1983; 2: 109–118.
21. Kokue E, Kurebayashi Y. Rat forestomach ulcer induced by drinking glucose solution as an experimental model of gastroduodenal ulcer in swine. Jpn J Vet Sci 1980; 42: 395–399.
22. Warwick R, Williams PL. Gray's anatomy. 35th ed. Edinburgh: Longmans, 1973.

23. Butler H. The veins of the oesophagus. Thorax 1951; 6: 276–296.
24. Kahn D, Terblanche J. A study of the venous drainage of the lower oesophagus using a resin-casting technique. S Afr J Surg 1979; 17: 136.
25. Vianna A, Hayes P, Moscoso G, Driver M, Portmann B, Westaby D, Williams R. Normal venous circulation of the gastroesophageal junction. Gastroenterology 1987; 93: 876–889.
26. de Carvalho CAF. Sur l'angio-architecture veineuse de la zone de transition oesophago-gastrique et son interpretation fonctionnelle. Acta Anat 1966; 64: 125–162.
27. Spence RAJ. The venous anatomy of the lower oesophagus in normal subjects and in patients with varices: an image analysis study. Br J Surg 1984; 71: 739–744.
28. von Luschka H. Der kehlkopf des menschen. Tubingen: Laupp H, 1871: p 143. (Cited by Butler [12]).
29. Davis MJ, Gore RW. Capillary pressure in rat intestinal muscle and mucosal villi during venous pressure elevation. Am J Physiol 1985; 249: H174–H187.
30. Elze C, Beck K. Die venosen wundernetze des hypopharynx. Ztschr fur Ohrenh 1919; 77: 185–194. (Cited by Butler [12])
31. Kegaries DL. The venous plexus of the oesophagus: its clinical significance. Surg Gynecol Obstet 1934; 58: 46–51.
32. Postlethwait RW, Sealy WC. Surgery of the oesophagus. Springfield: Thomas, 1961.
33. Enterline H, Thompson J. Pathology of the oesophagus. New York: Springer, 1984.
34. Sakata K. Ueber die lymphgefasse des oesophagus und uber seine regionaren lymphdrusen mit berucksichtigung der verbreitung des carcinoms. Med u Chir 1903; 11: 634–656.
35. Rouviere H. Anatomie des lymphatiques de l'homme. Paris: Masson, 1932.
36. Rouviere H. Anatomy of the human lymphatic system. Tobias MJ, Trans. Ann Arbour: Edwards, 1938.
37. Werner JA, Schunke M. Cerium-induced light microscopic demonstration of 5′-nucleotidase activity in the lymphatic capillaries of the proximal oesophagus of the rat. Acta Histochem 1989; 85: 15–21.
38. Szabo LE, Karacsonyi S, Pataki ZS. Uber den funktionellen lymphkrieslauf des osophagus. Acta Chir Hung 1963; 4: 85–91.
39. Kakegawa T, Yamana H, Fujita H, Machi J. Radical operation for thoracic esophageal carcinoma. In: Kasai M, ed. Esophageal cancer. Amsterdam: Exerpta Med, 1986: pp 122–125.
40. Zijlstra FG, Hynna-Liepert TT, Dinda PK, Beck IT, Paterson WG. Microvascular permeability increases early in the course of acid-induced esophageal injury. Gastroenterology 1991; 101: 295–302.
41. Stein BE, Schwartzman ML, Carroll MA, Stahl RE, Rosenthal WS. Role of arachadonic acid metabolites in acid-pepsin injury to rabbit oesophagus. Gastroenterology 1989; 97: 278–283.
42. Eastwood GL, Beck BD, Castell DO, Brown FC, Fletcher JR. Beneficial effects of indomethacin on acid-induced esophagitis in cats. Dig Dis Sci 1981; 26: 601–608.
43. Hashizume M, Kitano S, Sugimachi K, Sueishi K. Three-dimensional view of the vascular structure of the lower oesophagus in clinical portal hypertension. Hepatology 1988; 8: 1482–1487.
44. Beppu K, Inokuchi K, Koyanagi N et al. Prediction of variceal hemorrhage by esophageal endoscopy. Gastrointest Endosc 1981; 27: 213–218.
45. Spence RAJ, Sloan JM, Johnston GW, Greenfield A. Oesophageal mucosal changes in patients with varices. Gut 1983; 24: 1024–1029.
46. Spence RAJ, Sloan JM, Johnston GW. Oesophagitis in patients undergoing oesophageal transection for varices — a histological study. Br J Surg 1983; 70: 332–334.
47. Wagenknecht TW, Noble JF, Baronofsky ID. Nature of bleeding in esophageal varices. Surgery 1953; 33: 869–874.
48. Spence RAJ, Terblanche J. Venous anatomy of the lower oesophagus: a new perspective on varices. Br J Surg 1987; 74: 659–660.
49. McCormack TT, Rose JD, Smith PM, Johnson AG. Perforating veins and blood flow in oesophageal varices. Lancet 1983; II: 1442–1444.
50. Thorek P. Anatomy in surgery. 3rd ed. New York: Springer, 1985.
51. Okanobu K. The lymphatics of the osophagus — evaluation of endoscopic RI-lymphoscintigraphy with SPECT. (In Japanese). Nippon Gekka Gakkai Zasshi 1990; 91: 808–817.
52. Yu W, Whang I. Surgical implications of the posterior gastric artery. Am J Surg 1990; 159: 420–422.
53. Wheaton LG, Sarr MS, Schlossberg L, Bulkley AB. Gross anatomy of the splanchnic vasculature. In: Granger DN, Bulkley GB. Measurements of blood flow. Applications to the splanchnic circulation. Baltimore: Williams and Wilkins, 1981; pp 9–45.
54. Vandamme JPJ, Bonte J. The blood supply of the stomach. Acta Anat 1988; 131: 89–96.
55. Guth PH, Ballard KW. Physiology of the gastric circulation. In: Physiology of the gastrointestinal tract (1st edn.). Johnson LR, ed. New York: Raven, 1981; pp 17–27.
56. Guth PH, Leung FL. Physiology of the gastric circulation. In: Physiology of the gastrointestinal tract (2nd edn.) Johnson LR, ed. New York: Raven, 1987; Vol 2, pp 1031–1053.
57. Mall F. The vessels and walls of the dog's stomach. Johns Hopk Hosp Rep 1896; 1: 1–36.
58. Piasecki C. Blood supply to the human gastroduodenal mucosa with special reference to the ulcer bearing areas. J Anat 1974; 118: 295–335.
59. Piasecki C. Observations on the submucous plexus and mucosal arteries of the dog's stomach and first part of the duodenum. J Anat 1975; 119: 133–148.
60. Gannon B, Browning J, O'Brien P. The microvascular architecture of the glandular mucosa of rat stomach. J Anat 1982; 135: 667–683.
61. Matsuura T, Yamamoto T. An electron microscope study of arteriolar branching sites in the normal gastric mucosa of rats and in experimental ulcer. Virchows Arch A Pathol Anat Histopathol 1988; 413: 123–131.
62. Ohtani O, Kikuta A, Ohtsuka A, Takaguchi T, Murakami T. Microvasculature as studied by the microvascular casting/ scanning electronmicroscope method. 1. Endocrine and digestive system. Arch Histol Jpn 1983; 46: 1–42.
63. Ohtani O, Murakami T, Kobayashi Y. Lymphatics and myenteric plexus in the muscular coat in the rat stomach: a scanning electron microscopic study of corrosion casts made by intra-arterial injection. Arch Histol Jpn 1987; 50: 87–93.
64. Stach W, Hung N, Schoof S. Zur gefassversorgung des plexus myentericus (Auerbach) in dickdarm der katz. Z Microsc-Anat Forsch Leipzig 1977; 91: 522–530.
65. Gannon B, Browning S, O'Brien P, Rogers P. Mucosal microvascular architecture of the fundus and body of human stomach. Gastroenterology 1984; 86: 866–875.
66. Ohtsuka A, Ohtani O. The microvascular architecture of the rabbit stomach corpus in vascular corrosion casts. Scan Electron Microsc 1984; 4: 1951–1956.
67. Raschke M, Lierse H, van Ackeran H. Microvascular architectue of the mucosa of the gastric corpus in man. Acta Anat 1987; 130: 185–190.
68. Zabolot'ko LA. Vnutriorgannoe venoznoe ruslo kardial'nogo otdela Zheludka u detei pervykh trekh let zhizni. Arkh Anat Gistol Embriol 1990; 98: 42–47.
69. Prokopiw I, Hynna-Liepert TT, Dinda PK, Prentice RSA, Beck IT. The microvascular anatomy of the canine stomach. A comparison between the body and the antrum. Gastroenterology 1991; 100: 638–647.
70. Konig HE. Betraig zur blutversorgung des magens beim hund — eine korrosionsanatomische und rasterelektronenmikroskopische untersuchung. Tierarztl Prax 1992; 20: 429–433.
71. Imada M, Tatsumi H, Fujita H. Scanning electron microscopy of vascular architecture in the gastric mucosa of the golden hamster. Cell Tissue Res 1987; 250: 287–293.
72. Marais J. Microvasculature of the feline stomach. Acta Anat Basel 1988; 131: 262–264.

73. Marais J, Anderson BG, Anderson WG. Comparative mucosal microvasculature of mammalian stomach. Acta Anat Basel 1989; 134: 31–34.
74. Tsuchihashi Y, Tani T, Maruyama K, Yorioka S, Okada K, Sudo H, Ashihara T, Fujita S, Kawai K. Structural alterations of mucosal microvascular system in human chronic gastritis. In: Manabe H, Zweifach BW, Messmer K, eds. Microcirculation in circulatory disorders. Tokyo: Springer-Verlag, 1988; pp 161–169.
75. Piasecki C, Thrasivoulou C, Rahim A. Ulcers produced by ligation of individual gastric mucosal arteries in the guinea pig. Gastroenterology 1989; 97: 1121–1129.
76. Holm-Rutli L, Obrink KJ. Rat gastric mucosal microcirculation in vivo. Am J Physiol 1985; 248: G741–G746.
77. Barlow TE. Arterio-venous anastomoses in the human stomach. J Anat 1951; 85: 1–4.
78. Barlow TE, Bentley FH, Walder DN. Arteries, veins and arterio-venous anastomoses in the human stomach. Surg Gynecol Obstet 1951; 93: 651–671.
79. De Busscher G. Les anastomoses arterio-veineuses de l'estomac. Act Neerl Morph Norm Pathol 1948; 6: 1–19.
80. Boulter PS, Parks AG. Submucosal vascular patterns of the alimentary tract and their significance. Br J Surg 1959/60; 47: 546–550.
81. Nylander G, Olerud S. The vascular pattern of the gastric mucosa of the rat following vagotomy. Surg Gynecol Obstet 1961; 112: 475–480.
82. McMahan CA, Maxwell LC, Shepherd AD. Estimation of the distribution of blood vessel diameters from the arterio-venous passage of microspheres. Biometrics 1986; 42: 371–380.
83. Guth PH. The gastric microcirculation and gastric mucosal blood flow under normal and pathological conditions. In: Glass GBJ, ed. Progress in gastroenterology. New York: Grune and Stratton, 1977; Vol III, pp 323–347.
84. Hashizume M, Tanaka K, Inokuchi K. Morphology of gastric microcirculation in cirrhosis. Hepatology 1983; 3: 1008–1012.
85. Ohtani H. Glomeruloid structures as vascular reaction in human gastrointestinal carcinoma. Jpn J Cancer Res 1992; 83: 1334–1340.
86. Ohtani H, Nagura H. Differing microvasculature in the two major types of gastric carcinoma: a conventional, ultrastructural and ultrastructural immunolocalization study of von Willebrand factor. Virchows Arch A Pathol Anat Histopathol 1990; 417: 29–35.
87. Aozasa K, Matsumoto M, Tsujimoto M, Duijvestijn AM. Immunohistochemical detection of high endothelial venules in extranodal B-cell lymphomas. Jpn J clin Oncol 1991; 21: 82–86.
88. Kitajima M, Shimizu A, Sakai N, Otsuka S, Mogi M, Nakajima M, Kiuchi T, Ikeda Y, Oshima A. Gastric microcirculation and its regulating factors in stress. J Clin Gastroenterol 1991; 13 (Suppl 1): S9-S17.
89. Lehnen T, Erlandsen RA, Decoss JJ. Lymph and blood capillaries of the human gastric mucosa. A morphological basis for metastasis in early gastric carcinoma. Gastroenterology 1985; 89: 939–950.
90. Ezaki T, Matsuono K, Fujii H, Hayashi N, Miyakawa K, Ohmori J, Kotant M. A new approach for identification of rat lymphatic capillaries using a monoclonal antibody. Arch Histol Cytol 1990; 53 (Suppl): 77–86.
91. Kato S, Gotoh M. Application of backscattered electron imaging to enzyme histochemistry of lymphatic capillaries. J Electron Microsc Tokyo 1990; 39: 186–190.
92. Kato S. Enzyme histochemical identification of lymphatic vessels by light and backscattered image scanning electron microscopy. Stain Technol 1990; 65: 131–137.
93. Simionescu M, Simionescu N, Palade GE. Morphometric data on the endothelium of blood capillaries. J Cell Biol 1974; 60: 128–152.
94. Devenny JJ, Wagner RC. Transport of immunoglobulin G by endothelial vesicles in isolated capillaries. Microcirc Endoth Lymphat 1985; 2: 15–26.
95. Dikranian K, Stoinov N. Effect of vasoactive amines on Weibel-Palade bodies in capillary endothelial cells. Experientia 1991; 47: 830–832.
96. Gannon BJ, Browning J. Unpublished observations.
97. Tarnawski AS, Sarfeh IJ, Stachura J, Hajduczek A, Bui HX, Dabros W, Gergely H. Microvascular abnormalities of the portal hypertensive gastric mucosa. Hepatology 1988; 8: 1488–1494.
98. Teorell T. The acid base balance of the secreting isolated gastric mucosa. J Physiol 1951; 114: 267–276.
99. Puscas I, Busas G, Puscas JC, Persa F. Carbonic anhydrase inhibitors: antisecretory and cytoprotective properties. Acta Physiol hung 1989; 73: 167–177.
100. Oi M, Oshida K, Sugimura S. The location of gastric ulcer. Gastroenterology 1959; 36: 45–56.
101. Suzuki A, Kameyama J-I, Tsukamoto M, Suzuki Y. Bicarbonate secretion in isolated guinea pig antrum. J Clin Gastroenterol 1990; 12 (Suppl 1): S14–S18.
102. Guth PH. Local metabolism and circulation in mucosal defence. In: Allen A, Flemstrom G, Garner A, Silen W, Turnberg LA, eds. Mechanisms of mucosal protection in the upper gastrointestinal tract. New York: Raven, 1984; pp 253–258.
103. Szabo S, Trier JS. Pathogenesis of acute gastric mucosal injury: sulfhydryls as a protector, adrenal cortex as a modulator, and vascular endothelium as a target. In: Allen A, Flemstrom G, Garner A, Silen W, Turnberg LA, eds. Mechanisms of mucosal protection in the upper gastrointestinal tract. New York: Raven, 1984; pp 287–293.
104. Tarnawski A, Stachura J, Gergely H, Hollander D. Gastric microvascular endothelium: a major target for aspirin-induced injury and arachidonic acid protection. An ultrastructural analysis in the rat. Eur J Clin Invest 1990; 20: 432–440.
105. Hudson N, Hawthorne AB, Cole AT, Jones PD, Hawkey CJ. Mechanisms of gastric and duodenal damage and protection. Hepatogastroenterology 1992; 39 (Suppl 1): 31–36.
106. Tarnawski A, Stachura J, Krause WJ, Douglass TG, Gergely H. Quality of gastric ulcer healing: a new, emerging concept. J Clin Gastroenterol 1991; 13 (Suppl 1): S42–S47.
107. Konturek SJ, Brzozowski T, Majka J, Szlachcic A, Bielanski W, Stachura J, Otto W. Fibroblast growth factor in gastroprotection and ulcer healing: interaction with sucralfate. Gut 1993; 34: 881–887.
108. Tarnawski A, Hollander D, Stachura J, Krause WJ, Eltorai M, Dabros W, Gergely H. Vascular and microvascular changes — key factors in the development of acetic acid-induced gastric ulcers in rats. J Clin Gastroentrol 1990; 12 (Suppl 1): S148–S157.
109. Allen A, Flemstrom G, Garner A, Kivilaakso E. Gastroduodenal mucosal protection. Physiol Revs 1993; 73: 823–857.
110. Szabo S, Vattay P. Experimental gastric and duodenal ulcers. Advances in pathogenesis. Gastroenterol Clin North Am 1990; 19: 67–85.
111. Guth PH, Aures D, Paulsen G. Topical aspirin plus HCl gastric lesions in the rat. Cytoprotective effect of prostaglandin, cimetidine and probanthine. Gastroenterology 1979; 76: 88–93.
112. Meschter CL, Gilbert M, Krook L, Maylin G, Corradino R. The effects of phenylbutazone on the morphology and prostaglandin concentrations of the pyloric mucosa of the equine stomach. Vet Pathol 1990; 27: 244–253.
113. Carsson C, Jansson L. Bleeding gastric mucosal lesions in intensive care units. Scand J Gastroenterol 1984; (Suppl 105): 7–8.
114. Robert A, Negamis JE, Lancaster C, Hanchar AJ, Cytoprotection by prostaglandins in rats. Prevention of gastric necrosis produced by alcohol, HCl, NaOH, hypertonic NaCl and thermal injury. Gastroenterology 1979; 77: 433–443.
115. Trier JS, Szabo S, Allan CH. Ethanol-induced damage to mucosal capillaries of rat stomach. Gastroenterology 1987; 92: 13–22.
116. Pihan G, Majzoubi D, Haudenschild C, Trier JS, Szabo S. Early microcirculatory stasis in acute gastric mucosal injury in the rat and prevention by 16, 16-dimethyl prostaglandin E_2 or sodium thiosulphate. Gastroenterology 1986; 91: 1415–1426.
117. Dore M, Hawkins UK, Entman ML, Smith CW. Production of a monoclonal antibody against canine GMP-140 (P-selectin) and studies of its vascular distribution in canine tissues. Vet Pathol 1993; 30: 213–222.

118. O'Brien P, Schultz C, Gannon B, Browning J. Protective effects of the synthetic prostaglandin enprostil on the gastric microvasculature after ethanol injury in the rat. Am J Med 1986; 81 (Suppl 2A): 12–17.
119. Lacy ER, Hund P III, Tietge J. Effects of misoprostol, cimetidine, and ethanol on rat gastric plasma volume and morphology. J Clin Gastrenterol 1990; 12 (Suppl 1): S158–S169.
120. Lacy ER, Ito S. Microscopic analysis of ethanol damage to rat gastric mucosa after treatment with a prostaglandin. Gastroenterology 1982; 83: 619–625.
121. Livingston EH, Howard TJ, Garrick TR, Passaro EP Jr, Guth PH. Strong gastric contractions cause mucosal ischemia. Am J Physiol 1991; 260: G524–G530.
122. Ito M, Shichijo K, Sekine I. Gastric motility and ischemic changes in occurrence of linear ulcer formation induced by restraint–water immersion stress in rats. Gastroenterol Jpn 1993; 28: 367–373.
123. Cheung LY. Topical effects of 16, 16-dimethyl prostaglandin E_2 on gastric blood flow in dogs. Am J Physiol 1980; 238: G514–G519.
124. Szabo S. Critical and timely review of the concept of gastric cytoprotection. Acta Physiol Hung 1989; 73: 115–127.
125. Cherner JA, Brzozowski T, Naik L, Tarnawski A. Prostaglandin E_2 protects dispersed gastric chief cells from injury induced by ethanol: evidence for direct cytoprotection in vitro. Am Gastroenterol Assoc Ann Mtg, Dig Dis Wk, Chicago, May 1987, Abstract 148. Gastroenterology 1987; 93: 718.
126. Robert A, Nergamis JE, Lancaster C, Davis JP, Field SO, Hanchar AJ. Mild irritants prevent gastric necrosis through 'adaptive cyto-protection' mediated by prostaglandins. Am J Physiol 1983; 245: G113–G121.
127. Chaudhury TK, Robert A. Prevention by mild irritants of gastric necrosis produced in rats by sodium taurocholate. Dig Dis Sci 1980; 25: 830–836.
128. Litman A, Hascom DH. The course of recurrent ulcer. Gastroenterology 1971; 61: 585–591.
129. Tarnawski A, Hollander D, Krause WJ, Dabros W, Sthacura J, Gergely H. 'Healed' experimental gastric ulcers remain histologically and ultrastructurally abnormal. J Clin Gastroenterol 1990; 12 (Suppl 1): S139–S147.
130. Tarnawski AS, Stachura J, Krause WJ, Douglass TG, Gergely H. Quality of gastric ulcer healing: a new, emerging concept. J Clin Gastroenterol 1991; 13 (Suppl 1): S42–S47.
131. Nakata H, Guth PH. In vivo observation of the lymphatic system of the rat stomach. Gastroenterology 1984; 96: 1443–1450.
132. Listrom MB, Fenoglio-Preiser CM. Lymphatic distribution of the stomach in normal, inflammatory, hyperplastic, and neoplastic tissue. Gastroenterology 1987; 93: 506–514.
133. Donirli I. Sur la fine distribution des vaisseaux lymphatiques dans l'estomac humain. Acta Anat 1955; 23: 289–311.
134. Ohtani O, Murakami T. Lymphatics and myenteric plexus in the muscular coat in the rat stomach: a scanning electron microscopic study of corrosion casts made by intra-arterial injection. Arch Histol Jpn 1987; 50: 87–93.
135. Kobayashi S, Suzuki M, Endo T, Tsuji S, Daniel EE. Framework of the enteric nerve plexuses: an immunochemical study in the guinea pig jejunum using an antibody to S-100 protein. Arch Histol Jpn 1986; 49: 159–188.
136. Pissas A, Sarrazin R, Dyon J-F, Bouchet Y. The lymphatic vessels of the stomach in man. Folia Mophol 1982; 30: 363–365.
137. Jamieson JK, Dobson JF. The lymphatic system of the stomach. Lancet 1907; 1: 1060–1066.
138. Gray JH. The lymphatics of the stomach. J Anat (Lond) 1937; 72: 492–496.
139. Coller FA, Kay EB, McIntyre RS. Regional lymphatic metastases of carcinoma of the stomach. Arch Surg 1941; 43: 748–761.
140. Hagiwara A, Takahashi T, Sawai K, Iwamoto A, Shimotsuma M, Yoneyama C, Seiki K, Itoh M, Sasabe T, Lee M. Lymph nodal vital staining with newer carbon particle suspensions compared to India ink: experimental and clinical observations. Lymphology 1992; 25: 89–89.
141. Takahashi T, Sawai K, Hagiwara A, Takahashi S, Seiki K, Totsuda H. Type-oriented therapy for gastric cancer effective for lymph node metastasis: management of lymph node metastasis using activated carbon particles adsorbing an anticancer agent. Semin Surg Oncol 1991; 7: 378–383.
142. Natsugoe S. Experimental and clinical study on the lymphatic pathway draining from the distal esophagus and gastric cardia. (In Japanese). Nippon Geka Gakkai Zasshi 1989; 90: 364–376.
143. Bulkley GB, Womak WA, Downey JM, Kvietys PR, Granger DN. Characterization of segmental collateral blood flow in the small intestine. Am J Physiol 1985; 249: G228–G235.
144. Premen AJ, BaDchs V, Womal WA, Kvietys PR, Granger DN. Importance of collateral circulation in the vascularly occluded feline intestine. Gastroenterology 1987; 92: 1215–1219.
145. Ohashi Y, Kita S, Murakami T. Microcirculation of the rat small intestine as studied by the injection replica scanning electron microscope method. Arch Histol Jpn 1976; 39: 271–282.
146. Gershon MD, Bursztajn S. Properties of the enteric nervous system: limitation of access of intravascular macromolecules to the myenteric plexus and muscularis externa. J Comp Neur 1978; 180: 467–488.
147. Jacobs JM. Penetration of systematically injected horseradish peroxidase into ganglia and nerves of the autonomic nervous system. J Neurocytol 1971; 6: 607–618.
148. Stach W. Die vaskularization des plexus submucous externus (schabadasch) und des plexus submucous internus (meissner) in dunnddarm von schwein und katze. Acta Anat 1978; 101: 170–178.
149. Del'tsova EI. Vaskuliarizatsiia myshechno-kishechnogo nervnogo spleteniia tonkoi kishki golubia. Arkh Anat Gistol Embriol 1990; 99: 41–44.
150. Mall JP. Die blut- und lymphewege im dunndarm des hundes. Abh Kgl sachs Ges Wiss mathem-phys Klasse 1888; 14: 153–189.
151. Heller A. Uber die blutgefasse des dunndarmes. Ber Sachs Ges Wiss 1882; 24: 165–171.
152. Dart AJ, Snyder JR, Julian D, Hinds DM. Microvascular circulation of the small intestine in horses. Am J Vet Res 1992; 53: 995–1000.
153. Gannon BJ. Co-existence of fountain and tuft pattern of blood supply in intestinal villi of rabbit and man. Resolution of an old controversy. Bibl Anat 1981; 20: 130–133.
154. Krapat R, Schnorr B, Kressin M. Das blutgefasssystem des darmes von gallus domesticus. Anat Anz 1993; 175: 349–356.
155. Gannon BJ, Rogers PAW, O'Brien PAW. Two capillary plexuses in human intestinal villi. Micron 1980; 11: 447–448.
156. Casley-Smith JR, Gannon BJ. Intestinal microcirculation: spatial organization and fine structure. In: Shepherd AP, Granger DN, eds. Physiology of the intestinal circulation. New York: Raven, 1984; pp 9–31.
157. Hart TK, Pino RM. Variations in capillary permeability from apex and crypt in the villus of the ileo-jejunum. Cell Tissue Res 1985; 241: 305–315.
158. Florey HW, Wright RD, Jennings MA. The secretions of the intestines. Physiol Rev 1941; 21: 36–69.
159. Bellamy JEC, Latshaw WK, Nielsen NO. The vascular architecture of the porcine small intestine. Can J Comp Med 1983; 37: 57–62.
160. Nasset ES, Ju JS. Micropipet collection of succus entericus at crypt ostia of guinea-pig jejunum. Digestion 1973; 9: 205–211.
161. Welsh MJ, Smith PL, Fromm M, Frizzell RA. Crypts are the site of intestinal fluid and electrolyte secretion. Science 1982; 218: 1219–1221.
162. Gannon BJ, Perry MA. Histoanatomy and ultrastructure of the microvasculature of the alimentary tract. In: Handbook of physiology, Sect 6 (ed Schultz SG), Vol 1 (ed Wood JD), Pt 2: 1301–1334; Amer Physiol Soc 1989, Bethesda, MD.
163. Gannon BJ, Carati CJ. Intestinal microvascular organisation. In: Gastrointestinal microcirculation (eds Messmer K, Hammersen F) Vol 17: 55–89; Basel: Karger, 1990.
164. Lundgren O. Studies of blood flow distribution and countercurrent exchange in the small intestine. Acta Physiol Scand 1967; (Suppl 303): 1–42.
165. Lundgren O. Microcirculation of the gastrointestinal tract and

pancreas. In: Renkin EM, Michel CC, eds. Handbook of physiology. 2. The cardiovascular system, Vol IV pt 2, Microcirculation. Bethesda Md: Am Physiol Soc, 1984; pp 799–863.
166. Gannon BJ, Gore RW, Rogers PAW. Is there an anatomical basis for a vascular counter-current mechanism in rabbit and human intestinal villi? Biomed Res 1981; 2 (Suppl): 235–241.
167. Winne D. The influence of villous counter current exchange on intestinal absorption. J Theor Biol 1975; 53: 145–176.
168. Nichols K, Krantis A, Staines W. Histochemical localization of nitric oxide-synthesizing neurons and vascular sites in the guinea-pig intestine. Neuroscience 1992; 51: 791–799.
169. Leeds SE. Three centuries of history of the lymphatic system. Surg Gynecol Obstet 1977; 144: 927–934.
170. Ohtani O, Ohtsuka A. Three-dimensional organization of lymphatics and their relationship to blood vessels in rabbit small intestine. A scanning electron microscopic study of corrosion casts. Arch Histol Jpn 1985; 48: 255–268.
171. Revazov VS. Microtopographic relation between the lymphatic capillaries and glands of the small intestine. (In Russian). Arkh Anat Gistol Embriol 1987; 92: 53–57.
172. Nakamura S, Ohtani H, Watanabe Y, Fukushima K, Matsumoto T, Kitano A, Kobayashi K, Nagura H. In situ expression of the cell adhesion molecules in inflammatory bowel disease. Lab Invest 1993; 69: 77–85.
173. Ohtani O. Three dimensional organization of lymphatics and its relationship to blood vessels in rat small intestine. Cell Tissue Res 1987; 248: 365–374.
174. Ushiki T. The three-dimensional organisation and ultrastructure of the lymphatics of the rat intestinal mucosa as revealed by scanning electron microscopy after KOH-collagenase treatment. Arch Histol Cytol 1990; 53 (Suppl): 127–136.
175. Lee JS. Tissue fluid pressure, lymph pressure, and fluid transport in rat intestinal villi. Microvasc Res 1986; 31: 170–183.
176. Unthank JL, Bohlen HG. Lymphatic pathways and the role of valves in lymph propulsion from the small intestine. Am J Physiol 1988; 254: G389–G398.
177. Bohlen HG, Lash JM. Intestinal lymphatic vessels release endothelial-dependent vasodilators. Am J Physiol 1992; 262: H813–H818.
178. Zawieja DC, Davis KL, Schuster R, Hinds WM, Granger HJ. Distribution, propagation, and coodination of contractile activity in lymphatics. Am J Physiol 1993; 264: H1283–H1291.
179. Skalak TC, Schmid-Schonbein GW, Zweifach BW. New morphological evidence for a mechanism of lymph formation in skeletal muscle. Microvasc Res 1984; 28: 95–112.
180. Schmid-Schonbein GW. Mechanisms causing initial lymphatics to expand and compress to promote lymph flow. Arch Histol Cytol 1990; 53 (Suppl): 107–114.
181. Lee JS. Intraluminal distension pressure on intestinal lymph flow, serosal transudation and fluid transport in the rat. J Physiol 1983; 355: 399–409.
182. Barrowman JA. Physiology of the gastro-intestinal lymphatic system. Cambridge: Cambridge University Press, 1978.
183. De Franco S, Gelmetti M, Lampugnani R, Gamrelli M. Effect of lymph stasis on healing of rat intestinal anastomoses. Lymphology 1984; 17: 100–104.
184. Schmid T, Korozsi G, Klima G, Oberhuber G, Margreiter R, Regeneration of lymph drainage following transplantation of the small intestine. Lagenbecks Arch Chir 1989; 374: 299–302.
185. Huth F. Special pathology of the lymphovascular system. In: Foldi M, Casley-Smith JR, eds. Lymphangiology. Stuttgart: Schattauer, 1983; pp 414–433.
186. Fox U, Lucani G. Disorders of the intestinal mesenteric lymphatic system. Lymphology 1993; 26: 61–66.
187. Kovi J, Duong HD, Hoang CT. Ultrastructure of intestinal lymphatics in Crohn's disease. Am J Pathol 1981; 76: 385–394.
188. Simionescu M, Simionescu N. Ultrastructure of the microvascular wall: functional correlations. In: Renkin EM, Michel CC, eds. Handbook of physiology. 2. The cardiovascular system, Vol IV, pt 1, Microcirculation. Bethesda Md: Am Physiol Soc, 1984; pp 44–101.
189. Casley-Smith JR, Donoghue PJ, Crocker KWJ. The quantitative relationships between fenestrae in jejunal capillaries and connective tissue channels: proof of 'tunnel-capillaries.' Microvasc Res 1975; 9: 78–100.
190. Simionescu M, Simionescu N, Palade GE. Morphometric data on the endothelium of blood capillaries. J Cell Biol 1974; 60: 128–152.
191. Tso P, Balint JA. Formation and transport of chylomicrons by enterocytes to the lymphatics. Am J Physiol 1986; 25: G715–G726.
192. Harris MS, Kennedy JA. Effects of increasing intraluminal volume and flow rate on passive and carrier-mediated transport in the intact rat intestine. Am Gastroenterol Soc Ann Mtg, Dig Dis W, Abstract 282. Gastroenterology 1987.
193. Vogt C, Vogel A, Holliger C, Radzyner M, Anliker M, Knoblauch M. The microcirculatory system of the jejunal villus of the rat. Correlation of intravital microscopy, injection casts and electronmicroscopy. Bibl Anat 1981; 20: 69–70.
194. Knoblauch M, Vogt C, Hollinger C, Neff M, Metry J. The influence of hormones on the microcirculation of a single jejunal rat villus, with evidence for microfilament-mediated vasoconstriction. Microvasc Res 1981; 22: 232.
195. Takahashi S, Iwanaga T, Fujita T. Lamina propria of intestinal mucosa as a typical reticular tissue. A scanning electron microscopic study of the rat jejunum. Cell Tissue Res 1985; 242: 57–66.
196. Salmi M, Jalkanen S. Regulation of lymphocyte traffic to mucosa-associated lymphatic tissues. Gastroenterol Clin North Amer 1991; 20: 495.
197. Papp M, Rohlich P, Rusmyak I, Toro I. An electron microscopic study of the central lacteal in the intestinal villus of the cat. Z Zellforsch 1962; 57: 475–486.
198. Jeurissen SH, Duijvestijn AM, Sontag Y, Kraal G. Lymphocyte migration into the lamina propria of the gut is mediated by specialised HEV-like blood vessels. Immunology 1987; 62: 273–277.
199. Papp M, Rohlich P, Rusznyak I, Toro I. Central chyliferous vessel of intestinal villus. Fed Proc 1964; 23: T155–T158.
200. Wakefield AJ, Pittilo RM, Sim R, Cosby SL, Stephenson JR, Dhillon AP, Pounder RE. Evidence of persistent measles virus infection in Crohn's disease. J Med Virol 1993; 39: 345–353.
201. Tahara T, Yamamoto T. Morphological changes of the villous microvascular architecture and intestinal growth in rats with streptozotocin-induced diabetes. Virchows Arch A Pathol Anat 1988; 413: 151–158.
202. Magliocca FM, Bonamico M, Petrozza V, Correr S, Montuori M, Triglione P. Scanning electron microscopy of the small intestine during gluten-challenge in celiac disease. Arch Histol Cytol 1992; 55 (Suppl): 125–130.
203. Sibbons P, Spitz L, van Velsen D. The role of lymphatics in the pathogenesis of pneumatosis in experimental bowel ischemia. J Pediat Surg 1992; 27: 339–343.
204. Desaki J, Fujiwara T, Komoro T. A cellular reticulum of fibroblast-like cells in the rat intestine: scanning and transmission electron microscopy. Arch Histol Jpn 1984; 47: 179–186.
205. Joyce NC, Haire MF, Palade GE. Morphologic and biochemical evidence for a contractile cell network within the rat intestinal mucosa. Gastroenterology 1987; 92: 68–81.
206. Komuro T, Hashimoto Y. Three-dimensional structure of the rat intestinal wall (mucosa and submucosa). Arch Histol Cytol 1990; 53: 1–21.
207. Komuro T. Fenestrations of the basal lamina of intestinal villi of the rat: scanning and transmission electron microscopy. Cell Tiss Res 1985; 239: 183–188.
208. Cho Y, DeBruyn PPH. Internal structure of the postcapillary high-endothelial venules of rodent lymph nodes and Peyer's patches and the transendothelial lymphocyte passage. Am J Anat 1986; 177: 481–490.
209. Yamaguchi K, Schloefl GI. Blood vessels of the Peyer's patch in the mouse: III. High-endothelium venules. Anat Rec 1983; 206: 419–438.
210. Shikata JI, Shida T. Effects of tension on local blood flow in experimental intestinal anastomoses. J Surg Res 1986; 40: 105–111.

211. Falk P. The effect of elevated temperature on the vasculature of mouse jejunum. Br J Radiol 1983; 56: 41–49.
212. Herndon DN, Zeigler ST. Bacterial translocation after thermal injury. Crit Care Med 1993; 21 (Suppl): S50–S54.
213. Theuer CJ, Wilson MA, Steeb GD, Garrison RN. Microvascular constriction and mucosal hypoperfusion of the rat small intestine during bacteremia. Circ Shock 1993; 40: 61–68.
214. Koshi R, Mathan VI, David S, Mathan MM. Enteric vascular endothelial responses to bacterial endotoxin. Int J Exp Path 1993; 74: 593–601.
215. Mathan VI, Penny GR, Mathan MM, Rowley D. Bacterial lipopolysaccharide-induced intestinal microvascular lesions leading to acute diarrhea. J Clin Invest 1988; 82: 1714–1721.
216. Granger DN, Zimmerman BJ, Sekizuka E, Grisham MB. Intestinal microvascular exchange in the rat during luminal perfusion with Formyl-Methionyl-Leucyl-Phenylalanine. Gastroenterology 1988; 94: 673–681.
217. Fink MP, Antonsson JB, Wang H, Rothschild HR. Increased intestinal permeability in endotoxic pigs. Mesenteric hypoperfusion as an etiologic factor. Arch Surg 1991; 126: 211–218.
218. Osborne MP, Haddon SJ, Worton KJ, Spencer AJ, Starkey WG, Thornber D, Stephen J. Rotavirus-induced changes in the microcirculation of intestinal villi of neonate mice in relation to the induction and persistence of diarrhea. J Pediat Gastroenterol Nut 1991; 12: 111–120.
219. Madara JL, Kirkman RL. Structural and functional evolution of jejunal allograft rejection in rats and the ameliorating effects of cyclosporine therapy. J Clin Invest 1985; 75: 502–512.
220. Sonnino RE, Riddle JM, Besser AS. Small bowel transplantation in the rat: ultrastructural changes during the early phases of rejection. J Invest Surg 1988; 1: 181–191.
221. Hale DA, Waldorf KA, Kleinschmidt J, Pearl RH, Seyfer AE. Small intestinal transplantation in nonhuman primates. J Pediat Surg 1991; 26: 914–920.
222. Smith GJ, Ingham-Clark C, Crane P, Leap P, Wood RF, Fabre JW. Ex vivo perfusion of intestinal allografts with anti-T cell monoclonal antibody/ricin A chain conjugates for the supression of graft-versus-host disease. Transplantation 1992; 53: 717–722.
223. Lee KWW, Schraut WH. In vitro allograft irradiation prevents graft-versus-host disease in small-bowel transplantation. J Surg Res 1985; 38: 364–372.
224. Fajardo LF, Berthrong M. Vascular lesions following radiation. Pathol Annu 1988; 23: 297–330.
225. Buell MG, Harding RK. Proinflammatory effects of local abdominal irradiation on rat gastrointestinal tract. Dig Dis Sci 1989; 34: 390–399.
226. Eriksson B. Microangiographic pattern in the small intestine of the cat after irradiation. Scand J Gastroenterol 1982; 17: 887–895.
227. Ericksson B, Johnson L, Lundqvist PG. Ultrastructural aspects of capillary function in irradiated bowel. Scand J Gastroenterol 1983; 18: 473–480.
228. Granger DN, Hollwarth ME, Parks DA. Ischemia-reperfusion injury: role of oxygen-derived free radicals. Acta Physiol Scand 1986; (Suppl 548): 47–63.
229. Parks DA, Granger DN. Ischemia-induced vascular changes: role of xanthine oxidase and hydroxyl radicals. Am J Physiol 1983; 245: G285–G289.
230. Megison SM, Horton JW, Chao H, Walker P. Prolonged survival and decreased mucosal injury after low-dose enteral allopurinol prophylaxis in mesenteric ischemia. J Pediat Surg 1990; 25: 917–921.
231. Schoenberg MH, Poch B, Younes M, Schwartz A, Baczako K, Lundberg C, Haglund U, Beger HG. Involvement of neutrophils in postischemic damage to the small intestine. Gut 1991; 32: 905–912.
232. Suzuki M, Asako H, Kubes P, Jennings S, Grisham MB, Granger DN. Neutrophil-derived oxidants promote leucocyte adherence in postcapillary venules. Microvasc Res 1991; 42: 125–138.
233. Pitt RM, McKelvey TG, Saenger JS, Shah AK, Jones HP, Manci EA, Powell PW. A tungsten-supplemented diet delivered by transplacental and beast-feeding routes lowers intestinal xanthine oxidase activity and affords cytoprotection in ischemia-reperfusion injury to the small intestine. J Pediat Surg 1991; 26: 930–935.
234. Carati C, Rambaldo S, Gannon BJ. Changes in macromolecular permeability of microvessels in rat small intestine after total occlusion ischaemia/reperfusion. Microcirc Endoth Lymphat 1988; 4: 69–86.
235. Reinus JF, Brandt LJ, Boley SJ. Ischemic diseases of the bowel. Gastroenterol Clin North Am 1990; 19: 319–343.
236. Czyrko C, Steigman C, Turley DL, Drott HR, Zeigler MM. The role of reperfusion injury in occlusive intestinal ischemia of the neonate: malondialdehyde-derived fluorescent products and correlation of histology. J Surg Res 1991; 51: 1–4.
237. Stordahl A, Laerum F, Lunde OC, Aase S. The effects of water-soluble contrast media on luminal distention and blood flow in closed loops of small bowel in minipigs. Scand J Gastroenterol 1988; 23: 991–999.
238. Grisham MB, Hernandez LA, Granger DN. Xanthine oxidase and neutrophil infiltration in intestinal ischemia. Am J Physiol 1986; 251: G567–G574.
239. Petrone W F, English DK, Wong K, McCord JM. Free radicals and inflammation: superoxide-dependent activation of neutrophil chemotactic factor in plasma. Proc Natl Acad Sci USA 1980; 77: 1159–1163.
240. Kvietys PR, Morgan Smith S, Holm-Rutili L, Perry MA, Grisham MB, Arfors KE, Granger DN. The role of neutrophils in hemorrhagic shock-induced gastric mucosal injury. Gastroenterology 1987; Abstract.
241. Falcone J, Bohlen HG. EDRF from rat intestine and skeletal muscle venules causes dilation of arterioles. Am J Physiol 1990; 258: H1515–H1523.
242. Altura BM, Gebrewold A, Burton RW. Reactive hyperemic responses of single arterioles are attenuated markedly after intestinal ischemia, endotoxemia and traumatic shock: possible role of endothelial cells. Microcirc Endoth Lymphat 1985; 2: 3–14.
243. Altura BM, Gebrewold A, Burton RW. Failure of microscopic metarterioles to elicit vasodilator responses to acetylcholine, bradykinin, histamine and substance P after ischemic shock, endotoxemia and trauma: possible role of endothelial cells. Microcirc Endoth Lymphat 1985; 2: 121–127.
244. Cook AR. The glands of Brunner. In: Handbook of physiology, Section 6. Alimentary canal 2: Secretion (ed. Code CF). Washington: American Physiological Society, 1967: pp 1087–1095.
245. Flemstrom G, Garner A. Gastroduodenal HCO_3 transport: characteristics and proposed role in acidity regulation and mucosal protection. Am J Physiol 1982; 242: G183–G193.
246. Allen A, Flemstrom G, Garner A, Silen W, Turnberg LA. Mechanisms of mucosal protection in the upper gastrointestinal tract. New York: Raven, 1984.
247. Browning J, Gannon B. The microvascular architecture of rat proximal duodenum, with particular reference to Brunner's glands. Biomed Res 1984; 5: 245–258.
248. Aharinejad S, Lametschwandtner A. Microangioarchitecture of the guinea pig gall bladder and bile duct as studied by scanning electron microscopy of vascular corrosion casts. J Anat 1992; 181: 89–100.
249. Ichikawa S, Kyoda K, Iwanaga T, Fujita T, Uchino S. Nerve terminals associated with the central lacteal lymphatics in the duodenal and ileal villi of the monkey. Acta Anat Basel 1993; 146: 14–21.
250. Treasure T. The ducts of Brunner's glands. J Anat 1978; 127: 299–304.
251. Siddharth P, Ravo B. Colorectal neurovasculature and anal sphincter. Surg Clin Nth Am 1988; 68: 1185–1200.
252. Wolfram-Gabrel R, Maillot CL, Koritke JG. Systematisation del'angioarchitectonie du colon chez l'homme adulte. Acta Anat 1986; 125: 65–72.
253. Florey HW. The structure of normal and inflamed small blood vessels of the mouse and rat colon. Qt J Exp Physiol 1961; 46: 119–112.
254. Kvietys PR, Wilborn WH, Granger DN. Effects of rat

transmucosal volume flux on lymph flow in the canine colon. Gastroenterology 1981; 81: 1080–1090.
255. Browning J, Gannon B. Mucosal microvascular organization of the rat colon. Acta Anat 1986; 126: 73–77.
256. Aharinejad S, Gangler P, Hagen D, Firbas W. Studies on the microvascularisation of the digestive tract by scanning electron microscopy of vascular corrosion casts. 1. Large intestine in rats and guinea pigs. Acta Anat 1992; 144: 278–283.
257. Gannon B, Browning J. Unpublished observations.
258. Richardson PDI, Granger DN, Mailman D, Kvietys PR. Permeability characteristics of colonic capillaries. Am J Physiol 1980; 239: G300–G305.
259. Fenoglio CM, Kaye GI, Lane N. Distribution of lymphatics in normal, hyperplastic and adenomatous tissue. Gastroenterology 1973; 64: 51–66.
260. Hirashima T, Kuwahara D, Nishi M. Morphology of lymphatics in the canine large intestine. Lymphology 1984; 17: 69–72.
261. Hirai T, Nimura Y, Sakai H. The three dimensional microstructure of intramural lymphatics in the canine large intestine. Gastroenterol Jap 1990; 25: 169–174.
262. Jamieson JK, Dobson JF. The lymphatics of the colon; with special reference to the operative treatment of cancer of the colon. Ann Surg 1909; 50: 1077–1094.
263. Gilchrist RK, David VC. Lymphatic spread of carcinoma of the rectum. Ann Surg 1938; 108: 621–642.
264. Grinnell RS. The lymphatic and venous spread of carcinoma of the rectum. Ann Surg 1942; 116: 200–226.
265. Glover R, Waugh JM. The retrograde lymphatic spread of carcinoma of the 'rectosigmoid region': its influence on surgical problems. Surg Gynecol Obstet 1946; 82: 434–448.
266. Grinnell RS. Lymphatic metastases of carcinoma of the colon and rectum. Ann Surg 1950; 131: 494–506.
267. Clemente CD. Gray's anatomy of the human body. 30th Am ed. Philadelphia: Lea, Feibiger, 1985; pp 892–928.
268. Carr ND, Pullen BR, Schofield PF. Microvascular studies in non-specific inflammatory bowel disease. Gut 1986; 27: 542–549.
269. Carr ND, Pullen BR, Hasleton PS, Schofield PF. Microvascular studies in human radiation bowel disease. Gut 1984; 25: 448–454.
270. Flynn TC, Rowlands BJ, Gilliland M, Ward RE, Fischer RP. Hypotension-induced post-traumatic necrosis of the right colon. J Surg 1983; 146: 715–718.
271. Copron JP, Gineston JL, Remond A, Lallement PY, Delamarre J, Revert R, Veyssier P. Inferior mesenteric arteriovenous fistula associated with portal hypertension and acute ischaemic colitis. Successful occlusion by intraarterial embolization with steel coils. Gastroenterology 1984; 86: 351–355.
272. Dahlberg PJ, Kisken WA, Newcomer RL, Yutue WR. Mesenteric ischemia in chronic dialysis patients. Am J Nephrol 1985; 5: 327–332.
273. Dictor M. Kaposi's sarcoma. Origin and significance of lymphaticovenous connections. Virchow's Arch (A) Pathol Anat Histopathol 1986; 409: 23–35.
274. Shubik P. Vascularization of tumours: a review. J Cancer Res Clin Oncol 1982; 103: 211–226.
275. Wang W, Campiche M. Microvasculature of human colorectal epithelial tumors. An electron microscopic study. Virchows Arch (A) 1982; 397: 131–147.
276. Gabbert H, Wagner R, Hohn P. The relation between tumor cell proliferation and vascularization in differentiated and undifferentiated colon carcinomas in the rat. Virchows Archiv (B) 1982; 41: 119–131.
277. Ohtani H, Sasano N. Characterisation of microvasculature in the stroma of human colorectal carcinoma: an immunoelectron microscopic study on factor VIII/von Willebrand factor. J Electron Microsc 1987; 36: 204–212.
278. Skinner SA, Tutton PJM, O'Brien PE. Microvascular architecture of experimental colon tumors in the rat. Cancer Res 1990; 50: 2411–2417.
279. Grunt TW, Lametschwandtner A, Staindl O. The vascular pattern of basal cell tumors: light microscopy and scanning electron microscopic study on vascular corrosion casts. Microvasc Res 1985; 29: 371–386.
280. Lockwood CB. Note upon the lymphatics of the vermiform appendix. J Anat Physiol 1900; 34: 9–13.
281. Braithwaite LR. The flow of lymph from the ileocaecal angle, and its possible bearing on the course of duodenal and gastric ulcer. Br J Surg 1923/24; 11: 7–26.
282. Bockman DE. Functional anatomy of the appendix. Arch Histol Jpn 1983; 46: 271–292.
283. Crabb ED, Kensall MA. Organization of the mucosa and lymphatic structures in the rabbit appendix. J Morph 1940; 67: 351–367.
284. Ohtani O, Ohtsuka A, Owen RL. Three-dimensional organization of the lymphatics in the rabbit appendix. A scanning electron and light microscopic study. Gastroenterology 1986; 91: 947–955.
285. Therkelsen F. On the histological diagnosis of appendicitis. Acta Chir Scand 1942; 94 (Suppl 108): 1–49.
286. Hashimoto S, Ogata T. Blood vascular organisation of the human appendix: a scanning electron microscopic study of corrosion casts. Tohoku J Exp Med 1988; 154: 271–283.
287. Borchard A. Die primare lymphangitis des Wurmfortsatzes. Deutsche Med Wschr 1928; 54: 1074–1075.
288. Fischer E, Kaiserling H. Die experimentelle lympholene allergisch-hyperergische appendicitis. Virchows Arch 1936; 297: 146–176.
289. Frasher WG Jr, Wayland H. Repeating modular organization of the microcirculation of cat mesentery. Microvasc Res 1972; 4: 62–76.
290. Gannon BJ, Rosenberger SM, Versluis TD, Johnson PC. Autoregulatory patterns in the arteriolar network of cat mesentery. Microvasc Res 1983; 26: 1–14.
291. Ley K, Pries Are, Gaehtgens P. Topological structure of rat mesenteric microvessel networks. Microvasc Res 1986; 32: 315–332.
292. Oliver MG, Specian RD, Perry MA, Granger DN. Morphologic assessment of leucocyte-endothelial cell interactions in mesenteric venules subjected to ischemia and reperfusion. Inflammation 1991; 15: 331–346.
293. Gotloib L, Digenis GE, Rabinovich S, Medline A, Oreopoulos DG. Ultrastructure of normal rabbit mesentery. Nephron 1983; 34: 248–255.
294. Kato S, Miura M, Miyauchi R. Structural organisation of the initial lymphatics in the monkey mesentery and intestinal wall as revealed by an enzyme-histochemical method. Arch Histol Cytol 1993; 56: 149–160.
295. Cranshaw ML, Leak LV. Milky spots of the omentum: a source of peritoneal cells in the normal and stimulated animal. Arch Histol Cytol 1990; 53 (Suppl): 165–177.
296. Shimotsuma M, Shields JW, Simpson-Morgan MW, Sakuyama A, Shirasu M, Hagiwara A, Takahashi T. Morpho-physiological function and role of omental milky spots as omental-associated lymphoid tissue (OATL) in the peritoneal cavity. Lymphology 1993; 26: 90–101.
297. Ohtani Y, Ohtani O, Nakatani T. Microanatomy of the rat diaphragm: a scanning electron and confocal laser scanning microscopic study. Arch Histol Cytol 1993; 56: 317–328.
298. Oya M, Shimada T, Nakamura M, Uchida Y. Functional morphology of the lymphatic system in the monkey diaphragm. Arch Histol Cytol 1993; 56: 37–47.
299. Polak M, Mazza Faria R. Diseases of the lymphatic system and disturbances of the lymph flow in the abdominal region studied by means of laparoscopy and peritoneal biopsy. In: Foldi M, Casley-Smith JR. Lymphangiology. Stuttgart: Schattauer, 1983; pp 611–628.
300. Barber BJ, Babbitt RA, Dutta S, Parameswaran S. Changes in rat mesentery interstitial matrix due to superfusate. Am J Physiol 1993; 265: H852–H856.
301. Kredeit RT, Koomen GCM, Koopman MG, Hoek FJ, Struuk DG, Boeschoten EW, Arisz L. The peritoneal transport of serum proteins and neutral dextran in CAPD patients. Kidney Int 1989; 35: 1064–1072.
302. von Recklinghausen FT. Zur fettresorption. Virchows Arch Path Anat Physiol 1863; 26: 172–208.
303. Florey HW, Witts LJ. Absorption of blood from the peritoneal cavity. Lancet 1928; 1: 1323–1325.
304. Allen L. The peritoneal stomata. Anat Rec 1936; 67: 89–103.

305. Allen L, Vogt E. The mechanism of lymphatic absorption from serous cavities. Am J Physiol 1937; 119: 776–782.
306. Allen L, Weatherford T. Role of fenestrated basement membrane in lymphatic absorption from peritoneal cavity. Am J Physiol 1959; 197: 551–554.
307. Allen L. Lymphatics and lymphoid tissue. Ann Rev Physiol 1967; 29: 197–224.
308. Casley-Smith JR. Endothelial permeability. The passage of particles into and out of diaphragmatic lymphatics. Qt J Exp Physiol 1964; 49: 365–383.
309. Morris B, Murphy MJ, Bessis M (1970). Cited in Yoffey JM, Courtice FC. [183]; pp 302–303.
310. Namba Y. An electron microscopic demonstration of the invasion of tumor cells into the diaphragm. (In Japanese). J Jap Surg Soc 1989; 90: 1915–1921.
311. Di Paulo N, Sacchi G, De Mia M, Gaggiotti E, Capotondo L, Rosse P, Bernini M, Pucci AM, Orba L, Sabatelli P, Alessandrini C. Morphology of the peritoneal membrane during continuous peritoneal dialysis. Nephron 1986; 44: 204–211.
312. Yoffey JM, Courtice FC. Lymphatics, lymph and the lymphomyeloid complex. London: Academic, 1970.
313. Casparis HR. Lymphatics of the omentum. Anat Rec 1918/19; 15: 93–99.
314. Simer PH. Omental lymphatics in man. Anat Rec 1935; 63: 253–262.
315. Yamaguchi K, Schloefl Gl. Blood vessels of the Peyer's patch in the mouse: 1. Topographic studies. Anat Rec 1983; 206: 391–401.
316. Ohtani O, Murakami T. Organisation of the lymphatic vessels and their relationship to blood vessels in rabbit Peyer's patches. Arch Histol Cytol 1990; 53 (Suppl): 155–164.
317. McClugage SG, Low FN, Zimny ML. Porosity of the basement membrane overlying Peyer's patches in rats and monkeys. Gastroenterology 1986; 91: 1128–1133.
318. Yamaguchi K, Schloefl GL. Blood vessels of the Peyer's patch in the mouse: II. In vivo observations. Anat Rec 1983; 206: 403–417.
319. Fujita T, Miyoshi M, Murakami T. Scanning electron microscope observation of the dog mesenteric lymph node. Z Zellforsch 1972; 133: 147–162.
320. Anderson AO, Anderson ND. Studies on the structure and permeability of the microvasculature in normal rat lymph nodes. Am J Pathol 1975; 80: 387–418.
321. Pressman JJ, Simon MB. Experimental evidence of direct communications between lymph nodes and veins. Surg Gynecol Obstet 1961; 113: 537–541.
322. Dux K. Anatomy of the greater omentum and lesser omentum in the mouse with some physiological implications. In: Goldsmith H (Ed). The omentum. Research and clinical applications. New York: Springer-Verlag, 1990; pp 19–43.

CHAPTER

11

The gut-associated lymphoid tissue and immune system

M. N. Marsh   A. Ensari

The realm of intestinal, or mucosal, immunity has expanded considerably over the last 30 years. It was the description of the IgA immunoglobulin system that first led to the realization that mucus-secreting surfaces are endowed with unique properties designed to combat local invasion by microorganisms and other environmental antigens ingested in food, drugs or pulmonary and nasopharyngeal secretions. From this, the concept of a common mucosal immunological system, dependent on local IgA production and sustained by the constant migration and arrival of blood-borne precursors to intestinal, and extra-intestinal, sites emerged.

Initially, attention was focused mainly on the physiology of IgA and its role in mucosal protection. This came about partly for historical reasons but also because of the ease (i) of locating plasma cells by immunofluorescence, and later by immunoperoxidase, and (ii) of measuring antibodies produced to known immunogens.

More recently, considerable effort has been devoted towards the recognition and elucidation of mechanisms of local cell-mediated immunity and its role in mucosal protection and mucosal damage. Such mechanisms clearly relate to the vast quantity of lymphoid tissue occupying epithelial and subepithelial sites throughout the intestine comprising (i) organized tissues, such as Peyer's patches, mesenteric lymph nodes and discrete subepithelial lymphoid follicles, and (ii) a diffuse component, of which the plasma cell and intraepithelial lymphocyte (IEL) populations are notable examples.

Because of their strategic position within the intestinal mucosa, IEL have been the subject of intense study aimed at elucidating their range of activity and presumptive role in mucosal defence at this important frontier between host and environment.

Intestine that is shielded from the environment, either in animals maintained under germ-free conditions or fetal tissue transplanted under sterile conditions to sites of immunological privilege such as the renal capsule, fails to develop full immunological potential, its component tissues remaining rudimentary. These observations indicate that the intestinal immune apparatus constitutes a secondary organ which requires continued exposure to environmental antigens for full structural and developmental expression, and for the maintenance of 'memory'.

During normal development, the neonate is dependent on passive immunity derived from immunoglobulins, cells and other factors present within colostrum and milk. Milk immunoglobulin secretion is dependent on the enteromammary link whereby immunoblasts, primed to enteric organisms, recirculate to mammary epithelium and secrete appropriate antibody, thereby providing specific protection. The role of breast-feeding in reducing the prevalence and severity of diarrhoea in the newborn is sufficient demonstration of this physiological aspect of the gut-associated lymphoid tissue (GALT).

It is now evident that for complete maturity of expression, the local intestinal immune system is dependent on other inductive cells, particularly MHC class 2 expressing macrophages (dendritic cells) which process antigen for recognition by T-helper (inducer) lymphocytes. In addition, a population of non-immunological secondary effector cells such as macrophages, neutrophils, eosinophils, mast cells and basophils occupies the lamina propria, thus adding to the complexity of GALT and of its component lymphoid cells.

INTESTINAL MORPHOGENESIS AND MATURATION: ONTOGENY OF THE GUT-ASSOCIATED IMMUNE APPARATUS

Derived from an endodermal cell layer, the human small intestine is tubular and lined by an undifferentiated, stratified epithelium which, by 8 weeks gestation, is 2–4 cells thick:[1–3] during this period, all cell layers exhibit high mitotic activity. The second stage of intestinal morphogenesis (9–12 weeks) is marked by the formation of villi and crypts from the stratified cell layer. Villi, lined by a simple columnar epithelium, appear first while crypt formation subsequently evolves with the invagination of cords of epithelial-type cells into the underlying mesenchyme. This second stage is marked by cytodifferentiation of goblet cells, endocrine cells, Paneth cells and M cells. Differentiation of villous absorptive cells also continues with the formation of a microvillous brush border and increases in its membrane hydrolases — alkaline phosphatase, disaccharidases and oligopeptidases.

During the second trimester, there is characteristic differentiation of the endocytic system of the apical region of villous cells to form the apical tubular system, and of the lysosomal system to form the meconium corpuscle system. Both intracellular systems are most developed and evident in the mid and distal small intestine by 17 weeks, regressing by 22 weeks of gestation, during which time they appear to be involved in macromolecular uptake and degradation.

Intestinal development during the third trimester is the least well described phase due to lack of readily-available sequential tissue samples, but is marked by evolution of presumptive adult-type epithelium. Brush border enzymes have a slow rise except for lactase, whose activity begins to increase during the perinatal period.

Little is known about the postnatal development of the human small intestine because of the ethical difficulties in obtaining tissue. However, it has been asserted that there is growth of the small intestine in the postnatal period in comparison with other species,[4] as recently confirmed at autopsy.[5] Furthermore, there is a concomitant increase in surface area as indicated by the enhancement of xylose absorption.[6] The jejunum in 1–2 week old neonates has finger-like villi,[7] whereas older infants have broader, leaf-like villi. Lactase activity declines to some extent after weaning. Between 4 and 10 years of age, villi again may become narrower and finger-like. Growth maturation of the small intestine is influenced by many factors, including mesenchymal interactions,[8,9] systemic and neuropeptide hormones,[10,11] pancreatico-biliary secretions,[12] the presence of intraluminal nutrients,[13] microflora,[14] polyamine metabolism,[15] the influence of autonomic and enteric neural systems and mucosal T lymphocytes.[16,17]

Anatomically, the intestinal lymphoid system can be envisioned in terms of mesenteric lymph node, Peyer's patches and other subepithelial and submucosal aggregates, together with a diffuse collection of lymphocytes and plasma cells distributed within the lamina propria and epithelium. Although awaiting formal proof in humans, current animal-based dogma indicates that Peyer's patches function as antigen-sensing organs, while the remaining elements of the gut-associated lymphoid tissues (GALT) are essentially effector in nature, concerned with cytolytic, suppressor, inductive and humoral activities.[18]

In the human intestine, Peyer's patches are usually evident by 20 weeks gestation, with well-developed follicles.[19] They appear to arise from lymphoid aggregates containing T and B cells, seen as early as 11 weeks of gestation. The follicles contain IgM^+, IgD^+ B cells which also display the CD23 activation marker. The T lymphocyte cuff comprises $CD4^+$ and $CD8^+$ lymphocytes in a ratio of 3:1. Follicular dendritic cells ($R4/23^+$) are also evident at this time: all follicular cells express MHC Class 2 alloantigen (from 11 weeks of gestation).

After 20 weeks gestation, Peyer's patches are well-developed and continue to grow and expand along the length of the intestine, a process which continues to age 14–16 years.[20] Each patch is covered by a single layer of cuboidal epithelial cells lacking goblet cells but expressing MHC class 2 alloantigen:[21] secretion of interferon-γ (IFN-γ) by the numerous intraepithelial lymphocytes (IEL) that infiltrate the follicle-associated epithelium (FAE) may account for the induction and display of MHC alloantigen.[22] Unlike animals,[23] the human FAE contains few M cells, another difference being that human Peyer's patches contain mature plasma cells expressing cytoplasmic IgA, suggesting that dissemination of plasma cells may occur by local tissue migration, rather than by (or in addition to) the recirculatory mechanism demonstrated in animals.[21] Evidence for such a recirculatory pathway in the human is at best, indirect, such as the secretion of antibody to specific enteric organs in breast milk,[24] and the influence of breast feeding on reducing postnatal gastrointestinal infections.[25]

The diffuse cellular component of GALT has been less extensively studied in the newborn human infant. Limited studies of foetal ileum indicate that $CD3^+$ T lymphocytes migrate into the villi around 11–12 weeks gestation and increase in numbers to the 20th week.[19,26] At this time, the ratio of epithelial T lymphocytes (CD8:CD4) is 1.36/0.3 per 100 epithelial cell nuclei. In the lamina propria, the majority of cells express $CD4^+$ and comprise both macrophage-like cells ($CD3^-$), as well as bona fide T helper cells. Presumably these events take place in the absence of antigen stimuli (food or microbial). Few B cells are observable at this stage of fetal development. In contrast to the T cell population of the GALT prenatally, B cells populate and expand postnatally. After birth, there is considerable expansion of GALT, a clear reflection of exposure to luminal antigens.[27,28]

T CELL INFLUENCES ON INTESTINAL GROWTH AND DEVELOPMENT

The morphological changes in the small intestine of the rat at weaning have many similarities to a mucosal T cell-immune reaction, with hyperplasia of intestinal crypts, an increase in mesenteric lymph node weight, activation and degranulation of mucosal mast cells and a rise in the IEL population (Fig. 11.1).[16,29,30] These changes (excepting IEL) occur in a biphasic manner with an exponential peak at age 21–22 days, followed by a phase of stabilization (or decrease) thereafter. IEL increase until day 24 and stabilize at adult values. Similar changes occur in the evolution of the mucosal graft-versus-host reaction (GVHR) which is a prototypic example of a pure T cell mediated response and which provides the parallel for the involvement of mucosal T cells at weaning.

The activation of T cells at weaning was directly confirmed by high expression of IL-2R (a marker of activated T cells) on mesenteric node CD5-and CD4-positive T lymphocytes which peaked at day 22 before falling to adult levels.[29] Thus, the mucosal immune system was activated up to day 22, but was relatively suppressed after this time. Villous and crypt hyperplasia peaked at days 22–24 which indicated the accompanying morphological development of the small intestine, and coincided with the activation phase of the mucosal immune system. Treatment with cyclosporin A (which inhibits T cells) delayed small intestinal development:[30] thus, mucosal T cells may be major control factor for intestinal growth in the rat at weaning. The work of MacDonald and co-workers[31,32] showed that changes in human fetal small intestinal architecture in vitro (crypt hypertrophy) could be promoted by incubation with anti-CD3 antibody or with pokeweed mitogen (both of which activate lamina propria T cells as shown by their expression of IL-2R), and conversely that addition of cyclosporin A to the culture inhibited such growth. Studies of possible factors that could activate the mucosal immune system at this critical period in fetal/postnatal development have not been undertaken but are likely to include food antigens, luminal bacteria and engraftment of maternal milk-derived T cells.[33]

Activation in vivo of the mucosal immune system in the human at weaning could provide stimulus for the morphological development of the small intestine postnatally. In this respect, the local immune system could be viewed as specialized mesenchymal tissue and perceived as a factor, ancillary to the general mesenchyme, which supports and promotes growth of the intestine in foetal and neonatal life.

Failure to control or down-regulate T cell activation during the postnatal weaning period could be seen as a means whereby progressive damage to the intestinal mucosa could ensue, such as occurs with short-term dietary

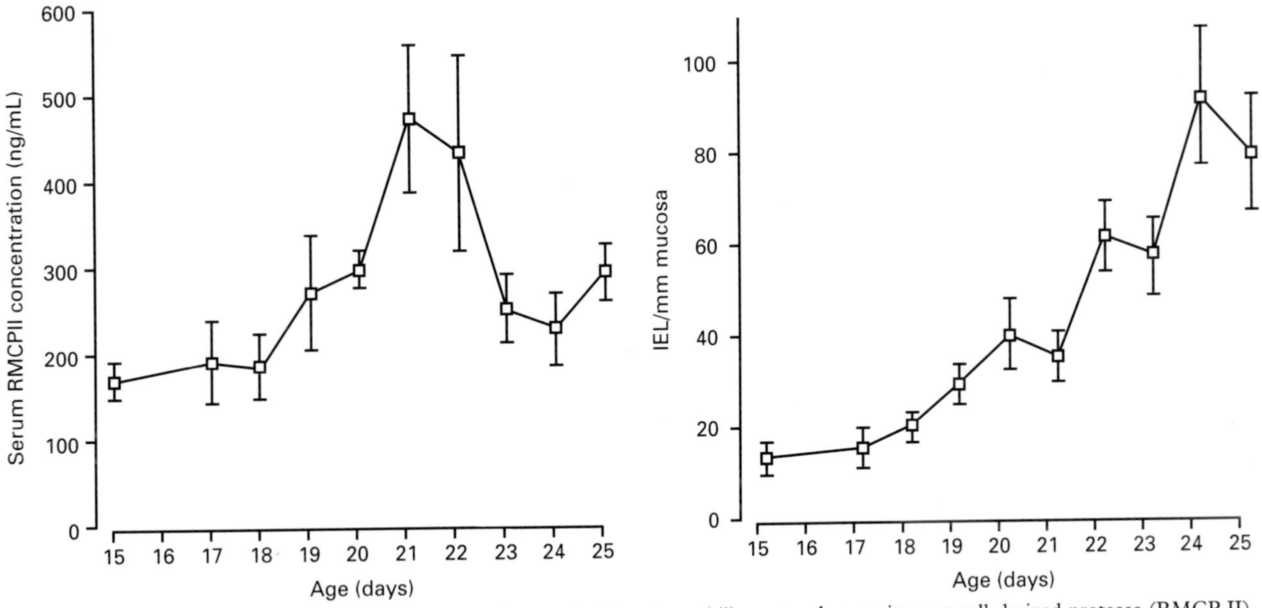

Fig. 11.1 Development of intestine at weaning in DA×PVG^c rats. Left hand panel illustrates changes in mast cell-derived protease (RMCP II) concentrations, compared with (right hand panel) changes in IEL density-counts (%) in jejunal epithelium. Each time-point refers to M ± SD of 6–8 animals.

sensitization to cow's milk protein, soya, egg and fish antigen. Alternatively, a failure of the mechanism of local T cell tolerance could also result in unwanted T cell priming for cell-mediated activity,[34] resulting in the characteristic Type 1 lesions which have been described in these conditions.[35] For example, in gluten-sensitive enteropathy, there seems to be a selective permanent defect in induction of oral tolerance to gluten at weaning in genetically susceptible (DR3 or DR7, DQw2) individuals. It is still difficult to explain why, in coeliac subjects, only 1 in 100 genetically susceptible individuals develop the disease. This would emphasize that environmental factors such as premature weaning, lack of breast feeding or possibly coincidental enteric infections could have an important role in the control of oral tolerance. On the other hand, the devastating syndrome of early-onset intractable diarrhoea of infancy[36] may represent a complete failure of oral tolerance, or even true GVHR caused by lymphocytes in maternal milk, although both of these mechanisms need confirmation.

That in some of these types of enteropathy (cow's milk protein intolerance) reactions are self-limited (rarely extending beyond the second year) indicates that compensatory mechanisms are available, or can be recruited, to reverse the earlier 'defect' and restore normal (immune) control, structure, and function.

ORAL TOLERANCE

The usual response of the immune system to systemic antigen encounter is induction of active immunity, which may be lifelong. However, specific immunological unresponsiveness may also occur, and this can be most effectively achieved through oral feeding of antigen. The precise mechanisms governing tolerance, although an observed phenomenon for over 70 years, are still poorly understood. It follows that occurrence of systemic, or local, immune responses to feeding of antigens implies that priming or sensitization occurred at first encounter. Furthermore, since food allergic symptomatology is more frequently encountered in youngsters, rather than adults, it follows that sensitization would, perhaps, result from imbalance, or some failure of normal maturation of the immune system at this period of growth.[37]

It has often been observed with various sensitizing agents, that systemic tolerance can easily be achieved in the neonate. Paradoxically, it appears that feeding of antigen to neonates does not result in (oral) tolerance, but priming for local humoral, and cell-mediated mucosal, events.

In older animals, regulatory T lymphocytes (Th:CD4) and (Ts:CD8) cells appear in Peyer's patches and mesenteric lymph node within 1–3 days, respectively, of oral challenge.[38] The cells migrate to the periphery and hence suppress the response to enterically-processed antigen.[38,39] Furthermore, if these Ts cells are separated, and infused into naive, syngeneic animals which are subsequently challenged with the same antigen, the systemic IgG response is dampened, while local IgA responses are heightened.[40] Thus, in normal physiological terms, tolerance suppresses the systemic response, although the local humoral response is amplified, and hence rapidly responsive to inhibition of further antigen potentiation via mucosae ('immune exclusion').[41,42]

Conversely, parenteral immunisation causes depression of local immune responses by suppressor cells which initially appear in spleen, and subsequently migrate to Peyer's patches via the circulation.[43,44]

Some of the factors involved in tolerogenesis, or priming, have been looked at in a more recent series of experiments. It was found that feeding ovalbumin to mice on day 1 of life consistently resulted in priming for local humoral immunity and cell-mediated immunity. Indeed, priming continued as far as day 7: after that interval (*c.* day 10) oral tolerance (adult-type) was assumed. Earlier introduction of antigen, by innoculation of amniotic fluid, also resulted in similar phenomena, with humoral and CMI responses extending into the early weeks of life.[45,46]

Some degree of tolerization could be achieved, however, if feeding, additional to the single dose given on day 1, was also repeated on successive days. This only affected humoral responses, and did not appear to influence CMI. On the other hand, CMI could be potentiated by inhibiting suppressor cells (cyclophosphamide) or by stimulating macrophages.[37] Even so, these mucosal responses were weak, and did not reproduce the changes that are seen in more severe and extensively developed lesions of GVH reactions, or adult (human)-type enteropathies.

It is evident, even from these limited studies, that the control of oral tolerance is an extremely complex affair, and it is regrettable that such an interesting series of experiments was not extended in order to dissect other variables, with use of anti-T cell subset monoclonals, defined oligopeptide antigens, Ig isotype responses and congenic mice. The interesting aspect of these observations was the apparent divarication between humoral and cell-mediated responses.

Such experiments are impossible to conduct in humans, and it is dangerous to extrapolate from animals. Little is known of the role that IgE could play in these responses and whether IgE might be involved in the short-term sensitivities to cereal, egg and milk proteins that are commonly seen in young children. It is noteworthy that in many of these reactions, the sensitivity may be lost by the age of two years, so clearly other mechanisms come into play, or other modulated effects of immune function occur at this time whose result is to suppress such abnormal reactivity. This is not the case with life-long gluten-sensitivity: with this condition, individuals behave as if tolerance did not occur, resulting in enhanced local mucosal humoral and CMI responses, and heightened systemic responses to gliadin proteins.

PEYER'S PATCHES

In adult humans (age range 40–95) abundant Peyer's patches are present, many containing more than 25 follicles. In middle-aged subjects, patches are sometimes 20–30 cm in length, while in the ninth decade, many patches approximately 10 cm in length are evident. Thus, at this period of life, Peyer's patches are still fairly extensively represented throughout the small intestine. In contrast, between 30–50 patches are observed throughout the intestinal tract in 20–40 week-old fetuses, and approximately one-half contain at least 25 follicles. In infants up to 2 months, the number of patches is around 100, increasing to between 150–250 thereafter.

Thus there are some important differences from experimental animals, in which patches tend to reside within the ileum: in humans, a considerable number of patches lie within the jejunum, and may exceed those in the ileum. Furthermore the largest patches (up to 10 cm in length) are invariably seen within the proximal ileum.[47,48]

Peyer's patches lie within the submucosa and lamina propria, extending upwards to cause protruberance of the luminal surface (Fig. 11.2). Here, each collection is covered by the villus-free, dome epithelium. In experimental animals, from which most of our current information derives, the follicle-associated epithelium is a region of specialized anatomical and functional significance in antigen-trapping.

Follicle-associated epithelium

In mice,[49] the follicle-associated epithelium (FAE) is a site of high metabolic activity, receiving oxygenated blood via the ascending central arteriole:[50] this activity is temperature-dependent and fluoride-sensitive.

Particulate antigens traverse the follicular epithelium rapidly and are subject to far less degradation than occurs in adjacent villous epithelia. Unlike the latter, contact between antigens and FAE is facilitated by the absence of mucus-producing goblet cells. Several studies indicate that a variety of antigens is taken up[51–54] by the specialized M ('micro-fold') cells (Fig. 11.3) which are an integral part of FAE in many species, including man.[55]

Substances shown to be taken up by M cells include horseradish peroxidase, lectins, *Vibrio cholerae* and reovirus subtypes. Other agents, such as *E. coli*, adhere to, but are not taken up by M cells, while others e.g. salmonella, giardia or *M. tuberculosi*, traverse FAE directly but

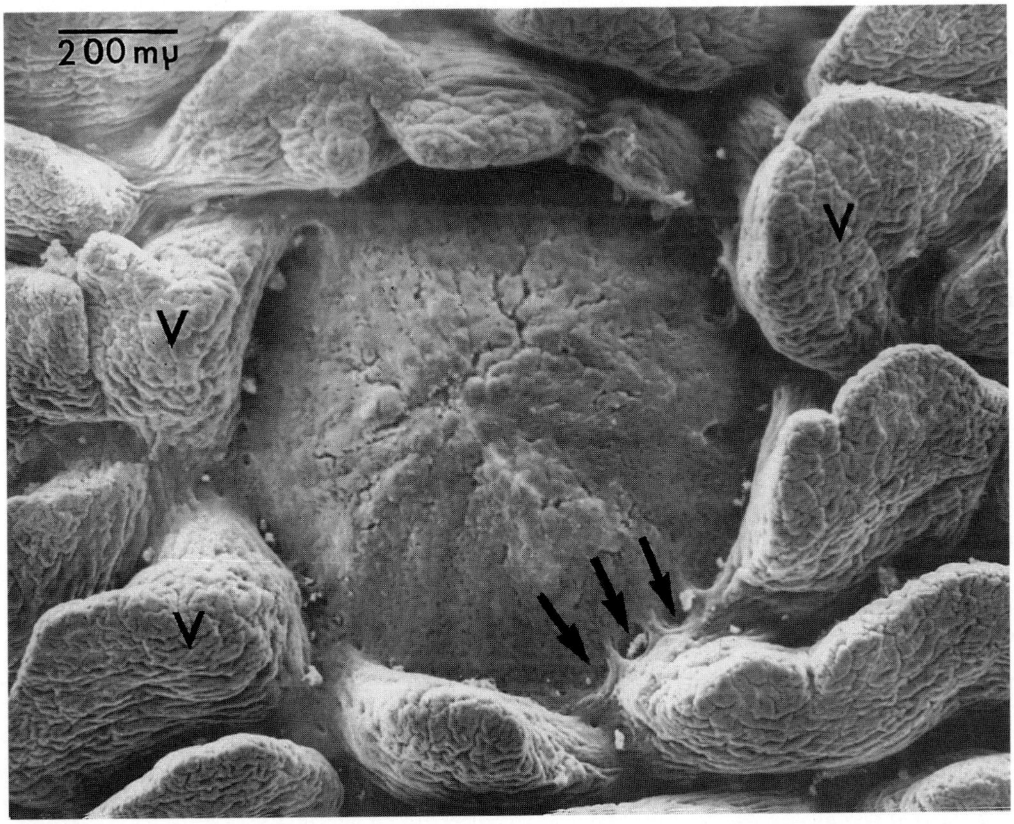

Fig. 11.2 This scanning electron micrograph of a lymphoid follicle of rat Peyer's patches reveals the dome-shaped epithelium encircled by crypt orifices and adjacent villous structures. (From Bhalla et al[50])

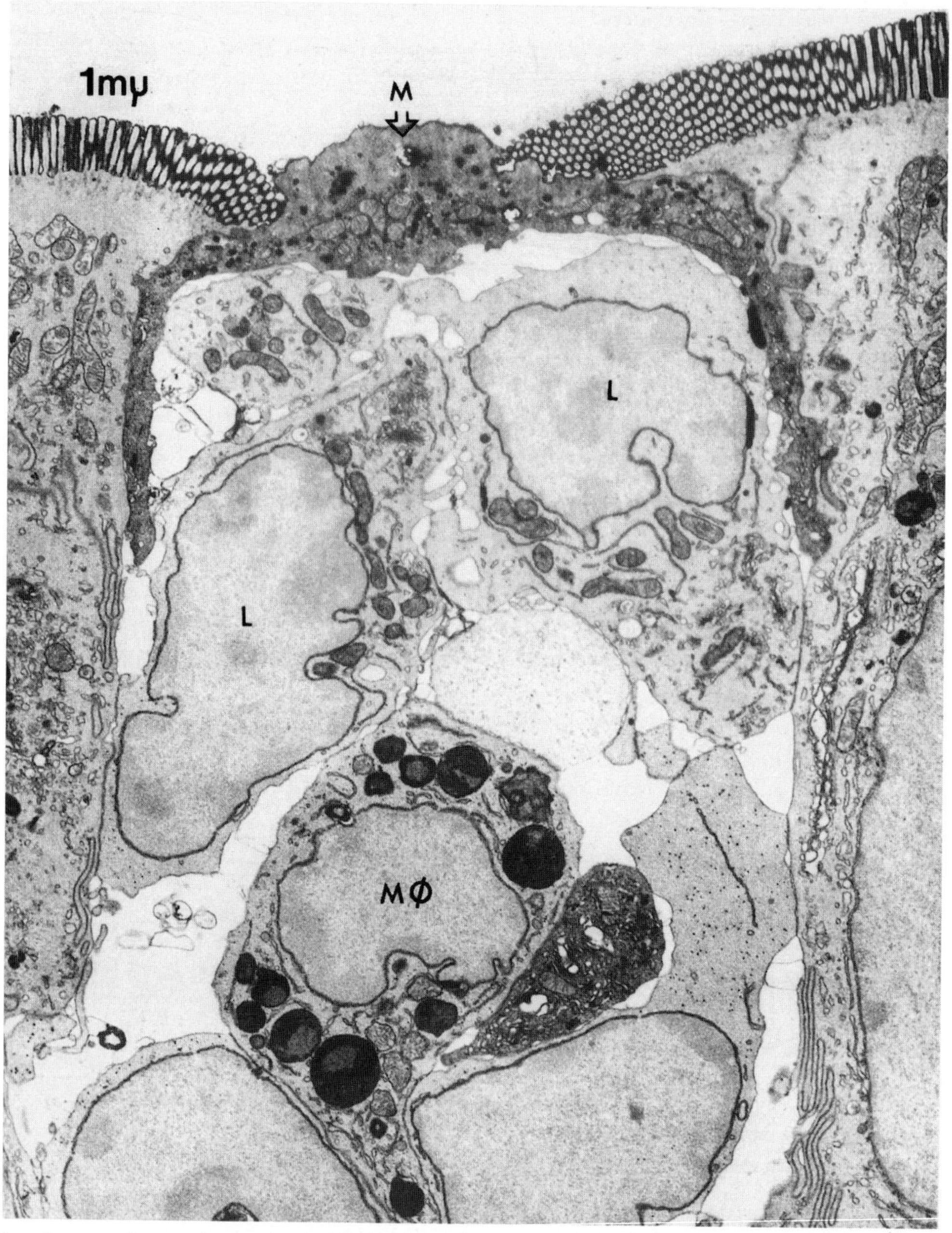

Fig. 11.3 Transmission electron micrograph of mouse jejunum showing the dark inverted U-shape of M cells, lying between the adjacent enterocytes. Note lack of microvilli. Beneath the M cell, and in intimate contact, are several lymphocytes, L, and macrophage, MØ. (From Owen et al,[51] with author's permission)

probably not via M cells.[49] Giardia organisms, for example, appear to be engulfed by macrophage processes that are extended upwards through FAE.[56]

Thus, uptake of a variety of molecular tracers and microorganisms may be a non-specific event: other factors either within GALT, or elsewhere, may ultimately determine immunogenicity, infectivity and hence access to distant (extra-intestinal) sites of cellular tropism, e.g. brain tissue. Furthermore, it is not clear whether antigen processing is a function of M cells, or whether they merely allow for rapid intake of antigen to other cells, such as macrophages, and dendritic cells[57,58] that lie close to the underside of FAE.[59] Evidence that the latter possibility is the more likely includes the observation that ferritin or giardia organisms[60] are taken up directly by macrophages and then presented to other lymphoid cells.

Lymphoid cells

There is highly suggestive evidence linking antigen-presenting function to the large, veiled Ia$^+$ dendritic cells that lie in close apposition to FAE, as well as in the paracortical areas.[59,61] These cells are capable of initiating MLR[62] and it has been proposed that they represent the physiological pathway for induction of immune responses.[63] Such function is potentially abrogated with anti-dendritic cell monoclonal antibody,[64] rather than by anti-Ia and complement, which is less specific for dendritic cells.

Architecturally, the structure of Peyer's patches is reminiscent of lymph nodes, comprising follicular B cell, and parafollicular T cell, zones. The subdome region comprises B lymphocytes, and T cells, predominantly the helper subset, together with Ia^+ macrophages and dendritic cells.[49,59,65] The FAE can be likened to the afferent lymphatic of a node in bringing antigenic material into contact with subjacent lymphoid cells.

In contrast to peripheral nodes, in which the follicles contain surface IgM- or IgG-bearing B cells, the Peyer's patch follicles comprise cells bearing sIgA. Approximately 60–70% of the B cell patch component resides in the follicles,[66] with $sIgM^+$, $sIgD^+$ B cells surrounding the follicles. Germinal centre B cells, which have high affinity for galactosyl-specific peanut agglutinin (PNA), develop after primary, or secondary, antigenic stimulation — indicating that germinal centres contain populations of Ig-switched, antigen-specific B cells. These can then migrate to mesenteric lymph nodes where final structural and functional development into plasmablasts and IgA-secreting plasma cells occurs. The resting $sIgM^+$, $sIgD^+$ B cells in the mantle region are the precursors for IgA plasma cells.[67,68]

MESENTERIC LYMPH NODES

Mesenteric lymph nodes (MLN), like their peripheral counterparts, comprise primary and secondary follicles interspersed by T cell-dependent (parafollicular) areas. They are secondary lymphoid structures and are dependent on antigen exposure for growth and full functional expression. The development of follicles is accompanied by the migration of T lymphocytes into the nodes.[69,70] Mesenteric nodes are also sites of intense mitotic activity, and newly-formed cells rapidly disperse to other sites, although with a preference for the lamina propria of the small intestine: the predominant contribution to this output is with T lymphocytes.

These nodes lie in the mesentery and receive cells and lymph from the intestinal mucosa and Peyer's patches. Efferent lymph drains into the thoracic duct, and thence to the circulation, thereby completing the anatomic pathway whereby lymphoid cells migrate between GALT and also gain access to other mucosal surfaces in mammary gland and genito-urinary tract.

Unlike Peyer's patches, MLN contain a larger proportion (70%) of T lymphocytes, the majority of which are Th cells: the remainder are $sIgM^+$ and $sIgA^+$ B cells. Presumably, $sIgA^+$ lymphocytes derive from migrating Peyer's patches 'post-switch' lymphocytes, as well as nodal lymphocytes stimulated by antigen, and antigen-primed dendritic cells, via afferent lymphatics in association with Th cells within the nodes, including many that are $Fc_\alpha R^+$.[71]

MLN are, like Peyer's patches, a rich source of gut-seeking immunoblasts that are destined to become IgA-secreting plasma cells within the lamina propria, and other mucosal sites, after circulation through the thoracic duct.[72–77]

The production of mature, immunoglobulin-secreting plasma cells involves the interplay of genetic and other factors including antigen and regulatory T lymphocytes acting sequentially within specialized micro-environments, especially Peyer's patches and mesenteric lymph nodes. Genes governing immunoglobulin production comprise three separate loci for heavy chains, κ and λ light chains on chromosomes 14, 2 and 22, respectively. Each DNA segment comprises constant (C) and variable (V) regions which undergo extensive rearrangement in establishing the presumptive isotype to be secreted by a given plasma cell, and are of cloned murine T cells has considerably advanced understanding of the way in which isotype (IgA) specificity is controlled within GALT (Fig. 11.4).

IgA responses are thymus-dependent, and hence subject to T lymphocyte regulation. One important set of lymphocytes, found circulating and antigen-inducible within Peyer's patches, is the Th α cell, bearing receptors for the α-heavy chain ($Fc_\alpha R^+$)[78–80] which promote IgA responses.

The clones isolated from murine Peyer's patches were $Thy1^+$, Lyt^+, $Lyt2^-$ and H-2 restricted. Those specific for sheep RBC[76] supported either IgA and IgM production, or polyclonal antibody responses; i.e., full differentiation to mature plasma cells occurred. In other studies,[81] clones of similar phenotype were shown to drive immunoglobulin production to the stage of sIgA in LPS-pulsed B cells; i.e., partial differentiation, or 'switch', from $sIgM^+$ to $sIgA^+$ status only. No mature plasma cells were generated by these switch clones, which likewise failed to further influence existing $sIgG^+$ or $sIgA^+$ B lymphocytes. Subsequent development to mature Ig-secreting plasma cells required influence of a further T cell subset ('post-switch' cells) together with other soluble factors,[82] particularly B cell differentiation factor (BCDF) and less so with macrophage-derived factor.

Effective 'post-switch' T lymphocytes were obtained either from uncloned splenic or mesenteric lymph nodes and comprised helper/inducer $Lyt\text{-}1^+$ cells. Macrophage factors were far less effective than BCDF in potentiating T cell-dependent terminal differentiation of IgA-committed, post-switch $sIgA^+$ Peyer's patch B cells: it is probable that the latter differentiation stages also remain class-specific in vivo, but this still requires formal demonstration. In addition to BCDF, it is clear that class-specific immunoglobulin binding factors (IBF), released by

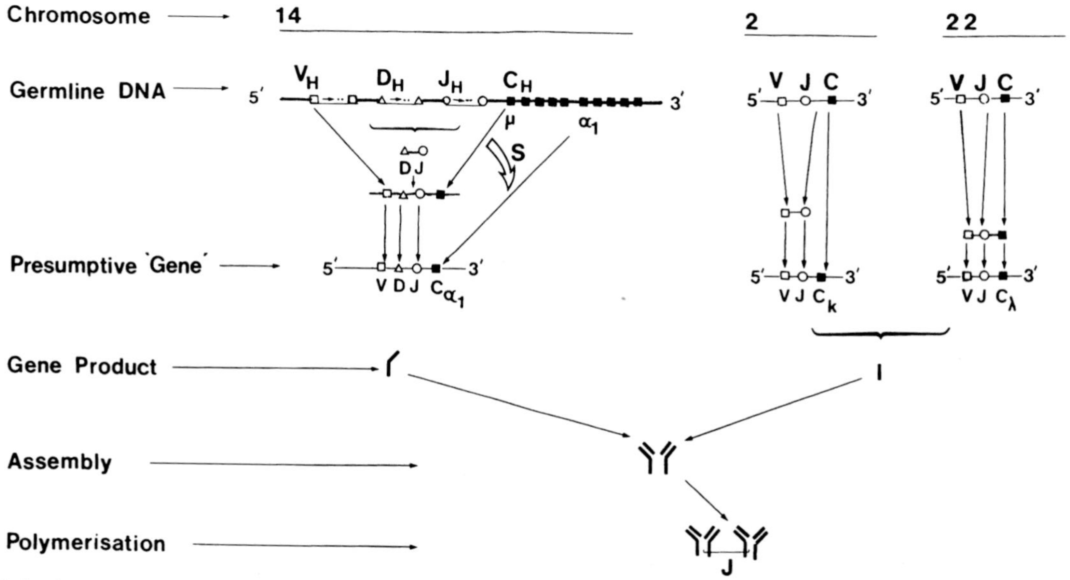

Fig. 11.4 B cell development: the heavy chains of human immunoglobulins are coded by four linked germ-line DNA regions on chromosome 14, each comprising multiple segments, collectively termed variable (V), diversity (D), joining (J) and constant (C) regions. These genes are progressively rearranged by various signals, beginning with the D-J region and followed by one of the V segments. The rearranged V-D-J gene, in association with the nearest C gene (Cμ), permits synthesis of cytoplasmic μ chains, which are thought to inhibit further rearrangement of H chain genes, and to signal V-J arrangement within the κ light chain gene segments on chromosome 2. The completed light chain gene (V-J-C) permits assembly of membrane IgM which identifies the pre-B cell. κ chains are rearranged before lambda chains, the latter located on chromosome 22. Finally, the presumptive isotype of the plasma cell destined to arise from these events, is achieved by translocation, or 'switch' (S), of the rearranged V-D-J_H segments to a point 5′ to the C gene concerned (α 1 as illustrated) probably by excision of the intervening exon-intron segments. α1 lies in the second group of 5 H-chain class-specific genes (α1, γ2, γ4, ϵ and α2).

$Fc_{\alpha}R^{+}$ T lymphocytes (IBF α), play an important role in augmenting, or suppressing, IgA responses.[83,84] Furthermore, these receptors are also subject to regulation by immunoglobulin or IFN-γ.[85]

LAMINA PROPRIA

The lamina propria, sandwiched between the intestinal epithelium and muscularis mucosae, contains a diffuse population of T and B lymphocytes, including fully-developed plasma cells of predominantly IgA-secreting type, together with other non-specific effectors like mast cells, eosinophils, neutrophils and basophils.[71] In addition, populations of macrophages[86] and dendritic cells have been identified within the lamina propria of various species, including man. In recent years techniques for the isolation of relatively pure populations of individual cell types have been developed and applied to elucidating their roles in local immunologically-mediated events.

The intrinsic structure and shape of the lamina propria is not entirely dependent on the presence of epithelium, since when the latter is removed, villous cores are preserved.[87,88] Important stuctural elements include the epithelial basement membrane, collagen and the subepithelial fibroblast sheath.[89,90] The inner muscle layer of the small intestine, or muscularis mucosae, is a thin layer of smooth muscle which acts as a foundation for the lamina propria and from which muscular extensions are inserted into the basement membrane throughout the villous cores.[91] Thirdly, the rich vascular network may also play a structural role in addition to bringing blood close to the epithelium for the nutritional support of enterocytes, absorbing transported materials from the lumen and permitting the emigration of newly-arrived cells into the mucosa. Receptors on endothelial cells influence this cellular traffic, rather than changes in mucosal blood flow,[92] as demonstrated for specialized venules within Peyer's patches and lymph nodes (Table 11.1).[93]

Important advances in our understanding of brain-gut homeostatic mechanisms throughout the neuro-endocrine system, of the influence of psychological[94] and neurological[95] factors on the expression of immunological competence and of alterations in lymphocyte behaviour by somatostatin, substance P, and vaso-intestinal peptide[96–99] indicate the potential for modulating immunological reactions within the micro-environment of the lamina propria. Such relationships are made more complicated by the knowledge that Ia induction on vascular endothelial cells[100] and even more unsuspected cells, such as fibroblasts, by γ-IFN[101,102] in the presence of other lymphokines (IL-2), may increase the available surfaces capable of presenting antigen, thereby serving to heighten local im-

Table 11.1

Family	Molecule	Receptor	Distribution	Role
INTERGRINS				
β_1 (VLA) family	VLA-1-10(?)	VCAM-1 Fibronectin	Lymphocytes	Lymphocyte-EC adhesion/tumour-EC adhesion Activation of lymphocytes (adhesion of cytotoxic T lymphocytes to target cells)
β_2 (LeuCAMs) family (CD 18)	LFA-1 (CD11a)	ICAM-1 ICAM-2	All leukocytes	Leukocyte-leukocyte and leukocyte-EC adhesion Non-organ specific strengthening of adhesion
	Mac-1 CD11b)	ICAM-1,iC3b, Fibrinogen, Factor X	Neutrophils, monocytes, some lymphocytes	Cell-cell adheson, phagocytosis, complement binding
β_3 (cytoadhesins) family	GP-150,95 (CD11c)	iC3b	Granulocytes, monocytes	Complement binding
IMMUNOGLOBULIN	ICAM-1	LFA-1, Mac-1	Many cell types induced by inflammation	Strong adhesion of leukocytes to activated EC Activation of naive T cells Enhances antigen-specific T cell activation Serves as a receptor for rhinovirus/malaria parasite
	ICAM-2	LFA-1	Resting endothelium	Binding of leucocytes to resting EC
	ICAM-3	LFA-1 (?)	?	?
	VCAM-1	VLA-4	Activated EC, macrophages, dendritic cells	Adhesion of memory T lymphocytes/monocytes
	LFA-3	CD2	Widespread	T cell adhesion
	CD2	LFA-3	All T cells	T cell adhesion
SELECTINS	L-Selectin	Sialic acid-containing oligosaccharide on EC	Leukocytes, malignant B and T cell lines	Initial neutrophil adhesion to EC (adjacent to inflammation)
	P-Selectin	Lewis-X	Platelets and EC	Adhesion of activated platelets to monocytes/ neutrophils
	E-Selectin	Sialyl-X Le	Activated EC	Neutrophilic/monocytic adhesion to activated Ec Adhesion to PLN and PP memory T cells
HOMING RECEPTORS	LECAM-1 (MECA 79)			Mediates homing
	LPAM-1	VCAM-1 (?)	Lymphocytes	Mediates homing
	LPAM-2		Melanoma cells and lymphocytes	Mediates homing
	HCAM (MECA 367)	EC mucosal addressin	Haematopoetic and non-haematopoetic cells, mesenchymal, epithelial cells, glial cells	Mediates homing to mucosal/lymphoid tissue Role in T cell activation
	$\alpha_4\beta_P$ (HML-1)		IELs	?homing receptor/activation marker for IEL
CADHERINS	E-Cadherin		Epithelial tissue	Responsible for cytoskeletal organization
	N-Cadherin		Brain, muscle, lens	Developmental cell-cell interactions/adhesions
	P-Cadherin		Placenta, epithelium, mesothelium	

Key: EC = endothelial cell; PLN = peripheral lymph node; PP = Peyer's patch; IEL = intra-epithelial space lymphocyte.

mune responses and attracting additional circulation lymphocytes into the lesion. It is within this wide context that local immunological interactions, and the cells participating in them within the lamina propria, must be viewed.

Antigen-presenting cells

T cell activation is dependent on antigen presentation by antigen-presenting cells (APC) in an MHC-restricted manner. The principle MHC-class restricted APC are macrophages, dendritic cells (DC) and B lymphocytes: other somatic cells, such as fibroblasts, epithelial and vascular endothelial cells induced to express Class II antigens by IFN-γ presumably also enjoy this property.

Class MHC class II (DR$^+$) APC are a heterogeneous collection of cells that comprise macrophage-like cells within the intestinal lamina propria, Langerhans cells in skin, thymic cortical cells and interdigitating dendritic cells of lymph nodes and spleen.[62] As described above, macrophages and DC play an important role in antigen sequestering within Peyer's patches, and are likely to be the primary cells concerned in initiating immune events[103] such as allogeneic lymphocyte stimulation in MLR or antigen presentation to CD4$^+$ inducer T cells.

How DC 'process' antigen is poorly understood[104] but they probably lack the intracellular lysosomal phase that has been so well characterized in marophages.[105] DC also differ from macrophages in their lack of Fc receptors,[62] lysosomes and lysosomal enzymes, and hence are not part of the secondary effector phase of immunological reactions.

DR^+ cells with the morphology and cytochemical features of DC are abundant within the lamina propria of the small intestine and colon in animals[58] and humans.[86]

Within human intestine, 90% of DR^+ lamina propria cells exhibit stellate morphology, express membrane ATPase activity, but lack lysosomal acid phosphatase and non-specific esterase, indicating marked differences from typical macrophages. Thus, by analogy derived from experimental animals, it seems certain that cells of this type may be involved with antigen presentation to T cells in areas of the intestine which are devoid of Peyer's patches. The origin and rate of turnover of these cells is also poorly documented, although it is likely that they derive from bone marrow and are delivered to the tissues via the circulation. The use of more specific monoclonal antibodies, such as were used in other studies of DC localization[106,107] will undoubtedly help to clarify the location and role of DC in local mucosal immune events, and what differences occur in diseases of the small intestine or colon.

Studies in animals have also shown that antigen-laden DC cells migrate from skin or intestine through lymphatic channels to regional lymph nodes,[108] suggesting that similar events are likely to occur in the human. Such a mechanism can be seen to be an effective way of mobilizing antigen from a larger mucosal surface, and enhancing contact with reactive T lymphocytes within paracortical areas of local mesenteric lymph nodes.

Macrophages are abundant within the lamina propria and contain acid phosphatase, exhibit considerable phagocytosis and on 'activation' take part in, and influence, other effector mechanisms. They extrude pseudopodia through the basement membrane into the interepithelial cell spaces, which both permits antigen-sampling (as in Peyer's patches) and closer contact with epithelial lymphocytes.[109] Thus, while macrophages present antigen[105] and hence take part in primary and secondary events on the 'afferent' side of the immune response, they also have diverse 'effector' functions and are markedly altered in inflammatory conditions of the intestine. The scope of macrophage involvement in the local immune response nevertheless requires considerably more investigation.

T lymphocytes

Of the lymphocytes within the small intestinal lamina propria (Fig. 11.5), approximately 30–40% comprise $CD3^+$ T lymphocytes.[18,71] Approximately 70% carry the CD4 phenotypic marker[110] which facilitate antigen recognition in the context of MHC class II markers. The remainder carry the CD8 surface molecule characterizing

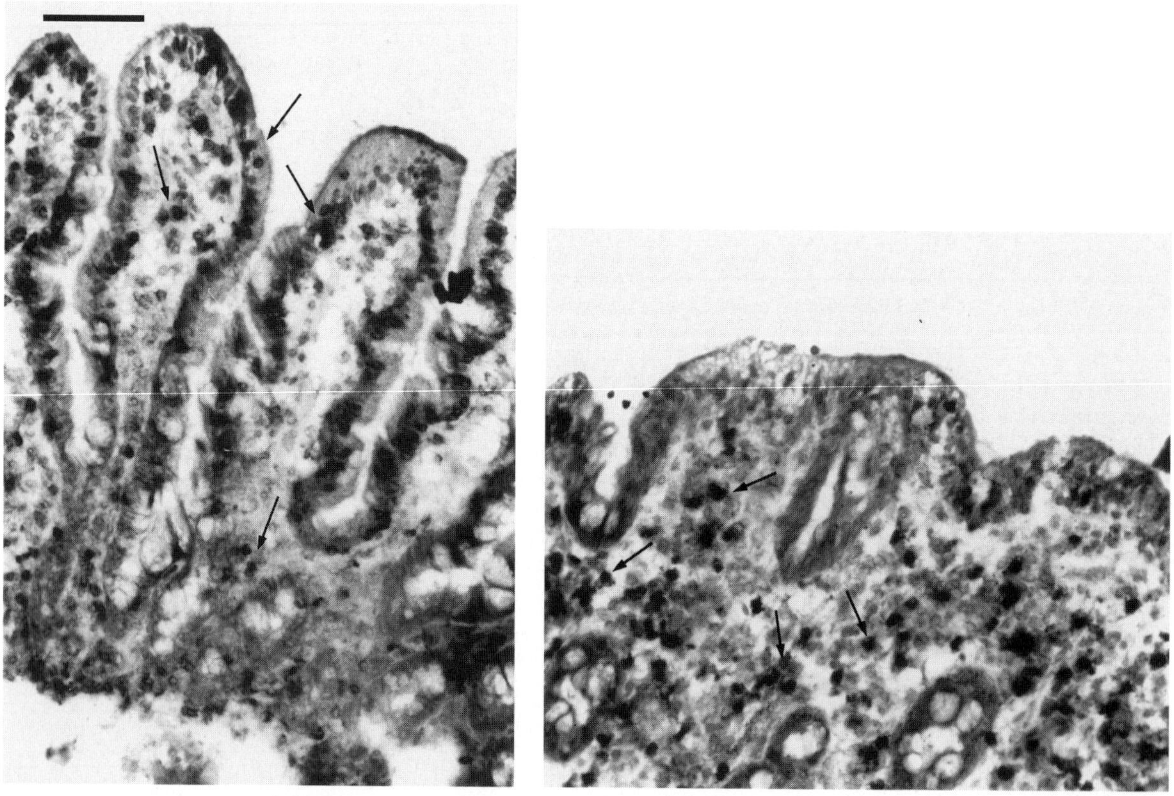

Fig. 11.5 Frozen sections stained with anti-CD3 monoclonal antibody for T cells. Left hand panel from disease-control with normal jejunal mucosal architecture, with occasional positive cells in epithelium and lamina propria (arrowed). Compare mucosa from untreated coeliac patient (right-hand panel) in which $CD3^+$ lymphocytic infiltration predominantly affects lamina propria. (Magnification bar: approx. 100 μm)

presumptive 'suppressor/cytolytic' cells that recognize antigens in association with MHC class I markers. Few lamina propria lymphocytes (LPL) contain granulated cytoplasm, so that there is a clear morphological, structural and phenotypic difference between cells in this compartment compared with those in the epithelium.

The functional role of LPL is not well defined. One problem to be explained is how idiotype (as opposed to isotype) expression is controlled within the lamina propria and what role T4$^+$ cells with α chain receptors ($Fc_\alpha R^+$) may play in this capacity, either within the lamina propria or at an earlier, and perhaps more critical, phase of clonal isotype expansion within mesenteric lymph nodes, or Peyer's patches.[111–113]

Progress in understanding the function and role of lamina propria T cells has been slow.[18] The majority of CD4 cells (60% total T cells) comprise two groups, CD45RO$^+$ cells (40%) which are 'memory' cells and are highly active in immunoglobulin synthesis, and CD45RA cells (60%) which are activated CD8$^+$ (suppressor-inducer) cells. Lamina propria T cells are highly activated by virtue of their generalized expression of IL2-R and MHC class 2 alloantigen, and because they also contain mRNA for IFN-γ and IL-4 and IL-5. However, IL-2R seems to be their main stimulatory factor for Ig synthesis, rather than IL-4 and IL-5, which are more characteristic of MLN lymphocytes. There appears to be no predilection for IgA synthesis: in other words, IgA synthesis depends on B blasts committed to this isotype before entering the lamina, as discussed above. This fact also explains why so few $Fc_\alpha R^+$ T cells are detectable within the lamina.[114] These difficulties are compounded by the presence of suppressor cells within the CD4$^+$ subset,[115] while some so-called 'suppressor' (CD8$^+$) T cells contain elements for a contra-suppressor circuit which actually facilitates augmentation of local immunoglobulin responses.[116] That this activity exists within the CD8$^+$ T lymphocyte subset of human intestine has recently been demonstrated.[117]

Evidence for cytolytic activity of lamina T cells is less certain, although ~50% CD8$^+$ cells are cytolytic (CD28$^+$: Tp44) while suppressor-inducers are CD11$^+$ (CR3R$^+$). A small minority of NK (NKH-1$^+$) cells has also been identified.

Antigen-specific T cells do apparently exist in lamina propria, but do not exhibit marked proliferative responses to specific antigen.[118] Clearly, these matters will need careful addressing in the future, especially if lamina propria is used as a source of cloned T cells for providing information on dietary or microbial sensitivities. Furthermore, more will be needed to be known in comparisons between control and diseased individuals.

Plasma cells

The majority of plasma cells in human intestine secrete IgA, followed by IgM, and lesser numbers are committed to IgG and IgE synthesis. Based on proper morphometric analyses, the percentage ratios of IgA:IgM:IgG are, respectively, 69:28:3.[119] The relative paucity of IgG-producing cells in the normal intestine contrasts markedly with the situation in spleen and peripheral lymph nodes.[120]

While the majority of circulating IgA in humans is of monomeric type and derived from bone marrow and other non-mucosal sites, mucosal IgA is a dimeric molecule derived from local mucosal synthesis[121] and joined by 15 000 MW glycoprotein, termed J chain (Fig. 11.5). Secreted by plasma cells,[122] J chain facilitates polymerization of IgA and IgM and their subsequent transport through epithelial cells via the specific polyclonal receptor, termed secretory component (SC).[123] SC is a transmembrane glycoprotein located to the basolateral membrane of human enterocytes[124,125] but, unlike other animals, not on hepatic sinusoidal membranes. It thus seems that recirculation of IgA through bile must have a different role in humans, compared with animals. What transport occurs seems to be via SC located on biliary duct epithelium[126] although SC-independent translocation mechanisms may also be important.[127] Human bile contains secretory IgA (IgA_2.J.SC), polymeric IgA (IgA_2.J) and monomeric IgA. The functional role of hepatobiliary IgA translocation is not clear; the fact that the concentration of polymeric IgA rises in the serum of patients with liver disease, however, suggests that this could be an important physiological process. There are some other curious paradoxes concerning the systemic and local (sIgA) immunoglobulin systems which still require further detailed analysis.[128]

There are two allotypes of IgA, IgA1 and IgA2, coded by different genes.[129] In serum 80–90% is monomeric IgA1, the remainder (10–20%) IgA2. In contrast, secretory IgA comprises 50–70% IgA1 and 30–50% IgA2, which roughly corresponds with the proportion of each type of plasma cell in the lamina propria. Two major allotypic forms of IgA2, A2m(1) and A2m(2), have been identified, of which the former is found in the majority of Caucasians.

Secretory IgA has a variety of important protective functions at the mucosal surface, such as:

(i) neutralization of viruses
(ii) neutralization of toxins and enzymes
(iii) possible inhibition of bacterial adherence
(iv) reduction of antigen uptake from the lumen
(v) enhancement of other antibacterial factors, such as lactoperoxidase and lactoferrin
(vi) suppression of complement-dependent and complement-independent activities, such as polymorphonuclear phagocytosis, cutaneous anaphylaxis, immune lysis and NK-cell activity.[128,130]

In serum, IgA1 antibodies are active against common environmental or dietary antigens, such as avian or bovine gammaglobulin, casein, beta-lactoglobulin, gliadin, soya and ovalbumin, together with lipopolysaccaride extracts from *E. coli*, *B. gingivalis* and *B. fragilis*; however, salivary antibody towards the latter is of IgA2 class.[128] Several bacteria produce anti-IgA1 proteases which may be related to their pathogenicity.[131] In general, the functions of circulating IgA are poorly defined, in comparison with studies of the local function and specificity of sIgA.[130]

In the normal intestine, IgG and IgE plasma cells are sparsely represented[129] but appear to arise from precursors within Peyer's patches. IgE responses mediate local allergic phenomena and are characteristically associated with worm infestations. IgE plasma cells are under T cell control and IgE immunoglobulin predominantly occupies high-affinity receptors on mast cells whose mediators, released on contact with the appropriate antigen, lead to mucosal oedema, smooth muscle contraction and vascular permeability.[132] Studies in allergic individuals, as well as Nippostrongylus-infested animals, show high levels of circulating regulatory T cells bearing receptors for the E heavy chain ($Fc_\varepsilon R^+$), similar to those specific for IgA.[79] Whether $Fc_\varepsilon R^+$ regulating T cells reside within the lamina propria, as occurs for $Fc_\alpha R^+$ cells,[133] is unclear.

Despite considerable advances into the immunobiology of IgE, and IgE-related phenomena,[134] we still lack knowledge of the way in which IgE may be involved in local allergic pathologies within the human small intestine in such conditions as food allergy, due to milk, egg, soya or other dietary antigens.[135] This difficulty is compounded by (i) the potentially dangerous effect of challenge in such sensitized individuals, and (ii) the very young age at which most of these patients present. Further studies with cloned cells, and purified immunogens, in vitro, may well help to delineate the immunopathology of these syndromes with a greater degree of clarity in the near future.

Mast cells

Virtually nothing is known of the functional attributes of human mast cells within intestinal tissues. For years, we have been conditioned to endless studies on rat peritoneal mast cells and to an equally restricted view that anything to do with mast cells must involve allergy, IgE or histamine. Only recently has it become obvious that mast cells exhibit considerable structural, cytochemical and functional heterogeneity, and that what happens with rat or mice cells does not necessarily hold for their human counterparts.[136]

Histological studies of human jejunum or colon[137–139] are consistent with a heterogeneous population of mast cells in these sites. The choice of fixative is critical, the largest counts being obtained with alcian blue (pH 0.5) staining of tissue in Carnoy's fluid or basic lead acetate. Conversely, considerably fewer mast cells are observed after formalin fixation alone. The difference is presumed to be due to the presence of so-called 'mucosal mast cells' (MMC) which are not resistant to the effects of formalin, unlike the remainder which have been termed 'connective tissue' mast cells (CTMC). Despite its widespread current usage, the terminology of MMC may require modification, since mucosal mast cells identified by the specific histological procedures noted above apparently occur in other non-mucosal sites. Thus the distinction, and the ontogenetic relationship between MMC and CTMC, if any, will be dependent on further detailed studies of a variety of tissues obtained from individual species, and compared in that context alone. This information is not yet available in humans.

Intestinal mast cells presumably derive from bone marrow and arrive within intestinal tissues via the circulation. Only relatively mature (granular) cells can, so far, be identified and these do not divide, even when analysed after administration of colchicine to human subjects.[140]

Rat intestinal mast cells show considerable differences in response to secretagogues and ionophores in comparison with peritoneal (CTMC) mast cells.[141] Similar kinds of differential responsiveness may also pertain to humans: this information is required for therapeutic reasons in controlling pathological conditions where mast cell mediator release is relevant, as in food allergy or intestinal mastocytosis.[142]

The mast cell has been aptly termed a pharmacological grenade. Its functions concern secretion of preformed mediators such as histamine, proteoglycans, enzymes with neutral protease, oxidative and acid hydrolase activities, chemotactic peptides for eosinophils, lymphocytes and neutrophils, and synthesis de novo of prostaglandin and leukotriene species via the cyclo-oxygenase and lipoxygenase pathways of arachidonic acid metabolism, respectively.[142–145]

It is clear from this formidable arsenal that mast cell secretion can cause profound changes in tissue structure and function, including smooth muscle contraction, increased microvascular permeability and tissue oedema. The enzymatic disruption of connective tissue components such as collagen (type IV) and proteoglycans could account for stripping of epithelium in asthma and intestinal allergic conditions. The mast cell may also play a role in adult enteropathies[146] and, by modulating collagen deposition, result in the longer term in generalized or localized fibrotic reactions.[147] It has an effect in recruiting other cells with inflammatory potential, such as neutrophils, eosinophils and basophils, which on activation augment both acute and chronic mucosal lesions.

Thus, early concepts of allergy being dependent on IgE-mediated release of mast cell histamine have been superseded by a new and extraordinarily complicated vista. This now is seen to involve widely diverse reactions operative within local micro-environments, particularly within lung, skin and intestinal tissues and to be concerned not only with classical immediate-type hypersensitivity, but also late-phase and delayed-type reactions, as well as in complement function.[148] The intimate relationship between mucosal mast cells and neural elements[149] adds a further dimension to the potential functions of these cells, especially in relation to changes in epithelial cell function.[150–151]

With such diversity of function and effects, it will be difficult to assign precise roles to mast cell mediators released in various immunopathological lesions of the intestinal tract. Extensive work in animals has provided a significant lead in our understanding of mast cell function, but much care is still needed in translating these results to intestinal disease in humans.

EPITHELIAL LYMPHOCYTES

In view of their strategic position between the lining cells of the intestinal mucosa, epithelial lymphocytes (EL) have been the subject of many studies[152–156] aimed at elucidating what functions they subserve at this important frontier between host and environment.

The cytological and ultrastructural features of EL in various species have been extensively documented[154,157–159] and revealed considerable heterogeneity which must presumably reflect their diversity of function. One of the most striking features of this compartmentalized population of cells is the high proportion (approximately 20–50%) containing 1–20 azurophilic granules that stain with alcian blue or PAS.[154,158,160–162] These are present in all mammalian species examined, including nude rats and mice, although not birds.[87,163]

Granular epithelial lymphocytes (gEL), despite earlier proposals,[164] are not mast cell precursors. Subsequent studies have shown that the mast cell deficient mouse strain (W/W^{v}) has a full complement of gEL.[165] Furthermore, analysis of the granules shows they are biochemically distinct and contain the specific mast cell proteinase RMCP II.[166] Moreover, the 'globule leucocyte' has no relationship to gEL, but represents a partially-discharged interepithelial space mast cell.[167,168] It thus seems clear that the ontogeny of mast cells and gEL proceeds along different pathways, deriving from separate progenitors.[169,170]

Apart from gEL, a smaller component of EL comprises cells larger than circulating leucocytes,[88,161,171] containing a variety of well-developed organelles consistent with an 'activated' state.[172] Some have 'blast-like' features with basophilic cytoplasm packed with polyribosomes or extensive endoplasmic reticulum. It is likely that the latter correspond to the 'large, degenerate ballooned cells' described by earlier histologists, whose interpretations engendered the false notion that the intestinal tract is a graveyard for effete lymphocytes as they pass through epithelium to lumen.[173–177]

In general, work from various laboratories has shown that EL:

1. arise from mitotic precursors outside the intestinal mucosa, notably Peyer's patches and mesenteric lymph nodes[75,164,178–180]
2. are a rapidly changing population of young cells[178,181–184]
3. exhibit mitotic activity within the epithelium as exemplified by ^{3}H-TdR labelling[185] or time-course colchicine blockade[178]
4. are increased in numbers by the appearance and presence of luminal antigen.[186,187]

The rate of loss and turnover of EL is unknown.[71,171] Some undoubtedly pass into the lumen, although it also seems likely that substantial numbers of EL return via the basement membrane and possibly recirculate through intestinal lymphatics.[178]

Progress in analysing the functions of human IEL (Fig. 11.6)(and or lamina propria lymphocytes) was previously limited by the inability to obtain sufficient cells to work with. However, the development,[188,189] with subsequent modifications by various workers, of methods for deriving enriched and relatively pure populations of cells from surgically-resected intestinal specimens, has helped considerably in bringing further insights into the physiological and immunopathological aspects of human intestinal mucosal immunology. Analysis of small biopsy fragments by morphological, immunohistological, or organ culture techniques also continues to provide vital information on this front. Nevertheless our views and concepts are still largely influenced and modified by observations derived from laboratory animals.

A high proportion (90–95%) of EL in human jejunum have been characterized as T 'cytolytic/suppressor' cells.[88,190–193] Although some workers have found the proportion of EL simultaneously expressing T cell markers (leu 1, UCHTI or HuTLA) to be approximately 30%, thus consistent with observations in mice (Thy1^{-}, CD8^{+}), other workers have found that the majority of EL express CD3 or leu-1 markers: the reason for this discrepancy is unclear. Few cells expressed NK markers (HNK-1) or other 'activation' antigens (DR, Tac or OKT10).

Granulated EL occur at a frequency of 20–50% and carry either CD3, CD4 or CD8 markers.[88,193] In pathological specimens, the percentage of gEL is higher than in the jejunum of young healthy volunteers: the highest proportion (65%) was seen in untreated coeliac patients, falling to around 50% after gluten restriction.[194] Thus mucosal inflammation clearly influences this structural subset of EL.

The average size of EL (range 5–8 5 μm)[193] parallels that of peripheral blood leucocytes (PBL), and is broadly in line with measurements by computerized image-analysis, both with surface, and crypt, epithelium.[171,195,196] Thus, in terms of surface phenotype and size distribution,

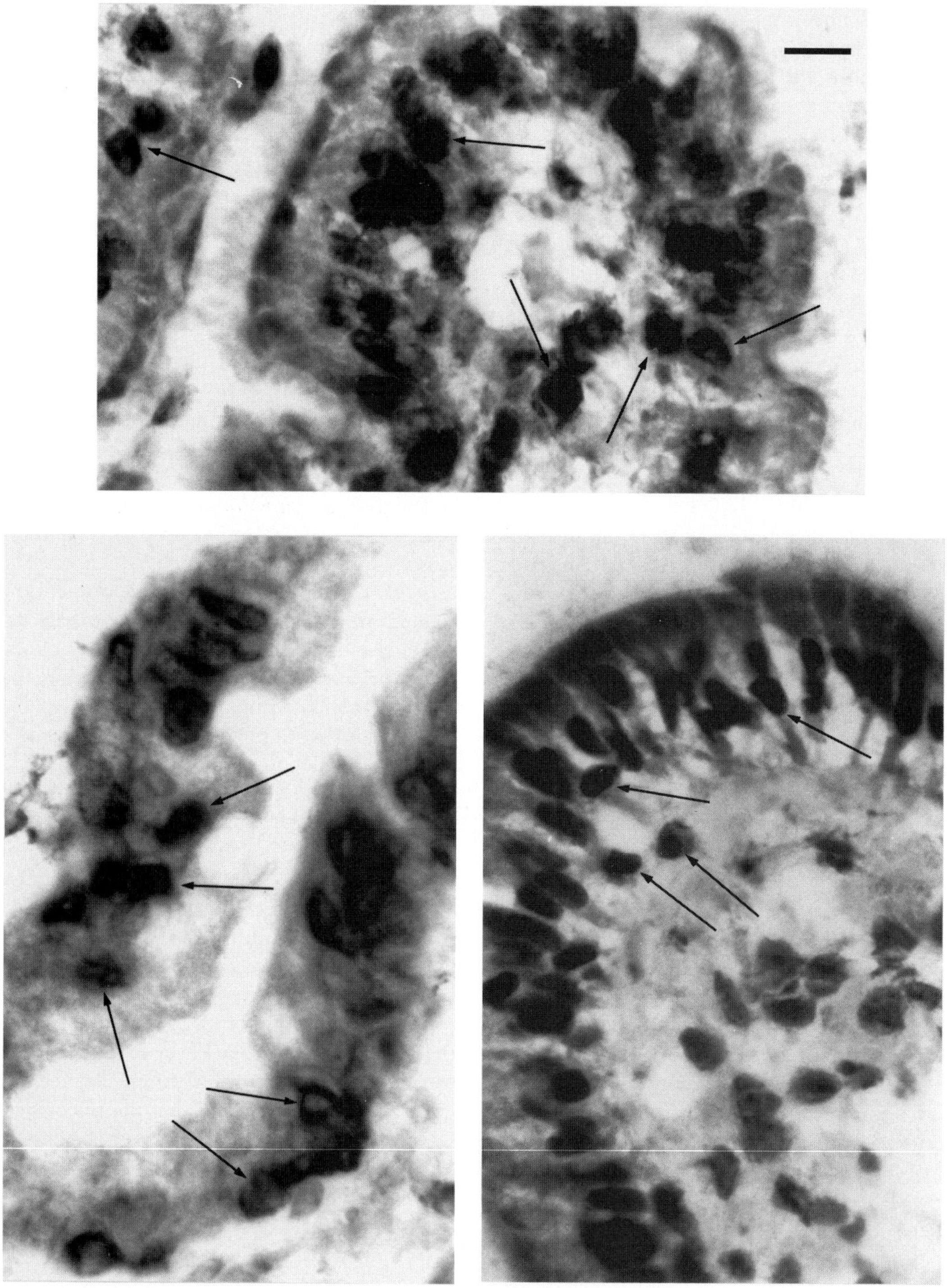

Fig. 11.6 Close-up micrographs of frozen-sections of control jejunal mucosae showing $CD3^+$ lymphocytes in epithelium (top panel), CD3+ lymphocytes in crypt epithelium (bottom left panel) and $\gamma\delta^+$ (TCR1) lymphocytes in epithelium (bottom right panel). (Magnification bar: approx. 15 μm)

EL are homogeneous throughout the entire epithelial cell column.

In vitro cultures of isolated human EL, in contrast to LPL or PBL, are unresponsive to the non-specific mitogens PHA, Con-A or PWN, even in the presence of exogenous TCGF.[88,197] That normal EL are non-proliferative cells was also shown by performing mitotic indices (% mitotic EL per 3000 EL per specimen) from control patients before and 4 hours after receiving hourly i.m. injections of colchicine (1.2 mg);[171,198,199] <20% mucosae showed evidence of low mitotic activity (range 0.03–0.1%).

Despite the failure of experimental attempts to induce EL proliferation, in untreated coeliac sprue[171,198,200] and endemic (Indian) tropical sprue[201] the mitotic activity of EL is considerably raised, and provides a useful marker to distinguish the untreated flat coeliac mucosa from other unrelated causes of mucosal flattening.[202,203] The mechanism of this striking proliferative response (Fig. 11.7) is unknown, although in the case of coeliac disease, it is dependent on gluten, which may be presented to sensitized EL by DR-bearing enterocytes.[204,205] Although not addressing this question specifically, it is noteworthy that presentation of antigen by I-A bearing rat enterocytes caused selection and proliferation of primed lymph node cells bearing the suppressor phenotype,[206] presumably through elaboration of lymphokine-like molecules.

Although in the human intestine the majority of IEL comprises $CD3^+$ $CD8^+$,[191–193] there are variations in certain enteropathies, notably gluten-sensitivity in which there is an expanded population of $CD3^+$ $CD4^-$ $CD8^-$ (double-negative IEL).[207] In regard to the former subsets ($CD3^+$ $CD8^+$) the majority, both in control and coeliac subjects, are CD45 RA^-.[208] However, an expanded population of $CD3^+$ (70%) and $CD8^+$ (62%) express the 180 kDa isoform CD45 RO compared with ≈50% for both populations in controls. All $CD3^+$ IEL express varying amounts of CD45 RB, often reciprocally in relation to RO. All IEL (controls and coeliacs) of the $CD4^+$ subset (≈5%) are also CD45 RO^{high}. Thus, in untreated coeliac patients there is an accumulation of CD45 RO^{high} RB^{low} IEL in the mucosa, regressing after treatment.[209] Since CD45 RA^+ cells (≈5% IEL) are naive or unprimed T cells, it is clear that the majority of $CD3^+$ IEL in untreated coeliacs are memory, or primed, lymphocytes.[210,211] The reason for this, and the way in which, and in what site, those cells

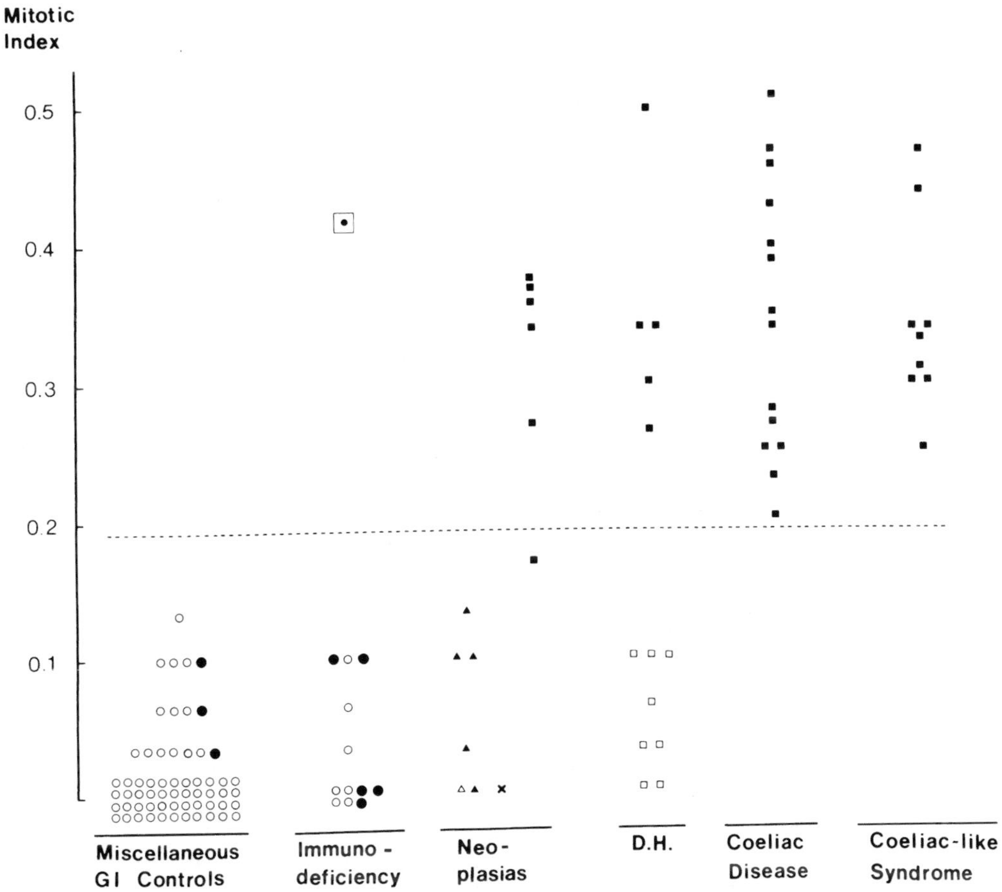

Fig. 11.7 These data reflect the mitotic activity of epithelial lymphocytes (EL) in a variety of human small intestinal biopsies. The index is derived from the percentage metaphase figures observed per 3000 EL per specimen. In the majority of control biopsies mitotic activity is rarely present. These observations contrast markedly with flat mucosae (■) obtained from gluten-sensitized patients (untreated coeliac disease: dermatitis herpetiformis (DH) and coeliac-associated lymphomas). DH patients without flat mucosae do not different from controls, neither do other patients with immunodeficiency (●) or non gluten-induced intestinal lymphomas (▲), or carcinoma (**X**), even with flat (solid symbols) mucosae. The patient with immunodeficiency and coeliac disease (boxed solid circle) behaved like coeliac patients and not like those with solitary immunodeficiency (Marsh & Haeney, 1983)[202]. Thus a high mitotic index (>0.20%) in a flat biopsy is a useful marker of presumptive coeliac disease. (Data from Marsh, J Clin Pathol 1982; 35: 517–525, by kind permission of the editor)

acquire memory in the intestinal mucosa require further analysis.

It is also of interest that such cells (CD45 RA⁻ RO⁺) are more sensitive to antigen stimulation and antigen recall, and secrete IFN-γ (gamma type interferon) in response to such stimulation.[212] Other evidence indicates that elaboration of IFN-γ by IEL results in upregulation and more extensive expression of MHC class 2 allospecificities among surface and crypt enterocytes[213] and is consistent with the observed relationship between MHC expression and IEL territory.[214,215]

At present data are scant, and it seems likely that some of the changes described are not exclusive to gluten-sensitivity, but may also be seen in other enteropathies in which architectural remodelling is a major feature.[209] It is also odd that if such cells are antigen-primed, they seem not to be responding to gluten antigen in the conventional manner:[216] this may be simply due to the fact that the majority of IEL is $CD8^+$. Clearly much more needs to be learned about these cells, their response to gluten challenge and withdrawal and their subsequent activation (cytokine) pathways dependent on the particular CD45 isoform expressed.

Considerable interest has recently been generated by the observation that in some species (i.e. mouse), a relatively high proportion of IEL express not the conventional α/β T cell receptor (TCR 2) but the γ/δ type (TCR 1) (Fig. 11.6). It is generally agreed that in the normal human intestine, about 90% IEL are TCR 2 (α/β) cells, while only about 10% carry TCR 2 (γ/δ) receptors.[217–220] A large proportion of γ/δ IEL (≈60%) characterize the expanded (≈30% of $CD3^+$ IEL) population of $CD3^+$ double negative ($CD3^+$ $CD4^-$ $CD8^-$) cells seen in coeliac mucosae, while the remainder are $CD3^+$ $CD8\alpha^+$, β^-; i.e. they express only the α chain of the expressed CD8 cell surface heterodimer. It is possible that the α chain expressed in such cells is induced by epithelium.[217] Up to 45% $CD3^+$ $CD8^+$ IEL express only the α chain of this dimeric molecule.

Of the γ/δ subset, ≈50% express V 9 gene-products in association with V 2, while the remainder express Vγ1/Vδ1 (δTCS-1⁺).[221] In untreated coeliac sprue patients with severe, flat (Type 3) lesions, the Vγ1/Vδ1 subset is increased, together with the $CD3^+$ $CD4^-$ $CD8^-$ subset (of which they comprise the majority) to upwards of 30%.[207,218,220] Interestingly, this subset gradually falls with prolonged gluten-withdrawal, suggesting that it may have nothing to do with gluten-sensitivity in general, or with the evolution of mucosal immunopathology in particular. Although it has been suggested that γ/δ cells may develop cytotoxicity towards enterocytes in the presence of gluten[217] it is still not explained how such activity would, or could be, selectively delivered to surface enterocytes alone, while those similar γ/δ gluten-activated IEL within crypt epithelium remain impotent. Finally, it should be noted that mucosal flattening can be brought about by activated lamina propria cells that are TCR α/β[222,223] and that in experimental GVH, in which mucosal flattening again can be brought about solely by $CD4^+$ cells, the increase in natural and NK-associated cytotoxicity appears to play no major role in the evolution of mucosal pathology.[224–227]

The heterogeneity of the IEL population is extremely intriguing, yet despite considerable interest and investigation, our ideas of their function and roles in the strategic epithelial frontier of the intestinal surface, which is constantly exposed to a variety of microbial and dietary antigens, is barely focussed.[228] Human IEL do appear to represent an antigen-experienced set of cells, and may also contain a small proportion of prethymic cells. However, they do not display the conventional markers developed by other (non-intestinal) lymphoid cells responding to specific antigen. The γ/δ recipient may be important in 'superantigen' recognition, and in the elimination of virally-infected or virally-damaged enterocytes. They may be increased in tropical forms of enteric disease, and in giardiasis and cryptosporidiosis, although the reason for the exaggerated epitheliotropic response in these circumstances is not known. More recently it has been shown that the activation antigen HML-1[229,230] is present on a very high proportion of IEL. The N-terminal of the smaller 105 kDa subunit of this heterodimer has homology with the integrin B_7,[231,232] which is likely, therefore, to play an important role in the mucosal localization (or activation) of these cells (Table 11.1).

MUCOSAL DEFENCE AND THE INTEGRATION OF THE LOCAL IMMUNE SYSTEM

At first sight, it seems paradoxical that such an elaborately-contrived local immune system evolved within the intestinal tract whose major function, in breaking down nutrients into absorbable form, would be expected to render antigenic substances innocuous to the host. There was also a view prevalent in the earlier part of this century, despite considerable evidence to the contrary,[233] that the intestinal mucosal 'barrier' was impervious to large and potentially-immunogenic molecules.

It is now known that this is not so, and that large molecules traverse the epithelium to reach the circulation intact.[234] In many pathological conditions, such as coeliac disease, the intestinal mucosa becomes extraordinarily permeable to macromolecules. A similar effect occurs during the recovery phase of acute enteric infections and may be the opportunity for systemic immunization to luminal antigens, particularly from foodstuffs. Hence the prevalence of transient food sensitivities following infantile 'gastroenteritis'.[235]

Experimentally, a variety of large molecular weight substances (Table 11.2) has been shown to pass through the intestinal mucosa of normal animals or man.[233] This may occur by receptor, or non-receptor-mediated mecha-

Table 11.2 Substances alleged to cross the intestinal mucosa intact.

(a) Transport of macromolecus	Molecular weight	(b) Particulate (persorption)
Lysine-vasopressin	1116	Corn
Insulin	6000	Maize
Trypsin	22 000	Starch
Bromelain	33 000	Pollen grain
β-lactoglobulin	35 000	Iron particles
Peroxidase	40 000	Sand
Ferritin	500 000	Spores

nisms.[236] Even larger particles, i.e. starch grains, pollen, and spores, may reach the circulation of humans by a process termed 'persorption'.

Unlike many small rodents, whose intestine is highly permeable to colostral-derived gammaglobulins until 'closure' takes place, the human intestine at birth is far less permeable to macromolecules, largely because passive immunity is derived from the maternal circulation via the placenta. Furthermore, the predominant antibody in human colostrum and milk is sIgA, which is specifically adapted to provide protection at mucosal surfaces. Nevertheless, full-term babies fed colostrum rich in IgA-antipolio virus antibody develop high blood levels,[237] indicating that some protein absorption does occur.

In contrast, human fetal intestine appears able to transfer large molecules because of enterocyte immaturity.[238] Prematurity is also a factor which leads to increased protein absorption, an event that may be facilitated by reduced proteolytic activity within the lumen, at the brush border, and within the cytoplasm.

Mucosal defence

From this, it is evident that the intestinal tract presents a site for the entry of a variety of substances capable of sensitizing the host and resulting in local or systemic disease. Various factors have now been identified which confer protection at the mucosal surface, while other circumstances that predispose to increased antigen penetration have also been defined. In addition to immunological processes, such as local sIgA secretion, other non-immunological processes contribute to mucosal defence, among which is the early establishment of a normal microbial flora. This acts to prevent colonization and invasion by pathogenic organisms, as is exemplified in people on powerful antibiotic regimens, or when germ-free mice are exposed to a normal environment: in both circumstances severe gastrointestinal, or systemic, infection may result.

Two factors limit the size of the microbial population: (i) gastric acid production and (ii) intestinal motility.

In the presence of achlorhydria, or hypochlorhydria, many more anaerobic bacterial colonies are found within the upper intestine.[239,240] The risk of cholera is appreciably increased in hypochlorhydric subjects, including those with gastrectomies. Low acid production may also predispose to salmonellosis and account for its endemicity in affected communities.[241] Other factors controlling bacterial growth include competition for substrates and metabolic production of inhibitory substances, such as short chain fatty acids in the colon, or other 'anti-bacterial' substances termed colicines.[239] Diet has little influence, qualitatively or quantitatively, on microbial flora.

Intestinal motility is perhaps of major importance in clearing the upper intestine of microorganisms and the nutritional effects of bacterial overgrowth when motility is impaired. Impairment either by primary neuronal degenerations, or secondarily, as occurs in scleroderma or amyloidosis, have been clearly recognized and documented.[242] In elderly patients without evidence of predisposing cause, malnutrition due to heavy bacterial overgrowth has been described,[243] although the raised intragastric bacterial overgrowth in patients receiving H_2 antagonists does not appear to cause problems; presumably peristaltic action is sufficient to control overgrowth, at least in most patients.[244]

Since Florey's classic studies on intestinal mucus, further functions concerning mucosal protection have been defined. During immunization of mucosal surfaces, antigen-antibody complexes can stimulate mucus release from goblet cells, and this may be a T lymphocyte-dependent phenomenon. Secreted antibody also becomes fixed to the extracellular glycoprotein of enterocytes where antigens are sequestered and degraded by adsorbed pancreatic peptidases, thereby preventing internalization of antigen and further immunization.[245,246] Glycoproteins within secreted mucus may also interfere with the attachment of microorganisms to receptors on gastric and intestinal epithelial cells.[234,236]

The uptake of macromolecules is also dependent on intestinal proteolytic activity. Protease inhibitors such as trasylol favour increased uptake of macromolecules,[236] while in neonates, failure of trypsinogen conversion to trypsin by a relative deficiency of brush border enterokinase is a cause of increased mucosal antigen uptake and sensitization. Acquired deficiency, as in severe chronic pancreatitis or following pancreatectomy, has been shown to facilitate insulin uptake with measurable effects on glucose homeostasis.[247]

Other studies point to changes in the lipid structure of enterocyte cell membranes, both as a function of position upon the villus, and age. Cholera toxin binds more rapidly to neonatal brush border membranes compared with those of adult animals.[248] Clearly, such developmental changes indicate in part why gastrointestinal infections are more frequent in the young individual; further analyses of structural changes in membrane composition may show how these influence host reactivity towards the environment.

Hepatic 'reticulo-endothelial' barrier

It should not be forgotten that the liver, and in particular the Kupffer cells,[249] which comprise approximately 30% of total liver mass, play an important role in sequestering antigen and antigen-antibody complexes circulating within portal venous blood, and thus in modulating the immune response to mucosal-transmitted immunogens. Blockade of these cells in experimental animals, or deviation of blood flow away from the sinusoids in cirrhosis leads to pathophysiological events such as fever or hyperglobulinaemia. Both humoral and cellular immune responses differ when the same antigen is introduced via the portal venous system, as opposed to a systemic vein.[250,251] The entero-hepatobiliary return of IgA to the intestinal tract presumably also performs an important role in clearing absorbed, but 'unwanted', antigen or antigen-antibody complexes from the circulation.

Thus mucosal defences can be seen as a multi-layered system of events which are:

1. operative at the mucosal surface or within the intestinal lumen
2. located within the lamina propria and concerned with the final elaboration of local antibody production, cell-mediated events towards foreign antigen and allergic phenomena (mediated by IgE and mast cells) and, finally
3. the hepato-biliary system filters absorbed antigens out of portal blood, and returns circulating antibody-antigen complexes to the intestinal tract.

Common mucosal immunological system

As well as providing local immunoglobulin production (sIgA) within the lamina propria, the concept of a widely divergent system of delivering gut-derived B immunoblasts to other extra-intestinal mucosal sites has become important, and is known as the common mucosal immune system.

The basis of this view was that mesenteric B blasts were capable of populating sites other than the intestinal lamina propria, e.g. the mammary gland,[252] salivary gland,[253] bronchus[254] and cervix.[17] Localization of blasts to mammary and genital mucosae was affected by cyclical changes in sex hormones. Furthermore, in lethally-irradiated animals, repopulation of mucosal sites could be respectively accomplished either by infusion of gut- or bronchus-associated lymphoid tissue (BALT).[255]

Nevertheless, good evidence exists for a local and restricted immune response, as shown in humans following specific immunization of the genital tract,[256] isolated intestinal loops,[257] nasal mucosa[258] and local oropharyngeal salivary glands (duct-associated lymphoid tissue, DALT).[259]

Clinically, the most obvious advantage of the recirculation of intestinal B blasts is to the mammary gland, resulting in passive immunization of the suckling infant against invasive gastrointestinal organisms. Possibly, migration to mammary glands also occurs from the respiratory and urinary tract.[260] Since lymphocyte transfer to the mammary gland is modulated by hormones, it is likely that the timing of antigen exposure during pregnancy and lactation will greatly influence the sIgA response in milk. Furthermore, in the human, $>95\%$ colostral protein comprises IgA, falling to $<30\%$ in mature milk, and epidemiological studies have shown that breast-fed infants are more effectively protected from infection, and possibly allergy, than formula-fed infants.[260]

INTEGRATION OF LYMPHOID TISSUE AND MUCOSAL FUNCTION

Although the major collections of lymphoid tissue within the intestinal tract have been considered separately, evidence from cell migration studies provides a glimpse of the inter-relationships between them in a way in which certain lymphocytes, after some kind of processing event, move to another domain where their mature functional capacities are expressed. In migrating to other sites within the territory of GALT, they may also be subject to further controls that direct and modulate both cellular structure and function.

Central to that understanding is the regulation of mucosal traffic, which is based on recognition elements expressed on lymphocytes, vascular endothelium and in connective tissue (Table 11.1). During inflammation, marked changes in the propensity of cells to migrate is seen and cytokines expressed during those events exert important influences in facilitating those altered patterns, and accumulation, of inflammatory cells into those sites.[261] Additional interplay comes from the influence of mucosal nerves and the secretory, immunomodulating effects of VIP, SP and somatostatin.[262] So far, we only have a glimpse of the complex patterns of influence which occur over short-ranges in tissue micro-environments.

However, it is also important to consider the relationship of lymphocytes to the structure of the tissues in which their acquired functional capacities are finally realized. Most obvious are the grosser structural changes in intestinal mucosa that accompany allergic, parasitic or other forms of cell-mediated immunopathology that characterize the lesions of coeliac disease, tropical sprue or graft-versus-host disease.[225,263,264]

A variety of studies indicate that villous flattening in these conditions is immunologically-mediated, and T cell-dependent. Furthermore, there are measurable effects revealing increased proliferation of crypt cells and a profound alteration of epithelial cell kinetics,[265] such as an increased rate of migration[266] and an enlarged population of goblet cells.[267] There are also alterations in the metabolism of enterocytes as witnessed by the development

profiles of brush border enzyme synthesis[268] and in their constitutive expression of MHC class II antigens.[205] Thus we see a curious circular pathway where antigen leads to stimulation of lymphocytes whose secretion of IFN-γ[213] leads to MHC class II expression by enterocytes which, in turn, presumably facilitate further presentation of antigen to lymphoid elements.[269,270]

However, recent studies have shown that antigen presentation by epithelium does not appear to follow the events characterized by dendritic (macrophage-like) cells, as is evident from Bland's thought-provoking review; again, the role of epithelial cells in the putative control of local immune functions, especially pertaining to maintenance or lifting of tolerance, is yet to be determined. Other alterations in epithelial function, induced by ongoing immune reactions within the mucosa, involve changes in electrolyte and sugar transport and alterations in potential difference and short circuit current.[150] Further changes in epithelial physiology, such as increased mucosal permeability or MHC class 2 expression, may reflect 'conserved' functions that evolved specifically for the expulsion of parasites. Such changes have been noted to accompany worm expulsion which permits transfer of circulating antibody to the intestinal lumen,[271] while increased epithelial fluid secretion may hinder establishment of worm larvae[272] in their specific intestinal niche.[264]

REFERENCES

1. Grand RJ, Watkins JB, Torti FM. Progress in Gastroenterology. Development of the human gastrointestinal tract. Gastroenterology 1976; 70: 790–810.
2. Colony PC. Successive phases of human fetal intestinal development. In: Kretchmer N, Minkowski A, eds. Nutritional Adaptation of the Gastrointestinal Tract of the Newborn. Nestlé Nutrition, Vevéy and Raven Press, New York, 1983; p 3–28.
3. Klein RM. Small intestinal proliferation during development. In: Lebenthal E, ed. Human Gastrointestinal Development. Raven Press, New York, p 367–392.
4. Weaver LT. Milk and the neonatal gut: comparative lessons to be learnt. Equine Vet J 1986; 18: 427–429.
5. Weaver LT, Austin S, Cole TJ. Small intestinal length: a factor essential for gut adaptation. Gut 1991; 32: 1321–1323.
6. Ducker DA, Hughes CA, Warren I, McNeish AS. Neonatal gut function, measured by the one hour blood D(+) xylose test: influence of gestational age and size. Gut 1980; 21: 133–136.
7. Walker-Smith JA. Variation of small intestinal morphology with age. Arch Dis Child 1972; 47: 80–83.
8. Mathan M, Hermos JA, Trier JS. Structural features of the epithelio-mesenchymal interface of rat duodenal mucosa during development. J Cell Biol 1972; 577–588.
9. Kedinger M, Simon-Assmann PM, Lacroix B, Marxer A, Hauri HP, Haffen K. Fetal gut mesenchyme induces differentiation of cultured intestinal endoderm and crypt cells. Dev Biol 1986; 113: 474–483.
10. Klein RM, Mackenzie JC. The role of cell renewal in the ontogeny of the intestine. I. Cell proliferation patterns in adult, fetal, and neonatal intestine. J Pediatr Gastroenterol Nutr 1983; 2: 10–43.
11. Klein RM, Mackenzie JC. The role of cell renewal in the ontogeny of the intestine. II. Regulation of cell proliferation in adult, fetal and neonatal intestine. J Pediatr Gastroenterol Nutr 1983; 2: 204–228.
12. Altmann GG. Influence of bile and pancreatic secretions on the size of the intestinal villi in the rat. Am J Anat 1971; 132: 167–178.
13. Castillo RO, Feng JJ, Stevenson DK, Kerner JA, Kwong LK. Regulation of intestinal ontogeny by intraluminal nutrients. J Pediatr Gastroenterol Nutr 1990; 10: 199–205.
14. Sprinz H. Morphological response of intestinal mucosa to enteric bacteria and its implication for sprue and Asiatic cholera. Gastroenterology 1962; 21: 57–64.
15. Alaron P, Lebenthal E, Lee PC. Effect of difluoromethyl ornithine (DFMO) on small intestine of adult and weaning rats. Dig Dis Sci 1987; 32: 883–888.
16. Cummins AG, Munro GH, Miller HRP, Ferguson A. Association of maturation of the small intestine at weaning with mucosal mast cell activation in the rat. Immunol Cell Biol 1988; 66: 417–422.
17. Cummins AG, Steele TW, Labrooy JT, Shearman DJC. Maturation of the small intestine of the rat at weaning: changes in epithelial cell kinetics, bacterial flora and mucosal immune activity. Gut 1988; 29: 1672–1679.
18. James SP. Mucosal T cell function. Gastroenterol Clin N America 1991; 20: 597–612.
19. Spencer J, MacDonald TT, Finn T, Isaacson PG. The development of gut-associated lymphoid tissue in the terminal ileum of foetal human intestine. Clin Exp Immunol 1986; 64: 536–543.
20. Walker-Smith J. Diseases of the Small Intestine in Childhood, 3rd ed, Butterworths, London, 1989.
21. Spencer J, Finn T, Isaacson PG. Human Peyer's patches: an immunohistochemical study. Gut 1986; 27: 405–410.
22. Spencer J, Finn T, Isaacson PG. Expression of HLA-DR antigens on epithelium associated with lymphoid tissue in the human gastrointestinal tract. Gut 1986; 27: 153–157.
23. Carlson JR, Owen RL. In: Marsh MN, ed. Immunopathology of the Small Intestine. Wiley, Chichester, 1987; p 21–40.
24. Goldblum RM. Antibody-forming cells in human colostrum after oral immunization. Nature 1975; 257: 797–799.
25. Mata L. Breast-feeding and host defense. In: Branski D, Dinari G, Rozen P, Walker-Smith JA, eds. Pediatric Gastroenterology — Aspects of Immunology and Infections. Frontiers in Gastroenterological Research, Vol 13. Karger, Basel, 1986; p 119–133.
26. Spencer J, Dillon S, Isaacson PG, MacDonald TT. T cell subclasses in foetal human ileum. Clin Exp Immunol 1986; 65: 553–558.
27. MacDonald T, Spencer J. Ontogeny of the mucosal immune response. Springer Seminar Immunopathol 1990; 12: 129–137.
28. MacDonald T, Spencer J. Gut Immunology. Baillières Clinical Gastroenterology 1990; 4: 291–313.
29. Cummins AG, Thompson FM, Mayrhofer G. A flow cytometric study of activation of mesenteric lymph node cells at weaning in the rat. In: MacDonald TT, ed. Advances in Mucosal Immunology. Kluwer Academic Publishers, Dordrecht, 1990; p 477–478.
30. Cummins AG, Labrooy JT, Shearman DJC. Effect of cyclosporin A in delaying maturation of the small intestine during weaning of the rat. Clin Exp Immunol 1989; 75: 451–456.
31. MacDonald TT, Spencer JM. Evidence that activated mucosal T cells play a role in the pathogenesis of enteropathy in human small intestine. J Exp Med 1988; 167: 1341–1349.
32. Ferreira RdC, Forsyth LE, Richman PI, Wells C, Spencer J, MacDonald TT. Changes in the rate of crypt epithelial cell proliferation and mucosal morphology induced by a T-cell-mediated response in human small intestine. Gastroenterology 1990; 98: 1255–1263.
33. Beer AE, Billingham RE, Head JR. Natural transplantation of leukocytes during suckling. Transpl Proc 1975; 7: 399–402 (suppl).
34. Strobel S, Ferguson A. Immune responses to fed protein antigens in mice. 3 — Systemic tolerance or priming is related to age at which antigen is first encountered. Ped Res 1984; 18: 588–593.

35. Marsh MN. The mucosal pathology in gluten-sensitivity. In: Marsh MN, ed. Coeliac Disease. Oxford, Blackwell Scientific Publications, 1992; p 136–191.
36. Cuenod B, Brousse N, Goulet O, et al. Classification of intractable diarrhoea in infancy using clinical and immunohistological criteria. Gastroenterology 1990; 99: 1037–1043.
37. Ferguson A. Immunological reactions in the small intestine. J Clin Nutr Gastroenterol 1988; 3: 109–113.
38. Ngan J, Kind LS. Suppressor T cells for IgE and IgG in Peyer's patches of mice made tolerant by the oral administration of ovalbumin. J Immunol 1978; 120: 861–865.
39. Mattingly JA, Waksman BY. Immunologic suppression after oral administration of antigen. I — Specific suppressor cells formed in rat Peyer's patches after oral administration of sheep erythrocytes and their systemic migration. J Immunol 1978; 121: 1898–1883.
40. Richman LK, Grafft AS, Yarchoan R, Strober W. Simultaneous induction of antigen-specific IgA helper T cells and IgG suppressor T cells in the murine Peyer's patch after protein feeding. J Immunol 1981; 126: 2079–2083.
41. Challacombe SJ, Tomasi TB. Systemic tolerance and secretory immunity after oral immunisation. J Exp Med 1980; 152: 1459–1472.
42. Koster FT, Pierce NF. Parenteral immunisation causes antigen-specific cell-mediated suppression of an intestinal IgA response. J Immunol 1983; 131: 115–119.
43. Elson CO. Induction and control of the gastrointestinal immune system. Scand J Immunol 1985; 20 (suppl 114): 163–177.
44. Kagnoff MF. Antigen handling by intestinal mucosa. In: Marsh MN, ed. Immunopathology of the Small Intestine. Chichester, Wiley, 1987; p 73–102.
45. Strobel S, Ferguson A. Immune responses to fed protein antigens in mice. III — Systemic tolerance or priming is related to age at which antigen is first encountered. Ped Res 1984; 18: 588–593.
46. Mowat A McI, Strobel S, Drummond HE, Ferguson A. Immunological responses to fed protein antigens in mice. I — Reversal of oral tolerance to ovalbumin by cyclophosphamide. Immunology 1982; 45: 105–113.
47. Cornes JS. Number, size and distribution of Peyer's patches in the human small intestine. I. The development of Peyer's patches. Gut 1956; 6: 225–229.
48. Cornes JS. Number, size and distribution of Peyer's patches in the human small intestine. II. The effect of age on Peyer's patches. Gut 1956; 6: 230–233.
49. Carlson JR, Owen RL. Structure and functional role of Peyer's patches. In: Marsh MN, ed. Immunopathology of the Small Intestine. London: Wiley 1987; p 21–40.
50. Bhalla DK, Murakami T, Owen RL. Microcirculation of intestinal lymphoid follicles on rat Peyer's patches. Gastroenterology 1977; 72: 440–451.
51. Owen RL. Sequential uptake of horseradish peroxidase by lymphoid follicle epithelium of Peyer's patches in the normal unobstructed mouse intestine: an ultrastructural study. Gastroenterology 1977; 72: 440–451.
52. Wolf JL, Rubin DH, Finberg R, Kauffman RS, Sharpe AH, Trier JS. Intestinal M cells: a pathway for entry of reovirus into the host. Science 1981; 212: 471–472.
53. Neutra MR, Guerina NG, Hall TL, Nicholson GL. Transport of membrane-bound macromolecules by M cells in rabbit intestine. Gastroenterology 1982; 82: Abstract 1137.
54. Owen RL, Pierce NF, Apple RT, Gray WD. Phagocytosis and transport by M cells of intact Vibrio cholerae into rabbit Peyer's patch follicles. J Infect Dis 1986; 153: 1108–1118.
55. Owen RL, Jones AL. Epithelial cell specialisation within human Peyer's patches: an ultrastructural study of intestinal lymphoid follicles. Gastroenterology 1974; 66: 189–203.
56. Owen RL, Allen CI, Stevens DP. Phagocytosis of Giardia muris by macrophages in Peyer's patch epithelium in mice. Infect Immunol 1981; 33: 591–601.
57. Spalding DM, Koopman WJ, Eldridge JH, McGhee JR, Steinman RM. Accessory cells in murine Peyer's patch. 1. Identification and enrichment of a functional dendritic cell. J Exp Med 1983; 157: 1646–1659.
58. Wilders MM, Drexhage HA, Weltevreden EF, Duijvestijn A, Meuwisse SGM. Large mononuclear Ia-positive veiled cells in Peyer's patches. I. Isolation and characterisation in rat, guinea pig and pig. Immunology 1983; 48: 452–460.
59. Ermak TE, Owen RL. Differential distribution of lymphocytes and accessory cells in mouse Peyer's patches. Anat Rec 1986; 215: 144–152.
60. Owen RL, Nemanic PC, Stevens DP. Ultrastructural observations on giardiasis in a murine model. I — Intestine distribution, attachment and relationship to the immune system of Giardia muris. Gastroenterology 1979; 76: 757–764.
61. Wilders MM, Sminia T, Plesch BEC, Drexhage HA, Weltevreden EF, Meuwisse SGM. Large mononuclear Ia-positive veiled cells in Peyer's patches. II. Locations in rat Peyer's patches. Immunology 1983; 48: 461–467.
62. Steinman RM, Nussenweig MC. Dendritic cells: features and functions. Immunol Rev 1980; 53: 127–147.
63. Steinman RM, Gutchinov B, Witmer MD, Nussenweig MC. Dendritic cells are the principal stimulators of the primary mixed leucocyte reaction in mice. J Exp Med 1983; 157: 613–627.
64. Nussenweig MC, Steinman RM, Witmer MD, Gutchinov B. A monoclonal antibody specific for mouse dendritic cells. Proc Natl Acad Sci USA 1983; 79: 161–165.
65. Mayrhofer G, Pugh CW, Barclay AN. The distribution, ontogeny and origin in the rat of Ia-positive cells with dendritic morphology and of Ia antigen in epithelia, with special reference to the intestine. Eur J Immunol 1983; 13: 112–122.
66. Kraal G, Weissman IL, Butcher EC. Germinal centre B cells: antigen specificity and changes in heavy chain class expression. Nature 1982; 298: 377–379.
67. Tseng J. A population of resting IgM-IgD double-bearing lymphocytes in Peyer's patches: the major precursor for IgA plasma cells in the gut lamina propria. J Immunol 1984; 132: 2730–2735.
68. Craig SW, Cebra JJ. Peyer's patches: an enriched source of precursors for IgA-producing immunocytes in the rabbit. J Exp Med 1971; 134: 188–200.
69. Chanana AD, Schaedeli J, Hess MW, Cottier H. Predominance of theta-positive lymphocytes in gut-associated and peripheral lymphoid tissues of newborn mice. J Immunol 1973; 110: 283–285.
70. Barg M, Draper LR. Migration of thymus cells to the developing gut-associated lymphoid tissues of the young rabbit. Cell Immunol 1975; 20: 177–186.
71. Mowat A McI. The cellular basis of gastrointestinal immunity. In: Marsh MN, ed. Immunopathology of the Small Intestine. London: Wiley 1987; p 41–72.
72. Gowans JL, Knight EJ. The route of recirculation of lymphocytes in the rat. Proc R Soc Lond B 1964; 159: 257–282.
73. Hall JG, Parry DM, Smith ME. The distribution and differentiation of lymph-borne immunoblasts after intravenous injection into syngeneic recipients. Cell Tissue Kinet 1972; 5: 269–281.
74. Guy-Grand D, Griscelli C, Vassalli P. The gut-associated lymphoid system: nature and properties of the large dividing cells. Eur J Immunol 1974; 4: 435–443.
75. Guy-Grand D, Griscelli C, Vassalli P. Peyer's patches, gut IgA plasma cells and thymic function: a study in nude mice bearing thymic grafts. J Immunol 1975; 115: 361–364.
76. McWilliams M, Phillips-Quagliata JM, Lamm Me. Characteristics of mesenteric lymph node cells homing to gut-associated lymphoid tissue in syngeneic mice. J Immunol 1975; 115: 54–58.
77. Husband AJ, Gowans JL. The origin and antigen-dependent distribution of IgA containing cells in the intestine. J Exp Med 1978; 148: 1146–1160.
78. Strober W, Hague NE, Lum LG, Henkart PA. IgA-Fc receptors on mouse lymphoid cells. J Immunol 1978; 121: 2440–2445.
79. Endoh M, Sakai H, Nomoto Y, Tomino Y, Kaneshiga H. IgA specific helper activity of T alpha cells in human peripheral blood. J Immunol 1981; 127: 2612–2626.
80. Kiyono H, McGhee JR, Mosteller LM, Eldridge JH, Koopman WJ, Kearney JF, Michalek SM. Murine Peyer's patch T cell

clones. Characterization of antigen-specific helper T cells for immunoglobulin A responses. J Exp Med 1982; 156: 1115–1130.
81. Kawanishi H, Saltzmann LE, Strober W. Mechanisms regulating IgA class-specific immunoglobulin production in murine gut-associated lymphoid tissues. I. T cells derived from Peyer's patches that switch sIgM B cells to sIgA B cells in vitro. J Exp Med 1983; 157: 433–450.
82. Kawanishi H, Saltzmann LE, Strober W. Mechanisms regulating IgA class-specific immunoglobulin production in murine gut-associated lymphoid tissues. II. Terminal differentiation of postswitch sIgA-bearing Peyer's patch B cells. J Exp Med 1983; 158: 649–669.
83. Kiyono H, Phillips JO, Colwell DE, Michalek SM, Koopman WJ, McGhee JR. Isotype-specificity of helper T cell clones: Fc alpha receptors regulate T and B cell collaboration for IgA responses. J Immunol 1984; 133: 1087–1089.
84. Kiyono H, Mosteller-Barnum LM, Pitts AM, Williamson SI, Michalek SM, McGhee JR. Isotype-specific immunoregulation. IgA-binding factors produced by Fc alpha receptor-positive T cell hybridomas regulate IgA responses. J Exp Med 1985; 161: 731–747.
85. Yodoi J, Adachi M, Teshigawara K, Masuda T, Fridman WH. T-cell hybridoma, co-expressing Fc receptors for different isotypes. I. Reciprocal regulation of Fc alpha R and Fc epsilon R expression by IgA and interferon. Immunology 1983; 48: 551–559.
86. Selby WS, Poulter LW, Hobbs S, Jewell DP, Janossy G. Heterogeneity of HLA-DR-positive histiocytes in human intestinal lamina propria: a combined histochemical and immunohistological analysis. J Clin Pathol 1983; 36: 379–384.
87. Arnaud-Battandier F, Lawrence EC, Blaese RM. Lymphoid populations of gut mucosa in chickens. Dig Dis Sci 1980; 25: 252–259.
88. Greenwood JH, Austin LL, Dobbins WO. In vitro characterisation of human intestinal epithelial lymphocytes. Gastroenterology 1983; 85: 1023–1025.
89. Marsh MN, Trier JS. Morphology and cell proliferation of subepithelial fibroblasts in adult mouse jejunum. I — Structural features. Gastroenterology 1974; 67: 622–635.
90. Marsh MN, Trier JS. Morphology and cell proliferation of subepithelial fibroblasts in adult mouse jejunum. II — Radioautographic studies. Gastroenterology 1974; 67: 636–645.
91. Wingate DL. The small intestine. In: Christensen J, Wingate DL, eds. A Guide to Gastrointestinal Motility. London: Wright, 1983; p 128–156.
92. Ottaway CA, Parrott DMV. Regional blood flow and the localisation of lymphoblasts in the small intestine of the mouse. I — Examination of normal small intestine. Immunology 1980; 41: 955–961.
93. Butcher EG, Scollay RG, Weissman IL. Organ specificity of lymphocyte migration: mediation by highly selective lymphocyte interaction with organ-specific determinants on high endothelial venules. Eur J Immunol 1980; 10: 556–561.
94. Black S, Humphrey JH, Nusin JSF. Inhibition of the mantoux reaction by direct suggestion under hypnosis. Br Med J 1963; 2: 1649–1652.
95. Kato K, Hamada N, Mizukoshi N, Yamamoto K-I, Kimura T, Ishihara C, Fujioka Y, Kato T, Fujieda K, Matsuura N. Depression of delayed-type hypersensitivity in mice with hypothalamic lesion induced by sodium monoglutamate: involvement of neuroendocrine system in immunomodulation. Immunology 1986; 58: 389–395.
96. Ottaway CA. In vitro alteration of receptors for vasoactive intestinal peptide change the in vivo localization of mouse T cells. J Exp Med 1984; 160: 1054–1069.
97. Ottaway CA, Greenberg GR. Interaction of vasoactive intestinal peptide with mouse lymphocytes: specific binding and the modulation of mitogen responses. J Immunol 1984; 132: 417–423.
98. Payan DG, Brewster DR, Missirian-Bistra A, Goetzl EJ. Substance P recognition by a subset of human T lymphocytes. J Clin Invest 1984; 74: 1532–1539.
99. Stanisz AM, Befus D, Bienenstock J. Differential effects of vasoactive intestinal peptide, substance P, and somatostatin on immunoglobulin synthesis and proliferations by lymphocytes from Peyer's patches, mesenteric lymph nodes, and spleen. J Immunol 1986; 136: 152–156.
100. Pober JS, Gimbrone MA, Cotran RS, Reiss CS, Burakoff SJ, Fiers W, Ault KA. Ia expression by vascular endothelium is inducible by activated T cells and by human gamma interferon. J Exp Med 1983; 157: 1339–1353.
101. Umetsu DT, Katzen D, Jabara HH, Geha RS. Antigen presentation by human dermal fibroblasts: activation of resting T lymphocytes. J Immunol 1986; 136: 440–445.
102. Pober JS, Collins T, Gimbrone MA, et al. Lymphocytes recognize human vascular endothelial and dermal fibroblast Ia antigens induced by recombinant immune interferon. Nature 1983; 305: 726–729.
103. Knight SC, Martin J, Stackpoole A, Clark J. Induction of immune responses in vivo with small numbers of veiled (dendritic) cells. Proc Natl Acad Sci USA 1983; 80: 6032–6035.
104. Chain BM, Kay PM, Feldmann M. The cellular pathway of antigen presentation: biochemical and functional analysis of antigen processes in dendritic cells and macrophages. Immunology 1986; 58: 271–276.
105. Unanue ER. Antigen-presenting function of the macrophage. Ann Rev Immunol 1984; 2: 395–428.
106. Wood GS, Turner RR, Shiurbe RA, Eng L, Warnke RA. Human dendritic cells and macrophages. In situ immunophenotypic definition of subsets that exhibit specific morphologic and microenvironmental characteristics. Am J Pathol 1985; 119: 73–82.
107. Van Voorhis WC, Steinman RM, Hair LS, Luban J, Witmer MD, Koide S, Cohn ZA. Specific antimononuclear phagocyte monoclonal antibodies. Application to the purification of dendritic cells and the tissue localization of macrophages. J Exp Med 1983; 148: 126–145.
108. Pugh CW, MacPherson GG, Steer HW. Characterisation of non-lymphoid cells derived from rat peripheral lymph. J Exp Med 1983; 157: 1758–1779.
109. Marsh MN. The morphologic expression of immunologically-mediated change and injury within the human small intestinal mucosa. In: Small Intestinal Function and Dysfunction in the Animal (Batt R, Lawrence TJ, eds) Liverpool: Liverpool University Press, 1983; p 167–198.
110. Selby WS, Janossy G, Bofill M, Jewell DP. Intestinal lymphocyte subpopulations in inflammatory bowel disease: an analysis by immunohistological and cell isolation techniques. Gut 1984; 25: 32–40.
111. Elson CO, Heck JA, Strober W. T-cell regulation of murine IgA synthesis. J Exp Med 1979; 49: 632–643.
112. Elson CO. T cells specific for IgA switching and for IgA B-cell differentiation. Immunol Today 1983; 4: 189–190.
113. Dunkley ML, Husband AJ. The induction and migration of antigen-specific helper cells for IgA responses in the intestine. Immunology 1986; 57: 379–385.
114. Elson CO, Kagnoff MF, Fiocchi C, Befus AD, Targan S. Intestinal immunity and inflammation: recent progress. Gastroenterology 1986; 91: 746–768.
115. Thomas Y, Rogozinski L, Chess L. Relationship between human T cell functional heterogeneity and human T cell surface molecules. Immunol Rev 1983; 74: 113–128.
116. Green DR, Gold J, St Martin S, Gershon R, Gershon RK. Microenvironmental immunoregulation: possible role of contrasuppressor cells in maintaining immune responses in gut-associated lymphoid tissues. Proc Natl Acad Sci USA 1982; 79: 889–892.
117. Lee A, Sugerman H, Elson CO. A comparison of the functional properties of the T8+ T cell subset in human intestinal lamina propria and peripheral blood. Gastroenterology 1985; 88: Abstract 1469.
118. Zeitz M, Quinn TC, Graeff AS, James SP. Mucosal T cells provide helper function but do not proliferate when stimulated by specific antigen in lymphogranuloma venereum proctitis in non-human primates. Gastroenterology 1988; 94: 353–366.
119. Dhesi I, Marsh MN, Kelly C, Crowe P. Morphometric analysis of

small intestinal mucosa. II. Determination of lamina propria volumes: plasma cell and neutrophil populations within control and coeliac disease mucosae. Virchows Archiv (A) 1984; 403: 173–180.
120. Kagnoff MF. Immunology and disease of the gastrointestinal tract. In: Gastrointestinal Disease (Sleisenger MH, Fordtran JS, eds). London: Saunders, 1983; p 20–44.
121. Jonard PP, Rambaud JC, Dive C, Vaerman JP, Galian A, Delacroix DL. Secretion of immunoglobulins and plasma proteins from the jejunal mucosa. Transport rate and origin of polymeric immunoglobulin A. J Clin Invest 1984; 74: 525–535.
122. Nagura H, Brandtzaeg P, Nakane PK, Brown WR. Ultrastructural localization of J chain in human intestinal mucosa. J Immunol 1979; 123: 1044–1050.
123. Koshland ME. Structure and function of the J chain. Advn Immunol 1975; 20: 41–69.
124. Brown WR, Isobe Y, Nakane PK. Studies on translocation of immunoglobulins across intestinal epithelium. II — Immunoelectron microscopic localization of immunoglobulins and secretory component in human intestinal mucosa. Gastroenterology 1976; 71: 985–995.
125. Brown WR, Kiyoko I, Nakane PK, Pacini B. Studies on translocation of immunoglobulins across intestinal epithelium. IV — Evidence for binding of IgA and IgM to secretory component in intestinal epithelium. Gastroenterology 1977; 73: 1333–1339.
126. Nagura H, Smith PD, Nakane PK, Brown WR. IgA in human bile and liver. J Immunol 1981; 126: 587–595.
127. Kutteh WH, Prince SJ, Phillips JO, Spenney JG, Mestecky J. Properties of immunoglobulin A in serum of individuals with liver diseases and in hepatic bile. Gastroenterology 1982; 82: 184–193.
128. Mestecky J, Russell MW, Jackson S, Brown TA. The human IgA system: a reassessement. Clin Immunol Immunopathol 1986; 40: 105–114.
129. Kagnoff MF. Antigen handling by intestinal mucosa: humoral and cell-mediated immunity, tolerance, and genetic control of local immune responses. In: Marsh MN, ed. Immunopathology of the Small Intestine. London: Wiley, 1987; p 73–102.
130. Underdown BJ, Schiff JM. Immunoglobulin A: strategic defense initiative at the mucosal surface. Ann Rev Immunol 1986; 4: 389–417.
131. Plaut N. Microbial IgA proteases. N Engl J Med 1978; 298: 1459–1463.
132. Lake AM, Kagey-Sobotka A, Jakubowicz T, Lichtenstein LM. Histamine release in acute anaphylactic enteropathy of the rat. J Immunol 1984; 133: 1529–1534.
133. Tseng J. Expression of immunoglobulin isotypes by lymphoid cells of mouse intestinal lamina propria. Cell Immunol 1982; 73: 324–326.
134. Katz DH. Recent studies on the regulation of IgE antibody synthesis in experimental animals and man. Immunology 1980; 41: 1–24.
135. Iyngkaran N, Yadav M. Food Allergy. In: Immunopathology of the Small Intestine (Marsh MN, ed). London: Wiley, 1987; p 415–449.
136. Schleimer RP, MacGlashan DW, Schulman ES, Peters SP, Adams GK, Adkinson NF, Lichtenstein LM. Human mast cells and basophils — structure, function, pharmacology and biochemistry. Clin Rev Allergy 1983; 1: 327–341.
137. Strobel S, Miller HRP, Ferguson A. Human intestinal mucosal mast cells: evaluation of fixation and staining techniques. J Clin Pathol 1981; 34: 851–858.
138. Strobel S, Busuttil A, Ferguson A. Human intestinal mucosal mast cells: expanded population in untreated coeliac disease. Gut 1983; 24: 222–227.
139. Befus D, Goodacre D, Dyck N, Bienenstock J. Mast cell heterogeneity in man. I. Histologic studies of the intestine. Int Arch Allergy Appl Immunol 1985; 76: 232–236.
140. Marsh MN, Hinde J. Inflammatory component of celiac sprue mucosae. I — Mast cells, basophils and eosinophils. Gastroenterology 1985; 89: 92–101.
141. Shanahan F, Denburg JA, Bienenstock J, Befus AD. Mast cell heterogeneity. Can J Physiol Pharmacol 1984; 62: 734–737.
142. Fox CC, Dvorak AM, Peters SP, Kagey-Sobotka A, Lichtenstein LM. Isolation and characterisation of human intestinal mucosal mast cells. J Immunol 1985; 135: 483–491.
143. Stenson WF, Parker CW. Metabolites of arachidonic acid. Clin Rev Allergy 1983; 1: 369–384.
144. Atkins PC, Wasserman SI. Chemotactic mediators. Clin Rev Allergy 1983; 1: 385–395.
145. Schwartz LB. Enzyme mediators of mast cells and basophils. Clin Rev Allergy 1983; 1: 397–416.
146. Marsh MN. Immunocytes, enterocytes and the lamina propria: an immunopathologic framework of coeliac disease. J R Coll Phys Lond 1983; 17: 205–212.
147. Claman HN. Mast cells, T cells and abnormal fibrosis. Immunol Today 1985; 6: 192–195.
148. Gervasoni JE, Conrad DH, Hugli TE, Schwartz LB, Ruddy S. Degradation of human anaphylatoxin C3a by rat peritoneal mast cells: a role for the secretory granule enzyme chymase and heparin proteoglycan. J Immunology 1986; 136: 285–292.
149. Newsom MB, Dahlstrom A, Enerback L, Ahlman H. Suggestive evidence for a direct innervation of mucosal mast cells. Neuroscience 1983; 10: 565–570.
150. Castro GA. Immunological regulation of epithelial function. Am J Physiol 1982; 243: G321–G329.
151. Miller RJ. New perspectives on gut peptides. J Med Chem 1984; 27: 1239–1245.
152. Ferguson A. Intra-epithelial lymphocytes of the small intestine. Gut 1977; 17: 921–937.
153. Bienenstock J, Befus AD. Mucosal Immunology. Immunology 1980; 41: 249–270.
154. Marsh MN. Functional and structural aspects of the epithelial lymphocyte with implications for coeliac disease and tropical sprue. Scand J Gastroenterol 1985; 20 (suppl 114): 55–75.
155. Ernst PB, Befus AD, Bienenstock J. Leukocytes in the intestinal epithelium: an unusual immunological compartment. Immunol Today 1985; 6: 50–55.
156. Dobbins WO. Human intestinal intraepithelial lymphocytes. Gut 1986; 27: 972–985.
157. Meader RD, Landers DF. Electron and light microscopic observations on relationships between lymphocytes and intestinal epithelium. Am J Anat 1967; 121: 763–774.
158. Collan Y. Characteristics of non-epithelial cells in the epithelium of normal rat ileum. Scand J Gastroenterol 1972; 7 (suppl 18): 5–66.
159. Toner PG, Ferguson A. Intraepithelial cells in the human intestinal mucosa. J Ultrast Res 1971; 34: 329–344.
160. Rudzik O, Bienenstock J. Isolation and characteristics of gut mucosal lymphocytes. Lab Invest 1974; 30: 260–266.
161. Marsh MN. Studies of intestinal lymphoid tissue. I — Electron microscopic evidence of 'blast-transformation' in epithelial lymphocytes of mouse small intestinal mucosa. Gut 1975; 16: 665–674.
162. Wilson AD, Stokes CR, Bourne FJ. Morphology and functional characteristics of isolated porcine intraepithelial lymphocytes. Immunology 1986; 59: 109–113.
163. Arnaud-Battandier F. Immunologic characteristics of isolated gut mucosal lymphoid cells. In: Recent Advances in Mucosal Immunity (Strober W, Hanson LA, Sell KW, eds). New York: Raven Press, 1982; p 289–299.
164. Guy-Grand D, Griscelli C, Vassalli P. The mouse gut T lymphocyte, a novel type of T cell. Nature, origin and traffic in mice in normal and graft-versus-host conditions. J Exp Med 1978; 148: 1661–1677.
165. Tagliabue A, Befus AD, Clark AD, Bienenstock J. Characteristics of natural killer cells in the murine intestinal epithelium and lamina propria. J Exp Med 1982; 155: 1785–1786.
166. Bland CE, Rosenthal KL, Pluznik DH, Dennert G, Hengartner H, Bienenstock J, Metcalfe DD. Glycosaminoglycan profiles in cloned granulated lymphocytes with natural killer function and in cultured mast cells: their potential use as biochemical markers. J Immunol 1984; 132: 1937–1942.
167. Huntley JF, McGorum BN, Newlands GFJ, Miller HRP. Granulated intraepithelial lymphocytes: their relationship to mucosal mast cells and globule leucocytes in the rat. Immunology 1984; 53: 525–535.

168. Miller HRP. Immunopathology of nematode infestation and expulsion. In: Immunopathology of the Small Intestine (Marsh MN, ed). London: Wiley, 1987; p 177–208.
169. Schrader JW, Lewis SJ, Clark-Lewis I, Culvenor JG. The persisting (P) cell histamine content, regulation by a T cell-derived factor, origin from a bone marrow precursor, and relationship to mast cells. Proc Natl Acad Sci USA 1981; 78: 323–327.
170. Guy-Grand D, Dy M, Luffan G, Vassalli P. Gut mucosal mast cells. Origin, traffic and differentiation. J Exp Med 1984; 160: 12–28.
171. Marsh MN. Studies of intestinal lymphoid tissue. III — Quantitative analyses of epithelial lymphocytes in the small intestine of human control subjects and of patients with celiac sprue. Gastroenterology 1980; 79: 481–492.
172. Douglas SD. Human lymphocyte growth in vitro. Morphologic, biochemical and immunologic significance. Int Rev Exp Pathol 1971; 10: 41–114.
173. Bunting CH, Huston J. Fate of the lymphocytes. J Exp Med 1921; 33: 593–600.
174. Schaffer J. Leucocyten in Epithel. In: Handbuch der Mikroscopischen Anatomie des Menschen, Bd II (Mollendorf von W, ed). Berlin: Springer, 1927; p 91–97.
175. Wolf-Heidegger G. Zur Frage der Lymphocytenwanderung durch das Darmepithel. Z Mikrosk.-Anat Forsch 1939; 45: 90–103.
176. Andrew W, Sosa JM. Mitotic division and degeneration of lymphocytes within cells of intestinal epithelium in young and in adult white mice. Anat Rec 1947; 97: 63–97.
177. Shields JW, Touchon RC, Dickson DR. Quantitative studies of small lymphocyte disposition in epithelial cells. Am J Pathol 1969; 54: 129–145.
178. Marsh MN. Studies of intestinal lymphoid tissue. II — Aspects of proliferation and migration of epithelial lymphocytes in the small intestine of mice. Gut 1975; 16: 674–682.
179. McDermott MR, Clark DA, Bienenstock J. Evidence for a common mucosal immunologic system. II — Influence of estrous cycle on B-immunoblast migration into genital and intestinal tissue. J Immunol 1980; 124: 2536–2539.
180. McDermott MR, Horsewood P, Clark DA, Bienenstock J. T lymphocytes in the intestinal epithelium and lamina propria of mice. Immunology 1986; 57: 213–218.
181. Lemmel EM, Fichtelius KE. Life span of lymphocytes within intestinal epithelium, Peyer's patch epithelium, epidermis and liver of mice. Int Arch Allergy 1971; 41: 716–728.
182. Glaister JR. Autoradiographic studies of lymphoid cells in the small intestinal epithelium of the mouse. Int Arch Allergy 1973; 545: 844–853.
183. Ropke C, Everett NB. Proliferative kinetics of large and small intraepithelial lymphocytes in the small intestine of the mouse. Am J Anat 1976; 145: 395–408.
184. Ropke C, Everett NB. Kinetics of intraepithelial lymphocytes in the small intestine of thymus-deprived mice and antigen-deprived mice. Anat Rec 1976; 185: 101–108.
185. Darlington D, Rogers AW. Epithelial lymphocytes in the small intestine of the mouse. J Anat 1966; 100: 813–830.
186. Ferguson A, Parrott DMV. The effect of antigen deprivation on thymus-dependent and thymus-independent lymphocytes in the small intestine of the mouse. Clin Exp Immunol 1972; 12: 477–488.
187. Glaister JR. Factors affecting the lymphoid cells in the small intestinal epithelium of the mouse. Int Arch Allergy 1973; 45: 719–730.
188. Bull DM, Bookman MA. Isolation and functional characterization of human intestinal lymphoid cells. J Clin Invest 1977; 59: 966–974.
189. Bartnick W, ReMine SG, Chiba M. Isolation and characterization of colonic intraepithelial and lamina propria lymphocytes. Gastroenterology 1980; 78: 976–985.
190. Selby WS, Janossy G, Goldstein G, Jewell DP. T lymphocyte subsets in human intestinal mucosa: the distribution and relationship to MHC-derived antigens. Clin Exp Immunol 1981; 44: 453–458.
191. Selby WS, Janossy G, Jewell DP. Immunohistological characterisation of intraepithelial lymphocytes of the human gastrointestinal tract. Gut 1981; 22: 169–176.
192. Selby WS, Janossy G, Bofill M, Jewell DP. Lymphocyte populations in the human small intestine. The findings in normal mucosa and in the mucosa of patients with adult coeliac disease. Clin Exp Immunol 1983; 53: 219–228.
193. Cerf-Bensussan N, Schneeberger EE, Bhan AK. Immunohistologic and immunoelectron microscopic characterization of the mucosal lymphocytes of human small intestine by the use of monoclonal antibodies. J Immunol 1983; 130: 2615–2622.
194. Marsh MN. Coeliac disease. In: Marsh MN, ed. Immunopathology of the Small Intestine. London: Wiley, 1987; p 371–399.
195. Niazi NM, Leigh RJ, Crowe P, Marsh MN. Morphometric analysis of small intestinal mucosa. I — Methodology, epithelial volume compartments and enumeration of inter-epithelial space lymphocytes. Virchows Archiv (Pathol Anat) 1984; 404: 49–60.
196. Marsh MN, Hinde J. Morphometric analysis of small intestinal mucosa. III — The quantitation of crypt epithelial volumes and lymphoid cell infiltrates, with reference to celiac sprue mucosae. Virchows Archiv (Pathol Anat) 1986; 409: 11–22.
197. Ebert EC. Jejunal intraepithelial lymphocytes (IEL): an examination of their low proliferative capacity. Gastroenterology 1986; 90: A1403.
198. Marsh MN. Studies of intestinal lymphoid tissue. V — The cytology and electron microscopy of gluten-sensitive enteropathy with particular reference to its immunopathology. Scand J Gastroenterol 1981; 16 (suppl 70): 87–106.
199. Marsh MN. Studies of intestinal lymphoid tissue. IV — The predictive value of raised mitotic indices among jejunal epithelial lymphocytes in the diagnosis of gluten-sensitive enteropathy. J Clin Pathol 1982; 35: 517–525.
200. Marsh MN. The small intestine — mechanisms of local immunity and gluten-sensitivity. Clin Sci Molec Med 1981; 61: 497–503.
201. Marsh MN, Mathan M, Mathan VI. Studies of intestinal lymphoid tissue. VII — The secondary nature of lymphoid cell 'activation' in the jejunal mucosa of Indian tropical sprue. Am J Pathol 1983; 112: 301–312.
202. Marsh MN, Haeney MR. Studies of intestinal lymphoid tissue. VI — Proliferative response of jejunal epithelial lymphocytes distinguishes gluten- from non-gluten-induced enteropathy. J Clin Pathol 1983; 36: 149–160.
203. Marsh MN, Miller V. Studies of intestinal lymphoid tissue. VIII — Use of epithelial mitotic indices in differentiating untreated celiac sprue mucosa from other childhood enteropathies. J Paediatr Gastroenterol Nutr 1985; 4: 931–935.
204. Scott H, Solheim BG, Brandtzaeg P, Thorsby E. HLA-DR-like antigens in the epithelium of the human small intestine. Scand J Immunol 1980; 12: 77–82.
205. Scott H, Brandtzaeg P, Solheim BG, Thorsby E. Relation between HLA-DR-like antigens and secretory component (SC) in jejunal epithelium of patients with coeliac disease or dermatitis herpetiformis. Clin Exp Immunol 1981; 44: 233–238.
206. Bland PW, Warren LG. Antigen presentation by epithelial cells of the rat small intestine. II — Selective induction of suppressor T cells. Immunology 1986; 58: 9–14.
207. Spencer J, MacDonald T, Diss T, Walker-Smith J, Ciclitira P, Isaacson P. Changes in intraepithelial lymphocyte subpopulations in coeliac disease and enteropathy associated T cell lymphoma. Gut 1989; 30: 339–346.
208. Brandtzaeg P, Bosnes V, Halstensen TS, Scott H, Sollid LM, Valnes K. T lymphocytes in human gut epithelium preferentially express the α/β antigen receptor and are often CD45/UCHL1 positive. Scand J Immunol 1989; 30: 123–128.
209. Halstensen TS, Scott H, Brandtzaeg P. Human $CD8^+$ intraepithelial T lymphocytes are mainly CD45 RA^-RB^+ and show increased co-expression of CD45 RO in celiac disease. Eur J Immunol 1990; 20: 1825–1830.
210. Streuli M, Murimoto C, Schreiber M, Schlossman SF, Saito H. Characterisation of CD45 and CD45R monoclonal antibodies using transfected mouse cell lines that express individual human common leukocyte antigens. J Immunol 1988; 141: 3910–3914.
211. Akbar AN, Timms A, Janossy G. Cellular events during memory

T-cell activation in vitro: the UCHL1 (180 000 MW) determinant is newly synthesized after mitosis. Immunology 1989; 66: 213–218.
212. Sanders ME, Makgoba MW, Sharrow SO, Stephany D, Springer TA, Young HA, Shaw S. Human memory T lymphocytes express increased levels of three cell adhesion molecules (LFA-3, CD2, and LFA-1) and three other molecules (UCHL1, CDw29 and Pgp-1) and have enhanced IFN-gamma production. J Immunol 1988; 140: 1401–1407.
213. Cerf-Bensussan N, Quaroni A, Kurnick JT, Bhan AK. Intraepithelial lymphocytes modulate la expression by intestinal epithelial cells. J Immunol 1984; 132: 2244–2252.
214. Scott H, Sollid LM, Fausa O, Brandtzaeg P, Thorsby E. Expression of MHC class II subregion products by jejunal epithelium of patients with coeliac disease. Scand J Immunol 1987; 26: 563–572.
215. Scott H, Sollid LM, Brandtzaeg P. Expression of MHC class II determinants by jejunal epithelium in coeliac disease. J Pediatr Gastroenterol Nutr 1988; 7: 145–146.
216. Malizia G, Trejdosiewicz LK, Wood G, Howdle PD, Janossy G, Losowsky MS. The microenvironment of coeliac disease: T cell phenotypes and expression of the T_2 'blast' antigen by small bowel lymphocytes. Clin Exp Immunol 1985; 60: 437–46.
217. Jarry A, Cerf-Bensussan N, Brousse N, Selz F, Guy-Grand D. Subsets of $CD3^+$ (T cell receptor α/β or γ/δ) and $CD3^-$ lymphocytes isolated from normal gut epithelium display phenotypical features different from their counterparts in peripheral blood. Eur J Immunol 1990; 20: 1097–103.
218. Viney J, MacDonald TT, Spencer J. Gamma/delta T cells in the gut epithelium. Gut 1990; 31: 841–844.
219. Spencer J, Diss TC, Isaacson PG, MacDonald TT. Expression of disulphide-linked and non-disulphide linked forms of the gamma/delta T cell receptor in human small intestinal epithelium. Eur J Immunol 1989; 19: 1335–1338.
220. Spencer J, Diss TC, Walker-Smith J, MacDonald TT, Cooke GC, Isaacson P. T cell receptor expression by intraepithelial lymphocytes in normal and coeliac jejunum. Gastroenterology, in press.
221. Halstensen TS, Scott H, Brandtzaeg P. Intraepithelial T cells of the TCR γ/δ^+ $CD8^-$ and $V\delta1/J\delta1^+$ phenotypes are increased in coeliac disease. Scand J Immunol 1989; 30: 665–672.
222. MacDonald TT, Spencer J. Evidence that activated mucosal T cells play a role in the pathogenesis of enteropathy in human small intestine. J Exp Med 1988; 167: 1341–1349.
223. Monk T, Spencer J, Cerf-Bensussan N, MacDonald TT. Stimulation of mucosal T cells in situ with anti-CD3 antibody: location of the activated T cells and their distribution within the mucosal micro-environment. Clin Exp Immunol 1988; 74: 216–622.
224. Ferguson A. Immunological reactions in the small intestine. J Clin Nutr Gastroenterol 1988; 3: 109–113.
225. Ferguson A. Models of immunologically-driven small intestinal damage. In: Marsh MN, ed. Immunopathology of the Small Intestine. Chichester, Wiley, 1987; 225–252.
226. Watret KC, Ferguson A. Lymphocyte-mediated intestinal damage — animal studies. In: Peters TJ, ed. The Cell Biology of Inflammation in the Gastrointestinal Tract. Hull: Corners Publications, 1989; 191–200.
227. Marsh MN. Lymphocyte-mediated intestinal damage — human studies. In: Peters TJ, ed. The Cell Biology of Inflammation in the Gastrointestinal Tract. Hull: Corners Publications, 1989; 203–229.
228. Cerf-Bensussan N, Guy-Grand D. Intestinal intraepithelial lymphocytes. Gastroenterol Clin North Am 1991; 20: 549–576.
229. Cerf-Bensussan N, Jarry A, Brousse N, Lisowska-Grospierre B, Guy-Grand D, Griscelli P. A monoclonal antibody (HML-1) defining a novel membrane molecule present on human intestinal lymphocytes. Eur J Immunol 1987; 17: 1279–1285.
230. Schieferdecker H, Ullrich R, Weiss-Breckwoldt A, Schwarting R, Stein H, Riecken E, Zeitz M. The HML-1 antigen of intestinal lymphocytes in an activation antigen. J Immunol 1990; 144: 2541–2549.
231. Parker CM, Cepek K, Russell GJ, Shaw SK, Posnett DN, Schwarting R, Brenner MB. A family of B7 integrins on human mucosal lymphocytes. Proc Natl Acad Sci USA 1992; 89: 1924–1928.
232. Yan Q, Jiang W, Hollander D, Lenng E, Watson JD, Krissansen GW. Identity between the novel integrin B7 subunit and an antigen found highly expressed on intraepithelial lymphocytes in the small intestine. Biochem Biophys Res Comm 1991; 176: 1443–1449.
233. Bazin H. The secretory antibody system. In: Ferguson A, MacSween RNM, eds. Immunological Aspects of the Liver and Gastrointestinal Tract. Lancaster: MTP, 1976, p 33–82.
234. Walker WA. Mechanisms of antigen handling by the gut. In: Brostoff J, Challacombe SJ, eds. Food Allergy. London: Saunders, 1982; p 15–40.
235. Hutchins P, Walker-Smith JA. The gastrointestinal system. In: Brostoff J, Challacombe SJ, eds. Food Allergy. London: Saunders, 1982; p 43–76.
236. Udall JN, Walker WA. Mucosal defence mechanisms. In: Marsh MN, ed. Immunopathology of the Small Intestine. London: Wiley, 1987; p 3–20.
237. Ogra SS, Weintraub D, Ogra PL. Immunologic aspects of human colostrum and milk. III — Fate of absorption of cellular and soluble components in the gastrointestinal tract of the newborn. J Immunol 1979; 119: 245–248.
238. Moxey PC, Trier JS. Structural features of the mucosa of human fetal small intestine. Gastroenterology 1975; 68: 1002–1009.
239. Simon GL, Gorbach SL. The human intestinal microflora. Dig Dis Sci 1986; 31 (suppl): 147S–162S.
240. Gianella RA, Broitman SA, Zamchek N. Influence of gastric acidity on bacterial and parasitic enteric infections. Ann Int Med 1973; 78: 271–276.
241. Gianella RA. The gastric barrier to intestinal infection. Gastroenterology 1979; 76: 1498–1499.
242. Gracey M. The contaminated small bowel syndrome: pathogenesis, diagnosis, and treatment. Am J Clin Nutr 1979; 32: 234–243.
243. McEvoy A, Dutton J, James OFW. Bacterial contamination of the small intestine is an important cause of occult malabsorption in the elderly. Br Med J 1983; 287: 789–793.
244. Ruddell WSJ, Losowsky MS. Severe diarrhoea due to small intestinal colonisation during cimetidine treatment. Br Med J 1980; 3: 273.
245. Walker WA, Isselbacher KJ. Intestinal antibodies. N Engl J Med 1977; 297: 767–773.
246. Lake AM, Block KJK, Neutra MR, Walker WA. Intestinal goblet cell mucus release. II — In vivo stimulation by antigen in the immunised rat. J Immunol 1979; 122: 834–837.
247. Crane CW, Luntz GR. Absorption of insulin from the human small intestine. Diabetes 1968; 17: 625–627.
248. Bresson JL, Pany KY, Walker WA. Microvillus membrane differentiation: Quantitative difference in cholera toxin binding to the intestinal surface of newborn and adult rabbits. Paed Res 1984; 18: 984–987.
249. Bjorneboe M, Prytz H. The mononuclear phagocytic functions of the liver. In: Ferguson A, MacSween RNM, eds. Immunological Aspects of the Liver and Gastrointestinal Tract. Lancaster: MTP, 1976; p 251–289.
250. Triger DR, Wright R. Studies on hepatic uptake of antigen. I — Comparison of inferior vena cava and portal vein routes of immunization. Immunology 1973; 25: 941–950.
251. Triger DR, Wright R. Studies on hepatic uptake of antigen. II — The effect of hepatotoxins in the immune response. Immunology 1973; 25: 951–956.
252. Roux ME, McWilliams M, Phillips-Quagliata JM, Weisz-Carrington P, Lamm ME. Origin of IgA-secreting plasma cells in the mammary gland. J Exp Med 1977; 146: 1311–1322.
253. Weisz-Carrington P, Roux ME, McWilliams M, Phillips-Quagliata JM, Lamm ME. Origin and isotype distribution of plasma cells producing specific antibody after oral immunization. J Immunol 1979; 123: 1705–1708.
254. McDermott MR, Bienenstock J. Evidence for a common mucosal immunologic system. I — Migration of B-immunoblasts into intestinal, respiratory and genital tissues. J Immunol 1979; 122: 1892–1898.

255. Bienenstock J. Bronchus-associated lymphoid tissue. In: Bienenstock J, ed. Immunology of the Lung and Upper Respiratory Tract. New York: McGraw-Hill, 1983; p 96–118.
256. Ogra PL, Ogra SS. Local antibody response to poliovaccine in the human female genital tract. J Immunol 1973; 110: 1307–1311.
257. Ogra PL, Karzon DT. The role of immunoglobulins in the mechanism of mucosal immunity of virus infection. Paediatr Clin North Am 1970; 17: 385–400.
258. Brandtzaeg P. Immune functions of human nasal mucosal and tonsils in health and disease. In: Bienenstock J, ed. Immunology of the Lung and Upper Respiratory Tract. New York: McGraw-Hill, 1983; p 28–95.
259. Nair PNR, Schroeder HE. Duct-associated lymphoid tissue (DALT) of minor salivary glands and mucosal immunity. Immunology 1986; 57: 171–180.
260. Hanson LA. The mammary gland as an immunological organ. Immunol Today 1982; 3: 168–172.
261. Salmi M, Jalkanen S. Regulation of lymphocyte traffic to mucosa-associated lymphatic tissues. Gastroenterol Clin North Am 1991; 20: 495–510.
262. Ottaway CA. Neuroimmunomodulation in the intestinal mucosa. Gastroenterol Clin North Am 1991; 20: 511–529.
263. Mowat A McI. The cellular basis of gastrointestinal immunity. In: Marsh MN, ed. Immunopathology of the Small Intestine. London: Wiley, 1987; p 41–72.
264. Miller HRP. Immunopathology of nematode infestation and expulsion. In: Marsh MN, ed. Immunopathology of the Small Intestine. London: Wiley, 1987; p 177–208.
265. Watson AJ, Wright N. Morphology and cell kinetics of the jejunal mucosa in untreated patients. In: Cooke WT, Asquith P, eds. Coeliac Disease. Clinics in Gastroenterology. London: Saunders, 1974: 3(1): 11–31.
266. Trier JS, Browning TH. Epithelial-cell renewal in cultured duodenal biopsies in celiac sprue. N Engl J Med 1970; 283: 1245–1250.
267. Miller HRP, Nawa Y. Immune regulation of intestinal goblet cell differentiation. Specific induction of non-specific protection against helminths? Nouv Rev Fr Haematol 1979; 21: 31–45.
268. Lund EK, Pickering MG, Smith MW, Ferguson A. Selective effects of graft-versus-host disease on disaccharidase expression by mouse jejunal enterocytes. Clin Sci 1986; 71: 189–198.
269. Bland PW, Warren LG. Antigen presentation by epithelial cells of the rat small intestine. I — Kinetics, antigen specificity and blocking by anti-Ia antisera. Immunology 1986; 58: 1–7.
270. Bland PW, Kambarage DM. Antigen handling by the epithelium and lamina propria macrophages. Gastroenterol Clin North Am 1991; 20: 577–596.
271. Murray M. Immediate hypersensitivity effector mechanisms. II — In vivo reactions. In: Soulsby EJL, ed. Immunity to Animal Parasites. New York: Academic Press, 1972; p 155–190.
272. Castro GA, Hessel JJ, Whalen G. Altered intestinal fluid movement in response to Trichinella spiralis in immunized rats. Parasite Immunol 1979; 1: 259–266.

CHAPTER 12

The alimentary tract in disorders of the immune system

P. Pavli *W. F. Doe*

THE ACQUIRED IMMUNODEFICIENCY SYNDROME (AIDS)

The acquired immunodeficiency syndrome (AIDS) was first recognized in early 1981 following reports of multiple cases of two rare diseases: *Pneumocystis carinii* pneumonia and Kaposi's sarcoma, occurring in young previously healthy homosexual men.[1,2] The aetiological agent, a human retrovirus — the human immunodeficiency virus (HIV) — has been identified[3] and the protean clinical manifestations have been described.

The United States Centers for Disease Control (CDC) have classified HIV infection to provide a means of grouping patients according to the clinical expression of disease[4] (see Table 12.1). Classification systems may also include the absolute number of $CD4^+$ T lymphocytes in the peripheral blood, which correlates well with the development of the various manifestations of HIV infection, and overall survival.

HIV is transmitted through intimate sexual contact or through parenteral contact with blood or blood products.[5] Over 70% of reported cases in the USA occurred in homosexual or bisexual men, and 15% in intravenous drug users. Other groups at risk include prostitutes, haemophiliacs, children born to HIV^+ mothers, other patients transfused with blood or blood products and heterosexual contacts of any of the above groups. Finally, HIV infection is endemic in certain areas of central Africa and Haiti.

Table 12.1 Human immunodeficiency virus infections: summary of classification system.

Group I	Acute infection	
Group II	Asymptomatic infection	
Group III	Persistent generalized lymphadenopathy	
Group IV	Other disease	
Subgroup	A	Constitutional disease
	B	Neurological disease
	C	Secondary infectious diseases
	D	Secondary neoplastic diseases
	E	Other conditions

HIV is tropic for the helper/inducer subset of T-lymphocytes which it infects following recognition of the helper cell CD4 surface antigen. The viral genome is integrated into the host genome, but may also replicate in a free extrachromosomal form. Following infection, the virus lies dormant until the T-cell undergoes immunological activation which triggers viral replication and a cytopathic effect.[6] Infected $CD4^+$ cells become functionally abnormal and a marked depletion occurs. The $CD8^+$ cytotoxic/ suppressor subset of T-cells is apparently uninfected and cell numbers are normal or elevated unless there is associated severe lymphopenia. The helper/inducer cell is central to the regulation of the immune system, and it is the loss of this function that is thought to result in the observed defects in cell-mediated immunity.[7]

Cells of the monocyte-macrophage lineage, which also bear the CD4 receptor, have also been identified as primary targets for infection, agents for virus dissemination (e.g. to the central nervous system) and reservoirs for reinfection.[8] Defects in humoral immunity include a typical polyclonal hypergammaglobulinaemia and defective primary and secondary antibody responses. Thrombocytopenia, leucopenia and neutropenia may also occur, especially in association with the febrile prodrome of AIDS or opportunistic infections.[7]

Homosexual males may suffer from a wide range of infections by recognized pathogens that have been termed collectively the 'gay bowel syndrome'. These have been reviewed elsewhere[9–11] and will be discussed only briefly here. When AIDS develops, however, gastrointestinal involvement occurs as (i) opportunistic infections or (ii) secondary malignancies, mainly Kaposi's sarcoma and non-Hodgkin's lymphoma. In addition, HIV infection may be associated with diarrhoea persisting for more than one month in the absence of any other apparent infection.

OPPORTUNISTIC INFECTIONS

The following section describes the more typical intestinal manifestations of opportunistic infections in HIV^+ patients. It is important to recognize, however, that 'normal' gut pathogens, such as Salmonella, Shigella and Campylobacter species and *Giardia lamblia* can cause significant disease in these patients. There is evidence that the rates of infections with Salmonella species are, in fact, 20 times more frequent than in the general population.[13] Conversely, pathogens normally affecting other systems present, albeit rarely, with gut manifestations. For example, *Pneumocystis carinii*, *Toxoplasma gondii*, cryptococcus and *Histoplasma capsulatum* have all been implicated in the development of colitis.

Candidiasis

Oropharyngeal candidiasis is one of the most frequent, and earliest, of the opportunistic infections seen in AIDS patients[12,14] and often spreads to involve the oesophagus.[15] Oesophageal involvement should be demonstrated by culture or biopsy. Like chronic mucocutaneous candidiasis there is no tendency for the infection to disseminate, though it is difficult to eradicate. Examination of the oesophagus may reveal characteristic 'cottage cheese' exudates or ulceration. Microscopy demonstrates 3–5 mm blastoconidia, pseudohyphae and hyphae (which are more prominent after periodic acid-Schiff or methenamine silver staining) throughout the mucosa and submucosa. The differential diagnosis of oesophageal ulceration in the immunocompromized patient should also include other infections (herpes simplex, varicella-zoster virus, cytomegalovirus, mycobacteria and cryptosporidia), hairy leukoplakia, non-Hodgkin's lymphoma and Kaposi's sarcoma.

Cytomegalovirus (CMV)

Evidence of CMV infection is a common finding amongst asymptomatic homosexual men; the prevalence of antibodies to CMV is over 90% and in 7–30% of these the virus can be isolated from urine or semen.[16–18] In AIDS patients, evidence of disseminated infection is found in 50–90% of cases,[19] but only a small proportion of patients have CMV-induced gastrointestinal disease on presentation.[20]

Histological or culture evidence of CMV infection may be demonstrated anywhere in the gastrointestinal tract where biopsies may show swollen cells that contain 'classical' dense, round, intranuclear inclusions surrounded by a halo. The CMV-infected cells more often contain atypical inclusions; there may be irregular smudge cells which have basophilic nuclear enlargement and elongated eosinophilic cytoplasm or cells containing small, granular cytoplasmic inclusions.[21] Inflammatory and stromal cells of the lamina propria show evidence of infection, particularly endothelial cells. Epithelial cells are commonly affected in the stomach, small intestine and colon, while the squamous epithelium of the oesophagus and anal canal rarely shows evidence of involvement.[21,22] Immunohistochemistry and in situ hybridization are more sensitive techniques for identifying CMV infection and can be used to confirm the presence of infection.

Concomitant inflammation may range from mild to severe and may be associated with ulceration. The presence of CMV vasculitis provides definitive evidence for a causative role for CMV in the development of oesophageal[23,24] or colonic[25] ulcers. In the first report, there was extensive tissue destruction in the base of the ulcer extending into the adventitia. CMV inclusions were noted in fibroblasts, degenerating smooth muscle, endothelial and submucosal nerve cells. In the non-ulcerated oesophagus, there were CMV inclusions in endothelial cells associated with vasculitis. In the reports of CMV colitis,[25,26] culture or histological evidence of CMV infection preceded the development of mucosal ulceration and the pathological changes of CMV colitis. CMV inclusions were found in the endothelial cells of the mucosal and submucosal capillaries. Enlarged CMV-infected cells, platelet thrombosis, and frank vasculitis characterized by neutrophil infiltration, vessel occlusion, associated necrosis and haemorrhage were observed. Although the pathogenesis of the mucosal lesions is unknown, CMV vasculitis and ischaemia probably contribute to tissue damage.

Herpes simplex virus

Herpes simplex virus (HSV) is a common cause of non-gonococcal proctitis in homosexual men. In AIDS patients, severe, enlarging mucocutaneous ulceration may occur in the perianal or intergluteal skin, the anal canal or the rectum.[27] Lesions are also found around the mouth or in the oesophagus. The diagnosis is generally made by viral culture, though the characteristic appearances of the herpetic vesicles themselves may be diagnostic. Histological examination of rectal biopsies may reveal intranuclear inclusion bodies, perivascular mononuclear cell infiltrates, giant cells and focal ulceration. Unlike CMV infection, which is rarely seen in squamous epithelium, cytomegaly and granular cytoplasmic inclusions are absent.[21] In progressive mucocutaneous herpes, areas of destructive ulceration will evolve. These lesions may respond to continuous acyclovir therapy.

Adenovirus

Adenovirus is an uncommon cause of intestinal illness in immunocompetent adults, but has been identified in 7% of HIV^+ homosexual men suffering from diarrhoea.[28] In affected patients the macroscopic mucosal appearances were normal or near normal, but microscopy showed foci of mucosal necrosis that contained chronic inflammatory cells and degenerating, necrotic epithelial cells with amphophilic nuclear inclusions. Electron microscopy demonstrated characteristic hexagonal particles within the epithelial cell inclusions; the cells in the lamina propria were spared, a point of contrast to cytomegalovirus infection.

Oral hairy leukoplakia

Oral hairy leukoplakia refers to the presence of flat or slightly raised white lesions which are usually found on the tongue, most commonly on the lateral borders.[29–31] Their size ranges from a few millimetres to over 3 cm and, unlike the similar lesions of candidiasis, they are firmly adherent. The majority of lesions are asymptomatic, but dysphagia may develop if extension into the oesophagus occurs.[32]

Originally described as another manifestation of HIV infection, it is found also in other immunosuppressed states; its presence in HIV positive individuals signifies progressive immunosuppression and presages the development of AIDS. Both papillomavirus and replicating Epstein-Barr virus have been demonstrated within the epithelial cells of hairy leukoplakia,[30] but only the latter appears to play a role in pathogenesis. The lesion is thought to develop by reactivation of latent EBV infection resulting in shedding of viral particles into the saliva. Access to EBV-specific receptors on the cells in the upper prickle layers of the parakeratinized oral epithelium may follow mechanical trauma to the tongue.[33]

The histological characteristics include hyperparakeratosis, acanthosis of epithelial cells, a characteristic ballooning of prickle cells, reduced numbers of Langerhans cells and minimal sub-epithelial inflammatory cell infiltration. *Candida* hyphae may be present in the parakeratin, but they are not associated with an inflammatory response. The ballooned cells are present as bands or nests in the prickle cell layers, and may extend into the parakeratin. The swollen cells generally have pale staining, glassy cytoplasm, and may show perinuclear vacuoles. Electron microscopy or in situ hybridization provides definitive confirmation of the EBV particles within the epithelial cells and should be carried out if there is any doubt about the diagnosis.[33]

Cryptosporidiosis

Cryptosporidium parvum is a coccidian protozoan parasite which is 4–6 µm in size and predominantly inhabits the microvillous region of epithelial cells. It produces an acute self-limited diarrhoea in immunocompetent patients,[34] but causes a protracted debilitating diarrhoea in AIDS patients.[35–37] Little is known about the pathogenesis of this infection.

Patchy involvement of the intestine is commonly found but evidence of mucosal injury is more variable.[38,39] There may be little reaction, or features of villous flattening with crypt hyperplasia of varying degree, and mild to moderate chronic inflammatory cell infiltration. Focal cryptitis, crypt abscesses, gland dilatation and rupture are also seen, whilst the presence of eosinophils, a predominantly neutrophilic infiltrate or extension of the inflammation across the muscularis mucosa should raise the possibility of concomitant infections.[21] Cryptosporidia manifesting as trophozoites, meronts, macro- and microgamonts or oocysts may be found in biopsy material anywhere from the pharynx to the rectum, with the small bowel being most heavily infected (Fig. 12.1). The diagnosis may be made in biopsy material by finding the organism associated with the microvillous border of the epithelial cell. In some cases an extension of the host cell membrane surrounding the organism[40] forms a parasitiferous vesicle. The cysts are usually visible following haemotoxylin and eosin staining, and may be differentiated from mucin, etc. using Giemsa, combined Alcian blue neutral red or a Best's mucicarmine stain.[21] The diagnosis of cryptosporidiosis is more reliably made, however, by isolating the organism from stool samples (with or without sugar flotation concentration techniques) and identification by iodine or acid-fast stains, bright field microscopy or indirect immunofluorescence.[38,41,42]

Isospora belli

Isospora belli is another coccidian parasite which is an uncommon finding in immunocompetent adults. It is frequently seen, however, in homosexual men suffering from enteritis, and, like cryptosporidiosis, is a cause of a severe diarrhoeal illness in AIDS sufferers. The diagnosis is made by stool examination where the organism can be demonstrated by acid-fast staining[42] or by the sugar flotation concentration assays. It may also be seen by careful histological examination of the duodeno-jejunal mucosa,[37] where there may be villous flattening and eosinophilia.[21]

Microsporidia

Microsporidians represent a protozoan order characterized by the presence of a polar filament inside the spore. They are obligate intracellular organisms which were

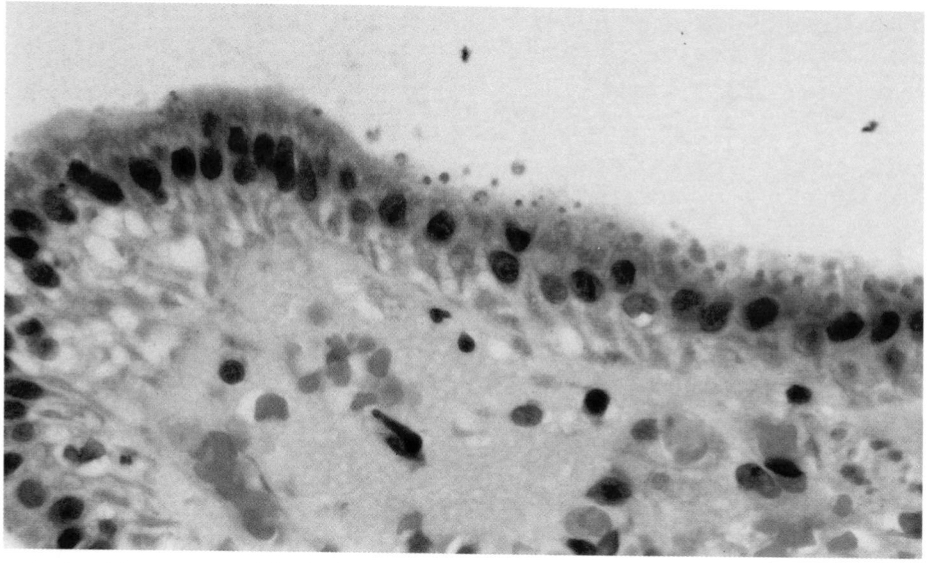

Fig. 12.1 Small bowel epithelium. Note cryptosporidia closely associated with luminal border of epithelial cells.

identified initially by electron microscopy in the enterocytes of two AIDS patients with enteritis.[37,40] The organisms, which contained multiple disc-shaped densities and nuclei but no mitochondria, were enclosed within a single plasma membrane without a cell wall. Subsequent studies using light microscopy and various standard and special stains have identified the histological features of the various stages of the life cycle in microsporidial infection — the meront, the sporont and mature spores. The spores are only 1–3 μm in size, tend to cluster and are found in a supranuclear distribution. Villi in affected areas may be blunted or bulbous, and the epithelial cells have irregular outlines, irregular hyperchromatic nuclei and cytoplasmic vacuolation. Spores are more easily seen as refractile objects when the microscope condenser is lowered or removed.[43] Identification of these microorganisms in direct smears of stools or duodenal aspirates and in tissue sections is facilitated by special staining techniques,[44,45] although standard methods including haemotoxylin and eosin, and Giemsa stains are also useful.

Microsporidia may cause diarrhoea and enteritis in up to 30% of immunocompromised HIV$^+$ patients who have no evidence of other intestinal pathogens.[44,46] The main species causing symptoms is *Enterocytozoon bieneusi*, although a new species has been identified.[47]

'Non-pathogenic' amoebae

Entamoeba histolytica is a frequent finding in asymptomatic homosexual men and may also be associated with a colitis of variable severity. A number of amoebae previously thought not to be pathogenic have been implicated as the cause of diarrhoea in 11 patients, 6 of whom had concurrent cryptosporidiosis.[48] These conclusions are based on the response of the diarrhoea to metronidazole therapy despite evidence of concurrent persistent cryptosporidiosis. The amoebae found included *Entamoeba coli, Entamoeba hartmanni, Endolimax nana* and *Iodamoeba buetschlli.* 'Non-pathogenic' zymodemes of *Entamoeba histolytica* occur frequently as commensal organisms in homosexual males.[49,50] The role of amoebae in the aetiology of chronic diarrhoea in AIDS patients, however, needs further clarification.

Mycobacterium avium-intracellulare infections

Atypical mycobacteria are ubiquitous organisms which have little virulence for the immunocompetent host. However, in the immunocompromized, the gastrointestinal tract is a frequent site of infection and may be the portal of entry. Disseminated atypical mycobacterial infections are common,[51] particularly in the late stages of HIV infection. Post-mortem isolation of the organism in patients with proven infection was possible in 60% of the colons cultured and 41% of small bowels. In live patients with disseminated infection, atypical mycobacteria were isolated in 36% of stool cultures as well as from bowel biopsy material.

The clinical syndromes include chronic diarrhoea with abdominal pain and a chronic malabsorption state with histological features resembling Whipple's disease. The small bowel may show thickened folds and periodic-acid Schiff (PAS)-positive foamy macrophages are found in the lamina propria. Unlike Whipple's disease, acid-fast stains may show large clusters of intracellular mycobacteria (Figs 12.2a & b). There may be associated sparse granuloma formation and a mild chronic inflammatory cell infiltrate. In addition, the draining mesenteric lymph nodes may also show infiltration by acid-fast bacteria.

Mycobacterium avium-intracellulare is most commonly

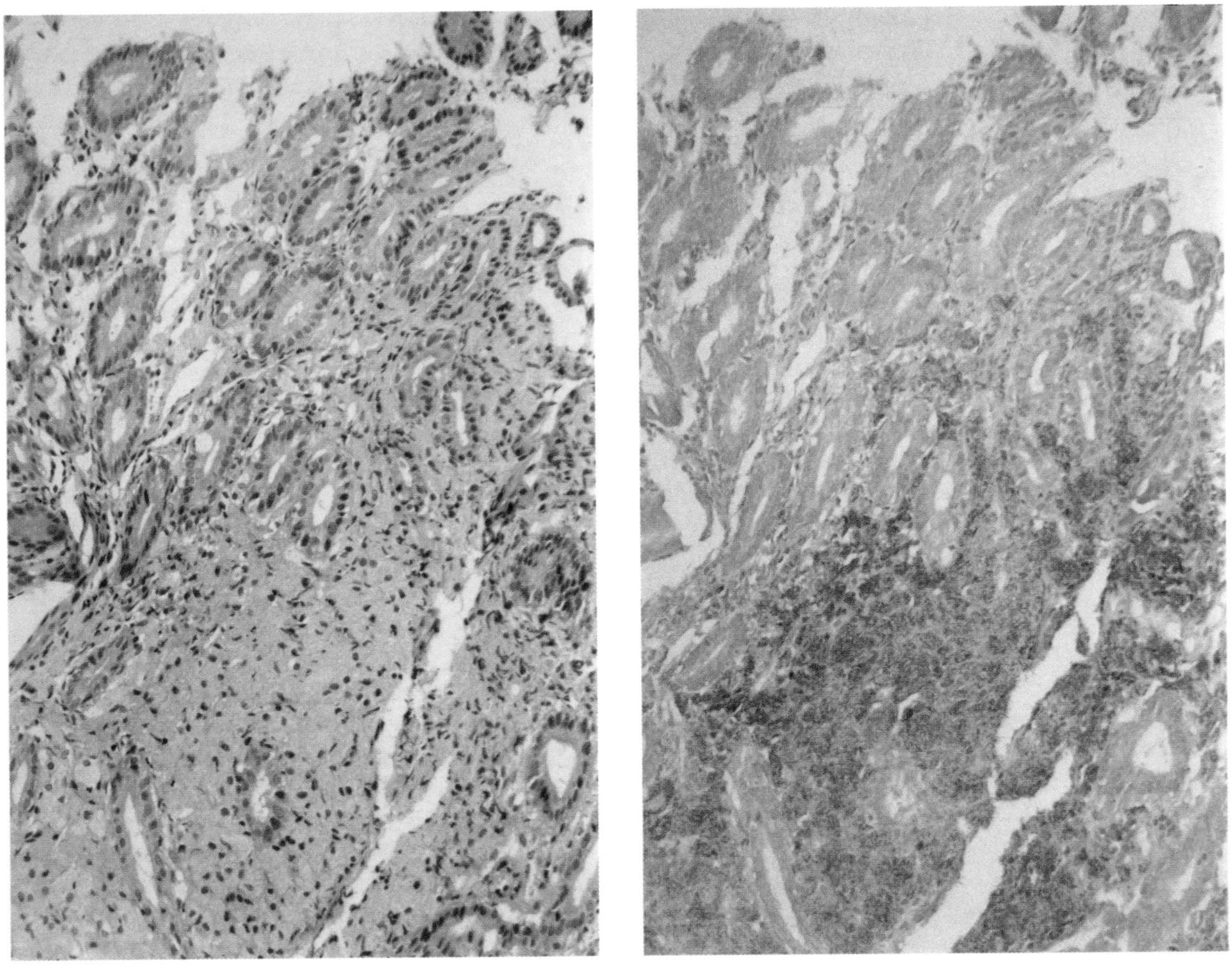

A B

Fig. 12.2A & B Rather autolysed small bowel with histiocytes filled with atypical mycobacteria. (H&E (A); PAS (B))

found, but molecular biological techniques are identifying new pathogenic species.[52] In spite of the demonstration of sensitivity in vitro to a number of anti-tuberculous drugs, no combination of therapy appears to be effective in eradicating the infection.

M. tuberculosis may also infect HIV$^+$ patients, often at an earlier phase of HIV infection, and particularly in environments where tuberculosis is prevalent. The typical histological features of giant cells and granulomata are often present, but as patients become more immunocompromized, there may be depletion of lymphocytes, large numbers of microorganisms and extensive tissue necrosis.

Although not described in the gastrointestinal tract, there is evidence of another organism causing histological changes resembling Whipple's disease.[53] *Rhodococcus equi (Corynebacterium equi)* are Gram-positive non-motile, non-spore-forming coccoid and coccobacillary bacteria which have been isolated from a bronchial lesion characterized by an organizing pneumonitis containing numerous macrophages filled with the organism. The macrophages had abundant granular cytoplasm and were strongly positive on staining with PAS, although acid-fast and silver methenamine stains were negative.

ENTEROPATHY ASSOCIATED WITH AIDS

A significant proportion of patients with AIDS and chronic diarrhoea, in whom neither enteric pathogens nor Kaposi's sarcoma has been found in spite of extensive investigation, has diffuse small bowel disease and malabsorption.[54,55]

Since the initial identification of epithelial cell infection by HIV, the role of HIV infection in the pathogenesis of diarrhoea has been debated. The main arguments for a direct cytopathic effect (reviewed in reference 56) are the demonstration of the virus (both viral DNA and the p24 antigen) in the epithelial cell, the absence of other pathogens, and questions concerning the relevance of 'non-pathogenic' microorganisms in HIV positive patients (where their presence did not correlate with symptoms).[57] Evidence that HIV could infect some epithelial cell lines and the effects of HIV infection in the nervous system (where it may cause encephalopathy or neuropathy in the absence of other infections or tumours) supported the concept of a cytopathic effect. Arguments against a direct pathogenic role include the inconsistent demonstration of HIV in the epithelium between different studies, the small numbers of infected epithelial cells even when infection is present, the suggestion that the virus is within intra-epithelial lymphocytes and macrophages rather than epithelial cells,[58] and the lack of a demonstrated cytopathic effect in cell lines.

A prospective, cross-sectional, histopathological analysis of the rectal mucosa from 75 HIV positive patients and 16 controls suggested that there was a progression through four histological phases which correlated with the various clinical stages of HIV infection.[59] The first or early phase, characterized by normal or nearly normal mucosa with scanty or absent HIV p24 protein, was seen mainly in patients who had peripheral blood CD4 counts >400 per cubic millimetre. The second, inflammatory phase was seen as the peripheral CD4 lymphocyte counts fell below 400. The main features were the presence of a marked inflammatory cell infiltrate (degranulated eosinophils, activated lymphocytes and plasma cells) and the presence of maximal HIV p24 content. A third, transitional phase in which the lymphocyte density was normal, preceded the final phase, lymphoid depletion, which occurred mainly in patients suffering from AIDS. In this phase, macrophage and eosinophil infiltrates occurred and apoptosis was observed commonly. The final two phases were associated with opportunistic infections which were characterized by eosinophilia, neutrophilia, greater degrees of apoptosis and evidence of tissue injury.

In patients without opportunistic infections, a correlation between histological inflammatory changes and symptoms is also described and there is evidence to suggest that these are the result of increased tissue cytokine levels and/or the products of degranulating eosinophils.

These observations suggest that there are at least two mechanisms for the development of diarrhoeal symptoms in HIV positive patients: in the earlier phases, there may be an 'inflammatory' diarrhoea, whilst symptoms in more advanced disease are due to opportunistic infections resulting from profound immunosuppression. The observations that patients found to have specific opportunistic infections have evidence of more severe mucosal injury and dysfunction[55] and a shorter survival than those in whom no pathogen is identified, also supports this concept of progressive phases of mucosal disease in HIV positive patients. Evidence presented in this paper argues against a direct cytopathic effect of HIV itself; in the later stages of HIV infection, even in the absence of opportunistic infections, HIV p24 levels in the mucosa were decreased when compared to those seen in the inflammatory phase.

Considerable experimental evidence suggests that there is a relationship between the mucosal inflammatory cell infiltrate and the normal mucosal architecture; this has been recognized since differences were observed in intestinal morphology between germ-free and conventional laboratory animals. Products of T cell activation appear to play a role in the induction of villous atrophy and crypt cell hyperplasia, whilst depletion or functional impairment of T cells may be expected to result in mucosal atrophy with hyporegeneration. Both patterns are described in morphometric studies of HIV infection[60–62] and probably reflect the degree of lymphocyte depletion together with the presence or absence of concomitant infection.

Previously unrecognized pathogenic micro-organisms or the presence of low-grade bacterial overgrowth[63] may also account for some cases of HIV enteropathy. A final suggestion is that the HIV causes diarrhoea as a result of autonomic neuropathy secondary to extensive axonal degeneration seen in the intrinsic nerves plexuses.[64]

The mechanism of HIV enteropathy is complex: it is possible that in the early phases of HIV infection, when the immune system is relatively intact, diarrhoea results from the release of the products of activated inflammatory cells (T cells, macrophages, eosinophils, etc.) in the intestinal mucosa; in the later phases, when immune deficiency is more profound, opportunistic infections by recognized, or perhaps as yet unrecognized, pathogens, or even low-grade bacterial overgrowth, may develop. Finally, other factors such as intestinal motility and the nutritional state of the patient may also contribute to the development of symptoms.

KAPOSI'S SARCOMA

Kaposi's sarcoma (KS) is found on presentation in over 30% of patients with the acquired immunodeficiency syndrome.[2] Of patients with skin or lymph node involvement, 40–50% or more will have gastrointestinal involvement at any site from the oropharynx to the rectum.[65] Multiple lesions are the rule. In a prospective study of 50 patients with KS,[66] 40% had visible lesions in the gastrointestinal tract. Combined upper and lower tract involvement occurred in 20% and upper or lower tract involvement in 12% and 8% respectively. Rarely, intestinal lesions develop before KS elsewhere in the body. These lesions may appear as red, pink or purple submucosal macules ranging in size from millimetres to centimetres. Larger lesions may appear as nodules or polyps with or without central umbilication. Because of the submucosal origin of the tumour, histological proof may be elusive, only 13% of visible lesions being confirmed following endoscopic forceps biopsy. Flexible sigmoidoscopic biopsies are more likely to be positive (36%).

Gastrointestinal involvement is clinically silent, and complications (ulceration, bleeding, perforation, obstruction and protein-losing enteropathy) are rare. Intestinal involvement with KS is associated with a poorer prognosis.[66]

The histological features of KS in AIDS are indistinguishable from those of classical KS. The lesions have two predominant features; interweaving bands of spindle cells, and the presence of vascular structures embedded in a network of reticular and collagen fibres. The vascular elements include erythrocyte-containing clefts or slit-like spaces, ectatic capillaries and lymphatics, and wide-lumen sinuses. Spindle cells are narrow and elongated and contain eosinophilic cytoplasm. They may show a wide range of nuclear pleomorphism. Histological patterns in the tumour may vary from lesion to lesion and may even vary in different sections of the same lesion. A sparse mononuclear cell infiltrate comprising mainly lymphocytes and plasma cells may be seen. Siderophages are not found in early lesions, but may be present in later lesions associated with prominent endothelial cells and extravasated erythrocytes. The gastrointestinal lesions are submucosal and involve the mucosa secondarily.

Extra-intestinal involvement occurs mainly in the dermis and the capsular area of lymph nodes. Tumours may involve all tissues in the body.[67,68]

Aetiology and pathogenesis

Factors other than the immunodeficient state and HIV infection appear to be necessary for the development of KS. The classical form of KS, an indolent, localized, nodular tumour found mainly on the lower extremities, is associated with neither immunodeficiency nor serological evidence of HIV infection. A more aggressive form of KS, resembling clinically the current epidemic KS, is seen in patients following iatrogenic immunosuppression, notably after renal allograft transplantation. Furthermore, although 30% of patients with AIDS will have KS, this may predate demonstrable immune deficiency.

Since KS does not occur equally in various risk groups, but primarily affects homosexual men,[69,70] these factors are most likely associated with the homosexual lifestyle. The fall in incidence of KS coincident with the adoption of safe-sex practices suggests that the development of KS is related to the transmission of a second infectious agent.[71] Further epidemiological evidence implies that this agent is a microorganism that is transmitted primarily by the faecal-oral route.[72]

The tissue of origin of KS (lymphatic or vascular endothelium) is not known[73] (see also Ch. 40, Part II). There is some evidence that KS results from an autocrine or paracrine growth loop: KS cells express a range of cytokines together with their receptors (such as platelet-derived growth factor), whilst their cellular extracts induce KS-like changes in normal vascular endothelial cells in vitro.[74,75]

GASTROINTESTINAL LYMPHOMAS AND OTHER MALIGNANCIES

Non-Hodgkin's lymphoma (NHL) is recognized as part of the clinical spectrum of infection with HIV,[76] and is found in all groups at risk. These tumours have been associated with unusual clinical features, including prodromal manifestations and a more aggressive course with a poor prognosis. Most patients present with extranodal involvement — predominantly of the CNS, bone marrow and the gastrointestinal tract. The median age and age range are similar to that of AIDS reported to the CDC, and the disease may either present in association with persistent generalized lymphadenopathy, Kaposi's sarcoma or opportunistic infection, or arise de novo. The demonstration of positive HIV serology in these patients suggests that the lymphomas develop secondarily to underlying immunosuppression from infection with HIV, rather than being the primary cause of the immunodeficiency. HIV-induced immunosuppression is thought to play a role in a manner analogous to that in immunosuppressed renal allograft recipients in whom lymphomas may also occur.

In a series of 90 homosexual males with NHL[76] intra-oral involvement occurred in 4, anorectal involvement in 3, and the bowel and liver were affected in 15 and 8 cases respectively. Virtually any site of the gastrointestinal tract or the hepatobiliary tree may be affected (reviewed in reference 78); the clinical manifestations are protean and depend on the size and location of the tumour.

Histological pictures include those of a diffuse, small noncleaved cell lymphoma, a large cell immunoblastic-plasmacytoid lymphoma and a large cell NHL. The latter are more commonly found in the gastrointestinal tract, and most are high grade. The lymphoma may be associated with chromosome (8,14) translocation identical to that seen in Burkitt's lymphoma. Cell marker studies indicate that the majority of lymphomas are of B or pre-B cell origin,[77] whilst analysis of immunoglobulin gene rearrangements demonstrates polyclonal B-cell proliferation[78] (reviewed in reference 66). This finding is common to NHL tissue from both AIDS patients and HIV-negative immunosuppressed patients. Presumably malignant transformation occurs in one of these clones, by an unknown mechanism. Co-infection with the Epstein-Barr virus has been implicated as a factor in the development of malignancy, but is not found as commonly as in endemic Burkitt's lymphoma.

Hodgkin's disease

Epidemiological studies examining the incidence of Hodgkin's disease in HIV-positive individuals do not show consistent effects, and do not establish an aetiological role for HIV in the development of this neoplasm (reviewed in reference 66); the diagnosis of Hodgkin's disease in HIV-positive patients is not included in the CDC criteria for the development of AIDS. The presence of HIV infection, however, modifies the clinical course of Hodgkin's disease, so that patients present with more widespread disease, are more likely to have systemic symptoms and have a poorer prognosis.

Squamous cell cancer of the anorectum

In an analogy with human papilloma virus (HPV) and female cervical cancer, the wart virus has been suggested as the aetiological agent in the development of squamous cell carcinoma of the anorectum. Supporting evidence is provided by studies showing that homosexual men with group IV HIV infection have a high prevalence of anal HPV infection and intraepithelial neoplasia (including carcinoma in situ).[79] The risk of developing anal neoplasia was dependent on the degree of immunosuppression. The low incidence of anal cancer among homosexual men with AIDS may be due to a long lead time for its development.

GRAFT-VERSUS-HOST DISEASE

Graft-versus-host disease (GVHD) arises when immunologically competent donor lymphoid cells bearing different histocompatibility antigens are transfused into an immunosuppressed recipient. Bone marrow transplantation (BMT) has developed over the last two decades as an effective form of treatment for a number of malignant and non-malignant disorders and it is in this context that GVHD has evolved as a significant cause of morbidity and mortality. The introduction of immunocompetent donor cells during the process of transplanting other organs, e.g. liver or heart-lung, may also result in GVHD. On rare occasions immunosuppressed, non-transplant patients may develop GVHD following transfusions of non-irradiated blood products. (For reviews, see references 80–88).

The risk of developing GVHD depends on the degree of matching of histocompatibility antigens and ranges from virtually zero for autologous grafts to 35% for HLA-matched transplantations and to 99% for HLA-non-identical transplantations. The incidence is also age-dependent with children having lower rates of GVHD.

Both acute and chronic forms of GVHD, which differ in target organ involvement, histology and response to treatment, have been described.

Acute GVHD

Acute GVHD generally starts 3–4 weeks after BMT (range 7–100 days) and affects the skin, the gut and the liver.[89] Skin involvement consists of an erythematous maculopapular rash which may progress to an exfoliative dermatitis (resembling toxic epidermal necrolysis).

Gastrointestinal tract involvement occurs in 30–60% of patients after allogeneic bone marrow transplantation and generally follows skin involvement. Clinical features range from mild diarrhoea to a large volume, watery diarrhoea associated with abdominal pain and distension and rarely, massive bleeding. A protein-losing enteropathy may also occur. A syndrome of upper gastrointestinal acute GVHD comprising anorexia, nausea, dyspepsia, food intolerance and vomiting may represent an early, more treatable manifestation of acute GVHD.[90] Associated hepatic involvement manifests as cholestatic jaundice, but progression to hepatocellular failure is rare.

Clinical grading schemes allow an assessment of prognosis and 10-30% of all engrafted allogeneic BMT recipients die of acute GVHD or its complications.[91]

Chronic GVHD

Chronic GVHD is a multisystem autoimmune-like disorder that develops 80–400 days after transplantation.[81,92] This syndrome affects 15–40% of long-term survivors and is generally preceded by acute GVHD which has resolved or evolved into chronic GVHD. In 20–30% of patients, however, there may have been no evidence of acute GVHD. Skin pigmentation, sclerodermatous infiltration and contractures, the sicca syndrome, cholestatic jaundice, oral mucositis, oesophagitis, malabsorption and polyserositis comprise the main clinical findings. Associated immunological abnormalities include hypergammaglobulinaemia, eosinophilia, circulating auto-antibodies in low titre and immune complexes. The development of antigen-specific antibody responses to bacterial antigens is impaired and hyposplenism may occur, making these patients susceptible to recurrent infections by encapsulated bacteria and opportunistic organisms. Varicella-zoster infections also are observed more frequently. The mucosal necrosis, characteristic of acute GVHD, is unusual after three months and is not a feature of chronic GVHD.

When clinical involvement is confined to the skin and the liver, the prognosis is good, whereas widespread organ involvement is associated with a poorer prognosis.[81,92] In retrospective analyses of leukaemic allogeneic BMT recipients, a significantly lower relapse rate occurred in patients with acute or chronic GVHD, the graft vs leukaemia effect.[93,94] These observations highlight the complex interrelationships between the four problems of BMT in leukaemias — graft rejection, leukaemic relapse, GVHD and sepsis.

Immunopathology

Early in the study of transplantation, disparities between the cell surface antigens coded for by the major histocompatibility complex (MHC) of the donor and recipient were found to be associated with graft rejection and GVHD. Although patients and donors are matched for the MHC antigens, GVHD still presents a major clinical problem — apparently due to differences in uncharacterized 'minor' histocompatibility antigens. Although these differences determine the T-cell response, the nature of the host (or donor) cell that expresses these antigens and initiates GVHD, the type of effector cell responsible for tissue injury and the actual mechanism of cellular damage in acute GVHD remain unclear.

The initiation of GVHD. Injection of allogeneic lymphocytes into neonatal or irradiated animals, or parental lymphocytes into first generation crossbred strains results in the graft-versus-host reaction (GVHR). In these models, the main stimulus to intestinal damage is a difference in the MHC class II antigens.[95] Normally, class II MHC expression on epithelial cells is restricted to the distal third of the villus in the small intestine; it is absent on the colonic epithelial cell. In GVHD and GVHR, however, expression of class II MHC-coded surface antigens is enhanced on the intestinal epithelium, as well as in other tissues.[96] This effect may be mediated by gamma-interferon which is released by activated T-cells in response to a variety of stimuli. Cells bearing allogeneic class II MHC determinants can stimulate sensitized T-cells, thereby amplifying the immune response; intestinal epithelial cells may have such a role in acute GVHD. In contrast, it has been proposed that donor bone marrow-derived cells bearing class II MHC antigens are necessary to stimulate intestinal GVHR and that they migrate to the mucosa where they stimulate precursor T-cells.[95] Alternatively, radioresistant host dendritic cells or macrophages may be involved in the induction of the immune response.[97]

The nature of the effector cell. Studies of T-cell depletion of donor marrow before BMT demonstrate a decreased incidence of both acute and chronic GVHD suggesting a central role for the T-lymphocyte. Immunohistochemical analysis of rectal biopsies of patients suffering from GVHD showed increased numbers of T lymphocytes, particularly $CD8^+$ (presumed cytotoxic-suppressor) cells in the lamina propria and epithelial regions early in the course of the disease. Furthermore, electron microscopy has demonstrated the presence of viable lymphocytes extending pseudopods towards the nuclear membranes of crypt cells adjacent to apoptotic bodies. These lymphocytes had the ultrastructural features of cytotoxic cells with dense lysosomal granules congregating in one pole of the cell. This evidence suggests that the $CD8^+$ cell is the effector of crypt cell necrosis, but does not explain the postulated role of cytokines in the pathogenesis of acute GVHD (see below). Previously, the CD8 antigen was thought to define class I MHC restriction and cytotoxic/suppressor cell function. Similarly, the CD4 antigen was thought to define cells with class II MHC restriction and helper/inducer or delayed-type hypersensitivity function. It is now known that there is not a constant relationship between restriction element (MHC class I or II), function and surface phenotype: $CD4^+$ T-cells can mediate cytotoxicity,[98] and $CD8^+$ T-cells can recognize class II MHC-restricted antigens and produce lymphokines essential for delayed-type hypersensitivity reactions.[99]

Mechanisms of tissue injury. Alterations in crypt cell proliferation resulting in crypt cell hyperplasia in the animal models of GVHR are thought to represent the initial responses of the mucosa and constitute the earliest phase of the developing enteropathy.[96,97] These effects are thought to be mediated by soluble 'enteropathic' cytokines which may directly stimulate crypt stem cell mitotic activity, alter the mucosal vasculature and recruit non-specific inflammatory effector cells, such as macrophages, polymorphs, eosinophils and natural killer cells. The villous atrophy characteristic of human GVHD may represent the later and more severe manifestations of this process. Release of toxic lymphokines may result from the interaction between donor and host lymphoid cells in the lamina propria and affect the epithelial cells as innocent bystanders. In experimental GVHR, this mechanism possibly explains the damage of epithelial cells histocompatible with donor lymphocytes.[100] In vivo experiments using antibodies directed against tumour necrosis factor alpha (TNFalpha) in an animal model of acute GVHD suggest that it is a major effector of tissue injury.[101] Similarly, gamma-interferon has been shown to play an important role in intestinal injury.[102] Experiments which minimized microbial colonization and invasion of the mucosa improved survival and decreased the incidence of GVHD following BMT in both animals[103] and in early studies in humans[104] (although subsequent work has not shown this effect). This raised the possibility of a causative role for infection in the development of GVHD. Furthermore, the observed depletion of lamina propria cells bearing IgA and IgM in GVHD patients suggests the development of a local immunodeficiency state.[105] Although infectious gastroenteritis is common in patients following BMT, severe acute GVHD need not be associated with clinical or histological evidence of infection. Other postulated mechanisms to explain these observations include the sharing of antigenic determinants between enteric bacteria and epithelial cells, hypersensitivity reactions to colonic bacterial antigens or the direct invasion of the mucosa by bacteria or their endotoxins in the absence of secretory immunoglobulins.[80] Against a causative role for the intestinal flora, however, are the observations that (i) the GVHR occurs in animals maintained under axenic conditions,[97] and (ii) that the incidence of GVHD has decreased since the routine use of therapy which does not affect the intestinal flora (e.g. immunosuppressive agents and T-cell depletion).

The elucidation of the mechanisms involved in GVHD is important in developing strategies for prevention. Immunosuppressive agents, such as prednisone, methotrexate and cyclosporine A, are given prophylactically following BMT; the combination of steroids and cyclosporine A reduces the incidence of GVHD in adults from 40% to 20% and results in more rapid haemopoietic recovery than combinations with methotrexate. The observation that removal of mature T-lymphocytes from murine donor bone marrow cells reduced the incidence of GVHD[106] raised the possibility of similar manoeuvres in man. Methods for T-cell depletion of bone marrow in man have involved the use of monoclonal antibodies directed against specific T-cell antigens used in combination with complement lysis or toxins to destroy the labelled cells. Utilization of the physical properties of T-cells, such as soybean lectin agglutination, or sheep red blood cell rosetting, has also been described.[80] T-lymphocyte depletion before BMT for adults suffering from leukaemia did reduce the incidence of both acute and chronic GVHD, but was associated with an increased rate of non-engraftment and leukaemic relapse. The overall survival rate of treated patients was decreased. The identification of cells responsible for the initiation of GVHD and their effective removal remains a major goal of research in this field, as does the development of methods for typing the more immunogenic 'minor' histocompatibility antigens. These problems, however, may be diminished by the widespread use of autologous bone marrow transplantation in malignant disease.

Histopathology

Gastrointestinal abnormalities following BMT may be due to the pretransplant bone marrow ablative regime, acute GVHD or superimposed infection.

Acute GVHD

The changes seen in acute GVHD range from individual intestinal crypt cell necrosis to diffuse mucosal ulceration. Apoptosis may occur anywhere in the gastrointestinal tract from the oesophagus to the rectum and is the sine qua non of intestinal GVHD.[107] Its presence in the proliferative zone of intestinal and colonic crypts after day 20 following BMT is specific, even in the absence of symptoms. Intraepithelial vacuoles filled with karyorrhectic debris ('exploding' crypt cells) may be found in the crypts, and there may be progression from these focal lesions to involvement of whole crypts resulting in crypt abscesses, crypt degeneration and obliteration. Colonic mucosal enterochromaffin cells are selectively spared from this process.[108] Intraepithelial lymphocyte numbers are increased, whilst the lamina propria and intestinal smooth muscle may be infiltrated with lymphocytes and plasma cells (although the infiltrate may be relatively scanty because of the lymphopenia after BMT). Depletion of IgA- and IgM-bearing plasma cells in the lamina propria is observed also. There may be progressive loss of villous architecture with submucosal oedema and fibrosis. In the advanced stages, the epithelium may be a cuboidal monolayer or there may be ulceration which can become confluent.

Demonstration of sites of involvement will depend on patient symptomatology; before the routine use of prophylactic immunosuppressive therapy, the common clinical presentation was with lower gastrointestinal tract manifestations. With the recognition of upper gastrointestinal tract acute GVHD, it is clear that the stomach and duodenum are commonly involved also.

In a study of patients who had proven gastrointestinal tract GVHD, simultaneous biopsies of the stomach, duodenum and rectum showed that the stomach was the tissue most commonly involved (64%); biopsies of the stomach and duodenum were positive in >90%, whilst the rectum was positive in only 56%.[86]

The cytoreductive therapy preceding transplantation may also be associated with diffuse mucosal abnormalities in the skin, rectum and duodenum. Abnormalities in the intestine include atypia of crypt cell nuclei, flattening of crypt epithelium, degeneration of crypt cells and abnormal surface cells. These effects mimic the changes in acute GVHD, but prospective studies indicate that these changes regress after transplantation, generally disappearing by day 20 in the colon if no other complications have arisen. These findings confound the diagnosis of GVHD in the early post-transplantation period.

Bone marrow transplant recipients are subject to the vast array of gastrointestinal infections of the immunocompromized, but particular difficulties arise with the diagnosis of acute GVHD in the presence of active cytomegalovirus (CMV) infections. Histopathological changes in concurrent CMV infections include single cell necrosis in the stomach and small intestine, suggesting that the diagnosis of GVHD of the gastrointestinal tract cannot be reliably made in the presence of active CMV (or herpes simplex)[86] infection. The final diagnosis must include consideration of the results of serology, stool examination and other microbiological and virological studies, and the use of immunohistochemical and in situ hybridization techniques, where available.

Chronic GVHD

The major gastrointestinal involvement of chronic GVHD occurs in the liver (in about 90%) and the oesophagus (in 13–30% of patients with extensive disease).[81,92] Clinical features include dysphagia, odynophagia, reflux symptoms, aspiration and weight loss associated with poor caloric intake. Lesions include upper and mid-oesophageal desquamation, upper oesophageal webs, rings and tapering strictures. Non-specific motor abnormalities have been described. Distal oesophageal involvement is generally related to gastro-oesophageal reflux.

Histological findings on oesophageal biopsy include infiltration of the mucosa by lymphocytes, plasma cells, neutrophils and eosinophils, necrosis of individual basal layer squamous cells and superficial epithelial desquamation. At autopsy, evidence of focal submucosal fibrosis without the muscle or nerve involvement typical of scleroderma has been reported. Hyalinization of serosal and submucosal blood vessels with subendothelial basal lamina replication is described also.[85,88]

Intestinal involvement in chronic GVHD is less common, although chronic GVHD, associated with diarrhoea, abdominal pain and malnutrition, has been reported. At autopsy, patchy fibrosis of the lamina propria and marked fibrosis of the submucosa and serosa extended from the stomach to the colon. The epithelium was normal. Multiple ulcerated fibrotic strictures of the small intestine have also been described,[81] as has a lymphocytic infiltration of the submucosal and myenteric nerve plexuses in a case of chronic GVHD of the duodenum.[86] These changes may account for the dysmotility problems seen in these patients. Early detection of chronic GVHD and treatment with prednisone, with or without azathioprine, is often effective.

PRIMARY IMMUNODEFICIENCY

Primary immunodeficiency states may affect antibody production, cell-mediated immunity or be associated with other specific defects. A classification of immunodeficiency syndromes is shown in Table 12.2 with the characteristic gastrointestinal sequelae. Reviews of the pathogenesis[109,110] and pathology[111] of these disorders have been published recently.

Predominant antibody defects

X-linked hypogammaglobulinaemia

This condition is characterized by recurrent pyogenic infections starting in infancy or early childhood, absent or very low levels of all classes of immunoglobulins, an inability to make antibodies and the absence of plasma cells from lymphoid tissue.[112]

Evidence suggests that the defect lies in the inability of the pre-B cell to differentiate into an immunoglobulin-bearing B cell and subsequently into an immunoglobulin-secreting plasma cell. The block appears to be due to the failure of translation of the V_H region genes during differentiation. Only a small proportion of bone marrow pre-B cells has demonstrable cytoplasmic mu chains. Light chain gene rearrangements do not occur, so neither K or L light chains, nor surface immunoglobulin, is expressed.[113] The abnormal gene has been mapped to chromosome Xq22–23 and has recently been shown to be a member of the *src* family of protein-tyrosine kinases.[114]

Clinical presentation often consists of acute gastrointestinal or respiratory tract infection.[115] Chronic gut infection is much less common, but *Giardia lamblia* or rotavirus infections cause diarrhoea, bacterial overgrowth, sprue-like syndromes or protein-losing enteropathy.[116–118] Bacteraemia due to enteric organisms, especially Salmonella, may also occur.[115]

The incidence of malignancy has been reported as increased in one study,[119] but unchanged in another.[115] Death is usually the result of disseminated viral infections or the cardiorespiratory complications of chronic respiratory infections.[115]

The main histological feature of this condition is the absence of primary follicles and germinal centres from mucosa-associated lymphoid tissues, including Peyer's patches, and, consequently, the absence of plasma cells from the intestinal lamina propria. In the rectum, this may be associated with early crypt abscesses and a polymorphonuclear infiltrate in the lamina propria.[116] The small bowel villous architecture may be normal or blunted.

X-linked hypogammaglobulinaemia has been reported in association with growth hormone deficiency in one family.[120] There are also rare reports of autosomal recessive agammaglobulinaemia,[121] but chronic gastrointestinal disease has not been recorded in these patients.

Common variable or acquired hypogammaglobulinaemia (CVH)[122]

CVH comprises a heterogeneous group of conditions characterized clinically by the onset of recurrent bacterial infections, most commonly in the respiratory tract, generally in the second or third decade. It may occur sporadically or as an autosomal recessive inheritance.

B-cell numbers vary, and the abnormality in immunoglobulin secretion may be due to intrinsic B-cell defects or imbalances in immunoregulatory T-cell subsets (absence of helper T-cells or presence of excessive suppressor T-cell activity). Rarely auto-antibodies to T- or B-cells are responsible.[110]

Gastric involvement is common. Achlorhydria affects some 50% of patients,[123,124] and the associated gastric atrophy may lead to a pernicious anaemia-like syndrome. This differs from classical pernicious anaemia in that the atrophic gastritis does not spare the antrum, plasma cells are absent from the mononuclear cell infiltrate[117] and anti-parietal cell antibodies are not seen. Intestinal involvement is also common with chronic or recurrent diarrhoea occurring in 60%, of whom two-thirds may have malabsorption.[124] Infestation by *Giardia lamblia is* common, and secondary disaccharidase deficiencies may result.[116,125] Varying degrees of damage to the villous architecture may result from giardiasis[116] or other infections such as cryptosporidiosis and strongyloidosis;[118] both gluten-sensitive (GSE) and gluten-insensitive enteropathy have been reported[117] In CVH, the histology may closely resemble that of GSE, except that plasma cells may be absent. Antigliadin antibodies are not seen. Ulcerative jejunitis[126] and protein-losing enteropathy[116] may also occur. A granulomatous enteropathy unresponsive to antibiotics or gammaglobulin therapy is another manifestation of CVH.[122] Crohn's disease and ulcerative colitis have both been

Table 12.2 Classifications of immunodeficiency diseases and their gastrointestinal sequelae.

Disorder	Gastrointestinal manifestations
A. *Predominant antibody defects*	
1. X-linked agammaglobulinaemia	Malabsorption and diarrhoea
	Giardiasis
	Rotavirus
	Disaccharidase deficiencies
	Malignancy
2. Common variable hypogammaglobulinaemia	
	Pernicious anaemia-like syndrome
	Pancreatic insufficiency
	Subtotal villous atrophy
	Nodular lymphoid hyperplasia
	Ulcerative jejunitis
	Disaccharidase deficiencies
	Infections due to giardia, salmonella, shigella, staphylococcus, campylobacter
	Inflammatory bowel disease
	Granulomatous enteropathy
3. Selective IgA deficiency	Pernicious anaemia
	Gluten-sensitive enteropathy
	Nodular lymphoid hyperplasia
	Disaccharidase deficiencies
	Inflammatory bowel disease
	Giardia lamblia infestation
B. *Predominant defects of cell-mediated immunity*	
1. Severe combined immunodeficiency	Childhood diarrhoea
	Candidiasis
	Disaccharidase deficiencies
	Mucosal abnormalities with PAS positive macrophages
	Infections due to salmonella, *E. coli*, coccidiosis, rotavirus
2. Chronic mucocutaneous candidiasis	Oropharyngeal/oesophageal candidiasis
	Diarrhoea sometimes due to candida
3. Nezelof's syndrome	Malabsorption
	Candidiasis
	Enterocolitis
	Subtotal villous atrophy
	Hepatosplenomegaly, lymphadenopathy
C. *Immunodeficiency associated with other defects*	
1. Di George's syndrome	Oesophageal atresia
	Chronic candidiasis
	Childhood malabsorption, diarrhoea
	Imperforate anus
2. Wiskott-Aldrich syndrome	Bloody diarrhoea
	Steatorrhoea
	Vitamin B_{12} malabsorption
3. Ataxia-telangiectasia	Mild Vitamin B_{12} malabsorption
4. Transcobalamin II deficiency	Malabsorption
5. Bare lymphocyte syndrome	Oral candidiasis
	Persistent viral infections
6. Leucocyte adhesion deficiency	Necrotizing enterocolitis
	Recurrent bacterial and fungal infections

recorded in CVH[117] Nodular lymphoid hyperplasia is often present (see below).

Pancreatic exocrine deficiency may contribute to malabsorption[124,127] Bacterial overgrowth is a common association of CVH, but does not appear to contribute to symptoms.[116]

There is an increased incidence of gastric and colonic cancer, lymphoma, especially non-Hodgkin's lymphoma, and other malignancies.[122]

Selective IgA deficiency[128]

Selective IgA deficiency is the commonest primary immunodeficiency syndrome, affecting up to 1:500 healthy adult blood donors.[129] The incidence is variable depending on the population being studied; published figures range from 1:400 in Finland to 1:15 000 in Japan.[128] It is likely that the majority of selective IgA-deficient subjects do not develop clinical symptoms, but some will develop immunological abnormalities with time.[130] Increased IgM production at mucosal surfaces may compensate for lack of IgA. In addition, there may be dissociation between the levels of serum and secretory IgA, as well as between the levels of the individual subclasses of IgA. This may result in adequate mucosal protection with secretory IgA_2 in the presence of low levels of serum IgA_1.[131] Rarely, the converse may occur. Serum IgA levels may be normal in patients with secretory IgA deficiency due to isolated secretory piece deficiency.[132]

Associated immunological abnormalities may also predispose to symptoms. Isolated IgG_2, IgG_3, IgG_4 and IgE deficiencies have all been described with IgA deficiency.[133-135] IgG_2 or IgG_3 deficiency is associated with impaired lung function, presumably due to an increased incidence of respiratory infections.[136]

IgA deficiency is probably the manifestation of a heterogeneous group of disorders, all of which affect the terminal differentiation of the B-cell.[128] Proposed mechanisms include intrinsic B-cell defects, inadequate T-cell help, and IgA-specific suppressor cells, e.g. following the administration of phenytoin[137] or penicillamine. The inheritance of IgA deficiency may be autosomal dominant or recessive, but the majority of patients do not have a family history. Genetically determined abnormalities have been linked to chromosomes 18, 14 and 6, although specific gene defects have not been identified (except for rare cases involving the deletion of alpha-1 or alpha-2 heavy chain genes on chromosome 14).[138]

Unlike hypogammaglobulinaemia, increased susceptibility to gastrointestinal pathogens is uncommon, although giardiasis may occur.

Autoimmune disorders, especially pernicious anaemia,[139] Addison's disease, thyroiditis, haemolytic anaemia and idiopathic thrombocytopenic purpura[128] occur with increased frequency, and systemic lupus erythematosus, rheumatoid arthritis, primary biliary cirrhosis and chronic active hepatitis are reported associations.[140]

The frequency of IgA deficiency in patients suffering from gluten-sensitive enteropathy is 10–12 times higher than in the general population, with a prevalence of approximately 1:40[117]–1:200[128] patients. The histological features of gluten-sensitive enteropathy are present, except that IgA plasma cells in the lamina propria are decreased in numbers or absent and there is an apparently compensatory increase in IgM-containing plasma cells. In most cases, there is a symptomatic and morphological response to a gluten-free diet.

An increased frequency of inflammatory bowel disease, especially Crohn's disease (1:73) has been reported.[117] Other gastrointestinal associations include disaccharidase deficiencies and nodular lymphoid hyperplasia. An increased risk of gastrointestinal and other malignancies (especially B-cell lymphomas) may also occur in this disorder.[128]

Transient IgA deficiency or hypogammaglobulinaemia may occur in children, with chronic diarrhoea a presenting feature.[141] The mechanism is unknown, but may reflect a delay in the terminal differentiation process, following the decline of placentally transferred maternal immunoglobulin.

Selective IgM deficiency is rare and is associated with meningococcal and other severe or recurrent infections.[110] Mild plasma IgM deficiency, however, is associated with gluten-sensitive enteropathy, but this defect resolves following treatment with a gluten-free diet.[142] The mechanisms of IgM deficiency are unknown.

Nodular lymphoid hyperplasia (NLH)

NLH describes the presence of multiple lymphoid nodules involving the entire small bowel and/or colon of patients with primary immunodeficiency syndromes. It is found in 20–60% of patients with CVH,[117] predominantly in the small bowel, but is less common in those suffering from selective IgA deficiency. In immunodeficient patients, giardiasis is a common association but effective elimination does not cause regression of the lesions.[117]

It may be found also in the terminal ileum or colon (or both) of children[143] and adults[144] without immunodeficiency. A retrospective study[145] on the patterns of presentation of 147 children with documented NLH showed an association with rectal bleeding and/or abdominal pain, although a clear cause and effect relationship was not proven — NLH is commonly an incidental finding, especially in children. In this study there were few associated conditions or alternative diagnoses made; ten were diagnosed subsequently as having Crohn's disease, only one had a low serum IgA and none developed lymphoma. There was no evidence of parasitic infestation or abnormal pathogens in the children studied.

Macroscopically, affected tissue may appear nodular or polypoid. The histological appearances are those of a benign or reactive lymphoid collection. If large, lymphoid follicles may produce distortion of the neighbouring villi. The overlying epithelium is not specialized. The germinal centres of the follicles are composed of proliferating B-cells and scattered tingible-body macrophages; the mantle zones contain both mature and immature B-cells, whilst the extramantle zones contain both B- and T-cells, plasma cells, macrophages, neutrophils and eosinophils. The germinal centres probably contain normally proliferating B-cells, although some reports have demonstrated a failure to switch from IgM to IgG antibody production.[146,147] The lamina propria may show a virtual absence of plasma cells in immunodeficient patients.[148] In both immunodeficient[124,149] and immunocompetent patients,[150] NLH has been associated with small or large bowel lymphoma, raising the possibility that NLH predisposes to malignancy (although this is very rare in immunocompetent children[145]). These hyperplastic lymphoid follicles may result from chronic antigenic stimulation in the absence of normal regulatory feedback control mechanisms.

Predominant defects of cell-mediated immunity

Severe combined immunodeficiency (SCID)

Inherited as an X-linked or autosomal recessive condition, SCID presents in the first few months of life with oropharyngeal candidiasis, intractable diarrhoea and pneumonia, often caused by *Pneumocystis carinii.*[110] Patients are also susceptible to viral infections and to systemic complications after inoculation with live virus vaccines. In the absence of successful bone marrow transplantation or enzyme replacement therapy, this condition is invariably fatal in the first few years of life.

Small intestinal biopsy may show absent or abnormally shaped villi, crypt abscesses and large PAS-positive vacuolated macrophages near the tips of the villi.[151] Plasma cells and lymphocytes are absent. Similarly, rectal biopsy may show crypt abscesses and damaged surface epithelium with absent plasma cells. Gastrointestinal infections may be due to salmonella, enteropathic *E. coli,* rotavirus, coccidiosis and cryptosporidiosis. Lactose intolerance may also develop. Sclerosing cholangitis,[152] large bile duct obstruction causing cirrhosis, and hepatomegaly[153] have been described in SCID.

The histological appearances of the thymus are characteristic and reveal islands and nests of endodermal cells that have not become lymphoid. Hassall's corpuscles are absent.[110,111]

A deficiency of the enzyme adenosine deaminase has been found in half of the autosomal recessive cases of SCID,[111,154] and prenatal diagnosis of this condition is now possible.[155] Another rare genetic defect of the enzyme purine-nucleoside phosphorylase results in susceptibility to opportunistic infections, leading to death from viral infections. The defect results in low T-cell numbers with normal immunoglobulin levels and B-cell numbers.[110] The gene associated with the X-linked form maps to chromosome Xq13; its product, however, although involved in B-cell differentiation, seems to be more important for normal T-cell function.[156]

Chronic mucocutaneous candidiasis[117,157,158]

A heterogeneous group of disorders cause persistent *Candida* infection of the mucous membranes, scalp, skin and nails which may occur at any time in the first two decades of life. The defects include selective disorders of T-cell immunity to *Candida* with variable B-cell involvement. Endocrine and/or autoimmune disorders such as hypoparathyroidism, hypoadrenalism, hypothyroidism, diabetes mellitus, pancreatic insufficiency, hypogonadism, pernicious anaemia, hepatitis, vitiligo and alopecia occur in 40–50% of patients. There is an association with thymoma, which may involve the other related disorders, e.g. myaesthenia gravis, aplastic anaemia, neutropenia and hypogammaglobulinaemia. In 20% of patients there is a family history, with both autosomal dominant and autosomal recessive inheritance being described. The endocrinopathies are more commonly associated with recessive patterns of transmission. Oral or oesophageal candidiasis may occur, but systemic spread is rare. *Candida albicans* can cause diarrhoea in these patients. Infections with organisms other than *Candida* (e.g. *Staph. aureus, Strep. pneumoniae, Haemophilus influenzae,* histoplasmosis and disseminated viral infections) cause significant clinical problems in up to 80% of patients.[157]

Nezelof's syndrome

Nezelof's syndrome is characterized by impaired T-cell immunity, normal immunoglobulin levels and a variable B-cell defect, resulting in variable antibody responses to antigen. The inheritance may be X-linked or autosomal recessive. In some cases it is associated with a deficiency of nucleoside phosphorylase.[111] Clinical features are similar to SCID, except that lymphadenopathy and hepatosplenomegaly may be present. Generalized malabsorption, candidiasis and enterocolitis occur.[159] Small intestinal biopsy may show blunting of villous architecture with increased numbers of plasma cells and polymorphonuclear leucocytes in the lamina propria.[117,160] Peyer's patches may be absent.[111]

Immunodeficiency associated with other defects

Congenital thymic aplasia (Di George's syndrome)[110,117,118]

This congenital malformation of the third and fourth pharyngeal pouch results in thymic and hypoparathyroid hypoplasia. Although an association with monosomy 22q11 has been described,[161] some authors argue that this anomaly represents a developmental field defect resulting from a number of different disorders, e.g. the autosomal dominant form of the Di George syndrome may be a manifestation of the velocardiofacial syndrome (which is characterized by the presence of cleft palate or velopharyngeal insufficiency, cardiac anomalies, characteristic facies and learning disabilities).[162]

Profound lymphopenia of T-cells may be seen, but with increasing age, cell-mediated immunity may be slowly acquired. B-cells are normal. Gastrointestinal involvement includes oesophageal atresia and imperforate anus, chronic candidiasis, watery diarrhoea (which may be related to the hypoparathyroidism) and malabsorption.

Wiskott-Aldrich syndrome[110,117]

Severe eczema, thrombocytopenia and susceptibility to opportunistic infections characterize the Wiskott-Aldrich syndrome which is inherited as an X-linked trait mapping to chromosome Xp11.[156] The presence of functional abnormalities of platelets, B- and T-cells, in association with the response to bone marrow transplantation,[163] suggests that the defective gene is one that is expressed early in haematopoiesis. Death usually occurs in the first decade as the result of infection, haemorrhage or lymphoreticular tumours.

T-cell numbers and function progressively decline with age, and T-cell-dependent areas of lymph nodes and spleen are depleted of cells. Immunoglobulin responses to polysaccharide antigens are absent, and isohaemagglutinins do not develop. Elevated IgA and IgE levels may be found in association with reduced IgM levels. The principal gut manifestations comprise bloody diarrhoea, steatorrhoea and vitamin B_{12} malabsorption.[116]

Chromosomal breakage syndromes including ataxia-telangiectasia[110,164,165]

A number of syndromes including ataxia-telangiectasia, Bloom's syndrome, Fanconi's anaemia, xeroderma pigmentosa and the Nijmegen breakage syndrome are characterized by chromosome instability associated with defects in DNA repair mechanisms.

Ataxia-telangiectasia (Louis-Bar syndrome) is inherited as an autosomal recessive trait characterized by the development of ataxia by the end of the second year of life and oculocutaneous telangiectasia by the fifth year. The thymus has a fetal appearance microscopically and a defect in helper T-cells is prominent. Immunoglobulin abnormalities include variable deficiencies of IgA, IgG and IgE. Secretory IgA function may be preserved in spite of low serum IgA. Autoantibodies to IgA may be found. Recurrent respiratory tract infections and bronchiectasis occur in approximately 70% of patients. The major cause of death, however, is malignancy, especially of the lymphoreticular system, but also of the liver, stomach and gonads. There is an increased risk of malignancy in assumed heterozygotes,[166] but the tumours seen in family members differ from those from which affected individuals suffer, e.g. breast cancer has a relative risk of 6.8 in female family members.[167] The condition may result in premature aging and death, but prenatal diagnosis is now available.[168]

Gastrointestinal involvement is uncommon, but mild vitamin B_{12} malabsorption has been described.[116] Small bowel and rectal biopsies are usually normal, except for decreased numbers of IgA-bearing cells.[117] Serum alpha-foetoprotein levels are elevated in approximately 90% of patients.

The defect appears to be related to a basic repair defect of DNA, with numerous chromosomal breaks and translocations being reported. Patients are very sensitive to ionizing radiation[169] and radiomimetic drugs, e.g. bleomycin and etoposide, making the treatment of malignancy difficult. Genetic linkage studies confirm an association between ataxia-telangiectasia and markers on chromosome 11q22.3; differences in clinical features suggest, however, that there may be more than one ataxia-telangiectasia gene.

Transcobalamin II deficiency

Genetic deficiency of the principal transport protein for vitamin B_{12} results in megaloblastic anaemia in infancy. If untreated, agammaglobulinaemia develops because of abnormal terminal B-cell differentiation.[170] Diarrhoea may also occur because of malformation or immaturity of the intestinal epithelium.[118]

Bare lymphocyte syndrome (major histocompatibility complex [MHC] deficiency)[111,171]

This syndrome, which has an autosomal recessive pattern of inheritance, is characterized by the absence of either class I or class II major histocompatibility complex (MHC) molecules as identified by immunohistochemistry; cells of the immune system are normally represented and there is no characteristic histopathology of the lymphoid organs or mucosa-associated lymphoid tissue. Given the importance of these molecules in presenting antigen to the immune system, it is not surprising that the clinical manifestations are characteristic of a combined immunodeficiency state and include oral candidiasis, *Pneumocystis carinii* pneumonia and persistent viral infections of the gastrointestinal tract. The functional effects of class II MHC deficiency are more severe than in class I MHC deficiency, and include absence of delayed-type hypersensitivity reactions and antigen-specific antibody responses. This condition appears to be a consequence of a defect in the regulation of expression of the class II MHC genes.

Leucocyte adhesion deficiency[111]

A family of leucocyte membrane proteins is formed by the non-covalent pairing of unique alpha chains (CD11a, CD11b and CD11c) to a common beta chain (CD18) to produce the cell surface molecules, lymphocyte function antigen (LFA)-1, CR3 complement receptor and p150,95 antigen respectively. Absence of the beta-subunit results in the failure to express all three heterodimers. The clinical features of the resultant defects in cell adhesion and adhesion-associated functions include delayed wound healing, and susceptibility to bacterial and fungal infections of the respiratory tract, skin and gut. The development of necrotizing enterocolitis with regions of mucosal ulceration and bacterial and fungal overgrowth together with a complete lack of an acute inflammatory infiltrate suggests an impairment of neutrophil emigration from blood vessels.[172] The leucocyte cell surface markers are absent when studied using immunohistochemistry.

IMMUNODEFICIENCY SECONDARY TO GASTROINTESTINAL DISEASE

Protein-losing enteropathy (PLE) and intestinal lymphangiectasia

A large number of diseases may be associated with plasma protein loss into the gut.[173] Whatever the cause of the protein loss, the effect may be a decrease in serum levels of all three major immunoglobulin sub-classes. Sometimes, only IgG levels may be reduced, reflecting a slower synthetic rate of IgG. If substantial losses of lymph occur, lymphopenia and a defect of cell-mediated immunity may result.[174] See also Chapter 26.

CHRONIC GRANULOMATOUS DISEASE (CGD)

Chronic granulomatous disease is an inherited disorder of oxidative metabolism in phagocytes, resulting in the failure to generate superoxide and activated oxygen derivatives following ingestion of microbes.[175,176] The clinical consequences comprise greatly impaired host defences against pathogens, particularly catalase-positive bacteria, such as *Staphylococcus aureus, Aspergillus* species and a number of other 'non-pathogenic' fungi. The lungs, lymph nodes, skin, liver and gastrointestinal tract are the commonest sites of infection, whilst infections of the genito-urinary tract, subcutaneous tissues, bone and brain may also occur.[177–179]

Gastrointestinal involvement may cause diarrhoea, steatorrhoea, vitamin B_{12} malabsorption or intestinal obstruction due to granulomata. The bowel wall may be thickened and biopsies usually show normal villous structure with collections of vacuolated PAS-positive macrophages containing lipofuscin pigment in the jejunal lamina propria.[180] A clinicopathological entity similar to Crohn's disease has been described, involving both small and large intestine or just colon alone. Colonic histology showed diffusely spread, non-caseating granulomata, associated giant cells, multiple crypt abscesses, and prominent lymphoid follicles,[181] which may represent a variant of chronic granulomatous disease or superimposed Crohn's disease.

The phenotypic expression of chronic granulomatous disease reflects at least four inherited disorders of phagocyte oxidative metabolism; since the localization and cloning of the abnormal gene in the X-linked disorder,[182] three other primary genetic abnormalities have been characterized.[175,176]

In phagocytic cells the generation of reactive oxygen intermediates is a function of an enzyme complex called the respiratory burst [nicotinamide adenine dinucleotide phosphate (NADPH)] oxidase. The components of this enzyme system include two plasma membrane-bound proteins which together form cytochrome b_{558} (gp91-phox and p22-phox; phox for *ph*agocyte *ox*idase) and several cytoplasmic proteins (including p47-phox and p67-phox) which are thought to assemble to form the enzyme complex upon activation of the cell. Functional defects in each of these proteins resulting in the clinical expression of CGD have been described. Their frequency and chromosomal localization is as follows: gp91-phox, 60-70%, chromosome Xp21; p22-phox, 5%, chromosome 16q24; p47-phox, 20–30%, chromosome 7q11,23; and p67-phox, 5%, chromosome 1q25. Even within these groups, genetic heterogeneity is described, e.g. there are at least three different types of mutations in the cytochrome b heavy-chain (gp91-phox). The three autosomal defects are inherited as recessive traits.

Treatment includes prophylactic antibiotics, the judicious use of steroids, leucocyte transfusions, together with aggressive surgery and antibiotic therapy for infections. Gamma-interferon also has a proven role in reducing the frequency of serious infections.[178,183] Its mechanism of action is unknown; it does not appear to enhance neutrophil oxidase activity to any significant degree.[184]

EOSINOPHILIC GASTROENTERITIS[185,186]

Eosinophilic gastroenteritis is a rare condition characterized by infiltration of the gastrointestinal tract with eosinophils, often affecting the gastric antrum and extending into the small bowel. Occasionally, the infiltrate is confined to the small bowel alone or, rarely, the colon. Affected bowel may be thickened and there is distortion of the mucosal pattern, but ulceration is not a prominent feature. Lymph node enlargement also occurs. The characteristic histological feature is a diffuse eosinophilic infiltration affecting mainly the submucosa, with associated oedema and some degree of inflammatory fibrosis. Capillary and lymphatic dilatation of the mucosa may be associated with oedema resulting in distortion of villous architecture and, rarely, effacement of the villi. Adjacent lymph nodes show reactive changes, although they too may show eosinophilic infiltration. Clinical features depend on the predominant site of infiltration. Major mucosal involvement is generally associated with nausea, vomiting and abdominal pain which may be related to the ingestion of specific foods. Weight loss, diarrhoea, protein-losing enteropathy and occult blood loss can also occur. Predominant muscular layer involvement results in symptoms of pyloric outlet obstruction or intermittent incomplete small bowel obstruction. Serosal involvement may result in an eosinophilic ascites. Other organs which can also be involved include the oesophagus, gall bladder, pancreas and bladder. Hepatomegaly, pleural effusions and prostatitis are other manifestations of this condition.

The pathogenesis of eosinophilic gastroenteritis is not understood, but evidence suggests an allergic aetiology. Most patients (70%) have a personal or family history of atopy, such as asthma, hay fever, eczema and drug hypersensitivity. Rarely, a specific food item causing symptoms can be identified. In other cases, a specific antigen may be implicated, e.g. larvae of the roundworm *Eustoma rotundatum,* a parasite of the North Sea herring, or hookworms (*Ancylostoma* species).[187] Blood eosinophilia is a common finding, affecting over 70% of patients. Finally, an immunological aetiology is also supported by the rapid clinical response to corticosteroids.

The differential diagnosis of eosinophilic infiltration of the gastrointestinal tract includes the systemic vasculitides, including polyarteritis nodosa and hypersensitivity vasculitis (the Churg-Strauss syndrome),[188] parasitic infestations including *Schistosoma* species, *Giardia lamblia* and hookworm, cow's milk intolerance, Crohn's disease, gastric antral carcinoma, intestinal lymphoma, histiocytosis X, systemic mastocytosis and the idiopathic hypereosinophilic syndrome.[189]

Inflammatory fibroid polyp[185,190]

Also known as localized eosinophilic granuloma, this lesion is a solitary sessile or polypoid lesion found in the gastric antrum, small bowel, oesophagus or colon. It generally presents with obstructive symptoms, but there is no blood eosinophilia or history of atopy.

Macroscopically, the polyp may be up to 5 cm in diameter, often has apical ulceration and may mimic the appearance of a leiomyoma. It arises in the submucosa and may project into the lumen. Additional serosal involvement may give it a dumb-bell appearance on sectioning.

Microscopically, the appearance is that of granulation tissue with a variable eosinophil infiltrate. The stroma consists of proliferating fibroblasts around arborizing capillaries and may be loosely collagenous or myxomatous. Other inflammatory cells may also be present. This structure probably represents a peculiar type of granulation tissue confined to the gut. There is no evidence that it is malignant or premalignant (See also Chapter 40).

REFERENCES

1. Centers for Disease Control: Pneumocystis pneumonia — Los Angeles. MMWR 1981; 30: 250–252.
2. Centers for Disease Control: Kaposi's sarcoma and Pneumocystis pneumonia among homosexual men — New York City and California. MMWR 1981; 30: 305–308.
3. Barre-Sinoussi F, Chermann JC, Rey F et al. Isolation of a T-lymphotropic retrovirus from a patient at risk for acquired immunodeficiency syndrome (AIDS). Science 1983; 220: 868–871.
4. Centers for Disease Control: Classification system for Human T-lymphotropic Virus Type III/Lymphadenopathy-Associated Virus Infections. MMWR 1986; 35: 334–339.
5. Castro KG, Hardy AM, Curran JW. The Acquired Immunodeficiency Syndrome: Epidemiology and risk factors for transmission. Med Clin North Am 1986; 70: 635–649.
6. Zagury D, Bernard J, Leonard R et al. Long-term cultures of HTLV III infected T cells: A model of cytopathology of T cell depletion in AIDS. Science 1986; 231: 850–853.
7. Gottlieb MS. Immunologic aspects of the Acquired Immunodeficiency Syndrome and male homosexuality. Med Clin North Am 1986; 70: 651–664.
8. Gartner S, Markovits P, Markovitz DM, Kaplan MH, Gallo RC, Popovic M. The role of mononuclear phagocytes in HTLV-III/LAV infection. Science 1986; 233: 215–219.
9. Baker RW, Peppercorn MA. Gastrointestinal ailments of homosexual men. Medicine 1982; 61: 390–405.
10. Quinn TC, Stamm WE, Goodell SE et al. The polymicrobial origin of intestinal infections in homosexual men. N Engl J Med 1983; 309: 576–582.
11. Weller IVD. The gay bowel. Gut 1985; 26: 869–875.
12. Fauci AS, Macher AM, Longo DL et al. Acquired Immunodeficiency Syndrome: Epidemiologic, Clinical, Immunologic and Therapeutic Considerations. Ann Intern Med 1984; 100: 92–106.
13. Bodey GP, Fainstein V, Garrant R. Infections of the gastrointestinal tract in the immunocompromised patient. Ann Rev Med 1986; 37: 271–281.
14. Klein RS, Harris CA, Small CB, Moll B, Lesser M, Friedland GH. Oral candidiasis in high-risk patients as the initial manifestation of the Acquired Immunodeficiency Syndrome. N Engl J Med 1984; 311: 354–358.
15. Tavitian A, Raufman J-P, Rosenthal LE. Oral candidiasis as a marker for oesophageal candidiasis in AIDS. Ann Intern Med 1986; 104: 54–55.
16. Drew WL, Mintz L, Miner RC, Sands M, Ketterer B. Prevalence of cytomegalovirus infection in homosexual men. J Infect Dis 1981; 143: 188–192.
17. Lange M, Klein EB, Kornfield H, Cooper LZ, Grieco MH. Cytomegalovirus isolation from healthy homosexual men. JAMA 1984; 252: 1908–1910.
18. Mintz L, Drew WL, Miner RC, Braff EH. Cytomegalovirus infections in homosexual men. An epidemiological study. Ann Intern Med 1983; 99: 326–329.
19. Jacobsen MA, Mills J. Serious cytomegalovirus disease in the acquired immunodeficiency syndrome (AIDS): clinical findings, diagnsosis and treatment. Ann Intern Med 1988; 108: 585–594.
20. Connolly GM. Cytomegalovirus disease of the gastrointestinal tract in AIDS. Gazzard BG. (Ed) Bailliere's Clinical Gastroenterology 1990; 4: 405–423.
21. Francis N. Light and electron microscopic appearances of pathological changes in HIV gut infection. Gazzard BG. (Ed) Bailliere's Clinical Gastroenterology 1990; 4: 495–527.
22. Schwartz DA, Wilcox CM. Atypical cytomegalovirus inclusions in gastrointestinal biopsy specimens from patients with the Acquired Immunodeficiency Syndrome. Hum Pathol 1992; 23: 1019–1026.
23. St Onge G, Bezahler GH. Giant oesophageal ulcer associated with cytomegalovirus. Gastroenterology 1982; 83: 127–130.
24. Laulund S, Visfeldt J, Klinken L. Patho-anatomical studies in patients dying of AIDS. Acta Pathol Microbiol Immunol Scand (A) 1986; 94: 201–221.
25. Foucar E, Mukai K, Foucar K, Sutherland DE, Van Buren CT. Colonic ulceration in lethal cytomegalovirus infection. Am J Clin Pathol 1981; 76: 788–801.
26. Meiselman MS, Cello JP, Margeretten W. Cytomegalovirus colitis: report of the clinical, endoscopic and pathologic findings in two patients with the Acquired Immunodeficiency Syndrome. Gastroenterology 1985; 88: 171–175.
27. Siegal FP, Lopez C, Hammer GS et al. Severe acquired immunodeficiency in male homosexuals, manifested by chronic perianal ulcerative herpes simplex lesions. N Engl J Med 1981; 305: 1439–1444.
28. Janoff EN, Orenstein JM, Manischewitz JF, Smith PD.

Adenovirus colitis in the Acquired Immunodeficiency Syndrome. Gastroenterology 1991; 100: 976–979.
29. Greenspan D, Greenspan JS, Conant M, Peterson V, Silverman S Jr, de Souza Y. Oral 'hairy' leukoplakia in male homosexuals: evidence of association with both papillomavirus and a herpes-group virus. Lancet 1984; ii: 831–834.
30. Greenspan JS, Greenspan D, Lennette ET et al. Replication of Epstein-Barr virus within epithelial cells of oral 'hairy' leukoplakia, an AIDS-associated lesion. N Engl J Med 1985; 313: 1564–1571.
31. Smith D, Croser D. Oral manifestations of HIV disease. Gazzard BG. (Ed) Bailliere's Clinical Gastroenterology 1990; 4: 315–337.
32. Weber J. Gastrointestinal disease in AIDS. Clin Immunol Allergy 1986; 6: 519–541.
33. Southam JC, Felix DH, Wray D, Cubie HA. Hairy leukoplakia — a histological study. Histopathology 1991; 19: 63–67.
34. Wolfson JS, Richter JM, Waldron MA, Weber DJ, McCarthy DM, Hopkins CC. Cryptosporidiosis in immunocompetent patients. N Engl J Med 1985; 312: 1278–1282.
35. Centers for Disease Control. Cryptosporidiosis: assessment of chemotherapy of males with acquired immunodeficiency syndrome (AIDS). MMWR 1982; 31: 589–592.
36. Current WL, Reese NC, Ernst JV, Bailey WS, Heyman MB, Weinstein WM. Human cryptosporidiosis in immunocompetent and immunodeficient persons. N Engl J Med 1983; 308: 1252–1257.
37. Modigliani R, Bories C, Le Charpentier Y et al. Diarrhoea and malabsorption in acquired immune deficiency syndrome: a study of four cases with specific emphasis on opportunistic protozoan infestations. Gut 1985; 26: 179–187.
38. Angus KW. Cryptosporidiosis and AIDS. Gazzard BG. (Ed) Bailliere's Clinical Gastroenterology 1990; 4: 425–441.
39. Godwin TA. Cryptosporidiosis in the Acquired Immunodeficiency Syndrome: A Study of 15 Autopsy Cases. Human Pathology 1991; 22: 1215–1224.
40. Dobbins WO III, Weinstein WM. Electron microscopy of the intestine and rectum in acquired immunodeficiency syndrome. Gastroenterology 1985; 88: 738–749.
41. Weller I. AIDS and the gut. Scand J Gastroenterol 1985; 20 (Suppl 114): 77–89.
42. De Hovitz JA, Pape JW, Boncy M, Johnson WD Jr. Clinical manifestations and therapy of *Isospora belli* infection in patients with the acquired immunodeficiency syndrome. N Engl J Med 1986; 315: 87–90.
43. Peacock CS, Blanshard C, Tovey DG, Ellis DS, Gazzard BG. Histological diagnosis of intestinal microsporidiosis in patients with AIDS. J Clin Pathol 1991; 44: 558–563.
44. Weber R, Bryan RT Owen RL et al. Improved light microscopical detection of microsporidia spores in stool and duodenal aspirates. N Engl J Med 1992; 326: 161–166.
45. van Gool T, Hollister WS, Schattenkerk JE et al. Diagnosis of *Enterocytozoon bieneusi* microsporidiosis in AIDS patients by recovery of spores from faeces. Lancet 1990; 336(8716): 697–698.
46. Orenstein JM, Chiang J, Steinberg W, Smith PD, Rotterdam H, Kotler DP. Intestinal microsporidiosis as a cause of diarrhoea in human immunodeficiency-infected patients: a report of 20 cases. Hum Pathol 1990; 21: 475–485.
47. Orenstein JM, Tenner M, Cali A, Kotler DP. A microsporidian previously undescribed in humans, infecting enterocytes and macrophages, and associated with diarrhea in an Acquired Immunodeficiency Syndrome patient. Hum Pathol 1992; 23: 722–728.
48. Rolston KVI, Hoy J, Mansell PWA. Diarrhoea caused by 'non-pathogenic amoebae' in patients with AIDS. N Engl J Med 1986; 315: 192.
49. Allason-Jones E, Mindel A, Sargeaunt P, Williams P. *Entamoeba histolytica* as a commensal intestinal parasite in homosexual men. N Engl J Med 1986; 315: 353–356.
50. Goldmeier D, Sargeaunt PG, Price AB et al. Is *Entamoeba histolytica* in homosexual men a pathogen? Lancet 1986: 641–644.
51. Hawkins CC, Gold JWM, Whimbrey E et al. Mycobacterium avium complex infections in patients with the acquired immunodeficiency syndrome. Ann Intern Med 1986; 105: 184–188.
52. Boettger EC, Teske, A Kirschner P et al. Disseminated 'Mycobacterium genavense' infection in patients with AIDS. Lancet 1992; 340: 76–80.
53. Wang HW, Tollerud D, Danar D, Hanff P, Gottesdiener K, Rosen S. Another Whipple-like disease in AIDS? N Engl J Med 1986; 314: 1577–1578.
54. Gillin JS, Shike M, Alcock N et al. Malabsorption and mucosal abnormalities of the small intestine in the acquired immunodeficiency syndrome. Ann Intern Med 1985; 102: 619–622.
55. Kotler DP, Gaetz HP, Lange M, Klein EB, Holt PR. Enteropathy associated with the acquired immunodeficiency syndrome. Ann Intern Med 1984; 101: 421–428.
56. Riecken EO, Zeitz M, Ullrich R. Non-opportunistic causes of diarrhoea in HIV infection. Gazzard BG. (Ed) Bailliere's Clinical Gastroenterology 1990; 4: 385–403.
57. Ullrich R, Heise W, Bergs C, L'Age M, Riecken EO, Zeitz M. Gastrointestinal symptoms in patients infected with human immunodeficiency virus: relevance of infective agents isolated from gastrointestinal tract. Gut 1992; 33: 1080–1084.
58. Jarry A, Cortez A, Rene E et al. Infected cells and immune cells in the gastrointestinal tract of AIDS patients: an immunohistochemical study of 127 cases. Histopathology 1990; 16: 133–140.
59. Clayton F, Reka S, Cronin WJ, Torlakovic E, Sigal SH, Kotler DP. Rectal mucosal pathology varies with human immunodeficiency virus antigen content and disease stage. Gastroenterology 1992; 103: 919–933.
60. Cummins AG, LaBrooy JT, Stanley DP, Rowland R, Shearman DJC. Quantitative histological study of enteropathy associated with HIV infection. Gut 1990; 31: 317–321.
61. Greenson JK, Belitsos PC, Yardley JH, Bartlett JG. AIDS enteropathy: occult enteric infections and duodenal mucosal alterations in chronic diarrhea. Ann Intern Med 1991; 114: 366–372.
62. Heise C, Dandekar S, Kumar P, Duplantier R, Donovan RM, Halsted CH. Human immunodeficiency virus infection of enterocytes and mononuclear cells in human jejunal mucosa. Gastroenterology 1991; 100: 1521–1527.
63. Smith PD, Quinn TC, Strober W, Janoff EN, Masur H. Gastrointestinal infections in AIDS. Ann Int Med 1992; 116: 63–77.
64. Griffin GE, Miller A, Batman P et al. Damage to jejunal intrinsic autonomic nerves in HIV infection. AIDS 1988; 2: 379–382.
65. Friedman SL. Kaposi's sarcoma and lymphoma of the gut in AIDS. Gazzard BG. (Ed) Bailliere's Clinical Gastroenterology 1990; 4: 455–475.
66. Friedman SL, Wright TL, Altman DF. Gastrointestinal Kaposi's sarcoma in patients with acquired imrnunodeficiency syndrome. Gastroenterology 1985; 89: 102–108.
67. Gottlieb MS, Groopman JE, Weinstein WM, Fahey JL, Detels R. The acquired immunodeficiency syndrome. Ann Intern Med 1983; 99: 208–220.
68. Safai B, Johnson KG, Myskowski PL et al. The natural history of Kaposi's sarcoma in the acquired immunodeficiency syndrome. Ann Intern Med 1985; 103: 744–750.
69. De Jarlais DC, Marmor M, Thomas P, Chamberland M, Zolla-Pazner, Spencer DJ. Kaposi's sarcoma among four different AIDS risk groups. N Engl J Med 1984; 310: 1119.
70. Haverkos H, Drotman DP, Morgan M. Prevalence of Kaposi's sarcoma among patients with AIDS. N Engl J Med 1985; 312: 1518.
71. Beral V, Peterman TA, Berkelman RL, Jaffe HW. Kaposi's sarcoma among persons with AIDS: a sexually transmitted infection? Lancet 1990; 335: 123–128.
72. Beral V, Bull D, Darby S, Weller I, Carne C, Beecham M, Jaffe H. Risk of Kaposi's sarcoma and sexual practices associated with faecal contact in homosexual or bisexual men with AIDS. Lancet 1992; 339: 632–635.
73. Millard PR, Esiri MM. The pathology of AIDS. Eds. Anthony

PP, MacSween RNM. Recent Advances in Histopathology 1992; 15: 67–92.
74. Ensoli M, Nakamura S, Salahuddin SZ et al. AIDS-Kaposi's sarcoma-derived cells express cytokines with autocrine and paracrine growth effects. Science 1989; 243: 223–226.
75. Werner S, Horschneider PH, Heldin C-H, Ostman A, Roth WK. Cultured Kaposi's sarcoma-derived cells express functional PDGF A-type and B-type receptors. Experimental Cell Research 1990; 187: 98–103.
76. Ziegler JL, Beckstead JA, Volberding PA et al. Non-Hodgkin's lymphoma in 90 homosexual men. Relation to generalized lymphadenopathy and the acquired immunodeficiency syndrome. N Engl J Med 1984; 311: 565–570.
77. Knowles DM, Chamulak GA, Subar M et al. Lymphoid neoplasia associated with the acquired immunodeficiency syndrome (AIDS). Ann Intern Med 1988; 108: 744–753.
78. Knowles DM, Chamulak GA, Subar M et al. Clinicopathologic, immunophenotypic, and molecular genetic analysis of AIDS-associated lymphoid neoplasia. In: Rosen PP, Fechner RE (Eds) Pathology Annual 1988 2: 33–67. Norwalk, CT: Appleton and Lange.
79. Palefsky JM, Gonzales J, Greenblatt RM, Ahn DK, Hollander H. Anal intraepithelial neoplasia and anal papillomavirus infection among homosexual males with group IV HIV disease. JAMA 1990; 263: 2911–2916.
80. McDonald GB, Shulman HM, Sullivan KM, Spencer GD. Intestinal and hepatic complications of human bone marrow transplantation. Part 1. Gastroenterology 1986; 90: 466–477.
81. McDonald GB, Shulman HM, Sullivan KM, Spencer GD. Intestinal and hepatic complications of human bone marrow transplantation. Part 2. Gastroenterology 1986; 90: 770–784.
82. Storb R, Thomas ED. Graft-versus-host disease in dog and man: the Seattle experience. Immunol Rev 1985; 88: 215–238.
83. McDonald GB. Graft-versus-host disease of the intestine and liver. Immunol Allerg Clin Nrth America 1988; 8: 543–557.
84. Witherspoon RP, Storb R. Immunologic aspects of marrow transplantation. Immunol Allerg Clin Nrth America 1989; 9: 187–208.
85. Cox GJ Jr, McDonald GB. Graft-versus-host disease of the intestine. Springer Semin Immunopathol 1990; 12: 283–299.
86. Snover DC. Graft-versus-host disease of the gastrointestinal tract. Am J Surg Pathol 1990; 14 (Suppl 1): 101–108.
78. Parkman R. Graft-versus-host disease. Annu Rev Med 1991; 42: 189–197.
88. Bombi JA, Palou J, Bruguera M et al. Pathology of bone marrow transplantation. Sem Diag Pathol 1992; 9: 220–231.
89. Glucksberg H, Storb R, Fefer A et al. Clinical manifestations of graft-versus-host disease in human recipients of marrow from HLA-matched sibling donors. Transplantation 1974; 18: 295–304.
90. Weisdorf DJ, Snover DC, Haake R et al. Acute upper gastrointestinal graft-versus-host disease: clinical significance and response to immunosuppressive therapy. Blood 1990; 76: 624–629.
91. Sullivan KM. Graft-versus-host disease. In: Blume KG, Petz LD, eds. Clinical bone marrow transplantation. New York: Churchill Livingstone 1983: 91–129.
92. Sullivan KM, Shulman HM, Storb R et al. Chronic graft–versus-host disease in 52 patients: adverse natural course and successful treatment with combination immunosuppression. Blood 1981; 57: 267–276.
93. Weiden PL, and the Seattle Marrow Transplant Team: Graft-vs-host disease in allogeneic marrow transplantation. In: Gale RP, Fox CF, eds. Biology of bone marrow transplantation. New York: Academic Press 1980: 37–48.
94. Weiden PL, Sullivan KM, Flournoy N et al. Antileukaemic effect of chronic graft-versus-host disease: Contribution to improved survival after allogeneic marrow transplantation. N Eng J Med 1981; 304: 1529–1533.
95. Mowat AM, Borland A, Parrott DMV. Hypersensitivity reactions in the small intestine. VII. Induction of the intestinal phase of murine graft-versus-host reaction by Lyt2$^-$ T cells activated by I-A alloantigens. Transplantation 1986; 41: 192–198.
96. Mason DW, Dallman M, Barclay AN. Graft-versus-host disease induces expression of Ia antigen in rat epidermal cells and gut epithelium. Nature 1981; 293: 150–151.
97. Guy-Grand D, Vassalli P. Gut injury in mouse graft-versus-host reaction: study of its occurrence and mechanisms. J Clin Invest 1986; 77: 1584–1595.
98. Spits H, Ijssel H, Thompson A, de Vries JE. Human T4$^+$ and T8$^+$ cytotoxic T lymphocyte clones directed at products of different Class II Major Histocompatibility Complex Loci. J Immunol 1983; 131: 678–683.
99. Mizuochi T, Ono S, Malex TR, Singer A. Characterisation of two distinct primary T cell populations that secrete interleukin 2 upon recognition of Class I or Class II Major Histocompatibility Antigens. J Exp Med 1987; 163: 603–619.
100. Mowat AM, Ferguson A. Hypersensitivity reactions in the small intestine. Vl. Pathogenesis of the graft-versus-host reaction in the small intestinal mucosa of the mouse. Transplantation 1981; 32: 238–243.
101. Piguet P-F, Grau GE, Allet B, Vassalli P. Tumor necrosis factor/cachectin is an effector of skin and gut lesions of the acute phase of graft-versus-host disease. J Exp Med 1987; 166: 1280–1289.
102. Mowat AM. Antibodies to interferon-gamma prevent immunologically mediated intestinal damage in murine graft-versus-host reaction. Immunology 1989; 68: 18–23.
103. Wagemaker G, Vriesendorp HM, Van Bekkum DW. Successful bone marrow transplantation across major histocompaability barriers in rhesus monkeys. Transplant Proc 1981; 13: 875–880.
104. Storb R, Prentice RL, Buckner CD et al. Graft-versus-host disease and survival in patients with aplastic anaemia treated by marrow grafts from HLA-identical siblings. Beneficial effect of a protected environment. N Engl J Med 1983; 308: 302–307.
105. Beschorner WE, Yardley JH, Tutschka P, Santos G. Deficiency of intestinal immunity with graft-versus-host disease in humans. J Infect Dis 1981; 144: 38–46.
106. Korngold R, Sprent J. Lethal GVHD across minor histocompatibility barriers: nature of the effector cells and role of the H-2 complex. Immunol Rev 1983; 71: 5–29.
107. Snover DC, Weisdorf SA, Vercellotti GM, Rank B, Hutton S, McGlove P. A histopathologic study of gastric and small intestinal graft-versus-host disease following allogeneic bone marrow transplantation. Hum Pathol 1985; 16: 387–392.
108. Lampert IA, Thorpe P, van Noorden S, Marsh J, Goldman JM, Gordon-Smith EJ, Evans DJ. Selective sparing of enterochromaffin cells in graft-versus-host disease affecting the colonic mucosa. Histopathology 1985; 9: 875–886.
109. Rosen FS, Cooper MD, Wedgwood RJP. The primary immunodeficiencies. (First of two parts.) N Engl J Med 1984; 311: 235–242.
110. Rosen FS, Cooper MD, Wedgwood RJP. The primary immunodeficiencies. (Second of two parts.) N Engl J Med 1984; 311: 300–310.
111. Huber J, Zegers BJM, Schuurman H-J. Pathology of congenital immunodeficiencies. Semin Diag Pathol 1992; 9: 31–62.
112. Rosen FS, Wedgwood RJ, Aiuti F et al. Primary immunodeficiency diseases: report prepared for the WHO by a Scientific Group on Immunodeficiency. Clin Immunol Immunopathol 1983; 28: 450–475.
113. Schwaber J, Molgaard H, Orkin SH, Gould HJ, Rosen FS. Early pre-B cells from normal and X-linked agammaglobulinaemia produce C*f* without an attached V_H region. Nature 1983; 304: 355–358.
114. Vetrie D, Vorechovsky I, Sideras P et al. The gene involved in X-linked agammaglobulinaemia is a member of the src family of protein-tyrosine kinases. Nature 1993; 361: 226–233.
115. Lederman HM, Winkelstein JA. X-linked agammaglobulinaemia: an analysis of 96 patients. Medicine 1985; 64: 145–156.
116. Ament ME, Ochs HD, Davis SD. Structure and function of the gastrointestinal tract in primary immunodeficiency syndromes. A study of 39 patients. Medicine 1973; 52: 227–248.
117. Ross IN, Asquith P. Primary immune deficiency. In: Asquith P, ed. Immunology of the gastrointestinal tract. New York: Churchill Livingstone, 1979: 152–182.

118. Ament ME. Immunodeficiency syndromes and the gut. Scand J Gastroenterol 1985; 20(Suppl 114): 127–135.
119. Kirkpatrick CH. Cancer and immunodeficiency diseases. Birth Defects: Original Article Series 1976; 12: 61–78.
120. Fleisher TA, White RM, Broder S et al. X-linked hypogammaglobulinaemia and isolated growth hormone deficiency. N Engl J Med 1980; 302: 1429–1434.
121. Hoffman T, Winchester R, Schulkind M, Frias JL, Ayoub EM, Good RA. Hypogammaglobulinaemia with normal T cell function in female siblings. Clin Immunol Immunopathol 1977; 7: 364–371.
122. Sperber KE, Mayer L. Gastrointestinal manifestations of common variable immunodeficiency. Immunol Allerg Clin North Amer 1988; 8: 423–434.
123. Twomey JJ, Jordan PH, Jarrold T et al. The syndrome of immunoglobulin deficiency and pernicious anaemia. Am J Med 1969; 47: 340–350.
124. Hermans PE, Diaz-Buxo JA, Stobo JD. Idiopathic late-onset immunoglobulin deficiency. Am J Med 1976; 61: 221–237.
125. Dubois RS, Roy CC, Fulginiti VA et al. Disaccharidase deficiency in children with immunologic defects. J Pediatr 1970; 76: 377–385.
126. Corlin RF, Pops MA. Nongranulomatous ulcerative jejunoileitis with hypogammaglobulinaemia. Gastroenterology 1972; 62: 473–478.
127. Doe WF, Booth CC. Two brothers with congenital pancreatic exocrine insufficiency, neutropenia and hypogammaglobulinaemia. Proc Roy Soc Med 1973; 66: 1125.
128. Cunningham-Rundles C. Selective IgA deficiency and the gastrointestinal tract. Immunol Allerg Clin North Amer 1988; 8: 435–449.
129. Holt PD, Tandy NP, Anstee DJ. Screening of blood donors for IgA deficiency: a study of the donor population of South-West England. J Clin Pathol 1977; 30: 1007–1010.
130. Koistinen J, Sarna S. Immunological abnormalities in the sera of IgA deficient blood donors. Vox Sanguinis 1976; 29: 203–213.
131. Andre C, Andre F, Fargier MC. Distribution of IgA_1 and IgA_2 plasma cells in various normal human tissues and in the jejunum of plasma IgA-deficient patients. Clin Exp Immunol 1978; 33: 327–331.
132. Strober W, Krakauer R, Klaeveman HL et al. Secretory component deficiency. A disorder of the IgA immune system. N Engl J Med 1976; 294: 351–356.
133. Cunningham-Rundles C, Oxelius V-A, Good RA. IgG_2 and IgG_3 subclass deficiencies in selective IgA deficiency in the United States. Birth Defects 1983; 19: 173–176.
134. Ugazio AG, Out TA, Plebani A et al. Recurrent infections with 'selective' IgA deficiency: association with IgG_2 and IgG_4 deficiency. Birth Defects 1983; 19: 169–172.
135. Polmar SH, Waldman TA, Balestra ST, Jost MC, Terry WD. Immunoglobulin E in immunologic deficiency diseases. 1. Relation of IgE and IgA to respiratory tract disease in isolated IgE deficiency, IgA deficiency, and ataxia-telangiectasia. J Clin Invest 1972; 51: 326–330.
136. Bjorkander J, Bake B, Oxelius V-A, Hanson LA. Impaired lung function in patients with IgA deficiency and low levels of IgG_2 or IgG_3. N Engl J Med 1985; 313: 720–724.
137. Dosch H-M, Jason J, Gelfand EW. Transient antibody deficiency and abnormal T suppressor cells induced by phenytoin. N Engl J Med 1982; 306: 406–409.
138. Cunningham-Rundles C. Genetic aspects of IgA deficiency. Adv Hum Genet 1990; 19: 235–266.
139. Ginsberg A, Mullinax F. Pernicious anaemia and monoclonal gammopathy in a patient with IgA deficiency. Am J Med 1970; 48: 787–791.
140. Ammann AJ. Immunodeficiency diseases. In: Stites DP, Stobo JD, Fudenberg HH, Wells JV, eds. Basic and Clinical Immunology. Fifth Edition. Los Altos: Lange 1984: 384–422.
141. Blum PM, Hong R, Stiehm ER. Spontaneous recovery of selective IgA deficiency. Clin Pediatr 1982; 21: 77–80.
142. Hobbs JR, Hepner GW. Deficiency of gamma-M-globulin in coeliac disease. Lancet 1968; i: 217–220.
143. Louw JH. Polypoid lesions of the large bowel in children, with particular reference to benign polyposis. J Pediatr Surg 1968; 3: 195–209.
144. Rambaud J-C, de Saint-Louvent P, Marti R et al. Diffuse follicular lymphoid hyperplasia of the small intestine without primary immunoglobulin deficiency. Am J Med 1982; 73: 125–132.
145. Colon AR, DiPalma JS, Leftridge CA. Intestinal lymphonodular hyperplasia of childhood: patterns of presentation. J Clin Gastroenterol 1991; 13: 163–166.
146. Johnson VL, Goldberg LS, Pops MA, Weiner M. Clinical and immunological studies in a case of nodular lymphoid hyperplasia of the small bowel. Gastroenterology 1971; 61: 369–374.
147. Kohler PF, Cook RD, Brown WR, Manguso RL. Common variable hypogammaglobulinaemia with T-cell nodular lymphoid interstitial pneumonitis and B-cell nodular lymphoid hyperplasia: different lymphocyte populations with a similar response to prednisone therapy. J All Clin Immunol 1979; 70: 299–305.
148. Hermans PE, Huizenga KA, Hoffman HN, Brown AL, Markowitz H. Dysgammaglobulinaemia associated with nodular lymphoid hyperplasia of the small intestine. Am J Med 1966; 40: 78–79.
149. Gonzalez-Vitale JC, Gomez LG, Goldblum RM, Goldman AS, Patterson M. Immunoblastic lymphoma of small intestine complicating late-onset immunodeficiency. Cancer 1982; 49: 445–449.
150. Matuchansky C, Touchard G, Lemaire M et al. Malignant lymphoma of the small bowel associated with diffuse nodular lymphoid hyperplasia. N Engl J Med 1985; 313: 166–171.
151. Horowitz S, Lorenzsonn VH, Olsen WA, Albrecht R, Hong R. Small intestinal disease in T cell deficiency. J Pediatr 1974; 85: 457–462.
152. Record CO, Eddleston AL, Shilkin KB, Williams R. Intrahepatic sclerosing cholangitis associated with a familial immunodeficieny syndrome. Lancet 1973; ii: 18–20.
153. Thomas IT, Ochs HD, Wedgwood RJ. Liver disease and immunodeficiency syndromes. Lancet 1974; i: 311.
154. Hirschhorn R, Vawter GF, Kirkpatrick JA Jr, Rosen FS. Adenosine deaminase deficiency: frequency and comparative pathology in autosomally recessive severe combined immunodeficiency. Clin Immunol Immunopathol 1979; 14: 107–120.
155. Carson DA, Goldblum R, Seegmiller JE. Quantative immunoassay for adenosine deaminase in combined immunodeficieny disease. J Immunol 1977; 118: 270–273.
156. de Saint Basile G, Fischer A. X-linked immunodeficiencies: clues to genes involved in T- and B-cell differentiation. Immunol Today 1991; 12: 456–461.
157. Herrod HG. Chronic mucocutaneous candidiasis in childhood and complications of non-*Candida* infection: A report of the Pediatric Immunodeficiency Collaborative Study Group. J Pediatrics 1990; 116: 377–382.
158. Kirkpatrick CH. Chronic mucocutaneous candidiasis. Eur J Clin Microbiol Infect Dis. 1989; 8: 448–456.
159. Lawler CJ, Ammann AJ, Wright WC, La Franchi SH, Bilstrom D, Stiehm ER. The syndrome of cellular immunodeficiency with immunoglobulins. J Pediatr 1974; 84: 183–192.
160. Ament ME. Immunodeficiency syndromes and gastrointestinal disease. Pediatr Clin North Am 1975; 22: 807–825.
161. Lupski JR, Langston C, Friedman R, Ledbetter DH, Greenberg F. Di George anomaly associated with a de novo Y;22 translocation resulting in monosomy del(22)(q11.2). Am J Med Genet 1991; 40: 196–198.
162. Stevens CA, Carey JC, Shigeoka AO. Di George anomaly and velocardiofacial syndrome. Pediatrics 1990; 85: 526–530.
163. Parkman R2, Rappaport J, Geha R et al. Complete correction of the Wiskott-Aldrich syndrome by allogeneic bone marrow transplantation. N Engl J Med 1978; 298: 921–927.
164. Gatti RA, Boder E, Vinters HV, Sparkes RS, Norman A, Lange K. Ataxia-telangiectasia: an interdisciplinary approach to pathogenesis. Medicine 1991; 70: 99–117.
165. Woods CG, Taylor AMR. Ataxia-telangiectasia in the British Isles: the clinical and laboratory features of 70 affected individuals. Quart J Med 1992; 298: 169–179.
166. Swift M, Sholman L, Perry M, Chase C. Malignant neoplasms in

the families of patients with ataxia-telangiectasia. Cancer Res 1976; 36: 209–215.
167. Swift M, Chase CL, Morrell D. Cancer predisposition of ataxia-telangiectasia heterozygotes. Cancer Genet Cytogenet 1990; 46: 21–27.
168. Shaham M, Voss R, Becker Y, Yarkoni S, Ornoy A, Kohn G. Prenatal diagnosis of ataxia-telangiectasia. J Pediatr 1982; 100: 134–137.
169. Gotoff SP, Amirmokri E, Liebner EJ. Ataxia-telangiectasia: neoplasia, untoward response to X-irradiation and tuberous sclerosis. Am J Dis Child 1967; 114: 617–625.
170. Hitzig WH, Kenny AB. The role of vitamin B_{12} and its transport globulins in the production of antibodies. Clin Exp Immunol 1975; 20: 105–111.
171. Touraine JL, Marseglia GL, Beteul H, Souilet G, Gebuhrer L. The bare lymphocyte syndrome. Bone Marrow Transplant 1992; 9 Suppl 1: 54–56.
172. Hawkins HK, Heffelfinger SC, Anderson SC. Leucocyte adhesion deficiency: clinical and postmortem observations. Pediatr Pathol 1992; 12: 119–130.
173. Jeffries GH. Protein-losing enteropathy. In: Sleisenger MH, Fordtran JS, eds. Gastrointestinal disease: pathophysiology, diagnosis, management. Third edition. Philadelphia, PA: WB Saunders 1983: 280–288.
174. Strober W, Wochner RD, Carbone PP, Waldman TA. Intestinal lymphangiectasia: a protein-losing enteropathy with hypogammaglobulinaemia, lymphocytopenia and impaired homograft rejection. J Clin Invest 1967; 46: 1643.
175. Smith RM, Curnutte JT. Molecular basis of chronic granulomatous disease. Blood 1991; 77: 673–686.
176. Dinauer MC. Chronic granulomatous disease. Annu Rev Med 1992; 43: 117–124.
177. Gallin Jl, Buescher ES, Seligmann BE, Nath J, Gaither T, Katz P. Recent advances in chronic granulomatous disease. Ann Intern Med 1983; 99: 657–674.
178. International Chronic Granulomatous Disease Co-operative Study Group. A controlled trial of interferon gamma to prevent infection in chronic granulomatous disease. N Engl J Med 1991; 324: 509–516.
179. Nakleh RE, Glock M, Snover DC. Hepatic pathology of chronic granulomatous disease of childhood. Arch Pathol Lab Med 1992; 116: 71–75.
180. Ament ME, Ochs HD. Gastrointestinal manifestations of chronic granulomatous disease. N Engl J Med 1973; 288: 382–387.
181. Werlin SL, Chusid MJ, Caya J, Oechler HW. Colitis in chronic granulomatous disease. Gastroenterology 1982; 82: 328–331.
182. Royer-Pokora B, Kunkel LM, Monaco AP et al. Cloning the gene for an inherited human disorder — chronic granulomatous disease — on the basis of its chromosomal location. Nature 1986; 322: 32–38.
183. Gallin JI. Interferon-gamma in the management of chronic granulomatous disease. Rev Infect Dis 1991; 13: 973–978.
184. Woodman RC, Erickson RW, Rae J, Jaffe HS, Curnutte JT. Prolonged recombinant interferon-gamma therapy in chronic granulomatous disease: evidence against enhanced neutrophil oxidase activity. Blood 1992; 79: 1558–1562.
185. Blackshaw AJ, Levison DA. Eosinophilic infiltrates of the gastrointestinal tract. J Clin Pathol 1986; 39: 1–7.
186. Johnstone JM, Morson BC. Eosinophilic gastroenteritis. Histopathology 1978; 2: 335–348.
187. Croese TJ. Eosinophilic enteritis — a recent North Queensland experience. Aust NZ J Med 1988; 18: 848–853.
188. Lanham JG, Elkon KB, Pusey CD, Hughes GR. Systemic vasculitis with asthma and eosinophilia: a clinical approach to the Churg-Strauss syndrome. Medicine 1984; 63: 65–81.
189. Fauci AS, Harley JB, Roberts WC, Ferrans VJ, Gralnick HR, Bjornson BH. The idiopathic hypereosinophilic syndrome: NIH Conference. Ann Intern Med 1982; 97: 78–92
190. Johnstone JM, Morson BC. Inflammatory fibroid polyp of the gastrointestinal tract. Histopathology 1978; 2: 349–361.

CHAPTER 13

Metabolic significance of the gut microflora

G. T. Macfarlane G. R. Gibson B. S. Drasar
J. H. Cummings

DISTRIBUTION OF BACTERIA IN THE INTESTINAL TRACT

In man, to a greater extent than in other animals, the areas of permanent bacterial colonization of the gastrointestinal tract are restricted to the lower ileum and large intestine. Intestinal physiology and host defence mechanisms play an important role in preventing invasion of the body by gut bacteria and influence the distribution of these organisms within the bowel. Environmental factors such as diet may also affect the activities and composition of the flora, as do ecological interactions between different species.

The stomach

The stomach receives bacteria from the mouth and the external environment. In man, unlike some other animals, it does not harbour a permanent flora and the bacteriocidal action of gastric juice results from secretion of hydrochloric acid. Immediately after a test meal, about 10^5 bacteria per ml of gastric juice can be isolated, but as pH falls, the bacterial count declines, and few viable cells can be recovered after a pH of about 3 has been attained.[1] Lactobacilli, which are particularly resistant to acid, persist longer than other bacteria. The achlorhydric stomach, whatever the cause, is usually heavily colonized by bacteria, indicating that gastric acid is an important factor in reducing the numbers of pathogenic bacteria entering the small bowel. Experimental evidence for this is afforded by studies of the infective dose of *Vibrio cholerae* in human volunteers, where neutralization of gastric acid with a solution of sodium bicarbonate enables an infection to be initiated by oral administration of a much smaller challenge dose compared to that needed for untreated subjects.[2,3]

The rate of gastric emptying also influences the survivability of bacteria in the stomach. It is controlled by a number of mechanisms of which the most important are pH, osmolarity and meal composition.[4] Gastric contents with an acid pH, high osmolarity and containing fat, empty most slowly. Liquids empty faster than solids and emptying follows an exponential pattern, with a relatively greater volume of material leaving the stomach in the initial period after a meal. Viable bacteria are best able to escape in the early post-meal period when the pH is in the region of 4–5 and substantial volumes of liquid are moving into the duodenum.

The small intestine

Although the restriction on bacterial proliferation in the small gut partly stems from the efficiency of gastric acid in reducing the bacterial load entering the bowel, small intestinal factors also play a role.[5] Samples of small gut contents obtained from fasting European and North American residents contain few if any cultivable bacteria. The viable count seldom exceeds 10^4 per ml of digesta, but for a short period after a meal, an increased number of bacteria, that are probably transients from the mouth, can be isolated from jejunal samples. Although relatively few bacteria can be cultured, microscopy of jejunal juice reveals large numbers of cells, usually exceeding 10^6 per ml of contents. The importance of these bacteria that can be seen but not grown has not yet been determined.

In healthy persons living in Western Europe and North America, the number of cultivable bacteria is lowest in the upper small bowel and greatest in the terminal ileum. Gram positive species predominate among those bacteria isolated and those observed microscopically. Streptococci and lactobacilli are most often isolated, though bacteroides and enterobacteria may be found in small numbers. The organisms seen but not identified are Gram-positive rods and cocci.

These results differ markedly from data obtained during studies of the small intestinal flora in residents of developing countries which show that they have a richer and more permanent flora. The relationship of this flora to nutritional status, nutrient utilization and subclinical disease may have important practical consequences.

The flow rate of gut contents contributes to control of bacterial colonization, being greatest at the top of the small intestine where microbial multiplication usually does not exceed the rate at which organisms are removed. Animal experiments have shown that bacteria are cleared from the small intestine wrapped in intestinal mucus. Among the roles that have been suggested for intestinal antibody is the binding of bacteria to this material. The anatomically normal animal can therefore only be colonized by adhesion to the epithelium, as occurs with some enteropathogenic serotypes of *E. coli*. In the ileum, water is absorbed, reducing the flow rate, which allows bacterial multiplication. The lower small intestine, the distal and terminal ileum contain many more cultivable bacteria than the proximal ileum. Although lactobacilli and streptococci are still prominent, bacteroides and enterobacteria occur more constantly. In the terminal ileum viable bacterial counts of 10^5–10^7 per ml are not uncommon, and the flora here qualitatively begins to resemble that of faeces.[6]

Disorders that interfere with the normal movement of gut contents result in an increased bacterial load in the ileum. Even in the absence of overt disease, slow transit of intestinal contents can allow development of a metabolic blind loop. Although impaired motility undoubtedly contributes to alterations in the distribution of bacteria within the intestine, the exact mechanism is not known. Changes in the distribution of the flora in animals can only be demonstrated as a result of gross alterations in the propulsion of intestinal contents.

The cleansing action of the movement of gut contents down the intestine is probably the most important determinant affecting the distribution of bacteria within the intestine, but in addition to flow rate, pH, redox potential (Eh), intestinal secretions and intestinal immunity also play a part.

No definite anti-bacterial agents have been demonstrated in the human intestine for the organisms that are usually present, and there is no evidence to suggest that intestinal bacteria are destroyed by the action of the succus entericus or pancreatic juice. The enzyme lysozyme is found in intestinal mucus and is able to digest bacterial cell walls. Similarly, bile salts are able to disperse the cell walls and membranes of some bacteria. However, bacteria susceptible to the action of these agents are not usually found in the intestine and it seems likely, therefore, that while lysozyme and bile salts may determine what can grow in the gut they do not control those bacteria that do.

Patients with immunoglobulin deficiencies have more cultivable small intestinal bacteria than normal and this cannot be explained solely on the basis of the achlorhydria often present in these conditions. There is little direct evidence that the immune system has a controlling influence on the indigenous flora, but it is assumed that locally produced secretory IgA (sIgA) antibody plays an important role. However, although increased levels of specific sIgA are produced in response to intestinal infection and are involved in the elimination of pathogens, the mechanism whereby this occurs is unclear. The suggestion has been made that sIgA is able to prevent adhesion of pathogens to the intestinal mucosa and it is possible that the normal mucosal flora is controlled by similar mechanisms.

Studies on germ-free animals show that acquisition of bacteria in the colon is accompanied by a cellular response within the lamina propria and epithelium of the villi.

The large intestine

In the United Kingdom, the adult colon contains approximately 220 g of contents. Bacteria are a major component and about 18 g consist of bacterial dry matter. Bacterial numbers, as estimated by direct microscope counts, increase progressively from the caecum to the rectum. This is shown in Figure 13.1, where samples of gut contents were taken from persons who had died suddenly, within a few hours of death. However, most studies on the colonic flora are made on faeces, which can provide some useful information, since the few investigations where viable

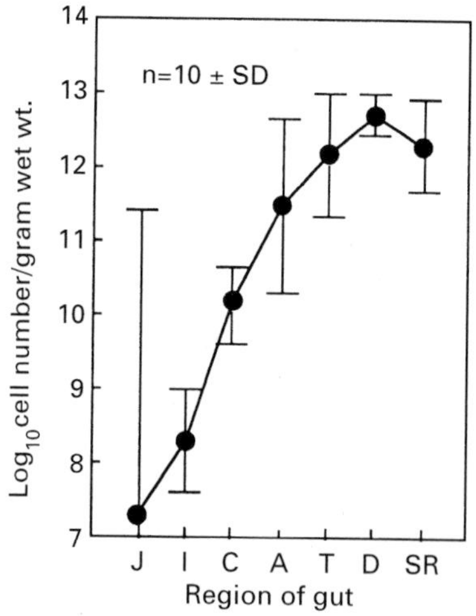

Fig. 13.1 Direct microscope counts of bacteria in human gut contents. J, jejunum; I, ileum; C, caecum; A, ascending colon; T, transverse colon; D, descending colon; S/R, sigmoid/rectum.

counts of bacteria were carried out with gut contents have indicated that with respect to the major taxonomic groups, the gut flora is qualitatively similar to faeces.[7] There is some evidence, however, for the existence of specific mucosa-associated populations, whose functional association with the mucus layer and intestinal wall may be of ecological and metabolic significance to the host.[8]

In colonic contents and faeces, bacterial counts usually exceed 10^{11} per gram dry weight of material. Several hundred different species are present, but some 30–40 species account for about 99% of bacterial mass, and most of these are strict anaerobes.[9] An important factor that facilitates the establishment of such a luxuriant flora is the increase in transit time of gut contents from about 3–4 hours in the small intestine to about 70 hours in the colon.[10]

Interactions between bacteria play an important role in determining both the total numbers and relative frequency of the various species. In any confined environment such as the colon, space and nutrients are limited, and bacteria that transform substrates into bacterial mass at the greatest rate will occur in highest numbers. Species that are able to utilize the waste products of other bacteria or nutrients that are not used by other microorganisms also possess an ecological advantage.

The large intestine is an open system in the sense that digesta from the small bowel enters at one end, and faeces is periodically excreted at the other. Because of this, the colon is often likened to a continuous culture system, but this is probably an oversimplification. Due to the way in which material moves through the gut, only the caecum and ascending colon can really be considered to exhibit characteristics of a continuous culture, since digesta in the remaining colon are frequently present as isolated masses and because there is no further input of substrates or removal of bacteria, gut contents in the distal colon are more likely to resemble batch or fed-batch systems. The proximal colon therefore effectively acts as the primary fermentation chamber and as a reservoir of bacteria.

Attempts have nevertheless been made to study a range of host/flora interactions in terms of continuous culture. In practical terms, this approach has led to the development of model systems that have allowed some of the factors controlling the flora to be identified.[11,12] Of interest has been the demonstration that interactions between bacteria play a dominant role. Although adhesion to specific receptors on the intestinal mucosa by the normal flora has been suggested as an important mechanism by which pathogens are excluded, investigations in continuous culture suggest that most adhesion is between different types of bacteria. These same studies indicate that metabolic poisons produced by bacteria, particularly H_2S may be more significant in their impact on bacterial populations than the fermentation acids previously implicated.[13]

Diet is an important factor that determines the quantitative and qualitative characteristics of the intestinal flora.[9] It probably accounts for the differences in microbial populations between man and herbivores, for example, and is related to the anatomical variations seen in ruminants and the horse, with its greatly enlarged caecum and colon. The role of diet is seen not only in the different microflora of the gut of different animals but also by differences in flora between the adult and neonate of the same species.[14,15,16]

The importance of diet can be demonstrated experimentally using laboratory animals, but similar experiments in man have produced equivocal results — largely because of the necessity of monitoring any changes by culturing the faecal flora.[9]

Studies on people living on different diets in varying environmental circumstances have shown numerical changes in some of the groups of bacteria present in their faeces. These variations may reflect diet, but this is by no means certain because attempts to alter the gut flora by manipulation of the diet have in general been unsuccessful.

Colonic bacteria

Many different types of bacteria representing most bacterial groups have at some time or other been isolated from the large intestine. Those detected most frequently can be considered as members of the resident flora or as regular contaminants from the environment. The number of bacterial groups that are found is related to the methods used for their isolation and characterization. Few researchers have ever attempted a systematic investigation to determine the composition of the gut microflora, and any list of species present must be incomplete.

Table 13.1 shows commonly isolated colonic bacteria. It can be seen that bacterial counts in different individuals range over several orders of magnitude, and that the nutrition and metabolic products of different bacterial groups vary considerably.

Most of the bacteria growing in the colon are non-sporing anaerobes and include members of the genera *Bacteroides*, *Bifidobacterium*, and *Eubacterium* among many others. Clostridia are also represented, though they are outnumbered by the non-sporing anaerobes, as are facultative anaerobes such as streptococci and enterobacteria. Quantitatively, the most important genera of intestinal bacteria in animals and man are the bacteroides and bifidobacteria, which can account for up to 30% and 25% of the total anaerobic counts respectively.[23,24,25] Amongst the Gram-positive, non-sporing rods, several genera are numerically significant. Obligate anaerobic types include eubacteria and bifidobacteria, such as *B. bifidum* and *B. infantis* which are isolated from the faeces of breast-fed infants. The genus *Lactobacillus* contains many species that occur in the guts of most warm-blooded animals. Although numerically important throughout the alimen-

Table 13.1 Cell population densities, nutrition and metabolism of human colonic bacteria.

Bacteria	Description	Numbers reported in faeces Log_{10}/g dry wt		Nutrition	Fermentation products
		Mean	Range		
Bacteroides	Gram negative rods	11.3	9.2–13.5	Saccharolytic	A,P,S
Eubacteria	Gram positive rods	10.7	5.0–13.3	Saccharolytic, some amino acid fermenting species	A,B,I
Bifidobacteria	Gram positive rods	10.2	4.9–13.4	Saccharolytic	A,l,f,e
Clostridia	Gram positive rods	9.8	3.3–13.1	Saccharolytic and amino acid fermenting species	A,P,B,L,e
Lactobacilli	Gram positive rods	9.6	3.6–12.5	Saccharolytic	L
Ruminococci	Gram positive cocci	10.2	4.6–12.8	Saccharolytic	A
Peptostreptococci	Gram positive cocci	10.1	3.8–12.6	As for the clostridia	A,L
Peptococci	Gram positive cocci	10.0	5.1–12.9	Amino acid fermenters	A,B,L
Methanobrevibacters	Gram positive coccobacilli	8.8	7.0–10.5	Chemolithotrophic	CH_4
Desulfovibrios	Gram negative rods	8.4	5.2–10.9	Various[a]	A
Propionibacteria	Gram positive rods	9.4	4.3–12.0	Saccharolytic, lactate fermenting	A,P
Actinomyces	Gram positive rods	9.2	5.7–11.1	Saccharolytic	A,L,S
Streptococci	Gram positive cocci	8.9	3.9–12.9	Carbohydrate and amino acid fermenting	L,A
Fusobacteria	Gram negative rods	8.4	5.1–11.0	Amino acid fermentation, carbohydrate also assimilated	B,A,L
Escherichia	Gram negative rods	8.6	3.9–12.3	As for streptococci	Mixed acid

[a]These bacteria can grow chemolithotrophically on H_2 and CO_2 fermentatively, or oxidatively on some organic acids using SO_4^{2-} as a terminal electron acceptor.
With the exception of the methanogenic bacteria (Miller & Wolin 1982[17]; Jones et al 1987[18]) and the sulphate-reducing bacteria (Gibson et al 1988a[19]; Gibson 1990[20]), the cell count results are taken from Finegold et al (1983)[21], and the fermentation product information from Holdeman et al (1977)[22].
A = acetate; P = propionate; B = butyrate; L = lactate, f = formate; e = ethanol

tary tract, their ecological significance has not been conclusively determined.

Several types of spore-forming rods and cocci are also normal inhabitants of the gut. The genus *Clostridium* is probably the most ubiquitous: *C. perfringens*, *C. bifermentans* and *C. tetani* are regularly isolated, albeit in relatively low numbers, from the lower gut of man and animals, and are of significance in human and veterinary medicine. The presence of aerobic members of the genus *Bacillus* is thought to result from contamination from the environment. Facultative and obligately anaerobic Gram-positive cocci are also numerically important. The strict anaerobes include *Peptostreptococcus*, *Ruminococcus*, *Megasphaera elsdenii* and *Sarcina ventriculi*. The facultatively anaerobic streptococci are well represented by many species from Lancefield group D including *S. faecalis*, *S. bovis* and *S. equinus* and some from group K such as *S. salivarius* which is usually associated with the mouth. Gram-negative anaerobic cocci include *Veillonella* and *Acidaminococcus*.

Although they are not numerous, the Gram-negative facultative anaerobic rods include a number of very important pathogens. Members of the Enterobacteriaceae, particularly *Escherichia coli*, are usually thought of as characteristic intestinal bacteria.

Several types of spirochaete can be seen in the gut of healthy animals, but their status in the human colon is uncertain.[8]

Although bacteria are distributed throughout the gastrointestinal tract, the vast majority occur in the large bowel. The major influences of the gut flora on host metabolism arise from bacterial metabolism of various substances in the colon. Of particular significance in the normal healthy bowel is the fermentation of proteins and carbohydrates.

FERMENTATION IN THE LARGE INTESTINE

In animal physiology the term fermentation is conventionally used to describe the complex series of anaerobic processes in which carbohydrates and proteins are broken down by the gut microbiota. The end products of these reactions are diverse, but quantitatively, ammonia, the short chain fatty acids (SCFA) acetate, propionate and butyrate, and the gases hydrogen, carbon dioxide and methane are the major metabolites formed. The breakdown of carbohydrate and protein in the large intestine by the flora is an integral part of digestion. Through fermentation, digestion is completed; the host gains energy and the orderly disposal of the end products of metabolism is facilitated. The control of fermentation is of major importance in determining colonic function in both health and disease.

Fermentation in the human large intestine has not been extensively studied and many concepts of large gut fermentation have by necessity been drawn from experiments carried out on ruminant animals. However, the rumen and the human large intestinal ecosystems are both functionally dissimilar and anatomically diverse, and although certain similarities do exist between the two systems, there are a number of significant differences that ultimately give rise to characteristically different fermentations.

From a microbiological perspective, the rumen is an energy and nutrient rich environment that receives an animal's total dietary intake. In marked contrast, much of the readily digestible material in the human diet is efficiently absorbed in the small gut and substrates entering the large intestine are therefore composed of materials that, for a variety of reasons, have escaped small intestinal digestion. The more readily fermentable of these substrates (particularly soluble polysaccharides) are rapidly broken down in the caecum, the main site of fermentation in the large gut. As a result, with distal progression along the colon, substantially less carbohydrate is available for fermentation. One consequence of this is that for saccharolytic organisms (bacteria requiring carbohydrate for energy and growth), the colon is frequently an extremely energy deficient environment. A further important point of difference between the rumen and human large intestinal ecosystems is that each contains different and quite distinct anaerobic bacterial populations, and the healthy large intestine, unlike the rumen, does not harbour large numbers of protozoa.

An outline of the major products of the human large gut fermentation is given in Figure 13.2. The major fermentable substrates of dietary origin are carbohydrates, in the form of starch and non-starch polysaccharides (dietary fibre) and protein. Endogenous substrates mainly consist of the polysaccharides and proteins that are present in sloughed epithelial cells and in small intestinal secretions such as mucins and the pancreatic hydrolytic enzymes (amylase, lipases, proteases and aminopeptidases). Like fermentation systems in other animals, acetate, propionate and butyrate are the major SCFA produced in the human large bowel.[26,27] Hydrogen, carbon dioxide and methane are the predominant gaseous products, whilst protein breakdown and amino acid fermentation, in addition, give rise to ammonia, branched chain fatty acids (mainly isobutyrate, isovalerate and 2-methyl-butyrate) and a range of phenols, indoles and amines.

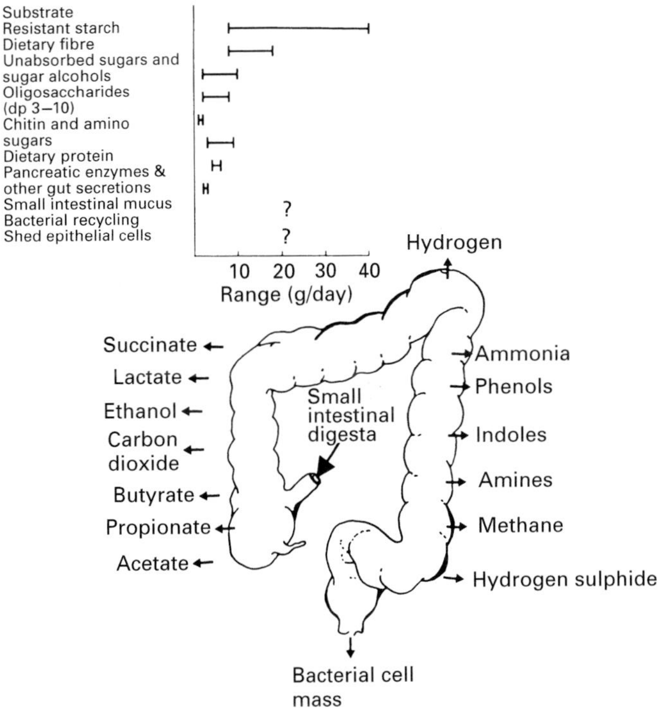

Fig. 13.2 Substrates available for fermentation in the colon and principal metabolic products formed by the microflora.

Carbohydrate fermentation

In the large intestine, saccharolytic bacteria metabolize carbohydrates in order to obtain energy and carbon for growth. One of the effects of fermentation therefore is to stimulate microbial growth in the large gut, so that when people are fed fermentable carbohydrate, faecal microbial mass increases (Fig. 13.3). In man, the yield of bacterial cells (dry weight) is probably about 20–30% of the weight of carbohydrate fermented. Whilst much is now known about carbohydrate breakdown by individual bacterial species, few data are available concerning the fermentation of carbohydrate by mixed populations of bacteria in the large intestine. However, a number of factors such as polymer solubility and chemical composition (see Fig. 13.4), together with the transit time of material through the large intestine (20–120 hours) are thought to be important determinants that affect the degradation of individual carbohydrates.

Available substrates

The majority of bacterial species that inhabit the colon are saccharolytic and until recently it was generally considered that non-starch polysaccharides such as pectin, cellulose and the hemicelluloses that occur in plant cell walls provided the major dietary sources of fermentable carbohydrate for these bacteria.[28] This was primarily because these polysaccharides were not digested by host secretions and so could enter the large gut virtually intact.[29] Recent work has shown however that between 15–20% of the starch in some foods such as potatoes, rice and maize can

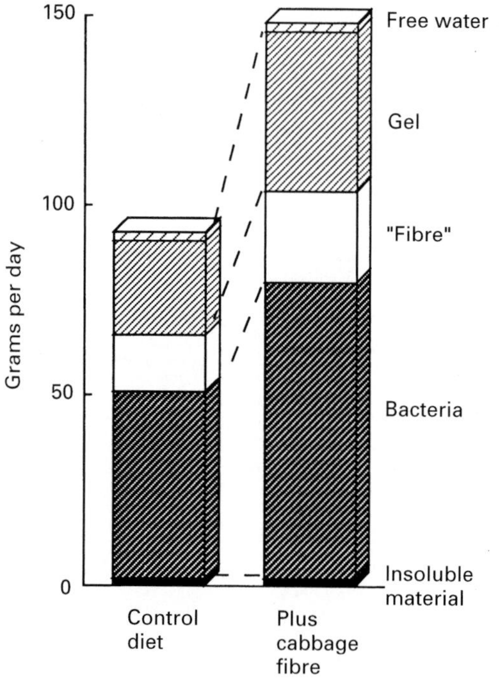

Fig. 13.3 Contribution of bacterial mass to faeces.

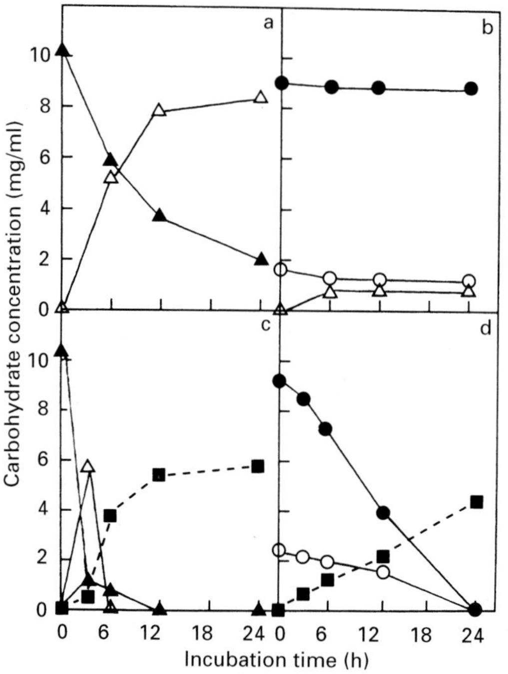

Fig. 13.5 Comparison of in vitro breakdown of readily digestible starch (RDS) and resistant starch (RS) by pancreatic and bacterial amylases associated with faecal water and washed bacteria respectively. Box a: hydrolysis of RDS by pancreatic amylase. Box b: incubation of RS with pancreatic amylase. Box c: breakdown of RDS by washed faecal bacteria. Box d: digestion of RS by washed faecal bacteria. RDS (▲); oligosaccharides (△); RS (●); unknown glucan fraction (○); short chain fatty acids (■).

escape hydrolysis in the small intestine and consequently this resistant starch is also available for fermentation in the large gut.[30] Figure 13.5 shows the relative abilities of pancreatic and bacterial amylases to digest different types of starch. Quantitatively, about 12 g/day of dietary fibre[31] and 3–4 g/day of endogenous carbohydrate[32] have been estimated to enter the colon from the upper gastrointestinal tract. Whilst the amount of starch that escapes digestion is at present largely unknown, values around 30–40 g/day are likely in people eating Western diets. In countries where the diet comprises a greater quantity of starchy foods and vegetables, as in many Third World populations, these amounts may be substantially greater. Table 13.2 shows the polysaccharides that are currently thought to be the major fermentable substrates in the large intestine.

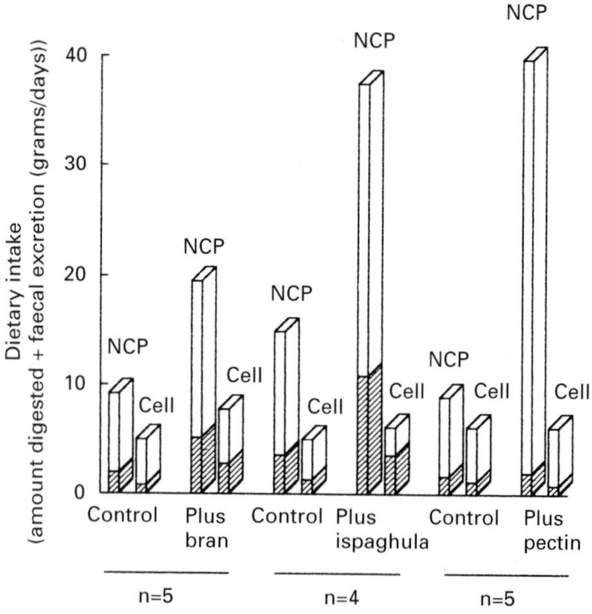

Fig. 13.4 Breakdown of different fibre sources by intestinal bacteria in three groups of healthy volunteers. Open areas show dietary intake and hatched areas show faecal excretion of non-cellulosic polysaccharides (NCP) and cellulose (cell).

Saccharolytic bacteria

Bacteria belonging to the genus *Bacteroides* are both numerically predominant and nutritionally the most versatile polysaccharide degrading organisms in the large gut. Other species belonging to the genera *Ruminococcus*, *Bifidobacterium*, *Clostridium*, *Eubacterium* and *Lactobacillus* also play a role in polysaccharide breakdown. The work of Hoskins and co-workers[33] has shown that ruminococci and some bifidobacteria are particularly important in the breakdown of host produced mucins and most-probable number studies by Miller and Hoskins[34] have suggested that these mucin degrading species can account for approximately 1% of total anaerobes in the colon.

Humans, and mammalian species in general, are not thought to secrete enzymes that can breakdown poly-

Table 13.2 Polysaccharides fermented by bacteria in the large intestine.

Polysaccharide	Constituents	Source	Bacterial genera reported to break down polysaccharide
Chondroitin sulphate	D-glucuronic acid, N-acetyl-D-galactosamine	Epithelial cells	*Bacteroides*
Heparin	D-glucosamine (some N-acetyl, some N-sulphate), D-glucuronic acid	Epithelial cells	*Bacteroides*
Mucins	D-galactose, N-acetyl-D-glucosamine N-acetyl-D-galactosamine, L-fucose	Endogenous secretions	*Bacteroides, Ruminococcus, Bifidobacterium*
Starch	D-glucose	Cereals and some vegetables	*Bacteroides, Bifidobacterium, Eubacterium, Clostridium, Lactobacillus*
Pectin	D-galacturonic acid, L-rhamnose, L-arabinose	Plant cell walls	*Bacteroides, Eubacterium, Lachnospira, Clostridium*
Cellulose	D-glucose	Plant cells walls	*Bacteroides*
Xylan	D-xylose, L-arabinose	Plant cell walls	*Bacteroides, Bifidobacterium*
Arabinogalactan	D-galactose, L-arabinose	Plant cell walls	*Bacteroides, Bifidobacterium*
Gum arabic	L-arabinose, L-rhamnose, D-galactose, D-glucuronic acid	From acacia	*Bifidobacterium*
Guar gum	D-mannose, D-galactose	From cluster beans	*Bacteroides, Ruminococcus*

saccharides other than starch in their gastrointestinal tracts, and so the complete degradation of a heterogeneous polysaccharide by a bacterium to its monomeric constituents requires that the organism produces a range of hydrolytic enzymes. Human intestinal bacteria primarily synthesize cell-associated polysaccharidases which initiate polymer breakdown by hydrolysing the polysaccharide backbone. Glycosidases hydrolyse the polysaccharide side chains and, in addition, further breakdown the backbone oligosaccharides.

The large intestinal ecosystem is an extremely complex environment where a range of cooperating and competing bacterial species is needed to complete the breakdown and metabolism of polymeric substrates. Although polysaccharide degrading bacteria are numerically predominant in the large gut, the cross feeding of products of polysaccharide hydrolysis provides substrates that enables substantial populations of saccharolytic species which cannot degrade polysaccharides themselves to be maintained in the gut. Because these bacteria depend upon substrates becoming available during polysaccharide hydrolysis, it follows that growth of the cross-feeding species is effectively controlled by the activities of the polysaccharide degraders. An outline of the major routes of carbon flow involved in polysaccharide breakdown is shown in Figure 13.6.

Short chain fatty acids (SCFA)

SCFA are the principal end products of fermentation in man and in all animal species. The major SCFA found in the human colon are the C_2 (acetic), C_3 (propionic) and C_4 (butyric) members of the aliphatic monocarboxylic acid series. SCFA are sometimes referred to as volatile fatty acids (VFA) because they are volatile in aqueous solutions at acid pH. It was this property that led to their identification in faeces more than 100 years ago.[35] However, the term VFA has never been clearly defined and it is preferable to call these acids SCFA, or better still by their individual names, since the borderline between short and medium chain fatty acids has not been defined.

Lactate, ethanol and to a lesser degree, succinate are important intermediates in gut fermentation (Fig. 13.6). Ethanol, succinate and lactate can be fermented to SCFA by some gut species such as sulphate-reducing bacteria (SRB) and propionibacteria, and, with the possible exception of ethanol, these metabolites do not accumulate to any extent in the adult large intestine under normal circumstances. These electron sink products are mainly formed by bacteria when fermentable carbohydrate is plentiful, and as is shown in Figure 13.7 occur in greatest amounts in the proximal bowel.

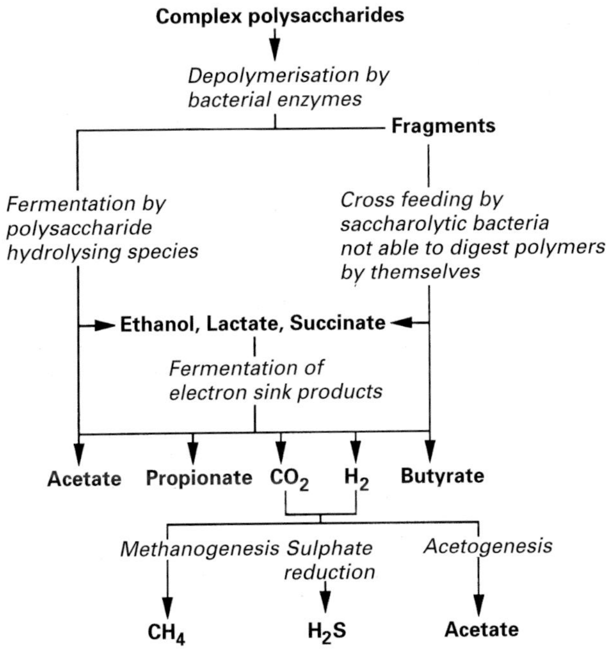

Fig. 13.6 Overview of processes involved in fermentation of polysaccharides by bacteria in the large bowel.

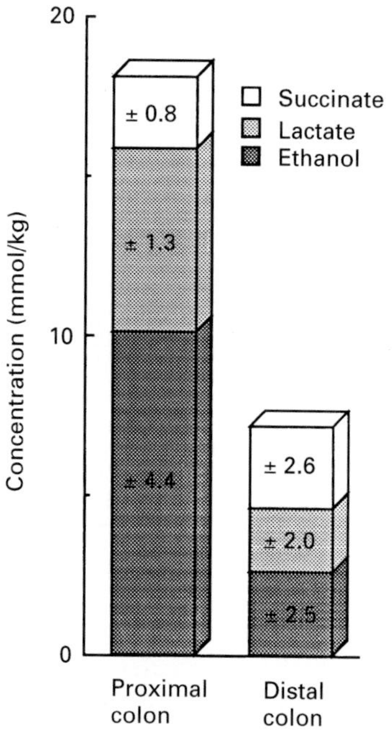

Fig. 13.7 Relative concentrations of electron sink products in different regions of the large intestine (N = 4 ± SD).

Table 13.3 summarises some of the chemical properties of the principal organic anions found in the human colon and lists others occasionally reported to be present. They are all low molecular weight substances with substantial or complete water solubility. Their pKs (dissociation constants) are approximately 4.8, so that at the pH of the small and large intestine they will be ionized and therefore present as fatty acid anions. The amounts and types of SCFA found in various regions of the human gut are shown in Table 13.4. Total SCFA concentrations are low in the small bowel (*c.* 10 mmol/kg contents), but in the colon they are the dominant anions,[36,37] with a total concentration of 80–131 mmol/kg contents.[38] SCFA levels are highest in the caecum and fall progressively towards the distal colon. By contrast, pH is lowest in the proximal colon (5.6) and rises in the distal bowel to 6.3–6.6. These changes in pH and SCFA concentration indicate maximal fermentation occurring in the proximal colon, where carbohydrate availability is greatest. pH may be important in controlling metabolism in different regions of the large bowel. Many microbial enzymes are sensitive to pH changes in the range 5.5–7.5, e.g. bile acid 7-α-dehydroxylase.[39] In all regions, acetate, propionate and butyrate account for 85–95% of total SCFA, with acetate being the principal anion. Molar ratios are similar irrespective of the concentration, at around 57:22:21 acetate:propionate:butyrate. The branched chain fatty acids (BCFA) isobutyrate and isovalerate are also present in human gut contents, together with some lactate and succinate. BCFA are produced by the deamination of branched chain amino acids and have been shown to account for about 3.4% of total SCFA in the proximal colon, rising to 7.5% in the distal bowel.[40] It was concluded from these data that SCFA production from protein could potentially account for about 17% of total SCFA produced in the caecum and up to 38% of the SCFA in the sigmoid/rectum.

In general, the concentrations of SCFA found in the human colon are very similar to those occurring in the rumen and hind gut of other animal species.[41]

Absorption

SCFA production by intestinal bacteria is beneficial to the host for a variety of reasons (Table 13.5). They are rapidly taken up from the human gut,[42,43] and absorption rates in the rectum, descending and transverse colon are comparable to those observed in animals:[44] e.g. human 6.1–12.6 μmol/cm²/h; cf. horse 8 μmol/cm²/h,[45] pig 8–10 μmol/cm²/h,[46] and from the cow's rumen 10.5 μmol/cm² /h.[47,48]

Table 13.3 Organic acids found in the human colon.

Common name	Proper name	Formula	Molecular weight	pk
Major acids				
Acetic acid	Acetic acid (ethanoic acid)	CH_3COOH	60	4.75
Propionic acid	Propanoic acid	CH_3CH_2COOH	74	4.87
Butyric acid	Butanoic acid	$CH_3(CH_2)_2COOH$	88	4.81
Other organic acids				
Formic acid	Formic acid (methanoic acid)	$HCOOH$	46	3.75
Lactic acid	2-hydroxy-propanoic acid	$CH_3CH(OH)COOH$	90	3.08
Isobutyric acid	2-methyl-propanoic acid	$(CH_3)_2CHCOOH$	88	4.84
Valeric acid	Pentanoic acid	$CH_3(CH_2)_3COOH$	102	4.82
Isovaleric acid	3-methyl-butanoic acid	$(CH_3)_2CHCH_2COOH$	102	4.77
Caproic acid	Hexanoic acid	$CH_3(CH_2)_4COOH$	116	4.83
Succinic acid	Butanedioic acid	$(CH_2COOH)_2$	118	4.21 5.64

Other organic acids may be present but at concentrations of less than 1.0 mmol/kg. Data from Wrong et al 1965;[38] Rubinstein et al 1969;[37] Cummings et al 1987.[36]

Table 13.4 pH short chain fatty acid and other organic anions* in the human intestine.

	Small intestine		Large intestine		
	Jejunum	Ileum	Caecum	Transverse	Sigmoid/Rectum
pH	5.9 (0.1)	6.3 (0.1)	5.6 (0.2)	6.2 (0.1)	6.3 (0.2)
Acetate	0.6 (0.6)	7.9 (4.1)	69.1 (5.0)	57.9 (5.4)	50.1 (16.2)
Propionate	—	1.5 (1.0)	25.3 (3.7)	23.1 (2.8)	19.5 (6.7)
Iso-butyrate	—	0.3 (0.2)	2.1 (0.4)	2.6 (0.5)	1.9 (0.8)
Butyrate	—	2.3 (1.3)	26.1 (3.8)	24.4 (2.2)	17.9 (5.6)
Iso-valerate	—	0.1 (0.1)	2.7 (0.5)	3.4 (0.4)	3.7 (0.9)
Valerate	—	0.2 (0.1)	4.5 (0.5)	4.2 (0.2)	4.3 (0.9)
Iso-caproate	—	0.1 (0.1)	0.6 (0.3)	—	0.9 (0.3)
caproate	—	0.3 (0.2)	1.4 (0.5)	1.7 (0.6)	1.5 (0.3)
Lactate	2.0 (1.2)	13.5 (5.5)	4.5 (1.4)	3.5 (2.2)	1.5 (1.5)
Succinate	3.7 (1.3)	8.3 (3.2)	0.9 (0.2)	1.7 (0.4)	2.1 (1.0)
N^+	6	6	6	5	5

*mmol/kg contents (±1 SEM)
†number of samples. In some cases areas of the large intestine did not contain enough material for analysis.
— none detected (less than 0.1 mmol/kg)
Samples obtained at autopsy from sudden death victims (Cummings et al 1987).[36]

Table 13.5 Importance of intestinal-derived short chain fatty acids in man.

1. Energy source
2. Preserve integrity of colonic mucosa
3. Stimulate sodium and water absorption
4. Lower intestinal pH
5. Aid resistance to bacterial infection

Net movement of SCFA out of the colonic lumen is more rapid than net sodium transport.[42,49]

The exact mechanism whereby these acids are absorbed requires further study in all species, but a number of general characteristics emerge from published reports. Transport from the lumen is associated with the appearance of bicarbonate ions and stimulation of sodium absorption, and is independent of bulk water flow.[49,50] A major route is by passive diffusion in the protonated form across the colonocyte membrane.[51,52] Hydrogen ions may be available from CO_2 conversion into carbonic acid, which would account for the bicarbonate accumulation; or from an electroneutral Na^+–H^+ exchange. This latter mechanism would explain the close relationship between Na^+ and SCFA absorption seen in most studies.[53] Significant regional differences in SCFA transport occur.[51]

In blood

As shown in Table 13.6, SCFA can be detected in human portal and peripheral blood.[36,54,56] Mean fasting peripheral blood acetate levels are in the range 40–80 μmol/l in healthy subjects with very little (< 5 μmol/l) propionate or butyrate. In portal blood, all three acids are found in a ratio of about 70:20:10 acetate:propionate:butyrate, and total concentrations of up to 500 or 600 μmol/l. The fall in the relative amount of butyrate compared with that

Table 13.6 Short chain fatty acids in human blood (μmol/l ± SEM).

	Acetate	Propionate	Butyrate	n
UK autopsy				
Portal:	258 (40)	88 (28)	29 (8)	6
Baragwanath surgical				
Portal:	271 (44)	96 (11)	56 (9)	6–11
Arterial:	134 (34)	16 (9)	11 (3)	6–11

Blood taken into heparin-lithium, centrifuged and frozen prior to analysis by freeze-transfer and gas-liquid chromatography as previously described (Pomare et al 1985).[54]

present in the colonic lumen is evidence of mucosal uptake of this particular fatty acid. The total SCFA concentration in the hepatic vein is only 40% of that in portal blood, at 140 μmol/l, indicating significant hepatic clearance of all three anions.

SCFA appear in portal blood very rapidly during fermentation. When lactulose (a non-absorbable, fermentable disaccharide) is instilled into the caecum, a substantial rise in portal blood levels is seen after only 15 minutes, with peak values occurring soon after.[56] In peripheral blood, only acetate levels respond to fermentation and vary according to the amount and type of substrate. After lactulose, peak levels are reached in 4–6 hours, whilst changes occur more slowly with complex carbohydrates such as pectin or oat bran (Fig. 13.8).[54,57]

Stoichiometry and production rates

The amounts of SCFA produced each day in the human colon can only be determined indirectly. In vitro studies (Fig. 13.9) show that the amount produced (net yield) per gram substrate fermented varies from 34% to 59%. Moreover, the molar ratios of acetate/propionate/butyrate differ markedly among these carbohydrates. Pectin produces almost all acetate (84%) and little butyrate (2%),

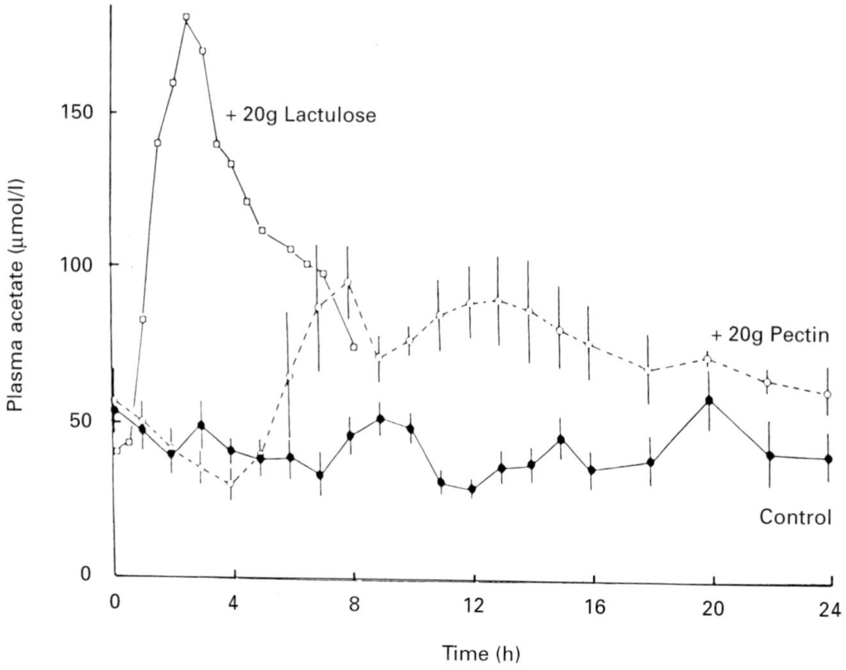

Fig. 13.8 Blood acetate after ingestion of lactulose and pectin.

whereas starch yields 50% acetate and 29% butyrate.[58,59] Since starch probably accounts for about 50% of total fermentable carbohydrate, for each 10 g of carbohydrate fermented, a yield of about 5.5 g SCFA and a molar ratio of 60:23:17 would be expected. Thus, total SCFA is about 80 mmol/10 g fermented, assuming virtually complete breakdown of all these polysaccharides in the colon. The total amount of all substrates fermented in the large bowel is of the order 20–60 g/day.[60] This gives a net yield of about 240–480 mmol SCFA.

An alternative approach to this calculation is to use A/V differences in SCFA across the human gut (Table 13.6). This shows that portal blood levels in two different human populations, although obtained under very different circumstances, are generally similar. A/V differences across the gut of the surgical patients average 262 µmol/l for total SCFA. Assuming a portal blood flow rate of about 1 l/min in man this gives a daily production rate of about 377 mmol (range 50–700), which is equivalent to the fermentation of about 45 g of carbohydrate in the colon. Some endogenous production of SCFA also occurs in man: ileostomy patients, who have no large intestine, have detectable levels of acetate in peripheral blood (*c.* 21±1 µmol/l), moreover, blood acetate levels increase during fasting, along with ketone bodies,[55] suggesting a hepatic source of SCFA in addition to the colon.

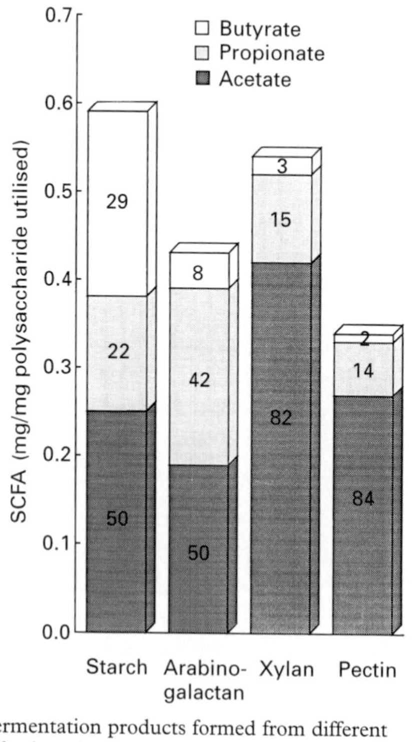

Fig. 13.9 Fermentation products formed from different polysaccharides by mixed populations of gut bacteria. Values in boxes show relative molar ratios.

Metabolism

Acetate, propionate and butyrate produced in the large intestine are each metabolized in different tissues. Butyrate is largely cleared by the colonic epithelium, which derives 60–70% of its energy from bacterial fermentation products generated in the colonic lumen.[61,62] SCFA are partly metabolised to CO_2 and ketone bodies and are precursors for lipid biosynthesis in the mucosa.[61] Roediger[62] has shown that more than 70% of oxygen consumption by colonocytes grown in vitro is due to butyrate metabolism, and that marked intracolonic regional differences in substrate utilization occur. For example, carbon dioxide production from butyrate is similar in both the proximal and distal colons, but ketone body formation is less in the proximal bowel. This suggests that more butyrate enters the TCA cycle in the distal gut and that butyrate is the primary respiratory fuel in this region. Conversely, glutamine metabolism and glucose oxidation appear to be more important in the proximal colon, and in this respect, it resembles the small bowel. Roediger[63] has suggested that the health of colonic epithelial cells is largely dependent on the availability and efficient metabolism of butyrate.

Propionate metabolism has been extensively studied in ruminants, where it is a major gluconeogenic precursor[64] but much less is known of the fate of this SCFA in monogastric species such as man. Propionate supplemented diets have been shown to lower serum cholesterol in rats[65,66] and pigs[67,68] either by inhibition of hepatic cholesterol synthesis or by redistribution of cholesterol from plasma to the liver.[66] In man, however, no change was seen in total cholesterol levels, although HDL cholesterol increased from 1.36 to 1.51 mmol/l when a group of female volunteers were fed 7.5 g sodium propionate per day.[69]

Acetate is usually present in peripheral blood but is rapidly oxidized and has a short half-life. It is metabolized by cardiac and skeletal muscle and by the brain. It is therefore a valuable fuel in tissues, where it is oxidized as the free fatty acid.[70–73]

Mucosal growth

Butyrate, apart from being an important respiratory fuel for the colonocyte, may also regulate gene expression and cell growth. This SCFA will reversibly change the in vitro properties of human colorectal cancer cell lines by prolonging doubling time and slowing down growth rate.[74] It affects a wide range of cellular enzymes,[75] induces the accumulation of acetylated histones in cell culture and may stabilize chromatin structure during cell division. Low concentrations reduce DNA synthesis in vitro and suppress proliferation of a variety of cell types.[76] Virus-induced cellular de-differentiation can be reversed by butyrate,[77] whilst in rat hepatoma cells, it induces the cell to revert to a more normal appearance and to its becoming anchorage-dependent for growth, a characteristic of non-transformed cells.[78] The effect on the nucleus is through its ability to inhibit histone deacetylase. Smith[79] has demonstrated that by inhibiting histone deacetylase, butyrate allows hyperacetylation of histones to occur. In turn, this 'opens up' DNA structure facilitating access of DNA repair enzymes. He has grown human adenocarcinoma cells at a range of butyrate concentrations of up to 10 mmol/l and shown inhibition of cellular proliferation, which was approximately concentration-dependent. Cells were blocked in GI phase. Cells grown in 5 mmol/l butyrate and exposed to various DNA damaging agents showed increased resistance to ultraviolet radiation damage and to adriamycin with butyrate, but surprisingly, increased sensitivity to X-irradiation. Accessibility of DNA to endonucleases was increased and a compensatory increase in ultraviolet repair incision rates seen.

A number of in vivo studies have also shown that SCFA may play a part in the maintenance of mucosal integrity and growth in the colon. Jacobs,[80] in a series of papers, has reported that when dietary fibre in various forms is added to the diets of rats, the colonic epithelial cell cycle is modified. The fraction of replicating cells increases and differentiation of goblet cell mucin and columnar cell membrane surfaces occurs. These changes are associated with variations in pH, but SCFA are the likely mediators. Sakata[81,82] has reported that SCFA are trophic to the colonic mucosa: using rats with ileal fistulae he instilled a mixture of SCFA into the colon daily and observed an increase in crypt cell production rate appearing within two days, which was independent of luminal pH. In a different series of studies, Rombeau[83] surgically divided the intestine of rats and showed that when SCFA are given intraluminally, healing of the anastomosis was more rapid and effective.

Thus, butyrate, and possibly other SCFA, appear to play a critical role in maintaining colonic epithelial integrity and health, and this may be particularly important in preventing large bowel cancer and in ulcerative colitis.

The rapid progress in our understanding of the genetics of bowel cancer since 1986[84,85] means that the activity of butyrate at a subcellular level can be related more directly to the genetic control of cell growth. Toscani et al[86] showed that the effects of butyrate are relatively specific, acting through a reduction in the expression of c-myc and p53, which are both involved in colorectal cancer, and the induction of the expression of c-fos and other genes. Equally importantly, Gibson et al[87] have shown contrasting effects on differentiation, expression of phenotypic markers and oncogenes between neoplastic and normal colonic epithelial cells induced by butyrate. Thus, a number of mechanisms apparently exist whereby carbohydrate fermentation may protect against large bowel cancer.

Ulcerative colitis

Roediger's work on SCFA has clearly established the important role these acids have in maintaining mucosal integrity.[62,88] He has gone on to suggest that ulcerative colitis may be a disorder of SCFA metabolism in the colonic epithelial cell; in particular, that failure to use butyrate effectively leads to mucosal damage in this condition.[89,90] Moreover, he has shown in rats that by impairing β-oxidation of fatty acids in colonocytes, lesions resembling those of ulcerative colitis can be induced.[91] Decreased faecal concentrations of SCFA have been reported in ulcerative colitis.[92]

These and other findings have led researchers to experiment with the clinical use of SCFA to treat various forms of colitis. One of the first reports concerned the successful resolution of inflammation in four patients with diversion colitis, in whom enemas of mixed SCFA had been instilled intrarectally for two weeks.[93] More recently, the value of SCFA in ulcerative colitis, either used as a mixture[94] or with butyrate alone[95] has shown improvement in both symptoms and histological appearance of the mucosae after two weeks. These studies further support the view that butyrate deficiency may be important in the pathogenesis of ulcerative colitis and other inflammatory conditions.

Homeostatic effects

SCFA may also be one of a number of factors maintaining the stability of the colonic microbial population and, in particular, its resistance to infection. Freter[96,97] gave antibiotics to mice and guinea-pigs and rendered them susceptible to antibiotic-resistant shigellas and vibrios. When an antibiotic resistant *E. coli* was introduced into the gut, the pathogens were eliminated. Similar work[98] showed that mice can be made susceptible to invasion by salmonella by administration of streptomycin. Subsequently, Meynell[99] demonstrated that resistance to invasion was due to the combined effect of low redox potential and SCFA produced by the normal flora. He found, in vitro, that growth of *Salmonella typhimurium* was inhibited by caecal contents and that this was largely due to SCFA. Later, Bohnhoff et al[100,101] showed that antibiotic administration to mice led to a rise in caecal pH, a fall in SCFA concentrations, and conditions which allowed the establishment of salmonella either in vitro or in vivo. Similar findings have been reported to regulate the invasion of pathogenic *E. coli*.[102,103]

Diarrhoea

It has been suggested that SCFA may contribute to diarrhoea, especially in certain malabsorptive states.[104] In children with diarrhoea due to carbohydrate malabsorption, stool output correlates with SCFA output[105,106] and similarly in adults with diarrhoea due to malabsorption,[107] lactose intolerance[108] and catharsis with magnesium sulphate.[109] In some circumstances, SCFA may even induce fluid secretion in the colon.[110] Other evidence for their laxative role comes from a series of studies on the effect of dietary fibre on stool composition in man.[111,112] Here, it was shown that stool weight correlated with SCFA output, and because breakdown of dietary fibre produced SCFA, these were thought to cause increased faecal weight. It is now clear however, that SCFA are absorbed from the colon and that the increase in faecal weight with dietary fibre is due to other factors (see later). Faecal SCFA concentrations remain more or less constant despite dietary changes, so any factor increasing stool weight will increase output of these acids, even laxatives. The change in stool output in diarrhoea caused by carbohydrate malabsorption is largely due to the osmotic effect of malabsorbed sugars.[113–116] Furthermore, it has been pointed out[117] that SCFA production from glucose results in only a small increase in theoretical osmotic pressure, some carbon dioxide is absorbed and bicarbonate reacts with short chain fatty acids as follows:

$$NaHCO_3 + CH_3COOH \rightleftharpoons CH_3COONa + CO_2 + H_2O$$

In addition, acetate stimulates absorption of sodium and water from the colon at pH 6.4.[118] The case against these acids being involved in diarrhoea is strong. However, where SCFA are rapidly generated, the colonic buffering system may not be able to deal with production of acid, and pH will fall. This may impair absorption of salt and water by the colonic mucosa[119] and, in addition, promote lactate (a less well-absorbed anion) formation by the bacteria. Lactate may be important in the diarrhoea of childhood malabsorption, since significant quantities are found in the stools of these children. In general, however, it is difficult to implicate SCFA directly in either the control of faecal output or the genesis of diarrhoea in man.

Gas

Gas production is an integral part of fermentation, and the presence of CO_2, H_2 and CH_4 has been well documented in the human large intestine. In man, about 80% of fermentation gas is excreted as flatus, which has an average composition of N_2 — 68%, O_2 — 1%, CO_2 — 9%, CH_4 — 6% and H_2 — 16%. However, considerable variability has been observed in the composition of flatus gas; e.g. CH_4 has been reported to reach 29% on occasions.[120–124]

The principal substrates for gas production are carbohydrates unabsorbed by the small intestine, protein, mucus and cellular debris which is shed into the gut. The total amount of gas produced each day from fermentation varies, mainly in relation to diet, with values of 0.5–4 l/day being reported.[120–126] A number of studies show that dietary intake of foods such as beans,[122,127,128] some fruit juices,[129] cereal fractions,[130–132] brussel sprouts,[130] and dietary fibre[133,134] substantially increases gas production, as does consumption of non-absorbable sugars such as lactitol and lactulose and other low molecular weight carbohydrates.[122,125,135,136] The precise stoichiometry of intestinal gas production in man is unknown at present, but for rapidly fermented sugars, values of around 45–50 ml H_2 per g carbohydrate have been reported.[135,136] Hourly production of flatus gas is usually less than 100 ml but has been reported to rise to 168 ml in subjects ingesting 51% of their calories as beans,[122] whilst a rate of 346 ml/h was recorded by Levitt et al[137] in a patient with lactose intolerance. In this subject, CO_2 and H_2 comprised 72% of total flatus gas at peak production times. Flatus gas is passed about 14 times a day in healthy subjects, with a volume of between 25–100 ml on each occasion.[120,137] A significant proportion (10–20%) of all gas produced in the large gut is also absorbed and excreted in breath. The major gases present in breath samples are H_2 and CO_2, as well as CH_4 in some individuals.[138–141] Lower amounts of mercaptans (methanediol, ethanediol),[142] ammonia[143] and H_2S[20] can also be detected. A proportion of the hydrogen that remains after absorption and excretion may be metabolized further by the gut microbiota to produce CH_4, H_2S and possibly, acetate.

Hydrogen

In the colon, H_2 is formed by bacteria to dispose of reducing equivalents generated during fermentation. Its formation is largely a result of the oxidation of pyruvate, formate, reduced pyridine nucleotides (NADH, NADPH) and reduced ferredoxins. However, high partial pressure of H_2 in some anaerobic ecosystems may have the effect of lowering the efficiency of fermentation by inhibiting re-oxidation of the reduced co-enzymes.[144]

The excretion of H_2 in breath has been used as a quantitative index of carbohydrate fermentation in man.[145–148] These studies assume that the proportion of H_2 produced is constant, irrespective of the chemical composition of the fermentable substrate, and that breath and flatus excretion are linearly related. However, the data of Christl et al[149] show that this is not necessarily the case. These authors used a whole body calorimeter to measure H_2 and CH_4 excretion in 10 volunteers, during a 36 hour period, in response to varying concentrations of lactulose, pectin and starch. The importance of this study was the use of near physiological conditions. The results conclusively demonstrated that in vivo, different carbohydrates did not give a constant amount of H_2 per unit of substrate fermented. This observation was probably connected with individual substrate preferences of bacteria involved in the fermentations. Christl et al[149] found that on average, 58% of H_2 gas produced was excreted in breath, but this value was variable (range 25–65%), depending on whether low (< 200 ml/day) or high (> 500 ml/day) production rates occurred. The situation is further complicated by the fact that H_2 may potentially be metabolized in the colon by sulphate-reducing,[19] methanogenic[17] or acetogenic bacteria.[150] The standard H_2 breath test is therefore not a particularly suitable method for accurately quantifying carbohydrate fermentation.

Timing of the first appearance of H_2 in breath following an oral dose of lactulose has also been used as a measure of gastrointestinal transit time.[151] The interval between ingestion of lactulose and first appearance of H_2 varies between 30–100 min and is related to the dose used; larger doses giving faster mean transit times (MTT).[151,152] Similarly, higher molecular weight substances also give slower apparent MTT.[133] It is not therefore a true measure of transit time, and other methods are required to determine the average rate of passage for complete meals to the caecum.[153,154] A small proportion (about 5%) of subjects do not produce any detectable H_2 in breath following ingestion of fermentable carbohydrate[155,156] and this may be related to changes in colonic luminal pH during fermentation.[157]

Methane

CH_4 formation in man is altogether more enigmatic than H_2 production. In studies of Western populations, only 30–50% of healthy subjects produce detectable CH_4 in their breath:[135,138,158–162] there is therefore always a number who apparently do not have any detectable CH_4. Table 13.7 shows the proportion of CH_4 producers in different ethnic and patient groups. These data show that clear differences exist: children under the age of 2 do not excrete CH_4, although the proportion of producers gradually rises until adult levels are reached at about the age of 10, and there is a strong association in CH_4 status amongst family members.[141] An unexpectedly high breath CH_4 level occurs in patients with large bowel cancer. Between 80–90% of these patients had detectable CH_4 in breath compared with only about 40% of controls.[159,160] Resection of the tumour causes the frequency of excretion to return to normal healthy population levels. Moreover, the proportion of CH_4 producers is also increased in patients with premalignant bowel conditions such as polyps or ulcerative colitis. Certain pathological conditions of the large intestine would therefore appear to promote CH_4 production. The presence of haem has been suggested as an important factor, but lumenal haemoglobin in the presence of tumour does not appear to influence CH_4 excretor status.[163]

Methanogenic bacteria (MB) in the large bowel have an obligate requirement for H_2. The principal CH_4-producing species is *Methanobrevibacter smithii* which reduces CO_2 with H_2, according to the following equation:[17,164,165]

$$(4H_2 + CO_2 \longrightarrow CH_4 + 2H_2O)$$

Methanosphaera stadtmaniae can also be isolated from some faecal samples and this species combines methanol with H_2 as shown in the equation:[166,167]

$$(H_2 + CH_3OH \longrightarrow CH_4 + H_2O)$$

Table 13.7 Proportion of different populations with detectable methane in breath.

Population	No. in Group	Sex	Age	% Producers	Source
Healthy subjects	100			35	Bond et al 1971[141]
Hospitalized patients	91			32	
Patients taking antibiotics	37			32	
Elderly veterans	35			33	
Mentally retarded	31			93	
Children	20		0–2	0	
Blacks	29	M	35	41	Pitt et al 1980[161]
	40	F	34	47	
Orientals	23	M	31	26	
	23	F	33	22	
Caucasians	51	M	30	35	
	65	F	29	58	
Indians	15	M	35	20	
	10	F	36	50	
Healthy subjects	56	26 M,31 F		61	McKay et al 1981[134]
Healthy subjects	100	50 M,50 F	34	34	Bjorneklett & Jensen 1982[155]
Nigerian adults	159			77	Drasar & Tomkins 1984[162]
older children	47			40	
younger children	49			8	
Healthy subjects	209	106 M,102 F	62.6	40	Haines et al 1977[159]
Large bowel cancer	30	17 M,13 F	61.0	80	
Non-malignant large bowel disease	64	31 M,33 F	61.7	39	
Healthy subjects	156	95 M,61 F	33.7	43	Pique et al 1984[158]
Large bowel cancer	47	23 M,24 F	65.2	91	
Large bowel cancer after surgery	36	19 M,17 F	62.0	47	
Non-malignant large bowel disease	29	13 M,16 F	47.7	41	
Ulcerative colitis	12	6 M,6 F	41.08	75	
Distal ulcerative colitis	12	5 M,7 F	37.0	25	
Colonic polyps	12	6 M,6 F	63.1	75	
Healthy subjects	142	74 M,68 F	35	54	McKay et al 1985[160]
Large bowel cancer	20			50	
Crohn's disease	40			13	
Ulcerative colitis	40	104 M,141 F	49	15	
Pneumatosis cystoides intestinalis	9			11	
Irritable bowel	42			40	
Non-specific diarrhoea	94			42	
Non-gastrointestinal disease	64			53	

In the rumen, methanogenesis has an important effect on the end products of fermentation, by removing H_2 produced from reduced pyridine nucleotides. This removal of H_2 results in an increase in the formation of more oxidized metabolites such as acetate and a decrease in propionate.[168] In contrast to the rumen, methanogenesis does not appear to significantly affect SCFA production in man. Although high concentrations of ethanol may be detected in the proximal colon, lactate and succinate do not accumulate in the large gut, and the molar ratios of acetate, propionate and butyrate are similar in methanogenic and non-methanogenic individuals.[169,170] In this case, the operation of alternative methods of hydrogen disposal may be of some significance (see later).

Unlike H_2, CH_4 production does not seem to change with variations in diet.[127,128,134,135,139,155] Intestinal intubation and sudden death victim studies indicate that CH_4 production predominantly occurs in the distal colon.[151]

From the host viewpoint, the reduction of 4 moles of H_2 to produce 1 mole of CH_4 which is relatively harmless and easily expelled, may be of some clinical importance in relation to reducing gas accumulation in the colon.

Hydrogen sulphide

An alternative pathway for disposal of the H_2 generated from colonic fermentation is through the activities of dissimilatory sulphate-reducing bacteria (SRB). They utilize H_2 according to the equation:[164]

$$4H_2 + SO_4^{2-} + H^+ \longrightarrow HS^- + 4H_2O$$

Faecal samples donated by healthy volunteers living in the United Kingdom and South Africa have been used to determine interactions between colonic SRB and MB.[19] Although the Africans were predominantly CH_4 producers, a strong inverse relationship between methanogenesis and SO_4^{2-} reduction was found to occur in samples from both populations. Subsequent studies with faecal slurries confirmed that the bacteria competed for the mutual growth substrate H_2.[171] In methanogenic individuals, H_2 did not accumulate during 48 h in vitro incubation of faecal slurries, however significant CH_4 production occurred. In their non-methanogenic counterparts, H_2 levels again remained low, but H_2S was a major product. Mixing of the two types of slurry demonstrated that colonic SRB were able to directly outcompete MB for the available H_2. Although many different electron donors are potentially available in the large gut to serve sulphate reduction, species belonging to the genera *Desulfovibrio* and *Desulfobulbus* are particularly efficient H_2 utilizing bacteria.[19] In a competitive environment such as the colon where H_2 is a limiting substrate, SRB are able to lower the partial pressure of H_2 to levels below those at which methanogens are able to effectively compete.[20] For this process to occur, a sufficient supply of electron acceptor (SO_4^{2-}) must be available.[172] Pure culture studies have shown that SRB have a much greater substrate affinity for H_2 than methanogens (Ks for *Desulfovibrio vulgaris* = 1 µmol l^{-1}; Ks for *Methanobrevibacter smithii* = 6 µmol l^{-1}).[173]

The critical role of SO_4^{2-} availability in this relationship was demonstrated by Christl et al.[174] In this study, six methanogenic volunteers were fed a SO_4^{2-} enhanced diet for 10 days (15 mmol/d). During this time, SO_4^{2-} reduction and methanogenesis were continuously monitored and compared with control periods (10 days) either side of the test. In half of the volunteers, the addition of SO_4^{2-} resulted in a rapid decrease in methanogenesis and concomitant stimulation of dissimilatory SO_4^{2-} reducing activities. In the other persons however, the increased availability of SO_4^{2-} had no effect on CH_4 production. These studies suggest that at least two types of methanogenic person exist: one group harbours populations of SRB that are apparently inactive and probably limited by a reduced supply of electron acceptor, although these bacteria are able to grow and outcomplete MB for H_2 when SO_4^{2-} becomes more available. In the other group, SRB are absent. Concentrations of SO_4^{2-} vary markedly in diet (range 2–9 mmol/d).[175] Foods with a high sulphate content include fermented beverages and dried fruits.[175] Endogenous sources of SO_4^{2-} may also make some contribution to the available pool. For example, some host secretions contain highly sulphated glycoproteins, particularly colonic mucins, which may be extensively degraded by the gut flora to release this anion in a free form.[176–181]

Studies by Strocchi et al[182] indicated that enhanced methanogenesis occurred when CH_4 producing faecal samples were mixed with those from non-producers. The explanation given for this observation was that excess H_2 was present in the non-methanogenic slurries, which served as an additional substrate for MB in the mixed environment. It seems therefore that SRB were either absent or inactive in the samples tested, since it is physiologically improbable that given an adequate supply of SO_4^{2-}, MB could outcompete SRB for H_2.

Dissimilatory sulphate reduction is a clinically undesirable method of hydrogen disposal. The common end product of SRB metabolism, H_2S, is highly toxic to the colonic mucosal barrier, and impairs cellular metabolism.[183,184] Coincidentally, the majority of gut disorders arise in the distal colon, where highest numbers and activities of SRB occur.[185] In a study by Florin et al,[186] 23 of 24 patients with ulcerative colitis harboured viable populations of colonic SRB and had elevated H_2S levels in their faeces. Although at present there is no direct evidence to implicate these bacteria in the aetiology of the disease, it is clear that they were able to adapt to some of the symptomatic conditions associated with the disease. Evidence for this arises from experiments with SRB isolated from faeces obtained from colitic patients.[187] Batch and continuous culture studies demonstrated that these bacteria were able to withstand certain clinical manifestations of the disease (high dilution rate, low substrate availability) that did not permit the growth of control cultures.

From the foregoing, it is clear that an inverse relationship between SO_4^{2-} reduction and methanogenesis exists in the large bowel. SO_4^{2-} availability undoubtedly plays a key role in hydrogen utilization. However, other factors such as pH, bacterial distribution in the colon and nutritional status of the individual are also likely to be significant.

The situation is further complicated by the existence of other potential pathways of H_2 disposal by colonic bacteria.[188] For example, homoacetogenic bacteria also grow in the large gut.[150] These organisms are able to combine 4 moles of H_2 with one mole of CO_2 to produce acetate.[164] Energetically however, acetogenesis ($\Delta Go'$ = −95 kJ per mole) is a less favourable route of hydrogen disposal than either sulphate reduction ($\Delta Go'$ = −152.2 kJ per mole) or methanogenesis ($\Delta Go'$ = −131 kJ per mole) and acetogenic bacteria, under normal circumstances, are outcompeted by SRB or MB for H_2.[164] Thus, significant levels of acetogenic activity would only be expected when conditions unfavourable for methanogenesis or sulphate reduction occur.

Gas production in the large bowel is frequently of some concern to patients with digestive disorders, or diseases such as pneumatosis cystoides intestinalis.[189] The underlying mechanisms that control both gas formation and utilization in the gut remain unsolved. However, it is clear that the colonic microflora plays a significant role and that gross physiological differences can occur both between and within distinct populations.

Nitrogen metabolism

Bacteria require nitrogen as well as carbon for growth, and potential sources of N reaching the large gut include urea, proteins and peptides. Ammonia is the preferred N source for many intestinal bacteria and consequently this metabolite plays a central role in the microbial cycling of nitrogen in the colon. High concentrations are found throughout the length of the large bowel (Table13.8) and until comparatively recently it was thought that the main source of this toxic metabolite was urea hydrolysis. However, infusion experiments by Wrong and co-workers[190] have demonstrated that urea hydrolysis does not occur to an appreciable extent in the colon and it is unlikely that this process contributes significantly to ammonia production. Another possible source of ammonia is from dissimilatory reduction of nitrate to ammonia, a process mediated by some clostridia and many facultative anaerobes in the colon. On a quantitative basis however, it is also unlikely that this pathway could account for the large amounts of ammonia found in the large gut and its primary route of formation therefore appears to be via deamination of amino acids that are produced during degradation of proteins. Figure 13.10 shows the principal transformations of nitrogen mediated by bacteria in the large intestine.

Current estimates suggest that about 12–13 g of proteinaceous material, from both dietary and endogenous sources, enter the large gut every day from the upper gastrointestinal tract.[191] As a result, substantial quantities of proteinaceous material are available for fermentation by the gut microflora. Protein degradation and amino acid turnover may therefore be a particularly important, although at present largely unstudied microbiological process in the large bowel.

Table 13.8 Soluble protein and ammonia concentrations in human intestinal contents.

Sampling location in gut	Soluble protein in gut (g/kg)	Ammonia (mmol/kg)
Small intestine:		
Jejunum	25.7	0.9
Ileum	11.7	4.9
Large intestine:		
Caecum	5.8	37.4
Ascending	7.3	26.5
Transverse	13.1	28.7
Descending	12.3	47.7
Sigmoid/rectum	14.4	38.0

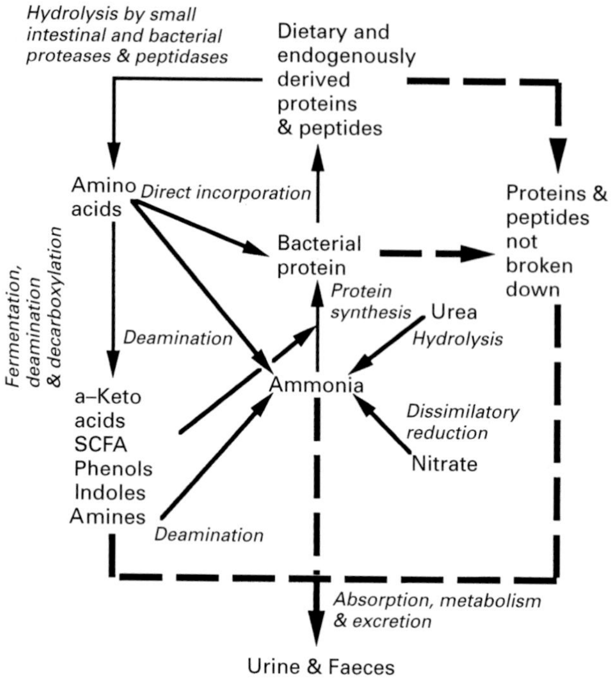

Fig. 13.10 Bacterial transformations of nitrogen in the large intestine.

Human colonic contents are intensely proteolytic[192] as a result of the combined activities of endogenous proteases (i.e. the pancreatic proteases trypsin, chymotrypsin and elastase that are secreted into the small intestine) and bacterial proteases. The distribution of proteolytic activity varies in different fractions of faeces. It can be seen from Table 13.9 that proteolytic activity in gut contents sharply decreases from the small bowel to faeces, due in part to adsorption of pancreatic proteases to epithelial cells and particulate materials, but mainly as a result of their breakdown by the microflora.[11] Comparison of the data from healthy persons and the pancreatectomy patient demonstrates that quantitatively, bacterial proteases contribute significantly to overall proteolysis in the distal colon and that these enzymes are both cell-associated and extracellular. Table 13.10 shows that bacterial proteases are qualitatively different from those produced by the pancreas, since faecal proteolysis results from the actions of serine, thiol and metalloproteases, whereas pancreatic enzymes are of the serine type.

The numerically predominant proteolytic species in the human colon belong to the *Bacteroides fragilis* group.[170] These bacteria, which are also the major fibre degraders in the colon, produce a number of proteases that are primarily cell-associated during active growth and it now appears increasingly likely that bacteroides may also play an important role in large intestinal protein breakdown.

The initial step in the breakdown of protein by gut bacteria is hydrolysis of the substrate to peptides. Some gut bacteria can assimilate these peptides directly, others, however, produce peptidases that degrade them further

Table 13.9 Significance of the microbial contribution towards proteolytic activities in the large intestine.[193]

Test material	Total protease activity in units/gram	% Recovery of activity			
		10% (w/v) faecal suspension	Washed particulate materials	Washed bacteria	Extracellular
Ileostomy effluent*	321 (157–619)	—	—	—	—
Faeces from healthy volunteers†	15.8 (3.3–49.5)	100	32	17	48
Faeces from a pancreatectomy patient‡	6.8 (4.5–8.8)	100	26	36	36

*Samples were taken directly from the ileostomy stoma from five patients and immediately assayed for protease activity.
†Results from 10 healthy persons.
‡Data from five consecutive daily samplings from one individual.
Values in parenthesis show the ranges of activities recorded.

Table 13.10 Characterization of small intestinal and colonic proteolytic activities using specific protease inhibitors.[193]

Protease inhibitor	Class of protease inhibited	% Inhibition of proteolytic activity		
			Faecal fraction†	
		Ileostomy effluent*	Washed bacteria	Extracellular
PMSF	Serine and some cysteine proteases	97.0 ± 5.8	47.8 ± 7.9	32.0 ± 16.7
STI	Trypsin	43.1 ± 4.9	24.2 ± 14.8	37.2 ± 10.0
Chymostatin	Chymotrypsin	53.3 ± 29.5	20.1 ± 7.8	40.9 ± 22.5
Pepstatin A	Aspartic proteases	11.0 ± 4.2	6.8 ± 4.5	5.0 ± 1.2
Thimerosal	Thiol proteases	15.1 ± 7.6	37.0 ± 5.9	28.0 ± 12.2
Iodoacetate	Thiol proteases	12.3 ± 3.7	7.8 ± 1.5	22.4 ± 9.8
EDTA	Metalloproteases	2.2 ± 0.2	4.6 ± 5.6	19.1 ± 5.4
Cysteine	Metalloproteases	1.0 ± 0.4	32.0 ± 7.3	22.0 ± 7.3

*Results are mean values from five persons ± SD.
†Results mean values from 10 persons ± SD.
PMSF, phenylmethylsulfonyl fluoride; STI, soybean trypsin inhibitor.

into dipeptides and amino acids. The amino acids are then metabolized to a wide range of end products. In vitro experiments have shown that when proteins are hydrolysed by suspensions of faecal bacteria, oligopeptides accumulate, but free amino acids do not,[194] which would suggest that in the large intestine, peptide breakdown is the rate limiting step in the bacterial degradation of protein. Although saccharolytic bacteria predominate in the colon, substantial populations of amino acid fermenting species are also present. These bacteria can obtain energy, carbon and nitrogen solely from amino acids and so are metabolically quite distinct from saccharolytic species such as, e.g. the bacteroides and the bifidobacteria, that can assimilate but not ferment certain organic nitrogen containing compounds. Not all amino acid fermenting bacteria are proteolytic, however, and so these species must depend on the proteolytic activities of other bacteria to provide amino acids and peptides.

Amino acids can be deaminated by either oxidative deamination, reductive deamination, hydrolytic deamination, deamination by removal of the elements of ammonia leaving an unsaturated product, and by the mixed amino acid or Stickland reaction, which is carried out by amino acid fermenting clostridia. On the basis of data obtained from in vitro fermentation studies of protein,[194] there is good evidence that the primary method of amino acid deamination by the large intestinal microflora is by reductive deamination, which forms SCFA and ammonia as end products. Dicarboxylic acids, α-keto acids and a range of phenolic compounds (from tyrosine and phenylalanine) are also produced by deamination of amino acids by intestinal bacteria, but quantitatively, the formation of these metabolites is less important than SCFA production.

The other major process involved in amino acid metabolism by intestinal bacteria involves decarboxylation of amino acids to produce amines and carbon dioxide. Amines can however be formed by N-dealkylation reactions,[195] degradation of polyamines[196] and by transamination of aldehydes.[197] Amino acid decarboxylases are optimally produced at acid pH values in some, but not all bacteria, and it is thought that synthesis of these enzymes represents an attempt by the microorganisms to buffer their local environment. Although many large intestinal species such as bacteroides, clostridia, entero-bacteria, streptococci and bifidobacteria are known to decarboxylate amino acids,[197] surprisingly little is known about the extent of amine production in the large gut or of the physiological and biochemical factors that control the process.

Importance for man

Faecal nitrogen was at one time thought to be either undigested dietary protein, or 'endogenous' arising from gastrointestinal secretion and sloughed epithelial cells. It is now clear however that active proteolysis is occurring in the large bowel and that the majority of faecal N is present in bacterial protein.[198–200] As already indicated, the main source of N for bacterial protein synthesis is ammonia. In the absence of active carbohydrate fermentation, much of the ammonia produced from amino acid deamination is absorbed by the colon and converted to urea in the liver. Given a suitable energy source however, the bacteria use ammonia for protein synthesis and bacterial growth is stimulated. In man, feeding dietary fibre increases faecal N while at the same time reducing faecal ammonia concentrations (Fig. 13.11).[201–205] In patients with hepatic cirrhosis, Weber[206] observed that urea production fell and faecal nitrogen excretion rose when the subjects were given lactulose, a non-absorbable disaccharide, suggesting reduction in ammonia recycling from the portal system and an increase in protein synthesis by the flora. Active fermentation therefore routes nitrogen into bacterial protein and in doing so lowers colonic and portal venous blood ammonia levels.[207]

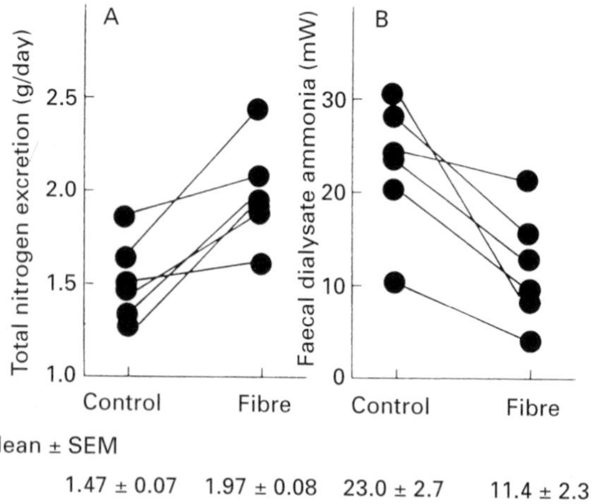

Fig. 13.11 A — Daily faecal nitrogen excretion in healthy subjects during the third week of either a standard diet (control) or the same diet with addition of 18 g dietary fibre from bran; B — Faecal NH_3 concentrations in stools from these subjects.

Ammonia affects the metabolism and morphology of colonic cells and may be a factor in tumour promotion.[208–211] Low concentrations (5–10 mM) alter intermediary metabolism and DNA synthesis, reduce the lifespan of intestinal cells, and induce faster cell turnover. In general, ammonia is more toxic for healthy than for transformed cells and thus a high concentration of ammonia in the bowel lumen may select for neoplastic growth. Ammonia, by increasing cell turnover, increases the probability of genetic damage occurring in the presence of oncogenic agents. Dividing cell populations are more susceptible to chemical carcinogenesis[212] and the concept of non-specific injury and cancer promotion is long-standing in medicine. Experimental evidence relating large bowel injury and dimethylhydrazine-induced tumours shows that cell kinetics are of fundamental importance during chemical carcinogenesis. Further evidence relating ammonia, cell turnover, and cancer is seen in ureterosigmoidostomy patients. These patients have very high lumenal ammonia concentrations (up to 100 mM)[213] and greatly increased risk of developing tumours distal to the site of the implantation.[214] Fermentation, by reducing ammonia levels, may therefore have important implications for cell division in addition to the effects brought about by butyrate production.

A number of other products of protein and amino acid fermentation are found in the human colon, including BCFA, dicarboxylic acids, amines, phenols and indoles. Little attention has been given to their metabolism in the gut or their importance to the host. It is most probable that they are absorbed and undergo varying fates. The branched chain and dicarboxylic acids are probably cleared by the liver since they are not found in significant amounts in human peripheral blood or urine. Other substances such as the phenols and indoles are excreted in urine where they serve as a further marker of colonic activity. Normal human urine contains 50–100 mg/day volatile phenols, mainly as phenol and p-cresol in the ratio 1:9 and, to a lesser extent, 4-ethyl phenol.[215,216] Phenol and p-cresol are produced by the flora from tyrosine, phenol by aerobes and p-cresol by anaerobes[217,218] and are absent from the urine of germ-free animals.[219] Bone et al[220] reported that p-cresol is produced mainly in the left colon whilst phenol originates in the ileum and caecum. In man, urinary phenol excretion is related both to protein intake and the presence of fibre in the diet. Urinary phenol increases with protein intake and falls when bran is added to the diet, suggesting that when fermentation is stimulated, tyrosine uptake by the flora may be increased for protein synthesis.[221]

Other compounds that are found in the gut that are derived from microbial metabolism include phenylacetic and phenylpropionic acids from phenylalanine[222] together with indole (indican) and indole 3-acetic acid, which are products of tryptophan breakdown. Urinary indican excretion has been used as an index of gut bacterial metabolism in man, and in particular in the diagnosis of the syndrome of small bowel bacterial overgrowth.[223,224] However, its value in these circumstances is limited since the amount excreted varies with diet, the occurrence of malabsorption, small bowel bacterial numbers, pH of intralumenal contents[225] and large bowel production and absorption of these metabolites.[226] A number of these products have been implicated in bladder and bowel cancer.[221,227]

Amino acid decarboxylation leads to the production of various amines in the gut, the importance of which is largely unknown. Histamine, 5-hydroxytryptamine, tyramine, piperidine, pyrrolidine, cadaverine, putrescine and agmatine have been identified in vivo.[197] They are all potentially important substances with pharmacological and physiological properties. For example, tyramine is a vasoconstrictor that can cause hypertensive crises in some individuals.[228] However, most amines are probably absorbed and deaminated by histaminase and monoamine and diamamine oxidases in the mucosa and liver.

Although the physiological significance of amine formation by bacteria in the large intestine remains to be established, amines have been implicated in the aetiology of hepatic coma[229] and psychological disorders such as migraine.[230] The direct relationship between dietary protein intake and amine excretion observed in infants[231] and adults indicate that some of the epidemiological findings relating protein in the diet to increased incidence to disease[195] might be explained by high levels of amine production by intestinal bacteria.

Amines may play a role in colon cancer as precursors of N-nitroso-compounds.[232,233] These substances can be formed chemically by condensation of a secondary amine with nitrite under acid conditions,[234] or the reactions can be catalysed by bacterial enzymes at neutral pH.[232,235,236] N-nitrosamines have been detected in faeces by many workers,[237,238] and several bacteria isolated from faeces possess the ability to carry out N-nitrosation of a variety of secondary amines.[232,235] The degree of nitrosamine formation in the colon depends on the availability of amines and nitrate/nitrite, as well as the pH of the local environment. Therefore, the acid pH of the proximal colon, together with relatively high nitrate availability may potentiate nitrosamine production.[232,238]

Bacteria, fermentation and the control of bowel habit

It is widely recognized that increased intakes of dietary fibre lead to changes in bowel habit, and in particular to increased stool output and the alleviation of constipation.[239] The mechanism by which fibre leads to changes in bowel habit is complex and probably involves a number of pathways, most of which are controlled by the microflora.

First, plant cell walls which resist breakdown by the microflora, e.g. because of lignification as in bran, are able to exert a physical effect on intestinal bulk by retaining water within their cellular structure. Increasing bulk stimulates colonic movement. Secondly, most forms of dietary fibre are extensively degraded by the microflora. The result of this is to stimulate microbial growth and increase excretion of microbial products in faeces.[240] This again contributes to the change in faecal mass. Thirdly, substances that increase bulk in the large intestine often speed up the rate of passage through the bowel. As transit time falls, so the efficiency with which the bacteria grow on dietary fibre improves.[241,242] Shortened transit time also leads to reduced water absorption by the colon and therefore wetter stools.[240] Fourthly, dietary fibre is an important source of gas in the colon. Gas trapped within gut contents again add to their bulk. These mechanisms together combine to increase stool mass.

THE PATHOLOGICAL SIGNIFICANCE OF BACTERIAL METABOLISM

Malabsorption

Few bacteria are usually isolated from the small intestine; but in patients with the blind or stagnant loop syndrome, numerous organisms may be present. There is some evidence to suggest that bacteria are important in the aetiology of tropical malabsorption, but their role requires further study. Undoubtedly, however, the presence of bacteria in the small intestine can influence host metabolism in many ways.

The composition of the bacterial flora of blind loops has been variously reported.[197] Animal investigations suggest that at least three or four species of bacteria are always involved. Studies in man have shown that *E. coli* is usually present, together with *Bacteroides fragilis*, *Clostridium perfringens* and *Streptococcus faecalis*. Some investigators have demonstrated the presence of bifidobacteria and other non-sporing anaerobes in addition to *B. fragilis*. Anaerobic bacteria are usually present in greater numbers than aerobic species, but the extent of this dominance varies at different locations within the intestine of an individual and the extent and type of colonization varies in different patients.[243]

Patients with tropical malabsorption, and many normal tropical residents, also have bacteria in the small intestine.[244,245] Some investigators have considered this 'contaminated bowel syndrome' to be analogous to the stagnant loop syndrome. However, the number of bacteria involved is not so large (Fig. 13.12) and it is unlikely that the direct metabolic effects observed in the blind loop syndrome occur. The type and number of bacteria found in blind loops determine their effect on host metabolism. Thus, strictures, fistulae, afferent loops, etc. that do not give rise to changes in the bacterial flora are often without

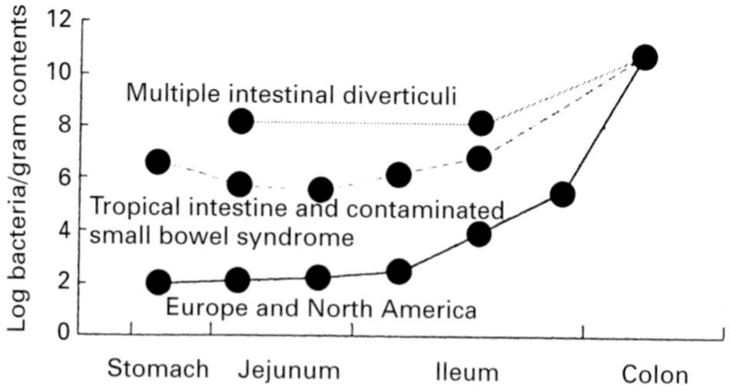

Fig. 13.12 Distribution of bacteria in the gastrointestinal tract of healthy individuals in Europe, North America and the tropics; in patients with contaminated bowel syndrome and in a patient with stagnant loop syndrome due to multiple intestinal diverticula.

metabolic impact. The degree of metabolic competition exerted by the bacteria depends in part on the total numbers present in the digestive and absorptive regions of the intestine, but the minimal effective bacterial mass has not been determined.

It is thought that many of the various types of malabsorption can be explained in terms of either (i) alteration in host metabolism brought about by the bacteria, or (ii) the result of the host's inability to compete for nutrients with its bacterial flora. The malabsorption of vitamin B_{12} — due to direct competition with bacteria — and malabsorption of fat — as a result of metabolism of bile acids by the bacteria — are the best understood examples of these interactions. Indeed, the metabolism of bile acids forms the basis of the non-invasive glycocholate breath test for bacterial colonization. Here, a sample of ^{14}C-labelled glycocholate is given to the patient by mouth and if the bacteria in the blind loop hydrolyse the substrate, $^{14}CO_2$ can be detected in expired air.

Bacteria present in blind loops are potentially able to metabolize a large number of chemicals including drugs, food additives, hormones, etc. Their possible influence is great. Effects that have been reported range from anomalous xylose absorption to infantilism. The significance of the bacteria in the contaminated bowel syndrome is less well understood and the mechanisms involved are certainly more subtle.

Large bowel cancer

The large intestine is the second most common site for the occurrence of carcinomas in man.[246] The role of the intestinal flora in the aetiology of large bowel cancer has been subject to active investigation since the late 1960s. Although there is no general agreement concerning the aetiology of these diseases, a number of factors such as diet, environment and genetics have all been implicated. The earliest published formulation of a testable hypothesis was that of Aries et al[247] and the theory has been modified by many investigators since then. Much of the available information has been extensively reviewed,[248] but the basic hypothesis is that the intestinal bacteria are able to produce carcinogens and that this process may be modified by diet.

Cancer of the large bowel is primarily a disease of developed communities. It is common in North America and Western Europe but rare among the indigenous populations of Africa, South America and Asia. These differences cannot be explained on the basis of differences of the genetic origins of the populations, since, in the United States, there are no marked differences in large bowel cancer incidence between the various established racial groups, although first generation immigrants maintain the pattern of incidence found in their country of origin. Similarly, studies in South Africa and Hawaii have shown that lifestyle and not geographical location determines cancer incidence. Changes in diet are an important part of the cultural adaptation associated with immigration. There is no agreement as to the contribution of various dietary components in the causation of large bowel cancer, but fibre and fat have been widely discussed. A major problem is the lack of adequate dietary data and estimates of cancer incidence for people living in low incidence areas. For example, such data are only available for three countries in Africa.

Major problems have also arisen in attempts to demonstrate the effects of diet on the gut flora. Although diet is often regarded as one of the most important factors controlling the intestinal flora in man, direct evidence is very difficult to obtain and the results of recent studies suggest that non-dietary factors may be more significant.

The relationship of the bacterial flora of the colon and rectum to diet has been examined in the faeces of populations with very different diets and cancer incidence in patients with large bowel cancer and in patients with various other diseases, including several non-neoplastic disorders. Populations with known dietary habits such as vegetarians and vegans have been studied in particular countries. In general, populations that consume the major part of their calories as fat are those with the highest cancer incidence.

Attempts to alter the gut flora by dietary manipulation, including supplementation of fibre, and studies — even when they are of the double-blind crossover type — are all open to the objection that uncontrollable changes may occur. Some of the problems can be overcome if subjects are maintained in a closely supervized metabolic ward, but at present no clear results linking particular bacteria with particular items of diet have emerged. Differences between the flora of individuals seem to be greater than any changes that may be induced. The bacterial flora of faeces includes several hundred distinct species of bacteria, but of these, perhaps 100 have been isolated with any regularity. The considerable methodological problems involved in studying large numbers of bacterial isolates makes it possible to identify only two or three dominant species in each of the individual groups under investigation. Consequently, fairly major changes in the gut flora probably remain undetected in such investigations.

It is the ability of bacteria to produce carcinogens, mutagens and co-carcinogens from substrates that include endogenous molecules such as tyrosine, tryptophan and bile acids, natural products such as cycasin, food additives such as cyclamate and tartrazine and environmental chemicals such as benzopyrene that has stimulated this type of research. *Bacteroides thetaiotaomicron* and some other bacteroides, for example, produce fecapentaenes[249] which are conjugated ether lipids with potent mutagenic activity. If further progress is to be made it will be necessary to show how carcinogen production is influenced by diet. This will in turn involve study of the events leading to the induction of cancer in the large gut mucosa. The development of improved bacteriological methodologies for the study of intestinal ecology will be an essential part of these advances.

REFERENCES

1. Drasar BS, Shiner M, McLeod GM. Studies on the intestinal flora. 1. The bacterial flora of the gastrointestinal tract in healthy and achlorhydric persons. Gastroenterology 1969; 56: 71–79.
2. Gianella RA, Broitman SA, Zamcheck N. The influence of gastric acidity on bacterial and parasitic infections. Ann Int Med 1973; 78: 271–276.
3. Hornick RB, Music SI, Wenzel R. The Broad Street pump revisited: response of volunteers to ingested cholera vibrios. Bull NY Acad Med 1971; 47: 1181–1191.
4. Kelly KA. Motility of the stomach and gastroduodenal junction. In: Johnson LR, ed. Physiology of the Gastrointestinal Tract. New York: Raven Press, 1981, pp. 393–410.
5. Justus PG, Martin JL, Goldberg DA, Taylor NS, Bartlett JG, Alexander RW, Matthias JR. Myoelectric effects of *Clostridium difficile*: motility-altering factors distinct from its cytotoxin and enterotoxin in rabbits. Gastroenterology 1982; 83: 836–843.
6. Gorbach SL, Plaut AG, Nahas L, Weinstein L, Spanknebel G, Levitan R. Studies of intestinal microflora. II. Microorganisms of the small intestine and their relations to oral and fecal flora. Gastroenterology 1967; 53: 856–867.
7. Bentley DW, Nichols R, Condon RE, Gorbach SL. The microflora of the human ileum and intra-abdominal colon: Results of direct needle aspiration at surgery and evaluation of the technique. J Lab Clin Med 1972; 79: 421–429.
8. Croucher SC, Houston AP, Bayliss CE, Turner RJ. Bacterial populations associated with different regions of the human colon wall. Appl Environ Microbiol 1983; 45: 1025–1033.
9. Finegold SM, Sutter VL, Mathisen GE. Normal indigenous intestinal flora. In: Hentges DJ, ed. Human Intestinal Microflora in Health and Disease. London: Academic Press 1983, pp. 3–31.
10. Cummings JH. Diet and transit through the gut. J Plant Foods 1978; 3: 83–95.
11. Macfarlane GT, Cummings JH, Macfarlane S, Gibson GR. Influence of retention time on degradation of pancreatic enzymes by human colonic bacteria grown in a 3-stage continuous culture system. J Appl Bacteriol 1989; 67: 521–527.
12. Macfarlane GT, Gibson GR. Co-utilization of polymerized carbon sources by *Bacteroides ovatus* grown in a two-stage continuous culture system. Appl Environ Microbiol 1991; 57: 1–6.
13. Freter R. Mechanisms that control the microflora in the large intestine. In: Hentges DJ, ed. Human Intestinal Microflora in Health and Disease. London: Academic Press 1983, pp. 33–54.
14. Ellis-Pegler RB, Crabtree C, Lambert HP. The faecal flora of children in the United Kingdom. J Hyg 1975; 75: 135–142.
15. Bullen CL, Tearle PV, Willis AT. Bifidobacteria in the intestinal tract of infants: An in vivo study. J Med Microbiol 1976; 9: 325–333.
16. Tomkins AM, Bradley AK, Oswald S, Drasar BS. Diet and the faecal microflora of infants, children and adults in rural Nigeria and urban UK. J Hyg 1981; 86: 285–293.
17. Miller TL, Wolin MJ. Enumeration of *Methanobrevibacter smithii* in human feces. Arch Microbiol 1982; 131: 14–18.
18. Jones WJ, Nasgle DP Jnr, Whitman WB. Methanogens and the diversity of archaebacteria. Microb Rev 1987; 56: 135–177.
19. Gibson GR, Macfarlane GT, Cummings JH. Occurrence of sulphate-reducing bacteria in human faeces and the relationship of dissimilatory sulphate reduction to methanogenesis in the large gut. J Appl Bacteriol 1988; 65: 103–111.
20. Gibson GR. Physiology and ecology of the sulphate-reducing bacteria. J Appl Bacteriol 1990; 69: 769–797.
21. Finegold SM, Sutter VL, Mathisen GE. Normal indigenous flora. In: Hentges DJ, ed. Human Intestinal Microflora in Health and Disease. London: Academic Press 1983, pp. 3–31.
22. Holdeman LV, Cato EP, Moore WEC. Anaerobe Laboratory Manual, 4th edn. Blacksburg: Virginia Polytechnic Institute Anaerobic Laboratory, 1977.
23. Macy JM, Probst I. The biology of gastrointestinal bacteroides. Ann Rev Microbiol 1979; 33: 561–594.
24. Mitsuoka T. Taxonomy and ecology of bifidobacteria. Bifid Microf 1984; 3: 11–28.
25. Scardovi V. Genus *Bifidobacterium*. In: Mair NS, ed. Bergey's Manual of Systematic Bacteriology, Vol. 2. New York: Williams & Wilkins 1986, pp. 1418–1434.
26. Kern AC, Slyter LL, Leffel EC et al. Ponies vs steers: microbial and chemical characteristics of intestinal digestion. J Anim Sci 1974; 38: 559–564.
27. Cummings JH. Short chain fatty acids in the human colon. Gut 1981; 22: 763–779.
28. Spiller GA, Chernoff MC, Gates JE et al. Effect of purified cellulose, pectin and a low-residue diet on faecal volatile fatty acids, transit time and faecal weight in humans. Am J Clin Nutr 1980; 33: 754–759.
29. Stephen AM. Effects of food on the intestinal microflora. In: Hunter JO, Jones VA, eds. Food and the Gut. London: Bailliere Tindall, 1985, pp. 57–77.
30. Anderson IH, Levine AS, Levitt MD. Incomplete absorption of the carbohydrate in all purpose wheat flour. New Eng J Med 1981; 304: 891–892.
31. Bingham SA, Williams PR, Cummings J. Dietary fibre consumption in Britain: new estimates and their relation to large bowel cancer mortality. Br J Cancer 1985; 52: 399–403.
32. Stephen AM, Haddad AC, Phillips SF. Passage of carbohydrate into the colon: direct measurements in humans. Gastroenterology 1983; 85: 589–595.
33. Hoskins LC, Augustines M, McKee WB et al. Mucin degradation in human colon ecosystems. J Clin Invest 1985; 75: 944–953.
34. Miller RS, Hoskins LC. Mucin degradation in human colon ecosystems. Fecal population densities of mucin-degrading bacteria estimated by a 'most probable number' method. Gastroenterology 1981; 81: 759–765.
35. Brieger L. Ueber die fluchtigen Bestandtheile der menschlichen Excremente. Journal fur praktische Chemie 1878; 17: 124–138.
36. Cummings JH, Pomare EW, Branch WJ, Naylor CPE, Macfarlane GT. Short chain fatty acids in human large intestine, portal, hepatic and venous blood. Gut 1987; 28: 1221–1227.
37. Rubinstein R, Howard AV, Wrong OM. In vivo dialysis of faeces as a method of stool analysis. IV. The organic anion component. Clin Sci 1969; 37: 549–564.

38. Wrong O, Metcalfe-Gibson A, Morrison BI, Ng ST, Howard V. In vivo dialysis of faeces as a method of stool analysis. I. Technique and results in normal subjects. Clin Sci 1965; 28: 357–375.
39. Midvedt T, Norman A. Parameters in 7-α-dehydroxylation of bile acids by anaerobic lactobacilli. Acta Pathol Microbiol Scand 1968; 72: 313–329.
40. Macfarlane GT, Gibson GR, Beatty E, Cummings JH. Estimation of short-chain fatty acid production from protein by human intestinal bacteria based on branched-chain fatty acid measurements. FEMS Microbiol Ecol 1992; 101: 81–88.
41. Cummings JH. Diet and short chain fatty acids in the gut. In: Hunter JO, Jones VA, eds. Food and the Gut. London: Bailliere Tindall, 1985, pp. 78–93.
42. McNeil NI, Cummings JH, James WPT. Short chain fatty acid absorption by the human large intestine. Gut 1978; 19: 819–822.
43. Ruppin H, Bar-Meir S, Soergel KH, Wood CM, Schmitt MG. Absorption of short chain fatty acids by the colon. Gastroenterology 1980; 78: 1500–1507.
44. McNeil NI. Short chain fatty acid absorption in the human large intestine. MD Thesis, University of Cambridge, 1980.
45. Argenzio RA, Southworth M, Lowe JE, Stevens CE. Interrelationship of Na, HCO_3 and volatile fatty acid transport by equine large intestine. Am J Physiol 1977; 233: E469–E478.
46. Argenzio RA, Southworth M. Sites of organic acid production and absorption in gastrointestinal tract of the pig. Am J Physiol 1974; 228: 454–460.
47. Stevens CE, Stettler BK. Factors affecting the transport of volatile fatty acids across rumen epithelium. Am J Physiol 1966; 210: 365–372.
48. Stevens CE, Stettler BK. Transport of fatty acid mixtures across rumen epithelium. Am J Physiol 1966; 211: 264–271.
49. Argenzio RA, Miller M, von Engelhardt W. Effect of volatile fatty acids on water and ion absorption from the goat colon. Am J Physiol 1975; 229: 997–1002.
50. Argenzio RA, Whipp SC. Interrelationship of sodium, chloride, bicarbonate and acetate transport by the colon of the pig. J Physiol 1979; 295: 315–381.
51. von Engelhardt W, Luciano L, Reale E, Gros G, Rechkemmer G. Transport of SCFA across the large intestinal epithelium of guinea pig. Acta Vet Scand 1989; Suppl 86: 103–106.
52. Soergel KH, Harig JM, Loo FD, Ramaswamy K, Wood CM. Colonic fermentation and absorption of SCFA in man. Acta Vet Scand 1989; Suppl 86: 107–115.
53. Bugaut M. Occurrence, absorption and metabolism of short chain fatty acids in the digestive tract of mammals. Comp Biochem Physiol 1987; 86B: 439–472.
54. Pomare EW, Branch WJ, Cummings JH. Carbohydrate fermentation in the human colon and its relation to acetate concentrations in venous blood. J Clin Invest 1985; 75: 1448–1454.
55. Scheppach W, Pomare EW, Elia M, Cummings JH. The contribution of the large intestine to blood acetate in man. Clin Sci 1991; 80: 177–182.
56. Peters SG, Pomare EW, Fisher CA. Portal and peripheral blood short chain fatty acid concentrations after caecal lactulose instillation at surgery. Gut 1992; 33: 1249–1252.
57. Bridges SR, Anderson JW, Deakins DA, Dillon DW, Wood CL. Oat bran increases serum acetate of hypercholesterolemic men. Am J Clin Nutr 1992; 56: 455–459.
58. Englyst HN, Hay S, Macfarlane GT. Polysaccharide breakdown by mixed populations of human faecal bacteria. FEMS Microbiol Ecol 1987; 95: 163–171.
59. Weaver GA, Krause JA, Miller TL, Wolin MJ. Cornstarch fermentation by the colonic microbial community yields more butyrate than does cabbage fiber fermentation; cornstarch fermentation rates correlate negatively with methanogenesis. Am J Clin Nutr 1992; 55: 70–77.
60. Cummings JH, Gibson GR, Macfarlane. Quantitative estimates of fermentation in the hind gut of man. In: Skadhauge E, Norgaard P, eds. Proceedings of the International Symposium on Comparative Aspects of the Physiology of Digestion in Ruminants and Hindgut Fermenters. Acta Vet Scand 1989, pp. 76–82.
61. Roediger WEW. Short chain fatty acids as metabolic regulators of ion absorption in the colon. Acta Vet Scand 1989; 86: 116–125.
62. Roediger WEW. Role of anerobic bacteria in the metabolic welfare of the colonic mucosa in man. Gut 1980; 21: 793–798.
63. Roediger WEW. Cellular metabolism of short-chain fatty acids in colonic epithelial cells. In: Roche AF ed. Short Chain Fatty Acids: Metabolism and Clinical Importance. Report of the Tenth Ross Conference on Medical Research, Columbus, Ohio, Ross Laboratories 1991, pp. 67–71.
64. Bergman DN, Roe WE, Kon K. Quantitative aspects of propionate metabolism and gluconeogenesis in sheep. Am J Physiol 1966; 211: 793–799.
65. Chen W-JL, Anderson JW, Jennings D. Propionate may mediate the hypocholesterolemic effects of certain soluble plant fibres in cholesterol-fed rats. Proc Soc Exp Biol Med 1984; 175: 215–218.
66. Illman RJ, Topping DL, McIntosh GH, Trimble RP, Storer GB, Taylor MN, Cheng B-Q. Hypocholesterolaemic effects of dietary propionate studies in whole animals and perfused rat liver. Ann Nutr Metab 1988; 32: 97–107.
67. Boila RJ, Salomons MD, Milligan LP, Aherne FX. The effect of dietary propionic acid on cholesterol synthesis in swine. Nutr Rep Internat 1981; 23: 1113–1121.
68. Thacker PA, Bowland JP. Effects of dietary propionic acid on serum lipids and lipoproteins of pigs fed diets supplemented with soybean meal or canola meal. Can J Anim Sci 1981; 61: 439–448.
69. Venter CS, Vorster HH, Cummings JH. Effects of dietary propionate on carbohydrate and lipid metabolism in healthy volunteers. Am J Gastroent 1990; 85: 549–553.
70. Skutches CL, Holroyde CP, Myers RM, Paul P, Reichard GA. Plasma acetate turnover and oxidation. J Clin Invest 1979; 64: 708–713.
71. Lindeneg O, Mellemgaard K, Fabricius J, Lundquist F. Myocardial utilization of acetate, lactate and free fatty acids after ingestion of ethanol. Clin Sci 1964; 27: 427–435.
72. Lundqvist F, Sestoft L, Damggard SE, Clausen JP, Trap-Jensen J. Utilization of acetate in the human forearm during exercise after ethanol ingestion. Clin Invest 1973; 52: 3231–3235.
73. Juhlen-Dannfelt A. Ethanol effects of substrate utilization by the human brain. Scand J Clin Lab Invest 1977; 37: 443–449.
74. Kim YS, Tsao D, Morita A, Bella A. Effect of sodium butyrate and three human colorectal adenocarcinoma cell lines in culture. In: Malt RA, Williamson RCN, eds. Colonic Carcinogenesis. Falk Symposium No 31. Lancaster: MTP Press, 1982: pp 317–323.
75. Prased KN. Butyric acid: a small fatty acid with diverse biological functions. Life Sci 1980; 27: 1351–1358.
76. Hagopian HK, Riggs MG, Swartz LA, Ingram VM. Effect of n-butyrate on DNA synthesis in chick fibroblasts and Hela cells. Cell 1977; 12: 855–860.
77. Leder A, Leder P. Butyric acid, a potent inducer of erythroid differentiation in cultural erythroleukemic cells. Cell 1975; 5: 319–322.
78. Borenfreund E, Schmid E, Bendich A, Franke WW. Constitutive aggregates of intermediate-sized filaments of the vimentin and cytokeratin type in cultured hepatoma cells and their dispersal by butyrate. Exp Cell Res 1980; 127: 215–235.
79. Smith PJ. n-Butyrate alters chromatin accessibility to DNA repair enzymes. Carcinogenesis 1986; 7: 423–429.
80. Jacobs L. Dietary fibre and the intestinal mucosa. In: Cummings JH, ed. The Role of Dietary Fibre in Enteral Nutrition, Abbott International Ltd 1989, pp. 24–35.
81. Sakata T. Effects of indigestible dietary bulk and short chain fatty acids on the tissue weight and epithelial cell proliferation rate of the digestive tract in rats. J Nutr Sci Vit 1986; 32: 355–362.
82. Sakata T. Stimulatory effect of short-chain fatty acids on epithelial cell proliferation in the rat intestine: a possible explanation for trophic effects of fermentable fibre, gut microbes and luminal trophic factors. Br J Nutr 1987; 58: 95–103.
83. Rombeau JL, Rolandelli RH, Kripke SA, Settle RG. Citrus pectin and short-chain fatty acids in intestinal dysfunction: experimental observations and potential clinical applications. In: Cummings JH, ed. The Role of Dietary Fibre in Enteral Nutrition, Abbott International Ltd 1989, pp. 75–84.
84. Herrera L, Kakati S, Gibas L, Pietrzak E, Sandberg AA. Brief

clinical report: Gardner syndrome in a man with an interstitial deletion of 5 q. Am J Med Genetics 1986; 25: 473–476.
85. Fearon ER. Genetic alterations underlying colorectal tumorigenesis. In: Cancer Surveys Vol 12, Tumour Suppressor Genes, the Cell Cycle and Cancer. Imperial Cancer Research Fund 1992, pp. 119–136.
86. Toscani A, Soprano DR, Soprano KJ. Molecular analysis of sodium butyrate-induced growth arrest. Oncogene Res 1988; 3: 223–238.
87. Gibson PR, Moeller I, Kagelari O, Folino M, Young GP. Contrasting effects of butyrate on the expression of phenotypic markers of differentiation in neoplastic and non-neoplastic colonic epithelial cells in vitro. J Gastroenterol Hepatol 1992; 7: 165–172.
88. Roediger WEW. Utilization of nutrients by isolated epithelial cells of the rat colon. Gastroenterology 1982; 83: 424–429.
89. Roediger WEW. The colonic epithelium in ulcerative colitis: an energy-deficiency disease? Lancet 1980; 2: 712–715.
90. Roediger WEW. The starved colon — diminished mucosal nutrition, diminished absorption and colitis. Dis Colon Rectum 1990; 33: 858–862.
91. Roediger WEW, Nance S. Metabolic induction of experimental ulcerative colitis by inhibition of fatty acid oxidation. Br J Exp Path 1986; 67: 773–782.
92. Vernia P, Gnaedinger A, Hauck W, Breuer RI. Organic anions and the diarrhea of inflammatory bowel disease. Dig Dis Sci 1988; 33: 1353–1358.
93. Harig JM, Soergel KH, Komorowski RA, Wood CM. Treatment of diversion colitis with short-chain fatty acid irrigation. N Engl J Med 1989; 320: 23–28.
94. Breuer RI, Buto SK, Christ ML, Bean J, Vernia P, Paoluzi P, DiPaolo MC, Caprilli R. Rectal irrigation with short-chain fatty acids for distal ulcerative colitis. Preliminary report. Dig Dis Sci 1991; 36: 185–187.
95. Scheppach W, Sommer H, Kirchner T, Paganelli G-M, Bartram P, Christl S, Richter F, Dusel G, Kasper H. Effect of butyrate enemas on the colonic mucosa in distal ulcerative colitis. Gastroenterology 1982; 103: 51–56.
96. Freter R. The fatal enteric cholera infection in the guinea pig, achieved by inhibition of normal enteric flora. J Infect Dis 1955; 97: 57–65.
97. Freter R. Experimental enteric *Shigella* and *Vibrio* infections in mice and guinea pigs. J Exp Med 1956; 104: 411–418.
98. Bohnhoff M, Drake BL, Miller CP. Effect of streptomycin on susceptibility of intestinal tract to experimental *Salmonella* infection. Proc Soc Exp Biol Med 1954; 86: 132–137.
99. Meynell GG. Antibacterial mechanisms of the mouse gut. II. The role of Eh and volatile fatty acids in the normal gut. Br J Exp Pathol 1963; 44: 209–219.
100. Bohnhoff M, Miller CP, Martin WR. Resistance of the mouse's intestinal tract to experimental *Salmonella* infection. I. Factors which interfere with the initiation of infection by oral inoculation. J Exp Med 1964; 120: 805–816.
101. Bohnhoff M, Miller CP, Martin WR. Resistance of the mouse's intestinal tract to experimental *Salmonella* infection. II. Factors responsible for its loss following streptomycin treatment. J Exp Med 1964; 120: 817–828.
102. Levison ME. Effect of colon flora and short chain fatty acids on growth in vitro of *Pseudomonas aeruginosa* and Enterobacteriaceae. Infect Immun 1973; 8: 30–35.
103. Abdul P, Lloyd D. Pathogen survival during anaerobic digestion: fatty acids inhibit anaerobic growth of *Escherichia coli*. Biotechnol Letts 1985; 7: 125–128.
104. Fordtran JS. Organic anions in feces. N Engl J Med 1971; 284: 329–330.
105. Torres-Pinedo R, Lavastida M, Rivera CL, Rodriguez H, Ortiz A. Studies on infant diarrhoea. I. A comparison of the effects of milk feeding and intravenous therapy upon the composition and volume of the stool and urine. J Clin Invest 1966; 45: 469–480.
106. Weijers HA, van de Kamer JH, Dicke WK, Ijsseling J. Diarrhoea cause by deficiency of sugar splitting enzymes. Acta paediat, Stockh 1961; 50: 55–71.
107. Bustos-Fernandez LB, Gonzalez E, Marzi A, Paolo MIL. Faecal acidorrhoea. N Engl J Med 1971; 284: 295–298.
108. McMichael HB, Webb J, Dawson AM. Lactose deficiency in adults. Lancet 1965; 1: 717–720.
109. Grove EW, Olmsted WH, Koenig K. The effect of diet and catharsis on the lower volatile fatty acids in the stools of normal men. J Biol Chem 1929; 85: 127–136.
110. Bustos-Fernandez LB, Gonzalez E, Paolo MIL, Celemer D, de Furuya KO. Organic anions induce colonic secretion. Am J Dig Dis 1976; 21: 329–332.
111. Williams RD, Olmsted WH. The effect of cellulose, hemicellulose and lignin on the weight of stool. A contribution to the study of laxation in man. J Nutr 1936; 11: 433–449.
112. Williams RD, Olmsted WH. The manner in which food controls the bulk of faeces. Ann Intern Med 1936; 10: 717–727.
113. Launiala K. The mechanisms of diarrhoea in congenital disaccharide malabsorption. Acta Paediat Scand 1968; 57: 425–432.
114. Launiala K. The effect of malabsorbed sucrose or mannitol-induced accelerated transit on absorption in the human small intestine. Scand J Gastroent 1969; 4: 25–32.
115. Christopher NL, Bayless TM. Role of the small bowel and colon in lactose induced diarrhoea. Gastroenterology 1971; 60: 845–852.
116. Saunders DR, Wiggins HS. Conservation of mannitol, lactulose and raffinose by the human colon. Am J Physiol 1981; 24: G397–G402.
117. Argenzio RA. Physiology of diarrhoea — large intestine. J Am Vet Ass 1978; 228: 454–460.
118. Crump MH, Argenzio RA, Whipp SC. Effects of acetate on absorption of solute and water from the pig colon. Am J Vet Res 1980; 41: 1565–1568.
119. Rousseau B, Sladen GC. Effect of luminal pH on the absorption of water, sodium and chloride by the rat intestine in vivo. Biochim Biophys Acta 1971; 233: 591–593.
120. Kirk E. The quantity and composition of human colonic flatus. Gastroenterology 1949; 12: 782–794.
121. Calloway DH, Murphy EL. The use of expired air to measure intestinal gas formation. Ann NY Acad Sci 1968; 150: 82–95.
122. Steggerda FR. Gastrointestinal gas following food consumption. Ann NY Acad Sci 1968; 150: 57–66.
123. Levitt MD. Volume and composition of human intestinal gas determined by means of an intestinal washout technic. N Engl J Med 1971; 284: 1394–1398.
124. Fleming SE, Calloway DH. Determination of intestinal gas excretion. In: Birch GG, Parker KJ, eds. Dietary Fibre. London: Applied Science Publishers, 1983: pp. 221–254.
125. Tadesse K, Smith D, Eastwood M A. Breath hydrogen (H_2) and methane (CH_4) excretion patterns in normal man and in clinical practice. Quart J Exp Physiol 1980; 65: 85–97.
126. Marthinsen D, Fleming SE. Excretion of breath and flatus gases by humans consuming high-fiber diets. J Nutr 1982; 112: 1133–1143.
127. Steggerda FR, Richards EA, Rackis JJ. Effects of various soybean products on flatulence in the adult man. Proc Soc Exp Biol Med 1966; 121: 1235–1239.
128. Calloway DH. Respiratory hydrogen and methane as affected by consumption of gas-forming foods. Gastroenterology 1966; 51: 383–389.
129. Hickey CA, Calloway DH, Murphy EL. Intestinal gas production following ingestion of fruits and fruit juices. Am J Dig Dis 1972; 17: 383–389.
130. Hickey CA, Murphy EL, Calloway DH. Intestinal gas production following ingestion of commercial wheat cereals and milling fractions. Cereal Chem 1972; 49: 276–282.
131. Meyer S, Calloway DH. Gastrointestinal response to oat and wheat milling fractions in older women. Cereal Chem 1977; 54: 110–119.
132. Bond JH, Levitt, MD. Effect of dietary fiber on intestinal gas production and small bowel transit time in man. Am J Clin Nutr 1978; 31: S169–S174.
133. Tadesse K, Eastwood MA. Metabolism of dietary fibre components in man assessed by breath hydrogen and methane. Br J Nutr 1978; 40: 393–396.
134. McKay L, Brydon WG, Eastwood MA, Smith JH. The influence of pentose on breath methane. Am J Clin Nutr 1981; 34: 2728–2733.

135. Fritz M, Kasper H, Schrezenmeir J, Siebert G. Effect of acarbose on the production of hydrogen and methane and on hormonal parameters in young adults under standardized low-fibre mixed diets. Z Ernahrungswiss 1985; 24: 1–18.
136. Fritz M, Siebert G, Kasper H. Dose dependence of breath hydrogen and methane in healthy volunteers after ingestion of a commercial disaccharide mixture, Palatinit. Br J Nutr 1985; 54: 389–400.
137. Levitt MD, Lasser RB, Schwartz JS, Bond JH. Studies of a flatulent patient. N Engl J Med 1976; 295: 260–262.
138. Levitt MD, Ingelfinger FJ. Hydrogen and methane production in man. Ann NY Acad Sci 1968; 150: 75–81.
139. Levitt MD. Production and excretion of hydrogen gas in man. N Engl J Med 1969; 281: 122–127.
140. Calloway DH, Colasito DJ, Mathews RD. Gases produced by human intestinal microflora. Nature; 212: 1238–1239.
141. Bond JH, Engel RR, Levitt MD. Factors influencing pulmonary methane excretion in man. An indirect method of studying the in situ metabolism of the methane-producing colonic bacteria. J Exp Med 1971; 133: 572–588.
142. Chen S, Zieve L, Mahadevan V. Mercaptans and dimethyl sulfide in the breath of patients with cirrhosis of the liver. J Lab Clin Med 1970; 75: 628–635.
143. Robin ED, Travis DM, Bromberg PA, Forkner CE, Tyler JM. Ammonia excretion by mammalian lung. Science 1959; 129: 270–271.
144. Wolin MJ. The rumen fermentation: a model for microbial interactions in anaerobic ecosystems. Adv Microbial Ecol 1979; 3: 49–77.
145. Bond JH, Levitt MD. Use of pulmonary hydrogen (H_2) measurements to quantitate carbohydrate absorption. Study of partially gastrectomized patients. J Clin Invest 1972; 51: 1219–1225.
146. Calloway DH, Murphy EL, Bauer D. Determination of lactose intolerance by breath analysis. Am J Dig Dis 1969; 14: 811–815.
147. Levitt MD, Donaldson RM. Use of respiratory hydrogen (H_2) excretion to detect carbohydrate malabsorption. J Lab Clin Med 1970; 75: 937–945.
148. Metz G, Jenkins DJA, Peters TJ, Newman A, Blendis LM. Breath hydrogen as a diagnostic method for hypolactasia. Lancet 1975, i: 1155–1156.
149. Christl SU, Murgatroyd PR, Gibson GR, Cummings JH. Production, excretion and metabolism of hydrogen in the large intestine. Gastroenterology 1992; 102: 1269–1277.
150. Lajoie SF, Bank S, Miller TL, Wolin MJ. Acetate production from hydrogen and [^{13}C] carbon dioxide by the microflora of human feces. Appl Environ Microbiol 1988; 54: 2723–2727.
151. Bond JH, Levitt MD. Investigation of small bowel transit time in man utilising pulmonary H_2 measurements. J Lab Clin Med 1974; 85: 546–559.
152. La Brooy SJ, Male P-J, Beavis AK, Misiewicz JJ. Assessment of the reproducibility of the lactulose H_2 breath test as a measure of mouth to caecum transit time. Gut 1983; 24: 893–896.
153. Read NW, Miles CA, Fisher D et al. Transit of a meal through the stomach, small intestine, and colon in normal subjects and its role in the pathogenesis of diarrhea. Gastroenterology 1980; 79: 1276–1282.
154. Read NW, Al-Janabi MN, Bates TE et al. Interpretation of the breath hydrogen profile obtained after ingesting a solid meal containing unabsorbable carbohydrate. Gut 1985; 26: 834–842.
155. Bjorneklett A, Jenssen E. Relationships between hydrogen (H_2) and methane (CH_4) production in man. Scand J Gastroenterol 1982; 17: 985–992.
156. Robb TA, Goodwin DA, Davidson GP. Faecal hydrogen production in vitro as an indicator for in vivo hydrogen producing capability in the breath hydrogen test. Acta Paediatr Scand 1985; 74: 942–944.
157. Perman JA, Modler S, Olson AC. Role of pH in production of hydrogen from carbohydrates by colonic bacterial flora. J Clin Invest 1981; 67: 643–650.
158. Pique JM, Pallares M, Cuso E, Vilar-Bonet J, Gassull MA. Methane production and colon cancer. Gastroenterology 1984; 87: 601–605.
159. Haines A, Metz G, Dilawari J, Blendis L, Wiggins H. Breath methane in patients with cancer of the large bowel. Lancet 1977; ii: 481–483.
160. McKay LF, Eastwood MA, Brydon WG. Methane excretion in man — a study of breath, flatus and faeces. Gut 1985; 26: 69–74.
161. Pitt P, de Bruijn KM, Beeching MF, Goldberg E, Blendis LM. Studies on breath methane: the effect of ethnic origins and lactulose. Gut 1980; 21: 951–959.
162. Drasar BS, Tomkins AM. Breath methane levels and intestinal methanogenesis among rural Nigerians on a local diet. Proc Nutr Soc 1984; 43: 86A.
163. Karlin DA, Mastromarino AJ, Jones RD, Stroehlein JR, Lorentz O. Fecal skatole and indole and breath methane and hydrogen in patients with large bowel polyps or cancer. J Cancer Res Clin Oncol 1985; 109: 135–141.
164. Thauer RK, Jungermann K, Decker K. Energy conservation in chemotrophic anaerobic bacteria. Bacteriol Rev 1977; 41: 100–180.
165. Miller TL, Wolin MJ. Methanogens in human and animal intestinal tracts. System Appl Microbiol 1986; 7: 223–229.
166. Miller TL, Wolin MJ. Oxidation of hydrogen and reduction of methanol to methane is the sole energy source for a methanogen isolated from human feces. J Bacteriol 1983; 153: 1051–1055.
167. Miller TL, Wolin MJ. *Methanosphaera stadtmaniae* gen. nov., sp. nov.: a species that forms methane by reducing methanol with hydrogen. Arch Microbiol 1985; 141: 116–122.
168. Wolin MJ. Metabolic interactions among intestinal microorganisms. Am J Clin Nutr 1974; 27: 1320–1328.
169. Wolin MJ, Miller TL. Carbohydrate fermentation. In: Hentges DJ, ed. Human Intestinal Microflora in Health and Disease. London: Academic Press, 1983, pp. 147–165.
170. Macfarlane GT, Cummings JH. The colonic flora, fermentation, and large bowel digestive function. In: Phillips SF, Pemberton JH, Shorter RG (eds). The large intestine: physiology, pathophysiology and disease. Raven Press Ltd, New York, 1991, pp. 51–92.
171. Gibson GR, Cummings JH, Macfarlane GT. Competition for hydrogen between sulphate-reducing bacteria and methanogenic bacteria from the human large intestine. J Appl Bacteriol 1988; 65: 241–247.
172. Postgate JR. The sulphate-reducing bacteria 2nd Edition. Cambridge University Press Cambridge 1984.
173. Kristjansson JK, Shonheit P, Thauer RK. Different Ks values for hydrogen of methanogenic bacteria and sulfate reducing bacteria: an explanation for the apparent inhibition of methanogenesis by sulfate. Arch Microbiol 1982; 131: 278–282.
174. Christl SU, Gibson GR, Cummings JH. Role of dietary sulphate in the regulation of methanogenesis in the human large intestine. Gut 1992; 33: 1234–1238.
175. Florin THJ, Neale G, Gibson GR, Christl SU, Cummings JH. Metabolism of dietary sulphate: absorption and excretion in humans. Gut 1991; 32: 766–773.
176. Macfarlane GT, Gibson GT. Formation of glycoprotein degrading enzymes by *Bacteroides fragilis*. FEMS Microbiol Ecol 1991; 77: 289–294.
177. Gibson GR, Cummings JH, Macfarlane GT. Use of a three-stage continuous culture system to study the effect of mucin on dissimilatory sulfate reduction and methanogenesis by mixed populations of human gut bacteria. Appl Environ Microbiol 1989; 54: 2750–2755.
178. Macfarlane GT, Hay S, Gibson GR. Influence of mucin on glycosidase, protease and arylamidase activities of human gut bacteria grown in a 3-stage continuous culture system. J Appl Bacteriol 1989; 66: 407–417.
179. Tsai HH, Sunderland D, Gibson GR, Hart CA, Rhodes JM. A novel mucin sulphatase from human faeces: its identification, purification and characterization. Clin Sci 1992; 82: 447–454.
180. Roberton AM, Stanley RA. In vitro utilization of mucin by *Bacteroides fragilis*. Appl Environ Microbiol 1982; 43: 325–330.
181. Vercellotti JR, Salyers AA, Bullard WS, Wilkins TD. Breakdown of mucin and plant polysaccharides in the human colon. Can J Biochem 1977; 55: 1190–1196.
182. Strocchi A, Furne JK, Ellis CJ, Levitt MD. Competition for

hydrogen by human faecal bacteria: evidence for the predominance of methane producing bacteria. Gut 1991; 32: 1498–1501.
183. Smith L, Kryszyna H, Smith RP. The effect of methaemoglobin on the inhibition of cytochrome c oxidase by cyanide, sulfide or azide. Biochem Pharmacol 1977; 22: 47–50.
184. Florin THJ, Neale G, Cummings JH. The effect of hydrogen sulphide on isolated rat colonic epithelium. Falk Symposium on Advances in the Treatment of Ulcerative Colitis 1990; (abstract).
185. Macfarlane GT, Gibson GR, Cummings JH. Comparison of fermentation reactions in different regions of the colon. J Appl Bacteriol 1992; 72: 57–64.
186. Florin THJ, Gibson GR, Neale G, Cummings JH. A role for sulfate reducing bacteria in ulcerative colitis? Gastroenterology 1990; 98: A170.
187. Gibson GR, Cummings JH, Macfarlane GT. Growth and activities of sulphate-reducing bacteria in gut contents of healthy subjects and patients with ulcerative colitis. FEMS Microbiol Ecol 1991; 86: 103–112.
188. Gibson GR, Cummings JH, Macfarlane GT, Allison C, Segal I, Vorster HH, Walker ARP. Alternative pathways for hydrogen disposal during fermentation in the human colon. Gut 1990; 31: 679–683.
189. Christl SU, Gibson GR, Murgatroyd PR, Scheppach W, Cummings JH. Impaired hydrogen metabolism in penumatosis coli. Gastroenterology 1993; 104: 392–397.
190. Wrong OM, Vince AJ, Waterlow JC. The contribution of endogenous urea to faecal ammonia in man, determined by ^{15}N labelling of plasma urea. Clin Sci 1985; 68: 193–199.
191. Chacko A, Cummings JH. Nitrogen losses from the human small bowel: obligatory losses and the effect of physical form of food. Gut 1988; 29: 809–815.
192. Macfarlane GT, Cummings JH, Allison C. Protein degradation by human intestinal bacteria. J Gen Microbiol 1986; 132: 1647–1656.
193. Macfarlane GT, Allison C, Gibson SAW, Cummings JH. Contribution of the microflora to proteolysis in the human large intestine. J Appl Bacteriol 1988; 64: 37–46.
194. Macfarlane GT, Allison C. Utilisation of protein by human gut bacteria. FEMS Microbiol Ecol 1986; 38: 19–24.
195. Johnson KA. The production of secondary amines by human gut bacteria and its possible relevance to carcinogenesis. Med Lab Sci 1977; 34: 131–143.
196. White Tabor C, Tabor H. Polyamines in microorganisms. Microbiol Rev 1985; 49: 81–99.
197. Drasar BS, Hill MJ. Human Intestinal Flora. London: Academic Press, 1974.
198. Mason VC. Some observations on the distribution and origin of nitrogen in sheep faeces. J Agri Sci (Cambridge) 1969; 73: 99–111.
199. Mason VC, Palmer R. The influence of bacterial activity in the alimentary canal of rats on faecal nitrogen excretion. Act Agric Scand 1973; 23: 141–150.
200. Stephen AM, Cummings JH. The influence of dietary fibre on faecal nitrogen excretion in man. Proc Nutr Soc 1979; 38: 141A.
201. Cummings JH, Hill MJ, Jenkins DJA, Pearson JR, Wiggins HS. Changes in fecal composition and colonic function due to cereal fiber. Am J Clin Nutr 1976; 29: 1468–1473.
202. Kelsay JL, Behall KM, Prather ES. Effect of fiber from fruits and vegetables on metabolic responses of human subjects. 1. Bowel transit time, number of defaecations, fecal weight, urinary excretions of energy and nitrogen and apparent digestibility of energy, nitrogen and fat. Am J Clin Nutr 1978; 31: 1149–1153.
203. Calloway DH, Kretsch MJ. Protein and energy utilization in men given a rural Guatemalan diet and egg formulas with and without added oat bran. Am J Clin Nutr 1978; 31: 1118–1126.
204. Prynne CJ, Southgate DAT. The effects of a supplement of dietary fibre on faecal excretion by human subjects. Br J Nutr 1979; 41: 495–503.
205. Cummings JH, Southgate DAT, Branch WJ et al. The digestion of pectin in the human gut and its effect on calcium absorption and large bowel function. Br J Nutr 1979; 41: 477–485.
206. Weber FL. The effect of lactulose on urea metabolism and nitrogen excretion in cirrhotic patients. Gastroenterology 1979; 78: 518–523.
207. Demigne C, Remesy C. Urea recycling and ammonia absorption in vivo in the digestive tract of the rat. Ann Biol Anim Biochim Biophys 1979; 19: 929–935.
208. Visek WJ. Effects of urea hydrolysis on cell life-span and metabolism. Fed Proc 1972; 31: 1178–1193.
209. Visek WJ. Diet and cell growth modulation by ammonia. Am J Clin Nutr 1978; 31: S216–S220.
210. Visek WJ, Clinton SK, Truex CR. Nutrition and experimental carcinogenesis. Cornell Vet 1978; 68: 3–39.
211. Topping DC, Visek WJ. Nitrogen intake and tumorigenesis in rats injected with 1,2-dimethylhydrazine. J Nutr 1976; 106: 1583–1590.
212. Warwick GP. Effect of the cell cycle on carcinogenesis. Fed Proc 1971; 30: 1760–1765.
213. McConnell JB, Morison J, Steward WK. The role of the colon in the pathogenesis of hyperchloraemic acidosis in ureterosigmoid anastomosis. Clin Sci 1979; 57: 305–312.
214. Tank ES, Krausch DN, Lapides J. Adenocarcinoma of the colon associated with ureterosigmoidostomy. Dis Colon Rect 1973; 16: 300–304.
215. Schmidt EG. Urinary Phenols. IV. The simultaneous determination of phenol and p-cresol in urine. J Biol Chem 1949; 179: 211–215.
216. Tamm A, Villako K. Urinary volatile phenols in patients with intestinal obstruction. Scand J Gastroent 1971; 6: 5–8.
217. Baumann E. Tyrosine metabolised to simple phenols. Ber dtsch Chem Ges 1879; 12: 1450.
218. Folin O, Denis W. Urinary phenols derived from protein metabolism. J Biol Chem 1915; 22: 309.
219. Bakke OM, Midtvedt T. Influence of germ-free status on the excretion of simple phenols of possible significance in tumour promotion. Experientia 1970; 26: 519.
220. Bone E, Tamm A, Hill M. The production of urinary phenols by gut bacteria and their possible role in the causation of large bowel cancer. Am J Clin Nutr 1976; 29: 1448–1454.
221. Cummings JH, Hill MJ, Bone ES, Branch WJ, Jenkins DJA. The effect of meat protein and dietary fiber on colonic function and metabolism. Part II. Bacterial metabolites in feces and urine. Am J Clin Nutr 1979; 32: 2094–2101.
222. Scott TW, Ward PFV, Dawson RMC. The formation and metabolism of phenyl-substituted fatty acids in the ruminant. Biochem J 1964; 90: 12–24.
223. Greenberger NJ, Saegh S, Ruppert RD. Urine indican excretion in malabsorptive disorders. Gastroenterology 1968; 55: 204.
224. Tomkin GH, Weir DG. Indicanuria after gastric surgery. Quart J Med 1972; 41: 191.
225. Neale G, Gompertz D, Schonsby H, Tabaqchali S, Booth CC. The metabolic and nutritional consequences of bacterial overgrowth in the small intestine. Am J Clin Nutr 1972; 25: 1409–1417.
226. Fordtran JS, Scroggie JB, Polter DE. Colonic absorption of tryptophan metabolites in man. J Lab Clin Med 1964; 64: 125–132.
227. Bryan GT. The role of urinary tryptophan metabolites in the etiology of bladder cancer. Am J Clin Nutr 1971; 24: 841.
228. Boulton AA, Cookson B, Carlton R. Hypertensive crisis in a patient on MAOI antidepressants following a meal of beef liver. Can Med Assoc J 1970; 102: 1394–1395.
229. Phear EA, Rubner B. The in vitro production of ammonium and amines by intestinal bacteria in relation to nitrogen toxicity as a factor in hepatic coma. Br J Exp Pathol 1956; 37: 253–262.
230. Anon. Headache, tyramine, serotonin and migraine. Nutr Rev 1968; 26: 40–44.
231. Murray KG, Adams RF, Earl JW, Shaw KJ. Studies of free faecal amines of infants with gastroenteritis and of healthy infants. Gut 1986; 27: 1173–1180.
232. Suzuki K, Mitsuoka T. N-nitrosamine formation by intestinal bacteria. In: O'Neill IK, ed. IARC Scientific Publication No. 57. Lyon: International Agency for Research on Cancer Scientific Publications, 1984, pp. 275–281.
233. Yamamoto M, Yamada T, Taminura A. Volatile nitrosamines in human blood before and after ingestion of a meal containing high concentrations of nitrate and secondary amines. Food Cosmet Toxicol 1980; 18: 287–299.

234. Shepard SE, Schlatter C, Luthy WK. N-Nitrosocompounds: relevance to human cancer. In: Bartels H, O'Neill IK, Herman RS, eds. IARC Scientific Publication No. 84. Lyon: International Agency for Research on Cancer Scientific Publications, 1987, pp. 328–332.
235. Calmels S, Ohshima H, Vincent P, Gourot AM, Bartsch H. Screening of microorganisms for nitrosation catalysis at pH7 and kinetic studies on nitrosamine formation from secondary amines by *E. coli* strains. Carcinogenesis 1985; 6: 911–915.
236. Thacker L, Brooks JN. In vitro production of N-nitrosodimethylamine and other amines by *Proteus* species. Infect Immun 1974; 9: 648–653.
237. Fine DH, Ross R, Roonbehler DP, Silvergleid A, Song L. Formation in vivo of volatile N-nitrosamines in man after ingestion of cooked bacon and spinach. Nature 1977; 265: 753–755.
238. Leach SA, Cook AR, Challis BC, Hill MJ, Thompson MH. Reactions and endogenous formation of N-nitrosocompounds. In: Bartels H, O'Neill IK, Herman RS, eds. IARC Scientific Publication No. 84. Lyon: International Agency for Research on Cancer Scientific Publications, 1987, pp. 396–399.
239. Cummings JH. Constipation, dietary fibre and the control of large bowel function. Postgrad Med J 1984; 60: 811–819.
240. Stephen AM, Cummings JH. Mechanisms of action of dietary fibre in the human colon. Nature 1980; 284: 283–284.
241. Stephen AM. Dietary fibre and human colonic function. Ph.D. Thesis, University of Cambridge, 1980.
242. Kotarski SF, Salyers AA. Effect of long generation times on growth of Bacteroides thetaiotaomicron in carbohydrate-limited continuous culture. J Bacteriol 1981; 146: 853.
243. Tabaqchali S. The pathophysiological role of the small intestine bacterial flora. Scand J Gastroenterol 1970; Suppl 6: 139.
244. Bhat P, Shantakumari S, Rajan D, Mathan VI, Kapadia CR, Swarnabai C, Baker SJ. Bacterial flora of the gastrointestinal tract in southern India; control subjects and patients with tropical sprue. Gastroenterology 1972; 62: 11–21.
245. Gracey M, Suharjono, Sunoto, Stone DE. Microbial contamination of the gut — another feature of malnutrition. Am J Clin Nutr 1973; 26: 1170–1174.
246. Morotomi M, Guillem JG, Zoberfo IP, Weinstein JB. Production of diacylglycerol, an activator of protein kinase C, by human intestinal microflora. Cancer Res 1990; 50: 3595–3599.
247. Aries V, Crowther JS, Drasar BS, Hill MJ, Williams REO. Bacteria and the aetiology of cancer of the large bowel. Gut 1969; 10: 334–335.
248. Rowland IR, ed. The Role of the Gut Flora in Toxicity and Cancer. London Academic Press, 1988.
249. Drasar BS, Cook PGS. Intestinal bacteria and the initiation of cancer. GANN Monograph on cancer research 1986; 31: 221–228.

SECTION

2

Congenital and developmental abnormalities

CHAPTER

14 The oesophagus

A. J. Bourne

ABNORMALITIES OF SIZE, POSITION AND SHAPE

Congenital absence

Congenital absence of the oesophagus is extremely rare and only seen in bizarre monsters, especially those with acardia.

Congenital short oesophagus

Congenital short oesophagus with a portion of the stomach within the thorax does occur, but is very rare. It must be distinguished from Barrett's oesophagus, where the lower portion of the oesophagus is lined by a special metaplastic type of columnar epithelium. Initially considered by Barrett and others to be a congenital short oesophagus, it is now generally believed to be an acquired metaplastic change (see Ch. 241).[1]

OESOPHAGEAL ATRESIA AND RELATED LESIONS

Tracheo-oesophageal fistula and oesophageal atresia

The oesophagus develops from the cranial end of the primitive foregut. Traditional embryological theories suggest that the respiratory system (larynx, trachea and lungs) begins its development as a median ventral diverticulum of the oesophageal portion of the foregut, with separation of the trachea and oesophagus taking place as a tracheo-oesophageal septum forms by the caudorostral fusion of lateral tracheo-oesophageal folds.[2,3] More recent evidence suggests that the respiratory system develops as a ventral outgrowth from the region of the pharyngeal floor with elongation proceeding in a caudal direction.[4,5]

The generic term 'tracheo-oesophageal fistula' is used to describe a variety of anomalies, usually also with associated oesophageal atresia, and which are traditionally attributed to failure of complete separation of the posteriorly located oesophagus from the anteriorly placed trachea. The newer theories of embryology deny that these anomalies occur as a result of partial failure of separation but suggest that they result from faulty development of the already separate and differentiating organs.[5,6] The variations within this complex of anomalies are many, but the majority of cases fall into five major groups. Various classifications, including those of Swenson[7] and Gross[8] have been devised, but since Kluth[9] described 97 types and subtypes there has been an increasing trend to describe the cases in anatomical terms.[10] The commonest forms are:

i) oesophageal atresia with distal trachea-oesophageal fistula (Swenson Type 1, Gross Type C): 86.5%[11]
ii) oesophageal atresia without trachea-oesophageal fistula (Swenson Type 2, Gross Type A): 7.7%
iii) tracheo-oesphageal fistula without oesophageal atresia (Swenson type 3, Gross type 4): 4.2% — commonly referred to as 'H' type
iv) oesophageal atresia with proximal tracheo-oesophageal fistula (Swenson Type 4, Gross type B): 0.8%
v) oesophageal atresia with proximal and distal tracheo-

oesophageal fistula (Swenson type 5, Gross type D): 0.7%.

While familial cases have been reported, the majority of cases are said to be sporadic, with a subsequent risk amongst siblings of 0.56%.[12] It should be noted, however, that although once a fatal condition, in recent years significant numbers of surgically corrected survivors have reached child-bearing age. The effect that this may have on genetic implications is still not clear.

Over 50% of affected patients have other associated, and often severe, anomalies. These are seen in the gastrointestinal tract, cardiovascular, renal or musculoskeletal systems. Indeed tracheo-oesophageal anomalies are the most common component of the **VACTERL** anomalad.[13] This acronym, expanded from the originally used term, VATER association,[14] describes a non-random concurrence of anomalies. Generically these anomalies are **V**ertebral or **V**ascular defects, **A**nal atresia, **C**ardiac anomalies, **T**racheo-**E**sophageal fistula with oesophageal atresia, **R**enal and **L**imb, especially radial, defects.

Laryngo-tracheo-oesophageal cleft

This condition is closely related to, and may occur together with, tracheo-oesophageal fistula and oesophageal atresia. In its simplest form (Type I) the cleft is restricted to the larynx and surgical correction is unnecessary. The more severe examples, when there is extension of the defect into the upper trachea (Type II), the whole length of the trachea to the carina (Type III) or into one or both main bronchi (Type IV), are almost invariably associated with life threatening disturbances, either because of aspiration or other congenital anomalies.[15,16]

Oesophageal bronchus

This is an uncommon condition, in which a main bronchus arises from the oesophagus. The lung receives its arterial supply from the pulmonary artery, unlike pulmonary sequestration where there is an anomalous systemic arterial blood supply. Various cardiac and non-cardiac anomalies have been described in association,[17] but notably, oesophageal atresia is not usually seen.

CYSTS AND DUPLICATIONS

Congenital cystic lesions derived from the primitive foregut are uncommon but well recognized entities. The classification and terminology of these lesions has been the source of much speculation, which has lead to confusion. Conclusions based on features of a single case have lead to classifications based upon anatomical site, embryology and epithelial lining. They have been referred to as enteric duplications, mediastinal cysts of foregut origin, gastrocytoma of the spinal cord, duplication cysts, tubular duplication, bronchogenic cysts, tracheobronchial cysts, oesophageal cysts, mediastinal gastric cysts, neurenteric cysts and enterogenic cysts. Since the 1952 paper of Bremer,[18] who developed the theory that a dorsal intestinal fistula was the cause, these lesions have been better understood. This theory was elaborated upon by Bentley and Smith,[19] who introduced the notion of the split notochord syndrome. A further paper[20] gathered these and other theories into an increasingly acceptable general classification which recognizes three basic groups: (i) bronchogenic cysts, (ii) intramural oesophageal cysts, and (iii) dorsal enteric cysts and duplications.[21]

Bronchogenic cysts

The respiratory system, as mentioned above, develops from the foregut. Abnormal budding of the bronchial tree may give rise to abnormal cystic structures which may, or may not, communicate with the bronchial tree. Such cysts are usually lined by ciliated columnar epithelium and contain cartilage in their walls. They are generally closely related to the bronchial tree, occuring in the mediastinum, along the tracheobronchial tree or within the lung. Rarely they are described in the abdomen[22] or the subcutaneous tissues of the neck or chest.[23] These cysts are most often isolated lesions and are not associated with vertebral anomalies.

Intramural oesophageal cysts

By definition, these lesions are contained within the wall of the oesophagus. They may bulge either into the lumen or externally. They are usually lined by ciliated columnar cells, but squamous, cuboidal or transitional epithelium or a mixture of these may be seen. This illustrates the difficulty involved in classifying these cysts on the basis of their epithelial lining. The usual explanation for their origin is a defect in the vacuolization process of the oesophageal epithelium. During development, the lining epithelium proliferates, converting the oesophagus into an almost solid tube. At a later stage vacuoles form between the cells and these coalesce to restore the lumen. It is worthwhile recalling that early in foetal development the oesophagus is lined by a simple pseudostratified columnar epithelium. These lesions are not accompanied by vertebral defects.

Dorsal enteric ('neurenteric') cysts and duplications

In the thorax, these lesions occur in the posterior mediastinum, while in the abdomen they are typically found in the mesentery. They may be either spherical cystic lesions or elongate cylindrical duplications which may or may not communicate with the lumen of the bowel. They have a muscular wall and a variable epithelial lining with foci of respiratory and gastric epithelium being commonly found.

It is postulated that during embryological development the notochord splits, allowing the closely related yolk sac or gut anlage to herniate and become adherent to the dorsal ectoderm. A similar, and not necessarily exclusive, proposal suggests that nests of endodermal cells may be drawn dorsally as the notochord is pinched off from the primitive gut at a slightly earlier stage of development. A variable degree of persistence of this herniated endoderm or the endodermal nests may give rise to a variety of abnormal endodermal remnants. These range from a complete dorsal enterocutaneous fistula with anterior and posterior spina bifida and diastematomyelia or diplomyelia to a simple mediastinal cyst. These lesions are commonly associated with vertebral anomalies such as butterfly and hemivertebrae, fusion of vertebrae or the presence of a bony spur in association with diastematomyelia, and they may be connected to the vertebrae by a fibrous cord. As a result of the differential growth rate between the spinal column and foregut, the cyst generally is found caudal to the corresponding abnormal vertebrae. By virtue of the same mechanism, the mediastinal lesion may further be in continuity or associated with similar lesions within the abdomen. Hence, infants found to have such apparently simple mediastinal cysts require extensive organ imaging, including computer assisted tomography, to exclude the possiblity of intraspinal or intra-abdominal cysts. Similary, the finding of an apparently isolated intra-abdominal cyst, lined by foregut derived epithelium, requires further examination of the mediastinum and vertebral column.[24] Because of the proposed method of origin, these lesions are best described by the terms dorsal enteric cysts or duplications, as this is a generic term covering virtually all of the described cases. The closely related term neurenteric cyst is in fairly common usage and perhaps acceptable, but certainly all other terms should be abandoned.

These lesions, especially if tubular, may be found fortuitously at any age, including the antenatal period,[24] during routine antenatal ultrasound or radiological investigations for other conditons. They may present in infancy by virtue of symptoms associated with a mass lesion, e.g. obstruction leading to respiratory distress or digestive symptoms, vascular compression, pain and haemorrhage, especially if the cyst contains acid secreting gastric mucosa.

An illustration of this latter complication is seen in Figure 14.1. An infant known to have a mediastinal cyst and abnormal vertebrae, died suddenly from exsanguination when a peptic ulcer in the cyst penetrated the aorta. The infant was also found to have cystic dilation of the central canal of the spinal cord, but there was no evidence of communication between the two lesions.

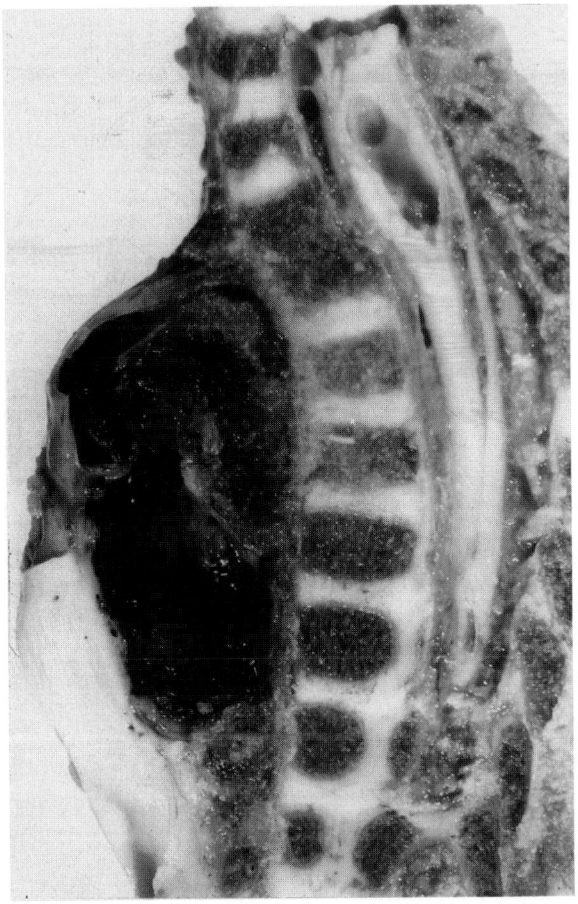

Figure 14.1 Prevertebral mediastinal cyst with erosion into aorta. Abnormal fused vertebrae at upper level of cyst and cystic dilation within the spinal cord.

Other bronchopulmonary foregut malformations

While pulmonary sequestrations are generally described in texts as anomalies of lung development[25,26] it is timely to reflect that examples that have retained a bronchial connection with the oesophagus or stomach are well described,[27] confirming that they are really best represented as foregut malformations. In addition, some sequestrations have been described in association with bronchogenic cysts that occur between the sequestration and the oesophagus, suggesting that they have a common embryological origin.[28] It has been suggested that the sequestrations develop as abnormal buds from the oesophagus and subsequently lose that connection, with occasional associated bronchogenic cysts resulting from residual nests of tissue along the migratory path. Extralobar sequestrations have a high incidence of associated congenital anomalies.[29] As there are a wide variety of related abnormalities it has been stated that no single embryologic theory can account for all cases.[27] Prenatal diagnosis by ultrasound is now documented.[30]

DIVERTICULA

Congenital diverticula of the oesophagus are very rare. They may be (i) hypopharyngeal-oesophageal, (ii) associated with other tracheo-oesophageal anomalies, or (iii) epiphrenic.[31]

Hypopharyngeal-oesophageal

These arise posteriorly from the same region as pulsion diverticula in adults, but in contrast they have a complete muscular wall. They become filled with food or saliva and may slowly increase in size, eventually causing symptoms due to compression of adjacent organs or producing an expansile swelling in the neck.

Diverticula associated with other tracheo-oesophageal anomalies

Very rare diverticula of the mid-oesophagus are usually associated with the tracheo-oesophageal fistula/oesophageal atresia complex.

Epiphrenic diverticula

Congenital diverticula of the lower oesophagus are considered to be part of the dorsal intestinal duplication complex referred to above.

STENOSIS

As acquired strictures resulting from peptic oesophagitis may develop very rapidly, it is difficult to establish that oesophageal stenosis is an independently occurring congenital anomaly.[32] However patients such as those described with a cartilaginous ring encircling the oesophagus are generally considered to have a congenital lesion.[33] They usually occur in the distal oesophagus, i.e. distal to the usual site in the tracheo-oesophageal fistula/oesophageal atresia complex, and have been regarded variously as variants of that complex, simple heterotopias or chondroepithelial choristomata. Since similar rings have been seen in patients that have communicating pulmonary sequestrations[27] and it has been suggested that isolated lesions may be regarded as oesophageal sequestrations,[33] it may be appropriate to consider such lesions as part of the bronchopulmonary foregut malformation complex.

IDIOPATHIC MUSCULAR HYPERTROPHY

While this condition is generally seen in males over the age of 40,[34] rare cases are seen in children and some of these are regarded as congenital. There is hypertrophy of the muscularis propria involving usually the lower third, but occasionally the whole length, of the oesophagus. It may occur in association with typical hypertrophic pyloric stenosis or segmental muscular hypertrophy elsewhere in the alimentary tract.[31]

HETEROTOPIA

The presence of heterotopic gastric mucosa in the upper oesophagus, initially described in post-mortem series, has been confirmed in 3.8% of 420 sequential endoscopies.[35] This is usually recognized as a pink patch in otherwise white mucosa. Patches of ciliated columnar cells, reflecting an early stage in embryogenesis, have been reported, especially in premature neonates. Sebaceous glands and thyroid tissue have also been described in the wall.[21] Ectopic cartilage, possibly associated with glandular elements and respiratory epithelium, has already been mentioned as a cause of true congenital oesophageal stenosis.

HAMARTOMAS

Haemangiomas and lymphangiomas present at birth are generally regarded as hamartomata and not as true neoplasms. While such lesions are extremely rare in the oesophagus, there may be involvement of this organ in the autosomally dominantly inherited disease, hereditary haemorrhagic telangiectasia (Osler-Rendu-Weber disease). Similarly infants having large cystic hygromata (cavernous lymphangioma) of the neck may show involvement of the oesophagus and other adjacent organs. The majority of benign intraluminal fibrovascular polyps occur in middle aged or elderly patients, but occasional examples are reported in children and thought to be hamartomas.[36]

REFERENCES

1. Spechler SJ, Goyal RK. Barrett's esophagus. N Engl J Med 1986; 315: 362–371.
2. Hamilton WJ. Human embryology. 4th ed. Baltimore: Williams & Wilkins, 1972.
3. Moore KL. The developing human: clinically oriented embryology. Philadelpia: Saunders. 1973.
4. Zaw-Tun HA. The tracheo-esophageal septum — fact or fantasy? Origin and development of the respiratory primordium and esophagus. Acta Anat 1982; 114: 1–21.
5. O'Rahilly R, Muller F. Respiratory and alimentary relations in staged human embryos. New embryological data and congenital anomalies. Ann Otol Rhinol Laryngol 1984; 93: 421–429.
6. Kluth D, Steding G, Seidl W. The embryology of foregut malformations. J Pediatr Surg 1987; 22: 389–393.
7. Swenson O, Lipman R, Fisher JH, DeLuca FG. Repair and complications of esphageal atresia and tracheoesophageal fistula. N Engl J Med 1962; 267: 960–963.
8. Gross RE. The surgery of infancy and childhood. Philadelphia, Saunders, 1953. Chapter 6.
9. Kluth D. Atlas of esophageal atresia. J Pediatr Surg 1976; 11: 901–919.
10. Editorial: Congenital esophageal anomalies : a plea for using anatomic descriptions rather than classifications. J Pediatr Surg 1978; 13: 355.

11. Holder TM, Cloud DT, Lewis JE, Pilling GP IV. Esophageal atresia and tracheoesophageal fistula — a survey of its members by the Surgical section of the American Academy of Pediatrics. Pediatrics 1964; 34: 542–549.
12. Chen H, Goei GS, Hertzler J. Family studies on congenital oesophageal atresia with or without tracheo-oesophageal fistula. Birth Defects 1979; 15: 117–144.
13. Baumann W, Greinacher I, Emmrich P et al. VATER-oder VACTERL-syndrom. Klin Padiatr 1976; 188: 328–337.
14. Quan L, Smith DW. The VATER association: vertebral defects, anal atresia, tracheoesophageal fistula with esophageal atresia, radial dysplasia. Birth Defects 1972; 8: 75–78.
15. Roth B, Rose K-G, Benz-Bohm G, Gunther H. Laryngo-tracheo-oesophageal cleft. Eur J Pediatr 1983; 140: 41–46.
16. Ryan DP, Muehrcke DD, Doody DD, Kim SH, Donahóe PK. Laryngotracheoesophageal Cleft (Type IV): management and repair of lesions beyond the carina. J Pediatr Surg 1991; 26: 962–970.
17. Lacina S, Townley R, Radecki L, Stockinger F, Wyngaarden M. Esophageal lung with cardiac abnormalities. Chest 1981; 79: 468–470.
18. Bremer JL. Dorsal intestinal fistula; accessory neurenteric canal; diastematomyelia. Arch Pathol 1952; 54: 132–138.
19. Bentley JFR, Smith JR. Developmental posterior enteric remnants and spinal malformations. The split notochord syndrome. Arch Dis Child 1960; 35: 76–86.
20. Kirwan WO, Walbaum PR, McCormack RJM. Cystic intrathoracic derivatives of the foregut and their complications. Thorax 1973; 28: 424–428.
21. Enterline H, Thompson J. Pathology of the esophagus. New York : Spinger-Verlag, 1984. Chapter 2.
22. Sumiyoshi K, Shimuzu S, Enjoji M, Iwashita A, Kawakami K. Bronchogenic cyst in the abdomen. Virchows Arch Pathol Anat 1985; 408: 93–98.
23. Bagwell CE, Schiffman RJ. Subcutaneous bronchogenic cysts. J Pediatr Surg 1988; 23: 993–995.
24. Sen S, Bourne AJ, Morris LL, Furness ME, Ford WDA. Dorsal enteric cysts — a study of eight cases. Aust NZ J Surg 1988; 58: 51–55.
25. Thurlbeck WM. Respiratory System. In Dimmick JE, Kalousek D. eds Developmental pathology of the embryo and fetus. New York: Lippincott, 1992. Chapter 15.
26. Stocker JT. The respiratory tract. In Stocker JT, Dehner LP. eds. Pediatric pathology. New York: Lippincott, 1992. Chapter 16.
27. Fowler CL, Pokorny WJ, Wagner ML, Kessler MS. Review of bronchopulmonary foregut malformations. J Pediatr Surg, 1988; 23: 793–797.
28. Stocker JT, Kagan-Hallet K. Extralobar pulmonary sequestration: analysis of 15 cases. Am J Clin Pathol, 1979; 72: 917–925.
29. Hruban RH, Shumway SJ, Orel SB, Dumler JS, Baker RR, Hutchins GM. Congenital bronchopulmonary foregut malformations: intralobar and extralobar pulmonary sequestrations communicating with the foregut. Am J Clin Pathol 1989; 91: 403–409.
30. Siffring PA, Forrest TS, Hill WC, Freick MP. Prenatal sonographic diagnosis of bronchopulmonary foregut malformation. J Ultrasound Med 1989; 8: 277–280.
31. Kissane JM. Pathology of infancy and childhood. 2nd ed. St. Louis: Mosby, 1975. Chapter 7.
32. Berry CL, Keeling JW. Gastrointestinal system. In Berry CL ed. Pediatric pathology. Berlin: Springer-Verlag, 2nd ed. 1989. Chapter 5.
33. Sneed WF, LaGarde DC, Kogutt MS, Arensman RM. Esophageal stenosis due to cartilaginous tracheobronchial remnants. J Pediatr Surg 1979; 14: 786–788.
34. Enterline H, Thompson J. Pathology of the esophagus. New York: Springer-Verlag, 1984. Chapter 4.
35. Jabbari M, Goresky CA, Lough J, Yaffe C, Daly D, Cote C. The inlet patch: heterotopic gastric mucosa in the upper oesophagus. Gastroenterology 1985; 89: 352–356.
36. Dieter RA Jr, Riker WL, Holinger P. Pedunculated esophageal hamartoma in a child. J Thorac Cardiovasc Surg 1970; 59: 851–854.

CHAPTER 15

The stomach

R. F. Carter

ABNORMALITIES OF SIZE, POSITION AND SHAPE

Congenital absence, dextroposition and microgastria

The stomach, together with all other structures derived from the embryonic foregut, may be absent in acardiac fetuses. In some severe forms of anencephaly it may be found completely within the thorax.[1] More commonly, part of the stomach may be found dislocated into the thorax through a congenital hernia of the left hemidiaphragm, where it is expanded by swallowed air after birth and can rapidly cause death from respiratory and circulatory compression.

Dextroposition is a functionally harmless congenital malformation that occurs in complete visceral situs inversus as well as other more complex syndromes of abnormal thoraco-abdominal visceral situs.[2] It may occur as a completely isolated phenomenon but this is very rare, occurring with an incidence of less than 1 in 100 000.[3]

Another very rare anomaly is microgastria, also known as tubular or foetal stomach, in which the greater and lesser curvatures fail to develop and the stomach remains as a much diminished tube-like structure associated with an incompetent cardiac sphincter and a dilated oesophagus.[4] It may be an isolated phenomenon or part of the Asplenia with Cardiovascular Anomalies Syndrome of Ivemark.[5]

CYSTS, DUPLICATIONS AND DIVERTICULA

The literature on this subject is confusing as some authors have tended to refer to all accessory structures lined by gastric mucosa as gastric 'cysts' if they are saccular and do not communicate with the stomach lumen, 'duplications' if they are tubular and non-communicating, and 'diverticula' if they communicate. The confusion can be eliminated if the term 'gastric duplication' is reserved for 'cystic or tubular' lesions intimately connected with the stomach, whether or not they are lined by gastric mucosa and whether or not they communicate with the definitive stomach.[6] 'Intimate connection' means that the lesion is surrounded by smooth muscle which is continuous with the muscle of the stomach.[7] This definition excludes those thoraco-abdominal lesions which have already been described in the foregoing section on the oesophagus as dorsal enteric or neurenteric cysts or duplications, which are lined usually by a mixture of epithelia, including gastric, and which may pass close by the stomach but are not 'intimately' connected with it.

Using the above criteria, Wieczorek et al[7] in a review of the literature to 1984 were able to find 109 genuine cases of gastric duplication. 39 cases were found in infants less than 3 months of age, and most of the remainder in childhood, with only 30 being discovered in patients older than 12 years. The commonest location is along the greater curvature (Fig. 15.1). Seven cases had duplications extending from various points in the oesophagus to the pylorus. Cystic lesions which did not communicate with the stomach accounted for 82%, whereas 18% were tubular and did communicate. Most of the cystic lesions ranged in size from 3–6 cm. In a subset of 55 of the cases reviewed, the mucosal lining was gastric in 31 and in 5 cases heterotopic pancreatic tissue was found. These lesions may also be lined by small or large intestinal mucosa or a non-specific glandular or simple columnar epithe-

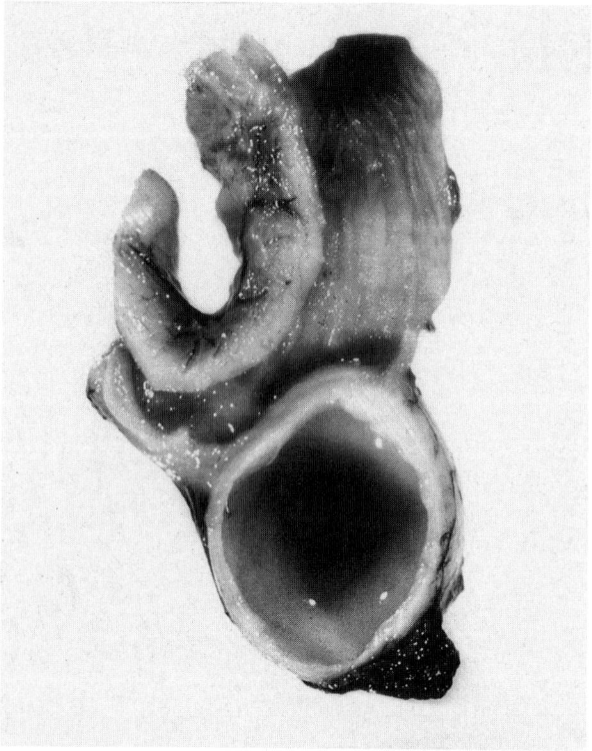

Fig. 15.1 A typical cystic, non-communicating duplication of the stomach located within the wall of the greater curvature (incidental finding at necropsy in a child dying soon after birth from tracheal atresia).

lium. Often the lining has been destroyed by inflammatory reaction. A wide variety of associated abnormalities of other organs was found in about half the cases, the commonest being duplication of the oesophagus. Treatment by either radical excision or dissection of the lesions was successful in most cases. Complications of the untreated lesion include obstruction of the pylorus, haemorrhage, and perforation into the peritoneal cavity, the gut or other adjacent organs, with the formation of fistulae or pseudocysts.

The most convincing theory of the embryogenesis of these lesions is that attributed to Bremer[8] which proposes that these lesions arise by fusion of the tips of the longitudinal multiple folds by which means the stomach grows in the 2nd and 3rd months of gestation. This contrasts with the solid epithelial proliferation and subsequent recanalization which occurs in the small and large intestines.

Diverticula are usually defined as cystic structures lined by alimentary mucosa that communicate with the stomach lumen. Most of these have a thin wall containing only a few attenuated strands of smooth muscle covered by serosa and are found almost always in adults. These are almost certainly acquired lesions or 'pulsion diverticula'. A few cases with proper muscular walls have been described in childhood. These are undoubtedly congenital lesions but as they comply with the definition of 'gastric duplications' of the communicating type they are best classified as such.[6]

Congenital double pylorus is also usually an acquired lesion most commonly attributed to complications of peptic ulceration. However cases with a complete fully formed dividing septum containing layers of mucosa and muscularis mucosae have been described and are probably congenital.[9] These are considered to be simply another form of gastric duplication with rather distinctive clinical and radiological features.

ATRESIAS AND OTHER OBSTRUCTIVE MALFORMATIONS

Pyloric atresia

Pyloric atresia is a very rare condition that is said to occur in approximately one in 1 million births.[10] It may take the form of an imperforate mucosal diaphragm at or just before the pylorus, two diaphragms isolating a cavity which can be mistaken for a gastric duplication, or a complete fibrous interruption which is sometimes referred to as pyloric aplasia.[6] Autosomal recessive inheritance has been reported[11] either for the isolated lesion or when it is associated with epidermolysis bullosa letalis.[12] Symptoms of complete pyloric obstruction occur soon after birth and treatment is by simple resection of the web or radical resection of the aplastic pylorus with gastro-duodenal anastomosis. The results are excellent if diagnosis and treatment is prompt. Theories of causation include fusion of the developing embryonic mucosal folds, or in the case of aplasia, a localized vascular injury.[11]

Antral web

This is an incomplete form of the diaphragmatic type of pyloric atresia in which there is a central or eccentric orifice in the diaphragm. Many of these are found in adults and some are probably acquired lesions secondary to peptic ulceration.[13] However, about half of the 180 cases reported by 1982 had occurred in children[14] and the condition can present in infancy if the orifice is very small and causes significant obstruction of gastric outflow.[15] Treatment is usually by simple resection with or without pyloroplasty, although successful conservative treatment by dietary modification has been reported in 4 infants with partially obstructing webs.[15]

Infantile hypertrophic pyloric stenosis

This is a relatively common disorder of young infants occurring in 2.5 per 1000 live births, although the incidence has been shown to vary considerably in time and place.[16] The term 'congenital' is often applied, but only a few cases have been described in new-born infants or fetuses and the main body of evidence suggests that the anatomical abnormality does not develop until on average about 3–4 weeks of age.[17] At this time a previously well infant will develop projectile, non-bilious vomiting associated with a voracious appetite and a distinctive hypochloraemia and alkalaemia. Confirmation of diagnosis is by palpation of the typical 'tumour' in the hypogastrium during a test feed or by radiological or ultrasonic investigation if the tumour cannot be felt. Treatment of choice is by laparotomy and pyloromyotomy, as described by Ramstedt in 1912, in which the hypertrophied circular muscle of the pylorus is incised to release the obstruction. Results are excellent with very low operative mortality and morbidity if careful attention is paid to pre and postoperative fluid and electrolyte balance. Return to completely normal function is the rule and there are rarely any longterm sequelae. Medical treatment with careful dietary management aided by anticholinergic drugs has some adherents but generally is not favoured as extended hospitalization is required and morbidity and mortality tend to be higher.

Pathologically, the pylorus is increased in length and diameter, the stomach is dilated and the antrum hypertrophic. The circular muscle is up to four times thicker than normal with, microscopically, a mixture of hypertrophy and hyperplasia, and a prominent leucocytic infiltration. The hypertrophy stops abruptly at the fibrous junction with the duodenum. Rarely in long-standing cases peptic ulcers may be present in the stomach and massive haemorrhage has been described. The aetiology of pyloric stenosis is still obscure despite numerous studies over the past 100 years. These have recently been reviewed extensively by Spicer.[17] Strikingly, it is 4 times more common in males than in females. A higher than expected association with oesophageal atresia, hiatus hernia, malrotation, dominantly inherited polycystic kidneys, Smith-Lemli-Opitz syndrome, XYY gonadal dysgenesis and X/XX chromosomal mosaicism occurs. The condition has a strong familial incidence with a polygenic pattern of inheritance and a disproportionately high incidence in children of an affected female. The condition is also much less common in non-Caucasian children. Environmental factors, such as breast feeding, appear to exert an effect on the expression of the condition, and there is also a strong seasonal effect with peaks in spring and autumn.

Theories of causation such as pylorospasm with work hypertrophy, changes in cardio/skeletal muscle enzyme ratios, effects of maternal gastrin, and abnormalities of the myenteric plexus and neurones have all been more or less discounted by detailed investigation. In particular, the observations of possibly degenerative or immature neurones are considered by many to be the result rather than the cause of the compression and inflammation[6] and in any case have not been supported by recent electron microscopic[18] and immunochemical[19,20] studies. Although gastrin has been discounted as a causal factor this is not the case for other intestinal peptides, and recent studies[20,21] have shown a deficiency of vasoactive intestinal peptide, enkephalin, neuropeptide Y and substance P in the circular muscle but not in the myenteric plexus.

Adult hypertrophic pyloric stenosis is a pathologically similar condition occurring in young to middle-aged adults and causing gastric outlet obstruction in the absence of inflammatory disease. The aetiology is unknown. Some authors consider that the condition represents a delayed presentation of the infantile variety[17] while others think this very unlikely, particularly in those cases with no previous symptoms and an onset in middle-age.[22]

HAMARTOMAS

Pancreatic heterotopia[6,23]

Pancreatic heterotopia occurs in a variety of sites but in approximately 25% of cases the stomach is involved. It is usually an incidental finding in children but is more commonly found in adults where it may also be asymptomatic or present as peptic ulcer or intermittent pyloric obstruction. The condition most commonly involves the pyloric antrum as a submucosal bulging mass 0.1–5 cm diameter with a characteristic central umbilication representing the opening of the rudimentary duct. Microscopically, the lesions consist of normal pancreatic acini and ducts often with islets of Langerhans as well. Whilst they are clearly developmental lesions, their embryogenesis is not certain. Complications include fat necrosis, diverticulum formation, cystic degeneration, inflammation, superficial ulceration, and the development of islet cell adenomas and carcinomas. Preferred treatment is local excision of the nodule.

Adenomyomas[24]

These are hamartomatous malformations of glands and smooth muscle which involve the mucosa and the submucosa. They may occur anywhere in the stomach and duodenum but are mostly in the lower part of the stomach and the pyloric antrum. They appear as sessile polyps usually no more than 1 cm diameter. They are liable to ulceration or may cause pyloric obstruction, particularly in a young child.

Peutz-Jeghers polyps

Benign gastric hamartomas similar to those which also occur in the small and large intestine are part of the Peutz-Jeghers syndrome.[24] Microscopically, their branching, polypoid structure with a central core of smooth muscle fibres and connective tissue is similar wherever they occur in the alimentary tract, but in the stomach gastric secretory cells and tubules of pyloric gland type are found as well.

Angiomas

Angiomas of the stomach are said to be very rare[24] but between 1965 and 1986 some 43 cases were reported in the literature which suggests that they need to be considered as an occasional cause of occult gastrointestinal blood loss. A recent report[25] described the finding of vascular malformations of the stomach in 9 patients out of 650 endoscoped for gastrointestinal bleeding and emphasized that these lesions are likely to remain undiagnosed by conventional radiology, biopsy and even laparotomy. A similar observation was made in a paper[26] describing a patient with an arteriovenous malformation of the stomach associated with 2 years of undiagnosed chronic anaemia in whom selective visceral angiography was used to demonstrate the lesion, which was then treated successfully during the same procedure by embolization, thus avoiding the need for a partial gastrectomy. The radiological demonstration of phleboliths may occasionally make the diagnosis obvious,[27] but in general it is likely that gastric angiomas are underdiagnosed.

Lymphangiomas

Lymphangiomas arising in the stomach appear to be genuinely quite rare. A review paper[28] published in 1978 was able to identify only 6 examples in the literature from 1879 to 1970 and described 2 new cases. A literature search for the period 1965 to 1986 revealed only 9 papers including the one just referred to. The lesions may be simple telangiectatic, cavernous or mixed in nature, and present with signs of obstruction, rupture or haemorrhage; simple drainage or local resection produces excellent results.[28]

MISCELLANEOUS

Spontaneous gastric perforation in infancy can be due to a number of causes, but in about one third of reported cases localized congenital deficiency in the muscle coat has been implicated.[6] This is disputed by some who claim that the appearances described are secondary to retraction of ruptured muscle fibres surrounding the perforation and are most likely the result of trauma from nasogastric tubes and the like. Some support for this explanation is provided by the observation that the perforation usually occurs as a long clean rent in the longitudinal axis of the stomach near the greater curvature. Whatever the causation, it is certain that prompt recognition and surgical repair is essential as the mortality otherwise is high.

Generalized neurofibromatosis may involve the stomach with the formation of large plexiform neurofibromas that may ulcerate and bleed.

Benign teratomas have been reported in infancy as being tumour-like lesions which usually present as a mass rather than because of bleeding or obstruction.[6]

REFERENCES

1. Willis RA. The Borderland of Embryology and Pathology. 2nd ed. London: Butterworths, 1962: 139, 161.
2. Landing BH, Wells TR. Tracheobronchial anomalies in children. In: Rosenberg HS, Bolande RP, eds. Perspectives in Pediatric Pathology. Chicago: Yearbook Medical Publishers, 1973; 1: 1–32.
3. Teplick JG, Wallner RJ, Levine AH, Haskin ME. Isolated dextrogastria: Report of two cases. Am J Radiol 1979; 132: 124–126.
4. Gorman B, Shaw DG. Congenital microgastria. Br J Radiol 1984; 57: 260–262.
5. Rose V, Izukawa T, Moes CAF. Syndromes of asplenia and polysplenia. A review of cardiac and non-cardiac malformations in 60 cases with special reference to diagnosis and prognosis. Br Heart J 1975; 37: 840–852.
6. Kissane JM. Pathology of Infancy and Childhood. St. Louis: Mosby, 2nd ed. 1975: 175–186.
7. Wieczorek RL, Seidman I, Ranson JHC, Ruoff, M. Congenital duplication of the stomach: Case report and review of the English literature. Am J Gastroenterol 1984; 79: 597–602.
8. Bremer JL. Dorsal intestinal fistula; accessory neurenteric canal; diastematomyelia. Arch Pathol 1952; 54: 132–138.
9. Sufian S, Ominsky S, Matsumoto T. Congenital double pylorus. A case report and review of the literature. Gastroenterol 1977; 73: 154–157.
10. Parrish RA, Kanavage CB, Wells JA, Moretz WH. Congenital antral membrane. Surg Gynecol Obstet 1968; 127: 999–1004.
11. Caglar MK, Ceyhan M, Dilmen U, Senses DA. Radiological case of the quarter. Turkish J Pediatr 1985; 27: 49–51.
12. Bull MJ, Norins AL, Weaver DD, Weber T, Mitchell M. Epidermolysis bullosa pyloric atresia. Am J Dis Child 1983; 137: 449–451.
13. Haddad V, Macon WL, Islami MH. Mucosal diaphragm of the gastric antrum in adults. Surg Gynecol Obstet 1981; 152: 227–233.
14. Sheinfeld A, Olsha O, Rivkin L, Dolberg M. Prepyloric diaphragm, an unusual case of gastric outlet syndrome. Isr J Med Sci 1982; 18: 1044–1047.
15. Tunell WP, Smith EI. Antral web in infancy. J Pediatr Surg 1980; 15: 152–155.
16. Editorial. Incidence of infantile hypertrophic pyloric stenosis. Lancet 1984; 1: 888–889.
17. Spicer RD. Infantile hypertrophic pyloric stenosis: A review. Br J Surg 1982; 69: 128–135.
18. Challa VR, Jona JZ, Markesbery WR. Ultrastructural observations of the myenteric plexus of the pylorus in infantile hypertrophic pyloric stenosis. Am J Pathol 1977; 88: 309–315.
19. Tam PKH. An immunochemical study with neuron-specific-enolase and substance P of human enteric innervation — the normal developmental pattern and abnormal deviations in Hirschsprung's disease and pyloric stenosis. J Pediatr Surg 1986; 21: 227–232.
20. Wattchow DA, Cass DT, Furness JB, Costa M, O'Brien PE, Little KE, Pitkin J. Abnormalities of peptide containing nerve fibres in infantile hypertrophic pyloric stenosis. Gastroenterol 1987; 92: 443–448.
21. Malmfors G, Sundler F. Peptidergic innervation in infantile hypertrophic pyloric stenosis. J Pediatr Surg 1986; 21: 303–306.

22. Dye TE, Vidals VG, Lockhart CE, Snider WR. Adult hypertrophic pyloric stenosis. Am Surg 1979; 45: 478–484.
23. Barrocas A, Fontenelle LJ, Williams MJ. Gastric heterotopic pancreas: A case report and review of literature. Am Surg 1973; 39: 361–365.
24. Morson BC. In: Payling Wright G, Symmers W StC, eds. Systemic Pathology. 1st ed. London: Longmans Green, 1966: 503–504.
25. Farup PG, Rosseland AR, Stray N, Pytte R, Valnes K, Rand AA. Localised telangiopathy of the stomach and duodenum diagnosed and treated endoscopically. Case reports and review. Endoscopy 1981; 13: 1–6.
26. Sellu DP, Fagan E, Allison DJ, Wood CB. Arteriovenous malformation of the stomach treated by embolization. Br J Surg 1981; 68: 39–40.
27. Simms SM. Gastric hemangioma associated with phleboliths. Gastrointest Radiol 1985; 10: 51–53.
28. Baumel H, Godlewski G, Deixonne B, Giraudon M, Raffanel C, Marty-Double C. Gastro-omental cystic lymphangiomas. General review and report of two cases. J Chir (Paris) 1978; 115: 533–540.

CHAPTER 16

The small intestine

J. W. Keeling

EMBRYOLOGY

The duodenum derives from the distal end of the primitive foregut, the jejunum and ileum from the midgut. The foregut region develops sequentially, so that at the 7 mm stage, when a small gastric expansion is recognizable, diverticuli appear from the anterior and posterior walls of the duodenum, which will become the biliary system and pancreas. By the 15 mm stage, gastric dorsal expansion has created the mature form of the stomach, and its relationship to the duodenum and biliary system and pancreas are virtually those observed in postnatal life. Rapid lengthening of the duodenum takes place and its lumen is temporarily obliterated in places by hyperplasia of the lining epithelium.

The midgut is that region of the intra-embryonic yolk sac between the foregut defined by the head fold and the hindgut defined by the tail fold. It has a broad communication with the extra-embryonic yolk sac which becomes progressively longer and narrower as the midgut region lengthens, becoming the omphalomesenteric duct. The intra-embryonic coelom on either side of the midgut becomes the peritoneal cavity. Rapid lengthening of the midgut takes place around the 15 mm stage and, at the same time, both liver and kidneys are growing rapidly and cannot all be contained by the intra-embryonic coelom. The midgut loop herniates into the extra-embryonic coelom with the omphalomesenteric connection at its apex and the superior mesenteric artery at its base.

During this period of physiological herniation, the cranial part of the loop increases in length much more rapidly than the distal part, giving rise to the jejunum and most of the ileum. The distal loop forms the terminal ileum, caecum, appendix, ascending colon and part of the transverse colon. The herniated loop rotates 180° in an anticlockwise direction whilst it is in the extra-embryonic coelom. At the 42–48 mm stage, approximately the 10th post-fertilisation week, the junctional region between mid- and hindgut moves to the left and, after rotation through a further 90° anticlockwise, the midgut returns to the abdominal cavity. The duodenum moves to the right, the caecum descends from the right upper quadrant below the liver to the right iliac fossa, and the ascending mesocolon fuses with the parietal peritoneum, thus stabilizing both ends of the small intestine. At this stage of development, small intestinal villi are short and few in number; they are covered by simple columnar epithelium. The muscularis propria is distinguishable from the inner supporting mesenchyme. By 20 weeks, villi are long and tapering and have increased in number. Glandular and villous epithelia are distinguishable, the latter having a brush border and being capable of mucus secretion. Further elaboration of villi continues until infancy.

ABNORMALITIES OF INTESTINAL ROTATION

Failure of intestinal rotation may be total (non-rotated) or, more commonly, incomplete (malrotation) when the 180° anticlockwise extra-abdominal rotation takes place but the caecum fails to descend to the right iliac fossa.

Non-rotation

When the intestines have failed to undergo rotation, the normal 'C' configuration of the duodenum is absent, the

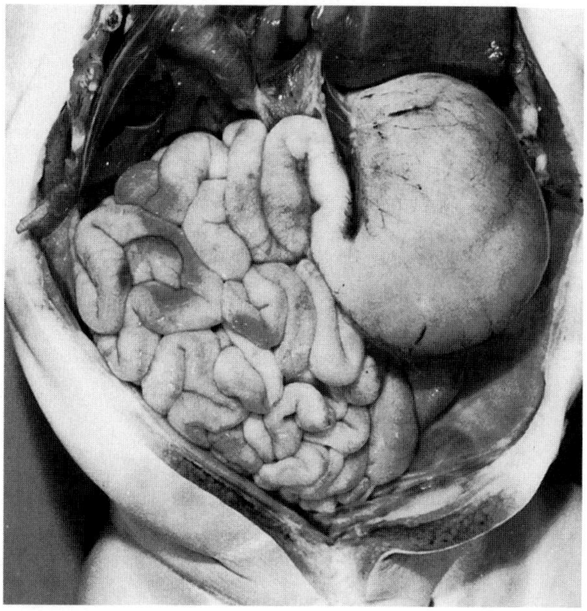

Fig. 16.1 Non-rotation of the intestine: small intestinal loops are crowded into the left side of the peritoneal cavity.

2nd to 4th parts of the duodenum run vertically downwards and all the small bowel loops lie in the right side of the abdominal cavity and the caecum and colon to the left. Failure of rotation of this type is the pattern which usually accompanies diaphragmatic hernia and exomphalos, although it may be the only abnormality (Fig. 16.1).

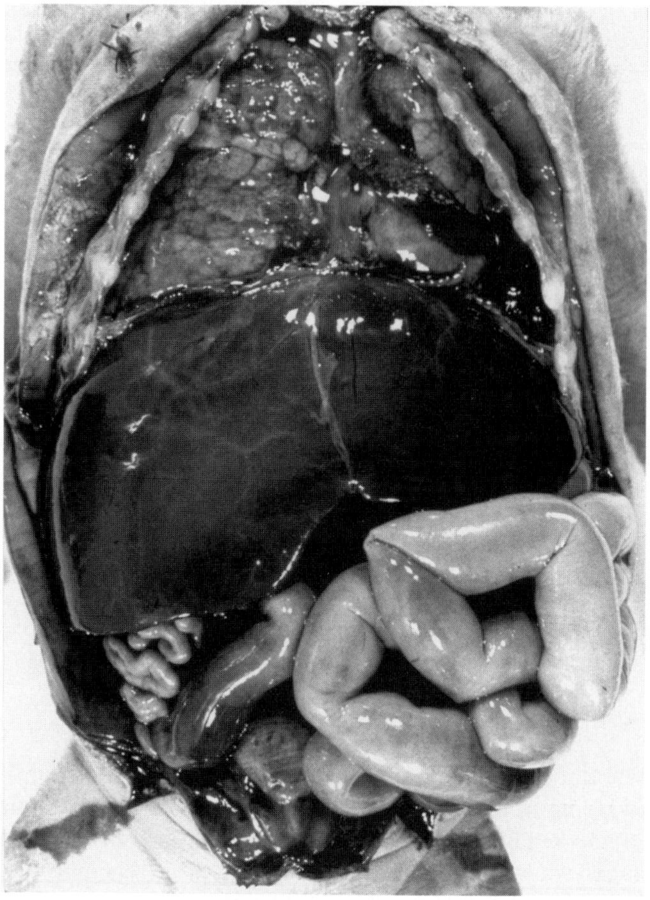

Fig. 16.2 Volvulus of incompletely rotated intestine giving rise to intestinal obstruction in a neonate.

Malrotation

With incomplete intestinal rotation, the position of the caecum is variable; it may lie in the upper, central part of the abdomen in front of the duodenum, immediately to the right of the duodenum beneath the liver or arrest at any point below this along its normal descent to the right iliac fossa. Failure of caecal descent renders the root of the small intestinal mesentery abnormally narrow.

Extrinsic obstruction of the duodenum can occur when the caecum lies in front of it.[1] Duodenal obstruction can also result from peritoneal bands (Ladd's bands) which run in front of the duodenum when the caecum is situated in the right upper quadrant.

The narrow mesenteric pedicle of the small intestine which accompanies malrotation renders small bowel loops unduly mobile and at risk of volvulus (Fig. 16.2). Diagnosis of malrotation can be made by ultrasonographic demonstration of alteration of the normal relationship of the superior mesenteric artery and vein,[2] or spiralling of intestinal loops around the mesenteric axis.[3] Malrotation is frequently symptomatic in the neonatal period. 25 of 45 symptomatic cases were seen in neonates in a Canadian study.[4] These authors record malrotation as an incidental finding at laparotomy or necropsy in a further 30 patients during the same period, 10 of whom had small intestinal anomalies and 14 had abdominal wall or diaphragmatic defects. In another study, 32 of 70 infants with symptomatic malrotation had other malformations, mainly intestinal atresia or duodenal web.[5] A further group found that of 102 infants and children with malrotation (half were neonates) 70 had congenital malformation including 15 abdominal wall defects and 25 anomalies of the small intestine or midgut derivitives.[6] Transient volvulus and local ischaemia in utero may explain some cases of intestinal atresia[7] and congenital short intestine.

Malrotation is seen in association with certain chromosome anomalies such as trisomies 21, 18 and 13 and in other malformation syndromes.[8]

Reversed rotation

Occasionally, intestinal rotation takes place in a clockwise, rather than anticlockwise, direction.[9] Both duodenum and superior mesenteric artery lie anterior to the transverse colon and may cause extrinsic colonic obstruction.

VITELLO-INTESTINAL REMNANTS

A group of anomalies is recognized which are derived from persistence of part of the vitello-intestinal duct, which normally becomes narrower and divides at around the 6.2 mm (35 days) stage and disappears before physiological intestinal herniation reduces at around the 45 mm stage (10 weeks' gestation). The different types of anomaly are illustrated diagrammatically in Figure 16.3.

Meckel's diverticula, with or without cord attachment to the abdominal wall, account for 90% of defects.[10]

Meckel's diverticulum

Meckel's diverticulum is the commonest congenital intestinal anomaly and is generally estimated to be present in about 2% of the population, although a careful search during consecutive appendicectomies revealed a Meckel's diverticulum in 3.2% of cases.[10]

It represents persistence of the intestinal end of the vitello-intestinal duct and is much more frequent than the other anomalies described below. The diverticulum is situated on the antimesenteric border of the terminal ileum. It is usually of the same diameter as the ileum from which it arises and its wall is of similar construction with muscle coats in continuity. The diverticulum is lined by small intestinal mucosa, but foci of heterotopic pan-

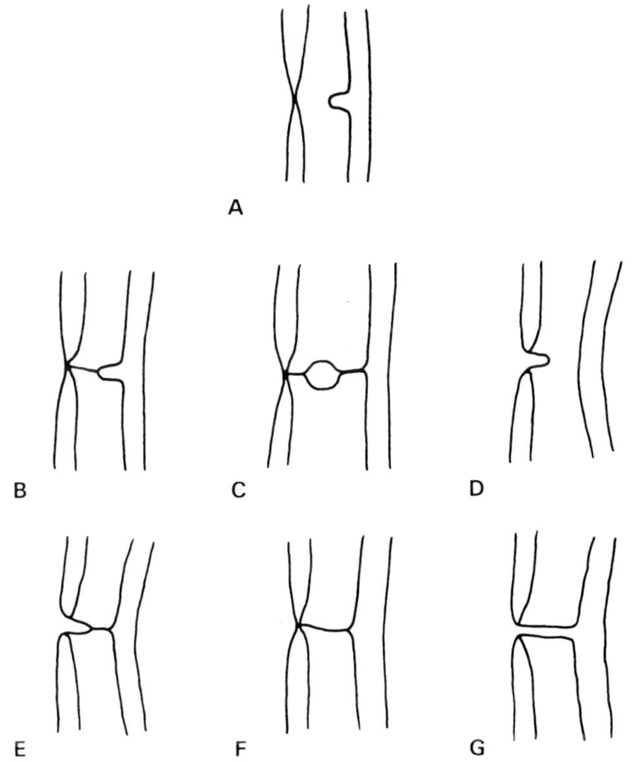

Fig. 16.3 Vitello-intestinal remnant. **A** Meckel's diverticulum; **B** with cord to abdominal wall; **C** enterocystoma; **D** vitelline sinus; **E** sinus with cord to terminal ileum; **F** obliterated duct; **G** persistent vitello-intestinal sinus.

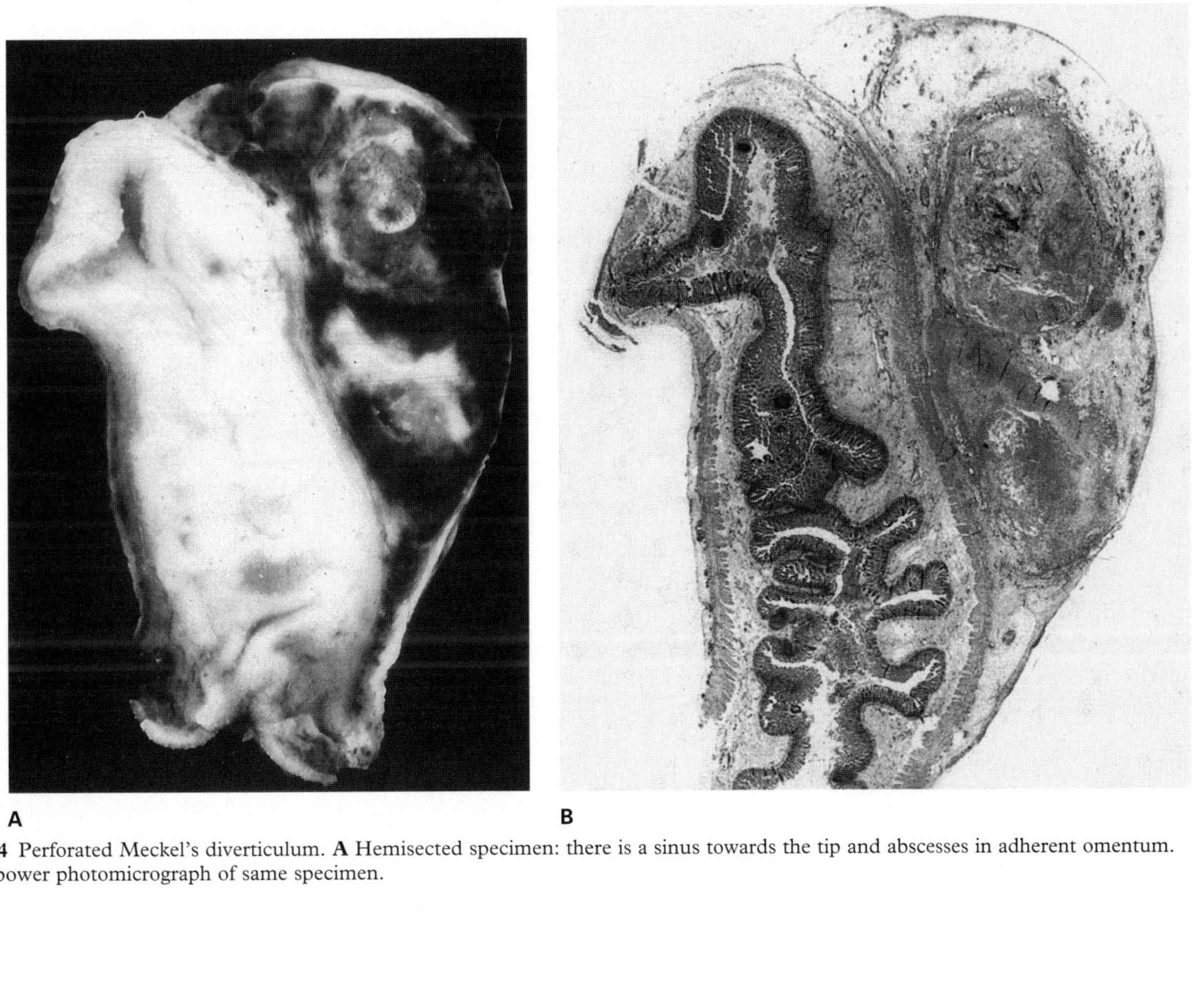

Fig. 16.4 Perforated Meckel's diverticulum. **A** Hemisected specimen: there is a sinus towards the tip and abscesses in adherent omentum. **B** Low-power photomicrograph of same specimen.

creas or gastric mucosa are present in about half of resected specimens and about 80% of symptomatic cases.[11] Gastrin-containing cells have been demonstrated histochemically in the mucosa of Meckel's diverticula[12] and may give rise to peptic ulceration either within the diverticulum or in the immediately distal ileum. These ulcers often bleed profusely. Less commonly, perforation (Fig. 16.4) with peritonitis or intestinal obstruction due to adhesions and diverticulitis are described. Meckel's diverticulum may interfere with peristalsis and become the apex of an intussusception. Complications of Meckel's diverticula from two studies are summarized in Table 16.1.

Neoplasms occasionally arise in Meckel's diverticula; in one review,[13] malignant tumours were encountered more commonly than benign ones. Carcinoid is the commonest type of tumour and a variety of sarcomata and adenocarcinomas are described. Both carcinoid tumour and sarcoma have been encountered in infants and older children.

Table 16.1 Complications of Meckel's diverticula.

Presentation	Soderlund 1959[10] Total	(children)	Weinstein et al 1962[11]
Peptic ulcer/haemorrhage	40	(36)	63
Bands/volvulus	40	(28)	28
Diverticulitis	24	(13)	29
Intussusception	19	(19)	15
Hernia	4	(4)	9
Umbilical fistula	15	(15)	8
Neoplasm	—		10
Total symptomatic	142	(115)	162
Incidental finding	271		560
Total	413		722

Vitello-intestinal duct

Persistence of patency of the vitello-intestinal duct is rare. It becomes apparent when meconium or faecal material appears at the umbilicus. Occasionally, the ileum may intussuscept through the duct, when its appearance has been confused with a ruptured exomphalos.[14]

Vitello-intestinal cysts

These cysts, which are lined by mucus-secreting epithelium, represent focally persistent patency of the vitello-intestinal duct. They can occur at any point along the length of the vitelline cord or be present within the fetal end of the umbilical cord (Fig. 16.5).

Umbilical sinus — enterocystoma

A mucosal lined sinus or mucosal covered polyp may be present at the umbilicus. Bleeding and local infection are common complications and necessitate excision or cautery.

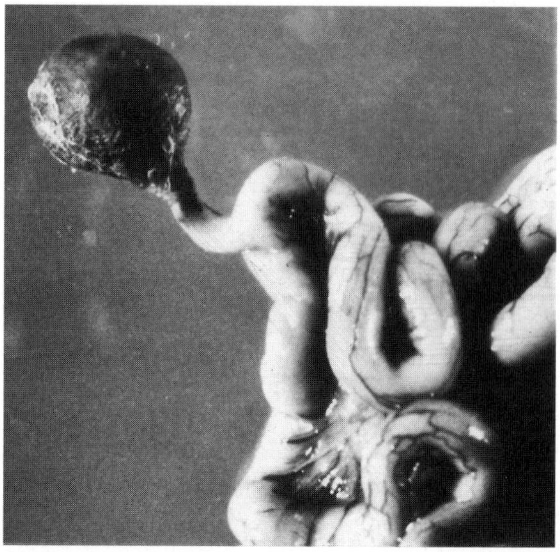

Fig. 16.5 Enterocystoma attached to ileum by a partly obliterated vitello-intestinal duct from neonate with trisomy 13. (By permission of Springer-Verlag[67])

Vitelline cord

A fibrous cord runs between the terminal ileum or a Meckel's diverticulum and the abdominal wall at the umbilicus. Such cords predispose the intestine to torsion. Persistence of a solid cord between the terminal small intestine is the least common vitello-intestinal remnant.

INTESTINAL DUPLICATION (DORSAL ENTERIC REMNANTS)

Intestinal duplications are cystic or tubular structures lined by functioning intestinal mucosa with a wall composed of smooth muscle. As their name implies, they lie on the dorsal aspect of the intestine and may be situated at any point from the spinal cord to the intestine. Many lie within the mesentery and some lie within the muscularis propria of the intestine. Duplications of the intestine may be found at any level in the gastrointestinal tract but more than 50% are related to the small intestine,[15] particularly the terminal ileum.

Duplications may be closed cystic, ovoid or spherical structures varying in size from a few millimetres to 10–15 cm in diameter, or tubular elongated structures. These often communicate with the lumen of the intestine and may achieve a length of more than 30 cm. Occasionally they extend the whole length of the small intestine.[16] Cystic duplications increase in size as mucus is secreted into the lumen, and present with symptoms of intestinal obstruction as the adjacent intestine is stretched over the surface of the cyst (Fig. 16.6). Intramural cysts may become the apex of an intussusception. Many small cysts are identified incidentally in infants at necropsy or during surgery. Tubular duplications usually lie close to the intestine and often run parallel to it, although this is not invariable. They may share their muscle coat with the intestine for the whole or part of their length. Tubular duplications often present with signs of intestinal obstruction as they impinge on the lumen of the intestine or provoke intussusception or volvulus. However symptoms do not always suggest intra-abdominal pathology[17] or be related to peptic ulceration caused by ectopic gastric mucosa in the duplication lining. Haemorrhage and occasionally perforation may complicate the peptic ulceration.

A number of theories have been advanced to explain the origin of duplication cysts, including errors of recanalization following the supposed obliteration of the intestinal lumen by epithelial proliferation before the 40 mm stage and persistence of outpouchings of the intestine which have been observed during embryogenesis and intra-uterine intestinal ischaemia.[18] The observation first made by Veeneklaas[19] that intrathoracic duplications were frequently associated with vertebral clefts and rib anomalies, and his suggestion that intestinal duplications might result from failure to complete separation of the foregut and notochord, is now generally accepted. This theory has been elaborated by Bentley & Smith[20] to encompass a variety of defects with vertebral, spinal and intestinal anomalies, including fistulous communications between the intestinal lumen and spinal canal and post-vertebral intestinal duplications.

Although intestinal duplications are usually single, abdominal and thoracic duplications co-exist.[21] Bizarre symptoms may result from intestinal duplications or their fibrous connections which traverse the diaphragm.[22]

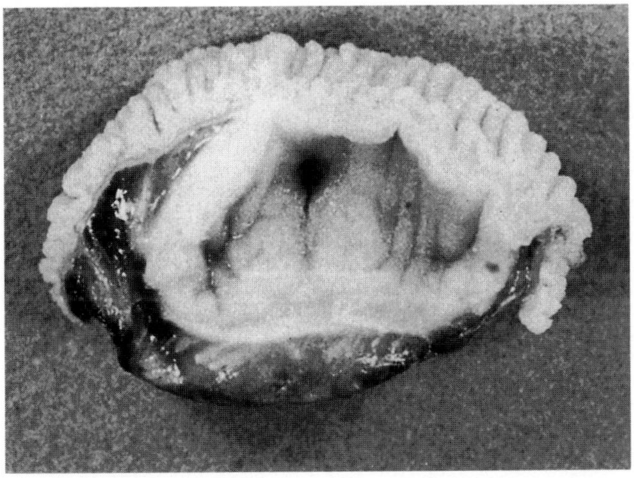

Fig. 16.6 Duplication cyst: the intestine is stretched over the surface of the cyst, which communicates with the intestinal lumen.

INTESTINAL ATRESIA AND STENOSIS

Intestinal atresia, in which there is a loss of continuity of the bowel lumen, may be due to deficiency of a segment of bowel or the lumen may be interrupted by a diaphragm internal to an intact muscularis propria. Atresia occurs most commonly in the duodenum, less commonly in the jejunum and ileum, where it is often multiple, and it is rare in the colon. Stenosis is less common at all sites in the small intestine and is usually the result of a diaphragm with a small meatus which may be a secondary phenomenon. Proximal myohypertrophy is usually greater in the presence of stenosis than of atresia.

Duodenal atresia

Duodenal atresia occurs in approximately 1:5000 live births. It is commonly associated with extra-abdominal defects, particularly cardiac anomalies and tracheo-oesophageal fistula, although anorectal anomalies are quite common.[23,24] Duodenal atresia occurs more commonly in Down's syndrome, in which it is described in one-third of patients in some centres.[24,25]

Duodenal atresia presents with vomiting when feeding is introduced and may be demonstrated radiographically by a 'double bubble' on a plain abdominal X-ray, when gas is seen in the distended stomach and proximal duodenum separated by the pylorus. Some cases of duodenal atresia are associated with increased maternal serum a-fetoprotein levels in the second trimester of pregnancy[26] or maternal polyhydramnios in the third trimester because of defective fetal swallowing. Survival is dependent on the nature of associated malformations. The commonest form of obstruction is atresia with loss of continuity of muscle, the gap between the bowel loops being occupied by pancreas. This type of obstruction comprises 49–65% of those reported in two large series.[24,25] A mucosal covered diaphragm (Fig. 16.7) was the cause of obstruction in 41% and 19% of the same series, whilst stenosis was identified in 10% and 15% respectively. Annular pancreas was noted in more than half of the cases with a diaphragm or stenosis. In two-thirds of 507 cases, the obstruction was situated beyond the ampulla of Vater, but in half of the remainder its relationship to the ampulla was not determined.[24]

Duodenal atresia is probably the result of defective embryogenesis when failure of complete recanalization of the viscus follows massive epithelial proliferation at the 8th week of gestation.[27] The association of annular pancreas points to this, as does the high incidence of other malformations.

Jejunal and ileal atresia

Atresias of the jejunum and ileum are encountered in approximately 1:6000 live births and are seen most fre-

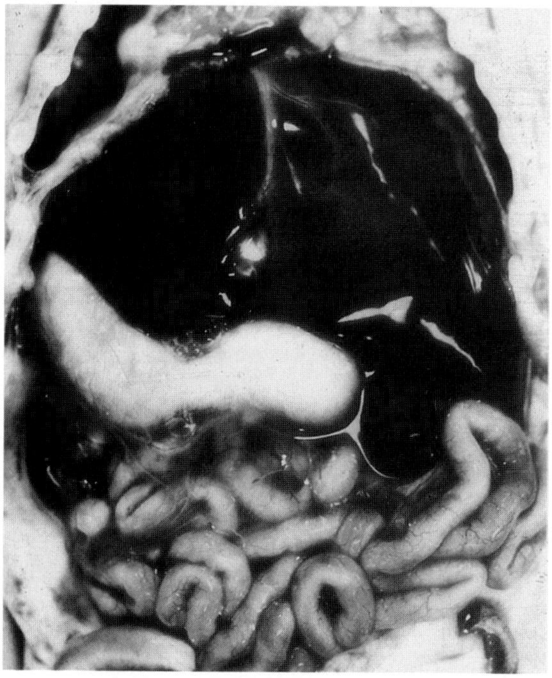

Fig. 16.7 Duodenal atresia: dilatation of the first part of the duodenum is apparent beyond the pylorus (fetus with trisomy 21).

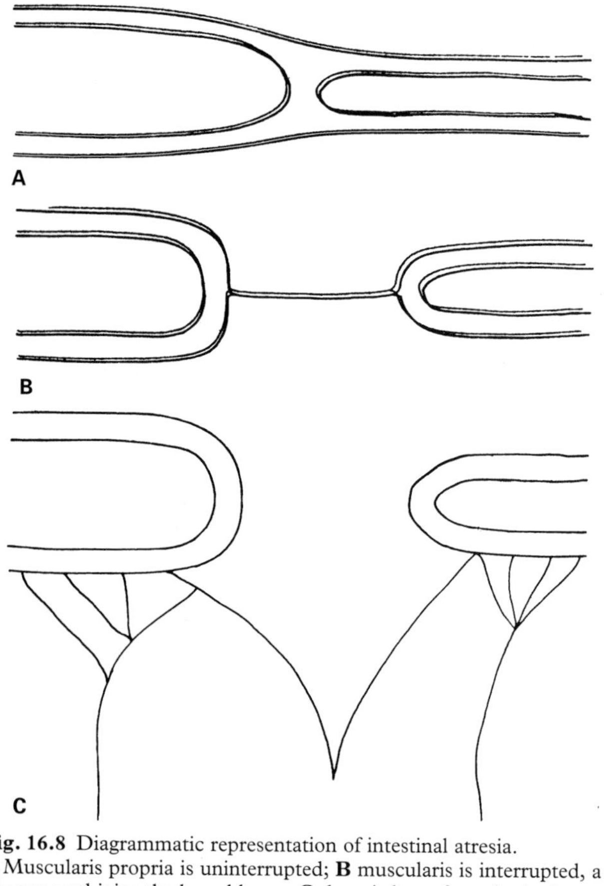

Fig. 16.8 Diagrammatic representation of intestinal atresia. **A** Muscularis propria is uninterrupted; **B** muscularis is interrupted, a fibrous cord joins the bowel loops; **C** there is loss of continuity between the bowel loops; a 'V' shaped defect is seen in the adjacent mesentery. (By permission of Springer-Verlag[67])

quently in the distal ileum (36%) and proximal jejunum (31%).[28] Three types of atresia are described (Fig. 16.8).

In type A, the lumen is occluded by a mucosa covered diaphragm, but the muscularis propria is intact (Fig. 16.9). Type B has loss of continuity of intestinal muscle, the two ends being joined by a fibrous cord, but the mesentery is uninterrupted. In type C, there is a gap between bowel loops (Fig. 16.10) and a 'V' shaped defect in the adjacent mesentery is usual.[29]

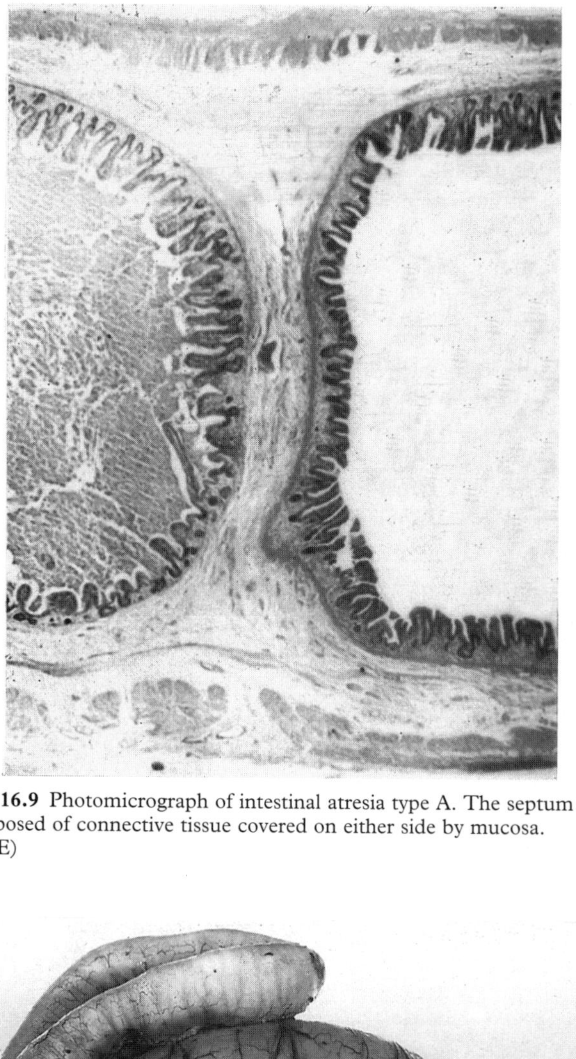

Fig. 16.9 Photomicrograph of intestinal atresia type A. The septum is composed of connective tissue covered on either side by mucosa. (H&E)

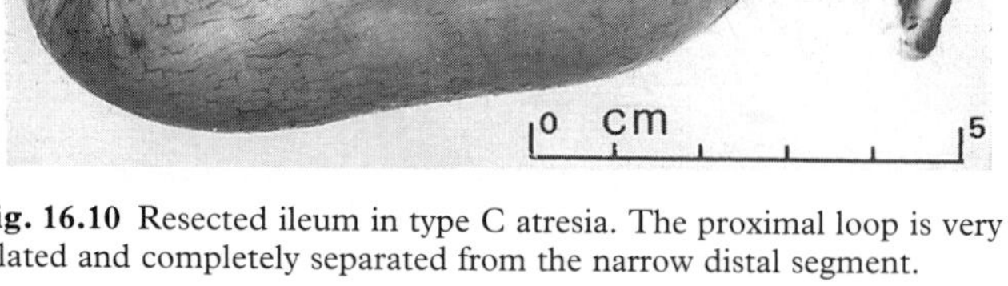

Fig. 16.10 Resected ileum in type C atresia. The proximal loop is very dilated and completely separated from the narrow distal segment.

For many years, failure of complete recanalization of the intestinal lumen after the 'solid' stage of mucosal hyperplasia was thought to be responsible for jejunal and ileal atresia, comparable to the development of duodenal atresia. It was subsequently shown that it is only in the duodenum that complete obliteration of the lumen occurs.[27] All three types of intestinal atresia and localized stenosis have been produced experimentally by interrupting intestinal blood supply by occluding branches of the superior mesenteric artery in fetal dogs and allowing pregnancy to continue.[30,31] Intestinal atresia has been produced in chicks by temporarily occluding a branch of the omphalomesenteric artery with a suture.[32]

Observations in human infants support the concept of development of intestinal atresia after the period of embryogenesis. Squamous debris and lanugo hairs are found in the intestinal lumen distal to the atretic segment in some cases,[29] indicating patency of the lumen until the second half of gestation. Intestinal infarction was present in 42 cases of intestinal atresia undergoing laparotomy.[28] Nearly half of a series of similar cases had evidence of peritonitis in the absence of intestinal perforation.[33] Occasional cases of intestinal atresia have evidence of in utero intussusception as the origin of ischaemic insult.[34] Intestinal atresia (and short small intestine) are recognized as disruptive effects following death in utero of a monozygous twin[35] and complicating congenital syphilis with mesenteric arteritis.[36] Extra-abdominal malformations rarely accompany jejunal or ileal atresia, although four infants who also had fetal akinesia deformation sequence have been described.[37] Local abnormalities such as malrotation, meconium ileus, omphalomesenteric remnants, gastroschisis or exomphalos are commonly found.[38] All are conditions which predispose to volvulus and thus to intestinal ischaemia. Exogenous insults, such as maternal hypotension during anaphylaxic shock[39] or iatrogenic insult during pregnancy, such as intestinal perforation during amniocentesis[40] and maternal Cafergot ingestion,[41] are described in association with fetal intestinal atresia. The development of intestinal atresia as a complication of necrotizing enterocolitis occurring in preterm neonates who had normal intestinal function in their immediate postnatal period is further evidence for an ischaemic aetiology for this condition.

Multiple intestinal atresias have been described in siblings in whom intestinal continuity was interrupted by a series of mucosal diaphragms at many sites from the pylorus to the sigmoid colon.[42] A failure of recanalization following epithelial hyperplasia was postulated as the cause, and defective embryogenesis may be the explanation here because they are not typical of the usual appearance of intestinal atresia.

Infants with jejunal or ileal atresia present with abdominal distension and vomiting. Peristalsis may be visible through the abdominal wall.

The commonest type of atresia is type C (Fig. 16.10). The proximal intestinal segment is distended, thick-walled and blind-ending. The immediate distal loop is of narrow diameter and separated from it. Atresia is frequently multiple, when there is a mixture of type II and type III lesions. Despite dilatation of the proximal loop by faecal material, the villi are not flattened unless meconium ileus is the predisposing factor.

Apple peel or maypole deformity

An unusual familial type of intestinal atresia has been reported and the possibility of an autosomal recessive mode of inheritance is suggested on the basis of similarly affected siblings.[43] However, in some families, siblings of babies with the 'apple peel' deformity have exhibited the more common form of multiple intestinal atresia.[44]

There is low duodenal or high jejunal atresia, marked reduction in length of the small intestine and a large defect in or absence of the dorsal mesentery. The remaining small intestine coils around the marginal artery

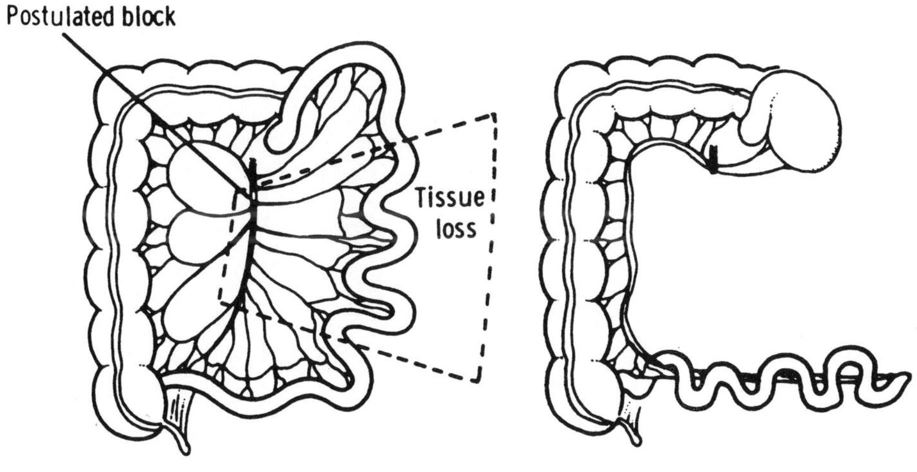

Fig. 16.11 Left: distribution of the superior mesenteric artery and the probable effect of a proximal arterial obstruction. Right: the end result of the obstruction with necrosis and resorption of bowel. (Courtesy of Mr JAS Dickson, Sheffield[46])

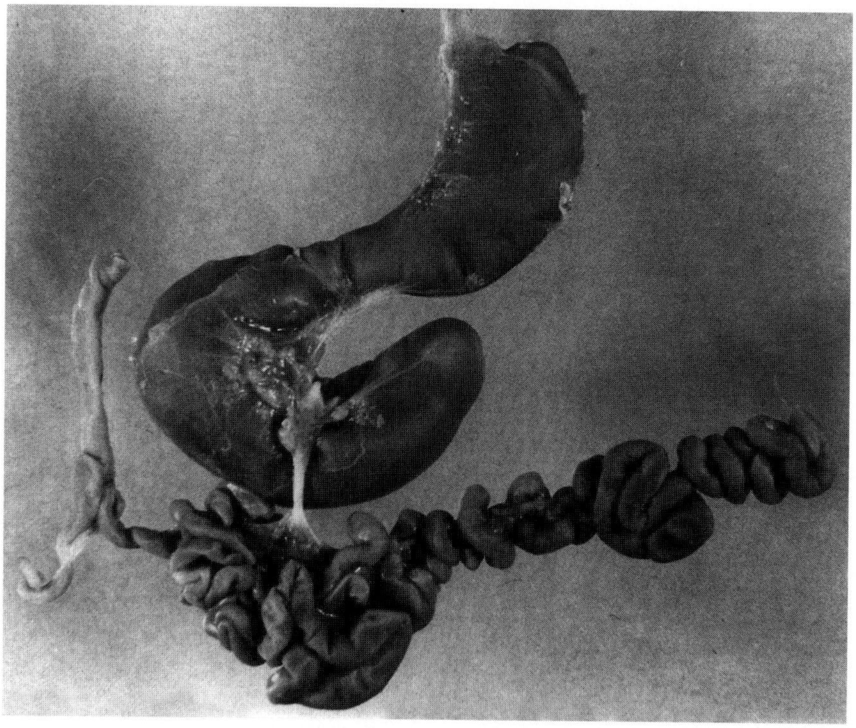

Fig. 16.12 'Apple peel' jejunal atresia. There is marked distension of the duodenum and loss of continuity between duodenum and jejunum. The distal small intestine is wrapped round the arterial axis.

(Figs 16.11, 16.12).[45,46] It has been suggested that volvulus (probably complicating short mesenteric attachment) initiates occlusion of the superior mesenteric artery distal to the origin of its first jejunal branches.[45]

VOLVULUS

Torsion of loops of intestine with interruption of their blood supply, ischaemia and gangrene of the bowel occur in infants and children as a complication of several congenital anomalies.

Malrotation renders bowel loops unduly mobile. In meconium ileus, bowel loops distended by abnormal putty-like contents are liable to volvulus, as are lengths of bowel where there is a congenital duplication. Torsion of bowel loops around intra-abdominal bands such as a vitello-intestinal remnant is also seen. Abdominal wall defects such as gastroschisis and exomphalos may also be complicated by volvulus.

Transient prenatal volvulus is one mechanism for development of intestinal atresia, short intestine and segmental absence of intestinal musculature.[47]

MECONIUM ILEUS

In meconium ileus, the small intestine is distended by an accumulation of abnormally viscid meconium during fetal life, so at birth the mature neonate has abdominal distension and intrinsic intestinal obstruction. This disorder accounts for about 15% of all forms of intestinal obstruction in the neonate. 90–95% of cases of meconium ileus are manifestations of mucoviscidosis, comprising 15% of cases of mucoviscidosis.[48]

Characteristically, the infant has a distended, doughy abdomen and does not pass meconium from birth. An

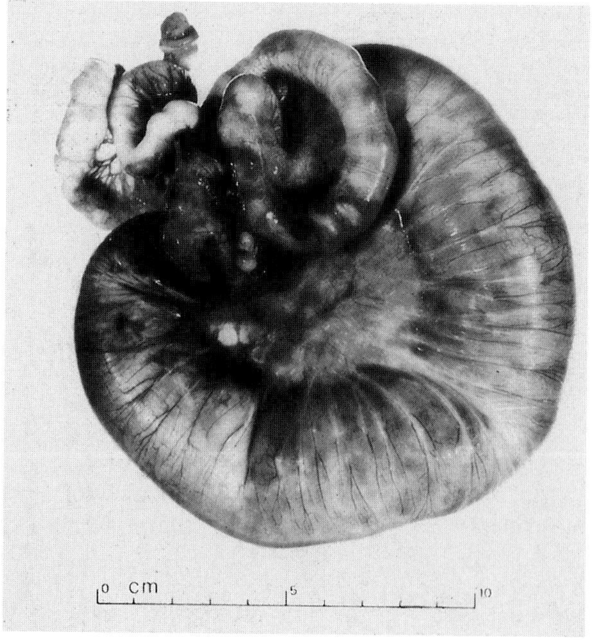

Fig. 16.13 Meconium ileus: a loop of small intestine is grossly distended by its abnormally viscid contents.

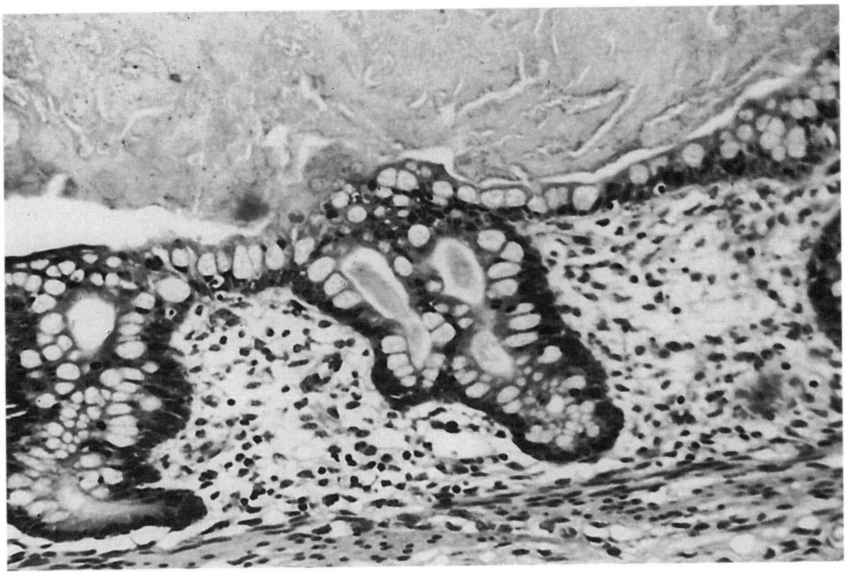

Fig. 16.14 Meconium ileus: intestinal villi are completely flattened by viscid meconium which fills and distends the lumen. (H&E)

abdominal radiograph has a characteristic ground glass appearance and may show focal calcification of bowel contents. There may also be intraperitoneal calcification as well as distension of bowel loops and a few fluid levels.[49] Maternal polyhydramnios can occur in the third trimester of affected pregnancies and sometimes the fetus is hydropic,[50] perhaps because of interference with venous return from the placenta during the last trimester because of increased intra-abdominal pressure.

The affected loops of small intestine are markedly distended (Fig. 16.13) by grey/green putty-like meconium, within which pale flecks of calcification may be present. The serosa is usually injected and dull; perforation with local adhesions is sometimes present. Volvulus or atresia of the intestine are frequent complications.[51] Histological examination of the bowel wall shows flattening of villi by the abnormal intestinal contents (Fig. 16.14). Goblet cells are conspicuous within the intestinal epithelium. When perforation occurs, peritonitis results. An inflammatory infiltrate, often with prominent eosinophils, is seen in muscle coats and serosa, and calcified flecks of meconium may be seen within the intestinal wall. Occasionally, diverticulosis is produced when intraluminal pressure rises due to the meconium plug (Fig. 16.15).

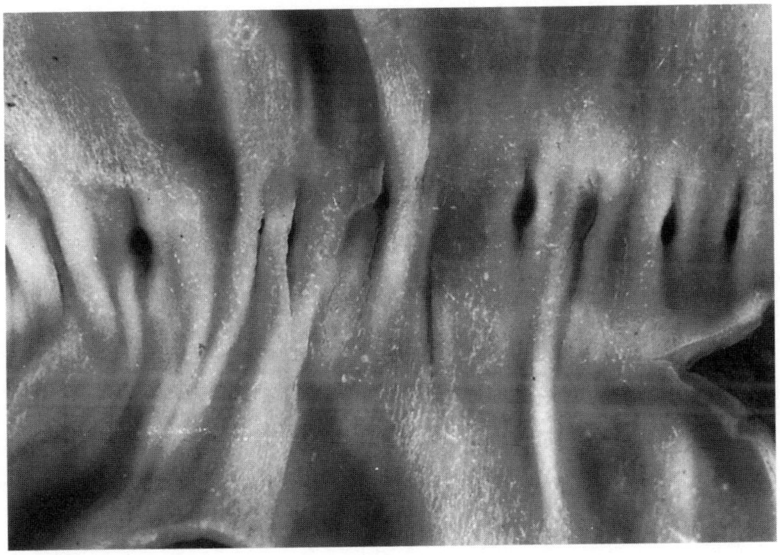

A

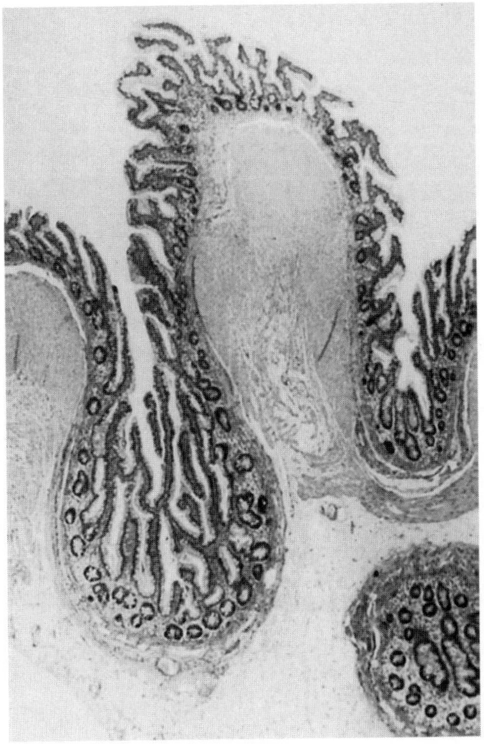

B

Fig. 16.15 A Meconium ileus: diverticula along the mesenteric border of the ileum. (Courtesty of Dr CH Mason, Oxford) **B** Photomicrograph of **A** showing diverticula, formed by herniation of the mucosa through the muscularis propria. (H&E)

Intestinal obstruction secondary to plugs of meconium is sometimes seen in preterm neonates, particularly when fluid restriction is instituted in order to prevent reopening of the ductus arteriosus.[52] Pancreatic changes similar to those of cystic fibrosis may be present, but immunoreactive trypsin levels are often normal. One distinguishing feature is that all the affected prematures described passed normal meconium prior to the onset of intestinal obstruction.

MICROVILLUS INCLUSION DISEASE

This condition, also known as congenital microvillus atrophy, is characterized by severe intractable diarrhoea from birth which is made worse by oral feeding. There is currently no curative treatment and parenteral nutrition is necessary throughout life.[53,54] Not only is glucose absorption impaired but there is net water and sodium excretion by the enterocyte.

Jejunal mucosa is morphologically abnormal. There is partial villus atrophy, crypt hypoplasia and variable loss of the microvillus brush border over the tips of villi. Vacuoles containing microvilli are present in the apical enterocyte cytoplasm. These and the loss of surface microvilli are demonstrated by PAS staining.[54] Electronmicroscopic examination demonstrates microvillus-packed vacuoles, an excess of secretory granules and loss or shortening of microvilli on apical enterocytes. The microvillus border of crypt enterocytes is normal although there is an excess of secretory granules.[54]

Whilst electron microscopy was originally considered essential for diagnosis of this condition, Lake[55] has clearly demonstrated brush border loss and the presence of apical cytoplasmic inclusions by alkaline phosphatase staining of routinely fixed and processed jejunal mucosa (Fig. 16.16). Others still consider that electron microscopy has an important role in the diagnosis of microvillus atrophy.[56] Their study demonstrates similar abnormalities in rectal epithelium. This is an important observation as rectal suction biopsy is an easier and safer procedure than jejunal biopsy in a very sick infant.

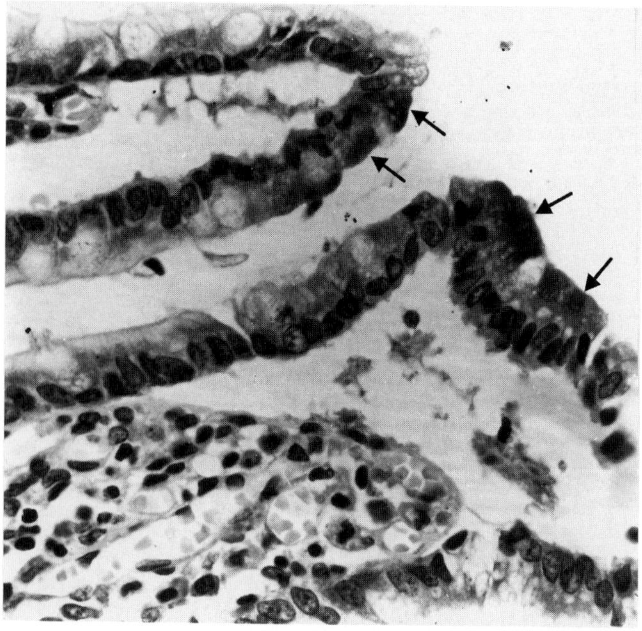

Fig. 16.16 Microvillus inclusion disease. There is loss of enterocyte brush border. Inclusions containing microvillus fragments are present in the apical cytoplasm (arrows). (Alkaline phosphatase/haematoxylin)

CONGENITAL SHORT SMALL INTESTINE

Reduction in length of the small intestine is sometimes observed at laparotomy or autopsy in the neonate. Occasionally it is the only anomaly,[57] but more commonly it accompanies other abdominal anomalies such as exomphalos,[58] gastroschisis, intestinal atresia,[7,35] enteric duplication[18] and malrotation.[59] Bowel ischaemia with subsequent reanastomosis and resorption of affected loops is postulated as the mechanism in most cases.

ABNORMALITIES OF INNERVATION

Abnormalities of innervation are seen less frequently in the small intestine than in the colon and are discussed fully in Chapter 22.

Hirschsprung's disease (see also Ch. 18)

Hirschsprung's disease can extend proximal to the ileocaecal valve, and in about 1% of cases the whole of the small intestine is aganglionic.[60] When aganglionosis

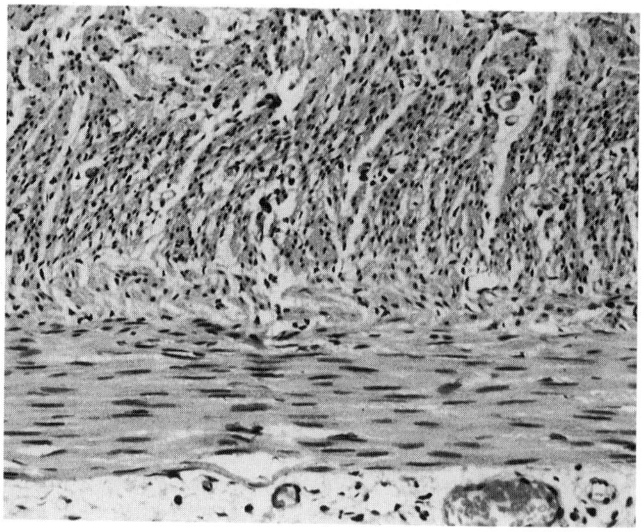

Fig. 16.17 Long segment Hirschsprung's disease: there are neither nerve trunks nor ganglion cells between the circular and longitudinal muscle coats. (H&E)

extends to the small intestine, myohypertrophy in the terminal region of the normally innervated gut is not pronounced, so that the 'cone' normally seen in the sigmoid colon in Hirschsprung's disease is absent. When histological examination of the bowel wall is undertaken in these babies, the plane of the myenteric plexus is empty (Fig. 16.17) for there is no hyperplasia of cholinergic nerves proximal to the region innervated by the sacral plexus.

Intestinal ganglioneuromatosis

A diffuse hyperplasia of nerves and ganglion cells involving both submicosal and myenteric plexus (Fig. 16.18) is present throughout the intestine in multiple endocrine adenoma syndrome type IIB.[61] Some affected individuals have symptoms related to disordered intestinal innervation which become apparent during infancy and childhood.

Intestinal neuronal dysplasia

Intestinal neuronal dysplasia is a recently recognized disorder of parasympathetic enteric innervation. It exists in localized and generalized forms. The former may coexist with short segment Hirschsprung's disease, the latter involves the small intestine and its mimicry of long segment Hirschsprung's disease has been described.[62]

Disseminated intestinal neuronal dysplasia presents in the neonatal period and early infancy with abdominal distension, contracted terminal ileum and microcolon.[63]

Histological features are hyperplasia of the submucosal and myenteric plexus which contain giant ganglion cells. Isolated ganglion cells lie free in the lamina propria and

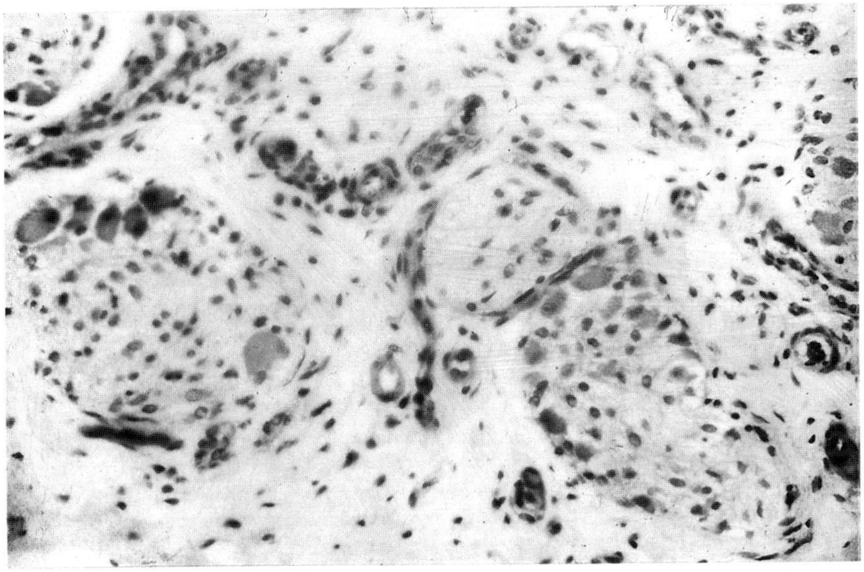

Fig. 16.18 Ganglioneuromatosis in the myenteric plexus of small intestine: 3 year old girl with multiple endocrine adenoma type IIB. (H&E)

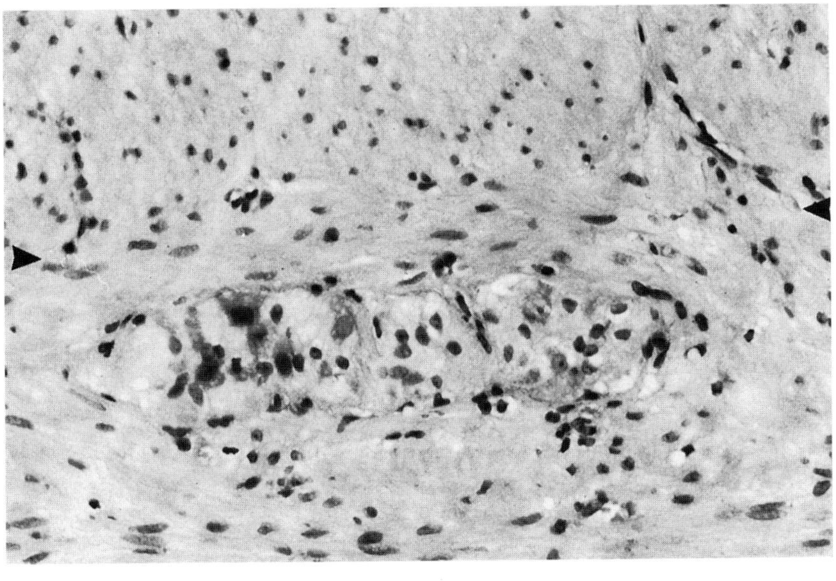

Fig. 16.19 Intestinal neuronal dysplasia: an abnormally large nerve containing ganglion cells is present within the longitudinal muscle. Arrowheads indicate the plane of the myenteric plexus, which contains tiny nerves.

within the muscularis propria distant from the plexus (Fig. 16.19). Increased numbers of nerves stain with the acetyl cholinesterase method in the lamina propria and circular muscle coats.[62]

HETEROTOPIAS

Nodules of heterotopic tissue, usually resembling pancreatic acinar glands, are sometimes visible through the serosa of the small intestine and stomach. They are commonly encountered in autosomal trisomy (particularly trisomy 13 and 18) (Fig. 16.20).

ANGIOMA

Angiomata of the small intestine are usually situated in the submucosa (Fig. 16.21), although infiltration of muscle may occur. They are usually multiple and come to attention because of anaemia or frank intestinal bleeding.[64] Intestinal obstruction resulting from intussusception of a cavernous angioma also is described.[65]

Most angiomata are cavernous, but capillary angiomata occur and may co-exist with angiomata in other sites, particularly cutaneous lesions,[65] or they are manifestations of the Klippel-Trenauny syndrome.[66,67]

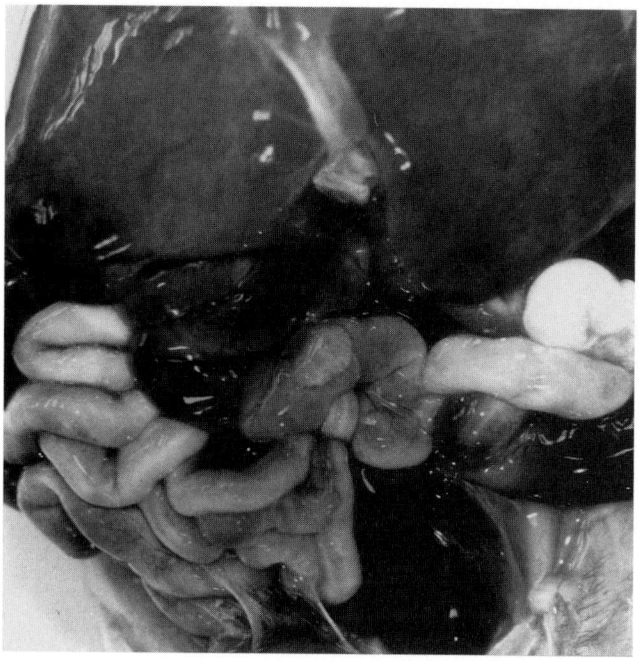

Fig. 16.20 Fetus, trisomy 18. A nodule of ectopic pancreatic tissue is present beneath the serosa of the small intestine.

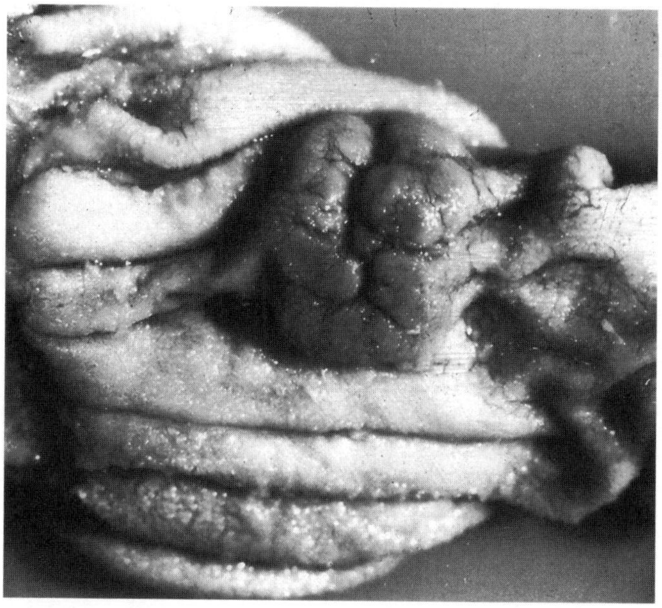

Fig. 16.21 A submucosal angioma protrudes into the intestinal lumen. Several similar lesions were identified at laparotomy in a 3-year-old boy with repeated intestinal haemorrhage.

REFERENCES

1. Snyder WH, Chaffin L. Embryology and pathology of the intestinal tract. Presentation of 40 cases of malrotation. Ann Surg 1954; 140: 368–379.
2. Weinberger E, Winters WD, Liddell RM, Rosenbaum DM, Krauter D. Sonographic diagnosis of intestinal malrotation in infants: importance of relative positions of the superior mesenteric vein and artery. Am J Roentgenology 1992; 159: 825–828.
3. Pracros JP, Sann L, Genin G. Ultrasound diagnosis of midgut volvulus: the 'whirlpool' sign. Pediatr Radiol 1992; 22: 18–20.
4. Spigland N, Brandt ML, Yazbeck S. Malrotation presenting beyond the neonatal period. J Pediatr Surg 1990; 25: 1139–1142.
5. Powell DM, Othersan HB, Smith CD. Malrotation of the intestines in children: the effect of age on presentation and therapy. J Pediatr Surg 1989; 24: 777–780.
6. Ford EG, Senac MO, Srikanth MS, Weitzman JJ. Malrotation of the intestine in children. Ann Surg 1992; 215: 172–178.
7. Benson CD, Lloyd JR, Smith JD. Resection and primary anastomosis in the management of stenosis and atresia of the jejunum and ileum. Pediatrics 1960; 26: 265–272.
8. Jones KL. Smith's recognizable patterns of human malformation. 4th ed. Philidelphia: Saunders, 1988.
9. Kiesewetter WB, Smith JW. Malrotation of the midgut in infancy and childhood. AMA Arch Surg 1958; 77: 483–491.
10. Soderlund S. Meckel's diverticulum. A clinical and histological study. Acta Chir Scand 1959; 118(Suppl 248).
11. Weinstein EC, Cain JC, ReMine WH. Meckel's diverticulum. JAMA 1962; 182: 251–253.
12. Capron J-P, Dupas J-L, Marti R, Descombes P. Gastrin cells in Meckel's diverticulum. N Eng J Med 1977; 297: 1126.
13. Weinstein EC, Dockerty MB, Waugh LJM. Neoplasms of Meckel's diverticulum. Int Abstr Surg 1963; 116: 103–111.
14. Moore TC, Schumacker HB. Intussusception of ileum through persistent omphalomesenteric duct. Surgery 1952; 81: 278–284.
15. Grosfeld JL, O'Neill JA, Clatworthy HW. Enteric duplications in infancy and childhood: an 18 year review. Ann Surg 1970; 172: 83–90.
16. Gdanietz K, Wit J, Heller K. Complete duplication of the small intestine in childhood. Z Kinderchir 1983; 38: 414–416.
17. Stringer MD, Dinwiddie R, Hall CM, Spitz L. Foregut duplication cysts: a diagnostic challenge. J Roy Soc Med 1993; 86: 174–175.
18. Favara BE, Franciosi RA, Akers DR. Enteric duplications. Thirty-

seven cases: a vascular theory of pathogenesis. Am J Dis Child 1971; 122: 501–506.
19. Veeneklaas GMH. Pathogenesis of intrathoracic gastrogenic cysts. Am J Dis Child 1952; 83: 500–507.
20. Bentley JFE, Smith JR. Developmental posterior enteric remnants and spinal malformations. Arch Dis Child 1960; 35: 76–86.
21. Fallon M, Gordon ARG, Lendrum AC. Mediastinal cysts of foregut origin associated with vertebral abnormalities. Br J Surg 1954; 41: 520–533.
22. McLetchie NGB, Purves JK, Saunders RL de CH. The genesis of gastric and certain intestinal diverticula and enterogenous cysts. Surg Gynecol Obstet 1954; 99: 135–141.
23. Dykstra G, Sieber WK, Kieswelter WB. Intestinal atresia. Arch Surg 1968; 97: 175–181.
24. Fonkalsrud EW, DeLorimier AA, Hays DM. Congenital atresia and stenosis of the duodenum. A review compiled from the members of the Surgical Section of the American Academy of Pediatrics. Pediatrics 1968; 43: 70–83.
25. Young DG, Wilkinson AW. Abnormalities associated with neonatal duodenal obstruction. Surgery 1968; 63: 832–836.
26. Weinberg AG, Milunsky A, Harrod MJ. Elevated amniotic fluid alphafetoprotein and duodenal atresia. Lancet 1975; ii: 496.
27. Moutsouris C. 'Solid' stage and congenital intestinal atresia. J Pediatr Surg 1966; 1: 446–450.
28. DeLorimier AA, Fonkalsrud EW, Hays DM. Congenital atresia and stenosis of the jejunum and ileum. Surgery 1969; 65: 819–827.
29. Santulli TV, Blanc WA. Congenital atresia of the intestine: pathogenesis and treatment. Ann Surg 1961; 154: 939–948.
30. Louw JH. Jejunoileal atresia and stenosis. J Pediatr Surg 1966; 1: 8–23.
31. Louw JH, Barnard CN. Congenital intestinal atresia. Lancet 1955; 2: 1065–1067.
32. Tibboel D, van Nie CJ, Molenaar JC. The effects of temporary general hypoxia and local ischaemia on the development of the intestines: an experimental study. J Pediatric Surg 1980; 15: 57–62.
33. Nixon HH, Tawes R. Etiology and treatment of small intestine atresia: analysis of a series of 127 jejunoileal atresias and comparison with 62 duodenal atresias. Surgery 1971; 69: 41–51.
34. Adejuyigbe O, Odesanmi WO. Intrauterine intussusception causing intestinal atresia. J Pediatric Surg 1990; 25: 562–563.
35. Hoyme HE, Higginbottom MC, Jones KL. Vascular etiology of disruptive structural defects in monozygotic twins. Pediatrics 1981; 67: 288–291.
36. Siplovich L, Davies MRQ, Kashchula ROC, Cywes S. Intestinal obstruction in the newborn with congenital syphilis. J Pediatr Surg 1988; 23: 810–813.
37. Collins DL, Kimura K, Morgan A, Johnson DG, Leonard C, Jones MC. Multiple intestinal atresia and amyoplasia congenita in four unrelated infants: a new association. J Pediatr Surg 1986; 21: 331–333.
38. Paterson-Brown S, Stalewski H, Brereton RJ. Neonatal small bowel atresia, stenosis and segmental dilatation. Br J Surg 1991; 78: 83–86.
39. Olson LM, Flom LS, Kierney CMP, Shermeta DW. Identical twins with malrotation and type IV jejunal atresia. J Pediatr Surg 1987; 22: 1015–1016.
40. Therkelsen AJ, Rehder H. Intestinal atresia caused by second trimester amniocentesis. Br J Obstet Gynaecol 1981; 88: 559–562.
41. Graham JN, Marin-Padilla N, Hoefnagel D. Jejunal atresia associated with Cafergot ingestion during pregnancy. Clin Pediatr 1983; 22: 226–228.
42. Puri P, Guiney EJ, Carroll R. Multiple gastro-intestinal atresias in three consecutive siblings: observations on pathogenesis. J Pediatr Surg 1985; 20: 22–24.
43. Blyth H, Dickson JAS. Apple peel syndrome (congenital intestinal atresia). A family study of seven index patients. J Med Genet 1969; 6: 275–277.
44. Seashore JH, Collins FS, Markowitz RI, Seashore MR. Familial 'apple peel' jejunal atresia: surgical, genetic and radiographic aspects. Pediatrics 1987; 80: 540–544.
45. Weitzman JJ, Vanderhoof RS. Jejunal atresia with agenesis of the dorsal mesentery. Am J Surg 1966; 111: 44–449.
46. Dickson JAS. Apple peel small bowel: an uncommon variant of duodenal and jejunal atresia. J Pediatr Surg 1970; 5: 595–600.
47. Alvarez SP, Greco MA, Genieser NB. Small intestinal atresia and segmental absence of muscle coats. Hum Pathol 1982; 13: 948–951.
48. Donnison AB, Schwachman H, Gross RE. A review of 164 children with meconium ileus seen at the Children's Hospital Medical Center, Boston. Pediatrics 1966; 37: 833–850.
49. Kopel FB. Gastrointestinal manifestations of cystic fibrosis. Gastroenterology 1972; 62: 483–491.
50. Hutchinson AA, Drew JH, Yu VYH, Williams ML, Fortune DW, Beischer NA. Nonimmunologic hydrops fetalis: a review of 61 cases. Obstet Gynecol 1982; 59: 347–352.
51. Oppenheimer EH, Esterley JR. Observations in cystic fibrosis of the pancreas. II. Neonatal intestinal obstruction. Bull Johns Hopkins Hosp 1962; 111: 1–13.
52. King A, Mueller RF, Heeley AR, Robertson NRC. Diagnosis of cystic fibrosis in premature infants. Pediatric Research 1986; 20: 536–541.
53. Davidson GP, Cutz E, Hamilton JR, Gall DG. Familial enteropathy: a syndrome of protracted diarrhoea from birth, failure to thrive and hypoplasic villus atrophy. Gastroenterology 1978; 75: 783–790.
54. Phillips AD, Jenkins P, Raafat F, Walker-Smith JA. Congenital microvillus atrophy: specific diagnostic features. Arch Dis Child 1985; 60: 135–140.
55. Lake BD. Microvillus inclusion disease: specific diagnostic features shown by alkaline phosphatase histochemistry. J Clin Pathol 1988; 41: 880–882.
56. Bell SW, Kerner JA Jr, Sibley RK. Microvillus inclusion disease. The importance of electron microscopy for diagnosis. Am J Surg Pathol 1991; 15: 1157–1164.
57. Yutani C, Sakurai M, Miyaji T, Okuno M. Congenital short intestine, a case report and review of the literature. Arch Pathol 1973; 96: 81–82.
58. Reiquam CW, Allen RP, Akers DR. Normal and abnormal small bowel lengths. An analysis of 389 autopsy cases in infants and children. Am J Dis Child 1965; 109: 447–451.
59. Shaw JRN, Rancroft L, Cook RCM, Gough DCS. Functional intestinal obstruction associated with malrotation and short small bowel. J Pediatr Surg 1984; 19: 172–173.
60. Bodian M, Carter CO. A family study of Hirschsprung's disease. Ann Hum Genet 1963; 26: 261–277.
61. Khairi MRA, Dexter RN, Burzynski NJ, Johnston CC Jr. Mucosal neuroma, pheochromocytoma and medullary thyroid carcinoma: multiple endocrine neoplasia type 3. Medicine 1975; 54: 89–112.
62. Scharli AR, Meier-Ruge W. Localised and disseminated forms of neuronal intestinal dysplasia mimicking Hirschsprung's disease. J Pediatr Surg 1981; 16: 164–170.
63. Berdon WE, Baker DH, Blanc WA, et al. Megacystis-microcolon-intestinal hypoperistalsis syndrome. AJR 1966; 126: 957–964.
64. Nader PR, Margolin F. Haemangioma causing gastrointestinal bleeding. Am J Dis Child 1966; 111: 215–222.
65. Browne AF, Katz S, Miser J, Boles ET Jr. Blue rubber bleb nevi as a cause of intussusception. J Pediatr Surg 1983; 18: 7–9.
66. Kuffer FR, Starzynsk EC, Girolan A, Murphy L, Grabstald H. The Klippel-Trenaunay syndrome, visceral anteriomatosis thrombocytopenia. J Pediatr Surg 1968; 3: 65–72.
67. Keeling JW, ed. Fetal and Neonatal Pathology. London: Springer-Verlag, 1993.

CHAPTER

17

The large bowel, rectum and anus

D. J. deSa

GENERAL FEATURES AND ANATOMY OF THE LARGE BOWEL

The large intestine includes the caecum, vermiform appendix, ascending, transverse, descending and sigmoid colon, rectum and anal canal. As reflected by their blood supply, these structures are derived from three distinct components.[1] The caecum, vermiform appendix, ascending colon and the proximal half to two-thirds of the transverse colon arise from the midgut, and are supplied by branches of the superior mesenteric artery. The remainder of the transverse colon distally to the lower third of the anal canal develops from the hindgut and is supplied by the inferior mesenteric artery. The lower third of the anal canal is derived from the proctodeum and receives its blood supply from the inferior rectal arteries, as well as branches of the (somatic) internal pudendal arteries. The exact point of transition between the midgut and hindgut derivatives may vary between patients, but the site is indicated by the zone of overlap between the territories of distribution of the superior and inferior mesenteric artery.

The anatomy of the colon and rectum reflects its primary physiological functions — the absorption of water and the expulsion of faeces. The general tubular structure of the bowel is maintained with a mucosal layer, a muscularis mucosa, a submucosal layer, a muscularis propria and serosa.

The mucosa is lined by a simple columnar absorptive epithelium that dips down into the lamina propria to produce simple tubular glands. From the caecum to the rectum there is a progressive increase in the proportion of goblet cells in the epithelium. The intervening columnar epithelial cells do not have zymogen granules, but in children, especially neonatal infants, occasional Paneth cells may be seen in the crypts. Argentaffin cells are also present. The lamina propria carries the mucosal plexus of vessels and a mixed population of inflammatory cells including plasma cells, lymphocytes, macrophages and variable numbers of mast cells and eosinophils. The muscularis mucosa is a well defined structure even in the developing fetal bowel and similar in structure to that seen in small bowel. In the junctional plane between the muscularis mucosa and the submucosa, lymphoid follicles are commonly present and the mucosa overlying them is attenuated. The dimpling of the mucosa over the lymphoid follicles produces the 'innominate grooves' seen on double-contrast radiographic studies of the colon.[2] In children lymphoid follicles can be particularly prominent.[3] Lymphoid follicles are largest and most numerous in the vermiform appendix. As in the small bowel, the submucosa contains the larger vessels. The circular muscle is a complete layer, but the longitudinal muscle is aggregated into three bundles — the taenia coli — over much of the large bowel, but these fuse together to form a complete layer in the appendix and rectum. Serosal covered tags of adipose tissue form the appendices epiploica and these nodules of fat are supplied by small inconsequential branches from the main vascular arcade. The innervation of the bowel is the subject of a separate section but a detailed report, based on microdissection of the plexuses of the bowel, is now available.[4] The neural network displayed in these 'flat-mount (circuit diagram)' preparations is more extensive than would be expected from a study of two dimensional histological slides.

The anatomy of the colon, rectum and anus is described well in most standard textbooks of anatomy and histology but some comments need to be made regarding the specialized nature of the anal anatomy. Since the anal canal is derived from both the cloaca and the proctodeum, the pectinate line — that defines the site of the anal membrane — is an important landmark. The line represents the approximate site of anastomosis between the branches of the superior, middle and inferior haemorrhoidal arteries. Similarly, the region of the pectinate line represents a watershed between the cephalad areas that drain to the portal system of veins and pararectal lymph nodes, and the caudal areas that drain to the systemic veins and inguinal lymph nodes. The line also represents the approximate lower end of the internal sphincter muscles (supplied by the autonomic nervous system's nervi erigentes derived from S2–3 or 3–4) and the junction between the subcutaneous and superficial muscles of the external sphincter muscle (supplied by inferior haemorrhoidal nerves derived from S3–4). Above the pectinate line the mucosa is relatively insensitive while below the line the mucosa is extremely sensitive. Low level fistula in ano open into the anus at the pectinate line, and when an abscess of the ischiorectal region bursts into the anal canal it usually does so at the pectinate line. These observations were made well over 50 years previously but their validity remains.[5]

The sphincter mechanism consists of the puborectalis sling of the levator ani muscle (supplied by S3–4) and the internal and external sphincters. The internal sphincter is a condensation and concentration of the circular smooth muscle, arranged in a spiral fashion around the anal canal's upper two-thirds. Above it is continuous with the circular muscle of the rectum. The external sphincter muscle has three components: the subcutaneous fibres, the superficial and the deep bands. The subcutaneous muscle lies around the anal verge and does not contribute greatly to sphincteric integrity. The superficial layer surrounds the internal sphincter, acting as a spiral constrictor of the anal canal. The deepest muscle bundles merge above with the puborectalis sling. The external sphincter receives its nerve supply from S3–4 segments.

The anal glands are small aggregates of ducts, lined by 'transitional' epithelium which open behind the cusps of the anal valves and pass into the submucosa and sometimes beyond the internal sphincter. The secretory component of the anal glands is a simple, mucus-secreting epithelium arranged in a simple acinar fashion, surrounded by variable amounts of lymphoid tissue.

Development of the large bowel

The components of the large intestine that are derived from the midgut are affected by the 'physiological hernia' that occurs when excessive growth of loops of midgut outstrip the capacity of the developing abdomen. Like the small intestinal derivatives of the midgut, the future caecum, vermiform appendix and colon prolapse into the sac of the omphalocele. The growth of the abdominal cavity is associated with the rotation of the bowel and the return of the midgut loops. The rotation of the midgut fixes the cephalad segment of the midgut to the right of the midline and, as a consequence, the caudad loops are displaced to the left. The caecum and the future ascending and transverse colon initially lie on the left of the midline following the return of the midgut. There now ensues a further period of rapid growth of both the developing small bowel colon, as well as the hindgut-derived segments of colon. This period of growth is associated with the repositioning of the caecum, first across the midline to the right and then caudally to its normal anatomical site in the right iliac fossa (Fig. 17.1).

Initially the large bowel retains a mesocolon but, eventually, as the pace of growth slows (and with it the consequent repositioning of the bowel), the mesocolon is fixed to the parietal peritoneum of the posterior abdominal wall. With the caecum in its normal anatomical position, the sites of fixation are the ascending colon and the descending colon since these are the areas in direct contact with the parietal peritoneum. There is, however, considerable variation in the degree of fixation of the large bowel, and a definite ascending mesocolon is not an uncommon variant in neonatal and adult autopsy material.

The development of the upper segment of the hindgut derivatives closely follows the general pattern of the midgut derivatives. The fixation of the descending colon has been referred to, and like the ascending colon, the degree of fixation can vary considerably in normal persons, and a small descending mesocolon is as unremarkable and as frequent as an ascending mesocolon. The sigmoid colon retains a mesocolon but, during the fixation of other segments, some reduction occurs in its overall length. The

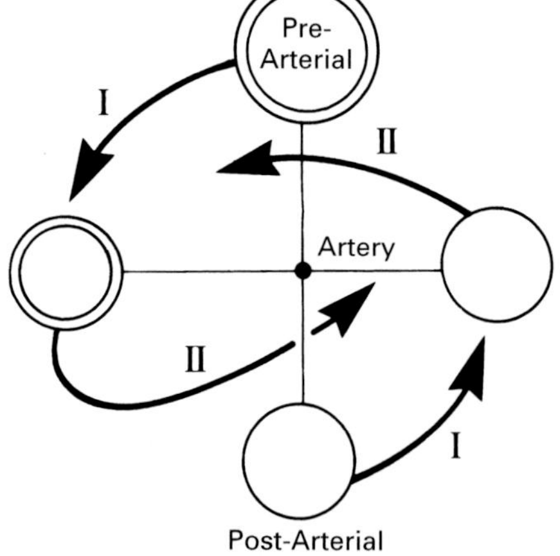

Fig. 17.1 A simplified scheme outlining the rotation of the midgut viewed from the ventral aspect. (Reproduced with permission from deSa 1991)[138]

length and redundancy of the sigmoid mesocolon varies considerably between different patients, however, and this may have an important bearing on the problem of volvulus of the sigmoid colon.

The early stages of the development of the large bowel are a relatively straightforward process of growth and repositioning of a tubular structure. However, the later development of the distal hindgut involves a complex series of steps with coordination of changes in many adjacent structures. Related to the development of the uterus and adnexal structures, differences exist between males and females. Many of the stages of development may be affected by the changes occurring in the sacrococcygeal region of the spine,[6] or by anomalies of the cloacal membrane that affect the external genitalia as well.[7] As a consequence, congenital anomalies of the anorectal region are frequent, and may form part of an extremely complex malformation sequence. Recognition of an anal anomaly is, therefore, an indication for a thorough investigation that must include the lower spine and the genitourinary system, as well as structures far removed from this area. From the pathologist's standpoint whole body radiographs are of inestimable value in studying these cases, and their importance cannot be overemphasized.

Development of the rectum and anal canal

The terminal portion of the hindgut is the *cloaca*. This cavity is lined by endoderm and comes in contact with the ectoderm in an area known as the *cloacal membrane*. The cloacal membrane forms the base of a shallow depression known as the *anal pit* or *proctodeum*. Ventrally, the cloaca is in continuity with the allantois, while the mesonephric ducts open into the lateral aspect of the cloaca. A short, blind prolongation of the hindgut into the tail fold is known as the *tailgut*, and this too communicates with the cloaca.

A sheet of mesenchyme develops in the coronal plane between the allantois and the hindgut. This *urorectal septum* grows caudally towards the cloacal membrane separating the dorsal (alimentary) structures from the ventral (genitourinary) derivatives. The alimentary derivatives are the rudimentary rectum and the upper two-thirds of the anal canal. In the female the paramesonephric ducts that are the progenitors of the fallopian tubes, uterus, cervix and upper vagina develop within the urorectal septum. Simultaneously with the development of the urorectal septum, the mesenchyme around the cloacal membrane proliferates leading to the development of the genital tubercles and the deepening of the anal pit, on the floor of which is the cloacal membrane. The deep anal pit so produced is now known as the proctodeal canal, and its development is accompanied by shrinkage and the ultimate disappearance of the tail fold and the tailgut (Fig. 17.2).

By the end of the 7th week the urorectal septum has reached and fused with the cloacal membrane. The point of fusion is marked by the perineal body or central perineal tendon. The cloacal membrane is now divided into

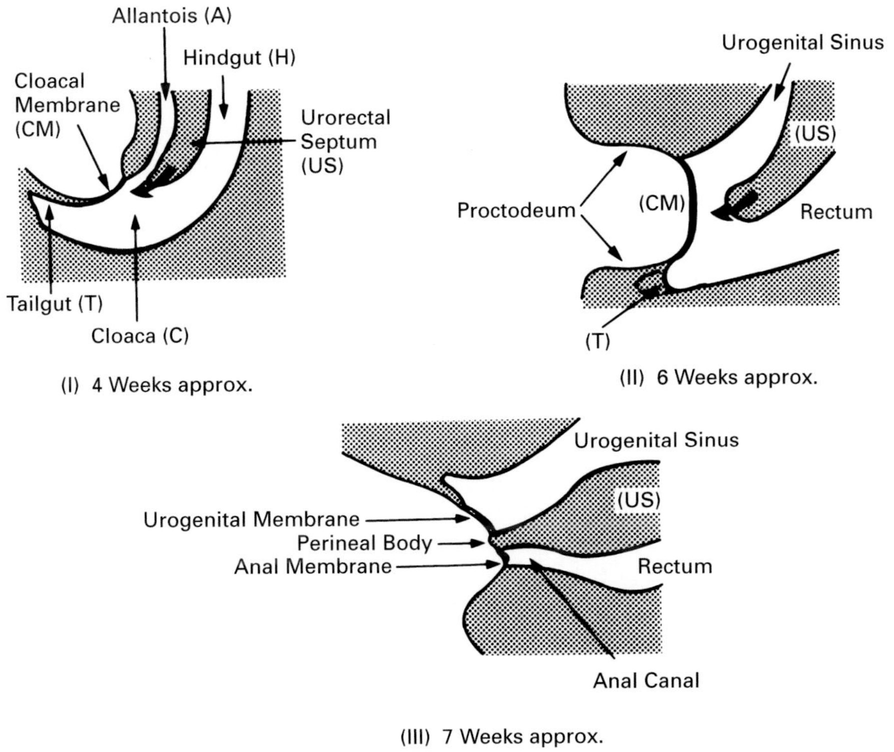

Fig. 17.2 Schematic representation of the partitioning of the cloaca and formation of the anal canal. (Reproduced with permission from deSa 1991)[138]

an anal membrane posteriorly and a larger urogenital membrane anteriorly. In the male the urogenital membrane, when it disintegrates, is incorporated into the urethral floor, while in the female it contributes to the hymen.

In the fetus, therefore, the hindgut communicates with the dorsal segment of the cloaca and is separated from the exterior only by the anal membrane. When the anal membrane breaks down the hindgut opens to the exterior, and this step is complete by 51 days.[8]

The anal canal of the fetus has two components. The cloacal component contributes to the upper two-thirds, while the proctodeal component forms the lower third. In the adult organ, their junction (the site of the anal membrane) is defined by the pectinate line and anal valves. The pectinate line should not be confused with the anocutaneous junction or 'white line' where the anal canal epithelium changes from stratified squamous to a keritinized type. The change from the mucus-producing columnar epithelium of the hindgut to the anal skin is not accomplished in a series of distinct clear-cut anatomical lines. In many infants the anal canal above the anal valves is lined by a narrow zone of 'transitional' mucosa with reduced numbers of goblet cells and islands of stratified squamous epithelium. However the epithelial lining can vary considerably, and in a few infants, areas of 'transitional' epithelium can be seen lining the upper anal canal. Transitional epithelium can be seen almost invariably lining the anal crypts. This 'transitional' epithelium shows an increase in the numbers of basally situated polygonal cells and no stratification. Some authors use the term 'cloacogenic epithelium' to describe the 'transitional' epithelium, but this appears tautologous since the upper two-thirds of the anal canal is cloacal in origin in its entirety, irrespective of the nature of its epithelial lining. Below the pectinate line the mucosa shows increasing keratinization, and at the anal margin, hair and sebaceous glands are seen.

From what has been described in the preceding paragraphs certain salient features emerge. The urorectal septum is the sole partition that separates the gastrointestinal tract from the genitourinary tract. The development of a normal anal canal depends on the coordinated development of the proctodeum with the urorectal septum. All the developmental anomalies that are associated with fistulae between the two systems, in either sex, are related to defects in the formation of the urorectal septum. The site of the fusion between the urorectal septum and the cloacal membrane is marked by the perineal body in both sexes, and the absence of a distinct perineal body indicates a failure of this process.

The normal development of the anal canal and lower rectum depends on at least two further factors: the regression of the tail and the tailgut, and the development of the sacrococcygeal vertebrae and lower spinal cord. Aberrant development of the lower spine or persistence of the tailgut and vestigial tail-like appendages, may be associated with malformations of the anal canal and rectum. The tailgut is a blind extension of the hindgut into the tail-fold just distal to the cloacal membrane. With the growth of the fetus and the development of the proctodeum, the tailgut is progressively resolved and taken up into the lower cloaca (Fig. 17.2). This process is complete by 56 days.[8] Remnants of this structure may persist, however, and form one variety of duplication or cyst of the presacral or retrorectal region. In their early developmental stages the anlages of the neural tube and the hindgut are anatomically adjacent to each other, becoming separated only later by the development of the notochord and somitic mesoderm. In association with abnormal development of the lower spinal cord and sacrococcygeal vertebrae, small columns of tissue linking the developing neural tube and hindgut may remain giving rise to neurenteric fistula and posterior enteric cysts.

Finally, anomalies of the anal canal and rectum may be part of malformation syndromes where abnormal development of many organ systems may result in a bewildering number of combinations of anomalies. While many of these syndromes are lethal, and do not pose problems in the realms of surgical pathology, *formes fruste* do exist and newer nonlethal combinations are added continually to the list. Since the anorectal anomalies in malformation syndromes have no unique, distinguishing features, it follows that all patients with anorectal anomalies require very detailed investigation.[9]

CONGENITAL ANOMALIES OF COLON

While the most frequent malformations of the large bowel are found in the anorectal region, the colon may be affected by many of the abnormalities seen in the small bowel and a brief discussion of these lesions seems appropriate.

Malrotation

If rotation of the bowel has been incomplete, the position of the large bowel is abnormal. As indicated earlier, the returning loops of large bowel that are derived from the midgut (appendix, caecum, ascending colon and proximal transverse colon) are initially found to the left of the midline and only reach their definitive anatomical sites following elongation of the bowel. The caecum and vermiform appendix may therefore be found in several different areas of the abdomen, depending on the extent to which bowel rotation has occurred. The most common aberrant site is the subhepatic caecum, but the caecum may be found in the left upper quadrant, and very rarely the entire colon may be found on the left side of the abdomen. A complete reversal of visceral situs can be seen in cases of complete *situs inversus*, and in syndromes such as Kartagener's triad where situs inversus is a feature. Minor degrees of malrotation may be encountered as an incidental finding in otherwise normal individuals, but malrotation is a common feature of many malformation syndromes.[10]

The malrotation anomalies of the large bowel assume importance in patients who develop appendicitis when the clinical localization of signs may be bizarre. Appendicitis developing in a subhepatic vermiform appendix has been misdiagnosed as acute pancreatitis, acute cholecystitis or acute pyelitis. A delay in accurate diagnosis may pose severe risks, especially in very old or very young patients where the clinical symptoms may be vague. The author has studied a fatal case of appendicitis in a child with a perforated subhepatic vermiform appendix and generalized peritonitis. In retrospect, the only clinical clue that might have provided the correct diagnosis was the abnormal distribution of the large bowel gas pattern on a plain film of the abdomen.

A further anomaly of fixation may be encountered in infants with massive bilateral renal enlargement for any reason, when the entire small and large bowel may be squeezed into a narrow band on either side of the midline.

Lack of fixation of large bowel

While it is not uncommon to find some mesocolon attached to the ascending and descending colon in addition to the normal sigmoid mesocolon, a large redundant mesocolon is not normal. In many instances, however, the condition is asymptomatic, but it may predispose the large bowel to volvulus, especially of the sigmoid colon, and less often, the caecum. The preferential involvement of the sigmoid colon in volvulus of the large bowel may be related to the increasingly solid nature of its contents; the combined effects of a redundant mesocolon, active peristalsis and inspissated faeces in the constipated patient, could lead to torsion of the bowel around its vascular pedicle. Lack of fixation often accompanies malrotation and thus may form part of many malformation syndromes.[10]

Stenosis and atresia of large bowel

While less frequent than similar lesions of the small bowel, stenosis and atresia do occur in the large bowel, and probably have the same ischemic origin.[11] Certainly the long-term follow-up of survivors of 'necrotizing enterocolitis' in infancy yielded many instances of stenotic and atretic lesions of the large bowel, as well as sealed perforations.[12]

Large bowel hamartomata

Hamartomatous ganglioneuromatous polyposis has now been described on many occasions, not only in association with von Recklinghausen's neurofibromatosis, but with juvenile polyposis,[13,14] or adenomatous polyps.[15] In neurofibromatosis, serosal lesions are common and diffuse plexiform involvement may be seen,[16,17,18] while in Multiple Endocrine Neoplasia IIB, ganglioneuromatous hyperplasia and polyposis is well recognized,[19,20] (Fig. 17.3). These polyps are usually small, sessile and asymptomatic.

Haemangiomas may be seen as incidental findings, but may be a source of bleeding, even when small.[16] Colonic mucosal lesions of diffuse neonatal angiomatosis,[21] blue rubber bleb nevus syndrome,[22] and hereditary haemorrhagic telangiectasia[23] have been reported, but in these rare conditions colonic involvement is only seen with extensive disease. When present, however, these lesions can bleed, and repeated episodes of bleeding may be life-threatening. The commonest angiomas of the colon are cavernous in type and though most cases show localized lesions, the entire colon may be involved.[24] These angiomas may present as small polyps. The abnormal vessels in larger lesions involve the pericolic and perirectal tissues, and resection of the lesion involves sacrificing the affected segment of gut.

Congenital fibromatosis may involve the large bowel causing obstruction in the neonatal period, and may even lead to perforation[25] (Fig. 17.4).

Cystic fibrosis and diverticula

In meconium ileus with cystic fibrosis the colon may be small (microcolon, hypoplastic colon). Intussusception may be a complication in older infants, as may rectal prolapse and colonic perforation.[26,27] Giant colonic diverticula have been seen in some older children with mucoviscidosis (Mancer, personal communication) (Fig. 17.5). In all patients, goblet cell hyperplasia and dilatation is a striking finding, and inspissation of mucus in the appendix of a newborn or infant can be a useful diagnostic finding.[28] Diverticula of the appendix may be present in some infants with meconium ileus.[29]

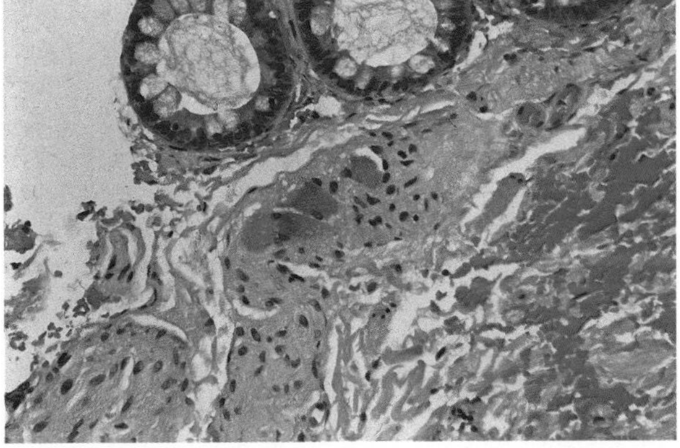

Fig. 17.3 Biopsy of rectal mucosal polyp showing thick nerve fibres and intramucosal ganglion cells in a 12 year old female with multiple endocrine neoplasia IIB. (H&E, ×400)

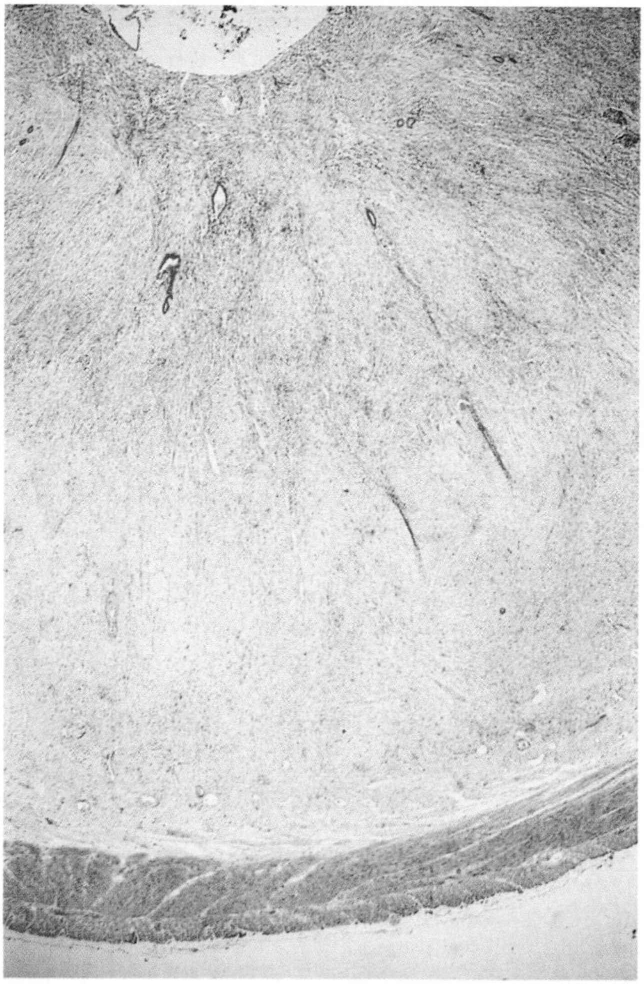

Fig. 17.4 Low power view of transverse section of swollen 3 cm segment of obstructed large bowel in a 4 week old infant, showing massive fibromatous replacement of mucosa and muscularis mucosa. Similar fibromatous change extended into the paracolic tissue (not shown). (H&E, ×10)

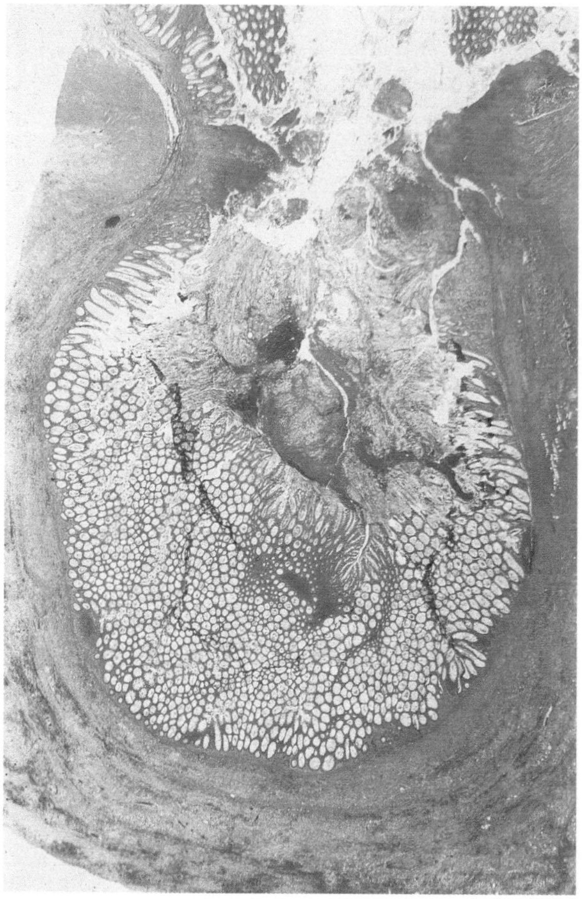

Fig. 17.5 Low power view of giant colonic diverticulum in a 3 year old male with cystic fibrosis. (H&E, ×32.5) (Slide courtesy of Dr Kent Mancer)

Congenital diverticula of the appendix have also been described in trisomy 13,[30] and the only personally studied example (Fig. 17.6A,B) was in an infant with trisomy 13. Trollope and Lindenauer[31] provide a very detailed review of diverticulosis of the appendix, with several examples of 'congenital' lesions, not all of which appear to be associated with trisomy 13 or cystic fibrosis; several of these diverticula were symptomatic in adult life. Most patients had a solitary diverticulum, and multiple diverticula were the exception.

Deficiency of smooth muscle

The initial report of this interesting condition described scattered sausage-shaped, non-perforated, ballooned segments of small bowel, which on histological examination had an apparent deficiency of the muscularis propria. Isolated examples have been described affecting the colon.[32] The pathogenesis of this lesion is not known. A curious feature is the persistence of a muscularis mucosa, normal mucosal morphology and absence of the myenteric plexus in the affected segments. The abnormal segments do not appear to be scarred or fibrosed. Since the muscularis mucosa develops after the muscularis propria,[33] a primary segmental deficiency of myogenesis does not seem to offer a likely explanation.

Duplications of the large bowel

Duplications of the large bowel fall into two separate categories:[34] those not associated with abnormalities of the bladder and urethra or anorectal region, and those that are.

By far the commonest variety consists of large, spherical or sausage-shaped mucus-filled cystic structures, with a muscular wall of varying thickness and completeness, lying within the mesocolon parallel to the normal segment of bowel. Only rarely do they communicate with the lumen of the bowel. The vascular supply to the normal bowel usually runs on the walls of the anomalous gut, so

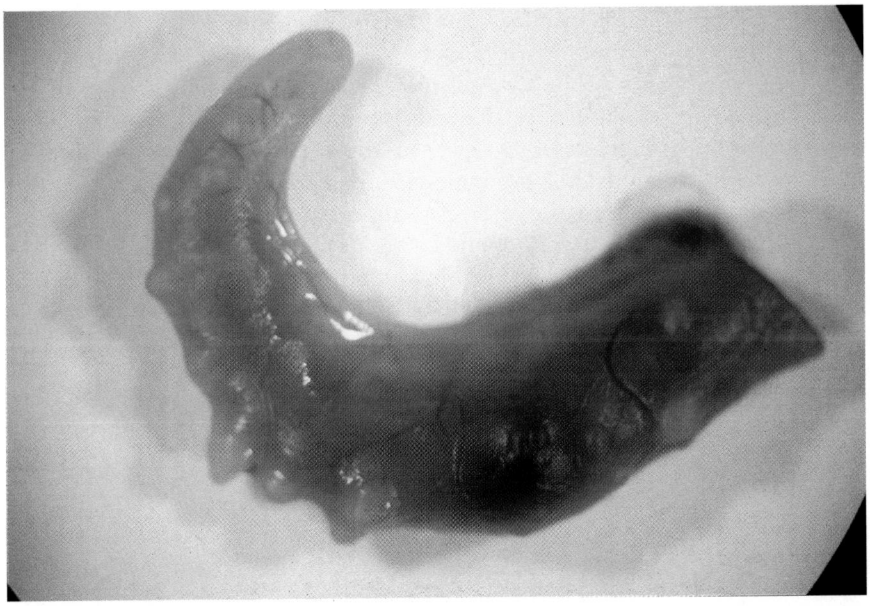

A

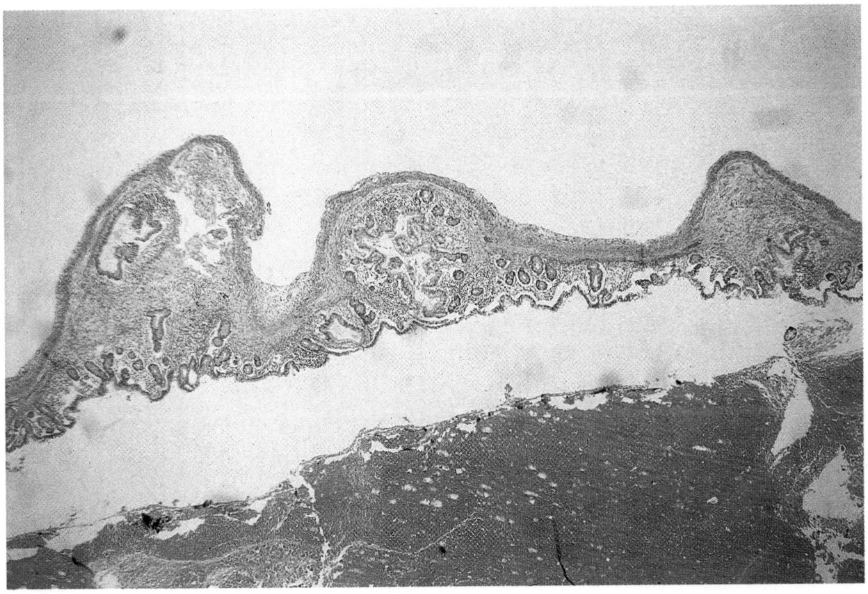

B

Fig. 17.6A Macroscopic view approximately 19.5 times enlarged, of vermiform appendix of female infant with Trisomy 13 (47XX,+13). Note the small diverticular protrusions. **B** Longitudinal section through diverticula showing the protrusion of mucosa covered by a thin layer of muscle. (H&E, ×325)

that surgical removal requires the removal of normal bowel as well. The duplicated segment is, usually, localized in extent, but the entire colon may be affected. Even when extensive, these simple duplications, are *not* associated with abnormalities of the bladder and urethra and there is normal rectal and anal anatomy. This is in sharp contradistinction to the next category.

In the second, rarer, variety of duplication of the colon the anorectal region is always involved and there are abnormalities of the bladder, Mullerian structures and external genitalia.[34,35] There is even a single case of triplication of the entire large intestine where two patent colonic structures emptied into the rectum and a normal anus, while a large dilated cul de sac, paralleling the double barrelled colon, ended blindly at the rectosigmoid junction. All three 'colons' received faecal material at the ileocaecal valve. Ovaries were present but no uterus and there was exstrophy of the bladder.[36]

This complex of malformations is the subject of an excellent review by Stephens and Smith[9] and their analysis of the 32 cases in the literature to that point remains unequalled and the conclusions are valid to this day. Females are affected more often than males (22:10) and while most cases present in the newborn period or early childhood, 6 of the 32 presented in adult life (one at 62 years of age!). Depending on the number of duplicated ani, three types of lesions were identified: double perineal ani opening externally (12 cases), double ani with fistulae of one or both duplicated segments to the genito-urinary tract (11 cases), and one external anus and one imperforate within the pelvis (9 cases). The female preponderance in the series is explained entirely by an increased number of cases in the first two categories; the third category appears to be common in males. However, the patterns are not exclusive to any one sex. The bladder may be duplicated or septate with double urethral openings. There may be two uteri and duplication of the vagina. There may be two penes or two clitora or combinations of the above. Anomalies outside the pelvis and pelvic area are frequent, and were found in 14 of the cases; in 5 reports no structures outside the pelvis were mentioned, and 13 infants were otherwise normal. The associated abnormalities ranged from a single instance of Meckel's diverticulum[34] to two examples of double headed monsters,[37,38] an example of double hemiliver with duplication of the lumbar spine but absent sacrum and anterior myelomeningocele,[39] and an infant with 4 lower limbs.[40] Somewhat surprisingly, associated renal anomalies were not too frequent: two examples of horseshoe kidneys, one draining with a single ureter to the left half of a double bladder,[41] while the other had 3 ureters;[42] two cases with unilateral absence of a kidney;[43,44] a single dysplastic kidney,[45] and a single example of unilateral bifid ureters draining a duplex kidney.[39] The anal component of the duplication may be separated from the normal bowel by a thin septum only and in Van Zwalenburg's case this had been resected in childhood. The anal openings may be on either side of the midline, but may also occur in the midline.[46]

Micturition appeared to be accomplished satisfactorily in those infants without neurological problems or fistulae, and menstrual flow did not appear to be impeded in those patients who presented in adult life.

The extent of duplicated bowel varies from duplication of the entire alimentary system,[37,38] to duplication of the entire colon from the caecum onwards (12 cases), or terminal ileum onwards (13) with the remainder showing lesser degrees of duplication. Fourteen of the infants are specifically mentioned as having double vermiform appendices.

The simpler, and fortunately commoner, variety of duplication, even though it may be extensive, is amenable to simple surgical removal. Infants with even more severe malformations pose more complex problems of management, and many of the malformation sequences are likely to be lethal. In the review of Stephens and Smith,[9] there were two stillbirths and 11 deaths related to the malformations occurred, despite attempted surgical correction.

Duplications of the large bowel are, therefore, a heterogeneous collection of abnormalities which share the common feature of their proximity to the large bowel and a lining of mucus producing epithelium similar to that seen in the normal large bowel. The very different characteristics of the two groups, however, makes it likely that their development depends on multiple factors that may vary from case to case. In those cases with double-headed monsters, an abnormal postzygotic event affecting the entire embryonic disc appears to be the most likely event. Infants with complicated malformation sequences in other organs as well as the hindgut have been subjected, clearly, to mutant stimuli of uncertain origin affecting several developmental areas either simultaneously or in sequence.

There is doubt even about the origin of the duplicated bowel itself. Lewis and Thyng,[47] described small diverticula and epithelial islands within the mesentery of developing small gut in the embryo of pig, rabbit and man, and these lesions have been used to explain the development of the isolated duplications of the bowel that are *not* associated with bladder anomalies.[34] However, these embryonic structures have not been seen in relation to the developing hindgut, and while they offer an attractive explanation for the development of duplications within the mesentery, they cannot be accepted unequivocally as the origin of the colonic lesions.

The development of an anomalous septum or sequestration of a tubular segment of bowel has been offered as an explanation of the duplications of the colon, but it is difficult to see how this would occur in an isolated segment of colon. The extensive duplication of the bowel seen in the second group of cases (with multiple associated anomalies including the bladder) are, conceivably, due to a teratogenic insult that exerts its influence over a diffuse segment of developing bowel including the caudal section of midgut (i.e. terminal ileum and colonic segments) as well as the entire hindgut including the cloaca.

Anorectal anomalies (other than duplications)

The development of the anal canal and rectum requires the successful completion of a complex and coordinated series of steps before the cloaca can be divided into the ventral genitourinary structures and the dorsal anorectal structures. These events involve the urorectal septum, the proctodeum, and, in the female, the Mullerian structures that are destined to form the female genital tract. It is not surprising that these steps may become deranged in their sequence or be executed incompletely, resulting in a wide range of anomalies.

To provide a rational approach to malformations in this area several attempts have been made at classifying the lesions. Historically, the earliest attempt was made by Ladd and Gross[48] who recognized four different types. This classification, while adopted by North American workers, was followed by other classifications in Europe and elsewhere.[49–54] In particular, Stephens[55] summarized the extensive experience of the Royal Children's Hospital of Melbourne which highlights the incomplete and unsatisfactory nature of all the classifications. His work was responsible in large measure for the development of an International Classification of Anorectal Anomalies that has received a wide measure of acceptance.[56] The descriptive classification recognizes several discriminants which include the level of the abnormality of the anus or rectum, the site of the anal opening, the presence of fistulae and the recording of the organs involved, and furthermore distinguishes between the patterns seen in the two sexes. Prior to the development of this classification the literature on the confusing subject of anorectal anomalies was confounded with different systems of nomenclature and incomplete descriptions, making a true assessment of prognosis and the effects of surgical procedures almost impossible. The descriptive terminology of the International Classification offers an accurate method for comparing the data from different areas (Table 17.1; Fig. 17.7). The classification does *not* include duplications with fistulae, nor does it attempt to cover lesions derived from tailgut remnants or those associated with agenesis of the cloacal membrane;[7] the classification restricts itself to the anorectal anomalies and the lesions directly related to them.

Table 17.1 International Classification* of anorectal anomalies.

	Female	Male
Low (Translevator)	1. *Normal anal site*	1. *Same*
	a) Anal stenosis	a) Same
	b) Covered anus complete	b) Same
	2. *Perineal site*	2. *Same*
	a) Anocutaneous fistula (covered anus incomplete)	a) Same
	b) Anterior perineal anus	b) Same
	3. *At vulvar site*	
	a) Anovulvar fistula	
	b) Anovestibular fistula	
	c) Vestibular anus	
Intermediate	1. *Anal agenesis*	1. *Same*
	a) Without fistula	a) Same
	b) Rectovestibular fistula	b) With rectobulbar fistula
	c) Rectovaginal fistula (low)	
	2. *Anorectal stenosis*	2. *Same*
High (Supralevator)	1. *Anorectal agenesis*	1. *Same*
	a) Without fistula	a) Same
	b) With rectovaginal fistula (high)	b) With rectourethral fistula
	c) Rectocloacal fistula	c) With rectovesical fistula
	2. *Rectal atresia*	2. *Same*
	Miscellaneous	
Imperforate anal membrane		
Cloacal exstrophy		
Others		

*Santulli TV, Kieswetter WB, Bill AH Jr (1970)[56]

The level of the anomaly is defined by the situation of the lesion relative to the levator ani muscle. The importance of this muscle lies in the bearing that it has on reconstructive surgery and sphincteric function.[9] The classification of the site of the lesion does not have any embryological significance, other than the fact that all lesions above the line of the anal valves occur in structures derived from the cloaca.

Low deformities

These lesions, occurring below the level of the levator ani musculature, are subdivided further into whether or not the anus is normally located. Lesions associated with a normal-sited anus include the 'completely covered anus' and 'anal stenosis'. The designation of lesions as being 'covered' indicates that no opening can be seen. Some of these lesions are seen in both sexes. The anus may be ectopically situated at the site of the perineal body and in both sexes two conditions are delineated: the anterior perineal anus and the covered anus with an anterior anocutaneous fistula (Fig. 17.8). A more anteriorly-sited anus in the female is known as the vestibular anus.

In females, additional 'low' malformations are seen: the anovulvar fistula where no anus is present and the anal canal opening may be hidden by a fold of the fourchette, and the anovestibular fistula where the anus opens above the vestibule. The last lesion is said to be the commonest variety of anal anomaly in the female.[9] From an embryological point of view, these lesions are predominantly related to the incomplete or inappropriate development of the anal canal and anal membrane, coupled with prominent genital folds that contribute to the 'covered' appearance. The persistence of the anal membrane in both covered anus and in anal stensosis is stressed by Magnus and Stephens,[57] whose detailed study of serial sections of a case of complete covered anus includes the interesting observation that part of the blind rectum (above the anal canal) was covered by an epithelium that many would regard as being of 'transitional type'. Anocutaneous, anovulvar and anovestibular fistule are associated with an upper anal canal of normal dimensions that tapers abruptly into a narrow tubular channel that runs forward to their ostia.

The sphincteric mechanisms in these low abnormalities are intact in both sexes, and these patients are continent.

Intermediate anomalies

These are anomalies where the blind segment ends at the level of the levator ani muscle and at the level of a line joining the ischial tuberosities (ischial line).[9] In males three types of lesions are seen: anal agenesis without fistula formation, anal agenesis with rectobulbar fistula and

Fig. 17.7 Line drawing representation of the spectrum of anorectal anomalies in males and females. (Based on data from Santulli et al 1970;[56] Stephens & Smith 1971[9])

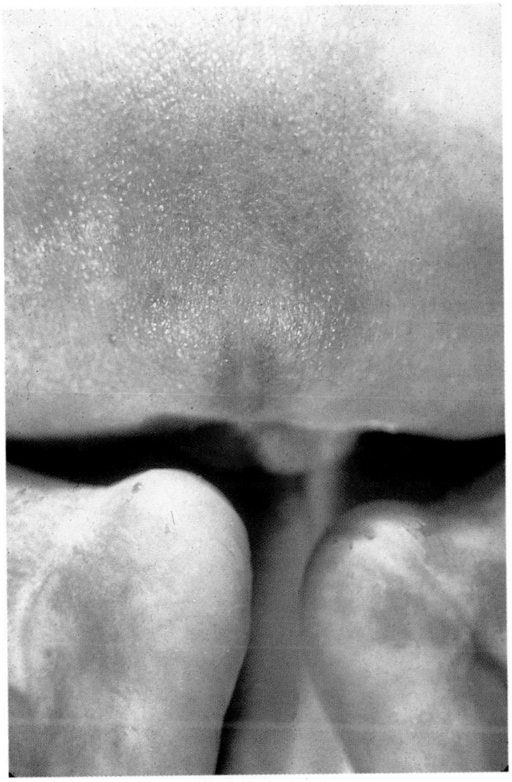

Fig. 17.8 View of perineal region of male infant showing a complete covered anus.

anorectal stenosis. In the female the general pattern of malformation is along similar lines, but instead of a rectobulbar fistula a low rectovaginal or rectovestibular fistulae may be seen. Anorectal stenosis is found in both sexes.

Anal agenesis (more correctly anal canal agenesis) occurs almost exclusively in male infants.[9] The blind and dilated rectal pouch often has a small anterior protrusion at its lower end. In addition, the anal dimple may be flattened or absent. With rectobulbar fistula (a much less frequent anomaly than agenesis without fistula) the dilated rectal pouch leads through a fistulous track to the cavernous tissue of the urethral bulb. Some fistulae may be relatively wide; others may be threadlike. In both these anomalies, the internal sphincter is absent, and the poorly formed external sphincter is not an effective control mechanism. In addition, the urethral floor is often very thin and friable and intimately attached to the anterior wall of the rectum. Penile hypospadias may occur in association with a rectobulbar fistula.

Anorectal stenosis occurring at a level of 4 cm above the anus is an extremely rare lesion and must be distinguished from the incomplete covered lesions mentioned earlier which are far more superficial. The bowel wall in this condition may show a tubular stenotic segment with variably increased amounts of connective tissue. Stephens and Smith[9] suggest that this lesion has an ischemic basis. The sphincters are intact in this anomalad.

In females the low rectovaginal and rectovestibular fistula are usually associated with a normal appearing vulva and hymen. Usually the fistulae open in the lower third of the vagina and vestibule and in the midline. With low rectovaginal fistulae the rectal opening into the vagina is usually wide, but the opening of a rectovestibular fistula may be a narrow, threadlike tube running downwards and anteriorly from the dilated rectal pouch. The internal sphincter is not present and the external sphincter is as poorly defined as it is in males with rectobulbar fistulae.

High anomalies

This group of anomalies is characterized by the presence of a blind rectal pouch with or without a fistulous track, above the level of the levator ani muscle's puborectalis sling. In addition to the blind rectal pouch the upper anal canal is absent as well. In the male, several patterns are seen. In the main group, that of anorectal agenesis, the large bowel ends blindly at the level of a line joining the lower end of the pubis with the coccyx (the pubococcygeal line) and there is no anal dimple. Anorectal agenesis may exist without a fistula but more commonly either a rectovesical or rectourethral fistula is present. Less frequently in rectal atresia an anal canal is connected by a membranous or stringlike cord of tissue with a blind rectal pouch that may even lie above the pubococcygeal line. This malformation may be a post-ischemic lesion.[52,58,59] In anorectal agenesis the internal and external sphincter muscles are not formed. In rectal atresia the sphincteric mechanisms are intact.

In females anorectal agenesis without fistula, or with a rectovesical fistula, are both described and these anomalies are identical to those seen in the male. However, in addition, several fistulae may be present in association with anorectal agenesis. A rectocloacal fistula may be found where rectal pouch, vagina and urethra all empty into a common cloacal channel with a single perineal opening. High rectovaginal fistula, usually near the posterior fornix, may be present. Variations on rectocloacal and rectovaginal fistulae of high type are encountered and may be the source of considerable confusion.[60] Much of the confusion centres around rectocloacal fistula formation. In some cases of this anomaly the cloaca may appear to be a direct continuation of the vagina whereas in others it may appear to be a direct continuation of the urethra. However, if a single perineal opening drains all these viscera, it satisfies the criteria for a cloacal opening, and any lesion with such a pattern is best regarded as a rectocloacal fistula.

Rectal atresia is found in females as in males. As in the male, rectal atresia is the only category of 'high' malformation that is associated with an intact sphincteric mechanism.

This review of the commoner malformations indicates

the importance of the level of the lesion and the complex nature of the fistulae that may be associated with anal anomalies. The International Classification scheme[56] is valuable and consistent but not complete. The 'Miscellaneous' and 'Other' categories[56] include imperforate anal membrane and anal membrane stenosis in both males and females, where the distinction from complete covered anus and incomplete covered anus are based solely on the relatively thinner membranes in the former pair of conditions. Stephens and Smith[9] also include perineal grooves and canals in their classification, lesions which are not described by other authors.

There are many other combinations of abnormalities that are well outlined and summarized by Stephens and Smith.[9] These vary from double fistulae (rectourethral and rectovesical, rectovesical and rectoperineal) to fistulae into ectopia vesicae and lesions as complicated as the vesico-intestinal fissure or exstrophy of the cloaca.[61]

In vesico-intestinal fissure the bladder, vagina and intestine all open onto the anterior abdominal wall. The bladder is usually bifid and in the central opening there is a 'double-barrel' opening of bowel, the rostral opening of which discharges intestinal contents while the lower end is usually blind. No hindgut or anus is present, but variable lengths of colon may be present (Fig. 17.9A,B). An omphalocele may be present above the exstrophy. There are often multiple renal anomalies such as hydronephrosis or dysplasia. The lesion is seen in both sexes, and in males there is a high incidence of cryptorchidism, and the phallus may be duplicated or very poorly formed. Magnus[62] has suggested that the lesion is due to a strangulation of the physiological hernia of the midgut combined with another insult to the hindgut. Clearly, the defect must involve the development of the anterior abdominal wall at an early stage of development, and many of the features are similar to those seen in the 'OEIS' syndrome[63] (see Table 17.2.)

The embryological explanation for the main anomalies outlined here centres on the urorectal septum. All the anomalies in the male can be explained by aberrations in the fusion of the urorectal septum with the cloacal membrane, or in the disordered formation of the urorectal septum. The anomalies in the female are more complex of a necessity, since the Mullerian ducts develop not just as offshoots of the anterior urinary chamber but within the urorectal septum.

The relative incidence of the various types of abnormalities is difficult to ascertain. Reported series, particularly in recent years, will tend to overemphasize the very rare anomalies. Large series collected in different centres are difficult to compare due to the several classifications used. The Melbourne series (168 cases) of Stephens and Smith[9] suggests that anal anomalies are commoner than rectal anomalies in male infants (95 to 64) with covered anus with anocutaneous fistula (37) and covered anal stenosis (23) as the commonest anal lesions. Rectourethral

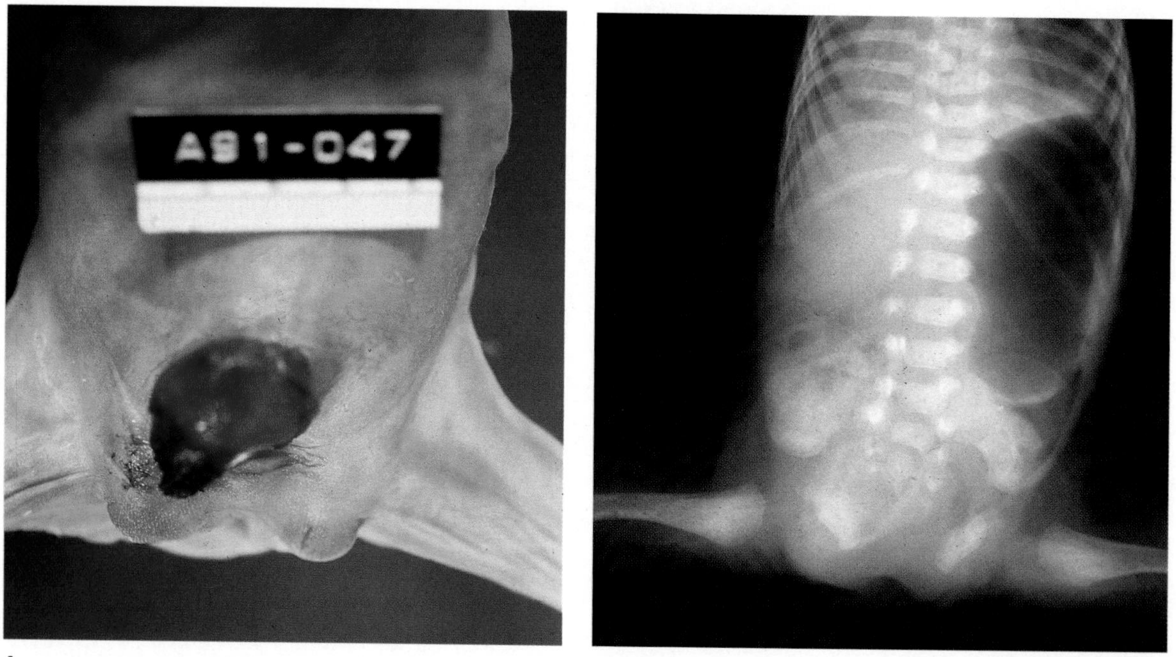

A

B

Fig. 17.9A A case of vitello-intestinal fissure in a 4 day old infant showing an abdominal wall defect into which the lower jejunum opened in the centre, and from the lower end of which a rudimentary length of rectum emerged which terminated blindly. The ureters opened in the lateral angles of the defect, but there was no urethra or phallus. The testes were undescended. **B** X-ray showing poorly developed sacral vertebrae and absence of ossification of pubic rami.

fistula with rectal agenesis, however, was the commonest single rectal high anomaly in males (44 cases). Their analysis of 92 female patients showed that anal anomalies were commoner than rectal anomalies (59 to 28) with ano-vestibular fistula by far the commonest lesion (22 cases). Of rectal anomalies, rectocloacal fistula and rectovaginal fistulae (both high and intermediate) were equally frequent (8 cases each). Stephens and Smith's analysis of the reports from 8 other authors in the literature suggests that the Melbourne series offers a good approximation of the general pattern seen throughout the world.

Agenesis of the cloacal membrane

In this unusual malformation sequence neither an anal opening nor an urethral opening is present, and in females the vagina ends blindly. All three structures end blindly or empty into a chamber of varying depth that does *not* communicate with the surface. The infants do not have a perineal body or median perineal raphe indicating that the most probable primary abnormality is agenesis of the cloacal membrane (Fig. 17.10A,B). Robinson and Tross[7] provide a detailed description of five infants with this pattern of anomaly, and cited reports of seven other affected infants between the years 1926 and 1980. Choisy[64] in turn cites additional cases from the early European literature. Other workers[65] have seen isolated cases in different North American centres while many more are unreported. This lesion has only been seen in autopsy material, and detailed dissections of these infants has yielded a remarkably precise and consistent pattern of anomalies that Robinson and Tross have classified into primary malformations of the cloaca, and deformations of the other organs due to the effects of external compression of the fetus and internal distension.

The primary malformations associated with the absence of a cloacal membrane include incomplete division of the cloaca (2 of 5 patients in Robinson & Tross' series), blind termination of the rectum and bladder, and by definition lack of a perineal body or median perineal raphe. The agenesis of the cloacal membrane is accompanied by failure to form a vaginal vestibule and labia minora (in female infants) or anus. Distal urethral development was rudimentary in all and there was no connection with the exterior. All infants (male and female) had a rudimentary phallic structure. The deformation sequences included massive bladder and ureteric distension with hydronephrosis and renal dysplasia in all except one infant who had renal agenesis and bladder hypoplasia; cephalad displacement of the massively dilated rectum and distension of the abdominal wall in all cases leading to rupture in one infant, and compression deformities of the limbs. In the three females the uterus and vagina were affected with vaginal duplication in one case, and vaginal hypoplasia and partial incorporation of the vaginal wall into the

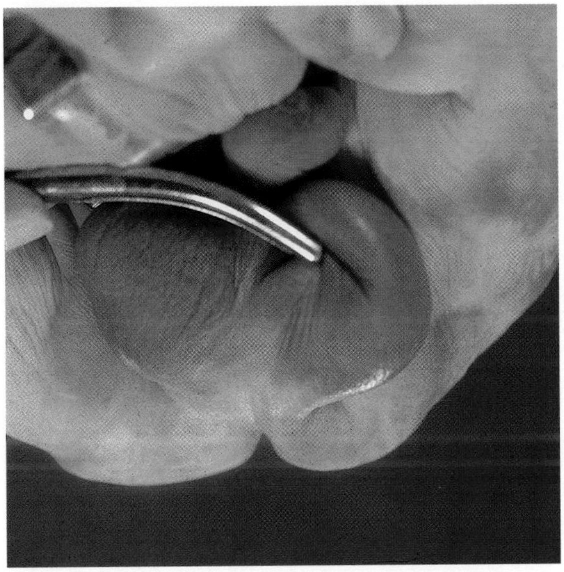

A

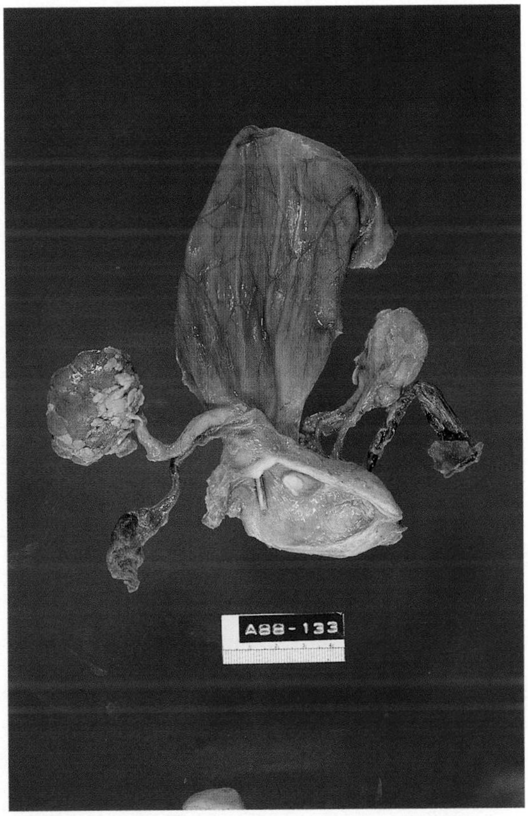

B

Fig. 17.10A An example of agenesis of the cloacal membrane, showing the perineal region without any evidence of an anal opening, rudimentary phallus and no perineal body. Prominent empty scrotal tubercles are seen. **B** Dissected organs of **A** showing probe in dilated hindgut opening into a bladder. No urethra was found. Both testes were in the inguinal canal. Both ureters were dilated, and there was cystic renal dysplasia bilaterally.

bladder in the other cases; bicornuate atrophic uteri with slit-like lumina were found in all three females.

Not surprisingly, anomalies in other sites were present. Three infants had sacrococcygeal dimples; one had multiple spina bifida of lumbar, thoracic and sacral vertebrae. All infants had abnormal umbilical arteries. In four infants, a single umbilical artery was present while in the fifth infant one artery was hypoplastic. Single examples of rectal duplication, oesophageal atresia and tracheo-oesophageal fistula, ventricular septal defect and septum primum defect were present.

This bizarre cluster of cases occurred over a 7½ month period in a relatively localized area of northeastern Ohio state, and Robinson and Tross[7] advance a plausible case for their suggestion that exposure to a single drug available in numerous proprietary, non-prescription 'cold and cough' remedies may have been implicated in their particular group of cases. Whatever the aetiology, this important series of cases illustrates the crucial importance of the cloacal membrane, and the bizarre pattern of malformations that may result when the development of the urorectal septum and the cloacal membrane is not coordinated. Personally studied cases have included overlaps with the 'OEIS' syndrome, hemisacrum syndrome, sacral vertebral anomalies, and even meningomyelocele (Figs 17.11, 17.12A,B, 17.13).

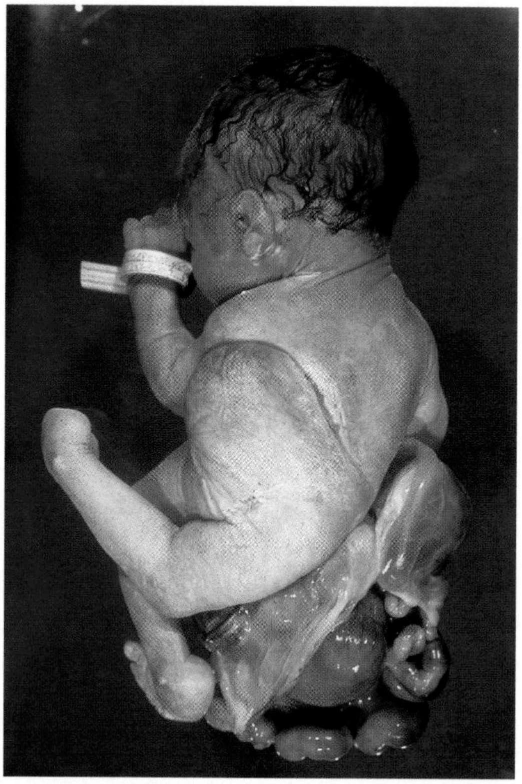

Fig. 17.11 Posterior view of female infant showing absence of anal, vaginal or urethral openings in association with massive omphalocoele, bladder exstrophy, kyphosis and multiple thoracolumbar and sacral hemivertebrae.

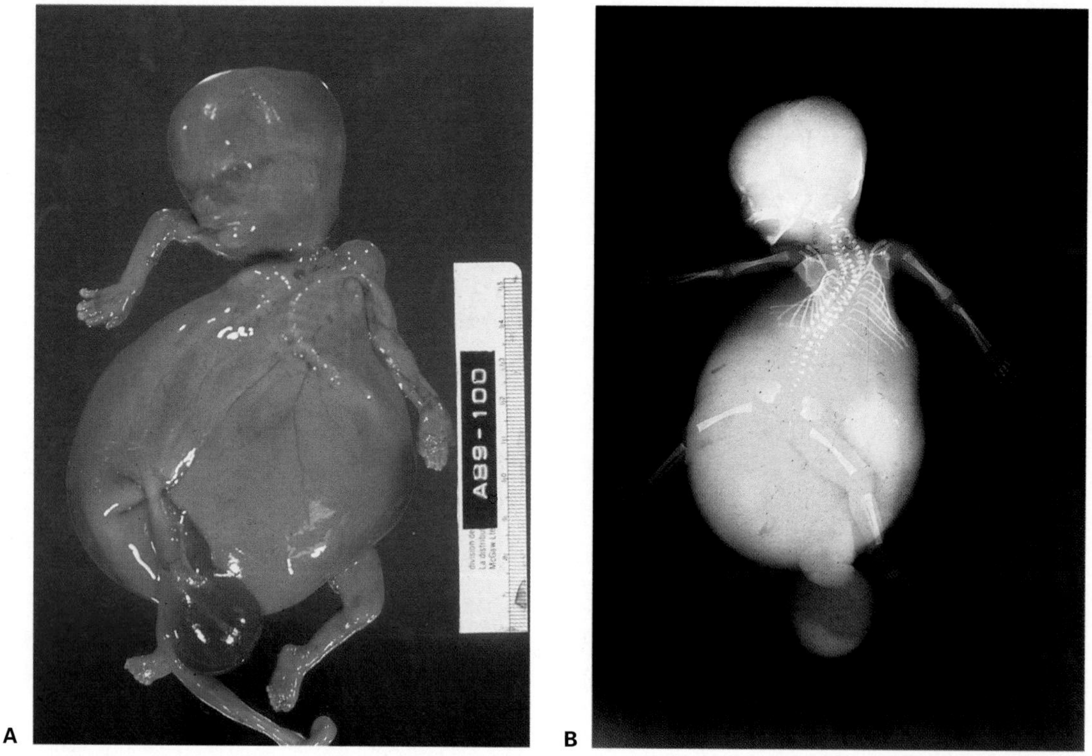

Fig. 17.12A Agenesis of cloacal membrane leading to massive abdominal distension in a 21 week fetus. **B** Radiograph of fetus shown in **A**, showing sacral agenesis and calcified meconium peritonitis due to rupture of ileum.

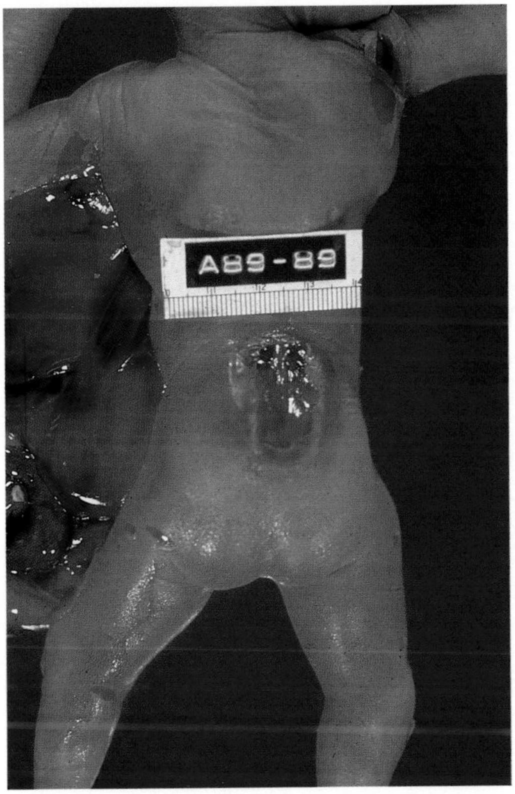

Fig. 17.13 Agenesis of cloacal membrane associated with massive omphalocoele and open meningomyelocoele in 22 week fetus.

Spinal defects and anorectal anomalies

Many of the anomalies discussed in the preceding sections may be associated with abnormalities of the lower half of the skeleton, especially spina bifida or hemivertebrae. Two important subgroups of anorectal anomalies however warrant special discussion. These are the lesions associated with defects of the sacrum and those associated with caudal dysplasia (or caudal regression) and homologous anomalies.[66]

Abnormalities of the sacral vertebrae, either in the form of large defects in bifid vertebrae or smaller defects in hemivertebrae, may coexist with a variety of hindgut enteric fistulae. Bale[6] has provided an outstanding review of these lesions based on material in the Royal Alexander Hospital for Children in Sydney, Australia. Loops of hindgut may herniate through sacral vertebral defects to open directly onto the skin surface with the distal limb of the loop opening at the anus, or the hindgut may end at the skin surface and the anus is imperforate. Rectal duplications associated with an otherwise normal rectum and anus are also described. Portions of a rectal duplication may persist as either presacral, intraspinal or postsacral enteric cysts, or a fistula between the rectum and the postsacral skin may be present. These uncommon malformations all pose the hazard of superadded meningitis in addition to the neurological and anorectal deficits that may be present.

The structure of these hindgut fistulae varies. They usually have a muscular wall of variable thickness and an epithelial lining that may contain epithelium identifiable as either colonic, small intestinal,[67] gastric[68] or mixed with some structures resembling oesophageal and bronchial epithelium.[69,70] Bale[6] describes tissue resembling pancreas in one instance. The presence of aberrant cartilaginous and adipose tissue nodules[71,72] has been noted. These enteric sinuses may be associated with a presacral teratoma,[73] but as can be seen, many of these hindgut-derived presacral cysts may be mistaken for a teratoma.[72]

The pathogenesis of these lesions is believed to be related to adhesions between ectoderm and endoderm developing in the caudal end of the early embryonic disc. This interferes with notochordal development and leads to splitting of the notochord to bypass the adhesion. In turn, the notochordal split is associated with a defect of mesenchyme that allows the endodermal and ectodermal adhesions to persist. This view[67,68] has gained considerable acceptance and is known as 'the split notochord syndrome'[69,74] The alternative view that the lesions are teratomatous in nature[70] should not be dismissed out of hand. Bale[6] cites an unusual case of a teenager with a probable presacral enteric cyst who developed a teratoma at the same site a year later. In addition to the already cited example of a presacral teratoma with an enteric sinus,[73] Bentley and Smith[67] include a case of a hindgut malformation associated with a postsacral dermoid with a rudimentary tooth! There is considerable overlap between teratogenesis and oncogenesis in all sites,[75] but nowhere greater than in the sacrococcygeal area.

Caudal dysplasia (regression) and anorectal anomalies

The syndrome of caudal dysplasia is associated with sacral vertebral anomalies, abnormalities in the pelvis and lower limbs and associated anomalies such as meningomyelocele, anal and genital defects, absent fibula and short femora.[76,77] The upper limbs are rarely involved. Congenital anomalies of the heart and great vessels may be present and tracheo-oesophageal fistula may be noted.[78,79] In its most extreme form sirenomelia may be present.[80,81,66] The mothers of affected infants may show minor sacral anomalies.[82] In this unusual constellation of anomalies, anal malformations figure prominently and several variants may be seen. The commonest lesions seen are complete covered anus with or without fistula, and rectal atresia, but any of the many varieties of anorectal anomalies described earlier may be seen[80] including agenesis of the cloacal membrane. The justification for the separate discussion of this group of anorectal anomalies is provided by the fact that many cases of caudal dysplasia may be associated with maternal diabetes or prediabetes.[76,77] Wilson and Vallance-Owen[83]

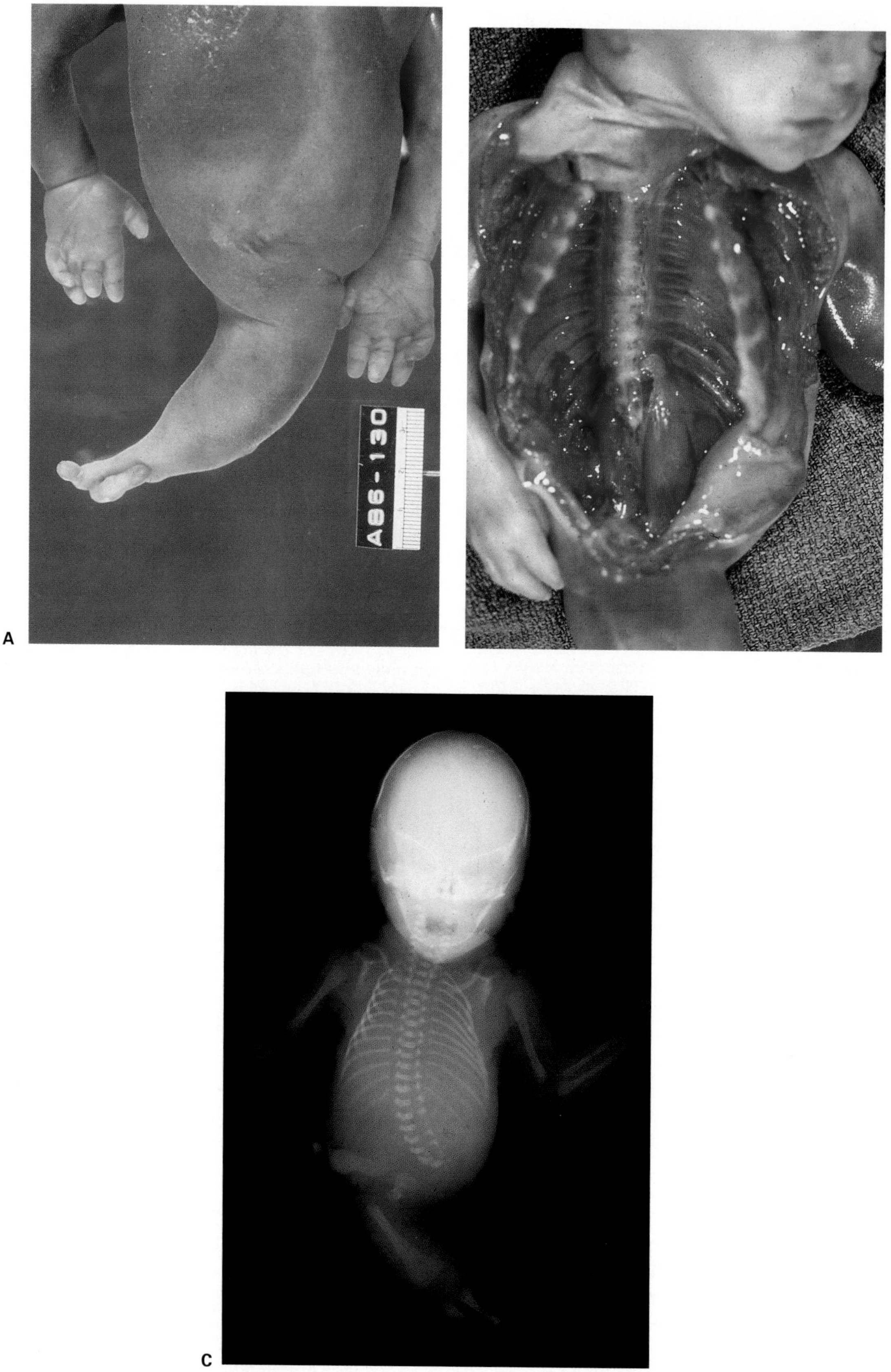

Fig. 17.14A A case of hemisacrum and hemipelvis, which when viewed from the posterior aspect had no cloacal openings and a single dysmorphic lower limb. **B** Dissection of the fetus shows asymmetry of the psoas major muscles and scoliosis due to traction of the lower spine to the left. **C** Radiograph of case showing sacral and pelvic abnormalities, and that the single limb represents an abnormally sited right lower limb.

have suggested that the syndrome is related to the presence of insulin antagonists in diabetics. Landauer and Clark[84] described the development of a syndrome superficially similar to caudal dysplasia called 'rumplessness' in chick embryos who received insulin. This argument was used to incriminate insulin therapy of gestational diabetics in the development of caudal dysplasia, but the occurrence of caudal dysplasia in prediabetic women argues against such a relationship. Studies in fetal rats suggest that fetal insulin production may have a role in the production of sacral defects,[85] but it is unlikely that these experimental results can be applied to humans since the dysmorphic lesions that are present indicate an intrauterine insult that predates the onset of fetal insulin production (which normally only begins at week 10).

The exact mechanisms that predispose infants of diabetic and prediabetic mothers to develop caudal dysplasia is unknown at present, but the association may be important.[82] The occurrence of very rare familial cases of caudal dysplasia syndrome[86,87] suggests that genetic factors may also play a 'conditioning role' in the development of caudal dysplasia. The overall low incidence of caudal dysplasia among infants of diabetic mothers (even though greater than in the nondiabetic population) and the rare occurrence of familial caudal dysplasia has led Welch and Aterman[82] to suggest that a combination of both a 'diabetogenic trend' and unrelated genetic factors that code for skeletal differentiation is required for the development of the fully developed caudal dysplasia syndrome. These two 'factors' may both be related to genes of the HLA-DR system.

A group of syndromes that are superficially very similar to the caudal dysplasia syndrome are grouped together under the heading of Familial Sacral Dysgenesis. These include the Cohn-Bay-Nielsen syndrome of familial hemisacrum (Type I) and the Aschcraft syndrome of familial hemisacrum (Type II).[82,88,89]

In familial hemisacrum I there is unilateral hemisacrum affecting all members of the family, and there may be abnormalities of the pelvic bones as well. Anal stenosis and rarely complete covered anus was seen in some of the affected siblings in some subsequent sibships. These affected members also had an anterior meningocele, and the inheritance pattern suggests an autosomal dominant gene. In Ashcraft's syndrome[89] the unilateral hemisacrum is associated with presacral teratomata (sometimes malignant) rather than anterior meningocele, but the distinction between the two hemisacral syndromes may not be an absolute one. Anal stenosis and complete covered anus were seen in the signal family. An example of hemisacrum and hemipelvis mimicking sirenomelia is shown in Fig. 17.14A,B,C, where the affected infant had no external opening of urethra or anus, and a reduction in spinal cord anterior horn cells in the affected side. Overlaps of sirenomelia and the small pelvic outlet syndrome[66] add to the overall complexity of malformations. In Currarino's series no assessment of the role of maternal diabetes was possible since glucose tolerance tests were not performed.[66]

Anorectal abnormalities and multiple malformation

Anorectal abnormalities are an important component of numerous multiple malformation syndromes (Table 17.2). It would be pointless to attempt to discuss them all or the multiplicity of fine points that differentiate between them. Detailed references are cited in most standard works on malformation syndromes[10] and many are available in the excellent review of Hall et al.[90] Certain general comments should be made. The list is not complete, and could not attempt to be, since there appears to be, on the one hand, an increasing number of syndromes, while on the other several syndromes have been collapsed into new entities. However, since the pattern of inheritance of these disorders varies from autosomal dominant to autosomal recessive to X-linked to sporadic, and is unknown in most, it is mandatory that individual cases are not placed arbitrarily in any one category. Only if the 'fit' is good with a detailed study of all the organ systems including the skeleton, and a karyotype has been obtained, should cases be assigned to any single category. Some syndromes merge with each other (e.g. Opitz-Frias and Opitz syndrome, Table 17.2, nos 10 and 11); many overlap with each other (e.g. the single umbilical artery associated malformation sequences overlap with VATER association; Table 17.2). Finally, some of these malformation syndromes may represent a possible teratogenic influence (e.g. fetal hydantoin effect) and may be preventable. The development of computerized banks of dysmorphic syndromes has helped considerably in classifying individual cases. We use the 'POSSUM' database of the Royal Children's Hospital of Melbourne, and the GDB-DMIM database of Johns Hopkins University.

In sirenomelia, the absence of hindgut derivatives as well as renal agenesis can be explained partly by the fact that the single umbilical artery represents the vitello-intestinal artery and arises from high up the dorsal aorta (Fig. 17.15A,B). Since the abnormal vessel represents the functional continuation of the aorta, and the distal vessels are rudimentary at best, all the distal elements (hindgut, cloaca and metanephros) are affected.

Enteric cysts, tailgut cysts of the anorectal region

In addition to hindgut duplications, and closely allied to them, a variety of cystic lesions can be seen in relation to the presacral and coccygeal region. These may be derived from sequestered duplications of the bowel, tailgut remnants or as part of the complex of neurenteric fistulae and sinuses associated with sacral anomalies. The presacral

Table 17.2 Anal anomalies in multiple malformation syndromes.

Syndrome	Other core anomalies	References
1. Rear [Townes] Syndrome	Radial and thumb anomalies Ear anomalies, renal anomalies	111 112
2. Schinzel's Syndrome	Ulnar deletion of hand, laryngeal stenosis, microphallus	113
3. Kaufman's Syndrome	Postaxial polydactyly, vaginal atresia, congenital heart disease	114
4. 'C' Syndrome	Postaxial polydactyly/syndactyly, fusion of metopic suture, multiple frenula; genu recurvatum; hypoplastic kidneys	115 116
5. 'FG' Syndrome	Broad thumbs, syndactyly, agenesis of corpus callosum, congenital heart disease, megacolon	117
6. Meckel-Gruber Syndrome	Postaxial polydactyly, renal dysplasia, hepatic fibrosis, occipital encephalocoele, congenital heart disease, microphthalmus	118 119 120
7. Noonan-Saldino Syndrome	Postaxial polydactyly, renal dysplasia, vaginal atresia, microphallus, congenital heart disease, hemivertebrae, chest abnormalities	121
8. Cryptophthalmos (Fraser's Syndrome)	Cryptophthalmos, laryngeal atresia/ stenosis, renal agenesis/ dysplasia, cleft lip/palate, deafness, syndactyly	122 123
9. Laurence-Moon-Bardet-Biedl Syndrome	Obesity, retinitis pigmentosa, postaxial polydactyly, syndactyly, nephritis and renal anomalies, hypogonadism, mental retardation	124
10. 'G' Syndrome (Opitz-Frias)	Short limbs, congenital heart disease, hypospadias, hypertelorism laryngeal cleft	125 126
11. Opitz Syndrome (BBB)	Hypospadias, hypertelorism, cryptorchidism	127
12. Johanson-Blizzard Syndrome	Hypothyroidism, deafness, hypoplastic alae nasi, absent permanent teeth, microcephaly, pancreatic insufficiency, scalp defects	128 129
13. '4H-RALPH-MISHAP' Syndrome	Hypothalamic hamartoblastoma, syndactyly, polydactyly, hypopituitarism, microphallus, abnormal lung lobulation	90
14. OEIS Complex	Omphalocele, extrophy of bladder, spinal abnormalities	63
15. VATER Complex & Single Umbilical Artery Syndrome	Vertebral, cardiac, tracheo-oesophageal, renal and radial anomalies	131
16. Aperts Syndrome	Irregular craniostenosis, cleft palate, syndactyly, fused fingers, congenital heart disease	132
17. Thanatophoric Dwarfism	Thanatophoric dwarfism, cloverleaf skull, pulmonary hypoplasia	10
18. Caudal Dysplasia Syndrome (Caudal Regression)	Variable absence of limb structures, absent external genitalia, absent internal genitalia, limb fusion, sacral veterbral anomalies	80 81
19. Familial Hemisacrum I & II	Hemisacrum, anterior meningocoele presacral teratoma	88 89
20. 13q Syndrome	Absent thumbs, eye anomalies, retinoblastoma, holoprosencephaly, hypertelorism	133
21. Trisomy 18 Syndrome	Polydactyly, syndactyly, meningomyelocoele, renal dysplasia, cardiac defects, cryptorchidism	133
22. Cateye Syndrome (Trisomy 22)	Colobomata of eye, hypertelorism, cardiac defects, renal agenesis	133 10
23. Fetal Hydantoin Effect	Rib anomalies, hypertelorism, umbilical and inguinal hernias, hip dislocation, cryptorchidism, duodenal atresia	134
24. Monozygous/Conjoined Malformation Sequence	Gastroschisis, porencephaly, aplasia cutis	135 10
25. Sling Pulmonary Artery	Abnormal trachea and bronchi, abnormal aortic arch, pulmonary artery anomalies	136
26. Small Pelvic Outlet Syndrome	Contracted lesser pelvis, rudimentary or absent urinary tract, defective external genitalia, vagina; sirenomelia	66
27. Right-sided Syndrome	Absent right testis, absent right kidney and rectum	137

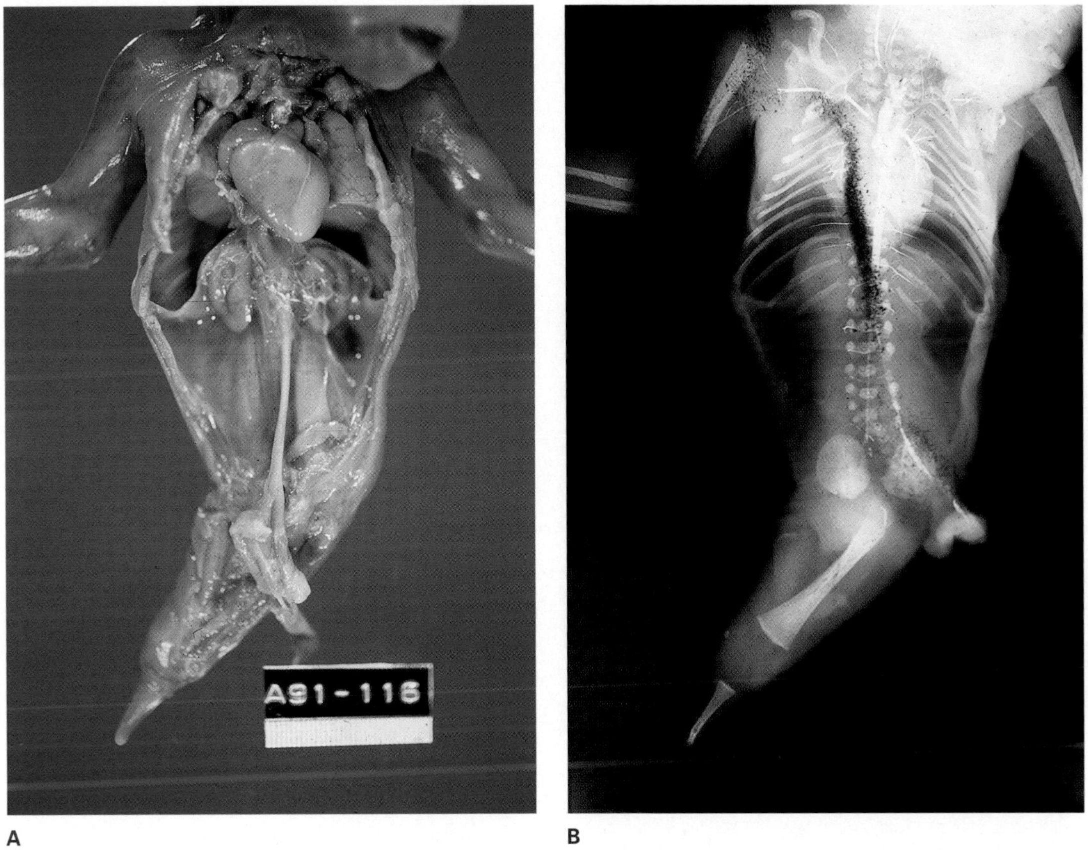

Fig. 17.15A Dissected example of a case of sirenomelia, showing symmetry of psoas major muscles and a high origin from the aorta of the single umbilical artery. No cloacal openings were seen. **B** Postmortem radiograph following barium injection of single umbilical artery and aorta, showing the high origin of the vessel from the aorta, the poorly developed lower abdominal aorta below the umbilical artery, the poorly developed sacrum, symmetrical iliac wings and the sympodium.

cysts may impinge on the anus and rectum or be intimately attached to the wall of these organs, and they may be associated with intraspinal and postsacral cysts as outlined earlier. The cysts may be multilocular single cysts or multiple small cysts may be present. The cysts contain mucin, but their lining may include ciliated and squamous epithelium. Cysts of the hindgut are said to be larger and unilocular while cysts derived from tailgut remnants are usually smaller and multilocular with satellite cysts.[6] Hindgut cysts are surrounded by a muscle layer of varying thickness and degree of completeness as befits a sequestered duplication (Fig. 17.16A,B). The example shown contained pancreatic tissue. Tailgut cysts may contain isolated bundles of muscle but a clearly defined wall of smooth muscle is not seen. Squamous epithelium when present has been attributed to metaplasia in the presence of inflammation, but Bale[6] has shown that it may be present in cysts found in infants without evidence of inflammation, and she suggests that it indicates differentiation towards an anal epithelium.

Unless they are large or associated with sacral defects, intraspinal lesions or posterior rectocutaneous fistula (all features of sequestered duplications of hindgut rather than simple cysts) cysts of the presacral area rarely present in children. The smaller tailgut cysts usually present in adult life as 'abscesses' in association with constipation, or as an incidental rectal mass during childbirth or a gynaecological examination.[91–99] These lesions have sometimes been designated as retrorectal cyst hamartomata,[100] and are usually benign; rarely an adenocarcinoma has developed in a precoccygeal tailgut cyst.[100–103]

Heterotopia

Heterotopic epithelium in the anorectal region is a rare finding, but the commonest variety seen is gastric epithelium in the rectum.[104,105] They may present in adults as a cause of rectal bleeding and may be polypoid or ulcerated.[106] The only personally studied case occurred in a 70 year old woman with rectal bleeding (Fig. 17.17), where gastric mucosa of body type was found. Gastric mucosa may line a duplication, and salivary gland tissue may be present either as a sole finding or in combination with gastric mucosa.[107–109] Sun et al[110] found immature re-

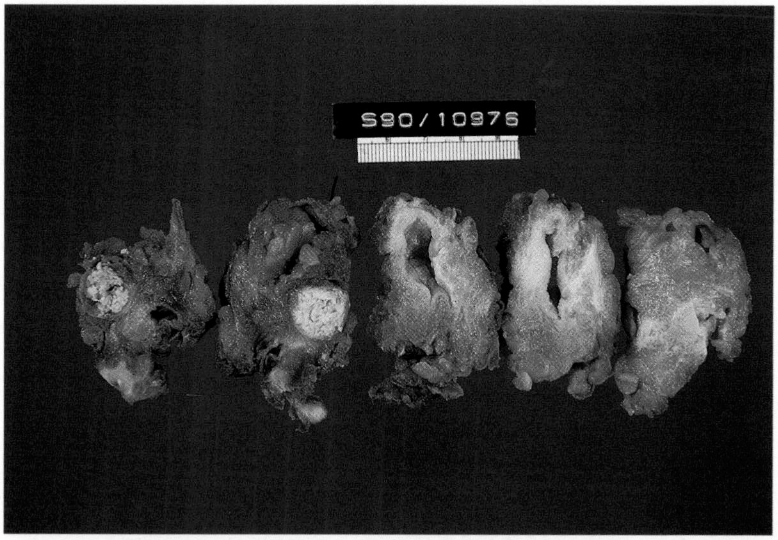

A

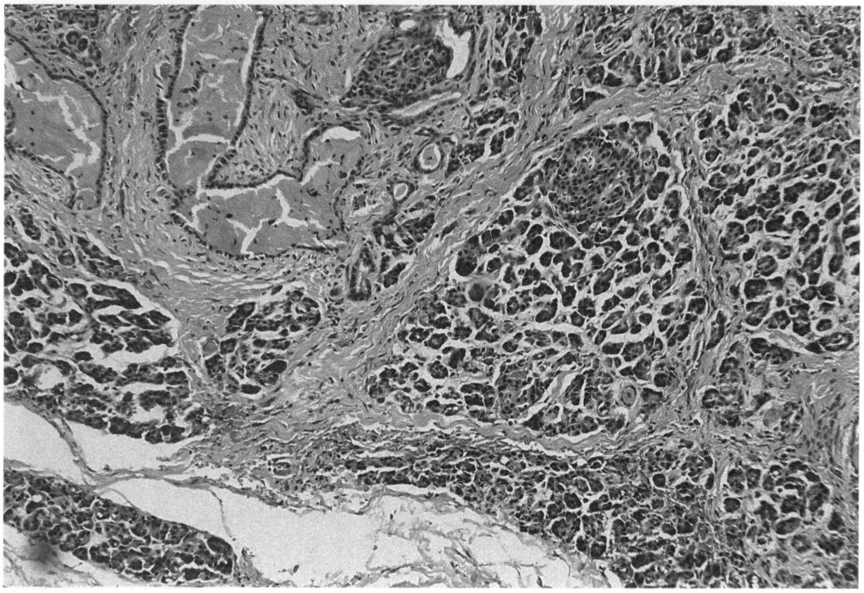

B

Fig. 17.16A Multiple transverse sections through an 8 × 5 cm presacral hindgut duplication cyst in a neonatal infant. A large thick-walled cyst is seen forming the bulk of the specimen, but microscopially smaller peripheral cysts were present. **B** Section through an area of the wall of the main cyst showing pancreatic exocrine and endocrine tissue. (H&E, ×487.5)

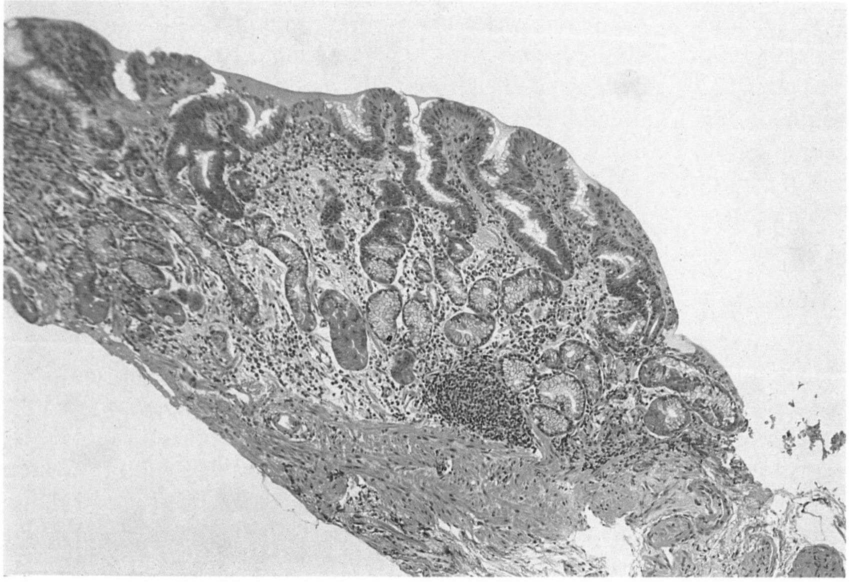

Fig. 17.17 Heterotopic gastric mucosa from a 70 year old woman who presented with rectal bleeding and proctoscopic evidence of ulceration. Parietal cells could be demonstrated in the speciment. (H&E, ×325)

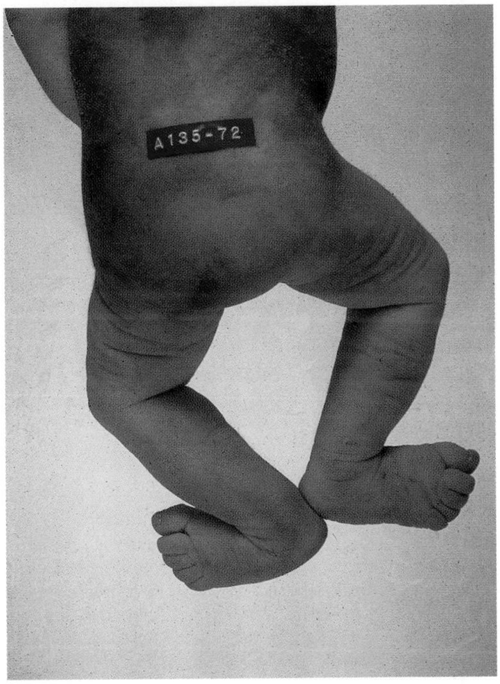

Fig. 17.18 Posterior view of a stillborn male with no anal opening and a presacral, smooth rounded mass filling the perineum, which proved to be a mature sacrococcygeal teratoma. The rectum terminated above the level of the levator ani muscles and a small rectovesical fistula was present.

nal tissue in the colon of a patient with caudal regression syndrome.

Sacrococcygeal tumours and anorectal lesions

A rare example of a dermoid cyst of the presacral region associated with rectal stenosis and rectovaginal fistula is recorded by Bale[6] and the author has autopsied a stillbirth with anorectal agenesis and rectovesical fistula with a large sacrococcygeal teratoma (Fig. 17.18).

Anorectal anomalies are complex and the finding of a single anomaly in this region is an indication for the most thorough examination of the infant. A systematic approach to the investigation of these infants is outlined by Stephens and Smith[9] whose monograph on the subject remains unrivalled. From a personal standpoint the value of photographic and radiographic studies of the entire fetus or infant cannot be overemphasized, and the use of these ancillary procedures needs to be stressed repeatedly. Quite apart from offering more information than would ordinarily be available, these ancillary studies offer the opportunity of a permanent record of the findings, supplementing and occasionally supplanting, any verbal description.

REFERENCES

1. Moore KL. The developing human: clinically oriented embryology. WB Saunders, Philadelphia, 3rd edn, 1982, p 204.
2. Cole FM. Innominate grooves of the colon: morphological characteristics and etiologic mechanisms. Radiology 1978; 128: 41.
3. Laufer I, deSa DJ. Lymphoid follicular pattern: a normal feature of the pediatric colon. Am J Roentgenol 1978; 130: 151.
4. Wells TR, Landing BH, Ariel I, Nadorra R, Garcia C. Normal anatomy of the myenteric plexus of infants and children: demonstration by flat-mount (circuit diagram) preparations. Perspect Pediatr Pathol 1987; 11: 152.
5. McGregor AL. A synopsis of surgical anatomy. John Wright, Bristol 8th edn, 1957, p 99.
6. Bale PM. Sacrococcygeal developmental abnormalities and tumours in children. Perspect Pediatr Pathol 1984; 8: 9.
7. Robinson HB Jr, Tross K. Agenesis of the cloacal membrane: a probable teratogenic anomaly. Perspect Pediatr Pathol 1984; 8: 79.
8. Bruyere HJ Jr, Arya S, Kozel JS, Gilbert EF, Fitzgerald JM, Reynolds JF Jr, Lewin SO, Opitz JM. The value of examining spontaneously aborted human embryos and placentas. Birth Defects: Orig Art Ser (National Foundation: March of Dimes) 1987; 23(1): 169.
9. Stephens FD, Smith ED. Anorectal malformations in children. Year Book Medical Publishers, Chicago, 1971.
10. Smith DW. Recognizable patterns of human malformation. (Major Problems in Clinical Pediatrics), WB Saunders, Philadelphia, 3rd edn, 1982.
11. deSa DJ. The spectrum of ischemic bowel disease in the newborn. Perspect Pediatr Pathol 1976; 3: 273.
12. Virjee J, Gill G, deSa D, Somers S, Stevenson G. Strictures and other long term complications of neonatal necrotizing enterocolitis. Clin Radiol 1979; 30: 25.
13. Donnelly WH, Sieber WK, Yunis EJ. Polypoid ganglioneurofibromatosis of the large bowel. Arch Pathol 1969; 87: 537.
14. Mendelsohn G, Diamond MP. Familial ganglioneuromatous polyposis of the large bowel: report of a family with associated juvenile polyposis. Am J Surg Path 1984; 8: 515.
15. Weidner N, Flanders DJ, Mitros FA. Mucosal ganglioneuromatosis associated with multiple colonic polyps. Am J Surg Path 1984; 8: 779.
16. Morson BC, Dawson IMP. Gastrointestinal pathology. Blackwells, Oxford, 2nd edn, 1979, pp 500,687.
17. Hochberg FH, Dasilva AB, Galdabini J, Richardson EP. Gastrointestinal involvement in von Recklinghausen's neurofibromatosis. Neurology 1974; 24: 1144.
18. Raszkowski HJ, Hufner RF. Neurofibromatosis of the colon: a unique manifestation of von Recklinghausen's disease. Cancer 1971; 27: 134.
19. Carney JA, Hayles AB. Alimentary tract malformations of multiple endocrine neoplasia, type 2B. Mayo Clin Proc 1977; 52: 543.
20. Carney JA, Go VLW, Sizemore GW, Hayles AB. Alimentary tract ganglioneuromatosis. A major component of the syndrome of multiple endocrine neoplasia, type 2B. N Engl J Med 1976; 295: 1287.
21. Holden KR, Alexander F. Diffuse neonatal hemangiomatosis. Pediatrics 1970; 46: 411.
22. Fretzin DF, Potter B. Blue rubber bleb nevus. Arch Intern Med 1965; 11: 624.
23. Halpern M, Turner AF, Citron BP. Hereditary hemorrhagic telangiectasia: an angiographic study of abdominal visceral angiodysplasias associated with gastrointestinal hemorrhage. Radiology 1968; 90: 1143.
24. Westerholm P. A case of diffuse haemangiomatosis of the colon and rectum. Acta chir Scand 1966; 133: 173.

25. Srigley JR, Mancer K. Solitary intestinal fibromatosis with perinatal bowel obstruction. Pediatr Pathol 1984; 2: 249.
26. Mullins F, Talamo R, di Sant'Agnese PA. Late intestinal complications of cystic fibrosis. JAMA 1965; 192: 741.
27. Lloyd-Still J, Klaw KT, Shwachman H. Problems of rectal prolapse. Br Med J 1971; 1: 110.
28. Esterly JR, Oppenheimer EH. Pathology of cystic fibrosis: review of the literature and comparison with 146 autopsied cases. Perspect Pediatr Pathol 1975; 2: 241.
29. George DH. Diverticulosis of the vermiform appendix in patients with cystic fibrosis. Hum Pathol 1987; 18: 75.
30. Favara BE. Multiple congenital diverticula of the vermiform appendix. Am J Clin Pathol 1968; 49: 60.
31. Trollope ML, Lindenauer SM. Diverticulosis of the appendix: a collective review. Dis Colon Rectum 1974; 17: 200.
32. Litwin A, Avidor J, Schujman E et al. Neonatal intestinal perforation caused by congenital defects of the intestinal musculature. Am J Clin Pathol 1984; 81: 77.
33. Semba R, Tanaka O, Tanimura T. Digestive system. In: Nishimura H, ed. Atlas of Human Prenatal Pathology. Igaku-Shoin, Tokyo, 1983, pp 171–225.
34. Van Zwalenburg BR. Double colon: differentiation of cases into two groups. Am J Roentgenol 1952; 68: 22.
35. Smith ED. Duplications of the anus and genitourinary tracts. Surgery 1969; 66: 909.
36. Gray AW. Triplication of the large intestine. Arch Pathol 1940; 30: 121.
37. Smith S, Boulgakov B. A case of dicephalus dibrachius, dipus showing certain features of embryologic interest. J Anat 1926; 61: 94.
38. Beischer NA, Fortune DW. Double monsters. Obstet Gynec 1968; 32: 158.
39. Mysorekar VR, Kolte DT, Shirole DB. A case of intestinal and urogenital duplication. J Obstet Gynaec Brit Cwlth 1967; 74: 596.
40. Rowe MI, Ravitch MM, Ranniger K. Operative correction of caudal duplication (dipygus). Surgery 1968; 63: 840.
41. Volpe M, Dell'asta Doppia. Il Policlin Roma 1903; 10: 46.
42. Smith ED. Urinary anomalies and complications in imperforate anus and rectum. J Pediat Surg 1968; 3: 337.
43. Weber HM, Dixon CF. Duplication of entire large intestine (colon duplex): report of a case. Am J Roentgenol 1946; 53: 319.
44. Van Velzer DA, Barrick CW, Jenkinson EL. Duplication of the colon: a case presentation. Am J Roentgenol 1956; 75: 349.
45. Ravitch MM, Scott WW. Duplication of the entire colon, bladder and urethra. Surgery 1953; 34: 843.
46. Abrami G, Dennison WM. Duplication of the stomach. Surgery 1961; 49: 794.
47. Lewis FT, Thyng FW. The regular occurrence of intestinal diverticula in embryos of the pig, rabbit and man. Am J Anat 1907–08; 7: 505.
48. Ladd WE, Gross RE. Congenital malformations of the anus and rectum: report of 162 cases. Amer J Surg 1934; 23: 167.
49. Browne D. Some congenital deformities of the rectum, anus, vagina and urethra. Ann Roy Coll Surg Eng 1951; 8: 173.
50. Browne D. Congenital deformities of the anus and rectum. Arch Dis Child 1955; 30: 42.
51. Gough MH. Congenital anomalies of the anus and rectum. Arch Dis Child 1961; 36: 146.
52. Nixon HH. Imperforate anus. British Surgical Practice (Surgical Progress). Butterworths, London 1961.
53. Louw JH. Congenital abnormalities of the rectum and anus. (Current Problems in Surgery) Year Book Medical Publishers, Chicago, 1965.
54. Romualdi P. Classification of the ano-rectal abnormalities. Riv Chir Pediat 1965; 7: 1.
55. Stephens FD. Congenital malformations of the rectum, anus and genitourinary tract. E&S Livingstone, Edinburgh, 1963.
56. Santulli TV, Kiesewetter WB, Bill AH Jr. Anorectal anomalies: a suggested international classification. J Pediatr Surg 1970; 5: 281.
57. Magnus RV, Stephens FD. Imperforate anal membrane: the anatomy and function of the sphincters of the anal canal. Austral Pediatr J 1966; 2: 165.
58. Partridge JP, Gough MH. Congenital abnormalities of the anus and rectum. Br J Surg 1961; 49: 37.
59. Magnus RV. Rectal atresia as distinguished from rectal agenesis. J Pediat Surg 1968; 3: 593.
60. Snyder WH Jr. Some unusual forms of imperforate anus in female patients. Amer J Surg 1966; 111: 319–325.
61. Johnston JH, Penn IA. Exstrophy of the cloaca. Brit J Urol 1966; 38: 302.
62. Magnus RV. Ectopia cloacae — a misnomer. J Pediat Surg 1969; 4: 511.
63. Carey JC, Greenbaum B, Hall BD. The OEIS Complex (Omphalocele, exstrophy, imperforate anus, spinal defects). Birth Defects: Orig Art Ser 1978; 14(6B): 252.
64. Choisy R. Sur l'absence des organes genitaux externes et la peritonite externe. Gynecol Obstet 1926; 13: 177.
65. Gale DH, Stocker JT. Cloacal dysgenesis with urethral, vaginal outlet, and anal agenesis and functioning internal genitourinary excretion. Pediatr Pathol 1987; 7: 457.
66. Currarino G, Weinberg A. From small pelvic outlet syndrome to sirenomelia. Pediatr Pathol 1991; 11: 195.
67. Bentley JFR, Smith JR. Developmental posterior enteric remnants and spinal malformations: 'the split notochord syndrome'. Arch Dis Child 1960; 35: 76.
68. Prop N, Frensdorf EL, van der Stadt FR. A post-vertebral endodermal cyst associated with axial deformities: a case showing the endodermal-ectodermal adhesion syndrome. Pediatrics 1967; 39: 555.
69. Burrows FGO, Sutcliffe J. The split notochord syndrome. Br J Radiol 1968; 41: 844.
70. Cameron AH. Malformations of the neuro-spinal axis, urogenital tract and foregut in spina bifida attributable to disturbances in the blastopore. J Pathol Bacteriol 1957; 73: 213.
71. Keen WW, Coplin ML. Sacrococcygeal tumour (teratoma) with an opening entirely thorugh the sacrum, and a sinus passing through this opening and communicating with the rectum, the sinus resembling a bronchus. Surg Gynecol Obstet 1906; 3: 661,
72. Rosselet PJ. A rare case of rhachischisis with multiple malformations. Am J Roentgenol 1955; 73: 235.
73. Esterly JR, Baghdassarian OM. Presacral neurenteric cyst. An unusual malformation resulting from persistence of the neurenteric canal. Johns Hopkins Hosp Bull 1963; 113: 202.
74. Faris JC, Crowe JE. The split notochord syndrome. J Pediatr Surg 1975; 10: 467.
75. Bolande RP. Neoplasia of early life and its relationship to teratogenesis. Perspect Pediatr Pathol 1976; 3: 145.
76. Blumel J, Evans EB, Eggers GWN. Partial and complete agenesis or malformation of the sacrum with associated anomalies. J Bone Jt Surg 1959; 41A: 497.
77. Passarge E, Lenz W. Syndrome of caudal regression in infants of diabetic mothers: observations of further cases. Pediatrics 1966; 37: 672.
78. Smith ED. Congenital anomalies of the sacrum. Austral NZ J Surg 1959; 29: 165.
79. Rusnak SL, Driscoll SG. Congenital spinal anomalies in infants of diabetic mothers. Pediatrics 1965; 35: 989.
80. Duhamel B. From the mermaid to anal imperforation: The syndrome of caudal regression. Arch Dis Child 1961; 36: 152.
81. Stocker JT, Heifetz SA. Sirenomelia. A morphological study of 33 cases and review of the literature. Perspect Pediatr Pathol 1987; 10: 7.
82. Welch JP, Aterman K. The syndrome of caudal dysplasia: a review including etiologic considerations and evidence of heterogeneity. Pediatr Pathol 1984; 2: 313.
83. Wilson JSP, Vallance-Owen J. Congenital deformities and insulin antagonism. Lancet 1966; 2: 940.
84. Landauer W, Clarke EM. Teratogenic interaction of insulin and 2-deoxy-D-glucose in chick development. J Exp Zool 1962; 151: 245.
85. Deuchar EM. Experimental evidence relating fetal anomalies to diabetes. In: HW Sutherland, JM Stowers, eds. Pregnancy and the newborn, 1978; Springer-Verlag, New York, 1979, p 21.
86. Stewart JM, Stoll S. Familial caudal regression anomalad and maternal diabetes. Lancet 1964; 2: 1124.

87. Finer NN, Bowen P, Dunbar LG. Caudal regression anomalad (sacral agenesis) in siblings. Clin Genet 1978; 13: 353.
88. Cohn J, Bay-Nielsen E. Hereditary defect of the sacrum and coccyx with anterior sacral meningocele. Acta Pediatr Scand 1969; 58: 268.
89. Ashcraft KW, Holder TM, Harris DJ. Familial presacral teratomas. Birth Defects: Orig Art Ser XV (National Foundation: March of Dimes), 1975; 11(5): 143.
90. Hall JG, Pallister PD, Clarren SK, Beckwith JB, Wiglesworth FW, Fraser FC, Cho S, Benke PJ, Reed SD. Congenital hypothalamic hamartoblastoma, hypopituitarism, imperforate anus, and post axial polydactyly — a new syndrome? Am J Med Genet 1980; 7: 47.
91. Uhlig BE, Johnson RL. Presacral tumors and cysts in adults. Dis Colon Rectum 1975; 18: 581.
92. Thomason TH. Cysts and sinuses of the sacrococcygeal region. Ann Surg 1934; 99: 585.
93. Hawkins WJ, Jackman RJ. Developmental cysts as a source of perianal abscesses and fistulas. Amer J Surg 1953; 86: 678.
94. Edwards M. Multilocular retrorectal cystic disease — cyst hamartoma: report of twelve cases. Dis Colon Rectum 1961; 4: 103.
95. Guillermo C, Grossman IW. Presacral cyst. Am Surg 1972; 38: 442.
96. Caropreso PR, Wengert PA Jr, Milford EH. Tailgut cyst — a rare retrorectal tumour. Dis Colon Rectum 1975; 18: 597.
97. Gius JA, Stout AP. Perianal cysts of vestigeal origin. Arch Surg 1938; 37: 268.
98. Campbell WL, Wolff M. Retrorectal cysts of developmental origin. Am J Roentogenol 1973; 117: 307.
99. Laird DR. Presacral cystic tumours. Amer J Surg 1954; 88: 793.
100. Marco V, Autonell J, Farre J, Fernandez-Layos M, Doncel M. Retrorectal cyst-hamartomas: report of two cases with adenocarcinoma developing in one. Am J Surg Path 1982; 6: 707.
101. Spencer RJ, Jackman RJ. Surgical management of pre-coccygeal cysts. Surg Gynecol Obst 1962; 115: 449.
102. Crowley LV, Page HG. Adenocarcinoma arising in presacral enterogenous cyst. Arch Pathol 1960; 69: 64.
103. Colin JF, Branfoot AC, Robinson KP. Malignant change in rectal duplication. J R Soc Med 1979; 72: 935.
104. Picard EJ, Picard JJ, Jorissen J, Jardon M. Heterotopic gastric mucosa in the epiglottis and rectum. Am J Dig Dis 1978; 23: 217.
105. Edouard A, Jouanelle A, Amar A, Doutone P, Maurice P, Galand A: Ulcerated heterotopic gastric mucosa located in the rectum. Gastroenterol Clin Biol 1983; 7: 39.
106. Castellanos D, Menchen P, Lopez de la Riva M et al. Heterotopic gastric mucosa in the rectum. Endoscopy 1984; 16: 197.
107. Schwarzenburg SJ, Whitington PF. Rectal gastric mucosa heterotopia as a cause of hematochezia in an infant. Dig Dis Sci 1983; 28: 470.
108. Shindo K, Bacon HE, Holmes EJ. Ectopic gastric mucosa and glandular tissue of a salivary type in the anal canal. Dis Colon Rectum 1972; 15: 57.
109. Weitzner S. Ectopic salivary gland tissue in submucosa of rectum. Dis Colon Rectum 1983; 26: 814.
110. Sun C-C J, Raffel LJ, Wright LL, Mergner WJ. Immature renal tissue in colonic wall of patient with caudal regression syndrome. Arch Pathol Lab Med 1986; 110: 653.
111. Townes PL, Brocks ER. Hereditary syndrome of imperforate anus with hand, foot and ear anomalies. J Pediatr 1972; 81: 321.
112. Kurnit DM, Steele MW, Pinsky L, Dibbins A. Autosomal dominant transmission of a syndrome of anal, ear, renal and radial congenital malformations. J Pediatr 1978; 93: 270.
113. Temtamy S. Schinzel syndrome of ulnar ray defects, hypogenitalism and anal atresia. Birth Defects: Orig Art Ser 1978; 14: 156.
114. Dungy C, Aptekar RG, Cann HM. Hereditary hydrometrocolpos with polydactyly in infancy. Pediatrics 1971; 47: 138.
115. Pinsky L. The community of human malformation syndromes that shares ectodermal dysplasia and deformities of the hands and feet. Teratology 1975; 11: 227.
116. Pinsky L. The syndromology of anorectal malformation (atresia, stenosis, ectopia). Am J Med Genet 1978; 1: 461.
117. Riccardi V, Hassler E, Lubinsky M. The FG syndrome: further characterization, report of a third family, and of a sporadic case. Am J Med Genet 1977; 1: 47.
118. Meckel S, Passarge E. Encephalocele, polycystic kidneys, and polydactyly as an autosomal recessive trait simulating certain other disorders. The Meckel Syndrome. Ann Genet (Paris) 1971; 14: 97.
119. Elliott GB, Tredwell J, Elliott K. The notochord as an abnormal organiser in production of congenital intestinal defect. Am J Roentgenol 1970; 110: 628.
120. Hsia YE, Bratu M, Herbordt A. Genetics of the Meckel syndrome (dysencephalia splanchnocystica). Pediatrics 1971; 48: 237.
121. Saldino RM, Noonan C. Severe thoracic dystrophy with striking micromelia, abnormal osseous development, including the spine, and multiple visceral anomalies. Am J Roentgenol 1972; 114: 254.
122. Fraser CR. Our genetical 'load'. A review of some aspects of genetical variation. Ann Hum Genet 1962; 25: 387.
123. Azvedo ES, Biondi J, Ramaldo LM. Cryptophthalmos in two families. J Med Genet 1973; 10: 389.
124. Toledo SA, Medeiros-Neto GA, Knobel M, Matler E. Evaluation of the hypothalamic-pituitary-gonadal function in Bardet-Biedl syndrome. Metabolism 1977; 26: 1277.
125. Little JR, Opitz JM. Case reports: the G syndrome. Am J Dis Child 1971; 121: 505.
126. Frias JL, Rosenbloom AL. Two new familial cases of the 'G' syndrome. Birth Defects: Orig Art Ser 1975; 11(2): 54.
127. Opitz JM, Summitt RL, Smith DW. The BBB syndrome, familial telecanthus with associated anomalies. Clinical Delineation of Birth Defects (National Foundation — March of Dimes) 1969; 5: 86.
128. Johanson A, Blizzard R. A syndrome of congenital aplasia of the alae nasi, deafness, hypothyroidism, dwarfism, absent permanent teeth, and malabsorption. J Pediatr 1971; 79: 782.
129. Daentl DL, Frias JL, Gilbert EF, Opitz JM. The Johanson-Blizzard syndrome: case report and autopsy findings. Am J Med Genet 1979; 3: 129.
130. Quan L, Smith DW.The VATER association: Vetebral defects, anal atresia, T-E fistula with esophageal atresia, radial and renal dysplasia: a spectrum of associated defects. J Pediatr 1973; 82: 104.
131. Heifetz SA. Single umbilical artery: a statistical analysis of 237 autopsy cases and review of the literature. Perspect Pediatr Pathol 1984; 8: 345.
132. Blank CE. Apert's syndrome (a type of acrocephalo-syndactyly) observations on British series of thirty-nine cases. Ann Hum Genet 1960; 24: 151.
133. Yunis J. New chromosomal syndromes. Academic Press, New York 1977, pp 69–71, 281–282.
134. Hanson JW, Myrianthopoulos NC , Harvey MAS, Smith DW. Risks to the offspring of women treated with hydantoin anticonvulsants, with emphasis on the fetal hydantoin effect. J Pediatrics 1976; 89: 662–668.
135. Tan KL, Tan R, Tan SH, Tan AM. The twin transfusion syndrome. Clin Pediatr 1979; 18: 111.
136. Wells TR, Gwinn JL, Landing BH. Sling left pulmonary artery: two diseases, one with bridging bronchus, absence of pars membranacea and high incidence of imperforate anus. Lab Invest 1987; 56: 7P.
137. Texter JF, Murphy GP. The right-sided syndrome: congenital absence of the right testis, right kidney and rectum. Johns Hopkins Med J 1968; 122: 224.
138. deSa DJ. The alimentary tract. In: Wigglesworth JS, Singer DB, eds. Textbook of Fetal and Perinatal Pathology. Blackwell Scientific Publications, Oxford, 1991; pp 923–954.

CHAPTER

18 Hirschsprung's disease and related disorders

B. D. Lake

Intestinal obstruction presenting in the neonatal or infantile period poses a problem in management. The diagnosis and consequently the management can be resolved by examination of a rectal biopsy which in a large proportion of cases shows Hirschsprung's disease or pseudo-Hischsprung's disease, although in some no diagnosis is reached.

Other causes of obstruction, including meconium plug syndrome, atresias, strictures following enterocolitis and anorectal anomalies, are also recognized. Pseudo-Hirschsprungs' disease is also considered under disorders of motility (see Ch. 22).

HIRSCHSPRUNG'S DISEASE

Hirschsprung's disease is characterized by absence of neurons in the distal portion of the intestine; their presence in proximal portions and can be divided into four main categories.

a) Short segment disease: the aganglionic segment extends no further than the sigmoid colon. The majority of patients (80–90%) have this form.

b) Long segment disease: the aganglionic segment extends beyond the sigmoid and involves a variable length of colon but does not extend beyond the caecum.

c) Total colonic aganglionosis: the whole colon is involved together with variable lengths of ileum, jejunum and even stomach in some cases. Its incidence varies in reported series from 2.6% to 14.9% of all Hirschsprung's disease.

d) Ultra-short segment disease: no aganglionic segment can be detected but the clinical symptoms are those of Hirschsprung's disease. The defect most probably lies in the anal sphincter and the disorder is best regarded as achalasia of the internal sphincter. The diagnosis cannot be made microscopically but is made on manometric evidence. Sometimes when only the distal third of the rectum is aganglionic this is also referred to as ultra-short segment disease, but there is no pathological justification for this although there may be surgical grounds for doing so.

Hirschsprung's disease primarily affects the neonate but infants, juveniles and adults can all have aganglionic segments which may extend as far as the terminal ileum. Length of segment is thus not necessarily related to severity of symptoms. For clinical, surgical and physiological details the reader is referred to Holschneider.[1]

Incidence and genetics

Hirschsprung's disease affects males more than females to the extent that 70–80% of patients are male,[2] but this ratio decreases as the length of segment increases,[3] and some report an equal incidence in total colonic aganglionosis. Hirschsprung's disease is seen in about 1 in 5000 live births and although its occurence appears to be genetically determined the nature of this is not clear. Mothers with Hirschsprung's disease are more likely to have affected children than are fathers, and in about 5–10% of cases there is an affected sibling. Genetic determination of the length of segment involved is unclear because short segment disease and cases of total colonic aganglionosis are reported in the same family.[4] However recent studies have revealed a series of mutations on chromosome 10 involving the receptor tyrosine kinase gene RET which gives rise to Hirschsprung's disease,[5,6] multiple endocrine neoplasia 2A and 2B, as well as familial medullary carcinoma of the thyroid. In Hirschsprung's disease, deletions are found as well as point mutations which result in loss of function of the gene. There is an increased incidence of Down's syndrome in association with Hirschsprung's disease and there are several reports of patients with Waardenberg's syndrome and Hirschsprung's disease.[7] A wide variety of other associations have been noted but these occur infrequently.[2]

Embryology

The studies by Okamoto and Ueda[8] on human fetuses indicated that by the 5th week vagal nerve trunks could be shown in the upper oesophagus and that neuroblasts were present alongside the vagal nerve in the pharynx. The nerve trunks extended on the outer surface of the gut wall, and neuroblasts were found along the nerves of the cardia of the stomach by the 6th week, the cephalic limb of the midgut by the 7th week and the whole gut, apart from the distal half of the colon and rectum, by the 8th week. By the 12th week they had migrated as far as the rectum. The myenteric plexus is formed first just outside the circular muscle coat which then develops its longitudinal coat. Neuroblasts migrate from the myenteric plexus to form the submucous plexuses which are completed during the third and fourth month. The rectum is also innervated by nerve fibres from the pelvic and pre-aortic plexus and this can be seen at about the 5th week.

Interruption of the orderly craniocaudal migration of nerve and neuroblasts can explain the variable length of the aganglionic segment in Hirschsprung's disease. Although this explanation provides a satisfactory pathophysiological basis for Hirschsprung's disease, it is not without its critics who point out that work on chick embryos indicates that cells at the trunk level of the neural crest can produce enteric ganglion cells.[9] This suggests that a caudocranial migration might be possible, at least under experimental conditions, but there is no evidence that this happens in the intact embryo. Changes in the embryonic gut microenvironment may also influence the development of enteric ganglia[10–13] and it has even been suggested that excessive rotation of the embryonic gut during the critical period between 5 and 10 weeks gestation could lead to ischaemia[14] and thus interfere with neural migration.

Innervation of the colon and rectum

The innervation of the colon has sympathetic, parasympathetic and peptidergic (purinergic) components. The ascending colon and small intestine are supplied by postganglionic sympathetic fibres derived from the coeliac plexus, while the descending colon and rectum are supplied by sympathetic preganglionic fibres from the lumbar segments (L1–L3) of the spinal cord.

The parasympathetic supply for the ascending colon is from the right vagal nerve but it is not clear whether this supply reaches the rectum. A parasympathetic supply from the sacral outflow (S2–S4) innervates the rectum and descending colon and there is evidence that the density of fibres is greatest in the rectum and least at the splenic flexure, the decrease being exponential. The peptidergic (purinergic/non cholinergic-non adrenergic) system appears to be mostly an intrinsic innervation[15] with communication between the ganglia in the three plexuses, there being little, if any, extrinsic connection. Nitric oxide and nitric oxide synthase appear to be important components of this system.

Normal histology

The normal intestine contains three neural plexuses which consist of neurons, nerve fibres and supporting Schwann cells. The nerves are almost exclusively unmyelinated but an occasional myelinated fibre, probably of extrinsic origin, can be found. The myenteric plexus of Auerbach is situated between the circular and longitudinal muscle coats, while the submucosal plexuses are present within the submucosa just below the muscularis mucosae (Meissner's plexus) and just above the circular muscle coat (Henle's plexus). The existence of a further plexus, of extrinsic origin, has become apparent in recent years. Using an Osmium tetroxide-zinc iodide technique, Stach[16] demonstrated the presence of a plexus within the outer quarter of the circular muscle coat (i.e. adjacent to the submucosa). This area has now been shown to be rich in interstitial cells of Cajal[17] and it is postulated to have a pacemaker role on smooth muscle activity.

In the normal colon of a child the ganglion cells in the submucosa are scattered in Meissner's plexus at intervals of about 1 mm and in clusters of 1–5 cells (Fig. 18.1). The density of ganglion cells[18] is of the order of 17 ganglion cells per mm^2. In the rectum there is a normal hypoganglionic zone[18] which extends from the pectinate line proximally for a distance which varies with each plexus and the age of the patient, being related to normal growth. The hypoganglionic zone for the myenteric plexus is about 4 mm, for Meissner's plexus about 10 mm, and for Henle's plexus about 7 mm. In Meissner's plexus ganglion cells are sparsely distributed in this region, their density may only be of the order of 1 ganglion cell per mm^2, and they may not be seen unless many serial sections are examined. The normal density of ganglion cells is found 2–3 cm from the pectinate line and does not vary much beyond that distance.

In the hypoganglionic zone prominent nerve trunks may be found in the submucosa and in the myenteric

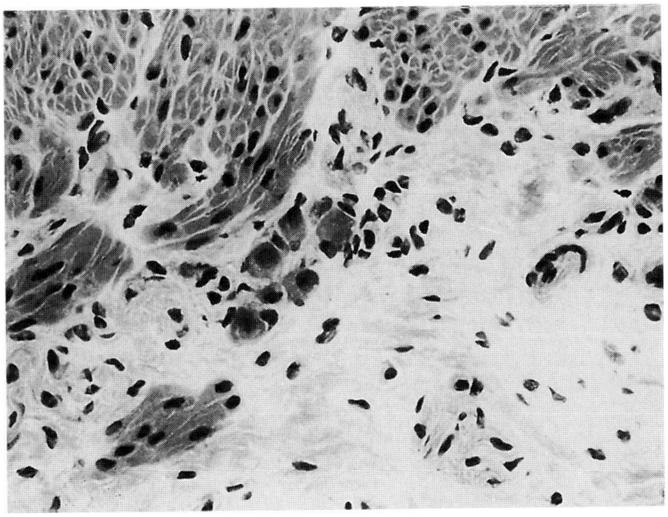

Fig. 18.1 Suction rectal biopsy: routine section, showing ganglion cells in the submucosa. (H&E)

plexus. Prominent submucosal blood vessels may also be present in this zone.[19]

In the neonate and premature infant the ganglia in Meissner's plexus can appear as small groups of neuroblasts rather than mature ganglion cells (Fig. 18.2). This is sometimes interpreted as a sign of immaturity of the plexus, which is held to account for dysfunction.[20] These immature ganglia consist of clusters of up to 10 cells in a circular, ovoid or horseshoe arrangement often associated with termination of a small nerve.[21] The nuclei have very little surrounding cytoplasm and the prominent nucleolus usually associated with mature ganglion cells is not found. Immature ganglion cells must be distinguished from blood vessels and transverse sections of small nerve trunks.

In sections treated to demonstrate catecholamines, adrenergic fibres visualized by one of the formaldehyde induced fluorescence (FIF) methods, are found in a network around the neurons in the myenteric and submucosal plexuses.[22–24] In addition a periadventitial arrangement of nerve fibres is found around blood vessels. Very few adrenergic fibres are detected in the muscle layers and no neurons contain fluorescent products.[23]

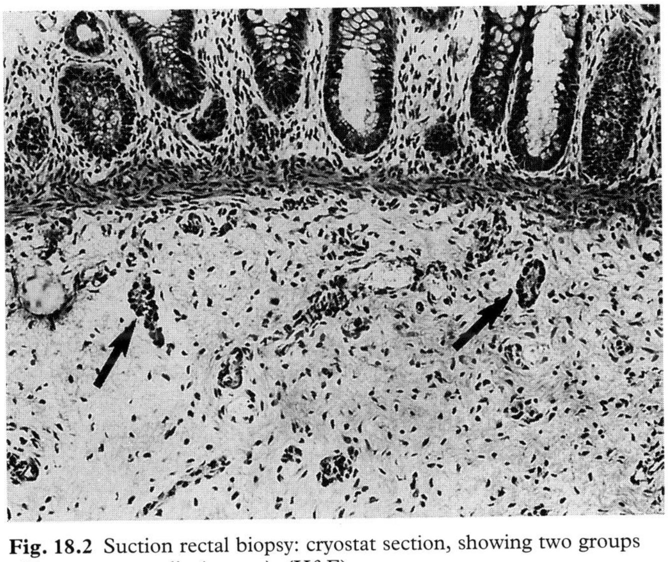

Fig. 18.2 Suction rectal biopsy: cryostat section, showing two groups of immature ganglia (arrows). (H&E)

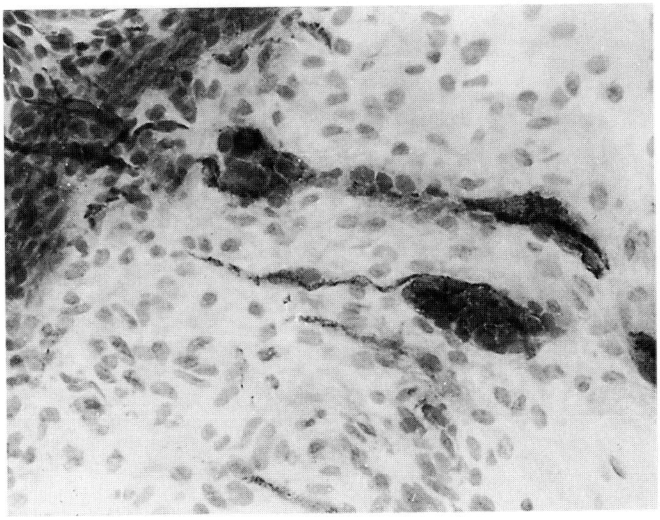

Fig. 18.3 Suction rectal biopsy: cryostat section stained for acetylcholinesterase activity showing immature ganglia and nerve fibres. The ganglia are readily identified by this method and are not confused with similar groups of cells (e.g. blood vessels) which are not stained. The muscularis mucosae is in the top left hand corner. A light nuclear stain has been added.

Acetylcholinesterase-positive nerve fibres (not all necessarily cholinergic) demonstrated by the Karnovsky and Roots method[25] or one of its variations,[26] form a network around and are seen to supply the neurons in the submucosal plexuses (Fig. 18.3). The ganglia of the myenteric plexus are also well demonstrated and have a profusion of nerve fibres and fewer neurons than the size of the ganglia in routinely stained sections would suggest. No positively stained neurons are found but the stippled appearance of their surface suggests terminal contact of individual fibres (Fig. 18.4).

In the longitudinal muscle coat a few nerve fibres can be demonstrated and there is a similar density in the circular coat. Very few acetylcholinesterase-positive nerve fibres are found in the muscularis mucosae and only scattered fine fibres are present in the lamina propria of the colon. However, in the small intestine there is a striking number of dense coarse acetylcholinesterase-positive fibres around the crypts. Neurons are readily recognized by their surrounding nerve fibres, and with this method the very occasional lamina propria neuron is well documented. Neurons in the lamina propria have been regarded as abnormal, and a reflection of some disturbance of orderly neuronal migration, but occasional examples are infrequently found in biopsies which are in all other respects quite normal. Acetylcholinesterase-positive nerve

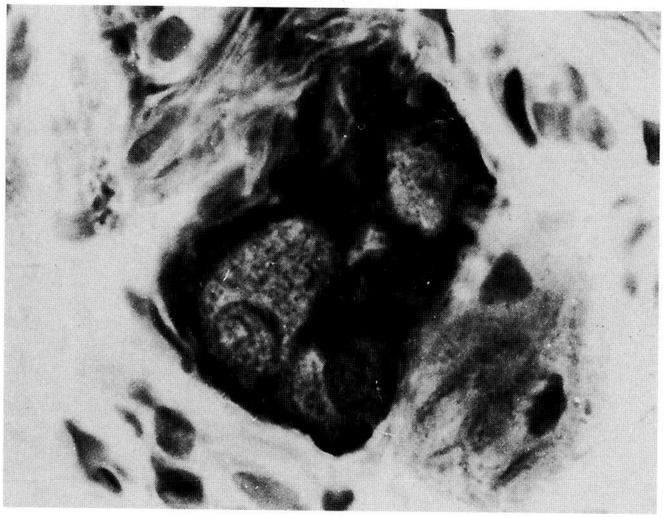

Fig. 18.4 Suction rectal biopsy: cryostat section stained for acetylcholinesterase activity. Ganglia are readily identified by the dense nerve network around the neurons, which have a stippled appearance.

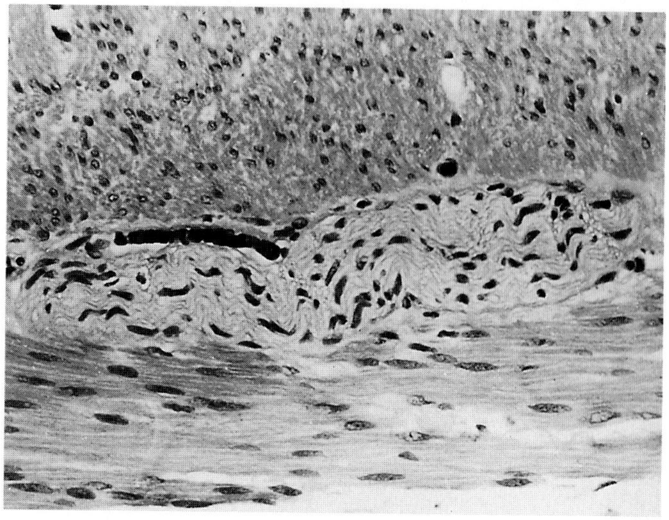

Fig. 18.5 Large nerve trunks in the myenteric plexus are found in the aganglionic segment of short and long segment Hirschsprung's disease. (Routine section, H&E)

fibres are also seen around blood vessels, particularly arterioles.

The distribution of peptidergic nerves is similar to that of the adrenergic and acetylcholinesterase-positive nerve fibres. Some difference between individual neuropeptide distributions is evident and some neurons contain one or more neuropeptide. Nitric oxide synthase can be shown within neurons of the myenteric plexus and in nerve fibres, particularly in the circular muscle coat, by application of antibodies to nitric oxide synthase or by the demonstration of NADPH dehydrogenase activity,[27] although this latter method may not be entirely specific.

DIAGNOSIS OF HIRSCHSPRUNG'S DISEASE

Since the recognition of the basic pathology of Hirschsprung's disease in the late 1940s the methods used in diagnosis have changed considerably. In the early days a full thickness biopsy of rectum which included mucosa, submucosa and both circular and longitudinal muscle coats was advocated. In haematoxylin and eosin (H&E) stained sections of formalin fixed wax-embedded tissue the nerve trunks in the myenteric and submucosal plexuses (Fig. 18.5) and the absence of ganglion cells were easy to interpret, but the surgical procedure was not without complications, particularly in neonates. Great skill was necessary in order to avoid subsequent bleeding, incontinence and stricture. Significant scarring could interfere with the subsequent pull through operation.

Bodian[28] later recommended the excision of a mucosal strip (including submucosa) measuring 0.5×2 cm and its examination in routinely stained serial H&E sections. Dobbins and Bill,[29] however, noted that they could exclude a diagnosis of Hirschsprung's disease in suction rectal biopsies of patients with ulcerative colitis. Since that time mucosal biopsy obtained by a suction biopsy machine[30] or with biopsy forceps[31] has been the established method and full thickness biopsy is only rarely undertaken under special circumstances.

It became usual for the biopsies to be taken at about 2 cm from the pectinate line and also at about 5 cm distance, but these are very approximate and depend upon the patient's age. In the very small neonate a biopsy just above the pectinate line and one as high as can be taken without risk of perforation are indicated, regardless of the distances involved. Two biopsies were preferred, first to increase the chances of an adequate biopsy, secondly to overcome the problem of the normal hypoganglionic segment, and thirdly to give some guidance as to the length of the segment. If, for some reason, only one biopsy is taken this should be at 2–3 cm from the pectinate line. It is not always readily recognized that because the rectal mucosal appearance may be altered due to digital examination, barium enemas, washouts and manometric studies, there may be difficulties in positioning the biopsy instrument with certainty. Occasionally biopsies confidently labelled as being at 5 cm prove to consist of anal epithelium and thus the distance quoted confidently by some surgeons cannot be relied upon.

The biopsy buttons were generally orientated with mucosa uppermost, routinely fixed and processed, and some 60 serial sections perpendicular to the mucosal surface were stained with H&E and examined for ganglion cells. Some advocated sectioning in a plane horizontal to the mucosal surface because the larger area of submucosa in each section meant that fewer serial sections need be examined. The diagnosis of both short and long segment Hirschsprung's disease can be made if there is an absence of submucosal ganglion cells and an increase in nerve trunks, some of which may be large.

In patients with total colonic aganglionosis an increase in submucosal nerve trunks is not always present and absence of ganglion cells in serial sections is the criterion for diagnosis.

This method of diagnosis was widely employed with success but in difficult cases involving short segment disease in neonates, and ganglion cell immaturity, uncertainty of the results led to the development of other techniques based upon histochemistry.

The demonstration of increased catecholamine containing nerves in the muscularis propria (the large nerve trunks are mainly negative) and in the muscularis mucosae and lamina propria led to the suggested use of the FIF technique in diagnosis.[32] However the increase is not a constant finding,[24] the method is exacting and can be capricious and proved unsuitable for routine use.

It was known that there was an elevated concentration of acetylcholine in the aganglionic segment and that the large nerve trunks present in Hirschsprung's disease showed acetylcholinesterase activity in histochemical preparations. However, the finer histological details only became apparent when Meier-Ruge[33,34] applied the Karnovsky and Roots direct staining method[25] and found that there was a consistent increase in acetylcholinesterase-positive nerve fibres in the lamina propria and muscularis mucosae. The histochemical diagnosis of Hirschsprung's disease thus became well established and is the most reliable method[26,35–40] and if applied correctly and interpreted with the following criteria, there should be no false positive and no false negative results.

Biopsies should be taken, as previously described, at 2 and 5 cm from the pectinate line or at around 3 cm if only one biopsy is taken. The biopsies should be kept moist on saline soaked filter paper in a small Petri dish and transported to the laboratory to arrive within 15 minutes. Longer than this may cause problems of interpretation due to autolysis. On arrival the biopsies are orientated on a block of animal liver or 10% gelatine, and frozen for cryostat sectioning in a plane perpendicular to the mucosal surface. Correct orientation of biopsies in OCT compound or similar products is not easily achieved. The tissue is trimmed until submucosa is visible in the sections, and sections are taken at 5 μm for haematoxylin and eosin and at 10 μm for acetylcholinesterase staining. With a careful H&E staining procedure (Harris haematoxylin 30–45 seconds, no differentiation) ganglion cells may be readily recognized by their amphiphilic cytoplasm and pale nuclei.

In the young child, juvenile and adult, with Hirschsprung's disease, there is a marked increase in coarse acetylcholinesterase-positive nerve fibres in the muscularis mucosae and lamina propria, the fibres in the lamina propria often travelling in a plane parallel to the mucosal surface (Fig. 18.6a,b,c). Numerous small nerve fibres, smaller and larger nerve trunks are also prominent in the submucosa. This pattern is evident even in the most distally taken biopsies which can include the mucocutaneous junction.

In the *neonate* the pattern is usually less dramatic with only the muscularis mucosae showing increased nerve fibres. In the lamina propria there may be an increase adjacent to the muscularis mucosae but in some neonates no increase may be seen in the lamina propria.[37] This has lead to false negative diagnoses through lack of appreciation of the natural history of the development of acetylcholinesterase-positive nerve fibres in Hirschsprung's disease. In one female neonate Hirsig et al[41] showed a progressive increase in nerve fibres in the lamina propria in biopsies taken on day 2, day 10, at 4 weeks and at 4½ months, although the pattern in the muscularis mucosae was clearly that of Hirschsprung's disease on day 2 (Fig. 18.7). Thus there may be a relationship between age and the number of fibres in the lamina propria,[42] but not between numbers of fibres and severity of disease. However severity may be related to the density of nerve fibres in the muscularis propria.

The increase in nerve fibres is found consistently in short and long segment Hirschsprung's disease but is not always present in total colonic aganglionosis. In this latter form, the pattern of staining may either be classic or may be normal.[43] In some there may be an increase in coarse fibres mainly at the submucosal aspect of the muscularis mucosae (Fig. 18.8). In general terms the longer the aganglionic portion of small bowel the less dramatic is the acetylcholinesterase staining pattern and the biopsy may appear normal, giving rise to a false negative result.

The reliability of the histochemical diagnosis depends on the quality of the stained preparations (a delicate nuclear counterstain is preferred because a heavy nuclear stain — Harris or Ehrlich — will mask the detail) and the strictness with which the criteria are observed. The infantile, juvenile and adult cases should pose no problem, but as indicated, the neonate, and especially those with total colonic aganglionosis, may give rise to false negative results.[43] In a series of biopsies from more than 1800 patients over a 15 year period at the Hospital for Sick Children, London, over 400 patients with Hirschsprung's disease were correctly diagnosed and there were no cases incorrectly identified as Hirschsprung's disease. False negative results were confined to one patient with total colonic aganglionosis.

The presence of acetylcholinesterase-positive nerves in the muscularis mucosae in Hirschsprung's disease makes it possible to make the diagnosis in biopsies which would otherwise be regarded as inadequate for assessment. Biopsies from patients without Hirschsprung's disease may show a variable increase in fine 'wispy' or 'knotty' nerve fibres in the muscularis mucosae, distinct from the coarse

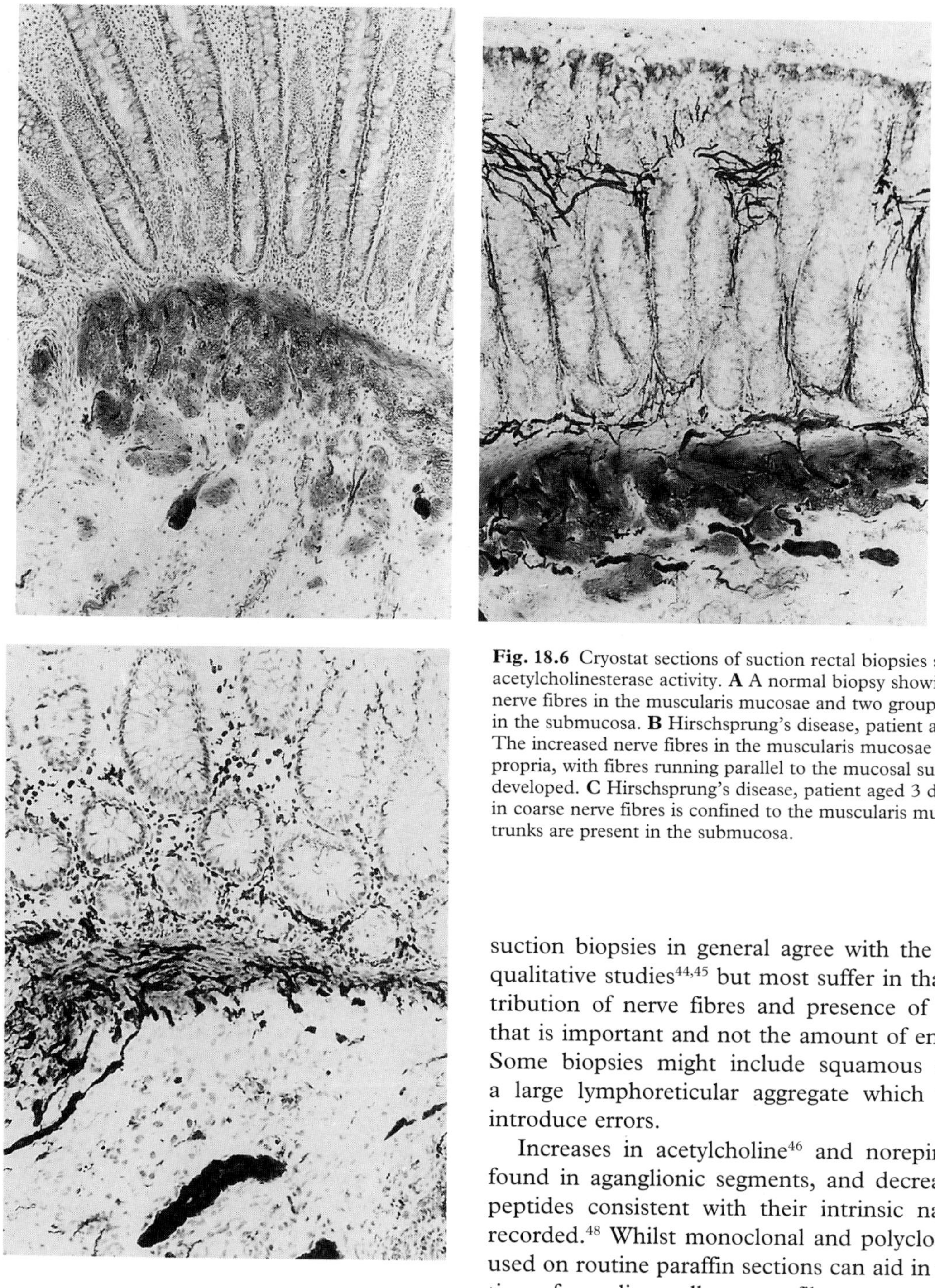

A B C

Fig. 18.6 Cryostat sections of suction rectal biopsies stained for acetylcholinesterase activity. **A** A normal biopsy showing a few fine nerve fibres in the muscularis mucosae and two groups of ganglion cells in the submucosa. **B** Hirschsprung's disease, patient aged 4 months. The increased nerve fibres in the muscularis mucosae and lamina propria, with fibres running parallel to the mucosal surface, are well developed. **C** Hirschsprung's disease, patient aged 3 days. The increase in coarse nerve fibres is confined to the muscularis mucosae. Nerve trunks are present in the submucosa.

fibres in Hirschsprung's disease (Fig. 18.9). These patients may have necrotizing enterocolitis, a high rectal anomaly where there may also be an increase in fine acetylcholinesterase-positive nerve fibres in the lamina propria[26] or constipation without recognized cause. The changes are not consistent, neither are they diagnostic features when present. There are no significant changes in ultra short segment disease as defined earlier.

Quantitative studies of acetylcholinesterase activity in suction biopsies in general agree with the histochemical qualitative studies[44,45] but most suffer in that it is the distribution of nerve fibres and presence of ganglion cells that is important and not the amount of enzyme present. Some biopsies might include squamous epithelium or a large lymphoreticular aggregate which would clearly introduce errors.

Increases in acetylcholine[46] and norepinephrine[47] are found in aganglionic segments, and decreases in neuropeptides consistent with their intrinsic nature are also recorded.[48] Whilst monoclonal and polyclonal antibodies used on routine paraffin sections can aid in the identification of ganglion cells, nerve fibres are more difficult to detect, although the use of antibodies to S100 protein and PGP 9.5 seems to be helpful in this respect.[49] It has been shown that microtubule associated protein (MAP5) is a good enteric neural marker[50] and will selectively demonstrate neurons and nerves in frozen sections. The authors suggested that the method might be used for the diagnosis of Hirschsprung's disease, but since it involves a special fixation protocol and immunofluorescence, it is better suited to research applications.

Intra-operative biopsies are taken during the definitive

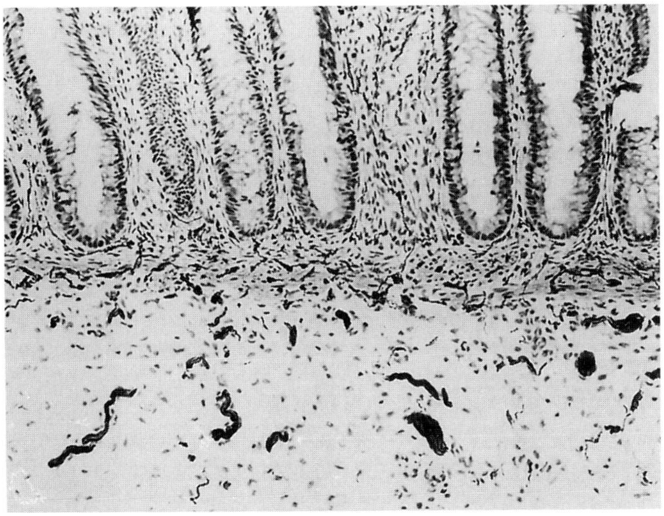

Fig. 18.7 In the neonate the increase in acetylcholinesterase-positive nerve fibres may not be seen in the lamina propria, and may only be mildly increased in the muscularis mucosae. The fibres are coarse and there is also an increased number of nerves in the submucosa. (Suction rectal biopsy, cryostat section: acetylcholinesterase and haematoxylin)

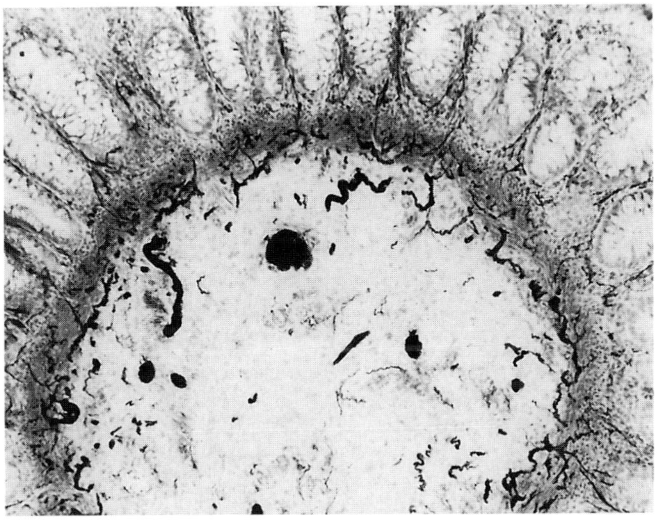

Fig. 18.8 Total colonic aganglionosis. Suction rectal biopsy stained for acetylcholinesterase activity showing the increased nerve fibres in the muscularis mucosae with accentuation at the submucosal side.

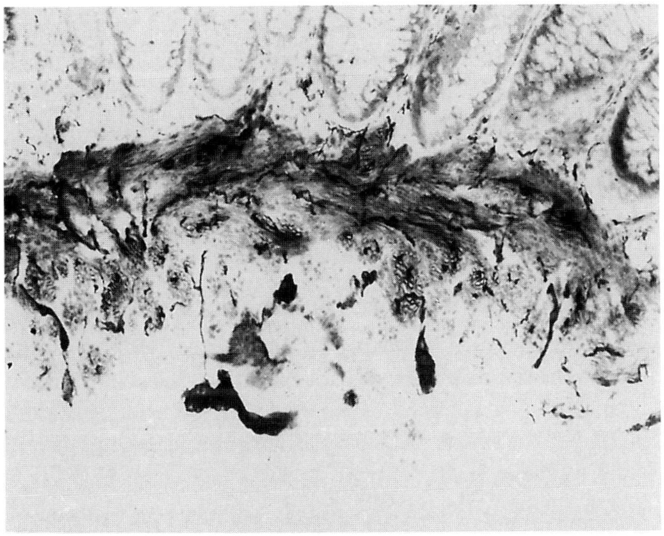

Fig. 18.9 Fine or knotty nerve fibres are sometimes found in the muscularis mucosae in non-Hirschsprung's disease. Ganglion cells are also shown in the submucosa in this figure. The fine nature of the nerve fibres serves to differentiate this non-specific finding from the coarse fibres in Hirschsprung's disease. (Cryostat section: acetylcholinesterase and haematoxylin.)

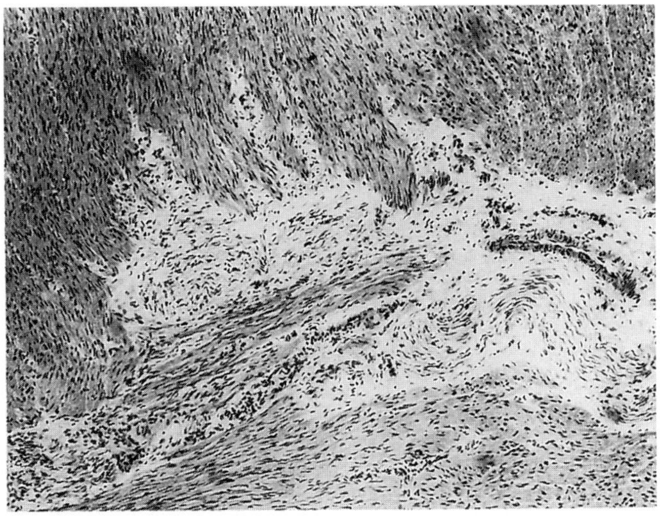

Fig. 18.10 Intraoperative seromuscular biopsy showing nerve trunks in the myenteric plexus. (Cryostat section: H&E)

pull-through operation to determine the length of the aganglionic segment. Seromuscular biopsies are orientated on edge, frozen and sectioned in a cryostat at 5–10 μm. An H&E stain (Harris haematoxylin for 30–45 seconds without differentiation gives the best result) is adequate to show the myenteric plexus. The presence of nerve trunks indicates the biopsy is from the aganglionic zone while adequate ganglia indicates the ganglionic portion (Fig. 18.10). If nerve trunks and neurons are present the biopsy is from the transitional zone (Fig. 18.11) and the surgeon should take a further biopsy proximally. In total colonic aganglionosis biopsies from the aganglionic portions show closely apposed muscle coats with no nerves. Rapid esterase staining, using a non-specific esterase method,[51] can be completed in less than five minutes and may be of help in showing positively stained neurons and nerve trunks, but good haematoxylin and eosin preparations are usually adequate. The length of time taken to

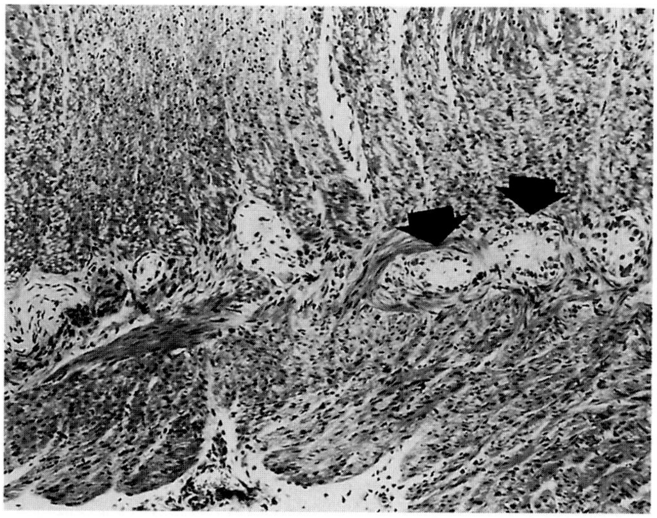

Fig. 18.11 Transitional zone in the colon in which nerve trunks (arrows) and groups of ganglion cells coexist. (Cryostat section: H&E)

produce an acetylcholinesterase stained slide (30 minutes or 2 hours) precludes its use at operation.

Resected segments from the pull-through operation should be sectioned longitudinally from end to end so that the extent of the aganglionosis can be determined and the status of the proximal portion ascertained. Transverse sections of the resected segment are inadequate and make it impossible to comment on the length of aganglionosis and the site of the appearance of ganglion cells.

In long and short segment disease the myenteric plexus contains many large nerve trunks and these are also prominent in the submucosa (Fig. 18.12). The transition between the aganglionic segment and normal bowel usually occurs over a short distance with ganglia appearing almost simultaneously, but not exclusively so, in the myenteric and submucosal plexuses. Some patients, however, have a longer transitional zone in which neurons and nerve trunks are present for several centimetres. Such areas can cause problems in biopsies taken during the pull-through operation. The colon from patients with total colonic aganglionosis usually shows no evidence of nerves in the region of the myenteric plexus or submucosa and hardly any acetylcholinesterase-positive nerve fibres are seen in the muscularis propria, a feature also found sometimes near to the transitional zone in other forms of Hirschsprung's disease.[23] The muscle coats are tightly apposed and the whole appearance is very bland (Fig. 18.13).

Some patients have symptoms after a pull-through operation which suggest a retained aganglionic segment, while others seem to acquire hyoganglionosis[52,53] which is possibly the result of ischaemia or infection.[54] Suction rectal biopsy with acetylcholinesterase staining is helpful in confirming a retained segment provided that the pulled through bowel is distal to the splenic flexure. This is because the acetylcholinesterase-positive fibres are derived from the sacral outflow and this innervation does not occur beyond the descending colon, although in the small intestine there is a pronounced acetylcholinesterase-positive network in the lamina propria in the normal subject. Biopsies taken after the Duhamel operation should be from the anterior wall (existing aganglionic rectum) as well as from the posterior wall (putative ganglionic bowel). It is noteworthy that in acquired aganglionosis[53] previously ganglionated bowel appears aganglionic and seems to acquire the increase in acetylcholinesterase-positive nerve fibres in the muscularis mucosae and lamina propria characteristic of Hirschsprung's disease. The possibility that the initial pull-through specimen might have different

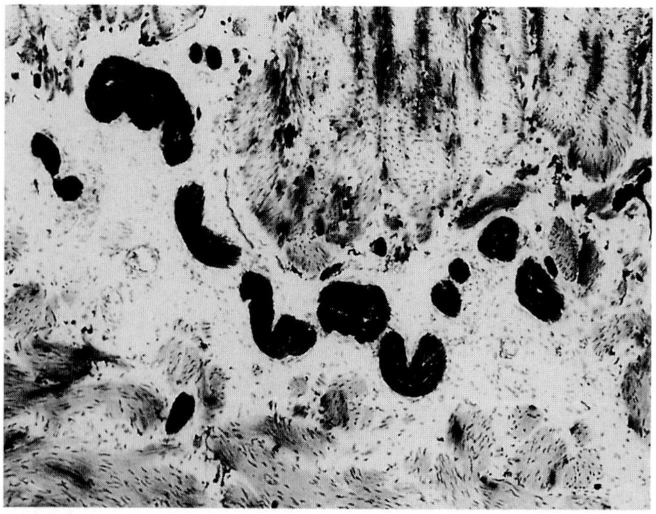

Fig. 18.12 The large nerve trunks in the myenteric plexus in short and long segment Hirschsprung's disease are strongly positive for acetylcholinesterase activity. (Cryostat section: acetylcholinesterase and haematoxylin)

Fig. 18.13 Colon in total colonic aganglionosis. The two muscle coats are closely apposed and there is no evidence of a myenteric plexus. No nerve trunks are present. (Routine section: H&E)

changes (ganglionic, transitional zone, aganglionosis) around the circumference was not considered, and this might be a factor.

Vascular abnormalities

Abnormal blood vessels are an infrequently observed feature of Hirschsprung's disease. Lister[55] commented on their occurrence in three patients with Hirschsprung's disease and in one with possible pseudo-Hirschsprung's disease. The abnormal arteries were most conspicuous in the transitional zone, were firm and thickened, and showed bizarre microscopical changes with marked proliferation of the muscle coats of the media and an obliterative endarteritis in others. Taguchi et al[56] found 8 of 25 patients with 'adventitial fibromuscular dysplasia' in which there was an increase in collagen around the arterial internal elastic lamina and marked hypertrophy of the medial muscle coat (Fig. 18.14). The changes were localized to the transitional zone in the submucosa, in the muscle layers and subserosa and were found in all types of Hirschsprung's disease. Earlam[14] has suggested that this change might be evidence for a vascular origin of the disease.

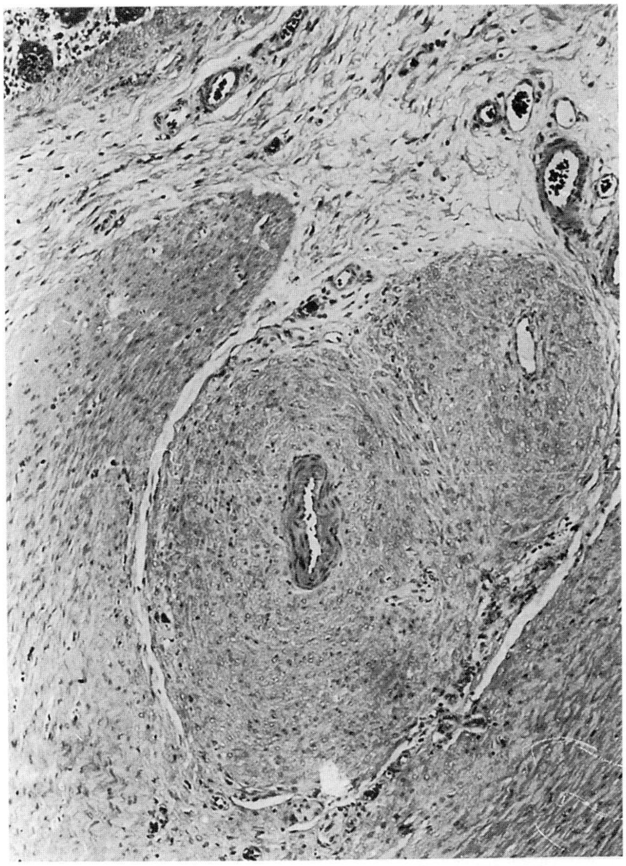

Fig. 18.14 Adventitial fibromuscular dysplasia involving arterial and venous vessels in the ileum in total colonic aganglionosis. This appearance was present in many vessels in an area near to the transitional zone. (Routine section: H&E)

Zonal aganglionosis

There are many reports of zonal aganglionosis, or skip segment Hirschsprung's disease, but when these are critically examined[57] most have been inadequately documented. It does appear however that genuine zonal changes occur in some patients with total colonic aganglionosis.[57–60] Variable lengths of hypoganglionic or normoganglionic transverse or ascending colon are found in otherwise classical total colonic aganglionosis. This finding should be borne in mind in the examination of intra-operative biopsies, and the colon in all cases of total colonic aganglionosis should be adequately sampled when resected. The occurence of zonal aganglionosis is difficult to explain in terms of the cranio–caudal embryonic migration of neuroblasts, and infective[61] and ischaemic origins have been proposed to account for its presence.

Pseudo-Hirschsprung's disease

The term pseudo-Hirschsprung's disease is a clinical term which refers to patients who have apparent intestinal obstruction or severe chronic constipation in whom ganglion cells are present in a rectal biopsy. The term chronic intestinal pseudo-obstruction is also used.

The 'condition' can be broadly divided into two groups:

a) Those with smooth muscle pathology
b) Those with neural abnormalities.

Smooth muscle pathology

In the majority of patients no morphological abnormalities can be detected in full thickness biopsies of bowel in spite of severe symptoms. One patient, whose biopsy samples were morphologically normal, was shown in immunohistochemical studies to have deficient alpha-smooth muscle actin in the circular muscle coat.[62] It is possible that abnormalities of other contractile proteins are the cause of pseudo-obstruction in at least some patients with morphologically normal bowel.

In a small proportion of patients, developmental abnormalities of the arrangement of muscle coats may be seen. Yamagiwa et al[63] reported muscular hypertrophy and an extra muscle layer under the longitudinal coat in the small intestine. Similar changes have been seen in our experience at The Hospital for Sick Children in London. The neuromuscular coordination of the abnormally arranged muscle layers may well be defective and sufficient to account for the pseudo-obstruction.

Patients with smooth muscle pathology (see also Ch. 22),

generally show symptoms of small bowel obstruction.[64–69] Ganglion cells are present in a suction rectal biopsy and acetylcholinesterase-positive nerves are normal in number in the lamina propria. The visceral myopathies show smooth muscle fibre atrophy with fibrous tissue replacement and an apparent increase in nerves within the affected muscle coat. The changes may be dramatic or subtle and occur either within the circular muscle coat, or the longitudinal muscle coat or both. There is minimal inflammation. The urinary tract may also be affected. Familial cases are reported with either autosomal dominant or recessive modes of transmission. A disorder essentially similar to visceral myopathy has been reported in Bantu African children and reviewed by Kaschula et al.[70]

Neural abnormalities

Of the disorders regarded as neural abnormalities, it is now apparent that those with neuronal nuclear inclusions[71] generally do not suffer from primary chronic constipation but have as their main problem progressive pyramidal and extrapyramidal signs and anterior horn cell dysfunction.[72]

The neural disorders can be regarded as neuronal dysplasias (of which Hirschsprung's disease is a special example) and can be broadly divided into those with hypoganglionosis and those with hyperganglionosis. In any assessment of number of ganglion cells in the myenteric plexus it may be necessary (although not proven) to take into account the degree of dilatation or contraction of the bowel. A grossly dilated bowel may show an apparent reduction in the numbers of ganglion cells per given length per section, while the converse may exist for the hypercontracted state. Studies on normal neuronal densities have been few and given conflicting results, and it is only recently that a systematic study has defined a baseline by which hypoganglionosis and hyperganglionosis can be assessed.[73] Smith's data, derived from studies of post mortem and surgically removed bowel, showed the normal colon contained 7 ganglion cells/mm in the myenteric plexus in a 3 μm section, with 3.6/mm in jejunum and 4.3/mm in ileum. There was no apparent difference with age.

Hypoganglionosis can be congenital with small ganglia consisting of immature neuroblast-like cells in the submucous and myenteric plexuses. This appearance extends throughout the gastrointestinal tract. In two reported cases[74,75] the outcome has been fatal while in a third the child survived.[76] Erdohazi[74] regarded the changes as a retarded development, while Munakata et al[75] and Ikeda et al[76] called the condition hypogenesis. Hypoganglionosis may also be acquired secondary to inflammation as in ulcerative colitis, Chagas' disease and in human immunodeficiency virus infection with or without cytomegalovirus being present.[77] Infiltration of the myenteric and submucosal plexuses by lymphocytes and the presence of autoantibodies to enteric neurons leading to hypoganglionosis is reported in a series of patients with small cell lung carcinoma who also had severe gastrointestinal dysmotility.[78] Patients with small-cell carcinoma of lung without symptoms of gastrointestinal dysmotility did not have such autoantibodies.

The presence of autoantibodies to enteric ganglia, and inflammatory changes in the myenteric plexus leading to severe hypoganglionosis/aganglionosis with glial preservation in a patient with pseudo-obstruction have also been seen at the Hospital for Sick Children, London. Inflammatory changes in the myenteric plexus leading to an axonopathy with preservation of ganglion cells have been reported in nonparaneoplastic chronic intestinal pseudo-obstruction of unknown aetiology.[79]

Hypoganglionosis can occur as part of the transitional zone in Hirschsprung's disease and is also reported to be acquired after pull-through procedures where damage to nerves or blood supply during surgery is implicated.[53,54] With milder degrees of hypoganglionosis[80,81] the ganglion cells of the myenteric and submucosal plexuses have a mature appearance but the ganglia in the myenteric plexus are small and contain only 10% of the normal number of ganglion cells.[34] A diagnosis of hypoganglionosis cannot be made on a suction rectal biopsy, and a full thickness sample is necessary to examine the myenteric plexus (Figs 18.15, 18.16). The muscle coats may have a reduced number of acetylcholinesterase-positive nerves.

Much confusion exists over the use of the term neuronal dysplasia. The disorder — described by Nezelov et al[82] and Meier-Ruge[83] and labelled neuronal colonic dysplasia, was recognized in biopsy samples by:[34]

a) hyperplasia of the submucosal and myenteric plexuses with formation of 'giant' ganglia

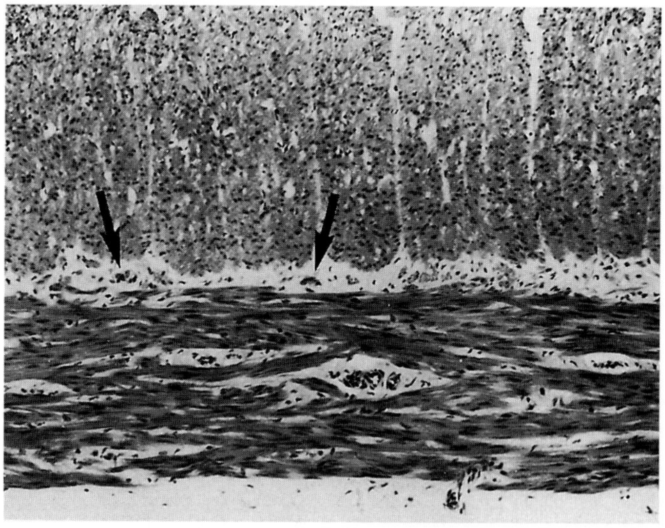

Fig. 18.15 In hypoganglionosis the ganglia are sparse and small (arrows). In contrast with total colonic aganglionosis the muscle coats are not closely apposed. (Routine section: H&E)

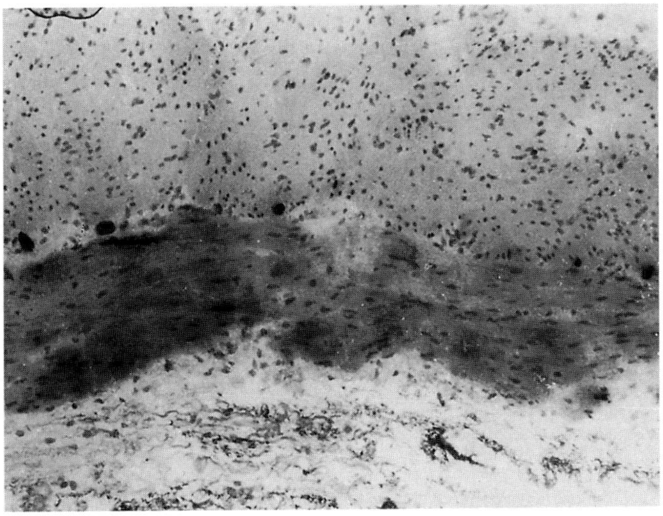

Fig. 18.16 The ganglia in hypoganglionosis are more easily found in acetylcholinesterase preparations. (Cryostat section: acetylcholinesterase and haematoxylin)

b) proliferation of fine nerve fibres in the lamina propria and circular muscle
c) ectopic ganglion cells in the lamina propria and within the muscularis mucosae; scattered islands of smooth muscle in the lamina propria may or may not be present (see Figs 18.17–18.19).

The criteria have been variably applied in the literature on neuronal colonic dysplasia, also referred to as intestinal neuronal dysplasia or as hyperganglionosis[81,84] and differing incidences have consequently been recorded. Meier-Ruge himself later commented[85] that the increase in the lamina propria was a more reliable indicator than the hyperplasia of the submucosal and myenteric plexuses. In 1983 a report on intestinal neuronal dysplasia[86] described absent adrenergic (sympathetic) innervation in a type A (early acute with an ulcerative colitis-like onset) and a type B (later onset with obstruction and megacolon) and the comment made that intestinal neuronal dysplasia was as common as Hirschsprung's disease. This high incidence was not found — or not recognized — in the UK[81,87] or in the USA.[88]

More recently the criteria have been reviewed and revised by Borchard and his colleagues[89] and applied by Scharli.[90] The criteria now comprised:

a) hyperplasia of the submucosal plexus
b) giant ganglia containing more than 7 small neurons
c) buds (buttons) of nerve cells on nerve fibres
d) increased acetylcholinesterase activity around arteries in the submucosa
e) the increase in acetylcholinesterase-positive fibres, previously considered as the most reliable indication, was now relegated as being helpful, if present, as were the presence of ectopic ganglion cells.

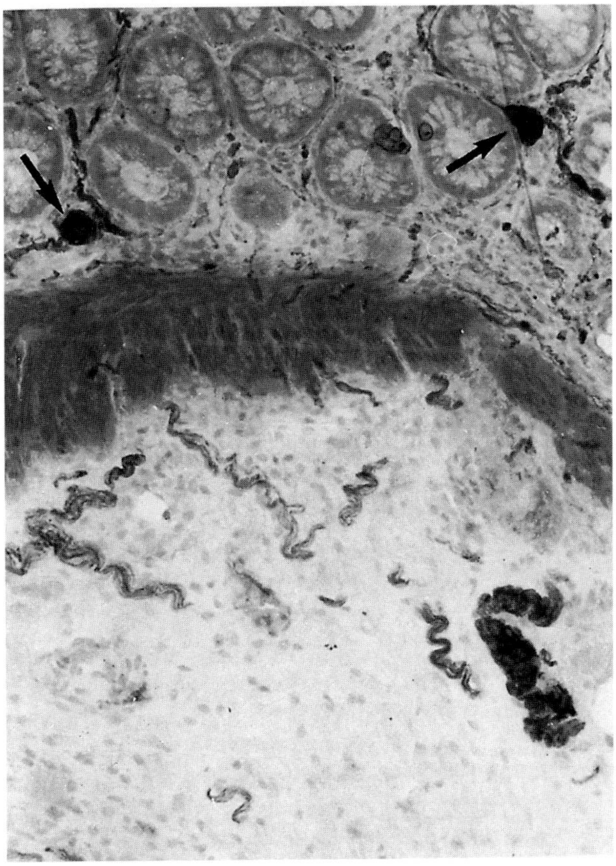

Fig. 18.17 Ganglion cells in the lamina propria (arrows) are sometimes found in intestinal neuronal dysplasia. There is also an increase in nerve fibres in the lamina propria and submucosa. The muscularis mucosae is usually normal. (Cryostat section: acetylcholinesterase and haematoxylin)

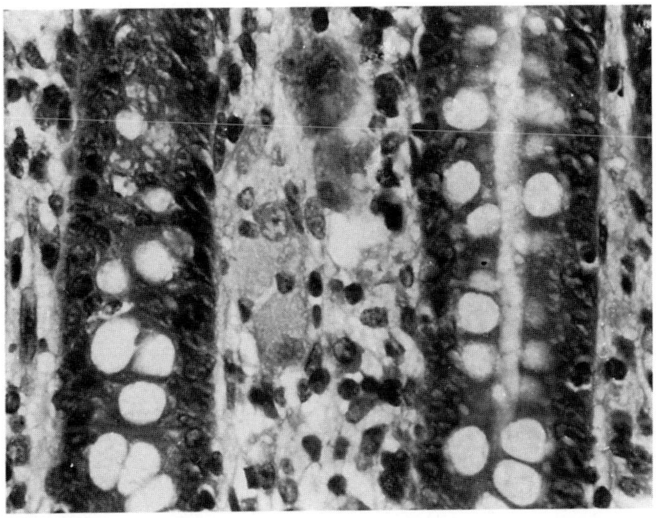

Fig. 18.18 Ganglion cells in the lamina propria can be identified with difficulty in routine sections. Their presence, without other features, is of doubtful significance. They are more easily seen in acetylcholinesterase preparations (see Fig. 18.17) when the number of nerve fibres can also be assessed. (Routine section: H&E)

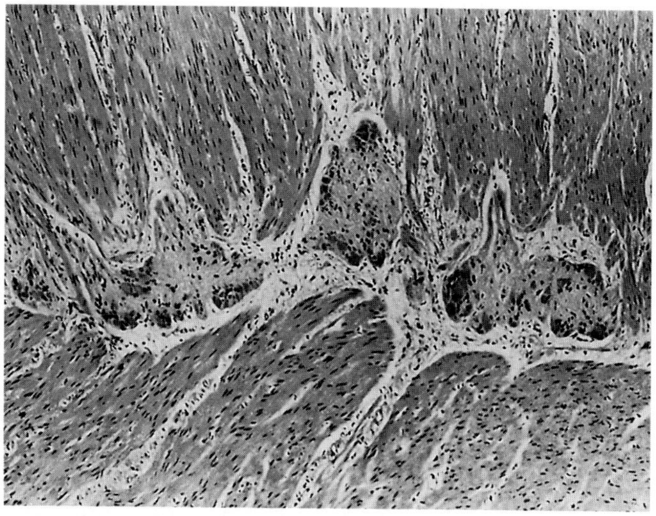

Fig. 18.19 In intestinal neuronal dysplasia the myenteric plexus can be almost continuous with excessive numbers of ganglion cells which push up into the circular muscle coat. (Routine section: H&E)

These criteria were applied to biopsies of mucosa and submucosa, and Scharli[90] reported that 62% of the 73 patients seen 1980–88 had intestinal neuronal dysplasia B, while 30% had aganglionosis. Meier-Ruge et al[91] quote a similar high incidence of intestinal neuronal dysplasia B. A significant proportion (18/45) of patients with a diagnosis of intestinal neuronal dysplasia B were managed conservatively,[90] and whether the microscopical changes noted were significant or were within the range of normality needs to be established.

From the practical point of view, it has long been our experience that, in rectal suction biopsies from neonates taken for the exclusion of Hirschsprung's disease, ganglion cells are plentiful and prominent in most sections, yet in similar biopsies taken for diagnosis of neuronal storage disorders in the infant and older child, ganglion cells are sparse. Smith[92] has evaluated the frequency of ganglia in suction rectal biopsies taken for the exclusion of Hirschsprung's disease and has shown that below the age of four weeks, ganglia were significantly more frequent than those in biopsies taken after the age of four weeks. The presence in the neonate of numerous prominent ganglia without other features (an acetylcholinesterase stain is always done) is therefore probably normal and represents an age related phenomenon. In addition it should be noted that up to 15 or so neurons in a single submucosal ganglion are not infrequently observed in post mortem colon from neonates dying from non-gastrointestinal disorders. It must be concluded (pending a long term clinical follow-up) that hyperplasia of the submucosal plexus without other features is a normal phenomenon in the neonate similar to that of nesidioblastiosis in the infant pancreas.

Smith[92] has also applied Borchard's criteria to a series of consecutive biopsies, previously regarded as within normal limits (having excluded those with Hirschsprung's disease), taken at The Hospital for Sick Children in London in the investigation of neonatal obstruction/constipation, and found in only about 10% could two of the four main criteria be recognized. None had giant ganglia. Thus the high incidences of IND reported,[86,90,91] are not confirmed in critical studies using Borchard's criteria in London and the existence of isolated intestinal neuronal dysplasia is doubtful. There is a need for a careful study which evaluates the clinical presentation, long term outcome and biopsy findings in patients who have any of the criteria of IND.

It has, however, been recognized that a condition which conforms to Meier-Ruge's 1974 description[34] does exist, appearing in association with Hirschsprung's disease, and this has been well documented.[91,92] In intestinal neuronal dysplasia associated with Hirschsprung's disease, there is always a marked increase in fine acetylcholinesterase-positive nerve fibres in the lamina propria, a hyperplasia of the myenteric plexus (hyperganglionosis) with up to three times the normal number of ganglion cells, and an increase in nerves in the circular muscle coat shown by the acetylcholinesterase staining method (Table 18.1). The ganglia in the myenteric plexus may be large and almost continuous with numerous readily identifiable neurons. This is in contrast to the appearance sometimes seen in resected bowel of large oedematous ganglia where neurons are less readily identified, and is probably related to a surgically induced hypoxia.

Table 18.1 Intestinal neuronal dysplasia (hyperganglionosis) proximal to aganglionosis.

Criteria for diagnosis

1. Hyperplasia of the *myenteric* plexus with more than 10 neurons per mm.
2. A marked increase in *fine* acetylcholinesterase-positive nerves in the lamina propria.
3. No increase in acetylcholinesterase-positive nerves in the muscularis mucosae.
4. Increased numbers of nerves in the circular muscle coat.
5. Neurons in the lamina propria are usually present, and may be prominent.

The diagnosis may be suspected from a suction rectal biopsy but must be confirmed in a full thickness biopsy.

The neuronal dysplasia associated with Hirschsprung's disease occurs in the zone between normal bowel and aganglionic bowel, and may account for the residual symptoms in some patients after a pull-through operation, and further resection of the affected bowel may be necessary to relieve the obstruction.[93] In Hirschsprung's disease the increase in acetylcholinesterase-positive nerve fibres is confined to the rectum and descending colon, but in the associated neuronal dysplasia the increase can be seen over the whole length of the affected bowel.[86] An acetylcholinesterase preparation, well stained and not over-interpreted appears to be a good reliable indicator for intestinal neuronal dysplasia and for many of the disorders of innervation.

The features of intestinal neuronal dysplasia (as originally described[34]), with ganglioneuromatosis and marked hyperplasia of submucosal nerve trunks are also found in the multiple endocrine neoplasia syndrome type 2B,[94,95] where the clinical presentation in the neonatal period may be indistinguishable from Hirschsprung's disease. The gastrointestinal symptoms often precede the appearance of the thyroid or adrenal tumours. Similar intestinal pathology may also be found in type 1 neurofibromatosis.[96]

Hyperplasia of the myenteric plexus with an excess of glial cells and fibres, usually accompanied by hypoganglionosis, is also a recognized change seen in patients presenting with pseudo-Hirschsprung's disease in the neonatal period.[95] The changes may be confined to the distal rectum or may be diffuse throughout the gastrointestinal tract. The appearances are similar to but more florid than the transitional zone in Hirschsprung's disease.

REFERENCES

1. Holschneider AM, ed. Hirschsprung's disease. Stuttgart: Hippokrates 1982.
2. Kaiser G, Bettex M. Clinical generalities. In: Holschneider AM, ed. Hirschsprung's disease. Stuttgart: Hippokrates 1982: chap IV pp 43–53.
3. Bodian M, Carter CO. A family study of Hirschsprung's disease. Ann Hum Genet 1963; 26: 261–277.
4. Fekete CN, Ricour C, Martelli H, Jacob SL, Pellerin D. Total colonic aganglionosis (with or without ileal involvement). A review of 27 cases. J Pediatr Surg 1986; 21: 251–254.
5. Romeo G, Ronchetto P, Luo Y, Barone V et al Point mutations affecting the tyrosine kinase domain of the RET photo-oncogene in Hirschsprung's disease. Nature 1994; 367: 377–378.
6. Edery P, Lyonnet S, Mulligan LM et al Mutations of the RET protooncogene in Hirschsprung's disease. Nature 1994; 367: 378–380.
7. Omenn GS, McKusick VA. The association of Waardenburg Syndrome and Hirschsprung megacolon. Am J Med Genet 1979; 3: 217–223.
8. Okamoto E, Ueda T. Embryogenesis of intramural ganglia of the gut and its relation to Hirschsprung's disease. J Pediatr Surg 1967; 2: 437–443.
9. Andrew A. The origin of intramural ganglia. IV. The origin of enteric ganglia: A critical review and discussion of the present state of the problem. J Anat 1971; 108: 169–184.
10. Le Douarin NM. Plasticity in the development of the peripheral nervous system. In: Development of the antonomic nervous system. Ciba Foundation Symposium 83. London: Pitman 1981: pp 19–50.
11. Gershon MD, Teitelman G, Rothman TP. Development of enteric neurons from non-recognizable precursor cells. In: Development of the antonomic nervous system. Ciba Foundation Symposium 83. London: Pitman 1981: pp 51–69.
12. Meijers JHC , Tibboel D, van der Kamp AWM, Van Haperen-Heuts CCM, Molenaar JC. Cell division in migratory and aggregated neural crest cells in the developing gut: An experimental approach to innervation-related motility disorders of the gut. J Pediatr Surg 1987; 22: 243–245.
13. Kapur RP. Contemporary approaches toward understanding the pathogenesis of Hirschsprung's disease. Pediatric Pathology 1993; 13: 83–100.
14. Earlam R. A vascular cause for Hirschsprung's disease? Gastroenterology 1985; 88: 1274–1276.
15. Hokfelt T, Johansson O, Ljungdahl A, Lundberg JM, Schultzberg M. Peptidergic neurons. Nature 1980; 284: 515–521.
16. Stach W. Der Plexus entericus extremus des Dickdarms und seine Beziehungen zuden Interstitiellen Zellen Cajal. Z. Mikrosk. Anat Forsch. 1972; 85: 245–272.
17. Rumessen JJ, Peters S, Thuneberg L. Light and electron microscopical studies of interstitial cells of Cajal and muscle cells at the submucosal border of human colon. Lab Invest 1993: 68: 481–495.
18. Aldridge RT, Campbell PE. Ganglion cell distribution in the normal rectum and anal canal. A basis for the diagnosis of Hirschsprung's disease by anorectal biopsy. J Pediatr Surg 1986; 3: 475–490.
19. Fenger C. Histology of the anal canal. Amer. J. Surgical Pathology 1988: 12: 41–55.
20. Smith B. Pre and post natal development of the ganglion cells of the rectum and its surgical implications. J Pediatr Surg 1968; 3: 386–391.
21. Yunis EJ, Dibbins AW, Sherman FE. Rectal suction biopsy in the diagnosis of Hirschsprung's disease in infants. Arch Pathol Lab Med 1976; 100: 329–333.
22. Bennett A, Garrett JR, Howard ER. Adrenergic myenteric nerves in Hirschsprung's disease. Br Med J 1968; 1: 487–489.
23. Garrett JR, Howard ER, Nixon HH. Autonomic nerves in rectum and colon in Hirschsprung's disease. Arch Dis Child 1969; 44: 406–417.
24. Tsuto T, Obata-Tsuto H, Kawakami F et al. New application of catecholamine fluorescence histochemistry using glyoxylic acid for diagnosis of Hirschsprung's disease by rectal biopsy. Z Kinderchir 1984; 39: 250–252.
25. Karnovsky MJ, Roots L. A 'direct coloring' thiocholine method for cholinesterases. J Histochem Cytochem 1964; 12: 219–221.
26. Lake BD, Puri P, Nixon HH, Claireaux AE. Hirschsprung's disease. An appraisal of histochemically demonstrated acetylcholinesterase activity in suction rectal biopsy specimens as an aid to diagnosis. Arch Pathol Lab Med 1978; 102: 244–247.
27. Dawson TM, Bredt DS, Fotuhi M, Hwang PM, Snyder SH. Nitric oxide synthase and neuronal NADPH diaphorase are identical in brain and peripheral tissues. Proc. Nat Acad Sci USA 1991: 88: 7797–7801.
28. Bodian M. Pathological aids in the diagnosis and management of Hirschsprung's disease. In: Dyke S C ed. Recent advances in clinical pathology. London: Churchill 1960: 3rd series p 384.
29. Dobbins WO, Bill AH. Diagnosis of Hirschsprung's disease excluded by rectal suction biopsy. N Engl J Med 1965; 272: 990–993.
30. Campbell PE, Noblett HR. Experience with rectal suction biopsy in the diagnosis of Hirschsprung's disease. J Pediatr Surg 1969; 4: 410–415.
31. Pease PWB, Corkery JJ, Cameron AH. Diagnosis of Hirschsprung's disease by punch biopsy of rectum. Arch Dis Child 1976; 51: 541–543.
32. Gannon BJ, Noblett HR, Burnstock G. Adrenergic innervation of bowel in Hirschsprung's disease. Br Med J 1969; 2: 338–340.
33. Meier-Ruge W. Das Megacolon. Seine Diagnose und Pathophysiologie. Virchows Arch (A) 1968; 344: 67–85.
34. Meier-Ruge W. Hirschsprung's disease: its aetiology, pathogenesis and differential diagnosis. In: Current Topics in Pathology, Vol 59. Berlin: Springer 1974: pp 131–179.
35. Meier-Ruge W, Lutterbeck PM, Herzog B, Morger R, Moser R, Scharli A. Acetylcholinesterase activity in suction biopsies of the rectum in the diagnosis of Hirschsprung's disease. J Pediatr Surg 1972; 7: 11–17.
36. Elema JD, de Vries JA, Vos LJM. Intensity and proximal extension of acetylcholinesterase activity in the mucosa of the rectosigmoid in Hirschsprung's disease. J Pediatr Surg 1973; 8: 361–368.
37. Chow CW, Chan WC, Yuc PCK. Histochemical criteria for the diagnosis of Hirschsprung's disease in rectal suction biopsies by acetylcholinesterase activity. J Pediatr Surg 1977; 12: 675–680.

38. Wakely PE, McAdams AJ. Acetylcholinesterase histochemistry and the diagnosis of Hirschsprung's disease. A 3½ year experience. Pediatr Pathol 1984; 2: 35–46.
39. Goto S, Ikeda K, Toyshara T. Histochemical confirmation of the acetylcholinesterase activity in rectal suction biopsy from neonates with Hirschsprung's disease. Z Kinderchir 1984; 39: 246–249.
40. Anonymous. Deformation of cholinergic (cholinesterase positive) nerves of rectal mucous membrane in Hirschsprung's disease. A histochemical diagnosis using mucosal biopsies. Chinese Med J 1979; 92: 93–100.
41. Hirsig J, Briner J, Rickham PP. Problems in the diagnosis of Hirschsprung's disease due to false negative acetylcholinesterase reaction in suction biopsy in neonates. Z Kinderchir 1979; 26: 242–247.
42. de Brits IA, Maksoud JG. Evolution with age of the acetylcholinesterase activity in rectal suction biopsy in Hirschsprung's disease. J Pediatr Surg 1987; 22: 425–430.
43. van der Staak FHJ. Reliability of the acetylcholinesterase (ACE) reaction in rectal mucosal biopsies for the diagnosis of Hirschsprung's disease. Z Kinderchir 1981; 34: 36–42.
44. Patrick WJA, Besley GTN, Smith II. Histochemical diagnosis of Hirschsprung's disease and comparison of the histochemical and biochemical activity of acetylcholinesterase in rectal mucosal biopsies. J Clin Pathol 1980; 33: 336–343.
45. Dale G, Bonham JR, Lowdon P, Wagget J, Rangecroft L, Scott DJ. Diagnostic value of rectal mucosal acetylcholinesterase levels in Hirschsprung's disease. Lancet 1979; 1: 347–349.
46. Ikawa H, Yokoyama J, Morikawa Y, Hayashi A, Katsumata K. A quantitative study of acetylcholine in Hirschsprung's disease. J Pediatr Surg 1980; 15: 48–52.
47. Nirasawa Y, Yokoyama J, Ikawa H, Morikawa Y, Katsumata K. Hirschsprung's disease: catecholamine content, Alpha-adreno-ceptors, and the effect of electrical stimulation in aganglionic colon. J Pediatr Surg 1986; 21: 136–142.
48. Bishop AE, Polak JM, Lake BD, Bryant MG, Bloom SR. Abnormalities of the colonic regulatory peptides in Hirschsprung's disease. Histopathology 1981; 5: 679–688.
49. Mackenzie JM, Dixon MF. An immunohistochemical study of the enteric neural plexus in Hirschsprung's disease. Histopathology 1987; 11: 1055–1066.
50. Tam PKH, Owen G. An immunohistochemical study of neuronal microtubule-associated proteins in Hirschsprung's disease. Hum Pathol 1993: 24; 424–431.
51. Garrett JR, Howard ER. Histochemistry and the pathology of Hirschsprung's disease. Proc R Micr Soc 1969; 4: 76–78.
52. Touloukian RJ, Duncan R. Acquired aganglionic megacolon in a premature infant. Report of a case. Pediatrics 1975; 56: 459–462.
53. Cohen MC, Moore SR, Noveling U, Kaschula ROC. Acquired aganglionosis following surgery for Hirschsprung's disease. A report of five cases during a 33 year experience with pull-through procedures. Histopathology 1993: 22: 163–168.
54. Dajani OM, Slim MS, Mansour A. Acquired hypoganglionosis after soave endorectal pull-through procedure. A case report. Z Kinderchir 1986; 41: 248–249.
55. Lister J. Abnormal arteries in Hirschsprung's disease. Arch Dis Child 1966; 41: 149.
56. Taguchi T, Tanaka K, Ikeda K. Fibromuscular dysplasia of arteries in Hirschsprung's disease. Gastroenterology 1985; 88: 1099–1103.
57. Yunis E, Sieber WK, Akers DR. Does zonal aganglionosis really exist? Report of a rare variety of Hirschsprung's disease and a review of the literature. Pediatr Pathol 1983; 1: 33–49.
58. Taguchi T, Tanaka K, Ikeda K, Hata A. Double zonal aganglionosis with a skipped oligoganglionic ascending colon. Z Kinderchir 1983; 38: 312–315.
59. DeChadarevian JP, Slim M, Akel S. Double zonal aganglionosis in long segment Hirschsprung's disease with a skip area in transverse colon. J Pediatr Surg 1982; 17: 195–197.
60. Seldenrijk CA, vander Harten HJ, Kluck P, Tibboel D, Moorman-Voestermans K, Meijer CJLM. Zonal aganglionosis. An enzyme and immunohistochemical study of two cases. Virchows Arch (A) 1986; 410: 75–81.
61. Dimmick JE. Cytomegalic inclusion virus and pseudo-Hirschsprung's disease. Lab Invest 1981; 44: 2P.
62. Smith VV, Lake BD, Kamm MA, Nicholls RJ. Intestinal pseudo-obstruction with deficient smooth muscle alpha-actin. Histopathology 1992: 21; 535–542.
63. Yamagiwa I, Ohta M, Obata K, Washio M. Intestinal pseudoobstruction in a neonate caused by idiopathic muscular hypertrophy of the entire small intestine. J Pediatr Surg 1988: 23: 866–869.
64. Schuffler MD, Beegle RG. Progressive systemic sclerosis of the gastrointestinal tract and hereditary hollow visceral myopathy: two distinguishable disorders of intestinal smooth muscle. Gastroenterology 1979; 77: 664–671.
65. Milla PJ, Lake BD, Spitz L, Nixon RH, Rarries JT, Fenton TR. Chronic idiopathic pseudo-obstruction in infancy. A smooth muscle disease. In: Labo G, Bortolotti M eds. Gastrointestinal motility. Verona: Cortina International 1983: pp 125–131.
66. Smith JA, Hauser SC, Madara JL. Hollow visceral myopathy. A light and electron-microscopic study. Am J Surg Pathol 1982; 6: 269–275.
67. Puri P, Lake BD, Gorman F, O'Donnell B, Nixon RH. Megacystis-microcolon-intestinal hypoperistalsis syndrome. A visceral myopathy. J Pediatr Surg 1983; 18: 64–69.
68. Smith B. The neuropathology of pseudo-obstruction of the intestine. Scand J Gastroenterol 1982; 71(Suppl.): 103–109.
69. Lake BD. Observations on the pathology of pseudo-obstruction. In: Milla PJ, Disorders of gastrointestinal motility in childhood. Chichester: Wiley 1988; ch 8, pp 81–90.
70. Kaschula ROC, Cywes S, Katz A, Louw JH. Degenerative leiomyopathy with massive megacolon. Perspectives in Pediatric Pathology 1987: 11: 193–213.
71. Schuffler MD, Bird TD, Sumi SM, Cook A. A familial neuronal disease presenting as intestinal pseudoobstruction. Gastroenterology 1978: 75: 889–898.
72. Goutieres F, Mikol J, Aicardi J. Neuronal intranuclear inclusion disease in a child. Diagnosis by rectal biopsy. Annals of Neurology 1990: 27: 103–106.
73. Smith VV. Intestinal neuronal density in Childhood. A baseline for the objective assessment of hypo- and hyperganglionosis. Pediatric Pathology 1993: 13: 225–237.
74. Erdohazi M. Retarded development of the enteric nerve cells. Dev Med Child Neurol 1974; 16: 365–368.
75. Munakata K, Okabe I, Morita K. Histologic studies of rectocolic aganglionosis and allied diseases. J Pediatr Surg 1978; 13: 67–75.
76. Ikeda K, Goto S, Nagasaki A, Taguchi T. Hypogenesis of intestinal ganglion cells. A rare cause of intestinal obstruction simulating aganglionosis. Z Kinderchir 1988: 43; 52–53.
77. Anderson VM, Greco MA, Recalde AL, Chandwani S, Church JA, Krasinski K. Intestinal cytomegalovirus ganglioneuronitis in children with human immunodeficiency virus infection. Pediatric Pathology 1990: 10: 167–174.
78. Lennon VA, Sas DF, Busk MF, Scheithauer B, Malagelada J-R, Camilleri M, Miller LJ. Enteric neuronal autoantibodies in pseudoobstruction with small-cell lung carcinoma.Gastroenterology 1991; 100: 137–142.
79. Krishnamurthy S, Schuffler MD, Belic L, Schweid AI. An inflammatory axonopathy of the myenteric plexus producing a rapidly progressive intestinal pseudoobstruction. Gastroenterology 1986; 90: 754–758.
80. Puri P, Lake BD, Nixon HH . Adynamic bowel syndrome. Report of a case with disturbance of the cholinergic innervation. Gut 1977; 18: 754–759.
81. Howard ER, Garrett JR, Kidd A. Constipation and congenital disorders of the myenteric plexus. J Roy Soc Med 1984; 77(Suppl. 3): 13–19.
82. Nezelov C, Guygrand D, Thomine E. Les megacolons avec hyperplasie du plexus myenterique. Nouv Press Med 1970; 78: 1501–1506.
83. Meier-Ruge W. Uber ein Erkrankungsbild des Colon mit Hirschsprung-Symptomatik. Verh. dtsch. Ges. Path 1971; 55: 506–510.
84. Garrett JR, Howard ER. Myenteric plexus of the hind-gut:

developmental abnormalities in human and experimental studies. In: Development of the antonomic nervous system. Ciba Foundation Symposium 83. London: Pitman 1981: pp 326–354.
85. Scharli AF, Meier-Ruge W. Localized and disseminated forms of neuronal intestinal dysplasia mimicking Hirschsprung's disease. J Pediatr Surg 1981; 16: 164–170.
86. Fadda B, Maier WA, Meier-Ruge W, Scharli A, Daum R. Neuronale intestinale Dysplasie. Eine kritische 10-Jahres-Analyse klinischer und bioptischer Diagnostik. Z Kinderchir 1983; 38: 305–311.
87. Lake BD, Malone MT, Risdon RA. The use of acetylcholinesterase (AChE) in the diagnosis of Hirschsprung's disease and intestinal neuronal dysplasia. Pediat Pathol 1989; 9: 351–354.
88. Schofield DE, Yunis EJ. Intestinal neuronal dysplasia. J Pediat Gastroenterol Nutr 1991; 12: 182–189.
89. Borchard F, Meier-Ruge W, Wiebecke B, Briner J, Muntefering H, Fodisch HF, Holschneider AM, Schmidt A, Enck P, Stolte M. Innervationsstorungen des Dickdarms. Klassification und Diagnostik. Pathologe 1991; 12: 171–174.
90. Scharli AF. Neuronal intestinal dysplasia. Pediatric Surgery Int 1992; 7: 2–7.
91. Meier-Ruge W, Kaufeler RE, Bronnimann P. Classification of inborn malformation of distal gut innervation. In Paediatric Gastroenterology. Inflammatory bowel diseases and morbus Hirschsprung. Eds. Hadziselimovic F, Herzog B. Kluwer, Dordrecht 1992, pp 177–201.
92. Smith VV. Isolated intestinal neuronal dysplasia. A descriptive histological pattern or a distinct clinicopathological entity? In: Paediatric Gastroenterology. Inflammatory bowel diseases and morbus Hirschsprung. Eds. Hadziselimovic F, Herzog B. Kluwer, Dordrecht 1992, pp 203–214.
93. Fadda B, Pistor G, Meier-Ruge W, Hofmann-von Kapherr S, Muntefering H, Espinoza R. Symptoms, diagnosis and therapy of neuronal intestinal dysplasia masked by Hirschsprung's disease. Pediatr Surg Int 1987; 2: 76–80.
94. Navarro J, Boccon-Gibod L, Sonsino E, Boureau M, Weisgerber G, Gruner M, et al. Demembrement du cadre 'pseudo-Hirschsprung'. A propos de 8 observation pediatrique. Arch Fr Pediatr 1980; 37: 437–444.
95. Navarro J, Sonsino E, Boige N, Nabarra B, Ferkadji L, Mashako LMN, Cezard JP. Visceral neuropathies responsible for chronic intestinal pseudo-obstruction syndrome in pediatric practice. Analysis of 26 cases. J Ped Gastro Nutr 1990; 11: 179–195.
96. Fuller CE, Williams GT. Gastrointestinal manifestations of type 1 neurofibromatosis (Von Recklinghausen's disease). Histopathology 1991; 19: 1–11.

CHAPTER 19

Storage disorders involving the alimentary tract

B. D. Lake

Lysosomal storage disorders are usually diagnosed by enzyme assay of leucocytes or fibroblasts following a clinical diagnosis of a specific disorder or group of disorders. However enzyme assays in experienced laboratories are not always readily available and a microscopic assessment is a valuable first indication that can be used as a screening or exclusion test. Microscopic diagnosis of the neuronal storage disorders now more usually involves a biopsy of the gastrointestinal tract rather than the brain, because it is a source of neurons which can be sampled without too much discomfort to the patient.

The early studies[1,2] showed that the neuronal pathology of the brain was mirrored in the neurons of the gastrointestinal tract and that a diagnosis could be made reliably by rectal biopsy. The observations by Pick[3] of the changes in the small and large intestine in Niemann-Pick disease type A included neuronal, smooth muscle, blood vessel and macrophage involvement and it is this range of cell types observed in a rectal biopsy which makes the intestine and particularly the rectum a preferred site. In some instances the electron microscopic examination of skin or conjunctival biopsies can be of value[4] but in any condition in which neuronal storage is the feature giving rise to symptoms, there is no substitute for a biopsy containing neurons because the diagnosis may have grave prognostic significance. For convenience either superficial or full thickness rectal biopsies are usually used, but surgical specimens such as the appendix obviously provide a greater abundance of tissue. Both light and electron microscopical assessments are usually advocated.

The stored substances are generally lipids of one type or another and thus frozen sections are necessary, which dictates that a portion of unfixed tissue is snap frozen when received. Sections of fixed paraffin wax embedded tissue are frequently of little help in diagnosis, one reason being the wide range in appearance of normal neurons as well as the extraction of stored material during processing. Transverse sections of appendix and longitudinal sections of full thickness rectal biopsies usually contain an adequate number of neurons in the submucosal and myenteric plexuses but suction rectal biopsies require extensive sectioning to ensure that neurons are found in each of the stained slides (see Fig. 19.1). Electron microscopy is also an im-

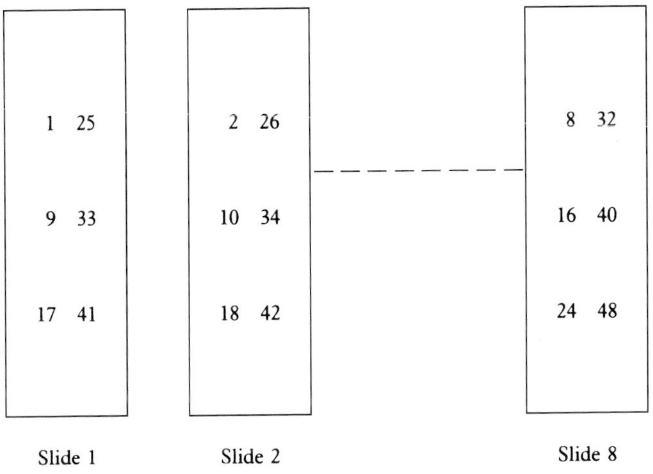

Fig. 19.1 Method of mounting serial (1–48) cryostat sections in diagnosis of storage diseases. Consecutive sections supported on liver or gelatin are mounted as shown and stained by the following methods: H&E, PAS, cell PAS, luxol fast blue, sudan black, acid phosphatase, Feyrter's thionin, and one is left unstained for autofluorescence. At least 8 slides are thus required but if the biopsy includes little submucosa many more may be necessary.

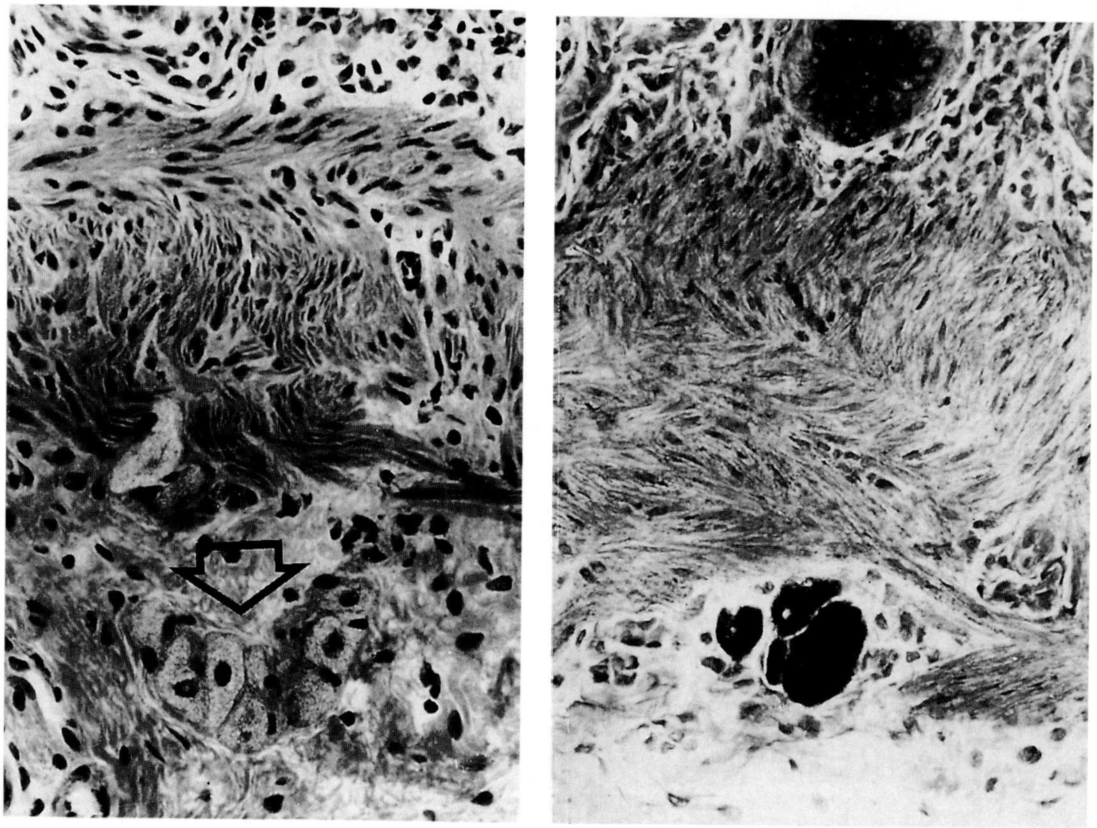

Fig. 19.2 Suction rectal biopsy: Tay-Sachs' disease. Cryostat section stained: **A** with haematoxylin and eosin showing enlarged ganglion cells in the submucosa (arrow); **B** with PAS showing the intense positivity of the stored ganglioside. A similar neuronal appearance is found in GMI-gangliosidosis and sialidosis.

portant investigation for confirmation of the nature and morphological appearance of the stored material, for detection of early storage and for confirmation of the absence of storage in some cases where clinical suspicion is not upheld by light microscopical observations.

Sections should be examined by a range of techniques so that the pattern of involvement of both neurons and other cell types can be identified. It is this pattern which characterizes a particular disease (Fig. 19.2). The methods should include the PAS (periodic acid-Schiff) reaction both with fixation and with protection by celloidin to contain the water soluble sugar compounds,[5] sudan black for lipids, Luxol fast blue, a reaction for acid phosphatase activity and an examination under ultraviolet light to determine autofluorescence. In children there is little lipofuscin in neurons which shows autofluorescence but in adults there may be significant amounts which can be misleading and give rise to a false diagnosis of Kuf's disease, an adult form of Batten's disease (neuronal ceroid lipofuscinosis). A reaction to show acid phosphatase activity is included since normal smooth muscle cells and normal endothelial cells show no activity, and their involvement in the lysosomal storage process is indicated by a positive

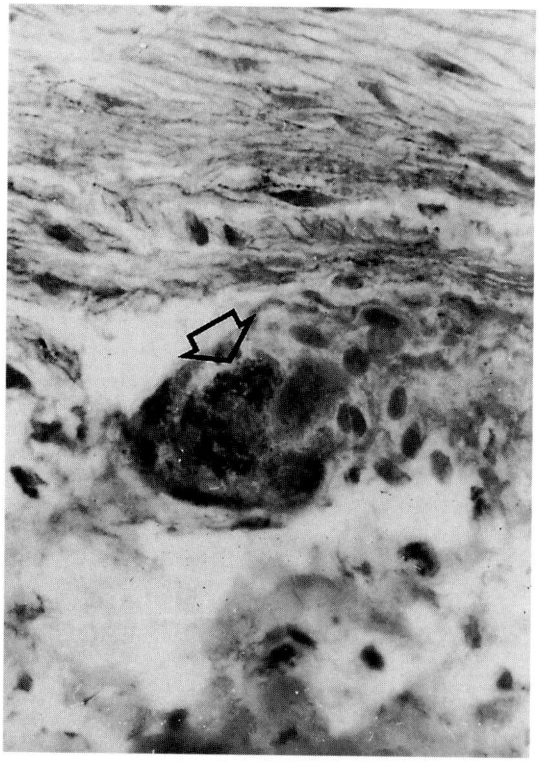

Fig. 19.3 Suction rectal biopsy: Niemann-Pick disease type C. Cryostat section stained by the protected PAS method (celloidinized PAS) showing the neuronal storage of a finely granular material (arrow). The material is extracted by fixation in aqueous media.

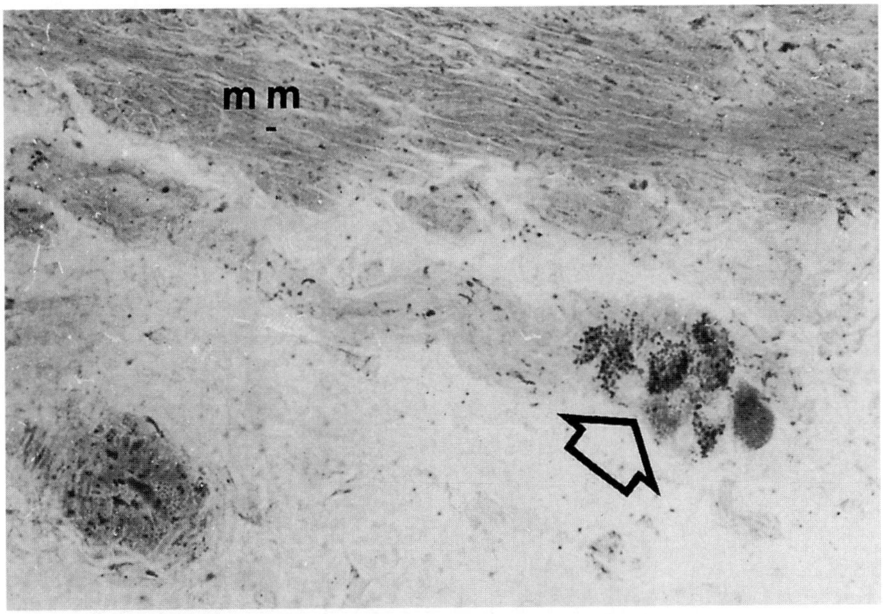

Fig. 19.4 Suction rectal biopsy: juvenile Batten's disease. Cryostat section stained with Sudan black showing granular neuronal storage (arrow) and storage in smooth muscle cells of the muscularis mucosae (MM) and in a small arteriole, bottom left. Some Sudanophilic storage material is seen in the nerve leading to the ganglion cells.

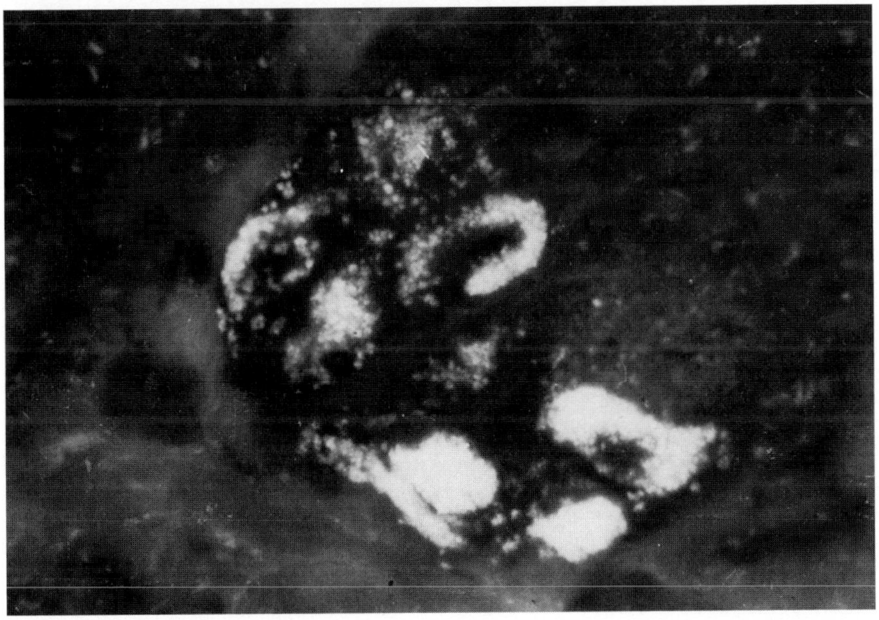

Fig. 19.5 Suction rectal biopsy, juvenile Batten's disease. Cryostat section, unstained, showing the neuronal storage of a granular material which exhibits strong autofluorescence. (Dark ground conditions; excite UG5, barrier 410 nm.)

reaction. Similarly, macrophages can be readily identified and the enhanced neuronal staining is not only useful in locating neurons but is an indication of storage (Figs 19.3, 19.4, 19.5). In those instances where a diagnosis is indicated on biopsy it should be confirmed by enzyme assay of a suitable tissue sample because prenatal diagnosis is possible for most lysosomal storage disorders. The detailed clinical, chemical and pathological features of these storage disorders can be found elsewhere.[6]

Tables 19.1 and 19.2 list the various disease states and both the site and nature of the staining reactions exhibited and Table 19.3 details the ultrastructural findings in cell types in a range of conditions. From these three tables it should be possible to achieve a diagnosis on biopsy of the gastrointestinal tract.

Some of the conditions listed would not normally be investigated by this type of biopsy although the pathologist should be aware of the possible changes and be prepared to exclude a particular disorder on the material presented. In metachromatic leucodystrophy the included unmyelinated nerves show metachromasia with cresyl fast violet or toluidine blue[2] and there is often a marked increase in PAS (protected with celloidin) positive muciphages in the lamina propria spilling over into the submucosa. In the mucopolysaccharidases of all types there is an accumulation of water soluble acidic mucopolysaccha-

Table 19.1 Cell types in storage diseases.

	Neurons	Smooth muscle cells	Endothelial cells	Mucosal & submucosal macrophages
Disease				
Tay-Sachs' disease (all types)	+	–	–	–
G_{M1}-gangliosidosis	+	–	+	+
Sialidosis (mucolipidosis I)	+	–	–	–
Niemann–Pick disease				
type A	+	+	+	+
type B	–	+	+	+
type C	+	–	–	+
Batten's disease				
infantile	+	+	+	–
late infantile	+	+	+	–
juvenile	+	+	+	–
Mucolipidosis IV	+	+	+	–
Mucopolysaccharidosis				
types I II III	+	–	+	+
types IV VI	–	–	+	+
Pompe's disease (glycogen storage II)	+	+	+	+
Fabry's disease	+	+	+	–
Wolman's disease	±	±	+	+
Krabbe's disease	–	–	–	–
Metachromatic leucodystrophy	–	–	–	–
Gaucher's disease	–	–	–	–
Cystinosis	–	+	–	+
Tangier disease	–	±	–	+

A + sign indicates stored material is present; – indicates no storage; ± indicates variable involvement.

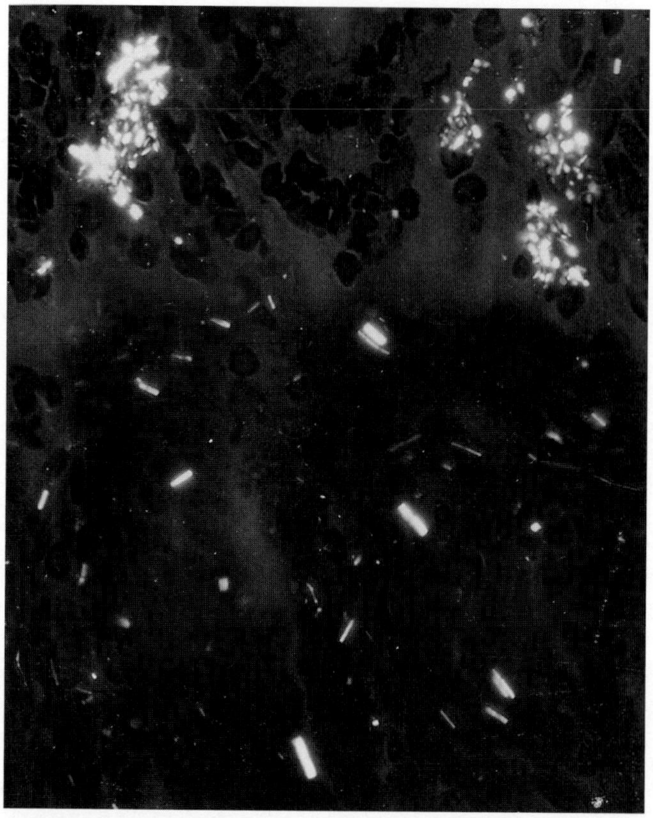

Fig. 19.6 Suction rectal biopsy: cystinosis. Cryostat section stained by alcoholic basic fuchsin and examined under polarized light. Macrophages containing cystine crystals are present in the lamina propria and single crystals are present within smooth muscle cells of the muscularis mucosae.

Table 19.2 Staining patterns of neuronal storage material. A + sign indicates a positive reaction without attempt to show intensity; a – sign shows no reaction, while ± indicates a variable weak reaction depending on a variety of factors, including length of fixation and age at which biopsy is taken.

	Stain					
	PAS	PAS cell.	Sudan black	Luxol fast blue	Feyrter's thionin	Auto-fluorescence
Disease						
Tay-Sachs' disease (all types)	+	+	+	+	+	–
G_{M1}-gangliosidosis	+	+	+	+	+	–
Sialidosis	+	+	+	+	+	–
Niemann-Pick A	±	±	+	–	±	–
Niemann-Pick C	±	+	–	–	+	–
Pompe's disease	±	+	–	–	–	–
Batten's disease						
Infantile	+	+	+	–	–	+
Late infantile	±	±	+	+	–	+
Juvenile	+	+	+	+	–	+
Mucolipidosis IV	+	+	+	–	–	+
Mucopolysaccharidosis I, II & III	+	+	+	+	±	–

Cell. = celloidinized

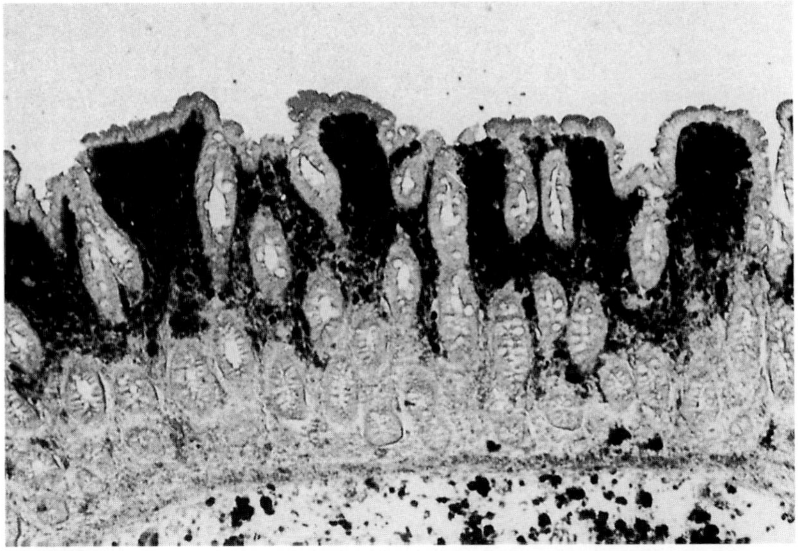

Fig. 19.7 Jejunal biopsy: Wolman's disease. Cryostat section stained by oil Red O showing massive lipid storage in the lamina propria and in the submucosa.

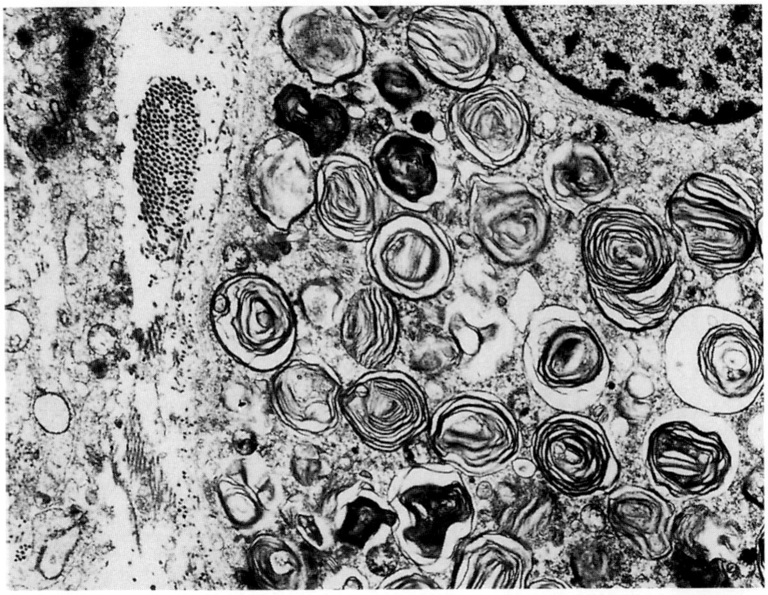

Fig. 19.8 Electron photomicrograph: Tay-Sachs' disease. Neurons in the submucosal plexus of a suction rectal biopsy showing numerous membranous cytoplasmic bodies (MCB) which are characteristic of ganglioside storage. (×8460)

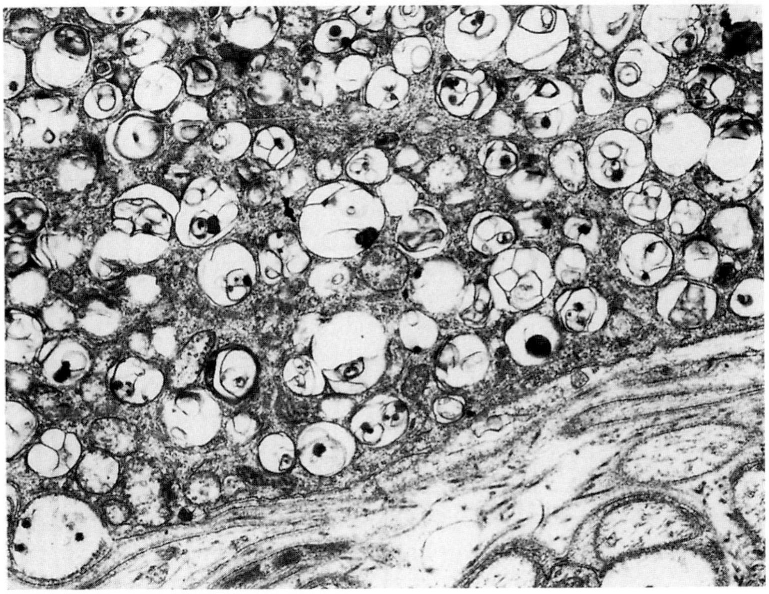

Fig. 19.9 Electron photomicrograph: Niemann-Pick disease type C. Pleomorphic lipid lamellae are present in a neuron in the submucosal plexus of a suction rectal biopsy. (×11 700)

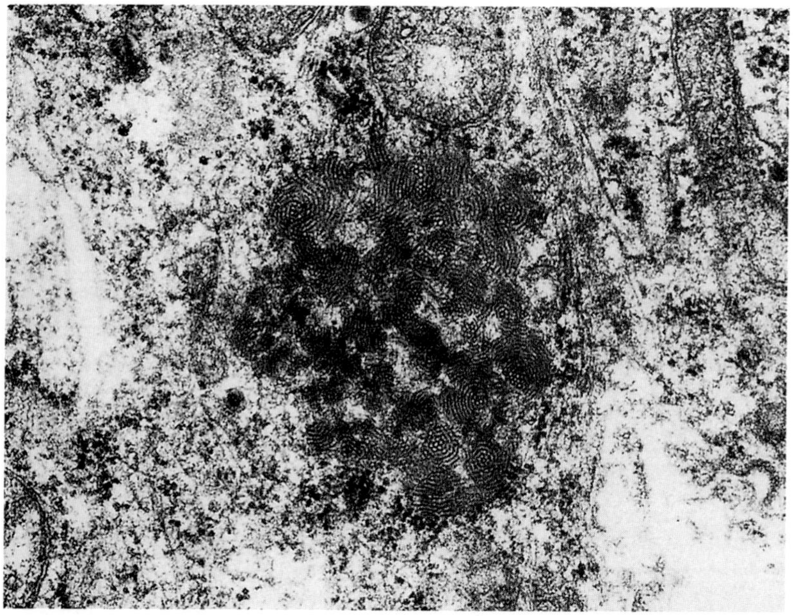

Fig. 19.10 Electron photomicrograph: juvenile Batten's disease. Fingerprint bodies are present in a neuron in the submucosal plexus of a suction rectal biopsy. Similar bodies are also present in smooth muscle cells and endothelial cells. (×48 600)

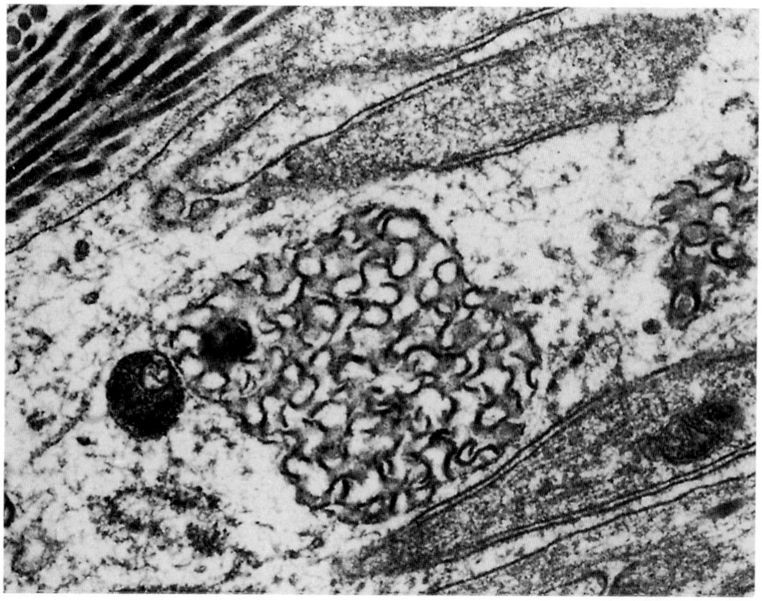

Fig. 19.11 Electron photomicrograph: late infantile Batten's disease. Curvilinear bodies are present in the Schwann cell cytoplasm of a nerve bundle in a suction rectal biopsy. Similar curvilinear bodies are present in neurons and smooth muscle cells. (×42 300)

ride shown by the metachromasia in the Haust & Landing toluidine blue method[5] and a similar accumulation is found in G_{M1}-gangliosidosis. The cystine crystals in cystinosis are widely distributed in the lamina propria and submucosa and are best demonstrated in the alcoholic basic fuchsin stained slide examined under polarized light (Fig. 19.6).[5] Contrary to popular belief the gut in Gaucher's disease is unremarkable.

Wolman's disease shows a marked accumulation of cholesteryl esters and triglycerides in macrophages in the lamina propria particularly in the jejunum (Fig. 19.7). A neutral fat stain shows these deposits as well as their accumulation in the enterocytes, but there is less severe lipid deposition in the large intestine.[7]

Electron microscopy serves to confirm the light microscopy changes and shows the characteristic ultrastructure for each disease or group of disorders (Figs 19.8–19.12 and Table 19.3). The gangliosidoses (G_{M1} and G_{M2}) show neuronal membranous cytoplasmic bodies, while pleomorphic lipid lamellae are found in Niemann–Pick disease type C. Fingerprint bodies are the hallmark of juvenile Batten's disease, curvilinear bodies in late infantile Batten's disease, and in the infantile form, the stored material is in the form of granular osmiophilic deposits (GROD). Less diagnostic findings include empty membrane bound vacuoles in a variety of cell types which are present in the mucopolysaccharidoses, fucosidosis, mannosidosis, aspartylglycosaminuria and G_{M1} gangliosidosis.[6]

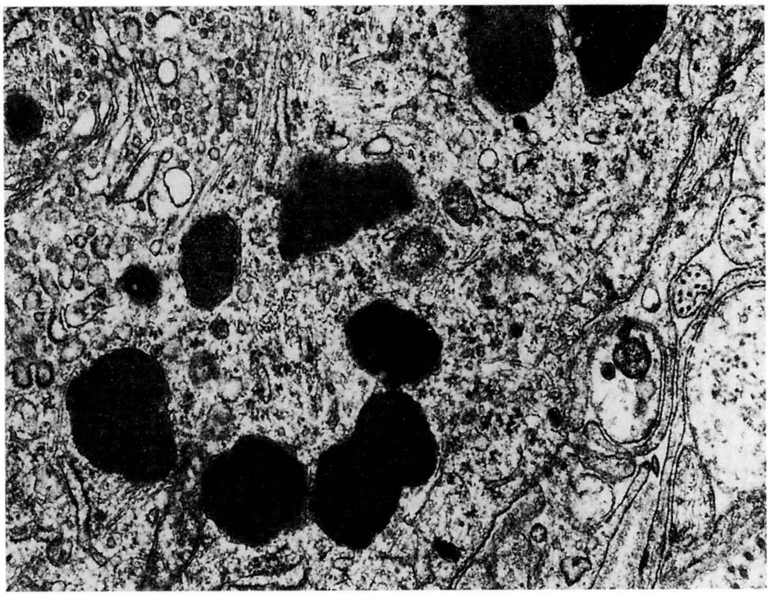

Fig. 19.12 Electron photomicrograph: infantile Batten's disease. Granular osmiophilic deposits (GROD) are present in a neuron in the submucosal plexus of a suction rectal biopsy. Similar bodies are also present in smooth muscle cells and endothelial cells. (×22 950)

Table 19.3 Electron microscopy appearances of the various cell types in a rectal biopsy.

Disease	Neurons	Smooth muscle	Endothelium	Fibroblasts
Tay-Sachs'	MCBs	–	–	–
G_{M1}-gangliosidosis	MCBs	Vacuoles	Vacuoles	Vacuoles
Sialidosis (MLI)	MCBs	–	–	?Vacuoles
Sialic acid storage	Vacuoles with some fibrillo-granular material	Vacuoles	Vacuoles	Vacuoles
Niemann-Pick type A	MCBs	MCBs	MCBs	–
Niemann-Pick type C	PLB	–	– occ. PLB	–
Batten, infantile	GROD	GROD	GROD	–
Batten, late infantile	Curvilinear bodies	Curvilinear bodies	Curvilinear bodies	–
Batten, early juvenile	Fingerprint bodies	Fingerprint and curvilinear bodies	Fingerprint and curvilinear bodies	–
Batten, juvenile	Fingerprint bodies	Fingerprint and curvilinear bodies	Fingerprint and curvilinear bodies	–
Mucopolysaccharidosis	MCB/zebra bodies	Vacuoles	Vacuoles	Vacuoles
Mucolipidosis IV	MCB-like bodies	Granular membrane-bound bodies	MCB-like bodies	–

GROD = granular osmiophilic material; MCB = membranous cytoplasmic bodies; PLB = pleomorphic lipid bodies; – = no storage material.

The rectal approach to neuropathology[2] has provided useful diagnostic information on which biochemical advances can be made, and still provides a definitive diagnosis where either the biochemistry is unknown or techniques are not immediately available. By providing light and electron microscopical evidence the rectal biopsy has considerable advantages over skin or conjunctival biopsies.

In spite of considerable involvement of neurons, smooth muscle cells and blood vessels there is no apparent effect on gastrointestinal function except in Wolman's disease, where the lipid deposition in the jejunum is so gross as to impair absorption.

REFERENCES

1. Nakai H, Landing BH. Suggested use of rectal biopsy in the diagnosis of neural lipidoses. Pediatrics 1960; 26: 225–228.
2. Bodian M, Lake BD. The rectal approach to neuropathology. Br J Surg 1963; 50: 702–714.
3. Pick L. Uber die lipoidzelligen Splenohepatomegalie Typus Niemann-Pick als Stoffwechsel erkrankung. Med Klin 1927; 23: 1483–1488.
4. Ceuterick C, Martin JJ. Diagnostic role of skin or conjunctival biopsies in neurological disorders. An update. J Neurol Sci 1984; 65: 179–183.
5. Filipe MI, Lake BD. Histochemistry in Pathology, 2nd edition. Edinburgh: Churchill-Livingstone (in press).
6. Lake BD. Lysosomal and peroxisomal enzyme deficiencies. In: Greenfield's Neuropathology, 5th edition. Hume Adams J, Duchen LW. eds. London: Edward Arnold 1992: pp 491–572.
7. Patrick AD, Lake BD. Wolman's disease. In: Hers HG, van Hoof F. eds. Lysosomes and storage diseases. New York: Academic Press 1973; pp 453–473.

SECTION

3

Mechanical and neuromuscular abnormalities

CHAPTER 20

The oesophagus

V. F. Eckardt

HIATAL HERNIA

The most distal 2–3 cm of the oesophagus, including a major proportion of the lower oesophageal sphincter, are normally located within the abdominal cavity. This position is secured by posterior fixation of the cardia to the periaortic fascia and by the phreno-oesophageal membrane. The latter anchors the distal oesophagus to both crura of the diaphragm (Fig. 20.1) and is composed mainly of elastic fibres which originate from the diaphragmatic fasciae and insert into the adventitia of the distal oesophagus.[1] However, these attachments are not firm and a limited longitudinal movement of the oesophagus may still occur without alteration of the normal anatomy of the diaphragmatic hiatus.[2]

With advancing age the attachment of the phreno-oesophageal membrane to the distal oesophagus becomes less firm as elastic fibres are gradually replaced by collagen.[2,3] In conjunction with a widened hiatus, other factors such as a chronic increase in intraabdominal pressure or a shortening of the oesophagus, may result in a protrusion of the stomach into the thoracic cavity. Depending on the degree of failure of the anchoring mechanisms and the diameter of the hiatus, several types of herniation may occur (Fig. 20.2). If the distal oesophagus remains fixed to the periaortic fascia, parts of the stomach may herniate alongside the oesophagus into the posterior mediastinum and a *paraoesophageal hernia* results. In contrast, a more complete detachment of the distal oesophagus from its infradiaphragmatic position leads to a cephalad displacement not only of the proximal stomach but also of the oesophagogastric junction. Since, in such instances, the protruded stomach is only incompletely covered by a peri-

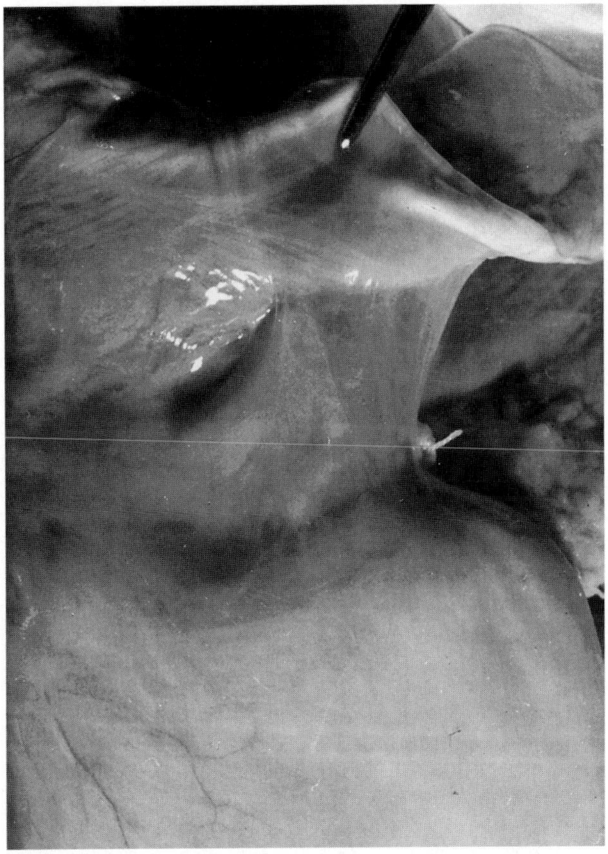

Fig. 20.1 Autopsy specimen demonstrating the phreno-oesophageal membrane which anchors the oesophagogastric junction to the diaphragm. (Courtesy of Dr D. Liebermann-Meffert, Department of Surgery, Kantonsspital Basel, Switzerland)

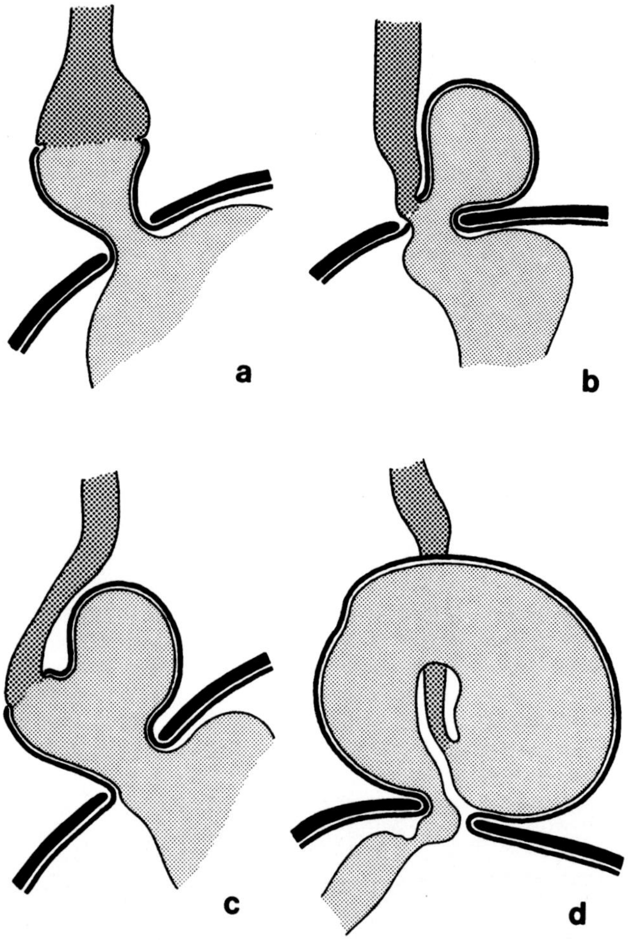

Fig. 20.2 Schematic drawings of the different types of hiatal hernias and their peritoneal margins (solid line). **A** sliding hiatal hernia; **B** paraoesophageal hiatal hernia; **C** combined hiatal hernia; **D** upside down stomach, representing the most extreme form of a combined hiatal hernia

toneal sac, the term *sliding hiatal hernia* is applied. However, a clear separation of paraoesophageal and sliding hiatal hernia is not always possible. For instance, in some patients with proximally displaced oesophagogastric junctions the proximal stomach may roll up alongside the oesophagus leading to its paraoesophageal position. Such *combined hiatal hernias* are more commonly observed when the displacement of the stomach into the chest is pronounced.

SLIDING HIATAL HERNIA

Incidence and aetiology

Sliding hiatal hernias are common; even in asymptomatic, healthy individuals an incidence ranging between 33–50% has been reported.[4–6] However, these figures are probably related to an all too vigorous attempt to demonstrate an upward migration of the oesophagogastric junction during radiographic studies. Furthermore, the physiological shortening of the oesophagus during the act of swallowing normally results in a transient supradiaphragmatic position of the lower oesophageal sphincter[7] which may also be misinterpreted as evidence for a sliding hiatal hernia. It is not surprising therefore that endoscopists observe herniations of the stomach with less frequency than do radiologists.[8]

The majority of sliding hiatal hernias occur beyond the fifth decade of life and the frequency then increases with advancing age.[9] These observations have led to the conclusion that almost all hiatal hernias have an acquired origin. Burkitt[10] has pointed out that hiatal hernias are exceedingly rare in the underdeveloped world and believes that a high residue diet is protective. In higher incidence areas the ingestion of a low residue diet leads to constipation and straining during defaecation, which in turn is associated with an increase in intra-abdominal pressure which facilitates the development of a hiatal hernia. Similar stretching of the diaphragmatic hiatus may occur with obesity, ascites and pregnancy, but age related morphological alterations, already referred to, also appear to be of importance.

Finally, but less commonly, an added factor is traction from a shortened oesophagus secondary to severe oesophagitis, or contraction abnormalities may cause an elevation of the oesophagogastric junction above the level of the diaphragm.[11,12]

Morphology and complications

The most characteristic morphological criteria for a sliding hiatal hernia are the intrathoracic displacement of the oesophagogastric junction (Figs 20.2A and 20.3) and the absence of a complete peritoneal sac. Since the proximal stomach is partially located in the retroperitoneum, its upward migration results in a hernia that is only anteriorly covered by a peritoneal sac. If gastric herniation is pronounced, as in combined hiatal hernias (Figs 20.2D and 20.6), an almost complete peritoneal sac may be demonstrated and the sliding nature of the hernia may only become evident by careful inspection of the peritoneal margins. Possibly the majority of giant hiatal hernias, which are often classified as para-oesophageal, are in fact combined hiatal hernias with a dislocation of the oesophagogastric junction and an incomplete peritoneal sac.[13–15]

A sliding hiatal hernia was for a long time used as a synonym for reflux disease of the oesophagus. This view was challenged first when it was recognized that the competence of the gastro-oesophageal anti-reflux mechanism is not solely dependent on its anatomical position.[16] In fact, most patients with sliding hiatal hernias are free of symptoms and have no evidence of reflux,[17] suggesting that a dislocation of the gastro-oesophageal junction does not necessarily equate to its malfunction. On the other hand, almost all patients with oesophagitis reveal evidence

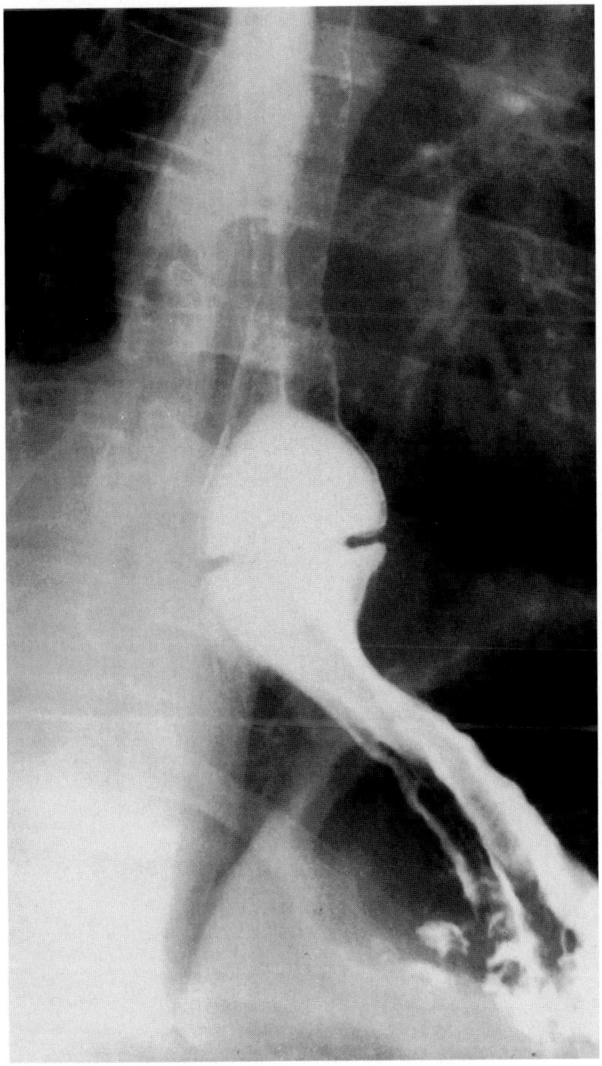

Fig. 20.3 Radiographic appearance of a sliding hiatal hernia. The oesophagogastric junction which is marked by a Schatzki ring has protruded into the chest.

of a sliding hiatal hernia,[18] indicating that this anatomical abnormality may be one of several factors that contribute to the development of reflux oesophagitis. It has been postulated, for example, that a large and nonreducing hernial sac interferes with oesophageal emptying and acid clearance.[19,20] More importantly, recent studies suggest that the crural diaphragm functions as an external sphincter that counteracts reflux promoting factors, such as deep inspiration and increases in intraabdominal pressure, by its simultaneous contraction.[21] Thoracic displacement of the oesophagogastric junction alters the preventive forces for gastro-oesophageal reflux in that it leaves the gastro-oesophageal junction unprotected by its 'second sphincter'. Finally, once oesophagitis and associated ulceration have occurred, the deep inflammatory reaction and fibrosis may cause shortening of the oesophagus which further complicates the disease by enlargement of the hernia and further impairment of mechanisms that prevent reflux or facilitate repair.

PARAOESOPHAGEAL HERNIA

Incidence and morphology

Paraoesophageal hernias are much less common than the sliding type and constitute approximately 5% of all gastric herniations.[9,22] They occur four times more often in female patients than in male patients.[23] As in the sliding type of hiatal hernias, increase of intra-abdominal pressure, such as occurs with obesity and constipation, is thought to be an aetiological factor.

In pure paraoesophageal hiatal hernia the oesophagogastric junction remains fixed posteriorly to the periaortic fascia. However, due to a widened hiatus and a stretched and weakened phreno-oesophageal membrane, the gastric fundus may protrude anterior to the oesophagus into the posterior mediastinum (Figs 20.2B and 20.4). Frequently

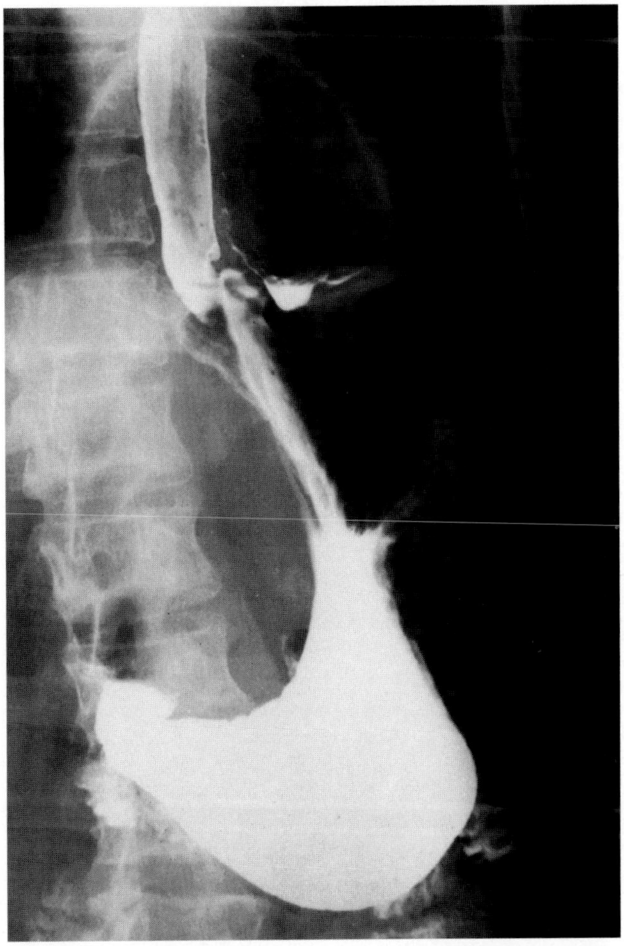

Fig. 20.4 Paraoesophageal hiatal hernia as demonstrated by a double contrast radiographic study. The gastric fundus is displaced into the chest but the oesophagogastric junction is still maintained in its normal subdiaphragmatic position.

the herniation is progressive[24] with migration of increasing amounts of the stomach into the chest. Since the greater curvature always protrudes first, large herniations result in an inversion of the stomach with its greater curvature lying uppermost. In extreme cases the entire stomach may enter the thorax and present as an 'upside down stomach' (Figs 20.2D and 20.5). This unusual condition is identical to an organoaxial volvulus in which the stomach has twisted along its longitudinal axis.[25] Regardless of the degree of herniation, the most characteristic finding in a paraoesophageal hiatal hernia, is its complete inclusion in a peritoneal sac. Whether this condition is fulfilled in giant 'paraoesophageal' hiatal hernias remains a matter of controversy. It appears more likely that these are in fact combined hiatal hernias with protrusion of the stomach and oesophagogastric junction (Figs 20.2C and 20.6), containing a peritoneal sac that spares the posterior aspect of the herniated viscus.

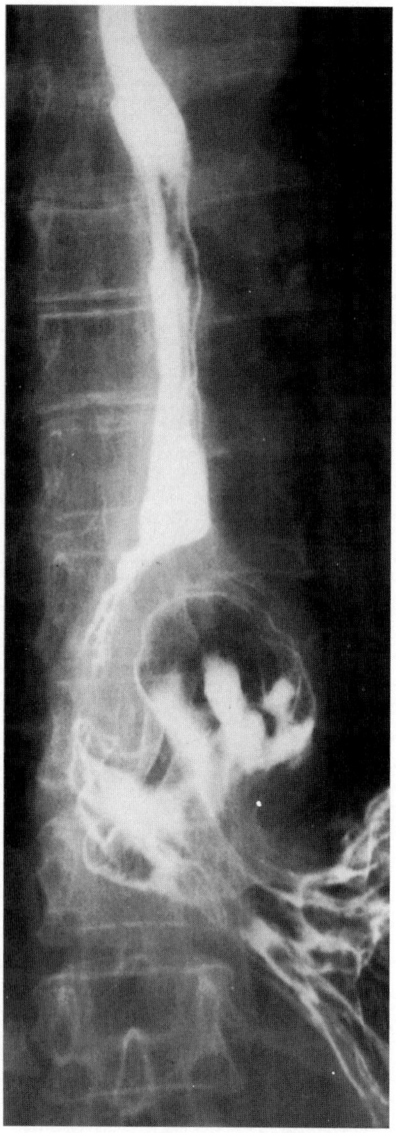

Fig. 20.5 Barium study demonstrating a combined hiatal hernia. The oesophagogastric junction is located above the diaphragm and parts of the stomach are pushed alongside the oesophagus.

Complications

In contrast to sliding hiatal hernias, reflux oesophagitis is uncommon in patients with paraoesophageal hernia.[13] However, significant complications are much more frequent and when they occur may pose a serious threat to the patient's life. Iron deficiency anaemia has been found in 7–30% of patients harbouring a paraoesophageal hiatal hernia.[26–29] Many patients have bleeding, presumably from congested and eroded mucosa or from ulcerations within the herniated pouch. Endoscopic studies have shown that more than 30% of patients with large diaphragmatic hernias may exhibit linear erosions on the crests of mucosal folds straddling the diaphragmatic hiatus.[29] Less frequently (1–5%) ulcerations may develop.[30,31] It is postulated that respiratory movements of the diaphragmatic crura leads to mechanical trauma and ischaemia of the herniated pouch[29,32] and that both of these factors contribute to the development of erosions and 'riding ulcer'. In addition to bleeding, ulcers may perforate and cause mediastinal inflammation and abscess.[33]

In patients with giant paraoesophageal hiatal hernias life threatening complications may occur. These include

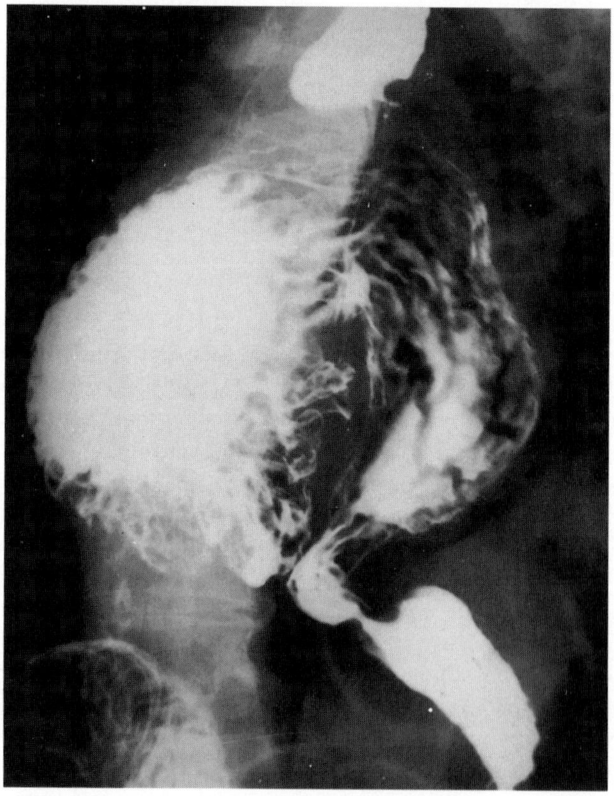

Fig. 20.6 Upside down stomach. The entire stomach is displaced into the chest and has undergone an organoaxial volvulus.

incarceration, obstruction and strangulation, all of which necessitate urgent surgical repair.[34] If left untreated these situations frequently result in a number of further complications ranging from respiratory embarassment to gangrene, bleeding and perforation.[14,15,34] Since this sequence of events may occur in up to one fourth of all patients with massive paraoesophageal hernias[14] a surgical approach has been recommended even for asymptomatic patients.[35]

WEBS AND RINGS

Oesophageal webs and rings are sharply demarcated membranous indentations which impinge on the lumen of the oesophagus at a right angle to its long axis. Both terms have been used interchangeably in the literature to describe many types of occlusive oesophageal abnormalities. Occasionally membranous structures are designated as rings if they are circumferential with a central or eccentric opening and as webs if they are segmented and only extend from a part of the wall. However, such a classification appears arbitrary since, with time, some webs may progress into rings. In addition the great majority of intraoesophageal diaphragms present with similar morphological characteristics regardless of whether they encircle the entire lumen or only a part of it. Only the lower oesophageal mucosal (Schatzki) ring is characterized by morphological findings which are sufficiently specific to allow its clear separation from all other oesophageal membranes. The term ring is reserved for the lower oesophageal mucosal ring, while all other membranous structures are designated as webs.

Although rings and webs of the oesophagus can be clearly distinguished on morphological grounds and may have different aetiologies, they both present with similar clinical manifestations. These consist of intermittent dysphagia which particularly occurs with the ingestion of meat. However, in most cases the membranous indentation of the oesophageal lumen represents an incidental finding. While dysphagia is highly unlikely to occur if the luminal opening exceeds 20 mm, this symptom becomes constant if the oesophageal lumen is compromised to a diameter of less than 12 mm.[36,37] The fact that most rings and webs never compromise the oesophageal lumen to such an extent explains why this relatively frequent abnormality only rarely gives rise to clinical symptoms.

Oesophageal webs

Based upon a study of nearly 5000 subjects, Elwood and coworkers[38] estimated the incidence of oesophageal webs as 0.7%. However, this figure represents the lowest possible incidence since only those subjects who complained of dysphagia were further investigated. Among patients who underwent cineradiographic studies for various reasons, 5.5% had oesophageal webs[39] and in an unselected autopsy series the incidence was as high as 16%.[40] Thus, although symptomatic webs are rare, asymptomatic membranes may be a frequent finding if careful radiographic and morphological studies are performed.

Most oesophageal webs are singular shelf-like defects that originate from the anterior wall of the proximal oesophagus. Occasionally they extend laterally or may become circumferential lesions.[41,42] The great majority are found within 2–3 cm of the postcricoid area while webs in the middle and distal oesophagus are distinctly unusual. Even less frequent are multiple webs which may be distributed along the entire length of the oesophagus (Fig. 20.7A, B, C). Only nine such cases have been reported in the English literature, all of whom presented with significant symptoms.[43–48] The more frequent upper oesophageal web has to be differentiated from the *postcricoid impression*[46,49,50] and the *cricopharyngeal indentation*.[40,46] The former represents a laxity of the mucosa over the ventrally located varicose plexus while the latter is formed by hypertrophic transverse fibres of the cricopharyngeal muscle. Both structures have to be considered as normal variants and, in contrast to webs, do not cause clinical symptoms.

Histological information on oesophageal webs is scanty. It is, however, generally agreed that these membranes rarely exceed a thickness of 2 mm and are always covered by squamous epithelium (Fig. 20.8). On transverse section they represent mucosal folds that do not incorporate the muscularis mucosa.[40] With the exception of one report, which mentioned submucosal infiltration of lymphocytes and plasma cells,[51] most authors have noted a lack of inflammation and have emphasized that webs are merely folds of essentially normal mucosa.[40,47,52] An exception to these findings may occur in patients with multiple webs. In two of these cases marked basal cell hyperplasia and elongation of the submucosal papillae (Fig. 20.7b) have been reported.[48] However, these findings may be secondary phenomena and related to the delay in bolus transport and stasis that may occur in patients with multiple webs.

Conjecture regarding the cause of oesophageal webs has focused mainly on inflammatory and congenital factors. The theory of an acquired and possibly inflammatory origin is mainly based on the observation that symptoms usually develop in adults and that some webs may decrease in diameter with age.[42] However, it is not unusual for congenital lesions such as antral and duodenal diaphragms to present with symptoms later in life. Furthermore the lack of significant inflammation on histological studies and the preferential location in the upper oesophagus, where exposure to gastric luminal contents rarely occurs, speaks strongly against inflammation as a causative factor for the development of oesophageal webs. In contrast, their association with other congenital abnormalities,[53,54] and the fact that webs have been described in infants[55] supports a congenital origin. It appears possible

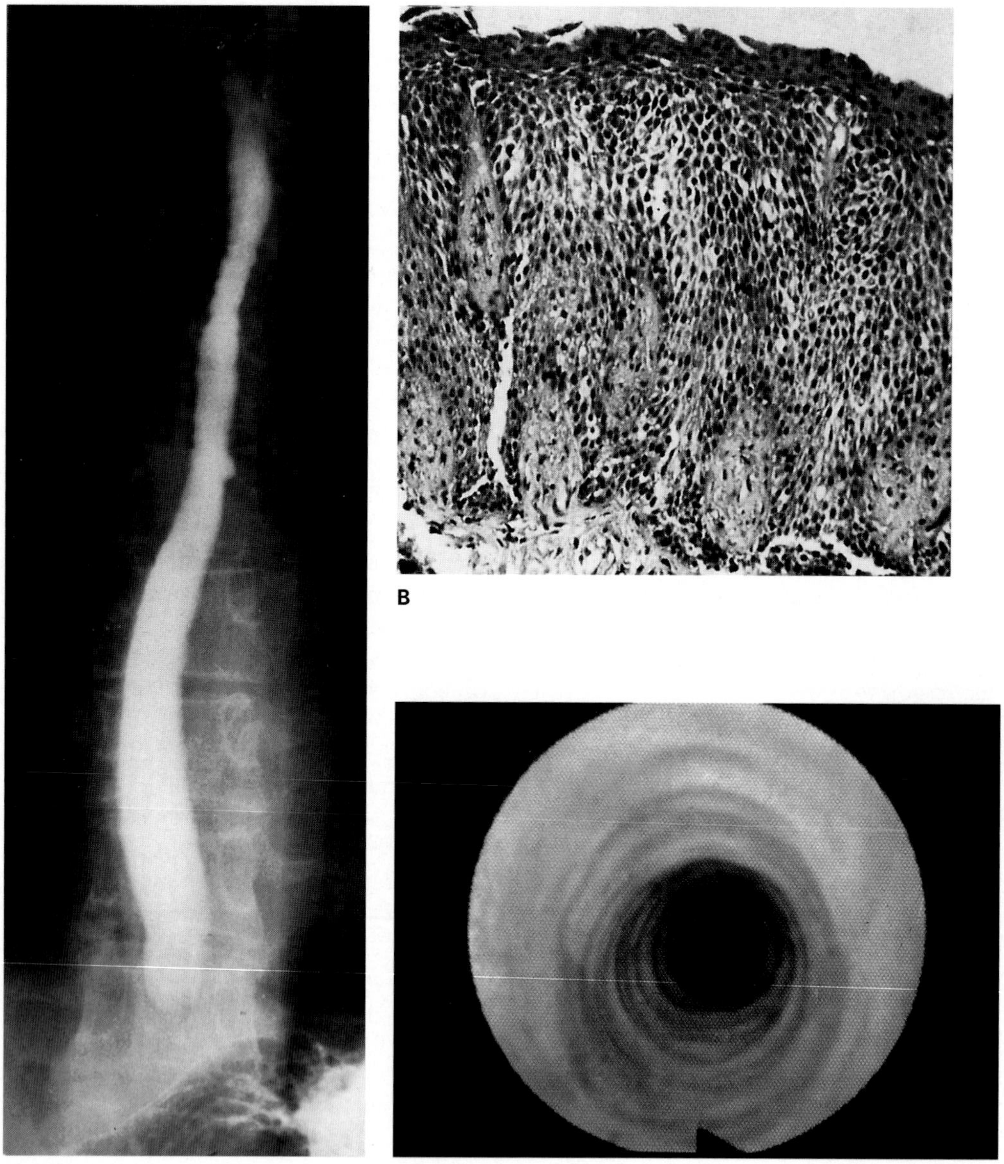

A B C

Fig. 20.7A Radiograph of the oesophagus in a patient with multiple oesophageal webs. **B** Oesophageal suction biopsy from the same patient, revealing elongation of the submucosal papillae and basal cell hyperplasia. **C** Endoscopic view of multiple oesophageal membranes.

that such 'congenital webs' are the result of incomplete vacuolation which appears to be the method by which the columnar oesophageal epithelium in the early embryo[56] is remodelled to become the usual stratified squamous lining normally present at both.

Plummer Vinson Paterson Kelly syndrome

In 1919 Kelly[57] and Paterson[58] independently described the frequent association of oropharyngeal dysphagia in middle-aged women with glossitis and mucosal changes in the mouth, pharynx and upper oesophagus. Vinson[59] later pointed out that anaemia is an important feature of this syndrome, but emphasized that Plummer was the first to notice such an association. It was later recognized that the anaemia was secondary to iron deficiency and the syndrome was also called 'sideropaenic dysphagia'.[60,61] Although the cause of dysphagia cannot be elucidated in all cases,[62] the great majority are found to have upper oesophageal webs.[38,63–65] However, it should be pointed out that postcricoid webs are not synonymous with the Plummer Vinson Paterson Kelly syndrome. Most patients with webs are not anaemic and do not have the characteristic oropharyngeal mucosal changes. In patients with the syndrome several other abnormalities have been reported. These include achlorhydria and vitamin B_{12} malab-

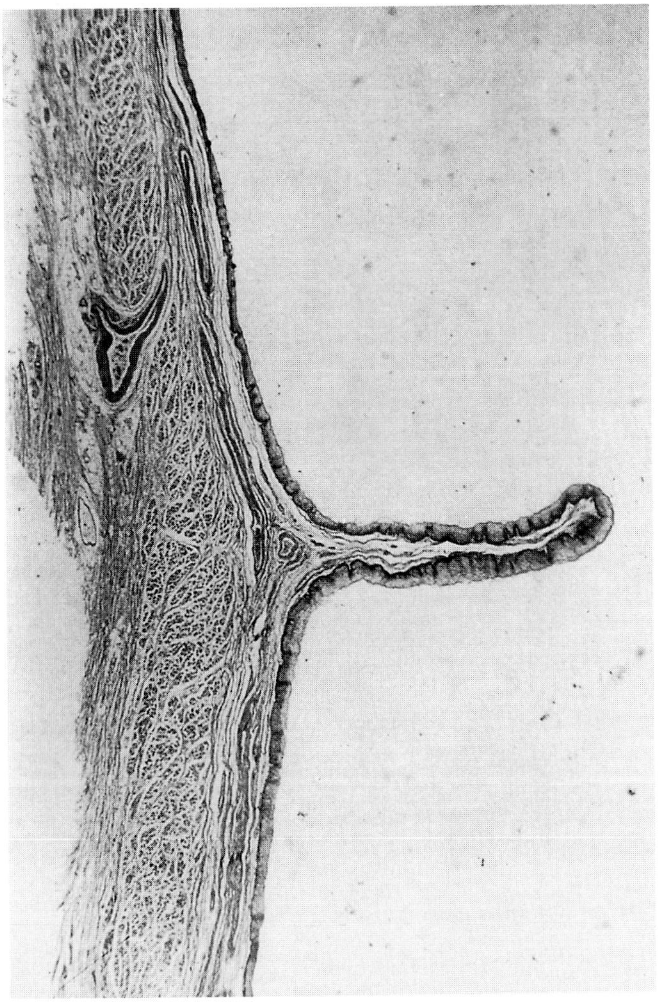

Fig. 20.8 Photomicrograph of an oesophageal web. The web does not contain a muscularis mucosae and is covered on its upper and lower surface by squamous epithelium. (Reproduced with permission from Clements et al 1974)

sorption,[60,66] ulcerative colitis,[67] thyroid disease,[47,68] and Sjogren's syndrome.[69] The fact that some of these diseases are considered autoimmune disorders and that autoantibodies may be detected in patients with iron deficiency anaemia and postcricoid webs, has led to speculations that autoimmune phenomena are important in the aetiology of the Plummer Vinson Paterson Kelly syndrome.[64]

Little information exists regarding the morphology of the postcricoid webs in patients with the syndrome. As with the common web they consist of a thin fold of the oesophageal mucosa, that does not contain a muscularis mucosa. However, in contrast to the former structure, webs that are associated with sideropaenic anaemia and oral mucosal changes often reveal marked epithelial alterations. These consist of atrophy of the epithelium with a chronic inflammatory reaction or hyperkeratinization.[70–72] Similar morphological changes exist in the mucosa of the mouth and pharynx and some authors believe that these changes extend into the upper oesophagus where they may predispose to the formation of the web.[53,73] A similar mechanism may finally underlie the frequent occurrence of cancer of the oral cavity, hypopharynx and oesophagus (Fig. 20.9) in these patients[74] which may be as high as 16%. Conversely, Wynder has shown that 70% of all cases of cancer of the hypopharynx had a history of the Plummer Vinson Paterson Kelly Syndrome.[75] These data suggest that patients with 'sideropaenic dysphagia' should be closely observed for the possible development of cancer in the oropharynx and oesophagus.

Postinflammatory webs

The great majority of oesophageal webs reveal little inflammation and are most likely of congenital origin.

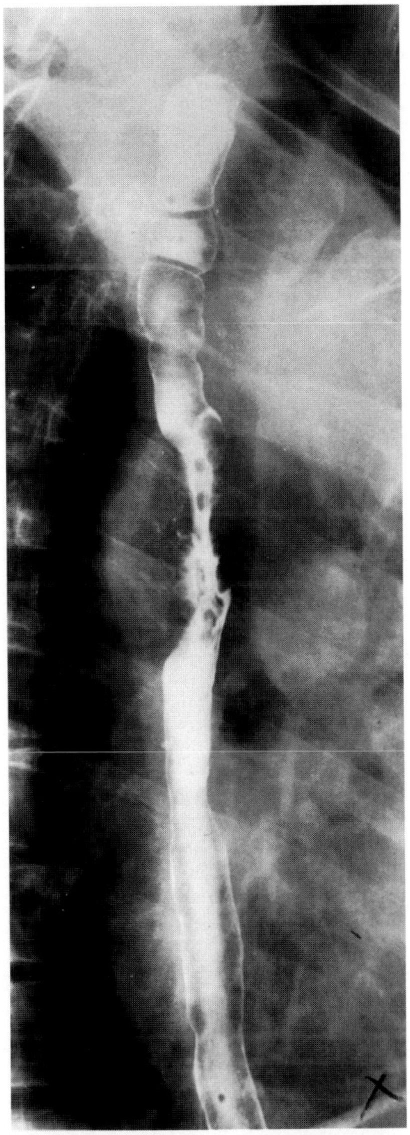

Fig. 20.9 Double oesophageal web in a patient with the Plummer-Vinson Paterson Kelly syndrome. In addition to the webs the patient's radiograph also shows a carcinoma of the upper oesophagus which most likely represents a complication of the syndrome.

However, in rare cases inflammatory factors have been firmly established in causing these membranous structures. Such inflammation is either caused by mucosal irritation through gastrointestinal contents or by intrinsic disease of the skin and mucous membranes.

Although peptic strictures secondary to gastro-oesophageal reflux usually have a tubular appearance, in rare instances they can become annular and may be confused with the lower oesophageal ring.[76] Most recently an unusual high frequency of such annular strictures has been described in progressive systemic sclerosis.[77] It appears possible that both the common occurrence of gastro-oesophageal reflux and the severe motility alterations of the oesophageal body in these patients contribute to the development of such inflammatory webs (Fig. 20.10). A similar mechanism may also explain the occasional formation of web-like strictures at the squamocolumnar junction in patients with columnar epithelial metaplasia (Barrett's oesophagus).[76,78] Such annular strictures are usually thicker than the more common oesophageal web and show some irregularity or asymmetry. On histological examination they are characterized by marked inflammation and subsequently fibrosis that extends between the muscle fibres, and it is this, with consequent narrowing of the lumen, which is responsible for the formation of these postinflammatory webs.[79]

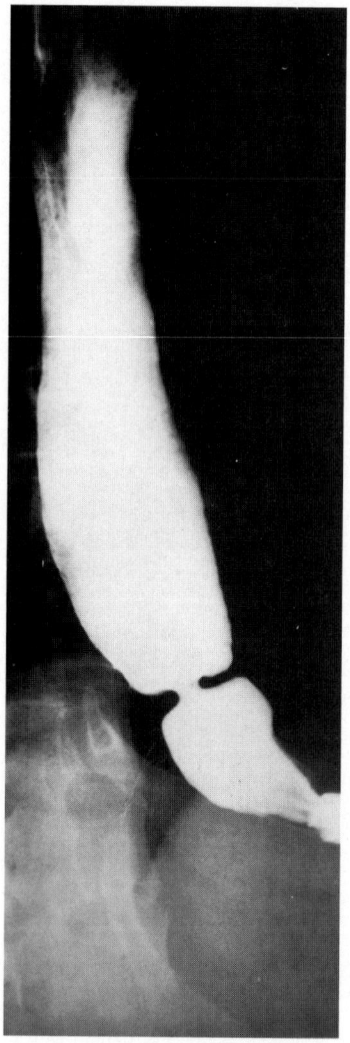

Fig. 20.10 Postinflammatory lower oesophageal web in a patient with scleroderma. Characteristic features are the thickness of the web and a dilated oesophagus as an expression of the underlying motility disorder.

Several dermatological illnesses are known to cause desquamative oesophagitis. Healing of these lesions may result in the formation of oesophageal strictures and webs. In epidermolysis bullosa collagen dissolution occurs in the lamina propria of the mucous membranes leading to recurrent blistering and eventually to the formation of strictures and webs which are most commonly located in the upper oesophagus.[80,81] Similarly, *benign mucous membrane pemphigoid* and *pemphigus vulgaris* frequently lead to oesophageal mucosal blisters and ulcerations which in the process of healing may form adhesive strictures and webs.[82,83] An additional form of desquamative oesophagitis has recently been described in graft-versus-host disease.[84] In these patients peeling of the mucosa and accretion of the resulting membranes led to the formation of eccentric oesophageal webs. Thus, it appears that any form of mucous membrane desquamation may result in membranous structures which are indistinguishable from the common oesophageal web.

Lower oesophageal mucosal (Schatzki) ring

Since its original description in 1944[85] the lower oesophageal mucosal ring has remained the most hotly debated subject of oesophageal pathology. For many years it has been a matter of controversy whether the ring is located at or above the oesophagogastric junction and whether it is a transient or constant phenomenon, but no consensus has been reached regarding its aetiology. However, at the present time most authors agree that the ring represents a thin supradiaphragmatic membrane of the lower oesophagus (Fig. 20.11) which on repeated examinations always appears to constrict the oesophageal lumen to the same diameter.[1,86–92] Morphologically the ring can be differentiated from oesophageal webs in that the free margin marks the squamocolumnar junction.[37,47,91,93–96]

Aetiological considerations

Although at the present time the aetiology of the ring remains unknown, speculation as to its development has centred on three different mechanisms. First, some authors believe that the ring is of inflammatory origin and secondary to gastro-oesophageal reflux. Secondly, it has been proposed that the ring represents merely an exuberant mucosal fold that develops as a consequence of oesophageal shortening, and finally a congenital origin has been proposed.

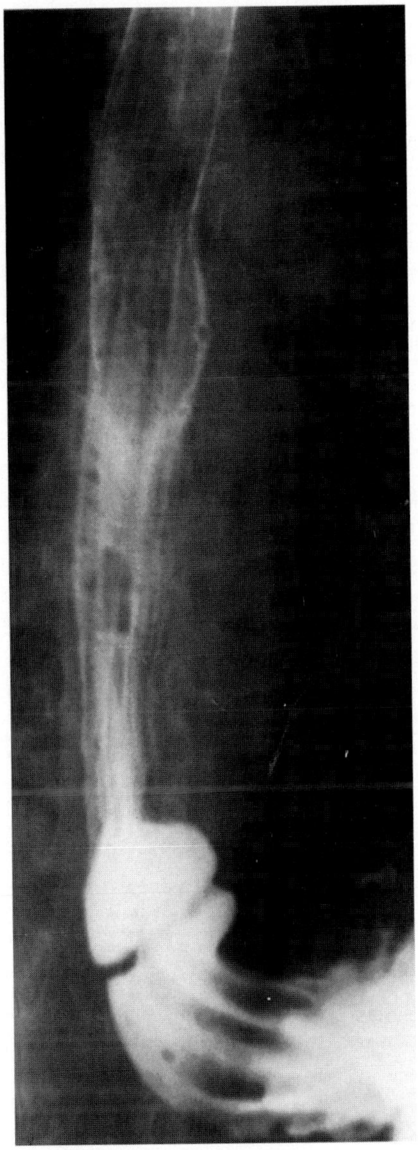

Fig. 20.11 Radiographic demonstration of a lower oesophageal mucosal ring. The membranous structure occurs at the junction of gastric and oesophageal mucosa.

The inflammatory theory is based upon the fact that symptoms of gastro-oesophageal reflux may co-exist with the presence of the ring[92,97] and that some morphological studies have shown mucosal inflammation at or near the ring.[88,92,98,99] Furthermore, the observation that the diameter of the ring can decrease with time[37] has been regarded as indicative of an acquired lesion related to gastro-oesophageal reflux. It has been postulated that progressive narrowing of the oesophagogastric junction may be a mechanism to protect the distal oesophagus from further reflux of gastric contents.[96] However, such speculations are weakened by the scarcity of morphological data supporting an inflammatory origin. In fact, careful morphological studies on autopsy material[95,100] or surgical specimens[101] have failed to reveal significant mucosal inflammation. In addition, more recent long term observations of symptomatic subjects have not revealed any correlation between the presence or absence of oesophagitis and further narrowing of the ring.[102]

An entirely different mechanism for the development of the lower oesophageal mucosal ring has been suggested by Stiennon.[103] Based on the assumption that the ring is always associated with a sliding hiatal hernia and thus a shortening of the oesophagus, he believes that the ring represents a fold of redundant mucosal tissue of a size which varies with the movement of the oesophagus during swallowing and respiration. A prerequisite for this theory is not only the presence of a hiatal hernia, but also a loose attachment of the oesophageal mucosal layer allowing the formation of such a plication. This, however, has not been proven by morphological studies.[104] Furthermore, it has been nearly universally shown that the ring is a fixed structure which, in the majority of subjects, occludes the oesophageal lumen to the same diameter when observed on repeated examinations.[37] Therefore, if the lower oesophageal mucosal ring develops from a plication of mucosal tissue, one would have to postulate that both leaflets of the fold become adherent to each other and do not attach and detach transiently.

Although most lower oesophageal mucosal rings become symptomatic beyond the fifth decade of life, a congenital origin cannot be excluded. Goyal suggests that a mucosal fold at the oesophagogastric junction is a rather frequent anatomic phenomenon that is found in many species other than man.[94] Whether these ridges may later develop into symptomatic rings remains unknown. However, such a developmental origin would be supported by the fact that symptomatic rings have been observed in members of the same family[105] and occasionally in infants.[55] This attractive hypothesis demands that the ring requires a preformed developmental background for its genesis.[94]

Incidence and morphology

The incidence of the lower oesophageal mucosal ring is unknown since systematic radiological studies in unselected subjects do not exist. However, radiographic studies in patients with upper gastrointestinal symptoms suggest that it is a rather frequent finding and may occur in 6–14% of such examinations.[87,106] In the majority of these patients the ring does not lead to oesophageal obstruction and in only 0.5% of patients with dysphagia can this symptom be attributed to the presence of a lower oesophageal mucosal ring.[106]

Although Templeton was the first to describe a ring-like diaphragm in the lower oesophagus,[85] Ingelfinger and Kramer deserve credit for pointing to its clinical significance.[36] These authors initially believed that symptoms and the morphological appearance were caused by an overactive inferior oesophageal sphincter which transiently obstructed the oesophageal lumen. Only a few months later Schatzki and Gary[86] challenged this view by pointing out that the ring is a fixed structure and believed that it is located at the oesophagogastric junction which has been displaced into the chest by a small sliding hiatal hernia. This hypothesis was later strongly supported by histological studies, which have nearly universally shown that the free margin of the ring represents the squamocolumnar junction.[93,95,100,101,107–109] However, confusion arose when simultaneous manometric and cineradiographic studies produced evidence that the lower oesophageal sphincter is located below the ring.[89,110] These differing findings can only be explained by an upward migration of the squamocolumnar junction in patients with lower oesophageal mucosal rings or a methodological error due to movement of the motility tube during simultaneous radiographic and manometric studies. More recently, simultaneous potential difference and manometric measurements have shown that the squamocolumnar junction in patients with lower oesophageal mucosal rings is located within the lower oesophageal sphincter.[111] Thus, although some controversy continues regarding the location of the ring,[112,113] the majority of experimental and morphological data indicate that the ring marks the oesophagogastric junction and is not associated with an upward migration of gastric mucosa into the tubular oesophagus. Therefore the radiographic demonstration of a lower oesophageal mucosal ring proximal to the diaphragm probably represents the most reliable evidence for the presence of a hiatal hernia.

In most patients the ring represents a thin circular membranous structure which constricts the oesophageal lumen to a varying extent (Fig. 20.12). A characteristic and unexplained finding is the demonstration of an almost straight squamocolumnar junction.[95] Similar to oesophageal webs, the ring is composed of a mucosal fold that may contain a muscularis mucosae, but the muscularis propria does not contribute to its structure.[95,100] Besides muscle fibres from the muscularis mucosae, the core of the ring contains a variable amount of fibrous tissue with little or no inflammatory infiltrates.[95,100,101] Occasionally the squamous epithelium covering the upper surface of the ring has been described as showing hyperkeratosis or irregular and hyperchromatic epithelial cells.[76,86,89] Severe mucosal changes are, however, usually absent and most authors have especially commented on the lack of inflammation.

The lower oesophageal mucosal ring has to be differentiated from *postinflammatory annular strictures* and the rare *muscular lower oesophageal ring*. While the former is due to acid pepsin regurgitation[107,114] and the resulting mucosal inflammation the latter represents a hypertrophy of the muscularis mucosae. Only a few of these cases have been reported in the English literature.[94,115,116] The ring is mainly composed of muscle bundles which are separated by thin septa of fibrous tissue and is covered on its upper and lower margins by squamous epithelium. In constrast to the lower oesophageal mucosal ring, muscular rings occur proximal to the oesophagogastric junction and may correspond to Lerche's 'inferior oesophageal sphincter'[117] or Wolf's 'A ring'.[118]

OESOPHAGEAL DIVERTICULA

Oesophageal diverticula are saccular outward protrusions from the oesophageal lumen. They may contain all layers of the oesophageal wall or only mucosa and submucosa

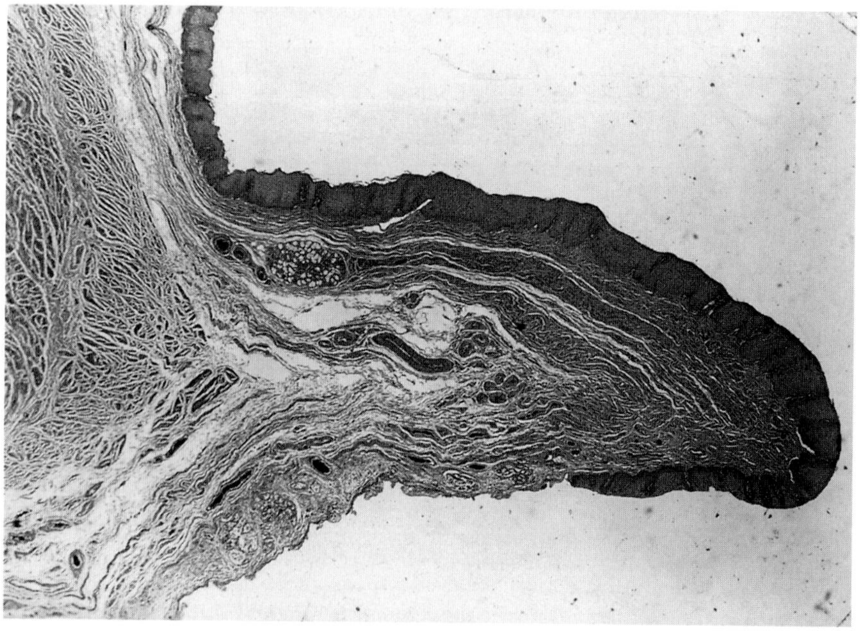

Fig. 20.12 Autopsy specimen of a lower mucosal ring. Its upper surface is covered by squamous epithelium while most of the under surface is covered by gastric mucosa. The core of the diaphragm consists mainly of connective tissue and muscularis mucosae. (Reproduced with permission from MacMahon et al 1958)

which herniate through areas of muscular weakness. In the past they have been classified as pulsion and traction diverticula according to their postulated aetiology. Using this nomenclature midoesophageal diverticula were referred to as traction diverticula while those occurring in the upper and lower oesophagus were termed pulsion diverticula. However, it is increasingly recognized that traction from inflamed lymph nodes play only a minor role in the development of midoesophageal diverticula and that pulsion forces cannot be demonstrated in all cases of lower oesophageal diverticula. It appears therefore more accurate to classify oesophageal diverticula according to their localization, namely as pharyngo-oesophageal (Zenker's), midoesophageal and epiphrenic diverticula.

On rare occasions radiographically and endoscopically demonstrated outpouchings of the oesophageal lumen do not fit either one of the above mentioned classifications. These exceptions include the so-called *intramural diverticulosis* and false *oesophageal diverticula*. The former represent saccular dilatations of oesophageal glandular ducts while the latter are diverticulum-like pouches produced by ulcerations, sinus tracts and partially occluded fistulas.

Little is known concerning the frequency with which oesophageal diverticula occur because many of them are asymptomatic and are incidental findings on radiographic, endoscopic or post mortem examinations. However, among symptomatic diverticula those occurring at the pharyngo-oesophageal junction are most frequent. In a large series they constituted 70% of all oesophageal diverticula while 21.5% were observed in the midoesophagus and 8.5% in the supradiaphragmatic region.[119] Most patients with pharyngo-oesophageal diverticula complain of dysphagia, regurgitation and frequent episodes of aspiration, whilst those with mid and lower oesophageal diverticula only rarely complain of symptoms related to disordered oesophageal motility.

Pharyngo-oesophageal (Zenker's) diverticulum

The first anatomic description of a pharyngo-oesophageal diverticulum was given by Ludlow in 1767.[120] He also described accurately the typical symptomatology, but his choice of therapy was unfortunate. In order to dilate the oesophagus the patient was asked to swallow a mouthful of mercury and succumbed two weeks later. In 1877 Zenker and Ziemssen published a lucid and expository review of 27 cases resulting in the association of Zenker's name with this entity.[121] It was pointed out that pulsion forces are responsible for its development, a view that is still widely held. Most diverticula are observed in patients beyond the sixth decade of life and occur slightly more commonly in the male sex.

Pathology

Zenker's diverticula protrude as narrow-necked sacculations from Kilians triangle,[122] a muscular dehiscence that is bordered by the oblique fibres of the inferior constrictor and the transverse fibres of the cricopharyngeus muscle (Fig. 20.13). Due to the sparsity of irregularly arranged muscle fibres in this area, the wall of the diverticulum contains only an attenuated muscularis propria. As the diverticulum progressively enlarges it protrudes between the posterior wall of the oesophagus and the vertebrae leading to an anterior displacement of the proximal oesophagus.

Little is known about the fine structure of oesophageal and hypopharyngeal muscular elements in patients with Zenker's diverticula. A recent investigation described alterations of the cricopharyngeal muscle that are suggestive of neurogenic as well as myogenic degeneration.[123] Evidence for the former included variation in fibre size and predominence for type I fibres while myogenic degeneration was suggested by the presence of necrosis, central nuclei and nemaline rods. Whatever lesion predominates,

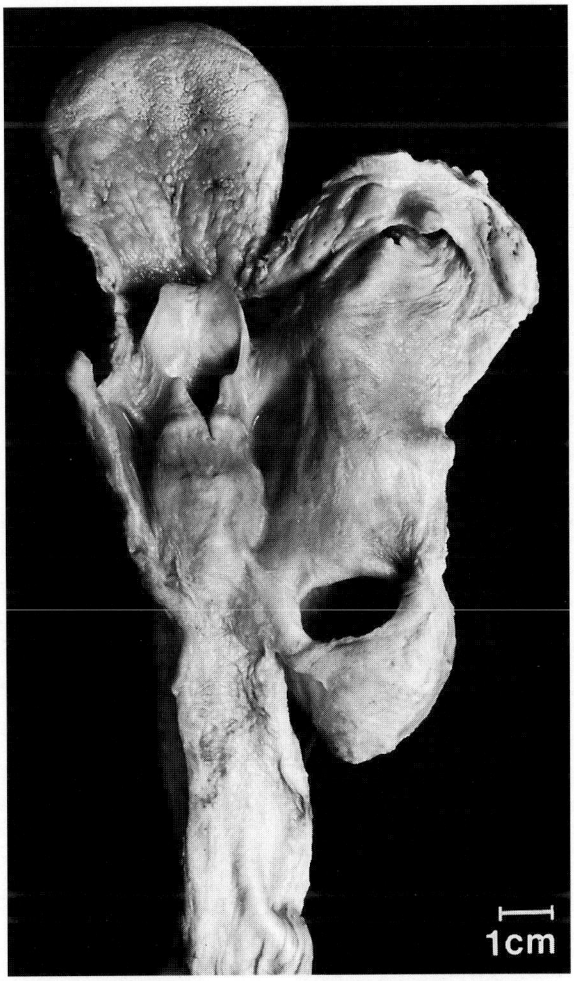

Fig. 20.13 Gross photograph of a Zenker's diverticulum which protrudes from Killian's triangle and involves all layers of the oesophageal wall. (Reproduced with permission from F. Borchard, in: Arnold, Laissue, Friedmann, Naumann: Histopathology of ENT-Diseases. Georg Thieme Verlag, Stuttgart, 1987)

the morphological alterations in the cricopharyngeal muscle appear to be important enough to explain some of the physiological alterations observed in Zenker's diverticula and perhaps even their genesis.

Complications such as significant inflammation and mucosal ulcerations rarely occur in the pharyngo-oesophageal diverticulum.[124] However, there may be a slightly increased risk for the development of squamous cell carcinoma, for Huang et al[125] reported a prevalence of 0.4% in 1249 treated cases — which is greater than that observed in the general population. The tumours were located in the apex of the diverticulum and the majority had already extended through its wall by the time the diagnosis was made.

Pathogenesis

Although it is generally accepted that the pharyngo-oesophageal diverticulum develops as a consequence of pulsion forces acting on an area of muscular weakness, the precise mechanism has long been debated. Most theories have centred on a disturbed coordination between pharyngeal contractions and upper oesophageal sphincter relaxation causing increased hypopharyngeal pressure during deglutition.[126–130] However, some of these observations possibly represented methodological artefacts inherent in early manometric techniques rather than true physiological alterations. Combined cineradiographic and manometric studies have now convincingly shown that the main defect in patients with Zenker's diverticula is not an abnormality in pharyngosphincteric coordination but a defect in sphincter opening that is either caused by a failure to completely inhibit cricopharyngeal muscle tone or by muscular fibrosis rendering the sphincter less compliant.[131] To maintain normal bolus flow through the upper oesophageal sphincter intrabolus pressure increases and eventually leads to the development of a pulsion diverticulum in an area where muscular elements are least developed. This sequence of events satisfactorily explains why diverticulectomy has to be combined with a myotomy

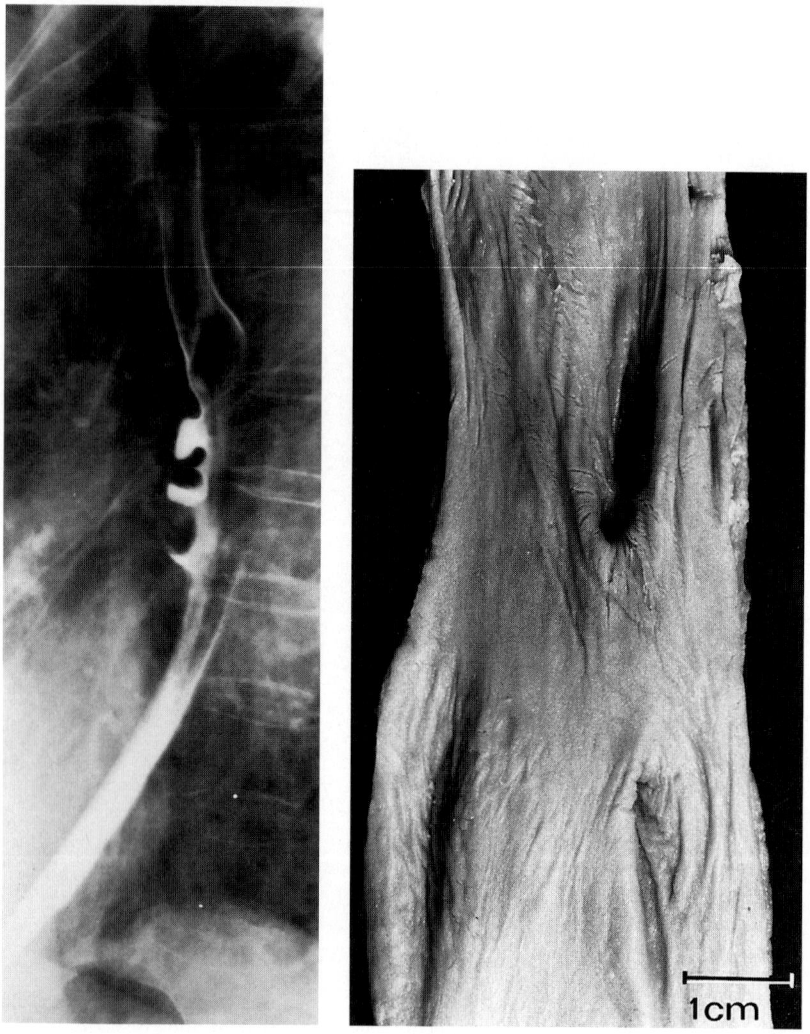

A B

Fig. 20.14 Multiple midoesophageal diverticula occurring in close proximity to the tracheal bifurcation. **A** Radiographic view. **B** Autopsy specimen. (Reproduced with permission from F. Borchard, in: Arnold, Laissue, Friedmann, Naumann: Histopathology of ENT-Diseases. Georg Thieme Verlag, Stuttgart, 1987) of the cricopharyngeal sphincter in order to achieve optimal treatment results.[132,133]

Lateral hypopharyngeal diverticula

In rare instances pharyngo-oesophageal diverticula may not originate in Kilian's triangle but from an area below the transverse portion of the cricopharyngeal muscle.[134] Such lateral diverticula protrude from a gap in the musculature which is found between the outer lateral border of the cricoid cartilage and the insertion of the cricopharyngeal muscle, corresponding to the route taken by the inferior laryngeal nerve.

Misoesophageal diverticula

Midoesophageal diverticula are almost always incidental findings on radiographic and endoscopic examinations. They may be single or multiple (Fig. 20.14A, B) and usually occur in immediate proximity to the tracheal bifurcation.[135,136] Most of them are wide mouthed and have a diameter of less than 2 cm. The wall of the diverticulum is mainly composed of mucosa and submucosa with only an attenuated muscularis.[137] Evidence of inflammation is usually lacking, but in rare instances localized transmural inflammation may occur and appears to be associated with related disease of neighbouring lymph nodes.[138,139]

For many years it was thought that all midoesophageal diverticula developed in association with mediastinal lymph node pathology.[121] Co-existent histoplasmosis or anthracosis is described, but the most common association is tuberculous infection. It has been postulated that the enlarged or inflamed lymph nodes adhere to the oesophagus and, in the stage of healing, progressively apply traction to localized portions of the wall. However, with the fall in tuberculous infections, it has become clear that many midoesophageal diverticula are unrelated to neighbouring lymphadenopathy. Some rare cases may develop on a congenital basis as a consequence of incomplete separation of the oesophagus and trachea during early embryonic life.[140] However, more recent observations suggest that the majority are associated with a wide spectrum of oesophageal motility disorders ranging from high amplitude contractions to diffuse oesophageal spasm and achalasia.[135,141–143] Similarly, as in Zenker's diverticulum, it is believed that pulsion forces acting on localized areas of muscular weakness are responsible for the development of these lesions. As a consequence, most surgeons recommend a myotomy in addition to diverticulectomy for the rare case in which surgery becomes unavoidable.[143,144]

Epiphrenic diverticula

Epiphrenic diverticula occur within the distal third of the oesophagus and most commonly project from the terminal 4 cm of the right posterior oesophageal wall.[145] They are usually wide mouthed, and in contrast to midoesophageal diverticula may become sizeable lesions (Fig. 20.15), reaching a diameter of up to 10 cm. Despite its often grotesque appearance symptoms and significant complications are exceedingly rare.

There is ample evidence to suggest that almost all epiphrenic diverticula are due to increased intraoesophageal pressure acting on areas of localized muscular weakness.[146–149] Up to 77% of patients are found to have motor abnormalities of the oesophageal body[150,151] and in some cases distal obstruction due to muscular hypertrophy may exist.[148] Thus, like the majority of midoesophageal diverticula, epiphrenic diverticula represent a morphological manifestation of an oesophageal motility disorder.

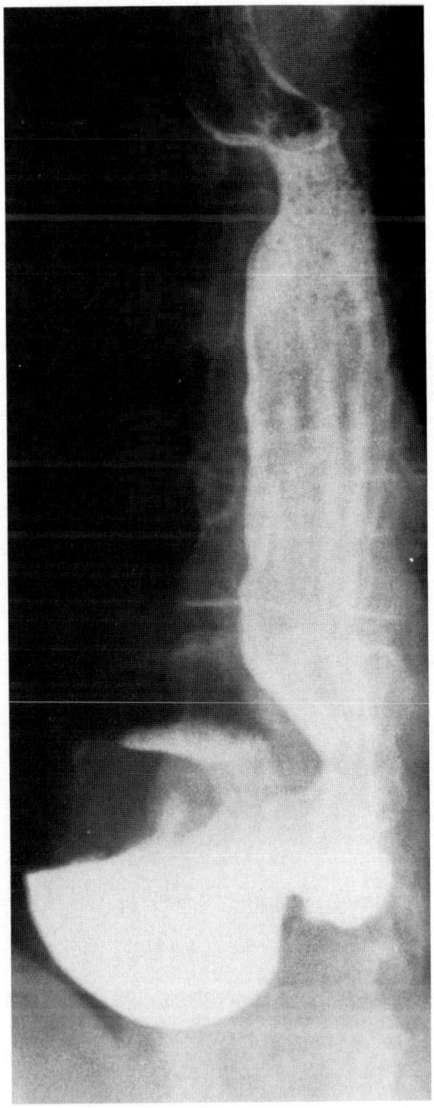

Fig. 20.15 X-ray appearance of an epiphrenic diverticulum in a patient with achalasia. The large diverticulum developed presumably as the consequence of the oesophageal motility disorder.

Oesophageal intramural diverticulosis

The first case of intramural oesophageal diverticulosis was described in 1960 by Mendl et al in the radiological literature.[152] Their patient presented with multiple collar button-like outpouchings of the oesophageal mucosa which all had a similar depth of only a few mm (Fig. 20.16). The authors believed that the lesions were caused by mucosal protrusions through areas of muscular weakness. Since then nearly 100 further cases have been reported and it has now been conclusively shown by morphological studies that the lesions develop as dilatations of preexisting oesophageal submucosal glands. Based upon these observations the term 'intramural oesophageal diverticulosis' appears the most appropriate for this rare morphological abnormality.

Oesophageal intramural diverticulosis is rarely diagnosed during conventional radiographic studies. It is found in only 0.15% of all patients undergoing radiographic examinations of the oesophagus.[153] However, precursor lesions such as duct dilations and cysts have been observed in up to 55% of randomly selected autopsy specimens.[154] The peak incidence occurs in the sixth and seventh decades of life[155,156] and only rare cases have been described in infancy and childhood.[157,158]

Although males may be affected more often than females the difference in sex distribution is not significant.

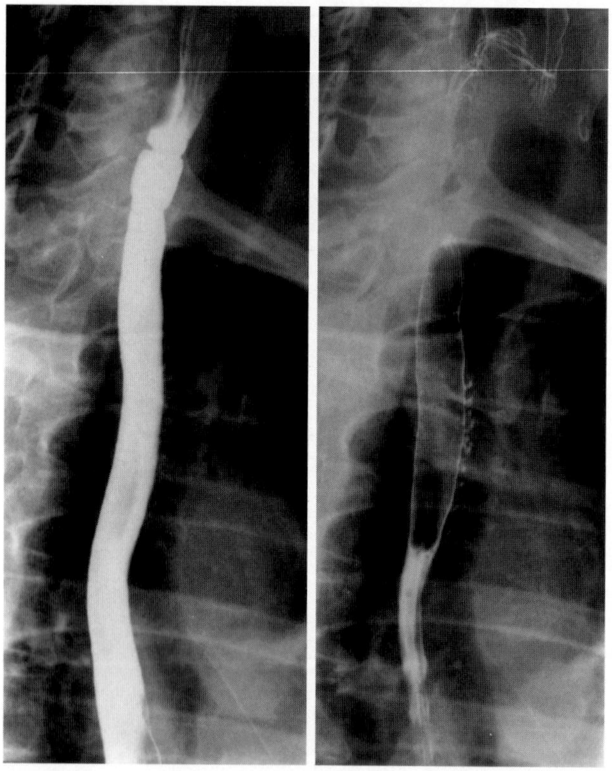

Fig. 20.16 Radiographic demonstration of oesophageal intramural diverticulosis. In this case, the collar button-like outpouchings of the mucosa are associated with web-like strictures of the upper oesophagus.

More than two thirds of all patients complain of dysphagia, a symptom that is directly related to the frequent association of intramural diverticulosis with stricture formation in the affected segment.[153,155,156,159,160] However, the disease usually runs a benign clinical course with little variation in its clinical expression, even on prolonged follow-up.[160–164]

Pathology

Postmortem examinations have led to a precise morphological definition (Figs 20.17 & 20.18) and have uniformly shown that the typical flask-like projections correspond to dilated excretory ducts of the deep submucosal oesophageal glands.[153,154,161,164] The dilations rarely exceed a diameter of 0.4 cm and are mostly confined to the submucosa. Extension to the lamina propria is rare and in no instance did they involve the muscularis propria.

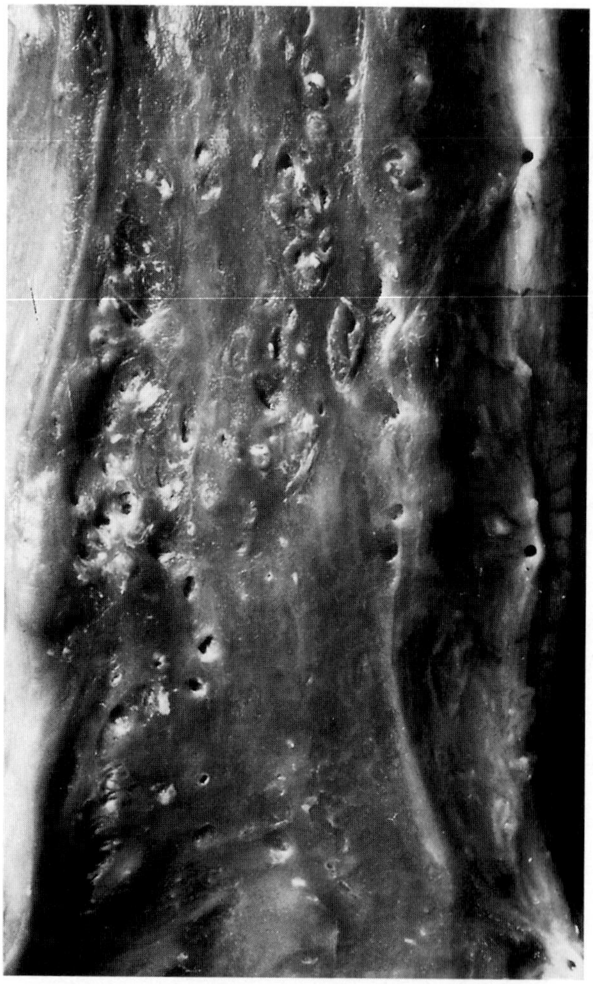

Fig. 20.17 Gross photograph of an autopsy specimen from a patient with oesophageal intramural diverticulosis. Numerous orifices of dilated submucosal glands are clearly demonstrated. (Reproduced with permission from Heinze et al 1985)

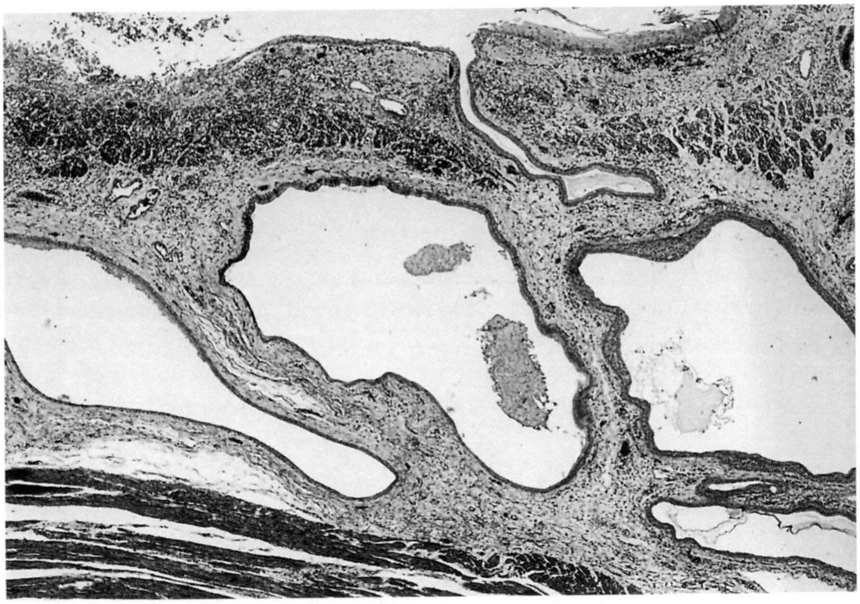

Fig. 20.18 Microscopic section showing glandular and ductal dilatation in an autopsy specimen from a patient with intramural diverticulosis. (Courtesy of Dr B. E. Kipreos, Department of Pathology, Veterans Administration Medical Center, Richmond, Virginia, USA)

It was initially suggested that the disease is not only characterized by cystic dilatations but also by a proliferation of the oesophageal submucosal glands.[165] However, careful histological studies have demonstrated that there are an average 4 ducts and glands in each 0.5 cm of normal oesophagus. This is comparable to the number of dilated ducts seen in patients with intramural diverticulosis.[164]

The lumen of the dilated ducts and glands often contains an abundance of polymorphonuclear leucocytes and desquamated epithelial cells and there is usually evidence of more chronic inflammation. Due to the accompanying submucosal fibrosis, marked thickening of the oesophageal wall may occur and is responsible for the frequently observed stricture formation.

Oesophageal intramural diverticulosis may be either diffuse or segmental, each type accounting for approximately half of all cases.[154] If only a portion of the oesophagus is affected, involvement of the proximal third is most common. The majority of associated strictures occur at the same location and have a reported incidence between 80–90%.[153,154,158,159,166] A possible reason for such preferential location of intramural diverticula and strictures may lie in a higher density of oesophageal glands in the proximal oesophagus.

Pathogenesis

The aetiology of oesophageal intramural diverticulosis remains speculative. Although a congenital origin cannot be totally dismissed,[167] its usual occurrence in elderly persons suggests it is acquired.

Several studies have shown that patients with intramural diverticulosis have isolated or generalized motility disturbances consisting in high amplitude and simultaneous contractions or aperistalsis at the level of the stricture.[153,158–160,168] Such motor abnormalities may lead to an increase of intraluminal pressure and consequently to dilatation of the submucosal glands. However, these functional abnormalities may be a consequence of deep fibrosing inflammation rather than a primary phenomenon. Furthermore, a number of patients have been reported in whom oesophageal peristalsis and intraluminal pressure were entirely normal.[159,163,168]

Submucosal inflammation and fibrosis which centres on the glands has been reported in the great majority of patients with intramural diverticulosis.[153,154,158,159,169,170] This has led to the theory that inflammatory infiltrates may lead to ductal obstruction with resultant dilatation of the ductular structures. Gastro-oesophageal reflux and invasion by *Candida albicans* have also been incriminated as responsible mechanisms. However, in view of the fact that the most pronounced inflammation occurs in the proximal oesophagus while distal regions are commonly spared, reflux is an unlikely aetiological factor. Similarly, although Candida has been frequently cultured from the oesophageal mucosa in patients with intramural diverticulosis[171–175] such findings are not consistent.[164,176,177] Finally, even inflammation may be totally absent, suggesting that at least in some patients some other factors may be involved in its pathogenesis. Whether these are abnormalities in oesophageal motility or in the composition of glandular secretions[178] awaits further clarification.

OESOPHAGEAL DISRUPTION

Oesophageal disruption may occur spontaneously during sudden increases of intraabdominal pressure or as a consequence of trauma, such as instrumentation, foreign body ingestion or blunt and penetrating injuries to the chest. The seriousness of the resulting clinical manifestations depends on whether the entire wall perforates or whether isolated mucosal or muscular disruptions occur. Disruption of the muscularis propria, as it occurs with oesophageal myotomies or dilatations, remains without serious sequelae as long as the mucosa remains intact. More frequent complications result from isolated mucosal perforations, which are commonly associated with massive upper gastrointestinal haemorrhage and may require surgical intervention. However, the most serious clinical event is a disruption of all layers of the oesophagus, resulting in infection of adjacent structures and commonly in death.

Mallory-Weiss syndrome

In 1879 Quincke[179] was the first to describe a mucosal laceration of the gastric cardia which was associated with severe upper gastrointestinal haemorrhage. Fifty years later Mallory and Weiss[180] noted its association with alcohol consumption and repeated episodes of vomiting. Since then it has been shown that the lesion is a rather frequent clinical event, accounting for approximately 10% of all acute upper gastrointestinal bleeding episodes.[181–184]

Aetiology

Mallory-Weiss tears are most commonly observed in male patients beyond the fifth decade of life. However, they may develop in almost every individual who experiences a sudden and often violent change in intraabdominal and intrathoracic pressure.

An increased pressure gradient between the abdomen and the chest causes ballooning of the distal oesophagus or herniated stomach and exposes these structures, according to Laplace's law, to the highest wall tension. If the pressure gradient reaches a certain level, structures of least distensibility such as mucosa and submucosa[185] will rupture first while the seromuscular layers may still remain intact. Such Mallory-Weiss tears are most commonly encountered with sudden increases in intraabdominal pressure as occurs with vomiting and retching or, less frequently, with lifting, defaecation, child birth and trauma to the abdomen.[186–189] Conversely, large decreases in intrathoracic pressure that are generated by thoracic expansions against a closed airway may occasionally result in similar lesions. This sequence of events has been described for patients with asthma, hiccups, protracted cough or even in those with intense snoring.[190–193]

Morphology and clinical course

The great majority of Mallory-Weiss tears are located in the upper stomach and immediately below the oesophagogastric mucosal junction (Fig. 20.19). This preferential location is possibly explained by the fact that most patients exhibit a hiatal hernia.[187] It has been postulated that oesophageal tears occur in subjects without hiatal hernias and junctional tears in those where the cardia does not remain in a fixed position in reference to the diaphragm.[194] Although multiple lesions occur, the majority are single and predominantly located at the lesser curvature of the stomach and the right lateral wall of the oesophagus. This location may result from its relative immobility and thus the higher shearing forces during forceful increases of intraabdominal pressure.[187] The tear is typically orientated parallel to the long axis of the cardia and has an average length of 1.5 cm but may occasionally extend up to 4.0 cm.

Macroscopically, the Mallory-Weiss tear appears as a cleft-like or linear lesion which in the acute stage is frequently covered with clotted blood. If the lacerations are

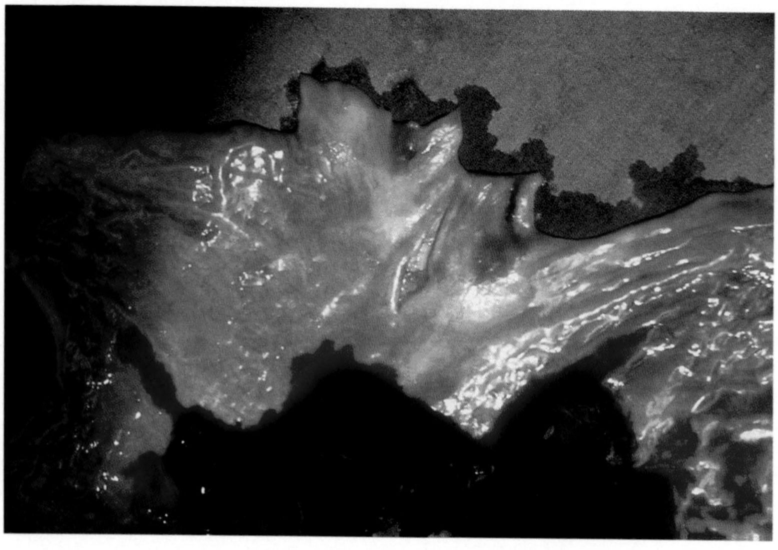

Fig. 20.19 Mallory-Weiss tear in its typical location at the lesser curvature immediately distal to the oesophagogastric junction. In this case death had occurred as a consequence of exsanguination from the mucosal tear. (Courtesy of Prof. W. Rosch, Nordwestkrankenhaus, Frankfurt, Germany)

observed later than 24 hours after their development, they may display the features of a linear ulceration with associated inflammatory reactions. On histologic examination the tear is always confined to the mucosa and submucosa, leaving the muscularis propria intact. At the base of the laceration numerous small veins and ruptured arterioles are usually observed, explaining the frequent occurrence of massive upper gastrointestinal haemorrhage. Some lesions convert into linear peptic ulcerations[195] which have the same morphological features as other peptic ulcers.

The great majority of patients with Mallory-Weiss syndrome run a benign clincial course and complete healing of the lesion usually occurs within 48–72 hours. Surgical intervention due to massive bleeding may be required in up to 10% of all patients, but mortality is exceedingly rare and in most series less than 3%.

Intramural oesophageal haematoma

Incomplete oesophageal disruption, such as occurs with Mallory-Weiss tears, may rarely be followed by the development of an intramural haematoma. The mucosal laceration results not only in intramural bleeding but also in intramural dissection of the oesophageal wall by blood. The dissection almost always develops in the plane of the submucosa of the lower oesophagus. Rarely, and especially after trauma to the distal oesophagus, such as pneumatic dilatation, the haematoma may spread between the inner and outer layers of the muscularis propria.[196] Although the lesion most often originates in the distal oesophagus, multiple haematomas and involvement of the entire oesophagus have been described.[197] It has been postulated that these more extensive haematomas more frequently occur in patients with impaired haemostasis as a consequence of thrombocytopaenia, haemophilia or treatment with anticoagulants.[198–200] On rare occasions and especially in elderly females, an intramural haematoma may develop spontaneously in the absence of any known trauma or coagulation defects.[201]

The collection of blood in the submucosa results in a protrusion of the oesophageal mucosa and incomplete obliteration of the oesophageal lumen (Fig. 20.20). If mucosal lacerations develop at both the proximal and distal end of the dissection, a 'double barrelled' oesophagus with a true oesophageal lumen and an additional intramural cavity may result.[200,202] Although the disorder may be associated with severe symptoms consisting of dysphagia, retrosternal pain and haematemesis, most patients run a benign clinical course and spontaneous resolution of the haematoma usually occurs within 1–3 weeks.[203]

Iatrogenic perforation

Perforation of the gastrointestinal tract carries the gravest prognosis if it occurs in the oesophagus.[204] Despite major

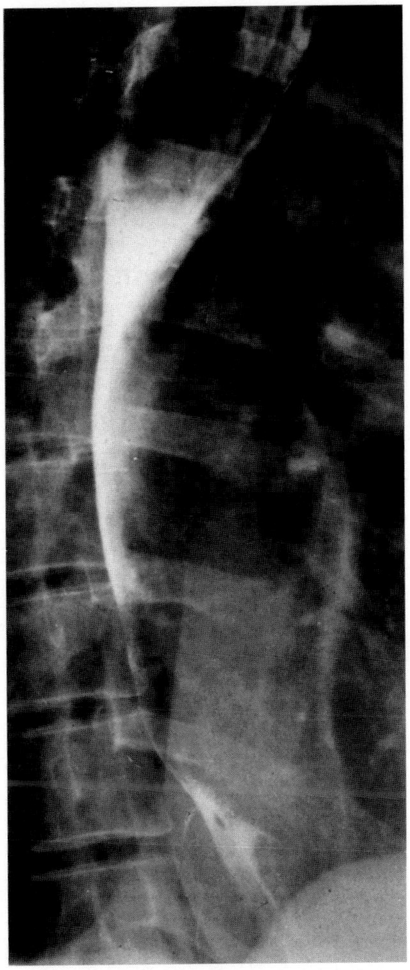

Fig. 20.20 Radiographic demonstration of an intramural haematoma occurring after sclerotherapy for oesophageal variceal bleeding. The haematoma had led to distal oesophageal obstruction. (Reproduced with permission from Van Steenbergen et al 1984)

advances in medical management and surgical technique, its mortality remains in excess of 20%.[205–207] Approximately 75% of all ruptures occur during instrumental manipulations such as endoscopy, dilatation, balloon tamponade and palliative intubation.[208] It has been estimated that 0.03% of all fibreoptic endoscopies[209] and up to 5% of pneumatic dilatations[210,211] of the cardia are associated with oesophageal perforation. Less commonly, the oesophagus may be injured during surgical manipulation of adjacent structures,[212] blunt or penetrating external trauma[213] or as a consequence of foreign body ingestion.[214,215] While instrumental perforations are usually immediately recognized, other causes may lead to delayed perforations secondary to ischaemia, transmural inflammation and pressure necrosis.

Most iatrogenic perforations occur at the site of anatomic narrowing, namely the cervical oesophagus at the thoracic inlet and the oesophagogastric junction. Each site accounts for 40% of all perforations.[216] Cervical perforations are most often located at the piriform sinus and at the level of the cricopharyngeal muscle where foreign bodies lodge and endoscopes have to be passed under limited luminal vision. At the cardia, perforations most frequently occur through the posterior wall of the oesophagus and, if the intraabdominal part is involved, into the retroperitoneal space and lesser sac.[217] One explanation for the common occurrence of perforations at this site is the fact that the distal oesophagus bends to the left and anteriorly prior to entering the stomach.[218]

Immediately following perforation acid, bile, food, saliva and air are freely disseminated into the fascial spaces of the neck, mediastinum and peritoneum. Although the leaked intraluminal material may remain localized, more frequently the contamination is widespread (Fig. 20.21). This is facilitated by the negative intrathoracic pressure which forces contaminated material during each inspiration into the mediastinum. Within a few hours there is pleuromediastinal inflammation, pneumothorax and pneumomediastinum.[219] Later on, massive pleural effusions, oesophagitis and pericarditis may result. At this stage the patient is often in respiratory failure and has septicaemia and shock and thus early recognition and treatment is essential.

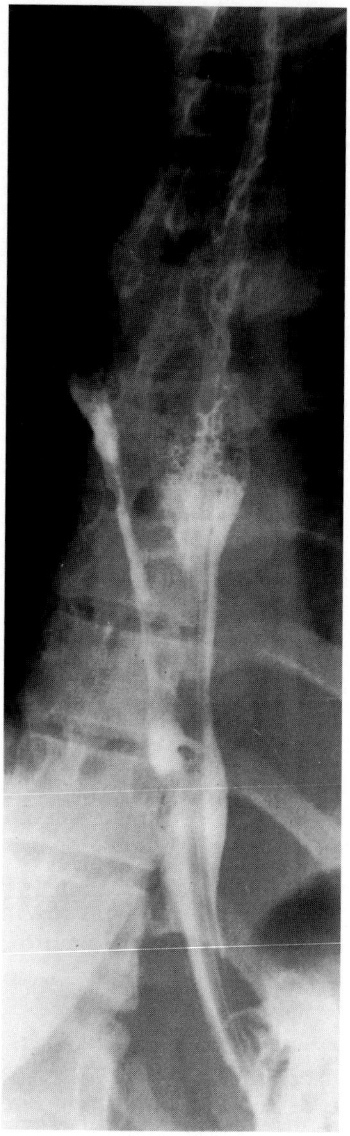

Fig. 20.21 Radiograph of a patient with instrumental perforation of the distal oesophagus, demonstrating leakage of the contrast material into the mediastinum.

Spontaneous perforation (Boerhaave syndrome)

The spontaneous perforation of an otherwise healthy oesophagus was first reported by Hermann Boerhaave in 1724.[220] He described the case of Baron von Wassenaer, the Grand Admiral of the Dutch Fleet, who suffered a lethal oesophageal perforation following an excessive meal which was terminated by self-induced vomiting. Since then more than 600 similar cases have been decribed.[221] However, misdiagnosis frequently occurs and it has been suspected that Boerhaave syndrome occurs more commonly than the literature suggests.[222] Most affected patients are middle-aged men who experience violent vomiting after heavy eating or alcohol intake or both. However, occasionally the syndrome has been observed in hyperemesis gravidarum,[223] during childbirth,[224] defecation[225] and seizures.[226] The common aetiological factor appears to be a sudden and violent increase in intraabdominal pressure. It has been proposed that such pressure changes preferentially occur when the upper oesophageal sphincter does not relax during the act of vomiting.[227] In any event the mechanism appears to be the same as that proposed for the Mallory-Weiss syndrome. The difference between the two diseases lies in the magnitude of intraluminal pressure elevation, which in Boerhaave's syndrome leads to a disruption not only of the mucosa, but all layers of the oesophageal wall.

More than 80% of all spontaneous perforations occur in the distal oesophagus and only a minority in the middle third.[221,228] In the distal oesophagus almost all lesions are located at the left posterior wall. Several explanations have been proposed for this preferential location. First, this area is characterized by a reduced number and size of the longitudinal smooth muscle fibres. Secondly, entrance of nerves and vessels into the oesophageal wall and the lack of buttressing structures such as the liver and aorta increase its distensibility, and thirdly, the abrupt anterior angulation of the oesophagus, due to the position of the diaphragm, may contribute to this weakness.[227,229,230] The laceration almost always runs in a longitudinal direction and extends between 2.5 and 6.0 cm (Fig. 20.22). A characteristic finding is that the length of the mucosal tear always exceeds that of the muscular rupture,[221] a fact that

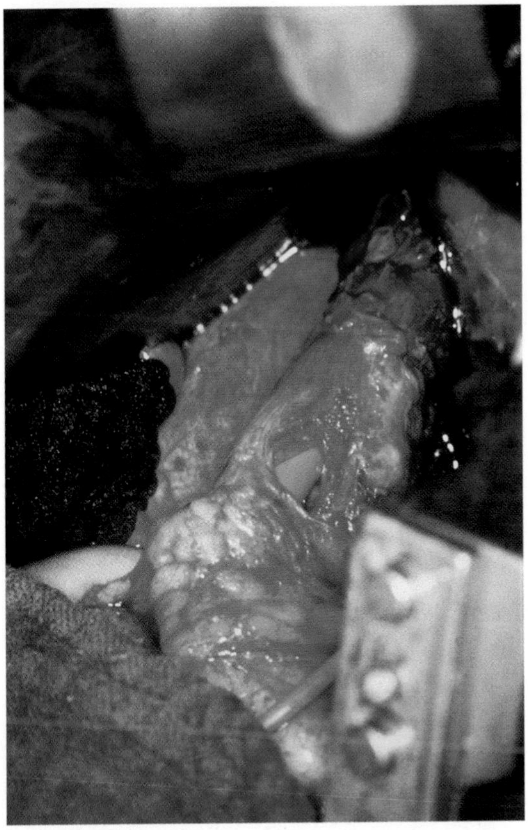

Fig. 20.22 Intraoperative view of a spontaneous perforation in the distal oesophagus. The transmural longitudinal tear is located immediately proximal to the diaphragm. (Reproduced with permission from Hirner et al 1982)

may be explained by differences in distensibility of both layers.

As in other forms of perforation the prognosis depends on the rapidity with which therapeutic measures are initiated. If surgery is performed within the first 12 hours, the mortality may be as low as 20%. Thereafter, a progressive increase in mortality occurs and reaches more than 95% in those who do not come to surgery.[231]

MOTILITY DISTURBANCES

The normal oesophageal function of transport of a swallowed bolus and the inhibition of its regurgitation is affected by a large number of neurological and muscular diseases. Depending upon their localization and severity, different syndromes may emerge, presenting as dysphagia, aspiration, chest pain or various combinations of these. Some abnormality may be confined to the striated muscle of the oesophagus, while others predominantly involve smooth muscle function. However, a clear separation of motor abnormalities according to the degree and localization of functional impairment is not always possible. For example, some diseases which preferentially alter the function of oesophageal striated muscle may also be associated with an inhibition of peristalsis in the distal part.[232,233] In contrast, 'smooth muscle disorders' such as scleroderma may occasionally affect oesophageal striated muscle.[234,235] Thus it appears more appropriate to classify oesophageal motor disorders according to their presumed aetiology rather than to the localization of the functional abnormalities.

Although the exact aetiologic mechanism for most oesophageal motor disorders remains unknown, a distinction between primary and secondary abnormalities can be made. In the former the oesophagus is the only organ known to be affected, while in the latter the functional abnormalities represent a manifestation of a systemic disease. A wide variety of such systemic illnesses[236] has been reported to cause oesophageal motor dysfunction (Table 20.1). However, only those with a morphological basis will be considered here.

Primary oesophageal motility disorders

In primary oesophageal motility disorders the functional and morphological changes are confined to the oesophagus or nerve structures that are directly related to this organ. Although a great variety of such motility disorders has been reported, that they interfere with the normal transport of a swallowed bolus is common to all. They may be caused by alterations in coordination and amplitude of oesophageal contractions, a compromised lower oesophageal sphincter function or a combination of these. In the mildest form, the 'nutcracker oesophagus', only the amplitude and duration of oesophageal contractions are affected, while patients with achalasia have serious alterations of both lower oesophageal sphincter function and oesophageal body contractions. Between these extremes several intermediate forms exist, which have been largely classified as 'nonspecific oesophageal motility disorders' and 'diffuse oesophageal spasm'.

Achalasia

Historical and clinical aspects

Although the first case description of a patient with a 'megaoesophagus' was in 1674 by Thomas Willis,[237] the term achalasia was first introduced into the medical literature by Sir Arthur Hurst in 1914.[238] He not only recognized that failure of the lower oesophageal sphincter to relax during deglutition is an important clinical feature of the disease, but also suggested that the lesion may be caused by a destruction of the normal oesophageal neuro-

Table 20.1 Causes of secondary oesophageal motility disorders. (Modified from Mukhopadyay A K, Graham D Y[236])

Neural, neuromuscular and primary muscular disorders	*Connective tissue disease*
Amyotrophic lateral sclerosis	Scleroderma
Pseudobulbar palsy	Systemic lupus erythematosus
Parkinsonism	Raynaud's phenomenon
Huntington's chorea	Polymyositis, dermatomyositis
Hepatolenticular degeneration (Wilson's disease)	Rheumatoid arthritis
Cerebrovascular disease	Mixed connective tissue disease
Brain stem involvement	
Multiple sclerosis	*Metabolic and endocrine disorders*
Poliomyelitis	Diabetes mellitus
Hereditary spinal ataxia (Friedreich's ataxia)	Thyrotoxicosis
Myotonic dystrophy	Myxoedema
Oculopharyngeal muscular dystrophy	Amyloidosis
Myasthenia gravis	Metabolic acidosis, alkalosis and electrolyte abnormalities
Familial dysautonimia (Riley-Day syndrome)	Alcoholism
Chronic intestinal pseudo-obstruction	
Botulism	*Miscellaneous*
	Presbyoesophagus
	Pernicious anemia
	Neoplastic invasion & distal oesophageal obstruction
	Monilial oesophagitis
	Sandifer syndrome
	Epidermolysis bullosa
	Radiation to the chest

anatomy. This view was soon substantiated by Rake's morphological descriptions of two autopsy cases in which ganglion cells of Auerbach's plexus were either reduced or completely absent.[239] The changes were not only observed at or near the oesophagogastric junction, but also in more proximal regions of the smooth muscle of the oesophagus. It has since been proven by physiological studies that achalasia is not only characterized by an impaired relaxation of a frequently hypertonic lower oesophageal sphincter, but also by a complete absence of peristalsis in the smooth muscle of the oesophagus.[240–242] These functional abnormalities lead to a marked delay of oesophageal emptying and clinically manifest as dysphagia, retrosternal fullness and pain as well as frequent episodes of regurgitation.

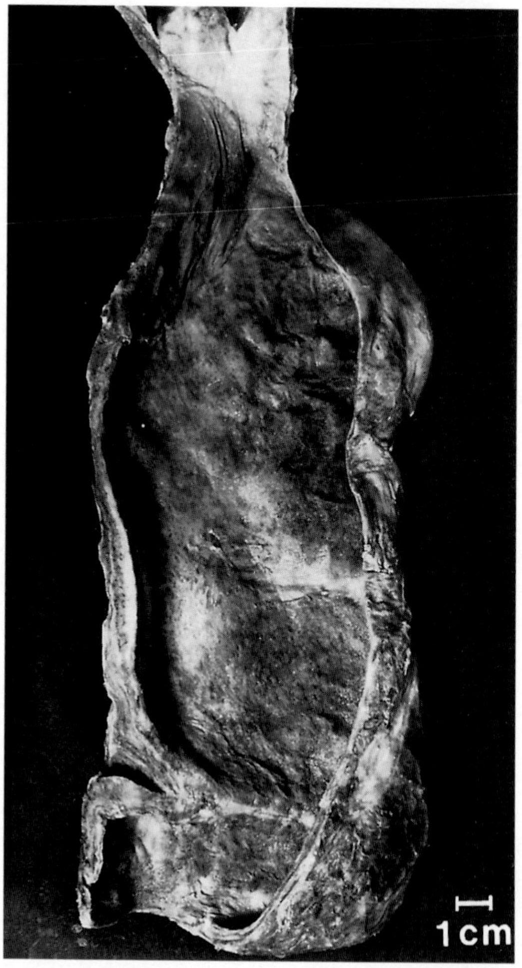

Fig. 20.23 Gross autopsy specimen of the oesophagus in a patient with achalasia. The oesophagus is dilated and elongated and its wall is markedly thickened. (Reproduced with permission from Borchard 1982)

Epidemiology

Achalasia is an uncommon disease with an estimated incidence of 1 case per 100 000 population.[243,244] Most patients in whom the diagnosis is made are between 35 and 45 years old. The disease is rare in children, and less than 5% of all cases present with symptoms before the age of 15 years.[245,246] Approximately a third of all newly diagnosed cases occur after the age of 60 years.[247] As it appears from the literature, the disease affects both sexes with similar frequency.

Aetiology

The exact cause of achalasia has not been established but several lines of evidence suggest that genetic factors as well as autoimmune and infectious processes may be involved in its pathogenesis. A genetic predisposition is supported by its occurrence among family members, a third of whom have consanguineous parents.[248] Although most of these cases appear to be transmitted via a rare autosomal recessive trait, a single family has been reported in whom an autosomal dominant mode of inheritance with complete penetrance was observed.[249] Further support for the importance of genetic factors comes from the observation that more than 80% of all patients with achalasia have the class II HLA antigen, DQw1.[250] Since class II antigens are frequently associated with autoimmune diseases, it could be speculated that a genetic predisposition exists that allows destruction of neural cells by an autoimmune process that is perhaps initiated by viral infections.

Pathology

Macroscopically, the most characteristic appearance of achalasia is an enormously dilated and lengthened oesophagus which tapers down at the level of the oesophagogastric junction (Fig. 20.23). In the distal oesophagus, the muscularis propria shows marked hypertrophy[251–253] that involves mainly the circular muscle (Fig. 20.24A) and occasionally presents as leiomyomatosis.[249] Such uneven distribution of muscular hypertrophy possibly explains the increased frequency of pulsion diverticula which usually occur in the distal oesophagus.[150] All of these changes seem to be a consequence of denervation[254] rather than a primary and independent phenomenon. If prolonged stasis of retained food has occurred, the oesophageal mucosa may reveal thickening, erosions and ulcerations. However, such findings are usually an indication of longstanding disease and may be totally absent in early cases of achalasia.

Since Rake's initial description[239] it has been confirmed by several authors that achalasia is associated with a loss of ganglion cells in the myenteric plexus.[254–259] These changes occur throughout the smooth muscle portion of the oesophagus, but are most pronounced in the dilated segment and show an inverse correlation with the degree of dilatation.[255,257,260] The layer of Auerbach's plexus is usually wider than normal, and neurons are replaced by fibrous tissue and small round cells (Fig. 20.24B). Since the latter resemble lymphocytes, these findings have often been interpreted as evidence for inflammation.[254,256] However, it appears that the majority of these mononuclear

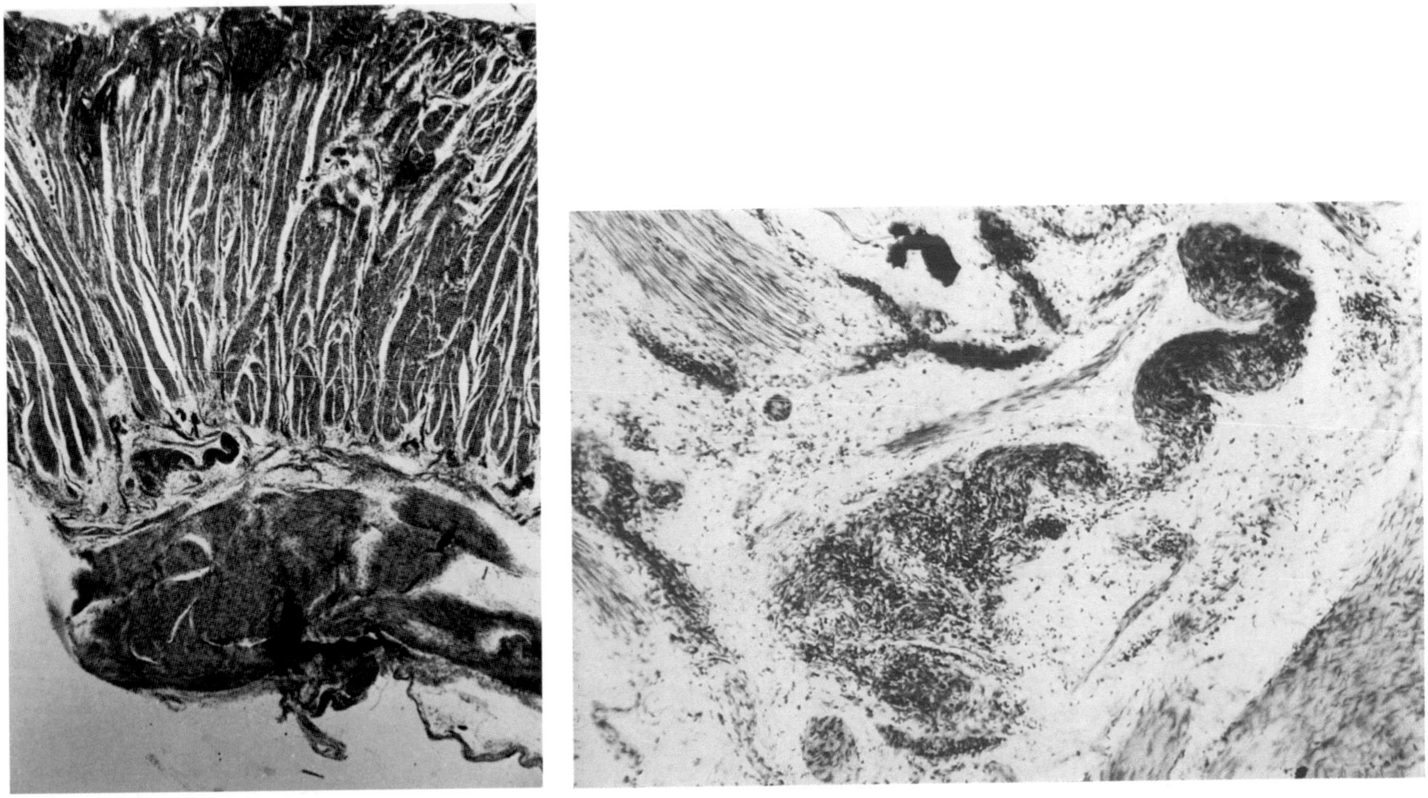

A B

Fig. 20.24 Longitudinal section of a surgical specimen from the distal oesophagus in a patient with achalasia. **A** The oesophageal wall shows marked thickening of the muscularis propria which is most pronounced in the circular muscle layers. **B** Greater magnification of the same specimen reveals a widened Auerbach's plexus in which neurones are largely replaced by fibrous tissue and small round cells.

cells are, in fact, satellite cells which are increased in number and difficult to distinguish from lymphocytes.[255] In addition, with the use of immunohistochemical methods, a varying degree of eosinophilic infiltration has been described and it was even suggested that such cells may contribute to the neuronal loss through activation and liberation of a highly toxic protein.[261]

In addition to marked alterations of the myenteric plexus, several authors have shown that such degenerative changes also affect the extrinsic innervation of the oesophagus. On light microscopy, occasional fragmentation of axons in parasympathetic nerves was observed.[262] Degeneration of fibres in the vagal trunk has also been demonstrated by electron microscopy.[263,264] Furthermore, Cassella et al described two cases of achalasia in which autopsy studies revealed a pronounced reduction in the number of cells in the dorsal motor nuclei of the vagus nerve.[265] These findings have led to speculation that the morphological alterations in the myenteric plexus are a secondary phenomenon and that denervation may be more extensive than previously recognized. Support for this theory comes from physiological studies which have shown that motor dysfunction is not confined to the oesophagus but may affect other organs such as the stomach[266] and the gallbladder.[267] In addition, a single study has shown that some patients with achalasia also exhibit a highly reduced ganglion cell count in the proximal stomach.[268] Thus, evidence is accumulating that the loss of myenteric ganglion cells is a consequence of centrally located neuronal degeneration rather than a primary phenomenon. The fibres predominantly affected are those releasing vasoactive intestinal polypeptide which, at the level of the cardia, are markedly reduced in patients with achalasia.[269] Since VIP possibly acts as the neurotransmitter for lower oesophageal sphincter relaxation,[270] this finding may explain the impaired sphincter relaxation that regularly occurs in this disease.

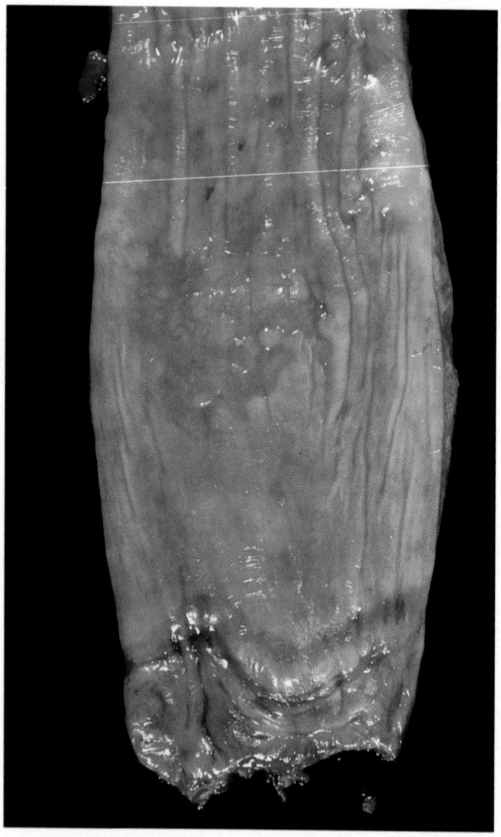

Fig. 20.25 Surgical specimen of the oesophagus in a patient with achalasia who was found to have early oesophageal cancer (eroded area in the upper oesophagus) during routine surveillance endoscopy.

Complications

Most complications in patients with achalasia are related to insufficient oesophageal emptying and prolonged stasis of retained food. Aspiration into the airways is frequent and up to 7.5% of patients have bronchopulmonary infections.[271] Rarely, bleeding may occur, and arises in varices that develop as a consequence of increased pressure in veins.[272]

The most serious complication, however, is the development of carcinoma in the dilated oesophagus. Autopsy studies have revealed a prevalence of oesophageal squamous carcinoma ranging from 20–29%.[273–275] With the exception of a single investigation,[276] clinical studies support these observations but have shown a somewhat lower prevalence ranging from 2–6%.[251,277] The most compelling evidence for an association between achalasia and squamous cell cancer comes from a recent long-term prospective investigation that found a 33 fold increase in the risk for oesophageal carcinoma.[278] If these tumors are detected by routine endoscopy in asymptomatic patients (Fig. 20.25) curative treatment may become possible.[278,279]

The localization of squamous cell cancers in patients with achalasia commonly corresponds to the level of the column of retained food in the middle oesophagus, but it may also occur in more distal and proximal regions.[280] Squamous carcinoma accounts for 90%, and less than 10% are adenocarcinomas.[251,277] The latter usually arise in Barrett's epithelium that may develop as a consequence of gastro-oesophageal reflux in patients who have been treated all too effectively by surgical myotomy.[281,282] The aetiological mechanism for squamous cell carcinoma remains unknown, but chronic irritation of the oesophageal mucosa resulting from stasis of retained food has been suggested as the most likely explanation. A similar mechanism may account for the increased occurrence of epithelial overgrowth and papillomas.

Diffuse oesophageal spasm and related motility disorders

Studies of oesophageal motor function have revealed a number of primary oesophageal motility disorders that can be clearly distinguished from achalasia. Clinically, they can closely resemble each other and a clear separation may not even be possible by the use of sophisticated manometric methods. That they are related is further strengthened by the fact that several forms of transition have been described.[283–286]

Diffuse oesophageal spasm (DOS)

Although diffuse oesophageal spasm is five times less frequent than achalasia[287] it represents one of the most thoroughly investigated primary oesophageal motility disorders. The characteristic clinical features of intermittent dysphagia and retrosternal pain were first described by Osgood in 1889.[288] Depending upon whether subsequent cases were described by radiologists, surgeons or gastroenterologists the disease was given numerous names including corkscrew oesophagus, curling, diffuse oesophageal spasm, giant or idiopathic muscular hypertrophy, segmental spasm as well as spastic pseudodiverticulosis. Among these, the term diffuse oesophageal spasm, which was introduced by Moersch and Camp in 1934,[289] has remained the most widely accepted and utilized. Although certain morphological features may suggest the presence of this disease, its final diagnosis depends upon the demonstration of characteristic alterations in oesophageal motor function. These have been defined manometrically as repetitive and simultaneous oesophageal body contractions in the presence of normal peristalsis and a normal relaxing lower oesophageal sphincter.[290]

The macroscopic appearance of autopsy specimens may resemble those of an achalasic oesophagus. Massive hypertrophy and hyperplasia of oesophageal smooth muscle has been the most impressive and consistent morphological finding.[291–296] Although the muscle thickening can involve all layers of the oesophageal wall it is usually most pronounced in the circular muscle. Lummert[297] has described several types of such muscular hypertrophy including diffuse, diffuse nodular and leimyomatous forms. These alterations may, in extreme cases, lead to enormous thickenings of the oesophageal wall reaching a diameter of more than 2 cm.[297] Diverticula have often been described as an associated abnormality, but most of these are transient radiological phenomena produced by abnormal oesophageal contractions (Fig. 20.26). However, if areas of muscular weakness occur in between the largely hypertrophied muscle, generating a high intraluminal pressure, true diverticula may result.[294,298–301] Although most of these macroscopic findings may also be observed in achalasia, dilatation of the oesophagus, which is a common feature of the latter disease, almost never occurs in diffuse oesophageal spasm.

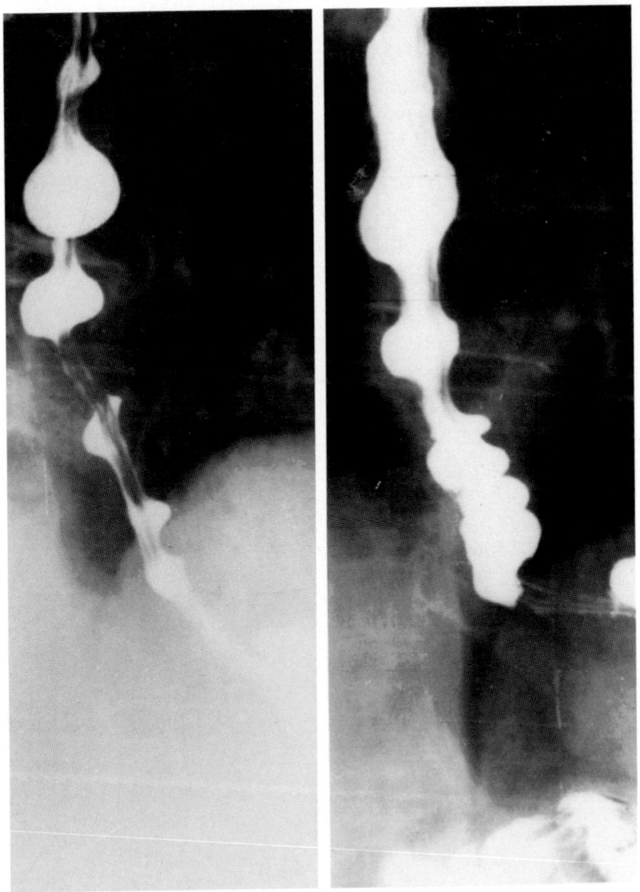

Fig. 20.26 Radiographic demonstration of diffuse oesophageal spasm. The powerful abnormal contractions lead to the formation of oesophageal pseudodiverticula.

In contrast to the findings in achalasia, most histological studies have not disclosed significant changes of Auerbach's plexus. A mild increase in the number of mononuclear cells has often been interpreted as evidence for inflammation,[292,293,298] but the possibility that these cells are Schwann cells remains. A single study of a small number of operative biopsy specimens described a neuronal loss in the myenteric plexus[260] and an electron microscopic investigation reported Wallerian degeneration of afferent vagal nerve fibres.[302] These findings, if confirmed by further studies, would support the theory that diffuse oesophageal spasm and achalasia are only different manifestations of the same disease process.

Related motility disorders

Many patients with oesophageal motility disorders, presenting with chest pain and dysphagia, can have their symptoms classified neither as achalasia nor as diffuse oesophageal spasm.[284] Such intermediate forms may either consist of oesophageal body dysfunction or an abnormality that is exclusively located at the level of the lower oesophageal sphincter. The most frequent abnormality of all of these has been defined as 'nutcracker oesophagus' or 'supersqueezer' and is characterized solely by an increase in duration and amplitude of oesophageal contractions.[303–305] With the exception of a single case in which thickening of the muscularis propria has been reported,[306] no morphological abnormality which would explain these functional disturbances seems to occur. However, a close association with achalasia and diffuse oesophageal spasm is suggested by the fact that transition into these disorders may occur.[285,286,307,308]

Secondary oesophageal motility disorders

If oesophageal motor dysfunction occurs in close association with a systemic illness or as a consequence of local pathology the motility disorder is referred to as secondary. In some of these illnesses the evidence for an association may only be circumstantial and are based upon clinical observations, while in others the structural abnormalities of the oesophagus are identical with those observed in other anatomic regions.

Secondary achalasia (pseudoachalasia)

2–4% of all motor abnormalities exhibiting the classical features of achalasia are due to neoplasms or benign diseases which either obstruct the oesophagus (Fig. 20.27) or interfere with its nerve supply.[309,310] That the motility disorder in these instances is caused by extrinsic disease and does not represent an association by chance is substatiated by the observation that the motor abnormalities usually resolve following treatment of the underlying illness.[311–313]

A wide variety of malignant and benign diseases (Table 20.2) have been reported to cause secondary achalasia[309–325] the most frequent of all being adenocarcinoma of the gastric cardia. The pathophysiology of the motor abnormality has not been precisely defined but suggested mechanisms include tumour infiltration of the myenteric plexus,[326,327] oesophageal obstruction causing neuromuscular damage,[313,316] and vagal dissection.[322] An alternative explanation was offered by the observation that patients with secondary achalasia may exhibit a massive eosinophilic infiltration of the muscularis propria and Auerbach's

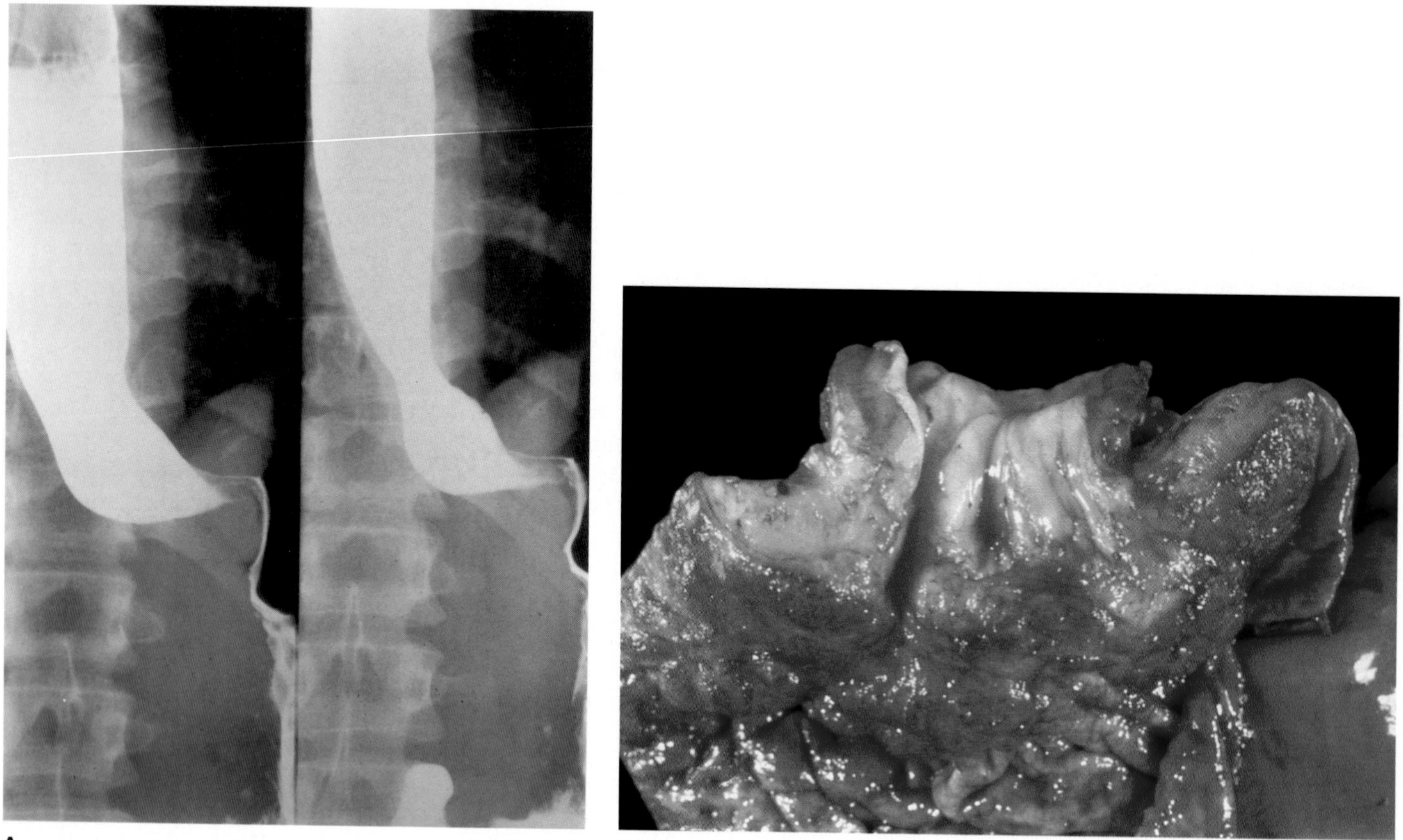

A B

Fig. 20.27 Secondary achalasia in a patient with low grade malignant lymphoma involving the gastric cardia. **A** Radiograph showing a dilated, aperistaltic oesophagus. **B** Surgical specimen from the same patient demonstrating infiltration of the oesophagogastric junction by malignant lymphoma.

Table 20.2 Causes of secondary achalasia.

Malignant tumours
Gastric adenocarcinoma
Lymphoma
Lung cancer
Hepatocellular carcinoma
Pancreatic adenocarcinoma
Oesophageal squamous cell carcinoma
Prostatic adenocarcinoma
Metastatic colon carcinoma
Mesothelioma
Benign lesions
Truncal vagotomy
Amyloidosis
Pancreatic pseudocyst
Lymphangioma

plexus.[328] Such activated eosinophils secrete a highly neurotoxic protein which leads to a reduction of neurotransmitters such as VIP and substance P, and in turn to a marked alteration in oesophageal motor function. A similar sequence of events was postulated by the same authors for the pathogenesis of primary achalasia.[261]

Megaoesophagus in Chagas' disease

An endemic form of megaoesophagus, which functionally and morphologically resembles achalasia, is commonly observed in certain parts of South America, with its highest incidence in central Brazil, Venezuela and northern Argentina.[329] The disease is caused by the protozoan haemoflagellate *Trypanosoma cruzi* and affects many hollow organs including the heart and gastrointestinal tract. Most gastrointestinal manifestations, among which dilatations of the oesophagus and colon are most frequent,[330] occur in the third and fourth decades of life as late manifestations of childhood infection.[331]

The functional abnormalities of Chagasic megaoesophagus are nearly identical to those of achalasia and consist of a complete absence of peristalsis in the smooth muscle of the oesophagus and an incomplete or absent relaxation of the lower oesophageal sphincter. However, hypertension of the lower oesophageal sphincter is less frequently observed, a finding that has been interpreted as evidence for more complete denervation occuring in patients with Chagas' disease.[332] Histological studies reveal marked degenerative changes of oesophageal smooth muscle and its innervation. The most notable feature is a decreased number of neurons in Auerbach's plexus. It has been estimated that the number of ganglion cells must be reduced to less than half to cause disturbances of oesophageal motor function and that the classical picture of aperistalsis develops only if more than 90% of the ganglion cell population is lost.[330] As in achalasia, the degenerative changes have not only been observed in Auerbach's plexus but also in fibres of the vagal trunk and in the dorsal motor nucleus of the vagus.[333] As a consequence of denervation, oesophageal smooth muscle hypertrophies and dilatation of the oesophagus occurs (Fig. 20.28), leading to the term megaoesophagus.

Although it has been firmly established that megaoesophagus of Chagas' disease is caused by a protozoan infection, the exact mechanism by which the morphological and functional alterations develop remains unknown. Theories to explain the selective destruction of autonomic innervation include a direct action of the parasite, destruction by local toxins, inflammation, allergy and ischaemia secondary to changes in the small arteries.[334] While these aetiological factors remain a matter of speculation, it appears likely that the increased incidence of oesophageal carcinoma in patients with Chagasic oesophagus is a consequence of stasis of oesophageal contents. As in achalasia, the frequency of this complication ranges in different series between 5 and 10%.[329,335]

Oesophageal motility disturbances in connective tissue disease

Progressive systemic sclerosis (PSS)

Visceral abnormalities are frequently found in scleroderma and may even precede or occur in the absence of skin changes. The first and most frequently affected internal organ is the oesophagus.[336] Up to 80% of all patients with scleroderma complain of oesophageal symptoms such as dysphagia and heartburn[234,337–340] and a similar proportion demonstrates a motor abnormality of the oesophagus if investigations are performed with sophisti-

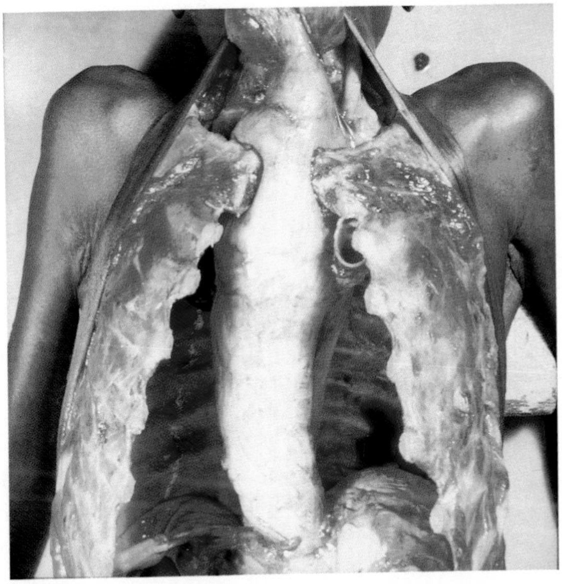

Fig. 20.28 Autopsy preparation from a patient with Chagas' disease demonstrating a massively dilated oesophagus. (Courtesy of Professor Dr Renato Alves de Godoy, Departmento de Clinica Medica, Faculdade de Medicina, Ribeirao Preto SP, Brasil)

cated diagnostic techniques.[233,337,340,341] Such studies reveal hypomotility, which predominantly affects the lower two thirds of the oesophagus including the lower oesophageal sphincter. Oesophageal contractions are markedly reduced in amplitude, and in advanced cases peristalsis may be entirely absent. Relaxation of the lower oesophageal sphincter is normal, but its resting tone is markedly decreased, leading to a high incidence of pathological reflux.[342] As a consequence of increased gastro-oesophageal reflux and poor oesophageal emptying, patients with scleroderma reveal an extraordinarily high incidence of oesophagitis, distal oesophageal strictures and Barrett's syndrome.[343]

Gross inspection of autopsy specimens show moderately dilated oesophagae with inflammatory mucosal changes in approximately half of them.[344] The inflammation is often severe and may have led to the development of longitudinal and annular strictures as well as Barrett's syndrome, which in turn may lead to the development of adenocarcinoma.[343,345] In rare instances atypical wide-mouthed diverticula may be found. Although histological proof is lacking, it has been suggested that such diverticula develop as outpouchings in diseased segments between intact strands of oesophageal smooth muscle.[346]

On histological examination the most prominent and consistent feature is smooth muscle atrophy, which occasionally leads to disappearance of the entire circular muscle coat.[337,344] Areas in which the muscle has atrophied are replaced by fibrous tissue. Intimal thickening and sclerosis of small arteries and arterioles within the oesophageal wall are also reported findings.[337,344] All of these changes are most prominent in the distal two thirds of the oesophagus, and despite the observation that motor dysfunction may occur in the proximal third, no structural abnormalities of oesophageal striated muscle have been reported.

With the exception of a mild increase in the number of round cells in Auerbach's plexus,[344] no histological abnormalities of the neural elements have been observed. However, these findings do not exclude the possibility that smooth muscle atrophy is only an associated event or even occurs as the consequence of neuronal damage. In fact, certain pieces of evidence exist that would support a neurogenic cause of oesophageal muscle dysfunction. First, the functional impairment often occurs prior to the development of muscular atrophy.[344] Secondly, there is a close association of motor abnormalities with the presence of Raynaud's phenomenon,[339,347,348] suggesting a common neurogenic cause. Finally, pharmacological studies have shown that the oesophageal smooth muscle responds abnormally to compounds that act indirectly through cholinergic nerves.[349] All of these observations support the theory that neural dysfunction may play a role in the aetiology of oesophageal motor abnormalities in scleroderma. A unifying but unproven concept for the functional and morphological changes in scleroderma of the oesophagus is that local ischaemia results in neural damage, which in turn causes smooth muscle atrophy.[349,350]

PSS-related collagen disorders

Oesophageal motility disturbances which are closely related to those occurring in scleroderma have also been described in patients with Raynaud's phenomenon, lupus erythematosus and mixed connective tissue disease. If investigated with sophisticated diagnostic techniques, approximately 20% of patients with lupus erythematosus, 40% with Raynaud's phenomenon and 60% with mixed connective tissue disease will have evidence of oesophageal smooth muscle dysfunction.[339,349,351,352] Although little is known of the pathogenesis of these abnormalities, in patients with Raynaud's phenomenon vascular spasm of oesophageal arterioles and abnormalities in serotonin degradation have been proposed as possible explanations.[353] The observation that some patients with oesophageal smooth muscle dysfunction in lupus erythematosus later develop features of scleroderma[339,351] suggests that these are transitional forms between both diseases. In contrast, the oesophageal manifestations of mixed connective tissue disease have features of scleroderma as well as polymyositis in that several patients show not only smooth muscle insuffiency but also upper oesophageal sphincter hypotension.[252] Finally, by definition, oesophageal motor disturbances regularly occur in the CREST syndrome which also consists of calcinosis, sclerodactylly and teleangiectasia. Although the disease usually runs a more benign and prolonged clinical course than scleroderma, its oesophageal manifestations may be more pronounced and occur with an even greater frequency.[343,354]

Dermatomyositis and polymyositis

20–30% of patients with dermatomyositis and polymyositis may have associated scleroderma.[355] In these cases oesophageal motor dysfunction affecting predominantly the smooth muscle may be present. However, in patients with 'pure' forms of polymyositis and dermatomyositis, both muscle types may be affected. Most patients with oesophageal manifestations complain of symptoms related to striated muscle involvement such as oropharyngeal dysphagia, nasal regurgitation and frequent episodes of laryngeal aspiration.[356,357] The most frequently reported finding in studies of motor function is a decreased amplitude of pharyngeal and proximal oesophageal contractions as well as weakness of the upper oesophageal sphincter.[358,359] However, more recent studies have shown that oesophageal smooth muscle may similarly be affected. A decrease in amplitude of distal oesophageal contractions may lead to impaired emptying and thus contribute to the frequently reported symptom of dysphagia.[357,360] Postmortem examinations have demonstrated a fragmentation of oesophageal striated muscle fibres with vacuolar, hyaline and granular changes.[361] Smooth muscle atrophy and fibrosis has only occasionally been reported.[362]

Muscular dystrophy

Oesophageal motor dysfunction may occur in three types of muscular dystrophy, namely myotonic, oculopharyngeal and Duchenne's muscular dystrophy. Although less than half of patients with myotonic muscular dystrophy complain of dysphagia, a motor abnormality can be demonstrated in all of them.[233,363–365] The most pronounced changes are a weakness of the upper oesophageal sphincter and poor peristaltic contractions. The oesophageal striated muscle is described as undergoing necrosis and regeneration. The fibres vary considerably in size and may show internalised nuclei, many of which are pyknotic.[233,366] In contrast, no evidence for degeneration or inflammation of oesophageal smooth muscle is found (Fig. 20.29).

Oculopharyngeal muscular dystrophy always involves the pharyngo-oesophageal junction. In addition to ptosis, by the age of 40 most patients also complain of oropharyngeal dysphagia which can lead to starvation and aspiration.[367] The most frequently reported functional abnormalities are a weakness of pharyngeal contractions and a diminished upper oesophageal sphincter pressure with prolonged relaxations.[368,369] Morphological studies in a single case revealed a variation in the size of striated muscle fibres and interstitial fatty infiltration.[370]

Duchenne's muscular dystrophy may occasionally involve gastrointestinal smooth muscle, including the oesophagus.[371,372] Autopsy studies have disclosed changes that are similar to progressive systemic sclerosis and consist of a replacement of smooth muscle fibres by collagen.[371] As a consequence oesophageal dilatation and diverticula may develop.

Chronic intestinal pseudo-obstruction

In chronic intestinal pseudo-obstruction there are invariably oesophageal abnormalities, and it has been suggested that the diagnosis becomes unlikely if oesophageal manometric studies prove to be normal.[373] Nine of 10 previously reported patients had marked oesophageal motor dysfunction consisting of aperistalsis, high amplitude oesophageal contractions and incomplete lower oesophageal sphincter relaxations.[373–375] The most significant finding in three cases studied at autopsy was a reduction in the number of neurons in Auerbach's plexus.[376,377] In silver stains deformed neurons with 'clubbed' dendrites and axonal swellings were observed. Thus it appears that oesophageal motor dysfunction is secondary to smooth muscle denervation.

Amyloidosis

In almost all patients with primary or secondary amyloidosis the gastrointestinal tract, including the oesophagus, is involved.[378] Oesophageal symptoms such as heartburn and dysphagia are common and are related to motor dysfunction.[379,380] Both striated and smooth muscle is affected and there may be weakness of both oesophageal sphincters as well as poor oesophageal peristalsis. In some cases abnormal oesophageal contractions and incomplete lower oesphageal sphincter relaxation resembling the motor pattern of achalasia may be observed.[323,381,382] It is therefore likely that the amyloid deposition not only leads to atrophy of striated and smooth muscle, but also interferes with their innervation.

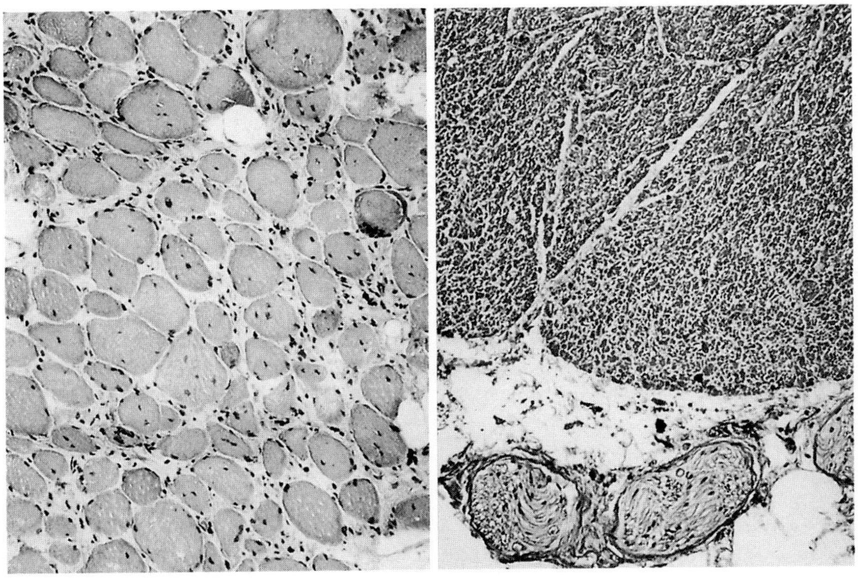

Fig. 20.29 Oesophageal striated (left) and smooth muscle (right) in a patient with myotonic muscular dystrophy. While smooth muscle appears normal, there is marked variation in the size of striated muscle fibres with internalization of nuclei and pyknotic clumps.

The amyloid deposition is mainly observed in its pericollagen or adventital form.[378,383] The extracellular homogenous, hyaline material is deposited around capillaries and in the outer layers of small and medium sized blood vessels. These changes may affect all layers of the oesophageal wall, but are most pronounced within the submucosa and muscularis propria. Massive infiltration of the latter is associated with degenerative changes in muscle fibres. Occasionally large areas of the oesophageal musculature may be replaced, leading to a loss of tone and dilatation of the entire organ (Fig. 20.30A,B). If amyloid is deposited in localized nodules, oesophageal obstruction which simulates neoplasia can result.[384,385] Only rarely is amyloid found in the myenteric plexus and nerve bundles are usually not infiltrated.[378] The mechanism by which neural dysfunction occurs is unknown, but ischemia of the neural elements is a possible explanation.

Diabetic neuropathy

Patients with diabetic neuropathy frequently exhibit a disturbance in oesophageal peristalsis. The most characteristic changes are spontaneous and multiphasic contractions which significantly interfere with oesophageal emptying.[386,387] The observation that the motility disturbance mainly affects the propagation of the peristaltic wave and is closely associated with the presence of a peripheral neuropathy[388] suggests that dysfunction of the autonomous nervous system is an important aetiological factor. Indeed, histological studies on autopsy material from patients with diabetes mellitus have disclosed a swelling and irregularity of the calibre of parasympathetic fibres within the myenteric plexus and trunks.[389] Although the number of neurons in the myenteric plexus appear normal, the number of non-neuronal cells is markedly increased.

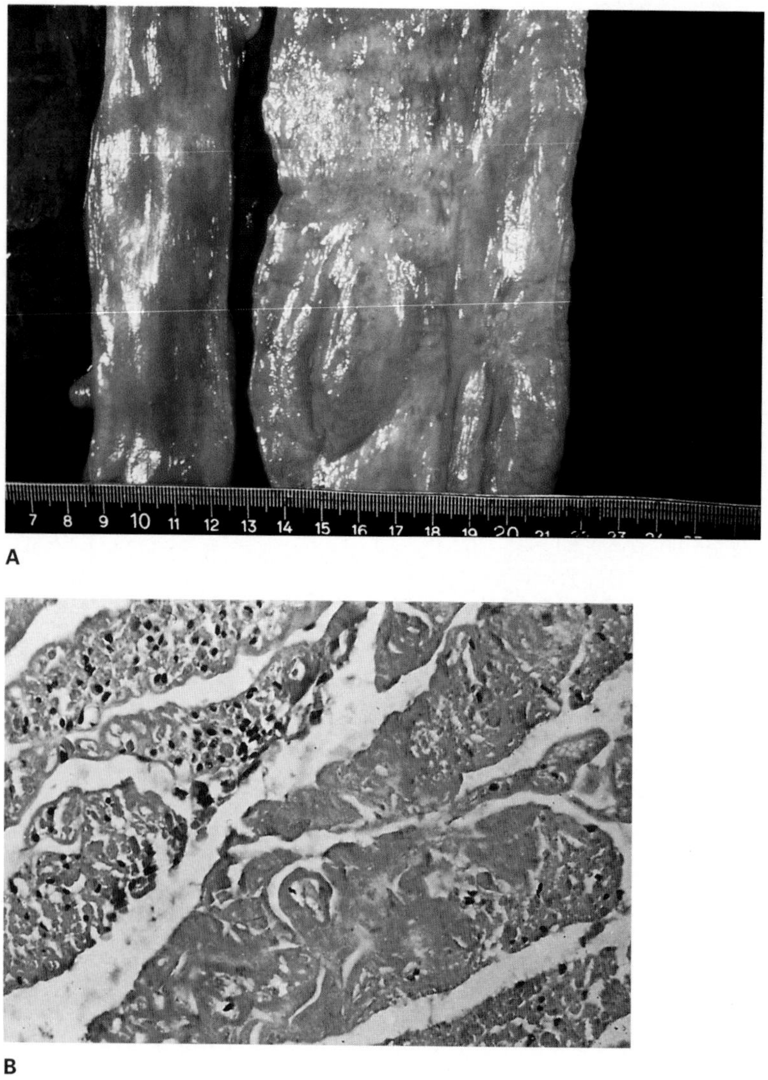

Fig. 20.30 Amyloidosis involving the oesophagus. **A** Gross autopsy specimen of a normal oesophagus (left) and an oesophagus in a patient with amyloidosis. Amyloid deposition has led to a marked dilatation of the entire oesophagus. **B** Histological examination of the same specimen reveals extensive amyloid deposition within the circular layer of oesophageal smooth muscle. Muscle fibres are largely replaced by homogenous hyaline material. (Courtesy of Dr H. D. John, Department of Pathology, University of Mainz, Germany)

A similar abnormality in oesophageal motor function may be demonstrated in patients with alcoholic neuropathy,[390] but it is not known whether these alterations have a morphological correlate.

Presbyoesophagus

Oesophageal motor function becomes abnormal with increasing age but controversy exists as to its nature. There is some evidence that peristalsis becomes disorganized[391] while in some cases a simple decrease in oesophageal contraction amplitude can be demonstrated.[392] In a histological study autopsy material from young persons was compared with that from elderly subjects but no evidence for oesophageal smooth muscle atrophy was found.[393] However, a quantitative analysis of the ganglion cell density in Auerbach's plexus revealed a significant decrease of the number of neurons, which is in keeping with previous observations.[255,394]

Radiation induced oesophageal motor dysfunction

Radiation to the mediastinum may cause oesophageal mucosal teleangiectasias with hyalinized vessel walls and injury to the muscularis propria.[395,396] As a consequence motor abnormalities may develop in the early post-treatment period as well as decades thereafter.[396,397] The functional abnormalities resemble those observed in scleroderma and consist in a marked reduction of the peristaltic amplitude.[396]

Idiopathic muscular hypertrophy

This unusual condition is frequently diagnosed only at autopsy and is symptomless (see Ch. 14).

REFERENCES

1. Liebermann-Meffert D. Chirurgische Anatomie des osophago-gastralen Ubergangssegmentes. Helv chir Acta 1980; 47: 667–677.
2. Liebermann-Meffert D. Anatomie des gastrooesophagealen Verschlussorgans. In: Blum AL, Siewert JR, eds. Refluxtherapie. Berlin: Springer Verlag, 1981; 10–39.
3. Eliska O. Phreno-oesophageal membrane and its role in the development of hiatal hernia. Acta Anat (Basel) 1973; 86: 137–150.
4. Dyer HH, Priedie RB. Incidence of hiatus hernia in asymptomatic subjects. Gut 1968; 9: 696–699.
5. Blum AL, Siewert JR. Hat die axiale Hiatushernie einen Krankheitswert? Schweiz med Wochenschr 1979; 109: 1977–1981.
6. Venkatachalam B, Dacosta LR, Beck IT. What is a normal esophagogastric junction? Gastroenterology 1972; 62: 521–527.
7. Killer-Walser R, Hess H, Wursch TG, et al. Fiberendoskopie und Radiologie bei Ulcus ventriculi, Magenkarzinom und Hiatushernie: Fragestellung, Zeitpunkt und Aussagekraft. Schweiz med Wochenschr 1979; 109: 3–6.
8. Dodds J, Stewart ET, Hodges D, et al. Movement of the feline esophagus associated with respiration and peristalsis. J Clin Invest 1973; 52: 1–13.
9. Siewert R, Rossetti M. Hiatushernien. In: Siewert R, Blum AL, Waldeck F, eds. Funktionsstorungen der Speiserohre. Berlin: Springer Verlag, 1976; 192–201.
10. Burkitt DP, James P . Low-residue diets and hiatus hernia. Lancet 1973; 1: 128–130.
11. Johnson HD. Active and passive opening of the cardia and its relation to the pathogenesis of hiatus hernia. Gut 1966; 7: 392–401.
12. Weiser HF, Lepsien G, Schattenman G, et al. Klinische Bedeutung der Hiatushernie. Zentralbl Chir 1978; 103: 20–29.
13. Walther B, DeMeester TR, Lafontaine E, et al. Effect of paraesophageal hernia on sphincter function and its implication on surgical therapy. Am J Surg 1984; 147: 111–115.
14. Pearson FG, Cooper JD, Ilves R, et al. Massive hiatal hernia with incarceration: a report of 53 cases. Ann Thorac Surg 1983; 35: 45–51.
15. Rossetti M, Geering P. Paraoesophagealer Magenvolvulus. Helv Chir Acta 1976; 43: 543–548.
16. Cohen S, Harris LD. Does hiatus hernia affect competence of the gastroesophageal sphincter? N Engl J Med 1971; 284: 1053–1056.
17. Rex JC, Andersen HA, Bartholomew LG. Esophageal hiatal hernia: A 10-year study of medically treated cases. JAMA 1961; 178: 271–274.
18. Wright RA, Hurwitz AL. Relationship of hiatal hernia to endoscopically proved reflux esophagitis. Dig Dis Sci 1979; 24: 311–313.
19. Mittal RK, Lange RC, McCallum RW. Identification and mechanism of delayed esophageal acid clearance in subjects with hiatus hernia. Gastroenterology 1987; 92: 130–135.
20. Sloan S, Kahrilas PJ. Impairment of esophageal emptying with hiatal hernia. Gastroenterology 1991; 100: 596–605.
21. Heine KJ, Mittal RK. Crural diaphragm and lower oesophageal sphincter as antireflux barriers. Gastroenterology International 1991; 4: 125–129.
22. Rossetti M. Les hernies hiatales. J Med Strasbourg 1976; 7: 29–30.
23. Allison PR. Hiatus hernia: a 20-year retrospective study. Ann Surg 1973; 178: 273–276.
24. Kunzli HF, Rossetti M. Inkarzerierter intrathorakaler Magenvolvulus als Komplikation asymptomatischer Hiatushernien. Helv Chir Acta 1971; 38: 262–264.
25. Tanner N. Chronic and recurrent volvulus of the stomach. Am J Surg 1968; 115: 505–515.
26. Cameron AJ. Incidence of iron deficiency anemia in patients with large diaphragmatic hernia: a controlled study. Mayo Clin Proc 1976; 51: 767–769.
27. Ozdemir IA, Burke WA, Ikins Ph M. Paraesophageal hernia: a life-threatening disease. Ann Thorac Surg 1973; 16: 547–553.
28. Gahagan T. Hiatal hernia without reflux. Arch Surg 1967; 95: 595–605.
29. Cameron AJ, Higgins JA. Linear gastric erosions. A lesion associated with large diaphragmatic hernia and chronic blood loss anemia. Gastroenterology 1986; 91: 338–342.
30. Windsor CWO, Collis JL. Anemia and hiatus hernia: experience in 450 patients. Thorax 1967; 22: 73–78.
31. Viard H, Klepping C, Barault JF, et al. Les ulceres du collet des hernies hiatales. Chirurgie 1977; 103: 518–531.
32. Davidson JS, Eadin MB. Gastric ulcer in association with a hiatal hernia. Lancet 1978; 2: 729–731.
33. Meredith HC, Seymour EQ, Vujic I. Hiatal hernia complicated by gastric ulceration and perforation. Gastrointest Radiol 1980; 5: 229–231.
34. Menguy. Surgical management of large paraesophageal hernia with complete intrathoracic stomach. World J Surg 1988; 12: 15–422.
35. Landreneau RJ, Johnson JA, Marshall JB, Hazelrigg SR, Boley TA, Curtis JJ. Clinical spectrum of paraesophageal herniation. Dig Dis Sci 1992; 37: 537–544.
36. Ingelfinger FJ, Kramer P. Dysphagia produced by a contractile

ring in the lower oesophagus. Gastroenterology 1953; 23: 419–430.
37. Schatzki R. The lower oesophageal ring. Long term follow-up of symptomatic and asymptomatic rings. AJR 1963; 90: 805–810.
38. Elwood PC, Jacobs A, Pitman RG et al. Epidemiology of the Paterson-Kelly syndrome. Lancet 1964; 2: 716–720.
39. Nosher JL, Campbell WL, Seaman WB. The clinical significance of cervical oesophageal and hypopharyngeal webs. Radiology 1975; 117: 45–47.
40. Clements JL, Cox GW, Torres WE et al. Cervical oesophageal webs — a roentgenanatomic correlation. AJR 1974; 121: 221–231.
41. Shauffer IA, Phillips HE, Sequeira J. The jet phenomenon: a manifestation of oesophageal web. AJR 1978; 129: 747–748.
42. Han SY, Mihas AH. Circumferential web of the upper oesophagus. Gastrointest Radiol 1978; 3: 7–9.
43. Kelly ML, Frazer JP. Symptomatic mid-esophageal webs. JAMA 1966; 197: 143–146.
44. Longstreth GF, Wolochow DA, Tu RT. Double congenital midesophageal webs in adults. Dig Dis Sci 1979; 24: 162–165.
45. Shifleet DW, Gilliam JH, Wu WC et al. Multiple esophageal webs. Gastroenterology 1979; 77: 556–559.
46. Seaman WB. The significance of webs in the hypopharynx and upper esophagus. Radiology 1967; 89: 32–38.
47. Shamma'a MH, Benedict EB. Esophageal webs. A report of 58 cases and an attempt at classification. N Engl J Med 1958; 259: 378–384.
48. Janisch HD, Eckardt VF. Histological abnormalities in patients with multiple esophageal webs. Dig Dis Sci 1982; 27: 503–506.
49. Pitman RG, Fraser GM. Post-cricoid impression on oesophagus. Clin Radiol 1965; 16: 34–39.
50. Friedland GW, Filly R. The postcricoid impression masquerading as an esophageal tumor. Am J Dig Dis 1975; 20: 287–291.
51. Gerami S, Cole FH. Dysphagia resulting from esophageal ring. Ann Thorac Surg 1970; 10: 223–226.
52. Ikard RW, Rosen HE. Midesophageal web in adults. Ann Thorac Surg 1977; 24: 355–358.
53. Waldman HK, Turnbull A. Esophageal webs. AJR 1957; 78: 567–573.
54. Kelley ML, Murtaugh J, McCarty Jr WC. Reduplication of the esophagus. Presenting as midesophageal web. JAMA 1968; 204: 171–173.
55. Goldenberg IS, Smith H. Congenital esophageal web. Report of a case. J Thorac Cardiovasc Surg 1961; 41: 733–736.
56. Johns BEA. Developmental changes in the oesophageal epithelium in man. J Anat 1952; 86: 431–442.
57. Kelly AB. Spasm of entrance to oesophagus. J Laryngol Otol 1919; 34: 285–289.
58. Paterson D . Clinical type of dysphagia. J Laryngol Otol 1919; 34: 289–291.
59. Vinson PO. Hysterical dysphagia. Minn Med 1921; 5: 107–108.
60. Waldenstrom J, Hallen L. Iron and epithelium. Some clinical observations. Acta Med. Scand (Suppl.) 1938; 90: 380–405.
61. Waldenstrom J, Kjellberg SR. The roentgenological diagnosis of sideropenic dysphagia (Plummer-Vinson's Syndrome). Acta Radiol 1938; 20: 618–638.
62. Anderson HA, Sanderson R. Webs, rings and rare types of esophagitis. In: Payne S, Olsen AM, eds. The esophagus. Philadelphia: Lea and Febiger, 1974: pp 147–157.
63. Chisholm M, Ardran GM, Callender ST et al. Follow-up study of patients with post-cricoid webs. QJ Med 1971; 40: 409–420.
64. Chisholm M, Srdran GM, Callender ST et al. Iron deficiency and autoimmunity in post-cricoid webs. QJ Med 1971; 40: 421–433.
65. Kramer P. Progress in Gastroenterology. The esophagus. Gastroenterology 1965; 49: 439–463.
66. Jacobs A, Kilpatrick GS. The Paterson-Kelly syndrome. Br Med J 1964; 2: 79–82.
67. Wright R, Whitehead R, Wangel AG, Salem SN, Schiller KFR. Autoantibodies and microscopic appearance of gastric mucosa. Lancet 1966; 1: 618–621.
68. Blendis LM, Sahay BM, Kreel L. The aetiology of 'sideropenic' web. Br J Radiol 1965; 38: 112–115.
69. Godtfredson E. Relation between Sjogren's disease, the Plummer-Vinson syndrome and ariboflavinosis. Acta Opthalmol 1947; 25: 95.
70. Jones RF Mc N. Paterson-Brown-Kelly syndrome. J Laryngol Otol 1961; 75: 529–561.
71. Entwistle CC, Jacobs A. Histological findings in the Paterson-Kelly syndrome. J Clin Pathol 1965; 18: 408.
72. Savilathi M. On the pathologic anatomy of the Plummer-Vinson syndrome. Acta Med Scand 1946; 125: 40.
73. Suzman MM. Syndrome of anemia, glossitis and dysphagia. Arch Intern Med 1933; 51: 1.
74. Ahlbom HE. Pradisponierende Faktoren fur Plattenepithelkarzinom in Mund, Hals und Speiserohre. Eine statistische Untersuchung am Material des Radiumhemmets, Stockholm. Acta Radiol 1937; 18: 163–185.
75. Wynder EL, Hultberg S, Jacobsson F et al. Environmental factors in cancer of the upper alimentary tract. A Swedish study with special reference to Plummer-Vinson (Paterson-Kelly) syndrome. Cancer 1957; 10: 470–487.
76. Goyal RK, Glancy JJ, Spiro HM. Lower esophageal ring (second of two parts). N Engl J Med 1970; 282: 1355–1364.
77. Lovy MR, Levine JS, Steigerwald JC. Lower esophageal rings as a cause of dysphagia in progressive systemic sclerosis — coincidence or consequence? Dig Dis Sci 1983; 28: 780–783.
78. Weaver GA. Upper esophageal web due to a ring formed by a squamocolumnar junction with ectopic gastric mucosa (another explanation of the Paterson-Kelly, Plummer-Vinson syndrome). Dig Dis Sci 1979; 24: 959–963.
79. Wolf BS, Marshak RH, Som ML. Peptic esophagitis and peptic ulceration of the esophagus. AJR 1958; 79: 741–759.
80. Hillemeier C. Touloukian R, McCallum R et al. Esophageal webs: a previously unrecognized complication of epidermolysis bullosa. Pediatrics 1981; 67: 678–682.
81. Mauro MA, Parker LA, Hartley WS, Renner JB, Mauro PM. Epidermolysis bullosa: Radiographic findings in 16 cases. Am J Radiol 1987;149: 925–927.
82. Benedict EB, Lever WF. Stenosis of esophagus in benign mucous membrane pemphigus. Ann Otol Rhinol Laryngol 1952; 61: 1121–1133.
83. Lever WF. Pemphigus and Pemphigoid. Springfield, Illinois: CC Thomas, 1965.
84. McDonald GB, Sullivan KM, Schuffler MD et al. Esophageal abnormalities in chronic graft-versus-host disease in humans. Gastroenterology 1981; 80: 914–921.
85. Templeton FE. X-ray examination of the stomach: a description of the roentgenologic anatomy, physiology and pathology of the esophagus, stomach and duodenum. Chicago: University of Chicago Press, 1944.
86. Schatzki R, Gary JE. Dysphagia due to a diaphragm like localized narrowing in the lower esophagus ('lower esophageal ring'). AJR 1953; 70: 911–922.
87. Kramer P. Frequency of the asymptomatic lower esophageal contractile ring. N Engl J Med 1956; 254: 292–294.
88. Bugden WF, Delmonico JE Jr. Lower esophageal web. J Thorac Surg 1956; 31: 1–18.
89. Harris LD, Kelly JE Jr., Kramer P. Relation of the lower esophageal ring to the esophagogastric junction. N Engl J Med 1960; 263: 1232–1235.
90. Mendl K, Evans CJ. Incomplete lower esophageal diaphragm. Br J Radiol 1962; 35: 165–171.
91. Postlethwait RW, Sealy WC. Experience with the treatment of 59 patients with lower esophageal web. Ann Surg 1967; 165: 786–795.
92. Scharschmidt BF, Watts HD. The lower esophageal ring and esophageal reflux. Am J Gastroenterol 1963; 69: 544–549.
93. Wilkins EW Jr, Bartlett MK. Surgical treatment of the lower esophageal ring. N Engl J Med 1963; 268: 461–464.
94. Goyal RK, Glancy JJ, Spiro HM. Lower esophageal ring (first of two parts). N Engl J Med 1970; 282: 1298–1305. 104–105
95. Goyal RK, Bauer JL, Spiro HM. The nature and location of lower esophageal ring. N Engl J Med 1971; 284: 1175–1180.
96. Johnston JH, Griffin JC. Anatomic location of the lower esophageal ring. Surgery 1967; 61: 528–534.

diospyrobezoar, due to eating persimmons or date fruit, which is a common custom in parts of North America and Isreal.[8] This fruit contains a tannin which, in contact with gastric acid, produces a sticky coagulum which traps pulp and seeds to form a bezoar. Any rapidly eaten, ill-chewed fruit or vegetable presents a risk, especially in patients with a gastrojejunostomy, when the mass can easily pass into the jejunum.

Trichobezoars, or hairballs, are composed of remarkable quantities of swallowed hair which enmesh food, and are encased in a mucoid coat. They are often of long standing, grow slowly and acquire the shape of the stomach. Extensions may occur into small bowel, and these can be difficult to extract when gastrotomy has to be undertaken to extract the bezoar for obstructive symptoms. By this time most trichobezoars are palpable. The underlying habit of trichophagia may be difficult to eradicate.

A peculiar form of concretion is seen in furniture finishers who drink a mixture of shellac and alcohol. The resinous shellac agglutinates when water is swallowed to form a solid mass, and this gradually grows as the patient takes further draughts of the shellac and alcohol mixture, followed by a drink of water.

Foreign bodies are usually swallowed by infants, the mentally retarded, or by prisoners hoping for a spell in a hospital bed. They form a highly diverse group, and many pass through the intestinal tract and are voided per rectum. Spoons and forks, and plastic sheeting, are more likely to remain in the stomach.

Yeast balls due to the proliferation of *Candida albicans* in vagotomized or gastrectomized patients living in Scandinavia have been described.[9]

Acute dilatation of the stomach

In the earlier years of this century surgeons were familiar with the patient who, following major abdominal surgery or injury, collapsed some 48 hours afterwards, became distended and began to vomit dark brown or black fluid: gastric aspiration then yielded as much as 5 l of this fluid, and much gas. The fluid was produced by gastric hypersecretion, with some bleeding, and this rapid loss of extracellular fluid produced the hypovolaemic shock. This complication was much feared and carried a mortality of about 40%. Nowadays it is rarely seen, probably because of the widespread use of nasogastric suction after major abdominal surgery, less toxic anaesthetics and better understanding of fluid and electrolyte balance. Nevertheless, its origin remains obscure.

A few postoperative cases still occur and because of their rarity and potential gravity need to be watched for. The 'body cast syndrome' has been known for a long time: acute dilatation coming on a day or two after a patient has been placed in a plaster bed or hip spica.[10] It is seen from time to time when a patient with anorexia nervosa, or a prisoner of war who has been on a meagre diet for a long time, eats more than is wise.[11,12] There is a risk of gastric rupture in these patients.[12] Acute dilatation occasionally complicates blunt abdominal trauma, when aspiration of the gas and fluid from the tense stomach can produce dramatic improvement in the patient's condition.[13]

Rupture of the stomach

The mobile stomach, protected by the thoracic cage, is rarely injured by blunt abdominal trauma, but not infrequently involved in penetrating injuries. Stabbings tend to affect the upper abdomen, and liver and stomach are the viscera most often injured.

The other ruptures of the stomach are described as 'spontaneous' and are very unusual. Most have followed excessive eating or drinking, sometimes associated with gastric outlet obstruction. Some cases of acute gastric dilatation go on to rupture and there are a few reports of rupture following the use of sodium bicarbonate to relieve indigestion, which are due to excessive release of carbon dioxide.

Perforation of the stomach in the newborn is a recognized cause of neonatal peritonitis, and is thought to be due to dehiscence of a congenital weakness, usually sited on the greater curvature.

SMALL INTESTINE

Obstruction

In 1884 Frederick Treves wrote a review of the many causes of intestinal obstruction which requires little amendment 100 years later. He ended with a plea to surgeons to be much readier than they had been to operate for intestinal obstruction. In the following year Thomas Bryant established the fundamental differences between stangulating and nonstrangulating obstruction, but it was in 1896 that John B. Murphy gave the first clear description of 'adynamic ileus'.

Since then, there have been innumerable papers published on the subject and the results of intestinal obstruction can be classified under four main headings.

1. Loss of alimentary secretions. The normal adult secretes 7–9 l of gastrointestinal juice each day, and voids only approximately 100 ml in faeces. Obstruction of the intestine interferes with this process of reabsorption. In a high jejunal obstruction the secretions of stomach, duodenum, pancreas and biliary tree will continue to be produced and will be lost in copious vomiting, but there will be little distension. In a low ileal obstruction the small bowel will gradually fill and distend with the gastric and intestinal secretions, and as much as 2 l of fluid may be

sequestrated in the distended small bowel before much vomiting occurs. Only minimal reabsorption of water occurs in the small intestine.

2. Distension. In all except high jejunal obstructions the bowel is distended with fluid secretions and swallowed air, which is reflected in the classical air/fluid levels seen in erect abdominal X-rays. The pressure rises within obstructed bowel, reaching 8–10 cm water in small bowel.[14] However, in distal colon obstructions, with a competent ileo-caecal valve, the pressure can rise to as much as 25 cm water and can, over a time, produce ischaemic changes, first in the mucosa but later involving the muscular wall, especially in the caecum which is particularly liable to disruption.[14]

3. Bacterial growth. The normal jejunum contains relatively few viable bacteria, but the population of aerobes and anaerobes rises steadily in samples taken progressively lower down the ileum. When small bowel is obstructed there is a rapid and large rise in bacterial counts above the blockage, with aerobes, especially coliforms, outnumbering anaerobes.[15] In large bowel, which normally has an enormous bacterial population, this also increases substantially in obstruction. This bacterial multiplication means that any contamination of the peritoneal cavity, either by perforation, or spillage during operation, constitutes a virulent inoculum.

4. Intestinal strangulation. The patient with strangulated bowel suffers all three of these effects, but additionally is exposed to the hazard of an impaired flow of blood to the strangulated gut.

The majority of strangulations involve bowel and its mesentery being caught under a fibrous adhesive band, or trapped by the narrow neck of a hernia. Generally this causes immediate venous occlusion and with continued arterial inflow into the strangulated loop a progressive venous engorgement occurs until finally there is interstitial haemorrhage, and useful arterial perfusion ceases. At some stage, depending on the time and the completeness of venous occlusion, viability of the bowel wall is lost. Mucosa is the most delicate tissue, and cannot survive much more than 4 hours of ischaemia. If the blood supply of the ileum of dogs is cut off for 6 hours and then re-established, most survive but fibrotic narrowing of the area develops.

Occlusion for more than 8 hours is followed by perforation and death from peritonitis.[16]

It has to be remembered that the bacterial population of faeces within a strangulated loop continues to multiply. This has an important effect, for, by potentiating the action of simple ischaemia on the gut wall, proteolysis is speeded up and an exudate is produced which, when shed into peritoneum, is highly toxic. Evidence suggests that a Gram-negative bacteraemia is responsible for most deaths in strangulating intestinal obstruction.[17]

On the rare occasions when a considerable length of bowel is strangulated, e.g. in mid-gut volvulus, a further important effect of strangulation is seen. With the venous drainage of the loop obstructed and arterial inflow continuing, as much as 50% of the blood volume can accumulate in the congested mesentery, causing severe hypovolaemic shock.

The incidence of the many different causes of intestinal obstruction show wide variations. When Treves was studying intestinal obstruction in the 1880s, strangulated hernias were much the commonest cause. In 1932 a review of 6000 British patients[18] showed that 55% had an obstructed external hernia, 25% had an adhesive or band obstruction and in 17% obstruction was due to malignant disease. As more and more individuals require a laparotomy whilst others have an elective hernia repair, the incidence of adhesive obstruction in Britain had risen by 1984[19] to 35–40%, large bowel carcinoma and obstructed hernias each caused 16–18%, and inflammatory bowel disease caused approximately 14%.

In countries with a less developed health service obstructed external hernias remain the principal cause of obstruction. In West Africa, for instance, approximately two-thirds of all obstructions are strangulated hernias,[20] adhesions account for only 10% and 33% of patients require a resection of gangrenous bowel; obstruction due to malignant disease is very unusual. In Eastern Europe and the Middle East the incidence is again different, with volvulus of the sigmoid colon producing 25–30% of all obstructions.[21]

The other major form of intestinal obstruction, known variously as neurogenic, adynamic or paralytic ileus, is due not to a mechanical blockage but to absence of normal peristaltic activity. It is most often secondary to generalized peritonitis.

Adhesions and bands

Some 9 out of 10 patients with an adhesive or band obstruction of small intestine have had a previous laparotomy.[22] Virtually every patient who has the peritoneum opened will form fibrinous adhesions between loops of bowel and between bowel and abdominal wall and other viscera. These adhesions are in many ways beneficial, limiting inflammatory processes, sealing anastomoses and enveloping ischaemic areas.[23] After about 8 days a process of fibrinolysis commences and most or all of these adhesions disappear. At appendicectomy, some 2 months after the conservative treatment of an appendicular abscess, there may be no sign of any adhesions. In some patients, possibly sensitive to stomach powder or gauze,[24] adhesions remain, whilst others have an intrinsic tendency to reform adhesions, even after operations to relieve adhesive obstructions.[25] Some operations, especially in the pelvis, carry a particular tendency to later adhesive obstruction.

So far, many experiments to prevent adhesion after laparotomy have failed to demonstrate a method which is safe as well as effective.[26]

About 10% of patients with an adhesive obstruction have never had a laparotomy. Some date from a previous inflammatory episode, e.g. untreated appendicitis, or they have a congenital band, e.g. a fibrous band connecting the umbilicus to a Meckel's diverticulum (persistent vitello-intestinal duct). Others have spontaneous adhesions of omentum or appendices epiploicae.

Adhesive obstructions due to fibrinous adhesions which kink the small bowel occur in the 2 weeks after laparotomy, but these usually settle as fibrinolysis occurs.

Late adhesive obstruction may occur at any time up to 20 or more years after laparotomy. A number of these resolve if the bowel is decompressed by starving the patient, applying nasogastric suction and giving fluids intravenously. The great concern of the surgeon is to identify promptly the patient who has a strangulated loop, caught under a rigid fibrous band: this can be difficult and is a classical problem in surgical management. Approximately 40% of all adhesive obstructions are strangulations[27] so patients treated conservatively require the closest supervision.

Abdominal hernias

The great majority of hernias which cause intestinal obstruction are visible or palpable herniations through the abdominal wall. Approximately 5% of all external hernia operations are performed as an emergency, and roughly equal numbers of inguinal and femoral hernias present with obstruction, although elective repairs of the former greatly exceed the latter. Males with an inguinal hernia outnumber females by about 6 to 1, whilst females with a femoral hernia outnumber the males by 5 to 1. Strangulated external hernias are seen throughout life. Irreducible and obstructed inguinal hernias are common in boys during the first year of life. They are then very unusual until about the age of 40, and the incidence rises sharply after 60 years to reach a peak between 70 and 76 years of age.[28]

The site of strangulation is almost always the neck of a femoral hernial sac, which is the point at the entrance to the femoral ring where the herniation broke through the peritoneum. In inguinal hernia the constriction may be at the neck, at the deep abdominal ring, but is often at the external abdominal ring.

A few inguinal hernias reduce with elevation of the legs and buttocks but most inguinal and all femoral obstructed hernias require urgent exploration because it is impossible to decide on clinical examination whether the loop is strangulated.

Richter's hernia is an abdominal hernia in which only part of the circumference of the bowel wall is incarcerated: consequently obstruction is not complete. Littre's hernia is any hernia containing a Meckel's diverticulum.

Paraumbilical hernia. This is the site of approximately 10% of strangulated hernias. They are important because these herniae are large, and occur mostly in elderly and obese patients in whom the signs of obstruction are often equivocal.

Incisional hernias. Once common, these are becoming increasingly unusual because much attention has been directed over the past 10 years to the sound repair of abdominal incisions. Burst abdomen is now a rarity and late dehiscence of an incision is uncommon, now that most incisions are securely closed with a non-absorbable suture instead of catgut. When strangulation occurs the same problems may arise as in paraumbilical hernias.

Obturator hernia. This is not visible, is rarely palpable, and is anyway very uncommon, so the occasional case of strangulation of bowel is usually only recognized at laparotomy for small bowel obstruction. Howship's classical symptom of this hernia is due to pressure on the obturator nerve, which is compressed by the hernia as it emerges through the foramen in the obturator membrane.

Internal hernias. Internal hernias of the abdominal cavity are numerous, but only rarely the site of small bowel obstruction. Much the most important are the various forms of diaphragmatic hernia. Some of these are congenital defects (e.g. the foramen of Bochdalek), others are the consequence of penetrating or blunt abdominal injuries, and a few are postoperative. All share the feature of being invisible and causing somewhat obscure abdominal and respiratory symptoms. Diagnosis may be delayed, which may have significant consequences because the incidence of strangulation is high.

Paraduodenal hernias. These are occasionally seen and are due to abnormalities of the rotation of the midgut which takes place at 8–11 weeks of foetal life. These are illustrated in Figures 21.4 and 21.5. A loop of small bowel may prolapse and strangulate or kink at the foramina where bowel enters and leaves the retroperitoneal sac. Other internal hernias are described around the ileocaecal valve, at the foramen of Winslow and alongside the bladder.

Iatrogenic hernias. These include parastomal herniations at the point where a colostomy or an ileostomy penetrates the abdominal wall and those which occur at defects in the abdominal wall which follow laparoscopy and peritoneal dialysis. Sometimes a loop of small bowel herniates through the space between colon and the afferent and efferent loops of an antecolic gastrojejunostomy.

Volvolus of small bowel

This is a rare cause of small bowel obstruction in Western Europe, North America and Australasia but is the cause

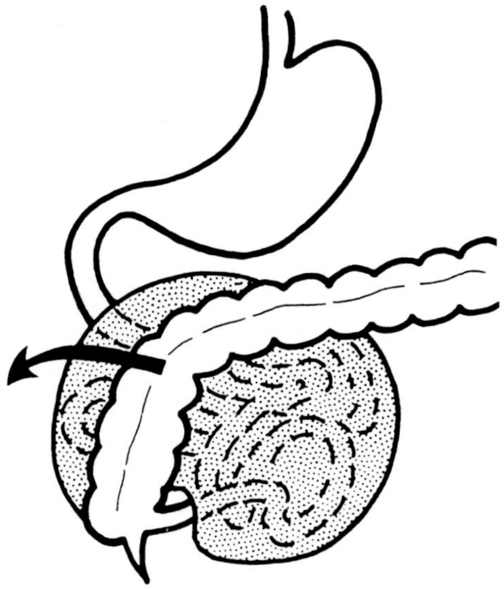

Fig. 21.4 Right paraduodenal hernia. Rotation of the prearterial loop of the midgut is incomplete and, as the postarterial loop migratges to the right (arrow), the small bowel is covered by an expanded ascending colon.

of 15–30% of obstructions in Iran, Northern India and Kenya.[29] These patients are mostly healthy farmers who work in the fields all day and return to a large meal in the evening which contains much whole grain flour. This passes speedily into the small bowel, to which it imparts a rotatory force.[30] At laparotomy the rotated loops are heavy with 1–2 l of thick undigested food.

Most cases of small bowel volvulus are spontaneous, but in a few a congenital malrotation or non-rotation means that the bowel hangs on a relatively unattached mesentery, and so is liable to volvulus.

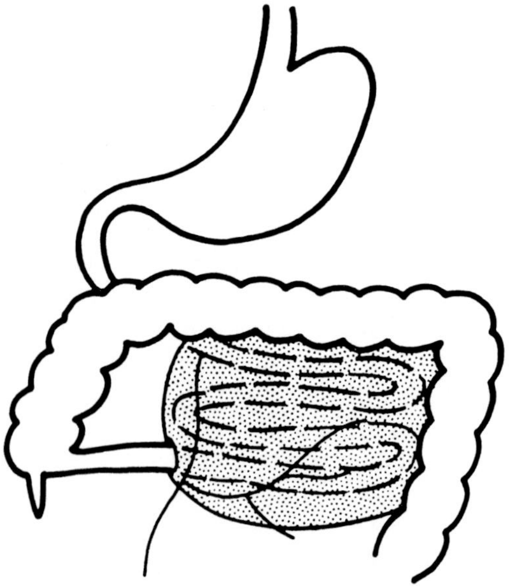

Fig. 21.5 Left paraduodenal hernia. The prearterial midgut loop has invaginated into the descending mesocolon, behind the inferior mesenteric vein, and is covered by the mesocolon.

A feature of small bowel volvulus is the severe pain and collapse suffered by the patient. The venous return of most of the small bowel is occluded by the twist in the mesentery whilst arterial perfusion continues and as much as 50% of the circulating blood volume is sequestrated.

Fortunately only a minority of patients require a major resection for gangrene.

Ileosigmoid knot. This is a peculiar form of volvulus, largely confined to the African continent.[31] The lower ileum winds itself around the root of the sigmoid loop (Fig. 21.6). As a consequence ileum becomes strangulated, and the sigmoid loop often becomes ischaemic also. There is no explanation for this curious syndrome, or for its geographical localization.

Stenosis

Some 15% of small bowel obstructions are due to intramural disease, and this may be inflammatory, neoplastic or iatrogenic in origin. Most patients present with a gradual onset of recurrent central abdominal pain, worse after meals, so at this stage the symptoms suggest peptic ulceration. Later, abdominal distention and visible intestinal peristalsis indicates the true state of affairs. Some

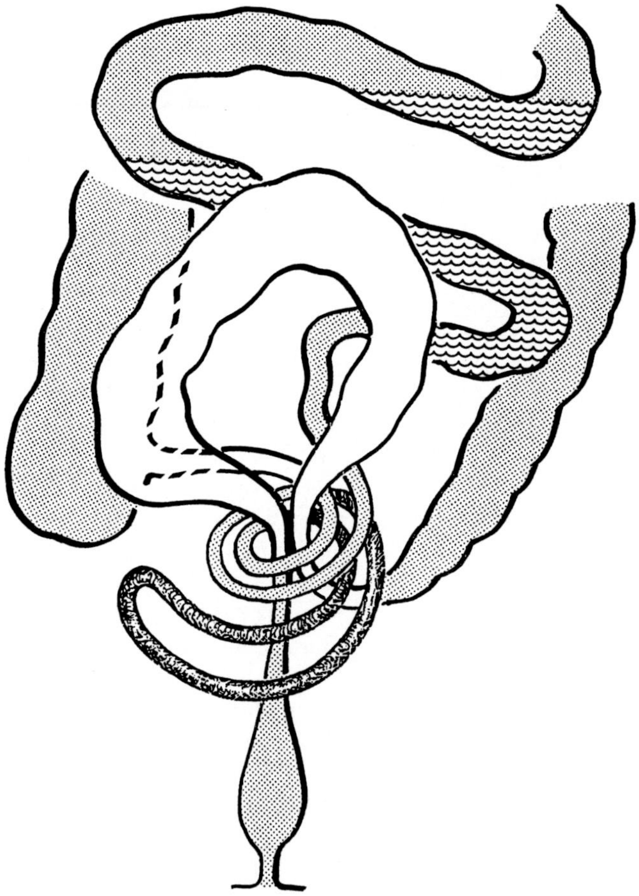

Fig. 21.6 Ileosigmoid knot.

present acutely, and this is usually due to impaction of food at the point of narrowing.

Inflammatory diseases

Of these, Crohn's disease is the usual cause in developed countries, and most patients will have typical Crohn's disease of the ileocaecal angle, although some will show a localized stenosis in small bowel. Approximately 25% of patients with small bowel Crohn's disease present with obstruction[32] which is due to active inflammation and oedema. Most respond quickly to starvation and a few days on intravenous fluids. Others may require corticosteroids and whilst some recover fully, others need semi-urgent or elective resection.

Tuberculous enteritis is rare in the West, except among immigrants from developing countries where tuberculosis is common. Approximately 10% of small bowel obstructions on the Indian subcontinent are due to tuberculosis.[33]

Endometriosis, usually due to direct involvement of adjacent ileum from the pelvic organs, occasionally causes small bowel obstruction.

Neoplasms

Neoplasms of the small bowel are fairly unusual, although they often present only when obstruction has occurred. Even so, one such case will occur for every 30–40 obstructed colonic carcinomas. Roughly equal numbers of primary adenocarcinomas (30%), carcinoids (30%) and lymphomas (30%) occur, the remainder being sarcomas. Approximately one in five small bowel neoplasms are benign, e.g. leiomyomas, and a few Peutz-Jeghers polyps, and these may present as the leading point of an intussusception. Sometimes metastatic deposits, due to transcoelomic or haematogenous spread, invade the bowel wall and cause obstruction.

Iatrogenic stenosis

Many people who have a full course of irradiation (4–6000 rads) to the pelvic organs experience some pain and diarrhoea, but only 0.5–1.0% suffer major bowel damage. If vasculitis predominates then ischaemia and perforation may occur, but if fibrosis predominates gradual stenosis develops and it may take years for obstruction to occur. In 93 radiation injuries to bowel seen at the Mayo Clinic, 76 were obstructed.[34]

When thiazide was introduced as a diuretic potassium chloride was given within an enteric coating. The coating quickly broke down and the high local concentration of the salt caused a local ulceration of small bowel, which healed by fibrosis, and a number of obstructions and perforations occurred. 'Slow release' capsules have made these complications very unusual.

Anticoagulant therapy may be complicated by an intramural intestinal haematoma, which can seriously narrow the lumen.

From the surgeon's point of view, many of these stenoses look very much alike at emergency laparotomy for intestinal obstruction. A short segment of Crohn's enteritis, a carcinoid, endometriosis, or a potassium-induced stenosis can be difficult to distinguish with the naked eye with any certainty. It is clearly helpful to know the diagnosis, because there is a strong case for radical resection of a neoplasm which has not visibly metastasized. There is thus a clear case for a histological diagnosis by frozen section or other means in such circumstances.

Another form of stenosis is so-called congenital intestinal atresia or stenosis which causes an obstruction in the newborn.

Obturation

A great variety of objects can impact in the lumen of the small bowel and cause occlusion. Probably the best known is gallstone ileus, which is responsible for approximately 1% of small bowel obstructions, and occurs almost entirely in elderly women. In most cases the gallbladder containing calculi adheres to and erodes into the duodenum producing a fistula. Calculus released into the small bowel will usually impact in the terminal ileum, but a number of temporary attacks of obstruction occur as the stone moves down the bowel. Now that endoscopic papillotomy is being practised, relatively large stones can be released from the bile duct, and may obstruct the bowel.[35] There is much speculation over the possibility that stones, once released into the bowel, can grow by accretion.

Many foods can obstruct the lumen of the bowel, including such exotica as turtle's eggs and grasshoppers eaten whole.[36] Masses of gobbled peanuts, poorly chewed, oranges and dried fruit eaten uncooked are among the commoner occluding foodstuffs. Local dietary customs provide many other examples e.g. persimmons in the United States and preserved ginger root in Hong Kong.[37] Impaction is particularly likely to occur at an adhesive kink, and patients with a gastrojejunostomy are especially at risk because ill-chewed food passes directly into the small bowel.

Obturation of the small bowel by masses of *Ascaris lumbricoides* is common throughout Africa and the East. It was responsible for 13% of over 700 African children admitted with acute abdominal pain in Cape Town.[38] The worms are sometimes palpable as a crepitant mass and can also cause pancreatitis and bile duct obstruction.

Cystic fibrosis is the cause of meconium ileus in newborn babies, and 'meconium ileus equivalent' later in life. In the latter a mass formed by a combination of unusually viscid intestinal mucus and undigested food, due to an insufficiency of pancreatic enzymes, impacts in the ileum.[39]

Intussusception

Intussusception occurs when a solid abnormality in the bowel wall is drawn into the lumen by peristalsis and then forms the leading point of a length of bowel which becomes ensheathed by the bowel distal to the point of intussusception.

The classical example of this condition is the intussusception of infancy. It is now generally accepted that a Peyer's patch enlarged in response to viral infection acts as the leading point (Figs 21.7 and 21.8). Viral studies on 64 infants with a proven intussusception were positive in 50%, 41% being due to adenovirus.[40] This condition is naturally restricted to the 1st and 2nd year of life during which time infants are first exposed to these viruses. The Peyer's patch, which may be 1.5–2.0 cm in diameter, is quite large enough to act as a leading point. Most cases are therefore ileocolic (60%), in approximately one third the ileocaecal valve forms the apex, and a few are colocolic, or remain ileoileal.

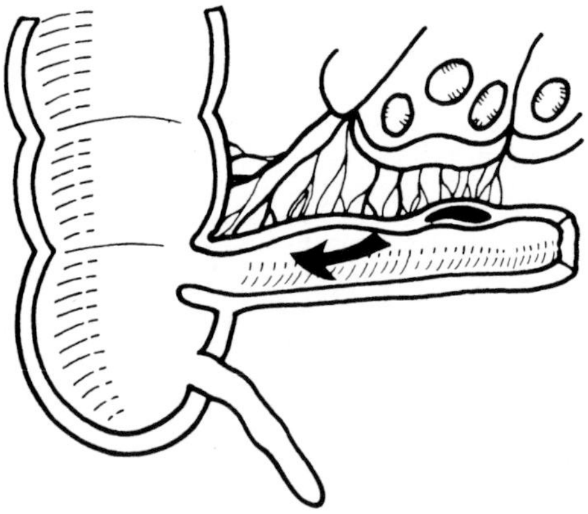

Fig. 21.7 Intussusception of infancy. The intussusception is initiated by the swollen Peyer's patch being drawn into the lumen of the terminal ileum by peristaltic activity (arrow). There is marked mesenteric adenitis.

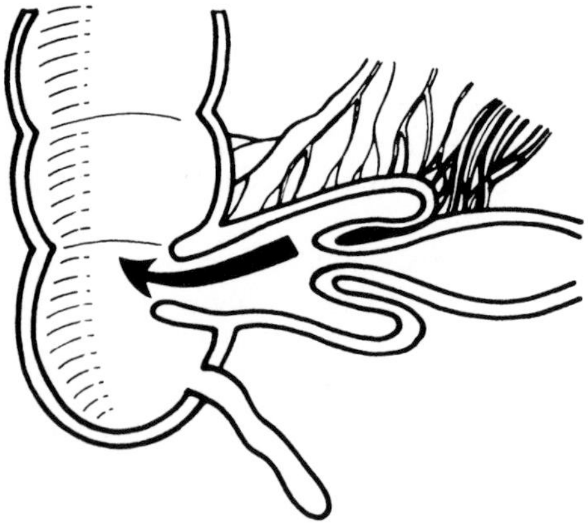

Fig. 21.8 Intussusception of infancy. The ileoileal intussusception is advancing, and is likely to pass through the ileocaecal valve to become an ileocolic intussusception. The mesentery is bunched, and progressively more compressed by the ensheathing layer: this pressure increases as the intussusception advances.

The main danger of intussusception is the constriction of the mesentery between the inner intussusceptium and the ensheathing intussuscipiens. This produces venous occlusion and consequent congestion, which is the source of the classical blood stained mucus passed per rectum. Later, oedema and constriction may obstruct arterial flow so gangrene is always a threat. Between 15–20% of cases require a resection because of irreducibility and there may be coincident gangrene. Four out of five children can be treated by simple reduction and, surprisingly, recurrence is very unusual.

In a few infants the intussusception is due to a congenital abnormality, such as a Meckel's diverticulum Once children have passed the age of 2 years, intussusception becomes uncommon, and is almost always initiated by an abnormality. Meckel's diverticulum is the commonest, but adenomata and lipomata, small duplications and the occasional case of Henoch-Schoenlein purpura are possibilities. After 5 years of age, intussusception is usually due to rarer lesions such as lymphoma and only 5–10% of intussusceptions occur after the age of 12 years. In the small bowel the leading point is usually an adenoma, a lipoma, a Peutz-Jegher polyp, a lymphoma or a carcinoid. Meckel's diverticulum still causes a few, and the inverted stump following appendicectomy is another unusual initiator. In the large bowel most intussusceptions are due to a polypoid carcinoma.

Rupture and perforation

This is an unusual cause of peritonitis in the developed countries, but it is familiar wherever typhoid fever is prevalent, because approximately 5% of patients develop a free perforation through the base of the ulcerated Peyer's patches.

There is a considerable range of diseases which can cause nontraumatic perforation of the small intestine, and they present in roughly equal numbers. The individual surgeon is unlikely to see more than 2 or 3 examples of each during a working lifetime, and most patients are likely to be operated on with a provisional diagnosis of perforated appendicitis.

Approximately two-thirds of small bowel lymphomas present with a perforation. It is important to establish an immediate histological diagnosis by frozen section or direct imprint, because prognosis is improved by proceeding to a radical resection. A liver biopsy should be taken.

Both Crohn's ileitis and tuberculous enteritis can perforate, but this is an unusual presentation[41] and tends to occur above a narrowed segment.

Diverticulosis of the jejunum, polyarteritis nodosa, Yersiniasis and radiotherapy are all occasional causes of perforation. If peptic ulceration occurs in a Meckel's diverticulum in childhood it is likely to bleed or perforate.

A swallowed foreign body occasionally penetrates the

wall of the small bowel, especially if it lodges in a diverticulum. Fishbones and toothpick splinters are the agents most often recovered at operation.

Enteritis necroticans is rare in temperate climes, but familiar in the Far East. The subjects are generally children who normally live on a vegetable-based diet, who partake of a feast of poorly cooked pig meat. This is contaminated with *Cl. welchii*; the B toxin which has been elaborated invades the mucosa of the jejunum, and consequent ulceration may go on to perforation.[42]

Ingested potassium chloride has occasionally caused small bowel perforation,[43] and ferrous sulphate and indomethacin may also cause focal necrosis.

Traumatic perforation of the small intestine is quite likely to occur in penetrating injuries because it lies beneath much of the anterior abdominal wall. Blunt abdominal trauma does not often result in perforation of small bowel, although it is liable to be disrupted when caught between a crushing force and the lumbar spine. This may directly injure bowel, or cause a blow-out in a loop closed at both ends.[44]

LARGE INTESTINE

Obstruction

Approximately one-third of all bowel obstructions occur in the large intestine. In developed Western countries, where colorectal cancer is second only to lung cancer in frequency, approximately 70% of large bowel obstructions are due to carcinoma, and approximately 10% are due to volvulus. In less developed parts of the world, where the diet contains much less processed food, volvulus of the colon is common, and neoplasms are rare.

Neoplastic obstructions

Most carcinomatous obstructions are due to an annular adenocarcinoma, which produces gradual narrowing: this allows a remarkable degree of proximal dilatation to occur before symptoms are experienced. Occasionally neoplastic obstruction develops from invasion by an adjacent neoplasm (e.g. ovary), and rarely it is due to growth of a blood-borne metastasis (e.g. from breast).

Between 15%–20% of patients with large bowel carcinoma only present when they have developed obstruction, and 50% will be over 70 years of age. About one-third of these carcinomas lie proximal to the splenic flexure, two-thirds at or beyond it. However, fewer than 10% are sited in the rectum even though 40% of colorectal carcinomas arise there.[45] The commonest sites for an obstructed carcinoma are the sigmoid colon, the caecum and ascending colon and the splenic flexure. It remains to be seen whether recent trends will result in a higher proportion of obstructions being seen in the proximal colon.[46]

Most of these obstructions generate a high level of intraluminal pressure because the lips of the ileocaecal valve are easily compressed, consequently a 'closed-loop' forms between the valve and the obstruction. This can have a serious effect on the viability of the colon, especially the caecum, and about 15% of obstructed patients present with a free perforation.[45]

Obstructed carcinomas tend to be more advanced than the non-obstructed, with only 50% of the obstructed being judged to be potentially curable at laparatomy, compared to 70% of the non-obstructed.[47] Long term survival is also impaired. The age-adjusted 5 year survival for the obstructed who have a radical resection is about 40% compared to 60% for the non-obstructed. There is a difference of opinion over whether this is largely due to deaths around and in the year after operation,[45] or whether obstructed carcinomas are intrinsically more aggressive.[47]

Volvulus

The sigmoid loop is the site of most volvuli, but volvulus of the caecum is a well recognized entity. Very occasionally volvulus of the transverse colon occurs.

Sigmoid volvulus shows a marked geographical variation in incidence. In Minsk 55% of 200 obstructed patients,[48] and in Iran 30% of 1000 patients[49] had a sigmoid volvulus. These figures can be compared with a series of 3380 obstructed patients in Edinburgh, of whom only 6% had a colonic volvulus.[50]

Diet is probably an important factor, because an unrefined diet is common to all places with high incidence. For example, Jews in Russia show a higher incidence than Jews in Western Europe. There is an association with mental abnormality in some, but by no means all cases.

The base of the sigmoid loop is usually very narrow, providing a pedicle for rotation, which may proceed through 180° up to 720°. The mesentery is often thick with large vessels, suggesting that recurrent episodes of rotation occur. This thickening may help to prevent ischaemic necrosis, which only occurs in approximately 10% of cases.

There is no indication of any precipitating factor. The main content of the rotated loop is gas, with some liquid faeces. Distention occurs very rapidly and the apex of the loop commonly lies under the costal margin.

Once a sigmoid volvulus has occurred there is a marked tendency towards recurrence. Approximately 4 patients out of 5 suffer subacute, slowly progressive attacks and often give a history of previous episodes; the other, smaller group are generally younger and suffer a short, severe illness, with much pain, which carries a high risk of gangrene in the loop.

Some 15–20% of colonic volvuli occur in the proximal colon. So-called caecal volvulus is something of a misnomer because in most cases the point of rotation lies in the mid-ascending colon. For this to occur the whole of the caecum and ascending colon must be unattached to the posterior abdominal wall and hanging free. This is due to a congenital failure of attachment at the time of midgut rotation in the 12th week of foetal life.

There is a tendency for caecal rotation to occur in pregnancy and the puerperium, and there is an important association with an obstructing lesion in the left colon. When rotation occurs, the caecum often swings up into the left hypochondrium, and becomes tensely distended: approximately 20% are infarcted at the time of laparotomy.

There are other unusual causes of large bowel obstruction. Some 3–5% are caused by severe diverticular disease, in which muscular thickening and inflammatory oedema has narrowed the lumen. Adhesions which so frequently cause small bowel obstruction only rarely obstruct the colon. Radiotherapy sometimes produces fibrotic narrowing, especially in the pelvic colon. Acute pancreatitis sometimes causes obstruction by pressure exerted on transverse colon from a pseudocyst or abscess.

Intussusception

Only some 5% of intussusceptions occur in adult life. In the colon the usual cause is a polypoid carcinoma, which is propelled forward by peristalsis, and forms the leading point of an intussusception.

A peculiar form of caecocolic intussusception is seen in Nigeria, and appears to be confined to that country.[51] The leading point is a firm dimple on the front of the caecum, and the intussusception is often of a chronic variety and gangrene is unusual. No explanation has been found for the origin of this form of intussusception.

Perforation

Perforation of the colon is always serious, because of the very high bacterial content of faeces and there are many causes.

Diverticular disease

Suppuration occurs in a diverticulum occluded by a faecolith, the pressure rises quickly and the abscess perforates into the general peritoneal cavity, causing a spreading purulent peritonitis. Less often, the abscess remains confined for longer, and the rising pressure causes ischaemic necrosis of the wall of the colon, resulting finally in a perforation 1–2 cm in diameter which allows faeces to escape and causes a particularly severe peritonitis.

Acute severe ulcerative colitis

This may progress to toxic dilatation or 'disintegrative colitis',[52] another cause of perforation. The perforation may occur into the free peritoneal cavity, but because much of the colon surface is retroperitoneal, perforation may occur here also.

Approximately 7% of colorectal carcinomas are complicated by perforation.[53] Most are perforations of the tumour itself, and these carry the risk of seeding tumour into the peritoneum. However, if this does not occur and the patient recovers from the peritonitis, long term survival does not appear to be prejudiced by perforation.

Some perforations are disruptions of the tensely distended caecum associated with a distal obstructing carcinoma.

Stercoral ulceration is a rare cause of perforation. A massive faecolith, usually in the distal colon, causes pressure ischaemia of the wall of the colon.

Acute infective colitis due to salmonella, campylobacter or amoebiasis or even a pseudomembraneous colitis, can all occasionally go on to perforation.

Necrotizing enterocolitis in the newborn quite often presents with evidence of peritonitis following perforation at one or more points.

Iatrogenic perforation of colon or rectum is only occasionally seen. It may follow endoscopic snare polypectomy, or it may occur during a difficult laparotomy in which an organ, e.g. uterus, is firmly adherent to the large bowel. Perforation during barium enema examination, and the taking of rectal temperature readings, are recorded but are unusual.

Blunt abdominal trauma is the cause of only 5% of colorectal injuries, and the great majority are caused by penetrating injuries. Stab injuries due to civilian street fighting only damage a small area. The missile injuries of modern sectarian and national wars are much more serious, the high velocity of the missile causing widespread damage.

Peritonitis

The hospital mortality for appendicitis with peritonitis in 1902, when King Edward VII suffered from a perforated appendix, was 75%. Now the overall mortality is less than 1%, although it is higher in the very young and those over 70 years of age and it may seem that the dangers of peritonitis have been overcome. This is not so, for the mortality of perforations of the large bowel is still as high as 50% and the mortality of peritonitis arising after elective alimentary tract surgery is 60%.[54]

Pathophysiology

The defensive properties of the peritoneal membrane are very considerable. Injury inhibits the normal fibrinolytic activity of the peritoneal secretions so that adjacent omentum and loops of bowel tend to adhere. When acute appendicitis develops gradually, this process effectively seals off the area, so that as and when the appendix perforates, the pus is localized, and an appendicular abscess forms. When, however, a virulent infection develops within the appendix or a colonic diverticulum, and there is a rapid development of gangrene with perforation within hours of onset, there is insufficient time for these fibrinous adhesions to form, and the released pus and exudate is able to spread freely through the peritoneum. When smaller quantities of infected exudate are released, it may travel along anatomical channels, e.g. pus from the appendix tends to spread upward along the paracolic gutter to contaminate the subphrenic space, and downwards into the pelvis, so residual abscesses are common in both these sites.

The bacteriology of peritonitis depends very much on the level of the perforation.[55] The sudden massive contamination of the peritoneal cavity which occurs when a peptic ulcer of stomach or duodenum perforates is intensely painful because the acid juice is a severe chemical insult to the peritoneal membrane. However, there are few organisms in the fluid which is released and bacterial contamination only becomes a problem when treatment is delayed for some reason beyond a day or two.

The bacterial population increases along the small bowel, and is quite high in the distal ileum, with *E. coli* predominating, which is why a Gram negative bacteraemia is a risk in perforations of the appendix. The bacterial population increases greatly in the colon, with one-third of the weight of faeces being made up of viable bacteria. Both aerobes and anaerobes abound, *Bacteroides* being the principal anaerobes. The risk of bacteraemia in large bowel perforation is particularly high. In 76 patients with peritonitis, 30% had a positive blood culture for *B. fragilis* or *E. coli*.[55] Unless treatment is started very quickly these patients are likely to show signs of 'septic shock' due largely to the vasodilatation and increased capillary permeability caused by the bacterial toxins.

Bacteria gain access to the peritoneal cavity via perforations of the alimentary tract, penetrating injuries, the female genital tract in, e.g. pelvic inflammatory disease, and through the bloodstream. Patients with ascites, due to cirrhosis or the nephrotic syndrome, are particularly prone to develop peritonitis.

Another important effect of peritonitis is to cause a marked loss of extracellular fluid. As infection spreads, a protein-rich exudate is formed, and extensive fibrinous plaques cause adjacent loops of bowel to adhere to each other. This introduces an element of mechanical obstruction due to kinking and to this is added the neurogenic ileus which is characteristic of peritonitis.

Consequently there is loss of extracellular fluid (a) through the formation of the exudate, (b) because obstructed bowel contains considerable volumes of intestinal juice which is not reabsorbed, and (c) because of repeated vomiting. Losses cannot be replaced orally and eventually signs of hypovolaemia develop if intravenous fluid therapy is not commenced.

The surface area of the peritoneum is roughly equal to the skin surface area, so the reaction of the peritoneum to infection can cause losses comparable to those seen in very extensive burns.

Neurogenic or paralytic ileus is the form of intestinal obstruction in which there is no mechanical block, but an absence of peristaltic propulsive activity in a part or the whole of the alimentary tract. It is essentially a secondary phenomenon and treatment has to be directed to the cause. The commonest of these is peritonitis. Arai[56] showed in 1922 that, in peritonitis in animals, the great delay in passage of a barium meal was abolished by division of the splanchnic nerves. This suggested that the sympathetic nervous system was exerting an inhibitory effect, and that the 'paralysis' was not due to any direct effect of infection on the intestinal wall.

This theory gains much support from the fact that another major cause of neurogenic ileus is retroperitoneal injury, and this may arise from a difficult nephrectomy, fracture of the lumbar spine, pancreatitis or retroperitoneal haemorrhage. There is clearly no direct action on the bowel wall in these situations, whilst interference with the balance of the autonomic nervous system provides a reasonable explanation. A number of drugs can also cause inhibition of intestinal function, e.g. some tricyclic antidepressants and anticholinergics such as propantheline.

Further support for a neurogenic origin is the rapid reversal of ileus by drugs such as guanethidine which prevent the release of noradrenaline.[57]

The clinical forms of peritonitis can be divided into generalized and localised.

Generalised peritonitis

This is occasionally primary, as in young females who develop diffuse peritonitis. *Str. pneumoniae* was commonly cultured in the early years of this century[58] and the infection was believed to have ascended from the vagina, via the fallopian tubes. Nowadays this is a rare condition and a number of cases are probably of viral origin.[59]

In the great majority of patients with generalized peritonitis, it is secondary to a perforation of the alimentary tract. This may be due to:

- —trauma, either blunt or penetrating. A particular form of this is the peritonitis which complicates peritoneal dialysis
- —disease, e.g. perforated peptic ulcer, perforated acute appendicitis, perforated colonic diverticulitis, perforated acute severe colitis, gangrene of the intestine due to stangulation or mesenteric artery obstruction, perforated neoplasms, typhoid fever
- —leakage after gastrointestinal surgery.

Localized peritonitis

Localized peritonitis generally takes the form of an abscess. This is the consequence of gradual development of sepsis in, e.g. appendix or a colonic diverticulum, which allows time for adhesions to develop among surrounding bowel, omentum, other organs or abdominal wall, before the organ perforates.

A special form of local peritonitis is the pelvic sepsis seen spreading from acute salpingitis. Residual pelvic and subphrenic abscesses are a particular form of local peritonitis, due to the tracking of infection along anatomical pathways.

REFERENCES

1. Wastell C, Ellis H. Gastric volvulus. Br J Surg 1971; 58: 557–562.
2. Hoffman E. Strangulated diaphragmatic hernia. Thorax 1968; 23: 541–549.
3. Kreel L, Ellis H. Pyloric stenosis in adults: a clinical and radiological study of 100 consecutive patients. Gut 1965; 6: 253–261.
4. Keynes WM. Simple and complicated hypertrophic stenosis in the adult. Gut 1965; 6: 240–252.
5. Simonian S J. Gallstone obstruction of the duodenal bulb. Lancet 1968; 1: 893–894.
6. Nugent FW, Richmond M, Park SK. Crohn's disease of the duodenum. Gut 1977; 18: 115–120.
7. Hudson CN. Congenital diaphragm of the duodenum causing intestinal obstruction in the adult. Br J Surg 1961; 49: 234–236.
8. Kaplan O, Klausner JM, Lelcuk S et al. Persimmon bezoars as a cause of intestinal obstruction: pitfalls in their surgical management. Br J Surg 1985; 72: 242–243.
9. Borg I, Heizkenskjold F, Nilehn B, Wehlin L. Massive growth of yeasts in resected stomach. Gut 1966; 7: 244–249.
10. Dorph MH. The cast syndrome. N Eng J Med 1950; 243: 440–442.
11. Brook GK. Acute gastric dilatation in anorexia nervosa. Br Med J 1977; 2: 499–500.
12. Saul SH, Dekker A, Watson CG. Acute gastric dilatation with infarction and perforation. Gut 1981; 22: 978–983.
13. Kasenally AT, Felice AG, Logie JRC. Acute gastric dilatation after trauma. Br Med J 1976; 2: 21.
14. Sperling L. Role of the ileocaecal sphincter in cases of obstruction of the large bowel. Arch Surg 1936; 32: 22–48.
15. Sykes PA, Boulter KH, Schofield PF. The microflora of the obstructed bowel. Br J Surg 1976; 63: 721–725.
16. Bussemaker JB, Lindeman J. Comparison of methods to determine viability of small intestine. Ann Surg 1972; 176: 97–101.
17. Powley JM. Unexpected deaths from small bowel obstruction. Proc R Soc Med 1965; 58: 870–873.
18. Vick RM. Statistics of acute intestinal obstruction. Br Med J 1932; 2: 546–548.
19. Bevan PG. Adhesive obstruction. Ann R Coll Surg Engl 1984; 66: 164–169.
20. Chiedozi LC, Aboh IO, Piserchia NE. Mechanical bowel obstruction: review of 316 cases in Benin City. Am J Surg 1980; 139: 389–393.
21. Boulvin R. L'intubation recto-sigmoidienne sous-controle rectoscopique dans le volvulus aigu du sigmoids. Lyon Chirurgical 1966; 62: 19–26.
22. Raf LE. Causes of abdominal adhesions in cases of intestinal obstruction. Acta Chir Scand 1969; 135: 73–76.
23. Ellis H. The aetiology of post-operative adhesions. Br J Surg 1962; 50: 10–16.
24. Myllarniemi H. Foreign material in adhesion formation after abdominal surgery. Acta Chir Scand 1967; (Suppl. 377): 6–48.
25. Krook SS. Obstruction of the small intestine due to adhesions and bands. Acta Chir Scand 1947; 95 (Suppl. 125): 1–200
26. Cade D. Adhesions — is drug prophylaxis feasible? In: Ellis H, Lennox M. eds. Adhesions — The Problems. London: Westminster Hospital Medical School 1983: pp 45–48.
27. Gough IR. Strangulating adhesive small bowel obstruction with normal radiographs. Br J Surg 1978; 65: 431–434.
28. Andrews NJ. Presentation and outcome of strangulated external hernia in a district general hospital. Br J Surg 1981; 68: 329–332.
29. Kerr WG, Kirkcaldy-Willis WH. Volvulus of the small intestine. Br Med J 1946; 1: 799–801.
30. Perry EG. Intestinal volvulus: a new concept. Aust NZ J Surg 1983; 53: 483–486.
31. Shepherd JJ. Ninety two cases of ileo-sigmoid knotting in Uganda. Br J Surg 1967; 54: 561–566.
32. Hellers G. Crohn's disease in Stockholm County 1955–1974. Acta Chir Scand 1979; (Suppl. 490): 5–84.
33. Vaidya MG, Sodhi JS. Gastrointestinal tract tuberculosis: a study of 102 cases. Clin Radiol 1978; 29: 189–195.
34. Schmitt EH, Symmonds RE. Surgical treatment of radiation induced injuries of the intestine. Surg Gynec Obstet 1981; 153: 896–900.
35. Taylor JD, Zaman K, Fossard DP, Carr Locke D. Gallstone ileus: a 12-year surgical review with special reference to ERCP and endoscopic sphincterotomy. Br J Surg 1984; 71: 992.
36. Stephens FO. Intestinal colic caused by food. Gut 1966; 7: 581–585.
37. Liu PHW, Ho HL. Ginger and drug bezoar-induced small bowel obstruction. JR Coll Surg Edinb 1983; 28: 397–398.
38. Louw JH. Abdominal complications of Ascaris lumbricoides infestation in children. Br J Surg 1966; 53: 510–521.
39. Hunton DB, Long WK, Tsumagari HY. Meconium ileus equivalent: an adult complication of fibrocystic disease. Gastroenterology 1966; 50: 99–102.
40. Nicolas JC, Ingrand D, Fortier B, Bricout F. A one-year virological survey of acute intussusception in childhood. J Med Virol 1982; 9: 267–271.
41. Steinberg DM, Cooke WT, Alexander-Williams J. Free perforation in Crohn's disease. Gut 1973; 14: 187–190.
42. Lawrence G, Walker PD. Pathogenesis of enteric necroticans in Papua New Guinea. Lancet 1976; 1: 125–126.
43. Leizonmark CE, Raf L. Ulceration of the small intestine due to slow-release potassium chloride tablets. Acta Chir Scand 1985; 151: 273–278.
44. Rouse T, Collin J, Dear A. Isolated injury to the intestine from blunt abdominal injury. Injury 1984; 16: 131–133.
45. Phillips RKS, Hittinger R, Fry JS, Fielding LP. Malignant large bowel obstruction. Br J Surg 1985; 72: 296–302.
46. Kee F, Wilson RH, Gilliland R, Sloan JM, Rowlands BJ, Moorehead RJ. Changing site distribution of colorectal cancer. BMJ 1992; 305: 158.
47. Serpell JW, McDermott FT, Katrivessis H, Hughes ESR. Obstructing carcinomas of the colon. Br J Surg 1989; 76: 965–969.
48. Perlmann J. Klinische Beitrage zur Pathologie und Chirurgischen Behandlung der Darmverschlusses. Arch f Klin Chir 1925; 137: 245.
49. Boulvin R. L'intubation recto-sigmoidienne sous-controle rectoscopique dans le volvulus aigu du sigmoide. Lyon Chirurgical 1966; 62: 19–26.
50. Anderson JR, Lee D. The management of acute sigmoid volvulus. Br J Surg 1981; 68: 117–120.
51. Cole GJ. Caeco-colic intussusception in Ibadan. Br J Surg 1966; 53: 415–419.
52. Brooke BN, Sampson PA. An indication for surgery in acute ulcerative colitis. Lancet 1964; 2: 1272–1273.
53. Goligher JC, Smiddy FG. The treatment of acute obstruction or perforation with carcinoma of the colon and rectum. Br J Surg 1957; 45: 270–274.
54. Bohnen J, Boulanger M, Meakins JL, McLean APH. Prognosis in generalised peritonitis. Arch Surg 1983; 118: 285–290.
55. Lorber B, Swenson RM. The bacteriology of intra-abdominal infections. Surg Clin N Amer 1975; 55: 1349–1354.
56. Arai K. Experimentalle Untersuchung uber die Magen —

Darmbewegungen bei akuter Peritonitis. Arch Exp Path Pharmak 1922; 94: 149.
57. Neely J, Catchpole B. Ileus: the restoration of alimentary tract mobility by pharmacological means. Br J Surg 1971; 58: 21–28.
58. McCartney JE, Fraser J. Pneumococcal peritonitis. Br J Surg 1922; 9: 479–484.
59. Fowler R. Primary peritonitis: changing aspects 1956–1970. Austr Paed J 1971; 7: 73–83.

PART II
The vermiform appendix

R. A. Williams

Intussusception

Reports of approximately 200 cases of intussusception of the vermiform appendix appear in the literature, the first of these being described in an autopsy examination by McKidd in 1859.[1] These reports probably do not reflect the true incidence, however it suffices to say that the condition is extremely uncommon. The intussusceptions occur more commonly in males, and in the adolescent age group, the age range being from 8 months to 75 years.[2]

Patients with appendiceal intussusception present with either signs and symptoms indistinguishable from those of acute appendicitis[3,4] or, more commonly, with a colicky right lower quadrant abdominal pain.[2–5]

It may be diagnosed preoperatively, and filling defects have been visualized during contrast radiological examination.[5–11] Levine and coworkers have described a 'coiled spring sign of appendiceal intussusception' in barium enema examinations.[12]

The intussusception is usually associated with other pathology in the appendix, with epithelial tumours, endometriotic deposits and lymphoid proliferations being the most common lead points.[2–6] References to causative foreign bodies have also been documented.[12] Occasionally, no obvious associated pathological lesion is found, and in these cases careful macroscopic examination sometimes reveals a wide-mouthed opening of the appendix into the caecum, which is a residual minor developmental abnormality. Such a case is illustrated in Figures 21.9a and b.

In 1941 McSwain classified intussusception of the appendix into four subtypes.[13] The macroscopic features are dependent on the type of intussusception (Figs 21.10–21.14). Other macroscopic and microscopic features are similar to those seen elsewhere in the gastrointestinal tract.

Complications of appendiceal intussusception are the result of inflammatory changes in the wall of the appendix. Rarely are cases of gangrenous necrosis described.[14] The treatment of the condition is surgical, the appendix being removed with a small cuff of caecum. Histological examination is mandatory to ensure that any associated pathological lesion, such as an epithelial tumour of the appendix, has been completely removed.

Torsion of the appendix

Torsion is another pathological process which rarely affects the appendix, with only approximately 30 cases

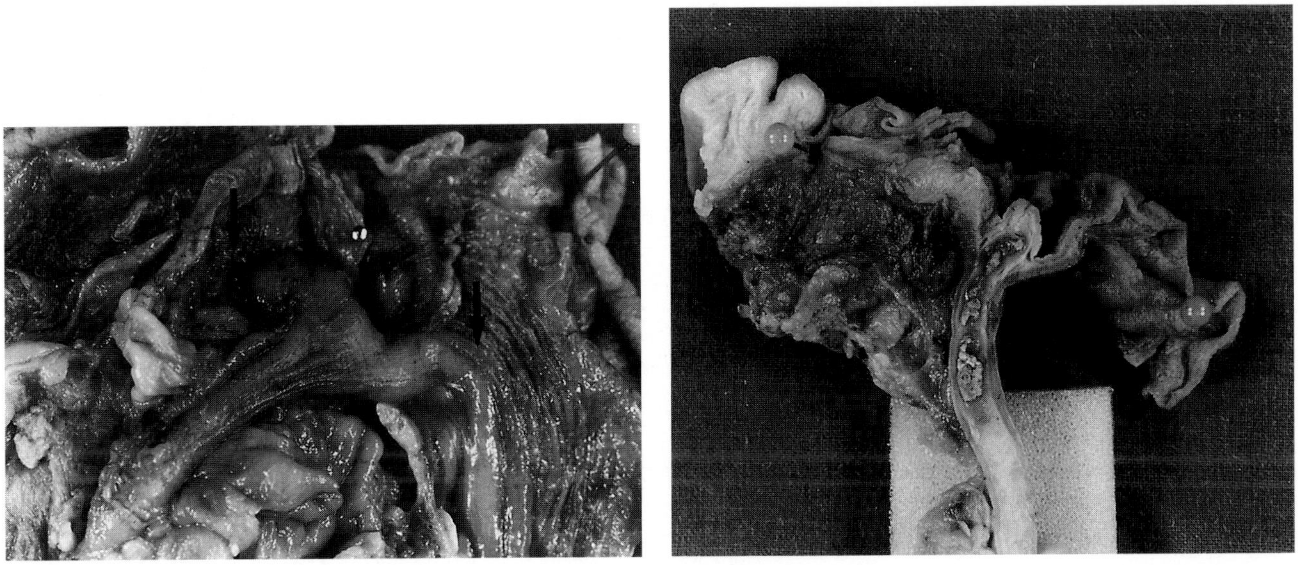

A B

Fig. 21.9A Shows a wide-based opening of the appendix into the caecum. The arrows indicate the extremities of the base. In **B** the specimen has been opened to show the early intussusception of the appendix into the caecum.

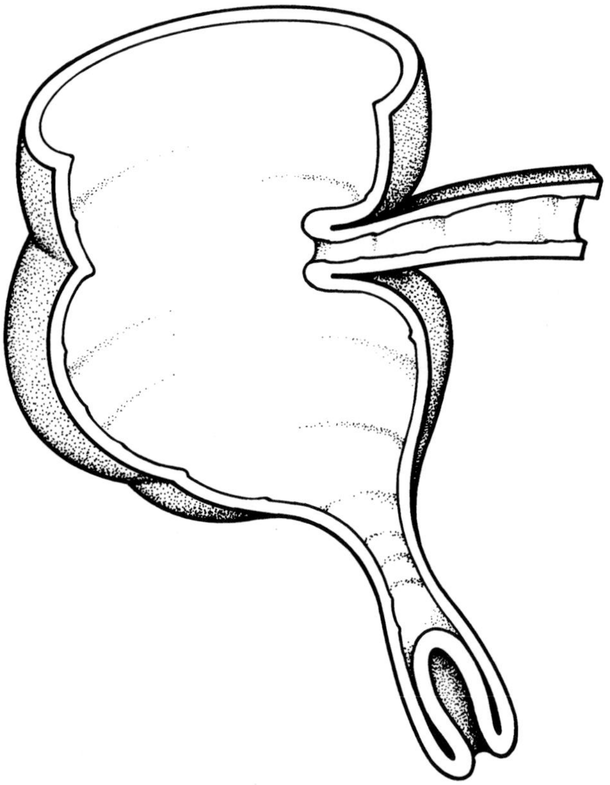

Fig. 21.10 McSwain Type I intussusception, where the tip of the appendix is the intussusceptum and the more proximal portion is the intussuscipiens.

being reported in the literature. Dilatation of the distal end of the appendix due to either a carcinoid or other epithelial tumour, with accompanying mucinous distension of the lumen, is present in some cases, and a case associated with mesoappendiceal lipoma is also recorded.[15] Associations with acute appendicitis and a mesoappendix with a short base are also recorded,[16] and an unusual case of torsion has been seen with a marked decidual change.[17]

The macroscopic and microscopic features are those seen in torsion of other regions of the gastrointestinal tract, with inflammatory changes being most severe in the distal part of the organ. Careful pathological examination of the specimen should be made to ensure that there has been adequate removal of any tumour which might be present (see Ch. 42 for discussion of treatment of tumours of the appendix).

Torsion has also been proposed as a possible cause of autoamputation of the appendix, and therefore one explanation for the apparrently 'congenitally absent' appendix.[18] Therefore, before congenital absence of the appendix is diagnosed either intraoperatively or at post mortem examination, a thorough search of the abdominal cavity for a separated, mummified appendix should be made.

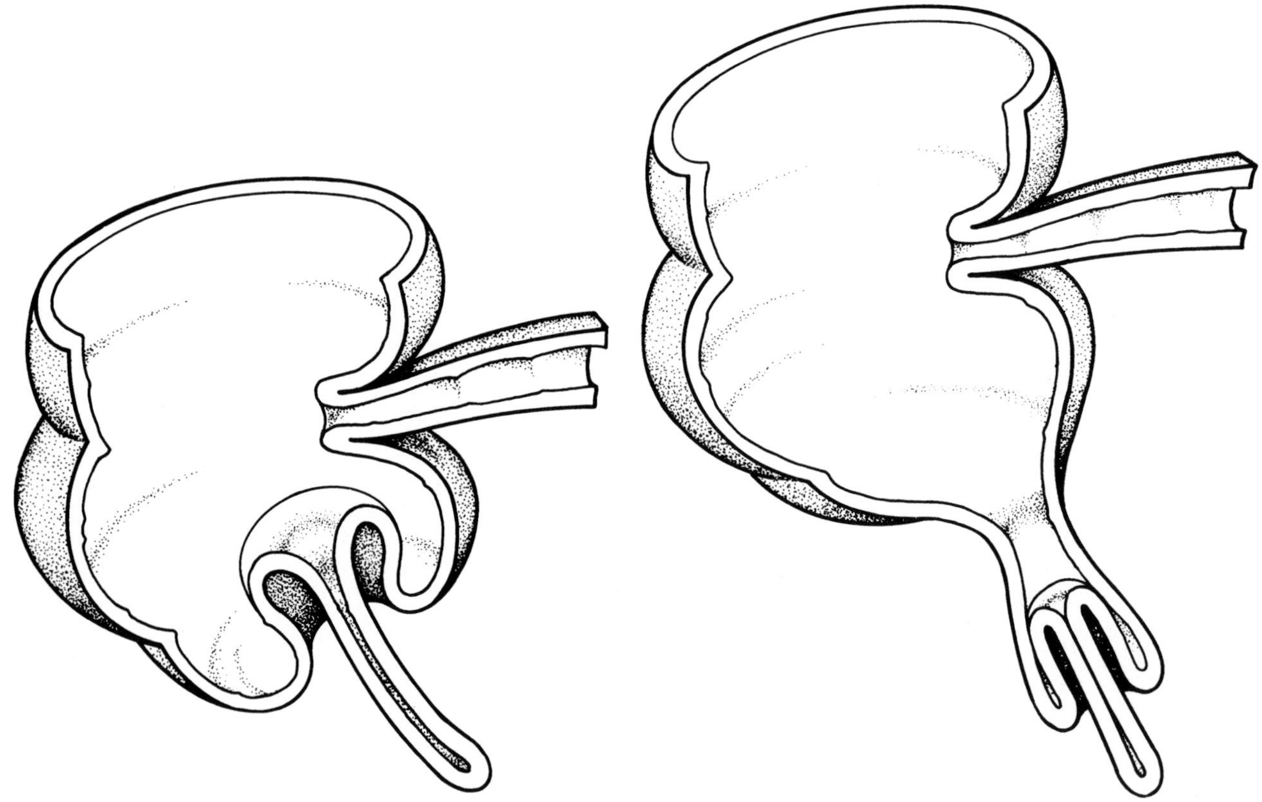

A B

Fig. 21.11 McSwain Type 2 intussusception. In **A** the intussusception begins at the appendicocaecal junction, whereas **B** illustrates the intussusception beginning near the base of the appendix.

A B

Fig. 21.12 The initial and the final stage of McSwain Type 3 intussusception.

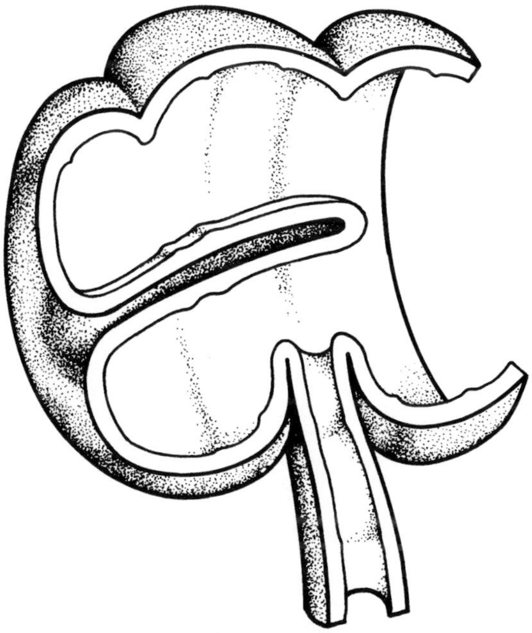

Fig. 21.13 This shows the complete inversion of the appendix into the caecum. McSwain designated this Type 4 appendiceal intussusception, pointing out that at this stage it is impossible to determine whether the process began as a Type I or Type 2 intussusception.

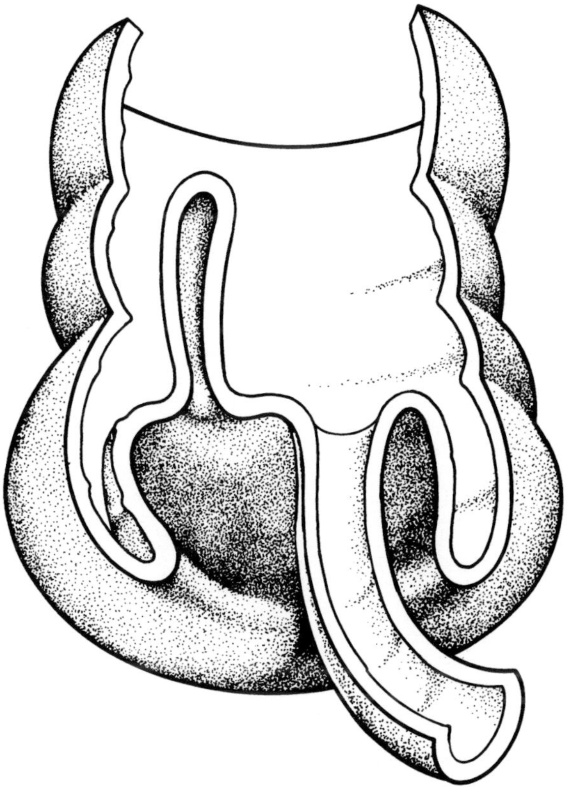

Fig. 21.14 In cases such as this, the intussusception is described as Type 4, combined. There is complete inversion of the appendix, accompanied by ileocaecal intussusception.

Diverticulosis

Diverticulosis of the vermiform appendix, in common with the same condition found elsewhere in the gastrointestinal tract, can be divided into congenital and acquired forms. Both types may have either single or multiple diverticula,[19] although multiple diverticula are more common.[20]

A diagnosis of congenital diverticulum cannot be made unless the muscularis propria is present around the diverticulum, whilst acquired diverticula are devoid of muscularis propria. This means simply that all layers of the wall are present in congenital diverticula, whilst in the acquired lesions there is herniation of the mucosa, including the muscularis mucosae, through the muscularis propria of the appendiceal wall.

The incidence of diverticular disease in the appendix varies in different series, and in the case of acquired diverticula probably reflects the investigator's thoroughness in searching for them. The incidence is around 0.2% of all resected specimens, with congenital diverticula making up only 3% of the total.[19]

Pathogenesis

The pathogenesis of congenital diverticula of the appendix is not well understood, and theories as to their development include failure of a distally placed yolk sac to obliterate completely, and that the diverticulum represents a duplication of the appendix which has been subjected to traction during development.[19] Favara[21] observed an association, in the case of multiple congenital diverticula, with the Dl (13–15) trisomy syndrome, based on findings in 3 of his own and 4 other reported cases.

Acquired diverticula may develop where inflammation weakens the wall, or where there is a congenital weakness. They may also occur as the result of pulsion with luminal obstruction, or traction due to external inflammation with reparative fibrosis.

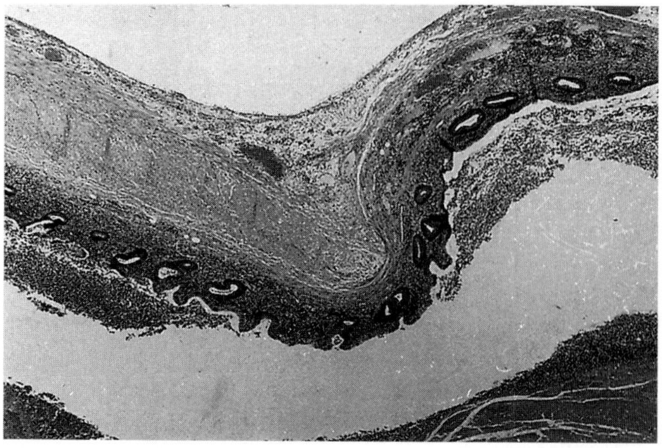

Fig. 21.15 Acquired diverticulum of the appendix. Note that the diverticulum is devoid of the muscularis propria layer of the wall. In this case, there was an accompanying acute suppurative appendicitis which involved the whole of the appendix including the diverticula.

An excellent review of the subject by Trollope and Lindenauer was published in 1974.[19] A case of diverticular disease of the appendix in a 22 year old female with cystic fibrosis is shown in Figure 21.15. In this case there was no mechanical obstruction of the appendiceal lumen; functional obstruction with pulsion changes due to the increased viscosity of the mucus was the probable cause.

Complications

Uncomplicated diverticulosis of the appendix may be detected during radiological examination;[22] diverticulitis, with or without perforation, may be present with or without a generalized acute suppurative appendicitis, and uncomplicated diverticulosis may be found in an acutely inflamed appendix where the inflammatory process does not involve the diverticula.[19,20]

REFERENCES

1. McKidd J. Case of invagination of caecum and appendix. Edinburgh Med J 1859; 4: 793–796.
2. Mann WJ, Fromowitz F, Saychek T, Madariaga JR, Chalas E. Endometriosis associated with appendiceal intussusception. J Reprod Med 1984; 29: 625–629.
3. Yates LN. Intussusception of the appendix. Int Surg 1983, 68: 231–233.
4. Langsam LB, Raj PK, Galang CF. Intussusception of the appendix. Dis Colon Rectum 1984; 27: 387–392.
5. Martin LF, Tidman MK, Jamieson MA. Appendiceal intussusception and endometriosis. J Can Assoc Radiol 1980; 31: 276–277.
6. Ho L, Rosenman LD. Complete invagination of the vermiform appendix with villous adenoma, intussuscepting to the splenic flexure of the colon. Surgery 1975; 77: 505–506.
7. Barry R, Visser JD, Nel CJC. Intussusception as a result of adenoma of the appendix. S Afr J Surg 1980; 19: 133–137.
8. Fullerton TE, Drabek GA, Lenz BT, Adams HP, Cavanaugh DJ. Appendiceal intussusception. SD J Med 1985; 38: 29–31.
9. Casteels M, Eggermont E, Kerremans R, Ponnette E. Intussusception of the vermiform appendix: a preoperative diagnosis in an adolescent girl. J Pediatr Gastroenterol Nutr 1986; 5: 159–162.
10. Myllarniemi H, Perttala Y, Peltokallio P. Tumor-like lesions of the cecum following inversion of the appendix. Am J Dig Dis 1974; 19: 547–556.
11. Gilsanz V. Displacement of the appendix in intussusception. AJR 1984; 142: 407–408.
12. Levine MS, Trenkner SW, Herlinger H, Mishkin JD, Reynolds JC. Coiled-spring sign of appendiceal intussusception. Radiology 1985; 155: 41–44.
13. McSwain B. Intussusception of the appendix. South Med J 1941; 34: 263–271.
14. McCafferty H. Isolated gangrene of the appendix complicating intussusception. Br J Clin Pract 1983; 37: 401, 403.
15. Legg NGM. Torsion complicating mucocele of the appendix. JR Coll Surg Edinb 1973; 18: 236.
16. De Bruin AJ. Torsion of the appendix. Med J Aust 1969; 1: 581.

17. Roikjaer O. Torsion of the vermiform appendix. Decidual reaction as a contributory cause. Ugeskr Laeger 1983; 145: 3496.
18. Fenoglio-Preiser CM, Lantz PE, Listrom MB, Davis M, Rilke FO. In: Gastrointestinal Pathology: An Atlas and Text. 1989. Raven Press, New York.
19. Trollope ML, Lindenauer SM. Diverticulosis of the appendix: a collective review. Dis Colon Rectum 1974; 17: 200–218.
20. Delikaris P, Stubbe Teglbjaerg P, Fisker-Sorensen P, Balslev I. Diverticula of the vermiform appendix. Alternatives of clinical presentation and significance. Dis Colon Rectum 1983; 26: 374–376.
21. Favara BE. Multiple congenital diverticula of the vermiform appendix. Am J Clin Pathol 1968; 49: 60.
22. Buffo GC, Clair MR, Bonheim P. Diverticulosis of the vermiform appendix. Gastrointest Radiol 1986; 11: 108–109.

CHAPTER

22

Neuromuscular abnormalities of small and large intestine

M. D. Schuffler

Intestinal motility is a complex process regulated by an interplay of intestinal smooth muscle, the enteric nervous plexuses, the autonomic nervous system extrinsic to the intestine, and hormones.[1,2] On theoretical grounds, abnormalities could be purely functional or they could be structural and recognizable microscopically.

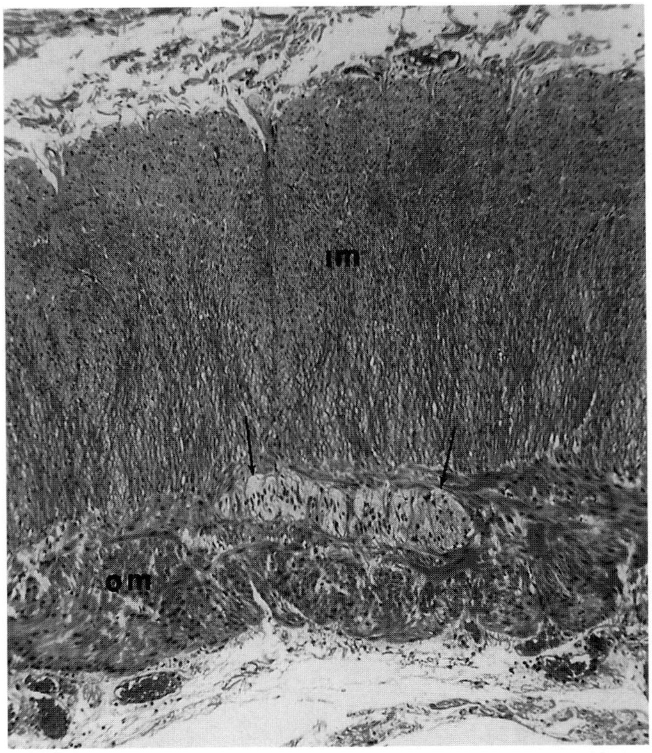

Fig. 22.1 Cross-section of colon. The arrows denote the myenteric plexus. im = inner muscle, om = outer muscle. (H&E, ×72. Reprinted with permission: Gastroenterology 1987; 93: 610–639)

In haematoxylin and eosin sections of the gastrointestinal tract, the myenteric plexus is visualized in cross-section between the two muscle layers (Fig. 22.1). Because the myenteric plexus is oriented in a longitudinal direction, and because its neurons are congregated within ganglia which are separated one from the other, conventional light microscopy is ill-suited to study this structure — because the perpendicularly cut sections allow only a

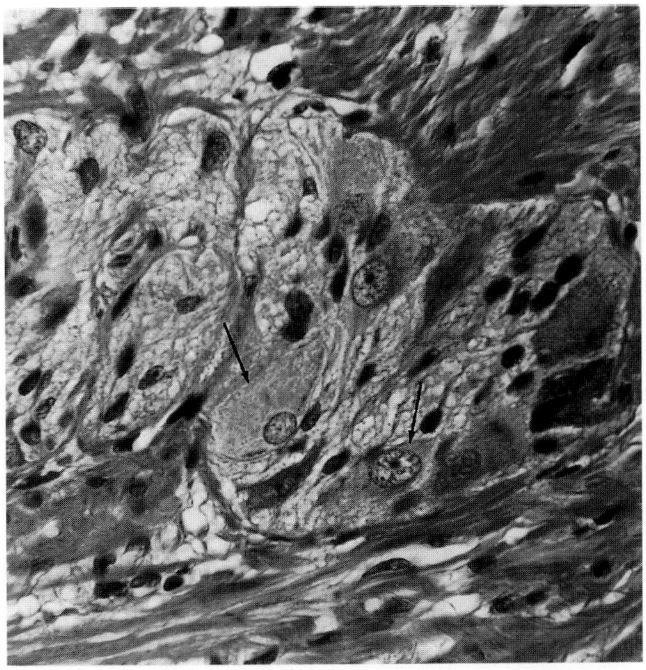

Fig. 22.2 Cross-section of myenteric plexus of colon, showing neurons (arrows), glial cell nuclei, and cross-sections of many axons. (H&E, ×288. Reprinted with permission: Gastroenterology 1987; 93: 610–639)

Fig. 22.3 Overview of the myenteric plexus of the duodenum. It has a mesh-like appearance and the neurons are black-staining bodies which tend to congregate at the intersections of the mesh. Strands of both the longitudinal and circular muscles can be noted around and between the arms of the mesh. (Silver, ×97. Reprinted with permission: Gastroenterology 1987; 93: 610–639)

fraction of the plexus to be visualized. Neuronal morphology is also difficult to evaluate with this technique and neuronal processes and nerve fibres remain unstained (Fig. 22.2).

If, on the other hand, thicker, larger sections are cut in the plane of the plexus, and then stained with silver, a large sample of neurons and processes is obtained. The layout of the mesh can be seen and nerve tracts followed from one ganglion to another (Figs 22.3 & 22.4). Neuron morphology is sharply defined and abnormalities can be readily appreciated. This technique[3] has been applied to the study of a large number of motility disorders and slight modification of it[4] will reveal neurons, axons, dendrites, and nerve fibres which vary from light tan to deep black in colour. The background muscle stains brown, and the two coats within the small intestine are oriented perpendicularly to each other. The nerve tracts between the small intestinal ganglia are fairly close together and each contains about 50–100 nerve fibres. Relatively few thick entrinsic nerve fibres are present in the small intestine and colon proximal to the rectosigmoid. Those which are present can sometimes be traced to a specific neuron body.

Neurons vary in stain uptake from intense (argyrophilic) to weak (argyrophobic). Argyrophobic neurons in the small intestine outnumber argyrophilic neurons by about two to one. The argyrophilic neurons vary widely in size, shape, and number of processes (Figs 22.5A,B & 22.6). Many are pyramidal or irregular in shape, and have slightly concave sides. Their processes are asymmetrically distributed around the borders of the neurons. The argyrophobic neurons are generally round to oval, vary in size, often have indistinct borders and usually have no visible

Fig. 22.4 Ganglion from the normal jejunum containing more than 50 neurons of varying stain intensity. Each nerve tract contains numerous thin nerve fibres, presumably of intrinsic origin. (Silver, ×194. Reprinted with permission: Gastroenterology 1987; 93: 610–639)

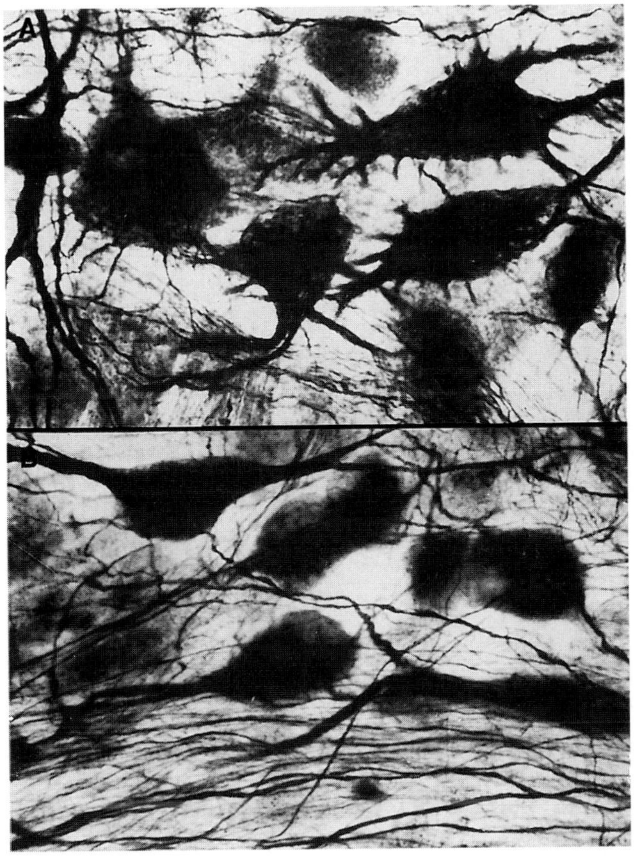

Fig. 22.5A (top)Argyrophilic neurons of the jejunum, showing heterogeneity of morphology. **B** (bottom) Argyrophilic neurons from different area of the same jejunum. These neurons are slightly smaller, have a variety of shapes and a smaller number of processes. (Silver, ×952. Reprinted with permission: Gastroenterology 1987; 93: 610–639)

processes (Fig. 22.7). In most patients there is a gradation of these neurons from argyrophobic with no visible processes, to neurons with some argyrophilia and one or two visible processes. The morphology of the plexus is basically the same throughout the small intestine except that in the lower ileum there are argyrophilic neurons which are smaller and 'spidery' in appearance (Fig. 22.6).

The colon is easily recognized because the smooth muscle is arranged differently. Instead of a distinct orientation of the circular and longitudinal muscles at approximately right angles, the smooth muscle fibres intersect the plexus at oblique angles and it often appears to be encased within one or the other muscle layer rather than being distinctly between the two (Fig. 22.8). The nerve tracts are harder to trace than in the small bowel and many fewer are found on any one slide. Visualization of the plexus is hardest in the ascending colon but easier in the transverse and descending colons. The nerve tracts in the sigmoid are wider and more distinct. As in the small bowel, there are relatively few thick extrinsic fibres in the plexus proximal to the sigmoid. In the sigmoid and rectum, some thick extrinsic fibres are seen (Fig. 22.9). It is likely that the presence of extrinsic fibres correlates with the fact that the parasympathetic outflow from the sacral cord innervates the lower colon and rectum.

As in the small intestine, both argyrophilic and argyrophobic neurons are seen (Fig. 22.10A,B). The relative number of the two types of neurons varies in different patients from about the same to an excess of argyrphobic neurons by about threefold. As in the small bowel, some neurons are intermediate in their staining characteristics. Compared with the small intestine, the argyrophilic neurons tend to be smaller, more irregular in shape, and contain a variable number of processes. Neurons vary from

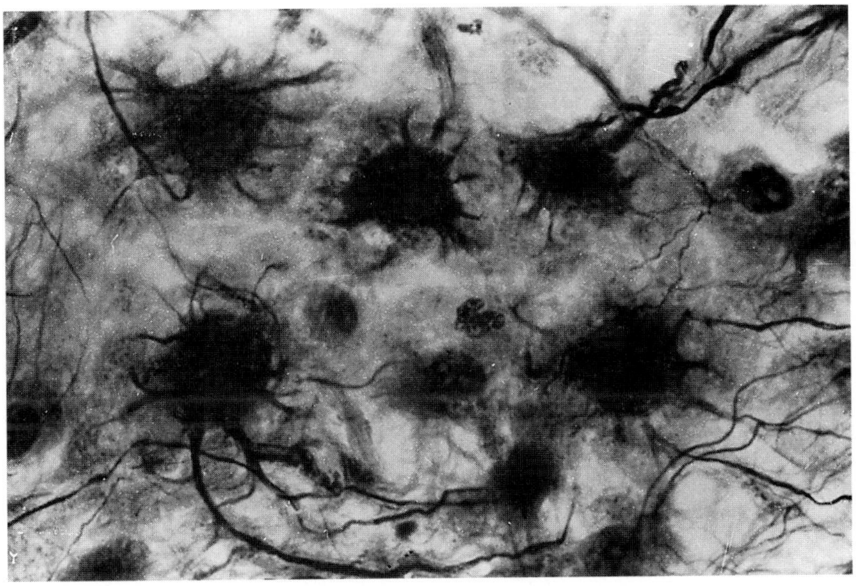

Fig. 22.6 Small, 'spidery' neurons from the ileum. Such neurons are not usually seen in the more proximal small intestine, but can be seen in the colon. (Silver, ×1292. Reprinted with permission: Gastroenterology 1987; 93: 610–639)

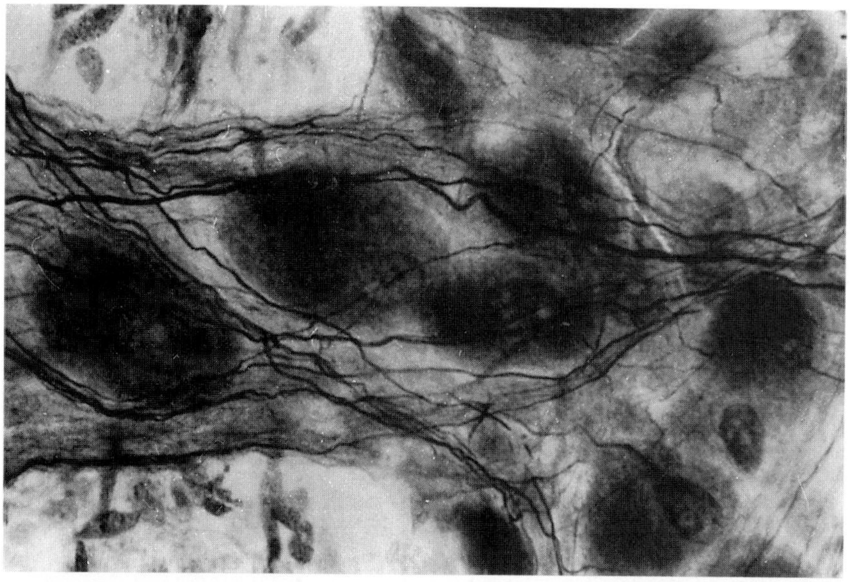

Fig. 22.7 Argyrophobic neurons from the jejunum. Although many axons are traversing this ganglion, the neurons themselves have no processes visible with this technique. (Silver, ×1292. Reprinted with permission: Gastroenterology 1987; 93: 610–639)

Fig. 22.8 The myenteric plexus of the colon. The arrangement is about the same as in the small intestine but many of the smooth muscle fibres (arrows) intersect the plexus at oblique angles. (Silver, ×97)

Fig. 22.9 Some thicker nerve fibres in the upper rectum which presumably are from the extrinsic innervation. (Silver, ×1292)

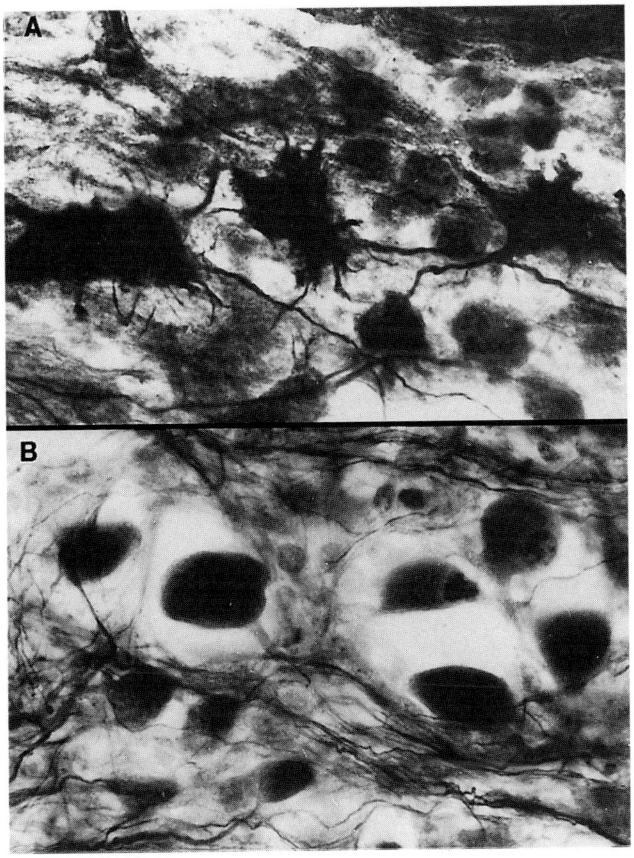

Fig. 22.10A Three argyrophilic neurons from a normal colon, which are quite irregular in shape. **B** 'Argyrophobic' neurons from the colon, which are smaller and more irregular in shape than those of the small bowel. (Silver, ×952. Reprinted with permission: Gastroenterology 1987; 93: 610–639)

oval to pear-shaped and dendrites tend to be short and stubby and the nuclei eccentric. As in the lower ileum, some neurons are spidery in shape. Other neurons are large, argyrophilic and have a great many processes. Compared with the more proximal intestine, the argyrophobic neurons are also smaller and more irregular in shape.

The muscularis propria of the small intestine and colon is organized into two layers: an inner circular muscle and an outer longitudinal muscle. The longitudinal muscle of the colon is thicker within the three taenia coli and may be quite thin between the taenia. When cut in cross section, smooth muscle fibres have distinct borders which vary from round to irregular, depending on the state of contractility at the time of fixation. If completely relaxed, they will be round, and if contracted, irregular. In post-mortem tissues autolysis alters appearances and fibres vary from being swollen and densely stained to ill-defined and poorly stained. When visualized in longitudinal section, the fibres are of variable length and smooth to irregular in contour.

There may normally be some strands of collagen dividing the circular muscle up into bundles. However, the collagen should be minimal in amount and have the appearance of septae. Collagen should not be present diffusely throughout the muscle.

Morphologic study of smooth muscle cells requires that the sections be thin (sectioned at 4 μm) and well-stained. Hollande's solution and a modified hematoxylin and eosin stain strong in eosin accentuates the muscle cells, and because collagen may be difficult to distinguish from smooth muscle cells, some sections should always be stained with Masson's trichrome. This distinguishes the scarlet staining muscle from the blue staining collagen. Proper interpretation of smooth muscle is impossible unless such techniques are used.

CLASSIFICATION AND DEFINITIONS

A classification of the neuromuscular disorders of the small intestine and colon which have recognizable abnormalities of the myenteric plexus or smooth muscle is presented in Table 22.1.

Intestinal pseudo-obstruction is a clinical syndrome characterized by symptoms and signs of intestinal obstruction in the absence of mechanical obstruction of the intestinal lumen.[5–7]

Acute intestinal pseudo-obstruction occurs in the context of underlying acute illness and is self-limited. Ileus, paralytic ileus and spastic ileus are synonymous terms. The pathogenesis is not understood but it is thought to be due to reflex mechanisms. Some of the illnesses associated with acute intestinal pseudo-obstruction include acute myocardial infarction, acute pancreatitis, renal colic, sepsis and acute respiratory failure. This type of pseudo-obstruction can involve the small intestine, the colon or both.

Ogilvie's syndrome is a term sometimes used synonymously with acute colonic pseudo-obstruction limited to the colon which may complicate any acute illness, especially of a severity necessitating admission to an intensive care unit.[8,9] This syndrome is named after Sir Heneage Ogilvie, a British surgeon who described two patients with colonic pseudo-obstruction associated with a distant carcinoma.[10] As used now, however, Ogilvie's syndrome denotes acute colonic pseudo-obstruction associated with any underlying acute illness.

Chronic intestinal pseudo-obstruction is not self-limited but persists for years.[5–7] Patients present with abdominal pain and distention, vomiting and weight loss. Abdominal radiographs show either an ileus or a picture mimicking mechanical obstruction.[11,12] The small bowel, the colon or both can be involved. Small intestinal pseudo-obstruction presents with a predominance of obstructive symptoms, steatorrhoea and diarrhoea, whereas colonic pseudo-obstruction presents primarily with abdominal distention and pain, often but not always accompanied by constipation.[13]

Table 22.1

I. Disorders of the myenteric plexus
  A. Familial visceral neuropathies
    1. Recessive, with intranuclear inclusions (neuronal intranuclear inclusion disease)
    2. Recessive, with mental retardation and calcification of the basal ganglia
    3. Dominant, with neither of above
  B. Sporadic visceral neuropathies
    1. Degenerative, non-inflammatory (at least two types)
    2. Degenerative, inflammatory
      a. Paraneoplastic
      b. Non-paraneoplastic (Chagas, cytomegalovirus, idiopathic)
    3. Inflammatory axonopathy
  C. Myotonic dystrophy
  D. Developmental abnormalities
    1. Hirschsprung's disease
    2. Total colonic aganglionosis (sometimes with small intestinal aganglionosis)
    3. Maturational arrest
      a. With mental retardation
      b. With other neurological abnormalities
      c. Isolated to myenteric plexus, without the above
    4. Neuronal intestinal dysplasia
      a. With neurofibromatosis
      b. With multiple endocrine neoplasia, type IIB
      c. Isolated to intestine, without above
      d. Severe, idiopathic constipation
      e. Cathartic damage
      f. Toxic damage

II. Disorders of the smooth muscle
  A. Primary
    1. Familial visceral myopathies
      a. Type I (autosomal dominant)
      b. Type II (autosomal recessive, with ptosis and external opthalmoplegia)
      c. Type III (autosomal recessive, with total GI tract dilatation)
  B. Secondary
    1. Progressive systemic sclerosis
    2. Progressive muscular dystrophy
    3. Amyloidosis
    4. Ceroidosis?
  C. Diffuse lymphoid infiltration

III. Small intestinal diverticulosis
  1. With muscle resembling visceral myopathy
  2. With muscle resembling progressive systemic sclerosis
  3. With visceral neuropathy and neuronal intranuclear inclusions
  4. Secondary to Fabry's disease

Chronic intestinal pseudo-obstruction is associated with a wide variety of systemic disorders, such as progressive systemic sclerosis, amyloidosis, myotonic dystrophy, and Duchenne's muscular dystrophy. These disorders are complicated by pseudo-obstruction because of changes they produce in either the smooth muscle or myenteric plexus. The term *chronic idiopathic intestinal pseudo-obstruction* was used in the past to categorize cases of pseudo-obstruction not associated with recognized systemic illness. In fact, many of the associated conditions listed in Table 22.1 now have more or less defined pathology and the word 'idiopathic' is less often used.[14]

Chronic intestinal pseudo-obstruction is sometimes associated with structural changes in the wall of the gastrointestinal tract which produce a marked enlargement. Megaoesophagus, megaduodenum, megajejunum and megacolon denote such an enlargement, but there are no agreed-upon criteria as to the minimal diameter an organ should measure to qualify for the designation.[15–31] They are secondary to abnormalities of the smooth muscle or myenteric plexus and can exist in the absence of symptoms. The megacolon of Hirschsprung's disease results from the absence of the myenteric plexus within the rectum or rectosigmoid. Non-Hirschsprung's megacolon, in many cases, results from abnormalities of the smooth muscle or myenteric plexus throughout the colon. A common cause of megacolon in South America is Chagas' disease, which destroys the myenteric plexus. When megacolon is present in the absence of such recognized association, it is referred to as an idiopathic megacolon. Patients with a megacolon have symptoms of constipation or pseudo-obstruction, or they may be asymptomatic.

Patients with megaduodenum are frequently thought to have the superior mesenteric artery syndrome.[15, 32–51] This is defined as a partial obstruction of the third part of the duodenum by the superior mesenteric artery which produces symptoms of intestinal obstruction. In fact, almost all such patients have primary pathologic abnormalities of the duodenal wall resulting in enlargement. Because the third part of the duodenum is held down by the overlying superior mesenteric artery, a picture of apparent obstruction is produced.

Visceral myopathy is the term used to denote degenerative changes consisting of smooth muscle cell degeneration and replacement fibrosis.[52–58] Either or both layers of the muscularis propria can be involved and when most severe, both are completely replaced. The smooth muscle of the bladder, uterus and iris of the eyes may also be involved. Visceral myopathy occurs at all ages, including infancy, and is either familial or sporadic.

Visceral neuropathy encompasses a number of different lesions of the myenteric plexus, and, occasionally, the submucosal plexus.[4,6,7,59–69] Any part of the gastrointestinal tract can be involved, and a variety of clinical syndromes may result. For instance, visceral neuropathy of the oesophagus produces achalasia or an achalasia-like syndrome; visceral neuropathy of the stomach produces gastroparesis; and visceral neuropathy of the small bowel and colon produces pseudo-obstruction, with or without enlargement of the bowel. Visceral neuropathy is characterized by a variety of degenerative changes in neurons, axons and both. These usually result in a reduction in neuron numbers within the myenteric plexus and are sometimes accompanied by an infiltration of mononuclear inflammatory cells. Visceral neuropathy can be confined to the gastrointestinal tract or associated with neural disease elsewhere, in the central, peripheral and autonomic nervous systems. Mental retardation, autonomic insufficiency and a neurogenic bladder are but three conditions which may be associated with some forms of visceral neuropathy.

Jejunal diverticulosis/Small intestinal diverticulosis describes the occurrence of multiple diverticula in the jejunum or throughout the small intestine. They are usually the result of structural changes produced in the wall of the small intestine by several types of visceral myopathies and neuropathies.[70] Patients may present with symptoms of intestinal pseudo-obstruction, bacterial overgrowth, perforation or haemorrhage.[71–77]

Severe idiopathic constipation denotes a clinical syndrome characterized by the passage of less than one stool per week despite the use of laxatives and enemas.[78,79] It is unassociated with any disease known to cause severe constipation, such as progressive systemic sclerosis or myxoedema. It is not associated with megacolon or symptoms of colonic pseudo-obstruction and its pathology is distinct from that of visceral myopathies and neuropathies.

DISORDERS OF THE MYENTERIC PLEXUS

Familial visceral neuropathies

Autosomal recessive, with intranuclear inclusions

This widespread neurological disorder, first described in a brother and sister in 1978,[63] is now referred to as 'neuronal intranuclear inclusion disease'[80–83] but the two siblings

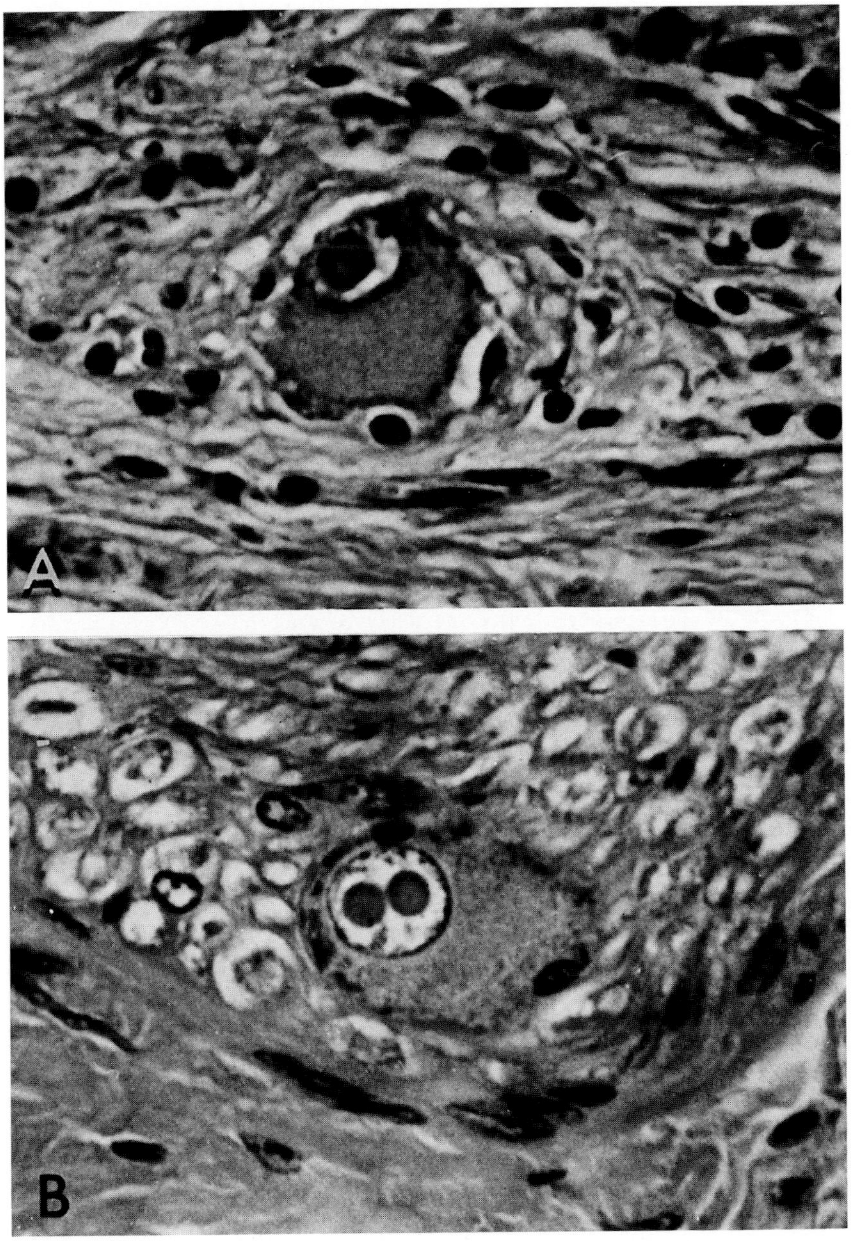

Fig. 22.11A A single intranuclear inclusion within a neuron of a patient with neuronal intranuclear inclusion disease. **B** Two intranuclear inclusions within a neuron of the patient's sibling. (H&E, ×1058. Reprinted with permission: Gastroenterology 1978; 75: 889–898).

presented with intestinal pseudo-obstruction. Subsequently reported cases, some misdiagnosed as Friedreich's ataxia, have manifested a variety of central, peripheral and autonomic nervous system abnormalities, including behaviour change, mental deterioration, multisystem atrophy, juvenile Parkinsonism and ataxia.

The first two cases, the only two children of a non-consanguineous marriage, had diffuse neurological abnormalities, mild autonomic insufficiency, and denervation hypersensitivity of the pupillary and oesophageal smooth muscles. By radiography, both had chaotic, repetitive and spontaneous contractions of the entire oesophagus; hyperactive, uncoordinated contractions of dilated small intestine, and extensive diverticular disease throughout the colon. One of them also had gastroparesis.

Both patients eventually died and at autopsy the myenteric plexus throughout the gastrointestinal tract was abnormal, whereas the smooth muscle was normal. In the oesophagus, stomach, small intestine and colon there was a significant reduction of neurons, approximately a third of which contained a prominent intranuclear inclusion which was mildly eosinophilic (Fig. 22.11A,B). These inclusions were shown to contain protein, but no DNA or RNA. By electron microscopy, they were composed of a random array of straight to slightly curving filaments, which were somewhat indistinct, but seemed to have beading at a periodicity of 15–30 nm and a diameter of 17–27 nm. There was no resemblance to any known viral particles. The inclusions were also present in the neurons of the submucosal plexus and thus would be found in mucosal rectal biopsies.

Examination of the brain, spinal cord, peripheral nerves and autonomic nervous system revealed the same type of neuronal inclusions which have been the key diagnostic features of all subsequent cases.

Silver stains of longitudinal sections of the myenteric plexus showed markedly decreased numbers of neurons and nerve fibres. Some nerve tracts contained only 1 or 2 axons whereas normal nerve tracts contain 50–100 axons (Fig. 22.12A,B). Most neurons were abnormally shaped and virtually none had a normal number of axons and dendrites. Particularly striking in the oesophagus was the presence of some neurons with swollen, clubbed dendrites (Fig. 22.13A,B,C,D). No inflammatory cells were seen within the plexus and no proliferation of glial cells was apparent.

In another family with chronic intestinal pseudo-obstruction, three of four siblings were affected and the diagnosis of neuronal intranuclear inclusion disease was made histologically by standard rectal biopsy into submucosa.[84] Discrete eosinophilic intranuclear inclusions were found in submucosal neurons. Because of involvement in multiple members of two generations, the familial visceral neuropathy in this pedigree was transmitted in an autosomal dominant manner. Furthermore, the definitive diagnosis of neuronal intranuclear inclusion disease could be made antemortem by standard rectal biopsy.

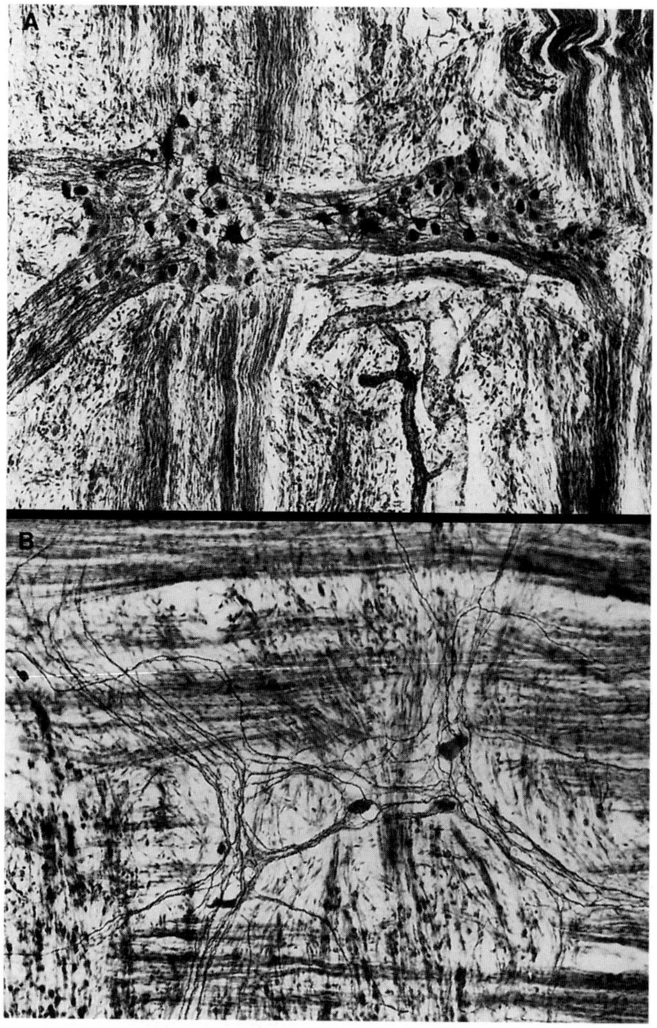

Fig. 22.12A Numerous neurons within a ganglion of a normal duodenum. There are many nerve fibres within the nerve tracts. **B** Ganglion from duodenum of patient with neuronal intranuclear inclusion disease, showing only three neurons and few axons within the nerve tracts. (Silver, ×86. Reprinted with permission: Gastroenterology 1978; 75: 889–898)

At least nine other cases of neuronal intranuclear inclusion disease have since been reported.[80–83] These cases have presented with extraintestinal neurological symptoms. This author has seen two other cases with typical inclusions in the myenteric plexus, one of whom had diffuse small intestinal diverticulosis.

Autosomal recessive, with mental retardation and calcifications of the basal ganglia

This syndrome was described in England in four siblings of a sibship of 16.[61] They all had malabsorption, mental retardation, calcifications of the basal ganglia and episodes of pseudo-obstruction. The smooth muscle was of

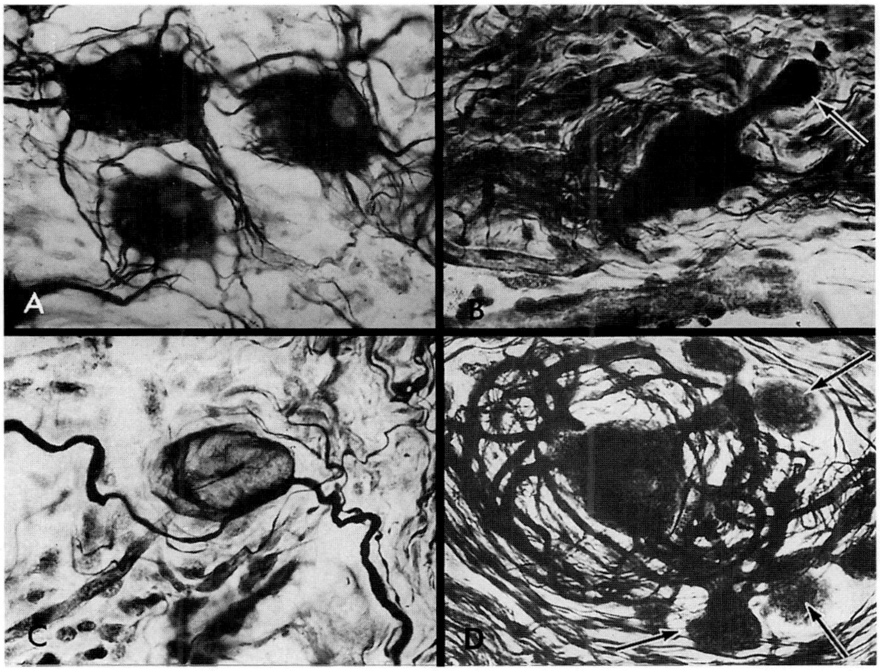

Fig. 22.13A Three neurons within a ganglion of a normal oesophagus. Note that they have multiple delicate processes. **B** An abnormal oesophageal neuron with a swollen dendrite (arrow) from a case of neuronal intranuclear inclusion disease. **C** Degenerated oesophageal neuron from same case. **D** Abnormal oesophageal neuron with many swollen dendrites (arrows) from same case. (Silver, ×345. Reprinted with permission: Gastroenterology 1978; 75: 889–898)

normal to reduced thickness. Although axons appeared normal on silver staining, argyrophilic neurons were reduced in number and argyrophobic neurons were degenerated.

Autosomal dominant

Two families have been studied, the first in Northern Ireland and the second in the United States.[59,85] Neither family had central, peripheral or autonomic nervous system abnormalities. Neither had oesophageal motor abnormalities and just one of four members of one family had a dilated, elongated colon. The predominant feature of gut involvement in both families was dilatation of the jejunum and ileum.

In haematoxylin and eosin sections, the smooth muscle coats were mildly thickened but otherwise unremarkable, and the neurons did not have intranuclear inclusions. By contrast, the 50 μm silver stained sections showed degenerative changes of argyrophilic neurons and axons. Many ganglia contained no argyrophilic neurons and others contained just one or two, whereas most ganglia normally contain eight or more. The argyrophilic neurons present had poor definition of cell borders, decreased argyrophilia and some were swollen, distorted and vacuolated. Large and intermediate sized axons were decreased in number and the smaller fibres had multiple swellings along their course. Several axons were abnormally hypertrophied and beaded and were distributed haphazardly within the smooth muscle, indicating non-specific fibre proliferation in response to neuronal injury. No inflammatory cells or glial cell proliferation was present.

Sporadic visceral neuropathies

Degenerative, non-inflammatory

In this form of visceral neuropathy there are at least two types of degenerative changes in the myenteric plexus which may involve the entire gastrointestinal tract.[4,60,64,65,67,86–88] They are not familial and do not involve the nervous system extrinsic to the gastrointestinal tract.

In Type I[4] the mean number of neurons within the colonic myenteric plexus is significantly decreased compared with controls. No inflammatory cells are present in the myenteric plexus and in haematoxylin and eosin sections it is difficult to be certain if morphological abnormalities of the neurons are present.

By contrast, silver stains demonstrate a number of abnormalities which are patchy in occurrence, with some sections containing a normal or near normal appearing plexus. Abnormalities consist of swelling, fragmentation and dropout of neurons, fragmentation and dropout of axons and replacement of areas of the plexus by a proliferation of glial cells (Figs 22.14–22.16) Such areas are devoid of neurons and only a few axons remain within what amounts to a glial cell scar. Normally by this technique, neurons are irregular and often have pyramidal and slightly concave shapes. Their cell boundaries are sharply defined and a number of distinct tapering processes emanate from the nerve bodies. In this disorder some neurons are swollen two to three times the normal size, their cell boundaries are rounded and indistinct and fewer processes are present. Many of the processes present are thickened and disposed in an haphazard fashion.

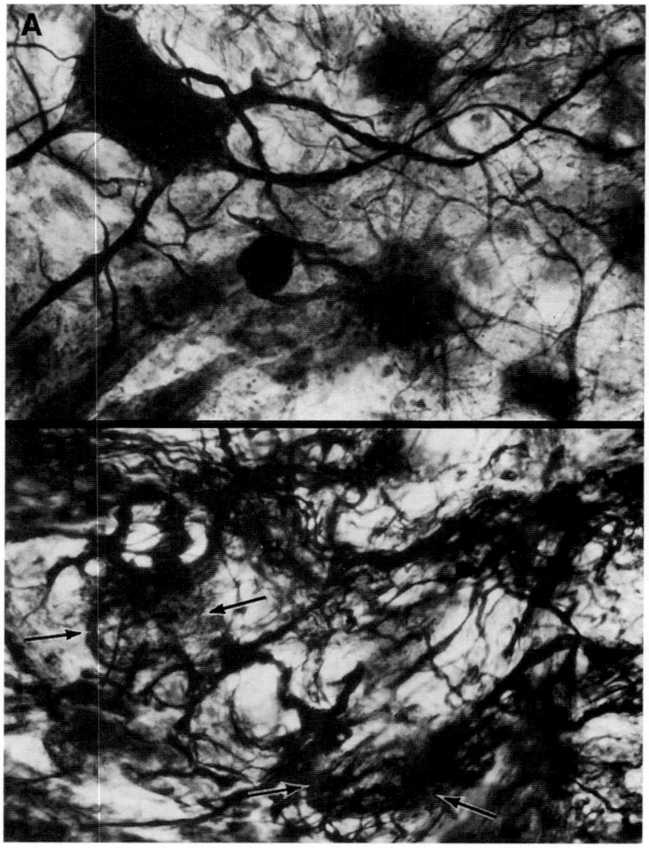

Fig. 22.14A Neurons and nerve processes from normal ileum showing distinct nerve bodies and fibres. **B** Same, but from ileum of a patient with a degenerative, non-inflammatory neuropathy. The nerve bodies (arrows) are indistinct and there is axonal disorganization. (Silver, ×1020. Reprinted with permission: Gastroenterology 1982; 82: 476–486)

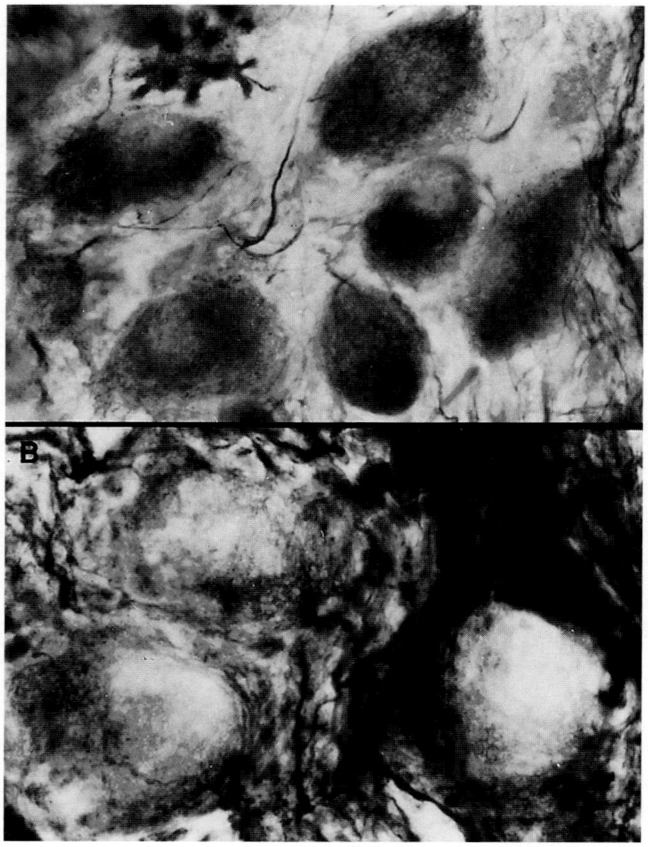

Fig. 22.15A Argyrophobic neurons from normal colon. **B** Three markedly swollen argyrophobic neurons from the same patients as in Figure 22.14. (Silver, both ×1020. Reprinted with permission: Gastroenterology 1982; 82: 476–486)

Electron microscopy confirms these findings, showing various stages of neuronal degeneration. The earliest stage consists of loss of neurotubules, imparting to the neuron a more electron lucent appearance. Mitochondria are swollen and the ribosomal network clumped together. More severe changes include vacuoles in the cytoplasm and fragmentation of the cell membrane. Axons vary in appearance from normal to severely abnormal. Abnormalities

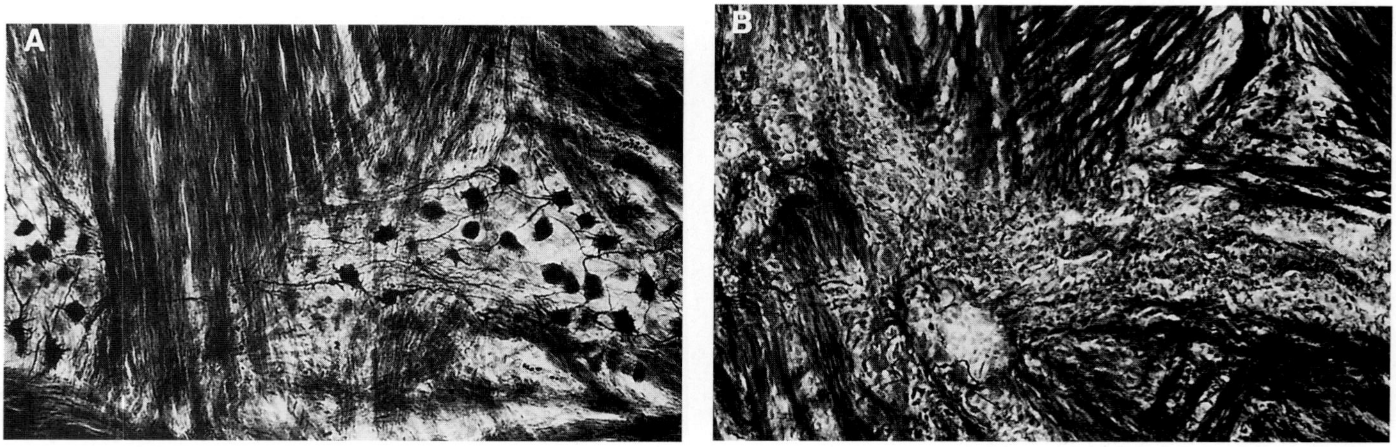

A B

Fig. 22.16A Myenteric plexus from control colon showing numerous neurons and nerve fibres. **B** Myenteric plexus from the same patient as in Figure 22.14, showing replacement by glial cells, denoted by multiple small nuclei. (Silver, both ×255. Reprinted with permission: Gastroenterology 1982; 82: 476–486) consist of swelling, loss of neurotubules, disappearance of organelles and fragmentation of axolemmas.

This disorder differs in appearance from neuronal intranuclear inclusion disease in several ways:

1) no intranuclear inclusions are present
2) dendrites are not clubbed
3) a proliferation of glial cells is present
4) neurons are more swollen and their cytoplasm more fragmented.

Type 2 non-inflammatory visceral neuropathy[67] is characterized by a degeneration of both the argyrophilic and argyrophobic neurons which results in a clearing of the neuronal cytoplasm, producing an appearance somewhat like signet ring cells (Fig. 22.17A,B). Neurons are swollen, with some argyrophobic almost twice normal size. Axonal degeneration is also present, but there are no intranuclear inclusions, no dendritic swellings, no inflammatory cells and no glial cell proliferation. There is dropout of neurons in some ganglia with apparent spaces created containing only traces of neuronal cytoplasm. This type of visceral neuropathy has been encountered in both the small intestine and colon.

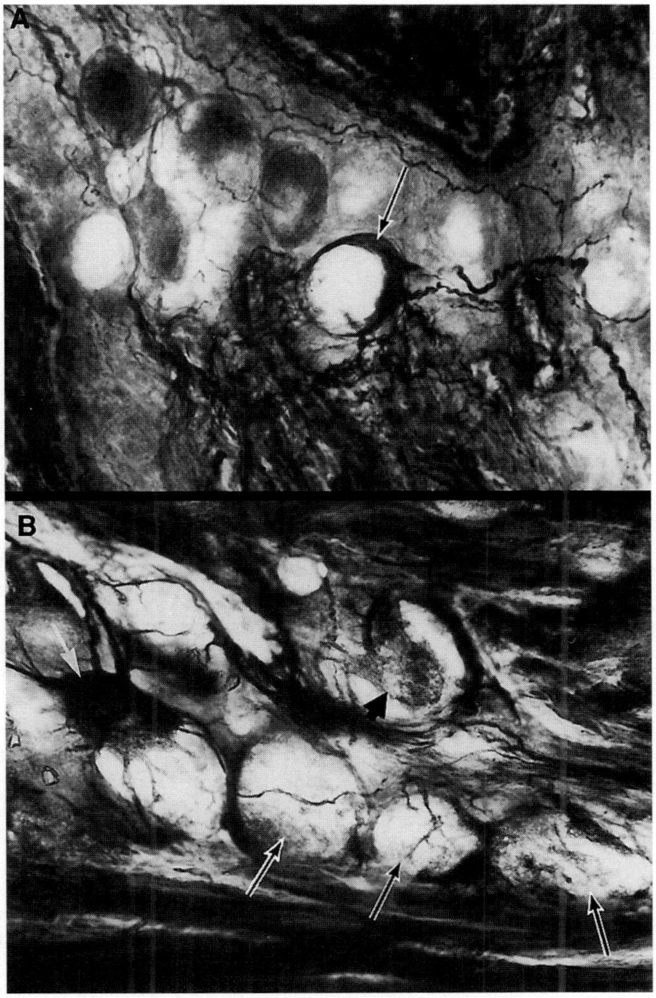

Fig. 22.17A Swollen neuron with complete absence of stainable cytoplasm except for a rim of argyrophilia (arrow), from a patient with a second type of degenerative, non-inflammatory visceral neuropathy. **B** Ganglionic area from same patient showing several spaces created by neuron degeneration and dropout (arrows). One degenerated neuron (short black arrow) and one normal argyrophilic neuron (white arrow) can still be discerned. (Silver, both ×353. Reprinted with permission: Gastroenterology 1985; 89: 1152–1156)

In some of the cases in this overall group which have been studied, clinical, radiographic and pathological details have been incomplete, thus it is possible that more than two subtypes of this form of neuropathy actually exist.

Degenerative, inflammatory

Paraneoplastic. Small cell carcinoma of the lung may produce a variety of paraneoplastic syndromes, and visceral neuropathy with severe gastrointestinal dysmotility has been reported several times, usually in association with other neurological manifestations.[66,89–91] Six cases associated with small cell carcinoma of the lung and one associated with metastatic carcinoid have been personally evaluated. All presented with intestinal pseudo-obstruction and severe obstipation; six of seven had gastroparesis and four had oesophageal peristaltic abnormalities. In two patients the carcinoma was only diagnosed at autopsy.

The first case presented at age 58 with an abrupt onset of intestinal pseudo-obstruction.[66] This left the patient incapacitated and totally dependent on parenteral nutrition. Several months later, a progressive neurological syndrome with autonomic insufficiency, a neurogenic bladder and generalized neurological abnormalities developed. At autopsy, nine months after onset, a small cell carcinoma of the lung was unexpectedly found. In haematoxylin and eosin sections of tissue from oesophagus to colon there was widespread degeneration of the myenteric plexus, a marked reduction of neurons and infiltration of the plexus by plasma cells and lymphocytes (Fig. 22.18). Silver stains showed a decrease in both argyrophilic and argyrophobic neurons throughout the gastrointestinal tract. Although some were normal, others were vacuolated and had cytoplasmic distortions and decreased numbers of processes. Nerve fibre abnormalities consisted of axonal swelling, fragmentation and dropout of axons (Fig. 22.19). In some nerve tracts, axons were completely replaced by a glial cell scar (Fig. 22.20A,B). In contrast to the extensive injury of the myenteric plexus, the submucosal plexus was unaffected.

Six other cases have been studied, and the cases reported in the literature have an identical pathology. This form of neuropathy produces extensive destruction of the myenteric plexus. The key finding is the presence of lymphoid cells and plasma cells within the plexus. It is hypothesized that they mediate the injury to the plexus.

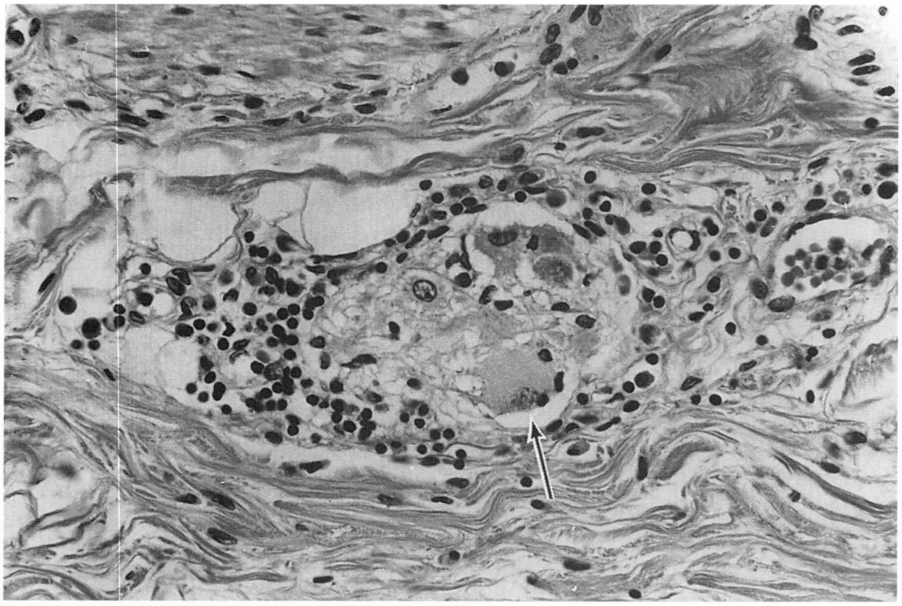

Fig. 22.18 Myenteric plexus from patient with paraneoplastic visceral neuropathy showing infiltration with many lymphocytes and plasma cells. The arrow denotes a neuron. (H&E, ×256)

This intestinal neuropathy may be the explanation for Ogilvie's syndrome as originally reported by Ogilvie in 1948 in association with metastatic cancer.[10] Its pathogenesis may be an antibody-associated neural injury due to shared antigens between small cell carcinoma and neural tissue.[92–96] In fact four of five patients in one study had immunoglobulin G antibodies reactive with neurons of the enteric nerve plexuses of the jejunum and stomach by an indirect immunofluorescence assay.[91] Antibodies in highly diluted serum bound selectively to neurons in the gut. The authors suggested that serological testing for the presence of this antibody could provide a means for diagnosing small cell carcinoma in patients with new onset of severe dysmotility.[91]

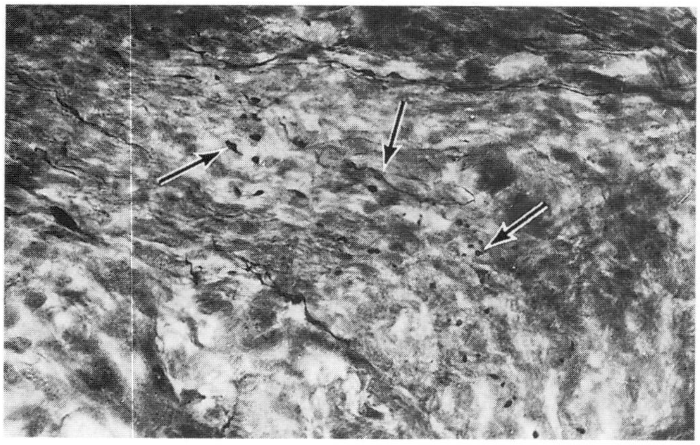

Fig. 22.19 Myenteric plexus from jejunum of same patient as in Figure 22.18, showing virtual absence of nerve fibres. Axon fragments (arrows) can be seen, the remaining evidence of severe axonal destruction. (Silver, ×642. Reprinted with permission: Annals of Internal Medicine 1983; 98: 129–134)

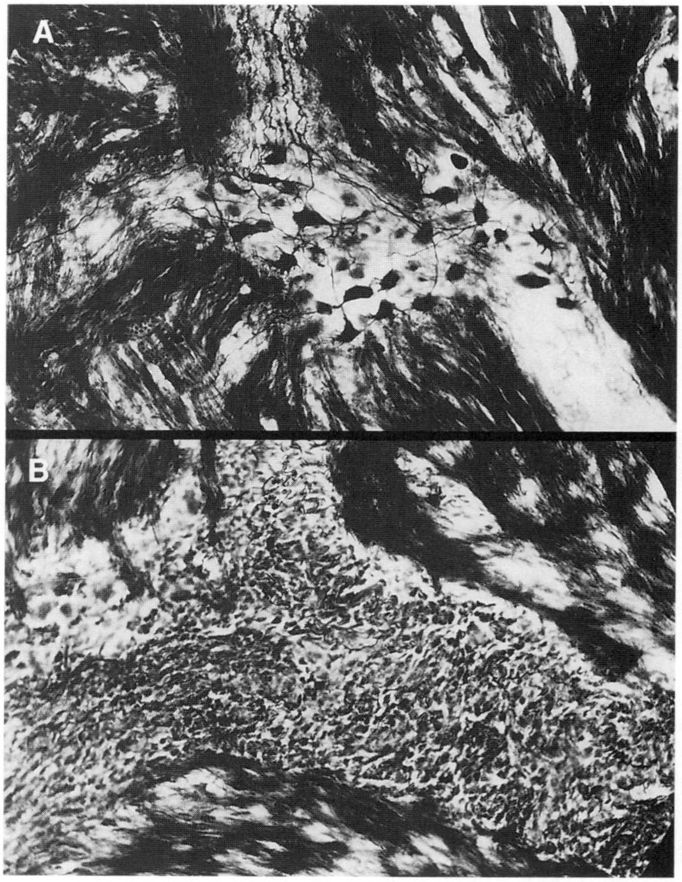

Fig. 22.20A Myenteric plexus of a normal colon shows numerous neurons and nerve fibres. **B** Myenteric plexus from colon of same patient as in Figure 22.18. Neurons and nerve fibres have been replaced by a proliferation of glial cells. (Silver, ×256. Reprinted with permission: Annals of Internal Medicine 1983; 98: 129–134)

Non-paraneoplastic — Chagas' disease. Chagas' disease is caused by the parasite *Trypanosoma cruzi*, which, like small cell carcinoma of the lung, can also elicit an immune cell response which cross reacts with the myenteric plexus and thereby injures it.[97,98] All areas of the intestine may be involved, with the oesophagus and colon being most frequently affected.[99–102] An achalasia-like illness results from the oesophageal involvement, intractable constipation and a megacolon from the colonic involvement and intestinal pseudo-obstruction from small intestinal involvement. The pathology is one of smooth muscle hypertrophy, infiltration of the myenteric plexus by lymphocytes and plasma cells, loss of both argyrophilic and argyrophobic neurons, degenerated argyrophilic neurons which have swollen and irregular processes, and axonal destruction and dropout. Thus, Chagas' disease produces an appearance similar to paraneoplastic visceral neuropathy.

Cytomegalovirus involvement of the myenteric plexus may rarely occur.[103,104] In one personally studied case, inflammatory cells and glial cell hyperplasia were present, along with typical neuronal intranuclear inclusions. Axons had degenerated and there was extensive dropout. Some of the remaining axons appeared hypertrophied and disorganized and showed sprouting. There was also some neuronal injury and dropout, but the major pathology was the axonopathy. This was a patchy process, with some ganglia remaining unaffected.

Encephalomyeloneuropathy and visceral neuropathy is also described in a 55-year-old woman with rapidly progressive brainstem dysfunction associated with severe constipation and ileus.[62] At autopsy within a month of onset there was neuronal degeneration and loss associated with a lymphocytic infiltrate in the brainstem, olivary nuclei, hypothalmus, dorsal root ganglia and myenteric plexus of the entire gastrointestinal tract. No neoplasm or viral particles were identified.

On occasion, the myenteric plexus alone or the myenteric and the submucosal plexus is involved in a chronic inflammatory process with lymphocytes and sometimes plasma cells and, rarely, eosinophils also, which is associated with marked neuronal and axonal loss and scarring.[15] The pathology is similar to that associated with small cell carcinoma and Chagas' disease, but no underlying disorder is present. In this idiopathic variant the abnormality is easily recognized in haematoxylin and eosin sections because the normal myenteric plexus never contains chronic inflammatory cells.

Inflammatory axonopathy

This is a disorder that proved fatal in a 39-year-old man just 3 months after initial symptoms of pseudo-obstruction.[68] Throughout the gastrointestinal tract the myenteric plexus contained lymphocytes and plasma cells (Fig. 22.21).

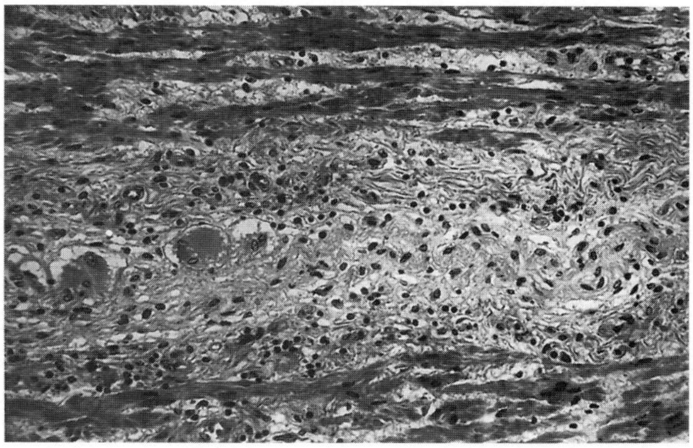

Fig. 22.21 Lymphoid cells within the myenteric plexus of a patient with an inflammatory axonopathy. (H&E, ×150. Reprinted with permission: Gastroenterology 1986; 90: 754–758)

Although both argyrophilic and argyrophobic neurons were normal in appearance and numbers, axons demonstrated beading, fragmentation, and dropout in all areas (Fig. 22.22A,B). Normally, 25–100 axons can be counted within a nerve tract, but the majority of nerve tracts in this patient contained 5–10 axons only. In addition, there were increased numbers of glial cell nuclei within the ganglionic areas and nerve tracts. Thus axonal destruction seemingly had occurred in the absence of significant damage to neuron bodies. The condition was not associated with coincident malignancy.

Myotonic dystrophy

Smooth muscle dysfunction in myotonic dystrophy can occur anywhere within the gastrointestinal tract, and patients may initially present with gastrointestinal symptoms.[105–107] Occasionally these symptoms become the most troublesome part of the illness, and patients may present with pseudo-obstruction or a megacolon.

Very little is known of the pathology other than from studies at autopsy which have limitations imposed by autolysis. One reported that smooth muscle cells were swollen, partially destroyed and replaced by fat[108] and in another study atrophy of individual muscle fibres and pericellular vacuolation was described.[109]

A personally studied case of megacolon secondary to myotonic dystrophy revealed a degenerative visceral neuropathy rather than, as expected, a visceral myopathy.[110] Neurons and axons were decreased in number and neuronal and axonal degeneration were present. The substance P/enkephalin innervation of the smooth muscle was deficient, whereas the VIP/neuropeptide Y innervation was normal, suggesting that the degeneration mainly affected neurons containing substance P and enkephalin. In contrast, the smooth muscles were normal by both light and electron microscopy.

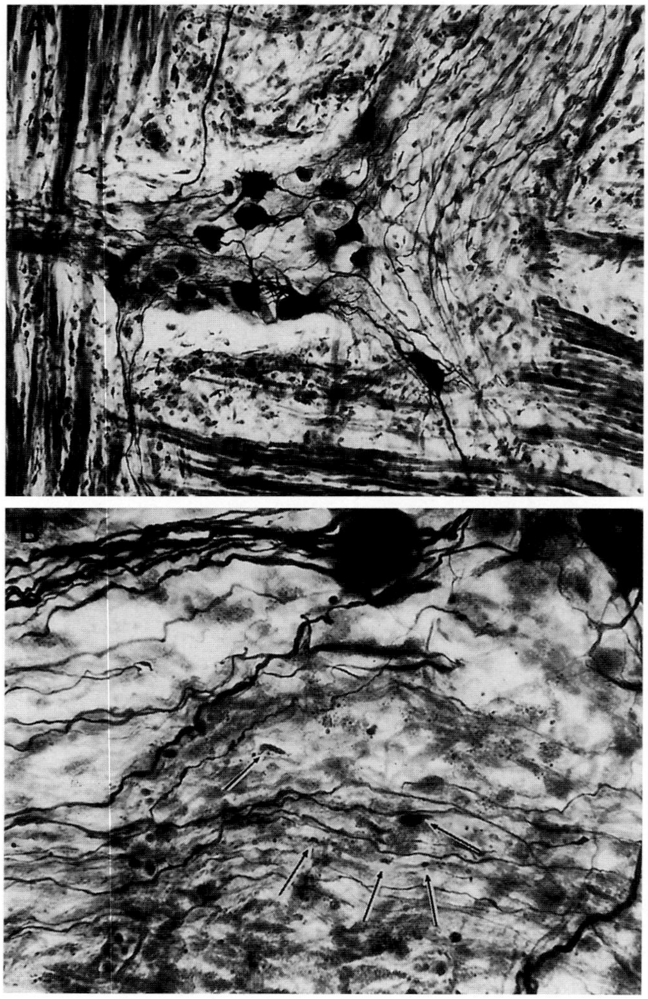

Fig. 22.22A Ganglionic area from ileum of same patient as in Figure 22.21 showing normal neurons but reduced number of axons. Inflammatory cell nuclei are seen in nerve tract. (Silver, ×150). **B** Different ganglion from ileum showing axonal beading, degeneration and axonal debris (arrows). (Silver, ×378. Reprinted with permission: Gastroenterology 1986; 90: 754–758)

DEVELOPMENTAL ABNORMALITIES

A variety of abnormalities of development can affect the myenteric plexus.[27,31,111–140] Some may be associated with other abnormalities, as in neurofibromatosis. Failure of neural crest cell migration into the intestine can result in Hirschsprung's disease and its variants. An abnormal proliferation of the enteric plexuses, *neuronal intestinal dysplasia*, can result in increased numbers of neurons and axons in both normal and abnormal locations, such as within the muscularis propria or lamina propria. These entities are discussed elsewhere.

It is less well appreciated that following neural crest cell migration into the gastrointestinal tract, cells proliferate and then neurons must mature and develop processes and synapses, allowing for communication within the same ganglia, between different ganglia and between the ganglia and smooth muscle. Interruption of this process results in abnormal intestinal motility which expresses itself at birth, infancy or early childhood. Those affected may present with pseudo-obstruction or with severe constipation mimicking Hirschsprung's disease and a definitive pathological diagnosis is often only possible utilizing the silver technique already referred to. In 26 personally studied cases, the findings have varied depending upon the stage at which development of the myenteric plexus ceased. In one subtype, clusters of bare nuclei or others with poorly developed cytoplasm are present in areas corresponding to ganglia. No cells recognizable as neurons are seen and nerve tracts are absent. The lesion suggests that either very few neural crest cells migrated in or that adequate proliferation did not occur or too many died off. In a second subtype, ganglia and nerve tracts are recognizable. However, although the ganglia are full of nuclei and some have associated cytoplasm, there are few argyrophilic neurons and few axons within the nerve tracts (Fig. 22.23). The argyrophilic neurons present are small and have only one or two processes. This appearance suggests an arrest of maturation of neuronal development. In a third sub-

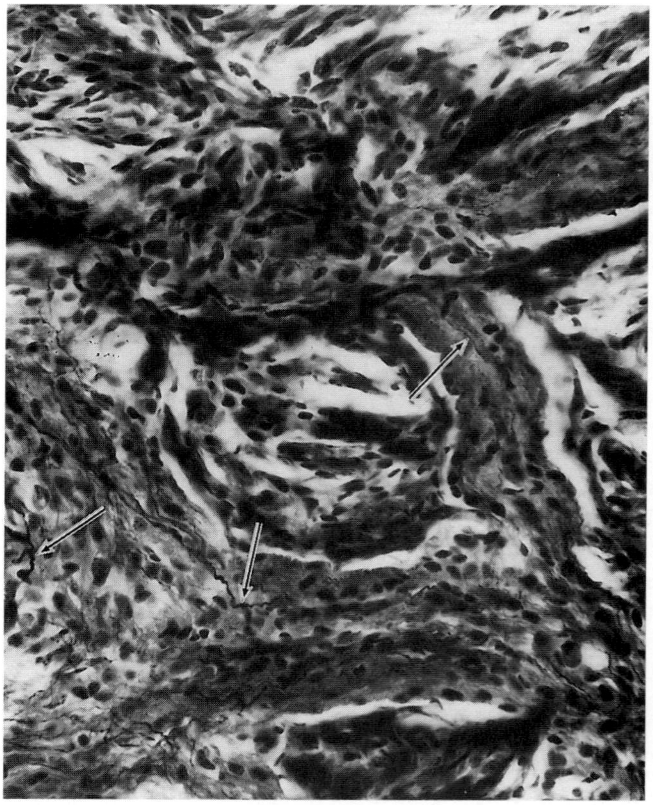

Fig. 22.23 Ganglionic area from an infant who was born with intestinal pseudo-obstruction. Many nuclei are seen within the nerve tracts. However, no argyrophilic neurons and only few axons (arrows) are present. (Silver, ×272)

type, there is greater development of argyrophilic neurons and axons, but their numbers are abnormally low compared with normal infants and children, so that this, too, probably represents an interruption of normal maturation.

These abnormalities are sometimes associated with other gastrointestinal, central and peripheral neurological disturbances, including a short, small intestine, malrotation, pyloric hypertrophy, failure of spontaneous respiration at birth, seizures, abnormal motor development and mental retardation. The more severe lesions of the myenteric plexus can be recognized in haematoxylin and eosin sections as a paucity of neurons and axons, but for the recognition of the more subtle lesions it is necessary to employ the silver stain, because argyrophilia and axon development are markers of maturation There are several reports which refer to problems caused by neuronal immaturity [112,119,131,139] or early neuronal damage.[123,140]

Antineurofilament antibodies have been used to study the bowel in congenital pseudo-obstruction, 'hypoganglionosis', and Hirschsprung's disease,[141,142] with the finding of unstained normal axon bundles in pseudo-obstruction, meaning that axons are present but lacking in neurofilament immunoreactivity. This would correlate with a deficiency of argyrophilia on silver stains, since normally, silver blackens neural elements by depositing on neurofilaments. With fewer neurofilaments, there is less blackening or argyrophilia. Thus, it appears that antineurofilament antibodies could be used as another method to diagnose abnormalities of the myenteric plexus.

SEVERE IDIOPATHIC CONSTIPATION

Of all patients who complain of constipation, there is a small number, all women, in whom it is severe, i.e. they may have only one stool every 1–4 weeks despite cathartics and enemas.[78,79] On barium enema, the colon in some of these patients is elongated and redundant; in others it is normal in appearance but fails to evacuate the barium.

The myenteric plexus shows a reduced number of argyrophilic neurons, which tend to be small and irregular and have fewer processes than normal.[78] They stain less intensely and more unevenly than usual and their margins tend to be indistinct. Ganglia contain numerous cells with nuclei of different sizes and prominent chromatin, but cell bodies which are indistinct (Fig. 22.24A,B,C). These may be glial cells or immature neurons. Axons are also decreased in number and in some nerve tracts there is slight axonal fragmentation and debris. These features are quite characteristic and have been identified in over 35 patients.

Some of these patients also have severe epigastric pain, nausea and vomiting in the absence of the dilatation of the small intestine characteristic of patients with intestinal pseudo-obstruction. However, they have abnormal gastric emptying and gastroduodenal motor function as recorded

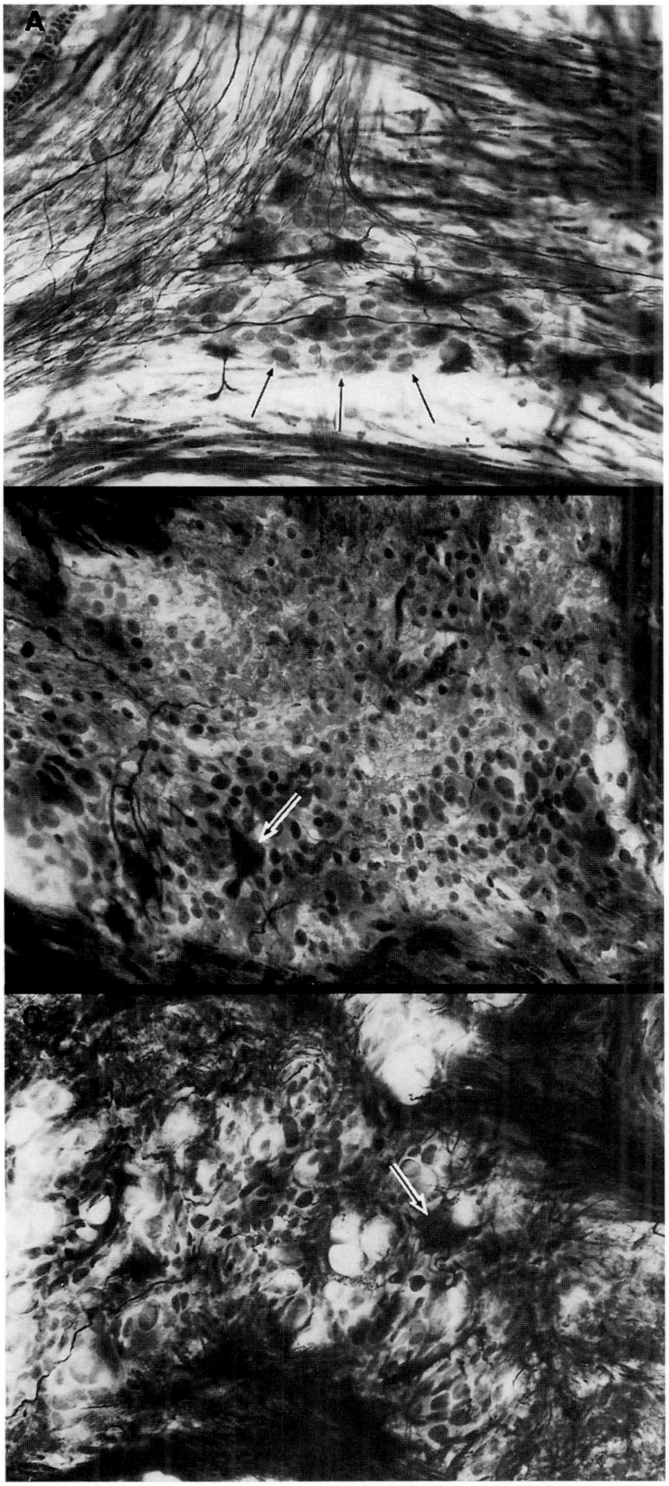

Fig. 22.24A Ganglionic area from the colon of a patient with severe idiopathic constipation. It shows argyrophilic neurons and nerve fibres, but with an increased number of nuclei, some of which have associated cytoplasm, identifying them as argyrophobic neurons (arrows). **B** Ganglionic area from the colon of another patient with severe idiopathic constipation, showing only one small argyrophilic neuron with a single process (arrow) within a background of numerous nuclei. **C** Ganglionic area from the colon of a third case of severe idiopathic constipation showing only one argyrophilic neuron (arrow) and numerous nuclei. (Silver, all ×377. Reprinted with permission: Gastroenterology 1985; 88: 26–34)

by manometry. Full thickness small intestinal biopsies in some of them show an abnormality of the myenteric plexus identical to that seen in the colon.[143]

Cathartic colon

It is fair to question whether the pathology of severe long standing idiopathic constipation is a primary disorder of the myenteric plexus or whether it represents an abnormality induced by abuse of cathartics. In cathartic induced injury of the colonic myenteric plexus, however, the pathology is different.

The chronic ingestion of anthraquinone cathartics, such as senna, cascara and danthrone, produce a brown to black discolouration of the mucosa known as melanosis coli.[144–148] This is due to the production of lipofuscin in the lysosomes of macrophages in the lamina propria and superficial submucosa. The pigmentation is usually most prominent in the right colon but may extend all the way down to the rectum. Although melanosis coli, by itself, is of no consequence, its presence serves as a marker of laxative use, a use which may be denied by some patients. The question is whether these laxatives ever produce injury of the enteric plexuses.

Mice given anthraquinones develop fragmentation of myenteric plexus axons and axonal and dendritic swelling.[149] According to Smith,[150] humans with melanosis coli may have injury of the myenteric plexus characterized by a loss of argyrophilic neurons, an increase of glial cells and remaining argyrophilic neurons which appear dark, shrunken and have clubbed or swollen processes. These changes have been confirmed in several personally studied cases of severe melanosis coli and are clearly different from those of severe idiopathic constipation.

In both, there are decreased argyrophilic neurons, but in cathartic colon many of the remaining argyrophilic neurons appear injured, i.e. they are shrunken and have abnormal or fewer processes (Fig. 22.25A,B) or they are swollen and pale. In severe idiopathic constipation, however, the argyrophilic neurons are small and indistinctly stained and have few processes, an appearance similar to that of normal neonates. Many of the background nuclei in severe idiopathic constipation are neuronal whereas in cathartic injury they are glial cells. Although, in both, there are decreased axons, in cathartic colon the remaining axons appear injured, being fragmented and swollen (Fig. 22.25A,B). In severe idiopathic constipation, the axons simply are not visible in normal numbers, an appearance somewhat similar to that of infants with arrested development of the myenteric plexus. In some patients with severe idiopathic constipation, there is mild axonal fragmentation which could be a secondary effect from cathartics used in treatment, but a majority of colons from these patients do not have melanosis coli.

Thus, the myenteric plexus in cathartic injury appears damaged whereas in severe idiopathic constipation, it has an appearance similar to immaturity.

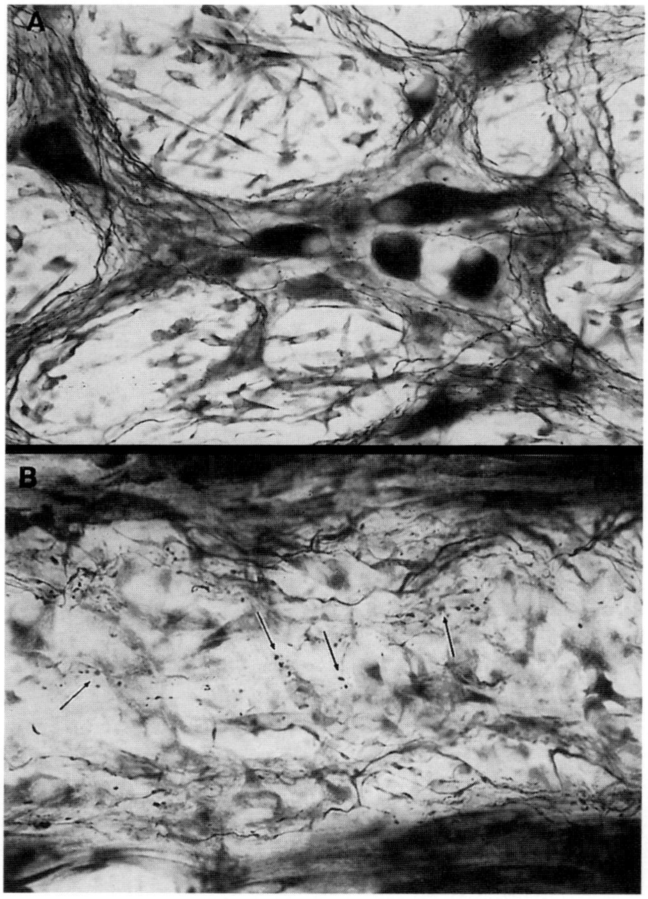

Fig. 22.25A Ganglionic area from the colon of a patient with melanosis coli and cathartic injury of the myenteric plexus. Argyrophilic neurons are present but they lack visible processes. There is a reduced number of axons.(Silver, ×224) **B** Nerve tract from adjacent area showing marked axon fragmentation (arrows) and reduced axon numbers. (Silver, ×353)

Ultrastructural studies of colonic biopsies from patients with chronic cathartic abuse are few but may show abnormalities of the submucosal plexus. Ballooning of axons, reduction of nerve-specific organelles, increased lysosomal activity, reduced numbers of neurofilaments and neurotubules and decreased amounts of neurosecretory granules within nerve endings are described.[151]

Toxic damage

There is evidence that mice given atropine, chlorpromazine or vinca alkaloids develop variable types of damage to the myenteric plexus.[3] It is well recognized that phenothiazines, vinca alkaloids, anticholinergics and tricyclic antidepressants can produce severe constipation in man. However, to what extent this constipation is caused by drug induced damage to the plexus is not known.

DISORDERS OF THE SMOOTH MUSCLE

Primary disorders

Familial visceral myopathies

Familial visceral myopathies are uncommon diseases characterized by degeneration and thinning of smooth muscle, changes readily appreciated in haematoxylin and eosin and trichrome stains.[52–58,152–154] The affected smooth muscle cells show loss of stain intensity, indistinct cell boundaries, fragmentation and their dropout creates apparent spaces containing cell debris (Fig. 22.26A,B,C). Associated with this process is a variable amount of collagen deposition. When this is marked, areas of muscle may be completely replaced. Collagen is sometimes deposited around degenerating cells in such a way that the muscle takes on a distinctly honey-combed appearance readily appreciated at low magnification; this is called 'vacuolar degeneration'. The severity of abnormality varies with site but in general the longitudinal muscle is more often affected than the circular. At electron microscopy[57] the earliest changes consist of dropout and disarray of myofilaments within the smooth muscle cells, such that the myofilaments do not align themselves in an orderly way with the dense bodies. This makes the cells appear electron-lucent. As cells degenerate, the mitochondria swell, cell membranes disintegrate and cells lyse so that the muscle layer is filled with cellular debris. These areas eventually come to contain collagen fibres.

Neurons, nerve processes and nerve terminals are all normal. No acute inflammatory cells, lymphocytes or plasma cells are seen in the muscle coats and vasculitis is absent. Thus, visceral myopathy seems to be a pure disorder of smooth muscle.

In some families the abnormality may affect smooth muscle in sites other than the gastrointestinal tract, such as the bladder and iris of the eyes[52] and has become known as 'familial visceral myopathy' rather than 'hereditary hollow visceral myopathy'. At least 12 families have been reported and although all have the same pathology,

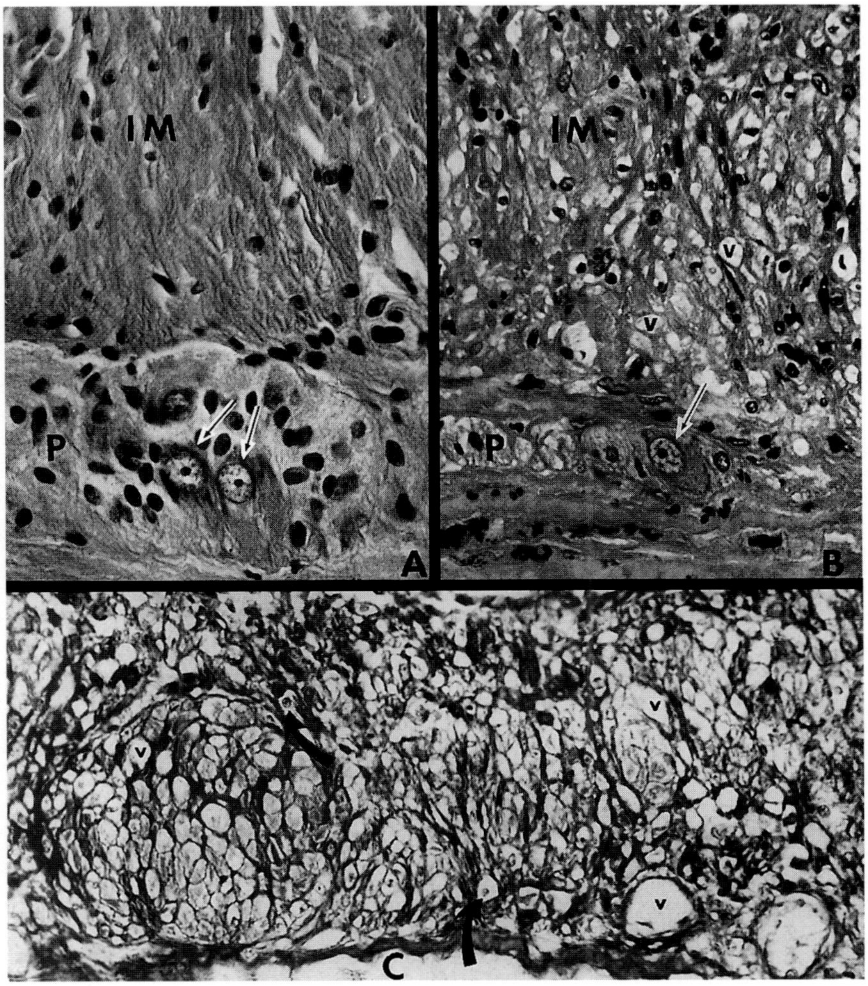

Fig. 22.26A Inner muscle (IM) and myenteric plexus (P) of a normal small intestine. The arrows point to neurons. **B** Inner muscle (IM) of the small intestine of a patient with familial visceral myopathy showing apparent vacuoles (v) and few distinct muscle fibres, i.e. vacuolar degeneration. The arrow indicates a normal neuron in the myenteric plexus (P). Both H&E, ×368). **C** Inner muscle of the patient's small intestine has a diffuse, lacy fibrosis which surrounds and accentuates the vacuoles, some of which contain poorly staining small muscle cells (arrows).(Masson's trichrome, ×368. Reprinted with permission: Gastroenterology 1977; 73: 327–338)

the pattern of involvement within the gastrointestinal tract and bladder and the mode of genetic transmission produces four different expressions of the illness.

Type I familial visceral myopathy is transmitted as an autosomal dominant trait.[52,53,55,57] It is characterized by oesophageal dilatation, a megaduodenum, redundant elongated colon and a megacystis. The stomach and the small intestine distal to the duodenum are usually normal, although the jejunum may occasionally be distended as well. One patient also had uterine inertia during labour.

Type II familial visceral myopathy is transmitted as an autosomal recessive trait.[56,152–154] It is characterized by gastric dilatation and slight dilatation and diverticulosis of the entire small intestine, while lacking the megaduodenum and megacystis seen in the Type I disorder. In addition, patients have ptosis and external ophthalmoplegia.

Type III familial visceral myopathy was reported in a family having marked dilatation of the entire gastrointestinal tract from the oesophagus to rectum.[155] No extraintestinal manifestations were observed and autosomal recessive transmission was probable. It is not clear whether this represents yet another form of familial visceral myopathy or whether it is but another expression of the autosomal recessive illnesses mentioned above.

Type IV familial visceral myopathy was described in two siblings who had gastroparesis, a tubular, narrow small intestine without diverticula and a normal oesophagus and colon.[54] These two cases had severe vacuolar degeneration and atrophy of the longitudinal muscle of the small intestine associated with striking hypertrophy of the circular muscle. It is this hypertrophy which probably produced the tubular narrowing of the small intestine. It is likely that this is also transmitted as an autosomal recessive trait.

One additional family has been reported in which members of three generations have the dysplastic naevus syndrome, visceral myopathy, and multiple basal cell carcinoma.[156] Affected family members have megaduodenum and bladder dysfunction. The authors suggest that the association between cutaneous disease and smooth muscle dysfunction may represent linkage between two genetic loci or pleiotropic expression of a single locus.

Nonfamilial visceral myopathy

Some patients with visceral myopathy have no evidence of familial involvement, either because they have a different disease which is not inherited, or because too few family members have been at risk to exclude the possibility of inheritance.[6] The pathology is identical to that in familial cases and involvement throughout the gastrointestinal tract and bladder occurs.

Nonfamilial visceral myopathy has been encountered in all age groups. Infants present within the first few months of life with pseudo-obstruction and involvement of the whole gastrointestinal tract. There is frequently a concomitant megacystis and megaloureters. Vacuolar degeneration and fibrosis of the smooth muscle are present in all these areas.

Undefined myopathies

Occasional patients have abnormal smooth muscle, but do not fall into the above categories because they do not have familial involvement or vacuolar degeneration. The smooth muscle coats of the bowel are thin and fibrotic, and there is no evidence for disorders such as progressive systemic sclerosis, polymyositis or myotonic dystrophy. Smooth muscle cells are hypereosinophilic, enlarged, hyalinized and have pyknotic, eccentric nuclei. Whether some of these cases represent progressive systemic sclerosis limited to the gastrointestinal tract or other undefined smooth muscle disorders remains to be determined.

Secondary disorders

Progressive systemic sclerosis/polymyositis

Progressive systemic sclerosis commonly involves intestinal smooth muscle and is probably the most common cause of intestinal pseudo-obstruction.[6,12] Although reports of gut involvement in dermatomyositis/polymyositis are rare,[157–159] the pathology appears to be identical.[160]

As in visceral myopathy, smooth muscle cells in progressive systemic sclerosis are fewer in number and the muscle layers are thinner than normal.[58,161] It can usually be differentiated from visceral myopathy, because it is characterized by fibrosis of intestinal smooth muscle in the absence of vacuolar degeneration (Fig. 22.27A,B); the muscle cells remaining are normal in appearance or are atrophied. In addition, it is the circular rather than the longitudinal muscle which is more commonly involved. Progressive systemic sclerosis is also characterized by more patchy involvement: normal muscle may exist immediately adjacent to severely fibrotic muscle.

Progressive muscular dystrophy

Gastrointestinal symptoms sometimes occur in progressive muscular dystrophy and in one personally studied case a 15-year-old boy had dysphagia and attacks of intestinal pseudo-obstruction.[162] Radiographs showed a noncontractile oesophagus, a lower oesophageal diverticulum and a dilated stomach and small intestine. At autopsy intestinal smooth muscle was replaced by collagen. This process was most prominent in the oesophagus and stomach, but also involved the small intestine and colon. The appearances were similar to those in progressive systemic sclerosis.

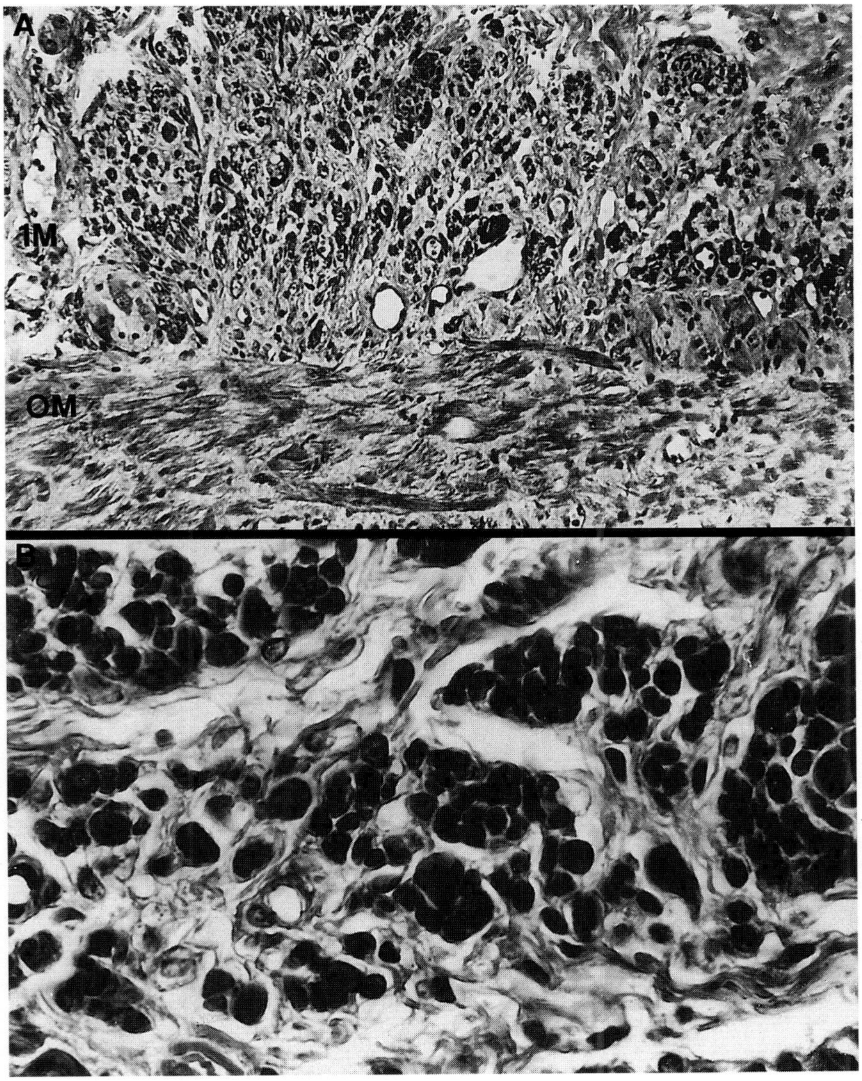

Fig. 22.27A Area of the small intestine of a patient with progressive systemic sclerosis. Even though there is extensive fibrosis, the residual muscle fibres are normal. The larger spaces within the muscle are capillaries and not vacuoles. IM = inner muscle; OM = outer muscle. (Masson's trichrome, ×256) **B** Higher magnification of inner muscle showing that the residual muscle cells are normal in appearance. (Masson's trichrome, ×1024. Reprinted with permission: Gastroenterology 1979; 77: 664–671)

Amyloidosis

Amyloidosis can involve the smooth muscle of the small intestine and colon.[163–165] Variable amounts of smooth muscle are replaced by amyloid, and the muscularis mucosa, submucosal blood vessels and both layers of the muscularis propria may all be involved. The affected intestine may be converted into an almost rigid tube, with walls measuring one or more centimeters in thickness. The myenteric and submucosal plexuses may also be involved, but less frequently than the smooth muscle.[166]

Ceroidosis

Whether the ceroid pigment in muscle cells actually causes smooth muscle degeneration and dysfunction is not known[167] but it is probably unlikely.

Diffuse lymphoid infiltration

Patients with this syndrome present with diarrhoea, malabsorption and intestinal pseudo-obstruction.[168] Full thickness intestinal biopsies show flat small intestinal mucosa, sparsity of crypts, and a widespread infiltration of lymphoid cells in the lamina propria, submucosa, serosa and muscularis propria (Fig. 22.28A,B). Although there are also scattered lymphoid cells in the myenteric plexus, there is no neuron or axon damage or loss. Absence of muscle cells in the vicinity of lymphoid cell infiltration in the muscularis propria probably accounts for the pathogenesis of pseudo-obstruction. An alternate hypothesis is that the lymphocytes secrete cytokines that inhibit smooth muscle contractility. Immunochemical stains show that the infiltrate is polyclonal, and none of four patients personally studied have developed lymphoma on clinical

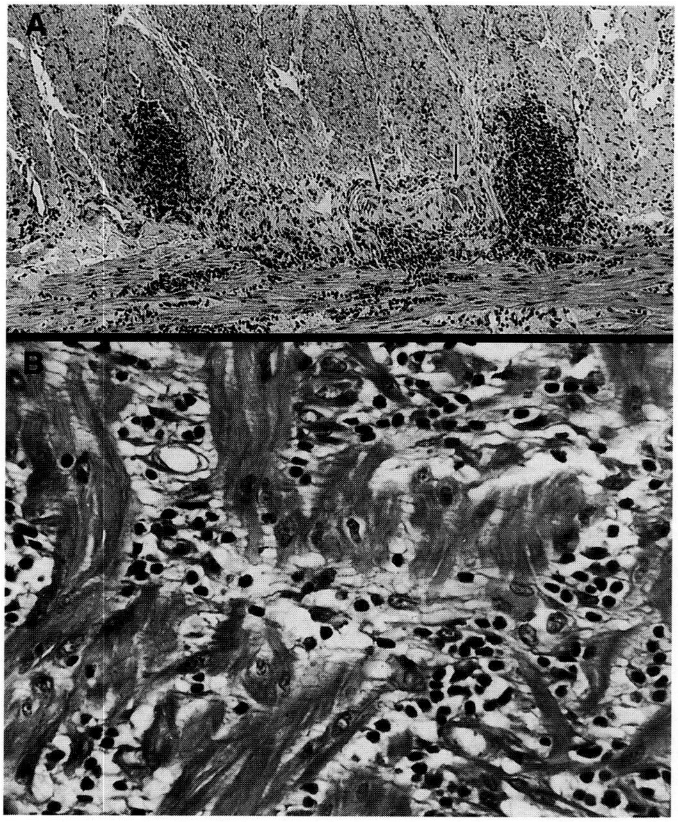

Fig. 22.28A Portions of circular and longitudinal muscles from the jejunum of a patient with diffuse lymphoid infiltration. There are increased lymphoid cells within both the circular and longitudinal muscles, with two particularly dense aggregates in the circular muscle, one of which is just to the right of a collection of neurons within the myenteric plexus (arrows). (H&E, ×68) B Higher magnification of the smooth muscle demonstrating muscle cell absence associated with the lymphoid cells. (H&E, ×330. Reprinted with permission: Gastroenterology 1985; 89: 882–889)

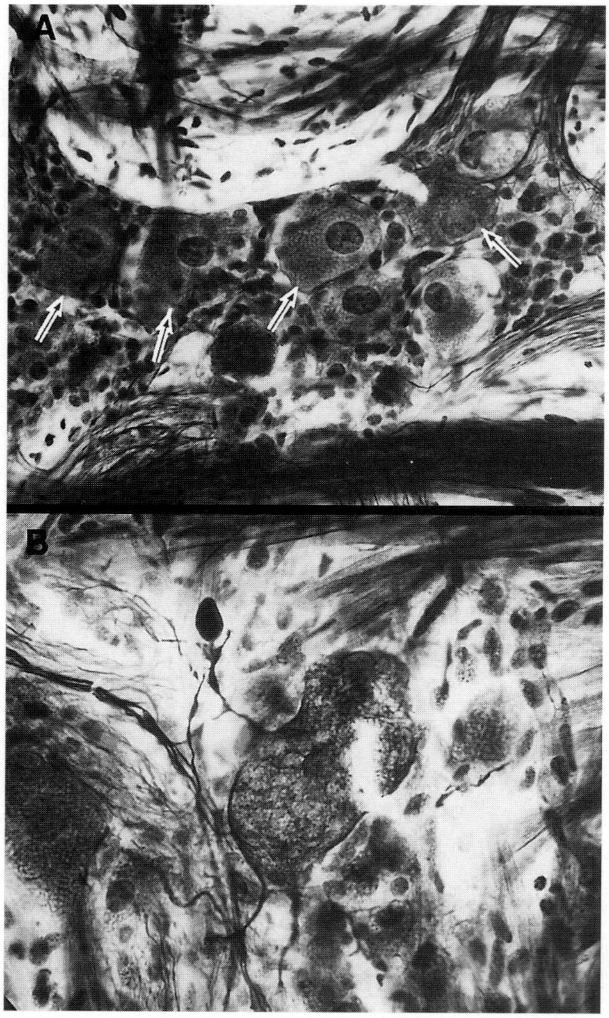

Fig. 22.29A Ganglionic area from the jejunum of a patient with jejunal diverticulosis secondary to Fabry's disease, showing a cluster of argyrophobic neurons with granular cytoplasm (arrows) caused by accumulation of ceramide trihexoside. (Silver, ×230) B Marked swelling and foamy cytoplasm of an argyrophilic neuron from an adjacent ganglion. (Silver, ×363)

follow up of up to 20 years. The mesenteric lymph nodes may be enlarged and contain hyperplastic germinal centres, but there is no evidence of lymphoma.

SMALL INTESTINAL DIVERTICULOSIS

Small intestinal diverticulosis is a heterogeneous disorder characterized by the presence of multiple diverticula throughout the small intestine.[70–77] Although most are located in the jejunum, they can also occur in the ileum and duodenum. They develop because of structural abnormalities of the intestinal wall, which also produce the clinical features of intestinal pseudo-obstruction. This is often associated with small bowel bacterial overgrowth, steatorrhea and vitamin B_{12} malabsorption, or may be complicated by perforation or haemorrhage from a diverticulum.

Small intestinal diverticulosis is caused by at least two disorders of the smooth muscle and two of the myenteric plexus.[70,169] One of the smooth muscle disorders resembles progressive systemic sclerosis and the other, visceral myopathy. Whether the muscle disorder resembling progressive systemic sclerosis is really this disorder in the absence of its other systemic manifestations, or whether it is another muscle disease is unknown. One familial form of visceral myopathy associated with small intestinal diverticulosis, gastroparesis, external ophthalmoplegia and ptosis was mentioned above.[56,152–154] Small intestinal diverticulosis secondary to visceral myopathy and not associated with external ophthalmoplegia or ptosis also occurs.[70]

Two types of disorders of the myenteric plexus are also associated with jejunal diverticulosis. In one, the myenteric plexus is degenerated and some of the neurons contain eosinophilic intranuclear inclusions identical to those described in the neuronal intranuclear inclusion disease discussed above.[70] The other is associated with Fabry's disease,[197] in which the neurons of the myenteric plexus contain ceramide trihexoside, a glycolipid which accumulates because of the enzyme deficiency causing this disease (Fig. 22.29A,B).

Diverticula result from one of two possible mechanisms. When the muscle is atrophied and both the circular and longitudinal muscle totally replaced by collagen, the bowel wall is very thin and being subject to intraluminal pressure, may balloon out. In contrast, the disorders of the myenteric plexus are characterized by smooth muscle coats which are thicker than normal, and it is theorized that this is associated with hypercontractility and areas of abnormally high pressure drive the mucosa and submucosa out along defects in the intestinal wall at the points of blood vessel penetration. Thus, the diverticula in muscle disorders are protrusions of the entire intestinal wall in places where the wall is weakened by muscle atrophy and fibrosis, whereas in myenteric plexus disorders the diverticula are composed of mucosa and submucosa which protrude through thickened smooth muscle at points of blood vessel penetration. This distinction is not invariably true, because some diverticula in muscle disorders also protrude at the points of blood vessel penetration.

It is not known whether the muscle diseases associated with jejunal diverticulosis are different from the muscle diseases already discussed or whether they are just different manifestations of the same disorders.

REFERENCES

1. Johnson LR. Physiology of the gastrointestinal tract. Volume 1. New York: Raven Press, 1981.
2. Christensen J, Wingate DL. A guide to gastrointestinal motility. Bristol: Wright, 1983.
3. Smith B. The neuropathology of the alimentary tract. London: Edward Arnold, 1972.
4. Schuffler MD, Jonak Z. Chronic idiopathic intestinal pseudo-obstruction caused by a degenerative disorder of the myenteric plexus: The use of Smith's method to define the neuropathology. Gastroenterology 1982; 82: 476–486.
5. Faulk DL, Anuras S, Christensen J. Chronic intestinal pseudo-obstruction. Gastroenterology 1978; 74: 922–931.
6. Schuffler MD, Rohrmann CA, Chaffee RG, et al. Chronic intestinal pseudo-obstruction: a report of 27 cases and review of the literature. Medicine 1981; 60: 173–196.
7. Schuffler MD. Chronic intestinal pseudo-obstruction syndromes. Med Clin North Am 1981; 65: 1331–1358.
8. Nanni G, Garbini A, Luchetti P, Nanni G, Ronconi P, Castagneto M. Ogilvie's syndrome (Acute colonic pseudo-obstruction). Dis Colon Rectum 1982; 25: 157–166.
9. Nakhgevany KB. Colonoscopic decompression of the colon in patients with Ogilvie's syndrome. Am J Surg 1984; 148: 317–320.
10. Ogilvie H. Large-intestine colic due to sympathetic deprivation. A new clinical syndrome. Br Med J 1948; 2: 671–673.
11. Schuffler MD, Rohrmann CA, Templeton FE. The radiologic manifestations of idiopathic intestinal pseudo-obstruction. AJR 1976; 127: 729–736.
12. Rohrmann CA, Ricci MT, Krishnamurthy S, Schuffler MD. Radiologic and histologic differentiation of neuromuscular disorders of the gastrointestinal tract: Visceral myopathies, visceral neuropathies and progressive systemic sclerosis. AJR 1984; 143: 933–941.
13. Anuras S, Shirazi SS. Colonic pseudo-obstruction. Am J Gastroenterol 1984; 79: 525–532.
14. Snape WJ. Taking the idiopathic out of intestinal pseudo-obstruction. Ann Intern Med 1981; 95: 646–648.
15. Erskine JM. Acquired megacolon, megaesophagus and megaduodenum with aperistalsis. A case report. Am J Gastroenterol 1963; 40: 588–600.
16. Bentley JFR. Some new observations on megacolon in infancy and childhood with special reference to the management of megasigmoid and megarectum. Dis Colon Rectum 1964; 7: 462–470.
17. Preston DM, Lennard-Jones JE, Thomas BM. Towards a radiologic definition of idiopathic megacolon. Gastrointest Radiol 1985; 10: 167–169.
18. Lane RHS, Todd IP. Idiopathic megacolon: a review of 42 cases. Br J Surg 1977; 64: 305–310.
19. Kune GA. Megacolon in adults. Br J Surg 1966; 53: 199–205.
20. Rosenberg RF, Caridi JG. Vincristine-induced megacolon. Gastrointest Radiol 1983; 8: 71–73.
21. Ryan P. Sigmoid volvulus with and without megacolon. Dis Colon Rectum 1982; 25: 673–679.
22. Zimmerman GR. Megacolon from large doses of chlorpromazine. Arch Pathol 1962; 74: 59–63.
23. Berenyi MR, Schwarz GS. Megasigmoid syndrome in diabetes and neurologic disease. Am J Gastroenterol 1967; 47: 311–320.
24. Nevin RW. Discussion on megacolon and megarectum with the emphasis on conditions other than Hirschsprung's disease. Proc R Soc Med 1961; 54: 1035–1037.
25. Duffy TJ, Erickson EE, Jordan GL et al. Megacolon and bilateral pheochromocytoma. Am J Gastroenterol 1962; 38: 555–563.
26. Scharer LL, Burhenne HJ. Megacolon, a nonspecific sign: clinical classification and roentgenologic differentiation. Radiol Clin Biol 1965; 34: 236–246.
27. Bentley JFR, Shepherd JJ, Katz A et al. Seminar on Pseudo-Hirschsprung's disease and related disorders. Arch Dis Child 1966; 41: 143–154.
28. Tobon F, Schuster MM. Megacolon: special diagnostic and therapeutic features. Hopkins Med J 1974; 135: 91–105.
29. Winkelman J. Coexistent megacolon and megaureter. Report of a case with normal vesical autonomic innervation. Pediatrics 1967; 39: 258–262.
30. Belliveau P, Goldberg SM, Rothenberger DA et al. Idiopathic acquired megacolon: the value of subtotal colectomy. Dis Colon Rectum 1982; 25: 118–121.
31. Ehrenpreis TH. Pseudo-Hirschsprung's disease. Arch Dis Child 1965; 40: 177–179.
32. Newton WT. Radical enterectomy for hereditary megaduodenum. Arch Surg 1968; 96: 549–553.
33. Weiss W. Zur atiologie des megaduodenums. Dtsch Z Chirurgie 1938; 251: 319–330.
34. Law DH, Eyck EAT. Familial megaduodenum and megacystis. Am J Med 1962; 33: 911–922.
35. Major JW, Ottenheimer EJ, Whalen WA. Duodenal obstruction at the ligament of Treitz. Report of a case treated by a plastic procedure. N Engl J Med 1960; 262: 443–446.
36. Strong EK. Mechanics of arteriomesenteric duodenal obstruction and direct surgical attack upon etiology. Ann Surg 1958; 148: 725–730.
37. Hearn JB. Duodenal ileus with special reference to superior mesenteric artery compression. Radiology 1965; 86: 305–310.
38. Ortiz VN, Major JE. Vascular compression of the duodenum. Am J Gastroenterol 1977; 67: 270–273.
39. Licht EF. Arteriomesenteric obstruction of the duodenum of adult life and adolescence. Acta Radiologica 1956; 45: 441–451.
40. Kaiser GC, McKain JM, Shumacker HB. The superior mesenteric artery syndrome. Surg Gynecol Obstet 1960; 110: 133–140.

41. Bitner WP. Arteriomesenteric occlusion of the duodenum. AJR 1958; 79: 807–814.
42. Burrington JD, Wane ER. Obstruction of the duodenum by the mesenteric artery — does it exist? J Pediatr Surg 1974; 9: 733–741.
43. Anuras S, Shirazi S, Faulk DL et al. Surgical treatment in familial visceral myopathy. Ann Surg 1979; 189: 306–310.
44. Fischer HW. The big duodenum. AJR 1960; 83: 861–875.
45. Nordentoft J. Two cases of megaduodenum. Acta Radiologica 1937; 18: 722–732.
46. Matzen P, Davidsen PM, Mathiasen MS. Megaduodenum. A case with bacterial overgrowth, deconjugation of bile salts, malabsorption, and polyneuropathy. Scand J Gastroenterol 1974; 9: 645–650.
47. Uncapher RP, Holder HG. Megaduodenum in the adult. A report case. AJR 1957; 77: 634–638.
48. Barnett WO, Wall L. Megaduodenum resulting from absence of the parasympathetic ganglion cells in Auerbach's plexus. Ann Surg 1955; 141: 527–535.
49. Anderson FH. Megaduodenum. Am J Gastroenterol 1974; 62: 509–515.
50. Kellogg EL, Kellogg WA. Chronic duodenal stasis. Radiology 1927; 9: 23–38.
51. Brown CH, Strittmatter WC. Obstructive lesions of the duodenum distal to the bulb. Radiology 1958; 70: 720–727.
52. Faulk DL, Anuras S, Gardner GD et al. A familial visceral myopathy. Ann Intern Med 1978; 89: 600–606.
53. Shaw A, Shaffer H, Teja K et al. A perspective for pediatric surgeons: chronic idiopathic intestinal pseudo-obstruction. J Pediatr Surg 1979; 14: 719–727.
54. Jacobs E, Ardichvili D, Perissino A et al. A case of familial visceral myopathy with atrophy and fibrosis of the longitudinal muscle layer of the entire small bowel. Gastroenterology 1979; 77: 745–750.
55. Schuffler MD, Pope CE. Studies of idiopathic intestinal pseudo-obstruction. II Hereditary hollow visceral myopathy: family studies. Gastroenterology 1977; 73: 339–344.
56. Anuras S, Mitros FA, Nowak TV et al. A familial visceral myopathy with external ophthalmoplegia and autosomal recessive transmission. Gastroenterology 1983; 84: 346–353.
57. Schuffler MD, Lowe MC, Bill AH. Studies of idiopathic intestinal pseudo-obstruction. I Hereditary hollow visceral myopathy: clinical and pathological studies. Gastroenterology 1977; 73: 327–338.
58. Mitros FA, Schuffler MD, Teja K, Anuras S. Pathology of familial visceral myopathy. Hum Pathol 1982; 13: 825–833.
59. Roy AD, Bharucha H, Nevin NC et al. Idiopathic intestinal pseudo-obstruction: a familial visceral neuropathy. Clin Genet 1980; 18: 291–297.
60. Dyer NH, Dawson AM, Smith BF et al. Obstruction of bowel due to lesion in the myenteric plexus. Br Med J 1969; 1: 686–689.
61. Cockel R, Hill EE, Rushton DI et al. Familial steatorrhoea with calcification of the basal ganglia and mental retardation. Q J Med 1973; 168: 771–783.
62. Horoupian DS, Kim Y. Encephalomyeloneuropathy with ganglionitis of the myenteric plexus in the absence of cancer. Ann Neurol 1982; 11: 628–631.
63. Schuffler MD, Bird TD, Sumi SM et al. A familial neuronal disease presenting as intestinal pseudo-obstruction. Gastroenterology 1978; 75: 889–898.
64. Shilkin KB, Gracey M, Joske RA. Idiopathic intestinal pseudo-obstruction. Report of a case with neuropathological studies. Aust Paediatr J 1978; 14: 102–106.
65. Smith B. The neuropathology of pseudo-obstruction of the intestine. Scand J Gastroenterol 1982; 17(Suppl. 71): 103–109.
66. Schuffler DM, Baird HW, Fleming CR et al. Intestinal pseudo-obstruction as the presenting manifestation of small cell carcinoma of the lung: a paraneoplastic neuropathy of the gastrointestinal tract. Ann Intern Med 1983; 98: 129–134.
67. Schuffler MD, Leon SH, Krishnamurthy S. Intestinal pseudo-obstruction caused by a new form of visceral neuropathy: Palliation by radical small bowel resection. Gastroenterology 1985; 89: 1152–1156.
68. Krishnamurthy S, Schuffler MD, Belic L, Schweid A. An inflammatory axonopathy of the myenteric plexus causing rapidly progressive intestinal pseudo-obstruction. Gastroenterology 1986; 90: 754–758.
69. Bogomoletz WV, Birembaut P, Gaillard D et al. Chronic idiopathic intestinal pseudo-obstruction with myenteric plexus damage. Lancet 1979; 1: 679–680.
70. Krishnamurthy S, Kelly MM, Rohrmann CA, Schuffler MD. Jejunal diverticulosis: a heterogeneous disorder caused by a variety of abnormalities of smooth muscle or myenteric plexus. Gastroenterology 1983; 85: 538–547.
71. Badenoch J, Bedford PD, Evans JR. Massive diverticulosis of the small intestine with steatorrhoea and megaloblastic anaemia. Q J Med, New Series XXIV 1955; 96: 321.
72. Knauer C, Svoboda AC. Malabsorption and jejunal diverticulosis. Am J Med 1968; 44: 606–610.
73. Schiffer LM, Faloon WW, Chodos RB, Lozner EL. Malabsorption syndrome associated with intestinal diverticulosis. Gastroenterology 1962; 42: 63–68.
74. Delaney WE, Hedges RC. Acquired diverticulosis and hemorrhagic diverticulitis. Gastroenterology 1962; 42: 56–59.
75. Bewes PC. Surgical complications of jejunal diverticulosis. Proc R Soc Med 1967; 60: 225–226.
76. Taylor MT. Massive hemorrhage from jejunal diverticulosis. Am J Surg 1969; 118: 117–120.
77. Donald JW. Major complications of small bowel diverticula. Ann Surg 1979; 190: 183–188.
78. Krishnamurthy S, Schuffler MD, Rohrmann CA, Pope CE, II. Severe, idiopathic constipation is associated with a distinctive abnormality of the myenteric plexus. Gastroenterology 1985; 88: 26–34.
79. Preston DM, Hawley RR, Lennard-Jones JE, Todd IP.Results of colectomy for severe idiopathic constipation in women (Arbuthnot Lane's disease). Br J Surg 1984; 71: 547–552.
80. Haltia M, Somer H, Palo J et al. Neuronal intranuclear inclusion disease in identical twins. Ann Neurol 1984; 15: 316–321.
81. Palo J, Haltia M, Carpenter S, Karpati G, Mushynski W. Neurofilament subunit-related proteins in neuronal intranuclear inclusions. Ann Neurol 1984; 15: 322–328.
82. Patel H, Norman MG, Perry TL, Berry KE. Multiple system atrophy with neuronal intranuclear hyaline inclusions. Report of a case and review of the literature. J Neurol Sci 1985; 67: 57–65.
83. Soffer D. Neuronal intranuclear hyaline inclusion disease presenting as Friedrich's ataxia. Acta Neuropathol (Berl) 1985; 65: 322–329.
84. Barnett J, McDonnell W, Appelman H, Dobbins W. Familial visceral neuropathy with neuronal intranuclear inclusions: Diagnosis by rectal biopsy. Gastroenterology 1992; 102: 684–691.
85. Mayer EA, Schuffler MD, Rotter JI, Hanna P, Mogard M. A familial visceral neuropathy with autosomal dominant transmission. Gastroenterology (in press).
86. Chousterman M, Phat VN, Petite J-P, Camilleri J-P et al. Pseudo-obstruction intestinale chronique de l'adulte. Gastroenterol Clin Biol 1980; 4: 326–332.
87. Hanks JB, Meyers WC, Andersen DK et al. Chronic primary intestinal pseudo-obstruction. Surgery 1981; 89: 175–182.
88. Nahai F. Pseudo-obstruction of the small bowel. Bristol Med Chir J 1969; 84: 209–212.
89. Lhermitte F, Gray F, Lyon-Caen O et al. Paralysie du tube digestif avec lesions des plexus myenteriques. Rev Neurol 1980; 136: 825–836.
90. Ahmed MN, Carpenter S. Autonomic neuropathy and carcinoma of the lung. Can Med Assoc J 1975; 113: 410–412.
91. Lennon V, Sas D, Busk M, Scheithauer B, Malagelada J, Camilleri M, Miller L. Enteric neuronal autoantibodies in pseudoobstruction with small-cell lung carcinoma. Gastroenterology 1991; 100: 137–142.
92. Croft PB, Henson RA, Urich H, Wilkinson PC. Sensory neuropathy with bronchial carcinoma: a study of four cases showing serological abnormalities. Brain 1965; 88: 501–514.
93. Wilkinson PC, Zeromski J. Immunofluorescent detection of

antibodies against neurones in sensory carcinomatous neuropathy. Brain 1965; 88: 529–538.
94. Bell CE Jr, Seetharam S, McDaniel RC. Endodermally-derived and neural crest-derived differentiation antigens expressed by a human lung tumor. J Immunol 1976; 116: 1236–1243.
95. Bell CE Jr, Seetharam S. Identification of the Swann cell as a peripheral nervous system cell possessing a differentiation antigen expressed by a human lung tumour. J Immunol 1977; 118: 826–831.
96. Bell CE Jr, Seetharam S. Expression of endodermally-derived and neural crest-derived differentiation antigens by human lung and colon tumors. Cancer 1979; 44: 13–18.
97. Wood JN, Hudson L, Jessell TM, Yamamoto M. A monoclonal antibody defining antigenic determinants on subpopulations of mammalian neurones and Trypanosoma cruzi parasites. Nature 1982; 296: 34–38.
98. Teixeira ML, Filho JR, Figueredo F, Teixeira ARL. Chagas' disease. Selective affinity and cytotoxicity of Trypanosoma cruzi immune lymphocytes to parasympathetic ganglion cells. Mem Inst Oswaldo Cruz, Rio de Janeiro. 1980; 75: 33–45.
99. Earlam RJ. Gastrointestinal aspects of Chagas' disease. Dig Dis Sci 1972; 17: 559–571.
100. Todd IP, Porter N H, Morson BC, Smith B, Friedmann CA, Neal RA. Chagas' disease of the colon and rectum. Gut 1969; 10: 1009–1014.
101. Raia A, Acquaroni D, Netto AC. Pathogenesis and treatment of acquired megaduodenum. Dig Dis Sci 1961; 6: 757–771.
102. Koberle F. Enteromegaly and cardiomegaly in Chagas' disease. Gut 1963; 4: 399–405.
103. Sonsino E, Mouy R, Foucaud P et al. Intestinal pseudo-obstruction related to cytomegalovirus infection of myenteric plexus. N Engl J Med 1984; 311: 196–197.
104. Press MF, Riddel RH, Ringus J. Cytomegalovirus inclusion disease: its occurrence in the myenteric plexus of a renal transplant patient. Arch Pathol Lab Med 1980; 104: 580–583.
105. Nowak T, Ionasescu V, Anuras S. Gastrointestinal manifestations of the muscular dystrophies. Gastroenterology 1982; 82: 800–810.
106. Kohn N, Faires J, Rodman T. Unusual manifestations due to involvement of involuntary muscle in dystrophia myotonica. N Engl J Med 1964; 271: 1179–1183.
107. Harper P. Myotonic dystrophy. Major Prob Neurol 1979; 9: 1–331.
108. Keschner M, Davidson D. Dystrophica myotonica: a clinicopathologic study. Arch Neurol Psychiatry 1933; 30: 1259–1275.
109. Pruzanski W, Huvos A. Smoooth muscle involvement in primary muscle disease. Arch Pathol 1967; 83: 229–233.
110. Yoshida M, Krishnamurthy S, Wattchow D, Furness J, Schuffler M. Megacolon in myotonic dystrophy caused by a degenerative neuropathy of the myenteric plexus. Gastroenterology 1988; 95: 820–827.
111. Taguchi T, Tanaka K, Ikeda K et al. Double zonal aganglionosis with a skipped oligoganglionic ascending colon. Z Kinderchir 1983; 38: 312–315.
112. Bughaighis AG, Emery JL. Funtional obstruction of the intestine due to neurological immaturity. Prog Pediatr Surg 1971; 3: 37–52.
113. Saul RA, Sturner RA, Burger PC. Hyperplasia of the myenteric plexus. Its association with early infantile megacolon and neurofibromatosis. Am J Dis Child 1982; 136: 852–854.
114. Cremin BJ, Golding RL. Congenital aganglionosis of the entire colon in neonates. Br J Radiol 1976; 46: 27–33.
115. Howard ER, Garrett JR, Kidd A. Constipation and congenital disorders of the myenteric plexus. J R Soc Med 1984; 77(Suppl 3): 13–19.
116. MacMahon RA, Moore CCM, Cussen LJ. Hirschsprung-like syndromes in patients with normal ganglion cells on suction rectal biopsy. J Pediatr Surg 1981; 16: 835–839.
117. Manakata K, Okabe I, Morita K. Histologic studies of rectocolic aganglionosis and allied diseases. J Pediatr Surg 1978; 13: 67–75.
118. Kapila L, Haberkorn S, Nixon HH. Chronic adynamic bowel simulating Hirschsprung's disease. J Pediatr Surg 1975; 10: 885–892.
119. Erdohazi M. Retarded development of the enteric nerve cells. Develop Med 1974; 16: 365–368.
120. Ravitch MM, Izant RJ, Bolande PR. Aganglionosis of the intestine in siblings. Surgery 1963; 53: 664–669.
121. Boggs JD, Kidd JM. Congenital abnormalities of intestinal innervation. Absence of innervation of jejunum, ileum and colon in siblings. Pediatrics 1958; 21: 261–265.
122. Stern M, Hellwege HH, Gravinghoff L et al. Total aganglionosis of the colon (Hirschspring's disease) and congenital failure of automatic control of ventilation (Ondine's curse). Acta Paediatr Scand 1981; 70: 121–124.
123. Puri FP, Lake BD, Nixon HH. Adynamic bowel syndrome. Report of a case with disturbance of the cholinergic innervation. Gut 1977; 18: 754–759.
124. Careskey JM, Weber TR, Grosfeld JL. Total colonic aganglionosis. Am J Surg 1982; 143: 160–168.
125. Demos TC, Blonder J, Schey WL et al. Multiple endocrine neoplasia (MEN) syndrome. Type IIB: Gastrointestinal manifestations. AJR 1983; 140: 73–78.
126. Davies MRQ. The newborn infant with intestinal aganglionosis. S Afr J Surg 1982; 20: 119–128.
127. Nixon HH, Lake B. 'Not Hirschsprung's disease' — rare conditions with some similarities. S Afr J Surg 1982; 20: 97–104.
128. Haney PJ, Hill JL, Sun CCJ. Zonal colonic aganglionosis. Pediatr Radiol 1982; 12: 258–261.
129. Farndon PA, Bianchi A. Waardenburg's syndrome associated with total aganglionosis. Arch Dis Child 1983; 58: 932–933.
130. Zizka J, Maresova J, Kerekes Z et al. Intestinal aganglionosis in the Smith-Lemli-Opitz syndrome. Acta Paediatr Scand 1983; 72: 141–143.
131. Tanner MS, Smith B, Lloyd JK. Functional intestinal obstruction due to deficiency of argyrophilic neurones in the myenteric plexus. Familial syndrome presenting with short small bowel malrotation, and pyloric hypertrophy. Arch Dis Child 1976; 51: 837–841.
132. Schnaufer L. Hirschsprung's Disease. Surg Clin North Am 1976; 56: 349–359.
133. Reynolds JF, Barber JC, Alford BA et al. Familial Hirschsprung's disease and Type D brachydactyly: A report of four affected males in two generations. Pediatrics 1983; 71: 246–249.
134. Liang JC, Juarez CP, Goldberg MF. Bilateral bicolored iride with Hirschsprung's disease. A neural crest syndrome. Arch Ophthalmol 1983; 101: 69–73.
135. Chadarevian JP, Slim M, Akel S. Double zonal aganglionosis in long segment Hirschsprung's disease with a 'skip area' in transverse colon. J Pediatr Surg 1982; 17: 195–197.
136. Verdy M, Weber AM, Roy CC et al. Hirschsprung's disease in a family with multiple endocrine neoplasia type 2. J Pediatr Gastroenterol Ntr 1982; 1: 603–607.
137. Currie ABM, Hemalatha AH, Doraiswamy NV et al. Colonic atresia associated with Hirschsprung's disease. J R Coll Surg Edinb 1983; 28: 31–34.
138. Bruyn R, Hall CM, Spitz L. Hirschsprung's disease and malrotation of the mid-gut. An uncommon association. Br J Radiol 1982; 55: 554–557.
139. Royer P, Ricour C, Nihoul-Fekete C, Pellerin D. Le syndrome familial de grele court avec malrotation intestinale et stenose hypertrophique du pylore chez le nourrisson. Arch Fr Pediatr 1974; 31: 223–229.
140. Mathe JC, Khairallah S, Phat Vuoung NP, Boccon-Gibod L, Rey A, Costil J. Dilatation segmentaire du grele a revelation neonatale. Nouv Presse Med 1982; 11: 265–266.
141. Kluck P, van Muijen G, van der Kamp A, Tibboel D, van Hoorn W, Warnaar S, Molenaar J. Hirschsprung's disease studied with monoclonal antineurofilament antibodies on tissue selections. Lancet 1984; 1: 653–53.
142. Kluck P, Tibboel D, Leendertse-Verloop K, van der Kamp A, ten Kate F, Molenaar J. Diagnosis of congenital neurogenic abnormalities of the bowel with monoclonal anti-neurofilament antibodies. J Pediatr Surg 1986; 21: 132–135.
143. Sninsky CA, Davis RH, Clench MH, Howard RJ, Schuffler MD, Jonak Z, Mathias JR. Severe idiopathic intestinal constipation:

comparison of histology and gastrointestinal tracing in human subjects. Gastroenterology 1984; 86: 1259.
144. Bockus HL, Willard JH, Bank J. Melanosis coli. JAMA 1933; 101: 1–6.
145. Wittoesch JH, Jackman RJ, McDonald JR. Melanosis coli: General review and a study of 887 cases. Dis Colon Rectum 1958; 1: 172–180.
146. Steer HW, Colin-Jones DG. Melanosis coli: studies of the toxic effects of irritant purgatives. J Pathol 1975; 115: 199–205.
147. Schrodt GR. Melanosis coli: a study with the electron microscope. Dis Colon Rectum. 1963; 6: 277–283
148. Ghadially FN, Parry EW. An electron-microscope and histochemical study of melanosis coli. J Pathol Bacteriol 1966; 92: 313–317.
149. Smith B. Effect of irritant purgatives on the myenteric plexus in man and the mouse. Gut 1968; 9: 139–143.
150. Smith B. Pathologic changes in the colon produced by arthraquinone purgatives. Dis Colon Rectum 1973; 16: 455–458.
151. Riemann JF, Schmidt H, Zimmermann W. The fine structure of colonic submucosal nerves in patients with chronic laxative abuse. Scand J Gastroenterol 1980; 15: 761–768.
152. Ionasescu V. Oculogastrointestinal muscular dystrophy. Am J Med Genet 1983; 15: 103–112.
153. Ionasescu V, Thompson SH, Ionasescu R, et al. Inherited ophthalmoplegia with intestinal pseudo-obstruction. J Neurol Sci 1983; 59: 215–228.
154. Ionasescu V, Thompson SH, Aschenbrener C, Anuras S, Risk WS. Late-onset oculogastrointestinal muscular dystrophy. Am J Med Genet 1984; 18: 781–788.
155. Anuras S, Mitros FA, Milano A, Kuminsky R, Decanis R, Green JB. A familial visceral myopathy with dilatation of the entire gastrointestinal tract. Gastroenterology 1986; 90: 385–390.
156. Foucar E, Lindholm J, Anuras S, Mitros F, Whitaker DC, Green JB. A kindred with dysplastic nevus syndrome associated with visceral myopathy and multiple basal cell carcinomas. Lab Invest 1985; 52: 23A.
157. Kleckner FS. Dermatomyositis and its manifestations in the gastrointestinal tract. Am J Gastroenterol 1970; 53: 141–146.
158. Feldman F, Marshak RH. Dermatomyositis with significant involvement of the gastrointestinal tract. AJR 1963; 90: 746–752.
159. Transfeldt EE, Morley JE, Segal F, Klein A, Bill P, Fancourt M. Polymyositis as a cause of malabsorption. S Afr Med J 1977; 51: 176–178.
160. Patterson M, Rios G. Disturbed gastrointestinal motility — an unusual manifestation of a systemic disorder: polymyositis or progressive muscular dystrophy. Texas Rep Biol Med 1959; 36: 261–268.
161. Schuffler MD, Beegle RG. Progressive systemic sclerosis of the gastrointestinal tract and hereditary hollow visceral myopathy: Two distinguishable disorders of intestinal smooth muscle. Gastroenterology 1979; 77: 664–671.
162. Leon SH, Schuffler MD. Intestinal pseudo-obstruction as a complication of Duchenne's muscular dystrophy. Gastroenterology 1986; 90: 455–459.
163. Wald A, Kichler J, Mendelow H. Amyloidosis and chronic intestinal pseudo-obstruction. Dig Dis Sci 1981; 26: 462–465.
164. Legge DA, Wollaeger EE, Carlson HC. Intestinal pseudo-obstruction in systemic amyloidosis. Gut 1970; 11: 764–767.
165. Symmers W, St C. Primary amyloidosis. A review. J Clin Pathol 1956; 9: 187–211.
166. French JM, Hall G, Parish DJ, Smith WT. Peripheral and autonomic nerve involvement in primary amyloidosis associated with uncontrollable diarrhea and steatorrhea. Am J Med 1965; 39: 277–284.
167. Boller M, Fiocchi C, Brown C H. Pseudo-obstruction in ceroidosis. AJR 1976; 127: 277–279.
168. McDonald GB, Schuffler MD, Kadin ME, Tytgat GNJ. Intestinal pseudo-obstruction caused by diffuse lymphoid infiltration of the small intestine. Gastroenterology 1985; 89: 882–889.
169. Friedman LS, Platika D, Thistlethwaite JR, Kirkham SE, Kolodny EH, Schuffler MD. Jejunal diverticulosis with perforation as a complication of Fabry's disease. Gastroenterology 1984; 86: 558–563.

CHAPTER 23

Diverticular disease of the colon and solitary ulcer syndrome; anorectal prolapse and incontinence

R. Whitehead C. E. H. du Boulay P. D. James

PART I

Diverticular disease of the colon and solitary ulcer syndrome

R. Whitehead C. E. H. du Boulay

DIVERTICULAR DISEASE

Diverticular disease is recognized as a common disorder of the 20th century Western world, but in the previous century it was considered a rare curiosity. The nomenclature of diverticular disease and its different forms can be confusing. Literally a 'little room', the diverticulum is a mucosal pouch which protrudes through a muscle coat. Diverticular disease or diverticulosis are the terms used for the presence of multiple colonic diverticula. Diverticulitis is a complication of diverticular disease. The 'pre-diverticular' state is considered by some radiologists to be present in colons which show the characteristic muscle abnormality (myochosis) in the absence of diverticula.[1,2]

Epidemiology

In the developed world diverticulosis is most common in the elderly population. It is estimated from autopsy studies that 30% of the adult population and over 50% of those over 40 years are affected.[3] Since the introduction of roller milled flour in the 1880s and the increased consumption of refined foods in economically developed countries, the incidence of diverticulosis has soared[4] and it is increasingly described in patients under 40 years of age, particularly obese males in whom it is more frequently complicated.[5,6] There is compelling evidence that lack of dietary fibre is a major contributing factor in the pathogenesis of diverticular disease[7,8] and this is associated with a striking geographical distribution. The disease was virtually unknown in rural Africa and Third World countries, although recent reports show an increasing incidence in parts of South Africa,[9] Israel,[10] and the Middle East where a Western diet has been adopted,[11] and it is now being described in black Africans.[12] The dietary-fibre hypothesis is further supported by evidence that vegetarians have a lower incidence of diverticulosis than matched controls but it is not entirely clear whether this is related to an increased fibre intake or to a reduced meat consumption.[13]

Pathogenesis

The development of colonic diverticula seems to be related to an interplay between an increased intraluminal pressure and the presence of points of relative weakness in the bowel wall through which mucosa can protrude. Anatomically, the latter lie between the taenia coli at sites of vascular penetration of the bowel wall. Several studies have shown raised intraluminal pressures and abnormal colonic motility in patients with diverticular disease, but by no means in all.[14,15] High intraluminal pressures and a raised motility index correspond closely to the presence of abdominal pain and distension often experienced by patients with diverticular disease, but they do not seem to be a prerequisite for the formation of diverticula.

A prominent and consistent feature of diverticular disease is the grossly abnormal appearance of the circular muscle and thickening of the taenia coli in affected portions of the large bowel.[16] This thickening is due to bunching of muscle fibres rather than a true hypertrophy or hyperplasia and has been studied in detail by Whiteway and Morson[17] who found a 200% increase in elastin in the taeniae, which is responsible for the shortening and concertina-like corrugation of the circular muscle and its overlying mucosa. It should be remembered, however, that both diverticula and the muscle abnormality may occur independently of each other.

The pathophysiological changes which occur in diverticular disease are complex but it seems that disorder of motility and raised intraluminal pressure, possibly related to a low residue diet, produces muscle changes as a secondary phenomenon. This could explain the clinical spectrum which is seen, ranging from patients with severe pain and hypermotility but no diverticula, to those with asymptomatic total diverticulosis.[18] However, a clinicopathological link between the pathogenesis of the irritable bowel syndrome and diverticular disease has yet to be established.[19]

Natural history of colonic diverticular disease

The majority of people with diverticulosis coli remain asymptomatic throughout life. A minority (10–25%) develop symptoms and complications.[20] In addition there are presumably an unidentified number of people with mild symptoms for which medical advice is not sought. Thus the natural history of diverticular disease has been assumed from radiological, endoscopic and pathological examinations of the colon in a minority of patients who are referred to hospital.

The majority (60%) of patients with symptomatic diverticula present between the ages of 50 and 70. The duration of symptoms is often surprisingly short, being less than one month in 50% of cases, and these patients show the highest mortality and morbidity rates.[20] Recurrence is common and is also associated with high morbidity and mortality.

From a clinical standpoint there are apparently two types of presentations, the more common with pain, bowel symptoms or fistulae, and the less common with bleeding.[21] There is also evidence that the severe complications of diverticular disease are more likely to occur in patients taking non-steroidal anti-inflammatory drugs.[22]

Anatomical distribution of diverticulosis

Diverticular disease in a western civilization most commonly affects the sigmoid colon (90% of cases) with 30% also involving the descending colon, 4% the transverse colon and 16% the whole colon. The rectum is virtually never involved. Only rarely is right sided diverticular disease seen, and when present is usually in a younger age group in the form of a solitary caecal diverticulum, which may have a congenital rather than acquired origin. The condition known as 'solitary ulcer' of the caecum is probably due to inflammation in a diverticulum. In contrast, multiple right sided diverticula is the commonest form of a diverticular disease in Japan[23] and Singapore[24] where it has been shown to be associated with an increase in luminal pressure in the caecum and ascending colon.[25] The reasons for the different patterns of disease in East and West are not understood.[26]

Macroscopical pathology

Colonic diverticula are of the acquired, pulsion type and are usually multiple. They protrude through the muscle coats of the bowel wall and lie in the pericolic fat and appendices epiploicae, forming two rows, one on each side of the bowel wall lying between the taenia coli on the anti mesenteric aspect. The herniations are often related to the sites of penetration of blood vessels. The colon affected by diverticular disease has thickened, hyaline circular muscle and is shortened. Consequently the mucosa falls in redundant folds over the corrugated muscle (Fig. 23.1) and pericolic fat appears to be increased in amount. Inspissated faecal material or faecoliths commonly accumulate in the diverticula (Fig. 23.2).

Microscopic pathology

Pouches of mucosa protrude through the circular muscle and are covered only by an attenuated layer of muscularis mucosae and longitudinal muscle (Fig. 23.3). They are lined by normal colonic mucosa and often lymphoid hyperplasia is present. The muscle is abnormal, with thick but not hypertrophied fibres of circular muscle.[27] An artery and vein can sometimes be seen at the neck of the diverticulum.

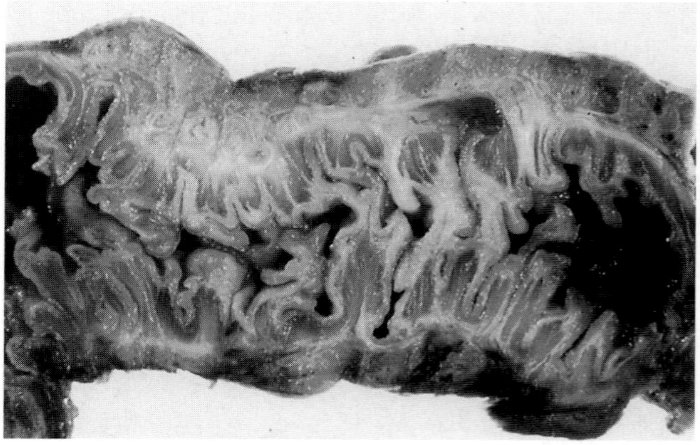

Fig. 23.1 Longitudinally cut segment of sigmoid colon affected by diverticulosis. Note the hyaline appearance of the circular muscle and the concertina effect of the mucosa.

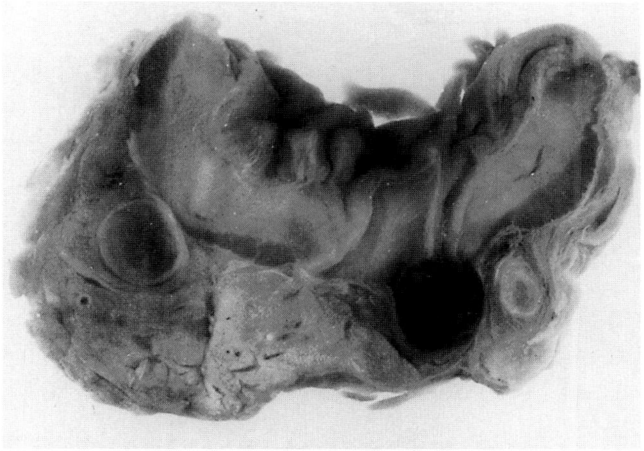

Fig. 23.2 Transverse section of sigmoid diverticular disease shows a dilated diverticulum containing a faecolith.

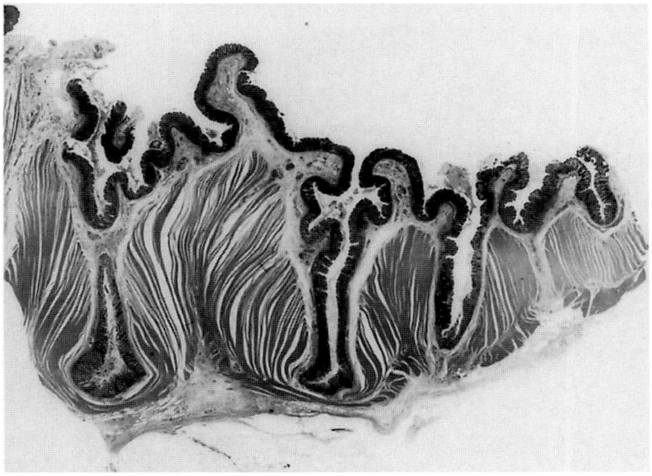

Fig. 23.3 Histology of diverticular disease. The circular muscle is thick with bunching of fibres. The diverticula are separated from pericolic fat only by an attenuated layer of longitudinal muscle. (H&E, ×2)

Complications

Inflammation

Diverticulitis is the commonest complication of diverticular disease and occurs as a secondary phenomenon, probably due to the presence of faecoliths. Acute or chronic inflammation of the diverticular mucosa, associated with prominent lymphoid tissue, develops and spreads outwards and longitudinally on the serosal surface of the bowel wall. It is surprisingly uncommon for more than one diverticulum to be involved in this process at any time. Because the mucosa of the diverticulum is separated from the pericolic tissues by only a thin layer of muscle, inflammation easily extends out into the pericolic fat and gives rise to a localized peritonitis which can then spread along the paracolic gutters to involve more distal areas of the sigmoid colon.

Histologically, there is inflammation of the diverticular mucosa often with foreign body giant cells associated with faecal material and barium. The luminal mucosa of the colon is rarely involved in diverticulitis, and if inflammation is seen at that site, the possibility of coexisting inflammatory bowel disease or the so-called colitis of diverticular disease should be considered. Resolution of the inflammatory process leads to the affected segment being ensheathed in fibrous tissue. It can be extremely difficult to distinguish macroscopically such a fibrous mass from carcinoma. It is important to take longitudinal sections when dissecting such a specimen in order that occult carcinoma is not missed. Primary surgical resection is the usual treatment of choice for diverticulitis[28,29] but initial colostomy and drainage of any abscess has been shown to produce slightly better results.[30]

Perforation and fistula formation

Rupture of a diverticulum can lead to localized abscess formation. Involvement of adjacent pelvic organs such as the bladder can then lead to fistula formation. Colovesical and colovaginal fistulae are the most common, but any two structures can be involved.

Haemorrhage

Bleeding from diverticular disease is common and manifests as fresh rectal haemorrhage. It is usually unrelated to diverticulitis. Severe blood loss can occur, but nearly always resolves spontaneously. It is not surprising that bleeding is a common complication of diverticulosis because the point of mucosal herniation is always near a vascular bundle (Fig. 23.4). The haemorrhage[31] is due to the eccentric rupture of small arteries at the neck of diverticula.[31] Any inflammation or ulceration caused by faecal material can therefore lead to bleeding and in the absence

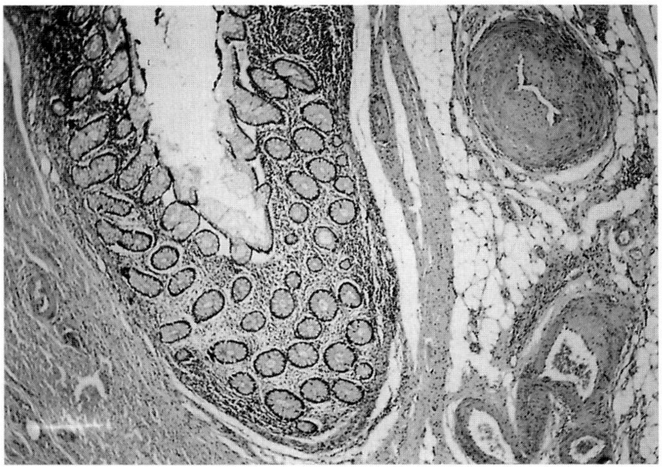

Fig. 23.4 Section shows the proximity of the diverticular lumen to large blood vessels. (H&E, ×80)

of carcinoma, brisk rectal bleeding was commonly ascribed to diverticular disease. This view has been revised in recent times with the recognition that such bleeding in elderly patients is often due to angiodysplasia.

Co-existent malignancy

It used to be thought that diverticulitis predisposed to the development of colorectal adenocarcinoma but this is now known to be a fallacy. If there is an association between the two conditions it is likely to be due to a common environmental factor such as diet. The incidence of adenomas and carcinoma in diverticular disease varies from 8–15% in different radiological studies and this is probably an underestimate. Preoperative assessment by colonoscopy has been shown to be diagnostically more accurate in such cases than is radiology alone.[32] However it is important to recognize this association and the pathologist should examine all specimens of complicated diverticular disease very carefully so as not to miss an occult carcinoma.

Adenocarcinoma arising in the mucosa of a diverticulum is extremely uncommon, warranting only sporadic case reports.[33]

Co-existent inflammatory bowel disease

Diverticulosis may coexist with both Crohn's disease and ulcerative colitis.[34,35] It can be difficult to distinguish between the granulomatous inflammation of diverticulitis and Crohn's colitis. The presence of a longitudinal, intramural fistulous tract is pathognomonic for granulomatous colitis and involvement of luminal large bowel mucosa is also a useful pointer to the diagnosis of inflammatory bowel disease (Figs 23.5 and 23.6).

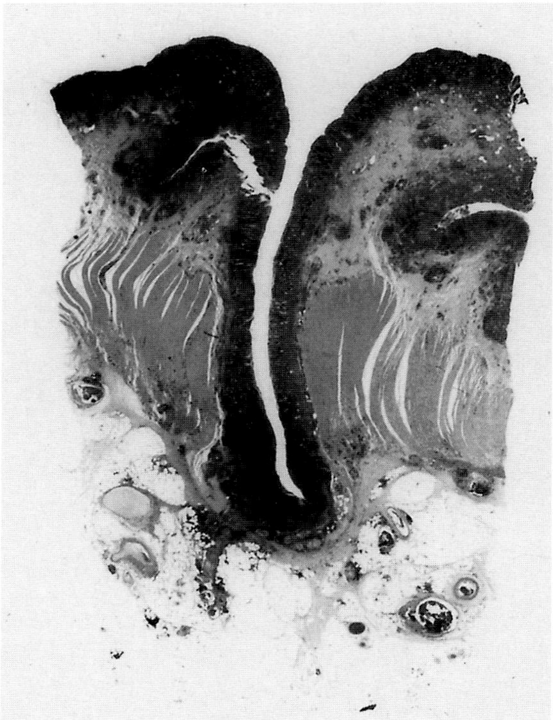

Fig. 23.5 Section of a diverticulum from a patient with coexisting diverticulosis and Crohn's disease. Note the inflammation of the luminal mucosa and fissures adjacent to the diverticulum. (H&E, ×2.8)

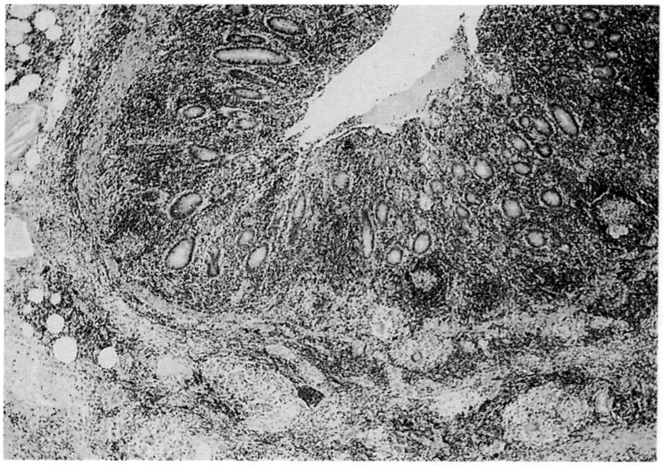

Fig. 23.6 Same case as Fig. 23.5. Section shows epithelioid granulomata adjacent to the diverticulum. (H&E, ×80)

MUCOSAL PROLAPSE (INCLUDING SOLITARY ULCER OF THE RECTUM)

Pathology

Solitary ulcer of the rectum syndrome (SURS) is a chronic benign condition characterized by rectal bleeding, the passage of mucus and rectal pain. It is poor nomenclature for a condition which, we will see, is by no means always associated with ulceration.[36] In its classical form it is a rare disorder which affects young adults, but is also described in old age and has even been reported in paediatric patients.[37]

Macroscopically, the lesions are typically seen as single or multiple shallow ulcers with hyperaemic margins usually situated on the anterior or anterolateral rectal wall. However, ulceration is not always apparent and the mucosa may appear polypoid or reddened and granular. In their review of 68 patients Madigan and Morson described single ulcers in 70% of cases, multiple lesions in 30% and showed that an ulcerative and a pre-ulcerative phase exist, thus emphasizing that solitary ulcer syndrome may not necessarily present clinically with either solitary or ulcerated lesions.[38]

Histologically, there is disorganization of the muscularis mucosae with extension of fibromuscular tissue into the lamina propria. The glandular epithelium is hyperplastic and may have a villous conformation with telangiectatic blood vessels beneath the surface epithelium (Figs 23.7 & 23.8). The hyperplastic crypts can appear almost adenomatous in some cases and it is important that a mistaken diagnosis of villous adenoma is not made. Mucin filled glands may become trapped deep in the submucosa giving rise to localised colitis cystica profunda. Histochemically, the mucin produced by the glands in this condition has been shown to be abnormal, with sialomucin predominance.[39]

Pathogenesis

Histological and histochemical features similar to those seen in SURS can be demonstrated in a variety of other conditions and sites, namely transitional mucosa adjacent to large bowel tumours, prolapsed colostomies and prolapsed haemorrhoids[40,41] (Figs 23.9 & 23.10) and in the mucosa between colonic diverticula.

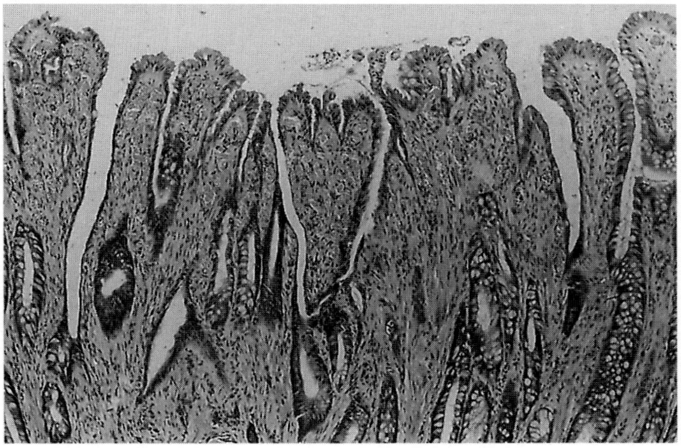

Fig. 23.7 Solitary ulcer of the rectum. Note villous epithelium with glandular hyperplasia and telangiectatic blood vessels. (H&E, ×120)

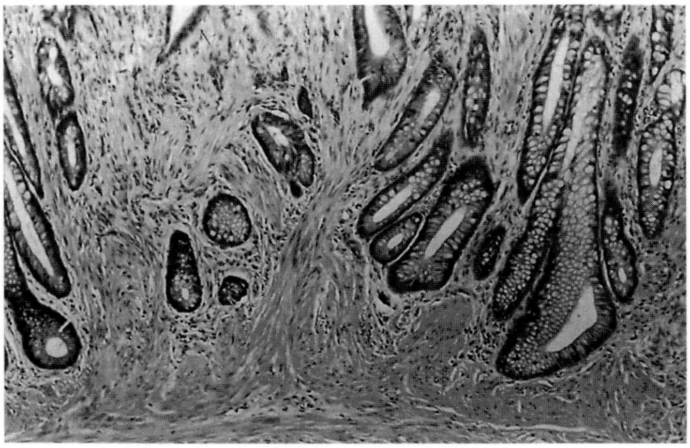

Fig. 23.8 Solitary ulcer of the rectum. The muscularis mucosae is disorganized and there is extension into the lamina propria. (H&E, ×240)

It appears that wherever mucosal prolapse occurs in the large bowel certain characteristic histological and histochemical features become manifest.[41] One explanation of this is the production of local ischaemia due to traction forces on submucosal vasculature secondary to prolapse of

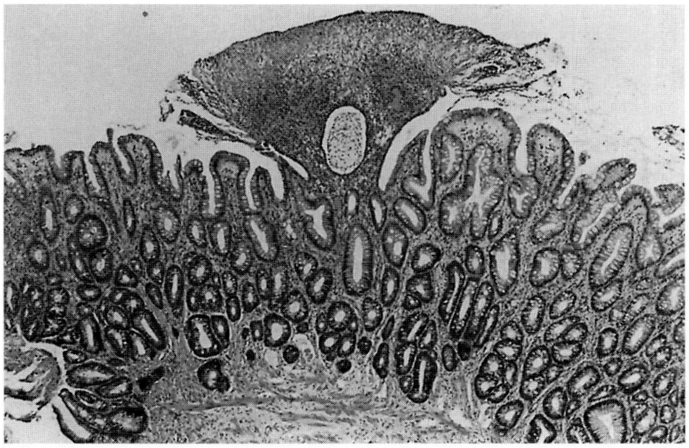

Fig. 23.9 Prolapsed mucosa adjacent to haemorrhoids showing histological features similar to SURS with surface ulceration and muscular disorganization. (H&E, ×45)

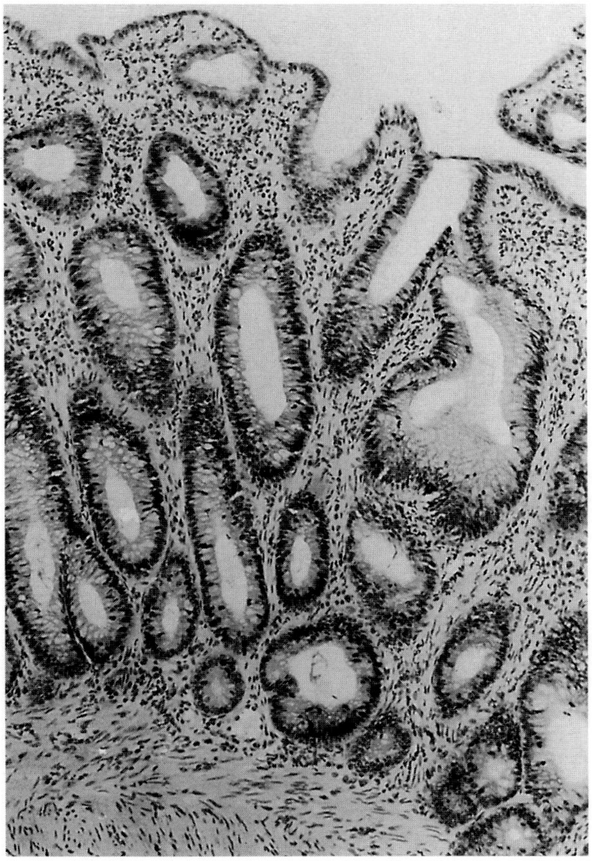

Fig. 23.10 Prolapsed mucosa shows disorganization of glands and smooth muscle hypertrophy. (H&E, ×60)

the rectal mucosa, as proposed by Rutter and Riddell.[42] This suggestion has been reinforced by the observation of a clinical association between SURS and rectal prolapse.[43] Abnormal EMG features of pelvic floor musculature have also been demonstrated in patients with SURS.[44] More recently, two studies have shown that internal procidentia or early prolapse is a relatively common clinical problem, particularly in elderly women with traumatic obstetric histories.[45] The diversity of terms previously used to describe this histologically similar group of conditions (hamartomatous inverted polyp, localized colitis cystica profunda and inflammatory cloacogenic polyp)[46–48] bear no relationship to the aetiology of the lesion and are frequently misused. A common clinicopathological term such as mucosal prolapse syndrome to embrace all these is preferable.[41,49,50] Certainly, surgical treatment of the associated mucosal prolapse will frequently effect a cure.[51,52]

REFERENCES

1. Almy TP, Howell DA. Diverticular disease of the colon. N Engl J Med 1980; 302: 324–331.
2. Marcus R, Watt J. The 'pre-diverticular state'. Br J Surg 1964; 51: 676–682.
3. Hughes LE. Post mortem survey of diverticular disease of the colon. Part I — Diverticulosis and diverticulitis. Gut 1969; 10: 336–351.
4. Painter NS, Burkitt DP. Diverticular disease of the colon: a deficiency disease of Western civilization. Br Med J 1971; 2: 450–454.
5. Acosta JA, Grebenc ML, Doberneck RC, McCarthy JD, Fry DE. Colonic diverticular disease in patients 40 years old or younger. Am Surg 1992; 58: 605–607.
6. Schauer PR, Ramos R, Ghiatas AA, Sirinek KR. Virulent diverticular disease in young obese man. Am J Surg 1992; 164: 443–446.
7. Burkitt D. Fiber as a protective agent against gastrointestinal diseases. Am J Gastroenterol 1984; 79: 249–252.
8. Painter NS, Burkitt DP. Diverticular disease of the colon — a 20th Century problem. Clin Gastroenterol 1975; 4: 3–22.
9. Segal I, Solomon A, Hunt JA. Emergence of diverticular disease in the urban South African black. Gastroenterology 1977; 72: 215–219.
10. Levy N, Stermer E, Simon J. The changing epidemiology of diverticular disease in Israel. Dis Colon Rectum 1985; 28: 416–418.
11. Manousos O, Day NE, Tzonou A, et al. Diet and other factors in the aetiology of diverticulosis: an epidemiological study in Greece. Gut 1985; 26: 544–549.
12. Ihekwaba FN. Diverticular disease in the colon in black Africa. J R Coll Surg (Edinb) 1992; 37: 107–109.
13. Heaton KW. Diet and diverticulosis — new leads. Gut 1985; 26: 541–543.
14. Painter NS, Truelove SC. The intraluminal pressure patterns in diverticulosis of the colon I. Resting patterns of pressure. Gut 1964; 5: 201–213.
15. Parks TG, Connell AM. Motility studies in diverticular disease of the colon. Gut 1969; 10: 534–542.
16. Hughes LE. Post mortem survey of diverticular disease of the colon Part II. The muscular abnormality in the sigmoid colon. Gut 1969; 10: 344–351.
17. Whiteway J, Morson BC. Elastosis in diverticular disease of the sigmoid colon. Gut 1985; 26: 258–266.
18. Weinreich J, Andersen D. Intraluminal pressure in the sigmoid colon. II Patients with sigmoid diverticula and related conditions. Scand J Gastroenterol 1976; 11: 581–586.
19. Parks TG. The possible aetiological link between the irritable bowel syndrome and diverticular disease of the colon. Ital J Gastroenterol 1984; 16: 240–246.
20. Parks TG. Natural history of diverticular disease of the colon. A review of 521 cases. Br Med J 1969; iv: 639–642.
21. Ryan P. Two kinds of diverticular disease. Ann R Coll Surg (Engl) 1991; 73: 73–79.
22. Campbell K, Steele RJ. Non-steroidal anti-inflammatory drugs in diverticular disease: a case-control study. Br J Surg 1991; 78: 190–191.
23. Sugihara K, Muto T, Morioka Y et al. Diverticular disease of the colon in Japan. A review of 615 cases. Dis Colon Rectum 1984; 27: 531–537.
24. Chia JG, Wilde CC, Ngoi SS, Goh PM, Ong CL. Trends of diverticular disease of the large bowel in a newly developed country. Dis Colon Rectum 1991; 34: 498–501.
25. Muto T, Sugihara K, Morioka Y. Motility study in right sided diverticular disease of the colon. Gut 1983; 24: 1130–1134.
26. Magness LJ, Sanfelippo PM, van Heerden JA, Judd ES. Diverticular disease of the right colon. Surg Gynecol Obstet 1975; 140: 30–32.
27. Morson BC. Pathology of diverticular disease of the colon. Clin Gastroenterol 1975; 4: 37–52.
28. Slack W. The anatomy, pathology and some clinical features of diverticulitis of the colon. Br J Surg 1962; 50: 185–189.
29. Weston Underwood J, Marks CG. The septic complications of sigmoid diverticular disease. Br J Surg 1984; 71: 209–211.
30. Peoples JB, Vilk DR, Maguire JP, Elliott DW. Reassessment of primary resection of the perforated segment for severe colonic diverticulitis. Am J Surg 1990; 159: 291–293.
31. Meyers MA, Alonso DR, Gray GF, Baer JW. Pathogenesis of bleeding colonic diverticulosis. Gastroenterology 1976; 71: 577–583.
32. Boulos PB, Karamanolis DG, Salmon PR, Clark CG. Is colonoscopy necessary in diverticular disease? Lancet 1984; 1: 95–96.
33. McCraw RC, Wilson SM, Brown FM, Gardner WA. Adenocarcinoma arising in a sigmoid diverticulum. Dis Colon Rectum 1976; 19: 553–556.
34. Marshak RH, Janowitz HD, Present DH. Granulomatous colitis in association with diverticula. N Engl J Med 1970; 283: 1080–1084.
35. Meyers MA, Alonso DR, Morson BC. Pathogenesis of diverticulitis complicating granulomatous colitis. Gastroenterology 1978; 74: 24–31.
36. Stolfi VM, Bacaro D, Rossi P, Forlini A et al. Solitary ulcer of the rectum: a report of a clinical case associated with rectal prolapse. G Chir 1991; 12: 389–392.
37. Eigenmann PA, Le-Coultre C, Cox J, Dederding JP, Belli DC. Solitary rectal ulcer: an unusual cause of rectal bleeding in children. Eur J Pediatr 1992; 151: 658–660.
38. Madigan MR, Morson BC. Solitary ulcer of the rectum. Gut 1969; 10: 871–881.
39. Ehsanullah M, Filipe MI, Gazzard B. Morphological and mucus secretion criteria for the differential diagnosis of the solitary ulcer of the rectum syndrome and non specific proctitis. J Clin Pathol 1982; 35: 26–30.
40. Isaacson P, Attwood PRA. Failure to demonstrate specificity of the morphological and histochemical changes in mucosa adjacent to colonic carcinoma transitional mucosa. J Clin Pathol 1979; 32: 214–218.
41. Du Boulay CEH, Fairbrother J, Isaacson PG. Mucosa prolapse syndrome — a unifying concept for solitary ulcer syndrome and related disorders. J Clin Pathol 1983; 36: 1264–1268.
42. Rutter KR, Riddell RH. The solitary ulcer syndrome of the rectum. Clin Gastroenterol 1975; 4: 505–530.
43. Schweiger M, Alexander Williams J. Solitary ulcer of the rectum. Its association with rectal prolapse. Lancet 1977; 1: 170–171.
44. Rutter KRP. Electromyographic changes in certain pelvic floor abnormalities. Proc R Soc Med 1974; 67: 53–56.

45. Johansson C, Ihre T, Ahlback SO. Disturbances in the defaecation mechanism with special reference to intussusception of the rectum (internal procidentia). Dis Colon Rectum 1985; 28: 920–924.
46. Lobert PF, Appelman HD. Inflammatory cloacogenic polyps. Am J Surg Pathol 1981; 5: 761–766.
47. Stuart M. Proctitis cystica profunda: incidence, etiology and treatment. Dis Colon Rectum 1984; 27: 153–156.
48. Martin JK, Culp CE, Weiland LH. Colitis cystica profunda. Dis Colon Rectum 1980; 23: 488–491.
49. Potet F, Bogomoletz WV, Fenzy A. Syndrome du prolapsus muqueux anorectal: un concept moderne et unitaire de l'ulcere solitaire du rectum et lesions du meme type. Gastroenterol Clin Biol 1985; 9: 561–563.
50. Bogomoletz WV. Solitary rectal ulcer syndrome. Mucosal prolapse syndrome. Pathol Ann 1992; 27: 75–86.
51. Costalat G, Garrigues JM, Alquier Y, Lopez P, et al. Solitary rectal ulcer syndrome: clinical features, clinical course and treatment. Ann Chir 1990; 44: 807–816.
52. Tjandra JJ, Fazio VW, Church JM, Lavery IC, Oakley JR, Milsom JW. Clinical conundrum of solitary rectal ulcer. Dis Colon Rectum 1992; 35: 227–234.

PART II

Anorectal prolapse and incontinence

P. D. James

ANORECTAL PROLAPSE

Rectal prolapse occurs when part or all of the rectal wall protrudes through the anal orifice. Mucosal prolapse may occur in children and adults while full thickness rectal prolapse (procidentia) is most frequently seen in elderly females.

Mucosal prolapse

In children, mucosal prolapse appears uncommon in westernized society, occuring most frequently in infants with cystic fibrosis. It may be associated with any disease causing diarrhoea, constipation, frequent cough or malnutrition, the latter being a major cause in developing countries. The prolapse is due to the loose mucosal attachment to the underlying muscle; the vertical course of the rectum, the relatively flat sacrum and coccyx, the low rectal position in relation to the other pelvic organs and the lack of levator support all make the rectal mucosa vulnerable to vertical shearing forces. Mucosal prolapse occurs under the age of 3, most frequently in the first year of life and usually disappears spontaneously with resolution of the underlying cause.[1]

In adults, mucosal prolapse may occur with prolapsing piles, in association with the descending perineum syndrome[2] and with the solitary ulcer of the rectum syndrome.[3]

Complete rectal prolapse (procidentia)

Prolapse of the full thickness of the rectal wall through the anal orifice is most common in the elderly nulliparous female who often has a coincident uterine prolapse.[4] Faecal incontinence and a descending perineum may be concurrent problems.

Early workers[5] believed that the prolapse represented a sliding hernia of a deep pouch of Douglas, but more recent cineradiographic studies suggest that it is an intussusception of the lower rectum.[6] However, it would seem that these two processes reflect different aspects of a single abnormality, the invagination of the anterior rectal wall described as a sliding hernia being interpreted as an intussusception which has not as yet involved the total bowel circumference.[7] The abnormal anatomy consistently found with procidentia includes a deep pouch of Douglas, diastasis of the levator ani muscles, a redundant sigmoid colon, elongated mesorectum, loss of the horizontal position of the rectum due to lax attachments to the sacrum and a patulous anus. These changes are secondary to the prolapse rather than its cause.

In common with the descending perineum syndrome and faecal incontinence, there is evidence of partial denervation damage to the pelvic musculature.[8] It is suggested that chronic straining at stool produces perineal descent which results in stretch injury to the nerve supply of the external sphincter and puborectalis muscles. The loss of tone in these muscles allows raised intra-abdominal pressure to initiate the process of rectal prolapse.[9] Other factors, including age related changes in muscle and connective tissue, may be important in some cases. Ischaemic damage to the prolapsing mucosa may occur as a result of traction on the submucosal vessels, resulting in changes of the solitary ulcer syndrome.[3]

A large number of operations have been devised for the treatment of complete rectal prolapse. These include anal encirclement procedures (Thiersch wire, nylon loop), fixation of the rectum (rectopexy, ivalon wrap) and resection of the redundant sigmoid colon.[10]

FAECAL INCONTINENCE

The important features of the pelvic anatomy which maintain normal faecal continence are the acute angulation between the rectum and anal canal together with the tonic contraction of the external sphincter muscle. A flap-valve mechanism is produced by the anorectal angulation which is maintained by the muscular sling formed by the puborectalis muscle.[11,12] The role of anal and rectal sensation in maintaining continence is controversial.[13] Incontinence may occur as a result of local disorders causing diarrhoea or faecal impaction, reduced rectal capacity and poor sphincter activity,[14] or neurological causes including peripheral neuropathies, spinal cord lesions or central nervous system diseases (multiple sclerosis, Parkinson's disease). Idiopathic faecal incontinence is more common in women who may give a history of difficult or prolonged labour. It is invariably associated with the descending perineum syndrome in which the pelvic floor occupies a lower position than normal, particularly on straining.[2] Some cases of rectal prolapse may be complicated by faecal incontinence.

It has been shown that idiopathic faecal incontinence is due to weakness of the pelvic musculature, particularly the external sphincter and puborectalis muscles, caused by damage to their nerve supply.[15] These muscles show loss of fibres with fibrous replacement and infiltration by adipose tissue. The presence of small angulated fibres and fibre-type grouping reflects denervation and reinnervation changes respectively.[8] The nerve supply of the external sphincter muscle is derived from branches of the pudendal nerve and that of the puborectalis muscle from a branch of the sacral nerve.[15] Electrophysiological studies have demonstrated damage to the distal parts of these nerves which appears due to repeated stretch injury occurring during perineal descent associated with chronic straining at defaecation.[16] In women this injury may be initiated by damage to the nerves during childbirth.[17] Stress incontinence of urine is an associated feature in some cases and similar neuromuscular abnormalities have been found in the peri-urethral sphincter muscles.[18]

Denervation may not be a factor in all cases of faecal incontinence. Other causes include direct trauma to the musculature during childbirth or following various surgical procedures and inflammatory bowel disease.[15]

REFERENCES

1. Corman ML. Rectal prolapse in children. Dis Colon Rectum 1985; 28: 535–539.
2. Parks AG, Porter NH, Hardcastle J. The syndrome of the descending perineum. Proc R Soc Med 1966; 59: 477–482.
3. Du Boulay CEH, Fairbrother J, Isaacson PG. Mucosal prolapse syndrome — a unifying concept for solitary ulcer syndrome and related disorders. J Clin Pathol 1983; 36: 1264–1268.
4. Kupfer CA, Goligher JC. One hundred consecutive cases of complete prolapse of the rectum treated by operation. Br J Surg 1970; 57: 481–487.
5. Moschcowitz AV. The pathogenesis, anatomy and cure of prolapse of the rectum. Surg Gynaecol Obstet 1912; 15: 7–21.
6. Broden B, Snellman B. Procidentia of the rectum studied by cineradiography: a contribution to the discussion of causative mechanism. Dis Colon Rectum 1968; 11: 330–347.
7. Goldberg SM, Gordon PH. The treatment of rectal prolapse. Clin Gastroenterol 1975; 4,3: 489–504.
8. Parks AG, Swash M, Urich H. Sphincter denervation in anorectal incontinence and rectal prolapse. Gut 1977; 18: 656–665.
9. Schoetz DJ Jr, Veidenheimer MC. Rectal prolapse A. Pathogenesis and clinical features. In: Henry MM, Swash M, eds. Coloproctology and the pelvic floor: pathophysiology and management. London: Butterworths, 1985.
10. Andrews NJ, Jones DJ. ABC of Colorectal Diseases. Rectal prolapse and associated conditions. Br Med J 1992; 305: 243–246.
11. Duthie HL. Progress report. Anal continence. Gut 1971; 12: 844–852.
12. Parks AG. Anal incontinence. Proc R Soc Med 1975; 68: 681–690.
13. Rogers J. Testing for and the role of anal and rectal sensation. Bailliere's Clin Gastroenterol 1992; 6,1: 179–191.
14. Kiff ES. ABC of Colorectal Diseases. Faecal incontinence. Br Med J 1992; 305: 702–704.
15. Swash M. Histopathology of the pelvic floor muscles. In: Henry MM, Swash M, eds. Coloproctology and the pelvic floor: pathophysiology and management. London: Butterworths, 1985.
16. Snooks SJ, Henry MM, Swash M. Anorectal incontinence and rectal prolapse: differential assessment of the innervation to puborectalis and external anal sphincter muscles. Gut 1985; 26: 470–476.
17. Snooks SJ, Setchell M, Swash M, Henry MM. Injury to innervation of pelvic floor sphincter musculature in childbirth. Lancet 1984; 2: 546–550.
18. Snooks SJ, Swash M. Abnormalities of the innervation of the urethral striated sphincter musculature in incontinence. Br J Urol 1984; 56: 401–405.

SECTION

4

Primary inflammatory disorders and disturbances of digestive function

CHAPTER 24

The oesophagus

H. Thompson R. Whitehead D. W. Day H. M. Gilmour

PART I

Reflux disease

H. Thompson

REFLUX DISEASE

Reflux oesophagitis has been defined as the response, subjective or objective, to the injurious effects of gastroduodenal contents on the oesophageal mucosa.[1] It is, basically, an inflammatory and reparative phenomenon. Reflux may consist of acid, pepsin, duodenal or intestinal contents, bile particularly being extremely damaging.

Gastro-oesophageal reflux is a normal physiological event and oesophagitis develops only in a proportion of patients with abnormal reflux. There is a complex defence mechanism which involves the lower oesophageal sphincter, oesophageal clearing, peristalsis, salivary and oesophageal gland secretions. There is also individual variation in oesophageal response and resistance to the effect of refluxed material but little is known about this. Once oesophagitis has been initiated, it is probable that the mucosa becomes more prone to further damage.

There is a poor correlation between symptoms and histological changes. Patients complain of heartburn, regurgitation or waterbrash, oesophageal pain or discomfort (odynophagia) in reponse to alcohol, hot food or beverage and in the more severe cases dysphagia and respiratory symptoms such as morning hoarseness, nocturnal cough or asthma. Some patients present with dysphagia due to peptic stricture or Barrett's oesophagus with little or no previous history. Mild and intermittent symptoms may be tolerated by the patient or controlled by antacids, H_2 antagonists, gaviscon or other treatment.

Clinical investigations involve endoscopic assessment, manometry and biopsy. Accurate endoscopic assessment of the severity of oesophagitis enables the physician to select the most appropriate treatment and to assess the likely prognosis. The most widely used endoscopic grading system is that of the Savary Miller system using 5 grades. In some cases more sophisticated tests may be employed such as Bernstein's acid perfusion test, scintigraphy, oesophageal pH monitoring, etc.

Certain conditions predispose towards the development of reflux oesophagitis, viz. obesity, fatty meals late in the day, cigarette smoking, hiatus hernia, duodenal ulcer, repeated vomiting, nasogastric intubation, diabetes, systemic sclerosis (Fig. 24.1) pemphigus, epidermolysis bullosa, surgery at the gastro-oesophageal junction including vagotomy, Zollinger-Ellison syndrome, delay in gastric emptying, duodenogastric reflux, recumbency, pregnancy, incompetent lower oesophageal sphincter, alcohol abuse, radiation and drugs, e.g. non steroidal anti-inflammatory drugs, oral contraceptives, aspirin, theophyllin, anticholinergic drugs used in Parkinson's syndrome or antidiarrhoeal drugs, tricyclic antidepressants and chemotherapeutic agents.

Biopsy technique is important for accurate interpretation of histological changes. Biopsies should be taken from levels more than 2.5 cm above the gastro-oesophageal junction. At least two biopsies should be obtained and additional biopsies improve the diagnostic accuracy. The biopsies should include the lamina propria and orien-

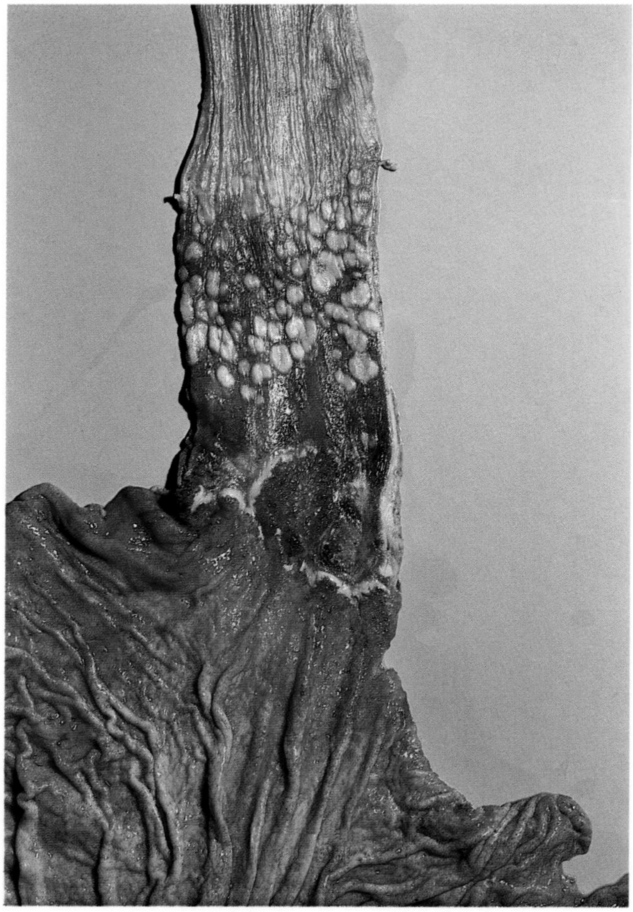

Fig. 24.1 Reflux oesophagitis. Erosive stage associated with pearly white foci of glycogenic acanthosis in a patient suffering from systemic sclerosis.

tation is desirable so that when flattened out on card or paper vertical sections through the mucosa can be obtained.

Grip or grasp forceps biopsies taken through a rigid oesophagoscope and suction biopsies using a Quinton suction biopsy instrument provide excellent specimens. Fibreoptic endoscopic suction or punch biopsies are smaller and have a more limited value.

The endoscopist must clearly identify the gastro-oesophageal junction, i.e. the ora serrata or in the case of Barrett's oesophagus the level of the squamocolumnar junction above the cardia or lower oesophageal sphincter. It is important also that the squamocolumnar junction and individual biopsy levels should be expressed in terms of distance from the incisor teeth.

NON-EROSIVE OESOPHAGITIS

In 1970 Ismail Beigi et al[2] drew attention to minor morphological changes which they considered characteristic of abnormal gastro-oesophageal reflux. These were basal cell hyperplasia, elongation of the papillae and sometimes the presence of neutrophils. Since that time the subject has been much debated. Because neutrophils are generally not regarded as essential for the diagnosis, the debate has largely concerned the other two parameters and particularly basal cell hyperplasia.

Basal cell hyperplasia (BCH)

The normal zone of basal cells (Fig. 24.2) occupies 10–15% of the epithelial layer thickness. Reparative hyperplasia due to gastro-oesophageal reflux leads to expansion of this zone so that it occupies 20–60% or more of the

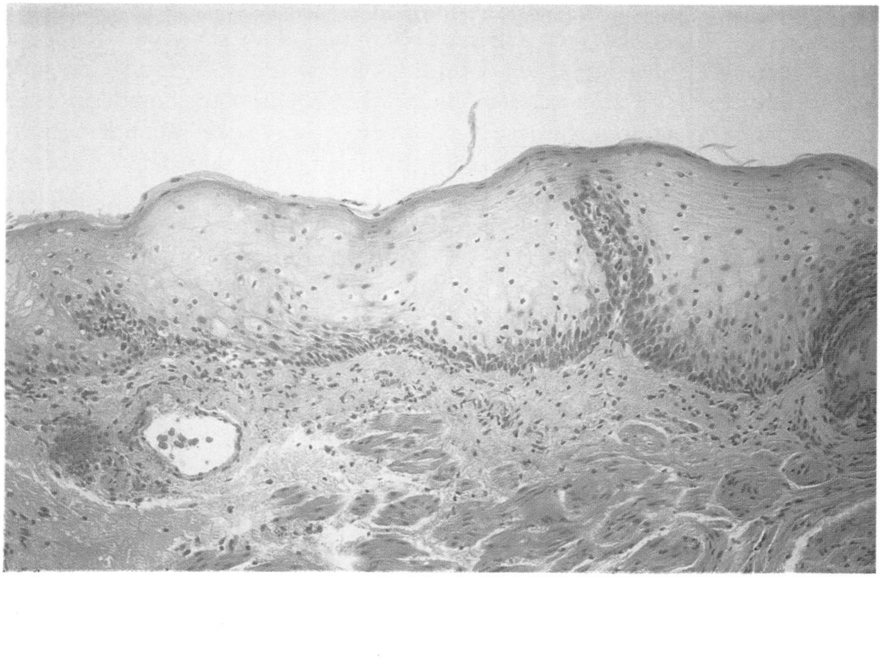

Fig. 24.2 Normal oesophageal mucosa. (×88)

mucosa (Figs 24.3 & 24.4). Glycogen staining by the PAS technique assists interpretation of the percentage thickness. Assessments are made in an area where there is no tangential cutting and in that part of the biopsy where the zone is thickest since the changes are often focal. They can be made by micrometer eyepiece or other morphometric techniques.

Recurrent reflux leads to chemical irritation of the oesophageal mucosa and accelerated desquamation of the superficial layers. Regenerative changes occur in the basal zone with an increased cell turnover rate[3] and are characterized by nuclear hyperchromatism and mitoses. Similar changes can also be seen in brush cytology specimens.

Elongation of papillae (Fig. 24.5) so that they are seen in the upper one-third of the mucosa is also said to be a feature of reflux[2] but Behar and Sheahan[4] suggest that papillary length greater than 50% in at least 2 biopsies is significant. It is not such a constant feature as basal cell hyperplasia but it is claimed nonetheless to have diagnostic value. The diameter of papillae also may appear to be increased.

Ismail-Beigi et al found a close agreement between the presence of BCH and both endoscopic and clinical evidence of reflux oesophagitis. It was shown later, however, that BCH occurs focally over the lower 8 cm of the oesophagus[5] and if two or more biopsies are examined up to 25% may prove to be normal. Furthermore, in so-called normal control subjects BCH may be seen in 10% of cases.

Basal cell hyperplasia probably represents a reversible change in the mucosa and it does not necessarily indicate progressive disease. Indeed Weinstein et al[6] found that biopsies from the distal 2.5 cm of the lower oesophagus showed BCH in 57% of asymptomatic subjects. At this

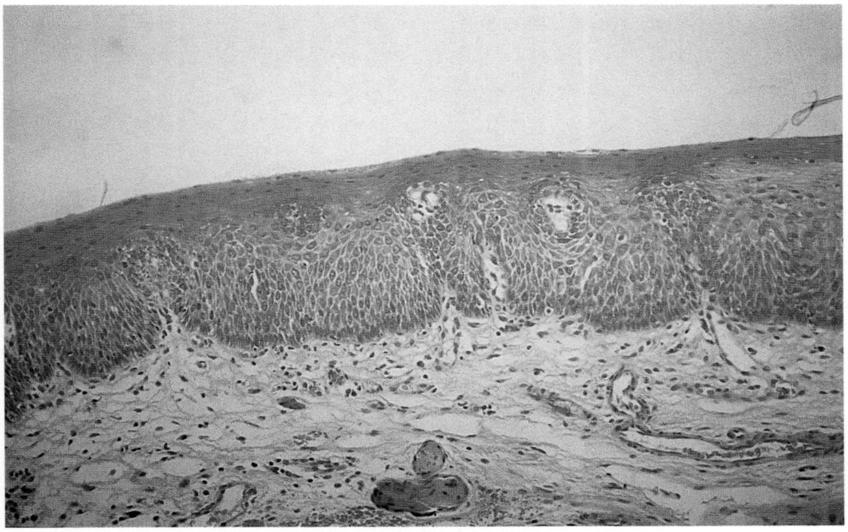

Fig. 24.3 Basal cell hyperplasia. (×88)

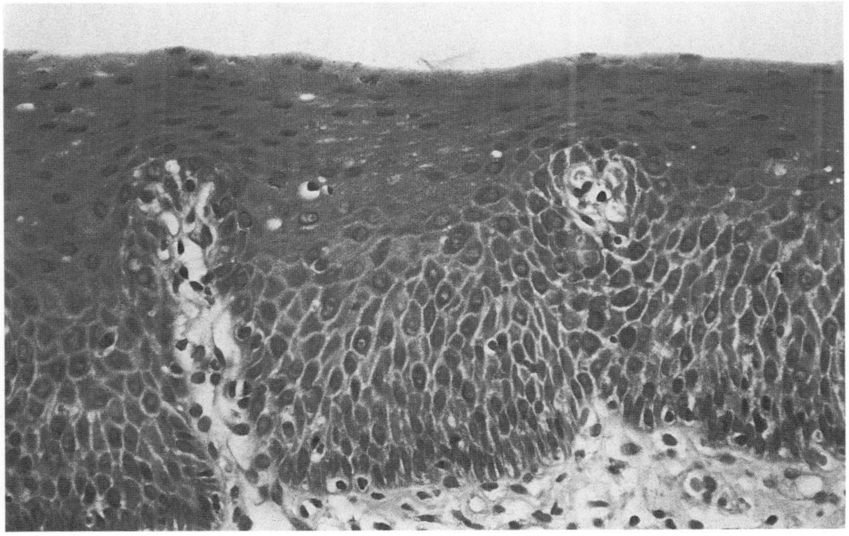

Fig. 24.4 Basal cell hyperplasia. (×210)

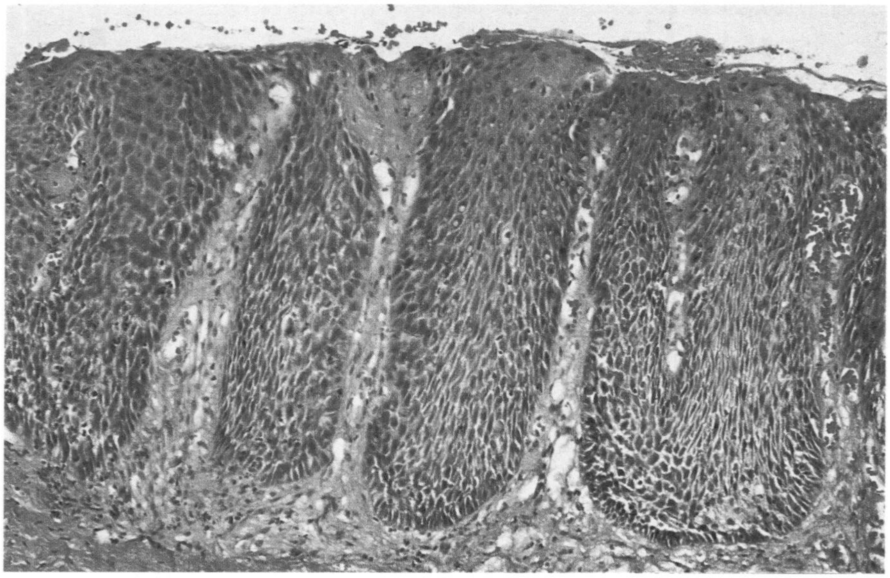

Fig. 24.5 Elongation of papillae. (×88; courtesy of Dr B Codling)

level, the changes reflect a physiological response to insignificant gastro-oesophageal reflux within the sphincter zone, but it is also seen in 19% of asymptomatic subjects at levels higher than 2.5 cm above the cardia. It is now generally agreed that changes in the lower 2 cm of the oesophagus are of little value in the histological assessment of non-ulcerative reflux.[7]

Thus there are grounds, it seems, for doubting the specificity and sensitivity of present histological criteria for reflux oesophagitis. It is perhaps pertinent that in a large study of 108 cases of sliding hiatus hernia in which reflux is known to occur, whilst endoscopic oesophagitis was found in 76.9%, conventional chronic inflammatory change of oesophagitis was only found in 56.2%.[8] This study was carried out prior to the establishment of current histological criteria, but in a second study in the same centre using the newest criteria histological evidence of reflux was found in 83% of a group of patients with endoscopic oesophagitis.[9]

Similar histological features, however, were observed in other types of oesophageal disease, viz. neuromuscular disorders such as achalasia of the cardia, carcinoma, radiation therapy, extrinsic lesion, Paterson Kelly syndrome, oesophageal diverticula, previous surgery (reflux and stricture) and columnar lined oesophagus.

It has been claimed, therefore, that BCH may be too sensitive an indicator and was identified in 20% of patients with no other positive features suggestive of oesophageal disease.[10] Furthermore, it also seems that normal squamous mucosa may be encountered in biopsy material from patients with symptomatic oesophagitis. Thus there are those who dispute the significance of these minor histological changes and have failed to confirm their diagnostic value using a morphometric technique.[11,12] Nevertheless

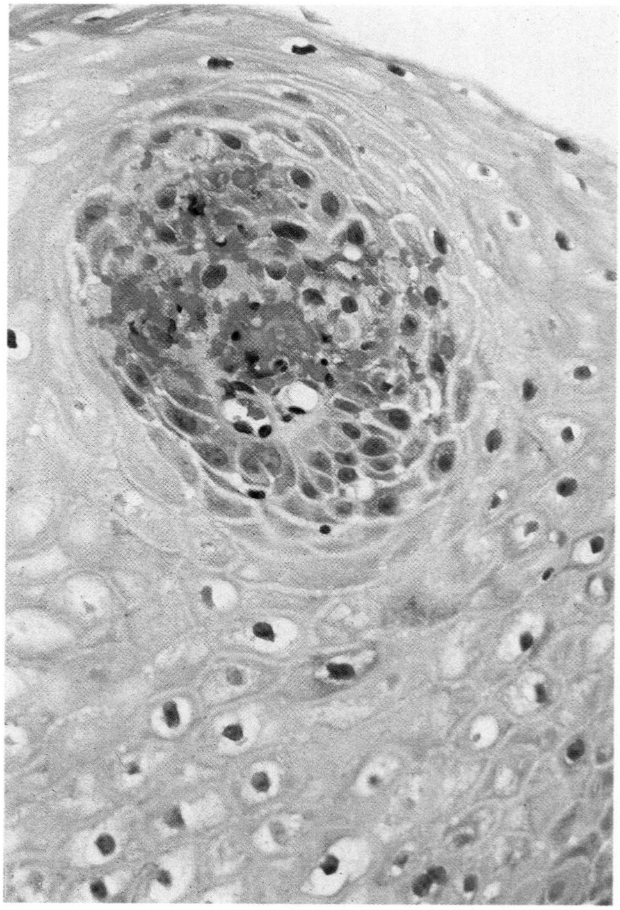

Fig. 24.6 Vascularization of papillae accompanied by haemorrhage. (Courtesy of Dr B Codling)

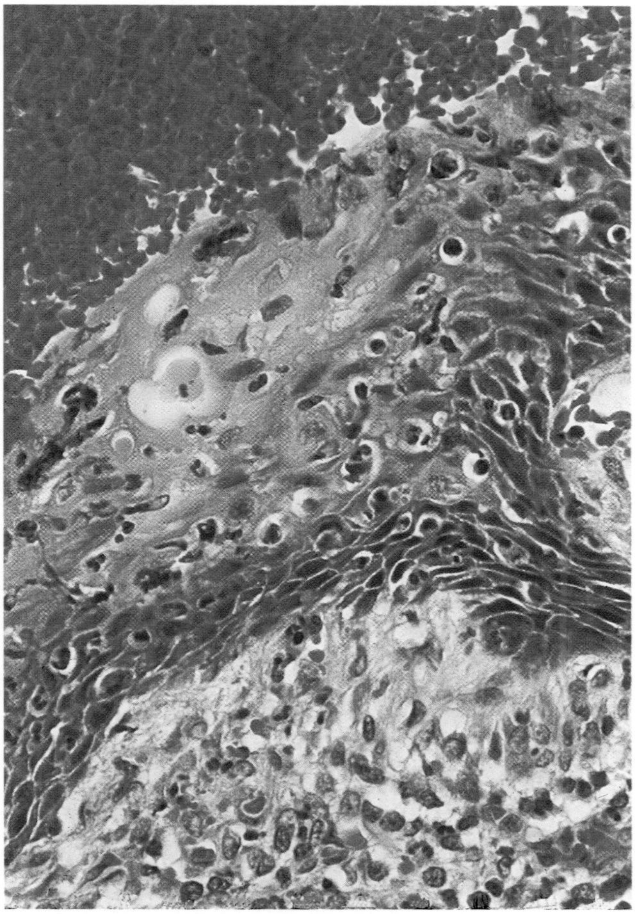

Fig. 24.7 Neutrophils in the papillae and epithelium.

other workers[13] still claim good correlation between minor histological changes and both clinical and endoscopic reflux. If they are to be used, there is strong argument for their being assessed objectively as advocated in a study by Jarvis and Whitehead.[14]

Other morphological features

Dilated capillaries and venules in the papillae which are sometimes associated with extravasated red cells (Fig. 24.6) are also thought to indicate reflux.[15] They are sometimes associated with an ingrowth of capillaries into the epithelium and there is margination and diapedesis of granulocytes. The transverse diameter of papillae is also increased. It appears that these features are in agreement with those seen in experimental feline oesophagitis.[16]

Polymorphonuclear leucocytes are not normally present in oesophageal mucosa. They may be found in 18–25% of mucosal biopsies from patients with symptoms suggestive of gastro-oesophageal reflux in a subepithelial (Fig. 24.7) or intra-epithelial location (Fig. 24.8). If the lamina propria is included then subepithelial neutrophils may be encountered in more than half of specimens showing basal cell hyperplasia. Collins et al[13] found subepithelial neutrophils in 38% of patients with erosive oesophagitis and also in one control patient. The presence of neutrophils where they normally do not occur is clearly a good indication of an inflammatory response but they have low sensitivity as a marker for reflux.

Winter et al[17] recently identified intra-epithelial eosinophils as a specific diagnostic criterion for reflux oesophagitis in children. Chromotrope 2R preparations assist the identification of eosinophils. However, in adults[13] eosinophils occur in only 52% of patients with erosive oesopha-

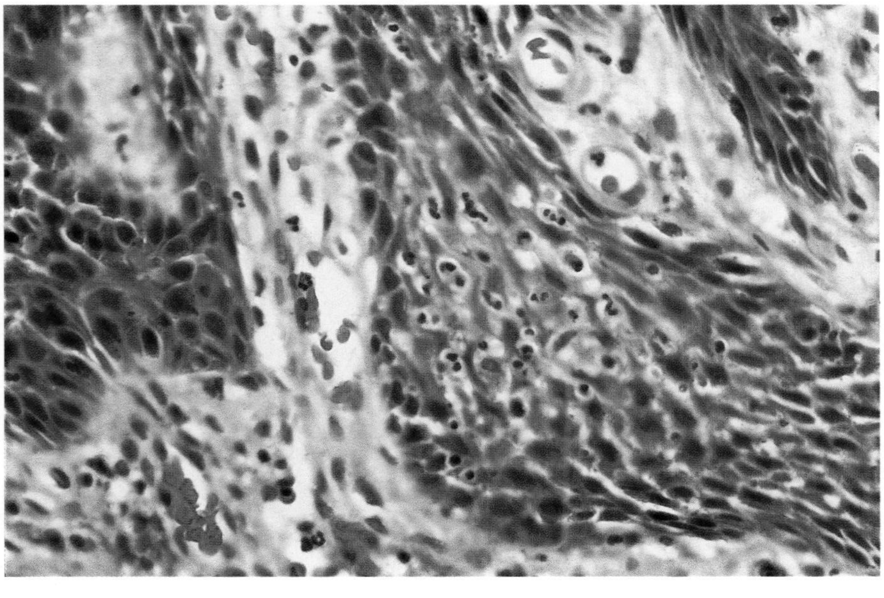

Fig. 24.8 Neutrophils in the epithelium. (×280)

gitis again indicating a low sensitivity in the adult. Two more recent studies[18,19] fail to support the view that eosinophils are a useful marker in oesophagitis.

Intra-epithelial cell nuclei other than neutrophils or eosinophils are often observed in biopsies.[20] These probably represent intra-epithelial lymphocytes which appear to be increased in oesophagitis. A monoclonal antibody study[21] showed that the number of Langerhans cells and cytotoxic T lymphocytes are increased in the epithelium in reflux oesophagitis

Jankowski et al[22] claim that epidermal growth factor receptors are increased in oesophagitis — 43.1% compared to normal mucosa 29.5%.

Lewis blood group antigens[23] in oesophageal mucosa are strongly correlated with the presence of oesophagitis. This technique can be automated by application to flow cytometry.[24]

Silver staining Nucleolar Organizer Regions (AGNORs)[25] can also be used to differentiate between normal, inflamed and dysplastic mucosa.

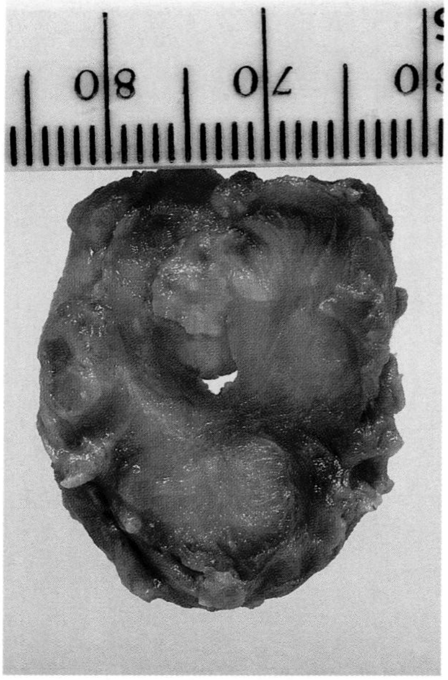

Fig. 24.9 Oesophageal peptic stricture due to chronic superficial oesophagitis.

Erosive or ulcerative oesophagitis

This stage can be clearly identified on endoscopy (Fig. 24.1) and mucosal biopsies may show erosions, ulcers, chronic inflammatory cellular infiltrations and in severe cases slight fibrosis. The biopsies however may only show the other minor features of gastro-oesophageal reflux, and in some patients who at endoscopy appear to have erosions the biopsies may show a normal histological appearance. This probably reflects a sampling phenomenon on most occasions.

Erosive or ulcerative oesophagitis may persist and progress over the years leading eventually to peptic stricture.

Peptic stricture

Recurrent or persistent ulceration leads to fibrosis in the submucosa, muscle coat and peri-oesophageal tissues. Peptic stricture (Fig. 24.9) can cause dysphagia due to fibrous stenosis, oedema and muscle spasm. The stricture may only be 1 cm or so in length but occasionally it is as long as 4 cm or more. Oedema and muscle spasm are reversible and strictures may disappear with healing of the oesophagitis or with treatment. Davidson[26] describes one patient in whom a stricture was seen to ascend the oesophagus over a period of 6 years and there is an apparent association with the use of non-steroidal anti-inflammatory drugs.[27]

Clinically there are two main varieties.[28] One is the more advanced stage of erosive or ulcerative oesophagitis. It is associated with circumferential fibrosis and gastric-type mucosa may extend up to a level of 2–4 cm above the cardia. Pearly white plaques of glycogenic acanthosis are frequently visible in the vicinity of the stricture.

Fig. 24.10 Barrett's ulcer. Autopsy case.

The other type is the stricture associated with a discrete ulcer crater. The ulcer has the typical structure of a simple peptic ulcer with zones of surface debris, fibrinoid necrosis, granulation tissue and collagenous fibrous tissue. There is a breach in the muscularis propria which is filled with scar tissue (Figs 24.10 & 24.11) and the ends of the muscle coat frequently end in the ulcer crater or merge with the muscularis mucosae. These ulcers are usually located at the junction between squamous and gastric-type epithelium or within gastric mucosa and are complicated by extensive, radiating cicatrical fibrosis. Two ulcers may coexist. Vessels in the base show endarteritis obliterans and neuromatous proliferation of nerve bundles is often an additional feature.

These ulcers are frequently referred to as Barrett's ulcers. Gastric mucosa may extend upwards to a level of 6 cm or more above the cardia. Interdigitation of squamous and gastric mucosa may be a feature associated with foci of glycogenic acanthosis. Both chronic superficial oesophagitis and chronic peptic ulcer are frequently present in the same patient.

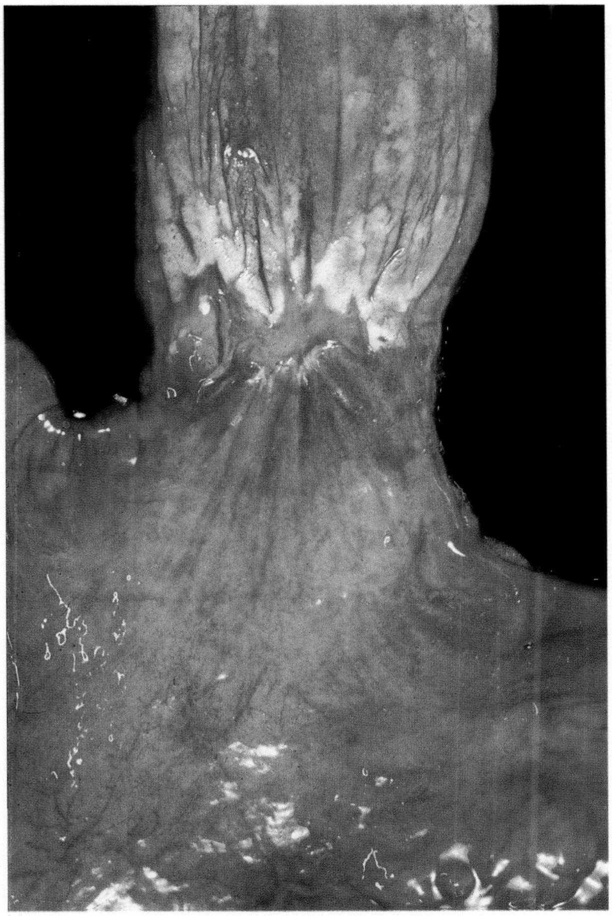

Fig. 24.11 Barrett's ulcer — surgically resected case showing a large peptic ulcer breaching the muscle coat.

Barrett's oesophagus (Columnar lined oesophagus — CLO, Columnar epithelial lined oesophagus — CELO, Gastric lined lower oesophagus, Barrett's metaplasia, Gastric metaplasia)

In this condition the lower oesophagus is lined by columnar epithelium of gastric or intestinal type (Fig. 24.12) and there is frequently a stricture at mid oesophageal or lower level. The columnar epithelium extends round the oesophagus in a circumferential manner. This was first thought to represent a congenital abnormality but evidence has accumulated that in the majority of adult cases it is acquired.

Acquired origin

Allison and Johnstone[29] were the first to suggest that gastro-oesophageal reflux could be responsible for this condition. They considered the possibility that the stratified squamous epithelium damaged by recurrent ulceration and regeneration had been replaced by overgrowth and upward extension of gastric columnnar epithelium.

It was then demonstrated in serial biopsies in a patient with reflux oesophagitis that glandular epithelium had appeared at levels previously occupied by squamous mucosa over a 32 month period.[30]

The experimental production of a columnar lining in the lower oesophagus[31] was followed by the demonstration that repeated mechanical injury to the stratified squamous epithelium of the rat forestomach could lead to healing by migration and overgrowth of columnar epithelial cells from adjacent gastric mucosa.[32]

Fig. 24.12 Barrett's oesophagus with columnar lined mucosa and squamocolumnar junction located at a high level. (Courtesy of Dr J Newman)

The development of Barrett's oesophagus by oral migration of the squamocolumnar junction with time,[33] and its development in patients who have had partial oesophagogastrectomy and anastomosis of the oesophagus to the fundus,[34] is well documented.

Although regression has been reported after antireflux surgery in four out of 10 patients[35] and also following Omeprazole[36] therapy the condition is frequently irreversible. Barrett's metaplasia has also been described complicating lye ingestion[37] with sparing of the distal oesophagus so that there was a band of ectopic gastric mucosa in the middle of the oesophagus. Barrett's oesophagus has recently been described following cytotoxic chemotherapy, viz. cyclophyosphamide,[38] methotrexate and 5 fluoro-uracil therapy.

Congenital origin

Although the majority of cases are acquired, rarely cases may be congenital or developmental in origin.

Barrett[39,40] interpreted the entity as a 'congenital short oesophagus' with a portion of gastric cardia and fundus being pulled up into the thorax. The developing oesophagus is initially lined by columnar epithelium and this is later replaced by squamous epithelium.[41] Starting in the mid oesophagus the change progresses in both oral and caudal directions. Barrett postulated that this transition may be halted, resulting in persistence of columnar epithelium within the oesophagus. However, columnar epithelium would be found in the upper oesophagus whenever it occurred in the lower oesophagus and this rarely ever occurs. Nevertheless, there are still those who attribute Barrett's to persistence of foetal type epithelium[42] and those who believe that both congenital and acquired factors are important, especially in children.[43]

Certainly the condition occurs in babies a few months old[44] and gastric heterotopia occurs occasionally in adults[45] and with an incidence as high as 7–8% at autopsy in children.[46] However, a relationship of oesophageal gastric heterotopia to Barrett's is doubtful.

Clinical presentation

Patients may have a history of reflux oesophagitis or dysphagia due to a stricture or ulcer and diagnosis is most easily achieved by oesophagoscopy and biopsy at specified levels measured from the incisor teeth.

Barrett's oesophagus secondary to severe gastro-oesophageal reflux has been reported in children[47] and as a complication of achalasia of the cardia in post-myotomy patients.[48]

It is interesting that Barrett's oesophagus is rare in black patients[49] in the USA. Genetic factors might be involved for there are also reports of Barrett's oesophagus in identical twins[50] and in three members of a family of five.[51]

An increased incidence of colorectal cancer has been recorded in patients with Barrett's oesophagus.[49]

The incidence of Barrett's oesophagus in patients with endoscopic oesophagitis is about 10% with a range of 8–20%.[52] Radigan et al[53] quote an incidence of almost 20% and its level will be determined to some extent by the manner in which the disorder is defined. The incidence of Barrett's oesophagus complicating peptic stricture is higher and quoted as 44% in one study.[54]

Distribution

Barrett's mucosa usually encircles the lower oesophagus (Fig. 24.13) and in the usual 'limited type'[55] may extent up to a distance of 30 cm from the incisor teeth, which is approximately one half its length. In a proportion of cases representing the 'extended type' columnar mucosa may involve virtually the whole oesophagus. Strictures can be located at any point but are not usually fibrous and the narrowing is due to muscular spasm. Ulceration is frequently present at the squamocolumnar junction but may be below it and there can be interdigitation of the two

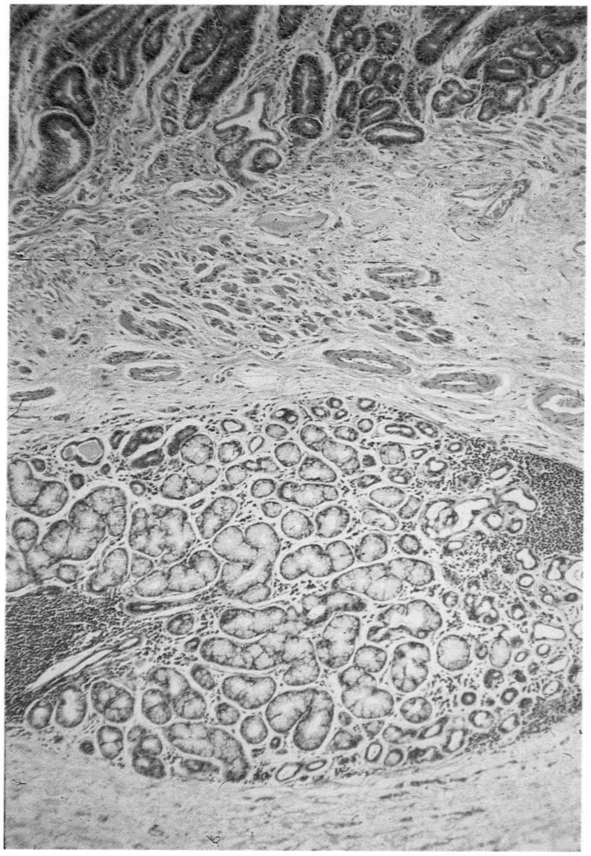

Fig. 24.13 Barrett's oesophagus with columnar lined mucosa and lobule of submucosal oesophageal glands (×94).

types of epithelium. Endoscopists also recognize an 'island' type of Barrett's oesophagus[52] in which there are a variable number of islands of gastric mucosa surrounded by stratified squamous epithelium and often associated with interdigitation of the two types of epithelium.

Dissecting microscopic examination of biopsies or excision specimens stained with trypan blue can be of value. Squamous mucosa is featureless, whereas columnar mucosa shows a mosaic pattern or convolutions while the presence of villi indicates an intestinalization.[56,57] Scanning electron microscopy achieves the same result.[58] Residual oesophageal submucous glands may be identified in the columnar lined segment (Fig. 24.13).[59]

Paull et al[60] described three varieties of columnar mucosa in this condition, a distal atrophic gastric fundal type (Fig. 24.14), a junctional type with cardiac mucous glands (Fig. 24.15) and proximally a specialized type with a villiform surface, mucous glands and intestinal type goblet cells (Figs 24.16 & 24.17). This is by and large correct, but in any one case mixtures of these types can occur in biopsies from approximately the same level.[61] Nevertheless, parietal cells, which can be found in about 50% of cases, tend to occur distally. Paneth cells, usually in association with intestinalized epithelium, are also relatively common and rarely ciliated cells which may be foetal in type are seen.

Argyrophil cells are represented in Barrett's mucosa and indeed may be prominent in some cases. Banner et al[62] describe the production of hormones indigenous to the gut, including gastrin, bombesin, substance P, but it is somatostatin and serotonin producing cells that predominate.

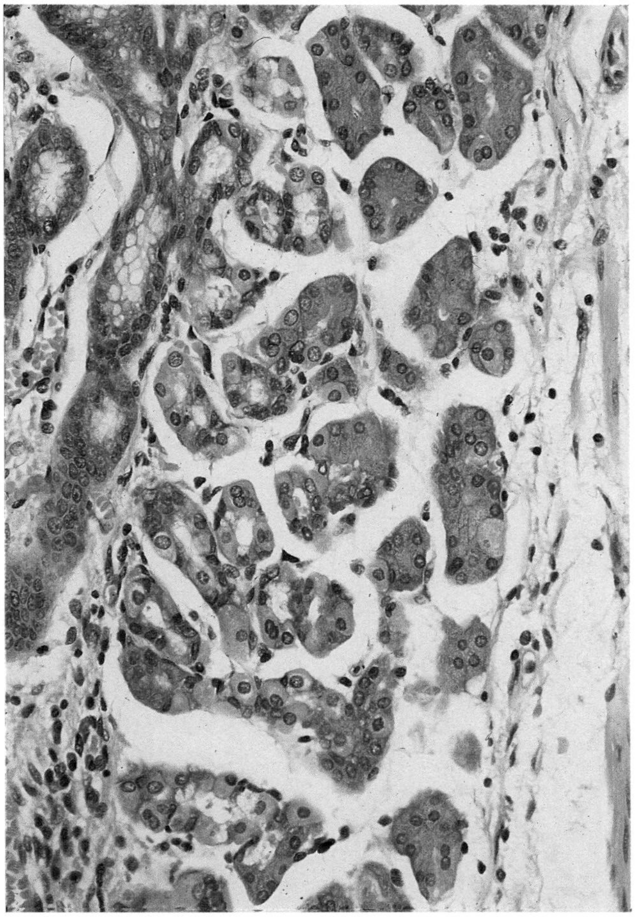

Fig. 24.14 Atrophic fundic mucosa with parietal cell glands (×787.5).

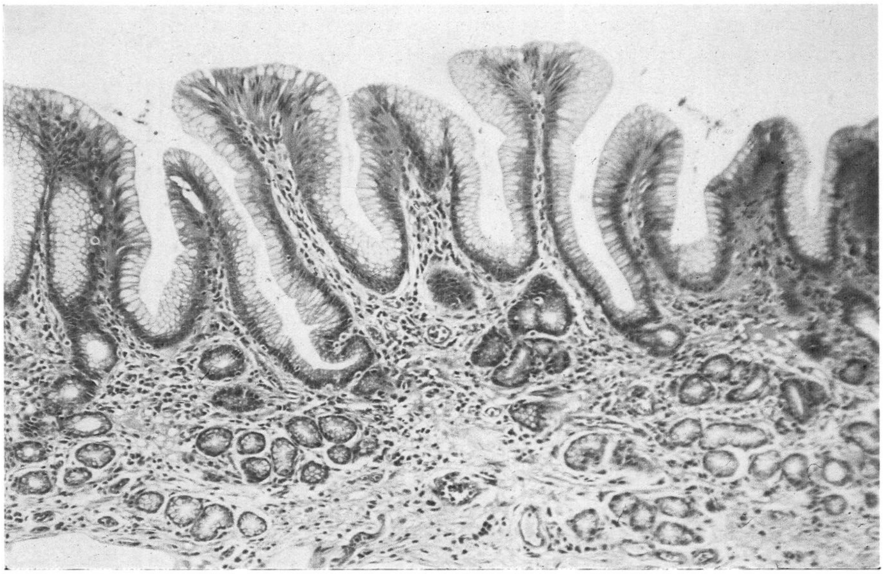

Fig. 24.15 Cardiac type mucosa in Barrett's oesophagus with mucin secreting glands (×305.5).

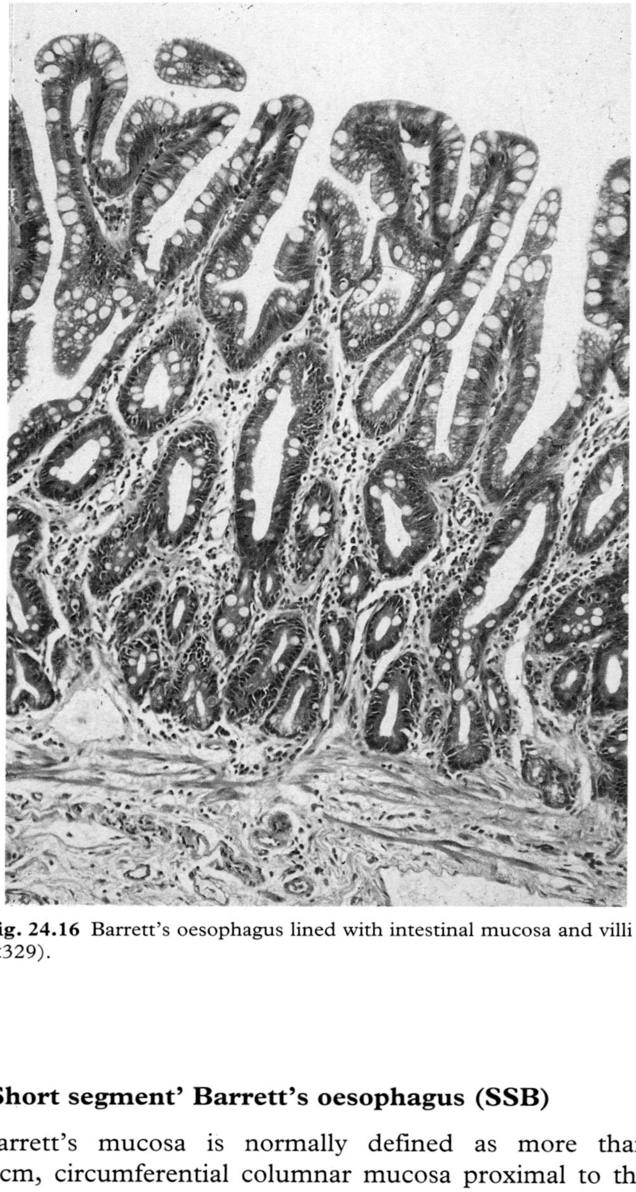

Fig. 24.16 Barrett's oesophagus lined with intestinal mucosa and villi (×329).

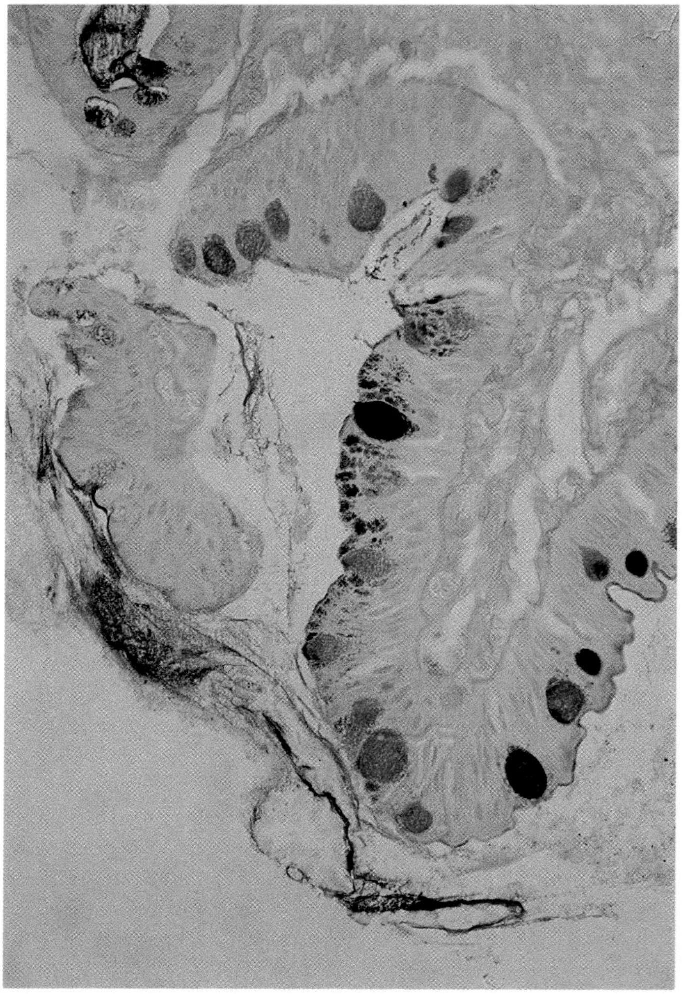

Fig. 24.17 Specialized epithelium with Type 2B (Type 3) intestinal metaplasia (×225).

'Short segment' Barrett's oesophagus (SSB)

Barrett's mucosa is normally defined as more than 3 cm, circumferential columnar mucosa proximal to the gastro-oesophageal junction. More recently a 'short segment' Barrett's oesophagus has been described as an undiagnosed condition by Williams et al[63] and others[64,65]. The columnar lined segment is shorter than 3 cm but it is frequently associated with intestinal metaplasia and specialized epithelium. The median length of the segment was 1.5 cm in a series of 32 patients.

REFERENCES

1. Pope CE. Pathophysiology and diagnosis of reflux esophagitis. Gastroenterology 1976; 70: 445–454.
2. Ismail-Beigi F, Horton PF, Pope CE. Histological consequences of gastroesophageal reflux in man. Gastroenterology 1970; 58: 163–174.
3. Livstone EM, Sheahan DG, Behar J. Studies of esophageal epithelial cell proliferation in patients with reflux esophagitis. Gastroenterology 1977; 73: 1315–1319.
4. Behar J, Sheahan DG. Histological abnormalities in reflux esophagitis. Arch Pathol 1975; 99: 387–391.
5. Ismail-Beigi F, Pope CE. Distribution of histologic changes of gastroesophageal reflux in the distal esophagus in man. Gastroenterology 1974; 66: 1109–1113
6. Weinstein WM, Bogoch ER, Bowes KL. The normal human esophageal mucosa: a histological reappraisal. Gastroenterology 1975; 68: 40–44.
7. Pope CE. Is section biopsy of the distal oesophagus useful in the diagnosis of oesophagitis. Gastroenterology 1975; 68: 202.
8. Ward AS, Wright DW, Leight-Collis J. The assessment of oesophagitis in hiatus hernia patients. Thorax 1970; 25: 519–572.
9. Codling BC. The modern histological grading of oesophagitis. Personal communication. Rotterdam, 1976.
10. Sladen GE, Riddell RH, Willoughby JMT. Oesophagoscopy, biopsy and acid perfusion test in diagnosis of 'reflux oesophagitis'. Br Med J 1975; i: 71–76.
11. Seefield U, Krejs GJ, Siebermann RE, Blum AL. Esophageal histology in gastroesophageal reflux. Morphometric findings in suction biopsies. Dig Dis 1977; 22: 956–964.

12. Adami B, Eckhardt VF, Paulini K. Sampling error and observer variation in the interpretation of esophageal biopsies. Digestion 1979; 19: 404–410.
13. Collins BJ, Elliot H, Sloan JM, McFarland RJ, Love AHG. Oesophageal histology in reflux oesophagitis. J Clin Pathol 1985; 38: 1265–1272.
14. Jarvis LR, Dent J, Whitehead R. Morphometric assessment of reflux oesophagitis in fibreoptic biopsy specimens. J Clin Pathol 1985; 38: 44–48.
15. Geboes K, Desmet V, Vantrappen G, Mebbis J. Vascular changes in the esophageal mucosa. An early histological sign of esophagitis. Gastrointest Endosc 1980; 26: 29–32.
16. Dodds WJ, Goldberg HJ, Montgomery CN, et al. Sequential gross microscopic and roentgenographic features of acute feline esophagitis. Invest Radiol 1970; 5: 209–219.
17. Winter HS, Madara JL, Stafford RJ, Grand RJ, Quinlan J, Goldman H. Intra-epithelial eosinophils: a new diagnostic criterion for reflux oesophagitis. Gastroenterol 1982; 83: 818–823.
18. Brown LF, Goldman H, Antonidi DA. Intraepithelial eosinophils in endoscopic biopsies of adults with reflux oesophagitis. Am J Surg Pathol 1984; 8: 899–905.
19. Tummala V, Sontag S, Vlahcevic R, Barwick K, McCullum RW. Are intraepithelial eosinophils helpful in the histological diagnosis of gastroesophageal reflux? (GER) Gastroenterology 1985; 88: 1619 (Abstract).
20. Whitehead R. Mucosal biopsy of the gastrointestinal tract. 3rd ed. Philadelphia: Saunders, 1985.
21. Geboes K, De Wolf-Peeters C, Rutgeerts P, Janssens J, Vantrappen G, Desmet V. Lymphocytes and Langerhans' cells in the human oesophageal epithelium. Virchows Arch (A) 1983; 401: 45–55.
22. Jankowski J, Coghill G, Murphy S, Hopwood D, Kerr M, Wormsley KG. Epidermal Growth Factor Receptors in the Oesophagus. Gut 1992; 33: 439–443.
23. Jankowski J, Sanders DSA, Coghill G, Wormsley KG, Hopwood D, Kerr M. The expression of Lewis blood group antigens in the oesophagus. J Pathol 1991; 163: 173A.
24. Hopwood D, Jankowski J. Flow cytometry of oesophageal mucosal biopsies. J Pathol 1992; 167: 321–326.
25. Jankowski J, Tregaskis B, Grant A, Correll C, Hopwood D, Kerr M, Wormsley KG. Nucleolar organiser regions in oesophageal diseases. Gullet 1992; 2: 85–90.
26. Davidson JS. High peptic stricture of the oesophagus. Thorax 1976; 31: 1–14.
27. Wilkins WE, Ridley MG, Pozniak AL. Benign stricture of the oesophagus: role of non-steroidal anti-inflammatory drugs. Gut 1984; 25: 478–480.
28. Sandry RJ. The pathology of chronic oesophagitis. Gut 1962; 3: 189.
29. Allison PR, Johnstone AS. The oesophagus lined with gastric mucous membrane. Thorax 1953; 8: 87.
30. Mossberg SM. The columnar lined oesophagus (Barrett's Syndrome) — an acquired condition. Gastroenterology 1966; 50: 671.
31. Bremner CG, Lynch VP, Ellis FH Jr. Barrett's esophagus: congenital or acquired? An experimental study of esophageal mucosal regeneration in the dog. Surgery 1970; 68: 209–221.
32. Wong J, Finckh ES. Heterotopia and ectopia of gastric epithelium produced by mucosal wounding in the rat. Gastroenterology 1971; 60: 279–287.
33. Naef AP, Ozzello L. Columnar-lined lower esophagus. An acquired lesion with malignant predisposition. J Thorac Cardiovasc Surg 1975; 70: 826–835.
34. Hamilton SR, Yardley JH. Regeneration of cardiac type mucosa and acquisition of Barrett mucosa after esophagogastrectomy. Gastroenterology 1977; 72: 669–675.
35. Brand DL, Ylvisaker JT, Gelfand M, Pope CE. Regression of columnar esophageal (Barrett's) epithelium after anti-reflux surgery. N Engl J Med 1980; 30: 844–848.
36. Gore S, Healey CJ, Sutton R, Shepherd NA, Wilkinson SP. Regression of Columnar lined Barrett's Oesophagus with continuous Omeprazole therapy. Supplement 1992; 33: 1 S32, T127.
37. Spechler SJ, Schimmel EM, Dalton JW, Doos W, Trier JS. Barrett's epithelium complicating Lye ingestion with sparing of the distal esophagus. Gastroenterology 1981; 81: 580.
38. Sartori S, et al. Barrett's oesophagus after chemotherapy with Cyclophosphamide, Methotrexate and 5-Fluoro-uracil (CMF): Iatrogenic Injury? Ann Intern Med 1991; 114: 210–211
39. Barrett NR. Chronic peptic ulcer of the oesophagus and 'oesophagitis'. Br J Surg 1950; 38: 175.
40. Barrett NR. The lower oesophagus lined by columnar epithelium. Surgery 1957; 41: 881–894.
41. Johns BAE. Developmental changes in the oesophageal epithelium in man. J Anat 1952; 86: 431–442.
42. Haque AK, Merkel M. Total columnar-lined oesophagus: a case for congenital origin? Arch Pathol Lab Med 1981; 105: 546–548.
43. Borrie J, Goldwater L. Columnar cell-lined esophagus: assessment of etiology and treatment. A 22 year experience. J Thorac Cardiovasc Surg 1976; 71: 825–834.
44. Heydenrych JJ, Keet AD. Giant lower oesophageal ulcer in a Bushman baby. A case report. S Afr Med J 1983; 63: 331–333.
45. Raine CH. Ectopic gastric mucosa in the upper esophagus as a cause of dysphagia. Otorhinolaryngology 1983; 92: 65–66.
46. Rector LE, Connerley ML. Aberrant mucosa in the oesophagus in infants and in children. Arch Pathol 1941; 31: 285–294.
47. Dahms BB, Rothstein FC. Barretts' esophagus in children: a consequence of chronic gastroesophageal reflux. Gastroenterology 1984; 86: 318–323.
48. Feczko PJ, Ma CK, Halpert RD, Batra SR. Barrett's metaplasia and dysplasia in postmyotomy achalasia patients. Am J Gastroenterol 1983; 781: 265–268.
49. Sontag SJ, Schnell TG, Chejfec G et al. Barretts oesophagus and colonic tumours. Lancet 1985; 1: 946–948.
50. Gelfand MD. Barrett's oesophagus in sexagenarian identical twins. J Clin Gastroenterol 1983; 5: 251–253.
51. Everhart CW Jr, Holtzapple PG, Humphries TJ. Occurrence of Barrett's oesophagus in three members of the same family. First report of a familial incidence. Gastroenterology 1978; 74: 1032 (Abstract).
52. Phillips RW, Wong RKH. Mucosal Diseases of the Oesophagus. Gastroenterology Clinics of North America, Mucosal Diseases of the Oesophagus (1991) Barrett's Oesophagus 20, 4: 791–816.
53. Radigan LK, Glover JL, Shipley FE, Shoemaker RE. Barrett's esophagus. Arch Surg 1977; 112: 486–491.
54. Spechler SJ, Sperber H, Doos WG, Schimmel EM. The prevalence of Barrett's oesophagus in patients with chronic peptic oesophageal stricture. Dig Dis Sci 1983; 28: 769–774.
55. Ransom JM, Patel GK, Clift SA, Womble NE, Read RC. Extended and limited types of Barrett's esophagus in the adult. Ann Thorac Surg 1982; 33: 19–27.
56. Thomson JJ, Zinsser KR, Enterline HT. Barrett's metaplasia and adenocarcinoma of the oesophagus and gastroesophageal junction. Hum Pathol 1983; 14: 42–60.
57. Ozzello L, Savary M, Roethlisberger B. Columnar mucosa of the distal esophagus in patients with gastro-esophageal reflux. Pathol Ann 1977; 12: 41–86.
58. Mangla JC, Lee CS. Scanning electron microscopy of Barrett's oesophageal mucosa. Gastrointest Endosc 1979; 25: 92–94.
59. Haggitt RC, Tryzelaar J, Ellis FH Jr, Colcher H. Adenocarcinoma complicating columnar epithelium-lined (Barrett's) oesophagus. Am J Clin Pathol 1978; 70: 1–5.
60. Paull A, Trier JS, Dalton MD, Camp RC, Loeb P, Goyal RK. The histological spectrum of Barrett's esophagus. N Engl J Med 1976; 295: 476–480.
61. Enterline H, Thompson JJ. Pathology of the Esophagus. New York: Springer-Verlag, 1984.
62. Banner BF, Memoli VA, Warren WH, Gould VE. Carcinoma with multidirectional differentiation arising in Barrett's esophagus. Ultrastruct Pathol 1983; 4: 205–217.
63. Williams AJK, Langman J, Rowland R, Dent J. Short segment Barrett's Oesophagus — an undiagnosed condition. Gut 1992; F245, S62 Suppl. Vol. 33, No. 1.
64. Hamilton SR, Smith RR, Cameron JL. Prevalence and characteristics of Barrett's oesophagus in patients with adenocarcinoma of the oesophagus or oesophagogastric junction. Hum Pathol 1988; 19: 942–948.
65. Schnell T, Sontag S, Miller T, et al. Are there identifiable risk factors for the presence of Barrett's oesophagus in patients with gastro-oesophageal reflux (abstract). Gastroenterology 1991; 100: A156.

PART II

Infective, physical and chemical oesophagitis

R. Whitehead D. W. Day

Although inflammation of the oesophagus is most often due to reflux of gastric contents, it can be due to infection, follow the ingestion of noxious material, or result from irradiation injury. Rarely, the oesophagus may be affected in Crohn's disease or in eosinophilic gastroenteritis, and several skin disorders may be accompanied by oesophageal involvement.

INFECTIVE OESOPHAGITIS

In the immune competent individual the oesophagus is normally very resistant to infection and although an oesophagitis can occur in the course of such infectious diseases as measles, scarlet fever, diphtheria and typhoid, primary infective disease is rare. The two exceptions to this are oesophagitis due to Candida species and that resulting from *Herpes simplex* virus infection.

Candidal (monilial) oesophagitis

Candidiasis is by far the most common oesophageal infection, which is not surprising because *Candida albicans*, the organism usually implicated, is a commensal of the mouth, oropharynx and lower gastrointestinal tract in man.[1,2] Although infection can occur in otherwise normal individuals,[3,4] it more often affects those with predisposing conditions. Concomitant oropharyngeal candidiasis may be present but is by no means invariable.[5,6] Early reports[7,8] emphasized the association with underlying malignant neoplastic disease, particularly myeloproliferative disorders, including leukaemias, myelomas and malignant lymphomas of Hodgkin's and non-Hodgkin's type. The immune system already altered by these disorders is often further compromised by the effects of chemotherapy and irradiation. Steroid therapy and antibiotics also increase the risk of infection, particularly after abdominal surgery[9] and in diabetics.[10] In the acquired immunodeficiency syndrome (AIDS), oesophageal candidiasis is common in the early stages of the disease or may arise in the course of treatment for other opportunistic infections.[11] It is not infrequently asymptomatic and patients with particularly low CD4/CD8 ratios appear most at risk.[12]

The condition of chronic mucocutaneous candidiasis[13] is characterized by recurrent and persistent infections of the skin, nails and mucous membranes, including the oesophagus. It incorporates several syndromes associated with deficiencies in cell-mediated immunity, some being genetically determined. The most common is subnormal production of lymphokines by T cells in response to Candida antigens. In some cases, within a few years adrenal, parathyroid and thyroid deficiency occurs, either alone or in combination.

Candida organisms are quite commonly seen in association with carcinoma or peptic ulcer, suggesting a secondary colonization following mucosal damage. In a prospective gastro-oesophageal endoscopic biopsy study there was a 4% prevalence of candidiasis, and in 17 of the 19 positive cases the organism was associated with other local pathology.[14]

Macroscopic appearances

The characteristic, but not specific, appearance of oesophageal candidiasis is of fairly discrete adherent white or creamy plaques which overlie a friable, erythematous mucosa in the middle and lower third (Fig. 24.18). Confluence of the plaques may lead to extensive pseudomembrane formation accompanied by erosion or superficial

Fig. 24.18 Candida oesophagitis. Discrete plaques are seen throughout the specimen which are becoming confluent in places. Post-mortem sample of oesophagus from patient with acute leukaemia.

ulceration. Occasionally, mushroom-like or polypoidal exophytic lesions may occur.[15,16]

Microscopic features

Organisms are seen in tissue sections as small (2–4 μm), oval or budding yeast-like cells along with a pseudomycelium of hyphal segments of varying thickness and length. Often these are incorporated within a pseudomembrane composed of fibrin, necrotic cells and a variable number of polymorphs. When inflammatory cells are numerous the fungal elements may be inconspicuous on H&E staining (Fig. 24.19) but are readily demonstrated if a PAS, Grocott or Gram stain is examined (Fig. 24.20). The acute inflammatory response is variable and in fatal disseminated candidiasis it correlates closely with the preterminal peripheral blood granulocyte count.[9] In many cases invasion of the oesophageal wall is limited and often affects the superficial epithelium only, but deeper extension with ulceration can occur and may give rise to complications (see below).

Endoscopic brush cytology smears are said to result in a higher detection rate than biopsy and a better correlation with serum agglutinin titres.[17] However the diagnostic value of serological tests for candidiasis is controversial.[18,19] In the past, final verification of suspected fungal infection in biopsy tissues required culture of the organism, but using immunoperoxidase techniques on smears, or sections this can now be achieved histologically.[20,21] Although *Candida albicans* is the species usually responsible for oesophageal disease, other organisms isolated have been *C. krusei*, *C. tropicalis*, *C. stellatoidea* and *Torulopsis glabrata*.

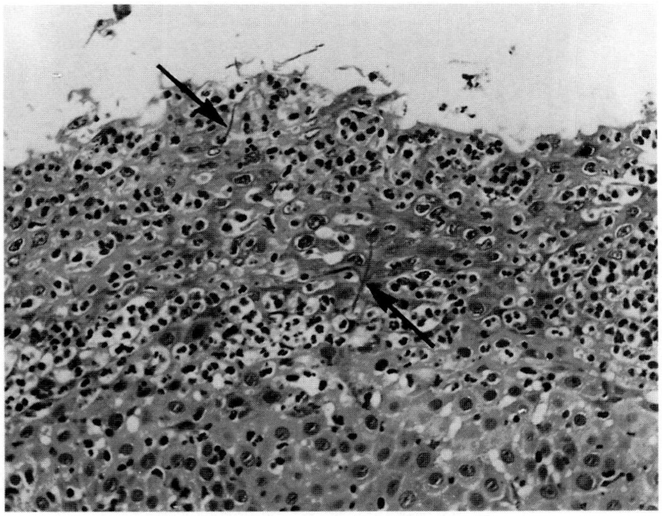

Fig. 24.19 Pseudomembrane of polymorphs, fibrin and degenerate cells overlying oesophageal epithelium. Linear fungal hyphae are just discernible in some areas (arrowed). (H&E, ×281)

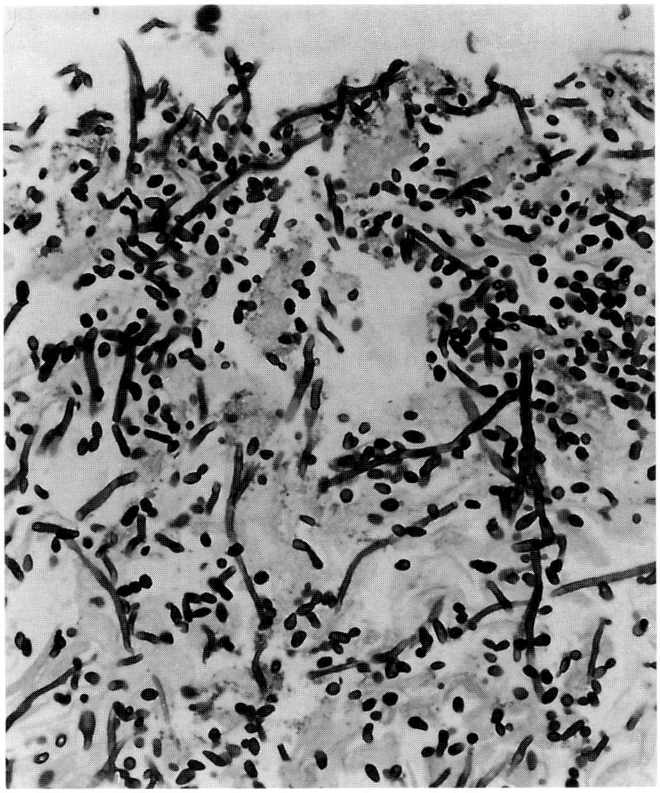

Fig. 24.20 Hyphae and spores of Candida. (Grocott-Gomori methenamine silver method, ×570)

Complications

Gross gastrointestinal bleeding is uncommon but its origin in oesophageal fungal lesions has been confirmed at autopsy.[15] Occasionally perforation occurs,[22] fistula formation,[23] and subacute or chronic Candida infections may result in benign strictures which occur most frequently in the upper oesophagus and may complicate intramural oesophageal pseudodiverticulosis,[24] an inflammatory disorder of unknown cause characterized by dilatation of the excretory ducts of submucosal oesophageal glands.[25] Mucosal bridges may also form and give rise to a fenestrated or multichannel oesophagus.[26]

Disseminated candidiasis originating in the gastrointestinal tract is a major cause of morbidity and mortality in cancer patients,[27] and is increasingly prevalent in patients with acute leukaemia, where the predisposing factors are antecedent myelosuppression, chemotherapy and antibiotic therapy.[9,28] Prolonged granulocytopenia during the induction of remission by the chemotherapy appears to be particularly important. *Candida albicans*, *C. stellatoidea* and *C. tropicalis* are the most frequently identified species.[9] *Candida tropicalis* appears to be particularly virulent and compared to *C. albicans* extends into the submucosa and penetrates submucosal blood vessels with greater frequency.[29] A band of necrosis at the advancing mycelial border as it invades the gut wall is a characteristic feature, and this is not seen with *C. albicans* infections.

Herpes simplex oesophagitis

Until comparatively recently herpetic oesophagitis was rarely suspected or diagnosed during life, although post-mortem studies have shown that it is quite frequent as a cause of oesophageal ulceration.[30] Thus in one study[31] approximately one quarter of such cases were considered to be due to *Herpes simplex*. The oesophagus is, in fact, the most common site of visceral infection.[32,33] The usual clinical setting for this infection is in immunosuppressed patients such as those with malignant disease, particularly malignant lymphoma and leukaemias.[34] It also occurs following transplantation,[35–37] or in the acquired immune deficiency syndrome (AIDS),[38,39] and all these situations are similar to those predisposing to Candida infection. Indeed, the two infections may co-exist.[40–43] Herpetic oesophagitis also occurs in otherwise healthy individuals as an acute self-limiting disease,[44,45] apparently with increasing frequency[46] and should be suspected in the presence of odynophagia, fever and chest pain[47] even in children.[48]

Occasional cases have been complicated by severe bleeding,[45,49] and spontaneous perforation followed by mediastinal suppuration is recorded.[50] Concomitant herpes labialis is present in a minority of cases and may be the source of oesophageal infection by contiguous spread.[51] An alternative pathogenesis is the reactivation of latent virus in sensory ganglion cells with axonal spread to the oesophagus. Indeed, virus has been detected in a latent form in the jugular portion of the vagus ganglion.[52]

Macroscopic features

The middle and distal thirds are most commonly involved and each appear endoscopically as discrete vesicles with an erythematous base.[45,53] These break down to form erosions covered by a fibrinopurulent exudate with slightly raised margins. With severe disease these areas may become confluent. At post-mortem, ulceration is often more severe and may appear to have 'punched out' margins. (Fig. 24.21).

Microscopic features

The typical changes of herpetic infection occur in the squamous epithelium at the margin of shallow ulcers or erosions (Fig. 24.22). The cells may contain intranuclear eosinophilic inclusions surrounded by a clear zone with the nuclear chromatin condensed to a peripheral ring (Cowdry's type A cells).[54] They are most frequent early in the course of infection. More commonly observed are cells showing ballooning degeneration with enlarged nuclei which have a faintly basophilic, opaque, ground glass appearance. Several of these may fuse to produce multinucleate forms with a characteristic moulding together of the nuclei. When inclusions and multinucleate cells are absent, a clue to the diagnosis is the presence of aggregates of mononuclear macrophages with convoluted nuclei in the inflammatory exudate.[55] Biopsies from the ulcer base will show only necrotic material and granulation tissue. However, it is not unusual for herpetic ulcers to become secondarily infected particularly by Candida organisms and the finding of fungal hyphae in oesophageal biopsies should alert the pathologist to examine any epithelial cells present for viral inclusions. Cytomegalovirus infection may co-exist with herpetic ulceration[30,35] but the characteristic inclusions occur in capillary endothelial cells and in granulation tissue fibroblasts and not in the epithelium. Aspergillus and Torula organisms have also been found as a superinfection of herpetic ulcers.

Electron microscopy[56,57] may reveal intranuclear virus particles of hexagonal shape consisting of a central electron-dense core and a capsid of similar electron density measuring approximately 100 nm in diameter (Fig. 24.23). Intranuclear particles, however, often appear empty. Envelopment of virions by the nuclear membrane may be present, with virus particles scattered throughout the cytoplasm of infected cells or lying in the intercellular

Fig. 24.21 Herpetic oesophagitis. Discrete shallow ulcers of varying size, some with 'punched-out' appearance, are present.

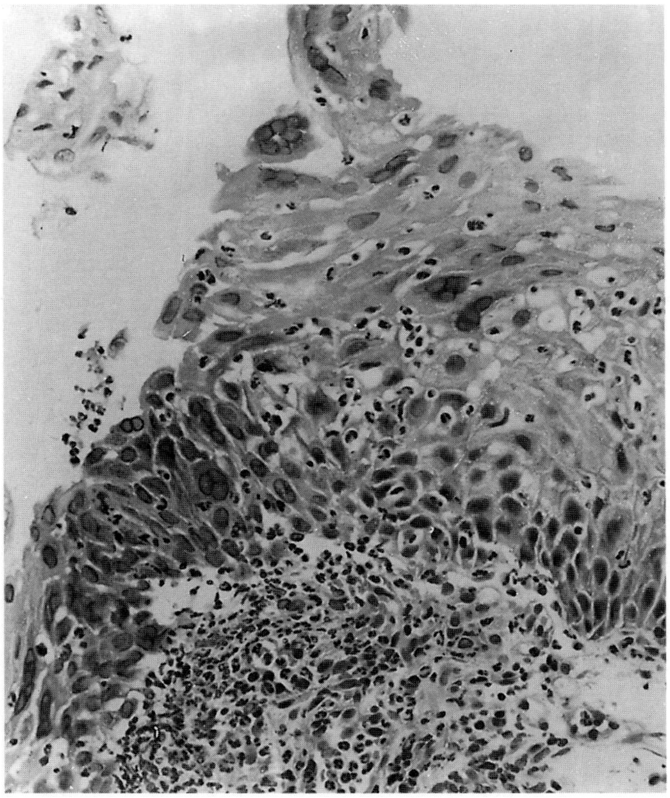

Fig. 24.22 Intranuclear viral inclusions of *Herpes simplex* are present in epithelial cells at left. Some cells are multinucleated. (H&E, ×356)

spaces. Definitive diagnosis is said to depend on culture of oesophageal brushings or biopsy tissue, but there is the theoretical possibility of contamination by oral secretions, since herpes virus is commonly present in the saliva of normal adults.[58,59] Confirmation may also be obtained using immunohistochemical methods.[56,57]

Other infections

Bacterial

Tuberculosis of the oesophagus is rare and nearly always secondary to pulmonary disease as a result of swallowed sputum, direct spread from tuberculous lymph nodes,[60] infected lung, or occasionally from Pott's disease of the spine.[61] Primary infection is described in adults with no signs of active disease elsewhere.[62,63] It may manifest itself macroscopically as a stenosing tumour, or as single or multiple ulcers. The mid-portion of the oesophagus in the region of the tracheal bifurcation is most commonly involved. Contrary to what might be expected, when the diagnosis is established pre-mortem, with appropriate therapy oesophageal tuberculosis has a favourable outcome.[64]

Tertiary syphilis of the oesophagus is also rare, taking the form of either a submucosal gumma or a diffuse inflammatory process resulting in scarring and stenosis.[65]

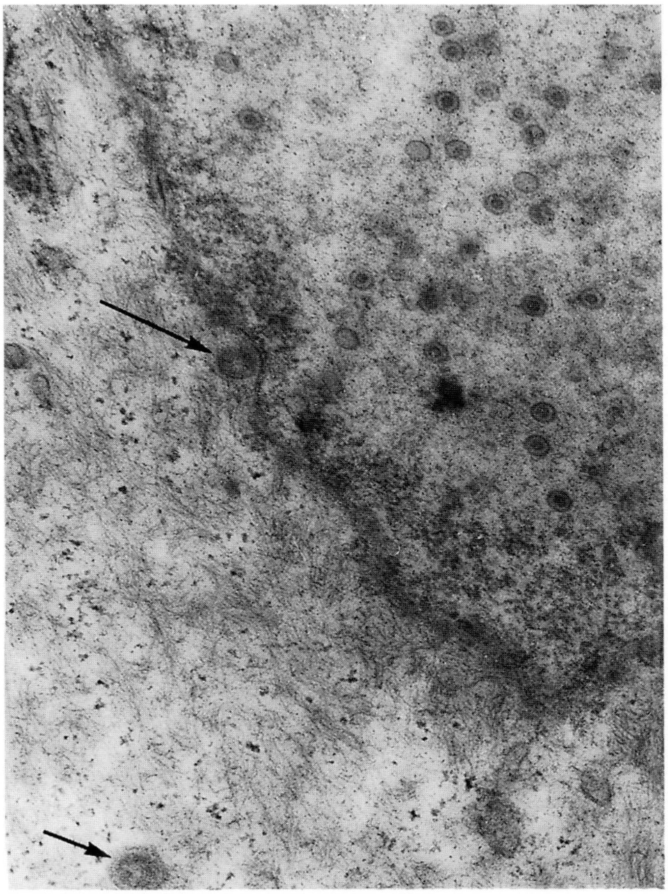

Fig. 24.23 Viral capsids, most of which have an electron-dense core, are present within the nucleus. Occasional enveloped particles are seen in the cytoplasm (arrowed). (EM, ×42 000)

Oesophagitis caused by *Lactobacillus acidophilus*, endoscopically and radiologically indistinguishable from moniliasis,[66] has been described and it has been stressed that in odynophagia bacterial oesophagitis should always be given consideration in the absence of other demonstrable agents even in the immunocompromized.[67]

Fungal

Fungi, other than candida which may infect the oesophagus include actinomycosis,[68,69] mucormycosis,[70] blastomycosis and histoplasmosis.[71–73]

Viral

Cytomegalovirus (CMV). Erosive oesophagitis due to CMV occurs predominantly, but not always,[74] in the context of immuno-suppression. This may be the result of primary malignancy of the immune system, the result of therapeutic immunosuppression,[36,75] or with increasing frequency the result of the acquired immune deficiency syndrome (AIDS),[76,77] when it may co-exist with other opportunistic infections or AIDS associated malignancy such as Kaposi's sarcoma and lymphoma.[78] Characteristic nuclear and cytoplasmic inclusions are present in fibroblasts and capillary endothelial cells within the granulation tissue of the ulcer base. Atypical inclusions also occur not infrequently and may be the only ones present. They can only be characterized with certainty by the use of in situ DNA hybridization.[79]

Other enveloped virus-like particles electron microscopically resembling human T lymphotropic retroviruses and distinct from *Herpes simplex* virus and CMV have also been described in the oesophageal ulcers of homosexual men seronegative for the human immunodeficiency virus who subsequently seroconverted.[80]

Human papillomavirus (HPV). There is increasing evidence that the HPV may be implicated in other forms of oesophageal disease. They have been demonstrated not only in oesophageal papilloma[81] but in oesophageal carcinoma[82,83] and in the entity known as clear cell acanthosis.[84]

Protozoal

Although cryptosporidiosis occurs most commonly in the small intestine in patients with AIDS it is also described in the oesophagus.[85]

The commonest protozoal infection of the oesophagus is due to *Trypanosoma cruzi* which is transmitted by triatomid (reduviid) bugs and results in Chagas' disease. It results in enormous dilatation of the viscera, particularly the oesophagus and colon, and may be associated with cardiopathy.[86] It affects individuals in parts of Brazil, Chile,[87] and Argentina. Pseudocysts containing amastigotes (leishmanial forms of the parasite) develop in the circular and longitudinal muscle coats of the bowel in the acute phase. Later they rupture and release a neurotoxin which gives rise to an inflammatory reaction and destruction of ganglion cells of the myenteric plexus. When reduced by 50% or more a functional disturbance can result, which proceeds inexorably to gross dilatation up to 8 or 10 cm as more ganglion cells are lost.[88] It is the smooth muscle of the lower two thirds of the oesophagus which is primarily affected. By the time the disease has become chronic, inflammatory changes are minimal, and organisms are not demonstrable. There also appears to be an increased risk of carcinoma in long-standing chagasic mega-oesophagus.[86]

CHEMICAL AND DRUG-INDUCED OESOPHAGITIS

Ingestion of corrosive chemicals is either accidental, occurring mainly in young children and generally involving small quantities, or purposeful in a suicide attempt, usually in adults, when large quantities are swallowed. Damage depends on the substance swallowed and its concentration, the amount and the contact time.

In general, the effects of ingestion of strong alkalis are seen in the oesophagus, and of acids in the stomach. Alkalis dissolve tissue and therefore penetrate more deeply, whereas acids give rise to a coagulative necrosis which has the effect of limiting penetration. Acute, subacute and chronic phases are distinguished. The acute phase of necrosis lasts 4 or 5 days, and is associated with oedema and acute inflammation with thrombosis of vessels. There may be secondary bacterial infection. The subacute phase follows sloughing of superficial necrotic tissue and ulceration with subsequent repair by granulation maturing to collagenous connective tissue. It is during the early part of this phase in the first 10–12 days after injury, that perforation is most likely.[89] The chronic phase, extending over the next 1–3 months, is associated with re-epithelialisation and fibrosis and may or may not lead to stricture formation. Apart from perforation, motility disturbances and strictures may occur. Strictures which usually follow lye ingestion are sometimes complicated by squamous carcinoma.[90,91]

A number of ingested drugs are capable of giving rise to oesophageal inflammation and ulceration when held up in the lumen.[92] The site of damage is at the anatomical site of narrowing and the mid point behind the left atrium predominates. The list of drugs that have been implicated is long and includes the anticholinergic emopromium, bromide, antibiotics such as doxycycline and tetracycline, quinidine, iron salts, non-steroidal anti-inflammatory drugs (NSAID) and slow release potassium preparations.[93–95] Drug induced injury is described in children as well as adults and similar substances appear to be involved.[96,97]

The injury and histological features are often nonspecific and the diagnosis is a clinical one based on history and endoscopic findings. However, it falls into two main groups.[98] The first is transient and self-limiting, as examplified by tetracycline and emepromium induced injury, whereas the second tends to be persistent and leads to stricture. In this subgroup there are those due to NSAID in which the injury appears to have a reflux component and those due to potassium chloride and quinidine sulphate where persistent injury is due to delayed transit.[98]

Radiation induced oesophagitis

This subject is discussed in greater detail in Chapter 44. Carcinoma of the oesophagus following therapeutic radiation has been described following a latent period ranging from 3 to 45 years.[99]

Crohn's disease

The oesophagus may be involved in patients with Crohn's disease and this is dealt with in greater detail later in this chapter. Usually the lower part of the oesophagus is affected and although on occasions endoscopic appearances are described as characteristic with aphthoid ulcers in a normal mucosa[100] or a cobblestone pattern, the changes are more often non-specific. This often applies as well to the biopsy findings although non-caseating granulomas have occasionally been seen[101] and are described in the paediatric age group[102] in whom it has been stressed that if changes are not to be missed, biopsies should be taken not only from ulcers, but from mucosa which appears normal.

Eosinophilic oesophagitis

Rarely the oesophagus may be infiltrated by large numbers of eosinophils in the absence of any parasitic infection vasculitis or malignancy. There is an associated peripheral eosinophilia and the condition may present with dysphagia and odynophagia and oesophageal motility disturbances.[103,104] Dysphagia may be intermittent and accompanied by attacks of asthma and hay fever. The small bowel may also be involved. The infiltrate may be deep and involve the entire thickness of the oesophageal wall and sometimes it is maximal in the muscularis, which may be hypertrophied.[105]

Oesophagitis in graft-versus-host disease

Oesophageal abnormalities are one of the consequences of chronic graft-versus-host disease and this is discussed in Chapter 12.

Oesophagitis and skin diseases

Many types of skin disease may involve the oesophagus including pemphigus vulgaris,[106] bullous pemphigoid,[107,108] benign mucosal pemphigoid, epidermolysis bullosa,[109] Stevens-Johnson syndrome,[110] lichen planus, Darier's disease, tylosis palmaris et plantaris and acanthosis nigricans. The subject has been well reviewed.[111] In Behcet's syndrome involvement of the right side of the colon[112,113] is usually described but oesophageal disease can also result.[114,115] A range of appearances has been described in individual cases including erosions, single or multiple ulcers which can lead to perforations, a widespread oesophagitis and severe stenosis. In systemic sclerosis, absent peristalsis and loss of lower oesophageal sphincter tone predispose to reflux and oesophagitis,[116,117] and co-existent candidiasis is common.[118]

REFERENCES

1. Gorbach S, Nahas L, Lerner P, Weinstein L. Studies of intestinal microflora. 1. Effects of diet, age, and periodic sampling on numbers of fecal micro-organisms in man. Gastroenterology 1967; 53: 845–855.
2. Cohen R, Roth F, Delgado E, Ahern DG, Kalser MH. Fungal flora of the normal human small and large intestine. N Engl J Med 1969; 280: 638–641.
3. Obrecht WF, Richter JE, Olympio GA, Gelfand DW. Tracheoesophageal fistula: a serious complication of infectious esophagitis. Gastroenterol 1984; 87: 1174–1179.
4. Orringer MB, Sloan H. Monilial esophagitis: an increasingly frequent cause of esophageal stenosis: Annals Thorac Surg 1978; 26: 364–374.
5. Holt JM. Candida infection of the oesophagus. Gut 1968; 9: 227–231.
6. Sheft DJ, Shrago G. Esophageal moniliasis.The spectrum of the disease. JAMA 1970; 213: 1859–1862.
7. Gruhn JG, Sanson J. Mycotic infections in leukemic patients at autopsy. Cancer 1963; 16: 61–73.
8. Jensen KB, Stenderup A, Thomsen JB, Bichel J. Oesophageal moniliasis in malignant neoplastic disease. Acta Med Scand 1964; 175: 455–459.
9. Myerowitz RL, Pazin GJ, Allen CM. Disseminated candidiasis. Changes in incidence, underlying diseases, and pathology. Am J Clin Pathol 1977; 68: 29–38.
10. Dutta SK, Al-Ibrahim MS. Immunological studies in acute pseudo-membranous esophageal candidiasis. Gastroenterology 1978; 75: 292–296.
11. Weinstein WM. The gastrointestinal tract as a target organ, pp. 210–212. In: Gottlieb MS, moderator. The acquired immunodeficiency syndrome. Ann Intern Med 1983; 99: 208–220.
12. Lopez-Dupla M, Mora-Sanz P, Pintado-Garcia V, et al. Clinical, endoscopic, immunologic, and therapeutic aspects of oropharyngeal and esophageal candidiasis in HIV-infected patients: a survey of 114 cases. Am J Gastroenterol 1992; 87: 1771–1776.
13. Kirkpatrick CH. Host factors in defense against fungal infections. Am J Med 1984; 77(Suppl. 4D): 1–12.
14. Scott BB, Jenkins D. Gastro-oesophageal candidiasis. Gut 1982; 23: 137–139.
15. Eras P, Goldstein MJ, Sherlock P. Candida infection of the gastro-intestinal tract. Medicine 1972; 51: 367–379.
16. Ho C-S, Cullen JB, Gray RR. An unusual manifestation of esophageal moniliasis. Radiology 1977; 123: 287–288.
17. Kodsi BE, Wickremesinghe PC, Kozinn PJ, Iswara K, Goldberg PK. Candida esophagitis. A prospective study of 27 cases. Gastroenterology 1976; 71: 715–719.
18. Mathieson R, Dutta SK. Candida esophagitis. Dig Dis Sci 1983; 28: 365–370.
19. Trier JS, Bjorkman DJ. Esophageal, gastric, and intestinal candidiasis. Am J Med 1984; 77 (Suppl. 4D): 39–43.
20. Saeed EN, Hay RJ. Immunoperoxidase staining in the recognition of Aspergillus infections. Histopathology 1981; 5: 437–444.
21. Moskowitz LB, Ganjei P, Ziegels-Weissman J, Cleary TJ, Penneys NS, Nadji M. Immunohistologic identification of fungi in systemic and cutaneous mycoses. Arch Pathol Lab Med 1986; 110: 433–436.
22. Gonzalez-Crussi IF, Iung OS. Esophageal moniliasis as a cause of death. Am J Surg 1965; 109: 634–638.
23. Weiss J, Epstsin BS. Esophageal moniliasis. AJR 1962; 88: 718–720.
24. Orringer MB, Sloan H. Monilial esophagitis: an increasingly frequent cause of esophageal stenosis? Ann Thor Surg 1978; 26: 364–374.
25. Umlas J, Sakhuja R. The pathology of esophageal intramural pseudodiverticulosis. Am J Clin Pathol 1976; 65: 314–320.
26. Simson JNL, Kinder RB, Isaacs PET, Jourdan MH. Mucosal bridges of the oesophagus in Candida oesophagitis. Br J Surg 1985; 72: 209–210.
27. Bodey GP. Candidiasis in cancer patients. Am J Med 1984; 77 (Suppl. 4D): 13–19.
28. Maksymiuk AW, Thongprasert S, Hopfer R, Luna M, Fainstein V, Bodey GP. Systemic candidiasis in cancer patients. Am J Med 1984; 77(Suppl. 4D): 20–27.
29. Walsh TJ, Merz WG. Pathologic features in the human

alimentary tract associated with invasiveness of Candida tropicalis. Am J Clin Pathol 1986; 85: 498–502.
30. Moses HL, Cheatham WJ. The frequency and significance of human herpetic esophagitis: an autopsy study. Lab Invest 1963; 12: 663–669.
31. Nash G, Ross JS. Herpetic esophagitis: a common cause of esophageal ulceration. Hum Pathol 1974; 5: 339–345.
32. Rosen P, Hajdu SI. Visceral herpesvirus infections in patients with cancer. Am J Clin Pathol 1971; 56: 459–465.
33. Buss DH, Scharyj M. Herpes virus infection of the esophagus and other visceral organs in adults: incidence and clinical significance. Am J Med 1979; 66: 457–462.
34. McBane RD, Gross JB Jr. Herpes esophagitis: clinical syndrome, endoscopic appearance, and diagnosis in 23 patients. Gastrointest Endosc 1991; 37: 600–603.
35. Montgomerie JZ, Becroft DMO, Croxson MC, Doak PB, North JDK. Herpes simplex virus infection after renal transplantation. Lancet 1969; 1: 867–871.
36. McDonald GB, Sharma P, Hackman RC, Meyers JD, Thomas ED. Esophageal infections in immunosuppressed patients after marrow transplantation. Gastroenterology 1985; 88: 1111–1117.
37. Mosimann F, Fontolliet C, Wauters JP. Herpetic esophagitis following renal transplantation. Schweiz Rundsch Med Prax 1990; 79: 391–393.
38. Dworkin B, Wormser GP, Rosenthal WS et al. Gastrointestinal manifestations of the acquired immunodeficiency syndrome: a review of 22 cases. Am J Gastroenterol 1985; 80: 774–778.
39. Parente F, Cernuschi M, Rizzardini G, Lazzarin A, Valsecchi L, Bianchi-Porro G. Opportunistic infections of the esophagus not responding to oral systemic antifungals in patients with AIDS: their frequency and treatment. Am J Gastroenterol 1991; 86: 1729–1734.
40. Mirra SS, Bryan JA, Butz WC, Miles ML. Concomitant herpes-monilial esophagitis: case report with ultrastructural study. Hum Pathol 1982; 13: 760–763.
41. Yacono JV. Type I herpes simplex esophagitis with candidal esophagitis in an immunocompetent host. NY State J Med 1985; 85: 656–658.
42. Bonacini M, Young T, Laine L. The causes of esophageal symptoms in human immunodeficiency virus infection. A prospective study of 110 patients. Arch Intern Med 1991; 151: 1567–1572.
43. Varsky CG, Yahni VD, Freire MC, et al. Esophageal pathology in patients with the AIDS virus. Etiology and diagnosis. Acta Gastroenterol Latinoam 1991; 21: 67–83.
44. Depew WT, Prentice RSA, Beck IT, Blakeman JM, Da Costa LR. Herpes simplex ulcerative esophagitis in a healthy subject. Am J Gastroenterol 1977; 68: 381–385.
45. Fishbein PG, Tuthill R, Kressel H, Freidman H, Snape WJ jr. Herpes simplex esophagitis: a cause of upper-gastrointestinal bleeding. Dig Dis Sci 1979; 24: 540–544.
46. Galbraith JC, Shafran SD. Herpes simplex esophagitis in the immunocompetent patient: report of four cases and review. Clin Infect Dis 1992; 14: 894–901.
47. Shortsleeve MJ, Levine MS. Herpes esophagitis in otherwise healthy patients: clinical and radiographic findings. Radiology 1992; 182: 859–861.
48. Chusid MJ, Oechler HW, Werlin SL. Herpetic esophagitis is an immunocompetent boy. Wis Med J 1992; 91: 71–72.
49. Rattner HM, Cooper DJ, Zaman MB. Severe bleeding from herpes esophagitis. Am J Gastroenterol 1985; 80: 523–525.
50. Cronstedt JL, Bouchama A, Hainau B, et al. Spontaneous esophageal perforation in herpes simplex esophagitis. Am J Gastroenterol 1992; 87: 124–127.
51. Pazin GJ. Herpes simplex esophagitis after trigeminal nerve surgery. Gastroenterology 1978; 74: 741–743.
52. Warren KG, Brown SM, Wroblewska Z, Gilden D, Koprowski H, Subak-Sharpe J. Isolation of latent herpes simplex virus from the superior cervical and vagus ganglions of human beings. N Engl J Med 1978; 298: 1068–1070.
53. Howiler W, Goldberg HI. Gastroesophageal involvement in herpes simplex. Gastroenterology 1976; 70: 775–778.
54. Strano AJ. Light microscopy of selected viral diseases (morphology of viral inclusion bodies). Pathol Ann 1976; 11: 53–75.
55. Greenson JK, Beschorner WE, Boitnott JK, Yardley JH. Prominent mononuclear cell infiltrate is characteristic of herpes esophagitis. Hum Pathol 1991; 22: 541–549.
56. McKay JS, Day DW. Herpes simplex oesophagitis. Histopathology 1983; 7: 409–420.
57. Burrig K-F, Borchard F, Feiden W, Pfitzer P. Herpes oesophagitis. II. Electron microscopical findings. Virchows Arch (A) 1984; 404: 177–185.
58. Buddingh GJ, Schrum DI, Lanier JC, Guidry DJ. Studies of the natural history of herpes simplex infections. Pediatrics 1953; 11: 595–610.
59. Douglas RG jr, Couch RB. A prospective study of chronic herpes simplex virus infection and recurrent herpes labialis in humans. J Immunol 1970; 104: 289–295.
60. Dow CJ. Oesophageal tuberculosis: four cases. Gut 1981; 22: 234–236.
61. Maillet P. Stenose oesophagienne consecutive au mal de Pott. Lyon chir 1960; 56: 924–926.
62. Laajam MA. Primary tuberculosis of the esophagus: pseudotumoral presentation. Am J Gastroenterol 1984; 79: 839–841.
63. Seivewright N, Feehally J, Wicks ACB. Primary tuberculosis of the esophagus. Am J Gastroenterol 1984; 79: 842–843.
64. Mokoena T, Shama DM, Ngakane H, Bryer JV. Oesophageal tuberculosis: a review of 11 cases. Postgrad Med J 1992; 68: 110–115.
65. Hudson TR, Head JR. Syphilis of the esophagus. J Thorac Surg 1950; 20: 216–221.
66. McManus JPA, Webb JN. A yeast-like infection of the esophagus caused by Lactobacillus acidophilus. Gastroenterology 1975; 68: 583–586.
67. Ezzell JH Jr, Bremer J, Adamec TA. Bacterial esophagitis: an often forgotten cause of odynophagia. Am J Gastroenterol 1990; 85: 296–298.
68. Pelemans W, Vantrappen G. Esophageal mycoses. In: Vantrappen GR, Hellemans JJ, eds. Diseases of the esophagus. New York: Springer-Verlag, 1974: pp 558–567.
69. Sebastian S, Parker JO, Lynn RB. Acquired esophagobronchial fistulas in adults. Can Med Assoc J 1969; 101: 517–519.
70. Neame P, Ragner D. Mucormycosis: a report of twenty-two cases. Arch Pathol 1960; 70: 261–268.
71. Schneider RP, Edwards W. Histoplasmosis presenting as an esophageal tumour. Gastrointest Endosc 1977; 23: 158–159.
72. Lee J-H, Neumann DA, Welsh JD. Disseminated histoplasmosis presenting with esophageal symptomatology. Dig Dis 1977; 22: 831–834.
73. Miller DP, Everett ED. Gastrointestinal histoplasmosis. J Clin Gastroenterol 1979; 1: 233–236.
74. Villar LA, Massanari RM, Mitros FA. Cytomegalovirus infection with acute erosive esophagitis. Am J Med 1984; 76: 924–928.
75. Allen JI, Silvis SE, Sumner HW, McClain CJ. Cytomegalic inclusion disease diagnosed endoscopically. Dig Dis Sci 1981; 26: 133–135.
76. Onge GS, Bezahler GH. Giant esophageal ulcer associated with cytomegalovirus. Gastroenterology 1982; 83: 127–130.
77. Freedman PG, Weiner BC, Balthazar EJ. Cytomegalovirus esophagogastritis in a patient with acquired immunodeficiency syndrome. Am J Gastroenterol 1985; 80: 434–437.
78. Theise ND, Rotterdam H, Dieterich D. Cytomegalovirus esophagitis in AIDS: diagnosis by endoscopic biopsy. Am J Gastroenterol 1991; 86: 1123–1126.
79. Schwartz DA, Wilcox CM. Atypical cytomegalovirus inclusions in gastrointestinal biopsy specimens from patients with the acquired immunodeficiency syndrome: diagnostic role of in situ nucleic acid hybridization. Hum Pathol 1992; 23: 1019–1026.
80. Rabeneck L, Boyko WJ, McLean DM, McLeod WA, Wong KK. Unusual esophageal ulcers containing enveloped virus-like particles in homosexual men. Gastroenterology 1986; 90: 1882–1889.
81. Winkler B, Capo V, Reumann W, et al. Human papillomavirus infection of the esophagus. Cancer 1985; 55: 149–155.

82. Williamson Al, Jaskiesicz K, Gunning A. The detection of human papillomavirus in oesophageal lesions. Anticancer Res 1991; 11: 263–265.
83. Hille JJ, Margolius KA, Markowitz S, Isaacson S. Human papillomavirus infection related to oesophageal carcinoma in black South Africans. South African Med J 1986; 69: 417–420.
84. Morris H, Price S. Langerhan's cells, papillomaviruses and oesophageal carcinoma. South African Med J 1986; 69: 413–417.
85. Kazlow PG, Shah K, Benkov KJ, Dische R, LeLeiko NS. Esophageal cryptosporidiosis in a child with acquired immunodeficiency syndrome. Gastroenterology 1986; 91: 1301–1303.
86. Bettarello A, Pinotti HW. Oesophageal involvement in Chagas' disease. Clin Gastroenterol 1976; 5: 103–117.
87. Atias A, Neghme A, Mackay LA, Jarpa S. Megaesophagus, megacolon, and Chagas' disease in Chile. Gastroenterology 1963; 44: 433–437.
88. Koberle F. Enteromegaly and cardiomegaly in Chagas' disease. Gut 1963; 4: 399–405.
89. Butler C, Madden JW, Davis WM. Morphologic aspects of experimental lye strictures. I. Pathogenesis and pathophysiologic correlations. J Surg Res 1974; 17: 232–244.
90. Kiviranta UK. Corrosion carcinoma of the esophagus: 381 cases of corrosion and 9 cases of corrosion carcinoma. Acta Oto-laryngol 1952; 42: 89–95.
91. Appelqvist P, Salmo M. Lye corrosion carcinoma of the esophagus. A review of 63 cases. Cancer 1980; 45: 2655–2658.
92. Kikendall JW, Friedman AC, Oyewole MA, Fleischer D, Johnson LF. Pill-induced esophageal injury. Case reports and review of the medical literature. Dig Dis Sci 1983; 28: 174–182.
93. Collins FJ, Mathews HR, Baker SE, Strakova JM. Drug-induced oesophageal injury. Br Med J 1979; 1: 1673–1676.
94. Ecker GA, Karsh J. Naproxen induced ulcerative esophagitis. J Rheumatol 1992; 19: 646–647.
95. Minocha A, Greenbaum DS. Pill-esophagitis caused by nonsteroidal antiinflammatory drugs. Am J Gastroenterol 1991; 86: 1086–1089.
96. Kato S. Komatsu K, Harada Y. Medication-induced esophagitis in children. Gastroenterol Jpn 1990; 25: 485–488.
97. Biller JA, Flores A, Buie T, Mazor S, Katz AJ. Tetracycline-induced esophagitis in adolescent patients. J Pediatr 1992; 120: 144–145.
98. Eng J. Sabanathan S. Drug-induced esophagitis. Am J Gastroenterol 1991; 86: 1127–1133.
99. Sherrill DJ, Grishkin BA, Galal FS, Zajtchuk R, Graeber GM. Radiation associated malignancies of the esophagus. Cancer 1984; 54: 726–728.
100. Huchzermeyer H, Paul F, Seifert E, Frohlich H, Rasmussen CW. Endoscopic results in five patients with Crohn's disease of the esophagus. Endoscopy 1976; 8: 75–81.
101. Miller LJ, Thistle JL, Payne WS, Gaffey TA, O'Duffy JD. Crohn's disease involving the esophagus and colon. Mayo Clin Proc 1977; 52: 35–38.
102. Schmidt-Sommerfeld E, Kirschner BS, Stephens JK. Endoscopic and histologic findings in the upper gastrointestinal tract of children with Crohn's disease. J Pediatr Gastroenterol Nutr 1990 11: 448–454.
103. Dobbins JW, Sheahan DG, Behar J. Eosinophilic gastroenteritis with esophageal involvement. Gastroenterology 1977; 72: 1312–1316.
104. Landres RT, Kuster GGR, Strum WB. Eosinophilic esophagitis in a patient with vigorous achalasia. Gastroenterology 1978; 74: 1298–1301.
105. Blei E, Gonzalez-Crussi F, Lloyd-Still JD. Eosinophilic infiltration of the esophageal muscle layer: a difficult diagnostic problem. J Pediatr Gastroenterol Nutr 1992; 15: 93–96.
106. Goldin E, Lijovetzky G. Esophageal involvement by pemphigus vulgaris. Am J Gastroenterol 1985; 80: 828–830.
107. Foroozan P, Enta T, Winship DH, Trier JS. Loss and regeneration of the esophageal mucosa in pemphigoid. Gastroenterology 1967; 52: 548–558.
108. Sharon P, Greene ML, Rachmilewitz D. Esophageal involvement in bullous pemphigoid. Gastrointest Endosc 1978; 24: 122–123.
109. Johnston DE, Koehler RE, Balfe DM. Clinical manifestations of epidermolysis bullosa dystrophica. Dig Dis Sci 1981; 26: 1144–1149.
110. Zweiban B, Cohen H, Chandrasoma P. Gastrointestinal involvement complicating Stevens-Johnson syndrome. Gastroenterology 1986; 91: 469–474.
111. Geboes K, Janssens J. The esophagus in cutaneous diseases. In: Vantrappen GR, Hellemans JJ, eds. Diseases of the esophagus. New York: Springer-Verlag, 1974: pp. 823–833.
112. Baba S, Maruta M, Ando K, Teramoto T, Endo I. Intestinal Behcet's disease: report of five cases. Dis Colon Rectum 1976; 19: 428–440.
113. Kasahara Y, Tanaka S, Nishino M, Umemura H, Shiraha S, Kuyama T. Intestinal involvement in Behcet's disease: review of 136 surgical cases in the Japanese literature. Dis Colon Rectum 1981; 24: 103–106.
114. Kikuchi K, Suga T, Senoue I, Nomiyama T, Miwa M, Miwa T. Esophageal ulceration in a patient with Behcet's syndrome. Tokai J Exp Clin Med 1982; 7: 135–143.
115. Mori S, Yoshihira A, Kawamura H, Takeuchi A, Hashimoto T, Inaba G. Esophageal involvement in Behcet's disease. Am J Gastroenterol 1983; 78: 548–553.
116. Atkinson M, Summerling MD. Oesophageal changes in systemic sclerosis. Gut 1966; 7: 402–408.
117. Cameron AJ, Payne WS. Barrett's esophagus occurring as a complication of scleroderma. Mayo Clin Proc 1978; 53: 612–615.
118. Cohen S, Laufer I, Snape WJ jr, et al. The gastrointestinal manifestations of scleroderma: pathogenesis and management. Gastroenterology 1980; 79: 155–166.

PART III
The oesophagus: Crohn's disease

H. M. Gilmour

Of the sites within the gastrointestinal tract which may be affected by Crohn's disease, the oesophagus has been suggested as the one least likely to be involved. However, involvement is almost certainly more common than has hitherto been recorded due to the difficulty of making a definitive diagnosis. Early or mild disease is unlikely to lead to major symptoms and could easily be ascribed to reflux oesophagitis. Few pathognomonic signs have been recorded either at endoscopy or by radiological investigation. Early changes, which include aphthous ulceration, may be seen in other conditions such as herpetic oesophagitis, and it is only the demonstration of granulomas in endoscopic biopsies from such aphthous ulcers which is evidence in favour of a diagnosis of Crohn's disease. Janssens et al[1] reported finding granulomas in endoscopic biopsies from seven of nine cases with aphthous ulceration, although this required serial sectioning of the biopsies from the margins of the ulcers. These nine cases were identified during a four-year period in 500 cases of known Crohn's disease and all nine developed the ulcers during an active phase of disease elsewhere in the gut when, in addition, other systems were commonly affected. Interestingly, the oesophageal symptoms and ulcers resolved relatively quickly with medical treatment.

A number of recent publications in the paediatric literature lend credence to the belief that oesophageal Crohn's disease is underdiagnosed.[2–5] There is often a poor correlation between symptoms and endoscopic and/or histological abnormalities although features such as dysphagia, pain when eating and oral aphthous ulcers correlate with upper gastrointestinal involvement in children with Crohn's disease elsewhere, particularly if both small and large bowel are affected.[4] In a number of patients thought to have ulcerative colitis, definite diagnosis of Crohn's disease may be obtained following investigation of the upper alimentary tract,[4] and upper gastrointestinal endoscopy with biopsies may be useful before surgery is contemplated in patients categorized as having ulcerative or indeterminate colitis. Histological abnormalities, including those diagnostic of Crohn's disease, may be found in biopsies from mucosa that was assessed as normal by the endoscopist,[5] emphasizing the importance of obtaining tissue for histological assessment.

More extensive disease of the oesophagus with ulceration and stricture formation, particularly if it occurred in the distal oesophagus, is likely to be diagnosed as either severe reflux oesophagitis or carcinoma.[6] Crohn's disease in the region of the cardia and lower oesophageal sphincter may lead to reflux through interference with normal sphincter function and the superimposition of inflammatory changes due to reflux oesophagitis. The presence of granulomas in biopsies from such an area of oesophagitis or association with aphthous ulceration in the proximal oesophagus should raise the possibility of Crohn's disease, although endoscopic biopsies are unlikely to be diagnostic in this situation. However, when Crohn's disease exists elsewhere in the gut a presumptive diagnosis of Crohn's disease may be made, and this is illustrated by some of the case reports in the literature.[7,8]

Fissuring ulceration or fistula formation is unusual in reflux oesophagitis although fistulae can occur in penetrating peptic ulcers. In a few cases of Crohn's disease of the oesophagus fissuring ulceration can lead to extensive intramural sinus tracts,[9] which may develop a lining of squamous epithelium. Where a resection of the distal oesophagus is performed, the identification of transmural focal lymphocytic inflammation, along with the other features mentioned above, should make diagnosis possible.

Should such inflammatory changes and stricturing be more widespread within the oesophagus or involve the proximal oesophagus, then Crohn's disease should enter the differential diagnosis at an earlier stage, and must be considered in any patient with known Crohn's disease who develops dysphagia, particularly when associated with pain or oral aphthous ulcers.[4,10]

Most cases of oesophageal Crohn's disease in the literature have been associated with Crohn's disease elsewhere in the gut, but there are a few reports of cases in which Crohn's disease initially presented in the oesophagus. The number of such cases, however, is likely to remain relatively small for the reasons outlined above unless the index of clinical suspicion can be raised and endoscopists are prepared to take multiple biopsies from multiple sites, including areas which appear endoscopically normal. The pathologist may also require to examine several levels from each biopsy in order to avoid missing focal lesions.

REFERENCES

1. Janssens J, Geboes K, Verhamme M, Rutgeerts P, Vantrappen G. Transient granulomatous aphthoid esophageal lesions in Crohn's disease. Gastrointest Endosc 1983; 29: 162 (abstract).
2. Mashako MN, Cezard JP, Navarro J et al. Crohn's disease lesions in the upper gastrointestinal tract: correlation between clinical, radiological, endoscopic and histological features in adolescents and children. J Paediatr Gastroenterol Nutr 1989; 8: 442–446.
3. Cameron DJS. Upper and lower gastrointestinal endoscopy in children and adolescents with Crohn's disease: a prospective study. J Gastroenterol Hepatol 1991; 6: 355–358.
4. Lenaerts C, Roy CC, Vaillancourt M, Weber AM, Morin CL, Seidman E. High incidence of upper gastrointestinal tract involvement in children with Crohn's disease. Paediatrics 1989; 83: 777–781.
5. Schmidt-Sommerfeld E, Kirschner BS, Stephens JK. Endoscopic and histological findings in the upper gastrointestinal tract of children with Crohn's disease. J Paediatr Gastroenterol Nutr 1990; 11: 448–454.
6. LiVolsi VA, Jaretzki III A. Granulomatous esophagitis: a case of Crohn's disease limited to the esophagus. Gastroenterology 1973; 64: 313–319.
7. Gelfand MD, Krone CL. Dysphagia and ulceration in Crohn's disease. Gastroenterology 1968; 55: 510–514.
8. Achenbach H, Lynch JP, Wright RW. Idiopathic ulcerative esophagitis. N Eng J Med 1956; 255: 456–459.
9. Freedman PG, Dieterich DT, Balthazar EJ. Crohn's disease of the esophagus: case report and review of the literature. Am J Gastroenterol 1984; 79: 835–838.
10. Dyer NH, Cook PL, Kemp Harper RA. Oesophageal stricture associated with Crohn's disease. Gut 1969; 10: 549–554.

CHAPTER

25 The stomach

J. M. Sloan P. Correa J. Lindeman
C. J. L. M. Meijer P. Sipponen

PART I

Acute haemorrhagic gastritis and acute infective gastritis; gastritis caused by physical agents and corrosives; uraemic gastritis

J. M. Sloan

ACUTE HAEMORRHAGIC GASTRITIS (Synonyms: acute stress ulceration of the stomach, acute erosive gastritis)

Acute haemorrhagic gastritis is a term used to describe the condition of haemorrhagic congestion, petechiae, localized erosions and acute ulcers of the gastric mucosa. It occurs in a variety of clinical situations which fall into two main groups:

1. Acute stress ulceration of the stomach which occurs in seriously ill patients after severe trauma, major surgery, sepsis or organ failure. It may also follow burns (Curling's ulcer) and/or head injury, neurosurgery or intracranial disease (Cushing's ulcer)
2. Acute erosive gastritis associated with therapeutic drugs and alcohol.

Acute stress ulceration of the stomach

The condition is characterized by congestion and oedema of the gastric mucosa, accompanied by petechial haemorrhages, focal erosions and acute ulcers. The erosions or ulcers are invariably multiple and give rise to bleeding. Clinical manifestations, if any, are haematemesis, melaena or, less often, perforation. These usually appear 3–6 days after onset of the stressful event.

There are numerous predisposing factors, including sepsis, widespread burns, severe trauma, major surgical procedures, renal failure, respiratory failure, hypotension, peritonitis, jaundice, head injuries or spinal injuries.[1] The development of new and successful forms of treatment has resulted in many patients suffering from the above conditions being kept alive. Stress ulceration has thus assumed a much greater clinical significance as it poses a further threat to life during the recovery phase.

The incidence of stress ulceration is especially high in critically ill patients. Endoscopic studies indicate that almost 85% of such patients have stress ulcers, although not all have clinical manifestations.[2] Ulceration is more common in patients over 35 years of age[3] but the incidence of bleeding from stress ulceration has fallen recently, largely due to the effect of prophylactic antacid therapy.[1,4] Despite this treatment, however, bleeding may in some cases merely be delayed and appear after an interval of 2–3 weeks.[5]

Macroscopic appearances

Macroscopic examination of the stomach shows congestion of the mucosa together with petechiae and localized

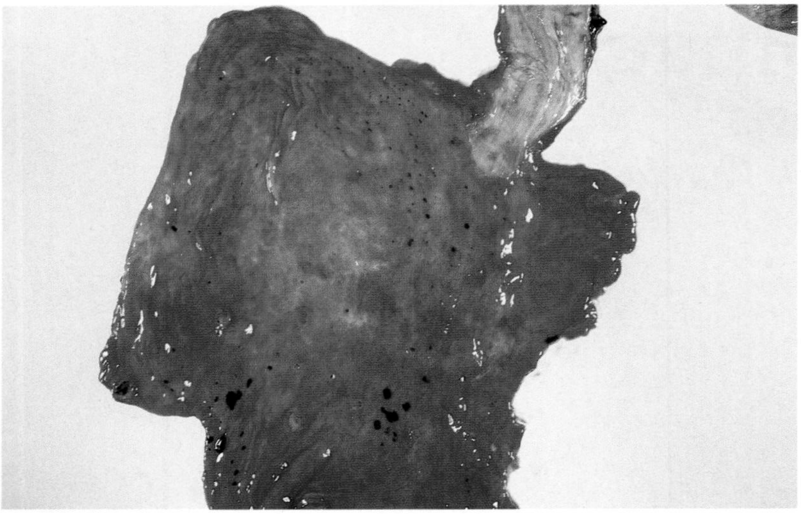

Fig. 25.1 Acute stress ulceration of the stomach. In contrast with the pale oesophageal mucosa, the gastric mucosa is congested and contains numerous dark erosions and acute ulcers within the fundus and body.

shallow erosions and ulcers (Fig. 25.1). Erosions are well-defined and contain fresh or altered blood. They are multiple, mostly round and measure 1–3 mm in diameter,[6] although some extend up to 2.5 cm diameter and these may be oval or linear. Larger lesions are especially likely in the presence of sepsis or multiple organ injury.[7] The lesions are distributed principally in the fundus and body of the stomach, the antrum is less frequently involved and may escape involvement entirely. Acute ulcers measure up to 2 cm in diameter. In the stomach they are more common in the body and occur mainly on the greater curvature and, like erosions, are usually multiple. In the duodenum they are less common, larger and often single. Occasionally there is diffuse involvement of the gastric mucosa resulting in a haemorrhagic and very friable gastric wall.[6]

Endoscopic studies indicate that erosions appear in the body of the stomach within 24 hours of severe trauma. They then spread distally, and antral involvement may occur when lesions are widespread throughout the body of the stomach. In contrast, erosive gastritis associated with alcohol or aspirin ingestion involves the antrum more often.[8]

Microscopic appearances

Histologically, erosions show focal necrosis and ulceration of the gastric mucosal surface. Depth of ulceration varies but it is often superficial. There is haemorrhage and necrotic slough within the crater of the erosion and extravasation of blood into adjacent intact mucosa; nearby capillaries are dilated and congested. In the initial stage little or no inflammatory cell infiltration takes place (Fig. 25.2A). This is composed of polymorphs, lymphocytes, plasma cells and eosinophils. Re-epithelialization of the surface of the erosion takes place with regenerating cells extending from adjacent intact mucosal surface (Fig. 25.2B). Healing takes place without fibrosis. If ulceration involves the full thickness of the mucosa and penetrates the muscularis mucosae the lesion is classified as an acute ulcer.

Curling's ulcer

This is the term applied to acute gastroduodenal ulceration in patients with burns. Curling originally described acute duodenal ulceration following severe burns, but gastric involvement is more common and the term is now generally accepted as referring to gastric, duodenal or lower oesophageal lesions. The distribution and morphological appearance of lesions are similar to those described in other forms of stress ulceration, with hyperaemic mucosa and multiple shallow erosions and small ulcers involving the fundus and, less often, the antrum or duodenum. These erosions are generally less than 5 mm in diameter, but occasionally larger irregular lesions occur.[9,10]

Duodenal ulceration is less common in adults although duodenitis is very common.[11] Duodenal lesions tend to be larger than those in the stomach and deeper, resulting in ulceration rather than erosion. Duodenal ulcers are usually single but multiple lesions are not uncommon; ulceration involving both stomach and duodenum is quite common.[9,10] In Curling's ulcer in children, duodenal ulcer is relatively more common[9,12] and is the usual cause of severe bleeding. Post burns ulceration of the gastrointestinal tract is not confined to stomach and duodenum and may involve oesophagus, small bowel or colon.[9]

The incidence of Curling's ulcer increases with the extent of the burns. Post-mortem studies indicate that lesions are rare in patients with less than 10% burns, but increasing area of involvement by burns is associated with increasing incidence of both gastric and duodenal lesions.[9,13] Endoscopic studies indicate that in patients with extensive burns (greater than 35% surface area) the incidence of gastric erosions is over 80%.[11]

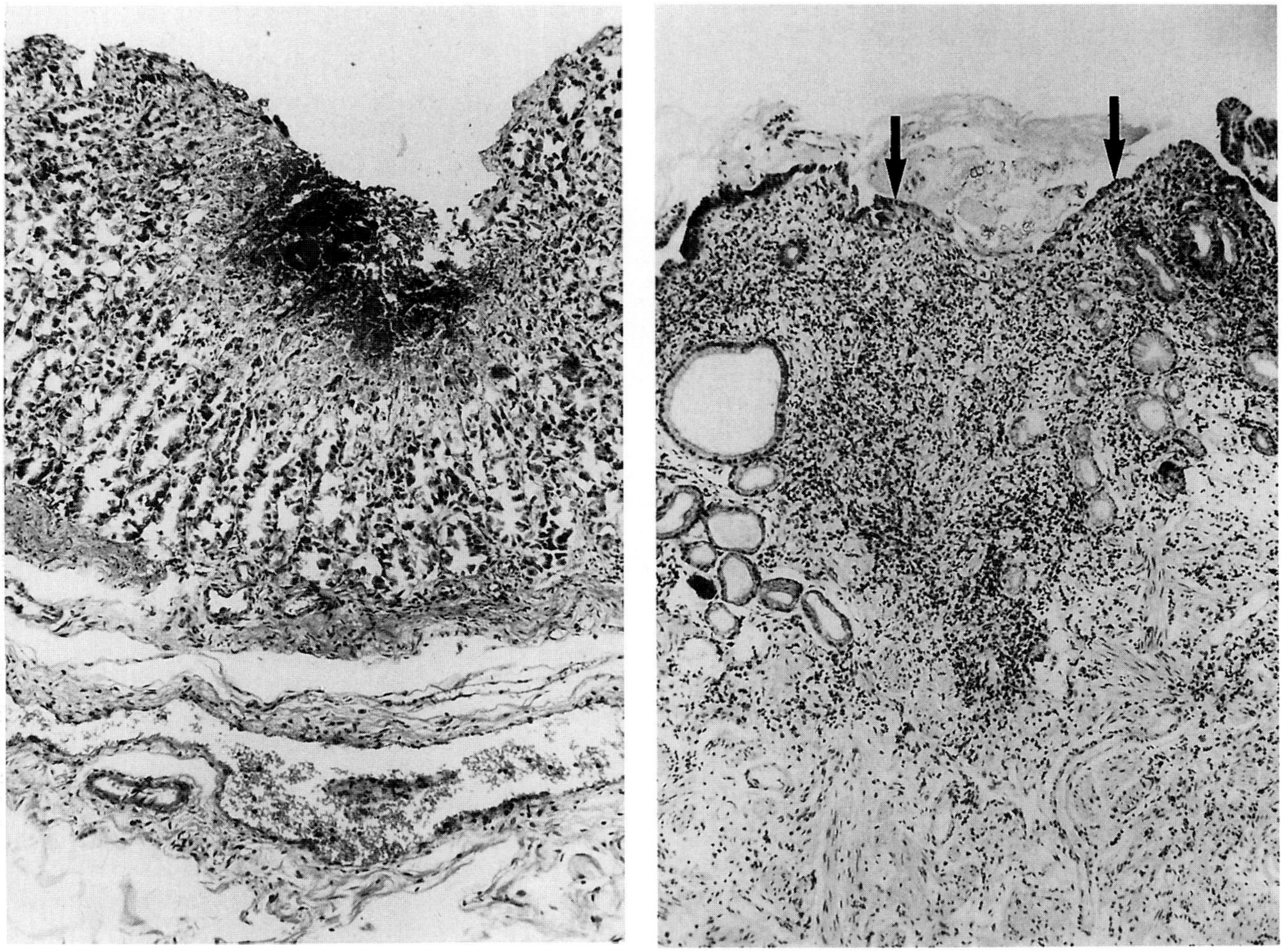

A B

Fig. 25.2A Acute gastric erosion. There is haemorrhagic necrosis of the superficial mucosa, congestion of adjacent capillaries and extravasation of RBCs. No significant inflammatory reaction is present. (H&E, ×50) **B** Healing gastric erosion. Re-epithelialization of the surface is taking place (arrows) and there is active inflammatory cell infiltration throughout the erosion. (H&E, ×50)

Sepsis in the burned patient significantly increases the risk and extent of Curling's ulcer;[13] this is especially so in children.[14] As in stress ulceration due to other causes, the advent of prophylactic antacid treatment has reduced the incidence of clinical manifestations.[15,16]

Cushing's ulcer

The term applies to acute ulceration of the stomach or duodenum in association with disease of, or injury to, the central nervous system. Cushing described a series of cases of acute erosion and perforation involving oesophagus, stomach and duodenum in patients following surgery for intracranial tumours and in malignant hypertension.[17] Unlike other forms of stress ulcer, Cushing's ulcer is often a single deep ulcer.[18]

The incidence of bleeding from such lesions is significant. In a study of a large series of cases of head injury of all degrees of severity, gastrointestinal bleeding occurred in 17% although endoscopy showed acute gastroduodenal lesions in 75%. The incidence of bleeding was significantly higher in severely injured patients.[19] A smaller study of patients with severe head injury indicates that the incidence of some degree of gastro-duodenal haemorrhage is almost 80%.[20] Patients with spasticity or paralysis due to spinal cord injury appear especially prone to gastroduodenal haemorrhage.[21]

Gastric erosions in patients who are not seriously ill are surprisingly common. In some cases there is associated peptic ulcer disease[22] but even in healthy asymptomatic volunteers endoscopy shows that erosions, haemorrhage or peptic ulceration are quite frequent.[23]

Mucosal defence mechanisms and pathogenesis of stress ulceration

The pathogenesis of stress ulceration is not fully understood but is multifactorial. Of importance is the nature of the gastric secretions and the mechanisms in the mucosa which protect against their injurious effects. These defence mechanisms can be divided into several components.

Surface mucus–bicarbonate barrier. The first line of defence is the layer of mucus adherent to the surface mucosal cells. Experimental evidence shows that bicarbonate ions are secreted by these cells at a rate of 2–10% of the maximal acid secretion and diffuse into the adherent mucus, thus forming an alkaline gel. The mucous layer provides an unstirred zone in which bicarbonate neutralizes acid diffusing towards the epithelium from the lumen.[24] In addition, it provides a barrier against luminal pepsin and protects against mechanical shearing damage caused by luminal contents.[25] The mucous layer in the human stomach is continuous, and estimates of the thickness of the layer vary from 200 μm[24] to around 550 μm,[26] although it varies under certain conditions such as gastric distension. Removal or thinning of the mucus layer by scraping or inhibition of mucus secretion leads to erosion of the underlying mucosa.[24]

Thus the mucous–bicarbonate barrier helps to maintain the surface epithelial cells at a pH in the region of 7, while the luminal contents of the stomach are much more acidic. The efficacy of this barrier is demonstrated by the significant pH gradient across the mucous layer. It has been demonstrated in rabbits[27] and in man[28] that there is a sharp rise in pH on the mucosal side of this layer. Depletion of mucus in isolated rat and dog gastric mucosa results in a marked increase in mucosal permeability to hydrogen ions.[29] While the structure of the mucus gel is unaffected by short term exposure to bile, ethanol or high acid levels, it does not prevent ions and small molecules reaching the underlying mucosa. Pepsin is a major factor in breakdown of the mucus gel and in the healthy state there is a balance between mucus secretion and erosion.[30]

Thus protection afforded by the mucous–bicarbonate barrier is limited. High acid concentration within the gastric lumen causes dissipation of the surface pH gradient thus exposing surface mucosal cells to acid luminal contents.[31,32]

Epithelial renewal. Further mucosal protection is provided by the ability of the surface epithelial cells of gastric mucosa to proliferate and replace desquamated or damaged cells rapidly. The proliferative zone from which cells are replaced lies at the junction of the base of the surface pits and the top of the glands.[33] The response of gastric mucosa to injury in experimental animals is very rapid. Damaged rat gastric mucosa shows evidence of restitution of the mucosal surface within 7 minutes of injury and widespread re-epithelialization of the surface within an hour.[34] In the frog, healing of the surface epithelium and restoration of normal functional activity takes place approximately 6 hours after NaCl-induced damage.[35]

Gastric mucosal barrier. The existence of a gastric mucosal barrier as another defence mechanism has been shown. The anatomical basis of this is the surface cell membranes and the tight junctions which exist between surface epithelial cells.[36] Under normal circumstances there is only a small amount of back diffusion of hydrogen ions from the acid luminal contents into gastric mucosa, some movement of sodium and potassium ions taking place in the opposite direction. A further component of this barrier is a transmucosal potential difference of about 50 mV, the lumen being negative.[37] Davenport showed that damage to the mucosal barrier by a variety of agents, notably aspirin in acid solution, leads to a decrease in luminal acid content. This is not due to inhibition of mucosal acid secretion by the drug but is instead caused by increased back-diffusion of acid from lumen to mucosa accompanied by a marked drop in transmucosal potential difference. The barrier thus appears to act as an important mucosal defence against the low pH levels in the gastric lumen.[36]

Mucosal blood flow. Perhaps the most essential defence mechanism of the gastric mucosa and the one on which other mechanisms depend is maintenance of adequate mucosal blood flow. This enables the gastric mucosa to dispose of hydrogen ions which have diffused in from the lumen,[38] and to maintain intramucosal acid-base balance. The HCO_3/CO_2 buffer system and carbonic anhydrase activity are essential to buffering of hydrogen ions within gastric mucosa.[39] In addition, adequate mucosal blood flow and delivery of oxygen, glucose and other nutrients is necessary for such a rapidly proliferating tissue as gastric mucosa. The importance of blood flow in dealing with hydrogen ions which have diffused into the mucosa from the lumen is reflected in increased gastric mucosal blood flow in response to increasing hydrogen ion concentration in the gastric lumen. Within limits, this maintains a constant physiological intramucosal pH. If blood flow is interrupted intramucosal pH falls sharply and ulceration occurs.[40]

Cytoprotective mechanisms. Numerous experimental studies have shown that gastric mucosa derives protection from the action of prostaglandins. Administration of exogenous prostaglandins protects the gastric mucosa of the rat against a variety of agents capable of inflicting severe damage, including boiling water.[41] This action of prostaglandins has been termed direct cytoprotection. Gastric mucosa can synthesize endogenous prostaglandins from the precursor arachidonic acid. Pretreatment of the mucosa with mild irritants provides protection against more noxious agents, and it is thought that this adaptive cytoprotection is mediated via endogenous prostaglandins.[42] Prostaglandins have a variety of actions within the gastric mucosa which contribute to mucosal protection.[43] These include stimulation of mucus secretion,[26] bicarbonate secretion by gastric and duodenal mucosa[44] and increasing gastric mucosal blood flow.[45] They also protect the mucosa against aspirin, which is a potent disruptor of the gastric mucosal barrier.[46–47] Much of the work on prostaglandins is experimental. However there is good evidence that prophylactic administration of a synthetic prostaglandin E1 analog (misoprostol) provides protection against development of gastric stress ulcers.[48]

In the absence of a single causative factor in pathogenesis of stress ulceration it is necessary to consider various aspects in relation to gastric defence mechanisms.

The presence of acid in the gastric lumen is thought to be essential for development of erosions and ulcers,[49] and the success of antacid prophylaxis in diminishing the incidence of the disease supports this. Nonetheless, it seems likely that defects in the protective mechanisms of the mucosa rather than a marked increase in acid and pepsin secretion are responsible for initiation of stress ulceration. In Cushing's ulcer, however, there is some evidence of increased gastric secretory activity.

Cushing[17] suggested that the pathogenesis of the lesions may be due to increased gastric motility, tonicity and acid secretion, secondary to central stimulation of the parasympathetic nervous system. Subsequent studies indicate that increased gastric acid secretion does indeed follow severe head injury although there is wide individual variation.[50,51] Increased pepsin and reduced mucus secretion have also been reported in association with hyperchlorhydria.[52] In general, patients who develop bleeding from gastric or duodenal lesions have especially high levels of acid secretion.[50,52] The level of gastric acid secretion in stress ulceration associated with CNS injury is reported to be higher than in patients with stress ulceration due to other causes.[51] These findings contrast with a study on seriously injured combat casualties which showed that those with cranial injuries have normal or decreased gastric acid output in the days following injury.[53]

No correlation has been noted between erosion or bleeding and sepsis, hypoxia or shock in patients with cranial injury.[20]

The morphology of Cushing's ulcers differs somewhat from other forms of stress ulceration, in that duodenal lesions are more common and in some cases ulcers penetrate deeply into the muscle wall and are more likely to perforate. For this reason, some workers contend that Cushing's ulcer should be considered separately from other forms of stress ulcer.[54] This view is not universally accepted[55] and in view of the broad similarity in distribution of lesions, histology and prophylaxis, it seems reasonable to group Cushing's ulcer alongside other forms of stress ulceration.

Gastric hypersecretion, however, is not peculiar to patients with CNS injury; it also occurs in patients with multiple organ injury or severe sepsis. Although gastric secretion is reduced and pH is high in the first two days following injury,[21] increased acid secretion follows and reaches a peak 3–5 days after injury.[7] This rise in secretory activity 24–36 hours following injury has been reported as being more marked in severely injured patients.[53] Pepsin secretion also increases at this time, especially following severe abdominal injury.[52,53]

To summarize, it seems unlikely that initiation of mucosal damage occurs because of increased acid or pepsin secretion in most cases of stress ulceration. Nonetheless, the presence of acid appears necessary for ulceration to occur ('no acid no ulcer' is a well-known maxim) and increased secretory activity 2 or 3 days following onset of stress exacerbates existing mucosal damage and increases the likelihood of ulceration and bleeding. The importance of acid is underlined by the prophylactic effect of neutralization of gastric acid either by antacids or H_2 receptor antagonists. A review of a large number of trials indicated that bleeding from stress ulceration is significantly reduced by either of these agents when compared with placebo.[56]

The defence mechanisms of the gastric mucosa have been outlined above, and defects in these mechanisms are closely connected with the pathogenesis of stress ulcer.

Pathogenetic mechanisms

Many patients suffering from stress ulceration undergo a period of hypotension or hypovolaemic shock, and most authorities consider that under-perfusion of gastric mucosa and subsequent ischaemia plays an important part in the development of lesions. There are isolated reports of gastric ischaemia secondary to occlusion of the coeliac axis giving rise to lesions very similar to stress ulceration[57,58] but in most cases ischaemia is less obvious and is only one of a series of aetiological factors. Considerable experimental evidence exists that hypovolaemic shock gives rise to gastric lesions closely resembling stress ulceration.[59,60] In rabbits rendered hypovolaemic by bleeding, focal areas of anoxic mucosa develop during the shock phase and subsequently ulcerate when blood volume is restored.[59] Local impairment of gastric mucosal blood flow in combination with topical application of bile salts and acid is a potent cause of ulceration in the dog.[61] The corollary is true: enhancement of blood flow tends to protect the mucosa.[62]

Haemorrhagic shock in dogs causes a significant reduction in gastric mucosal blood flow, which is more pronounced in the fundus than the antrum,[63] which may explain the propensity for stress ulcers to occur in the proximal part of the stomach. In the rat there is correlation between falling blood pressure and decreasing gastric and duodenal mucosal blood flow. Haemorrhagic erosions in the corpus of the stomach do not appear, however, until mucosal blood flow is markedly reduced.[64]

Stress ulceration of the stomach following shock and subsequent resuscitation is probably an example of an ischaemic-reperfusion type of injury. The importance of oxygen-derived free radicals in inducing tissue damage in such injury is now apparent.[65] In addition, leucocytes (neutrophils) appear to contribute to the damage by production of proteases, elastase, tissue oxygen products and leukotrienes which increase vascular permeability and contribute to cell lysis.[66] Increased neutrophil adhesiveness to capillary endothelial cells and neutrophil aggregation leading to microvascular occlusion, also appears to be a contributory factor. In the experimental situation, prevention of neutrophil adhesion provides protection against haemorrhagic gastritis in rabbits subjected to haemorhagic shock and resuscitation.[67]

Reduction in gastric mucosal blood flow is considered to be the first in a series of events which leads to stress ulceration.[68] However there is evidence to suggest that ischaemia is not the sole aetiological factor. Studies on sepsis-induced stress ulceration in pigs indicate increased rather than decreased gastric blood flow[69] and ischaemia alone fails to disrupt the gastric mucosal barrier in dogs.[70] In similarly induced stress ulceration in cats, gastric lesions could not be explained by mucosal ischaemia, and the protective action of synthetic prostaglandin was not mediated via an effect on blood flow.[71] Studies in man are limited but endoscopy in seriously injured patients shows focal pallor in the proximal stomach followed by development of erosions in these areas after 36 hours.[7]

Thus ischaemia appears to be only one of a series of aetiological factors in stress ulceration, but is probably the most important. In the presence of ischaemia other defence mechanisms such as buffering of acid within the mucosa, bicarbonate secretion and disposal of hydrogen ions are compromised.

The importance of the buffering capacity of the mucosa in protecting against luminal acid has been well demonstrated experimentally.[39,72] Acid-base balance within the mucosa depends on availability of bicarbonate ions and carbonic anhydrase activity. Reduction in either of these results in severe impairment of the protective mechanisms against luminal acid. In normal circumstances there is back-diffusion of small amounts of hydrogen ion from lumen into mucosa. Impairment of the buffering capacity will render even this amount of back-diffusion pathogenic.[73,74]

The effect of haemorrhagic shock on the buffering capacity of the gastric mucosa has been investigated in dogs and rabbits.[75] Under conditions of shock the intramucosal pH decreases significantly, especially in the presence of luminal acid. The drop in pH is more marked in fundic than antral mucosa and is particularly marked in the region of localized ischaemic spots in the mucosa. It was concluded that this drop is due to back-diffusion of luminal acid into the mucosa and inability of the latter to buffer and dispose of this. Ischaemia upsets intramucosal acid-base balance thus compromising the mucosal capacity to cope with acid.[74]

The gastric mucosal barrier described above is another important defence mechanism. It is not broken by ischaemia alone[70] but is sensitive to 'barrier breakers,' including bile salts. Experimental studies show that a combination of bile salts, acid and ischaemia is highly ulcerogenic.[61]

In dogs, stress ulceration of the stomach induced by hypovolaemic shock can be prevented by occluding the pylorus and protecting the stomach from reflux of duodenal contents.[76] Extrapolation of these studies to the human situation is uncertain but is is quite likely that bile reflux occurs in shocked patients, especially in association with paralytic ileus.

The high metabolic rate of gastric fundic and body mucosa is reflected in its energy requirement. Hypovolaemic shock leads to depletion of ATP levels within the mucosa. This is more marked in fundus than antrum[77] and deficiency of such an energy source may explain the prevalence of lesions in that area. Energy deficiency alone may give rise to necrosis within mucosal cells without involvement of other mechanisms.[4]

The components of mucosal defence and ways in which they are compromised have been considered separately but biological systems within the body do not act in isolation and there is no reason to believe that the stomach is different. Thus the various aspects of mucosal defence act in unison, and compromise of one aspect is likely to have a 'knock-on' effect which is reflected in the remainder and eventually results in morphological damage and clinical manifestations.

To summarize the likely sequence of events in acute stress ulceration, most evidence points to shock and hypoperfusion of the gastric mucosa, albeit transient, as the precipitating factor resulting in focal mucosal ischaemia. In a highly energy dependent tissue such as gastric mucosa, necrosis may occur and, in addition, important defence mechanisms are impaired. These include impairment of surface bicarbonate and mucus secretion, intramucosal buffering capacity and endogenous prostaglandin synthesis. Furthermore, there is excessive hydrogen ion diffusion from gastric lumen into the mucosa. If mucosal blood flow is insufficient to dispose of these ions, they cause vasodilatation, a fall in local vascular resistance, histamine release, increased vascular permeability, oedema and localized haemorrhage.[36,78] Later in the patient's recovery phase regeneration of mucosal cells and resumption of acid and pepsin secretion take place. This further damages focal areas of mucosa already rendered vulnerable, resulting in ulceration and in some cases gastrointestinal haemorrhage or perforation. In addition, production of oxygen-derived free radicals associated with reperfusion probably plays a significant part in tissue damage.

Acute erosive gastritis induced by drugs

This condition bears a close morphological resemblance to stress ulceration. It is common and is likely to increase in incidence because the causative substances are freely available and are increasingly consumed for social and therapeutic purposes. The drugs principally associated with gastric toxicity are salicylates which include acetyl salicylic acid (aspirin), sodium salicylate and salicylic acid and other non-steroidal anti-inflammatory drugs (NSAID). In addition, corticosteroids are often implicated in gastric toxicity and there are occasional reports involving other drugs. Alcohol (ethanol) is also considered under this heading.

Salicylates have been recognized as a potent cause of gastric mucosal irritation, haemorrhage and ulceration for some time.[79,80] The great majority of cases cause no significant clinical symptoms, but endoscopic studies indicate that the incidence of acute drug-induced gastritis is higher than generally realized. Plain unbuffered salicylate taken in therapeutic doses for 8 days induced focal mucosal haemorrhage or ulceration in all volunteers.[81] Patients receiving long-term salicylate therapy are likely to suffer mucosal erythema and erosions, and run a real risk of developing gastric ulcer.[82] There is evidence that tolerance to continued dosage occurs and initial mucosal damage subsides.[83] Enteric-coated salicylate is reported to cause considerably less damage than plain or buffered salicylate.[81]

There is convincing evidence that alcohol taken simultaneously potentiates gastric damage caused by salicylates and other NSAIDs.[84–86]

A number of non-salicylate non-steroidal anti-inflammatory drugs are also widely used. These include indomethacin, sulindac, ibuprofen, fenoprofen, napoxen, tolmetin, mefenamic acid. Although they are less damaging to gastric mucosa than salicylates, they are all gastric irritants[87] and there are reports of these drugs causing ulceration, acute gastritis, petechiae and erosions or gastrointestinal haemorrhage.[88–91] Similar drugs including azaproprazone, piroxicam and diflunisal cause a significant increase in acute and chronic gastro-duodenal lesions in elderly patients, especially women.[92]

The scope of this problem has become apparent in recent years. Adverse reactions to NSAIDs are among the most frequently reported of drug side effects and of these gastrointestinal effects are most common.[93] NSAIDs are very widely prescribed accounting for over 20 million prescriptions per year in UK.[94] In addition, many are available without prescription. While there may be some variation in patient response and in the occurrence of side effects to different types of NSAID,[95] all drugs of this type, including phenylbutazone, are associated with a risk of serious gastrointestinal haemorrhage or perforation. The incidence of these reactions varies considerably between different drugs.[96] In addition to the stomach, the small intestine and colon may also be affected.[97–99]

While dyspepsia is the most common side effect and is usually of little consequence, it is estimated that NSAIDs are a contributory factor in almost one-third of the 10 000 cases of haematemesis and melaena occurring each year in patients aged over 60 in UK.[100] The magnitude of the problem is emphasized by Freis et al[101] who consider that gastropathy associated with NSAIDs is the most frequent and severe drug side effect in the United States. Patients with rheumatoid arthritis receiving NSAIDs are six times more likely to be hospitalized for gastrointestinal disorders than those not taking NSAIDs. The increased risk among the elderly is again strongly emphasized.

The role of steroids in the aetiology of erosive gastritis is problematical. Most investigations relate to the problem of chronic peptic ulceration following steroid therapy. The long-held view that steroids are potent ulcerogens is probably exaggerated, due to the fact that most patients receiving steroid therapy are also receiving other gastrotoxic drugs. A survey of a large number of controlled trials did not indicate that steroids are ulcerogenic.[102] A more recent study did, however, identify a small but definite increase in risk of gastrointestinal haemorrhage and peptic erosions and ulceration in association with steroid therapy.[103]

There is experimental evidence that low doses of corticosteroids can actually protect against the ulcerogenic effect of indomethacin in rats.[104] A recent survey involving a large number of elderly patients indicated that a combination of relatively low dose corticosteroids and NSAIDs carried a markedly increased risk for peptic ulceration. However patients receiving steroids alone did not appear to be at any increased risk.[105]

The observation that alcohol causes acute gastritis will not be hailed as a major scientific breakthrough by the drinking classes. Petechial mucosal haemorrhages were reported many years ago in patients dying of acute alcoholism.[106] Transient mucosal damage is probably more common than is generally realized. Palmer noted gastroscopic evidence of gastritis in 90% and erosions in almost 60% of young men following a bout of heavy drinking.[107] Even a single dose of alcohol, albeit in concentrated form, taken on an empty stomach led to mucosal erythema in all subjects examined and erosions or microscopic intramucosal haemorrhage in stomach and duodenum in over half.[108] Healing appeared to be rapid.

Macroscopic appearances

Erosive gastritis caused by anti-inflammatory drugs is similar in many ways to that due to stress ulceration except that the mucosa is generally not so congested and haemorrhagic. Erosions occur in body and antrum but tend to be fewer and less florid, and antral lesions are more common.[8,82] Erosions are often situated along the lesser curvature.[109] Drug-induced erosions tend to involve all parts of the stomach simultaneously while stress ulcers involve the fundus first and spread distally over the body over a period of 48 hours.[8] Chronic peptic ulcer is quite a common accompaniment to drug-induced disease, especially in long-term salicylate therapy.[82] Erosion and ulceration may extend into the duodenal mucosa, and haemorrhage may occur in the base of erosions. Penetration by an acute ulcer through the gastric wall, giving rise to perforation, takes place over a few days during which time many of the other erosions may have healed. In such cases the more florid appearances of acute erosive gastritis may not be seen.

Microscopic appearances

Histologically, acute drug-induced gastritis is similar to other forms of acute erosive gastritis described under stress ulceration. Erosions and ulcers are usually small and sharply demarcated. Gastritis is common in the adjacent mucosa but in the early stages of an acute ulcer there is often surprisingly little inflammatory reaction, even in the ulcer base which contains haemorrhage (Fig. 25.3). Healing occurs in a similar fashion to stress ulcers with inflammatory cell infiltration taking place within a few days, re-epithelialization of the ulcer surface and minimal fibrosis. The relative lack of inflammation related to acute lesions is reflected in chronic drug-induced ulcers. Chronic gastric ulcers with no surrounding gastritis are likely to be due to chronic salicylate use.[110]

Recently the effects of long term NSAID administration on gastric mucosal histology have been clarified. Dixon and his colleagues in Leeds[111] identified the features of foveolar hyperplasia, lamina propria oedema and paucity of inflammatory cell infiltration as being associated with bile reflux. Since then these workers have identified similar but more subtle changes in association with long-term NSAID therapy.[112] Histological changes include elongation and tortuosity of foveolae, some lamina propria oedema, relative paucity of inflammatory cells, vascular

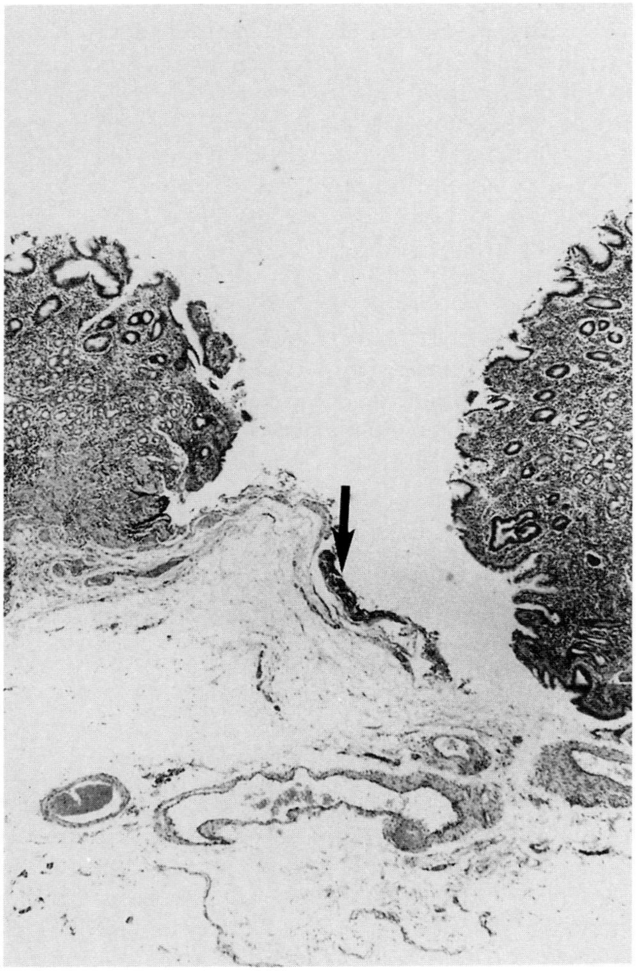

Fig. 25.3 Acute gastric ulcer following self-medication with aspirin for pain caused by a nearby chronic gastric ulcer which subsequently bled. There is some haemorrhage in the ulcer base (arrow) but no inflammatory response. The adjacent mucosa shows pre-existing mild chronic gastritis. (H&E ×20).

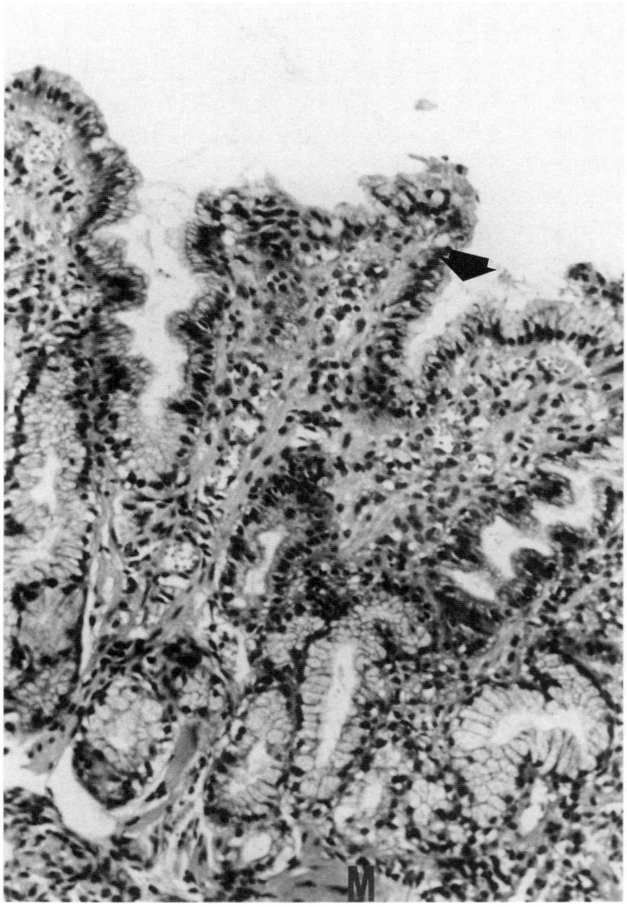

Fig. 25.4 Histological appearances in a patient taking NSAID who had concomitant *Helicobacter pylori* infection. There is foveolar hyperplasia and tortuosity, capillary congestion and nuclear crowding on the surface. Despite the presence of *Helicobacter pylori* (arrow) there is relative paucity of inflammatory cells and prominence of mesenchymal spindle cells in the lamina propria. (M = muscularis mucosa) (H&E, ×150)

congestion, nuclear crowding at the mucosal surfaces and a villiform appearance of the mucosa (Fig. 25.4). The microscopic features of alcohol-induced gastritis have also been described.[113] Approximately 20% of actively drinking alcoholics had small subepithelial mucosal haemorrhages in the proximal stomach on gastroscopy. Biopsy revealed haemorrhages in the region of the mucosa between the pits, together with mucosal oedema, regenerative changes in surface epithelium and no increased inflammatory cell infiltrate. With the exception of the haemorrhage, these changes are similar to those described in NSAID-associated reactive gastritis.

Pathogenesis of drug-induced gastritis

Salicylates in acid solution damage the alkaline mucous barrier on the surface of the gastric mucosa, thus reducing the pH gradient across the mucous layer and exposing surface epithelial cells to significantly lower pH levels.[32] It has been suggested that salicyates cause increased exfoliation of cells from gastric mucosa and that ulceration may occur when the rate of exfoliation exceeds regeneration.[109] Experimental evidence shows that chronic aspirin ingestion stimulates epithelial cell proliferation in the rat fundus but not the antrum. This has been postulated as evidence of a protective adaptive process in fundic mucosa.[114]

The effects of salicylates on the gastric mucosal barrier have been extensively investigated and it is well established that they act as 'barrier breakers', increasing back-diffusion of hydrogen ions from the lumen into the mucosa.[36] Topical application of salicylates and hydrochloric acid to dog gastric mucosa causes vasodilatation via histamine release and possibly via direct action of the acid upon mucosal vessels.[78] The role of focal ischaemia is uncertain. Studies in dogs show no evidence of mucosal ischaemia following application of salicylates in hydrochloric acid.[115] In contrast, other work on rats indicates local cessation of blood flow through mucosal microcirculation under similar circumstances.[116]

The effect of drugs on prostaglandin formation probably plays an important part in development of erosive gastritis. Prostaglandins are formed within gastric mucosa and their protective effects have already been mentioned. Salicylates and other NSAIDs all appear to inhibit endogenous prostaglandin secretion.[87] The possibility that damage caused by NSAIDs is mediated via inhibition of endogenous prostaglandin synthesis is underlined by the protective effect of prostaglandin treatment against salicylate-induced gastric injury.[46,47] This theory is supported by evidence that in man the extent of gastric mucosal damage by NSAIDs is correlated with the degree of inhibition of prostaglandin synthesis.[117]

Pre-existing gastritis may play a part in the development of drug-induced acute gastritis. An association exists between gastritis, intestinal metaplasia and NSAID-induced lesions.[118] This raises the possibility that gastritis may render the mucosa more susceptible to damage by anti-inflammatory drugs. Recent evidence supports this in that chronic active gastritis associated with *Helicobacter pylori* infection appears to increase the severity of NSAID-induced gastropathy as manifested by mucosal haemorrhage and increased activity of gastritis.[119]

There is some evidence that in animal models NSAIDs reduce gastric mucosal blood flow and this may be another important pathogenetic factor.[120] Reduction in gastroduodenal mucosal blood flow has also been recorded in humans receiving NSAIDs over a long period.[121] NSAIDs influence leucocyte aggregation and adherence to blood vessel endothelium.[122] Kitahora and Guth[123] suggested that thrombus formation within mucosal capillaries and capillary constriction may contribute to slowing of blood flow within the mucosa and observed white thrombus formation in small vessels before cessation of blood flow. The importance of neutrophils in initiating NSAID-induced mucosal injury has been supported by experimental evidence. In rabbits subjected to intragastric instillation of indomethacin, pretreatment with monoclonal antibody against adhesion molecules on leucocytes and vascular endothelial cells reduced margination of leucocytes in mucosal capillaries, vaso-congestion and gastric mucosal damage.[124] Similarly in rats indomethacin-induced damage to gastric mucosa was reduced by oral dexamethasone and it was postulated that this was due to inhibition of neutrophil infiltration and of leukotriene B_4 release (a chemotactic agent) by antral mucosa.[104]

Experimental studies indicate that alcohol-induced gastric damage increases in proportion to the concentration of alcohol applied to the gastric mucosa[125,126] as well as the dose ingested.[127] Alcohol in concentration of 10% or less appears to cause little damage, but in the dog 12.5% alcohol applied to the stomach produces hyperaemia and occasional petechial haemorrhages. The extent of mucosal haemorrhage increases when higher concentration is applied. At concentrations of 40% and above, alcohol causes destruction of surface epithelium and separation of cell junctions in focal areas, accompanied by capillary disruption and haemorrhage[126] with outpouring of mucus and fibrin on to the damaged mucosal surface.[34,126] Alcohol also stimulates gastric acid secretion[125] and the presence of acid increases alcohol-induced mucosal damage.[128] In animals restitution of the mucosal surface following alcohol-induced damage appears to be remarkably rapid.[34,127,128]

Parallel with morphological damage there is evidence that alcohol in concentrations of 14% or higher damages the gastric mucosal barrier[125] causing altered fluxes of sodium, potassium and hydrogen ions. This concentration of alcohol is exceeded in many popular drinks. The synergistic effect of salicylates and alcohol is underlined by the severe effect which the two drugs have on potential difference across the gastric mucosa in man.[129]

In addition to damaging surface mucosal cells it has been suggested that alcohol or its metabolites may have a direct damaging effect on mucosal vasculature.[128] This is supported by a study on rats in which application of high concentrations of alcohol causes focal increase in vascular permeability within the gastric mucosa. Mucosal haemorrhage and erosion subsequently develop within these areas of vascular damage.[130]

Of necessity much of the investigative work on the pathogenesis of ethanol-induced mucosal damage has been carried out in experimental animals and in many cases very high concentrations of alcohol, beyond the range of even the most ardent human tippler, have been instilled. Thus a question mark must remain over the extrapolation of these studies to the human situation. However, endoscopic studies have indicated mild hyperaemia and occasional erosions even after ingestion of modest amounts of alcohol.[86,108]

There is also experimental evidence that concentrations of alcohol in the stomach similar to those achieved during acute intoxication can increase neutrophil adherence to endothelial cells of the gastric mucosal microvasculature. In addition release of neutrophil proteases is induced. Thus neutrophil-mediated cell injury may play a part in alcohol-induced injury to the gastric mucosa as well as NSAID-induced injury.[131]

While alcohol and anti-inflammatory drugs are those most often studied in association with gastritis, other types of medication may affect the stomach. Cytotoxic drugs have a profound effect on the gut, especially the small intestine. Sequential chemotherapeutic regimens using a variety of cytotoxic agents may, however, cause gastric ulceration and erosion in a significant proportion of patients, probaby due to the action of cytosine arabinoside, which appears more toxic to the gut than cyclophosphamide, duanorubicin or vincristine.[132] Histological changes are centred around the proliferating zone at the base of gastric mucosal pits, and loss of mucus secretion, bizarre regenerating cells and glandular dilatation may be seen in addition to ulceration. Differentiated parietal and chief cells are spared.

Oral ferrous sulphate has long been known to cause transient nausea. In therapeutic doses it causes mucosal erythema and occasional erosions.[133]

GASTRITIS ASSOCIATED WITH INFECTIVE AGENTS

Helicobacter pylori-associated gastritis

There has been a vast amount of recent investigation into *Helicobacter pylori* (*H. pylori*) and its role in gastritis. Intragastric bacteria have been noted periodically over a number of years.[134–136] However, Warren[137] described an association between the presence of small curved and S-shaped bacilli on the surface of gastric mucosa and active chronic gastritis. At the same time his colleague Marshall described culture of the bacteria and their morphology showing them to be spiral shaped and flagellated.[138] More details of events surrounding identification of the organism have recently been published.[139] The organism was originally named *Campylobacter pyloridis* then *Campylobacter pylori*. It was subsequently shown that it is not a member of the campylobacter genus[140] and the name *Helicobacter pylori* was suggested by Goodwin et al.[141] This has now been universally accepted.

Following the initial report implicating *H. pylori* as a cause of chronic gastritis the same workers reported that it is also frequently present in patients with peptic ulcer.[142] These associations have subsequently been confirmed in numerous studies from different parts of the world.[143–147]

Microscopic appearances

H. pylori is a curved or spiral shaped organism measuring 2–4 μm in length with marked urease activity. The organisms may be present anywhere in the stomach but are found most consistently in the antrum.[137,148] Histological examination shows chronic gastritis involving the superficial mucosa. The lamina propria contains increased numbers of plasma cells and lymphocytes. Variable numbers of polymorphs — indicators of active inflammation — are seen within the lamina propria mainly around the base of the mucosal pits and in severe cases infiltrating between epithelial cells of the gastric pits or the surface mucosa (Fig. 25.5). Quantitative studies have confirmed the subjective impression of increased inflammatory cell infiltration in the presence of *Helicobacter pylori*.[149] The inflammation seldom extends deeply into the mucosa and in the early stages at any rate parietal cells, pyloric glands and neuroendocrine cells are largely unaffected.[150] Thus *H. pylori* gastritis is more often superficial than atrophic. Lymphoid follicle formation (Fig. 25.6) in the deeper parts of the mucosa is frequently found in *H. pylori* gastritis. The intensity of the superficial gastritis is very variable and there is poor correlation between *H. pylori* gastritis, symptoms and endoscopic appearances, in that many patients are asymptomatic and appear to have normal mucosa on endoscopy. Thus the diagnosis of this type of gastritis is often dependent on histology.

It is the author's subjective impression that in children the mucosal inflammatory response to *H. pylori* infection is often less intense than in adults. This is supported to some extent by others who found that the active component, i.e. the polymorph response, is minimal in the younger age group.[151]

The organisms are often visible on H&E staining. However they are more easily seen with a Giemsa stain, which is useful in detecting small numbers. The Warthin-Starry silver stain demontrates *H. pylori* well (Fig. 25.7)

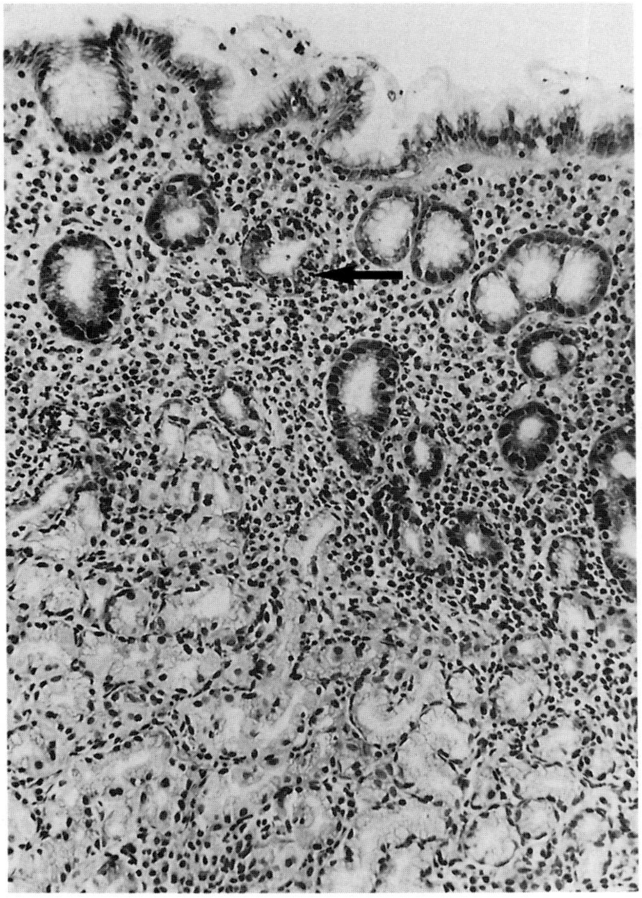

Fig. 25.5 *Helicoabcter pylori*-associated gastritis. There are increased numbers of lymphocytes and plasma cells in the lamina propria of the superficial mucosa. Polymorphs, indicating active gastritis, are seen infiltrating between the epithelial cells of the gastric pits (arrow) as well as in the lamina propria. (H&E, ×128)

but is capricious and expensive and seldom used in routine work. The curved or spiral configuration of the organisms is best illustrated on scanning electron microscopy (Fig. 25.8). Transmission electron microscopy shows them to measure approximately 2.5 μm × 0.5 μm with 4–7 sheathed flagellae at one, and occasionally at both, ends.[138,152]

While *H. pylori* are found most frequently within the mucus layer and especially in the gastric pits,[153] electron microscopy shows that organisms may become adherent to the surface epithelial cells,[154,155] and may also invade between these cells. Bacterial adherence and intercellular colonization tends to be associated with increased epithelial damage ranging from loss of mucin to surface erosions.[155,156] These findings support a pathogenic role for the organism.

While there is a strong association between active superficial gastritis and the presence of *H. pylori* some workers have reported the organism in small numbers of patients in whom the mucosa is histologically normal.[157,158]

H. pylori is not found on normal small intestinal mucosa nor on foci of intestinal metaplasia within the stomach although it may be present on adjacent gastric mucosa. Colonization may be patchy and increasing degrees of atrophic gastritis (characterized by intestinal metaplasia) are associated with decreasing prevalence of *H. pylori* in both body and antrum.[158] The organism is seldom found in the stomach following gastric surgery and subsequent development of bile reflux.[159] Even in the absence of previous gastric surgery, bile reflux leads to clearing of the organism from mucosa and replacement of the typical histology of *H. pylori* gastritis with that of reactive gastritis. *H. pylori* are not commonly seen in these circumstances.[160] A combination of *H. pylori* infection and bile reflux in the stomach may favour the formation of intestinal metaplasia.[161]

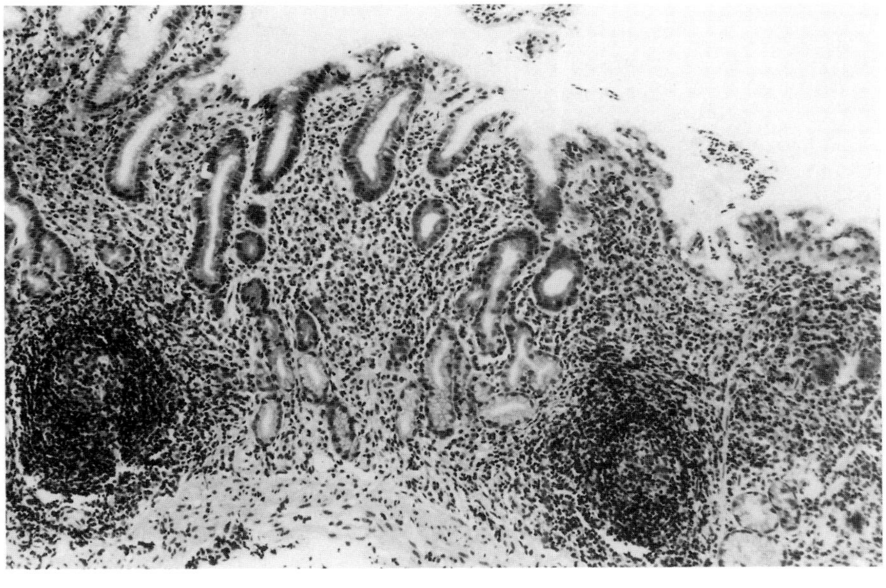

Fig. 25.6 *Helicobacter pylori* gastritis showing prominent lymphoid follicles in the deeper part of the mucosa. (H&E, ×75)

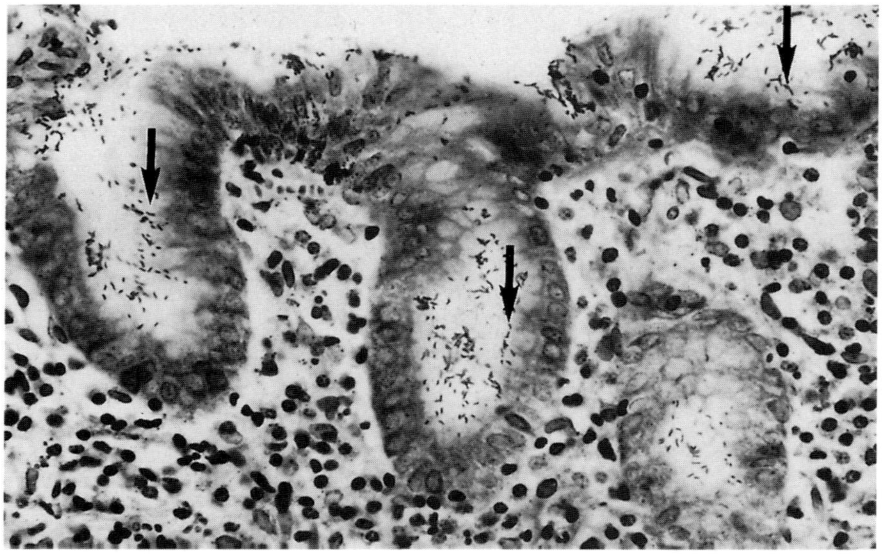

Fig. 25.7 *Helicobacter pylori*-associated gastritis. Typical distribution of organisms on the surface of the mucosa and within gastric pits. Organisms are present on the surface of epithelial cells and within the adherent mucus layer (arrows). At this magnification, the S-shaped or curved configuration of the organisms is not discernible. (Warthin-Starry, ×300)

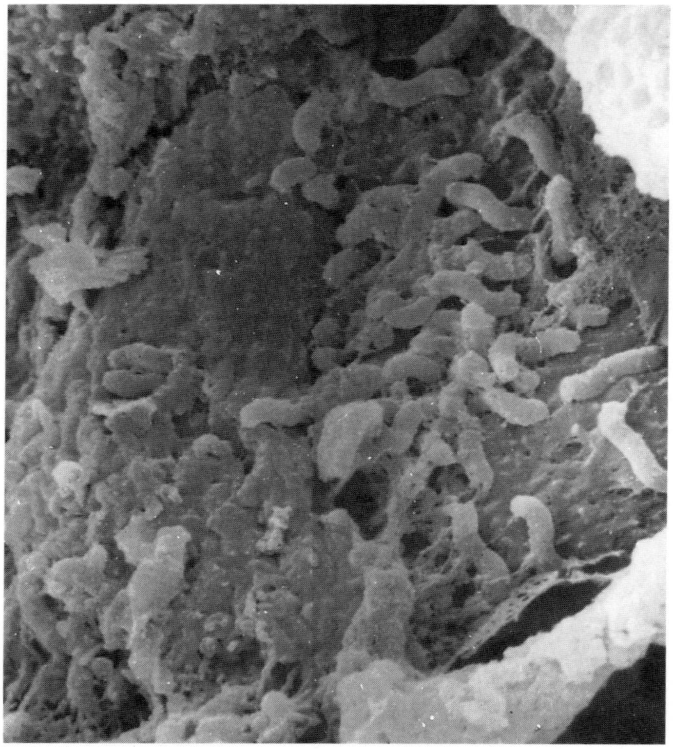

Fig. 25.8 *Helicobacter pylori*-associated gastritis. Scanning electron micrograph showing bacilli on the surface of inflamed gastric mucosa. Their S-shaped configuration is clearly seen. (×8075) (Courtesy of Dr HMH Kamel, Pathology Department, Royal Victoria Hospital, Belfast)

Epidemiology of H. pylori infection and evidence for pathogenetic effect

The presence of bacteria on gastric mucosa does not prove that they are pathogenic, but a considerable body of evidence has accumulated to this effect. The close association between *H. pylori* infection and peptic ulcer and chronic gastritis in adults has already been discussed. The same associations apply in children and teenagers with regard to gastritis.[162–164] In childhood the association between *H. pylori* infection and duodenal ulcer is less strong than in adults.[165] In the elderly (over 70 years of age) the association between *H. pylori* infection and peptic ulceration is also less strong. Use of NSAIDs appears to be an important risk factor for peptic ulcer in this age group.[166]

Peptic ulceration is however, a multifactorial disease and *H. pylori* infection is only one of the pathogenic factors. The majority of people infected with the organism appear to suffer little or no clinical disease. This is indicated by epidemiological surveys showing that infection is exceedingly widespread and that many patients are asymptomatic. Studies on healthy asymptomatic volunteers indicate that 32% are infected by *H. pylori* with increased prevalence of infection in older age groups.[167] A strong association between infection and chronic gastritis was confirmed despite lack of symptoms. Some recent larger studies found overall rates of seroprevalence of antibodies to *H. pylori* in the region of over 50%.[168,169] These studies were carried out in developed countries and again showed increased prevalence of infection with increasing age. Studies in some developing nations indicate higher rates of infection. Seventy-five percent of patients examined in Rawanda had *H. pylori* infection.[170] Serological surveys in other developing countries also indicate that well over half the population carry *H. pylori* and that infection among young people is often much more prevalent in these regions.[171,172,173] In northern Nigeria over 80% of the population have serological evidence of infection yet the incidence of peptic ulcer is low.[174]

Thus in the great majority of cases *H. pylori* infection appears to be associated with few or no clinical symptoms and while the prevalence of infection is very high in patients with peptic ulcer, only a small proportion of infected patients appear to develop this condition. Cynics may well suggest the organism is not pathogenic and merely an innocent bystander on inflamed gastric mucosa.

However the weight of evidence in favour of pathogenicity is very considerable and even 'non-believers' have accepted this view to some extent.[175] Perhaps the most convincing evidence that *H. pylori* infection is indeed important in the pathogenesis of chronic gastritis and peptic ulcer is the effect of eradication of the organism on the disease process. Eradication is associated with significant improvement in histologically assessed gastritis (Fig. 25.9).[143,154,176] This has been confirmed using the detailed and semi-quantitative Sydney system of histological classification of gastritis.[177] Eradication of bacteria for 6 months abolished polymorph infiltration within the mucosa and markedly reduced lymphoid follicle formation.

Duodenal ulcer can frequently be healed by use of gastric acid suppression therapy. When treatment is discontinued, however, there is a very high rate of recurrence. When *H. pylori* are eradicated, not only do the ulcers heal but the rate of recurrence is greatly reduced. Rauws and Tytgat[178] reported no cases of ulcer recurrence after elimination of the organism while others have noted a significant reduction in longterm recurrence rate[179,180,181] or recurrence only in patients reinfected with *H. pylori*.

There are reports indicating that gastritis can be transmitted between patients undergoing gastroscopy via contaminated instruments.[182,183] The illness is characterized by nausea, vomiting, upper abdominal pain and hypochlorhydria and there is histological evidence of gastritis. No infective organism was identified at the time but retrospective examination of gastric biopsy material from some of the patients revealed *H. pylori* organisms.[184] Iatrogenic spread of *H. pylori* during repeated endoscopy and possibly via biopsy forceps has more recently been confirmed and infection was again associated with transient hypochlorhydria.[185] On this occasion the organisms were present two years after infection and were accompanied by chronic active gastritis with lymphoid follicle formation.

Further evidence of pathogenicity of *H. pylori* is derived from volunteer studies. Not surprisingly, these are limited. Administration of a culture of *H. pylori* to a healthy volunteer resulted in histological gastritis and temporary colonization of gastric mucosa by identical organisms. However the organisms disappeared and gastritis subsided after 10–14 days. Thus chronic gastritis did not ensue.[184] The authors postulate that if the bacteria are not eradicated by immune processes, hypochlorhydria and chronic gastritis may develop. This is borne out by a similar study[186] in which ingestion of bacteria led to upper abdominal pain and vomiting. This was followed by active gastritis and transient hypochlorhydria. In this case bacteria and gastritis persisted for some years despite repeated treatments with single antibiotics. The organism was finally eradicated using triple therapy — bismuth, metronidazole and tetracycline. This was followed by progressive resolution of the gastritis which disappeared over a period of several months.[187]

Patients with *H. pylori* infection have circulating antibodies (usually IgG) to the organism. There is good correlation between serology and histological findings and thus serology provides a useful alternative means of detecting

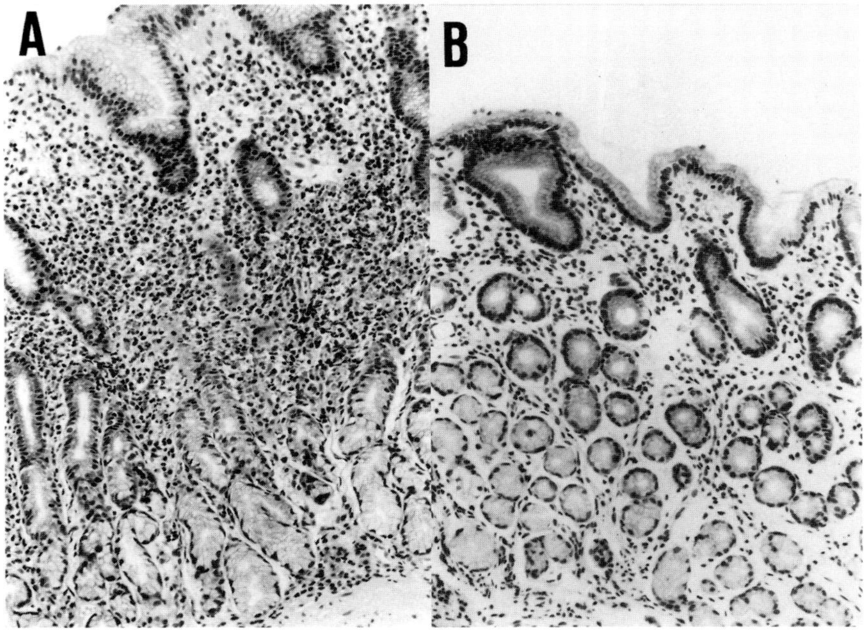

Fig. 25.9 Effect of treatment on *Helicobacter pylori* gastritis. **A** shows active chronic gastritis before treatment; **B** shows a biopsy from the same patient two months later after eradication of the organism. Polymorphs have disappeared from the mucosa and chronic inflammatory cell infiltration is much reduced. (both H&E, original magnification ×150)

infection and screening.[188–190] Raised levels of IgA antibodies are found in gastric juice and coating of organisms by IgA in all cases and by IgM and IgG in the presence of neutrophils, i.e. active gastritis, has been demonstrated, providing evidence of stimulation of inflammtory response by the organism.[191] It was notable that bacteria lying deep within gastric pits were not coated by immunoglobulin and may thus be protected from the host immune response.

Mechanisms of pathogenicity

While there is considerable evidence of the association between *H. pylori* infection and gastritis and peptic ulceration, the pathogenetic mechanisms are not well understood. Bacterial colonization of gastric mucosa can be associated with little or no morphological evidence of damage to underlying mucosal cells.[153] However there are a number of reports of damage to surface epithelium resulting in loss of mucin, loss of single cells and microerosions in addition to the more common inflammatory cell infiltration.[192–194] This appears to occur only in a minority of cases but such damage to mucosal surface cells is likely to increase the risk of subsequent ulceration. Degenerative changes in surface epithelium are shown in Figure 25.10.

There is in vitro evidence that *H. pylori* can damage the integrity of the gastric mucous gel and diminish its protective effect.[195] Mucus secretion in response to secretagogues such as inflammatory mediators may be significantly impaired and consequently the protection afforded by mucus to the mucosal surface may be diminished.[196] *H. pylori* has marked urease activity but there is little evidence that this or the resulting breakdown products such as ammonia or mono-N-chloramine have a toxic effect.[197] Very high levels of gastric juice ammonia are reached in uraemic patients infected with *H. pylori* but this is not associated with increased mucosal inflammation or damage.[198]

Although *H. pylori* does not colonize normal duodenal mucosa, plausible theories have been put forward to explain the strong association between infection and duodenal ulceration. There is evidence of diffuse acute inflammation in the duodenal mucosa in patients with duodenal ulcer even where the mucosa is endoscopically normal.[199] Goodwin has put forward the 'leaking roof' theory,[200] suggesting that islands of gastric metaplasia in duodenal mucosa become colonized by *H. pylori* already present in the stomach. The resulting inflammation and impaired mucus secretion allows gastric acid and pepsin to initiate erosion and subsequent ulceration. Gastric metaplasia is common, it was found in almost one-third of a large series of dyspeptic patients.[201] It occurs in randomly placed foci in duodenal mucosa close to the pylorus and the area involved by metaplasia appears to be increased in the presence of *H. pylori* infection. Colonization of these foci by the organism is likely to increase duodenitis and thereby increase the likelihood of mucosal damage and ulceration.

Why only a tiny proportion of patients infected with *H. pylori* develop peptic ulcers remains unsolved. The organism shows an unusual degree of genomic heterogeneity and there is a possibility that some strains are more pathogenic or ulcerogenic than others. This may be associated with cytotoxin release by some strains of organism resulting in degeneration of surface epithelium.[202] The expression of a protein of molecular weight 120 kDa by some strains of *H. pylori* have been related to more severe

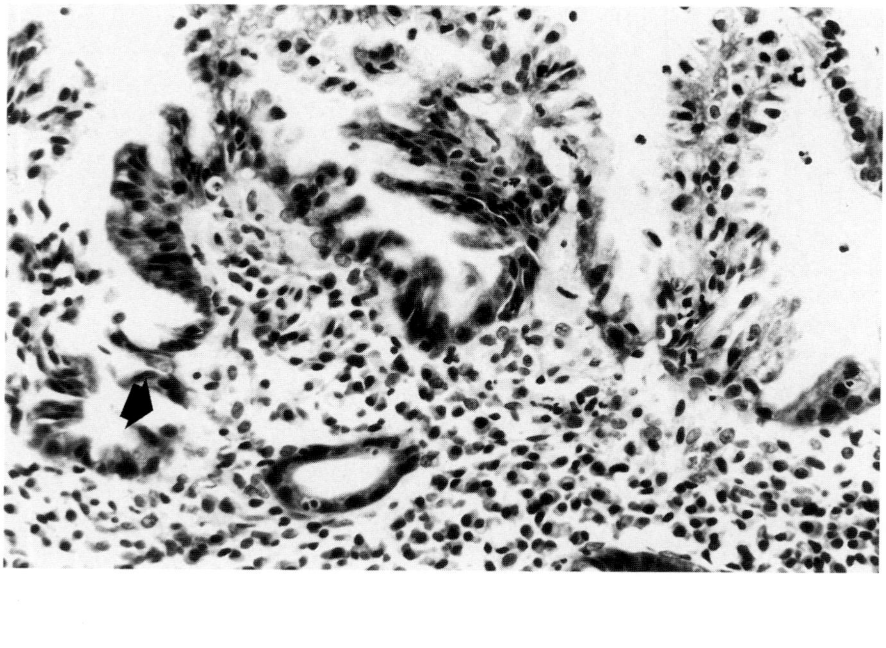

Fig. 25.10 Degenerative changes in the surface epithelium in *Helicobacter pylori* gastritis. There is reduction in mucin secretion, tufting of epithelial cells and loss of individual surface cells (arrow). (H&E, ×180)

gastritis, epithelial cell degeneration and increased tendency to peptic ulceration.[203] Other workers[204] do not support the idea that some strains are more ulcerogenic than others and contend that the tendency to develop ulcers is due to host factors which are as yet uncertain. Failure to secrete ABO blood group antigens is one such factor which is associated with increased tendency to duodenal ulceration but this is not related to susceptibility to *H. pylori* infection.[205]

Patients infected with *H. pylori* have slightly raised basal and markedly raised post-prandial serum gastrin levels.[206,207] This may be mediated via mononuclear cells involved in the gastritis rather than by the bacteria or bacterial products.[208] Hypergastrinaemia may be important in the pathogenesis of peptic ulcer and may explain the increased gastric acid output which is a feature of duodenal ulcer disease. There is evidence that while healthy patients with *H. pylori* have increased gastrin-mediated acid release, those with *H. pylori* and duodenal ulcer have even higher acid levels. Eradication of the organism markedly reduces both gastrinaemia and acid secretion.[209]

Spread of the organism

The mode of spread of *H. pylori* is undetermined. There is some evidence that bacterial contamination of water supply is an important source of infection, at least in developing countries, although infection is also correlated with low socio-economic status.[210] Faecal-oral spread is also likely. This is supported by isolation and culture of the organism from faeces.[211]

There is considerable evidence of person to person and intrafamilial spread. Parents and siblings of infected children are much more likely to have serological evidence of *H. pylori* infection than those of non-infected children.[212,165] Use of DNA typing showed an identical strain of organism in at least two members of three out of four families studied in which the child was the index patient,[213] thus suggesting a degree of intrafamilial spread. In an ulcer-prone family three out of nine members harboured variants of a single strain of *H. pylori*.[214] The organism has also been cultured from dental plaque.[215]

Conclusions

In conclusion, *H. pylori* infection of the human gastric mucosa is widely recognized. Histological identification of the organism is the 'gold standard' method of diagnosis but serological detection of *H. pylori* antibodies and breath testing after ingestion of C^{14} labelled urea are satisfactory alternative methods of diagnosis.

Infection is common especially in developing countries and prevalence of infection increases with age. Only a small proportion of children are affected in developed nations but this is much higher in developing countries where infection appears to occur early. The mode of spread of the organism is uncertain but there is evidence of faecal-oral and intrafamilial spread.

H. pylori is found throughout the stomach but especially in the antrum. It does not occur in normal duodenal mucosa or on islands of intestinal metaplasia in the stomach. The majority of infected patients are asymptomatic or have only mild symptoms. However the organism appears to be an important pathogenic factor in active chronic superficial gastritis and peptic ulceration. Over 90% of adults with duodenal ulcer harbour the organism, the association with chronic gastric ulcer is less strong in that 60–70% of patients carry *H. pylori*. In children and in the elderly a smaller proportion of patients with peptic ulcer are infected and in the latter group NSAID ingestion is an important pathogenic factor in ulceration.

Much investigation is at present being carried out into the possible association between chronic *H. pylori* infection and development of gastric cancer. There is evidence to support such a link. Comparison of areas with high and low gastric cancer mortality rates showed significant correlation between prevalence of *H. pylori* antibodies and gastric cancer mortality.[216] Serological evidence of long-standing *H. pylori* infection is associated with increased risk of gastric carcinoma (excluding tumours of the gastro-oesophageal junction).[217,218] The possibility of a link between the two conditions has been discussed in detail[219,220] and likely pathogenic pathways have been suggested. Histological studies support a link suggesting a relatively small increased risk of gastric cancer with chronic non-atrophic gastritis and greater risk in atrophic gastritis with intestinal metaplasia. Both types of gastritis are associated with long-term *H. pylori* infection.[221]

However there is no doubt that, like peptic ulcer, gastric cancer is a multifactorial disease and some evidence does not support a link beween *H. pylori* infection and malignancy. The close association between the infection and peptic ulceration, especially duodenal ulceration, is well accepted. There is however no recognized association between peptic ulcer and gastric cancer, indeed peptic ulceration appears to be associated with decreased risk of carcinoma.[217] In some areas of Africa where *H. pylori* infection is almost universal and childhood infection, which is quoted as a significant risk factor, is rife, the incidence of gastric cancer is very low.[222] These topics are discussed in more detail in the chapters on chronic gastritis and gastric carcinoma.

The relatively common presence of lymphoid follicles in *H. pylori* gastritis has already been mentioned and is considered to be a manifestation of immune response to the presence of the organism.[223,224] This mucosa-associated lymphoid tissue (MALT) may be the background from which low-grade B cell gastric malignant lymphoma arises.[225] *H. pylori* infection is very common in gastric lymphoma. The postulated associated is also supported by evidence that cells from such a lymphoma are stimulated by the presence of *H. pylori* via activation of T cells[226] and that eradication of *H. pylori* may lead to regression of these low-grade lymphomas.[227]

Gastrospirillum hominis

Another spiral organism has been reported in the human stomach which, like *H. pylori*, is associated with active chronic gastritis.[228] The name suggested for this bacterium by the team who first identified it is *Gastrospirillum hominis*.[229] Morphologically similar organisms have also been cultured.[230] These workers pointed out that similar organisms are commonly found in the stomachs of cats and dogs.

Gastrospirillum hominis is larger than *H. pylori*, measuring up to 7.5 μm in length with up to 8 easily identified spirals (Fig. 25.11). It may be found on gastric antral or body mucosa and in the human is associated with dyspepsia and active gastritis. Like *H. pylori* it is found within or beneath the mucus layer close to the mucosal surface. It is usually visible on H&E staining. Electron microscopy shows that this organism also possesses flagellae.[229,231] *Gastrospirillum hominis* infection is rare in humans in comparison with the widespread *H. pylori*. While spread from infected pets is suspected, there is little evidence for this in many of the reported cases. Eradication of the organism has been achieved following antibiotic therapy and this was followed by alleviation of symptoms and return of the gastric mucosal histology to normal.[231]

Phlegmonous (suppurative) gastritis

Phlegmonous gastritis is the term used to describe acute suppurative inflammation of the stomach wall. The disease was much more common in the pre-antibiotic era and the largest reported series date from that time.[232,233] The condition is rare but reports continue to appear.[234–236] With the spread of AIDS, it is likely that the number of cases may increase. Recent reports involve a patient likely to have had AIDS-related complex and another associated with HIV seroconversion.[237,238]

Most cases involve patients in the 30–60 age group, but there is a wide age range. Clinical features are usually of rapid onset with nausea, vomiting and upper abdominal pain and tenderness, accompanied by fever, signs of peritoneal irritation, polymorphonuclear leucocytosis and sometimes positive blood culture. Concomitant bacterial infection is often present in a variety of sites including septicaemia, appendix, peritoneum, kidneys and meninges. Streptococcus is the organism most frequently implicated[233] but staphylococcus, *E. coli*, *H. influenzae* and other organisms have also been isolated. Infection with gas-forming organisms resulting in gas within the stomach wall may occur. This variant of phlegmonous gastritis is known as emphysematous gastritis.

Inflammation within the stomach wall may be localized, in which case it is usually limited to the pyloric canal, or diffuse involving the entire stomach.[234] On macroscopic examination, the inflamed area of the wall is thickened. The mucosa is usually intact, although the longitudinal folds may be lost and the serosal surface covered with a fibrinous exudate.[233,234] Pus may exude from the gastric wall on slight pressure. The inflammation and thickening of the wall rarely extends beyond the cardia or pylorus.

Histology shows acute inflammation, principally in the submucosa of the stomach wall (Fig. 25.12) but often extending into the muscle coat and the serosa. The submucosa in particular is oedematous, and intramural abscesses

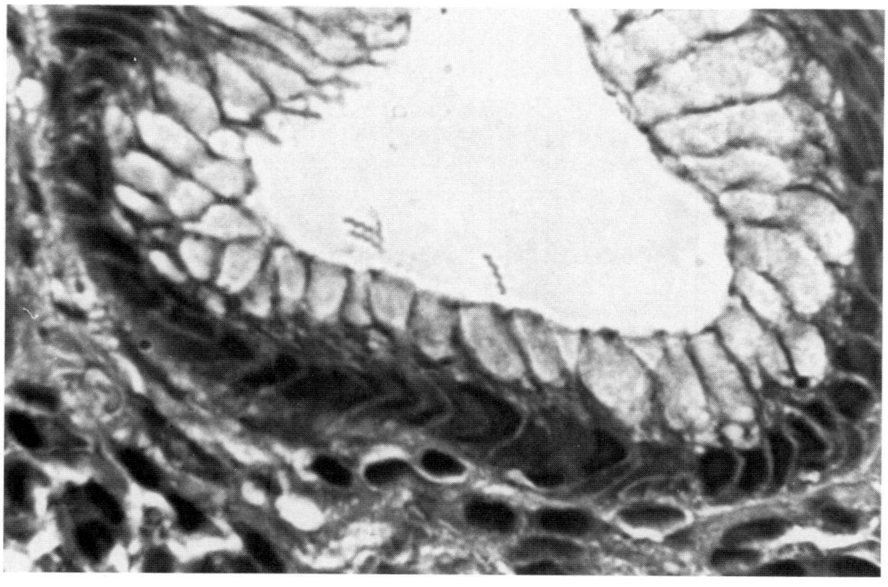

Fig. 25.11 *Gastrospirillum hominis* on the surface of gastric mucosa. The organism is larger and has more obvious spirals than *H. pylori*. (H&E oil immersion, ×800)

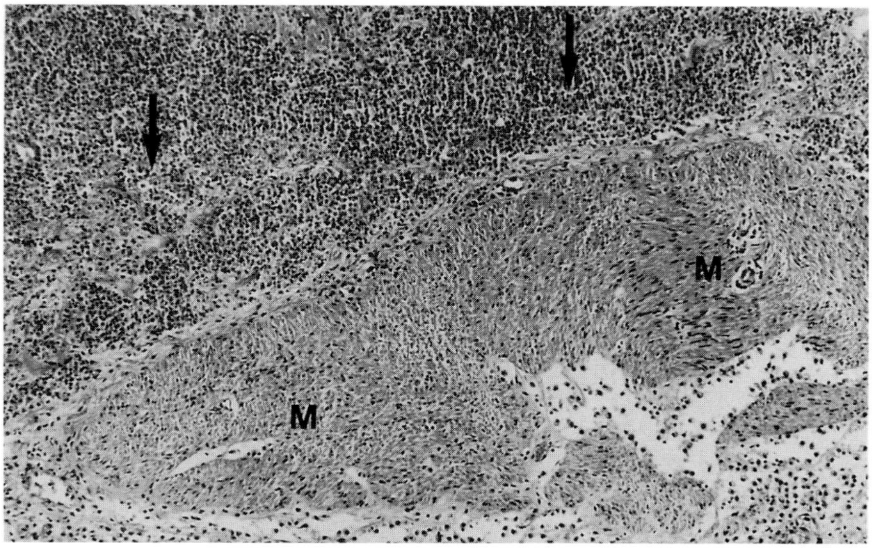

Fig. 25.12 Phlegmonous gastritis. Pus (arrow) within the submucosa and muscle wall (M) of the stomach. The inflammatory infiltrate contains many macrophages as well as polymorphs and lymphocytes. (H&E, ×60).

may form. The gastric mucosa is usually intact and shows relatively little inflammation.[234,239] Occasionally a chronic form develops within the stomach wall due to organization of the acute inflammatory exudate and fibrosis.[240]

The pathogenesis of the condition is variable. In some cases there is pre-existing gastric pathology which might permit entry of microorganisms.[233,239] In others the gastritis appears to arise in association with systemic infection, or as a complication of infection elsewhere, such as endocarditis,[241] puerperal sepsis[239] or pharyngitis.[234] In some patients, however, no predisposing factors are apparent.

The condition is rare and clinical diagnosis is difficult. Mortality is high[234,235] but surgical intervention with drainage of pus or partial gastrectomy involving the affected area, accompanied by antibiotic therapy, appears to be the most effective form of treatment.

Opportunistic infections

The incidence of infection by unusual opportunistic organisms has increased markedly recently, largely because of increasing numbers of patients who are immunocompromized due to a variety of reasons, such as malignancy, diabetes, immunosuppressive therapy, primary immunodeficiency and spread of the acquired immunodeficiency syndrome (AIDS). The majority of AIDS patients develop gastrointestinal infection at some stage. The oesophagus, small intestine and colon are the usual sites but the stomach is also affected.

Opportunistic infections most often encountered in the stomach in such cases are candida, phycomycosis and cytomegalovirus (CMV). Fungal infection is discussed later. While oesophageal ulceration is the commonest manifestation of CMV infection in the upper gastrointestinal tract in AIDS patients, the stomach may also be involved. The virus is common in patients with HIV infection and has been identified in gastrointestinal biopsies in 13% of patients with AIDS.[242]

CMV infection in the stomach is associated with erosions and ulcers[243,244] and occasionally with perforation and fistula formation.[245] Erosions and ulcers may be single or multiple. Clinical manifestations in such patients are often dominated by diarrhoea, due to infection of small intestine or colon, but upper abdominal pain and haematemesis may suggest gastric involvement.[246] Gastric involvement is usually secondary to disseminated CMV infection, but this is not always so.[244] Furthermore, while most patients who contract CMV infection are immunocompromized, this is not invariable.[247]

Histological examination shows that infected cells are markedly enlarged. The nucleus contains a characteristic large inclusion which is amphiophilic. In some cells the intranuclear inclusion is surrounded by a clear halo, but this is often absent. The nucleolus may be retained. Intracytoplasmic inclusions are also visible but are less prominent; they are much smaller than intranuclear inclusions and are usually basophilic (Fig. 25.13). Inclusions are found within mucosal cells adjacent to ulcers and in more distant intact mucosa. They are also found within endothelial cells and fibroblasts in granulation tissue in the ulcer base. Gastric biopsy is of great value in reaching the diagnosis[244] but may require painstaking search before pathognomonic inclusion bodies are detected. The problem is compounded in AIDS patients who may carry the virus without normal antibody response and in whom evidence of infection in tissue may be very difficult to find.[248] In many cases, the classic large intranuclear inclusions are not seen and infected cells may show a variety of less obvious changes. Immunocytochemistry using anti CMV antibody is invaluable in identifying infected cells

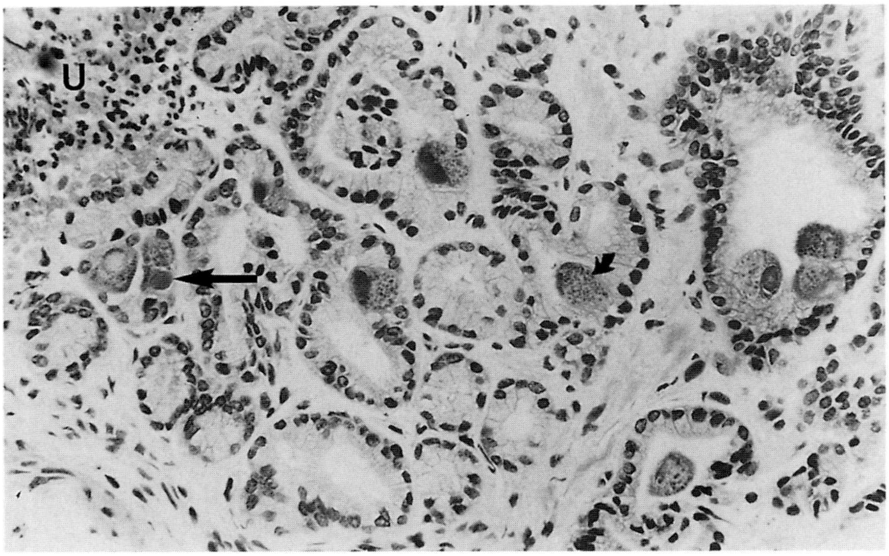

Fig. 25.13 Cytomegalovirus infection of gastric mucosa adjacent to acute ulcer (U). Infected epithelial cells are markedly enlarged and large intranuclear inclusions are present, some of which are surrounded by a clear halo (straight arrow). Much smaller intracytoplasmic inclusions are also seen (curved arrow). (H&E, ×192).

and the polymerase chain reaction (PCR) may also be useful.[242]

Apart from fungal and cytomegalovirus infection, the stomach is not frequently affected by the myriad opportunistic agents which may infect the immunocompromized patient. Other herpes viruses most frequently affect the oesophagus and may cause pain and ulceration. In AIDS patients this is associated with more common buccal or peri-oral herpetic infection.[248] Occasional cases of herpes simplex and herpes zoster gastritis occur in patients who are terminally ill.[249,250] Examination reveals small superficial plaque-like or linear ulcers in gastric mucosa, but the characteristic eosinophilic intranuclear inclusion bodies surrounded by a zone of pallor may be difficult to find on histological examination. Immunohistochemistry using specific antiviral antibody is very useful in identifying infected cells. Cytological examination of gastric mucosal brushings may also facilitate the diagnosis.[249]

Cryptosporidiosis frequently infects the small intestine in immunocompromized patients but on occasion may be found in other sites such as biliary tract and stomach.[251] Haemorrhagic gastritis and gastric involvement by *Toxoplasma gondii* in a case of generalized toxoplasmosis in a patient with AIDS has been noted.[252]

GASTRITIS ASSOCIATED WITH PHYSICAL AND CORROSIVE CHEMICAL AGENTS

Effects of freezing

For a short period after 1960 the technique of gastric freezing was used as a treatment for chronic pyloric or duodenal ulcer. Ethyl alcohol at a temperature of –17°C to –20°C was circulated through a balloon placed in the stomach for one hour.[253] In a study of partial gastrectomy specimens obtained due to recurrence of symptoms or bleeding, little evidence of damage was seen following an interval of two weeks or longer after freezing. Occasionally the technique itself caused acute gastric ulceration with necrosis which extended down to the muscle coat of the stomach. Mucosa adjacent to the ulcer showed necrosis gradually merging with regenerating viable mucosa.[254]

Experimental studies in dogs indicate that a few days after freezing there is goblet-cell metaplasia of the mucosal surface, necrosis of parietal cells and inflammation of the submucosa. Unless ulceration occurs, healing is well advanced after six weeks.[255] The technique is no longer used, and in view of the development of more effective means of treatment for peptic ulcer it seems unlikely to be revived in this form.

Effects of corrosive poisons

The stomach is severely affected by a variety of corrosive poisons ingested accidentally or with suicidal intent. These are widely used in cleaning and disinfectant products and as corrosive or caustic agents such as oven cleaners, metal polish, kettle descalers and drain cleaners. The list is extensive but includes the mineral acids, organic acids such as carbolic acid (phenol) from which are derived many commercial disinfectants, lysol, acetic acid, sodium or potassium hydroxide, sodium hypochlorite (bleach), ammonia, sodium acid sulphate (widely used as a toilet cleaner). Heavy metal salts such as zinc or mercuric chloride or ferrous sulphate taken in excess also have a corrosive effect.

The effect of ingestion of these substances is rapid and severe, and the pathologist may only encounter such cases at post mortem. Corrosive burns are usually visible on the skin around the mouth, oral mucosa and oesophagus as well as the stomach. Fuming substances such as nitric acid or ammonia also cause severe irritation of the upper respiratory passages and bronchi due to inhalation of corrosive fumes. Readers are referred to textbooks of forensic pathology for more detailed description. The gastric mucosa is very haemorrhagic and oedematous. These changes may not be uniform throughout the stomach, as some parts may escape direct contact with the corrosive agent, depending upon the amount taken and on the patient's posture at the time of ingestion. There is also necrotic slough on the mucosal surface, and in many instances the mucosa is black due to altered blood, especially in the presence of acid corrosives.

The gastric and oesophageal walls are extremely friable, although the oesophagus is said to be less severely affected by acids than alkalis. There is sloughing necrosis of the mucosa often extending into the muscle wall, depending upon the amount of corrosive ingested. Perforation is common. The development of emphysematous gatritis with appearance of gas within the stomach wall due to infection by gas-forming organisms following corrosive ingestion has been reported.[256,257]

Gastric changes in chronic renal failure

Lesions involving all parts of the gastrointestinal tract occur in uraemia. Mucosal and submucosal haemorrhage is the most common lesion, accompanied in some cases by ulceration and bleeding. Sites frequently affected include stomach, duodenum, ileum, caecum and colon. In the stomach multiple small petechial mucosal haemorrhages may give an appearance similar to that of acute haemorrhage gastritis.[258,259] The cause of these lesions is uncertain but there is experimental evidence that in the rat, chronic renal failure is accompanied by both increased gastric acid secretion and increased gastric mucosal blood flow. The latter is probably mediated via increased synthesis of the vasodilator nitric oxide (NO) by endothelial cells.[260] This hyperaemia may account for the mucosal haemorrhages. Gastric and duodenal erosions are found in 16–17% of patients undergoing regular dialysis treatment or following successful renal transplantation.[261] The incidence of chronic peptic ulcer (mainly duodenal) has been reported as considerably increased during chronic dialysis[262,263] but more recent studies indicate only a small increase[264] or none at all.[261,265] Mucosal erythema and petechiae frequently persist however. Following renal transplantation the incidence of peptic ulceration is reported to be increased.[266–268]

Other workers found that gastric erosions or ulcers were the commonest source of serious bleeding in the upper gastrointestinal tract in patients with chronic renal failure and that in the majority of patients who bled, the use of ulcerogenic drugs such as anti-inflammatory drugs was an important additional risk factor.[269]

Histological examination shows that superficial gastritis involving antrum and fundus is common in uraemic patients[270–271] but the incidence may diminish after successful renal transplantation.[271] Heterotopic calcification within the fundus may occur in association with secondary hyperparathyroidism, and cytomegalovirus inclusions may occasionally be seen in transplant patients receiving immunosuppressive therapy.[272]

More severe atrophic gastritis is seen in a minority of uraemic patients[270] but is quite rare in patients undergoing dialysis or following successful renal transplantation.[272,264] The incidence of atrophic gastritis is reported to be less in successfully treated uraemic patients than in age-matched controls.[271] Indeed, in these patients there is frequently evidence of mucosal hypertrophy with enlarged mucosal folds and hyperplasia of Brunner's glands.[272,264] Histology shows thickening of the fundic mucosa, foveolar hyperplasia, increase in parietal cell mass with multinucleated parietal cells and expansion of parietal cells into the antrum and duodenum. These hypertrophic changes diminish with time following transplantation.[272]

Patients with chronic renal failure also show increased incidence of gastric metaplasia of the duodenum and chronic duodenitis. Colonization of islands of gastric metaplasia by *H. pylori* is, however, uncommon.[273]

The hypertrophic mucosal changes may explain the high levels of gastric acid secretion seen in some patients following onset of dialysis treatment.[263,274,275] After successful renal transplantation acid secretion tends to fall with time.[268,275] Serum gastrin levels are also increased in chronic renal failure. The increase is proportional to the degree of renal dysfunction and is not affected by dialysis.[265] Gastrin levels return to normal following successful renal transplantation.[268,265]

Mucosal hypertrophic changes in dialysis patients may be explained by the trophic effect of gastrin.[264] Two possibilities may explain increased serum gastrin levels: the kidneys are a major site of gastrin removal from the circulation[276] and removal is likely to be impaired in renal failure; in addition, there is hyperplasia of gastrin cells within the antral mucosa and expansion of these cells into fundic mucosa within areas of pseudopyloric and intestinal metaplasia in patients undergoing chronic dialysis.[277,278]

In post-transplantation patients receiving immunosuppressive therapy in whom serum gastrin levels are not raised, the hypertrophic gastric mucosa described is not so readily explained. Franzin et al[272] suggest that steroids may increase parietal cell mass and acid secretion, and cite experimental evidence to support this.[279]

REFERENCES

1. Hastings PR, Skillman JJ, Bushnell LS, Silen W. Antacid titration in the prevention of acute gastrointestinal bleeding. N Engl J Med 1978; 298: 1041–1045.
2. Bank S, Misra P, Mausner D et al. The incidence, distribution and evolution of stress ulcers in surgical intensive care units. Am J Gastroenterol 1980; 74: 76.
3. Bank S. Stress ulcers — prevention of gastrointestinal bleeding in critical care units. Med J Aust 1985; 142 (Special Suppl): S17–S21.

4. Menguy R. The prophylaxis of stress ulceration. N Engl J Med 1980; 302: 461–462.
5. Bowen JC, Rees M. Acute stress ulcerations of the stomach: clinical correlates. Scand J Gastroenterol 1984; 19 (Suppl 105): 29–31.
6. Lev R, Molot MD, McNamara J, Stremple JF. 'Stress' ulcers following war wounds in Vietnam. Lab Invest 1971; 25: 491–502.
7. Lucas CE, Sugawa C, Riddle J, Rector F, Rosenberg B, Walt AJ. Natural history and surgical dilemma of 'stress' gastric bleeding. Arch Surg 1971; 102: 266–272.
8. Sugawa C, Lucas CE, Rosenberg BF, Riddle JM, Walt AJ. Differential topography of acute erosive gastritis due to trauma or sepsis, ethanol and aspirin. Gastrointest Endosc 1973; 19: 127–130.
9. Sevitt S. Duodenal and gastric ulceration after burning. Br J Surg 1967; 54: 32–41.
10. Pruitt BA, Goodwin CW. Stress ulcer disease in the burned patient. World J Surg 1981; 5: 209–222.
11. Czaja AJ, McAlhany CJ, Pruitt BA. Acute gastroduodenal disease after thermal injury. N Engl J Med 1974; 291: 925–929.
12. Williams JW, Pannell WP, Sherman RT. Curling's ulcer in children. J Trauma 1976; 16: 639–644.
13. Pruitt BA, Foley FD, Moncrief JA. Curling's ulcer: a clinical pathology study of 323 cases. Ann Surg 1970; 172: 523–539.
14. Bruck HM, Pruitt BA. Curling's ulcer in children: a 12 year review of 63 cases. J Trauma 1972; 12: 490–494.
15. Solem LD, Strate RG, Fischer RP. Antacid therapy and nutritional supplementation in the prevention of Curling's ulcer. Surg Gynaecol Obstet 1979; 148: 367–370.
16. McAlhany JC, Czaja AJ, Pruitt BA. Antacid control of complications from acute gastroduodenal disease after burns. J Trauma 1976; 16: 645–649.
17. Cushing H. Peptic ulcers and the interbrain. Surg Gynaecol Obstet 1932; 55: 1–34.
18. Cheung LY. Pathogenesis, prophylaxis and treatment of stress gastritis. Am J Surg 1988; 156: 437–440.
19. Kamada T, Fusamoto H, Kawano S et al.Gastrointestinal bleeding following head injury: a clinical study of 433 cases. J Trauma 1977; 17: 44–47.
20. Gudeman SK, Wheeler CB, Miller JD, Halloran LG, Becker DP. Gastric secretory and mucosal injury response to severe head trauma. Neurosurgery 1983; 12: 175–179.
21. Lucas CE. Stress ulceration: the clinical problem. World J Surg 1981; 5: 139–151.
22. Karvonen AL. Occurrence of gastric mucosal erosions and their association with other upper gastrointestinal disease: a study of patients examined by elective gastroscopy. Ann Clin Res 1981; 13: 159–163.
23. Woltjen JA, Barber GB, Leese PF, Burger AE. Prevalence of abnormal oesophageal, gastric and duodenal mucosa in normal healthy males. Gastroenterology 1986; 90: 1695.
24. Turnberg LA. Gastric mucosal defence mechanisms. Scand J Gastroenterol 1985; Suppl 110: 37–40.
25. Garner A, Flemstrom G, Allen A. Gastroduodenal alkaline and mucus secretions. Scand J Gastroenterol 1983; 18(Suppl 87): 25–41.
26. Bickel M, Kauffman GL. Gastric gel mucus thickness: effect of distention 16, 16-dimethyl prostglandin E2 and carbenoxolone. Gastroenterology 1981; 80: 770–775.
27. Williams SE, Turnberg LA. Demonstration of a pH gradient across mucous adherent to rabbit gastric mucosa: evidence for a 'mucus-bicarbonate' barrier. Gut 1981; 22: 94–96.
28. Bahari HMM, Ross IN, Turnberg LA, Irving MH. The mucous-bicarbonate barrier: demonstration of a pH gradient within the mucous layer of the human stomach. Br J Surg 1981; 68: 365.
29. Slomiany BL, Piasek A, Sarosiek J, Slomiany A. The role of the surface and intracellular mucus in gastric mucosal protection against hydrogen ion. Scand J Gastroenterol 1985; 20: 1191–1196.
30. Bell AE, Sellers LA, Allen A et al. Properties of gastric and duodenal mucus: effect of proteolysis, disulfide reduction, bile acid, ethanol and hypertonicity on mucus gel structure. Gastroenterology 1985; 88: 269–280.
31. Kivilaakso E, Flemstrom G. Surface pH gradient in gastroduodenal mucosa. Scand J Gastroenterol 1984; 19 (Suppl 105): 50–52.
32. Ross IN, Bahari HMM, Turnberg LA. The pH gradient across mucus adherent to rat fundic mucosa in vivo and the effect of potential damaging agents. Gastroenterology 1981; 81: 713–718.
33. Eastwood GL. Gastrointestinal epithelial renewal. Gastroenterology 1977; 72: 962–975.
34. Ito S, Lacy ER. Morphology of rat gastric mucosal damage, defence and restitution in the presence of luminal ethanol. Gastroenterology 1985; 88: 250–260.
35. Svanes K, Ito S, Takeuchi K, Silen W. Restitution of the in vitro frog gastric mucosa after damage with hyperosmolar sodium chloride: morphoogic and physiologic characteristics. Gastroenterology 1982; 82: 1409–1426.
36. Davenport HW. Salicylate damage to the gastric mucosal barrier. N Engl J Med 1966; 276: 1307–1312.
37. Kauffman GL. The gastric mucosal barrier: component control. Dig Dis Sci 1985; 30 (Suppl): 69S–76S.
38. Kaufman GL. Mucosal damage to the stomach: how, when and why? Scand J Gastroenterol 1984; 19 (Suppl 105): 19–26.
39. O'Brien P, Bushell M. Role of acid-base status in the response of the isolated amphibian gastric mucosa to back diffusion of H^+. Gastroenterology 1980; 79: 439–446.
40. Starlinger M, Schiessel R, Hung CR, Silen W. H^+ back diffusion stimulating gastric mucosal blood flow in the rabbit fundus. Surgery 1981; 89: 232–236.
41. Robert A, Nezamis JE, Lancaster C, Hanchar AJ. Cytoprotection by prostaglandins in rats. Gastroenterology 1979; 77: 433–443.
42. Chaudhury TK, Robert A. Prevention by mild irritants of gastric necrosis produced in rats by sodium taurocholate. Dig Dis Sci 1980; 25: 830–836.
43. Konturek SJ. Gastric cytoprotection. Scand J Gastroenterol 1985; 20: 543–553.
44. Konturek SJ, Tasler J, Bilski J, Kaminska A, Laskiewicz J. Role of prostaglandins in alkaline secretion from gastroduodenal mucosa exposed to acid and taurocholate. Scand J Gastroenterol 1984; 19 (Suppl 92): 69–74.
45. Konturek SJ, Robert A. Cytoprotection of canine gastric mucosa by prostacyclin: possible mediation by increased mucosal blood flow. Digestion 1982; 25: 155–163.
46. Konturek SJ, Piastuki I, Brzozowski T et al. Role of prostaglandins in the formation of aspirin-induced gastric ulcers. Gastroenterology 1981; 80: 4–9.
47. Bertko R, Davidovich A, Finckenor B, Gaginella T. Protection by the synthetic prostanoid RO 22–1327 against aspirin-induced gastric mucosal damage in dogs. Gastroenterology 1986; 90: 1345.
48. Zinner MJ, Rypins EB, Martin LR et al. Misoprostol versus antacid titration for preventing stress ulcers in postoperative surgical ICU patients. Ann Surg 1989, 210: 590–595.
49. Guldvog I. Stress ulceration: possible pathogenic mechanisms. Scand J Gastroenterol 1984; 19 (Suppl 105): 9–13.
50. Watts CC, Clarke K. Gastric acidity in the comatose patient. J Neurosurg 1969; 30: 107–109.
51. Gordon MJ, Skillman JJ, Zervas NT, Silen W. Divergent nature of gastric mucosal permeability and gastric acid secretion in sick patients with general surgical and neurosurgical disease. Ann Surg 1973; 178: 285–294.
52. Idjadi F, Robbins R, Stahl WM, Essiet G. Prospective study of gastric secretion in stressed patients with intracranial injury. J Trauma 1971; 11: 681–686.
53. Stremple JF. Prospective studies of gastric secretion in trauma patients. Am J Surg 1976; 131: 78–85.
54. Bowen JC, Fleming WH, Thompson JC. Increased gastrin release following penetrating central nervous system injury. Surgery 1974; 75: 720–724.
55. Stremple JF. Stress ulceration — revisited. Surgical rounds 1979; 2: 40–52.
56. Shuman RB, Schuster DP, Zuckerman GR. Prophylactic therapy for stress ulcer bleeding: a reappraisal. Ann Intern Med 1987; 106: 562–567.
57. Force T, MacDonald D, Eade OE, Doane C, Krawit EL. Ischaemic gastritis and duodenitis. Dig Dis Sci 1980; 25: 307–310.

58. Talansky AL, Katz S, Naidich J. Aphthous ulcers in ischaemic gastroenterocolitis: a case report. Am J Gastroenterol 1985; 80: 257–259.
59. Harjola P-T, Sivula A. Gastric ulceration following experimentally induced hypoxia and haemorrhagic shock: in vivo study of pathogenesis in rabbits. Ann Surg 1966; 163: 21–28.
60. Goodman AA, Osborne MP. An experimental model and clinical definition of stress ulceration. Surg Gynecol Obstet 1972; 134: 563–571.
61. Ritchie WP. Acute gastric mucosal damage induced by bile salts, acid and ischaemia. Gastroenterology 1975; 68: 699–707.
62. Ritchie WP, Shearburn EW. Influence of isoproterenol and cholestyramine on acute gastric mucosal ulcerogenesis. Gastroenterology 1977; 73: 62–65.
63. Shirazi S, Mueller TM, Hardy BM. Canine gastric acid secretion and blood flow measurement in hemorrhagic shock. Gastroenterology 1977; 73: 75–78.
64. Leung FW, Itoh M, Hirabayashi K et al. Role of blood flow in gastric and duodenal mucosal injury in the rat. Gastroenterology 1985; 88: 281–289.
65. McCord JM. Oxygen derived free radicals in post ischaemic tissue injury. N Engl J Med 1985; 312: 159–163.
66. Harlan JM. Neutrophil-mediated vascular injury. Acta Med Scand 1987; Suppl 715: 123–129.
67. Vedder NB, Winn RK, Rice CL, Chi EY, Arfors K-E, Harlan JM. A monoclonal antibody to the adherence-promoting leucocyte glycoprotein CD18 reduced organ injury and improves survival from haemorrhagic shock and resuscitation in rabbits. J Clin Invest 1988; 81: 931–944.
68. Durham RM, Shapiro MJ. Stress gastritis revisited. Surg Clins of N America 1991; 71: 791–810.
69. Lucas CE, Ravikant T, Walt AJ. Gastritis and gastric blood flow in hyperdynamic septic pigs. Am J Surg 1976; 131: 73–77.
70. Davenport HW, Barr LL. Failure of ischaemia to break the dog's gastric mucosal barrier. Gastroenterology 1973; 65: 619–624.
71. Arvidsson S, Haglund U. On the pathogenesis of acute gastric mucosal lesions in septic shock. Scand J Gastroenterol 1984; 19 (Suppl 105): 67–70.
72. Kivilaakso E, Barzilai A, Shiessel R, Crass R, Silen W. Ulceration of isolated amphibian gastric mucosa. Gastroenterology 1979; 77: 31–37.
73. Silen W, Merhav A, Simson JN. The pathophysiology of stress ulcer disease. World J Surg 1981; 5: 165–174.
74. O'Brien P. The pathogenesis, prevention and treatment of stress ulceration. In: Gastrointestinal haemorrhage. Hunt PS ed. Edinburgh: Churchill Livingstone 1986; 60–67.
75. Kivilaakso E, Fronn D, Silen W. Relationship between ulceration and intramural pH of gastric mucosa during haemorrhagic shock. Surgery 1978; 84: 70–78.
76. Guilbert J, Bounous G, Gurd FN. Role of intestinal chyme in the pathogenesis of gastric ulceration following experimental haemorrhagic shock. J Trauma 1969; 9: 723–724.
77. Menguy R, Masters YF. Mechanism of stress ulcer. Gastroenterology 1974; 66: 509–516.
78. Bruggeman TM, Wood JG, Davenport HW. Local control of blood flow in the dog stomach: Vasodilatation caused by acid back-diffusion following topical application of salicyclic acid. Gastroenterology 1979; 77: 737–744.
79. Douthwaite AH, Lintott GAM. Effect of aspirin and certain other substances on the stomach. Lancet 1938; 2: 1222–1225.
80. Muir A, Cossar IA. Aspirin and ulcer. Br Med J 1955; 2: 7–12.
81. Lanza FL, Rack MF, Wagner GS, Balm TK. Reduction in gastric mucosal haemorrhage and ulceration with chronic high level dosing of enteric coated aspirin granules 2 and 4 times a day. Dig Dis Sci 1985; 30: 509–512.
82. Silvoso GR, Ivey KJ, Butt JH et al. Incidence of gastric lesions in patients with rheumatic disease on chronic aspirin therapy. Ann Intern Med 1979; 91: 517–520.
83. Graham DY, Smith JL, Dobbs SM. Gastric adaption occurs with aspirin administration in man. Dig Dis Sci 1983; 28: 1–6.
84. Goulston K, Cooke AR. Alcohol, aspirin and gastrointestinal bleeding. Br Med J 1968; 4: 664–665.
85. Needham CD, Kyle J, Jones PF, Johnston SJ, Kerridge EF. Aspirin and alcohol in gastrointestinal haemorrhage. Gut 1971; 12: 819–821.
86. Lanza FL, Royer GL, Nelson RS, Rack MF, Seckman CC. Ethanol, aspirin, Ibuprofen and the gastroduodenal mucosa: an endoscopic assessment. Am J Gastroenterol 1985; 80: 767–769.
87. Simon LS, Mills JA. New non-steroidal anti-inflammatory drugs. N Engl J Med 1980; 302: 1179–1185 and 1237–1243.
88. Taylor RT, Huskisson EC, Whitehouse DH, Hart FD, Trapnell DH. Gastric ulceration occurring during indomethacin therapy. Br Med J 1968; 4: 734–737.
89. McIntyre RLE, Irani MS, Piris J. Histological studies on the effects of three anti-inflammatory preparations on the gastric mucosa. J Clin Pathol 1981; 34: 836–842.
90. Chernish SM, Rosenik BD, Brunelle RL, Crabtree R. Comparison of gastrointestinal effects of aspirin and fenoprofen. Arthritis Rheum 1979; 22: 376–383.
91. Hart FD. Naproxan (naprosyn) and gastrointestinal haemorrhage. Br Med J 1974; 2: 51–52.
92. Clinch D, Banerjee AK, Ostick G, Levy DW. Non-steroidal inflammatory drugs and gastrointestinal adverse effects. J R Coll Physicians Lond 1983; 17: 228–230.
93. Brooks PM. Clinical management of rheumatoid arthritis. Lancet 1993; 341: 286–291.
94. CSM Update. Non-steroidal anti-inflammatory drugs and serious gastrointestinal adverse reactions — I Br Med J 1986; 292: 614.
95. Brooks PM, Day RO. Non steroidal anti-inflammatory drugs — differences and similarities. N Engl J Med. 1991; 324: 1716–1725
96. CSM update. Non-steroidal anti-inflammatory drugs and serious gastrointestinal adverse reactions — 2. Br Med J 1986; 292: 1190–1191.
97. Bjarnason I, Zanelli G, Prowse P et al. Blood and protein loss via small intestinal inflammation induced by non-steroidal anti-inflammatory drugs. Lancet 1987; 2: 711–714.
98. Lang J, Price AB, Levi AJ, Burke M, Gumpel JM, Bjarnason I. Diaphragm disease: pathology of disease of the small intestine induced by non-steroidal anti-inflammatory drugs. J Clin Pathol 1988; 41: 516–526.
99. Riddell RH, Tanaka M, Mazzoleni G. Non-steroidal anti-inflammatory drugs as a possible cause of collagenous colitis: a case controlled study. Gut 1992; 33: 683–686.
100. Haslock I. Prevalence of NSAID induced gastrointestinal morbidity and mortality. J Rheumatol 1990; 17 Suppl 20: 2–6.
101. Freis JF, Miller SR, Spitz PW, Williams CA, Hubert HB, Bloch DA. Toward an epidemiology of gastropathy associated with non-steroidal anti-inflammatory drug use. Gastroenterology 1989; 96: 607–655.
102. Conn HO, Blitzer BL. Non association of adrenocorticosteroid therapy and peptic ulcer. N Engl J Med 1976; 294: 473–479.
103. Messer J, Reitman D, Sacks HS, Smith H, Chalmers TC. Association of adrenocorticosteroid therapy and peptic ulcer disease. N Engl J Med 1983; 309: 21–24.
104. Trevethick MA, Clayton NM, Strong P, Harman IW. Do infiltrating neutrophils contribute to the pathogenesis of indomethacin induced ulceration of the rat gastric mucosa? Gut 1993; 34: 156–160.
105. Piper JM, Ray WA, Daugherty JR, Griffin MR. Corticosteroid use and peptic ulcer disease: role of non steroidal anti-inflammatory drugs. Ann Intern Med 1991; 114: 735–740.
106. Hirsch EF. The gastric mucosa in delirium tremens. Arch Intern Med 1916; 17: 354–362.
107. Palmer ED. Gastritis: a revaluation. Medicine 1954; 33: 199–200.
108. Gottfried EB, Korsten MA, Lieber CS. Alcohol induced gastric and duodenal lesions in man. Am J Gastroenterol 1978; 70: 587–592.
109. Croft DN, Wood PHN. Gastric mucosa and susceptibility to occult gastrointestinal bleeding caused by aspirin. Br Med J 1967; 1: 137–141.
110. Hamilton SR, Yardley JH. Endoscopic biopsy diagnosis of aspirin associated chronic gastric ulcers. Gastroenterology 1980; 78: 1178.
111. Dixon MF, O'Connor HJ, Axon ATR, Keane RFJG, Johnston D. Reflux gastritis: distinct histopathological entity? J Clin Pathol 1986; 39: 524–530.
112. Sobala GM, Keane RFG, Axon ATR, Dixon MF. Reflux gastritis in the intact stomach. J Clin Pathol 1990; 43: 303–306.

113. Laine L, Weinstein WM. Histology of alcoholic haemorrhagic gastritis: a prospective evaluation. Gastroenterology 1988; 94: 1254–1262.
114. Eastwood GL, Quimby GF. Effect of chronic aspirin ingestion on epithelial proliferation in rat fundus, antrum and duodenum. Gastroenterology 1982; 82: 852–856.
115. McGreevy JM, Moody FG. Focal microcirculatory changes during the production of aspirin induced gastric mucosal erosions. Surgery 1981; 89: 337–341.
116. Kitahora T, Guth PH. Effect of aspirin on the rat gastric microcirculation. Gastroentrology 1986; 90: 1494.
117. Lange S, Hench V, Malagelada J-R. Drug-induced gastric injury in man is directly related to inhibition of mucosal prostaglandin synthesis. Gastroenterology 1986; 90: 1511.
118. Carsson D, Garber E, Weinstein W, Grossman M, Bluestone R, Guth P. Drug-associated gastroduodenal lesions in rheumatoid arthritis: an endoscopic and histologic study. Gastroenterology 1980; 78: 1147.
119. Heresbach D, Raoul JL, Bretagne JF et al. Helicobacter pylori: a risk and severity factor of non-steroidal anti-inflammatory drug induced gastropathy. Gut 1992; 33: 1608–1611.
120. Gana TJ, Huhlewych R, Foo J. Focal gastric mucosal blood flow in aspirin induced ulceration. Ann Surg 1987; 205: 399–403.
121. Taha AS, Angerson W, Nakshabendi I et al. Gastric and duodenal mucosal blood flow in patients receiving non-steroidal anti-inflammatory drugs — influence of age, smoking, ulceration and Helicobacter pylori. Aliment Pharmacol Ther 1993; 7: 41–45.
122. Brooks PM. Clinical management of rheumatoid arthritis. Lancet 1993; 341: 286–290.
123. Kitahora T, Guth PH. Effect of aspirin plus hydrochloric acid on the gastric mucosal microcirculation. Gastroenterology 1987; 93: 810–817.
124. Wallace JL, Arfors K-E, McKnight GW. A monoclonal antibody against the CD18 leucocyte adhesion molecule prevents indomethacin-induced gastric damage in rabbits. Gastroenterology 1991; 100: 878–883.
125. Davenport HW. Ethanol damage to canine oxyntic glandular mucosa. Proc Soc Exp Biol Med 1967; 126: 657–662.
126. Dinoso VP, Ming Si-Chem, McNiff J. Ultrastructural changes of the canine gatric mucosa after topical application of graded concentrations of ethanol. Dig Dis 1976; 21: 626–632.
127. Kawashima K, Jerzy Glass GB. Alcohol injury to gastric mucosa in mice and its potentiation by stress. Dig Dis 1975; 20: 162–172.
128. Morris GP, Wallace JL. The roles of ethanol and of acid in the production of gastric mucosal erosions in rats. Virchows Arch (A) 1981; 38: 23–28.
129. Murray HS, Strottman MP, Cooke AR. Effect of several drugs on gastric potential difference in man. Br Med J 1974; 1: 19–21.
130. Szabo S, Trier JS, Brown A, Schnoor J. Early vascular injury and increased vascular permeability in gastric mucosal injury caused by ethanol in the rat. Gastroenterology 1985; 88: 228–236.
131. Kvietys PR, Twohig B, Danzell J, Specian RD. Ethanol-induced injury to the rat gastric mucosa. Role of neutrophils and xanthine oxidase-derived radicals. Gastroenterology 1990; 98: 909–92.
132. Slavin RE, Dias MA, Saral R. Cytosine arabinoside induced gastrointestinal toxic alterations in sequential chemotherapeutic protocols. Cancer 1978; 42: 1747–1759.
133. Laine L, Bentley E, Chandrasoma P. The effects of oral iron therapy on the upper gastrointestinal tract. A prospective evaluation. Gastroenterology 1986; 90: 1509.
134. Doenges JL. Spirochetes in the gastric glands of macacus rhesus and of man without related disease. Arch Path 1939; 27: 469–477.
135. Freedberg AS, Barron LE. The presence of spirochetes in human gastric mucosa. Am J Dig Dis 1940; 7: 443–445.
136. Steer HW. Ultrastructure of cell migration through the gastric epithelium and its relationship to bacteria. J Clin Pathol 1975; 28: 639–646.
137. Warren JR. Unidentified curved bacilli on gastric epithelium in active chronic gastritis. Lancet 1983; 1: 1273.
138. Marshall B. Unidentified curved bacilli on gastric epithelium in active chronic gastritis. Lancet 1983; 1: 1273–1275.
139. Goodwin CS. Helicobacter pylori. 10th Anniversary of its culture in April 1982. Gut 1993; 34: 293–294.
140. Editorial. C. pylori becomes H. pylori. Lancet 1989; 1: 1019–1020.
141. Goodwin CS, Armstrong JA, Chilvers T et al. Transfer of Campylobacter pylori and Campylobacter mustelae to Helicobacter gen. nov. and Helicobacter pylori comb. nov and Helicobacter mustelae comb. nov. respectively. Int J Syst Bacteriol 1989; 39: 397–405.
142. Marshall BJ, Warren JR. Unidentified curved bacilli in the stomach of patients with gastritis and peptic ulceration. Lancet 1984; 1: 1311–1314.
143. Humphreys H, Bourke S, Dooley C et al. Effect of treatment on Campylobacter pylori in peptic disease: a randomised prospective trial. Gut 1988; 29: 279–283.
144. Rauws EAJ, Langenberg W, Houthoff HJ, Zanen HC, Tytgat GNJ. Campylobacter pyloridis associated chronic active antral gastritis. Gastroenterology 1988; 94: 32–40.
145. Blaser MJ. Gastric Campylobacter-like organisms, gastritis and peptic ulcer disease. Gastroenterology 1987; 93: 371–383.
146. Ormand JE, Talley NJ, Shorter RG et al. Prevalence of Helicobacter pylori in specific forms of gastritis. Dig Dis Sci 1991; 36: 142–145.
147. Kang JY, Wee A, Math MV et al. Helicobacter pylori and gastritis in patients with peptic ulcer and non-ulcer dyspepsia: ethnic differences in Singapore. Gut 1990; 31: 850–853.
148. Steer HW. The gastroduodenal epithelium in peptic ulceration. J Pathol 1985; 146: 355–362.
149. Collins JSA, Sloan JM, Hamilton PW et al. Investigation of the relationship between gastric antral inflammation and Campylobacter pylori using graphic tablet planimetry. J Pathol 1989; 159: 281–285.
150. Sloan JM, Buchanan KD, McFarland RJ, Titterington P, Sandford JC. Histological study of the effect of chronic gastritis on gastrin cell distribution in the human stomach. J Clin Pathol 1979; 32: 201–207.
151. Mitchell HM, Bohane TD, Tobias V et al. H. pylori infection in children: potential clues to pathogenesis. J Paed Gastroent & Nutr 1993; 16: 120–125.
152. Hazell SL. Microbiology and taxonomy of Helicobacter pylori and related bacteria. In: Helicobacter pylori in peptic ulceration and gastritis. Marshall BJ, McCallum MC, Callum RW, Guerrant RL eds. Publ by Blackwell Scientific Publications, Oxford 1991; 19–33.
153. Thomsen LL, Gavin JB, Tasman-Jones C. Relation of Helicobacter pylori to the human gastric mucosa in chronic gastritis of the antrum. Gut 1991; 31: 1230–1236.
154. Goodwin CS, Armstrong JA, Marshall BJ. Campylobacter pyloridis, gastritis and peptic ulceration. J Clin Pathol 1986; 39: 353–365.
155. Hessey SJ, Spence RJ, Wyatt JI et al. Bacterial adhesion and disease activity in Helicobacter associated chronic gastritis. Gut 1990, 31: 134–138.
156. Chan WY, Hui PK, Leung KM, Thomas TMM. Modes of Helicobacter colonisation and gastric epithelial damage. Histopathology 1992; 21: 521–528.
157. Loffeld RJLF, Potters HVPS, Arends JW, Stobbering HE, Flendrig JA, Van Spreeuwel JP. Campylobacter associated gastritis in patients with non-ulcer dyspepsia. J Clin Path 1988; 41: 85–88.
158. Siurala P, Sipponen P, Kekki M. Campylobacter pylori in a sample of Finnish population: relations to morphology and functions of the gastric mucosa. Gut 1988; 29: 909–915.
159. O'Connor HK, Wyatt JL, Dixon MF, Axon ATR. Campylobacter-like organisms and reflux gastritis. J Clin Pathol 1986; 39: 531–534.
160. Sobala GM, King RFG, Axon ATR, Dixon MF. Reflux gastritis in the intact stomach. J Clin Pathol 1990; 43: 303–306.
161. Sobala GM, O'Connor HJ, Dewar EP, Keane RFG, Axon ATR, Dixon M F. Bile reflux and intestinal metaplasia in gastric mucosa. J Clin Pathol 1993; 46: 235.
162. Hill R, Pearman J, Worthy P, Caruso V, Goodwin S, Blincow E. Campylobacter pyloridis and gastritis in children. Lancet 1986; 1: 387.
163. Drumm B, O'Brien A, Cutz E, Sherman P. Campylobacter pyloridis associated with primary antral gastritis in the paediatric population. Gastroenterology 1986; 90: 1399.

164. Oderda G, Dell'olio D, Morra I, Ansaldi N. Campylobacter pylori gastritis: long term results of treatment with amoxycillin. Arch Dis Child 1989; 64: 326–329.
165. Oderda G, Vaira D, Holton J et al. Helicobacter pylori in children with peptic ulcer and their families. Dig Dis Sci 1991; 76: 572–576.
166. Wyatt JI, Shallcross TM, Crabtree JE, Heatley RV. H. pylori, gastritis and peptic ulceration in the elderly. J Clin Pathol 1992; 45: 1070–1074.
167. Dooley CP, Cohen H, Fitzgibbons PL et al. Prevalence of Helicobacter pylori infection and histologic gastritis in asymptomatic persons. N Engl J Med 1989; 321: 1562–1566.
168. Sitas F, Forman D, Yarwell JWG et al. Helicobacter pylori infection rates in relation to age and social class in a population of Welsh men. Gut 1991; 32: 25–28.
169. Graham DY, Malaty HM, Evans DG, Evans DJ, Klein PD, Adam E. Epidemiology of Helicobacter pylori in an asymptomatic population in the United States. Gastroenterology 1991; 100: 1495–1501.
170. Rouvray D, Bogaerts J, Nsengiumva O, Omar M, Versailles L, Haot J. Campylobacter pylori, gastritis and peptic ulcer disease in Central Africa. Br Med J. 1987; 295: 1174.
171. Megraud F, Brassens-Rabbe M-P, Denis F, Belbouri A, Hoa DQ. Seroepidemiology of Campbylobacter pylori infection in various populations. J Clin Microbiol 1989; 27: 1870–1873.
172. Perez-Perez GI, Taylor DN, Bodhgidatta L. Prevalence of Helicobacter pylori infections in Thailand. J Infect Dis 1990; 161: 1237–1241.
173. Taylor DN, Blaser MJ. The epidemiology of H. pylori infection. In: H. pylori in peptic ulceration and gastritis. Marshall B J, McCallum RW, Guerrant RL eds. Publ by Blackwell Scientific, Oxford 1991; 46–54.
174. Holcombe C, Omotara BA, Eldridge J, Jones DM. H. pylori the most common bacterial infection in Africa: a random serological study. Am J Gastroenterol. 1992; 87: 28–30.
175. Blum AL. The role of Campylobacter pylori in gastroduodenal diseases. A 'non-believer's' point of view. Gastroenterol Clin Biol 1989; 13: 122b–126b.
176. McNulty CAM, Gearty JC, Crump B et al. Campylobacter pyloridis and associated gastritis: investigator blind, placebo controlled trial of bismuth salicylate and erythromycin ethylsuccinate. Br Med J 1986; 293: 645–649.
177. Di Napoli A, Petrino R, Boero M, Bellis D, Chiandussi L. Quantitative assessment of histological changes in chronic gastritis after eradication of Helicobacter pylori. J Clin Pathol 1992; 45: 796–798.
178. Rauws EAJ, Tytgat GNJ. Cure of duodenal ulcer with eradication of Helicobacter pylori. Lancet 1990; 335: 1233–1235.
179. Graham DY, Lew GM, Klein PD et al. Effect of treatment of Helicobacter pylori infection on the long-term recurrence of gastric or duodenal ulcer. Am Int Med 1992; 116: 705–708.
180. Coghlan JG, Humphries H, Dooley C et al. Campylobacter pylori and recurrence of duodenal ulcers — a 12 month follow-up study. Lancet 1987; 2: 1109–1111.
181. Patchett S, Beattie S, Leen E, Keane C, O'Morain C. Helicobacter pylori and duodenal ulcer recurrence. Am J Gastroenterol 1992; 87: 24–27.
182. Gledhill T, Leicester RJ, Addis B et al. Epidemic hypochlorhydria. Br Med J 1985; 290: 1383–1386.
183. Ramsey EJ, Carey KV, Peterson WL et al. Epidemic gastritis with hypochlorhydria. Gastroenterology 1979; 76: 1449–1457.
184. Marshall BJ, Armstrong JA, McGechie DB, Glancy RJ. Attempt to fulfil Koch's postulates for pyloric campylobacter. Med J Aust 1985; 142: 436–439.
185. Graham DY, Albert LC, Smith JL, Yoshimura HH. Iatrogenic Campylobacter pylori infection is a cause of epidemic achlorhydria. Am J Gastroenterol 1988; 83: 974–980.
186. Morris A, Nicholson C. Ingestion of Campylobacter pyloridis causes gastritis to raised factor L H. Amer J Gastroenterol 1987; 82: 192–199.
187. Morris AJ, Rafiq Ali, Nicholson GI et al. Longterm follow-up of voluntary ingestion of H. pylori. Ann Int Med 1991; 114: 662–663.
188. Mitchell HM, Lee A, Berkowicz J, Brody T. The use of serology to diagnose active Campylobacter pylori infection. Med J Aust 1988; 149: 604–609.
189. Mosgrove C, Bolton FJ, Krypczyk AM et al. Campylobacter pylori: clinical, histological and serological studies. J Clin Pathol 1988; 41: 1316–1321.
190. Collins JSA, Bamford KB, Sloan JM, Collins BJ, Moorhead RJ, Love AHG. Screening for Helicobacter pylori antibody could reduce endoscopy workload in young dyspeptic patients. Eur J Gastroenterol and Hepatol 1992; 4: 991–993.
191. Wyatt JI, Rathbone BJ, Heatley RV. Local immune response to gastric Campylobacter in non-ulcer dyspepsia. J Clin Pathol 1986; 39: 863–870.
192. Chen XG, Correa P, Offerhaus J et al. Ultrastructure of the gastric mucosa harboring Campylobacter-like organisms. Am J Clin Pathol 1986; 86: 575–582.
193. Chan WY, Hui PK, Chan JKC et al. Epithelial damage by Helicobacter pylori in gastric ulcers. Histopathology 1991; 19: 47–53.
194. Hui PH, Chan WY, Cheung PS, Chan JKC, Ng CS. Pathologic changes of gastric mucosa colonised by Helicobacter pylori. Hum Pathol 1992; 23: 548–556.
195. Sarosiek J, Slomiany A, Slomiany BL. Evidence for weakening of gastric mucus integrity by Campylobacter pylori. Scand J Gastroenterol 1988; 23: 585–590.
196. Micots I, Augeron C, Laboisse CL, Muzeau F, Mgraud F. Mucin exocytosis: a major target for Helicobacter pylori. J Clin Pathol 1993; 46: 241–245.
197. Graham DY, Go MF, Evans DJ. Review article: urease, gastric ammonia/ammonium and Helicobacter pylori — the past, the present and recommendations for future research. Aliment Pharmacol Ther 1992; 6: 659–669.
198. Nujumi AM, Rowe PA, Dahill S, Dorrian CA, Neithercut WD, McColl KEL. Role of ammonia in the pathogenesis of the gastritis hypergastrinaemia and hyperpepsinogenaemia caused by Helicobacter pylori infection. Gut 1992; 33: 1612–1616.
199. Collins JSA, Hamilton PW, Watt PCH, Sloan JM, Love AHG. Quantitative histological study of mucosal inflammatory cell densities in endoscopic duodenal biopsy specimens from dyspeptic patients using computer linked image analysis. Gut 1990; 31: 858–861.
200. Goodwin CS. Duodenal ulcer, Campylobacter pylori and the 'leaking roof' concept. Lancet 1988; 2: 1467–1469.
201. Wyatt JI, Rathbone BJ, Soballa GM et al. Gastric epithelium in the duodenum: its association with Helicobacter pylori inflammation. J Clin Pathol 1990; 43: 981–986.
202. Dixon MF, Sobala GM. Gastritis and duodenitis: the histopathological spectrum. Eur J Gastroenterol and Hepatol 1992; 4 (Suppl 2): S17–S23.
203. Crabtree JE, Taylor JD, Wyatt JI. Mucosal IgA recognition of Helicobacter pylori 120 kDa protein, peptic ulceration and gastric pathology. Lancet 1991; 338: 332–335.
204. Lee A. Peptic ulceration. H. pylori — initiated ulcerogenesis: look to the host. Lancet 1993; 341: 280–281.
205. Dickey W, Collins JSA, Watson RGP, Sloan JM, Porter KG. Secretor status and H. pylori infection are independent risk factors for gastroduodenal disease. Gut 1992; 33 (Suppl 2): S5.
206. Levi S, Berdshall K, Haddad G, Playford R, Ghosh P, Calam J. Campylobacter pylori and duodenal ulcers: the gastrin link. Lancet 1989; 1: 1167–1168.
207. McColl KEL, Fullarton GM, Chittajalu R et al. Plasma gastrin, daytime intragastric pH and nocturnal acid output before and at 1 and 7 months after eradication of Helicobacter pylori in duodenal ulcer subjects. Scand J Gastroent 1991; 26: 339–346.
208. Calam J, Golodner EH, Walsh JH, Soll AH. Mononuclear cells, but not H. pylori, release gastrin from cultured G-cells via diffusable factors. Gut 1993; 34 (Suppl 1): S3.
209. El-Omar E, Penman I, Dorrian CA, Ardill JES, McColl KEL. Eradication of H. pylori lowers gastrin-mediated acid secretion by 70% in DU patients. Gut 1993; 34: 1060–1065.
210. Kline PD. Gastrointestinal Physiology Working Group, Graham DY, Giallour A, Odekun AR, Smith EO'B. Water spores as risk factor for H. pylori infection in Peruvian children. Lancet 1991; 337: 1503–1506.
211. Thomas HE, Gibson GR, Darboe MK, Dale A, Weaver LT.

Isolation of H. pylori from human faeces. Lancet 1992; 340: 1194–1195.
212. Drumm B, Perez-Perez GI, Blaser MJ, Sherman PM. Intrafamilial clustering of Helicobacter pylori infection. N Engl J Med 1990; 322: 359–363.
213. Bamford KB, Bickley J, Collins JSA et al. Helicobacter pylori: comparison of DNA fingerprints provide evidence for intrafamilial infection. Gut 1993; 34: 1348–1350.
214. Nwokolo CU, Bickley J, Attard AR, Owen RJ, Costas M, Fraser IA. Evidence of clonal variants of Helicobacter pylori in three generatins of a duodenal ulcer disease family. Gut 1992; 33: 1323–1327.
215. Shames B, Krajden S, Fuksa M, Babida C, Penner JL. Evidence for the occurrence of the same strain of Campylobacter pylori in the stomach and dental plaque. J Clin Microbiol 1989; 27: 2849–2850.
216. Forman D, Sitas F, Newell DG et al. Geographic association of Helicobacter pylori antibody prevalence and gastric cancer mortality in rural China. Int J Cancer 1990; 46: 608–611.
217. Parsonett J, Friedman GD, Vandersteen DP et al. Helicobacter pylori infection and the risk of gastric carcinoma. N Engl J Med 1991; 325: 1127–1131.
218. Nomura A, Stemmermann GN, Chyou P-H, Kato I, Perez-Perez GI, Blaser MJ. Helicobacter infection and gastric carcinoma among Japanese Americans in Hawaii. N Engl J Med 1991; 325: 1132–1136.
219. Correa P. Is gastric carcinoma an infectious disease? N Engl J Med 1991; 325: 1170–1171.
220. O'Connor HJ. Helicobacter pylori and gastric cancer: a review and hypothesis. Eur J Gastroenterol and Hepatol 1992; 4: 103–109.
221. Sipponen P. Long term consequences of gastro-duodenal inflammation. Eur J Gastroenterol and Hepatol 1992; 4 (Suppl 2): S25–S29.
222. Holcombe C, Thom C, Kaluba J, Lucus SB, Eldridge J, Jones DM. Helicobacter pylori and gastric pathology in northern Nigeria. Gut 1992; 33 (Suppl 1): S41.
223. Wyatt JI, Rathbone BJ. Immune response of gastric mucosa to Campylobacter pylori. Scand J Gastroenterol 1988; 23 (Suppl 142): 44–49.
224. Stolte M, Eidt S. Lymphoid follicles in antral mucosa: immune response to Campylobacter pylori. J Clin Pathol 1989; 42: 1269–1271.
225. Wotherspoon AC, Ortiz-Hidalgo C, Falzon MR, Isaacson PG. Helicobacter pylori-associated gastritis and primary B-cell gastric lymphoma. Lancet 1991; 338: 1175–1176.
226. Hussell T, Isaacson PG, Crabtree JE, Spencer J. Responsive cells from low-grade B-cell gastric lymphomas of mucosa-associated lymphoid tissue to Helicobacter pylori. Lancet 1993; 342: 571–574.
227. Wotherspoon AC, Doglioni C, Diss TC, et al. Regression of primary low-grade B-cell gastric lymphoma of mucosa-associated lymphoid tissue type after eradication of Helicobacter pylori. Lancet 1993; 342: 575–577.
228. Dent JC, McNulty CAM, Uff JC, Wilkinson SP, Gear MWL. Spiral organisms in the gastric antrum. Lancet 1987; 2: 96.
229. McNulty CAM, Dent JC, Curry A et al. New spiral bacterium in gastric mucosa. J Clin Pathol 1989; 42: 585–591.
230. Lee A, Dent J, Hazell S, McNulty C. Origin of spiral organisms in human gastric antrum. Lancet 1988; 1: 300–301.
231. Dye KR, Marshall BJ, Frierson HF, Guerrant RL, McCallum RW. Ultrastructure of another spiral organism associated with human gastritis. Dig Dis Sci 1989; 34: 1787–1791.
232. Sundberg HH. Uber Gastric phlegmone. Nord Med Arkiv 1919; 11: 303–468.
233. Eliason EL, Wright VWM. Phlegmonous gastritis. Surg Clin North Am 1938; 18: 1553–1564.
234. Nevin NC, Eakins D, Clarke SD, Carson DJL. Acute phlegmonous gastritis. Br J Surg 1969; 56: 268–270.
235. Cowan SS, Sarlin JG, Mori K. Phlegmonous gastritis: report of a case. Mt Sinai J Med 1983; 50: 417–419.
236. O'Toole PA, Morris JA. Acute phlegmonous gastritis. Postgrad Med J 1988; 64: 315–316.
237. Mittleman RE, Suarez RV. Phlegmonous gastritis associated with the acquired immunodeficiency syndrome/pre-acquired immunodeficiency syndrome. Arch Pathol Lab Med 1985; 109: 765–767.
238. Zazzo J-F, Troche G, Millat B, Aubert A, Bedossa P, Keros L. Phlegmonous gastritis associated with HIV-I seroconversion. Dig Dis Sci 1992; 37: 1454–1459.
239. Pritchard JE, McRoberts JW. Phlegmonous gastritis. Can Med Assoc J 1931; 25: 183–187.
240. Starr A, Wilson JM. Phlegmonous gastritis. Ann Surg 1957; 145: 88–93.
241. LaForce FM. Diffuse phlegmonous gastritis. Arch Intern Med 1967; 120: 230–233.
242. Francis ND, Boylston AW, Roberts AHG, Parkin JN, Pinching AJ. Cytomegalovirus infection in gastrointestinal tracts of patients infected with HIV-I or AIDS. J Clin Pathol 1989; 42: 1055–1064.
243. Henson D. Cytomegalovirus inclusion bodies in the gatrointestinal tract. Arch Pathol 1972; 93: 477–482.
244. Andrade JDES, Bambirra EA, Lima GF, Moreira EF, De Olivera CA. Gastric cytomegalic inclusion bodies diagnosed by histologic examination of endoscopic biopsies in patients with gastric ulcer. Am J Clin Pathol 1983; 79: 493–496.
245. Aqel NM, Tanner P, Drury A, Francis ND, Henry K. Cytomegalovirus gastritis with perforation and gastrocolic fistula formation. Histopathology 1991; 18: 165–168.
246. Strayer DS, Phillips GB, Barker KH, Winokur T, DeSchryver-Kecskemeti K. Gastric cytomegalovirus infection in bone marrow transplant patients. Cancer 1981; 48: 1478–1483.
247. Levine RS, Warner NE, Johnston CF. Cytomegalic inclusion disease in the gastrointestinal tract of adults. Ann Surg 1964; 159: 37–48.
248. Gazzard BG. HIV disease and the gastroenterologist. Gut 1988; 29: 1497–1505.
249. Sperling HV, Reed WG. Herpetic gastritis. Dig Dis 1977; 22: 1033–1034.
250. Khilnani MT, Keller RJ. Roentgen and pathological changes in the gastrointestinal tract in Herpes Zoster Generalizata. Mt Sinai J Med 1971; 38: 303–310.
251. Guarda LA, Stein SA, Cleary KA, Ordonez NG. Human cryptosporidiosis in the Aquired Immune Deficiency Syndrome. Arch Pathol Lab Med 1983; 107: 562–566.
252. Garcia LW, Hemphill RB, Marasco WA, Ciano PS. Acquired immunodeficiency syndrome with disseminated toxoplasmosis presenting as an acute pulmonary and gastrointestinal illness. Arch Pathol Lab Med 1991; 115: 459–463.
253. Peter ET, Bernstein EF, Sosin H, Madsen AJ, Walder AI, Wangensteen OH. Technique of gastric freezing in the treatment of duodenal ulcer. JAMA 1962; 181: 760–764.
254. Barner HB, Collins CH, Jones TI, Garlick TB. Morphology of human stomach after therapeutic freezing. Arch Surg 1965; 90: 358–362.
255. Allcock EA, Carpenter A-M, Bernstein EF, Peter ET, Wangensteen OH. Structural changes following gastric freezing. Surgery 1963; 53: 764–777.
256. Clearfield HR, Shin YH, Schreibman BK. Emphysematous gastritis secondary to lye ingestion. Am J Dig Dis 1969; 14: 195–199.
257. Han SY, Collins LC, Petrany Z. Emphysematous gastritis. JAMA 1965; 192: 914–916.
258. Jaffe RH, Laing DR. Changes of the digestive tract in uremia. Arch Intern Med 1934; 53: 851–864.
259. Mason EE. Gastrointestinal lesions occurring in uremia. Ann Intern Med 1952; 37: 96–105.
260. Quintero E, Guth PH. Renal failure, increased gastric mucosal blood flow and acid secretion in rats: role of endothelium-derived nitric oxide. Am J Physiol 1992; 263: G75–G80.
261. Musola R, Franzin G, Mora R, Manfrini C. Prevalence of gastroduodenal lesions in uremic patients undergoing dialysis and after renal transplantation. Gastrointest Endosc 1984; 30: 343–346.
262. Goldstein H, Murphy D, Sokol A, Rubina ME. Gastric acid secretion in patients undergoing chronic dialysis. Arch Intern Med 1967; 120: 645–653.

263. Shepherd AMM, Stewart WK, Wormsley KG. Peptic ulcertion in chronic renal failure. Lancet 1973; 1: 1357–1359.
264. Franzin G, Musola R, Mencarelli R. Morphological changes of the gastroduodenal mucosa in regular dialysis uraemic patients. Histopathology 1982; 6: 429–437.
265. Kang JY, Wu AYT, Sutherland IH, Vathsala A. Prevalence of peptic ulcer in patients undergoing maintenance haemodialysis. Dig Dis Sci 1988; 33: 774–778.
266. Hadjiyannakis EJ, Evans DB, Smellie WAB, Calne RY. Gastrointestinal complications after renal transplantation. Lancet 1971; 2: 781–785.
267. Rasmussen K, Christiansen J, Nielsen OV, McNair A, Sorensen MB. Gastroduodenal ulcer in kidney transplanted patients receiving immunosuppressive therapy. Acta Chir Scand 1975; 141: 61–64.
268. Muolo A, Ghidini O, Ancona G et al. Gastroduodenal mucosal changes, gastric acid secretion and gastrin levels following successful kidney transplantation. Transplant Proc 1979; XI: 1277–1279.
269. Boyle JM, Johnston B. Acute upper gastrointestinal haemorrhage in patients with chronic renal disease. Am J Med 1983; 75: 409–412.
270. Cheli R, Dodero M. Etude biopsique et secretoire de la muqueuse gastrique au cours de l'uremie chronique. Acta Gastro-Enterologica Belgica 1958; 21: 193–201.
271. Paimela H, Stenman S, Kekki M, Sipponen P, Tallgren LG, Scheinin TM. Chronic gastritis and gastric acid secretion in uraemic and renal transplant patients. Hepatogastroenterology 1985; 32: 15–19.
272. Franzin G, Musola R, Mencarelli R. Changes in the mucosa of the stomach and duodenum during immunosuppressive therapy after renal transplantation. Histopathology 1982; 6: 439–449.
273. Shousha S, Keen C, Parkins RA. Gastric metaplasia and C. pylori infection of duodenum in patients with chronic renal failure. J Clin Pathol 1989; 42: 348–351.
274. McConnell JB, Thjodleifsson B, Steward WK, Wormsley KG. Gastric function in chronic renal failure. Lancet 1975; 2: 1121–1123.
275. Doherty CC. Gastric secretion in chronic uraemia and after renal transplantation. Irish J Med Sci 1980; 149: 5–9.
276. Walsh JH, Grossman MI. Gastrin. N Engl J Med 1975; 292: 1324–1334.
277. Caruso U, Lezoche E, Ruscitto G et al. Distribution of G-cells in the gastrointestinal mucosa of the uremic patient. Mt Sinai J Med 1983; 50: 85–86.
278. Carlei F, Caruso U, Lezoche E et al. Hyperplasia of antral G-cells in uraemic patients. Digestion 1984; 29: 26–30.
279. Clarke SD, Neill DW, Welbourn RB. The effects of corticotrophin and corticoids on secretion from denervated gastric pouches in dogs. Gut 1960; 1: 36–43.

PART II

Chronic Gastritis

P. Correa

CHRONIC GASTRITIS

The gastric mucosa is a specialized organ and in the lifespan of most individuals is exposed to a variety of injurious agents. Some may be found in the diet, others include, under special circumstances, hydrochloric acid, bile and duodenal juice and injury may be induced by autoimmune circulating antibodies. The gastric mucosa responds to these agents in a rather limited number of ways and on most occasions, initially at least, the structure and function is restored 'ad integrum'. The first line of defence against external injury is the mucus barrier which prevents contact between the epithelial cell and potential irritants or toxins. If that fails and injury is inflicted, inflammatory changes occur, cell replication is stimulated and a remarkable regenerative capacity is displayed. When repair mechanisms are impaired and injury persists, atrophy and metaplasia are observed which probably represent an adaptation to the unfavourable ecological situation. Another element in the evolution of gastritis is genetic susceptibility to injury and this may determine susceptibility to gastritis induced by environmental agents; in some cases this is the overriding aetiological factor.

Given such a complex aetiological background, it is not surprising that our understanding of chronic gastritis is far from complete. The observations available, however, support the view that gastritis progresses in severity from superficial inflammation through progressive stages of deeper inflammation and mucosal atrophy and is associated with an increasing degree of intestinal metaplasia. These histologically identifiable lesions vary in their topographical distribution and with other clinico-pathological associations which indicates that chronic gastritis is not a homogeneous nosological entity. At least four sets of aetiological factors are identifiable in chronic gastritis. These are associated with peptic ulcer disease, pernicious anaemia, chemical irritation and diet. Thus each form of gastritis can be recognized on the basis of its distribution in the stomach, but when more than one aetiological factors operates, mixed forms result. It is assumed that superficial gastritis is the initial stage of most chronic gastritis.

Because the topographical distribution of gastritic lesions is important, it is necessary to clarify certain anatomical terminology. The antrum is that part of the stomach which is limited distally by the pyloric sphincter and proximally by the junction of the specialized pyloric mucus-producing glands and the oxyntic mucosa. The corpus or body is the middle portion of the mucosa limited distally by the junction of pyloric and oxyntic mucosa and proximally by an imaginary horizontal line drawn at the level of the cardia. The fundus is that part which lies above this imaginary line. It is worth stressing that in the literature antral mucosa is also frequently referred to as 'pyloric' and the oxyntic mucosa as 'fundic'.

Our understanding of chronic gastritis has been acquired very gradually and was determined by the increasing sophistication of investigative methods. Many misunderstandings have been corrected, but the two most prominent were that chronic gastritis was an integral part of the normal process of ageing and that chronic gastritis constituted one homogeneous disease entity.

A comprehensive review of the developments is not the purpose of this chapter. Main events will be briefly mentioned in the hope that they will give the readers enough perspective to make their own judgement when interpreting the presently available medical literature.

Cruveilhier[1] associated it with gastric ulcer in 1862 and Fenwick[2] with pernicious anaemia in 1870. In 1883 Kupfer described intestinal metaplasia which is now recognized as part of the spectrum of chronic gastritis.[3] He interpreted it as a heterotopia, but this was challenged by Schmidt in 1896 and it is now accepted that it represents a metaplastic process triggered by chronic atrophic gastritis.[4]

In the first decades of this century chronic gastritis received attention mostly as a clinical entity described among others by Ostler and McRae as loss of appetite, painful feeling, nausea, eructation of gas, vomiting and other signs and symptoms of 'dyspepsia'.[5] He recognized that 'the disease itself probably does not cause many symptoms', pointing to a lack of correlation between clinical and pathological findings which has been reported by many recent investigators.[6,7] A link between chronic gastritis and cancer was suspected by Bonne et al[8] who in 1938 reported that Chinese immigrants had a higher frequency of gastric cancer and chronic atrophic gastritis with 'goblet cell metaplasia' than native Malays. At that time most observations were made on autopsy material, the problem of autolysis being overcome by the instillation of formalin into the stomach soon after death. At approximately this time also, the gastritis associated with pernicious anaemia was noted to have a different topographical distribution than that associated with gastric ulcer.[9,10] Jarvis and Lauren in 1951[11] discussed the relationships between certain types of gastric carcinoma and the presence of intestinal type glands in the gastric mucosa. Apparently the idea that the 'tumour has its origin in the numerous islands of intestinal epithelium' was first proposed by Schmidt in 1896[2] and later by Gosset and Masson in 1912.[12] When Finnish investigators[13] described diffuse and so-called intestinal type carcinomas, Morson[14] documented gastric carcinomas arising from areas of intestinal metaplasia. The relationship of the 'intestinal type' of carcinoma to intestinal metaplasia[15] was further strengthened. Further progress in the understanding of this relationship has been made recently and will be reviewed later.

The realization that chronic gastritis is not a homogeneous entity came mainly from observations of its variable severity and of differences in its topographic distribution. Motteram[16] in 1951 pointed out that in some cases the inflammatory infiltrate is limited to the superficial layers while the deeper glandular component of the mucosa is preserved (superficial gastritis) while in others the mucosa is atrophic (atrophic gastritis). Observations on the topographical distribution of the lesions was for a long time misunderstood because it was linked to peptic ulcer, considered by some investigators as the primary lesion[17] and therefore determining the location of gastritis in its vicinity. The school of thought which places gastritis as the primary lesion and peptic ulceration as secondary, postulates that duodenal and prepyloric ulcers represent one syndrome preceded by antral gastritis while a higher gastric ulcer is part of a different nosological complex characterized by multifocal gastritis in the antrum and corpus.[18] The latter was then recognized as a different disease from the pernicious anaemia related chronic gastritis which had been described as occupying the corpus and fundus in a diffuse manner and is not significantly associated with peptic ulceration.[19] The available observations thus made it possible to divide gastritis into superficial and atrophic types with antral, corporal and multifocal distribution.

In the 1970s a wealth of information became available and was the subject of a scholarly review by Lambert.[20] It was by then well documented that the diffuse corporal gastritis with pernicious anaemia was characterized by autoantibodies against parietal cells and intrinsic factor, hypergastrinaemia and low output of hydrochloric acid and pepsinogen. Antral gastritis associated with duodenal ulcer was mostly associated with excessive secretion of acid and pepsin and often occurred in a distinct clinical setting in which psychomatic and neurogenic mechanisms could operate. Multifocal gastritis was less well-defined, mostly because the physiopathological parameters appear to change with the progression of the disease. In the early stage there are minimal changes in hydrochloric acid and pepsin secretion, but both tend to decrease in the later stages. Recently information concerning enzymes, gastric antigens, cell kinetics, histochemistry and molecular biology has allowed refinements in the characterization of gastritis.

Strickland and Mackay[21] combined morphological information and physiopathological parameters in proposing the term Type A gastritis for the corporal lesion associated with the pernicious anaemia syndrome. All other gastritis were called Type B, which led some authors to apply the term to the gastritis associated with duodenal ulcer[22] and others to multifocal gastritis.[23] Glass and Pitchumoni[24] proposed the term pangastritis for cases not classifiable as Type A or B, also called type AB gastritis. Superficial gastritis is not clearly identified with a specific set of aetiological factors and may represent initial stages of the other forms.

There are two terms — which frequently appear in the relevant medical literature — which could be abandoned with benefit. The first is 'simple gastritis' because it means 'not atrophic' to some, not associated with pernicious anaemia to others and not associated with focal lesions (i.e. ulcers) to still others. The second is 'gastric atrophy' which is widely used to describe the lesion in pernicious anaemia and for advanced stages of atrophic gastritis. It is meant to convey the message of scant or absent leucocytic infiltrate and advanced metaplasia; however, these changes are legitimately covered by the term atrophic gastritis which implies a specific tissue response to injury. The term gastric atrophy has little if any clinical usefulness since chronic atrophic gastritis is one and the same lesion.[25]

In an attempt to clarify the terminology of chronic gastritis, the organizers of the 1990 World Congress of Gastroenterology devised the so-called Sydney System which takes into account the endoscopic and histological information and adds a prefix to indicate the aetiological and pathogenic associations.[26] The Sydney System recommends uniform grading of each morphological parameter within each location (antrum and corpus). The system is an acceptable outline to grade chronic gastritis but has short-comings as a classification because it does not clearly describe separate nosological entities.[27]

The classification proposed here, shown in Table 25.1, is derived from an attempt to reconcile morphology, physiopathology, aetiology and the clinical setting in which it occurs.[28] Although describing prototypes of gastritis, it leaves room for the recognition of mixed forms which are probably present in populations where more than one set of aetiological factors are in operation.

It recognizes five basic kinds of gastritis: two which are atrophic and three which are non-atrophic. Four of them represent well defined clinical entities whilst the fifth (superficial gastritis) probably represents the initial stages of the others. All are well described in the relevant medical literature, but as yet a consensus has not been reached on the terminology used. Recognizing this, the classification is given together with alternative terminology for each of three entities (Table 25.1). One alternative is based on morphological or nosological grounds which gave origin to the original name assigned and the other on mechanistic considerations.

It should be understood that the mechanistic classification does not imply aetiological certainty but it is based upon statistical associations which suggest aetiological relevance. Parietal cell autoantibodies are usually associated with diffuse corporal gastritis but not all investigators believe that they are the cause of the gastritis. Likewise, hypersecretion is frequently, but not always, present in patients with duodenal ulcer and an antral gastritis.

Table 25.1 Classification of chronic gastritis.

Name: Morphological	Name: Mechanistic	Synonyms
Not atrophic		
Superficial	*H. Pylori*	Simple (?)
Diffuse antral (DAG)	Hypersecretory & *H. pylori*	Antral Type B Follicular Diffuse interstitial
Reflux (CIG)	Chemical irritational	Type C (chemical) Reactive
Atrophic		
Diffuse corporal	Autoimmune	Type A
Multifocal (MAG)	Environmental & *H. pylori*	Dietary Type B Pangastritis Type AB

Superficial gastritis

Morphology

This is a well recognized histopathological lesion characterized by a band-like infiltrate of lymphocytes and plasma cells in the superficial portion of the lamina propria (Fig. 25.14). The intensity of the infiltrate is variable, but frequently it is very compact, expanding the lamina propria and increasing the distance between the epithelial structures of the mucosa. Although lymphocytes and plasma cells predominate, they may be accompanied by other inflammatory cells (Fig. 25.15). Eosinophils are found frequently scattered among the mononuclear cells. Neutrophilic polymorphonuclear leukocytes may be found and

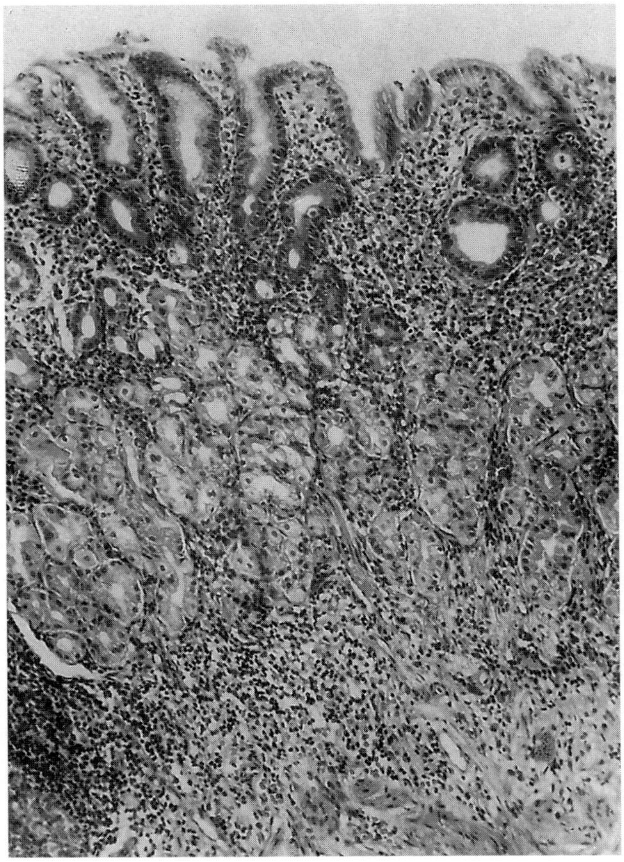

Fig. 25.14 Superficial gastritis. Chronic inflammatory changes are confined to the superficial portion of the mucosa. Note depletion of foveolar cell mucus, hyperplasia of glandular necks and mononuclear infiltrates of the lamina propria. The deeper glands are well preserved.

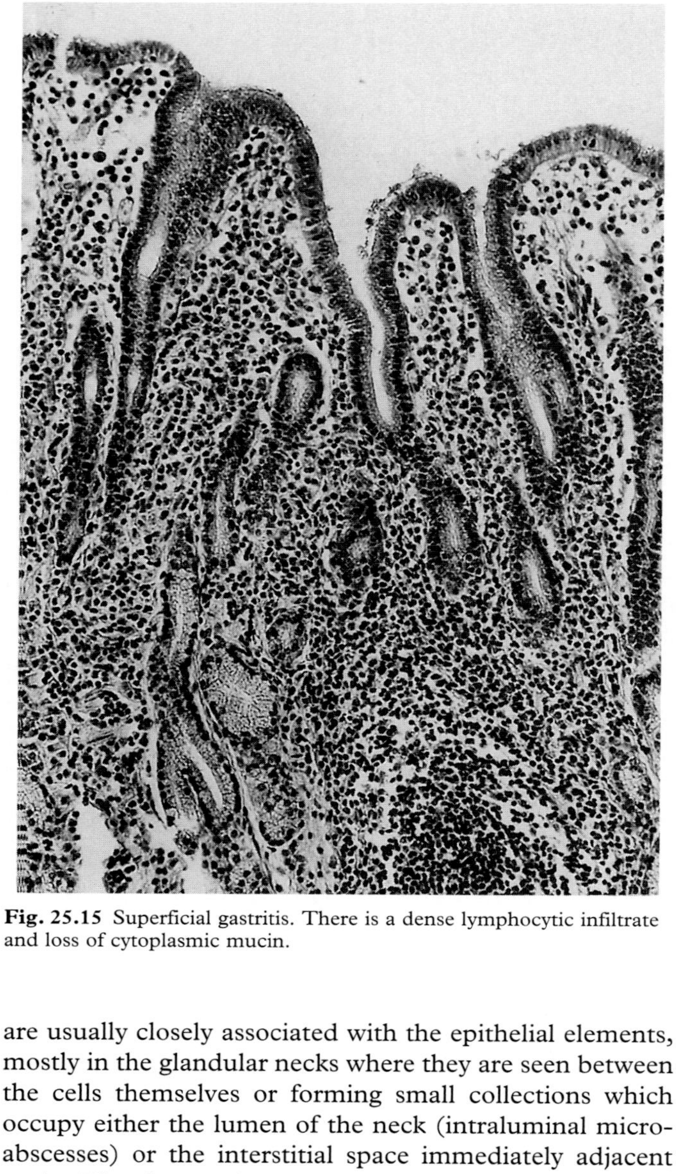

Fig. 25.15 Superficial gastritis. There is a dense lymphocytic infiltrate and loss of cytoplasmic mucin.

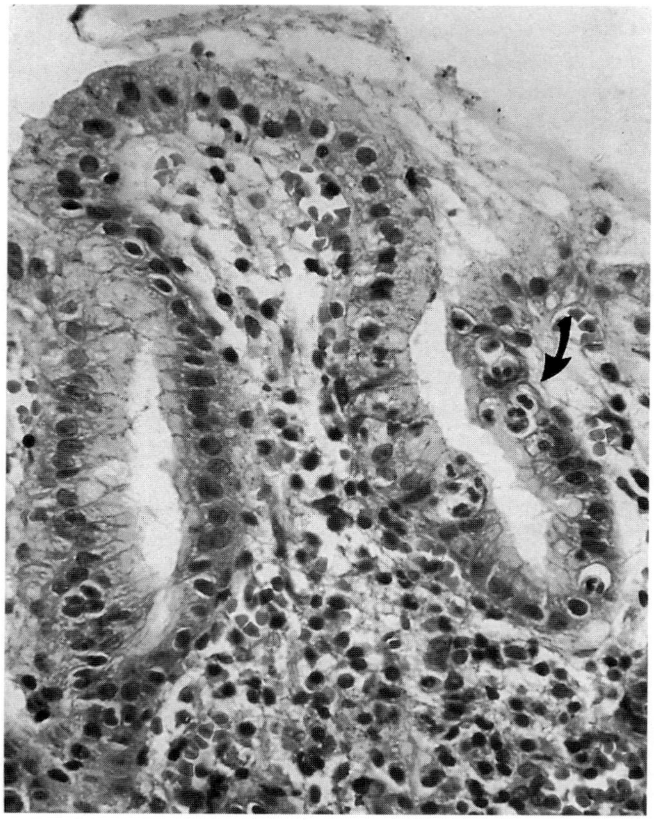

Fig. 25.16 Active changes in superficial gastritis. Note the small collections of polymorphonuclear leucocytes in the foveolar epithelium (arrow). There is infiltration of lymphocytes and plasma cells in the lamina propria.

are usually closely associated with the epithelial elements, mostly in the glandular necks where they are seen between the cells themselves or forming small collections which occupy either the lumen of the neck (intraluminal micro-abscesses) or the interstitial space immediately adjacent to it. The latter changes indicate active gastritis and recent injury and are a good marker of *H. pylori* infection (Fig. 25.16).

The inflammatory infiltrate is accompanied by depletion of intracytoplasmic mucin, which may vary in degree and by cell degeneration and glandular neck hyperplasia. The latter results in elongation and distortion of the shape of the necks as well as increase in the size, number and staining intensity of the nuclei. This regenerative hyperplasia may occasionally be severe enough to simulate dysplasia. The inflammatory changes may occupy between ⅕ and ⅓ of the mucosa but characteristically, the deeper glands are morphologically intact.

Topography

Superficial gastritis may be found in any portion of the gastric mucosa. It is frequent to find it in antral biopsies in patients with a normal corpus and the contrary situation of a normal antrum and an inflamed corpus is infrequent.

There is a well known lack of correlation between endoscopic and histopathological findings in superficial gastritis, and therefore, it is difficult to define its distribution with any accuracy, except in multiple biopsies. It would appear to be multifocal in some patients and diffuse in others.

Physiopathology

Little is known of the functional disturbances, if any, which are due to superficial gastritis. There may be marked inter-population differences in both aetiology and significance. The most comprehensive data are available for the Finnish population (Fig. 25.17).[29] Subjects with superficial gastritis who were relatives of pernicious anaemia patients have been compared to similar subjects with a normal mucosa and with subjects having more severe atrophic gastritis. The maximal acid output was lower than normal but higher than in patients with atrophic gas-

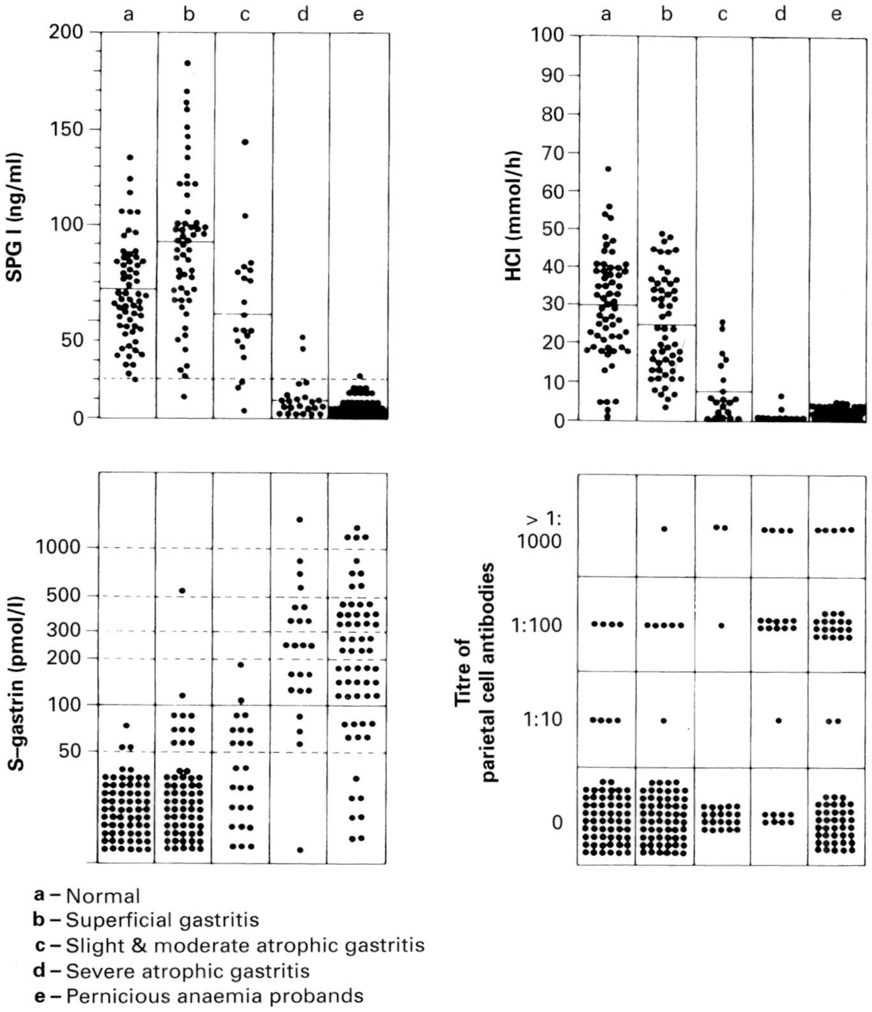

Fig. 25.17 Serum pepsinogen I (SPG I), maximal acid output (HCl), serum gastrin (S-gastrin) and parietal cell antibodies (PCA) in patients with overt pernicious anemia and their first degree relatives according to the histological findings in the gastric body mucosa. (Reproduced with permission: Varis & Isokoski 1981)

tritis. Serum gastrin levels were slightly above normal. Studies of parietal cell antibodies did not show higher levels in subjects with superficial gastritis than in those with a normal mucosa, but it should be pointed out that in both groups approximately 12% of the subjects had detectable levels of parietal cell antibodies. Serum pepsinogen I levels in those with superficial gastritis were slightly higher than normal, which may indicate *H. pylori* infection. Table 25.2 outlines the main clinical features of chronic gastritis and Fig. 26.19 depicts the topographic localization of inflammatory lesions.

Clinical significance

No clear clinical syndrome has been associated with superficial gastritis and there is a lack of correlation between symptoms and gastric mucosal histology.[6,20] According to Lambert[20] the term gastritis is often incorrectly used in a clinical sense to account for the symptomatology in non-ulcer dyspepsia. However it is reported that epigastric pain, feelings of 'fullness', 'heartburn', nausea and vomiting are more frequent in populations with a high incidence of chronic gastritis.[30] On the other hand the lesion is frequently found in asymptomatic patients. It has been postulated that pain arises from distention of an inflamed mucosa, but this is pure speculation.

Aetiology and pathogenesis

Chronic superficial gastritis is a frequent finding in patients with diseases unrelated to the stomach and in patients with anaemia being investigated for suspected carcinoma. Thus it may be the initial phase of atrophic gastritis or it may represent non-specific self-healing episodes of inflammation. Its localization in the superficial layers of the mucosa indicates an injury induced by the gastric contents. The agents responsible appear to overcome the protective mucous barrier and it is notable that the lesion is characterized by a depletion in the mucus of foveolar and surface epithelial cells. It has been associated in humans

Table 25.2 Characteristics of chronic gastritis.

	Diffuse corporal (Autoimmune)	Diffuse antral (DAG)	Multifocal (MAG)	Chemical irritational (CIG)
Topography	Oxyntic mucosa	Antrum	Antrum, body	Diffuse
Histopathology	Atrophy, metaplasia, endocrine-cell hyperlasia	Lymphoid infiltrate	Atrophy, metaplasia, dysplasia	Oedema, foveolar hyperlasia
Genetic predisposition	Autosomal dominant	Heterogeneous	Autosomal recessive	Not relevant
Blood group	A more frequent	More frequent	Same as population	Same as population
Geographical distribution	Northern Europe	Urban centres	China, Japan, Northern Europe, Andes	Universal
Peptic ulcer	No	Duodenal or pyloric	High gastric	No
Aetiology	Genetic	Helicobacter & excessive acid	Diet & Helicobacter	Bile reflux; NSAIDs
Acid-pepsin secretion	Diminished	Increased or normal	Decreased	?
Gastrinaemia	Very elevated	Normal or high	Variable	?
Cancer risk	Questionable	No effect	Elevated	?

with the ingestion of spicy and salty foods,[31] alcohol[32] and analgesic drugs.[33]

The acid environment of the stomach probably plays a role in preventing most forms of bacterial growth and possible injury to the mucosa. The identification of *Helicobacter pylori* as a gastric pathogen in 1983[34] has led to its recognition as the major cause of several types of chronic gastritis, including superficial gastritis. This bacteria has the capacity to damage the mucus substances contained in the cytoplasm of the foveolar cells and can also compete favourably with other bacteria in the acid gastric microenvironment. Even though *Helicobacter pylori* displays negative chemotaxis to acid, it can survive in acid environment. This is accomplished by its potent urease, which splits the urea that leaks through the intercellular spaces into the gastric lumen. This enzyme splits the urea into ammonium and CO_2. The ammonium forms a neutral pH cloud around the bacteria which gives protection from the acid environment. The CO_2 is rapidly absorbed into the peripheral circulation and exhaled in the breath. Ingested urea tagged with C_{13} or C_{14} can be detected within minutes in the exhaled air of individuals infected with *Helicobacter pylori*. C_{13} and C_{14} breath urea tests are very useful to detect Helicobacter-associated gastritis (of all types).[35,36]

Diffuse antral (hypersecretory) gastritis (DAG)

Morphology

This type of chronic gastritis is characterized by an intense interstitial mononuclear infiltrate in the antral region of the gastric mucosa. The infiltrate consists mainly of mature lymphocytes but some plasma cells also occur especially in the superficial layers. Lymphoid follicles with prominent germinal centres are also frequently seen in the deeper aspect of the mucosa. These expand the lamina propria and separate the epithelial structures from each other (Fig. 25.18). This may give a false impression of epithelial atrophy, but the number of glands is probably not reduced and their separation from each other is compensated by an increase in the thickness of the mucosa. The epithelial changes consist of a decrease in the amount of mucin in the cytoplasm and an elongation of the suprafoveolar portion of the mucosa. Epithelial changes, mucus depletion and foveolar hyperplasia vary in intensity, probably reflecting different degrees of injury.

Small foci of intestinal metaplasia may occasionally be found but they are usually found in association with multifocal gastritis and probably represent this entity rather than being an integral part of diffuse antral gastritis.

Topography

This is primarily a diffuse antral lesion (Fig. 25.19) and the corpus mucosa is usually normal but occasionally shows small superficial foci of mononuclear infiltrate.

Physiopathology

Diffuse interstitial antral gastritis is part of the nosological entity of peptic ulcer of the duodenum and pyloric ring.[18,20,37] It is generally characterized by excessive acid and pepsin secretion and gastrin hypersecretion may also

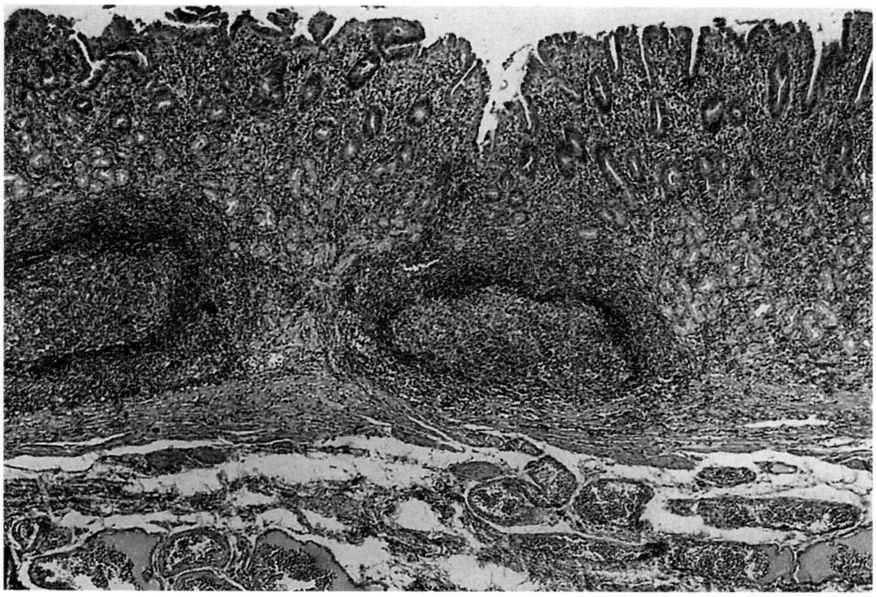

Fig. 25.18 Diffuse antral (hypersecretory) gastritis. A dense mononuclear infiltrate is present diffusely throughout the mucosa. Several lymphoid follicles are present. An adequate number of glands is seen. Decreased mucus secretion and glandular neck hyperplasia are observed in the superficial layers.

be present. It is well established that hyperacidity is not present in all patients with duodenal and pyloric ulcers which probably indicates that such ulcers may be induced in other ways. Aspirin and similar drugs have been associated with ulcers, but the type of mucosal lesion associated with it is not DAG but rather the chemical irritational gastritis described below.

Clinical significance

The signs and symptoms associated with this type of gastritis are basically those of duodenal peptic ulcer.

Aetiology and pathogenesis

It is now recognized that the overriding cause of DAG is *Helicobacter pylori* infection. The bacteria can be detected in approximately 90% of the cases.[38] The same bacteria are associated with superficial gastritis and MAG. The reasons for the different morphological expressions associated with Helicobacter infection are poorly understood. It has been proposed that when the acid output is abundant, bacterial colonization is not favourable in the corpus and, therefore, the colonization and the gastritis remain confined to the antrum. It is also possible that dietary factors play a role in determining the outcome of *Helicobacter pylori* infection. At present, the cofactors involved in the causation of this desease complex are unknown, but it is widely believed that they are present.

Helicobacter infection brings about marked alterations of the feedback mechanism of hydrochloric acid secretion. This was first shown in volunteers recruited to study gastric secretion who accidentally became infected with Helicobacter and developed 'epidemic' hypochlorhydria.[39] It is now known that *Helicobacter pylori*, probably via soluble products ,make parietal cells less responsive to gastrin stimulation and may lead to moderate hypergastrinemia.[40]

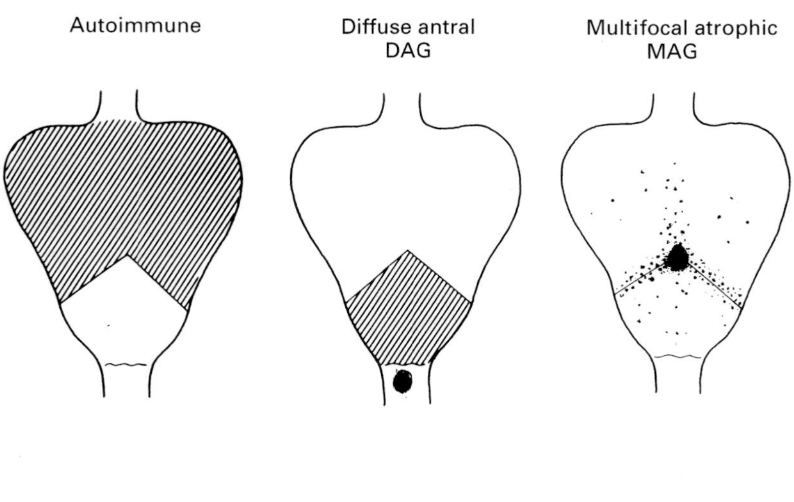

Fig. 25.19 Schematic representation of the topographical distribution of the three main types of chronic gastritis. Diffuse antral gastritis is localized to the antrum and may be associated with duodenal ulcer. Autoimmune gastritis affects the corpus and body diffusely. Multifocal environmental gastritis first appears as discrete foci in the area of the incisura angularis and the junction between corpus and antrum. It then spreads up and down the lesser curvature and finally to other portions of the mucosa. It may be associated with high gastric peptic ulcer. (Reproduced with permission: S. Karger AG, Basel).

Chemical irritational gastritis (CIG)

This new entity was first recognized in patients with previous gastric surgery who had enterogastric reflux, which gave it the name of 'reflux gastritis'.[41] It was later realized that the same histological changes are seen in patients taking aspirin or other non-steroid anti-inflammatory drugs (NSAIDS).[42] It is also suspected that alcohol may elicit a similar response. It thus appears that this type of gastritis may be very prevalent in populations where the above factors are common. Because chemical irritations may be the common link between the aetiological factors, other names have been proposed, such as 'chemical' or 'reactive' gastritis. The search for an appropriate name continues for this 'irritational' gastritis.

Chemical irritations may be due to compounds ingested or regurgitated, such as aspirin, alcohol or biliary components. They damage the surface epithelium, disrupt the mucus barrier, induce capillary dilatation and oedema of the superficial portions of the lamina propria. Foveolar hyperplasia is a prominent feature of the reaction of these irritants. The inflammatory cellular infiltrate is minimal and consists mainly of scarce lymphocytic and plasma cells. In long-standing cases smooth muscle bundles are seen in the lamina propria (Figs 25.20 & 25.21).

Pure cases of this type of gastritis are usually negative for Helicobacter infection. It is possible however, that irritation from bile, NSAID and alcohol is present in patients with Helicobacter-associated gastritis. In such cases a mixture of histological features is expected.

Diffuse corporal (autoimmune) gastritis

Morphology

Typically in this entity there is a diffuse involvement of the mucosa of the corpus and fundus by chronic atrophic gastritis. The prevalence and the severity of the gastritis increases with age, suggesting a chronically progressive disease. Superficial gastritis, representing the early lesion, may be present in both the corpus and antrum, but the more advanced lesion, namely atrophy and intestinal metaplasia, characteristically involve the oxyntic mucosa and spare the antrum.

The inflammatory infiltrate is mostly composed of lymphocytes and plasma cells. It is more intense in early lesions and becomes less conspicuous in the advanced metaplasia observed in the elderly. These advanced lesions are sometimes called 'gastric atrophy' but this is

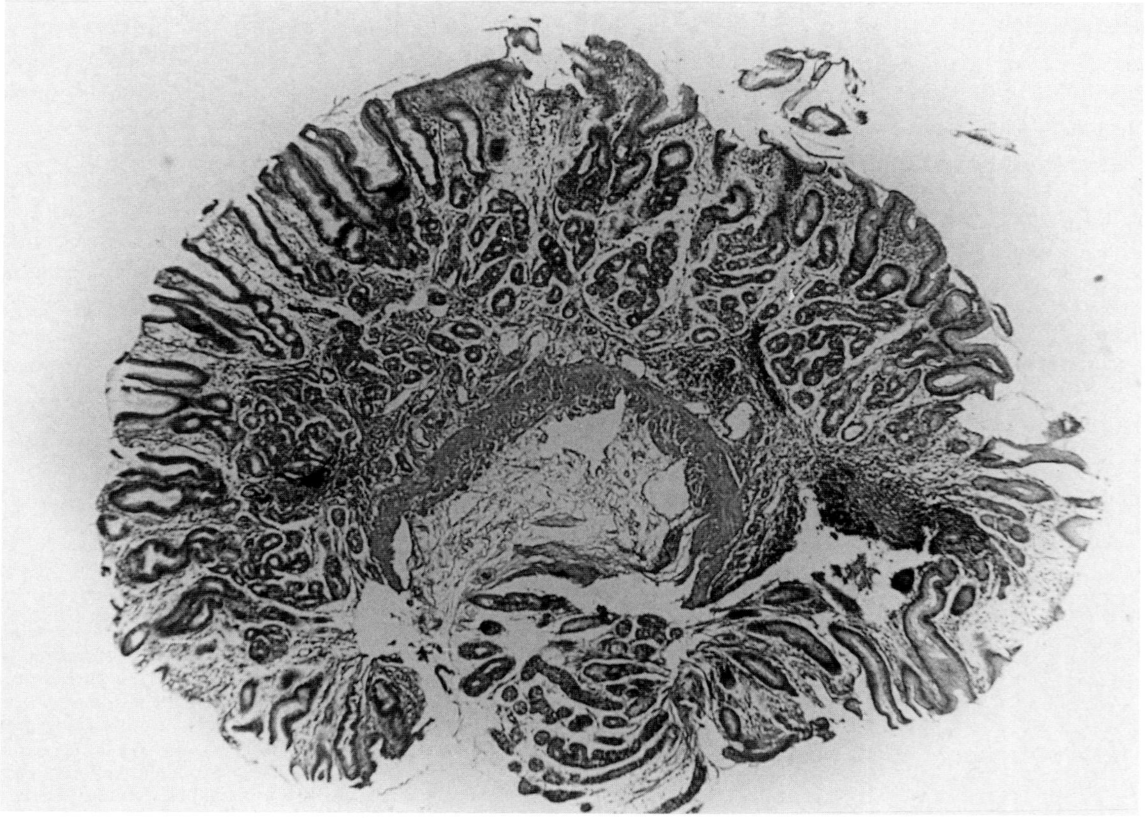

Fig. 25.20 Chemical irritational gastritis (CIG), also called reflux or reactive gastritis. Interstitial oedema compresses the glands. Foveolar hyperplasia results in elongation and irregularity of the foveolae.

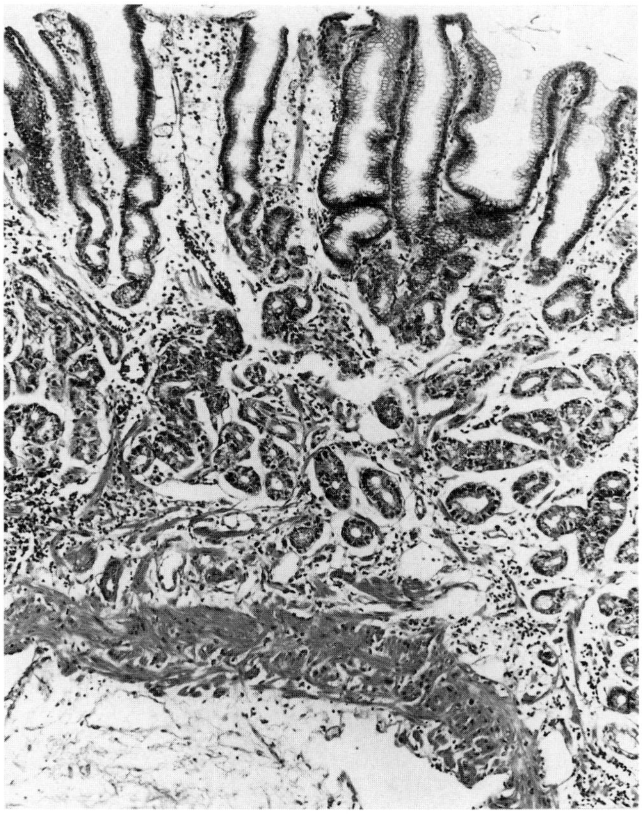

Fig. 25.21 Chemical irritational gastritis. Note also capillary dilatation and smooth muscle bundles and the scant infiltrate by lymphocytes in the stroma.

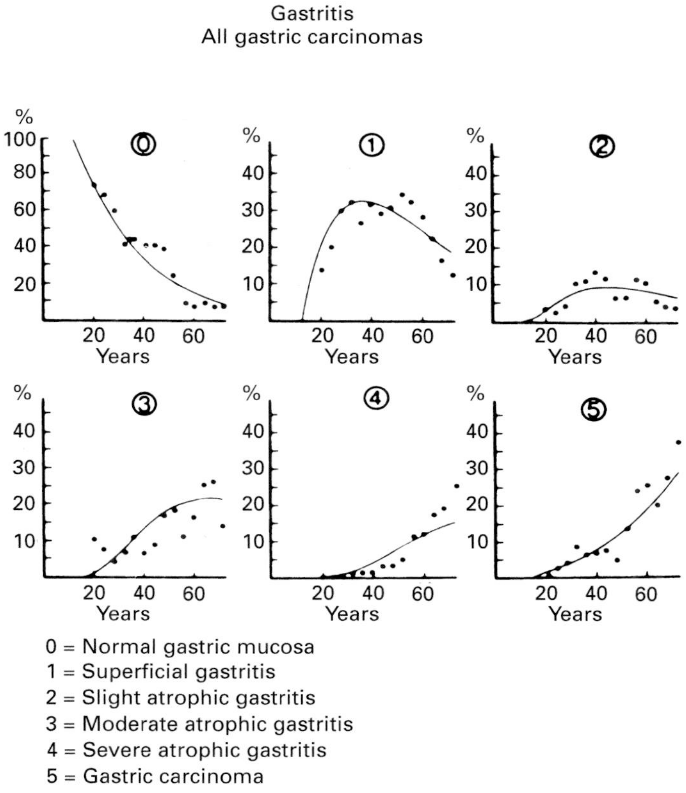

Fig. 25.22 Prevalence of gastritis by age in relatives of patients with atrophic gastritis, pernicious anaemia and gastric carcinoma. The statistical model suggests that superficial gastritis peaks around age 40 and is an intermediate stage in the progression from normal mucosa to atrophic gastritis. Reproduced with permission: Varis et al 1978; Siurala 1980)

not a separate entity and there is no real line of demarcation between advanced atrophic gastritis and so-called gastric atrophy.

The spectrum of lesions associated with the development of atrophic gastritis has been well illustrated in first degree relatives of patients with gastric carcinoma.[43] The prevalence of superficial gastritis peaks around age 40 and then gradually declines with age whereas the prevalence of atrophic gastritis steadily increases after age 20. (Fig. 25.22.)

Topography

As stated, this type of gastritis involves in a diffuse manner the oxyntic mucosa of corpus and fundus. This classical description has been challenged by investigators who report antral lesions in patients with pernicious anaemia.[44] The controversy appears at least partially settled by the elegant studies of Finnish investigators[45–47] who have followed-up patients with repeated gastric biopsies for periods up to 34 years and have also applied mathematical models to cross-sectional data. Both methodological approaches show that oxyntic mucosa gastritis progresses steadily over the years whereas antral gastritis decreases in frequency after age 50–60. The older patient will usually show a normal antrum and a severely damaged corpus and fundus, while the younger patient may have superficial antral gastritis and only a moderate atrophic gastritis in the corpus and fundus.

The lesions in the antrum usually do not include atrophic changes but when they do, it probably represents the effect of additional aetiological factors associated with multifocal atrophic gastritis.

Physiopathology

Diffuse corporal gastritis is frequently associated with autoantibodies to parietal cells and intrinsic factor — components of the pernicious anaemia complex.[21] Some patients with diffuse corporal and fundic gastritis, however, do not have pernicious anaemia, but if followed-up for approximately 15 years, many will be found to have developed the disease.[48] Very rarely, patients with pernicious anaemia do not have parietal cell antibodies and cellular immune mechanisms may be involved.[49] Congenital deficiency of intrinsic factor and immune deficiency may be involved in cases where there are discrepancies between morphology and immunological status. Another factor to be considered is that very small amounts of vitamin B_{12} stored in the liver may suffice to prevent the development of megaloblastic anaemia for some time.

Patients with diffuse autoimmune gastritis usually have progressively decreasing secretion of hydrochloric acid and pepsin, with complete achlorhydria in the final stages. This progressive damage of the oxyntic mucosa is well reflected in the low levels of pepsinogen I and II in the blood and urine[29] (Fig. 25.25). Gastrin levels in the blood are elevated, due to hypochlorhydria in the presence of an intact antrum and its G cells. The combination of high serum gastrin levels and low serum pepsinogen I has in the past been considered specific for diffuse autoimmune gastritis but this has recently been challenged.

The mucous secretions of patients with intestinal metaplasia are markedly altered with abnormal sialo- and sulfomucins replacing partially or totally the normally neutral glycoproteins. A foetal sulfoglycoprotein antigen, apparently related to blood group antigens, and not normally present in the gastric juice, has been demonstrated in patients with clinically undetected gastric cancer, chronic atrophic gastritis, gastric polyps and ulcers. It has been used as a screening technique for gastric cancer and precancerous lesions.[50]

Clinical significance

No specific clinical signs and symptoms have been related to diffuse autoimmune gastritis. In fact, most patients discovered by means of endoscopic surveys of a population have been asymptomatic.[6] Advanced lesions are, of course, usually associated with anaemia, but non-ulcer dyspepsia, gastric pain and fullness are no more commonly seen than in patients who have no gastritis.

Aetiology and pathogenesis

This disease primarily affects subjects of northern European extraction and is more frequent in persons of blood group A who have light blue eyes and premature gray hair. It is rare in other populations. The tendency to form parietal cell auto-antibodies appears to be transmitted in an autosomal dominant fashion with incomplete penetrance.[48] Some members of pernicious anaemia families who have parietal cell antibodies do not have gastritis, but this often develops with increasing age.

In most populations where diffuse autoimmune gastritis and pernicious anaemia are prevalent there is also a high incidence of multifocal gastritis. Mixed forms then occur with extensive atrophy and metaplasia of corpus and antrum.

Multifocal atrophic gastritis (MAG)

This is the most frequent form of chronic atrophic gastritis in all populations studied, but in those of northern European extraction it is frequently combined with diffuse corporal (autoimmune) gastritis. The description is based upon observations in populations in which autoimmune gastritis is so rare that it can be considered non-existent.[15,51]

Morphology

Multifocal atrophic gastritis is a disease complex characterized at one time or another by superficial gastritis, regenerative epithelial changes, loss of glands, pseudopyloric metaplasia, intestinal metaplasia of small intestinal and colonic types, erosions, gastric peptic ulcers, epithelial dysplasia and adenocarcinomas. The lesions follow a pattern of progression in severity and extension, but it is apparent that the advance from one stage to the next may or may not take place and is not predictable.

The early stages of this complex are represented by superficial gastritis already described. When the main feature of this lesion is lymphoplasmocytic infiltrate, a quiescent stage is presumed. When polymorphonuclear infiltrate is superimposed, the gastritis is considered active. The intensity of the polymorphonuclear infiltrate correlates with the presence of *Helicobacter pylori*. This bacterial infection is highly prevalent in MAG. In different series it has been reported in 65% to 100% of cases.[52] It has been postulated that *H. pylori* infection is a cause of atrophy. In a cohort study a rate of progression from non-atrophic to atrophic gastritis of 3.3 per 100 person years was reported.[53] It is strongly suspected that *H. pylori* is an important causal factor in such progression. Other factors, however, most probably act in concert with *H. pylori* infections.

Atrophy is recognized by the loss of gastric glands, a gradual process which may lead to total loss of glands in the antrum and corpus. The glands are replaced by crypts lined by intestinal type cells. From population studies it has been inferred that this metaplastic change is also progressive, first manifested by the presence of absorptive enterocytes, alternating with goblet cells which secrete sialomucin. Since this is the normal appearance of the small intestine, this pattern is called 'small intestinal' or type I metaplasia. In older, more extensive and more advanced lesions the enterocytes disappear and are replaced by columnar cells with abundant mucous droplets in their cytoplasm which lack a well-developed brush border. In this pattern, sulphomucins are detected in both columnar and goblet cells. Since this is typical of the large intestine, this pattern has been called 'colonic' or type III metaplasia. Colonic metaplasia is associated with dysplasia and carcinoma more frequently than small intestinal metaplasia. This pattern of change from normal mucosa to carcinoma has been interpreted as a progressive loss of differentiation. Adenomatous polyps may be observed in advanced stages of autoimmune gastritis. Well-differentiated adenocarcinomas are the final stage of this complex and may arise in the polyps or in the flat mucosa.

Atrophy, or loss of glands brings about drastic changes in the gastric micro-environment (Fig. 25.23). Progressive loss of glands results in diminished acid and pepsin secretions. The resulting hypochlorhydria allows bacterial colonization.

Atrophy is recognized by thinning of the mucosa, characteristically multifocal or 'patchy' in this condition. Microscopically, the loss of glands results in relative widening of the lamina propria and collapse of the reticulum fibres. As the atrophy advances, the leukocytic infiltrate decreases.

The loss of glands and superficial epithelium brings about hyperplastic changes in the glandular neck cells, the only ones with replicating capacity in the normal gastric mucosa. The proliferative compartment is expanded. Glandular neck hyperplasia results in elongated and distorted tubular or pseudopapillary structures composed of cells with nuclei that are large, oval or elongated but have a regular and smooth nuclear membrane, which helps to differentiate the appearance from dysplasia.

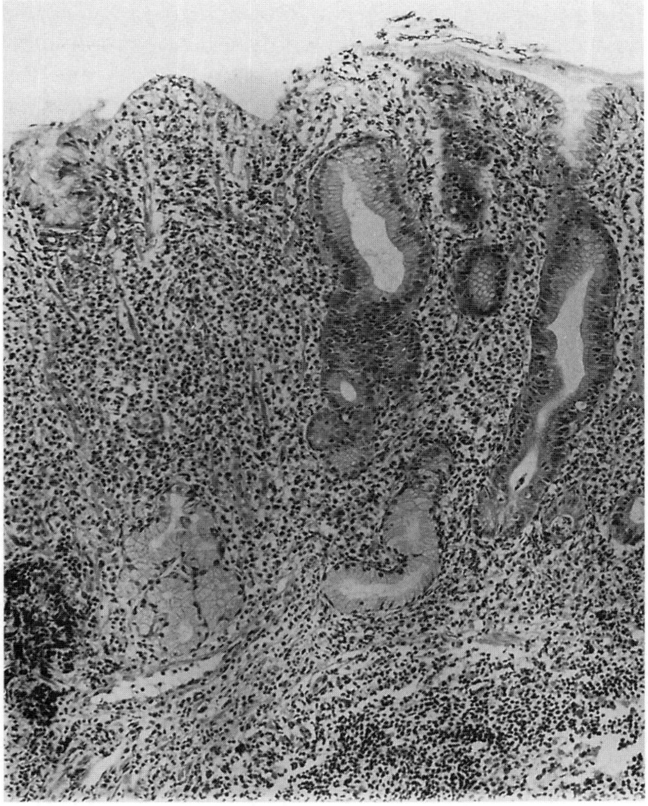

Fig. 25.23 Chronic atrophic gastritis. Loss of glands is the hallmark of this condition. Of the normal antral glands only a small cluster remains on the left side of the photograph. The lamina propria displays a mononuclear infiltrate. The remaining glands are widely separated from each other. Some glandular necks are hyperplastic.

The foci of atrophy and the altered mucous secretions make the mucosa more vulnerable to damage by the acid and pepsin secretions and this may lead to erosions and peptic ulceration. Ulcers tend to heal as acid secretion decreases due to progressive atrophy of the gastric glands. Most peptic ulcers associated with chronic gastritis are located near the incisura angularis, where atrophic changes appear earlier in the process and are more intense.[54]

As the atrophy advances, some of the glands lost in the corpus and the corpus-antrum junction are replaced by mucus-secreting glands, a phenomenon known as pseudopyloric metaplasia.[55] This is associated with an expansion of the antral mucosa at the expense of the corporal mucosa, sometimes referred to as upward migration of the antrum-corpus junction.

The inflammatory and atrophic phases are followed by a change of the phenotype of the gastric epithelial cells. The normal gastric epithelium is replaced by cells with morphological features of intestinal epithelia (Fig. 25.24). In most patients, intestinal metaplasia does not progress to more advanced lesions but in a few progression to dysplasia occurs (Fig. 25.25). Frequently, a biopsy showing dysplasia is followed by further endoscopic or surgical procedures which reveal the presence of invasive adenocarcinoma. It is impossible to tell if the dysplasia preceded or developed in parallel with the carcinoma, but its presence is always an ominous sign which should lead to thorough investigation of the patient.

Most dysplasias are observed in populations at high risk for intestinal type of gastric carcinoma and occur on a background of intestinal metaplasia.[56] Occasionally, dysplasia appears to originate in non-metaplastic epithelium. Diffuse carcinomas as a rule are not seen where there is a background of mucosal metaplasia or dysplasia. Some diffuse carcinomas, especially the signet ring type, are accompanied by a special form of dysplastic metaplasia called 'globoid dysplasia'.[57] It consists of the presence of foveolar cells whose cytoplasm is overdistended by a large mucous vacuole which compresses the nucleus to the periphery of the cell. The nucleus is frequently seen in the superficial side of the mucosa, and for that reason such cells are called 'inverted' goblet cells. The mucin is neutral and usually of gastric foveolar type, but the morphology is similar to the cells of the intestine. These changes are seen late in the development of the carcinoma.

It is customary to subdivide dysplasias according to the degree of severity, but different investigators use two, three or more subdivisions.[58–61] The more advanced degrees are also known as borderline lesion, atypical epithelium Type IV (Japanese classification), pre-invasive carcinoma or intraepithelial carcinoma. In the absence of a consensus and of internationally accepted criteria for the subdivisions, each pathologist should use a nomenclature which conveys a clear message to the clinician submitting biopsy material. When assessed subjectively it is natural

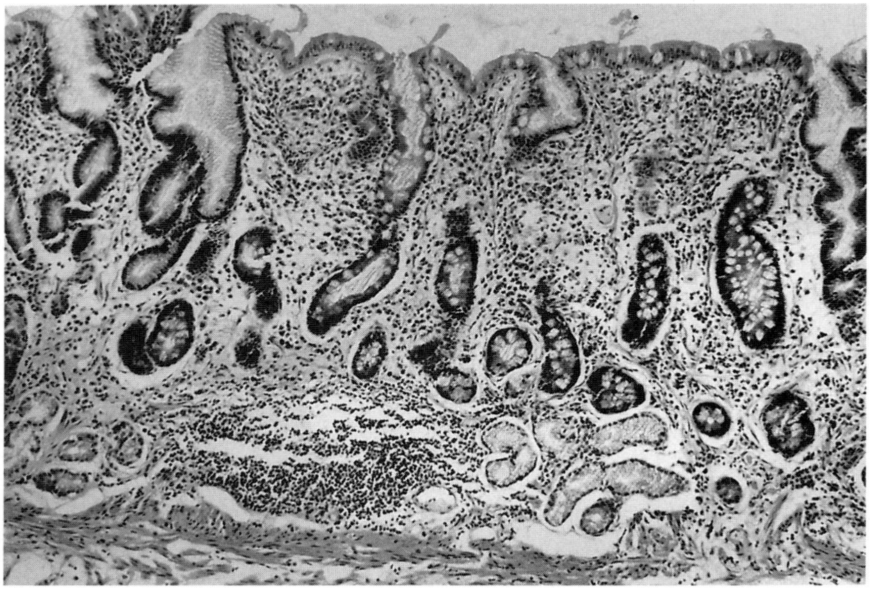

Fig. 25.24 Chronic atrophic gastritis and intestinal metaplasia. Most antral glands have disappeared. The glands that remain and part of the surface epithelium are replaced by intestinal type epithelium lined by alternating goblet and absorptive cells.

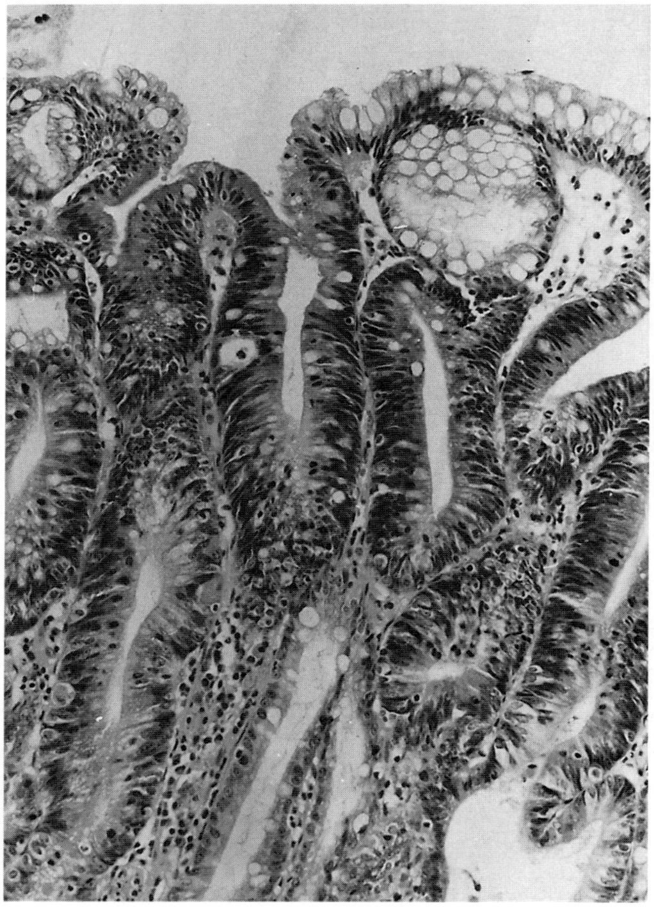

Fig. 25.25 Adenomatous dysplasia of the region of the gland necks in a background of mature intestinal metaplasia. The nuclei are elongated, hyperchromatic and crowded.

for pathologists to be cautious in diagnosing dysplasia and it has been suggested that the nomenclature developed for assessing large bowel dysplasia be adopted.[62] When in doubt 'dysplasia indefinite' can be used and repeat biopsy performed after a time interval. Objective parameters such as nuclear size, variability, crowding and elongation, DNA content, nucleocytoplasmic ratio, mitotic index and thymidine labelling have all been examined and there are computer-assisted morphometric techniques which simplify these procedures. Nuclear size has proven the main discriminating variable when this technique is utilized and this procedure makes it possible to clarify more accurately cases of so-called 'dysplasia indefinite'.[63]

Proliferative and antigenic abnormalities

Multifocal atrophic gastritis leads to loss of glands and decrease in tissue mass, although kinetic studies reveal increased turnover. Incubation of gastric biopsies with tritiated thymidine followed by autoradiography shows an expansion of the zone of cell replication which is normally confined to the gland necks and an increase of the labelling index in all compartments of the gastric pit. Given the multifocal character of the gastritis, this phenomenon occurs in both antrum and corpus. The increased cell replication is accompanied by an expression of fetal antigens, reflecting a loss of cell differentiation. Figure 25.26 compares the antral labelling index of each pit compartment with its reactivity to lambda fetal antigen.[64] This antigen is expressed in human fetal, but not in normal adult gastric mucosa. A high labelling index is seen in antigen positive but not in antigen negative compartments. The very superficial foveolar cells are the only exception to this rule. Such discrimination was not found in

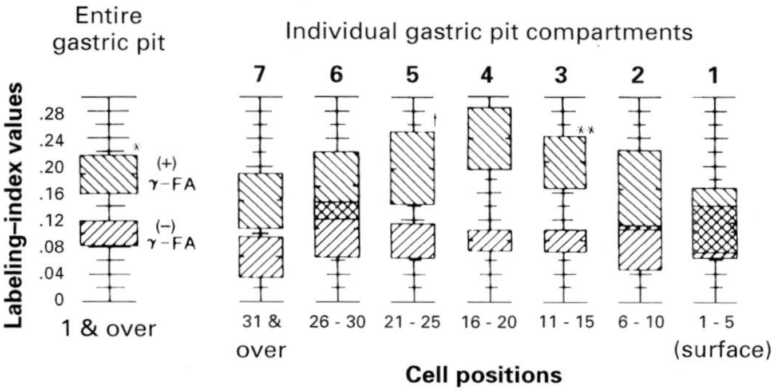

Fig. 25.26 Tritiated thymidine incorporation in gastric antral biopsies with chronic atrophic gastritis. ——— indicates cases of atrophic gastritis; ▨ indicates cases positive for gamma fetal antigen (γ-FA⊕); ▧ indicates cases negative for gamma fetal antigen (γ-FA⊖). The labelling index (thymidine incorporation) is higher at all levels of the gastric pit for cases positive for the fetal antigen (Lipkin et al 1985).

the corpus and fundic mucosa of the same patients, indicating a more advanced loss of differentiation in the antrum. There is also a correlation between tritiated thymidine labelling and the expression of alkaline phosphatase, a marker of metaplasia.[65]

Other fetal antigens have also been found in multifocal environmental gastritis. Table 25.3 shows an increase in the prevalence of expression of second trimester fetal antigen in accordance with the degree of progression of the lesions.[66]

Nardelli and co-workers have identified three separate antigens in human goblet cells: M3SI found in the small intestine, M3D found in the duodenum and M3C in the colon.[67] The intestinal metaplasia adjacent to gastric carcinomas contained all three antigens, which is the pattern found in fetal duodenum and is the equivalent of what is also called 'colonic' metaplasia.

Skinner and Whitehead have studied the behavior of fetal and tumour antigens in intestinal metaplasia and gastric cancer.[68] Interestingly, metaplasia associated with cancer, but not itself distinguishable on routine staining from metaplasia not associated with cancer, had a pattern of antigen expression similar to that of cancer tissue itself. Tumour-associated antigens obtained from colon carcinoma (rCSA) and pregnancy specific beta-glycoprotein (SPI) were detected in carcinomas and in intestinal metaplasia associated with carcinomas but not in intestinal metaplasia associated with chronic gastritis only. Carcinoembryonic antigen (CEA), alpha-fetoprotein and human placental lactogen (HPL) were found in carcinomas and also in both types of metaplasia. These studies again point to a gradual loss of differentiation leading to cancer development and also indicate that the expression of certain fetal antigens may signal premalignancy in intestinal metaplasia earlier than other morphological or histochemical parameters.

Table 25.3 Antibodies against second trimester fetal antigen detected with immunoperoxidase techniques (Higgins et al 1984).

Histology	Percent Positive
Normal and superficial gastritis	10
Chronic atrophic multifocal gastritis	38
Intestinal metaplasia	50
Dysplasia	86

Present advances in molecular biology point to the identification of amino-acid sequences in the DNA molecule which may be meaningful in our understanding of the premalignant role of intestinal metaplasia. A product of the ras oncogene has been identified in metaplastic intestinal cells[69] which indicates the expression of amino-acid sequences with malignant potential before the invasive stage of cancer.

Specific translocation involving the Translocated Promotor Regin (TPR) of chromosome 1 and the met oncogene of chromosome 7 has been found frequently in gastric carcinomas and its precursor lesions.[70]

Abnormalities of p53 suppressor gene have been reported in dysplasia and carcinoma.[71] Abnormal expression of Lewis antigens have also been detected, as well as several other molecular lesions.[72] The timing and the relevance of these molecular lesions has not been well characterized.

Topography

Detailed studies of the distribution of MAG have revealed a clear pattern of progression. In young persons the lesions first appear on the lesser curvature or the incisura angularis.[15] Later new foci of atrophy appear along the lesser curvature and on both sides of the antrum-corpus junction and take on the form of inverted 'V' as shown in Figure 25.27. The foci coalesce and in advanced cases cover extensive areas of the mucosa. In extreme cases metaplastic glands may occupy almost all the gastric mucosa.

Other intestinal enzymes and Paneth cells have similar distribution but colonic metaplasia and dysplasia, which are also multifocal, occur in more irregular fashion tending to be more intense around the incisura and in the vicinity of carcinomas.

Physiopathology

As expected from the progressive mucosal involvement, a gradual decrease of hydrochloric acid and pepsin secretion is observed in this disease but total achlorhydria is not a frequent phenomenon. A fasting gastric juice pH of 5 or higher occurs in moderate to advanced cases and this allows bacterial and fungal colonization with the production of nitrites. The latter results from the action of bacterial reductases on nitrate present in the normal diet. As a rule parietal cell antibodies, intrinsic factor deficiency,

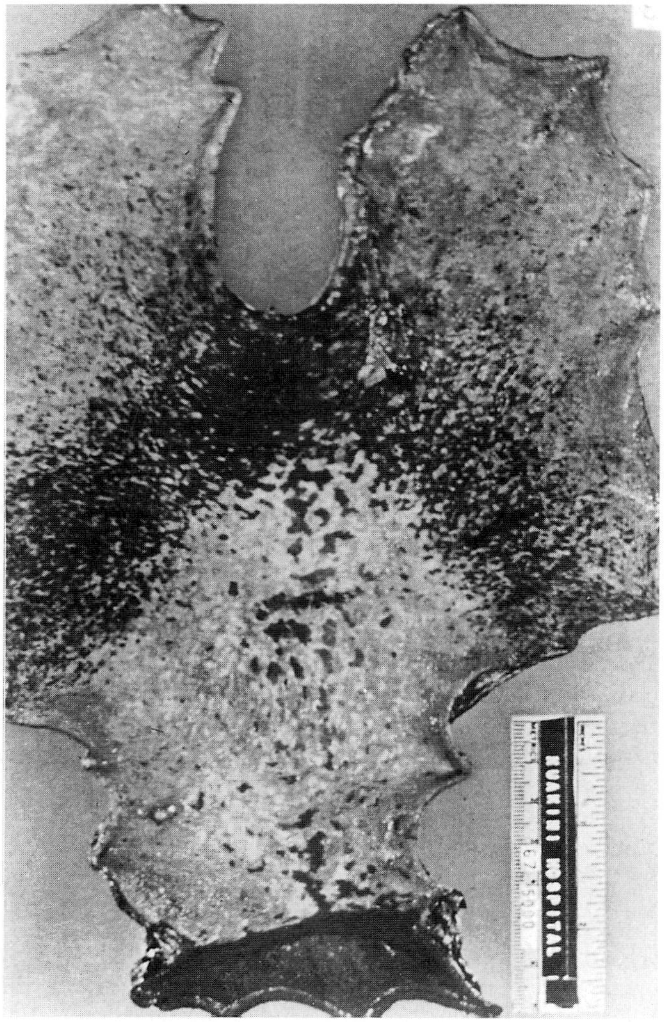

Fig. 25.27 Gastrectomy specimen stained for alkaline phosphatase. Positive areas appear in red as shown in the duodenum, where the enzyme is normally present. The multifocal distribution of the lesion with preponderance in the antrum-corpus junction and the area of the incisura angularis is clearly seen. Several foci are also seen along the lesser curvature and to a lesser degree in other areas. (Photograph courtesy of Dr Grant N. Stemmermann)

vitamin B_{12} deficiency and megaloblastic anaemia do not occur in spite of the rather extensive loss of parietal cells.

If the gastritis and metaplasia have progressed to the stage of partial or total loss of differentiation, markers of such changes such as foetal suphoglycoprotein,[50] beta-glucuronidase and lactic dehydrogenase may appear in the gastric juice. These markers correlate with the presence of sulphomucin-containing colonic type intestinal metaplasia.[73]

Low pepsinogen I (PG-I) values in blood or urine as well as low PG-I/PG-II ratios are good indicators of the extent of atrophic gastritis.[74] In a population in which pernicious anaemia is extremely rare, as atrophy progresses gastrin levels rise (Table 25.4). In fact antral G cells do

Table 25.4 Serum gastrin levels and histology (Cuello 1986).

Histology	Number of cases with serum gastrin levels 48–172 (pg/ml)	>172 (pg/ml)
Normal	13	2
Superficial gastritis	22	4
Chronic atrophic multifocal gastritis and intestinal metaplasia	36	16
Dysplasia	8	11

not participate in the atrophic process and may indeed be hyperfunctional or hyperplastic.[75] This also means that a diagnosis of diffuse corporal (autoimmune) gastritis cannot be based solely on low pepsinogen and high gastrin values, as previously proposed.

Clinical significance

Although the correlation between clinical signs, endoscopic findings and histopathology is poor, most patients with this disease have a very prolonged history of vague gastrointestinal complaints. Anecdotal information gathered from patients in Narino, Colombia, where this disease is extremely prevalent, reveals that as young adults they begin to complain of heartburn which is accentuated by gastric irritants such as alcohol and tobacco.[30] The symptoms remit and relapse but generally become accentuated as years advance. At some point some patients develop classic symptoms of peptic ulcer which in the past was often treated by surgical procedures. As years pass, the heartburn and ulcer symptoms tend to disappear and they complain only of a feeling of post-prandial 'fullness'. In a few cases gastric carcinoma develops which may lead to a further change in symptomatology.

This clinical pattern of disease has a morphological basis. Early on, the atrophic mucosa is vulnerable to the acid-pepsin secretion emanating from the areas where the mucosa is intact. As the atrophy progresses, the secretion of acid decreases and the ulcers tend to heal. The feeling of fullness may be related to an abundant mucus and food residues which are found even in the fasting state.

The correlation between histopathology and the endoscopic findings depends upon the experience of the endoscopist. Areas of atrophy and intestinal metaplasia are described as resembling duodenal mucosa[76] or are slightly depressed and pale or grey.[7] Metaplastic areas can be stained by the use of a methylene blue spray[77] or identified by use of a Congo red spray which stains the secreting mucosa black.[7]

Aetiology and pathogenesis

Although it cannot be said at the present time that the exact cause of multifocal gastritis is known, some factors seem to be important. Helicobacter infection and the

Fig. 25.28 World map with bars indicating the age-adjusted (world population) incidence rates of gastric cancer. Two or more distinct groups living in the same country show contrasting cancer incidence in Hawaii, California, New Mexico, Detroit, Israel, Singapore and New Zealand.

diet, especially salt intake, stand out as the overriding aetiological factors.

Gastritis, atrophy, metaplasia, dysplasia and ultimately carcinoma are part of a disease complex which has a geographical distribution depicted in Figure 25.28.[78] The highest rates occur in Japan, northern Europe and the Andean part of South and Central America.

The aetiological hypothesis for this disease complex is outlined in Figure 25.29. In the initial stages of superficial gastritis Helicobacter infection most probably plays a key role. The infection persists throughout the entire process of atrophy, metaplasia and dysplasia, but in the later stages the colonies remain only in the areas of the mucosa where the normal foveolar epithelium remains. The next stage, atrophy or gland loss, has been related to excessive salt intake in humans[79] and experimental animals.[80] One key event in the hypothesis is the formation of N-nitroso compounds in the gastric cavity, many of which are toxic and carcinogenic. They may be formed because of the high levels of nitrate resulting from bacterial reductases acting on dietary nitrate. Nitrite is a very reactive molecule which may interact with amines, amides, ureas and other nitrogen containing molecules abundant in foods.[81] Two prominent examples of these events have been investigated. Nitrosation of fish which is a major component of the Japanese diet results in substances which experimentally induce gastric cancer in rats.[82] Similarly nitrosation of dietary fava beans in the high-risk Colombian population results in the formation of a very potent mutagen.[83]

Another source of mutagenic compounds may be the macrophages and polymorphonuclear leukocytes which infiltrate the lamina propria, most probably as a result of the presence of *Helicobacter pylori* in the lumen, which produce soluble substances toxic to the cells. These white blood cells produce nitric oxide (NO) which may alter DNA in several ways, resulting in mutations such as those of the p53 gene.[84]

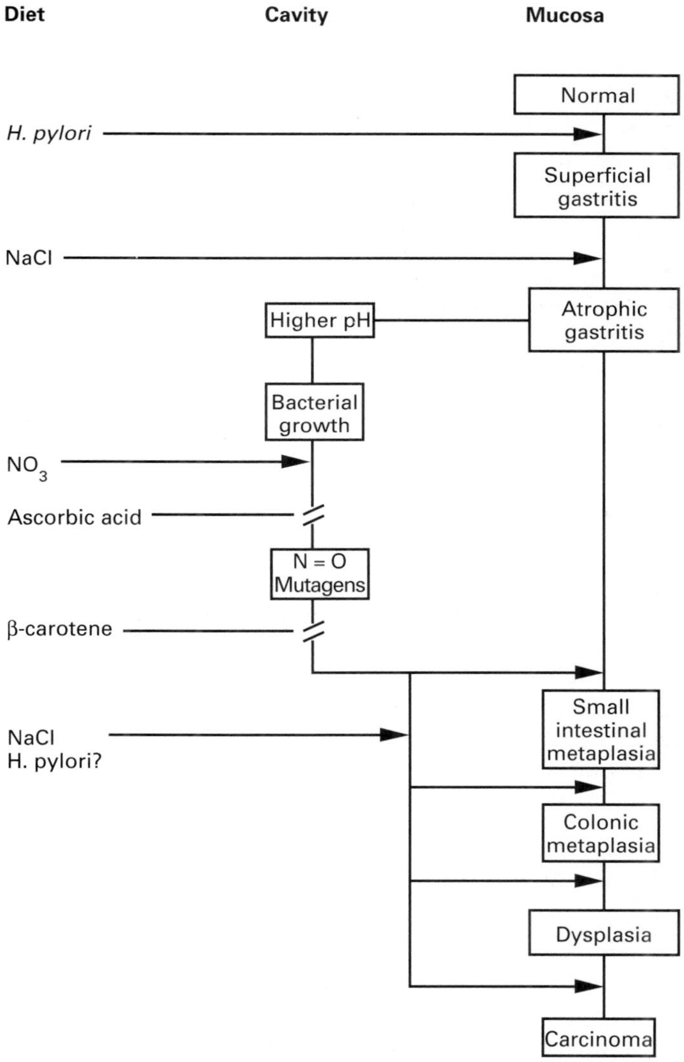

Fig. 25.29 Schematic representation of a hypothetical model of gastric carcinogenesis. Progressive changes in the morphology of the gastric mucosa are determined by micro-environmental changes of the gastric cavity reflecting dietary peculiarities of the population.

The molecular alterations connected with successive mutations may be brought about by oxidants from foods, cigarette smoke or white blood cells. These noxious influences may be avoided or diminished by antioxidants such as ascorbic acid, alpha-tocopherol and beta-carotene.

Vitamin C is a potent antioxidant and in some but not all case-controlled studies it has been found to be relatively deficient.[85] Modern methods of food preservation utilize antioxidants which may also play a protective role. There is also a report that vitamin E, which is also an antioxidant, may be deficient in severe gastritis which shows dysplasia.[86]

There is a relative deficiency of carotenoids in the diet of populations with high incidence of gastritis and serum levels are also low in subjects with gastric dysplasia.[87] The significance of this is not clear but these substances are not only vitamin A precursors, they also act as antioxidants and scavengers of free radicals.

All these protective dietary substances are abundant in fresh fruits, vegetables and salads. Given the international dietary diversity, there is likely to be quite a complex interplay of irritants, toxins and protectors in the different populations with a high prevalence of MAG and gastric carcinoma.

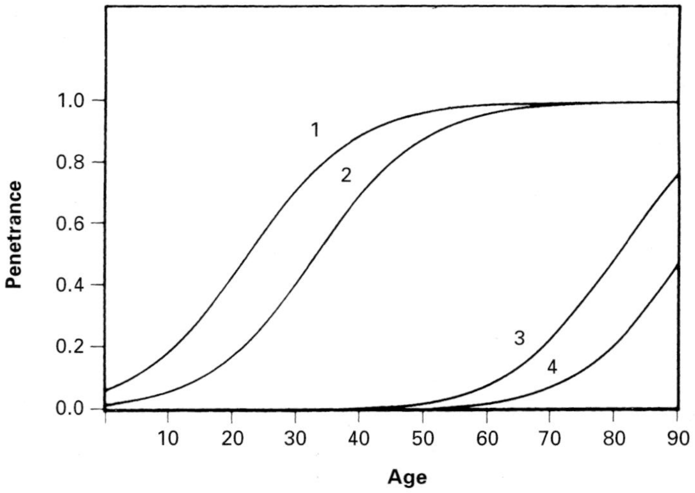

Fig. 25.30 Prevalence of gastritis (penetrance) in four subpopulations of Narino, Colombia. **1** Homozygous (AA) with mother affected; **2** Homozygous (AA) with mother unaffected; **3** Carrier (AB) or non-carrier (BB) with mother affected; **4** Carrier (AB) or non-carrier (BB) with mother unaffected. The effect of age and having an affected mother is illustrated for each group. A single locus autosomal recessive gene determining susceptibility to atrophic gastritis is postulated. (Reproduced with permission: Bonney et al 1986)

Genetic factors

The role of genetics has long been suspected and Siurala and co-workers, after extensive studies in Finnish populations, have postulated the existence of three different genetic traits respectively associated with diffuse corporal (autoimmune) gastritis, antral gastritis and multifocal (environmental) gastritis.[45–47] The genetic pattern of pernicious anaemia and autoimmune gastritis has been well described.[47] A genetic predisposition to antral gastritis and duodenal ulcer is suspected, but the heterogeneity of the disease points to the existence of several independent genetic traits.[88]

The role of genetics in multifocal atrophic gastritis families in Narino, Colombia has been studied utilizing segregation analysis.[89] Age and having an affected mother are important risk factors. The analysis suggests a single locus autosomal recessive major gene with age-dependent penetrance. The gene occurs in approximately 70% of the Columbian population (Fig. 25.30).

The biopsy in the diagnosis of gastritis

Biopsies should supply the maximum information concerning leukocytic infiltration, activity of inflammatory changes, cellular hyperplasia, atrophy, metaplasia and dysplasia. This can only be achieved if biopsies are of adequate size and are properly identified as to the exact location in the stomach from which they were taken. The presence of intestinalization and pseudopyloric metaplasia makes the correct labelling of containers as to site absolutely mandatory and each specimen should be individually submitted. Superficial biopsies cannot be properly oriented but may still provide useful information when their location is known.

REFERENCES

1. Cruveilhier J. Traite d'anatomie pathologique generale. Paris: Balliere 1862: p. 484.
2. Fenwick S. On atrophy of the stomach. Lancet 1870; 2: 78.
3. Kupfer C. Festschrift. Arz Verein Munch 1883; p 7.
4. Schmidt A. Untersuchungen ulcer des menschliche Magenepitel unter normalen und pathologischen Verhaltnissen. Virchows Arch (A) 1896; 143: 477–508.
5. Osler W, McRae T. Diseases of the stomach. In: The principles and practice of medicine. New York: Appleton, 1920.
6. Siurala M, Isokoski M, Varis K. Prevalence of gastritis in a rural population. Scand J Gastroenterol 1968; 3: 211–223.
7. Vilardell F. Gastritis. In: Besk JE, ed. Bockus Gastroenterology. Philadelphia: Saunders, 1985; 941–974.
8. Bonne L, Hartz Ph, Clerks JV. Morphology of the stomach and gastric secretions in Malays and Chinese and the different incidence of gastric ulcer and gastric cancer in those races. Am J Cancer 1938; 3: 265–279.
9. Faber K, Bloch CE. Uber die pathologischen Verenderungen am digestion tractus bei die perniciosen anemia und ulcer die Sogennante. Dermat Z Klin Med 1900; 40: 98.
10. Magnus HA. A re-assessment of the gastric lesion in pernicious anaemia. J Clin Path 1958; 11: 289–295.
11. Jarvis O, Lauren P. On the role of heterotopias of intestinal epithelium in the pathogenesis of gastric cancer. Acta Path Microbiol Scand 1951; 29: 26–44.
12. Gosset A, Masson P. Cancer intestinal de l'estomac. Presse Med 1912; 20: 225–228.
13. Lauren P. The two histological main types of gastric carcinoma: diffuse and the so-called intestinal-type carcinoma. An attempt at a histological classification. Acta Path Microbiol Scand 1965; 64: 31–49.
14. Morson BC. Carcinoma arising from areas of intestinal metaplasia in the gastric mucosa. Br J Cancer 1955; 9: 377–385.

15. Correa P, Cuello C, Duque E. Carcinoma and intestinal metaplasia in Colombian migrants. JNCI 1970; 44: 297–306.
16. Motteram RA. A biopsy study of chronic gastritis and gastric atrophy. J Path Bact 1951; 63: 389–394.
17. Schindler R. Gastritis. London: Heinemann, 1947.
18. Gear MWL, Truelove SC, Whitehead R. Gastric ulcer and gastritis. Gut 1971; 12: 639–645.
19. Walker IR, Strickland PG, Ungar B, McKay IR. Simple atrophic gastritis and gastric carcinoma. Gut 1971; 12: 906–911.
20. Lambert R. Chronic gastritis. Digestion 1972; 7: 83–126.
21. Strickland RG, Mackay IR. A reappraisal of the nature and significance of chronic atrophic gastritis. Am J Dig Dis 1973; 18: 426–440.
22. Siurala, M, Varis K. Gastritis. In: Sircus and Smith, eds. Scientific Foundations of Gastroenterology. Philadelphia: Saunders, 1980; pp 357–369.
23. Bins M, Burgers ICJ, Selbach SGM et al. Is discrimination between Type A and B atrophic gastritis clinically useful in achlorhydria? J Clin Gastroenterol 1983; 5: 17–19.
24. Glass GBJ, Pitchumoni CS. Atrophic gastritis. Hum Pathol 1975; 6: 219–250.
25. Cheli R, Giacosa A. Chronic atrophic gastritis and gastric mucosal atrophy — one and the same. Gastrointest Endosc 1983; 29: 23–25.
26. Misiewicz J J. The Sydney System: a new classification of gastritis. J Gastroenterol Hepatol 1991; 6: 207–208.
27. Correa P, Yardley JH. Grading and classification of chronic gastritis: one American response to the Sydney System. Gastroenterology 1992; 102: 355–359.
28. Correa P. The epidemiology and pathogenesis of chronic gastritis. Three etiologic entities. Front Gastroenterol Res 1980; 6: 98–108.
29. Varis K, Isokoski M. Screening of Type A gastritis. Ann Clin Res 1981; 13: 133–138.
30. Correa P, Bolanos O, Garcia FT, Gordillo C, Duque E, Cuello C. The cancer registry of Cali, Colombia — epidemiologic studies of gastric cancer. Recent Results. Cancer Res 1975; 50: 155–169.
31. MacDonald WC, Anderson FH, Hashimoto S. Histological effect of certain pickles on the human gastric mucosa. A preliminary report. Can Med Assoc J 1967; 96: 1521–1523.
32. Palmer ED. Gastritis. A reevaluation. Medicine 1954; 33: 199–290.
33. Edwards FC, Coghill NF. Aetiological factors in chronic atrophic gastritis. Br Med J 1966; 2: 1409–1415.
34. Warren JR, Marshall B. Undifferentiated curved bacilli on gastric epithelium in active chronic gastritis. Lancet 1983; 1: 1273–1275.
35. Graham DY, Klein PD, Evans DJ et al. Campylobacter pylori detected non-invasively by ^{13}C urea breath test. Lancet 1987; 2: 1174–1177.
36. Bell GD, Weil J, Harrison G. Detection of Helicobacter pylori by the ^{14}C urea breath test. In: Rathbone BJ and Heatley RV. Helicobacter pylori and Gastrointestinal Desease: Second Edition. Blackwell Publications, London, 1992.
37. Stemmermann G, Haenszel W, Locke F. Epidemiologic pathology of gastric ulcer and gastric carcinoma among Japanese in Hawaii. JNCI 1977; 58: 13–20.
38. Sobala GM, Axon ATR, Dixon MF. Morphology of chronic antral gastritis: relationship to age, Helicobacter pylori status and peptic ulceration. European J Gastroenterol Hepatol 1992; 4: 825–829.
39. Ramsey EJ, Carey KV, Peterson WL et al. Epidemic gastritis with hypochlorhydria. Gastroenterology 1979; 76: 1449–1457.
40. Cave D, Vargas M. Effect of a Campylobacter pylori protein on acid secretion by parietal cells. Lancet 1989; 2: 187–189.
41. Dixon MF, O'Connor HJ, Axon AT et al. Reflux gastritis: distinct histopathologic entity: J Clin Pathol 1986; 39: 524–530.
42. Hamilton SR, Yardley JH. Endoscopic biopsy diagnosis of aspirin-associated chronic gastric ulcers. Gastroenterology 1980; 78: Abstract 1178.
43. Siurala M, Villako K, Ihamaki T, Kekki M, Lehtola J, Sipponen P. Atrophic gastritis: Its genetic and dynamic behaviour and its relations to gastric carcinoma and pernicious anemia. In: Farber E, ed. Physiopathology of carcinogenesis in the digestive organs. Tokyo: University of Tokyo Press, 1977.
44. Lewis KJ, Dowling F, Wright JP, Taylor KB. Gastric morphology and serum gastrin levels in pernicious anaemia. Gut 1976; 17: 551–560.
45. Kekki M, Varis K, Pohjanpelo H, Isokoski M, Ihamaki T, Siurala M. Course of antrum and body gastritis in pernicious anemia families. Dig Dis Sci 1983; 28: 698–704.
46. Sipponen P, Kekki M, Siurala M. Age-related trends of gastritis and intestinal metaplasia in gastric carcinoma patients and controls representing the population at large. Br J Cancer 1984; 49: 521–530.
47. Varis K, Ihamaki T, Lehtola J et al. Genetic aspects of gastritis-cancer relationship. Dtsch Z Verdau u Stoffwechselk 1978; 38: 51–54.
48. Wangel AG, Callender ST, Spray GH, Wright R. A family study of pernicious anemia. Br J Haematol 1968; 14: 183–204.
49. Uibo R, Salupere V. Immunology of chronic gastritis. J Clin Res 1981; 13: 130–132.
50. Hakkinen PT. A population screening for fetal sulfoglycoprotein antigen in gastric juice. Cancer Res 1974; 34: 3069–3072.
51. Correa P, Cuello C, Duque E et al. Gastric cancer in Colombia. III. Natural history of precursor lesions. JNCI 1976; 57: 1027–1035.
52. Correa P, Munoz N, Cuello C, Fox J, Zavala D, Ruiz B. The role of Campylobacter pylori in gastro-duodenal disease. In: Progress in Surgical Pathology, Vol. X, Fenoglio-Preiser, ed. Philadelphia; Field & Wood, 1989: 191–210.
53. Correa P, Haenszel W, Cuello C, et al. Gastric precancerous process in a high risk population: a cohort follow-up. Cancer Res 1990; 50: 4737–4740.
54. Stemmermann GN, Hayashi T. Intestinal metaplasia of the gastric mucosa: A gross and microscopic study of its distribution in various disease states. JNCI 1976; 57: 1027–1035.
55. Whitehead R. Mucosal biopsy of the gastrointestinal tract. 3rd ed. Philadelphia: Saunders, 1985.
56. Cuello C, Correa P, Zarama G, Lopez J, Murray J, Gordillo G. Histopathology of gastric dysplasia. Am J Surg Pathol 1979; 3: 491–500.
57. Borchard F, Mittestaedt A, Stux G. Dysplasien im Resektionmagen und Klassifikationproblem verschiedenes Dysplasieformen. Verh Dtsch Ges Path 1979; 63: 250–257.
58. Morson BC, Sobin LH, Grundmann E, Johansen A, Nagayo T, Serck-Hanssen A. Precancerous conditions and epithelial dysplasia in the stomach. J Clin Path 1980; 33: 711–721.
59. Nagayo T. Dysplasia of the gastric mucosa and its relation to the precancerous state. Gann 1981; 72: 813–823.
60. Grundmann E. Histologic types and possible initial stages in early gastric carcinoma. Beitr Pathol 1975; 154: 256–280.
61. Oehlert W, Keller P, Henke M, Strauch M. Die Dysplasien der Magenschleimhaut. Dtsch Med Wochenschr 1975; 100: 1950–1956.
62. Ransohoff DF, Riddel RH, Levin B et al. Ulcerative colitis and colon cancer: Problems in assessing the diagnostic usefulness of mucosal dysplasia. Dis Colon Rectum 1985; 28: 383–388.
63. Jarvis LR, Whitehead R. Morphometric analysis of gastric dysplasia. J Path 1985; 147: 133–138.
64. Lipkin M, Correa P, Mikol YB et al. Proliferative and antigenic modifications of human epithelial cells in chronic atrophic gastritis. JNCI 1985; 75: 613–619.
65. Hashimoto M, Tokunaga A, Nishi K et al. H3-thymidine auto-radiographic and alkaline phosphatase histochemical studies of intestinal metaplasia of the human stomach. Histochem J 1983; 15: 953–959
66. Higgins PJ, Correa P, Cuello C, Lipkin M. Fetal antigens in the precursor stages of gastric cancer. Oncology 1984; 41: 73–76.
67. Nardelli J, Bara J, Rosa B, Burtin P. Intestinal metaplasia and carcinomas of the human stomach: An immunohistologic study. J Histochem Cytochem 1983; 31: 366–375.
68. Skinner JM, Whitehead R. Tumour markers and premalignant states of the stomach in humans. Eur J Cancer 1982; 18: 227–235.
69. Karayiannis M, Yiagnisis M, Papadimitrion K et al. Evaluation of the ras and myc oncoproteins in benign gastric lesions. Anticancer Res 1990; 10: 1127–1134.
70. Soman NR, Correa P, Ruiz B, Wogan GN. The TPR-MET oncogenic re-arrangement is present and expressed in human gastric carcinoma and precursor lesions. Proc Natl Acad Sci 1991; 88: 4892–4896.
71. Rugge M, Shiao YH, Correa P et al. Immunohistochemical evidence of p53 overexpression in gastric epithelial dysplasia. Cancer Epid Biomarkers Prev 1992; 1: 551–554.
72. Torrado J, Correa P, Ruiz B et al. Prospective study of Lewis

antigen alterations in the gastric precancerous process. Cancer Epid Biomarkers Prev 1992; 1: 199–205.
73. Williams GT, Rogers K. Elevated gastric juice enzymes. A marker for increased gastric cancer risk? Clin Oncol 1984; 10: 319–323.
74. Stemmermann GN, Heilbrun LK, Nomura A, Samloff IM. The relation of serum pepsinogen to gastric cancer and its precursors in Hawaiian Japanese men: a progress report. In: Kreuning J ed. Pepsinogens in man: clinical and genetic advances. 1985: 213–220.
75. Bordi C, Ravazzola M, De Vita O. Pathology of endocrine cells in the gastric mucosa. Ann Pathol 1983; 3: 19–28.
76. Kohli K, Hattoris S, Kodama T, Kawai K. Endoscopic diagnosis of intestinal metaplasia in asymptomatic (control) volunteers. Gastroenterol Jap 1979; 14: 15–17.
77. Fennerty MB, Emerson JC, Sampliner RE et al. Gastric intestinal metaplasia in ethnic groups in the southwestern United States. Cancer Epid Biomarkers Prev 1992; 1: 293–296.
78. Correa P, Tannenbaum SR. The microecology of gastric cancer. In: N-nitroso compounds. Am Chem Soc Symposium #174. ACS Washington 1981: 319–329.
79. Correa P. The gastric precancerous process. Cancer Surveys 1983; 2: 437–450.
80. Kodama M, Kodama T, Susuki H. Effect of rice and salty rice diet on the structure of mouse stomach. Nutr Cancer 1984; 6: 135–147.
81. Mirvish S. The etiology of gastric cancer. JNCI 1983; 71: 631–647.
82. Weisburger JH, Marquardt H, Hirota N, Mori H, Williams SM. Induction of cancer of the glandular stomach in rats by an extract of nitrite-treated fish. JNCI 1980; 64: 163.
83. Yang D, Tannenbaum SR, Buchi G, Lee G. 4-Chloro-6-methoxy-indole is the precursor of a potent mutagen (4-chloro-6-methoxy-2-hydroxy-1-nitroso-indolin-3-one oxime) that forms during nitrosation of the fava bean (Vicia faba). Carcinogenesis 1984; 5: 1219–1224.
84. Correa P. Human gastric carcinogenesis: a multistep and multifactorial process. Cancer Res 1992; 52: 6735–6740.
85. Fontham E, Zavala D, Correa P et al. Diet and chronic atrophic gastritis: A case-control study. JNCI 1986; 76: 621–627.
86. Graham S, Schotz W, Martins P. Alimentary factors in the epidemiology of gastric cancer. Cancer 1972; 30: 927–938.
87. Haenszel W, Correa P, Lopez A et al. Serum micronutrients in relation to gastric pathology. Int J Cancer 1985; 36: 43–48.
88. Taylor IL, Calam J, Rotter JI et al. Family studies of hypergastrinemia hyperpepsinogenic I duodenal ulcer. Ann Intern Med 1981; 95: 421–425.
89. Bonney GE, Elston RC, Correa P et al. Genetic etiology of gastric carcinoma: I. Chronic atrophic gastritis. Genetic Epidemiology 1986; 3: 213–214.

PART III

Chronic hyperplastic gastritis and specified forms including Crohn's disease

J. Lindeman C. J. L. M. Meijer

HYPERPLASTIC STATES

Circumscribed, multifocal and diffuse areas of hyperplasia of the gastric mucosa have a confusing nomenclature that lacks uniformity.[1–6] The term hyperplasia is applied to lesions which are macroscopically obvious and to those just of sufficient size to be visible using radiographic and endoscopic techniques (i.e. 2–3 mm). They are believed to arise in response to a chronic persistent stimulus. In general it is assumed that they are reactive and potentially reversible if the abnormal stimulus is removed.

The endogenous or exogenous local or generalized factors that cause a hyperplastic reaction are largely unknown, as is the physiological controlling mechanism for gastric cell turnover. Hyperplasia can occur in the foveolar layer, glandular layer, muscularis mucosae and the submucosa, or a combination of these. However, in most cases involvement of the muscularis mucosae and submucosa is secondary to gastritis.

In giant fold disease there is hypertrophy of the submucosal cores under the hyperplastic mucosa, and the folds follow the normal pattern of gastric rugae. They can reach a height of 0.5–3 cm and a width of 0.7–2.2 cm,[7] resembling cerebral convolutions,[1,4] but the hyperplastic epithelium itself rarely exceeds a fourfold increase in thickness (normal <1 mm).[8] The basic mechanism leading to a polypoidal mucosa is the proliferation of foveolar, glandular and metaplastic mucous (pseudopyloric) epithelial cells, all of which arise from a common precursor in the base of the gastric pit.[9] In most lesions the superficial foveolar cells show the most marked hyperplasia.

There are some similarities with the reaction seen in chronic superficial and atrophic gastritis, for the ratio of foveolar to glandular epithelium in chronic non-specific gastritis can change from 1:4 up to 5:1 in favour of the foveolar layer.[2] One can also recognize a polypoid foveolar hyperplasia in the margin of a peptic ulcer.

From a clinical standpoint, in the early stage hyperplastic lesions usually have no accompanying clinical symptoms. Later, however, symptoms due to bleeding and obstruction of the cardia and pylorus can occur. In giant fold and diffuse giant fold disease the symptoms often resemble those of peptic ulcer disease and there may be associated hypergastrinaemia and protein losing gastroenteropathy with a fairly low gastric acid secretion even after stimulation. Endoscopically, the conditions which resemble hyperplastic states include polyposis syndromes, benign mesenchymal and epithelial tumours of the mucosa and submucosa, granulomatous inflammations, diffuse carcinoma and lymphoma. In many hyperplastic lesions a full thickness mucosal biopsy is essential for definitive diagnosis.[4]

While the basic tissue reactions for all hyperplastic polypoidal lesions are the same, various clinical, macroscopic and microscopic features allow several different types to be recognized.

Focal foveolar hyperplasia

The lesions measure up to 5 mm in diameter and, as seen at endoscopic examination, usually occur in the antrum and are frequently multiple.[10] The foveolae are elongated and the foveolar cells are either normal or slightly hyperplastic. The surface may be eroded and shows both degenerative and regenerative changes. These lesions are seen in association with duodenal and gastric ulcer, gastric carcinoma and gastrojejunostomy.[10,11] The mucosa next to the lesions often shows chronic atrophic gastritis.[12]

Fundic gland hyperplasia

Fundic gland hyperplasia produces polyps which are usually sessile and up to 5 mm high. They are confined to the body or fundus and are characteristically multiple. The foveolar layer is normal, and the lesion is due to the presence of mucous epithelial lined or fundic gland epithelial lined cysts and fundic gland hyperplasia. There is no known relationship with other pathology and the lesions can regress spontaneously.[13] The aetiology is unknown[14] but there is an association with familial polyposis coli and Gardner's syndrome.[12]

Focal foveolar glandular hyperplasia

These focal hyperplasias are probably related to foveolar hyperplastic polyps. They are usually not more than 5 mm high, and are often multifocal. An association with carcinoma of the stomach and both gastric and duodenal ulcer is described.[11] The hyperplastic glandular layer is usually composed of pseudopyloric metaplastic glands and evidence of coexistent chronic atrophic gastritis.

Hyperplastic polyps

The most common polyp is the hyperplastic polyp (Fig. 25.31A), which accounts for 75–90% of all gastric polyps.[15,16] It is also referred to as regenerative polyp,[17] 'hyperplasiogenous polyp'[18] or hyperplastic adenomatous polyp.[1] They are usually sessile and vary in size from 0.5 cm up to 2 cm and occasionally up to 4 cm. The lesions are usually located in the antrum and are occasionally multiple.

Histologically, there is a marked elongation and distortion of the pits, often with cystic dilatation. The foveolar mucous cells are frequently hyperplastic at the surface with basal nuclei and a huge amount of cytoplasm. The surface can be ulcerated with degenerative and regenerative changes in association with a mixed cellular infiltrate. In the uninflamed areas there is oedema and a scattered infiltrate of lymphocytes, plasma cells and eosinophils. Characteristically, strands of smooth muscle extend from the muscularis mucosae between the basal gastric glands. The basal gastric glands are usually metaplastic pseudopyloric mucous glands, but occasionally residual chief and parietal cells are found in polyps arising in the gastric body region. There is rarely a hyperplasia of body type glands (Fig. 25.32B). Sometimes the polyp epithelium shows elongated basal nuclei resembling low grade dysplasia such as that seen in adenomas, but the presence of inflammation, erosion and typical regenerating epithelium indicates the reactive nature of the atypia. In a long-term follow-up study of patients with hyperplastic gastric polyps[19] only 2 cases of carcinoma were found in more than 2000 lesions. In another long-term follow-up study[20] the incidence of subsequent carcinoma was 1.4%. These results indicate that polypectomy is adequate therapy and that they have a low malignant potential. Often, however, they occur in combination with various conditions associated with an increased risk of gastric carcinoma such as chronic atrophic gastritis, pernicious anaemia and also at the sites of gastroenterostomy stomas.[16,21]

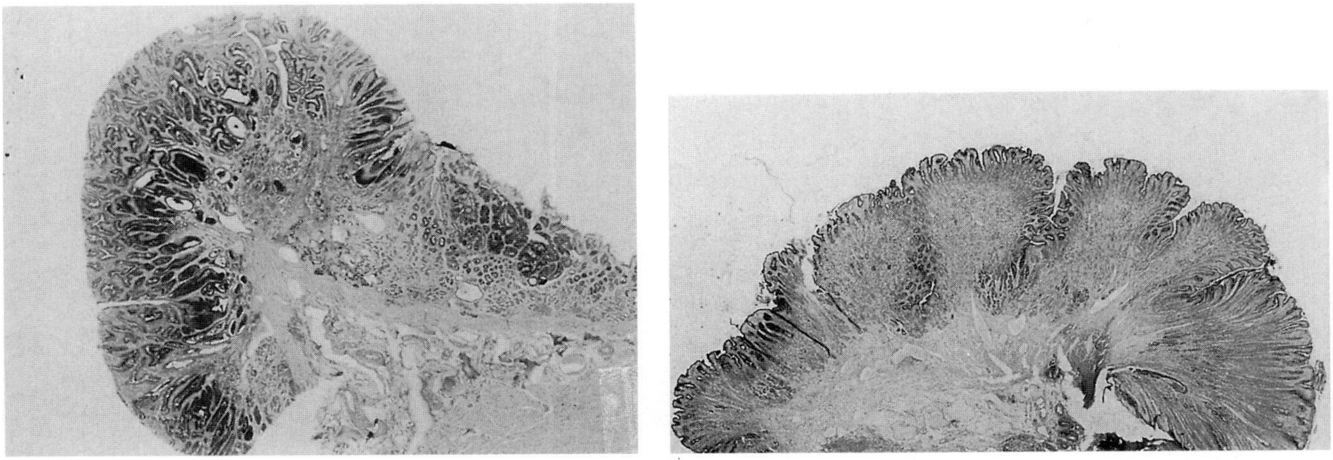

A B

Fig. 25.31A Hyperplastic polyp with hyperplastic foveolar layer and cystic distorted mucous glands. (PAS) **B** Hyperplastic polyp with hyperplastic fundic glandular layer. (PAS)

In a recent study[12] a higher degree of assocation of carcinoma with atrophic gastritis than with hyperplastic polyps was shown.

Gastritis polyposa et cystica

Gastritis polyposa et cystica is a hyperplastic polyp with cystic transformation and herniation of the glands into the submucosa and tunica muscularis propria.[22–24] This is associated with marked hyperplasia and splitting of the muscularis mucosae (Fig. 25.32). These lesions occur at gastroenterostomy stomas, at the margins of peptic ulcers and in association with carcinoma.[25] Similar appearances occur in the diffuse hyperplastic gastropathy described by Menetrier.[26] Lesions at a gastroenterostomy stoma can be quite large, sessile, up to 4 cm high and are normally single. When multiple, they can completely encircle the stoma in a line of several individual polyps. They are reactive and regenerative in nature, presumably a hyperplastic response to the prolonged mucosal injury of bile reflux.

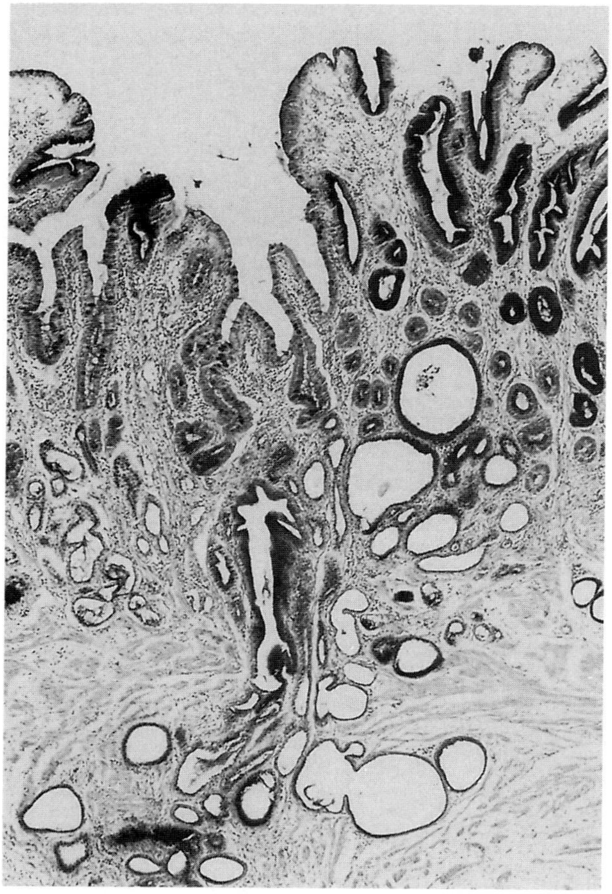

Fig. 25.32 Hyperplastic lesion with herniation of the glands in the markedly hyperplastic muscularis mucosae. (PAS; courtesy of Dr S Gratama)

Cronkhite-Canada syndrome

This non-familial polyposis syndrome is characterized by generalized intestinal polyposis involving the stomach, small and large bowel. Often there are associated ectodermal changes of alopecia, onychodystrophy and hyperpigmentation. Patients may suffer weight loss, diarrhoea, hypokalaemia and hypoalbuminaemia.[27–30]

The syndrome occurs mainly in women during the sixth decade of life. It is a non-neoplastic condition which shares histological features with the juvenile polyp, the hyperplastic polyp and diffuse hyperplastic states.[5,6,31] In the stomach, as in the rest of the intestine, the lesions appear to be the result of a functional disorder of the mucous glands. There is a progressive loss of specialized cells by a process of mucous cell transformation. The glands become cystic, are lined by hypertrophic and bizarre mucous cells, and are filled with mucus. The lamina propria is oedematous and contains a variable number of different inflammatory cells. Due to rupture of the mucus-filled cysts there is a secondary histiocytic inflammatory response. There is a probable relationship with Menetrier's disease; they share clinical and histological similarities and both are known to be completely reversible.[31]

Diffuse giant fold hyperplastic states (hyperplastic gastropathy)

In diffuse giant fold hyperplastic states — also called hyperplastic gastropathy,[1,32] hypertrophic gastritis,[8] giant hypertrophy of gastric mucosa,[7] or hypertrophic gastropathy[29,33] — markedly enlarged mucosal folds grossly resembling cerebral convolutions are found.[1] The enlarged folds follow the normal rugal pattern of the stomach, sparing more or less the antrum and lesser curvature (Fig. 25.33). Uneven hyperplasia can result in focal nodularity.

Histologically there are three main types:[1]

1. A glandular type: hyperplasia involves mainly the parietal and chief cells, and the foveolar layer is normal
2. A mucous type: hyperplasia of the foveolar layer occurs and the glands are atrophic or normal (Fig. 25.34)
3. A mixed type: hyperplasia involves both foveolar and glandular layers.

Clinically these histological types are recognized as:

a. Zollinger Ellison syndrome
b. Hypertrophic hypersecretory gastropathy
c. Menetrier's syndrome.

Zollinger-Ellison syndrome

This syndrome was first described in 1955[34] and consists

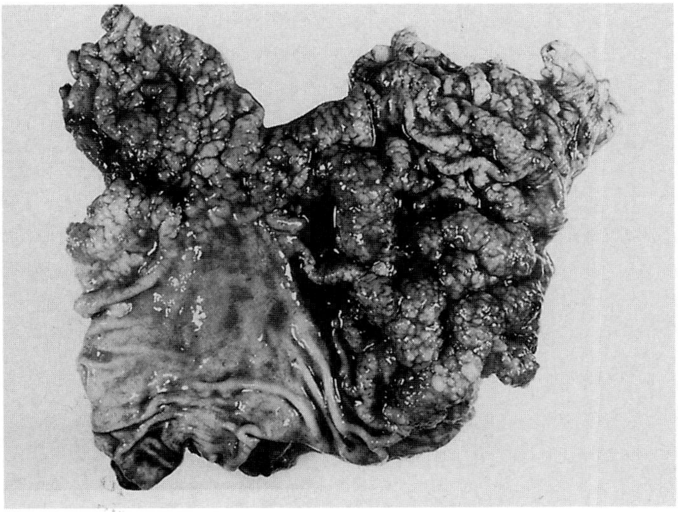

Fig. 25.33 Macroscopic picture of a hyperplastic gastropathy sparing the antrum. (Courtesy of Dr C Cuvelier)

of peptic ulceration, which is often multiple and in atypical location, together with high gastric acid secretion due to hypergastrinaemia. The hypergastrinaemia is the result of a gastrin-producing tumour or hyperplasia of antral G cells. It causes a diffuse hyperplasia and hypertrophy of both parietal and argyrophilic endocrine (mainly enterochromaffin-like) cells in the body and fundic gland area[35] but the foveolar layer remains normal.

Hypertrophic hypersecretory gastropathy

This clinical syndrome is characterized by acid hypersecretion and epigastric pain, and there is nodular hyperplasia of the glandular layer with prominent gastric rugae. The foveolar layer is again normal. There is a strong association with peptic ulcer disease, but hypergastrinaemia does not occur.[33,36,37] Sometimes there is cystic transformation of the glands in the submucosa and muscularis mucosae. Intestinal metaplasia and dysplasia are often also present.

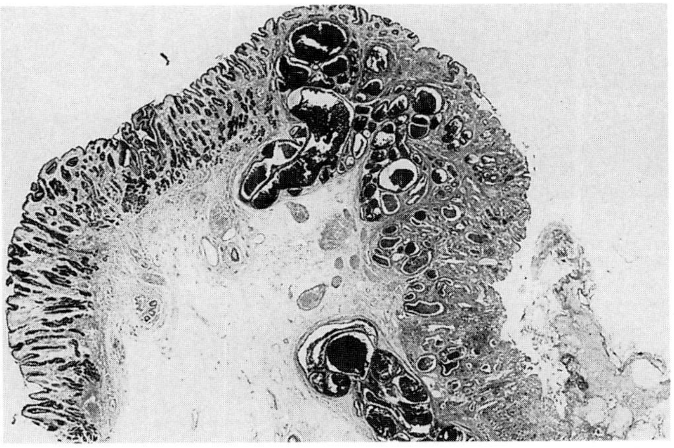

Fig. 25.34 Hyperplastic fold with dilated mucous glands with herniation into the submucosa and some atrophic glands. (H&E; courtesy of Dr S Gratama)

Menetrier's disease (hyperplastic gastropathy)

In Menetrier's disease[26] there is marked thickening of the gastric mucosa and rugae which involves mainly the body and fundus. The foveolae are elongated, tortuous and dilated and there is an excess of mucus covering the surface.[26,31] Sometimes there is cystic transformation of the glands, which may penetrate through the muscularis mucosae into the submucosa. Intestinal metaplasia and dysplasia are often associated features.

In the complete form there is low acid secretion even after stimulation, due to loss of the parietal cell mass, and severe protein loss leading to hypoalbuminaemia and hypoproteinaemia. The exact mechanism of the protein leakage is not known, but there is evidence that the cause is passive diffusion through 'leaky tight junctions', possibly due to a cholinergic mechanism.[38] Other proposed mechanisms include active secretion through intracellular routes and disturbances of mucous cell metabolism.[32]

In the clinically incomplete forms there is more or less normal acid output and a protein loss which is partially compensated by increased production. The outcome of these cases is not known with certainty because follow-up studies have been limited.[5] The disease occurs more commonly in middle-aged men than women, but it has been described in children.[32] Some reports indicate that Menetrier's disease is reversible and in adults it develops into chronic atrophic gastritis.[39–41]

Children having conditions resembling Menetrier's disease, with protein loss and giant rugae, may apparently spontaneously recover.[42,43] There is also an association with cytomegalovirus infections, eosiniphilic gastritis and lymphocytic gastritis.[44,45]

In giant fold disease generally there is quite a variation in the degree of the individual histological features present. The degree and distribution of hyperplasia, cyst formation and inflammation varies between individual cases. In two literature surveys of Menetrier's disease an incidence of carcinoma in 10% of 155 cases[46] and in 13% of 236 cases[47] has been reported. As yet no long-term follow-up studies of patients have been made, so the causal relationship between Menetrier's disease and carcinoma remains obscure.[32,33]

SPECIFIC FORMS OF GASTRITIS

Some types of gastritis, which may or may not be associated with erosion, have macroscopic or microscopic characteristics which are more or less typical or characteristic.

Chronic erosion (Synonyms: varioliform gastritis, chronic erosive gastritis, 'dellen' gastritis, superficial hypertrophic gastritis, aphthous ulcers)

Chronic erosions are round or oval, usually multiple, lesions of the gastric mucosa 5–10 mm in diameter. They consist of a central erosion surrounded by an elevated border, which is in contrast to acute erosions. Chronic erosions are located predominantly in the gastric antrum along the greater curvature[48,49] but may occur diffusely throughout the stomach. The prevalence in patients subjected to diagnostic gastroduodenoscopy varies from 3–8%.[50,51]

These lesions are more common in males than females and their incidence reaches a maximum in the fifth and sixth decades, which is similar to that of gastric and duodenal ulcer disease. In 30–40% of the patients peptic ulceration of the duodenum or the stomach is diagnosed simultaneously[49] or during follow-up.[49,52,53] Gastrointestinal bleeding, common in acute erosions, is rare. Occasionally chronic erosions are complicated by protein losing enteropathy.[54] In some patients with multiple lesions, the hyperplastic foveolar reaction fuses to form large hyperplastic folds, usually in the gastric antrum. Whilst chronic erosions can heal over a period of several days they are more usually persistent.[48,51,55]

Histopathology

Chronic erosion is characterized by a central area of fibrinoid necrosis of the mucosa which does not involve muscularis mucosae. The mucosa at the margins of the erosion shows marked foveolar hyperplasia with a remarkable infiltration of intraepithelial T-lymphocytes (Fig. 25.35) and especially in the pangastric cases there is an association with lymphocytic gastritis.[56] Intestinal metaplasia may also be found as well as atrophy of the glandular layer. Sometimes the glands are cystic; occasionally they penetrate the submucosa and there may be marked hyperplasia of the muscularis mucosae.[6]

Roesch and Warnatz[57] demonstrated a decrease of IgM and an increase in IgG-bearing cells in the lesion, whereas Andre et al[58] demonstrated a marked increase of IgE-positive plasma cells and activated mast cells; other studies, however, have failed to confirm these findings.[59] As in chronic non-specific gastritis, *Helicobacter pylori* organisms can regularly be demonstrated.[60]

Crohn's disease may also produce varioliform aphthous erosions in the stomach,[61] and histological differentiation depends upon the demonstration of granulomas. It has been shown that they are present in two-thirds of the patients with clinically suspected disease.[61,62] In their absence, the diagnosis depends upon the demonstration of Crohn's disease in either the small or large bowel.[63] When fused hyperplastic folds are seen, gastric carcinoma and lymphoma can usually be excluded in the gastric biopsy, but differentiation from other hyperplastic states can be difficult. This is especially true of Menetrier's disease when there is marked inflammation in the hyperplastic foveolar layer.

Pathogenesis

There is uncertainty as to whether or not the pathogenesis of chronic erosion is uniform. It is suggested that Type I IgE-mediated hypersensitivity plays a primary role. This idea is supported by the increase of IgE-containing cells

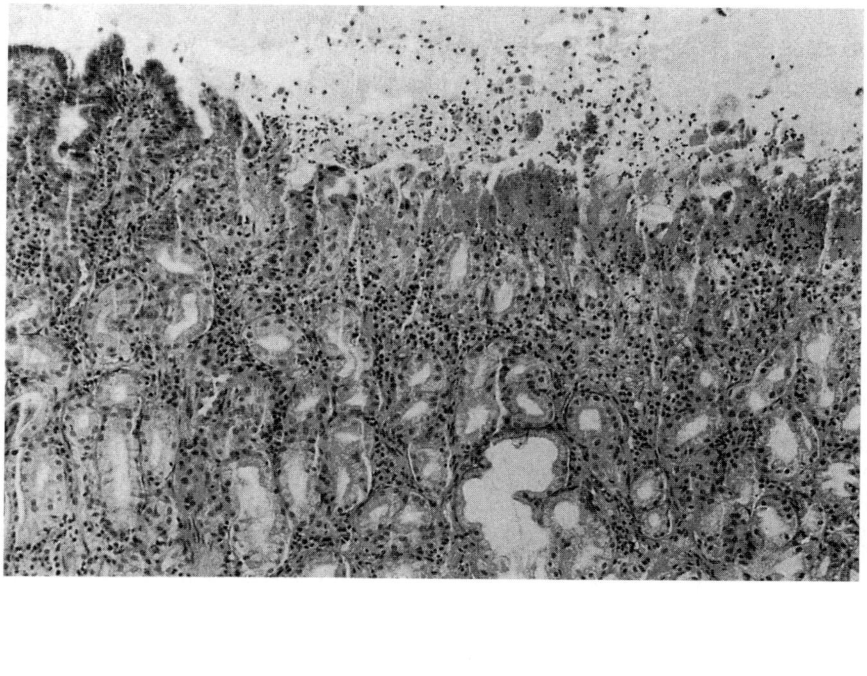

Fig. 25.35 Chronic erosion with fibrinoid necrosis of superficial mucosa and underlying mucous glands. (H&E)

in the lesions and the favourable response to disodium cromoglycate and prednisolone.[64,65]

However, an increase of IgE-containing cells occurs in equal frequency in a variety of chronic inflammatory disorders of the stomach.[59] It is suggested that it is an epiphenomenon, i.e. an allergic reaction, caused by prolonged or repeated exposure of the intestinal mucosa to certain food constituents and is secondary to chronic non-specific inflammation. An ischaemic origin of chronic erosion has also been suggested.[53] The frequent association with benign gastric and duodenal ulcers suggests that the two disorders are related. In view of the association between peptic ulcer and chronic non-specific gastritis, perhaps chronic erosion is a morphological variant of the latter.

Lymphocytic gastritis

Lymphocytic gastritis is a rare form of chronic gastritis characterized by a marked increase of intraepithelial T-cells in the surface epithelium of the foveolar region. Lymphocytic gastritis occurs in 0.1% of patients with routine gastric biopsies.[66] There is an association with coeliac disease,[67] chronic erosion[56] and Menetrier's disease.[44,45]

Granulomatous gastritis

This type of gastritis is characterized by a granulomatous inflammatory infiltrate. However, what constitutes a granuloma has been the subject of some discussion.[68–72] Granulomas can differ histologically, from compact collections of mature mononuclear phagocytes, with or without additional features such as necrosis or other inflammatory cells,[68,73] to epithelioid or sarcoid granulomas (Fig. 25.36), i.e. epithelioid mononuclear cells, often with giant cells admixed and surrounded by lymphocytes, plasma cells and, in the healing phase, fibroblasts.[74]

The granulomatous process is thought to be an inflammatory response to the presence of poorly degradable agents. An aetiological classification of granulomatous gastritis is given in Table 25.5.

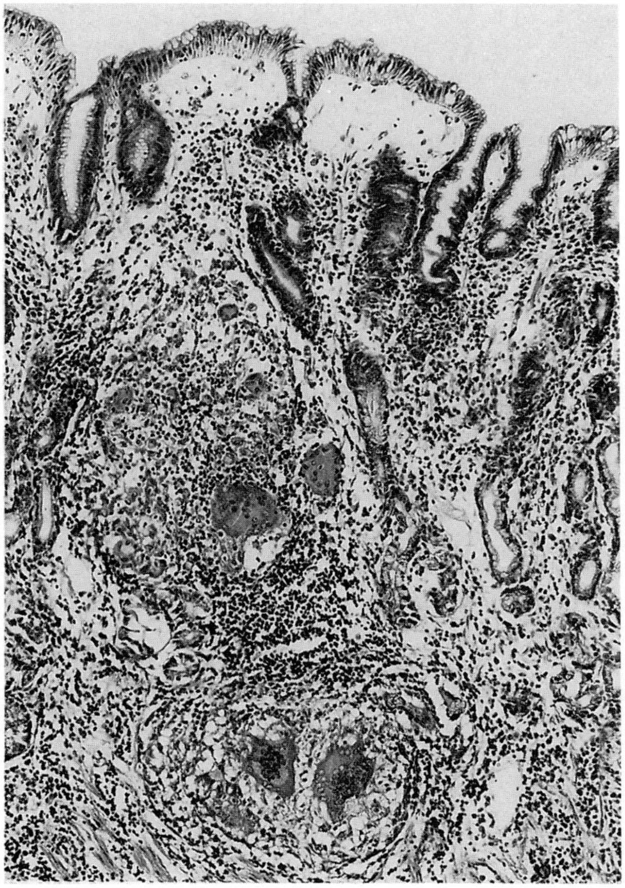

Fig. 25.36 Granulomatous gastritis with two epithelioid (sarcoid) granulomas with several giant cells. (H&E)

Table 25.5 Granulomatous disorders of the stomach.

Idiopathic	Crohn's disease Sarcoidosis Isolated granulomatous gastritis
Foreign body granulomas	Food granulomas Suture granulomas Barium granulomas Kaolin granulomas Beryllium granulomas Endogenous granulomas
Infectious granulomas	Tuberculosis Syphilis Mycobacteriose (avium) Whipple's disease Histoplasmosis Phycomycosis Paracoccidiodomycosis (South American blastomycosis) Anasakiasis
Miscellaneous	Chronic granulomatous disease of childhood Allergic granulomatosis and vasculitis Granulomas as reaction to malignancy

Idiopathic granulomatous disorders

Crohn's disease

Clinically, patients with gastric involvement in extensive Crohn's disease have symptoms of non-ulcer dyspepsia or signs of gastric outlet obstruction. In two-thirds of these patients granulomas can be found histologically.[61,62] Besides typical epithelioid cell granulomas the wall may also show transmural, often focal, lymphoid infiltrates. In addition lymphangiectasis, submucosal and subserosal fibrosis, fissures and ulceration can be seen. In mucosal biopsies a focal chronic or active chronic non-specific inflammation is often all that is seen, and in the usual patients with small and/or large bowel disease, gastric involvement with histological evidence of granulomatous infiltration is rare (2–7%).[63,75] In general, gastric Crohn's is associated with disease in more typical sites in the gastrointestinal tract.[76] More than 80% of patients with Crohn's disease located in the stomach also have duodenal bulb involvement.[75] However, in cases where no gastric involvement was suspected on clinical grounds, the gastric biopsy showed abnormalities in 16%.[75]

A significant increase of macrophages and IgM-containing cells may be found in the gastric mucosa[63,76] and it is thus proposed that Crohn's disease is a generalized disorder of the gastrointestinal tract. From a practical standpoint, if granulomas are found in gastric biopsies, the differential diagnosis between sarcoidosis, isolated granulomatous gastritis, food granulomas without recognizable food elements and tuberculosis without acid-fast bacilli has to be considered.

In Crohn's disease there is often also a diffuse or focal active inflammation in the lamina propria. In sarcoidosis and isolated granulomatous gastritis, however, there is usually no associated inflammation. In tuberculosis the granulomas tend to aggregate and fuse; they have more giant cells and may also show central necrosis. Most patients with Crohn's disease and sarcoidosis are younger than 40 years. In general, however, a full laboratory and clinical investigation is necessary in order to reach a final diagnosis.

Sarcoidosis

Sarcoidosis is a multisystem disorder of unknown aetiology, most commonly affecting young adults and frequently presenting with bilateral hilar lymphadenopathy, pulmonary infiltrations, and less often with ocular and skin lesions. The diagnosis is most frequently established when typical clinical and radiological findings are supported by histological evidence of widespread epithelioid cell granulomas in more than one system.[72]

Stomach involvement in sarcoidosis is rare, usually incidental and symptomless, and is only exceptionally of clinical importance.[72,77,78] Although asymptomatic gastric involvement in as high as 10% of cases has been claimed,[79] this appears high in the experience of others.[80] The usual clinical symptoms are non-ulcer dyspepsia and gastric outlet obstruction,[81] and there appears to be a predilection for antral and pyloric involvement. The diagnostic hallmark is the sarcoid granuloma, necrosis being typically absent.

In older lesions, the granuloma is infiltrated by fibroblasts with deposition of reticulin fibres and hyalinized collagen. Schaumann's and asteroid bodies are frequent and increase in number with ageing. Their presence is not diagnostic for they occur within epithelioid and giant cells in many other granulomatous disorders such as Crohn's disease, tuberculosis and isolated granulomatous gastritis.[82] In active disease the granulomas contain numerous T-helper cells, especially towards the centre.[83–86]

A firm diagnosis of sarcoidosis can only be made on radiological and clinical grounds.

Isolated granulomatous gastritis

When other forms of granulomatous gastritis are excluded, the term isolated granulomatous gastritis is used. The aetiology is unknown despite a suggested relationship with duodenal ulcer.[87] The clinical symptoms of non-ulcer dyspepsia and epigastric pain, nausea, vomiting, weight loss, and sometimes pyloric obstruction and its localization in the distal part of the stomach are similar to sarcoidosis and Crohn's disease.[82]

On morphological grounds alone, isolated granulomatous gastritis cannot be distinguished from sarcoidosis or Crohn's disease. The granulomas occur throughout the whole gastric wall, but are commonest in the submucosa and the mucosa. In general, patients with isolated granulomatous disease are more than 40 years old. In contrast to Crohn's disease, the lesions are confined to the antrum and pyloric region and do not involve the duodenal bulb.

Isolated granulomatous gastritis should not be confused with food granulomas and endogenous granulomas due to the peptic digestion of muscle coats. Spontaneous resolution without surgical intervention is reported.[88]

Foreign body granulomas

Food granulomas are caused in general by food particles (e.g. insoluble cereal husks) which become embedded in the mucosa, submucosa, muscle layers and serosa, usually in association with an active or healed peptic ulcer. Vegetable matter in the centre of the granulomas should not be mistaken for parasites.[89,90] If no foreign material is found, the diagnosis can only be made by exclusion of other granulomatous diseases. Other foreign materials that cause granulomatous inflammation in the stomach are barium sulphate, kaolin (trialuminiumsilicate), beryllium and suture material.[90] Sometimes foreign body granulomas will form around degenerated areas of gastric muscle, usually in association with peptic ulcers and mucus.[89]

Infectious granulomatous disorders

Tuberculosis

Since the availability of effective antibiotic therapy, , tuberculosis of the stomach has become extremely rare.[91,92] In earlier studies, however, an incidence of 0.6% of gastric involvement was reported.[92] Tuberculous lesions have a predilection for the pylorus, antrum and lesser curvature of the corpus. Caseation is usual, but diagnosis is made by the demonstration of acid-fast rod-shaped bacilli in the lesions; they may be difficult to demonstrate and sometimes the diagnosis must be based on clinical features. Confluent granulomata may break down and form serpiginous ulcers.

Syphilis

Involvement of the gastric mucosa in secondary and tertiary syphilis is rare.[71] In secondary syphilis, erosions and enlargement of the folds may be seen[59] and there is marked plasma cell infiltration and endarteriolitis. Spirochaetes can be demonstrated either by silver stains or by immunohistochemistry.[93–96] In secondary syphilis, there is a predilection for the antrum. Granulomatous and gummatous lesions, such as those seen in tertiary syphilis, are uncommon. The diagnosis in these cases is mainly based on gastroscopy and clinical history[97] rather than on biopsy. There is more severe involvement of the muscularis propria and submucosa and the stomach may become fibrotic with an 'hourglass' appearance.

Histoplasmosis

Gramulomatous lesions in the stomach due to disseminated infection with histoplasma capsulatum are rare also, although an incidence of 5% is claimed.[98] The organisms can easily be identified using the Grocott silver stain and are found in the necrotic granulomas. In non-necrotizing granulomas they are much more difficult to demonstrate.

Phycomycosis

Mucormycosis is caused by fungi of the class phycomycetes. The fungi have broad-branching non-septate hyphae easily identified by a suitable silver stain. It may be a primary gastrointestinal infection or part of a disseminated disease.[99] Stomach involvement is rare, but the lesions are ischaemic due to fungal invasion of blood vessels which causes thrombotic occlusion. At the base and margins of the infected lesions there is a granulomatous inflammatory reaction with multinucleate giant cells. It is a rare opportunistic infection in immunosuppressed individuals and patients with debilitating diseases.

Paracoccidioidomycosis (South American blastomycosis)

Paracoccidioides brasiliensis is a dimorphic fungus endemic to South America which does not occur beyond Mexico and Central America.[100] The parasitic form is an oval round yeast cell 5–40 μm in diameter. The stomach is seldom involved, but histological examination when lesions occur reveals a suppurative inflammation with a reaction of epithelioid cell granulomas and giant cells. The yeast can often be found in the giant cells.

Non-granulomatous opportunistic fungal infections include candidiasis and aspergillosis. There is a high incidence of secondary colonization of benign and malignant gastric ulcers by these fungi.[100–102]

Anisakiasis

Anisakiasis is an infection by larval nematodes of the family anisakidae and is encountered in people who eat inadequately cooked saltwater fish. The types of anisakine larvae that infect humans are those that use marine mammals as a host. Acute infections show a phlegmonous inflammation of the gastric wall with many eosinophils and neutrophils, lymphocytes, plasma cells, histiocytes and occasionally giant cells.[103] In chronic lesions granulomas occur around distorted fragments of cuticle.[104]

Granulomatous gastritis occurs also in Whipple disease[105,106] and in *Mycobacterium avium* infection in immunosuppressed patients.

Miscellaneous granulomatous disorders

Chronic granulomatous disease of childhood

Chronic granulomatous disease of childhood is an inherited and commonly X-linked disease of children and infants. It is characterized by an inherited enzymatic defect that results in the failure of production of H_2O_2 during phagocytosis through inhibition of the H_2O_2 myeloperoxidase halide killing system.[107,108] The recurrent infections are caused by catalase-positive microorganisms. Tuberculoid granulomas, varying from noncaseating tuberculoid lesions to the more common large necrotic abscesses, are frequent. Patients with gastric involvement present with outlet obstruction, for the antrum is narrowed by granulomatous inflammation simulating Crohn's disease or peptic ulcer disease.[109]

Allergic granulomatosis and vasculitis

The syndrome is related to the polyarteritis nodosa group. However, there is a strong association with bronchial asthma and eosinophilia, frequent involvement of pulmonary and splenic vessels and the presence of intra and extravascular granulomas. The lesions show a striking infiltration by eosinophils. Gastric involvement is rare.[97,110,111]

Granulomas in relation to malignant tumours

The presence of sarcoid-like granulomas within and at the periphery of malignant tumours, as well as in the draining lymph nodes, is well recognized.[112] Such granulomas can occasionally be seen in relation to gastric carcinoma and malignant lymphoma.

REFERENCES

1. Ming SC. Tumors of the oesophagus and stomach. Washington: Armed Forces Institute of Pathology 1973: 115–119.
2. Oehlert W. Klinische Pathologie des Magen-Darm Traktes. Stuttgart: Schattauer Verlag, 1978.
3. Morson BS, Dawson IMP. Gastrointestinal Pathology, 2nd Ed. Oxford: Blackwell Scientific Publications, 1979.
4. Rotterdam H, Sommers SC. Biopsy diagnosis of the digestive tract. New York: Raven Press, 1981.
5. Appelman HD. Pathology of the esophagus, stomach and duodenum. New York: Churchill Livingstone, 1984.
6. Whitehead R. Mucosal biopsy of the gastrointestinal tract. Philadelphia: Saunders, 1985.
7. Kennedy FD, Dockerty MB, Waugh JM. Giant hypertrophy of gastric mucosa. Cancer 1954; 7: 671–681.
8. Schindler R. On hypertrophic glandular gastritis, hypertrophic gastropathy and parietal cell mass. Gastroenterology 1963; 45: 77–83.
9. Lipkin M. Proliferation and differentiation of gastrointestinal cells in normal and diseased states. In: Physiology of the gastrointestinal tract. New York: Raven Press, 1981.
10. Koch AK, Lesch R, Cremer M, Oehlert W. Polyps and polypoid foveolar hyperplasia in gastric biopsy specimens and their precancerous prevalence. Front Gastrointest Res 1979; 4: 183–191.
11. Monroe LS, Boughton GA, Sommers SC. The association of gastric epithelial hyperplasia and cancer. Gastroenterology 1964; 46: 267–272.
12. Snover DC. Benign epithelial polyps of the stomach. Pathol Ann 1985; 1: 303–329.
13. Iida M, Yao T, Watanabe H, Imamura K, Fuyuno S, Omae T. Spontaneous disappearance of fundic gland polyposis. Report of these cases. Gastroenterology 1980; 79: 725–728.
14. Elster K, Eidt H, Ottenjann R, Roesch W, Seifert E. Druesenkoerperzystem, eine polypoide Lesion der Magenschleimhaut. Dtsch Med Wschr 1977; 6: 183–187.
15. Tomasulo J. Gastric polyps: Histologic types and their relationship to gastric carcinoma. Cancer 1971; 27: 1346–1355.
16. Ming SC. The classification and significance of gastric polyps. In: Yardley BL. ed. The Gastrointestinal Tract. Baltimore: Williams & Wilkins, 1977: 149–175.
17. Ming SC, Goldman H. Gastric polyps: A histogenetic classification and its relation to carcinoma. Cancer 1965; 18: 721–726.
18. Elster K. Histologic classification of gastric polyps. Curr Top Pathol 1976; 63: 78–93.
19. Kamiya T, Morishita T, Asakura H, Munakata Y, Miura S, Tsuchiya M. Histological long-standing follow-up study of hyperplastic polyps of the stomach. Am J Gastroenterol 1981; 75: 275–281.
20. Seifert E, Gail K, Weismueller J. Gastric polypectomy long-term results (survey of 23 centres in Germany). Endoscopy 1983; 15: 8–11.
21. Janunger KG, Domelloef L. Gastric polyps and precancerous mucosal changes after partial gastrectomy. Acta Chir Scand 1978; 144: 293–298.
22. Franzin G, Novelli P. Gastritis cystica profunda. Histopathology 1981; 5: 535–547.
23. Jablokow VR, Aranha GV, Reyes CV. Gastric stomal hyperplasia. Report of four cases. J Surg Oncol 1982; 19: 106–108.
24. Littler ER, Gleibermann E. Gastric cystica polyposa. Cancer 1972; 29: 205–209.
25. Mori K, Shinya H, Wolff WI. Polypoid reparative mucosal proliferation at the site of a healed gastric ulcer. Sequential gastroscopic, radiological and histological observations. Gastroenterology 1971; 61: 523–529.
26. Menetrier P. Des polyadenomes gastriques et de leur rapports avec le cancer de l'estomac. Archives de Physiologie Normale et Pathologique 1888; I: 32–55 and II: 236–262.
27. Cronkhite LW, Canada WJ. Generalized gastrointestinal polyposis. N Engl J Med 1955; 252: 1011–1015.
28. Johnson GK, Soergel KH, Hensley GT, Dodds Wj, Hogan WJ. Cronkhite-Canada syndrome. Gastrointestinal pathophysiology and morphology. Gastroenterology 1972; 63: 140–151.
29. Scharschmidt BF. The natural history of hypertrophic gastropathy (Menetrier's disease). Am J Med 1977; 63: 644–652.
30. Daniel ES, Ludwig SL, Lewis KJ, Ruprecht RM, Rajacich GM, Schwabe AD. The Cronkhite-Canada Syndrome: an analysis of clinical and pathologic features and therapy in 55 patients. Medicine 1982; 61: 293–309.
31. McRussell D, Bhathal PS, St John DJB. Complete remission in Cronkhite-Canada Syndrome. Gastroenterology 1983; 85: 180–185.
32. Fieber SF, Richert RR. Hyperplastic gastropathy. Am J Gastroenterol 1981; 76: 321–329.
33. Stempien SJ, Dagradi AE, Reingold IM et al. Hypertrophic hypersecretory gastropathy: analysis of 15 cases and a review of the pertinent literature. Am J Dig Dis 1964; 9: 471–493.
34. Zollinger RM, Ellison EH. Primary peptic ulcerations of the jejunum associated with islet cell turnover of the pancreas. Ann Surg 1955; 142: 709–728.
35. Solcia E, Capella C, Buffa R, Frigeria B, Fiocca R. Pathology of the Zollinger-Ellison Syndrome. Progress in Surgical Pathology 1980; 1: 119–133.
36. Palmer ED. What Menetrier really said. Gastrointest Endosc 1968; 15: 83–90.
37. Tan DTD, Stempien SJ, Dagradi AE. The clinical spectrum of hypertrophic hypersecretory gastropathy. Report of 50 patients. Gastrointest Endosc 1971; 18: 69.
38. Kelly DG, Miller EJ, Malagelada JR, Huizenga KA, Markowitz H. Giant hypertrophic gastropathy (Menetrier's disease): Pharmacologic effects on protein leakage and mucosal ultrastructure. Gastroenterology 1982; 83: 581–589.
39. Frank BW, Kern F, Jr. Menetrier's disease. Spontaneous metamorphosis of giant hypertrophy of gastric mucosa to atrophic gastritis. Gastroenterology 1967; 53: 953–960.
40. Berenson MM, Sannella J, Freston JW. Menetrier's disease. Serial morphological secretory and serological observations. Gastroenterology 1976; 70: 257–263.
41. Walker FB. Spontaneous remission in hypertrophic gastropathy (Menetrier's disease). South Med J 1981; 74: 1273–1276.
42. Kraut JR, Powell R, Hruby MA, Lloyd-Still JD. Menetrier's disease in childhood: report of two cases and a review of the literature. J Ped Surg 1981; 16: 707–711.
43. Stillmann AE, Sieber O, Manther U, Pinnas J. Transient protein losing enteropathy and enlarged rugae in childhood. Am J Dis Child 1981; 135: 29–33.
44. Haot J, Bogomoletz WV, Jouret A, Mainguet P. Menetrier's disease with lymphocytic gastritis: an unusual association with possible pathogenic implications. Hum Pathol 1991; 22: 379–386.
45. Wolber RA, Owen DA, Anderson FH, Freeman HJ. Lymphocytic gastritis and giant gastric folds associated with gastrointestinal protein loss. Mod Pathol 1991; 4: 13–15.
46. Martin E, Potet F, Debray C et al. Etude anatomo-pathologique de la gastrite hypertrophique geante. Acta gastroenterol Belg 1962; 25: 514–551.
47. Dottrens Y. Maladie de Menetrier et carcinome gastrique. Etude de 4 cas. Geneve: These no. 3611 Medicine et Hygiene, 1977.
48. Roesch W. Erosions of the upper gastrointestinal tract. Clin Gastroenterol 1978; 7: 623–634.
49. Freise J, Hofmann R, Gebel M, Huchzermeyer H. Follow-up study of chronic gastric erosions. Endoscopy 1979; 1: 13–17.
50. Roesch W, Ottenjahn R. Gastric erosions. Endoscopy 1970; 2: 93–98.
51. Oehlert W. Klinische Pathologie des Magen-Darm-Traktes. Stuttgart: Schattauer Verlag, 1978.
52. Kawai K, Shimamoto K, Misaki F, Murakami K, Masuda M. Erosions of gastric mucosa: Pathogenesis, incidence and classification of the erosive gastritis. Endoscopy 1970; 3: 168–174.
53. Franzin G, Manfrini C, Musola R, Rodella S, Fratton A. Chronic erosions of the stomach. A clinical, endoscopic and histological evaluation. Endoscopy 1984; 16: 1–5.
54. Clarke AC, Lee Sp, Nicholson GI. Gastritis varioliformis.

Chronic erosive gastritis with protien losing gastropathy. Am J Gastroenterol 1977; 68: 599–602.
55. Walk L. Polyps caused by gastric erosions. Radiologe 1975; 15: 354–355.
56. Haot J, Jouret A, Willette M, Gossnin A, Mainguet P. Lymphocytic gastritis — prospective study of its relationship with varioliform gastritis. Gut 1990; 31: 282–285.
57. Roesch W, Warnatz H. Immunofluorescenzmikroskopische Untersuchungen bei Magenerosionen. In: Lindner H. ed. Fortschritte in der gastroenterologische Endoscopie. Baden-Baden: Witzstrock, 1974: 194–251.
58. Andre C, Moulinier B, Lambert R, Bugnon B. Gastritis varioliformis, allergy and disodium cromoglycate. Lancet 1976; 1: 964–965.
59. Spreeuwel JP van, Lindeman J, Maanen J van, Meijer CJLM. Increased numbers of IgE containing cells in gastric and duodenal biopsies. An expression of food allergy secondary to chronic inflammation? J Clin Pathol 1984; 37: 601–606.
60. Walinga H. Varioliforme erosies. Amsterdam: Thesis, 1985.
61. Rutgeerts P, Onette E, Vantrappen G, Geboes K, Broeckart L, Talloen L. Crohn's disease of the stomach and duodenum: a clinical study with emphasis on the value of endoscopy and endoscopic biopsies. Endoscopy 1980; 12: 288–294.
62. Haggitt RC, Meissner WA. Crohn's disease of the upper gastrointestinal tract. Am J Clin Pathol 1973; 59: 613–622.
63. Spreeuwel JP van, Lindeman J, Wal AM van der, Weterman I, Kreuning J, Meijer CJLM. Morphological and immunohistochemical findings in upper gastrointestinal biopsies of patients with Crohn's disease of the ileum and colon. J Clin Pathol 1982; 35: 934–940.
64. Farthing MJG, Fairclough PD, Hegarthy JE, Swarbrick ET, Dawson AM. Treatment of chronic erosive gastritis with prednisolone. Gut 1981; 22: 759–762.
65. Andre G, Gillon J, Moulinier B, Martin A, Fargier MC. Randomised placebo-controlled double blind trial of two dosages of sodium cromoglycate in treatment of varioliform gastritis: comparison with cimetidine. Gut 1982; 23: 348–352.
66. Jaskiewicz K, Price SK, Zak J, Lourens HD. Lymphocytic gastritis in non ulcer dyspepsia. Dig Dis Sci 1992; 36: 1079–1083.
67. Wolber R, Owen D, Delbuono L, Appelman H, Freeman H. Lymphocytic gastritis in patients with celiac sprue or sprue-like intestinal disease. Gastroenterology 1990; 98: 310–315.
68. Adams DO. The granulomatous inflammatory response. Am J Pathol 1976; 84: 164–191.
69. Warren KS. A functional classification of granulomatous inflammation. Ann New York Ac Sci 1976; 278: 7–18.
70. Epstein WL. Granuloma formation in man. Pathol Biol Ann 1977; 7: 1–30.
71. Haggitt RC. Granulomatous diseases of the gastrointestinal tract. In: Joachim H L, ed. Pathology of granulomas. New York: Raven Press, 1983: 257–306.
72. James DG, Williams JW. Sarcoidosis and other granulomatous disorders. Philadelphia: Saunders, 1985.
73. Adams DO. The structure of mononuclear phagocytes differentiating in vivo. Am J Pathol 1975; 80: 101–116.
74. Williams WJ. Sarcoidosis. Beitr Pathol 1977; 160: 325–336.
75. Korelitz BI, Waye JD, Kreuning J et al. Crohn's disease in endoscopic biopsies of the gastric antrum and duodenum. Am J Gastroenterol 1981; 76: 103–109.
76. Pryse-Davies J. Gastro-duodenal Crohn's disease. J Clin Pathol 1964; 17: 90–94.
77. Longcope WT, Freiman DG. A study of sarcoidosis. Medicine. Baltimore: Williams & Wilkins, 1952; 31: 1–132.
78. Maycock RL, Bertrand P, Morrison E, Scott JH. Manifestation of sarcoidosis. Am J Med 1963; 35: 67–89.
79. Palmer ED. Note on silent sarcoidosis of the gastric mucosa. J Lab Clin Med 1958; 52: 231–234.
80. Konda J, Ruth M, Sassaris M, Hunter FM. Sarcoidosis of the stomach and rectum. Am J Gastroenterol 1980; 73: 516–518.
81. Orie NGM, Rijssel TG van, Zwaag GL van der. Pyloric stenosis in sarcoidosis. Acta Med Scan 1950; 138: 139–143.
82. Fahimi HD, Deren JJ, Gottlieb LS, Zamcheck N. Isolated granulomatous gastritis: its relationship to disseminated sarcoidosis and regional enteritis. Gastroenterology 1963; 45: 161–175.
83. Semenzato G, Pezzuto A, Chisoli M, Pizzolo G. Redistribution of T-lymphocytes in the lymph nodes of patients with sarcoidosis. N Eng J Med 1982; 306: 48–49.
84. Oord JJ van den, Wolf-Peeters C de, Facchetti F, Desmet V. Cellular composition of hypersensitivity-type granulomas: immunohistochemical analysis of tuberculous and sarcoid lymphadenitis. Hum Pathol 1984; 15: 559–565.
85. Daniele RP. Cell-mediated immunity in pulmonary disease. Hum Pathol 1986; 17: 154–160.
86. Maarsseveen ACMT van, Mullink H, Alons CL, Stam J. Distribution of T-lymphocyte subsets in different portions of sarcoid granulomas: immunohistologic analysis of monoclonal antibodies. Hum Pathol 1986; 17: 493–500.
87. Schinella RA, Ackert J. Isolated granulomatous disease of the stomach. Am J Gastroenterol 1979; 72: 30–35.
88. Weinstock JV. Idiopathic isolated granulomatous gastritis. Dig Dis Sci 1980; 25: 233–235.
89. Sherman FE, Moran TJ. Granulomas of stomach. I. Response to injury of muscle and fibrous tissue of wall of human stomach. Gastrointest Pathol 1954; 24: 415–421.
90. Moran TJ, Sherman FE. Granulomas of stomach. II. Experimental production by intramural injection of foreign material including gastric juice. Gastrointest Pathol 1954; 24: 422–433.
91. Palmer ED. Tuberculosis of the stomach and the stomach in tuberculosis. Am Rev Tuberculosis 1950; 61: 116–130.
92. Bentley G, Webster JHH. Gastrointestinal tuberculosis. Br J Surg 1967; 54: 90–96.
93. Sachar DB, Klein RS, Swerdlow F et al. Erosive syphilic gastritis: dark-field and immunofluorescence diagnosis from biopsy specimen. Ann Intern Med 1974; 80: 512–515.
94. Reisman TN, Leverett FL, Hudson JR et al. Syphilitic gastropathy. Am J Dig Dis 1975; 20: 588–593.
95. Butz WC, Watts JC, Rosales-Quintana S, Hicklin MD. Erosive gastritis as a manifestation of secondary syphilis. Am J Clin Pathol 1975; 63: 895–900.
96. Morin ME, Tan A. Diffuse enlargement of gastric folds as a manifestation of secondary syphilis. Am J Gastroenterol 1980; 74: 170–172.
97. Goldgraber MB, Kirsner JB, Raskin HF. Nonspecific granulomatous disease of the stomach. AMA Arch Intern Med 1958; 102: 10–24.
98. Schulz DM. Histoplasmosis: a statistical morphologic study. Am J Clin Pathol 1954; 24: 11–26.
99. Calle S, Klatsky S. Intestinal phycomycosis (mucormycosis). Am J Clin Pathol 1966; 45: 264–272.
100. Smith JMB. Mycoses of the alimentary tract. Gut 1969; 10: 1035–1040.
101. Brown JR. Human actinomycosis. Hum Pathol 1973; 4: 319–330.
102. Scott BB, Jenkins D. Gastro-oesophageal candidiasis. Gut 1982; 23: 137–139.
103. Yokogawa M, Yoshimura H. Clinicopathologic study on larval anisakiasis in Japan. Am J Trop Med & Hyg 1967; 16: 723—728.
104. Dooley JR, Neafie RC. Anisakiasis. Armed Forces Institute. In: Pathology of tropical and extraordinary diseases. Washington: Binford & Connor. 1976; Chapter 15: 475–481.
105. Ectors N, Geboes K, Desmet V. Gastrite granulomateuse. Acta Endosc. 1990; 20: 453–463.
106. Ectors N, Geboes K, Wijnants P, Desmet V. Granulomatous Gastritis and Whipple's disease. Am J Gastroenterol 1992; 87: 509–513.
107. Johnston RB, Newman SL. Chronic granulomatous disease. Pediatr Clin North Am 1977; 24: 365–376.
108. Segal AW, Cross AR, Garcia RC et al. Absence of cytochrome b-245 in chronic granulomatous disease. A multicenter European evaluation of its incidence and relevance. N Eng J Med 1983; 308: 245–251.
109. Griscom NT, Kirkpatrick JA, Girdany BR, Berdon WE, Grand RJ, Mackie GG. Gastric antral narrowing in chronic granulomatous disease of childhood. Pediatrics 1974; 54: 456–460.

110. Abell MR, Limond RV, Blamey WE, Martel W. Allergic granulomatosis with massive gastric involvement. N Engl J Med 1970; 282: 665–668.
111. Lie JT. Disseminated visceral giant cell arteritis. Am J Clin Pathol 1978; 69: 299–305.
112. Gregori HB, Othersen HB, Moore MP. The significance of sarcoid-like lesions in association with malignant neoplasms. Am J Surg 1962; 104: 577–586.

PART IV

Peptic ulcer disease

P. Sipponen

PEPTIC ULCER DISEASE

Peptic ulcer disease is arguably the most important upper gastrointestinal disorder. Approximately 10% of the population is affected during their lifetime, and the economic costs of this are high. It is not an homogeneous group of disorders despite the fact that the ulcers affect the same sites of the stomach and duodenum. There are marked differences in the pathogenetic mechanisms and genetic background between ulcer patients.[1,2]

Peptic ulcer patients are nowadays almost always subjected to endoscopy and biopsy, procedures that provide the opportunity for histological examination of the entire gastric and duodenal mucosa and allows the exclusion of malignancy.

Peptic ulcers are caused by an imbalance between the action of factors such as acid and pepsin digestion and those which tend to preserve mucosal integrity. The normality of the gastric mucosa is probably essential in regulating these actions. Chronic atrophic gastritis inevitably causes a loss of normal cell elements and may thereby impair mucosal functions. The role of *Helicobacter pylori* (*Hp*) as an aetiological cause of chronic gastritis has thus added a new dimension to discussions and studies on the pathogenesis of peptic ulcer disease. New possibilities for the treatment of peptic ulcer and gastritis with antimicrobial drugs have therefore been introduced.

Acute ulcer

By convention, lesions that penetrate the muscularis mucosa are considered to be ulcers, in contrast to erosions, in which the lesion is limited to the mucosa. Ulcers are designated acute if they are new and heal rapidly, even though they extend down to the muscular layer. Acute ulcers are frequently multiple and probably represent variants of acute mucosal erosions. They seem to be related to mucosal ischaemia and mechanisms mediated following shock or stress.[3,4] They occur in association with chronic lung disease, lesions of the central nervous system (Cushing's ulcers), severe burns (Curling's ulcers), but also after the ingestion of acetosalicylic acid, indomethacin or related anti-inflammatory drugs and alcohol, either alone or in combination.[2,5]

Experimentally, similar ulcers are easily and rapidly induced by specific chemicals, e.g. by cysteamine or propionitrile.[6] Acute ulcers commonly bleed and may respond to antisecretory treatment. This suggests that similar pathogenetic mechanisms operate in both acute and chronic ulcers. In contrast to chronic peptic ulcer, however, acute ulcers tend not to recur after successful elimination of the precipitating cause.

Chronic ulcer

Recurrent or stable ulcers are classified as chronic and can be either duodenal (DU) or gastric (GU), or occur simultaneously at both sites. Pathogenetically and with respect to associated mucosal morphology, however, there seem to be fundamental differences between the two apart from their differing sites.

Johnson et al[7] classified gastric ulcers into three types (Fig. 25.37). It was claimed that Type 1 represents ordinary GU, whereas ulcers of Type 2 and 3 might be variants of DU disease. It has, however, been proposed that chronic gastritis and duodenogastric reflux are the most important factors in the pathogenesis of Type 1 body ulcers, gastric stasis in Type 2 combined ulcers, and that Type 3 prepyloric ulcers resemble DU disease.[8]

Other workers[9] have divided GU into those seen in the upper, middle or lower third of the stomach and related them to differences in acid secretion and in the topography and grade of the associated chronic gastritis. The more severe the grade of gastritis of the body mucosa, the higher is the location of ulcer in the stomach. Patients with such ulcers are also more likely to be female and to be in the older age group.

Ulcers in the cardia are probably a separate clinical entity, but little attention has been given to this subgroup. They may be related more closely to disease of the oesophagus rather than the stomach.

Zollinger-Ellison syndrome

This syndrome is characterized by:

(i) recurrent duodenal ulcers that are commonly multiple, either in the bulb or beyond, and even in the proximal jejunum
(ii) high basal acid output (>15 mEq/h)
(iii) high fasting serum gastrin (in most cases >1000 pg/ml) secreted by a gastrinoma.[10]

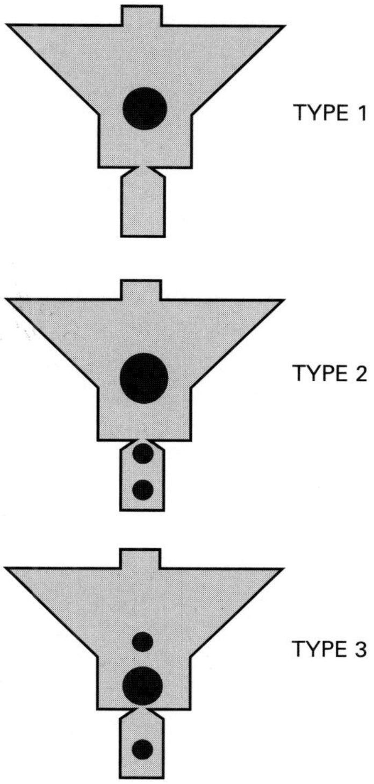

Fig. 25.37 Schematic presentation of classification of gastric ulcer according to Johnson et al.[7] Type 1 ulcer is localized in the body (most often at the angulus) of the stomach. There are no abnormalities in the duodenum, pylorus or prepyloric region. Type 2 ulcer is localized in the body of the stomach and exists combined with an ulcer or ulcer scar in the duodenum or at the pylorus. Type 3 is a prepyloric (antral) ulcer with or without coexisting ulcer or ulcer scar in the duodenum or gastric body (angulus).

The Zollinger-Ellison syndrome (ZES) is a rare disorder compared to ordinary DU disease[2] but it represents a variant in which the pathogenesis is based purely upon the aggressive effects of acid and pepsins. Ulceration or erosion in the stomach is unusual, but may occur and the gastric body mucosa is thick and exhibits pronounced rugal folds. The mucosa is hyerplastic and there is an increased parietal cell mass.

In two thirds of ZES cases gastrinomas are sporadic but in the remainder they are a part of the Type 1 multiple endocrine neoplasia syndrome (MEN-1). Over one half of MEN-1 patients have ZES.[10] Most gastrinomas in both types of ZES occur in the pancreas, but also occur in the stomach, duodenal wall, jejunum, other abdominal organs and even the parathyroid.[10] Gastrinomas are potentially malignant especially if they arise where gastrin containing cells (G cells) are ectopic, i.e. the pancreas and sites other than stomach, duodenum and upper jejunum.

Hypergastrinaemia, although not present in the same levels as in ZES, also occurs in hyperfunction and hyperplasia of antral G cells.[2] The significance of this phenomena is, however, controversial and is not regarded as ZES.

EPIDEMIOLOGY

The incidence of DU in most western countries is currently higher than that of GU; although the ratio is approximately 2–3:1, there is considerable variation.[11–13] In a population sample of subjects over 15 years of age from Finland, the point prevalence of active DU and GU was 1.4% and 0.3%, respectively. If the history of previous ulcer operations and endoscopic ulcer scars were included the total lifetime prevalence of peptic ulcer disease was calculated as 5.9%.[14] In the United States, in any one year period the prevalence of peptic ulcer disease has been estimated at 1.7–1.9%.[15]

The published annual incidence rates for DU and GU probably indicate a true geographic variation. In Denmark[16] the incidence (per 10^5 persons at risk) of DU, GU and combined ulcers (Johnson Types 2 and 3) was 132, 31 and 16 new cases respectively, which is similar to that reported from England.[17] In a corresponding study from the United States, however, the annual incidence of DU and GU was 62 and 24 new cases per 10^5 persons at risk.[15] Based upon these figures, Kurata and Haile[15] estimated that 350 000 new cases are to be expected annually in the United States and that about 4 million Americans simultaneously have active peptic ulcer disease.

The incidence of peptic ulcer shows an increase with increasing age.[11] This increase is somewhat slower in GU than in DU, and a peak incidence may occur in males with GU in the age group of 60–64 years.[11,12,18]

Several investigations have indicated considerable variation in incidence and location of peptic ulcer disease during different time periods. In the beginning of the present century DU was said to be a rare disorder in comparison to GU and in comparison to the situation at present. In addition, peptic ulcer disease might have been more common in females decades ago. For a time it become more common in males and then during the past few decades of this century there has been a rise in incidence in females and a decrease in males.[11,15]

PATHOPHYSIOLOGY

Acid secretion

Hydrochloric acid secretion has an important role in ulcer pathogenesis. Although less than half of DU patients and only a small proportion of GU patients show hypersecretion of acid,[19,20] its presence is necessary for ulcer development. Peptic ulcer cannot develop in a pentagastrin-resistant achlorhydric stomach and if ulceration is demonstrated, malignancy should be suspected. In a recent survey of the literature, Lam[21] reports that the percentage of DU patients with maximal or peak acid output greater than the upper normal limit varied between 16–56%. The frequency of higher than expected basal acid output varied between 11–38%.

For DU, Baron[22] introduced the concept of threshold value of acid secretion that represents the lowest possible value of peak (approximately 15 mmol/h) or maximal (12 mmol/h) acid output. DU may occur in subjects with acid output higher than these limits but is most unlikely in those with lower output. GU, on the other hand, may exist in such a hypoacidic stomach but does not develop in an achlorhydric stomach.

There is a positive linear correlation between acid output and parietal cell mass,[23–25] and an increased number of parietal cells in a biopsy specimen may indicate a risk for DU. Correspondingly, ulcer risk is probably low if the number of parietal cells is reduced. In practice, this will occur in persons with a degree of atrophic body gastritis. This is rarely seen in biopsy specimens from patients with active or healed DU.[26–29] The relationship between acid secretion and the degree of chronic gastritis in biopsies from the gastric body is presented in Figure 25.38; the mean maximal acid output in patients with slight atrophic gastritis is reduced to half compared to that in subjects with normal mucosa.

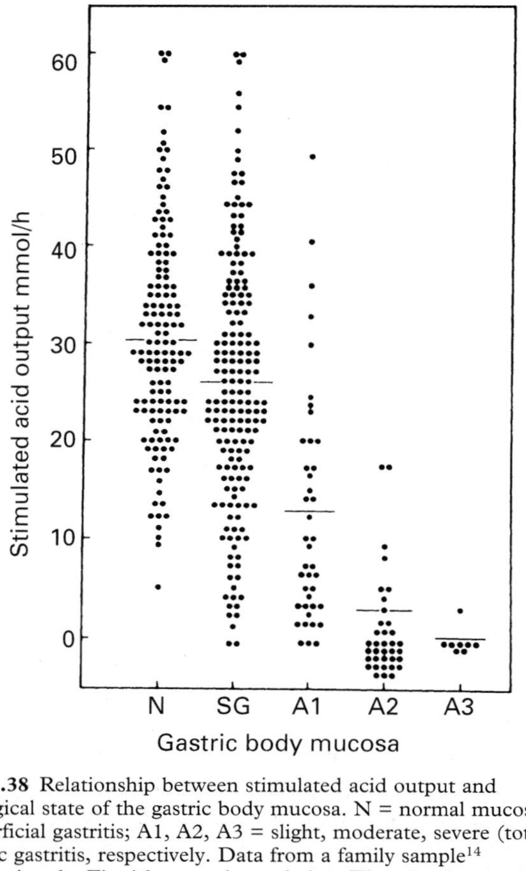

Fig. 25.38 Relationship between stimulated acid output and histological state of the gastric body mucosa. N = normal mucosa; SG = superficial gastritis; A1, A2, A3 = slight, moderate, severe (total) atrophic gastritis, respectively. Data from a family sample[14] representing the Finnish general population. The stimulated acid output was determined as follows: after administration of 6 μg/kg of body weight of pentagastrin, the stomach was emptied for 10 min by continuous suction. The gastric aspirate was collected during the following 30 min and was used for measurement of the acid output.

Gastroduodenal defence mechanisms

Several mechanisms operate to maintain the integrity of the gastroduodenal mucosa (see Ch. 10).

Influence of H. pylori *infection and gastritis on the defence mechanisms*

Mucus forms an insoluble gel layer adherent to the mucosal surface[30] and several functions are proposed for it. Because the mucus consists of polymerized glycoproteins, it is easily permeable to hydrogen ions but impermeable to pepsins. It acts as an unstirred layer of water that provides a compartment for neutralization of acid by bicarbonate secreted from underlying epithelial cells.[31] The physical gel-like property of the mucus layer is a prerequisite for its proper functioning. The breakdown of the gel to soluble glycoprotein subunits impairs its protective function. The breakdown can be induced by external agents, drugs and possibly by luminal endogenous pepsins, but it can, in addition, be affected by impaired synthesis and secretion by surface epithelial cells.[32,33]

Another mucosal barrier complex consists of cellular, metabolic and circulatory mechanisms, and factors that are considered to counteract and neutralize the influence of back-diffused H^+ ion in the duodenal and gastric wall or to counteract the damaging effects of external agents.[34] The concept of cytoprotection is applied to defence mechanisms that protect the gastric mucosa through mechanisms other than acid inhibition.[35] Postaglandins seem to have a significant role in this cytoprotection by exerting a positive influence on mucus and bicarbonate secretion in surface epithelial cells, on mucosal circulation, on prevention of haemorrhagic lesions and by having a trophic effect on the gastric mucosa.[35–37] A significant trophic effect is provided also by several other hormones, such as gastrin and glucagon and possibly steroid hormones. The epidermal growth factor, secreted by salivary and Brunner's glands, also significantly stimulates cell renewal and repair.[38]

Genetic influences

An hereditary tendency to peptic ulcer disease does not conform to a simple Mendelian principle but is seemingly heterogeneous and multifactorial.[39] Approximately 30% of patients with DU are reported to have one or more close relatives affected with DU or dyspepsia. Gastric disease is also more common than expected by chance in parents, as well as siblings of GU patients.[40] The risk of peptic ulcer disease in sibs of probands with ulcer disease is calculated to be 2–2.5 times as high as the risk in the population at large.

A higher than expected frequency of blood group O is found among DU patients. Non-secretors with blood group O seem to have a 2.5 times higher risk of getting

DU than secretors with other blood groups.[41,42] The relationship between peptic ulcer risk and some HLA antigens has also been suggested, but is not firmly established.[21] A specific genetic link is exhibited by a relationship between DU and MEA-1 in some cases,[10,43] and between DU and other even rarer syndromes.[44] In these syndromes, the heredity of DU can be mediated through a single gene.

The size of the parietal cell mass differs between populations and ethnic groups: both the parietal cell counts and the maximal stimulated acid output in Chinese DU patients, for example, are lower than those in Scots.[21,25] This suggests heterogeneity in DU disease but might also indicate that the size of cell populations in the mucosa might be genetically determined. Supporting this view are the high serum levels of pepsinogen I, a serum marker for acid and pepsin-secreting body glands which occur in siblings of hyperpepsinogenic DU patients. This suggests an autosomal-dominant pattern of inheritance.[43] In addition, a significant increase in levels of acid output can be demonstrated among the family members with a histologically normal stomach,[45] suggesting that the functional capacity and size of the parietal cell population could, in fact, be genetically determined.

Drugs

Aspirin, phenylbutazone, indomethacin and related anti-inflammatory drugs (NSAIDs), when taken regularly, may result in peptic ulcer,[46,47] particularly of the duodenum or lower stomach. Experimentally, aspirin-induced lesions can be inhibited by prostaglandins and cimetidine, indicating that these drugs are ulcerogenic because they promote an imbalance between the aggressive effects of acid secretion and prostaglandin-mediated cytoprotection.

Experimentally, a long list[6] of defined chemical compounds can be used to produce acute ulcers that resemble peptic ulcer disease in humans. A single oral or subcutaneous dose of cysteamine or propionitrile may cause an acute ulcer within a few hours. After exposure to such drugs, profound changes are seen in the metabolism of neurotransmitter compounds in gastric and duodenal mucosa, in the adrenals and in the brain. Changes also occur in the metabolism of prostaglandins, acid and bicarbonate secretion, and in the motility of both duodenum and stomach.[6] The ulcerogenic potency of such simple compounds emphasizes a vulnerability of the gastroduodenal mucosa. However, to date no single general environmental ulcerogenic chemical or toxin has been identified.

Diet, smoking, alcohol

Diet is believed to have a limited influence in the prevention or promotion of mucosal damage.[48] On the other hand, the large geographic differences in peptic ulcer incidence could logically be explained by differences in diet. Fresh vegetables may protect against DU, whereas dietary fat or proteins are probably of limited significance. In a controlled trial, DU patients on a high fibre diet have been found to experience fewer ulcer recurrences than patients on a low fibre diet.[49] Smoking and alcohol are probably strongly ulcerogenic.[50]

Duodeogastric reflux

Scintigraphic, endoscopic and biochemical studies indicate a higher than expected frequency of duodenogastric reflux in GU patients.[13,51] The role and significance of reflux in the pathogenesis of chronic ulcer is, however, a subject of controversy.[52] Reflux is common in non-ulcer diseases, and it is not known whether the reflux could be secondary to the motility abnormalities that are associated with the development of gastric ulcer, or whether they are a direct consequence of the disease.[51] According to experimental studies and indirect observations in human beings, bile salts, lysolecithin and taurocholate, as well as pancreatic enzymes, may cause acute damage to the gastro-oesophageal mucous membrane.[53,54]

MORPHOLOGY AND SITE OF THE ULCER

The mucosa at ulcer margins shows non-specific inflammatory and regenerative changes. Individual features including metaplasia are no different from those seen in other conditions. Four different layers are detected in the ulcer base. The uppermost layer consists of a purulent exudate and is succeeded by layers of necrosis, granulation tissue and fibrotic scar tissue. The muscle layer is often completely replaced at the base of a chronic penetrating ulcer (Fig. 25.39).

Peptic ulcer is usually a solitary lesion, but two active ulcers or, infrequently, an ulcer accompanying an ulcer scar occurs in 2–8% of GU and 20% of DU cases.[55] 'Kissing ulcer', or ulcer twins, usually in the duodenal bulb or the prepyloric antrum, represents the simultaneous ulceration of the anterior and posterior walls.

In the duodenal bulb peptic ulcer occurs within the first 2 cm, usually in the anterior or the posterior wall. In the stomach, ulceration becomes less frequent as the distance from the pylorus increases. The percentage of cases per 1 cm on the lesser curvature drops from 16.7 at a distance less than 11 mm from the pylorus to 3.7 at 91–120 mm.[55] GU appears in the upper, middle and lower thirds of the stomach in 17%, 42% and 41% of cases, respectively.[9]

Approximately 80% of gastric ulcers are situated on the lesser curvature of the stomach.[56,57] They are rare in the gastric fundus (1% of cases) and relatively rare on the greater curvature (5%), anterior wall (1%) and posterior wall (6%).

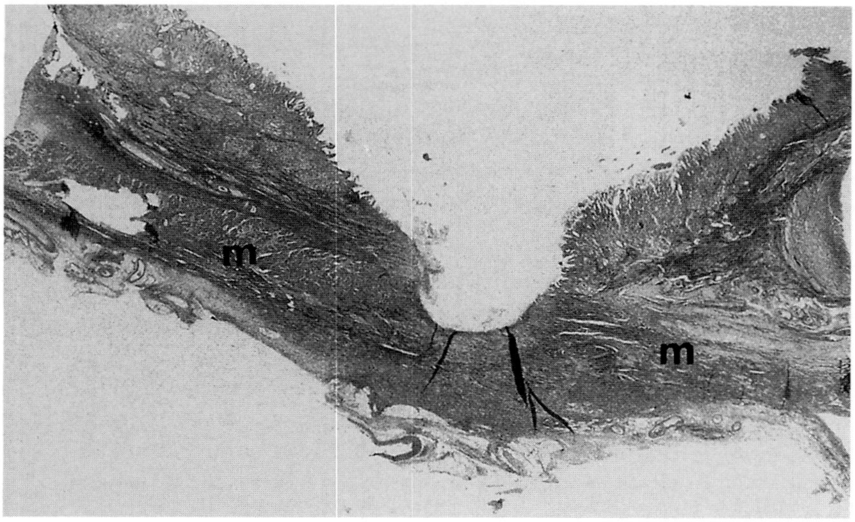

Fig. 25.39 Chronic gastric ulcer that penetrates the muscular layer. Ulcer base is formed of tight collagenous scar. The muscle layer (m) is penetrated. (Trichrome, ×3.6)

There is a significant negative correlation between acid output and the distance of a GU from the pylorus.[58] In addition, the higher the mean age of the patient, the higher the ulcer tends to be localized and the more likely is the patient to be female.[9,58] Ulcers in the lower third of the stomach tend to be smaller than ulcers in the upper third. By contrast, no age or sex-related differences exist with respect to localization or multiplicity of DU.

The relatively specific localization of peptic ulcer to the lesser smaller curvature, angulus, prepyloric antrum and anterior and posterior walls of the proximal duodenal bulb is considered to indicate areas of greatest vulnerability. The 'Magenstrasse', which constitutes less than 5% of the whole gastric mucosa, is said to be the most susceptible to chronic ulcer.[56,58] Differences in microcirculation and vascular architecture between the lesser and greater curvatures have been muted as the basis for ulcer susceptibility but there are no real grounds for this.

It has been hypothesized by Oi and colleagues[59] that the prevalence of GU at the angulus is due to a triangular area of relative muscular weakness of the wall. The high susceptibility being apparently due to secondary changes in the circulation consequent upon altered motility. In the duodenum, on the other hand, jet effects due to the emptying of acid gastric contents into the duodenal bulb are said to be factors determining the particular location of DU to the anterior or posterior wall of the bulb.[60]

Chronic gastritis may have some influence on the determination of the site of ulcer in the stomach. Gastritic mucosa probably forms an area with reduced resistance and with a liability to develop ulcer. Indeed, the GU is most frequently located in areas where the extent and grade of chronic gastritis is highest, i.e. distal to the antrofundal mucosal border and on the lesser curvature of the stomach.[61]

DUODENITIS

Duodenitis has been a subject of controversy, but objective criteria for the histological diagnosis and grading of duodenitis are established. Although there are some differences in methods of grading (Table 25.6), the histological criteria are based on similar features. These include the structure and architecture of the duodenal mucosa and villous processes, changes in surface epithelium, and on the inflammatory reaction (Table 25.6, Figs 25.40–25.42).

Whitehead and colleagues[62] separated three grades of duodenitis. Grade 1 represents a mild duodenitis with increase of number of mucosal lymphocytes and plasma cells, and Grades 2 or 3 moderate or severe duodenitis with abnormal surface epithelium and later with erosions. A grading of duodenitis into mild or severe degrees is recommended by Jenkins and colleagues[63]. These authors suggest that incipient epithelial erosions distinguish

Table 25.6 Criteria for histological diagnosis and grading of duodenitis.

1. *Mucosal architecture and villous processes*
   — irregularity and shortening of villi
   — oedema in lamina propria
   — high number of Brunner's glands above the muscularis mucosae
2. *Superficial epithelium*
   — flattening and basophilia of epithelial cells
   — disappearance of brush border
   — stratification of epithelial cells
   — bud-like syncytial processes
   — 'gastric metaplasia'
   — invasion of polymorphs
   — erosions
3. *Inflammation*
   — increased number of lymphocytes, plasma cells
   — increased number of polymorphs

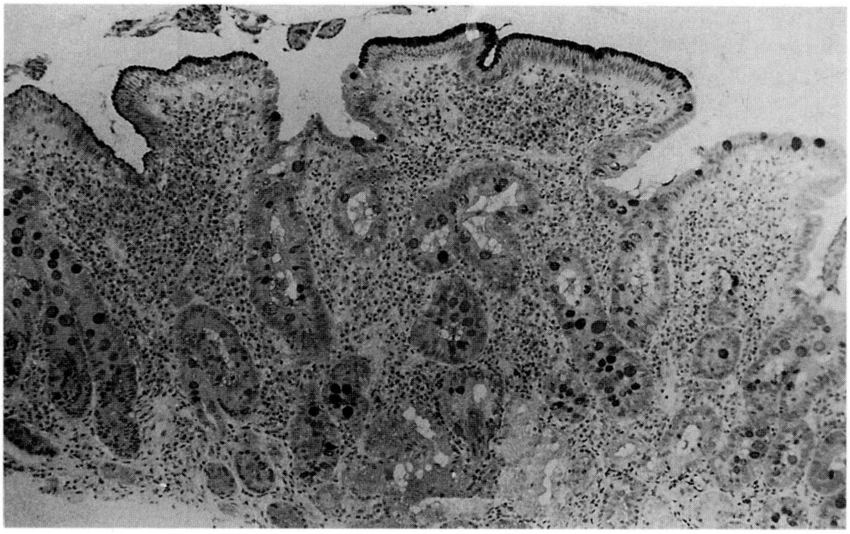

Fig. 25.40 Duodenitis (bulbitis) of moderate degree according to Whitehead et al[62] and of slight degree according to Jenkins et al.[63] The surface epithelium is abnormal, duodenal villi are short and deformed. Gastric metaplasia occurs focally in the surface epithelium. Lamina propria shows increased cellularity, and is composed mainly of lymphocytes and plasma cells. (AB (pH 2.5)-PAS, ×270)

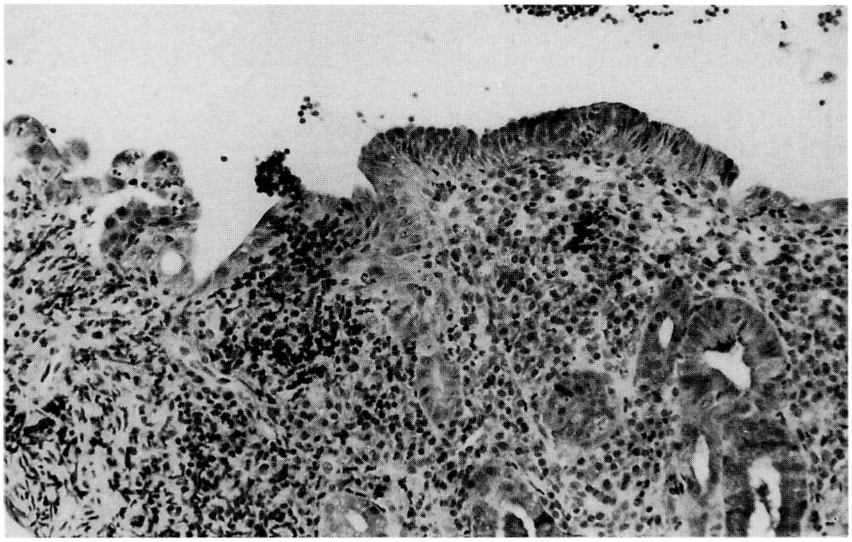

Fig. 25.41 Duodenitis (bulbitis) of severe degree. Villi are absent. Surface epithelium abnormal and eroded. Inflammation is composed of lymphocytes, plasma cells and polymorphs. (H&E, ×405)

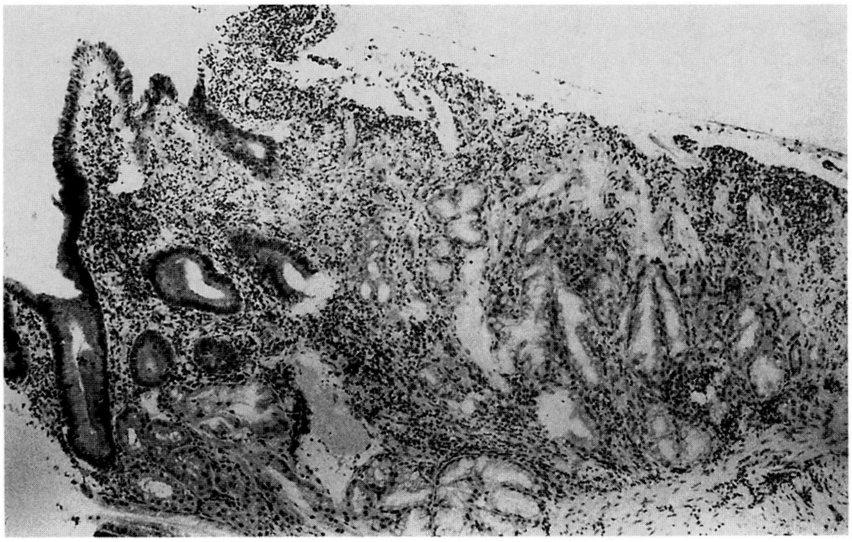

Fig. 25.42 Duodenitis with erosion. Architecture of the mucosa and villous processes is destroyed. Surface epithelium is abnormal and metaplastic. Large erosion with intense polymorph reaction. (H&E, ×270)

between mild and severe duodenitis. It is characterized by a decrease in number of lymphocytes but an increase in number of polymorphs in the lamina propria and surface epithelium. There is an accompanying metaplasia in the surface epithelium and distortion of the villi. Most would now recommend that cases with an increase in cellularity of the duodenal mucosa, but normal mucosal architecture, should be included within the range of normal biological variation.[64]

The question whether duodenitis is a cause, a co-existing, a subsequent or an independent lesion in DU has often been asked. Divergence of opinions also exists concerning the relationship between endoscopic and histological duodenitis. Although the recognition of mild degrees of duodenitis (bulbitis) may have limited value, duodenitis of moderate or severe degree is a highly reliable sign of the propensity to develop active DU disease. In experimental DU, all stages from histological duodenitis to overt ulcer occur during both the induction and the healing phases of the ulcer. Follow-up studies of DU patients have shown that duodenitis precedes the active ulcer and remains after the ulcer has healed.[63]

Johansen and Hansen[65] have shown that there is a significant positive correlation between the presence of gastric metaplasia and an acid load in the duodenal bulb. Moreover, experimental installation of acid into the duodenal bulb causes gastric metaplasia.[66]

Histological duodenitis tends to be focal and patchy. The changes are limited to the duodenal bulb and are rarely seen in the postbulbar duodenum. Inflammation, erosions or ulcers in the postbulbar duodenum should prompt the suspicion of a Zollinger-Ellison syndrome, but they can be due to duodenal Crohn's disease or a non-specific ulcerative jejunitis.

HELICOBACTER PYLORI

Helicobacter pylori (*Hp*) infection and subsequent chronic gastritis (see below) appear to be important risk factors for peptic ulcer disease.[67–69] This is possibly because of a decrease of gastroduodenal defence mechanisms in *Hp* infected subjects. Such a decrease may be dependent on injury of the surface epithelium caused by the bacterium itself and/or on damage of the mucosa mediated by the gastritis and host responses that are directed toward the colonizing *Hp* organisms.[70–72] Potentially injurous substances (ammonia, acetaldehyde, proteolotylic and lipolytic enzymes, toxins, etc.) are produced by the bacterium locally. In addition, several cascades of immunological reactions are triggered in the gastric lamina.

Successful eradication of the *Hp* infection appears to lead to healing of peptic ulcer disease, to a low rate of ulcer relapse, and to a rapid disappearance of acute gastritis ('activity' of gastritis), and, ultimately, to a slow healing of the chronic gastritis itself.[73–75]

The *Hp* gastritis seems to increase the risk of peptic ulcer in both relative and cumulative terms.[76–78] According to case control studies, the relative risk of peptic ulcer may be 10–30 times higher in subjects with an *Hp* gastritis than in controls with a normal stomach. Cumulatively, every third or quarter of middle-aged males with *Hp* gastritis (antral gastritis or pangastritis) have been estimated to develop symptomatic peptic ulcer in a follow-up of 10 years.

In the pathogenesis of DU, an extension of the *Hp* infection from the stomach into the duodenum (duodenal bulb) is considered a critical step in the development of duodenitis and DU (Fig. 25.43).[79–81] A prerequirement is, however, an occurrence of acid-induced gastric metaplasia on the duodenal epithelium, thereby forming a suitable niche for the bacterial growth and colonization. It has been suggested that the mechanisms operating in an infected stomach also play a role in the development of mucosal injuries in the duodenal bulb.[79,80]

The strong association of *Hp* gastritis and bulbitis with peptic ulcer disease has been convincingly proven in several epidemiological and clinical studies in the last decade. In the multifactorial background of peptic ulcerations,[82] *Hp* gastritis and hydrochloric acid seem to be two known major factors which markedly increase the risk of peptic ulceration. Other important factors still exist, however. Acid secretion and *Hp* infection alone do not explain many of the features of peptic ulceration, e.g. its focal nature or its occurrence at particular and specific sites in the stomach and duodenum. In addition, only a proportion of infected subjects will ever contract a peptic ulcer and in some racial groups, particularly in Africa, *Hp* infection rates are high but peptic ulceration is a rarety.

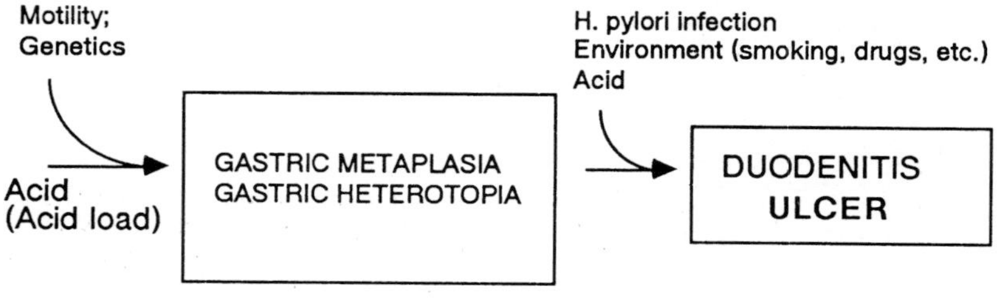

Fig. 25.43 A scheme on proposed mechanisms and participation of *H. pylori* infection in the pathogenesis of duodenitis and duodenal ulcer. Modification from references 79 & 80.

CHRONIC GASTRITIS

DU and GU are virtually always associated with the *Hp* +ve gastritis in gastric biopsies from antrum and corpus.[76,81,83–86] This is the case in DU patients in particular. *Hp* associated gastritis can be found in up to 100% of patients with DU if cases are excluded which are associated with the use of NSAIDs. The frequency of *Hp* infection is lower in GU than in DU and the bacteria are typically infrequent and the degree of colonization is low in atrophic gastritis and in subjects with a low acid output,[87] as is often the case in the GU disease. Antibodies may be found in those patients,[88] however, indicating an association of *Hp* with gastritis in these cases also.

Atrophic gastritis of the gastric corpus inevitably decreases the output of acid and pepsins.[58] The decrease of acid output correlates well with the histological grade of mucosal atrophy (Fig. 25.38), and this is the logical explanation for the negative relationship between body mucosal atrophy and ulcer risk. Atrophy in the antral mucosa may influence the release of gastrin or other hormones,[78] thereby modulating the physiological or patho-physiological functions of the stomach, and exerting, correspondingly, positive or negative influences on the pathogenesis of peptic ulcerations.

There are remarkable differences between the occurrence of DU and GU disease with regard to the time-related course and extent of chronic gastritis.[76,78,84,89–93] In DU patients, development of atrophic body gastritis is exceptional, or does not occur at all: the body mucosa seems to retain its normal structure and function for decades. This is a possible explanation for the chronicity of the DU disease.[26] It is possible that the integrity of the body mucosa in DU patients may be maintained by trophic action of antral gastrin. After removal of the antrum at partial gastrectomy, a rapidly progressive atrophic gastritis develops in the remnant of DU patients. This progression follows the same time-dependent course as is seen in the development of body gastritis in the population at large (Fig. 25.44).

At the time of diagnosis, the pattern of gastritis in GU, Johnson Type 1, is similar to that seen in DU, i.e. there is a mild pangastritis or mild antral gastritis.[76] However, in contrast to DU, a rapidly progressive atrophic gastritis develops, particularly in the body mucosa in a high proportion of GU patients in the following 5–15 years (Fig. 25.45).[94,95]

In GU, the gastritis may affect the body mucosa or both antrum and body, i.e. it is of Type A or AB. The autoantibodies that commonly accompany gastritis of Type A are not usually found, although they may occur. In addition the extent of intestinal metaplasia tends to be high in the gastritis of GU patients, but the gastritis itself is more patchy in distribution than the gastritis of Type A in non-ulcer subjects.

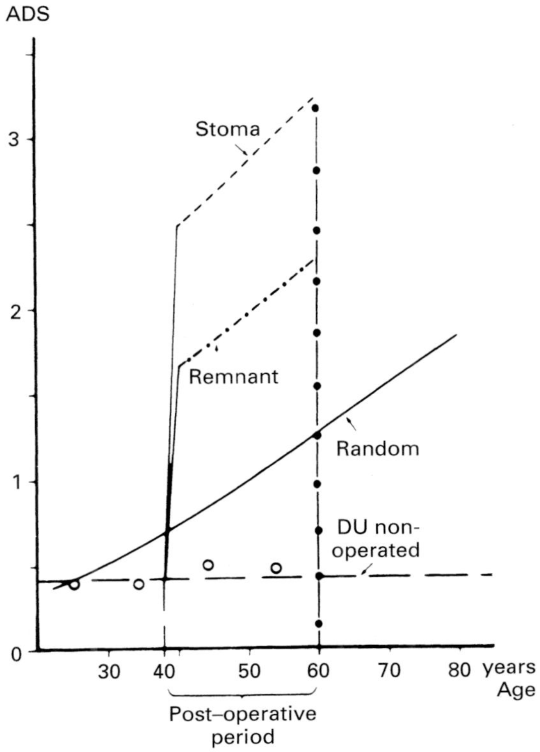

Fig. 25.44 A schematic presentation of progression of chronic body gastritis in patients with duodenal ulcer disease. The age-specific score lines of mean body gastritis in non-operated DU patients and in the remnant of operated DU patients is compared with the progression of gastritis in a population sample ('Random'). After operation there is a rapid initial progression of gastritis and thereafter a slowing down of the process both in the stoma and remnant mucosa. The later progression of gastritis equals that in the population sample 2 years after operation. In contrast, virtually no progression is seen in non-operated DU patients. (From Siurala et al[91])

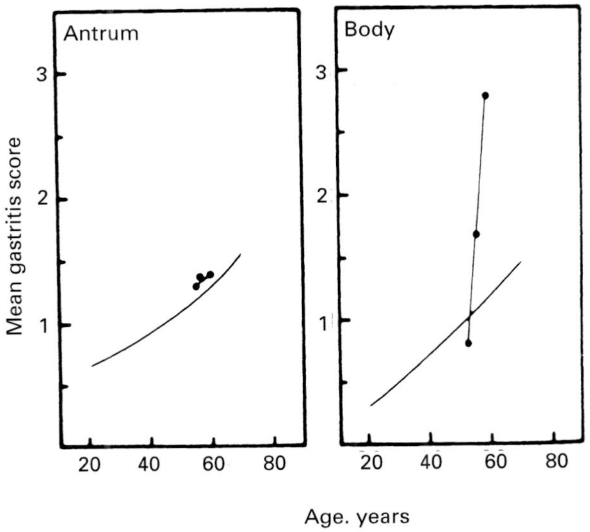

Fig. 25.45 A schematic presentation of progression and behaviour of chronic atrophic gastritis in antrum and body mucosa in patients with gastric ulcer (Johnson Type 1 ulcer). A rapidly progressive atrophic body gastritis develops. The mean progression of gastritis in the antrum follows the same course as is seen in the population at large. (From Maaroos et al[94])

Gear et al[84] found that patients with a long history of GU tend to have an ulcer in the upper stomach with a coexisting widespread and severe gastritis of the gastric corpus. Mackay and Hislop[97] have reported follow-up data of 9 patients with chronic or recurrent GU and long-standing dyspepsia. Within a follow-up period ranging from 3 months to 14 years, all patients developed a severe impairment in stimulated acid secretion. Furthermore, all showed advanced atrophic body gastitis and 4 developed achlorhydria. Using an endoscopic Congo red test and gastric biopsy in 160 patients with active or healed GU, Tatsuta and Okuda[95,96] found that ulcers were more proximal in the stomach when the gastritis in the gastric body was more active. In a further study of 106 patients with GU[84] it was shown that corpus gastritis progressed and became more extensive in 25% of patients followed between 1 and 10 years. The progression resembled gastritis (the Type A or Type AB) that is also seen in patients with gastric polyps.

Atrophic changes in the gastric body mucosa are accompanied by a progressive loss of parietal cells and, hypoacidity. Thus a Johnson Type 1 ulcer may be a self-limiting disease and, according to Maaroos et al,[94] between 5–15 years of progressive atrophic gastritis of the gastric body results in levels of acid secretion which permit ulcer healing. The degree of atrophy was significantly higher in patients with healed GU than in those with active ulcer.

In a further study[83] 86% of GU patients with atrophic corpus gastritis healed within 3 months compared to 63% of those without severe atrophic gastritis. Although a rapid healing rate of GUs can occur in an atrophic and hypoacidic stomach, such ulcers are also reported to recur easily.[83]

The close relationship of duodenitis and chronic gastritis to DU and GU has practical applications in the endoscopic evaluation of patients with dyspepsia (Table 25.7). The presence of histological duodenitis with coexisting chronic antral gastritis and non-atrophic gastric body is compatible with a DU diathesis.[29,86,97–99] On the other hand, the risk of future DU or GU disease would be low in subjects who have a histologically normal stomach and duodenum. The presence of atrophic corpus gastritis would suggest that DU is improbable but would be compatible with GU disease. An advanced atrophic gastritis in body mucosa of patients with active GU indicates a late phase in the 'life-span' of the disease.

Table 25.7 Clinical significance of histological biopsy findings in gastroduodenal peptic ulcer disease.

Histological biopsy finding	Interpretation
Normal stomach	DU or GU improbable. If an ulcer exists, it is probably caused by NSAIDs
Chronic antral or pangastritis with non-atrophic corpus (+ bulbitis)	DU or GU disease possible or even probable; ulcer risk is increased
Chronic pangastritis with corpus atrophy	DU improbable, GU possible even though unlikely
Chronic pangastritis or corpus gastritis with severe corpus atrophy	DU or GU impossible; if an ulcer exists it is probably malignant

DU = duodenal ulcer; GU = gastric ulcer

PEPTIC ULCER AND CANCER

In practice, the cancer risk in peptic ulcer disease applies exclusively to GU. There is, however, the problem of the ulcer which appears macroscopically benign but which is in fact malignant. Approximately 10% of gastric cancers (GCA) are endoscopically indistinguishable from benign peptic ulcer. The proportion is still higher in cases of early GCA, more than half of which present as ulcers. Up to 14% of endoscopically benign gastric ulcers are later proven to be malignant.[98–101] In approximately half the cases the tumour is limited to mucosa and submucosa and has a favourable prognosis, the mean 5 year survival time being approximately 60%, in contrast to approximately 20% in gastric cancer in general.[102]

The location of benign and malignant ulcers in the stomach is roughly similar,[101] but the latter tend to be larger (>2 cm in diameter). Multiplicity and irregularity of ulcer shape may also indicate malignancy. The diagnosis of malignant ulcers is largely dependent on the number of biopsies and is facilitated by simultaneous cytological examination. Diagnostic accuracy depends upon the number of biopsies taken: a rate of diagnosis of 70% when only one or two biopsies are examined[103] rises to 100% if the number taken is 6 or more.

Estimation of the cancer risk in peptic ulcer disease is difficult because most studies are short-term investigations that probably reflect false negative diagnoses of originally existing cancer. A large proportion of ulcer cases have also been operated upon which introduces further risk factors in any group of cases studied over a long term, and it interferes with the natural history of the disease. Moreover, it is possible and even probable that GUs of different locations may vary with respect to cancer risk. This is suggested by the close relationship between location of ulcer and the type, progression and severity of chronic gastritis.

The few available long-term (>5 years) follow-up studies indicate that the precancerous property of GU is low.[104,105] The relative risk of cancer in GU disease hardly exceeds the expected risk or is estimated to be at the most two-fold compared to the population at large. In a study of 78 patients with endoscopically verified GU, Rollag and Jacobsen[104] did not find a single GCA on endoscopic re-examination 5 years later.

Epidemiological data on the incidence of the two diseases suggest that ulcer disease cannot be an important precursor of gastric cancer. However, possible links between the two are suggested by a similar relationship with chronic gastritis. Severe grades of chronic atrophic gastritis, both in the antrum and in the body, are probably a precancerous condition.[106] A proportion of GU patients show such severe atrophic gastritis in the antrum, and some also develop severe atrophic gastritis in the gastric body.

THE POSTOPERATIVE STOMACH

Although there has been rapid progress in the medical treatment of peptic ulcer, a proportion of peptic ulcer patients are still subjected to partial gastrectomy, vagotomy or other surgical procedures.

The prevalence of cancer in the postoperative stomach has been a subject of some controversy. Most of the literature indicates an increased frequency of cancer in the stump 15–20 years after the operation, the frequency before that time being lower than expected.[107–109] The degree of cancer risk in the remnant is 3–4 times that in the general population. Antrectomy results in resection of that part of the stomach which is a site of predilection for gastric cancer. Thus if a correction is made to take this into consideration, and comparison is made with peptic ulcer patients not subjected to surgery, practically all available studies would indicate a cancer risk in the postoperative stomach which is clearly increased. The line of anastomosis would appear to be the site of predilection.

Partial gastrectomy is followed by a rapidly progressive chronic atrophic gastritis and intestinal metaplasia of the remnant mucosa, particularly at the site of anastomosis.[110–112] Antrum-dependent serum gastrin levels are decreased after partial gastrectomy (antrectomy) and removal of the gastrin-mediated trophic influence may well help to cause this atrophy.[108] Damage is also caused by reflux of duodenal contents,[113–116] particularly by pancreatic juice. In addition to features of chronic atrophic gastritis, the remnant mucosa shows some specific morphological alterations. The number and size of parietal cells is diminished to a greater extent than the other epithelial elements. The mucosal pits appear hyperplastic, elongated and tortuous, and the inflammation appears less intense than expected.[117–120]

A small proportion of patients get a recurrent peptic ulcer after partial gastric resection. Usually these are associated with histologically normal acid secreting oxyntic mucosa in the remnant which is an indication of a poor surgical result.[120] Sometimes a recurrent ulcer, hypergastrinaemia and features resembling the Zollinger-Ellison syndrome occur. This is the result of retained antral mucosa, either in the duodenal stump or in the gastric remnant. It may function as an autonomous gastrin-secreting 'pseudotumour' and induces a trophic effect on body mucosa of the remnant.[2] Only a small number of patients exhibit such an effect after partial gastrectomy.[2]

REFERENCES

1. Grossman MI, Kurata JH, Rotter JI et al. Peptic ulcer: new therapies, new diseases. Ann Intern Med 1981; 95: 609–627.
2. Brooks FP. The pathophysiology of peptic ulcer: an overview. In: Brooks FP, Cohen S, Soloway RD. eds. Peptic ulcer diseases. New York: Churchill Livingstone, 1985: pp 45–149.
3. Kivilaakso E, Silen W. Pathogenesis of experimental gastric mucosal injury. N Engl J Med 1979; 301: 364–369.
4. Silen W, Merhev A, Simson JNL. The pathophysiology of stress ulcer disease. World J Surg 1981; 5: 165–172.
5. Siurala M, Kivilaakso E, Sipponen P. Gastritis. In: Demling L, Domschke S. eds. Klinische Gastroenterologie. Band I. Stuttgart: Georg Thieme Verlag, 1984: pp 321–337.
6. Szabo S. Pathogenesis of duodenal ulcer disease. Lab Invest 1984; 51: 121–147.
7. Johnson HD, Love AHG, Rogers NC, Wyatt AB. Gastric ulcer, blood groups and acid secretion. Gut 1964; 5: 402–412.
8. Baron JH. Current view on pathogenesis of peptic ulcer. Scand J Gastroenterol 1982; 80: 1–10.
9. Thomas J, Greig M, McIntosh J, Hunt J, McNeil D, Piper DW. The location of chronic gastric ulcer. A study of the prevalence of ulcer size, age, sex, alcohol, analgesic intake and smoking. Digestion 1980; 20: 79–84.
10. McCarthy DM, Jensen RT. Zollinger-Ellison syndrome — current issues. In: Cohen S, Soloway RD. eds. Hormone-producing tumors of the gastrointestinal tract. New York: Churchill Livingstone, 1985: pp 25–55.
11. Bonnevie O. Changing demographics of peptic ulcer disease. Dig Dis Sci 1985; 30: 8S–14S.
12. Kurata JH. Ulcer epidemiology: an overview and proposed research framework. Gastroenterology 1989; 96: 569–580.
13. Sonnenberg A. Geographic and temporal variations in the occurrence of peptic ulcer disease. Scand J Gastroenterol 1985; (suppl 110): 11–24.
14. Ihamaki T, Varis K, Siurala M. Morphological, functional and immunological state of the gastric mucosa in gastric carcinoma families. Comparison with a computer-matched family sample. Scand J Gastroenterol 1979; 14: 801–812.
15. Kurata JH, Haile BM. Epidemiology of peptic ulcer disease. Clin Gastroenterol 1984; 13: 289–307.
16. Bonnevie O. Peptic ulcer in Denmark. Scand J Gastroenterol 1980; (suppl 15): 163–174.
17. Pulvertaft CN. Comments on the incidence and natural history of gastric and duodenal ulcer. Postgrad Med J 1968; 44: 597–602.
18. Kawai K, Shirakawa K, Misaki F, Hayashi K, Watanabe Y. Natural history and epidemiologic studies of peptic ulcer disease in Japan. Gastroenterology 1989; 96: 581–585.
19. Wormsley KG, Grossman MI. Maximal histological test in control subjects and patients with peptic ulcer. Gut 1965; 6: 427–435.
20. Kirkpatrick JR, Lawrie JL, Forrest APM, Campbell H. The short pentagastrin test in the investigation of disease. Gut 1969; 10: 760–762.
21. Lam S-K. Pathogenesis and pathophysiology of duodenal ulcer. Clin Gastroenterol 1984; 13: 447–472.
22. Baron JH. Pathophysiology of gastric acid and pepsin secretion. In: Domschke W, Wormsley KG, eds. Magen und Magenkrankheiten. Stuttgart: Georg Thieme Verlag, 1981: pp 131–149.
23. Cox AJ. Stomach size and its relation to chronic peptic ulcer. Arch Pathol 1952; 54: 407–422.

24. Card WI, Marks IN. The relationship between the acid output of the stomach following 'maximal' histamine stimulation and parietal cell mass. Clin Sci 1960; 19: 47–63.
25. Cheng FCY, Lam SK, Omg GB. Maximal acid output to graded doses of pentagastric and its relation to parietal cell mass in Chinese patients with duodenal ulcer. Gut 1977; 18: 827–832.
26. Kekki M, Sipponen P, Siurala M. Progression of antral and body gastritis in patients with active and healed duodenal ulcer and duodenitis. Scand J Gastroenterol 1984; 19: 382–388.
27. Ihamaki T, Kekki M, Sipponen P, Siurala M. The sequelae and course of chronic gastritis during a 30 to 34-year follow-up study. Scand J Gastroenterol 1985; 20: 485–491.
28. Sipponen P, Varis K, Fraki O, Korri U-M, Seppala K, Siurala M. Cumulative 10-year risk of symptomatic duodenal and gastric ulcer in patients with or without gastritis. A clinical follow-up of 454 patients. Scand J Gastroenterol 1990; 25: 966–973.
29. Sipponen P. Helicobacter pylori and chronic gastritis: an increased risk of peptic ulcer? A review. Scand J Gastroenterol 1991; 26(Suppl 186): 6–10.
30. Allen A. Structure and function of gastro-intestinal mucus glycoproteins and the viscous and gel forming properties of mucus. Br Med Bull 1978; 34: 28–33.
31. Allen A, Garner A. Mucus and bicarbonate secretion in the stomach and their role in mucosal protection. Gut 1980; 21: 249–262.
32. Davenport HW. Gastric mucosal injury by fatty acid and acetylsalicylic acids. Gastroenterology 1965; 46: 245–253.
33. Flemstrom G, Turnberg LA. Gastroduodenal defence mechanisms. Clin Gastroenterol 1984; 13: 327–354.
34. Miederer SE. The gastric mucosal barrier. Hepatogastroenterol 1986; 33: 88–91.
35. Robert A. Cytoprotection by prostaglandins. Gastroenterology 1979; 77: 761–767.
36. Lacy ER. Prostaglandins and histological changes in the gastric mucosa. Dig Dis Sci 1985; 30: 83S–94S.
37. Willems G. Cellular kinetics and gastric mucosal disease. In: Domschke E, Wormsley KG, eds. Magen und Magenkrankheiten. Stuttgart: Georg Thieme Verlag, 1981: pp 195–204.
38. Konturek SJ, Radecki T, Dembinski A, Brzozowski T. Gastric cytoprotective properties of the epidermal growth factor. Gastroenterology 1981; 80: 4–9.
39. Rotter JI, Rimon DL, Samloff IM. Genetic heterogeneity in peptic ulcer. Lancet 1979; 1: 1088–1089.
40. Wolf G, Berndt H. Zur analytischen Epidemiologie des Ulcus ventriculi. Z Klin Med 1986; 41: 611–613.
41. Clarke CA, Edwards JW, Haddock DRW et al. ABO blood groups and secretor character in duodenal ulcer. Br Med J 1965; 2: 725–731.
42. Langman MJS. Blood groups and alimentary disorders. Clin Gastroenterol 1973; 2: 497–506.
43. Rotter JI, Petersen G, Samloff IM et al. Genetic heterogeneity of hyperpepsinogenemic I and normopepsinogenemic I duodenal ulcer disease. Ann Intern Med 1979; 91: 372–377.
44. Ellis A. The genetics of peptic ulcer. Scand J Gastroenterol 1985; 20(suppl 110): 25–27.
45. Kekki M, Sipponen P, Siurala M. Hypersecretion of gastric acid in a representative Finnish family sample. Scand J Gastroenterol 1985; 20: 478–484.
46. Langman MJS. Epidemiological evidence on the association between peptic ulceration and anti-inflammatory drug use. Gastroenterology 1989; 96: 640–646.
47. Soll AH, Kurata J, McGuigan JE. Ulcers, nonsteroidal anti-inflammatory drugs, and related matters. Gastroenterology 1989; 96: 561–568.
48. Kirk RM. Factors determining the site of chronic gastroduodenal ulcers. Hepatogastroenterol 1982; 29: 75–85.
49. Ryding A, Berstad A, Aaland E, Odegaard B. Prophylactic effect of dietary fibre in duodenal ulcer disease. Lancet 1982; 2: 736–739.
50. Piper DW, Nasiry R, McIntosh J et al. Smoking, alcohol, analgesics and chronic duodenal ulcer. A controlled study of habits before first symptoms and before diagnosis. Scand J Gastroenterol 1984; 19: 1015–1021.
51. Alexander-Williams J, Wolverson RL. Pathogenesis and pathophysiology of gastric ulcer. Clin Gastroenterol 1984; 13: 601–619.
52. Blum AL, Sonnenberg A, Muller-Lissner S. Der duodenogastrale Reflux, ein Grenzphanomen zwischen Physiologie und Pathophysiologie des Magens. In: Domschke W, Wormsley KG. Magen und Magenkrankheiten. Georg Thieme Verlag, 1981: pp 58–69.
53. Davenport HW. Effect of lysolecithin, digitonin and phospholipase A upon the dog's gastric mucosal barrier. Gastroenterology 1970; 59: 505–509.
54. Duane WC, Wiegand DM. Mechanism by which bile salt disrupts the gastric mucosal barrier in the dog. J Clin Invest 1980; 66: 1044–1049.
55. Kang JY, Nasiry R, Guan R et al. Influence of the site of the duodenal ulcer on its mode of presentation. Gastroenterology 1986; 90: 1874–1876.
56. Oi M, Oshida K, Sugimura S. The location of gastric ulcers. Gastroenterology 1959; 36: 45–56.
57. Kirk RM. Site and localization of duodenal ulcers: a study at operation. Gut 1968; 9: 414–419.
58. Stadelmann O, Elster K, Stolte M et al. The peptic gastric ulcer — histotopographic and functional investigations. Scand J Gastroenterol 1971; 6: 613–623.
59. Oi M, Ito Y, Kumagai F et al. A possible dual control mechanism in the origin of peptic ulcer. A study on ulcer location as affected by mucosa and musculature. Gastroenterology 1969; 57: 280–293.
60. Kirk RM. Does the jet emerging through the pylorus determine the site of the duodenal bulbar ulcers? Br Med J 1975; 3: 629–630
61. Kimura K. Chronological transition of the fundic pyloric border determined by stepwise biopsy of the lesser and greater curvatures of the stomach. Gastroenterology 1972; 63: 584–592.
62. Whitehead R, Roca M, Meikle DD, Skinner J, Truelove SC. The histological classification of duodenitis in fibreoptic biopsy specimens. Digestion 1975; 13: 129–136.
63. Jenkins D, Goodall A, Gillet FR, Scott BB. Defining duodenitis: quantitative histological study of mucosal responses and their correlations. J Clin Pathol 1985; 38: 1119–1126.
64. Whitehead R. Mucosal biopsy of the gastrointestinal tract. 1990; Ed. Saunders p 178.
65. Johansen A, Hansen OH. Heterotopic gastric epithelium in the duodenum and its correlation to gastric disease and acid level. Acta Pathol Microbiol Immunol Scand (A) 1973; 81: 679–680.
66. Rhodes J. Experimental production of gastric epithelium in the duodenum. Gut 1964; 5: 454–458.
67. Lee A. Helicobacter pylori: causal agent in peptic ulcer. Microbiological aspects. J Gastroenterol Hepatol 1991; 6: 115–120.
68. Graham DY. Campylobacter pylori and peptic ulcer disease. Gastroenterology 1989; 96: 615–625.
69. Graham DY. Helicobacter pylori: it epidemiology and its role in duodenal ulcer disease. J Gastroenterol Hepatol 1991; 6: 105–113.
70. Marshall BJ. Virulence and pathogenicity of Helicobacter pylori. J Gastroenterol Hepatol 1991; 6: 121–124.
71. Blaser MJ. Hypothesis on the pathogenesis and natural history of Helicobacter pylori-induced inflammation. Gastroenterology 1992; 102: 720–727.
72. Graham DY. Pathogenic mechanisms leading to Helicobacter pylori-induced inflammation. Eur J Gastroenterol Hepatol 1992; 4(Suppl 2): S9–S16.
73. Axon ATR. Helicobacter pylori therapy: effect on peptic ulcer disease. J Gastroenterol Hepatol 1991; 6: 131–137.
74. Valle J, Seppala K, Sipponen P, Korsunen T. Disappearance of gastritis after eradication of Helicobacter pylori. Scand J Gastroenterol 1991; 26: 1057–1065.
75. Kosunen TU, Seppala K, Sarna S, Sipponen P. Diagnostic value of decreasing IgG, IgA and IgM antibody titers after eradication of Helicobacter pylori. Lancet 1992; 339: 893–895.
76. Sipponen P, Seppala K, Aarynen M, Helske T, Kettunen P. Chronic gastritis and gastroduodenal ulcer: a case control study on risk of coexisting duodenal or gastric ulcer in patients with gastritis. Gut 1989; 30: 922–929.

77. Sipponen P, Aarynen M, Kaariainen I, Kettunen P, Helske T, Seppala K. Chronic antral gastritis, Lewis a+ phenotype and male sex as factors in predicting coexisting duodenal ulcer. Scand J Gastroenterol 1989; 24: 581–588.
78. Sipponen P, Valle J, Varis K, Kekki M, Ihamaki T, Siurala M. Fasting levels of serum gastrin in different functional and morphological states of the antrofundal mucosa. An analysis of 860 subjects. Scand J Gastroentrol 1990; 25: 513–519.
79. Wyatt J, Rathbone BJ, Dixon MF, Heatley RV. Campylobacter pyloridis and acid-induced gastric metaplasia in the pathogenesis of duodenitis. J Clin Pathol 1987; 40: 841–848.
80. Goodwin CS. Duodenal ulcer, Campylobacter pylori and the 'leaking roof' concept. Lancet 1988; 2: 1467–1469.
81. Dixon MF. Helicobacter pylori and peptic ulceration: histopathological aspects. J Gastroenterol Hepatol 1991; 6: 125–130.
82. Sipponen P, Kekki M, Siurala M. The Sydney System: epidemiology and natural history of chronic gastritis. J Gastroenterol Hepatol 1991; 6: 244–251.
83. Schrager J, Spink R, Mitra S. The antrum in patients with duodenal and gastric ulcers. Gut 1967; 8: 497–508.
84. Gear MWL, Truelove SC, Whitehead R. Gastric ulcer and gastritis. Gut 1971; 12: 639–645.
85. Earlam RJ, Amerigo J, Kakavoulis T, Pollock DJ. Histological appearances of oesophagus, antrum and duodenum and their correlation with symptoms in patients with a duodenal ulcer. Gut 1985; 26: 95–100.
86. Sipponen P. Chronic gastritis and ulcer risk. Scand J Gastroenterol 1990; 25: 193–196.
87. Siurala M, Sipponen P, Kekki M. Campylobacter pylori in a sample of Finnish population: relation to morphology and functions of the gastric mucosa. Gut 1988; 29: 909–916.
88. Karnes WE, Samloff IM, Siurala M, Kekki M, Sipponen P, Kim SWR, Walsh JH. Positive serum antibody and negative tissue staining for Helicobacter pylori in subjects with atrophic gastritis. Gastroenterology 1991; 101: 167–174.
89. Correa P. Chronic gastritis: a clinico-pathological classification. Am J Gastroenterol 1988; 83: 504–509.
90. Yardley JH. Pathology of chronic gastritis and duodenitis. In Gastrointestinal Pathology, eds. Goldman H, Appelman HD, Kaufman N. Baltimore: Williams and Wilkins, 1990: pp 69–143.
91. Siurala M, Sipponen P, Kekki M. Chronic gastritis: dynamic and clinical aspects. Scand J Gastroenterol 1985; 20 (suppl 109): 69–79.
92. Price AB. Histological aspects of Campylobacter pylori colonization and infection of gastric and duodenal mucosa. Scand J Gastroenterol 1988; 23: 21–24.
93. Dixon MF, Sobala GM. Gastritis and duodenitis: the histopathological spectrum. Eur J Gastroenterol Hepatol 1992; 4 (suppl 2): S17–S23.
94. Maaroos H-I, Salupere V, Uibo R, Kekki M, Sipponen P. Seven-year follow-up study of chronic gastritis in gastric ulcer patients. Scand J Gastroenterol 1985; 20: 198–204.5
95. Tatsuta M, Okuda S. Location, healing, and recurrence of gastric ulcers in relation to fundal gastritis. Gastroenterology 1975; 69: 897–902.
96. Tatsuta M, Iishi H, Iishi M, Okuda S. Chromoendoscopic observations on extension and development of fundal gastritis and intestinal metaplasia. Gastroenterology 1985; 88: 70–74.
97. Mackay IR, Hislop IG. Chronic gastritis and gastric ulcer. Gut 1966; 7: 228–233.
98. Meikle DD, Taylor KB, Truelove SC, Whitehead R. Gastritis, duodenitis and circulating levels of gastrin in duodenal ulcer before and after vagotomy. Gut 1976; 17: 719–728.
99. Sipponen P. Long-term consequences of gastroduodenal inflammation. Eur J Gastroenterol hepatol 1992; 4 (suppl 2): S25–S29.
100. Graham DY, Schwartz JT, Cain GD, Gyorkey F. Prospective evaluation of biopsy number in diagnosis of esophageal and gastric carcinoma. Gastroenterology 1982; 82: 228–231.
101. Ming S-C. Relationship between gastric carcinoma and chronic gastric ulcer. In: Ming S-C. ed. Precursors of Gastric Cancer. New York: Praeger, 1984: pp 265–284.
102. Sipponen P, Hakkiluoto A, Lempinen M. Ulcer simulating gastric cancer. Ann Clin Gyn Fenn 1975; 64: 10–17.
103. Dekker W, Tytgat GN. Diagnostic accuracy of fiberendoscopy in the detection of upper intestinal malignancy. A follow-up analysis. Gastroenterology 1977; 73: 710–714.
104. Rollag A, Jacobsen CD. Gastric ulcer and risk of cancer. Acta Med Scand 1984; 216: 105–109.
105. Mowat NAG, Needham CD, Brunt PW. The natural history of gastric ulcer in a community: a four-year study. Q J Med 1975; 44: 45–56.
106. Sipponen P, Kekki M, Haapakoski J, Ihamaki T, Siurala M. Gastric cancer risk in chronic atrophic gastritis: statistical calculations of cross-sectional data. Int J Cancer 1985; 35: 173–177.
107. Domellof L, Janunger K-G. The risk for gastric carcinoma after partial gastrectomy. Am J Surg 1977; 134: 581–584.
108. Offerhaus GJA, Stadt J, Huibregtse K, Tytgat GNJ. Endoscopic screening for malignancy in the gastric remnant: the clinical significance of dysplasia in gastric mucosa. J Clin Pathol 1984; 37: 748–754.
109. Kivilaakso E, Hakkiluoto A, Kalima TV, Sipponen P. Relative risk to stump cancer following partial gastrectomy. Br J Surg 1977; 64: 336–338.
110. Gjeruldsen ST, Myren J, Fretheim B. Alterations of gastric mucosa following a graded partial gastrectomy. Scand J Gastroenterol 1968; 3: 465–470.
111. Schrumpf E, Serck-Hanssen A, Stadaas J, Aune S, Myren J, Osnes M. Mucosal changes in the gastric stump 20–25 years after partial gastrectomy. Lancet 1977; 2: 467–469.
112. Saukkonen M, Sipponen P, Varis K, Siurala M. Morphologic and dynamic behaviour of the gastric mucosa after partial gastrectomy with special reference to the gastroenterostomy area. Acta Hepato-Gastroenterol 1980; 27: 48–56.
113. Willems G, Gepts W, Bremer A. Endogenous hypergastrinemia and cell proliferation in the fundic mucosa in dogs. Am J Dig Dis 1977; 22: 419–423.
114. JanungerK-G, Domellof L, Eriksson S. The development of mucosal changes after gastric surgery for ulcer disease. Scand J Gastroenterol 1978; 13: 217–223.
115. Mason RC, Brame KG, Filipe MI, Owen WJ. Longterm effects of duodenogastric reflux on rat gastric mucosa. Gut 1986; 27: A634.
116. Dixon MF, O'Connor HJ, Axon ATR, King RFGJ, Johnston D. Reflux gastritis — distinct histological entity? J Clin Pathol 1986; 39: 524–530.
117. Sipponen P, Hakkiluoto A, Kalima TV, Siurala M. Selective loss of parietal cells in the gastric remnant following antral resection. Scand J Gastroenterol 1976; 11: 813–816.
118. Sipponen P, Saukkonen M, Varis K, Siurala M. Morphometric analysis of the loss of chief and parietal cells after partial gastrectomy for duodenal ulcer. Acta Hepato-Gastroenterol 1979; 26: 493–498.
119. Capoferro R, Nygaard K. Effects of antrectomy on the gastric mucosa of the rat. Scand J Gastroenterol 1973; 8: 347–352.
120. Johnston DH. A biopsy study of the gastric mucosa in postoperative patients with and without marginal ulcer. Am J Gastroenterol 1966; 46: 103–118.

CHAPTER 26

The small intestine

M. M. Mathan H. M. Gilmour J. Piris

PART I
Specific infections and tropical sprue

M. M. Mathan

The epithelial lining of the gastrointestinal mucosa is one of the primary barriers which separates the body from the external environment in the lumen of the gastrointestinal tract.[1] The lumen contains a variety of bacteria, viruses, fungi and parasites in addition to food and secretions. Although the luminal flora is considered to be commensal, in tropical developing countries recognized enteropathogenic microbes can be identified in apparently asymptomatic individuals.[2,3] In keeping with the differences in the microbial flora and other factors, it has also been shown that the mucosal lining of the gastrointestinal tract of healthy people in tropical developing countries is different from that in temperate countries.[4,5]

In contrast to the finger and leaf shaped villi of the small intestinal mucosa in temperate climates, in the tropics the mucosa consists of more broad structures which may even be long ridges thrown into convolutions.[6] This is accompanied by an increase in the length of the crypts, reduced villus height and increased mononuclear cells in the lamina propria and epithelium (Fig. 26.1). The epithelial cells are shortened, contain increased numbers of lysosomes and scattered cells are degenerate.[7] This is also associated with minor abnormalities of intestinal function in apparently healthy people. In southern India, 40% of the population have malabsorption of D-xylose and about 10% mild steatorrhoea.[4] This minimal lesion, or tropical enteropathy, is widely prevalent and roughly parallels poor environmental sanitation and low economic status.[8] It may influence pathological changes due to specific infections.

Infection of the small intestine may result in acute, persistent or chronic diarrhoea. Identification of as yet unrecognized enteric pathogens, microbial pathogenic mechanisms and opportunistic infections in immunocompromized hosts, has led to a better understanding of the pathology of host response to enteric infections, several of which affect both the small and the large intestine.

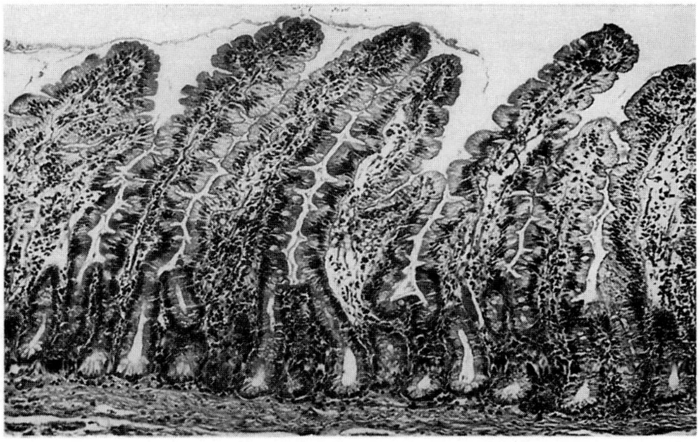

Fig. 26.1 Jejunal biopsy from a healthy asymptomatic southern Indian volunteer. Note the increase in cellularity of lamina propria and crypt height compared to temperate zone biopsies. (H&E, ×79)

ACUTE INFECTION

Bacterial pathogens

Vibrio cholerae

The classic example of enterotoxigenic acute diarrhoea is that due to *Vibrio cholerae*, a highly motile, coma shaped organism, first described by Robert Koch in 1885. The attachment of *Vibrio cholerae* to the surface of enterocytes is necessary for colonization and proliferation.[9,10] The classic cholera toxin is a heat labile protein with two subunits, first described by De in 1959.[11] The toxin binds to a receptor, GM1 ganglioside, on the luminal surface of enterocytes and stimulates the adenyl cyclase enzyme via ADP-ribosylation of its G-protein catalytic subunit, resulting in increased cellular cyclic AMP, which in turn stimulates secretion of water and electrolytes by crypt enterocytes.[12,13] The fluid secretion results in acute diarrhoea and, if uncorrected, can lead to death by dehydration. Recently, two other toxins, the zonula occludens toxin (ZOT)[14] and the accessory cholera enterotoxin (ACE),[15] have been recognized, but their clinical significance is not known.

Vibrio cholera colonizes the surface of the proximal small intestine, but does not invade the mucosa. The epithelial lining is intact, with a high turnover. The goblet cells are empty and there is mild oedema and vascular dilatation in the lamina propria. In contrast to several reports from the tropical developing world, where no significant differences from appropriate controls were found in jejunal biopsies at light microscopy,[16–18] studies from temperate climates[19–21] report an inflammatory infiltrate of mononuclear cells subjacent to an intact epithelium.

At the ultrastructural level, in addition to oedema of the lamina propria, the intercellular spaces and the apical junctional complexes in the epithelial layer are irregularly widened. There are also minor changes in cellular organelles.[16]

Escherichia coli

Diarrhoea associated with *E. coli* may be due to enterotoxins, enteropathogenicity, enteroadhesion, enteroinvasiveness, enterohaemorrhagic effects, or due to as yet unknown mechanisms.[22,23] Enteroinvasive and enterohaemorrhagic *E. coli* predominantly affect the colon and result in dysentery with blood and mucus in the stool.

Enterotoxigenic *E. coli* colonize the small intestine and produce two distinct enterotoxins, the heat-labile toxin which is similar in action to cholera toxin, and the heat-stable toxin, which acts through activation of cyclic GMP.[24,25] Several *E. coli* serotypes are identified as enteropathogenic; they elaborate a cytotoxin, and are capable of adhering to the surface of enterocytes.[26] Adhesion of the bacteria to the intestinal mucosa cause destruction of microvilli, disruption of associated cytoskeleton with cup-like depressions or pedestal formations of the cell membrane where bacteria are intimately attached[27] (Fig. 26.2). This characteristic lesion is termed the 'attaching effacing lesion'.[28] Jejunal mucosal biopsies from children with heavy colonization show shortening of villi and increased inflammatory cell infiltrate in the lamina propria and electron microscopy shows the attaching effacing lesions.[29–31] These findings are similar to the changes in rabbit intestine on colonization by the diarrhoeagenic RDEC-1 *E. coli* organism.[32]

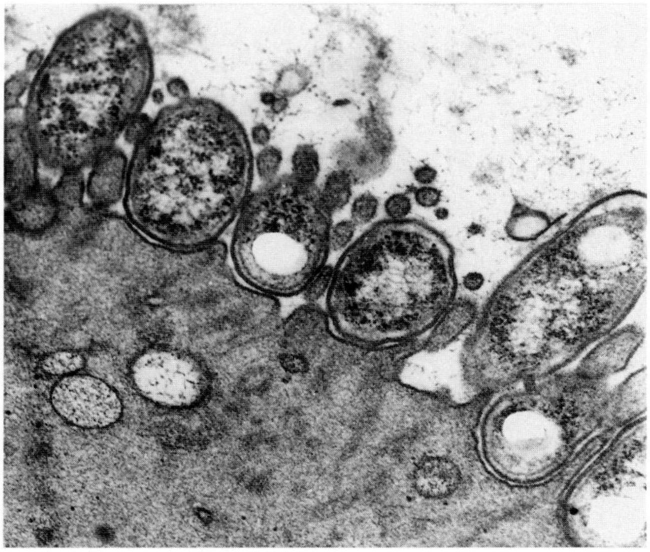

Fig. 26.2 Electron micrograph of luminal border of a colonocyte showing *E. coli* attached to cup like formation with effacement of microvilli on the luminal border. (×40 200)

Clostridia

The clostridial group of organisms are anaerobic commensals usually found in the terminal part of the ileum and colon. They can invade the mucosa when the intestinal barrier function is compromized. A segmental necrotizing enteritis associated with clostridia, noticed either at surgery or at autopsy, has been reported from different geographic locations. In Papua New Guinea, detailed studies of this acute, patchy necrotizing inflammatory disease of the small intestine called 'pig-bel' has shown a relationship to a trypsin inhibitor in sweet potatoes which allows the B toxin of *Clostridium welchii* in contaminated pig meat to initiate the lesion.[33,34] The small intestine shows segmental necrosis which appears to start at the tips of the villi with oedema and vascular congestion in the adjacent submucosa. There is infiltration by polymorphonuclear leukocytes, mononuclear cells and eosinophils in varying proportions with perivascular cuffing (Fig. 26.3).

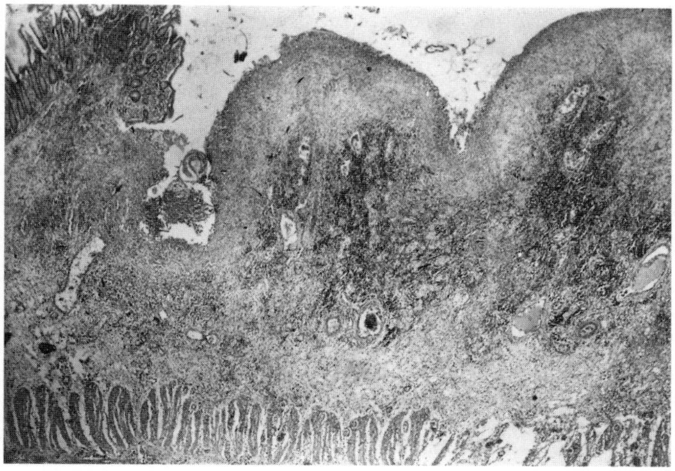

Fig. 26.3 Necrotizing enteritis: segmental ulceration and infarction of small bowel mucosa and submucosa which is congested and infiltrated with lymphocytes, plasma cells and eosinophils. (H&E, ×16)

A striking finding is a vascular lesion in the smaller submucosal arteries with relatively normal veins. The arterial wall is oedematous and infiltrated by inflammatory cells and has a homogeneous or granular eosinophilic appearance of fibrinoid necrosis.[35] A similar lesion has been reported from Sri Lanka[36] primarily in children. It is suggested that a hypersensitivity reaction to parasitic antigen is the initiating factor with clostridia acting as a promoting factor for the necrotizing lesion. However, in a similar syndrome reported from Bangladesh no association with clostridia was established.[37]

Campylobacter

Campylobacter can cause jejunitis and enterocolitis with haemorrhagic lesions in the jejunum, more often in the ileum and also in the colon.[38,39] Multiple superficial ulcers up to 1 cm in diameter can be present in the ileum, proximal to the ileocaecal valve and may involve the valve itself. The ulcer bases have acute inflammatory granulation tissue with prominent vascularity and absence of fibrosis.[40,41] This invasive lesion is in addition to the campylobacter toxin which can give rise to watery diarrhoea.[42]

Salmonella

In the small intestine invasion by *Salmonella typhimurium* and *Salmonella enteritidis*, which predominantly cause infective colitis, can also be responsible for food poisoning and traveller's diarrhoea.[43,44] The pathological changes in this condition are similar to that produced in primates and include mild enteritis or shallow ulcers in the ileal mucosa with enlarged Peyer's patches.[45,46] There are reports that *Salmonella typhimurium* may also evoke fluid secretion through enterotoxins.[47–51]

Viral pathogens

A variety of viruses which cause acute diarrhoea have been identified since 1973.[52–55] There are only limited studies of intestinal morphology in these infections in humans but much work has been done in animal models. Viruses such as the cytomegalovirus and the herpes virus, which are not primary intestinal pathogens, are now recognized as important opportunistic infections.

Rotavirus

Rotavirus is one of the major aetiological agents associated with acute diarrhoea in children below the age of 3 years, with the highest incidence in the 6–18 months age group. This virus occurs world wide and, whilst in temperate zones the disease occurs primarily in the colder months of the year,[56] it occurs in summer and winter in tropical countries. The virus is shed in the stool in large amounts and can be detected by electron microscopy, polyacrylamide gel electrophoresis for viral RNA, or by a variety of immunological techniques.[57]

The virus was first described in jejunal biopsies from infants with acute nonbacterial gastroenteritis[58] and was subsequently shown to be present in diarrhoeal faeces.[59] The pathology of the small intestine in this disease has been described in limited studies of biopsies from children with acute diarrhoea[60] and in experimental animals using a related virus. Rotavirus primarily infects the mature absorptive enterocytes on the villi of the small intestine. These cells are rapidly destroyed and are shed into the lumen, with shortening of villi. The immature dividing cells in the crypts, which appear to be unaffected, replace the surface cells. The diarrhoea appears to be due the loss of surface area due to the loss of mature enterocytes and their replacement by immature cells which are not fully functional. There is also an osmotic component due to unabsorbed carbohydrates in the lumen of the bowel.[61,62] Intracytoplasmic viruses or viral antigen can be demonstrated in villus enterocytes and in occasional colonocytes.[58,63] Children usually recover rapidly and in two to three weeks the small intestinal biopsy is normal by both light and electron microscopy.

Norwalk agent

The Norwalk and related viral agents cause acute gastroenteritis mainly in adolescents and adults. Villus shortening, damage to absorptive enterocytes, crypt cell proliferation and increased neutrophil polymorphs and mononuclear cells in the lamina propria were the pathological changes in small intestinal biopsies from volunteers infected with Norwalk and Hawaii agents.[64,65] Viral particles have not been demonstrated in affected enterocytes.

Other viruses associated with acute infectious diarrhoea

The enteric adenoviruses, calicivirus, astrovirus, coronavirus and small round viruses have also been associated with acute diarrhoea and evidence of mucosal damage.[66] Coronavirus infection causes diarrhoea in new born animals and there are reports of human infection causing acute diarrhoea and necrotizing enterocolitis.[67,68]

PERSISTENT AND CHRONIC INFECTION

Bacterial pathogens

Enteroadherent and Enteroaggregative E. coli

Escherichia coli are associated with acute, persistent and chronic diarrhoea. Two subgroups of *E. coli* which cannot always be identified by the EPEC serotype have been designated as enteroadherent *E. coli* (EAEC)[22,24] and enteroaggregative *E. coli* (EAggEC).[69] These organisms are identified by their ability to adhere to HEp-2 cells in tissue culture. Such organisms are positive for the EPEC adherence factor (EAF). EAEC are associated with acute diarrhoea and in biopsies of jejunal mucosa adhere to pedestals on the enterocyte surface membrane. Of special interest in persistent diarrhoea in young children are the EAggEC, which adhere to HEp-2 cells with a characteristic stacked brick appearance.[70,71] The intestinal pathology of this persistent diarrhoea is not known. EAggEC may also affect the colon, and bloody diarrhoea has been reported in some children from whom EAggEC have been isolated as the sole pathogen.[72–74]

Salmonellae

Typhoid (enteric) fever is a systemic infection, due to organisms belonging to the salmonella group which proliferate in reticuloendothelial (RE) cells and produce a febrile illness. Severe illness is caused by *S. typhi*, while *S. paratyphi* A, B and C, are less severe. The disease is transmitted through faecal-oral spread. With improvements in sanitation and hygiene, enteric fever is now seldom encountered in the industrialized countries of the temperate regions. It is still a major problem in most tropical developing countries, although mortality has been reduced by effective antibiotic therapy.

After entry, through the Peyer's patches, the organisms spread throughout the body, particularly to the RE cells in the liver, the spleen and the bone marrow. In about two weeks, septicaemia with release of bacteria from necrosed RE cells leads to high fever and other constitutional symptoms.[75,76] The organisms are excreted through the bile, colonize the gall bladder and enter the small intestine. At this point, they re-enter the Peyer's patches and since these are already sensitized by the prior entry of the organism, they become markedly inflamed and ulcerate. The exact mechanism of this hypersensitivity reaction is not fully established.

Oedema and hyperaemia of Peyer's patches and lymphoid follicles in the ileum and caecum, which become well demarcated and raised above the surrounding mucosa, is the initial lesion. The mucosa in these areas undergoes necrosis in the second week of illness and sloughing produces ulcers by the third week. Typhoid ulcers are oval with their long diameter in the long axis of the bowel (Fig. 26.4). The base of the ulcers are haemorrhagic and they usually extend to the submucosa or even the muscle layer. Erosion of blood vessels by these ulcers causes haemorrhage and deeper penetration may cause perforation.[76,77] The intestinal mucosa between ulcers is hyperaemic. The lesion does not extend proximally and peroral biopsies of the jejunum are normal.[78]

Microscopically the lesions are infiltrated by macrophages (typhoid cells), which often contain ingested bacilli, red blood cells and nuclear debris (Fig. 26.5A & B). A few plasma cells and lymphocytes are also present but neutrophil polymorphs are characteristically absent. The regional lymph nodes are enlarged, soft and hyperaemic with areas of necrosis. Their rupture can give rise to peritonitis. Histologically there is reticuloendothelial hyperplasia with sinusoids filled with macrophages containing

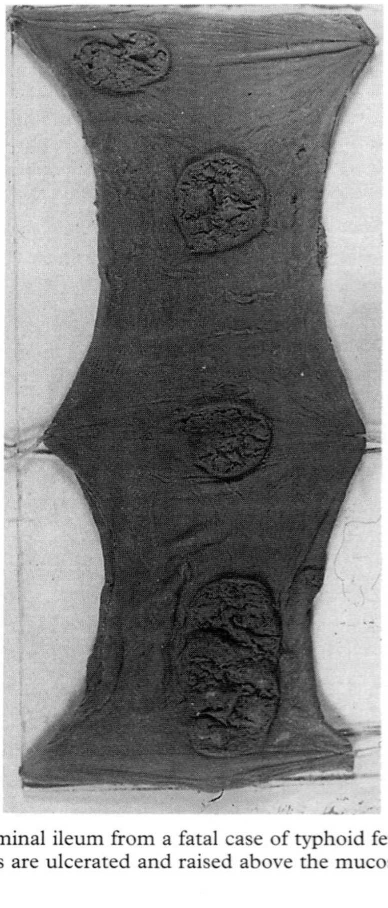

Fig. 26.4 Terminal ileum from a fatal case of typhoid fever. The Peyer's patches are ulcerated and raised above the mucosal surface.

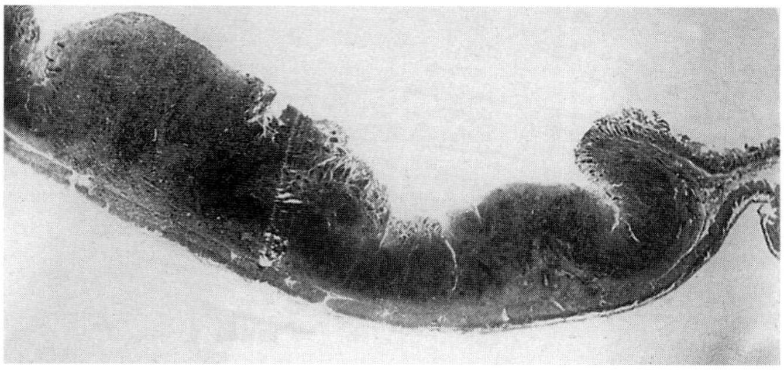

A

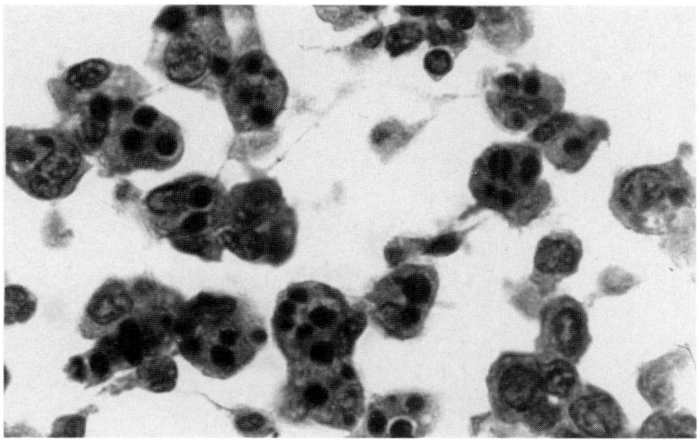

B

Fig. 26.5 **A** Sections of Peyer's patch in a patient who died of typhoid with marked histiocytic infiltration, hyperaemia and oedema of the submucosa. (H&E, ×56) **B** Typhoid macrophages adjacent to area of ulceration with ingested nuclear debris. (H&E, ×1050)

bacilli. A variety of local (perforation, bleeding) and systemic (typhoid hepatitis, encephalopathy, arthritis) complications can occur in patients with enteric fever.[79–82]

Yersinia enterocolitis

Intestinal infection with yersinia organisms, *Y. enterocolitica* and, rarely, *Y. pseudotuberculosis*, occurs mainly in industrialized countries of the temperate zones.[83] The preference of this organism for lower temperatures and its ability to preferentially infect iron replete populations may be responsible for this distribution. Clinically, yersinia infections produce acute enteritis with fever and diarrhoea in children, and terminal ileitis, mesenteric adenitis and pseudoappendicular syndrome in older age groups.[84–88] A variety of other systemic manifestations, including erythema nodosum and polyarthritis have also been reported.[86,89] *Y. enterocolitica* produces an enterotoxin similar to the heat stable toxin of *E. coli* and this may play a role in the pathogenesis of diarrhoea.[84]

The infection primarily involves the terminal ileum, caecum and ascending colon and at surgery, the serosal surface of the affected bowel is dull and hyperaemic with thickening of the muscularis.[90] Mucosal ulceration, with longitudinally oriented ulcers up to 5 cm in length most numerous and large in the terminal ileum, and scattered punctate aphthous ulcers throughout the colon, are characteristic. Ileal ulcers are covered by fibrinopurulent exudate and surrounded by mucosa which is oedematous and inflamed. Large colonies of gram negative coccobacilli can usually be demonstrated below the surface exudate and also in microabscesses in the intestinal tissue. The microabscesses and the ulcers are surrounded by neutrophils and macrophages. Though the lesion mainly involves the mucosa and the submucosa, the muscular wall and serosa of the intestine are thickened with an inflammatory infiltrate, predominantly eosinophils and mononuclear cells. The mucosa adjacent to aphthous ulcers is less inflamed. The lymphoid tissue, both in the intestinal walls and in the draining mesentery are hyperplastic, the germinal centres are prominent and usually microabscesses are scattered throughout.[90,91] Severe terminal ileitis due to Crohn's disease, tuberculosis and typhoid have to be differentiated from yersiniosis. If the infection is due to *Y. pseudotuberculosis* granulomas may be present in mesenteric nodes.[92,93]

Mycobacterium tuberculosis

Gastrointestinal tuberculosis is still a major problem in most tropical developing countries. In India, intestinal tuberculosis is the second most common cause of malabsorption after tropical sprue, because of bacterial overgrowth following intestinal strictures.[94] It was rarely encountered in industrialized nations since the prevalence of tuberculosis has decreased markedly due to BCG inoculation, pasteurization of milk and the availability of antituberculous chemotherapy. However, the emergence of immunocompromized populations and migrants from tropical countries has led to an increase in the prevalence of tuberculosis.[95–97]

Enteric infection in an individual who has not been previously infected gives rise to primary intestinal tuberculosis. The primary complex may occur in the intestinal wall with a minute ulcer or more often in the regional lymph nodes. Infection of the regional lymph nodes, especially in children, can give rise to massive enlargement (tabes mesenterica) (Fig. 26.6A & B) and lead to peritonitis and systemic dissemination, as miliary tuberculosis. Ulceration and stenosis of the small intestine can occur by retrograde spread from infected regional nodes. Secondary intestinal tuberculosis occurs in individuals who had primary complexes elsewhere with reinfection of the intestinal tract or, more commonly, in association with pulmonary tuberculosis with ingestion of infected sputum, retrograde lymphatic spread or contiguous spread from pelvic organs. Most cases of intestinal tuberculosis in India are due to the human strain of the bacillus.[98]

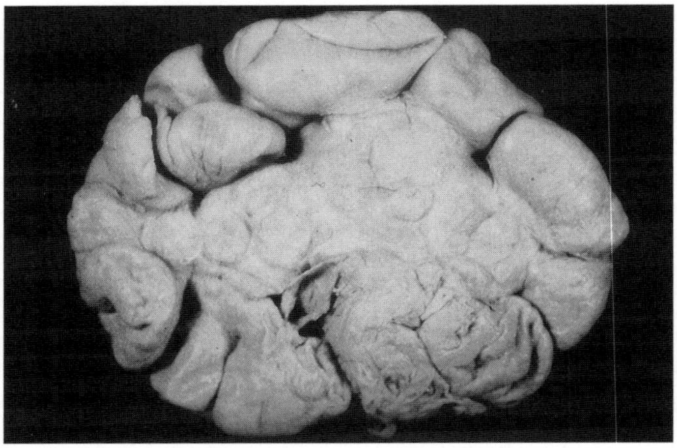

A

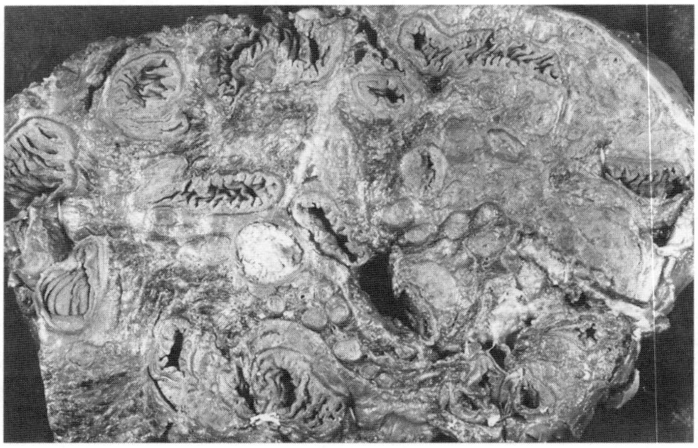

B

Fig. 26.6 **A** Mesenteric lymph nodes are markedly enlarged and caseous (tabes mesenterica) and loops of small intestine are plastered together due to tuberculous peritonitis. **B** Cut section showing plastering of loops of intestine and enlarged caseous mesenteric lymph nodes.

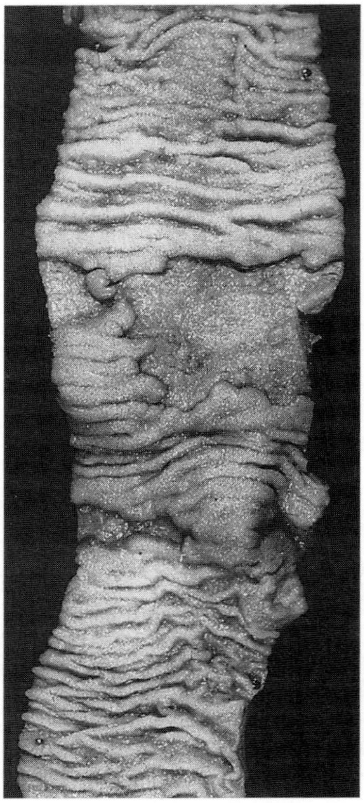

Fig. 26.7 Tuberculous ulcers. Two transverse ulcers with clearcut margins encircling the bowel wall of the proximal ileum.

Ulcers and stenotic lesions are the common macroscopic findings in intestinal tuberculosis. Lesions are usually present in the terminal ileum and ileocaecal region, where lymphoid tissue is abundant and may also be associated with relative stagnation of intestinal contents. Morphologically, intestinal tuberculosis can be of three varieties: ulcerative, hypertrophic and ulcerohypertrophic.[99] Tuberculous intestinal ulcers are placed transversely and may be annular as infection spreads through lymphatic channels in the intestinal wall (Fig. 26.7). The ulcers are small or large, single or multiple and have thick, sloping or overhanging edges with minimal induration. Caseous material may be present in these ulcers on sectioning and small white tuberculous nodules are usually present over the serosa. The regional lymph nodes are invariably enlarged and may contain caseous foci. The deposition of fibrous tissue in ulcerated lesions with progressive narrowing of the lumen can give rise to intestinal obstruction with 'napkin-ring' lesions. Secondary infection with pyogenic bacteria may further contribute to fibrosis. Pseudopolyp formation may occur in the mucosa adjacent to areas with much fibrosis.[100,101]

'Hypertrophic' tuberculosis most commonly occurs in the ileocaecal region.[102] Infection starts in the Peyer's patches of the terminal ileum and caecal lymphoid tissue.[103] A large inflammatory mass, usually palpable in the right iliac fossa, is made up of adhesions, mesenteric fat, fibrous tissue, abundant granulation tissue and caseous lymph nodes. The fibrosis shortens the ascending colon and the caecum is usually pulled up to the lumbar region. Ulceration superimposed on such lesions gives rise to the ulcerohypertrophic variety (Fig. 26.8). These lesions have to be differentiated from carcinoma of the caecum, Crohn's disease and chronic appendicular abscess.[99,104]

The characteristic tuberculous granuloma is an agglomeration of many tubercles composed of epithelioid cells, which are oval or spindle shaped with abundant pale foamy cytoplasm and oval vesicular nucleus, Langhans' type of giant cells and a prominent mantle of lymphocytes. The centre of such lesions are usually caseous, pale pink staining with scattered nuclear debris (Fig. 26.9A & B). Tubercle bacilli can be demonstrated by the Ziehl-Nielsen stains or by DNA amplification methods.[105,106] Granulomas of different sizes and caseation and confluence may be present in all layers of the intestine. This tissue reaction

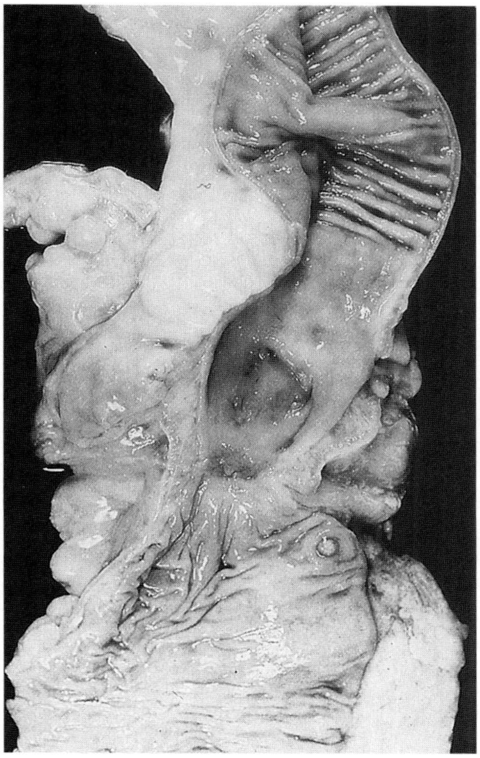

Fig. 26.8 Ileocaecal tuberculosis. Ulcerohypertrophic variety — ulceration of terminal ileum and caecum with flattened mucosa and narrowing at the ileocaecal valve.

varies according to the infective dose, virulence of the organism, immunological response of the host, the duration of infection and response to therapy. With healing, fibrosis, hyalinization or calcification can occur. Caseous granulomas are almost always present in the regional lymph nodes and this is of particular value when the intestinal lesion is 'burnt out' with only dense fibrous tissue. The detection of caseous granulomas in biopsy material obtained through the colonoscope facilitates the diagnosis of ileocaecal tuberculosis.[107]

The distinction of tuberculous lesions from Crohn's disease is particularly important. Miliary tubercles on the serosa, the relative absence of deep fissures and internal fistulae, varying size of caseous granulomas with a peripheral cuff of lymphocytes, the confluent nature of the granulomas, extensive hyalinization and fibrosis and the presence of granulomas in the regional nodes when absent in the intestinal mucosa indicate tuberculosis.[100,108–110] The demonstration of tubercle bacilli in the lesion and the growth of epithelium inward from the edges of the ulcer in response to antituberculous therapy in colonoscopic biopsies are useful in confirming the diagnosis.

Other mycobacterial infections

The emergence of a large number of immunocompromized individuals, particularly those with the acquired immunodeficiency syndrome (AIDS), has led to the recognition of the importance of non-tuberculous mycobacterial disease of the gastrointestinal tract. Such infections have been found in up to 75% of AIDS patients who have been examined at autopsy in the United States of America. The most frequently identified mycobacterium is *M. avium-intracellulare* (MAC), although infection with *M. kansasii* also occurs. Ingestion of these microbes from the environment by immunocompromized individuals causes the infection, rather than by person-to-person spread. MAC infection has been reported infrequently from sub-Saharan Africa. Disseminated MAC infection involves almost all tissues of the body and MAC can be cultured from blood or stool. A poorly defined granuloma consisting of pale blue striated histiocytes due to large number of mycobacteria is the distinctive pathological feature of MAC infection in patients with AIDS. The bacilli can be demonstrated by Ziehl-Nielsen stain. Typical granulomas with caseous necrosis, epithelioid cells and Langhans' giant cells are found only in a minority of cases.[111–113]

Viral pathogens

Human immunodeficiency virus

Infections of the gastrointestinal tract have been a major focus of interest in the study of human immunodeficiency virus (HIV) infection and the acquired immunodeficiency syndrome. The recognition of large numbers of opportunistic infections with their distinctive gastrointestinal pathology obscured the question of whether there was a primary HIV enteropathy. A jejunal enteropathy characterized by villus atrophy and crypt hyperplasia was described in male homosexuals at different clinical stages of HIV infection without associated secondary opportunistic infections.[114,115] Many of the patients were found to have fat malabsorption and diarrhoea and the degree of villus atrophy correlated with the degree of steatorrhoea. Some of the features of the duodenal mucosal changes in these patients suggested features of the human graft-versus-host disease associated with bone marrow transplantation, and the possibility was raised that these abnormalities could be due either to the effect of HIV or that they could be secondary to immunological changes.

A detailed electron microscopic examination of jejunal mucosal biopsies from HIV infected individuals with no detectable intestinal microbial infection showed definite abnormalities involving the enterocytes as well as several lamina propria elements. In the enterocytes, the most striking finding was the proliferation of the smooth endoplasmic reticulum (SER) which occupied almost half the area of the enterocytes, with dilated tubules of the endoplasmic reticulum at the periphery containing electron

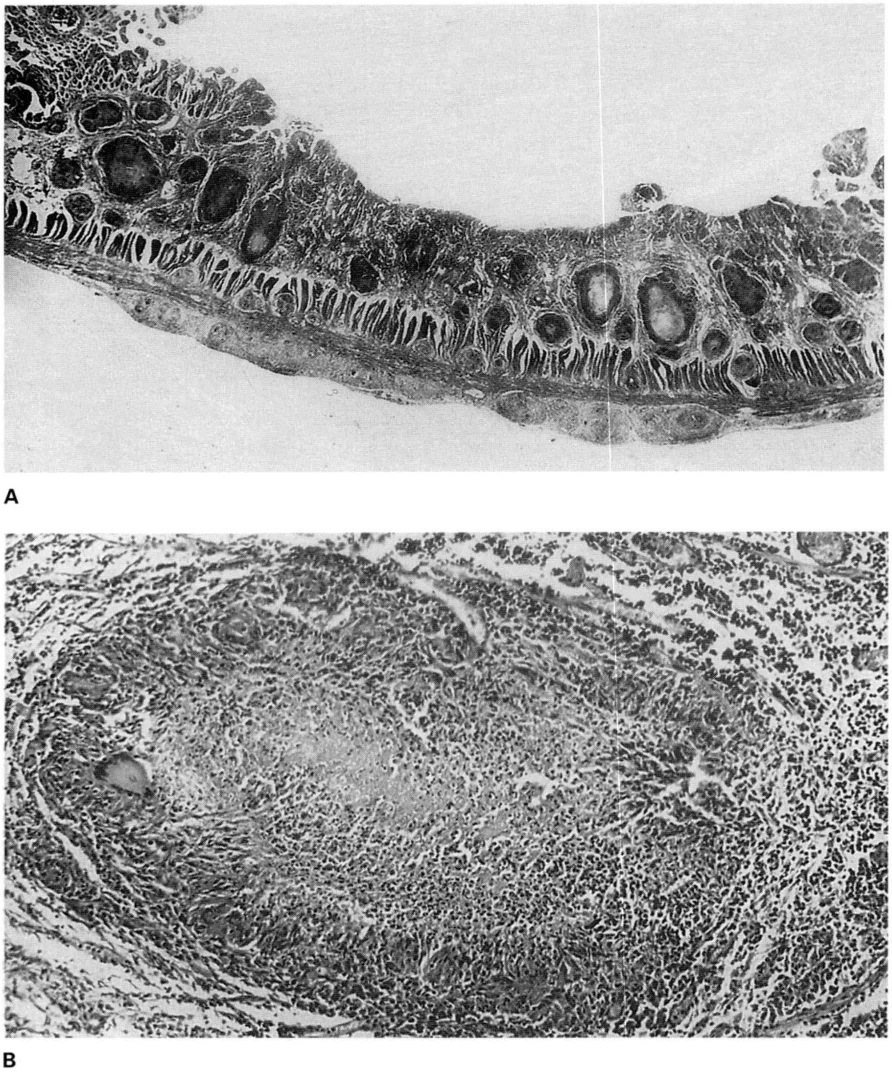

Fig. 26.9 **A** Sections of a tuberculous ulcer containing many caseating granulomas in the mucosa and submucosa of the ileum. Smaller granulomas are present in the muscle coat and serosa. (H&E, ×8) **B** Higher magnification of a confluent tuberculous granuloma with central caseation and peripheral cuff of lymphocytes. (H&E, ×100)

dense inclusions and occasional tubular structures. The SER proliferation was found maximally in patients with full blown AIDS and was much less marked in patients with asymptomatic HIV infection. There was a decrease in mitochondria, which showed morphological abnormalities, and scattered degenerated enterocytes. Degenerative changes were seen in enteric nerves and in the microvasculature of the lamina propria.[116,117] These observations suggest a primary HIV enteropathy and were supported by the demonstration of HIV genome by hybridization techniques in argentaffin cells and in macrophages in the lamina propria,[118,119] HIV protein in epithelium and lamina propria cells[120,121] and by the demonstration of HIV particles in duodenal biopsy specimens.[122]

Cytomegalovirus

Asymptomatic infection by this virus is widespread in immunocompetent subjects.[123] Symptomatic intestinal infection usually occurs as an opportunistic infection in immunocompromized subjects or as a secondary invader of ulcerated mucosa, mainly in the large intestine.[124,125] In the small intestine cytomegalovirus infection causes single cell infection without inflammatory response, or ulcerations with or without perforation,[126–129] with characteristic cytomegaly and acidophilic intranuclear inclusion with a clear surrounding halo, giving an owl's eye morphology. Granular basophilic cytoplasmic inclusions are found mainly in cells of mesenchymal origin.

Fungal pathogens

Fungal infections of the small intestine are usually opportunistic infections in immunocompromized subjects or associated with prolonged antibiotic therapy, diabetes or malignancy.

Fig. 26.10 Candidiasis. PAS stain of an ulcerated lesion in ileum from an immunocompromized patient with many yeast forms and filamentous pseudohyphae invading the mucosa. (H&E, ×209)

Candidiasis

Candida are yeast-like fungi and are part of the normal intestinal flora which can cause diarrhoea and superficial inflammation of the mucosa.[129,130] Overgrowth of candida, when cell mediated immunity is defective, causes oral, oesophageal or gastric lesions.[131] The small intestine is involved infrequently with ulcerating or penetrating lesions and rarely perforation.[132–134] In tissue sections, candida appear as 4–6 μm budding yeast-like forms in the surface exudate and non-septate pseudohyphae extending from the yeast form which stain with PAS and Gomori-methaneamine silver technique. Tissue invasion by pseudohyphae is pathognomonic of the infection (Fig. 26.10).

Mucormycosis or phycomycosis

Fungi of the genus mucor produce superficial erosions or deep necrotic haemorrhagic ulcers which may lead to perforation. In tissue section the hyphae of mucor are broad, aseptate 10–20 μm in diameter, pleomorphic and show irregular branching at right angles. The hyphae stain better in haematoxylin and eosin stain than classical fungal stains. The predilection of the hyphae to invade blood vessels and cause thrombosis leads to ischaemic infarction which is associated with deep haemorrhagic ulceration (Fig. 26.11A & B).[135–137]

A

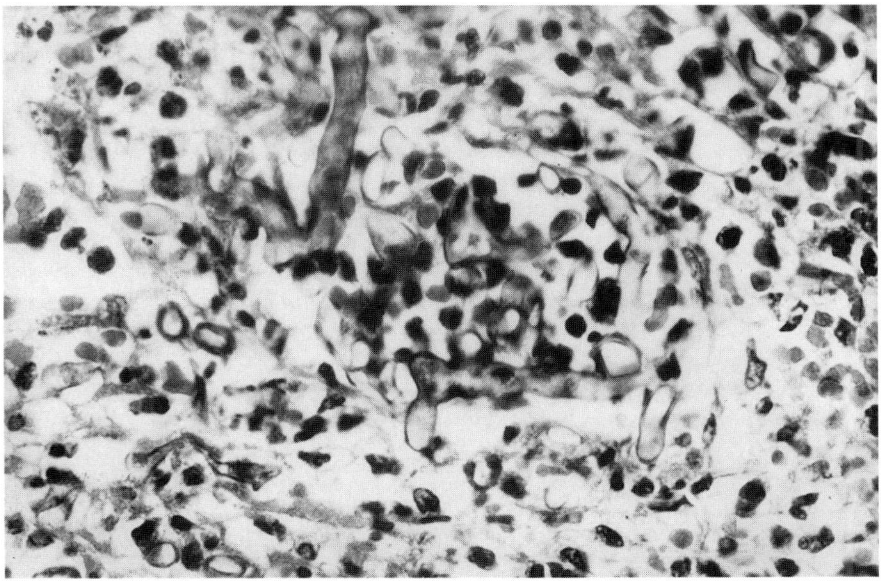

B

Fig. 26.11 A Ulcerated small intestine in a fatal case of mucormycosis in an immunocompromised individual. Large thrombosed blood vessel is present in the submucosa. (×11) **B** Higher magnification of **A** to show the haemotoxyphilic broad irregular pleomorphic aseptate hyphae branching at right angles, characteristic of mucormycosis. (H&E, ×690)

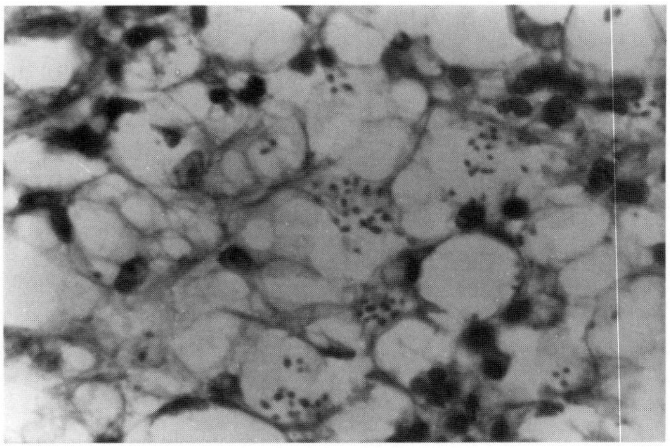

Fig. 26.12 Mesenteric lymph node with yeast-like fungi of *Histoplasma capsulatum* within macrophages. (H&E, ×576)

Other fungi

Histoplasmosis, a primary respiratory infection, may affect the gastrointestinal tract due to haematogeneous spread, presenting as diarrhoea and malabsorption.[134–140] Nodular or ulcerative lesions are mainly seen in the ileum. Budding yeast forms of *Histoplasma capsulatum* are seen in large numbers in histiocytes in the lamina propria (Fig. 26.12). In immunocompetent subjects a granulomatous response may be seen.

Aspergillosis involving the gastrointestinal tract predominantly affects the oesophagus. In the small intestine, ulcerative lesions and infarcts may occur due to its predilection to invade blood vessels.[136,141] In tissue sections septate hyphae of uniform diameter running in the same direction has dichotomous branching at 45° (Fig. 26.13).

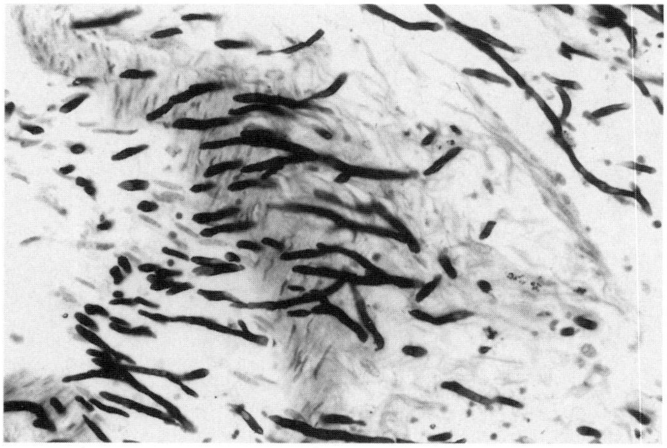

Fig. 26.13 Hyphae of *Aspergillus* with dichotomous branching oriented in some directions to invade a blood vessels. (GMS ×216)

PARASITES

Protozoa

Giardia lamblia

Giardia lamblia, the most common human intestinal protozoan parasite, causes giardiasis, defined as an acute or persistent diarrhoeal illness.[142] Infection occurs through the faecal-oral route and through contaminated water supplies. In the faeces, except during acute diarrhoeal episodes, the parasite is found predominantly as cysts. After ingestion of the cyst, there is excystation which is triggered by the gastric acid or by the pancreatic exocrine secretions. The parasite then colonizes the duodenum and proximal jejunum and an important step in this process is the attachment of the parasite to the surface of the enterocyte, possibly through a combination of hydrodynamic and mechanical forces in which the ventral disc of the parasite is important. Lectin mediated attachment with a trypsin-cleaved lectin with affinity for the mannose-6-phosphate residues on enterocyte surface membrane has been postulated.[143] The parasites proliferate by binary fission and bile is probably an important factor influencing multiplication.

Endemic cases of acute and persistent giardiasis are found mainly in children. Large epidemics due to contaminated water sources have been described from industrialized countries.[144] In tropical developing countries, although the prevalence in apparently healthy asymptomatic individuals may be as high as 30–40%,[145,146] clinical illness occurs predominantly in children.[147] There are several theories regarding the pathogenesis of diarrhoea and malabsorption in giardia infestation.[148] These include the formation of a mechanical barrier by a large number of organisms,[149] tissue invasion,[150] microvillus damage by the suction disk[151] or a mucoid pseudomembrane.[152] None of these mechanisms has yet been confirmed and it is likely that a complex interaction between the parasite, the host and other flora of the gut lumen is involved.

There are conflicting reports regarding the pathological changes in the small intestinal mucosa in giardial infestation. In jejunal mucosal biopsies from immunocompetent children, there are reports of normal mucosal structure or varying degree of villus atrophy with increased numbers of intraepithelial lymphocytes and lamina propria plasma cells.[153] However, in a detailed morphometric study of 80 patients and appropriate controls,[154] no abnormality was detected in giardia infested individuals. In proximal small intestinal biopsies giardia organisms can be seen on the luminal surface of villi, mainly in the intervillus space. Detection is facilitated by Giemsa stain. Parasites are pear shaped with a broad round anterior end containing two nuclei (Fig. 26.14A & B). Electron microscopy reveals the suction discs (Fig. 26.15) and evidence of occasional

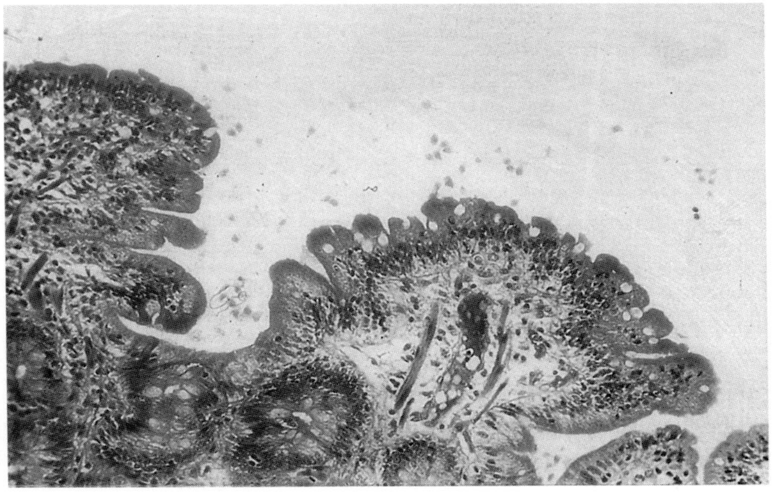

A

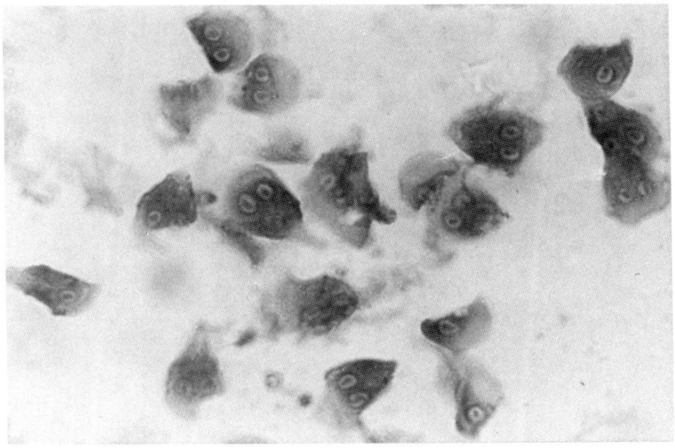

B

Fig. 26.14 **A** Jejunal biopsy with *Giardia lamblia* trophozoites in the intervillous space and luminal mucus. (H&E, ×150) **B** Higher power of **A** showing pear-shaped binucleate trophozoites which are sickle-shaped in lateral profile. (H&E, ×980)

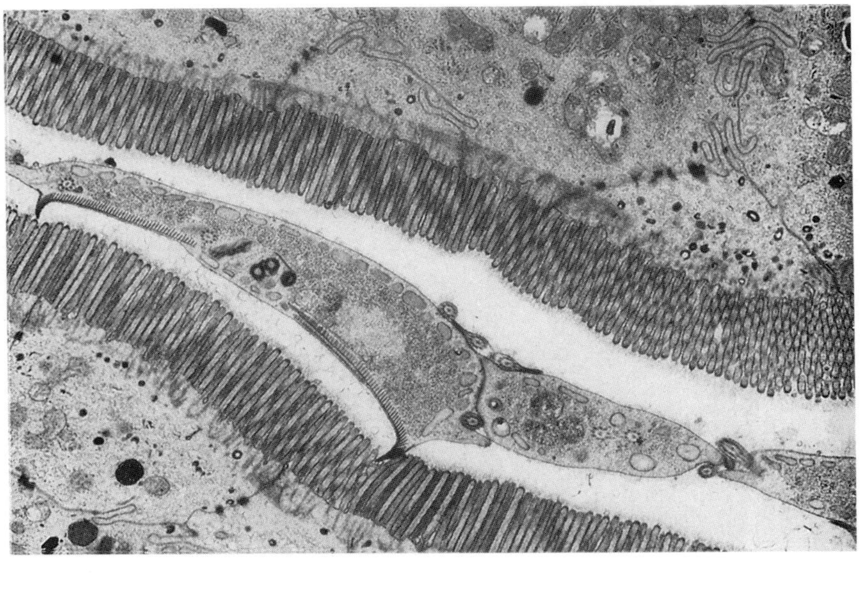

Fig. 26.15 Electron micrograph with a giardia trophozoite attached to the luminal border by the concave striated adhesive disc. (×10 260)

invasion of epithelium.[149,155] A syndrome of nodular lymphoid hyperplasia of the intestinal mucosa with hypogammaglobulinaemia and IgA deficiency, is associated with severe giardia infestation.[156]

Coccidia

Coccidia are intracellular protozoa, belonging to the class sporozoa, and include toxoplasma, cryptosporidia, isospora, microsporidia and sarcocystis. In their general life cycle, ingested oocysts from the contaminated environment excyst in the duodenum with release of sporozoites which invade enterocytes and undergo merogony (asexual multiplication). New merozoites invade other enterocytes and can multiply asexually or form gametes (gametogony). Fertilized gametes give rise to zygotes, which develop a cyst wall to form oocysts; these undergo maturation to form infective sporozoites (sporogony). These parasites have been reported occasionally from tropical countries in immunocompetent patients, but the wide prevalence of immunodeficiency associated with AIDS has made coccidia the most important opportunistic gut infection, since cell mediated immunity seems to be particularly important for resisting colonization.

Cryptosporidiosis

Cryptosporidium is a widely prevalent parasite that infects human and many animal species and can cause chronic diarrhoea.[157–159] *Cryptosporidium parvum*, the species that infects humans, can complete its life cycle in a single host.[160,161] Infection occurs due to ingestion of oocysts. 80% of the oocysts have thick walls, are environmentally resistant and are excreted in the stool and transmit the infection, while 20% of the oocysts have thin walls which rupture, releasing the infective sporozoites within the host, leading to autoinfection. In industrialized countries, cryptosporidium is usually detected only in patients with diarrhoea, but in contrast, in several tropical areas prospective studies showed that the prevalence of cryptosporidium was similar in children with acute diarrhoea and in matched controls.[162] While cryptosporidium can infect all parts of the gastrointestinal tract from the oesophagus to the rectum, the major site of infection is the small intestine. The mucosa may be granular or nodular, oedematous and hyperaemic. There is shortening of villi with crypt hyperplasia and infiltration of the lamina propria with mononuclear cells. The severity of the mucosal change correlates with the number of organisms that are present. In haematoxylin and eosin stained sections, the organisms can be seen attached to the epithelial microvillus border as small basophilic, spherical or oval structures measuring 2–5 μm in diameter, arranged in rows or clusters (Fig. 26.16). This appearance has to be distinguished from cytoplasmic blebs or yeast like organisms.[163] All

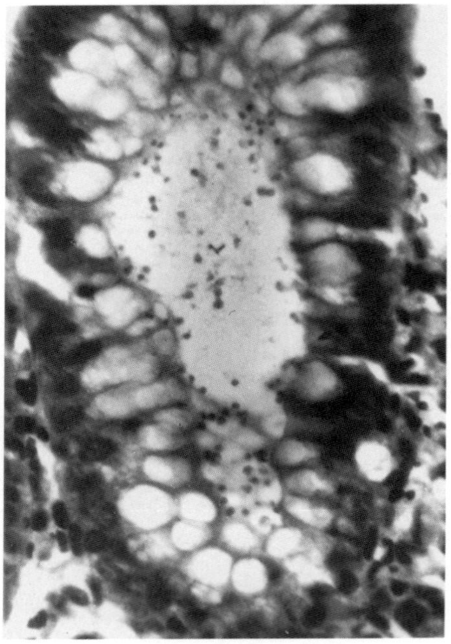

Fig. 26.16 Colonic crypt with oval or spherical cryptosporidia attached to the luminal border and free within the lumen. (H&E, ×216)

stages of the life cycle of the parasite can be readily identified by electron microscopic examination of infected small intestinal biopsies. The location of the parasite is in the parasitophorous vacuoles of the host microvillous membrane, intracellular but external to the perinuclear cytoplasm. The parasitic membrane in contact with host cytoplasm shows complicated infolding to form a 'feeder organelle' (Fig. 26.17).[164,165]

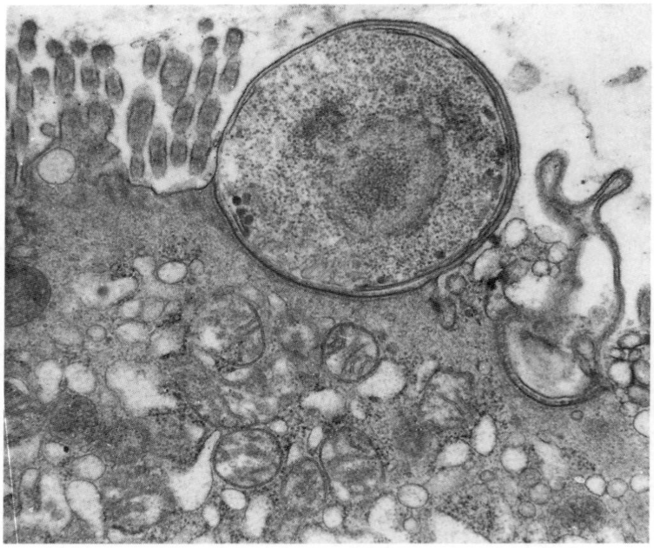

Fig. 26.17 Electron micrograph of jejunal enterocyte with a trophozoite of a cryptosporidia within the parasitophorous vacuole formed by microvillus membrane. A 'feeder organelle' is seen at the site of attachment to the apical cytoplasm. (×26 800)

Coccidiosis

Isospora is an intracellular parasite widely prevalent in Africa, South America and Southeast Asia. In these regions, the infection is by *Isospora belli*, but in temperate zone countries *Isospora hominus* is more prevalent. Infection causes chronic diarrhoea with abdominal pain and weight loss and can be diagnosed by detecting the oocyst in jejunal biopsies, jejunal aspirate or stool.[166,167] The jejunal mucosal villi are blunted with crypt hyperplasia and marked increase in cellularity of the lamina propria with plasma cells, lymphocytes and neutrophil polymorphs. There is a striking increase in eosinophils. Various stages of the life cycle of the parasite can be identified within the enterocytes in haematoxylin and eosin sections but detection is facilitated by the Giemsa or PAS stain (Fig. 26.18) or by electron microscopy.[168,169]

Microsporidiosis

Four genera of this coccidian have been identified and human enteric infection is caused by *Enterocytozoon bienuesi*.[170] Microsporidia infection can cause severe diarrhoea and has been reported especially in patients with AIDS from Europe, North America and Africa. The jejunum is the preferred site of infection, with villus shortening and villous enterocyte damage paralleling the severity of the infection. Infection is initiated by the ingestion of spores of microsporidia. After ingestion, the polar filament in the sporozoites uncoils and penetrates the host cell membrane with inoculation of sporoplasm into the cell. All stages of merogony and sporogony can be identified in the supranuclear cytoplasm of villous enterocytes. In haematoxylin and eosin stained paraffin sections many spores measuring 2–3 μm can be identified in a single cell, as supranuclear refractile bodies. These spores stain with Brown and Brenn acid fast stains, and fluorescent stains.[171] Sporozoites and merozoites show characteristic empty clefts and measure 3–5 μm in size. These can be better demonstrated in 1 μm sections stained with the Giemsa stain or by electron microscopy (Fig. 26.19), which is particularly useful in identifying the polar filaments in the spores.[172,173] A new species has been described which does not have the characteristic polar disc and clear clefts.[174]

Sarcosporidiosis

Sarcocystis species require two hosts with a carnivorous animal as the definitive host, where the sexual cycle occurs, and a herbivorous animal as intermediate host. Man is a definitive host for *Sarcocystis hominis* and *Sarcocystis sui hominis* and segmental necrotizing enteritis with heavy eosinophilic infiltration of the lamina propria has been reported from Thailand, in people who eat uncooked beef.[175]

Another coccidian parasite which can give rise to enteric infection is *Toxoplasma gondii* which usually causes extraintestinal infection.[176]

Trypanosomiasis

Infection by *Trypanosoma cruzi* causes Chagas' disease and is mainly reported from South America. The major clinical presentation is involvement of the colon and oesophagus with destruction of large numbers of ganglion cells

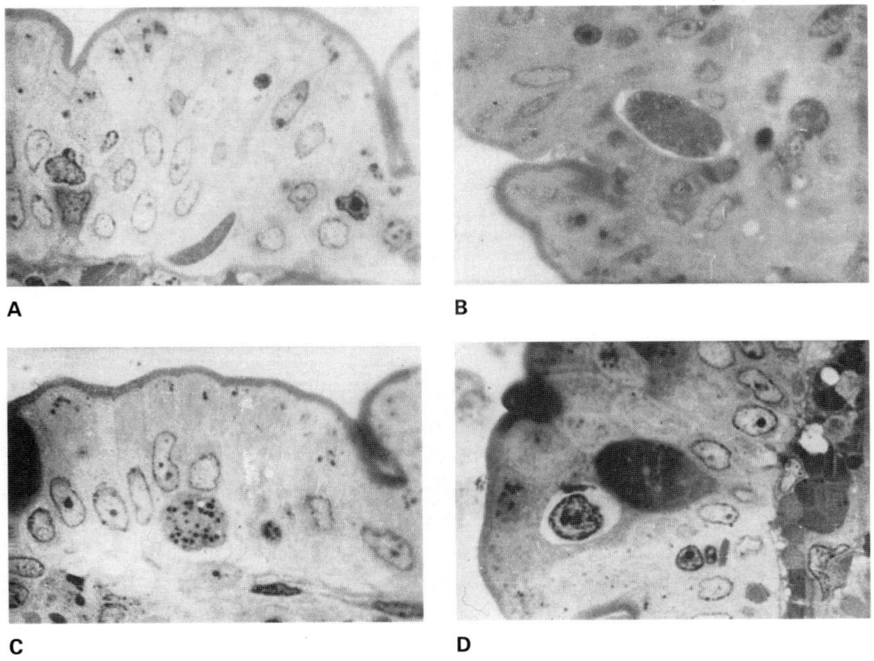

Fig. 26.18 Epon-embedded toluidine blue stained sections of jejunal biopsy from a patient with *Isospora belli*. (×855) **A** Merozoite which is elliptical in shape is seen in the basal epithelial cytoplasm; **B** Immature schizont in a vacuole; **C** Microgametocyte, subnuclear in position; **D** Unsporulated oocyst in a parasitophorous vacuole

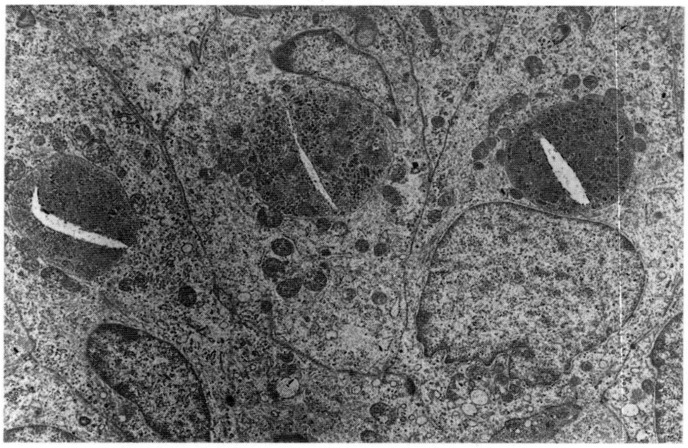

Fig. 26.19 Electron micrograph of jejunal villus cells showing microsporidia in the supranuclear cytoplasm with characteristic central cleft. (×2880)

from the Auerbach's plexus and focal inflammatory lesions in the muscle layer. Clinically apparent small bowel dilatation is rare, but in most patients with American trypanosomiasis many ganglion cells of the Auerbach's plexus of the small intestine are destroyed.[177,178]

Visceral leishmaniasis

Visceral Leishmaniasis, particularly in the Indian subcontinent, causes a febrile illness which is chronic with marked hepatosplenomegaly. An enteric infection by *Leishmania donovani* has been reported in this condition.[179,180] The diagnosis is made by detection of the Leishman-Donovan bodies in macrophages in the lamina propria of the intestine. However, the parasite is usually first detected in bone marrow smears rather than in small bowel mucosal biopsies. Recently, Leishmaniasis of the intestine has also been reported in patients with AIDS.[181,182]

Helminths

Hookworm disease

Infestation of the upper gastrointestinal tract of man by the nematode hookworm is one of the most common causes of severe iron deficiency anaemia in the tropics. There are two major species: *Ancylostoma duodenale* and *Necator americanus*. Infective larva from soil contaminated by faeces enter through the exposed skin of the feet (ground itch). The larvae migrate through the lung and ultimately arrive in the duodenum and upper small bowel where they grow to adult forms.[183] The adult hookworm attaches itself by its mouth parts to the mucosa and can suck between 0.03–0.15 cm^3 of blood each day. When the worm load is heavy the loss of blood leads to anaemia.[184]

Since the worm attaches itself to the duodenal mucosa, structural and functional abnormalities might be expected and there are some reports of hookworm enteropathy[185] and suggestions that mucosal trauma may result from the feeding activities of ancylostomes in animal models.[186] In humans, however, no structural or functional abnormalities have been detected in jejunal biopsies in several clinical studies in patients with heavy hookworm infestation.[187–189]

Strongyloidiasis

Infestation of the small intestine by the nematode *Strongyloides stercoralis* may be asymptomatic, produce chronic diarrhoea with malabsorption or result in fatal hyperinfection in immunocompromized individuals.[190–192] The parasite is prevalent throughout the world and infestation is diagnosed by detecting larvae in stool or small intestinal aspirates, or eggs, larvae and adult worms in jejunal biopsies. This parasite primarily infects man and has a complex life cycle. Infective filariform larvae from the soil penetrate the skin of the foot, transit through the lung and reach the intestine, where the adults usually colonize the duodenum and proximal jejunum; however adults can be found throughout the small and large intestine in heavy infestation. The adult female worm burrows into the mucosal crypts to lay eggs which release rhabditiform larvae. When these larvae reach the intestinal lumen, they can either be excreted in the faeces to continue the cycle of infection or they can metamorphose into filariform larvae in the intestinal lumen itself and give rise to autoinfection, which, in immunocompromized individuals, can lead to hyperinfection.[193–195]

The intestines may appear normal or be oedematous and hyperaemic. Oedema and extensive ulceration occurs in hyperinfection and in chronic cases there may be fibrosis. On histological examination the adult female worms can be seen penetrating the epithelium and in the crypts. Many segmented eggs and numerous larvae may also be present in the tissues (Fig. 26.20A & B). The lamina propria is infiltrated with mononuclear cells and eosinophils. There may be a granulomatous reaction around dead worms. Atrophy of the mucosa and ulceration is seen in severe cases, who can present with a malabsorption syndrome.[196]

Capillariasis

Detailed studies of an epidemic of severe diarrhoea and malabsorption which resulted in many deaths in the northern Philippines in 1967 identified a new species of round worm, *Capillaria philippinensis*.[197] This parasite is endemic in the Philippines, Thailand and Japan and has recently been detected in Iran[198] and India. The eggs of *Capillaria philippinensis* in human faeces resemble that of another worm, *Trichuris trichura*, which has a much wider geographical distribution.

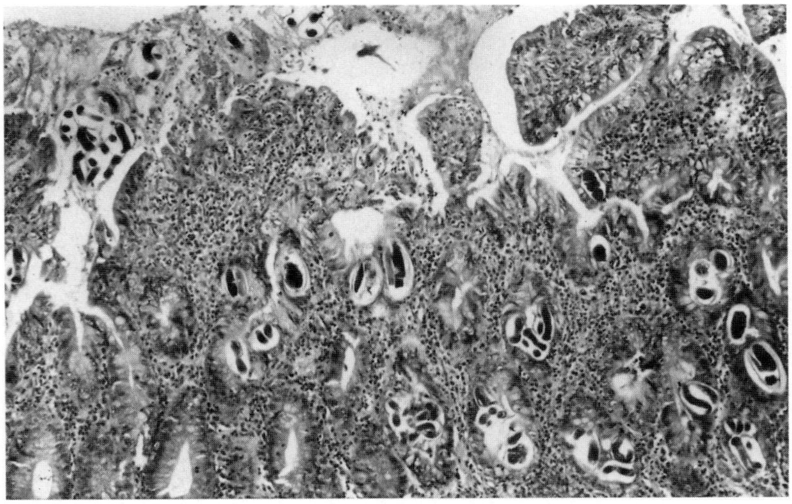

A

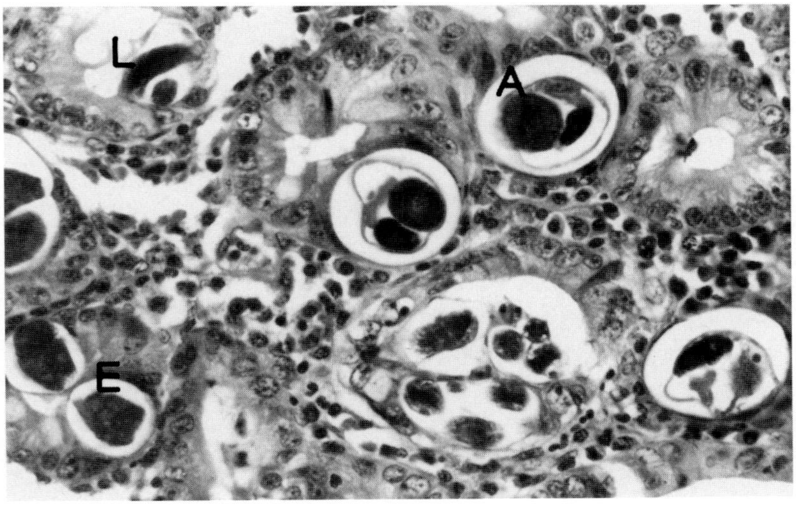

B

Fig. 26.20 **A** Jejunal mucosa in hyperinfection due to *Strongyloides stercoralis* with surface ulceration and increased cellularity of lamina propria. Adult worm, larvae and eggs are seen. (H&E, ×85) **B** Higher power to show the cross section of adult worm (A), larvae (L) and eggs (E) within the crypt epithelium compressing the cells. (H&E, ×170)

C. philippinensis eggs can be distinguished by their flatter polar plugs and the presence of fully developed larvae. Although the full life cycle of the parasite is not yet known, it is likely that part of it is in fish. Patients with severe capillariasis have many worms embedded in the small bowel mucosa and develop severe diarrhoea, malabsorption, protein losing enteropathy and die due to malnutrition and electrolyte abnormalities. The jejunum is thickened and congested with shortening of villi and sloughing of epithelium. There is marked infiltration of the lamina propria by lymphocytes, plasma cells and neutrophil polymorphs; many adult worms and larvae can be seen (Fig. 26.21A & B).[199–202] At electron microscopy, there are degenerative changes in the enterocytes and compressive degeneration of the cells surrounding the worms (Fig. 26.22). From autopsy samples and animal experiments it has been suggested that the worm gives rise to microulceration of the jejunal mucosa by lifting off the epithelial layer.[203]

Anisakiasis

Anisakiasis is an illness caused by the accidental infection of humans by the larvae of a nematode belonging to the subfamily anisakinae which is a parasite of sea mammals. Since infection occurs due to consumption of raw or improperly cooked fish,[204] it has been reported from countries where raw fish is considered a delicacy. The larvae are released from the fish in the stomach and penetrate the mucosa of the stomach and the upper small intestine, giving rise to localized inflammation and ulcers. There is diffuse interstitial oedema of the tissues accompanied by phlegmonous infiltration in which numerous eosinophils are present along with neutrophil polymorphs.

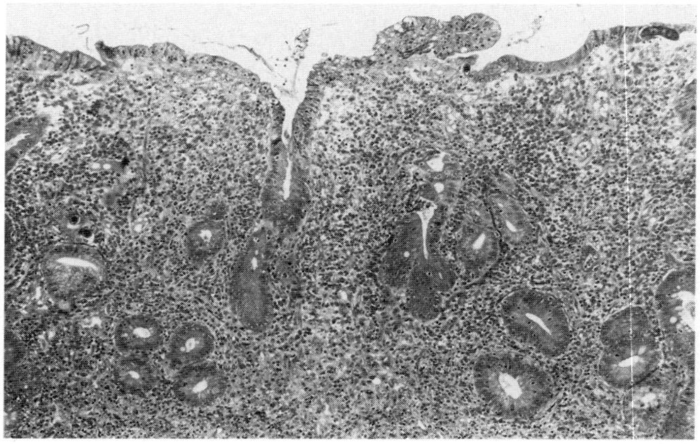

A

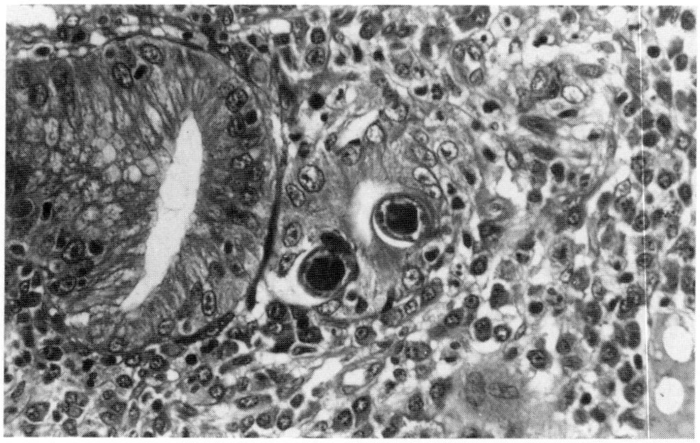

B

Fig. 26.21 **A** Jejunal mucosal biopsy in a case of malabsorption with villus atrophy and marked increase in lamina propria cellularity. Cross sections of capillaria parasites can be seen in surface and crypt cells. (H&E, ×70) **B** Higher power of crypt epithelium showing cross section of the worm within the basal lamina. (H&E, ×364)

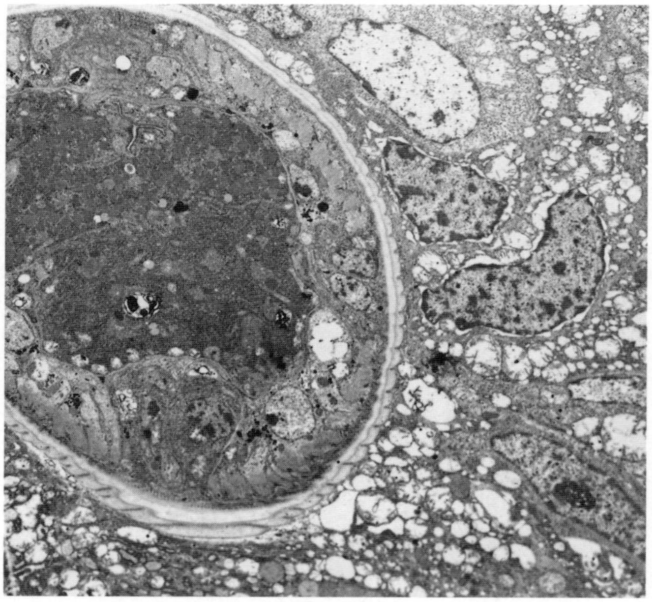

Fig. 26.22 Electron micrograph of the crypt epithelium harbouring capillaria. The worm is seen to be in direct contact with enterocytes which show degenerative changes. (×3440)

The parasite may be seen in the tissues in eosinophilic abscesses. In chronic cases, epithelioid cell granulomata with foreign body giant cells can also be present.[205] Occasionally the larvae can penetrate through the muscularis into the peritoneum and give rise to generalized peritonitis.[206]

Ascariasis

Ascaris lumbricoides is one of the most common intestinal parasites in humans and it has been estimated that approximately 9×10^{14} ascarid eggs contaminate the soil of the world per day![207] Large numbers of the round worms can colonize the small intestine and most of the pathology which results from ascariasis is due to mechanical blockade of the small intestine, which can lead to acute intestinal obstruction. Rarely, perforation and peritonitis has been reported.[208] The worms can also travel from the small intestine into biliary and pancreatic ducts and the appendix, giving rise to cholangitis, pancreatitis and appendicitis (Fig. 26.23).[209]

Angiostrongyliasis

Abdominal angiostrongyliasis is caused by a nematode, *Angiostrongylus costaricensis*, first described from Costa Rica in 1971 and prevalent in Central and South America. The life cycle of the worm involves two hosts: wild rodents (definitive host) and a slug (intermediate host). Man is an accidental host due to ingestion of slug contaminated food. Larvae penetrate the gut wall and mature in lymphatics and lymph nodes and migrate to arterioles of the

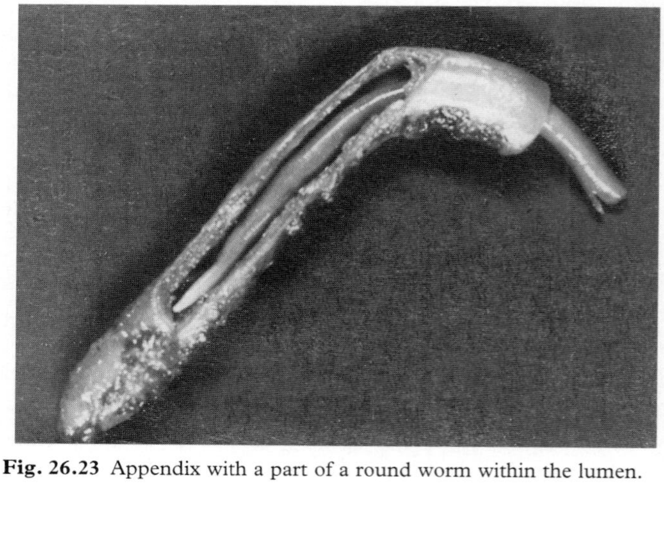

Fig. 26.23 Appendix with a part of a round worm within the lumen.

ileocaecal region. Histologically, massive eosinophil infiltration in all layers of the intestinal wall with granulomatous reaction and eosinophilic vasculitis of arteries, veins, capillaries and lymphatics is characteristic.[210–212]

Schistosomiasis

Trematodes (flukes) belonging to the genus schistosoma cause schistosomiasis which is endemic in many tropical regions. *S. mansoni* and *S. japonicum* can give rise to intestinal schistosomiasis. The major lesions which give rise to a bloody diarrhoea occur in the colon, but jejunal involvement can give rise to malabsorption[213] and in the duodenum, duodenitis[214] or polyps[215] may occur. Diagnosis can be made by endoscopic biopsy when granulomas containing the eggs of the parasite can be recognized.

Cestodes

The adult tapeworms which may infect the intestinal tract are *Taenia saginata* (beef tapeworm), *Taenia solium* (pork tapeworm) and *Diphyllobothrium latum*, the fish tapeworm which is found in certain Scandinavian countries. These are flat worms with a scolex for attachment, a neck which is the region of growth, and segments or proglottids which are the organ of reproduction. Man is the definitive host for *Taenia saginata* and *Taenia solium*. No pathological changes are usually found in the intestinal mucosa with infestation with this worm, but occasionally intestinal obstruction due to tangled masses of worms occurs (Fig. 26.24).[216] *D. latum* is associated with megaloblastic anaemia due to Vitamin B_{12} deficiency. The diagnosis is made by identification of proglottids or eggs in faeces.

UNKNOWN BUT PRESUMABLY INFECTIOUS AETIOLOGIES

Whipple's disease

Whipple's disease is a chronic systemic illness[217,218] of probable bacterial origin[219] Patients, usually middle-aged males, present with migratory polyarthralgia, steatorrhoea and wasting. The major manifestations are due to small intestinal involvement, but rarely extraintestinal forms of Whipple's disease have been described. Electron microscopic demonstration of bacterial bodies in foamy macrophages and the clinical response to antibiotic therapy supports a bacterial aetiology.[220,221]

Endoscopic examination of the proximal small intestinal mucosa has shown a granular yellow elevated appearance which is due to enlarged villi infiltrated by foamy macrophages.[222,223] These are the hallmark of the disease; the cytoplasm is finely granular and greyish and contains PAS positive and diastase resistant granules and rods.[224] These macrophages are present in large numbers in the lamina propria of the subepithelial area at villus tips and decrease towards the muscularis. The villus architecture may be distorted by the macrophage infiltration, but the crypt enterocytes appear to be normal. In some patients, an early manifestation may be a sarcoid-like lesion in the small intestine and other organs.[225] A defect of cell-mediated immunity has now been demonstrated in patients with Whipple's disease.[226]

The Whipple bacillus is an intracellular pathogen difficult to culture. It is rod shaped and surrounded by an approximately 20 nm thick cell wall, with a unique outer plasma membrane.[227] Bacilli in macrophages show variable degenerative changes. They are also found free in

Fig. 26.24 Segment of small intestine resected for intestinal obstruction containing a tangled adult tapeworm within the lumen.

the lamina propria and may invade enterocytes, vascular endothelium, neutrophil polymorphs, plasma cells and smooth muscle.[227] Response to therapy is coincident with reduction and disappearance of the bacteria.[221] Molecular biological techniques have enabled the cloning of a 16S ribosomal RNA sequence of the bacterial genome and resulted in the identification of the organism as a Gram positive actinomycete which has been named *Tropheryma whippelli*.[228,229] This exciting discovery is likely to lead to a better understanding of this rare disease.

Tropical sprue

Tropical sprue is a primary malabsorption syndrome which affects residents and visitors to many tropical countries.[230] The patients present with chronic diarrhoea and malabsorption and suffer from severe malnutrition as a result. Although the disease was initially thought to be confined to expatriates from temperate climates resident in certain tropical areas, it is now known that the prevalence of tropical sprue in indigenous populations is high.[231]

The jejunal mucosal changes have been studied in several regions where the disease is endemic.[232–234] The total thickness of the mucosa is not usually reduced, but crypt length is increased with reduction in villus height. The cellularity of the lamina propria is increased with infiltration of lymphocytes and plasma cells (Fig. 26.25). The epithelial lymphocytes are also increased[235] and it has been shown that this is secondary to enterocyte damage.[236]

The primary lesion in tropical sprue is enterocyte damage in both the surface and the crypt epithelium. In fact, apart from patients treated with antimitotic drugs or radiation therapy, tropical sprue appears to be the only

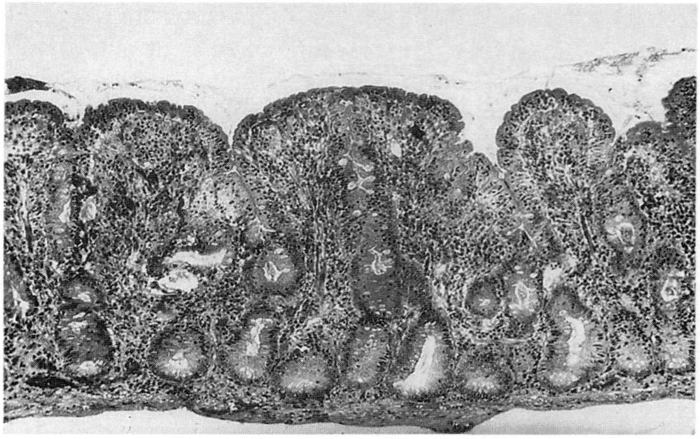

Fig. 26.25 Jejunal biopsy from a patient with tropical sprue showing crypt hyperplasia, shortened villi covered with shortened enterocytes. Lamina propria has increased mononuclear cells. (H&E, ×78)

condition where there is primary damage to the crypt cells. Using techniques of morphometry and in vitro organ culture, combined with ultrastructural studies, it has been possible to postulate a pathogenetic model of the disease.[237] The agent causing tropical sprue damages groups of enterocyte stem cells, this progeny is lost from the surface and crypt epithelium well before they reach the zone of extrusion at the tips of villi. This leads to reduction in the villus height and compensatory crypt hypertrophy as the stem cells try to replace the lost functional cells. The nature of the damaging agent is not known, although epidemiological investigations in southern India have suggested that it might be an unusual virus.[238] It is not yet clear whether patients with tropical sprue in other regions, such as the Caribbean or expatriates in temperate zones, have similar crypt cell lesions.

REFERENCES

1. Gebbers J, Laissrue JA. Functional morphology of the mucosal barrier. Microecology and Therapy 1984; 14: 137–168.
2. Mathan VI, Rajan DP. The prevalance of bacterial enteric pathogens in a healthy rural population in southern India. Med Microbiol 1986; 22: 93–96.
3. Moe K. Epidemiology of acute childhood diarrhoea in Burma. In: Infectious diarrhoea in the young. Tzipori S, ed. Excerpta Medica, Amsterdam, 1985: p 99.
4. Baker SJ, Mathan VI. Tropical enteropathy and tropical sprue. Am J Clin Nutr 1972; 25: 1047–1050.
5. Lindenbaum J, Kent TH, Spring H. Malabsorption and jejunitis in American Peace Corps volunteers in Pakistan. Ann Intern Med 1966; 65: 1201–1207.
6. Baker SJ, Ignatius M, Mathan VI, Vaish SK, Chacko CJ. Intestinal biopsy in tropical sprue. Intestinal Biopsy. Ciba Foundation Study Group No.14. eds, GEW Wolstenholme, MP Cameron. Boston: Little Brown, 1962: p 84.
7. Mathan M, Mathan VI, Baker SJ. An electron microscopic study of jejunal mucosal morphology in control subjects and in patients with tropical sprue in southern India. Gastroenterology 1975; 68: 17–32.
8. Baker SJ. Geographical variations in the morphology of the small intestinal mucosa in apparently healthy individuals. Pathol Microbiol 1973; 39: 222–237.
9. Rabbani GH. Cholera. Clin Gastroenterol 1986; 15: 507–528.
10. Jones GW. The adhesive properties of Vibrio cholerae and other Vibrio species. In: Beachey EH, ed. Bacterial Adherence. London: Chapman and Hall, 1980.
11. De SN. Enterotoxicity of bacteria free culture filtrate of Vibrio cholerae. Nature 1959; 183: 1533–1534.
12. Field M. Modes of action of enterotoxins from Vibrio cholera and Escherichia coli. Rev Infect Dis 1979; 1: 918–925.
13. Cassel D, Pfeuffer T. Mechanism of cholera toxin action: covalent modification of the guanyl nucleotide-binding protein of the adenylate cyclase system. Proc Natl Acad Sci USA 1978; 75: 2669–2673.
14. Fasano A, Baudry B, Pumplin DW, Wasserman SS, Tall BD, Ketley JM, Kaper JB. Vibrio cholerae produces a second enterotoxin, which affects intestinal tight junctions. Proc Natl Acad Sci, USA 1991; 88: 5242–5246.
15. Kaper J. Toxic factors produced by V. cholerae. In: Frontier Conference on Cholera Toxin, The Wellcome Trust, London, 1993: p 11.
16. Asakura H, Tsuchiya M, Watanabe Y, et al. Electron microscopic study on the jejunal mucosa in human cholera. Gut 1974; 15: 531–544.
17. Gangarosa EJ, Beisel WR, Benyajati C, Sprinz H, Piyartn P. The nature of the gastrointestinal lesion in Asiatic cholera and its

relation to pathogenesis: a biopsy study. Am J Trop Med 1960; 9: 125–135.
18. Sprinz H, Sribhibhadh R, Gangarosa EJ, Benyajati C, Kundel D, Halstead S. Biopsy of small bowel in Thai people, with special reference to recovery from Asiatic cholera and to an intestinal malabsorption syndrome. Am J Clin Pathol 1962; 38: 43–51.
19. Fresh JW, Versage P, Reyes V. Intestinal morphology in human and experimental cholera. Arch Pathol 1964; 77: 529–537.
20. Sheehy TW, Sprinz H, Augerson WS, Formal SB. Laboratory vibrio cholera infection in the United States. JAMA 1966; 197: 321–326.
21. Pastore G, Schiraldi G, Fera G, Sforza E, Schiraldi O. A bioptic study of gastrointestinal mucosa in cholera patients during an epidemic in southern Italy. Dig Dis 1976; 21: 613–617.
22. Levine MM. Escherichia coli that cause diarrhea: Enterotoxigenic, enteropathogenic, enteroinvasive, enterohemorrhagic and enteroadherent. J Infec Dis 1987; 155: 377–389.
23. Hart CA, Batt RM, Fletcher J, Embaye H, Saunders JR. Interactions between enterocytes and enteropathogenic Escherichia coli. Biochem Soc Trans 1989; 17: 466–469.
24. Levine MM. Adhesion of enterotoxigenic Escherichia coli in humans and animals. In: Adhesion and microorganism pathogenicity. Ciba Foundation Symposium 80, London, Pitman, 1981: p 142.
25. Wanke CA, Guerrant RL. Enterotoxigenic Escherichia coli. In: Enteric Infection. eds, Farthing MJG, Keusch GT. London: Chapman Hall, 1989: p 253.
26. Boedeker EC. Enteroadherent (enteropathogenic) Escherichia coli. In: Enteric Infection. eds, Farthing MJG, Keusch GT. London: Chapman Hall, 1989: p 123.
27. Knutton S, Lloyd DR, McNeish AS. Adhesion of enteropathgenic Escherichia coli to human intestinal enterocytes and cultured human intestinal mucosa. Infec Immun 1987; 55: 69–77.
28. Moon HW, Whipp SC, Argenzio RA, Levine MM, Giannella RA. Attaching and effacing activities of rabbit and human enteropathogenic Escherichia coli in pig and rabbit intestines. Infec Immun 1983; 41: 1340–1351.
29. Ulshen MH, Rollo JL. Pathogenesis of Escherichia coli. Gastroenteritis in man — another mechanism. N Eng J Med 1980; 302: 99–101.
30. Rothbaum RJ, McAdams AJ, Giannella RA, Partin JC. A clinicopathologic study of enterocyte-adherent Escherichia coli: A cause of protracted diarrhea in infants. Gastroenterology 1982; 83: 441–454.
31. Rothbaum RJ, Partin JC, Saalfield K, McAdams AJ. An ultrastructural study of enteropathogenic Escherichia coli infection in human infants. Ultrastructural Pathology 1983; 4: 291–304.
32. Cantey JR, Lushbaugh WB, Inman LR. Attachment of bacteria to intestinal epithelial cells in diarrhea caused by Escherichia coli strain RDEC-1 in the rabbit: stages and role of the capsule. Infec Immun 1981; 143: 219–230.
33. Murrell TGC, Roth L, Egerton J, Samels J, Walker PD. Pig-Bel: enteritis necroticans. A study in diagnosis and management. Lancet 1966; 1: 217–222.
34. Lawrence G, Walker PD. Pathogenesis of enteritis necroticans in Papua New Guinea. Lancet 1976; 1: 125–126.
35. Murrell TGC, Walker PD. The pigbel story of Papua New Guinea. Trans Roy Soc Trop Med Hyg 1991; 85: 119–122.
36. Arseculeratne SN, Padabokke RG, Navaratnam C. Pathogenesis of necrotising enteritis with special reference to intestinal hypersensitivity reactions. Gut 1980; 21: 265–278.
37. Butler T, Dahms B, Lindpaintner K, Islam M, Azad MAK, Anton P. Segmental necrotising enterocolitis: Pathological and clinical features of 22 cases in Bangladesh. Gut 1987; 28: 1433–1438.
38. Butzler JP, Skirrow MB. Campylobacter enteritis. Clin Gastroenterol 1979; 8: 737–765.
39. Karmali MA, Fleming PC. Campylobacter enteritis. CMA J 1979; 120: 1525–1532.
40. Michalak DM, Perrault J, Gilchrist MJ, Dozois RR, Carney JA, Sheedy PF. Campylobacter fetus ss. jejuni: A cause of massive lower gastrointestinal hemorrhage. Gastroenterology 1980; 79: 742–745.
41. Coffin CM, Heureaux PL, Dehner LP. Campylobacter associated enterocolitis in childhood. Am J Clin Pathol 1982; 78: 117–123.
42. Walker RI, Caldwell MB, Lee EC, Guerry P, Trust TJ, Ruiz-Palacios GM. Pathophysiology of campylobacter enteritis. Microbiol Rev 1986; 50: 81–94.
43. Boyd JF. Pathology of the alimentary tract in Salmonella typhimurium food poisoning. Gut 1985; 26: 935–944.
44. Merson MH, Morris GK, Sack DA, et al. Traveller's diarrhea in Mexico. N Engl J Med 1976; 294: 1299–1305.
45. Rout WR, Formal B, Dammin GJ, Giannella RA. Pathophysiology of salmonella diarrhea in the Rhesus monkey: Intestinal transport, morphologic and bacteriologic studies. Gastroenterology 1974; 67: 59–70.
46. Dammin GJ. Salmonellosis. In: Pathology of tropical and extraordinary diseases. Eds, Binford CH, Connor DH. Armed Forces Institute of Pathology, Washington, 1976: Vol. 1, p 150.
47. Stephen J, Wallis TS, Starkey WG, Candy DCA, Osborne MP, Haddon S. Salmonellosis: in retrospect and prospect. In: Microbial toxins and diarrhoeal disease. Ciba Foundation Symposium 112. London: Pitman, 1985: p 175.
48. Candy DCA, Stephen J. Salmonella. In: Enteric Infection: Mechanisms, manifestations and management. Eds, Farthing MJG, Keusch GT. London: Chapman and Hall, 1989: p 289.
49. Finkelstein RA, Marchlewicz BA, McDonald RJ et al. Isolation and characterisation of a cholera-related enterotoxin from Salmonella typhimurium. FEMS Microbiol Lett 1983; 17: 239.
50. Giannella, Gots RE, Charney AN, Greenough WB III, Formal SB. Pathogenesis of salmonella-mediated intestinal fluid secretion. Gastroenterology 1975; 69: 1238–1245.
51. Giannella RA, Formal SB, Dammin GJ. Pathogenesis of salmonellosis: Studies of fluid secretion, mucosal invasion and morphologic reaction in the rabbit ileum. J Clin Invest 1973; 52: 441–453.
52. Holmes IH. Viral Gastroenteritis. Prog Med Virol 1979; 25: 1–36.
53. Christensen ML. Human viral gastroenteritis. Clin Microbiol Rev 1989; 2: 51–89.
54. Flewett TH, Beards GM. Recent advances in the study of viral gastroenteritis. Sci Prog Oxf 1989; 73: 33–51.
55. Blacklow NR, Greenberg HB. Viral gastroenteritis. NEJM 1991; 325: 252–264.
56. Holmes IH. Rotaviruses. In: The Reoviridae. Joklik WK ed. New York: Plenum, 1983: p 359.
57. Kjeldsberg E, Mortensson-Egnund K. Comparison of solid-phase immune electron microscopy, direct electron microscopy and enzyme-linked immunosorbert assay for detection of rotavirus in faecal samples. J Virol Meth 1982; 4: 45–53.
58. Bishop RF, Davidson GP, Holmes IH, Ruck BJ. Viruses particles in epithelial cells of duodenal mucosa from children with acute non-bacterial gastroenteritis. Lancet 1973; 2: 1281–1283.
59. Flewett TH, Bryden AS, Davies H. Virus particles in gastroenteritis. Lancet 1973; 2: 1497.
60. Davidson GP, Barnes GL. Structural and functional abnormalities of the small intestine in infants and young children with rotavirus enteritis. Acta Paediatr Scand 1979; 68: 181–186.
61. Hamilton JR, Gall DG, Butler DG, Middlelan PJ. Viral gastroenteritis: recent progress, remaining problems. Ciba Foundation Symposium 1976; 42: 209–222.
62. Guerrant RL. Pathophysiology of the enterotoxic and viral diarrhoeas. In: Diarrhoea and malnutrition. eds. Chen LC, Scrimshaw NS. New York: Plenum Press, 1982: p 23.
63. Davidson GP, Goller I, Bishop RF, Townley RRW, Holmes IH, Ruck BJ. Immunofluorescence in duodenal mucosa of children with acute enteritis due to a new virus. J Clin Pathol 1975; 28: 263–266.
64. Agus SG, Dolin R, Wyatt RG, Tousimis AJ, Northrup RS. Acute infectious nonbacterial gastroenteritis: Intestinal histopathology. Histologic and enzymatic alterations during illness produced by the Norwalk agent in man. Ann Int Med 1973; 79: 18–25.
65. Scheiber DS, Blacklow NR, Trier JS. The small intestinal lesion induced by Hawaii agent acute infectious nonbacterial gastroenteritis. J Infect Dis 1974; 129: 705–708.
66. Philips AD. Mechanisms of mucosal injury: human studies. In: Farthing MJG, ed. Viruses and the Gut. (Proceedings of the Ninth International Workshop) London: Smith, Kline & French, British Society of Gastroenterology, 1988: p 30.

67. Caul EO, Paver WK, Clarke SKR. Coronavirus particles in faeces in patients with gastroenteritis. Lancet 1975; 1: 1192.
68. Resta S, Luby JP, Rosenfeld CR, Siegel JD. Isolation and propagation of a human enteric coronavirus. Science 1985; 229: 978–981.
69. Vial PA, Robbins-Browne R, Lior H et al. Characterization of enteroadherent aggregative Escherichia coli, a putative agent of diarrheal disease. J Infec Dis 1988; 158: 70–79.
70. Yamamota T, Endo S, Yokota T, Echeverria P. Characteristics of adherence of enteroaggregative Escherichia coli to human and animal mucosa. Infec Immun 1991; 59: 3722–3739.
71. Knutton S, Shaw RK, Bhan MK et al. Ability of enteroaggregative Escherichia coli strains to adhere in vitro to human intestinal mucosa. Infec Immun 1992; 60: 2083–2091.
72. Haider K, Faruque SM, Shahid NS et al. Enteroaggregative Escherichia coli infections in Bangladeshi children: clinical and microbiological features. J Diarrheal Dis Res 1991; 4: 318–322.
73. Bhan MK, Raj P, Levine MM, Kaper JB et al. Enteroaggregative Escherichia coli associated with persistent diarrhoea in a cohort of rural children in India. J Infect Dis 1989; 159: 1061–1064.
74. Cravioto A, Tello A, Navarro A et al. Association of Escherichia coli HEp-2 adherence patterns with type and duration of diarrhoea. Lancet 1991; 337: 262–264.
75. Stuart BM, Pullen RL. Typhoid. Arch Intern Med 1946; 78: 629–661.
76. Rowland HAK. Typhoid fever and other salmonella infections. Br J Hosp Med 1974; 10: 54–62.
77. Smith JH. Typhoid fever. In: Pathology of tropical and extraordinary diseases. eds, Binford CH, Connor DH. Armed Forces Institute of Pathology, Washington, 1976: p 123.
78. Chuttani HK, Jain K, Misra RC. Small bowel in typhoid fever. Gut 1971; 12: 709–712.
79. Butler T, Islam A, Kabir I, Jones PK. Patterns of morbidity and mortality in typhoid fever dependent on age and gender: Review of 552 hospitalized patients with diarrhea. Rev Inf Dis 1991; 13: 85–90.
80. Khosla SN. Typhoid perforation. J Trop Med Hyg 1977; 80: 83–87.
81. Khosla SN. Typhoid hepatitis. Postgrad Med J 1990; 66: 923–925.
82. Osuntokun BO, Bademosi O, Ogunremi K, Wright SG. Neuropsychiatric manifestations of typhoid fever in 959 patients. Arch Neurol 1972; 27: 7–13.
83. Vantrappen G, Agg HO, Ponette E, Geboes K, Bertrand Ph. Yersinia enteritis and enterocolitis: Gastroenterological aspects. Gastroenterology 1977; 72: 220–227.
84. Swaminathan B, Harmon MC, Mehlman IJ. Yersinia enterocolitica. J Appl Bacteriol 1982; 52: 151–183.
85. Vantrappen G, Geboes K, Ponette E. Yersinia enteritis. Med Clin North Amer 1982; 66: 639–653.
86. Cover TL, Aber RC. Yersinia enterocolitica. N Eng J Med 1989; 321: 16–24.
87. O'Loughlin EV, Gall DG, Pai CH. Yersinia enterocolitica: Mechanisms of microbial pathogenesis and pathophysiology of diarrhoea. J Gastroenterol Hepatol 1990; 5: 173–179.
88. Doyle MP. Pathogenic Escherichia coli, Yersinia enterocolitica and Vibrio parahaemolyticus. Lancet 1991; 336: 1111–1115.
89. Rabson AR, Koornhof HJ. Yersinia enterocolitica infections in South Africa. S Afr Med J 1972; 46: 798–803.
90. Gleason TH, Patterson SD. The pathology of Yersinia enterocolitica ileocolitis. Am J Surg Pathol 1982; 6: 347–355.
91. Bradford WD, Noce PS, Gutman LT, Durham NC. Pathologic features of enteric infection with Yersinia enterocolitica. Arch Pathol 1974; 98: 17–21.
92. El-Maraghi NRH, Mair NS. The histopathology of enteric infection with Yersinia pseudotuberculosis. Am J Clin Pathol 1979; 71: 631–639.
93. Bohm N, Wybitul K. Different histologic types of mesenteric lymphadenitis in Yersinia pseudotuberculosis type I and type II infection. Path Res Pract 1978; 162: 301–315.
94. Chuttani HK. Intestinal tuberculosis. In: Modern Trends in Gastroenterology. ed. Card WI, Creamer B. London: Butterworth 1970: p 308.
95. Styblo K. The global aspects of tuberculosis and HIV infection. Bull Internat Union Tub Lung Dis 1990; 65: 28–32.
96. Palmer KR, Patil DH, Basran GS, Riordan JF, Silk DBA. Abdominal tuberculosis in urban Britain — a common disease. Gut 1985; 26: 1296–1305.
97. Schofield PF. Abdominal tuberculosis. Gut 1985; 26: 1275–1278.
98. Wig KL, Chitkara NL, Gupta SP, Kishore K, Manchanda RL. Ileocaecal tuberculosis with particular reference to isolation of Mycobacterium tuberculosis. Am Rev Resp Dis 1961; 84: 169–178.
99. Hoon JR, Dockerty MB, Pemberton J, De J. Ileocaecal tuberculosis including a comparison of this disease with nonspecific regional ileitis and noncaseous tuberculated colitis. Int Abstr Surg 1950; 91: 417–440.
100. Tandon HD, Prakash A. Pathology of intestinal tuberculosis and its distinction from Crohn's Disease. Gut 1972; 13: 260–269.
101. Tandon HD, Prakash A, Rao VB, Prakash O, Nair SK. Ulceroconstrictive disorders of the intestine in Northern India: a pathologic study. Indian J Med Res 1966; 54: 129–141.
102. Anand SS. Hypertrophic ileo-caecal tuberculosis in India with a record of fifty hemicolectomies. Ann R Coll Surg 1956; 19: 205–222.
103. Gaffney EF, Condell D, Majmudar B, Nolan N, Mcdonald GSA, Griffin M, Sweeney EC. Modification of caecal lymphoid tissue and relationship to granuloma formation in sporadic ileocaecal tuberculosis. Histopathology 1987; 11: 691–704.
104. Addison NV. Abdominal tuberculosis — a disease revived. Ann Roy Coll Surg Eng 1983; 65: 105–111.
105. Churukian CJ. Demonstration of mycobacteria: a brief review with special emphasis on fluorochrome staining. J Histochem 1991; 14: 117–121.
106. Shibata NM, Togashi M, Kobayashi T. Polymerase chain reaction for detection of Mycobacterium tuberculosis. Acta Paediatr 1992; 81: 141–144.
107. Shah S, Thomas V, Mathan M, Chacko A, Chandy G, Ramakrishna BS, Rolston DDK. Colonoscopic study of 50 patients with colonic tuberculosis. Gut 1992; 33: 347–351.
108. Chuttani HK, Sarin SK. Intestinal tuberculosis. Ind J Tub 1985; 32: 117–125.
109. Tandon HD. The pathology of intestinal tuberculosis and distinction from other diseases causing stricture. Trop Gastroenterol 1981; 2: 77–93.
110. Tonghua L, Guozong P, Minhang C. Crohn's disease. Clinicopathologic manifestations and differential diagnosis from enterocolonic tuberculosis. Chinese Med J 1981; 94: 431–440.
111. Collins FM. Mycobacterium avium-complex infections and development of the acquired immunodeficiency syndrome: Casual opportunist or causal cofactor? Int J Lep 1986; 54: 458–474.
112. Perfect JR. Mycobacterium avium-intracellulare complex infections in the Acquired Immunodeficiency Syndrome. J Electron Microsc Tech 1988; 8: 105–113.
113. Pitchenik AE, Fertel D. Tuberculosis and nontuberculous mycobacterial disease. Med Clin N Amer 1992; 76: 121–171.
114. Batman PA, Miller ARO, Forster SM, Harris JRW, Pinching AJ, Griffin GE. Jejunal enteropathy associated with human immunodeficiency virus infection: quantitative histology. J Clin Pathol 1989; 42: 275–281.
115. Ullrich R, Zeitz M, Heise W, L'age M, Hoffken G, Riecken EO. Small intestinal structure and function in patients infected with human immunodeficiency virus (HIV): Evidence for HIV-induced enteropathy. Ann Int Med 1989; 111: 15–21.
116. Griffin GE, Miller A, Batman P, Forster SM, Pinching AJ, Harris JRW, Mathan MM. Damage to jejunal intrinsic autonomic nerves in HIV infection. AIDS 1988; 2: 379–382.
117. Mathan MM, Griffin GE, Miller A, Batman P, Forster S, Pinching A, Harrow W. Ultrastructure of the jejunal mucosa in human immunodeficiency virus infection. J Pathol 1990; 161: 119–127.
118. Nelson JA, Wiley CA, Reynolds-Kholer C, Reese CE, Margaretten W, Levy JA. Human immunodeficiency virus detected in bowel epithelium from patients with gastrointestinal symptoms. Lancet 1988; 1: 259–262.

119. Fox CH, Kotler DP, Tierney AR, Wilson CS, Fauci AS. Detection of HIV-1 RNA in intestinal lamina propria of patients with AIDS and gastrointestinal disease. J Infect Dis 1989; 159: 467–471.
120. Kotler DP, Reka S, Borcich A, Cronin WJ. Detection, localization, and quantitation of HIV-associated antigens in intestinal biopsies from patients with HIV. Am J Pathol 1991; 139: 823–829.
121. Jarry A, Cortez A, Rene E, Muzeau F, Brousse N. Infected cells and immune cells in the gastrointestinal tract of AIDS patients. An immunohistochemical study of 127 cases. Histopathology 1990; 16: 133–140.
122. Ehrenpreis ED, Patterson BK, Brainer JA et al. Histopathologic findings of duodenal biopsy specimens in HIV-infected patients with and without diarrhea and malabsorption. Am J Clin Pathol 1992; 97: 21–28.
123. Sommerville RG. Cytomegalovirus — an update. Scot Med J 1984; 29: 2–3.
124. Fiala M, Payne JE, Berne TV et al. Epidemiology of cytomegalovirus infection after transplantation and immunosuppression. J Infect Dis 1975; 132: 421–433.
125. Rosen PP. Opportunistic fungal infections in patients with neoplastic diseases. Pathol Annu 1976; 11: 255–315.
126. Henson D. Cytomegalovirus inclusion bodies in the gastrointestinal tract. Arch Pathol 1972; 93: 477–482.
127. Knapp AB, Horst DA, Eliopoulos G et al. Widespread cytomegalovirus gastroenterocolitis in a patient with acquired immunodeficiency syndrome. Gastroenterology 1983; 85: 399–402.
128. Frank D, Raicht RF. Intestinal perforation associated with cytomegalovirus infection in patients with acquired immune deficiency syndrome. Am J Gastroenterol 1984; 79: 201–205.
129. Maartens G, Wood MJ. The clinical presentation and diagnosis of invasive fungal infections. J Antimicrob Chemother 1991; 28: 13–22.
130. Kane JG, Chretein JH, Garagusi VF. Diarrhoea caused by candida. Lancet 1976; i: 335–336.
131. Eras P, Goldstein MJ, Sherlock P. Candida infection of the gastrointestinal tract. Medicine (Baltimore) 1972; 51: 367–379.
132. Schlossberg D, Devig PM, Travers H, Kovalcik PJ, Mullen JT. Bowel perforation with candidiasis. JAMA 1977; 238: 2520–2521.
133. Walsh TJ, Merz WG. Pathologic features in the human alimentary tract associated with invasiveness of candida tropicalis. Am J Clin Path 1986; 85: 498–502.
134. Daar ES, Meyer RD. Bacterial and fungal infections. Med Clin N Amer 1992; 76: 173–203.
135. Lyon DT, Schubert TT, Mantia AG, Kaplan MH. Phycomycosis of the gastrointestinal tract. Am J Gastroenterol 1979; 72: 379–394.
136. Smith JMB. Mycoses of the alimentary tract. Gut 1969; 10: 1035–1040.
137. Calle S, Klatsky S. Intestinal phycomycosis (mucor- mycosis). Am J Clin Pathol 1966; 45: 264–272.
138. Schwarz J, Baum GL. Histoplasmosis. Arch Intern Med 1963; 111: 710–718.
139. Wheat LJ, Slama TG, Norton JA. Risk factors for disseminated or fatal histoplasmosis. Ann Intern Med 1982; 96: 159–163.
140. Johnson PC, Hamill RJ, Sarosi GA. Clinical Review: Progressive disseminated histoplasmosis in the AIDS patient. Semin Respir Infect 1989; 4: 139–146.
141. Scully RE, Galdabini JJ, McNeely BU. Case records of the Massachusetts General Hospital. Weekly clinicopathological exercises. N Engl J Med 1976; 295: 608–614.
142. Farthing MJG. New perspectives in giardiasis. J Med Microbiol 1992; 37: 1–2.
143. Ward HD, Lev BI, Kane AV, Keusch GT, Pereira MEA. Identification and characterization of taglin: a trypsin activated mannose-6-phosphate binding lectin from Giardia lamblia. Biochemistry 1987; 26: 8669–8675.
144. Brady PG, Wolfe JC. Waterborne giardiasis. Ann Intern Med 1974; 81: 498–499.
145. Gilman RH, Brown KH, Visvesvara GS et al. Epidemiology and serology of Giardia lamblia in a developing country: Bangladesh. Trans R Soc Trop Med Hyg 1985; 79: 469–473.
146. Islam A. Giardiasis in developing countries. In: Giardiasis, Ed. Meyer EA. Amsterdam: Elsevier, 1990: p 236.
147. Hartong WA, Gourley WK, Arvanitakis C. Giardiasis: clinical spectrum and functional-structural abnormalities of the small intestinal mucosa. Gastroenterology 1979; 77: 61–69.
148. Smith JW, Wolfe MS. Giardiasis. Annu Rev Med 1980; 31: 373–383.
149. Morecki R, Parker JG. Ultrastructural studies of the human Giardia lamblia and subjacent jejunal mucosa in a subject with steatorrhoea. Gastroenterology 1967; 52: 151–164.
150. Brandberg LL, Tankersley CB, Gottlieb S, Barancik M, Sartor VE. Histological demonstration of mucosal invasion by Giardia lamblia in man. Gastroenterology 1967; 52: 143–150.
151. Tandon BN, Puri BK, Gandhi PC, Tewari SG. Mucosal surface injury of jejunal mucosa in patients with giardiasis: An electron microscopic study. Indian J Med Res 1974; 62: 1838–1842.
152. Poley JR, Rosenfield S. Malabsorption in giardiasis: presence of a luminal barrier (Mucoid Pseudomembrane). J Pediat Gastroenterol Nutr 1982; 1: 63–80.
153. Dupont HL, Sullivan PS. Giardiasis: the clinical spectrum, diagnosis and therapy. Ped Infec Dis 1986; 5: S131–138.
154. Oberhuber G, Stolte M. Giardiasis; Analysis of histological changes in biopsy specimens of 80 patients. J Clin Pathol 1990; 43: 641–643.
155. Owen RL. The ultrastructural basis of giardia function. Trans Roy Soc Trop Med Hyg 1980; 74: 429–443.
156. Webster ADB. Giardiasis and immunodeficiency diseases. Trans Roy Soc Trop Med Hyg 1980; 74: 440–443.
157. Tzipori S. Cryptosporidiosis in animals and humans. Microbiol Rev 1983; 47: 84–96.
158. Angus KW. Cryptosporidiosis in man, domestic animals and birds: a review. J Roy Soc Med 1983; 76: 62–70.
159. Navin TR, Juranek DD. Cryptosporidiosis: Clinical, epidemiologic and parasitologic review. Rev Infec Dis 1984; 6: 313–327.
160. Crawford FG, Vermund SH. Human Cryptosporidiosis. CRC Crit Rev Microbiol 1988; 16: 113–159.
161. Current WL, Garcia LS. Cryptosporidiosis. Clin Microbiol Rev 1991; 4: 325–358.
162. Mathan M, Venkatesan S, George R, Mathew M, Mathan VI. Cryptosporidium and diarrhoea in southern Indian children. Lancet 1985; ii: 172–175.
163. Godwin TA. Cryptosporidiosis in the Acquired Immunodeficiency Syndrome. A study of 15 autopsy cases. Hum Pathol 1991; 22: 1215–1224.
164. Bird RG, Smith MD. Cryptosporidiosis in man. Parasite life cycle and fine structural pathology. J Path 1980; 132: 217–233.
165. Lefkowitch JH, Krumholz S, Feng-Chen KC, Griffin P, Despommier D, Brasitus TA. Cryptosporidiosis of the human small intestine. A light and electron microscopic study. Hum Pathol 1984; 15: 746–752.
166. Liebman WM, Thaler MM, DeLorimier A, Brandborg LL, Goodman J. Intractable diarrhea of infancy due to intestinal Coccidiosis. Gastroenterology 1980; 78: 579–584 .
167. Curry A, Turner AJ, Lucas S. Opportunistic protozoan infections in human immunodeficiency virus disease: Review highlighting diagnostic and therapeutic aspects. J Clin Pathol 1991; 44: 182–193.
168. Brandborg LL, Goldberg SB, Breidenbach WC. Human coccidiosis — A possible cause of malabsorption. The life cycle in small bowel mucosal biopsies as a diagnostic feature. N Engl J Med 1979; 283: 1306–1313.
169. Trier JS, Moxey PC, Schimmel EM, Robles E. Chronic intestinal coccidiosis in man: intestinal morphology and response to treatment. Gastroenterology 1974; 66: 923–935.
170. Canning EU, Hollister WS. Microsporidia of Mammals — Widespread pathogens or opportunistic curiosities? Parasitol Today 1987; 3: 267–273.
171. Weir GO, Sullivan JT. A fluorescence screening technique for microsporida in histological sections. Trans Am Microsc Soc 1989; 108: 208–210.

172. Orenstein JM, Chiang J, Steinberg W, Smith PD, Rotterdam H, Kotler DP. Intestinal microsporidiosis as a cause of diarrhea in human immunodeficiency virus infected patients: A report of 20 cases. Hum Pathol 1990; 21: 475–481.
173. Peacock CS, Blanshard C, Tovey DG, Ellis DS, Gazzard BG. Histological diagnosis of intestinal microsporidiosis in patients with AIDS. J Clin Pathol 1991; 44: 558–563.
174. Orenstein JM, Tenner M, Cali A, Kotler DP. A microsporidian previously undescribed in humans, infecting enterocytes and macrophages, and associated with diarrhea in an acquired immunodeficiency syndrome patient. Hum Pathol 1992; 23: 722–728.
175. Bunyaratvej S, Bunyawongwiroj P, Nitiyanant P. Human intestinal sarcosporidiosis: Report of six cases. Am J Trop Med Hyg 1982; 31: 36–41.
176. Canning EU. Protozoan infections. Trans Roy Soc Trop Med Hyg 1990; 84: 19–24.
177. Smith B. The myenteric plexus in chagas' disease. J Path Bact 1967; 94: 462–463.
178. Andrade ZA, Andrade SG. Chagas' disease (American trypanosomiasis). In: Pathology of protozoal and helminthic diseases. Ed. Marcial-Rojas RJ. New York: Krieger, 1975: p 69.
179. Banerjee M, Pal A, Ghosh S, Maitra TK. Small intestinal involvement in visceral Leishmaniasis. Am J Gastroenterol 1990; 85: 1433–1434.
180. Altes J, Salas A, Llompart A, Obrador A. Small intestinal involvement in visceral Leishmaniasis. Am J Gastroenterol 1991; 86: 1283.
181. Smith D, Gazzard B, Lindley RP, Darwish A, Reed C, Bryceson ADM, Evans DA. Visceral leishmaniasis (kala azar) in a patient with AIDS. AIDS 1989; 3: 41–43.
182. Peters LS, Fish D, Golden R, Evans DA, Bryceson ADM, Pinching AJ. Visceral Leishmaniasis in HIV infection and AIDS: Clinical features and response to therapy. Quart J Med 1990; 77: 1101–1111.
183. Rep BH. The topographic distribution of Necator americanus and Ancylostoma duodenale in the human intestine. Trop Geogr Med 1975; 27: 169–176.
184. Mahamood A. Blood loss caused by helminthic infections. Trans Roy Soc Trop Med Hyg 1966; 60: 766–769.
185. Sheehy TW, Meroney WH, Cox RS, Soler JE. Hookworm disease and malabsorption. Gastroenterology 1962; 42: 148–156.
186. Kalkofen UP. Intestinal trauma resulting from feeding activities of Ancylostoma caninum. Am J Trop Med Hyg 1974; 23: 1046–1053.
187. Chuttani HK, Puri SK, Misra RC. Small intestine in hookworm disease. Gastroenterology1967; 53: 381–388.
188. Banwell JG, Marsden PD, Blackman V, Leonard PJ, Hutt MSR. Hookworm infection and intestinal absorption amongst Africans in Uganda. Am J Trop Med Hyg 1967; 16: 304–308.
189. Tandon BN, Kohli RK, Saraya AK, Ramachandran K, Om Prakash. Role of parasites in the pathogenesis of intestinal malabsorption in hookworm disease. Gut 1969; 10: 293–298.
190. Marcial-Rojas RA. Strongyloidiasis. In: Pathology of protozoal and helminthic diseases. Ed. Marcial- Rojas R A. New York: Krieger, 1975: p 711.
191. Milder JE, Walzer PD, Kilgore G, Rutherford I, Klein M. Clinical features of Strongyloides stercoralis infection in an endemic area of the United States. Gastroenterology 1981; 80: 1481–1488.
192. Igra-Siegman Y, Kapila R, Sen P, Kaminski ZC, Louria DB. Syndrome of hyperinfection with Strongyloides stercoralis. Rev Infect Dis 1981; 3: 397–407.
193. De Paola D, Dias LB, Da Silva JR. Enteritis due to Strongyloides stercoralis. Am J Digest Dis 1962; 7: 1086–1098.
194. Genta RM, Miles P, Fields K. Opportunistic strongyloides stercoralis infection in lymphoma patients. Report of a case and review of the literature. Cancer 1989; 63: 1407–1411.
195. Boran LH, Keller KF, Justus DE, Collins JP. Strongyloidiasis in immunosuppressed patients. Am J Clin Pathol 1981; 76: 778–781
196. Meyers WM, Connor DH, Neafie RC. Strongyloidiasis. In: Pathology of tropical and extraordinary diseases. Eds. CH Binford, DH Connor. Armed Forces Institute of Pathology, Washington. 1976: vol 2: p 428.
197. Whalen GE, Rosenberg EB, Strickland GT, et al. Intestinal capillariasis. A new disease in man. Lancet 1969; i: 13–16.
198. Hoghooghi-Rad N, Maraghi S, Narenj-Zadeh A. Capillaria philippinensis infection in Khoozestan province, Iran: Case report. Am J Trop Med Hyg 1987; 37: 135–137.
199. Watten RH, Becksner WM, Cross JH, Gunning JJ, Jarimillo J. Clinical studies of Capillariasis philippinesis. Trans Roy Soc Trop Med Hyg 1972; 66: 828–834.
200. Fresh JW, Cross JH, Reyes V, Whalen GE, Uylangco CV, Dizon JJ. Necropsy findings in intestinal capillariasis. Am J Trop Med Hyg 1972; 21: 169–173.
201. Cross JH, Bhaibulaya M. Intestinal capillariasis in the Philippines and Thailand. In: Human Ecology and Infectious Diseases. Eds. Croll NA, Cross JA. Orlando: Academic Press, 1983: p 103.
202. Cross JH. Intestinal capillariasis. Clin Microbiol Rev 1992; 5: 120–129.
203. Sun SC, Cross JH, Berg HS, Kau SL, Singson CN, Banzon TC, Watten RH. Ultrastructural studies of intestinal capillariasis Capillaria philippinesis in human and gerbil hosts. Southeast Asian J Trop Med Public Health 1974; 5: 524–533.
204. Van Thiel PH. The present state of anisakiasis and its causative worms. Trop Geogr Med 1976; 28: 75–85.
205. Dooley JR, Neafie RC. Anisakiasis. In: Pathology of tropical and extraordinary diseases. Eds. Binford CH, Connor DH. Armed Forces Institute of Pathology, Washington. 1976: vol. 2: p 475.
206. Valdiserri RO. Intestinal anisakiasis. Report of a case and recovery of larvae from market fish. Am J Clin Pathol 1981; 76: 329–333.
207. Pawlowski ZS. Ascariasis: Host-pathogen biology. Rev Infect Dis 1982; 4: 806–814.
208. Walter N, Krishnaswami H. Granulomatous peritonis caused by Ascaris eggs: a report of three cases. J Trop Med Hyg 1989; 92: 17–19.
209. Arean VM, Crandall CA. Ascariasis. In: Pathology of Protozoal and Helminthic Diseases. Ed. Marcial-Rojas RA. New York: Krieger, 1975: p 769.
210. Graeff-Teixeira C, Camillo-Coura L, Lenzi HL. Histopathological criteria for the diagnosis of abdominal angiostrongyliasis. Parasitol Res 1991; 77: 606–611.
211. Graeff-Teixeira C, Camillo-Coura L, Lenzi HL. Clinical and epidemiological aspects of abdominal angiostrongyliasis in southern Brazil. Rev Inst Med Trop Sao Paulo 1991; 33: 373–378.
212. Hulbert TV, Larsen RA, Chandrasoma PT. Abdominal angiostrongyliasis mimicking acute appendicitis and Meckel's diverticulum: Report of a case in the United States and review. Clin Inf Dis 1992; 14: 836–840.
213. Sherif SM. Malabsorption and schistosomal involvement of jejunum. Br Med J 1970; 1: 671–672.
214. Witham RR, Mosser RS. An unusual presentation of schistosomiasis duodenitis. Gastroenterology 1979; 77: 1316–1318.
215. Thatcher BS, Fleischer D, Rankin GB, Petras R. Duodenal schistosomiasis diagnosed by endoscopic biopsy of an isolated polyp. Am J Gastroenterol 1984; 79: 927–929.
216. Faust EC, Beaver PC, Jung RC. In: Animal Agents and Vectors of Human Diseases. IV edition. Philadelphia: Lea and Febiger, 1975: p 187.
217. Sieracki JC, Fine G. Whipple's disease — observations on systemic involvement. II. Gross and histologic observations. Arch Pathol 1959; 67: 81–93.
218. Dobbins WO. Whipple's disease: An historical perspective. Quart J Med 1985; 221: 523–531.
219. Yardley JH, Hendrix TR. Combined electron and light microscopic studies in Whipple's disease: demonstration of 'bacillary bodies' in the intestine. Bull Johns Hopkins Hosp 1961; 109: 80–98.
220. Trier JS, Phelps PC, Eidelman S, Rubin CE. Whipple's disease: light and electron microscope correlation of jejunal mucosal histology with antibiotic treatment and clinical status. Gastroenterology 1965; 48: 684–707.
221. Denholm RB, Mills PR, More IAR. Electron microscopy in the long-term follow up of Whipple's disease. Am J Surg Pathol 1981; 5: 507–515.
222. Volpicelli NA, Salyer WR, Milligan FD, Bayless TM, Yardley JH. The endoscopic appearance of the duodenum in Whipple's disease. Johns Hopkins Med J 1976; 138: 19–23.

223. Mayberry J, Furness P, Austin M, Toghill T. Endoscopic appearances in Whipple's disease. J Roy Soc Med 1986; 79: 483–485.
224. Morningstar WA. Whipple's disease — an example of the value of electron microscopy in diagnosis, follow up and correlation of pathological process. Hum Pathol 1975; 6: 443–454.
225. Cho C, Linscheer WG, Hirschkorn MA, Ashutosh K. Sarcoidlike granulomas as an early manifestation of Whipple's disease. Gastroenterology 1984; 87: 941–947.
226. Ectors N, Geboes K, De Vos R et al. Whipple's disease: a histololgical, immunocytochemical and electronmicroscopic study of the immune response in the small intestinal mucosa. Histopatholgy 1992; 21: 1–12.
227. Dobbins WO III, Kawanishi H. Bacillary characteristics in Whipple's disease: an electron microscopic study. Gastroenterology 1980; 80: 1468–1475.
228. Relman DA, Schmidt TM, MacDermott RP, Falkow S. Identification of the uncultured bacillus of Whipple's disease. NEJM 1992; 327: 293–301.
229. Donaldson RM. Whipple's disease — rare malady with uncommon potential. N Eng J Med 1992; 327: 346–347.
230. Baker SJ, Mathan VI. Syndrome of tropical sprue in South India. Am J Clin Nutr 1968; 21: 984–993.
231. Baker SJ, Mathan VI. Tropical sprue in southern India. In: Tropical sprue and megaloblastic anaemia. The Wellcome Trust. Edinburgh: Churchill Livigstone, 1971: p 189.
232. Schenk EA, Samloff IM, Klipstein FA. Morphologic characteristics of jejunal biopsies in celiac disease and tropical sprue. Am J Pathol 1965; 47: 765–780.
233. Swanson VL, Thomassen RW. Pathology of the jejunal mucosa in tropical sprue. Am J Pathol 1965; 46: 511–551.
234. Mollin DL, Booth CC. Chronic tropical sprue in London. In: Tropical Sprue and Megaloblastic Anaemia. The Wellcome Trust. London: Churchill Livingstone, 1971: p 61.
235. Ross IN, Mathan I. Immunologic alterations in tropical sprue. Quart J Med 1981; 50: 435–449.
236. Marsh MN, Mathan M, Mathan VI. Studies of intestinal lymphoid tissue. VII. The secondary nature of lymphoid cell 'Activation' in the jejunal lesion of tropical sprue. Am J Pathol 1983; 112: 302–312.
237. Mathan M, Ponniah J, Mathan VI. Epithelial cell renewal and turnover and its relationship to morphologic abnormalities in the jejunal mucosa in tropical sprue. Dig Dis Sci 1986; 31: 586–592.
238. Mathan VI, Baker SJ. The epidemiology of tropical sprue. In: Tropical Sprue and Megaloblastic Anaemia. The Wellcome Trust. Edinburgh: Churchill Livingstone, 1971: p 159.

PART II

The small intestine: Crohn's disease

H. M. Gilmour

This chronic, granulomatous, inflammatory condition, which may affect any part of the gastrointestinal tract from mouth to anus, is named after the first author of a paper published in 1932.[1] A series of cases of an inflammatory disease affecting the terminal ileum was described, and the disease was called 'regional ileitis' by Crohn and his colleagues, Ginzburg and Oppenheimer. This was not the first description of the disease, which Shapiro in a historical review[2] suggests may have been as early as 1806, but Kyle[3] argues persuasively that the first description and recognition of this 'new disease' was by Dalziel in 1913.[4] Dalziel reported nine cases with disease affecting both small and large intestine. Not only did he operate on all nine cases but he also appreciated that there was a spectrum of severity within the disease which he named 'chronic interstitial enteritis.' Ginzburg has indicated that while Crohn publicized the disease he, Ginzburg, had in fact recognized the disease in the 1920s.[5] Although on several counts the eponymous title is perhaps not deserved, there seems little chance of the disease, which is now named after Crohn, being re-christened Dalziel's disease.

Despite Dalziel's description of colonic involvement in 1913, it was not until 1959 when Brooke[6] and Morson and Lockhart-Mummery[7] distinguished colonic Crohn's disease from ulcerative colitis clinically and pathologically, and Marshak and colleagues described the radiological features,[8] that it was finally accepted that Crohn's colitis existed. Follow-up papers from both groups of authors in the early 1960s further confirmed and defined the features of colonic disease.[9–11] It is now recognized that Crohn's disease may affect any part of the gastrointestinal tract, including several areas at any one time, and may be associated with effects in organs and tissues outside the gut.

EPIDEMIOLOGY

The disease is more common in North America and northern Europe, possibly emerging in southern Europe, and has a low incidence elsewhere in the world, although it is difficult to be sure in developing countries, where information is difficult to come by. There is a range in incidence within the United Kingdom from 1–11.6 cases/10^5/year with a prevalence of 9–147 cases/10^5.[12,13] There is some north to south bias, and it appears to be more common in urban than country dwellers. There are differences even in areas where the disease is prevalent although comparisons are difficult due to differences in case definition, case ascertainment and study periods. Some of these difficulties should be solved by the prospective European Collaborative Study on the Epidemiology of IBD, which involves defined populations in 20 countries and will be completed by the end of 1993. However, with these provisos, there has been a six fold increase in incidence in Copenhagen between 1962–87,[14] a steady increase in northeast Scotland over a similar period,[13] a relatively constant incidence of about six cases/10^5/year in Sweden[15,16] and a suggestion of a recent decline in New York.[17] In the Swedish reports of an at-risk cohort, the increase is seen in those born in the first six months of the years 1945–54 but this pattern has not been confirmed in other countries. The sex incidence shows a male to female ratio of 1:1.1–1.5, being higher in the Scottish series.[13] Although said to be uncommon in children and the elderly, this may not be the case.[18,19] Kyle reported an increased incidence and younger age of onset, with the incidence in teenagers nearly doubling and colorectal disease increasing.[13] In Denmark, for ages 15–19 years, the incidence was 11 cases/10^5/year in girls and six cases/10^5/year in boys.[14] About 16% of patients with Crohn's disease (range 7–26%) are over 60 years of age and in this age group females outnumber males, and colonic disease, particularly left-sided in women, is more frequent.[19] There also seems to be a real increase in the elderly which is not just due to better diagnostic accuracy. Migrant communities in the UK appear to be prone to an increasing incidence of Crohn's disease, with Asians in Leicester showing an increase from 1.2 to 3.1 cases/10^5/year between the 1970s and 1980s and Bangladeshis in London showing a similar doubling in incidence.[20,21] The concomitant drop in cases of abdominal tuberculosis is not the explanation for this change.

AETIOLOGY

Despite all that has been written about possible causes of the disease and associated environmental, dietary and genetic factors, there is, as yet, no unified concept of aetiology and pathogenesis.[22] Microbiological studies continue to raise hopes of finding a possible causative organism but Pounder and colleagues have suggested that a vascular lesion initiated by endothelial cell damage and leading to multiple infarcts is a likely mechanism for many of the features seen in Crohn's disease.[23] This has at least stimulated some novel thinking and opened new avenues for exploration.

Diet

In many alimentary diseases the possibility of an aetiological dietary factor warrants consideration. Infant feeding habits could be important, and although an association with shorter periods of breast feeding has been found in Sweden, this may be due to factors such as postnatal infection, which may also have a role in pathogenesis.[24] 'Agents' such as toothpaste, cornflakes, sugar and food additives have been suggested to be, if not causative, associated with an adverse effect on the disease, but such studies are fraught with difficulties. Most are retrospective, and the problems are well summarized by Urban[25] commenting on a Swedish survey on the consumption of sugar by patients with inflammatory bowel disease. There is little evidence that food allergy or intolerance plays a major role either in the initiation of the disease process or in its continuing evolution.[26] However, Levine in a recent review expresses support for the concept of an exogenous factor such as silicates playing a role in the aetiology of Crohn's disease.[27]

Smoking

Meta-analysis of the results from a number of studies has shown a direct association between Crohn's disease and smoking and indicated it to be the single most important variable with a clearly defined risk relationship to inflammatory bowel disease.[28] One such study also included the relationship to the use of oral contraceptives but was unable to demonstrate any significant association,[29] although other studies have shown a slight risk with their use. Wakefield has attempted to support the concept of a vascular pathogenesis by relating possible vascular mechanisms to both smoking and oral contraceptive use.[30] In a Swedish study, those who smoked more than 10 cigarettes a day were more likely to require surgery and had more abscesses and fistulae.[31] It will be of interest to see if changes in incidence and pattern of disease will follow alterations in smoking habits and studies are beginning to look at the influence of passive smoking in childhood. Overall, it appears that smoking habits may influence the presentation and form of inflammatory bowel disease in susceptible individuals.[32]

Genetic

A wide range of genetic factors seem to influence an individual's liability to develop Crohn's disease. Many family studies have shown an increased risk of inflammatory bowel disease in relatives of patients, particularly siblings. While studies are seldom directly comparable, pooling of results gives an idea of the overall position.[33] The relatively reduced prevalence in the children of patients could be due to the lag time before evidence of disease develops or to a parent's reduced fertility as a result of disease or its treatment, rather than to genetic effects. Spouses are rarely affected but familial cases sometimes develop disease at an earlier age. There seems to be an association between psoriasis and Crohn's disease and Crohn's disease is more common than expected in patients with ankylosing spondylitis, and vice versa, suggesting a genetic link, but so far there has been no identification of specific HLA markers, although Biemond et al showed a relative risk of 1.25 for Crohn's disease in those with HLA-A2.[34] Various but inconsistent HLA Dr associations have been described although a positive association with Dr4 has been reported in several studies from Japan and some HLA types have been associated with certain features of the disease, including granuloma formation. Altered frequency distribution of IgG markers[35] and an excess of certain phenotypes for the C3 component of complement[36] have been described in Crohn's disease cases. It is difficult to separate the effects of possible recessive genes from environmental factors and while the evidence supports a genetic susceptibility, it has not been possible to demonstrate a specific genetic marker.

Infection

There has been a strong suspicion that an infectious agent is the cause of Crohn's disease, but there have been considerable difficulties in the identification and culture of a putative organism and demonstration of its pathological effect. The latent period, which could be lengthy, between infection and the development of symptoms may mean that the organism is no longer present or has been altered by the host defence mechanisms so that it is unable to behave 'normally' when studied. Many papers were published in the 1970s on transmissible agents from Crohn's tissue and the tissue response produced in experimental animals, but no consistent results emerged.[37] The demonstration that organisms such as *Clostridium difficile*, *Camplyobacter jejuni* and *Helicobacter pylori* could cause gastrointestinal disease helped fuel a resurgence of interest in the search for an infective aetiology of inflammatory bowel disease. A further stimulus has been the widespread introduction of molecular biology techniques such as the polymerase chain reaction (PCR). However the extreme sensitivity of this technique may lead to problems in the interpretation of results. Evidence for a viral aetiology is unconvincing and Yoshimura et al failed to demonstrate any evidence of virus particles in material from 95 cases of Crohn's disease.[38] Wakefield et al demonstrated measles virus RNA utilizing an in situ hybridization technique in an attempt to find an aetiology for the early vascular changes which they propose as a pathogenic mechanism for Crohn's disease.[39] Evidence has been found of a humoral response to a number of enteric organisms but this is likely to represent secondary invasion following mucosal damage.[40,41] Organisms which may lead to a granulomatous response are obvious candidates but a study of *Yersinia enterocolitica* has shown no evidence of a relationship with Crohn's disease[42] and the same can be said for *Campylobacter jejuni*.[43] A recent study from the UK using PCR and serology has failed to find evidence to support Chlamydia as a cause.[44] Because of a number of factors, including the resemblance of the tissue reaction in Crohn's disease to tuberculosis, mycobacteria have been sought in Crohn's disease patients. Chiodini et al identified a mycobacterium in three patients with Crohn's disease; the organism produced a granulomatous reaction in the liver, spleen and lymph nodes in mice and ileitis in neonatal goats.[45] This organism resembles *Mycobacterium paratuberculosis*, which causes Johne's disease, a chronic granulomatous ileitis in ruminants, and a number of investigations have centred on this and related mycobacteria. Results have been confusing and inconclusive and are summarized in an editorial by Ciclitira who concludes that proof of a definitive role for mycobacteria in Crohn's disease is still awaited.[46] This is also the case for any other organism studied so far and suggests a cautious approach to the idea that there is a single causative organism of Crohn's disease.

Immune mechanisms and inflammatory responses

The study of the complex interrelationship between the immune system, with its production of modulators of the inflammatory response, and the resulting inflammatory reaction poses innumerable problems which are illustrated only too well in the confusing results from many of the reported studies. These include differences in methodology, particularly when attempting to compare results, the choice of whether to look at circulating or tissue-based cells, the separation of cause and effect and primary and secondary responses and the inherent complexity when many of the responses are part of cascade reactions. It is therefore not surprising that in this area conflicting results abound but it is gratifying that some progress has been made. A number of novel ideas regarding therapeutic options have been formulated and are starting to be put into practice.

The question of what part autoimmune mechanisms play is one that is difficult to answer in a chronic condition such as Crohn's disease. A number of autoantibodies have been identified in the serum of Crohn's disease patients, including antibodies directed against cytoskeleton components.[47] Anti-neutrophil cytoplasmic antibodies have been found in many patients with ulcerative colitis but in very few with Crohn's and, perhaps disappointingly for supporters of a vascular pathogenesis, anti-endothelial cell antibodies are present in only 15% of Crohn's disease cases compared to 53% in ulcerative colitis. However many of these are likely to be epiphenomena, and it seems there is more evidence for an element of autosensitization in ulcerative colitis.[48]

Progress depends on an understanding of the normal immune function of the GI tract and while there may be disagreement over details regarding the characterization of certain immune cells and their distribution, there is little argument that there is an exaggeration of the normal response.[49] This involves activation of most competent immune cells in active disease including intraepithelial T lymphocytes, lamina propria and circulating B and T lymphocytes, macrophages and natural killer cells. Mucosal epithelial cells which can express MHC class II molecules may act as antigen presenting cells and similar molecules have also been demonstrated on glial cells in the enteric neural plexuses in Crohn's disease.[50] Many studies have attempted to categorize the alterations in the distribution of various immunologically competent cells and their relation to disease activity, but it is proving difficult to achieve concordant results. However particular interest has centred on the products resulting from this activation, which include a variety of cytokines and related products. In order to implicate any of these agents in Crohn's disease it is necessary to show (i) increased production in diseased tissue (ii) the effects of the mediator resemble the pathological lesion, and (iii) inhibitors are effective in altering the response.

The interleukins and their receptors have a variety of pro-inflammatory actions and are mainly derived from activated mononuclear cells but there is a lack of consistency in many of the studies. Several growth factors are involved including transforming growth factor beta (TGF β) which is a chemoattractant, promotes the synthesis and expression of adhesion molecules and stimulates the release of other cytokines. When used to stimulate fibroblasts from Crohn's disease in vitro, more type III collagen was produced from cells derived from strictured areas than from non-strictured or normal areas. This suggests that the response to locally produced growth factors may vary.[51] Other mediators may be released by inflammatory cells and these include oxygen radicals or reactive oxygen metabolites (ROM), platelet-activating factor and other lipid derivatives from eicosanoids through the arachidonic acid pathway. These latter mediators include thromboxanes, prostaglandins and leucotrienes. ROM, probably derived from leucocyte phagocytes, are increased in active inflammatory bowel disease and have been implicated in ischaemia and reperfusion injury. It is known that hydrogen peroxide can cause mucosal damage and aminosalicylates can scavenge ROM in vitro, perhaps explaining some of their therapeutic effect.[52] Thromboxanes derived from platelets, which are increased in active Crohn's, damaged endothelial cells, neutrophils or mononuclear cells have both direct and indirect pro-inflammatory effects, probably stimulated by a variety of cytokines.[53] Corticosteroids and aminosalicylates inhibit thromboxane synthesis but perhaps more selective inhibitors may prove useful in reducing mucosal inflammation in inflammatory bowel disease. Leukotriene B4, which may be an important attractant and activator of neutrophils, is increased in Crohn's colitis.[54] While abnormalities of neutrophil function have been reported, including alterations in post-phagocytic metabolic activity, it is uncertain whether this reflects secondary effects or an intrinsic defect. The role of adhesion molecules is attracting growing interest both in their involvement in the activation of lymphoid cells and also in the relationship between endothelial cells and inflammatory cells. Endothelial leucocyte adhesion molecule-1 (ELAM-1) plays a significant role in the latter reaction and its expression in mucosal vascular endothelium is increased in the colon of patients with active inflammatory bowel disease.[55] There may well be active synthesis and secretion of ELAM-1 into the vascular lumen in active inflammation.[56]

Many studies, with varying degrees of contradiction, have sought to identify and quantify the populations of immunoglobulin-bearing cells in the lamina propria of the gut in inflammatory bowel disease. There seems to be a disproportionate increase in cells bearing IgG and a reduction in IgA secretion has been found in apparently uninvolved jejunum, suggesting a possible primary defect in local immunity.[57] The study of immune complexes in relation to local disease of the gut and extra-intestinal complications is particularly difficult, and conflicting results make interpretation of their role problematical. The production of a B-cell lymphoma or lymphoid hyperplasia in 'nude' mice by the injection of Crohn's tissue has led to speculation regarding both immune mechanisms and aetiological agents. The demonstration of reactivity between the serum of patients with Crohn's disease and cells from the lymphoma or hyperplastic nodes suggested antigenic proteins in Crohn's tissue recognized in this murine model. However this seroreactivity may not be specific and further work in this area continues.[58–60]

In any granulomatous condition the study of macrophage function[61] is relevant and it is possible to produce a monocytopoietic proliferative activity index, which is 1.4 in Crohn's disease. This compares with an index of 3.5 in active tuberculosis and 1.1 in sarcoidosis, suggesting that Crohn's disease is a low turnover granulomatous condition more analogous to sarcoid. No major defect has been described in macrophage function, but circulating monocytes are functionally more active and release of cytokines and other inflammatory mediators may promote local tissue damage. Stamp, using in situ hybridization, has shown strong staining for lysozyme in granulomas and macrophages in the mucosa in Crohn's disease.[62] It is suggested that such staining of aggregates of mucosal macrophages, even without macroscopic disease, should suggest Crohn's disease.

Studies in Crohn's disease patients will continue to be bedevilled by the multiplicity of secondary effects on the system and the variations occurring in different stages of disease activity.

Mucosal defects

It has been suggested that mucosal abnormalities leading to increased permeation of antigens across the mucosa might potentiate a state of chronic inflammation. Although altered permeability has been demonstrated in other diseases such as coeliac disease, it has been shown in both diseased and apparently normal bowel in patients with Crohn's disease.[63] This suggests a widespread defect but does not prove a primary role in pathogenesis. A leaking mucosa, apart from allowing ingress of bacterial antigens, might also be responsible for loss of protein into the gut, leading to a protein-losing enteropathy. Mucus abnormalities have been sought in Crohn's disease and it was postulated that the increased activity of bacterial enzymes responsible for mucus degradation in the stool might lead to mucosal damage by reducing the amount of mucus in the colon. However, studies of sulphatase[64] in the stools of patients with Crohn's disease have not shown significant differences from normal, and there does not appear to be any correlation with disease activity suggesting that defective synthesis of mucin may be more important than increased breakdown. Excretion of alpha-1-antitrypsin by the gut correlates well with the presently accepted indices of Crohn's disease activity.[65] It is normally found in a deglycosylated form but in some patients with active Crohn's more remains glycosylated due to a decrease in glycosidase activity in the stool, possibly due to changes in gut flora.[66]

O'Morain et al[67] have reported an increase in vasoactive intestinal polypeptide (VIP) throughout the mucosa of the gastrointestinal tract in Crohn's disease, despite normal serum levels, and the recognition of a close relationship between the neuroendocrine system and modulation of inflammation in the gut by neuropeptides should lead to a greater interest in 'gut-brain' interactions.[68] Hyaluronic acid production from apparently normal bowel is increased in active disease and this, together with the demonstration of a diffuse defect in colonic microanatomy, widespread permeability defects and the role of neuropeptides, points to a more extensive abnormality in Crohn's disease than is evident from the macroscopic appearances.

PATHOLOGY

Sites of disease

Since the recognition of colonic Crohn's disease in the 1960s, a number of reported studies from both high and low incidence areas have shown that the small intestine is involved in 30–35% of cases, the colon alone in 25–35% and both these sites in 30–50% of cases.[69] Colonic involvement tends to be reported less in low incidence areas, although in Stockholm, which has a high incidence, only 17% of cases involved the colon, and this has changed little over the years studied. In several other countries, however, there has been a gradual increase in the detection of colonic disease, which is commonly found in the elderly.[19] Significant gastroduodenal involvement occurs in only some 5% of patients with Crohn's disease elsewhere in the gut[70] but careful radiological and endoscopic[71] examination has shown that about half of all patients have minor mucosal abnormalities in the stomach or duodenum (see Ch. 25).

Macroscopic features

Although the pathology of Crohn's disease is basically the same whatever area of the gastrointestinal tract is involved, classical descriptions of its gross appearances commonly refer to the small intestine. They combine observations made at laparotomy, after resection, and abnormalities detected by radiology. Although endoscopic

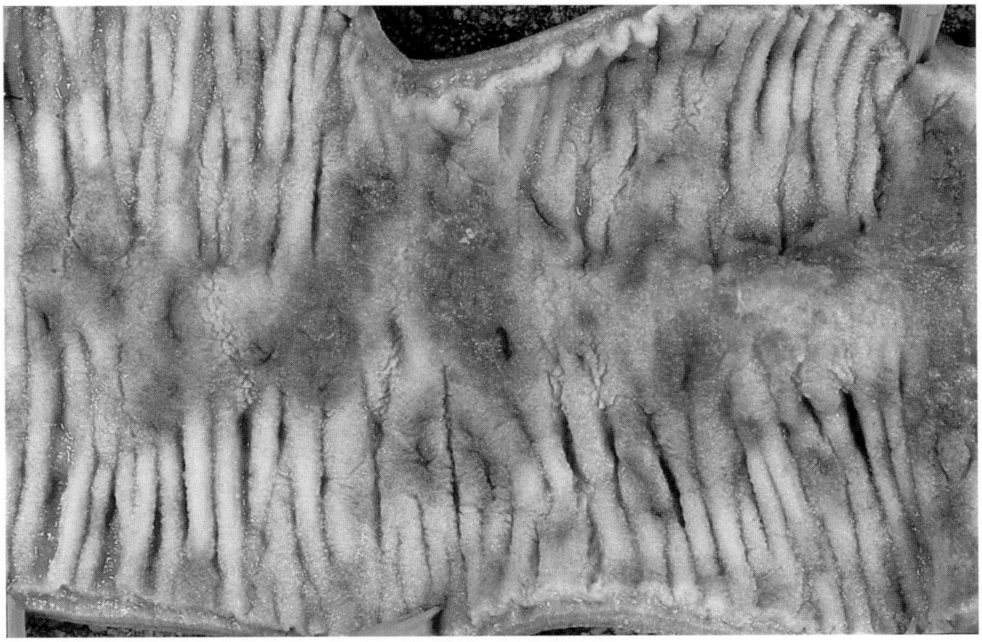

Fig. 26.26 Crohn's disease. Several discrete, irregular ulcers are present in the ileal mucosa.

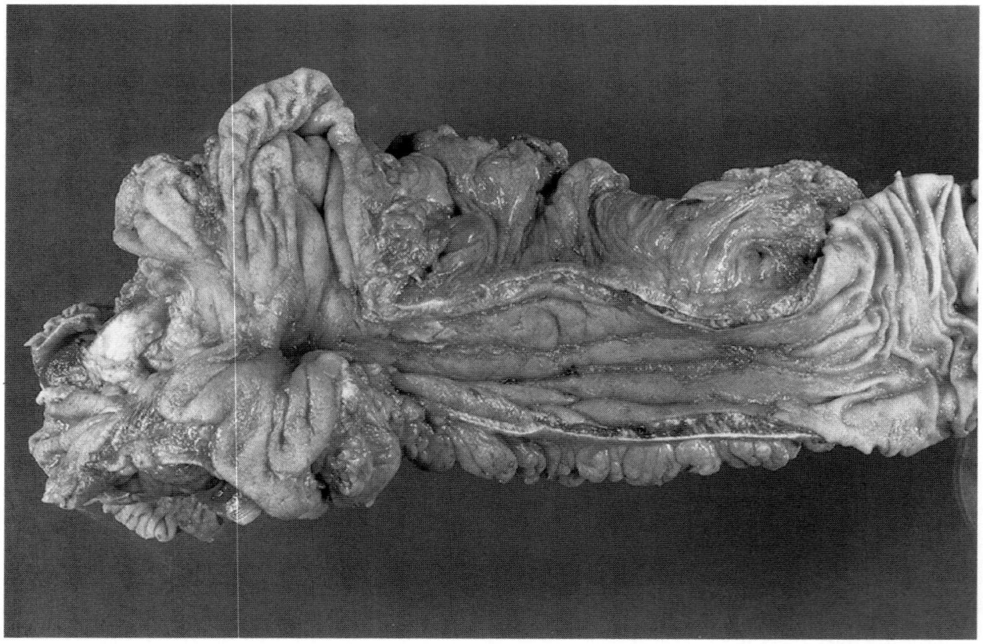

Fig. 26.27 Crohn's disease. Longitudinal linear ulcers in the terminal ileum.

examination and biopsy of the proximal small bowel may have a role in the detection of early proximal disease, it has a lesser role in the investigation of ileal disease.[71]

It is difficult to better Dalziel's original description of an affected segment of intestine: 'The affected bowel gives the consistence and smoothness of an eel in a state of rigor mortis, and the glands, though enlarged, are evidently not caseous.'[4] The affected bowel has also been likened to a hosepipe due to its rigid unyielding consistency, the result of marked mural thickening. The luminal surface may show a variety of patterns, the classical being the so-called 'cobblestone' appearance produced by a combination of submucosal oedema and inflammation, delineated by narrow linear ulcers. This pattern, however, is seldom seen in isolation and is usually combined with areas of stricture and ulceration of a more irregular, serpiginous character (Fig. 26.26). The ulceration may be longitudinal (Fig. 26.27) and may involve a considerable length of bowel in linear fashion, often on the mesenteric side, and this is a pattern commonly seen in Japan.[72] A characteristic feature of Crohn's involvement of the gastrointestinal tract is the presence of 'skip' lesions, where apparently isolated segments of disease are separated by macroscopically normal intestine. The ulcers commonly have a fissuring character (Fig. 26.28), are often particularly well visualized by barium examination, and are probably the

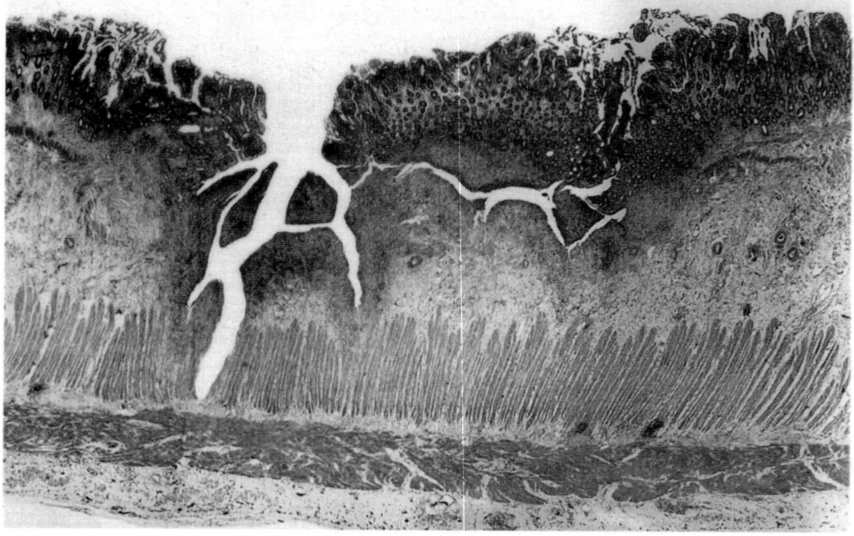

Fig. 26.28 Crohn's disease. Complex fissuring ulcer which penetrates to the level of the myenteric nerve plexus. (H&E, ×8) (Reproduced with permission from Shearman & Finlayson)[102]

forerunners of the fistulae which may form between adjacent loops of bowel, between the bowel and other intra-abdominal organs, or between bowel and skin. Fissuring ulcers penetrating the complete thickness of the bowel wall, aided by serosal inflammation which is common in Crohn's disease, lead to the formation of adhesions and fistulae. Sheehan identified 'fat wrapping' around affected segments of bowel as a useful diagnostic feature indicative of transmural involvement which correlated with other connective tissue changes.[73] It was not, however, a marker of disease extent and while specific for Crohn's in small bowel resections it would not help in the diagnosis of early superficial mucosal disease which may present a problem at laparotomy.[74] Mucosal polyps are rarely seen in Crohn's disease of the small intestine but when present are the result of inflammation,[75] regeneration and possible lymphoid hyperplasia, but the identification of a polypoid lesion within the small bowel should also raise the possibility of malignant change.

A not uncommon feature of ileal Crohn's disease as indicated by Dalziel is lymphadenopathy of the regional ileocolic lymph nodes, which can be markedly enlarged but seldom have the appearance of the matted, caseous nodes seen in tuberculosis or the firm, indurated nodes of lymphoma.

Microscopic features

A major feature of the disease is the transmural nature of the inflammatory infiltrate. This is usually evident from the focal lymphocytic aggregates which are seen in all layers of the intestinal wall, although they tend to be particularly numerous in the subserosal fat and submucosa. The submucosa usually appears oedematous (Fig. 26.29) and in addition to the lymphoid aggregates there is commonly dilatation and ectasia of lymphatics and the blood vessels. Vascular changes have been noted as part of the spectrum of histological changes in Crohn's disease for many years[76] but Pounder et al have proposed that vascular changes play a major role in the pathogenesis of Crohn's disease and have described a vasculitis associated with the development of granulomas.[23,77]

Proliferation of fibrous tissue may be present in areas of stricturing. This is usually maximal in the submucosa but can impinge on the muscularis propria and may also affect the subserosal adipose tissue. The muscularis mucosae can be destroyed but may show marked hyperplasia or fusion with the muscularis propria, resulting in obliteration of the submucosa. This latter change probably occurs in areas of previous ulceration (Fig. 26.29). The thickened muscularis mucosae may comprise 10% of the thickness of the bowel wall in areas of strictures and contribute to their causation.[78] Neural hyperplasia may affect the myenteric plexus but can also be seen to a striking degree in the submucosa of a small number of cases, where it produces a ramification of nerve fibres associated with fibrosis. Axonal degeneration as shown by electron microscopy has been claimed as a useful diagnostic feature of Crohn's disease[79] but a further study suggests this is also seen in ulcerative colitis and controls and is not specific for Crohn's.[80] However, Strobach, utilizing immunohistochemistry, has shown intense staining of small mucosal nerve fibres for anti-nerve growth factor receptor in Crohn's and suggested this may be of diagnostic value in mucosal biopsies.[81]

The mucosa may show considerable variation in the degree and extent of features including inflammatory cell infiltration, villous abnormalities, pyloric metaplasia of the crypts of Lieberkuhn and ulceration (Fig. 26.30). Early changes described in Crohn's disease include alterations

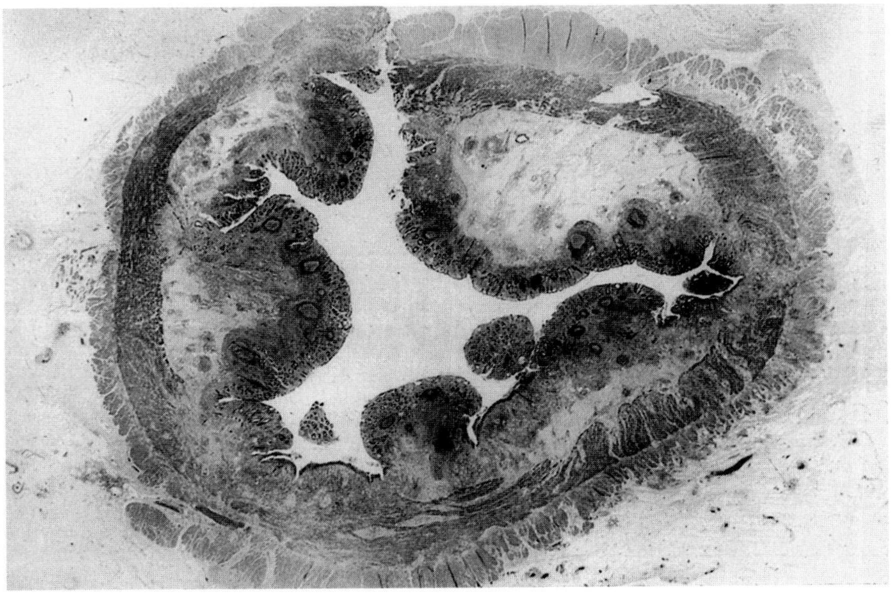

Fig. 26.29 Crohn's disease. Cross-section of bowel showing submucosal oedema, and focal ulcers which extend down to the muscularis propria. (H&E, ×4)

in villous morphology, goblet-cell hyperplasia, increased mucus secretion as demonstrated by scanning electron microscopy[82] and focal necrosis of mucosal epithelium as shown by both light and electron microscopy.[83] Aphthous ulceration remains the most readily identifiable early change of Crohn's disease although unfortunately this cannot by itself be regarded as diagnostic. This erosive or ulcerating lesion is often related to a mucosal or submucosal lymphoid aggregate. There is loss of epithelium in the base of a crypt, acute inflammatory exudate within the crypt lumen and macrophage accumulation in the exposed lamina propria or submucosa (Fig. 26.31). Sanky et al describe very early damage to mucosal capillaries leading to intramucosal haemorrhage which it is suggested leads to the development of aphthoid ulcers.[84] It is presumably by extension and expansion of these early ulcerating lesions that the more extensive fissures and fistulae develop. Granulomas formed by aggregation of macrophages, often with giant cells, and associated with small numbers of lymphocytes and plasma cells, are a characteristic feature of Crohn's disease (Fig. 26.32). Unfortunately, they can only be found in about two-thirds of cases but nevertheless are an important diagnostic feature of the disease. Granulomas may be seen throughout the bowel wall and within lymph nodes, although lymphadenopathy can occur in the absence of granulomas as a result of oedema, congestion and lymphoid hyperplasia.

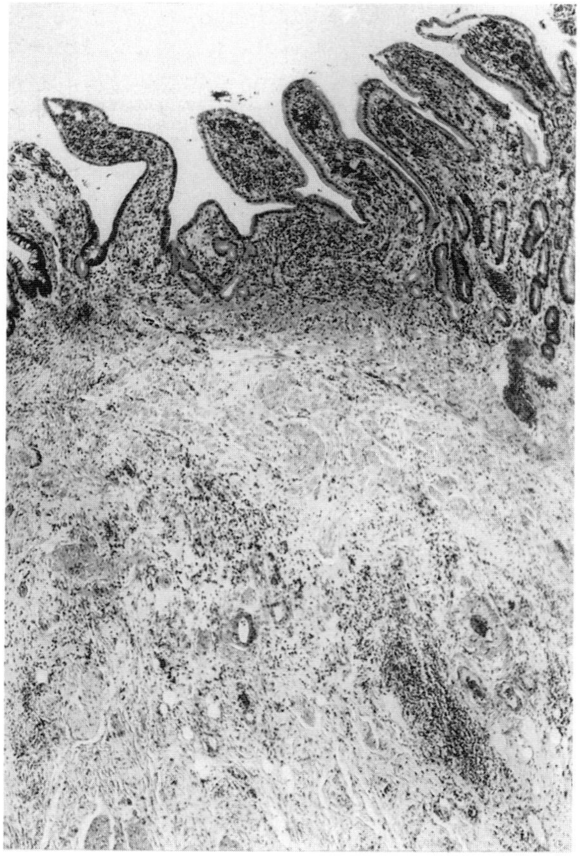

Fig. 26.30 Crohn's disease. The villi are abnormal with atrophy of crypts, focal pyloric metaplasia, increased numbers of mononuclear cells and submucosal fibrosis. (H&E, ×35)

Complications

Small bowel obstruction is seldom complete and usually takes the form of episodes of subacute intestinal obstruction. Marshak amusingly describes his early worries about causing complete intestinal obstruction by impaction of barium in patients with small bowel Crohn's disease,[85] but

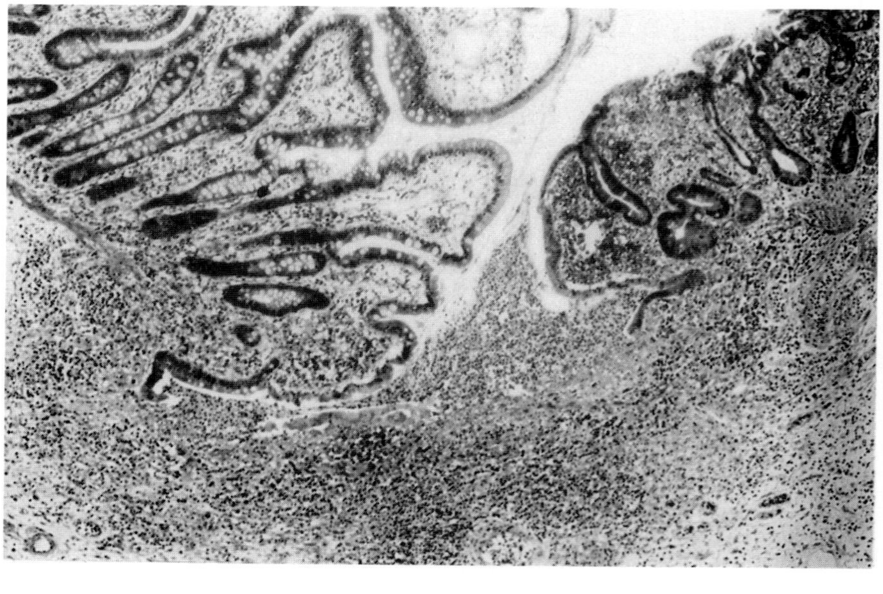

Fig. 26.31 Aphthous ulcer in Crohn's disease. Loss of epithelium overlying an atrophic lymphoid aggregate with inflammatory exudate in the distended crypt. (H&E, ×50)

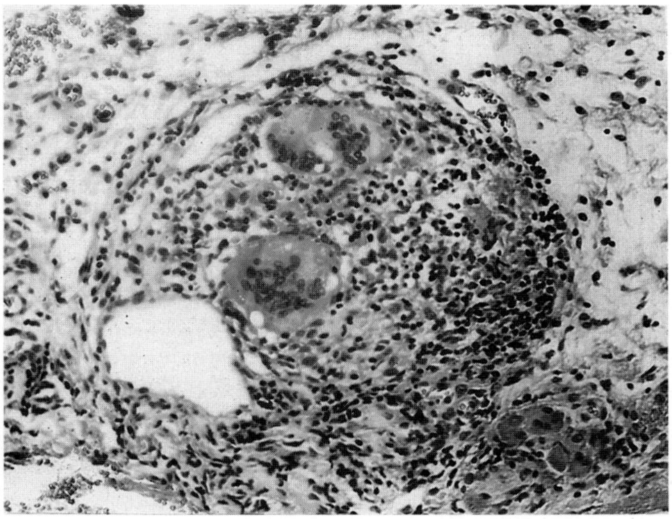

Fig. 26.32 Crohn's disease. Submucosal granuloma composed of giant cells, macrophages and lymphocytes in relation to vessels and to a small lymphatic. (H&E, ×157)

experience showed that it was virtually impossible to produce complete obstruction by this means. Subacute obstruction is produced by active disease causing transmural, and particularly submucosal, thickening but is likely to be more persistent and troublesome where fibrous strictures form. Obstructive symptoms are one indication for surgical intervention.

Malabsorption may result from extensive, terminal ileal disease with production of a megaloblastic anaemia due to reduced absorption of vitamin B12. This problem may also follow surgical resection of ileal Crohn's disease. Terminal ileal disease may interfere with the enterohepatic circulation of bile salts, which may further exacerbate symptoms of diarrhoea and predispose to gallstones.[86] Fistulae may cause malabsorption due to re-routing of bowel content, and bacterial colonization of the small bowel may compound the problem. Ulceration and, as discussed earlier, a 'leaky' mucosal epithelium, may be responsible for a protein-losing enteropathy.

Perforation of the bowel is uncommon in Crohn's disease, and, while becoming increasingly recognized as a complication of toxic dilatation in colonic disease, free perforation is probably still commoner in the small bowel. Although jejunal perforation occurring early in the course of the disease was found in a significant number of cases in one series,[87] most perforations occur in the ileum. It is uncertain what predisposes to free perforation in small intestinal Crohn's disease and although active fissuring ulceration early in the disease, before adhesions and fibrosis have formed, may be a precipitating factor, Tonelli related mural thickening to perforation in the ileum.[88]

Direct extension of inflammation to adjacent organs may occur, as in the development of salpingitis in female patients with terminal ileal disease. The inflammatory reaction is usually non-specific but in a few cases granulomas can be identified in the wall of the Fallopian tube. The ureters may also be involved by this mechanism. Abscesses may form and Ribeiro reported 129 abscesses in 610 cases of small bowel Crohn's from 1960–84.[89] Of these 109 were intraabdominal while 20 were retroperitoneal, nearly all of the latter occurring in males. The high incidence in this series may reflect the referral nature of many of the cases. Recurrence of disease following surgical treatment is common although it is debatable whether this is truly recurrence since it is more likely to reflect residual disease not clinically apparent at the time of treatment. Intraoperative frozen sections of resection margins, not unexpectedly, does not reduce the likelihood of recurrence.[90] There are few reliable pathological indicators of recurrence but this is more likely after ileocolic resection, particularly if a long segment is involved. Granulomas are not related to recurrence rates.[91] Following ileal resection recurrence usually occurs on the proximal side of the anastomosis and early changes may be seen at endoscopy within a short time of surgery.[92] These changes seem to be related to the faecal stream only appearing after this is restored following diversion.[93] An increased risk of malignancy in both small and large intestine is recognized in Crohn's disease and risk factors, dysplasia and detection are discussed in Chapter 27.

DIFFERENTIAL DIAGNOSIS

When gastrointestinal disease presents acutely, Crohn's disease will seldom be responsible, but when patients present with chronic symptoms Crohn's disease merits serious consideration in the differential diagnosis. Both Dalziel and Crohn were at pains to point out the distinction between Crohn's disease and gastrointestinal tuberculosis, and this remains an important distinction, particularly in patients from areas where abdominal tuberculosis is common. Primary alimentary tuberculosis seldom produces a major lesion within the bowel wall, the predominant feature being prominent mesenteric lymphadenopathy with caseation. Post-primary gastrointestinal tuberculosis may show a hyperplastic pattern with scarring and fibrosis usually of the caecum, with or without significant lymphadenopathy, or small bowel ulceration which tends to be circumferential or transverse.[94] The classic feature of the tuberculous granuloma is central caseous necrosis, but this may not be a prominent feature and small foci of central necrosis can be seen in occasional granulomas in Crohn's disease. Identification of tubercle bacilli will distinguish the two conditions, but organisms are commonly few in number in post-primary gastrointestinal tuberculosis and the appropriate specimen may not have been sent for culture at the time of resection. A history of contact with tuberculosis or evidence of pulmonary tuberculosis is circumstantial evidence in favour of this diagnosis, and there are a number of pathological features which can be useful in distinguishing Crohn's disease from tuberculosis.[94] Other organisms which have been considered as possible aetiological agents of Crohn's disease, such as *Yersinia enterocolitica*, may cause lesions in the ileocaecal region which can mimic Crohn's disease. Positive yersinia serology with a rising antibody titre can be used as evidence of infection with this organism, and if resection is carried out the typical features of necrotizing granulomatous inflammation within lymphoid tissue in the intestinal wall and mesenteric lymph nodes should suggest this diagnosis.[95]

Neoplasia within the small bowel is rare, but non-Hodgkin's lymphoma of the small intestine may present with multifocal involvement including strictures and ulceration. This pattern may be seen in the condition first described as malignant histiocytosis of the intestine[96] although now recognized as a T cell lymphoma.[97,98] This can be a difficult diagnosis to make and, like Crohn's disease, enters the differential diagnosis of the condition known by a variety of names including non-specific jejunoileitis, non-specific small bowel ulceration or idiopathic chronic ulcerative enteritis,[99,100] which, as the name suggests, is characterized by ulceration within the small intestine. The aetiology of this condition is unknown and it is in essence a diagnosis of exclusion. It is possible that some of these cases represent an atypical form of Crohn's disease but there is also an association in some series with lymphoma and/or coeliac disease. Strictures can be seen following chronic ischaemia and radiation enteritis and may be associated with drugs such as NSAIDs[101,102] but the history should be helpful in these cases. However, the finding of a strictured segment in the distal small bowel of a young patient in North America or northern Europe is much more likely to be due to Crohn's disease than any of the conditions discussed above.

REFERENCES

1. Crohn BB, Ginzburg L, Oppenheimer GD. Regional ileitis: a pathologic and clinical entity. J Am Med Assoc 1932; 99: 1323–1329.
2. Shapiro R. Regional ileitis: a summary of the literature. Am J Med Sci 1939; 198: 269–292.
3. Kyle J. Dalzeil's disease — 66 years on. Br Med J 1979; 1: 876–877.
4. Dalziel TK. Chronic interstitial enteritis. Br Med J 1913; 2: 1068–1070.
5. Ginzburg L. Regional enteritis: historical perspective. Gastroenterology 1986; 90: 1310–1311.
6. Brooke BN. Granulomatous diseases of the intestine. Lancet 1959; 2: 745–749.
7. Morson BC, Lockhart-Mummery HE. Crohn's disease of the colon. Gastroenterologica (Basel) 1959; 92: 168–173.
8. Marshak RH, Wolf BS, Eliasoph J. Segmental colitis. Radiology 1959; 73: 707–716.
9. Lockhart-Mummery HE, Morson BC. Crohn's disease (regional enteritis) of the large intestine and its distinction from ulcerative colitis. Gut 1960; 1: 87–105.
10. Lockhart-Mummery HE, Morson BC. Crohn's disease of the large intestine. Gut 1964; 5: 493–509.
11. Lindner AE, Marshak RH, Wolf BS, Janowitz HD. Granulomatous colitis: a clinical study. N Eng J Med 1963; 269: 379–385.
12. Mayberry JF, Rhodes J. Epidemiological aspects of Crohn's disease: a review of the literature. Gut 1984; 25: 886–899.
13. Kyle J. Crohn's disease in the Northeastern and Northern Isles of Scotland: an epidemiological review. Gastroenterology 1992; 103: 392–399.
14. Munkholm P, Langholz E, Haagen NO, Kreiner S, Binder V. Incidence and prevalence of Crohn's disease in the county of Copenhagen 1962–87: a sixfold increase in incidence. Scand J Gastroenterol 1992; 27: 609–614.
15. Ekbom A, Helmick C, Zack M, Adami H-O. The epidemiology of inflammatory bowel disease: a large population based study in Sweden. Gastroenterology 1991; 100: 350–358.
16. Lindberg E, Jarnerot G. The incidence of Crohn's disease is not decreasing in Sweden. Scand J Gastroenterol 1991; 26: 495–500.
17. Stow SP, Redmond SR, Stormont JM et al. An epidemiologic study of inflammatory bowel disease in Rochester, New York: hospital incidence. Gastroenterology 1990; 99: 1032–1036.
18. Sanderson IR, Walker-Smith JA. Crohn's disease in childhood. Br J Surg 1985; 72 (Suppl): S87–90.
19. Grimm IS, Friedman LS. Inflammatory bowel disease in the elderly. Gastroenterol Clin North Am 1990; 19: 361–389.
20. Probert CSJ, Jayanthi V, Hughes AO, Thompson JR, Wicks ACB, Mayberry JF. Prevalence and family risk of ulcerative colitis and Crohn's disease: an epidemiological study among Europeans and South Asians in Leicestershire. Gut 1993; 34: 1547–1551.
21. Probert CSJ, Jayanthi V, Pollock DJ, Baithun SI, Mayberry JF, Ramotin DS. Crohn's disease in Bangladeshis and Europeans in Britain: an epidemiological comparison in Tower Hamlets. Postgrad Med J 1992; 68: 914–920.
22. Gitnick G. Etiology of inflammatory bowel diseases: where have we been? Where are we going?. Scand J Gastroenterol 1990; 25 (Suppl 175): 93–96.
23. Wakefield AJ, Sawyerr AM, Dhillon AP et al. Pathogenesis of Crohn's disease: multifocal gastrointestinal infarction. Lancet 1989; ii: 1057–1062.
24. Ekbom A, Adami H-O, Helmick CG, Jonzon A, Zack MM. Perinatal risk factors for inflammatory bowel disease: a case control study. Am J Epidemiology 1990; 132: 1111–1119.
25. Urban E. Selected summaries. Gastroenterology 1984; 87: 978–979.
26. Hodgson HJF. Inflammatory bowel disease and food intolerance. J R Coll Physicians Lond 1986; 20: 45–48.
27. Levine J. Exogenous factors in Crohn's disease. J Clin Gastroenterol 1992; 14: 216–226.
28. Calkins BM. A meta-analysis of the role of smoking in inflammatory bowel disease. Dig Dis Sci 1989; 34: 1841–1854.
29. Vessey M, Jewell D, Smith A, Yeates D, McPherson K. Chronic inflammatory bowel disease, cigarette smoking, and use of oral contraceptives: findings in a large cohort study of women of child bearing age. Br Med J 1986; 292: 1101–1103.
30. Wakefield AJ, Sawyerr AM, Hudson M, Dhillon AP, Pounder RE. Smoking, the oral contraceptive pill, and Crohn's disease. Dig Dis Sci 1991; 36: 1147–1150.
31. Lindberg E, Jarnerot G, Huitfeldt B. Smoking in Crohn's disease: effect on localisation and clinical course. Gut 1992; 33: 779–782.
32. Tobin MV, Logan RFA, Langman MJS, McConnell RB, Gilmore IT. Cigarette smoking and inflammatory bowel disease. Gastroenterology 1987; 93: 316–321.
33. Sofaer J. Crohn's disease: the genetic contribution. Gut 1993; 34: 869–871.
34. Biemond I, Burnham WR, D'Amaro J, Langman MJS. HLA-A and -B antigens in inflammatory bowel disease. Gut 1986; 27: 934–941.
35. Kagnoff MF, Brown RJ, Schanfield MS. Associations between Crohn's disease and immunoglobulin heavy chain (Gm) allotypes. Gastroenterology 1983; 85: 1044–1047.
36. Elmgreen J, Sorenson H, Berkowicz A. Polymorphism of complement C3 in chronic inflammatory bowel disease: predominance of the C3F gene in Crohn's disease. Acta Med Scand 1984; 215: 375–378.

37. Sacher DB, Taub RN, Janowitz HD. A transmissible agent in Crohn's disease? New pursuit of an old concept. N Engl J Med 1975; 293: 354–355.
38. Yoshimura HH, Estes MK, Graham DY. Search for evidence of a viral aetiology in inflammatory bowel disease. Gut 1984; 25: 347–355.
39. Wakefield AJ, Pittilo RM, Sim R et al. Evidence of persistent measles virus infection in Crohn's disease. J Med Virol 1993; 39: 345–353.
40. Blaser MJ, Miller RA, Lacher J, Singleton JW. Patients with active Crohn's disease have elevated serum antibodies to antigens of seven enteric bacterial pathogens. Gastroenterology 1984; 87: 888–894.
41. Bull K, Matthews N, Rhodes J. Antibody response to anaerobic coccoid rods in Crohn's disease. J Clin Pathol 1986; 39: 1130–1134.
42. Persson S, Danielsson D, Kjellander J, Wellensten S. Studies on Crohn's Disease. 1. The relationship between Yersinia enterocolitica infection and terminal ileitis. Acta Chir Scand 1976; 142: 84–90.
43. Blaser MJ, Hoverson D, Ely IG, Duncan DJ, Wang W-LL, Brown WR. Studies of Campylobacter jejuni in patients with inflammatory bowel disease. Gastroenterology 1984; 86: 33–38.
44. McGarity BH, Robertson DAF, Clark IN, Wright R. Deoxyribonucleic acid amplification and hydridisation in Crohn's disease using a chlamydial plasmid probe. Gut 1991; 32: 1011–1015.
45. Chiodini RJ, Van Kruiningen HJ, Thayer WR, Merkal RS, Coutu JA. Possible role for mycobacteria in inflammatory bowel disease. 1. An unclassified Mycobacterium species isolated from patients with Crohn's Disease. Dig Dis Sci 1984; 29: 1073–1079.
46. Ciclitira PJ. Does Crohn's disease have a mycobacterial basis? Br Med J 1993; 306: 733–734.
47. Zauli D, Crespi C, Dall'Amore P, Bianchi FB, Pisi E. Antibodies to the cytoskeleton components and other autoantibodies in inflammatory bowel disease. Digestion 1985; 32: 140–144.
48. Snook J. Are the inflammatory bowel diseases autoimmune disorders? Gut 1990; 31: 961–963.
49. Brandtzaeg P, Halstensen TS, Kett K et al. Immunobiology and immunopathology of human gut mucosa: humoral immunity and intraepithelial lymphocytes. Gastroenterology 1989; 97: 1562–1584.
50. Geboes K, Rutgeerts P, Ectors N et al. Major histocompatibility class II expression on the small intestinal nervous system in Crohn's disease. Gastroenterology 1992; 103: 439–447.
51. Stallmach A, Schuppan D, Riese HH, Matthes H, Riecken EO. Increased collagen type III synthesis by fibroblasts isolated from strictures of patients with Crohn's disease. Gastroenterology 1992; 102: 1920–1929.
52. Simmonds NJ, Rampton DS. Inflammatory bowel disease — a radical view. Gut 1993; 34: 865–868.
53. Rampton DS, Collins CE. Review article: thromboxanes in inflammatory bowel disease — pathogenic and therapeutic implications. Aliment Pharmacol Ther 1993; 7: 357–367.
54. Sharon P, Stenson WF. Enhanced synthesis of leukotriene B4 by colonic mucosa in inflammatory bowel disease. Gastroenterology 1984; 86: 453–460.
55. Koizumi M, King N, Lobb R, Benjamin C, Podolsky DK. Expression of vascular adhesion molecules in inflammatory bowel disease. Gastroenterology 1992; 103: 840–847.
56. Ohtani H, Nakamura S, Watanabe Y et al. Light and electron microscopic localisation of endothelial leucocyte adhesion molecule-1 in inflammatory bowel disease: morphological evidence of active synthesis and secretion into vascular lumen. Virchows Archiv A Pathol Anat 1992; 420: 403–409.
57. Marteau P, Colombel JF, Nemeth J, Vaerman JP, Dive JC, Rambaud JC. Immunological study of histologically non-involved jejunum during Crohn's disease: evidence for reduced in vivo secretion of secretory IgA. Clin Exp Immunol 1990; 80: 196–201.
58. Walvoort HC, Fazzi GE, Pena AS. Seroreactivity of patients with Crohn's disease with lymph nodes of primed nude mice is independent of the tissue used for priming. Gastroenterology 1989; 97: 1097–1100.
59. Zuckerman MJ, Williams SE, Bura R, Das KM, Sachar DB. Sera-reactivity in inflammatory bowel disease: frequency of recognition of Crohn's disease tissue primed nude mouse lymphoid tissue in an interinstitutional blinded study. J Clin Gastroenterol 1989; 11: 639–644.
60. Das KM, Vecchi M, Novikoff A, Mazumdar S, Novikoff PM. Hybridomas using athymic nude mice injected with Crohn's disease (CD) tissue filtrate: immunoreactivity of the hybridomas with CD sera. Am J Pathol 1990; 136: 1375–1382.
61. Tanner AR, Arthur MJP, Wright R. Macrophage activation, chronic inflammation and gastrointestinal disease. Gut 1984; 25: 760–783.
62. Stamp GWH, Poulsom R, Chung LP et al. Lysozyme gene expression in inflammatory bowel disease. Gastroenterology 1992; 103: 532–538.
63. Olaison G, Tagesson C. Abnormal intestinal permeability in Crohn's disease: a possible pathogenic factor. Scand J Gastroenterol 1990; 25: 321–328.
64. Rhodes JM, Gallimore R, Elias E, Kennedy JE. Faecal sulphatase in health and in inflammatory bowel disease. Gut 1985; 26: 466–469.
65. Meyers S, Wolke A, Field SP, Feuer EJ, Johnson JW, Janowitz HD. Faecal alpha-1-antitrypsin measurement: an indicator of Crohn's disease activity. Gastroenterology 1985; 89: 13–18.
66. Yamani JE, Mizon C, Capon C et al. Decreased faecal exoglycosidase activities identify a subset of patients with active Crohn's disease. Clin Sci 1992; 83: 409–415.
67. O'Morain C, Bishop AE, McGregor GP et al. Vasoactive intestinal polypeptide concentrations and immunohistochemical studies in rectal biopsies from patients with inflammatory bowel disease. Gut 1984; 25: 57–61.
68. Shanahan F, Anton P. Neuroendocrine modulation of the immune system: possible implications for inflammatory bowel disease. Dig Dis Sci 1988; 33 (Suppl): 41S–49S.
69. Bozdech JM, Farmer RG. Diagnosis of Crohn's disease. Hepatogastroenterology 1990; 37: 8–17.
70. Fielding JF, Toye DKM, Beton DC, Cooke WT. Crohn's disease of the stomach and duodenum. Gut 1970; 11: 1001–1006.
71. Korelitz BI, Wayne JD, Kreuning J et al. Crohn's disease in endoscopic biopsies of the gastric antrum and duodenum. Am J Gastroenterol 1981; 76: 103–109.
72. Crohn's Workshop: a global assessment of Crohn's disease. Lee ECG, ed. London: Heyden, 1981; p 136–144.
73. Sheehan AL, Warren BF, Gear MWL, Shepherd NA. Fat wrapping in Crohn's disease: pathological basis and relevance to surgical practice. Br J Surg 1992; 79: 955–958.
74. Butterworth RJ, Williams GT, Hughes LE. Can Crohn's disease be diagnosed at laparotomy? Gut 1992; 33: 140–142.
75. Kahn E, Daum F. Pseudopolyps of the small intestine in Crohn's disease Hum Pathol 1984; 15: 84–86.
76. Knutson H, Lunderquist A, Lunderquist A. Vascular changes in Crohn's disease. Am J Roentg 1968; 103: 380–385.
77. Wakefield A J, Sankey EA, Dhillon AP et al. Granulomatous vasculitis in Crohn's disease. Gastroenterology 1991; 100: 1279–1287.
78. Lee EY, Stenson WF, DeSchryver-Kecskemeti K. Thickening of muscularis mucosae in Crohn's disease. Mod Pathol 1991; 4: 87–90.
79. Dvorak AM, Silen W. Differentiation between Crohn's disease and other inflammatory conditions by electron microscopy. Ann Surg 1985; 201: 53–63.
80. Brewer DB, Thompson H, Haynes IG, Alexander-Williams J. Axonal damage in Crohn's disease is frequent, but non-specific. J Pathol 1990; 161: 301–311.
81. Strobach RS, Ross AH, Markin RS, Zetterman RK, Linder J. Neural patterns in inflammatory bowel disease: an immunohistochemical survey. Mod Pathol 1990; 3: 488–493.
82. Dvorak AM, Connell AB, Dickersin GR. Crohn's disease: a scanning electron microscopic study. Hum Pathol 1979; 10: 165–177.
83. Dourmashkin RR, Davies H, Wells C et al. Epithelial patchy necrosis in Crohn's disease. Hum Pathol 1983; 14: 643–648.
84. Sanky EA, Dhillon AP, Anthony A et al. Early mucosal changes in Crohn's disease. Gut 1993; 34: 375–381.
85. Marshak RH. Granulomatous disease of the intestinal tract (Crohn's disease). Radiology 1975; 114: 3–22.

86. Whorwell PJ, Hawkins R, Dewbury K, Wright R. Ultrasound survey of gallstones and other hepatobiliary disorders in patients with Crohn's disease. Dig Dis Sci 1984; 29: 930–933.
87. Greenstein AJ, Mann D, Sachar DB, Aufses Jr AH. Free perforation in Crohn's disease: I. A survey of 99 cases. Am J Gastroenterol 1985; 80: 682–689.
88. Tonelli F, Ficari F. Pathological features of Crohn's disease determining perforation. J Clin Gastroenterol 1991; 13: 226–230.
89. Ribeiro MB, Greenstein AJ, Yamazaki Y, Aufses Jr AH. Intraabdominal abscess in regional enteritis. Ann Surg 1991; 213: 32–36.
90. Hamilton SR, Rees J, Pennington L, Boitnott JK, Bayless TM, Cameron JL. The role of resection margin frozen section in the surgical management of Crohn's disease. Surg Gynecol Obstet 1985; 160: 57–62.
91. Williams JG, Wong WD, Rothenberger DA, Goldberg SM. Recurrence of Crohn's disease after resection. Br J Surg 1991; 78: 10–19.
92. Rutgeerts P, Geboes K, Vantrappen G, Beyls J, Kerremans R, Hiele M. Predictability of the postoperative course of Crohn's disease. Gastroenterology 1990; 99: 956–963.
93. Rutgeerts P, Goboes K, Peeters M et al. Effect of faecal stream diversion on recurrence of Crohn's disease in the neoterminal ileum. Lancet 1991; 338: 771–774.
94. Tandon HD, Prakash A. Pathology of intestinal tuberculosis and its distinction from Crohn's disease. Gut 1972; 13: 260–269.
95. Morson BC et al. Morson and Dawson's gastrointestinal pathology. 3rd ed. Oxford: Blackwell, 1990: pp 248–250.
96. Isaacson PG, Wright DH. Malignant histiocytosis of the intestine: its relationship to malabsorption and ulcerative jejunitis. Hum Pathol 1978; 9: 661–677.
97. Isaacson PG, Spencer J, Connolly CE et al. Malignant histiocytosis of the intestine: a T-cell lymphoma. Lancet 1985; 2: 688–691.
98. Salter DM, Krajewski AS, Dewar AE. Immunophenotype analysis of malignant histiocytosis of the intestine. J Clin Pathol 1986; 29: 8–15.
99. Jewell DP. Ulcerative enteritis. Br Med J 1983; 287: 1740–1741.
100. Thomas WEG, Williamson RCN. Non-specific small bowel ulceration. Postgrad Med J 1985; 61: 587–591.
101. Lang J, Price AB, Levi AJ, Burke M, Gumpel JM, Bjarnason I. Diaphragm disease: pathology of disease of the small intestine induced by non-steroidal anti-inflammatory drugs. J Clin Pathol 1988; 41: 516–526.
102. Shearman DJC, Finlayson NDC. Diseases of the gastrointestinal tract and liver. 2nd ed. Edinburgh: Churchill Livingstone, 1989.

PART III

Malabsorption and protein intolerance

J. Piris

MALABSORPTION

Malabsorption can be simply defined as a failure to absorb nutritive substances from the food or to reabsorb endogenous substances such as bile salts. Malabsorption syndrome refers to a clinical syndrome in which malabsorption of fat results in bulky, loose stools, high in fatty acid content — steatorrhoea — as well as failure to gain weight, usually accompanied by anorexia and deficiences of the fat-soluble vitamins (A, D, E and K).

The clinical presentation of malabsorption is variable but usually includes gastrointestinal symptoms of diarrhoea, steatorrhea, borborygmi, distension and abdominal discomfort and nutritional disturbances. The nutritional disturbances may be quite specific, such as anaemia due to vitamin B12, folate or iron deficiency, or vitamin K deficiency with associated bleeding, or they may be more generalized, presenting with anorexia and weight loss due to negative protein or fat balance. Severe degrees of malabsorption may be associated with oedema due to hypoproteinaemia and electrolyte deficiency and bone disease related to vitamin D or calcium absorption deficiencies.

In a significant number of patients there may be manifestations of the underlying cause of the malabsorption such as dermatological features in scleroderma or the result of an ileocolic fistula in Crohn's disease.

Digestion and absorption of nutrients

Digestion is defined as the process of converting food into an assimilable form whilst absorption refers to the passage of the products of digestion through the gastrointestinal mucosa and ultimately into the bloodstream. The limitation of such broad definitions is easily demonstrated by the fact that some 'digestion' — as reduction in molecular size — occurs within the enterocytes after absorption. It must also be remembered that transport across the small intestinal mucosa occurs in two directions and that in certain pathological conditions, such as in protein-losing enteropathy, the movement towards the lumen may well be a more important factor in the protein deficiency than the lack of absorption.

Absorption of carbohydrates

In the diet of Western countries, these are mostly ingested in the form of starch, sucrose and lactose. Although salivary amylase contributes to the digestion of starch in the mouth and stomach, it is the pancreatic amylase that hydrolyses starch to maltose, maltotriose and alpha-limit dextrins. These substances, together with sucrose and lactose, are further hydrolysed to their constituent monosaccharides, glucose, galactose and fructose, by disaccharidase enzymes present at the microvilli of enterocytes. Active, energy-dependent transport of glucose to the interior of the cell occurs against a gradient, is dependent on the presence of Na^+ ions and involves a carrier mechanism. Deficiencies in disaccharidase activity, either primary — as a rare congenital disorder — or, more commonly, secondary deficiencies, may cause clinical symptoms such as abdominal cramps, bloating and diarrhoea.

Absorption of proteins

Hydrolysis of proteins of dietary and endogenous origin commences in the stomach by the action of pepsin, but hydrolysis is mostly the domain of the pancreatic proteases, trypsin, chymotrypsin, elastase and carboxypeptidases. These enzymes are released as proenzymes into the duodenum and have an optimal pH of about 6.5; they are activated by enterokinase, which is itself produced at the brush border of the enterocytes and converts trypsinogen to trypsin. Trypsin further activates trypsinogens and the other proenzymes. In this manner, proteins are broken down into oligopeptides and amino acids; further digestion of oligopeptides into amino acids takes place at the brush border through the action of peptidases but significant amounts of dipeptides and tripeptides are absorbed directly into the cells where they are further hydrolysed by the enzymes of the cytosol. Once again, amino acids on the luminal side of the membrane are transported into the cells by means of energy-dependent active mechanisms requiring a variety of carrier molecules. It is also clear that there are four distinct transport systems, each responsible for the absorption of a particular group of amino acids:

1. neutral amino acids: alanine, serine, valine, leucine cysteine, histidine, tyrosine, etc.
2. dibasic (diamino) amino acids: ornithine, arginine, lysine and cystine
3. dicarboxylic (acidic) amino acids: glutamic and aspartic acids
4. glycine, proline and hydroxyproline.

Within each group, the members compete with each other for transport but no competition exists between members of different groups. A common carrier molecule may be responsible for the transport of amino acids of one group. This concept is supported by the existence of genetic disorders in man in which there is a defect of absorption of only one group of amino acids while the transport of other groups is unaffected, e.g. in Hartnup disease there is reduced transport of neutral amino acids.

Absorption of fat

Most dietary fat consists of triglycerides and small amounts of cholesterol and fat-soluble vitamins. An initial stage in the digestion of fat takes place in the stomach where a coarse emulsion is formed. As the chyle passes into the duodenum, pancreatic lipase, a specific esterase present in the duodenal juice, hydrolyses triglycerides; the products of this hydrolysis — fatty acids and monoglycerides — are then combined with water-soluble bile salts to form large molecular aggregates termed micelles. These are also water-soluble and reach the brush border of the enterocytes where the lipids are absorbed by incorporation into the lipid phase of the cell membrane. The bile salts are released downstream to be reabsorbed in the terminal ileum. Monoglycerides and fatty acids which have entered the mucosal cells are reconverted into triglycerides, aggregated and coated with phospholipid, lipoprotein and cholesterol ester to form chylomicrons; these are released into the mucosal lymphatics, the lacteal ducts and ultimately into the circulating blood. Beta-lipoprotein is necessary for the formation of chylomicrons, and a specific deficiency syndrome exists in which lipid droplets accumulate in enterocytes.[1] Deficiencies in the production of pancreatic lipase (as in chronic pancreatitis) or bile salts (as in biliary disease), or interference with the flow through the lacteals, may cause abnormal absorption of fat in man.

A broad classification of the causes of malabsorption is given in Table 26.1. It will be appreciated that many of the conditions listed are not accompanied by a structural abnormality of the small intestinal mucosa.

Small intestinal biopsy in the investigation of malabsorption

It is now widely agreed that small intestinal biopsy is a safe, readily available and invaluable means of obtaining tissue samples for diagnostic and investigative purposes. The exploration of the duodenum with a flexible fibreoptic endoscope is a routine clinical investigation in most hospitals and it provides the opportunity for obtaining small biopsy specimens of the duodenal mucosa. Such specimens often provide sufficient information for the diagnosis of primary duodenal pathology, such as peptic ulcer or duodenitis, or some forms of generalized small intestinal diseases, such as giardiasis; however they frequently show a degree of chronic inflammation and distortion of the morphology of villi which are not related to any underlying enteric pathology and which are seen in clinically asymptomatic individuals. In addition, it is known that the mucosa of the duodenal bulb normally shows a higher proportion of leaf-shaped villi than other more distal parts of the small intestine.[2] For these reasons, it is preferable that one or more samples of jejunal mucosa are obtained, and usually by means of a suction biopsy instrument (such as the Crosby capsule) placed under fluoroscopic control at the duodenojejunal junction. Hydraulically operated instruments are used when more than one sample is necessary since the capsule remains in the jejunum while the specimen is retrieved. All these instruments have been adapted for use in children.

Small intestinal biopsy is mandatory in any patient suspected of suffering from coeliac disease, and during the investigation of malabsorption which is not obviously due to extraintestinal causes. Many patients with coeliac disease have only a mild illness or one which is often not of a digestive nature, such as anaemia or osteomalacia. A high degree of awareness is required from the physician to ensure that a malabsorption syndrome is not overlooked.

Table 26.1 Classification of malabsorption

I INADEQUATE DIGESTION
- A. Gastric disorders
  - i Post-gastrectomy
  - ii. Vagotomy
  - iii. Gastrinoma
- B. Hepatic and biliary disorders
  - i. Hepatitis
  - ii. Chronic extrahepatic biliary obstruction
- C. Pancreatic disorders
  - Cystic fibrosis
  - Chronic pancreatitis
  - Hypoplasia (Shwachman–Diamond)
  - Carcinoma
  - Zollinger–Ellison syndrome
  - Other endocrine tumours
- D. Enterokinase deficiency

II INADEQUATE ABSORPTION
- A. Reduced absorptive area
  - i. Small intestinal resection
  - ii. Fistulae
  - iii. Congenital short bowel
- B. Small intestinal mucosal disease
  - i. Infective enteritis
    - a. Acute
      - — bacterial
      - — viral
      - — fungal
      - — parasitic
    - b. Chronic
      - — tuberculous
      - — tropical sprue
      - — Whipple's disease
    - c. Aquired immunodeficiency
  - ii. Unknown aetiology
    - a. Coeliac disease
    - b. Refractory sprue
    - c. Collagenous sprue
    - d. Ulcerative jejunoileitis
    - e. Crohn's disease
    - f. Cow's milk protein intolerance
    - g. Soy protein intolerance
    - h. Other food intolerance
    - i. Intractable diarrhoea of infancy

III LYMPHATIC OBSTRUCTION
- A. Primary intestinal lymphangiectasia
- B. Secondary intestinal lymphangiectasia

IV INHERITED DISORDERS OF ABSORPTION
- A. Amino acids
  - i. Aminoglycinuria
  - ii. Hartnup disease
  - iii. Cystinuria
  - iv. Lysinuric protein intolerance
  - v. Blue diaper syndrome
  - vi. Lowe's syndrome
- B. Fat
  - i. Abetalipoproteinaemia
  - ii. Bile salt deficiencies
- C. Carbohydrates
  - i. Lactase
  - ii. Glucose-galactose malabsorption
  - iii. Disaccharidase deficiencies

V MALABSORPTION IN SYSTEMIC DISEASES
- A. Skin diseases
- B. Endocrine
- C. Malignancy
- D. Others
  - Amyloidosis
  - Collagenosis
  - Drugs
  - Eosinophilic gastroenteritis

INADEQUATE DIGESTION

Gastric disorders

Total gastrectomy is not now commonly performed but even following a partial gastrectomy, patients may develop a degree of malabsorption due to stasis in the efferent loop and subsequent bacterial overgrowth. This can be demonstrated as excessive faecal fat but patients may be clinically asymptomatic. Iron malabsorption often develops many years after the gastrectomy and is related to abnormal mixing of pancreatic and biliary secretions with food. Vitamin B12 malabsorption may occur if atrophic gastritis in the residual gastric mucosa results in intrinsic factor deficiency. Some types of gastrectomy, e.g. Billroth II, bypass the duodenum and this may result in a decrease in the stimulus for the release of secretin and cholecystokinin-pancreozymin from the small intestine and a 'functional' pancreatic insufficiency.

Vagotomy

Although diarrhoea can be severe after vagotomy for peptic ulcer disease, it is a rare complication, particularly of the more selective forms of vagotomy performed nowadays. Malabsorption of fat due to inefficient micelle formation and low bile salt concentration is seen in some patients after truncal vagotomy, but is rare after total gastric vagotomy and almost non-existent after highly selective vagotomy.

Gastrinoma

Gastrin-secreting tumours are usually situated within the pancreas but may originate in the duodenum or stomach. The excessive secretion of the hormone gastrin is associated with the Zollinger–Ellison syndrome in which excessive gastric acid secretion causes extensive peptic ulceration in the stomach or duodenum and occasionally in the jejunum. In a significant proportion of patients diarrhoea is a major problem which can be accompanied by steatorrhoea. The excessive amounts of acid secreted cannot be neutralized by duodenal bicarbonate, resulting in a decreased pH of the intestinal content, inactivation of some pancreatic enzymes and precipitation of bile salts. Abnormalities of the jejunal mucosa, usually mild and of patchy distribution, are seen in some patients with gastrinoma; the surface epithelium covering the villi may show erosions and acute inflammatory changes and there may be some acute inflammation of the lamina propria. Brunner's glands are commonly present in the proximal jejunum in these patients.[3]

Hepatic and biliary disorders

Interference with the synthesis or excretion of bile salts resulting in a significantly low concentration of bile in the intestinal lumen (below 4 mmol/l) results in defective formation of micelles with reduction of fat absorption and mild steatorrhoea. Absorption of carbohydrates is unaffected, the D-xylose test is normal and jejunal biopsy specimens show no histological abnormality. Vitamin D and calcium absorption is also affected with resulting metabolic bone disease.

In the absence of liver or biliary disease, the enterohepatic circulation of bile salts may be abnormal when there is extensive ileal mucosal disease, as in Crohn's disease, and a malabsorptive syndrome may occur. It has been estimated that over 100 cm of ileal mucosa must be affected before the bile salt depletion is sufficient to cause severe steatorrhoea; less extensive lesions are associated with mild malabsorption but often with diarrhoea which is caused by the effect of the unabsorbed bile salts on the colonic transport of water and electrolytes.

A similar pathogenetic mechanism for malabsorption is seen in the blind loop syndrome and other circumstances leading to enteric bacterial overgrowth (i.e. diverticulosis of small intestine and coloenteric fistulae). Bacteria can deconjugate bile salts and interfere with micelle formation and lipid absorption. In these situations, vitamin B12 malabsorption is also common and is due to competition by the bacteria for vitamin B12 even when bound to intrinsic factor. These abnormalities are usually corrected by appropriate antibiotic treatment.

Pancreatic disorders

The failure of pancreatic enzymes to reach the small intestine, which may be due to obstruction of the outflow or impaired capacity to secrete them, results in malabsorption. Pancreatic carcinoma is an important cause of obstruction of major ducts and is usually accompanied by obstructive jaundice which may itself contribute to the malabsorption. Chronic pancreatitis in adults and cystic fibrosis in children are the commonest causes of pancreatic insufficiency. In both conditions, in addition to the enzyme deficiencies, additional factors are of importance. In children with cystic fibrosis the secretion of bile is abnormal, and gastric hypersecretion is often seen in chronic pancreatitis. Pancreatic hypoplasia (Shwachman–Diamond syndrome) is an inherited disorder in which trypsin and lipase are absent from the pancreatic secretion and there is also neutropenia and thrombocytopenia. The infants present with steatorrhoea and failure to thrive, and, in some, small intestinal biopsy specimens show blunting of the villi and inflammation in the lamina propria.[4]

Pancreatic endocrine tumours

Such tumours may release one or more peptide hormones and are associated with clinical syndrome in which malabsorption can be present; the Zollinger–Ellison syndrome has already been mentioned and is commonly due to a primary pancreatic neoplasm. The Verner–Morrison syndrome, or watery diarrhoea, hypokalaemia and achlorhydria (WDHA) syndrome, is due to a pancreatic endocrine tumour or hyperplasia with secretion of high quantities of vasoactive intestinal peptide (VIP); faecal fat excretion is increased in some patients but small intestinal mucosal morphology is normal in the majority.[5]

Enterokinase deficiency

Enterokinase is an enzyme produced by the duodenal mucosa and localized in the brush border of the enterocytes; its function is to convert pancreatic trypsinogen — an inactive proenzyme — into trypsin. Activation of other proteolytic enzymes is dependent upon the action of trypsin. Deficiency of enterokinase is a rare inborn error of metabolism which prevents hydrolysis of proteins and polypeptides, a necessary step for their absorption. Affected infants present with failure to thrive, oedema and hypoproteinaemia. No abnormalities of the morphology of duodenal or jejunal mucosa have been described in this condition.

INADEQUATE ABSORPTION

Reduced absorptive area

Reduction of mucosal surface area is commonly due to surgical resection and more rarely to extensive mucosal disease such as Crohn's jejunoileitis. The minimum length of small intestine required for survival in humans is unknown but the literature records many instances of recovery after what has become known as 'massive small intestinal resection.' In one such publication[6] the author described three cases and reviewed a total of 257 cases from the literature. The most common conditions underlying the need for surgery were intestinal volvulus and intussusception, strangulated hernia and mesenteric thrombosis; the average length of bowel resected in these patients was about 300 cm, representing approximately 45–47% of the normal length of the adult small intestine. The average length of resection for the 86 cases with subsequent good clinical recovery was 310 cm; but the outcome of 21 cases was described as only fair with resection of an average of 367 cm. Amongst 15 cases in whom the entire terminal ileum was resected the outcome was poor despite an average length of resection of 348 cm. The author concluded that resection of 50% of small intestine constitutes the upper limit of safety. Loss of the ileum is more important in relative terms to its length because bile salt resorption is abolished and vitamin B12 malabsorption is inevitable. Preservation of the ileocaecal valve seems to hold an equally important role in functional recovery and is thought to be due to its ability to slow down the transit of intestinal contents.

A similar functional defect to that seen in patients after small intestinal resections occurs in cases of fistula formation and in operations for the treatment of obesity which result in bypass of the absorptive areas. Once again, bypass of the terminal ileum leads to malabsorption. Resection of the terminal ileum and ascending colon is relatively commonly performed in Crohn's disease and may be followed by diarrhoea, steatorrhea and vitamin B12 malabsorption. It is interesting that 'massive intestinal resection' in the newborn baby is associated with a much greater chance of recovery than that in adults.[7] This has stimulated a longstanding debate regarding the existence of a compensatory adaptation of the residual bowel. The few studies in humans indicate that compensatory longitudinal growth occurs only in some cases in older children and adults, but dilatation of the residual small intestine is common in this situation. Small intestinal biopsy studies of patients after massive small bowel resection demonstrate evidence of hypertrophy of the villi in most cases and a significant increase in the number of enterocytes per unit length of villus.[8] This morphological adaptation is accompanied by functional recovery. However after ileal resection, the jejunum does not acquire the ability to absorb vitamin B12 or reabsorb bile salts. Conversely the small intestinal mucosa undergoes a degree of functional 'atrophy' in bypassed segments, situations of food deprivation and total parenteral nutrition.

Congenital short bowel syndrome

This rare condition is associated with malrotation of the bowel and presents with symptoms similar to those following massive intestinal resection.

Small intestinal mucosal disease

Infective enteritis

The majority of acute diarrhoeal illnesses are due to viral infections and in developed countries most resolve within a few days.[9] However, a proportion of patients fail to improve rapidly and some may develop a chronic malabsorptive syndrome (which is sometimes called postinfective malabsorption). A large variety of aetiological agents have been implicated as the cause of the initial acute illness the most important of which are listed in Table 26.2.

Histological abnormalities are not always present and usually there is return to complete normality after the acute episode. However, in a small proportion of patients in whom the symptoms persist and progress, malabsorption may be mild and specific to only one test substance or more serious and accompanied by deficient absorption of various substances. Children, in particular, may develop transient intolerance to cow's milk or gluten, and others may develop disaccharidase deficiency. Following treatment with an appropriate diet, reintroduction of the offending food is usually harmless, indicating complete functional recovery. Rare cases occur, both in children and adults, however, in which true gluten-sensitive enteropathy develops after the acute episode, requiring continuous treatment with a gluten-free diet. In such cases, the damage caused to the mucosa during the acute infection may result in sensitization to gluten in a susceptible individual.

In other cases, particularly those suffering from parasitic infections such as giardiasis or amoebiasis, the initial acute enteritis may be followed by a persistent low-grade infection with damage to the absorptive mucosa and malabsorption. The pathologist must be alert to this possibility and conduct a careful examination of biopsy material in order to confirm such a diagnosis. Adequate antimicrobial therapy can then be established.[10]

In developing countries, the appearances of the small intestinal mucosa in asymptomatic individuals may be different from those considered normal in the developed countries, and often show mild or moderate villous atrophy and increased inflammatory infiltration of the lamina propria. However a recent comparative study, using morphometric methods, between individuals from North India and the UK failed to show significant differences in the crypt/villus ratio or plasma cell numbers in the lamina

Table 26.2 Infective agents which may cause absorption

	Agent	Clinical syndrome
I	*Viruses*	
	Rotavirus	Enteritis in older children and adults
	Norfolk agent	Acute infantile gastroenteritis
II	*Bacteria*	
	Shigella	Bacilliary dysentery
	E. coli (enterotoxigenic)	Traveller's diarrhoea
	Campylobacter	Acute dysentery
	Salmonella	Cholera
	Staphylcocci, etc.	Food poisoning
	V. cholerae	
	Enterobacteria	
III	*Parasites*	? Tropical sprue
	Giardia lamblia	Diarrhoea ± steatorrhoea
	Strongyloides	Rarely severe malabsorption
	Coccidia	Chronic malabsorption
	Entamoeba histolytica	Bloody diarrhoea
IV	*Fungus*	
	Candida	

propria.[11] Some abnormalities of absorption to nutrients in these subjects are not uncommon and it is thought that the damage may be caused by repeated infection. Frank malabsorption is also encountered in patients with similar histological appearances and in whom no consistent evidence of concurrent intestinal infection is demonstrated. This is referred to as 'tropical sprue' and can affect both individuals living in endemic areas, such as India and the Carribean, and those who have visited these areas and present with malabsorption on return to their own countries. Small intestinal mucosal biopsy should always be performed in such patients to exclude gluten-sensitive enteropathy and giardiasis.

Chronic enteritis

Specific infections such as tuberculous enteritis may affect the ileocaecal region and cause weight loss, abdominal pain and diarrhoea with malabsorption.

Whipple's disease

In 1907 Whipple described the first case of a disease he named 'intestinal lipodystrophy'. The patient, a 36-year-old physician, complained of symptoms which began insidiously with attacks of arthritis involving every joint of the body and of a few hours duration, consisting of swelling, tenderness or pain. He also noted an evening fever, weight loss and marked lassitude; diarrhoea appeared later with three of four motions of fluid or semi-solid consistency.[12]

Incidence

The true incidence is unknown but it is a rare disease with only several hundred cases reported in the English literature, most of them since 1950. The disease has been recognized all over the world but most cases are reported from the USA and Europe, with a few cases from South America. Approximately 90% of patients are Caucasian males, mostly between 30–70 years of age but females and children with the disease are described. It only occasionally affects members of the same family.

Pathology

All cases so far reported have shown diffuse involvement of the small bowel, primarily the jejunum. The intestinal wall is often thickened and oedematous and sometimes shows a serosal fibrinous exudate. Enlarged lymph nodes and small peritoneal nodules are seen. The villi are club-shaped, bloated and show a white-yellow appearance at endoscopy. Under the light microscope, the villi are distorted due to the accumulation of foamy macrophages with a granular basophilic cytoplasm which stains a bright magenta with PAS and resists digestion by diastase (Fig. 26.33A,B). The lamina propria also shows rounded 'empty' spaces which contain neutral fat and are believed by some to represent distended lymphatics. However lymphatic obstruction has not been demonstrated and similar fat deposits are seen in extraintestinal tissues, a finding which formed the basis of the name 'intestinal lipodystrophy' given by Whipple. The accumulation of fat in the intestinal mucosa may be related to a disturbance of fat absorption. There is a remarkable absence of inflammatory response other than by macrophages, and intraepithelial lymphocytes are not usually increased in numbers.

The characteristic macrophages with strong PAS-positive material have been found in numerous other tissues of the body including the lymph nodes, heart, brain, lung and skin and the fat-filled cystic spaces can be very prominent in mesenteric lymph nodes.

The formation of sarcoid-like granulomata within the intestinal wall of treated and untreated patients has been recorded and recently a case was reported showing epithelioid granulomas within the liver.[13]

Ultrastructural studies demonstrate the characteristic bacilliform bodies — $0.25\ \mu m \times 1.3\ \mu m \times 1.5\ \mu m$ — within macrophages and lying free in the lamina propria from where they invade enterocytes and endothelial cells. Organisms at different stages of degeneration are seen within phagosomes in macrophages which also contain abundant irregular membranous inclusions representing remnants of the bacterial capsule, which are the equivalent of the PAS-positive material seen at light microscopy.

The pathological features seen in the small bowel mucosa in untreated patients show regression with successful antibiotic treatment; in particular, the number of PAS-positive macrophages in the lamina propria gradually decreases and the viable bacteria disappear slowly after the introduction of antibiotics, providing further evidence of the infective nature of the disease. However the membranous inclusions within macrophages have been seen two years after treatment and much later than the disappearance of viable organisms.[14]

Pathogenesis

The presence of bacteria within the macrophages in the small intestinal mucosa and other affected tissues provides strong support for the hypothesis of an infective aetiology in Whipple's disease. Morphologically similar bacteria are seen in every case but have not been clearly identified; they appear as encapsulated bacilliform bodies and are often seen dividing, particularly in the lamina propria where they are present extracellularly. Although the disease has not been reproduced in experimental animals, it has been reported that a cell wall deficient bacterium was isolated from a jejunal biopsy specimen from a patient with Whipple's disease and grown in cell monolayers

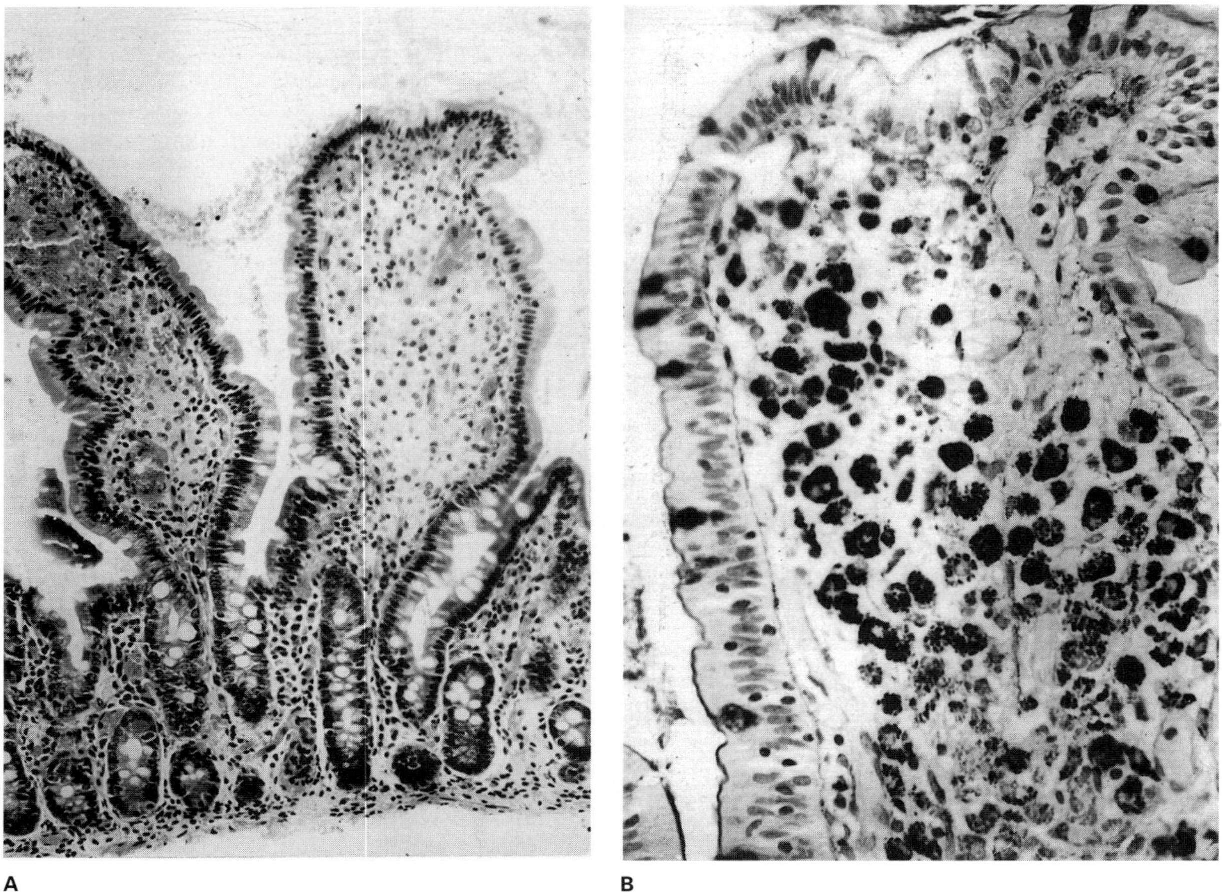

Fig. 26.33 **A** Jejunal biopsy specimen of Whipple's disease. The lamina propria contains numerous macrophages. (H&E, ×125) **B** The macrophages are filled with strongly PAS-positive granules. (PAS, ×320)

of human fibroblasts. Parenteral injection into a rabbit caused systemic disease characterized pathologically by accumulation of PAS-positive material within macrophages, from which a streptococcus could be isolated.[15] Many other organisms have been isolated from affected tissues including corynebacteria, haemophilus, klebsiella, streptococci, nocardia, etc. but it is almost certain that these are contaminants and not aetiologically relevant. Recent studies using immunocytochemical methods have demonstrated cross-reactivity between the macrophage granules and different antibacterial sera. A strong positive immunofluorescence with antisera to streptococci of groups B and G and shigella of group B was demonstrated.[16] A recent study of tissues from six cases confirmed that an antiserum specific for group B streptococci stains the typical PAS-positive macrophages of Whipple's disease but not similar cells such as colonic muciphages or macrophages in a case of malakoplakia. It claimed that the staining is due to the presence of rhamnose in the polysaccharides of the bacterial wall.[17]

There is inconclusive evidence that a primary immunological abnormality is the underlying cause of Whipple's disease but many such abnormalities have been described in these patients. The majority have reverted to normal with successful treatment and are considered secondary to the disease. However there may exist a subtle defect of cell-mediated immunity which may explain the ability of the intracellular pathogen to penetrate and disseminate widely within the body and to persist for long periods even after apparent successful eradication by antibiotics.[18] An association with HLA-B27 has been found in only about one third of patients.

In conclusion, there is strong evidence that Whipple's disease is caused by a bacterium of similar antigenic characteristics to streptococci of groups B and G, which shows features of a cell wall deficient organism and behaves as an intracellular pathogen; the case for a primary immunological deficit remains unproven.[19]

Acquired immune deficiency syndrome (AIDS) and Whipple's Disease

The case of a Haitian woman suffering from AIDS and found at autopsy to have the intestinal changes of

Whipple's disease was reported in a letter to the Lancet in 1983.[20] It seems most likely that she suffered instead from an infection with *Mycobacterium avium-intracellulare*, an ubiquitous organism found in the soil and carried by birds and domestic farm animals. Several cases or mycobacteriosis in AIDS sufferers have now been reported[21,22] and all show a similar endoscopic and histological pattern of blunt, abnormal villi distended by the presence of PAS-positive macrophages in the lamina propria which, on electron microscopy, are shown to contain rod-like bacillary bodies. Unlike those in Whipple's disease, the organisms in mycobacteriosis are strongly acid-fast, and both Ziehl-Neelsen and Fite stains are positive. Since antibiotic treatment may be ineffective in mycobacteriosis, it is important that such infection is ruled out before the diagnosis of Whipple's disease is offered in AIDS sufferers.

COELIAC DISEASE

The earliest available written account of intestinal malabsorption which, with all probability, was due to gluten sensitivity dates back to Aretaeus of Cappadocia in the second century AD and accurately describes the clinical features of affected children and women, and the appearances of the faeces. The realization of the association of the disease with the ingestion of farinaceous foods had to wait until the late nineteenth century, when Samuel Gee gave a most accurate description of the disease in patients who had never left the British Isles and compared it with the condition of 'diarrhoea alba' seen in India. At autopsy, he was unable to detect any structural abnormality and concluded that 'naked-eye examination of dead bodies throws no light upon the nature of the coeliac affection: nothing unnatural can be seen in the stomach, intestines or other digestive organs. Whether atrophy of the glandular crypts of the intestines be ever or always present, I cannot tell'.[23]

Only two years later Thin (1890) gave perhaps the first account of the pathological appearances of the small intestine in 'sprue' and described inflammatory changes and destruction of the crypts of Lieberkuhn of the jejunum and ileum.[24] A number of other reports describing the postmortem appearances in coeliac disease followed, and in some the procedure was performed after injection of the abdominal cavity with formalin soon after death, to avoid the effect of autolysis. Some of these reports, such as the one by Blumgart,[25] were in agreement — perhaps because many failed to appreciate the distinction between tropical and coeliac sprue — and some authors failed to find *any* significant abnormality. This prepared the ground for Thysen who, in 1932, reviewed the existing literature and described one case of his own. The autopsy, performed after injection of fixative into the abdomen, demonstrated a normal small intestine. Thysen concluded that all abnormalities ascribed to the sprue were, in fact, postmortem artefacts and that in this condition, the small intestine is normal; he also held the view that tropical sprue, non-tropical sprue and the 'coeliac affection of Gee' were identical and grouped them together under the name of 'idiopathic steatorrhoea'.[26] Thysen's opinion was widely shared until challenged by Paulley in 1954,[27] who described the appearances of the jejunal mucosa in biopsy specimens obtained at laparotomy from four coeliac patients. Only a year after Paulley's paper appeared, Royer and his colleagues in Argentina described a technique for peroral duodenal biopsy by aspiration[28] and the following year saw the first of a series of articles by Margot Shiner from England describing the appearances of duodenal and jejunal biopsy specimens obtained through endoscopes.[29] Since then, jejunal biopsy has become a routine procedure in the investigation of coeliac patients and the appearances of the intestinal mucosa at the light and electron microscopic level are now well known.

Definition

Our incomplete understanding of the precise cause of coeliac disease is well reflected by the absence of a universally accepted precise definition of the condition. Most of the widely used working definitions refer to the key features, i.e. malabsorption, the salient pathological characteristic of the jejunal mucosa and the essential relation to the ingestion of gluten. All these elements are notoriously variable and, whilst in some patients malabsorption may be sufficiently severe to cause clinically evident malnutrition, in others malabsorption may be asymptomatic and diagnosed only incidentally in the course of other investigations for anaemia or other complaints. Some are identified by family studies of relatives of affected patients.

Similarly, the pathological changes are not constant in their degree of severity or the extent of their distribution and, whilst some authors require a total atrophy of the villi in untreated subjects, others will offer the diagnosis of coeliac disease in subjects showing partial villous atrophy but suffering from the typical clinical picture. Controversy remains also with respect to the role of gluten in the disease. Most workers consider it essential to diagnosis that the clinical condition be considerably improved after withdrawal of gluten from the diet. This need not apply to the pathological changes in the jejunal mucosa however. Others require in addition, that symptoms return after gluten challenge.

Perhaps one of the most widely used definitions of coeliac disease is that which was adopted by the European Society of Paediatric Gastroenterology in 1970. As a literary effort it has little to commend it but it is certainly comprehensive: 'A permanent condition in which there is a flat mucosa in upper small intestine, a gluten-free diet results in complete restoration of normal mucosal architecture and in which the reintroduction of gluten into the diet will be followed by recurrence of mucosal abnormalities.'[30]

Recently it has become apparent that the clinical condition, as well as the morphological appearances seen on small intestinal biopsy, are one part of a spectrum and that insistence on rigid diagnostic criteria may lead to under-diagnosis of gluten-sensitive enteropathy and its possible complications.[31]

Incidence and geographical distribution

Perhaps not surprisingly, coeliac disease is common in those parts of the world where wheat constitutes a significant component of the diet. Europe and countries with a western life style, such as the USA and Australia, show the greatest incidence in the general population, but the disease is known to occur in most other parts of the world (e.g. Northern India, Central and South America, Sudan and China). The precise incidence is not known in those areas where the disease is relatively rare but in Western Europe it is estimated at between 0.52 per 100 000 per year in the general population in France, to as high as 170 per 100 000 in the West of Ireland. In the UK there is some variation between England and Wales, and Scotland, where it is commoner. The figure of 50 per 100 000 of the general population is often quoted. There is some evidence of a decline in recent years.[32]

Age and sex distribution

The disease is much more commonly diagnosed in children than in adults but occasionally patients are discovered while in their eighties. In children, the initial introduction of gluten into the diet 'triggers' the presenting symptoms so that the majority are diagnosed before the age of two years.

There is a tendency for young patients to experience a spontaneous remission around adolescence, and a second peak of incidence occurs during the third decade. Claims have been made that pregnancy may precipitate the appearance or exacerbation of clinical symptoms; however such cases are rare and constitute a very small proportion of those at first diagnosis.

Whilst discrepancies between reports have also occurred with regard to the sex incidence, there is in general a female preponderance of 1.3:1.

Familial incidence

Coeliac disease occurs with greater frequency among relatives of patients than in the general population. Whilst many of the studies of family incidence had been based on clinical histories, some used evidence provided by the study of jejunal biopsy specimens of the probands and relatives. One such study found that among 96 relatives of 17 index cases, four siblings out of a total of 31 had the disease and five children of index cases, out of a total of 26, were also found to have flat jejunal mucosa.[33] Other studies confirm this and show that about 154% of first degree relatives of coeliac patients may have the disease, even though many are asymptomatic.[34]

Twin studies incorporating histological evidence of jejunal mucosal abnormalities show 75% concordance for the disease in monozygous twins. This emphasizes the existence of other environmental factors for the development of gluten-sensitive enteropathy.

Genetic markers

There is a strong association between coeliac disease and certain major histocompatibility complex (MHC) antigens. The genes controlling the expression of MHC products are situated on the short arm of chromosome 6 and occupy four loci known as HLA-A, -B, -C and -D. They are closely linked and are inherited together. Their precise function is unknown but the expression of certain HLA antigens is associated with abnormalities of immunoregulation, coeliac disease and many other disorders.[2] Coeliac disease is primarily associated with a combination of an HLA-DQA1 and an HLA-DQB1 alleles, which results in the expression of a particular DQ alpha/beta protein heterodimer. Such molecules can be recognized by the intestinal mucosal T cells. HLA class II molecules are known to bind $CD4^+$ T cells (T-helper cells) with subsequent production of cytokines IL2, IL4 and gamma interferon. HLA DR3 and DR7 are in linkage disequilibrium with DQ alleles and therefore also commonly associated with coeliac disease. As all these HLA antigens are seen in a significant percentage of normal individuals, it is clear that their presence confers susceptibility to coeliac disease rather than being its cause.[35–37] The strength of the association can be expressed as the relative risk of developing coeliac disease for an individual expressing a particular HLA antigen in relation to an individual lacking that antigen. This relative risk seems to be greater for DR3 than for DR7. Data pooled from a number of published reports on 58 sibling pairs with coeliac disease suggests a recessive mode of inheritance.[34]

There are other possible inherited markers of coeliac disease which have no relation to the major histocompatibility complex. A specific B lymphocyte surface antigen has been described in the great majority of patients with coeliac disease and those with dermatitis herpetiformis (but not in normal subjects two being HLA-B8 positive). This antigen is recognized by maternal antisera and is known as GSE-associated B cell antigen. It has been shown to be independent of the HLA antigens and it is suggested that coeliac patients are homozygous for this cell marker.[38] The relationship between HLA-DR antigens and the immunological response in coeliac disease has been further explored in a recent study of 80 Spanish children with coeliac disease. It was found that certain phenotypes — such as DR3/DR7 and DR7/DR5 — were accompanied by significantly higher serum titres of antibody to gliadin when the children were on a normal diet than when on a gluten-free diet. These results suggest that genetic factors in the DR region influence the immune response to gliadin in coeliac disease.[39]

Finally, the association between specific immunoglobulin allotype markers on the heavy chain of the IgG molecule — GM (f; n; b) — and coeliac disease has been reported. All patients lacking the HLA-B8 and HLA-DR3 express this particular allotype in their immunoglobulin. This suggests that the controlling genes may influence susceptibility to coeliac disease.[40]

Environmental factors

Gluten toxicity

Samuel Gee, in his lucid description of the coeliac affection, demonstrated his awareness of the importance of environmental factors in the causation of the symptoms and categorically stated: 'If the patient can be cured at all, it must be by means of a diet'. Also, when describing the diet he considered appropriate for coeliacs he said: 'The allowance of farinaceous food must be small; highly starchy food, rice, sago, cornflour are unfit'. The Second World War caused a severe shortage of food in Europe and in Holland, Dicke and his colleagues noted that as a result of the lack of wheat in the diet, many of the children with coeliac disease showed a remarkable clinical improvement, and after further experiments discovered that a protein component of wheat was responsible for the harmful effects in coeliac patients.[41]

Further advances have been made since the development of small intestinal peroral biopsy studies. The improvement of the jejunal mucosa after the withdrawal of gluten from the diet and the reappearance of the characteristic lesion following its reintroduction has proven beyond doubt that gluten, or some of its constituents, have a major role in the pathogenesis of coeliac disease.

Gluten consists of a group of insoluble proteins which are separated from the soluble components — albumin, globulins and starch — after aqueous extraction from wheat fluor. It has been known from the early works of Dicke that the toxicity of wheat resided in the gluten and not in the starch of flour. Subsequent work has attempted to further isolate the toxic fraction of gluten; treatment with 70% ethanol produces two fractions, an insoluble one, glutenin, and a soluble one, gliadin. Gliadin has a high content of glutamine and proline and is known to contain some 40 different constituents which, on the basis of their electrophoretic mobility, are classified as alpha, beta, gamma and omega. A recent study has shown that all these gliadin fractions are toxic to coeliac mucosa in vitro although, based on less convincing evidence provided by mostly uncontrolled clinical experiments, it is widely believed that only alpha-gliadin is toxic to patients.[42] Another approach was that of Frazer and his colleagues who, in 1959, submitted gluten to digestion with first pepsin and then trypsin and obtained their fraction III, which was proven to be toxic to patients by feeding experiments.[43]

Fraction III was submitted to ultrafiltration by Truelove's group at Oxford and three subfractions, A, B and C were obtained. Fraction A contained electrolytes and small peptides of less than 1000 mw and was non-toxic to the jejunal mucosa of volunteer coeliac patients in biopsy studies. Fractions B and C containing peptides of 8000 and 13 000 mw respectively were found to cause light and electron microscopical abnormalities, as well as pronounced disaccharidase derangement in jejunal biopsy specimens.[44] Following on from these studies, the Oxford group have recently been able to demonstrate toxic damage to small intestinal mucosa caused by a polymer of alpha-gliadin consisting of 266 amino acids.[45]

These studies and many others available in the literature are marred by lack of comparability — some are based on feeding experiments, others on toxicity to in vitro cultured jejunal mucosa, others still on immunological responses to the fractions tested. There is a clear need for a reliable testing method.

Other cereal toxicity

The close taxonomic relationship between wheat and the other major cereals consumed by humans is illustrated in Table 26.3.[46] Based on the recommendations from the early work of the Dutch group, it had been assumed that not only wheat but other cereals, particularly rye and oats, should be excluded from the diet of coeliac patients. The evidence regarding the toxicity of oats is contradictory and numerous studies have failed to confirm its toxicity. Feeding 40–60 g of oats daily for one month to four coeliac volunteers who had a complete mucosal recovery on a gluten-free diet resulted in no morphological change by light or electron microscopy, no alteration of the mucosal surface to volume ratio and no significant depression of disaccharidase activity.[47]

A similar study was conducted to investigate the toxicity of barley, rye, maize and rice. The conclusion reached was that wheat, rye and barley (the three most closely related botanically, see Table 26.3) are toxic and their products such as beer and malts should be avoided, whereas oats, rice and maize are probably harmless. Many of the subjects in the study remained well even though their jejunal mucosa showed frank deterioration. Also, there was very considerable individual variability in response to the same amount of toxic cereals, indicating

Table 26.3 Taxonomic relationships of major cereal grains (from Kasarda[46])

Family	Gramineae					
Subfamily	Festucoideae					Panicoideae
Tribe	Triticeae			Aveneae	Oryzeae	Tripsaceae
Subtribe	Triticinae					
Genus	Triticum	Secale	Hordeum	Avena	Oryza	Zea
Species	Wheat	Rye	Barley	Oat	Rice	Maize

the varying susceptibility so clearly manifested by the differences in severity of symptoms encountered in coeliac patients.[48]

Other food toxicity

A small number of patients with the characteristic clinical symptoms of coeliac disease and corresponding jejunal mucosal abnormalities fail to achieve a complete remission of their symptoms or to show a significant morphological improvement of the intestinal lesion when gluten is excluded. It is well recognized that many such cases represent a failure of the patients to adhere to a strict diet. There are nonetheless a number of well documented patients who suffer intolerance to foods other than cereals, of which milk is the commonest. In these patients, which are mostly children, restoration to normal histology of the jejunal mucosa does not take place until both milk and gluten are removed from the diet. In some, the milk intolerance may be transient and in two reported cases, the children became tolerant to milk when they reached the age of 8½ years.[49,50] Other dietary components, such as eggs, chicken and tuna fish have also been found to be harmful in some patients.[51]

Morphological considerations

Dissecting microscopy

This technique of observation affords a valuable opportunity of assessing villous morphology of biopsy specimens prior to tissue processing. Its contribution to the overall assessment after light microscopy is perhaps of less significance. This is well illustrated by a remarkable change of opinion by one of the earliest groups advocating the value of the procedure.[52] One of the authors of the original publication has recently stated: 'The dissecting microscope ceremony is essentially a waste of time' and the correlation between the gross surface appearances and those seen on serial sections of the specimen is poor.[53] There are, nonetheless, abnormalities of the gross appearances easily distinguished from the normal, digitate and leaf villi:

Ridges. Shorter than the digitate or leaf villi, they have a longer axis and the breadth of several normal villi. The significance of their presence is probably very limited since they are found in normal individuals from all areas of the world.

Convolutions. These resemble the gyri of the cerebral cortex and are thought to represent a degree of abnormality corresponding to partial villous atrophy.[54] However it is clear that this pattern can be encountered in apparently healthy, asymptomatic individuals, particularly in tropical zones of the world.

Flat mucosa. There are no visible villi and the openings of the crypts are clearly visible; the surface is often broken by deep interconnecting clefts giving rise to a 'mosaic' appearance. This is the most commonly seen pattern in untreated coeliac disease and is rarely seen in other disease entities.

Cell kinetics

The morphological abnormalities associated with coeliac disease are best understood as alterations of the dynamics of the processes involved in mucosal cell renewal.[55]

The significantly increased rate of cell division, which is thought to be a response to an increased rate of cell loss from the damaged surface epithelium of the villi, requires a corresponding expansion of the proliferative compartment and, therefore, of the maturation compartment. This results in lengthening of the crypts, which also enlarge their diameter to accommodate the calculated sixfold increase in cell output and the consequential reduction of the height of the villi. By this process, the surface area exposed to the bowel lumen is greatly reduced and the loss of surface epithelial cells is thus minimized. Cytokinetic studies of crypts in jejunal biopsy specimens showing convolutions are of interest in that in severe cases, they resemble the cytokinetic profile of that of the flat avillous coeliac mucosa just described, but with crypt cell production rates which are not as high.[56]

Histological appearance

In severe cases, and in the majority of untreated coeliac patients, the biopsy specimens will show a 'flat' surface without villi (Fig. 26.34A); the picture is usually labelled 'subtotal villous atrophy', a particularly inept term since, as has been said, far from the inactivity implied by atrophy, the intestinal mucosa shows a six-fold increase in cell production and a marked crypt hyperplasia, and its overall thickness is normal or only slightly decreased. The term 'crypt hyperplastic villous atrophy' is therefore much more appropriate, and can be refined by adding subtotal or partial to indicate the degree of severity of the villous atrophy. Crypt hyperplastic villous atrophy, rather than the complete absence of villous processes, is characteristic of subtotal atrophy. This is encountered in some cases of untreated coeliac disease and in many patients with a partial response to treatment, who display intestinal mucosa with stunted, blunt, fused villi often of differing height and shape. This histological picture usually corresponds to the dissecting microscopical appearances of convolutions.

Surface epithelium

The covering cells are cuboidal with a basophilic cytoplasm and densely staining nuclei, often irregularly placed, giving rise to an appearance of stratification or palisading. The brush border is attenuated or absent as demonstrated with PAS staining. Intraepithelial lymphocytes are prominent and the ratio of lymphocytes to surface epithelial cells is higher than in the normal mucosa, although the total number of these lymphocytes may not be increased.

Basement membrane

Although by no means a constant finding, thickening of the epithelial basement membrane is seen and in some

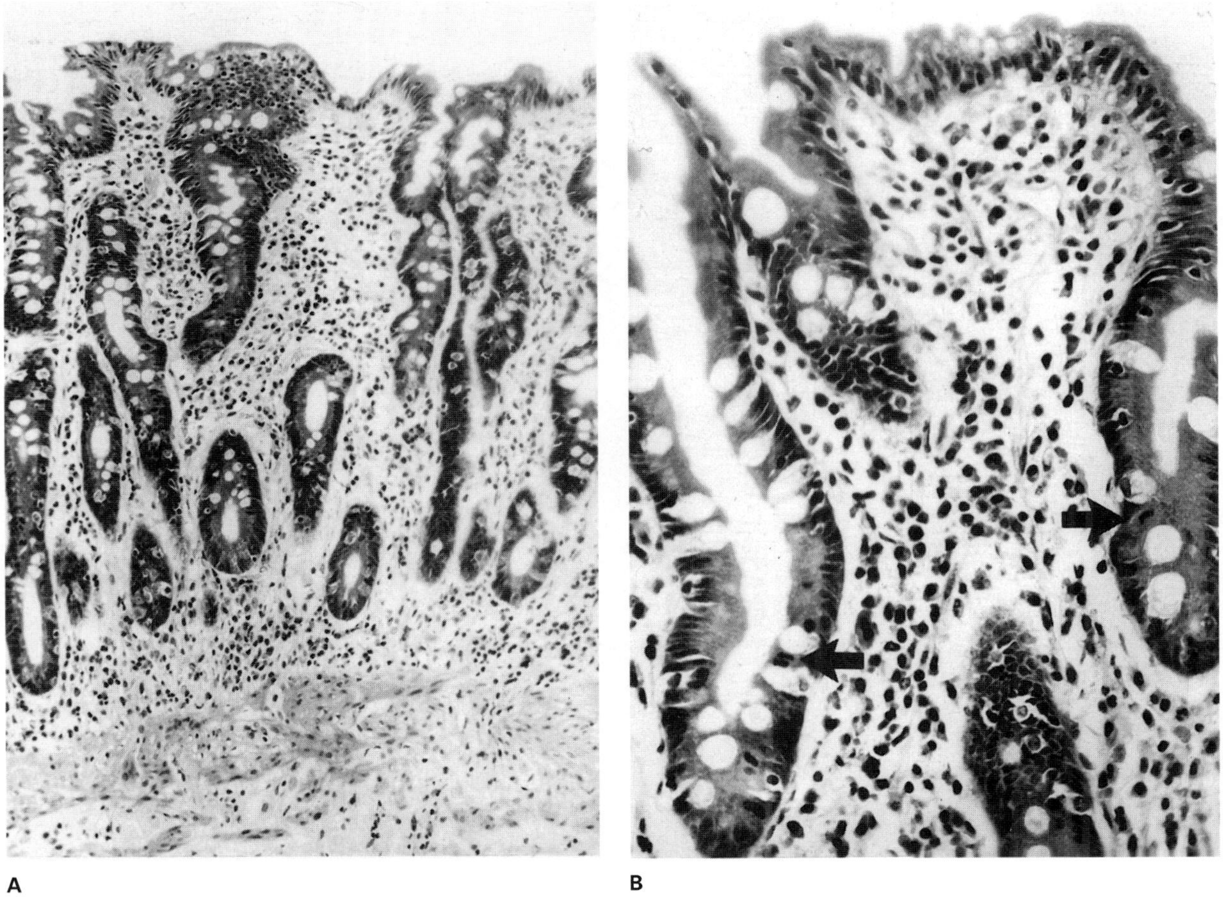

A B

Fig. 26.34 A Jejunal mucosa showing crypt hyperplasia, subtotal villous atrophy. (H&E, ×125) **B** Detail illustrating the lack of maturation of enterocytes; mitotic figures (arrows) are seen in the upper zones of crypts. Intraepithelial lymphocytes are easily identified. (H&E, ×320)

cases collagen may be demonstrated as a thin deposition on the membrane. Occasionally, this deposition may be exaggerated and the term collagenous sprue is sometimes used to describe these cases.

Crypts

In addition to the abnormalities of the shape and height of the villi, the crypts are elongated and increased in diameter. Sometimes the crypts are tortuous and show branching; they appear to open directly on to the surface. The number of mitoses per crypt is often obviously higher than in the normal mucosa and they can be seen at a much higher position within the crypt than is normal (Fig. 26.35B).

Paneth cells

It remains in doubt whether Paneth cells are increased in number since accurate information derived from proper quantitative studies based on reliable methods of identification is lacking.[57] It has been show, however, that their absence makes no difference to the clinical course of the disease,[54] despite some earlier reports suggesting that an increase in their numbers was associated with a good response to a gluten-free diet.

Endocrine cells

An increased number of enterochromaffin (EC) cells and increased tissue concentration of 5-hydroxytryptamine (5-HT) has been found in the duodenal tissues of children with coeliac disease. This is seemingly a reflection of the crypt hyperplasia but may have some importance since 5-HT appears to have a stimulatory effect on the cell growth of jejunal mucosa.[58] The number of EC cells have been found to be both increased and decreased in different studies and it is unlikely that these findings have any pathogenetic relevance.

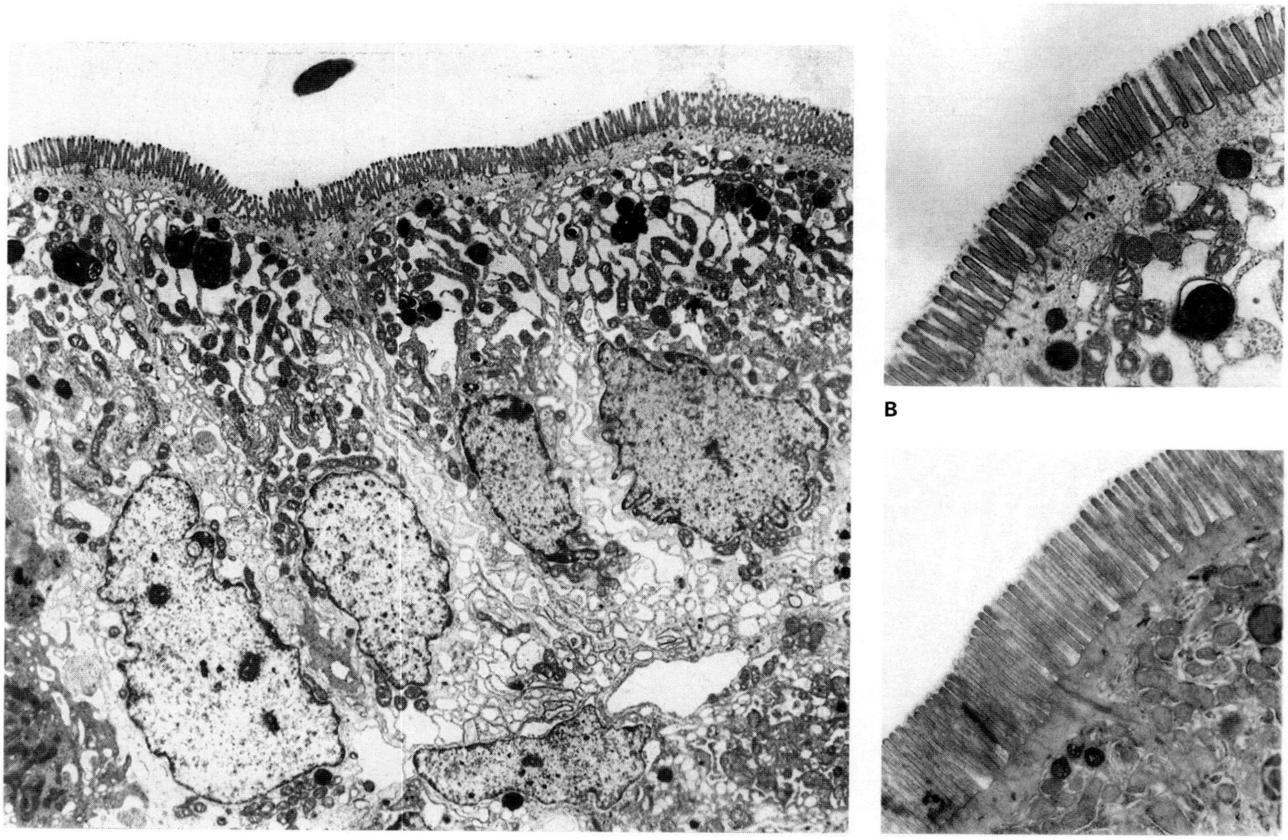

A B C

Fig. 26.35 A Transmission electron micrograph of jejunal mucosa in a patient with coeliac disease. The mitochrondria are swollen and there is noticeable cytoplasmic vacuolation of the enterocytes; lysosomes are also prominent. (×4200) **B** Detail of abnormal microvilli. **C** Normal microvilli for comparison. (×21 450).

Lamina propria

A major feature of the typical histological abnormality of coeliac disease is the increased inflammatory cell population of the lamina propria. This is made up of a variety of cells, the most significant of which are lymphocytes, plasma cells, histiocytes, eosinophils and mast cells. The lymphoid component of the infiltrate has been the object of much study since the immunological reactions of lymphocytes and plasma cells may be involved in the pathogenesis of the disease. The plasma cells are mostly of IgA type followed in frequency by IgM and IgE and fewer IgG. IgD-producing plasma cells are only occasionally found.[59]

Using tissue culture techniques, it has been found that most of the IgA produced in the lamina propria is reactive with gliadin. The lymphocytes in the lamina propria are mostly helper T cells and B lymphocytes, contrasting with the intraepithelial lymphocyte population, the vast majority of which are cytotoxic T cells. Macrophages may also be involved in immune mechanisms in their role as antigen-presenting cells. Although contradictory results have been reported, it appears that mast cells are increased in most cases of coeliac disease.[60] Their role in an immunological response mediated through IgE remains speculative. Similarly, eosinophils are present in excessive numbers but their function or significance is obscure.

The increased cellularity of the lamina propria in active coeliac disease returns to normal in patients who respond to a gluten-free diet. Correspondingly, an incomplete response to treatment is reflected by an intermediate degree of inflammatory infiltration of the lamina propria between that of normal controls and untreated coeliacs. This feature, together with the changes in the villous morphology and the degree of crypt hyperplasia, is of very considerable help in assessing response to treatment.

Morphometric methods of assessment of mucosal reactions

The recognition and assessment of the pathological features mentioned above involves subjective judgement by the pathologist. This may be of relatively minor importance when the objective is to establish a diagnosis of coeliac disease in an untreated patient whose biopsy specimen displays flat avillous mucosa. However the severity of the mucosal changes may not be uniform, and although a flat mucosa is the commonest finding on presentation, not all patients show it. It is common practice to perform a second biopsy after an interval on treatment to confirm that improvement of the mucosal structure has indeed occurred. In the case of children, it is also common practice to subject the patient to a gluten challenge to confirm the initial diagnosis and to exclude a transient state of gluten intolerance (see below). In these circumstances, as well as those in which the mucosal changes are used as an 'objective' means of comparing different treatments, it is essential that sound and reproducible methods are used. The degree of reduction of villous height is usually graded as subtotal (flat mucosa) and partial, the latter subdivided into mild, moderate or severe. Nevertheless, a continuous spectrum of changes exists and relatively minor changes may not be appreciated. Dunnill and Whitehead in 1972 described a point-counting morphometric method for the accurate measurement of the ratio between surface area and volume of the small intestinal mucosa. The volume is measured by counting the number of points of a grid interposed in the microscope eyepiece that 'fall' on the tissue. The grid also has evenly-distributed lines of a constant length and the number of times that these lines 'cut' the surface epithelium covering the villi or the mucosal surface on a flat specimen is proportional to the length of that surface.[61]* This method has the advantage of minimizing intra- and inter-observer variability.

Similar methods based on the point counting principle have been used to quantify objectively the number of inflammatory cells in the lamina propria of biopsy specimens, which are expressed as a ratio of cells per unit area.[62]

The need for such methods is well illustrated by the controversy which has arisen concerning intraepithelial lymphocytes (IEL) in coeliac disease. Following reports of their markedly increased numbers in the mucosa of untreated coeliac disease, and their return to more normal values after successful treatment,[63] speculation followed as to their role in the pathogenesis of the disease, and any possible prognostic or diagnostic value.[64]

The method used by these and other workers relates the number of IEL to a fixed number of enterocytes (usually 100). This ignores the fact that both the number of IEL and the number of surface epithelial cells are affected by the activity of the disease. When the numbers are related to a fixed parameter not altered by the disease (such as the length of muscularis mucosae), the number of IEL have been shown to be normal[65] or even decreased.[66]

Several authors have been able to apply computerized image analysis systems to the study of jejunal biopsy specimens and have reported a high degree of accuracy in detecting minor abnormalities by these quantitative methods.[67,68]

Electron microscopical studies

Ultrastructural studies are of limited value in the routine investigation of biopsy specimens of jejunal mucosa (Figs

*The mathematical basis for these and other morphometric methods is well established and can be found in a variety of specialized publications such as: Aherne and Dunnill. Morphometry. London: Edward Arnold, 1982.

26.35A, B, C) A number of consistent features are, however, seen in specimens from adults with untreated coeliac disease. The number of immature or undifferentiated cells is greater and they occupy a larger proportion of the crypts. The upper parts of the crypts are lined by cells showing a varying degree of morphological differentiation, and those on the surface, while fully mature, show irregular apical surfaces with short, irregular microvilli. These are often fused at their base into small 'bunches'. The cytoplasm shows varying degrees of vacuolation, increased lysosomal bodies and disruption and dilatation of mitochondria.[69,70] Other features seen are the disruption of the epithelial basal lamina with patchy deposition of collagen fibres among the reticulin framework. In the lamina propria, there are increased numbers of inflammatory cells, particularly plasma cells, which also show features of secretory activity with distension of the cysternae.

The electron microscopical features seen in response to gluten challenge under experimental conditions have also been the subject of detailed study.[44,62]

Brush border enzymes

Histochemistry applied to fresh tissue from jejunal biopsies has demonstrated deficiencies in content of a variety of enzymes in the absorptive cells on the surface of the flat mucosa, such as succinic dehydrogenase, esterase and acid phosphatase. By contrast, aminopeptidases and alkaline phosphatase activity is found in normal concentrations.[71]

Other methods involving subcellular fractionation techniques have shown that brush border enzymes are markedly reduced but with some increase in lysosomal enzymes reflecting increased lysosomal fragility. These changes tend to return to normal with successful treatment but beta-glucosidase usually remains low even in patients whose jejunal mucosa is histologically normal.[72]

Peptidases have also been the subject of detailed studies, particularly since it was claimed that their deficiency could be the cause of coeliac disease. There are many different types and not all are located in the brush border, some being found in the cytosol and lysosomes. The activity of brush border peptidases is reduced in untreated CD but usually returns to normal after a gluten-free diet is started. However a recent study which used a fluorometric assay to measure the hydrolysis by jejunal cell brush borders of a peptic-tryptic digest of gluten showed that the brush borders of coeliac patients were as efficient as those from normal controls in hydrolysing gliadin. There was no depression of any specific peptidase activity in the coeliac patients in remission.[73]

The disaccharidases, trehalase, lactase, sucrase, maltase and invertase, are confined to the brush border mainly at the apical parts of the villi, with lower activity in the basal part of the villi and are absent from the crypts. The activity of these enzymes is always greatly reduced in untreated coeliacs but returns to normal levels with treatment, except for lactase which may remain low. Disaccharidase activity appears to be a very sensitive marker for mucosal damage and in experimental studies is significantly reduced soon after gluten challenge.[44,62]

Distribution of the mucosal reaction

The most constant and severe damage in coeliac disease is seen in the proximal parts of the small intestine, the duodenum and jejunum, and decreases in intensity distally. Conversely, studies with multiple peroral biopsy specimens have shown that the improvement with gluten-free diet is seen more rapidly in the ileum and distal jejunum.[74]

Postmortem studies on 24 cases of coeliac disease, carried out within 2–4 h of death and using a technique of whole small intestinal fixation by distension with 10% formalin solution, have been reported by Thompson.[54,75] They show that the most severe mucosal changes are seen in the proximal jejunum and duodenum. In untreated coeliacs, the upper third of the small intestine shows a flat mucosa or severe partial villous atrophy. Less severe changes are seen in the middle third of the intestine and the terminal ileum is usually covered by finger-like villi but of small height.

Occasionally there are areas of degenerate and leaf-shaped villi in an otherwise extensively flat mucosa, supporting the notion that multiple biopsy specimens should be obtained to avoid false-negative results. The mucosal changes after gluten-free diet are much less extensive and in some case the villous pattern returns to normal.

Detailed postmortem examination of the small intestine may uncover undiagnosed malignant tumours, especially of lymphoreticular type.[54]

In general, endoscopic duodenal biopsies are small, rarely contain an intact muscularis mucosae and often include Brunner's glands. Good orientation of the specimen can be more a question of luck than skill, and ideal orientation is necessary for the proper assessment of relatively minor alterations of the height and shape of the villi. However, such specimens are readily obtained during an upper gastrointestinal endoscopic examination and, in most instances, several specimens can be produced safely and quickly. Step sections of each specimen often results in some of the levels displaying an acceptably good orientation. There are attractions to the clinician of endoscopic biopsy as an early investigation in cases of malabsorption and there are then increasing requests for diagnosis of coeliac disease on such material. Recent studies comparing the value of endoscopic duodenal biopsy and capsule jejunal biopsy indicate a very high degree of correlation between the diagnoses arrived at by both methods. Thus, in 27 patients with suspected coeliac disease, 24 (89%)

were correctly diagnosed by duodenal biopsy. It was concluded that although not an acceptable means of definitively diagnosing villous atrophy, duodenal biopsy specimens are a useful screening test in patients undergoing gastroduodenoscopy.[76]

A more recent study included 48 patients with dermatitis herpetiformis (DH) and compared the findings in three endoscopic duodenal bulb biopsies, three to six specimens from the second part of the duodenum and one suction biopsy specimen from the jejunum. Mucosal abnormalities confined to the duodenum when the jejunum was normal were present in 17% of patients. These findings are in accord with the reputed patchy nature of the mucosal abnormality associated with DH, and suggest that it is detected with the same degree of probability by multiple endoscopic duodenal biopsies as by a single jejunal one.[77]

Timing of the mucosal reaction

In the establishment of a firm diagnosis of coeliac disease there are two important aspects:

a) the time taken for a gluten-free diet to result in a significant improvement of the intestinal lesion, and
b) the time required for the mucosal changes to reappear after reintroduction of dietary gluten.

The majority of patients show a good response both clinically and histologically within six months on a gluten-free diet. In a number of cases there is no response or even a deterioration, and noncompliance with a strict gluten-free diet should be suspected; observation in hospital may be required. Because of the marked variation in sensitivity to gluten, even very small amounts inadvertently included in the diet may be responsible for an apparent lack of response. A small but significant proportion may be found to have an underlying malignancy complicating their coeliac disease.

Mention has already been made that in children gluten intolerance may be transient and that, because of this, it is prudent to submit children to a gluten challenge to confirm that sensitivity persists and continuous treatment is required. Unfortunately, the time taken for recurrence of symptoms and signs after reintroduction of dietary gluten is variable. In a study of 40 children whose duodenal or jejunal mucosa had returned to normal on a gluten-free diet, and who were then given a normal diet, relapse occurred between four months and more than six years (mean 16.9 months) in 37 of them. The three remaining patients still had normal mucosal morphology when last biopsied after 70, 85, and 65 months respectively. Although many patients may have actually relapsed before the definitive biopsy was taken, and thus the mean duration of 16.9 months may be an overestimate, several children took a very long time to show signs of recurrence. Although absence of evidence of relapse for two years is accepted by the European Society of Paediatric Gastroenterology as indicating that coeliac disease can be excluded, in view of the results of this study perhaps these requirements should be modified.[78] Similar experiences are reported in children by others who, however, found that most adults (18 out of 19) relapsed within seven weeks.[79] It may be that not only is there a great variability in the individual sensitivity of the jejunal mucosa to gluten, but that this might vary with time in the same individual.

The aetiology of coeliac disease

Coeliac disease is a protean disorder with a variable clinical expression and a complex pathogenesis in which local, systemic and genetic factors play important roles.

Enzyme deficiency hypothesis

From an historical perspective, the first hypothesis proposed to explain the toxic effect of the gluten in wheat and other cereals was prompted by the important discovery by Dicke and his Dutch colleagues that: 'The harmful factor [in the diet] must be situated in a component of wheat flour other than starch'.[41]

This pioneering work was followed by Frazer's fractionation of gluten and his discovery that his toxic fraction III — a peptic trypsin digest of gluten — could be rendered harmless by incubation with hog's intestinal mucosa. He postulated that this could be due to the absence of a peptidase from the jejunal mucosa, leading to incomplete digestion of gluten and accumulation and absorption of toxic peptides. The confirmation of peptidase deficiencies in the mucosa of coeliacs lent temporary support to this theory, but it was soon realized that the peptidase activity returned to normal with the mucosal improvement following a gluten-free diet, thus indicating that the peptidase deficiency was secondary to the mucosal damage rather than the underlying cause of it. Moreover, there are up to half a dozen peptidases in the jejunal brush border with such broad specificity that it is inconceivable that the failure of one of them could result in such a severe disturbance. More recent work has further reduced the credibility of the 'missing peptidase' hypothesis by proving that brush border preparations of coeliac jejunal mucosa from coeliacs were as efficient in hydrolysing gliadin as preparations from normal controls.[73]

The possibility that the toxic moiety of the gluten may not reside in the peptide chain but in glycoproteins in side chains has been investigated. Enzymatic removal of carbohydrate components of gliadin and administration to three coeliac patients in remission caused no morphological change in their jejunal mucosa.[80] There is little evidence that this suspected lack of a carbohydrase is the cause of coeliac disease, particularly since A-gliadin, an alpha-gliadin component which is toxic to coeliac patients, has no carbohydrate side chains. Confirmation of the initial studies has not been forthcoming. Lactase deficiency, an almost invariable finding in active coeliac disease in children, persists in many even after considerable improvement on a gluten-free diet and some of these children recover fully only after cow's milk has also been excluded from their diets. The importance of lactase deficiency as a precipitating factor in coeliac disease has not been fully explored.

Immunological hypothesis

It is beyond reasonable doubt that many of the features of the mucosal reaction represent manifestations of an immunological response, which may involve both humoral and cell-mediated immune reactions.

Humoral immunity. Both abnormal and normal levels of circulating immunoglobulins have been reported on numerous occasions. Many of the abnormalities may be related to associated disorders, such as milk protein intolerance, commonly found in coeliac patients, particularly in children. Because some 20% of patients with hypogammaglobulinaemia have a sprue-like syndrome and may respond to a gluten-free diet, it is unlikely that humoral antibodies are important in the pathogenesis. There is also an association between coeliac disease and selective IgA immuodeficiency.[81] Using immunohistochemical techniques, it has been shown that numbers of plasma cells of all five heavy-chain classes (A, G, M, D and E) in treated coeliac patients are not significantly different from those found in controls.[82]

Antibodies. Anti-reticulin antibodies were thought to be of importance in the pathogenesis of coeliac disease since they are found in 30–40% of patients and also in 20% of their first degree relatives. However, IgG class anti-reticulin antibodies are also found in about 25% of patients with Crohn's disease and other forms of inflammatory enteropathy. There may be some cross-reactivity between reticulin and fractions of gluten. More recently, IgA class anti-reticulin antibodies have been found which are more specific for coeliac disease, being present only in untreated patients and disappearing with treatment. They are also seen in 75% of relatives of coeliac patients who had villous atrophy in small intestinal biopsy specimens, but not in those with normal villous morphology.[83,84]

Serum antibodies to gluten and to gliadin fractions are found in the majority of coeliac subjects and their presence can be detected even after many symptom-free years on a gluten-free diet.[84] It is possible that these anti-gliadin antibodies may combine with gluten in food and give rise to immune complexes, which may deposit on the capillary basement membrane. This may activate complement and cause an Arthus-type hypersensitivity reaction leading to tissue damage. Evidence for such a reaction was provided by feeding experiments on coeliac subjects with toxic fractions of gluten.[62] Three to seven hours after the challenge, significant light and electron microscopical abnormalities were present in biopsy specimens from coeliac patients. The inflammatory response included a significant increase in the numbers of plasma cells and acute inflammatory cells with accompanying oedema and epithelial cell damage (Fig. 26.36A,B).

Cell-mediated immunity. As indicated above, the architectural abnormality of the intestinal villi is accompanied by a lymphocytic response within the lamina propria and among the surface epithelial cells — the intraepithelial lymphocytes (IEL). These lymphocytes differ in that those in the lamina propria are of helper type (CDA4) while most IEL are cytotoxic (CD8).

The ratio of $CD4^+/CD8^+$ appears to change little even in the active phase of the disease. Natural killer (NK) cells do not seem to play a significant role in coeliac disease.[85]

It is of considerable interest that recently the definitive T cell lineage marker, the T cell antigen receptor (TCR), has been studied in coeliac patients. There are two defined types of TCR: TCR-2 is a heterodimer of two polypeptides named alpha and beta; TCR-1 is similar but its two polypeptides are gamma and delta. Both receptors are associated with the CD3 complex, thus originating the T cell receptor complex (TCR-CD3 complex). Some 85–95% of blood T cells express TCR-2; however, it has been discovered that amongst the IEL in coeliac patients, the percentage expressing the TCR-1 (gamma/delta) is much higher — up to 30% — and of these, 75% are both CD4 and CD8 negative.[45,8] The function of these gamma/delta T cells is unknown, but they may act as memory cells and recognize antigens presented both by MHC class II and CD1 cystems. Cytotoxic T cells sensitized to gliadin have been demonstrated in coeliac patients and an inverse correlation between circulating T cell numbers and jejunal IEL have also been claimed, indicating that cytotoxic/suppressor T cells are attracted to the small intestine during the active phase of the disease and may mediate the tissue damage.[85] Other features which suggest the involvement of cell-mediated immunological mechanisms in coeliac disease are the well-known association with other 'autoimmune' diseases such as dermatitis herpetiformis, IgA nephropathy, rheumatoid arthritis, sarcoidosis, etc.[87]

There is therefore some evidence to suggest that an abnormal activation of cell-mediated immunity occurs in coeliacs. It is reasonable to assume that the 'trigger' for all this sequence of events may well be the breakdown of the mechanism by which 'tolerance' to ingested proteins is established, resulting in the immunogenicity of gliadin. The presence of sensitized lymphocytes to alpha-gliadin in cell-culture systems has been documented and the possibility that such T cells may mediate the epithelial damage

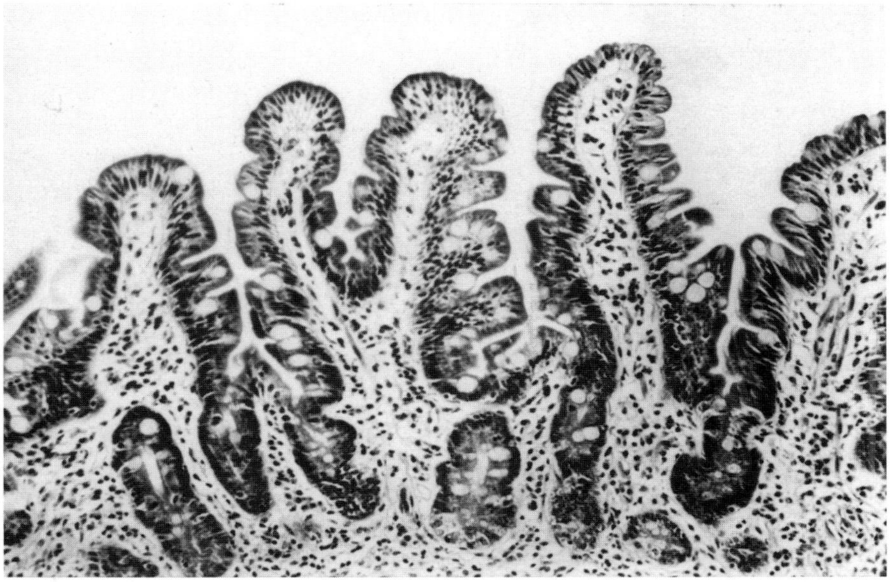

A

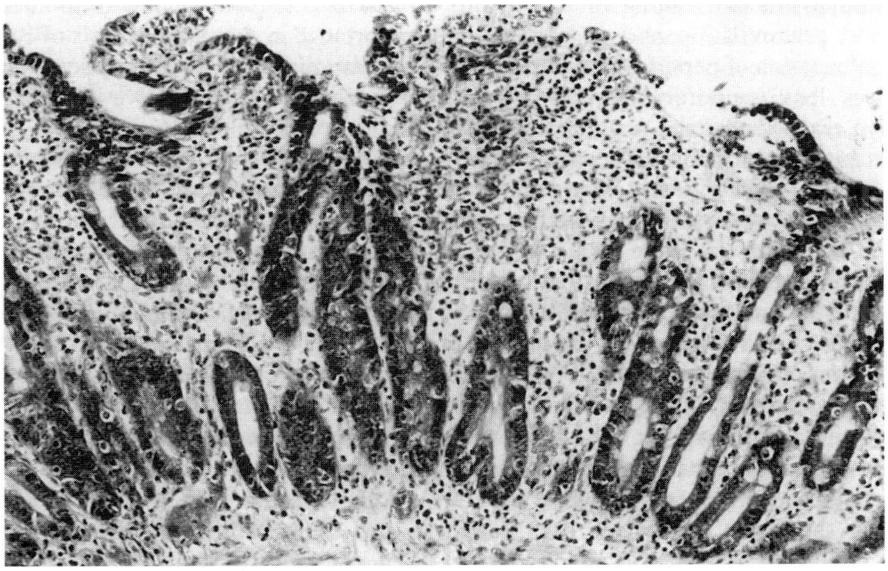

B

Fig. 26.36 Jejunal mucosa from a coeliac patient on gluten-free diet immediately before (**A**) and four hours after (**B**) a gluten challenge. (H&E, ×125)

through the release of cytokinases, such as leukocyte migration factor (LIF), interleukin-2, alpha-interferon, tumour necrosis factor (TNF), etc. appears to be high.

The role of T cells with the gamma/delta TCR is intriguing and their presence has also been documented in other autoimmune disorders.[88]

Another aspect of the involvement of cell-mediated immune reactions has been exposed by the reaction of experimental models in which villous atrophy and crypt hyperplasia were induced by allograft rejection of small intestine, infection by parasites and graft-versus-host disease.[89]

Genetic theory

Mention has already been made of the importance of major histocompatibility complex (MHC) components in antigen recognition by some T cells; also, the D region of the human MHC contains genes for class 2 products which are involved in interactions and cooperation between cells of the immune system. Certain class II MHC products are strongly associated with CD, in particular HLA-DR3, HLA-DR7 and HLA-DQW2 which are found in the phenotype of almost all coeliac patients. Recently it has been claimed that the enterocytes of children with coeliac disease show abnormally strong positive reactions with monoclonal antibodies to class II antibodies, particularly at the crypt level. It is possible that this increased expression of class II antigen may, in the presence of gluten, activate sensitized T lymphocytes in coeliac patients thus initiate an immune response.[90]

Possible role of adenovirus

It has been shown that there exists a region of homology between A-gliadin and the early region E1b protein of human adenovirus type 12 (Ad12), which is usually isolated from the gastrointestinal tract. Antibodies which react with the Ad12 E1b protein specifically cross-react with A-gliadin.[91] It is possible that the occurrence of specific HLA haplotypes in coeliac disease may reflect the presence of genes associated with these haplotypes that govern the host's immune response to specific viral infection. After exposure to infection with Ad12 virus, the immune system responds by producing antibodies which can cross-react with alpha-gliadin — the major antigenic fraction of crude gliadin — and this cross-reaction may perpetuate the reaction and cause the mucosal damage.

Gluten as a lectin

Lectins are glycoproteins found in a wide variety of plant seeds; they display the property of binding to some human cells, particularly immature, transformed or tumour cells, with an antibody–antigen-like specificity. This binding results in toxicity to the cell in some circumstances, and is due to the specificity of the lectin for a carbohydrate component of the cell membrane. It has been postulated that there may be an increase in incomplete glycoproteins in the cell surface membrane of enterocytes in coeliac disease which results in gluten binding to the cell surface and, acting as a lectin, causes cell damage. This damage results in increased cell turnover and lengthened crypts, covered by immature enterocytes which are themselves more susceptible to binding by the lectin (gluten), thus completing a cycle of increasing damage. Only the absence of gluten breaks this cycle and allows the mucosa to recover. This hypothesis could also explain the common observation of gluten-intolerance appearing after a gastrointestinal infection — which causes the initial damage to the enterocytes — and the reversal of this intolerance after the recovery from the infection when gluten is no longer toxic. Similar mechanisms may operate in other food intolerances such as soy protein, since lectins have been isolated from soy beans.[92]

These theories are not mutually exclusive and it seems more than likely that all pathogenetic mechanisms explained above may contribute, in some measure, to the manifestation of the disease.

Coeliac disease complications

There are a number of clinical manifestations of coeliac disease, the cause of which is far from understood; many of these improve with treatment but others persist even when the malabsorption syndrome is well controlled. Among the commoner and most troublesome are glossitis and oral ulceration, which may be severe in up to a third of patients. Recurrent aphthous ulcers may sometimes be the only manifestation of the disease. Abnormalities of small bowel motility and distension may lead to volvulus or intussusception, which may be transient or lead to intestinal obstruction. Occasionally these manifestations present in the absence of a prior diagnosis.

Cholecystitis, peptic ulceration and pancreatitis are more common in coeliac patients than in the general population. Anaemia may be due to iron or vitamin B12 malabsorption and is a very common presenting sign; it is usually easily corrected with appropriate treatment. Vitamin K deficiency may cause bleeding into subcutaneous tissues or mucous membranes and into the gut lumen.

Disturbances of calcium metabolism result in a variety of skeletal abnormalities of which osteomalacia in adults and rickets in children are the most important. Once again, these may occur as presenting signs of coeliac disease.

Eight out of 34 young patients, between 2–17 years of age, presenting because of short stature but complaining of no gastrointestinal symptoms were found to have subtotal or severe partial villous atrophy of the jejunal mucosa, and seven of them showed a significant acceleration of growth on a gluten-free diet.[93] This finding confirms the well known fact that perhaps 20% of coeliac patients show retardation of growth, which, in children, is reversed with treatment. In adults, coeliacs have been found to be significantly shorter than non-coeliacs.

Hyposplenism, often accompanied by splenic atrophy, is demonstrated by the presence of Howel-Jolly bodies, acanthocytes and thrombocytosis in the peripheral blood. It is commonly found in adults but not in children with coeliac disease. The spleen weighed less than 100 g in 13 of 31 consecutive autopsies of coeliacs and in four of these 13, lymphoma was demonstrated.[54] Lymphadenopathy with progressive lymphoid hyperplasia leading to the development of malignant lymphoma in the small intestine, was described by Whitehead in 1968 who proposed the term 'steatorrhoea lymphadenopathy' for this condition.[94] While the occurrence of lymphoma in coeliac disease has repeatedly been confirmed, it seems that in some patients the lymphadenopathy improves or disappears following gluten withdrawal.[95] A few reports describe patients with a flat mucosa, splenic atrophy and cavitation of the mesenteric lymph nodes.[96–98] In some, a gluten-free diet causes a reversion to normal of both mucosa and nodes. However, it is more usual in patients with gluten-sensitive

Table 26.4 Malignancy in coeliac disease

Type of tumour	Cases	Percent
Lymphoma	133	51.4
Carcinoma of GI tract	64	24.7
Carcinoma elsewhere	61	23.6
Total	258	

enteropathy who fail to continue to respond to dietary treatment and who develop lymphoma.

Malignancy in coeliac disease

A collaborative study was set up at the Clinical Research Centre in London in 1978 and received information from 70 centres throughout the UK. A register was established of 400 patients with coeliac disease and definite or suspected malignancy, and 235 patients with 259 tumours were eventually found to fulfill the acceptance criteria. Table 26.4 shows the types of tumours encountered amongst these patients.

In 156 patients the diagnosis of coeliac disease preceded that of malignancy with a mean interval between the two diagnoses of 7.3 years. Both malignancy and coeliac disease were diagnosed at the same time in 44 patients and in 35 malignancy was first discovered (up to 16 years earlier). Of the 235 patients, 215 had single malignant tumours, 18 had two tumours and the remaining two had three and five respectively. Eleven patients had a lymphoma and a carcinoma. Among the 133 lymphomas (107) 90% were of the so-called malignant histiocytosis type; the remainder were mostly of large cell undifferentiated type (9) or unclassified (14). Coeliac patients who did not respond to a gluten-free diet were apparently at no higher risk of developing lymphoma; the majority of lymphomas arose in the small intestine in patients who presented with weight loss and diarrhoea, or with acute intestinal perforation or obstruction. The prognosis of this type of lymphoma is poor and only 9.5% of patients were alive five years after the diagnosis, which was an improvement on previously available data.

The epithelial malignancies were preferentially located within the small intestine, 19 patients developing such tumours, which represents a relative risk of 82.6 compared with the general population. Oesophageal (10) and pharyngeal (4) malignancies were also found with a small but significantly raised incidence.[99]

The importance of lymphoma as a major complication in coeliac disease cannot be overemphasized because its diagnosis is often missed, as is illustrated in several studies. The possible relationship with abdominal lymphadenopathy in coeliac patients has already been mentioned. Otherwise the presenting symptoms are weight loss, which affects 80% of patients and is associated with lethargy, abdominal pain and/or diarrhoea. These symptoms are often mistaken for dietary indiscretions. Palpable lymph nodes are seen only in a minority.[100]

The pathological features of the tumour are described in Chapter 37 of this book. Initially thought to be of histiocytic cell derivation and consequently named malignant histiocytosis of the intestine,[101] it is now known that the malignant cells are derived from T cells.[102] The mucosa not involved by the tumour appears to show changes in the subsets of intraepithelial lymphocytes present which mimic the markers expressed by the tumour cells.[103]

It is of considerable interest that adherence to a strict gluten-free diet appears to confer some protection against the occurrence of the currently-termed enteropathy-associated T cell lymphoma. Probably close to 50% of death in coeliacs are due to malignancy, of which lymphomas are by far the commonest; the small intestine is the site of the primary lesion in over 75% of cases. Unfortunately, the prognosis of this type of tumour is poor, with most patients dying within a year of diagnosis.[104] The involvement of the Epstein-Barr virus in four out of eleven recently reported cases is supported by the presence of viral DNA demonstrated by in situ hybridization.[105]

Coeliac disease-associated disorders

Dermatitis herpetiformis (DH)

This skin disorder is characterized by a papulovesicular itchy rash, usually symmetrical and involving the limbs, face, scalp or trunk. It may occur at any age but is uncommon in childhood. Although almost all patients show an intestinal mucosal lesion similar to that of coeliac disease; symptoms of malabsorption are very unusual. The incidence of DH amongst coeliacs is approximately 1%.

Jejunal mucosal abnormalities in patients with DH were first demonstrated in 1966.[106] The importance of taking more than one sample of the jejunal mucosa in those patients was emphasized in a study which showed mucosal abnormalities in 21 out of 22 DH patients of which 15 showed a flat mucosa. It was concluded that the distribution of the lesion was patchy, with areas of normal appearances between frankly abnormal mucosa. It was thought initially that this patchiness was characteristic of DH. However some studies have found no difference in the degree of abnormalities and distribution between patients with coeliac disease with and without DH.[107]

The vast majority of patients with DH will experience a considerable improvement of both their skin condition and gastrointestinal symptoms on a gluten-free diet.

The cause of DH is not well understood but a characteristic feature is the deposition of IgA along the basement membrane of the epidermis. A recent study of seven patients with DH has suggested that this immunoglobulin is of small intestinal origin since it was found to be dimeric and to possess J-chain, features which are not found in circulating IgA.[108] There is also a marked concordance with respect to the histocompatibility phenotype. About 80% of DH patients are HLA-B8 positive and have a similar frequency of HLA-DW3 to that found in coeliac disease. Other diseases of the skin, such as psoriasis or eczematous dermatitis, have also been reported in coeliacs. Furthermore, it has been shown that gluten challenge (in the form of *increased* amount of gluten in a normal diet) in DH patients with 'normal' intestinal mucosal morphology may result in gross histological abnormalities;[109] this finding supports the concept of 'latent coeliac disease' which is seen also amongst relatives of patients with coeliac disease.[89]

Pulmonary disorders

A form of diffuse fibrosing alveolitis has been described in patients with coeliac disease and the high titres of autoantibodies found in these subjects was thought to indicate an autoimmune aetiology. Again an association with HLA-B8 and HLA-DW3 have been found in some cases of fibrosing alveolitis and coeliac disease. The finding of serum antibodies against avian-derived antigens lead to the suggestion that this form of pulmonary disorder was identical to bird fancier's lung. However the precipitins in coeliacs were shown to be different from those found in bird fancier's lung, and probably of dietary origin rather than acquired by inhalation. A study designed to clarify this possible association found that in 12 patients with bird fancier's lung none had jejunal mucosal abnormalities, and only one patient out of 61 with coeliac disease showed a positive result to an inhalation provocation test.[110]

The multisystem granulomatous disorder, sarcoidosis, has also been linked to coeliac disease and some patients have raised levels of anti-gliadin antibodies and increased numbers of IEL in the jejunal mucosa.[87]

Ulcerative jejunoileitis

This rare condition has been described under a variety of names such as idiopathic chronic ulcerative enteritis, chronic ulcerative jejunitis, non-granulomatous ulcerative jejunoileitis, chronic nonspecific ulcerative enteritis, etc., reflecting the underlying lack of understanding of its aetiology and pathogenesis.

The clinical picture emerging from approximately 50 cases published in the English literature is fairly well defined. Most patients are in their sixth or seventh decade and present with a chronic history of abdominal pain and distention, fever, weight loss, diarrhoea and often steatorrhoea. The diagnosis should be considered only after exclusion of other well known causes of small intestinal ulceration such as Crohn's disease, ischaemic enteritis, polyarteritis, irradiation enteritis, lymphoma and drugs — particularly enteric-coated potassium tablets. In addition, rarer infective processes such as tuberculosis, fungal infections, typhoid fever, bacillary dysentery, etc., should be ruled out. Jejunal biopsy, when performed, is unhelpful or shows features consistent with coeliac disease. The majority of the patients undergo exploratory laparotomy.

Pathology. At operation, the small intestine may show one or more abnormal areas; the wall is thickened and oedematous and there may be strictures with proximal dilatation. Perforation of the small bowel is not infrequent and enlarged mesenteric lymph nodes are often seen. Inspection of the mucosal lining reveals multiple ulcers always in the jejunum but commonly in the ileum and rarely in the colon. These ulcers may be superficial, involving the mucosa and submucosa and of varying size and outline, or may be sharp and penetrating to the muscularis propria or serosa. The ulcer bed is made up by granulation tissue infiltrated by lymphoid cells, histiocytes and acute inflammatory cells in different proportions (Fig. 26.37A,B); eosinophils may be prominent. There may be underlying fibrosis in the chronic type of lesions causing narrowing of the lumen. In some cases the flat mucosa adjacent to the ulcer may show pseudopyloric metaplasia. The intervening mucosa almost invariably shows villous atrophy and crypt hyperplasia similar to the lesion in coeliac disease. The mucosa in areas distant from the ulcers may be normal.

The relationship of ulcerative jejunoileitis to coeliac disease remains controversial. One of the largest series available, based on 36 previously published cases and 9 new ones, concludes that 12 patients could be classified as being coeliacs whilst 11 others with a long history of malabsorption had a similar jejunal mucosal lesion but did not respond to a gluten-free diet.[111] None of five cases in another report showed a response to a gluten-free diet in spite of the fact that four showed subtotal villous atrophy and crypt hyperplasia of the jejunal mucosa.[112]

The evidence available suggests that this may be a heterogenous group of patients who could be separated into three subgroups:

a. patients who are clearly coeliacs, improve on a gluten-free diet and in whom ulcerative jejunoileitis may supervene while under control on treatment
b. as above but do not respond to gluten withdrawal
c. non-coeliac patients — with normal jejunal mucosa between the ulcers.[113]

Whatever the underlying pathology, the prognosis of these patients is poor with a mean survival of 37 months (15–120 months). The best form of treatment appears to be surgical resection of the segment or segments of the affected small intestine.

An interesting and equally controversial aspect of

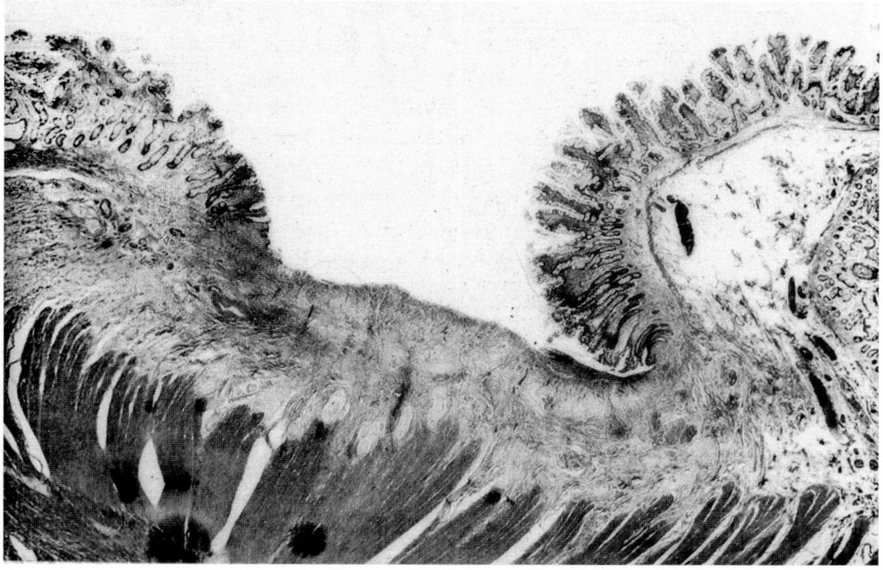

A

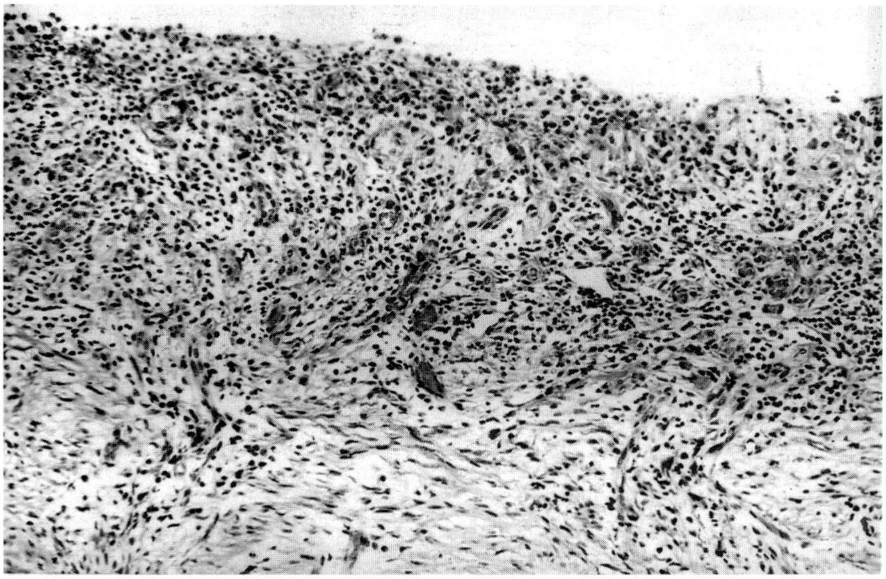

B

Fig. 26.37 A Ulcerative jejunoileitis. The ulcer penetrates to the submucosa only. (H&E, ×11) **B** The ulcer is lined by granulation tissue. (H&E, ×125)

ulcerative jejunoileitis is its relationship to malignant lymphoma. The association of a flat mucosa with areas of ulceration and lymphoid infiltration of the lamina propria with atypical cells which in some cases progressed to 'reticulum cell sarcoma' was highlighted by Whitehead in 1968.[94] Isaacson and Wright described seven cases considered to show the clinical and pathological features of ulcerative jejunoileitis in whom the presence of underlying malignant histiocytosis of the intestine was demonstrated by careful histological and electron microscopical examination of the intestinal lesions and similar infiltrates in liver, spleen and bone marrow. They considered their cases to be similar to those of Whitehead but believed the neoplasia to be a malignant histiocytosis.[114] However Isaacson and his colleagues have recently provided new evidence indicating that the malignant cells in many, if not all, cases of so-called malignant histiocytosis of the intestine are of T cell origin.[102]

The contention that *all* cases of ulcerative jejunoileitis are simply occult or overt forms of intestinal lymphoma[115] has little support in recent publications and appears to be almost certainly untenable.[125] On the other hand, the absolute necessity of a detailed study of the infiltrate at the ulcer base and in adjacent areas, and, when available, accompanying lymph nodes, cannot be overemphasized. An extensive search for neoplastic cells, which may not be overtly atypical, must be carried out over several blocks from resected specimens. Repeated biopsy may be required to confirm the diagnosis.

Collagenous sprue

The presence of an amorphous hyaline band under the surface epithelial basement membrane, later identified as collagen, has been recorded in many early descriptions of the pathology of coeliac disease. Rarely this collagen band is quite conspicuous and can be seen to progress in sequential biopsies. It has been proposed that patients with malabsorption and whose jejunal mucosa shows this change suffer from a disease named collagenous sprue. This claim is based on the study of a single case in which, following an initial response to gluten withdrawal, there was a steady deterioration of health and persistent diarrhoea which could only be controlled by steroids. The postmortem study demonstrated large deposits of collagen throughout the intestine associated with avillous mucosa.[116]

Although further cases have been reported, seemingly accepting the hypothesis of the separate standing of collagenous sprue, it has also been made clear that collagen deposition occurs not infrequently in coeliac patients. One study of patients with adult coeliac disease demonstrated subepithelial collagen deposition in 36% of biopsy specimens from 146 coeliac patients. Furthermore, a similar deposit was noted in three out of seven patients with tropical sprue and, in some coeliacs, there was regression of the amount of collagen following treatment.[117] It is therefore clear that the subepithelial collagen deposition does not define a separate clinical entity. In a study of 50 coeliac patients, collagen was found in 42% of jejunal biopsy specimens and on reviewing progress 22 years later there was no difference in the prognosis between those with and those without subepithelial collagen deposition.[118] Nevertheless, a number of cases are described in whom the response to gluten exclusion from the diet is very poor and steroids are required to control the diarrhoea and malabsorption. Whitehead, noting the advanced age of most patients, and the fact that usually they have been suffering from coeliac disease for a long time, points out that when the deposit is marked, the mucosa shows a crypt hypoplastic villous atrophy. This pattern is suggestive of decreased cell turnover which is also seen in association with malignancy, untreated pernicious anaemia and severe tropical sprue. He postulated that the findings may represent a state of unresponsiveness of the mucosa which may precede jejunal ulceration.[119]

Nonspecific ileal ulcer

Ulceration and spontaneous jejunoileal perforation is common in those parts of the world where typhoid fever and tuberculous enteritis are still prevalent. In developed countries, however, these diseases are seldom encountered and in the majority of cases, no cause for ileal ulceration can be found. A recent retrospective study of 54 cases of spontaneous (nontraumatic) perforation has been retrieved from the files of the Department of Pathology of Edinburgh University during the period 1966–1982. Table 26.5 shows the underlying causes of ulceration of 44 of these cases. In the remaining ten cases no cause could be identified and in eight there was no history of drug taking. The specimens showed localized ulceration with neighbouring chronic and acute inflammation but normal appearances of the remaining small bowel. Two of the patients in this group of ten had recently taken drugs and, characteristically in one, a thiazide diuretic and slow release potassium had been ingested. Enteric-coated potassium tablets are known to lead to nonspecific ileal ulceration.[120] It is important to exclude the diagnoses listed in Table 26.5 since the mortality for this group of usually elderly patients is high. However when the ulceration and/or perforation of the ileum is not due to an underlying cause, resection of the affected segment of ileum is usually curative.[121]

Ulcerative enteritis in graft-versus-host disease (GVHD)

In recent years allogeneic marrow transplant has been used with increasing frequency for various bone marrow diseases. A report of 13 cases in which a laparatomy was performed for symptoms of severe enteritis described five of these cases in whom ulcerative enteritis was thought to be due to GVHD.[122]

Cow's milk protein intolerance

Intolerance to cow's milk with malabsorption is a temporary condition affecting young infants. It causes a variety of symptoms among which the commonest are diarrhoea and vomiting, eczema, recurrent respiratory infections and, occasionally, colitis. The infants present within ten weeks, having had symptoms usually from the second week after birth, and show signs of malabsorption and

Table 26.5 Aetiology of jejunoileal perforation

Cause of perforation	No.
Secondary to an obstructing lesion	13
Lymphoma	9
Crohn's disease	5
Localized ischaemia/infarction	3
Polyarteritis nodosa	3
Radiation enteritis	3
Small bowel carcinoma	2
Post-tubal diathermia	1
Others	5
Total	44

dehydration which may be severe and require parenteral nutrition. There is no difference in sex incidence. The majority of cases reported come from Europe and North America but the condition has also been encountered in developing countries such as Indonesia, where it is estimated that up to 20% of children develop chronic diarrhoea following acute infantile gastroenteritis and many of these are intolerant to cow's milk.[123]

Pathology. Most infants with cow's milk protein intolerance (CMPI) show an enteropathy which resembles closely that seen in coeliac disease. As in the latter condition, there is a significant alteration of the cell kinetics of the jejunal mucosa, with an increase in the number of cells in the proliferative and maturation compartments and a higher mitotic index. These changes return to normal values with treatment and are, in general, milder than those seen in coeliac disease. In one series 10 out of 17 children had only partial villous atrophy as opposed to all of 47 with coeliac disease, who showed subtotal villous atrophy.[124] The crypts, while hyperplastic, are shorter than those of coeliac children and the mitotic response more vigorous, which suggests that the rate of cell loss is higher and may explain why recovery is usually quicker. The similarity between the enteropathy seen in CMPI and coeliac disease was also emphasized in a more recent morphometric study of jejunal biopsy specimens from 12 children with CMPI and 11 with coeliac disease. The villous height was found to be significantly shorter in untreated children with both diseases but those with cow's milk intolerance, while improving with milk withdrawal, did not reach control values. Another important finding in this study was that, in contrast to previous reports, the number of eosinophils in the lamina propria in cases of CMPI was no different from that in controls, but following cow's milk challenge the number of intraepithelial eosinophils did rise significantly in five out of seven cases. Several of the biopsy specimens obtained from children after milk challenge showed a patchy distribution of the changes.[125]

Pathogenesis. The aetiology of this temporary disorder is not known. In a significant proportion of cases the condition begins after an acute episode of gastroenteritis and it is possible that the damage caused by this infection to the small intestinal mucosa may increase its permeability to proteins in the cow's milk, which can then stimulate an immune response with further damage and sensitization. In such circumstances the enterocytes may become deficient in lactase and thus maintain the intolerance to the milk. Evidence to support this hypothesis is provided by the finding of higher than normal levels of serum IgA, which return to normal when cow's milk is excluded from the infants' diet and rise sharply again after milk challenge. However, the immediacy with which some children respond to milk challenge and the systemic and severe character of this response, which in some cases resembles anaphylaxis, has given rise to theories of an allergic mechanism involving IgE antibodies or antigen–antibody reaction with fixation of complement. The search for IgE-containing plasma cells in the small intestinal mucosa or changes in the serum levels of IgE have, in general, been fruitless, but in a later report, all eight babies with cow's milk protein intolerance were found to have significantly higher numbers of IgE-containing plasma cells per square millimetre of lamina propria than children with coeliac disease and controls.[126] The significance of this unconfirmed finding is not clear.

Course and prognosis. The withdrawal of cow's milk and cow's milk-based foods, such as ice-cream, is followed by a rapid improvement of the clinical symptoms and mucosal changes within four weeks. Following this treatment, most children will develop tolerance to cow's milk by the age of one-and-a-half years and the intestinal mucosa becomes normal 6–18 months after the start of treatment. A very small number of cases will fail to show such a positive response, and among these some are shown to have gluten-sensitive enteropathy as well which may also be transient. Conversely, there is evidence that a significant number of coeliac children also have cow's milk intolerance. More recently, there have been two reports of children with a 'combined cow's milk protein and gluten-induced enteropathy'. In both patients the diagnosis of coeliac disease was followed by a failure to improve on a gluten-free diet. Further investigations proved that the children's enteropathy was also induced by cow's milk and only when both foods were removed from the diet was there a jejunal mucosa recovery. Unlike most cases of CMPI, both of these children remained intolerant to cow's milk until they were eight years old. Both reports highlight the fact that while on a gluten-free diet, and in spite of the existence of marked jejunal mucosal abnormalities, the patients remain asymptomatic.[49,50]

Soy and other protein intolerance

It seems paradoxical that while soy bean food prepared in a milk-like fluid has been used in children allergic to cow's milk, over the last years there have been several reports of intolerance to soy proteins. The conditions was well documented in a report of a child with clinical intolerance to soy protein in whom a challenge with soy produced a reversal of the initial response to its exclusion from the diet. Jejunal biopsy specimens showed abnormalities identical to those of coeliac subtotal villous atrophy which disappeared within a few days of dietary treatment and recurred after challenge.[127] It may not always be appreciated that soy is very extensively used in manufactured foods and that its avoidance is therefore quite difficult.

Vitoria and colleagues have reported three children with proven CMPI who were also found to be intolerant to fish, rice and chicken respectively. Each of these foods was shown to induce abnormalities in the jejunal mucosa, identical to those of CMPI, while the children were kept on a cow's milk-free diet, and all remained asymptomatic while the appropriate food was excluded from their diet. Like the CMPI, the fish rice and chicken intolerance was temporary in two of the children. The authors believe that CMPI is not a specific entity but part of a broader intolerance to various dietary proteins.[128]

Transient gluten intolerance

It has already been mentioned that recurrence after gluten challenge in patients with documented gluten-sensitive enteropathy may in some rare cases take several years to occur.[78] It is therefore questionable whether or not transient or temporary gluten intolerance exists and when the diagnosis should be contemplated. What seems unquestionable is that rare cases have been described, as far back as 1952, in whom tolerance to gluten develops after a period of coeliac disease. One such case was described in 1976; the patient, an 8-week-old infant was shown to have gluten-sensitive enteropathy by jejunal biopsy and gluten challenge studies. Nine months after the last positive challenge, gluten was once again introduced into the diet, without symptoms, and a jejunal biopsy specimen taken after the child had been eating a normal diet for 26 months showed normal features. The authors considered that the child did not have coeliac disease and that temporary gluten sensitivity is more akin to cow's milk protein intolerance following gastroenteritis. They also laid down strict criteria which need to be met before the diagnosis is entertained.[129]

Persistent postenteritis diarrhoea

This entity, also known as postinfective malabsorption syndrome or postenteritis syndrome, is a well recognized complication of infantile gastroenteritis. One study of 168 children admitted to the Royal Children's Hospital in Brisbane with acute gastroenteritis showed that 32 (19%) went on to develop postenteritis diarrhoea. Further studies demonstrated persistence of pathogens in the stools in seven and ten more had evidence of carbohydrate intolerance. In the remaining 15 children, no cause for the persistent symptoms could be found. All the cases recovered within 14–40 days of onset. Comparison between the group of 32 children with those who recovered from the acute gastroenteritis in less than seven days indicated the existence of several possible predisposing factors. Persistent diarrhoea occurred in a younger age, was commoner amongst aboriginals and Asians and those with a history of previous diarrhoeal disease, and was more likely to occur with enteritis caused by bacteria rather than a virus. It is postulated that the recovery of the damage caused to the jejunal mucosa by the initial infection may depend on a variety of environmental, age and immunological factors and may not be complete, resulting in decreased absorptive area and deficient disaccharidase activity.[130]

This condition has also been documented in adults following acute bacterial and viral enteritis. The disease often follows an acute episode of infective diarrhoea contracted while visiting other countries in temperate areas of the world and in the majority no pathogens are isolated. The jejunal mucosa shows a well preserved morphology but an increased chronic inflammatory infiltration of the lamina propria and apparent increase in the numbers of intraepithelial lymphocytes. The most severe cases are often associated with folate deficiency. Montgomery and associates, in a number of publications, have drawn attention to the fact that when compared with 'tropical sprue' (postinfective tropical malabsorption) the only significant difference was the tendency for spontaneous resolution.[131–133]

Intractable (protracted) diarrhoea of infancy

Intractable diarrhoea of infancy was defined as a condition presenting in the first three months of life, for greater than two weeks duration, and with three or more stools negative for enteric pathogens. The reason why certain infants progress from an acute episode of diarrhoea to a prolonged and sometimes fatal disease is unknown. There is evidence that the syndrome is due to a variety of causes and some familial forms have been described.[134]

Pathology

The appearance of the jejunal mucosa varies greatly from normal to a severe degree of villous atrophy, which in some cases is associated with a crypt hypoplasia.[135] The majority of cases show a partial or subtotal villous atrophy with varying degrees of round cell infiltrate of the lamina propria. This mucosal lesion, which in many respects resembles the changes seen in some cases of the 'classical' acute self-limited gastroenteritis, persists for an undefined period of time. However while the mucosal lesion in the acute form is seen to improve markedly within a few days, many of the infants with protracted diarrhoea continue to have very abnormal jejunal mucosal morphology months or even years after the commencement of the symptoms.[136] It seems that the high mortality associated with this condition can now be reduced significantly by the use of parenteral nutrition. No death occurred among 30 cases recently reported.[136]

Malabsorption due to lymphatic obstruction

Intestinal lymphangiectasia (IL)

This rare condition was first recognized by Waldman et al

who, in 1961, described some patients with idiopathic hypoalbuminaemia and a protein-losing enteropathy associated with dilated small intestinal mucosal lymphatics.[137] The disease forms part of a wide spectrum of disorders of lymphatic development which can be inherited or acquired. These may involve mostly the extremities of the body, as in idiopathic lymphoedema, or mainly the intestinal tract, as in intestinal lymphangiectasia (IL), in which no peripheral involvement is seen. There are some intermediate forms but in these the intestinal abnormalities usually predominate. IL can also be secondary to many systemic diseases and in this setting is usually reversible. Cardiac diseases, such as constrictive pericarditis, cardiomyopathy or right-sided rheumatic heart disease, by restricting the drainage of lymph into the venous system, result in obstruction of the lymphatics. Chronic inflammatory diseases, such as systemic lupus erythematosus, are occasionally accompanied by IL. Infiltration or fibrosis of intestinal lymphatics may cause obstruction and IL may occur in rare cases of infective enteritis, Crohn's disease, Whipple's disease or malignancy.

Several forms of the primary disease are recognized and all affect young persons before the age of 30. The neonatal form is usually fatal and is characterized by massive oedema, diarrhoea, malabsorption and overwhelming infection. In childhood, IL interferes with physical and mental growth. The commonest form, however, affects adolescents and young adults, and causes chronic oedema,

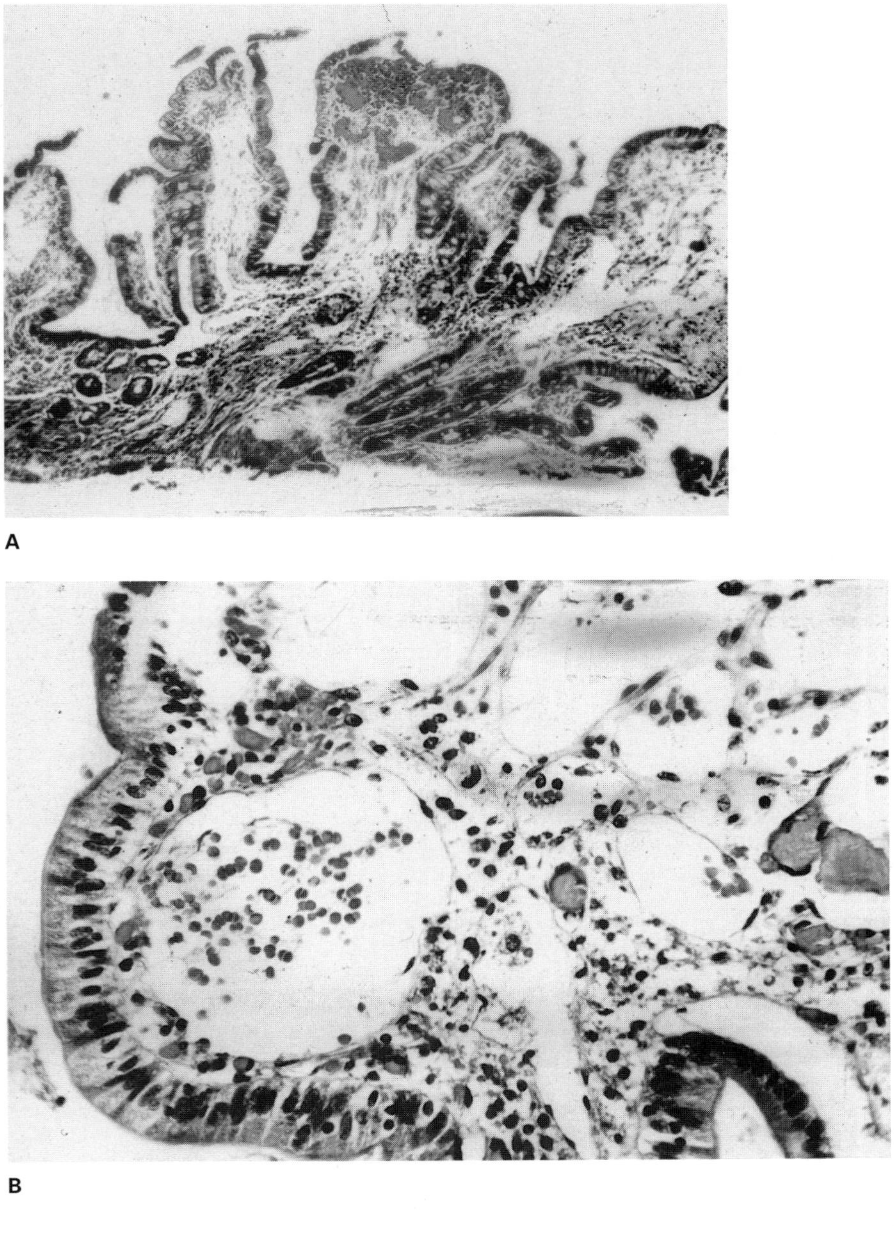

A

B

Fig. 26.38 A Jejunal mucosa from a child with intestinal lymphangiectasia. (H&E, ×70) **B** higher power detail of villus tip. (H&E, ×320)

fatigue and abdominal symptoms. The oedema may be due to local blockage of lymphatics and thus may be asymmetrical. More commonly, as the result of hypoproteinaemia due to intestinal loss, it is generalized with peritoneal and pleural chylous effusions. The gastrointestinal symptoms include diarrhoea in a small number of patients and steatorrhoea only in those with massive protein-loss.

Immunological abnormalities. Lymphopenia, particularly of T cells, and low serum IgG are caused by the intestinal loss of proteins and cells and result in a secondary cell-mediated immune deficit. Serum IgA and IgM proteins, of much shorter half life, are not profoundly deficient.[138]

Pathology. The affected bowel shows an oedematous and rigid wall sometimes displaying a brown discolouration due to accumulation of lipofuscin in the muscular coat. The serosa shows dilated lymphatics and small yellow nodules in which lipid-laden macrophages accumulate. The intestinal folds are enlarged and this change is particularly noticeable in the ileum. Microscopically, the most characteristic feature is the lymphatic dilatation at the tips of villi which gives them a bloated, club shape (Fig. 26.38A,B). Dilated lymphatics are also present in the submucosa and serosa. These distended lymphatics are almost invariably intact and no evidence of rupture is noted. The villi are covered by normal absorptive cells which, on electron microscopy, are seen to have a normal brush border and may contain small lipoprotein droplets in the cytoplasm.[139] The lamina propria contains no excess of inflammatory cells but some authors describe the presence of weakly PAS-positive, foamy macrophages and occasional multinucleated giant cells.[140] The lesion has a patchy and variable distribution, changing in sequential biopsy specimens from the same patients from a severe abnormality to an almost normal appearance.[141]

Malignancy complicating IL may be the result of the impaired immunity in these patients and three out of a series of 60 patients were found to suffer from malignant lymphoma.[142] Recently, it has been reported that an association may exist between IL and macroglobulinaemia and that the increased viscosity of the lymph caused by its high content of IgM may play a pathogenetic role.[143] Intestinal lymphangiectasia should not be confused with the localized, discrete lymphangiectatic cysts which are not infrequently encountered in routine autopsy examinations of the jejunum. These cysts, normally of less than 1 cm in size, may be multiple and are caused by dilatation of submucosal lymphatics, which raises the mucosa into a polyp-like fold protruding into the lumen (Fig. 26.39). The adjacent bowel wall is normal.

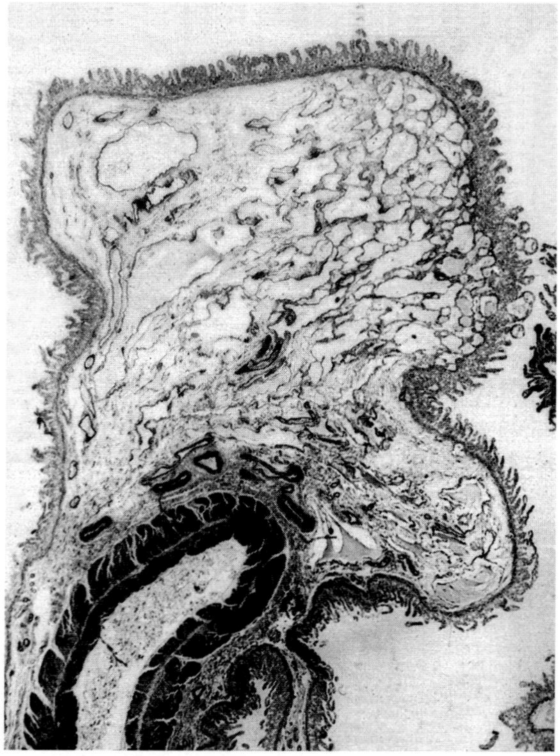

Fig. 26.39 Small intestinal lymphangiectatic cyst. (H&E, ×9)

REFERENCES

1. Variend S, Placzec M, Raafat F, Walker-Smith JA. Small intestinal mucosal fat in childhood enteropathies. J Clin Pathol 1984; 37: 373–377.
2. Whitehead R. Duodenal and ileal biopsy. In: Mucosal biopsy of the gastrointestinal tract. 3rd ed. Philadelphia: Saunders, 1985: p 128.
3. Shimoda SS, Saunders DR, Rubin CE. The Zollinger–Ellison syndrome with steatorrhoea. II. The mechanisms of fat and vitamin B12 malabsorption. Gastroenterology 1968; 55: 705–723.
4. Potter EL, Craig JM. Pathology of the fetus and the infant. 3rd ed. Chicago: Year Book Medical Publishers, 1976: p 353.
5. Rambaud JC, Matuchansky C. Diarrhoea and digestive endocrine tumours. Clin Gastroenterol 1974; 3: 657–670.
6. Haymond HE. Massive resection of the small intestine. An analysis of 257 collected cases. Surg Gynecol Obstet 1935; 61: 693–705.
7. Rickham PP. Massive small intestinal resection in newborn infants. Ann R Coll Surg 1967; 41: 480–492.
8. Hughes CA, Ducker DA. Adaptation of the small intestine — does it occur in man? In: Polak JM, Bloom SR, Wright NA, Daly MJ, eds. Basic science in gastroenterology: structure of the gut. London: Glaxo Group Research, 1982: p 465–474.
9. Agus SG, Dolin R, Wyatt RG, Tousimis AJ, Northup RS. Acute infectious nonbacterial gastroenteritis: intestinal histopathology. Ann Intern Med 1973; 79: 18–25.
10. Stolte M. Giardiasis: analysis of histological changes in biopsy specimens of 80 patients. J Clin Pathol 1990; 43: 641–643.
11. Bennett MK, Sachdev GK, Jewell DP, Anand BS. Jejunal mucosal morphology in healthy north Indian subjects. J Clin Pathol 1985; 38: 368–371.
12. Whipple GH. A hitherto undescribed disease characterised anatomically by deposits of fat and fatty acids in the intestinal and

mesenteric lymphatic tissues (intestinal lipodystrophy). Johns Hopkins Hosp Bull 1907; 18: 382–391.
13. Saint-Marc Girardin M-F, Zafrani ES, Chaumette M-T, Delchier J-C, Metreau J-M, Dhumedux D. Hepatic granulomas in Whipple's disease. Gastroenterology 1984; 86: 753–756.
14. Lamberty J, Varela PY, Font RG, Jarvis BW, Coover J. Whipple disease: light and electron microscopy study. Arch Pathol 1974; 98: 325–330.
15. Clancy RL, Tompkins WAF, Muckle TJ, Richardson H, Rawls WE. Isolation and characterisation of an aetiological agent in Whipple's disease. Br Med J 1975; 3: 568–570.
16. Bhagavan BS, Hofkin GA, Cochran BA. Whipple's disease: morphologic and immunofluorescence characterization of bacterial antigens. Hum Pathol 1981; 12: 930–936.
17. Kent SP, Kirkpatrick SM. Whipple's disease: immunological and histochemical study of 8 cases. Arch Pathol Lab Med 1980; 104: 544–547.
18. Evans DJ, Ali MF. Immunocytochemistry in the diagnosis of Whipple's disease. J Clin Pathol 1985; 38: 372–374.
19. Dobbins WO. Is there an immune deficit in Whipple's disease? Dig Dis Sci 1981; 26: 247–252.
20. Autran BR, Gorin I, Leibowitch M et al. AIDS in a Haitian woman with cardiac Kaposi's sarcoma and Whipple's disease. Lancet 1983; i: 767–768.
21. Kooijman CD, Poen H. Whipple-like disease in AIDS. Histopathology 1984; 8: 705–708.
22. Roth RI, Owen RL, Keren DF, Volberding PA. Intestinal infection with Mycobacterium avium in acquired immune deficiency syndrome (AIDS). Dig Dis Sci 1985; 30: 497–504.
23. Gee S. On the coeliac affection. St Bartholomew's Hosp Rep 1888; 24: 17–20.
24. Thin G. Psilosis (linguae et mucosae intestini). Br Med J 1890; 1: 1358–1361.
25. Blumgart HL. Three fatal adult cases of malabsorption of fat with emaciation and anaemia and in two, acidosis and tetany. Arch Intern Med 1923; 32: 113–128.
26. Thaysen TEH. Pathological anatomy of the intestinal tract in tropical sprue. Trans R Soc Trop Med Hyg 1931; 24: 539–546.
27. Paulley JW. Observations on the aetiology of idiopathic steatorrhea. Br Med J 1954; 2: 1318–1321.
28. Royer M, Croxatto O, Biempica L, Balcazar-Morrison AJ. Biopsia duodenal por aspiracion bajo control radioscopico. Prensa Medica Argentina 1955; 42: 2515–2519.
29. Shiner M. Duodenal biopsy. Lancet 1956; i: 17–19.
30. Meeuwisse GW. Diagnostic criteria in coeliac disease. Acta Paediatr Scand 1970; 59: 461–463.
31. Marsh MN. Gluten, major histocompatibility complex, and the small intestine. Gastroenterology 1992; 102: 330–353.
32. Logan RFA, Rifkind EA, Busuttil A, Gilmour HM, Ferguson A. Prevalence and 'incidence' of coeliac disease in Edinburgh and the Lothian region of Scotland. Gastroenterology 1986; 90: 334–342.
33. MacDonald WC, Dobbins WO, Rubin CE. Studies of the familial nature of coeliac sprue using biopsy of the small intestine. N Engl J Med 1965; 272: 448–456.
34. Pena AS, Genetics of coeliac disease. In: Jewell DP, Lee EG, eds. Topics in gastroenterology 9. Oxford: Blackwell's, 1981: p 69–81.
35. Kagnoff MF. Role of environmental and genetic factors in coeliac disease. Front Gastrointest Res 1992; 19: 15–28.
36. Sollid LM, Markussen G, Ek G, Gjerde H, Vartbal F, Thoresby E. Evidence for a primary association of coeliac disease to a particular HLA-DQ alpha/beta heterodimer. J Exp Med 1989; 169: 345–350.
37. Kelleher D. The genetics of coeliac disease. Europ J Gastroenterol Hepatol 1991; 3: 115–118.
38. Pena AS, Mann DL, Hague NE et al. Genetic basis of gluten-sensitive enteropathy. Gastroenterology 1978; 75: 230–235.
39. Mearin ML, Koninckx CR, Biemond I, Polanco I, Pena AS. Influence of genetic factors of the serum levels of antigliadin antibodies in celiac disease. J Pediatr Gastroenterol Nutr 1984; 3: 373–377.
40. Kagnoff MF, Weiss JB, Brown RJ, Lee T, Schanfield MS. Immunoglobulin allotype markers in gluten-sensitive enteropathy. Lancet 1983; i: 952–953.
41. Dicke WK, Weijers HA, Van der Kamer JH. Coeliac disease. II. The presence in wheat of a factor having a deleterious effect in cases of coeliac disease. Acta Paediatr 1953; 42: 34–42.
42. Howdle PD, Ciclitira PJ, Simpson FG, Losowsky MS. Are all gliadins toxic in coeliac disease? Scand J Gastroenterol 1984; 19: 41–47.
43. Frazer AC, Fletcher RF, Ross CAC, Shaw B, Sammons HG, Schneider R. Gluten induced enteropathy. The effect of partially digested gluten. Lancet 1959; ii: 252–255.
44. Dissanayake AS, Jerrome DW, Offord RE, Truelove SC, Whitehead R. Identifying toxic fractions of wheat gluten and their effect on the jejunal mucosa in coeliac disease. Gut 1974; 15: 931–946.
45. Rosenberg WMC, Mantzaris GJ, Jewell DP. In: Front Gastrointest Res. 2nd ed. Basel: Karger, 1992; 19: 29–43.
46. Kasarda DD, Qualset CO, Mecham DK, Goodenberger DM, Strober W. A test of toxicity of bread made from wheat lacking alpha-gliadins code by the 6A chromosome. In: McNicholl B, McCarthy CF, Fottrell PF, eds. Perspectives in coeliac disease. Lancaster: MTP, 1978: p 55–61.
47. Dissanayake AS, Truelove SC, Whitehead R. Lack of harmful effect of oats on small-intestinal mucosa in coeliac disease. Br Med J 1974; 4: 189–191.
48. Anand BS, Piris J, Truelove SC. The role of various cereals in coeliac disease. Q J Med 1978; 47: 101–110.
49. Watt J, Pincott JR, Harries JT. Combined cow's milk protein and gluten-induced enteropathy: common or rare? Gut 1983; 24: 165–170.
50. Vitoria JC, Sojo A, Camarero C. Combined cow's milk protein and gluten induced enteropathy. Gut 1984; 25: 103.
51. Baker AL, Rosenberg IH. Refractory sprue: recovery after removal of non-gluten dietary proteins. Ann Intern Med 1978; 89: 505–508.
52. Rubin CE, Brandborg LL, Phelps PC, Taylor HC. Studies of coeliac disease. I. The apparent identical and specific nature of the duodenal and proximal jejunal lesion in coeliac disease and idiopathic sprue. Gastroenterology 1960; 38: 28–49.
53. Perera DR, Weinstein WM, Rubin CE. Small intestinal biopsy. Hum Pathol 1975; 6: 157–217.
54. Thompson H. Pathology of coeliac disease. In: Morson BC, ed. Current topics in pathology. Pathology of the gastrointestinal tract. Berlin: Springer-Verlag, 1976: p 49–75.
55. Watson DJ, Appleton DR, Wright NA. Adaptive cell-proliferative changes in the small intestinal mucosa in coeliac disease. In: Polak JM, Bloom SR, Wright NA, Daly MJ, eds. Basic science in gastroenterology: structure of the gut. Herts: Glaxo Group Research, 1982: p 431–443.
56. Wright NA, Appleton DR, Marks J, Watson AJ. Cytokinetic studies of crypts in convoluted human small-intestinal mucosa. J Clin Pathol 1979; 32: 462–470.
57. Sandow M J, Whitehead R. The Paneth cell. Gut 1979; 20: 420–431.
58. Sjolund K, Aluments H, Berg NO, Hakanson R, Sundler F. Enteropathy of coeliac disease in adults: increased number of enterochromaffin cells in the duodenal mucosa. Gut 1982; 23(1): 42–48.
59. Scott BB, Goodall A, Stephenson R, Jenkins D. Small intestinal plasma cells in coeliac disease. Gut 1984; 25: 41–46.
60. Marsh MN. Morphology an immunopathology of the jejunal lesion in gluten-sensitivity. Europ J Gastroenterol Hepatol 1991; 3: 108–114.
61. Dunnill MS, Whitehead R. A method for the quantitation of small intestinal biopsy specimens. J Clin Pathol 1972; 25: 243–246.
62. Anand BS, Piris J, Jerrome DW, Offord RE. Truelove SC. The timing of histological damage following a single challenge with gluten in treated coeliac disease. Q J Med 1981; 50: 83–94.
63. Ferguson A, Murray D. Quantitation of intraepithelial lymphocytes in human jejunum. Gut 1971; 12: 988–994.
64. Lancaster-Smith M, Packer S, Kumar PJ, Harries JT. Cellular infiltrate of the jejunum after re-introduction of dietary gluten in

children with treated coeliac disease. J Clin Pathol 1976; 29: 587–591.
65. Guix M, Skinner JM, Whitehead R. Measuring intraepithelial lymphocytes, surface area, and volume of lamina propria in the jejunal mucosa of coeliac patients. Gut 1979; 20: 275–278.
66. Marsh MN. Studies of intestinal lymphoid tissue. III. Quantitative analysis of epithelial lymphocytes in the small intestine of human control subjects and of patients with coeliac sprue. Gastroenterology 1980; 79: 481–492.
67. Slavin G, Sowter C, Robertson K, McDermott S, Paton K. Measurement in jejunal biopsies by computer-aided microscopy. J Clin Pathol 1980; 33: 254–261.
68. Corazza GR, Frazzoni M, Dixon MF, Gasbarrini G. Quantitative assessment of the mucosal architecture of jejunal biopsy specimens: a comparison between linear measurement, stereology and computer aided microscopy. J Clin Pathol 1985; 38: 765–770.
69. Rubin WL, Ross L, Sleisenger MH, Weser E. An electron microscope study of adult coeliac disease. Lab Invest 1966; 15: 1720–1747.
70. Shiner M. Electron microscopy of jejunal mucosa. Clin Gastroenterol 1974; 3: 33–53.
71. O'Grady JG, Stevens FM, Keane R, Cryan EM, Egan-Mitchell B, McNicholl B, McCarthy CF, Fottrell PF. Intestinal lactase, sucrase, and alkaline phosphatase in 373 patients with coeliac disease. J Clin Pathol 1984; 37: 298–301.
72. Peters TJ, Jones PE, Wells G. Analytical subcellular fractionation of jejunal biopsy specimens: enzyme activities, organelle pathology and response to gluten withdrawal in patients with coeliac disease. Clin Sci 1978; 55: 285–292.
73. Bruce G, Woodley JF, Swan CHJ. Breakdown of gliadin peptides by intestinal brush border from coeliac patients. Gut 1984; 25: 919–924.
74. MacDonald WC, Brandborg LL, Flick AL, Trier JS, Rubin CE. Studies of coeliac sprue. IV. The response of the whole length of the small bowel to a gluten free diet. Gastroenterology 1964; 47: 573–589.
75. Thompson H. The small intestine at autopsy. Clin Gastroenterol 1974; 3: 171–181.
76. Holdstock G, Eade OE, Isaacson P, Smith CL. Endoscopic duodenal biopsies in coeliac disease and duodenitis. Scand J Gastroenterol 1979; 14: 717–720.
77. Gillberg R, Kastrup W, Mobacken H, Stockbrugger R, Ahren C. Endoscopic duodenal biopsy compared with biopsy with the Watson capsule from the upper jejunum in patients with dermatitis herpetiformis. Scand J Gastroenterol 1982; 17: 305–308.
78. McNicholl B, Egan-Mitchell B, Fottrell PF. Variability of gluten intolerance in treated childhood coeliac disease. Gut 1979; 20: 126–132.
79. Kumar PJ, O'Donoghue DP, Stenson K, Dawson AM. Reintroduction of gluten in adults and children with treated coeliac disease. Gut 1979; 20: 743–749.
80. Phelan JJ, Stevens FM, McNicholl B, Fottrell PF, McCarthy CF. Coeliac disease: the abolition of gliadin toxicity by enzymes from aspergillus niger. Clin Sci 1977; 53: 35–43.
81. Webster ADB, Slavin G, Shiner M, Platts-Mills TAE, Asherson GL. Coeliac disease with severe hypogammaglobulinaemia. Gut 1981; 22: 153–157.
82. Scott H, Fausa O, Ek J, Brandtzaeg P. Immune response patterns in coeliac disease. Serum antibodies to dietary antigens measured by an enzyme linked immunoabsorbent assay. Clin Exp Immunol 1984; 57: 25–32.
83. Cooke WT, Holmes GKT. Coeliac disease. Edinburgh: Churchill Livingstone, 1984: pp 247–263.
84. Arranz E, Ferguson A. Intestinal antibody pattern of coeliac disease: occurrence in patients with normal jejunal biopsy histology. Gastroenterol 1993; 104: 1263–1272.
85. Selby WS, Janossy G, Bofill M, Jewell DP. Lymphocyte subpopulations in the human small intestine. Clin Exp Immunol 1983; 52: 219–228.
86. Feighery C. Immune responses in coeliac disease. Europ J Gastroenterol Hepatol 1991; 3: 119–124.
87. O'Farrelly C. The spectrum of gluten sensitive disease. Europ J Gastroenterol Hepatol 1991; 3: 129–135.
88. Rust C, Kooy Y, Pena S, Mearin ML, Kluin P, Koning F. Phenotypical and functional characterisation of small intestinal T-cell receptor gamm delta (+) T-cells in coeliac disease. Scand J Immunol 1992; 35: 459–468.
89. Neild GH. Coeliac disease: a graft-versus-host-like reaction localised to the small bowel wall? Lancet 1981; i: 811–812.
90. Ferguson A, Arranz E, O'Mahony S. Definitions and diagnostic criteria of latent and potential coeliac disease. Dyn Nutr Res 1992; 12: 119–127.
91. Kagnoff MF, Paterson YJ, Kumar PJ, Kasarda DD, Carbone FR, Unsworth DJ, Austin RK. Evidence for the role of a human intestinal adenovirus in the pathogenesis of coeliac disease. Gut 1987; 28: 995–1001.
92. Weiser MM, Douglas AP. An alternative mechanism for gluten toxicity in coeliac disease. Lancet 1976; i: 567–569.
93. Groll A, Candy DCA, Preece MA, Tanner JM, Harries JT. Short stature as the primary manifestation of coeliac disease. Lancet 1980; ii: 1097–1099.
94. Whitehead R. Primary lymphadenopathy complicating idiopathic steatorrhoea. Gut 1968; 9: 569–575.
95. Simmonds JP, Rosenthall FD. Lymphadenopathy in coeliac disease. Gut 1981; 22: 756–758.
96. Matuchansky C, Colin R, Hemet J et al. Cavitation of mesenteric lymph nodes, splenic atrophy and a flat small intestinal mucosa. Report of six cases. Gastroenterology 1984; 87: 606–614.
97. Freeman HJ, Chiu BK. Small bowel malignant lymphoma complicating coeliac sprue and the mesenteric lymph node cavitation syndrome. Gastroenterology 1986; 90: 2008–2012.
98. Holmes GKT. Mesenteric lymph node cavitation in coeliac disease. Gut 1986; 27: 728–733.
99. Swinson C, Slavin G, Coles EC, Booth CC. Coeliac disease and malignancy. Lancet 1983; i: 111–115.
100. Cooke WT, Holmes GKT. Coeliac disease. Edinburgh: Churchill Livingstone, 1984: pp 173–180.
101. Isaacson P, Wright DH. Intestinal lymphoma associated with malabsorption. Lancet 1978; i: 67–70.
102. Isaacson PG, Spencer JO, Connolly CE et al. Malignant histiocytosis of the intestine: a T-cell lymphoma. Lancet 1985; ii: 688–691.
103. Spencer J, MacDonald T, Diss T, Walker-Smith J, Ciccitira P, Isaacson P. Changes in intraepithelial lymphocyte subpopulations in coeliac disease and enteropathy associated T-cell lymphoma. Gut 1989; 30: 339-346.
104. McCarthy CF. Malignancy in coeliac disease. Europ J Gastroenterol Hepatol 1991; 3: 125–128.
105. Pan L, Diss TC, Peng H, Lu Q, Wotherspoon AC, Alero Thomas, Isaacson PG. Epstein-Barr virus (EBV) in enteropathy-associated T-cell lymphoma (EATL). J Pathol 1993; 170: 137–143.
106. Marks JM, Shuster S, Watson AJ. Small bowel changes in dermatitis herpetiformis. Lancet 1966; ii: 1280–1282.
107. Scott BB, Losowsky MS. Patchiness and duodenal-jejunal variation of the mucosal abnormality in coeliac disease and dermatitis herpetiformis. Gut 1976; 17: 984–992.
108. Unsworth DJ, Payne AW, Leonard JN, Fry L, Holborow EJ. IgA in dermatitis-herpetiformis skin is dimeric. Lancet 1982; i: 478–479.
109. O'Mahoney S, Vestey JP, Ferguson A. Similarities in intestinal humoral immunity in dermatitis herpetiformis without enteropathy and in coeliac disease. Lancet 1990; 335: 1487–1490.
110. Hendrick DJ, Faux JA, Anand B, Piris J, Marshall R. Is bird fancier's lung associated with coeliac disease? Thorax 1978; 33: 425–428.
111. Baer AN, Bayless TM, Yardley JH. Intestinal ulceration and malabsorption syndromes. Gastroenterology 1980; 79: 754–765.
112. Mills PR, Brown IL, Watkinson O. Idiopathic chronic ulcerative enteritis. Q J Med 1980; 49: 133–149.
113. Jewell DP. Ulcerative enteritis. Brit Med J 1983; 3: 1740–1741.
114. Isaacson PG, Wright DH. Malignant histiocytosis of the intestine. Its relationship to malabsorption and ulcerative jejunitis. Hum Pathol 1978; 9: 661–677.

115. Robertson DAF, Dixon MF, Scott BB, Simpson FG, Losowsky MS. Small intestinal ulceration: diagnostic difficulties in relation to coeliac disease. Gut 1983; 24: 565–574.
116. Weinstein WN, Saunders DR, Tygat GN, Rubin CE. Collagenous sprue — an unrecognised type of malabsorption. N Engl J Med 1970; 283: 1297–1301.
117. Bossart R, Henry K, Booth CC, Doe WF. Subepithelial collagen in intestinal malabsorption. Gut 1975; 16: 18–22.
118. Cooke WT, Holmes GKT. The jejunal mucosa. In: Coeliac disease. Edinburgh: Churchill Livingstone, 1984; p 51.
119. Whitehead R. In: Mucosal biopsy of the gastrointestinal tract. 3rd ed. Philadelphia: Saunders, 1985: p 161.
120. Baker DR, Shrader WH, Hitchcock CR. Small bowel ulceration apparently associated with thiazide and potassium therapy. JAMA 1969; 190: 586–590.
121. Dixon JM, Lumsden AB, Piris J. Small bowel perforation. J Roy Coll Surg Edinb 1985; 30: 43–46.
122. Spencer GD, Shulman HM, Myerson D, Thomas ED, McDonald GB. Diffuse intestinal ulceration after marrow transplantation. Hum Pathol 1986; 17: 621–633.
123. Manuel PD, Soeparto P, Walker-Smith JA, Cow's milk allergy in chronic diarrhoea and malnutrition in Indonesian infants. In: Jackson W, ed. Food allergy workshop. Oxford: The Medicine Publishing Foundation, 1983.
124. Kosnai I, Kuitunen P, Savilahti E, Rapola J, Kohegyi J. Cell kinetics in the jejunal crypt epithelium in malabsorption syndrome with cow's milk protein intolerance and in coeliac disease in childhood. Gut 1980; 21: 1041–1046.
125. Maluenda C, Phillips AD, Briddon A, Walker-Smith JA. Quantitative enteropathy. J Pediatr Gastroenterol Nutr 1984; 3: 349–356.
126. Rosekrans PCM, Meijer CJLM, Cornelisse CJ, Wal AM, Lindeman J. Use of morphometry and immunohistochemistry of small intestinal biopsy specimens in the diagnosis of food allergy. J Clin Pathol 1980; 33: 125–130.
127. Ament ME, Rubin CE. Soy protein — another cause of the flat intestinal lesion. Gastroenterology 1972; 62: 227–234.
128. Vitoria JC, Camarero C, Sojo A, Ruiz A, Rodriguez-Soriano J. Enteropathy related to fish, rice and chicken. Arch Dis Child 1982; 57: 44–48.
129. McNeish AS, Rolles CJ, Arthur LJH. Criteria for diagnosis of temporary gluten intolerance. Arch Dis Child 1976; 51: 275–278.
130. Halliday K, Edmeades R, Shepherd R. Persistent post-enteritis diarrhoea in childhood. Med J Aust 1982; 1: 18–20.
131. Montgomery RD, Beale DJ, Sammons HG, Schneider R. Postinfective malabsorption: a sprue syndrome. Br Med J 1973; ii: 265–268.
132. Montgomery RD, Shearer ACI. The cell population of the upper jejunal mucosa in tropical sprue and postinfective malabsorption. Gut 1974; 15: 387–391.
133. Montgomery RD, Chesner IM. Post-infective malabsorption in the temperate zone. Trans R Soc Trop Med Hyg 1985; 79: 322–327.
134. Candy DCA, Larcher VF, Cameron DJS et al. Lethal familial protracted diarrhoea. Arch Dis Child 1981; 56: 15–23.
135. Fisher SE, Boyle JT, Holtzapple P. Chronic protracted diarrhoea and jejunal atrophy in an infant. Dig Dis Sci 1981; 25: 181–186.
136. Rossi T, Lebenthal E, Nord KS, Falizi RR. Extent and duration of small intestinal mucosal injury in intractable diarrhoea of infancy. Pediatrics 1980; 66: 730–735.
137. Waldmann TA, Steinfeld JL, Dutcher TF et al. The role of the gastrointestinal system in idiopathic hypoproteinemia. Gastroenterology 1961; 41: 197–207.
138. Strober W, Wochner RD, Carbone PP, Waldmann TA. Intestinal lymphangiectasia: a protein-losing enteropathy with hypogammaglobulinemia, lymphopenia and impaired homograft rejection. J Clin Invest 1967; 46: 1643–1656.
139. Asakura H, Miura S, Morishita T et al. Endoscopic and histopathological study of primary and secondary intestinal lymphangiectasia. Dig Dis Sic 1981; 26: 312–320.
140. Whitehead R. Mucosal biopsy of GI tract. Philadelphia: Saunders, 1985: p 182.
141. Vardi AA, Lebenthal E, Shwachman H. Intestinal lymphangiectasia: a reappraisal. Paediatrics 1975; 55: 842–851.
142. Strober W. Intestinal lymphangiectasia. In: Bouchier IAD, Allan RN, Hodgson HJF, Keighley MRB, eds. Textbook of gastroenterology. London: Balliere Tindall, p 605.
143. Harris M, Burton IE, Scarffe JH. Macroglobulinaemia and intestinal lymphangiectasia: a rare association. J Clin Pathol 1983; 36: 30–36.

CHAPTER

27 The large intestine

M. M. Mathan   H. M. Gilmour   R. Whitehead

PART I

Specific infections of the large intestine

M. M. Mathan

The lumen of the large intestine, with its abundant microbial flora, is analogous to a fermenter in steady state, the growth of the microbes maintained by the entry of nutrients in unabsorbed chyme, with removal of contents as faeces. The colonic mucosa is adapted to containing this microbial flora and in temperate zone countries no abnormalities attributable to this flora have been noted even at the ultrastructural level.[1] Although light microcopic examination of healthy colonic mucosal biopsies revealed no adaptive changes to the luminal environment in tropical countries, there were ultrastructural changes which suggested a tropical colonopathy with nonspecific damage to luminal colonocytes. These colonocytes were shorter with irregularly placed nuclei, short irregular microvilli, variation in staining density and vacuolated cytoplasm. Electron dense bodies, vesicles and lysosomes were increased in crypt and luminal colonocytes. The mucus granules of the goblet cells showed variation in electron density. Mononuclear cells were increased in the lamina propria, the subepithelial 'reticulohistiocytic complex' was prominent and there were changes in the microvasculature.[2] The histopathological changes in the colonic mucosa in response to infection, seen mainly in tropical countries, should be interpreted in the light of this tropical colonopathy.

ACUTE INFECTIONS OF THE LARGE INTESTINE

A variety of bacteria with the ability to invade tissues gives rise to inflammation of the colon, usually associated with acute bloody mucoid diarrhoea (dysentery). With the worldwide increase in the prevalence of inflammatory bowel disease, histological differentiation of acute infectious colitis from the first episode of inflammatory bowel disease is a challenge to the pathologist. A variety of terms — acute infectious colitis, acute self limiting colitis and transient colitis — have been used to indicate the histological changes in the rectal and colonic mucosa in infectious conditions and to distinguish them from the changes in inflammatory bowel disease. In analysing the significance of these descriptive terms, one of the problems is that even in epidemics due to virulent organisms such as *Shigella dysenteriae* serotype 1, under ideal conditions the organism can be cultured from the stool or rectal biopsy in only around 80% of the patients, while in endemic cases culture is possible in only about 60%.[3] Infections due to *Shigella dysenteriae* type 1 and campylobacter can also give rise to chronic dysentery. Furthermore, infections, particularly due to the salmonella group of organisms, can occur more frequently in patients with inflammatory bowel disease.[4] The diagnosis of the individual patient therefore has to be based on a combination of the clinical features, the response to therapy, the progress on follow up, as well as histological changes.[5–9] It has been suggested in reports from the temperate zones that crypt atrophy,

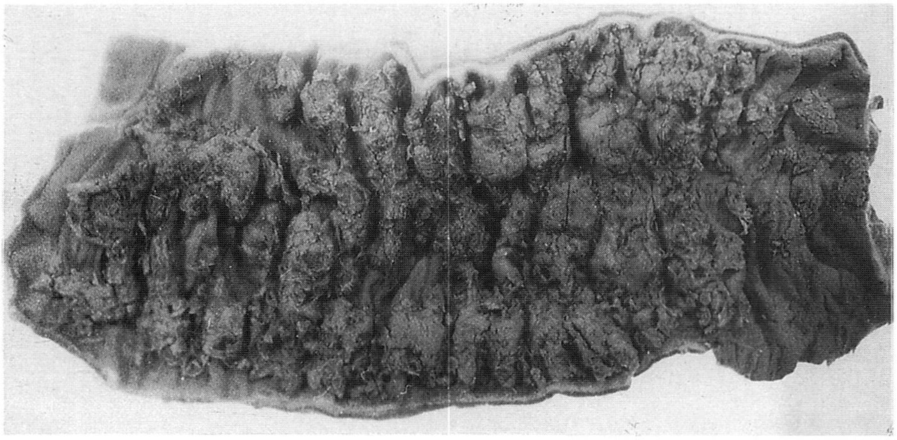

Fig. 27.1 Fatal shiga dysentery. Segment of colon with marked hyperaemia and oedema covered by a pseudomembrane of inflammatory exudate and necrotic tissue beneath which there were mucosal ulcerations.

distorted crypt architecture, increased numbers of round cells and neutrophils in the lamina propria, a villus surface epithelium and basal lymphoid aggregations are characteristic of nonspecific ulcerative colitis, while granulomas and isolated giant cells are additional features of granulomatous colitis.[10–14] The diagnosis of acute infectious colitis is considered easier in patients with a disease of shorter duration because of diffuse mucosal oedema with groups of neutrophils infiltrating the superficial lamina propria and the crypts.[10] While most of these features are applicable in tropical countries the lamina propria infiltrate is seldom predominantly neutrophilic, but usually consists of a mixture of round cells and neutrophils.[15–17]

Bacterial infections

Shigellae

Acute bacillary dysentery is the result of invasion of the colonic mucosa by organisms belonging to the shigella group: *Shigella shigae* (dysenteriae 1), *S. flexneri*, *S. sonnei* and *S. boydii*. Of these, *Shigella dysenteriae* serotype 1 or the Shiga bacillus produces the most severe infection and has been responsible for large pandemics, in Central America in the late 1970s and the Indian subcontinent in the 1980s.[18–20] The small frequent bloody mucoid stools of acute shigella dysentery is the result of destruction of the epithelial lining of the colon by this invasive organism which produces a cytotoxin.[21,22] Shigellae also elaborate an enterotoxin and some cases may present with watery diarrhoea.[23] Although the disease is usually self limited and of short duration, infections with the shiga bacillus can develop into chronic persistent dysentery and give rise to major complications, intestinal perforation, Gram negative septicaemia, paralytic ileus, toxic megacolon, endotoxaemia and the haemolytic uraemic syndrome with renal shut down.[20,24,25]

Extensive ulceration and pseudomembrane formation in the colon is found in patients who die due to severe bacillary dysentery (Fig. 27.1).[26] Beneath this necrotic layer the mucosa is diffusely congested and oedematous as though covered by a bright red eruption. There are circumscribed or diffuse areas of haemorrhage with irregular margins and superficial areas of ulceration. Solitary lymphoid follicles are often swollen and congested (Fig. 27.2). At colonoscopy the changes mainly affect the rectosigmoid region, but may extend to involve the whole colon, with severity decreasing towards the caecum. The main changes are mucosal oedema and erythema, with loss of normal vascular pattern, focal haemorrhages, mild friability and mucopurulent exudates. Small aphthoid ulcers may also be present as in Crohn's disease or yersinia infection.[27]

Histological abnormalities in infective colitis range from minimal to severe abnormalities, related to the virulence of the organism, the host response and the duration

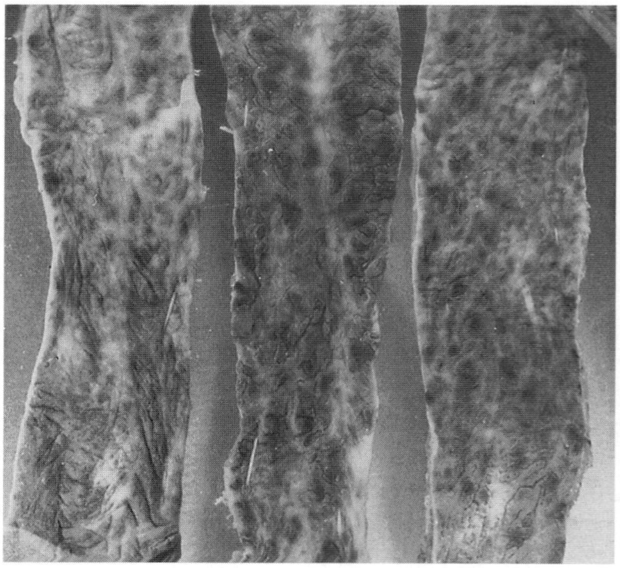

Fig. 27.2 Segments of colon from a fatal case of shigella dysentery showing diffusely hyperaemic haemorrhagic oedematous mucosa with superficial ulceration.

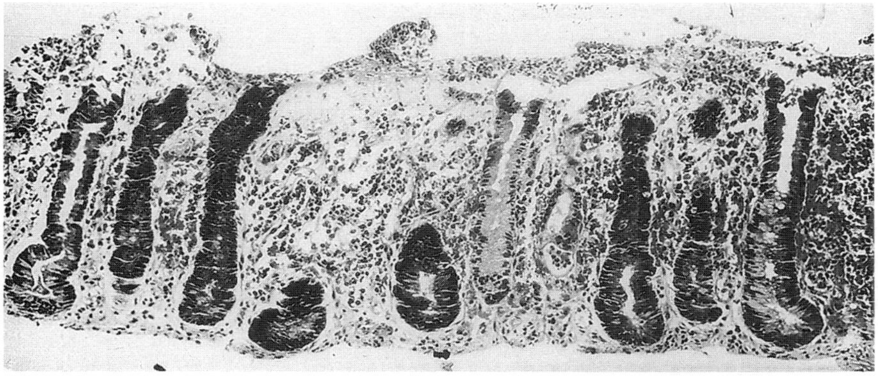

Fig. 27.3 Colonic biopsy from a patient with acute shiga dysentery. Ulcerated, mucus depleted epithelium covered by inflammatory exudate. Lamina propria with many plasma cells and neutrophil polymorphs. (H&E, ×15)

of illness. These responses include goblet cell depletion, epithelial degeneration and shedding with microulceration and compensatory crypt hyperplasia, occasional crypt abscesses and oedema of the lamina propria with increase in neutrophil polymorphs initially and, later, plasma cells, lymphocytes and eosinophils. The capillaries are congested with margination of neutrophils (Fig. 27.3). There are focal areas of haemorrhage associated with capillary thrombosis. This inflammation is more pronounced in the subepithelial area but may extend to the submucosa.[15,17] The initial lesions are often present over lymphoid follicles since the follicles with their overlying M cells are a portal of entry of infectious agents.[28,29] The few reports of rectal biopsies in patients with shigellosis from temperate countries indicate that the inflammatory infiltrate is predominantly neutrophilic.[3]

Ultrastructural examination of rectal mucosal biopsies show that colonocyte damage leading to ulceration in the rectal mucosa is the result of bacterial invasion (Fig. 27.4).[30] Cell lysis is a consequence of shut down of protein synthesis by the shiga toxin which acts on a 60S ribosomal subunit and is the possible mechanism in patients infected with *S. shigae*.[22] There was also evidence of isolated mitochondrial damage in colonic crypt cells which suggested that bacterial endotoxins may also play a role in the pathogenesis of the disease. A vascular lesion was present in the lamina propria of the rectal mucosa which resembled endothelial damage secondary to bacterial endotoxin. In a few patients with longer duration of symptoms, the basis of chronicity appeared to be relative vascular insufficiency, activated lymphocytes, and eosinophil and mast cell degranulation.[30]

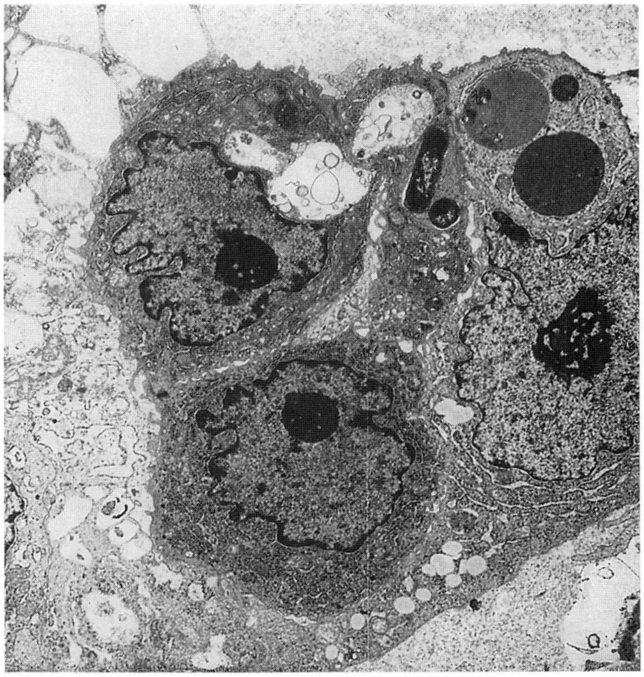

Fig. 27.4 Electron micrograph of the colonic surface epithelial cells in a mucosal biopsy from a patient with shigellosis. The colonocytes have scanty microvilli and have degenerative changes. Bacteria are seen invading the epithelium. (×4200)

Enteroinvasive Escherichia coli

Certain serotypes of *E. coli* produce two distinct cytotoxins, one similar to shiga toxin, (shiga-like toxin 1 or verocytotoxin, since its effects were initially demonstrated on cultured verocells) and the other serologically distinct cytotoxin with similar action, designated shiga-like toxin 2. *E. coli* serotype 0157:H7, which produces these two toxins, is now recognized as the commonest cause of haemorrhagic colitis and the haemolytic uraemic syndrome in temperate zone countries.[31] The right colon is usually severely affected and the lesion can extend to the terminal ileum. There is mucosal and submucosal oedema, haemorrhage and occasionally pseudomembranous colitis. Haemorrhages and vascular microthrombosis is more prominent than inflammatory changes.[32–37]

Other acute infective colitis

Salmonella infections of the gastrointestinal tract were originally thought to be associated with food poisoning and predominantly small intestinal, but it is now well established that *S. enteritidus* can cause acute infectious colitis.[38–41] *Campylobacter jejuni*, in addition to causing acute infectious colitis,[42–45] can give rise to watery diarrhoea since it produces an enterotoxin.[46] *C. jejuni* has also been associated with a nonspecific ulcerative colitis-like syndrome of chronic persistent dysentery,[47] and may result in toxic megacolon.[48] Demonstration of campylobacter organisms either by culture or by immunofluorescent studies of rectal mucosal biopsies are diagnostic in this condition[49] and appropriate antibiotic therapy promptly cures the patients. The sigmoidoscopic appearance of an inflamed erythematous, oedematous mucosa and the histological appearance of acute colitis is similar to that of other infectious colitis conditions.[50]

Clostridium difficile colitis

The colonic luminal ecology and its normal flora are an important protective barrier against colonization by several pathogenic bacteria. Alteration of the flora, especially by antibiotic therapy, can give rise to a variety of diarrhoeal syndromes, the most important of which is associated with the organism *Clostridium difficile*. *C. difficile* has a carrier rate in healthy adults in temperate countries of around 3%[51] and is found also in the stools of healthy neonates and infants.[52]

C. difficile is an anaerobe known to secrete at least four toxins which can cause fluid secretion, tissue damage, inflammatory response and gut motility abnormalities.[53] *C. difficile* infection can cause self limited diarrhoea, a transient colitis which mimics infective colitis, or it may infrequently produce severe dehydration and a pseudomembranous colitis which can be life threatening with toxic megacolon, peritonitis and sepsis.[54] Clostridial toxin A can be detected in high titre in the stool of patients with established *C. difficile* colitis and in tissue sections the organism can be identified immunohistochemically.[55] The lesions are patchy and multiple biopsies may be necessary to identify them.[56] The mucosa shows yellowish mucosal plaques, of pinpoint size to over 1 cm in diameter, with larger plaques coalescing to form pseudomembranes. Histologically three types of lesions have been described.[56,57] The type 1 lesion is a small surface erosion between crypts with a luminal spray of nuclear debris, polymorphs and mucus. Intact surface epithelial cells are often grouped in tufts, but other abnormalities are of a minor nature with oedema of the immediate adjacent lamina propria with clusters of polymorphs and capillary ectasia. Unless care is taken in the interpretation, these lesions can be misinterpreted as nonspecific erosions.

The type 2 lesion is the classical picture of pseudomembranous colitis detected by biopsy of the yellow plaque seen on sigmoidoscopic or colonoscopic examination. There are focal groups of disrupted crypts which are dilated and have shed the superficial half of the crypt epithelium. Mucin, fibrin and polymorphs stream out of these damaged crypts and sit as a cap over the surface, giving rise to the yellow plaque (Fig. 27.5). The adjacent mucosa shows only minimal inflammation but the submucosa is oedematous and capillary microthrombi with margination of polymorphs may be observed.

Type 3 lesions have extensive and complete mucosal ulceration with a covering of inflammatory slough forming a continous pseudomembrane over large areas of the colonic mucosa.

Staphylococcal colitis

Fatal shock and diarrhoea with colonization by antibiotic resistant enterotoxin producing staphylococci has usually been associated with antibiotic therapy.[58,59] The colonic epithelium is covered by a pseudomembrane in which staphylococci can be demonstrated and there is severe inflammation of the mucosa of the ileum, appendix and colon. The shock is thought to be due to the absorption

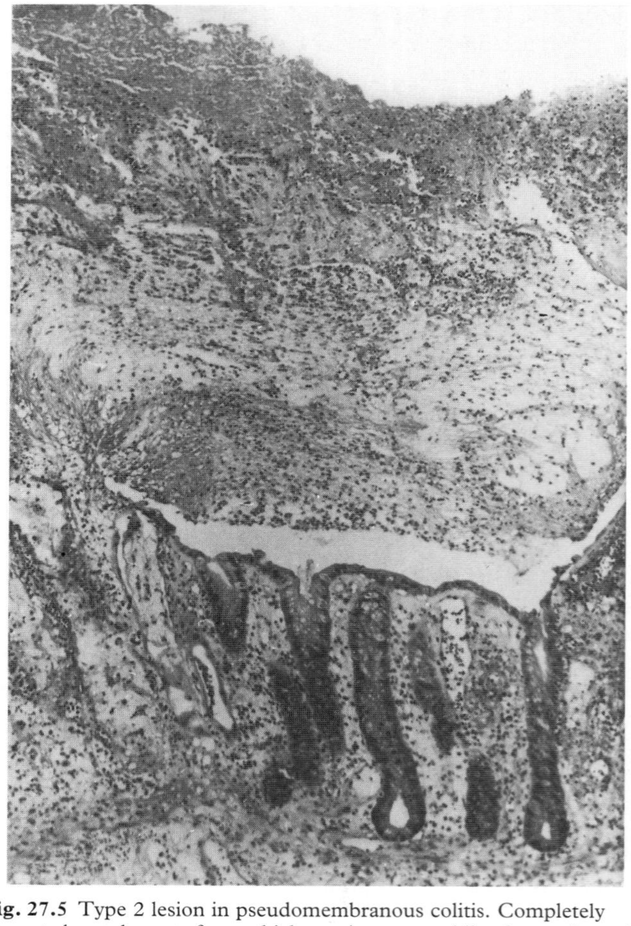

Fig. 27.5 Type 2 lesion in pseudomembranous colitis. Completely disrupted rectal crypts from which mucin, neutrophil polymorphs and cellular debris enmeshed in fibrin are seen to stream out to form a pseudomembrane over the mucosa. Adjacent rectal crypts appear intact. (H&E, ×80)

of staphylococcal toxin. This condition is seldom encountered now, because of more appropriate antibiotic therapy.

Rectal mucosal changes in acute diarrhoea in tropical countries

In rectal mucosal biopsies obtained from adults with acute infectious diarrhoea in southern India, with or without pathogens isolated, a vascular lesion in the lamina propria associated with deep pericryptal haemorrhages has been demonstrated in addition to other changes.[16] This vascular lesion and haemorrhage was the result of endothelial damage, resembling a bacterial lipopolysaccharide induced local Schwartzman reaction.[60] The lesions correlated with the clinical severity of illness and not with the type of pathogen that was isolated from the stool.[16] These findings suggested that in addition to other recognized factors, bacterial endotoxins may also play a role in the pathogenesis of the diarrhoea and may be a determinant of the severity of illness. The role of the vascular lesion in diarrhoea was confirmed by a murine model of acute watery diarrhoea induced by endotoxin challenge of appropriately conditioned mice,[61] in which similar vascular changes in the small and large intestinal mucosal lamina propria were present.

Parasitic infections

Entamoeba histolytica

Although amoebiasis has been defined as the harbouring of *E. histolytica* in the gastrointestinal tract with or without clinical manifestations,[62] the demonstration of zymodeme related virulence of *E. hystolytica* strains, as well as antigenic and genomic variations, suggested that this definition and current epidemiological data may need to be reconsidered.[63–66] Only less than 10% of the individuals who harbour *E. histolytica* in their gastrointestinal tract develop disease, while in others it exists as a commensal with asymptomatic passage of cysts.[67] Only two stages of the multistage life cycle, trophozoites and cysts, are seen in man. Trophozoites 20–40 μm in diameter are spherical or oval with a single nucleus, a central karyosome and a thin surface membrane with many pseudopods.[68] Trophozoites are present in tissue in the invasive phase and are also excreted in the stool. Cysts are spherical with thick walls, 8–20 μm in diameter and are seen only in the stool.[69] Transmission of the disease occurs by faecal-oral route with ingestion of cysts. The pathogenicity and virulence of this primitive eukaryote, without any exotoxin, depends on contact mediated killing of target cells by adhesion and cytolysis. This is followed by phagocytosis of lysed cells and intracellular degradation.[67–70] Diagnosis is by detecting trophozoites in tissue sections, stool samples or sigmoidoscopic smears. Serological tests are of value in detecting invasive amoebiasis.[71]

Amoebiasis can produce lesions in the entire colon, appendix and terminal ileum but the commonest sites affected are the caecum, rectosigmoid and hepatic flexures. Five types of morphological abnormalities have been described at sigmoidoscopy.[72] The mild change shows only oedematous, moderately friable mucosal folds with increased mucus production. The lobular change, which is frequently found, is characterized by oedematous, very friable, pale pinkish mucosa, with superficial erosions and irregular, slightly raised lobules of varying sizes and shapes separated by clefts forming a reticular pattern. The lobular change forms the background on which either necrotic ulcers, which are irregular and covered with slough, or open ulcers, which are round with a clear dark red granular floor, are found (Fig. 27.6). The fifth abnormality, which is rare, is the development of a mucosal cast where the entire surface is covered by a tough, tenacious whitish pseudomembrane.

The histological lesions can also be quite varied.[73] A nonspecific minimal lesion without ulceration, but with stromal oedema and congestion with increased neutrophil polymorphs and prominent goblet cells, appears to be the earliest lesion. Amoebae are not usually found within the tissues at this stage, but may be present in the exudate or

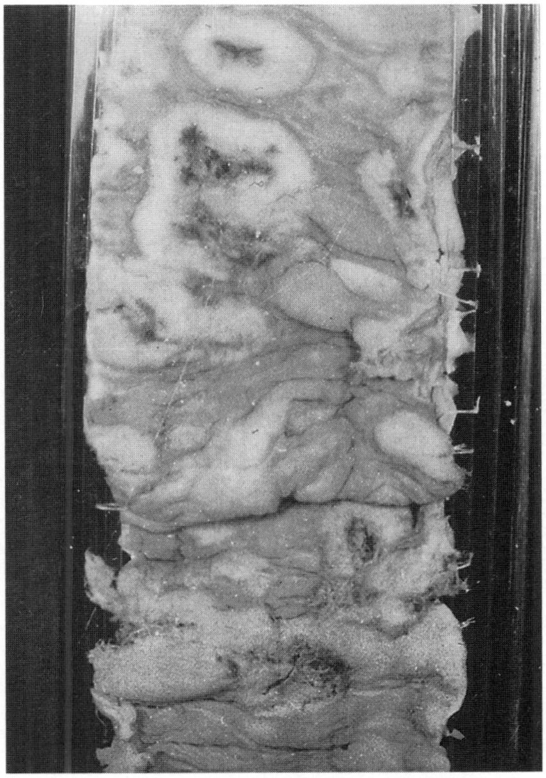

Fig. 27.6 Segment of colon with multiple amoebic ulcers with undermined ragged edges raised by exudate and necrotic base.

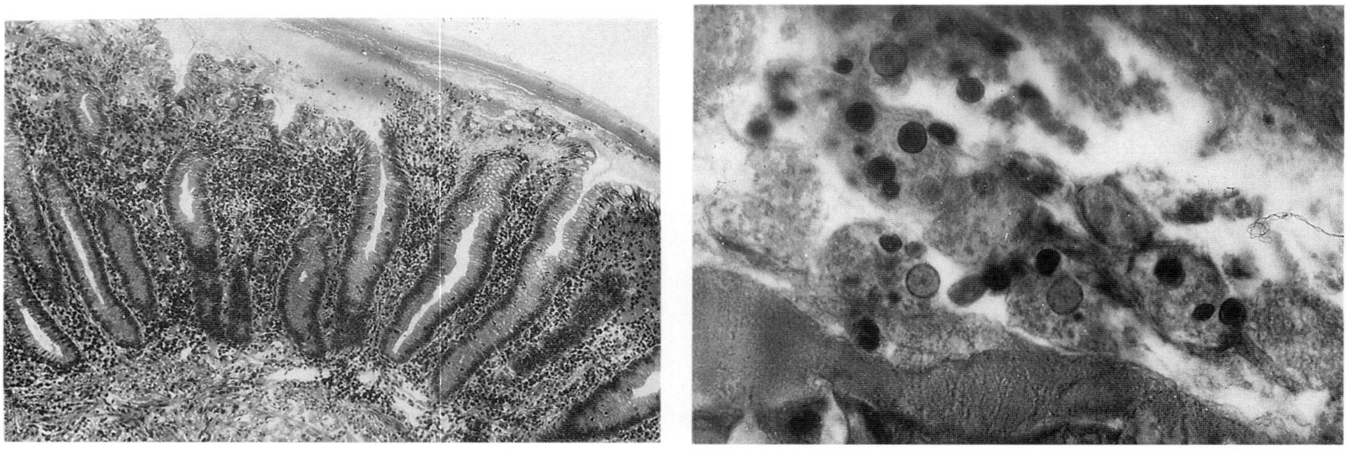

A B

Fig. 27.7A Rectal biopsy with mucus depletion, microulceration and increased neutrophil polymorphs, plasma cells and lymphocytes in the lamina propria of a patient with amoebic colitis. (H&E, ×87) **B** Surface mucus in a field adjacent to **A** showing amoebic trophozoites with ingested red blood cells. (H&E, ×846)

mucus that is associated with the specimen. Characteristic erythrophagocytosis and a round nucleus with a central karyosome, clearly shown by an iron haematoxylin stain, and cytoplasmic glycogen which is strongly PAS positive, distinguishes *E. histolytica* from macrophages and cell debris.

The next stage has been called the mucopenic depression phase which shows depletion of goblet cell mucus and later microulceration due to focal erosions of the surface epithelium, covered by inflammatory exudate containing many amoebae (Fig. 27.7A,B). In the next stage two types of early invasive lesions are present with either small interglandular foci or larger areas of superficial ulceration (Fig. 27.8). Amoebae are present in these ulcers but are separated from surviving tissue by a thin zone of necrosis. The subjacent lamina propria is usually congested and infiltrated by neutrophils. The muscularis mucosa is intact. Deep ulceration produces the classical flask shaped ulcer with undermining at the level of the submucosa (Fig. 27.9A). There is considerable acellular necrotic debris and proteinacious exudation. Amoebae can usually be found deep within these ulcers, as large round cells with surrounding clear zones (Fig. 27.9B). The surrounding tissue is infiltrated mainly by plasma cells and lymphocytes. Secondary bacterial infection can produce neutrophil polymorph infiltration. The last stage is the granulating ulcer, which does not have overhanging edges and has only minimal necrosis. Amoebae are usually

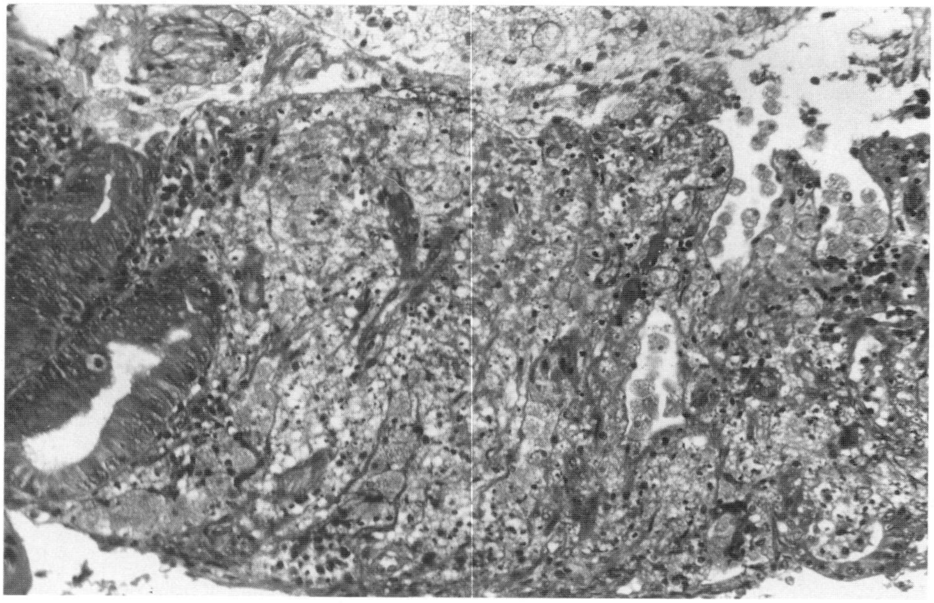

Fig. 27.8 Amoebic colitis showing numerous amoebae invading the mucosa up to the muscularis mucosae with scanty inflammatory response and necrosis. (H&E, ×190)

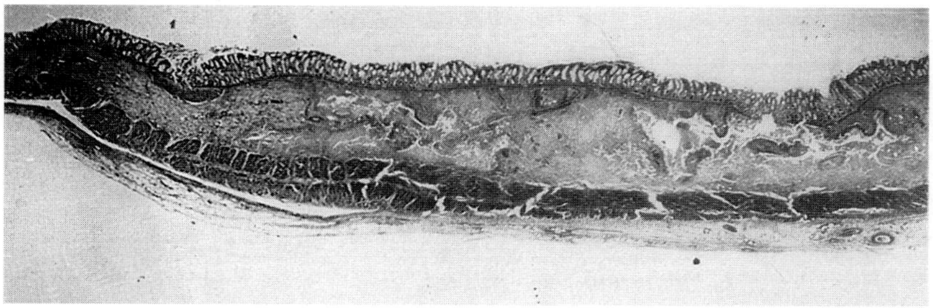

A

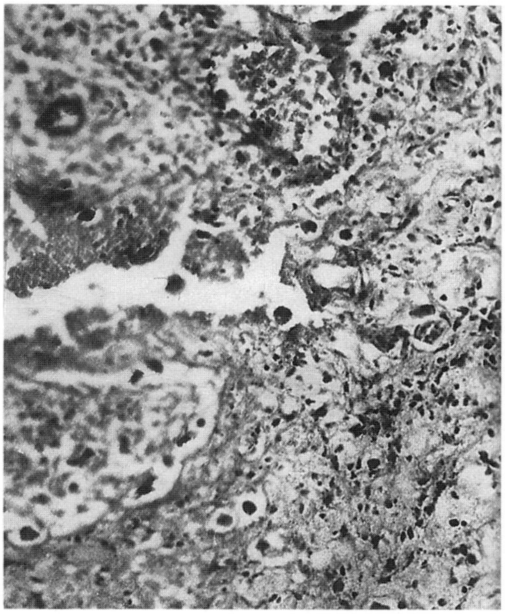

B

Fig. 27.9A Section of amoebic ulcer with undermined edges extending into the submucosa. Necrotic tissue at the border of the ulcer evokes very little inflammatory response. (H&E, ×5) **B** High power photomicrograph of the edge of the ulcer in **A**. Many amoebae surrounded by a clear zone are present in the necrotic tissue adjacent to the zone of inflammation. (H&E, ×175)

not present in such ulcers. On endoscopic examination the mucosa in between ulcers appears normal, but microscopic lesions can be demonstrated in this apparently normal mucosa.[74,75]

Although amoebic ulceration is usually stopped by the muscular layer, amoebic perforation of the bowel has been reported from hyperendemic countries.[76] Fulminating amoebic colitis can even present with toxic dilatation of the colon.[77] Colonic pseudopolyposis[78] and amoebic granulomas, also called amoebomas, can occur and may mimic carcinoma of the colon.[79,80] Experimental studies have shown that the amoebic granuloma results from hypersensitivity to *E. histolytica*.[81] The most serious complication of amoebiasis, which may or may not be associated with dysentery, is distant metastasis, initially to the liver and from there to other systemic areas, particularly the brain. The factors which determine such systemic spread in immunocompetent individuals are not yet understood.

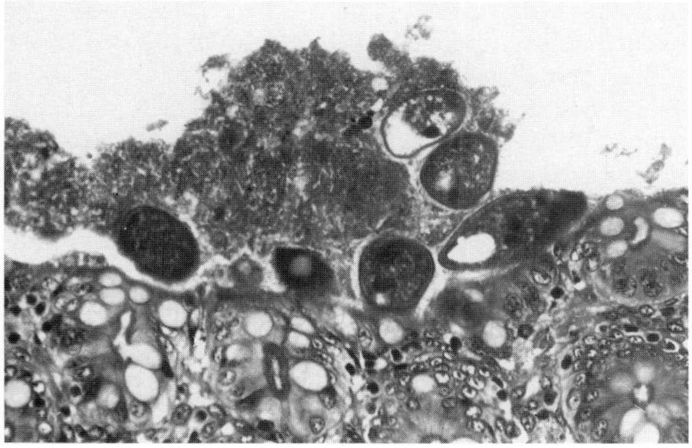

A

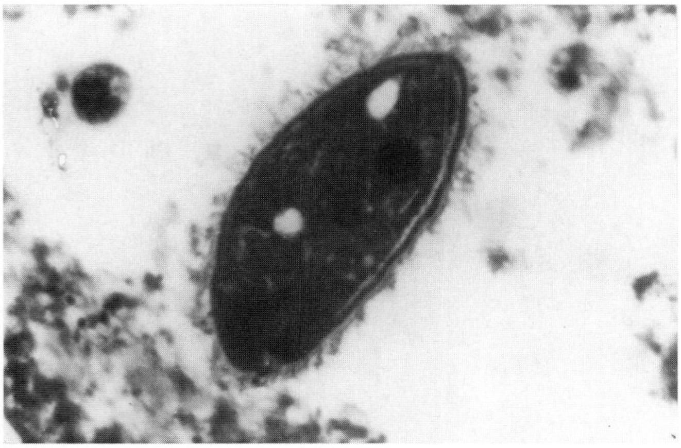

B

Fig. 27.10A Colonic mucosa with many trophozoites of *Balantidium coli* adjacent to the luminal cells. (H&E, ×308) **B** Trophozoite of *Balantidium coli* with large nucleus and surface cilia. (H&E, ×816)

Balantidium coli

Balantidium coli is the only pathogenic ciliate of man. It is a parazoonotic infection, with a high rate of infestation in a variety of animals. Colonization of man is usually without apparent ill effects. In symptomatic balantidial dysentery the pathological changes in the colon are similar to amoebic dysentery.[82,83] The parasite is easily identified by its large size, large reniform nucleus and numerous surface cilia (Fig. 27.10A,B). Chronic balantidiasis can cause inflammatory polyposis and invasive lesions.[84]

CHRONIC INFECTIONS OF THE LARGE INTESTINE

Bacterial infections

Tuberculous colitis

The predominant form of intestinal infection by *Myco-*

bacterium tuberculosis is considered to be ileocaecal tuberculosis (described in Ch. 26). However, with increasing availability of colonoscopic techniques, segmental or diffuse colonic tuberculosis is diagnosed more frequently[85–87] (Fig. 27.11A,B). The caecum is still the most commonly affected area, but segmental colonic involvement is mostly seen in the ascending and transverse colon. Diffuse ulcerative and polypoidal lesions and isolated strictures can occur in tuberculous infection of the colon[88,89] and these have to be distinguished from carcinoma[90] and Crohn's disease.[91] With the increasing incidence of tuberculosis in AIDS patients, colonic tuberculosis is likely to become a diagnostic challenge to the gastrointestinal pathologist.

Anorectal tuberculosis can present as a cold abscess of the ischiorectal fossa or as anal ulcers.[92]

Yersinia infection

Infection of the gastrointestinal tract by *Yersinia enterocolitica* can involve the colon, although classically the disease is in the ileocaecal region.[93,94] The mucosa may appear normal, have aphthoid ulcers or be diffusely oedematous, erythematous and friable. The lesions can be segmental or involve the whole colon. The histological appearance shows inflammatory changes similar to that in the small intestine.

Colonic spirochaetosis

Large numbers of spirochaetes may be found attached to the luminal border of colonocytes, but their clinical significance is not yet fully established. Several reports from the industrialized countries of the temperate zones suggest that this infestation may have clinical significance and may be assoiated with rectal symptoms, especially in homosexual males.[95–100] However, in a detailed study of rectal biopsies from asymptomatic healthy controls in southern India, spirochaetes were found to infest the luminal border of colonocytes in 60%, without associated symptoms.[2] Histologically, spirochaetes can be identified as a haematoxyphilic zone at the luminal brush border and the mouth of crypts and can be demonstrated by silver stains.[101] Ultrastructurally the microorganisms are attached end on, parallel to the microvilli, to depressions on the luminal surface membrane (Fig. 27.12). Occasionally, spirochaetes may penetrate epithelial cells and lamina propria. These spirochaetes have now been cultivated and the group characteristics and morphology differs from other spirochaetes, the name *Brachyspira aalborgi*, has been proposed.[102] Further characterization of the organisms and assessment of functional alterations in the colon correlated with clinical symptoms are necessary before ascribing aetiology.[103,104]

A

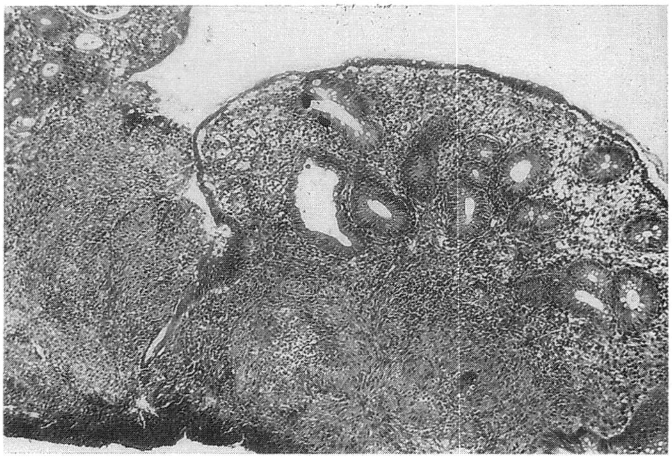

B

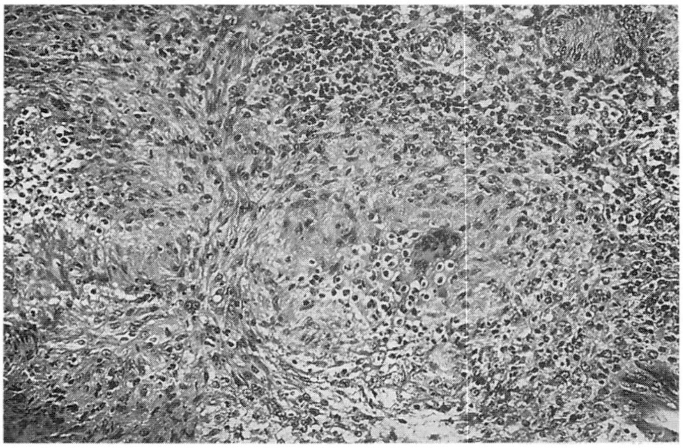

Fig. 27.11A Colonoscopic biopsy from a patient with segmental tuberculosis. The crypt architecture is distorted and granulomas are present in the mucosa. (H&E, ×90) **B** High power of **A** showing early necrotic changes in the centre of granulomas with epithelioid cells and giant cells. (H&E, ×198)

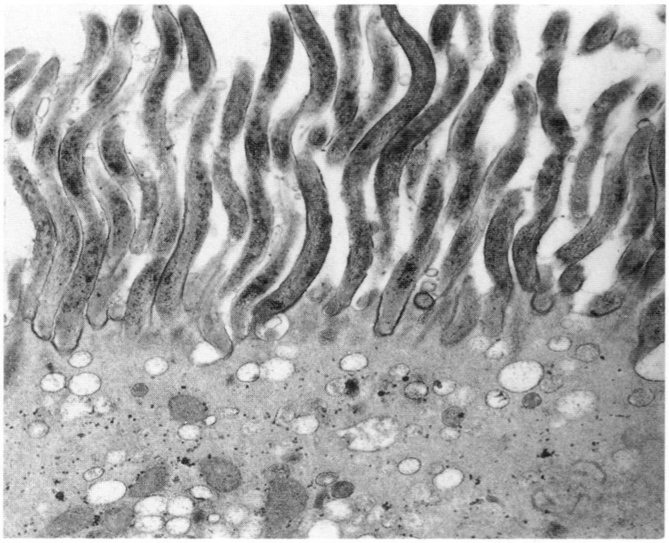

Fig. 27.12 Electron micrograph of part of a luminal colonocyte with many adherent spiral organisms. (×9600)

Viral infections

Cytomegalovirus (CMV) is a ubiquitous herpes virus which can produce latent infection and can be reactivated when cell mediated immunity is depressed. Clinically significant CMV infection of the gastrointestinal tract has been described even in normal subjects,[105,106] but is more common in immunocompromized patients, especially with AIDS, and can cause persistent diarrhoea, oesophagogastritis, enteritis, colitis, colonic ulceration, bleeding and perforation.[107–113] The pathogenesis of the mucosal disease in CMV is thought to be virus induced vasculitis with thrombosis and ischaemia. On sigmoidoscopy haemorrhagic mucosal lesions can be visualized. Histologically characteristic changes of CMV infection are cytomegaly and an acidophilic intranuclear inclusion with a clear halo, giving an 'owl's eye' morphology associated with a granular basophilic cytoplasm (Fig. 27.13). The inclusions mainly occur in cells of mesenchymal origin, endothelial cells, fibroblasts, smooth muscle cells and macrophages. Colonocytes are occasionally involved and may have viral inclusions, but the cellular morphology is relatively well preserved, unlike cells of mesenchymal origin.[114–116] Atypical inclusions have been described in AIDS patients[117] and in situ DNA hybridization confirms and increases sensitivity of detection.[118]

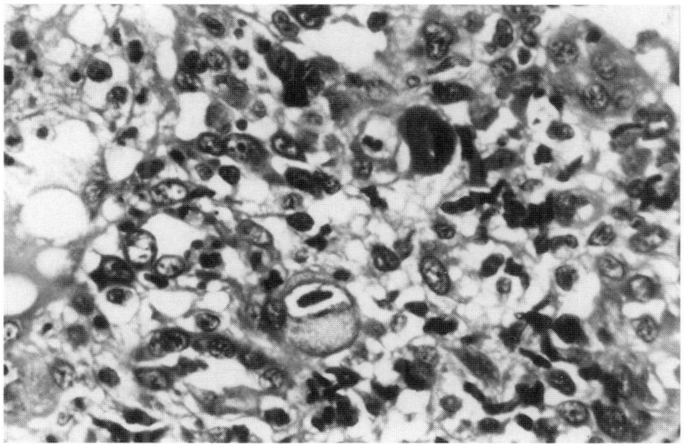

Fig. 27.13 Colonic mucosal lamina propria with a CMV infected endothelial cell with characteristic 'owl's eye' appearance. (H&E, ×520)

Fungal infections

Fungi and yeasts can infect the mucosa of the rectum and colon, especially in individuals whose defences against infection are compromized.[119] *Actinomyces israeli*, an anaerobic filamentous organism of the order Actinomycetae, is a normal commensal of the mouth. It can produce chronic suppurative lesions of the caecum and rectum, especially when there is a break in the epithelial lining. The lesions present in the caecum as a palpable mass, which may be associated with multiple sinuses in the abdominal wall[120] and in the rectum as an area of induration which is often associated with anal fistulae.[121] The diagnostic feature is the presence of colonies of actinomycetes in the abscess cavities. The colonies are haematoxyphilic and when Gram stained contain many Gram positive filaments surrounded by pink amorphous material. The peripheries of such colonies have club shaped Gram negative fringes (Fig. 27.14).

Candidiasis,[122] mucormycosis,[123,124] blastomycosis,[125] histoplasmosis[126,127] and aspergillosis[128] have also been reported to affect the colon and rectum.

Parasitic infections

Trypanosoma cruzi

In American trypanosomiasis (Chagas' disease), caused by *Trypanosoma cruzi*, the major pathology occurs in the oesophagus and colon, as well as in the heart. Chronic

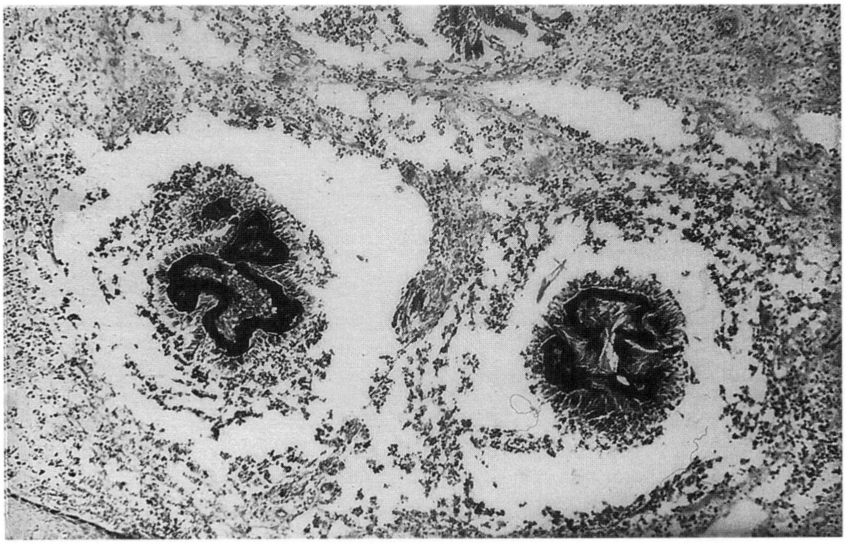

Fig. 27.14 Actinomycosis of the caecum with granules surrounded by purulent exudate. Granules stain deep purple with H&E, with eosinophilic centre and peripheral fringe. (H&E, ×60)

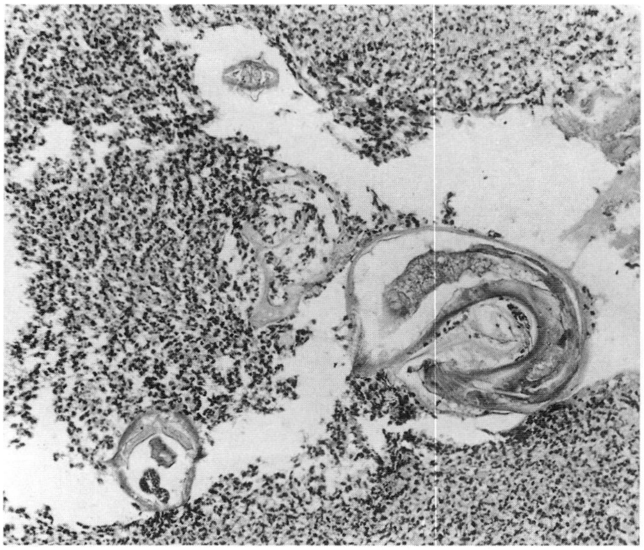

Fig. 27.15 Pin worm in an ulcerative lesion. Cross section of the worm shows characteristic lateral alae of the cuticle. (H&E, ×85)

Chagas' disease patients may present as adult cases of megacolon. The number of ganglion cells in Auerbach's plexus of the colon is markedly decreased. The pathogenesis of neuronal destruction is not fully understood. The walls of the viscera are distended and thinned out and scarring with minimal inflammation is present.[129]

Blastocystis hominis

Blastocystis hominis is a protozoan parasite of the order Amoebida. Its role as an enteric pathogen and pathogenic mechanisms are not clear.[130] The parasite inhabits the caecum and colon and invades superficial layers and produces an inflammatory response. Infection may cause diarrhoea and abdominal discomfort.[131,132] Its varied cell forms and size makes detection in stool difficult.[133]

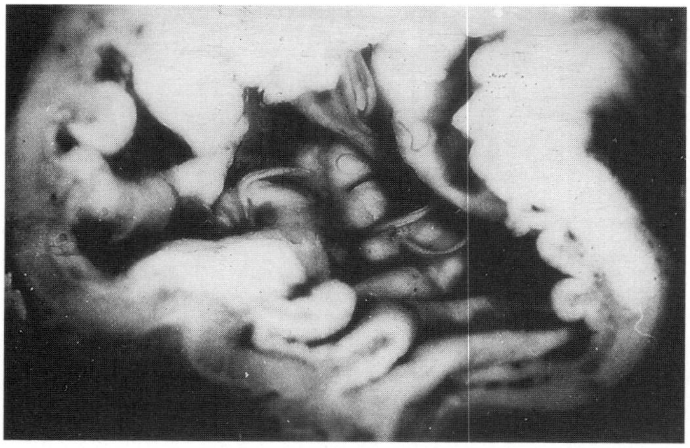

Fig. 27.16 A surgical specimen resected for perforation of the caecum. The wall is markedly oedematous and the lumen contains many whipworms.

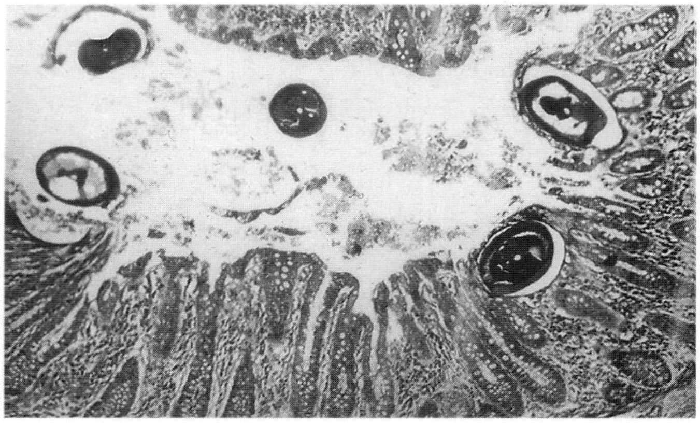

Fig. 27.17 Section of the mucosa of the caecum in Fig. 27.16 showing cross section of the anterior segment of whipworms embedded in the superficial mucosa. (H&E, ×52)

Enterobius vermicularis

Infection due to *Enterobius vermicularis*, or pin worm, seldom produces severe clinical illness. The usual habitat of the adult worm is the caecum and appendix. Deposition of eggs around the perianal skin gives rise to an intensely itchy reaction and leads to autoinfection. In the rare instances where the worms invade the caecum, appendix, lower ileum or the anal canal there may be small hae-

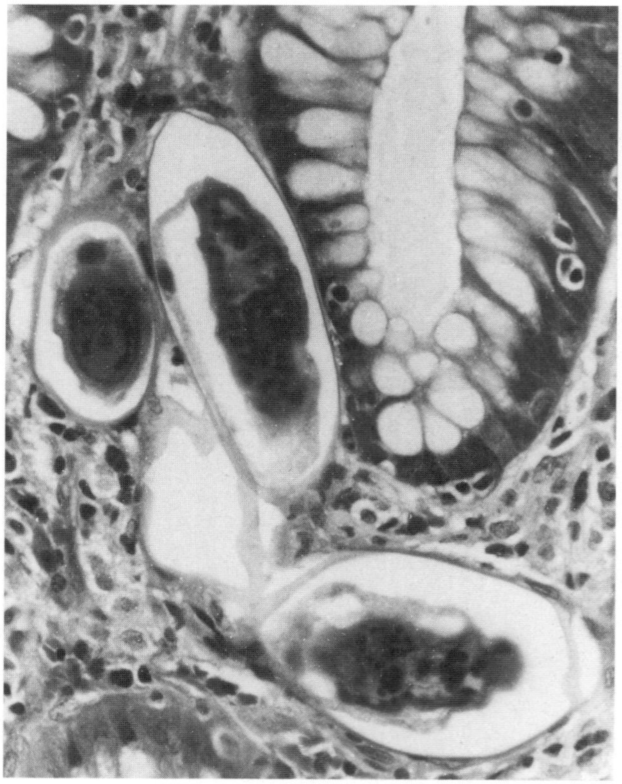

Fig. 27.18 Schistosomal egg with miracidia in the colonic mucosal lamina propria. (H&E, ×360)

morrhagic foci, ulceration and abscesses containing adult parasites (Fig. 27.15). Chronic granulomatous lesions (oxyuris nodule) characterized by abundant eosinophils can develop when the adult parasite invades the superficial mucosa or adjacent structures.[134–136]

Trichuris trichura

Trichuris trichura, or the whip worm, is a nematode which embeds itself in the superficial mucosa of the caecum (Fig. 27.16) colon and appendix and may cause no symptoms. Severe infestation with trichuris gives rise to chronic diarrhoea with loss of fluid and electrolytes and can result in rectal prolapse.[137,138] Large worm loads are associated with malnutrition and iron deficiency anaemia. With low or moderate worm loads, no definite histopathological changes occur but in heavy infestation hyperaemia, oedema and diffuse eosinophilic and lymphocytic infiltration throughout the affected colon has been reported (Fig. 27.17). Colonic penetration with granulomatous reaction,[139] perforation and obstruction occur very rarely.[140]

Schistosoma

Schistosomiasis is a major parasitic disease estimated to affect 200 million people in tropical countries. The three common species of schistosoma that infect man are *S. mansoni* (Middle East, Africa and the Caribbean), *S. haematobium* (Africa and Middle East) and *S. japonicum* (China, Japan and south-east Asia).

Infection of humans occurs by exposure to infective cercariae released in snail infested water. These cercariae penetrate the skin and migrate via the lung and liver, where they mature. Mature *S. mansoni* and *S. japonicum* migrate to the venous plexus of the intestine, and *S. haematobium* to the vesical plexus, and deposit their eggs in the tissues. The majority of the eggs are retained in the tissues (Fig. 27.18) while some penetrate the intestine or urinary tract and are excreted. In water, the eggs hatch and release ciliated miracidia which infect the intermediate host, a snail.

The clinical symptoms are the result of tissue reaction to the eggs and depend on the strain of the parasite, density of infection and the host response. In the tissues, the

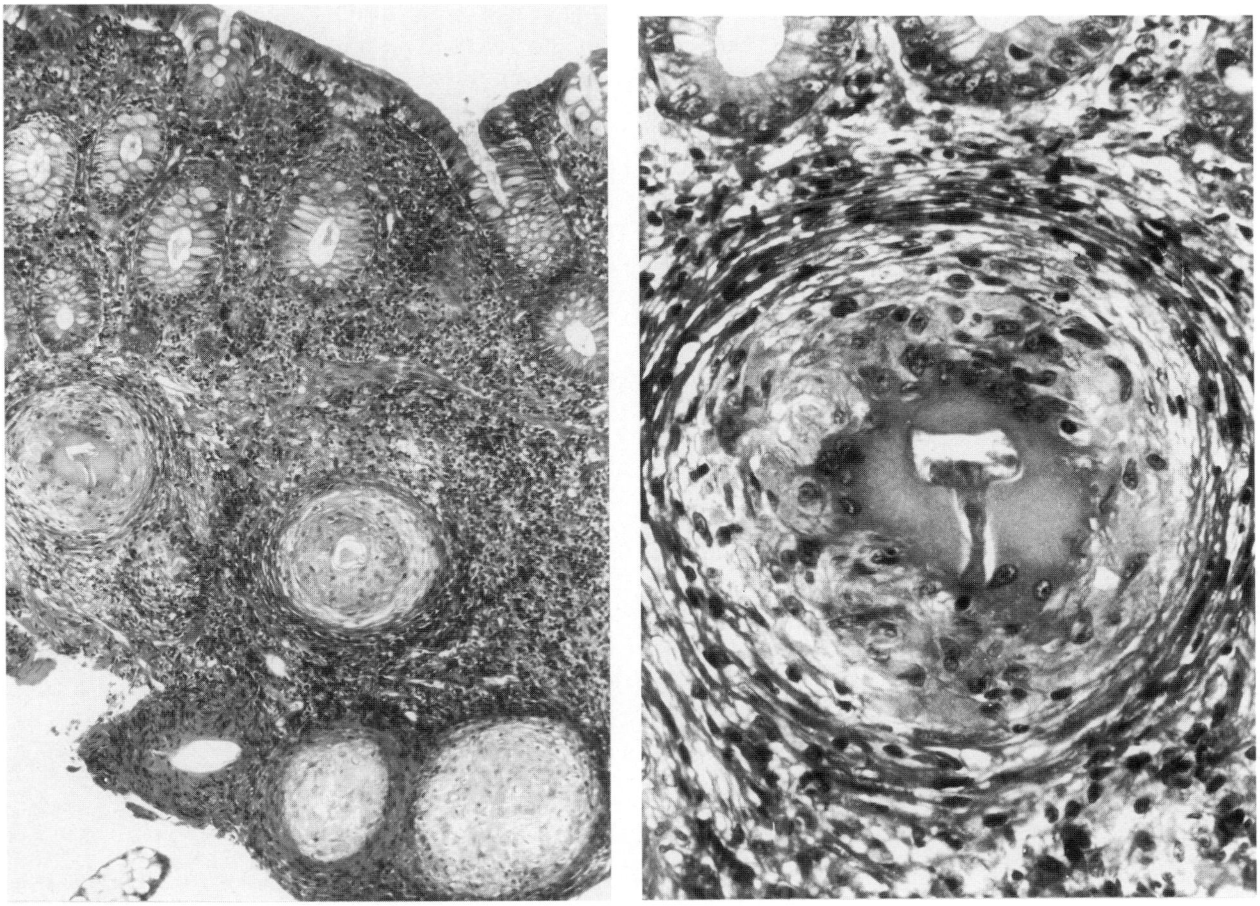

A B

Fig. 27.19A Rectal biopsy from patient with chronic schistosomiasis with multiple submucosal granulomas. (H&E, ×140) **B** Schistosomal granuloma with surrounding concentric fibrosis showing degenerating egg. (H&E, ×500)

eggs evoke a granulomatous reaction with lymphocytes, eosinophils and macrophages and subsequent fibrosis (Fig. 27.19A,B) or a diffuse exudative lesion. Degenerating eggs, which appear refractile and brown coloured, can be seen at the centre of the granuloma. The pathogenesis of this complex immunological response is not fully understood.[141–143] Mild infestation can be asymptomatic. Severe chronic infestation by *S. mansoni* and *S. japonicum* causes protein losing enteropathy, bloody diarrhoea and polyps in the distal colon. This is the result of submucosal granuloma formation around the eggs with hyperplasia of the overlying mucosa. Large collections of eggs can cause mass lesions, especially in the pelvic colon, and ulcerations in the rectum.[143,144] It is not yet proven that chronic schistosomiasis can lead to cancer of the colon.[145,146]

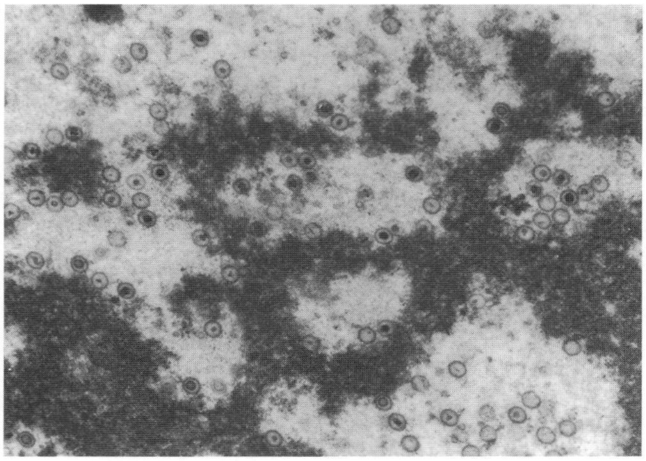

Fig. 27.20 Electron micrograph with HSV nucleocapsids in the nucleus of a rectal crypt cell. (×12620)

Venereal colitis

Anorectal and intestinal infections occurring in homosexually active males are now well recognized, with the wide prevalence of Human Immunodeficiency Virus infections and a better understanding of the sexual transmission of enteric pathogens. Important sexually transmitted anorectal infections are due to *N. gonorrhoea*, herpes virus, *Chlamydia trachomatis* and *T. pallidum*.[147–150] Gonorrhoea presents as an acute or chronic proctitis and is diagnosed by culturing the organism.[151,152] Anorectal lesions of early syphilis due to *T. pallidum* infection include polyps, lobulated masses, mucosal ulcerations and proctitis.[153] Syphilitic chancres with endothelial proliferation and perivascular plasma cell cuffing can be confirmed by demonstrating spirochaetes by silver impregnation[154] or immunofluorescence.[153] In secondary syphilis in addition to condyloma lata, an inflammatory proctitis with perivascular granulomata may be seen.[155] Lymphogranuloma venereum is caused by *Chlamydia trachomatis* L1, L2, and L3 immunotypes. It can be asymptomatic or can present as extensive necrotizing granulomatous lesions with marked induration,[156] rectal mass[157] or rectal bleed.[158] Rectal involvement can lead to stricture formation, especially in women where the involvement is usually by contiguous spread from the genital tract.[159,160] Diagnosis can be confirmed by culture and immunofluorescence using specific antibody.[157] Proctitis due to herpes simplex virus (types 1 or 2) is a well recognized gastrointestinal problem in the AIDS syndrome. It can also occur in other immunosuppressed populations.[161] These are usually spreading superficial ulcers which can extend to the gluteal clefts and the diagnosis is confirmed by culturing the virus from rectal swabs. Histologically, there may be multinucleation of the epithelium with intranuclear inclusions due to the 100 nm nucleocapsids (Fig. 27.20).[162,163] Sexual transmission of a variety of other enteric pathogens has been reported in homosexual men.[164,165] In patients with AIDS, without opportunistic infection, diffuse colitis with mucosal ulceration is reported[166] and the HIV nucleic acid has been demonstrated in epithelial cells of rectal crypts, neuroendocrine cells and in the lamina propria[167,168] with depletion of neuroendocrine cells,[169] suggesting primary damage to the colonic epithelium by HIV infection.

REFERENCES

1. Shamsuddin AM, Phelps PC, Trump BF. Human large intestinal epithelium: Light microscopy, histochemistry and ultrastructure. Human Pathol 1982; 13: 790–803.
2. Mathan M, Mathan VI. Rectal mucosal morphologic abnormalities in normal subjects in southern India: a tropical colonopathy? Gut 1985; 26: 710–717.
3. Jewkes J, Larson HE, Price AB, Sanderson PJ, Davies HA. Aetiology of acute diarrhoea in adults. Gut 1981; 22: 388–392.
4. Day DW, Mondal BK, Morson BC. The rectal biopsy appearances in Salmonella colitis. Histopathology 1978; 2: 117–131.
5. Dickinson RJ, Gilmour HM, McClelland DBL. Rectal biopsy in patients presenting to an infectious disease unit with diarrhoeal disease. Gut 1979; 20: 141–148.
6. Holdsworth CD. Acute self limited colitis. Br Med J 1984; 289: 270–271.
7. Goldman H. Acute versus chronic colitis: How and when to distinguish by biopsy. Gastroenterology 1984; 86: 199–200.
8. Surawicz CM. The role of rectal biopsy in infectious colitis. Am J Surg Pathol 1988; 12: 82–88.
9. Mandal BK, Schofield PF, Morson BC. A clinicopathological study of acute colitis: The dilemma of transient colitis syndrome. Scand J Gastroenterol 1982; 17: 865–869.
10. Kumar NB, Nostrant TT, Appelman HD. The histopathologic spectrum of acute self limited colitis (acute infectious-type colitis). Am J Surg Pathol 1982; 6: 523–529.
11. Surawicz CM, Belic L. Rectal biopsy helps to distinguish acute

self-limited colitis from idiopathic inflammatory bowel disease. Gastroenterology 1984; 86: 104–113.
12. Nostrant TT, Kumar NB, Appleman HD. Histopathology differentiates acute self-limited colitis from ulcerative colitis. Gastroenterology 1987; 92: 318–328.
13. Surawicz CM. Diagnosing colitis. Biopsy is best. Gastroenterology 1987; 92: 538–539.
14. Allison MC, Hamilton-Dutoit SJ, Dhillon AP, Pounder RE. The value of rectal biopsy in distinguishing self-limited colitis from early inflammatory bowel disease. Quart J Med 1987; 248: 985–995.
15. Anand BS, Malhotra V, Bhattacharya SK et al. Rectal histology in acute bacillary dysentery. Gastroenterology 1986; 90: 654–660.
16. Choudari CP, Mathan M, Rajan DP, Raghavan R, Mathan VI. A correlative study of etiology, clinical features and rectal mucosal pathology in adults with acute infectious diarrhea in southern India. Pathology 1985; 17: 443–450.
17. Mathan MM, Mathan VI. Morphology of rectal mucosa of patients with shigellosis. Rev Infec Dis 1991; 13: S314–318.
18. Mata LJ, Caceres A, Torres MF. Epidemic shiga dysentery in Central America Lancet 1971; 1: 600–601.
19. Mathan VI, Bhat P, Kapadia CR, Ponniah J, Baker SJ. Epidemic dysentery caused by the Shiga bacillus in a southern Indian village. J Diar Dis Res 1984; 1: 27–32.
20. Rahaman M, Azis KMS. The emergence and the decline of epidemics due to Shigella dysenteriae type 1 and S. flexneri in Bangladesh between 1971 and 1978: Some new lessons learned. In: Shigellosis: A continuing problem. ICDDRB, Dhaka: 1981; pp 8–13.
21. Levine MM, DuPont HL, Formal SB et al. Pathogenesis of Shigella dysenteriae type 1 (Shiga) dysentery. J Infect Dis 1973; 127: 261–270.
22. Keush GT, Donohue-Rolfe A, Jacewicz M. Shigella toxin(s): Descriptive and role in diarrhoea and dysentery. Pharmacol Ther 1982; 15: 403–438.
23. Keusch GT, Grady GF, Takeuchi A, Sprinz H. The pathogenesis of Shigella diarrhoea. II. Enterotoxin-induced acute enteritis in the rabbit ileum. J Infect Dis 1972; 126: 92–95.
24. Raghupathy P, Date A, Shastry JCM, Sudarsanam A, Jadhav M. Haemolytic-uraemic syndrome complicating shigella dysentery in south Indian children. Br Med J 1978; 1: 1518–1521.
25. Bennish ML. Potentially lethal complications of Shigellosis. Rev Infec Dis 1991; 13: S319–324.
26. Dammin GJ. Shigellosis. In: Binford CH, Connor DH, eds. Pathology of tropical and extraordinary diseases. Washington: Armed Forces Institute of Pathology, 1976; Vol. 1: 145–149.
27. Speelman P, Kabir I, Islam M. Distribution and spread of colonic lesions in shigellosis: A colonoscopic study. J Infect Dis 1984; 150: 899–903.
28. Jacob E, Baker SJ, Swaminathan SP. 'M' cells in the follicle-associated epithelium of the human colon. Histopathology 1987; 11: 941–952.
29. O'Leary AD, Sweeny EC. Lymphoglandular complexes of the colon: structure and distribution. Histopathology 1986; 10: 267–283.
30. Mathan MM, Mathan VI. Ultrastructural pathology of the rectal mucosa in Shigella dysentery. Am J Pathol 1986; 123: 25–38.
31. Karmali MA, Petric M, Lim C et al. The association between idiopathic hemolytic uremic syndrome and infection by verotoxin-producing Escherichia coli. J Infect Dis 1985; 151: 775.
32. Riley LW, Remis RS, Helgerson SD et al. Hemorrhagic colitis associated with a rare Escherichia coli serotype. N Engl J Med 1983; 308: 681–685.
33. Pai CH, Gordon R, Sims HV, Bryan LE. Sporadic cases of hemorrhagic colitis associated with Escherichia coli. Ann Intern Med 1984; 101: 738–742.
34. Morrison DM, Tyrrell DLJ, Jewell LD. Colonic biopsy in Verotoxin-induced hemorrhagic colitis and thrombotic thrombocytopenic purpura (TTP). Am J Clin Pathol 1986; 86: 108–112.
35. Kelly JK, Pai CK, Jadusingh IH, MacInnis ML, Shaffer EA, Hershfield NB. The histopathology of rectosigmoid biopsies from adults with bloody diarrhoea due to verotoxin-producing Escheridia coli. Am J Clin Pathol 1987; 88: 78–82.
36. Richardson SE, Karmali MA, Becker LE, Smith CR. The histopathology of the hemolytic uremic syndrome associated with verocytotoxin-producing Escherichia coli infection. Hum Pathol 1988; 19: 1102–1108.
37. Kelly J, Oryshak A, Wenetsek M, Grabiec J, Handy S. The colonic pathology of Escherichia coli 0157:H7 infection. Am J Surg Pathol 1990; 14: 87–92.
38. Boyd JF. Pathology of the alimentary tract in Salmonella typhimurium food poisoning. Gut 1985; 26: 935–944.
39. McGovern VJ, Slavutin LJ. Pathology of salmonella colitis. Am J Surg Pathol 1979; 3: 483–490.
40. Murphy TF, Gorback SL. Salmonella colitis. NY State J Med 1982; 82: 1236–1239.
41. Vender RJ, Marignani P. Salmonella colitis presenting as a segmental colitis resembling Crohn's disease. Dig Dis Sci 1983; 28: 848–851.
42. Lambert ME, Schofield PF, Ironside AG, Mandal BK. Campylobacter colitis. Br Med J 1979; 1: 857–859.
43. Colgan T, Lambert JR, Newman A, Luk SC. Campylobacter jejuni enterocolitis. Arch Pathol Lab Med 1980; 104: 571–574.
44. Blaser MJ, Parsons RB, Wang WLL. Acute colitis caused by Campylobacter fetus ss. jejuni. Gastroenterology 1980; 78: 448–453.
45. van Spreeuwel JP, Duursma GC, Meijer CJLM, Bax R, Rosekrans PCM, Lindeman J. Campylobacter colitis: histological immunohistochemical and ultrastructural findings. Gut 1985; 26: 945–951.
46. Walker RI, Caldwell MB, Lee EC, Guerry P, Trust TJ , Ruiz-Palacios GM. Pathophysiology of Campylobacter enteritis. Microbiol Rev 1986; 50: 81–94.
47. Loss RW Jr, Mangla JC, Pereira M. Campylobacter colitis presenting as inflammatory bowel disease with segmental colonic ulcerations. Gastroenterology 1980; 79: 138–140.
48. Kalkay MN, Ayanian ZS, Lehaf EA, Baldi A. Campylobacter induced toxic megacolon. Am J Gastroenterology 1983; 78: 557–559.
49. Price AB, Dolby JM, Dunscombe PR, Stirling J. Detection of Campylobacter by immunofluorescence in stools and rectal biopsies of patients with diarrhoea. J Clin Pathol 1984; 37: 1007–1013.
50. Price AB, Jewkes J, Sanderson PJ. Acute diarrhoea: Campylobacter colitis and the role of rectal biopsy. J Clin Pathol 1979; 32: 990–997.
51. George RH. The carrier state: clostridium difficile. J Antimicrob Chemother 1986; 18: 47–58.
52. Bolton RP, Tait SK, Dear PRF, Losowsky MS. Asymptomatic neonatal colonization by Clostridium difficile. Arch Dis Child 1984; 59: 466–472.
53. Griffin GE. Clostridium difficile. In: Enteric Infection: Mechanisms, Manifestation and Management. eds. Farthing MJR, Keusch GT. London: Chapman and Hall, 1989.
54. Gerding DN, Olson MM, Peterson LR, Teasley DG, Gebhard RL, Schwarts ML, Lee JT. Clostridium difficile associated diarrhoea and colitis in adults. Arch Intern Med 1986; 146: 95–100.
55. Qualman SJ, Petric M, Karmali MA, Smith CR, Hamilton SR. Clostridium difficile invasion and toxin circulation in fatal pediatric pseudomembranous colitis. Am J Clin Pathol 1990; 94: 410–416.
56. Price AB, Day DW. Pseudomembranous and infective colitis. In: Recent Advances in Histopathology, eds. Anthony PP, MacSween RNM. London: Churchill Livingstone, 1981; p. 99.
57. Price AB, Davies R. Pseudomembranous colitis. J Clin Pathol 1977; 30: 1–12.

58. Gardner RJ, Henegar GC, Preston FW. Staphylococcus enterocolitis. Arch Surg 1963; 87: 58–64.
59. Brown WJ, Winston R, Sommers SC. Membranous staphylococcal enteritis after antibiotic therapy. Am J Dig Dis 1953; 20: 73–75.
60. Mathan MM, Mathan VI. Local Schwartzman reaction in the rectal mucosa in acute diarrhoea. J Pathol 1985; 146: 179–187.
61. Mathan VI, Penny GR, Mathan MM, Rowley D. Bacterial lipopolysaccharide-induced intestinal microvascular lesions leading to acute diarrhoea. J Clin Invest 1988; 82: 1714–1721.
62. WHO 1969. WHO Technical report series 421.
63. Sargeaunt PG, Williams JE, Grene JD. The differentiation of invasive and non-invasive Entamoeba histolytica by isoenzyme electrophoresis. Trans R Soc Trop Med Hyg 1978; 72: 514–521.
64. Sargeaunt PG, Williams JE, Bhojnani R, Kumate J, Jimenez E. A review of isoenzyme characterization of Entamoeba histolytica with particular reference to pathogenic and non-pathogenic stocks isolated in Mexico. Arch Invest Med (Mex) 1982; 13(Suppl. 3): 89–94.
65. Strachan WD, Chiodini PL, Spice WM, Moody AH, Ackers JP. Immunological differentiation of pathogenic and nonpathogenic isolates of Entamoeba histolytica. Lancet 1988; i: 561–562.
66. Tannich E, Hortsmann RD, Knobloch J, Arnold HH. Genomic DNA differences between pathogenic and nonpathogenic Entamoeba histolytica. Proc Natl Acad Sci USA 1989; 86: 5118–5122.
67. Gitler C, Mirelman D. Factors contributing to the pathogenic behaviour of Entamoeba histolytica. Ann Rev Microbiol 1986; 40: 237–261.
68. Sepulveda B. Progress in Amebiasis. Scand J Gastroenterol 1982; 77: 153–164.
69. Martinez-Palomo A. Entamoeba histolytica. In: Enteric Infection: Mechanisms, Manifestations and Management. eds. Farthing MJG, Keusch GT. London: Chapman and Hall Medical, 1989; p. 381.
70. Martinez-Palomo A. The pathogenesis of amoebiasis. Parasitol Today 1987; 3: 111–118.
71. Pillai S, Mohimen A. A solid-phase sandwich radioimmunoassay for Entamoeba histolytica proteins and the detection of circulating antigens in amoebiasis. Gastroenterology 1982; 83: 1210–1216.
72. Gilman RH, Prathap K. Acute intestinal amoebiasis — proctoscopic appearances with histopathological correlation. Ann Trop Med Parasitol 1971; 65: 359–365.
73. Prathap K, Gilman R. The histopathology of acute intestinal amebiasis. A rectal biopsy study. Am J Pathol 1970; 60: 229–246.
74. Pittman FE, El-Hashimi WK, Pittman JC. Studies of human amebiasis. II. Light and electron-microscopic observations of colonic mucosa and exudate in acute amebic colitis. Gastroenterology 1973; 65: 588–603.
75. Pittman FE, Hennigar GR. Sigmoidoscopic and colonic mucosal biopsy findings in amebic colitis. Arch Pathol 1974; 97: 155–158.
76. Eggleston FC, Verghese M, Handa AK. Amoebic perforation of the bowel: experiences with 26 cases. Br J Surg 1978; 65: 148–151.
77. Wig JD, Talwar BL, Bushnurmath SR. Toxic dilatation complicating fulminant amoebic colitis. Br J Surg 1981; 68: 135–136.
78. Berkowitz D, Bernstein LH. Colonic pseudopolyps in association with amebic colitis. Gastroenterology 1975; 68: 786–789.
79. Spicknall EG, Pierce EG. Amebic granulomata — report of 4 cases with review of literature. N Engl J Med 1954; 250: 1055–1062.
80. Kaushik SP, Perianayagam WJ, Budhraja SB. Amebic granuloma of the large bowel. Int Surg 1973; 58: 715–720.
81. Trissl D. Immunology of Entamoeba histolytica in human and animal hosts. Rev Infect Dis 1982; 4: 1154–1184.
82. Arean VM, Echevarria R. Balantidiasis. In: Marcial-Rojas RA, ed. Pathology of protozoal and helminthic diseases. New York: RE Krieger, 1975; pp 234–253.
83. Castro J, Vazquez-Iglesias JL, Arnal-Monreal F. Dysentery caused by Balantidium coli — Report of two cases. Endoscopy 1983; 15: 272–274.
84. Ladas SD, Savva S, Frydas A, Kaloviduris A, Hatzioannou J, Raptis S. Invasive balantidiasis presented as chronic colitis with lung involvement. Dig Dis Sci 1989; 34: 1621–1623.
85. Franklin GO, Mohapatra M, Perrillo RP. Colonic tuberculosis diagnosed by colonoscopic biopsy. Gastroenterology 1979; 76: 362–364.
86. Bhargava DK, Tandon HD, Chawla TC, Shriniwas? Tandon BN, Kapur BML. Diagnosis of ileocaecal and colonic tuberculosis by colonoscopy. Gastrointestinal Endos 1985; 31: 68–70.
87. Shah S, Thomas V, Mathan M, Chacko A, Chandy G, Ramakrishna BS, Rolston DDK. Colonoscopic study of 50 patients with colonic tuberculosis. Gut 1992; 33: 347–351.
88. Vaidya MG, Sodhi JS. Gastrointestinal tract tuberculosis: a study of 102 cases including 55 hemicolectomies. Clin Radiol 1978; 29: 189–195.
89. Chawla S, Mukerjee P, Bery K. Segmental tuberculosis of the colon. Clin Radiol 1971; 22: 104–109.
90. Gadwood KA, Bedetti CD, Herbert DL. Colonic tuberculosis mimicking annular carcinoma: Report of a case. Dis Colon Rectum 1981; 24: 395–398.
91. Brenner SM, Annes G, Parker JG. Tuberculous colitis simulating nonspecific granulomatous disease of the colon. Am J Dig Dis 1970; 15: 85–92.
92. Jali HM. Tuberculosis anal ulcer. J Roy Soc Med 1989; 82: 629–630.
93. Vantrappen G, Agg HO, Ponette E, Geboes K, Bertnard PH. Yersinia enteritis and enterocolitis: Gastroenterological aspects. Gastroenterology 1977; 72: 220–227.
94. Bradford WD, Noce PS, Gutman LT, Durham NC. Pathologic features of enteric infection with Yersinia enterocolitica. Arch Pathol 1974; 98: 17–22.
95. Crucioli V, Busuttil A. Human intestinal spirochaetosis. Scand J Gastroenterol 1981; 70: 177–179.
96. Douglas JG, Crucioli V. Spirochaetosis: a remediable cause of diarrhoea and rectal bleeding? Br Med J 1981; 283: 1302.
97. Antonakopoulos G, Newman J, Wilkinson M. Intestinal spirochaetosis: an electron microscopic study of an unusual case. Histopathology 1982; 6: 477–488.
98. Nielsen RH, Orholm M, Pedersen JO, Hovind-Hougen K, Teglbjaerg PS, Thaysen EH. Colorectal spirochetosis: clinical significance of the infestation. Gastroenterology 1983; 85: 62–67.
99. Cotton DWK, Kirkham N, Hicks DA. Rectal spirochaetosis. Br J Vener Dis 1984; 60: 106–109.
100. Tomkins DS, Waugh MA, Cooke EM. Isolation of intestinal spirochaetes from homosexuals. J Clin Pathol 1981; 34: 1385–1387.
101. Burns PA. Staining intestinal spirochaetes. Med Lab Sci 1982; 39: 75–77.
102. Hovind-Hougen K, Andersen AB, Nielsen RH, Orholm M, Pedersen JO, Teglbjaerg PS, Thaysen EH. Intestinal spirochetosis: Morphological characterisation and cultivation of the spirochete Brachyspira aalborgi gen. nov. sp. nov. J Clin Microbiol 1982; 16: 1127–1136.
103. Editorial. Intestinal spirochaetosis. Lancet 1984; i: 720.
104. Teglbjaerg PS. Intestinal spirochaetosis. In: Gastrointestinal Pathology. William GT ed. Berlin: Springer-Verlag, 1990; p. 247.
105. Kinney JS, Onorato IM, Stewart JA. Cytomegalovirus infection and disease. J Infec Dis 1985; 151: 772–774.
106. Starr SE. Cytomegalovirus. Pediat Clin North Am 1979; 26: 283–293.
107. Underwood JCE, Corbett CL. Persistent diarrhea and hypoalbuminemia associated with cytomegalovirus enteritis. Br Med J 1978; 1: 1029–1030.
108. Foucar E, Mukai K, Foucar K, Sutherland DER, van Buren CT. Colon ulceration in lethal cytomegalovirus infection. Am J Clin Pathol 1981; 76: 788–801.
109. Knapp AB, Horst DA, Eliopoulos G et al. Widespread

cytomegalovirus gastroenterocolitis in a patient with Acquired Immunodeficiency Syndrome. Gastroenterology 1983; 85: 1399–1402.
110. Frank D, Raicht RF. Intestinal perforation associated with cytomegalovirus infection in patients with Acquired Immune Deficiency Syndrome. Am J Gastroenterol 1984; 79: 201–205.
111. Meiselman MS, Cello JP, Margaretten W. Cytomegalovirus colitis: Report of the clinical, endoscopic and pathologic findings in two patients with the acquired immune deficiency syndrome. Gastroenterology 1985; 88: 171–175.
112. Tatum ET, Sun PCJ, Cohn DL. Cytomegalovirus vasculitis and colon perforation in a patient with Acquired Immunodeficiency Syndrome. Pathology 1989; 21: 235–238.
113. Dieterich DT, Rahmin M. Cytomegalovirus colitis in AIDS: Presentation in 44 patients and a review of the literature. J Acquired Immune Deficiency Syndrome 1991; 4: S29–35.
114. Rotterdam H. Tissue diagnosis of selected AIDS related opportunistic infections. Amer J Surg Pathol 1987; 11: 3–15.
115. Miller SE, Howell DN. Viral infections in the Acquired Immunodeficiency Syndrome. J Electron Microsc Tech 1988; 8: 41–78.
116. Buckley RM, Braffman MN, Stern JJ. Opportunistic infections in the Acquired Immunodeficiency Syndrome. Seminars Oncol 1990; 17: 335–349.
117. Schwartz DA, Wilcox CM. Atypical cytomegalovirus inclusions in gastrointestinal biopsy specimens from patients with the Aquired Immunodeficiency Syndrome. Hum Pathol 1992; 23: 1019–1026.
118. Rasing LAJ, Weger RAD, Verndonck LF et al. The value of immunohistochemistry and in situ hybridization in detecting cytomegalovirus in bone marrow transplant recipients. APMIS 1990; 98: 479–488.
119. Rosen PP. Opportunistic fungal infections in patients with neoplastic diseases. Pathol Ann 1976; 11: 255–315.
120. Mahant TS, Kohli PK, Mathur JM, Bhushurmath SR, Wig JD, Kaushik SP. Actinomycosis caecum. A case report. Digestion 1983; 27: 53–55.
121. Morson BC. Primary actinomycosis of the rectum. Proc R Soc Med 1961; 54: 723–724.
122. Cairns MR. Fungal infections in the Acquired Immunodeficiency Syndrome. J Electron Microsc Tech 1988; 8: 115–131
123. Moore M, Anderson WAD, Everett HH. Mucormycosis of large bowel. Am J Pathol 1949; 25: 559–567.
124. Horowitz A, Dinabar A, Tulcinsky DB. Isolated primary intestinal mucormycosis. A case report. Israel J Med Sci 1974; 10: 1143–1147.
125. Penna FJ. Blastomycosis of the colon resembling clinically ulcerative colitis. Gut 1979; 20: 896–899.
126. Kirk ME, Lough J, Warner HA. Histoplasma colitis: An electron microscopic study. Gastroenterology 1971; 61: 46–54.
127. Lee SH, Barnes WG, Hodges GR, Dixon A. Perforated granulomatous colitis caused by Histoplasma capsulatum. Dis Col Rect 1985; 28: 171–176.
128. Kinder RB, Jourdan MH. Disseminated aspergillosis and bleeding colonic ulcers in renal transplant patient. J Roy Soc Med 1984; 78: 338–339.
129. Andrade ZA, Andrade SG. Chagas' disease (American trypanosomiasis). In: Marcial-Rojas RA, ed. Pathology of protozoal and helminthic diseases. New York: RE Krieger, 1975: pp 69–85.
130. Editorial. Blastocystis hominis: commensal or pathogen? Lancet 1991; 337: 521–522.
131. Kain KC, Noble MA, Freeman HJ, Barteluk RL. Epidemiology and clinical features associated with Blastocystis hominis infection. Diagn Microbiol Infect Dis 1987; 8: 235–244.
132. Vannatta JB, Adamson D, Mullican K. Blastocystis hominis infection presenting as recurrent diarrhea. Ann Int Med 1985; 102: 495–496.
133. Zierdt CH. Blastocystis hominis — past and future. Clin Microbiol Rev 1991; 4: 61–79.
134. Mayers CP, Purvis RJ. Manifestations of pinworms. CMA J 1970; 103: 489–493.
135. Symmers WSC. Pathology of oxyuriasis. Arch Pathol 1950; 50: 475–516.
136. Vafai M, Mohit P. Granuloma of the anal canal due to Enterobius vermicularis. Dis Col Rect 1982; 40: 349–350.
137. Ramirez-Weiser RR. Trichuriasis. In: Marcial-Rojas RA, ed. Pathology of protozoal and helminthic diseases. New York: Krieger, 1975; pp 658–665.
138. Kamath KR. Severe infection with Trichuris trichiura in Malaysian children. A clinical study of 30 cases treated with stilbazium iodide. Am J Trop Med Hyg 1973; 22: 600–605.
139. Kojima Y, Sakum H, Izumi R, Nakagawara G, Miyazaki I, Yoshimura H. A case of granuloma of the ascending colon due to penetration of Trichuris trichiura. Gastroenterol Jpn 1981; 16: 193–196.
140. Fishman JA, Perrone TL. Colonic obstruction and perforation due to Trichuris trichiura. Am J Med 1984; 77: 154–156.
141. Nash TE, Cheever AW, Ottesen EA, Cook JA. Schistosome infections in humans: Perspectives and recent findings. Ann Intern Med 1982; 97: 740–754.
142. Mahmoud AA. Schistosomiasis. N Engl J Med 1977; 297: 1329–1331.
143. Geboes K, El-Dosoky I, El-Wahab A, Almagd KA. The immunopathology of Schistosoma mansoni granulomas in human colonic schistosomiasis. Virchows Archiv (A) 1990; 416: 527–534.
144. Gambescia RA, Kaufman B, Noy J, Young J, Tedesco FJ. Schistosoma mansoni infection of the colon: A case report and review of the late colonic manifestations. Dig Dis 1976; 21: 988–991.
145. Bessa SM, Helmy I, Mekky F, Hamam SM. Colorectal schistosomiasis: clinicopathologic study and management. Dis Col Rectum 1979; 22: 390–395.
146. Chen MC, Chuang CY, Chang PY, Hu JC. Evolution of colorectal cancer in schistosomiasis. Transitional mucosal changes adjacent to large intestinal carcinoma in colectomy specimens. Cancer 1980; 46: 1661–1675.
147. Quinn TC, Stamm WE, Goodell SE et al. The polymicrobial origin of intestinal infections in homosexual men. NEJM 1983; 309: 576–582.
148. Aral SO, Holmes KK. Sexually transmitted diseases in the AIDS era. Sci Amer 1991; 264: 62–69.
149. Sohn N, Robilotti JG. The Gay Bowel Syndrome. A review of colonic and rectal conditions in 200 male homosexuals. Am J Gastroenterol 1977; 67: 478–484.
150. Weller IVD. The gay bowel. Gut 1985; 26: 869–875.
151. Kilpatrick ZM. Gonorrheal proctitis. N Engl J Med 1972; 287: 967–969.
152. McMillan A, McNeillage G, Gilmour HM, Lee FD. Histology of rectal gonorrhoea in men, with a note on anorectal infection with Neisseria meningitidis. J Clin Pathol 1983; 36: 511–514.
153. Quinn TC, Lukehart SA, Goodell S, Mkrtichian E, Schuffler MD, Holmes KK. Rectal mass caused by Treponema pallidum: confirmation by immunofluorescent staining. Gastroenterology 1982; 82: 135–139.
154. Gluckman JB, Kleinman MS, May AG. Primary syphilis of rectum. NY State J Med 1974; 74: 2210–2211.
155. McMillan A, Lee FD. Sigmoidoscopic and microscopic appearance of the rectal mucosa in homosexual men. Gut 1981; 22: 1035–1041.
156. Quinn TC, Goodell SE, Mkrtichian E et al. Chlamydia trachomatis Proctitis. NEJM 1981; 305: 195–200.
157. Mindel A. Lymphogranuloma venereum of the rectum in a homosexual man. Br J Vener Dis 1983; 59: 196–197.
158. Klotz SA, Drutz DJ, Tam MR, Reed KH. Hemorrhagic proctitis due to lymphogranuloma venereum serogroup L2. Diagnosis by fluorescent monoclonal antibody. NEJM 1983; 308: 1563–1565.
159. Geller SA, Zimmerman MJ, Cohen A. Rectal biopsy in early lymphogranuloma venereum proctitis. Am J Gastroenterol 1980; 74: 433–435.
160. Smith FB, Custer RP. The histopathology of lymphogranuloma venereum. J Urol 1950; 63: 546–563.

161. Boulton AJM, Slater DN, Hancock BW. Herpesvirus colitis: a new cause of diarrhoea in a patient with Hodgkin's disease. Gut 1982; 23: 247–249.
162. Rose AG, Becker WB. Disseminated herpes simplex infection: retrospective study by light microscopy and electron microscopy of paraffin embedded tissues. J Clin Pathol 1972; 25: 79–87.
163. Goodell SE, Quinn TC, Mkrtichian E, Schuffler MD, Holmes KK, Corey L. Herpes simplex virus proctitis in homosexual men. Clinical, sigmoidoscopic and histopathologic features. NEJM 1983; 308: 868–871.
164. Quinn TC, Goodell SE, Fennell C, Wang S, Schuffler MD, Holmes KK, Stamm WE. Infection with Campylobacter jejuni and Campylobacter-like organisms in homosexual men. Ann Int Med 1984; 101: 187–192.
165. Quinn TC. Gay bowel syndrome. The broadened spectrum of nongenital infection. Postgrad Med 1984; 76: 201–210.
166. Hing MC, Goldschmidt C, Mathijs JM, Cunningham AL, Cooper DA. Chronic colitis associated with human immunodeficiency virus infection. Med J Aust 1992; 156: 683–687.
167. Jarry A, Cortez A, Rene E, Muzeau F, Brousse N. Infected cells and immune cells in the gastrointestinal tract of AIDS patients. An immunohistochemical study of 127 cases. Histopathology 1990; 16: 1330–1340.
168. Nelson JA, Wiley CA, Reynolds-Kohler C, Reese CE, Margaretten W, Levy JA. Human immunodeficiency virus detected in bowel epithelium from patients with gastrointestinal symptoms. Lancet 1988; i: 259–262.
169. McCullough JB, Batman PA, Miller ARO, Sedgwick PM, Griffin GE. Depletion of neuroendocrine cells in rectal biopsy specimens from HIV positive patients. J Clin Pathol 1992; 45: 524–527.

PART II

The large intestine: Crohn's disease

H. M. Gilmour

It is only since the early 1960s that Crohn's disease has been recognized as a cause of colitis[1–3] and this has resulted in an increasing awareness of Crohn's disease of the colon, both in isolation and in association with disease elsewhere in the gut. Crohn's colitis — alone or in combination with ileal disease — is now probably as common as ileal involvement alone. The rising incidence of colonic Crohn's disease seems to be real and is not simply a reflection of increasing recognition, although there are countries where isolated colonic Crohn's disease has shown little increase in incidence over the years, or indeed forms only a very small proportion of cases of Crohn's disease. The reason for such differences is unclear, but while patterns of referral or methods of investigation may account for some discrepancies, this is unlikely to be the complete answer. Colonic Crohn's disease is seen at all ages, particularly in the peak age range of 15–30 years, but there have been suggestions of an increased incidence in the elderly.[4,5] This applies particularly to the distal colon, where it seems to be associated with a favourable prognosis.

HISTOPATHOLOGY

Macroscopic

Crohn's disease may affect any part of the colon or rectum and cause a total colitis or a segmental colitis which may or may not spare the rectum (Fig. 27.21). The appearances of colonic Crohn's disease are similar to those seen in the small intestine. The classical cobblestone pattern (Fig. 27.22) is uncommon, the more usual picture being one of ulceration (Fig. 27.23) or a combination of these two patterns (Fig. 27.24). Ulceration in Crohn's colitis may be difficult, if not impossible, to distinguish from idiopathic ulcerative colitis using endoscopy and radiology. Even with biopsy or resection specimens, a small proportion of cases justify the label of indeterminate colitis, since it is impossible to be certain of the nature of the disease

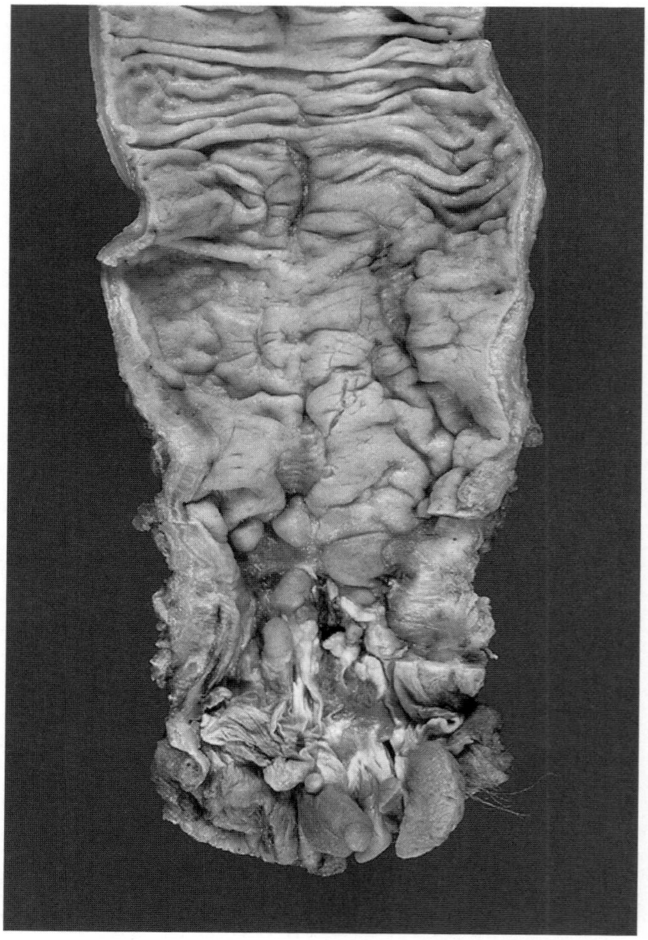

Fig. 27.21 Rectal Crohn's disease with ulceration and marked mural thickening extending into the anal canal. The sigmoid colon is spared but ileal disease was present.

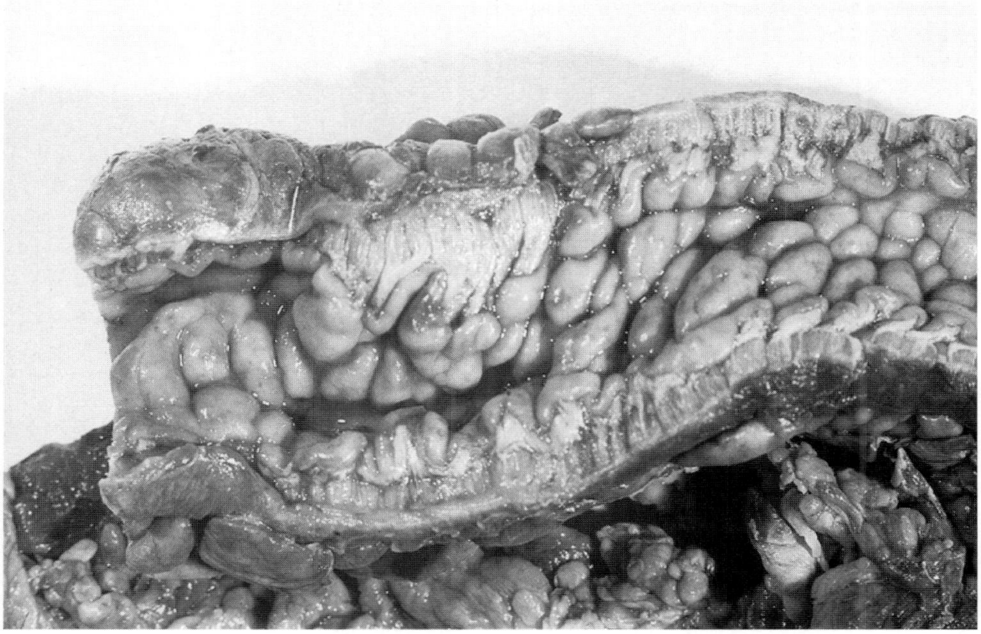

Fig. 27.22 Crohn's disease. 'Classical' cobblestone mucosal pattern in the colon. (Reproduced with permission from Shearman & Finlayson)[83]

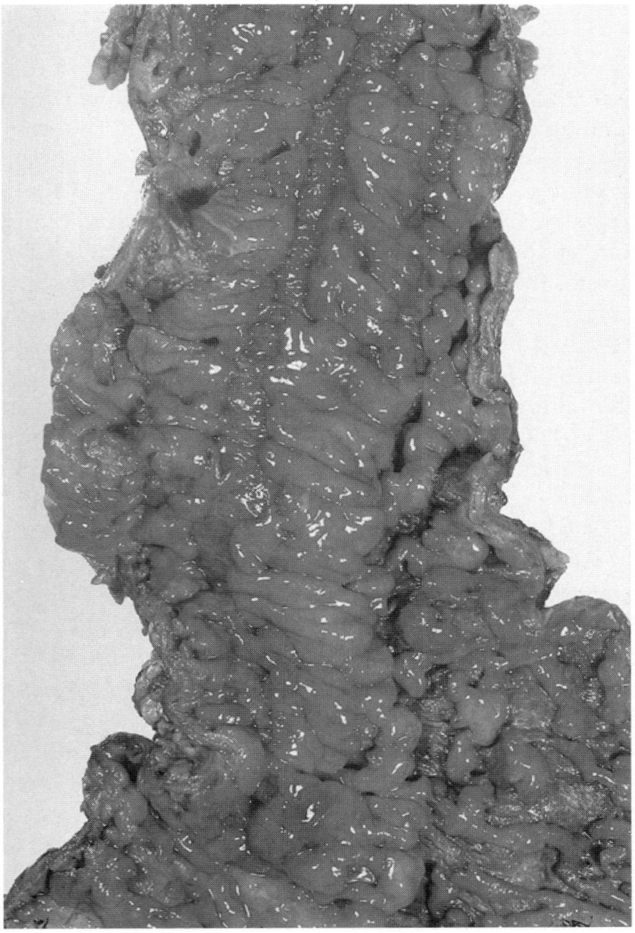

Fig. 27.23 Crohn's disease. Serpiginous ulceration of the distal colonic mucosa which appears oedematous and non-granular between the ulcers. (Reproduced with permission from Shearman & Finlayson)[83]

process.[6] This problem is probably most likely to arise following colectomy for an active colitis, early in the course of the disease.

In a series of colectomy and proctocolectomy specimens from Denmark, an attempt was made to distinguish ulcerative colitis from Crohn's disease using gross pathology only.[7] Of the 198 specimens studied 52% were classified as ulcerative colitis, 37% as Crohn's disease and 11% as indeterminate. There was, however, such an overlap in the features that even skip lesions and strictures could not discriminate and the conclusion reached was that in the colon it was not possible to separate the two diseases on macroscopic features alone.

Attempts have been made at endoscopy to identify early lesions utilizing a spray of indigocarmine dye[8] or magnifying endoscopy.[9] The dye spray allowed visualization of minute lesions, the majority described as aphthoid ulcers, in 90% of 20 patients whose main site of disease was proximal to the transverse colon, while magnification revealed 'worm-eaten appearances' of the mucosa in about 75% of 27 patients. The latter appearances were seen more frequently in active disease in patients with disease for more than 5 years. These two studies further illustrate the widespread involvement of the large bowel in Crohn's disease even when, grossly, it may appear 'segmental'.

Anal lesions, which are common in Crohn's disease, are seen particularly in association with colonic disease and include fissures, ulcers, oedematous skin tags and fistulae.[10,11] In children this is particularly common; indeed it may antedate involvement elsewhere in the bowel, although the perianal disease itself tends to have a benign

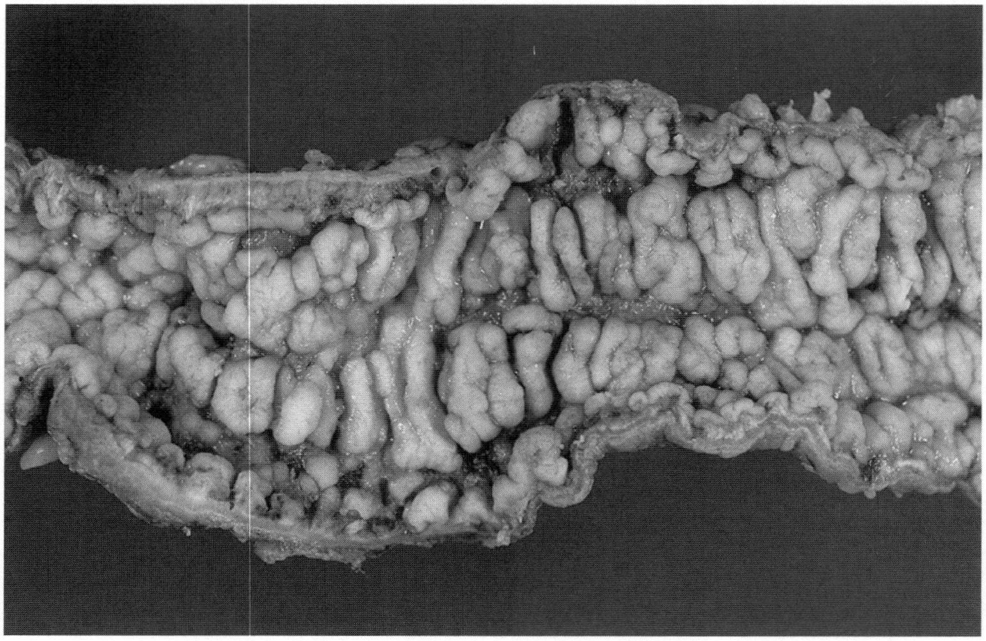

Fig. 27.24 Crohn's colitis. Combined pattern of ulceration with 'cobblestoning' of the intervening mucosa.

course.[12] Biopsy of anal skin tags may provide evidence of Crohn's disease either alone or in combination with rectal biopsy.[13]

Microscopic

The histological features of colonic Crohn's disease are similar to those seen in other sites of the alimentary tract, but the histopathologist has been given the opportunity to study the disease process without reliance on resection specimens by the advent of endoscopic biopsy. These biopsies include mucosa, muscularis mucosae and possibly an element of superficial submucosa, thus eliminating the ability to assess transmural inflammation. However, the relative ease of obtaining these small biopsies allows the endoscopist to sample widely from macroscopically normal and abnormal mucosa, and to repeat the biopsies in different phases of disease activity. This is particularly valuable in inflammatory bowel disease as it may take more than one biopsy, perhaps on more than one occasion, to reach even a presumptive diagnosis of Crohn's disease.

Features which suggest Crohn's disease in mucosal biopsies include granulomas, lymphoid hyperplasia, particularly extending into the submucosa, variations in the degree and extent of chronic inflammatory cell infiltration within the lamina propria and focal aggregation of neutrophil polymorphs in a pericryptal position (Fig. 27.25).[14] None of these features, however, is pathognomonic for Crohn's disease, as even granulomas can be found in other diseases of the alimentary tract. Granulomas, as indicated, are not always present in patients with Crohn's disease and may not be a constant feature in individual cases.[15] Crohn's colitis may present acutely, at which time granulomas may not be found even in resected specimens, only to appear in large numbers in subsequent biopsies or resections. Granulomas have been looked at in a number of paediatric studies. In a large series of colorectal biopsies from children, granulomas were found in 26% of the biopsies from 42% of the patients.[16] Compared to adults, granulomas were twice as common in children, but they tended to be larger in adults. Numbers were less in the left side of the colon compared to the right side but diminished after the second year of illness and after the age of 16 years. Comparison between children with granulomas in rectosigmoid biopsies on first presentation and children without granulomas showed a similar age of onset of disease but those with granulomas had more extensive disease, and perianal fistulae, perianal abscesses and anal stenoses were more common.[17]

In another study, 37 children who had clinical symptoms and were found to have granulomas without diagnostic radiology were followed up for a mean of 3 years.[18] All were investigated by radiology and some by endoscopy, which showed evidence of Crohn's disease in 22. In one patient a diagnosis of chronic granulomatous disease was made but 13 were still unclassified, indicating that prolonged follow-up may be required to determine the significance of finding granulomas. The actual granulomas may vary considerably in appearance, ranging from the typical rather oedematous, loosely aggregated collection of macrophages through sarcoid-like densely cellular aggregates to large tuberculoid granulomas (Fig. 27.26).

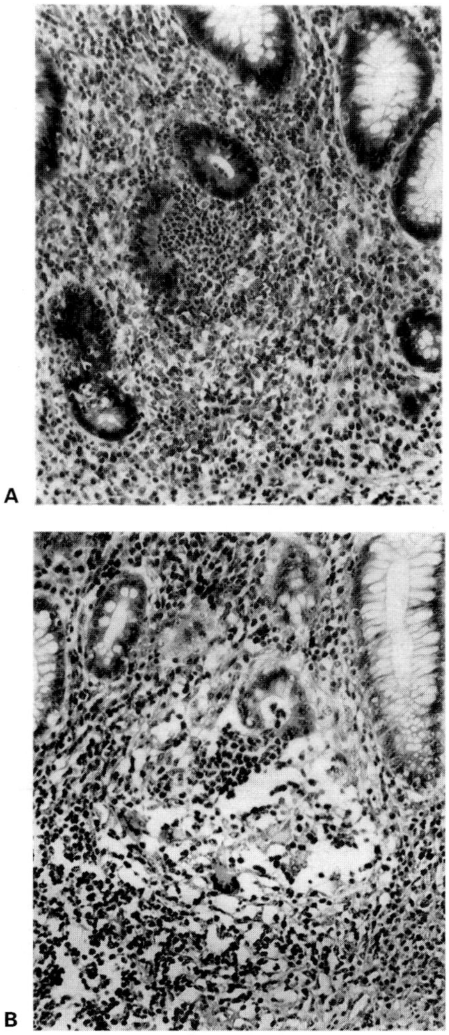

Fig. 27.25 Crohn's disease. Rectal biopsies showing **A** inflammatory cell infiltrate in the lamina propria with focal pericryptal aggregate of neutrophil polymorphs; **B** similar inflammatory infiltrate with pericryptal aggregate of macrophages and early giant cell formation. (H&E, ×112)

COMPLICATIONS

The development of toxic dilatation in a patient with inflammatory bowel disease can no longer be taken as an indication that the likely diagnosis is ulcerative colitis since it has become increasingly recognized as a complication of colonic Crohn's disease.[19] Indeed, it may occur during an acute episode or first presentation. The danger, as in ulcerative colitis, is of perforation as a result of extensive ulceration and necrosis, which may be induced, at least in part, by ischaemic changes, although the exact aetiology of toxic dilatation in inflammatory bowel disease remains uncertain. In the absence of toxic dilatation free perforation is uncommon, usually occurring in patients already diagnosed as having Crohn's disease.[20] Tonelli and Ficari in a series of 94 cases indicated that perforation was usually related to stenosis and while in the ileum perforation was associated with mural thickening, in the colon there was a direct relationship to the length of the stricture.[21] There was, however, no relationship to steroid therapy, duration of disease, toxic dilatation or obstruction in a series of 33 cases reported by Katz.[22]

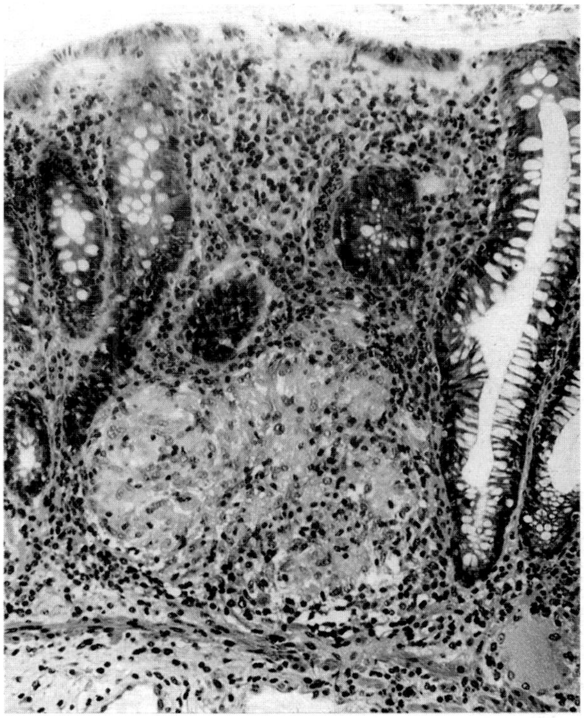

Fig. 27.26 Crohn's disease. Discrete granuloma in the colonic mucosa composed of histiocytic cells. (H&E, ×125)

Fistulae, which are said to occur in about 10% of Crohn's disease cases, include ileocolic and enterovesical communications. Fistulae may rarely involve the upper gastrointestinal tract,[23] where only a minority will present with the pathognomonic sign of faecal vomiting, but undoubtedly the most common site is in the perianal region. Soeters et al, reporting from Massachusetts, described a series of gastrointestinal fistulae in which both the number and the percentage due to Crohn's disease increased after 1960, with more fistulae being seen in the five years from 1970 when compared to the preceding decade.[24] In a report from St Mark's Hospital, over half of the fistulae were between the ileum and sigmoid colon or rectum and about 20% involved either small or large intestine and bladder.[25] In another series of 236 resections for Crohn's disease, there were 60 fistulae excluding those at the anus.[26] Fistulae were more common in first excisions, predominantly affected the ileum and tended to occur at the proximal end of strictures. In the re-excisions, 10 of the 16 arose at the site of anastomosis and communication with the skin was very much commoner in re-excision specimens. Crohn's disease accounted for 23% of the 64 anal and non-anal fistulae recorded in the diagnostic codes of the Edinburgh University Department of Pathology from 1980–84 and was suspected in a further 20%.[27] All the suspected cases were perianal lesions, illustrating the difficulty of making a definite diagnosis on biopsy tissue from this region. This survey also demonstrated that Crohn's fistulae form a significant proportion of those treated surgically and submitted to histopathologists for diagnosis. Colonic fistulae tend to be more indolent and less life-threatening than small bowel fistulae, and although intra-abdominal abscess formation may be associated with large bowel fistulae this is not always the case. In ileocolic Crohn's, most abscesses are related to the ileum while in colonic Crohn's the sigmoid colon is where most abscesses seem to arise.[28] Despite longstanding chronic inflammation in many cases of Crohn's disease, amyloid is only rarely seen as a complication, being reported in only 0.5% of cases in a large series from England and in 1% of a comparable series in North America.[29]

Although almost all patients with active Crohn's disease will have positive tests for faecal occult blood, severe acute haemorrhage from Crohn's disease is rare. It is estimated to occur with the same frequency as in ulcerative colitis, ranging from 0–6% but in a series of 1526 cases seen between 1960–86 at Mount Sinai, only 21 cases (1.4%) had 26 episodes of severe bleeding.[30] This occurred more commonly with colonic involvement and the precise site was only identified by angiography in two cases. Although three patients died, only one death was directly due to a third episode of haemorrhage many years after the first. If seems that fissuring ulceration seldom penetrates a large vessel within the gut wall and Crohn's disease is ranked low in the order of causes of life-threatening acute lower gastrointestinal haemorrhage.

Malignancy in Crohn's disease

The first case report of a malignant intestinal tumour arising in a patient with Crohn's disease was by Ginzberg in 1956 and during the late 1960s and early 1970s the suspicion that there was an increased risk of malignancy in patients with Crohn's disease was growing. It is now recognized that there is an increased risk of malignancy developing in both small and large intestine in patients with Crohn's disease, but quantification of this risk has proved difficult. Most of the cases have been reported from North America[31] and the risk may have been underestimated due to the surgical resection of 'at risk' bowel. It will be of interest to see whether any changes follow the current more conservative approach to surgical management.

The problems in determining the risk of small bowel neoplasia are compounded by the very low incidence of 'spontaneously' occurring malignancies, but a feature of some of the early case reports of small bowel tumours in Crohn's disease was their origin in segments of bowel by-passed as a result of surgical intervention.[32] This form of carcinoma is difficult to diagnose and has a poor prognosis, although Collier et al, in reporting three cases and reviewing the literature, showed that 72% of 75 cases of small bowel carcinoma arising from Crohn's disease had not had previous by-pass surgery.[33] While most cases arising in by-passed segments tend to have a long history of Crohn's disease, in other cases the tumour may be detected at the same time as Crohn's disease is diagnosed, usually in a resected specimen.

Colonic carcinomas may arise in macroscopically uninvolved bowel (Fig. 27.27), and this raises difficulties for the surgical management of cases. While recent recommendations have included the avoidance of by-pass operations, carcinoma, when it arises in segments of active disease, particularly when strictured, may be extremely difficult to diagnose, and even in resection specimens the presence of a tumour may be difficult or impossible to recognize on macroscopic inspection.[35] However, when a surgeon suspects such a tumour at the time of laparotomy, there is considerable value in utilizing frozen section examination of lymph nodes, suspicious areas of bowel and resection margins.

The association of epithelial dysplasia related to carcinomas both locally and at a distance[35–37] has lent support to the idea of a dysplasia–carcinoma sequence, although not all series demonstrate this.[38,39] This raises the question of surveillance and long-term follow-up of patients with colonic Crohn's disease but a consensus is still awaited as to whether surveillance is justified and, if so, how it is to be carried out. Attempts to define a high-risk group suggest that early onset, long duration of disease, by-passed segments, strictures and fistulae raise the likelihood of intestinal malignancy.[40] Lashner, reviewing the risk factors for small intestinal cancer, adds proximal small bowel disease, use of 6-mercaptopurine and the hazardous occupations associated with increased risk of colorectal cancer.[41] While some authors have suggested a similar surveillance programme to that employed in the follow-up of cases of ulcerative colitis, the recent report from the Leeds group casts doubt on the effectiveness of such programmes.[42] Technical difficulties would be greater in Crohn's disease if colonoscopy was to be contemplated and even regular proctoscopy/sigmoidoscopy with multiple biopsies would only identify a small proportion of patients harbouring carcinoma. Allowing for the difficulty of recognizing and grading dysplasia,[43] the detection of high grade dysplasia would be particularly important, but the problems would then be to identify the site of the carcinoma, which could be in the small bowel, determine how widespread the dysplasia was, decide if surgical management was justified and what surgery to perform.

It is difficult to place a numerical value on the increased risk of malignancy. This is demonstrated in the

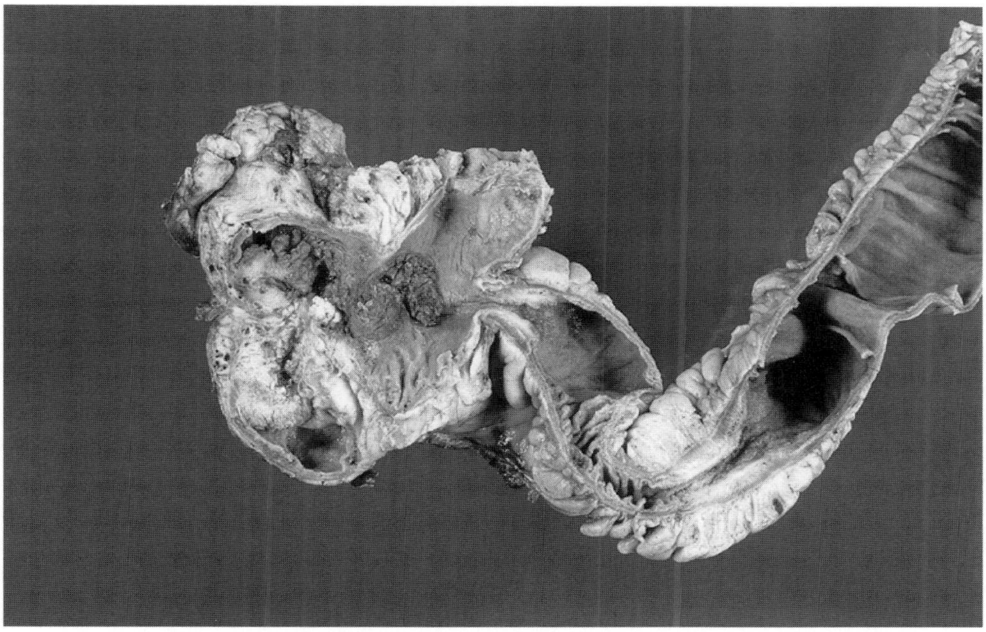

Fig. 27.27 Ileocolic resection with large caecal carcinoma and two strictured segments of Crohn's disease in the terminal ileum.

variation in reported series, which ranges from no excess risk to estimates of a 4–26.6-fold increased risk over the expected in patients with Crohn's disease. Hordijk, in suggesting this is likely to be due to selection bias and problems of generalization and validation of results, calls for the adoption of more rigorous standards in reporting cases.[44] A prevalence of 0.45% of malignancy in Crohn's disease has been suggested, and most of these tumours appear to develop within the colon.

Tumours have been described at other sites within the alimentary tract; these include carcinomas arising in the anal canal,[45] carcinosarcoma in the small intestine,[46] carcinoid tumours in the ileum[47] and lymphoma.[48]

While there is no overall excess of extra-intestinal tumours in patients with Crohn's disease in most series,[49,50] a Danish study which found no increase in intestinal tumours over a 20-year period did report an excess of extra-intestinal malignant tumours in women.[51] Squamous skin cancers were increased following Crohn's disease in the Swedish study[50] and there also seems to be an excess of lymphomas over the expected number.[52] This is of interest in relation to the experimental induction of lymphomas in 'nude' mice using Crohn's tissue, and an excess in immunosuppressed patients. The question is whether this is an effect of immunosuppressive therapy in patients with Crohn's disease, or whether it reflects an abnormality of immune function.

DIFFERENTIAL DIAGNOSIS

Since the early descriptions of Crohn's disease affecting the colon, the major problem has been to distinguish Crohn's colitis from ulcerative colitis. This has already been alluded to in the discussion on the role of biopsy in Crohn's disease, but the features of particular value in the distinction between these two major causes of chronic inflammatory colonic disease are the distribution of the disease within the colon and the rectum, the involvement of anus and perianal region, including fistula formation, the character of the ulceration, the diffuse or patchy distribution of inflammation within the mucosa and the extent of disease within the bowel wall.[53] There remains, however, a significant minority of cases of about 5–10% which are difficult to place with certainty into one or other of these disease entities.[6] Continued follow-up will allow a definitive diagnosis in a number of these difficult cases if, for example, the patient subsequently develops recurrent disease in another part of the gastrointestinal tract indicating a diagnosis of Crohn's disease.

Apart from ulcerative colitis, there are many other conditions which may cause difficulty in making a definitive diagnosis of Crohn's disease.[54–56] Increasing awareness of the role of infecting organisms in producing colonic mucosal abnormalities has increased the pathological problems in trying to distinguish not only Crohn's disease from ulcerative colitis,[57] but also from infective proctitis/colitis.[58–60] This can cause particular problems in patients who present acutely with inflammatory disease within the colon. However, there are relatively few bacterial causes of chronic inflammation within the colon, and persistence of inflammation beyond two or three weeks suggests that the patient is likely to be suffering from idiopathic inflammatory disease. In the acute case, it can be difficult to distinguish infection due to organisms such as *Campylobacter jejuni* from inflammatory bowel disease, and indeed in some cases of infective aetiology granulomas may be identified in rectal biopsies.[61] Features suggestive of an infective aetiology include superficial mucoid crypt abscesses and superficial infiltration of the lamina propria by neutrophil polymorphs, whereas distorted crypts, crypt atrophy, basal lymphoid aggregates and granulomas are strongly suggestive of Crohn's disease or ulcerative colitis.[58] Other causes of infection within the colon such as amoebiasis and tuberculosis require to be considered in the differential diagnosis, but these are more likely to be a problem in areas where parasitic infestation and tuberculosis are still rife. In both instances, search for organisms in stool or tissue is important in reaching the correct diagnosis.

There are a number of circumstances when mucosal inflammation and/or ulceration may cause confusion in diagnosis. These include changes induced by drugs including non-steroidal anti-inflammatory drugs and methyldopa, pseudomembranous colitis following antibiotic use and microscopic and lymphocytic colitis. The latter may well form part of a spectrum which includes collagenous colitis.[62] The history and pattern of the inflammatory changes should enable these diagnosis to be made.

When a segment of colon or rectum is deprived of the normal faecal flow through it, a so-called diversion colitis results. While this more often resembles ulcerative colitis macroscopically,[63] it can result in features suggestive of Crohn's disease and this is particularly likely in the defunctioned rectum of patients with ulcerative colitis. In these circumstances, classification should be based on examination of the colon.[64]

Inflammation in the ileal reservoir created after colectomy, so called 'pouchitis', can lead to similar diagnostic difficulties. Most cases respond to antibiotic therapy but a small group are refractory to treatment, raising suspicions of Crohn's disease. Subramani et al studied 24 cases of 'refractory pouchitis' but found no evidence to suggest that Crohn's disease was responsible.[65]

Diverticula are common in the distal colon in the elderly, and many patients with distal colonic Crohn's disease have coexistent diverticulosis. The problem usually occurs either due to segmental inflammation in the sigmoid colon[66] or when a patient with suspected diverticular disease undergoes resection of the sigmoid colon and granulomas are found on histological examination. In diverticulitis, these are usually of foreign body type, but if other features of Crohn's disease are present, this diagnosis should be suspected and evidence sought elsewhere in the gastrointestinal tract. However, as in the mouth and appendix, a number of these cases show no tendency to develop any other evidence of Crohn's disease despite prolonged follow-up, suggesting this is unlikely to be true Crohn's disease.

Ischaemic colitis, particularly in the chronic phase when granulation tissue and fibrosis can produce a stricture, may mimic Crohn's disease[67] and this can be difficult to diagnose if the patient has no predisposing cause of ischaemic damage to the colon and radiological or endoscopic examination is equivocal. While there may be features suggestive of ischaemia in biopsies, it may be difficult or impossible to make a definite diagnosis on such biopsy material.

Previous abdominal irradiation can produce areas of stricturing and ulceration within the gastrointestinal tract but the history of previous treatment, usually for neoplastic disease, is an important factor in the diagnosis. 'Solitary ulcer' of the rectum may present with an area of apparent inflammation in the rectum and can be mistaken for a localized area of Crohn's disease, but there are typical histological changes in the mucosa.[68]

Tumours within the colon are seldom confused with inflammatory bowel disease, except when the tumour arises in a patient with inflammatory bowel disease or the presentation is of an irregular, ill-defined area of stricturing due to a diffusely infiltrating neoplasm. This pattern may occasionally be seen in patients with metastatic lobular carcinoma of the breast.

Associated diseases

Crohn's disease commonly affects the anus and perianal region, but fortunately it is only occasionally that this process extends to involve the neighbouring skin of the genitalia, groins or natal cleft. The oedema, induration and ulceration are usually in continuity with perianal disease, but so-called 'metastatic' Crohn's disease of the skin has been described at a number of sites including the umbilicus, submammary and retroauricular regions and on the anterior abdominal wall. The lower limbs are frequently affected, biopsy usually reveals a granulomatous inflammatory reaction and most cases have been associated with gastrointestinal and particularly perianal disease.[69,70] The possibility of Crohn's disease of the skin should be considered in patients who present with indolent, indurated and sometimes ulcerated nodules or plaques which do not resemble the lesions seen in pyoderma gangrenosum, erythema nodosum or polyarteritis nodosa, dermatological diseases seen more commonly in patients with Crohn's disease.

Aphthous ulceration has been described within the gastrointestinal tract related to areas of active Crohn's disease, and oral aphthous ulceration may also be a manifestation of gastrointestinal Crohn's disease. However, the majority of aphthous ulcers occurring in the general population are not associated with more serious disease elsewhere, although a number of patients with recurrent and severe oral ulceration may be suffering from conditions such as coeliac disease, Crohn's disease or Behcet's. In Crohn's disease, the inflammatory process may involve lips, gingiva or buccal mucosa. There may be diffuse swelling, oedema, ulcers, a cobblestone mucosa or polypoid mucosal hyperplasia and biopsy demonstrates a granulomatous reaction in a high proportion of cases.[71,72]

Abnormalities of liver function tests are common in patients with inflammatory bowel disease, but it is probably only in those who have persistent abnormalities that significant chronic liver disease exists.[73] Cholelithiasis, which is likely to be a problem in ileal Crohn's, was reported in 13% of cases of regional enteritis[29] and in a series from Southampton 34% of patients with small bowel Crohn's disease had gallstones demonstrated by ultrasound scans.[74] Minor histological changes are not uncommonly seen in liver biopsies, and these include fatty change and very mild inflammatory cell infiltration usually confined to the portal tracts.[75,76] However, major hepatic pathology is rare and in a large series from Birmingham less than 1% of patients with Crohn's disease had cirrhosis.[73] Pericholangitis was diagnosed in about 20% of patients with persistent liver function test abnormalities, but the significance and rate of progression of these changes remains uncertain. The cause of chronic liver disease in these patients is unknown as it seems unrelated to such aspects as blood transfusion, drug treatment including anaesthetics, or other systemic complications. It is also difficult to determine the effect of resection of affected bowel on the progression or resolution of significant hepatic abnormalities.

A number of skeletal and joint abnormalities have been described in Crohn's disease.[77–80] A peripheral, asymmetric, self-limited and non-deforming arthritis affects large joints in 15–20% of cases. This is seronegative and its activity corresponds to that of the bowel disease. Ankylosing spondylitis is found in 3–6% of cases of inflammatory bowel disease or there may be a bilateral symmetrical sacroiliitis. These two patterns do not show clear links with HLA type or the activity of bowel disease. The fourth group includes the many connective tissue abnormalities seen in 4–18% of cases of bowel disease and range from granulomas to finger clubbing. A few patients show some of the features of Marfan's syndrome. Eye problems including episcleritis, keratitis, conjunctivitis and macular haemorrhage have been described, although anterior uveitis is probably the commonest, occurring in some 2–3%. Both joint and eye problems seem to be commoner in patients with Crohn's colitis than in those with ileal disease.[29] While the recently recognized association with pulmonary disease has been regarded as a rare event, recent reports have described bronchiectasis, granulomatous lung disease, interstitial fibrosis and cases of drug toxicity in patients with inflammatory bowel disease.[81] Relatively few patients with Crohn's disease have been studied by sophisticated pulmonary function tests, but a report from France described abnormalities in pulmonary function measured by broncho-alveolar lavage, estimation of serum angiotensin-converting enzyme and demonstration of increased physiological dead space in the upper part of the lung in half of the 12 patients studied.[82] The results from this small group of patients without pulmonary symptoms or chest X-ray abnormalities suggest that many more patients with Crohn's disease may have latent pulmonary disease. It is likely that as other systems are looked at in more detail further alterations of structure and function will come to light in patients with Crohn's disease.

The pathogenesis of these systemic manifestations remains a mystery. Bacterial antigens or antigen–antibody complexes have both been suggested as possible causes, but the link is tenuous and so far remains unproven.

REFERENCES

1. Brooke BN. Granulomatous disease of the intestine. Lancet 1959; 2: 745–749.
2. Morson BC, Lockhart-Mummery HE. Crohn's disease of the colon. Gastroenterologica (Basel) 1959; 92: 168–173.
3. Marshak RH, Wolf BS, Eliasoph J. Segmental colitis. Radiology 1959; 73: 707–716.
4. Fabricius PJ, Gyde SN, Shoulder P, Keighley MRB, Alexander-Williams J, Allan RN. Crohn's disease in the elderly. Gut 1985; 26: 461–465.
5. Grimm IS, Friedman LS. Inflammatory bowel disease in the elderly. Gastroenterol Clin North Am 1990; 19: 361–389.
6. Price AB. Overlap in the spectrum of non-specific inflammatory bowel disease — 'colitis indeterminate'. J Clin Pathol 1978; 31: 567–577.
7. Palnaes-Hanson C, Hegnhoj J, Moller A, Brauer C, Hage E, Jarnum S. Ulcerative colitis and Crohn's disease of the colon: is there a macroscopic difference? Ann Chir Gynaecol 1990; 79: 78–81.
8. Okada M, Maeda K, Yao T, Iwashita A, Nomiyama Y, Kitahara K. Minute lesions of the rectum and sigmoid colon in patients with Crohn's disease. Gastrointest Endosc 1991; 37: 319–324.
9. Makiyama K, Tanaka T, Senju M, Itsuno M, Murata I, Hara K. Clinical course and magnifying endoscopic findings of fine lesions of the large intestinal mucosa in Crohn's disease. Gastro Jap 1989 24: 120–126.
10. Lockhart-Mummery HE. Anal lesions in Crohn's disease. Br J Surg 1985; 72 (Suppl): S95–96.
11. Markowitz J, Daum F, Aiges H, Kahn E, Silverberg M, Fisher SE. Perianal disease in children and adolescents with Crohn's disease. Gastroenterology 1984; 86: 829–833.
12. Palder SB, Shandling B, Bilik R, Griffiths A M, Sherman P. Perianal complications of pediatric Crohn's disease. J Pediatr Surg 1991; 26: 513–515.
13. Taylor BA, Williams GT, Hughes LE, Rhodes J. The histology of anal skin tags in Crohn's disease: an aid to confirmation of the diagnosis. Int J Color Dis 1989; 4: 197–199.
14. Whitehead R. Mucosal biopsy of the gastrointestinal tract. 3rd ed. Philadelphia: Saunders, 1985: p 227–237.
15. Chambers TJ, Morson BC. The granuloma in Crohn's disease. Gut 1979; 20: 269–274.
16. Schmitz-Moormann P, Schag M. Histology of the lower intestinal

tract in Crohn's disease of children and adolescents: multicentric paediatric Crohn's disease study. Pathol Res & Pract 1990; 186: 479–484.
17. Markowitz J, Kahn E, Daum F. Prognostic significance of epithelioid granulomas found in rectosigmoid biopsies at the initial presentation of pediatric Crohn's disease. J Pediatr Gastroenterol Nutr 1989; 9: 182–186.
18. Keller KM, Bender SW, Kirchmann H et al. Diagnostic significance of epithelioid granulomas in Crohn's disease in children. J Pediatr Gastroenterol Nutr 1990; 10: 27–32.
19. Whorwell PJ, Isaacson P. Toxic dilatation of colon in Crohn's disease. Lancet 1981; ii: 1334–1337.
20. Bundred NJ, Dixon JM, Lumsden AB, Gilmour HM, Davies GC. Free perforation in Crohn's colitis: a ten year review. Dis Colon Rectum 1985; 28: 35–37.
21. Tonnelli F, Ficari F. Pathological features of Crohn's disease determining perforation. J Clin Gastroenterol 1991; 13: 226–230.
22. Katz S, Schulman N, Levin L. Free perforation in Crohn's disease: a report of 33 cases and review of literature. Am J Gastroenterol 1986; 81: 38–43.
23. Pichney LS, Fantry GT, Graham SM. Gastrocolic and duodenocolic fistulas in Crohn's disease. J Clin Gastroenterol 1992; 15: 205–211.
24. Soeters PB, Ebeid AM, Fischer JE. Review of 404 patients with gastrointestinal fistulae. Ann Surg 1979; 190: 189–202.
25. Glass RE. The management of internal fistulae in Crohn's disease. Br J Surg 1985; 72 (Suppl): S93–95.
26. Kelly JK, Preshaw RM. Origin of fistulas in Crohn's disease. J Clin Gastroenterol 1989; 11: 193–196.
27. Piris J. Personal communication, 1986.
28. Greenstein AJ, Sachar DB, Greenstein RJ, Janowitz HD, Aufses Jr AH. Intraabdominal abscess in Crohn's (ileo) colitis. Am J Surg 1982; 143: 727–730.
29. Greenstein AJ, Janowitz HD, Sacher DB. The extra-intestinal complications of Crohn's disease and ulcerative colitis: a study of 700 patients. Medicine 1976; 55: 401–412.
30. Robert JR, Sachar DB, Greenstein AJ. Severe gastrointestinal haemorrhage in Crohn's disease. Ann Surg 1991; 213: 207–211.
31. Rubio CA, Befritz R, Poppen B, Svenberg T, Slezak P. Crohn's disease and adenocarcinoma of the intestinal tract: report of four cases. Dis Colon Rectum 1991; 34: 174–180.
32. Greenstein AJ, Sachar DB, Smith H, Janowitz HD, Aufses Jr AH. Patterns of neoplasia in Crohn's disease and ulcerative colitis. Cancer 1980; 46: 403–407.
33. Collier PE, Turowski P, Diamond DL. Small intestinal adenocarcinoma complicating regional enteritis. Cancer 1985; 55: 516–521.
34. Thompson EM, Clayden G, Price AB. Cancer in Crohn's disease — an 'occult' malignancy. Histopathology 1983; 7: 365–376.
35. Hamilton SR. Colorectal carcinomas in patients with Crohn's disease. Gastroenterology 1985; 89: 398–407.
36. Petras RE, Mir-Madjlessi SH, Farmer RG. Crohn's disease and intestinal carcinoma: a report of 11 cases with emphasis on associated epithelial dysplasia. Gastroenterology 1987; 93: 1307–1314.
37. Korelitz BI, Lauwers G, Sommers SC. Rectal mucosal dysplasia in Crohn's disease. Gut 1990; 31: 1382–1386.
38. Warren R, Barwick KW. Crohn's colitis with carcinoma and dysplasia: report of a case and review of 100 small and large bowel resections for Crohn's disease to detect incidence of dysplasia. Am J Surg Pathol 1983; 7: 151–159.
39. Glotzer DJ. The risk of cancer in Crohn's disease. Gastroenterology 1985; 89: 438–441.
40. Stahl TJ, Schoetz Jr DJ, Roberts PL et al. Crohn's disease and carcinoma: increasing justification for surveillance? Dis Colon Rectum 1992; 35: 850–856.
41. Lashner BA. Risk factors for small bowel cancer in Crohn's disease. Dig Dis Sci 1992; 37: 1179–1184.
42. Lynch DAF, Lobo AJ, Sobala GM, Dixon MF, Axon ATR. Failure of colonoscopic surveillance in ulcerative colitis. Gut 1993; 34: 1075–1080.
43. Simpson S, Traube J, Riddell RH. The histologic appearance of dysplasia: precarcinomatous change in Crohn's disease of the small and large intestine. Gastroenterology 1981; 81: 492–501.
44. Hordijk ML, Shivananda S. Risk of cancer in inflammatory bowel disease: why are the results in the reviewed literature so varied? Scan J Gastro 1989; 24 (Suppl 170): 70–74.
45. Preston DM, Fowler EF, Lennard-Jones JE, Hawley PR. Carcinoma of the anus in Crohn's disease. Br J Surg 1983; 70: 346–347.
46. Radi MF, Gray GF, Scott HW. Carcinosarcoma of ileum in regional enteritis. Hum Pathol 1984; 15: 385–387.
47. Kortbeek J, Kelly JK, Preshaw RM. Carcinoid tumors and inflammatory bowel disease. J Surg Oncol 1992; 49: 122–126.
48. Glick SN, Teplick SK, Goodman LR, Clearfield HR, Shanser JD. Development of lymphoma in patients with Crohn's disease. Radiology 1984; 153: 337–339.
49. Greenstein AJ, Gennuso R, Sachar DB et al. Extra-intestinal cancer in inflammatory bowel disease. Cancer 1985; 56: 2914–2921.
50. Ekbom A, Helmick C, Zack M, Adami H-O. Extracolonic malignancies in inflammatory bowel disease. Cancer 1991; 67: 2015–2019.
51. Kvist N, Jacobsen O, Norgard P et al. Malignancy in Crohn's disease. Scand J Gastroenterol 1986; 21: 82–86.
52. Greenstein AJ, Mullin GE, Strauchen JA et al. Lymphoma in inflammatory bowel disease. Cancer 1992; 69: 1119–1123.
53. Morson BC et al. Morson and Dawson's gastrointestinal pathology. 3rd ed. Oxford: Blackwell, 1990: p 514–525.
54. Tanaka M, Riddell RH. The pathological diagnosis and differential diagnosis of Crohn's disease. Hepatogastroenterology 1990; 37: 18–31.
55. Talbot IC, Price AB. The differential diagnosis of inflammatory bowel disease. In: Biopsy pathology in colorectal disease. London: Chapman Hall, 1987: p 201–217.
56. Shepherd NA. Pathological mimics of chronic inflammatory bowel disease. J Clin Pathol 1991; 44: 726–733.
57. Goldman H, Antonioli DA. Mucosal biopsy of the rectum, colon and distal ileum. Hum Pathol 1982; 13: 981–1012.
58. Surawicz CM, Belic L. Rectal biopsy helps to distinguish acute self-limited colitis from idiopathic inflammatory bowel disease. Gastroenterology 1984; 86: 104–113.
59. Goldman H. Acute versus chronic colitis: how and when to distinguish by biopsy. Gastroenterology 1984; 86: 199–201.
60. Allison MC, Hamilton-Dutoit SJ, Dhillon AP, Pounder RE. The value of rectal biopsy in distinguishing self-limited colitis from early inflammatory bowel disease. Q J Med 1987; 248: 985–995.
61. Dickinson RJ, Gilmour HM, McClelland DBL. Rectal biopsy in patients presenting to an infectious disease unit with diarrhoeal disease. Gut 1979; 20: 141–148.
62. Lazenby A, Yardley J, Giardiello F, Jessurun J, Bayless T. Lymphocytic ('microscopic') colitis: a comparative histopathologic study with particular reference to collagenous colitis. Hum Pathol 1989; 20: 18–28.
63. Ma CK, Gottlieb C, Haas PA. Diversion colitis: a clinicopathological study of 21 cases. Hum Pathol 1990; 21: 429–436.
64. Warren BF, Shepherd NA. Diversion proctocolitis. Histopathology 1992; 21: 91–93.
65. Subramani K, Harpaz N, Bilotta J et al. Refractory pouchitis: does it reflect underlying Crohn's disease? Gut 1993; 34: 1539–1542.
66. Gore S, Shepherd NA, Wilkinson SP. Endoscopic crescentic fold disease of the sigmoid colon: the clinical and histopathological spectrum of a distinctive endoscopic appearance. Int J Colorectal Dis 1992; 7: 76–81.
67. Marston A. Vascular disease of the gut. 2nd ed. London: Arnold, 1986: p; 152–173.
68. Rutter KRP, Riddell RH. The solitary ulcer syndrome of the rectum. Clin Gastroenterol 1975; 4: 505–530.
69. Sutphen JL, Cooper PH, Mackel SE, Nelson DL. Metastatic cutaneous Crohn's disease. Gastroenterology 1984; 86: 941–944.
70. Shum DT, Guenther L. Metastatic Crohn's disease: case report and review of the literature. Arch Dermatol 1990; 126: 645–648.
71. Williams AJK, Wray D, Ferguson A. The clinical entity of orofacial Crohn's disease. Q J Med 1991; 79: 451–458.
72. Plauth M, Jenss H, Meyle J. Oral manifestations of Crohn's disease: an analysis of 79 cases. J Clin Gastroenterol 1991; 13: 29–37.

73. Dew MJ, Thompson H, Allan RN. The spectrum of hepatic dysfunction in inflammatory bowel disease. Q J Med 1979; 48: 113–115.
74. Whorwell PJ, Hawkins R, Dewbury K, Wright R. Ultrasound survey of gallstones and other hepatobiliary disorders in patients with Crohn's disease. Dig Dis Sci 1984; 29: 930–933.
75. Perrett AD, Higgins G, Johnston HH, Massarella GR, Truelove SC, Wright R. The liver in Crohn's disease. Q J Med 1971; 40: 187–209.
76. Eade MN, Cooke WT, Williams JA. Liver disease in Crohn's disease: a study of 100 consecutive patients. Scand J Gastroenterol 1971; 6: 199–204.
77. Haslock I, Wright V. The musculo-skeletal complications of Crohn's disease. Medicine 1973; 52: 217–225.
78. Enlow RW, Bias WB, Arnett FC. The spondylitis of inflammatory bowel disease: evidence for a non-HLA linked axial arthropathy. Arthritis Rheum 1980; 23: 1359–1365.
79. Gravallese EM, Kantrowitz FG. Arthritic manifestations of inflammatory bowel disease. Am J Gastro 1988; 83: 703–709.
80. Gran JT, Husby G. Joint manifestations in gastrointestinal disease 1. Pathophysiological aspects, ulcerative colitis and Crohn's disease. Dig Dis 1992; 10: 274–294.
81. Kayser K, Probst F, Gabius HJ, Muller KM. Are there characteristic alterations in lung tissue associated with Crohn's disease? Pathol Res and Pract 1990; 186: 485–490.
82. Bonniere P, Wallaert B, Cortot A et al. Latent pulmonary involvement in Crohn's disease: biological, functional, bronchoalveolar lavage and scintigraphic studies. Gut 1986; 27: 919–925.
83. Shearman DJC, Finlayson NDC. Disease of the gastrointestinal tract and liver. 2nd ed. Edinburgh: Churchill Livingstone, 1989.

PART III

Other forms of colitis and non-specific ulcers

R. Whitehead

FORMS OF COLITIS

Diarrhoea is a common affliction and, especially if prolonged or associated with bleeding, is ever likely to be fully investigated and this will often include biopsy. Depending upon the sophistication of the available means of diagnosis, less then 50% of cases will prove to have a microbiological cause[1] Of the remainder, a proportion will have or eventually develop a spectrum of features which will substantiate a diagnosis of ulcerative colitis or Crohn's disease. The rest will continue to pose a significant problem, even although within this group entities such as antibiotic-associated colitis and collagenous colitis have been defined. There remain a significant group of cases of acute colitis for which no apparent cause is found. However, even within this group, it is becoming evident that the horizon of suspicion for implicating a greater variety of microorganisms and drugs must be widened. This is supported by reports of acute colitis caused by sulphasalazine,[2] salicylates[3] and organisms of the Aeromonas species[4] and others such as enteropathogenic *E. coli*.[5,6] *Escherichia coli* 0157:H7 is described as causing a particularly haemorrhagic colitis which may be related to the production to one or more cytotoxins.[7,8] Rarely, colitis due to *Edwardsiella tarda*[9] occurs and cases of neonatal mucormycosis colitis in the absence of apparent immunodeficiency have been described recently, but it is unclear whether or not the infection was complicating necrotizing enterocolitis.[10] Commonplace organisms such as group A streptococci are thought to cause protocolitis on occasion in otherwise immune competent individuals,[11,12] and experience with AIDS patients has shown us that in circumstances of altered immunity and changes in mode of transmission, a vast new field of colorectal infections, bacterial, viral, fungal and parasitic, will be recognized. Toxoplasma, for example, which normally affects the central nervous system, has recently been reported as a cause of colitis in this condition.[13] However, it also seems that the AIDS virus itself, as demonstrated by in situ hybridization, may infect that colonic mucosa and result in a diffuse low-grade colitis which can last for up to four years.[14] There can thus be no doubt that even in the group of colitis cases which endoscopically are typical of idiopathic inflammatory bowel disease, an increasing proportion will be found to be due to infectious or other agents.[15]

In our present state of knowledge, colitis other than idiopathic ulcerative colitis and Crohn's colitis can be subdivided into the following clinicopathological subtypes: acute self-limited, microscopic, antibiotic-associated, colitis indeterminate, collagenous and allergic.

Acute self-limited colitis

This entity has also been described under the transient colitis syndrome.[16] Essentially, it is that group of cases of acute colitis for which no aetiological agent is recognized which is different from first attack ulcerative colitis because it is transient and resolves permanantly. The histological features nevertheless are suggestive of an infective origin. There is lack of atrophy and architectural distortion other than that due to oedema, a mixed inflammatory infiltrate with an obvious acute component more noticeable in the luminal aspect of the mucosa. The superficial epithelium tends to be thin and degenerate and crypt abscesses, if they occur, are small and poorly formed. Despite this, it is not always possible to differentiate the appearances from first attack ulcerative colitis. Furthermore, although there are claims to the contrary,[17] the differences between ulcerative colitis and transient or self-limited colitis are particularly difficult in the healing phase. The goblet cell population in both tends to be replaced by primitive proliferating crypt cells, the inflammatory infiltrate is more predominantly chronic and some crypt dilatation may be seen.[1] The importance of recognizing a group of 'self-limited colitis' cases is clear when one recalls that it was only after Skirrow[18] developed selective culture media for campylobacter species that we recognized that these organisms are a common cause of colitis and may mimic ulcerative colitis.[19]

Antibiotic-associated colitis (pseudomembranous)

The colitis which may follow the use of antibiotics is morphologically variable. It may be pseudomembranous but more commonly is not, although this type might represent an early or less severe form. Pseudomembranous colitis was described long before the antibiotic era and this should have provided a clue that the pathogenesis of this striking lesion involved a final common pathway which could perhaps be triggered by more than one set of circumstances. In the early descriptions of pseudomembranous colitis,[20] it was noted that developing lesions involved the luminal surface and that they extended deeper into mucosa and submucosa only as they advanced. This distribution suggested that the condition was due to a toxic agent, but it was 13 years later that a toxin somehow involved in the pathological process was identified.[21,22] It now seems that it is one of the four toxins produced by *Clostridium difficile* (toxin A) which plays a central role in the pathogenesis of antibiotic-associated colitis.[23]

Antibiotics with a wide range of activity can seemingly alter gut flora in a way which promotes the growth of *C. difficile*. Whether the organism is acquired from the environment or whether the antibiotic promotes growth of organisms already in the bowel is not clear in all cases. Whereas, for example, neonates frequently harbour *C. difficile*, in adults it is detectable in only 2% of cases. These differences may, however, be manifestations of the widely differing microbial populations in these two age groups and the effect that this has on the result of culture, even when selective media are used. Clustering of cases of *C. difficile* colitis would indicate cross-infection[24] whereas isolated cases unassociated with the use of antibiotics in patients who are severely ill for a variety of reasons points to the importance of other factors. One of these may be ischaemia, for it is known that obstructed bowel with a raised intraluminal pressure and decreased mucosal blood flow due to splanchnic shunting is particularly prone to the development of pseudomembranous colitis.[25] As a manifestation of the complexity of the pathogenetic mechanisms involved in this condition, it is notable that it can also occur spontaneously in otherwise young healthy patients.

Currently this disease is still posing questions as to precise pathogenesis. For example, in patients who do not have colitis, the toxin can be demonstrated and it may be absent in those with typical pseudomembranous lesions.[26,27] Other organisms and toxins may be involved and indeed this would appear to include other clostridial species.[28,29]

The spectrum of pathological changes also appears to be broadening. It has long been known that the small as well as the large bowel may show typical lesions, which presumably means that in some circumstances the organisms concerned also flourish in sites where there is no permanent bacterial population. The lesions may also be quite localized, confined to or sparing the rectum or causing a segmental colitis; they vary in severity from a mild inflammation which is self-limiting to a severe necrotizing diease associated with toxic dilatation. The disease can be chronic and relapsing[30,31] and apparently a cause of exacerbation of activity in idiopathic inflammatory bowel disease,[32] although this is disputed.[33] In view of the proposed aetiology of this condition, successful treatment of refractory cases by using faecal enemas is of interest.[34] Presumably the ecological circumstances of the colon are affected by this manoeuvre in such a way that they become hostile to the clostridial organisms responsible for the ongoing disease.

Fig. 27.28 Typical varying-sized plaques in severe pseudomembranous colitis. In one area they are almost confluent.

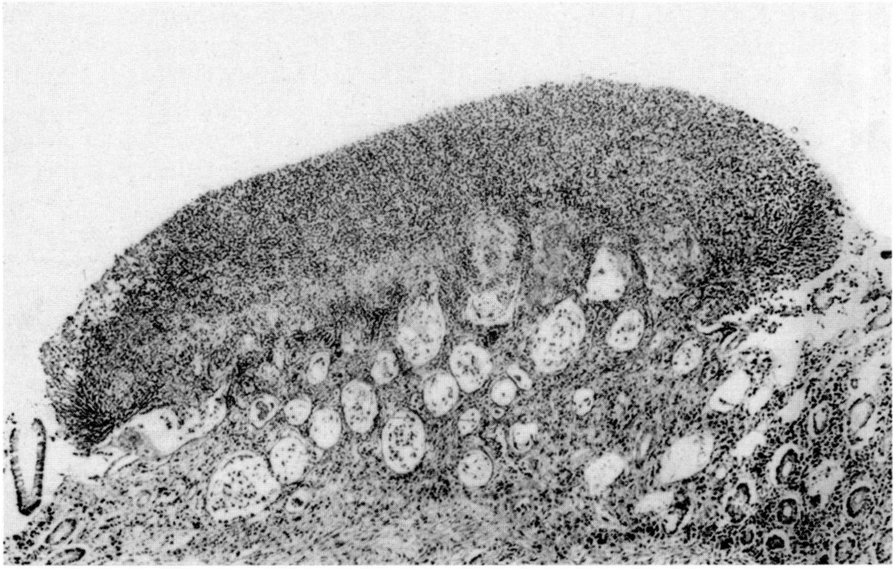

Fig. 27.29 Typical lesion in pseudomembranous colitis. The exudate of fibrin, mucus and inflammatory cells is continuous with underlying inflammation involving dilated thin-walled and degenerate tubules. (H&E, ×38)

Histopathology: Gross appearances

Mention has already been made of the variable pathology of pseudomembranous and antibiotic-related colitis. Fully developed pseudomembranous colitis is macroscopically unmistakable (Fig. 27.28), but there is a spectrum of appearances from patchy or diffuse erythema, superimposed adherent purulent spots, to classical diffuse, yellow or whitish membranes. When these slough during the healing phase, shallow congested ulcers are left behind which finally heal. These varied lesions may be localized or generalized and there is no characteristic distribution. In severe cases, the small intestine may also be involved. Occasionally, if the disease is severe, surgical intervention is necessary and usually the bowel then also shows some dilatation and the changes of toxic megacolon.

Microscopic appearances

These are as varied as the gross appearances. The classical membranous lesions are composed of a plaque of fibrin, mucus and acute inflammatory cells which is continuous on its deep aspect with exudate of similar material into the thin-walled degenerating cystic gland tubules of the underlying mucosa (Fig. 27.29). Fibrin plugs are occasionally present in the mucosal capillaries. The spectrum of appearances from early to late ulcerated and healing lesions has been described in detail in biopsy tissues.[35] The first changes are a focal, mild superficial, mainly acute inflammation of a group of adjacent tubules, principally affecting their upper parts and the associated luminal epithelium (Fig. 27.30). The tubular and surface epithelium shows degenerative changes and a polymorph infiltrate, there is a fibrin and mucous exudate into the lumen and this, mixed with inflammatory cells, begins to

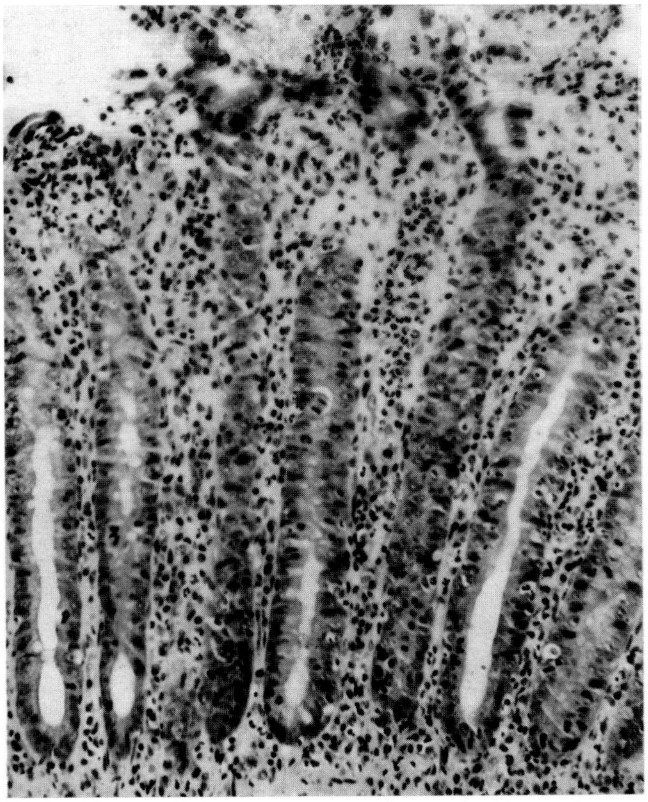

Fig. 27.30 Early lesion in *C. difficile* toxin-associated colitis. The inflammatory and degenerative epithelial changes are maximum in the luminal aspect of the mucosa. Exudation of fibrinopurulent material is just commencing. (H&E, ×90)

burst onto the surface due to focal areas of necrosis. This release of fibrinomucoid exudate, creating an appearance that has been likened to firework display, is arguably the first truly diagnostic feature of the condition. In severe lesions, these features occur in a full thickness fashion and there is an obvious element of structural necrosis of the abnormal mucosa which underlies the dome-shaped plaques of exudate. It is these changes which have drawn attention to the possible role of ischaemia in this condition and which, due to increased depth of the lesion, determine residual mucosal abnormalities in the healed phase.[34] When the condition is protracted, as occasionally happens, an element of regenerative hyperplasia is superimposed. Then a mixture of the features seen above, together with abnormal elongated branched tubules, can produce quite a complex appearance.

Antibiotic-associated colitis (haemorrhagic)

Sometimes, following the use of oral penicillins, an acute illness characterized by abdominal pain and bloody diarrhoea occurs.[36,37] There follows the classical radiological signs of thumb-printing which characterize acute ischaemic colitis. The condition is transient and complete recovery is the rule. The right half of the colon is involved and thus the detailed pathology is inadequately documented in most cases. The toxin of *Clostridium difficile* has not been implicated and the precise pathophysiology of the disorder is not understood. It is basically similar in many respects, except for its location in the proximal colon, to acute transient ischaemic colitis and some form of ischaemia thus appears to be the underlying cause.

Colitis and other drugs

Sometimes, during the course of drug therapy with gold,[38] methyldopa[39] or methotrexate,[40] a related colitis develops. When the offending drugs is discontinued the symptoms abate and they recur if the drug is reintroduced, thus a true causal relationship is established. A mild non-specific colitis is described in biopsy tissue under these circumstances and is characterized by an eosinophil infiltration. A peripheral eosinophilia occurs in gold-associated disease but the exact pathogenesis of this colitis is not known. Of a different nature is the inflammatory reaction that may occur in response to trauma or the use of enemas.[41]

Colitis indeterminate

In 1978 Price[42] drew attention to the overlap which occurs in the spectrum of idiopathic inflammatory bowel disease. He coined the term 'colitis indeterminate' for a group of cases which were neither typical of ulcerative colitis nor Crohn's disease. Clinically, these cases are associated with acute severe symptoms and a total colitis frequently necessitating colectomy (Fig. 27.31). Rectal sparing is often a feature and the ulceration is severe, deep and histologically non-specific. The intervening mucosa is surprisingly well preserved, but in relation to the ulceration some myocytolysis may be seen. There are reports in the literature[43] of similar but less clinically severe forms of inflammatory bowel disease. Multiple deep collar-stud colonic ulcerations, lacking histological specificity, associated with preservation of haustra, a normal ileum and rectum and a spontaneous recovery with return to normality at follow-up for periods of up to 5 years are described. This is seemingly an entity quite distinct from Crohn's disease or ulcerative colitis and, apart from severity, appears similar to indeterminate colitis. There would appear to be more to this category of colitis than its being a variant of ulcerative colitis or Crohn's disease and it is important that the temptation to regard them so be resisted. For example, Rhodes et al[44] appear to have characterized a segmental colonic inflammatory disease resembling Crohn's but which is non-granulomatous and related to the use of oral contraceptives. Cessation of contraceptive therapy brings

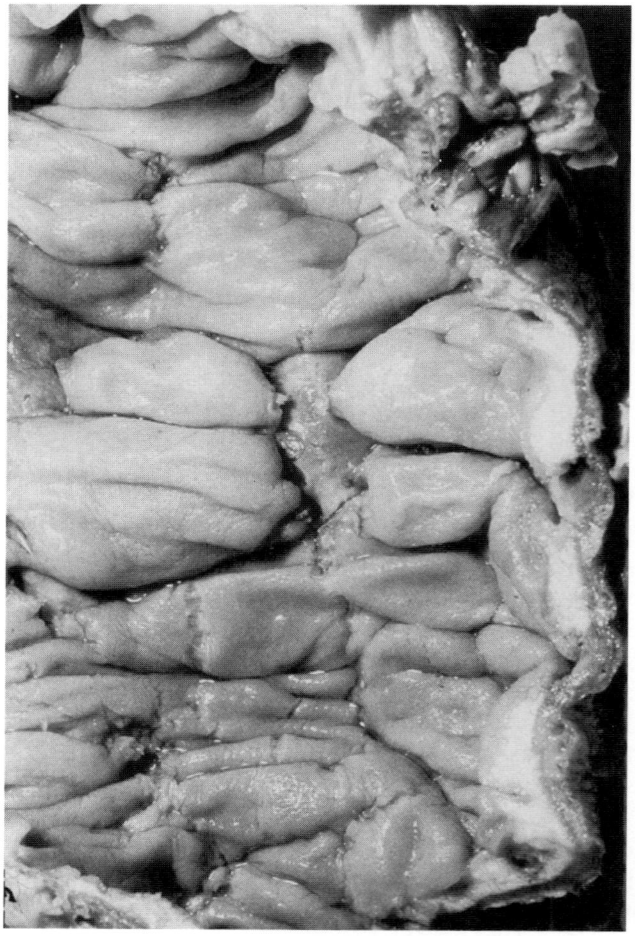

Fig. 27.31 Operative specimen of indeterminate colitis. Deep severe undermining ulceration superimposed on a mucous membrane which appears surprisingly normal.

about termination of the disease process which does not recur in follow-up periods varying from 12 months to 10 years. There is very little information concerning the long term outcome of patients diagnosed as having indeterminate colitis and thus it continues to be a somewhat unsatisfactory diagnosis. In one such study[45] patients were followed up for a minimum of 2–5 years, during which time only four of 16 cases of indeterminate colitis could be reclassified. Crohn's disease was the new diagnostic category in one case and ulcerative colitis in three cases. It is of interest, however, that no case classified as indeterminate colitis required small intestinal surgery.

Microscopic colitis

A small proportion of patients with large-volume diarrhoea and normal barium radiology and endoscopic appearances prove to have a colitis on microscopic examination of colonic biopsies.[46] This colitis is without known cause and relatively distinctive morphologically.[47] That the mucosal abnormality is indeed associated with impaired function has also been documented and it seems that, in addition to decreased large intestine absorptive function, a small intestinal abnormality may also be implicated at least in a small proportion of cases.[48]

In biopsy material, there is a total colitis and the mucosa shows a range of abnormality, including a generalized increase in usual lamina propria cells, typically with some neutrophil polymorphs, degenerative epithelial cell changes with minimal loss of goblet cells, flattening of superficial epithelium and a variable degree of cryptitis (Fig. 27.32). Sometimes but not always, a striking feature is an increase in intraepithelial lymphocytes and hence the alternative terminology of lymphocytic colitis which has been recommended.[49] The relative preservation of overall mucosal structure readily accounts for the lack of abnormal radiological and endoscopic features.

The cause of this inflammation is unknown but extensive and repeated culture studies have proved negative. Some patients respond to sulphasalazine therapy but even in patients followed up for as long as 10 or more years no stigmata of ulcerative colitis or Crohn's disease developed. Clearly this entity is yet another indication of the need for biopsy investigation of patients with chronic diarrhoea of unknown cause even if the mucosa appears normal at endoscopy. Occasionally patients with microscopic (lymphocytic) colitis develop a thickening of the subepithelial collagen plate and a possible relationship between this entity and collagenous colitis has been the subject of debate.[50] Yardley et al,[51] however, believe them to be separate entities, though possibly both may represent an immune response to luminal antigens. Patients with lymphocytic colitis have a significant excess of HLA A1 and unlike collagenous colitis, the sex incidence is equal and lymphocytic colitis is described in children.[52]

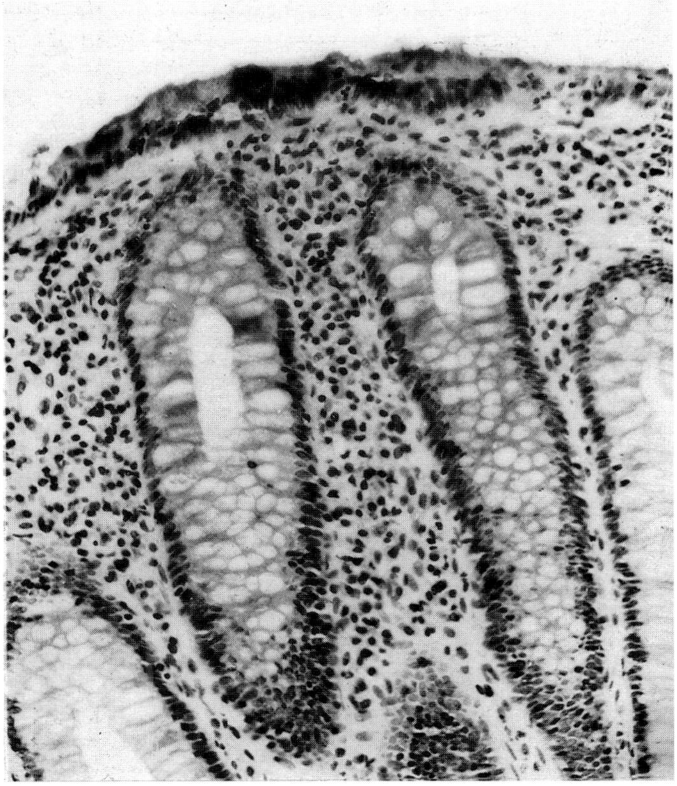

Fig. 27.32 Microscopic colitis. There is definite but slight overall increase in cellularity of the lamina propria with a polymorphonuclear leukocyte component. Invasion of the degenerate superficial epithelium, which has lost its goblet population, is evident intraepithelial lymphocytes are only minimally increased. (H&E, ×250)

Diversion colitis

It has been observed that the mucosa of segments of colon excluded from the faecal stream by diversion operations may become inflamed.[53] Following colostomy or jejunostomy for conditions other than inflammatory bowel disease the by-passed colonic mucosa may become inflamed to a degree which mimics mild ulcerative colitis, although ulceration itself is not a feature. The change is most commonly confined to the distal rectum but sometimes the whole excluded segment is involved. Macroscopically the bowel is shrunken and the lumen is barely visible. The microscopic changes include crypt abscesses, increased lamina propria inflammatory cells and epithelial regenerative changes, but they tend to be focal. They can, on occasion, simulate ulcerative colitis[54–56] and granulomas have been described[54] which could cause confusion with Crohn's disease. The inflammation, however, persists for as long as the mucosa is bypassed by the bowel contents but subsides otherwise. Diversion colitis associated with ulceration and rectal bleeding usually occurs in association with severe diverticular disease of the excluded segment,[57,58] although 'aphthous' ulceration of the excluded mucosa unassociated with diverticula is also on record.[59] Lymphoid follicular hyperplasia is also part of the histological spectrum of diversion colitis[60] and some workers claim that it is the most striking and constant histological feature[61] and is also described in a paediatric patient.[62] Diversion colitis is occasionally associated with the formation of multiple submucosal carcinoids.[63]

The colitis of diverticular disease

In diverticular disease, a segmental sigmoid colitis may occur.[64,65] This can result in rectal bleeding and is recorded as responding to sulphasalazine therapy. The colitis may seemingly be a more or less diffuse inflammation of the mucosa between the diverticula and has no histological specificity, being a mixed acute and chronic inflammation with crypt abscess formation.[65] In other cases[64] histological features similar to the changes in solitary rectal ulcer syndrome occur. This could be the end result of recurrent mucosal prolapse of the mucosa between the diverticula. Of late, attention has been drawn to a pre-diverticular sigmoid disease in which colonic motor abnormalities lead to a polypoidal mucosal appearance which is red and hyperaemic and presumably due to recurrent partial prolapse.[66] The condition can be mistaken for mucosal polyps and it appears entirely possible that such a condition could lead to inflammatory changes and ulceration. Indeed, Kelly[67] describes eight cases in which the swollen folds, sometimes in two rows between the diverticula, showed congestion, vascular thrombosis, oedema, haemorrhage and haemosiderin deposition. The colonic gland pattern was distorted and the lamina propria muscularized. A superimposed diffuse mucosal ulceration was also present and differentiating the changes from ulcerative colitis could be difficult.

Collagenous colitis

Since Lindstrom[68] described the first case of collagenous colitis, there have been numerous other reports in the literature. No doubt many more cases exist which have not been published or have not been diagnosed. The entity that has emerged is one affecting females much more commonly than males with an age range between 23–86 years. A familial occurrence is also described.[69] Patients complain of persistent watery diarrhoea over a period varying from weeks to years. Up to 20 bowel actions a day may occur and, characteristically, the stool contains neither mucus nor blood and has been shown in some cases at least to be of secretory origin.[70] At colonoscopy the mucosa is nondescript or sometimes pale, friable and oedematous and there are no radiological features. In biopsy specimens, however, there is a characteristic zone of hyaline collagen situated immediately underneath the superficial epithelium (Fig. 27.33). When this has been measured, it has varied between 11.5–100 μm and in it there are capillaries, plump or spindle-celled fibroblasts and apoptotic bodies. At electron microscopy, the collagen encases capillaries which show reduplication of their basal lamina and endothelial cell hyperplasia with loss of normal fenestration.[71] The basal lamina of the epithelial cells themselves is normal but they show a variety of degenerative changes and few if any remaining goblet cells. By immunohistochemistry, the collagen has been shown to be of types I and III.[72] The lamina propria shows a varying cellularity, usually more dense than normal and sometimes a few polymorphs are present, occasionally within the epithelium of tubules. Two patients have even been recorded in which the collagenous colitis was preceded by a mild nonspecific colitis.[73]

Although Lindstrom's case was described in a rectal biopsy subsequently it seems that total colonic involvement is usual. The degree of collagenous thickening may vary with site and it tends to be maximum in the proximal bowel with a thinner band distally and the rectum may

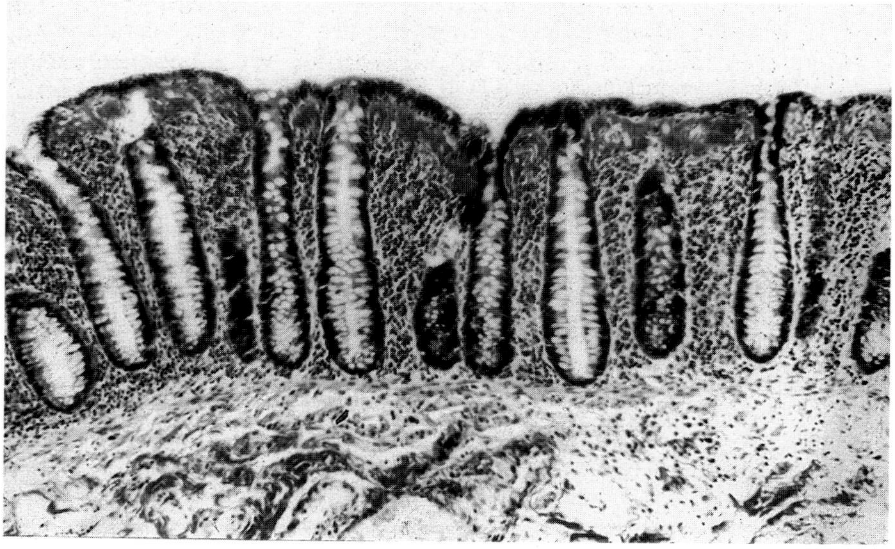

Fig. 27.33 Collagenous colitis with a conspicuous subepithelial zone of dense hyaline collagen. A moderate increase in round cells is apparent in the lamina propria. (H&E, ×60)

even be spared.[74,75] This could account in part for reports that the collagenization may be reversible.[76–78] The aetiology of the disease is obscure and although it has been suggested that the deposition of immune complexes may be important,[68] neither immunoglobulin, complement nor fibrinogen has been demonstrated in the subepithelial zone.[79] It seems not to be the end result of an inflammatory response because it is not a feature of even longstanding inflammatory bowel disease, although coincident Crohn's disease and collagenous colitis is described.[80] This probably has the same significance as coincident occurrence of collagenous colitis and coeliac disease[81,82] although there are claims that their coexistence is more than fortuitous.[83] Involvement of the stomach, duodenum[84] and the terminal ileum[85] is recorded. A recent case of combined collagenous colitis and collagenous sprue is described with resolution of the collagen band following a gluten exclusion diet.[86]

Food protein-induced colitis

Bloody diarrhoea in some infants given cow's milk, which disappeared when the milk was withdrawn from the diet, was first recorded almost 50 years ago[87] and highlighted again some 14 years later.[88] Food protein-induced colitis is now a well established entity which commonly occurs in the early weeks or months of life, but can present in infants up to 2 years of age.[89–92] There is evidence that other areas of the gastrointestinal tract from oesophagus downwards may also be involved in the inflammatory process which has features of an allergy. The commonest allergen is cow's milk protein, but soya and beef protein have also been implicated, as has human breast milk. Patients have bloody diarrhoea, frequently with mucus, which begins shortly after the first feed of allergen and all become symptom-free when the offending agent is removed from the diet. The colitis induced is either total or segmental and tends to become left-sided. It is patchy at endoscopy with scattered erythematous areas and sometimes small ulcerations. Biopsy specimens also show a patchy inflammation characterized by oedema and a predominantly eosinophil infiltration.[93,94] A significant increase in IgE-containing plasma cells is also described which, like the eosinophil infiltration, disappears with manipulation of the diet to exclude the allergen. Re-challenge with the offending food substance will induce recurrence of symptoms and the histological changes. In some cases of longer standing, more severely affected foci, especially if ulcerated, show increased cellularity involving other cell types and some architectural changes with decreased mucin and regenerative features.[89]

The long term prognosis of these infants appears good in that the intestinal allergy tends to disappear but a general predilection to allergic disorders may exhibit itself in the form of eczema, asthma or hay fever. The relationship of this infant form of disease to the allergic proctitis described by Rosekrans et al[95] is not clear. They described adults with localized rectal and sigmoid colitis who presented with bloody diarrhoea. In immunoperoxidase preparations, there was a markedly increased number of IgE-containing plasma cells. Dietary antigens, however, were not identified and only three of 12 cases had atopy or a family history of allergic disease. In eight of the 12 cases, however, treatment with disodium chromoglycate, an inhibitor of chemical mediators of inflammation such as histamine, resulted in clinical improvement and return of histological appearances to near normality, although the IgE cell population remained unchanged.

A colitis resembling ulcerative colitis has also been described in the hypereosinophilic syndrome. Mimicking inflammatory bowel disease with primary sclerosing cholangitis, the patients' condition and eosinophil count returned promptly to normal with hydroxyurea therapy.[96]

Autoimmune colitis of childhood

Whereas some children with protracted diarrhoea and small bowel villous atrophy have been shown to have circulating antibodies against enterocytes, it is only recently that evidence of a colitis has been demonstrated as a concommitant lesion.[97] These children often have blood and mucus in their stools. There are other poorly understood enterocolic intractable, ulcerating conditions of infancy which often require colectomy. An association ulcerative stomatatis is often present and the small bowel may show partial villous atrophy. Large colonic ulcers characterize the colitis and severe perianal disease is often present. The aetiology is obscure but there is some evidence for an inherited susceptibility.[98]

Nonspecific ulcers of the colon

Cruveilhier[99] was the first to describe nonspecific ulceration of the colon in 1832. The condition is unusual and quite distinct from ulceration of the rectum associated with mucosal prolapse (see Ch. 22). These ulcers should also be regarded as distinct from stercoral ulcers seen in association with impacted scybalous faeces. Normally these occur in the distal colon and rectum and are probably ischaemic in origin and due to local pressure effects of the luminal mass and bowel distension. Nonspecific colonic ulcers are usually single and most commonly seen in the caecum in an age range of 12–80.[100] They tend not to be diagnosed except at operation and, because they often perforate, are associated with peritonitis. They may also bleed and cause abdominal pain. The ulcers vary in size from a few millimetres to several centimetres and histologically are well demarcated and entirely nonspecific, showing surface necrosis and underlying acute and chronic inflammation. Although the question of ischaemia is often raised in the context of their aetiology,[101] when evidence of this is found the ulcers are obviously no longer nonspecific and ischaemic ulcers should be thus classified. As to their aetiology, nothing is certain and a relationship to diverticular disease has been both raised and discounted.[102] It is likely that local trauma due to foreign body and subsequent tissue breakdown secondary to infection is the cause, but this is hard to reconcile with their prediliction for the right half of the colon. If any foreign body capable of damaging the intestinal mucosa were to be involved, it seems more likely that this would occur predominantly in the small bowel and, failing that, the more distal large bowel where the contents would tend to favour such a mechanical event. Nevertheless, even in children this does not seem to apply, for the caecum is also the common location for nonspecific colonic ulceration.[103]

Colitis cystica profunda

This is a rare disorder in which cystic glandular inclusions of colonic epithelium occupy the submucosa. It can occur in a localized form, affect the rectum, one or more segments of colon or the whole of the large bowel. The cysts contain mucin and the epithelial lining is not always intact. On occasions lakes of mucin appear to be free in the submucosa where there is then an attendant reactive inflammatory cell and histiocyte infiltration and fibrosis. Clearly, the lesions can produce a variety of symptoms including haemorrhage if they ulcerate, intestinal obstruction, or diarrhoea and abdominal pain. The condition occurs in childhood and during adult life and the rectal lesion has incorrectly been thought of as the cause of solitary rectal ulcers[104] (see Ch. 23). There appear to be two categories of this disease. One complicates ulcerative conditions of the bowel and represents a healing or reparative phenomenon described in association with inflammatory bowel disease or chronic dysentery.[105–109] The other occurs without antecedent bowel disease and the lesion is often thus considered of congenital origin and hamartomatous in nature.[110–113] Because of the situation of the glandular elements in this type of case, emphasis has been placed upon the need to avoid the erroneous diagnosis of adenocarcinoma, but the histological character of the epithelium seldom warrants such a mistake. However, when misplaced epithelium occurs in the colon of patients with ulcerative colitis and Crohn's disease, the fact that both conditions may be complicated by dysplasia and malignancy makes this difficulty a real possibility.[114] This is accounted by the fact that in these two conditions the misplaced glands can be found more deeply situated in the muscularis propria.

Colitis cystica superficialis

This histological lesion, in which the glands of the colonic mucosa form multiple cysts and there is an associated colitis, is the classical lesion seen in the colon in Pellagra[115] but lesser degrees can be seen in other inflammatory states of the colonic mucosa, especially as a healing phase; they probably do not merit this rather grand nomenclature.

REFERENCES

1. Kumar NB, Nostrant TT, Appleman HD. The histopathologic spectrum of acute self-limited colitis (acute infectious-type colitis). Am J Surg Pathol 1982; 6: 523–529.
2. Ruppin H, Domschke S. Acute ulcerative colitis — a rare complication of sulfasalazine therapy. Hepatogastroenterol 1984; 31: 192–193.
3. Pearson DJ, Stones NA, Bentley SJ, Reid H. Proctocolitis induced by salicylate and associated with asthma and recurrent nasal polyps. Br Med J 1983; 287: 1675.
4. George WL, Nakata MM, Thompson J, White ML. Aeromonas-related diarrhea in adults. Arch Intern Med 1985; 145: 2207–2211.
5. Pai CH, Gordon R, Sims HV, Bryan LE. Sporadic cases of hemorrhagic colitis associated with Escherichia coli 0157:H7. Ann Intern Med 1984; 101: 738–742.
6. Remis RS, MacDonald KL, Riley LW, Puhr ND, Wells JG, Davis BR, Blake PA, Cohen ML. Sporadic cases of hemorrhagic colitis associated with Escherichia coli 0157:H7. Ann Intern Med 1984; 101: 624–626.
7. Kelly J, Oryshak A, Wenetsek M, Grabiec J, Handy S. The colonic pathology of Escherichia coli 0157:H7 infection. Am J Surg Pathol 1990; 14: 87–92.
8. Cohen MB, Giannella RA. Hemorrhagic colitis associated with Escherichia coli 0157:H7. Adv Intern Med 1992; 37: 173–175.
9. Marsh PK, Gorbach SL. Invasive enterocolitis caused by Edwardsiella tarda. Gastroenterology 1982; 82: 336–338.
10. Woodward A, McTigue C, Hogg G, Watkins A, Tan H. Mucormycosis of the neonatal gut: a 'new' disease or a variant of necrotizing enterocolitis? J Pediatr Surg 1992; 27: 737–740.
11. Figueroa-Colon R, Grunow JE, Torres-Pinedo R, Rettig PJ. Group A streptococcal proctitis and vulvovaginitis in a prepubertal girl. Pediatr Infect Dis 1984; 3: 439–442.
12. Guss C, Larsen JG. Group A beta-hemolytic streptococcal protocolitis. Pediatr Infect Dis 1984; 3: 442–443.
13. Pauwels A, Meyohas MC, Eliaszewicz M et al. Toxoplasma colitis in the acquired immunodeficiency syndrome. Am J Gastroenterol 1992; 87: 518–519.
14. Hing MC, Goldschmidt C, Mathijs JM, Cunningham AL, Cooper DA. Chronic colitis associated with human immunodeficiency virus infection. Med J Aust 1992; 156: 683–687.
15. Tedesco FJ, Hardin RD, Harper RN, Edwards BH. Infectious colitis endoscopically simulating inflammatory bowel disease: a prospective evaluation. Gastrointest Endosc 1983; 29: 195–197.
16. Mandal BK, Schofield PF, Morson BC. A clinicopathological study of acute colitis: the dilemma of transient colitis syndrome. Scand J Gastroenterol 1982; 17: 865–869.
17. Nostrant TT, Kumar NB, Appelman HD. Histopathology differentiates acute self-limited colitis from ulcerative colitis. Gastroenterology 1987; 92: 318–328.
18. Skirrow MB. Campylobacter enteritis: a 'new' disease. Br Med J 1977; 3: 9–11.
19. Cooper R, Murphy S, Midlick D. Campylobacter jejuni enteritis mistaken for ulcerative colitis. J Fam Pract 1992; 34: 357, 361–362.
20. Goulston SJM, McGovern VJ. Pseudo-membranous colitis. Gut 1965; 6: 207–212.
21. Bartlett JG, Chang TW, Gurwith M et al. Antibiotic associated pseudomembranous colitis due to toxin producing clostridia. N Eng J Med 1978; 298: 531–534.

22. Larson HE, Price AB, Honour P. Clostridium difficile and aetiology of pseudomembranous colitis. Lancet 1978; 1: 1063–1066.
23. Mitchell TJ, Ketley JM, Haslam SC, Stephen J, Burdon DW, Candy DCA, Daniel R. Effect of toxin A and B of clostridium difficile on rabbit ileum and colon. Gut 1986; 27: 78–85.
24. Bender BS, Bennett R, Laughon BE et al. Is clostridium difficile endemic in chronic-care facilities? Lancet 1986; 2: 11–13.
25. Whitehead R. The pathology of ischaemia of the intestines. In: Sommers SC, ed. Pathology annual 1976; 1–52.
26. George WL, Rolfe RD, Finegold SM. Clostridium difficile and its cytotoxin in feces of patients with antimicrobial agent-associated diarrhoea and miscellaneous conditions. J Clin Microbiol 1982; 15: 1049–1053.
27. Dickinson RJ, Rampling A, Wight DGD. Spontaneous pseudomembranous colitis not associated with clostridium difficile. J Infection 1985; 10: 252–255.
28. Chiu AO, Abraham AA. Pseudomembranous colitis associated with an unidentified species of clostridium. Am J Clin Pathol 1982; 78: 398–402.
29. Borriello SP, Larson HE, Welch AR et al. Enterotoxigenic Clostridium perfringens: a possible cause of antibiotic-associated diarrhoea. Lancet 1984; 1: 305–307.
30. Vesikari T, Maki M, Baer M et al. Pseudomembranous colitis with recurring diarrhoea and prolonged persistence of Clostridium difficile in a 10-year-old girl. Acta Paediatr Scand 1984; 73: 135–137.
31. Schwarz RP, Ulshen MH. Pseudomembranous colitis presenting as mild chronic diarrhea in childhood. J Pediatr Gastroenterol Nutr 1983; 2: 570–573.
32. LaMont JT, Trnka Y. Therapeutic implications of Clostridium difficile toxin during relapse of chronic inflammatory bowel disease. Lancet 1980; 1: 381–383.
33. Keighley MRB, Youngs D, Johnson M et al. Clostridium difficile toxin in acute diarrhoea complicating inflammatory bowel disease. Gut 1982; 23: 410–414.
34. Bowden TA, Mansberger AR, Lykins LE. Pseudomembranous enterocolitis: mechanism of restoring floral homeostasis. Am Surg 1981; 47: 178–183.
35. Whitehead R. Mucosal biopsy of the gastrointestinal tract. 3rd edition. Philadelphia: Saunders, 1985: pp 248–256.
36. Toffler RB, Pingoud EG, Burrell MI. Acute colitis related to penicillin and penicillin derivatives. Lancet 1978; 2: 707–709.
37. Sakurai Y, Tsuchiya H, Ikegami F et al. Acute right-sided hemorrhagic colitis associated with oral administration of ampicillin. Dig Dis Sci 1979; 24: 910–915.
38. Martin DM, Goldman JA, Gilliam J, Nasrallah SM. Gold-induced eosinophilic enterocolitis: response to oral cromolyn sodium. Gastroenterology 1981; 80: 1567–1570.
39. Graham CF, Gallagher K, Jones JK. Acute colitis with methyldopa. N Engl J Med 1981; 304: 1044–1045.
40. Atherton LD, Leib ES, Kaye MD. Toxic megacolon associated with methotrexate therapy. Gastroenterology 1984; 86: 1583–1588.
41. Whitehead R. Mucosal biopsy of the gastrointestinal tract. 3rd edition. Philadelphia: Saunders, 1985: p 212.
42. Price AB. Overlap in the spectrum of non-specific inflammatory bowel disease — 'colitis indeterminate'. J Clin Pathol 1978; 31: 567–577.
43. Bonfils S, Hervoir P, Girodet J et al. Acute spontaneously recovering ulcerating colitis (ARUC). Report of 6 cases. Am J Dig Dis 1977; 22: 429–436.
44. Rhodes JM, Cockel R, Allan RN et al. Colonic Crohn's disease and use of oral contraception. Br Med J 1984; 288: 595–596.
45. Wells AD, McMillan I, Price AB, Ritchie JK, Nicholls RJ. Natural history of indeterminate colitis. Br J Surg 1991; 78: 179–181.
46. Kingham JGC, Levison DA, Ball JA, Dawson AM. Microscopic colitis — a cause of chronic watery diarrhoea. Br Med J 1982; 285: 1601–1604.
47. Fasoli R, Talbot I, Reid M, Prince C, Jewell DP. Microscopic colitis: can it be qualitatively and quantitatively characterized? Ital J Gastroenterol 1992; 24: 393–396.
48. Bo-Linn GW, Vendrell DD, Lee E, Fordtran JS. An evaluation of the significance of microscopic colitis in patients with chronic diarrhea. J Clin Invest 1985; 75: 1559–1569.
49. Lazenby AJ, Yardley JH, Giardiello FM, Jessurun J, Bayless TM. Lymphocytic ('microscopic') colitis: a comparative histopathologic study with particular reference to collagenous colitis. Hum Pathol 1989; 20: 18–28.
50. Giardello FM, Bayless TM, Jessurun J, Hamilton SR, Yardley JH. Collagenous colitis: physiologic and histopathologic studies in seven patients. Ann Intern Med 1987; 106: 46–49.
51. Yardley JH, Lazenby AJ, Giardiello FM, Bayless TM. (Editorial) Collagenous, 'microscopic', lymphocytic and other gentler and more subtle forms of colitis. Hum Pathol 1990; 21: 1089–1091.
52. Mashako MN, Sonsino E, Navarro J, Mougenot JF et al. Microscopic colitis: a new cause of chronic diarrhea in children? J Pediatr Gastroenterol Nutr 1990; 10: 21–26.
53. Glotzer DJ, Glick ME, Goldman H. Proctitis and colitis following diversion of the fecal stream. Gastroenterology 1981; 80: 438–441.
54. Ma CK, Gottlieb C, Haas PA. Diversion colitis: a clinico-pathologic study of 21 cases. Hum Pathol 1990; 21: 429–436.
55. Komorowski RA. Histologic spectrum of diversion colitis. Am J Surg Pathol 1990; 14: 548–554.
56. Geraghty JM, Talbot IC. Diversion colitis: histological features in the colon and rectum after defunctioning colostomy. Gut 1991; 32: 1020–1023.
57. Ona FV, Boger JN. Rectal bleeding due to diversion colitis. Am J Gastroenterol 1985; 80: 40–41.
58. Bosshardt RT, Abel ME. Proctitis following fecal diversion. Dis Colon Rectum 1984; 27: 605–607.
59. Lusk LB, Reichen J, Levine JS. Aphthous ulceration in diversion colitis. Gastroenterology 1984; 87: 1171–1173.
60. Warren BF, Shepherd NA. Diversion proctocolitis. Histopathology 1992; 21: 91–93.
61. Yeong ML, Bethwaite PB, Prasad J, Isabister WH. Lymphoid follicular hyperplasia — a distinctive feature of diversion colitis. Histopathology 1991; 19: 55–61.
62. Hague S, Eisen RN, West AB. The morphologic features of diversion colitis: studies of a pediatric population with no other disease of the intestinal mucosa. Hum Pathol 1993; 24: 211–219.
63. Griffiths AP, Dixon MF. Microcarcinoids and diversion colitis in a colon defunctioned for 18 years. Report of a case. Dis Colon Rectum 1992; 35: 685–688.
64. Cawthorn SJ, Gibbs NM, Marks GG. Segmental colitis: a new complication of diverticular disease. Gut 1983; 24: A500.
65. Sladen GE, Filipe MI. Is segmental colitis a complication of diverticular disease? Dis Colon Rectum 1984; 27: 513–514.
66. Mathus-Vliegen EMH, Tytgat GNJ. Polyp-simulating mucosal prolapse syndrome in (pre-) diverticular disease. Endoscopy 1986; 18: 84–86.
67. Kelly JK. Polypoid prolapsing mucosal folds in diverticular disease. Am J Surg Pathol 1991; 15: 871–878.
68. Lindstrom CG. 'Collagenous colitis' with watery diarrhoea — a new entity. Pathol Eur 1976; 11: 87–89.
69. Van Tilburg AJ, Lam HG, Seldenrijk CA, Stel HV et al. Familial occurrence of collagenous colitis. A report of two families. J Clin Gastroenterol 1990; 12: 279–285.
70. Rask-Madsen J, Grove O, Hansen MGJ et al. Colonic transport of water and electrolytes in a patient with secretory diarrhoea due to collagenous colitis. Dig Dis Sci 1983; 28: 1141–1146.
71. Teglbjaerg PS, Thaysen EH. Collagenous colitis: an ultra-structural study of a case. Gastroenterology 1982; 82: 561–563.
72. Birembaut P, Adnet JJ, Feydy P et al. Colite collagene: Approche immunomorphologique de la lesion. Gastroenterology Clin Biol 1982; 10: 833.
73. Teglbjaerg PS, Thaysen EH, Jensen HH. Development of collagenous colitis in sequential biopsy specimens. Gastroenterology 1984; 87: 703–709.
74. Mason CH, Jewel DP. Collagenous colitis: a review of five cases. Gut 1985; 26: A1152.
75. Tanaka M, Mazzoleni G, Riddell RH. Distribution of collagenous colitis: utility of flexible sigmoidoscopy. Gut 1992; 33: 65–70.
76. Bamford MJ, Matz LR, Armstrong JA et al. Collagenous colitis: a case report and review of the literature. Pathology 1982; 14: 481–484.

77. Eaves ER, McIntyre RLE, Wallis PL et al. Collagenous colitis: a recently recognised reversible clinicopathological entity. Aust NZ J Med 1983; 13: 630–632.
78. Pieterse AS, Hecker R, Rowland R. Collagenous colitis: a distinctive and potentially reversible disorder. J Clin Pathol 1982; 35: 338–340.
79. Bogomoletz WV. Collagenous colitis: a clinicopathological review. Surv Dig Dis 1983; 1: 19–25.
80. Chandratre S, Bramble MG, Cooke WM, Jones RA. Simultaneous occurance of collagenous colitis and Crohn's disease. Digestion 1987; 36: 55–60.
81. Hamilton I, Sanders S, Hopwood D, Bouchier IAD. Collagenous colitis associated with small intestinal villous atrophy. Gut 1986; 27: 1394–1398.
82. O'Mahoney S, Nawroz IM, Ferguson A. Coeliac disease and collagenous colitis. Postgrad Med J 1990; 66: 238–241.
83. Armes J, Gee DC, Macrae FA, Schroeder W, Bhathal PS. Collagenous colitis: jejunal and colorectal pathology. J Clin Pathol 1992; 45: 784–787.
84. Stolte M, Ritter M, Borchard F, Koch-Scherrer G. Collagenous gastroduodenitis on collagenous colitis. Endoscopy 1990; 22: 186–187.
85. Lewis FW, Warren GH, Goff JS. Collagenous colitis with involvement of terminal ileum. Dig Dis Sci 1991; 36: 1161–1163.
86. McCashland TM, Donovan JP, Strobach RS, Linder J, Quigley EM. Collagenous enterocolitis: a manifestation of gluten-sensitive enteropathy. J Clin Gastroenterol 1992; 15: 45–51.
87. Rubin MI. Allergic intestinal bleeding in the newborn: a clinical syndrome. Am J Med Sc 1940; 200: 385–390.
88. Clein NW. Cow's milk allergy in infants. Pediatr Clin N Am 1954; 1: 949–962.
89. Lake AM, Whitington PF, Hamilton SR. Dietary protein-induced colitis in breast-fed infants. J Pediatrics 1982; 101: 906–910.
90. Jenkins HR, Pincott JR, Soothill JF, Milla PJ, Harries JT. Food allergy: the major cause of infantile colitis. Arch Dis Child 1984; 59: 326–329.
91. Goldman H, Proujansky R. Allergic proctitis and gastroenteritis in children. Clinical and mucosal biopsy features in 53 cases. Am J Surg Pathol 1986; 10: 75–86.
92. Powell GK. Food protein-induced enterocolitis of infancy: differential diagnosis and management. Comprehensive Therapy 1986; 12: 28–37.
93. Winter HS, Antonioli DA, Fukagawa N, Marcial M, Goldman H. Allergy-related proctocolitis in infants: diagnostic usefulness of rectal biopsy. Mod Pathol 1990; 3: 5–10.
94. Hill SM, Milla PJ. Colitis caused by food allergy in infants. Arch Dis Child 1990; 65: 132–133.
95. Rosekrans PCM, Meijer CJL, Van der Wal AM et al. Allergic proctitis, a clinical and immunopathological entity. Gut 1980; 21: 1017–1023.
96. Hill SM, Milla PJ, Bottazzo GF, Mirakian R. Autoimmune enteropathy and colitis: is there a generalised autoimmune gut disorder? Gut 1991; 32: 36–42.
97. Sanderson JR, Risdon RA, Walker-Smith JA. Intractable ulcerating enterocolitis of infancy. Arch Dis Child 1991; 66: 295–299.
98. Scheurlen M, Mork H, Weber P. Hypereosinophilic syndrome resembling chronic inflammatory bowel disease with primary sclerosing cholangitis. J Clin Gastroenterol 1992; 14: 59–63.
99. Cruveilhier J. Un beau cas de cicatrisation d'un ulcere de l'intestin gaele datant d'une douzaine d'annees. Bull Soc Anat 1832; 7: 102.
100. Barron ME. Simple, non-specific ulcer of the colon. Arch Surg 1928; 17: 355–407.
101. Mahoney TJ, Bubrick MP, Hitchcock CR. Nonspecific ulcers of the colon. Dis Colon Rectum 1978; 21: 623–626.
102. Shah NC, Ostrov AH, Cavallero JB, Rodgers JB. Benign ulcers of the colon. Gastrointest Endosc 1986; 32: 102–104.
103. Iuchtman M, Heldemberg D, Auslaeder L. Perforated nonspecific ulcer of the colon in children. Eur J Pediatr Surg 1991; 1: 372–373.
104. Madigan MR, Morson BC. Solitary ulcer of the rectum. Gut 1969; 10: 871–881.
105. Carstens PHG, Gonzalez R. Colitis cystica profunda. Acta Pathol Microbiol Scand 1969; 75: 273–281.
106. Castleman B. Case records of the Massachusetts General Hospital. N Engl J Med 1972; 286: 147–153.
107. Tedesco FJ, Summer HW, Kassens WD. Colitis cystica profunda. Am J Gastroenterol 1976; 65: 339–343.
108. Wayte DM, Helwig EB. Colitis cystica profunda. Am J Clin Pathol 1967; 48: 159–169.
109. Magidson JG, Lewin KJ. Diffuse colitis cystica profunda. Am J Surg Pathol 1981; 5: 393–399.
110. Nagasako K, Nakae Y, Kitao Y, Aoki G. Colitis cystica profunda: report of a case in which differentiation from rectal cancer was difficult. Dis Colon Rectum 1977; 20: 618–624.
111. Yashiro K, Murakami Y, Iizuka B, Hasegawa K, Nagasako K, Yamada A. Localized colitis cystica profunda of the sigmoid colon. Endoscopy 1985; 17: 198–199.
112. Krummel TM, Bell S, Kodroff MB, Berman WF, Salzberg AM. Colitis cystica profunda: a pediatric case report. J Pediatr Surg 1983; 18: 314–315.
113. Bentley E, Chandrasoma P, Cohen H, Radin R, Ray M. Colitis cystica profunda: presenting with complete intestinal obstruction and recurrence. Gastroenterology 1985; 89: 1157–1161.
114. Allen DC, Biggart JD. Misplaced epithelium in ulcerative colitis and Crohn's disease of the colon and its relationship to malignant mucosal changes. Histopathology 1986; 10: 37–52.
115. Pinkerton H. In: Anderson WAD, ed. Pathology. 4th ed. St Louis: Mosby, 1961; p 431.

PART IV

Ulcerative colitis

R. Whitehead

Ulcerative colitis is a disease of unknown aetiology and, with Crohn's disease, is included in the term idiopathic inflammatory bowel disease. This term is often shortened to inflammatory bowel disease which is so nondescript that it can be a source of confusion. Furthermore, with the recognition of relatively newer entities, such as lymphocytic colitis, there are good reasons why the term should be dropped. Although ulcerative colitis itself is also poor terminology for a condition that may be localized to the rectum and unassociated with ulceration, its use is entrenched. In short, ulcerative colitis is initially at least a primary, often recurrent, occasionally persistent mucosal inflammatory condition which affects the rectum and a variable length of contiguous colon in continuity. When the whole colon is involved, the appendix is frequently affected and in about 25% of cases a 'field' effect involves the terminal ileum in the inflammatory process but this has no pathological or clinical importance.

Aetiology and pathogenesis

Despite exhaustive investigations, the cause of ulcerative colitis remains elusive. There are natural animal models in the boxer dog, the horse, pig and the rodent. A similar disease has been induced in animals by carageenin, which is a polysaccharide found in seaweed, by a variety of bacterial products or toxins and by manipulating the immune or the vascular system.[1,2] None of these models has led to anything other than a reinforcement that the aetiology is probably complicated and many of the observations made in humans are the result of the disease rather than being related to its cause. Thus, suggestions that ulcerative colitis has an allergic basis, is the result of antibodies to gut flora which are cytotoxic for gut epithelial cells, is due to a reaction to the deposition of immune complexes, or is related to abnormalities of lymphocyte function, have all foundered.[3,4] The chances are that recent evidence for a specific defect in mucin, which appears to be associated with ulcerative colitis, will also prove to be effect rather than cause.[5]

Incidence

Ulcerative colitis presents most frequently between the second and fifth decade. It can occur in infancy and childhood but a first attack in senescence is very unusual. The sexes are roughly equally affected with perhaps a slight predominance of males in juveniles. It is claimed that whites have a greater incidence than blacks and Jews the highest incidence of all the races.

Macroscopic features

The gross appearance of colon affected by ulcerative colitis is extremely varied. It is determined by the fact that the disease process may be a continuous one despite treatment or it may follow a pattern of remission and exacerbation. The disease intensity also varies markedly from a mild mucosal inflammation without ulceration to one with severe inflammation and/or widespread deep ulceration. The abnormalities may be limited to the most distal parts of the large intestine or involve increasing lengths of it in continuity. The whole large intestine may be obviously diseased. Alternatively the disease process may vary in severity in different parts. Thus it may be relatively quiescent and macroscopically unremarkable in the rectum whilst active and producing ulceration more proximally. This accounts for a false impression of segmental involvement. Different appearances in different segments of bowel may also be due to variations in the time of onset of the disease. Chronic disease in the rectum, for example, may be associated with very recent involvement of more proximal bowel. In very acute severe disease it is usual for the more proximal segments to be severely involved when the rectum may show only minor changes.

Thus the mucosa involved may appear simply hyperaemic and granular (Fig. 27.34) or it may also show ulceration. The ulceration can be inconspicuous or multiple and punctate (Fig. 27.35) or more severe and irregular with undermining of the edges. The ulceration may be linear, following the taeniae coli, which produces a conspicuous 'tram-line' effect (Fig. 27.36). Intervening mucosa usually appears granular and inflamed but sometimes seems more normal although histologically it is involved. The non-ulcerated mucosa may appear polypoidal due to regenerative attempts and thus a polyposis is produced (Fig. 27.37). This most commonly affects the more proximal bowel leaving the rectum uninvolved.

In quiescent phases, the mucosa may appear relatively normal but more usually has a featureless atrophic or bland appearance (Fig. 27.38). There may be mucosal bridges or tags as the result of resolved ulceration (Fig. 27.39). Overall the bowel is frequently shortened and of decreased calibre. Smooth tubular strictures may occur and these have been shown to be due to fibromuscular thickening of the muscularis mucosa.[6] The radiological equivalent of this form of disease is the short featureless narrowed bowel with loss of the sigmoid loop. Sometimes in chronic mild unremitting disease, lymphoid

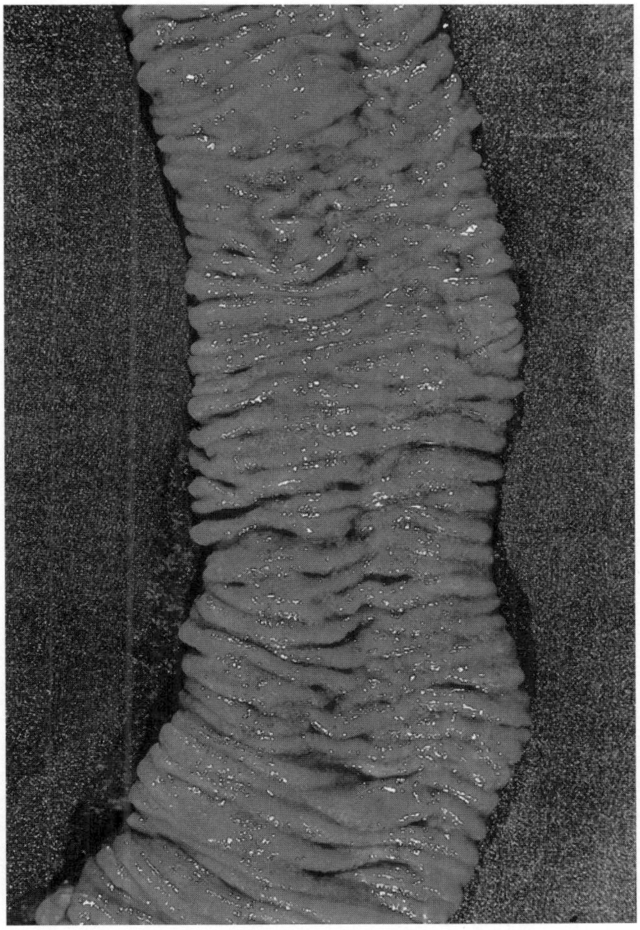

Fig. 27.34 Typical granular appearance in ulcerative colitis unassociated with ulceration.

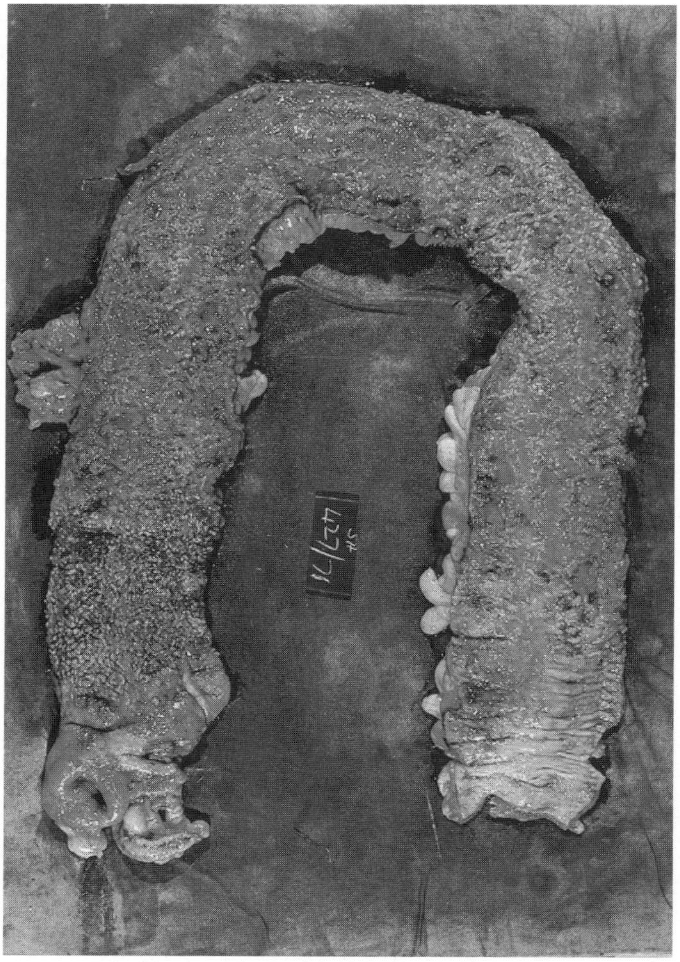

Fig. 27.35 Ulcerative colitis with diffuse punctate ulceration. Note the apparent rectal sparing and the rigid pouting ileocolic valve.

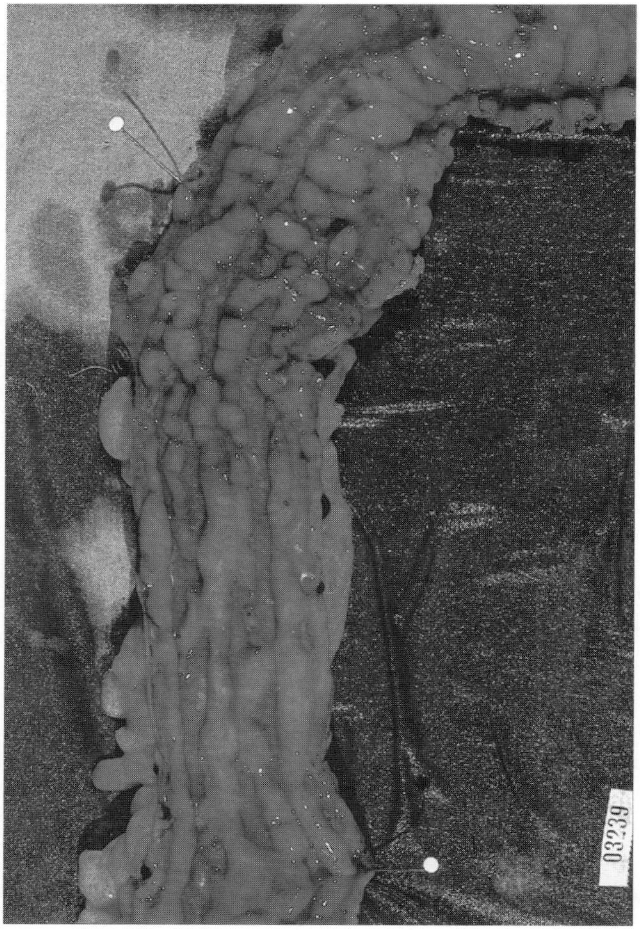

Fig. 27.36 So-called tram-line ulceration in chronic ulcerative colitis.

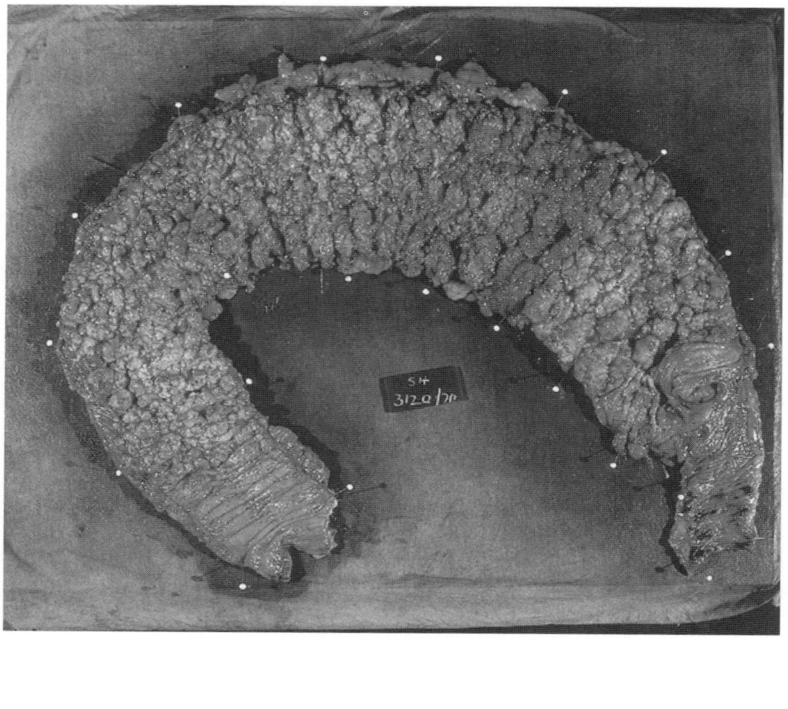

Fig. 27.37 Ulcerative colitis with numerous regenerative or inflammatory pseudopolyps.

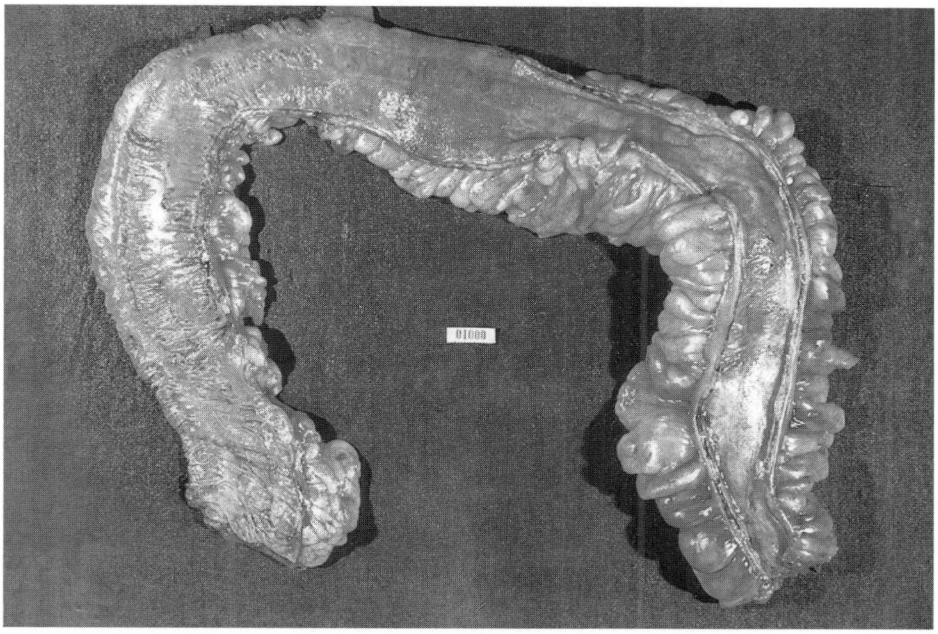

Fig. 27.38 Colectomy specimen in chronic ulcerative colitis. Note the featureless atrophic mucosa in most areas and the smooth tubular stricture in the region of the arrows.

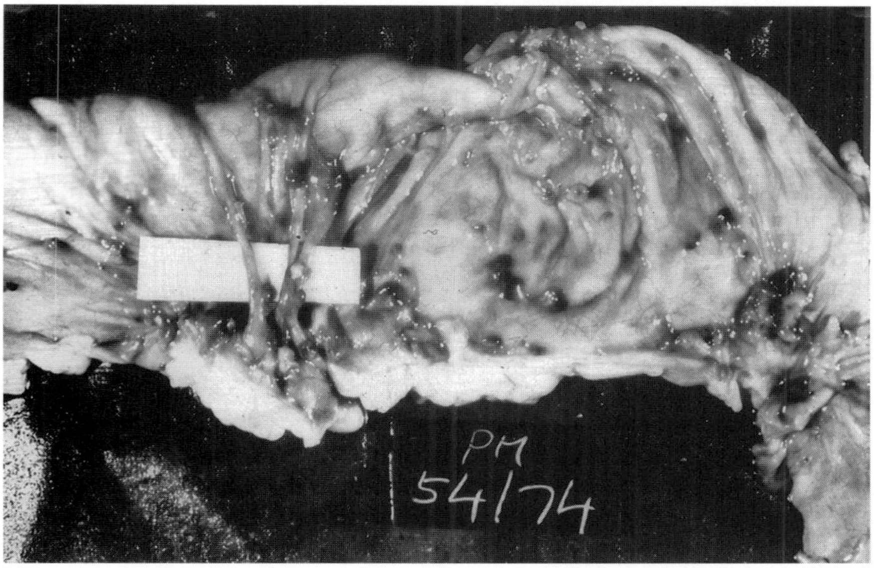

Fig. 27.39 Autopsy specimen from a patient with known ulcerative colitis in remission. The atrophic mucosa is the site of mucosal bridges and pseudopolyps.

follicular hyperplasia imparts to the mucosal aspect a multiple diffuse polyposis appearance. The protrusions are quite unlike inflammatory epithelial regenerative polyps for they tend to be small, uniform in size and have a regular surface.

Superimposed upon these changes may be the severe disease associated with toxic megacolon. The bowel is dilated and thin-walled, particularly in the sigmoid and transverse segments which do not have the girding support of being retroperitoneal. It appears friable and deeply congested and there is gross mucosal ulceration. Perforations may be apparent with evidence of early faecal peritonitis.

Microscopic features

Just as macroscopic features vary according to the stage of the disease process and its severity, so do the microscopic appearances, which have been described in detail.[7] During the first attack there is mucosal oedema and a prominent congestion of small vessels. Capillary thrombi, which can be demonstrated in more than half of all cases, have no diagnostic importance, because they also occur in Crohn's colitis and in self-limited colitis of infective type.[8] The lamina propria contains increased numbers of plasma cells and lymphocytes. Neutrophil polymorphs show margination of the endothelium of capillaries, migrate into the lamina propria where they are less conspicuous and then invade the tubular epithelium. Entering the lumen and in association with the degenerative epithelial cell lining, they constitute crypt abscesses. These may rupture into the lamina propria or discharge onto the surface and are associated with a tendency for the goblet cell population to be replaced by more immature basophilic cells, a manifestation of increased cell turnover. This inflammatory process is almost exclusively mucosal if there is no ulceration (Fig. 27.40) and as the disease goes into remission, chronic inflammation and architectural mucosal distortion characterizes the picture (Fig. 27.41). However with further attacks and with increasing degrees of epithelial cell destruction the mucosa breaks down and ulcers are produced. These vary from small surface erosions to large areas of complete mucosal denudation and there is a tendency for tunnelling of the ulcerating process underneath marginal mucosa. This produces the collar-stud abscesses described radiologically. Clearly at this stage, vascular dilatation and some inflammatory cell infiltration appears in the submucosa but in the absence of penetrating ulcers the density of inflammation remains maximum in the mucosa.

Either as the result of therapy or spontaneously, the inflammatory process may resolve. Diminishing cellularity

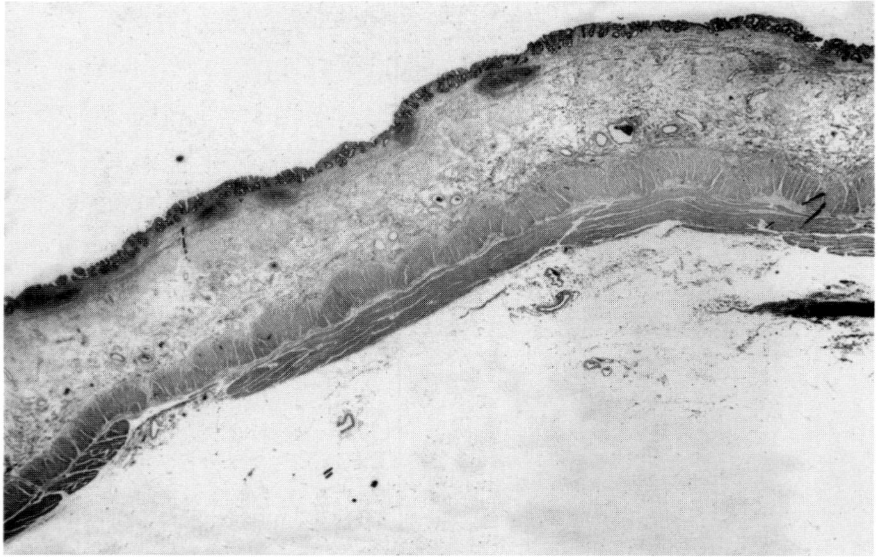

Fig. 27.40 Chronic ulcerative colitis. The exclusively mucosal site of the disease process is evident. Note the gross glandular architectural alterations. (H&E, ×16)

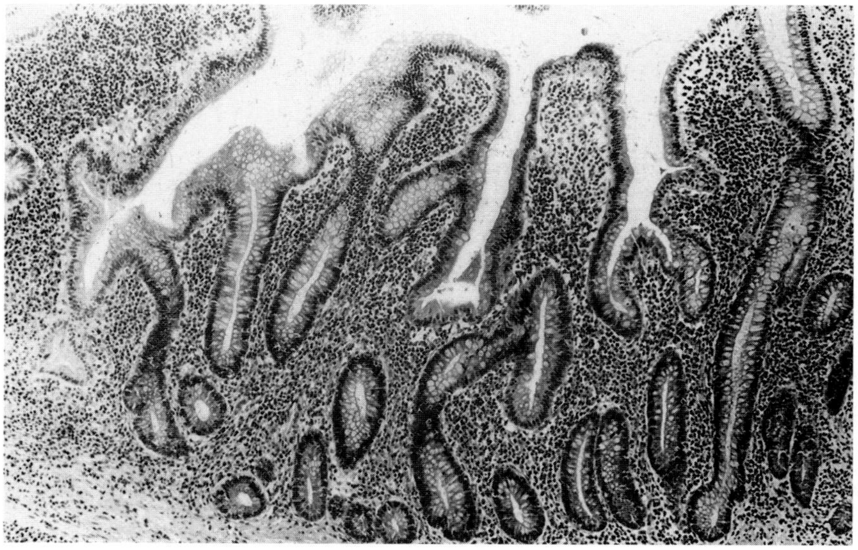

Fig. 27.41 Ulcerative colitis in resolving phase manifested as mainly chronic inflammation, but with gross mucosal architectural abnormality. (H&E, ×52)

of the lamina propria coupled with regenerative epithelial features now dominates the picture. Complete restoration of the mucosa is possible after a mild first attack, but usually resolution leaves some slight abnormalities. Regenerated tubules often fall short of the muscularis mucosae and may be abnormal in shape or orientation. With recurrences, architectural abnormality increases and a relative loss of tubular glands occurs. They tend to become irregular in size and shape and the mucosa overall has an atrophic appearance. At this stage there may be a significant fibromuscular hyperplasia of the muscularis mucosa. This has already been referred to in the context of producing strictures, which are often radiological rather than functional. Depending when in relation to the course of the disease one examines the mucosa, it can vary from one with a nearly normal appearance to one that is distorted, atrophic and with a variable residual inflammatory cell infiltration of the lamina propria. There is evidence that in clinically chronic quiescent ulcerative colitis the tendency to relapse is related to the persistence of crypt abscesses, mucin depletion and breaches of the surface epithelium, as seen in rectal biopsies.[9] In the reactive chronic remitting form of the disease, a more or less dense collagenosis of the deep aspect of the lamina propria develops as successive generations of regenerating tubules fail to reach the muscularis mucosa (Fig. 27.42).

In patients who have a chronic persistent form of the disease, the mucosa always shows features of inflammation. Thus those changes which characterize the acute phase are superimposed upon an architecturally abnormal mucosa showing chronic inflammation. Ulceration and healing proceed side by side and through this interplay, inflammatory pseudopolyps are produced, due to a combination of granulation tissue and regenerative epithelial hyperplasia. Usually the presence of inflammatory polyps does not alter the clinical picture, but sometimes if they are of giant proportions they can produce symptomatology due to bowel obstruction and can mimic neoplasms.[10,11] If low grade chronic activity characterizes the disease process, lymphoid follicular hyperplasia may occur to a degree which is macroscopically polypoidal.

Lymphoid hyperplasia is much more frequently seen in the distal localized form of the disease and there are claims that so-called proctocolitis may be a different entity or represents a more intense reaction which results in localization.[12] One of the histological features of longstanding disease is the presence of Paneth cell metaplasia.[13] Argentaffin cells, however, are usually decreased in number and found in abnormal situations.[14,15] On occasions, endocrine cell hyperplasia occurs and carcinoid tumours may arise.[16] Whereas the number of eosinophils appears to be increased in chronic disease,[17] a normal population is seen in a first attack.[18] Although claims have been made for the significance of changes in plasma cell populations in the lamina propria, it has been shown that in a comparison of ulcerative colitis with Crohn's disease and infective colitis they are a nonspecific response to mucosal damage and in no way differentiate the type of inflammation.[19] Repeated histological examinations over a fairly extended period is the only certain way of distinguishing infective colitis from ulcerative colitis.[20]

During the course of any attack of ulcerative colitis, even the first, a fulminant course may supervene. This is

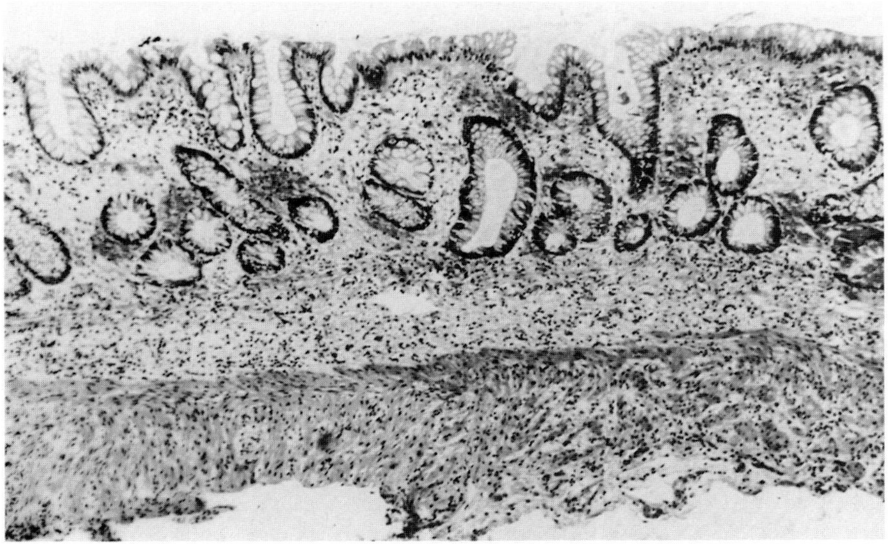

Fig. 27.42 Chronic quiescent ulcerated colitis. The glandular architecture is abnormal and they fall short of the muscularis mucosa being separated from it by a fibrosis of the lamina propria. (H&E, ×50)

characterized by severe clinical disease and increasing abdominal girth due to dilatation of the colon. Severe systemic disturbances are associated phenomena and if surgical intervention is delayed a fatal outcome is inevitable due to colonic perforation. The histological appearances of the grossly dilated necrotic bowel are often disappointing. Ulceration tends to be widespread and deep, involving both submucosa and muscle, but the mucosal features of ulcerative colitis may be minimal, especially if the complication occurs early during a first attack. A characteristic feature is the presence of myocytolysis, an appearance of ischaemic necrosis of the muscularis propria, coupled with intense vascular congestion of the thinned colonic wall. Toxic megacolon, as this condition is usually referred to, occurs not only as a complication of ulcerative colitis and Crohn's colitis but is described in salmonella colitis,[21,22] amoebic colitis,[23–26] campylobacter colitis[27] and antibiotic-associated colitis.[28] It can almost certainly supervene in any form of severe colitis and has even been described in colitis due to toxic drugs such as methotrexate.[29]

Reference has already been made to involvement of the terminal ileum in ulcerative pan-colitis. Depending upon how it is defined, it occurs in up to 25% of colectomy specimens, but is severe enough to be an obvious feature in less than half of these. It is of no clinicopathological significance except that it may be related to incompetence of the ileocaecal valve, although this has never been proven. Lesser degrees are probably the result of the regional colonic inflammatory process affecting the neighbouring small bowel. The vermiform appendix, on the other hand, is embryologically and histologically similar to colon and is affected by the disease process because of this. Both these inflammatory lesions are unrelated to so-called pouch ileitis. Treatment of ulcerative colitis with total colectomy and creation of a continent ileostomy is not uncommonly accompanied by inflammation of the ileal pouch. It is generally a local problem but occasionally is severe enough to cause a systemic illness. Histologically, there is normally slight mucosal inflammation, but occasionally one sees crypt abscess formation, ulceration and blunting of villi. The aetiology of this condition is unknown but it is important in that a diagnosis of recurrent Crohn's disease may be entertained. However pouch ileitis usually responds to antibiotic therapy[30] and is thought in some way to be related to all altered microflora in the pouch and the mucosal response to it.

ULCERATIVE COLITIS DYSPLASIA AND ADENOCARCINOMA

There can be no doubt that as a group, patients with ulcerative colitis are more than usually prone to develop adenocarcinoma of the large bowel. A total colitis and a history of more than 10 years duration appear to be particularly predisposing factors. Thus, an onset of colitis in childhood would seem to designate a group at high risk, but this view has been challenged.[31] There is also disagreement whether patients with continuous symptomatic disease or those in which the colitis is quiescent are most prone. The incidence may well be modified by the type of surveillance of colitis patients. Patients attending different clinics may well be subject to different sets of criteria for colectomy for other reasons. It is now accepted that most, if not all, cases of carcinoma of the large bowel in ulcerative colitis arise through a sequence of increasing dysplasia. In effect, this is no different from the sequence which occurs in the adenoma–carcinoma sequence in non-colitic patients, except that the dysplastic lesion in the latter is generally polypoidal. Indeed, there is increasing evidence that carcinomas in many other sites evolve through a sequence of increasing in situ dysplasia before becoming invasive. Based upon the assumption that cancer in ulcerative colitis is preceded by dysplasia, one could predict that cases would occur in which the mucosa showed one or more areas of dysplasia but no carcinoma, carcinoma or carcinomas and dysplasia occurring together but not necessarily in the same part of the bowel and carcinoma without dysplasia. In the latter case, the malignancy obliterates the preceding dysplasia just as occurs in the majority of ordinary colon carcinomas in which no predisposing dysplastic adenomatous areas can be found. This is, in fact, the spectrum of changes that occur in ulcerative colitis.[32,33] Thus, earlier recommendations that sequential rectal biopsy would be a valuable screening procedure for colitis patients deemed at risk for dysplasia and carcinoma[34] are no longer regarded as valid. Indeed, for the at-risk patient it is now suggested[35] that colonoscopic step-wise biopsy of the whole colon at 10 cm intervals be performed when the mucosa is flat and further biopsies of areas taken if they are raised. Depending on resources, it is suggested that the procedure should be performed on an annual basis.[36] There is still, however, controversy relating to the efficacy of surveillance programmes based upon repeated colonoscopic biopsies. Some claim that even low-grade dysplasia is predictive of future carcinoma and warrants follow-up,[37] others express concern that random colonoscopic biopsies cannot be relied upon to detect dysplasia in the at-risk patient,[38] whilst others believe colonoscopic surveillance is an entirely safe alternative to prophylactic colectomy.[39]

Macroscopic features

Dysplasia in ulcerative colitis can occur in a mucosa which appears atrophic or featureless. One is tempted to speculate, however, that with increasing experience and improved endoscopic techniques dysplasia of the colonic mucosa will be as accurately recognized as it is in the uterine cervix by colposcopists. One macroscopic type of dysplasia that certainly can be recognized in operative

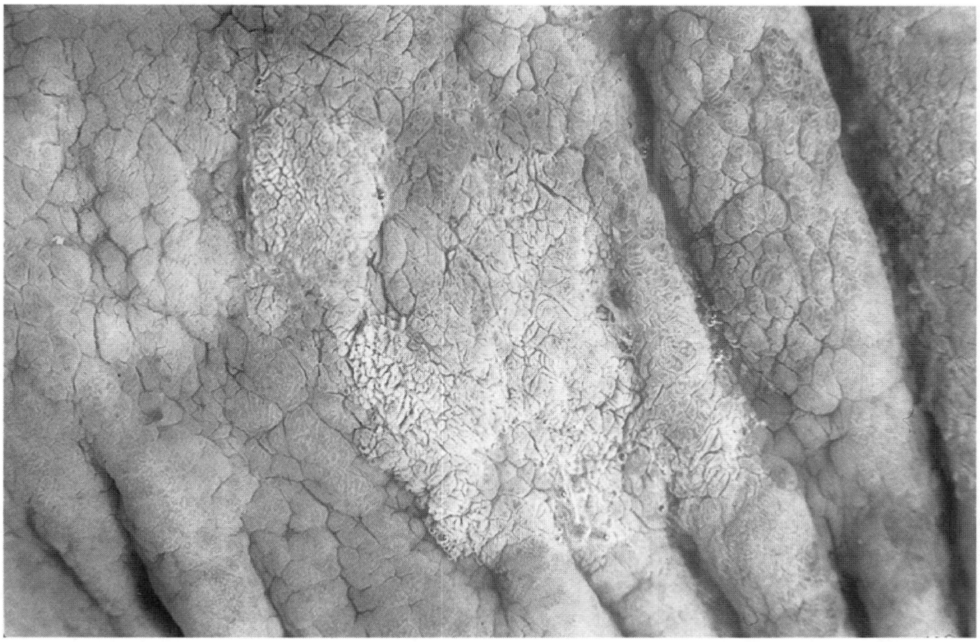

Fig. 27.43 Quiescent longstanding ulcerative colitis with typical velvety macroscopic appearance denoting microscopic villous dysplasia.

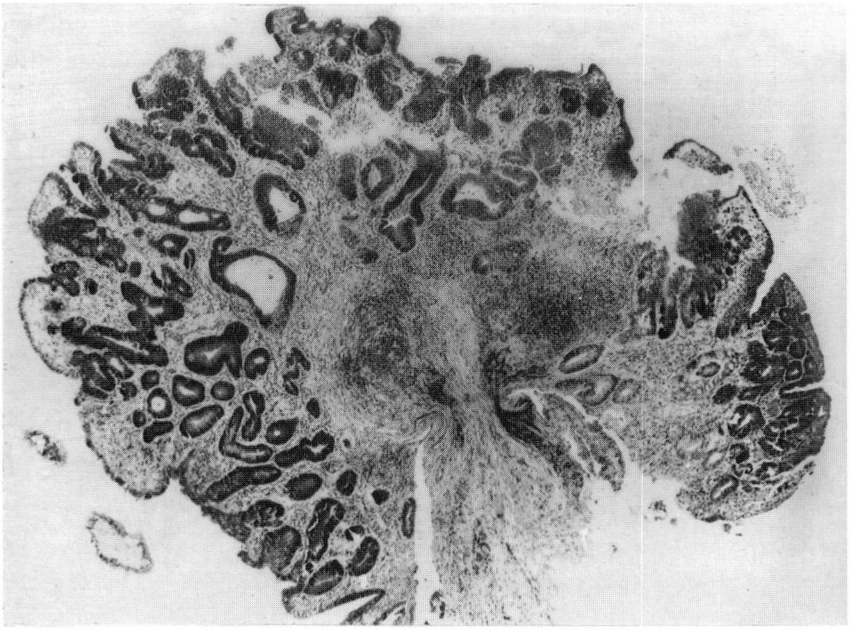

Fig. 27.44 A polypoidal area of dysplasia removed endoscopically from a patient with a 12-year history of ulcerative colitis. (H&E, ×18)

specimens is the velvety lesion which is due to an underlying villous microscopic structure (Fig. 27.43). Polypoidal lesions (Fig. 27.44) or plaques also occur[40] and are likely to be chronologically older lesions,[41] but raised lesions generally in ulcerative colitis are more likely to be solely inflammatory.

When invasive carcinoma supervenes, the lesions are often multiple, they are as often flat as they are raised or diffusely infiltrating and frequently grossly mucinous. It is often stated that when carcinoma complicates ulcerative colitis the prognosis is grave. However, with increasingly successful surveillance and earlier treatment this may no longer be true in all cases.[42] The fact that many of the tumours are of mucinous type and often poorly differ-

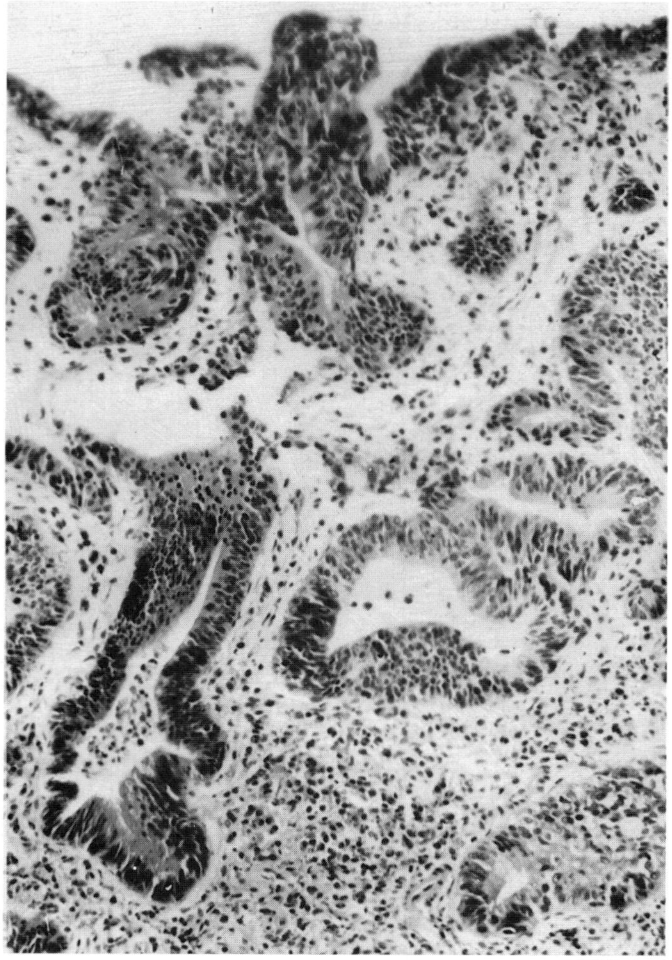

Fig. 27.45 Dysplasia in the polypoid lesion shown in Fig. 27.44. Note the hyperchromasia and multilayering of nuclei in epithelium which is largely non-mucus-producing. (H&E, ×170)

entiated (see below) does mean, though, that they tend to be more aggressive as a group than those arising in non-colitic colons.

Microscopic features

The microscopic features of dysplasia, whether it be in the uterine cervix or the bowel, are basically the same. The cells involved show variations in size, shape and staining characteristics of both nucleus and cytoplasm with evidence of increased mitotic rate (Figs 27.45, 27.46). They also exhibit variations in their total numbers and in their organization into the epithelial unit. In the colon, not only may this process involve the goblet cell, which constitutes most of the epithelial unit, but it may include other cells such as those of endocrine type, which are also normally present, and cells such as the Paneth cells, which are not. Much has been made of subjectively characterizing the many different patterns of dysplasia thus created by the combinations of various features outlined above,[43] but just as in the enormously varied appearances of dysplasia in adenomatous colonic polyps, the exact significance of the subdivisions is in doubt. Furthermore, minor degrees of nuclear and cytoplasmic morphological abnormality together with an increased mitotic rate occur in epithelium which is turning over rapidly in response to inflammation and cell damage. A pragmatic approach has been advocated by a large international working group.[44] Dysplasia is defined as epithelial change which is unequivocally neoplastic based upon its variation from normal outlined above. Biopsy specimens are then categorized as either positive, indefinite or negative for dysplasia. The negative category includes inflammatory and regenerative appearances whereas the positive and indefinite are either clearly dysplastic or highly suspicious. Thus there is a

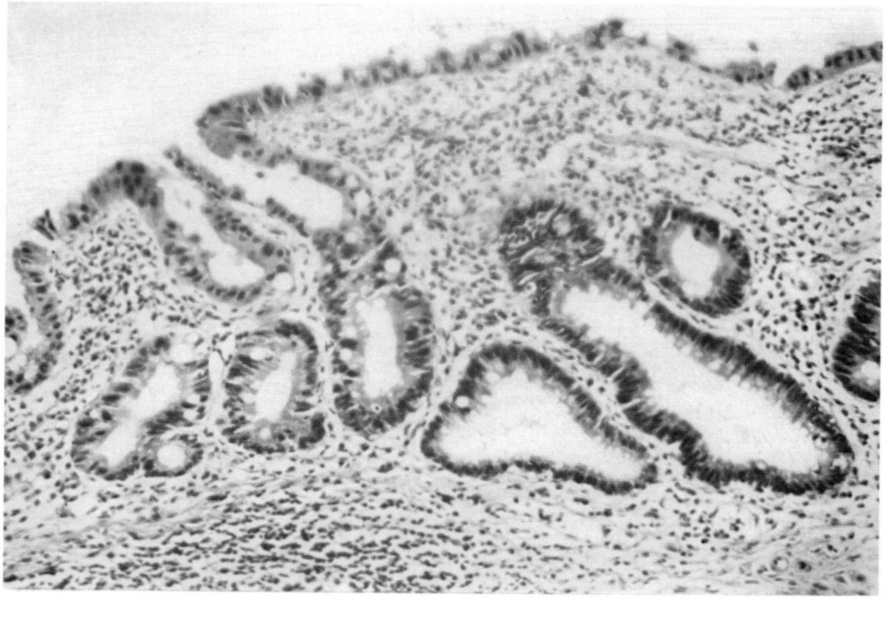

Fig. 27.46 Dysplasia in an atrophic flat mucosa. Mucus production is still in evidence, but nuclear pleomorphism and hyperchromasia is marked and there is a particularly pronounced atypia of the goblet cell population. (H&E, ×160)

basis for establishing guidelines for management, but difficulties still abound because of uncertainty of the behaviour of dysplasia and the complex decision-making involved in advocating total colectomy, sometimes for patients with few symptoms. One of the problems for most pathologists, however, is that they see so few biopsies from cases such as these that decision-making despite these guidelines still creates difficulties. Although there is at the moment no histochemical or other marker for dysplasia other than routine light microscopy,[45] estimates of DNA aneuploidy are being advocated. There are claims that changes in nuclear DNA may be an earlier phenomenon than dysplasia in the malignant process.[46] Recently, attention has been drawn to the difficulties in interpretation with respect to dysplastic changes occurring in the outlying glands of colitis cystica profunda when this complicates ulcerative colitis (see Ch. 27).

Invasive carcinomas arising in ulcerative colitis are capable of reduplicating any of the appearances seen in carcinomas in non-colitic bowel. As already noted, as a group they tend to be less well differentiated and more frequently mucinous. Atypical argyrophic cell components are described[47] as are frankly malignant carcinoids,[48] and mixed mucinous and Paneth cell tumours occur as in non-colitic carcinomas of the colon.

Ulcerative colitis versus Crohn's colitis

Much has been written during the last 10 or 15 years of the difficulties in differential diagnosis between ulcerative colitis and Crohn's colitis.[7] It is true that this may pose a problem in the interpretation of colonic biopsies or the assessment of colectomy specimens. However with greater awareness of the variations of pathology that both conditions may exhibit, the diagnostic dilemma is becoming rarer. Moreover, the realization that there are a significant number of other forms of colitis has placed the differentiation between Crohn's and ulcerative colitis properly in perspective. In fact, it could be argued that pressure to utilize too few diagnostic categories acts to limit the increase in our understanding of inflammatory bowel disease.

The relationship between Crohn's disease and ulcerative colitis is nonetheless intriguing. The earlier view,[49] which may still prevail, that they are both simply different tissue expressions of the same disease process, is largely unfounded. Of course, they have many common features, both clinical and pathological, but there are too many dissimilarities for these not to be regarded as separate entities. It is claimed that of prime importance in differentiating the two diseases in biopsies are a villous surface in ulcerative colitis mucosa and a histiocytic inflammatory cell component and granulomas in Crohn's colitis.[50] There are also now rare but well documented cases of the coexistence of Crohn's disease and ulcerative colitis in the same patient.[51,52] This makes the assertion that they are one and the same disease process most unlikely.

Table 27.1 The extraintestinal manifestations of ulcerative colitis

Hepatobiliary	Steatosis, pericholangitis, cirrhosis, sclerosing cholangitis, hepatitis, liver abscess, amyloidosis
Musculoskeletal	Peripheral arthritis, sacroiliitis, ankylosing spondylitis, finger clubbing
Skin and mucous	Erythema nodosum, pyoderma gangrenosum, aphthous ulceration, conjunctivitis, iritis, episcleritis
Genitourinary	Nephrolithiasis
Thromboembolic	Leg vein thromboembolism, cerebral vein thrombosis, (rarely) arterial thrombosis
Growth retardation	In Childhood-onset disease (?steroid therapy)

Extracolonic manifestations

One of the reasons that Crohn's and ulcerative colitis were thought possibly to be different expressions of a single disease process was the similarities that they show in their extracolonic manifestations. These include hepatobiliary disorders, musculoskeletal complications, skin, mucous membrane and eye lesions, genitourinary conditions, thromboembolic disease and growth retardation (see Table 27.1). For a detailed description see Kern.[53]

Quite apart from the above, there is mounting evidence that patients with ulcerative colitis also have an increased incidence of extraintestinal cancer, particularly of the central nervous system and connective tissues.[54] This may be related to the immunosuppression secondary to prolonged use of steroids or to a basic immune defect in patients prone to ulcerative colitis. It is curious that there should be a notable increase in squamous carcinoma of the perianal and vaginal skin.[55] With respect to a possible immune deficit, it is of interest that patients with ulcerative colitis also appear more than usually susceptible to malignant lymphoma of both Hodgkins and non-Hodgkins type.[56] Non-Hodgkins lymphoma affecting the large intestine primarily seems to be a particular risk and is more commonly of large-cell high grade type.[57] The disease is also described in the rectum many years after ileorectal anastomosis.[58]

REFERENCES

1. Onderdonk AB. Experimental models for ulcerative colitis. Dig Dis Sci 1985; 30: 40S–44S.
2. Strober W. Animal models of inflammatory bowel disease — an overview. Dig Dis Sci 1985; 30 (Suppl): 3S–10S.
3. Kraft SC, Kirsner JB. The immunology of ulcerative colitis and Crohn's disease: clinical and humoral aspects. In: Kirsner JB, Shorter RG, eds. Inflammatory bowel disease. 2nd ed. Philadelphia: Lea and Febiger, 1980: pp 86–120.
4. Waston DW, Bartnik W, Shorter RG. Lymphocyte function and chronic inflammatory bowel disease. In: Kirsner JB, Shorter RG,

eds. Inflammatory bowel disease. 2nd ed. Philadelphia: Lea and Febiger, 1980: pp 121–137.
5. Editorial: Ulcerative colitis: a specific mucin defect. Gastroenterology 1984; 87: 1193–1195.
6. Goulston SJM, McGovern VJ. The nature of benign strictures in ulcerative colitis. N Engl J Med 1969; 281: 290–295.
7. Whitehead R. Mucosal biopsy of the gastrointestinal tract. 3rd ed. Philadelphia: Saunders, 1985: pp 237–238.
8. Dhillon AP, Anthony A, Sim R et al. Mucosal capillary thrombi in rectal biopsies. Histopathology 1992; 21: 127–133.
9. Riley SA, Mani V, Goodman MJ, Dutt S, Herd ME. Microscopic activity in ulcerative colitis: what does it mean? Gut 1991; 32: 174–178.
10. Balazs M. Giant inflammatory polyps associated with idiopathic inflammatory bowel disease. An ultrastructural study of five cases. Dis Colon Rectum 1990; 33: 773–777.
11. Kelly JK, Langevin JM, Price LM, Hershfield NB, Share S, Blustein P. Giant and symptomatic inflammatory polyps of the colon in idiopathic inflammatory bowel disease. Am J Surg Pathol 1986; 10: 420–428.
12. Jenkins D, Goodall A, Scott BB. Ulcerative colitis: one disease or two? (Quantitative histological differences between distal and extensive disease). Gut 1990; 31: 426–430.
13. Watson AJ, Roy AD. Paneth cells in the large intestine in ulcerative colitis. J Pathol Bacteriol 1960; 80: 309–316.
14. Skinner JM, Whitehead R, Piris J. Argentaffin cells in ulcerative colitis. Gut 1971; 12: 636–638.
15. Kyosola K, Penttila O, Salaspuro M. Rectal mucosal adrenergic innervation and enterochromaffin cells in ulcerative colitis and irritable colon. Scand J Gastroenterol 1977; 12: 363–367.
16. Haidar A, Dixon MF. Solitary microcarcinoid in ulcerative colitis. Histopathology 1992; 21: 487–488.
17. Anthonisen P, Riis P. Eosinophilic granulocytes in the rectal mucus of patients with ulcerative colitis and Crohn's disease of the ileum and colon. Scand J Gastroenterol 1971; 6: 731–734.
18. Willoughby CP, Piris J, Truelove SC. Tissue eosinophils in ulcerative colitis. Scand J Gastroenterol 1979; 14: 395–399.
19. Scott BB, Goodall A, Stephenson P, Jenkins D. Rectal mucosal plasma cells in inflammatory bowel disease. Gut 1983; 24: 519–524.
20. Schumacher G, Sandstedt B, Mollby R, Kollerg B. Clinical and histologic features differentiating non-relapsing colitis from first attacks of inflammatory bowel disease. Scand J Gastroenterol 1991; 26: 151–161.
21. Schofield PF, Mandal BK, Ironside AG. Toxic dilatation of the colon in salmonella colitis and inflammatory bowel disease. Br J Surg 1979; 66: 5–8.
22. Gonzalez A, Vargas V, Guarner L, Accarino A, Guardia J. Toxic megacolon in typhoid fever. Arch Intern Med 1985; 145: 2120.
23. Stein D, Bank S, Louw JH. Fulminating amoebic colitis. Surgery 1979; 85: 349–352.
24. Wig JD, Talwar BL, Bushnurmath SR. Toxic dilatation complicating fulminant amoebic colitis. Br J Surg 1981; 68: 135–136.
25. Vajrabukka T, Dhitavat A, Kichananta B, Sukonthamand Y, Tanphiphat C, Vongviriyatham S. Fulminating amoebic colitis: a clinical evaluation. Br J Surg 1979; 66: 630–632.
26. Saltzberg DM, Hall-Craggs M. Fulminant amebic colitis in a homosexual man. Am J Gastroenterol 1986; 81: 209–212.
27. Kalkay MN, Ayanian ZS, Lehaf EA, Baldi A. Campylobacter-induced toxic megacolon. Am J Gastroenterol 1983; 78: 557–559.
28. Keighley MRB. Antibiotic-associated pseudomenbranous colitis: pathogenesis and management. Drugs 1980; 20: 49–56.
29. Atherton LD, Leib ES, Kaye MD. Toxic megacolon associated with methotrexate therapy. Gastroenterology 1984; 86: 1583–1588.
30. Klein K, Stenzel P, Katon RM. Pouch ileitis: report of a case with severe systemic manifestations. J Clin Gastroenterol 1983; 5: 149–153.
31. Sachar DB, Greenstein AJ. Cancer in ulcerative colitis: good news and bad news. Ann Intern Med 1981; 95: 642–644.
32. Evans DJ, Pollock DJ. In situ and invasive carcinoma of the colon in patients with ulcerative colitis. Gut 1972; 13: 566–570.
33. Cook MG, Goligher JC. Carcinoma and epithelial dysplasia complicating ulcerative colitis. Gastroenterology 1975; 68: 1127–1136.
34. Morson BC, Pang LS. Rectal biopsy as an aid to cancer control in ulcerative colitis. Gut 1967; 8: 423–434.
35. Lennard-Jones JE, Morson BC, Ritchie JK, Williams CB. Cancer surveillance in ulcerative colitis. Lancet 1983; ii: 149–152.
36. Yardley JH, Ransohoff DF, Riddell RH, Goldman H. Cancer in inflammatory bowel disease: how serious is the problem and what should be done about it. (Editorial) Gastroenterology 1983; 85: 197–200.
37. Woolrich AJ, DaSilva MD, Korelitz BI. Surveillance in the routine management of ulcerative colitis: the predictive value of low-grade dysplasia. Gastroenterology 1992; 103: 431–438.
38. Taylor BA, Pemberton JH, Carpenter HA et al. Dysplasia in chronic ulcerative colitis: implications for colonoscopic surveillance. Dis Colon Rectum 1992; 35: 950–956.
39. Leidenius M, Kellokumpu I, Husa A, Riihela M, Sipponen P. Dysplasia and carcinoma in longstanding ulcerative colitis: an endoscopic and histological surveillance programme. Gut 1991; 32: 1521–1525.
40. Blackstone MO, Riddell RH, Rogers BHG, Levin B. Dysplasia-associated lesion or mass (DALM) detected by colonoscopy in long-standing ulcerative colitis: an indication for colectomy. Gastroenterology 1981; 80: 366–374.
41. Butt JH, Morson B. Dysplasia and cancer in inflammatory bowel disease. Gastroenterology 1981; 80: 865–868.
42. Leading Article. Colorectal carcinoma in ulcerative colitis. Lancet 1986; 2: 197–198.
43. Riddell RH. The precarcinomatous phase of ulcerative colitis. In: Current topics in pathology: pathology of the gastrointestinal tract. Morson BC, ed. New York: Springer, 1976: p 179.
44. Riddell RH, Goldman H, Ransohoff DF et al. Dysplasia in inflammatory bowel disease. Hum Pathol 1983; 14: 931–968.
45. Riddell RH. Cancer and dysplasia in ulcerative colitis: an insoluble problem. Progress in Clinical and Biological Research 1985; 186: 77–90.
46. Lofberg R, Brostrom O, Karlen P, Ost A, Tribukait B. DNA aneuploidy in ulcerative colitis: reproducibility, topographic distribution, and relation to dysplasia. Gastroenterology 1992; 102: 1149–1154.
47. Miller RR, Sumner HW. Argyrophilic cell hyperplasia and an atypical carcinoid tumor in chronic ulcerative colitis. Cancer 1982; 50: 2920–2925.
48. Owen DA, Hwang WS, Thorlakson RH, Walli E. Malignant carcinoid tumor complicating chronic ulcerative colitis. Am J Clin Pathol 1981; 76: 333–338.
49. Shorter RG, Huizenga KA, Spencer RJ. A working hypothesis for the etiology and pathogenesis of inflammatory bowel disease. Am J Dig Dis 1972; 17: 1024–1032.
50. Seldenrijk CA, Morson BC, Meuwissen SGM, Schipper NW, Lindeman J, Meijer CJLM. Histopathological evaluation of colonic mucosal biopsy specimens in chronic inflammatory bowel disease: diagnostic implications. Gut 1991; 32: 1514–1520.
51. White CL III, Hamilton SR, Diamond MP, Cameron JL. Crohn's disease and ulcerative colitis in the same patient. Gut 1983; 24: 857–862.
52. Jones BJM, Gould SR, Pollock DJ. Coexistent ulcerative colitis and Crohn's disease. Postgrad Med J 1985; 61: 647–649.
53. Kern F. Extraintestinal complications. In: Kirsner JB, Shorter RG, eds. Inflammatory bowel disease. 2nd ed. Philadelphia: Lea and Febiger, 1980: pp 217–240.
54. Ekbom A, Helmick C, Zack M, Adami HO. Extracolonic malignancies in inflammatory bowel disease. Cancer 1991; 67: 2015–2019.
55. Greenstein AJ, Gennuso R, Sachar DB et al. Extraintestinal cancers in inflammatory bowel disease. Cancer 1985; 56: 2914–2921.
56. Greenstein AJ, Mullin GE, Strauchen JA et al. Lymphoma in inflammatory bowel disease. Cancer 1992; 69: 1119–1123.
57. Shepherd NA, Hall PA, Williams GT et al. Primary malignant lymphoma of the large intestine complicating chronic inflammatory bowel disease. Histopathology 1989; 15: 325–337.
58. Teare JP, Greenfield SM, Slater S. Rectal lymphoma after colectomy for ulcerative colitis. Gut 1992; 33: 138–139.

CHAPTER 28

The appendix

R. A. Williams   H. M. Gilmour

PART I

Specific infections

R. A. Williams

For over a century the vermiform appendix has been the intra-abdominal organ most subject to surgical exploration and removal, and the literature abounds with discussions on the diagnosis of acute appendicitis and the surgical procedures undertaken to remove the organ.[1,2] Little has changed, however, with respect to the pathological findings in the excised appendix.[3,4]

Acute appendicitis is slightly more common in males than females and the condition is more prevalent in the young, with the majority of cases occurring before 30 years of age.[4,5] The most consistent explanation for the higher incidence of histologically normal appendices being removed from females is the mimicry by other pelvic inflammatory diseases of appendicitis.[4] It is therefore important that pathological examination of the appendicectomy specimen is thorough. Purely serosal or other extra-appendiceal pathology might indicate the need for further investigation of the patient. Classical extra-appendiceal pathology which mimics acute appendicitis includes yersinial infection with mesenteric adenitis,[6,7] acute salpingitis, ovarian cysts, urinary tract infection and an inflamed Meckel's diverticulum.[8] Other pathology in the appendix may also mimic acute appendicitis, and a resected specimen should be carefully examined for the presence of these processes, which include localized organ arteritis,[4,9] pinworm (*Enterobius vermicularis*) infestation, endometriotic deposits and tumours arising in the appendix.[10,11]

With an appendix of average length, the best possible yield from routine pathological examination is gained by a thorough external examination of the specimen, noting the state of the serosal surface and mesoappendix, and inspecting the muscular layers and mucosa on the cut surface. In practice a block should be taken to include a longitudinal section of the distal 2 cm of the appendix through the lumen,[11] and the remainder of the specimen should be sectioned transversely to the proximal resection margin at 3 mm intervals, with at least one section from the mid-body region and one from the proximal end of the specimen being processed for microscopic examination. Further blocks may be processed at a later stage, depending upon the initial histopathological findings.

In the case of an appendix which is partially dilated along its length, it is important to examine a longitudinal section from the junction of the dilated and non-dilated portions of the organ, as this may be the site of an obstruction caused by a small epithelial tumour and the pathology may be missed in the routine transverse sections.

The technique can be modified for unusual cases such as the presence of a malignant tumour, or an anatomical or developmental anomaly.

ACUTE APPENDICITIS

Aetiology

The aetiology of acute appendicitis has been the subject of numerous investigations and reports. Probably the most readily acceptable explanation for the development of acute appendicitis, because of its appealing simplicity, is obstruction and secondary infection. The obstruction may be due to extraluminal adhesions, or luminal due to faecoliths or lymphoid hyperplasia in the wall. However, faecoliths are not found in many cases in which an acute appendicitis is confirmed[4] and the amount of lymphoid tissue present is often not more than that expected according to age. Indeed, if there is some degree of reactive lymphoid hyperplasia, then it may well be secondary to the primary inflammation in the appendix, rather than a causative factor.

There is experimental and epidemiological evidence to support the view that appendicitis is secondary to luminal obstruction, and this is the commonly held view.[12,13] Manometric measurements of appendiceal intraluminal pressure prior to operative removal have led others to the view that any obstruction is a sequel of the inflammatory process.[14] References are also made to low bulk, low cellulose diets in affluent societies leading to increased transit time of faecal material through the bowel, with an altered bacterial flora and stasis increasing susceptibility to infection. Whilst this is a possibility, it is not proven.

Vascular factors may also play a part in the development of appendicitis. The fact that the appendicular artery is an end artery, and that acute suppurative appendicitis is most commonly distributed towards the distal end of the organ, would tend to support the proposal that ischaemia may play a role in the genesis of appendicitis. Similarly, the complex submucosal and intramucosal vascular plexus of the appendix could be extremely susceptible to insult and compromise from a number of agents, given the small luminal volume of the organ. Focal ischaemia leading to areas of mucosal ulceration would then allow entry of microorganisms into the mucosa, with the possibility of secondary infection and the sequelae.

Sisson, Ahlvin and Harlow (1971) proposed that viral induced mucosal ulceration could be the earliest feature of acute appendicitis. Whilst this must remain a possibility, it is, like many of the other postulates, difficult to prove.[15]

Occasional very rare cases of appendicitis appear to be due to haematogenous spread of infection from other organs. It has been postulated that the cause of appendiceal pain in a noninflamed appendix is neurogenic, and Dhillon and Rode, as a result of immunohistochemical studies, proposed that it was related to serotonin release.[16]

The definitive cause of acute appendicitis remains obscure and it may be multifactorial. A large range of bacteria have been cultured from acutely inflamed appendices and commonly there is a mixed growth in which normal commensals predominate. Where there are 'pure' growths, *Bacteroides fragilis* and *Escherichia coli* are the most common organisms cultured.[17–19] Most series include the full range of gut commensals, including the Clostridium group, with *C. perfringens* being present in a small but significant group of cases. Lau and co-authors in 1984,[18] in a study of appendicitis and its septic complications, concluded that aerobic infection is common in early appendicitis, but that as the inflammation spreads the bacterial culture profile changes, and mixed aerobic and anaerobic infection predominates in late cases. In a different age group, Madden and Hart suggest that *Streptococcus milleri* is a significant infecting organism in appendicitis in children.[20] Many organisms have thus been identified, but perhaps of prime importance is the therapeutic implication of the possibility of the presence of both aerobic and anaerobic species should there be complications, or if preoperative prophylactic antibiotic cover is used.[18,19,21]

Other specific bacterial infections of the appendix occur in association with a more generalized enteritis/colitis. These include typhoid and paratyphoid infection, shigellosis,[22] and *Helicobacter jejuni* infection.[23] Tuberculous infection in the appendix highlights the need to culture and stain for acid-fast bacilli in cases of granulomatous appendicitis. Actinomycosis may also cause an appendicitis but, as the organism is a gut commensal, the finding of the organism within the wall of the appendix is necessary before making this diagnosis and instituting any long-term antibiotic therapy (Fig. 28.1).[4]

Other associations

Inflammation of the vermiform appendix may be associated with infestation of a host by other organisms including spirochaetes (*Brachyspiria aalborgi*),[24] schistosomes, toxoplasma, amoebae and pinworms (*Enterobius vermicularis*). Sometimes it is involved in rare infestations with balantidia[25] and *Echin. granulosus*.[26] Involvement of the appendix in a case of Rocky Mountain spotted fever (*Rickettsia rickettsia* infection) is documented.[27]

Acute appendicitis is described in association with mechanical abnormalities such as intussusception and torsion. It occurs in appendices in unusual sites such as subhepatic,[28] and intracaecal,[29] and in an appendix found projecting from the ascending colon about 10 cm from the junction of the taeniae of the caecum.[30] Acute appendicitis also occurs in neonates,[31,32] and a case of prenatal appendiceal perforation leading to meconium peritonitis has been described.[33] The presence of foreign bodies, including vegetable seeds, pins and fragments of ingested animal bones, may be coincident with appendiceal inflammation. Interestingly, the first recorded appendicectomy was performed by Claudius Amayand in St George's Hospital, London, in 1735, as a result of complications of a pin lodging in the appendix.[34] Rarely, cases of appendicitis associated with displaced intra-uterine contraceptive devices have also been recorded.[35–37] Even malakoplakia in the appendix has been described.

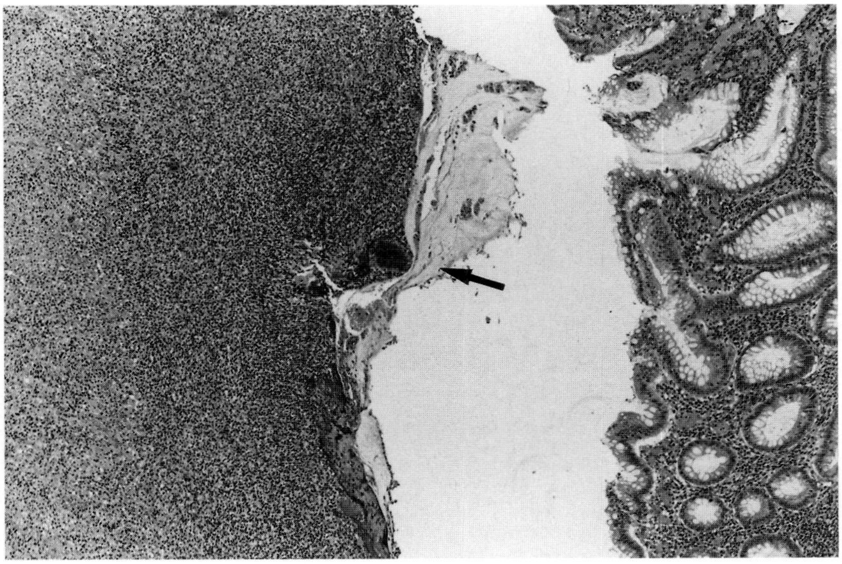

Fig. 28.1 Colonies of *Actinomyces israeli* (arrowed) in the wall of the appendix. The overlying epithelium is ulcerated and an acute inflammatory reaction is present in the wall. (H&E, ×120)

Macroscopic appearances

In acute appendicitis the appearance of the serosal coat may vary from apparently normal, through suffused and congested, to a dull grey-white appearance with an inflammatory exudate (Fig. 28.2), and in complicated cases abscess formation around the site of a perforation may be present. As the inflammation spreads, the mesoappendix becomes involved. On the cut surface the mucosa classically has a reddened congested appearance, and in the case of acute suppurative appendicitis, a pasty grey-brown liquid mixture of pus and faecal material is present in the lumen. Gangrenous areas may be obvious in the wall in advanced cases.

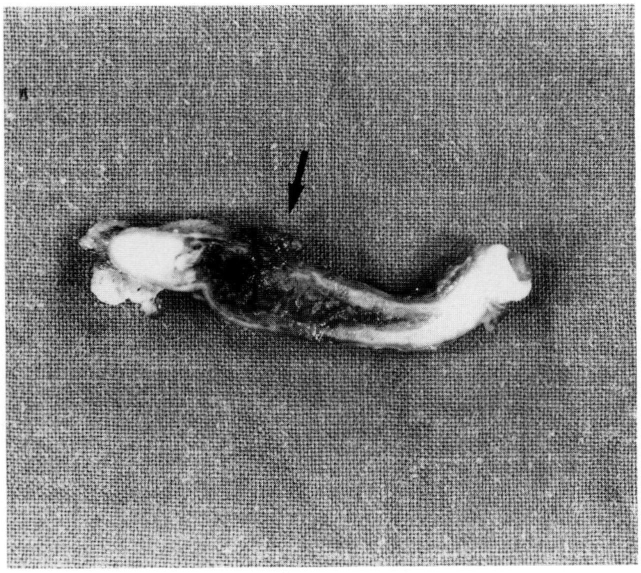

Fig. 28.2 Acute appendicitis. Ulceration of the mucosa is seen, and the inflammatory reaction extends through the wall and into the serosal tissues (arrow).

Intra-operative manipulation of the appendix can cause some suffusion of the serosal coat, with small focal traumatic haemorrhages, but in these cases there are only minimal changes found on microscopic examination (see below).

Microscopic appearances

Many pathologists will not diagnose acute appendicitis unless there is at least a transmucosal infiltration of polymorphonuclear inflammatory cells. Others require a transmural acute inflammatory cell infiltrate (Fig. 28.3). In the histological assessment it is important to remember that acute appendicitis may be focal. The initial sections may not include the main area of pathology.[4,11]

The presence of mucosal inflammation with crypt abscesses should dictate that more tissue be examined. In a retrospective study of 1000 appendices in our laboratory, we found that examination of more tissue, in cases where only superficial mucosal inflammation was present in the initial sections examined, led, in the majority of cases, to us finding infiltration of polymorphonuclear inflammatory cells through the muscularis mucosae in other areas. Therefore the minimal diagnostic criteria for an early acute appendicitis are mucosal congestion and oedema, together with an infiltrate of polymorphonuclear inflammatory cells in the mucosa. If the diagnosis is still in doubt, then further tissue should be examined. Microabscesses, submucosal inflammation and a transmural inflammatory cell infiltrate are seen later. Following this phase, areas of reparative granulation tissue are present in

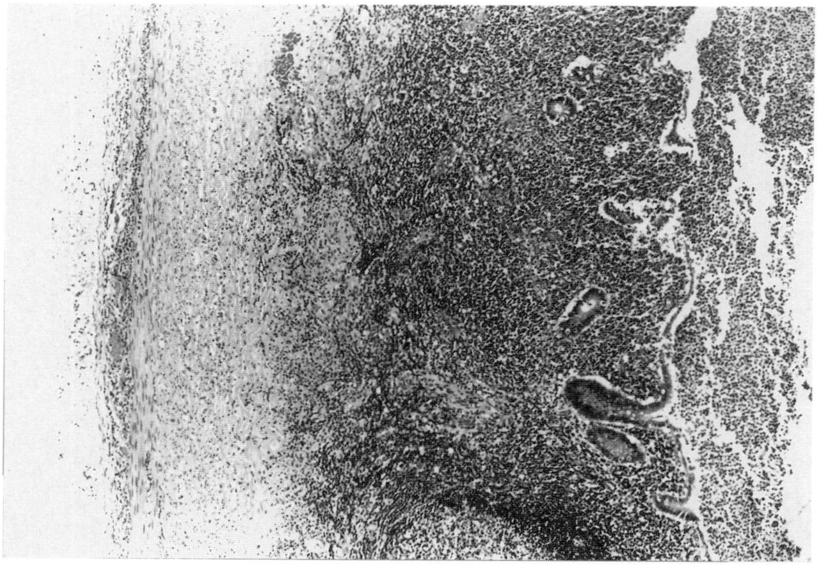

Fig. 28.3 Acute suppurative appendicitis. An inflammatory cell infiltrate is evident throughout all layers of the wall of the appendix. (H&E, ×25)

the wall of the appendix, with an accompanying infiltrate of mononuclear and eosinophil polymorphonuclear inflammatory cells throughout all layers. The final stage of the reparative process is fibrosis. This can involve all layers including the mucosa and submucosa, and is dependent on the extent of the previous inflammation. An interpretation of the amount of fibrous tissue in the appendix should take into account the patient's age, as the amount of fibrous tissue in the appendix generally increases in middle and old age, just as the prominence and amount of lymphoid tissue decreases along with that in the rest of the body. Involution and luminal obliteration, however, may occur in young people.[38] At the end of the resolution phase the epithelial lining either returns to normal, or the appendix may be lined by a single layer of simple cuboidal epithelium.[4,11]

In assessing very superficial inflammatory changes, it must be remembered that focal mucosal ulceration in the presence of faecoliths may be the result of localized mechanical trauma.

Exclusively serosal inflammatory change in sections should alert the pathologist to possible extra-appendiceal causes for the patient's symptoms, e.g. a perforated caecal carcinoma. To ascribe microscopic changes to intra-operative manipulation, the changes should be minimal with, at the most, margination of polymorphs in blood vessels in association with vascular congestion and perhaps occasional small traumatic capillary ruptures in the serosa. Emigration of polymorphonuclear inflammatory cells through the walls of blood vessels may occur within 2–3 hours, and therefore an appendix removed, en passant, during a lengthy pelvic operation may already show polymorphs in the tissues.

CHRONIC APPENDICITIS

The diagnostic label of 'chronic appendicitis' is confusing and not universally accepted.[39] Although much is written about its existence, little attempt has been made to define it precisely. The term is used to describe the appendix in which there is fibrous obliteration of the lumen or one in which a mononuclear inflammatory cell infiltrate is seen throughout the wall. Both these are probably resolving, or the end stage of an acute inflammatory process. Thus it is difficult to ascribe any further significance to them. However, if chronic inflammation is defined in terms such as proposed by Walter and Israel,[40] who describe it as 'a prolonged process in which destruction and inflammation are proceeding at the same time as attempts at healing', and there is a supportive clinical history of ongoing or prolonged symptoms, then it is reasonable for a diagnosis of chronic ongoing appendicitis to be made. In practice this situation rarely arises.

OTHER CONDITIONS OF THE APPENDIX

Enterobius vermicularis and the appendix

The presence of pinworms (*Enterobius vermicularis*) in the lumen of the appendix represents a stage in the life cycle of the organism (Fig. 28.4).[41] The adult forms live in the lumen of the human colon where they copulate, after which the male of the species soon dies and the gravid female migrates to the anal verge, depositing eggs on the skin in the perianal region. Ano-oral transmission of the eggs is effected either directly, via fingers or oro-genito-anal contact, or indirectly by ingestion of dust. The eggs

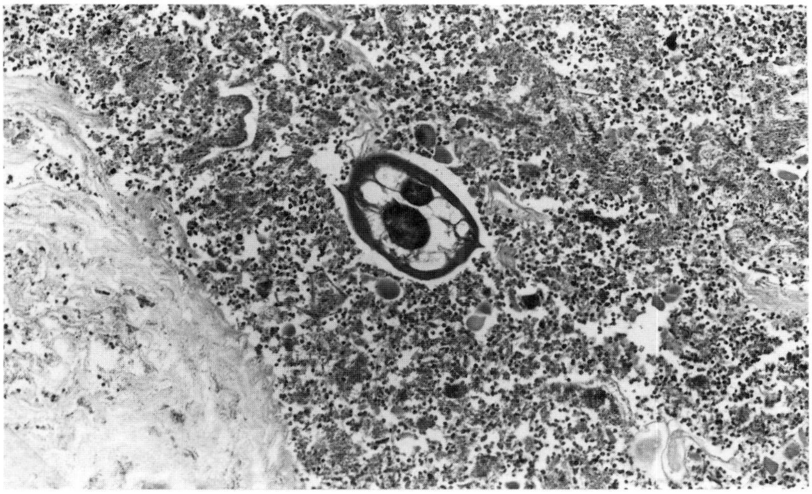

Fig. 28.4 *Enterobius vermicularis* in the lumen of the appendix. A transverse section through one organism is obvious amongst the faecal material. (H&E, ×60)

release larvae in the duodenum which develop into mature adult worms in the caecum and appendix. The adult worms (which have no obligatory tissue phase) penetrate tissues rarely, but they can migrate into the peritoneum and omentum, or other organs such as the fallopian tubes, causing tissue reactions in these sites. When penetration into the wall of the appendix occurs, a granulomatous foreign-body type inflammatory reaction is seen around the organism.[41,42]

The causal association of pinworms with acute appendicitis is tenuous, and it is highly unlikely that an associated appendicitis is secondary to obstruction by the worms, as they are seldom present in sufficient numbers.[4] Nevertheless it is clearly important to report their presence.

Yersinial infection

Yersinia enterocolitis affects not only the intra-abdominal lymph nodes, but may also cause lesions in the ileum and the submucosal region of the appendix. Histologically, the changes induced are those of a reactive lymphoid hyperplasia, with or without the characteristic irregular granulomas, with a central zone of necrotizing inflammation containing polymorphs, surrounded by palisaded histiocytic cells.

Amoebiasis and the appendix

Occasional reports of infestation of the appendix by *Entamoeba histolytica* are found in the literature. Their presence

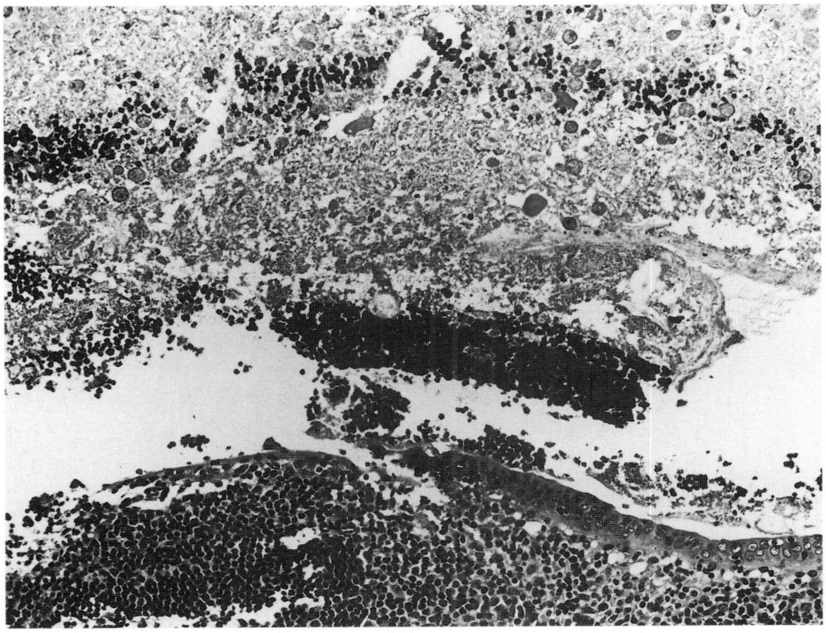

Fig. 28.5 *Entamoeba coli* in the lumen of the appendix. The organism is a gut commensal and does not invade the wall. No evidence of appendicitis was present in this specimen. (H&E, ×54)

in association with acute appendicitis is very rare. In identifying the organism histologically, the pathologist must be aware of the similarity in appearance between the amoebae and phagocytes with ingested red blood cells. Careful examination, paying attention to the sizes of the respective structures, should allow easy differentiation.[43] If amoebic organisms are seen in the lumen of an appendicectomy specimen, bacteriological studies of the patient's gut flora may be indicated in order to differentiate between *E. histolytica* and the non-pathogenic gut commensal *Entamoeba coli* (Fig. 28.5).

Schistosomiasis and the appendix

Schistosomiasis involves the appendix in association with infection elsewhere in the body.[44] The species of organism in the sections is usually easily determined by the position of the spines of the ova. Ova often cause a granulomatous inflammatory reaction in the wall of the appendix, and calcified foci may be present (Fig. 28.6).[39]

Viral infections

The appendix may show changes in generalized viral infection in the body which are usually non-specific: a reactive follicular lymphoid hyperplasia being all that is seen. In the case of measles, the presence of the characteristic Warthin-Finkeldey giant cells confirms the diagnosis. Dymock cites the finding of adenovirus inclusions in the appendix,[11] and O'Brien and O'Briain have reported a

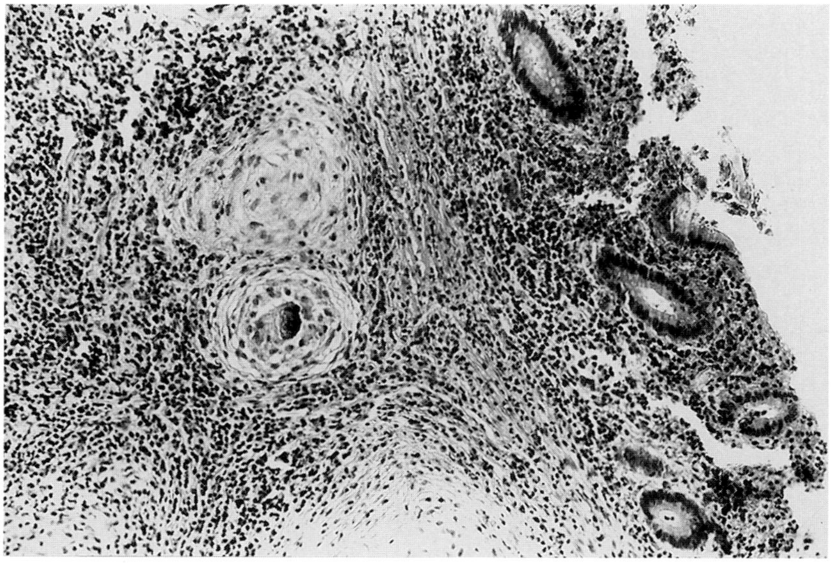

Fig. 28.6 *Schistosoma mansoni* in the wall of the appendix. Note the prominent granulomatous reaction to the organism. (H&E, ×114)

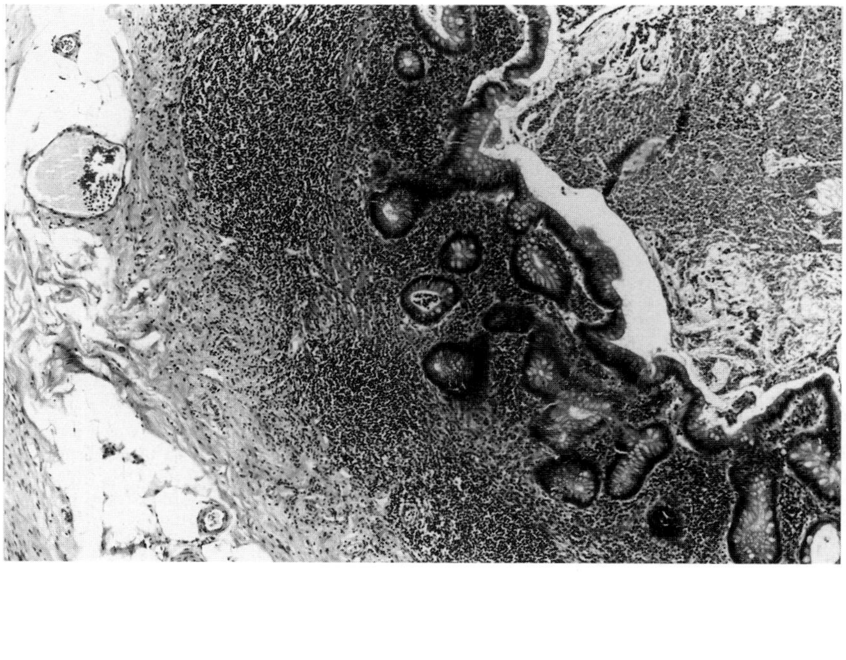

Fig. 28.7 In this case of longstanding ulcerative colitis, the typical glandular architectural abnormalities seen elsewhere in the colon are also evident in the appendix. The inflammation, as elsewhere, was predominantly mucosal. (H&E, ×96)

case of infectious mononucleosis showing characteristic changes in the appendiceal lymphoid tissue.[45]

Other non-granulomatous inflammatory conditions

Ulcerative colitis involves the appendix as mucosal inflammation in the majority of cases where a pancolitis is present. The histological features are the same as those seen in other parts of the colon (Fig. 28.7). Rupture and perforation have not been described.

COMPLICATIONS OF APPENDICITIS

The complications of acute appendicitis include rupture of the organ with the formation of localized abscesses or a generalized peritonitis. Heltberg et al suggest that acute appendicitis with pneumococcal infection may be the underlying pathology in so-called 'primary' pneumococcal peritonitis, and that the appendix should be examined in all these cases.[46] Fibrous adhesions are a late sequel.

The most common complications are wound and pelvic abscesses. Subphrenic abscess secondary to acute appendicitis also occurs,[47] and other rarer complications include gas gangrene of the abdominal wall following appendicectomy,[48] pyogenic liver abscess,[49] lumbar abscess,[50] and appendicocutaneous and appendicovesical fistula.[51,52] Infective thrombophlebitis, if present, may lead to hepatic abscess formation. Septicaemia, shock, disseminated intravascular coagulation and all their sequelae may also follow acute appendicitis.

REFERENCES

1. Berry J Jr, Malt RA. Appendicitis near its centenary. Ann Surg 1984; 200: 567–575.
2. Waldron R, Johnston JG. Appendicitis: 357 consecutive cases. Ir Med J 1983; 76: 446–448.
3. Collins DC. A study of 50,000 specimens of the human vermiform appendix. Surg Gynecol Obstet 1955; 437–445.
4. Chang AR. An analysis of the pathology of 3003 appendices. Aust NZ J Surg 1981; 51: 169–178.
5. Detmer DE, Frisch C. Improved results in acute appendicitis care following areawide review. Med Decis Making 1984; 3: 217–227.
6. Olinde AJ, Lucas JF Jr., Miller RC. Acute yersiniosis and its surgical significance. South Med J 1984; 77: 1539–1540.
7. Paris MF, Fraire AE, Pollack DS. Yersinia pseudoappendicitis — case report. Penn Med 1983; 86: 52–53.
8. Grussner R, Pistor G, Engelskirchen R, Hofmann-von Kapherr S. Appendicius in childhood. Monatsschr Kinderheilkd 1985; 133: 158–166.
9. Vinther S, Nielsen PL. Arteritis in the vermiform appendix. Report of a case interpreted as acute appendicitis. Ugeskr Laeger 1984; 146: 3132–3133.
10. Thompson JE Jr, Livesay JV, Dainko EA. Common pitfalls of the appendix. Am J Proctol Gastroenterol Colon Rectal Surg 1980; 31: 28–30.
11. Dymock RB. Pathological changes in the appendix: a review of 1000 cases. Pathology 1977; 9: 331–339.
12. Wangansteen OH, Bowers WF. Significance of the obstructive factor in the genesis of acute appendicitis. An experimental study. Arch Surg 1937; 496–562.
13. Burkitt DP. The aetiology of appendicitis. Br J Surg 1971; 58: 695–699.
14. Arnbjornsson E, Bengmark S. Role of obstruction in the pathogenesis of acute appendicitis. Am J Surg 1984; 147: 390–392.
15. Sisson RG, Ahlvin RC, Hartlow MC. Superficial mucosal ulceration and the pathogenesis of acute appendicitis in childhood. Am J Surg 1971; 122: 378–380.
16. Dhillon AP, Rode J. Serotonin and its possible role in the painful noninflamed appendix. Diagn Histopathol 1983; 6: 239–246.
17. Jess P. Acute appendicitis: epidemiology, diagnostic accuracy, and complications. Scand J Gastroenterol 1983; 18: 161–163.
18. Lau WY, Teoh-Chan CH, Fan ST, Yam WC, Lau KF, Wong SH. The bacteriology and septic complication of patients with appendicitis. Ann Surg 1984; 200: 576–581.
19. Miholic J, Riezinger F, Wurnig P. Metronidazole plus cefazolin versus cefazolin in gangrenous and perforated appendicitis in childhood — a prospective randomised trial. Z Kinderchir 1983; 38: 159–162.
20. Madden NP, Hart CA. Streptococcus milleri in appendicitis in children. J Pediatr Surg 1985; 20: 6–7.
21. O'Rourke MG, Wynne JM, Morahan RJ, Green AJ, Walker RM, Wilson ME. Prophylactic antibiotics in appendicectomy: a prospective double blind randomized study. Aust NZ J Surg 1984; 54: 535–541.
22. Tovar JA, Trallero EP, Garay J. Appendiceal perforation and shigellosis. Z Kinderchir 1983; 38: 419.
23. Chan FT, Stringel G, MacKenzie AM. Isolation of campylobacter jejuni from an appendix. J Clin Microbiol 1983; 18: 422–424.
24. Henrik-Nielsen R, Lundbeck FA, Stubbe Teglbjaerg P, Ginnerup P, Hovind-Hougen K. Intestinal spirochetosis of the vermiform appendix. Gastroenterology 1985; 88: 971–977.
25. Dorfman S, Rangel O, Bravo LG. Balantidiasis: report of a fatal case with appendicular and pulmonary involvement. Trans R Soc Trop Med Hyg 1984; 78: 833–834.
26. Scaramuzza P, Vincenti R, Valenti G, Sodaro AA. A case of primary Echinococcus cyst of the ileo-cecal appendix. Minerva Chir 1985; 40: 997–999.
27. Walker DH, Lesesne HR, Varma VA, Thacker WC. Rocky Mountain spotted fever mimicking acute cholecystitis. Arch Intern Med 1985; 145: 2194–2196.
28. Izimbergenov NI, Forafonova LN, Ostrovskii GK. Acute appendicitis of a subhepatic appendix. Khirurgiia (Moskva) 1984; 8: 32–35.
29. Abramson DJ. Vermiform appendix located within the cecal wall. Anomalies and bizarre locations. Dis Colon Rectum 1983; 26: 386–389.
30. Prabhu M, McCleary G, Tiwara AK. An unusual case of appendicitis. Med J Aust 1986; 144: 43.
31. Lassiter HA, Werner MH. Neonatal appendicitis. South Med J 1983; 76: 1173–1175.
32. Schorlemmer GR, Herbst CA Jr. Perforated neonatal appendicitis. South Med J 1983; 76: 536–537.
33. Martin LW, Glen PM. Prenatal appendiceal perforation: a case report. J Paediatr Surg 1986; 21: 73–74.
34. Amayand C. Of an inguinal rupture, with a pin in the appendix caeci, incrusted with stone, and some observations on wounds in the guts. Philos Trans R Soc London 1736; 39: 329–342.
35. McWhinney NA, Jarrett R. Uterine perforation by a Copper 7 intrauterine contraceptive device with subsequent penetration of the appendix. Case report. Br J Obstet Gynaecol 1983; 90: 774–776.
36. Goldman JA, Peleg D, Feldberg D, Dicker D, Samuel N. IUD appendicitis. Eur J Obstet Gynecol Reprod Biol 1983; 15: 181–183.
37. Moodley TR. Unusual displacement of an intrauterine contraceptive device: A case report. S Afr Med J 1984; 66: 110.
38. Soave F, D'Anna F, Magillo P, Pesce C. Histochemical enzymatic assessment of the human appendix at different ages. Arch Anat Histol Embryol (Strasb) 1984; 67: 43–56.
39. Weiland LH. Afflictions of the pesky appendix. Postgrad Med 1977; 61: 54–57, 60–62.

40. Walter JB, Israel MS. General Pathology, 5th Ed. Edinburgh: Churchill Livingstone, 1979: 125.
41. Binford CH, Connor DH, eds. Pathology of Tropical and extraordinary diseases. Vol. 2. AFIP Fasicle Series, 1976. Washington DC.
42. Sterba J, Vlcek M. Appendiceal enterobiasis — its incidence and relationships to appendicitis. Folia Parasitol (Praha) 1984; 31: 311–318.
43. Whitehead R. Mucosal biopsy of the gastrointestinal tract. 3rd Ed. Vol. 3 in the series: Major Problems in Pathology. Philadelphia: Saunders, 1985: pp 259–261.
44. Onuigbo WI. Appendiceal schistosomiasis. Method of classifying oviposition and inflammation. Dis Colon Rectum 1985; 28: 397–398.
45. O'Brien A, O'Briain DS. Infectious mononucleosis. Appendiceal lymphoid tissue involvement parallels characteristic lymph node changes. Arch Pathol Lab Med 1985; 109: 680–682.
46. Heltberg O, Korner B, Schouenborg P. Six cases of acute appendicitis with secondary peritonitis caused by Streptococcus pneumoniae. Eur J Clin Microbiol 1984; 3: 141–143.
47. van der Sluis RF. Subphrenic abscess. Surg Gynecol Obstet 1984; 158: 427–430.
48. Milani H, Lebec JC. Gas gangrene of the abdominal wall following appendicectomy. Acta Chir Belg 1983; 83: 266–268.
49. Sorensen MR, Baekgaard N, Kirkegaard P. Pyogenic liver abscess. A case report with a short review of current concepts of diagnosis and management. Acta Chir Scand 1983; 149: 437–439.
50. Turner G, Daniell SJ. Lumbar abscess resulting from appendicitis. J R Soc Med 1984; 77: 884–887.
51. Uccheddu A, Murgia C, Licheri S, Dazzi C, Cagetti M. Primary appendiculocutaneous fistula caused by appendicitis. Description of a case and review of the literature. Ann Chir 1984; 38: 216–219.
52. Haas GP, Shumaker BP, Haas PA. Appendicovesical fistula. Urology 1984; 24: 604–609.

PART II
The appendix: Crohn's disease

H. M. Gilmour

The appendix shows evidence of inflammation in about a quarter of patients with Crohn's disease of the neighbouring ileum or caecum, although Kahn et al[1] have reported abnormalities in all the appendices of 24 children with Crohn's disease and 17 with ulcerative colitis. This may take the form of a nonspecific inflammatory reaction resembling a rather indolent acute appendicitis, or, in a proportion of cases, the features will be typical of Crohn's disease. The appendix may also show features of Crohn's disease in the absence of local disease but with evidence of disease elsewhere in the gut, e.g. the anus or rectum.

In a small number of cases,[2] patients with symptoms of acute appendicitis have histological features in the operative specimens which suggest Crohn's disease when there is no evidence of concurrent involvement of other areas of the gastrointestinal tract. The first such case was reported by Meyerding and Bertram[3] in 1953, and in 1983 Allen and Biggart[4] reported a series of 19 cases seen over a 20-year period in Belfast. In 10 out of the 15 cases where information was available, the clinical diagnosis was acute appendicitis, and Ruiz et al[5] drew attention to a more prolonged clinical presentation of appendicitis in patients with Crohn's disease affecting the appendix. In the Belfast series, there were no findings at laparotomy which could predict the diagnosis, but histological examination in all revealed increased appendiceal diameter, ulceration, transmural inflammation and granulomas. Indeed, these were the principal features used in reaching the diagnosis.

Granulomas may be seen in the appendix in a number of circumstances other than Crohn's disease, including sarcoidosis, tuberculosis and foreign body reactions, such as may occur in response to parasites or their ova. They can also be found occasionally, especially in children, as an apparently isolated phenomenon, in that there is no association with other causes of granulomas, and follow-up is uneventful.[1]

Transmural inflammation is common in acute appendicitis but the inflammatory infiltrate is predominantly of neutrophil polymorphs, whereas the inflammation in Crohn's disease is usually lymphocytic, often focal and associated with mural thickening (Fig. 28.8). It is the latter feature, leading to an increased appendiceal diameter, which should make the surgeon or pathologist think of Crohn's disease.

It is somewhat surprising that in the above series from Belfast, a similar series of 14 cases from North America,[6] 22 cases from Israel[7] and the three cases from Copenhagen[2] so few patients developed further evidence of Crohn's disease elsewhere in the gastrointestinal tract. This seems at variance with the experience of Crohn's disease elsewhere in the gut and it is also of interest that none of the cases in these four series developed a fistula

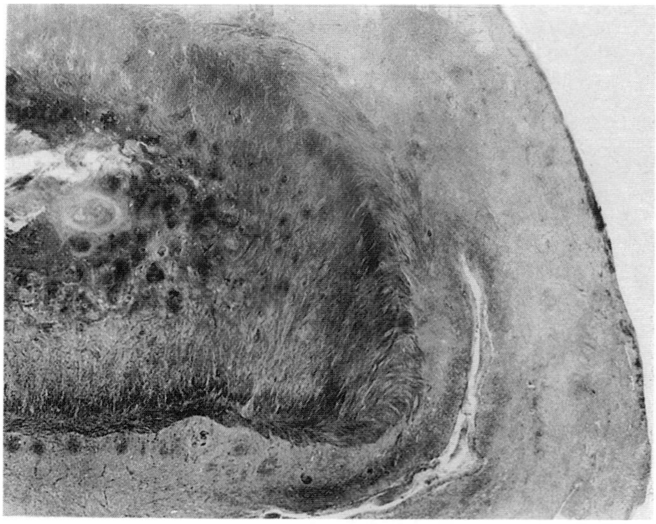

Fig. 28.8 Section from the tip of the appendix showing mural thickening with marked subserosal inflammation including fibrosis, lymphocytic aggregates and a tracking fissuring ulcer. (H&E, ×5.4)

at the operation site, a complication which has been the reason, in the past, for the reluctance to perform appendicectomy in ileocaecal Crohn's disease.

While it is possible that there is another aetiological agent which in the appendix results in a histological appearance mimicking Crohn's disease, there is at present no evidence to support this contention, although the failure to develop Crohn's disease elsewhere in the alimentary tract adds some credence to this view.[7] However, although the diagnosis of primary Crohn's disease of the appendix should continue to be made on the basis of the features described, other causes of a similar inflammatory response should be considered and, where possible, excluded.

REFERENCES

1. Kahn E, Markowitz J, Daum F. The appendix in inflammatory bowel disease in children. Mod Pathol 1992; 5: 380–383.
2. Wettergen A, Munkholm P, Larsen LG et al. Granulomas of the appendix: is it Crohn's disease? Scand J Gastro 1991; 26: 961–964.
3. Meyerding EV, Bertram HF. Non specific granulomatous inflammation (Crohn's disease) of the appendix. Surgery 1953; 34: 891–894.
4. Allen DC, Biggart JD. Granulomatous disease in the vermiform appendix. J Clin Pathol 1983; 36: 632–638.
5. Ruiz V, Unger SW, Morgan J, Wallack MK. Crohn's disease of the appendix. Surgery 1990; 107: 113–117.
6. Yang SS, Gibson P, McCaughey RS, Arcari FA, Bernstein J. Primary Crohn's disease of the appendix. Ann Surg 1979; 189: 334–339.
7. Ariel A, Vinograd I, Hershlag A et al. Crohn's disease isolated to the appendix: truths and fallacies. Hum Pathol 1986; 17: 1116–1121.

CHAPTER 29

The anal region: specific and nonspecific inflammatory lesions

F. D. Lee

An awareness of the anatomical characteristics of this region is essential to understanding the inflammatory and circulatory disturbances with which it is all too often afflicted. There are several reasons for this high rate of morbidity. First, conditions which affect other parts of the intestinal tract, and in particular inflammatory bowel disease, often involve the anorectal region and indeed may initially declare their presence in this area; secondly, the trauma accompanying disorders of defaecation is a common source of nonspecific inflammation; and thirdly, the anal canal, by virtue of its termination in a mucocutaneous junction, is unduly susceptible to the infections which complicate neutropenic states and, in particular, acute leukaemia of granulocytic type.[1]

A further factor of increasing importance is the recognition that active male homosexuals are unduly susceptible to anorectal disease. This is mainly due to trauma which is associated with proctogenital sexual contact or the introduction into the anal canal of a variety of foreign bodies for the purposes of sexual gratification, and produces a high incidence of nonspecific lesions such as anal fistula, anorectal abscess, haemorrhoids, anal fissure and ulcerative lesions both in the anal canal and rectum, including the solitary ulcer syndrome.[2,3] There is, however, also a high risk of sexually transmitted infection including not only the classical venereal diseases such as syphilis, gonorrhoea and lymphogranuloma venereum (LGV), but also other infections not usually included in this category, such as amoebiasis[4,8] shigellosis,[2] salmonellosis,[5] campylobacter infections,[6] non-LGV chlamydial infection[7] and giardiasis.[8] The incidence of intestinal spirochaetosis is also greatly increased in male homosexuals.[9] Of even greater importance is the transmission of viral diseases including those due to human papilloma virus (condyloma acuminatum), herpes simplex,[10] hepatitis B[9] and HIV.[5] The last mentioned, of course, is now recognized to be the cause of the acquired immune deficiency syndrome (AIDS) which in turn may predispose the affected individual to opportunistic intestinal infections, with, for example, cytomegalovirus[11] or atypical mycobacteria.[12] Moreover, infections such as cryptosporidiosis, which are usually mild in normal people, tend to be much more severe in immunocompromized individuals.[13] This remarkable spectrum of anorectal disease (which may also include anal neoplasia)[14] in male homosexuals is sometimes referred to as the 'gay bowel syndrome' — an indelicate term which nonetheless draws the attention of clinicians to the wider social and epidemiological implications of disease of this kind in the community.

ANAL ULCERATION

The most common form of ulcer found in the anal canal is the condition referred to clinically as anal fissure. Unqualified, this term is usually taken to indicate a form of ulceration which is probably related to trauma, has a distinctive appearance and location and shows nonspecific histological changes as described in greater detail below. Even if an ulcer exhibits all the pathological features of a fissure, however, the possibility that it might be caused by some other aetiological factor or related to some recognized clinical syndrome must always be borne in mind and both clinician and pathologist must be aware of the diagnostic alternatives — the more so with the advent of the 'gay bowel syndrome' in recent years. A summary of these alternatives is therefore considered to be appropriate here: the more important are discussed in separate sections.

Infective anal ulceration has undergone mixed fortunes in recent years. Tuberculosis, formerly a troublesome cause of anal ulceration, is now uncommon, nevertheless it should always be considered in the diagnosis of ulcers which are irregular in shape, discoloured or undermined and may or may not be associated with fistula formation. On the other hand, the classic sexually transmitted diseases such as syphilis and gonorrhoea have re-emerged as important causes of anorectal erosion or ulceration and chlamydial infection, including lymphogranuloma venereum, is also becoming more prevalent. In tropical or subtropical zones, it has to be remembered that granuloma inguinale, caused by the Gram negative bacillus *Calymmatobacterium* (formerly *Klebsiella*) *granulomatis* may produce ulcerating nodular lesions in the distal anal canal or perianal region, especially in male homosexuals. Histologically, the lesions show lymphoplasmacytic infiltration associated with swollen histiocytes which can, in some instances, be shown with stains such as Giemsa to contain intracytoplasmic encapsulated organisms (Donovan bodies). Chancroid, another venereal infection rarely seen outside the tropics, is caused by *Haemophilus ducreyi* and may likewise produce ulcerating or vesicular perianal lesions; the inflammatory changes, however, are histologically nonspecific. Of the viral infections, herpes simplex is undoubtedly pre-eminent as a cause of anal and perianal ulceration, the latter being especially severe in immunocompromized individuals.[15]

The importance of idiopathic inflammatory bowel disease as a cause of anorectal disturbance cannot be overemphasized. In Crohn's disease, the incidence of anorectal complications is nearly 50%[16] and may take the form of either anal ulcers or perianal fistulae. The ulcers tend to be larger than traumatic fissures, are more often multiple or randomly distributed, and show oedematous undermined edges with purplish discolouration of the surrounding anal skin. Perianal skin tags also tend to be unusually prominent. The mucosa of the upper anal canal and lower rectum may also be clearly abnormal, as discussed elsewhere. Anal complications are less common in ulcerative colitis, the incidence being about 18%.[16] Ulcers and fistulae may nonetheless be troublesome. The pathological features, however, are nonspecific; the diagnosis must therefore rest upon the appearances in rectal biopsies.

It should be recalled that anal or perianal ulceration may be a feature of the mucocutaneous syndromes, especially Behcets disease,[17] which may also cause extensive ulceration in the small or large intestine, and the Stevens Johnson syndrome.[18] Fissuring of the anal verge may also develop in skin diseases such as intertrigo or lichen sclerosus et atrophicus.

Of the remaining causes of anal ulceration, two deserve special mention. First, there is neutropenia, most often related to acute granulocytic leukaemia, which may provoke perianal or perirectal infective lesions, such as abscesses, fistulae and fissures.[1,19] Secondly, of course, there is neoplasia, discussed in detail elsewhere. Suffice to say here that this should be suspected in any instance where ulceration is either unexplained or proves refractory to treatment and, in particular, when the ulcer margins are indurated, raised nodular or pigmented.

Many of the conditions mentioned above are capable of producing ulceration in the distal rectum as well as in the anal canal. There are, however, some additional forms of ulceration which more selectively involve the distal rectum and are worth mentioning here since they may enter into the diagnostic assessment of the 'gay bowel syndrome' and anorectal inflammation generally. Of particular importance is the solitary ulcer syndrome which is closely associated with mucosal prolapse but may also be related to trauma, and has been observed in active male homosexuals.[3] The diagnosis rests upon the characteristic histological appearance in a rectal biopsy. Drugs administered in the form of suppositories are also capable of producing rectal ulceration, indomethacin being the most notable example (Fig. 29.1).

NONSPECIFIC INFLAMMATORY LESIONS

Anal fissure

This term is reserved for a nonspecific longitudinally disposed type of ulcer which commonly arises in the distal part of the anal canal and usually extends from the pectinate line to the anal verge. In over 70% of cases it is located posteriorly. While a specific cause has not been identified, it is generally assumed that the lesion is a traumatic tear produced by stretching of the distal anal canal during the passage of hard bulky faeces. There is frequently a history of constipation. Anal intercourse and the introduction of foreign material may have a similar effect. Sometimes fissures arise in the postpartum state (when they tend to be located anteriorly) or follow anal operations such as haemorrhoidectomy.[20] As described above, ulcerating lesions resembling anal fissures may also be secondary to known conditions, especially inflammatory bowel disease; in such instances they may develop in any quadrant of the anal canal.

While the ulcerative process tends initially to be superficial, in chronic cases it may penetrate to a depth such as to expose transverse fibres of the internal sphincter. Consequent spasm of this muscle may be an important factor in the delayed healing which typifies the condition. The distal extremity of a fissure involves anal skin which may become swollen and inflamed to produce the so-called sentinel pile; this may undergo fibrosis at a later phase to leave a permanent skin tag. The proximal end may likewise be capped by an inflamed anal papilla. The edges of a

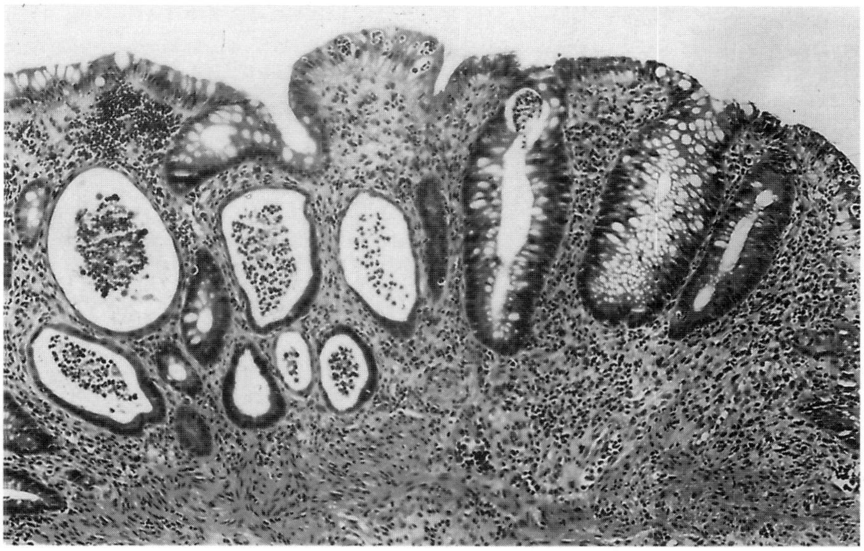

Fig. 29.1 Drug-induced proctitis. Acute mucosal inflammation with crypt abscess formation in a rectal biopsy taken following the administration of an indomethacin suppository. (×121)

fissure may, to some extent, be undermined and this reflects a tendency for infection to spread from the fissure with the formation of perianal abscesses or sinuses, especially at the distal edge. Occasionally this process goes further with the development of a posteriorly located subcutaneous fistula.

Histologically, the appearance of the usual type of fissure is entirely nonspecific: the ulcerating surface showing a thin layer of fibrinopurulent exudate while the margins show lymphoplasmocytic infiltration with fibrosis of variable degree. When biopsies are taken from fissures, however, the possibility that the lesion might be of a secondary nature, e.g. to Crohn's disease, must always be considered; this problem is discussed in greater detail in relation to fistulae.

Anorectal abscesses

Foci of suppuration commonly develop in the anorectal region, especially in males in the third or fourth decades of life. While an obvious precipitating cause can seldom be demonstrated, it is reasonable to suppose that the initial event, in some instances at least, is probably a breach in the epithelial lining of the anal canal which becomes exploited by enteric microorganisms, notably *Eschericha coli*. Some abscesses are related, e.g. to anal fissures, ruptured anal haematomas or ulcerated haemorrhoids. The most prevalent, if not universally accepted, hypothesis, however, is that the usual initial event is either infection of the lymphoid tissue of an anal gland[21] or trauma-related inflammation of an anal crypt (cryptitis) with ascending infection of an anal gland; either event enables an inflammatory process not only to persist but to gain access to the deeper layers of the anal wall. Individuals with impairment of the inflammatory response, most notably due to diabetes mellitus or neutropenia, are, as one might expect, unduly susceptible to lesions of this kind.

Of course, in a minority of cases perianal abscesses are related to idiopathic inflammatory bowel disease (especially Crohn's disease) or to infective diseases such as tuberculosis, lymphogranuloma venereum or actinomycosis. The tendency of these conditions to involve the anal region may also be explained by their predilection for lymphoid tissue.[21]

Anorectal abscesses may be found in a variety of sites. Most appear to originate in the intersphincteric plane and spread downwards into the perianal space (perianal abscess). Occasionally, spread takes place proximally beyond the pectinate line and even into the rectal wall. Another important type is the ischiorectal abscess, which develops outside the external sphincter in the ischiorectal fossa, a space within the deep tissues of the buttock beneath the levator ani.

Anorectal abscesses and fistulae are intimately associated and probably represent differing expressions of the same basic disease process. The histological features are thus similar and are discussed in detail below.

Perianal fistula

By definition, a fistula is a pathological track or channel linking two epithelial surfaces. In a perianal fistula, the surfaces involved are those of the perianal skin and the lower rectum or anal canal. Since it is thought that in most instances the lesion arises as a consequence of anorectal suppuration, the same aetiological considerations apply.

The various types of fistulae and the pathways they pursue are intimately related to the sites of the anorectal abscesses from which they usually develop. Most common are the low (intersphincteric) fistulae. These arise internally at the level of the pectinate line or more distally and reach the perianal skin by penetrating the distal part of the internal sphincter, passing down the intersphincteric plane and tracking below the subcutaneous part of the external sphincter. Less common are high (transsphincteric) fistulae; these have an internal opening at the pectinate line or higher in the anal canal but penetrate both sphincters and traverse the ischiorectal fossa before reaching the perianal skin. Occasionally, fistulous tracts extend above the anorectal ring, usually as blind sacs from high fistulae; only rarely is there an internal opening into the rectum (anorectal fistulae). Subcutaneous fistulae, which lie just below the mucosa or cutaneous lining of the distal anal canal, are rare; if they occur at all they are usually related to anal fissures.

In the common nonspecific types of perianal fistula, histological examination shows a track lined by a layer of neutrophils and incorporating faecal debris and some fibrin overlying granulation tissue which is infiltrated by lymphocytes and plasma cells to a variable degree. Eosinophils may also be quite numerous. More peripherally, there is fibrous scar tissue within which it is often possible to find evidence of muscle damage with a sarcolemmal reaction. There may also be a good deal of foreign body giant cell formation in response to the presence of faecal matter (Fig. 29.2) and occasionally a histiocytic reaction to lubricating materials introduced inadvertantly by clinicians. Reactions of this kind usually take place close to the surface of a fistulous tract but may arise more deeply. In either event they must be distinguished from the granulomatous lesions of Crohn's disease, which are characterized by the aggregation of epithelioid histiocytes in addition to giant cells. The latter may contain inclusions such as conchoid (Fig. 29.3) or asteroid bodies which are usually distinctive enough to avoid being mistaken for faecal matter. Even so it cannot be over-stressed that Crohn's disease can only be confidently diagnosed in the perianal region when the epithelioid cell granulomas can be demonstrated at some distance from fistulous tracts and preferably beneath an intact epithelial covering (Fig. 29.4).

The same remarks apply, of course, to tuberculosis. This may well have been mistaken for Crohn's disease in the past and more so in the absence of caseation. It is always important nevertheless to look diligently for acid fast bacilli (AFB) in granulomatous lesions and if there is good reason to suspect tuberculosis, even in the absence of AFB or caseation, culture of fresh biopsy material is advised.

Actinomycosis should be suspected when (a) granulomas show central suppuration, and (b) there is an unusual abundance of foamy histocytes. If necessary serial sections should be examined with the appropriate stains in order to exclude the presence of the diagnostic bacterial colonies.

Chlamydial disease may also show a granulomatous reaction in fistulae, but this is unusual; when suspected, serological studies are advocated since the organisms are difficult to find histologically.

Perianal fistulae may be mistaken clinically for the condition known as suppurative hidradenitis, an infective process related to the perianal apocrine sweat glands. The distinction can also be difficult histologically; the presence of abscess formation plainly related to sweat glands may help to resolve the difficulty. Moreover, the sinuses that complicate this process may be lined by squamous epithelium. Occasionally a pilonidal sinus may extend close to the anus and resemble a perianal fistula: the histological demonstration of hair shaft remnants embedded within the sinus tract is regarded as diagnostic of the former condition.

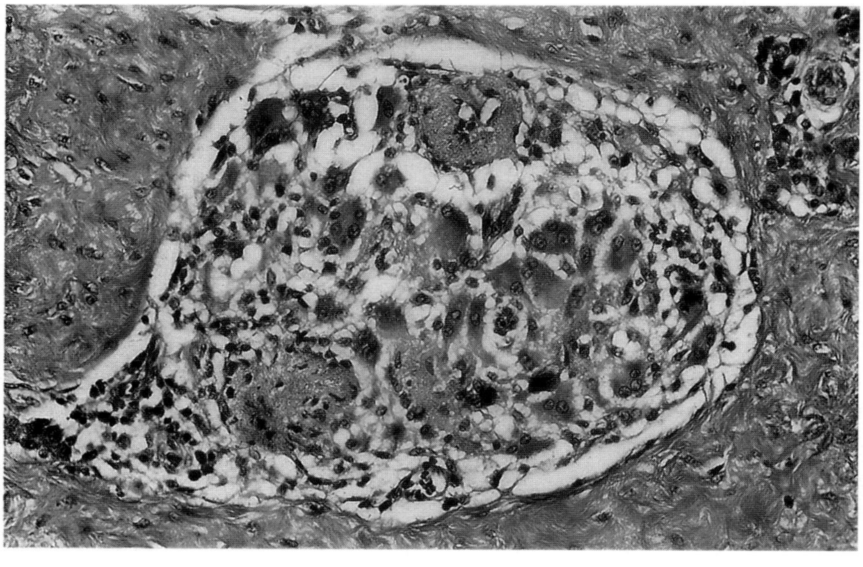

Fig. 29.2 Perianal fistula. Pronounced foreign body giant cell reaction in the scar tissue surrounding a fistulous tract. Note the absence of epithelioid cells (cf. Crohn's disease, Fig. 29.3). (×192)

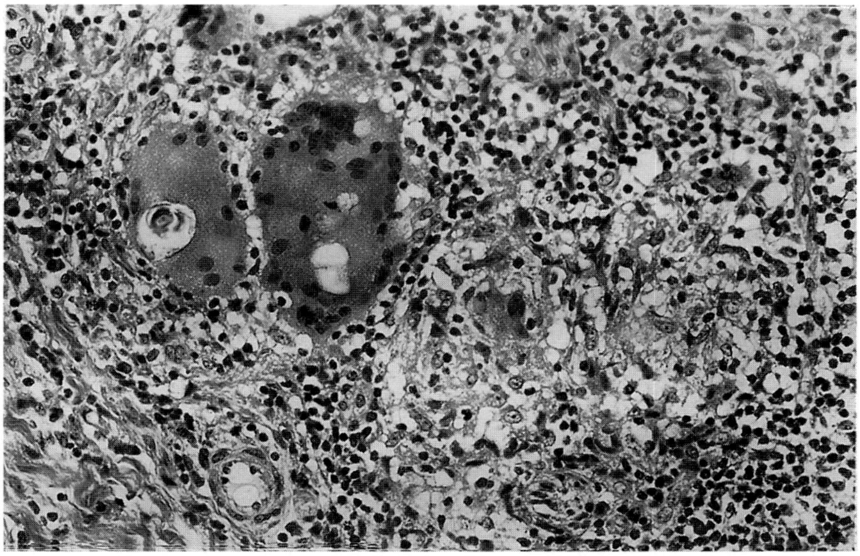

Fig. 29.3 Crohn's disease. In this epithelioid granuloma related to fistulous tract there is a giant cell of Langhans type containing a conchoid body. (×247)

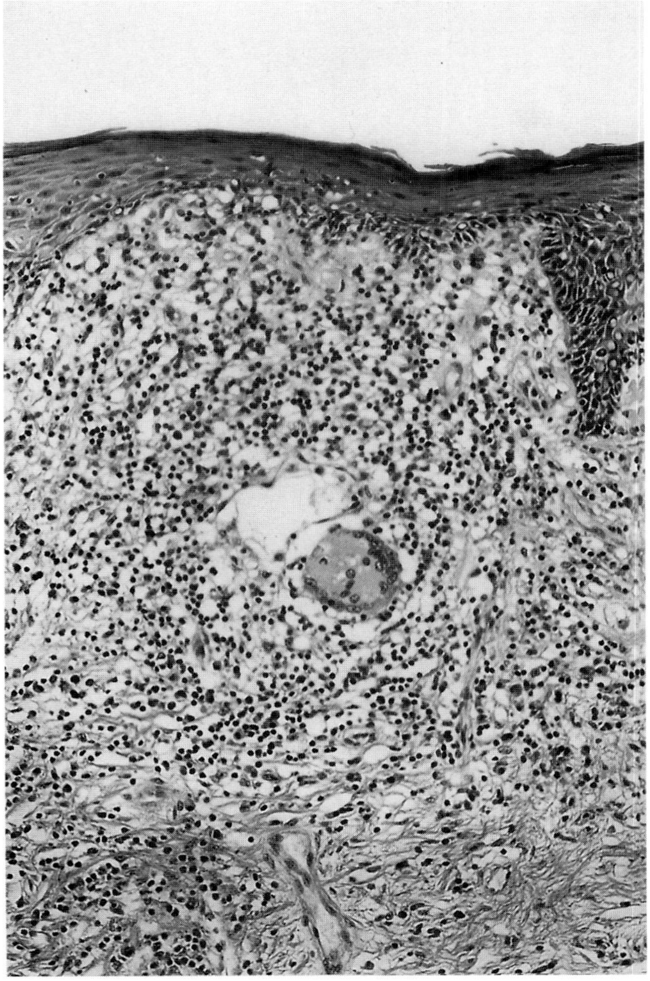

Fig. 29.4 Crohn's disease. An epithelioid granuloma is seen just beneath the epithelial lining of the distal anal canal. (×138)

Lastly, it should be mentioned that there is a distinctive form of anorectal adenocarcinoma which is characterized by the formation of multiple perianal fistulae which leak mucin in large quantities from the perineum. The unexpected presence of unusually well differentiated glandular epithelium within a fistulous tract should lead one to suspect this condition.

SPECIFIC INFECTIONS

Anorectal gonorrhoea

This is perhaps the commonest sexually transmitted infection in homosexual males. In both clinical and pathological terms the condition is often unimpressive in the anorectal region and many patients are asymptomatic. Proctoscopically, the anorectal mucosa appears normal in over 80% of cases,[22] and the generalized redness of the mucosa with superficial erosions (but not frank ulceration), as initially described by Harkness,[23] is not often seen. When present, changes are confined to the distal rectum and upper anal canal within a distance of 10 cm from the anal margin.[21]

Histologically, Harkness[23] described severe changes such as epithelial disorganization and degeneration in the rectal mucosa, the anal canal being affected to a lesser extent and probably secondarily. Recent biopsy studies have failed to reveal such changes.[9,22] In one of these, the rectal mucosa was found to be normal in over 50% of cases, the remainder usually showing only an increase in plasma cells (mainly of IgA secreting type) and lymphocytes in the lamina propria or, at most, neutrophil infiltration extending into the cryptal or surface epithelium.[22] The latter changes are essentially similar to those seen in other infective forms of colitis which may also, of course, be sexually transmitted. They may also resemble early inflammatory bowel disease; the importance of microbiological investigation of any inflammatory process in the anorectal mucosa thus cannot be overemphasized. It is worth noting that not all anorectal infections caused by Gram negative cocci are gonococcal in origin: *Neisseria meningitidis* has been implicated on occasion.[22,24]

Syphilitic proctitis

It is probable that in western societies most cases of syphilis are homosexually transmitted and it is therefore not surprising that the primary chancre is commonly encountered either at the anal verge or within the lower rectum or anal canal.[25] These sites, including rectum, may also be affected during the secondary stage.[9] Proctoscopically, the appearances in rectum vary: in the primary form the changes may be diffuse or multifocal and they are usually indurative, and if there is accompanying ulceration neoplasia may be suspected. Mucosal oedema and loss of vascular pattern for a distance of up to 20 cm may be seen in the secondary stage.[9] The anal lesions are similar and may on occasion resemble anal fissure. Of course, the classical condyloma lata of the secondary stage may also be seen in the perianal region.

Histologically, the appearances in a rectal biopsy during the early stages of syphilis are distinctive (Fig. 29.5). Most notably, there is intense lymphoplasmocytic infiltration of the lamina propria with the development of small aggregates of epithelial histiocytes. These microgranulomatous lesions may be related to vascular channels which often show pronounced endothelial swelling. An inflammatory vasculitis may also be found in the submucosa.[26] The crypts tend to be compressed and there may be neutrophil infiltration into both the cryptal and surface epithelium.[9] Crypt abscesses are not usually seen and when found may indicate the presence of infective agents other than *Treponema pallidum*.[26] Occasionally *T. pallidum* can be identified in sections stained by the Warthin-Starry technique.

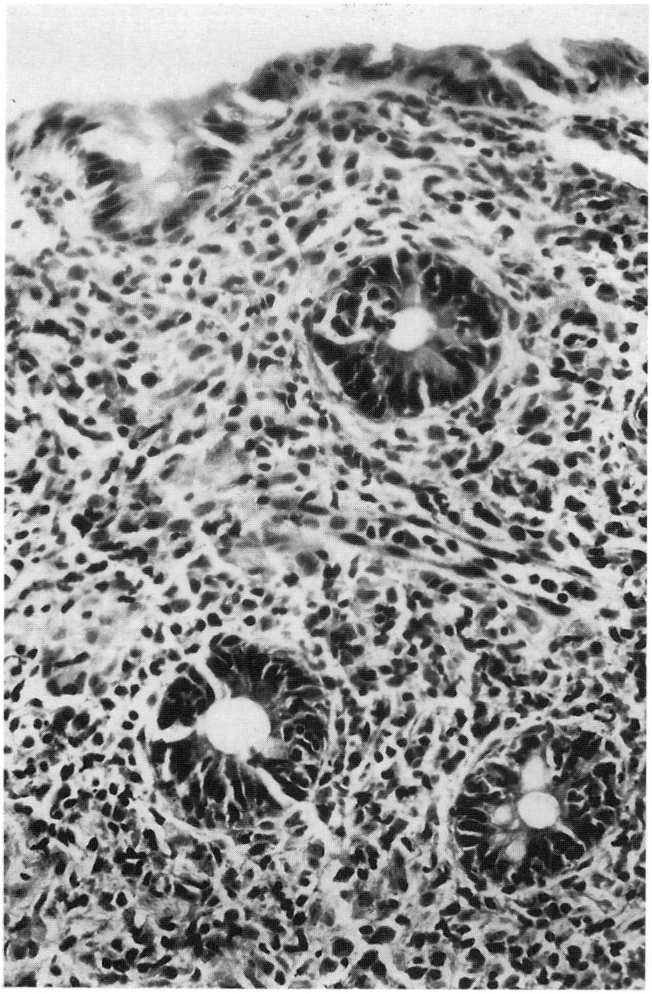

Fig. 29.5 Syphilitic proctitis. There is intense lymphoplasmocytic infiltration of the rectal mucosa with the formation of small epithelioid granulomas related in places to blood vessels. (×250)

Chlamydial infections

Chlamydia trachomatis is an important cause of sexually transmitted proctogenital disease. The immunotypes L1, L2 and L3 are responsible for lymphogranuloma venereum (LGV), which in the past was recognized mainly as an infection of the genital tract with, as a rule, only secondary involvement of the anorectal region, especially in women. It was generally thought that this was due to perirectal lymphatic spread from the vulva or vagina or to direct extension of the disease from the vagina. The introduction into the rectum of infected vaginal discharge as a result of anal intercourse or, indeed, primary infection by the same mechanism now seems a more probable explanation, the more so since it has become apparent that LGV immunotypes of *C. trachomatis* can also cause a severe primary proctitis in male homosexuals.[27] Non-LGV immunotypes D–K may also cause proctitis in similar circumstances but this tends to be less severe than LGV and is sometimes asymptomatic.[7]

Proctoscopically, the rectum in the acute phase of LGV may be severely inflamed with friable haemorrhagic and ulcerated mucosa. In the later phase, the rectal wall becomes thickened and fibrotic leading to progressive narrowing with eventual stricture formation. Perirectal abscesses with fistula formation involving adjacent structures such as bladder or vagina may also be observed in untreated cases.[28] In non-LGV chlamydial proctitis, the mucosal changes are less severe with perhaps some oedema and congestion and, at most, superficial erosions.[7]

Histologically, rectal biopsies in LGV have shown diffuse inflammatory infiltration of the lamina propria with crypt abscess formation which in some instances is related to pericryptal epithelioid-cell granuloma formation. Giant cells can be conspicuous and the appearances closely resemble the mucosal lesions of colorectal Crohn's disease.[7] This resemblance may be reinforced by the presence of rectal strictures or fistula formation, emphasizing the need for microbiological or serological investigation of putative IBD.

Lymph nodes, usually in the inguinal region but sometimes elsewhere, are commonly involved in LGV and may present histological features which are distinctive if not diagnostic. Most notable is the presence of irregularly shaped granulomatous lesions in which there is a central zone of necrosis and suppuration bordered by a mantle of palisaded epithelioid histiocytes, an appearance similar to that observed in yersinial infections and cat scratch disease. In non-LGV chlamydial proctitis, the mucosal lesions are less impressive, with often only a few neutrophils in the lamina propria and at most the occasional crypt abscess.[7]

Intestinal spirochaetosis (IS)

This condition is characterized by the presence of spirochaetal organisms located on the epithelial surface of the human large intestine. These organisms have not been formally identified. At first they were tentatively assigned to the species Borrelia:[29] more recently, however, it has been suggested that at least two different organisms might be implicated,[30] the small (and more common) being identified as *Brachyspira aalborgii*.[31] While the incidence of this phenomenon in normal individuals is difficult to assess, it has been found in approximately 7% of unselected rectal biopsies from both males and females in the West of Scotland[32] and more recently in 3% of normal rectal biopsies from males aged 50 years or less. In a comparable population of active male homosexuals, the incidence was found to be twelve times greater, i.e. 36%.[9] Presumably in this context, at least, IS is sexually transmitted. There is no convincing evidence, however, that the phenomenon has any pathogenic effect despite occasional reports of spirochaetes being isolated from homosexuals with rectal symptoms.[33,34] The main importance of IS is that if it is found in a biopsy, it may indicate that the patient has a lifestyle which might be associated with more clinically important sexually transmitted infection.

Histologically, IS can be readily recognized in H&E paraffin sections of colorectal biopsies as a distinct haematoxyphilic zone, in most instances measuring approximately 3 μm in depth, occupying the site of the brush border of the surface epithelium but seldom extending more deeply than the upper parts of the crypts (Fig. 29.6). Occasionally, a broader zone penetrating more deeply into the crypts is observed.[35] With some haematoxylins, the brush border itself stains blue but is seldom more than 1 μm in depth. Electron microscopy shows that the organisms are sustained in an upright position (i.e. at right angles to the epithelial surface) by the embrace of surrounding microvilli and it is notable that the organisms do not flourish on the abnormal surface of dysplastic epithelium. It is yet to be clearly shown that the epithelium is transgressed by the organisms or that any mucosal abnormality can be attributed to their presence. Even so, it is worth mentioning that luminal (but not systemic) antibiotics rapidly eradicate IS, thus accounting for the virtual absence of IS in 'cold' large bowel resections.

Viral infection

As mentioned above, several viruses gain entrance into the body by penetrating the anorectal mucosa; others produce

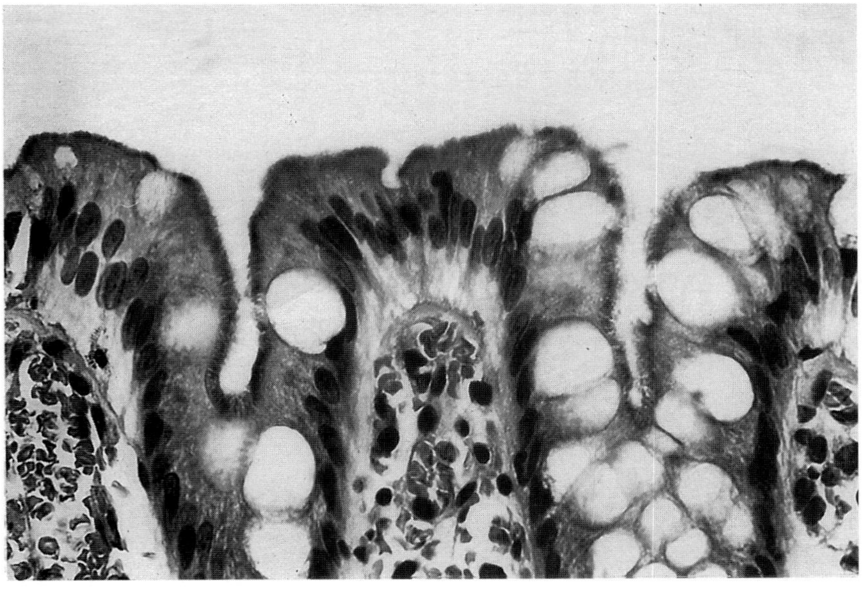

Fig. 29.6 Intestinal spirochaetosis. The condition is recognized by a thick furry haematoxyphilic zone occupying the site of the brush border of the surface epithelium in this rectal biopsy. (×483)

distinctive lesions in this area and four of these are of particular importance.

The herpes simplex virus (especially type 2) is becoming increasingly recognized as a cause not only of perianal ulceration, but also of proctitis, especially in young sexually active male homosexuals. In most cases, the disease process is confined to the distal 10 cm of the rectum and is not associated with lesions elsewhere, apart from the inguinal lymph nodes. Sigmoidoscopically, the most notable feature is mucosal friability; less often, diffuse ulceration develops and only occasionally are discrete vesicular lesions found.[10]

Histologically, rectal biopsies as a rule are either normal[9] or show only minor non-specific changes with a diffuse increase in plasma cells and lymphocytes in the lamina propria mucosae. More acute changes have been described in some cases and, in particular, neutrophil emigration into the lamina propria with crypt abscess formation and perivascular lymphocyte cuffing. Only in a minority of instances is the viral nature of the lesions revealed by the presence of either multinucleated cells or intranuclear inclusions.[10] In the diagnosis of this condition, it must be borne in mind that it is frequently accompanied by other infections.

Lesions caused by the cytomegalovirus are frequently found throughout the alimentary tract in homosexual men[36] and in immunocompromized individuals generally, and are especially common in the anorectal region in patients with AIDS. Both perianal ulcers[37] and proctitis have been described. In the latter location there are ulcerative lesions which may penetrate deeply into the bowel wall, and some may be covered by a pseudomembrane.[38] Histologically, the characteristic CMV inclusions are usually to be found in epithelial cells in the vicinity of ulcerative lesions. Inclusions may also be seen in endothelial cells, especially in deeply penetrating ulcers. In cases where the diagnosis is in doubt, immunocytochemistry using CMV antibodies is unquestionably of value, even in paraffin sections.

Condyloma acuminatum is a highly infectious lesion which is now known to be caused by the human papilloma viruses (HPV) of the subtypes 6, 11, 16 and 18, which are apparently specific for the urogenital tract.[39] The condition is usually sexually transmitted and subtype 6 commonly affects the perianal skin. It may, however, arise within the squamous epithelium of the distal part of the anal canal and even as high as the squamocolumnar junction, particularly in homosexuals. To the naked eye it appears as a soft knuckle-like papule which may enlarge into a vegetative mass.

Histologically, the lesion is characterized by pronounced thickening of the rete ridges with acanthosis and papillomatosis (Fig. 29.7). This is associated with parakeratosis if the condition arises in the lower part of the anal canal or slight thickening of the corneal zone if the anal skin itself is involved. The maturation of the affected epithelium is usually orderly although this may to some extent be obscured by basal cell hyperplasia or the presence of koilocytotic atypia in cells of the malpighian layer. This last feature is important diagnostically and identified by irregular crumpling of the nuclear outline associated with perinuclear clearing or vacuolation (Fig. 29.8). It must not be confused with the normal basket-weave appearance of non-keratinizing squamous epithelium in which the nuclei are normal. The epithelial cells may also show multinuclearity and focal dyskeratosis and eosinophilic intranuclear inclusions may be detectable in some cases. There is usually some subepithelial inflammatory infil-

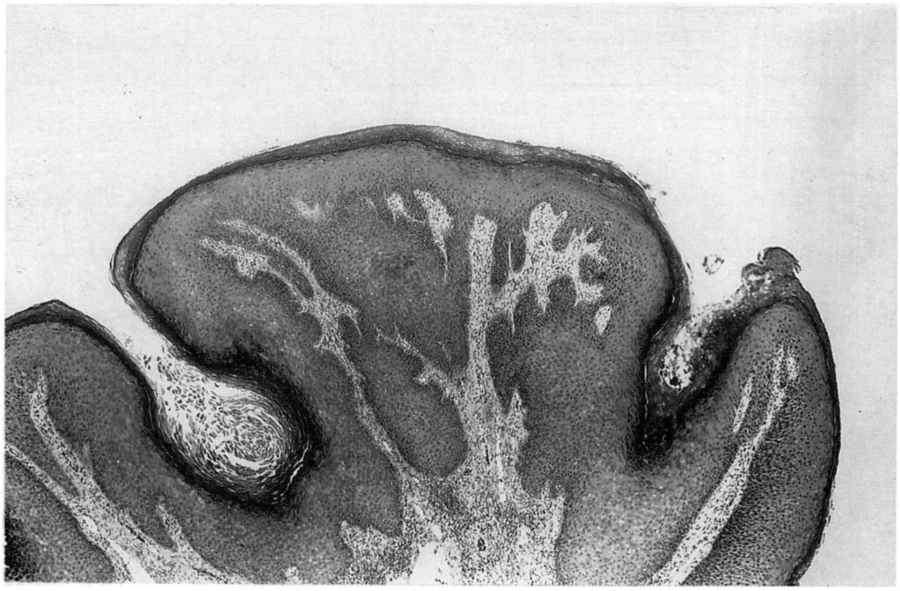

Fig. 29.7 Condyloma acuminatum. There is marked thickening of the rete ridges of the mucosa of the distal anal canal, with acanthosis, and papillomatosis. (×144)

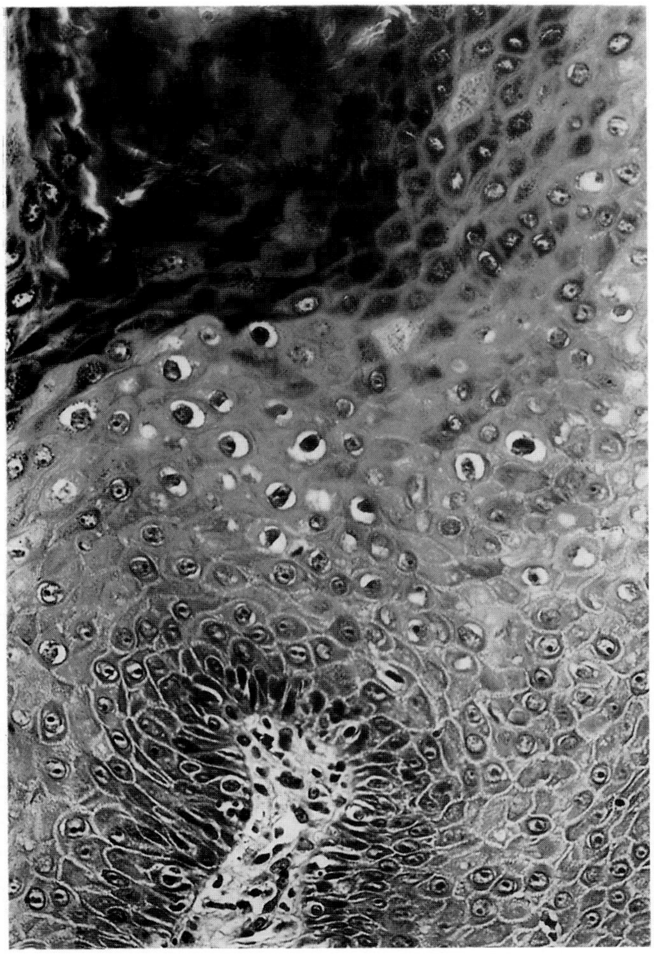

Fig. 29.8 Condyloma acuminatum. A small focus of koilocytosis is present. (×280)

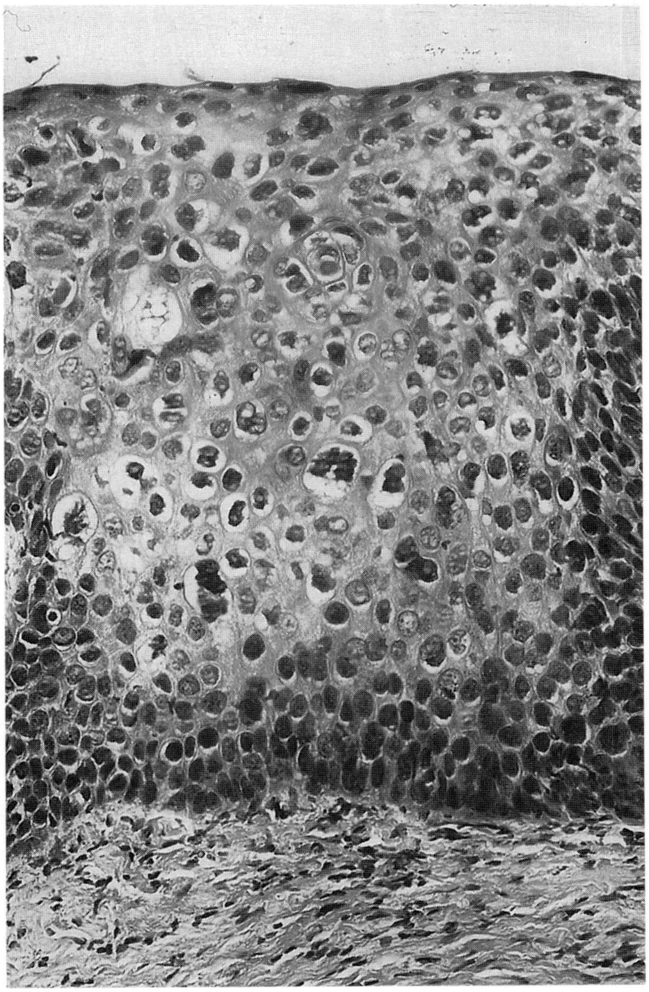

Fig. 29.9 Condyloma acuminatum. In this instance koilocytosis and epithelial multinuclearity are associated with severe epithelial atypia and maturation disturbance, suggestive of intraepithelial neoplasia. (×252)

tration. While it is unlikely that the irregular acanthosis which typifies condyloma acuminatum would be mistaken for a malignant process, squamous carcinoma does occasionally arise as a complication.[40] Sometimes one may also encounter epithelial alterations such as hyperchromatism, pleomorphism, maturation disturbance and atypical mitotic activity (Fig. 29.9), the appearances closely resembling the intra-epithelial neoplasia or carcinoma in situ,[41] often associated with HPV infection in the cervix uteri. Careful follow-up is advocated in cases of this kind. It is to be noted that infections associated with HPV subtypes 6 and 11 have little if any malignant potential: at most they might be associated with low grade dysplasia.[42] High grade lesions are more likely to be associated with HPV16.[42,43] The condition sometimes referred to as 'giant condyloma' of Buschke and Loewenstein is, despite its bland histiological features, clinically aggressive and in at least some instances may be a verrucous variant of squamous carcinoma ab initio.[40] In the latter condition an orderly maturation of squamous epithelium is retained and its distinction from a true condyloma acuminatum may be very difficult. The exceptionally deep penetration of the acanthotic prolongations which typify this tumour, the absence of viral changes and the clinical features suggestive of involvement of adjacent structures may be helpful in this regard.

As mentioned previously, HIV infection is an important component of the 'gay bowel syndrome', i.e. the spectrum of disease associated with proctogenital sexual contact.[1] The converse is, of course, also true: individuals suffering from HIV infection commonly exhibit other features of the 'gay bowel syndrome'.[44] In addition, they eventually become unduly susceptible to 'opportunistic' organisms typified by CMV[11] and *Mycobacterium avium-intracellulare*,[12] or develop unusually severe reactions to organisms such as HSV[15] or cryptosporidia.[13] There is also accumulating evidence that HIV itself is capable of producing pathological changes in the rectal mucosa. The nature of these changes tends to vary with the clinical stage of HIV infection.[45] Initially, there may be little abnormality. As the disease progresses there may be an increase in lymphocytes, plasma cells and eosinophils in the superficial part of the lamina propria. With further progression, a phase of lymphocyte depletion supervenes, often associated with the presence of apoptotic bodies in the cryptal epithelium. It has been suggested that this last feature is related to HIV infection of endocrine cells.[46] Abnormalities in the lymphoid aggregates, most notably fragmentation of the cell processes of follicular dendritic cells, has been reported in some studies.[47] None of these changes, however, can be regarded as in any way specific for HIV infection.[48]

REFERENCES

1. Sehdev MK, Dowling MD, Seal SH, Stearns MW. Perianal and anorectal complications in leukaemia. Cancer 1973; 31: 149–152.
2. Kazal HL, Sohn N, Carrasco JI, Robilotti JG, Delaney WE. The gay bowel syndrome: clinico-pathologic correlation in 260 cases. Ann Clin Lab Sci 1976; 6: 184–192.
3. Sohn N, Robilotti JG. The gay bowel syndrome. A review of colonic and rectal conditions in 200 male homosexuals. Am J Gastroenterol 1977; 67: 478–484.
4. Schmerin MJ, Gelston A, Jones TC. Amoebiasis: an increasing problem among homosexuals in New York City. JAMA 1977; 238: 1386–1402.
5. Weller IVD. The gay bowel. Gut 1985; 26: 869–875.
6. Quinn TC, Corey L, Chaffee RG, Schuffler MD, Holmes KK. Campylobacter proctitis in a homosexual man. Ann Intern Med 1980; 93: 458–459.
7. Quinn TC, Goodell SE, Mkrtichian E et al. Chlamydia trachomatis proctitis. N Engl J Med 1981; 305: 195–200.
8. Phillips SC, Mildvan D, William DC, Gelb AM, White MC. Sexual transmission of enteric protozoa and helminths in a venereal-disease-clinic population. N Engl J Med 1981; 305: 603–606.
9. McMillan A, Lee FD. Sigmoidoscopic and microscopic appearance of the rectal mucosa in homosexual men. Gut 1984; 23: 1035–1041.
10. Goodell SE, Quinn TC, Mkrtichian E, Schuffler MD, Holmes KK, Corey L. Herpes simplex proctitis in homosexual men: Clinical, sigmoidoscopic and histopathological features. N Engl J Med 1983; 308: 868–871.
11. Knapp AB, Horst DA, Eliopoulos G et al. Widespread cytomegalovirus gastroenterocolitis in a patient with acquired immunodeficiency syndrome. Gastroenterology 1983; 85: 1399–1402.
12. Strom RL, Gruninger RO, Roth RI, Owen RL, Keren DF (letters). AIDS with mycobacterium avium-intra cellulare lesions resembling those of Whipple's disease. N Engl J Med 1983; 309: 1323–1325.
13. Casemore DP, Sands RL, Curry A. Cryptosporidium species: a 'new' human pathogen. J Clin Pathol 1985; 38: 1321–1336.
14. Daling JR, Weiss NS, Klopfenstein LL, Cochran LE, Chow WH, Daifuku R. Correlation of homosexual behaviour and the incidence of anal cancer. JAMA 1982; 247: 1988–1990.
15. Siegal FO, Lopez C, Hammer GS et al. Severe acquired immunodeficiency in male homosexuals manifested by chronic perianal ulcerative herpes simplex lesions. N Engl J Med 1981; 305: 1439–1440.
16. Goligher J. Surgery of anus, rectum and colon. 5th ed. London: Bailliere Tindall, 1984.
17. Lockhart-Mummery HE. Non-venereal lesions of the anal region. Br J Vener Dis 1963; 39: 15–17.
18. Ashby DW, Lazar T. Erythema multiforme exudativum major (Stevens-Johnson syndrome). Lancet 1951; 1: 1091–1095.
19. Barnes SG, Sattler FR, Ballard JO. Perirectal infections in acute leukaemia: improved survival after excision and debridement. Ann Intern Med 1984; 100: 515–518.
20. Hughes E, Cuthbertson AM, Killingback MK. Colorectal surgery. Edinburgh: Churchill Livingstone, 1983.
21. Parks AG, Morson BC. Fistula-in-ano. Proc R Soc Med 1962; 53: 751–754.
22. McMillan A, McNeillage G, Gilmour HM, Lee FD. Histology of rectal gonorrhoea in man, with a note on anorectal infection with Neisseria meningitidis. J Clin Pathol 1983; 36: 511–514.
23. Harkness AH. Anorectal gonorrhoea. Proc R Soc Med 1948; 41: 476–478.
24. Janda WM, Bohnhoff M, Morello JA, Lerner SA. Prevalence and site-pathogen studies of Neisseria meningitidis and N. gonorrhoeae in homosexual men. JAMA 1980; 244: 2060–2064.
25. Samenius B. Primary syphilis of anorectal region. Dis Colon Rectum 1968; 11: 462–466.
26. Akdamar K, Martin RJ, Ichinose H. Syphilitic proctitis. Dig Dis 1977; 22: 701–704.
27. Levine JS, Smith PD, Brugge WR. Chronic proctitis in male homosexuals due to lymphogranuloma venereum. Gastroenterology 1980; 79: 563–565.
28. Levin I, Romano S, Steinberg M, Welsh RA. Lymphogranuloma venereum: rectal stricture and carcinoma. Dis Colon Rectum 1964; 7: 129–134.
29. Harland WA, Lee FD. Intestinal spirochactosis. Brit Med J 1967; 3: 718–719.
30. Antonakopoulo G, Newman J, Wilkinson M. Intestinal spirochactosis: An electron microscopic study of an unusual case. Histopathology 1981; 6: 477–488.
31. Hovind-Hougan K, Birch-Anderson A, Henrik-Nielsen R, Orholn M, Petersen JO, Peglbjarg PS et al. Intestinal spirochactosis: Morphological characterisation and cultivation of the spirochaete Brachyspira aalborgii gen. nov. sp. nov. J Clin Microbiol 1982; 16: 1127–1136.
32. Lee FD, Kraszewski A, Gordon J, Howie JGR, McSeveney D, Harland WA. Intestinal spirochaetosis. Gut 1971; 12: 126–133.
33. Anonymous. Intestinal spirochaetes. Lancet 1984; 1: 720.
34. Rodgers FS, Rodgers C, Sheldon AP, Hawkey CJ. Proposed pathogenic mechanisms for the diarrhoea associated with human intestinal spirochotes. Am J Clin Pathol 1986; 86: 679–682.
35. Lewin KJ, Riddell RH, Weinstein WM. Enteric infections and associated diseases. In: Gastrointestinal Pathology and its Clinical Implications. Igaku-Shoin: New York, 1992: p. 1047.
36. Drew WL, Mintz L, Miner RC, Sands M, Ketterer B. Prevalence of cytomegalovirus infection in homosexual males. J Infect Dis 1981; 143: 188–192.
37. Puy-Montbrun T, Ganansia R, Lemarchand N, Delechenault P, Denis J. Anal ulcerations due to cytomegalovirus in patients with AIDS. Report of 6 cases. Dis Colon Rectum 1990; 33: 1041–1043.
38. Wexner SD. Sexually transmitted diseases of the colon, rectum and anus. The challenge of the nineties. Dis Colon Rectum 1990; 33: 1048–1062.
39. Singer A, Walker P, McCance DJ. Genital wart virus infections: nuisance or potentially lethal? Br Med J 1984; 288: 735–736.
40. Dawson DF, Duckworth JK, Bernhardt H, Young JM. Giant condyloma and verrucous carcinoma of the genital area. Arch Path 1965; 79: 225–231.
41. Oriel JD, Whimster IW. Carcinoma-in-situ associated with virus containing anal warts. Br J Dermatol 1971; 84: 71–73.
42. Duggan MA, Boras VF, Inoue M, McGregor SE, Robertson DI. Human papillomavirus DNA determination of anal condylomata, dysplasias and squamous carcinomas with in situ hybridisation. Amer J Clin Pathol 1989; 92: 16–21.
43. Palefsky JM, Holly EA, Gonzales J, Berline J, Aha DK, Greenspan JS. Detection of human papilloma virus DNA in anal intraepithelial neoplasia and anal cancer. Cancer Res 1991; 51: 1014–1019.

44. Orkin BA, Smith LE. Perineal manifestations of HIV infection. Dis Colon Rectum 1992; 35: 310–314.
45. Clayton F, Reka S, Cronin WJ, Torlakovic E, Sigal SH, Kotlet DP. Rectal mucosal pathology varies with human immunodeficiency virus antigen content and disease stage. Gastroenterology 1992; 103: 919–933.
46. McCullough JB, Batman PA, Miller ARD, Sedgwick PM, Griffin GE. Depletion of neuroendocrine cells in rectal biopsy specimens from HIV positive patients. J Clin Pathol 1992; 45: 524–527.
47. Bishop PE, McMillan A, Gilmour HM. Immunological study of the rectal mucosa of men with and without human immunodeficiency virus infection. 1987; 28: 1619–1624.
48. Stamm B, Grant JW. Biopsy pathology of the gastrointestinal tract in human immunodeficiency virus-associated disease: a 5-year experience in Zurich. Histopathology 1988; 13: 531–540.

SECTION

5

Vascular disorders, abnormalities, ischaemia and vasculitis

CHAPTER

30

The oesophagus and stomach

J. D. Davies B. F. Warren

INTRODUCTION

The pathological classification of vascular lesions of the oesophagus and stomach is best considered in general terms. An outline of their nature is shown in Table 30.1. Helpful clinically-based reviews of these conditons have been made by Colin-Jones[1] and Camilleri and his colleagues.[2,3] One important difficulty lies in making a clear distinction between developmental vascular malformations, age related changes and the genuinely neoplastic, if benign, vascular tumours. Such problems are not confined to the gastrointestinal tract but they have given rise to especial confusion in the nomenclature of gastric and oesophageal vascular lesions. Accurate diagnosis is nowadays an important aspect of pathology, in that consistency[4] is necessary in order to facilitate the assessment of clinical trials.[5,6]

The normal vasculature of the oesophagus and stomach is rather different from the rest of the bowel. Unlike the large bowel, the stomach possesses recognizable, if small, arteries and veins within the admittedly sparse[7,8] lamina propria. In addition, there are lymphatic channels and elastic fibres[7] which are not normal components of the colonic lamina propria.[9,10] The subepithelial veins of the lower 2–5 cm of the normal oesophagus occupy more space than in the proximal stomach wall or the upper part of the oesophagus.[11]

Table 30.1 Comparative frequency and clinical importance of the upper gastrointestinal vascular abnormalities.

	Oesophagus	Stomach	Intestine
Genetic conditions	0	++	+
varices	++	+	0
External compression	+	0	+
Angiodysplasias	0	++	++
Dieulafoy's disease	0	+	0
Infarction	0	+	++
Vasculitis	0	+	+
Phlebectasia	+	0	+

0 = very rare; + = only very occasional occurrence, or clinically unimportant; ++ = not infrequent, or may present serious clinical problems.

OESOPHAGUS

Genetic vascular abnormalities

Clinically, the oesophagus is infrequently affected by genetically determined[3] vascular malformations that can affect other parts of the gastrointestinal tract, including the stomach (see below).

Hypertensive varices

Any cause of portal venous hypertension leads to distension of the portal veins, and later the establishment of portosystemic anastomoses. The distended veins or their radicles in the oesophagus are especially likely to rupture and cause life-threatening haemorrhage.[12]

The site of especial distension of the veins in the lower oesophagus has been quantitatively identified, using morphometry, and is limited to the last 2–5 cm.[11] Varicose veins of the oesophagus display the changes associated with venous hypertension elsewhere; these consist of a marked proliferation of the medial smooth muscle cells and associated elastic fibres, with subsequent fibrosis, a change called phlebosclerosis.[13] The elastic fibres in oesophageal varices appear to be newly synthesized in that they contain not only immunoreactive elastin and amyloid P component, which are codistributed with lysozyme[14,15] in all elastic fibres, but also several of the principal plasma protease inhibitors which are markers of recently formed elastic fibres.[16–18] The pathogenetic mechanisms underlying haemorrhage from oesophageal varices is contentious. Acid reflux from the stomach and passive expansion of the veins due to the portal venous pressure is a cause favoured by some views. Spence, Sloan and Johnson[19] have shown that oesophagitis, as assessed by the criteria of Ismail-Beigi et al[20] or Goldman and Antonioli,[21] is not especially related to variceal bleeding. Spence et al[19] implicated the formation of distended intraepithelial blood-filled spaces, which are not true vessels, within the oesophageal squamous epithelium. These distended spaces were shown to be lined only by epithelium, and thus it is reasonable to expect that they should be liable to rupture.

Macroscopically, the veins of the lower oesophagus, which bear the main brunt of portal hypertension, are readily visible in the oesophagus when inspected by endoscopy,[22] barium swallow, or on portal venography. At post-mortem, however, they are inconspicuous unless thrombosis has occurred and the use of chemical sclerosants[23,24] during life may provoke this. Usually only a faint bluish discolouration of the oesophagus over the varices is visible and an inconspicuous punctum may mark the site of haemorrhage.

Microscopically, the changes in the vein walls are much more obvious. They show an increase in wall thickness and a reduplication of the lamellae of elastic fibres in the media. These alterations in medial elastic fibres differ fundamentally from those in tumoural venous elastosis, which particularly affects the adventitia of veins.[10,17,18]

An updated radiological classification of oesophageal and paraoesophageal varices[25] divides oesophageal varices into pallisading and bar types, and paraoesophageal veins into intraabdominal and thoracoabdominal types. The thoracoabdominal veins may be predominantly left or right sided. Thus, using selective left gastric venography, it is proposed that treatment should be determined according to these radiological appearances.

Recently, the anatomy of the normal circulation at the gastrooesophageal junction has been delineated more clearly.[26] Vianna et al have employed the three complimentary techniques of radiology, corrosion casting and morphometry and have established four distinct zones of venous drainage: a gastric zone with a longitudinal venous distribution, a palisade zone with parallel vessels arranged in groups within the lamina propria, a perforating zone of treble clef-shaped veins to collect and channel blood into external veins, and, finally, a truncal zone of deep descending veins. They have shown that venous flow is bidirectional at the palisade zone area, which presents a region of high resistence between the portal and azygos systems, and the increased flow in portal hypertension overcomes this high resistence, producing varices.

Sclerotherapy results in thicker stronger collagen in the oesophageal perivenous connective tissue[27] and may sometimes result in the appearance of varices lower down the gut,[28,29] or a mosaic like pattern in the gastric mucosa as the result of congestive gastropathy.[30]

Inflammation

The increased vascularity of the oesophageal connective tissue papillae of the squamous epithelium is of diagnostic help in recognizing low-grade oesophagitis in small endoscopic biopsies. The presence of a thin surrounding rim of connective tissue distinguishes these from the vascular spaces described by Spence et al[19] in portal hypertension.

Cardiac and aortic lesions

The oesophagus is liable to external compression due to atrial distension of the heart, as in severe mitral stenosis, or from syphilitic, dissecting or atherosclerotic aneurysms of the thoracic aorta, and this may mimic intrinsic obstructions.

Torsion

Normally the oesophagus is sufficiently tethered to prevent rotation but after surgical reconstruction with colonic anastomosis for malignancy it may become liable and this produces ischaemia.

Mallory-Weiss syndrome

Severe haemorrhage may follow vomiting or retching (the Mallory-Weiss syndrome). The mucosal tear usually occurs at the lower end of the oesophagus and appears to be traumatic, without evidence of a pre-existing vascular abnormality. Postoperative death due to haemorrhage from a Mallory-Weiss tear without associated vomiting has also been described.[31]

Irradiation

After therapeutic irradiation for intrinsic tumours or bronchogenic carcinoma, a wide variety of vascular damage, including capillary telangiectasia, connective tissue and occlusive alterations of larger blood vessels may occur.

Haemangioma-like lesions

The oesophagus may also be involved in a variety of connective tissue disorders, either directly or due to ischaemia.

True haemangiomas and angioma-like lesions of the oesophagus are extremely uncommon.[32] In surgical pathology practice it is very unlikely that such benign vascular lesions will reach the histopathologist, since it is inadvisable to biopsy them.[1] They include the curious venous lesions, often multiple in the lower bowel, called 'phlebectasia' which are unrelated to portal hypertension. They do not show sclerosis and consist simply of grossly dilated veins that may give rise to severe haemorrhage. They are reviewed by Camilleri and colleagues[2,3] and by Gentry et al.[33]

Another cause of haemorrhage unrelated to angiomas or phlebectasia is the development of arteriooesophageal fistulae[34] due to foreign bodies.

STOMACH

There is a heterogeneous group of vascular lesions of the stomach which include capilllary venous and arterial and combined abnormalities. Some have relatively recently been described and not all completely delineated.[4,35] The recent developments in endoscopic laser[36] and surgical treatment for such vascular lesions, however, now necessitates a more accurate histopathological diagnosis from biopsy and resected tissue.

Gastric 'angiodysplasias'

Unfortunately, the term 'dysplasia' has been used in different contexts. It can refer to various developmental abnormalities, reactive conditions, or to potentially neoplastic lesions. In the gastrointestinal tract, 'angiodysplasia', whilst not having many of the other connotations, does not distinguish between developmental vascular malformations and the proliferative and ectactic changes associated with ageing. It denotes lesions in which there is an abnormal proliferation of small and ectatic blood vessels.[37] They may be situated in the mucosa or in the submucosa. The lack of understanding as to their origin is still reflected in the varied terminology used to categorize such vascular lesions in the stomach. However, certain clinical associations are beginning to clarify the situation.

It has been suggested that some angiodysplasias of the stomach, on account of their morphology, clinical presentation and age incidence are similar to caecal and colonic angiodysplasias.[37,38] Other superficially similar vascular lesions, also confusingly termed 'angiodysplasias', have been related to portal hypertension associated with cirrhosis,[39–41] but are probably best regarded separately.[42] Yet other cases occur in patients on long-term haemodialysis for renal failure,[43,44] or with von Willebrand's disease.[45] Sometimes they are part of the infantile haemorrhagic angiodysplasia syndrome.[46]

How these 'angiodysplastic' lesions produce their clinical effects is not at all well understood. Possibly, coexistent pathological processes, such as atrophic gastritis, aortic stensosis,[47–49] mitral valve disease[50] and as yet unrecognized circumstances may actually predispose to the bleeding with which they are associated.

Antral vascular malformations ('watermelon stomach')

Recently, an endoscopically and pathologically distinctive lesion of the gastric antrum has emerged, imaginatively called 'watermelon stomach' by Jabbari and colleagues.[51] Patients are predominantly adult and the abnormality is usually detected on account of intermittent upper gastrointestinal haemorrhage.[1,52–54] The bleeding can give rise to a severe iron deficient anaemia. On endoscopy, the gastric antrum shows striated hyperaemic lesions, which are the basis of the descriptive title.[51] This appearance is not always seen and the antrum may appear to be affected by gastritis instead.[55] Biopsies do not always contain characteristic diagnostic features, which may only be seen in the resected stomach.[55]

There is still debate about the nature of the antral vascular malformations and it is possible that they are another form of angiodysplasia. Rare cases have been associated with primary biliary cirrhosis.[56] It is not clear whether the hypertrophic antral gastritis described by Stamp et al[48] is or is not the same 'watermelon stomach'.[57]

Although the 'watermelon stomach' is often accepted as a gastric vascular malformation, Gardiner and collegues have postulated that it is the result of mucosal prolapse,[58] thus resembling so-called 'solitary' ulcer of the rectum. These are thought to be manifestations of the ischaemic consequences of mucosal prolapse.[59] Intramucosal elastosis is a constant histological feature of rectal mucosal prolapse,[60] and this feature is also seen in the mucosa in 'watermelon stomach'.[61]

Histologically, the lesions consist of dilated capillaries in the lamina propria of the distal stomach, associated with patchy thrombosis in the capillaries. In addition, the mucosa is thickened, more folded than normal and contains vertically orientated tongues of smooth muscle. The deeper tissues of the stomach wall are also involved. The submucosa is also often described as containing distended vessels, and the muscularis propria of the pylorus may be hypertrophic.[51] Clearly, therefore, there are some morphological resemblances in 'watermelon stomach' and mucosal prolapse found elsewhere in the gastrointestinal tract. The biopsy appearances have been subjected to repeated scrutiny and a scoring system has been described by Gilliam et al[62] which claims to produce more reliable diagnosis. Other authors suggest that the larger volume of capillaries available for study in a snare biopsy specimen, rather than a pinch biopsy specimen, is important for a more reliable diagnostic yield.[63]

'Watermelon stomach' in cirrhosis may be associated with hypergastrinaemia and low serum levels of pepsinogen I.[64] Endoscopically visible red spots[65] composed of ectatic capillaries and red cell extravasation are also described in cirrhosis even in the absence of the features of 'watermelon stomach'.

Dieulafoy's disease

It is very likely that the small lesions of Dieulafoy's disease[66] are still being unrecognized both by clinicians and pathologists. Nonetheless, over 100 reported cases of the condition have now been comprehensively reviewed by Veldhuyzen van Zanten and his colleagues in Amsterdam,[67] who also provide an extensive bibliography of the earlier descriptions. It seems that the first account of the condition was, in fact, also made in France by Gallard in 1884,[68] 14 years before Dieulafoy.[66]

Patients with Dieulafoy's disease often present with a massive, usually repeated and potentially fatal haematemesis. The age range of those affected is wide, but most patients are in their fifth decade or older. Men are affected twice as frequently as women.[67]

The gastric lesion of Dieulafoy's disease is not always easily detected on endoscopy. However, it is almost invariably situated in the proximal part of the stomach, within 6 cm of the gastro-oesophageal junction. An absence of overt bleeding lesions in the distal stomach or duodenum should alert an endoscopist to the possibility of this particular lesion. A sharply localized bleeding point in the upper stomach may be found, with or without an adherent blood clot. The clot itself on the surface of the mucosa may have a very distinctive peaked appearance. The abnormal vessel responsible for the haemorrhage can sometimes be identified, even at endoscopy in occasional cases.

The preferred method of treatment in Dieulafoy's disease is surgical excision of the wedge of the proximal stomach wall containing the bleeding site. A 'blind' Billroth II gastrectomy is unsatisfactory, because it may fail to include the lesion.[67] Before the advent of endoscopy, the mortality rate of Dieulafoy's disease was very high, and even now the early mortality rate approaches 25%.[67]

The pathological lesion in Dieulafoy's disease consists of abnormally dilated and tortuous arteries which are present in the submucosa and also penetrate the mucosa (Figs 30.1 & 30.2). Their origin has been variously interpreted. They have been previously regarded as acquired aneurysms, in association with atherosclerosis, or as vascular malformations. It has also been postulated that the lesions are a reflection of the normal developmental processes involved in the postnatal involution of the vasculature of the upper part of the stomach,[69] thus explaining their peculiar anatomical distribution. Molnar and Miko[70] believe that these lesions represent an abnormal lack of involution in superficial mucosal arteries ('calibre persistence'), a view supported earlier by Chapman and Lapi,[71] Goldman,[72] and Krasznai and Szokoly.[73] Similar vascular lesions of the lower lip also appear to result from incomplete involution of immature arteries.[74] A case of Dieulafoy's disease presumed to be due to an intra-abdominal vascular abnormality has been described.[75]

Microscopically, the gastric lesions of Dieulafoy's disease invariably show an unusually large and tortuous artery in the base of an ulcer. The superficial wall of the artery may be entirely lost or just display fibrinoid necrosis. The overlying mucosal ulcer itself is unusually small,

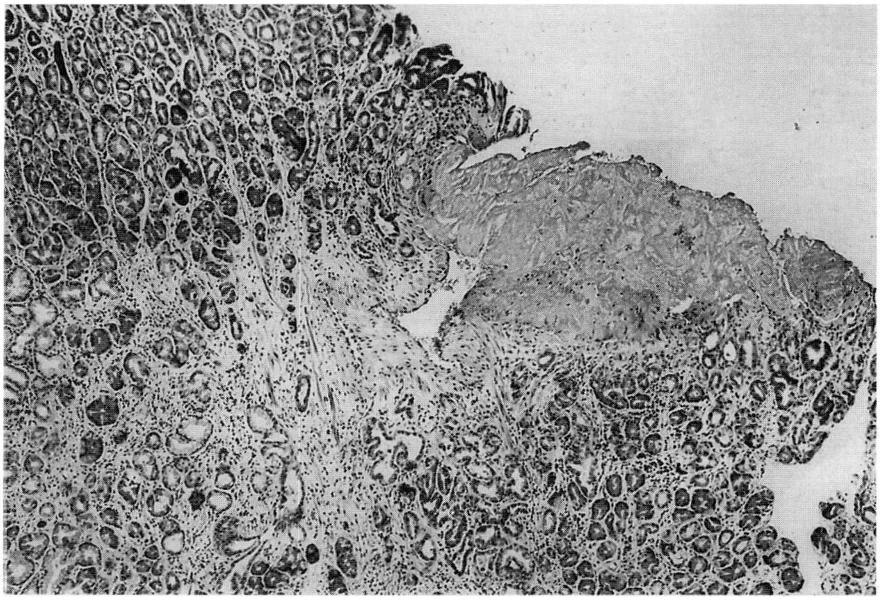

Fig. 30.1 Dieulafoy's disease of stomach. Thick-walled artery within gastric lamina propria underlies fresh clot adherent to surface of mucosa. (H&E, ×60).

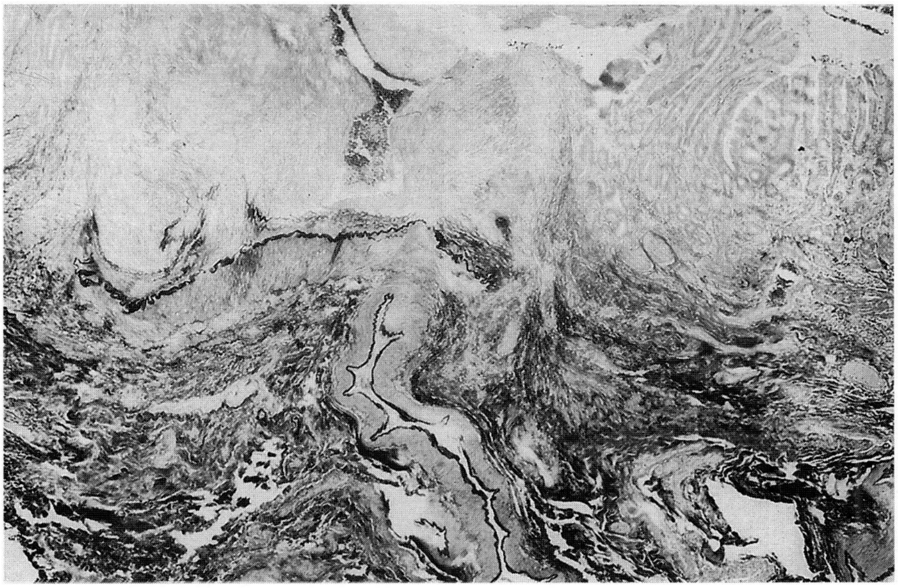

Fig. 30.2 Dieulafoy's disease of stomach. Elastic stain shows the ruptured and incomplete superficial aneurysm in the vascular lesion. (Lawson's elastic–van Giesen, ×60)

being only 2–5 mm in diameter, and it is surrounded by an entirely normal gastric mucosa which exhibits neither inflammation, dysplasia nor intestinal metaplasia.[76] The mucosa immediately above the abnormal artery is lost, and the vessel is often partially thrombosed. The ulcer differs from the 'ordinary' chronic peptic ulceration in being entirely superficial, and by showing no breach in the muscularis propria or any significant associated mural fibrosis. Within the submucosa, the abnormal tortuosity of the exposed artery is usually very obvious.[77] Recognition of the classic Dieulafoy lesion clinically may be extremely difficult but the diagnosis should always be considered in unidentified causes of gastric haemorrhage.[78]

The lesions in Dieulafoy's disease thus differ both in site and histological appearance from angiodyplasias of the stomach, which display a more prominent capillary component, as do true gastric angiomas. Whatever the real nature of Dieulafoy lesions, it has been proposed that gastric aneurysm, Dieulafoy and submucosal arterial malformation should all be grouped as so-called calibre persistent artery of the stomach in order to raise awareness of this potentially fatal, under-recognized condition.[79]

Occasionally in Dieulafoy's disease, intramural haemorrhage,[70] instead of the more common lumenal bleeding, occurs and an association with cirrhotic venous phlebosclerosis is described, but this association appears to be entirely coincidental.

Hypertensive varices in the stomach

The vascular lesions in the stomach associated with portal hypertension are similar to those in the oesophagus, although the venous distention is predominantly submucosal in the stomach.[11] Similar dilatation of small intramucosal vessels is also found in the upper stomach in patients with cirrhosis.

Gastric volvulus

Despite the potential mobility of the stomach, volvulus is rare but it leads to ischaemia as a result of occlusion of the lymphatic vessels, the veins and, ultimately, the arteries. Usually the rich vascularity of the stomach[80] protects it against infarction. However, if the vascular occlusion is sufficiently widespread the lesions can be extensive and ischaemic necrosis, when it takes place, can be very severe, involving all layers.

Atherosclerosis

The stomach is infrequently the site of the ischaemic complications of atherosclerosis. The main reason for this appears to be its generous arterial blood supply from five separate sources.[80] Nonetheless, necrosis and subsequent haemorrhage can occur as a complication of thromboembolism from atherosclerosis.[81]

Rarely, expansile atherosclerotic aneurysms of neighbouring arteries may rupture into the gastric lumen,[82] usually with fatal results.

Amyloidosis

The main vessels affected by amyloid in the stomach are the submucosal arteries. The use of polarized light to demonstrate birefringence, and acidified Congo red[83,84] are recommended procedures in order to distinguish amyloid from elastic fibres, which often have similar tinctorial properties.

A rare case of vascular amyloid deposition in an arteriovenous vascular malformation of the stomach is described.[85]

For the biopsy diagnosis of amyloidosis, samples from the gum and the rectum have been used, but the stomach is now the preferred site. In the diagnosis of amyloid at light microscopic level, the use of several stains is mandatory[83] thus obviating the need for further and expensive ultrastructural examination.

Polyarteritis and other gastric vasculitides

Classical polyarteritis nodosa and its variants[86] rarely affect the stomach.[87,88] In contrast to amyloidosis, rectal, rather than gastric, biopsies are of more diagnostic use in seeking arteritic lesions. In gastric ateritis there is usually an active inflammation with both polymorphonuclear leucocytes and eosinophils infiltrating the arterial wall. In the gastric lesions of the Kohlmeier-Degos arteriopathy,[89] there is no active inflammation, but characteristic mural fibrosis of the arteries may be found. The arteritis may be limited to certain organs, or occur with a systemic distribution. In the Churg-Strauss type of granulomatous arteritis, the stomach is usually only one part of the gastrointestinal tract involved.[90]

A similar widespread distribution of gastrointestinal lesions is also found in systemic lupus erythematosus,[91,92] the vasculitic variants of rheumatoid disease,[93,94] and the other 'collagen-vascular' diseases. All these vasculitides may give rise to gastrointestinal complications which require surgical intervention.

In Henoch-Scholein purpura, which mainly affects the small vessels in children, the stomach may also be affected.[95,96]

Haemangiomas of the stomach

Genuine haemangiomas of the stomach are rare. In a litereature search Bongiovi and Duffy[97] found only 35 cases by 1967, and only rather less than 50 had been reported by the mid 1980s.[56] These benign vascular tumours often present as a result of chronic haemorrhage but tend, in contrast to gastric angiodysplasias, to be protuberant or polypoid lesions.[45] Microscopically, they are distinguishable from angiodysplasias by the presence of cellular endothelial and vascular proliferation. The exact reason for the susceptibility of gastric mucosa to damage by nonsteroidal anti inflammatory agents is unknown,[98] but the microvascular endothelium seems to be a major target site for its initiation[99] and is preventable by arachidonic acid administration.

Incidental vascular thrombosis

Thrombosis of the gastric vessels may occur in conditions which are not of vascular origin. It is seen most frequently in peptic ulceration, in which a secondary endarteritis obliterans is commonplace. In addition it may be found in the less common conditions of 'antral hypertrophic gastritis' of Stamp et al 1985[48] and 'watermelon stomach'.[51]

Iatrogenic fistulae

Arteriodigestive fistulae are a recognized complication of postoperative radiotherapy for gastric carcinoma,[100] and probably have a basis in vascular occlusion and ischaemic damage.

Shock and infarction

Circulatory shock can produce ischaemic lesions in many organs. At first sight, the gastric mucosa appears to be no exception. However, although mucosal necrosis certainly occurs, there are doubts as to whether this is a direct result of ischaemia.[102] Gastric blood flow in hypotensive cats is well maintained, and it is thought that changes in gastric acidity and bile may, in fact, be responsible for the gastric mucosal necrosis. Chemical insults to the gastric mucosa[103] can simulate ischaemia closely.

Other chemical damage, notably produced by ethanol[104,105] and aspirin[106] possibly also evoke their effects by impairment of local mucosal blood flow.

Frank infarction of the whole stomach wall by any cause is much less common than in the small or large intestine, although it undoubtedly does occur. The infrequency of gastric ischaemia is due also to its abundant vascular supply.

REFERENCES

1. Colin-Jones DG. Upper gastrointestinal lesions. In: Salmon PR ed. Gastrointestinal Endoscopy: advances in diagnosis and therapy. London: Chapman and Hall. 1984; pp 89–96.
2. Camilleri M, Chadwick VS, Hodgson HJF. Vascular anomalies of the gastrointestinal tract. Hepato-gastroenterol (Stuttgart) 1984; 31:149–153.
3. Camilleri M. Vascular abnormalities of the intestine: genetic and congenital disorders. In: Bouchier IAD, Allan RN, Hodgson HJF, Keighley MRB, eds. Textbook of gastroenterology. London: Balliere Tindall, 1984; 247–259.
4. Underwood JCE. Introduction to biopsy interpretation and surgical pathology. Berlin: Springer-Verlag. 1981; 7–12.
5. Langman MJS. Upper gastrointestinal bleeding: the trial of trials. Gut 1985; 26: 217–220.
6. Dykes PW. Bleeding from the stomach and duodenum. Curr Opinion Gastroenterol 1985; 1: 865–873.
7. Plenk H. Der Magen. In: von Mollendorf W, ed. Handbuch der mikroskopischen Anatomie des Menschen, Volume 5; Part 2. Berlin: Springer, 1932; 184–189.
8. Palmer ED. Histology of the normal gastric mucosa: an

investigation into the state of normalcy of the stomachs of persons without gastrointestinal complaints. Gastroenterology 1952; 21: 12–23.
9. Platzelt V. Der Darm. In: Von Mollendorf W, ed. Handbuch der Mikroskopischen Anatomie des Menschen, Volume 5; Part 3. Berlin: Springer, 1936; 1–448.
10. Davies JD, Wharton B. Elastosis in the large bowel. J Pathol 1983; 141: 514.
11. Spence RA. The venous anatomy of the lower oesophagus in normal subjects and in patients with varices: an image analysis study. Br J Surg 1984; 71: 739–744.
12. Hunt AH. An analysis of 584 cases of portal obstruction. St Barts Hosp J 1965; 69(Suppl 11): 1–15.
13. Crawford T. Arteries, veins and lymphatics. In: Wright GP, Symmers WStC, eds. Systemic Pathology, vol 1. London: Longmans, Green, 1966; 91–140.
14. Davies JD, Young EW, Mera SL, Barnard K. Lysozyme is a component of human vascular elastic fibres. Experientia 1983; 39: 382–383.
15. Mera SL, Lovell C, Russell Jones R, Davies JD. Elastic fibres in normal and actinic-damaged skin: an immunohistochemical study. Br J Dermatol 1987; 117: 21–27.
16. Davies JD, Barnard K, Whicher JT, Young EW. Breast elastosis: the association with lysozyme and certain protease inhibitors. J Pathol 1982; 138: 505.
17. Mera SL, Lovett F, Davies JD. The effects of preliminary proteolysis on the immunohistochemical and dye staining properties of elastic fibres. Histochem J 1985; 17: 243–257.
18. Davies JD, Mera SL. Elastosis in breast carcinoma. II: Immaturity of elastic fibres shown by immunohistochemistry and lectins. J Pathol 1987; 153: 317–324.
19. Spence RAJ, Sloan JM, Johnston GW. Histologic factors of the esophageal transection ring as clues to the pathogenesis of bleeding varices. Surg Gynecol Obstet 1984; 159: 253–259.
20. Ismail-Beigi F, Horton PF, Pope CE. Histological consequences of gastro-esophageal reflux in man. Gastroenterology 1970; 58: 163–174.
21. Goldman H, Antonioli DA. Mucosal biopsy of the esophagus, stomach and proximal duodenum. Human Pathol 1982; 13: 423–448.
22. Inokuchi K. The general rules for recording endoscopic findings on oesophageal varices. Jpn J Surg 1980; 10: 84–87.
23. Terblanche J, Bornman PC, Kirsch RE. Injection of oesophageal varices. In: Salmon PR, ed. Gastrointestinal Endoscopy: advances in diagnosis and therapy. London: Chapman and Hall. 1984; pp 37–48.
24. Leader. Bleeding oesophageal varices. Lancet 1984; 1: 139–141.
25. Hashizume M, Kitano S, Yamaga H, Higashi H, Sugimachi K. Angioarchitectural classification of esophageal varices and paraesophageal veins in selective left gastric venography. Arch Surg 1989; 124: 961–966.
26. Vianna A, Hayes PC, Moscoso G, Driver M, Portmann B, Westaby D, Williams R. Normal venous circulation of the gastroesophageal junction. A route to understanding varices. Gastroenterology 1987; 93: 876–889.
27. Paluszkiewicz R, Rozga J, Kwiatowski J, Zieniewicz K, Krus S, Szczerban J. Morphology of oesophageal wall after repeated sclerotherapy of varicose veins. Scand J Gastroenterol 1987; 22: 743–749.
28. Lewis P, Warren BF, Bartolo DCC. Massive gastro-intestinal haemorrhage due to ileal varices. Brit J Surg 1990; 77: 1277–1278.
29. Kitajima M, Kenmizaki H, Nakajima M, et al. Gastric lesions in surgical patients with oesophageal transection for oesophageal varices. J Gastroenterol Hepatol 1989; 4: 129–131.
30. Kotzampassi K, Eleftheriadis E, Aletras H. The mosaic-like pattern of portal hypertensive gastric mucosa after variceal eradication by sclerotherapy. J Gastroenterol Hepatol 1990; 5: 659–663.
31. Humphrey GM, Benbow E, Tait WF. Sudden postoperative death caused by unheralded Mallory Weiss tears. J Clin Pathol 1991; 44: 787–788.
32. Foster CA, Yomihiro EG, Benjamin RB. Oesophageal haemangioma. ENT J 1978; 57: 455–459.
33. Gentry R, Dockerty M Clagett OT. Vascular malformations and vascular tumors of the gastrointestinal tract. Int Abstr Surg 1949; 88: 281–323.
34. Mok CK, Chiu CS, Cheung HH. Left subclavian arterioesophageal fistula induced by a foreign body. Ann Thorac Surg 1989; 47: 458–460.
35. Davies JD. In support of the colonoscopist: the pathologist. In: Salmon PR ed. Gastrointestinal Endoscopy: advances in diagnosis and therapy. London: Chapman and Hall. 1984; pp 263–273.
36. Bown SG, Swain CP, Storey DW et al. Endoscopic laser treatment of vascular anomalies of the upper gastrointestinal tract. Gut 1986; 26: 1338–1348.
37. Hunt RH. Angiodysplasia of the colon. In: Salmon PR, ed. Gastrointestinal Endoscopy: advances in diagnosis and therapy. London: Chapman and Hall, 1984; pp 97–114.
38. Boley SJ, Sammartano R, Adams A, Di Biase A, Kleinhaus S, Sprayregen S. On the nature and etiology of vascular ectasia of the colon. Gastroenterology 1977; 72: 650–660.
39. Testart J, Hemet J, Metayer P. Gastrite hemorrhagique par coagulation intravasculaire localisee au cours de l'evolution d'une cirrhose inflammatoire cryptogenetique. Sem Hop Paris 1975; 51: 1235–1241.
40. Van Vliet ACM, Ten Kate FJW, Dees J, Van Blankenstein M. Abnormal blood vessels of the prepyloric antrum in cirrhosis of the liver as a cause of chronic gastrointestinal bleeding. Endoscopy 1978; 10: 89–94.
41. Haboubi NY, Asquith P. Gastric angiodysplasia associated with primary biliary cirrhosis. Lancet 1988; 2: 972.
42. Cairns HS, Bevan G, Rees H. Aetiology of antral vascular malformation. J Roy Soc Med 1986; 79: 434.
43. Cunningham JT. Gastric telangiectasia in chronic hemodialysis patients: a report of six cases. Gastroenterology 1981; 81: 1131–1133.
44. Dave PB, Romen J, Antonelli A, Eiser AR. Gastrointestinal telangiectasias: a source of bleeding in patients receiving hemodialysis. Arch Int Med 1984; 144: 1781–1786.
45. Duray PH, Marcal JM, LiVolsi VA, Fisher R, Scholmacher C, Brand MH. Gastrointestinal dysplasia: a possible component of von Willebrand's disease. Human Pathol 1984; 15: 539–544.
46. Odell JM, Haas JE, Tapper D, Nugent D. Infantile haemorrhagic angiodysplasia. Paediatr Pathol 1987; 7: 629–636.
47. Cairns HS, Rees H, Bevan G. Iron deficiency anaemia, gastritis and antral vascular malformation. J Roy Soc Med 1986; 79: 46–47.
48. Stamp GWH, Palmer K, Misiewicz JJ. Antral hypertrophic gastritis: a rare cause of iron deficiency. J Clin Pathol 1985; 38: 390–392.
49. Weaver GA, Alpern HD, Davis JS, Ramsey WH, Reichelderfer M. Gastrointestinal angiodysplasia associated with aortic valve disease: part of a spectrum of angiodysplasia of the gut. Gastroenterology 1979; 77: 1–11.
50. Theodore C, Leymarious J, Molas G, Paolaggi JA. Gastroduodenal angiodysplasias: endoscopic study of 40 cases. Scand J Gastroenterol 1982; 17(suppl 78): 4.
51. Jabbari M, Cherry R, Lough JO, Daly DS, Kinnear DG, Gorelsky CA. Gastric antral vascular ectasia: the watermelon stomach. Gastroenterology 1984; 87: 1165–1170.
52. Lewis TD, Laufer I, Goodacre RL. Arteriovenous malformation of the stomach. Dig Dis 1978; 23: 467–471.
53. Wheeler MH, Smith PM, Cotton PB, Evans DMD, Lawrie BW. Abnormal blood vessels in the gastric antrum: a cause of upper gastrointestinal bleeding. Dig Dis Sci 1979; 24: 155–158.
54. Lee FI, Costello F, Flanagan N, Vasudev K. Diffuse antral vascular ectasia. Gastrointest Endosc 1984; 30: 87–90.
55. Kruger R, Ryan ME, Dickson KB, Nunez JF. Diffuse vascular ectasia of the gastric antrum. Am J Gastroenterol 1987; 82: 421–426.
56. Hunt RH. Angiodysplasia of the gut. In: Bouchier IAD, Allan RN, Hodgson HJF, Keighley MRB, eds. Textbook of gastroenterology. London: Balliere Tindall, 1984: 259–267.
57. Heaton N. Aetiology of antral vascular malformation. J Roy Soc Med 1986; 79: 434.

58. Gardiner GW, Murray D, Prokipchuk EJ. Watermelon stomach, or antral gastritis. J Clin Pathol 1985; 38: 1317–1318.
59. DuBoulay C, Fairbrother J, Isaacson PG. Mucosal prolapse syndrome: a unifying concept for solitary ulcer syndrome and related disorders. J Clin Pathol 1983; 36: 1264–1268.
60. Warren BF, Dankwa EK, Davies JD. Diamond shaped crypts and mucosal elastin: helpful diagnostic features in biopsies of rectal prolapse. Histopathology 1990; 17: 129–134.
61. Warren BF, Milroy CM, Davies JD. Elastosis in watermelon stomach. J Pathol 1992; 165: 20A.
62. Gilliam JH, Geisinger KR, Wu WC, Weidner N, Richter JE. Endoscopic biopsy is diagnostic in gastric antral vascular ectasia. The watermelon stomach. Dig Dis Sci 1989; 34: 885–888.
63. Saperas E, Pique JM, Perez-Ayuso R, Bombi JA, Bordas JM, Sentis J, Rhodes J. Comparison of snare and large forceps biopsies in the histological diagnosis of gastric vascular ectasia in cirrhosis. Endoscopy 1989; 21: 165–167.
64. Quintero E, Pique JM, Bombi JA, Bordas JM, Sentis S, Elena M, Bosch J, Rodes J. Gastric mucosal vascular ectasias causing bleeding in cirrhosis. A distinct entity associated with hypergastrinaemia and high serum levels of Pepsinogen I. Gastroenterol 1987; 93: 1054–1061.
65. Iwao T, Toyonaga A, Tanikawa K. Gastric red spots in patients with cirrhosis: subclinical condition of gastric mucosal haemorrhage? Gastroenterol 1990; 25: 685–692.
66. Dieulafoy G. Exulceratio simplex: L'intervention chirurgicale dans les hematemeses foudroyantes consecutives a l'exulceration simple de l'estomac. Bull Acad Med 1898 49: 49–84.
67. Veldhuyzen van Zanten SJO, Bartelsman JFWM, Schipper MEI, Tytgart GNJ. Recurrent massive haematemesis from Dieulafoy vascular malformations: a review of 101 cases. Gut 1986; 27: 213–222.
68. Gallard T. Anevrysmes miliares de l'estomac, donnant lieu a des hematemeses mortelles. Bull Soc Med Hop Paris 1884; 1: 84–91.
69. Voth D. Das architektonische Prinzip der Magenarterien in seiner Bedeutung fur die Magenblutung. Zentralbl Allg Pathol 1962; 103: 553–554.
70. Molnar P, Miko T. Multiple arterial caliber persistence resulting in hematomas and fatal rupture of the gastric wall. Am J Surg Pathol 1982; 6: 83–86.
71. Chapman I, Lapi N. A rare cause of gastric hemorrhage. Arch Intern Med 1963; 112: 347–352.
72. Goldman RL. Submucosal arterial malformation ('aneurysm') of the stomach with fatal hemorrhage. Gastroenterology 1964; 46: 589–594.
73. Krasznai G, Szokoly V. Congenital vascular malformation (calibre persistence) as a pathogenic factor of lethal gastric hemorrhage. Acta Chir Acad Sci Hung 1968; 9: 137–142.
74. Miko T, Adler P, Endes P. Simulated cancer of the lower lip attributed in 'caliber persistent' artery. J Oral Pathol 1980; 9: 137–144.
75. Louwerens JW, Gratama S, Zwaan A, van der Schaar H. Dieulafoy's erosion in the stomach as a result of an intra-abdominal vascular anomaly. Brit J Surg 1988; 75: 489–490.
76. Mortensen NJ, Mountford RA, Davies JD, Jeans WD. Dieulafoy's disease: a distinctive arteriovenous malformation causing massive gastric haemorrhage. Br J Surg 1983; 70: 76–78.
77. Kung T-M, Wong J. Arterial malformation of stomach: a cause of massive bleeding. Pathology 1982; 14: 81–84.
78. Welch M, Hoare EM. The Dieulafoy gastric malformation: an under-recognised cause of massive upper gastro-intestinal haemorrhage. Postgrad Med J 1991; 66: 581–583.
79. Miko TL, Thomazy VA. The calibre persistent artery of the stomach: a unifying approach to gastric aneurysm, Dieulafoy's lesion, and submucosal arterial malformation. Hum Pathol 1988; 19: 914–921.
80. Owen DA. Normal histology of the stomach. Am J Surg Pathol 1986; 10: 48–61.
81. Anderson WR, Richards AM, Weiss L. Hemorrhage and necrosis of the stomach and bowel due to atheroembolism. Am J Clin Pathol 1967; 48: 30–38.
82. Bottiglieri NG, Palmer ED, Ylitalo EW. Rupture of a splenic artery aneurysm into the stomach. Gastroenterology 1964; 46: 474–476.
83. Tribe CR, Perry VA. Diagnosis of amyloid. ACP Broadsheet 1979; 92: 1–9.
84. Davies JD, Young EW. Congo blue: a rapid stain for elastic fibres. J Clin Pathol 1982; 35: 789–791.
85. Walley VM. Amyloid deposition in a gastric arteriovenous malformation. Arch Pathol Lab Med 1986; 110: 69–71.
86. Fauci AS, Haynes BF, Katz P. The spectrum of vasculitis: clinical, pathologic, immunologic and therapeutic implications. Ann Intern Med 1978; 89: 660–676.
87. Lee HC, Kay S. Primary polyarteritis nodosa of the stomach and small intestine as a cause of gastro-intestinal haemorrhage. Ann Surg 1958; 147: 714–725.
88. Morson BC, Dawson IMP. Gastrointestinal pathology. 1st ed. Oxford: Blackwells 1972; p 102.
89. Strole WE, Clark WH, Isselbacher KJ. Progressive arterial occlusive disease (Kohlmeier-Degos): a frequently fatal cutaneosystemic disorder. N Engl J Med 1967; 276: 195–201.
90. Modigliani R, Muschart JM, Galian et al. Allergic granulomatous vasculitis (Churg-Strauss syndrome): report of a case with digestive involvement. Dig Dis Sci 1981; 26: 264–270.
91. Hoffman BI, Katz WA. The gastrointestinal manifestations of systemic lupus erythematosus: a review of the literature. Sem Arth Rheum 1980; 9: 237–247.
92. Weiser MM, Andres GA, Brendtjens JR et al. Systemic lupus erythematosus and intestinal venulitis. Gastroenterology 1981; 81: 570–579.
93. Sun DCH, Roth SH, Mitchell CS, England DWW. Upper gastrointestinal diseases in rheumatoid arthritis. Am J Dig Dis 1974; 19: 405–412.
94. Marcolongo R, Bayell PF, Montagnani M. Gastrointestinal involvement in rheumatoid arthritis: a biopsy study. J Rehumatol 1979; 6: 163–173.
95. Balf CL. The alimentary lesions in Henoch-Schonlein purpura. Arch Dis Childh 1951; 26: 20–27.
96. Feldt RH, Stickler GB. The gastrointestinal manifestations of anaphylactoid purpura in children. Staff Meet Mayo Clin 1962; 37: 465–473.
97. Bongiovi JH, Duffy JL. Gastric Haemangioma associated with upper gastrointestinal bleeding. Arch Surg 1967; 95: 93–98.
98. Safe A, Warren BF, Mountford RA. The elderly stomach and NSAIDs (in preparation).
99. Tarnawski A, Stachura J, Gergely H, Hollander D. Gastric microvascular endothelium: a major target for aspirin induced injury and arachidonic acid protection. An ultrastructural analysis in the rat. Eur J Clin Invest 1990; 20: 432–440.
100. de Villa VH, Calvo FA, Bilbao JI, Azinovic I, Balen E, Hernandez JL, Pardo F, Cienfuegos J. Arteriodigestive fistula: a complication associated with intraoperative and external beam radiotherapy following surgery for gastric cancer. J Surg Oncol 1992; 49: 52–57.
101. de Faria JL, Trevisan MAS. Necrosis of gastric mucosa following orthostatic collapse in rabbits. Virchows Arch (A) 1973; 358: 105–112.
102. Arvidsson S, Falt K, Haglund U. Acute gastric mucosal ulceration in septic shock: an experimental study on pathogenic mechanisms. Acta Chir Scand 1984; 150: 541–547.
103. Stamm B, Mirkovitch V, Winistorfer B, Robinson JWL, Ozzello L. Regeneration and functional recovery of canine intestinal mucosa following injury caused by formalin. Virchows Arch (B) 1974; 17: 137–148.
104. Guth PH, Paulsen G, Nagata H. Histologic and microcirculatory changes in alcohol-induced gastric lesions in the rat: effect of prostaglandin cytoprotection. Gastroenterology 1984; 87: 1083–1090.
105. Szabo S, Trier J S, Brown A, Schnoor J. Early vascular injury and increased vascular permeability in gastric mucosal injury caused by ethanol in the rat. Gastroenterology 1985; 88: 228–236.
106. Ashley SW, Sonnenschein LA, Cheung LY. Focal gastric mucosal blood flow at the site of aspirin-induced ulceration. Am J Surg 1985; 149: 53–59.

CHAPTER 31

The small intestine

M. F. Dixon

Until relatively recently, mesenteric vascular disease was thought of in terms of sudden occlusion and intestinal infarction, which was almost uniformly fatal. The past 25 years have seen an upsurge of interest in small intestinal ischaemia, in part a response to an increase in incidence and advances in the surgical management of acute occlusion, but equally because of a realization that interference with intestinal blood flow can produce a wide variety of clinical manifestations. The concept of 'non-occlusive' ischaemia is now firmly established and this has necessitated radical revision of previously held views on pathogenesis, indeed it has prompted much needed research into the physiology of the intestinal circulation. Furthermore, the recognition that some intestinal strictures are longer-term sequelae of ischaemia, and definition of the syndrome of 'intestinal angina', have aroused interest in the causes of chronic ischaemia and their management by restorative surgery. Before discussing the causes of ischaemia and their consequences, it is necessary to take account of these recent developments and briefly review the physiological control of the small intestinal circulation and the implications this has for the pathogenesis of ischaemic injury.

PHYSIOLOGICAL CONTROL

The small intestine receives the majority of its blood supply from the superior mesenteric artery (SMA). There are small collateral contributions from the dorsal pancreatic branch of the coeliac artery, and the upper left colic branch of the inferior mesenteric artery, but from a functional point of view, the superior mesenteric can be considered an 'end-artery'. However, the presence of a complex anastomosing network of arcades, both in the mesentery and within the bowel wall, means that occlusion of peripheral branches is unlikely to be followed by ischaemic damage.

The mucosa receives over half the total resting blood flow to the small intestine, while the muscularis propria, although accounting for half the mass of the wall, receives only 10–15% of total flow.[1] SMA blood flow increases dramatically during the process of digestion, rising by more than 100% after a mixed meal; conversely, exercise reduces both resting and postprandial blood flow.[2] The collateral arcades between adjacent segments of small bowel can maintain blood flow in a short occluded segment at about 55% of its control level. Approximately two-thirds of this collateral flow is carried by extramural or marginal vessels and the remainder by intramural channels.[3]

Blood flow through the intestinal wall is under the control of arterial smooth muscle and the muscle tone of the muscularis propria, while flow to the mucosa is governed by pre-arteriolar sphincters in the submucosal plexus. In contrast, the veins are thin-walled, deficient in smooth muscle and offer little resistance to blood flow. It is claimed that they contain most of the intestinal blood volume and have been designated 'capacitance' vessels, as opposed to the arteriolar 'resistance' vessels, but experiments on the cat indicate that a relatively small proportion of intestinal blood volume is pooled in veins.[4]

Although tonic muscular contractions and gut distension usually decrease total wall blood flow, their effects may be greatly modified by intrinsic metabolic and neural alterations. Likewise, the net effect of chemical agents on blood flow is determined by their relative potency with regard to actions on vessels, as opposed to actions on gut motility and contractility.[5]

Most of the resistance of the small intestinal circulation is governed by the pre-arteriolar sphincters, and it is their responsiveness to local pO_2, pCO_2 and metabolites which dictates whether or not mucosal capillaries are perfused. Since it has been estimated that only one-fifth of the mucosal capillaries are open at any one time, it is possible for an agent to constrict pre-arteriolar sphincters and arterioles without reducing the diffusion of oxygen into cells so long as total blood flow does not decrease by more than 75%.[6] However, oxygen diffusion within the villus is not determined simply by blood flow rates and the 'openness' of mucosal capillaries, so that other explanations have had to be invoked. Most notably, the close proximity of the artery and vein of the villus and the permeability of their walls has led to the proposition that there exists a counter-current exchanger in the villus, similar to that described in the kidney.[7] Such an exchanger would permit the direct transfer of oxygen between artery and vein at the base of the villus without perfusing the capillaries, and thereby establish an oxygen gradient up the villus. This could explain the increased susceptibility to hypoxic injury of cells at the tip of the villus when compared to epithelial cells at the base.[8] The exchanger could also facilitate the 'shunting' of lipid soluble nutrients absorbed from the intestinal lumen from capillaries to artery, and act as a brake on such absorption. A further extension of this hypothesis is that a countercurrent multiplier could exist which would markedly increase the absorption of water and ions from the gut lumen, for which the fenestrated mucosal capillaries are particularly adapted.[6]

In addition to the muscular and local redistributive factors already mentioned, intestinal blood flow is subject to a complex interplay of extrinsic and intrinsic controlling mechanisms (Table 31.1).

Table 31.1 Factors influencing intestinal blood flow.

1. General haemodynamic factors
2. Autonomic nervous system
   - Sympathetic
   - Parasympathetic
3. Circulating factors
   - Catecholamines
   - Vasopressin
   - Angiotensin II
   - Opiates
4. 'Gut' hormones
   - VIP
   - GIP
   - Glucagon
   - Secretion
   - Somatostatin
5. Locally produced mediators
   - Prostaglandins
   - Vasoactive amines
   - Kinins
   - Nucleotides

General haemodynamic factors

In so far as the blood flow through any vascular bed is determined by the pressure gradient across it, as well as the resistance offered by the vessels, general haemodynamic factors such as cardiac output, systemic arterial pressure, central venous pressure and blood viscosity are crucially involved in perfusion of the small intestine.

Autonomic nervous system

Stimulation of the sympathetic nerve supply to the gut produces vasoconstriction and marked reduction in blood flow. As a consequence, capillary pressure falls and interstitial fluid re-enters the vascular compartment. Thus the reflex sympathetic response to haemorrhage has the effect of enhancing capillary absorption of fluid and thereby expanding the depleted blood volume.[9] Until recently, such effects were thought to be transient, but Granger et al[10] have shown that reduced capillary filtration and lymph flow are sustained throughout sympathetic stimulation and appear to be mediated by increased 'shutting down' of mucosal capillaries. However, sympathetic stimulation may also bring about considerable distributional changes of blood flow within the intestinal wall, so that decreased supply to the mucosa might be balanced by increased blood flow to the muscularis propria. In this way, the overall blood flow through the intestine may be little changed but supply to the mucosa can be severely compromised.[6] Parasympathetic stimulation has little effect on the vessels themselves but muscular contraction restricts blood flow through the penetrating arteries.

Circulating factors

In so far as ligation of adrenal vessels has no effect on total small intestinal blood flow, the role of circulating catecholamines in regulation is dubious.[11] Nevertheless, the development of small intestinal infarction in a case of propanolol overdosage[12] demonstrates that severe splanchnic vasoconstriction can result from unopposed adrenergic stimulation. Circulating vasopressin and angiotensin II do have vasoconstrictive effects and prior blockade of the renin-angiotensin axis can protect the small intestine from ischaemic injury.[13]

Opiate peptides such as enkephalin and met-enkephalin relax intestinal arterioles and pre-capillary sphincters thereby bringing about an increase in intestinal oxygen consumption and blood flow.[14]

Gut hormones

Notwithstanding the potent effects of the autonomic nervous system on intestinal blood flow, it has been established that the hyperaemia of the mucosa observed during digestion is not mediated via an adrenergic or cholinergic reflex. The main candidate as mediator is vasoactive intestinal polypeptide (VIP).[15] Immunohistology has demonstrated that most, if not all, VIP in the gut is localized to synaptosomes in the intrinsic neurons and is therefore likely to act as a neurotransmitter. Other gut hormones affecting intestinal blood flow are gastric inhibitory polypeptide (GIP), glucagon and secretin, which stimulate mesenteric flow, and somatostatin, which exerts an inhibitory effect.

Local metabolites

Blood flow through the mucosal capillaries is particularly susceptible to the concentration of metabolites in the interstitium of the lamina propria. Indeed, there is an element of autoregulation in that accumulation of metabolites leads to a relaxation of the precapillary sphincters, and the ensuing vasodilatation brings more nutrients to the deprived mucosa. Thus, in conditions of mucosal hypoxia, the build-up of CO_2, lactic acid, and K^+ and H^+ ions leads to a relaxation of arteriolar smooth muscle, and the resultant increase in mucosal perfusion tends to restore the oxygen supply. Furthermore, conditions which bring about accumulation of metabolites also result in the secondary release or production of other vasodilators such as serotonin (5-hydroxytryptamine), prostaglandins, kinins and cyclic nucleotides, which in turn also increase mucosal blood flow. Serotonin might have a more fundamental role as a regulator of vascular tone, as serotoninergic nerves have been demonstrated in the mesentery. Excessive release of 5-HT from these nerves, or dysregulation of the indoleamine uptake system, might underlie some ischaemic disorders.[16]

Overall regulation

When the primary disturbance is a reduction in flow, the ability of the mucosa to compensate by recruitment of additional capillaries means that oxygen uptake remains constant over a wide range. Only when blood flow falls by more than 35% of control values is this compensatory mechanism defeated, and oxygen uptake becomes flow dependent.[3]

EVOLUTION OF ISCHAEMIC INJURY

Ischaemic injury to the small intestine occurs as a consequence either of obstruction of the SMA (occlusive ischaemia), or when, despite patency of the vessels, reduction in blood supply results in a level at which adequate nutrition of the mucosa cannot be maintained (non-occlusive ischaemia).

Structural damage develops soon after the onset of ischaemia, but the rapidity with which the changes occur has probably been exaggerated with respect to the human intestine. Animal experimentation has certainly indicated a very rapid time course, ultrastructural changes in the enterocytes at the villous tips having been detected as little as 3–5 min after complete cessation of the circulation to isolated intestinal loops.[17] More recently, however, Wagner and Gabbert[18] have described a much slower onset and sequence of changes in human small intestine subjected to absolute ischaemia, as compared to those observed in the rat. Ultrastructural changes comprising loss of cytoplasmic organelles from the basal parts of the surface enterocytes at the villus tip were first seen after 1 h ischaemia. After 2 h, separation of the enterocytes from their basement membrane was seen as discrete blebs, and at 4 h shedding of individual or cohesive groups of epithelial cells was observed. Over the following hours, a progressive loss of villous epithelial cells occurred in a downward direction so that at 16 h they were completely denuded. Necrosis of the lamina propria led to collapse and disappearance of villi at about 30 h, and by 44 h there was complete mucosal necrosis. A similar state was reached in rat mucosa after 7 h complete ischaemia, but as the former observations were based on maintenance of samples of small intestine in a moist chamber at 37°C, it seems likely that ischaemic mucosa in contact with bowel contents, including digestive enzymes bile and bacteria, would show accelerated degeneration.

Animal studies indicate that non-occlusive ischaemia produces qualitatively similar changes to those seen following total occlusive ischaemia, but the time required for the same morphological damage to occur is much longer. It has recently been established, however, that mucosal damage increases after the period of hypotension is terminated indicating a 'reperfusion' injury[19] (see below).

Mucosal regeneration is also claimed to be remarkably rapid but its rate will inevitably depend on the extent of the ischaemic injury. Thus a transient injury which results in damage to the surface enterocytes alone will be quickly restored by crypt cell proliferation and migration up the villus. Such regeneration is under feedback control by the functional villus cells. A more severe injury which affects the crypt cells will take longer to restore. For example, regeneration of villi in dog ileum subjected to 1 h total ischaemia was almost complete by 24 h,[20] but when full-thickness mucosal necrosis was produced in segments of dog intestine by ligation of branches of the SMA, it took about 30 days for well-developed villi to appear.[21]

When the ischaemic injury extends deeper than the mucosa, complete regeneration and restoration to normality is impossible. Partial thickness involvement frequently gives rise to a fibrous stricture, while sustained transmural ischaemia leads to potentially irreparable infarction and gangrene.

PATHOGENESIS OF ISCHAEMIC INJURY

The root cause of the cellular degeneration seen in ischaemic injury is clearly hypoxia. Several mechanisms have bee invoked to explain how hypoxia causes degeneration of enterocytes, and these fall into three main categories (reviewed by Robinson et al[20]).

First, it is suggested that hypoxia causes membrane degeneration leading to lysosomal rupture. Subsequent release of hydrolytic enzymes brings about 'autodigestion' of the enterocytes, which are shed into the lumen. While lysosomal enzymes are undoubtedly released during intestinal ischaemia,[22] lysosomal rupture is a late event in cell injury and probably accompanies frank necrosis. This does not accord with the finding of only minor ultrastructural abnormalities in the detached cells.[18]

A second possibility assumes that under normal circumstances there is a very rapid turnover of enterocyte brush border proteins, their digestion at the cell surface by luminal pancreatic proteases being balanced by equally rapid synthesis. Under hypoxic conditions, however, the necessary high rate of protein synthesis for replacement cannot be maintained and the protection afforded by the trypsin-resistant glycoproteins is lost, so that digestion by pancreatic endopeptidases ensues.[23]

The third hypothesis, and one more in keeping with morphological and functional observations, is that altered membrane permeability and diminished activity of ATPase-dependent ionic pumps brings about disturbed osmoregulation and an influx of fluid into the epithelial cells, i.e. hydropic degeneration. The existence of a countercurrent exchanger with extravascular short-circuiting of oxygen explains the appearance of the earliest hypoxic injury at the villus tip.[24]

Whatever the precise mechanism, it has been generally assumed that the severity of the injury is proportional to the prevailing degree of hypoxia. Thus total occlusion leads to cellular anoxia and ultimately to cell death (probably mediated by a lethal ingress of Ca^{2+} ions through the damaged plasma membrane), while non-occlusive ischaemia produces varying degrees of injury depending on the severity and duration of the diminished blood flow. Recent work indicates that this represents a considerable oversimplification. It is now appreciated that much of the mucosal injury in non-occlusive ischaemia develops after the period of hypoperfusion, that is when normal perfusion and oxygenation have been restored.[25] This is therefore an example of a 'reperfusion injury' of the kind described after myocardial and cerebral ischaemia, and following iatrogenic ischaemia in organ transplantation.[26]

Reperfusion injury in the intestine, as elsewhere, is thought to result from 'free radical' formation. Free radicals are molecules containing an odd number of electrons and are therefore highly reactive moieties, capable of initiating long chain reactions or peroxidation of unsaturated fatty acids. By this means, they produce lethal membrane alterations within cells. The most noteworthy free radical in the context of postischaemic injury is the superoxide radical (O^{-2}), produced by the one electron reduction of molecular oxygen. Its role in the pathogenesis of small intestinal ischaemia has been well reviewed by Granger and Parks[27] and by Schoenberg et al,[28] on which the following account is based.

Faced with increasing hypoxia and diminished energy levels, the cell attempts to maintain homeostasis by discharging adenosine triphosphate (ATP) and accumulating AMP. AMP is catabolized to adenosine, which diffuses out of the cell where it is broken down to inosine and hypoxanthine. Hypoxanthine is normally further catabolized by the NAD-reducing enzyme, xanthine dehydrogenase (which is present in high concentration in intestinal villi), to form xanthine and uric acid, but under hypoxic conditions this enzyme is rapidly converted into xanthine oxidase. However, oxidation of hypoxanthine and the resulting formation of superoxide radicals will only proceed in the presence of an additional substrate molecular oxygen. Thus, in hypoxia there is an accumulation both of hypoxanthine and the associated enzyme xanthine oxidase. This explains why with restoration of blood flow and oxygen supply, oxidation of hypoxanthine commences and superoxide radicals are formed. The superoxide anions may undergo further reduction to hydrogen peroxide and hydroxyl radicals (OH^-). These oxygen-derived free radicals are then responsible for the membrane injuries in epithelial and endothelial cells which bring about mucosal disintegration and increased vascular permeability in the reperfusion phase. Bounous[29] has attempted to reconcile his pancreatic protease theory with the superoxide mechanism by suggesting that trypsin may be responsible for the conversion of xanthine dehydrogenase to the free radical forming oxidase, but this is an unnecessary and probably irrelevant proposition.

The liberation of free radicals, particularly superoxides, brings about lipid peroxidation. The consequent membrane disruption provokes an inflammatory response and has numerous secondary effects which tend to increase tissue injury. Platelet-activating factor mediates adhesion between granulocytes and microvascular endothelium[30] and the consequent accumulation of polymorphs with release of neutrophil-derived superoxides and proteases may exaggerate tissue damage.[31] It also seems likely that tumour necrosis factor, which is liberated during ischaemia, has a role in polymorph activation.[32] The reperfusion phase is also characterized by increased production of eicosanoids, both leukotrienes and prostaglandin precursors, which further diminish blood flow.[33] Thus free radical formation is considered to be the principal initiator of a cascade of chemically mediated effects which end in tissue destruction.

Strong support for a major role of oxygen-derived free

radicals in intestinal reperfusion injury is given by the finding that xanthine oxidase inhibitors such as allopurinol[34] and pterin aldehyde[35] largely prevent mucosal damage. Similarly, free radical anion 'scavengers', such as thiopental[36] and dimethyl sulphoxide,[37] have also been shown to be cytoprotective in experimental ischaemia in the small intestine.

To summarize, total vascular occlusion results in segmental anoxic or hypoxic injury, the extent of which depends on the adequacy of the collateral supply. Free radical formation appears to play little or no part in anoxic injury, but pancreatic proteases appear to be operative. Non-occlusive ischaemia or hypoperfusion sets in train a complex series of biochemical changes which, on restoration of an oxygenated blood supply, result in the formation of cytotoxic free radicals. The fact that the ensuing mucosal injury can be modified or even prevented by xanthine oxidase inhibitors or free radical scavengers opens up the intriguing possibility of prophylactic treatment in conditions which produce intestinal hypoperfusion, such as systemic hypotension and other shock states.

Table 31.2 Causes of small intestinal ischaemia.

Occlusive
- (i) Atherosclerosis
- (ii) Arterial thrombosis
- (iii) Mesenteric embolism
  - (a) Thromboembolism
  - (b) Atherosclerotic debris
  - (c) Foreign matter, e.g. 'Gelfoam'
- (iv) Arteritis
- (v) Miscellaneous arterial causes
  - (a) Hypertension
  - (b) Dissecting aneurysm
  - (c) Amyloidosis
  - (d) Radiation injury
  - (e) Fibroelastosis
- (vi) Small vessel diseases and microthrombosis
  - (a) Henoch-Schonlein purpura
  - (b) Leucocytoclastic vasculitis
  - (c) Disseminated intravascular coagulation
- (vii) Venous thrombosis and microthrombosis
- (viii) Mechanical obstruction
  - (a) Volvulus
  - (b) Strangulation
  - (c) Intussusception

Non-occlusive
- (i) Vasoconstriction
- (ii) Systemic hypotension
- (iii) Viscosity disturbances
- (iv) Arterial narrowing
  - (a) Atherosclerosis
  - (b) Hypertension
  - (c) Intimal proliferation in distal mesenteric arteries
- (vi) Drugs

TYPES AND CAUSES OF SMALL INTESTINAL ISCHAEMIA

Occlusion of the SMA may be sudden or gradual, partial or complete, and therefore may result in a wide spectrum of changes which defy precise categorization. However, from a clinicopathological viewpoint, it is conventional to think in terms of acute and chronic ischaemia. While this is the most useful division, it must be borne in mind that there is much overlap between the two processes, and, of necessity, chronic ischaemia will embrace changes attributable to continuing acute injury. A useful concept in considering the consequences of acute ischaemia is separation of the forms of infarction based on the depth of involvement of the wall, such that mucosal, mural and transmural categories are recognized.[38]

In considering the causes of small intestinal ischaemia, it has become increasingly apparent that in many cases there is no associated large vessel occlusion. A few, however, do have demonstrable lesions in small vessels, but the majority are assumed to be due to non-occlusive ischaemia resulting from splanchnic vasoconstriction. Thus the causes can be considered as either 'occlusive' or 'non-occlusive' (Table 31.2).

Occlusive causes of small intestinal ischaemia

Atherosclerosis

Although atherosclerosis is the most common mesenteric vascular disease, its relationship to intestinal ischaemia is far from clear-cut. Older autopsy studies have generally yielded a high incidence of stenosis of the SMA by atherosclerosis (35–70% of cases), but in the vast majority such narrowing is not accompanied by ischaemic damage (Fig. 31.1). The frequency with which significant stenosis is encountered is probably much smaller, however, as a careful study by Marston's group[39] revealed that only 4.9% of 203 consecutive autopsies had 'critical' stenosis (i.e. >50% reduction in intraluminal diameter). Nevertheless, they did reaffirm the lack of correlation between arterial occlusion and symptoms of digestive disease experienced during life.

Arterial narrowing by atherosclerosis is the usual cause of chronic ischaemic syndromes, but they are comparatively rare. On the other hand, in acute ischaemia occlusion by superimposed thrombosis is a frequent cause. While these patients almost inevitably have atherosclerotic involvement of the thrombosed artery, its role as a major causative factor is frequently obscured by the presence of low cardiac output, increased blood viscosity and other hypercoagulable states. In addition to superimposed thrombosis, atherosclerosis can lead to intestinal ischaemia through mesenteric artery aneurysm formation,[40] involvement of the ostium of the SMA in an aortic aneurysm, or by rupture of an aortic plaque and microembolisation of cholesterol-rich debris (see below).

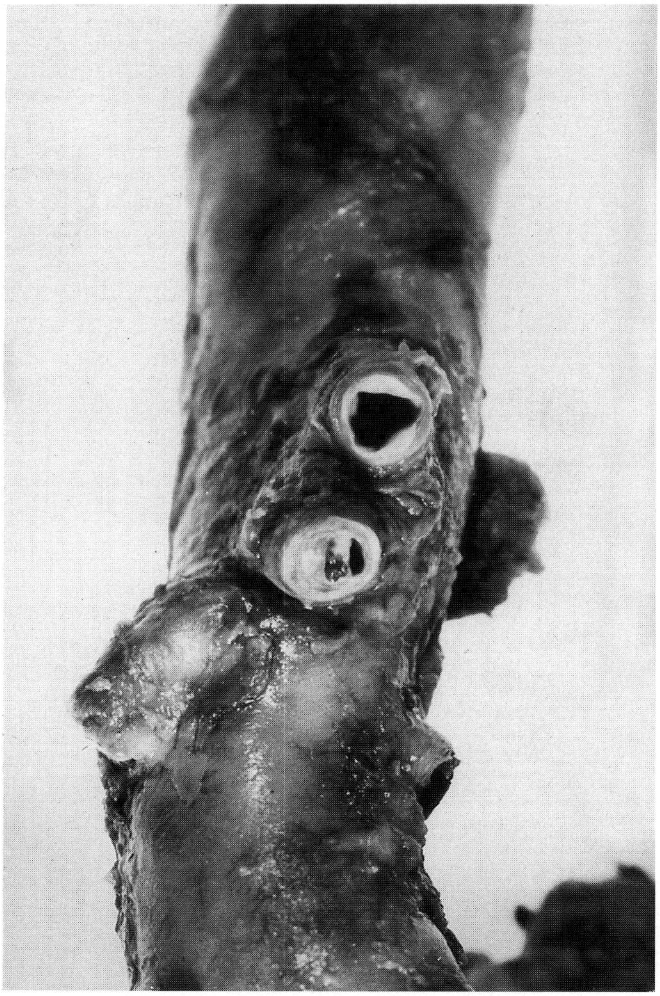

Fig. 31.1 Marked superior mesenteric artery narrowing by atherosclerosis found at post mortem in a man of 84 years who had suffered from severe systemic hypertension and ischaemic heart disease but had no symptoms referable to mesenteric ischaemia.

Arterial thrombosis and embolism

Taken together, thrombosis and embolism are the commonest causes of mesenteric arterial occlusion, accounting for 74% and 88% of cases in two recent surveys.[41,42] Thromboembolism appears to be increasing in incidence and accounts for three to four times as many cases as in situ thrombosis.[43]

SMA thrombosis is almost always superimposed on severe atherosclerotic narrowing, indeed most patients have severe widespread atherosclerosis and frequently have a history of cerebral or peripheral arterial ischaemia.[43]

Thromboemboli usually originate from atrial or cardiac mural thrombus. Formerly, rheumatic valvular disease was an important cause of intracardiac thrombosis, but this has been replaced by atherosclerotic ischaemic heart disease as the major source of emboli. Brandt and Boley[43] found that ischaemic heart disease was the cause in all but 3 of their 47 patients with SMA embolization. Many of these patients had a history of previous embolization, and approximately 20% had synchronous emboli in other arteries. A somewhat unusual example of coeliac artery embolization occurred in a 23-year-old man who sustained a myocardial infarct following a hockey injury to his chest. The embolism resulted in severe upper abdominal pain but fortunately did not produce intestinal infarction.[44] The importance of cholesterol emboli as a cause of intestinal ischaemia is gaining increasing attention.[45,46] While this can occur spontaneously,[47] others arise subsequent to surgery to the proximal aorta or following the introduction of cannulae for aortography.

Intestinal infarction has also been reported after iatrogenic embolization of foreign matter injected for the control of haemorrhage. Shapiro et al[48] reported infarction of the duodenum in a 67-year-old diabetic following 'Gelfoam' embolization for a bleeding duodenal ulcer, and we have seen infarction of the terminal ileum following a similar procedure carried out for bleeding angiodysplasia of the caecum (Fig. 31.2A,B,C).

Arteritis

While involvement of the mesenteric arteries in polyarteritis nodosa is well known, arteritis leading to ischaemia can be seen in a variety of other, frequently multisystem, disorders. Thus recent case reports describe intestinal ischaemia resulting from arteritis in rheumatoid disease,[49–51] in malignant hypertension,[52,53] systemic lupus erythematosus,[54] giant cell arteritis,[55,56] and Takayashu's disease.[57] Intestinal ischaemia has also been reported in Buerger's disease.[58] An interesting development in the more recent reports has been an increasing emphasis on small vessel disease and obliterative endarteritis, rather than the necrotizing arteritis of muscular arteries typified by polyarteritis nodosa. In particular, McCurley and Collins[50] describe three cases of rheumatoid disease in which there was marked intimal proliferation without vessel wall necrosis or inflammation, a finding also described in a case of Kohlmeier-Degos disease (a variant of polyarteritis nodosa)[59] and previously reported in SLE and systemic sclerosis.[50]

Miscellaneous arterial causes

A dissecting aneurysm involving the SMA is a recognized cause of acute intestinal ischaemia and constituted 4% of Haglund's series.[60] There are occasional cases of dissection of the SMA itself.[61]

The intimal proliferation and medial sclerosis associated with systemic hypertension may exacerbate intestinal ischaemia, and other arteriopathies result from irradiation, fibro-elastosis (sometimes seen adjacent to carcinoid tumours)[62] and amyloidosis (Fig. 31.3). Fibromuscular

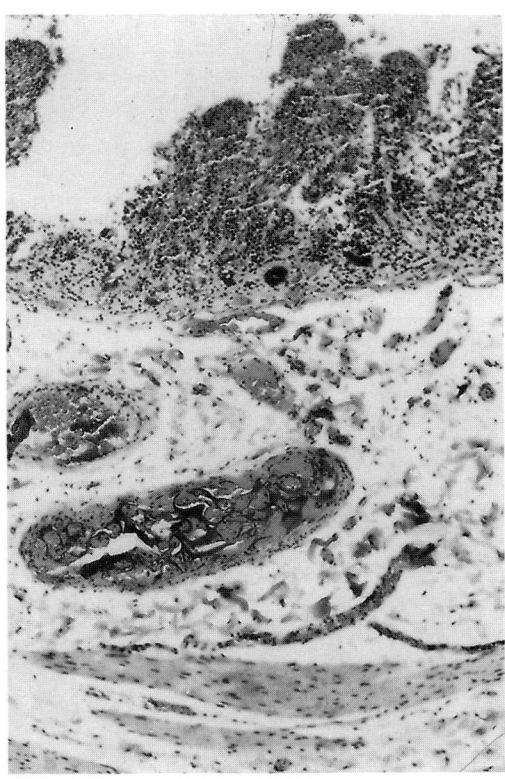

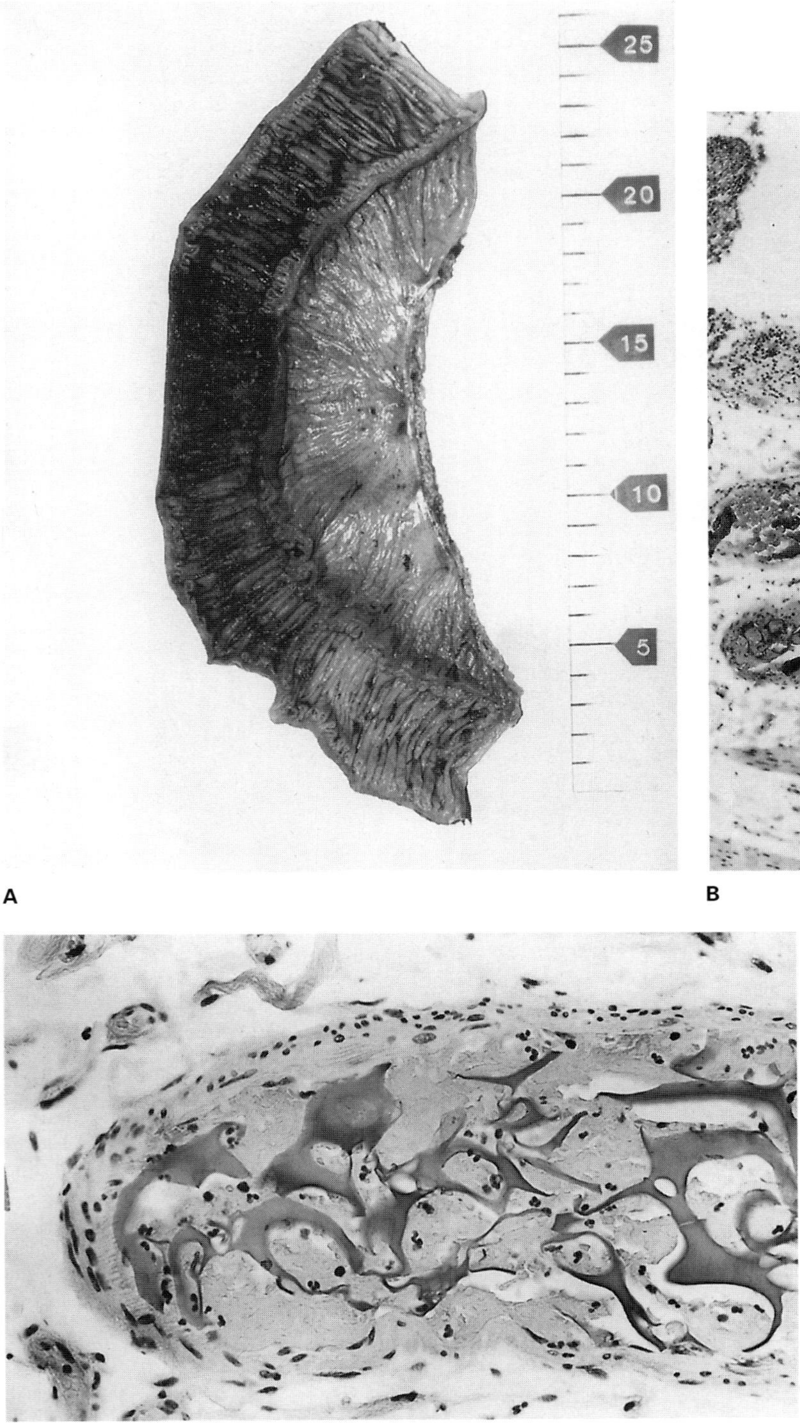

Fig. 31.2A Small bowel infarction following 'Gelfoam' embolization. The patient, a man of 85 years, presented with bleeding per rectum and an angiogram revealed caecal angiodysplasia. He underwent selective angiography with attempted 'Gelfoam' embolization of the ileocaecal supply. Shortly afterwards he developed abdominal pain and this infarcted loop was later removed. **B & C** A submucosal artery blocked by 'Gelfoam' in an area of mucosal infarction. (H&E, ×25, ×64)

dysplasia of mesenteric arteries may also contribute to intestinal ischaemia.[63]

Small vessel diseases and microthrombosis

Henoch-Schonlein purpura and leucocytoclastic vasculitis (hypersensitivity angiitis) are conditions characterized by vasculitis affecting postcapillary venules. Gastrointestinal involvement in the former is well known,[64] but there have also been reports of small intestinal mucosal necrosis and haemorrhage resulting from leucocytoclastic vasculitis.[65] A vasculitis affecting submucosal vessels was the cause of

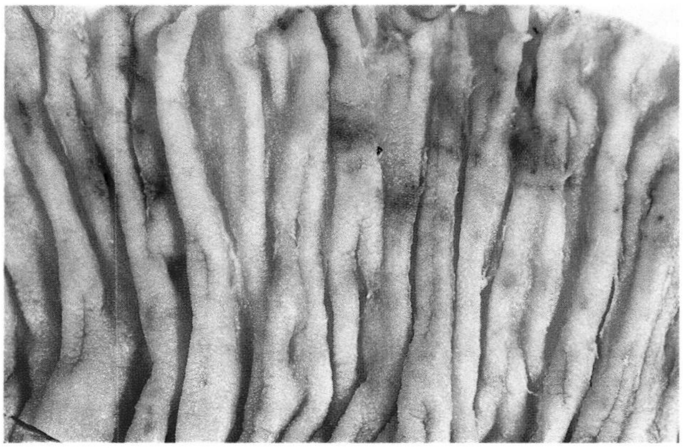

A

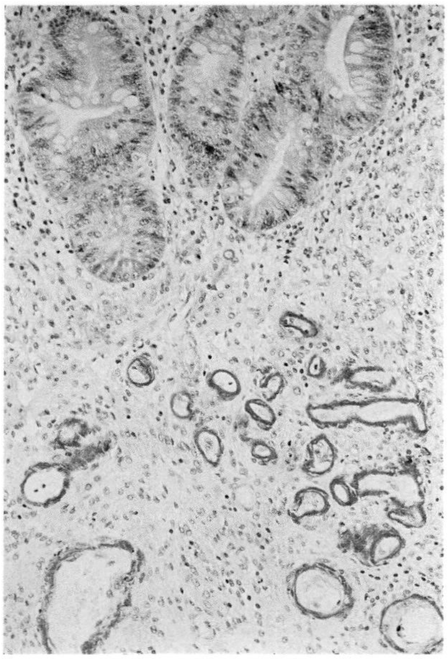

B

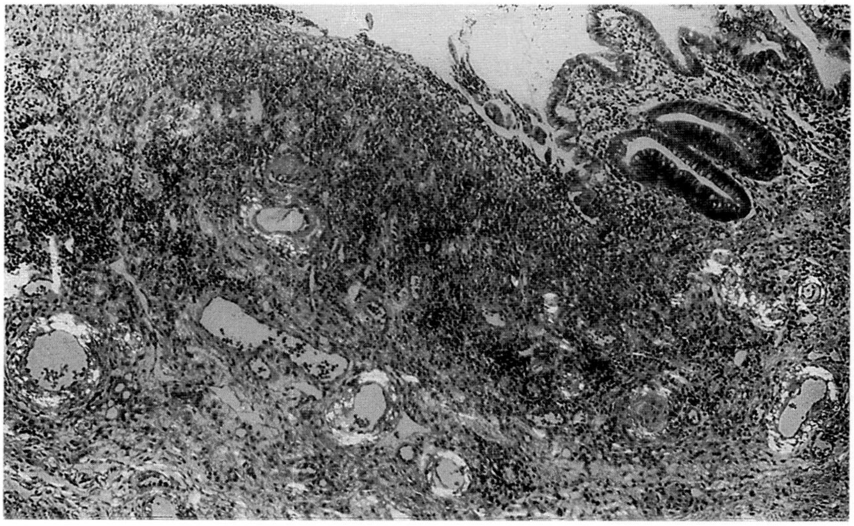

C

Fig. 31.3A Multiple ischaemic ulcers complicating systemic amyloidosis. The patient, a man of 32 years with primary (idiopathic) amyloidosis, developed massive intestinal haemorrhage and underwent small bowel resection. **B** Amyloid deposition in a leash of thin walled blood vessels in the superficial submucosa in a non-ulcerated area of the jejunum. (Congo Red stain, ×135) **C** Margin of a jejunal ulcer showing inflamed granulation tissue in the base and amyloid deposition in blood vessels in the ulcer base and submucosa. (Congo Red stain, part polarized light, ×20)

small intestinal infarction which developed 3 weeks after a 'successful' bone marrow transplant for chronic myeloid leukaemia.[66]

Thrombosis in small intramural veins and mucosal capillaries is a feature of disseminated intravascular coagulation (DIC) which may itself complicate septicaemia, endotoxic shock, obstetric emergencies, the haemolytic-uraemic syndrome and neoplasia. The resultant widespread fibrin thrombi have been claimed to lead to intestinal infarction, but their precise role is in dispute because similar microthrombi are found more frequently in straightforward cases of occlusive ischaemia than in patients with DIC and non-occlusive ischaemia.[67]

Mesenteric venous thrombosis

Venous thrombosis was formerly considered to be a frequent cause of small intestinal ischaemia. However, many cases previously diagnosed as venous thrombosis were secondary to arterial or mechanical occlusion, or were unrecognized cases of non-occlusive ischaemia. Grendell and Ocker,[68] in an excellent review, claim that 5–15% of cases of intestinal ischaemia (without mechanical bowel obstruction) result from venous thrombosis. The accuracy of their estimate is borne out by a subsequent analysis of 98 patients with mesenteric infarction in which 13 cases were attributed to mesenteric venous thrombosis.[69] Such thrombosis may be a consequence of portal hypertension, intra-abdominal sepsis,[70] hypercoagulable states,[71] surgical operations (especially splenectomy) and abdominal trauma.[72] An unusual cause of venous thrombosis is lymphocytic phlebitis, a condition of unknown aetiology in which the intramural veins (but not arteries or arterioles) of the small intestine are surrounded by a dense infiltrate of lymphocytes. Superimposed thrombosis can lead to intestinal infarction.[73]

Mechanical causes

Mechanical obstruction of the vascular supply to the small intestine may be a consequence of torsion of the mesentery in a volvulus, or of compression of the pedicle in a strangulation or intussusception (Fig. 31.4), or by a tumour.[74] In general, compression produces an initial venous thrombosis resulting in a 'pure' venous infarction, whereas torsion is equally liable to produce arterial occlusion. Malrotation and volvulus are important in the causation of ischaemic bowel disease in neonates.[75]

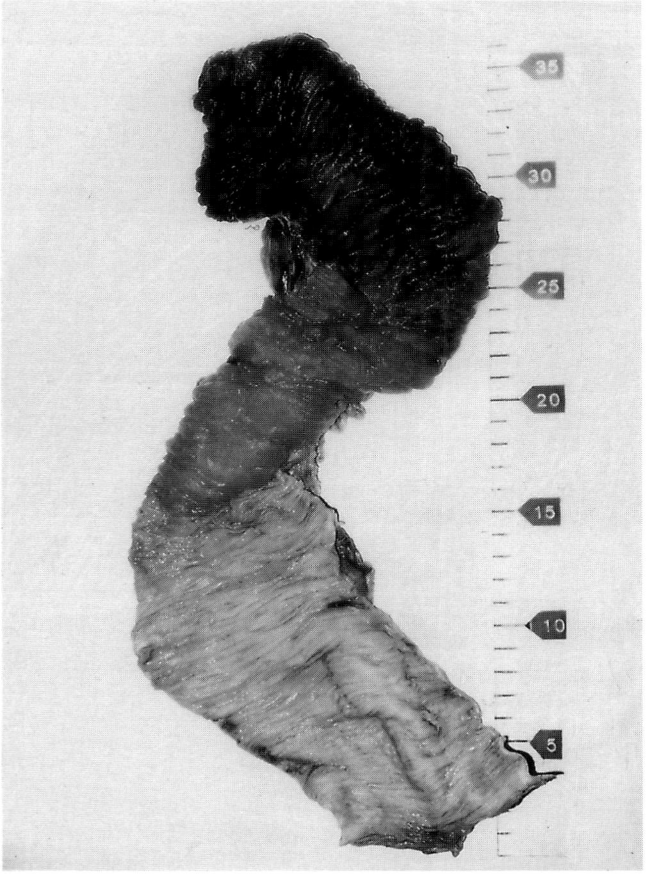

Fig. 31.4 Infarction following intussusception. This specimen was removed from a woman of 43 years who one year before had undergone small bowel by-pass for morbid obesity. At laparotomy, the blind end of the small intestine had intussuscepted back into itself and produced full thickness infarction.

Non-occlusive causes of small intestinal ischaemia

Recognition of non-occlusive ischaemia has been a relatively recent development, credit for the first description going to Ende in a study published in 1958.[76] Non-occlusive ischaemia encompasses those cases where ischaemic damage is found in the presence of a patent vascular supply. Thus Renton[77] defined non-occlusive infarction as necrosis of some part of the bowel due to ischaemia where there is no organic block to the vessels. This concept may be an oversimplification.

Non-occlusive ischaemia is claimed to be the cause of between 25%[60] and 50%[43] of all cases of intestinal infarction, and its incidence appears to be rising. While the precise cause is frequently obscure, it has been generally assumed that vasoconstriction in response to decreased cardiac output, hypovolaemia, dehydration and hypotension together with arterial atherosclerosis are the major factors. In addition, the vasoconstrictor effects of digitalis have been incriminated. Haglund and Lundgren[60] compared 'occlusive' and 'non-occlusive' groups of patients with intestinal infarction to examine the validity of these suggested associations. They found that patients with non-occlusive intestinal infarction showed a tendency to be younger, to have associated myocardial infarction, and to have had a preceding period of systemic hypotension, more frequently than those with vessel obstruction. A history of atrial fibrillation and digitalis therapy was present with equal frequency in the two groups. These authors postulated that reduced intestinal perfusion pressure in the first place causes mucosal damage and that this damage, leading as it does to release of proteolytic enzymes and increased permeability to toxic substances, brings about further cardiovascular deterioration and gradual progression of the intestinal lesion to transmural infarction. Although Haglund and Lundgren's study casts doubt on the role of digitalis in non-occlusive ischaemia, a recent case report[78] in which small bowel infarction followed immediately after an intravenous injection of a digitalis preparation, appears to reaffirm a direct link.

Some re-assessment of the concept of non-occlusive intestinal infarction has been prompted by the finding of obstructive lesions in distal mesenteric arteries in two patients labelled as 'non-occlusive'.[79] This study revealed narrowing by intimal fibromuscular proliferation, medial hypertrophy, and peri-arterial fibrosis. The normal practice of gross inspection of the major arterial tree at autopsy, and histological examination of intramural vessels in sections of the intestinal wall, would not reveal these lesions in the peripheral arcades. Hence, this form of obliteration might be widespread in cases of non-occlusive ischaemia, and their presence would explain why a 'critical' reduction in mesenteric blood flow could readily bring about intestinal infarction. Substantiation of these findings by study of a large series of patients is crucial to our further understanding of this entity.

Drugs and non-occlusive ischaemia

Small bowel infarction has been reported after administration of certain drugs and poisons, but their relationship to non-occlusive ischaemia is variable. Intestinal ischaemia has been found in drug addicts who have consumed large quantities of cocaine,[80,81] an effect attributable to the drug's sympathomimetic action on intestinal vessels, and there has been a recent report of small intestinal infarction induced by 'crack'.[82] However, intestinal infarction in a case of selenium poisoning[83] was probably a consequence of profound systemic hypotension and not a primary drug effect. Indeed, some cases of infarction in drug addicts represent occlusive ischaemia brought about by embolization of particulate matter following injection of crushed tablets.[84]

ACUTE ISCHAEMIA

Mucosal necrosis

Acute ischaemic injury confined to the mucosa has been termed 'transient' or 'reversible' because the lesion is usually followed by complete regeneration. However, as already discussed, mucosal necrosis, particularly in non-occlusive ischaemia, may be simply the first step in a 'vicious circle' of events leading to transmural infarction.

The earliest lesion encountered in human material is epithelial separation, which commences in a matter of minutes after the onset of ischaemia. The surface epithelial layer remains intact, but a clear bleb or vesicle develops at the tips of the villi between the elevated epithelial cell and the underlying basement membrane (Fig. 31.5). This is a difficult lesion to evaluate because identical appearance may be seen in any surgical resection specimen of small intestine, especially if there has been a long 'warm ischaemic' time. Furthermore, epithelial separation is considerably exaggerated by fixation in 10% formalin, presumably because of its hypertonicity,[23] so that preoperative ischaemic changes are difficult, if not impossible, to distinguish from intraoperative and fixation artefacts. The finding of proteinaceous exudation and inflammatory cells within the subepithelial cleft is in favour of preoperative ischaemia.

Macroscopically, the first change is one of intense congestion, which later gives way to the development of small shallow ulcers. On histological examination, there is disintegration of the surface epithelium. The underlying capillaries of the oedematous lamina propria are widely dilated, congested and show focal breakdown of their walls with interstitial haemorrhage.

Although the connective tissue cells also undergo necrosis, the denuded villi are frequently preserved so that by 24–36 h there is an eosinophilic ghost outline of the mucosa. Later the necrotic mucosa may slough away and be replaced by a pseudomembrane of fibrin and enmeshed necrotic cells. At first, the acute inflammatory cell infiltrate is sparse but between 24–48 h, probably in response to bacterial invasion, neutrophil polymorphs accumulate, especially at the margins of the infarcted mucosa. Fibrin thrombi may be found in mucosal capillaries but no assumptions can be made as to their causal role in mucosal necrosis.

If the patient survives, healing is achieved through macrophage ingestion and clearing of necrotic material and by regeneration of the mucosa by proliferation and migration of epithelial and connective tissue cells from the viable margins. Epithelial integrity is restored, although there is permanent crypt distortion in the regenerated mucosa.

Mural necrosis

Mural necrosis reaches into the submucosa or into, but

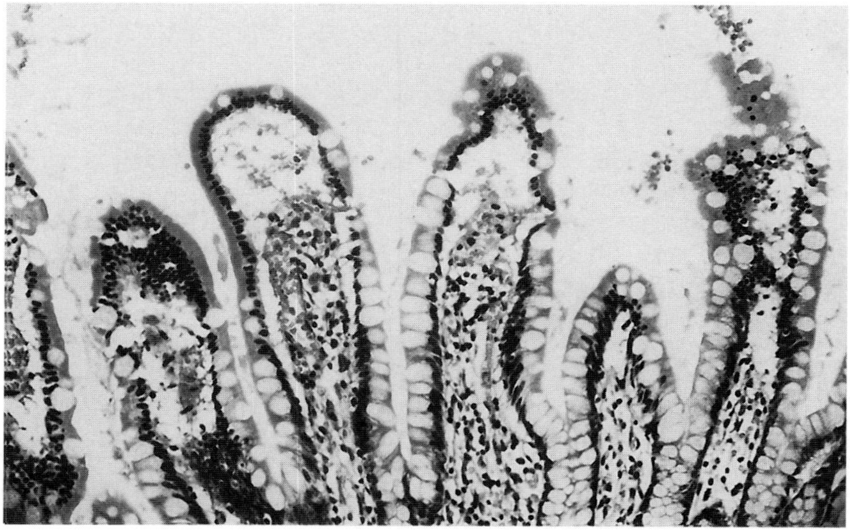

Fig. 31.5 Epithelial separation in mucosa adjacent to an infarcted segment from a man of 40 years who earlier underwent highly selective vagotomy for duodenal ulcer. The abdominal wound had been closed with wire sutures and 6 days later he required small bowel resection after a small loop of bowel had become strangulated in a hernia between two of the sutures. (H&E, ×51)

not through, the muscularis propria.[38] In such cases, the deeper extension of the necrosis necessitates granulation tissue formation and a more prolonged reparative process. The importance of this lesion lies in its tendency towards chronicity and the possibility of stricture formation. Thus mural necrosis may either evolve into a transmural infarct, in which case early operation is the only hope for survival, or can retain partial thickness and heal with insignificant fibrosis and no untoward effects, or with greater fibrosis and produce a stricture.[38] As Whitehead[85] has pointed out, the healing of ischaemic lesions is governed by simple principles, and the only lesion which produces a permanent morphological abnormality is one involving a segment of bowel short enough to be compatible with survival, at a depth of less than the full thickness of the bowel, but including more than the whole of the mucosa. Healing is thus achieved by a combination of mucosal regeneration and fibrous repair in the wall. The viable margins around the necrotic zone show endothelial cell and fibroblast proliferation, and these cells infiltrate the base to form granulation tissue. There is lysis of red blood cells, and macrophages take up the haemosiderin that forms. Epithelial cells proliferate from the margins, cover the granulation tissue, and finally close the breach in continuity (Fig. 31.6A). However the final crypt pattern is at best irregular and distorted, and frequently there is merely a single covering layer of flattened epithelium.

The breach in the muscularis mucosae does not regenerate, so that even with complete healing, the site is always marked by interruption of the muscularis and a fibrous scar in the submucosa. Several days or even a few weeks after mural infarction, the occlusive vascular lesion may be relieved (by recanalization of a thrombus, for example) or the segment may become revascularized through an opening up of collaterals. If this occurs, the healing but still ulcerated infarct may be the source of substantial and life-threatening secondary haemorrhage (Fig. 31.6B).

Transmural necrosis

Transmural infarction of the intestine extends through the muscularis propria, with or without involvement of the serosa, and is synonymous with 'gangrene'.[38] The macroscopic appearances are well known. The bowel becomes flaccid, dilates, and the serosal aspect is deeply congested and 'frosted' by a thin layer of fibrin (Fig. 31.7A). On opening, the lumen contains heavily blood-stained fluid and the mucosa is intensely congested. There may be elevation and distortion of the mucosa by haemorrhage and oedema. In established transmural infarcts, frank ulceration of the mucosa will be evident, and the wall may be so friable that perforation has occurred.

On microscopy soon after infarction, the full extent of necrosis will not be apparent, but by 24–36 h eosinophilic necrosis of smooth muscle cells is recognizable, and

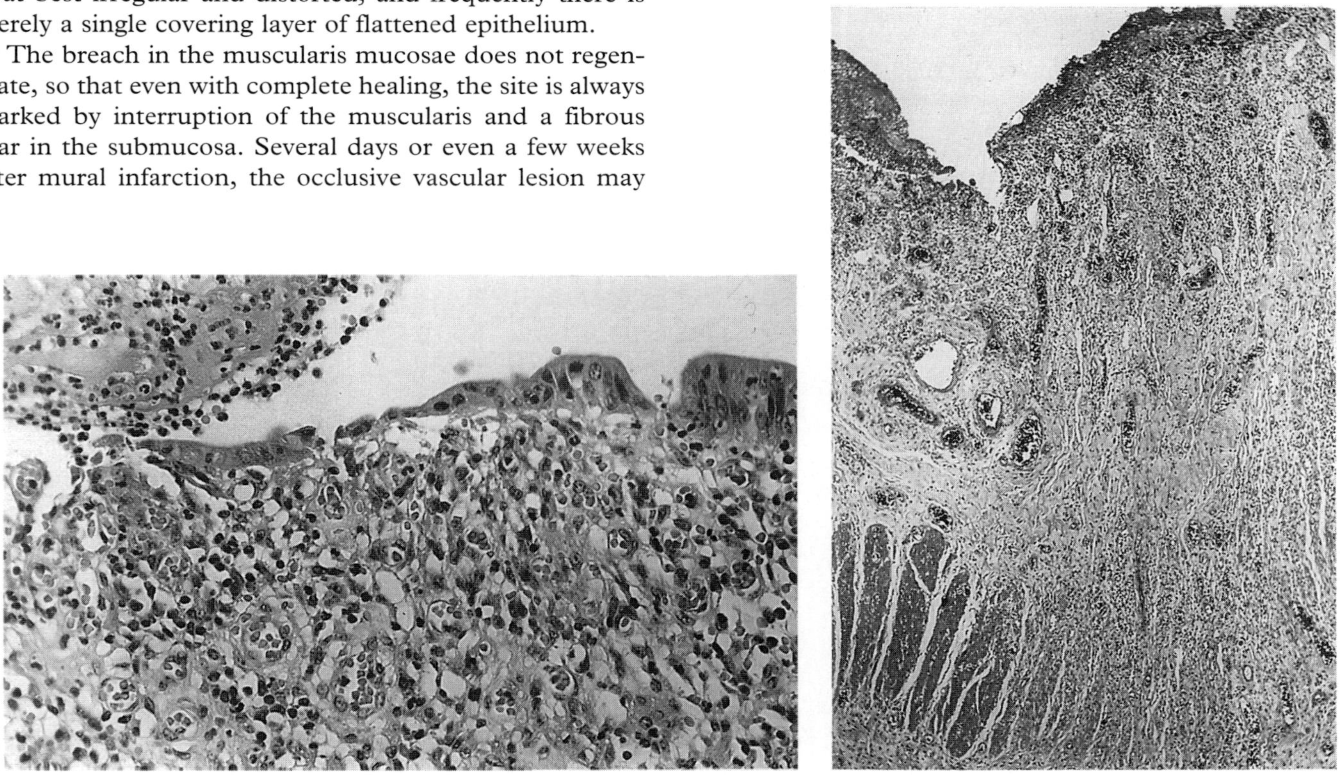

A B

Fig. 31.6A Margin of ulcerated segment showing re-epithelialization extending over inflamed granulation tissue. (H&E, ×75) **B** Infarction complicated by secondary haemorrhage. A 72-year-old woman underwent aortic valve replacement. Three weeks later she developed massive intestinal bleeding and at laparotomy a segment of thickened, oedematous ileum was removed. This representative field shows ulceration and transmural involvement with fibrosis and granulation tissue formation consistent with onset 3 weeks before. (H&E, ×12)

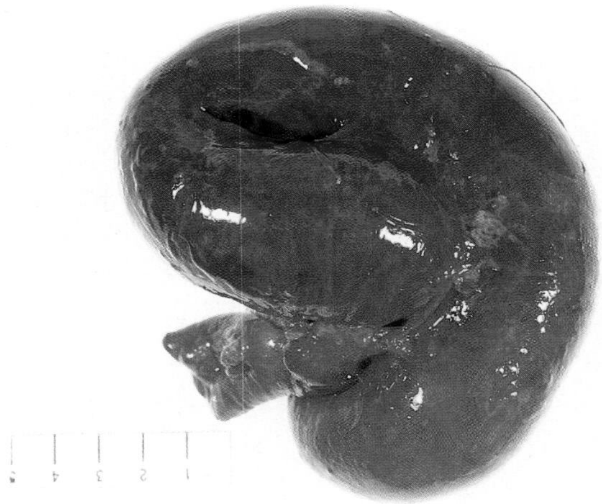

A

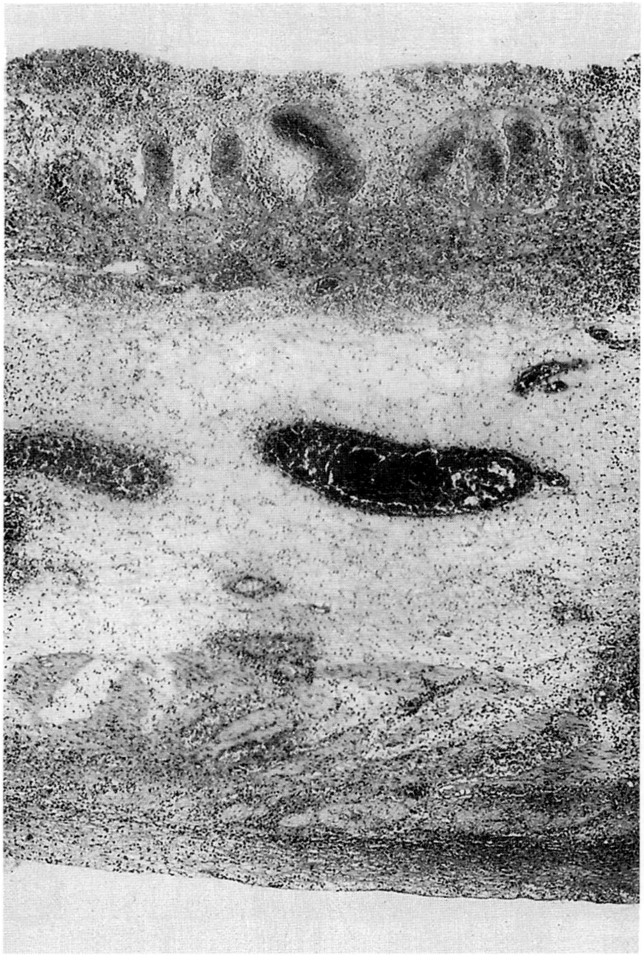

B

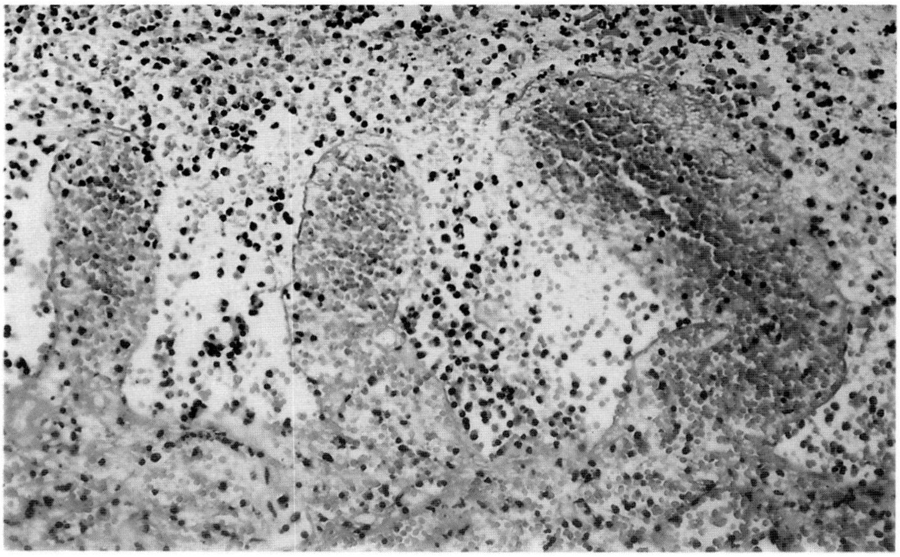

C

Fig. 31.7A Infarction resulting from volvulus. The patient was a woman of 48 years who developed a small bowel volvulus around a fibrous adhesion between the omentum and sigmoid colon. She had undergone a previous small bowel resection one year earlier for strangulation through a defect in the broad ligament following a vaginal hysterectomy. **B** Microscopy from the same case confirms the transmural infarction. All layers of the wall are infiltrated by moderate numbers of polymorphs and there is marked submucosal oedema and congestion of vessels. There is considerable haemorrhage into the mucosa and superficial submucosa. (H&E, ×15) **C** 'Ghost' villi surrounded by fibrin and neutrophils of the coating pseudomembrane. (H&E, ×54) oedema and congestion involves the main muscle coat and subserosa (Fig. 31.7B,C). Thrombosis may be seen in adjacent mesenteric arteries and veins but this is frequently a secondary phenomenon related to stasis and only rarely will these vessels reveal the primary occlusive lesion.

Infarction of the small intestine can be described in terms of segmental or massive involvement. Segmental infarction results either from occlusion of distal mesenteric vessels which is sufficiently widespread to impair the collateral supply, or by mechanical obstruction of the supply to a loop of intestine. This type of involvement is readily amenable to surgical treatment, but many patients already have peritonitis, endotoxaemia and severe circulatory disturbances at the time of diagnosis, so that operative results remain poor. Nevertheless, there is a definite relationship between survival and the length of bowel resected.[60]

Massive small intestinal infarction, usually resulting from complete occlusion of the SMA, has a hopeless prognosis with only occasional survivors after resection who are dependent on intravenous alimentation. If ischaemia is diagnosed early, i.e. before development of total infarction, it is occasionally possible to undertake embolectomy or reconstruction of the SMA, but as one would anticipate the results are uniformly poor.[42,86,87]

Venous infarction

Venous thrombosis results in marked congestion and oedema of the affected segment of intestine. The wall, and the adjacent mesentery, are generally a dark plum colour, and blood-stained fluid is present in the peritoneum. Microscopically, there is diffuse and severe interstitial haemorrhage in the wall with necrosis varying from mucosal to transmural in extent. The veins contain thrombi of variable age as the lesion is frequently progressive. The arteries are patent.

CHRONIC ISCHAEMIA

Chronic ischaemic lesions of the small intestine fall into two categories. One, already mentioned, is the ischaemic ulcer or stricture that follows segmental mural infarction. The other is the syndrome of chronic mesenteric insufficiency or 'intestinal angina'.

Chronic mesenteric insufficiency

This term is used to describe a condition where there is insufficient intestinal blood flow to satisfy the demands of increased motility, secretion and absorption that develop after meals.[43] The insufficiency is usually manifest as abdominal pain, and other features attributed to this syndrome, such as chronic blood loss,[88] diarrhoea and malabsorption are seldom seen,[89] although it should be emphasized that symptomatic mesenteric insufficiency is itself distinctly rare.

While chronic insufficiency is occasionally due to aortic aneurysms or traumatic or congenital anomalies of the SMA, atherosclerotic narrowing is by far the most common cause of this form of intestinal ischaemia.[43] Interestingly, however, there is no relationship between intestinal function and the degree of potential ischaemia suggested by angiography.[90]

Although the postprandial pain is patently a response to ischaemia akin to coronary angina, nothing is known of the nature of any pathological changes. One must conclude from the dearth of information that any lesions, if present, are restricted to the mucosa and are 'transient'. It is known, however, that if left untreated the majority of patients will go on to develop frank transmural infarction.

Ischaemic ulceration and strictures

In some patients who develop a segmental mural infarct, there is continuing ischaemia because of persistence of the occlusive lesion and an inadequate collateral supply. In such patients, complete healing is thwarted, there is continuing mucosal ulceration allowing access of bacteria to underlying tissues, and excessive fibrosis. Thus there develops a chronic ulcer with eventual fibrous stricture formation. This gives rise to a clinical picture of crampy abdominal pain, diarrhoea, weight loss and occasional fever which may be indistinguishable from Crohn's disease.[43] Even the gross appearances — a segment of concentrically thickened bowel with mucosal ulceration and prominent submucosal fibrosis — can be identical. The greater tendency for Crohn's disease to involve the terminal ileum is of some diagnostic assistance. Features of subacute obstruction may be accompanied by anaemia, diarrhoea and steatorrhoea if there is bacterial overgrowth in the dilated proximal loops, and there may be an antecedent history of abdominal trauma, pain or a strangulated hernia.[43]

Microscopically, inflamed granulation and fibrous tissue underlie an area of ulceration. At the margins, regenerative epithelial hyperplasia is evident, and a single layer of deeply-staining cuboidal epithelial cells extends for a variable distance over the granulation tissue. The deeper parts are occupied by dense fibrous tissue in which scattered collections of lymphocytes and neuronal hyperplasia may again cause confusion with Crohn's disease. Apart from finding the diagnostic granulomas, Crohn's disease is indicated by the presence of mucosal inflammation away from the ulcerated area, and by dense aggregated chronic inflammatory cells extending through to the subserosa. On the other hand, ischaemia is suggested by the finding of haemosiderin-laden macrophages and fibrous replacement of the muscle layers.

Apart from Crohn's disease, there are several less common conditions which enter into the differential diagnosis of chronic ischaemic ulceration. Irradiation, tuberculosis, actinomycosis, Zollinger-Ellison syndrome, carcinoma and malignant lymphoma should be readily distinguishable on the basis of the clinical history and on microscopic examination. There are other conditions, however, which invariably present considerable diagnostic difficulty and confusion. Three of these entities deserve brief consideration, namely drug-induced small bowel ulceration primary non-specific ulceration and chronic ulcerative enteritis.

Drug-induced ulceration

In the 1960s there was a sudden increase in the incidence of non-specific stenosing ulcers of the small intestine and it soon became apparent that most of these patients were taking enteric-coated potassium preparations.[91] The ulcers, which are generally small (about 1.5 cm diameter) are most commonly located in the ileum. The surrounding mucosa is oedematous and hyperaemic and there is frequently extensive submucosal fibrosis resulting in stricture formation. The muscularis propria is rarely involved except in the few cases which have perforated. The mechanism of injury probably relates to the high concentration of the irritant potassium salt released on breakdown of its coating.

The number of cases was such, and the link with this medicament so incontrovertible, that the preparation was withdrawn. It was replaced by a 'slow release' form, in which the salt was incorporated into a wax or plastic matrix to aid its dispersal and release at lower concentration. However, soon after its introduction further cases of small bowel ulceration were encountered and, although the numbers of patients are small in relation to the widespread use of slow release preparations, the problem is far from eliminated.[92]

More recently, other drugs have been incriminated and there are reports in the literature relating intestinal ulceration and fibrous strictures to non-steroidal anti-inflammatory drugs in general,[93] and to salicylates[94] and indomethacin[95] in particular.

Primary non-specific ulceration

When the acknowledged causes of small bowel ulceration have been eliminated, there is a residuum of patients in whom the only possible diagnosis is 'primary non-specific ulceration'. Such ulcers may be single, in which case the term 'solitary ulcer of the small intestine' has been applied, or they can be multiple. Common presentations are intestinal bleeding, either overt or causing iron-deficiency anaemia, intestinal obstruction and perforation.[96] Most of these patients respond completely to surgical resection, but a few develop further ulcers and clinical relapses.

The pathological features are indistinguishable from those found in drug-induced ulceration.[97] The aetiology of this condition remains a mystery. Some patients will have villous atrophy and malabsorption, and the ulceration is probably a manifestation of coeliac disease (see below). Other patients placed in this diagnostic category will be unrecognized cases of chronic ischaemia (Fig. 31.8) and non-granulomatous Crohn's disease. It seems likely that 'primary non-specific ulceration' is not a distinct entity but embraces a variety of conditions in which the his-

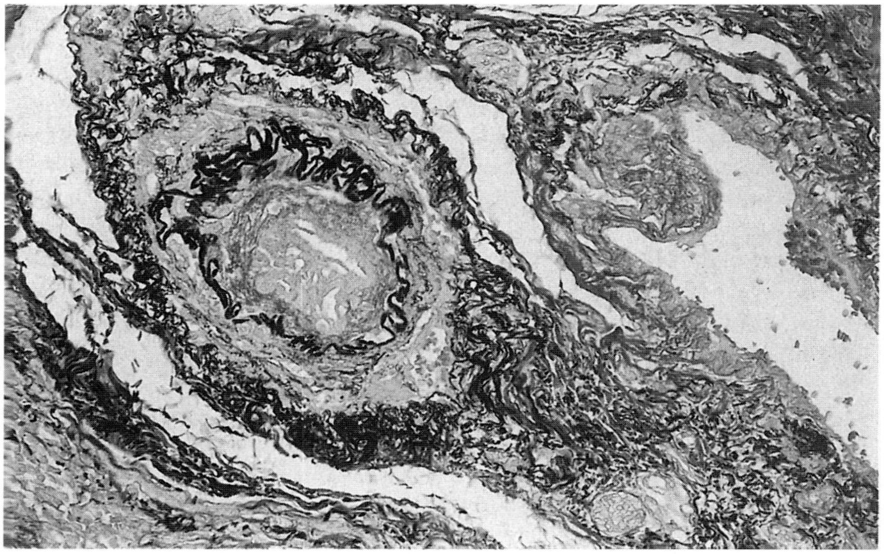

Fig. 31.8 Extramural artery seen on review of a lesion originally diagnosed as 'primary non-specific ulcer' of the ileum. The finding of total atherosclerotic occlusion indicates an ischaemic origin. (Elastic-van Gieson, ×53)

topathological changes are not sufficiently distinctive to permit proper categorization.

Chronic ulcerative enteritis (see also Ch. 26)

The term 'chronic ulcerative enteritis' should be reserved for small intestinal ulceration arising in the context of a malabsorption state. Its separation from primary non-specific ulceration is to a large extent artificial, as the cause of chronic ulcerative enteritis is also unknown, but their distinction serves to lessen the confusion over this subject.

The association between small bowel ulceration and malabsorption was first described by Nyman in 1947,[98] and a comprehensive review of the subject covering data from patients has been provided by Baer et al,[99] but there remain a number of controversies. The existence of this entity has been doubted by some authors[100] and interpretative problems relate to villous atrophy, malabsorption and the nature of the ulcers.

First, villous atrophy restricted to the immediate vicinity of the ulcer should not be considered significant; the diagnosis should be based on its finding in remote mucosa. Secondly, villous atrophy is not synonymous with malabsorption and the latter diagnosis should be substantiated by the relevant tests of intestinal function. Thirdly, malabsorption is not synonymous with coeliac disease; this diagnosis can only be established by a demonstrable histological response to a gluten-free diet. There are considerable difficulties involved in fulfilling these criteria in ulcerative enteritis.[101] Finally, the presence of a 'covert' lymphoma, particularly a T-cell lymphoma, must be carefully considered and excluded before concluding that the ulceration is simply a form of non-specific chronic inflammation. Bearing all these points in mind, there remains a strong argument that simple, inflammatory ulcers do occur in patients with malabsorption states, including coeliac disease, and that the term 'chronic ulcerative enteritis' can be usefully retained for this condition (Fig. 31.9A,B).

NECROTIZING ENTERITIS

Necrotizing enteritis (or enterocolitis) represents a complex, multifactorial condition in which intestinal ischaemia plays at least some part, and occasionally a major one. The disease manifests itself as severe abdominal pain, distension and diarrhoea. Paralytic ileus rapidly supervenes and progresses to intestinal infarction, sepsis and shock, often with a fatal outcome. Cases of necrotizing enteritis seem to fall into two age related clinicopathological groups.

Neonatal necrotizing enterocolitis

Neonatal necrotizing enterocolitis (NNEC) occurs in more than 2% of admissions to neonatal intensive care units,[102] and the vast majority of those affected are premature and have other serious illnesses.[103] NNEC is considered in more detail in Chapter 32.

Necrotizing enteritis in adults

In adolescence and adults, bacterial infection appears to be paramount in the causation of necrotizing enteritis. Hence the older texts laid emphasis on staphylococcal enterocolitis developing in postoperative patients or those treated with broad spectrum antibiotics, but this is a rare condition judging from the paucity of reports in the literature. Of much more importance is the role of clostridia in the causation of necrotizing enteritis.

A notable example of necrotizing enteritis resulting from clostridial infection is the disease 'pig-bel' found among natives of Papua/New Guinea, a disease which follows feasting on undercooked pork and is associated with beta toxin producing strains of *Clostridium perfringens* type C.[104] The same organism was responsible for the 'Darmbrand' necrotizing enteritis in post-World War II Germany.[105] Acute clostridial enteritis was the cause of death of a 23-year-old fashion model who suffered from bulimia nervosa — an irresistible urge to overeat. She developed acute gastric dilatation and a fatal enteritis after eating a prodigious meal.[106]

Sporadic cases of necrotizing enteritis are not uncommon in Sri Lanka, and Arseculeratne et al[107] have reported on their experience with 83 patients. In this series, however, of 12 patients in whom *C. welchii* (*perfringens*) were cultured, the majority were the non beta toxin producing type A. These authors argue that clostridia may act either as initiators of mucosal necrosis, or as colonizers of previously established necrotic foci, to produce intestinal gas gangrene. Thus clostridia which produce the beta toxin (type C organisms) are capable of initiating necrosis, whereas the type A strain requires synergistic factors such as stasis, altered bowel flora, or a pre-existing focus of necrosis before colonization leading to enteritis will occur. Certainly, *C. perfringens* type A is increasingly accepted as a cause of necrotizing enteritis[108] and we have recently encountered two fatal cases following food poisoning with the type A organism (Dr J. Hopkinson, personal communication).

The pathology of clostridial necrotizing enteritis is essentially that of a coagulative necrosis commencing in the mucosa and extending into and through the wall. In Sri Lankan patients who had been previously healthy, there was usually a perivascular infiltrate of polymorphs and mononuclear cells, suggesting the possibility of a type II hypersensitivity reaction, whereas patients with a preceding illness showed a paucity of inflammatory cells and no vasculitis.[107] Gram-positive bacilli can be demonstrated in tissue sections in most cases.

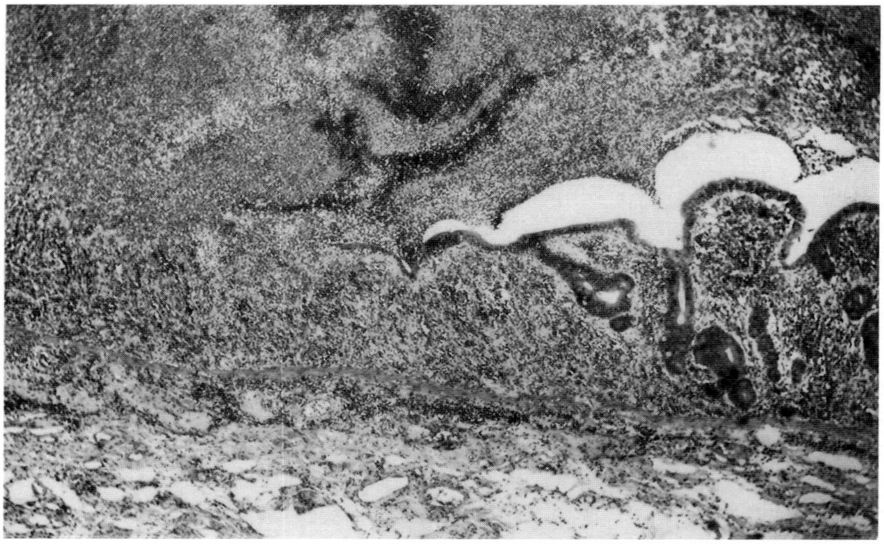

A

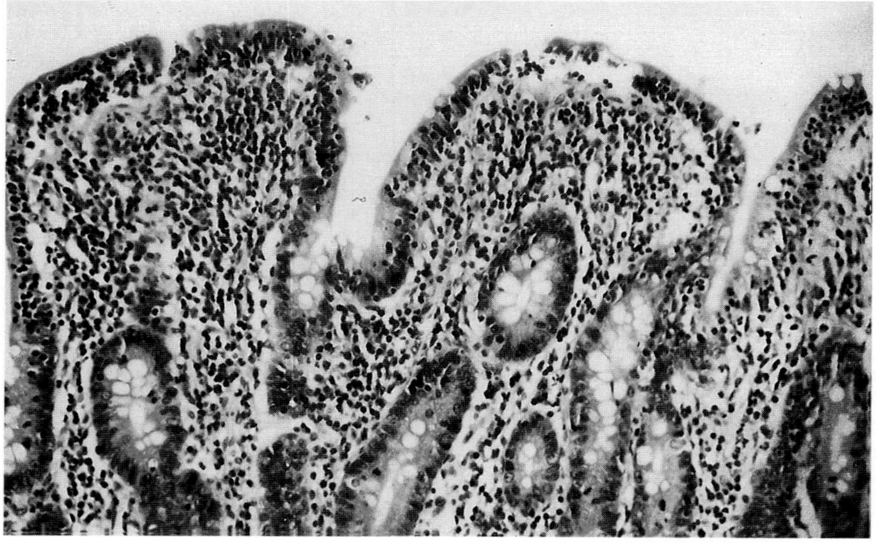

B

Fig. 31.9A Small intestinal ulceration of 'non-specific' type in a patient with undiagnosed coeliac disease. The resection was carried out 3 days after the onset of colicky abdominal pain. The patient, a man of 49 years, passed 5–6 motions each day and had been diagnosed as having a 'dietary deficiency' 15 years before. (H&E, ×31), **B** Mucosa from proximal resection margin showing blunting of villi and a marked increase in intra-epithelial lymphocytes. The patient made a good response to a gluten-free diet. (H&E, ×53)

VASCULAR ANOMALIES

Vascular anomalies of the small intestine are rare but when present may give rise to haemorrhage which can be life threatening and difficult to diagnose. A review of the pathology of such lesions, however, is bedevilled by the profusion of terms used to describe them. Thus arteriovenous malformations, vascular ectasias, telangiectasias and angiodysplasia have all been used to describe very similar, if not identical, lesions of the gastrointestinal tract. Rees and Wright,[109] in an excellent review of angiodysplasia of the colon, make the claim that it constitutes a distinct pathological entity and is due to telangiectasia or dilatation of pre-existing vessels, but the same term has been used to describe apparently identical lesions in the stomach and small intestine,[110] while others have labelled the same lesions in the colon (and elsewhere) arteriovenous malformations,[111] telangiectasias,[112] or vascular ectasias. Under these circumstances, certainly as far as the small intestine is concerned, it seems preferable to classify these lesions under the descriptive heading of 'vascular ectasias' and to avoid such ambiguous terms as 'dysplasia' and 'malformation'. Thus, although the present classification (Table 31.3) is based on that given by Camilleri et al[113] in their comprehensive review, the categories of 'angiodysplasia' and 'telangiectasia' are amalgamated under vascular ectasias, rather than categorizing the former as an arteriovenous malformation. The term arteriovenous malformation is reserved for lesions composed of an inter-

Table 31.3 Vascular anomalies of the small intestine.

1. Vascular ectasias (including angiodysplasias and telangiectasias)
(a) Associated with inherited or congenital diseases
(i) Osler-Rendu-Weber disease
(ii) von Willebrand's disease
(iii) Turner's syndrome
(b) Associated with acquired diseases
(i) Systemic sclerosis (especially CRST variant)
(ii) Haemodialysis for renal failure (?)
(iii) Aortic stenosis
(c) Sporadic
2. Venous ectasia (phlebectasia)
3. Haemangiomas
(a) Associated with cutaneous abnormalities
(i) Blue rubber bleb naevus syndrome
(ii) Klippel-Trenaunay-Weber syndrome
(iii) Peutz-Jeghers' variant
(b) Sporadic
4. Arteriovenous malformation

woven leash of enlarged thick-walled arteries, veins and sinusoidal capillaries, as described in other sites in the body, and which are presumed to be of congenital origin.

Vascular ectasias

Histology of these lesions reveals dilated and distorted vessels lined by flattened endothelium whose thin walls contain scanty smooth muscle fibres. They appear to be made up, therefore, of ectatic veins, venules and capillaries and involve both mucosal and submucosal vessels. The dilated mucosal capillaries come to lie very close to the surface, and where the epithelium is denuded, appear to be separated from the gut lumen by only a single layer of endothelium; presumably this layer is readily disrupted and leads to haemorrhage.

Although the vast majority of these lesions are found in the right side of the colon, they are an occasional source of bleeding from the small intestine. Meyer et al,[111] in a review of 218 'arteriovenous malformations' of the bowel, identified 10.5% in the jejunum, 5.5% in the ileum and 2.3% in the duodenum. Some instances of small intestinal vascular ectasias are undoubtedly of inherited or congenital origin, notably those that occur in Osler-Rendu-Weber disease,[114] von Willebrand's disease,[115] and Turner's syndrome.[116] Others are acquired lesions but have certain disease associations. Intestinal vascular ectasias form part of the Calcinosis-Raynaud's-Sclerodactyly-Telangiectasia (CRST) variant of systemic sclerosis, where the telangiectasias are largely confined to the stomach and small intestine.[113] It has been claimed that a higher incidence of intestinal vascular ectasias is found in patients on haemodialysis[112] and those with aortic stenosis,[112] but in both instances the association may well be spurious. In the former, anticoagulation may increase the incidence of bleeding from ectasias that would otherwise go unnoticed; in aortic stenosis, it is argued that bleeding is due to the low perfusion pressure and ischaemia.[117] A further consideration of 'angiodysplasia' is given in Chapter 32.

Venous ectasia

Venous ectasia is distinguished from the generality of vascular ectasias because the dilatation in this condition is restricted to the larger submucosal veins. Such varicosities are akin to those found in the rectum or oesophagus, but are of course a comparative rarity in the small intestine. Nevertheless varicosities may develop in the duodenum in portal hypertension and can be a source of life-threatening haemorrhage.[118,119] Diffuse phlebectasia occurring apart from portal hypertension appears as multiple, compressible, dark bluish-red nodules varying from a few millimetres to several centimetres in diameter.[120] These lesions are not associated with any other somatic or cutaneous abnormality.

Haemangiomas

In contrast to the dilatation of pre-existing vessels which characterizes the vascular ectasias, haemangiomas are tumour-like lesions better regarded as hamartomas than true neoplasms. They appear to develop within the submucosal vascular plexus and are conventionally described as either capillary, cavernous or mixed.

The lesions are similar to those described in other sites. The capillary haemangiomas consist of a tortuous network of variably dilated capillaries lined by a single, generally flattened, layer of endothelium. The vascular channels are usually tightly packed with only a little intervening connective tissue stroma. Cavernous lesions are composed of larger irregular spaces, some with papillary infoldings, lined by flattened endothelium, but separated by a more substantial fibrocellular stroma, sometimes containing scanty smooth muscle cells. Haemangiomas of the small intestine may be single or multiple, when the term 'haemangiomatosis' has been employed. Occasional reports refer to 'diffuse haemangiomas' affecting long segments or the entire small intestine, but these cases are invariably accompanied by diffuse lymphangiectasia[121] and are better termed diffuse vascular ectasias. Malignant change is extremely rare, but an acceptable case of malignant haemangioendothelioma complicating multiple haemangiomas of the intestine has been reported.[122]

The relationship of haemangiomas to various cutaneous syndromes has been well reviewed by Golitz.[123] The blue rubber bleb naevus syndrome is characterized by cavernous haemangiomas of the skin and gastrointestinal tract with recurrent episodes of bleeding. The gastrointestinal haemangiomas are usually multiple and principally affect the small intestine, followed by the colon and stomach. Haemangiomas may be found at other sites, including liver, spleen, subcutaneous tissue and synovium.[123] Cavernous haemangiomas and other vascular anomalies of the small intestine may be found in the Klippel-Trenaunay-Weber syndrome, a sporadic disorder characterized by soft tissue and bony hypertrophy of limbs associated with cutaneous haemangiomas and varicose veins.[113] A variant of Peutz Jegher's syndrome, in which the mucocutaneous pigmentation is associated with gastrointestinal haemangiomas but not epithelial polyposis, has been described, but one of these rare cases[124] is another example of a 'diffuse cavernous haemangioma' affecting the entire small intestine.

Arteriovenous malformations

Reports of vascular malformations are confused by problems over nomenclature and difficulties in distinguishing congenital from acquired. A lesion fulfilling the definition of arteriovenous malformation given above is the so-called cirsoid aneurysm which, when it occurs in the stomach, is usually referred to as Dieulafoy's malformation. Such lesions do occur in the small intestine and can give rise to massive haemorrhage.[125]

HAEMORRHAGE

It is self evident that haemorrhage is a frequent complication of any gastrointestinal lesion involving the mucosa, but three aspects of small intestinal haemorrhage deserve specific mention, namely the role of non-steroidal anti-inflammatory drugs (NSAIDs), bleeding in long-distance runners, and intramural haemorrhage, resulting in haematoma formation.

Drug-induced haemorrhage

While the role of NSAIDs in gastric mucosal injury and haemorrhage is well known, their potential for effects on the small intestine has received much less attention. It is true that the acid milieu of the stomach is much more conducive to mucosal injury than the alkaline pH of the small intestine, but high doses of NSAIDs, particularly indomethacin and phenylbutazone, are capable of producing perforating small bowel lesions in rats.[126] The ability of NSAIDs to produce chronic ulcers and strictures in humans has already been mentioned[93–95] and it has to be assumed that these lesions arise on the basis of an acute injury which, although asymptomatic, must undoubtedly give rise to intestinal bleeding. Studies using 5Cr-labelled red blood cells have shown that gastrointestinal bleeding is a frequent occurrence in patients taking NSAIDs,[127] and Langman et al[128] have shown that a significant number of patients admitted to hospital with small bowel and colonic perforation or haemorrhage were receiving NSAIDs.

Bleeding in long-distance runners

The medical consequences of a recreational activity in which an estimated 10–30 million people regularly participate must be of wide concern. A complication recently added to the growing list of medical complaints developing in long-distance runners is that of gastrointestinal haemorrhage.[129] The source of this haemorrhage is not known; it may be gastric rather than intestinal, and its causation is obscure, but the fact that it occurs is indisputable. Stewart and colleagues[130] found a significant increase in faecal haem concentration in 83% of tested athletes when comparing pre- and post-race samples, while McMahon et al[131] found a 22% incidence of clinically detectable bleeding in runners after a marathon. Much speculation surrounds the pathogenesis, but intestinal ischaemia and repetitive 'trauma' to the abdominal organs have been proposed as possible mechanisms.[129]

Intramural haematoma

Intramural haematoma of the gastrointestinal tract has been well reviewed by Hughes et al,[132] and Table 31.4 showing the causes and sites of 260 small intestinal haematomas, is drawn from their results. Intramural haematomas frequently present with intestinal obstruction, but perforation, intraperitoneal or intestinal haemorrhage and intussusception are all recognized complications.

Most haematomas result from blunt abdominal trauma which may be major, or minor and overlooked by the patient. As an example of the latter, the history given in a report[133] of a duodenal haematoma in a 34-year-old alcoholic male is worthy of repetition. Two weeks before presentation the patient had become intoxicated after drinking with a group of friends and had scaled the fence of a zoo and proceeded to ride one of the camels. The patient was thrown from the camel, and, although he had no personal recollection of subsequent events, his friends told him that the camel had stepped on his abdomen! The frequency with which the duodenum is involved in traumatic haematomas is explained by its relative fixity and its proximity to the vertebral column.

The other major causes of intramural haematoma are anticoagulant therapy, Henoch-Schonlein purpura and blood dyscrasias. The great majority of these haematomas are in the small intestine, particularly the jejunum. There is a high incidence of intussusception related to intra-

Table 31.4 Intramural haematomas of the duodenum and small intestine.

Cause	No.	Site: Duodenum	Site: Small intestine
Trauma	105	102	3
Anticoagulant therapy	93	5	88
Henoch-Schonlein/blood dyscrasias	25	9	16
Pancreatic disease	16	16	0
Iatrogenic	7	3	4
Unknown	14	14	0

Data from Hughes, Conn & Sherman 1977[109]

mural haematomas in Henoch-Schonlein disease.[132] Pancreatic disease, notably pancreatitis but also carcinoma and pseudocysts, have been complicated by duodenal intramural haematomas.

Haematomas can also arise, albeit very rarely, from spontaneous rupture of intramural or mesenteric arteries affected by atherosclerotic aneurysm[134] or Ehlers–Danlos syndrome.[135]

REFERENCES

1. Parks DA, Jacobson ED. Physiology of the splanchnic circulation. Arch Intern Med 1985; 145: 1278–1281.
2. Qamar MI, Read AE. Intestinal blood flow. Q J Med 1985; 220: 417–419.
3. Bulkley GB, Womack WA, Downey JM, Kvietys PR, Granger DN. Characterisation of segmental collateral blood flow in the small intestine. Am J Physiol 1985; 249: G228–G235.
4. Haglund U, Lundgren O. The effects of vasoconstrictor fibre stimulation on consecutive vascular sections of cat small intestine during hemorrhagic hypotension. Acta Physiol Scand 1973; 88: 95–108.
5. Chou CC, Gallavan RH. Blood flow and intestinal motility. Federation Proc 1982; 41: 2090–2095.
6. Jacobson EO, Lanciault G. The gastrointestinal vasculature. In: Duthie HL, Wormsley KG, eds. Scientific Basis of Gastroenterology. Edinburgh: Churchill Livingstone, 1979; p 26–48.
7. Lundgren O. The circulation of the small bowel mucosa. Gut 1974; 15: 1005–1013.
8. Marston A. Basic structure and function of the intestinal circulauon. Clin Gastroenterol 1972; 1: 539–546.
9. Redfors S, Hallback DA, Sjovall H, Jodal M, Lundgren O. Effects of hemorrhage on intramural blood flow distribution, villous tissue osmolality and fluid and electrolyte transport in the cat small intestine. Acta Physiol Scand 1984; 121: 211–222.
10. Granger DN, Barrowman JA, Harper SL, Kvietys PR, Korthuis RJ. Sympathetic stimulation and intestinal capillary fluid exchange. Am J Physiol 1984; 247: G279–283.
11. Falk A, Myrvold HE, Haglund U. Sympathetico-adrenergic influences on the small intestinal vascular reactions in experimental septic shock. Acta Physiol Scand 1983; 119: 373–379.
12. Pettei MJ, Levy J, Abramson S. Nonocclusive mesenteric ischaemia associated with propanolol overdosage: implications regarding splanchnic circulation. J Paed Gastroenterol Nutr 1990; 10: 544–547.
13. Bailey RW, Bulkley GB, Hamilton SR, Morris JB, Haglund UH. Protection of the small intestine from nonocclusive mesenteric ischemic injury due to cardiogenic shock. Amer J Surg 1987; 153: 108–116.
14. Konturek SJ. Action of enkephalins on the digestive system. In: Bloom SR, Polak JM, eds. Gut Hormones. 2nd ed. Edinburgh: Churchill Livingstone, 1981; p 439.
15. Eklund S, Jodal M, Lundgren O, Sjoqvist A. Effects of vasoactive intestinal polypeptide on blood flow, motility and fluid transport in the gastrointestinal tract of the cat. Acta Physiol Scand 1979; 105: 461–468.
16. Griffith SG, Burnstock G. Immunohistochemical demonstration of serotonin in nerves supplying human cerebral and mesenteric blood vessels. Lancet 1983; 1: 561–562.
17. Varkonyi T, Wittman T, Varro V. Effect of local circulatory arrest on the structure of the enterocytes of the isolated intestinal loop. Digestion 1977; 15: 295–302.
18. Wagner R, Gabbert H. Morphology and chronology of ischemic mucosal changes in the small intestine: A light and electron microscopic investigation. Klin Wochenschr 1983; 61: 593–599.
19. Schoenberg MH, Muhl E, Sellin D, Younes M, Schildberg FW, Haglund U. Posthypotensive generation of superoxide free radicals — possible role in the pathogenesis of the intestinal mucosal damage. Acta Chir Scand 1984; 150: 301–309.
20. Robinson JWL, Mirkovitch V, Winistorfer B, Saegesser F. Response of the intestinal mucosa to ischaemia. Gut 1981; 22: 512–527.
21. Si-Chun Ming, Bonakdarpour A. Evolution of lesions in intestinal ischaemia. Arch Pathol Lab Med 1977; 101: 4–43.
22. Polson H, Mowat C, Himal HS. Experimental and clinical studies of mesenteric infarction. Surg Gynecol Obstet 1981; 153: 360–362.
23. Bounous G. Acute necrosis of the intestinal mucosa. Gastroenterology 1982; 82: 1457–1467.
24. Redfors S, Hallback DA, Haglund U, Jodal M, Lundgren O. Blood flow distribution, villous tissue osmolality and fluid and electrolyte transport in the cat small intestine during regional hypotension. Acta Physiol Scand 1984; 121: 193–209.
25. Parks DA, Grogaard B, Granger N. Comparison of partial and complete arterial occlusion models for studying intestinal ischemia. Surgery 1982; 92: 896–901.
26. McCord JM. Oxygen-derived free radicals in post ischemic tissue injury. N Engl J Med 1985; 312: 159–163.
27. Granger DN, Parks DA. Role of oxygen radicals in the pathogenesis of intestinal ischemia. The Physiologist 1983; 26: 159–164.
28. Schoenberg MH, Fredholm BB, Haglund U, Jung H, Sellin D, Younes M, Schildberg FW. Studies on the oxygen radical mechanism involved in the small intestinal reperfusion damage. Acta Physiol Scand 1985; 124: 581–589.
29. Bounous G. Pancreatic proteases and oxygen-derived free radicals in acute ischaemic enteropathy. Surgery 1986; 99: 92–94.
30. Kubes P, Ibbotson G, Russell J, Wallace Jl, Granger DN. Role of platelet-activating factor in ischemia/reperfusion-induced leukocyte adherence. Amer J Physiol 1990; 259: G300–305.
31. Kubes P, Hunter J, Granger DN. Ischemia/reperfusion-induced feline intestinal dysfunction; importance of granulocyte recruitment. Gastroenterology 1992; 103: 807–812.
32. Caty MG, Guice KS, Oldham KT, Remick DG, Kunkel SI. Evidence for tumour necrosis factor-induced pulmonary microvascular injury after intestinal ischemia-reperfusion injury. Ann Surg 1990; 212: 694–700.
33. Mangino MJ, Anderson CB, Murphy MK, Brunt E, Turk J. Mucosal arachidonate metabolism and intestinal ischemia-reperfusion injury. Amer J Physiol 1989; 257: G299–307.
34. Siems W, Kowalewski J, Werner A, Schimke I, Gerber G. Nucleotide degradation and radical formation in ischemic and reperfused small intestine. Biomed Biochim Acta, 1989; 48: S16–19.
35. Granger DN, McCord JM, Parks DA, Hollwarth ME. Xanthine oxidase inhibitors attenuate ischemia-induced vascular permeability changes in the cat intestine. Gastroenterology 1986; 90: 80–84.
36. Dalsing MC, Sieber P, Grosfeld JL, Hasewinkel J, Hull M, Weber TR. Ischemic bowel: The protective effect of free-radical anion scavengers. J Pediat Surg 1983; 18: 360–364.
37. Ravid M, Van-Dyk D, Bernheim J, Kedar I. The protective effect of dimethyl sulfoxide in experimental ischemia of the intestine. Ann N Y Acad Sci 1983; 411: 100–104.
38. Swerdlow SH, Antonioli DA, Goldman H. Intestinal infarction: a new classification. Arch Pathol Lab Med 1981; 105: 218.
39. Croft RJ, Menon GP, Marston A. Does 'intestinal angina' exist? A critical study of obstructed visceral arteries. Br J Surg 1981; 68: 316–318.
40. Rogers DM, Thompson JE, Garrett WV, Talkington CM, Patman RD. Mesenteric vascular problems. A 26 year experience. Ann Surg 1982; 195: 554–565.
41. Socinski MA, Frankel JP, Morrow PL, Krawitt EL. Painless diarrhoea secondary to intestinal ischaemia. Diagnosis of

atheromatous emboli by jejunal biopsy. Dig Dis Sci 1984; 29: 674–677.
42. Sachs SM, Morton JH, Schwartz SI. Acute mesenteric ischaemia. Surgery 1982; 92: 64–653.
43. Andersson R, Parsson H, Isaksson B, Norgren L. Acute intestinal ischemia. A 14 year retrospective investigation. Acta Chir Scand 1984; 150: 217–221.
44. Brandt LJ, Boley SI. Ischemic intestinal syndromes. Adv Surg 1981; 15: 1–45.
45. Fratesi SJ, Barber GG. Celiac artery embolism: case report. Can J Surg 1981; 24: 512–513.
46. Rosman HS, Davis TP, Reddy D, Goldstein S. Cholesterol embolization: clinical findings and implication. J Am Coll Cardiol 1990; 15: 1296–1299.
47. Smith FC, Boon A, Shearman CP, Downing R. Spontaneous cholesterol embolism: a rare cause of bowel infarction. Eur J Vasc Surg 1991; 5: 581–582.
48. Shapiro N, Brandt L, Sprayregan S, Mitsudo S, Glotzer P. Duodenal infarction after therapeutic Gelfoam embolization of a bleeding duodenal ulcer. Gastroenterology 1981; 80: 176–180.
49. Mosley JG, Desai A, Gupta I. Mesenteric arteritis. Gut 1990; 31: 956–957.
50. McCurley TI, Collins RD. Intestinal infarction in rheumatoid arthritis. Three cases due to unusual obliterative vascular lesions. Arch Pathol Lab Med 1984; 108: 125–128.
51. Wisher M, Smeeton WM, Koelmeyer TD, Roche AH. Complete heart block and bowel infarction secondary to rheumatoid disease. Ann Rheum Dis 1985; 44: 425–428.
52. Soares VA, Franco MF. Perforation of small intestine after treatment for malignant hypertension. Lancet 1980; 2: 97.
53. Chi JG, Suh YL, Choi Y, Choi H, Ko KW. Necrotizing arteritis of ileum, as the initial manifestation of malignant hypertension in childhood. Child Nephr Urol 1988; 9: 112–115.
54. Prouse PJ, Thompson EM, Gumpel JM. Systemic lupus erythematosus and abdominal pain. Br J Rheumatol 1983; 22: 172–175.
55. Srigley JR, Gardiner GW. Giant cell arteritis with small bowel infarction. A case report and review of the literature. Am J Gastroenterol 1980; 73: 157–161.
56. Ljungstrom KG, Strandberg O, Sandstedt B. Infarction of the small bowel caused by giant cell arteritis. Case report. Acta Chir Scand 1989; 155: 361–363.
57. Esato K, Noma F, Kurata S, Oda E, Mohri H. Mesenteric infarction in Takayashu's arteritis treated by thromboendarterectomy and intestinal resection. Jpn J Surg 1982; 12: 130–134.
58. Herrington JL, Grossman LA. Surgical lesions of the small and large intestine resulting from Buerger's disease. Ann Surg 1968; 168: 1079–1087.
59. Barcelli U, Crissman J, First MR, Pollak VE. Rapidly progressing arteri-occlusive syndrome in a patient receiving long-term hemodialysis. Kohlmeier-Degos disease? Arch Intern Med 1981; 141: 1331–1335.
60. Haglund U, Lundgren O. Non-occlusive acute intestinal vascular failure. Br J Surg 1979; 66: 155–158.
61. Krupski WC, Effeney DJ, Ehrenfeld WK. Spontaneous dissection of the superior mesenteric artery. J Vasc Surg 1985; 2: 731–734.
62. Anthony PP, Drury RAB. Elastic sclerosis of mesenteric blood vessels in argentaffin carcinoma. J Clin Path 1970; 23: 110–118.
63. Roodnat JI, Bolk JH, van Unnik JG, Thompson J. Intestinal necrosis in a patient with fibromuscular dysplasia and digoxin poisoning. Ned V Geneeskunde 1988; 132: 2159–2162.
64. Gaskell H, Searle M, Dathan JR. Henoch-Schonlein purpura with severe ileal involvement responding to plasmapheresis. Int J Artif Organs 1985; 8: 163–164.
65. Agha FP, Nostrant TT, Keren DF. Leucocytoclastic vasculitis (Hypersensitivity angiitis) of the small bowel presenting with severe gastrointestinal hemorrhage. Am J Gastroenterol 1986; 81: 195–198.
66. Jafri FM, Mendelow H, Shadduck RK, Sekas G. Jejunal vasculitis with protein losing enteropathy after bone marrow transplantation. Gastroenterology 1990; 98: 1689–1692.
67. Brandt LJ, Gomery P, Mitsudo SM, Chandler P, Boley SJ. Disseminated intravascular coagulation in non-occlusive mesenteric ischaemia: the lack of specificity of fibrin thrombi in intestinal infarction. Gastroenterology 1976; 71: 954–957.
68. Grendell JH, Ockner RK. Mesenteric venous thrombosis. Gastroenterology 1982; 82: 358–372.
69. Clavien PA, Durig M, Harder F. Venous mesenteric infarction: a particular entity. Brit J Surg 1988; 75: 252–255.
70. Witte CL, Brewer ML, Witte MH, Pond GB. Protean manifestations of pylethrombosis. A review of thirty-four patients. Ann Surg 1985; 202: 191–202.
71. Klar E, Buhr H, Zimmermann R. Protein C deficiency with recurrent infarct of the small intestine. Chirurg 1990; 61: 59–62.
72. Bryner UM, Longerbeam JK, Reeves CD. Post-traumatic ischaemic stenosis of the small bowel. Arch Surg 1980; 115: 1039–1041.
73. Saraga EP, Costa J. Idiopathic entero-colic lymphocytic phlebitis. A cause of ischemic intestinal necrosis. Amer J Surg Pathol 1989; 13: 303–308.
74. Ray R, Agarwal P, Vaiphei, Bose SM, Datta BN. Malignant fibrous histiocytoma of mesentery with ischemic gangrene of small bowel. Indian J Gastroenterol 1992; 11: 145.
75. Howell CG, Vozza F, Shaw S, Robinson M, Srouji MN, Krasna I, Ziegler MM. Malrotation, malnutrition, and ischaemic bowel disease. J Pediatr Surg 1982; 17: 469–473.
76. Ende N. Infarction of the bowel in cardiac failure. N Engl J Med 1958; 258: 879–881.
77. Renton CJC. Non-occlusive intestinal infarction. Clin Gastroenterol 1972; 1: 656.
78. Kirkeby OJ, Risoe C. Intestinal ischaemia after a single intravenous injection of declanoside. A case report. Acta Chir Scand 1984; 150: 91–92.
79. McGregor DH, Pierce GE, Thomas JH, Tilzer LL. Obstructive lesions of distal mesenteric arteries. Arch Pathol Lab Med 1980; 104: 79–83.
80. Nalbandian H, Sheth N, Dietrich R, Georgiou J. Intestinal ischaemia caused by cocaine ingestion: report of two cases. Surgery 1985; 97: 374–376.
81. Garfia A, Valverde JL, Borondo JC, Candenas I, Lecena J. Vascular lesions in intestinal ischemia induced by cocaine and alcohol abuse: report of a fatal case due to overdose. J Forensic Sci 1990; 35: 740–745.
82. Hon DC, Salloum LJ, Hardy HW, Barone JE. Crack-induced enteric ischemia. New Jersey Med 1990; 87: 1001–1002.
83. Pentel P, Fletcher D, Jentzen J. Fatal acute selenium toxicity. J Forensic Sci 1985; 30: 556–562.
84. Taggart DP, Gunn IG. Lower limb amputation and small bowel infarction following parenteral diconal abuse. Br J Addict 1985; 80: 101.
85. Whitehead R. The pathology of intestinal ischaemia. Clin Gastroenterol 1972; 1: 613–637.
86. Ottinger LW, Austen WG. A study of 136 patients with mesenteric infarction. Surg Gynecol Obstet 1967; 124: 251–261.
87. Hansen HJB, Christoffersen JK. Occlusive mesenteric infarction: a retrospective study of 83 cases. Acta Chir Scand 1976; 472: 103–108.
88. Pollak JS, Bennick M, Denny DF, Markowitz D. Chronic intestinal bleeding due to mesenteric vascular insufficiency. Amer J Roentg 1991; 157: 1203–1204.
89. Dick AP, Graff R, Gregg D McC, Peters N, Sarner M. An arteriographic study of mesenteric arterial disease. Gut 1967; 8: 206–219.
90. Marston A, Clarke JMF, Garcia Garcia J, Miller AL. Intestinal function and intestinal blood supply: a 20 year surgical study. Gut 1985; 26: 656–666.
91. Wilson IH, Cooley NV, Luibel FJ. Nonspecific stenosing small bowel ulcers. Am J Gastroenterol 1968; 50: 449–455.
92. Leijonmarck CE, Raf L. Ulceration of the small intestine due to slow-release potassium chloride tablets. Acta Chir Scand 1985; 151: 273–278.
93. Lang J, Price AB, Levi AJ, Burke M, Gumpel JM, Bjarnason I. Diaphragm disease: pathology of disease of the small intestine induced by non-steroidal anti-flammatory drugs. J Clin Pathol 1988; 41: 516–526.

94. Souza Lima MA. Ulcers of the small bowel associated with stomach by-passing salicylates. Arch Intern Med 1985; 145: 1139.
95. Waisman Y, Dinan G, Marcus H, Ligumsky M, Rosenbach Y, Zahavi I, Nirzan M. Naloxone is protective against indomethacin-induced intestinal ulceration in the rat. Gastroenterology 1985; 89: 86–91.
96. Thomas WEG, Williamson RCN. Nonspecific small bowel ulceration. Postgrad Med J 1985; 61: 587–591.
97. Davies DR, Brightmore T. Idiopathic and drug-induced ulceration of the small intestine. Br J Surg 1970; 57: 134–139.
98. Nyman E. Ulcerative jejuno-ileitis with symptomatic sprue. Acta Med Scand 1947; 134: 275–283.
99. Baer AN, Bayless TM, Yardley JH. Intestinal ulceration and malabsorption syndromes. Gastroenterology 1980; 79: 754–765.
100. Isaacson P, Wright DH. Malignant histiocytosis of the intestine: its relationship to malabsorption and ulcerative jejunitis. Hum Pathol 1978; 9: 661–677.
101. Robertson DAF, Dixon MF, Scott BB, Simpson FG, Losowsky MS. Small intestinal ulceration: diagnostic difficulties in relation to coeliac disease. Gut 1981; 24: 565–574.
102. Brown EG, Sweet AY. Neonatal necrotizing enterocolitis. Pediatr Clin North Am 1982; 29: 1149–1170.
103. Cikrit D, Mastandrea J, West KW, Schreiner RL, Grosfield JL. Necrotizing enterocolitis: factors affecting mortality in 101 surgical cases. Surgery 1984; 96: 648–655.
104. Lawrence G, Walker PD. The pathogenesis of enteritis necroticans in Papua, New Guinea. Lancet 1976; 1: 125–126.
105. Zeissler J, Rassfeld-Sternberg L. Enteritis necroticans due to Clostridium welchii type F. Br Med J 1949; 1: 267–269.
106. Devitt PG, Stamp GWH. Acute clostridial enteritis — or pig-bel? Gut 1983; 24: 678–679.
107. Arseculeratne SN, Panabokke RG, Navaratnam C. Pathogenesis of necrotising enteritis with special reference to intestinal hypersensitivity reactions. Gut 1980; 21: 265–278.
108. Van Kessel LJP, Verbrugh HA, Stringer MF, Hoekstra JBL. Necrotising enteritis associated with toxigenic Type A Clostridium perfringens. J Inf Dis 1985; 151: 974–975.
109. Rees HC, Wright NA. Angiodysplasia of the colon. In: Recent Advances in Histopathology, 12. Anthony PP, MacSween RNM, eds. Edinburgh: Churchill Livingstone, 1984; p 178–188.
110. Weaver GA, Alpern HD, Davis JS, Ramsey WH, Reichelderfer M. Gastrointestinal angiodysplasia associated with aortic valve disease: part of a spectrum of angiodysplasia of the gut. Gastroenterology 1979; 77: 1–11.
111. Meyer CT, Troncale FJ, Galloway S, Sheahan DG. Arteriovenous malformations of the bowel: an analysis of 22 cases and a review of the literature. Medicine (Balt) 1981; 60: 36–48.
112. Dave PB, Romeu J, Antonelli A, Eiser AR. Gastrointestinal telangiectasis: a source of bleeding in patients receiving hemodialysis. Arch Intern Med 1984; 144: 1781–1783.
113. Camilleri M, Chadwick VS, Hodgson HJF. Vascular anomalies of the gastrointestinal tract. Hepato-gastroenterol 1984; 31: 149–153.
114. Shepherd JA. Angiomatous conditions of the gastrointestinal tract. Br J Surg 1953; 40: 409–421.
115. Conlon CL, Weinger RS, Cimo PL, Moake JL, Olson JD. Telangiectasia and von Willebrand's disease in two families. Ann Intern Med 1978; 89: 921–924.
116. Schultz LS, Assimacopoulos CA, Lillehei RC. Turner's syndrome with associated gastrointestinal bleeding: a case report. Surgery 1970; 68: 485–488.
117. Galloway SJ, Casarella WJ, Shimkin PM. Vascular malformations of the right colon as a cause of bleeding in patients with aortic stenosis. Radiology 1974; 113: 11–15.
118. Heaton ND, Khawaja H, Howard ER. Bleeding duodenal varices. Brit J Surg 1991; 78: 1450–1451.
119. Chandra-Sekhar HB, Alstead EM, Kumar PJ, Farthing MJ. Duodenal varices. A neglected cause of massive, recurrent gastrointestinal bleeding. Dig Dis Sci 1992; 37: 449–451.
120. Peoples JB, Kartha R, Sharif S. Multiple phlebectasia of the small inestine. Am Surg 1981; 47: 373–376.
121. Velascquez G, D'Souza VJ, Glass TA, Turner CS, Formanek AG. Diffuse intestinal arteriovenous malformation. AJR 1984; 143: 1339–1340.
122. Murray-Lyon IM, Doyle D, Philpott RM, Porter NH. Haemangiomatosis of the small and large bowel with histological malignant change. J Pathol 1971; 105: 295–297.
123. Golitz LE. Heritable cutaneous disorders that affect the gastrointestinal tract. Med Clin N Am 1980; 64: 829–846.
124. Bandler M. Hemangiomas of the small intestine associated with mucocutaneous pigmentation. Gastroenterology 1960; 38: 641–645.
125. Vetto JT, Richman PS, Kariger K, Passaro E. Cirsoid aneurysms of the jejunum. An unrecognized cause of massive gastrointestinal bleeding. Arch Surg 1989; 124: 1460–1462.
126. Shriver DA, Dove PA, White CB, Sandor A, Rosenthale ME. A profile of the gastrointestinal toxicity of aspirin, oxaprozin, phenylbutazone, and fentiazac in arthritic and Lewis normal rats. Toxicol Appl Pharmacol 1977; 42: 75–83.
127. Rainsford KD. An analysis of the gastro-intestinal side effects of nonsteroidal anti-inflammatory drugs, with particular reference to comparative studies in man and laboratory species. Rheumatol Int (Berlin) 1982; 2: 1–10.
128. Langman MJS, Morgan L, Worrall A. Use of anti-inflammatory drugs by patients admitted with small or large bowel perforations and haemorrhage. Br Med J 1985; 290: 347–349.
129. Buckman MT. Gastrointestinal bleeding in long distance runners. Ann Intern Med 1984; 101: 127–128.
130. Stewart JG, Ahlquist DA, McGill DB, Ilstrup DM, Schware S, Owen RA. Gastrointestinal blood loss and anemia in runners. Ann Intern Med 1984; 101: 843–845.
131. McMahon LF, Ryan MJ, Larson D, Fisher RL. Occult gastrointestinal blood loss in marathon runners. Ann Intern Med 1984; 101: 846–847.
132. Hughes CE, Conn J, Sherman JO. Intramural hematoma of the gastrointestinal tract. Am J Surg 1977; 133: 276–279.
133. Alsop WR, Burt RW, Tolman KG. Intramural duodenal hematoma. Gastrointest Endosc 1985; 31: 32–34.
134. Skudder PA, Craver WL. Mesenteric hematoma suggests rupture of visceral artery aneurysm. Arch Surg 1984; 119: 863.
135. Beighton PH, Murdoch JL, Votteler T. Gastrointestinal complications of the Ehlers-Danlos syndrome. Gut 1969; 10: 1004–1008.

CHAPTER

32 The large intestine

R. Whitehead S. Gratama

ISCHAEMIC COLITIS

Bowel ischaemia, either temporary or permanent, may be arterial or venous in origin and the colon is the commonest site of involvement.[1] Its pathological features have been extensively reviewed[1–16] and changes similar to those observed in man have been produced experimentally in animals.[4,11,14–21] Nevertheless, it still represents a challenge to the clinician because the diagnosis is often delayed and even following treatment the prognosis is poor.[22,23]

Causative factors

There are numerous causes for colonic ischaemia, (Fig. 32.1) and not infrequently the pathogenesis is multifactorial.[24,25] Thus a large vessel stenosis or an angiopathy of vessels in or near the bowel wall may compromise the intramural ciculation, but it may be a fall in blood pressure that actually precipitates a massive necrosis.[2,4,7] Furthermore, ischaemia may play an additive role in circumstances where the major pathology is due to other causes such as amyloid bowel involvement or bowel distension due to myxoedema.[26,27] Claims are made that ischaemia may complicate the use of immunotherapy for metastatic carcinoma,[28] but the mechanisms involved are not clear. They may be similar to those causing ischaemic colitis described following renal transplantation.[29] Despite an element of uncertainty there are, however, certain aetiological factors which are better understood.

Mechanical factors

Ischaemia of the large bowel due to mechanisms such as torsion or hernia strangulation are uncommon due to its largely retroperitoneal location. However, the nature of its blood supply makes it prone to primary vascular causes of ischaemia and its contents ensure that the pathological consequences of this will be severe.[9] Its relatively low blood flow is also substantially decreased during motor activity, an effect enhanced by straining at stool.[1]

Large vessel occlusions

The inferior mesenteric artery (IMA) is less prone to embolization than the superior branch (SMA) because of its smaller calibre and its more acute angle of take off. Thrombosis of its ostium occurs frequently in the course of aortic atherosclerosis but adequate perfusion is usually maintained via a good collateral circulation.[7] Ligation of the IMA in the course of aortic reconstruction or abdominoperineal surgery may lead to ischaemia of the left colon, particularly in the presence of stenosing lesions of the hypogastric artery.[6,11] The right colon will usually be involved in extensive bowel ischaemia when the SMA is occluded by thrombosis or emboli. Abdominal aortic surgery, however, which leaves the coeliac and SMA intact results in ischaemic colitis in less than 1% of cases.[30]

Other forms of large artery stenosis (Fig. 32.1) are rare causes of colonic ischaemia. The same applies to the venous occlusion that may occur in cirrhosis of the liver, septic intra-abdominal conditions and hypercoagulable states.[1,7,12]

Small vessel disease

Microangiopathy may also impede the intramural circulation of the colon.[9,12,31,32] Proliferative intimal hyperplasia of

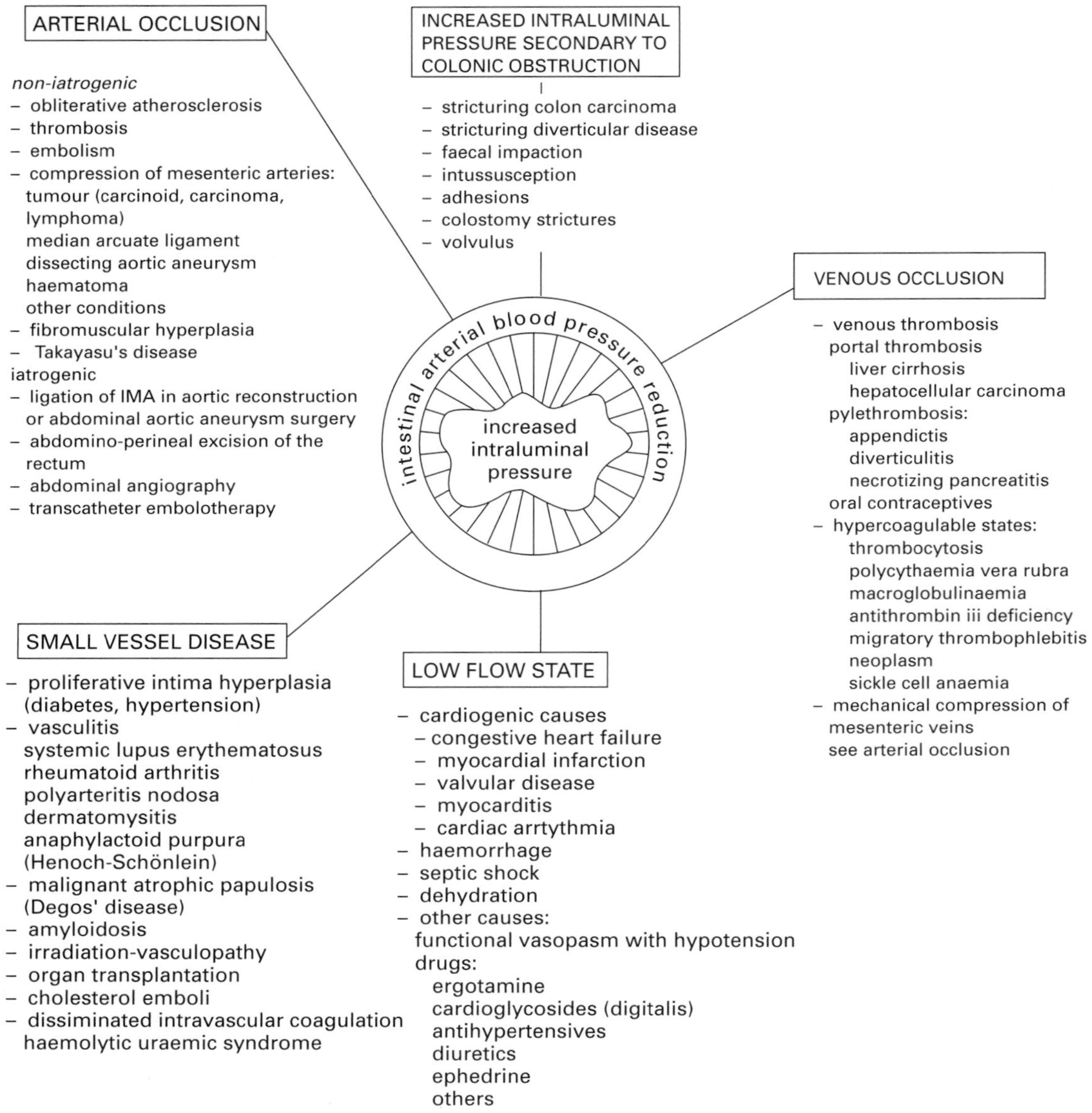

Fig. 32.1 Causative factors in ischaemic necrosis. (Reproduced with permission from Reeders et al 1984)[12]

small arteries is a frequent finding in the elderly patient,[33,34] particularly in association with hypertension and diabetes mellitus. Vasospasm, hypoxia and the release of platelet growth-stimulating factor may also be contributory.[35,36] Obliterative microangiopathy also occurs in collagen diseases, vasculitic disorders,[37] diffuse intravascular coagulation, thrombotic states such as antithrombin III deficiency and in amyloidosis, radiation vascular damage and as a result of vasoconstrictive drugs like ergotamine.[12]

Non-occlusive factors

Ischaemia may also occur in the absence of vessel occlusion. Low flow states due to a sustained decrease in left ventricular output such as occurs in arrythmias, myocardial infarction, myocarditis, etc., or by depletion of intravascular volume during shock or severe dehydration, cause a shunting of blood from the splanchnic circulation to more vital organs.[16] Contraction of the muscularis of the bowel wall and its arteries will further impede circulation, while absorption of bacterial endotoxins and vasoactive substances through a damaged mucosa may illicit a Shwartzman reaction.[2,9,25] The resulting endothelial damage and activation of factor XII of the coagulation cascade may then lead to diffuse intravascular coagulation.[38]

Obstruction

Elevation of intraluminal pressure and distension occur proximal to stenosing lesions of the colon in the presence of a competent ileocaecal valve. At first this interferes with the venous outflow, causing stasis and hypoxia, and with further increase in the pressure the arterial flow is also affected. Blood is shunted away from the oxygen consuming tissues like the mucosa and muscularis through arteriovenous communications. The serosal circulation is maintained even at extremely high intraenteric pressure.[11,18] Hypermotility of the proximal colon, straining and muscle spasm in the course of a gradually increasing stenotic process will also contribute to compromise the intramural circulation.[39]

The increase in susceptibility to intestinal microorganisms coupled with the favoured growth of anaerobic species, such as clostridia, may thus result in invasion of the devitalized tissues and a severe phlegmonous transmural inflammation with gas formation.[1,11]

Distribution of ischaemic lesions; extent and severity of involvement of the bowel wall

The effect of an ischaemic period varies with the rapidity of its onset, its duration and severity. The latter depends on the cause, the level of arterial occlusion, the state of the collateral circulation and on the virulence of the intestinal flora. It is reflected by the degree of the ensuing tissue damage.[1,16,40] The location and extent of ischaemic lesions are related to the anatomy of the blood supply in the occlusive form, to the decrease in the circulating blood volume and state of the microvasculature in the non-occlusive form, and to the level of the intraluminal pressure and rapidity of its increase in the obstructive form of ischaemic colitis.[12]

Anatomical distribution of lesions

Ischaemia may involve any part of the entire colon, but is commonest by far on the left and in the so-called watershed areas, at the splenic flexure (Griffith's point) and in the rectosigmoid region (Sudeck's point). The anastomotic circulation between the inferior mesenteric artery (IMA), the superior mesenteric artery (SMA) and the hypogastric arteries is least effective in these areas and it is these sites that are most commonly involved, even in hypotensive states.[7,11,16] Ligation of the IMA may result in ischaemia of the sigmoid[1] and irradiation vasculopathy commonly affects this area. Thus ischaemic proctitis, once thought to be rare, is being recognized with increasing frequency.[1,9,41]

Ischaemia of the right side of the colon occurs after occlusion of the SMA or its ileocolic branch. It is also the area frequently involved in obstructive colitis, its greater diameter, according to LaPlace's law, leading to a higher wall tension, which is an important factor in perfusion failure. A transient form of colonic ischaemia in young adults also occurs most frequently in the right colon.

Reeders et al[12] analyzed published data in 1024 patients with ischaemic colitis and the anatomical distribution is depicted in Figure 32.2.

Extent of disease

Lesions vary in extent and may involve almost the whole large bowel. Focal lesions are relatively rare and may be multiple. Occlusion of small vessels by cholesterol emboli or vasculitis is the usual cause.[5]

Occlusion of larger proximal vessels by emboli, thrombosis or vasculitis produce short lesions. When distal vessels near the bowel wall are affected, segmental damage may also develop if the involvement is extensive enough to cancel the effect of local anastomoses.[5] A variable length of colon ischaemia may be present proximal to a stenosing process and the largest lesions occur in the watershed areas in the elderly with cardiovascular disease and are often associated with a fall in blood pressure.[16] Early lesions of this type are often encountered at autopsy and are the result of preterminal circulatory collapse in patients with a compromised splanchnic circulation.[3,9]

Massive involvement of the colon is usually the consequence of embolic or, more frequently, of thrombotic occlusion of the SMA, but it may be associated with non-occlusive ischaemia.

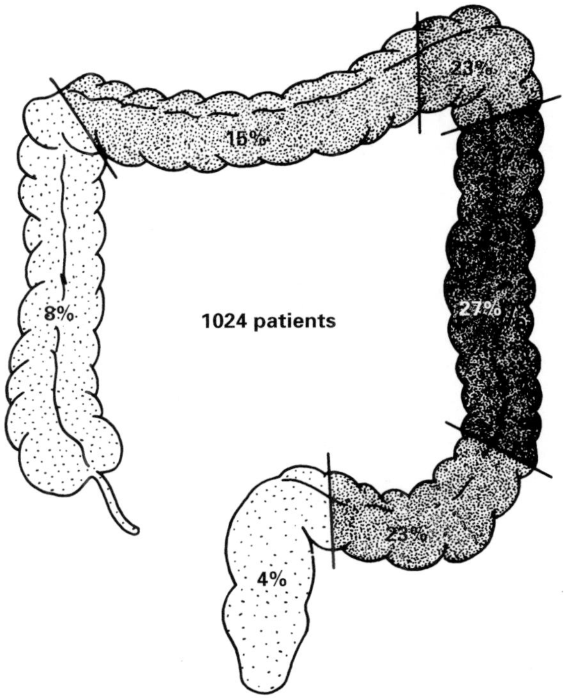

Fig. 32.2 Anatomical distribution of ischaemic lesions in the colon of 1024 patients from the literature (1956–82). (Reproduced with permission from Reeders et al 1984)[12]

Severity of the anoxic insult (Fig. 32.3)

Mild ischaemia of short duration produces transient oedema, haemorrhage and sometimes superficial ulceration of the mucosa and submucosa. In the presence of an adequate collateral circulation, complete recovery takes place in 1–2 weeks.[16]

More severe deprivation of oxygen results in damage to deeper structures, and a persistent type of colitis with ulceration or fibrous scarring, with or without stenosis, will ensue in the course of 4 weeks to several months.[1,42]

Total deprivation of oxygen leads to complete transmural necrosis and gangrene, with or without perforation.

The evolution of these ischaemic lesions cannot be predicted early in their onset and originally mild and superficial damage may extend in depth and extent. Different stages of ischaemia may coexist in adjacent segments. A mixed pattern of haemorrhagic, ulcerative and pseudomembranous lesions may thus be present.[5] Progress towards transmural necrosis is indicated by dilatation on X-ray examination.[12]

Transient lesions are commonest and 67 of the 150 cases described by Boley[1] fell into this category, against 28 with persistent ulcerating colitis, 19 with strictures and 28 with gangrene or perforation. Of Saegesser's[11] 124 patients, 52 had lesions of transient nature, 43 developed a stenosis and 22 became gangrenous, but in this series there were more cases associated with aortic and abdominoperineal surgery.

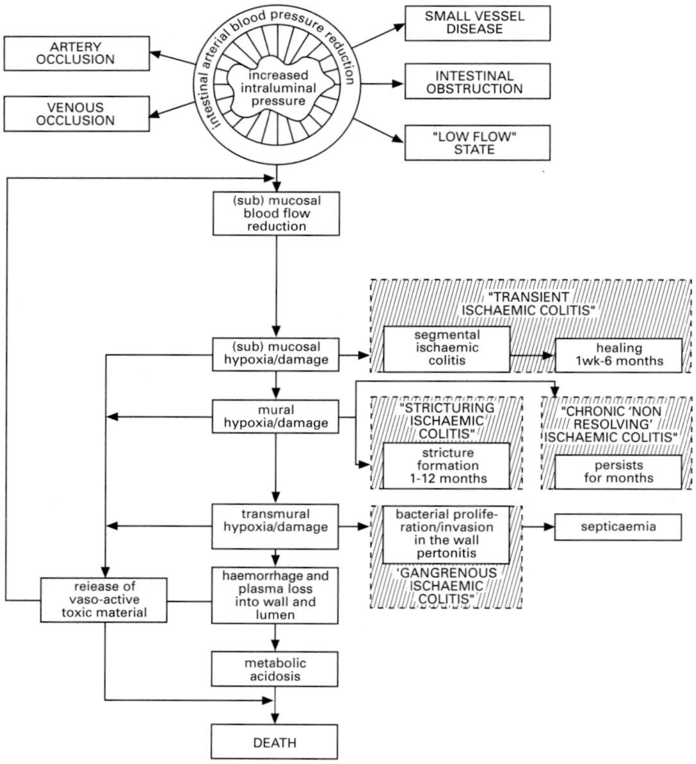

Fig. 32.3 Classification and extent of ischaemic lesions. (Reproduced with permission from Reeders et al 1984)[12]

Clinical symptoms and diagnosis

Not surprisingly, colonic ischaemia occurs predominantly in the older age groups with a peak incidence in the 6th and 7th decades[12,16] (Fig. 32.4). Clinical symptoms vary with the aetiology, the extent and depth of the lesions and their duration.[1,16,40,43,44] A rapidly developing, mild to moderate colicky or more continuous pain in the left lower abdomen in elderly patients with no previous bowel disease, followed by abdominal distension, nausea and vomiting and rectal bleeding or bloody diarrhoea are clinical features suggesting bowel ischaemia, particularly in the presence of chronic cardiovascular disease and a preceding period of hypotension.[6,45–48] Symptoms, however, may be relatively mild, but occasionally there may even be signs of intestinal obstruction in the acute phase due to submucosal oedema and haemorrhage or to spasm resulting from muscle involvement which interferes with the distensibility and motility of the colon.[43]

Nearly half the patients show a complete resolution of symptoms within 4 weeks[48] but recurrence is reported in 5–12% of cases.[6,47]

A gradual decline of disease activity over several months may result in a stricture. This may remain stable or show marked improvement in the course of many months, and some do not require surgical resection.[44] The clinical course of the disease can be varied and may even simulate carcinoma.[45] In some patients, a chronic persistent ulcerative condition evolves and needs to be differentiated from Crohn's disease or ulcerative colitis.[43,44,47]

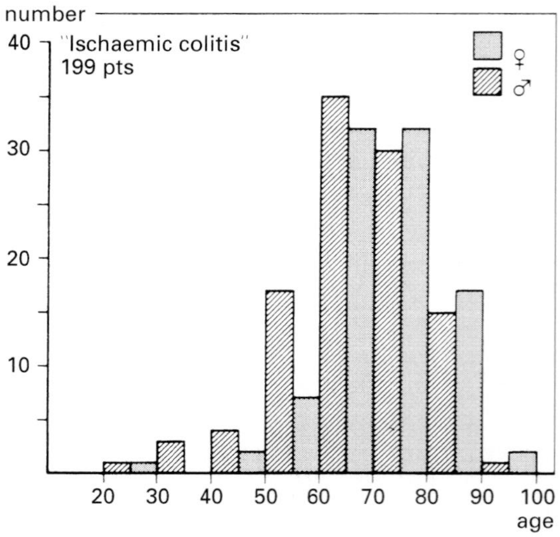

Fig. 32.4 Age and sex distribution of 199 patients with ischaemic colitis. (Reproduced with permission from Reeders et al 1984)[12]

Acute fulminant disease with progression to transmural necrosis is rare. It may follow ligation of the IMA or occurs in sustained low flow states. Severe dilatation, usually of the transverse colon, comparable to toxic megacolon of chronic inflammatory bowel disease, is then associated with symptoms of shock and peritonitis.[11,43,48]

The tendency of many cases to follow a transient course with complete recovery emphasizes the need for an accurate diagnosis.[1,12,48,49] So-called thumbprinting pseudotumours, spastic narrowing, loss of haustration and ulceration are early radiological signs.[12] Early endoscopic examination[49,50] shows oedema and haemorrhage and towards the end of the first week there is ulceration. Stricturing may develop 3 weeks to 12 months after the first ischaemic episode. In some 10–12% of patients[6,12,48] there is an obstruction due to carcinoma, diverticulitis or faecal impaction and the acute illness due to ischaemic colitis may lead to recognition of a stenosis.[43] Likewise, in cases of overt obstruction an associated ischaemic colitis may remain unnoticed. A deceptively normal looking serosa at operation may mask even extensive mucosal damage and this has obvious implications for the surgeon involved in resecting an obstructing bowel lesion.[1]

Pathology

Gross lesions

The macroscopic appearance of the ischaemic colon varies with the severity and depth of the necrotic process and with the stage of healing (Figs 32.5 & 32.6).

Early ischaemia appears as a pale contracted bowel segment in which the mucosa shows patchy, red, granular or purple, swollen areas. Later there is more severe

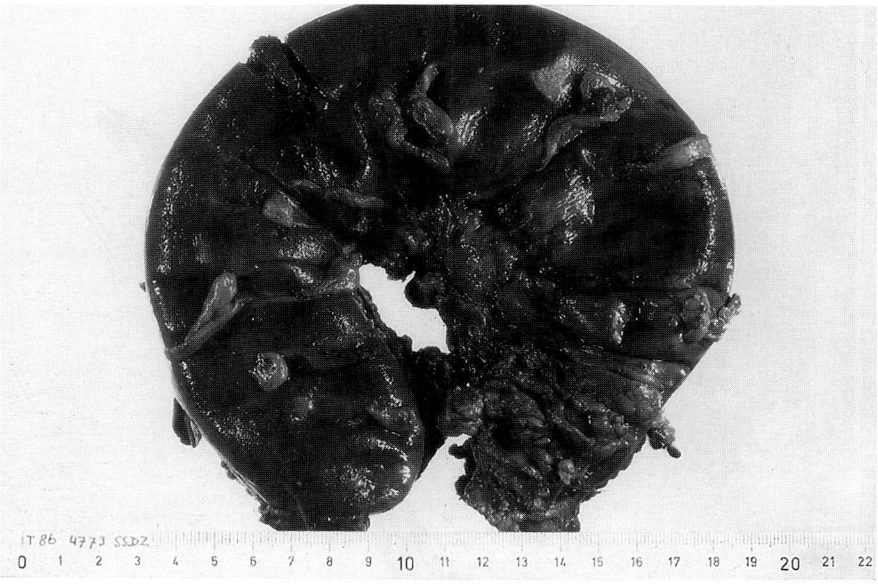

Fig. 32.5 Gangrenous colonic necrosis which followed aortic reconstruction surgery.

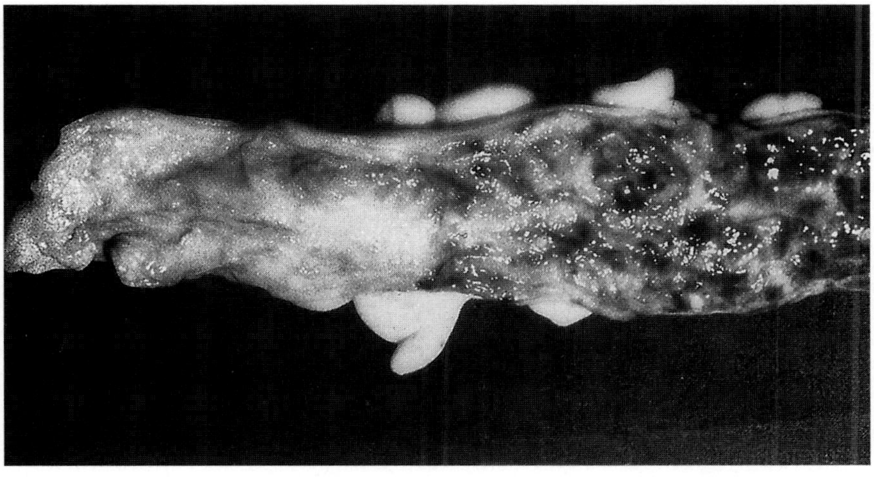

Fig. 32.6 Ulcerated ischaemic colitis in a patient with rheumatoid arthritis.

congestion, often associated with focal massive oedema and haemorrhage into the submucosa, forming blebs. In a more advanced stage the mucosa has a purplish cobblestone appearance. When ischaemia persists, areas of greenish-grey mucosal necrosis develop and after sloughing longitudinal and serpiginous ulcers with a yellow or grey base can be seen. A picture of pseudomembranous colitis is the result of extensive superficial mucosal necrosis in more slowly progressing milder forms.

The depth of the bowel wall damage will frequently not be apparent from the serosal appearance.

Transmural necrosis can be either pale, turning to black, with thinning of the dilated wall, or haemorrhagic, in which case the colon appears purple and congested, the wall being thickened by blood extravasation and oedema.

Strictures appear as pale, contracted, thick-walled, smoothly contoured tubular or more fusiform segments with a granular, ulcerated lining. Sacculation of the wall may be the consequence of irregular fibrosis that involves only the antimesocolic side of the circumference.

The hallmark of ischaemic lesions is their sharp demarcation from the uninvolved bowel.

Microscopy

Acute lesions. The earliest change may occur in the submucosa, which becomes oedematous. Lymphatics,

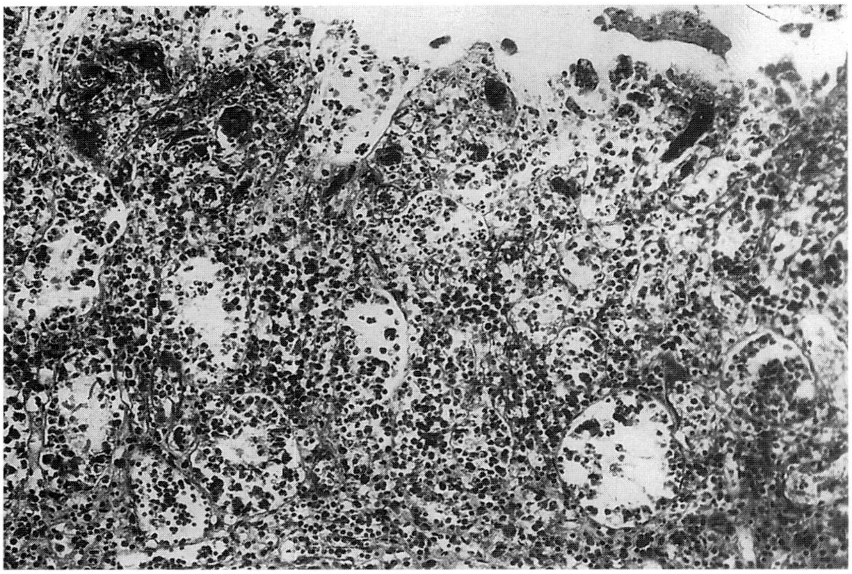

Fig. 32.7 Early mucosal ischaemia Dissolving crypt and surface epithelium is invaded by granulocytes. Superficial capillaries contain fibrin thrombi. (×114)

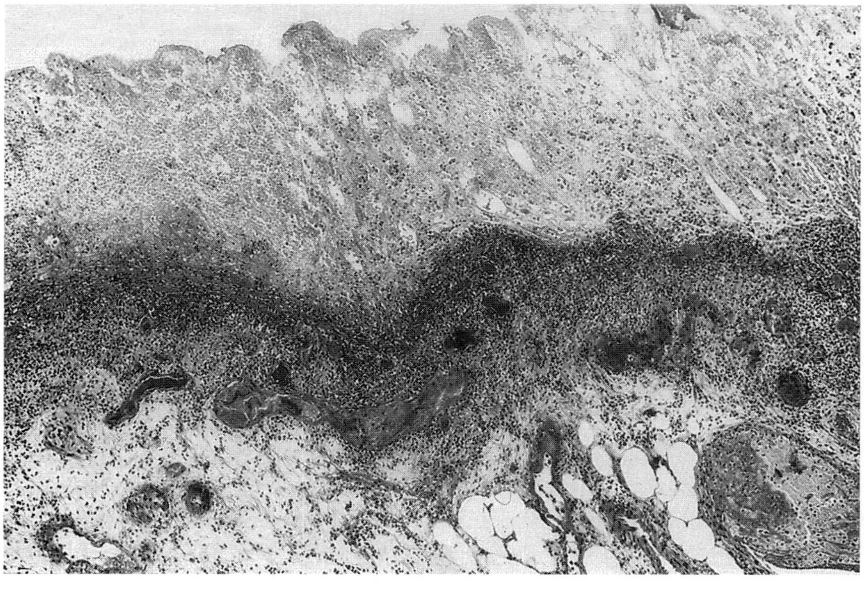

Fig. 32.8 Ghost-like appearance of necrotic mucosa. Demarcation zone of granulocytes along the muscularis mucosae. Dilated vessels with early thrombosis in submucosa. (×48)

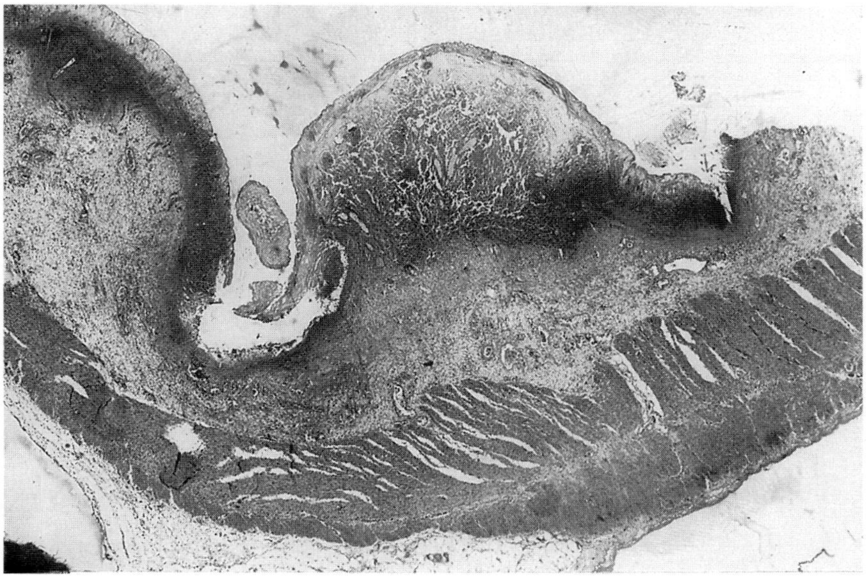

Fig. 32.9 Oedema and haemorrhage cause ballooning of the submucosa — the histologic substrate of thumbprint lesions of the barium enema (×9). Compare with Figure 32.10.

veins and capillaries dilate; sludging and stasis are followed by thrombosis and haemorrhage.[42] The mucosa may still be intact[9] but later it shows dilatation of capillaries, oedema and haemorrhage in the lamina propria. The surface-epithelium and distal parts of the crypt-lining become necrotic (Figs 32.7, 32.8). As a reaction to necrosis and invasion by bacteria, a demarcation zone of polymorphonuclear leucocytes forms between the necrotic inner zone and the hyperaemic, still viable parts of the bowel wall. Following lysis of cells, the necrotic mucosa assumes a ghost-like appearance in which outlines of crypts and vessels are still faintly visible. Fibrin thrombi are frequently present in mucosal and submucosal capillaries and veins.[1,5,12] The presence of areas of intact mucosa between foci of necrosis is typical of ischaemic damage.[9]

Sometimes a mushroom-like layer of mucus, fibrin and granulocytes can be seen covering the mucosal surface that seems to originate in dilated crypt remnants, the top of which has become necrotic.[2,5,9] Bacterial colonization may be evident on the surface. This pseudomembranous type of early ischaemic colitis may represent a more slowly progressing form of ischaemia,[5] or possibly be connected with a particular type of intraluminal flora (*Clostridiium difficile* produces a toxin that causes a superficial necrosis).

The thumbprint lesions seen radiologically arise when the submucosa has become greatly widened by oedema and haemorrhage. The covering mucosa may be necrotic. There is extensive granulocytic infiltration and the dilated submucosal veins frequently contain thrombi. A demarcation zone of polymorphs form the base of such lesions (Figs 32.9 & 32.10).

Phlegmonous transmural inflammation may develop when the invasive flora is particularly virulent and intramural gas formation may occur. A thickening of the serosa

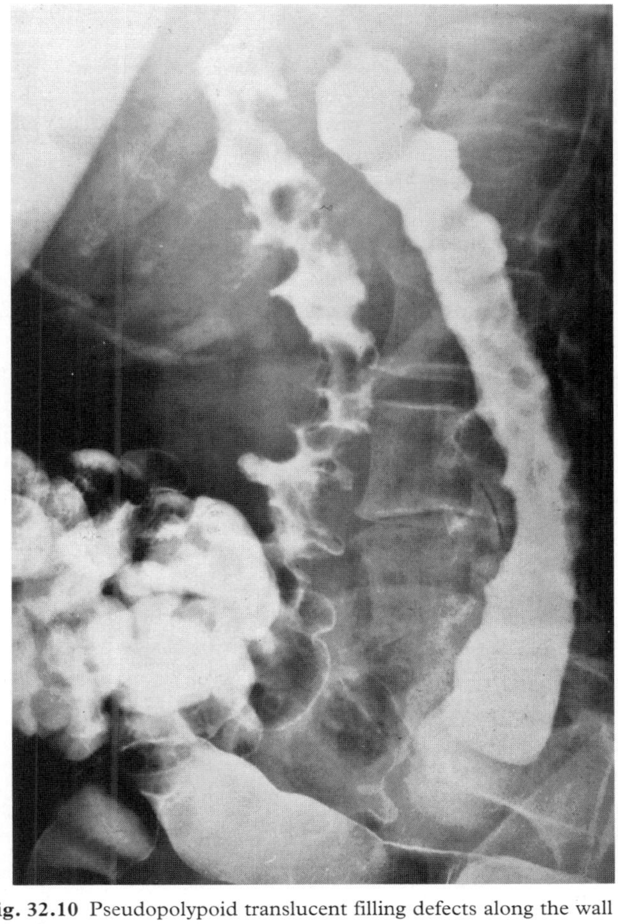

Fig. 32.10 Pseudopolypoid translucent filling defects along the wall of the colon.

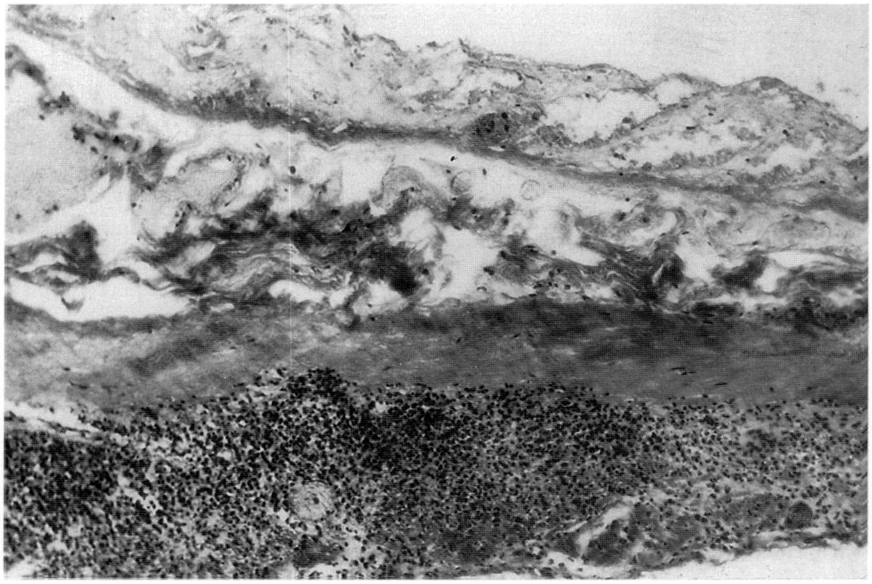

Fig. 32.11 Ischaemic transmural necrosis with demarcating granulocytic infiltration in the serosa. The collapsed wall is much thinner than normal. (×48)

due to lymphangiectasia, oedema, congestion, fibrin deposits and small haemorrhages may also be observed at this early stage.[9,42]

With increasing severity and duration of ischaemia, the necrosis progresses to deeper layers and will involve the muscularis, which is more resistant to hypoxia than the mucosa. In severe lesions, transmural necrosis results and the subserosal layer is also affected (Fig. 32.11).

In the pale ischaemic type, the bowel wall is thinned due to collapse of necrotic tissue. Haemorrhagic necrosis is a more slowly progressive process in which blood and plasma escape from damaged and ruptured vessels.[12]

Subacute lesions, ulcerative phase. Sloughing of the necrotic layers results in ulcer formation. The ulcer base is at first covered with fibrin and polymorphs. These will be gradually replaced by plasma cells, lymphocytes and histiocytes. There is marked proliferation of capillaries with swollen endothelium (Fig. 32.12) and a hyperplasia of neural elements occurs. The ulcer base may have a flat surface, or at points of deeper anoxic damage, wedge-shaped ulcers (Fig. 32.13) may penetrate the muscularis propria, or the ulcer undermines adjacent undamaged mucosa (Fig. 32.14). Ischaemic damage to the muscularis propria results in vacuolization of myocytes and cell lysis, usually in the inner layer of the circular muscle, followed by patchy replacement with granulation tissue and fibrosis.[3]

Chronic lesions. The inflammatory reaction diminishes gradually and a fibrosis occurs (Fig. 32.15). There may be residual siderophages and if there is a good deal of fibrosis, ulceration persists and is usually associated with a stricture. A striking obliterative vasculopathy is seen in the base of such chronic ulcers.[4,12]

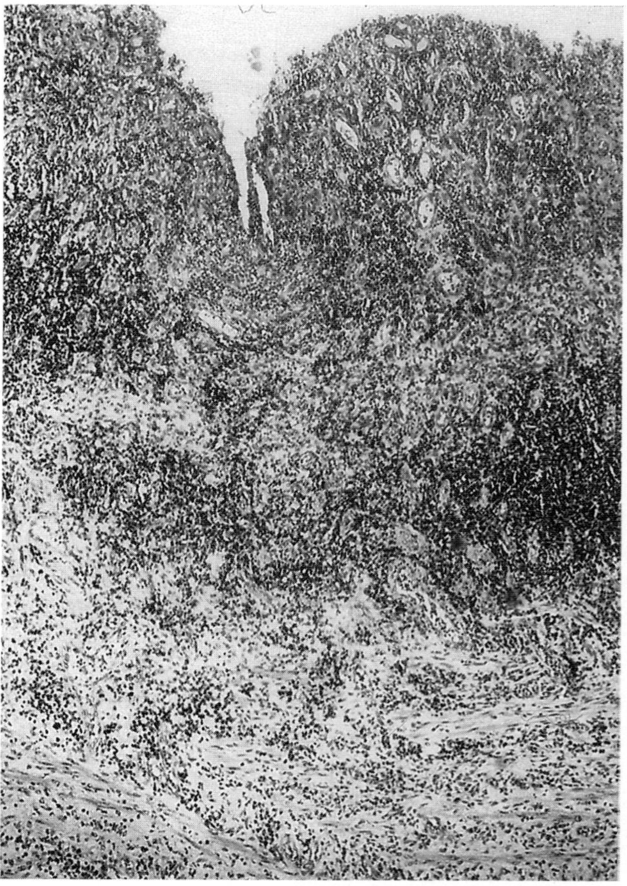

Fig. 32.12 After sloughing of necrotic mucosa, the ulcer base contains a dense mononuclear infiltrate and proliferating capillaries. (×50)

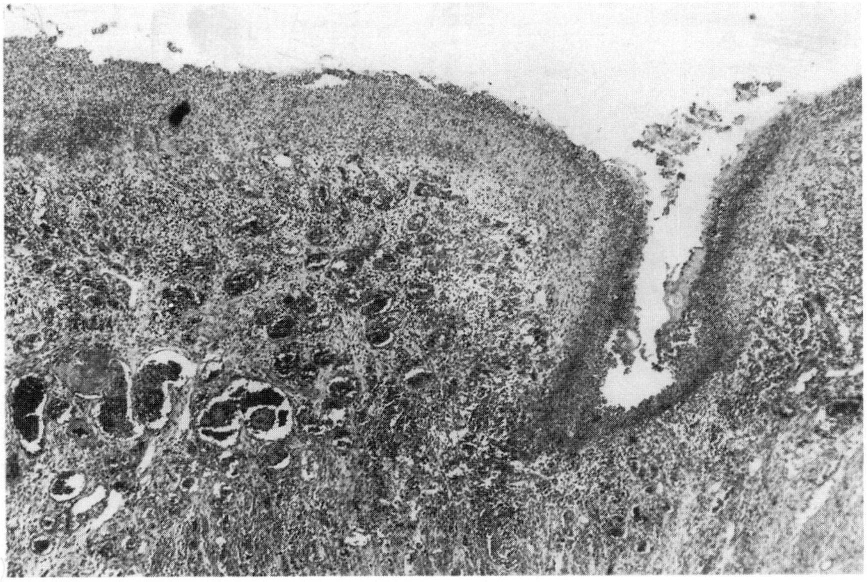

Fig. 32.13 Wedge-shaped ulcer penetrating the inner muscularis. (×48)

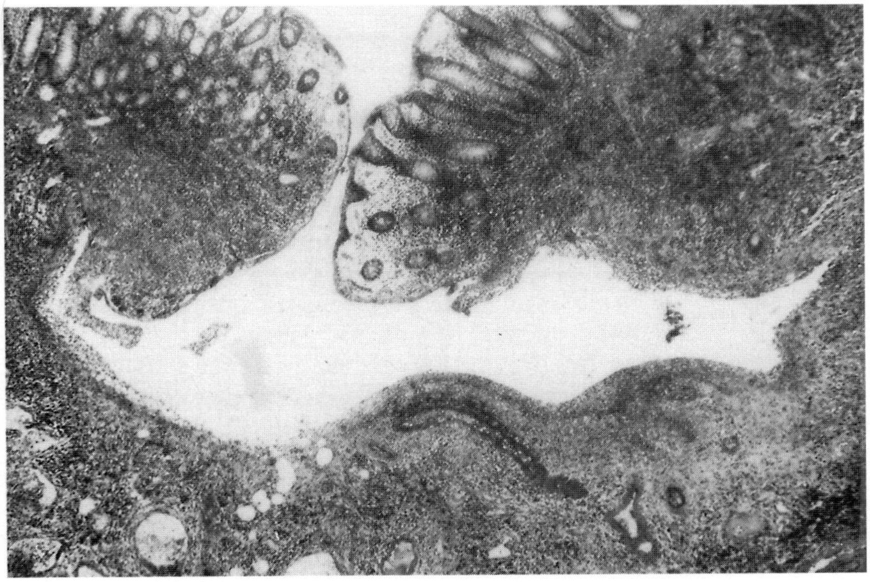

Fig. 32.14 Undermining ulcers may be evident in chronic persisting ulceration as well as in obstructive colitis. (×29)

Transmural lymphocytic aggregates may be present, especially near ulcers which penetrate the muscularis propria and the appearances can mimic Crohn's disease.[5,9,12] (Figs 32.16, 32.17) Crypt abscesses can be found in the mucosa adjoining the ulcers, but the epithelium usually does not show mucus depletion.[47]

Regeneration

Acute superficial lesions will revert to normal when the ischaemic insult is short-lived and the collateral supply is sufficient for repair to take place. The necrotic tissue is sloughed off, remnants are removed by macrophages and re-epithelialization takes place from the still viable parts of remaining crypts and from the surface epithelium at the margin of the ulcerated area (Fig. 32.18). The lamina propria is reconstituted by a proliferation of capillaries and fibroblasts. Newly formed crypts are distorted and often show bizarre appearances due to crowding and pleomorphism of nuclei.[3,4,12]

Deeper lesions will show an irregular type of healing in which there are residual abnormalities, such as an ulcer base covered by only a flat layer of undifferentiated cells, pseudopolyps with distorted regenerated glands (Figs 32.19, 32.20) and pseudopyloric or Paneth cell metaplasia.[5,12]

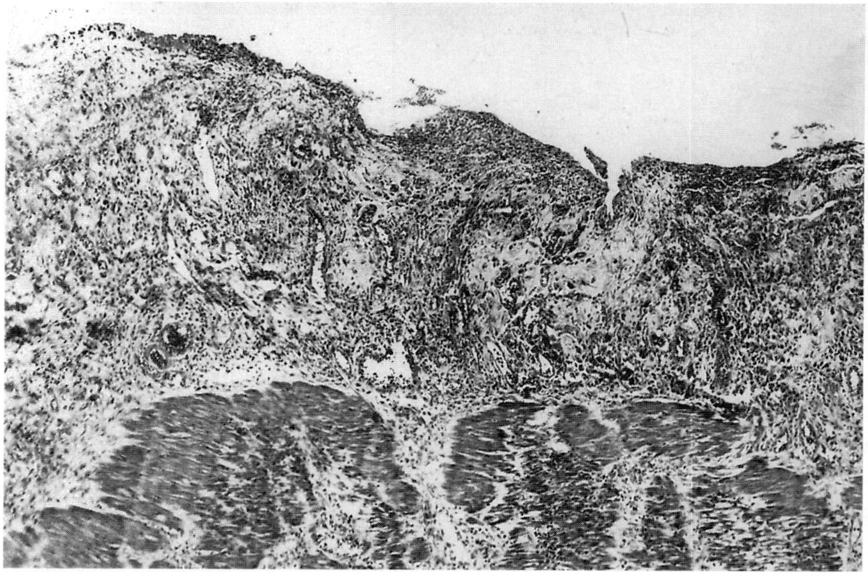

Fig. 32.15 Chronic persistent ulceration with onset of fibrosis in the submucosa and inner aspect of the muscularis propria. (×114)

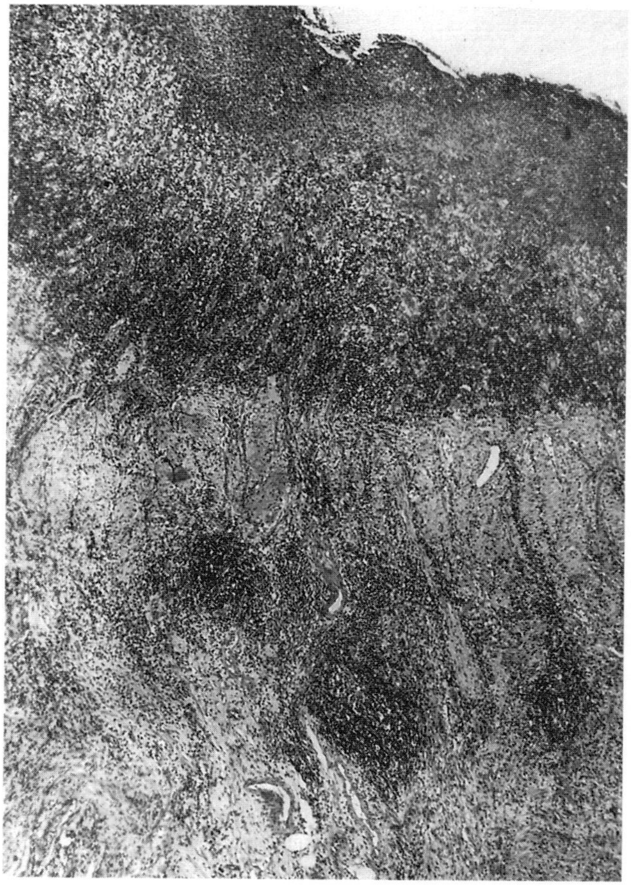

Fig. 32.16 Aggregates of lymphocytes are present in the muscularis. (×48)

The lesions in obstructive colitis

In this form, the complete spectrum of colonic ischaemia may be seen. Early lesions comprise marked oedema and haemorrhage of the submucosa, superficial mucosal necrosis and ulceration.

In a slowly progressive stenosis, there will be a gradual rise of the intraluminal pressure, resulting in a chronic superficial ulcerating colitis in which shallow linear ulcerations are separated by a near-normal or by a haemorrhagic cobblestone-type of mucosa. However, wedge-shaped ulcers (see Fig. 32.13) that penetrate the muscularis may develop and perforate, and undermining ulcers may give rise to the formation of pseudopolyps (Fig. 32.21). The appearances can closely mimic ulcerative colitis, except that they are segmental.

A rapid increase in pressure leads to distension and thinning of the wall with more or less acute arrest of the intramural circulation and transmural necrosis. This may be patchy and occurs by preference in the caecum and ascending colon. Lysis of muscle fibres in a 'vanishing' muscularis is a frequent finding[12] (Fig. 32.22).

Transmural phlegmonous colitis with or without the formation of mucosal and submucosal gas blebs (Fig. 32.23) is caused by the invasion of particularly virulent microbes.

Stricturing lesions with submucosal fibrosis may result from repair in a quiescent phase. In most cases a segment of normal colon is present between the stenosis and the segment of colitis.[39,51]

Ischaemic colitis in elderly patients

The role played by ischaemia in the pathogenesis of colitis in the elderly has been underestimated in the past. In

Fig. 32.17 Aggregates of lymphocytes, one with a germinal centre, appear along the outer border of the muscularis. (×48)

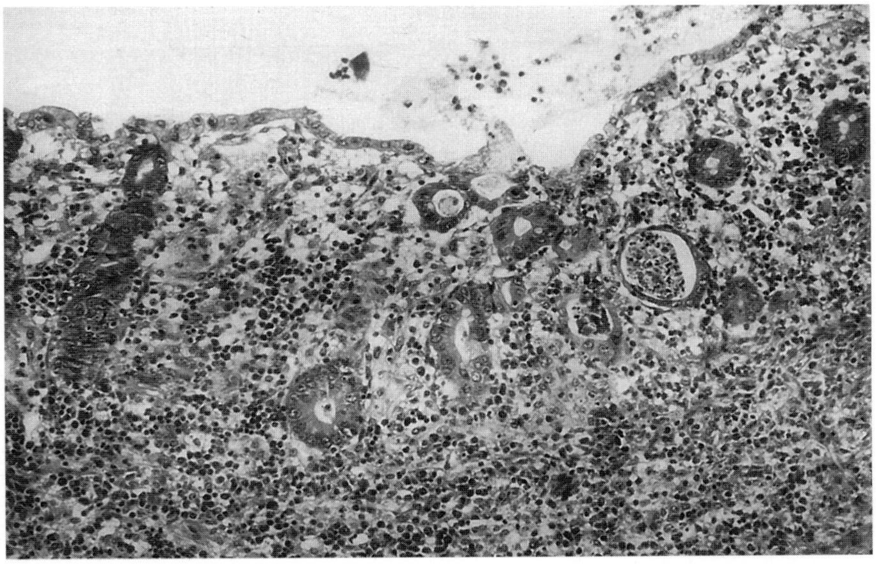

Fig. 32.18 Reconstitution of the mucosa. Regeneration of abnormal surface epithelium and crypts.

studies of patients with an onset of colitis after the age of 50 years, ischaemic colitis is found to be the cause in approximately two-thirds of cases and frequently these are misdiagnosed as ulcerative colitis.[46,47]

The histological appearances in ischaemia may include crypt abscesses, pseudopolyps, undermining and superficial ulceration with a proliferation of capillaries and a normal thickness of the bowel wall, all mimicking ulcerative colitis (see Fig. 32.21). When fissuring and transmural ulcers surrounded by aggregates of lymphocytes occur, they will easily suggest Crohn's disease[46,48] (see Figs 32.16, 32.17).

Toxic megacolon may be encountered in all three conditions. In such cases it is particularly difficult to define the exact nature of the underlying process. In obstructive ischaemic colitis with dilatation, for example, wedge-shaped and cleft-like ulcers and intense transmural vascular engorgement, in association with lymphoid infiltrates along the muscular layer and myocytolysis can be observed. These are identical to lesions that have been described as colitis indeterminate.[52,53]

It is clear that the radiological and pathological appearances may not allow a definitive diagnosis and the appearances need to be considered in the light of the clinical presentation and course of the disease.[46] Early colonoscopic and radiological examination are essential in the investigation, but features which suggest an ischaemic origin for colitis include:

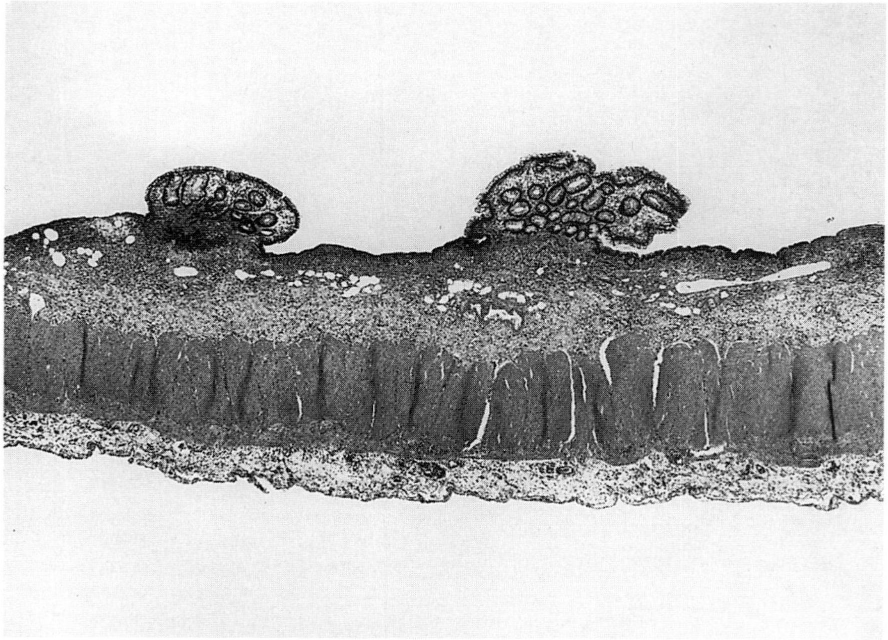

Fig. 32.19 Incomplete regeneration following chronic ischaemic ulceration resulting in a tubular stricture. The surface is covered by a flat layer of epithelial cells which is interrupted by mucosal pseudopolyps showing glandular deformity. (×15)

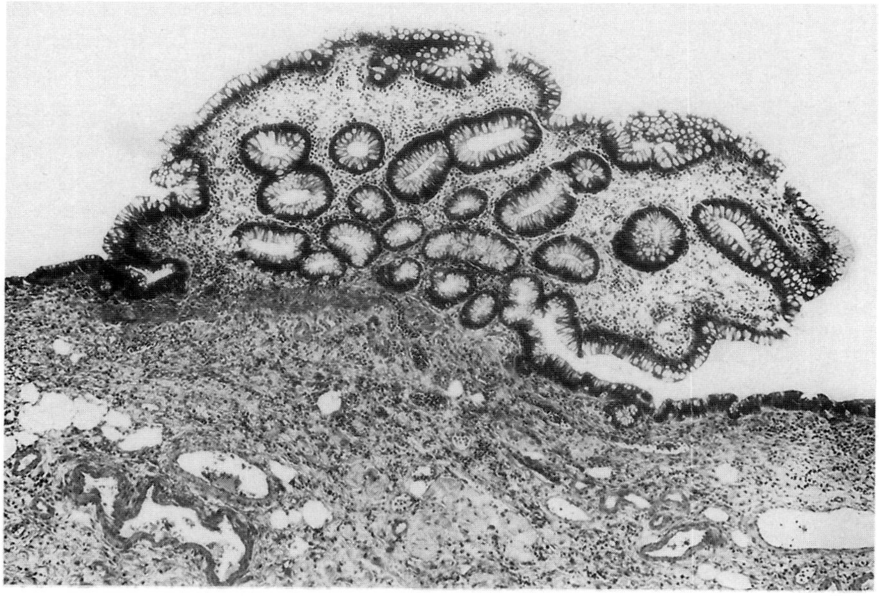

Fig. 32.20 Detail of Figure 32.19. Note destruction of the right half of the muscularis mucosae. (×114)

—characteristic clinical symptoms
—a high incidence of spontaneous resolution
—segmental distribution of lesions
—less frequent involvement of the rectum.

A form of ischaemic colitis that is both rontgenologically and microscopically similar to inflammatory bowel disease occurs in younger patients who are recipients of renal transplants. The condition affects large segments or even the entire colon. Rejection, prolonged hypotension, uraemia and coprostasis have been implicated as precipitating factors in the absence of vascular changes.[54]

Transient colon ischaemia of young adults

This is often a transient colitis and it occurs more frequently in the right half of the colon.[55,56] It has been associated with periods of severe hypotension following trauma[57] and the use of intravenous drugs,[58] clostridial infections with production of necrotizing exotoxins,[59] hypersensitivity vasculitis due to penicillin derivatives,[60] prolonged usage of high doses of ergotamine in migraine patients,[61] thrombotic states associated with oral contraceptives,[56,62] antithrombin III deficiency,[63] and in premature obliterative vascular disease occurring in homo- and

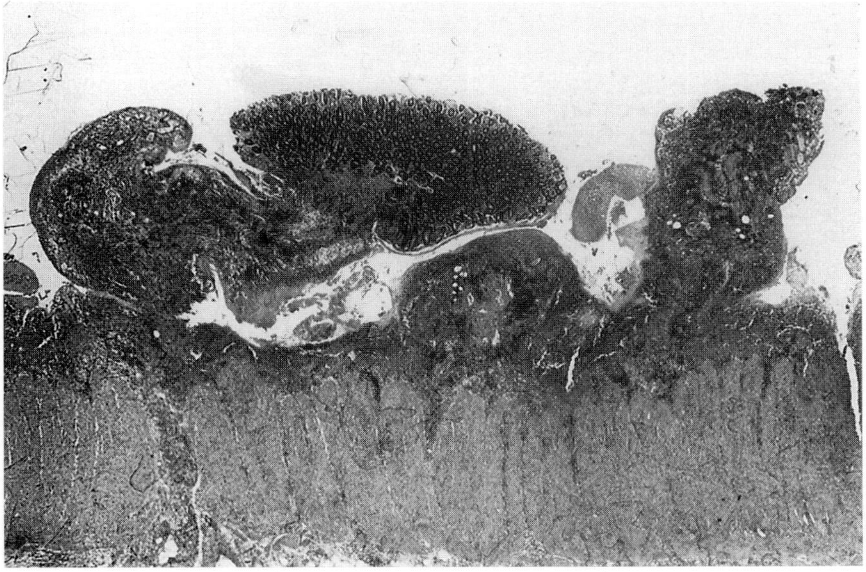

Fig. 32.21 Bizarre pseudopolyps of mucosal remnants in chronic obstructive colitis caused by a gradual increase of intraluminal pressure. (×13)

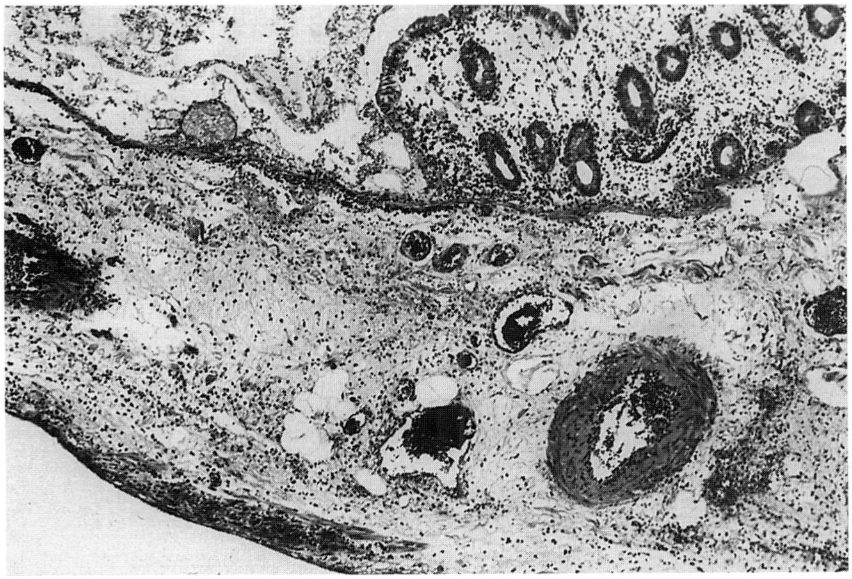

Fig. 32.22 Early focal transmural necrosis. Note almost complete lysis of the muscularis propria and sharp demarcation of the mucosal necrosis. (×48)

heterozygous homocysteinuria.[64] More recently, transient ischaemic colitis is being described in association with the use of drugs of addiction such as cocaine and amphetamines.[65–67]

Stercoral ulcers

These occur in the dilated rectum of elderly constipated patients, particularly in those heavily sedated and institutionalized. They are ischaemic in nature. Distension of the rectal wall and pressure on the mucosa by a faecal mass interferes with the intramural circulation. The ulcers may be single or multiple and occur in a swollen mucosa which often has a purple discolouration. Transmural necrosis and perforation sometimes lead to a phlegmonous periproctitis. Stercoral ulceration is also more likely if the blood supply is already compromised, such as may occur in scleroderma colon.[68]

NECROTIZING ENTEROCOLITIS OF THE NEWBORN

Neonatal necrotizing enterocolitis (NNEC) is a serious and frequently fatal condition with pathological features that closely resemble those of non-occlusive bowel ischaemia, pseudomembranous colitis and toxin-induced bowel disease in animals and man.[69–72]

It is most commonly associated with prematurity[73] and

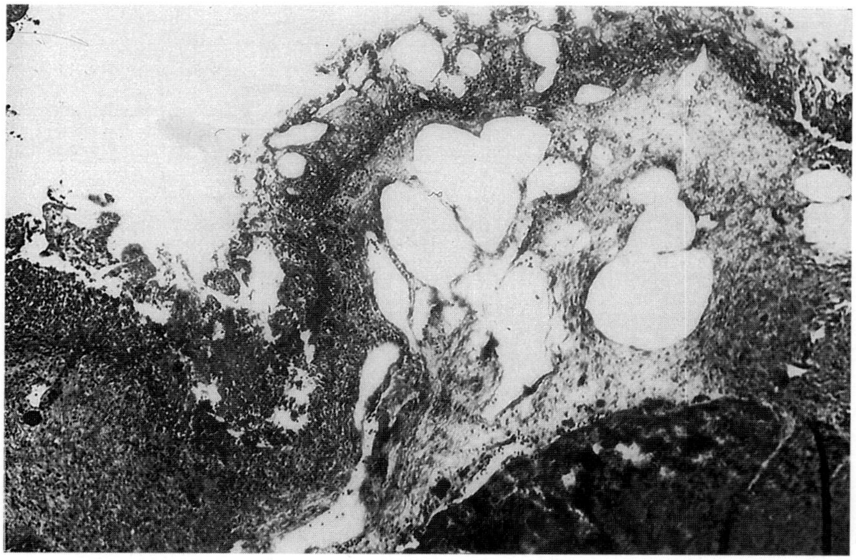

Fig. 32.23 Gas spaces in a necrotic mucosa and in the widened oedematous submucosa dominate the picture. Ischaemic ulceration with fibrinopurulent surface layer is present to the left. (×48)

a birthweight below 1500 g, but also occurs in term infants. The incidence varies between 1–5% of admissions to neonatal intensive care units and is found in 3% of autopsies of premature infants.[74]

Successful neonatal intensive care has probably contributed to an increase of reported cases in the last decade and perinatal hypoxia, respiratory distress syndrome and temperature instability often precede its onset. Increasing abdominal distension, gastric retention, bile emesis and bloody stools herald the onset, usually between the 3rd and 10th day of life. The disease varies from a mild gastrointestinal disturbance to a rapidly lethal, fulminant illness with septic shock.[75–77]

Radiological evidence of the diagnosis includes the demonstration of gas in the intestinal wall and in the portal vein within the liver. Toxic dilatation of the colon, perforation and pneumoperitoneum may occur in severe cases.

Pathology

Gross lesions

Lesions occur in all parts of the gastrointestinal tract, but most commonly involve the terminal ileum and right colon. Grossly, the bowel shows increasing vascular congestion and mural thickening and as the condition progresses it leads to ulceration and necrosis. Non-ulcerated mucosa may have a cobblestone appearance or the bowel may be dilated and haemorrhagic or grey, necrotic and friable. Numerous gas cysts are usually present in the submucosa and subserosa and perforation with peritonitis may occur.[74–77]

Microscopic lesions

Microscopically, the basic lesion is a coagulative necrosis of the bowel wall. At first there is a ghost-like appearance of the mucosa and little inflammatory reaction, but with haemorrhage and oedema of the submucosa which shows markedly distended vessels that may contain thrombi. In more severe lesions, sloughing of the necrotic layers is followed by ulceration which may be focal or confluent and extensive. The ulcers are covered by a pseudomembrane of fibrin and necrotic cell debris. Inflammation is a later reaction and characteristically very variable consisting of lymphocytes, plasma cells, neutrophils, histiocytes and eosinophils that may be prominent. Gas-filled cystic spaces are often present in the bowel wall. The gas, which consists largely of hydrogen, is probably produced by the proliferation of clostridial organisms originating in the bowel.[78] Frank necrosis of the entire bowel wall results in perforation and peritonitis.[74,76,77,79] Microscopic features often vary within the same specimen.

With healing within 1–6 months, intestinal strictures occur as a result of fibrosis in 11% of cases and over 80% are found in the colon. Over 50% occur in the left colon,[80] whereas the majority of acute lesions involve the ascending colon. Sometimes complete or partial disappearance of the muscularis occurs and the appearances mimic intestinal atresia, which is itself thought to be a consequence of intra-uterine intestinal hypoxia.

Aetiology and risk factors

The aetiology of NNEC remains unknown and it probably has a complex pathogenesis but 75–80% of cases occur in stressed premature infants.[71,77,81]

Important in the development of the disease seems to be an element of mucosal abnormality or injury. Injury to the mucosa by hyperosmolar feeds, oral drugs, bacterial endotoxins, toxic plasticizers leaking from catheters and tubes, and allergic or Shwartzman-type reactions have all been implicated. Ischaemia is the most consistent factor and probably occurs as a consequence of shunting of splanchnic blood to vital organs during adverse conditions. There is no doubt that NNEC occurs when there is poor cardiac and respiratory function and in association with polycythaemia and other causes of altered haemodynamics.

More recently, it has been suggested that immaturity of the intestinal secretory immune system may play a role. Arends et al[82] were unable to demonstrate secretory component in the colonic epithelium of two term infants with NNEC, whereas it is normally present at 38 weeks.

Epidemiological studies in recent years have demonstrated the importance of both bacterial and viral infection. Clustering of cases in place and time, positive cultures of blood, faeces, peritoneal fluid and resected bowel specimens and the possible protection of oral aminoglycosides are evidence implicating infectious agents. Toxin-producing clostridial species are the organisms most commonly associated with this condition even though an acute inflammatory reaction is often absent histologically.[72]

Lawrence et al[81] have proposed that the aseptic environment of neonatal intensive care units is responsible for a delayed colonization of the gut and by fewer strains of microorganisms that are then able to multiply without the interference of competing strains. There is certainly evidence that changes in faecal microflora occur prior to the onset of the disease.[83,84] Thus colonization of the gut by a single clostridial species may produce levels of exotoxin sufficient to cause mucosal necrosis. The ability of the immature mucosa, especially of the terminal ileum and proximal colon to absorb complete macromolecules, such as bacterial toxins, may explain the preferential occurrence of lesions in these areas. Even if the flora is not abnormal, absorption of lipopolysaccharide endotoxin coupled with a compromised detoxifying capability of the liver could lead to endotoxinaemia and resulting damage to endothelial cells and platelets and the activation of vasoactive kinins, complement and coagulation.[85]

Enteric feeding may play an important part in causing NNEC, although non-fed prematures may also suffer from the disease.[86] Commercial formulae lack secretory IgA and macrophages that are protective components of mother's milk, and may form a substrate for the proliferation of intestinal bacteria.

Deficiency of pancreatic proteolytic enzymes in the immature infant may cause impaired proteolysis. This might result in a tendency to obstruction and also a diminished degradation of bacterial toxins.[71]

Vascular phenomena may be involved. Immune complexes have been demonstrated in the diseased bowel of infants with NNEC,[87] but whether they are an epiphenomenon or play a role in the patho-genesis is yet to be demonstrated. Certainly, changes in blood flow in the superior mesenteric artery seem to be important[88,89] and rarely the condition is complicated by intravascular haemolysis.[90] (See also necrotizing enteritis in adults: Ch. 31).

VASCULITIS

The spectrum of ischaemic bowel lesions that may occur in patients with vasculitis depend on the type, size, location and degree of involvement of the affected vessels. Solitary or multiple ulcers, if deep enough, may lead to perforation. Ulceration may be segmental and the infarction may be transmural. Stricture formation follows recovery from more superficial damage.[91]

Involvement of the aorta and its major branches may occur in giant cell (temporal) arteritis[92,93] and also occurs in Takayasu's disease.

Medium-sized arteries are affected in polyarteritis nodosa, in the eosinophilic granulomatous angiitis of Churg and Strauss, and in Wegener's granulomatosis, but may also be involved in Buerger's thromboangiitis and collagen disease associated vasculitis, systemic lupus erythematosus (SLE), rheumatoid arthritis and mixed connective tissue disease (MCTD).

The vasa recta and intramural vessels are more often the site of lesions in the vasculitides of the leukocytoclastic type.

Rectal biopsy may aid in the diagnosis of disseminated small vessel vasculitis, but not always.[94]

The various types of vasculitis are basically reaction patterns of vessels to a variety of insults which are frequently the result of hypersensitivity or disordered immunological reactivity. Identification of offending antigens, such as hepatitis B virus, other infectious agents, drugs and immunoglobulins has demonstrated a considerable overlap in the type of vasculitic response and a precise classification of the various vasculitis syndromes is difficult.[92]

Two categories which affect the gastrointestinal tract most frequently are the polyarteritis nodosa group of systemic necrotizing vasculitis and hypersensitivity angiitis. Gastrointestinal symptoms usually occur in the presence of systemic manifestations of the disease.[95]

Polyarteritis nodosa

Classic polyarteritis nodosa is characterized by segmental inflammation and fibrinoid necrosis of small and medium-sized arteries with formation of microaneurysms. Immune complexes, which may contain hepatitis B antigen in up to 30% of patients[92] but may also be the result of bacterial and fungal infections, have been demonstrated in the vascular lesions of many of the patients. Of the cases described by Cohen et al,[96] 25% had gastrointestinal tract involvement. Serious complications including transmural necrosis, perforation and bleeding were present in 15%.

Granulomatous arteritides

Asthma, allergic rhinitis and eosinophilia are characteristic features in patients with eosinophilic granulomatous angiitis of Churg and Strauss. Necrotizing vasculitis of small and occasional medium-sized arteries (Fig. 32.24) and veins with a prominent eosinophilic infiltration occurs and necrotizing extravascular granulomas may be seen. Involvement of the gastrointestinal tract is uncommon, but ulceration and pseudopolyp formation have been described.[97] Rarely, multiple colonic ulcers occur and it seems that this is a form seen particularly in Japan.[98] It is also unusual to see bowel involvement in Wegener's granulomatosis.[94]

Hypersensitivity vasculitis

In allergic, hypersensitivity or leukocytoclastic vasculitis the skin, musculoskeletal tissues, kidney and gastrointestinal tract are frequently involved. Small vessels, like arterioles, small arteries and capillaries are predominantly affected and venulitis is a prominent feature. Fibrinoid necrosis of the vessel wall and thrombosis are frequently present in addition to perivascular infiltrates.

This type of small vessel vasculitis occurs in a large and heterogeneous group of syndromes in which immune complex deposition can frequently be demonstrated. Distinct syndromes in this group comprise Henoch-Schonlein purpura, Cryoglobinaemia syndrome and connective tissue disease associated vasculitis.

Henoch-Schonlein purpura

The Henoch-Schonlein (anaphylactoid) purpura, which is primarily a disease of children, frequently follows an upper respiratory tract infection. IgA deposits and circulating IgA-containing immune complexes are frequently demonstrable. Gastrointestinal tract manifestations occurred in 66% of children under the age of 16 and in 26% of patients over that age in one large series studied.[99] Any bowel segment may be involved, but the jejunum and ileum are most frequently affected. Damage to blood vessels in the form of a perivenulitis is a prominent feature and leads to exudation of blood and the formation of submucosal haemorrhagic blebs and focal oedema. Focal peritonitis may result from inflammation of subserosal vessels.

Cryoglobulinaemia syndrome

Cold precipitable protein complexes, usually consisting of IgM with rheumatoid factor activity and IgG, may occur in the serum of patients with infectious, collagen and lymphoproliferative diseases. They are considered to be immune complexes which may interact with complement components to give rise to systemic vasculitis, in the cryoglobulinaemia syndrome. Hepatitis B antigen or antibody has been found in the cryoprecipitate of more than 50% of patients with the essential type.[95] Precipitates in the lumen of small blood vessels may induce a low grade vasculitis, primarily involving the intima, while deposition of C1q-binding complexes in the vessel wall are responsible for the occurrence of necrotizing vasculitis.[100] Severe obliterative inflammation of submucosal vessels may lead to haemorrhage, ulceration and perforation and to stenosing lesions in the small and large intestine.[100,101]

Connective tissue disease associated vasculitis

Vasculitis associated with connective tissue disease, such

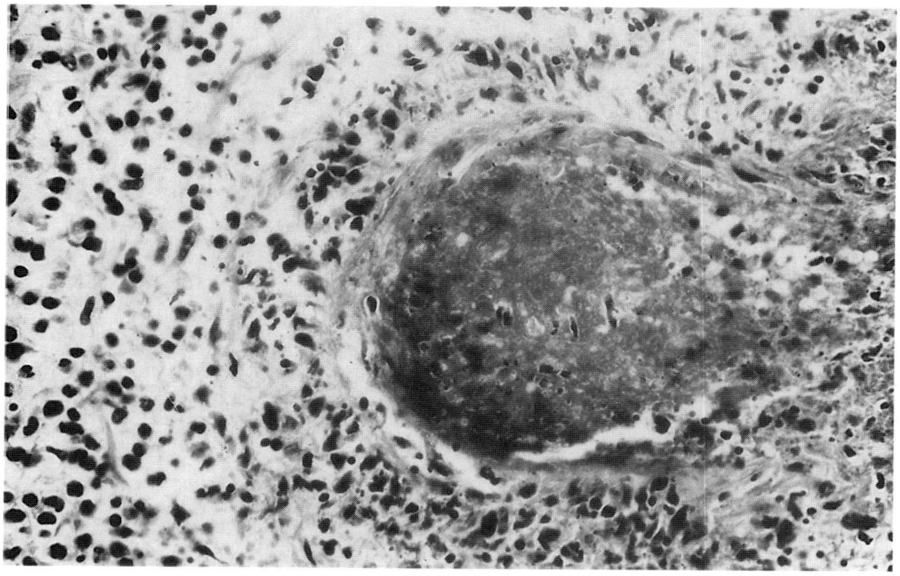

Fig. 32.24 Churg-Strauss vasculitis. The vessel wall and surrounding tissue is densely infiltrated by eosinophilic granulocytes. The lumen is occluded by thrombus. (×114)

as SLE and rheumatoid arthritis, is most commonly of low grade leukocytoclastic type with obliteration of small vessels and little inflammation. However, a fulminant, disseminated, PAN-like, necrotizing vasculitis involving arterioles, medium-sized muscular arteries and larger veins may occur.[91,102] It is believed that immune complex deposition is the causative factor. Extensive ischaemic lesions with ulceration and gangrene may involve the entire colon[103–108] due to the very widespread character of the vasculitis. Arteriolitis[109] as well as venulitis[110] may cause ischaemic ulcers in the colon and perforation can follow or, when larger vessels are affected, segmental necrosis may ensue. Ischaemic gastrointestinal tract manifestations may occur in 20–30% of patients,[95] although they are not always clinically apparent.[107] Extensive deposits of amyloid in the wall of intra- and extramural blood vessels can also give rise to bowel ischaemia in patients with rheumatoid arthritis.

Intimal proliferation and occlusion of small-sized arteries may lead to bowel ischaemia in systemic sclerosis but this is a rare complication.[111] In mixed connective tissue disease medium-sized arteries are affected (Fig. 32.25).

Miscellaneous vasculitis

Behcet syndrome

Gastrointestinal lesions in the Behcet syndrome occur in over 50% of patients, especially from Japan.[112–115] Multiple scattered ulcers, which may be aphthoid or round, deep and undermined, and tend to perforate, occur in the ileum and caecum, but less frequently in the more distal colon. Inflammation of arterioles, venules and capillaries with perivascular lymphocytic infiltration, focal fibrinoid necrosis and thrombosis of vessel walls is described.

Thromboangiitis obliterans (Buerger's disease)

This rare vasculopathy, presumably of inflammatory nature, affects intermediate and small-sized arteries as well as their accompanying veins and nerves in a segmental fashion. It is associated with thrombus formation and evolves through acute and subacute phases to a chronic stage with fibrosis and recanalization, during which the internal elastic lamina remains intact.[92] The disease affects mainly the vessels of the extremities and is frequently associated with superficial thrombophlebitis. Involvement of the mesenteric vasculature has been described[116,117] and segments of ulcerating and transmural ischaemic colitis can occur in the ascending, transverse or sigmoid colon.[118–120] Vascular lesions in the burnt out stage should be differentiated from thrombotic vessel occlusion that occurs in patients with antithrombin III and protein C deficiency, which may also occur in the same age group and likewise be associated with superficial thrombophlebitis.

Malignant atrophic papulosis

Ulceration and perforation of small and large bowel commonly occurs in patients with malignant atrophic papulosis of Degos. This is a rare disease of young adults. Crops of red papules that develop a porcelain-white sunken centre usually precede intestinal lesions by weeks or months. Recurring attacks of abdominal pain may remit spontaneously or end in perforation. Occlusive lesions of small and medium sized arteries are the result of thrombosis or a progressive fibrotic obliteration of the lumen. The internal elastic lamina and the outer vessel wall remains intact. Small vessels show endothelial swelling with vacuolization and fibrinoid necrosis of the entire wall.[121] Segmental ischaemic colitis due to idiopathic myointimal hyperplasia

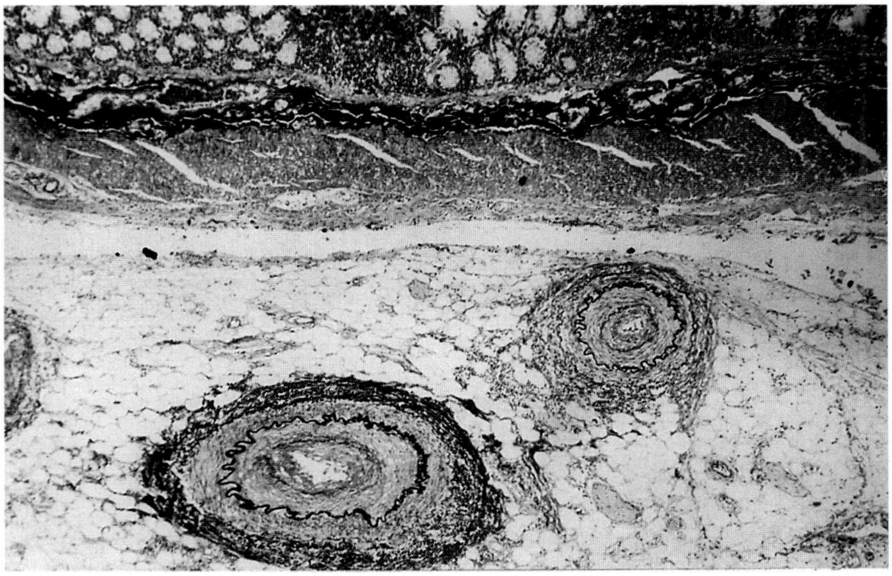

Fig. 32.25 Mixed connective tissue disease associated obliterative type of low grade vasculitis. Note early ischaemic haemorrhage in colonic mucosa. (×28)

of small mesenteric veins has also been reported; the aetiology is unknown.[122]

Vasculitis of both large (Takayasu), middle sized and small vessels (giant cell arteritis) has been reported in association with chronic inflammatory bowel disease but probably occurs by chance.[123–125]

ANGIODYSPLASIA

The variable nomenclature of vascular malformations in the gastrointestinal tract reflects uncertainty as to their exact nature.[126] Lesions may evolve through various stages and thus explain different pathological findings.[127]

Arteriovenous malformations, which consist of enlarged, tortuous and dilated, often thin-walled blood vessels, usually occur in the submucosa or mucosa. They have been described in children[128] and may be so small that they are not easily detected without angiography. Nevertheless they can cause recurrent and even massive haemorrhage.

Moore et al[129] have proposed their classification into three types according to the age of the patient, their localization in the gastrointestinal tract and the presence or absence of hereditary factors.

Type I lesions usually occur in the right side of the colon in patients over 55 years of age.

Type II lesions are seen in younger patients with a mean age of onset of symptoms of 29 years, and are usually present in the stomach and proximal bowel.

Type III is characterized by a family history and punctate telangiectatic lesions in the proximal gastrointestinal tract, on the skin of face and fingers and in the oral and nasal mucosa.

It is type I lesions which are called angiodysplasis and are by far the most common vascular malformations of the colon. They are now recognized with increasing frequency as a source of recurrent and chronic blood loss in elderly patients, especially since the introduction of selective angiography by Baum[130] and the increased use of colonoscopic examination in the investigation of intestinal bleeding. Few young patients are affected, the youngest being 19 years of age.[131] Bleeding may occur over many years and varies from occult to acute exsanguinating episodes.[132] The early lesions occur most commonly in the caecum and ascending colon and appear as one or more sharply delineated areas of the mucosa, which are red and flat or slightly raised with scalloped edges and have a prominent draining vein. Later they increase in size and become confluent. The incidence and multiplicity of lesions increase with age, but only a small percentage will bleed.

At routine colonoscopy between 1–2% of patients harbour such lesions.[132,133]

Histopathology

The earliest morphological changes[134] occur in the submucosal veins, which become dilated, tortuous and thin walled (Fig. 32.26). The mucosal venules and capillaries surrounding the crypts then become dilated and connect with distended branches which pierce the muscularis mucosae (Fig. 32.27). Finally, the entire width of the submucosa and mucosa may be filled by ectatic vessels and vascular spaces. At this stage they can be recognized at endoscopy as the cherry-red coral reef lesion with its prominent central vessel surrounded by radiating smaller branches. Small arteriovenous communications are formed due to incompetence of precapillary sphincters and these are responsible for the large early draining veins seen at angiography. Arteries and arterioles are not involved until

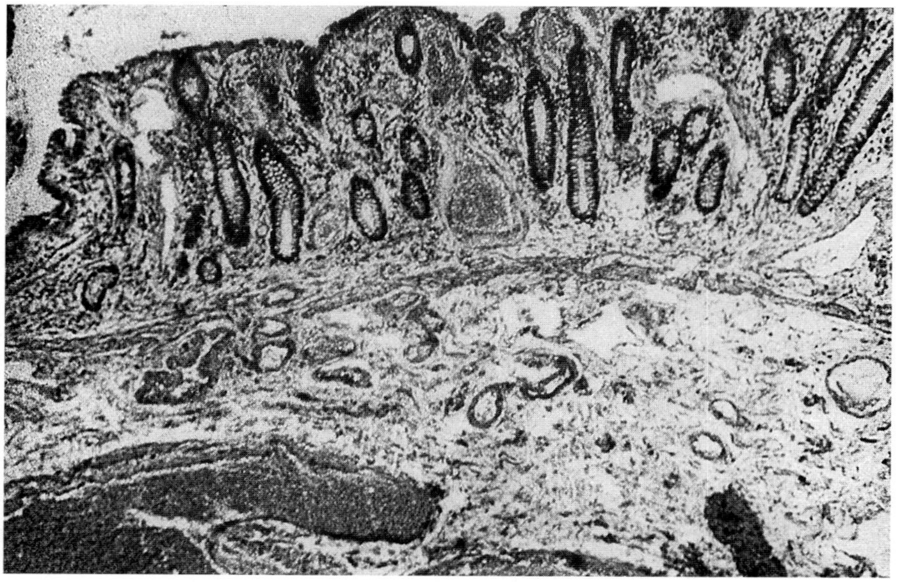

Fig. 32.26 A group of dilated veins with accompanying normal arteries is present in the submucosa. Note distended capillaries in the mucosa. (×46)

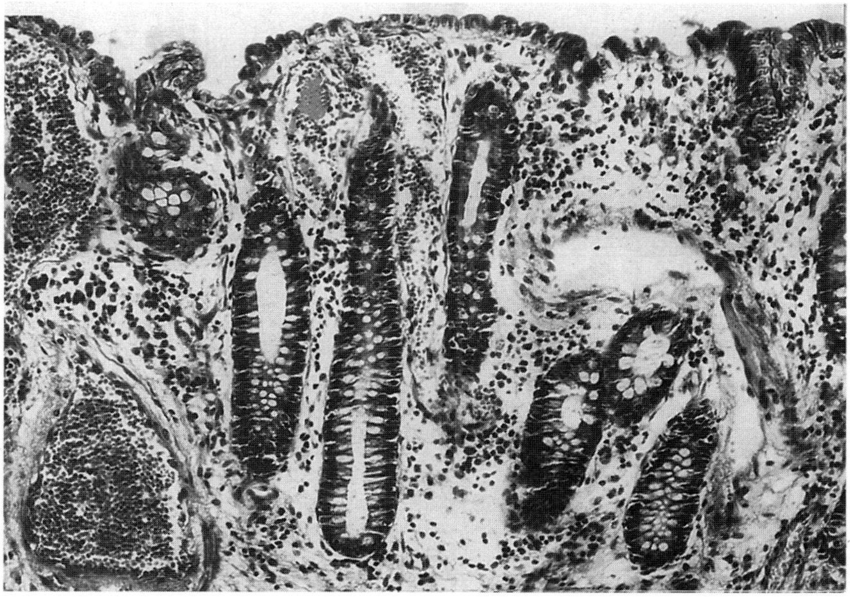

Fig. 32.27 Dilated venules and capillaries alongside mucosal crypts extend towards the often flimsy layer of surface epithelium. (×114)

late in the process, and the vessels of the serosa and muscular layers retain a normal appearance.[135] Early lesions may be difficult to demonstrate unless the resected specimen is injected with silicone rubber or radiopaque substances.[127,136] A more recently described technique employs intraluminal formalin fixation followed by dissection of the mucosa from the muscle wall. By transilluminating the bowel wall, lesions are readily seen on gross direct inspection.[137]

Pathogenesis

Boley et al[134] postulate, on the basis of their elegant studies of silicone rubber injected, cleared specimens, that these lesions represent an acquired ectasia of pre-existing vessels which is associated with aging (Fig. 32.28). Repeated chronic partial intermittent obstruction of submucosal veins occurs in their course through the muscularis propria. They are compressed by surrounding muscle in conditions of increased intraluminal pressure brought on by repeated episodes of right colon distension. This is the result of increased peristalsis and straining in constipated elderly patients. A prevalence of these lesions in the caecum and ascending colon may be explained by the greater tension in the bowel wall in these areas.

Angiodysplastic lesions in adolescents and young adults are possibly congenital, but may enlarge with duration under the same influences as apply in the older age group.

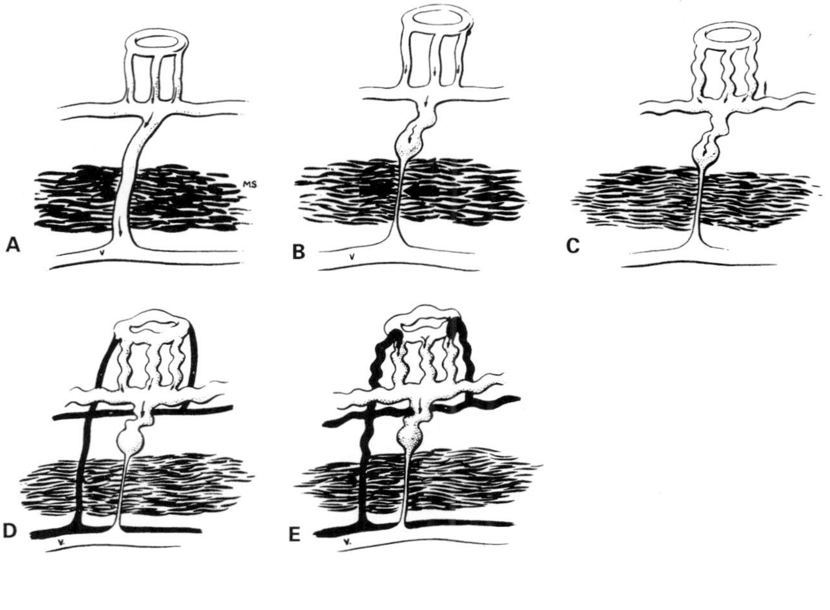

Fig. 32.28 Diagrammatic illustration of the development of caecal vascular ectasias. **A** Normal state of vein perforating muscular layers; **B** With muscular contraction or increased intraluminal pressure the vein is partially obstructed; **C** After repeated episodes over many years the submucosal vein becomes dilated and tortuous; **D** Later, the veins and venules draining into the abnormal submucosal vein become similarly involved; **E** Ultimately, the capillary ring becomes dilated, the precapillary sphincter becomes incompetent and a small arteriovenous communication is present through the ectasia. Reprinted with permission from Boley S J et al. On the nature and etiology of vascular ectasias of the colon. Degenerative lesions of aging. Gastroenterology 1977; 72: 650–660. (Copyright 1977 by the American Gastroenterological Association)

There seems to be an association with aortic stenosis which is difficult to explain, but it may be through an increased tendency to bleeding due to a low perfusion pressure, resulting in superficial ischaemic necrosis which would result in their detection.[134,138–140]

Cholesterol emboli are regularly found in the submucosal arteries related to angiodysplastic lesions. They possibly originate spontaneously in the aortic wall or be the result of angiographic procedures.[141] There also seems to be an association with cirrhosis of the liver[142,143] and hypertrophic obstructive cardiomyopathy.[144]

Bleeding and coagulation disorders such as von Willebrand disease may also play a role in unmasking silent lesions.[145]

Other vascular malformations

Acquired angiodysplasia must be distinguished from other forms of ectatic vascular malformations which comprise a heterogenous group.

Congenital lesions occur in younger patients and more often in the small bowel and stomach rather than colon. When associated with fat, smooth muscle and fibrous tissue, they assume a hamartomatous aspect. In general, congenital malformations are characterized by a localized increase in the number and size of blood vessels without the architectural features of a haemangioma.[146] Both arteries and veins are thick-walled, the veins show hypertrophy of muscle fibres and eccentric fibrous intimal thickening with a narrowed lumen. Organizing thrombi may be present.

In hereditary telangiectatic lesions, the dilatation affects vessels throughout the entire wall and is not confined to the mucosa and submucosa. Patients with the Osler-Rendu-Weber syndrome do not usually bleed until late in life. Small punctate lesions occur with greatest frequency in the stomach, duodenum and jejunum.

Acquired angioectatic lesions may also be present in association with inflammatory and neoplastic bowel disease[1] and especially in the wall of diverticula, where they may account for the origin of bleeding.[147]

REFERENCES

1. Boley SJ, Brandt TJ, Veith FJ. Ischemic disorders of the intestines. Current problems in surgery 1978; 15: 1–85.
2. McGovern VJ, Goulston SJM. Ischaemic enterocolitis. Gut 1965; 6: 213–220.
3. Morson BC. Histopathology of intestinal ischaemia. In: Vascular disorders of the intestine. Boley SJ, Schwartz SG and Williams LF, eds. (New York: Appleton-Century-Crofts) 1971; 6: 103–123.
4. Whitehead R. The pathology of intestinal ischaemia. Clin Gastroenterol 1972; 1: 613–637.
5. Whitehead R. The pathology of ischaemia of the intestines. Pathol Ann 1976; 11: 1–52.
6. Marcuson RW. Ischaemic colitis. Clin Gastroentrol 1972; 1: 745–763.
7. Fagin RR, Kirsner JB. Ischaemic diseases of the colon. Adv Int Med 1973; 17: 343–362.
8. Norris HT. Ischemic bowel disease: its spectrum. In: Yardley JH, Morson BC, Abell MR, eds. The gastrointestinal tract. Int Acad Pathol Monograph. Baltimore: Williams and Wilkins, 1977.
9. Alschibaja I, Morson BC. Ischaemic bowel disease. J Clin Pathol 1977; 11(suppl 30): p 68–77.
10. Marston A. Intestinal ischaemia. London: Edward Arnold, 1977.
11. Saegesser F, Loosli H, Robinson JWL, Roenspies H. Ischemic diseases of the large intestine. Int Surg 1981; 66: 103–117.
12. Reeders JWAJ, Tytgat GNJ, Rosenbusch G, Gratama S. Ischaemic colitis. Boston: Martinus Nijhoff, 1984.
13. Berger RL, Byrne JJ. Intestinal gangrene associated with heart disease. Surg Gynecol Obstet 1961; 112: 529–533.
14. Boley SJ, Schwartz S, Lash J, Sternhill V. Reversible vascular occlusion of the colon. Surg Gynecol Obstet 1963; 116: 53–60.
15. Marston A. The bowel in shock; the role of mesenteric arterial disease as a cause of death in the elderly. Lancet 1962; 2: 365–370.
16. Marston A, Pheils MT, Thomas ML, Morson BC. Ischaemic colitis. Gut 1966; 7: 1–15.
17. Marston A, Marcuson RW, Chapman M, Arthur JF. Experimental study of devascularization of the colon. Gut 1969; 10: 121–130.
18. Boley SJ, Agrawal GP, Warren AR, et al. Pathophysiologic effects of bowel distension on intestinal blood flow. Am J Surg 1969; 117: 228–234.
19. Marcuson RW, Stewart JO, Marston A. Experimental venous lesions of the colon. Gut 1972; 13: 1–7.
20. Rausis C, Robinson JWL, Mirkovitz V, Saegesser F. Desordres vasculaires du gros intestin: donnees experimentales et correlations cliniques. Helv Chir Acta 1973; 40: 295–305.
21. Robinson JWL, Mirkovitz V, Winistoerfer B, Saegesser F. Progress report: Response of the intestinal mucosa to ischaemia. Gut 1981; 22: 512–527.
22. Parish KL, Chapman WC, Williams LF Jr. Ischemic Colitis. An ever-changing spectrum? Am Surg 1991; 57: 118–121.
23. Longo WE, Ballantyne GH, Gusberg RJ. Ischemic colitis: patterns and prognosis. Dis Colon Rectum 1992; 35: 726–730.
24. Ming SC. Haemorrhagic necrosis of the gastrointestinal tract and its relation to cardiovascular status. Circulation 1965; 32: 332–340.
25. Renton CJC. Non-occlusive intestinal infarction. Clin Gastroenterol 1972; 1: 655–673.
26. Trinh TD, Jones B, Fishman EK. Amyloidosis of the colon presenting as ischemic colitis: a case report and review of the literature. Gastrointest Radiol 1991; 16: 133–136.
27. Patel R, Hughes RW Jr. An unusual case of myxedema megacolon with features of ischemic and pseudomembranous colitis. Mayo Clin Proc 1992; 67: 369–372.
28. Sparano JA, Dutcher JP, Kaleya R, et al. Colonic ischemia complicating immunotherapy with interleukin-2 and interferon-alpha. Cancer 1991; 68: 1538–1544.
29. Hellstrom PM, Rubio C, Odar-Cederlof I, Slezak P. Ischemic colitis of the cecum after renal transplantation masquerading as malignant disease. Dig Dis Sci 1991; 36: 1644–1648.
30. Noirhomme P, Buche M, Louagie Y, et al. Ischemic complications of abdominal aortic surgery. J Cardiovasc Surg Torino 1991; 32: 451–155.
31. Williams LF, Bosniak MA, Wittenberg J, Manuel B, Grimes H, Byrnes JJ. Ischemic colitis. Am J Surg 1969; 117: 254–264.
32. Feller E, Reichert R, Spiro HM. Small vessel disease of the gut. In: Boley SJ, Schwartz SS, Williams LF, eds. Vascular disorders of the intestine. New York: Appleton-Century-Crofts 1971: 483–507.
33. Arosemena E, Edwards JE. Lesions of the small mesenteric arteries underlying intestinal infarction. Geriatr 1967; 22: 122–137.

34. Aboumrad MH, Fine G, Horn RC. Intimal hyperplasia of the small mesenteric arteries. Arch Pathol 1963: 75: 196–200.
35. McGregor D, Pierce GE, Thomas JH, Tilzer LL. Obstructive lesions of the distal mesenteric arteries. Arch Lab Med 1980; 104: 79–83.
36. Rao RN, Hilliard K, Wray CH. Widespread intimal hyperplasia of small arteries and arterioles. Arch Pathol Lab Med 1983; 107: 254–257.
37. Kumar PJ, Dawson AM. Vasculitis of the alimentary tract. Clin Gastroenterol 1972; 1: 719–743.
38. Whitehead R. Ischaemic enterocolitis. An expression of the intravascular coagulation syndrome. Gut 1971; 12: 912–917.
39. Boley SJ, Schwartz SS. Colitis complicating carcinoma of the colon. In: Boley SJ, Schwartz SS, Williams LF, eds. Vascular disorders of the intestine. New York: Appleton-Century-Crofts, 1971: 631–642.
40. Swerdlow SH, Antonioli DA, Goldman H. Intestinal infarction: A new classification. (Letter to the editor). Arch Path Lab Med 1981; 105: 218.
41. Kilpatrick ZM, Farman J, Yesner R, Spiro HM. Ischemic proctitis. JAMA 1968; 205: 74–80.
42. Allan AC. The vascular pathogenesis of enterocolitis of varied etiology. In: Boley SJ, Schwartz SS, Williams LF, eds. Vascular disorders of the intestine. New York: Appleton-Century-Crofts 1971: 57–102.
43. Williams LF, Wittenberg J. Ischemic colitis: A useful clinical diagnosis, but is it ischemic? Ann Surg 1975; 182: 439–446.
44. Brown AR. Non-gangrenous ischemic colitis. A review of 17 cases. Br J Surg 1972; 59: 463–472.
45. Brandt LJ, Katz HJ, Wolf EL, Mitsudo S, Boley SJ. Simulation of colonic carcinoma by ischemia. Gastroenterology 1985; 88: 1137–1142.
46. Eisenberg RL, Montgomery CK, Margulis AR. Colitis in the elderly: ischaemic colitis mimicking ulcerative and granulomatous colitis. AJR 1979; 133: 1113–1118.
47. Brandt LJ, Boley SJ, Goldberg L, Mitsudo S, Berman A. Colitis in the elderly: a reappraisal. Am J Gastroenterol 1981; 76: 239–245.
48. Brandt LJ, Boley SJ, Mitsudo S. Clinical characteristics and natural history of colitis in the elderly. Am J Gastroenterol 1982; 77: 382–386.
49. Dawson MA, Schaeffer JW. The clinical course of reversible ischaemic colitis. Observations on the progression of sigmoidoscopic and histological changes. Gastroenterol 1971; 60: 577–580.
50. Tytgat GNJ, Reeders JWAJ. Die ischaemische kolitis unter besondere Berucksichtigung der Endoskopie. Internist 1983; 24: 75–80.
51. Toner M, Condell D, O'Briain DS. Obstructive colitis. Ulceroinflammatory lesions occurring proximal to colonic obstruction. Am J Surg Pathol 1990; 14: 719–728.
52. Price AB. Difficulties in the differential diagnosis of ulcerative colitis and Crohn's disease. In: Yardley JH, Morson BC, Abell MR, eds. The gastrointestinal tract. Int Acad Pathol Monograph. Baltimore: Williams and Wilkins, 1977: 1–14.
53. Rowland R, Pounder DJ. Crohn's colitis. Pathol Ann 1982; 17: 267–290.
54. Komorowski RA, Cohen EB, Kauffman HM, Adams AB. Gastrointestinal complications in renal transplant patients. Am J Clin Pathol 1986; 86: 161–167.
55. Duffy TJ. Reversible ischaemic colitis in young adults. Br J Surg 1981; 68: 34–37.
56. Barcewicz PA, Welch JP. Ischaemic colitis in young adult patients. Dis Colon Rectum 1980; 23: 109–114.
57. Reickert RR, Johnson RG, Wignarajan KR. Ischaemic colitis in a young adult patient: report of a case. Dis Colon Rectum 1974; 17: 112–116.
58. Turnbull AR, Isaacson P. Ischaemic colitis and drug abuse. Br Med J 1977; 2: 1000.
59. Sakurai Y, Isuchiya H, Ikegami F et al. Acute rightsided haemorrhagic colitis associated with oral administration of Ampicillin. Dig Dis Sci 1979; 24: 910–915.
60. Toffler RB, Pingoud EG, Burell ML. Acute colitis related to penicillin and penicillin derivates. Lancet 1978; 2: 707–709.
61. Stillman AE, Weinberg M, Mast WC, Palpant S. Ischemic bowel disease attributable to Ergotamine. Gastroenterology 1977; 72: 1336–1337.
62. Kilpatrick ZM, Silverman JF, Betancourt E, Farman J, Lawson JP. Vascular occlusion of the colon and oral contraceptives. Possible relation. N Engl J Med 1968; 278: 438–440.
63. Britton BJ, Royle G. Mesenteric venous thrombosis. Br J Surg 1982: 69: 117–118.
64. Boers GHJ, Smals AGH, Trybels FJM, et al. Heterozygosity for homocysteinuria in premature peripheral and cerebral occlusive arterial disease. N Engl J Med 1985; 313: 709–715.
65. Yang RD, Han MW, McCarthy JH. Ischemic colitis in a crack abuser. Dig Dis Sci 1991; 36: 238–240.
66. Beyer KL, Bickel JT, Butt JH. Ischemic colitis associated with dextroamphetamine use. J Clin Gastroenterol 1991; 13: 198–201.
67. Johnson TD, Berenson MM. Methamphetamine-induced ischemic colitis. J Clin Gastroenterol 1991; 13: 687–689.
68. Robinson JC, Teitelbaum SC. Stercoral ulceration and perforation of the sclerodermatous colon. Report of 2 cases and review of the literature. Dis Colon Rectum 1974; 17: 622–632.
69. Lawrence G, Walker PD. Pathogenesis of enteritis necroticans in Papua New Guinea. Lancet 1976; 1: 125–126.
70. Arseculeratna SN, Panabokke RG, Navaratnam C. Pathogenesis of necrotizing enteritis with special reference to intestinal hypersensitivity reaction. Gut 1980; 21: 265–278.
71. Kosloske AM. Pathogenesis and prevention of necrotizing enterocolitis: A hypothesis based on personal observation and a review of the literature. Pediatrics 1984; 74: 1086–1092.
72. Kliegman RM, Fanaroff AA. Necrotizing enterocolitis. N Engl J Med 1984; 310: 1093–1103.
73. Beeby PJ, Jeffery H. Risk factors for necrotising enterocolitis: the influence of gestational age. Arch Dis Child 1992; 67: 432–435.
74. Hopkins GB, Gould NE, Stevenson JK, Oliver TK. Necrotizing enterocolitis in premature infants. Am J Dis Child 1970; 120: 229–232.
75. Stevenson JK, Graham EB, Oliver TK, Goldenberg VE. Neonatal necrotizing enterocolitis. A report of twenty-one cases with fourteen survivors. Am J Surg 1969; 118: 260–272.
76. Berdon WE. Necrotizing enterocolitis of the newborn. In: Boley SJ, Schwartz SS, Williams LF, eds. Vascular disorders of the intestine. New York: Appleton-Century-Crofts 1971: 613–629.
77. Santulli TV, Schullinger JN, Heird VC, et al. Acute necrotizing enterocolitis in infancy: a review of 64 cases. Pediatrics 1975; 55: 376–387.
78. Tait RA, Kealy WF. Neonatal necrotizing enterocolitis. J Clin Pathol 1979; 3: 1090–1099.
79. Joshi VV, Winston YE, Kay S. Neonatal necrotizing enterocolitis: Histologic evidence of healing. Am J Dis Child 1973; 126: 113–116.
80. Janik JS, Ein SH, Mancer K. Intestinal stricture after necrotizing enterocolitis. J Pediatr Surg 1981; 16: 438–443.
81. Lawrence S, Bates J, Gaul A. Pathogenesis of neonatal necrotizing enterocolitis. Lancet 1982; 1: 137–139.
82. Arends JW, Walther FJ, Forget PP, Huber J, Bosman FT. Abnormal expression of secretory component in term newborns with bowel perforation. A report of two cases. J Pediatr Gastroenterol Nutr 1986; 5: 310–313.
83. Hoy C, Millar MR, MacKay P, et al. Quantitative changes in faecal microflora preceding necrotising enterocolitis in premature neonates. Arch Dis Child 1990; 65: 1057–1059.
84. Millar MR, MacKay P, Levene M, Langdale V, Martin C. Enterobacteriaceae and neonatal necrotising enterocolitis. Arch Dis Child 1992; 67: 53–56.
85. Scheifele DW, Olsen EM, Pendray MR. Endotoxemia and thrombocytopenia during neonatal necrotizing enterocolitis. Am J Clin Pathol 1985; 83: 221–229.
86. Marchildon MB, Buch BE, Abdenour S. Necrotizing enterocolitis in the unfed infant. J Pediatr Surg 1982; 17: 620–624.
87. Gray ES, Lloyd DJ, Miller SS, et al. Evidence for an immune complex vasculitis in neonatal necrotizing enterocolitis. J Clin Pathol 1981; 34: 759–763.
88. Coombs RC, Morgan ME, Durbin GM, Booth IW, McNeish AS. Abnormal gut blood flow velocities in neonates at risk of

necrotising enterocolitis. J Pediatr Gastroenterol Nutr 1992; 15: 13–19.
89. Kempley ST, Gamsu HR. Superior mesenteric artery blood flow velocity in necrotising enterocolitis. Arch Dis Child 1992; 67: 793–796.
90. Squire R, Kiely E, Drake D, Lander A. Intravascular haemolysis in association with necrotising enterocolitis. J Pediatr Surg 1992; 27: 808–810.
91. Feller E, Rickert R, Spiro HM. Small vessel disease of the gut. In: Boley SJ, Schwartz SS, Williams LF, eds. Vascular disorders of the intestine. New York: Appleton-Century-Crofts 1971: 483–507.
92. Fauci AAS, Haynes Br, Katz P. The spectrum of vasculitis: clinical, pathologic, immunologic and therapeutic considerations. Ann Intern Med 1978; 89: 660–676.
93. Klein RG, Hunter GG, Stanson AW, Sheps SG. Large artery involvement in giant cell (temporal) arteritis. Ann Int Med 1975; 83: 806–812.
94. Camilleri M, Pusey CD, Chatwick VS, Rees AJ. Gastrointestinal manifestations of systemic vasculitis. Quart J Med 1983; 52: 141–149.
95. Luzar MJ. Systemic vasculitis. In: Cooperman M, ed. Intestinal ischaemia. New York: Futura, 1983.
96. Cohen RD, Conn DL, Ilstrup DM. Clinical features, prognosis and response to treatment in polyarteritis. Mayo Clin Proc 1980; 55: 146–155.
97. Chumbley LC, Harrison EG, DeRemee RA. Allergic granulomatosis and angiitis (Churg-Strauss syndrome). Report and analysis of 30 cases. Mayo Clin Proc 1977; 52: 477–484.
98. Shimamoto C, Hirata I, Ohshiba S, Fujiwara S, Nishio M. Churg-Strauss syndrome (allergic granulomatous angiitis) with peculiar multiple colonic ulcers. Am J Gastroenterol 1990; 85: 316–319.
99. Lopez LR, Schocket AL, Stanford RE, Claman HN, Kohler PF. Gastrointestinal involvement in leukocytoclastic vasculitis and polyarteritis nodosa. J Rheumatol 1980; 7: 677–684.
100. Gorevic PD, Kassab MJ, Levo Y, Kohn R et al. Mixed cryoglobulinemia: Clinical aspects and long term follow up of 40 patients. Am J Med 1980; 69: 287–308.
101. Reza MJ, Roth BE, Pops MA, Goldberg LS. Intestinal vasculitis in essential, mixed cryoglobulinemia. Ann Intern Med 1974; 81: 632–634.
102. Christian CL, Sergent JS. Vasculitic syndromes: Clinical and experimental models. Am J Med 1976; 61: 385–392.
103. Whitehead R. The pathology of ischaemia of the intestines. Pathol Ann 1976; 11: 1–52.
104. Kistin MG, Kaplan MM, Harrington JT. Diffuse ischaemic colitis associated with systemic lupus erythematosus. Response to subtotal colectomy. Gastroenterology 1978; 75: 1147–1151.
105. Stoddard CJ, Kay PJ, Simms JM, Kennedy A, Hughes P. Acute abdominal complications of systemic lupus erythematosus. Br J Surg 1978; 65: 625–628.
106. Prouss PJ, Thompson EM, Gumpel JM. Systemic lupus erythematosus and abdominal pain. Br J Rheumatol 1983; 22: 172–175.
107. Burt RW, Berenson MM, Samuelson CO, Cathey WJ. Rheumatoid vasculitis of the colon presenting as pancolitis. Dig Dis Sci 1983; 28: 183–188.
108. Ferrari BT, Ray JE, Robertson HD, Bonaer RJ, Guthright JB. Colonic manifestations of collagen vascular diseases. Dis Colon Rectum 1980; 23: 473–477.
109. Zizic TM, Shulman LE, Stevens MB. Colonic perforations in systemic lupus erythematosus. Medicin 1975; 54: 411–426.
110. Helliwell TR, Flook D, Whitworth J, Day DV. Arteritis and venulitis in systemic lupus erythematosus resulting in massive lower intestinal haemorrhage. Histopathology 1985; 9: 1103–1113.
111. Edwards DH, Lennard-Jones JF. Diffuse systemic sclerosis presenting as infarction of the colon. Proc R Soc Med 1960; 53: 877–879.
112. Roenspies U, Saegesser R. Morbus Behcet und toxisches megakolon. Schweiz Med Wochenschr 1975; 105: 199–204.
113. Eng K, Ruoff M, Bystrym JC. Behcet's syndrome. An unusual cause of colonic ulceration and perforation. Am J Gastroenterol 1981; 75: 57–59.
114. Baba S, Maruta M, Ando K, Teramoto T, Endo J. Intestinal Behcet's disease: Report of 5 cases. Dis Colon Rectum 1976; 19: 428–440.
115. Lakhanpal S, Tani K, Lie JT, Katoh K, Ishigatsubo Y, Ohokubo T. Pathologic features of Behcet's syndrome: A review of Japanese autopsy registry data. Hum Pathol 1985; 16: 790–795.
116. Deitch EA, Sikkema WW. Intestinal manifestations of Buerger's disease: Case report and literature review. Am Surgeon 1981; 47: 326–328.
117. Rosen N, Sommer S, Knobel B. Intestinal Buerger disease. Arch Path Lab Med 1985; 109: 962–963.
118. Herrington L, Grossmen LA. Surgical lesions of the small and large intestine resulting from Buerger's disease. Ann Surg 1968; 168: 1079–1087.
119. Guay A, Janower ML, Bain RW, McCready FJ. A case of Buerger's disease causing ischaemic colitis with perforation in a young male. Am J Med Sci 1976; 271: 239–240.
120. Sachs JL, Klima T, Frankel NB. Thromboangiitis obliterans of the transverse colon. JAMA 1977; 238: 336–337.
121. Melski JW, Murphy GF. Progressive neurologic disorder and abdominal pain in an 18 year old woman. N Engl J Med 1980; 303: 1103–1111.
122. Genta RM, Haggitt RC. Idiopathic myointimal hyperplasia of mesenteric veins. Gastroenterology 1991; 101: 533–539.
123. Yassinger S, Adelman R, Cantor D, Hasted CH, Bolt RJ. Association of inflammatory bowel disease and large vascular lesions. Gastroenterology 1976; 71: 844–846.
124. Owyang C, Miller LJ, Lie JT, Fleming CR. Takayasu's arteritis in Crohn's disease. Gastroenterology 1979; 70: 825–828.
125. Teja K, Crum P, Friedman C. Giant cell arteritis and Crohn's disease. An unreported association. Gastroenterology 1980; 78: 796–802.
126. Fowler DL, Fortin D, Wood WC, Pinkerton JA, Koontz PG. Intestinal vascular malformations. Surgery 1979; 86: 377–385.
127. Pounder DJ, Rowland R, Pieterse AS, Freeman R, Hunter R. Angiodysplasia of the colon. J Clin Pathol 1982; 35: 824–829.
128. Sasaki K, Nakagawa H, Takahashi T, Sato E. Bleeding ectatic vascular lesion involving the sigmoid colon, endoscopically indistinguishable from angiodysplasia in an 8-year-old boy. Am J Gastroenterol 1991; 86: 105–108.
129. Moore JD, Thompson NW, Appelman HD, Foley D. Arteriovenous malformations of the gastrointestinal tract. Arch Surg 1976; 111: 381–389.
130. Baum S, Athanasoulis CA, Waltman AC, et al. Angiodysplasia of the right colon. AJR 1977; 129: 789–794.
131. Allison DJ, Hemingway AP. Angiodysplasia: Does old age begin at nineteen? Lancet 1981; 4: 979–980.
132. Richter JM, Hedberg SE, Athanasoulis CA, Shapiro RH. Angiodysplasia. Clinical presentation and colonoscopic diagnosis. Dig Dis Sci 1984; 29: 481–485.
133. Stamm B, Heer M, Buehler H, Ammann R. Mucosal biopsy of vascular ectasia (angiodysplasia) of the large bowel detected during routine colonoscopic examination. Histopathology 1985; 9: 639–646.
134. Boley SJ, Sammartano R, Adams A, DiBiase A, Kleinhaus S, Sprayregen S. On the nature and etiology of vascular ectasias of the colon. Degenerative lesions of aging. Gastroenterology 1977; 72: 650–660.
135. Mitsudo SM, Boley SJ, Brandt LJ, Montefusco CM, Sammartano RJ. Vascular extasias of the right colon in the elderly. A distinct pathologic entity. Hum Pathol 1979; 10: 585–600.
136. Margulis AR, Baum S, Galdabini JJ. Selective angiographic study in a patient with recurrent melena (case record). N Engl J Med 1974; 291: 569–575.
137. Thelmo WL, Vetrano JA, Wibowo A, et al. Angiodysplasia of colon revisited: pathologic demonstration without the use of intravascular injection technique. Hum Pathol 1992; 23: 37–40.
138. Weaver GA, Alpern HD, Davis JS, Ramsey WH, Reicheldorfer M. Gastrointestinal angiodysplasia associated with aortic valve disease: part of a spectrum of angiodysplasia of the gut. Gastroenterology 1979; 77: 1–11.

139. Meyer CI, Troncale FJ, Galloway S, Sheehan DG. Arteriovenous malformations of the bowel: An analysis of 22 cases and a review of the literature. Medicine 1981; 60: 36–48.
140. Apostolakis E, Doering C, Kantartzis M, Winter J, Schulte HD. Calcific aortic-valve stenosis and angiodysplasia of the colon: Heyde's syndrome — report of two cases. Thorac Cardiovasc Surg 1990; 38: 374–376.
141. Bank S, Aftalion B, Anfang C, Altman M, Wise L. Acquired angiodysplasia as a cause of gastric hemorrhage: A possible consequence of cholesterol embolization. Gastroenterology 1983; 78: 206–209.
142. Jakab F, Balazs M, Faller J, Kiss S. Gastrointestinal angiodysplasia. Acta Chir Hung 1991; 32: 57–68.
143. Naveau S, Bedossa P, Poynard T, Mory B, Chaput JC. Portal hypertensive colopathy. A new entity. Dig Dis Sci 1991; 36: 1774–1781.
144. Banerjee AK. Angiodysplasia associated with hypertrophic obstructive cardiomyopathy. Br J Clin Pract 1990; 44: 326–327.
145. Duray PH, Marcal JM, LiVolsi VA, et al. Gastrointestinal angiodysplasia. A possible component of von Willebrand's disease. Hum Pathol 1984; 15: 539–544.
146. Ottinger LW, Vickery AL. A 30 year history of recurrent gastrointestinal bleeding. N Engl J Med 1981; 305: 211–218.
147. Meyers MA, Volberg F, Katzen B, Alonso D, Abbott G. The angioarchitecture of colonic diverticula. Significance in bleeding diverticulosis. Radiology 1973; 108: 249–261.

CHAPTER 33

The anal canal

P. D. James

HAEMORRHOIDS

The terms haemorrhoids (from the Greek words *haima* = blood, and *rhois* = flowing) and piles (from the Latin *pila* = a ball) are used synonymously to describe a disease of the anus which has been known to man for over 4000 years.[1] Despite its antiquity, the precise pathogenesis of this very common condition remains speculative; the vascularity of the anal canal, with its communications between portal and systemic venous systems, the absence of valves in the portal vein and its tributaries, along with the upright posture of man led to the belief that piles were varicose anal veins caused by increased venous pressure. The hydrostatic pressure produced by straining at stool is still thought to be an essential factor in the production of piles.[2] However, the pathogenesis is probably multifactorial and other mechanisms provide more likely explanations.

The vascular anal submucosa with its plentiful arterio-venous anastomoses represents a type of erectile tissue[3] which forms localized vascular cushions within the anal canal.[4] These are part of the normal anatomy of the anus providing an 'adjustable washer' for anal continence and their position corresponds to the sites of symptomatic piles.[5] The two factors responsible for converting normal cushions into a pathological state are laxity of mucosal fixation to the bowel wall, which leads to prolapse, and a tight anal canal, which compresses the prolapsing cushions causing vascular engorgement.[6] The perianal connective tissue forms a network which anchors the anal mucosa and submucosa to the internal sphincter and conjoint longitudinal muscle.[7] Muscle fibres from the sphincter and longitudinal muscles may provide additional support, as well as helping to retract the mucosa.[4] This connective tissue degenerates with age,[7–9] leading to prolapse which becomes congested in a tight anal canal. Functional narrowing of the anal canal due to fibrosis of the internal sphincter is described[10] and fibrous anorectal bands may lead to a tight anal canal.[11,12] Manometric studies in patients with symptomatic haemorrhoids show a high resting anal pressure caused by increased tonic activity of the internal[13] or external[14] anal sphincters and leading to expansion of the anal cushions by impairing venous drainage. The high anal pressure may be reduced following treatment, suggesting that these changes are secondary to the presence of haemorrhoidal masses, rather than a primary abnormality in the anal sphincters.[15] The abnormally high anal pressure may be related to an increased vascular pressure within the vascular anal cushions.[16] Histometric studies of the external anal sphincter have shown increased type 1 fibre predominance as well as hypertrophy of both type 1 and type 2 fibres.[14] This and the neuronal hyperplasia seen in haemorrhoids[17] may be secondary effects caused by the presence of prolapsed piles within the anal canal.

Genetic factors are important in the development of piles and may be mediated through the variable speed and degree of deterioration of perianal connective tissue.[7] Epidemiological studies show that piles are uncommon in populations with a high fibre diet.[18] Low residue diets produce small hard stools which require excessive straining to evacuate, leading to raised venous pressure and vascular dilatation.[19] While some believe that poor defaecatory habits (straining, length of time defaecating) are associated with haemorrhoids,[20] others suggest that these habits are caused by the swollen anal cushions which may occlude the anal canal and obstruct defaecation.[21] Epidemiological studies cast doubt upon the hypothesis that haemorrhoids are caused by chronic constipation.[22,23]

Symptomatic piles may begin with or be aggravated by pregnancy due to the mechanical effect of the gravid uterus and the hormonal influence on vein walls.[24] However, despite this, piles are more common in men.[25] Pelvic tumours may present with piles but their relationship with carcinoma of the rectum is probably coincidental.[26] The prevalence of piles in patients with cirrhosis and portal hypertension is the same as in the general population but when they do coexist, bleeding may be a problem due to the associated coagulopathy.[27] The prevalence of anorectal varices rises with progression of portal hypertension but anorectal varices occur less often and bleed less frequently than oesophageal varices.[28] Anorectal varices with dilated veins extending into the buttocks[29] may occur and simulate cavernous haemangiomas (see Ch. 43).

The position of the piles correspond to the sites of the major vascular cushions in the left lateral, right posterior and right anterior positions around the anal canal.[4] Large piles may have an internal component, covered by rectal mucosa, and an external part, lying below the mucocutaneous junction, with overlying squamous mucosa. Haemorrhoidectomy specimens show dilated thick-walled submucosal veins with accompanying arteries and dilated capillaries in the mucosa (Fig. 33.1). Bleeding may occur from these mucosal vessels and the bright red colour is due to the abundant arteriovenous anastomoses; less often larger submucosal vessels may become ulcerated. Connective tissue fibres are present in the submucosa as well as muscle fibres.

The overlying mucosa may show changes of the solitary ulcer syndrome (Fig. 33.2A,B). Unsuspected carcinoma in surgical specimens taken at haemorrhoidectomy is a rare occurrence[30] and some cases of high grade intraepithelial neoplasia present in haemorrhoidal tissue have been shown to be a clinically non-aggressive lesion associated with human papilloma virus infection.[31] Other unexpected findings include anal duct carcinoma, carcinoid tumours, lymphomas, melanomas and condylomata. Primary Kaposi's sarcoma simulating haemorrhoids has also been reported.[32] Localized thrombosis within sacculations of the dilated veins in the anal submucosa may produce an acute painful swelling, incorrectly termed a perianal haematoma.[33] True perianal haematomas may occur after pelvic trauma and are a rare presentation of a leaking aortic aneurysm.[34] Redundancy of the perianal skin may occur in association with internal haemorrhoids, producing skin tags, whilst organization of thrombosed and ulcerated lesions results in fibrous polyps.

Successful treatment should produce either fixation of the prolapsing anal mucosa or relief of a tight anal sphincter and there are a number of options available.[35] The injection of sclerosing agents (5% phenol in arachis

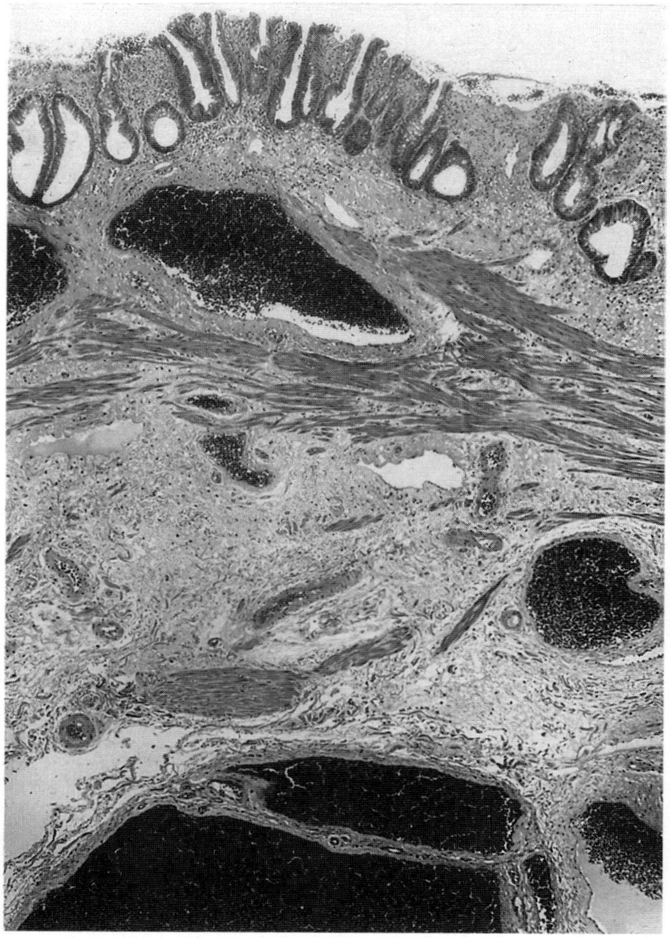

Fig. 33.1 Surgically resected haemorrhoid showing large, dilated blood vessels in the submucosa and in the overlying mucosa. (H&E, ×41)

oil) into the base of a pile produces submucosal fibrosis and fixation of the mucosa to the anal wall. More recent lines of therapy include rubber band ligation, cryosurgery and infrared coagulation. Anal outlet stenosis or spasm may be ameliorated by maximal anal dilation or internal sphincterotomy and large redundant piles can be removed by haemorrhoidectomy. Minor complications due to infection or secondary haemorrhage occasionally occur but more serious sequelae (anal stenosis, pelvic infection and septicaemia) are very rare.

OLEOGRANULOMAS

Oleogranulomas (oleomas, paraffinomas) represent a granulomatous tissue reaction to extraneous vegetable or mineral oils and are rare lesions in the anorectal region. They usually present as localized submucosal nodules proximal to the dentate line in the lower rectum[36] but circumferential lesions may occur and clinically they mimic tumours.[37,38] The reaction is usually a sequel to the injection of vegetable oils in sclerotherapy for piles[39] but may

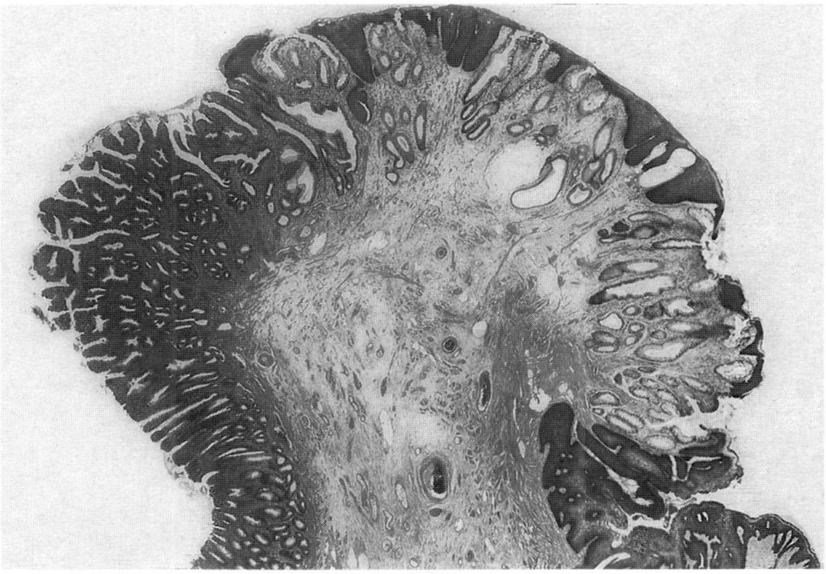

A

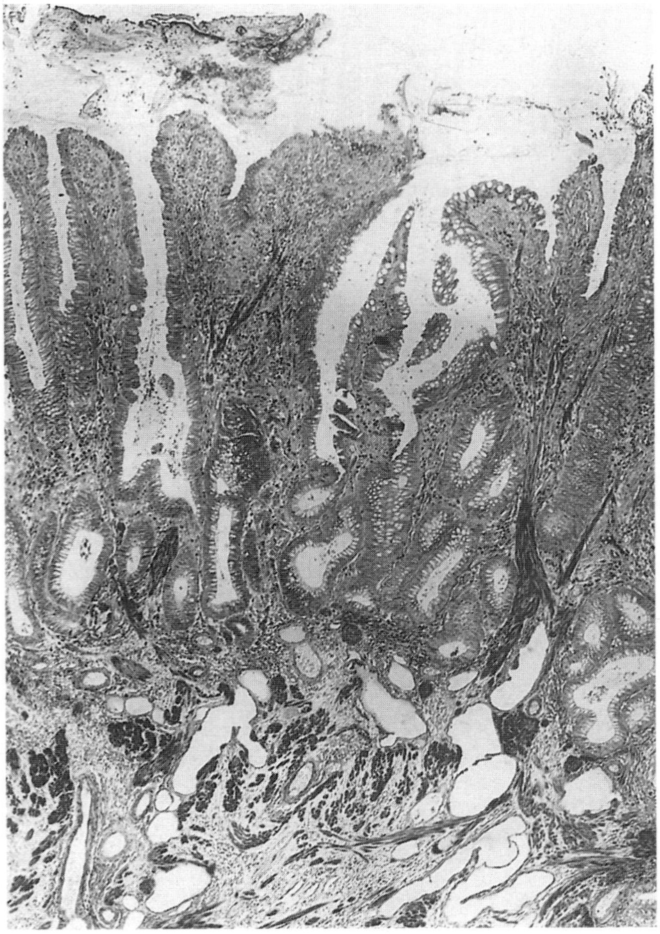

B

Fig. 33.2A Polypoid mucosa at the squamocolumnar junction of a surgically resected haemorrhoid. The junctional glandular epithelium is hyperplastic and villous. (H&E, ×12)

Fig. 33.2B Higher magnification of junctional epithelium from a similar case. The glandular epithelium is hyperplastic, villous and shows surface erosions. There is disorganization of the muscularis mucosae with extension into the lamina propria, changes typical of mucosal prolapse. (Phosphotungstic acid haematoxylin, ×41)

occur after the local application of paraffin-containing ointments,[40] installation of oil dressings following anorectal surgery,[41] accidental introduction of oil into the rectum,[42] chronic ingestion of liquid paraffin, or for no apparent reason.[43] There can be a long latent period before a lesion develops and the process may be extensive due to the tracking of oil.[44]

In routine haematoxylin and eosin stained sections, oleogranulomas contain rounded spaces, representing the site of the oil removed during histological preparation; the spaces are variable in size and although predominantly submucosal, may extend into the overlying mucosa. The spaces lack an endothelial lining and are surrounded by a fibrous stroma which contains lipid-laden macrophages and occasional giant cells. Macrophages and giant cells are also seen actually lining some of the spaces (Fig. 33.3). There is an acute inflammatory response in the early stages which is followed by increasing fibrosis.[44] Frozen sections of fresh tissue stained with oil red O demonstrate lipid within the spaces. The nature of the oil can be more precisely determined by chromatography and spectrometry following tissue extraction.[45]

The histological appearances may be confused with sclerosing liposarcoma, lymphangioma, pneumatosis in-

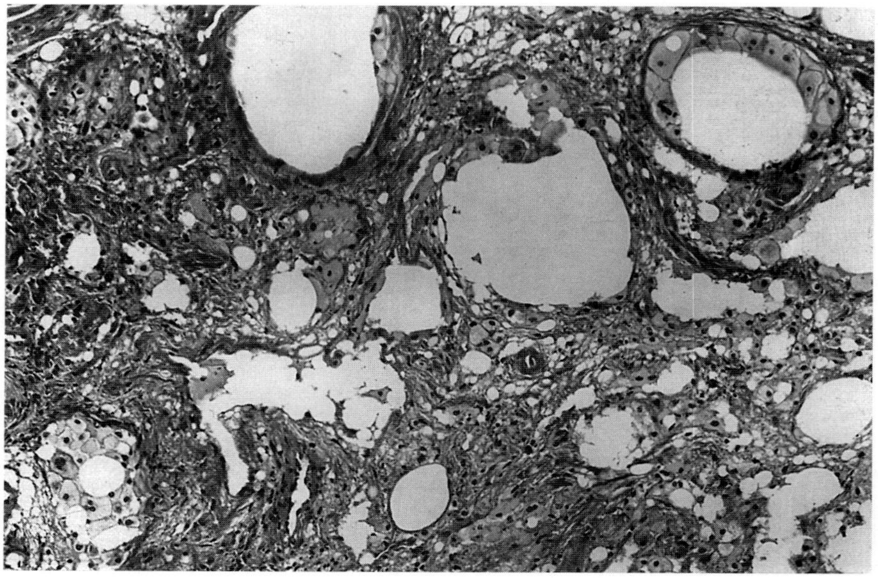

Fig. 33.3 An oleogranuloma showing a histiocytic reaction with these cells apparently lining some of the variably sized spaces. (H&E, ×96)

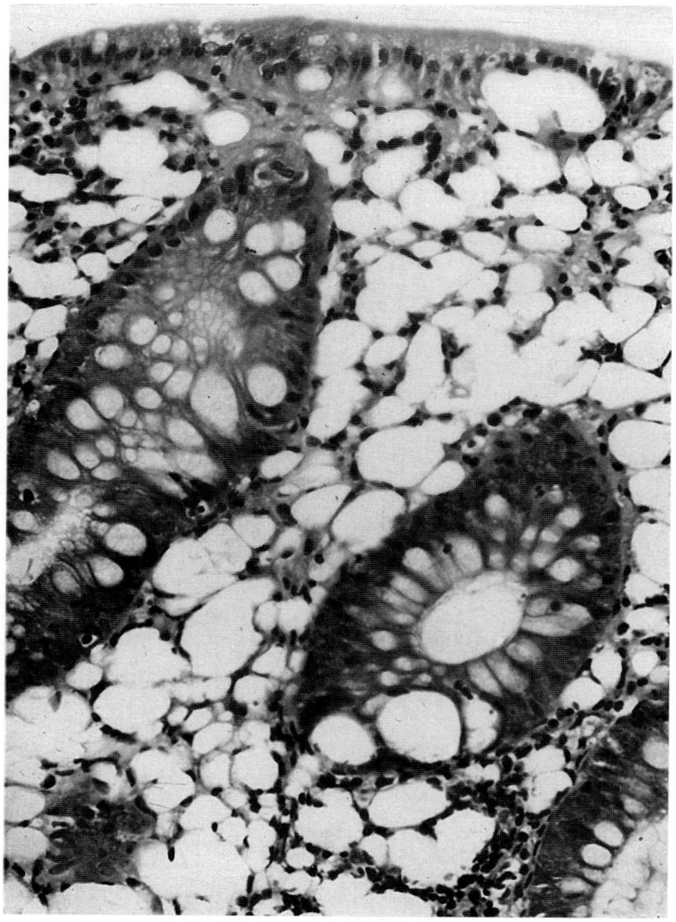

Fig. 33.4 'Incidental' finding of numerous spaces within the lamina propria in an otherwise normal rectal biopsy. This condition is best termed mucosal pseudolipomatosis but may be a mucosal manifestation of pneumatosis intestinalis. (H&E, ×260)

testinalis and mucosal lipomatosis. Liposarcoma cells have intracellular fat vacuoles and show atypia whilst lymphangiomas are distinguished by the presence of endothelial-lined spaces which lack fat on frozen section[46] In pneumatosis, the gas spaces are commonly large, submucosal and surrounded by a prominent giant cell reaction; lipid laden macrophages and interstitial fibrosis are not prominent features.[44] Mucosal lipomatosis is an uncommon condition in which the lamina propria contains vacuoles thought to be adipocytes (Fig. 33.4).[47] Histochemical and ultrastructural studies have failed to demonstrate fat in such lesions and it is suggested that they represent gas spaces within the lamina propria.[48] This is supported by a study of the mucosal changes in pneumatosis intestinalis, which describes small spaces within the lamina propria distinguishable from fat cells by their variable size and absence of nuclei.[49] It is thus suggested that lipomatosis or pseudolipomatosis is an early manifestation of pneumatosis intestinalis and may indicate the portal of entry of gas into the intestine in this condition, but this is controversial (see Ch. 46).

REFERENCES

1. Parks AG. De Haemorrhoids. Guy's Hosp Rep 1955; 104: 135–156.
2. Wannas HR. Pathogenesis and management of prolapsed haemorrhoids. J R Coll Surg Edinb 1984; 29: 31–37.
3. Thulesius O, Gjores JE. Arterio-venous anastomoses in the anal region with references to the pathogenesis and treatment of haemorrhoids. Acta Chir Scand 1973; 139: 476–479.
4. Thomson WHF. The nature of haemorrhoids. Br J Surg 1975; 62: 542–552.
5. Thomson H. Haemorrhoids and all that. Practitioner 1982; 226: 619–628.

6. Alexander-Williams J. The nature of piles. Br Med J 1982; 285: 1064–1065.
7. Haas PA, Fox TA, Haas GP. The pathogenesis of haemorrhoids. Dis Colon Rectum 1984; 27: 442–450.
8. Gass OC, Adams J. Haemorrhoids: aetiology and pathology. Am J Surg 1950; 79: 40–43.
9. Haas PA, Fox TA. Age-related changes and scar formation of perianal connective tissue. Dis Colon Rectum 1980; 23: 160–169.
10. Haqqani MT, Hancock BD. Internal sphincter and haemorrhoids: a pathological study. J Clin Pathol 1978; 31: 268–270.
11. Lord PH. A day-case procedure for the cure of third-degree haemorrhoids. Br J Surg 1969; 56: 747–749.
12. Shafik A. A new concept of the anatomy of the anal sphincter mechanism and the physiology of defaecation. Treatment of haemorrhoids: report of a technique. Am J Surg 1984; 148: 393–398.
13. Hancock BD. Internal sphincter and the nature of haemorrhoids. Gut 1977; 18: 651–655.
14. Teramoto T, Parks AG, Swash M. Hypertrophy of the external anal sphincter in haemorrhoids: a histometric study. Gut 1981; 22: 45–48.
15. El-Gandi MA. Abdel-Bakey N. Anorectal pressure in patients with symptomatic haemorrhoids. Dis Colon Rectum 1986; 29: 388–391.
16. Sun WM, Read NW, Shorthouse AJ. Hypertensive anal cushions as a cause of the high anal canal pressure in patients with haemorrhoids. Br J Surg 1990; 77: 458–462.
17. Fenger C, Schroder HD. Neuronal hyperplasia in the anal canal. Histopathology 1990; 16: 481–485.
18. Burkitt DP. Varicose veins, deep vein thrombosis, and haemorrhoids: epidemiology and suggested aetiology. Br Med J 1972; 2: 556–561.
19. Burkitt DP, Graham-Stewart CW. Haemorrhoids: postulated pathogenesis and proposed prevention. Postgrad Med J 1975; 51: 631–636.
20. Dehn TC, Kettlewell MG. Haemorrhoids and defaecating habits. Lancet 1989; 1: 54–55.
21. Read NW, Sun WM. Haemorrhoids, constipation and hypertensive anal cushions. Lancet 1989; 1: 610.
22. Gibbons CP, Bannister JJ, Read NW. Role of constipation and anal hypertonia in the pathogenesis of haemorrhoids. Br J Surg 1988; 75: 656–660.
23. Johanson JF, Sonnenberg A. The prevalence of haemorrhoids and chronic constipation. An epidemiologic study. Gastroenterology 1990; 98: 380–386.
24. Gallagher PG. Varicose veins of the vulva. Br J Sex Med 1986; 13: 12–14.
25. Haas PA, Haas GP, Schmaltz S, Fox TA. The prevalence of haemorrhoids. Dis Colon Rectum 1983; 26: 435–439.
26. Thomson JPS, Leicester RJ. Haemorrhoids A. Pathophysiology and clinical features. In: Henry MM, Swash M, eds. Coloproctology and the pelvic floor: pathophysiology and management. London: Butterworth, 1985.
27. Bernstein WC. What are haemorrhoids and what is their relationship to the portal venous system? Dis Colon Rectum 1983; 26: 829–834.
28. Hosking SW, Smart HL, Johnson AG, Triger DR. Anorectal varices, haemorrhoids, and portal hypertension. Lancet 1989; 1: 349–352.
29. McCormack TT, Bailey HR, Simms JM, Johnson AG. Rectal varices are not piles. Br J Surg 1984; 71: 163.
30. Cataldo PA, MacKeigan JM. The necessity of routine pathologic evaluation of hemorrhoidectomy specimens. Surg Gynecol Obstet 1992; 174: 302–304.
31. Foust RL, Dean PJ, Stoler MH, Moinuddin SM. Intraepithelial neoplasia of the anal canal in hemorrhoidal tissue: a study of 19 cases. Hum Pathol 1991; 22: 528–534.
32. Khan AA, Ravalli S, Vincent RA, Chabon AB. Primary Kaposi's sarcoma simulating hemorrhoids in a patient with acquired immune deficiency syndrome. Am J Gastroenterol 1989; 84: 1592–1593.
33. Thomson H. The real nature of 'perianal haematoma'. Lancet 1982; 2: 467–468.
34. Antrum RM. Perianal haematoma: an unusual feature of a leaking aortic aneurysm. Br J Surg 1984; 71: 649.
35. Hancock BD. ABC of colorectal diseases. Haemorrhoids. Br Med J 1992; 304: 1042–1044.
36. Mazier WP, Sun KH, Robertson WG. Oil induced granuloma (oleoma) of the rectum: report of four cases. Dis Colon Rectum 1978; 21: 292–294.
37. Symmers W StC. Simulation of cancer by oil granulomas of therapeutic origin. Br Med J 1955; 2: 1536–1539.
38. Webb AJ. Oleocysts presenting as rectal tumours. Br J Surg 1966; 53: 410–413.
39. Graham-Stewart CW. Injection treatment of haemorrhoids. Br J Med 1962; 1: 213–216.
40. Greaney MG, Jackson PR. Oleogranuloma of the rectum produced by Lasonil ointment. Br Med J 1977; 2: 997–998.
41. Susnow DA. Oleogranulomas of the rectum. Am J Surg 1952; 83: 496–499.
42. Nairn RC, Woodruff MFA. Paraffinoma of the rectum. Ann Surg 1955; 141: 536–540.
43. Bennett DHJ. Rectal paraffinoma. Proc R Soc Med 1969; 62: 818.
44. Morson BC, Dawson IMP. Gastrointestinal Pathology. 2nd ed. London: Blackwell, 1979.
45. Winslow PH, Parks S, Whetstone C. Lipogranulomatosis of the genitalia caused by topical application of 'baby oil'. J Urol 1980; 123: 127–128.
46. Oertel IC, Johnson FB. Sclerosing lipogranuloma of male genitalia. Arch Pathol Lab Med 1977; 101: 321–326.
47. Whitehead R. Mucosal Biopsy of the Gastrointestinal Tract. 2nd ed. Philadelphia: WB Saunders, 1985.
48. Snover DC, Sandstad J, Hutton S. Mucosal pseudolipomatosis of the colon. Am J Clin Pathol 1985; 84: 575–580.
49. Pieterse AS, Leong ASY, Rowland R. The mucosal changes and pathogenesis of pneumatosis cystoides intestinalis. Hum Pathol 1985; 16: 683–688.

CHAPTER 34

Gut-associated lymph nodes

J. D. Davies

INTRODUCTION

Thirty years ago, primary vascular abnormalities of lymph nodes were scarcely recognized and there was scanty information relating to regional variations, normal vascular anatomy and physiology. The intervening years, however, have seen a two to three-fold increase in the related literature.[1]

It is now well established that there is an organized system of lymphoid tissue in the wall of the gastrointestinal tract, usually called the gut-associated lymphoid tissue (GALT). Tumours arising from the GALT, and their physiological basis, are described in Chapter 37.

It is also recognized that the deeply situated lymph nodes, including those draining the gastrointestinal tract, possess their own distinctive characteristics, differing fundamentally from superficial lymph nodes in the axillae and the groin.[2,3] Human cervical, intrathoracic, lumbar, intramammary, mesenteric, popliteal, antecubital, paragastric, paracolonic and salivary gland associated lymph nodes are often of this deep type. Many of the lmph nodes in these sites do not contain an invaginated hilum; instead, they are solid ovoid structures and display a more complex arrangement of the B and T cell areas.[4] For these reasons, the term gut-associated lymph nodes, implying a distinctive anatomy and blood supply, is used here. However, there is also evidence that there is considerable interspecies variation in the blood supply of lymph nodes, even in equivalent sites.[5,6]

Although certain lymph node lesions in man have only recently been recognized as having a vascular aetiology, the lymph nodes draining the gastrointestinal tract show some of the vascular changes more commonly than nodes elsewhere. Not infrequently, both the gut-associated lymph nodes and the gastrointestinal tract itself are affected by vascular lesions of the same type. Such 'field' effects[7,8] may well result from ischaemia and other vasoproliferative stimuli.

VASCULAR DERANGEMENT OF GUT-ASSOCIATED LYMPH NODES

Normal vasculature of lymph nodes

All lymph nodes are richly endowed with both blood and lymphatic vessels. They are supplied by arteries and afferent lymphatic vessels, and are drained by veins and efferent lymphatics.[9] The rates of flow in these four types of vessels and their anatomy are variable in different parts of the body, and they are also affected by local factors such as vascular disease, inflammation and the increased flow of lymph after the ingestion of food. It also appears that these vessels are not independent, and that there are physiological communications between the arteries, veins and the lymphatic vessels and between veins and lymphatics in pathological circumstances.[10]

Arteries and veins

The classical description of the arterial supply of lymph nodes in man was made by Calvert,[11] who described a fan-like arrangememt of the nodal arteries. A single main artery in this model enters the lymph node at its hilum, and then centrifugally sends branches to supply the surrounding shell of lymphoid tissue. Arteriography of inguinal nodes supports this model.[12] A separate, relatively small artery may supply the capsule of the lymph node and also penetrates its outer part.[13] More recently it has been shown in man[13,14] and animals[15–17] that mesenteric and other deep lymph nodes, which often lack a hilum, receive branches from several arteries. In these nodes, the arteries penetrate the capsule, and supply the lymph node through the trabeculae in a centripetal manner (Fig. 34.1). In sheep[16] the arteries form anastomosing rings around the individual lymph nodes. The same is probably true in man. It is generally thought that the veins follow the same pathways.

Lymphatic vessels

The afferent lymphatic vessels supplying lymph nodes are multiple and pass through the capsule to enter the marginal sinus. Within the node there is a network of intermediate sinuses which ultimately emerge as the efferent lymphatic vessels in the hilum of the lymph node. Smooth muscle cells are present in the walls of the lymphatic vessels, to a certain extent in the nodal capsule,[18] and in the connective tissue of the hilum.[19]

Pathology

Basically, vascular abnormalities in any organ can produce two main effects. These are ischaemia and vasoproliferation. Morphologically, the effects of ischaemia and vasoproliferation are not necessarily distinct, because ischaemia itself, or vascular stasis, can lead to vasoproliferation and may merely reflect release of angioactive stimuli in a variety of pathological circumstances (see the sections below).

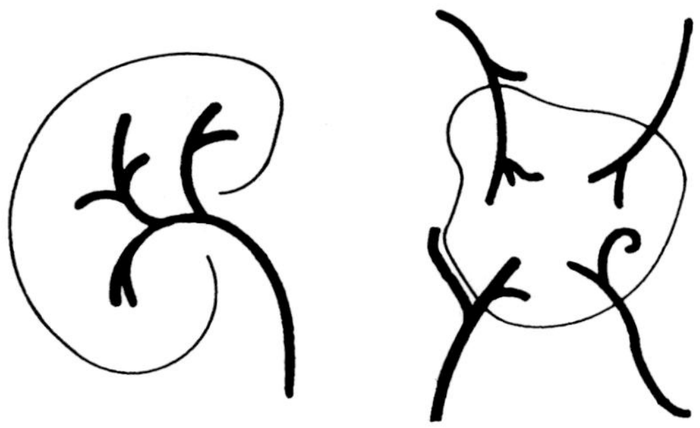

Fig. 34.1 Superficial (left) lymph nodes have a different blood supply to mesenteric (deep) nodes. A single artery branches in centrifugal manner to superficial nodes. Several arteries penetrate the capsule of mesenteric nodes and branch in centripetal fashion. (Reproduced with permission from the Journal of Anatomy)

Vascular proliferation in lymph nodes

Proliferation of vessels in the gut-associated lymph nodes is almost invariably benign, and either reactive or apparently autonomous. The precise stimuli underlying such vasoproliferation are still ill-characterized, but it is becoming evident that inflammation, ischaemia, or possibly local neoplasia, may be responsible.[7,8,20]

Inflammatory reactive vascular proliferation

Inflammation is always associated with vascular proliferation and vascular responses are part of reactive lymphadenopathies. The vascular changes may be generalized throughout the node (Fig. 34.2), as is common in the paracolonic lymph nodes of patients with active ulcerative colitis,[21] or restricted to selected areas of the nodes. The proliferation of postcapillary venules in the paracortex of gut-associated lymph nodes is commonplace. The cystic duct lymph nodes beside the gall bladder frequently display vascularization of their follicles, and it appears that the vascular response is related to earlier B cell activity.[22] In addition to these types of vascular change, the focal vascular proliferation in intensely reactive lymph nodes described by Diebold et al may rarely lead to an angiomatous appearance.[23] Although similar focal vascular proliferation may occur in lymph nodes in patients with viral hepatitis,[20] there is no indication that the nodes draining the gastrointestinal tract are particularly liable to this vascular reaction.

An inflammatory pseudotumour of lymph nodes[24,25] affects mesenteric, retroperitoneal or mandibular lymph nodes in about a quarter of reported cases. There is a marked vascular proliferation accompanied by a storiform spindle-cell element, and a mixed inflammatory infiltrate. Focal infarction and fibrinoid vascular necrosis are also features of some cases.[25] Obstruction of both large extranodal and involvement of small intranodal vessels may be seen. The precise aetiology and pathogenesis of this curious condition remains uncertain.

Reactive vascular proliferation associated with ischaemia of gut-associated lymph nodes is considered together with the other ischaemic lesions (see below).

Benign vascular tumours, hamartomas and related lesions

Although not appreciated until relatively recently, it is now clear that benign vascular tumours can occur in lymph nodes of both man and animals,[20,26] and that the lymph nodes associated with the gastrointestinal tract are affected. Haemangiomas had been described in the mesenteric nodes in some ageing laboratory rats[27] (Fig. 34.3) but early sceptical reservations of the existence of the reported benign angiomas, or angioma-like lesions in lymph nodes, were undoubtedly fair; some lesions were not even

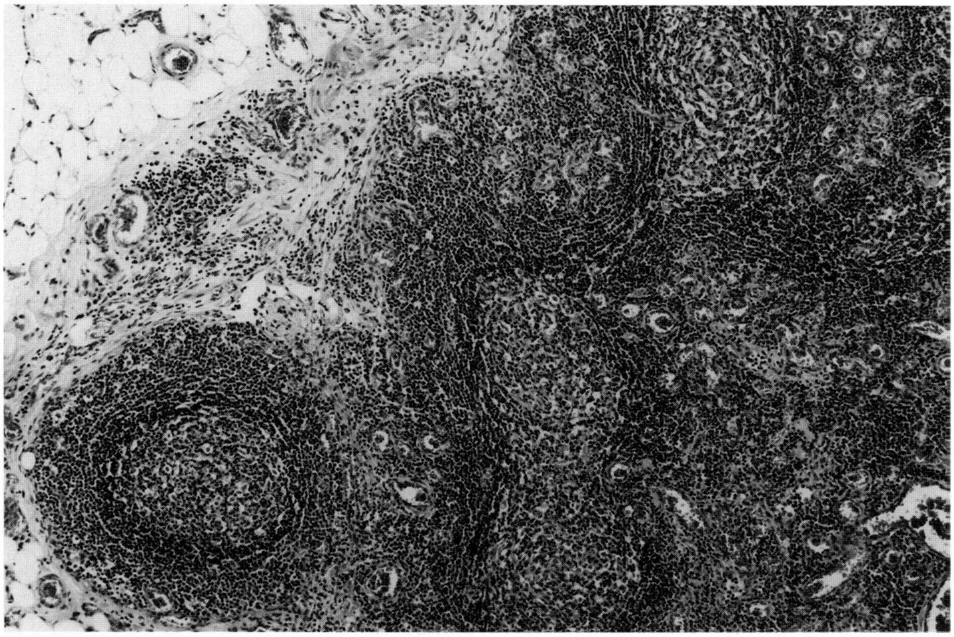

Fig. 34.2 Vascular dilatation (all the circular target-like spheres, centre and right) is present throughout the paracolonic lymph node from a patient with ulcerative colitis, and is accompanied by a periadenitic mononuclear infiltrate (top left).

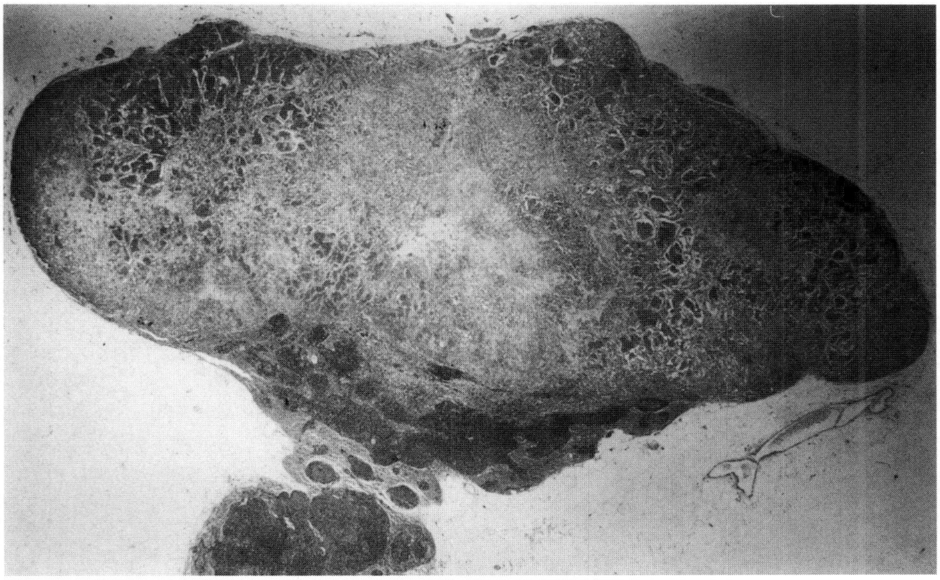

Fig. 34.3 Haemangioma of a mesenteric lymph node of an ageing laboratory rat. The haemangioma, giving a variegated and mottled appearance (top three quarters of field), although confined to the nodal capsule, bulges outwards and upwards in dramatic fashion. The original size of the affected node may be gauged from the normal node (bottom left) included in the figure.

nodal,[28,29] or if in lymph, some were thought to be extreme variants of cervical cystic hygromas.[30]

Despite these views, there are undoubtedly lymph nodal lesions which have the characteristics of genuine angiomas or epithelioid (histiocytic) angiomas. The first of these to be reported were in extra-abdominal sites[21,31–34] but subsequently a similar lesion in the lower abdomen was found by Satge et al.[35] Angioma-like lesions in gut-associated lymph nodes have also been recorded in the last few years. An expansile haemangioma in a paracaecal lymph node from a man with associated angiodysplasia of the ascending colon was described by Almagro et al.[36] One of two personal cases involving paraoesophageal lymph nodes occurred in a 61-year-old man with a vascular oesophageal polyp. Its histological appearance was similar to the rat mesenteric lesion (Fig. 34.3) and the case no. 3 illustrated by Chan et al.[26] Bleeding from the local oesophageal lesion itself was responsible for the exploratory surgery that led to the resection of the otherwise asymptomatic node. Such a case certainly suggests that the gut-associated lymph nodes may be affected by vasoproliferative stimuli similar to those affecting the segment of the gastrointestinal tract which they drain.

Primary spindle-cell epithelioid haemangioendotheliomas of lymph nodes[33,34] may simulate[22] lymph nodal leiomyomatosis,[37] a lesion which particularly occurs in intra-abdominal lymph nodes and can be associated with endometriosis.[38]

A separate, but distinctive benign spindle-cell tumour of lymph nodes, the palisaded myofibroblastoma,[39] alternatively called spindle-cell tumour with myoid differentiation,[40] or haemorrhagic spindle-cell tumour with 'amianthoid' fibres[41] was initially thought to be restricted to the inguinal lymph nodes of men. It has since[42,43] been detected in the submandibular and cervical regions and in the groin of both men (Padfield CJH & Davies JD, unpublished observations 1992) and women.[26] The demonstration of type I and III collagen and their electron microscopic characteristics distinguish such nodal lesions from those in other soft tissues with 'giant' collagen fibres.[44] For reasons of prior usage, therefore, the term 'with "amianthoid" fibres' for nodal deposits of this type may be inappropriate. Both Suster and Rosai[41] and Michal et al[43] consider that these tumours may well originate from vascular-associated smooth muscle in lymph nodes. These tumours need distinction from the even rarer intranodal neurilemmomas.[45]

The precise status of Castleman's angiofollicular hyperplasia[46] remains debatable nearly 40 years later. As indicated in the early reports, most of these lesions occur in the thorax. However, there are at least three types of lesions.[47] Two of these, which may be accompanied by systemic manifestations (the localized hyaline-vascular and plasma cell types), are especially liable to affect the mesenteric, mesocolic and retroperitoneal regions (in over a quarter and a half of cases, respectively, in Frizzera's survey).[47] Morphologically, these variants of Castleman's disease are characterized by distorted and vascularized follicles, interfollicular vascularity and plasma cell infiltration of the interfollicular regions. In contrast, the preservation or distension of the sinusoidal and follicular structure in the third type of Castleman's disease (the multicentric form, which uncommonly affects abdominal nodes) is not seen in the first two variants.[24,47,48] All these lesions may become clinically apparent as the result of a variety of systemic manifestations,[47] including those which may result from abdominal surgery.

A further rarer proliferative lesion involving both blood and lymphatic vessels which results in a consumptive coagulopathy with thrombocytopaenia in children is Kasabach's syndrome. Involvement of the coeliac perivascular axis, with upper intestinal obstruction due to a prominent concomitant perivascular lymphoid infiltration, has recently been reported.[49] Such lesions, because of the intimate lymphoid investment, can closely simulate a vascular proliferation in lymph nodes.

Smooth muscular proliferation

Proliferation of smooth muscle, apparently of reactive character, may occur in the immediate vicinity of the hilum of lymph nodes.[50] This muscular proliferation may involve the capsule or the perinodal vessels. Deposition of lipofuscin in smooth muscle cells, as is found in malabsorption states resulting in the 'brown bowel syndrome', may make hyperplastic smooth muscle in and around gut-associated lymph nodes more obvious.[51]

Malignant vascular tumours of gut-associated lymph nodes

Primary malignant vascular tumours of lymph nodes were very uncommon in Europe and North America until the advent of the Acquired Immune Deficiency Syndrome (AIDS).[52] Their differential diagnosis from Kaposi's sarcoma has been the subject of innumerable reports and reviews. Even so, vasoformative malignancies arising in gut-associated lymph nodes still remain extremely rare.

ISCHAEMIA AND CONGESTION

It is now accepted that human lymph nodes, like those in experimental animals,[53,54] are liable to ischaemic damage. Infarction of human nodes may follow massive surgical procedures,[55] be spontaneous and affect non-neoplastic nodes (so-called 'banal' infarction)[56] or take place in neoplastic lymph nodes.[57]

General morphology

Most 'banal' or non-neoplastic infarction is accompanied by demonstrable combined occlusion of veins, arteries or lymphatic channels.[54,56,57] Arterial thrombosis alone is less common.[20]

The differences in vascular supply (see above) is responsible for differences between lesions in superficial and deep lymph nodes (Fig. 34.4). In superficial nodes, subtotal infarction, with sparing of only a very superficial rind of the cortex, is the usual pattern.[56,58] In this subtotal type of infarction almost the entire core of the node and the

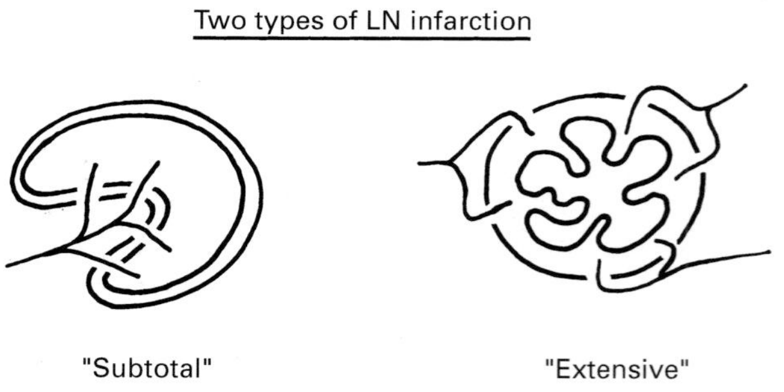

Fig. 34.4 Occlusion of the different blood supplies to superficial (left) and mesenteric (right) lymph nodes (LN) lead to subtotal (left) and extensive (right) infarction of the nodal substance. The surviving subcortical rind is supplied by ancillary arteries (left; see section on normal vasculature). The necrotic core and its radial extensions (right) are furthest from the centripetal vessels.

deeper parts of the cortex, cortical follicles included, are lost.[56] On the other hand, the necrosis of tissue in infarcts of deep lymph nodes, including those lying close to the gastrointestinal tract, tends to be extensive (Fig. 34.4). In this extensive type of necrosis there are surviving follicles or even complete trabeculae of lymphoid pulp (Fig. 34.5) well within the substance of the node.[59] Such changes are found both in human and bovine lymph nodes subject to vascular derangement as a result of intussusception, torsion or primary vascular infarction.

In both types of 'banal' lymph node infarction, the reticulin architecture of the original node is preserved. Within the necrosis it is either entirely normal, or merely shows distension of the intermediate[56] and marginal sinuses.[56,59] With the later development of granulation tissue around the infarct, the marginal sinus tends to become lost. This preservation of normal reticulin architecture is often of practical importance in attempting to distinguish 'banal' lymph node infarction from complete necrosis of lymphomas.[57]

Necrotic patterns associated with arterial and microvascular occlusion[20] differ from the subtotal and extensive infarcts outlined above. Arteries and small vessels are not infrequently implicated in gut-associated lymph node infarction. In the infarction following damage to these vessels the ischaemic loss tends to be focal or polar. In many instances there is a frank necrosis of the lymphoid cells, leaving only the coagulated ghost-like remnants of cells, as is characteristic of subtotal and extensive lymph node infarction. However, particularly after arterial occlusion, nodes tend to show merely a depletion of lymphoid cells, often accompanied by a local influx of polymorphonuclear leucocytes. It is possible to demonstrate quantitatively this decrease of small lymphocytes in gut-associated lymph nodes by densitometry.[60]

The commonest causes of lymph node infarction or ischaemia are undoubtedly volvulus, or intestinal infarction resulting from occlusion of large blood vessels. The vessels involved may be arteries or veins. Volvulus and vascular occlusion of the bowel are seemingly associated with ischaemia of draining mesenteric nodes to a disproportionate degree when compared with similar lesions in nodes related to other anatomical structures. It is true that the lesions are easily overlooked and the incidence of involvement has not hitherto been adequately recognized.

With the introduction of small bowel transplantation, it is almost predictable that ischaemia of mesenteric lymph nodes, similar to those documented by Ren et al[55] in hilar lymph nodes associated with heart-lung transplants, will result.

Infarction of gut-associated lymph nodes also occurs in malignant lymphomas and in nodes replaced by metastatic carcinoma. The demonstration of vascular thrombosis in such cases is much more difficult than in 'banal' infarcts.[57] It is likely that the necrosis in neoplastic lymph nodes results not from frank occlusion of the vessels by thrombus, but from impaired vascular flow.[57] Malignant lymphomas displaying infarction are varied in type, although tumours of centrocytic origin are especially liable.[57] Gastrointestinal (T cell) lymphomas associated with coeliac disease[61] also have a particular tendency to exhibit widespread necrosis.

The diagnosis of necrotic malignant lymphomas usually presents no problem since some viable tumour is found either in the infarcted node itself or in another node resected at the same time. On occasion, however, reticulin

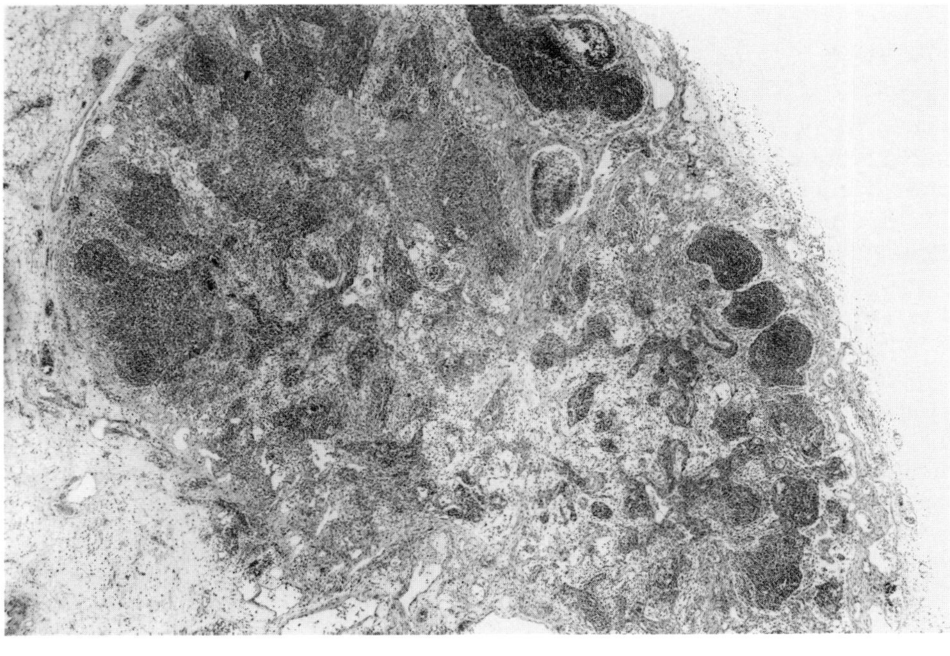

Fig. 34.5 Extensive necrosis of a mesenteric lymph node in a patient with volvulus. The surviving lymphoid trabeculae and discrete cortical nodules are dark staining. The serpiginous pale areas, extending outwards from the core (lower centre), are not sinus histiocytosis but infarcted necrotic tissue. For explanation see also Fig. 34.4.

stains can be helpful in at least suspecting the true nature of the underlying lesion.[20,62] More recently it has been shown that immunohistochemistry can be useful in detecting the residue of malignant lymphomas in infarcts of lymphomatous lymph nodes.[63]

Necrosis in metastatic carcinomas of lymph nodes is common and sometimes involves the whole node, masking its nature. The use of reticulin stains, in all but the most anaplastic carcinomas of the large bowel, can thus be helpful diagnostically.[64,65] There are lymph nodes which lack a well defined marginal sinus and these are not uncommon in the paracolic region (Davies & Jass JR, unpublished observations 1988–91). Massive necrosis of tumour in such nodes is not always easily recognizable as a nodal metastasis.

A special type of necrosis in gut-associated lymph nodes now uncommon in Europe and North America, but still seen in underdeveloped countries, occurs in bovine tuberculous lymphadenitis. The pathogenesis of necrosis in tuberculous caseation remains uncertain. Initially, at least, it appears to result from cell-mediated immunity.[66,67] In the early caseous necrosis there is commonly loss of the reticulin framework of the node,[65] an effect which is probably brought about by a diffusion of lymphokines and leucocytic proteases. There may, in fact, be an interaction between lymphokines and the endothelium of vessels.[68] A later stage in caseation of lymph nodes is the formation of widespread necrosis, in which much of the pre-existing reticulin is preserved. This second phase of caseation may be due to ischaemia. In the absence of demonstrable acid-fast bacilli, examination of the reticulin pattern of an extensively necrotic lymph node can thus be a diagnostic aid.[22,64,65] Indeed a reticulin preparation in such circumstances is an effective complement to a Ziehl-Neelsen stain.

Secondary vascular changes following nodal ischaemia

There is a brisk inflammatory reaction to lymph node infarction. This takes the form of an initial acute inflammation, with the subsequent formation of granulation tissue.[56] The vascular proliferation in the granulation tissue can be very marked, and in places completely replaces the former marginal sinuses.[57]

Another lesion, originally described as 'vascular transformation of lymph node sinuses',[69] is also probably usually of ischaemic origin. In the three cases originally described by Haferkamp et al[69] there was patchy loss of lymphoid tissue and its replacement by a network of small capillary blood vessels. Venous obstruction appeared to precede their development; indeed it has been suggested that the term 'stasis lymphadenopathy' is appropriate.[70] A related vascular lesion of mesenteric lymph nodes described[71,72] under the same name involves capillary proliferation in marginal and peripheral intermediate sinuses of the nodes,[72] but without the focal loss of lymphoid tissue seen in the series of Haferkamp et al.[69] A further case, with vasoproliferation in both the ischaemic ileal wall and a mesenteric lymph node, has been highlighted by DiBlasi and Ferbo.[73] The distinctive intrasinusoidal vascular proliferation described closely resembles that seen in some cases of frank lymph node infarction.[57]

More recently, in an impressively large series of 94 cases of vascular transformation of sinuses or 'nodal angiomatosis', almost half were intra-abdominal.[7] Even allowing for the previously fashionable biopsy of mesenteric lymph nodes in the course of staging for Hodgkin's disease, which may have weighted the retrospective series of Chan et al (1991),[7] this series clearly demonstrates the frequent involvement of gut-associated lymph nodes by vascular transformation of sinuses.

Another morphologically related lesion occurring in cats has been called, for the want at the time of a more satisfactory name, 'plexiform vascularization'.[74] This particular change found in biopsies of the superficial (axillary and inguinal) lymph nodes has since been demonstrated in intra-abdominal nodes in man.[7]

The precise relationship of the lymph node lesions resembling vascular transformation of sinuses is currently uncertain, despite attempts to unify them.[7,8,75,76] However, in this author's opinion nodal 'angiomatosis',[32] nodal 'haemangiomatoids',[21] and nodal 'angiomas'[31–36] are better currently regarded as separate entities[26] rather than being grouped [7] with lesions which seem to have an ischaemic or possible congestive pathogenesis. This is based upon extensive personal experience with both animal and human lesions. The confusing profusion of terminology in the field, however, may now have the paradoxical beneficial effect of restraining further speculation until further study leads to more precise definition.

Lymphangiectasia of the small bowel may also be associated with mesenteric lymph node abnormalities. Lymphoid atrophy and fibrosis in the nodes, possibly of ischaemic origin,[20] have been recorded by Belaiche et al.[77] Distension of the lymphatic vessels in small bowel lymphangiectasia occurring in combination with macroglobulinaemia leads to a striking dilatation of the sinuses in mesenteric lymph nodes.[77,78] In these two series of cases, further emphasis is given to the intimate relationship between abnormalities of vasculature in the gastrointestinal tract and in its associated lymph nodes. The exact nature of the cavitating necrosis of mesenteric lymph nodes found in association with coeliac disease[79] remains unknown. Evidently, no frank vascular occlusion has been demonstrable in such cases (Thompson H, personal communication 1990). The rare occurrence of skeletal muscular necrosis in coeliac disease, also in the absence of vascular abnormality (Moss TH, personal communication 1992), further compounds the problem of the pathogenesis of systemic idiopathic necrosis of tissue in coeliac disease.

REFERENCES

1. Cross SS, Macgillivray F. Has there been an information explosion in histopathology? J Clin Pathol 1992; 45: 724–725.
2. Denz FA. Age changes in lymph nodes. J Pathol Bacteriol 1947; 59: 576–591.
3. Luscieti P, Hubschmid T, Cottier H, Hess MW, Sobin LH. Human lymph node morphology as a function of age and site. J Clin Pathol 1980; 33: 454–461.
4. Belisle C, Sainte-Marie G. Topography of the deep cortex of the lymph nodes of various mammalian species. Anat Rec 1981; 201: 553–561.
5. Spalding HJ, Heath TJ. Blood vessels within lymph nodes: a comparison between pigs and sheep. Res Vet Sci 1989; 46: 43–48.
6. Belisle C, Sainte-Marie G. Blood vascular network of the rat lymph node: tridimensional studies by light and scanning electron microscopy. Am J Anat 1990; 189: 111–126.
7. Chan JKC, Warnke RA, Dorfman RF. Vascular transformation of sinuses in lymph nodes: a study of its morphological spectrum and distinction from Kaposi's sarcoma. Am J Surg Pathol 1991; 15: 732–743.
8. Papadimitriou JD, Drachenberg CB. Vascular transformation of lymph node sinuses. Am J Surg Pathol 1992; 16: 730–731.
9. Kowala MC, Schloefl GI. The popliteal lymph node of the mouse: internal architecture, vascular distribution and lymphatic supply. J Anat 1986; 148: 25–46.
10. Dictor M. Kaposi's sarcoma: origin and significance of lymphaticovenous connections. Virchows Arch (A) 1986; 409: 23–35.
11. Calvert WJ. On the blood vessels of the human lymphatic gland. Johns Hopk Hosp Bull 1901; 12: 177–178.
12. Bjork L, Leven H. Intra-arterial DSA and duplex-Doppler ultrasonography in detection of vascularized inguinal lymph node. Acta Radial 1990; 31: 106–107.
13. Semeraro D, Davies JD. The arterial supply of human inguinal and mesenteric lymph nodes. J Anat 1986; 144: 221–233.
14. Sasaki K. Arterial supply to the lumbar lymph nodes in man. J Anat 1990; 168: 229–233.
15. Heath T, Brandon R. Lymphatics and blood vessels of the popliteal node in sheep. Anat Rec 1983; 207: 461–472.
16. Heath T, Brandon RB, Fogarty SJP. The arterial supply to lymph nodes in sheep. J Anat 1985; 141: 41–62.
17. Hoshi N, Hashimoto Y, Kitagawa H, Kon Y, Kudo N. Blood supply and microvasculature in pigs. Jpn J Vet Res 1988; 36: 15–29.
18. Folse DS, Beathard GA, Granholm NA. Smooth muscle in lymph node capsule and trabeculae. Anat Rec 1975; 183: 517–521.
19. Pinkus GS, Warhol MJ, O'Connor EM, Etheridge CL, Fujiwara K. Immunohistochemical localization of smooth muscle myosin in human spleen, lymph node, and other lymphoid tissue. Am J Pathol 1986; 123: 440–453.
20. Davies JD. Vascular disturbances in lymph nodes. In: Lymph node biopsy interpretation. 2nd edn. Stansfeld AG, d'Ardenne AJ, eds. Edinburgh: Churchill Livingstone, 1992: 117–141.
21. Lott MF, Davies JD. Lymph node hypervascularity: haemangiomatoid lesions and pan-nodal vasodilatation. J Pathol 1983; 140: 209–219.
22. Davies JD. Gut-associated lymph nodes. In: Gastrointestinal and oesophageal pathology. 1st ed. Whitehead R. ed. Edinburgh: Churchill Livingstone, 1989: 611–616.
23. Diebold J, Tulliez M, Bernadou A, Audouin J, Tricot G, Reynes M, Bilski-Pasquier G. Angiofollicular and plasmacytic lymphadenopathy: a pseudotumourous syndrome with dysimmunity. J Clin Pathol 1980; 33: 1068–1076.
24. Perrone T, De Wolf-Peeters C, Frizzera G. Inflammatory pseudotumor of lymph nodes: a distinctive pattern of nodal reaction. Am J Surg Pathol 1988; 12: 351–361.
25. Davis RE, Warnke RA, Dorfman RF. Inflammatory pseudotumor of lymph nodes: additional observations and evidence for an inflammatory etiology. Am J Surg Pathol 1991; 15: 744–756.
26. Chan JKC, Frizzera G, Fletcher CDM, Rosai J. Primary vascular tumors of lymph nodes other than Kaposi's sarcoma: analysis of 39 cases and delineation of two new entities. Am J Surg Pathol 1992; 16: 335–350.
27. Graves P, Faccini JM. Rat histopathology: a glossary for use in toxicology and carcinogenicity studies. Amsterdam: Elsevier, 1984: p 41.
28. Enzinger FM. Angiomatoid malignant fibrous histiocytoma. Cancer 1979; 44: 2147–2157.
29. Wright DH, Padley NR, Judd MA. Angiolymphoid hyperplasia with eosinophilia simulating lymphadenopathy. Histopathology 1981; 5: 127–140.
30. Davies JD. Vascular disturbances. In: Stansfeld AG, ed. Lymph node biopsy interpretation. Edinburgh: Churchill Livingstone. 1985; pp 142–158.
31. Gupta IM. Haemangioma in a lymph node. Ind J Pathol Bacteriol 1964; 7: 108–111.
32. Fayemi AO, Toker C. Nodal angiomatosis. Arch Pathol 1975; 99: 170–172.
33. Silva EG, Phillips MJ, Langer B, Ordonez NG. Spindle and histiocytoid (epithelioid) hemangioendothelioma: primary in lymph node. Am J Clin Pathol 1986; 85: 731–735.
34. Ellis GL, Kratochvil FJ. Epithelioid hemangioendothelioma of the head and neck: a clinicopathologic report of twelve cases. Oral Surg Oral Med Oral Pathol 1986; 61: 61–68.
35. Satge D, Pusel J, Albert A, Trabold G. Hemangiomatoide ganglionnaire iliaque. Arch Anat Cytol Pathol 1985; 33: 277–280.
36. Almagro UA, Choi H, Rouse TM. Haemangioma in a lymph node. Arch Pathol Lab Med 1985; 109: 576–578.
37. Horie A, Ishii N, Matsumoto M, Hashizume Y, Kawakami M, Sato Y. Leiomyomatosis in the pelvic lymph node and peritoneum. Acta Pathol Jpn 1984; 34: 813–819.
38. Channer JL, Davies JD, Scarritt W. Leiomyomatosis and endometrial glands in a pelvic lymph node: a possible manifestation of of endometriosis. Histopathology 1987; 11: 770–771.
39. Weiss SW, Gnepp DR, Bratthauer GL. Palisaded myofibroblastoma: a benign mesenchymal tumor of lymph node. Am J Surg Pathol 1989; 13: 341–346.
40. Lee JY-Y, Abell E, Shevechick GJ. Solitary spindle cell tumor with myoid differentiation of the lymph nodes. Arch Pathol Lab Med 1989; 113: 547–550.
41. Shuster S, Rosai J. Intranodal hemorrhagic spindle-cell tumor with 'amianthoid' fibers. Am J Surg Pathol 1989; 13: 347–357.
42. Fletcher CDM, Stirling RW. Intranodal myofibroblastoma presenting in the submandibular region: evidence of a broader clinical and histological spectrum. Histopathology 1990; 16: 287–294.
43. Michal M, Chlumska A, Povysilova V. Intranodal 'amianthoid' myofibroblastoma: report of six cases — immunohistological and electron microscopical study. Pathol Res Pract 1992; 188: 199–204.
44. Skalova A, Michal M, Chlumska A, Leivo I. Collagen composition and ultrastructure of the so-called amianthoid fibres in palisaded myofibroblastoma: ultrastructural and immunohistochemical study. J Pathol 1992; 167: 335–340.
45. Enzinger FM, Weiss SW. Soft-tissue tumors. 2nd edn. St Louis: Mosby CV, 1988: 734.
46. Castleman B, Iverson L, Menendez VP. Localized mediastinal lymph node hyperplasia resembling thymoma. Cancer 1956; 9: 822–830.
47. Frizzera G. Castleman's disease and related disorders. Seminars Diagnost Pathol 1988; 5: 346–364.
48. Paradinas FJ. Primary and secondary immune disorders. In: Biopsy interpretation of lymph nodes. 2nd edn. Stansfeld AG, d'Ardenne AJ, eds. Edinburgh: Churchill Livingstone, 1992; 143–186.
49. Davenport M, Salisbury J, Karani J, Tan KC. Retroperitoneal haemangiolymphangioma presenting with projectile vomiting and thrombocytopaenia at 2 weeks of age. J Roy Soc Med 1990; 83: 591–502.
50. Channer JL, Davies JD. Smooth muscle proliferation in superficial lymph nodes. Virchows Arch (A) 1985; 406: 261–270.
51. Al-Okati D, Ibrahim NBN, Davies JD. Brown bowel syndrome associated with chronic oesophagitis and oesophageal stricture. J Roy Soc Med 1992; 85: 511.
52. Millard PR. AIDS: histopathological aspects. J Pathol 1984; 143: 223–239.

53. Osogoe B, Courtice FC. The effects of occlusion of the blood supply to the popliteal lymph node of the rabbit on the cell and protein content of the lymph and on the histology of the node. Austr J Exp Biol Med Sci 1968; 46: 515–524.
54. Steinmann G, Foldi E, Foldi M, Racz P, Lennert K. Morphologic findings in lymph nodes after occlusion of their efferent lymphatic vessels and veins. Lab Invest 1982; 47: 43–50.
55. Ren H, Hruban RH, Baumgartner WA, Reitz BA, Baker RR, Hutchins GM. Hemorrhagic infarction of hilar lymph nodes associated with combined heart-lung transplantation. J Thoracic Cardiovasc Surg 1990; 99: 861–867.
56. Davies JD, Stansfeld AG. Spontaneous infarction of superficial lymph nodes. J Clin Pathol 1972; 25: 689–696.
57. Maurer R, Schmid U, Davies JD, Mahy NJ, Stansfeld AG, Lukes RJ. Lymph node infarction and malignant lymphoma: a multicentre study of European, English and American cases. Histopathology 1986; 10: 571–588.
58. Schwartz A, Horacek J, Sterba K. Infarkt minzi uzliny nezname etiologie. Cas lek Cez 1976; 115: 524–526.
59. Mahy NJ, Davies JD. Ischaemic changes in human mesenteric lymph nodes. J Pathol 1984; 144: 257–267.
60. Davies JD, Jeal CC, Holton AR. Linear track scanning of tissue sections: an interdisciplinary approach to microscopy. J Pathol 1987; 40: 694–696.
61. Isaacson PG, O'Connor NTJ, Spencer J et al. Malignant histiocytosis of the intestine: a T-cell lymphoma. Lancet 1985; 2: 688–691.
62. Mackenzie DH. Reticulin patterns in the diagnosis of carcinomas and sarcomas. Br J Cancer 1958; 12: 14–19.
63. Norton AJ, Ramsay AD, Isaacson PG. Antigen preservation in infarcted lymphoid tissue: a novel approach to the infarcted lymph node using monoclonal antibodies effective in routinely processed tissues. Am J Surg Pathol 1988; 12: 759–767.
64. Channer JL, Davies JD. Necrotic lymph nodes and their connective-tissue framework. Bristol Med-Chir J 1986; 101: 42–43.
65. Channer JL, Tettey Y, Davies JD. The preservation of connective-tissue fibres in necrotic lymph node lesions. J Pathol 1986; 148: 121A–122A.
66. Poole JCF, Florey HW. Chronic inflammation and tuberculosis. In: Florey HW, ed. General Pathology, 4th ed. London: Lloyd-Luke, 1970; pp 1195–1200.
67. Dustin P, Dourov N. Lecons d'anatomie pathologique generale, 3rd ed. Paris: Maloine, 1981; p 222.
68. Flanagan AM, Chambers TJ . In: Chronic inflammation. McGee JO'D, Isaacson PG, Wright NA, eds. Oxford Textbook of Pathology. 1992; 389–406.
69. Haferkamp O, Rosenau W, Lennert K. Vascular transformation of lymph node sinuses due to venous obstruction. Arch Pathol 1971; 92: 81–83.
70. Michal M, Koza V. Vascular transformation of lymph node sinuses — a diagnostic pitfall: histopathologic and immunohistochemical study. Pathol Res Pract 1989; 185: 441–444.
71. Borisch B, Racz P. Die Vaskulare Sinustransformation des Lymphknotens: ein Indiz fur eine Tumorabsiedlung im Abflussgebiet. Verhand dtsch Ges Path 1984; 68: 77–80.
72. Scherrer C, Maurer R. La transformation vasculaire sinusienne du ganglion lymphatique: analyse morphologique et immunohistochemique de six cas. Ann Pathol (Paris) 1985; 5: 231–238.
73. DiBlasi A, Ferbo U. Stenosi ischemica dell'ileo con iperplasia reattiva angioendotheliomatosa parietale e linfonodale. Pathologica 1989; 81: 63–69.
74. Lucke VM, Davies JD, Wood C, Whitbread TJ. Plexiform vascularisation of lymph nodes: an unusual but distinctive lymphadenopathy in cats. J Comp Pathol 1987; 97: 109–119.
75. Bedrosian SA, Goldman RL. Nodal angiomatosis: relationship to vascular transformation of lymph nodes. Arch Pathol Lab Med 1984; 108: 864–865.
76. Ostrowski ML, Siddiqui T, Barnes RE, Howton MJ. Vascular transformation of lymph node sinuses: a process displaying a spectrum of histologic features. Arch Pathol Lab Med 1990; 114: 656–660.
77. Belaiche J, Vesin P, Chaumette MT, Julien M, Catten D. Lymphangiectasies intestinales et fibrose des ganglions mesenteriques. Gastroenterol Clin Biol 1980; 4: 52–58.
78. Harris M, Burton IE, Scarffe JH. Macroglobulinaemia and intestinal lymphangiectasia. J Clin Pathol 1983; 36: 30–36.
79. Holmes GKT. Mesenteric lymph node cavitation in coeliac disease. Gut 1986; 27: 728–733.

SECTION

6

Tumours

CHAPTER 35

Gastrointestinal stromal (smooth muscle) tumours

R. L. Kempson M. R. Hendrickson

Non-epithelial and non-lymphoid mesenchymal tumours of the gastrointestinal (GI) tract are relatively uncommon, but when they occur, they frequently cause diagnostic problems. One problem relates to the direction of differentiation of these tumours. Historically, most of the mesenchymal neoplasms arising in the GI tract had been referred to as 'leiomyomas' if benign and 'leiomyosarcomas' if malignant, because Stout and his coworkers, who performed the early studies of GI mesenchymal tumours, believed, for largely unstated reasons, that most such neoplasms were of smooth muscle 'origin' even though smooth muscle differentiation was not always obvious.[1–4] Indeed, many of the spindle cell neoplasms they reported were largely undifferentiated and a sizable number, the 'leiomyoblastomas' had a distinctly epithelial appearance.[3] Subsequent study confirmed that the vast majority of GI mesenchymal tumours are undifferentiated when examined with conventional light microscopic techniques although there is a small subset of tumours that are composed of smooth muscle cells. Moreover, ultrastructural examination of the constituent cells of GI mesenchymal tumours that are undifferentiated using conventional light microscopy failed to reveal consistent evidence of smooth muscle or other lines of differentiation. Investigators using immunohistochemical reagents have reported, with some exceptions, that only a small number of GI mesenchymal tumours contain cells that express desmin, while another subset contain cells that express S-100 protein, usually focally. These failures to establish an unambiguous directional differentiation have led to the suggestion that these tumours be classified as GI stromal tumours (GIST) rather than smooth muscle tumours. More recently, investigators using panels of antibodies have found that over three quarters of GI stromal tumours express one or another antigen found in smooth muscle cells, although the specificity for muscle of two of the antibodies is low and sometimes staining with these reagents has been reported to be weak and focal. This problem is further discussed below. In addition to tumours that are undifferentiated by light microscopy (stromal tumours) and those that display light microscopic evidence of smooth muscle differentiation, there is a small subset of other mesenchymal tumours, some of which demonstrate neural differentiation by light microscopy, electron microscopy or immunohistochemistry. The subject of this chapter is the tumours that fall into the stromal or smooth muscle categories; distinction of these from other mesenchymal tumours is addressed in the Assessment of cell type section.

A second, and more serious, diagnostic problem concerning GI stromal or smooth muscle tumours is the well known difficulty of predicting clinical behaviour because morphologically, benign stromal tumours of the GI tract can recur and metastasize. Much of this chapter is devoted to an analysis of the features that have been proposed as predictors of aggressive behaviour for this group of neoplasms.

Stromal and smooth muscle neoplasms of the GI tract are relatively uncommon. Malignant stromal neoplasms do account for about 20% of all small bowel malignancies, but less than 0.1% of all malignant neoplasms of the large intestine.[5] Between 1–3% of gastric malignancies are of smooth muscle or stromal type, while malignant oesophageal stromal neoplasms are vanishingly rare.[6] Benign stromal neoplasms are unusual in all parts of the gastrointestinal tract except the oesophagus but their precise incidence, as we shall see, depends upon how their malignant counterparts are defined morphologically. Because the behaviour of stromal neoplasms in different parts of the GI tract varies considerably, despite having a similar appearance, diagnostic criteria for one site may not be applicable in another.[4,7]

GI stromal tumours occur at all ages although they are distinctly unusual in children and teenagers. The peak incidence is from the 5th to the 7th decade. GI stromal tumours with smooth muscle differentiation have been reported in the gastrointestinal tract in children with AIDS.[8]

The evidence for and against smooth muscle differentiation[2–4,6,7,9–22]

Classification of neoplasms is based on cellular differentiation as determined by light microscopic or ultrastructural features or from the immunohistochemical profile of the tumour cells. Most mesenchymal tumours of the GI tract are composed of spindle cells, and because these spindle cell tumours arose within the muscularis propria, it was assumed by early investigators that the cells were differentiated along smooth muscle lines, even though many tumours were composed of cells with scant cytoplasm, unlike normal smooth muscle cells.[2,3] At the time of these investigations, the only positive identification of cells as of smooth muscle type was a light microscopic appearance similar or identical to normal smooth muscle. Another difficulty was noted early on in that many of the tumours arising in the muscularis propria of the GI tract were composed of cells with a distinct epithelioid appearance. In spite of this epithelioid appearance, Stout considered these to be demonstrating smooth muscle differentiation, possibly as embryonic smooth muscle cells. Consequently, he labelled GI mesenchymal tumours composed of such as 'leiomyoblastoma'.[3]

With the advent of electron microscopy, many investigators undertook ultrastructural examination of GI mesenchymal tumours and most reported that, by and large, the tumour cells demonstrated few smooth muscle characteristics.[9,13,16,20,23,24] The normal smooth muscle cell has a constellation of ultrastructural features — large numbers of cytoplasmic filaments, dense contractile bodies, clustering of organelles around the nucleus, cytoplasmic membrane plaques, pinocytotic vesicles and basal lamina. In only a few tumours did the constituent cells demonstrate all of these features and in most they were absent or only a few were represented. As a result, it was generally considered that most of the GI mesenchymal neoplasms that were undifferentiated at the light microscopic level were also undifferentiated at the ultrastructural level, with only a minority showing convincing smooth muscle differentiation and an even smaller minority demonstrating neural differentiation.

Immunohistochemical studies have not solved the problem because desmin is expressed by only a small number of GI stromal tumours (usually reported range 0–20%).[11] Actin is expressed by the tumour cells in approximately 70% of GI stromal tumours. To further confuse the issue, the cells in GI mesenchymal tumours have been reported to express S-100 protein in 0–80% of cases (usually reported range 0–15%).[11] However, the S-100 positive cells in most GI stromal tumours are scattered and focal, suggesting the possibility of trapping of non-neoplastic neural cells.

One consequence of these immunohistochemical and ultrastructural results was a call to change the name of these mesenchymal gastrointestinal neoplasms from 'smooth muscle tumours' to 'gastrointestinal stromal tumours'.[4,6] The latter label was meant to encompass all mesenchymal neoplasms arising in the muscularis propria of the GI tract, including smooth muscle tumours, that did not demonstrate specific and recognizable differentiation along a non-smooth muscle line, e.g. neural. This terminology has gained widespread acceptance and is the most commonly employed today.

More recently, immunohistochemical studies utilizing a panel approach have reported a high incidence of expression of one or another muscle antigen by GI stromal tumours. Franquemont and Frierson reported that while only nine of 45 GI stromal tumours from all parts of the GI tract were positive for desmin, 36 of 46 stained with muscle specific actin (MSA), and the cells in 34 of 46 tumours were reactive with alpha smooth muscle actin (SMA).[11] 85% of the tumours stained with at least one of these three antibodies and the staining pattern was unrelated to the site of the tumour within the GI tract. Desmin staining was focal in half of the positive cases, MSA staining was focal in eight of the 36 positive cases while SMA was focal in 2/34. The intensity of staining 'varied'. This raises the spectre that some of the positive cells may be entrapped normal muscle cells. In this study, six of 46 tumors were positive for S-100 protein and in five of these, the staining was only focal. Hagan and associates reported at least one of these three antibodies (desmin, muscle specific actin or alpha smooth muscle) was positive in 88% of gastric epithelioid tumours.[12] However, muscle specific actin (in spite of its name) and smooth muscle actin are not specific for smooth muscle cells because they also decorate myofibroblasts and fibroblasts. The more specific antibody, desmin, is expressed by only a small percentage of GI stromal tumours. Most recently it has been found that the CD34 monoclonal antibody reacts with the cells of 80–90% of GI stromal tumours.[12a,12b] In our opinion, these more recent immunohistochemical results do not provide the clarion call that would warrant return to the older smooth muscle nomenclature; we continue to use the GI stromal tumour terminology. When the tumour cells have smooth muscle features by light microscopy we use the term GI stromal tumour, smooth muscle type. The malignant potential of such differentiated tumours is evaluated in the same manner as for undifferentiated GI stromal tumours.

Benign vs. malignant: morphological features to be assessed in gastrointestinal stromal neoplasms[4–7,25–34]

The histopathological evaluation of a gastrointestinal neoplasm thought on initial examination to be a stromal neoplasm has two main goals:

1) to establish that the neoplasm is appropriately placed in this group by ruling out other diagnostic possibilities, and
2) to determine the neoplasm's likelihood of behaving in a clinically malignant fashion. The results of the second determination are captured by the labels benign GI stromal tumour, GI stromal tumour of uncertain malignant potential ('intermediate,' 'borderline') and high/low-grade malignant GI stromal tumour. To achieve these two goals we think the following should be done in addition to examining the specimen:

1) *Determine what segment of the GI tract gave rise to the neoplasm*. The criteria used to classify gastrointestinal stromal tumours as benign, uncertain malignant potential and malignant vary depending on the location of the tumour within the GI tract.[4,7] An accurate assessment of these neoplasms cannot be made without this information.

2) *Be aware of the clinical features*. Certain clinical features are of importance in classifying gastrointestinal stromal tumours. The pathologist should be acquainted with the findings at the time of surgery; in particular, should know about the presence or absence of metastases and spread of the tumour to contiguous organs (of course, both are malignant features). Also of importance is a history of a previous or coexistent neoplasm. This is important because the putative gastrointestinal stromal tumour may be a metastasis, or, extremely rarely, part of the multicentric neoplastic syndrome known as Carney's triad (extra-adrenal paragangliomas, stromal neoplasms of the stomach and pulmonary chondromas).[35–40] This syndrome occurs predominantly in young women with an average age of around 15 years. The gastric tumours are not all characteristic stromal tumors, as some have a distinctly neural appearance. Whatever their appearance, the gastric tumours tend to be multiple. The paragangliomas are usually found near the adrenals or the abdominal aorta, although a few are found around the great vessels in the mediastinum; they also may be multiple. The syndrome is diagnosed whenever at least two of the three tumours in the triad are present. Because isolated paragangliomas and gastric stromal tumours are rare in young people, anyone under 40 who is found to have a paraganglioma or a gastric stromal tumour should be evaluated to determine if they have other tumours. GI stromal tumours have been reported in HIV-infected children and in patients with neurofibromatosis.[8,41]

Gross appearance[4–7,42]

It is important to thoroughly section gastrointestinal stromal tumours to ensure that all areas have been sampled. This is particularly important if the neoplasm appears inhomogeneous. We recommend obtaining a minimum of one section per centimetre of tumour diameter. Important gross features which should be evaluated are dealt with below.

Size

Several different series have shown that larger tumours are more frequently aggressive.[6] Stromal tumours greater than 10 cm should be viewed with great caution, regardless of how bland and mitotically inactive the cells. Appelman has reported that 75% of gastric stromal tumours >10 cm metastasized and the figure is at least as high for intestinal tumours.[6] GI stromal tumours >5 cm but <10 cm also metastasize frequently enough to be labelled either as of 'uncertain malignant potential' or malignant, depending on the histological features and location. Histologically bland stromal tumours in the intestine can metastasize when they are >3 cm so we utilize this size criterion rather than 5 cm outside the stomach and oesophagus. Some investigators have found that patients whose sarcomas measure less than 10 cm have a longer mean survival than patients whose sarcomas are greater than 10 cm.

Invasion

Invasion of contiguous organs is, of course, an absolute indication that a stromal tumour is malignant. Infiltration of the muscularis alone, however, can be found in both benign and malignant stromal tumours. Infiltration of stromal neoplastic cells between residual mucosal glands, spreading them apart, is a feature reported to be limited to malignant stromal tumours.[4]

Ulceration and necrosis

Ulceration of the surface of a stromal tumor with subsequent necrosis of the tumor itself is found in both clinically benign and clinically malignant stromal neoplasms. In fact, surface ulceration with cavitary necrosis is relatively common in these tumours and is a helpful radiographic finding. However, in our experience tumour cell necrosis away from areas of ulceration is rather frequent in stromal sarcomas and unusual in benign stromal tumors.[7] Therefore, sections should be taken from areas grossly suggestive of necrosis, particularly if they are away from areas of surface ulceration.

Microscopic appearance[4–7,42]

H&E sections

Assessment of cell type and differential diagnosis. The focus here should be on excluding other types of diseases which figure in the differential diagnosis of gastrointestinal stromal tumours: inflammatory or reactive lesions, lymphoma, carcinoma, endocrine neoplasms, neural neoplasms, glomus tumours, gangliocytic paraganglioma, mesenteric fibromatosis and metastases (particularly melanoma).

A panel of immunohistochemical stains is often useful to exclude these other neoplasms. Although a few GI stromal tumours contain keratin-positive cells, the staining is typically focal and weak; most carcinomas stain diffusely and more intensely with keratin.[11,43,44] Endocrine neoplasms frequently express synaptophysin or chromogranin or both. Gangliocytic paragangliomas occur in the duodenum.[45–48] They contain polygonal epithelioid cells resembling those of an epithelioid GI stromal tumour but spindle cells, ganglion cells and a carcinoid element are also present. The latter is chromogranin-positive while the spindled elements often stain with S-100 and GFAP.

Whether some intestinal tumours demonstrate neural differentiation is contentious because S-100 positivity is occurs in about 5–15% of otherwise characteristic GI stromal tumours (range 0–80%), but in most of the tumours the positive cells are focal or nuclear staining is absent.[16,49] However, a rare subset of GI neoplasms composed of spindled cells in bundles with variably developed nuclear palisading are characterized by diffuse intense nuclear staining with S-100 and the cells are positive for GFAP. These have been designated as schwannomas and all have been clinically benign.[50] GI schwannomas almost always occur in the stomach and are associated with a lymphoplasmacytic infiltrate that helps identify them when H&E sections are examined. Because of their non-aggressive behaviour these tumours should be distinguished from GI stromal tumours. Gastrointestinal autonomic nerve tumours (GANT) or plexosarcomas are defined ultrastructurally: the constituent cells have interdigitating cytoplasmic processes, membrane bound dense core granules and intracytoplasmic vesicular structures.[40,51,52] By light microscopy they may resemble epithelioid stromal tumours by virtue of the round shape and often cleared cytoplasm of the constituent cells. By immunohistochemistry, most GANTs are synaptophysin-positive with variably positive chromogranin and S-100 protein staining. GANTs may recur and metastasize so distinction from the usual GI stromal tumour is less critical than for schwannomas. Criteria for malignancy for GANTs are not standardized, but using the size and mitotic index criteria applied to other GI stromal tumours with the statement that experience is limited, is probably the best way to proceed.

Intestinal glomus tumours are rare; they are almost exclusively limited to the stomach.[53,54] They most often grow as small polyps and have not been reported to be larger than 5 cm. Rare examples have been reported in the jejunum and colon.[55,56] The histological pattern is that of glomus tumour elsewhere and the cells demonstrate smooth muscle features. They are all clinically benign and thus should be distinguished from the GI stromal tumours.

Mesenteric fibromatosis may be composed of spindled cells similar to those in GI stromal tumours and they can involve the muscularis, although the bulk of the tumour is usually in the serosa or in the mesentery. Unlike GI stromal tumours, the stroma is usually myxoid and the tumour is less cellular than the usual GI stromal tumour. Even though bland and relatively paucicellular, mesenteric fibromatosis can recur relentlessly. Inflammatory fibrous polyps are usually less than 3 cm, they are well circumscribed and the stroma is myxoid to sclerotic and usually hypocellular. They contain inflammatory cells, including the almost inevitable eosinophils, but mast cells and plasma cells also may be found. Granular cell tumours can occur in the intestine but the histological pattern should allow distinction from epithelioid stromal tumours.[57]

Having established that the process is neoplastic and that it falls into the category of gastrointestinal stromal tumours, finer subdivision into spindled, epithelioid and mixed categories is possible. Whether this is of value is controvesial. Appelman maintains that such subdivision is important for two reasons: 1) Nuclear pleomorphism is generally a feature of malignancy in spindled neoplasms, whereas, paradoxically, malignant epithelioid stromal tumours tend to be composed of cells with uniform nuclei, although such tumours are cellular.[4] We think application of the predictors of malignancy discussed in the next section works equally well for spindled or epithelioid stromal neoplasms[7,58] 2) Given that a gastric stromal neoplasm is malignant, a more favourable prognosis seems to attach to those containing epithelioid areas (median survival 5 years) than those without that feature (median survival 9 months).[27]

Spindled GI stromal tumours are composed of cells with elongated nuclei, often arranged in bundles. In most, and particularly if they are cellular, cytoplasm is scant and hard to discern. Because of this, the cells do not resemble normal smooth muscle cells, which have rather abundant and often fibrillary cytoplasm. The nuclei may be either blunt or pointed and they are not infrequently arranged in a palisading fashion similar to that found in neural tumours. The stroma of the spindled tumours may be myxoid, hyalinized, fibrotic or necrotic or a combination of these. Some tumours are composed of spindled cells arranged in packets surrounded by delicate connective tissue. Such tumours have a predilection for the duodenum and jejunum.

Epithelioid tumours feature rounded cells with abundant or cleared eosinophilic cytoplasm. The cytoplasmic clearing may be partial or complete and sometimes the clearing is perinuclear. The tumour cell nuclei of epithelioid stromal tumours tend to be central and rounded. Mixtures of spindled and epithelioid cells are common, raising the suspicion that at least sometimes an epithelioid appearance results from transverse sectioning of elongate cells. Epithelioid cells are often arranged in packets surrounded by connective tissue. A perivascular arrangement of epithelioid tumour cells is also not uncommon.

Evaluation of predictors of clinical malignancy[4,5,7,34]

Predicting the future behaviour of a gastrointestinal stromal tumour requires evaluation of several different morphological features. Although some sarcomas are obviously malignant using standard nuclear features, most malignant stromal tumours are only subtly or not at all histologically different from their benign counterparts. Prediction of future behaviour is not possible for a few stromal tumours because their morphological features are not sufficiently deviated from benign stromal tumours to be certain of their potential. These we label 'of uncertain malignant potential'. The morphological features we find most useful in predicting future behaviour of gastrointestinal stromal tumours are: metastasis, invasion of surrounding organs, the mitotic index, tumour cell necrosis in the absence of mucosal ulceration, the degree of cellularity, nuclear pleomorphism and nuclear anaplasia.

Invasion of surrounding structures. See Gross appearance.

Mitotic index: the number of mitotic figures found in a specified number of high-power fields (HPF). Assessing the mitotic index of a GI stromal tumour is essential because almost all investigators have found that the mitotic index is a powerful prognostic indicator. Mitotic counts have been given in some studies as the number of mitotic figures/**10** HPF, while in others, as the number of mitotic figures/**50** HPF. The reader should take care to be sure which scheme is used when reading this literature. Tumours with >5 MF/10 HPF (>25 MF/50 HPF) regardless of their site within the GI tract metastasize frequently enough to be considered malignant neoplasms.[7] The outcome for patients whose tumours contain <5 MF/10 HPF is less certain. In a recent report that utilized multivariate analysis, it was found that, next to the presence of metastasis at the time of diagnosis, the mitotic index was the single best indicator of prognosis.[29] In this study, site of tumour, size of tumour and epithelioid versus spindled cell histology had some prognostic value in the univariate analysis, but had no independent predictive power when analyzed together with the mitotic index. These investigators concluded that any GI stromal tumour with a mitotic index of >10 MF/50 HPF (>2 MF/10 HPF) should be considered to have significant malignant potential. Whether this degree of predictive power is retained when the mitotic index is based on a 10-field count rather than a 50-field count has not been tested to our knowledge.

Obtaining an accurate mitotic index requires that thin, well-stained sections be available. Care should be taken to only count structures that are unambiguously mitotic figures. Lymphocytes, pyknotic nuclei, karyorrhectic fragments and chunks of haematoxylin can mimic mitotic figures. For division figures, we require hair-like extensions from a central chromatin clot in a cell with no nuclear membrane. In order to exclude degenerative cells, the cytoplasm of the putative dividing cell should not be eosinophilic. We suggest that at least four sets of 10 high-power fields, or 50 high-power fields if desired, in the most active areas of the tumour be examined for mitotic figures. The highest number of mitoses in any one count should be used as the final mitotic count. Although the reproducibility of mitotic counting by different observers has been questioned,[59] we have found counting of mitoses reliable when the precautions listed above are utilized.[7]

Tumour cell necrosis in the absence of mucosal ulceration. See Gross appearance.

Cellularity. (Fig. 35.1) Evaluation of cellularity is fraught with subjectivity and the observer needs some point of reference. We use the normal muscularis propria as the standard for cellularity and define hypercellularity as increased numbers of nuclei per unit area when compared to the normal muscularis. Obviously, not all hypercellular tumours are malignant, but nearly all malignant tumours are hypercellular, using this definition. Appelman and Helwig report hypercellularity to be a more significant finding in epithelioid stromal neoplasms because so few hypercellular epithelioid tumours are benign, while benign hypercellular spindle stromal cell tumours are relatively common.[25]

Pleomorphism. (Fig. 35.2) Many malignant stromal tumours contain cells with nuclei of varying sizes and shapes, but some do not. Moreover, benign stromal tumours, particularly spindled ones, may demonstrate pleomorphism. Paradoxically, pleomorphism is often absent in clinically malignant epithelioid gastric tumours.

Nuclear enlargement and nuclear anaplasia. (Fig. 35.3) These are features of many different types of malignant neoplasms, of course, and may also be found in gastrointestinal stromal tumours. However, the cells in a disproportionate number of malignant gastrointestinal stromal sarcomas do not display sufficient nuclear aberration to be recognized as cytologically malignant.

It should be apparent to the reader that predicting the behaviour of a gastrointestinal stromal tumour requires the assessment of all of the microscopic features discussed above, plus a knowledge of the size of the tumour and whether it has invaded other organs or metastasized. As

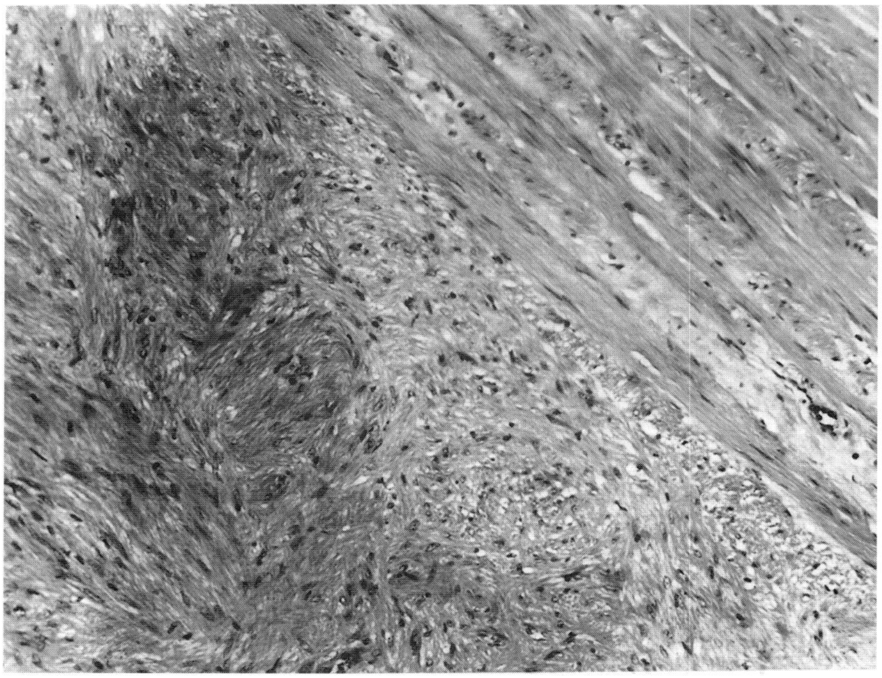

Fig. 35.1 Leiomyoma of the oesophagus. Note that the cellularity of the tumour is the same as the muscularis propria in the upper right hand portion of the photomicrograph. Use of the muscularis propria as the point of reference for evaluating the cellularity of gastrointestinal stromal tumours is advocated. Although this tumour was 6 cm in diameter, it is normocellular, contains no mitotic figures and the cells are bland. (H&E, ×125)

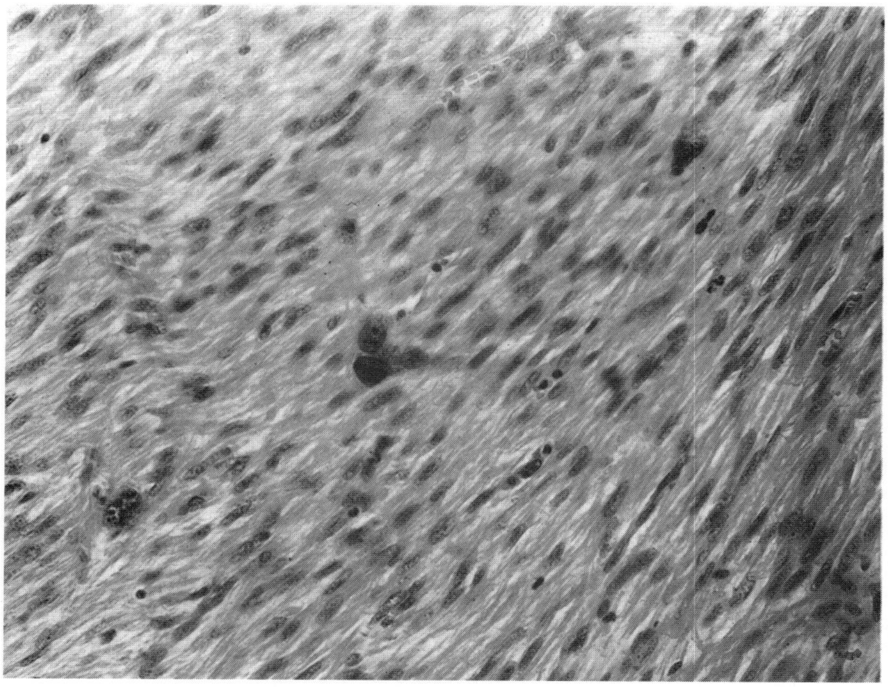

Fig. 35.2 This photomicrograph demonstrates pleomorphism in a spindled stromal sarcoma arising in the small bowel. Pleomorphism may be found in both benign and malignant gastrointestinal stromal tumours, but this tumour is malignant based on the following features: size (10 cm), mitotic counts (8–10MF/10HPF) and location (almost all small intestinal stromal tumours of this size behave in a malignant fashion). Paradoxically, malignant gastrointestinal epithelioid stromal tumours often do not demonstrate pleomorphism. (H&E, ×250)

noted, several studies emphasize the central role of the mitotic index in predicting outcome. Moreover, knowledge of the site is critical since the weight-given size is the specific. The interpretation of these features in each part of the GI tract is provided below.

Special techniques

Trichrome

Brick-red cytoplasm with faint longitudinal fibrils is the feature usually associated with smooth muscle cells, but

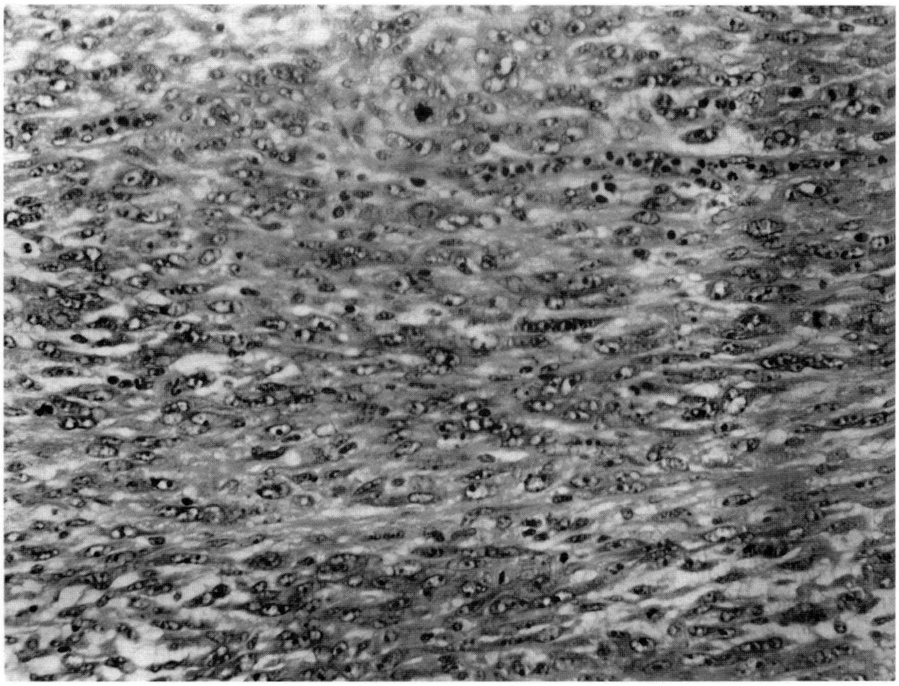

Fig. 35.3 This jejunal spindle cell stromal sarcoma is malignant on cytological grounds. In addition, there were numerous mitotic figures with abnormal forms and the tumour was 10 cm in diameter. The main differential diagnoses for malignant gastrointestinal stromal tumours are metastasis (particularly melanoma), spindle-cell carcinoma and lymphoma. In this case, the common leukocyte antigen, S-100 and monoclonal keratin immunohistochemical stains were negative. (H&E, ×250)

this will not be found in the majority of cells composing gastrointestinal neoplasms. In fact, many spindled GI stromal neoplasms are composed of cells with sparse cytoplasm. Epithelioid neoplasms of the stomach will often possess a moderate amount of cytoplasm, but it does not usually have a fibrillar character.

Immunohistochemistry

As noted above, some but not all GI stromal tumours express antigens found in normal smooth muscle cells and recent studies have found that 80–90% of the tumours contain cells that decorate with one or more of the following antibodies: muscle specific actin, smooth muscle actin or desmin.[11,12] Although these results indicate that some GI stromal tumours do not express any of these antigens, and thus a negative result does not exclude the diagnosis, we think negative staining for all three antibodies suggests the need for a careful differential diagnosis and consideration for other immunohistochemical stains. On the other hand, in spite of their names, MSA and SMA are not specific for smooth muscle cells and are present in myofibroblasts and other mesenchymal cells. The antibody more specific for muscle, desmin, is present in only a small minority of GI stromal tumours.[11,12,60,61] Recent investigation has revealed that 80–90% of GI stromal tumours contain cells that react with the CD34 antibody. Moreover CD34 is often positive for stromal tumours negative for MSA, SMA and desmin.[12a] Immunohistochemistry is also of use to eliminate relevant diseases in the differential diagnosis such as lymphoma, carcinoma, endocrine tumors and metastatic melanoma. So far, although lymphoblastic lymphoma and some granulocytic and lymphocytic leukaemias contain CD34 positive cells, only 1% of carcinomas are positive and melanomas are negative.[12b] We suggest a panel approach with the caution that S-100 protein is expressed by some cells in some GI stromal tumours. However, if large numbers of S-100 positive cells are present and the staining is intense and nuclear, the tumour may well be neural or melanoma (see above, Assessment of cell type).

Flow cytometry and morphometry

Several groups of investigators have reported that the nuclear DNA content of the tumour cells correlates with outcome for patients with GI stromal tumours.[29,62,63] Furthermore, some investigators have found a correlation between DNA ploidy, the size of the tumour, the histological grade of the tumour and the patient's survival. Others have reported that morphometry is useful in predicting outcome.[64] However, it is questionable whether flow cytometry provides independent prognostic information beyond that provided by clinical and morphological evaluation. In fact, a recent study found that when clinical information about the presence or absence of metastases was available and a mitotic index was determined, morphometry, image cytometry and flow cytometry did not prove to be independent predictors of patient outcome.[29] These procedures are expensive and to justify their routine use, they should yield information not provided by clinical and morphological parameters. To date, this is not the case in our opinion.

Some investigators have suggested that DNA ploidy be

utilized for tumours whose morphological predictors are indeterminate, presumably with the idea that aneuploid tumours would be deemed malignant. This also may not be cost effective, because there is no efficacious adjuvant therapy for patients with malignant GI stromal tumours and any patient with a tumour deemed indeterminate for malignancy on morphological grounds should have as complete a removal of tumour as possible and be followed carefully, regardless of the ploidy of the tumour cells.

Ultrastructural evaluation

This technique is of very limited diagnostic usefulness for this group of neoplasms. In the past, its chief use has been to attempt to eliminate carcinoma, neural tumours and melanoma from the differential diagnosis. Today, this is most effectively accomplished with immunohistochemical stains.

GASTROINTESTINAL STROMAL NEOPLASMS INVOLVING SPECIFIC REGIONS OF THE GI TRACT

Oesophagus[6,65–67]

Oesophageal stromal neoplasms are rare, with the exception of the small 'seedling leiomyomas' encountered as incidental findings in the region of the cardio-oesophageal junction. Most oesophageal stromal tumours are composed of cells with the features of smooth muscle cells and the terms 'leiomyoma' and 'leiomyosarcoma' or GI stromal tumour, smooth muscle type are appropriate. Benign neoplasms outnumber malignant ones in a ratio of about 5:1.[6]

Presenting symptoms of leiomyoma include dysphagia and pain, but bleeding due to ulceration is common. Most neoplasms are less than 5 cm, single, they involve any portion of the oesophagus and histologically they have the appearance of the usual uterine leiomyoma (Fig. 35.1). Rarely, leiomyomas may be multiple and when most of the oesophagus is involved the condition is known as leiomyomatosis. Leiomyomatosis usually affects women in their second and third decades and may be associated with vulvar leiomyomas.[68–70]

Leiomyosarcoma of the oesophagus is extremely rare, and the diagnosis in many reported cases is doubtful since many of these appear to be large leiomyomas or spindle-cell carcinomas.[65,71] The latter are bulky, exophytic, spindle-cell lesions associated with zones of invasive or in situ squamous cell carcinoma (see Ch. 38).

Because of the rarity of oesophageal stromal neoplasms, criteria for separating benign from malignant lesions are not well defined, but those over 5 cm in diameter with greater than 2 MF/10 HPF (i.e. 10 MF/50 HPF) should be considered malignant. Tumors of 3–4 cm diameter which contain 1–2 MF/10 HPF are of uncertain malignant potential.

Stomach[1,4,6,7,9,25,26,29–33,58,72–76]

Over half of all gastrointestinal stromal neoplasms occur in the stomach, and roughly three-quarters of them are benign. Most patients are adults, although rarely stromal neoplasms occur in children and young adults (see Carney Triad, above).[8,75,77] The typical patient presents with melena or haematemesis due to ulceration of the mucosa overlying the neoplasm. Clinical features favouring malignancy include weight loss, abdominal pain and the presence of a palpable mass.

Grossly, stromal neoplasms involving the stomach range from asymptomatic neoplasms less than 1 cm in maximum dimension to bulky 20 cm masses. Malignant neoplasms tend to be larger than benign ones, but not always, and some clinically benign lesions are larger than 10 cm. In one reported series no tumour less than 5.5 cm in diameter metastasized, whereas those between 6–10 cm and over 10 cm had a metastatic rate of approximately 30% and over 60% respectively.[6] Gastric stromal tumours with five or more MF/10 HPF are regarded as 'leiomyosarcoma'.[7,30] A recent series has demonstrated that stromal tumours from all parts of the GI tract, including those from the stomach, with >10 MF/50 HPF (>2 MF/10 HPF) behave aggressively often enough to be considered malignant. Tumours less than 5 cm in diameter and with <5 MF/50 HPF (<1 MF/10 HPF) are considered benign while those with 5–9 MF/50 HPF (1–2 MF/10 HPF) are placed in the category of uncertain malignant potential as are tumours >5 cm and with <9 MF/50 HPF. These criteria are used for both epithelioid and spindle-cell tumours because in this study multivariate analysis revealed that epithelioid histology was not a significant variable.

Of several different histological patterns encountered in gastric stromal tumours, lesions consisting of spindle cells are commonest.[26,27,73] A few of these contain cells that demonstrate smooth muscle differentiation and in classic nomenclature are 'leiomyomas' 'cellular leiomyoma' or 'leiomyosarcoma' (Fig. 35.4); however most are undifferentiated. Not infrequently, the tumour cell nuclei composing the undifferentiated tumours are stratified, resulting in a pattern reminiscent of neurilemmoma (Fig. 35.5). Spindled tumours occur primarily in the proximal stomach and when bland, <5 cm and mitotically inactive, only rarely behave in a clinically malignant fashion. Only one such neoplasm in Appelman and Helwig's series of 47 patients metastasized, and that was greater than 17 cm in maximum diameter.[25]

Many otherwise spindle-celled gastric stromal neoplasms contain a variable component of epithelioid cells, featuring clear to eosinophilic cytoplasm, centrally placed

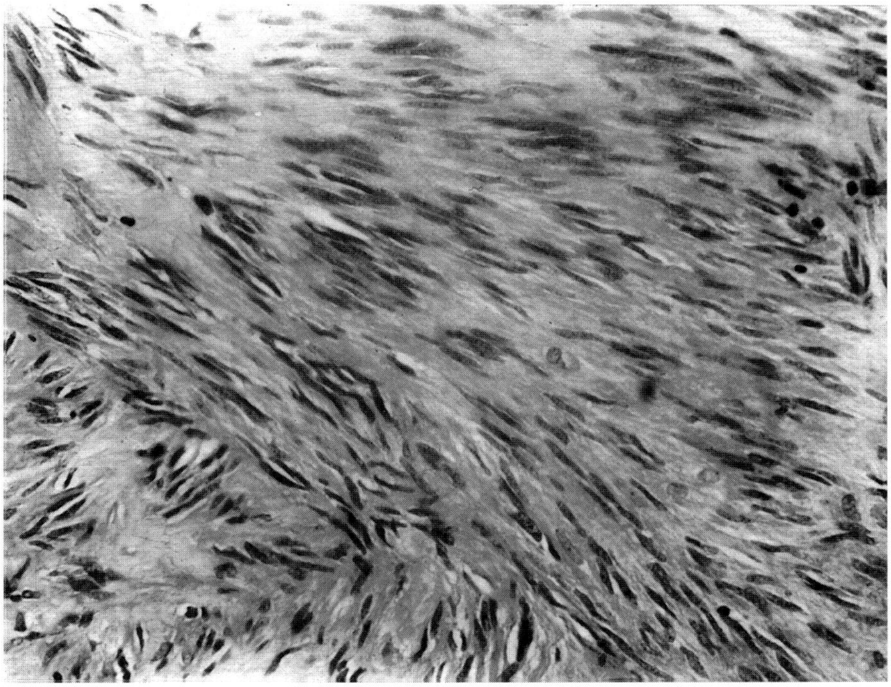

Fig. 35.4 This 2 cm gastric spindle cell stromal tumour does not contain identifiable mitoses and it is not hypercellular. Consequently, it can be confidently interpreted as benign. Note that the tumour cell nuclei do not particularly resemble those found in normal smooth muscle cells, hence the suggestion that these be classified as gastric stromal tumours. (H&E, ×250)

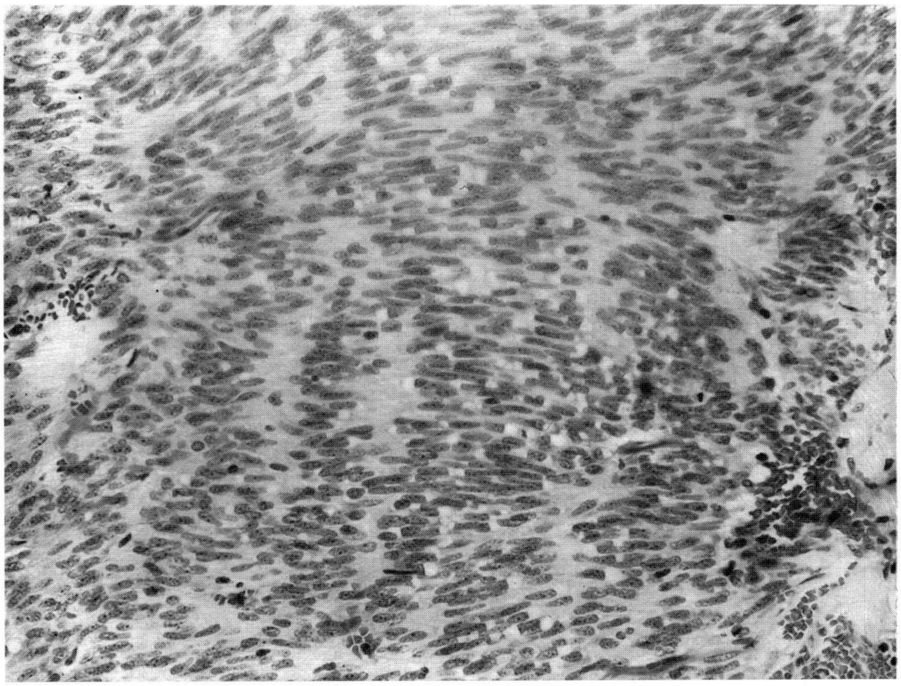

Fig. 35.5 A gastric spindle-cell stromal tumour in which the nuclei are stratified in the manner often seen in neural tumours. However, such tumours in the gastrointestinal tract rarely demonstrate other evidence of neural differentiation. This cellular neoplasm measured 6 cm in diameter, and it contained 1–2 mitotic figures/10 HPF. Consequently, it is of uncertain malignant potential (see text). (H&E, ×200)

nuclei and often perinuclear vacuoles and some gastric stromal tumours are purely epithelioid.[9,25,73] (Fig. 35.6A,B). Investigators found that some 90% of gastric epithelioid stromal tumours contained cells that were decorated with at least one of the following antibodies: muscle specific actin, smooth muscle actin, CD34 or desmin.[12,12a,12b] Tumours composed partially or completely of these round cells have in the past been labelled 'leiomyoblastoma' and, more recently, 'epithelioid gastrointestinal stromal tumours'.

Management and treatment of gastric stromal neoplasms[6,72,78,79]

In most cases, the diagnosis of a gastric stromal neoplasm is suspected preoperatively because imaging studies or

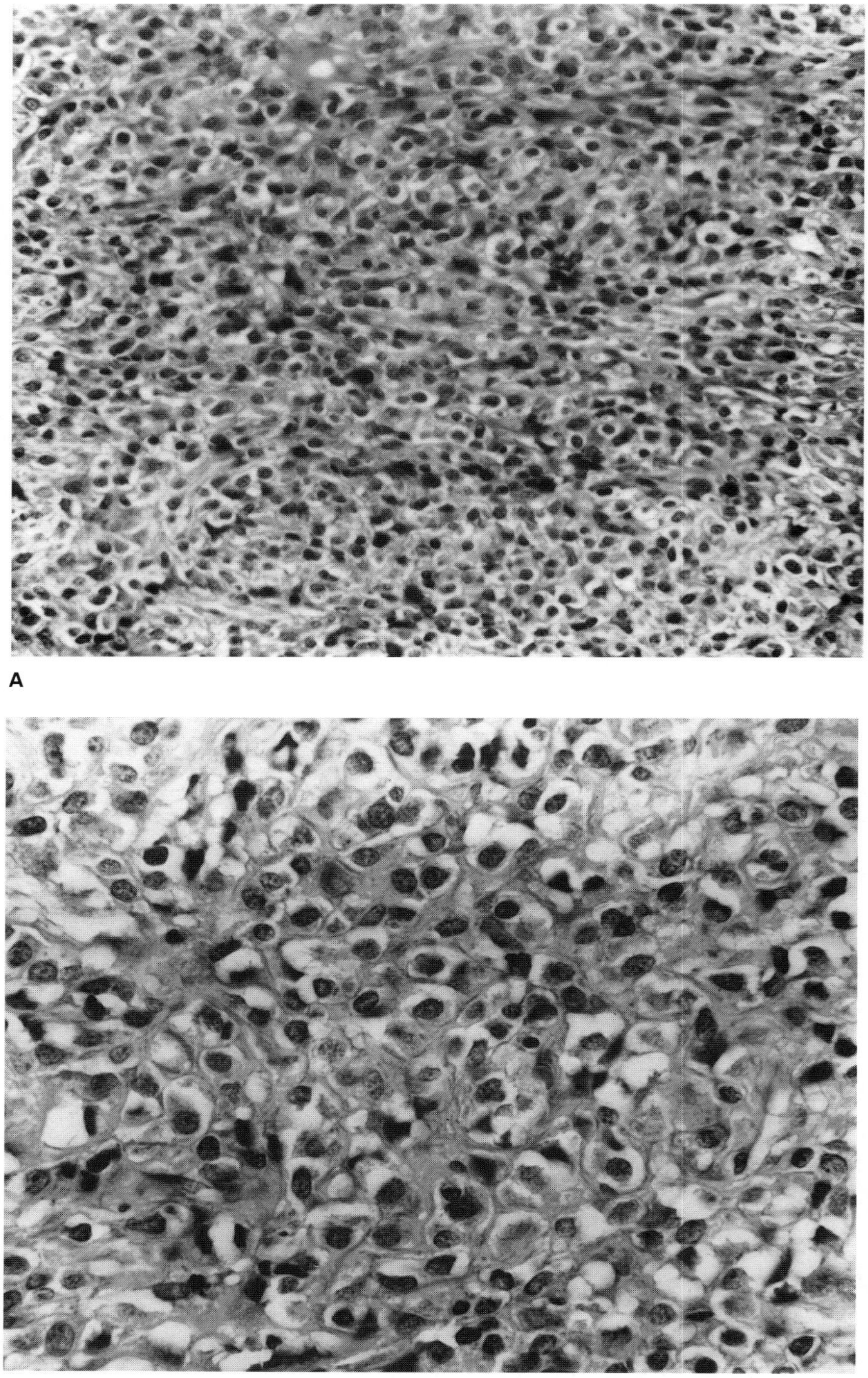

A

B

Fig. 35.6A,B This malignant epithelioid stromal tumour is involving the jejunum. Note the perinuclear clearing. This tumour is malignant on the basis of hypercellularity, high mitotic counts and its large size. S-100, cytokeratin and common leukocyte antigen immunohistochemical stains were negative. (**A** — H&E, ×125; **B** — H&E, ×450)

radiographs are distinctive or the diagnosis has been established by endoscopy and biopsy.

Malignant stromal neoplasms metastasize to lymph nodes with insufficient frequency to warrant lymph node dissections. Indeed, there is no evidence to suggest that procedures more extensive than removal of all gross neoplasm prolong survival or delay recurrences.[42] However, if there is still doubt whether the tumour is a stromal neoplasm or a carcinoma after biopsy or at the time of frozen section, an operation suitable for the treatment of carcinoma should be performed. If the neoplasm is clearly in the 'stromal' group at frozen section, some preliminary prognostic information (based on an assessment of size, location and the frozen section appearance of the neoplasm) can be given to the surgeon. However, determining whether an individual tumour is benign, of uncertain malignant potential or malignant is most often not possible until permanent sections are examined. As a result, the surgeon should carefully explore all patients with stromal tumours greater than 1 cm for evidence of spread and obtain appropriate biopsies to document his suspicions; but he should be discouraged from performing excessively wide or radical excisions.[79]

Small and large intestine and anus[4,5,7,11,28,29,31,32,34,58,62,76,80–85]

Most intestinal stromal tumours arise in the jejunum and ileum, although the number occurring in the duodenum is higher than would be expected given its short length. The next largest group occurs in the rectum. Anal stromal neoplasms are vanishingly rare and almost all have occurred in women. Rarely, GI stromal tumours may be multiple.[85]

Patients with intestinal stromal neoplasms most commonly present with bleeding, usually due to ulceration of the overlying mucosa. Other common symptoms include epigastric pain, weight loss and jaundice. The latter is more common in duodenal neoplasms. Large neoplasms may be palpated on physical examination and some have a characteristic dumb-bell appearance on radiological examination, reflecting growth on both sides of the muscularis propria.

Some of the clinically malignant neoplasms in these study groups were large, contained atypical cells with easily found mitotic figures and had zones of necrosis. In short, they were obviously malignant. Unfortunately, 45% of the tumours in the Ranchod and Kempson study did not contain areas of tumour cell necrosis and mitotic counts were less than 5 MF/10 HPF.[7] In a similar vein, Appelman asserts that stromal neoplasms in the intestine with as few as 1 MF/20 HPF should be regarded as 'probably malignant'.[6] A recent multivariate analysis has suggested that a MI of >10 MF/50 HPF should be considered evidence of malignancy. Thus it is apparent that while high values of the usual predictors are well correlated with clinical malignancy, low values are very poor at picking out clinically malignant neoplasms. Or, to put it another way, low cellularity, small size and difficult-to-find mitotic figures are no guarantee of a benign clinical course when dealing with intestinal stromal tumours. As a result, we do not think any *intestinal* stromal tumour arising in the muscularis propria greater than 1 cm in diameter should be interpreted as unequivocally benign. A study from St Mark's Hospital found that most rectal stromal tumours involving the muscularis propria behaved in an aggressive fashion regardless of their histological appearance or size.[34] In this study, rectal tumours as small as 1 cm recurred. On the other hand, rectal stromal tumours arising from the muscularis mucosa (leiomyomatous polyps) almost always were composed of cells demonstrating smooth muscle differentiation and were cured by excision.

In Table 35.1 guidelines for the clinical behaviour of duodenal stromal neoplasms are presented[6] and it is probable that these are also applicable to tumours of the small and large bowel that arise from the muscularis propria. The following guidelines are also proposed:

Table 35.1 Guidelines for clinical behaviour of duodenal stromal neoplasms (modified from Appelman 1984)[6]

Size	
<4 cm:	metastases unlikely
4–9 cm:	about 50% malignant
>10 cm:	75% or more malignant
Cellularity	
Not crowded:	benign
Crowded:	malignant
Mitoses	
1 per 20 HPF or more:	probably malignant
Easily found:	malignant

1. Tumours up to 4 cm in diameter are diagnosed as of uncertain malignant potential if bland, hypocellular and mitotically inactive. If cellular and mitotically active, i.e. they have a MI >10 MF/50 HPF (i.e. >2 MF/10 HPF), they are regarded as gastrointestinal stromal sarcoma.
2. Tumours more than 4 cm in diameter are diagnosed as gastrointestinal stromal sarcoma and designated as low grade or high grade on the basis of mitotic counts of <10 MF/10 HPF (low grade) or >10 MF/10 HPF (high grade).
3. The only stromal neoplasms regarded as unequivocally benign are the small polypoid lesions arising from, and limited to, the muscularis mucosae (leiomyomatous polyps).[34]

Two somewhat distinctive microscopic features of small intestinal stromal neoplasms deserve special comment. In some an organoid pattern reminiscent of paraganglioma is seen, and others possess focal aggregates of collagen. In one series eight neoplasms also contained areas with an appearance of gastric 'leiomyoblastomas'.[5]

There have been a few reports of multiple benign stromal tumours of the small and large bowel, some of which have been associated with pregnancy. This has been labelled as leiomyomatosis. The small size of the multiple tumours and the clinical setting provide clues to the diagnosis but metastasis from a primary malignant GI stromal tumour or the uterus must be excluded.

After attempted curative resection the 5 and 10 year survival rates for patients with malignant intestinal stromal tumors are 50% and 35% respectively, but late recurrences are relatively common.[5] The site of the primary as long as it is within the intestine is not prognostically important. If a simplified grading scheme is employed, based solely upon mitotic index, tumours with counts greater than 10 MF/10 HPF are associated with a median survival of 25 months while those with fewer have a median survival of 98 months.[58]

Intestinal stromal sarcomas tend to metastasize primarily to the peritoneal surfaces, the liver and the lungs.

REFERENCES

1. Golden T, Stout A. Smooth muscle tumors of the gastrointestinal tract and retroperitoneal tisses. Surg Gynecol Obstet 1941; 73: 784–810.
2. Stout A. Tumors of the stomach. In: Atlas of tumor pathology. Washington, DC: Armed Forces Institute of Pathology, 1953: Vol (Section 6, fasc 21).
3. Stout A. Bizarre smooth muscle tumors of the stomach. Cancer 1962; 15: 400–409.
4. Appelman H. Smooth muscle tumors of the gastrointestinal tract. What we know now that Stout didn't know. Am J Surg Pathol 1986; 10 (Suppl 1): 83–99.
5. Akwari O, Dozois R, Weiland L, Beahrs O. Leiomyosarcoma of the small and large bowel. Cancer 1978; 43(3): 1375–1384.
6. Appelman H. Stromal tumors of the esophagus, stomach and duodenum. In: HD A, ed. Pathology of the esophagus, stomach and duodenum. New York: Churchill Livingstone, 1984: 195–242.
7. Ranchod M, Kempson R. Smooth muscle tumors of the gastrointestinal tract and retroperitoneum: a pathologic analysis of 100 cases. Cancer 1977; 39(1): 255–262.
8. Chadwick E, Connor E, Hanson I et al. Tumors of smooth-muscle origin in HIV-infected children. JAMA 1990; 263(23): 3182–3184.
9. Cornog J Jr. Gastric leiomyoblastoma. A clinical and ultrastructural study. Cancer 1974; 34(3): 711–719.
10. Evans D, Lampert I, Jacobs M. Intermediate filaments in smooth muscle tumours. J Clin Pathol 1983; 36(1): 57–61.
11. Franquemont D, Frierson HJ. Muscle differentiation and clinicopathologic features of gastrointestinal stromal tumors. American Journal of Surgical Pathology 1992; 16(10): 947–954.
12. Hogan C, Zuckerberg LR, Bhan AK, Dickinsen GR. Epithelioid 'smooth muscle' tumors: an immunohistochemical and ultrastructural profile. Mod Pathol 1991; 4: 5A.
12a. van de Rijn M, Rouse RV. CD34: a review. Appl Immunohistochem 1994; 2(2): 71–80.
12b. van de Rijn M, Hendrickson MR, Rouse RV. CD34 expression by gastrointestinal tract stromal tumours. Human Pathol 1994, in press.
13. Hajdu S, Erlandson R, Paglia M. Light and electron microscopic studies of a gastric leiomyoblastoma. Arch Pathol 1972; 93(1): 36–41.
14. Kahn H, Marks A, Thom H, Baumal R. Role of antibody to S-100 protein in diagnostic pathology. Am J Clin Pathol 1983; 79(3): 341–347.
15. Knapp R, Wick M, Goellner J. Leiomyoblastomas and their relationship to other smooth-muscle tumors of the gastrointestinal tract. An electron-microscopic study. Am J Surg Pathol 1984; 8(6): 449–461.
16. Mazur M, Clark H. Gastric stromal tumors. Reappraisal of histogenesis. Am J Surg Pathol 1983; 7(6): 507–519.
17. Nakajima T, Watanabe S, Sato Y et al. An immunoperoxidase study of S-100 protein distribution in normal and neoplastic tissues. Am J Surg Pathol 1982; 6(8): 715–727.
18. Pike A, Appelman H, Lloyd R. Differentiation of gut stromal tumors: an immunohistochemical study. Lab Invest 1986; 54: 50A.
19. Salazar H, Totten R. Leiomyoblastoma of the stomach. An ultrastructural study. Cancer 1970; 25(1): 176–185.
20. Weiss R, Mackay B. Malignant smooth muscle tumors of the gastrointestinal tract: an ultrastructural study of 20 cases. Ultrastruct Pathol 1981; 2(3): 231–240.
21. Weiss S, Langloss J, Enzinger F. Value of S-100 protein in the diagnosis of soft tissue tumors with particular reference to benign and malignant Schwann cell tumors. Lab Invest 1983; 49(3): 299–308.
22. Welsh R, Meyer A. Ultrastructure of gastric leiomyoma. Arch Pathol 1969; 87(1): 71–81.
23. Mackay B, Ro J, Floyd C, Ordonez N. Ultrastructural observations on smooth muscle tumors. Ultrastruct Pathol 1987; 11(5–6): 593–607.
24. Min K-W. Small intestinal stromal tumors with skeinoid fibers. Clinicopathological, immunohistochemical, and ultrastructural investigations. Am J Surg Pathol 1992; 16(2): 145–155.
25. Appelman H, Helwig E. Gastric epithelioid leiomyoma and leiomyosarcoma (leiomyoblastoma). Cancer 1976; 38(2): 708–728.
26. Appelman H, Helwig E. Cellular leiomyomas of the stomach in 49 patients. Arch Pathol Lab Med 1977; 101(7): 373–377.
27. Appelman H, Helwig E. Sarcomas of the stomach. Am J Clin Pathol 1977; 67(1): 2–10.
28. Chiotasso P, Fazio V. Prognostic factors of 28 leiomyosarcomas of the small intestine. Surg Gynecol Obstet 1982; 155(2): 197–202.
29. Cunningham RE, Federspiel BH, McCarthy WF, Sobin LH, O'Leary TJ. Predicting prognosis of gastrointestinal smooth muscle tumors. American Journal of Surgical Pathology 1993; 17(6): 588–594.
30. Lindsay P, Ordonez N, Raaf J. Gastric leiomyosarcoma: clinical and pathological review of fifty patients. J Surg Oncol 1981; 18(4): 399–421.
31. McGrath P, Neifeld J, Lawrence W Jr, Kay S, Horsley J III, Parker G. Gastrointestinal sarcomas. Analysis of prognostic factors. Ann Surg 1987; 206(6): 706–710.
32. Morgan B, Comptom C, Talbert M, Gallagher W, Wood W. Benign smooth muscle tumors of the gastrointestinal tract. A 24-year experience. Ann Surg 1990; 211(1): 63–66.
33. Morrissey K, Cho E, Gray G Jr, Thorbjarnarson B. Muscular tumors of the stomach: clinical and pathological study of 113 cases. Ann Surg 1973; 178(2): 148–155.
34. Walsh T, Mann C. Smooth muscle neoplasms of the rectum and anal canal. Br J Surg 1984; 71(8): 597–599.
35. Carney J. The triad of gastric epithelioid leiomyosarcoma, functioning extra-adrenal paraganglioma, and pulmonary chondroma. Cancer 1979; 43(1): 374–382.
36. Carney J. The triad of gastric epithelioid leiomyosarcoma, pulmonary chondroma, and functioning extra-adrenal paraganglioma: a five-year review. Medicine (Baltimore) 1983; 62(3): 159–169.
37. Cardwell R, Solaiman A, Kim K, Thomford N. Carney's triad with recurrent gastric leiomyoblastoma. Am Surg 1990; 56(6): 355–359.
38. McLaughlin S, Dodge E, Ashworth J, Connors J. Carney's triad. Aust N Z J Surg 1988; 58(8): 679–681.
39. Raafat F, Salman W, Roberts K, Ingram L, Rees R, Mann J. Carney's triad: gastric leiomyosarcoma, pulmonary chondroma and extra-adrenal paraganglioma in young females. Histopathol 1986; 10(12): 1325–1333.
40. Tortella B, Matthews J, Antonioli D, Dvorak A, Silen W. Gastric autonomic nerve (GAN) tumor and extra-adrenal paraganglioma in Carney's triad. A common origin. Ann Surg 1987; 205(3): 221–225.
41. Cox J, Royston C, Sutton D. Multiple smooth muscle tumours in neurofibromatosis presenting with chronic gastrointestinal bleeding. Postgrad Med J 1988; 64(748): 149–151.
42. Shiu M, Farr G, Papachristou D, Hajdu S. Myosarcomas of the stomach: natural history, prognostic factors and management. Cancer 1982; 49(1): 177–187.
43. Brown D, Theaker J, Banks P, Gatter K, Mason D. Cytokeratin expression in smooth muscle and smooth muscle tumours. Histopathol 1987; 11(5): 477–486.
44. Norton AJ, Thomas JA, Isaacson PG. Cytokeratin-specific monoclonal antibodies are reactive with tumours of smooth muscle derivation. An immunocytochemical and biochemical study using antibodies to intermediate filament cytoskeletal proteins. Histopathol 1987; 11(5): 487–499.
45. Anders KH, Glasgow BJ, Lewin KJ. Gangliocytic paraganglioma associated with duodenal adenocarcinoma. Case report with immunohistochemical evaluation. Arch Pathol Lab Med 1987; 111(1): 49–52.
46. Inai K, Kobuke T, Yonehara S, Tokuoka S. Duodenal gangliocytic paraganglioma with lymph node metastasis in a 17-year-old boy Cancer 1989; 63(12): 2540–2545.
47. Perrone T. Duodenal gangliocytic paraganglioma and carcinoid. Am J Surg Pathol 1986; 10(2): 147–149.
48. Scheithauer BW, Nora FE, LeChago J et al. Duodenal

gangliocytic paraganglioma. Clinicopathologic and immunocytochemical study of 11 cases. Am J Clin Pathol 1986; 86(5): 559–565.
49. Hjermstad BM, Sobin LH, Helwig EB. Stromal tumors of the gastrointestinal tract: myogenic or neurogenic? [published erratum appears in Am J Surg Pathol 1987 Aug; 11(8): 660]. Am J Surg Pathol 1987; 11(5): 383–386.
50. Daimaru Y, Kido H, Hashimoto H, Enjoji M. Benign schwannoma of the gastrointestinal tract: a clinicopathologic and immunohistochemical study. Hum Pathol 1988; 19(3): 257–264.
51. Herrera GA, Cerezo L, Jones JE et al. Gastrointestinal autonomic nerve tumors. 'Plexosarcomas'. Arch Pathol Lab Med 1989; 113: 846–853.
52. Walker P, Dvorak AM. Gastrointestinal autonomic nerve (GAN) tumor. Ultrastructural evidence for a newly recognized entity. Arch Pathol Lab Med 1986; 110(4): 309–316.
53. Almagro UA, Schulte WJ, Norback DH, Turcotte JK. Glomus tumor of the stomach. Histologic and ultrastructural features. Am J Clin Pathol 1981; 75(3): 415–419.
54. Appelman HD, Helwig EB. Glomus tumors of the stomach. Cancer 1969; 23(1): 203–213.
55. Barua R. Glomus tumor of the colon. First reported case. Dis Colon Rectum 1988; 31(2): 138–140.
56. Hamilton CW, Shelburne JD, Bossen EH, Lowe JE. A glomus tumor of the jejunum masquerading as a carcinoid tumor. Hum Pathol 1982; 13(9): 859–861.
57. Johnston J, Helwig EB. Granular cell tumors of the gastrointestinal tract and perianal region: a study of 74 cases. Dig Dis Sci 1981; 26(9): 807–816.
58. Evans H. Smooth muscle tumors of the gastrointestinal tract. A study of 56 cases followed for a minimum of 10 years. Cancer 1985; 56(9): 2242–2250.
59. Silverberg S. Reproducibility of the mitosis count in the histologic diagnosis of smooth muscle tumors of the uterus. Hum Pathol 1976; 7(4): 451–454.
60. Hurlimann J, Gardiol D. Gastrointestinal stromal tumours: an immunohistochemical study of 165 cases. Histopathol 1991; 19: 311–320.
61. Pike AM, Lloyd RV, Appelman HD. Cell markers in gastrointestinal stromal tumors. Hum Pathol 1988; 19(7): 830–834.
62. Cooper P, Quirke P, Hardy G, Dixon M. A flow cytometric, clinical, and histological study of stromal neoplasms of the gastrointestinal tract. Am J Surg Pathol 1992; 16(2): 163–170.
63. El-Naggar A, Ro JY, McLemore D, Garnsey L, Ordonez N, Mackay B. Gastrointestinal stromal tumors: DNA flow-cytometric study of 58 patients with at least five years of follow-up. Mod Pathol 1989; 2(5): 511–515.
64. Federspiel B, Sobin L, Helwig E, Mikel U, Bahr G. Morphometry and cytophotometric assessment of DNA in smooth-muscle tumors (leiomyomas and leiomyosarcomas) of the gastrointestinal tract. Anal Quant Cytol Histol 1987; 9(2): 105–114.
65. Gray S, Skandalakis J, Shepard D. Collective review: smooth muscle tumors of the esophagus. Int Abstr Surg 1961; 113: 205.
66. Seremetis M, Lyons W, DeGuzman V, Peabody JJ. Leiomyomata of the esophagus. An analysis of 838 cases. Cancer 1976; 38(5): 2166–2177.
67. Takubo K, Nakagawa H, Tsuchiya S, Mitomo Y, Sasajima K, Shirota A. Seedling leiomyoma of the esophagus and esophagogastric junction zone. Hum Pathol 1981; 12(11): 1006–1010.
68. Fernandes J, Mascarenhas M, Costa C, Correia J. Diffuse leiomyomatosis of the esophagus: a case report and review of the literature. Am J Dig Dis 1975; 20(7): 684–690.
69. Kabuto T, Taniguchi K, Iwanaga T, Terasawa T, Tateishi R, Taniguchi H. Diffuse leiomyomatosis of the esophagus. Dig Dis Sci 1980; 25(5): 388–391.
70. Schapiro R, Sandrock A. Esophagogastric and vulvar leiomyomatosis: a new radiologic syndrome. J Can Assoc Radiol 1973; 24(2): 184–187.
71. Rainer W, Brus R. Leiomyosarcoma of the esophagus: review of the literature and report of 3 cases. Surgery 1965; 58: 343–350.
72. Choen S, Rauff A. Gastric leiomyosarcomas: a general surgical experience. Aust N Z J Surg 1990; 60(8): 607–611.
73. Kay S. Smooth muscle tumors of the stomach. Surg Gynecol Obstet 1964; 119: 842–846.
74. Kieffer R, McSwain B, Adkins R Jr. Sarcoma of the gastrointestinal tract: a review of 40 cases. Am Surg 1982; 48(4): 167–169.
75. Lack E. Leiomyosarcomas in childhood: a clinical and pathologic study of 10 cases. Pediatr Pathol 1986; 6(2–3): 181–197.
76. Lavin P, Hajdu S, Foote F Jr. Gastric and extragastric leiomyoblastomas: clinicopathologic study of 44 cases. Cancer 1972; 29(2): 305–311.
77. Rogers B, Grishaber J, Mahoney D, McGill C, Wagner M. Gastric leiomyoblastoma (epithelioid leiomyoma) occurring in a child: a case report. Pediatr Pathol 1989; 9(1): 79–85.
78. Lee Y. Leiomyosarcoma of the gastro-intestinal tract: general pattern of metastasis and recurrence. Cancer Treat Rev 1983; 10(2): 91–101.
79. Lehnert T, Sinn H, Waldherr R, Herfarth C. Surgical treatment of soft tissue tumors of the stomach. Eur J Surg Oncol 1990; 16(4): 352–359.
80. Barkan A, Wolloch Y, Dintsman M, Yeshurun D. Leiomyosarcoma of the duodenum. Two cases reports and a literature review. Am J Proctol Gastroenterol Colon Rectal Surg 1981; 32(8): 18–21.
81. Berkley KM. Leiomyosarcoma of the large intestine, excluding the rectum. Int Surg 1981; 66(2): 177–179.
82. Berridge D. Leiomyosarcoma of the rectum. Report of two cases illustrating an unusual presentation and the need for repeated biopsy. Dis Colon Rectum 1987; 30(9): 721–722.
83. Kusminsky R, Bailey W. Leiomyomas of the rectum and anal canal: report of six cases and review of the literature. Dis Colon Rectum 1977; 20(7): 580–599.
84. Moyana TN, Friesen R, Tan LK. Colorectal smooth-muscle tumors. A pathobiologic study with immunohistochemistry and histomorphometry. Arch Pathol Lab Med 1991; 115: 1016–1021.
85. Nagar R, Mehta J, Bhargava K. Multiple leiomyomas of small intestine. J Indian Med Assoc 1982; 78(3): 49–50.

CHAPTER 36

Endocrine cell tumours

E. Wilander

In the mucosa of the entire gastrointestinal canal there are scattered endocrine cells which synthesize, store and secrete biogenic amines or peptide hormones, or both, and they are considered to be the origin of carcinoid tumours. The endocrine cells have a defined topographic distribution, their type and frequency varying in different areas. This is reflected in the type and distribution of the tumours that arise from them. It is usual to classify gastrointestinal carcinoids according to their topography as foregut, midgut and hindgut tumours.[1] These areas are defined according to their blood supply. The stomach and duodenum comprise the foregut and is the area supplied by the coeliac artery; the small intestine, ascending colon and proximal transverse colon comprise the midgut, being supplied by the superior mesenteric artery, and the hindgut, which consists of the remaining colon and rectum, is supplied by the inferior mesenteric artery.

Location and frequency

Carcinoids represent about 2% of all malignant tumours in the gastrointestinal canal. Their topographic distribution is illustrated in Figure 36.1. Approximately 50% are found in the small intestine and the next commonest site is the appendix, where they are most frequently located distally. Except for the caecum and rectum, carcinoids are rare in the colon, as they are in the stomach and duodenum. The carcinoid is the most common type of tumour in the appendix, accounting for some 90% and in the small intestine, they occur more often than adenocarcinomas and malignant lymphomas. In the stomach and colon, less than 1% of the malignant tumours are of the carcinoid type (Table 36.1).

At the time of diagnosis of a carcinoid tumour, the mean age is in general just less than that of patients with adenocarcinomas at corresponding sites. One exception is the appendiceal carcinoid, which is found in considerably younger persons, with an average age of about 30 years, but this may only reflect that they are often incidental findings. In patients with foregut carcinoids, the mean age is about 60 years and for midgut carcinoids about 56 years.[2]

Gross pathology

Appendiceal carcinoids are round, regular and mostly located in the distal part of the appendix. They are frequently less than 1 cm in diameter. Small intestinal carcinoids are larger, often 1–2 cm in diameter, and covered with intact mucosa. They tend to be multiple and in a recent study were found in 41% of the patients examined.[3] Carcinoids of the caecum are relatively large, more than 2 cm in diameter, possibly because they are present for a longer period before giving rise to clinical symptoms. Foregut and hindgut carcinoids are mostly less than 2 cm in diameter. Gastric carcinoids, also, tend to be multiple

Table 36.1 Frequency of carcinoid tumours in relation to the total number of malignant tumours at various locations in the gastrointestinal canal.

Stomach	0.2%
Duodenum	30%
Small intestine	60%
Appendix	90%
Colon	0.5%
Rectum	0.5%

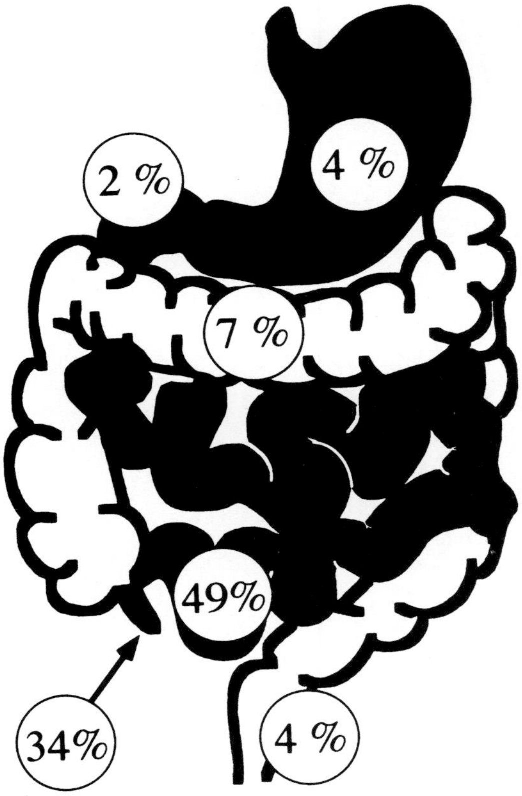

Fig. 36.1 Topographical distribution of carcinoid tumours of the gastrointestinal canal according to the Swedish National Cancer Registry.

when they are located in the body and fundus of the stomach.[4]

Light microscopy

Although carcinoids at different locations vary with respect to their biology and morphology, they share some common features, such as a regular growth pattern and the fact that the tumour cells are monomorphous. As a rule, there are few mitotic figures. Mostly the differential diagnosis from adenocarcinoma presents no difficulties.

Within the midgut, carcinoid tumours arising in the small intestine and proximal colon are surprisingly similar. They are composed of regular insular groups of tumour cells which sometimes anastomose with one another and are surrounded by a relatively prominent fibrovascular stroma (Fig. 36.2). However, some tumour areas may display tubular structures and cystic formations. The appendiceal carcinoids may exhibit a picture similar to that of other midgut carcinoids, but they may also show more solid, trabecular structures or grow in small cords in a condensed stroma.

The hindgut carcinoids, especially rectal carcinoids, are trabecular, solid or tubular and the differential diagnosis

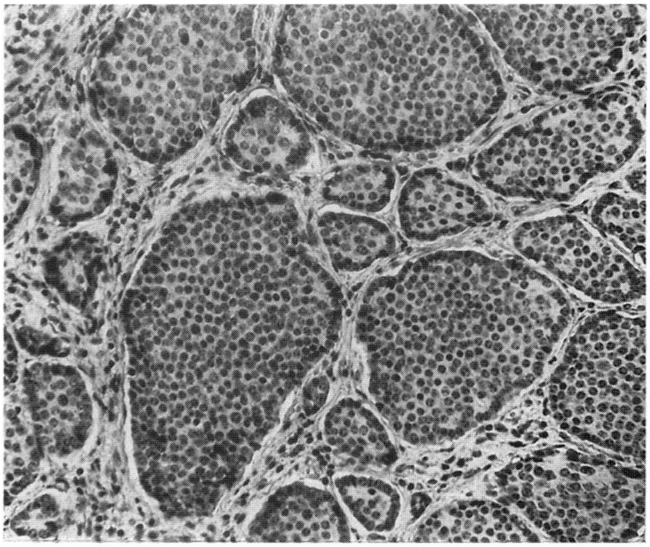

Fig. 36.2 Micrograph of a classical carcinoid tumour of the small intestine. The tumour cells are monomorphous and arranged as regular insular structures. (H&E, ×188)

from highly differentiated adenocarcinoma is very occasionally difficult (Fig. 36. 3).

In the foregut, mixed growth patterns are frequently observed in different areas of the tumour. Solid, insular, trabecular or ribbon-like, and tubular structures may be seen (Fig. 36.4). About 15% of gastric carcinoids are atypical and exhibit poor differentiation, are highly cellular, have an increased number of mitotic figures and occasional areas of necrosis[4] (Fig. 36.5). These tumours are larger, with a mean diameter of 5 cm, whereas the average diameter of the remainder is 1.8 cm. Atypical carcinoids

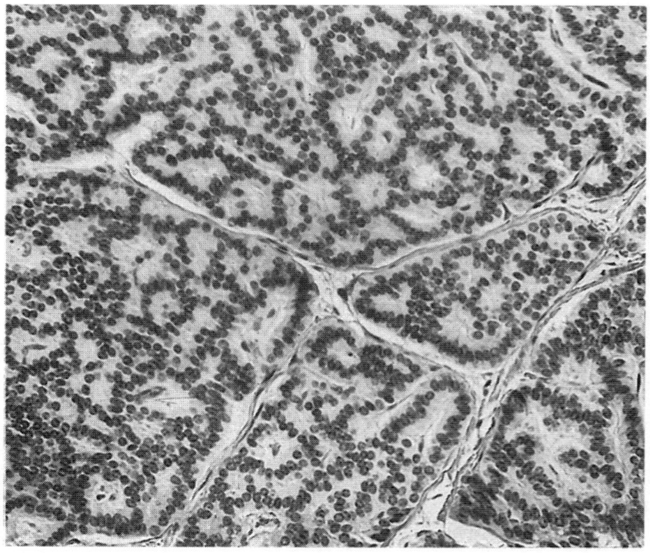

Fig. 36.3 Micrograph of a rectal carcinoid. The regular tumour cells are growing as ribbon and rosette-like structures. (H&E, ×188)

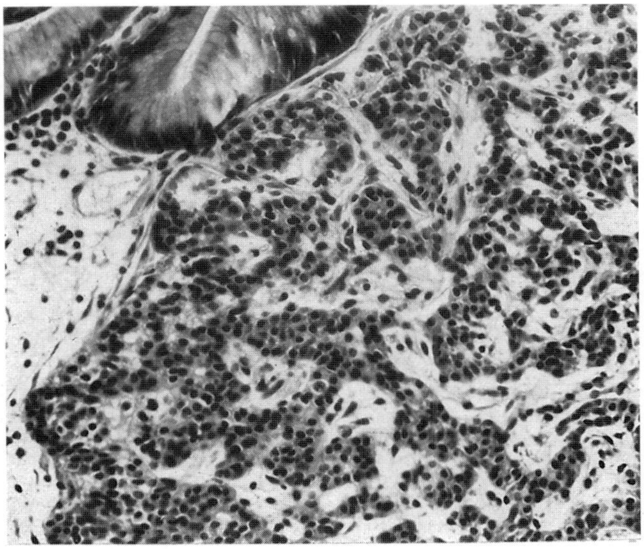

Fig. 36.4 Carcinoid tumour of the mucosa of the body of the stomach. The tumour cells are arranged in trabecular structures and surrounded by a loose fibrovascular stroma. (H&E, ×188)

occur in both the acid-secreting and antral areas of the stomach[4] and in the past some have been diagnosed as adenocarcinoma. A spectrum of endocrine neoplasia analogous to that observed in the bronchus has been postulated, and 'atypical carcinoids' are considered to hold an intermediate position both in terms of histological appearance and biological aggressiveness.[5–7] The differential diagnosis between carcinoids and carcinomas in the stomach can be difficult and borderline tumours occur. The situation is quite different in the midgut, in particular, where a corresponding spectrum of tumours is not encountered.

The fibrous stroma which surrounds the carcinoid tumour aggregates is particularly prominent in midgut carcinoids. Although the reason for this is somewhat unclear, it is worthy of note that in a recent in vitro study it was observed that peptides of the tachykinin family, such as substance P and substance K, caused stimulation of connective tissue cell growth.[8] Since tachykinin has been found in small intestinal carcinoid tumours, a biological explanation for this stroma proliferation is offered.[9,10]

Rarely, tumours with a mixture of carcinoid and adenocarcinoma growth pattern (*adenocarcinoids*) occur in the gut. The so-called goblet cell carcinoid of the appendix is probably the most distinct type. It is made up of an admixture of exocrine and endocrine tumour cells. The exocrine cells often contain copious amounts of neutral and acid mucopolysaccharides and appear as signet ring forms. The endocrine cells, which are in close contact and surround the exocrine cells, are often both argentaffin and argyrophil, may display serotonin-immunoreactivity, and contain hormonal secretory granules at electron microscopy.[11–13]

Argentaffin reaction

In 1914 Gosset and Masson[14] found that carcinoid tumours possessed the ability to reduce ammoniacal silver to metallic silver, and coined the term argentaffinoma (Fig. 36.6). The argentaffin nature of the tumour cells is due to their content of serotonin.[15] However, the reaction is not a characteristic attribute of all carcinoids but only of

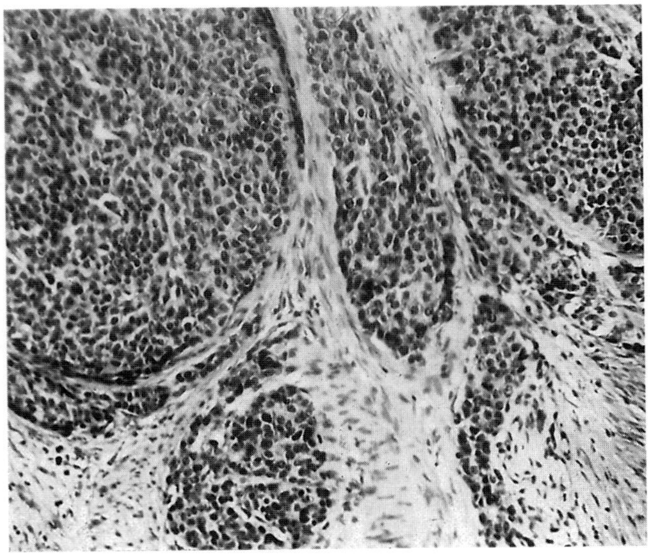

Fig. 36.5 Micrograph of an atypical carcinoid tumour of the stomach. The tumour cells appear to show a lesser degree of differentiation and the cytoplasm is relatively sparse. (H&E, ×120)

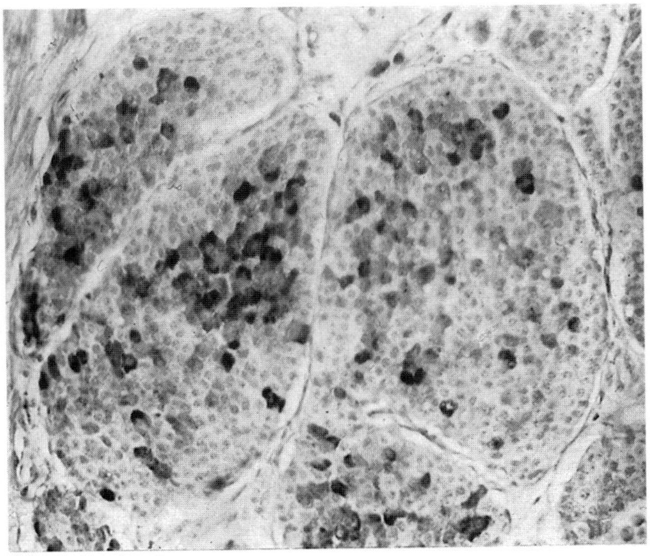

Fig. 36.6 Classical carcinoid tumour of the small intestine stained with an argentaffin stain. Both argentaffin and unreactive tumour cells are present. (Masson's stain, ×188)

those located in the midgut.[1,16] Carcinoid tumours of the small intestine, appendix and caecum are almost without exception argentaffin, with the proportion of positive cells being highest in the outer rather than the inner aspect of the tumours.[17] In foregut carcinoids, argentaffin cells occur in about 15%.[4] However, the stained cells are scattered and constitute the minority of the tumour cell population. A similar frequency of argentaffin cells is found in hindgut carcinoids.[18] The argentaffin method is a simple staining technique that will often differentiate midgut from foregut and hindgut carcinoids.

The argentaffin staining properties of carcinoids are, as a rule, preserved in their metastatic deposits and consequently liver metastases of small intestinal carcinoids will usually display an argentaffin reaction, while metastases originating from tumours in more proximal or distal parts of the bowel do not.[19]

Argyrophil reaction of Grimelius

The Grimelius silver technique has proved very useful in the identification of endocrine cells in normal tissues and in determining the endocrine value of tumours, irrespective of their hormone or amine content (Fig. 36.7). Although the chemical basis of the argyrophil reaction is somewhat unclear, it has been repeatedly shown at electron microscopy that it is localized exclusively to the hormonal secretory granules. Thus it permits light microscope visualization of the endocrine cell granules (Fig. 36.8) and it has become the routine method for the identification of carcinoid tumours.[20,21]

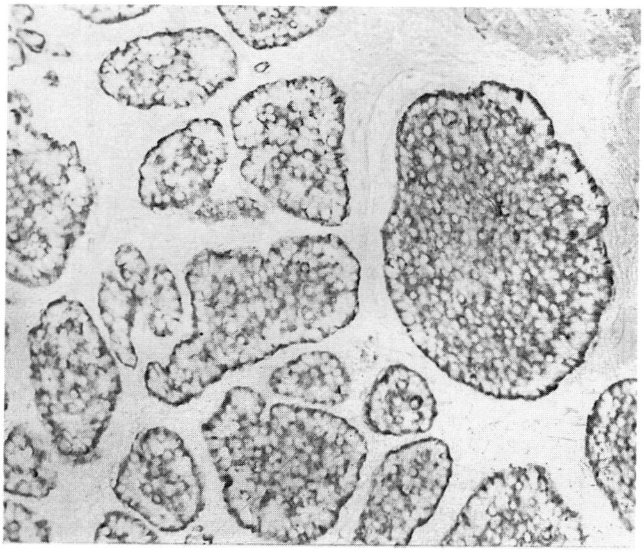

Fig. 36.7 Classical carcinoid tumour of the small intestine stained with the argyrophil silver nitrate stain of Grimelius. An accumulation of silver grains is seen in the cytoplasm of most tumour cells. (×188)

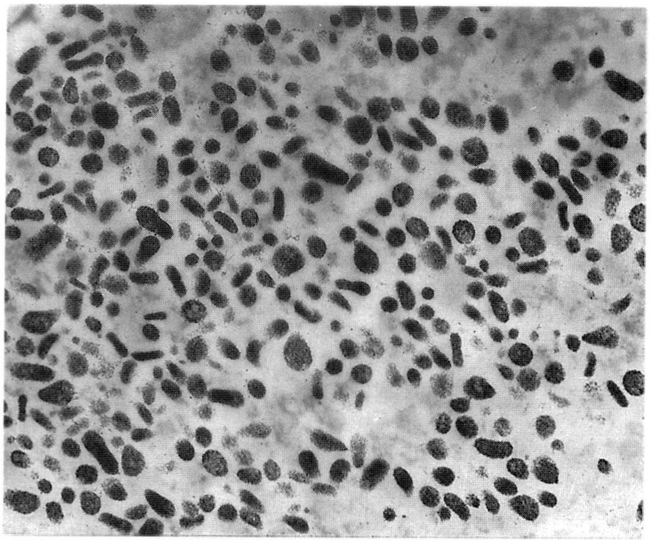

Fig. 36.8 Electron micrograph of a classical carcinoid tumour. An abundance of pleomorphic hormonal secretory granules are present in the cytoplasm of the tumour cells. These granules accumulated silver particles after staining, both with argentaffin and with the argyrophil staining technique. (Grimelius silver stain ×12 000)

Since argentaffin cells are also argyrophil, midgut carcinoid tumours contain three types of tumour cells, namely:

1. argentaffin cells
2. argyrophil but non-argentaffin cells
3. unreactive cells.

In most tumours the argentaffin cell population is the predominant one while the argyrophil but non-argentaffin cells are in the minority.[17] The argentaffin cells presumably store serotonin, while the non-argentaffin but argyrophil cells may store other hormonal products. Thus, with silver stains indirect evidence that carcinoid tumours contain several hormones can be obtained. It should be emphasized that most of the cells of foregut carcinoid tumours with an atypical morphology may fail to stain with the argyrophil technique,[4] indicating that they are morphologically dedifferentiated and biologically nearer to gastric carcinomas.

There is controversy concerning the staining reaction of hindgut carcinoids with the argyrophil technique of Grimelius. Some claim that these tumours are almost never positive, whereas others find that a significant proportion are. However, most rectal carcinoids display argyrophil cells if a slightly modified Grimelius silver stain is used, although the reaction is sometimes weak and occurs only in a minority of the tumour cell population.[22]

Argyrophil reaction of Sevier-Munger

With the Sevier-Munger technique, argentaffin cells and

some non-argentaffin endocrine cell types are stained. It is mainly the enterochromaffin-like (ECL) cells of the body and fundus of the stomach that are visualized.[18,23–25] This cell type is the predominant one of the various endocrine cells in the acid-secreting part of the stomach. In patients with atrophic gastritis and achlorhydria, proliferation of ECL cells is frequently encountered.[24,26,27] This proliferation can be both diffuse and nodular and is considered to precede the development of infiltrating carcinoid tumours of the body and fundus of the stomach.[28] It is easily demonstrated by the Sevier-Munger technique. Most foregut carcinoids arising in the non-antral part of the stomach are non-argentaffin but argyrophil with this technique[4] (Fig. 36.9). Because it is not known which peptide hormone ECL cells store, immunocytochemical methods with hormone-specific antisera cannot be used for their identification.

Serotonin in carcinoids

Carcinoid tumours of midgut origin characteristically synthesize, store and secrete serotonin[29] while those arising in the foregut and hindgut lack or infrequently produce it.[1] The serotonin content of carcinoid tumours can be demonstrated by the argentaffin reaction,[30] formalin-induced fluorescence as described by Falck-Hillarp,[31] and by an immunocytochemical method using antibodies against serotonin.[32–34]

The majority of small intestinal carcinoids that are formalin-fixed and paraffin-embedded, display formalin-induced fluorescence and a pristine argentaffin reaction, but some lack serotonin immunoreactivity. Furthermore, the number of argentaffin positive tumour cells usually exceeds that of serotonin-immunoreactive cells. In appendiceal carcinoid tumours, however, there is much better correlation.[35,36]

In foregut and hindgut carcinoids, serotonin-immunoreactivity is more frequent than a positive argentaffin reaction and formalin-induced fluorescence. Furthermore, when all are positive the majority of cells are serotin-immunoreactive.[37] The reason for this is not completely understood. The use of antibodies against serotonin seems to be a sensitive and useful method for visualizing normal endocrine cells, but the results when applied to tumours seem to be less reliable.

Peptide hormone content

During the last decade it has become evident that endocrine tumours may produce multiple hormones. This is also true for carcinoid tumours, in which a wide variety of peptide hormonal substances have recently been identified. However, the type of peptide varies with the topographic location of the carcinoids. Typical midgut carcinoids storing and secreting serotonin also frequently display substance P immunoreactivity[38] (Fig. 36.10). Serotonin and substance P are probably stored in the same tumour cells, as has been presumed for some of the normal mucosal enterochromaffin (EC) cells. The plasma concentration of substance P is elevated in most patients with midgut carcinoids. Chemical characterization of immunoreactive substance P in carcinoids by high pressure liquid chromatography shows it to be indistinguishable from synthetic undeca peptide substance P.[39] Recent

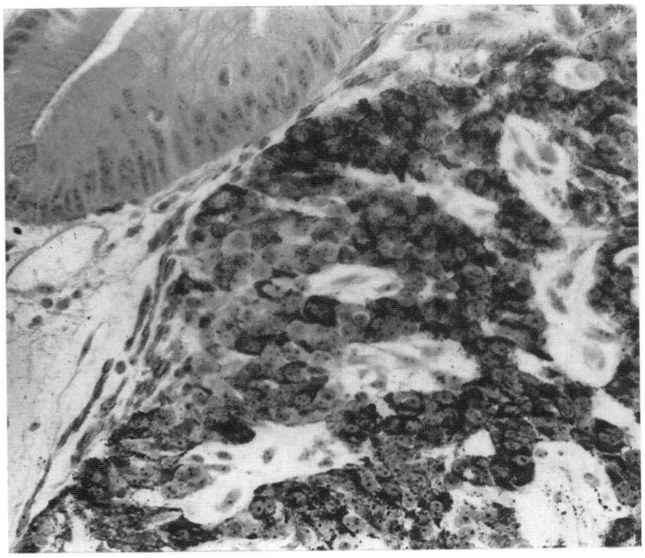

Fig. 36.9 Micrograph of a carcinoid tumour of the body of the stomach. The tumour cells are argyrophilic (dark cytoplasm) after staining with the Sevier-Munger argyrophil stain (×300)

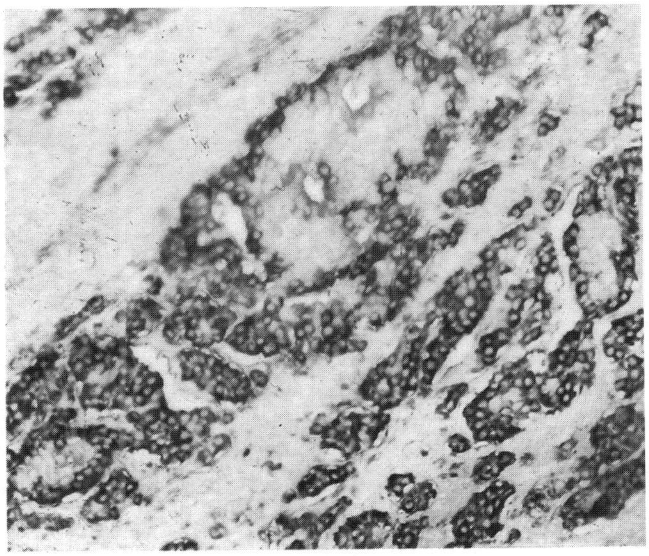

Fig. 36.10 Micrograph of a midgut carcinoid tumour displaying immunoreactivity — tumour cells with dark cytoplasmic staining — after application of a substance P antiserum. (Peroxidase-antiperoxidase (PAP) staining, ×188)

results indicate that substance P, which belongs to a group of structurally closely related peptides of the tachykinin family, is not the only substance of this family that is stored and secreted in carcinoids.[9,10] In addition to tachykinins, various peptides in minor cell populations can be detected immunocytohemically, e.g. gastrin, gastrin-releasing peptide, somatostatin and enkephalin.[40–47]

Rectal carcinoids show immunoreactivity mainly with polypeptide YY (PYY) glucagon/glicentin, pancreatic polypeptide and somatostatin antiserum, although other peptide hormones may also be present.[15,48–51] The tumours may display immunoreactivity with one or several hormone antisera, but sometimes lack identifiable hormonal substances. It is noteworthy that serotonin, which is stored in one of the most frequently found endocrine cell types in the human rectum, is only occasionally observed in rectal carcinoids and mostly in minor cell populations. The foregut carcinoids located in the antrum of the stomach and the duodenum most frequently store gastrin and somatostatin, but other hormonal substances have also been identified.[52,53] In the non-antral area of the stomach the ECL-cell tumours predominate. However, minor tumour cell populations with immunoreactivity to serotonin, pancreatic polypeptide and gastrin, for instance, may be found.

Neuron-specific enolase in carcinoids

In 1965 Moore and McGregor[54] reported that a protein, 14–3–2, appeared during development of the brain. Further studies revealed that it was located in neurons and it was renamed neuron-specific protein.[55] Later,[56] a new immunologically distinct form of enolase was described in rat brain and later still[57] three enolase isoenzymes, designated alpha/alpha, alpha/gamma and gamma/gamma were demonstrated. It was shown, further, that the concentration of the gamma/gamma-enolase form increased during development of the brain. Structural and immunological studies revealed that the gamma/gamma-enolase was identical to the 14–3–2 protein,[57–59] which was redesignated neuron-specific enolase (NSE). NSE was first considered to be located exclusively in central nervous system neurons but later it was also found in peripheral peptidergic endocrine cells.[59–61] Moreover, it has further been suggested that NSE is a specific marker for tumours derived from peptidergic endocrine cells.[62–66]

Carcinoid tumours of the small intestine as well as other carcinoids are stained with NSE antiserum. The intensity of the staining and the number of reactive cells vary between individual cases. NSE is a metabolic enzyme and is not related to the secretory granules. Application of silver staining and NSE antibodies on the same section reveals that the NSE immunoreactivity does not correlate with the argentaffin or agyrophil reaction.[67] The occurrence of NSE immunoreactivity in these tumours indicates their neuroendocrine differentiation and functional activity, while positive staining with the silver stains implies the presence of hormonal secretory granules. For identification of endocrine tumours with a low granule content, therefore, NSE immunocytochemistry would seem to be a more useful histological technique. However, caution is required when interpreting a positive NSE immunoreaction, since tumours that are generally considered to be non-endocrine may exhibit a positive reaction. Furthermore, NSE may be expressed in non-endocrine human cell lines. In general, endocrine tumour specimens and derived tumour cell lines contain more NSE than non-endocrine tumour specimens and cell lines, but some cultured haematopoietic cell lines have been shown to display NSE levels comparable to those found, for instance, in neuroblastoma and small-cell lung carcinoma cell lines. Consequently, NSE appears not to be exclusively expressed in endocrine tumour cells.[68]

Chromogranin in carcinoids

The chromogranins represent a family of acidic polypeptides constituting the major part of the soluble proteins in the secretory granules of many, but not all, endocrine cell types. Originally, the peptides were isolated from the chromaffin granules of the adrenal medulla.[69–72] One of the major compounds of the peptide family is chromogranin A, a molecule of 431 amino acids with the gene code on chromosome 14.[73–76] The physiological role of the chromogranins is unclear, but the concentration of chromogranin A is elevated in plasma in patients with a variety of tumours of endocrine type.[77] Polyclonal and monoclonal antibodies against chromogranin are now available and can be applied for immunocytochemical studies of endocrine tumours. Mostly, the chromogranin A immunoreactivity corresponds to the argyrophil reaction of Grimelius in endocrine cells and tumours. Thus, the peripheral A (glucagon) cells of the pancreatic islets, the EC cells and several other hormonal peptide-producing cells of the gastrointestinal mucosa are chromogranin A immunoreactive. Furthermore, foregut and midgut carcinoids are chromogranin positive, while rectal carcinoids are either reactive or unstained.

The obvious correspondence between chromogranin A immunoreactivity and the argyrophil reaction has led to the proposal that chromogranin has an affinity for silver ions and is one component responsible for argyrophilia. In accordance with this view, pure chromogranin has been found to correspond to an argyrophil reaction in vitro.[78–79] Both chromogranin A and the argyrophil reaction are useful adjuncts for demonstration of endocrine cells and tumours producing biogenic amines and/or peptide hormones. Since they do not give exactly identical staining results, they can be recommended to be applied in combination.

S-100 protein and carcinoids

S-100 protein is a highly acidic protein with a molecular weight of 21 000, which was first isolated from bovine brain extract by Moore.[80,81] The substance contains a number of molecular species, structurally built up of two polypeptide chains which associate as dimers with subunit compositions of alpha/alpha, alpha/beta and beta/beta respectively. Until recently, S-100 protein was regarded as a neural-specific protein occurring mainly in glial and Schwann cells, but it is now known to be also present in several non-neural cells, such as melanocytes and Langerhans cells of the skin, interdigitating reticulum cells of lymphoid tissues, chondrocytes, satellite cells of the adenohypophysis, and interstitial cells of the pineal body.[82–88]

Most appendiceal carcinoid tumours show S-100 protein immunoreactivity. The reaction occurs predominantly in slender cells with long cytoplasmic processes which are located mainly in the periphery of small tumour aggregates, but may also be seen between unreactive tumour cells (Fig. 36.11). Small intestinal and caecal carcinoid tumours and those of fore and hindgut are devoid of S-100 protein immunoreactive cells either within or in close contact with the tumour growth. The biphasic pattern, with endocrine differentiated tumour cells in close contact or intermingled with S-100 protein immunoreactive cells with long cytoplasmic extensions, seems to be a phenomenon exclusive to appendiceal tumours.[89,90] It is presumed that the S-100 protein immunoreactive cells are of Schwann cell origin, on the basis of their morphology but also because a Schwann cell component has been observed electron microscopically in carcinoid tumours of the appendix.[91]

Electron microscopy

Carcinoid tumours store peptide hormones and/or biogenic amines and, as seen ultrastructurally, these are stored in cytoplasmic secretory granules which, in comparison with other intracytoplasmic organelles, are relatively electron dense, abundant and are easily identified by their morphology. Often, the ultrastructure of an endocrine tumour will allow recognition of the hormone being produced. However, sometimes tumours may show granule structures which are atypical for the hormones they contain.[92–94]

The type of hormone being produced by a tumour may also be revealed at the light microscope level. Argentaffin areas of midgut carcinoids, for example, will exhibit a predominance of cells with both large and small pleomorphic granules of the EC cell type storing serotonin (Fig. 36.12). They all accumulate silver after staining both with the argentaffin and with the argyrophil methods.[95] Liver metastases from primary small intestinal carcinoid tumours also show an argentaffin reaction and possess an abundance of tumour cells with pleomorphic granules. In areas with argyrophilia, the granules are mainly round and covered with silver grains and do not react or are only very weakly stained with the argentaffin method. In addition, some tumour cells contain a mixture of round and pleomorphic granules. They are argyrophil and show variable staining characteristics with the argentaffin stain.

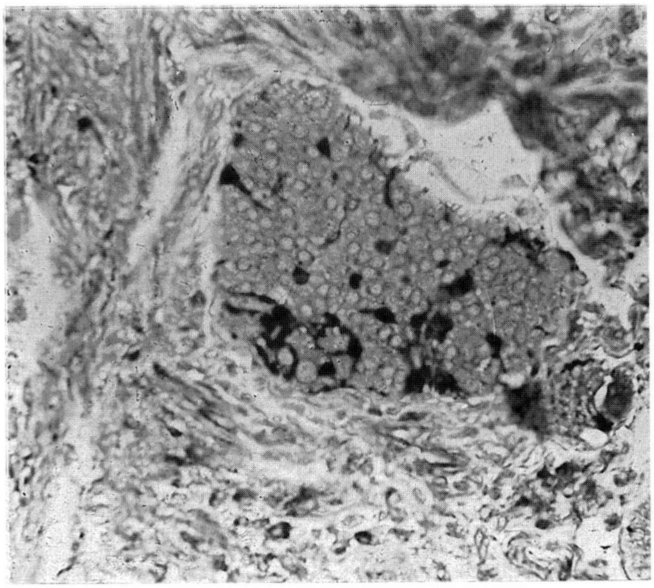

Fig. 36.11 Micrograph of a tumour aggregate of an appendiceal carcinoid. Intermingled with the tumour cells, S-100 protein (Schwann-like) cells with long cytoplasmic processes are seen. (PAP stain, S-100 protein antiserum, ×300)

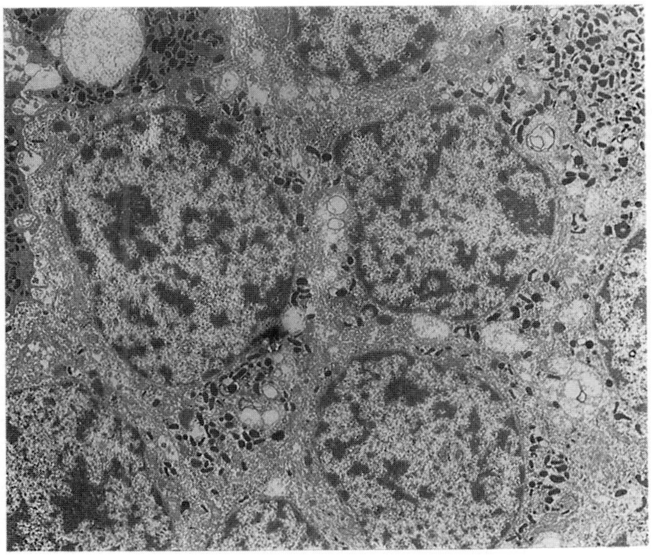

Fig. 36.12 Electron micrograph of classical carcinoid tumour of the small intestine. In the tumour cells pleomorphic hormonal secretory granules similar to those seen in the mucosal enterochromaffin (EC) cells are observed. (Osmium fixation, ×4875)

Electron microscopic examination of hindgut carcinoid tumours reveals pleomorphic secretory granules in the few tumours displaying argentaffinity, while those which are argyrophilic or unstained contain tumour cells with round granules.[18,92] Thus, the ultrastructure of carcinoids is correlated to their silver staining properties. This is further emphasized by the fact that Sevier-Munger argyrophil carcinoids of the body and fundus of the stomach often exhibit an ultrasturctural morphology comparable to that observed in the normal ECL cells of the gastric mucosa, which also are characteristically argyrophil with the Sevier-Munger stain[93] (Fig. 36.13).

Histogenesis of carcinoids

The histogenesis of intestinal carcinoid tumours has not yet been established. An origin in both epithelial and subepithelial endocrine cells or their more undifferentiated progenitors has been considered.[14,91,96] Preneoplastic alterations have been observed only in relation to gastric carcinoids, exclusively those located in the body and fundic area of the stomach. The occurrence of diffuse and/or nodular hyperplasia of mucosal endocrine cells preceding or in association with gastric carcinoids is well documented and it has been postulated that carcinoid tumours of the ECL cell type arise from proliferating ECL cells in the non-antral area of the glandular stomach.[28,97–100]

The intestinal carcinoids are presumed to be derived from the mucosal endocrine cells because, at light microscopy, a continuous growth has been observed from the mucosal endocrine cells to the carcinoid tumour.[101] Further, both mucosal epithelial cells and small intestinal and most rectal carcinoids express intermediate filament of cytokeratin type. The only exception are the appendiceal carcinoids, which mostly are cytokeratin negative. Appendiceal carcinoids alone contain elongated S-100 protein immunoreactive cells which are probably of Schwannic origin.[36,89,90] The morphology of appendiceal carcinoids is closely related to the population of endocrine cells in the lamina propria of the appendix. Both contain cells which are argentaffin positive, contain immunoreactive serotonin,[91,102–104] are ultrastructurally similar and are also accompanied by nerve fibres and Schwann cells. The subepithelial endocrine cells have thus been regarded as the origin of appendiceal carcinoids, or at least some of them.[89–91,96,102–104]

Pathogenesis of carcinoids

The pathogenesis of most carcinoids is not known. However, the carcinoid tumours that arise in the non-antral area of the stomach in atrophic gastritis appear to arise from a gastrin driven proliferation of mucosal ECL cells[99,100,105–107] (Fig. 36.14). Patients with the Zollinger-Ellison syndrome, who also have high serum gastrin levels, may develop non-antral gastric carcinoids of the ECL-cell type.[107,108] Moreover, omeprazole, which inhibits the proton pump and the acid secretion, also produces diffuse and nodular hyperplasia of the ECL cells in the non-antral area of the gastric mucosa in rats. This proliferation may continue and become an infiltrative carcinoid

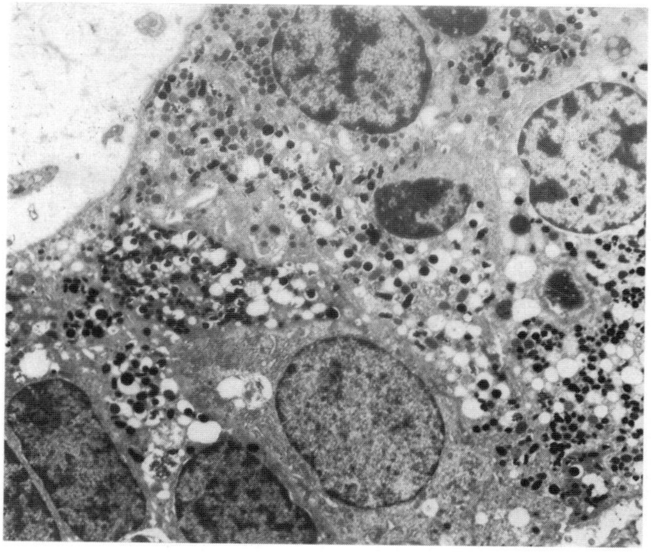

Fig. 36.13 Electron micrograph of a carcinoid tumour of the gastric body of the enterochromaffin-like (ECL) cell type. The hormonal secretory granules have a central electron dense core and an empty halo surrounded by a limiting membrane. (Osmium fixation, ×4875)

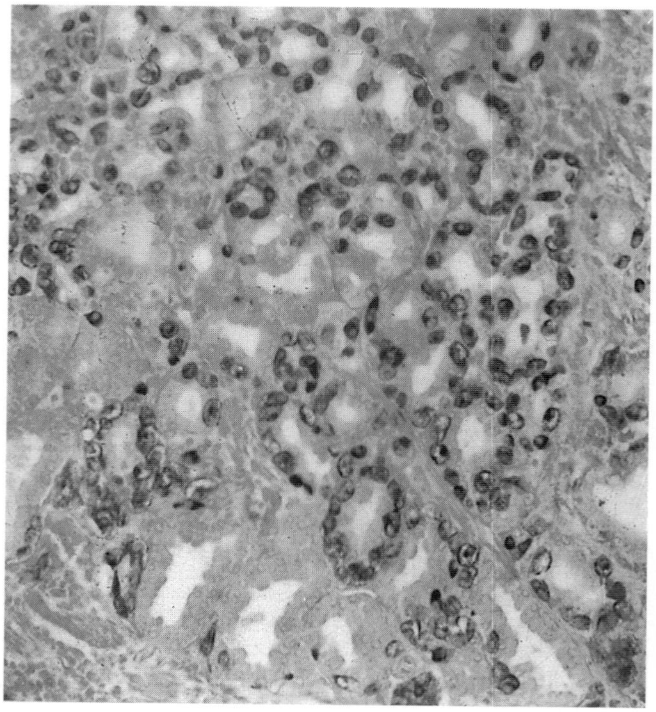

Fig. 36.14 Micrograph of mucosa of the gastric body with chronic atrophic gastritis and a marked proliferation of argyrophil endocrine cells, mainly in the basal area of the epithelial crypts. (Grimelius stain, ×340)

tumour when the substance is administered in large doses for a long period. The ECL cell hyperplasia is prevented by antrectomy prior to the drug administration, corroborating the stimulating effect of hypergastrinaemia on the ECL cells.[107]

It has also been observed that the mean nitrate concentration in gastric juice from fasting patients with atrophic gastritis and pernicious anaemia is nearly 50-fold greater than that in age-matched controls. Nitrate is essential for the formation of volatile nitrosamines, which possess carcinogenic properties, and it has been suggested that a high concentration of nitrosamines in the achlorhydric stomach may be an important factor in the development of gastric cancer.[109] It is possible that hypergastrinaemia promotes the development of gastric carcinoids by inducing proliferation of the endocrine cells of the mucosa, and that the tumour transformation is initated by the presence of high concentrations of carcinogenic nitrosamines in the achlorhydric stomach.[100] In rats, oral administration of the nitroso compound, N-methyl-N-nitroso-N-nitrosoguanidine, results in a carcinoid tumour in the fundic portion of the glandular stomach. The tumour cells display argentaffin and/or argyrophil staining properties and are ultrastructurally loaded with secretory granules of the endocrine type.[110] Thus, both hypergastrinaemia and carcinogenic nitrosamines are able to cause non-antral gastric carcinoids in experimental animals.

Since the incidence of both non-antral gastric carcinoids of the ECL-cell type and carcinoma of the stomach is increased in achlorhydria and pernicious anaemia, similarities in the pathogenetic mechanisms are possible.[4] It is worthy of mention in this context that atypical carcinoids occur in the stomach and that both morphologically and biologically they are borderline between carcinoids and carcinomas.[4–7]

Symptomatology

Carcinoid tumours of the appendix seldom give rise to clinical symptoms. They are mostly incidental findings in appendicectomy specimens. A carcinoid of the appendix may possibly obstruct the lumen and cause retention and the development of faecal stones, which may contribute to the initiation of an inflammatory reaction.

Carcinoids of the small intestine and caecum sometimes give rise to symptoms of intestinal obstruction or melaena and frequently diarrhoea. Indeed, preoperatively, they are often not distinguishable from adenocarcinoma. Rectal carcinoids may cause rectal bleeding, but are often observed by chance at endoscopy and the histopathological diagnosis is usually unexpected.[111]

In foregut carcinoids, the symptoms are almost invariably non-specific and consist of pain (33%), melaena (31%), haematemesis (24%), weight loss (21%), tiredness (21%), vomiting (19%) and diarrhoea (12%).[112]

However, carcinoids can cause a more specific clinical syndrome which may be present at the time of admission to hospital, or develop later as a result of tumour progression and metastases.

Carcinoid syndrome

The carcinoid syndrome is by far the most frequently observed clinical syndrome associated with gastrointestinal carcinoids. It occurs almost exclusively in patients with midgut carcinoids which have metastasized to the liver, although a few cases have been reported in association with gastric carcinoids and rarely a rectal carcinoid. The syndrome is characterized by attacks of flushing and wheezing or asthma-like attacks, diarrhoea, and right-sided heart failure due to stenosis of the bicuspid and pulmonary valves. Several additional features such as pellagra-like skin lesions, peptic ulcers and malabsorption are also sometimes present.[113–116]

Various active biological substances, such as gastrin, substance P, calcitonin, glucagon, somatostatin, gastrin-releasing peptide and several biogenic amines have been identified in the tumours and some of them are considered to contribute to the clinical symptoms.[40–47,117,118] However, since the carcinoid syndrome occurs almost exclusively in association with malignant midgut carcinoids, serotonin is probably of most importance. Recently, serum levels of serotonin and sutstance P were assayed in patients with midgut carcinoid tumours by Ahlman et al 1985.[119] Following provocation with either intravenous pentagastrin or calcium infusion they concluded, among other things, that serotonin may be responsible for the gastrointestinal symptoms in carcinoid patients, but that it does not seem to play any role in flushing. Further, they found that substance P may possibly contribute to the mediation of flushing, but that it cannot be the only agent responsible.

Antisera raised against the tachykinins eledoisin and kassinin have been used to measure their serum levels by radioimmunoassay in patients with malignant carcinoid tumours.[9,10] Elevated concentrations were found in 75% of the carcinoid patients but not in healthy controls or patients with endocrine pancreatic tumours. The antisera did not cross-react with substance P. Exchange chromatography of plasma samples and tumour tissue extracts indicated the presence of several molecular forms of the tachykinin family and also components different from those of all currently known mammalian tachykinins. Although all the biologically active substances contributing to the carcinoid syndrome are not completely known, it must be emphasized that hormone secretion from the tumour tissue plays a major role in the development of the syndrome and that the plasma concentrations of several hormonal peptides in combination with serotonin are elevated in these patients.

ECL-OMA syndrome

There is a distinct clinicopathological syndrome in which carcinoid tumours of the body and fundus of the stomach are involved.[106,107] By analogy with terminology used for syndromes caused by other hormone-producing endocrine tumours of the gastrointestinal canal, this syndrome may be called the ECL-oma syndrome, since the gastric tumours involved are mainly of ECL cell type. The features of the ECL-oma syndrome are: gastric carcinoid tumours, often multiple and located in the body and fundus of the stomach, atrophic gastritis, achlorhydria and hypergastrinaemia, often in association with pernicious anaemia. Atrophic gastritis of the acid-secreting area of the stomach results in parietal cell loss and achlorhydria. This causes increased secretion of gastrin, due to inhibition of a negative acid feedback machanism. Hyperplasia of the antral G cells is often observed[120,121] and the parietal cell loss leads to a decrease in the production of intrinsic factor, resulting in vitamin B_{12} malabsorption which promotes pernicious anaemia.

A diffuse or nodular hyperplasia of the ECL cells in the gastric body mucosa is frequently seen before or in association with the growth of an ECL-cell carcinoid.[28,97–100] The ECL-cell hyperplasia is probably directly due to hypergastrinaemia.[26,27,105,122,123]

A comprehensive review of the ECL-oma syndrome has been published by Carney et al 1983.[106] In a total of 61 cases 69% of patients presented with multiple carcinoids and 49% were associated with mucosal argyrophil endocrine cell hyperplasia. Concomitant pernicious anaemia was observed in 56% and hypergastrinaemia was found in all patients in whom serum gastrin measurements were performed.

In two endoscopic studies of a large number of patients with pernicious anaemia, gastric carcinoids were found in 1–4%;[124,125] Thus they are at an increased risk of developing not only carcinoma of the stomach but also gastric carcinoids.[125–127]

Zollinger-Ellison syndrome

Zollinger-Ellison syndrome was initially characterized by the triad of peptic ulcer disease, gastric acid hypersecretion and the presence of non-beta islet cell tumours of the pancreas. Patients have elevated levels of serum gastrin which is secreted by an endocrine tumour in most cases.[128–131] However, the tumour may occur outside the pancreas, especially the distal part of the duodenum, and a few cases with a primary tumour in the stomach have been described.[40,132–134]

Gastrinomas display the same morphological features as foregut carcinoids, and they can only be distinguished from them by the detection of intracellular gastrin. Thus, gastrinomas can be regarded as a specialized subtype of carcinoids. Indeed, ordinary carcinoids may contain gastrin-immunoreactive cells, and peptic ulcer disease appears as a minor feature of the carcinoid syndrome. This is possibly due to secretion of gastrin or a gastrin-releasing peptide from the carcinoid tumour.[45,46]

Somatostatinoma syndrome

The clinical symptoms in the somatostatinoma syndrome comprise diabetes mellitus, diarrhoea, steatorrhoea, hypo- or achlorhydria, weight loss and anaemia. All these features are explained by hypersecretion of somatostatin.[135–138] The syndrome is rare and although usually associated with pancreatic tumours, a few somatostatinomas are located in the duodenum.[40,139] They show the same morphology as other foregut carcinoids. Owing to their hormone content, they display no or very few argyrophil cells with the Grimelius technique, but are argyrophil positive with the Hellerstrom-Hellman stain.[137]

Although there are few carcinoids in which somatostatin-containing cells are in the majority, they occur as minor cell populations relatively frequently in other gastrointestinal carcinoids.[43,140]

Cushing's syndrome

The secretion of ACTH by carcinoid tumours sufficient to cause Cushing's syndrome is extremely rare and only a few cases are documented in the literature. Nevertheless, they are testimony to the enormous variety of hormones that carcinoids may synthesize and secrete.[141,142]

Carcinoid tumour metastases

Patients with carcinoid tumours may have liver metastases at the time of presentation. Even if these can be recognized as being of endocrine type, it is frequently difficult to determine the topographic location of the primary.

A positive Grimelius argyrophil reaction will be obtained in most carcinoids irrespective of their hormone content. The argentaffin reaction of Masson, on the other hand, is relatively specific for carcinoid tumours with a content of serotonin, a characteristic of midgut carcinoids. On occasions, therefore, the silver-staining properties of carcinoid metastases are of value in the identification of site of the primary tumour.[19]

Survival and prognosis

Carcinoid tumours are biologically malignant, they infiltrate locally and give rise to metastases. However, they are considerably slower growing than gastrointestinal adenocarcinomas, and the prognosis and survival are much more favourable. In exception, carcinoid tumours of the appendix, although infiltrative, are almost invariably clinically benign, and metastases from these tumours are very uncommon.

The frequency of metastases at the time of diagnosis and surgery is related to the diameter of the primary tumour. Gastric carcinoids with a mean diameter of 1.8 cm will be associated with metastases in 15%. In comparison, in atypical gastric carcinoids with a mean diameter of 5 cm, about 80% exhibited metastatic spread at the time of surgery.[4] Small intestinal carcinoids with a mean diameter of less than 1 cm metastasize to the liver in 22% of patients, while tumours larger than 1 cm metastasize in 58%.[3] The figures are approximately similar for hindgut carcinoids.

In a study of patients with gastric carcinoids followed up for a period of 5 years or longer, 80% were still alive and symptom-free, whereas in five patients with atypical tumours followed up for the same length of time, only 20% were alive and free from recurrence.[112] For midgut tumours, excluding appendiceal carcinoids, the average 5 year survival is 53% and in patients with liver metastases at the time of diganosis the five year survival is 43%. When no metastases are present, the survival is 80%.[3]

REFERENCES

1. Williams ED, Sandler M. The classification of carcinoid tumours. Lancet 1963; 1: 238–239.
2. The Cancer Registry of the National Board of Health and Welfare. Cancer Incidence in Sweden 1959–1965. Stockholm 1971: pp 19–25.
3. Martensson H, Nobin A, Sundler F. Carcinoid tumours in the gastrointestinal tract — An analysis of 156 cases. Acta Chir Scand 1983; 149: 607–616.
4. Wilander E, El-Salhy M, Pitanen P. Histopathology of gastric carcinoids: a survey of 42 cases. Histopathology 1984; 8: 183–193.
5. Chejfec G, Gould VE. Malignant gastric neuroendocrinomas. Ultrastructural and biochemical characterization of their secretory activity. Human Pathol 1977; 8: 433–440.
6. Rogers LW, Murphy RC. Gastric carcinoid and gastric carcinoma. Morphologic correlates of survival. Am J Surg Pathol 1979; 3: 195–202.
7. Sweeney EC, McDonnell L. Atypical gastric carcinoids. Histopathology 1980; 4: 215–224.
8. Nilsson J, von Euler AM, Dalsgaard C-J. Stimulation of connective tissue cell growth by substance P and substance K. Nature 1985; 315: 61–63.
9. Norheim I, Theodorsson-Norheim E, Brodin E, Oberg K, Lundqvist G, Rosell S. Antisera against eledoisin and kassinin detect elevated levels of immunoreactive material in plasma and tumour tissue from patients with carcinoid tumours. Reg Pept 1984; 9: 245–257.
10. Theodorsson-Norheim E, Norheim I, Oberg K, Brodin E, Lundberg JM, Tatemoto K, Lindgren PG. Neuro-peptide K: a major tachykinin in plasma and tumour tissues from carcinoid patients. Biochem Biophys Res Commun 1985; 131: 77–83.
11. Abt A, Carter SL. Goblet cell carcinoid of the appendix. An ultrastructural and histochemical study. Arch Pathol Lab Med 1976; 100: 301–306.
12. Chen V, Qizilbash AH. Goblet cell carcinoid tumour of the appendix. Report of five cases and review of the literature. Arch Pathol Lab Med 1979; 103: 180–182.
13. Warner TFCS, Seo IS. Goblet cell carcinoid of appendix. Ultrastructural features and histogenic aspects. Cancer 1979; 44: 1700–1706.
14. Gosset A, Masson P. Tumeurs endocrines de l'appendice. Presse Med 1914; 22: 237–240.
15. Barter R, Pearse AGE. Detection of 5-hydroxy-tryptamine in mammalian enterochromaffin cells. Nature 1953; 171: 810.
16. Wilander E, Portela-Gomes G, Grimelius L, Westermark P. Argentaffin and argyrophil reaction of human gastrointestinal carcinoids. Gastroenterol 1977; 73: 733–736.
17. Lundqvist M, Wilander E. Majority and minority cell populations in small intestinal carcinoids. Acta Pathol Microbiol Immunol Scand (A) 1982; 90: 317–321.
18. Wilander E, Portela-Gomes G, Grimelius L, Lundqvist G, Skoog V. Enteroglucagon and substance P-like immunoreactivity in argentaffin and argyrophil rectal carcinoids. Virchows Arch (B) 1977; 25: 117–124.
19. Lindgren PG, Lundqvist M, Norheim I, Wilander E, Oberg K. Silver stains and immunocytochemical analysis with monoclonal serotonin antibodies for liver metastases of endocrine tumours. A study on percutaneous biopsy specimens. Am J Surg 1984; 148: 353–356.
20. Grimelius L. A silver nitrate stain for A_2-cells of human pancreatic islets. Acta Soc Med Upsal 1968; 73: 243–270.
21. Grimelius L, Wilander E. Silver stains in the study of endocrine cells of the gut and pancreas. Invest Cell Pathol 1980; 3: 3–12.
22. Wilander E, El-Salhy M, Lundqvist M. Argyrophil reaction in rectal carcinoids. Acta Pathol Microbiol Immunol Scand (A) 1983; 91: 85–87.
23. Sevier A, Munger B. A silver method for paraffin sections of neural tissue. J Neuropathol Exp Neurol 1965; 24: 130–135.
24. Solcia A, Capella C, Vassallo G, Buffa R. Endocrine cells of the stomach and pancreas in states of gastric hypersecretion. Rendic Gastroenterol 1970; 2: 147–158.
25. Vassallo G, Capella C, Solcia E. Endocrine cells of the human gastric mucosa. Z Zellforsch 1971; 118: 49–67.
26. Rubin W. A fine structural characterization of the proliferated endocrine cells in atrophic gastric mucosa. Am J Pathol 1973; 70: 109–118.
27. Bordi C, Costa A, Missale G. ECL cell proliferation and gastrin levels. Gastroenterol 1975; 68: 205–206.
28. Black WC, Haffner HE. Diffuse hyperplasia of gastric argyrophil cells and multiple carcinoid tumours. Cancer 1968; 21: 1080–1099.
29. Lembeck F. 5-hydroxytryptamine in carcinoid tumour. Nature 1953; 172: 910–911.
30. Masson P. La glande endocrine de l'intestine chez l'homme. CR Acad Sci Paris 1914; 15: 59–61.
31. Falck B, Hillarp N-A, Thieme G, Torp AV. Fluorescence of catecholamines and related compounds condensed with formaldehyde. J Histochem Cytochem 1962; 10: 348–354.
32. Facer P, Polak JM, Jaffe BM, Pearse AGE. Immuno-cytochemical demonstration of 5-hydroxytryptamine in gastrointestinal endocrine cells. Histochem J 1979; 11: 117–121.
33. Consolazione A, Milstein C, Wright B, Cuello AC. Immunocytochemical detection of serotonin with monoclonal antibodies. J Histochem Cytochem 1981; 29: 1425–1430.
34. Cuello AC. Serotonin immunoreactivity in carcinoid tumours demonstrated with a monoclonal antibody. Lancet 1982; 1: 771–773.
35. Lundqvist M, Wilander E. Small intestinal chromaffin cells and carcinoid tumours — a study with silver stains, formalin-induced fluorescence and monoclonal antibodies to serotonin. Histochem J 1984; 16: 1247–1256.
36. Wilander E, Lundqvist M, Movin T. S-100 protein in carcinoid tumours of the appendix. Acta Neuropathol 1985; 66: 306–310.
37. Wilander E, Lundqvist M, El-Salhy M. Serotonin in fore-gut carcinoids. A survey of 60 cases with regard to silver stains, formalin-induced fluorescence and serotonin immunocytochemistry. J Pathol 1985; 145: 251–258.
38. Alumets J, Hakanson R, Ingemansson S, Sundler F. Substance P

and 5-HT in granules isolated from an intestinal argentaffin carcinoid. Histochemistry 1977; 52: 217–222.
39. Emson PC, Gilbert RFT, Martensson H, Nobin A. Elevated concentrations of substance P and 5-HT in patients with carcinoid tumours. Cancer 1984; 54: 715–718.
40. Alumets J, Ekelund G, Hakanson R, Ljungberg O, Ljungqvist U, Sundler F, Tibblin S. Jejunal endocrine tumour composed of somatostain and gastrin cells and associated with duodenal ulcer disease. Virchows Arch (A) 1978; 378: 17–22.
41. Wilander E, Grimelius L, Portela-Gomes G, Lundqvist G, Skoog V, Westermark P. Substance P and enteroglucagon-like immunoreactivity in argentaffin and argyrophil mid-gut carcinoid tumours. Scand J Gastroenterol 1979; 14 (suppl 53): 19–25.
42. Dayal Y, O'Briain DS, Wolfe HJ, Reichlin S. Carcinoid tumours: A comparison of their immunocytochemical hormonal profile with morphological and histochemical characteristics. Lab Invest 1980; 42: 1111.
43. Dayal Y, O'Briain DS, DeLellis RA, Wolfe HJ. Carcinoid tumours in gastrointestinal and extra intestinal sites. A comparative study of peptide hormonal profile. Reg Peptides 1980; 1: 22.
44. Goedert M, Otten U, Suda K, et al. Dopamine, norepinephrine and serotonin production by an intestinal carcinoid tumour. Cancer 1980; 45: 104–107.
45. Wilander E, El-Salhy M. Immunocytochemical staining of mid-gut carcinoid tumours with sequence specific gastrin antisera. Acta Pathol Microbiol Immunol Scand (A) 1981; 89: 247–250.
46. Bostwich DG, Roth KA, Barchas ID, Bensch KG. Gastrin-releasing peptide immunoreactivity in intestinal carcinoids. Am J Clin Pathol 1984; 82: 428–431.
47. Dayal Y, Lin HD, Tallberg K, Reichlin S, DeLellis RA, Wolfe HJ. Immunocytochemical demonstration of growth hormone-releasing factor in gastrointestinal and pancreatic endocrine tumours. Am J Clin Pathol 1985; 85: 13–20.
48. Fiocca R, Capella C, Buffa R, et al. Glucagon-like, glicentin-like and pancreatic polypeptide-like immunoreactivities in rectal carcinoids and related colorectal cells. Am J Pathol 1980; 100: 81–92.
49. Taxy JB, Mendelsohn G, Gupta PK. Carcinoid tumours of the rectum. Silver reactions, fluorescence, and serotonin content of the cytoplasmic granules. Am J Clin Pathol 1980; 74: 791–795.
50. O'Briain DS, Dayal Y, DeLellis RA, Tischler AS, Bendron R, Wolfe HJ. Rectal carcinoids as tumours of the hindgut endocrine cells. A morphological and immunohistochemical analysis. Am J Surg Pathol 1982; 6: 131–142.
51. Iwafuchi M, Watanabe H, Ishihara N, Shimoda T, Iwashita A, Ito S. Peptide YY immunoreactive cells in gastrointestinal carcinoids. Immunohistochemical and ultrastructural studies of 60 tumors. Human Pathol 1986; 17: 291–296.
52. Wilander E, Grimelius L, Lundqvist G, Skoog V. Polypeptide hormones in argentaffin and argyrophil gastroduodenal endocrine tumours. Am J Pathol 1979; 96: 519–530.
53. Dayal Y. Endocrine cells of the gut and their neoplasms. In: Pathology of the colon, small intestine and anus. Norris HT, ed. Edinburgh: Churchill-Livingstone 1983: pp 267–302.
54. Moore BW, McGregor D. Chromatographic and electro-phoretic fractionation of soluble proteins of brain and liver. J Biol Chem 1965; 240: 1647–1653.
55. Pickel VM, Reis DJ, Marangos PJ, Zomzely-Neurath C. Immunocytochemical localization of nervous system specific protein (NSP-R) in rat brain. Brain Res 1976; 105: 184–187.
56. Rider CC, Taylor CB. Enolase isoenzymes in rat tissues. Electrophoretic, chromatographic, immunological and kinetic properties. Biochim biophys Acta 1974; 365: 285–300.
57. Fletcher L, Rider CC, Taylor CB. Enolase isoenzymes. Chromatographic and immunological characteristics of rat brain enolase. Biochim biophys Acta 1976; 452: 245–252.
58. Bock E. Demonstration of enolase activity connected to the brain-specific protein 14–3–2. Scand J Immunol 1975; 4 (suppl 2): 31–36.
59. Schmechel D, Marangos PJ, Brightman M. Neuron-specific enolase is a molecular marker for peripheral and central neuroendocrine cells. Nature 1978; 276: 834–836.
60. Schmechel DE, Marangos PJ, Zis AP, Brightman MW, Goodwin FK. Brain enolase as a specific marker of neuronal and glial cells. Science 1978; 199: 313–315.
61. Facer P, Polak JM, Marangos PJ, Pearse AGE. Immunohistochemical localization of neuron specific enolase (NSE) in the gastro-intestinal tract. Proc Microsc Soc 1980; 15: 113–114.
62. Tapia FJ, Polak JM, Barbosa AJA, Bloom SR, Marangos PJ, Dermody C, Pearse AGE. Neuron-specific enolase is produced by neuroendocrine tumours. Lancet 1981; 1: 808–811.
63. Marangos PJ, Polak JM, Pearse AGE. Neuron specific enolase. A probe for neurons and neuroendocrine cells. TINS 1982; 5: 193–196.
64. Printz RA, Bermes EW, Kinnal JR, Marangos PJ. Serum markers for pancreatic islet cell and intestinal carcinoid tumours: A comparison of neuron-specific enolase beta-human chorionic gonadotropin and pancreatic polypeptide. Surgery 1983; 94: 101–123.
65. Printz RA, Marangos PJ. Serum neuron-specific enolase: A serum marker for nonfunctioning pancreatic islet cell carcinoma Am J Surg 1983; 145: 77–81.
66. Pahlman S, Esscher T, Bergh J, Steinholz L, Nou E, Nilsson K. Neuron-specific enolase as a marker for neuroblastoma and small-cell carcinoma of the lung. Tumour Biol 1984; 5: 119–126.
67. Lundqvist M, Wilander E, Esscher T, Pahlman S. Neuron-specific enolase in mucosal endocrine cells and carcinoid tumours of the small intestine: a comparative study with neuron-specific enolase immunocytochemistry and silver stains. Histochem J 1985; 17: 323–331.
68. Esscher T. Neuron-specific enolase and its clinical use as a diagnostic marker for neuroblastoma and small cell carcinoma of the lung. Acta Universitatis Upsaliensis. Abstracts of Uppsala Dissertations from the Faculty of Medicine. No. 530, 1985.
69. Smith AD, Winkler H. Purification and properties of an acidic protein from chromaffin granules of bovine adrenal medulla. Biochem J 1967; 103: 483–492.
70. Blaschko H, Comline RS, Schneider FH, Silver M, Smith AD. Secretion of a chromaffin granule protein, chromogranin, from the adrenal gland after splanchnic stimulation. Nature 1983; 215: 58–59.
71. Fischer-Colbrie R, Lassmann H, Hagn C, Winkler H. Immunological studies on the distribution of chromogranin A and B in endocrine and nervous tissues. Neuroscience 1985; 16: 547–555.
72. O'Connor DT, Frigon FP, Sokoloff RF. Human chromogranin A: Purification and characterization from catecholamine storage vesicles of pheochromocytoma. Hypertension 1983; 6: 2–12.
73. Deftos LJ, Murray SS, Burton DW, Parmer RJ, O'Connor DT. A cloned chromogranin A (CgA) cDNA detects a 2.3 Kb mRNA in diverse neuroendocrine tissues. BBRC 1986; 137: 418–423.
74. Icangelo A, Affolter H-U, Eiden LE, Herbert E, Grimes M. Bovine chromogranin A. Sequence and distribution of its messenger RNA in endocrine tissues. Nature 1986; 323: 82–84.
75. Benedum UM, Baeerle PA, Koneck DS et al. The primary structure of bovine chromogranin A. EMBO J 1987; 142: 141–146.
76. Murray SS, Deaven LL, Burton DW, O'Connor DT, Mellon PL, Deftos LJ. The gene for human chromogranin A (CgA) is located on chromosome 14. Biochem Biophys Res Commun 1987; 142: 141–146.
77. O'Connor DT, Deftos LJ. Secretion of chromogranin A by peptide producing endocrine neoplasms. N Engl J Med 1986; 314: 1145–1151.
78. Wilson BS, Lloyd RV. Detection of chromogranin in neuro-endocrine cells with a monoclonal antibody. Am J Pathol 1984; 115: 458–468.
79. Rindi G, Buffa R, Sessa F, Tortora O, Solcia E. Chromogranin A, B and C immunoreactivities of mammalian endocrine cells. Distribution, distinction from costored hormones/prohormones and relationship with the argyrophil component of secretory granules. Histochemistry 1986; 85: 19–28.
80. Moore BW. A soluble protein characteristic of the nervous system. Biochem Biophys Res Commun 1965; 19: 739–744.

81. Moore BW, Perez VJ. Specific acidic proteins of the nervous system. In: Carlson FD, ed. Physiological and biochemical aspects of nervous integration. Inglewood Cliffs NJ: Prentice Hall, 1968: pp 343–360.
82. Perez VJ, Olney JW, Cicero TJ, Moore BW, Bahn BA. Wallerian degeneration in rabbit optic nerve: cellular localization in the central nervous system of the S-100 and 1432 proteins. J Neurochem 1970; 17: 511–519.
83. Matus A, Mughal S. Immunohistochemical localization of S100 protein in brain. Nature 1975; 258: 746–748.
84. Ludwin SK, Kosek JC, Eng LF. The topographic distribution of S-100 and GFA proteins in the adult rat brain: An immunohistochemical study using horseradish peroxidase-labelled antibodies. J Comp Neurol 1976; 165: 197–208.
85. Cocchia D, Michetti F. S-100 antigen in satellite cells of the adrenal medulla and the superior cervical ganglion of the rat. Cell Tissue Res 1981; 215: 103–112.
86. Konda H, Iwanaga T, Nakajima T. Immunocytochemical study on the localization of neuronspecific enolase and S-100 protein in the carotid body of rats. Cell Tissue Res 1982; 227: 291–295.
87. Stefansson K, Wollmann RL, Moore BW. Distribution of S-100 protein outside the central nervous system. Brain Res 1982; 234: 309–317.
88. Kahn HJ, Marks A, Thom H, Baumal R. Role of antibody to S-100 protein in diagnostic pathology. Am J Clin Pathol 1983; 79: 341–347.
89. Toshiaki S, Takamori A, Kazuo H. S-100 protein immunoreactive cells in the lamina propria and carcinoid tumours of the appendix. Biomed Res 1984; 5: 157–164.
90. Lundqvist M, Wilander E. Subepithelial neuroendocrine cells and carcinoid tumours of the human small intestine and appendix. A comparative immunohistochemical study with regard to serotonin, neuron-specific enolase and S-100 protein reactivity. J Pathol 1986; 148: 141–147.
91. Aubock L, Hofler H. Extraepithelial intraneural endocrine cells as starting points for gastro-intestinal carcinoids. Virchows Arch (A) 1983; 401: 17–23.
92. Black WC III. Enterochromaffin cell types and corresponding carcinoid tumours. Lab Invest 1968; 19: 473–486.
93. Solcia E, Capella C, Buffa R, Usellini L, Frigerio B, Fontana P. Endocrine cells of the gastrointestinal tract and related tumours. In: Joachim H L, ed. Pathology Annual. New York: Raven Press, 1979: 163–204.
94. Capella C, Polak JM, Timson CM, Frigerio B, Solcia E. Gastric carcinoids of argyrophil ECL cells. Ultrastruct Pathol 1980; 1: 411–418.
95. Lundqvist M, Wilander E. Majority and minority cell populations in small intestinal carcinoids. Acta Pathol Microbiol Immunol Scand (A) 1982; 90: 317–321.
96. Masson P. Carcinoids (argentaffin-cell tumours) and nerve hyperplasia of the appendicular mucosa. Am J Pathol 1928; 4: 181–212.
97. Capella C, Solcia E, Snell CK. Ultrastructure of endocrine cells and argyrophil carcinoids of the stomach of Praomys (Mastomys) natalensis. J Natl Cancer Inst 1973; 50: 1471–1485.
98. Soga J, Kohro T, Tazawa K, et al. Argyrophil cell microneoplasia in Mastomys' stomach — an observation on early carcinoid formation. J Natl Cancer Inst 1975; 55: 1001–1006.
99. Hodges JR, Isaacson P, Wright R. Diffuse entero-chromaffin-like (ECL) cell hyperplasia and multiple gastric carcinoids: a complication of pernicious anaemia. Gut 1981; 22: 237–241.
100. Wilander E. Achylia and the development of gastric carcinoids. Virchows Arch (A) 1981; 394: 151–160.
101. Lundqvist M, Wilander E. A study of the histopathogenesis of carcinoid tumours of the small intestine and appendix. Cancer 1987; 60: 201–206.
102. Rode J, Dhillon AP, Papadaki L, Griffith D. Neuro-secretory cells of the lamina propria of the appendix and their possible relationship to carcinoids. Histopathology 1982; 6: 69–70.
103. Rode J, Dhillon AP, Papadaki L. Serotonin-immuno-reactive cells in the lamina propria plexus of the appendix. Hum Pathol 1983; 14: 464–469.
104. Millikin PD. Extraepithelial enterochromaffin cells and Schwann cells in the human appendix. Arch Pathol Lab Med 1983; 107: 189–194.
105. Larsson L-I, Rehfeld J, Stockbrugger R, et al. Mixed endocrine gastric tumours associated with hypergastrinaemia of antral origin. Am J Pathol 1978; 93: 53–68.
106. Carney JA, Go VLW, Fairbansk VF, Moore SB, Alport EC, Nora FE. The syndrome of gastric argyrophil carcinoid tumours and nonantral gastric atrophy. Ann Intern Med 1983; 99: 761–766.
107. Harvey RF, Bradshaw MJ , Davidsson CM, Wilkinson SP, Davies PS. Multifocal gastric carcinoid tumours, achlorhydria and hypergastrinaemia. Lancet 1985; I: 951–953.
108. Bordi L, Cocconi G, Togni R, Vezzadini P, Missale G. Gastric endocrine cell proliferation in association with the Zollinger-Ellison syndrome. Arch Pathol 1974; 98: 274–279.
109. Ruddell WS, Bone S, Hill MJ, Walters CL. Patho-genesis of gastric cancer in pernicious anaemia. Lancet 1978; I: 521–523.
110. Tahara E, Ito H, Nakagami K, Shimamato F. Induction of carcinoids in the glandular stomach of rats by N-methyl-N-nitro-N-nitrosoguanidine. J Cancer Res Clin Oncol 1981; 100: 1–12.
111. Marks C. Carcinoid tumours. A clinicopathologic study. Boston: GK Hall, 1979.
112. Johansson H, Wilander E. A clinical study of 30 gastric carcinoids. Upsala J Med Sci 1982; 87: 135–142.
113. Pernow B, Waldenstrom J. Paroxysmal flushing and other symptoms caused by 5-hydroxytryptamine and histamine in patients with malignant tumours. Lancet 1954; II: 951
114. Thorson A, Bjork G, Bjorkmann G, Waldenstrom J. Malignant carcinoid of small intestine with metastases to liver, valvular disease of the right side of the heart (pulmonary stenosis and tricuspid regurgitation without septal defects), peripheral vasomotor symptoms, bronchoconstriction and an unusual type of cyanosis. Am Heart J 1954; 44: 795–817.
115. Thorson A. Studies on carcinoid disease. Acta Med Scand 1958; (suppl 334): 1–132.
116. Grahame-Smith DG. The carcinoid syndrome. London: Heinemann, 1972: pp 76–82.
117. Sandler M, Snow PJD. An atypical carcinoid tumour secreting 5-hydroxytryptophan. Lancet 1958; I: 137–139.
118. Oates IA, Butler TC. Pharmacological and endocrine aspects of carcinoid syndrome. Adv Pharmacol Chemother 1967; 5: 109–128.
119. Ahlman H, Dahlstrom A, Gronstad K, Tisell LE, Oberg K, Zinner MJ, Jaffe BM. The pentagastrin test in the diagnosis of the carcinoid syndrome. Blockade of gastrointestinal symptoms by Ketanserin. Ann Surg 1985; 201: 81–86.
120. Polak JM, Hoffbrand AV, Reed PI, Bloom S, Pearse AGE. Quantitative and qualitative studies of antral and fundic G cells in pernicious anaemia. Scand J Gastro-enterol 1973; 8: 361–367.
121. McGuigan JE, Trudeau WL. Serum gastrin concentrations in pernicious anaemia. N Engl J Med 1970; 282: 358–361.
122. Wilander E. Achylia, pernicious anaemia, ECL cells and gastric carcinoids. Virchows Arch (A) 1980; 387: 371–373.
123. Hodges JR, Isaacson P, Wright R. Diffuse enterochromaffin-like (ECL) cell hyperplasia and multiple gastric carcinoids: a complication of pernicious anaemia. Gut 1981; 22: 237–241.
124. Stockbrugger RW, Menon GG, Beilby JOW, Mason RR, Cotton PB. Gastroscopic screening in 80 patients with pernicious anaemia. Gut 1983; 24: 1141–1147.
125. Borch K, Renvall H, Liedberg G. Gastric endocrine cell hyperplasia and carcinoid tumours in pernicious anaemia. Gastroenterology 1985; 88: 638–648.
126. Borch K, Liedberg G. Prevalence and incidence of pernicious anaemia. An evaluation for gastric screening. Scand J Gastroenterol 1984; 19: 159–160.
127. Borch K. Intrinsic factor deficiency gastritis (Pernicious anaemia). A study on cost and benefit of gastric screening and on possible mechanisms and risk-factors on gastric neoplasia development. Linkoping University Medical Dissertations No. 213, 1985.
128. Zollinger RM, Ellison EM. Primary peptic ulceration of the jejunum associated with islet cell tumours of the pancreas. Ann Surg 1955; 142: 709–728.

129. Zollinger RM, Coleman DW. The influences of pancreatic tumours of the stomach. Springfield: Charles C Thomas 1974; pp 1–181.
130. Creutzfeldt W, Arnold R, Creutzfeldt C, Track NS. Pathomorphologic, biochemical and diagnostic aspects of gastrinomas (Zollinger-Ellison syndrome). Human Pathol 1975; 6: 47–76.
131. Walsh JH, Grossman MI. Gastrin. N Engl J Med 1975; 292: 1324–1332, 1377–1384.
132. Hoffman JE, Fox PS, Wilson SD. Duodenal wall tumour and the Zollinger-Ellison syndrome. Arch Surg 1973; 107: 334–339.
133. Roystone CMS, Brew DSJ, Garnham JR, Stagg BH, Polak JM. The Zollinger-Ellison syndrome due to an infiltrating tumour of the stomach. Gut 1972; 13: 638–642.
134. Larsson L-I, Ljungberg O, Sundler F, et al. An antropyloric gastrinoma associated with pancreatic nesidioblastosis and proliferation. Virchows Arch (A) 1973; 360: 305–314.
135. Kovacs K, Horvath E, Ezvin C, Sepp H, Elkan I. Immunoreactive somatostatin in pancreatic islet-cell carcinoma accompanied by ectopic ACTH syndrome. Lancet 1977; 1: 1365–1366.
136. Larsson LI, Hirsch MA, Holst JJ, et al. Pancreatic somatostatinoma. Clinical features and physiological implications. Lancet 1977; 1: 666–668.
137. Ganda OD, Weir GC, Soeldner JS, et al. Somatostatinoma: A somatostatin containing tumour of the endocrine pancreas. N Engl J Med 1977; 296: 963–967.
138. Pipeleers D, Somers G, Gepts W, De Nutle N, DeVroede M. Plasma pancreatic hormone levels in a case of somatostatinoma. Diagnostic and therapeutic implications. J Clin Endo Metab 1979; 49: 572–579.
139. Kaneko H, Yanaihara N, Ito S, et al. Somatostatinoma of the duodenum. Cancer 1979; 44: 2273–2279.
140. Lundqvist M, Wilander E. Somatostatin-like immuno-reactivity in mid-gut carcinoids. Acta Pathol Microbiol Scand (A) 1981; 89: 335–337.
141. Hirata Y, Sakamoto N, Yamamoto H, Matsukura S, Imura H, Okada S. Gastric carcinoid with ectopic production of ACTH and beta MSH. Cancer 1976; 37: 377–385.
142. Marcus FS, Friedman MA, Callen PW, Chung A, Harbour J. Successful therapy of an ACTH-producing gastric carcinoid APUD tumour. Report of a case and review of the literature. Cancer 1980; 46: 1263–1269.

CHAPTER 37

Gut-associated lymphoid tumours

P. G. Isaacson   D. H. Wright

GUT-ASSOCIATED LYMPHOID TUMOURS

The gastrointestinal tract is the commonest site of extranodal lymphoma.[1] Gastrointestinal lymphomas are almost exclusively of non-Hodgkin's type, primary Hodgkin's disease of the gastrointestinal tract being extremely rare. The incidence of primary gastrointestinal lymphoma shows considerable geographical variation, with a very high incidence in the Middle East[2] and pockets of high incidence in western Europe.[3]

Since nodal lymphoma often spreads to involve the gastrointestinal tract,[4] strict criteria for a diagnosis of primary gastrointestinal lymphoma are required. Those laid down by Dawson et al in 1961,[5] which require that the lymphoma is limited to the gastrointestinal tract and its contiguous lymph nodes, are still applicable but do not take account of modern staging procedures which can detect small foci of disease in the liver and bone marrow. A satisfactory operational definition is that the lymphoma has presented with the main bulk of disease in the gastrointestinal tract, necessitating direction of treatment to that site. Recognition that most primary gastrointestinal lymphomas are pathologically distinctive has, to a certain extent, circumvented the problem of definition.

The stomach is the commonest site of primary gastrointestinal lymphoma in western countries but in the Middle East, most lymphomas arise in the small intestine, closely followed by the stomach. In both areas oesophageal and colorectal lymphomas are very rare.

B cell gastrointestinal lymphoma and mucosa associated lymphoid tissue (MALT) (the MALT lymphoma concept)

In 1983 Isaacson and Wright[6] noted features in common between low grade B cell gastric lymphoma and immunoproliferative small intestinal disease (IPSID), an unusual variety of small intestinal lymphoma which occurs in the Middle East. The histology of these lymphomas was unlike that of comparable low grade nodal lymphomas, which tend to be described in the context of normal peripheral lymph nodes, but, instead, was similar to that of mucosa associated lymphoid tissue (MALT). These observations were later extended to include similar lymphomas of salivary gland, thyroid and lung.[7] The morphological and clinical homogeneity of these lymphomas was thought to reflect their origin from MALT. Unlike low grade B cell lymphomas arising in lymph nodes, MALT lymphomas tend to remain localized and seldom involve the bone marrow. Low grade MALT lymphoma may undergo transformation to a high grade lesion and residual low grade foci are often seen in apparently primary high grade MALT lymphomas.

At first sight, the MALT lymphoma concept seems illogical since there is normally no lymphoid tissue in the stomach[8] and the other sites where MALT lymphomas arise, such as the salivary gland[9] and thyroid.[10] However, in the salivary gland and thyroid, lymphoma is always preceded, respectively, by myoepithelial sialadenitis,[9] usually a consequence of Sjogren's syndrome, and Hashimoto's thyroiditis.[10] The B cell component of the lymphoid tissue that accumulates in these two autoimmune conditions shows the features of MALT as typified by Peyer's patches. In the stomach, the commonest site of MALT lymphoma, a similar sequence of events occurs following *Helicobacter pylori* infection[8,11] and it is from this so-called acquired MALT that lymphoma may arise. Autoimmune phenomena are probably also involved in the formation of MALT following *H. pylori* infection.[12]

THE CLASSIFICATION OF PRIMARY GASTROINTESTINAL LYMPHOMA

With the exception of cerebriform T-cell lymphoma (mycosis fungoides), any of the lymphomas listed in the Kiel classification may occur as a primary tumour of the gastrointestinal tract. Such cases are the exception, however, and most primary gastrointestinal lymphomas are distinctive entities that do not arise in peripheral lymph nodes and do not form a part of any current lymphoma classification. It is necessary, therefore, to formulate a separate classification for primary gastrointestinal lymphomas, as shown in Table 37.1.

B cell lymphomas of MALT type are the commonest and low grade B cell MALT lymphomas have been studied most intensively. When these low grade lymphomas transform to high grade tumours, they lose most of the histological hallmarks of MALT lymphoma. Unless there are residual foci of low grade disease, which is frequently the case, it is problematical whether a high grade B cell lymphoma of the gut is of MALT type or not. However, evidence is emerging which supports immunophenotypic[13] and molecular genetic[14] differences between high grade B cell lymphomas of MALT and nodal types. Immunoproliferative small intestinal disease (IPSID) is a specific subtype of MALT lymphoma[15] distinguished by its epidemiology and the synthesis of an abnormal alpha heavy chain by the tumour cells. Burkitt's or Burkitt-like lymphoma is an especially common primary small intestinal lymphoma in the Middle East, where it occurs in children and young adults.[16] While any of the nodal B cell lymphomas may occur as a primary gastrointestinal tumour, the only one that does so with any frequency is mantle cell lymphoma which manifests in the gut as lymphomatous polyposis.[17] The increasingly important group of B cell lymphoproliferative conditions associated with immunodeficiency commonly present in the gastrointestinal tract, but a full discussion of this entity is beyond the scope of this chapter.

Gastrointestinal T cell lymphomas are much less common but include the important entity of enteropathy associated T cell lymphoma (EATL), which appears to arise from a gut committed T cell. A number of rare entities including histiocytic neoplasms and granulocytic sarcoma (myeloid leukaemia) may also occur as primary gastrointestinal tumours.

Table 37.1 Primary gastrointestinal non-Hodgkin's lymphoma.

B cell
1. Lymphomas of mucosa-associated lymphoid tissue (MALT):
   a. Low grade B cell lymphoma of MALT
   b. High grade B cell lymphoma of MALT with or without a low grade component
   c. Immunoproliferative small intestinal disease (IPSID), low grade, mixed or high grade
2. Malignant lymphoma mantle cell type (lymphomatous polyposis)
3. Burkitt's or Burkitt-like lymphoma
4. Other types of low or high grade lymphoma corresponding to peripheral lymph node equivalents

T cell
1. Enteropathy associated T cell lymphoma (EATL)
2. Other types unassociated with enteropathy

Rare types

B CELL LYMPHOMA OF MALT TYPE

In western countries, this type of lymphoma occurs most commonly as a primary gastric tumour. Identical intestinal lymphomas do occur but are much less frequent, while oesophageal MALT lymphomas are very rare. Because it is the prototype of MALT lymphoma, gastric lymphoma will form the basis for the discussion that follows. The intestinal MALT lymphomas will be described separately.

Low grade B cell gastric lymphoma of MALT type

As mentioned previously in this chapter, the normal stomach contains no organized lymphoid tissue.[8] Following infection with *Helicobacter pylori*, lymphoid follicles accumulate in gastric mucosa[8] and B cells surrounding these follicles can be seen selectively infiltrating gastric epithelium to form a lymphoepithelium comparable with that seen in MALT[11] (Fig. 37.1). Gastric MALT lymphomas appear to arise from this 'acquired MALT' and this is supported by the finding of *H. pylori* in almost all cases.[11]

Low grade B cell gastric lymphoma occurs predominantly in older patients but a substantial number of cases have been reported in younger individuals. The clinical presentation is similar to that of gastritis or peptic ulcer disease and is usually not suggestive of a neoplasm.

Pathology

Low grade gastric lymphoma usually arises in the antrum, where it appears as an ill-defined, thickened, inflamed area, often with one or more ulcers and superficial erosions (Fig. 37.2). Microscopically, the ulcers are usually not associated with significant underlying fibrosis and the muscularis propria is preserved. This can be useful in differentiating between lymphoma and a reactive lymphoid infiltrate in the case of a peptic ulcer (Fig. 37.3).

The histological features of low grade B cell lymphoma of MALT type closely simulate those of MALT.[18] Re-

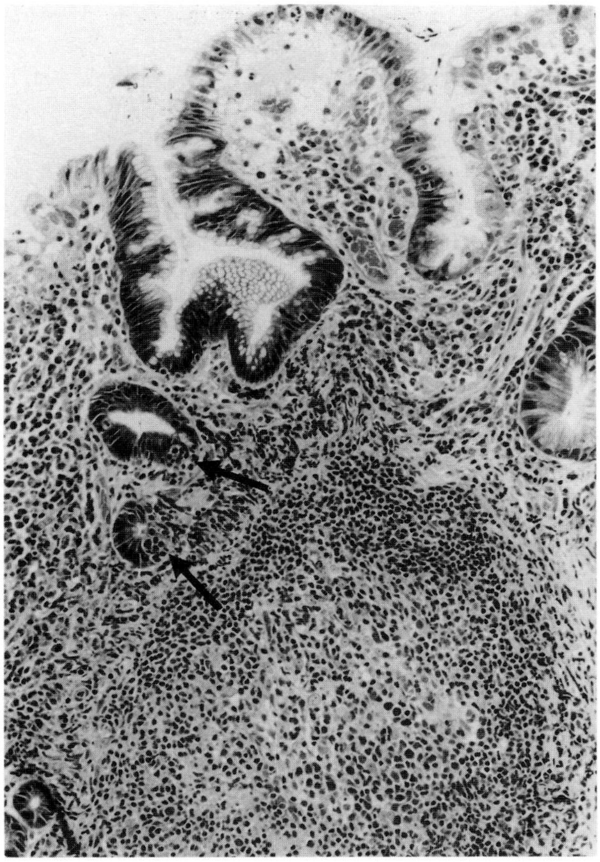

Fig. 37.1 Gastric biopsy from a case of chronic gastritis caused by *Helicobacter pylori*. There is a prominent lymphoid follicle and adjacent gastric glands show infiltration by lymphocytes (arrows).

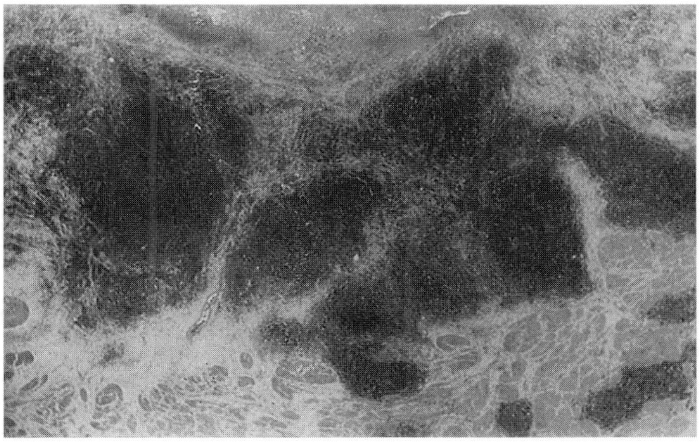

A

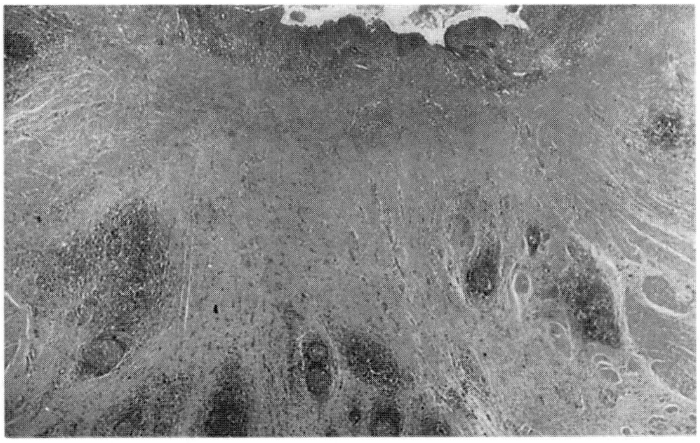

B

Fig. 37.3A Primary gastric lymphoma showing a heavy lymphoid infiltrate in the base of an ulcer and intact muscularis propria; **B** Peptic ulcer with a lymphoid infiltrate in its base. Note interruption of muscularis propria by scar tissue containing lymphoid nodules. (H&E, ×11)

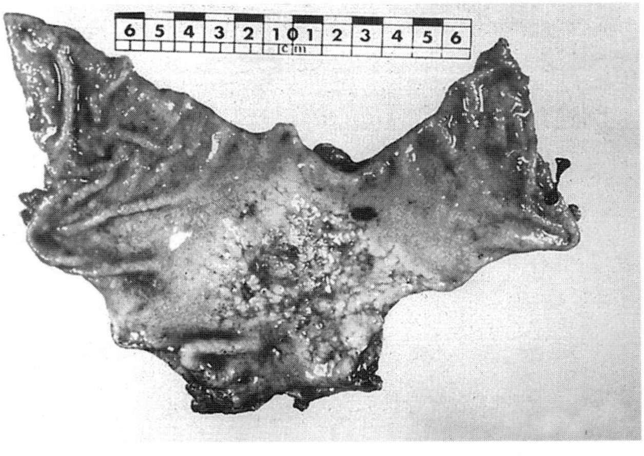

Fig. 37.2 Macroscopic appearance of typical primary gastric lymphoma. There is a flat, irregular, ulcerating infiltrate involving the antrum of the stomach.

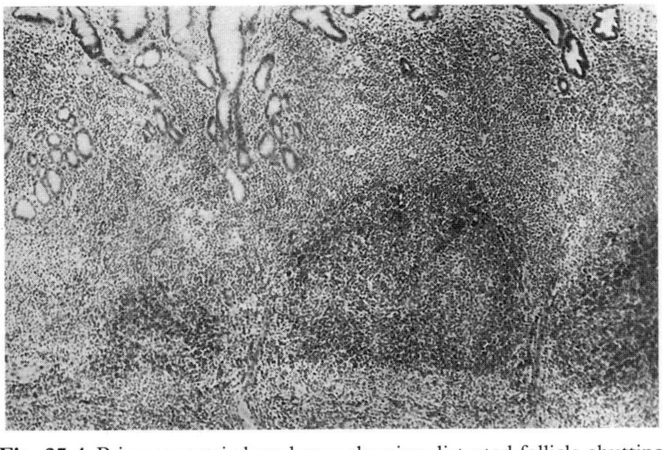

Fig. 37.4 Primary gastric lymphoma showing distorted follicle abutting muscularis mucosae. The mucosa is infiltrated by CCL cells. (H&E, ×45)

active non-neoplastic follicles are an integral component and may greatly influence the appearance of the tumour, as will be discussed in greater detail below. The neoplastic cells infiltrate around the follicles in the region corresponding to the Peyer's patch marginal zone, spreading out into surrounding tissue (Fig. 37.4). The tumour cells are small to medium sized with moderately abundant cytoplasm and nuclei that have an irregular outline, bearing a close resemblance to the nuclei of centrocytes. The detailed cytology of these centrocyte-like (CCL) cells covers a spectrum (Fig. 37.5); some resemble small lymphocytes, others more closely resemble small or larger centrocytes while others show the features of so-called monocytoid B cells, with abundant pale-staining cytoplasm and well defined cell margins. A small to moderate number of transformed blasts are characteristically present. An important feature of low grade MALT lymphomas is the presence of lymphoepithelial lesions formed by invasion of epithelium lining glands, ducts or crypts, by aggregates of CCL cells, often associated with epithelial destruction[19] (Fig. 37.6). Care must be taken not to over-interpret the presence of lymphoepithelial lesions out of context since

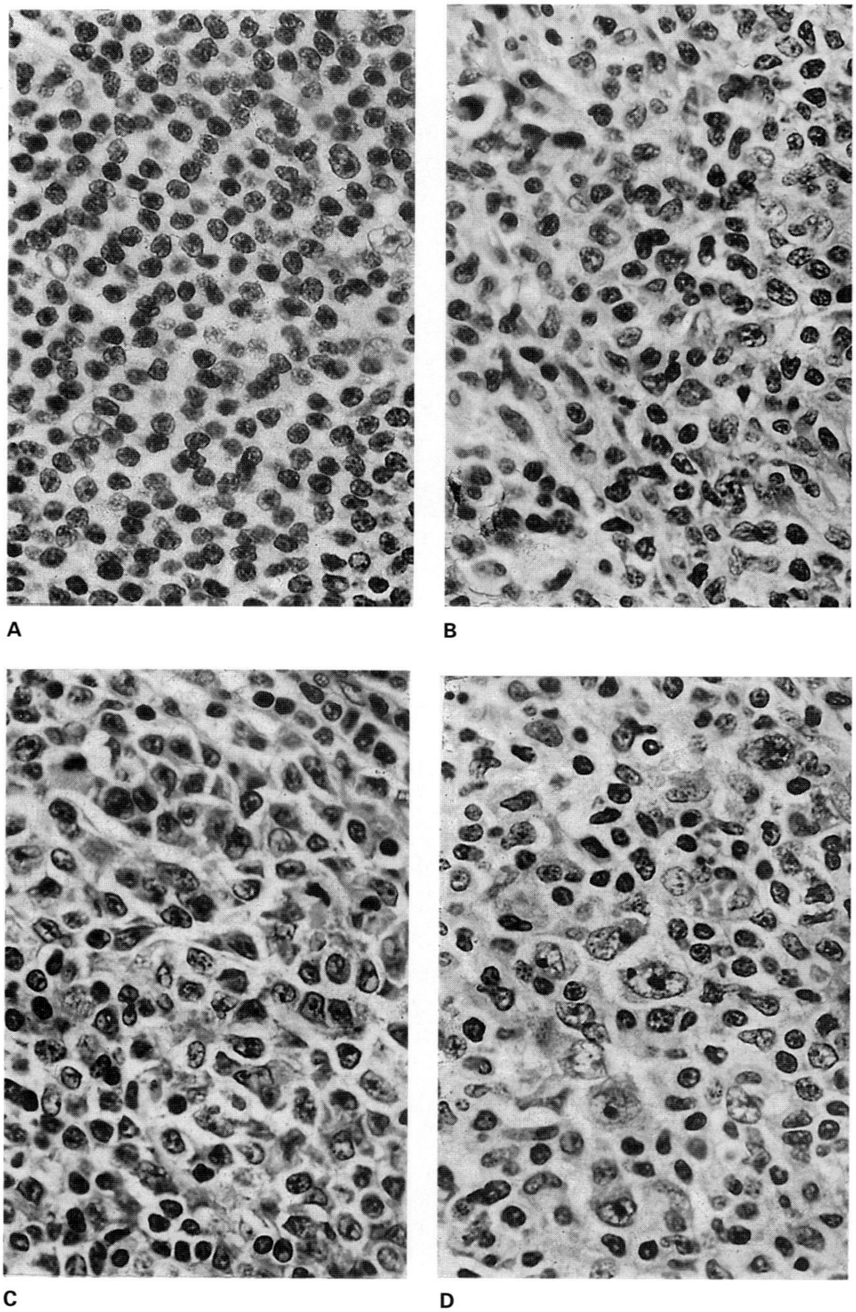

Fig. 37.5 Variation in morphology of CCL cells. **A** Monocytoid, variety; **B** typical appearances of CCL cells; **C** larger CCL cells with prominent nucleoli; **D** focal transformation into large blast forms with prominent nucleoli. (H&E, ×420)

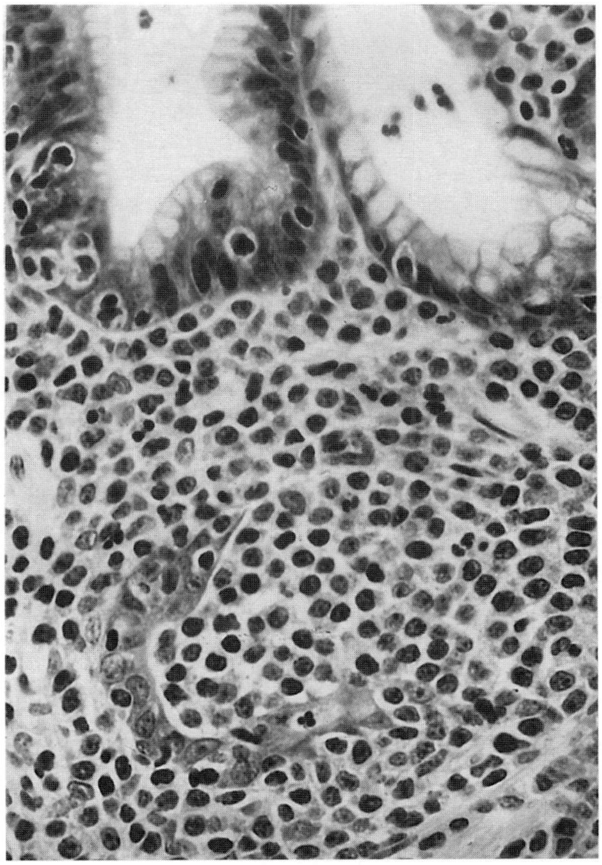

Fig. 37.6 Partial destruction of a gland by CCL cells in gastric lymphoma forming characteristic 'lymphoepithelial lesions'. Isolated intraepithelial lymphocytes in gland epithelium are probably T cells. (H&E, ×400)

intraepithelial B cells are a normal component of MALT and may be quite prominent in the presence of florid *H. pylori* gastritis, so-called follicular gastritis. Plasma cell differentiation is a feature of MALT lymphoma but is often masked by reactive plasmacytic infiltration from which it can only be distinguished by immunohistochemical demonstration of immunoglobulin light chain restriction (Fig. 37.7). In some instances, the plasma cell component of the lymphoma may be dominant and differential diagnosis from a plasmacytoma may be difficult.

Low grade B cell gastric lymphoma is frequently a multifocal disease.[20] Small foci of tumour may be present remote from the main site tumour, the smallest of these consisting of a single follicle surrounded by an expanded marginal zone of tumour cells. This has to be taken into account when assessing resection margins if the lymphoma is treated by gastrectomy.

B cell follicles in gastric MALT lymphoma

Non-neoplastic follicles are an integral component of MALT lymphoma. Even the smallest focus of lymphoma appears to be accompanied by a reactive follicle, suggesting that the formation of follicles is a precondition to the development of the lymphoma. In established MALT lymphomas, the number of such follicles can be dramatic and in those cases where follicles appear to be absent, immunostaining reveals numerous aggregates of follicular dendritic cells representative of follicles which have been overrun by tumour. While follicles precede the growth of the lymphoma, the lymphoma itself seems to induce follicle formation as shown, for example, by the presence of follicles in gastric MALT lymphoma which has extended

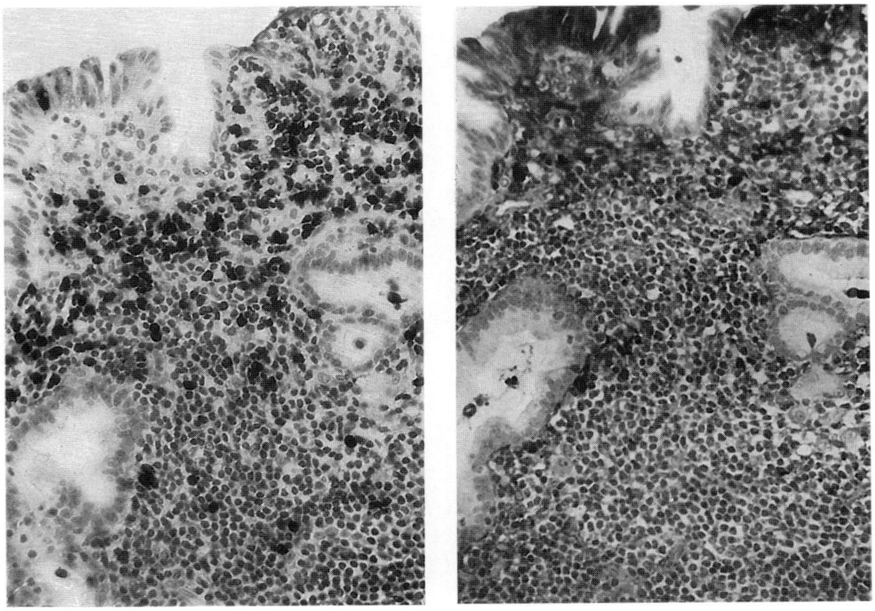

A B

Fig. 37.7 Primary gastric lymphoma stained **A** for kappa light chain and **B** for lambda light chain. Note presence of plasma cells showing kappa light chain restriction and increasing in concentration beneath surface epithelial layer. (Immunoperoxidase, ×175)

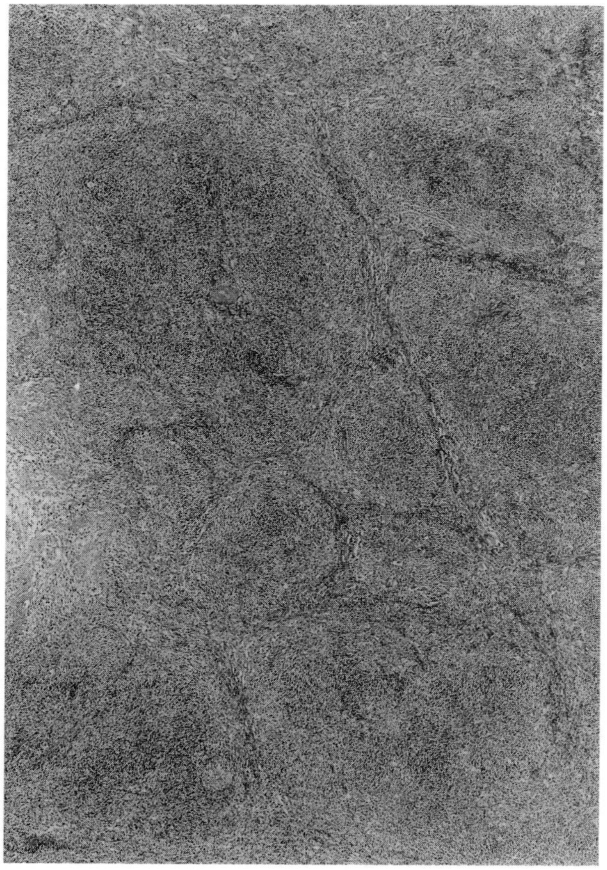

Fig. 37.8 Low grade B cell gastric MALT lymphoma showing type I follicular colonization producing a nodular pattern.

into the peritoneum (unpublished observations). The neoplastic CCL cells interact with the reactive follicles in a complex way that may lead to an appearance closely resembling follicular (centroblastic/centrocytic [cb/cc]) lymphoma. This interaction, known as follicular colonization,[21] can be divided into three types. In the first type (Fig. 37.8), reactive follicles are replaced by CCL cells resulting in confluent but poorly defined follicles in which broken up residues of follicle centre cells remain. In the second type (Fig. 37.9), follicle centres are selectively replaced by CCL cells while the mantle zone may remain intact. The intrafollicular CCL cells are larger and more 'active' than the surrounding diffuse interfollicular infiltrate and occasionally undergo blast transformation. This type of follicular colonization may lead to appearances almost indistinguishable from cb/cc follicular lymphoma; the immunophenotype and genotype of the tumour, however, remains that of MALT lymphoma (see below). Finally, in the third type, the intrafollicular CCL cells undergo plasma cell differentiation.

Biopsy appearances

In small endoscopic biopsies, the classical features of low grade MALT lymphoma may not be as easily observed as they are in resection specimens. Reactive follicles may not be as obvious, especially in the presence of crush artefact. Equally, the cytological features of CCL cells may not be as clear for the same reasons. A diffuse dense lymphoid infiltrate in a gastric biopsy should always raise the suspicion of lymphoma and the cytology should be carefully evaluated together with a search for lympho-epithelial lesions. In borderline cases immunohistochemistry or molecular genetic studies are indicated (see below).

Lymph node involvement

The characteristic pattern of lymph node involvement consists of an interfollicular infiltrate of CCL cells which surround follicles occupying the area corresponding to the marginal zone[22] (Fig. 37.10). This infiltrate may extend to form broad confluent sheets with eventual replacement of the node. Follicular colonization, as described above, may occur. If the CCL cells are monocytoid in appearance, the lymph node histology can be indistinguishable from that of monocytoid B cell lymphoma.[23]

The phenotype and genotype of low grade gastric MALT lymphoma

The CCL B cells of MALT lymphoma express surface and, to a lesser extent, cytoplasmic immunoglobulin (usually IgM) which shows light chain restriction.[24] The cells are CD5 and CD10 negative, Cdw32 (KB61) and KiB3 positive and express Bcl-2 protein. They usually express both CD21 and CD35. This immunophenotype, which is maintained in those cases showing follicular colonization,[21] is homologous with that of marginal zone B cells, which also share cytological and functional properties (e.g. follicular colonization) with CCL cells.[22] This suggests that CCL cells may be the neoplastic equivalent of marginal zone B cells.

Genotypic investigations[24] show monoclonal immunoglobulin gene rearrangement in all cases and usually this can successfully be shown in formalin fixed material. Unlike follicular (cb/cc) lymphoma, MALT lymphomas, including those with a follicular appearance, do not show rearrangement of the Bcl-2 gene[25] (t[14;18] translocation) and likewise the bcl-1 gene is not rearranged (t[11;14) translocation).

High grade gastric MALT lymphoma

Reference has already been made to the presence of larger transformed blast cells in low grade MALT lymphoma and to blast transformation in colonized follicles. More obvious foci of high grade transformation may be seen in low grade MALT lymphoma and in many high grade B cell lymphomas of the stomach; careful examination may

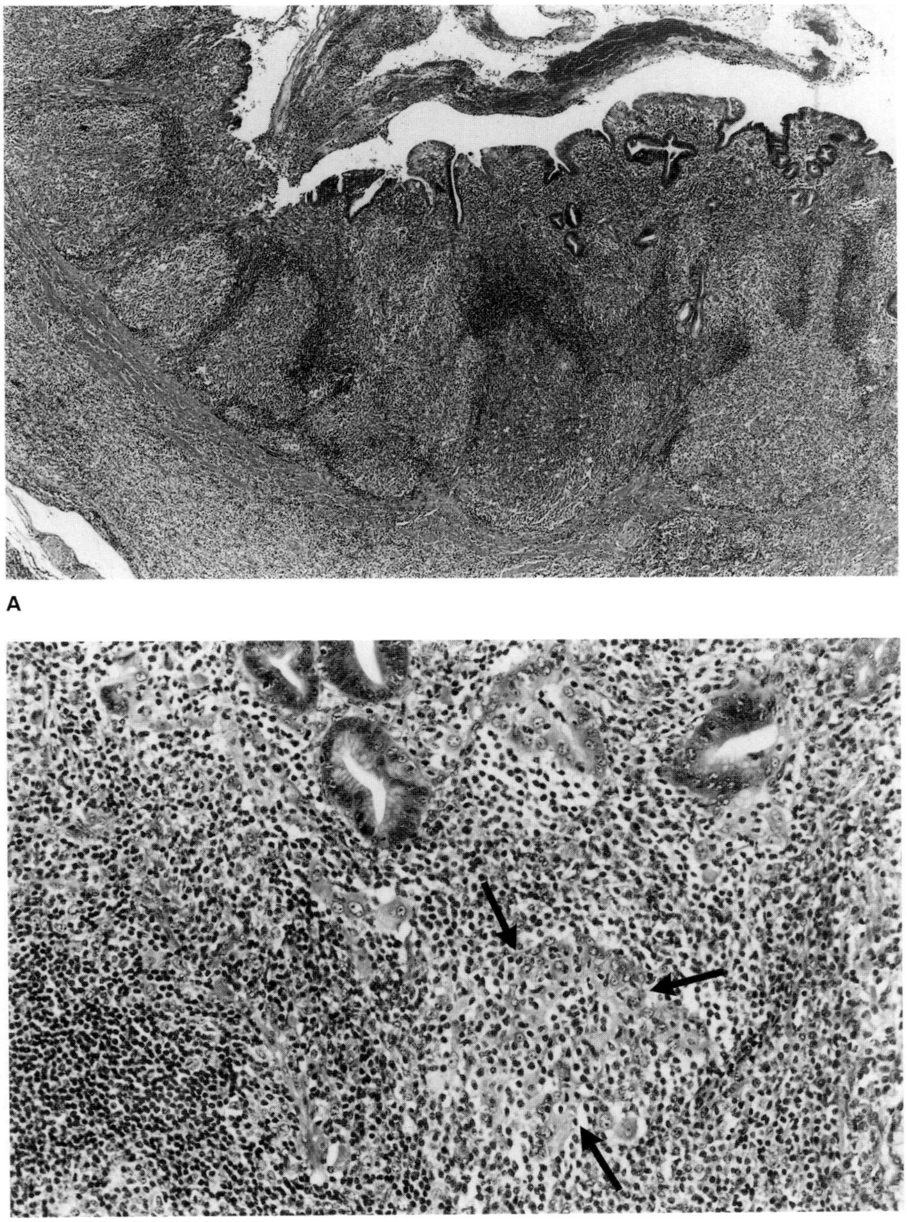

A

B

Fig. 37.9A Low grade B cell gastric MALT lymphoma showing type II follicular colonization. **B** Higher magnification of interfollicular infiltrate showing lymphoepithelial lesions (arrows).

reveal evidence of preceding low grade disease.[26] Because this mixture of grades is so common, it can sometimes be difficult to decide whether a gastric lymphoma is low grade with high grade foci or high grade. There is general agreement that the presence of confluent clusters or sheets of transformed cells outside colonized follicles serves to define a gastric MALT lymphoma as high grade (Fig. 37.11).

There are no histological or cytological features whereby high grade MALT lymphoma can reliably be differentiated from other high grade B cell tumours. The characteristic features of low grade MALT lymphoma, such as the presence of reactive follicles and lymphoepithelial lesions, are lost together with high grade transformation. Cytologically, the tumour cells may resemble centroblasts or plasmablasts and sometimes they are bizarre with numerous multinucleated forms.

Immunohistochemistry is not distinctive, with the possible exception of the expression of Bcl-2 protein which, while usually present in high grade lymphomas of FCC origin, is usually not found in high grade MALT lymphomas.[13] Molecular studies have suggested that c-myc rearrangement may also be a distinguishing feature of high grade MALT lymphoma.[14]

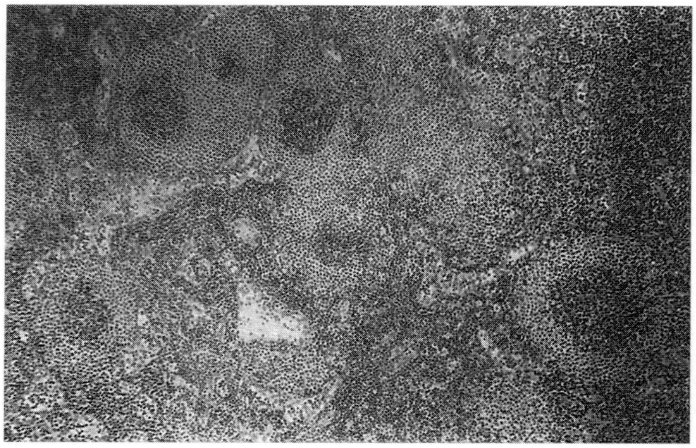

Fig. 37.10 Lymph node from a case of gastric lymphoma showing perifollicular infiltration of CCL cells. (H&E, ×45)

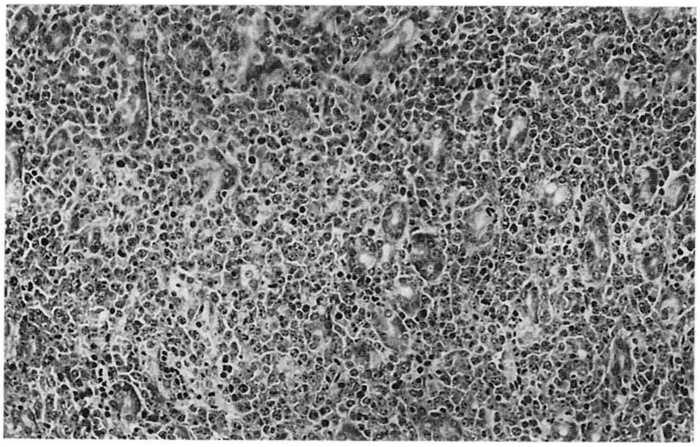

A

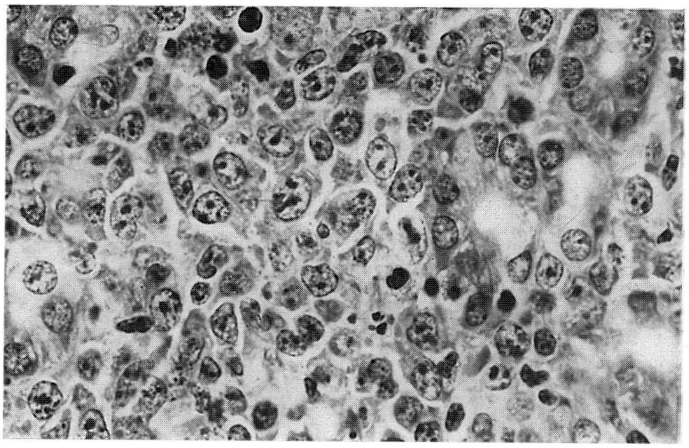

B

Fig. 37.11A Primary gastric lymphoma composed predominantly of blast-like cells infiltrating between glands without formation of lymphoepithelial lesions. **B** High power magnification shows nuclear detail of cells resembling centroblasts and immunoblasts. (H&E: **A**, ×112; **B**, ×450)

The clinical behaviour of gastric MALT lymphoma

In comparision with nodal low grade B cell lymphoma, which, at the time of diagnosis, characteristically involves multiple lymph node sites and the bone marrow (stage IV), low grade MALT lymphoma is usually confined to the site of origin (stage I or IIE) when diagnosed and is slow to disseminate, especially to the bone marrow.[27] Hence low grade MALT lymphoma responds favourably to local measures and the survival curve, unlike that of low grade nodal lymphoma which is essentially incurable, approximates that of the general population. The prognosis of high grade MALT lymphoma is also more favourable than equivalent nodal disease and, interestingly, the presence or absence of synchronous low grade foci appears to make no difference.[27]

INTESTINAL LYMPHOMA OF MALT TYPE ('WESTERN' TYPE)

Like gastric lymphoma, most intestinal B cell lymphomas are of MALT type.[28,29] The majority arises in the small intestine, colorectal lymphomas being distinctly uncommon. Distinction must be made between intestinal B cell lymphomas, which occur throughout the world (so-called 'western' type)[30] and immunoproliferative small intestinal disease (IPSID) (see below), which is a special subtype of MALT lymphoma distinguished by its restricted epidemiology and the synthesis of alpha heavy chain paraprotein (alpha chain disease). Intestinal lymphomas tend to occur in the elderly and present with obstruction or melaena. In colorectal cases, there may be a history of inflammatory bowel disease.[31,32] Most are single lesions and any part of the intestine can be involved. Mesenteric lymph node involvement is common but extra-abdominal spread is unusual at presentation.

Pathology

The microscopic features are identical to those of gastric MALT lymphoma. In low grade tumours, reactive B cell follicles are prominent and there is a surrounding infiltrate of CCL cells which often show plasma cell differentiation. Lymphoepithelial lesions are characteristic but may be more difficult to find in comparison to gastric lymphoma. Follicular colonization may lead to confusion with follicular lymphoma.

High grade lymphomas are much commoner and in a proportion of these a low grade MALT component is present. These high grade lymphomas again resemble their gastric counterparts. Both the high and low grade intestinal MALT lymphomas exhibit the same immunophenotypic and molecular genetic features as gastric MALT lymphomas.

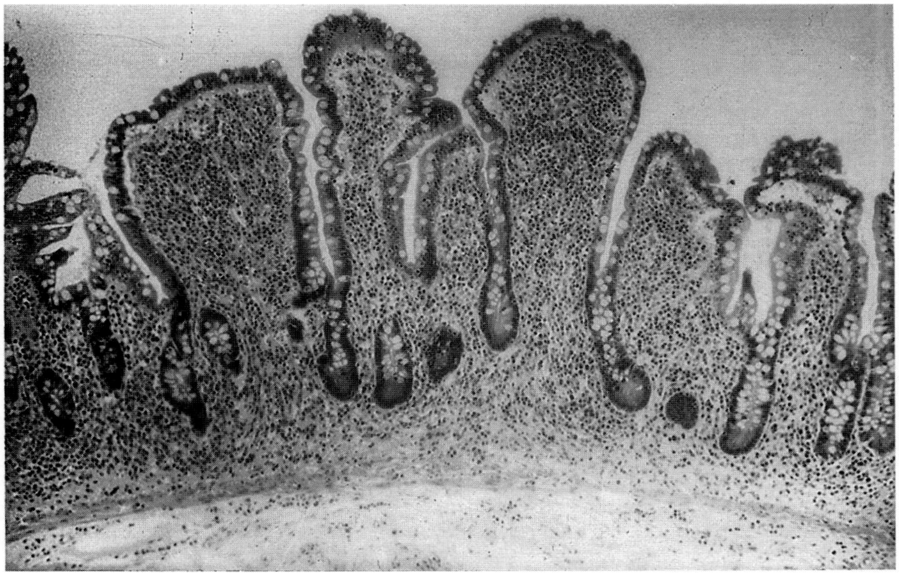

A

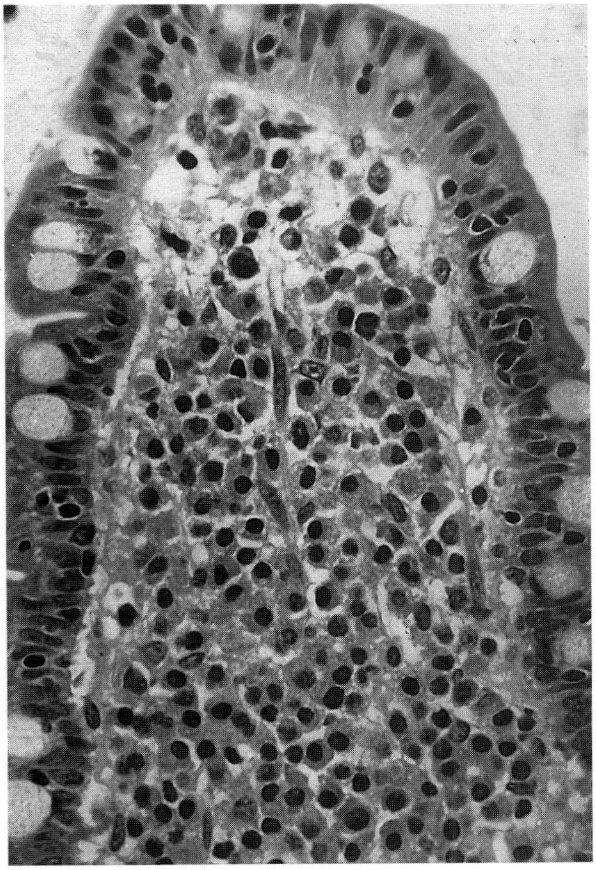

B

Fig. 37.12 IPSID Stage A. In **A** there is expansion of villi by cellular infiltrate which is confined above the muscularis mucosae. Detail of this infiltrate is shown in **B** where it can be seen to consist of mature plasma cells. (H&E: **A**, ×60; **B**, ×400)

Clinical behaviour

The clinical behaviour of intestinal MALT lymphoma is not as favourable as that of gastric lymphoma.[28,29] Five year survival rates of 44%–75% and 25%–37% are reported for low and high grade lymphoma respectively. Histological grade, stage and resectability are all significant factors.

IMMUNOPROLIFERATIVE SMALL INTESTINAL DISEASE (IPSID)

This condition is a subtype of MALT lymphoma which occurs almost exclusively in the Middle East, although a small number of cases have been reported from elsewhere.[15,33] IPSID is characterized by a diffuse lymphoplasmacytic infiltrate of the small intestinal mucosa and synthesis of abnormal alpha heavy chain, without light chain, by the plasma cells. IPSID is a disease of young adults and usually presents with profound malabsorption. In the early stages, this malabsorption may be responsive to broad spectrum antibiotics which may also cause the lymphoplasmacytic infiltrate to resolve.[34]

Pathology

In most cases, there is diffuse even thickening of the proximal small intestine and enlarged mesenteric lymph nodes but circumscribed, often multiple, lymphomatous masses may be present.

The histology of IPSID exhibits all the features of low grade B-cell lymphoma of MALT with marked plasma cell differentiation. Three stages are recognized.[35] In stage A, the lymphoplasmacytic infiltrate is confined to the mucosa and mesenteric lymph nodes (Fig. 37.12). In stage B, nodular mucosal lymphoid infiltrates are present and the infiltrate extends below the muscularis mucosae

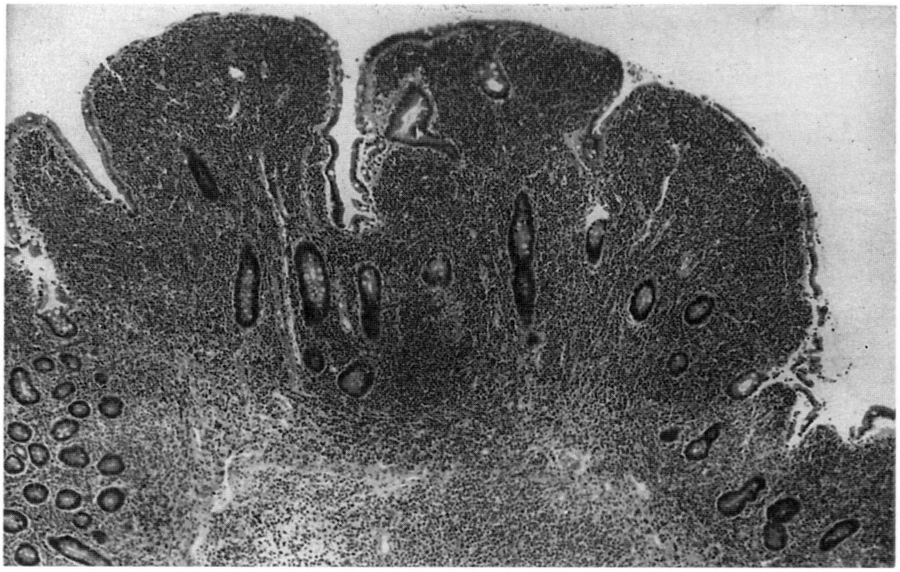

Fig. 37.13 IPSID stage B, showing extension of cellular infiltrate beneath the muscularis mucosae. (H&E, ×60)

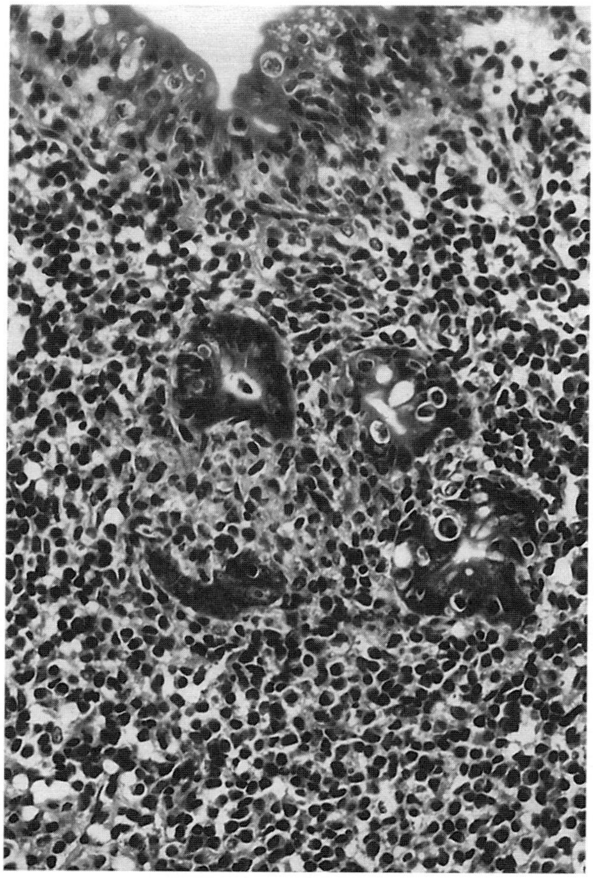

Fig. 37.14 Lymphoepithelial lesion in IPSID showing partial destruction of gland by an infiltrate of CCL cells. (H&E, ×250)

(Fig. 37.13). Stage C is characterized by the presence of lymphomatous masses and transformation to high grade lymphoma. The plasma cell infiltrate in the mucosa causes broadening, but not shortening, of the villi. These cells are not invasive and show no evidence of mitotic division.

Already present in stage A IPSID, and increasing in prominence in stage B, are aggregates of CCL B cells, which cluster around epithelial crypts and form lymphoepithelial lesions (Fig. 37.14). Reactive follicles vary in number and it is colonization of these by CCL cells that results in the lymphoid nodules of stage B IPSID[15] and may lead to the so-called follicular lymphoma variant.[36] Intrafollicular blast transformation and plasma cell differentiation also occur. Transformation to high grade lymphoma occurs in the same way as in gastric lymphoma except that the high grade cells more frequently show bizarre cytological features (Fig. 37.15).

Lymph node involvement

The mesenteric lymph nodes are involved early in the course of IPSID. Initially there is filling of the sinusoids by mature plasma cells but later the characteristic marginal zone infiltrate of CCL cells is seen (Fig. 37.16). Follicular colonization may occur in the lymph nodes.

Phenotype and genotype of IPSID

Immunohistochemical studies of IPSID confirm the synthesis of alpha heavy chain, without light chain, by the plasma cells, centrocyte-like cells and transformed blasts (Fig. 37.17). The IgA is always of subclass IgA1 except

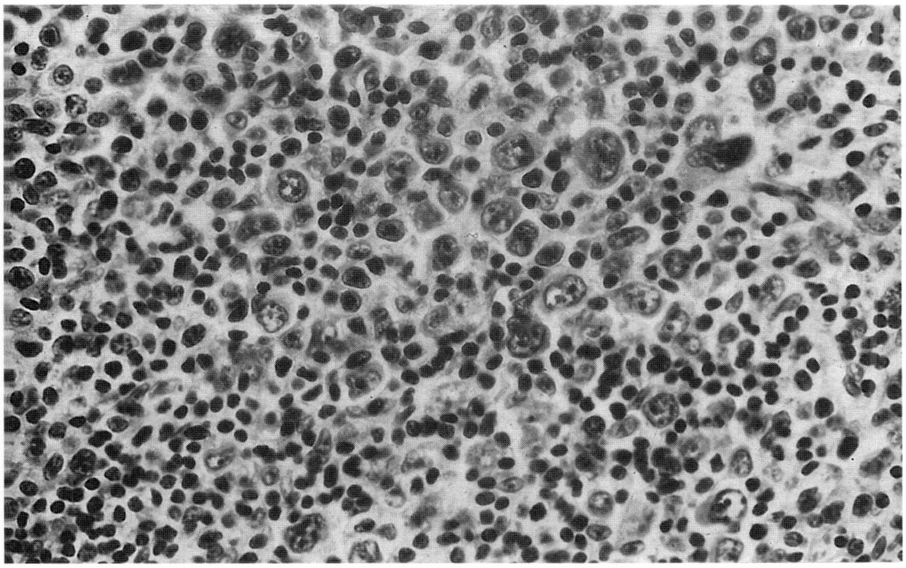

Fig. 37.15 IPSID stage C, showing an infiltrate consisting both of CCL cells and large transformed blast forms. (H&E, ×400)

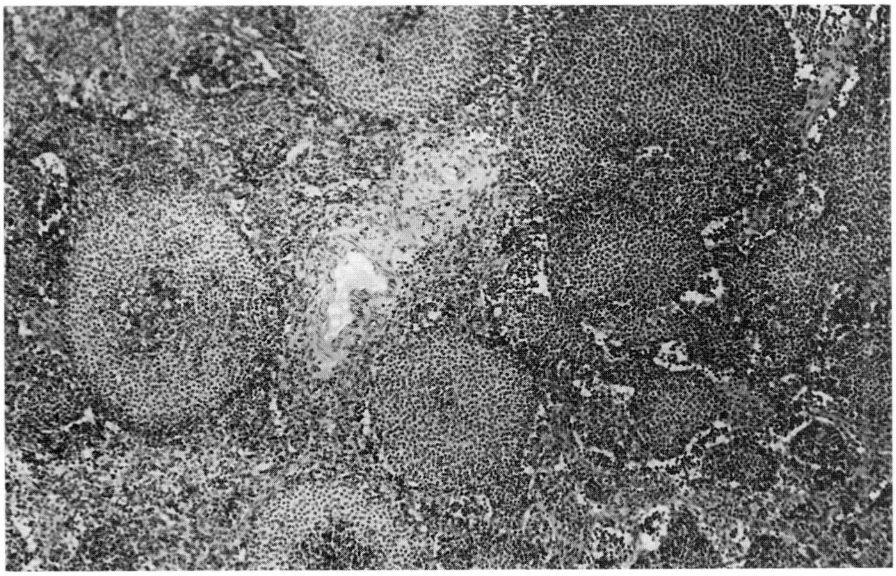

Fig. 37.16 Lymph node involvement in a case of IPSID showing perifollicular infiltrate by CCL cells. Compare with Figure 37.10. (H&E, ×60)

for occasional cases in which synthesis of both IgA1 and IgA2 has been observed. In a minority of cases Ig light chain is synthesised and when this occurs there is light chain restriction. In cases in which the infiltrate appears to consist only of plasma cells, staining with anti-CD20 will often reveal clusters of B cells concentrated around small intestinal crypts and forming lymphoepithelial lesions. Gene rearrangement studies have shown monoclonal heavy and light chain gene rearrangement which are present even in stage A, when the lymphoplasmacytic infiltrate is still responsive to antibiotics.

Clinical behaviour

IPSID runs a prolonged course, often over many years, and rarely spreads out of the abdomen until the terminal stages, following high grade transformation.

MALIGNANT LYMPHOMA, MANTLE CELL TYPE (LYMPHOMATOUS POLYPOSIS)

Lymphomatous polyposis is an uncommon disease, but well described in western countries; whether it occurs as part of the increased incidence of gastrointestinal lymphoma in the Middle East is uncertain. Most cases occur in patients over 50 years. The presenting symptoms are those of abdominal pain, sometimes accompanied by melaena, and barium studies or endoscopy reveal multiple polyps which prove to be lymphomatous. Any part of the gastrointestinal tract may be involved but in many of the cases the largest tumours are in the ileocecal region.

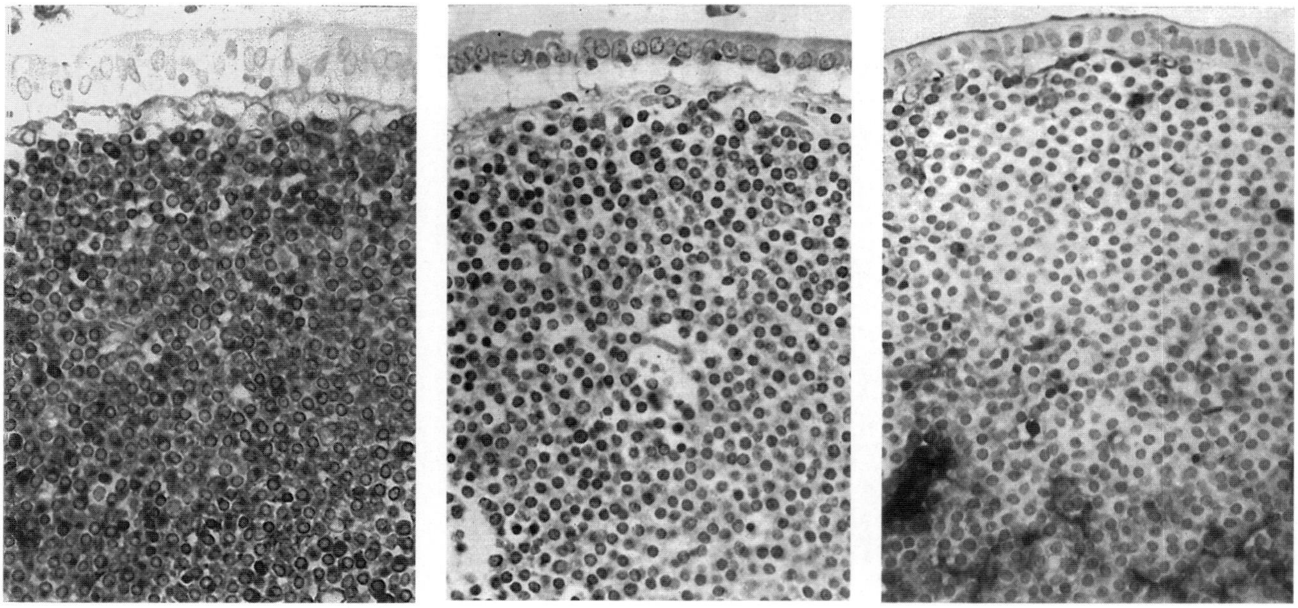

Fig. 37.17 Plasma cell infiltrate in IPSID, **A** stained for alpha-1 heavy chains, **B** stained for alpha-2 heavy chains, **C** stained for both kappa and lambda light chains. (Immunoperoxidase, ×280)

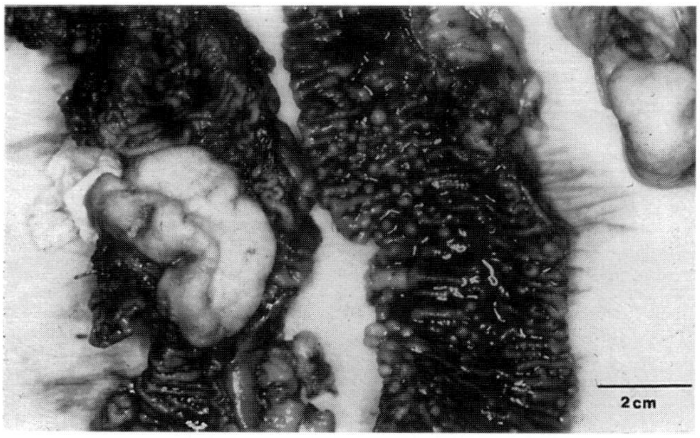

Fig. 37.18 Ileum from case of lymphomatous polyposis showing carpeting of a mucosa by small polyps together with a much larger fleshy tumour.

Pathology

Macroscopically, the intestinal mucosa is peppered with multiple white fleshy polyps ranging in size from 0.5–2 cm; much larger tumours may be present, especially in the ileocecal region (Fig. 37.18). The mesenteric lymph nodes are usually obviously involved.

The smallest histological lesions consist of a single mucosal lymphoid nodule which is diffusely replaced by lymphoma, sometimes with preservation of the reactive follicle centre (Fig. 37.19). The larger polyps may show either a diffuse or nodular lymphoid infiltrate which may, in some cases, be so nodular as to resemble follicular lymphoma (Fig. 37.20). Characteristically, reactive follicle centres are trapped in the lymphomatous infiltrate which appears selectively to replace their mantle zones (Fig. 37.21). Intestinal glands are displaced and obliterated but lymphoepithelial lesions are not present.

The cells in lymphomatous polyposis are very similar to centrocytes (Fig. 37.22) and the lymphoma conforms to the entity previously known by a number of terms, including centrocytic lymphoma, intermediate lymphocytic lymphoma and mantle zone lymphoma and, more recently, characterized as mantle cell lymphoma.[37] The immunophenotype is in keeping with a derivation from a subpopulation of CD5 positive mantle zone B cells. In addition to CD5, the cells also express mature B cell markers. Other distinctive features of this type of lymphoma include expression of CD35, absence of CD10 and the presence of a rather loose nodular network of follicular dendritic cells.

Clinical behaviour

Lymphomatous polyposis can be regarded as the intestinal form of mantle cell lymphoma, which more commonly arises in peripheral lymph nodes. Like nodal mantle cell lymphoma, lymphomatous polyposis disseminates widely early in its course and involvement of liver, spleen, bone marrow and peripheral lymph nodes soon follows identification of the polyps or may be present at the time of diagnosis. This type of clinical behaviour is quite different

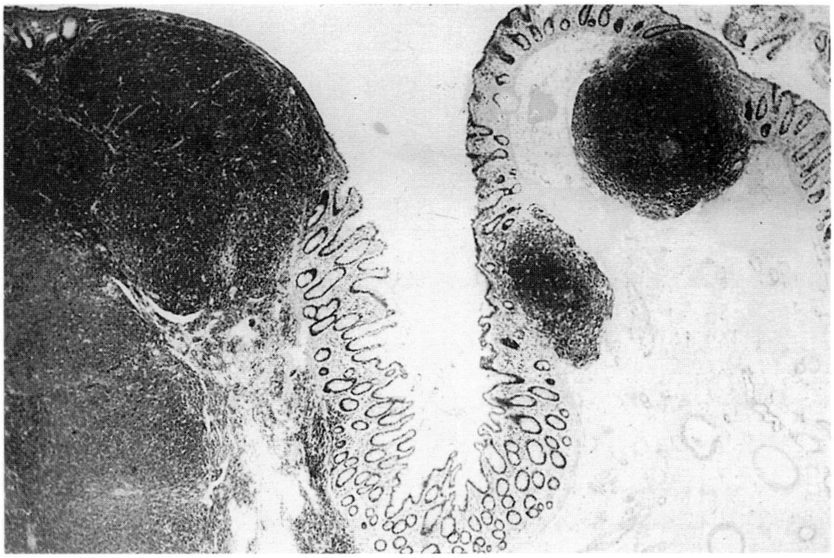

Fig. 37.19 Lymphomatous polyposis showing involvement of single lymphoid follicles together with larger focus of tumour at left. (H&E, ×15)

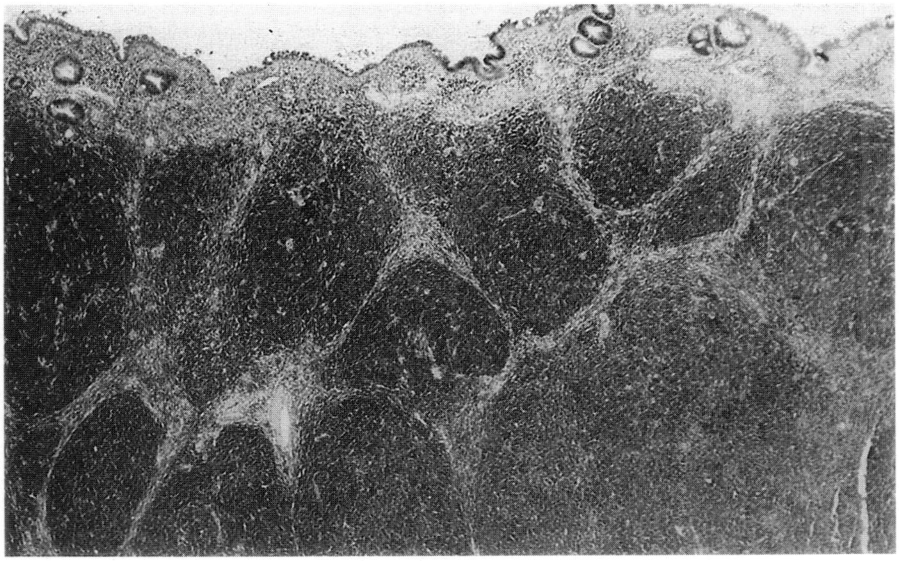

Fig. 37.20 Lymphomatous polyposis showing marked nodularity of infiltrate. (H&E, ×25)

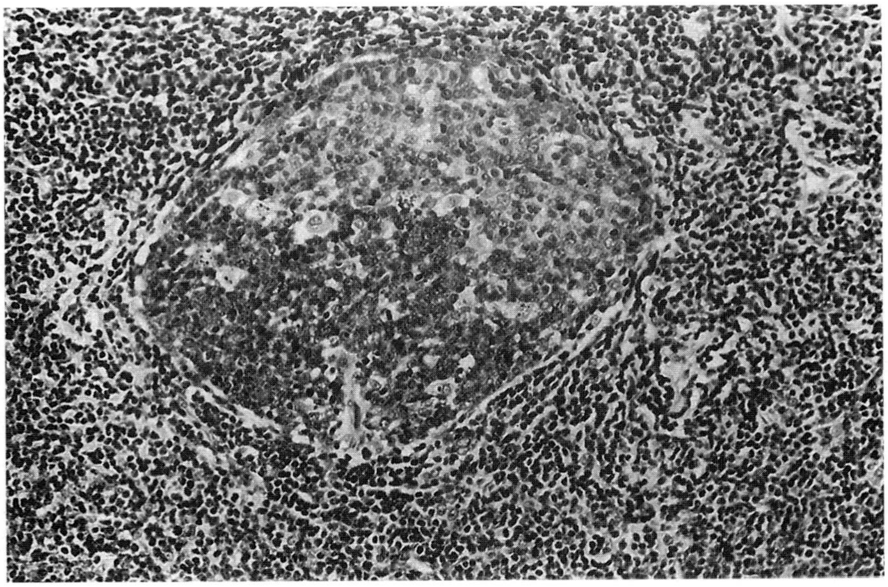

Fig. 37.21 Lymphomatous polyposis showing infiltrate surrounding and replacing the mantle of a reactive lymphoid follicle. (H&E, ×50)

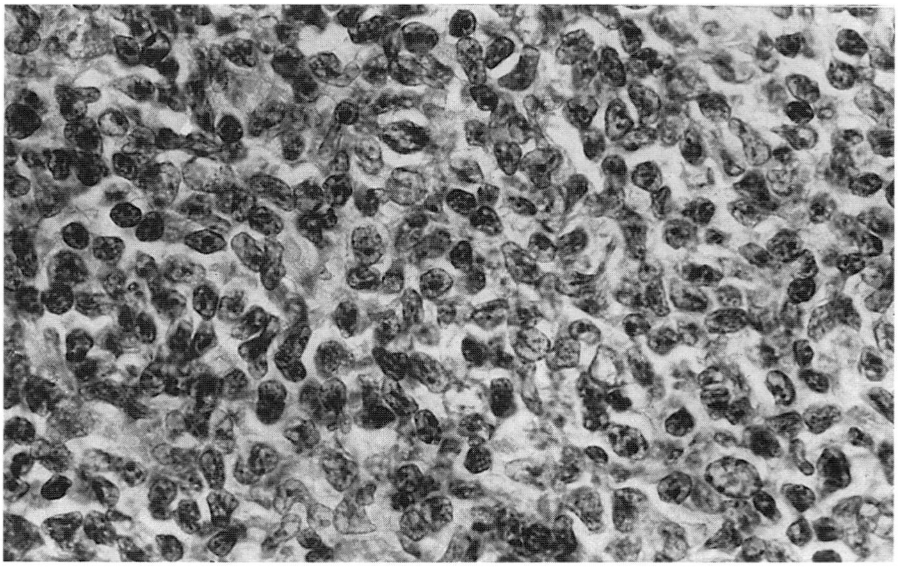

Fig. 37.22 Detail of lymphoid infiltrate in lymphomatous polyposis showing uniform centrocytic morphology of tumour cells. (H&E, ×600)

from that of MALT lymphoma and distinction between the two conditions is, therefore, important.

BURKITT LYMPHOMA AND BURKITT-LIKE LYMPHOMAS

Endemic Burkitt lymphomas often present with abdominal swelling and involvement of the gastrointestinal tract may contribute to this feature. Presentation with gastrointestinal disease, such as obstruction or intussusception is, however, uncommon.[38] In contrast, Burkitt-like or sporadic Burkitt's lymphoma in the western world, and particularly in areas of the Middle East,[39] show involvement of the intestine, frequently of the ileocaecal region, and often present with abdominal pain and obstructive features. In the UK, Burkitt-like lymphoma is the most common non-Hodgkin's lymphoma of childhood and most frequently presents with gastrointestinal disease.

Pathology

Endemic Burkitt's lymphoma and Burkitt-like or sporadic Burkitt lymphoma are high grade lymphomas that may be indistinguishable from each other in histological sections (Fig. 37.23). The tumour cells have been categorized as small, non-cleaved cells.[40] They have granular nuclear chromatin, 3–4 nucleoli and a well defined rim of deeply basophilic cytoplasm. Small lipid droplets may be seen in this cytoplasm in cytological preparations and in good quality histological sections.

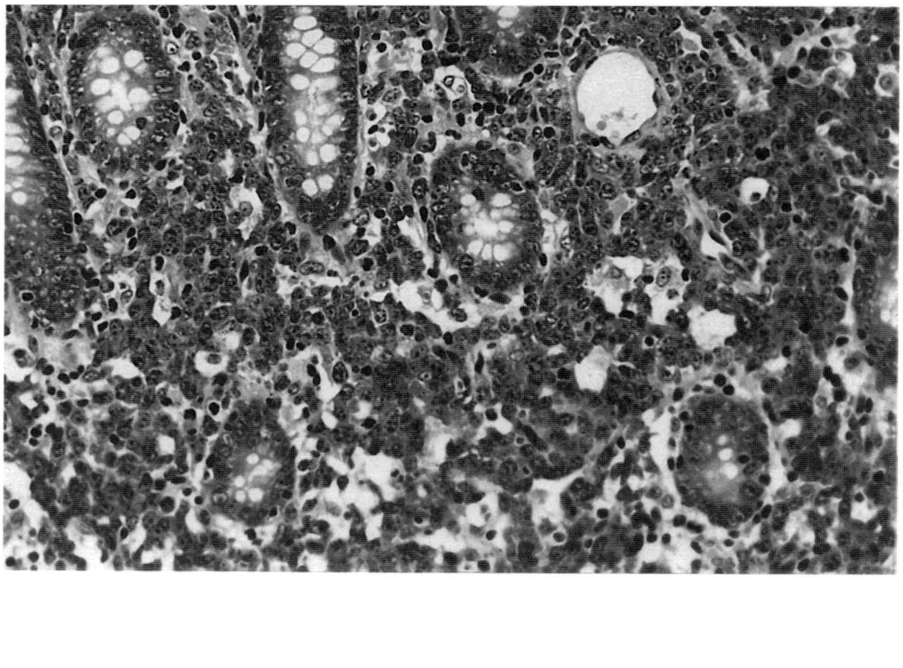

Fig. 37.23 Mucosal infiltrate from a case of Burkitt-like lymphoma of terminal ileum. Burkitt-like cells accompanied by abundant foamy macrophages infiltrate between crypts. (H&E, ×250)

Molecular genetics

EBV genomes are found within the tumour cells of all cases of endemic Burkitt's lymphoma but in only approximately one-third of sporadic cases, despite the seropositivity of 75% of these cases. Both endemic and sporadic tumours show characteristic chromosomal translocations involving the c-myc oncogene locus on chromosome 8 and the immunoglobulin genes on chromosomes 14, 2 or 22. The breakpoints involved in these translocations are, however, different in the endemic and sporadic tumours.[41] The translocation results in disregulation of the c-myc oncogene and is probably responsible for the rapid proliferation of these tumours. The consequent high rate of apoptosis and presence of large numbers of 'tingible body macrophages' give the tumours a characteristic 'starry-sky' appearance.

RELATIONSHIP OF BURKITT'S LYMPHOMA TO MALT

There is some evidence which suggests that endemic Burkitt's lymphoma is a tumour of mucosa-associated lymphoid tissue, since it shows a predilection for mucosal sites and relative sparing of peripheral lymph nodes.[42] The pattern of breast involvement in patients with Burkitt's lymphoma who are pregnant or lactating parodies the physiological behaviour of mucosal B cells.[43] The clinicopathological features of Burkitt's lymphoma are very different from those of MALT lymphomas, described earlier in this chapter. This presumably relates to the different aetiopathology of these tumours and perhaps, in particular, to the disregulation of the c-myc oncogene in Burkitt's lymphoma. Sporadic Burkitt's lymphoma or Burkitt-like lymphomas most frequently arise from the lymphoid tissue of the oropharynx and terminal ileum and may be follicle centre cell derived.[44]

OTHER TYPES OF PRIMARY B CELL LYMPHOMA CORRESPONDING TO PERIPHERAL LYMPH NODE EQUIVALENTS

There is no reason why any type of lymphoma cannot arise from mucosa associated lymphoid tissue but, in practice, entities common in peripheral lymph nodes, such as centroblastic/centrocytic lymphoma, only rarely arise in the gastrointestinal tract. The reasons for this are obscure.

ENTEROPATHY ASSOCIATED T CELL LYMPHOMA

The first account of the association of malabsorption and gastrointestinal lymphoma, over half a century ago, attributed the malabsorption to the lymphoma.[45] However, in 1962, Gough et al[46] reported several cases in which the malabsorption preceded the diagnosis of lymphoma by many years. Isaacson and Wright[47] reported a study of 12 cases of intestinal lymphoma associated with malabsorption and concluded that the tumours were of a single histogenetic type.

Morphological characteristics of the tumour cells, and the limited immunohistochemistry available at the time, led them to conclude that the tumours were of histiocyte origin. Subsequent reports, based on immunohistochemistry and gene rearrangement studies, indicated that these tumours are of T cell origin.[48,49] Farrelly et al[50] coined the now widely used term, 'enteropathy associated T cell lymphoma' (EATL) to designate these tumours.

Clinical features

The median age at diagnosis of EATL is in the region of 60. There is a wide age range, but the disease is rare under the age of 30. There is a slight male preponderance, which contrasts with the female preponderance of uncomplicated coeliac disease.[50] The majority of patients have a history of a few months to a few years of abdominal pain and weight loss. A small proportion of patients have a history of malabsorption dating back to childhood. Presentation as an acute emergency with perforation, obstruction or haemorrhage is common.

All patients with EATL should, by definition, show villous atrophy and excess intra-epithelial lymphocytes in the small bowel mucosa, giving the appearances of coeliac disease. However, whereas a clinical response to gluten withdrawal has been recorded in a proportion of reported cases of EATL, cases with a histologically confirmed response are rare.

Pathology

EATL occurs most commonly in the jejunum, either alone or in combination with other sites in the gastrointestinal tract. Lesions are frequently multiple and most commonly take the form of circumferential ulcers without the formation of large tumour masses, although these can occur. The ulcers are often more frequent than is at first apparent and may be buried in the plicae of the oedematous intestinal mucosa. Enlargement of mesenteric lymph nodes may be due to tumour or reactive changes. At autopsy, the small intestine remains the major site of involvement, although microscopic tumour may be found at other sites, including the liver, spleen and bone marrow.

The histological appearances of EATL are variable, both between cases and between different sites of tumour in the same patient. Using the Kiel classification, these tumours have been categorized both as pleomorphic, small cell and pleomorphic, medium and large cell lymphomas.[51] The most frequently encountered type is composed of medium to large blast cells with moderately

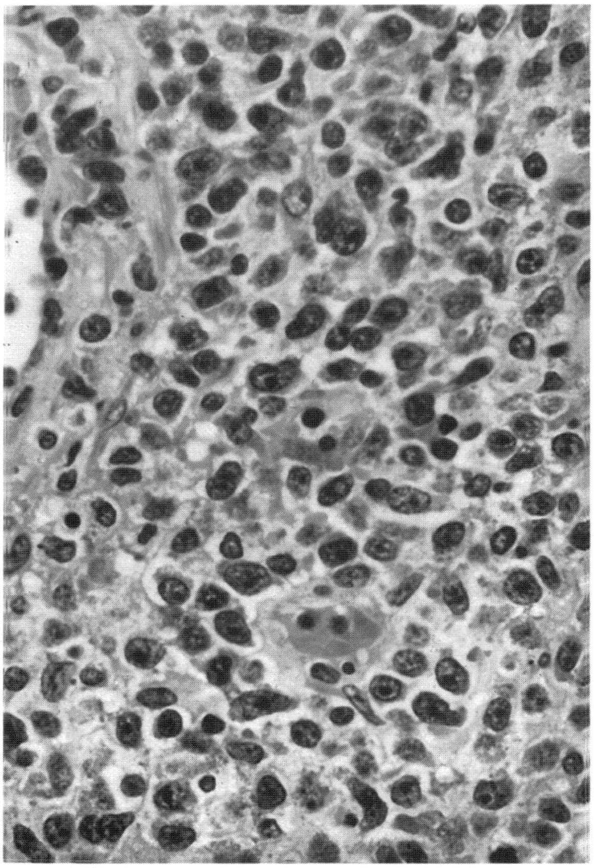

Fig. 37.24 Enteropathy associated T cell lymphoma showing tumour cells with irregular indented nuclei and a moderate amount of cytoplasm. (H&E, ×500)

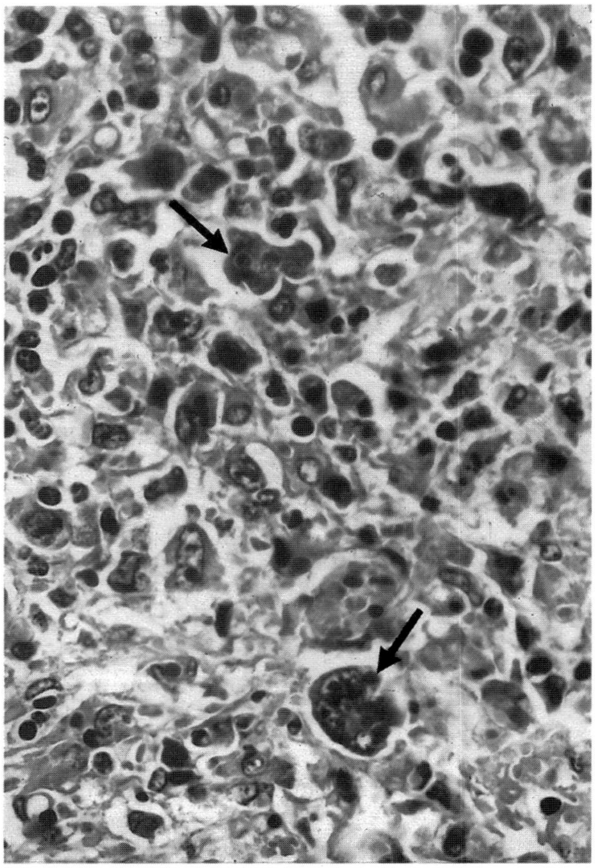

Fig. 37.25 Enteropathy associated T cell lymphoma showing marked pleomorphism of tumour cells and erythrophagocytosis (arrows). (H&E, ×500)

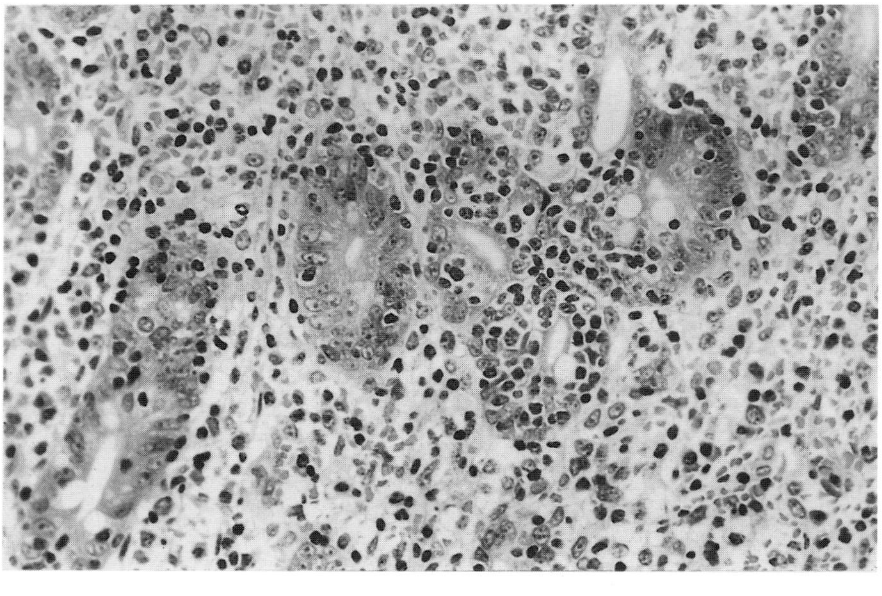

Fig. 37.26 Mucosal infiltrate from a case of enteropathy associated T cell lymphoma showing intra-epithelial tumour cells. (H&E, ×250)

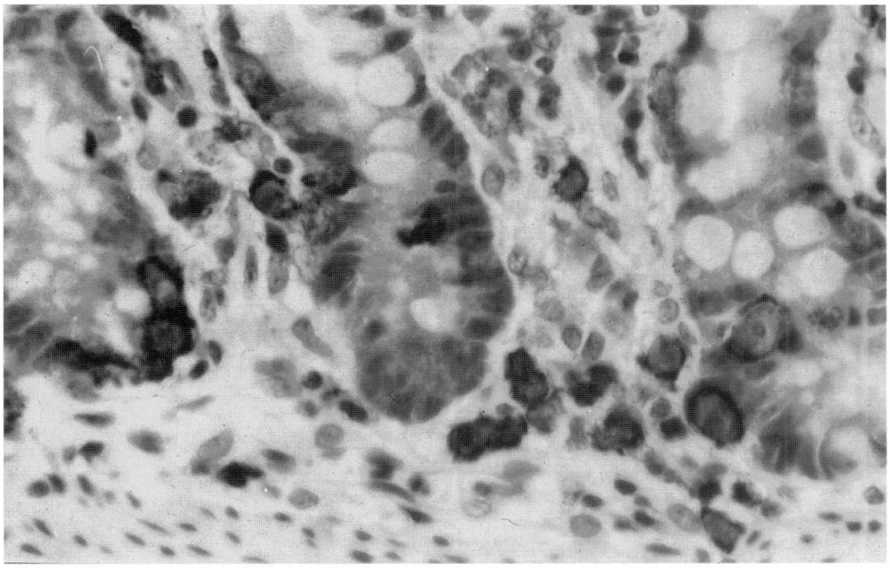

Fig. 37.27 Mucosal infiltrate from a case of enteropathy associated T cell lymphoma stained with the monoclonal antibody recognizing T cells. Note apparently selective infiltration of crypts by large nucleolated tumour cells. (Immunoperoxidase, ×500)

abundant cytoplasm (Fig. 37.24). Their nuclei are vesicular and often have a single eosinophilic nucleolus. Many more pleomorphic tumours with multinucleated cells may, in the past, have been misdiagnosed as Hodgkin's disease. These pleomorphic lymphomas (Fig. 37.25) may represent tumour progression from more monomorphic lymphomas, as may be seen in other non-Hodgkin's lymphomas. Neoplastic cells occasionally show erythrophagocytosis, but this is more frequently seen in the accompanying benign histiocytes (Fig. 37.25). Tumour cells infiltrate the epithelium of the surviving mucosa, either as single cells or small clusters (Fig. 37.26). This feature is highlighted if the tumour cells are labelled with antibodies to T cells (Fig. 37.27) or if the surviving epithelium is visualized using immunohistochemical markers for EMA or cytokeratin. Involved lymph nodes characteristically show infiltration of the sinusoids and the paracortex (Fig. 37.28).

Tumour cells may appear as easily identifiable aggregates and sheets. In ulcerated tumours, however, the intense inflammatory cell infiltrate, often including large numbers of eosinophils and histiocytes, may obscure the isolated malignant cells present. In such cases, the sectioning of multiple blocks of tissue may be necessary before the malignant cells can be identified. The neoplastic cells may be highlighted by immunohistochemical stains for CD30. It is easy to see why such lesions may be labelled as ulcerative jejunitis.

If the tumour has been resected from the jejunum, the uninvolved mucosa characteristically shows villous atro-

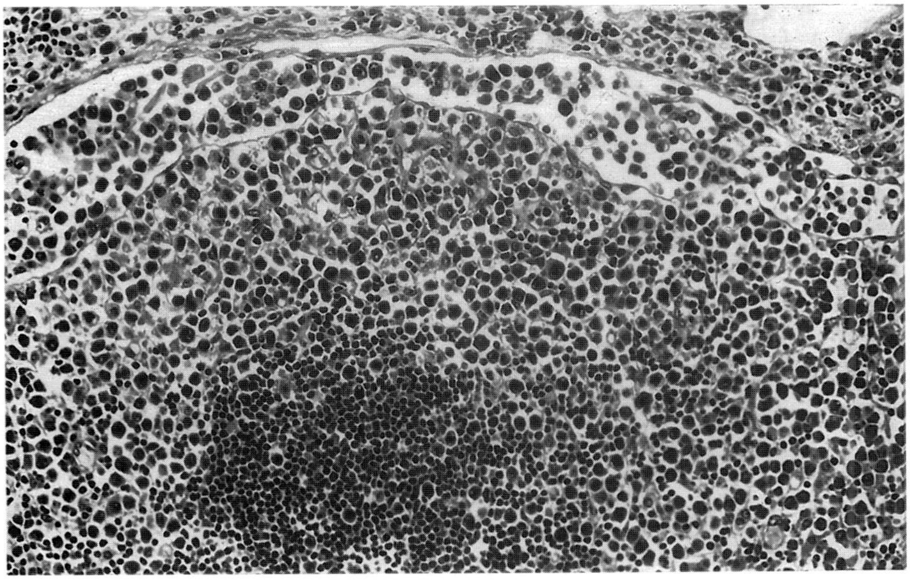

Fig. 37.28 Lymph node from a case of enteropathy associated T cell lymphoma showing intrasinusoidal infiltration by tumour cells. (H&E, ×150)

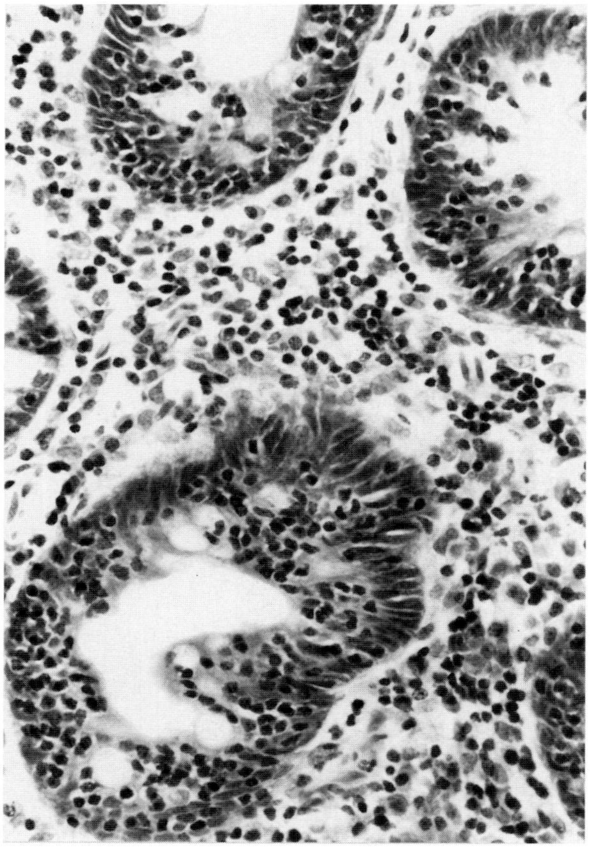

Fig. 37.29 Mucosa from a patient with malabsorption and intestinal ulceration showing intense intra-epithelial lymphocytosis. These lymphocytes showed monoclonal T cell receptor gene rearrangement.

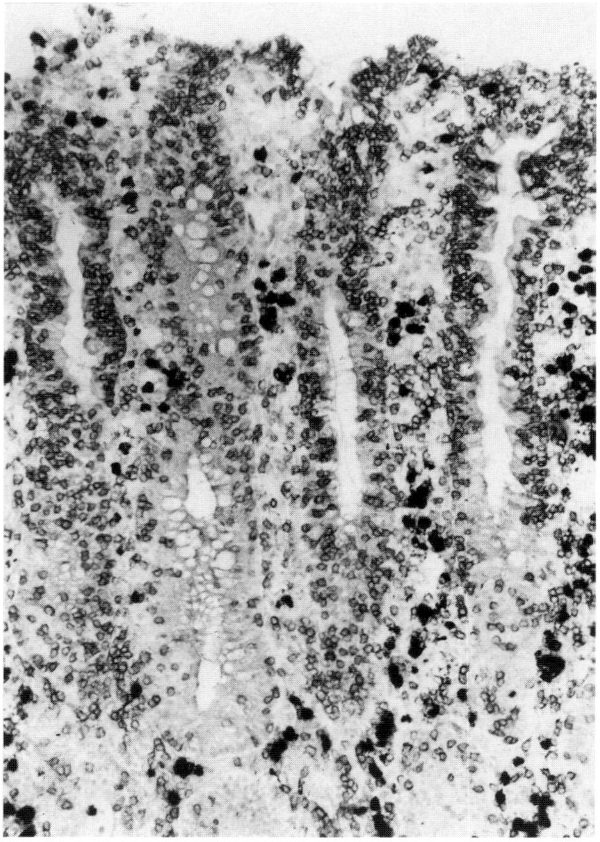

Fig. 37.30 Cryostat section of mucosa from same case illustrated in Figure 37.29 stained with HML-1. The intra-epithelial T cells are HML-1 positive (immunoperoxidase).

phy and intra-epithelial lymphocytosis. This may not be the case if the patient has been on a gluten-free diet, or if the tumour has been resected from the ileum where only minimal changes may be evident. In a study of 27 T cell lymphomas of the intestine, Chott et al[51] categorized nine as EATL, with characteristic changes in the adjacent bowel, five as EATL-like, in that they showed epitheliotropism at the margins of the tumour but no evidence of enteropathy in the uninvolved bowel; seven cases were categorized as non-EATL on the grounds that they did not show intramucosal spread and were not associated with enteropathy. Apart from the criteria used to separate these groups, they showed no difference in their clinical or pathological features and their significance is uncertain.

In recent years, we have seen a small number of patients with clinical features of malabsorption, ulceration of the jejunum and an intense intra-epithelial lymphocytosis (Figs 37.29, 37.30). The lymphocytes in these cases did not show morphological atypia but did show monoclonal T cell receptor gene rearrangement and, in one case, cytogenetic abnormalities.[52] These cases may represent low-grade (cytic) variants of EATL and it will be of interest to see if any progress to high grade tumours.

ULCERATIVE JEJUNITIS

We believe that ulcerative jejunitis occurring in a patient with coeliac disease is a manifestation of EATL. In the majority of cases, a careful search, perhaps of multiple blocks, will reveal clusters of isolated neoplastic cells (Fig. 37.31). Immunohisto-chemical staining for CD30 may aid this search. In those cases in which only small lymphocytes are identified, it is possible that these represent 'low grade' EATL. The identification of clonal rearrangements of the T cell receptor, which can now be performed using PCR on single paraffin sections, may, in future, help to resolve such cases.

IS EATL A TUMOUR OF INTRA-EPITHELIAL LYMPHOCYTES?

EATL very rarely presents as extra-intestinal disease, presumably following dissemination of the tumour. The majority of cases present in the small intestine where, like B cell lymphomas of MALT, they may remain without evidence of extra-intestinal spread for a prolonged period. Recurrences occur most frequently in the small intestine

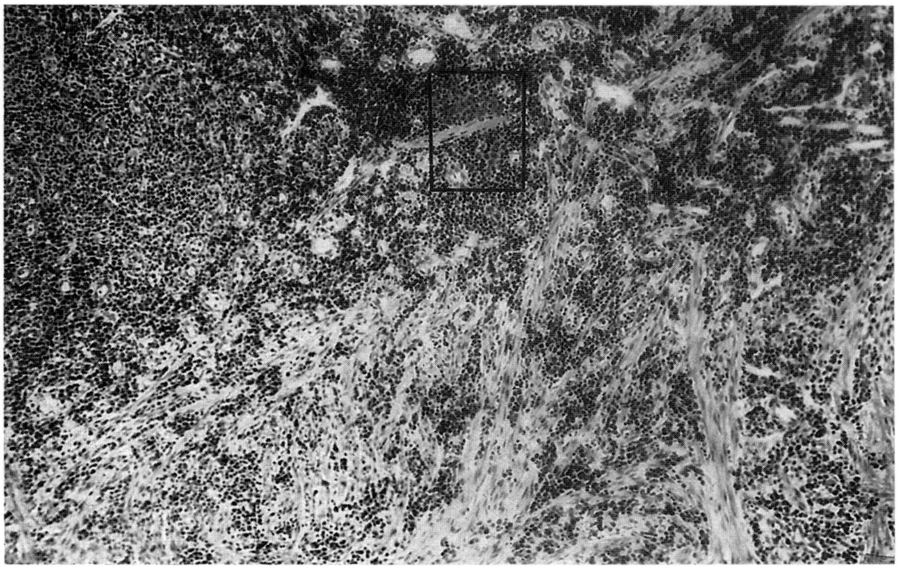

A

Fig. 37.31A Infiltrate in the base of one of many ulcers in a case of ulcerative jejunitis; **B** Detail of hatched area in **A** showing a small collection of malignant cells. (H&E: **A**, ×25; **B**, ×400)

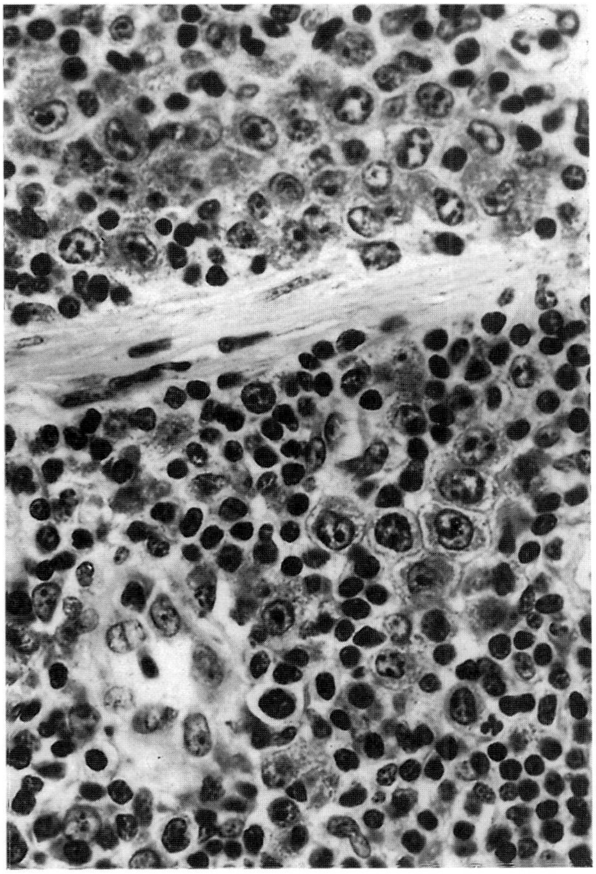

B

and, even in autopsied cases, the predominant involvement is at this site.[51] The tumour cells of EATL frequently show epitheliotropism, a feature that is particularly striking in the more recently described low grade tumours.

The majority of intra-epithelial lymphocytes express a membrane antigen defined by the monoclonal antibody, HML-1.[53] The expression of this antigen on the cells of EATL is consistent with origin from intra-epithelial lymphocytes,[54,55] although it should be noted that it is also expressed on a variety of extra-intestinal non-Hodgkin's lymphomas.[55–59] Intra-epithelial T lymphocytes in the small intestine display a number of different phenotypes. The majority are $CD3^+$, $CD4^-$, $CD8^+$, with minority populations expressing $CD3^+$, $CD4^+$, $CD8^-$ and $CD3^+$, $CD7^+$, $CD4^-$, $CD8^-$. The majority of EATLs express the $CD3^+$, $CD7^+$, $CD4^-$, $CD8^-$ phenotype consistent with derivation from this subpopulation of intra-epithelial lymphocytes.[60] Although the proportion of gamma-delta T cells is increased in the jejunal mucosa of patients with active coeliac disease,[61] immunohistochemical and gene rearrangement studies indicate that EATL is derived from intra-epithelial lymphocytes expressing the alpha-beta T cell receptor.[51]

COELIAC DISEASE AND EATL

The exact relationship between coeliac disease and EATL remains controversial. Some cases of EATL have a clear history of coeliac disease with biopsy evidence of gluten sensitivity. Splenic atrophy and dermatitis herpetiformis, both strongly associated with coeliac disease, may also occur. The HLA type in patients with uncomplicated coeliac disease and EATL have been shown to be similar in two studies[62,63] but different in a third.[50] However, in many cases of EATL there is no history of coeliac disease or objective findings of gluten sensitivity. O'Farrelly et al[50] found that antibodies to wheat proteins present in patients with uncomplicated coeliac disease are absent in patients with EATL. These authors also noted a marked difference in the sex incidence and in the incidence of the DR3 antigen in patients with uncomplicated coeliac disease and patients with EATL. They propose two possible scenarios for the pathogenesis of EATL. The first is that it may occur in patients with coeliac disease, but that its development is influenced by other factors, such as sex and DR status. The second is that a slowly progressive T cell lymphoma may cause the enteropathy and eventually transforms into a high grade lymphoma in a manner analogous to mycosis fungoides.[64] The identification of clonal T cells in the enteropathic bowel, not involved by lymphoma, can be taken as evidence in support of the latter hypothesis.[52,65] However, our own studies have shown that if multiple blocks are taken from the enteropathic bowel, clonal T cell populations are found in a minority and that most are polyclonal, consistent with evolution of the clonal populations within a reactive process.

CONCLUSIONS

The central theme of this chapter is that the majority of malignant lymphomas of the gastrointestinal tract have specific clinicopathological features and appear to be derived from populations of lymphocytes that home to the gastrointestinal tract. Other non-Hodgkin's lymphomas, such as follicle centre cell lymphomas, are occasionally encountered in the gastrointestinal tract. The relationship of these tumours to their nodal counterparts is as yet uncertain. Most reported cases of lymphoplasmacytic lymphoma of the gastrointestinal tract are probably examples of low grade MALT lymphomas, although occasional examples of plasmacytic lymphoma, sometimes associated with amyloid deposition, are encountered. Metastatic tumours to the bowel, particularly malignant melanoma, may closely mimic high grade non-Hodgkin's lymphoma.

REFERENCES

1. Freeman C, Berg JW, Cutler SJ. Occurrence and prognosis of extranodal lymphomas. Cancer 1972; 29: 252–260.
2. Salem P. El-Hashimi L, Anaissie E, et al. Primary small intestinal lymphoma in adults: A comparative study of IPSID versus non-IPSID in the Middle East. Cancer 1987; 59: 1670–1676.
3. Doglioni C, Wothespoon AC, Moschini A, De Boni M, Isaacson PG. High incidence of primary gastric lymphoma in northeastern Italy. Lancet 1992; 339: 834–835.
4. Fischbach W, Ketel W, Kirchner T, Mossner J and Wilms K. Malignant lymphomas of the upper gastrointestinal tract. Cancer 1992; 70: 1075–1080.
5. Isaacson PG. Extranodal lymphomas: the MALT concept. Verh Dtsch Ges Path 1992; 76: 14–23.
6. Isaacson PG, Wright DH. Malignant lymphoma of mucosa-associated lymphoid tissue. A distinctive type of B cell lymphoma. Cancer 1983; 52: 1410–1416.
7. Isaacson PG and Wright DH. Extranodal malignant lymphoma arising from mucosa-associated lymphoid tissue. Cancer 1984; 53: 2515–2524.
8. Genta RM, Hamner HW, Graham DY. Gastric lymphoid follicles in Helicobacter pylori infection: frequency, distribution and response to triple therapy. Hum Pathol 1993 (in press).
9. Hyjek E, Smith WJ, Isaacson PG. Primary B cell lymphoma of salivary gland and its relationship to myoepithelial sialadenitis. Hum Pathol 1988; 19: 766–776.
10. Hyjek E, Isaacson PG. Primary B cell lymphoma of the thyroid and its relationship to Hashimoto's thyroiditis. Hum Pathol 1988; 19: 1315–1326.
11. Wotherspoon AC, Ortiz-Hidalgo C, Falzon MR, Isaacson PG. Helicobacter pylori-associated gastritis and primary B cell gastric lymphoma. Lancet 1991; 338: 1175–1176.
12. Negrini R, Lisato L, et al. Helicobacter pylori infection induces antibodies cross-reacting with human gastric mucosa. Gastroenterology 1991; 101: 437–445.
13. Villuendas R, Piris MA, Orradre JL, et al. Different bcl-2 protein expression in high-grade B cell lymphomas derived from lymph node or mucosa-associated lymphoid tissue. Am J Pathol 1991; 139: 989–993.
14. Raghoebier S, Kramer MHH, van Krieken JHJM, et al. Essential differences in oncogene involvement between primary nodal and extranodal large cell lymphoma. Blood 1991; 78: 2680–2685.
15. Isaacson PG, Dogan A, Price SK, Spencer J. Immunoproliferative small intestinal disease: An immunohistochemical study. Am J Surg Pathol 1989; 13: 1023–1033.
16. Ladjadj Y, Philip T, Lenior GM, et al. Abdominal Burkitt-like lymphomas in Algeria. Br J Cancer 1984; 49: 503–512.
17. Isaacson PG, MacLennan KA, Subbuswamy SG. Multiple lymphomatous polyposis of the gastrointestinal tract. Histopathology 1983; 8: 641–656.
18. Isaacson PG, Spencer J. Malignant lymphoma of mucosa associated lymphoid tissue. Histopathology 1987; 11: 445–462.
19. Papadaki L, Wotherspoon AC, Isaacson PG. The lymphoepithelial lesion of gastric low-grade B cell lymphoma of mucosa-associated lymphoid tissue (MALT): an ultrastructural study. Histopathology 1992; 21: 415–421.
20. Wotherspoon AC, Doglioni C, Isaacson PG. Gastric B cell lymphoma of mucosa-associated lymphoid tissue is a multifocal disease. Histopathology 1992; 20: 29–34.
21. Isaacson PG, Wotherspoon AC, Diss TC, Pan LX. Follicular colonization in B cell lymphoma of mucosa associated lymphoid tissue. Am J Surg Pathol 1991; 15: 819–828.
22. MacLennan ICM, Lui Y J, et al. The evolution of B cell clones. Current Topics Microbiol Immunol 1990; 159: 37–63.
23. Traweek ST, Sheibani K, et al. Monocytoid B cell lymphoma: Its evolution and relationship to other low-grade B cell neoplasms. Blood 1989; 73: 573–578.
24. Spencer J, Diss TC, Isaacson PG. Primary B cell gastric lymphoma and 'pseudolymphoma': A genotypic analysis. Am J Pathol 1989; 135: 557–564.
25. Pan L, Diss TC, Cunningham D, Isaacson PG. The bcl-2 gene in primary B cell lymphomas of mucosa associated lymphoid tissue (MALT). Am J Pathol 1989; 135: 7–11.
26. Chan JKC, Ng CS, Isaacson PG. Relationship between high grade lymphoma and low grade B cell mucosa associated lymphoid tissue lymphoma (MALToma) of the stomach. Am J Pathol 1990; 136: 1153–1164.
27. Cogliatti SB, Schmid U, Schumacher U, et al. Primary B cell gastric lymphoma: A clinicopathological study of 145 patients. Gastroenterology 1991; 101: 1159–1170.
28. Radasziewicz T, Dragosics B, Bauer P. Gastrointestinal malignant lymphomas of the mucosa-associated lymphoid tissue: Factors relevant to prognosis. Gastroenterology 1992; 102: 1628–1638.
29. Domizio P, Owen RA, Shepherd NA, Talbot IC, Norton AJ. Primary lymphoma of the small intestine: A clinicopathological study of 119 cases. Am J Surg Pathol (in press).
30. Lewin KJ, Kahn LB, Novis BH. Primary intestinal lymphoma of 'Western' and 'Mediterranean' type, Alpha chain disease and massive plasma cell infiltration. A comparative study of 37 cases. Cancer 1976; 38: 2511–2528.
31. Shepherd NA, Hall PA, Coates PJ, Levison DA. Primary malignant lymphoma of the colon and rectum. A histopathological and

immunohistochemical analysis of 45 cases with clinicopathological correlations. Histopathology 1988; 12: 235–252.
32. Greenstein AJ, Mullin GE, Strauchen JA, et al. Lymphoma in inflammatory bowel disease. Cancer 1992; 69: 1119–1123.
33. Price SK. Immunoproliferative small intestinal disease: a study of 13 cases with alpha heavy-chain disease. Histopathology 1990; 17: 7–17.
34. Ben-Ayed F, Halphen M, Najjar T, et al. Treatment of alpha chain disease — results of a prospective study in 21 Tunisian patients by the Tunisian-French intestinal lymphoma study group. Cancer 1989; 63: 1251–1256.
35. Galian A, Lecester MJ, Scott J, Bogwel C, Mutuchansky C, Rambaud JC. Pathological study of alpha-chain disease, with special emphasis on evolution. Cancer 1977; 39: 2081–2101.
36. Nemes Z, Thomazy V, Steifert G. Follicular centre cell lymphoma with alpha heavy chain disease: a histopathological and immunohistochemical study. Virchows Arch [A] 1981; 394: 119–132.
37. Banks PM, Chan J, Cleary ML, et al. Mantle cell lymphoma. A proposal for unification of morphologic, immunologic, and molecular data. Am J Surg Pathol 1992; 16: 637–640.
38. Wright DH. Burkitt's tumour in England: A comparison with childhood lymphosarcoma. Int J Cancer 1966; 1: 503–514.
39. Anaissie E, Geha S, Allam C, Jabbour J, Khakyk M, Salem P. Burkitt's lymphoma in the Middle East: A study of 34 cases. Cancer 1985; 56: 2539–2543.
40. The non-Hodgkin's lymphoma pathologic classification project: National Cancer Institute sponsored study of non-Hodgkin's lymphomas: Summary and description of a working formulation for clinical usage. Cancer 1982; 49: 2112–2135.
41. Magrath I. The pathogenesis of Burkitt's Lymphoma. In: Vande Woude G F, Klein G, eds. Advances in Cancer Research. Academic Press 1990; 55: 133–270.
42. Wright DH. Histogenesis of Burkitt's lymphoma: A B cell tumour of mucosa-associated lymphoid tissue. In: Lenoir G, O'Conor G, Olweny CLM, eds. Burkitt's lymphoma, A human cancer model (IARC Scientific Publications No. 60). Lyon, International Agency for Research on Cancer, 1985.
43. Shepherd JJ, Wright DH. Burkitt's tumour presenting as bilateral swellings of the breast in women of child bearing age. Br J Surg 1967; 54: 776–780.
44. Mann RB, Jaffe ES, Braylin RC, Nanba K, Frank MM, Ziegler JL, Berard CW. Non-endemic Burkitt's lymphoma. A B-cell tumor related to germinal centers. New Engl J Med 1976; 295: 685–691.
45. Fairley NH, Mackie FP. The clinical and biochemical syndrome in lymphadenoma and allied disease involving the mesenteric lymph glands. Br Med J 1937; 1: 3972–3980.
46. Gough KR, Read AE, Naish JM. Intestinal reticulosis as a complication of idiopathic steatorhoea. Gut 1962; 3: 232–239.
47. Isaacson P, Wright DH. Malignant histiocytosis of the intestine: Its relationship to malabsorption and ulcerative jejunitis. Hum Pathol 1978; 9: 661–677.
48. Isaacson PG, O'Connor NTJ, Spencer J, et al. Malignant histiocytosis of the intestine: A T-cell lymphoma. Lancet 1985; 2: 688–691.
49. Salter DM, Krajewski AS, Dewar AE. Immunophenotype analysis of malignant histiocytosis of the intestine. J Clin Path 1986; 39: 8–15.
50. O'Farrelly C, Feighery C, O'Brien DS, et al. Humoral response to wheat protein in patients with coeliac disease and enteropathy associated T cell lymphomas. Br Med J 1986; 293: 908–910.
51. Chott A, Dragosics B, Radaszkiewicz T. Peripheral T cell lymphomas of the intestine. Am J Path 1992; 141: 1361–1371.
52. Wright DH, Jones DB, Clark H, Mead GM, Hodges E, Howell WM. Is adult onset coeliac disease due to a low-grade lymphoma of intraepithelial T-lymphocytes? Lancet 1991; 337: 1373–1374.
53. Cerf-Bensussan N, Jarry A, Brousse N, Lisowska-Grospierre B, Guy-Grand D, Griscelli C. A monoclonal antibody (HML-1) defining a novel membrane molecule present on human intestinal lymphocytes. Eur J Immunol 1987; 17: 1279–1285.
54. Spencer J, Cerf-Bensussan N, Jarry A, Brousse N, Guy-Grand D, Krajewski AS, Isaacson PG. Enteropathy-associated T cell lymphoma (malignant histiocytosis of the intestine) is recognised by a monoclonal antibody (HML-1) that defines a membrane molecules on human mucosal lymphocytes. Am J Path 1988; 132: 1–5.
55. Stein H, Dienemann D, Sperling M, Zeitz M, Riecken EO. Identification of a T cell lymphoma category derived from intestinal mucosa-associated T cells. Lancet 1988; 2: 1053–1054.
56. Pallesen G, Hamilton-Dutoit SJ. Monoclonal antibody (HML1) labelling of T-cell lymphomas. Lancet 1989; 1: 223.
57. Sperling M, Kaudewitz P, Braun-Falco O, Stein H. Reactivity of T cells in mycosis fungoides exhibiting marked epidermotropism with the monoclonal antibody HML1 that defines a membrane molecules on human mucosal lymphocytes. Am J Path 1989; 134: 955–960.
58. Moller P, Mielke B, Moldenhauer G. Monoclonal antibody HML1, a marker of intraepithelial T cells in lymphomas derived thereof, also recognises hairy cell leukaemia and some B cell lymphomas. Am J Path 1990; 136: 509–512.
59. Falini B, Flenghi L, Fagioli M, Pelicci PG, Stein H, Bigerna B, Pileri S, Martelli MF. Expression of the intestinal T-lymphocytes-associated molecule HML1: Analysis of 75 non-Hodgkin's lymphomas and description of the first HML1 positive lymphoblastic tumour. Histopathology 1991; 18: 421–426.
60. Spencer J, MacDonald TT, Diss TC, Walker-Smith JA, Ciclitira PJ, Isaacson PG. Changes in intraepithelial lymphocyte sub-populations in coeliac disease and enteropathy-associated T cell lymphoma (malignant histiocytosis of the intestine). Gut 1989; 30: 339–346.
61. Holm K, Macki M, Savilahti E, Lipsanen V, Laippala P, Koskimies S. Intraepithelial T cell-receptor lymphocytes and genetic susceptibility to coeliac disease. Lancet 1992; 339: 1500–1503.
62. Swinson CM, Slavin G, Coles EC, Booth CC. Coeliac disease and malignancy. Lancet 1983; 1: 111–115.
63. O'Driscoll BRC, Stevens FN, O'Gorman TA, et al. HLA type of patients with coeliac disease and malignancy in the west of Ireland. Gut 1982; 23: 662–665.
64. Hourihane DO'B, Weir DG. Malignant celiac syndrome. Gastroenterology 1970; 29: 130–139.
65. Alfsen GC, Beiske K, Bell H, Martin Per F. Low-grade intestinal lymphoma of intraepithelial T-lymphocytes with concomitant enteropathy-associated T cell lymphoma: Case report suggesting a possible histogenetic relationship. Hum Pathol 1989; 20: 909–913.

CHAPTER

38 Other tumours of the oesophagus

A. M. Mandard R. Whitehead L. Li
S. R. Hamilton W. V. Bogomoletz

PART I

Tumours of the squamous epithelium

A. M. Mandard

EPIDEMIOLOGICAL AND AETIOLOGICAL FACTORS

Oesophageal cancer is generally rapidly progressive and thus there is little difference between incidence and mortality rates. In the most recent epidemiological studies,[1–4] the highest incidence is reported in the black population of South Africa (63.8:10^5), in China (31.7:10^5) and in Central Asia (where rates range from 10:10^5 to over 80:10^5). High rates also occur in the Chinese of Singapore (20:10^5) and in India in the region of Bombay (15:10^5). In Europe, the highest incidence is found in France (14:10^5). It is generally an uncommon disease in the Americas, except among certain black male populations of the United States and the Caribbean (14.8:10^5) and in Brazil (13.1:10^5). Elsewhere in the world, oesophageal cancer remains uncommon.[5]

Sharp gradients in incidence have been demonstrated in the countries where the disease is most common, and rates can vary from one to ten within a few miles. Cancer of the oesophagus occurs in both sexes but with the exception of Scandinavia, the United Kingdom, India and certain peoples of Central Asia, there is a marked male predominance.[1,4]

Aetiological factors

The demonstration of marked variations in incidence of oesophageal cancer has directed epidemiological research to the role of environmental factors. Alcohol and tobacco are currently considered to be the essential aetiological factors in France, the United States, Japan and certain Latin American countries, where they are estimated to account for 80% of male cases.[5] The combined effect of both fits with a multiplicative model.[6] In South Africa and India, tobacco has been found to play a greater role than alcohol.[5] Nutritional deficiencies (especially of vitamins A and C and riboflavine) have been observed in the oesophageal cancer populations of the United States, France, Puerto Rico and Japan. Dietary deficiency may thus potentiate the effects of alcohol and tobacco.[5]

On the other hand, in north-eastern Iran and northern China, where the risk of oesophageal cancer is highest, alcohol and tobacco are not major aetiological factors. In northern Iran, oesophageal cancer is associated with a markedly restricted diet and the eating of opium pipe residues which are both mutagenic and carcinogenic. The effect of these carcinogens on an oesophageal mucosa made susceptible by dietary deficiencies, and the frequent use of hot tea, could explain most cases of oesophageal cancer.[5] In northern China, another suggested aetiological factor is the consumption of mouldy foodstuffs. Laboratory experiments have shown that extracts of these foodstuffs have a mutagenic and weak carcinogenic activity. In addition, nitroso compounds which have been identified in these foodstuffs and in cornbread made of wheat flour inoculated with *Fusarium moniliform*[5] can induce oeosophageal cancer in experimental animals.[7]

Some studies have suggested that human papillomavirus infection may be implicated in the development of oesophageal squamous-cell carcinoma.[8–10]

Individual susceptibility

In addition to environmental factors, there are other predisposing conditions[11]

Tylosis, or keratosis palmaris et plantaris, a genodermatosis characterized by abnormal keratinization, can be associated with oesophageal carcinoma,[12,13] but accounts for a minimal proportion of cases.[1]

Oesophageal cancer can develop after chemical burning of the oesophagus. The precise incidence of associated carcinoma varies, according to the series studied, from 0 to 16%.[14] The incidence of lye corrosion in series of oesophageal carcinoma varies from 0.8–7.2%;[15] there is often a latent period of several decades and it can exceed 40 years.[14,16]

Achalasia is another risk factor and in a recent review of 1388 cases, occurred in 3.8%.[14]

The Patterson-Kelly or Plummer-Vinson syndrome (postcricoid dysphasia associated with hypochromic anaemia) is also a predisposing factor. This syndrome occurs particularly in Scandinavia, where it has been shown that correction of the factors associated with it has caused a decrease in the incidence of upper alimentary tract cancer.[11]

An increased incidence of oesophageal cancer is also found in patients with Barrett's oesophagus but it is usually adenocarcinoma and occurs in less than 10%.[17] In rare cases, a squamous cell carcinoma can arise from Barrett's oesophagus.[18]

Oesophageal diverticula have been linked to cancer of the oesophagus,[19] and in 45 cases collected from the literature the incidence varied between 0.3–0.8%. Radiation-induced oesophageal neoplasms appear to be extremely rare, for in 1984 only 13 cases had been published, the majority being squamous cell carcinomas.[20]

BENIGN TUMOURS OF THE SQUAMOUS EPITHELIUM

The only benign tumour of the squamous epithelium of the oesophagus is the papilloma, and it is rare,[21] only two papillomas being found in 19 982 autopsies.[22] Only three were reported in 6157 endoscopic examinations and only 17 documented cases appear in the literature up to 1980[23] and more than 60 cases up to 1992.[24] Oesophageal papilloma is predominantly a tumour of adult males, although exceptional cases have been reported in young subjects. It may be located in any region of the oesophagus, but a predominance of lower-third lesions has been noted. Clinically, the tumour is most frequently asymptomatic, and is an incidental finding at endoscopy. It presents as a smooth, round, pink, sharply demarcated, sessile tumour, varying in size from 0.4–1.5 cm.[25] It is generally single, but can be multiple,[26] and a giant form is described, but is extremely rare.[27]

Histologically, the papilloma consists of finger-like projections of delicate fibrous tissue supporting layers of stratified squamous epithelium.[28] It is now usual practice to resect the lesion via an endoscope.[29,30]

Aetiological studies in cattle, in which the tumour is common and known to precede carcinoma, have demonstrated a viral origin.[31,32] It can also be induced in the rodent by nitrosamines,[7] and appears to be one stage in the development of carcinoma.[33] In humans, the human papilloma virus antigen has been identified by immunoperoxidase[34,35] and by in-situ hybridization.[24]

PRECANCEROUS LESIONS OF THE HUMAN OESOPHAGUS

Although the different stages of oesophageal carcinogenesis have been well documented in animals,[36,37] fewer studies of precancerous lesions of the oesophagus in humans have been made. The oesophageal mucosa in autopsy or surgical specimens that harbour carcinoma has been examined for lesions comparable to those known to be precancerous in histologically similar tissue, such as the squamous epithelium of the uterine cervix.

A second approach has involved the screening of high risk populations with follow-up studies aimed at detecting precancerous conditions. The first screening studies were conducted in northern China using cytological examination,[38] but more recently, in Iran and northern China, endoscopy and biopsies have been used.[39,40]

Oesophageal dysplasia and in situ carcinoma

Although to date no specific terminology has been accepted, recent work seems to show that oesophageal dysplasia and in situ carcinoma may be classified in a manner similar to that used for the intra-epithelial neoplasia of other squamous mucosae.[41–45]

In an autopsy study in Japan, in different risk areas, the lower two-thirds of the oesophagus was assessed for dysplasia. A higher rate of severe dysplasia in the high risk regions was demonstrated and subsequently evaluated in a cytofluorometric study.[46–47] Oesophageal dysplasia has also been found at autopsy in South Africa,[48] which is also a high risk area.

In China, systematic cytological screening of high risk populations using the balloon technique,[38] and more recently also utilizing histological methods,[49] revealed that there was a similarity between the incidence of dysplasia and mortality from oesophageal cancer within a given region. The average age of the population with dysplasia was five years younger than that of the cancer patients. Follow-up of cases with dysplasia shows that the rate of progression to cancer increases with the time and that the more severe the dysplasia at detection, the greater the potential for malignant transformation.

Endoscopic and biopsy examinations have been conducted among the high and low risk populations of Iran and China. Oesophageal dysplasia was encountered in high risk populations only and was found in 4.7–7.9% of males and 2.9–8.1% of females.[40,50] In a recent report from China, the rate of dysplasia was 38% in a high risk region and 4% in a low risk region.[51]

An in situ carcinoma is frequently found bordering on, or distant from, the invasive carcinoma in surgical or autopsy specimens.[42,52,53] The endoscopic appearance of in situ carcinomas associated with micro-invasive neoplasms has also been described.[54] In a French study, oesophagectomy specimens from 56 cancer patients were examined in semi-serial sections, and in 14% an in situ carcinoma was found distant from the invasive cancer. In this population, oesophageal cancer is linked to alcohol and tobacco consumption, and is associated with a high incidence of a second oesophageal malignancy or other tumours of the upper digestive tract.[42]

The macroscopic features of in situ carcinoma have been defined in a report on 20 cases by Mandard et al[55] as: mucosal erosion, the most frequent (Fig. 38.1); mosaic patterns; hypervascularisation; and occult. The in situ carcinoma is characteristically iodine-negative.[42,55] Toluidine blue appears to give a positive result in the majority of cases and vital staining can be helpful to endoscopists when screening high risk populations for early oesophageal cancer, particularly in its occult forms.[54]

Histologically, dysplasia once in situ carcinoma of the oesophagus does not differ from that arising in other squamous mucosae (Fig. 38.2).

In addition, studies of high risk populations in Iran and China have highlighted the possible role of oesophagitis as a precursor to cancer.[40] The endoscopic and histological appearances of the oesophagitis in these countries have been characterized.[39,40,56,57] In China, moderate and severe oesophagitis have been found more frequently among people in the high risk areas for oesophageal carcinoma than in the low risk areas.[51] Chronic oesophagitis was associated with cigarette smoking in a high risk population for oesophageal cancer.[58]

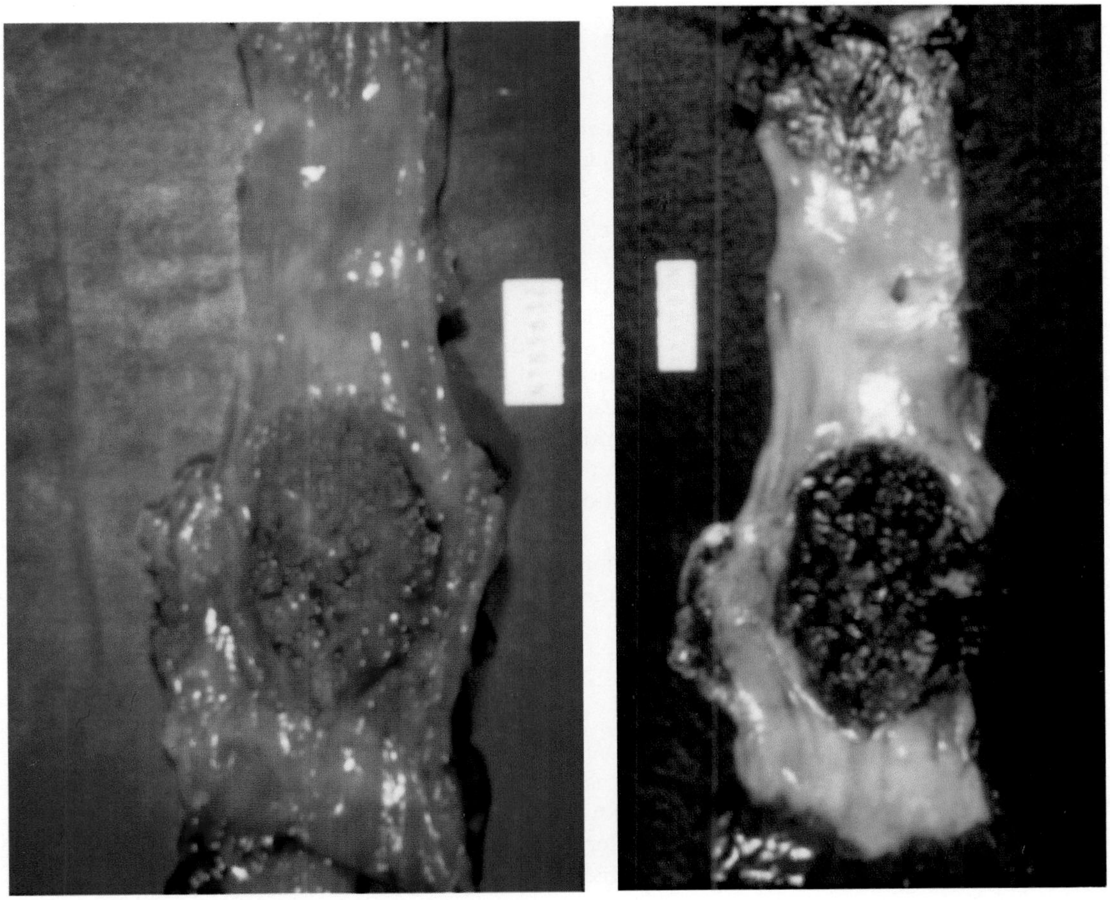

Fig. 38.1 Oesophageal in situ carcinoma erosive type (1) at a distance from squamous carcinoma fungating type (2). (Fresh specimen (left); toluidine blue dye test (right)).

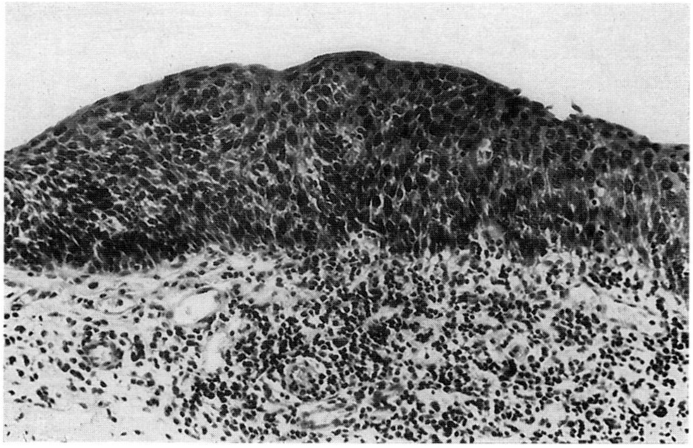

Fig. 38.2 Oesophagus: in situ squamous cell carcinoma. (H&E, ×138)

MALIGNANT TUMOURS OF THE SQUAMOUS EPITHELIUM

The average age at diagnosis of squamous carcinoma is 55–65 years. About 50% are located in the middle third, 31% in the lower third, and 15% in the upper third of the oesophagus.[59]

Endoscopy and gross pathology

The gross appearance of oesophageal cancer will vary according to whether it is detected early or at an advanced stage, as is usually the case in populations without screening procedures.

Invasive carcinomas limited to the mucosa and submucosa may appear endoscopically as an area of localized congestion and oedema, more commonly as a superficial erosion, or as a focus of coarse granularity or a polypoid protrusion.[60] In surgical specimens, they may occur as erosions or plaques, or be papillary.[50,61] The Japanese have described similar morphological and endoscopic appearances.[62] Advanced oesophageal carcinomas are most commonly fungating but may be ulcerative and infiltrating.[28] Verrucous and polypoid types are far less common and, rarely, carcinomas are multifocal.[63–65]

After preoperative chemoradiotherapy, the oesophagus may have a sclerocicatricial or ulcerosclerocicatricial appearance.

Histology

Histologically, squamous cell carcinomas represent between 72–96% of the published cases of oesophageal malignancy.[42,66–68] According to the WHO classification, squamous cell carcinoma is usually graded as well, moderately and poorly differentiated.[21] The appearance may vary markedly from one area to another, from well differentiated to relatively undifferentiated.[42] The verrucous carcinoma is a rare but particular variant of squamous cell carcinoma,[63] and is histologically comparable to verrucous carcinoma arising in other sites.[69,70] Only a few cases have been reported as arising in the oesophagus, where they present as an exophytic, papillary, warty, fungating mass. Histologically, it is a malignant papillary tumour composed of well differentiated squamous epithelium with minimal cytologic atypia, and blunt, pushing rather than infiltrating margins[21] (Fig. 38.3). Differential diagnosis from benign papilloma and pseudo-epitheliomatous hyperplasia requires adequate biopsy specimens and close collaboration between endoscopist and histopathologist.

What is now recognized as another variant of squamous cell carcinoma is spindle cell carcinoma, also described as pseudosarcoma or carcinosarcoma. This is considered in detail later in this chapter.

DNA analysis

Abnormal nuclear DNA content has been found in oesophageal carcinoma[71–73] and DNA analyses have been reported as prognostically relevant.[74–78] DNA aneuploidy was correlated with histological grading and postoperative recurrences.[79] Proliferative antigen (Ki67) and proliferative cell nuclear antigen can be immunolocalized in cytology smears from oesophageal carcinoma and may be helpful in assessing the proliferative activity.[80]

Immunohistochemistry of cancerous and precancerous lesions in comparison with the normal uninvolved oesophageal epithelium

Human chorionic gonadotrophin, human placental lactogen, alpha-fetoprotein, carcino-embryonic antigen and non-specific cross-reacting antigen may be tumour-associated antigens in oesophageal cancer.[81] p53 mutation has been described in oesophageal precancerous lesions as well as in oesophageal carcinoma.[82–84] Epidermal growth factor over-expression has been observed and correlates with a bad prognosis.[85,86]

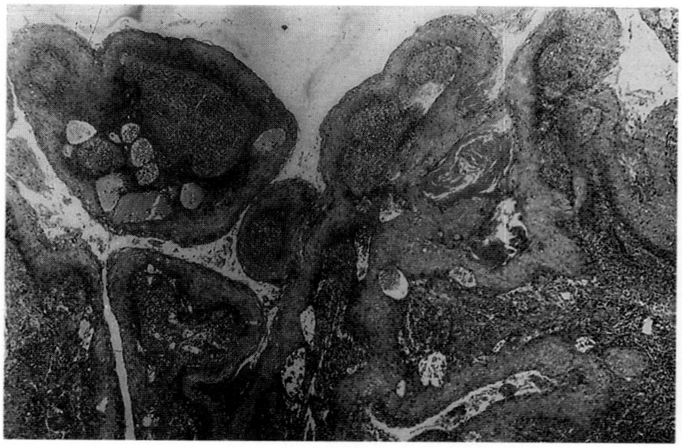

Fig. 38.3 Oesophagus: verrucous carcinoma (H&E, ×21).

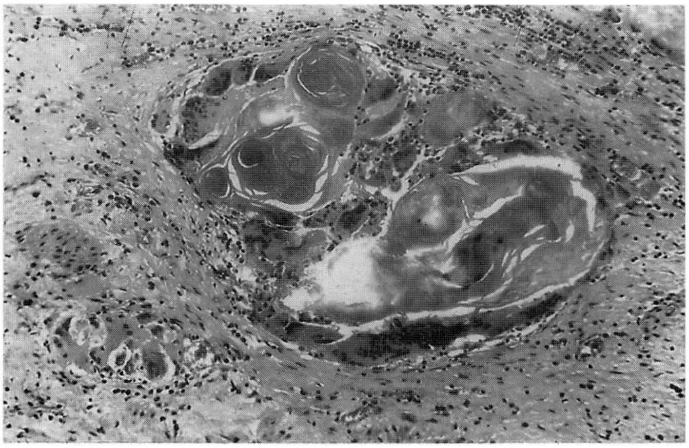

Fig. 38.4 Oesophageal squamous cell carcinoma: tumour regression after irradiation and chemotherapy — giant cell granuloma around ghost cells and keratin. (H&E, ×86)

Morphological alterations of oesophageal cancer after irradiation and/or chemotherapy

Radiation therapy and chemotherapy can induce partial or, more rarely, complete tumour regression. This regression is observed macroscopically, as the cancer loses its fungating appearance and becomes an ulcer or a scar. Histologically, giant cell granulomas appear around ghost cells or keratin (Fig. 38.4), and then give way to fibrous scar tissue.

Experimental cancer

Oesophageal cancer can be induced in various animal species and these tumours have been compared to human oesophageal cancer.[36,37] The majority of experimental cancers have been induced in rodents, particularly in the rat. The tumours produced are generally papillomas or well-differentiated keratinizing papillary carcinomas which do not metastasize.[7,33,36,87] Tumours produced in the monkey and the dog seem to most closely resemble those found in humans,[36] however it is difficult to establish a sufficiently large experimental series, and the more recent work on carcinogenesis of the oesophagus concerns experiments in transplantation to the nude mouse and cell transformation in tissue cultures.[88–91]

Natural history and patterns of spread of malignant tumours of the squamous epithelium of the oesophagus

In China it has been shown that asymptomatic patients with in situ carcinoma develop advanced cancer within 3–4 years.[60] In most other countries without screening programmes, cancer of the oesophagus is diagnosed when symptomatic, i.e. at an already advanced stage. In 1939, Dormanns[92] reported that the average interval from onset of symptoms to autopsy was 7.3 months. A much more recent autopsy study shows that this has changed little in populations where there are no attempts at early detection, with the interval from first symptoms to autopsy being 10.6 months.[53] Thus it can also be surmised that the local and metastatic spread of symptomatic disease at diagnosis will be similar to that found at post-mortem. Cancer of the oesophagus spreads locally to the oesophageal wall, peri-oesophageal tissues, mediastinum, trachea, aorta, pleura, bronchi, lung and pericardium. The organs involved will obviously depend on the region of the oesophagus in which the cancer is located. Curative surgery can be envisaged in only 10% of cancers diagnosed when symptomatic.[93] Curative surgical specimens studied in semi-serial sections show extension to the adventitia in 72% of cases and lymph node metastases in 76% of cases. In autopsy series,[28] extension beyond the oesophagus occurs in 60% of cases. More recent post-mortem studies show that local spread is associated with metastases to the cervical, mediastinal or abdominal lymph nodes in more than 70% of cases.[53,94] Lymph node metastases do not necessarily reflect the site of the cancer because 40% of the cancers in the upper third of the oesophagus metastasize to the abdominal lymph nodes and 38% of lower third cancer to cervical lymph nodes.[53]

Metastases to the viscera are observed in 39%–75% of autopsied cases.[28,53,91,95] The most commonly involved organs are the liver (18–47%) and the lung (15–52%), but the cancer can spread to almost any viscera. Undifferentiated carcinomas and squamous cell carcinomas with an undifferentiated component demonstrate the highest rate of visceral and lymph node metastases.[28,53,94]

The most common cause of death appears to be bronchopulmonary, i.e. bronchopneumonia, interstitial pneumonitis, lymphangitic carcinomatosis and Mendelsohn's syndrome.[53] In the geographic areas where alcohol and tobacco are the recognized aetiological factors, autopsy reveals that 10% of patients with oesophageal carcinoma have a second cancer of the upper digestive tract, and the incidence of malignant tumours originating in sites other than the upper digestive tract is also significant.[53]

Treatment and results

A detailed study of the results of the various therapeutic modalities used in the treatment of cancer of the oesophagus has been made.[59] Choice of the treatment depends on the stage at which the disease is diagnosed. Patients with superficial oesophageal squamous carcinoma can benefit from early diagnosis and prompt surgery.[96] When the cancer is detected at an advanced stage in symptomatic subjects, attempted curative excision (oesophagectomy or oesophagogastrectomy) may not be possible. Radiotherapy and chemotherapy can be used as adjuncts, especially when indicated by peroperative observations of the extent of disease and by the results of histopathological examination of the specimen. Radiotherapy and chemotherapy may also be given prior to surgery, and studies are currently being conducted in order to assess the precise roles for these methods. The results obtained with surgery for carcinoma of the oesophagus and cardia range from 14–34.6% survival at 5 years.[97] The Chinese report survival rates after surgery which reach 44% in Linxian county,[98] and can apparently be as high as 90.3% at five years for cancer detected at an early stage because of routine cytological screening. In the absence of lymph node metastases, survival at five years reaches 47.9%, whereas when metastases are present the rate is only 6.3%. Similarly, when involvement is limited to the oesophageal wall, survival at five years is 32.6%, whereas when the cancer has spread beyond the oesophageal wall, the rate drops to 7.3%. Oesophageal cancer arising within the circumstances which prevail in China renders comparison with cancer arising in Western countries difficult. In the latter, the role of alcohol and tobacco in aetiology may constitute a poorer prognostic factor. Thus, the percentage of resectable tumours reported by the Chinese authors before the introduction of screening tests was 39.1%,[98] whereas in France, where there is also no screening, it was only 10%.[93] Survival at five years in the patient populations treated prior to 1975 with radiation therapy only rarely exceeds 7%.[59]

REFERENCES

1. Day NE, Munoz N, Ghadirian P. Epidemiology of esophageal cancer: a review. In: Correa P, Haenszel W, eds. Epidemiology of Cancer of the digestive tract. The Hague: Martinus Nijhoff, 1982: pp 21–57.
2. Day NE. The geographic pathology of cancer of the oesophagus. Br Med Bull 1984; 40: 329–334.
3. Parkin DM, Stjernsward J, Muir CS. Estimates of the worldwide frequency of twelve major cancers. Bull WHO 1984; 62: 163–182.
4. Schottenfeld D. Epidemiology of Cancer of the esophagus. Semin Oncol 1984; 11: 92–100.
5. Munoz N, Crespi M. Studies in the aetiology of oesophageal carcinoma. In: Watson A, Celestin LP, eds. Disorders of the esophagus — Advances and controversies. London: Pitman Publishing, 1984: pp 147–154.
6. Tuyns AJ, Pequignot G, Jensen OM. Le cancer de l'oesophage en Ille-et-Vilaine en fonction des niveaux de consommation d'alcool et de tabac. Des risques qui se multiplient. Bull Cancer 1977; 64: 45–60.
7. Druckrey H, Preussmann R, Ivankovic S, Schmahl D. Organotrope carcinogene Wirkungen bei 65 verschiedenen N-Nitroso-Verbindungen an BD-Ratten. Z Krebsforsch 1967; 69: 103–201.
8. Benamouzig R, Pigot F, Quiroga G, et al. Human papillomavirus infection in esophageal squamous-cell carcinoma in western countries. Int J Cancer 1992; 50: 549–552.
9. Chang F, Syrjanen S, Shen Q, Ji H, Syrjnen K. Human papillomavirus (HPV) DNA in esophageal precancer lesions and squamous cell carcinomas from China. Int J Cancer 1990; 45: 21–25.
10. Toh Y, Kuwano H, Tanaka S, et al. Detection of human papillomavirus DNA in esophageal carcinoma in Japan by polymerase chain reaction. Cancer 1992; 70: 2234–2238.
11. Warwick GP, Harington JS. Some aspects of the epidemiology and etiology of esophageal cancer with particular emphasis on the Transkei, South Africa. In: Klein G, Weinhouse S, eds. Advances in cancer research, vol 17, New York: Academic Press, 1973: pp 81–229.
12. O'Mahony MY, Ellis JP, Hellier M, Mann R, Huddy P. Familial tylosis and carcinoma of the oesophagus. J R Soc Med 1984; 77: 514–517.
13. Ritter SB, Petersen G. Esophageal cancer, hyperkeratosis, and oral leukoplakia. Occurrence in a 25-year-old woman. JAMA 1976; 235: 1723.
14. Nakamura T, Nakayama K. Malignant esophageal tumors concomitant with benign esophageal diseases. Int Adv Surg Oncol 1984; 7: 33–46.
15. Applequist P, Salmo M. Lye corrosion carcinoma of the esophagus. A review of 63 cases. Cancer 1980; 45: 2655–2658.
16. Hopkins RA, Postlethwait RW. Caustic burns and carcinoma of the esophagus. Ann Surg 1981; 194: 146–148.
17. Spechler SJ, Robbins AH, Bloomfield Rubins H, et al. Adenocarcinoma and Barrett's esophagus. An overrated risk. Gastroenterology 1984; 87: 927–933.
18. Resano CH, Cabrera N, Gonzalez Cueto D, Sanchez Basso AE, Rubio HH. Double early epidermoid carcinoma of the esophagus in columnar epithelium. Endoscopy 1985; 17: 73–75.
19. Fujita H, Kakegawa T, Shima S, Kumagaya Y. Carcinoma within a middle esophageal (para-bronchial) diverticulum: a case report and the review of the literature. Jpn J Surg 1980; 10: 142–148.
20. Sherrill DJ, Grishkin BA, Galal FS, Zajtchuk R, Graeber GM. Radiation associated malignancies of the esophagus. Cancer 1984; 54: 726–728.
21. Watanabe H, Jass JR, Sobin LH. Histological typing of oesophageal and gastric tumours. WHO International Histological Classification of Tumours, 2nd ed., Springer-Verlag, Berlin, 1990: pp 1–109.
22. Plachta A. Benign tumors of the esophagus — Review of the literature and report of 99 cases. Am J Gastroenterol 1962; 38: 639–651.
23. Colina F, Solis JA, Munoz MT. Squamous papilloma of the esophagus — A report of three cases and a review of the literature. Am J Gastroenterol 1980; 74: 410–414.
24. Politoske EJ. Squamous papilloma of the esophagus associated with the human papillomavirus. Gastroenterol 1992; 102: 668–673.
25. Javdan P, Pitman ER. Squamous papilloma of esophagus. Dig Dis Sci 1984; 29: 317–320.
26. Nuwayhid NS, Ballard ET, Cotton R. Esophageal papillomatosis. Case report. Ann Otol Rhinol Laryngol 1977; 86: 623.
27. Walker JH. Giant papilloma of the thoracic esophagus. Am J Roentgenol 1978; 131: 519–520.
28. Si-Chun Ming. Benign epithelial tumors. In: Tumors of the esophagus and stomach. Washington, DC: Armed Forces Institutes of Pathology, 1973: pp 22–23. (Atlas of Tumor Pathology, 2nd series, fascicle 7).
29. Ravry MJR. Endoscopic resection of squamous papilloma of the esophagus. Am J Gastroenterol 1979; 71: 398–400.
30. Toet AE, Dekker W, Odo Op den Orth J, Block P. Squamous cell papilloma of the esophagus: report of four cases. Gastrointest Endosc 1985; 31: 77–79.
31. Saveria Campo M, Moar MH, Jarrett WFH, Laird HM. A new papillomavirus associated with alimentary cancer in cattle. Nature 1980; 286: 180–182.
32. Jarrett WFH, Saveria Campo M, Blaxter ML, et al. Alimentary fibropapilloma in cattle: a spontaneous tumor, nonpermissive for papillomavirus replication. JNCI 1984; 73: 499–504.
33. Pozharisski KM. Tumours of the oesophagus. In: Turusov VS, ed. Pathology of tumours in laboratory animals, vol. 1, part I. Lyon: International Agency for Research on Cancer, 1973: pp 87–100. (IARC Scientific publication No. 5).
34. Syrjanen K, Pyrhonen S, Aukee S, Koskela E. Squamous cell papilloma of the oesophagus: a tumour probably caused by human papilloma virus (HPV). Diagn Histopathol 1982; 5: 291–296.
35. Winkler B, Capo V, Reumann W, et al. Human papillomavirus infection of the esophagus. A clinicopathologic study with demonstration of papillomavirus antigen by the immunoperoxidase technique. Cancer 1985; 55: 149–155.
36. Stinson SF, Reznik G. Comparative pathology of experimental esophageal carcinoma. In: Pfeiffer CJ, ed. Cancer of the esophagus, vol. II, Boca Raton, Fl: CRC Press, 1982: pp 139–168.
37. Peto R, Gray R, Branton P, Grasso P. Dose and time relationships for tumor induction in the liver and esophagus of 4080 inbred rats

by chronic ingestion of *N*-Nitrosodiethylamine or *N*-Nitrosodimethylamine. Cancer Res 1991; 51: 6452–6469.
38. The Coordinating Groups for the Research of Esophageal Carcinoma, Honan Province and Chinese Academy of Medical Sciences. Studies on the relationship between epithelial dysplasia and carcinoma of the esophagus. Chin Med J 1975; 1: 110–116.
39. Crespi M, Munoz N, Grassi A, et al. Oesophageal lesions in Northern Iran: a premalignant condition? Lancet 1979; 2: 217–220.
40. Munoz N, Crespi M, Grassi A, Wang Guo Qing, Shen Qiong, Li Zhang Cai. Precursor lesions of oesophageal cancer in high-risk populations in Iran and China. Lancet 1982; 1: 876–879.
41. Sato E, Mukada T, Sasano N. Dysplasia as related to esophageal carcinoma in Japan. In: Pfeiffer CJ, ed. Cancer of the esophagus, vol. I. Boca Raton, Fl: CRC Press, 1982: pp 125–138.
42. Mandard AM, Marnay J, Gignoux M, et al. Cancer of the esophagus and associated lesions: detailed pathologic study of 100 esophagectomy specimens. Hum Pathol 1984; 15: 660–669.
43. Rubio CA, Liu FS, Zhao HZ. Histologic classification of intraepithelial neoplasias and microinvasive squamous carcinoma of the esophagus. Am J Surg Pathol 1989; 13: 685–690.
44. Kuwano H, Morita M, Matsuda H, Mori M, Sugimachi K. Histopathologic findings of minute foci of squamous cell carcinoma in the human esophagus. Cancer 1991; 68: 2617–2620.
45. Nagamatsu M, Mori M, Kuwano H, Sugimachi K, Akiyoshi T. Serial histologic investigation of squamous epithelial dysplasia associated with carcinoma of the esophagus. Cancer 1992; 69: 1094–1098.
46. Mukada T, Sato E, Sasano N. Comparative studies on dysplasia of esophageal epithelium in four prefectures of Japan (Miyagi, Nara, Wakayama and Aomori) with reference to risk of carcinoma. Tohoku J Exp Med 1976; 119: 51–63.
47. Mukada T, Sasano N, Sato E. Evaluation of esophageal dysplasia by cytofluorometric analysis. Cancer 1978; 41: 1399–1404.
48. Jaskiewicz K, Banach L, Mafungo V, Knobel GJ. Oesophageal mucosa in a population at risk of oesophageal cancer: post-mortem studies. Int J Cancer 1992; 50: 32–35.
49. Yi-Jing Shu. The Cytopathology of esophageal carcinoma. Precancerous lesions and early cancer. Koss LG, ed. New York: Masson, 1985.
50. Fu-Sheng Liu, Song-Liang Qu. Pathological study of early human esophageal cancer in the People's Republic of China. In: Pfeiffer CJ, ed. Cancer of the esophagus, vol. I. Boca Raton, Fl: CRC Press 1982, pp 97–109.
51. Qiu S, Yang G. Precursor lesions of esophageal cancer in high-risk populations in Henan province, China. Cancer 1988; 62: 551–557.
52. Mandard AM. Precancerous lesions of the human esophagus. In: Pfeiffer CJ, ed. Cancer of the esophagus, vol. I. Boca Raton, Fl: CRC Press 1982, pp 91–95.
53. Mandard AM, Chasle J, Marnay J, et al. Autopsy findings in 111 cases of esophageal cancer. Cancer 1981; 48: 329–335.
54. Monnier Ph, Savary M, Pasche R, Anani P. Intra-epithelial carcinoma of the oesophagus: endoscopic morphology. Endoscopy 1981; 13: 185–191.
55. Mandard AM, Tourneux J, Gignoux M, Segol P, Blanc L, Mandard JC. In situ carcinoma of the esophagus. Macroscopic study with particular reference to the Lugol test. Endoscopy 1980; 12: 51–57.
56. Crespi M, Munoz N, Grassi A, Shen Qiong, Wang Kuo Jing, Lin Jing Jien. Precursor lesions of oesophageal cancer in a low-risk population in China: comparison with high-risk populations. Int J Cancer 1984; 34: 599–602.
57. Crespi M, Grassi A, Munoz N, Guo-Quing W, Guanrei Y. Endoscopic features of suspected precancerous lesions in high-risk areas for esophageal cancer. Endoscopy 1984; 16: 85–91.
58. Jacob JH, Riviere A, Mandard AM, et al. Prevalence survey of precancerous lesions of the oesophagus in a high-risk population for oesophageal cancer in France. Europ J Cancer Prev 1993; 2: 53–59.
59. Roth JA, Lichter AS, Putnam JB Jr, Forastiere AA. Cancer of the esophagus. In: De Vita VT Jr, Hellman S, Rosenberg SA, eds. Cancer Principles and Practice of Oncology, 4th ed. Philadelphia: Lippincott JB, 1993: vol. 1, pp 776–817.
60. Guanrei Y, He H, Sungliang Q, Yuming C. Endoscopic diagnosis of 115 cases of early esophageal carcinoma. Endocopy 1982; 14: 157–161.
61. Tumor Prevention, Treatment and Research Group, Chengchow, Honan; Esophageal Cancer Research Group, Chinese Academy of Medical Sciences, Peking; and Linhsien County People's Hospital, Honan. Pathology of early esophageal squamous cell carcinoma. Chin Med J 1977; 3: 180–192.
62. Endo M, Yamada A, Ide H, Yoshida M, Hayashi T. Nakayama K. Early cancer of the esophagus: diagnosis and clinical evaluation. Int Adv Surg Oncol 1980; 3: 49–71.
63. Minielly JA, Harrison EG, Fontana RS, Payne WS. Verrucous squamous cell carcinoma of the esophagus. Cancer 1967; 20: 2078–2087.
64. Cho SR, Henry DA, Schneider V, Turner MA. Polypoid carcinoma of the esophagus: a distinct radiological and histopathological entity. Am J Gastroenterol 1983; 78: 476–480.
65. Tekeste H, Latour F. Squamous cell carcinoma of esophagus presenting as multiple pedunculated polyps. Dig Dis Sci 1986; 31: 433–437.
66. Cederquist C, Nielsen J, Berthelsen A, Hansen HS. Cancer of the oesophagus. I. 1002 cases: survey and survival. Acta Chir Scand 1978; 144: 227–231.
67. Suzuki H, Nagayo T. Primary tumors of the esophagus other than squamous cell carcinoma. Histologic classification and statistics in the surgical autopsied materials in Japan. Int Adv Surg Oncol 1980; 3: 73–109.
68. Turnbull AD, Goodner JT. Primary adenocarcinoma of the esophagus. Cancer 1968; 22: 915–918.
69. Ackerman LV. Verrucous carcinoma of the oral cavity. Surgery 1948; 23: 670–678.
70. Kraus FT, Perez-Mesa C. Verrucous carcinoma. Clinical and pathologic study of 105 cases involving oral cavity, larynx and genitalia. Cancer 1966; 19: 26–38.
71. Robaszkiewicz M, Reid BJ, Volant A, Cauvin JM, Rabinovitch PS, Gouerou H. Flow-cytometric DNA content analysis of esophageal squamous cell carcinomas. Gastroenterol 1991; 101: 1588–1593.
72. Rubio CA, Auer GU, Kato Y, Liu FS. DNA profiles in dysplasia and carcinoma of the human esophagus. Analyt Quant Cytol Histol 1988; 10: 207–210.
73. Sugimachi K, Koga Y, Mori M, Huang GJ, Yang K, Zhang RG. Comparative data on cytophotometric DNA in malignant lesions of the esophagus in the Chinese and Japanese. Cancer 1987; 59: 1947–1950.
74. Sugimachi K, Matsuoka H, Ohno S, Mori M, Kuwano H. Multivariate approach for assessing the prognosis of clinical oesophageal carcinoma. Br J Surg 1988; 75: 1115–1118.
75. Jin-Ming Y, Li-hua Y, Guo-Qian, et al. Flow cytometric analysis DNA content in esophageal carcinoma. Correlation with histologic and clinical features. Cancer 1989; 64: 80–82.
76. Kaketani K, Saito T, Kobayashi M. Flow cytometric analysis of nuclear DNA content in esophageal cancer. Aneuploidy as an index for highly malignant potential. Cancer 1989; 64: 887–891.
77. Edwards JM, Jones DJ, Wilkes SJ, Hillier VF, Hasleton PS. Ploidy as a prognostic indicator in oesophageal squamous carcinoma and its relationship to various histological criteria. J Pathol 1989; 159: 35–41.
78. Matsuura H, Kuwano H, Morita M, et al. Predicting recurrence time of esophageal carcinoma through assessment of histologic factors and DNA ploidy. Cancer 1991; 67: 1406–1411.
79. Ruol A, Segalin A, Panozzo M, et al. Flow cytometric DNA analysis of squamous cell carcinoma of the esophagus. Cancer 1990; 65: 1185–1188.
80. Sasano H, Miyazaki S, Nishihira T, Sawai T, Nagura H. The proliferative cell fraction in cytology specimens. A study of human esophageal carcinoma. Am J Clin Pathol 1992; 98: 161–166.
81. Burg-Kurland CL, Purnell DM, Combs JW, Hillman EA, Harris CC, Trump BF. Immunocytochemical evaluation of human esophageal neoplasms and preneoplastic lesions for beta-chorionic gonadotropin, placental lactogen, alpha-fetoprotein, carcinoembryonic antigen, and nonspecific cross-reacting antigen. Cancer Res 1986; 46: 2936–2943.
82. Bennett WP, Hollstein MC, Metcalf RA, et al. p53 mutation and protein accumulation during multistage human esophageal carcinogenesis. Cancer Res 1992; 52: 6092–6097.
83. Sasano H, Miyazaki S, Goukon Y, Nishihira T, Sawai T, Nagura H. Expression of p53 in human esophageal carcinoma: an

immunohistochemical study with correlation to proliferating cell nuclear antigen expression. Hum Pathol 1992; 23: 1238–1243.
84. Hollstein MC, Peri L, Mandard AM, et al. Genetic analysis of human esophageal tumors from two high incidence geographic areas: frequent p53 base substitutions and absence of ras mutations. Cancer Res 1991; 51: 4102–4106.
85. Yano H, Shiozaki H, Kobayashi K, et al. Immunohistologic detection of the epidermal growth factor receptor in human esophageal squamous cell carcinoma. Cancer 1991; 67: 91–98.
86. Iihara K, Shiozaki H, Tahara H, et al. Prognostic significance of transforming growth factor-alpha in human esophageal carcinoma. Indication for the autocrine proliferation. Cancer 1993; 71: 2902–2909.
87. Reuber MD. Experimental neoplasms of the esophagus in Buffalo strain rats. In: Pfeiffer CJ, ed. Cancer of the esophagus, vol. II, Boca Raton, Fl: CRC Press 1982, pp 169–183.
88. Banks-Schlegel SP, Harris CC. Tissue-specific expression of keratin proteins in human esophageal and epidermal epithelium and their cultured keratinocytes. Exp Cell Res 1983; 146: 271–280.
89. Kitamura M, Suda M, Nishihira T, Watanabe T, Kasai M. Heterotransplantation of human esophageal carcinoma to nude mice. Tohoku J Exp Med 1981; 135: 259–264.
90. Nishihira T, Kasai M, Mori S, et al. Characteristics of two cell lines (TE-1 and TE-2) derived from human squamous cell carcinoma of the esophagus. GANN 1979; 70: 575–584.
91. Robinson KM, Maistry L, Evers P, Bux S. Morphology of a human esophageal carcinoma cell line before and after transplantation into nude mice. Scan Electron Microsc 1980; II: 231–238.
92. Dormanns E. Das Oesophaguscarcinom. Ergebnisse der unter Mitarbeit von 39 Pathologischen Instituten Deutschlands durchgefuhrten Erhebung uber das Oesophaguscarcinom (1925–33). Z Krebsforsch 1939; 49: 86–108.
93. Roussel A, Gignoux M, Verwaerde JC, Segol Ph, Abbatucci JS, Valla A. Le cancer de l'oesophage dans l'Ouest de la France. Analyse retrospective d'une population de 1400 cas. Bull Cancer 1977; 64: 61–66.
94. Anderson LL, Lad TE. Autopsy findings in squamous-cell carcinoma of the esophagus. Cancer 1982; 50: 1587–1590.
95. Bosch A, Frias Z, Caldwell WL, Jaeschke WH. Autopsy findings in carcinoma of the esophagus. Acta Radiol 1979; 18: 103–112.
96. Bogomoletz WV, Molas G, Gayet B, Potet F. Superficial squamous cell carcinoma of the esophagus. A report of 76 cases and review of the literature. Am J Surg Pathol 1989; 13: 535–546.
97. Ellis, Jr FH. Carcinoma of the esophagus. Cancer J Clin 1983; 33: 264–281.
98. Wu Ying-K'Ai, Huang Kuo-Chun. Chinese experience in the surgical treatment of carcinoma of the esophagus. Ann Surg 1979; 190: 361–365.

PART II

Tumours of the cardia and oesophageal glands

R. Whitehead L. Li

BENIGN TUMOURS

Adenoma

True adenomas are extraordinarily rare lesions although areas that could be described as adenomatous hyperplasia are occasionally seen in Barrett's oesophagus. True adenomas originate in the oesophageal glands in heterotopic or in metaplastic columnar epithelium and may be cystic.[1] Histologically, they resemble either gastric[2,3] or, more rarely, bronchial adenomas.[4] They are usually single but a case of multiple villous adenomas in a patient with Barrett's oesophagus has been reported.[3]

MALIGNANT TUMOURS

Carcinomas arising from glandular epithelium account for 0.8–8% of malignant epithelial tumours of the oesophagus.[5–11] The most common site is in the lower third, and before a diagnosis of primary oesophageal adenocarcinoma is made it is often necessary to exclude the possibility that the lesion is not a cardiac carcinoma extending upwards to involve the lower oesophagus. There is increasing evidence that the incidence of lower oesophageal adenocarcinoma is rising,[12–14] but it does not seem to be related to the use of either cigarettes or alcohol.[15]

Gross appearances

Grossly, oesophageal adenocarcinomas are similar to squamous carcinoma and can be fungating or ulcerative, scirrhous or medullary, and sometimes polypoidal.[16] They usually produce some thickening of the wall and may be covered completely or incompletely by intact mucosa.

Histological appearances

Adenocarcinomas of the oesophagus may arise from gastric type mucosa in two situations. The columnar-lined oesophagus or metaplastic Barrett's oesophagus is closely associated with adenocarcinomas of the oesophagus and cardia.[17–23] The adenocarcinoma arises in Barrett's mucosa and is probably the commonest type of oesophageal carcinoma of glandular origin. There is now good evidence that in most, if not all, cases carcinoma arises through a stage of increasing dysplasia.[24–26] The dysplastic epithelium as seen in histological preparations has also been shown to express both transforming growth factor alpha, which is a growth promoting peptide, and proliferating cell nuclear antigen.[27]

Others may arise in heterotopic epithelium of either cardiac or fundic type, which occurs most commonly in the upper oesophagus, but this is extremely rare.[25]

There are two other types of glandular elements in the oesophagus which may give rise to carcinoma. These are the so-called cardiac glands, which are situated at the lower end of the oesophagus and are composed of simple mucous glands similar to the gastric cardiac glands. A few are also found at the upper oesophagus. There are also the oesophageal submucous glands which have a structure similar to the minor salivary glands. Their ducts have a cuboidal cell lining near the glands which becomes squamous nearer to the lumen. Carcinomas arising from the cardiac and oesophageal glands show differing patterns of differentiation which reflects these histological variations. Thus, in addition to anaplastic tumours, there are adenocarcinomas, adenosquamous carcinoma, mucoepidermoid carcinoma adenoid cystic carcinoma and rare composite tumours.

Adenocarcinoma

Adenocarcinoma of the oesophagus is identical to adenocarcinoma of the cardia.[22] Most consist of cuboidal or columnar cells which form tubular or acinar structures (Fig. 38.5). A small proportion are mucinous carcinomas and rarely, a signet-ring cell tumour occurs.[23,28,29] The diagnosis of oesophageal adenocarcinoma should only be made if this histological appearance is combined with a tumour situated at a distance above the oesophagogastric junction, and preferably contiguous with one or other types of glandular epithelium of the oesophagus.

Figure 38.6 depicts a well-differentiated adenocarcinoma which showed contiguity with surrounding glandular epithelium thought to be heterotopic.

The prognosis for oesophageal adenocarcinoma is poor.[5–7,23]

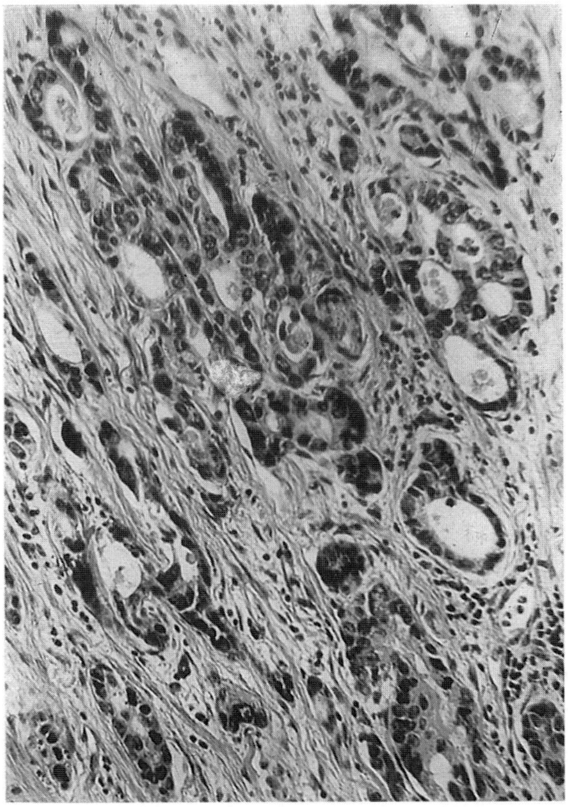

Fig. 38.5 Adenocarcinoma of the oesophagus. The tumour cells are moderately differentiated and are arranged in the form of tubular structures. (H&E, ×160)

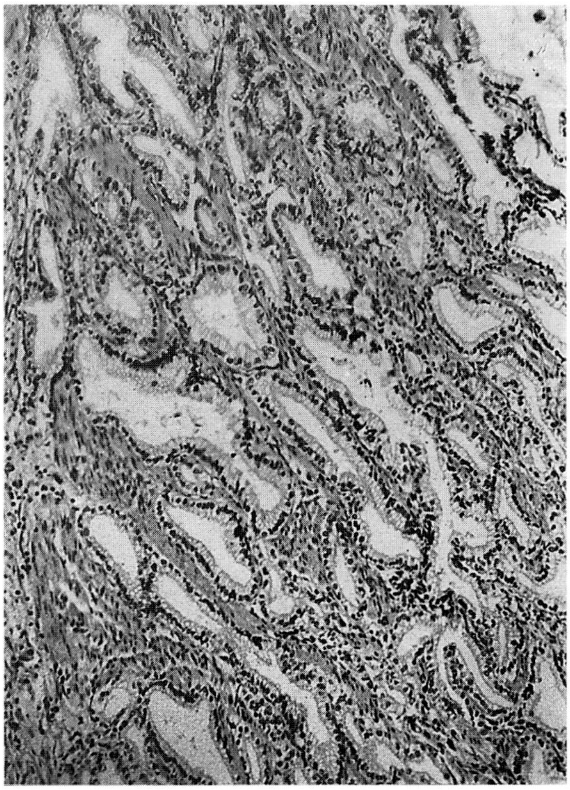

Fig. 38.6 Adenocarcinoma of the oesophagus. The tumour is very well differentiated and mimics dysplasia of cardiac glands. (H&E, ×100)

Adenosquamous carcinoma

Adenosquamous carcinoma arising from oesophageal glands is rare, but not as uncommon as it was once thought to be.[30] The prognosis is poor.

Histologically, both malignant squamous and glandular elements are present and often intimately intermingled (Fig. 38.7). Structures mimicking the ducts of submucosal glands are usually evident (Fig. 38.8). Sometimes the squamous component can be very well differentiated, and the term of adenoacanthoma or adenocarcinoma with squamous metaplasia has been used. The differentiation may also be very poor and such tumours can be confused with small cell undifferentiated carcinoma. If the two elements are not intimately mixed, the possibility of collision tumours needs to be considered.

Mucoepidermoid carcinoma

Mucoepidermoid carcinoma is rare,[31–37] and usually occurs in the elderly. Most arise in the lower and middle third of the oesophagus.

Histologically, it is identical to mucoepidermoid carcinoma arising in salivary glands, having mucinous, squamous and intermediate cells in varying proportions

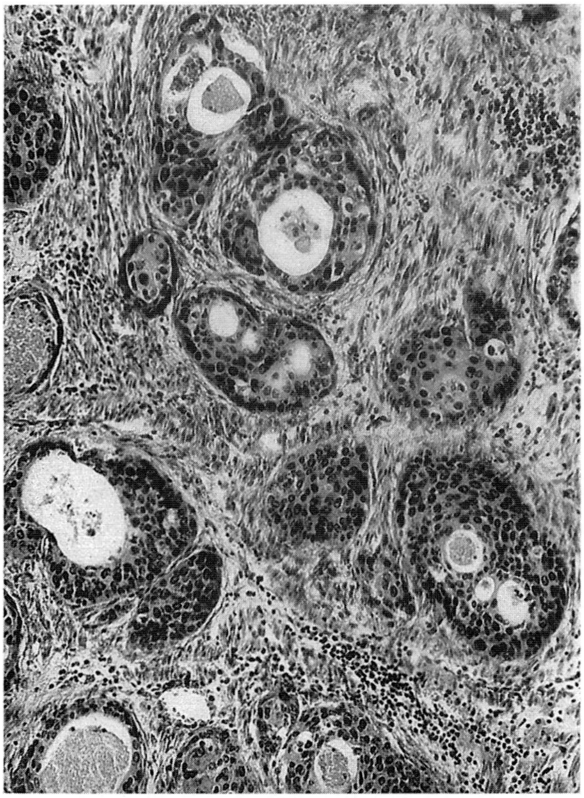

Fig. 38.7 Well differentiated adenosquamous carcinoma of the oesophagus. (H&E, ×100)

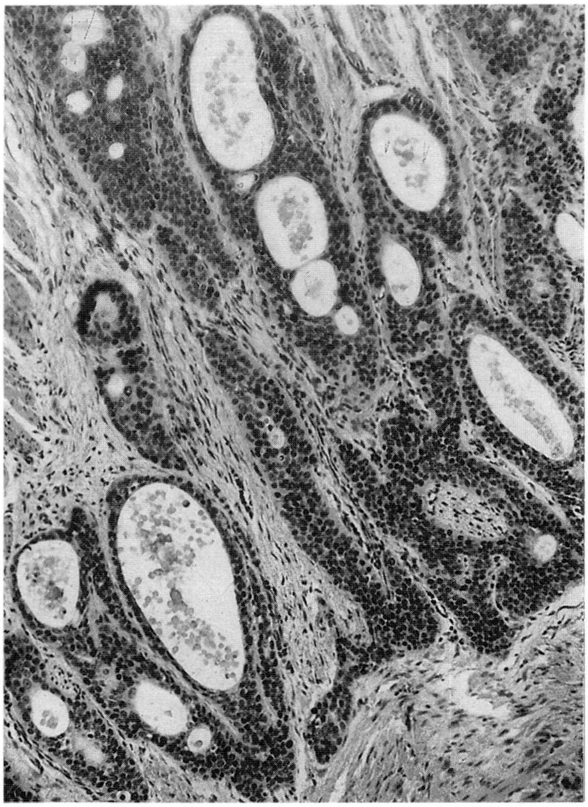

Fig. 38.8 Adenosquamous carcinoma of the oesophagus, exhibiting solid cell masses and structures resembling the ducts of oesophageal glands. (H&E, ×100)

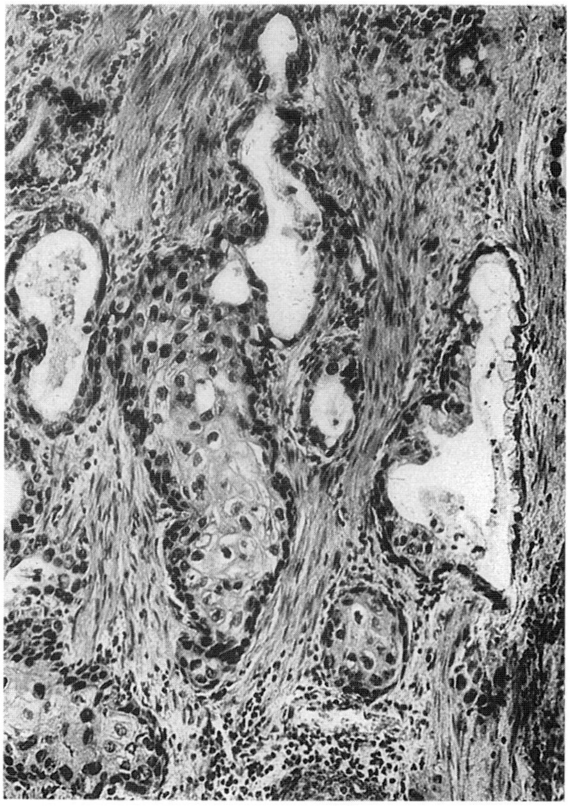

Fig. 38.9 Mucoepidermoid carcinoma of the oesophagus. The tumour cells form solid squamous foci with glandular spaces containing mucinous material. (H&E, ×100)

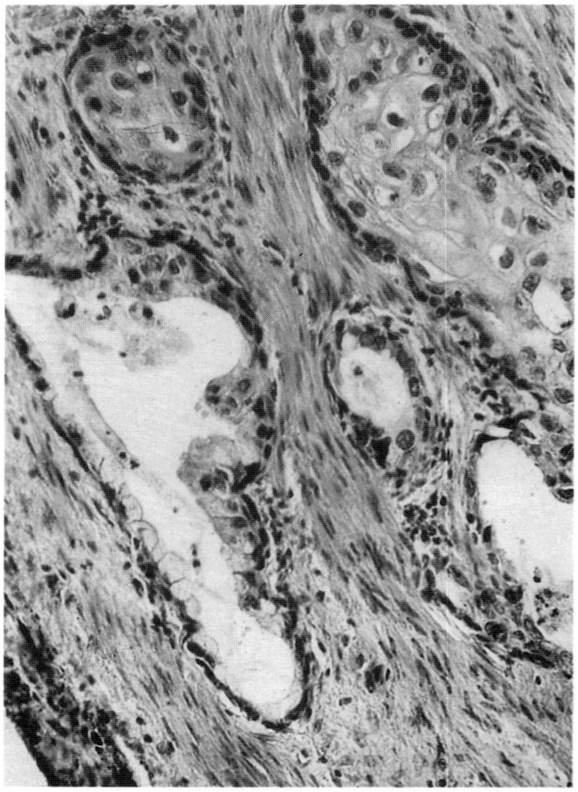

Fig. 38.10 Higher magnification of Figure 38.9, revealing mucin-secreting cells, squamous cells and intermediate cells. (H&E, ×200).

(Figs 38.9, 38.10). The mucin-secreting cells may be columnar, cuboidal or goblet shaped and they often form gland spaces. The squamous cells exhibit intercellular bridges and keratinization with occasional pearl formation. The overlying squamous epithelium is usually normal.

Despite its sometimes well differentiated histological appearance, most of the reported cases have been aggressive and the prognosis is poor.[31–33]

Electron microscopy demonstrates tumour cells with numerous cell junctions, tonofibrillar aggregates, microvilli, basal lamina and secretory vacuoles, all of which are features of both squamous and adenocarcinoma.[34]

Adenoid cystic carcinoma

This tumour is also relatively rare.[38–47] Most are located in the middle and lower third of the oesophagus. Elderly males predominate, with a mean age of 62 years. In the majority of the cases, the tumours show more aggressive behaviour than those of salivary glands.

Adenoid cystic carcinoma of the oesophagus has similar histological features to those seen in salivary glands. It is characterized by the presence of the cells of myoepithelial and glandular duct types, forming cribriform, pseudoacinar and small duct-like structures with stromal and intraluminal PAS and alcian blue positive mucus (Fig. 38.11). There are usually more solid and basaloid areas with more cellular pleomorphism and mitotic figures than in the salivary gland counterparts. The overlying epithelium, like that in mucoepidermoid carcinoma, is usually uninvolved (Fig. 38.12). However, in a proportion of cases, it shows hyperplasia, sometimes carcinoma in situ, and there are foci of squamous carcinoma in addition to the adenoid cystic areas.[43]

It has been suggested, because of the close resemblance to its counterpart in salivary glands and the upper respiratory tract, that the adenoid cystic carcinoma of the oesophagus originates in tracheobronchial rests.[48] However, most authors believe that it arises in the oesophageal submucosal glands.[43–45,49] Ultrastructural study reveals that the tumour cells have the features of myoepithelial and epithelial cells with microvilli, lumina and cystic spaces containing replicated basement membrane. The findings suggest that the intercalated ducts of oesophageal glands is the probable site of origin,[44] and this would be in keeping with the occasional occurrence of a squamous component.

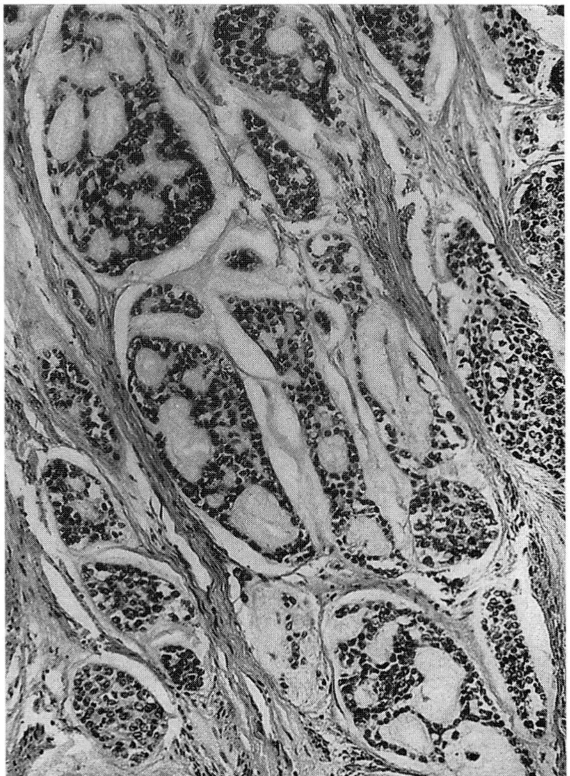

Fig. 38.11 Adenoid cystic carcinoma of the oesophagus, showing multiple cystic spaces and a cribriform arrangement, with intercellular and intraluminal mucus. (H&E, ×100)

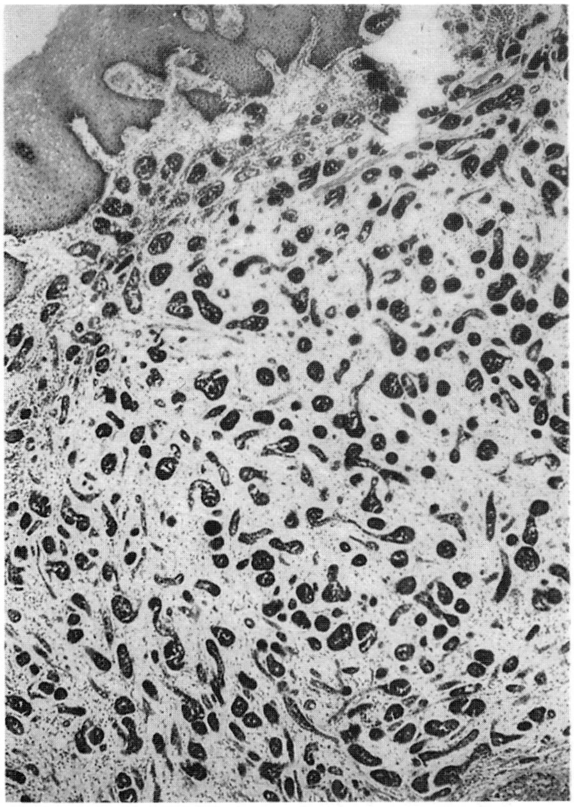

Fig. 38.12 A lower power view of the edge of the tumour in Figure 38.11. The tumour cells are mainly arranged in small cribriform groups. The overlying squamous epithelium is mildly hyperplastic. (H&E, ×40)

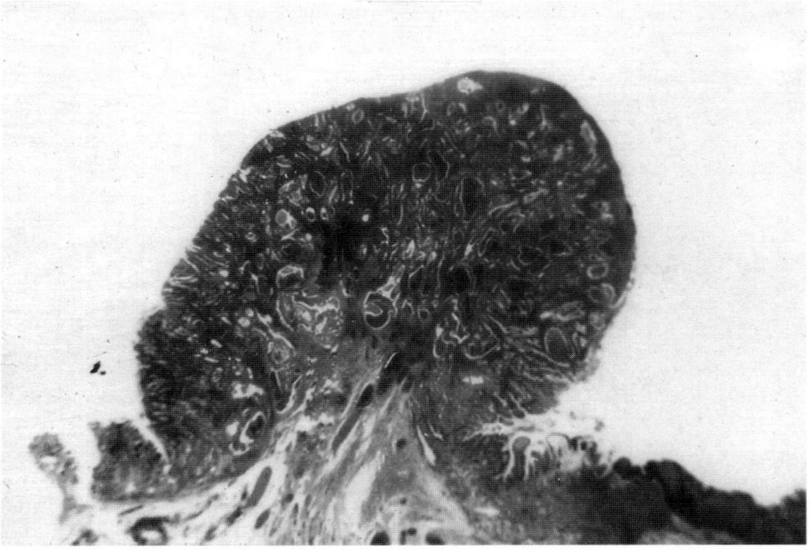

Fig. 38.13 An early adenocarcinoma arising from an adenoma on the greater curvature of the cardia of a 50-year-old man. The patient was alive and well 10 years after operation. (H&E, ×10)

Composite tumours

Oesophageal adenocarcinoma may, on rare occasions, be a component of a so-called composite tumour.

A combination of adenocarcinoma and choriocarcinoma with gonadotropic secretion is described,[50] and the mucin-producing adenocarcinoma and carcinoid reported by Chong et al[51] is another example.

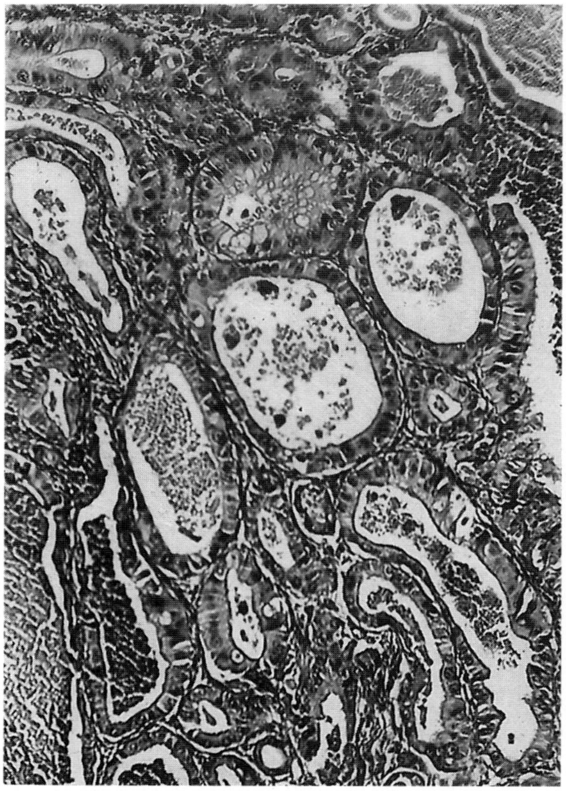

Fig. 38.14 Detail of the well differentiated adenocarcinoma in Figure 38.13. (H&E, ×150)

Early detection of oesophageal adenocarcinoma

In the past two decades, as a result of the extensive use of fibreoptic endoscopy and cytological techniques, a number of minute adenocarcinomas of oesophageal glands despite their location, have been detected.[52–54]

BENIGN EPITHELIAL TUMOURS OF THE GASTRIC CARDIA

Adenoma

Adenomas, with morphological features of a tubular or villous adenoma, are less frequently seen in the cardia than elsewhere in the stomach. One such lesion removed from a 50-year-old male also contained an early infiltrating well differentiated adenocarcinoma (Figs 38.13, 38.14). The patient was alive and well 10 years later.[55]

MALIGNANT EPITHELIAL TUMOURS OF THE CARDIA

Although carcinoma of the cardia is widely regarded as a gastric cancer, others believe that it is better regarded as a tumour of the lower oesophagus.[56] Still others regard it as a separate entity.[57,58]

Difficulty in its definition is partly due to the fact that many cardiac cancers are seen at an advanced stage. If the designation is reserved for those tumours arising in the 2–2.5 cm below the oesophagogastric junction line,[59,60] and entirely restricted to the area of cardiac mucosa, then it appears that adenocarcinoma of the cardia is a separate entity.

Unlike carcinoma in other parts of the stomach, adenocarcinoma of the cardia is closely related to oesophageal cancer epidemiologically, clinically and pathologically.

Macroscopic appearances

Borrmann's system of classification can be applied so that four main types are recognized, i.e. fungating, localized ulcerating, ulcero-infiltrating and infiltrating.

Fungating type

The tumour forms a nodular, fungating, cauliflower-like, polypoid or bulky mass which protrudes into the lumen, usually with a regular margin and occasionally with shallow ulceration.

Localized ulcerating type

The tumour has a conspicuous deep ulcer with a sharply demarcated and raised margin.

Ulcero-infiltrating type

The tumour appears as an infiltrating and ulcerating lesion without clear demarcation from the surrounding mucosa.

Infiltrating type

The cancer cells diffusely infiltrate all layers of the cardia, resulting in generalized thickening of the diseased cardiac wall.

Bulky fungating tumoours, by and large, tend to have a better prognosis than infiltrating lesions.[59,60]

Histology

Although there have been previous attempts at classification of carcinoma of the cardia, they have generally been simple.[61–66] Some favoured division into adenocarcinoma, adenoacanthoma and squamous carcinoma,[61–63] whilst others[64] recognized a papillary adenocarcinoma and undifferentiated and mixed types.[67] Most are adenocarcinomas and may be mucinous. In both categories, there is a histological spectrum, ranging from very well differentiated to very poorly differentiated forms. However, each tumour can usually be placed into one of three groups: well differentiated, poorly differentiated and diffuse.

Well differentiated adenocarcinoma

Highly columnar cancer cells form glandular and occasionally papillary or acinar structures (Fig. 38.15).

Well differentiated mucinous adenocarcinoma

There is conspicuous mucin secretion by the cancer cells.

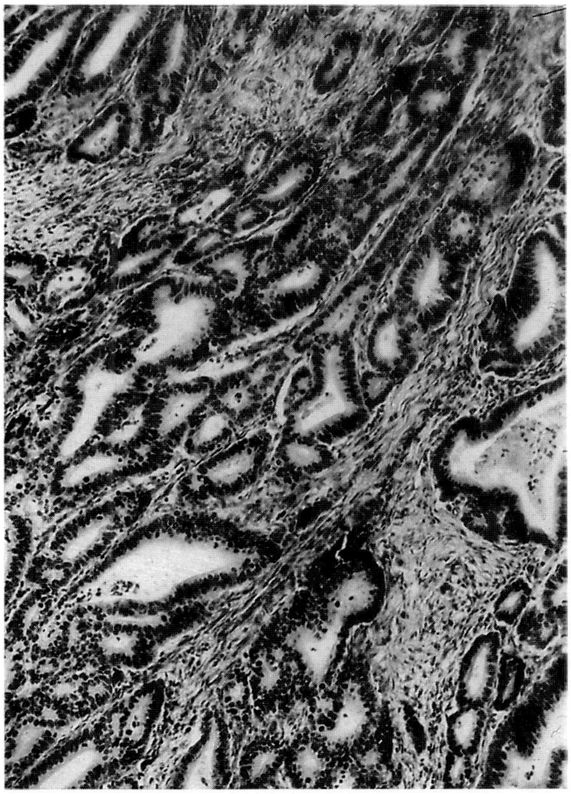

Fig. 38.15 Well differentiated adenocarcinoma of the cardia. (H&E, ×100)

The cancer cells are well differentiated, some forming glandular structures and others floating in mucous pools (Fig. 38.16).

Poorly differentiated adenocarcinoma

The cancer cells are mostly low columnar, cuboidal, flat, polyhedral, or irregular in shape, and are often small with scanty cytoplasm. They are arranged in small irregular tubules or strands, and form 'simplex', 'medullary', or 'cribriform' patterns (Fig. 38.17).

Poorly differentiated mucinous adenocarcinoma

The histological appearance of this type is between well differentiated and diffuse mucinous adenocarcinomas (Fig. 38.18).

Diffuse adenocarcinoma

The cancer cells are mostly small with irregular, deeply stained nuclei and scanty cytoplasm. They tend to infiltrate the tissue individually or in groups of three to five. Some of the cells contain varying amounts of mucus and few present as typical signet-ring cells (Fig. 38.19).

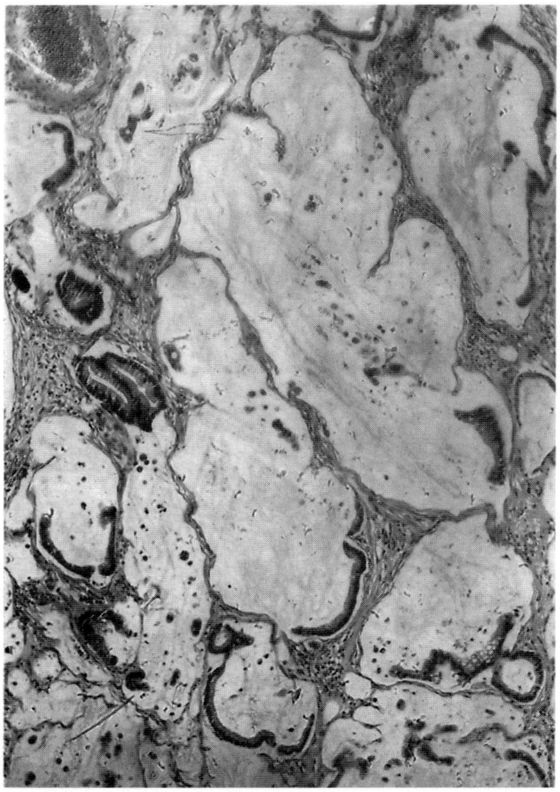

Fig. 38.16 Well differentiated mucinous adenocarcinoma of the cardia, with well developed mucinous pools lined partly by a single layer of columnar cancer cells. (H&E, ×50)

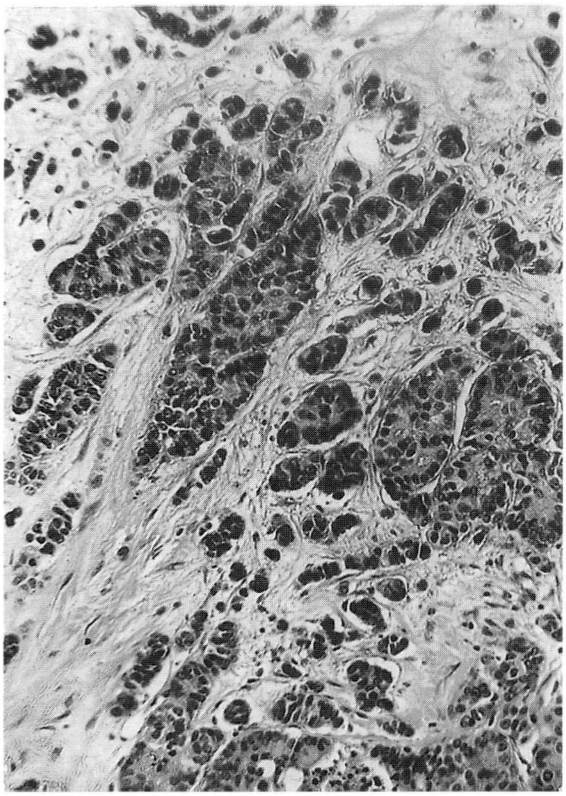

Fig. 38.17 Poorly differentiated adenocarcinoma of the cardia. The cancer cells are mainly arranged in small groups and are of 'simplex' carcinoma type. (H&E, ×150)

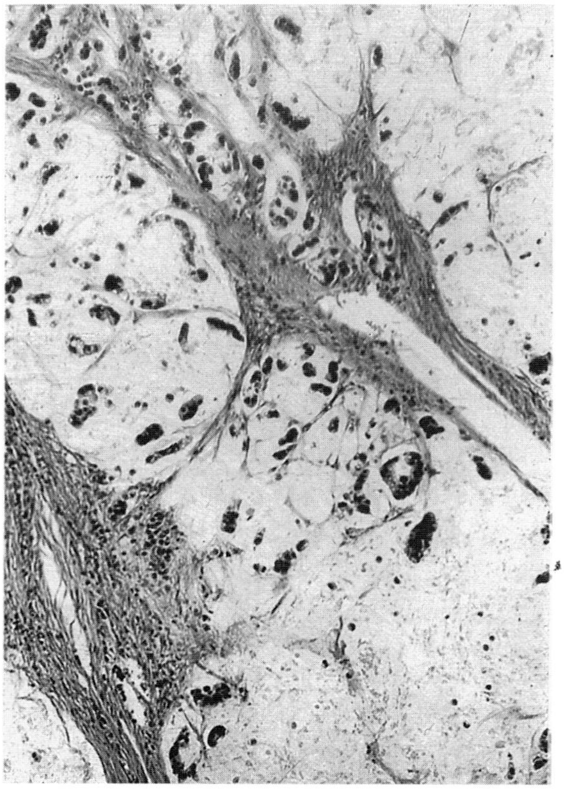

Fig. 38.18 Poorly differentiated mucinous adenocarcinoma of the cardia. The cancer cells are less well differentiated, floating in mucinous pools or scattered in fibrous stroma. (H&E, ×100)

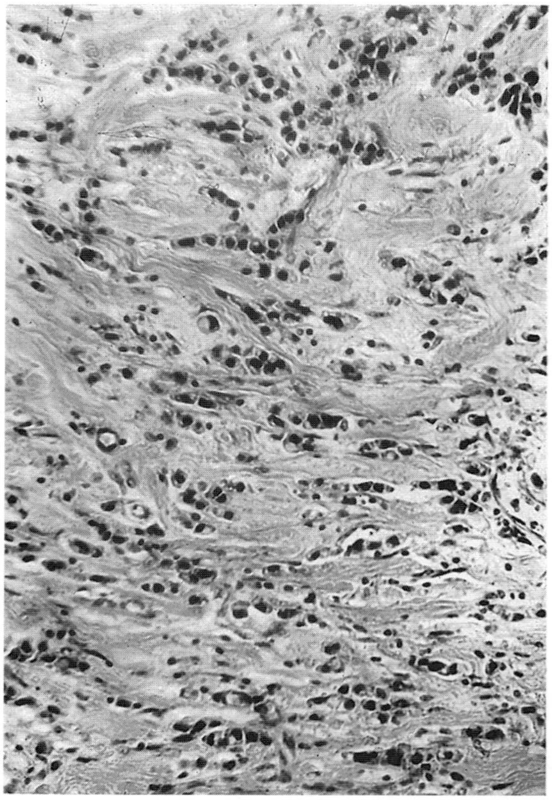

Fig. 38.19 Diffuse adenocarcinoma of the cardia. The cancer cells are mostly anaplastic with deeply stained small nuclei and scanty cytoplasm. Intermingled are a few mucin-secreting cells and signet-ring cells. (H&E, ×180)

Diffuse mucinous adenocarcinoma

The tumour is mainly composed of signet-ring cells which infiltrate the tissue diffusely and are frequently mixed with varying numbers of anaplastic cells (Fig. 38.20). The presence of mucin appears to make no significant difference to prognosis,[61,62] which is best for well differentiated tumours. A small number of cases are so well differentiated that they can be mistaken for dysplasia (Fig. 38.21). The prognosis for this group is far better than that for other well differentiated adenocarcinomas. The 10 year survival rate after surgery can be as high as 40%.[61]

The diffuse tumours, by comparison, have a 0% survival rate after 3 years.[61,62]

Other histological variants exist, but they account for less than 5% of all cases. Rarely, one sees adenocarcinomas with squamous components closely intermingled and sometimes present in the same nest of cells. Although there are claims for the occurrence of pure squamous carcinoma of the cardia,[63–65,67] most are probably squamous carcinomas of the lower oesophagus and some metastatic.[61,68]

Anaplastic tumours composed of cells with little evidence of differentiation toward squamous carcinoma or adenocarcinoma are also decidedly rare.

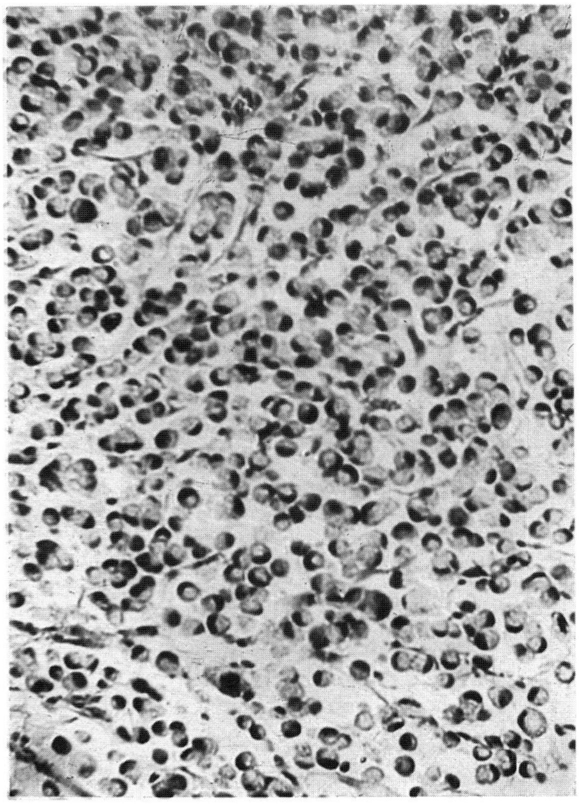

Fig. 38.20 Diffuse mucinous adenocarcinoma of the cardia. Nearly all the cancer cells are signet-ring cells. (H&E, ×200)

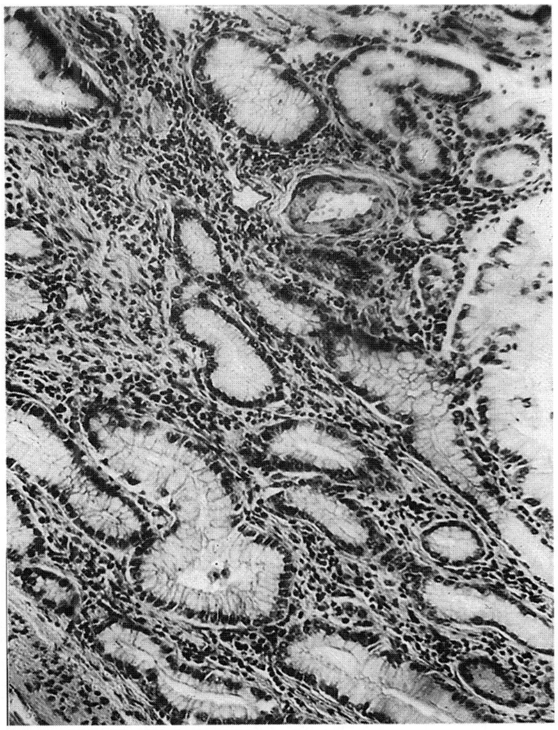

Fig. 38.21 Very well differentiated adenocarcinoma of the cardia. The cancer cells form regular tubes. They are so well differentiated that they closely resemble mild dysplasia of cardiac glands. The tumour, however, extended to the serosa and there were metastasis in local lymph nodes. The patient died 2 years and 6 months after operation. (H&E, ×140)

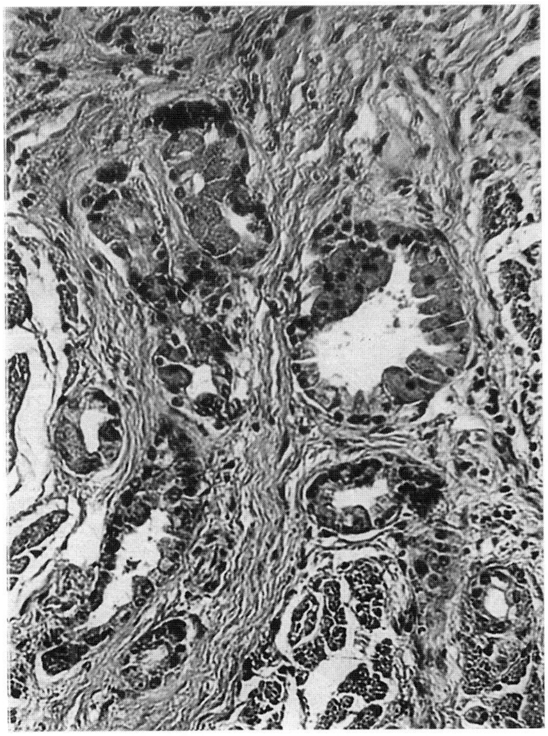

Fig. 38.22 Well differentiated adenocarcinoma of the cardia containing neoplastic Paneth cells. (H&E, ×200)

Neoplastic Paneth cells occasionally occur in adenocarcinomas of the bowel,[69–72] and rarely in the urinary bladder and nasal mucosa.[70–72] They are rare in adenocarcinoma of the cardia (Fig. 38.22).

Adenocarcinoma with acanthosis nigricans

Acanthosis nigricans may accompany visceral adenocarcinomas, particularly those of the stomach.[73–76] It is generally considered that the cutaneous lesions are related to metastases in the adrenals and in the sympathetic nerve plexus. Recently, it has been postulated that the cause is an ectopic release of peptides such as epidermotrophic factor, melanocyte stimulating hormone and growth hormone from the neoplasm.[74,75]

Carcinosarcoma of the cardia has rarely been reported in the literature. Wu and Sun described one case in which adenocarcinoma and rhabdomyosarcoma were closely intermingled.[77]

There have been several reports of double primaries in the oesophagus and cardia.[78–81] The so-called collision carcinoma occurs when a primary squamous carcinoma in the lower segment of the oesophagus and a primary adenocarcinoma of the cardia intermingle and fuse to form one tumour mass.[82–85] Double primary carcinomas of the oesophagus and cardia at a very early stage are also described,[86] and would no doubt give rise to so-called collision carcinoma if their evolution had not been interrupted.

Pathology of early carcinoma of the cardia

Because of its peculiar anatomical location, the discovery of early malignancy at the cardiac region poses a problem. Nevertheless, recent progress in diagnostic technology has resulted in the detection of quite a few early cases of cardiac adenocarcinoma.[60,87–90] Shen used a large balloon inflated with 60–80 ml air in order to collect cytological specimens in mass screening programmes.[91] Early cases of cardiac adenocarcinomas have been demonstrated by this technique (Fig. 38.23) and include carcinoma in situ, lesions which have not invaded the muscularis propria and have not metastasized.

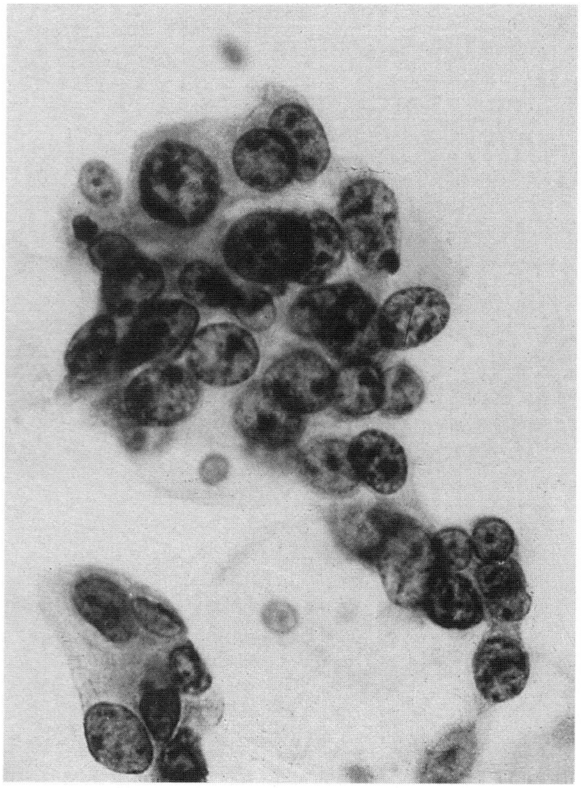

Fig. 38.23 Balloon cytology smear from an early carcinoma of the cardia, with eccentric nuclei and prominent nucleoli. The background is relatively clear, with little inflammatory cells. (H&E, ×550)

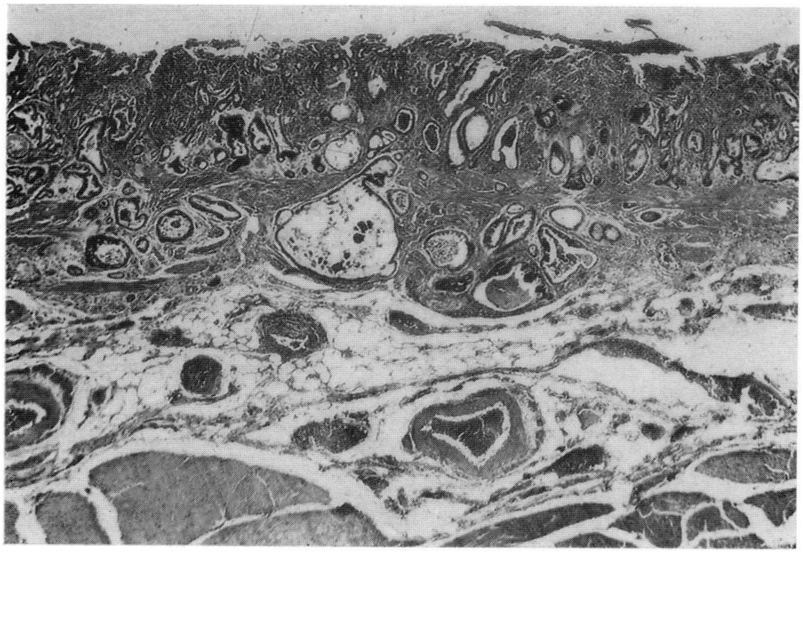

Fig. 38.24 Submucosal adenocarcinoma of the cardia, presenting pleomorphic patterns. (H&E, ×25)

The macroscopic morphology of early carcinomas of the cardia is similar to that of early carcinomas in the oesophagus or elsewhere in the stomach. They may be slightly depressed or slightly elevated and some are hardly perceptible to the naked eye, or not at all.

Early adenocarcinomas of the cardia are histologically identical to their advanced counterparts. The two categories of adenocarcinoma and mucinous adenocarcinoma are further subdivided in the same way. By and large, submucosal tumours will display a greater variety of subtypes and are histologically more similar to advanced carcinoma (Figs 38.24, 38.25).

Intramucosal carcinomas are usually of the better differentiated types (Figs 38.26, 38.27) and patterns such as mucinous adenocarcinoma with well developed mucinous pools are hardly seen at this stage.

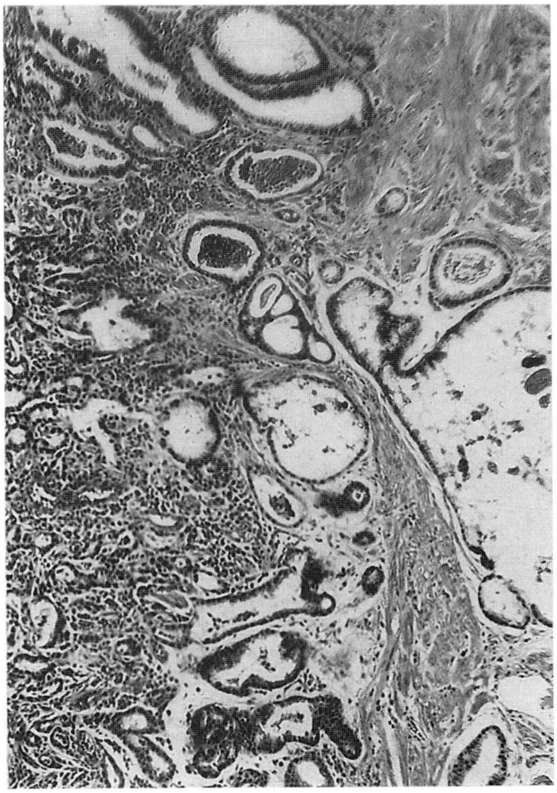

Fig. 38.25 Higher magnification of Figure 38.24. Some of the cancer cells are well differentiated and arranged in the shape of regular glands, others are poorly differentiated and take the form of small tubes or clusters. (H&E, ×60)

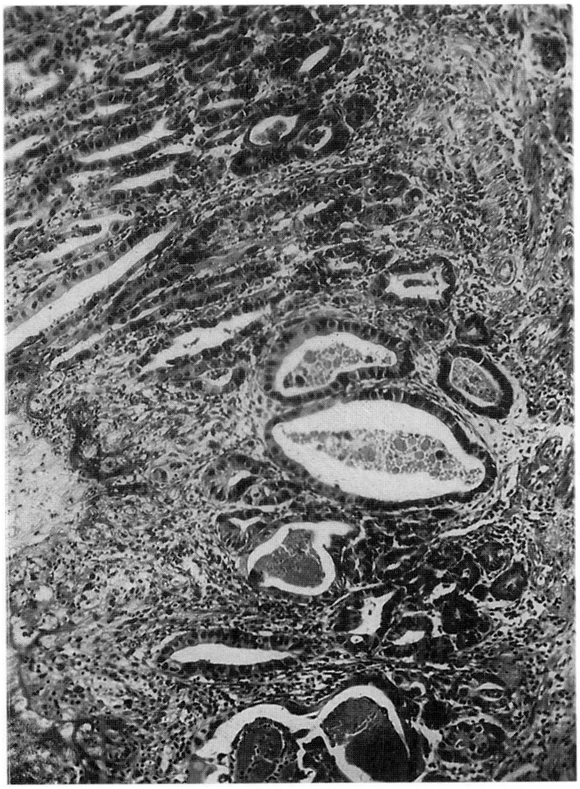

Fig. 38.27 Higher magnification of the minute adenocarcinoma in Figure 38.26. The cancer cells show obvious atypism and form irregular tubes. (H&E, ×100)

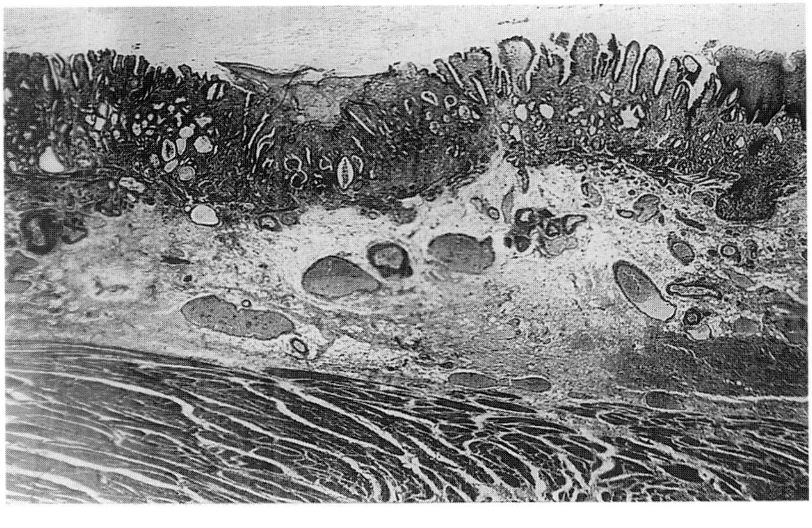

Fig. 38.26 A minute adenocarcinoma of the cardia. The tumour is limited to the mucosa, 0.3 cm from the oesophagogastric junction, and 0.2 cm in diameter. (H&E, ×15)

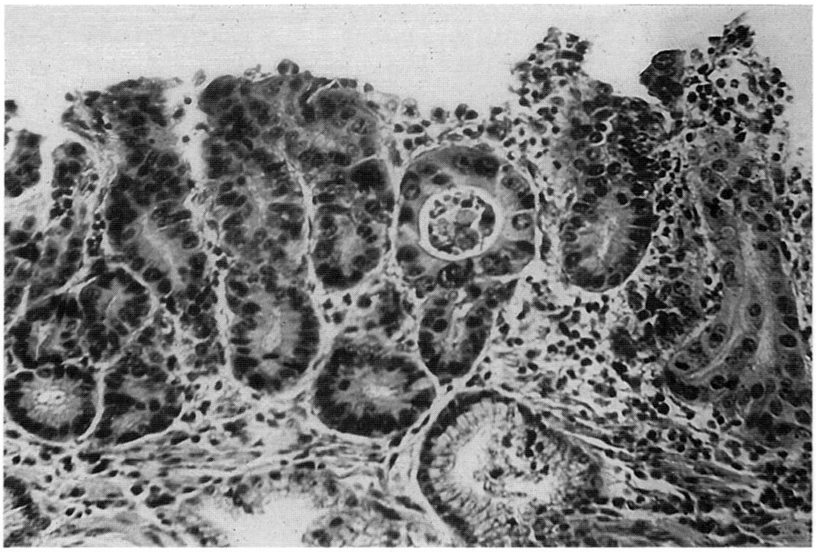

Fig. 38.28 Histologic view of the tumour in Figure 38.23 showing the earliest malignant change. There is adenocarcinoma in situ in at least one gland of the cardia with surrounding dysplasia. (H&E, ×200)

The earliest stage of malignancy is adenocarcinoma in situ (Fig. 38.28). Although some doubt the value in its identification,[92] and believe it would be better avoided,[93,94] most argue that it is a carcinoma in which the malignant cells are confined to glands by a basement membrane.[95–98] Nevertheless, it is a diagnosis which is difficult to make in practice, especially on biopsy samples. However, if carcinoma can be diagnosed at this stage it is surely desirable because of its curability.

REFERENCES

1. Tsutsumi M, Mizumoto K, Tsujiuchi T, et al. Serous cystadenoma of the esophagus. Acta Pathol Jpn 1990; 40: 153–155.
2. Spin FP. Adenomas of the esophagus: a case report and review of the literature. Gastrointest Endosc 1973; 20: 26–27.
3. McDonald GB, Brand DL, Thorning DR. Multiple adenomatous neoplasms arising in columnar-lined (Barrett's) esophagus. Gastroenterology 1977; 72: 1317–1321.
4. Lesbros F, Berger F, Berger G, et al. Adenome des glandes oesophgiennes ressemblant a un adenoma mucipave bronchique. Arch Anat Cytol Pathol 1980; 29: 55–58.
5. Rapbael HA, Ellis FH, Dockerty MB. Primary adenocarcinoma of the esophagus: 18 year review of the literature. Ann Surg 1966; 164: 785–796.
6. Turnbull ADM, Goodner JT. Primary adenocarcinoma of the esophagus. Cancer 1968; 22: 915–918.
7. Bosch A, Frias Z, Caldwell WL. Adenocarcinoma of the esophagus. Cancer 1979; 43: 1557–1561.
8. Appelqvist P. Carcinoma of the esophagus and gastric cardia at autopsy in Finland. Ann Clin Res 1975; 7: 334–340.
9. Suzuki H, Nagayo T. Primary tumours of the esophagus other than squamous cell carcinoma: histologic classification and statistics in the surgical and autopsied materials in Japan. Int Adv Surg Oncol 1980; 3: 73–109.
10. Sons HU, Borchard F. Esophageal cancer: autopsy findings in 171 cases. Arch Pathol Lab Med 1984; 108: 983–988.
11. Dodge OG. Intraesophageal adenocarcinoma. Gut 1960; 1: 351–356.
12. Powell J, McConkey CC. The rising trend in oesophageal adenocarcinoma and gastric cardia. Eur J Cancer Prev 1992; 1: 265–269.
13. Moller H. Incidence of cancer of oesophagus, cardia and stomach in Denmark. Eur J Cancer Prev 1992; 1: 159–164.
14. Blot WJ , Devesa SS, Kneller RW, Fraumeni JF Jr. Rising incidence of adenocarcinoma of the esophagus and gastric cardia. JAMA 1991; 265: 1287–1289.
15. Gray JR, Coldman AJ, MacDonald WC. Cigarette and alcohol use in patients with adenocarcinoma of the gastric cardia or lower esophagus. Cancer 1992; 69: 2227–2231.
16. Liu FS, Zhou CN. Pathology of carcinoma of the esophagus. In: Huang GJ, Wu YK, eds. Carcinoma of the esophagus and gastric cardia. Berlin: Springer-Verlag 1984: pp 81–84.
17. Enterline H, Thompson J. Barrett's metaplasia and adenocarcinoma. In: Pathology of the esophagus. New York: Springer-Verlag 1984: pp 109–126.
18. Smith RR, Boitnott JK, Hamilton SR, Rogers EI. The spectrum of carcinoma arising in Barrett's esophagus: a clinicopathologic study of 26 patients. Am J Surg Pathol 1984; 8: 563–573.
19. Lee RG. Dysplasia in Barret's esophagus: a clinicopathologic study of six patients. Am J Surg Pathol 1985; 9: 845–852.
20. Goodwin WJ, Larson DL, Sajjad SM. Adenocarcinoma of the cervical esophagus in a patient with extensive columnar cell-lined (Barrett's) esophagus. Otolaryngol Head Neck Surg 1983; 91: 446–449.
21. Naef AP, Savary M, Ozzello L. Columnar-lined lower esophagus: an acquired lesion with malignant predisposition: report on 140 cases of Barrett's esophagus with 12 adenocarcinomas. J Thorac Cardiovasc Surg 1975; 70: 826–835.
22. Kalish RJ, Clancy PE, Orringer MB, Appelman HD. Clinical, epidemiologic, and morphologic comparison between adenocarcinomas arising in Barrett's esophageal mucosa and in the gastric cardia. Gastroenterology 1984; 86: 461–467.
23. Haggitt RC, Tryzelaar J, Ellis FH, Colcher H. Adenocarcinoma complicating columnar epithelium-lined (Barrett's) esophagus. Am J Clin Pathol 1978; 70: 1–5.
24. Tytgat GN, Hameeteman W. The neoplastic potential of columnar-lined (Barrett's) esophagus. World J Surg 1992; 16: 308–312.
25. Altorki NK, Sunagawa M, Little AG, Skinner DB. High-grade dysplasia in the columnar-lined esophagus. Am J Surg 1991; 161: 97–99.
26. Geisinger KR, Teot LA, Richter JE. A comparative cytopathologic and histologic study of atypia, dysplasia and adenocarcinoma in Barrett's esophagus. Cancer 1992; 69: 8–16.
27. Jankowski J, McMenemin R, Yu C, Hopwood D, Wormsley KG. Proliferating cell nuclear antigen in oesophageal diseases,

correlation with transforming growth factor alpha expression. Gut 1992; 33: 587–591.
28. Yan PS, Li WH. Adenocarcinoma of the esophagus arising in ectopic gastric mucosa (in Chinese). Cancer Res Prev Treat 1986; 13: 142.
29. Symonds DA, Ramsey HE. Adenocarcinoma arising in Barrett's esophagus with Zollinger-Ellison syndrome. Am J Clin Pathol 1980; 73: 823–826.
30. Bombi JA, Riverola A, Bordas JM, Cardesa A. Adenosquamous carcinoma of the esophagus. A case report. Pathol Res Pract 1991; 187: 514–519.
31. Emoto I, Chihara T, Tamai M, et al. A patient with double carcinoma of the esophagus-squamous cell carcinoma and mucoepidermoid carcinoma. Jpn J Cancer Clin 1982; 28: 1754–1757.
32. Matsufuji H, Kuwano H, Ueo H, et al. Mucoepidermoid carcinoma of the esophagus: a case report. Jpn J Surg 1985; 15: 55–59.
33. Osamura RY, Sato S, Miwa M, Mita T. Mucoepidermoid carcinoma of the esophagus: report of an unoperated autopsy case and review of the literature. Am J Gastroenterol 1978; 69: 467–470.
34. Woodard BH, Shelburne JD, Vollmer RT, Rostlethwait RW. Mucoepidermoid carcinoma of the esophagus: a case report. Hum Pathol 1978; 9: 352–254.
35. Kay S. Mucoepidermoid carcinoma of the esophagus: report of two cases. Cancer 1968; 22: 1053–1059.
36. Bell-Thomson J, Haggitt RC, Ellis FH. Mucoepidermoid and adenoid cystic carcinomas of the esophagus. J Thorac Cardiovasc Surg 1980; 79: 438–446.
37. Sasajima K, Watanabe M, Takubo K, Takai A, Yamashita K, Onda M. Mucoepidermoid carcinoma of the esophagus: report of two cases and review of the literature. Endoscopy 1990; 22: 140–143.
38. Allard M, Farkouh E, Atlas H, Paquin JG. Primary adenoid cystic carcinoma of the esophagus. Can J Surg 1981; 24: 405–406.
39. Kabuto T, Taniguchi K, lwanaga T, et al. Primary adenoid cystic carcinoma of the esophagus: report of a case. Cancer 1979; 43: 2452–2456.
40. Rouzand A, Freant L, Levin R, et al. Primary adenoid cystic carcinoma of the esophagus: report of a case and review of the literature. J Thorac Cardiovasc Surg 1975; 69: 785–789.
41. Nelms DC, Armando-Luna M. Primary adenocystic carcinoma (cylindromatous carcinoma) of the esophagus. Cancer 1972; 29: 440–443.
42. Jacobsohn WZ, Libson Y, Dollberg L. Adenoid cystic carcinoma of the esophagus. Gastrointest Endosc 1980; 26: 102–104.
43. Epstein JI, Sears DL, Tucker RS, Eagan JW. Carcinoma of the esophagus with adenoid cystic differentiaton. Cancer 1984; 53: 1131–1136.
44. Sweeney EC, Cooney T. Adenoid cystic carcinoma of the esophagus: a light and electron microscopic study. Cancer 1980; 45: 1516–1525.
45. O'Sullivan JP, Cockburn JS, Drew CE. Adenoid cystic carcinoma of the esophagus. Thorax 1975; 30: 476–480.
46. Blaauwgeers JL, Allema JH, Bosma A, Brummelkamp WH. Early adenoid cystic carcinoma of the upper oesophagus. Eur J Surg Oncol 1990; 16: 77–81.
47. Cerar A, Juterserk A, Vidmar S. Adenoid cystic carcinoma of the esophagus. A clinicopathologic study of three cases. Cancer 1991; 67: 2159–2164.
48. Bergmann M, Charnas RM. Tracheobronchial rests in the esophagus: their relation to some benign structures and certain types of cancer of the esophagus. J Thorac Surg 1958; 35: 97–104.
49. Kuwano H, Ueo H, Sugimachi K, et al. Glandular or mucus-secreting components in squamous cell carcinoma of the esophagus. Cancer 1985; 56: 514–518.
50. McKechnie JC, Fechner RE. Choriocarcinoma and adenocarcinoma of the esophagus with gonadotropic secretion. Cancer 1971; 27: 694–702.
51. Chong FK, Graham JH, Madoff IM. Mucin producing carcinoid ('composite tumour') of the upper third of the esophagus — a variant of carcinoid tumour. Cancer 1979; 44: 1853–1859.
52. Belladonna JA, Hajdu SI, Bains MS, Winawer SJ. Adenocarcinoma in situ of Barrett's esophagus diagnosed by endoscopic cytology. N Engl J Med 1974; 291: 895–896.
53. Liu FS, Li L, Qu SL. Clinical and pathological characteristics of early esophageal cancer. In: Burghardt E, Holzer E (guest editors). Clinics in Oncology. Vol. 1, No 2. 'Minimal invasive cancer'. London: Saunders 1982: pp 539–550.
54. Shima S, Sugiura Y, Yonekawa H, et al. Adenocarcinoma of the esophagus (early stage) concomitant with lung cancer: a case report (in Japanese). Jpn J Cancer Clin 1985; 31: 193–198.
55. Pan GL, Li L, Liu FS. An early adenocarcinoma arising from an adenoma of gastric cardia (in Chinese). Chin J Oncol 1984; 6: 312.
56. Griffith JL, Davis JT. A twenty-year experience with surgical management of carcinoma of the esophagus and gastric cardia. J Thorac Cardiovasc Surg 1980; 79: 447–452.
57. Nishi M, Nomura H, Kajisa T, et al. Surgical problem of carcinoma in the esophagogastric junction (in Japanese). Stomach Intestine 1978; 13: 1497–1507.
58. Takagi K, Mochizuki T, Okashima K, et al. Carcinoma of esophagogastric junction (panel discussion) (in Japanese). Stomach Intestine 1978; 13: 1517–1528.
59. Kato Y, Sugano H, Wada J, Nakamura K. Histogenesis of cardiac carcinoma (adenocarcinoma) in comparison with that of antral carcinoma (in Japanese). Stomach Intestine 1978; 13: 1509–1515.
60. Li L, Pan GL, Shen Q. Pathological study of early carcinoma of gastric cardia (in Chinese). Chin J Oncol 1982; 4: 93–97.
61. Li L, Pan GL, Huang GJ, Lu X. Pathological features of carcinoma of the gastric cardia (in Chinese). Chin J Oncol 1984; 6: 37–40.
62. Pan GL, Li L, Huang GJ, et al. Prognostic significance of histologic host response in cancer of the gastric cardia. Acta Acad Med Sin 1983; 5: 97–101.
63. Sun SQ, Wu X, Liu TW. A study of gross classification of carcinoma of the gastric cardia (in Chinese). Chin J Pathol 1963; 7: 173–179.
64. Ellis FH. Surgical aspects of malignant lesions of the esophagogastric junction. In: Cancer of the stomach. Philadelphia: Saunders 1964: pp 127–140.
65. Gunnlaugsson GH, Wychulis AR, Roland C. Analysis of the records of 1657 patients with carcinoma of the esophagus and cardia of the stomach. Surg Gynecol Obstet 1970; 130: 997–1005.
66. McPeak E, Warren S. Histological features of carcinoma of the cardioesophageal junction and cardia. Am J Pathol 1948; 24: 971–991.
67. Dodge OG. The surgical pathology of gastro-esophageal carcinoma. Br J Surg 1961; 49: 121–125.
68. Talerman A, Woo-Ming MO. The origin of squamous cell carcinoma of the gastric cardia. Cancer 1968; 22: 1226–1232.
69. Shousha S. Paneth cell-rich papillary adenocarcinoma and a mucoid adenocarcinoma occurring synchronously in colon: a light and electron microscopic study. Histopathology 1979; 3: 48–501.
70. Heitz PU, Wegmann W. Identification of neoplastic Paneth cells in an adenocarcinoma using lysozyme as a marker, and electron microscopy. Virchows Arch (A) 1980; 386: 107–116.
71. Pallesen G. Neoplastic Paneth cells in adenocarcinoma of the urinary bladder. Cancer 1981; 47: 1834–1837.
72. Schmid KO, Aubock L, Albegger K. Endocrine-amphicrine enteric carcinoma of the nasal mucosa. Virchows Arch (A) 1979; 383: 329–343.
73. Arora A, Choudhuri G, Tandon RK. Acanthosis nigricans associated with adenocarcinoma of the gallbladder. Am J Gastroenterol 1985; 80: 896–897.
74. Jacobs MI, Rigel DS. Acanthosis nigricans and the sign of Leser-Trelat associated with adenocarcinoma of the gall-bladder. Cancer 1981; 48: 325–328.
75. Yao BL, Shen DW. Acanthosis nigricans associated with carcinoma of gastric cardia: a case report (in Chinese). Tianjin Med J (Spec. Issue Cancer) 1965; 3: 153–154.
76. Department of Pathology, Cancer Institute, Chinese Academy of Medical Sciences. The atlas of tumour pathology (in Chinese). Beijing: People's Medical Publishing House 1975: p 59.
77. Wu X, Sun SQ. Adenocarcinoma and rhabdomyosarcoma of the gastric cardia (in Chinese). Chin J Oncol 1979; 1: 314.
78. Sun SQ, Liu FS, Wu X, et al. Five cases of double primary carcinomas of the esophagus and gastric cardia (in Chinese). Tianjin Med J (Spec. Issue Cancer) 1964; 2: 297–298.
79. Liu FS. Double primary carcinomas of the esophagus and stomach:

a pathological study of nine cases (in Chinese). Acta Acad Med Sin 1979; 1: 67–70.
80. Zhang ZY, Ge K, Yao SC. Double primary carcinomas of the esophagus and cardia: report of four cases (in Chinese). Chin J Oncol 1984; 6: 330.
81. Wang ZH, Gu YZ. Double primary carcinomas of the esophagus and gastric cardia (in Chinese). Chin J Surg 1955; 3: 459–460.
82. Dodge OG. Gastro-esophageal carcinoma of mixed histological type. J Pathol Bacterial 1961; 81: 459–471.
83. Wanke M. Collision tumour of the cardia. Virchows Arch (A) 1972; 357: 81–86.
84. Majmudar B, Dillard R, Susann PW. Collision carcinoma of the gastric cardia. Hum Pathol 1978; 9: 471–476.
85. Spagnolo DV, Heenan PJ. Collision carcinoma at the esophagogastric junction: report of two cases. Cancer 1980; 46: 2702–2708.
86. Li L. Double primary early carcinomas in the esophagus and gastric cardia (in Chinese). Chin J Oncol 1981; 3: 142–143.
87. Suzuki S, Nagayo T, Murakami H, Takemoto T. Minute early carcinoma on the esophago-gastric junction (in Japanese). Stomach Intestine 1976; 11: 697–704.
88. Endo M, Suzuki S, Kawada A, Yoshida K. Endoscopic diagnosis of esophagocardial cancer (in Japanese). Stomach Intestine 1978; 13: 1489–1495.
89. Matsue H, Hirota T, Itabasi M, et al. Pathological features and X-ray diagnosis of cancer of the esophagocardiac region (in Japanese). Stomach Intestine 1978; 13: 1477–1488.
90. Kumagai K, Maekawa K, Urabe M, et al. Clinicopathological study of early gastric carcinoma of the cardiac portion (in Japanese). Jpn J Cancer Clin 1985; 31: 31–36.
91. Shen Q. Diagnostic cytology and early detection. In: Huang GJ, Wu YK, eds. Carcinoma of the esophagus and gastric cardia. Berlin: Springer-Verlag 1984: pp 187–189.
92. Kraus B, Cain H. Is there a carcinoma in situ of gastric mucosa? Pathol Res Pract 1979; 164: 342–355.
93. Grundmann E. Histologic types and possible initial stages in early gastric carcinoma. Beitr Pathol 1975; 154: 256–280.
94. Morson BC, Sobin LH, Grundmann E, et al. Precancerous conditions and epithelial dysplasia in the stomach. J Clin Pathol 1980; 33: 711–721.
95. Whitehead R. Mucosal biopsy of the gastrointestinal tract (3rd edition). Philadelphia: Saunders 1985: p 65.
96. Ming SC, Bajtai A, Correa P, et al. Gastric dysplasia: significance and pathologic criteria. Cancer 1984; 54: 1794–1801.
97. Machado G, Davies JD, Tudway AJC, et al. Superficial carcinoma of the stomach. Br Med J 1976; 2: 77–79.
98. Schade ROK. The borderline between benign and malignant lesions in the stomach. In: Grundmann E, Grune H, Witte S, eds. Early gastric cancer, current status of diagnosis. Berlin: Springer 1974: pp 45–53.

PART III

Carcinoma and dysplasia in Barrett's oesophagus

R. Whitehead   S. R. Hamilton

Barrett's oesophagus is the eponym for columnar epithelial replacement of squamous epithelium in the lower oesophagus, usually as a consequence of chronic gastro-oesophageal reflux.[1–7] The predisposition of Barrets's oesophagus to develop adenocarcinoma is one of the major reasons that it has attracted such great interest in recent years.

The first published case of carcinoma arising in Barrett's oesophagus was reported by Morson and Belcher[8] in 1952, less than three years after Barrett's seminal paper appeared. In 1955, McCorkle and Blades published the first case from the United States.[9] Subsequently, case reports and small series of patients appeared frequently in the literature as recognition of Barrett's carcinoma

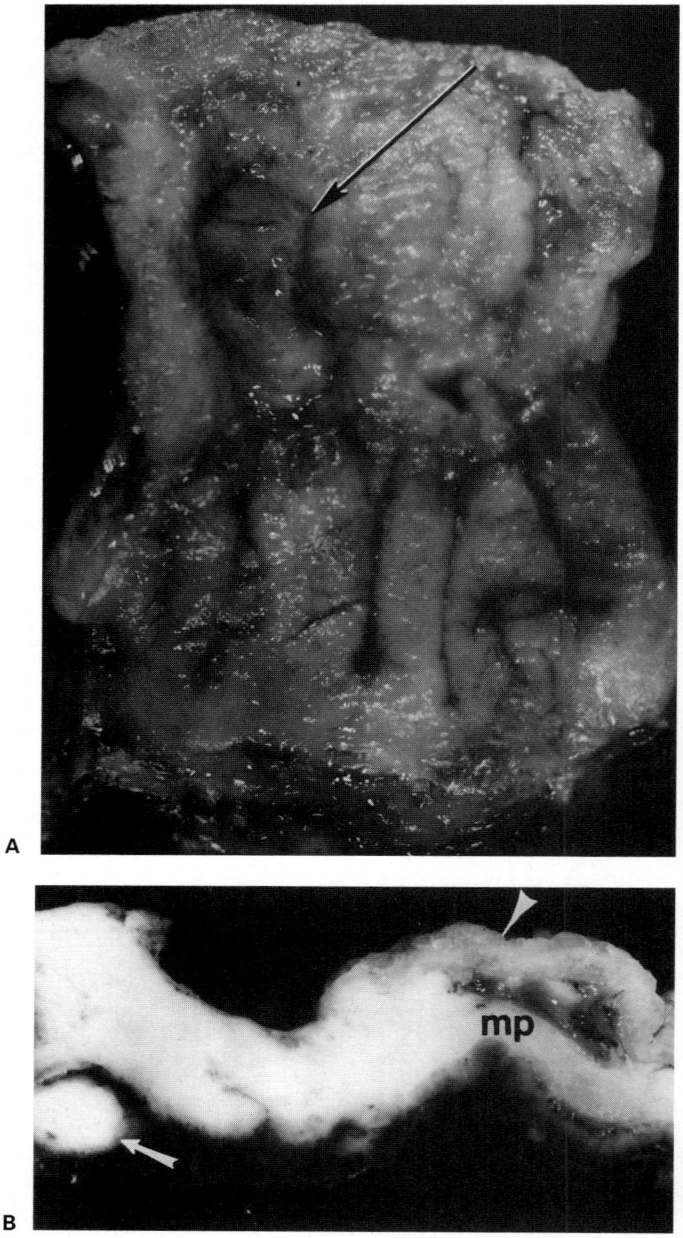

Fig. 38.29 Specimen from palliative resection of mid-oesophagus with Barrett's adenocarcinoma. **A** The endophytic tumour is deeply ulcerated (arrow) and narrows the oesophagus. The entire mucosal surface surrounding the tumour is granular due to the presence of Barrett's mucosa rather than squamous epithelium (×1.3)
B Transverse section through the tumour shows extension through the muscularis propria (mp) to involve the perioesophageal soft tissue and metastasis to a regional lymph node (arrow). Barrett's mucosa (arrowhead) adjoins the tumour. (×2.2)

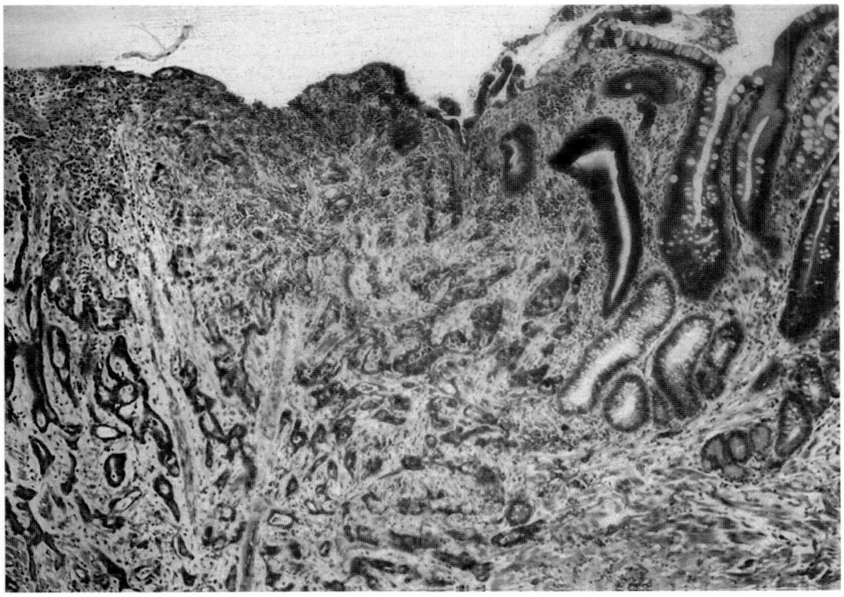

Fig. 38.30 Barrett's adenocarcinoma. Histopathological section from the periphery of the tumour mass shows Barrett's mucosa of the distinctive type adjoining the infiltrating adenocarcinoma. (H&E, ×50)

increased. It is now apparent that Barrett's carcinoma accounts for the majority of adenocarcinomas of the oesophagogastric junction and the lower oesophagus. Furthermore, the incidence of this tumour appears to be increasing.

BARRETT'S ADENOCARCINOMA

Definition

The definition of Barrett's adenocarcinoma would seem to be self-evident: a malignant epithelial neoplasm with glandular differentiation or mucin production arising in the columnar epithelium-lined lower oesophagus which is usually acquired as a consequence of chronic gastro-oesophageal reflux. Application of the definition to individual cases, however, is a source of controversy with implications for research on Barrett's carcinoma, as well as clinical management.

When adenocarcinoma arises within a long segment of Barrett's mucosa, its recognition is usually easy due to the presence of residual columnar-lined mucosa of the distinctive type (Figs 38.29, 38.30). Occasionally, a large tumour will obliterate nearly all of a long segment of Barrett's mucosa, but obliteration is more likely with carcinoma near or in a short segment (Fig. 38.31). Although the pathogenetic definition of Barrett's esophagus is straightforward, the pathological definition of short-segment Barrett's oesophagus is controversial, particularly when the anatomy is distorted by tumour.

The oesophagogastric junction is a complex anatomical region with different landmarks for endoscopy, manometry, radiology, surgery and pathology which do not correspond (Table 38.1). For example, the squamocolumnar

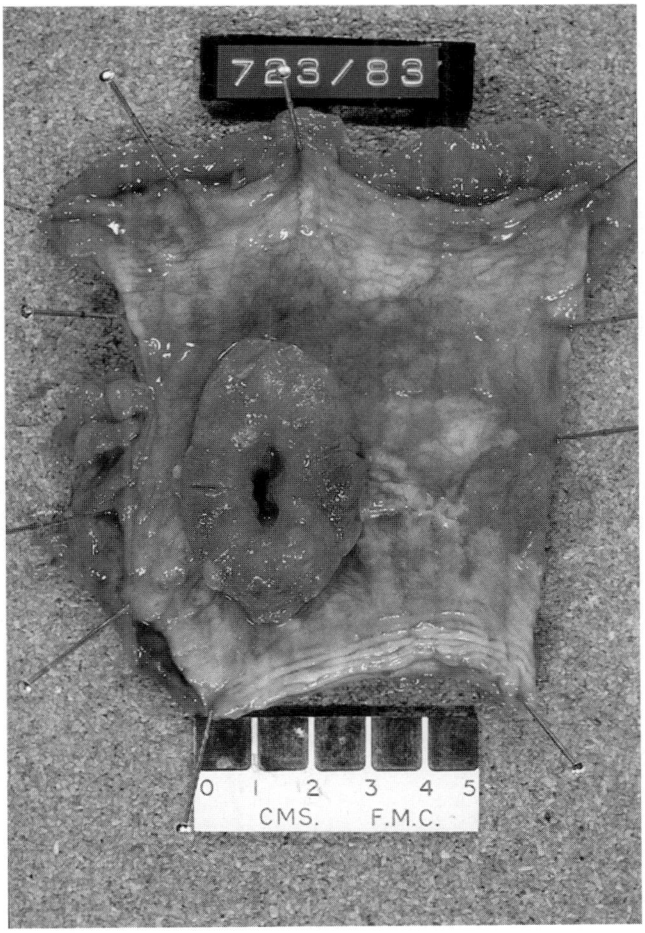

Fig. 38.31 Resection of adenocarcinoma at oesophagogastric junction. Oesophageal (grey) epithelium above and smooth (yellow) gastric mucosa below. Barrett's mucosa is not evident macroscopically, but histopathology revealed typical mucosa and areas of dysplasia were slightly nodular.

Table 38.1 Landmarks of the normal oesophagogastric junction

Luminal surface	
	Squamocolumnar junction
	Contraction of lower oesophageal sphincter zone
Mural structure	
	Distal extent of oesophageal submucosal glands
	Change in configuration of muscularis propria
External surface	
	Tubular appearance of oesophagus
	Peritoneal covering of stomach
	Diaphragmatic hiatus
Manometry	
	Lower extras of lower oesophageal sphincter zone

junction is said to occur normally 1–2 cm proximal to the peritoneal reflection of the stomach.[4,10–12] If this definition is accepted, columnar epithelium can occur in the lower portion of the oesophagus. As a result, some authors require that columnar-lined mucosa extend more than 2 cm or more than 3 cm into the oesophagus to be considered Barrett's mucosa.[12,13] However, comparison of the appearance of the squamocolumnar junction in stillborns and adults suggests that the junction is not static, as the Z-line is often much less pronounced in neonates. Thus, short-segment Barrett's oesophagus appears to be common, but difficult to recognize unless the columnar-lined mucosa occurs in finger or tongues extending above the native squamocolumnar junction on the remainder of the circumference. The development of a hiatal hernia may obscure the anatomy in some patients and heterotopic gastric mucosa can occur in the oesophagus,[14–16] providing potential for confusion with Barrett's mucosa. Endoscopic biopsy specimens include only mucosa so that some structures evident in the oesophageal wall in resection specimens cannot be seen in biopsy specimens. With these various limitations in mind, criteria for recognition of Barrett's carcinoma are shown in Table 38.2.

These criteria for Barrett's carcinoma can result in 'false negatives' and 'false positives,' as shown in Table 38.2. Clinical symptoms of gastro-oesophageal reflux are not helpful, as a large minority of patients presenting with Barrett's carcinoma deny antecedent symptoms.[12,13,17] 'False positives' may not be a great problem, however, as recent studies suggest that Barrett's carcinoma and

Table 38.2 Pathological criteria for Barrett's adenocarcinoma

Adenocarcinoma of the oesophagus or oesophagogastric junction associated with:

1. Columnar-lined (Barrett's) mucosa of the distinctive type, in the oesophagus

or

2. Dysplastic columnar-lined mucosa with the histochemical characteristics of distinctive-type Barrett's mucosa (intestinal-type mucin) in the oesophagus.[a]

[a] Evidence for localization in the oesophagus may be provided by subjacent oesophageal submucosal glands with squamous-lined ducts and/or native squamous epithelium present more distally.

Table 38.3 Potential causes of 'false negative' and 'false positive' classification of Barrett's carcinoma

False negative
1. Tumour obliteration of Barrett's mucosa
2. Biopsy sampling at endoscopy
3. Insufficient histopathological sections of resection specimen

False positive
1. Misinterpretation of cardiac fundic or heterotopic gastric mucosa as Barrett's mucosa
2. Carcinoma of oesophagogastric junction region or oesophagus in a patient with incidental Barrett's oesophagus

carcinoma of the oesophagogastric junction region have epidemiological and pathological similarities.[12,18–22]

Prevalence, incidence and risk

Ascertainment of the frequency of Barrett's carcinoma is influenced by the definitions used by various investigators and the inherent bias toward recognition of patients who develop cancer over those who are asymptomatic, do not seek medical attention or do not undergo endoscopy with biopsy. In the past, adenocarcinoma of the oesophagogastric junction region was assumed generally to represent gastric carcinoma involving the lower oesophagus. As a result, there is a paucity of studies which provide useful data on the prevalence of Barrett's carcinoma among oesophageal carcinomas. In one series, adenocarcinoma arising in Barrett's oesophagus accounted for 11/35 (31%) consecutive oesophageal cancers.[20] Based on the prevalence of adenocarcinoma among all oesophageal cancers, other authors have suggested that Barrett's carcinoma accounts for 5–10%.[12] In another series, adenocarcinoma accounted for 11% of all oesophageal cancers, and 62% of these adenocarcinomas (7% of total) were accompanied by Barrett's mucosa.[23] When cancer of the lower oesophagus is considered, the prevalence of Barrett's carcinoma is undoubtedly much higher accounting for 25/54 (65%) consecutively resected adenocarcinomas of the oesophagus and oesophagogastric junction region.[24] The problem of clinical recognition is illustrated by the finding that only 10/29 (35%) has been recognized endoscopically as Barrett's carcinoma.[24] Incidence data in populations are scant, as most statistics for oesophageal cancer do not consider the histological types.

The prevalence of Barrett's carcinoma in patients with Barrett's oesophagus varies widely from series to series.[13, 25–33] Based on the available data, 10% appears to be a reasonable estimate,[34] but many patients are found to have Barrett's oesophagus when they present with symptoms of the complicating carcinoma and the rate of diagnosis of Barrett's oesophagus at autopsy is approximately 20 times higher than during life.[35] As a result, the prevalence data do not give a meaningful assessment of risk in patients known to have Barrett's oesophagus. Incidence data in patients with known Barrett's oesophagus who did not have carcinoma at presentation are available from a few series and range from 1/81 to 1/441 cases/ patient-year of follow-up.[36–38] These series cannot include patients who have not had Barrett's oesophagus recognized. Risk of oesophageal carcinoma was reported as 30–40 times that of the general population in two of the series.[36–37] Although these risks are substantially increased, the incidence of oesophageal carcinoma in the general population is low[39] so that only a relatively small number of Barrett's carcinoma cases would be expected.[4] Based on the estimate cited above, that Barrett's carcinoma accounts for 5–10% of all oesophageal cancers, fewer than 1000 new cases would be expected each year in the United States. Although this figure may be an underestimate due to inclusion of some Barrett's carcinomas in the statistics for gastric cancer, and although the incidence appears to be rising, the estimate contrasts sharply with the expected 150 000 colorectal carcinomas. More importantly, the overall survival rate in Barrett's patients was not decreased as compared to the general population in one study.[37] Furthermore, not all patients with Barrett's oesophagus are at equal risk for carcinoma. Recognition of predisposing factors, as discussed below, may allow identification of patients at particular risk.

Predisposing factors and implications for patient management

Gastro-oesophageal reflux predisposes to Barrett's carcinoma by resulting in the oesophageal columnar-lined mucosa from which the tumour develops. Whether or not continued gastro-oesophageal reflux in a patient with already established Barrett's oesophagus predisposes to carcinoma is controversial. Effective anti-reflux therapy produces regression of Barrett's mucosa in some patients,[31,33,40–43] thus potentially reducing the risk of cancer. Complete regression, however, is rare and pseudoregression with squamous epithelium overlying Barrett's mucosa has been documented. Furthermore, many cases of Barrett's carcinoma after anti-reflux surgery have been reported,[17,29,40,44,45] and success of the operation in preventing reflux has been well-documented in some.[45] Although effective anti-reflux therapy is desirable in reducing peptic complications, the evidence that cancer risk is reduced by surgical or medical therapy is not convincing.

White males appear to be particularly predisposed to Barrett's carcinoma.[12,13,17,36,46,47] The explanation of this finding is uncertain, but is of considerable interest. First, squamous carcinoma of the oesophagus is much more common in blacks than whites in the United States, whereas Barrett's oesophagus and carcinoma is uncommon in blacks.[4,36] Secondly, the male predominance among patients with Barrett's carcinoma is far higher than for Barrett's oesophagus without carcinoma.[32] The implication of these findings is that white males known to have Barrett's oesophagus may comprise a suitable group for surveillance for cancer detection and prevention.

The association of squamous carcinoma of the oesophagus with the use of tobacco and alcohol is well-known. Available data suggest that the same may hold true for Barrett's carcinoma,[13,19,36,46–48] although some authors have not reported such an association.[12,18,49–51] Nonetheless, Barrett's patients with heavy tobacco and/or alcohol usage may help to define a higher risk group. There is some evidence for a genetic predisposition.[52]

Extent and duration of Barrett's oesophagus could be expected logically to influence the predisposition to Barrett's carcinoma: the greater the area of Barrett's mucosa and the longer the mucosa has been present, the higher the risk would seem to be. Studies show, however, the majority of Barrett's carcinomas occur in relatively short-segment Barrett's oesophagus. The relative risk in patients with longer as compared to shorter segments is not well studied at present.

Data on the duration of Barrett's oesophagus are difficult to obtain in patients with Barrett's carcinoma. A substantial minority give no antecedent history of reflux symptoms.[12,13,17] This finding may be accounted for by remission of symptoms due to the relative acid insensitivity of the acquired columnar-lined mucosa as compared to the native squamous-lined mucosa.[53] Studies in children with Barrett's oesophagus indicate that the prevalence of distinctive-type mucosa, the incompletely intestinalized type usually associated with Barrett's carcinoma, is lower than in adults.[54,55] However, in other studies there is ample evidence of a higher cancer risk in children with Barrett's oesophagus, especially in those with intestinalized mucosa.[56,57] Thus, there appears to be a sequence of columnar replacement of squamous epithelium (metaplasia), intestinalization and dysplasia preceeding the development of invasive adenocarcinoma. This sequence has been evident in serial specimens from occasional patients.[45] The time interval from biopsy documentation of cardiac-type Barrett's mucosa until adenocarcinoma accompanied by distinctive-type mucosa was nine years, but Barrett's mucosa could have been present for as long as 19 years because of a 10-year interval from oesophagoscopy with biopsy showing only ulceration. The interval from demonstration of dysplasia to Barrett's carcinoma was eight years, despite partial oesophagectomy and elimination of reflux by colonic interposition. At present, the available data on extent and duration appear insufficient to identify individual patients at particular risk for Barrett's carcinoma.

Gross and histopathological appearances of Barrett's carcinoma

The heterogeneity of Barrett's carcinoma is impressive.[17]

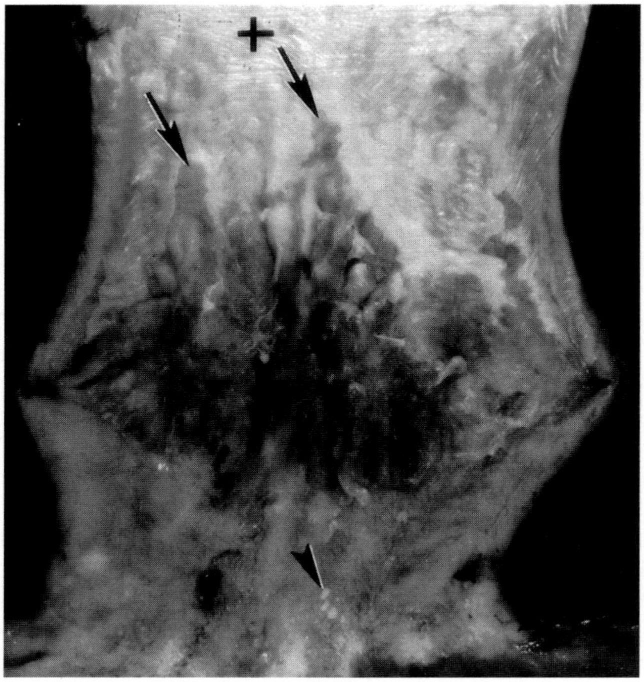

Fig. 38.32 Resection specimen of Barrett's adenocarcinoma. The nodular area of tumour has fingers of Barrett's mucosa (arrows) above it. Islands of squamous-lined mucosa (arrowhead) remain within the columar-lined segment, the highest point of which (arrow with plus sign) is about 6 cm above the oesophagogastric junction. (×1.3)

The gross appearances in individual cases vary from large exophytic masses and ulcers (Fig. 38.29) to more subtle endophytic tumours (Fig. 38.32). More than one grossly evident primary site occurs in a small minority of cases.[17,49] The vast majority of carcinomas are adenocarcinomas. There is, however, a broad spectrum from well to poorly differentiated tumours, which can be classified into three grades similar to gastric carcinoid. Adenosquamous carcinoma, adenocarcinoma with neuroendocrine carcinoid differentiation, and occasional cases of squamous carcinoma have been reported in Barrett's oesophagus.[12,17,58–60]

The spectrum of differentiation of Barrett's carcinomas is apparent with transmission electron microscopy and immunohistochemistry.[61] Among six Barrett's adenocarcinomas studied with these techniques, four tumours showed endocrine features (neurosecretory granules or peptide hormones) and two had squamous differentiation. The authors raised the possibility that the multidirectional tumours behaved more aggressively than 'pure' adenocarcinomas.

Diagnosis and staging of Barrett's carcinoma in resection specimens

The criteria for recognition of Barrett's carcinoma are shown in Table 38.2. A staging system analogous to the Dukes' classification of large bowel carcinoma has been reported.[47] With this system, the depth of infiltration into or through the oesophageal wall as well as the status of the regional lymph nodes are used. At present, the vast majority of patients presents with symptomatic, advanced tumours which have a poor prognosis.[12,13,17,46] As a result, the utility of staging in assessment of prognosis has not been verified in large numbers of cases. A few cases of superficially invasive Barrett's carcinoma have been reported in the literature; these patients appear to have a better prognosis.[47,62–66] As additional cases are accumulated in surveillance programmes, the potential importance of staging should be clarified.

Diagnosis of Barrett's carcinoma in endoscopic biopsies

As is apparent from Table 38.2, the best evidence for origin of a carcinoma in Barrett's mucosa is residual, distinctive-type Barrett's mucosa accompanying the tumour in the biopsy specimens. The presence of dysplastic villiform columnar-lined mucosa with histochemical characteristics of incomplete intestinalization (Fig. 38.33) is most useful in our experience.[66] In the absence of these two features, presumptive recognition of Barrett's carcinoma is dependent upon the endoscopic localization of biopsy specimens containing cardiac-type mucosa to the oesophagus and the exclusion of gastric heterotopia, all this in a patient whose anatomy may be greatly distorted by the presence of a tumour mass. The difficulty of obtaining Barrett's mucosa if it is present in biopsies as opposed to locating it in resection specimens is illustrated in the finding of only 10/29 (35%) Barrett's carcinomas by endoscopy in one series reported.[24] Distinctive-type epithelium can sometimes be identified in oesophageal brush cytology specimens, and cytopathology may play a role in clinical recognition of Barrett's carcinoma by improving sampling.[67,68]

Differential diagnosis of Barrett's carcinoma

Carcinoma involving the gastro-oesophageal junction region and oesophagus has the potential to arise in various structures.[12,18] Differentiation does not equate to 'cell of origin' since cancer is pathogenetically a disease of stem cells. Nevertheless, squamous carcinoma is generally assumed to arise from native squamous-lined mucosa, although a few cases of squamous carcinoma have been observed in patients with Barrett's oesophagus,[12,17,58–60] In one case, the tumour arose in an histopathologically identifiable squamous-lined remnant in the midst of Barrett's mucosa.[17] There are a variety of columnar epithelium-lined structures in the vicinity of the oesophagogastric junction such that malignant transformation could be expected to produce adenocarcinomas. Demonstration of origin in oesophageal cardiac glands, submucosal glands

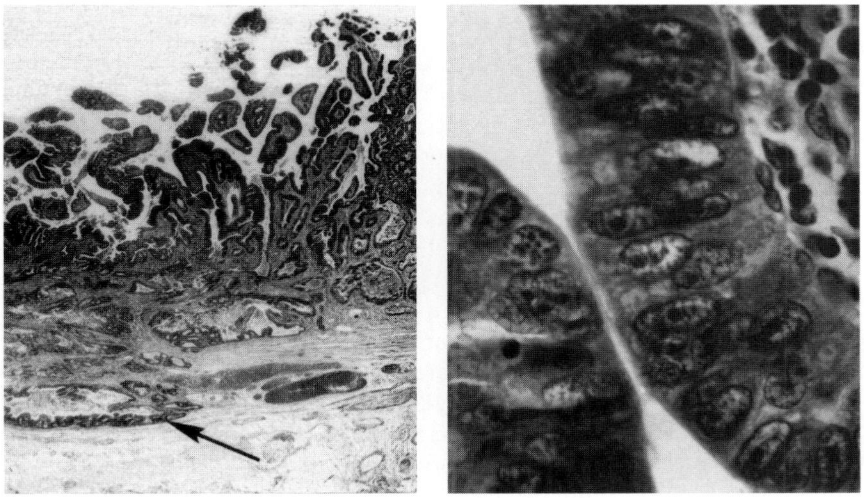

A B

Fig. 38.33 Barrett's adenocarcinoma. **A** Well-differentiated adenocarcinoma infiltrates through the muscularis mucosae into the submucosa (arrow). The overlying columnar epithelial-lined mucosa shows bizarre villous architecture and had intestinal-type mucin by histochemistry, suggesting antecedent Barrett's mucosa of the distinctive type. (H&E, ×195) **B** The Barrett's epithelium is dedifferentiated with prominent nuclear stratification and cytological abnormalities. (H&E, ×638)

or gastric heterotopia is difficult due to obliteration of the primary site as the tumour grows. Carcinoma arising in embryonic ciliated epithelial rests has not been reported. The site of origin of neuroendocrine carcinoma may also be difficult to localize (Table 38.4). There are occasional reports of carcinosarcomas[69] and combined adenocarcinomas and carcinoids.[70]

COLUMNAR EPITHELIAL DYSPLASIA IN BARRETT'S MUCOSA

Definition

Barrett's oesophagus is now recognized as a predisposing (premalignant) condition for oesophageal carcinoma, i.e. a clinical state occurring in a patient which results in a higher risk of cancer than in an unaffected person,[71] and it arises via a stage of columnar epithelial dysplasia.

'Dysplasia' is used variably in pathology but in this context it refers to epithelial abnormalities that are regarded as unequivocally neoplastic.[72] It must be recognized that invasive carcinoma may have developed already when dysplasia is the only identifiable pathological finding, particularly in a biopsy specimen. Dysplasia is synonymous with terms used in the literature on Barrett's oesophagus including carcinoma in situ,[44,47,49,73–75] dysplastic changes,[76] adenomatous neoplasms,[77] adenomatous hyperplasia,[77] adenomatous changes,[75] adenoma[75,78,79] and oesophageal columnar intraepithelial neoplasia.[80] The latter term may be preferable due to its analogy with intraepithelial neoplasia in other organ systems, but dysplasia[12,13,44,47,64,73–75,77,81–83] is ingrained in the literature. 'Adenoma' is probably an inappropriate term when applied to dysplasia in Barrett's mucosa, due to a possible perception of benignity and the potential for polypectomy as in the large bowel. Rather, such lesions are better termed nodular or polypoid dysplasia in Barrett's oesophagus, analogous to dysplasia in chronic colitis,[72] although reports of adenomas, sessile and pedunculated are still to be found in the literature.[84]

Table 38.4 Differential diagnosis of Barrett's carcinoma

Gastric adenocarcinoma involving lower oesophagus
Adenocarcinoma arising in oesophageal cardiac glands
Adenocarcinoma arising in oesophageal submucosal glands
Adenocarcinoma arising in oesophageal gastric heterotopia
Adenocarcinoma arising in oesophageal ciliated epithelial rest (embryonic)
Squamous carcinoma of oesophagus
Oesophageal neuroendocrine (oat-cell) carcinoma
Carcinoma of indeterminate origin, including metastatic

Diagnostic criteria for dysplasia

Dysplasia in Barrett's mucosa is similar to that in other columnar-lined mucosae such as the stomach.[71] Mucosal architecture,[85] epithelial morphology and cytology of individual epithelial cells are the basis for identification and classification of dysplasia. Mucosal architecture is characterized by thickening due to elongation of glands and, when present, villi, along with abnormal configuration due to irregularity of size and shape. In the case of glands, there are increased numbers, crowding with back-to-back configuration, loss of orientation, irregularity of shape with budding, branching and dilatation and intraluminal epithelial cell proliferation producing bridging and a cribriform pattern. Villous structures may be widened, blunted, branched and contorted.

The epithelial morphology of dysplasia is characterized by increased cellularity; stratification, loss of polarity and pleomorphism of nuclei, increased numbers of mitotic figures and abnormal position in the upper portions of the crypt or villous epithelium and reduced numbers of goblet cells or columnar mucous cells.

The cytological features of dysplasia include nuclear enlargement with increased nuclear-to-cytoplasmic ratio, nuclear irregularity, abnormal chromatin pattern with hyperchromatism and clumping, increased number, size and irregularity of nucleoli especially in epithelium of the luminal surface, abnormal morphology of mitotic figures and reduced mucin content in goblet and columnar mucus cells with cytoplasmic basophilia.

The histopathological features of dysplasia generally involve either the entire depth of the epithelium or the luminal portions with transitions from cardiac-type or distinctive-type epithelium in the subjacent crypts.

Table 38.5 Classification lexicon for columnar epithelial dysplasia in Barrett's oesophagus

Negative for dysplasia
Indefinite for dysplasia
Probably negative
Unknown significance
Probably positive
Positive for dysplasia
Low-grade
Intermediate-grade[a]
High-grade

[a]Included in high-grade category in classification lexicons using two grades (low-grade and high-grade).

Classification and grading of dysplasia

The nomenclatures which can be used for classification and grading of dysplasia are shown in Table 38.5. The 'indefinite for dysplasia' category[72] is particularly useful in dealing with histopathological abnormalities of Barrett's mucosa occurring in the setting of ongoing reflux oesophagitis. In some cases, the distinction between dysplasia and reactive epithelial changes consequent to inflammation is difficult. The 'Indefinite for dysplasia' category allows pathologists to communicate their concern to the clinician in the context of a formalized lexicon. In the positive category, carcinoma in situ, manifested by cribriform back-to-back glands and full-thickness stratification of nuclei with marked cytological abnormality, is included within the category of high-grade dysplasia. If invasion of the lamina propria is identified, the lesion is termed invasive adenocarcinoma rather than dysplasia (Figs 38.34, 38.35).

Examples of the three grades of dysplasia are shown in Figures 38.36–38.40. This classification system divides the 'Positive for dysplasia' category into three grades, in contrast to use of two grades modelled after dysplasia in chronic colitis (Table 38.6).[62,63,72,81–83] Use of three grades was based on the international classification of gastric dysplasia[71] as well as on the relationship between the grades of dysplasia in Barrett's mucosa and the presence of invasive carcinoma.[66,80,86] Greater intra- and interobserver variation would be expected with three grades of dysplasia rather than two.[72,83] However, three grades may provide a more accurate reflection of the relationship between

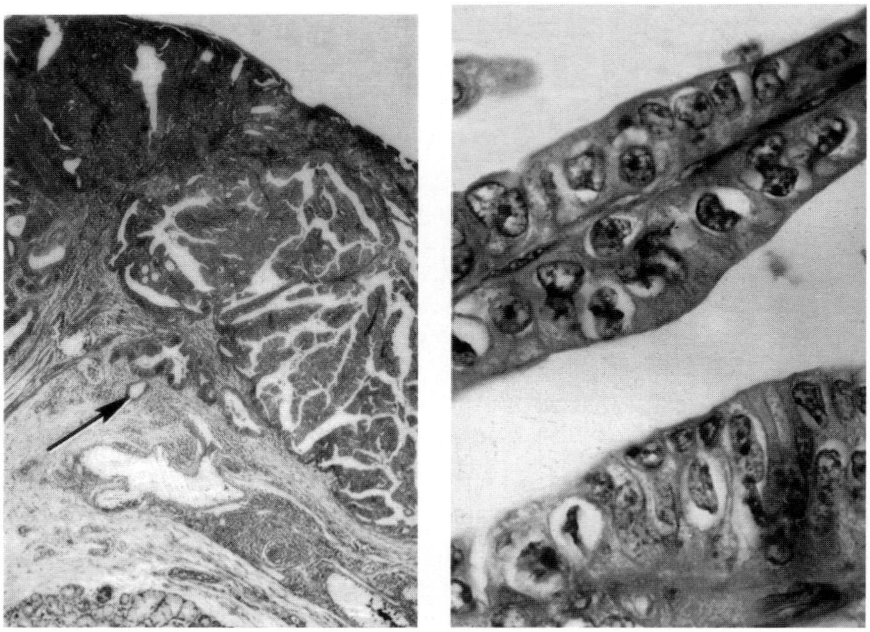

A B

Fig. 38.34 Intramucosal invasive adenocarcinoma in Barrett's mucosa with focal submucosal extension. **A** The papillary architecture of the intramucosal carcinoma is evident. Focal extension through the muscularis mucosae into the submucosa (arrow) is present. (H&E, ×30) **B** The epithelium of the papillary structures shows stratification of nuclei, loss of nuclear polarity and marked cytological abnormalities. (H&E, ×563)

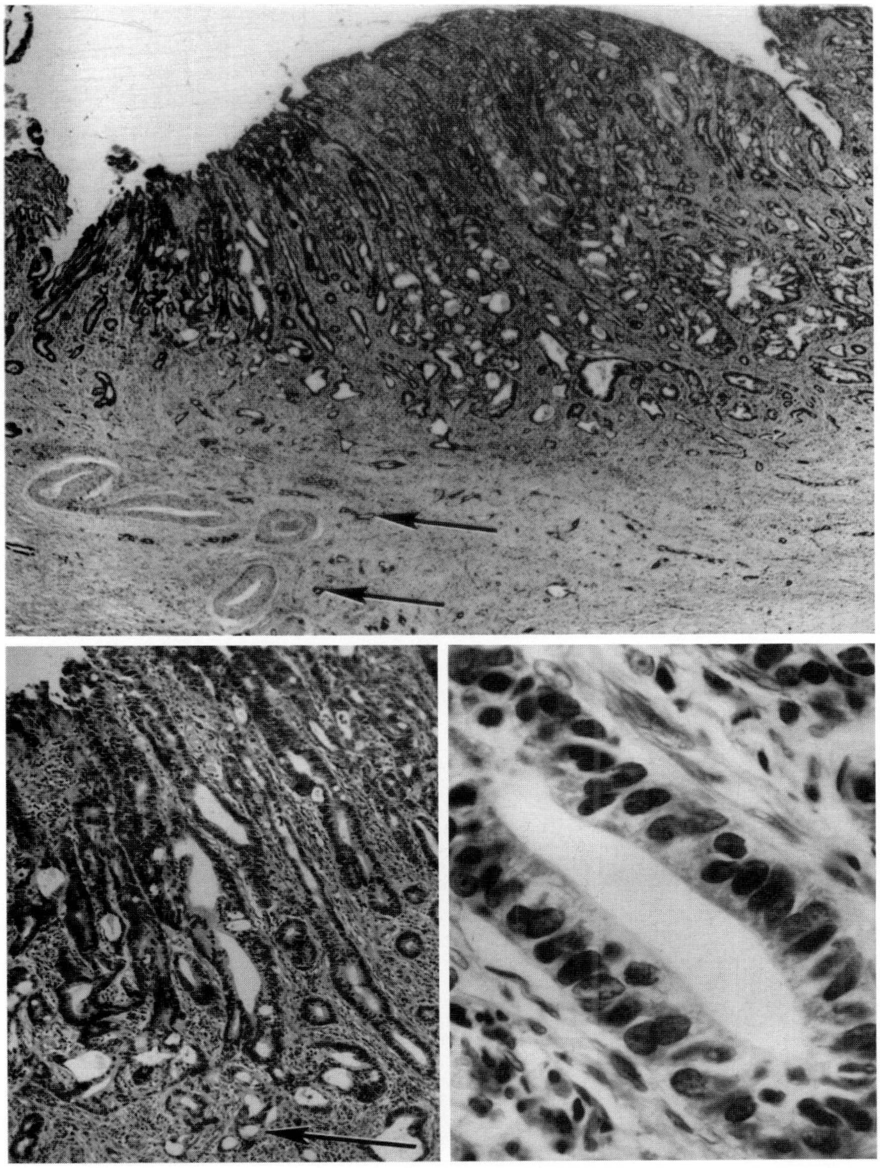

A B C

Fig. 38.35 Intramucosal invasive adenocarcinoma in Barrett's mucosa with submucosal extension. **A** The mucosa is markedly thickened due to extensive infiltration by gland-forming adenocarcinoma. Invasion through the muscularis mucosae into the submucosa (arrows) is evident. (H&E, ×29) **B** The lamina propria is invaded by adenocarcinoma (arrow). Identification of the glands of the Barrett's mucosa among those of the adenocarcinoma is difficult. (H&E, ×80) **C** The epithelium of the glands shows modest cytological abnormalities. (H&E, ×640)

morphology and biological behaviour. The specificity for invasive carcinoma and predictive value of a positive in the high-grade dysplasia category appear to be improved if three grades are used. The implications for management of patients are discussed below.

Dysplasia has been subcategorized by Riddell et al into Type 1 and type 2.[81,82] Type 1 dysplasia resembled adenomatous epithelium with enlarged, elongated, hyperchromatic nuclei which are crowded and stratified. By contrast, Type 2 dysplasia showed rounded or pleomorphic vesicular nuclei without crowding or stratification. Type 1 tended to occur in intestinalized mucosa while Type 2 did not, but the two forms of dysplasia were frequently found together. Invasive carcinoma, when found, seemed to arise mainly from Type 2 dysplasia in their study.

Dysplasia–carcinoma sequence in Barrett's mucosa

Invasive carcinoma arising in Barrett's oesophagus is frequently accompanied by multifocal dysplasia in the

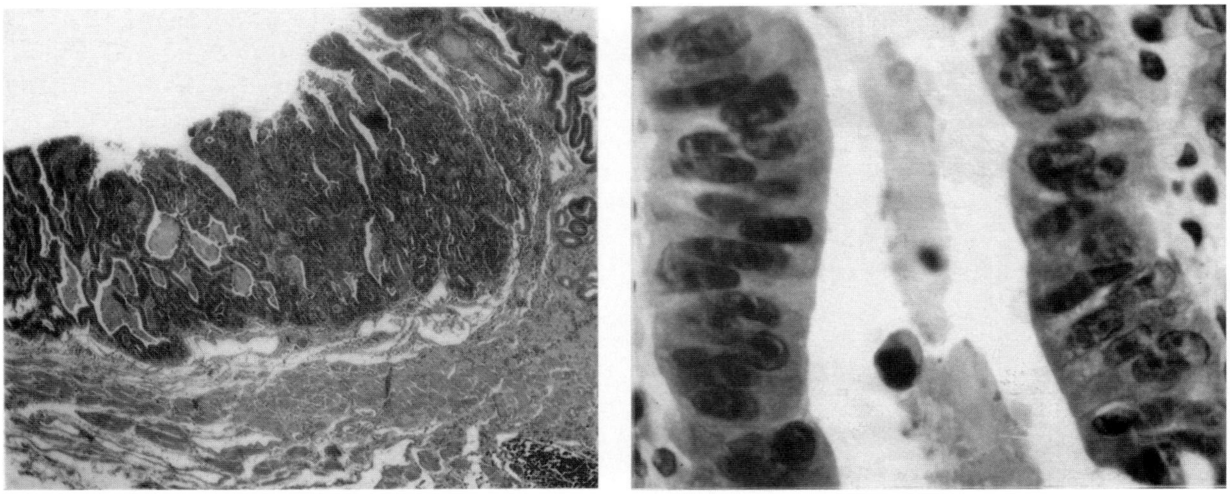

A B

Fig. 38.36 High-grade dysplasia in Barrett's mucosa. **A** The bizarre villous architecture contrasts with that of non-dysplastic distinctive-type Barrett's mucosa. No invasive carcinoma is evident. (H&E, ×30) **B** High-grade dysplasia is characterized by hypercellular epithelium with stratified elongated nuclei showing loss of polarity and reduced cytoplasmic mucin. (H&E, ×850)

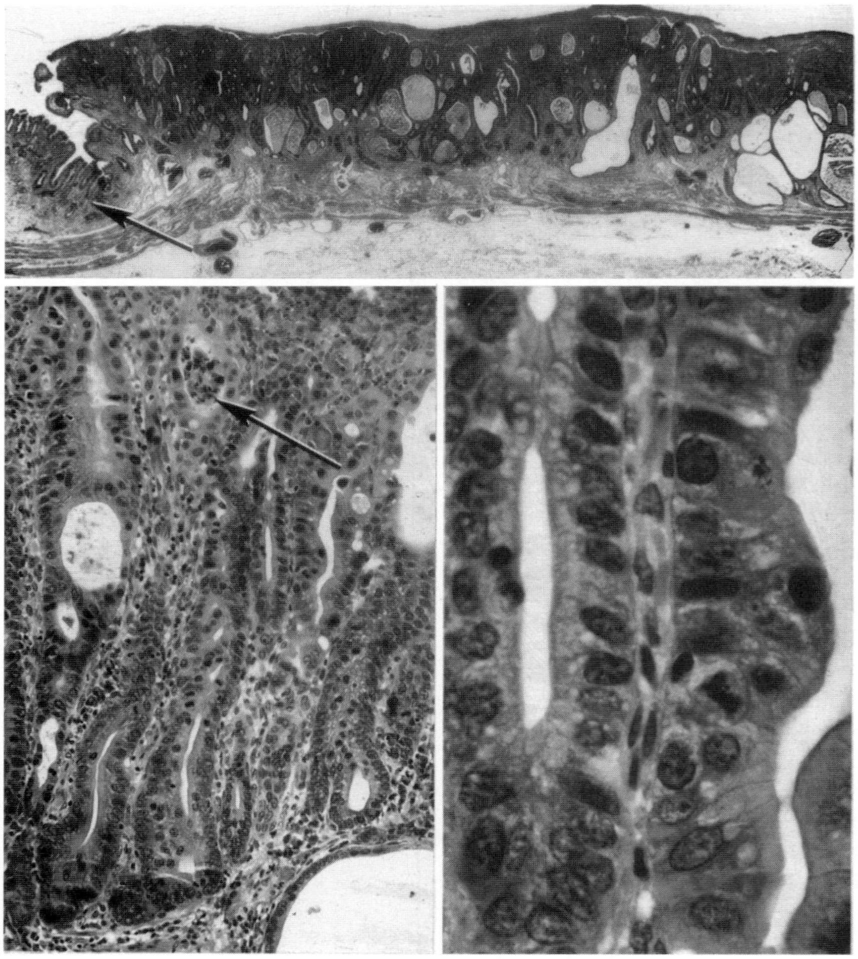

Fig. 38.37 Plaque-like area of high-grade dysplasia in Barrett's mucosa. **A** The plaque-like area is elevated above the adjoining distinctive-type Barrett's mucosa (arrow). The bizarre glandular architecture includes numerous dilated glands. (H&E, ×9.6) **B** The glands are strikingly elongated with irregular outlines. No invasive carcinoma is evident. A gland abscess (arrow) is present. (H&E, ×144) **C** The epithelium shows enlarged nuclei with loss of polarity and striking cytological abnormalities, but little nuclear stratification. Epithelial mucin is markedly reduced. (H&E, ×720)

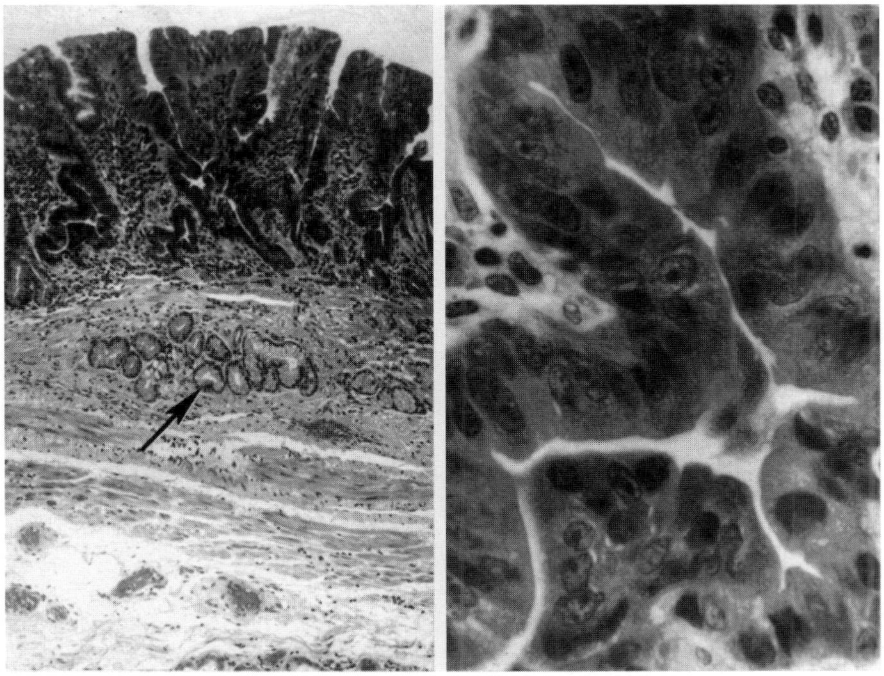

A B

Fig. 38.38 Intermediate-grade dysplasia in Barrett's mucosa. **A** The villous architecture of the distinctive-type mucosa is only modestly distorted and the mucosa is of usual thickness, but epithelial mucin is markedly reduced. An oesophageal cardiac gland (arrow) underlies the Barrett's mucosa. (H&E, ×110) **B** The epithelium of a gland shows enlarged nuclei with prominent nucleoli. Less severe abnormalities were present in the villous epithelium. (H&E, ×700)

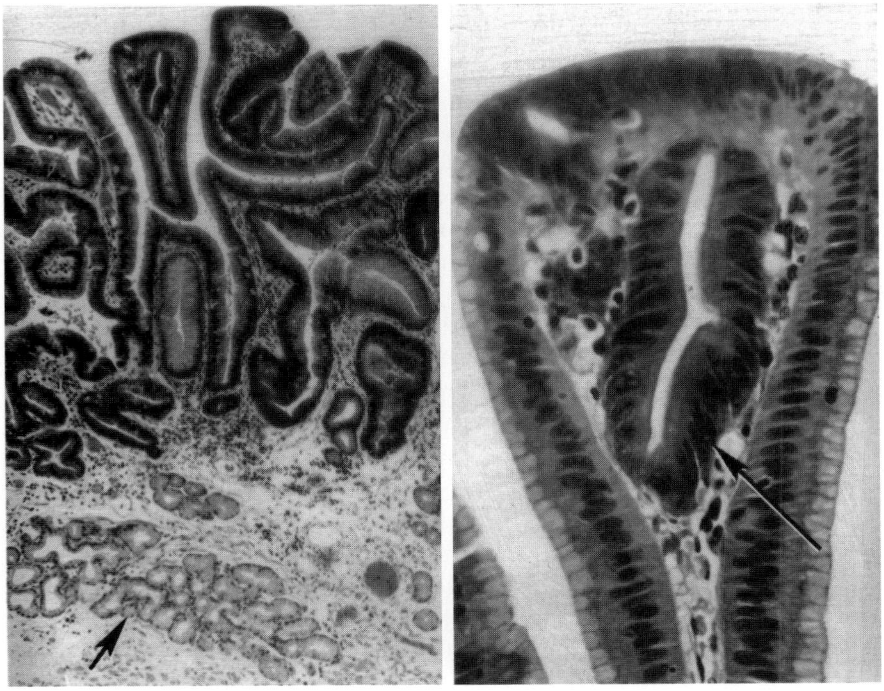

A B

Fig. 38.39 Low-grade dysplasia in Barrett's mucosa. **A** The Barrett's mucosa has bizarre villiform architecture but generally bland-appearing epithelium. An oesophageal cardiac gland (arrow) underlies the Barrett's mucosa (H&E, ×76) **B** The villous epithelium is cardiac-type with columnar mucous cells containing abundant mucin. Hypercellularity of the epithelium with mild enlargement and stratification of nuclei characterizes the low-grade dysplasia. In some foci (arrow), the epithelial abnormalities are more prominent, equivalent to intermediate-grade dysplasia. (H&E, ×336)

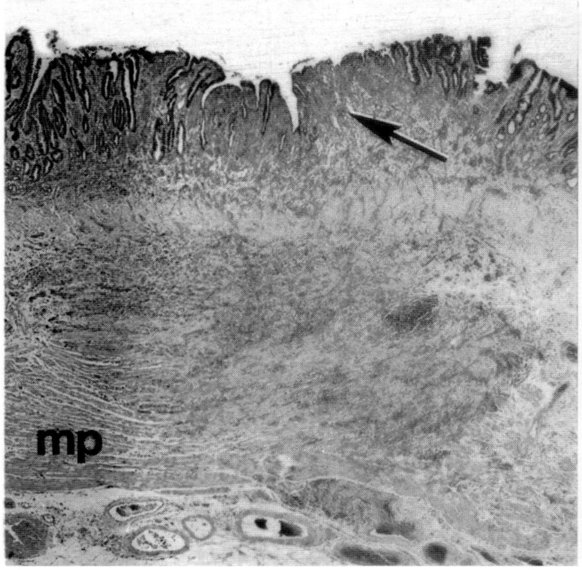

A

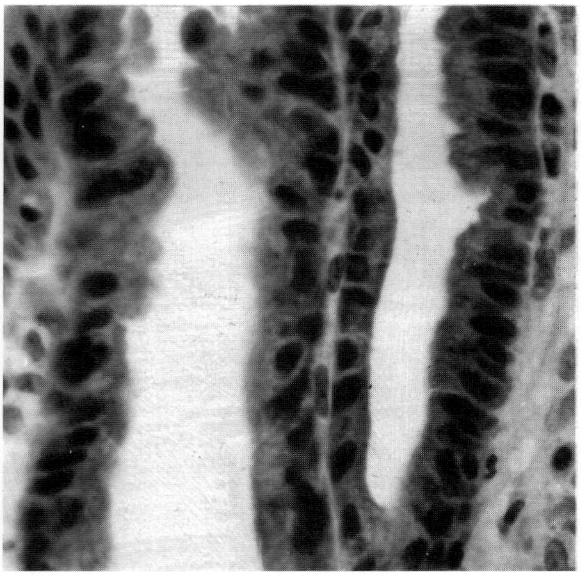

B

Fig. 38.40 Low-grade dysplasia in Barrett's mucosa associated with invasive adenocarcinoma. **A** Poorly differentiated adenocarcinoma fills the lamina propria (arrow) of distinctive-type Barrett's mucosa and invades into the muscularis propria (mp). This area was found incidentally in flat Barrett's mucosa of a 'mapped' resection specimen in which the entire specimen was embedded for histopathological examination (H&E, ×16)
B Low-grade dysplasia in the Barrett's mucosa adjoining the carcinoma is characterized by nuclear enlargement, hyper-chromatism, irregularity and loss of polarity. Epithelial mucin is markedly reduced. (H&E, ×400)

Table 38.6 Comparison of grading systems of dysplasia

Spectrum of abnormality	Dysplasia in Barrett's mucosa	Dysplasia in Barrett's mucosa based on dysplasia in IBD[a]	International classification of gastric dysplasia
Least	Low-grade	Low-grade	Mild
	Intermediate-grade	High-grade	Moderate
Most	High-grade[b,c,d]	High-grade[b,d]	Severe[c,d]

[a]See reference nos 62, 63, 81–83; [b]Includes carcinoma in situ (confined within basement membrane); [c]Excludes intramucosal carcinoma (invasion of lamina propria); [d]Does not use 'carcinoma in situ'.

residual mucosa.[49,65,66,75] As a result, a *morphological* sequence of Barrett's mucosa–dysplastic mucosa–invasive carcinoma is frequently demonstrable in resection specimens (Fig. 38.41). Interpretation of such findings, however, is limited in that the patients represent the end of the *temporal* dysplasia–carcinoma sequence, since resection is generally done because of malignancy. Endoscopic biopsies at sequential examinations during the natural history of a patient's Barrett's oesophagus, despite the problem of sampling, provide data which suggest that Barrett's mucosa of the distinctive type is that which is susceptible to the development of dysplasia. This interpretation is based on the high frequency of distinctive-type mucosa in association with Barrett's carcinoma and dysplasia in both resection and biopsy specimens.[12,18,65,66,73,76,77,82,87]

The more severe the dysplasia, the stronger the association with invasive carcinoma appears to be.[62,63,66,81,82] The natural history of the Barrett's mucosa–dysplasia–carcinoma sequence remains to be defined in large populations of patients evaluated sequentially with endoscopic biopsies. Initial studies of small numbers of patients have shown evolution from Barrett's mucosa through dysplasia into carcinoma over periods of a few years and high grade dysplasia has been followed by adenocarcinoma after relatively short time intervals of as little as a few months. This has been substantiated in more recent studies.[87,88]

Surveillance and implications of dysplasia for patient management

The high prevalence of adenocarcinoma in patients with Barrett's oesophagus (about 10%) and poor survival rate in those patients who present with symptomatic tumours (median survival about 2 years,[17] 5-year survival about 25%)[13] have led to proposals for surveillance in order to permit early intervention in the dysplasia–carcinoma sequence and thereby attempt to improve outcome.[5–7,44,48,73,89] These proposals are supported by the relatively high prevalence of dysplasia in Barrett's oesophagus. Although admirable from a humanistic standpoint, such proposals require careful consideration, particularly in

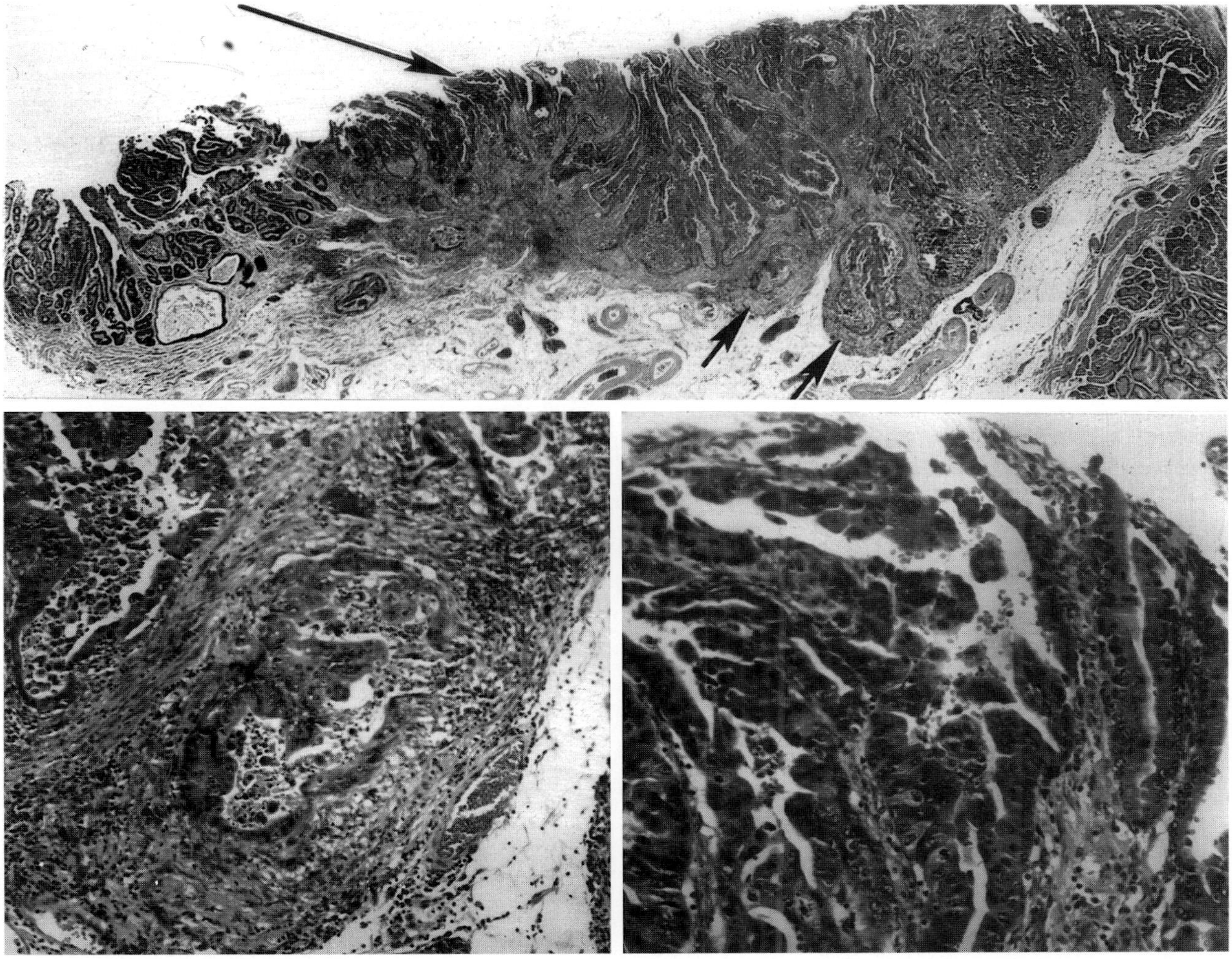

Fig. 38.41 Morphological Barrett's mucosa–dysplasia–invasive adenocarcinoma sequence in resection specimen of Barrett's oesophagus. **A** Small flat adenocarcinoma invades only into the superficial submucosa (short arrows). The Barrett's mucosa adjoining the invasive carcinoma shows high-grade dysplasia (long arrow) while distinctive-type Barrett's mucosa without dysplasia is present further away from the tumour (left margin of photograph). Preoperative biopsies showed only high-grade dysplasia. (H&E, ×17) **B** Area of superficial submucosal invasion indicated by short arrow in **A** shows moderately differentiated adenocarcinoma with desmoplastic and inflammatory reaction. (H&E, ×110) **C** Area of high-grade dysplasia indicated by long arrow in **A** shows bizarre villous architecture with strikingly abnormal epithelial morphology. (H&E, ×165)

light of fiscal constraints on delivery of health care. Successful surveillance programmes in general have three requirements:

1. Satisfactory identification of a high-risk population
2. Availability of satisfactory surveillance techniques
3. Availability of suitable interventional therapy.

At present, successful surveillance for early detection of invasive Barrett's carcinoma or for cancer prevention based on detection of dysplasia poses major problems. Data to address these problems are currently provisional at best.

The high-risk population for Barrett's carcinoma appears to be white males with reflux who use tobacco and consume alcoholic beverages. In at least three series, however, a sizable minority (about 40%) of patients with Barrett's carcinoma gave no antecedent reflux history.[12,13,17] In another study, none of the patients was known to have Barrett's oesophagus until they presented with the complicating carcinoma.[49] Such patients provided no clinical evidence of their antecedent Barrett's oesophagus and as a result could not have been included in a surveillance programme. Thus, even totally successful surveillance of known Barrett's patients may prevent no more than approximately two-thirds of all Barrett's carcinomas as we see from the incidence of Barrett's carcinoma diagnosed at autopsy.[35]

Thus the high prevalence of Barrett's carcinoma appears in large part attributable to patients with occult Barrett's oesophagus who present with the complicating

Table 38.7 Summary of reported patients with high-grade dysplasia in Barrett's mucosa by biopsy

Reference	No. of patients with high-grade dysplasia	No. undergoing oesophagectomy	No. found to have invasive carcinoma	No. with carcinoma through wall	No. of operative deaths	No. with recurrent carcinoma	Length of follow-up in survivors (months)
Hamilton et al[66]	6	5[a]	3 (60%)	0	0	0	4, 5, 8, 18, 30
Lee[62]	4	4	3 (75%)	2	1 (25%)[b]	1[c]	26, 27
Reid et al[63]	4	4	0	NA[d]	1 (25%)[e]	NA[d]	13, 43
Womach et al[64]	3	2	0	NA[d]	1 (50%)	NA[d]	4
Riddell et al[81,82]	2	2	2 (100%)	1	0	NS[f]	NS[f]

[a]One patient underwent fundoplication after no radiographic or surgical evidence of carcinoma was found; [b]Patient with carcinoma through oesophageal wall; [c]Patient died of metastatic carcinoma 6 months after oesophagectomy; NA[d] = not applicable; A[e] second patient died of a stroke 9 months after oesophagectomy; NS[f] = not stated.

carcinoma. By contrast, the incidence of carcinoma during follow-up of patients known to have Barrett's oesophagus alone on initial evaluation is relatively low (1/81, 1/175 and 1/441 cases/patient-year of follow-up in three studies). These data suggest that substantial medical resources would be required to identify a relatively small number of cases of carcinoma by surveillance. The incidence of dysplasia is unknown at present.

A second consideration in surveillance is the techniques to be used. Endoscopy with biopsies and brush cytology appears to be the best approach. Brush cytology has the advantage of reducing sampling problems inherent to biopsies.[67,68,90] Endoscopic techniques to improve identification and localization of dysplasia, such as use of indigo carmine dye,[65] or toluidine blue[91] may be helpful. Recognition of the occurrence of intra- and interobserver variation among pathologists in interpretation of histopathological and cytological findings is important.[72,83] As a result, confirmation of the diagnosis of dysplasia or invasive carcinoma by a second experienced pathologist is recommended before decisions on therapy are made. The optimal endoscopic protocol (e.g. frequency of examination and number of biopsies) is uncertain at present. It has been recommended[92] that jumbo biopsies be taken from all quadrants at 2 cm intervals at the time of examination, but this approach may not be practical for routine management.

The final consideration in surveillance is the mode of therapy. Decisions regarding treatment depend on the histopathological and cytological findings. If the patient is confirmed to have invasive carcinoma and is a suitable surgical candidate, oesophagectomy is indicated. However, data showing that survival is improved by early detection and resection of Barrett's carcinoma are sketchy at present (Table 38.7).

If dysplasia without invasive carcinoma is found and confirmed, the decisions become much more difficult. The probability of synchronous and metachronous carcinoma must be considered relative to the morbidity and mortality of oesophagectomy. Operative mortality of as much as 15% can be expected with thoracic oesophagectomy, but is lower with the transabdominal approach. These mortalities are substantial for a prophylactic procedure, and as a result 'prophylactic oesophagectomy' appears to be an oxymoron. Nonetheless, confirmed biopsy identification of high-grade dysplasia in Barrett's mucosa is currently an indication for prophylactic oesophagectomy in suitable surgical candidates. This recommendation is based on the data shown in Table 38.8, which suggest that a substantial number of patients with only high-grade dysplasia in biopsies already have invasive carcinoma in their Barrett's oesophagus (Fig. 38.41). Thus, high-grade dysplasia appears to be a marker for high probability of synchronous invasive carcinoma, as well as a precursor for metachronous adenocarcinoma. It is important, however, that the risks and potential benefits of prophylactic oesophagectomy are explained carefully to the patients and their families, as a large proportion of the resection specimens will not contain invasive carcinoma. In addition, the operative mortality in the small number of patients reported in the literature is distressingly high (Table 38.7).

Table 38.8 Provisional recommendations for surveillance of patients with Barrett's oesophagus

Population
Patients with Barrett's oesophagus who are *suitable surgical candidates* for oesophagectomy
Emphasis on white males with tobacco and alcoholic beverage usage

Surveillance techniques
Yearly to tri-yearly oesophago-gastroduodenoscopy by an experienced endoscopist
Multiple biopsies and brush cytology of any lesions
'Mapping' of the Barrett's mucosa by biopsies of each quadrant at about 2 cm intervals
Brush cytology from entire Barrett's mucosa

Recommended therapy
All patients: aggressive antireflux therapy with cessation of tobacco and alcoholic beverage usage
Invasive carcinoma or high-grade dysplasia patients: if patient is suitable surgical candidate, oesophagectomy after confirmation of diagnosis
Intermediate-grade or low-grade dysplasia patients: repeat surveillance examination in 3 months with careful review of all findings.

The optimal management of patients found to have intermediate or low-grade dysplasia is even less certain than with high-grade dysplasia. No cases with only low-grade dysplasia in preoperative biopsy have been reported to show invasive adenocarcinoma in resection specimens.[62,81,82] In resection specimens, however, invasive carcinoma arising from occasional areas of intermediate-grade and even low-grade dysplasia can occur (Fig. 38.40).[66] On the other hand, the natural history of dysplasia in Barrett's mucosa is unknown at present, such that the optimal time for surgical intervention in the dysplasia–carcinoma sequence is unknown. The risks of oesophagectomy currently outweigh the potential benefits for cancer prevention in patients with intermediate and low-grade dysplasia unless the dysplasia is associated with a mass or is extensive and persistent.

Regression of dysplasia with anti-reflux therapy has been reported.[41] Regression of the Barrett's mucosa itself and replacement by squamous epithelium has also been reported,[31,33,40–43] although this phenomenon may be pseudoregression: one report showed that the squamous epithelium overgrew but did not replace the Barrett's mucosa.[81] Nonetheless, all patients with Barrett's oesophagus should have aggressive anti-reflux therapy, as the peptic complications are ameliorated. Both medical and surgical modalities have been recommended.[4–7,93–95] Cessation of tobacco and alcoholic beverage usage is also recommended, in view of a proposed association of their use with Barrett's carcinoma in some studies.[13,19,36,46–48] The possible role of laser or thermal ablation in Barrett's oesophagus combined with complete acid inhibition remains to be examined.

The issues of surveillance in patients with Barrett's oesophagus are similar to those in patients with chronic idiopathic colitis (ulcerative colitis and Crohn's disease involving the colon).[96] The options are to:

1. Ignore the risk
2. Carry out prophylactic resection, or
3. Carry out surveillance.

Despite the many unanswered questions, surveillance as described in Table 38.8 is usually recommended currently. These provisional recommendations will probably require modification as additional data become available. There is possibly a case, for example, of giving priority to patients with Barrett's mucosa greater than 8 cm in length.[97] Others believe the risk of adenocarcinoma in Barrett's overrated.[98]

POTENTIAL MARKERS FOR DYSPLASIA AND CARCINOMA IN BARRETT'S MUCOSA

Discovery of a marker for dysplasia and carcinoma in Barrett's mucosa has the potential to improve surveillance by allowing identification of patients at particular high risk. Alternatively, the markers could identify those of very low risk. There are several potential markers which have been studied or are currently under investigation.

Altered epithelial proliferation

Measurements of DNA synthesis as a marker of epithelial proliferation in Barrett's mucosa has been studied due to the association of abnormal epithelial proliferation with premalignant conditions of the large bowel and stomach.[99] Published studies of Barrett's mucosa present disparate results not of diagnostic value in assessing dysplasia.[100,101] Similarly, estimates of growth regulatory peptides, epidermal growth factor, transforming growth factor alpha and epidermal growth factor receptor, whilst aiding in the understanding of pathogenesis of Barrett's oesophagus and dysplasia, have no diagnostic implication for the individual case assessment. The same applies for Ki 67 reactivity, and proliferating cell nuclear antigen.[102–105] Thus, at present, there are no data to suggest that epithelial proliferation assessed by a variety of methods will provide a marker for risk of dysplasia and carcinoma in Barrett's mucosa.

Abnormal mucin histochemistry

Alterations in epithelial mucins of Barrett's mucosa as assessed by methods utilizing Alcian blue, high iron diamine and lectins have also been explored as potential markers, again with discouraging results.[106–112] At present it seems that abnormalities of mucin histochemistry appear unlikely to be sufficiently specific to provide a useful marker for dysplasia and adenocarcinoma in Barrett's oesophagus.

Carcinoembryonic antigen (CEA) expression

In several studies[113–115] the marked heterogeneity in CEA staining led to the conclusion that its use in biopsy specimens was likely to be limited. Thus, at present CEA immunohistochemistry does not provide a marker for dysplasia and carcinoma in Barrett's mucosa.

Altered DNA content and cytogenetic aneuploidy

It has been suggested that dysplasia and carcinoma in Barrett's mucosa arise in association with a process of genetic instability and that flow cytometry may be an objective adjunct to histopathology in assessing nuclear abnormalities associated with these changes.[116,117] In a more recent study[118] it has been shown prospectively that in a subset of patients with Barrett's oesophagus who developed dysplasia and adenocarcinoma, there is an acquired genomic instability which manifests as increased

G2/tetraploid DNA and the development of aneuploid clones which may lead to the evolution of invasive carcinoma. Further work in this field is clearly needed.

Elevated ornithine decarboxylase activity

Ornithine decarboxylase (ODC) converts the amino acid ornithine to the polyamine putrescine and is the first and rate-limiting enzyme in polyamine biosynthesis.[119] Polyamines appear to play important roles in regulation of cell proliferation, including neoplasia. Elevated ODC activity in colonic mucosa has been shown to be a marker for increased risk of colorectal carcinoma in the form of adenomatous polyposis.[120] A recent study showed elevated ODC activity in Barrett's mucosa of 14/20 patients (70%).[121] Further work, however, has failed to substantiate that measurement of ODC is a practical method of assessing dysplasia.[92]

p53 gene product overexpression

There is some evidence that p53 gene product overexpression may be a relatively late event in the dysplasia–carcinoma sequence,[122,123] and it may have a role in the management of Barrett's patients.

Histological examination is still arguably the best current method of assessing dysplasia and high-grade dysplasia. In its presence there is a significant risk of synchronous or metachronous invasive carcinoma. This is arguably an indication for oesophagectomy in suitable surgical candidates. Many questions regarding surveillance of Barrett's patients and appropriate management of those found to have dysplasia, particularly intermediate-grade or low-grade dysplasia are, however, unanswered at present. Studies of mucosal laser and thermal ablation therapy are in progress and there is clearly hope for the better management of patients with Barrett's oesophagus in terms of their cancer risk.

REFERENCES

1. Barrett NR. Chronic peptic ulcer of the oesophagus and 'oesophagitis'. Br J Surg 1950; 38: 175–182.
2. Hamilton SR, Yardley JH. Regeneration of cardiac-type mucosa and acquisition of Barrett mucosa after esophagogastrostomy. Gastroenterology 1977; 72: 669–675.
3. Hamilton SR. Pathogenesis of columnar cell-lined (Barrett's) esophagus. In: Spechler SJ, Goyal RK, eds. Barrett's esophagus: pathophysiology, diagnosis and management. New York: Elsevier, 1985: p 29–37.
4. Spechler SJ, Goyal RK. Barrett's esophagus. N Engl J Med 1986; 315: 362–371.
5. Bozymski EM, Herlihy KJ, Orlando RC. Barrett's esophagus. Ann Intern Med 1982; 97: 103–107.
6. Sjogren RW Jr, Johnson LF. Barrett's esophagus: a review. Am J Med 1983; 74: 313–321.
7. Berardi RS, Devaiah KA. Barrett's esophagus. Surg Gynecol Obstet 1983; 156: 521–538.
8. Morson BC, Belcher JR. Adenocarcinoma of the oesophagus and ectopic gastric mucosa. Br J Cancer 1952; 6: 127–130.
9. McCorkle RG, Blades B. Adenocarcinoma of the esophagus arising in aberrant gastric mucosa. Am J Surg 1955; 21: 781–785.
10. Goyal RK, Glancy JJ, Spiro HM. Lower esophageal ring. N Engl J Med 1970; 282: 1298–1305.
11. Hayward J. The lower end of the esophagus. Thorax 1961; 16: 36–41.
12. Haggitt RC, Dean PJ. Adenocarcinoma in Barrett's epithelium. In: Spechler SJ, Goyal RK eds. Barrett's esophagus: pathophysiology, diagnosis, and management. New York: Elsevier, 1985: p 153–166.
13. Skinner DB, Walther BC, Riddell RH, Schmidt H, Iascone C, DeMeester TR. Barrett's esophagus: comparison of benign and malignant cases. Ann Surg 1983; 198: 554–566.
14. Rector LE, Connerley ML. Aberrant mucosa in the esophagus in infants and in children. Arch Pathol 1941; 31: 285–294.
15. de la Pava S, Pickren JW, Adler RH. Ectopic gastric mucosa of the esophagus: a study on histogenesis. NY State J Med 1964; 64: 1831–1835.
16. Jabbari M, Goresky CA, Lough J, Yaffe C, Daly D, Cote C. The inlet patch: heterotopic gastric mucosa in the upper esophagus. Gastroenterology 1985; 89: 352–356.
17. Smith RRL, Hamilton SR, Boitnott JK, Rogers EL. The spectrum of carcinoma arising in Barrett's esophagus: a clinicopathologic study of 26 patients. Am J Surg Pathol 1984; 8: 563–573.
18. Appelman HD, Kalish RJ, Clancy PE, Orringer MB. Distinguishing features of adenocarcinoma in Barrett's esophagus and in the gastric cardia. In: Spechler SJ, Goyal RK, eds. Barrett's esophagus: pathophysiology, diagnosis, and management. New York: Elsevier, 1985: p 167–187.
19. Kalish RJ, Clancy PE, Orringer MB, Appelman HD. Clinical, epidemiologic, and morphologic comparison between adenocarcinomas arising in Barrett's esophageal mucosa and in the gastric cardia. Gastroenterology 1984; 86: 461–467.
20. Wang HH, Antonioli DA, Goldman H. Comparative features of esophageal and gastric adenocarcinomas: recent changes in type and frequency. Hum Pathol 1986; 17: 482–487.
21. MacDonald WC. Clinical and pathologic features of adenocarcinoma of the gastric cardia. Cancer 1972; 29: 724–732.
22. Rogers E, Iseri O, Bustin M, Goldkind L, Goldkind SF. Adenocarcinoma of the esophago-gastric junction — a distinct entity. Gastroenterology 1981; 80: 1264 (abstract).
23. Rogers EL, Goldkind SF, Iseri OA, Bustin M, Goldkind L, Hamilton SR, Smith RRL. Adenocarcinoma of the lower esophagus: a disease primarily of white males with Barrett's esophagus. J Clin Gastroenterol 1986; 8: 613–618.
24. Hamilton SR, Smith RRL, Cameron JL. Prevalence and extent of Barrett esophagus in adenocarcinoma of the esophagus and esophagogastric junction. Human Pathology 1988; 19: 942–948.
25. Borrie J, Goldwater L. Columnar cell-lined esophagus: assessment of etiology and treatment: a 22 year experience. J Thorac Cardiovasc Surg 1976; 71: 825–834.
26. Hawe A, Payne WS, Weiland LH, Fontana RS. Adenocarcinoma in the columnar epithelial lined lower (Barrett) oesophagus. Thorax 1973; 28: 511–514.
27. Messian RA, Hermos JA, Robbins AH, Friedlander DM, Schimmel EM. Barrett's esophagus: clinical review of 26 cases. Am J Gastroenterol 1978; 69: 458–466.
28. Bremmer CG. Benign strictures of the esophagus. Curr Prob Surg 1982; 19: 402–489.
29. Naef AP, Savary M, Ozzello. Columnar-lined lower esophagus: an acquired lesion with malignant predisposition: report on 140 cases of Barrett's esophagus with 12 adenocarcinomas. J Thorac Cardiovasc Surg 1975; 70: 826–835.
30. Mengkuy R. On the malignant potential of acquired short esophagus. Arch Surg 1979; 114: 260–263.
31. Ransom JM, Patel GK, Clift SA, Womble NE, Read RC. Extended and limited types of Barrett's esophagus in the adult. Ann Thorac Surg 1982; 33: 19–27.

32. Sarr MG, Hamilton SR, Marrone GC, Cameron JL. Barrett's esophagus: its prevalence and association with adenocarcinoma in patients with symptoms of gastroesophageal reflux. Am J Surg 1985; 149: 187–193.
33. Radigan LR, Glover JL, Shipley FE, Shoemaker RE. Barrett esophagus. Arch Surg 1977; 112: 486–491.
34. Li H. Malignant Barrett's oesophagus. Eur J Cancer Prev 1993; 2: 47–52.
35. Cameron AJ, Zinsmeister AR, Ballard DJ, Carney JA. Prevalence of columnar-lined esophagus — comparison of population based clinical and autopsy findings. Gastroenterology 1990; 99: 918–922.
36. Spechler SJ, Robbins AH, Rubins HB et al. Adenocarcinoma and Barrett's esophagus: an overrated risk? Gastroenterology 1984; 87: 927–933.
37. Cameron AJ, Ott BJ, Payne WS. The incidence of adenocarcinoma in columnar-lined (Barrett's) esophagus. N Engl J Med 1985; 313: 857–859.
38. Sprung DJ, Ellis FH Jr, Gibb SP. Incidence of adenocarcinoma in Barrett's esophagus. Am J Gastroenterol 1984; 79: 817 (abstract).
39. Silverberg E, Lubera J. Cancer statistics, 1986. CA 1986; 36: 9–25.
40. Brand DL, Ylvisaker JT, Gelfand M, Pope CE II. Regression of columnar esophageal (Barrett's) epithelium after anti-reflux surgery. N Engl J Med 1980; 302: 844–848.
41. Patel GK, Clift SA, Schaefer RA, Read RC, Texter EC Jr. Resolution of severe dysplastic changes with regression of columnar epithelium in Barrett's esophagus on medical treatment. Gastroenterology 1982; 82: 1147 (abstract).
42. Sprung DJ, Ellis FH Jr, Gibb SP. Regression of Barrett's epithelium after anti-reflux surgery. Am J Gastroenterology 1984; 79: 817 (abstract).
43. Pope CE II. Regression of Barrett's epithelium. In: Spechler SJ, Goyal RK, eds. Barrett's esophagus: pathophysiology, diagnosis, and management. New York: Elsevier, 1985: p 224–229.
44. Haggitt RC, Tryzelaar J, Ellis FH, Colcher H. Adenocarcinoma complicating columnar epithelium-lined (Barrett's) esophagus. Am J Clin Pathol 1978; 70: 1–5.
45. Hamilton SR, Hutcheon DF, Ravich WJ, Cameron JL, Paulson M. Adenocarcinoma in Barrett's esophagus after elimination of gastro-esophageal reflux. Gastroenterology 1984; 86: 356–360.
46. Sanfey H, Hamilton SR, Smith RRL, Cameron JL. Carcinoma arising in Barrett's esophagus. Surg Gynecol Obstet 1985; 161: 570–574.
47. Rosenberg JC, Budev H, Edwards RC, Singal S, Steiger Z, Sundareson AS. Analysis of adenocarcinoma in Barrett's esophagus utilizing a staging system. Cancer 1985; 55: 1353–1360.
48. Harle IA, Finley RJ, Belsheim M et al. Management of adenocarcinoma in columnar-lined esophagus. Ann Thorac Surg 1985; 40: 330–336.
49. Witt TR, Bains MS, Zaman MB, Martini N. Adenocarcinoma in Barrett's esophagus. J Thorac Cardiovasc Surg 1983; 85: 337–345.
50. Gray MR, Donnelly RJ, Kingsnorth AN. The role of smoking and alcohol in metaplasia and cancer risk in Barrett's columnar-lined oesophagus. Gut 1993; 34: 727–731.
51. Menke-Pluymers MB, Hop WC, Dees J, van Blankenstein M, Tilanus HW. Risk factors for the development of an adenocarcinoma in columnar-lined (Barrett) esophagus. The Rotterdam Esophageal Tumour Study Group. Cancer 1993; 72: 1155–1158.
52. Fahmy N, King JF. Barrett's esophagus: an acquired condition with genetic predisposition. Am J Gastroenterol 1993; 88: 1262–1265.
53. Iascone C, DeMeester TR, Little AG, Skinner DB. Barrett's esophagus: functional assessment, proposed pathogenesis, and surgical therapy. Arch Surg 1983; 118: 543–549.
54. Dahms BB, Rothstein FC. Barrett's esophagus in children: a consequence of chronic gastroesophageal reflux. Gastroenterology 1984; 86: 318–323.
55. Hassal E, Weinstein WM, Ament ME. Barrett's esophagus in childhood. Gastroenterology 1985; 89: 1331–1337.
56. Hassall E, Dimmick JE, Magee JF. Adenocarcinoma in childhood Barrett's esophagus: case documentation and the need for surveillance in children. Am J Gastroenterol 1993; 88: 282–288.
57. Cheu HW, Grosfeld JL, Heifetz SA, Fitzgerald J, Rescorla F, West K. Persistence of Barrett's esophagus in children after antireflux surgery: influence on follow-up care. J Pediatr Surg 1992; 27: 260–264 (discussion: p 265–266).
58. Tamura H, Schulman SA. Barrett-type esophagus associated with squamous carcinoma. Chest 1971; 59: 330–333.
59. Allan NK, Weitzner S, Scott L, Khalil KG. Adenocarcinoma arising in Barrett's esophagus with synchronous squamous cell carcinoma of the esophagus. South Med J 1986; 79: 1036–1039.
60. Burke EL, Sturm J, Williamson D. The diagnosis of microscopic carcinoma of the esophagus. Am J Dig Dis 1978; 23: 148–151.
61. Banner BF, Memoli VA, Warren WH, Gould VE. Carcinoma with multi-directional differentiation arising in Barrett's esophagus. Ultrastruct Pathol 1983; 4: 205–217.
62. Lee GR. Dysplasia in Barrett's esophagus: a clinical pathologic study of six patients. Am J Surg Pathol 1985; 9: 845–852.
63. Reid BJ, Lewin K, VanDeventer G et al. Barrett's esophagus: high-grade dysplasia and intramucosal carcinoma detected by endoscopic biopsy surveillance. Gastroenterology 1986; 90: 1601 (abstract).
64. Womack C, Harvey L. Columnar epithelial lined oesophagus (CELO) or Barrett's oesophagus: mucin chemistry, dysplasia, and invasive adenocarcinoma. J Clin Pathol 1985; 38: 477–478 (letter).
65. Saubier EC, Gouillat C, Samaniego C, Guillaud M, Moulinier B. Adenocarcinoma in columnar-lined Barrett's esophagus. Analysis of 13 esophagectomies. Am J Surg 1985; 150: 365–369.
66. Hamilton SR, Smith RRL. The relationship between columnar epithelial dysplasia and invasive adenocarcinoma arising in Barrett esophagus. Am J Clin Pathol 1987; 87: 301–312.
67. Doos WG, Stilmant MS, Murphy JL, Robbins AH, Vincent ME, Spechler SJ. The cytologic characteristics of Barrett's epithelium. Gastroenterology 1985; 88: 1368 (abstract).
68. Robey S, Hamilton S, Gupta PK, Erozan YS. Diagnostic value of cytopathology in Barrett esophagus and associated carcinoma. Am J Clin Pathol 1988; 89: 493–498.
69. Dworak O, Koerfgen HP. Carcinosarcoma in Barrett's oesophagus: a case report with immunohistological examination. Virchows Arch A 1993; 422: 423–426.
70. Carey NR, Barron DJ, McGoldrick JP, Wells FC. Combined oesophageal adenocarcinoma and carcinoid in Barrett's oesophagitis: potential role of enterochromaffin-like cells in oesophageal malignancy. Thorax 1993; 48: 404–405.
71. Morson BC, Sobin LH, Grundmann E, Johansen A, Nagayo T, Serck-Hanssen A. Precancerous conditions and epithelial dysplasia in the stomach. J Clin Pathol 1980; 33: 711–721.
72. Riddell RH, Goldman H, Ransohoff DF et al. Dysplasia in inflammatory bowel disease: standardized classification with provisional clinical applications. Hum Pathol 1983; 14: 931–968.
73. Berenson MM, Riddell RH, Skinner DB et al. Malignant transformation of esophageal columnar epithelium. Cancer 1978; 41: 554–561.
74. Levine MS, Caroline D, Thompson JJ et al. Adenocarcinoma of the esophagus: relationship to Barrett mucosa. Radiology 1984; 150: 305–309.
75. Thompson JJ, Zinsser KR, Enterline HT. Barrett's metaplasia and adenocarcinoma of the esophagus and gastroesphageal junction. Hum Pathol 1983; 14: 42–61.
76. Wesdorp ICE, Bartelsman J, Schipper MEI, Offerhaus J, Tytgat GN. Malignancy and premalignancy in Barrett's esophagus: a clinical, endoscopical and histological study. Acta Endoscopica 1981; 11: 317–322.
77. McDonald GB, Brand DL, Thorning DR. Multiple adenomatous neoplasms arising in columnar-lined (Barrett's) esophagus. Gastroenterology 1977; 72: 1317–1321.
78. Lee RG. Adenomas arising in Barrett's esophagus. Am J Clin Pathol 1986; 85: 629–632.
79. Kalsbeek HL, van der Wouden A. Barrett-oesophagus with papillomatous tumor. Arch Chir Nerl 1971; 23: 287–296.
80. Hamilton SR, Smith RRL. Esophageal columnar intraepithelial

neoplasia: relationship to invasive adenocarcinoma occurring in Barrett esophagus. Lab Invest 1985; 52: 27A–28A (abstract).
81. Riddell RH. Dysplasia and regression in Barrett's epithelium. In: Spechler SJ, Goyal RK, eds. Barrett's esophagus: pathophysiology, diagnosis, and management. New York: Elsevier, 1985: p 143–152.
82. Schmidt HG, Riddell RH, Walther B, Skinner DB, Rieman JF. Dysplasia in Barrett's esophagus. Cancer Res Clin Oncol 1985; 110: 145–152.
83. Reid BJ, Haggitt RC, Rubin CE et al. Criteria for dysplasia in Barrett's esophagus: a cooperative consensus study. Gastroenterology 1985; 88: 1552 (abstract).
84. Paraf F, Flejou JF, Potet F, Molas G, Fekete F. Adenomas arising in Barrett's esophagus with adenocarcinoma. Report of three cases. Pathol Res Pract 1992; 188: 1028–1032.
85. Takahashi T, Iwama N. Three dimensional microstructure of gastro-intestinal tumours: gland pattern and its diagnostic significance. Pathol Annual 1985; 20: 419–440.
86. Hamilton SR, Smith RRL. Epithelial dysplasia in Barrett esophagus. Relationship to invasive carcinoma. Gastroenterology 1984; 86: 1105 (abstract).
87. Bartlesman JF, Hameeteman W, Tytgat GN. Barrett's oesophagus. Eur J Cancer Prev 1992; 1: 323–325.
88. Miros M, Kerlin P, Walker N. Only patients with dysplasia progress to adenocarcinoma in Barrett's oesophagus. Gut 1991; 32: 1441–1446.
89. Skinner DB. The columnar-lined esophagus and adenocarcinoma. Ann Thorac Surg 1985; 40: 321–322.
90. Belladonna JA, Hajdu SI, Bains MS, Winawer SJ. Adenocarcinoma in situ of Barrett's esophagus diagnosed by endoscopic cytology. N Engl J Med 1974; 291: 895–896.
91. Contini S, Consigli GF, Di Lecce F, Chiapasco M, Ferri T, Orsi P. Vital staining of oesophagus in patients with head and neck cancer: still a worthwhile procedure. Ital J Gastroenterol 1991; 23: 5–8.
92. Dent J, Bremner CG, Collen MJ, Haggitt RC, Spechler SJ. Working Party Report to the World Congresses of Gastroenterology, Sydney 1990. J Gastroenterol Hepatology 1991; 6: 1–22.
93. Skinner DB, Walther BC, Little AG. Surgical treatment of Barrett's esophagus. In: Spechler SJ, Goyal RK, eds. Barrett's esophagus: pathophysiology, diagnosis, and management. New York: Elsevier, 1985: p 211–221.
94. Castell DO. Medical management of the patient with Barrett's esophagus. In: Spechler SJ, Goyal RK, eds. Barrett's esophagus: pathophysiology, diagnosis, and management. New York: Elsevier, 1985: p 199–209.
95. Attwood SE, Barlow AP, Norris TL, Watson A. Barrett's oesophagus: effect of antireflux surgery on symptom control and development of complications. Br J Surg 1992; 79: 1050–1053.
96. Yardley JH, Ransohoff DF, Riddell RH, Goldman H. Cancer in inflammatory bowel disease: how serious is the problem and what should be done about it? Gastroenterology 1983; 85: 197–200 (editorial).
97. Iftikhar SY, James PD, Steele RJ, Hardcastle JD, Atkinson M. Length of Barrett's oesophagus: an important factor in the development of dysplasia and adenocarcinoma. Gut 1992; 33: 1155–1158.
98. Van der Veen AH, Dees J, Blankensteijn JD, Van Blankenstein M. Adenocarcinoma in Barrett's oesophagus: an overrated risk. Gut 1989; 30: 14–18.
99. Deschner EE. Early proliferative changes in gastrointestinal neoplasia. Am J Gastroenterol 1982; 77: 207–211.
100. Pellish LJ, Hermos JA, Eastwood GL. Cell proliferation in three types of Barrett's epithelium. Gut 1980; 21: 26–31.
101. Eastwood GL. Cell proliferation in Barrett's epithelium. In: Spechler SJ, Royal RK, eds. Barrett's esophagus: pathophysiology, diagnosis, and management. New York: Elsevier, 1985: p 39–47.
102. Jankowski J, McMenemin R, Hopwood D, Penston J, Wormsley KG. Abnormal expression of growth-regulatory factors in Barrett's oesophagus. Clin Sci 1991; 81: 663–668.
103. Jankowski J, Hopwood D, Wormsley KG. Flow cytometric analysis of growth-regulatory peptides and their receptors in Barrett's oesophagus and oesophageal adenocarcinoma. Scand J Gastroenterol 1992; 27: 147–154.
104. Iftikhar SY, Steele RJ, Watson S, James PD, Dilks K, Hardcastle JD. Assessment of proliferation of squamous, Barrett's and gastric mucosa in patients with columnar lined Barrett's oesophagus. Gut 1992; 33: 733–737.
105. Jankowski J, McMenemin R, Yu C, Hopwood D, Wormsley KG. Proliferating cell nuclear antigen in oesophageal diseases: correlation with transforming growth factor alpha expression. Gut 1992; 33: 587–591.
106. Jass JR. Mucin histochemistry of the columnar epithelium of the oesophagus: a retrospective study. J Clin Pathol 1981; 34: 866–870.
107. Jass JR. Role of intestinal metaplasia in the histogenesis of gastric carcinoma. J Clin Pathol 1980; 33: 801–810.
108. Sheahan DG, West AB. Sulfated mucosubstances in Barrett's (columnar cell) esophageal mucosa. Gastroenterology 1981; 80: 1282 (abstract).
109. Peutchmaur M, Potet F, Goldfain D. Mucin histochemistry of the columnar epithelium of the oesophagus (Barrett's esophagus): a prospective biopsy study. J Clin Pathol 1984; 37: 607–610.
110. Lee RG. Mucins in Barrett's esophagus: a histochemical study. Am J Clin Pathol 1984; 81: 500–503.
111. Zwas F, Shields HM, Doos WG et al. Scanning electron microscopy of Barrett's epithelium and its correlation with light microscopy and mucin stains. Gastroenterology 1986; 90: 1932–1941.
112. Jacobs LR, Huber PW. Regional distribution and alterations of lectin binding to colorectal mucin in mucosal biopsies from controls and subjects with inflammatory bowel disease. J Clin Invest 1986; 75: 112–118.
113. Geboes K, Vanstapel MJ, Desmet VJ. Tissue demonstration of carcinoembryonic antigen (CEA) in columnar esophageal epithelium. Hepatogastroenterology 1981; 28: 324–336.
114. Smith RRL, Hamilton SR. Carcinoembryonic antigen in Barrett esophagus: an immunohistochemical study of Barrett carcinoma and columnar-lined mucosa. Lab Invest 1985; 52: 63A (abstract).
115. Hamilton SR, Smith RRL. Carcinoembryonic antigen (CEA) in Barrett esophagus and associated adenocarcinoma: an immunohistochemical study. Gastroenterology 1985; 88: 1411 (abstract).
116. Reid BJ, Haggitt RC, Rubin CE, Rabinovitch PS. Barrett's esophagus. Correlation between flow cytometry and histology in detection of patients at risk for adenocarcinoma. Gastroenterology 1987; 93: 1–11.
117. James PD, Atkinson M. Value of DNA image cytometry in the prediction of malignant change in Barrett's oesophagus. Gut 1989; 30: 899–905.
118. Pegg AE. Polyamine metabolism and its importance in neoplastic growth and as a target for chemotherapy. Cancer Res 1988; 48: 759–774.
119. Luk GD, Baylin SB. Ornithine decarboxylase as a biological marker in familial colonic polyposis. N Engl J Med 1984; 311: 80–83.
120. Garewal HS, Sampliner R, Gerner E, Steinbronn K, Alberts D, Kendall D. Ornithine decarboxylase activity in Barrett's esophagus. A potential marker for dysplasia. Gastroenterology 1988; 94: 819–821.
121. Reid BJ, Blount PL, Rubin CE, Levine DS, Haggitt RC, Rabinovitch PS. Flow cytometric and histological progression to malignancy in Barrett's esophagus: prospective endoscopic surveillance of a cohort. Gastroenterology 192; 102: 1212–1219.
122. Ramel S, Reid BJ, Sanchez CA, Blount PL, Levine DS, Neshat K et al. Evaluation of p53 protein expression in Barrett's esophagus by two parameter flow cytometry. Gastroenterology 1992; 102: 1220–1228.
123. Flejou JF, Potet F, Muzeau F, Le Pelletier F, Fekete F, Henin D. Overexpression of p53 protein in Barrett's syndrome with malignant transformation. J Clin Pathol 1993; 46: 330–333.

PART IV

Rare and secondary (metastatic) tumours

W. V. Bogomoletz

Despite their rarity, oesophageal tumours such as malignant melanoma, small-cell carcinoma, spindle-cell (squamous) carcinoma, adenoid cystic carcinoma or granular-cell tumour are being recognized with increasing frequency since the advent of endoscopy. Previously confined to individual case reports, small series have now been published. Consequently, meaningful data on incidence, sex ratio, clinical presentation, pathological aspects or response to treatment are progressively emerging. However, some of these tumours continue to be the subject of controversy and pose problems in nomenclature, classification and histogenesis. Moreover, because many of these rare neoplastic lesions tend to show great variation in their histological appearances, caution is recommended in their diagnosis, particularly in small biopsy samples which may not be entirely representative.

Finally, it is of interest that many examples of these rare tumours of the oesophagus have been recorded in Japan. This observation raises the possibility of some peculiar, but as yet unexplained, geographical distribution of these neoplasms.

Malignant melanoma

(Synonyms and related terms: melanosarcoma, melanocarcinoma)

Primary malignant melanoma of the oesophagus is now a recognized entity,[1–3] but prior to the demonstration of melanocytes in the oesophageal mucosa,[4] its existence was doubted in earlier classifications.[5]

Well over 130 documented cases of primary malignant melanoma of the oesophagus have been published,[6–9] approximately half of which are from Japan.[7] The reported incidence varies from 0.1[10]–6%[7] of all primary malignant tumours of the oesophagus other than typical squamous cell carcinoma.

Malignant melanoma of the oesophagus shows a fairly consistent clinical presentation. Patients are generally in their 6th to 8th decades; the case reported by Basque et al[11] in a 7-year-old boy is unusual. Men outnumber women by 2 to 1. Most patients present with symptoms of oesophageal obstruction such as dysphagia, retrosternal discomfort or pain, weight loss, haemorrhage and pulmonary complications. Barium swallow usually shows a large polypoid filling defect. The tumour generally arises in the mid or lower third of the oesophagus and may be pigmented (Fig. 38.42) or non-pigmented. If the lesion is pigmented, endoscopy may be strongly suggestive of the nature of the lesion.[12] There is usually a single tumour but they are occasionally multiple growths. The mean survival is 7 months and patients die with metastatic dissemination despite surgery, chemotherapy or radiotherapy, which at best are palliative.

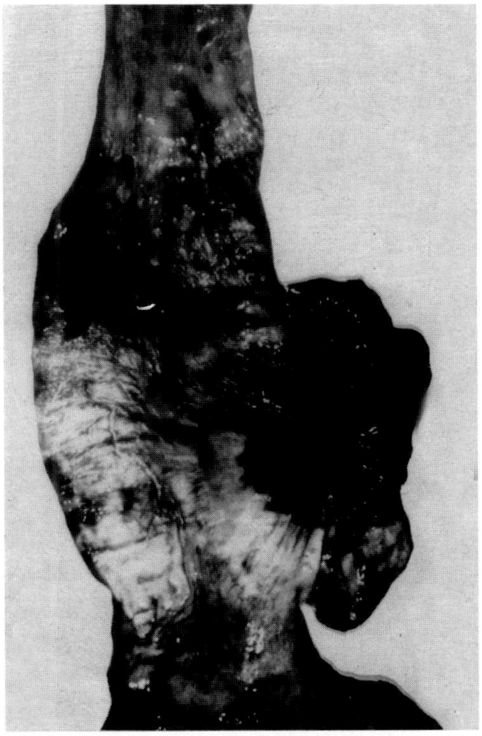

Fig. 38.42 Malignant melanoma of oesophagus. Surgical specimen showing a characteristic large polypoid and pigmented mass.

Microscopic examination shows the characteristic features of malignant melanoma arising in other mucosal sites. The tumour is composed of uniform, pleomorphic and poorly adhesive cells, containing varying amounts of melanin pigment (Fig. 38.43). The latter can be easily identified by the usual histochemical methods including the Masson Fontana silver method and bleaching by oxidizing agents. In case of haemorrhage, haemosiderin pigment may also be present and should be distinguished from melanin pigment with the Perls's reaction. The growth pattern of the neoplasm tends to be nodular with a 'pushing' edge. In surgical specimens, the depth of tumour invasion is variable but submucosal spread is usually more marked than transmural infiltration.

An important microscopic feature is the presence of junctional activity in the squamous epithelium adjacent to

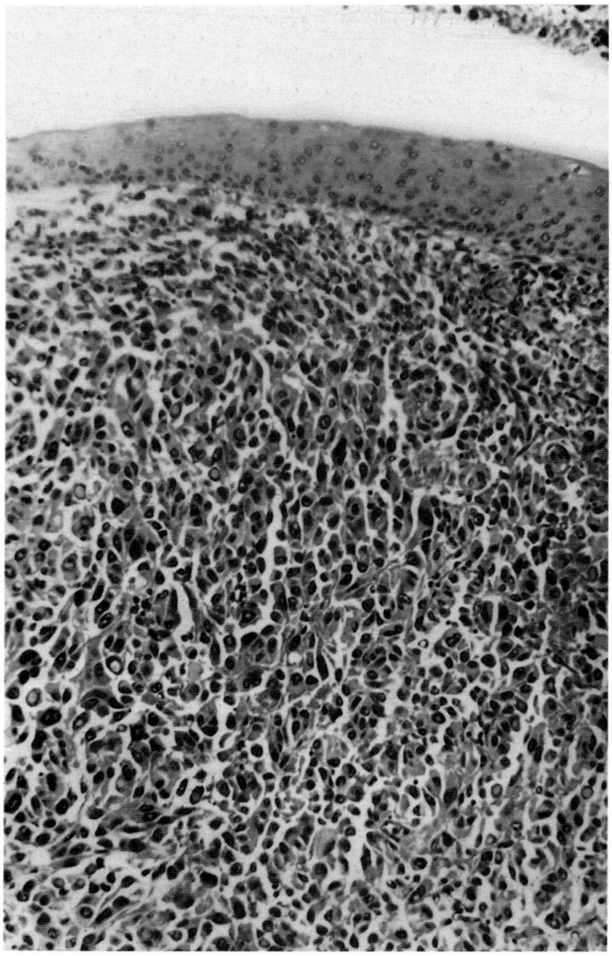

Fig. 38.43 Malignant melanoma of oesophagus (same case as Fig. 38.42). Mucosal spread by typical pleomorphic and poorly cohesive tumour cells. (×125)

the tumour (Fig. 38.44). This has also been referred to as 'lentigenous radial component' and is a characteristic of malignant melanoma originating in mucosal sites.[13] Some authors believe that the demonstration of such junctional changes is a prerequisite for the diagnosis. However, in a review of 64 published cases, Kreuser pointed out that junctional changes had been identified in only 40%.[6]

Some cases of primary malignant melanoma of the oesophagus have been associated with melanosis of the oesophageal mucosa.[6,14] This melanosis can be a focal or diffuse change and is characterized by the presence of melanocytes in the basal layer of the squamous epithelium.[4,14] Microscopically, these melanocytes usually appear benign. However Guzman et al[15] described a case combining oesophageal malignant melanoma and diffuse melanosis, the latter showing melanocytic proliferation ranging from benign junctional activity to melanocytic dysplasia to malignant melanoma in situ.

Clearly the presence of a malignant melanoma, bland or atypical junctional activity and melanosis is strong evidence of a primary tumour at that site.

Transmission electron microscopic study of a few cases has shown ultrastructural features identical to those of malignant melanomas arising in other sites, particularly the presence of premelanosomes and melanosomes.[9,16,17] In a series of six cases of malignant melanoma of the oesophagus, DiConstanzo et al[9] found all six tumours to be immunoreactive for S-100 protein, and none reacting with anti-cytokeratin.

Despite an apparent lack of reason for being there, melanocytes can be demonstrated in the oesophagus in 3.7% to 11% of unselected autopsies, depending upon the histochemical method used.[4,18,19] During embryogenesis, melanocytes originate in the neural crest and migrate to various other sites, such as the epidermis, hair follicles,

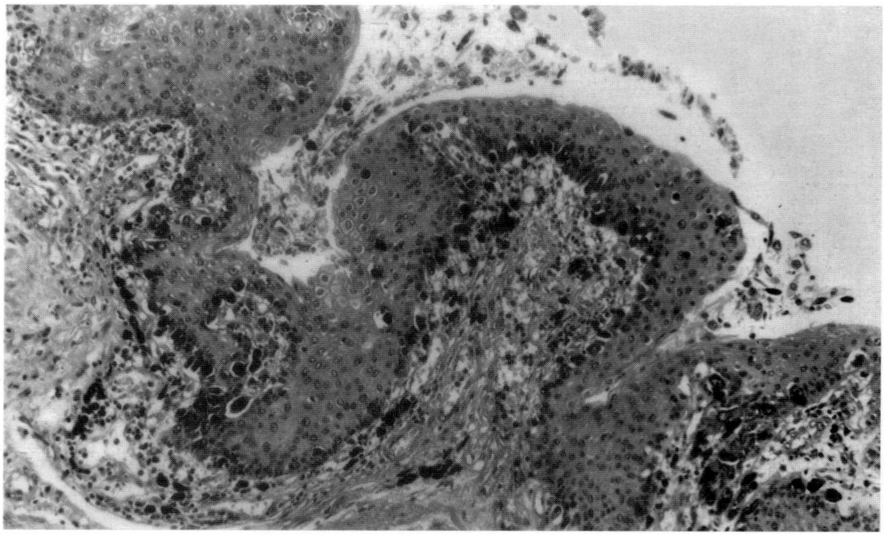

Fig. 38.44 Malignant melanoma of oesophagus (same case as Fig. 38.42). Marked junctional activity of adjacent squamous epithelium with atypical melanocytes heavily laden with melanin pigment. (×113)

uvea, choroid, leptomeninges, substantia nigra, oral cavity, nasopharynx and conceivably such seemingly ectopic sites as the oesophageal mucosa.[4] However, another possibility that they are formed in situ, as the result of differentiation from totipotential cells in the basal layer of the squamous epithelium, cannot be entirely ruled out.

Interestingly, there are few well documented reports of metastatic melanoma of the oesophagus[20,21] and secondary involvement appears to be even rarer than cases of genuine primary growth.[22]

The extreme rarity of benign melanocytic naevi in the oesophagus is in marked contrast to their high incidence in the oral mucosa.[23] A good example of a slowly-growing, intramural and encapsulated benign melanocytic tumour arising in the upper oesophagus was described by Assor.[24]

Small-cell carcinoma

(Synonyms and related terms: oat-cell carcinoma, anaplastic carcinoma, undifferentiated carcinoma, argyrophilic-cell carcinoma, apudoma, apudocarcinoma, carcinoid tumour, neuroendocrine carcinoma)

Primary small-cell carcinoma of the oesophagus has also recently gained significant recognition[1–3,25] as a malignant epithelial neoplasm differing from the more common squamous carcinoma. However, its true nature and histogenesis have only been partially resolved and some controversy still prevails.[26–30] Primary small-cell carcinoma of the oesophagus can be best defined as a highly malignant tumour consisting of small anaplastic cells which are histologically and cytologically indistinguishable from the cells in small-cell carcinoma of the bronchus. Histochemically and ultrastructurally many but not all of these oesophageal tumours also show evidence of being related to the diffuse endocrine cell system.

Small-cell carcinoma of the oesophagus accounts for between 0.05[10]–18%[7] of all treated carcinomas of the oesophagus. Well over 130 cases have been reported,[30] about half the number from Japan,[31] with some large series.[7,26,32] Criterion for diagnosis is the absence of any other primary small-cell carcinoma outside the oesophagus, particularly in the tracheobronchial tree.

Most patients with small-cell carcinoma of the oesophagus are in their 5th and 6th decades. A higher incidence has been reported in males,[30,32] particularly in the Japanese series[7] and this is not unlike the male predominance observed in small-cell carcinoma of the bronchus. However, a rather higher incidence of female patients was noted in one British series.[26] The major clinical presentation is dysphagia and most cases occur as a single tumour mass in the lower or middle third of the oesophagus, more rarely in the upper third.[32] Few instances of multiple small-cell carcinoma of the oesophagus have been described.[33]

Macroscopically, they present as a large and fleshy exophytic growth, with or without ulceration (Fig. 38.45). The size of the tumour is usually between 1–14 cm long, with a mean value of 5.8 cm.[30] Regional lymph nodes are often invaded at the time of operation.

The histological features resemble those of its bronchial counterpart. The small anaplastic cells show scanty cytoplasm, hyperchromatic nuclei with coarse chromatin and absent nucleoli. Mitotic figures are frequent. 'Crush' artifact is readily encountered. An attempt should be made to distinguish the different cell types, as for small-cell carcinoma of the bronchus: oat-cell type, intermediate-cell type and composite-cell type. The commonest pattern

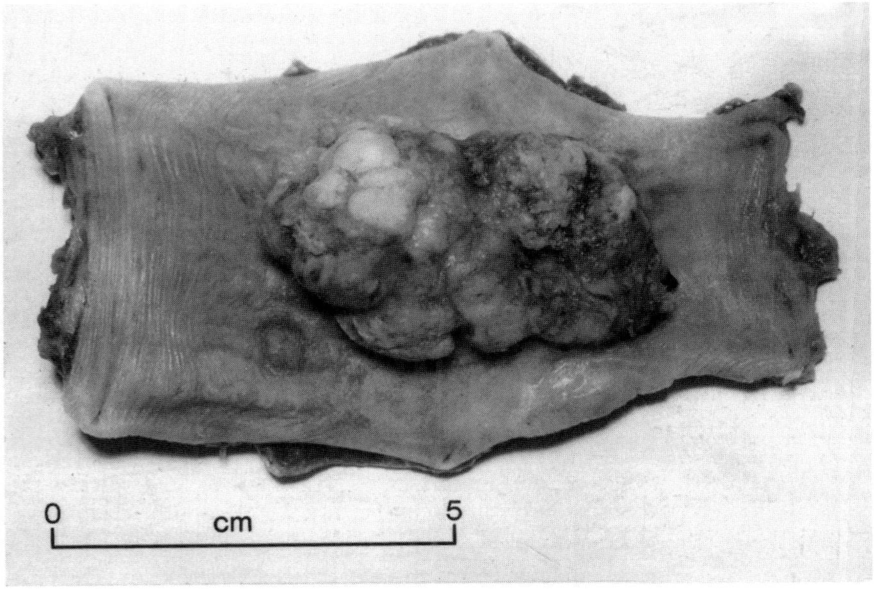

Fig. 38.45 Small-cell carcinoma of oesophagus. Surgical specimen showing a large exophytic tumour.

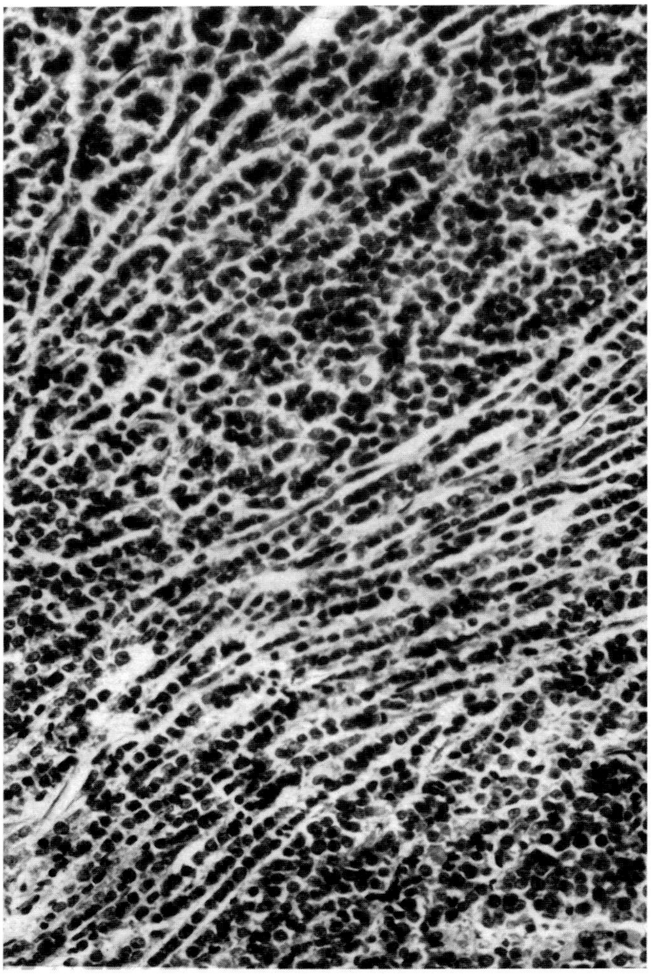

Fig. 38.46 Small-cell carcinoma (same case as Fig. 38.45). Ribbons and anastomosing cords of small anaplastic cells. (×270)

consists of cells arranged in irregular sheets. As in bronchial small-cell carcinoma, however, other growth patterns can be encountered such as nests, anastomosing cords or ribbons (Fig. 38.46). Rosettes as well as carcinoid differentiation can be found. Some cases may also contain foci of squamous and/or glandular differentiation.[26,32] Necrosis is frequently noted. The Grimelius and other stains for argyrophilic granules are usually positive, but the degree of this positivity is variable and some cases are entirely negative. The Masson Fontana argentaffin reaction has been consistently reported as negative. Amyloid has been described in rare instances.[26]

Electron microscopic examination often discloses the presence of membrane-bound neurosecretory granules within tumour cells.[27,30,31,34–36] When identified ultrastructurally, neurosecretory granules are present in 3–50%[5] of the tumour cells, but they may be absent in some cases. The presence of intracytoplasmic filaments and desmosomes, both features of squamous cells, has also been reported by some[27] but not all investigators.[36]

A recent immunoperoxidase study of 10 cases of small-cell carcinoma of the oesophagus has shown positive immunostaining of tumour cells for ACTH and calcitonin in, respectively, six and three cases.[31] Serotonin, peptide YY, somatotropin and gastrin have also been demonstrated in some cases.[3]

The nature and origin of small-cell carcinoma of the oesophagus remains uncertain. In the mid-seventies they were considered to represent poorly differentiated squamous carcinoma.[2,37] This view was based on the fact that areas of squamous carcinoma or adenocarcinoma could be found in some cases. Confusion was caused by subsequent reports of so-called 'anaplastic' or 'undifferentiated' carcinomas of the oesophagus. Later reports, referring to their histochemical properties, ultrastructural features and hormonal status have been more in favour of an origin from an endocrine cell. The tumour could obviously arise from argyrophilic cells, which have been demonstrated in the oesophageal mucosa as well as in oesophageal glands.[23,32,34] This would be in keeping with the common origin of oesophageal and tracheobronchial mucosae from the embryonic foregut. On the other hand, totipotential 'reserve' cells, located in the squamous epithelial basal layer of the oesophageal mucosa, could be responsible.[26,27] This latter hypothesis would account for cases showing dual or multiple differentiation such as mixtures of small cells, squamous cells or glandular elements. In order to avoid terminology and classification problems, it would probably be better to separate 'pure small-cell carcinoma' from 'combined' or 'mixed small-cell carcinoma'.[26,38] One should probably only classify as pure small-cell carcinoma of the oesophagus those cases showing histochemical and ultrastructural evidence of a neuroendocrine origin. However, this would still leave a small group of 'non-small-cell anaplastic or undifferentiated carcinoma' lacking evidence of either squamous differentiation or neuroendocrine features.[9,29] So-called tripartite differentiation, i.e. typical small-cell carcinoma intermingled with foci of squamous and glandular differentiation, has been described in the oesophagus as well as in the bronchus.[27]

Small-cell carcinoma of the oesophagus behaves in the same aggressive fashion as small-cell carcinoma of the bronchus, with rapid and widespread tumour dissemination, despite surgery, radiotherapy or chemotherapy.[33,39]

Spindle-cell (squamous) carcinoma

(Synonyms and related terms: pseudosarcoma, carcinosarcoma, polypoid carcinoma)

Spindle-cell (squamous) carcinoma of the oesophagus is now generally considered to be a special variant of primary squamous-cell carcinoma, with spindle-cell metaplasia and possibly phenotype change.[3,25] It is characterized grossly by a large polypoid and intraluminal tumour mass.

The nature of spindle-cell (squamous) carcinoma was, until fairly recently, controversial. Because of its spindle-cell component it was considered as either a 'carcinosarcoma' or a pseudosarcoma'.[5,40] 'Carcinosarcoma' implied a malignant neoplasm showing both carcinomatous and sarcomatous elements, both proliferating as a single tumour mass and both possessing metastatic potential (a so-called 'collision' tumour).[40,41] In contrast, 'pseudosarcoma' was felt to be a squamous carcinoma capable of metastases, but associated with a florid spindle-cell component presumed to be non-specific.[5,42] Furthermore, it was believed that pseudosarcoma represented a relatively benign lesion. Argument sustaining the distinction between carcinosarcoma and pseudosarcoma rested largely on the 'intermingling' or 'non-intermingling' of the two components in the primary tumour, as well as the predominantly carcinomatous or sarcomatous appearances of any metastases. In 1976, Matsusaka and coworkers carefully compared the cases described as carcinosarcomas with those recorded as pseudosarcomas, and found essentially similar clinicopathological features.[43] This unifying concept of spindle-cell (squamous) carcinoma of the oesophagus has since been supported by the findings of other workers.[44–46]

The exact incidence of spindle-cell (squamous) carcinoma of the oesophagus is difficult to evaluate with precision because of the early confusion as to whether it was a single entity, but there appears to be a strong association with alcoholism and cigarette smoking.[47] Patients are aged between 50–60, show a male predominance and present clinically with progressive dysphagia and marked weight loss. Endoscopically, the tumour is polypoid and often pedunculated, projecting into the lumen of the oesophagus (Fig. 38.47). Tumours measuring up to 15 cm have been recorded[46] and most cases have been described as arising from the middle and lower thirds of the oesophagus.

Microscopic examination shows what appears to be at first sight two separate neoplastic cell components: epithelial and spindle. The epithelial component is usually represented by a squamous in situ or invasive carcinoma, occasionally by adenocarcinoma and sometimes by undifferentiated carcinoma. This carcinomatous component is frequently found at the base of the pedicle of the polypoid growth. The spindle-cell or 'mesenchymal-like' component' which usually composes the bulk of the tumour, consists of mixtures of bland-looking or pleomorphic spindle elements. On light microscopy, the growth pattern of the spindle cells can be fascicular and may strikingly mimic myofibroblasts or muscle elements. Myxoid changes may be present. Cartilaginous and osseous features have also been described. Careful study of multiple blocks and sections may show transition-like areas between the islands of squamous carcinoma and the spindle cell proliferation (Figs 38.48, 38,49).

The squamous nature of the spindle-cell component has been supported by several ultrastructural studies, which have demonstrated the presence of desmosomes and tonofilaments within the spindle cells.[45,48,49] Positive immunostaining for keratin of both the squamous carcinomatous component and the spindle-cell 'sarcomatous-like' component has been demonstrated by several authors.[50,51] However, negative immunostaining of the spindle-cell component for keratin has been recorded by two groups,[52,53] but such contradictory results could be explained by phenotype change.

This variant of squamous carcinoma with spindle-cell metaplasia is not restricted to the oesophagus and similar tumours have been described in the uterine cervix, upper respiratory tract, oral cavity and skin. In the past, the prognosis of spindle-cell (squamous) carcinoma of the oesophagus was considered to be better than that of squamous-cell carcinoma with conventional histology.

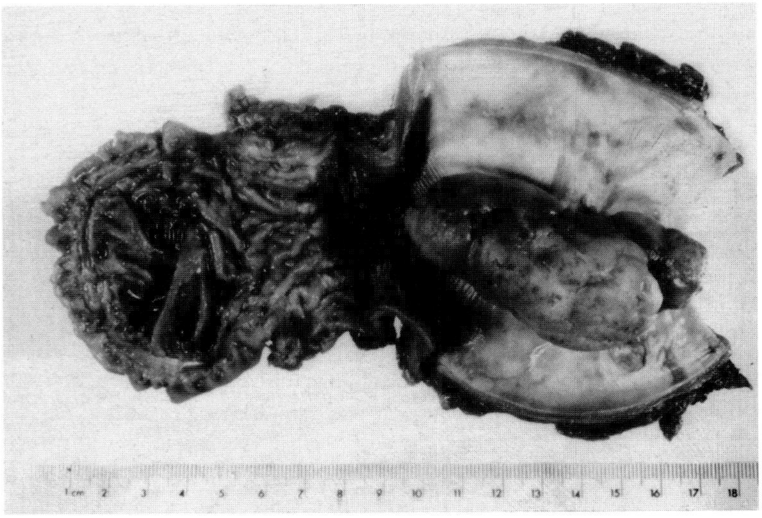

Fig. 38.47 Spindle-cell (squamous) carcinoma of oesophagus. Surgical specimen showing a characteristic polypoid tumour projecting into the lumen.

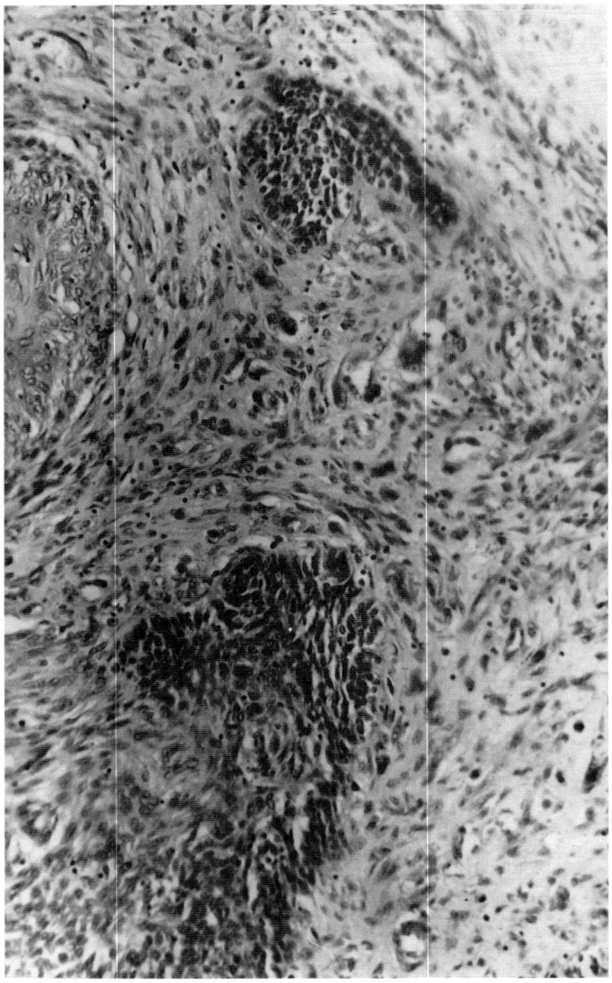

Fig. 38.48 Spindle-cell (squamous) carcinoma of oesophagus (same case as Fig. 38.47). Note nests of obvious squamous cells with an intervening neoplastic spindle-cell proliferation. (×125)

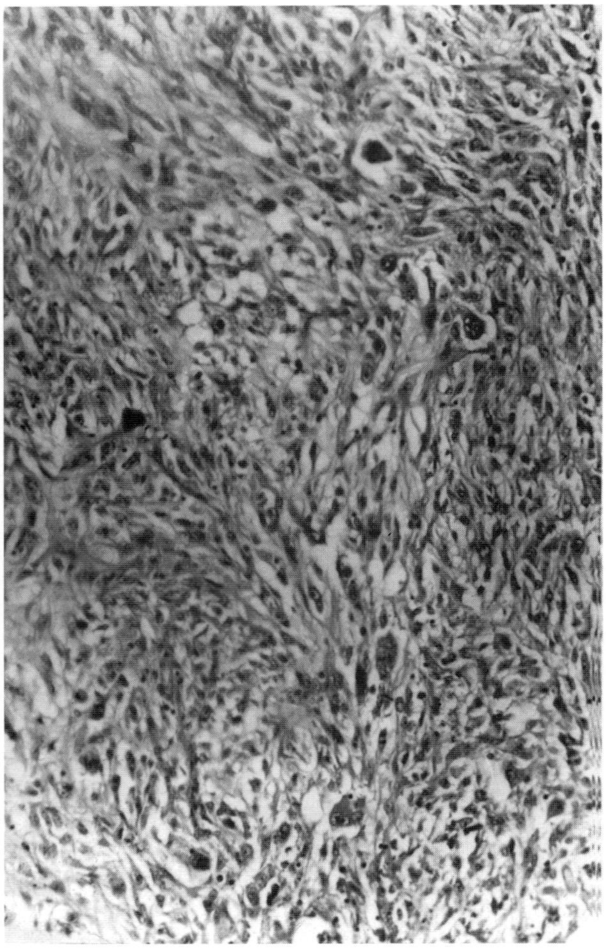

Fig. 38.49 Spindle-cell (squamous) carcinoma of oesophagus (same case as Fig. 38.47). 'Sarcomatous'-looking areas of metaplastic spindle-cell component. Note presence of giant tumour cells resembling rhabdomyoblassts. (×125)

However, critical analysis shows that there are few fundamental differences between these two types of tumour in terms of age, sex, localization and survival.[44] Treatment of spindle-cell (squamous) carcinoma of the oesophagus has usually consisted of surgical resection followed by palliative radiotherapy.[46]

Adenoid cystic carcinoma

More than 50 cases of adenoid cystic carcinoma of the oesophagus have been described.[9,54–58] They are characterized histologically by a 'cribriform' pattern of variable degree, thus resembling adenoid cystic carcinoma of salivary gland origin, but have a greater biological aggressiveness. Adenoid cystic carcinoma of the oesophagus should be distinguished from adenocarcinoma arising from heterotopic gastric mucosa or from columnar-lined oesophagus (Barrett's oesophagus).

Patients are mostly in their sixties, show a male predominance (76%) and present with progressive dysphagia and obstruction. The majority of cases of adenoid cystic carcinoma of the oesophagus are in an advanced state at the time of diagnosis. Survival is less than 2 years, with widespread metastases to distant organs. The overall incidence has been recorded as 0.75[56]–5%[9] of all primary oesophageal carcinomas. A few cases of 'superficial' adenoid cystic carcinoma, i.e. carcinoma with invasion confined to mucosa or submucosa irrespective of lymph node status, have also been described.[59]

Its histogenesis has not been entirely resolved. Earlier workers had suggested that the tumour originated from the squamous epithelium of the oesophageal mucosa. However, most authors now believe that it probably arises from the ducts or possibly even from the acini of the submucosal glands in the oesophagus.[56,57]

Macroscopically, adenoid cystic carcinoma of the

oesophagus appears as a large and fungating growth which may ulcerate or become infiltrative, and arises most frequently from the middle and lower thirds.[55]

Histologically, the tumour displays a spectrum of appearances, from a well-developed cribriform pattern with pseudocysts to a more solid or basaloid pattern. The uniform and small epithelial cells are arranged in trabeculae and sheets, frequently disposed around cystic spaces (Fig. 38.50). These cells have scanty cytoplasm and hyperchromatic nuclei. The material contained in the cystic spaces stains positively with PAS before and after diastase digestion, negatively with mucicarmine and variably with Alcian blue. The trabeculae and sheets of cells can also be separated by interstitial hyaline material, thus resembling the pattern of cylindroma of the skin. Some of the solid cellular areas of the tumour may resemble small-cell carcinoma.[57] In general, adenoid cystic carcinoma of the oesophagus shows a greater tendency to solid and basaloid patterns than is seen in the typical salivary gland lesions, with focal areas of necrosis, greater nuclear pleomorphism and increased mitotic rate. Some direct continuity is often identified between the tumour and the overlying squamous epithelium after step sectioning; this squamous epithelium tends to be dysplastic. Genuine primary adenoid cystic carcinoma of the oesophagus should be distinguished from adenoid cystic differentiation which may be present to a varying degree in most oesophageal adenocarcinomas.[55] Recently, it has been suggested that cases of adenoid cystic carcinoma of the oesophagus showing prominent basaloid pattern and pleomorphic nuclei could be related to the so-called 'basaloid-squamous carcinoma' of the upper aerodigestive tract.[60]

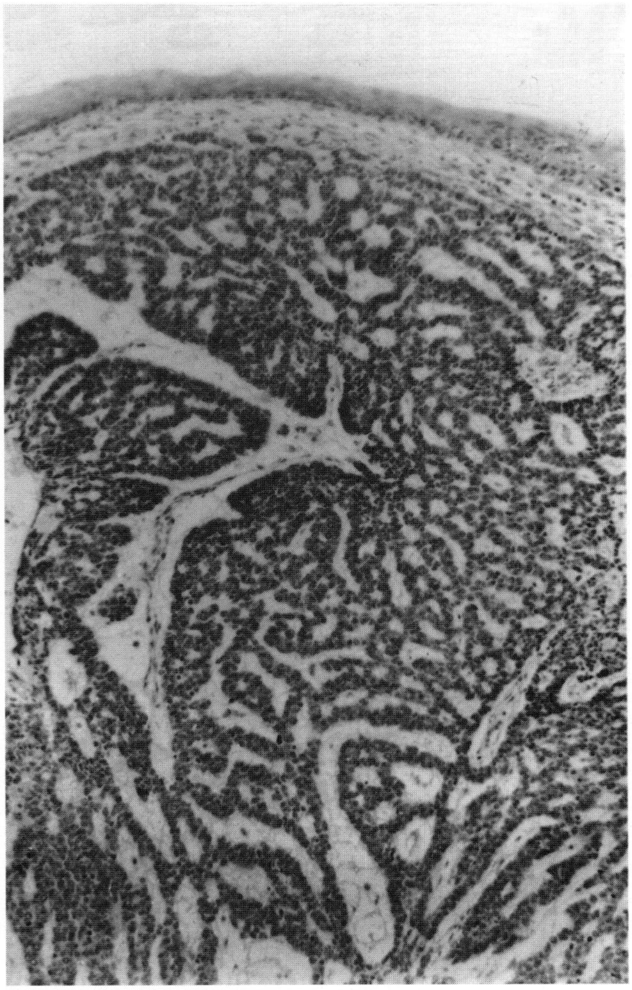

Fig. 38.50 Adenoid cystic carcinoma of oesophagus. Trabeculae and sheets of uniform small epithelial cells arranged around cystic spaces. (×125)

Earlier writers on adenoid cystic carcinoma of the oesophagus have usually assumed that it was an exact counterpart of the common adenoid cystic carcinoma of salivary glands. However, apart from histological differences, adenoid cystic carcinoma of the oesophagus is a much more aggressive tumour, with a median survival of only 9 months following diagnosis.[55] It has more clinical similarities and similarities in gross configuration and location with the more common oesophageal squamous carcinoma. For instance, adenoid cystic carcinoma of the oesophagus also occurs in male patients in their sixties. This is in contrast with adenoid cystic carcinoma of salivary glands, which occurs mostly in female patients within the 40–50 year age range.

Malignant lymphoma

Lewin and colleagues found no case of oesophageal primary in their review of 117 cases of gastrointestinal malignant lymphomas.[61] There are, however, a few case reports of authentic primary oesophageal malignant lymphoma, usually arising in the distal oesophagus.[62–64] Primary malignant lymphoma of the oesophagus must be distinguished from a secondary direct extension to the distal oesophagus by an extranodal malignant lymphoma arising in the cardia of the stomach[65,66] and secondary involvement of the oesophagus as part of systemic malignant lymphoma.[67,68] Different histological types of non-Hodgkin malignant lymphomas have been described as primary tumours of the oesophagus. Two cases of primary extramedullary plasmactyoma localized to the oesophagus have also been described.[69,70] One case of Hodgkin's disease apparently localized only to the oesophagus, and thus considered as a primary growth, has been reported.[71]

Two unusual cases of focal lymphoid hyperplasia or 'pseudolymphoma' have been reported, one involving the distal oesophagus and associated with Barrett's oesophagus[72] and the other limited to the mucosa and submucosa of the middle third.[73] Finally, a few cases of so-called 'inflammatory pseudotumour' of the oesophagus have also been described, chartacterized histologically by inflammatory cells and proliferating fibroblasts.[74]

Granular-cell tumour

(Synonyms and related terms: granular-cell myoblastoma, granular-cell neurofibroma, Abrikossoff's tumour)

Granular-cell tumours of the oesophagus are usually small and histologically resemble granular-cell tumours in other sites, tending to run a benign course.

Granular-cell tumours are being recognized in the oesophagus with increasing frequency, since the advent and development of endoscopy. More than 100 cases of oesophageal granular-cell tumour have been reported,[75–78] representing a 2% incidence of all reported granular-cell tumours. The largest series is the 24 cases studied by Johnston and Helwig.[76]

The mean age of patients with granular-cell tumour of the oesophagus is approximately 40 years, with a wide range from adolescence to old age.[77] Although they are found more frequently in sites such as the tongue and subcutaneous tissues, twice as commonly in women than in men, there has been no such significant sex ratio in reports of granular-cell tumour of the oesophagus. In more than 50% of cases, granular-cell tumour is located in the lower third of the oesophagus but cases are equally distributed in the upper and middle thirds. It is usually solitary but several examples of multiple oesophageal tumours have been reported[76,77,79] as well as cases of granular-cell tumours arising simultaneously in the oesophagus and other sites.[77] The majority of patients are asymptomatic. If the tumour becomes large enough, it can cause symptoms of obstruction such as dysphagia, substernal discomfort, heartburn, regurgitation and, more rarely, weight loss.[77] Barium swallow usually shows a circumscribed filling defect. On endoscopy they appear as a raised, firm, yellowish nodule with a smooth surface covered by fairly normal mucosa. However, some cases have presented as an annular constriction.[80] In general, they measure under 1–2 cm but larger tumours up to 10 cm have been described.

Histologically, they show a characteristic pattern and are seldom a diagnostic problem. Sharply circumscribed but not encapsulated, the growth is usually confined to the mucosa. A few cases are submucosal and may even show deeper extension into the muscularis mucosae.[76] They consist of plump cells with a granular eosinophilic cytoplasm and small centrally located nuclei. These granules can be stained with the PAS reaction (after prior diastase digestion) or show positive immunostaining with S-100 protein (Fig. 38.51). Ultrastructurally, the granules are bound by basement membrane-like material and may contain myelin figures.[80] A frequent feature of granular-cell tumour is a pseudocarcinomatous hyperplasia of the overlying squamous epithelium which can be mistaken for infiltrating squamous carcinoma, particularly in superficial biopsies.

For many years, the histogenesis of the granular-cell tumour was controversial and this resulted in the tumour being given more than 20 synonyms. Abrikossoff, reporting on the first granular-cell tumour, favoured a muscle origin.[81] Other authors have postulated a fibroblastic or a histiocytic origin. Recently the concept of Schwann cell origin,[82,83] supported by electron microscopic studies and immunohistochemistry of S-100 protein of granular-cell tumours from different sites, has gained recognition.

Granular-cell tumour tends, as a rule, to behave in a benign fashion. Usual treatment has been endoscopic removal when feasible or surgical excision. A malignant oesophageal granular-cell tumour infiltrating the trachea has been reported.[79]

Secondary (metastatic) tumours

Metastatic carcinoma of the oesophagus is distinguished from direct invasion of the stomach, the hypopharynx, the thyroid and the tracheobronchial tract. Carcinoma of the gastric cardia often invades the distal oesophagus and carcinoma of the hypopharynx or larynx may extend into the upper oesophagus in a similar fashion.[2] Moreover, reported cases of oesophageal metastases from pharyngeal tumours may, in effect, be examples of multiple primary tumours.[1] True metastatic carcinoma to the oesophagus should also be distinguished from metastases of carcinoma to paraoesophageal lymph nodes with subsequent invasion of the oesophagus.

Metastatic carcinoma of the oesophagus is reckoned to occur in approximately 1%[85]–3% of patients dying with carcinoma, particularly those with lung and breast carcinoma.[85] However, it also occurs with primary tumours of the pancreas, testis, eye, prostate, bone, liver, bladder, rectum, kidney, synovium, skin, cervix and endometrium.[86]

Metastatic carcinoma of the oesophagus generally produces clinical and radiological findings suggestive of primary oesophageal disease, benign or malignant.[87,88]

Over 60 case reports deal exclusively with secondary involvement by breast cancer.[89] The average interval was eight years between mastectomy for breast cancer and the start of oesophageal symptoms. The presenting symptoms were those of a progressive onset of dysphagia and dysphonia. Metastatic carcinoma usually occurred from the middle third of the oesophagus. Radiological and endoscopic investigations showed a short concentric stricture covered by normal mucosa, suggesting an extrinsic compression. There was usually an associated pleural effusion, skin recurrences and metastases in supraclavicular lymph nodes. At autopsy, mediastinal carcinomatosis usually accounted for metastatic involvement of the oesophagus, via the perioesophageal lymph nodes.

REFERENCES

1. Morson BC, Dawson IMP, Jass JR, Price AB, Williams GT. Gastrointestinal pathology. Oxford: Blackwell, 1990.
2. Ming SG. Tumors of the esophagus and stomach. Washington: Armed Forces Institute of Pathology, 1973.
3. Watanabe H, Jass JR, Sobin LH. Histologic typing of gastric and oesophageal tumours. Berlin: Springer Verlag, 1990.
4. De La Pava S, Nigogosyan G, Pickren J, Cabrera A. Melanosis of the esophagus. Cancer 1963; 16: 48–50.
5. Stout AP, Lattes R. Tumors of the esophagus. Washington: Armed Forces Institute of Pathology, 1957.
6. Kreuser ED. Primary malignant melanoma of the esophagus. Virchows Arch (A) 1979; 385: 49–59.
7. Suzuki H, Nagayo T. Primary tumors of the esophagus other than squamous cell carcinoma — histologic classification and statistics in the surgical and autopsied material in Japan. Int Adv Surg Oncol 1980; 3: 73–109.
8. Chalkiadakis C, Wihlm JM, Morand G, Weill-Bousson M, Witz JP. Primary malignant melanoma of the esophagus. Ann Thorac Surg 1985; 39: 472–477.
9. DiConstanzo DP, Urmacher C. Primary malignant melanoma of the esophagus. Am J Surg Pathol 1987; 11: 46–52.
10. Turnbull AD, Rosen P, Goodner JT, Beattie EJ. Primary malignant tumors of the esophagus other than typical epidermoid carcimona. Ann Thorac Surg 1973; 15: 463–473.
11. Basque GJ, Boline JE, Holyoke JB. Malignant melanoma of the esophagus. First reported case in a child. Am J Clin Pathol 1970; 53: 609–611.
12. Roesch W, Rohner HG. Primary malignant melanoma of the oesophagus. Endoscopy 1984; 16: 186–188.
13. Takubo K, Kanda Y, Ishii M et al. Primary malignant melanoma of the esophagus. Hum Pathol 1983; 14: 727–730.
14. Piccone VA, Klopstock R, LeVeen HH, Sika J. Primary malignant melanoma of the esophagus associated with melanosis of the entire esophagus. First case report. J Thorac Cardiovasc Surg 1970; 59: 864–870.
15. Guzman RP, Wightman R, Ravinsky E, Unruh HW. Primary malignant melanoma of the esophagus with diffuse melanocytic atypia and melanoma in situ. Am J Clin Pathol 1989; 92: 802–804.
16. Frable WJ, Kay S, Schatzki P. Primary malignant melanoma of the esophagus: an electron microscopic study. Am J Clin Pathol 1972; 58: 659–667.
17. Kyosola K, Harjula A, Heikkinen L, Timonen T, Miettinen M. Primary malignant melanoma of the oesophagus. Scand J Thorac Cardiovasc Surg 1984; 18: 267–270.
18. Tateishi R, Taniguchi H, Wada A, Horai T, Taniguchi K. Argyrophil cells and melanocytes in esophageal mucosa. Arch Pathol 1974; 98: 87–89.
19. Ohashi K, Kato Y, Kanno J, Kasuga T. Melanocytes and melanosis of the oesophagus in Japanese subjects — analysis of factors affecting their increase. Virchows Archiv (A) 1990; 417: 137–143.
20. Butler ML, Van Heertum RL, Teplick SK. Metastatic malignant melanoma of the esophagus: a case report. Gastroenterology 1975; 69: 1334–1337.
21. Wood CB, Wood RAB. Metastatic malignant melanoma of the esophagus. Am J Dig Dis 1975; 20: 786–789.
22. Das Gupta TK, Brasfield RD. Metastatic melanoma of the gastrointestinal tract. Arch Surg 1964; 88: 969–976.
23. Trodahl JN, Sprague WG. Benign and malignant melanocytic lesions of the oral mucosa. An analysis of 135 cases. Cancer 1970; 25: 812–823.
24. Assor D. A melanocytic tumor of the esophagus. Cancer 1975; 35: 1438–1443.
25. Ming SC. Tumors of the esophagus and stomach. Supplement. Washington: Armed Forces Institute of Pathology, 1985.
26. Briggs JC, Ibrahim NBN. Oat cell carcinoma of the oesophagus: a clinicopathological study of 23 cases. Histopathology 1983; 7: 261–277.
27. Ho KJ, Herrera GA, Jones JM, Alexander CB. Small cell carcinoma of the esophagus: evidence for a unified histogenesis. Hum Pathol 1984; 15: 460–468.
28. Ibrahim NBN, Briggs JC, Corbishley CA. Extrapulmonary oat cell carcinoma. Cancer 1984; 54: 1645–1661.
29. Sato T, Mukai M, Ando N et al. Small cell carcinoma (non-oat cell type) of the esophagus concomitant with invasive squamous cell carcinoma and carcinoma in situ. A case report. Cancer 1986; 57: 328–332.
30. Beyer KL, Marshall JB, Diaz-Arias AA, Loy TS. Primary small-cell carcinoma of the esophagus. Report of 11 cases and review of the literature. J Clin Gastroenterol 1991; 13: 135–141.
31. Mori M, Matsukama A, Adachi Y et al. Small cell carcinoma of the esophagus. Cancer 1989; 63: 564–573.
32. Reyes CV, Chejfec G, Jao W, Gould VE. Neuroendocrine carcinomas of the esophagus. Ultrastruct Pathol 1980; 1: 367–376.
33. Rosenthal SN, Lemkin JA, Multiple small cell carcinomas of the esophagus. Cancer 1983; 51: 1944–1946.
34. Reid HAS, Richardson WW, Corrin B. Oat cell carcinoma of the esophagus. Cancer 1980; 45: 2342–2347.
35. Rivera F, Matilla A, Fernandez-Sanz J, Galera H. Oat cell carcinoma of the oesophagus. Case description and review of the literature. Virchows Arch (A) 1981; 391: 337–344.
36. Johnson FE, Clawson MC, Bashiti HM, Silverberg AB, Brown Jr GO. Small cell undifferentiated carcinoma of the esophagus. Case report with hormonal studies. Cancer 1984; 53: 1746–1751.
37. Rosen Y, Moon S, Kim B. Small cell epidermoid carcinoma of the esophagus. An oat cell-like carcinoma. Cancer 1975; 36: 1042–1049.
38. Drut R. Oat-cell carcinoma and mixed oat-cell epidermoid carcinoma of the esophagus. Patologia 1978; 16: 99–107.
39. Nichols GL, Kelsen DP. Small cell carcinoma of the esophagus. The Memorial Hospital experience 1970–1987. Cancer 1989; 64: 1531–1533.
40. Gowing NFC. The pathology of oesophageal tumours. In: Tanner NC, Smithers DW, eds. Tumours of the oesophagus. Edinburgh: E & S Livingstone, 1961: p 91–133.
41. Lin MH, Luna-Munoz MI, Kraft JR, Marks LM. Carcinosarcoma of the esophagus. Am J Gastroenterol 1972; 55: 249–256.
42. Enrile FT, De Jesus PO, Bakst AA, Baluyot R. Pseudosarcoma of the esophagus (polypoid carcinoma of the esophagus with pseudosarcomatous features). Cancer 1975; 31: 1197–1202.
43. Matsusaka T, Watanabe H, Enjoji M. Pseudosarcoma and carcinosarcoma of the esophagus. Cancer 1976; 37: 1546–1555.
44. Osamura RY, Shimamura K, Hata J et al. Polypoid carcinoma of the esophagus. A unifying concept for 'carcinosarcoma' and 'psuedosarcoma'. Am J Surg Pathol 1978; 2: 201–208.
45. Du Boulay CEH, Isaacson P. Carcinoma of the oesophagus with spindle cell features. Histopathology 1981; 5: 403–414.
46. Cho SR, Henry DA, Schneider V, Turner MA. Polypoid carcinoma of the esophagus: a distinct radiological and histopathological entity. Am J Gastroenterol 1983; 78: 476–480.
47. Nichols T, Yokoo H, Craig RM, Shields TW. Pseudosarcoma of the esophagus. Three new cases and review of the literature. Am J Gastroenterol 1979; 72: 615–622.
48. Battifora H. Spindle cell carcinoma. Ultrastructural evidence of squamous origin and collagen production by the tumor cells. Cancer 1976; 37: 2275–2282.
49. Takubo K, Tsuchiya S, Nakagawa H, Futatsuki K, Ishibashi I, Hirata F. Pseudosarcoma of esophagus. Hum Pathol 1985; 13: 503–505.
50. Kuhajda FP, Sun TT, Mendelsohn G. Polypoid squamous carcinoma of the esophagus. A case report with immunostaining for keratin. Am J Surg Pathol 1983; 7: 495–499.
51. Gal AA, Martin SE, Kernen JA, Patterson MJ. Esophageal carcinoma with prominent spindle cells. Cancer 1987; 60: 2244–2250.
52. Melato M, Lazzini C, Strami G, Bortul M, Tendella E. Carcinosarcoma vs pseudosarcoma. Am J Surg Pathol 1985; 9: 388–389.
53. Linder J, Stein RB, Roggli VL et al. Polypoid tumor of the esophagus. Hum Pathol 1987; 18: 692–700.
54. Petursson SR. Adenoid cystic carcinoma of the esophagus.

Complete response to combination chemotherapy. Cancer 1986; 57: 1464–1467.
55. Epstein JI, Sears DL, Tucker RS, Eagan Jr JW. Carcinoma of the esophagus with adenoid cystic differentiation. Cancer 1984; 53: 1131–1136.
56. Kabuto T, Taniguchi K, Iwanaga T et al. Primary adenoid cystic carcinoma of the esophagus. Report of a case. Cancer 1979; 43: 2452–2456.
57. Sweeny EC, Cooney T. Adenoid cystic carcinoma of the esophagus. A light and electron microscopic study. Cancer 1980; 45: 1516–1525.
58. Cerar A, Jutersek A, Vidmar S. Adenoid cystic carcinoma of the esophagus. A clinicopathologic study of three cases. Cancer 1991; 67: 2159–2164.
59. Bogomoletz WV, Molas G, Gayet B, Potet F. Superficial squamous cell carcinoma of the esophagus. A report of 76 cases and review of the literature. Am J Surg Pathol 1989; 13: 535–546.
60. Tsang WYW, Chan JKC, Lee KC, Leung AFK, Fu YT. Basaloid-squamous carcinoma of the upper aerodigestive tract and so-called adenoid cystic carcinoma of the esophagus: the same tumour? Histopathology 1991; 19: 35–36.
61. Lewin KJ, Ranchod M, Dorfamn RF. Lymphomas of the gastro-intestinal tract. Cancer 1978; 42: 693–697.
62. Berman MD, Falchuk KR, Trey C, Gramm HF. Primary histiocytic lymphoma of the esophagus. Dig Dis Sci 1979; 24: 883–886.
63. Doki T, Hamada S, Murayama H, Suenaga H, Sannohe Y. Primary malignant lymphoma of the esophagus. A case report. Endoscopy 1984; 16: 189–192.
64. Matsuura H, Saito R, Makajima S, Yoshira W, Enomoto T. Non-Hodgkin's lymphoma of the esophagus. Am J Gastroenterol 1985; 80: 941–946.
65. Carnovale RL, Goldstein HM, Zornoza J, Dodd GD. Radiologic manifestations of esophageal lymphoma. AJR 1977; 128: 751–754.
66. Hricak H, Thoeni RF, Margulis AR, Eyler WR, Francis IR. Extension of gastric lymphoma into the esophagus and duodenum. Radiology 1980; 135: 309–312.
67. Nissan S, Bar-Moar JA, Levy E. Lymphosarcoma of the esophagus: a case report. Cancer 1974; 34: 1321–1323.
68. Taube M, Waldron JA, McCallum RW. Systemic lymphoma initially presenting as an esophageal mass. Am J Gastroenterol 1982; 77: 835–837.
69. Morris WT, Pead JL. Myeloma of the oesophagus. J Clin Pathol 1972; 25: 537–538.
70. Ahmed N, Ramos S, Sika J, Leveen HH, Piccone VA. Primary extramedullary esophageal plasmocytoma. First case report. Cancer 1986; 38: 943–947.
71. Stein HA, Murray D, Warner HA. Primary Hodgkin's disease of the esophagus. Dig Dis Sci 1981; 26: 457–461.
72. Sheahan DG, West AB. Focal lymphoid hyperplasia (pseudolymphoma) of the esophagus. Am J Surg Pathol 1985; 9: 141–147.
73. Gervaz E, Potet F, Mahe R, Lemasson G. Focal lymphoid hyperplasia of the oesophagus: report of a case. Histopathology 1992; 21: 187–189.
74. Wolff BC, Khetty O, Leonardi HK, Neptune WB, Bhattacharyya AK, Legg MA. Benign lesions mimicking malignant tumours of the esophagus. Hum Pathol 1988; 19: 148–154.
75. Lack EE, Worsham GF, Callihan MD et al. Granular cell tumor: a clinicopathologic study of 110 patients. J Surg Oncol 1980; 13: 301–316.
76. Johnston J, Helwig EB. Granular cell tumors of the gastrointestinal tract and perianal region. A study of 74 cases. Dig Dis Sci 1981; 26: 807–816.
77. Rubesin S, Herlinger H, Sigal H. Granular cell tumors of the esophagus. Gastrointest Radio 1985; 10: 11–15.
78. Brady PG, Nord HJ, Connar RG. Granular cell tumor of the esophagus: natural history, diagnosis and therapy. Dig Dis Sci 1988; 33: 1329–1333.
79. Cone JB, Wetzel WJ. Esophageal granular cell tumors. Report of two multicentric cases with observations on their natural histories. J Surg Oncol 1982; 20: 14–16.
80. Vuyk HD, Snow GB, Tiwari RM, Van Velzen D, Veldhuizen RW. Granular cell tumor of the proximal esophagus. A rare disease. Cancer 1985; 55: 445–449.
81. Abrikossof AJ. Uber Myome, ausgehend von der quergestneiften willkurlichen Muskulatur. Virchows Arch (A) 1926; 260: 214–233.
82. Enzinger FM, Weiss Sw. Soft tissue tumors. St Louis: Mosyb, 1983: pp 745–756.
83. Stefansson K, Wollman RL. S-100 protein in granular cell tumors (granular cell myoblastomas). Cancer 1982; 49: 1834–1838.
84. Phadke M, Rao U, Taikta H. Metastatic tumors of esophagus. NY State J Med 1976; 76: 963–965.
85. Anderson MF, Harell GS. Secondary esophageal tumors. AJR 1980; 135: 1243–1246.
86. Zarian LP, Berliner L, Redmond P. Metastatic endometrial carcinoma to the esophagus. Am J Gastroenterol 1983; 78: 9–11.
87. Fisher MS. Metastasis to the esophagus. Gastrointest Radiol 1976; 1: 249–251.
88. Gore RM, Sparberg M. Metastatic carcinoma of the prostate to the esophagus. Am J Gastroenterol 1982; 77: 358–359.
89. Boccardo F, Merlano M, Canobbio L, Rosso R, Aste H. Esophageal involvement in breast cancer. Report of 6 cases. Tumori 1982; 68: 149–153.

CHAPTER

39 Other tumours of the stomach

R. Whitehead A. Johansen C. A. Rubio

PART I

Epithelial tumours

R. Whitehead A. Johansen

EPITHELIAL GASTRIC TUMOURS

Epithelium derived tumours, in particular adenocarcinoma, are relatively common in Japan, Columbia, Chile and in many East European countries,[1] but infrequent in the United States and comparatively rare in Egypt and Thailand. In Denmark, the number of newly diagnosed cases of gastric cancer in 1980 was 930, and the incidence rate per 100 000 adjusted to the world standard population was 14.1% for men and 6.3% for women. The prevalence of gastric cancer on 1 January 1981 was 1801; 78 (4.3%) were under 50 years, and 1753 (95.7%) were 50 years or more.[2] There is evidence that, except for Portugal, the incidence and mortality rates in most countries have fallen markedly since the 1930s,[2] and even in Japan it has decreased.

The worldwide decrease in incidence cannot be fully explained, because certain aspects of the aetiology of gastric cancer are still obscure. However, epidemiological studies,[3–5] and particularly studies on migrants,[6–8] have shown that environmental factors play an important role. It is likely that the falling incidence of gastric cancer is related to changes in diet. Food preservation methods, such as salting and smoking, have disappeared since the introduction of refrigerators and legislation restricting the nitrite content of food and other improvements in the standard of living[9] may have also played a role. There is no doubt that genetic factors also play a role in gastric carcinogenesis,[10,11] but these would not change significantly with time.

The prognosis of gastric cancer is generally very poor, although in Japan it has been improved, mainly because of early diagnosis. Indeed, since irradiation and adjuvant chemotherapy are without significant effect, this is the likely way that improvement in prognosis will occur in the foreseeable future. Thus, in recent times, the focus of attention has been on premalignant or dysplastic lesions.[12]

The precancerous changes of dysplasia are histological alterations of the epithelium, including cellular atypia, abnormal differentiation and disorganized architecture. Nagayo[13] graded dysplasia subjectively into mild, moderate and severe categories, but from a practical standpoint the recognition of low and high grade dysplasia might be better. In any event, the recognition of dysplasia in patients such as those with pernicious anaemia or, for example, those who have undergone a Billroth II resection 20 years previously,[14–16] is important. If management guidelines can be derived for patients with dysplasia, improvements in survival in gastric cancer disease can be expected to ensue. Follow-up studies of large groups of patients with gastric dysplasia have shown that whilst up to 50% may regress, nearly 10% develop adenocarcinoma.[17] Severe dysplasia has also been defined more objectively in morphometric and by ploidy analysis,[18] and this may result in the future as a means of case selection for determining therapy.

Apart from mucosal dysplasia, there are other potentially precancerous lesions. One is intestinal metaplasia of the gastric mucosa and this is a controversial subject discussed in greater detail in Chapters 7 and 8. Of the remainder, adenomatous polyps constitute the most important. These can only be defined after consideration of polypoidal lesions as a whole.

POLYPS

Most epithelial gastric polyps can be subdivided into hyperplastic and adenomatous, according to their histological characteristics. The remainder are a miscellaneous group of lesions.

Hyperplastic polyps

Elster[19,20] subdivides hyperplastic polyps into focal foveolar hyperplasia and larger lesions, which he terms hyperplasiogenous. This is arguably overelaborate terminology for lesions which are basically the same, differing only in size and possibly duration. The smallest and earliest hyperplastic polyp is a small elevation (Fig. 39.1) with elongated tortuous pits and papillary crests in between. The pits are composed of normal epithelium, and the glands, which are of usual dimensions, are also normal. The lamina propria is often no different from that of the surrounding mucosa and may or may not contain inflammatory cells. These polyps correspond to the type II of Nakamura,[21] and have been called regenerative polyps by others.[22,23]

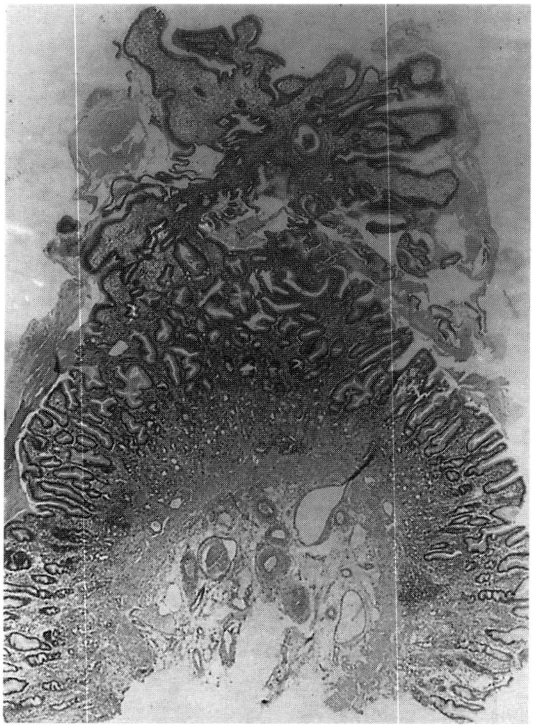

Fig. 39.1 A small hyperplastic polyp.

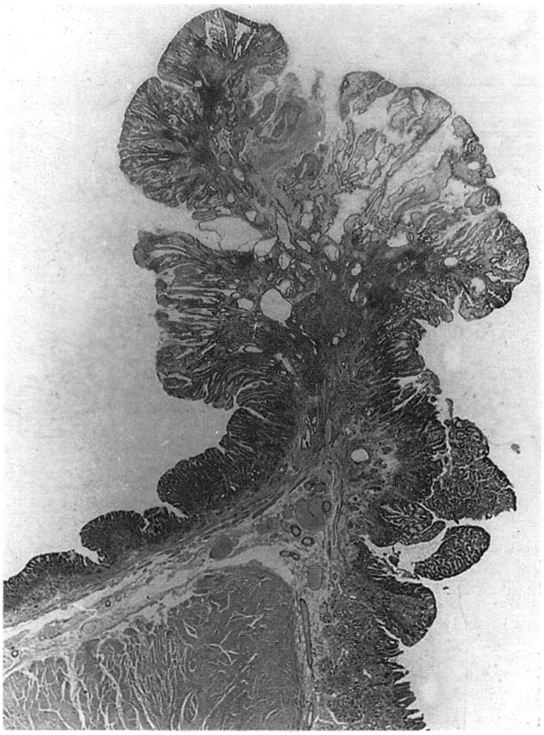

Fig. 39.2 A large hyperplastic (hyperplasiogenous) polyp located at the pyloric ring. The duodenum is to the right.

Larger lesions (Fig. 39.2) have a more obvious polyp-shape with a head and a stalk,[24] but may be sessile. The foveolae are elongated and often cystic-dilated. Normal glands may be present, but usually there are a number which are cystic. Serial sections have shown that some of the cysts are connected with the foveolae and some are not. Intestinal metaplastic epithelium is not usually present but it is sometimes seen in larger lesions. The epithelium shows evidence of increased mucus secretion and the cells are often enlarged globular or goblet cell-like. They are usually PAS positive and Alcian-blue negative. Incomplete metaplasia of the type described by Jass[25] is absent. The stroma is characteristically congested and oedematous, and there may be superficial inflammation and erosion. It also contains bundles of fan-shaped smooth muscle which grow up from the muscularis mucosae. Larger lesions may rarely contain adenomatous areas and it is now generally accepted that it is mixed lesions which give rise to adenocarcinoma.[26–28]

Adenomatous polyps

The other main group are the neoplastic or adenomatous polyps. These are real neoplasms caused by an abnormal differentiation of the foveolar cells. Irrespective of the form they take they will, by definition, show dysplasia of varying degrees.

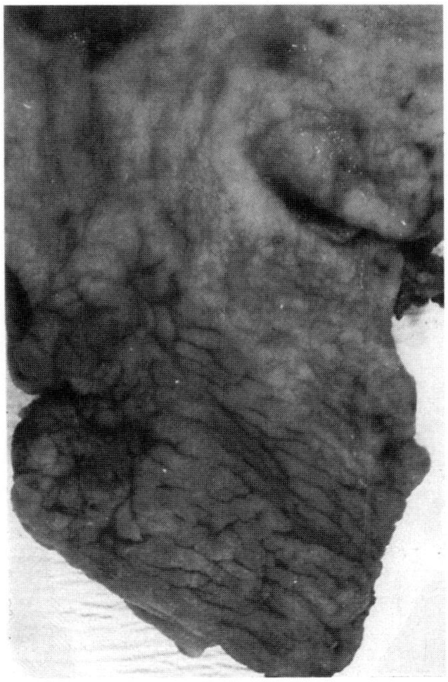

Fig. 39.3 A flat, sessile, adenomatous polyp in the pyloric part of the stomach.

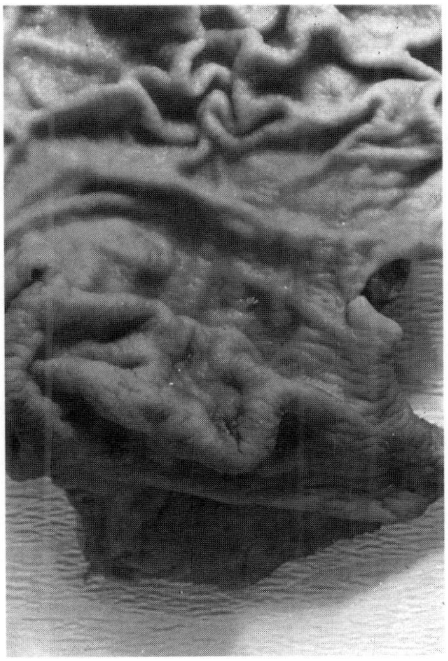

Fig. 39.4 A fold-like adenoma extending across the pyloric ring.

The entire lesion is composed of proliferating tubules composed of dysplastic epithelium. This is often of the intestinal metaplastic-type,[29] with evidence of differention to enterocytes and goblet cells. It is obvious that most adenomas originate from metaplastic mucosa. Tubes with dysplastic epithelium rarely appear to arise from PAS-positive foveolar epithelium, suggesting that this also can be a starting point. However in the adjacent mucosa atrophic gastritis of some degree is always present.[30] Adenomas appear never to develop from a normal gastric mucosa or from a mucosa with only superficial chronic gastritis. Cysts which are common in the basal part of adenomas may be lined by epithelium which is normal, intestinalized or dysplastic. The stroma is sparse and may contain inflammatory cells and muscle fibres from the muscularis mucosae.

Adenomatous polyps seldom have the shape typical of colonic adenomas. Few are pedunculated and most are sessile (Fig. 39.3), wart-like or appear as thickened mucosal folds (Fig. 39.4).[31] Adenomatous polyps are commonly located in the prepyloric region and occasionally prolapse into the duodenum. Commonly mainly tubular, both tubulovillous and villous adenomas occur, but wholly villous lesions are rare.[32]

The incidence of gastric polyps is difficult to assess, but according to a German survey,[24] they occur in 8–9% of gastroscoped patients. In resected stomachs, 91.3% are hyperplastic polyps and 8.7% adenomatous polyps.[33]

It has been shown that in about 40% of the patients who have a polyp removed, another develops.[34] Sometimes this is at the same site (6.1%) and sometimes in another (32.5%). Approximately 90% of the new polyps have the same histological structure as the one removed.

Polyposis

Gastric polyps are often single, but they may be multiple. In elderly people, several polyps are occasionally found at the transitional zone between the pyloric and the body mucosa.[21,35] Gastric polyposis is the term used when more than 50 polyps are present.[36] It is a rare condition and the polyps are nearly always of the hyperplastic type,[37–39] and usually the patient has no other disease. However, multiple hyperplastic polyps are described in Cowden's disease,[40] and some consider that the polyps of Cronkhite-Canada's syndrome are hyperplastic. Occasionally hyperplastic gastric polyps are seen in familial polyposis coli.

Miscellaneous polyps (see next section)

In familial adenomatosis coli, a large number of small polypoid lesions, hemispheric, and one or a few millimetres in diameter occur in the body mucosa.[41–43] They are caused by cystic dilation of the body glands and were at first thought to be specific for familial colonic adenomatosis. However it is now known that they occur quite commonly without this association.[44–46]

Both single or multiple juvenile polyps and Peutz-Jegher's polyps, which are regarded as hamartomatous, may also be found in the stomach.

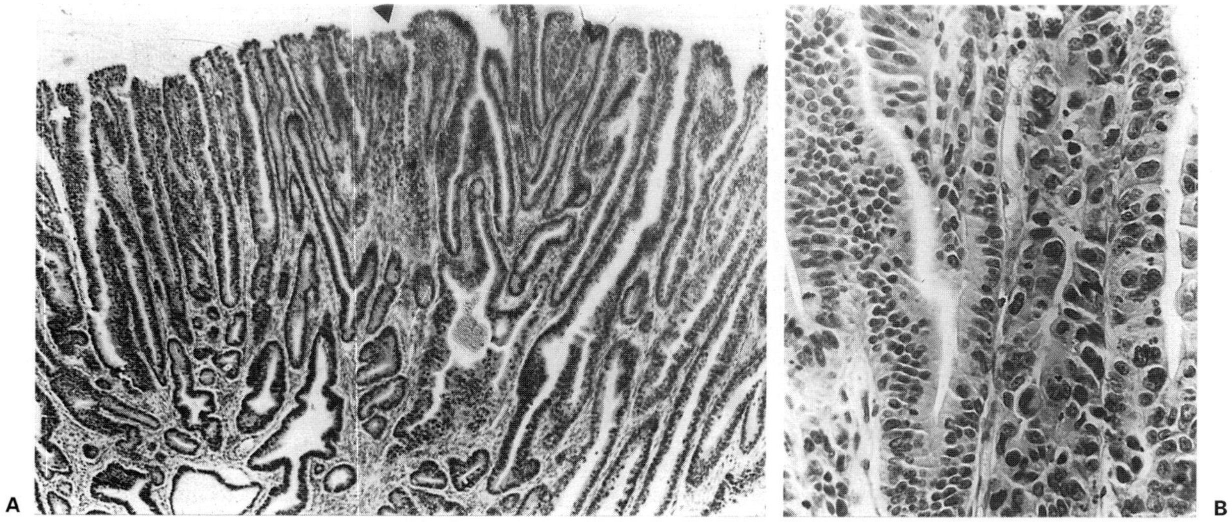

Fig. 39.5 **A** A tubular adenoma with transition into carcinoma. **B** The carcinomatous area in high magnification.

THE ADENOMA-CARCINOMA SEQUENCE

There is evidence that gastric adenomas can develop into carcinomas and adenomas occur more frequently if the stomach also contains a carcinoma.[13,47,48] However, the age range of patients with adenomas does not appear to be any lower than that of patients with carcinomas. Nevertheless, as in the colon, one can find histological evidence of early carcinoma in tumours which are still quite clearly adenomas (Fig. 39.5). More often, one can find evidence of residual adenoma in advanced carcinomas. Of 455 carcinomas examined, there was evidence that 25 (5.5%) had originated from adenomas.[33]

Rarely, hyperplastic polyps also appear to give rise to gastric carcinoma;[49,50] certainly, as we have seen, dysplasia

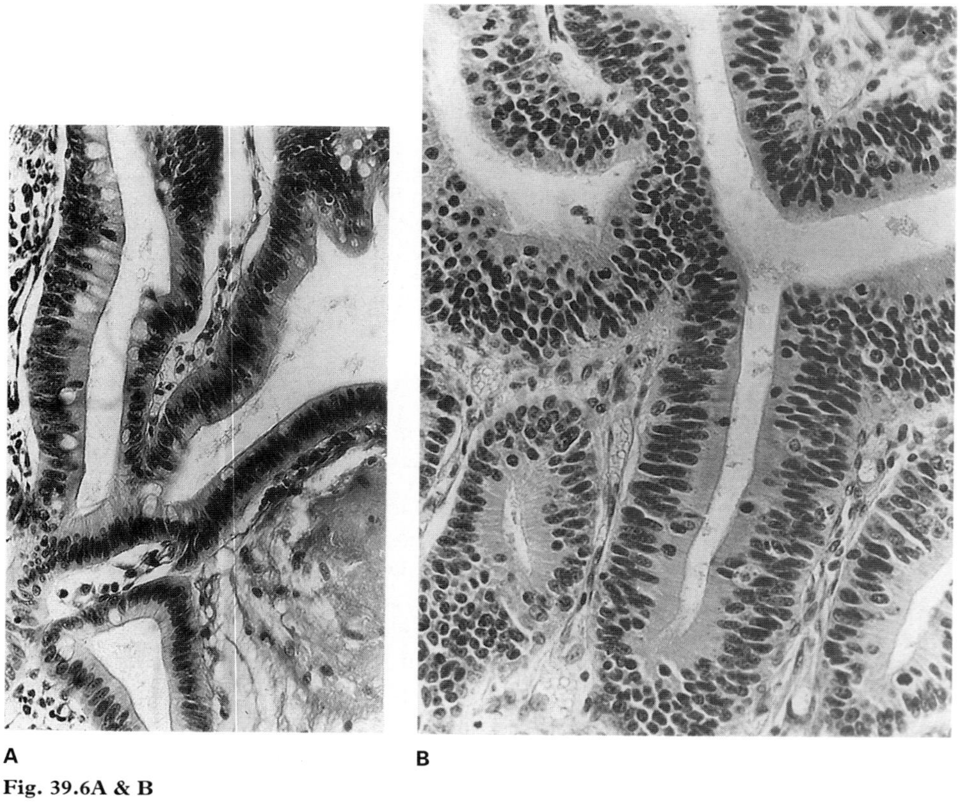

Fig. 39.6A & B

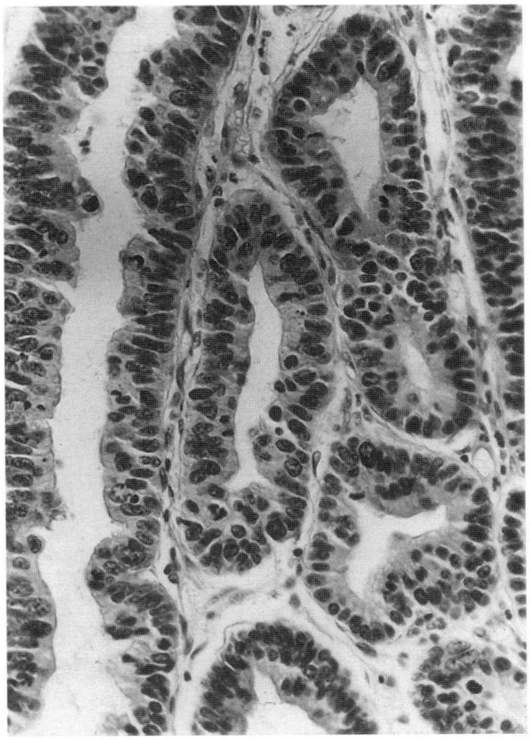

Fig. 39.6 Dysplasia. **A** Mild; **B** moderate; **C** severe.

may occur in hyperplastic polyps and so the occasional occurrence of carcinoma is to be expected. Generally speaking, the dysplasia seen in adenomatous polyps, and which is a prerequisite for diagnosis, is frequently more severe (Fig. 39.6).

A lesion which also shows moderate dysplasia is that which has been called the border-line lesion (Fig. 39.7).[51–53] Macroscopically, it is a sessile elevation, which was named before the lesion of gastric dysplasia was developed. Border-line was simply meant to define a lesion which lay somewhere between benign and malignant. It is probably now redundant but as a term it characterizes a lesion which has remarkable similarities from case to case. The epithelium usually shows moderate dysplasia, and the lesion is most often stable, although transitions into carcinoma have been reported.[48]

Whilst it can be said in conclusion that compared with the colorectum only a small percentage of gastric carcinomas originate in polyps, there can be no doubt these occur and nearly always in adenomatous polyps with a high degree of dysplasia.

EARLY GASTRIC CANCER

Early gastric cancer[54] is defined as a carcinoma limited to the mucosa or submucosa. The definition is based entirely on the depth of invasion and not on the size or the shape of the tumour. The final diagnosis can only be made by histological examination of the resected stomach, although sophisticated radiology and endoscopy with biopsy often allow the diagnosis to be made with a high degree of certainty. Penetration of the muscularis mucosa is the criterion for subdividing early gastric cancer into intramucosal and submucosal types.

Originally, there was some debate as to whether submucosal carcinoma should be included, because of its capacity to metastasize to the regional lymph nodes. However, follow-up studies have shown that most submucosal carcinomas also have an excellent prognosis.

The term early gastric cancer is not ideal because it implies the temporal state of the lesion and there is, of course, no evidence as to how long they have been present when discovered. Other terms such as superficial carcinoma or surface carcinoma have been proposed but the most satisfactory are intramucosal or mucosal and submucosal, since they are anatomical and unambiguous.

A

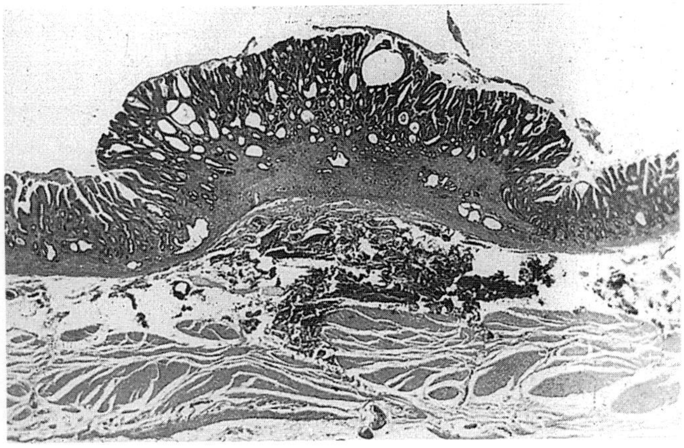

B

Fig. 39.7 Borderline lesion. **A** The macroscopic appearance; **B** section through the lesion.

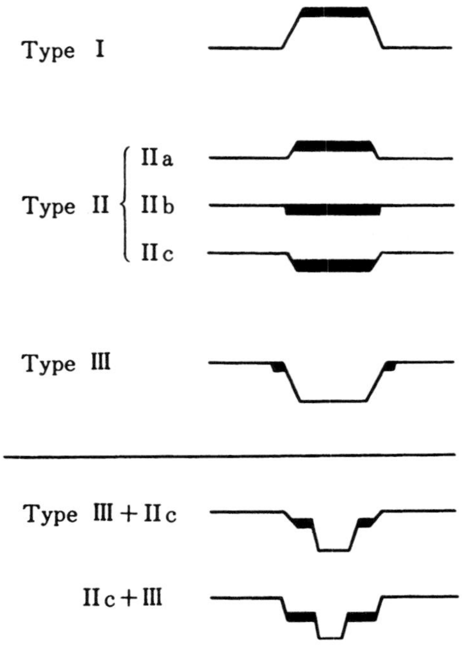

Fig. 39.8 The classification sketch given by the Japanese Endoscopic Society.

Macroscopic classification of early gastric cancer

Early gastric cancer has been known for many years, but it was the introduction of the widespread use of fibre-gastroscopy which caused the Japanese Endoscopical Society to propose a classification which was adopted by the Japanese Research Society of Gastric Cancer in 1962.[55] Early gastric cancers are divided into three principal groups (Fig. 39.8). In Type I, the protruded type, the tumours project clearly into the lumen. Type II, is the superficial type, where unevenness of the surface is inconspicuous. The last, or Type III, shows excavation of the gastric wall. Type II is further divided: Type IIa, the elevated type, where the elevation of the tumour is less than the thickness of the adjacent mucosa; Type IIb, the flat type, where virtually no elevation or depression is seen; and Type IIc, the depressed type, where the surface is only slightly depressed.

Tumours are, however, often compound: Type III carcinomas, especially, are often combined with the subtypes IIc and IIb. The classification is based exclusively on the macroscopic appearance and its value is limited. It is, however, useful in drawing attention to the fact that early cancer of the stomach can take the form of minor surface irregularities of the mucosa and this will tend to lead to biopsy.

Protruding carcinomas often appear as a hemispherical nodule (Fig. 39.9). It is usually sessile but many have a short broad stalk. Some are flat, plateau-like, and well demarcated. The surface may be smooth, but is often nodular or uneven. The colour is usually different from that of the surrounding mucosa, the flat ones being lighter. The majority of tumours have a diameter of less than 3 cm but some are much larger. Large tumours show submucosal, often quite extensive, invasion. Most often antral, they can also occur in the body of the stomach.

The depressed carcinoma of Type IIc[1] (Fig. 39.10) is small, usually less than 2 cm in diameter. It is well demarcated with a slightly irregular margin. The margins may also be elevated and would be designated IIc + IIa

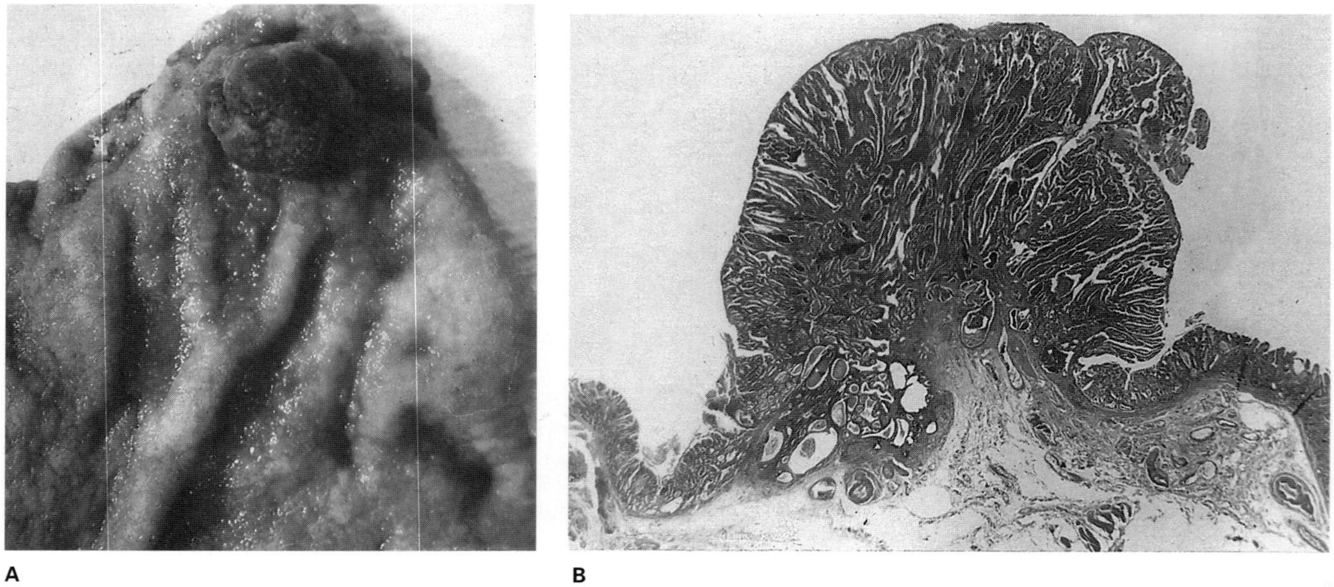

Fig. 39.9 EGC, elevated type. **A** Small, polyp-like lesion at the proximal border of a resection specimen; **B** section through **A**: the carcinoma invades the submucosa.

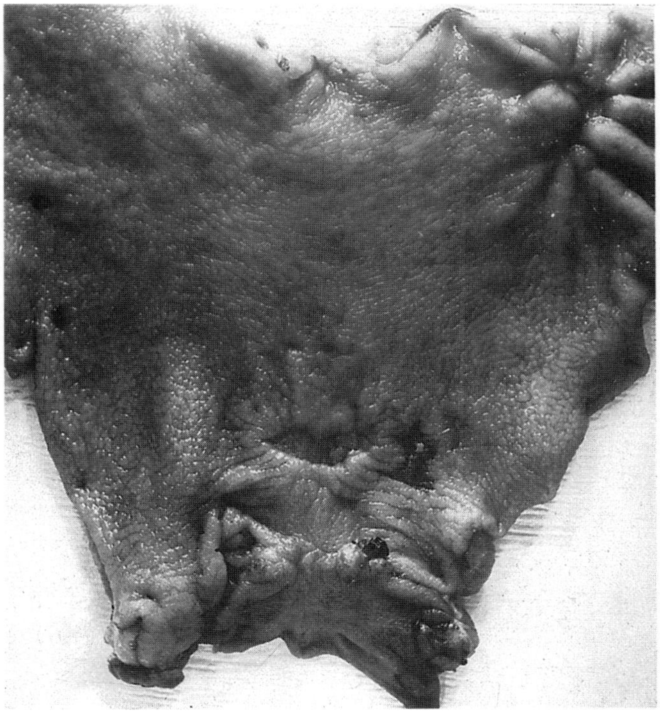

Fig. 39.10 EGC, depressed type (IIc′) located proximally to the pyloric ring. An erosion is seen beside the carcinoma.

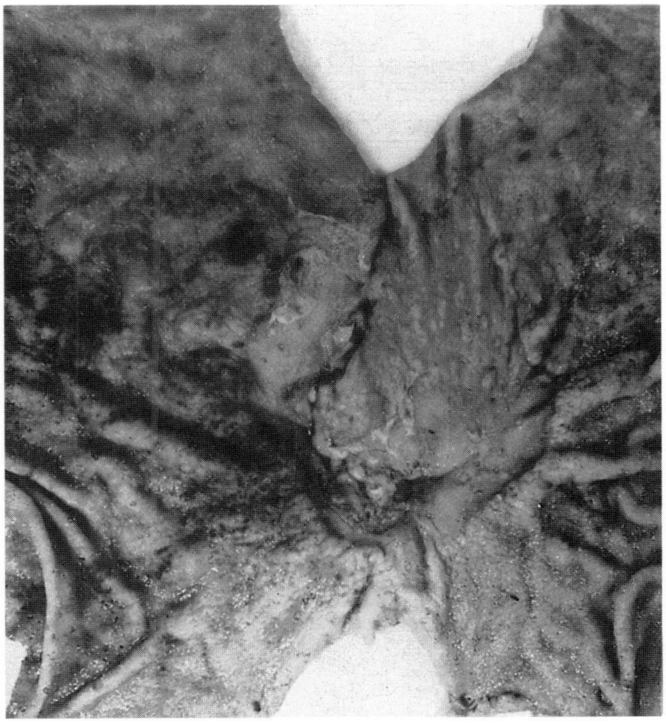

Fig. 39.11 EGC, depressed type (IIc″). A large, eroded area on the lesser curvature side. A specimen for frozen section has been taken.

in the Japanese nomenclature. The larger lesions of this type show submucosal spread, but most are mucosal carcinomas.

The depressed carcinoma of Type (IIc^{11}) (Fig. 39.11) has the character of a large erosion; it is red, or grey if covered with fibrin. There may be residual small islands of non-eroded mucosa and the margins are not so sharply demarcated as those of Type IIc,′ and show convergent mucosal folds. The carcinoma is very superficial and purely mucosal, and is often localized to the body of the stomach, whereas Type IIc′ is often localized to the antral part.

The imperceptible carcinoma, IIb (Fig. 39.12), has no macroscopic characteristics although in the endoscopic classification it is defined as an 'almost non-recognizable elevation or depression'.

The ulcer-associated carcinoma is naturally characterized by an ulcer. This has the same appearance as an ordinary, benign peptic ulcer. The carcinoma is localized to the margin, and if it is not macroscopically noticeable the lesion is a Type III + IIb. If the surrounding mucosa shows a depression, it is a Type III + IIc-carcinoma. If the depression is small and well demarcated, the lesion can be

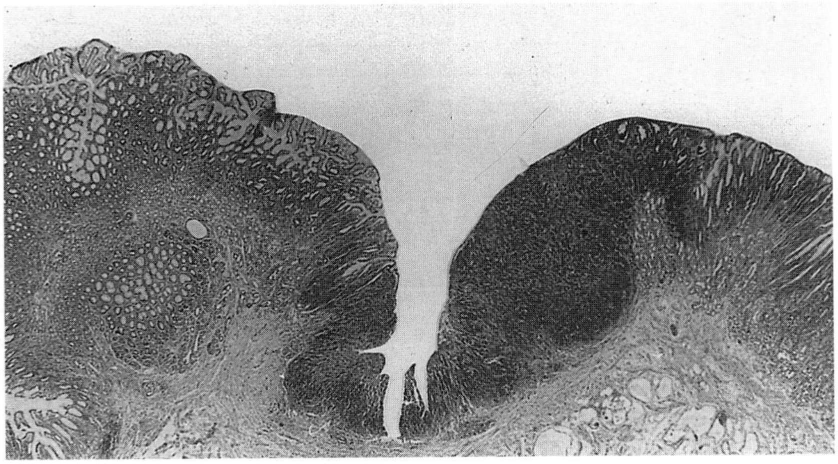

Fig. 39.12 EGC, imperceptible type, an incidental finding in the pyloric mucosa.

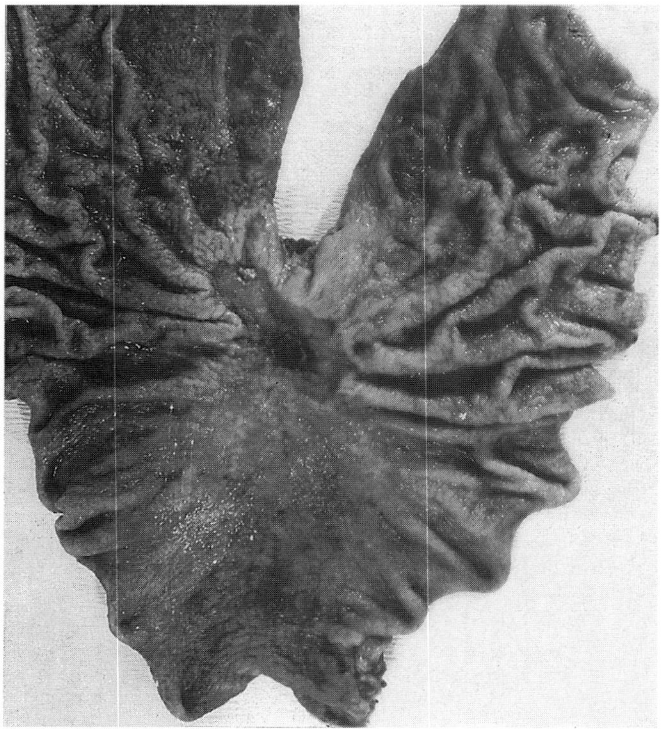

Fig. 39.13 EGC, ulcer-associated type. The ulcer is surrounded by a small, well demarcated depression.

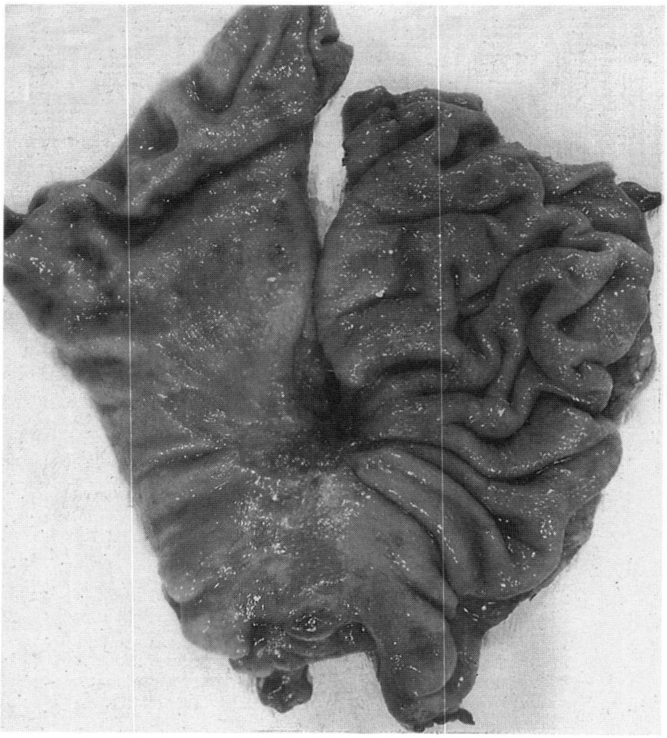

Fig. 39.14 EGC, ulcer-associated type. The ulcer is surrounded by a large, eroded area.

designated III + IIc′ (Fig. 39.13). If the depression is a large erosion the designation is IIc″ + III (Fig. 39.14). Histogenetically, it is held that the carcinoma is the primary lesion, and the ulcer develops in it owing to its vulnerability.

Early gastric cancer accounts for a variable percentage of all gastric cancers ranging from 6.2–40%,[54,56] but the trend will be for more to be diagnosed because of the implementation of screening programmes, and the increasing sophistication of detection techniques.

ADVANCED GASTRIC CARCINOMA

The macroscopic appearance of advanced gastric cancer varies and it is argued that it has little value.[37] Two common features used for classification are the direction of tumour growth and whether it is demarcated or diffusely infiltrative.

These features are utilized in Borrmann's classification,[57] which, although in common use in Germany and Japan, has never gained acceptance in English-speaking countries. Advanced gastric cancers are divided into four types. Type I, or the fungating type (Fig. 39.15), is a polypoid protrusion with a broad base and an uneven surface. It is usually soft and red in colour. It may be slightly ulcerated and it is well demarcated. Type II, the excavated carcinoma (Fig. 39.16), is dominated by a deep crater with elevated margins. The floor of the ulcer is often necrotic and covered with grey exudate. This type is also well demarcated and there is no infiltration of the surroundings. Type III, the ulcerated, infiltrating type

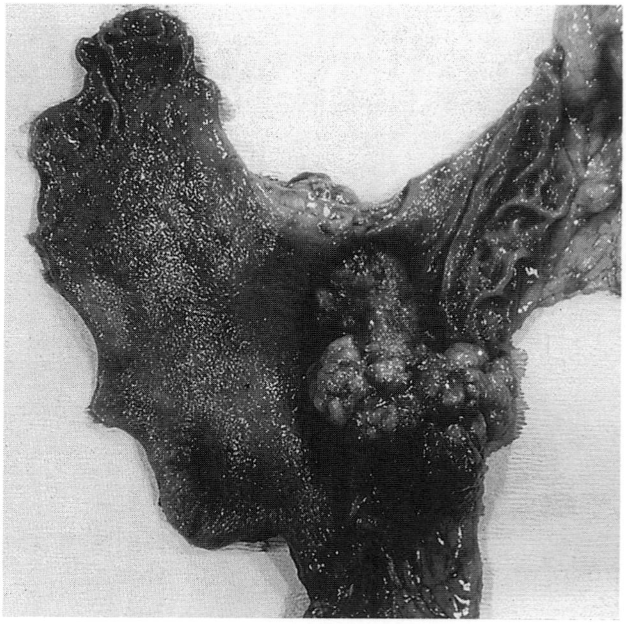

Fig. 39.15 A fungating carcinoma of the Borrmann Type I.

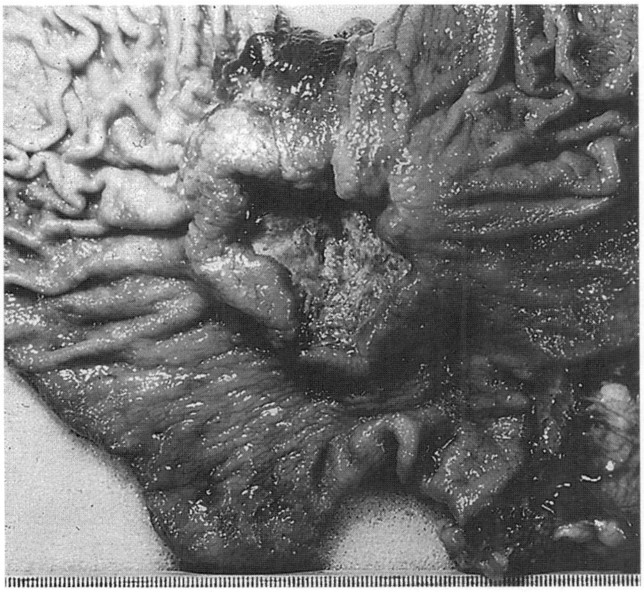

Fig. 39.16 An excavated carcinoma of the Borrmann Type II.

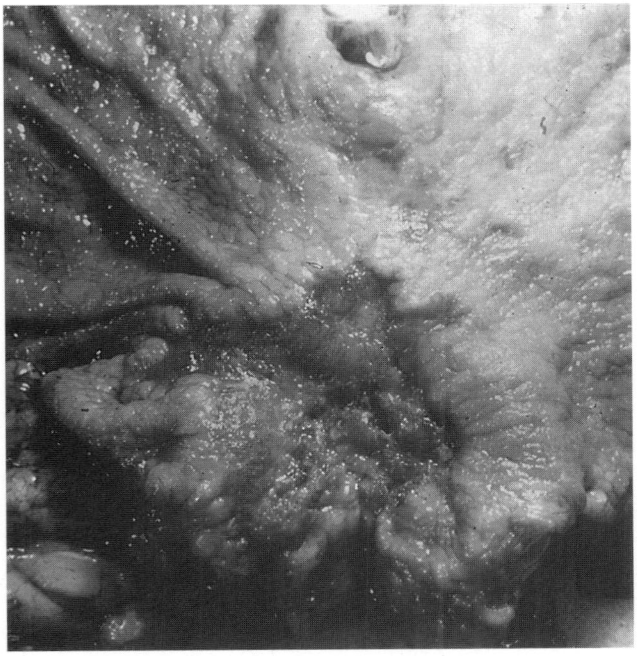

Fig. 39.17 An infiltrative, ulcerating carcinoma of the Borrmann Type III.

(Fig. 39.17), has flat or only slightly elevated margins in contrast to Type II. The ulcer is not very deep, has an irregular shape, and the surrounding mucosa is indurated and clearly infiltrated by tumour tissue. Type IV, the diffusely thickened or schirrous type (Fig. 39.18), shows no circumscribed lesion, but shallow, superficial ulcerations may be seen on the surface. If the entire stomach wall is involved, the tumour is called linitis plastica.

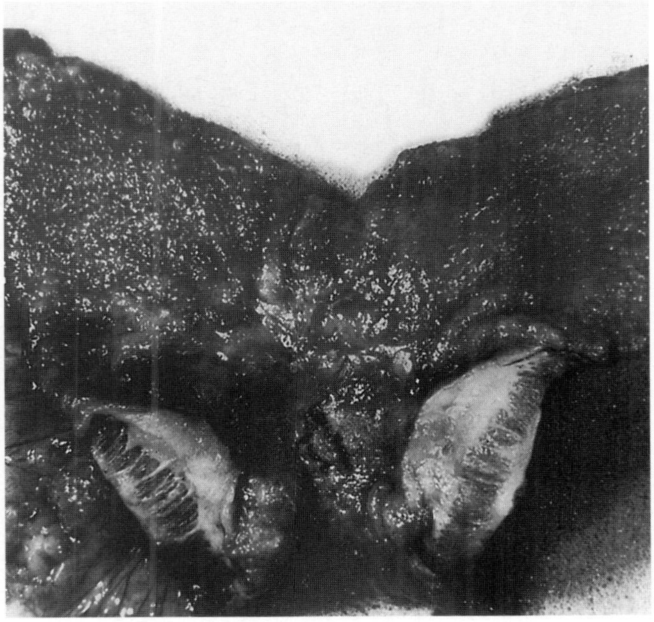

Fig. 39.18 A diffuse thickened carcinoma of the Borrmann Type IV.

All four types are most often found in the antrum, but Type III and Type IV are also seen at the angulus and in the body.

There is a great difference between the frequencies of the four types. Type II is far the most common followed by Type III and Type IV. The most infrequent tumour is the protruding Type I tumour. The practical importance of Borrmann's classification is limited, for it is unrelated to prognosis. It does, however, allow for communication and studies concerning changes in the natural history of the disease.

HISTOLOGY OF GASTRIC CANCER

The microscopic appearance of gastric carcinoma is fundamentally the same whether the carcinoma is early or advanced. There is no reason to believe that an early carcinoma is a special type. However, the early carcinomas often disclose purer forms of the various microscopic types.

In practice, all gastric carcinomas are adenocarcinomas, but a complete classification[58] includes rarities such as adenosquamous and pure squamous carcinoma (see next section). Completely undifferentiated carcinoma is, in our experience, extremely rare because a thorough search of most tumours will usually reveal cells with small mucous droplets. If it does not, then a lymphoma should be carefully considered.

In the WHO classification[58] four types of adenocarcinoma are recognized: the papillary, the tubular, the mucinous and the signet ring cell. They are classified according to their degree of differentiation (Fig. 39.19). In well dif-

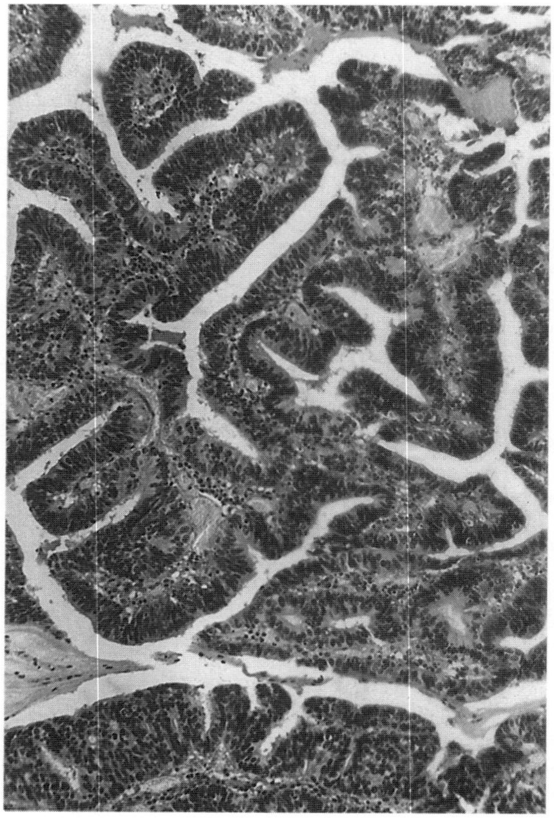
A

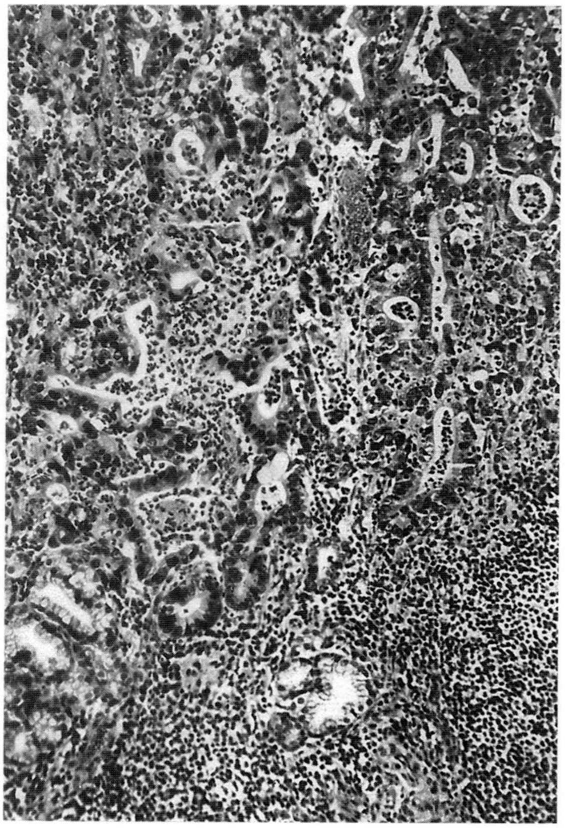
B

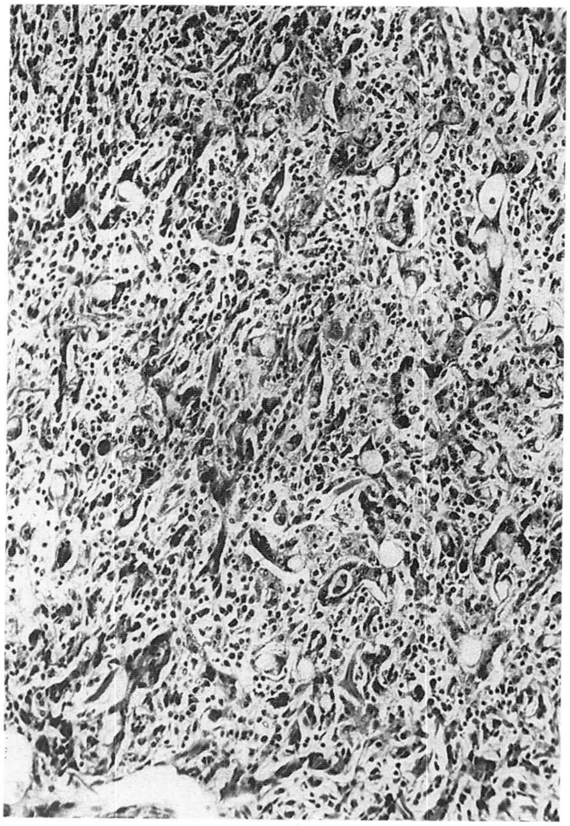
C

Fig. 39.19 **A** Well, **B** moderately, and **C** poorly differentiated adenocarcinomas.

ferentiated carcinomas the glandular or cellular structure in most cases closely resembles metaplastic intestinal epithelium. A poorly differentiated carcinoma has a glandular or cellular structure which can be recognized only with difficulty, and the moderately differentiated carcinoma is one with features which are intermediate between these groups.

In the Japanese literature,[59,60] the various degrees of differentiation are sometimes illustrated by a range of symbols: closed lines, open lines, dashes and dots. Closed lines symbolize the highly differentiated carcinoma with its glandular, tubular and acinar structures. The open lines symbolize the moderately differentiated carcinoma with its trabeculae, and the dashes and dots, poorly differentiated carcinoma with its small cell clusters and solitary cells.

The appearance of carcinoma also depends on the amount of collagen or mucus, both of which may dominate.

In advanced cancer, various degrees of differentiation are seen in the same tumour. Quite often, there are also differences in appearance between the primary and the secondaries and thus classification can be somewhat arbi-

Table 39.1 The prevalence of degree of differentiation according to Borrmann's macroscopic types. ($p < 0.005$)

Type of Borrman	Degree of differentiation (No. of tumours) Well	Moderate	Poor	Total
I	12	1	0	13
II	92	57	17	166
II	7	14	18	39
IV	3	5	44	52
Total	114	77	79	270

trary. The figures of Table 39.1 are based on the predominant degree of differentiation because if each tumour were classified according to its poorest differentiated area, nearly every tumour would be classified as poorly differentiated.

Table 39.1 shows that the elevated and well demarcated Borrmann I and II tumours are most often well differentiated, and that tumours of the Borrmann Type III and IV are most often poorly differentiated.

Table 39.2 gives the relation between the degree of differentiation and the macroscopic main types of early gastric cancer. Elevated carcinomas are significantly most often well differentiated, while the ulcer-associated and, in particular, the imperceptible IIb carcinomas are most often poorly differentiated. In Nagayo's series,[60] the most remarkable finding was the large difference in differentiation between the focal, depressed Type IIc′ and the large, eroded Type IIc″. The former showed a clear predominance of well differentiated tumours whereas the latter was dominated by poorly or moderately differentiated tumours. This seems to be the justification for dividing depressed carcinomas into two main groups, but more recent work on early gastric cancer refutes this.[61] With the trend towards strip biopsy excision of early gastric cancer[62] this assumes greater importance.

The classification of Lauren[63] also gained wide acceptance. He was influenced by work published by Jarvi[64–66] and divided gastric carcinomas into two types: the diffuse type and the so-called intestinal type carcinoma. Fundamentally histogenetic, it presumes that a proportion of gastric carcinomas originate in metaplastic intestinal epithelium. The evidence for this is that certain intestinal epithelial features are also found in the tumour cells. Intestinal-type carcinomas are usually also surrounded by a mucosa which is intestinalized. The diffuse type purportedly takes its origin from non-metaplastic epithelium but even Jarvi and Lauren have shown by histochemistry, immunohistochemistry and electron microscopy that many similar features occur in both main types of carcinomas.[63,67–70]

Nevertheless, the classification appears to divide gastric cancer into two broad groups which show differences in biological behaviour. The intestinal type is most common in men and in the elderly and has a slightly better prognosis than the diffuse type, which is most commonly found in women and in the younger age group.[63,70] The classification has been used particularly in epidemiological studies with apparent success.[71–73] It is of interest that very small signet-ring cell carcinomas are rarely associated with intestinal metaplasia of the surrounding mucosa, and are considered by some to originate from non-metaplastic epithelium.[59]

As a group, however, early small carcinomas are more uniform in morphology. In advanced carcinoma, on the other hand, both Lauren types are often present and intestinalized mucosa invaded by signet-ring cells is not infrequently seen. This may be explained by the evolution of intestinalization after a signet-ring cell carcinoma had developed.

Another classification was proposed by Ming in 1977,[74] who divides gastric cancer into expanding (67%) and infiltrating (33%), which show differences in sex, age distribution and in prognosis and are similar to the intestinal and the diffuse types of Lauren respectively. Some of Ming's infiltrative carcinomas would be classified as Lauren's intestinal type.

A classification which perhaps supplements that of Lauren is that of Mulligan and Rember,[75] and Mulligan[76] describes two groups which are similar to the intestinal and diffuse but adds a third: the pylorocardiac gland carcinoma. This is supposed to originate in pyloric or cardiac glands but some tumours in this group could be classified as intestinal-type carcinoma. It is clear from all this that adenocarcinomas of the stomach can be broadly classified into two main groups and that this has shown itself to be of value in epidemiological studies. However, they are clearly far more diverse and this probably relates to the factors which are concerned in the neoplastic process and the degree to which this determines the properties of the resulting malignant cells.

Some tumours which do not fit neatly into the groups have rather distinct morphological features. One is a small celled anaplastic lymphoma-like tumour described by Grundmann.[77] This probably corresponds to the small cell carcinoma reported by others.[78] It is an aggressive tumour similar to small cell carcinoma of the lung.

Table 39.2 The prevalence of degree of differentiation according to the macroscopic types of early gastric cancer (EGC). ($p < 0.005$)

EGC-type	Degree of differentiation (No. of tumours) Well	Moderate	Poor	Total
Elevated	15	4	1	20
Depressed	8	5	10	23
Imperceptible	3	0	9	12
Ulcer associated	11	4	20	35
Total	37	13	40	90

Another, known as the indolent mucoid carcinoma,[79] is characterized by a large amount of extracellular mucus and is well demarcated. It is probably related histologically to the intestinal type but it has a fairly good prognosis.

Steiner et al[80] have also described a 'blue cell carcinoma', composed of uniformly distributed polygonal cells arranged in sheets or trabeculae. Its characteristic feature is a stroma composed of large numbers of lymphocytes and plasma cells and it is similar in this respect to medullary breast carcinoma,[81] and also has a good prognosis.

Multiplicity

Since carcinomas are always found in the stomach, which shows a degree of generalized gastritis, it is not surprising that multiple gastric cancers are common.[82–85]

Coexistent peptic ulcer is also a common finding, being present in 18% of specimens with early gastric cancer.[54,84]

Growth pattern and spread

Most gastric cancers are incurable at presentation, but in early carcinoma observed for over a period just in excess of 7 years, approximately one third developed advanced disease, whereas about one fifth remained as early tumours.[86]

Ignoring carcinomas that develop in polyps and ulcers, it thus seems reasonable to assume that the more usual carcinomas start as so-called early carcinomas. Even at the intramucosal stage, a carcinoma may give rise to lymph node metastases, but when the growth has reached the submucosal stage, about one fifth will have spread to lymph nodes and nodal metastases are three or more times as common when the tumour grows expansively rather than infiltratively.[87] When the growth extends beyond the submucosa, node involvement increases proportionately and 75% of carcinomas penetrating the serosa will have metastases.

The terminal stage of gastric carcinoma is dominated by remote metastases, both lymphatic and blood borne. Metastatic phenomena such as Virchows's gland and Krukenberg ovarian tumours are well known and widespread but the liver and peritoneum are particularly frequently involved.

Prognosis

The prognosis of gastric cancer is poor. The five year survival rate is between 5–10% in most Western countries.[54,88–90] The five year survival rate for those having a so-called curative operation rises to approximately 20%.[91,92] Of patients with incurable gastric cancer, which make up approximately half of all gastric cancer patients admitted to hospital, few will live more than one year.

Prognostic parameters are systematized in the well known TNM-classification.[93] Consequently, the prognosis is best for early gastric cancer and better for intramucosal cancer than for those with submucosal spread. Early gastric cancer without lymph node metastases has a five year survival rate of over 90% and even in advanced gastric cancer limited to the muscularis propria without lymph node metastases, the prognosis is almost as good.

Early diagnosis and treatment clearly results in a better prognosis[94] and with ever increasing knowledge and even earlier diagnosis, further improvements in the results of therapy can be predicted.

REFERENCES

1. Aoki K, Tominaga S, Kuroishi T. Age-adjusted death rates for cancer by site in 50 countries. GANN Monogr 1981; 26: 251–274.
2. Haenszel W. Variation in incidence of and mortality from stomach cancer with particular reference to the United States. J Natl Cancer Inst 1958; 21: 213–262.
3. Hirayama T. Changing patterns in the incidence of gastric cancer. In: Fielding J, Newman C, Ford C, Jones B, eds. Gastric Cancer. Oxford: Pergamon, 1981: pp 1–16.
4. Tominaga S, Ogawa H, Kuroishi T. Usefulness of correlation analyses in the epidemiology of stomach cancer. Natl Cancer Inst Monogr 1982; 2: 135–140.
5. Joossens JV, Geboers J. Epidemiology of gastric cancer: A clue to etiology. In: Sherlock P, Morson BC, Barbara L, Veronesi U, eds. Precancerous lesions of the gastrointestinal tract. New York: Raven, 1983: pp 97–114.
6. Munoz N, Correa P, Cuello C, Duque E. Histologic types of gastric carcinoma in high- and low-risk areas. Int J Cancer 1968; 3: 809–818.
7. Haenszel W, Kurihara M. Studies of Japanese migrants. I. Mortality from cancer and other diseases among Japanese in the United States. J Natl Cancer Inst 1968; 42: 43–68.
8. Correa P, Sasano N, Stemmermann G. Pathology of gastric carcinoma in Japanese populations: Comparisons between Miyagi Prefecture, Japan, and Hawaii. J Natl Cancer Inst 1973; 51: 1449–1459.
9. Clemmesen J, Nielsen A. The social distribution of cancer in Copenhagen 1943 to 1947. Br J Cancer 1951; 5: 159–171.
10. Hill MJ. Environmental and genetic factors in gastro-intestinal cancer. In: Sherlock P, Morson BC, Barbara L, Veronesi U, eds. Precancerous lesions of the gastro-intestinal tract. New York: Raven, 1983: pp 1–22.
11. Ogawa H, Kato I, Tominaga S. Family history of cancer among cancer patients. GANN 1985; 76: 113–118.
12. Morson BC, Sobin LH, Grundmann E, Johansen A, Nagayo T, Serck-Hanssen A. Precancerous conditions and epithelial dysplasia in the stomach. J Clin Pathol 1980; 33: 711–721.
13. Nagayo T. Precursors of human gastric cancer: Their frequencies and histological characteristics. In: Farber E et al, eds. Pathophysiology of carcinogenesis in digestive organs. Tokyo: University of Tokyo Press, 1977: pp 151–161.
14. Balfour DC. Factors influencing the life expectancy of patients operated on for gastric ulcer. Ann Surg 1922; 76: 405–408.
15. Domellof L, Eriksson S, Janunger K-G. Carcinoma and possible precancerous changes of the gastric stump after Billroth II resection. Gastroenterology 1977; 73: 462–468.
16. Schrumpf E, Serck-Hanssen A, Stadaas J, Aune S, Myren J, Osnes M. Mucosal changes in the gastric stump 20–25 years after partial gastrectomy. Lancet 1977; 2: 467–469.

17. Coma del Corral MJ, Pardo-Mindan FJ, Razquin S, Ojeda C. Risk of cancer in patients with gastric dysplasia. Follow-up study of 67 patients. Cancer 1990; 65: 2078–2085.
18. Bearzi I, Ranaldi R, Santinelli A, Mannello B, Mariuzzi GM. Epithelial dysplasia of the gastric mucosa. A morphometric and ploidy pattern study. Pathol Res Pract 1992; 188: 550–555.
19. Elster K. A new approach to the classification of gastric polyps. Endoscopy 1974; 6: 44–47.
20. Elster K. Histologic classification of gastric polyps. In: Morson BC, ed. Current topics in pathology. Vol. 63. Berlin: Springer, 1976: pp 77–93.
21. Nakamura T. Pathohistologische Einteilung der Magenpolypen mit spezifischer Betrachtung ihrer malignen Entartung. Chirurg 1970; 41: 122–130.
22. Ming S-C, Goldman H. Gastric polyps. A histogenetic classification and its relation to carcinoma. Cancer 1965; 18: 721–726.
23. Muto T, Oota K. Polypogenesis of gastric mucosa. GANN 1970; 61: 435–442.
24. Remmele W, Phannkuche S. Epitheliale Polypen und Drusen-korperzysten der Magenschleimhaut. Untersuchungen an 352 Polypen und Literaturubersicht. Pathologe 1979; 1: 25–39.
25. Jass JR. Role of intestinal metaplasia in the histogenesis of gastric carcinoma. J Clin Pathol 1980; 33: 801–810.
26. Daibo M, Itabashi M, Hirota T. Malignant transformation of gastric hyperplastic polyps. Amer J Gastroenterol 1987; 82: 1016–1025.
27. Mitsufuji S, Tsuchihashi Y, Isetani K, et al. A ten year observation of malignant changes in a hyperplastic polyp of the stomach — a cellular kinetic study using bromodeoxyuridine (BrdU). Gan No Rinsho 1990; 36: 1035–1041.
28. Cristallini EG, Ascani S, Bolis GB. Association between histologic type of polyp and carcinoma in the stomach. Gastrointest Endosc 1992; 38: 481–484.
29. Morson BC. Gastric polyps composed of intestinal epithelium. Br J Cancer 1955; 9: 550–557.
30. Nakano H, Persson B, Slezak P. Study of the gastric mucosal background in patients with gastric polyps. Gastrointest Endosc 1990; 36: 39–42.
31. Johansen A. Elevated early gastric carcinoma. Differential diagnosis as regards adenomatous polyps. Pathol Res Pract 1979; 164: 316–330.
32. Burnett KR, Keyser B, Tomasulo J, Edwards KC. Giant gastric villous adenoma. Am J Gastroenterol 1980; 74: 368–373.
33. Johansen A. Gastric polyps: pathology and malignant potential. In: Sherlock P, Morson BC, Barbara L, Veronesi U, eds. Precancerous lesions of the gastrointestinal tract. New York: Raven, 1983; pp 171–188.
34. Seifert E, Gail K, Weismuller J. Gastric polypectomy — Long term results (survey of 23 centres in Germany). Endoscopy 1983; 15: 8–11.
35. Konjetzny GE. Der Magenkrebs. Stuttgart: Enke, 1938.
36. Bettendorf U, Klinge O, Morgenroth K, Remmele W. Pathologie. 2. Verdauungsorgane. Ein Lehr-und Nachschla-gebuch. Berlin: Springer, 1984: p 203.
37. Morson BC, Dawson IMP. Gastrointestinal pathology. Oxford: Blackwell, 1972.
38. Tatsuta M, Okuda S, Tamura H, Taniguchi H. Gastric hamartomatous polyps in the absence of familial polyposis coli. Cancer 1980; 45: 818–823.
39. Weaver GA, Kleinman MS. Gastric polyposis due to multiple hyperplastic adenomatous polyps. Dig Dis Sci 1978; 23: 346–352.
40. Weinstock JV, Kawanishi H. Gastrointestinal polyposis with orocutaneous hamartomas (Cowden's disease). Gastroenterology 1978; 74: 890–895.
41. Watanabe H, Enjoji M, Yao T, Ohsato K. Gastric lesions in familial adenomatosis coli: their incidence and histologic analysis. Human Pathol 1978; 9: 269–83.
42. Bulow S, Lauritsen KB, Johansen AA, Svendsen LB, Sondergaard JO. Gastroduodenal polyps in familial polyposis coli. Dis Col Rect 1985; 28: 90–93.
43. Domizio P, Talbot IC, Spigelman AD, Williams CB, Phillips RK. Upper gastrointestinal pathology in familial adenomatous polyposis: results from a prospective study of 102 patients. J Clin Pathol 1990; 43: 738–743.
44. Nishiura M, Hirota T, Itabashi M, Ushio K, Yamada T, Oguro Y. A clinical and histopathological study of gastric polyps in familial polyposis coli. Am J Gastroenterol 1984; 79: 98–103.
45. Zeuzem S, Lembcke B, Hubner K, Schwab V, Caspary WF. Cystic polyposis of the stomach. Dtsch Med Wochenschr 1990; 115: 653–656.
46. Haruma K, Sumii K, Yoshihara M, Watanabe C, Kajiyama G. Gastric mucosa in female patients with fundic glandular polyps. J Clin Gastroenterol 1991; 13: 565–569.
47. Tomasulo J. Gastric polyps. Histologic types and their relationship to gastric cancer. Cancer 1971; 27: 1346–1355.
48. Sugano H, Nakamura K, Takagi K. An atypical epithelium of the stomach. GANN Monogr 1971; 11: 257–269.
49. Laxen F, Sipponen P, Ihamaki T, Hakkiluoto A, Dortscheva Z. Gastric polyps: their morphological and endoscopical characteristics and their relation to gastric carcinoma. Acta Path Microbiol Immunol Scand 1982; A90: 221–228.
50. Remmele W, Kolb E. Malignant transformation of hyperplasiogenic polyps of the stomach. Endoscopy 1978; 10: 63–65.
51. Nagayo T. Dysplasia of the gastric mucosa and its relation to the precancerous state. GANN 1981; 72: 813–823.
52. Nagayo T. Histological diagnosis of biopsied gastric mucosa with special reference to that of borderline lesions. GANN Monogr 1971; 11: 245–256.
53. Fukuchi S, Hiyama M, Mochizuki T. Endoscopic diagnosis of IIa-subtype of polypoid lesions which belong to borderline lesions between benignancy and malignancy. Stomach Intestine 1975; 10: 1487–1493.
54. Johansen AA. Early Gastric Cancer. A contribution to the pathology and to gastric cancer histogenesis. Copenhagen: Bispebjaerg Hospital, 1981.
55. Murakami T. Pathomorphological diagnosis. Definition and gross classification of early gastric cancer. GANN Monogr 1971; 11: 53–55.
56. Miller G, Kaugmann M. Das Magenfruhkarzinom in Europa. Dtsch Med Wschr 1975; 100: 1946–1949.
57. Borrmann R. Makroskopische Formen des vorgeschritteten Magenkrebses. In: Henke F, Lubarsch O, eds. Handbuch der speziellen pathologischen Anatomie und Histologie. Vol. 4/1. Berlin: Springer, 1926.
58. Oota K, Sobin LH. Histological typing of gastric and oesophageal tumours. International histological classification of tumours, No. 18. Genf: WHO, 1977.
59. Nakamura K. Histogenesis of gastric cancer and its clinical applications. Tsukuba International Center: Japan International Cooperation Agency, 1983.
60. Nagayo T, Komagoe T. Histological studies of gastric mucosal cancer with special reference to relationship of histological pictures between the mucosal cancer and the cancer-bearing gastric mucosa. GANN 1961; 52: 109–119.
61. Olivera P, Nobre-Leitao C, Chaves P. Early gastric cancer: an analysis of 44 cases with emphasis on the prognostic significance of the macroscopic and microscopic growth patterns. J Surg Oncol 1992; 51: 118–121.
62. Fujimori T, Nakamura T, Hirayama D, et al. Endoscopic mucosectomy for early gastric cancer using modified strip biopsy. Endoscopy 1992; 24: 187–189.
63. Lauren P. The two histological main types of gastric carcinoma: diffuse and so-called intestinal-type carcinoma. Acta Path Microbiol Scand 1965; 64: 31–49.
64. Jarvi O, Lauren P. On the role of heterotopias of the intestinal epithelium in the pathogenesis of gastric cancer. Acta Path Microbiol Scand 1951; 29: 26–44.
65. Jarvi O. Heterotopic tumours with an intestinal mucous membrane structure in the nasal cavity. Acta Oto-laryng (Stockh) 1945; 33: 471–485.
66. Jarvi O. A review of the part played by gastro-intestinal heterotopias in neoplasmogenesis. Proc Finn Acad Sci Lett 1961: 151–187.

67. Lauren P. Histochemical study on enzyme distribution in diffuse and intestinal-type gastric carcinoma. Acta Path Microbiol Scand 1967; (suppl 187): 62.
68. Hakkinen I, Jarvi O, Gronroos J. Sulphoglycoprotein antigens in the human alimentary canal and gastric cancer. An immunohistological study. Int J Cancer 1968; 3: 572–581.
69. Nevalainen T, Jarvi O. Ultrastructure of intestinal and diffuse type gastric carcinoma. J Pathol 1977; 122: 129–136.
70. Jarvi O, Nevalainen T, Ekfors T, Kulatunga A. The classification and histogenesis of gastric cancer. Proceedings of XI International Cancer Congress, Florence 1974. Excerpta Med (Amst) 1975; 6: 228–234.
71. Correa P, Cuello C, Duque E. Carcinoma and intestinal metaplasia of the stomach in Colombian migrants. J Nat Cancer Inst 1970; 44: 297–306.
72. Munoz N, Conelly R. Time trends of intestinal and diffuse types of gastric cancer in the United States. Int J Cancer 1971; 8: 158–164.
73. Munoz N, Asvall J. Time trends of intestinal and diffuse types of gastric cancer in Norway. Int J Cancer 1971; 8: 144–157.
74. Ming S-C. Gastric carcinoma. A pathobiological classification. Cancer 1977; 39: 2475–2485.
75. Mulligan RM, Rember RR. Histogenesis and biologic behaviour of gastric carcinoma. Arch Pathol 1954; 58: 1–25.
76. Mulligan RM. Histogenesis and biologic behaviour of gastric carcinoma. Pathol Ann 1972; 7: 349–415.
77. Grundmann E. Histologic types and possible initial stages in early gastric carcinoma. Beitr Pathol 1975; 154: 256–280.
78. Hussein AM, Otrakji CL, Hussein BT. Small cell carcinoma of the stomach: case report and review of the literature. Dig Dis Sci 1990; 35: 513–518.
79. Brander WL, Needham PRG, Morgan AD. Indolent mucoid carcinoma of stomach. J Clin Pathol 1974; 27: 536–541.
80. Steiner PD, Maimon SN, Palmer WL, Kirsner JB. Gastric cancer: morphologic factors in five-year survival after gastrectomy. Am J Pathol 1948; 24: 947–969.
81. Watanabe H, Enjoji M, Imai T. Gastric carcinoma with lymphoid stroma. Its morphological characteristics and prognostic correlations. Cancer 1976; 38: 232–243.
82. Moertel CG, Bargen A, Soule EH. Multiple gastric cancers. Gastroenterology 1957; 32: 1095–1103.
83. Nakamura K, Sugano H, Takagi K. Carcinoma of the stomach in incipient phase: Its histogenesis and histological appearances. GANN 1968; 59: 251–258.
84. Ostertag H, Georgii A. Early Gastric Cancer: A morphological study of 144 cases. Pathol Res Pract 1979; 164: 294–315.
85. Elster K, Thomasko A. Klinische Wertung der histologischen Typen des Magenfruhkarzinoms. Eine Analyse von 300 Fallen. Leber Magen Darm 1978; 8: 319–327.
86. Tsukuma H, Mishima T, Oshima A. Prospective study of 'early' gastric cancer. Int J Cancer 1983; 31: 421–426.
87. Kodama Y, Inokuchi K, Soejima K, Matsusaka T, Okamura T. Growth patterns and prognosis in early gastric carcinoma. Superficially spreading and penetrating growth types. Cancer 1983; 5: 320–326.
88. Inberg MV, Vuori J, Viikari SJ. Carcinoma of the stomach. A follow up study of 1963 patients. Acta Chir Scand 1972; 138: 195–201.
89. Buchholtz TW, Welch CE, Malt RA. Clinical correlates of resectability and survival in gastric carcinoma. Ann Surg 1978; 188: 711–715.
90. Dupont JB, Lee JR, Burton GR, Cohn I Jr. Adenocarcinoma of the stomach: review of 1497 cases. Cancer 1978; 41: 941–947.
91. Ohman V, Wetterfors J, Moberg A. Primary gastric cancer and its prognosis. Acta Chir Scand 1972; 138: 378–383.
92. Nielsen SAD, Amdrup E, Christiansen P, Fenger C, Jensen H-E, Nielsen J. Carcinoma of the stomach, an analysis of 385 cases treated 1955–64. Acta Chir Scand 1974; 140: 313–320.
93. Die Klassifizierung der malignen Tumoren nach dem TNM System. Berlin: Springer-Verlag, 1970.
94. Miwa K. Evaluation of the TNM classification of stomach cancer and proposal for its rational stage-grouping. Jpn J Clin Oncol 1984; 14: 385–410. Quoted after Nagayo (5).

PART II
Rare and secondary (metastatic) tumours

C. A. Rubio

Perceptions of what constitutes rarity differ widely. For example, gastric adenocarcinoma is rare in parts of Africa[1,2] and in children.[3] Asbestos exposure is a well-known but uncommon association,[4] and the tumour will rarely be reported as occurring in twins.[5]

Recent advances in histochemistry, immunohistochemistry and ultrastructure have resulted in reevaluation and reclassification of several tumours. The recent finding of six different types of normal exocrine pyloric cells in the human stomach,[6] for example, may well influence future classification of tumours arising there.

EPITHELIAL TUMOURS

Squamous cell papilloma

A single case of squamous cell papilloma of the stomach is on record.[7] It was described as a large mass involving almost the entire stomach from the oesophagus to the pylorus on the lesser curvature. Histologically, it consisted of mature hyperkeratotic squamous epithelium and, because of its extent, was described as squamous 'papillomatosis'. There were no metastases or signs of local invasion.

Brunner's gland adenoma

Gastric adenomas composed of Brunner's gland type are sometimes multiple.[8] They tend to be well circumscribed and are entirely benign, without cellular atypia.

Fundic gland polyp

These lesions are often seen as slight elevations in the fundic mucosa. The polyps are characterized by cystically dilated glands composed of parietal cells and chief cells. Fundic gland polyps are sometimes observed in patients with familial adenomatous polyposis[9,10] but are more common in patients without any genetic association. They have no malignant potential.

Villous adenoma

True villous adenomas of the stomach are uncommon.[11–14] Of all gastric tumours seen at the Armed Forces Institute of Pathology,[15] only 0.2% were villous adenomas. Of the 88 gastric adenomas reviewed at the Cancer Institute, Tokyo,[16] 3 were pure villous adenomas. The increased degree of epithelial dysplasia in gastric adenomas and the presence of foci of invasive adenocarcinoma have been found to correlate well with other non-histological parameters, such as abnormal DNA values[17] and increased nuclear area.[18]

Adenocarcinoma in hyperplastic polyps

Adenocarcinomas arising in hyperplastic gastric polyps may occur in about 2% of the cases.[19–21] It seems to be reported more frequently in the Japanese literature, and this may be due to differences in diagnostic criteria. Nevertheless, it does seem that malignancy may occasionally be seen in hyperplastic polyps of the stomach.

Small cell carcinoma

Small cell carcinomas, characterized by a monotonous proliferation of small fusiform to polygonal cells, hyperchromatic nuclei and scanty cytoplasm, have been described only recently in the gastric mucosa. These tumours are usually of so called 'intermediate cell type' and occasionally of 'oat cell type'. They are often mixed or composite with glandular or squamous cell differentiation but they can also be 'pure' small cell carcinomas. Histochemical analyses have shown argyrophilic granules in about half these tumours and many contain cells positive for chromogranin, neuron-specific enolase, CEA and keratin. Electron microscopical studies indicate that some of the tumours contain electron-dense core granules. So far, a total of 26 cases of small cell carcinoma of the stomach have been reported in the literature.[22,23]

Parietal cell adenocarcinoma

These invasive gastric tumours are composed of round and/or polygonal cells with abundant eosinophilic granular cytoplasm.[24] By transmission electron microscopy, the tumour cells were shown to contain abundant mitochondria, tubulovesicles, intracellular canaliculi and intracellular lumina containing microvilli. Histochemically, the abundant mitochondria can be demonstrated in Luxol fast blue and PTAH preparations. Strong cytoplasmic Vimentin positivity is usually demonstrated histochemically. A total of 9 cases have been reported so far in the literature. Adenocarcinomas with parietal cell differentiation have been reported to have a more favourable prognosis.[25]

Paneth cell adenoma

One case of Paneth cell adenoma of the stomach has been reported.[26] The dysplastic Paneth cells dominated the cell population in the adenoma (>95% of the cells). The coarse cytoplasmic granules stained red with eosin and PAS but remained unstained with Alcian-blue pH 2.5.[27] Paneth cell dysplasia of the stomach, without an exophytic adenomatous lesion, has also been recorded.[28]

Paneth cell adenocarcinoma

Gastric adenocarcinomas will uncommonly contain numerous Paneth cells showing typical light and electron microscopic granules and lysozyme immunoreactivity.[29] The cells are also present in the lymph node metastases.

Hepatoid gastric adenocarcinoma

There are several reported cases of adenocarcinomas of the stomach with histological and immunohistochemical features of hepatocellular differentiation.[30] They display a solid pattern with masses, nests and trabecula of large polygonal-shaped cells separated by fibrous stroma. Most of the tumour cells are positive for albumin, alpha-1-antitrypsin (AAT), alpha-fetoprotein (AFP), alpha-1-antichymotrypsin, albumin, prealbumin and transferrin. The immunohistochemical profiles are, however, not entirely specific since AFP is produced by other embryonal tumours and occurs in 6% of all gastric carcinomas.[31] The prognosis for hepatoid gastric carcinoma seems to be poor.

Adenocarcinoma with zymogen granules

A medullary gastric carcinoma containing zymogenic granules is also on record. The observation was made at electron microscopy.[32]

Adenocarcinoma in heterotopic pancreas

While pancreatic heterotopias are not uncommon in the human stomach, gastric adenocarcinomas arising in such foci are rare. They are of ductular type with considerable desmoplastic reaction. An important diagnostic feature is the presence of uninvolved ductular, acinar and islet pancreatic tissue. Since only 3 cases of adenocarcinoma in heterotopic pancreas have been reported,[33] it would appear that the heterotopic tissue has a low malignant potential.

Adenocarcinoma in a pyloric adenomyoma

Gastric adenomyomas are rare gastric tumours characterized by benign Brunner glands and antral type mucosa, embedded within a smooth muscle stroma. Most tumours occur in the antrum (85%). There are 3 cases of adenocarcinoma arising within a pyloric adenomyoma in the literature.[34]

Adenocarcinoma in a gastroduodenal fistula

The first case of adenocarcinoma occurring in a gastroduodenal fistula or 'double channel pylorus' was reported by Friehling and Rosenthal.[35] Endoscopic examination revealed two ulcers in the antrum along the lesser curvature and one ulcer in the duodenal bulb. The gastric carcinoma extended through the wall of the distal antrum and invaded the pancreas.

Squamous cell carcinoma

To establish a diagnosis of squamous cell carcinoma of the stomach, the tumour has to be unrelated to the cardiac region, and the cells should show evidence of keratinization and intercellular bridges. Moreover, the presence of keratin with high concentrations of sulphydryl or disulphide groups should be demonstrated histochemically. There is uncertainty regarding the origin of these tumours. They are thought to arise from areas of squamous metaplasia, induced either by chemicals or by peptic ulceration. Some 82 cases of squamous cell carcinoma of the stomach have appeared in the literature,[36] including 2 cases of squamous cell carcinoma in the remnant following Billroth II gastrectomy for peptic ulcer disease.[37]

Choriocarcinoma

A total of 67 cases of choriocarcinoma of the stomach have been documented, mainly in Japanese patients.[38–41] Only 28% of these had choriocarcinomatous tissue exclusively, the remaining cases being mixed with adenocarcinomatous components. In 13% of the choriocarcinomas reported, the trophoblastic elements were present only at the site of the metastases. Beta-human chorionic gonadotrophin, human placental lactogen, and pregnancy-specific beta-s-glycoprotein may be demonstrated in syncytial trophoblastic and even in cytotrophoblastic tumour cells. The origin of this malignant epithelial tumour is debated, but it probably simply manifests the differentiation potential of the malignant cells.

Epithelial tumours in children

Benign epithelial gastric tumours in children are very rare and include single case reports of giant solitary hyperplastic polyps. A tubular adenoma arising at the umbilicus in ectopic gastric mucosa is also on record.[42] Malignant neoplasms of the stomach are particularly uncommon in children, even in high incidence areas, and the majority are lymphomas or sarcomas.[43] There are only 62 reported gastric malignancies in Japanese children.[44] Histologically, the majority are undifferentiated or unclassifiable, and only 7 cases were diagnosed as signet-ring cell adenocarcinoma. In the English literature, a mucinous adenocarcinoma was reported in a 20-month-old child[45,46] and an adenocarcinoma histologically resembling linitis plastica in a 15-year-old.

Ciliated metaplasia in adenomas and adenocarcinomas

Ciliated gastric cells may occur in the non-neoplastic dilated pyloric glands which occur beneath gastric adenomas or early adenocarcinomas. In one study, 43% of 87 consecutive gastric adenomas or intestinal type adenocarcinoma in Japanese patients living in Japan[47] or in Hawaii[48] were shown to contain ciliated cells. Similar cells also occurred, although less frequently, in association with intramucosal diffuse gastric cancer and benign peptic ulcers. Interestingly, ciliated gastric cells are uncommon in Europeans,[49] in mainland Americans[51] and Mexicans.[52] It has been claimed that the proliferation of dysplastic or malignant cells in the neck region of the pyloric glands leads to glandular mucous retention with cyst formation. Ciliated metaplasia may be an adaptative phenomenon, aiming to expel the retained mucus. Although ciliated dysplastic or malignant gastric cells have not yet been demonstrated, a case of glandular tumour cells with cilia was found in a Barrett's adenocarcinoma.[53]

ENDOCRINE TUMOURS

These are described in detail in Chapter 36.

Gastrinoma

Extrapancreatic gastrinomas usually occur near the lesser curve, in lymph nodes or in extranodal tissue near the stomach, but not in the gastric mucosa proper.[54] Occasionally, they are in the wall,[55] sometimes multiple and associated with Menetrier's disease. Both benign and malignant tumours express a subunit of human chorionic gonadotropin protein (alpha-HCG). However, only malignant gastrinomas express adrenocorticotrophic hormone protein or propiomelanocortin (POMC) mRNA. In addition, in-situ and northern hybridization analyses may reveal a chromogranin A mRNA as the most common member of the chromogranin/secretogranin family.

Non-chromaffin paragangliomas (chemodectomas)

Four cases of non-chromaffin paragangliomas of the stomach have appeared in the literature.[56,57] Only one of these behaved aggressively and metastasized to the bones.

MESODERMAL TUMOURS (see Chapter 35)

Mesodermal tumours are a heterogenous group whose behaviour is often difficult to assess. Histologically, the tumours are usually classified as smooth muscle, probably smooth muscle, probably nerve sheath tumours or tumours of undetermined differentiation.[58] Immunohistochemical techniques have shown that mesenchymal tumours of the stomach react with a variety of antibodies to smooth muscle, neural and even histiocyte antigens.[59]

Since tumours with similar histological features prove to have disparate final outcomes, other methods of categorizing them have been applied. DNA flow cytometry, for example, has shown that DNA ploidy is an independent parameter in predicting the clinical outcome for patients with gastric stromal neoplasms.[60,61]

Lipomas

Three-quarters of all gastric lipomas are located in the antrum and 95% originate in the submucosa, the remainder being subserosal. They are usually sessile, with smooth contours, and appear yellow through the overlying gastric mucosa.[62–64] Gastric lipomas are today being removed by endoscopic procedures.

Angiolipomas

A single case of angiolipoma which was removed endoscopically has been reported.[65]

Liposarcomas

These locally aggressive tumours tend to become large and, of three treated by gastrectomy,[66] there was no recurrence.

Histiocytosis X

In histiocytosis X of the stomach, the tumors are characterized by a proliferation of histiocytes showing interdigitating cytoplasmic projections and Birbeck granules at electron microscopy. The tumour derives from the histiocytes of the dendritic cell system, namely from Langerhans cells or interdigitating reticulum cells of the T-zone. The case reported by Iwafuchi et al[67] showed a spontaneous regression after 5 years of follow-up.

Malignant fibrous histiocytoma

Gastric malignant fibrous histiocytoma may be multicentric with tumours in other parts of the bowel. By and large, they exhibit the same histological features as similar tumours in other sites.[68,69]

Alveolar soft-part sarcoma

Only one case of alveolar soft-part sarcoma of the stomach has been described.[70] The large eosinophilic cells showed the characteristics of alveolar compartmentalization and contained intracytoplasmic periodic acid-Shiff-positive granules and typical elongated crystals. At electron microscopy, numerous electron-opaque secretory granules as well as crystals of 9 nm periodicity are found. Immunohistochemistry showed methionin, kefalin and neuropeptide Y in tumour cells. This suggests that gastric alveolar soft-part sarcoma may be of neuroendocrine origin; the tumour gave positive reactions to NSE, S-100, NPY and M-INK in addition to showing argyrophilia. Thus it would appear to have similarities to pargangliomas and a paraganglial origin has been suggested.

Inflammatory fibrosarcoma

Inflammatory fibrosarcomas in the stomach are usually composed of fibroblasts, myofibroblasts and plasma cells with variable degrees of fibrosis and calcification. Immunostains indicate myofibroblastic differentiation.[71] Similar differentiation can be observed at ultrastructural level. The tumours show local aggressive behaviour and usually metastasize.

MUSCLE TUMOURS

Smooth muscle tumours are discussed in detail in Chapter 35.

Striated muscle tumours

Striated muscle tumours may occur, not only in the oesophagus but also in the stomach.[72,73] The submucosal tumours are composed of closely packed, oval, round and elongated cells with abundant eosinophilic cytoplasm. Strap-like cells with transverse parallel cytoplasmic bridges, long fibres with two to three peripheral eccentric nuclei, myofibrils and faint but distinct cross-striations are present. The cells may contain irregular, elongated narrow structures resembling myosin crystals. Each individual cell is surrounded by reticulin fibres. An embryonal rhabdomyosarcoma (sarcoma botryoides) occurred in a 5-year-old female child[43] which, at autopsy, appeared as an ulcerated pedunculated polyp on the anterior and posterior wall. It had metastasized to the liver, ovaries, lungs, bone marrow and cerebellum. A further case is described in a 3-year-old male negro child.[73]

VASCULAR TUMOURS

Using immunohistochemical techniques, it is now possible to assess the vascular nature of gastric tumours. The presence of cells of endothelial origin in routine material can be determined by using a small panel of three reagents (factor VIII-related antigen, CD31 (JC70) and CD34 (QBend 10).[74]

Haemangioma

Only 59 of 10 079 gastric tumours reviewed by Palmer[75] were vascular. The majority were cavernous haemangiomas, capillary haemangiomas being rare. The histological appearances are similar to haemangiomas in other organs. Recently, a case of calcified cavernous haemangioma of the stomach was reported.[76] A review of the literature by Yamaguchi et al[77] indicates that a total of 53 cases were recorded up to 1991.

Angiosarcoma

Angiosarcomas are decidedly rare; only a few cases are described.[78]

Lymphangioma

Gastric lymphangiomas are even less common than haemangiomas,[79] and occasionally occur in childhood. They are often classified histologically as lymphangioma simplex, cavernous lymphangioma or cystic lymphangioma.

Glomus tumours (glomangioma)

Although usually relatively small, gastric glomangiomas are often larger than their cutaneous counterpart and draw attention because of their propensity to ulcerate and bleed.[80] They arise usually in the antrum, either in the submucosa or muscular layer, and have histological appearances typical of glomangiomas in other sites.

At electron microscopy, glomus tumour cells have features of smooth muscle. They are immunoreactive for alpha-smooth muscle actin, Vimentin, laminin and type IV collagen, but they do not express desmin. In the stomach, glomus tumours contain histologically solid areas, areas with mucoid-hyalin differentiation and with angiomatous differentiation. These tumours should be distinguished from epitheloid leiomyoblastoma, haemangiopericytoma, carcinoid, lymphoma and carcinoma. Approximately 75 cases of glomangiomas of the stomach have been reported in the literature.[80] No case of glomangiosarcoma has been reported in the stomach.

Haemangiopericytomas

These rare gastric tumours are usually composed of epithelioid or spindle cells which surround thin-walled blood vessels. The presence of such concentrically arranged pericytes is crucial for the diagnosis. While extragastric haemangiopericytomas behave as malignant neoplasms prone to develop local recurrence and metastases in up to 45% of cases, in the stomach they appear to be less aggressive: local recurrences or metastases are much less frequent. Recently, a case of haemangiopericytoma of the stomach in a neonate has been reported.[81]

LYMPHOID TUMOURS

These are discussed in detail in Chapter 37.

Plasmacytoma

Plasmacytoma of the stomach is a rare disease and amounts to about 5% of all cases of extramedullary plasmacytomas reported in the Japanese and English literature.[82–84] Immunohistochemically, some cases are positive for IgM and others for IgA. The majority are positive for anti-epithelial membrane antibody and a monoclonal population of B-cells can be demonstrated.

NEUROGENIC TUMOURS

Tumours of nervous tissue account for only 0.2% of all gastric tumours and tumour-like conditions.[85–88] They originate in the elements of Auerbach's and, less frequently, Meissner's plexus. Those that arise in the nerve sheath are schwannomas, neurofibromas, which may be plexiform and ganglionated neurofibromas, or granular cell tumours (granular cell myoblastoma); all are benign.

The malignant counterparts are the neurogenic sarcomas and the plexosarcomas. Another group is neuroblastic and includes ganglioneuroma and neuroblastoma.

Benign tumours

Schwannomas (neurilemmomas)

From a total of 194 neurogenic tumours, 128 (66%) were schwannomas.[87–89] Schwannomas are usually solitary, mainly submucosal and often ulcerated on their luminal surface. They may achieve considerable size, but are usually encapsulated, and they must be distinguished from leiomyomas. Schwannomas are, however, positive for S-100 neuronspecific enolase and microfilament proteins, whereas smooth muscle tumours can contain myoglobin, desmin and Vimentin.

Neurofibromas

Recently, a case of rapidly growing gastric myxoid neurofibroma was reported. Immunohistochemically, the tumour was positive for S-100 protein and NSE. These tumours may occur as solitary primary lesions or, less frequently, as a part of generalized systemic neurofibromatosis (von Recklinghausen's disease).[86] Generalized neurofibromatosis with gastric involvement was reviewed by Petersen and Ferguson,[90] who compiled only 16 cases. In only one of these was a sarcomatous change present. Patients with gastric neurofibromas may have high serum levels of nerve growth stimulating factor and may also show hyperplasia of Auerbach's plexus in other parts of the gastrointestinal tract.

Granular cell tumour (granular cell myoblastoma)

According to recent studies.[91–94] granular cell tumours of the stomach arise in Schwann cells surrounding small vessels in the submucosa.

The lesions are firm, poorly circumscribed, with a yellow-white cut surface, and are composed of nests of typical polygonal cells with a centrally located dark nucleus. The relatively abundant cytoplasm contains diastase-resistant PAS-positive granules. At electron microscopy, a multilayered basal lamina is often seen around islands of tumour cells, and non-myelinated axons in contact with their cytoplasm may also be present. These mainly submucosal tumours may extend into the muscularis propria, but despite this apparently 'invasive' pattern, granular cell tumours in the stomach are benign and are found incidentally at endoscopy or at autopsy. Malignant granular cell tumours of the stomach do, however, exist but it is vascular invasion and size, rather than cytological features which are the important indicators of malignant behaviour. Immunochemistry is valuable in the diagnosis of these tumours, since they react with S-100 antisera, a fact which also supports the neurogenic nature of these neoplasms.

Malignant tumours

Plexosarcoma

Plexosarcomas are unique gastrointestinal neoplasms that appear to form a distinct subset of gastrointestinal tumours.[88] These tumours are also known as gastrointestinal autonomic nerve tumours (GANT), showing neuroaxonal differentiation including interdigitating cytoplasmic processes and scattered aggregates of membrane-bound dense core granules and empty vesicles. They immunoreact for Vimentin, NSE, synaptophysin and neurofilament with variable positivity for S-100 protein and chromogranin, and are focally positive for neurofilament triplet protein (NFTP) 160. Tumours with a diffuse positive reaction for S-100 protein indicate a Schwann cell origin. Although gastric autonomic nerve tumours have been reported to have a deceptively low-grade malignant appearance by light microscopy, they follow an aggressive clinical course.

Neurogenic sarcomas

In 1981, Shivshanker and Bennetts[95] claimed to have reported the first case of primary neurogenic sarcoma of the stomach in the English literature. However, Ransom and Kay[96] had already reported 3 cases some 40 years earlier. Neurogenic sarcomas would appear to be only locally aggressive tumours and do not give rise to distant metastases. Whether such tumours arise in neurilemmomas or arise de novo is uncertain. The development of immunohistochemical techniques have demonstrated that many gastrointestinal stromal tumours show a neural differentiation and about 13%[72] have a neural differentiation with positivity for S-100 protein. In another series[73] 36% of 60 stromal tumours showed neural differentiation, 31% smooth muscular differentiation, 20% manifested B-directional differentiation and 13% were negative for all markers used. Interestingly, tumours with a neural phenotype have the best prognosis of all gastrointestinal stromal tumours.

Ganglioneuroma and ganglioneuroblastoma

Relatively few cases of ganglioneuroma have been reported in the literature.[97–99] Ganglioneuromas tend to be well circumscribed and encapsulated tumours which appear yellowish and semitranslucent, thus resembling adipose tissue. The tumours are usually lobulated due to the presence of fibrous septae, and between these septae, ganglion cells of variable size, sometimes multinucleated, are observed. The cells, which in toluidine blue preparations show Nissl substance, are surrounded by a compact fibrillar neurogenic stroma. Like ganglioneuromas in other sites, these gastric tumours are benign.

In contrast, ganglioneuroblastomas frequently metastasize. These tumours have the typical histological appearances of similar tumours in other sites, and a variable neuroblastomatous component. However, the neuroblasts are arranged in trabeculae or round clusters and tend not to form the characteristic rosettes present in neuroblastomas in other organs.

MIXED TUMOURS

On occasions, tumours of the stomach are found to contain more than one type of tissue. Others are collision tumours in which two (or more) separate tumours are seen to collide within one tumour mass. Finally, coexistant tumours are those growing synchronously in the same organ but separated by non-neoplastic gastric mucosa.

Teratomas

These occur in children under one year old and almost exclusively in males.[100–104] Some attain considerable size, with displacement of the diaphragm resulting in respiratory distress. They often occur in the greater curvature, and commonly contain neural tissue. Squamous epithelium and its derivatives, together with transitional and cuboidal epithelium, are found, as are a variety of connective tissue and bone. Gastric teratomas are mature benign lesions, with an excellent prognosis after excision. Approximately 59 cases of gastric teratomas have been reported, including 1 case in an infant which was malignant.

Carcinosarcomas

In the past, much has been written concerning tumours in which both epithelial and stromal elements appear malignant. So-called carcinosarcomas of the stomach are more common in middle-aged men, and localize predominantly in the pyloric region. They are associated with a high mortality rate due to aggressive local behaviour, but metastases are seldom seen.[105,106] Attempts have been made to subdivide carcinosarcomas according to whether they have arisen by collision or whether they are true mixed tumours. When the combination of malignancies is lymphoma and adenocarcinoma, then collision or coincidental association is the usual interpretation. Some tumours, however, have a distinctive adenocarcinomatous component and a sarcomatous stromal element, and in such cases divergent differentiation of a single stem cell is implicated. Differentiation with more than two patterns is seen on occasions. Some carcinosarcomas show areas resembling oat cell carcinoma with intracytoplasmic endocrine granules. Such divergent differentiation potential is certainly described in experimental situations. Some 43 mixed tumours have been recorded, and whilst some were of collision type, others clearly represent aberrations of differentiation. This phenomenon is also illustrated by tumours which exhibit features of carcinoid and adenocarcinoma.

Adenosquamous carcinoma

These tumours have adenocarcinomatous and squamous carcinomatous elements,[107] both components being capable of metastasis. By convention, this property is said to differentiate adenosquamous carcinomas from adenoacanthomas, in which the squamous component is well differentiated and does not metastasize. Both, however, simply represent different degrees of expression of the same disturbance in differentiation and one further example of the disturbances of differentiation inherent in the malignant process.

Coexisting tumours

The coexistence of adenocarcinomas and lymphomas is a not uncommon event which has been reviewed by Lin et al.[108] Other coexisting tumours which have been reported are adenocarcinoma and leiomyosarcoma, adenocarcinoma and rhabdomyosarcoma,[109] adenocarcinoma of the cardiac end colliding with a squamous carcinoma of the oesophagus and gastric adenocarcinoma colliding with carcinoid tumours.

Composite tumours

Exocrine-endocrine cell carcinoma of the stomach are rare, only 21 well-documented cases being reported up to 1991,[110] They usually have a poor prognosis and sometimes they show an amphicrine differentiation.[111,112] The fundamental feature is that the tumour is discreetly separated into adenocarcinoma and carcinoid parts. They are juxtaposed but not admixed. Tumours are classified as truly mixed only if both components are present in significant proportions, i.e. endocrine cells must comprise at least one third to one half of an adenocarcinoma. Using this strict definition, few gastric carcinomas with endocrine cells qualify as truly mixed. The tumours show distinctive immunoreactivity. Neuroendocrine markers (Cga and NSE) are expressed in the carcinoid cells but are largely absent from the adenocarcinomatous epithelium. In contrast, immunoreactivity for CEA and BD-5 is found in the non-endocrine glands.

MISCELLANEOUS TUMOURS, TUMOUR ASSOCIATIONS AND TUMOUR-LIKE CONDITIONS (INCLUDING PESUDOTUMOURS)

Adenocarcinoma with lymphoid stroma

A marked stromal lymphoid reaction was observed in 42 of 1049 consecutive gastric adenocarcinomas and appears to be associated with a higher survival rate.[113]

Kaposi's sarcoma

Gastric involvement when there is disseminated Kaposi's sarcoma is well documented[114–116] and the lesions appear to have the same histological features as in other organs.

The gastric sarcoma of Carney's triad

Carney[117,118] described the simultaneous occurrence of multiple gastric epithelioid sarcoma, pulmonary chondroma and extra-adrenal paraganglioma. The gastric lesion has a propensity for local recurrence, but does not metastasize and has light and electron microscopic features of a smooth muscle tumour.

Adenocarcinomas in multicentric reticulohistiocytosis

Multicentric reticulohistiocytosis is a rare skin disease characterized by papulonodular lesions in the skin and a progressive destructive arthropathy in approximately half of the cases. It is a chronic disease in which malignant tumours may occur. Three cases of adenocarcinoma of the stomach in patients with multicentric reticulohistiocytosis have appeared in the literature.[117,118]

Adenocarcinoma and acanthosis nigricans

The most common malignancy associated with acanthosis nigricans is gastric adenocarcinoma[119] a tumour which also sometimes occurs in patients with acanthosis palmares.[120]

Amyloid tumours

These lesions, usually located at the antrum, may be associated with diffuse infiltration of the gastric mucosa and present as a mass, often with central ulceration.[121,122] The cut surface is either homogeneous or displays confluent nodules. The amorphous eosinophilic material in H&E-stained preparations is often surrounded by a foreign-body reaction. Amyloid deposits may also be present in medium-sized blood vessels in other organs.

Inflammatory lesions

The so-called fibroid polyp[123] and plasma cell granuloma[124] are basically inflammatory lesions which, although they may mimic tumours clinically, are easily differentiated at histological examination.

Parasitic eosinophilic granuloma

Parasitic eosinophilic granulomas of the stomach may resemble a submucosal tumour. The histological examination may reveal an abscess surrounded by eosinophilic granulocytes in the submucosal layer and in the upper part of the muscle layer. The granulomatous eosinophilic reaction of the submucosal layer may be due to the presence of parasitic larvae (Anisakis-like).[125]

Other inflammatory reactions giving rise to false tumour diagnosis are due to rare examples of primary gastric tuberculosis.[126]

Gastric bezoars

Gastric bezoars are foreign bodies composed of vegetable fibres or hair and result from poor motility or altered gastric anatomy. Gastric bezoars can also be caused by lecithin (in a patient ingesting large amounts of lecithins believed to lower cholesterol levels and improve memory). One rare case of bezoar developed after a gastric stapling procedure following partial gastrectomy.[127,128]

Thorotrast-induced adenocarcinoma

One rare case of gastric cancer 47 years after thorotrast injection has been described.[129]

SECONDARY (METASTATIC) TUMOURS

20% of melanomas are said to metastasize to the stomach.[130] and as many as 15% of mammary carcinomas. Bronchial carcinomas and germ cell tumours also metastasize to the gastric wall, but others such as thyroid, uterine, ovarian and pancreatic cancers do so rarely.

A rare manifestation of myeloid leukaemia was recorded in two instances, when a granulocytic sarcoma of the stomach preceeded the signs of haematological malignancy.

Recently, a case of Merckel cell carcinoma metastasizing to the stomach, resulting in profuse gastrointestinal bleeding, was reported.[131] Finally, an oesophageal carcinoma metastasizing to an early gastric cancer was noted in a Japanese.[130]

The subject of gastrointestinal metastatic disease is covered in depth in Chapter 40.

REFERENCES

1. Cook PJ, Burkitt DP. Cancer in Africa. Br Med Bull 1971; 27: 14–20.
2. Oettle AG. Cancer in Africa, especially in regions south of the Sahara. J Natl Cancer Inst 1964; 33: 383–439.
3. Magazzu G, Familiari L, Ruggeri C, Germanotta G, Bonica M, Sperlazzas SC. Case of solitary hyperplastic polyp of the stomach in a child (abstract). I Corso Internationale de Aggiornamento. In Diagnostica e Chirurgia Endoscopia. December 2–4, 1984, Catania, Sicily. Societa Italiana di Endoscopia Digestiva 1982: pp 304.
4. Selikoff IJ, Churg J, Cuyler-Hammond E. Asbestos exposure and neoplasia. CA J Clin 1984; 34: 48–56.
5. Cwern N, Garcia RL, Davidson MI, Friedman IM. Simultaneous occurrence of gastric carcinoma in identical twins. Am J Gastroenterol 1981; 75: 41–47.
6. Rubio CA. Five types of pyloric cells in the antral mucosa of the stomach. Path Res Pract 1992; 188: 157–161.
7. Carr GL, Squires G. Squamous papillomatosis of the stomach. A new pathologic entity: Report of a case. Am Surg 1962; 28: 790–793.
8. Williams WA, Michie W. Adenomatosis of the stomach of Brunner gland type. Br J Surg 1957; 45: 259–263.
9. Watanabe H, Enjoji M, Yao T, Ohsato K. Gastric lesions in familial adenomatosis coli. Their incidence and histologic analysis. Hum Pathol 1978; 9: 269–283.
10. Domizio P, Talbot IC, Spigelman AD, Williams CB, Phillips RKS. Upper gastrointestinal pathology in familial adenomatous polyposis: results from a prospective study of 102 patients. J Clin Pathol 1990; 43: 738–743.
11. Fieber SS, Boden RE. Polypoid villous adenoma of the stomach. Am J Gastroenterol 1977; 68: 286–289.
12. Freeny PC, Vimont TR. Villous tumours of the stomach and small bowel. Arch Surg 1978; 113: 255–259.
13. Rotterdam H, Sommers SC. Biopsy diagnosis of the digestive tract. New York: Raven Press, 1981.
14. Miller JH, Gisvold JJ, Weiland LH, McIlrath DC. Upper gastrointestinal tract: villous tumours. AJR 1980; 134: 933–936.
15. Ming SC. Atlas of tumour pathology. Fasc 7: Tumours of the esophagus and stomach. Armed Forces Inst Pathol 1973.
16. Rubio CA, Kato Y, Sugano H. The intramucosal cysts of the stomach. VI. Their quantitative and qualitative characteristics in focal (elevated) neoplastic lesions. Pathol Res Pract 1984; 179: 105–109.
17. Rubio CA, Kato Y. DNA profiles in mitotic cells from gastric adenomas. Am J Pathol 1988; 130: 485–488.
18. Rubio CA, May I. A method for quantitating the nuclear area of gastric polyps using image analysis. Analyt Quant Cytol Histol 1990; 12: 117–121.
19. Daibo M, Itabashi M, Hirota T. Malignant transformation of gastric hyperplastic polyps. Am J Gastroenterol 1987; 82: 1016–1025.
20. Yamaguchi K, Shiraishi G, Maeda S, Kitamura K. Adenocarcinoma in hyperplastic polyp of the stomach. Am J Gastroenterol 1990; 85(3): 327–328.

21. Ichiyoshi Y, Saku M, Maekawa S, Ikejiri K, Muranaka T, Iwashita A. Poorly differentiated adenocarcinoma developed in a hyperplastic polyp of the stomach; Report of a case. Stomach and Intestine (Tokyo) 1992; 27(6): 695–699.
22. Matsui K, Kitagawa M, Miwa A, Kuroda Y, Tsuji M. Small cell carcinoma of the stomach: A clinicopathologic study of 17 cases. Am J Gastroenterol 1991; 86: 1167–1174.
23. Hussein AM, Otrakji CL, Hussein BT. Small cell carcinoma of the stomach. Case report and review of the literature. Dig Dis Sci 1990; 35: 513–518.
24. Rychterova V, Hagerstrand I. Parietal cell carcinoma of the stomach. APMIS 1991; 99: 1008–1012.
25. Gaffney EF. Favourable prognosis in gastric carcinoma with parietal cell differentiation. Histopathol 1987; 11: 217–218.
26. Rubio CA. Paneth cell adenoma of the stomach. Am J Surg Pathol 1989; 13: 325–328.
27. Rubio CA, Porwit-McDonald A, Rodensj M, Duvander A. A method of quantitating Paneth cell metaplasia of the stomach by image analysis. Analyt Quant Cytol Histol 1989; 11: 115–118.
28. Falck VG, Wright NA. Paneth cell dysplasia in the stomach. Am J Surg Pathol 1990; 14: 200–201.
29. Heitz PU, Wegmann W. Identification of neoplastic Paneth cells in an adenocarcinoma of the stomach using lysozyme as a marker, and electron microscopy. Virchows Arch (A) 1980; 386: 107–116.
30. Matias-Guiu X, Guix M. Hepatoid gastric adenocarcinoma. Path Res Pract 1989; 185:397–400.
31. Caruso RA. Hepatoid gastric adenocarcinoma. A histological and immunohistological study of a case. Eur J Basic Appl Histochem 1991; 35: 203–209.
32. Sasano N, Nakamura K, Arai M, Akazaki K. Ultrastructural cell patterns in human gastric carcinoma compared with non-neoplastic gastric mucosa — histogenetic analysis of carcinoma by mucin histochemistry. J Natl Cancer Inst 1969; 43: 783–802.
33. Goldfarb WB, Bennett D, Monafo W. Carcinoma in heterotopic gastric pancreas. Am Surg 1963; 158: 56–58.
34. Kneafsey PD, Demetrick DJ. Malignant transformation in a pyloric adenomyoma: a case report. Histopathol 1992; 20: 433–435.
35. Friehling JS, Rosenthal LE. Gastric carcinoma presenting as double-channel pylorus on upper gastrointestinal series. Dig Dis Sci 1985; 30: 269–273.
36. Ruck P, Wehrmann M, Campbell M, Horny HP, Breucha G, Kaiserling E. Squamous cell carcinoma of the gastric stump. A case report and review of the literature. Am J Surg Pathol 1989; 13: 317–324.
37. Piper MH, Ross JM, Bever FN, Shartsis JM, Mohammadi D. Primary squamous cell carcinoma of a gastric remnant. Am J Gastroenterol 1991; 86: 1080–1092.
38. Yakeishi Y, Mori M, Enjoji M. Distribution of beta-human chorionic gonadotropin-positive cells in noncancerous gastric mucosa and in malignant gastric tumours. Cancer 1990; 66: 695–701.
39. Matsunaga N, Hayashi K, Futagawa S, Fukuda T, Takahara O, Yoshida K, Maeda H. Primary choriocarcinoma of the stomach presenting as gastrointestinal hemmorhage: report of a case. Radiat Med 1989; 7: 220–222.
40. Gorczyca W, Woyke S. Endoscopic brushing cytology of primary gastric choriocarcinoma. A case report. Acta Cytol 1992; 36: 551–554.
41. Lombard F, Burtin P, Ketani S, Delaby J, Cales P, Boyer J. Mediastinal poserior choriocarcinoma with hemmorhagic gastric metastasis: endosonographic features. Gastrointest Endosc 1992; 38: 187–190.
42. Bambirra EA, Miranda D. Gastric polyp of the umbilicus in an 8-year-old boy. Clin Pediatr 1980; 19: 430–432.
43. Mahour GH, Isaacs H, Chang L. Primary malignant tumors of the stomach in children. J Pediatr Surgery 1980; 15: 603–608.
44. Siegel SE, Hays DM, Romansky S, Isaacs H. Carcinoma of the stomach in childhood. Cancer 1976; 38: 1781–1784.
45. Goto S, Ikeda K, Ishii E, Miyazaki S, Shimizu S, Iwashito A. Carcinoma of the stomach in a 7-year-old boy — a case report and a review of the literature on children under 10 years of age. Z Kinderchir 1984; 39: 137–140.
46. Black RE. Linitis plastica in a child. J Pediatr Surg 1985; 20: 86–87.
47. Rubio CA, Kato Y. Ciliated metaplasia in the gastric mucosa. Studies on Japanese patients. Jpn J Cancer Res 1986; 77: 282–286.
48. Rubio CA, Stemmermann GN, Hayashi T. Ciliated gastric cells among Japanese living in Hawaii. Jpn J Cancer Res 1991; 82: 86–89.
49. Rubio CA, Serck-Hanssen A. Ciliated metaplasia in the gastric mucosa. II. In a European patient with gastric carcinoma. Pathol Res Pract 1986; 181: 382–384.
50. Rubio CA. Ciliated metaplasia in a gastric carcinoma in a Swedish patient. APMIS 1988; 96: 895–897.
51. Rubio CA, Antonioli D. Ciliated metaplasia in the gastric mucosa in an American patient. Am J Surg Pathol 1988; 12: 786–789.
52. Rubio CA, Jessurun J, Alonso de Ruiz P. Geographic variations in the histologic characteristics of the gastric mucosa. Am J Clin Pathol 1991; 96: 330–333.
53. Rubio CA, •berg B. Barrett's mucosa in conjunction with squamous carcinoma of the esophagus. Cancer 1991; 68: 583–586.
54. Wolfe MM, Alexander RW, McGuigan JE. Extrapancreatic, extraintestinal gastrinoma. N Engl J Med 1982; 306: 1533–1536.
55. Perkins PL, McLeod MK, Jin L, Fukuuchi A, Cho KJ, Thompson NW, Lloyd RV. Analysis of gastrinomas by immunohistochemistry and in situ hybridization and histochemistry. Diagn Mol Pathol 1992; 1: 155–164.
56. Delamare J, Potet F, Capron JP, Minh HN, Lorriaux A. Chemodectome gastrique. Etude d'un cas et revue de la litterature. Arch Fr Mal App Dig 1975; 64: 339–346.
57. Westbrook KC, Bridger WM, Williams GD. Malignant nonchromaffin paraganglioma of the stomach. Am J Surg 1972; 124: 407–409.
58. Ueyama T, Guo K-J, Hashimoto H, Daimaru Y, Enjoji M. A clinicopathologic and immunohistochemical study of gastrointestinal stromal tumors. Cancer 1992; 69: 947–955.
59. Hurlimann J, Gardiol D. Gastrointestinal stromal tumours: an immunohistochemical study of 165 cases. Histopathology 1991; 19: 311–320.
60. El-Naggar AK, Ro JY, McLemore D, Garnsey L, Ordonez N, MacKay B. Gastrointestinal stromal tumors: DNA flow-cytometric study of 58 patients with at least five years of follow-up. Modern Pathol 1989; 2: 511–516.
61. Cooper PN, Quirke P, Hardy GJ, Dixon MF. A flow cytometric clinical and histological study of stromal neoplasms of the gastrointestinal tract. Am J Surg Pathol 1992; 16: 163–170.
62. Bruneton JN, Guoy AM, Dageville X, Lecomte P. Les lipomes du tube digestif. Revue de la litterature a propos de 5 cas. Ann Gastroenterol Hepatol 1984; 20: 27–32.
63. Maderal F, Hunter F, Fuselier G, Gonzales-Rogue P, Torres O. Gastric lipomas — an update of clinical presentation, diagnosis and treatment. Am J Gastroenterol 1984; 79: 964–967.
64. Nakamura S, Iida M, Suekane H, Matsui T, Yao T, Fujishima M. Endoscopic removal of gastric lipoma: Diagnostic value of endoscopic ultrasonography. Am J Gastroenterol 1991; 86: 619–623.
65. DeRidder PH, Levine AJ, Katta JJ, Catto JA. Angiolipoma of the stomach as a cause of chronic upper gastrointestinal bleeding. Surg Endosc 1989; 3: 106–108.
66. Hawins PE, Terrell GK. Liposarcoma of the stomach. JAMA 1965; 191: 154–155.
67. Iwafuchi M, Watanabe H, Shiratsuka M. Primary benign histiocytosis X of the stomach: A report of a case showing spontaneous remission after 5½ years. Am J Surg Pathol 1990; 14: 489–496.
68. Shibuya H, Azumi N, Onda Y, Abe F. Multiple malignant fibrous histiocytoma of the stomach and small intestine. Acta Pathol Jpn 1985; 35: 157–164.
69. Wolf HK, Harrelson JM, Bossen E H. Multicentric malignant fibrous histiocytoma of soft tissue. Case Report. Am J Surg Pathol 1990; 14: 188–193.
70. Yagihashi S, Yagihashi N, Hase Y, Nagai K, Alguacil-Garcia A. Primary alveolar soft-part sarcoma of stomach. Case report. Am J Surg Pathol 1991; 15: 399–406.

71. Meis JM, Enzinger FM. Inflammatory fibrosarcoma of the mesentery and retroperitoneum: A tumor closely simulating inflammatory pseudotumor. Am J Surg Pathol 1991; 15: 1146–1156.
72. Franquemont DW, Frierson HF. Muscle differentiation and clinicopathologic features of gastrointestinal stromal tumors. Am J Surg Pathol 1992; 16: 947–954.
73. Newman PL, Wadden C, Fletcher CDM. Gastrointestinal stromal tumours: Correlation of immunophenotype with clinicopathological features. J Pathol 1991; 164: 107–117.
74. Kuzu I, Bicknell R, Harris AL, Jones M, Gatter KC, Mason DY. Heterogeneity of vascular endothelial cells with relevance to diagnosis of vascular tumours. J Clin Pathol 1992; 45: 143–148.
75. Palmer ED. Benign intramural tumors of the stomach: A review with special reference to gross pathology. Medicine 1951; 30: 81–181.
76. Torricelli P, Furno A, Baldoni C, Tomasini A. Calcified cavernous hemangioma of the stomach. A case report. Radio Med (Torino) 1989; 78: 112–114.
77. Yamaguchi K, Kato Y, Maeda S, Kitamura K. Cavernous hemangioma of the stomach: A case report and review of the literature. Gastroenterol Jpn 1990; 25: 489–493.
78. Pack GT. Unusual tumors of the stomach. Ann NY Acad Sci 1964; 114: 985–1011.
79. Yamaguchi K, Maeda S, Kitamura K. Lymphangioma of the stomach: Report of a case and review of the literature. Jpn J Surg 1989; 19: 485–488.
80. Haque S, Modlin IM, West AB. Multiple glomus tumors of the stomach with intravascular spread. Am J Surg Pathol 1992; 16: 291–299.
81. Quinn FM, Brown S, O'Hara D. Hemangiopericytoma of the stomach in a neonate. J Pediatr Surg 1991; 26: 101–102.
82. Shapira I, Isakov A, Werbin N, Marmor S, Wiznitzer T, Almog C. Plasmacytoma of the stomach. Eur J Surg Oncol 1989; 15: 165–167.
83. Ishido T, Mori N. Primary gastric plasmacytoma: A morphological and immunohistochemical study of five cases. Am J Gastroenterol 1992; 87: 875–878.
84. Kinoshita Y, Watanabe M, Takahashi H, Itoh T, Kawanami C, Kishi K, Kitajima N, Nakamura T, Inatome T, Inoh T, Chiba T. A case of gastric plasmacytoma: Genetic analysis and immunofixation electrophoresis. Am J Gastroenterol 1991; 86: 349–352.
85. Roseanu M, Obersnu F. Benign tumors of the stomach of neurogenic origin. Ann Ital Chir 1990; 61: 147–151.
86. Saito M, Tominaga S, Suzuki R, Sugimasa T, Fujii T, Inoue S, Takamura Y. Unusual rapidly growing gastric myxoid neurofibroma: A case report. Gastroenterol Jpn 1992; 27: 240–245.
87. Genova G, Maiorana AM, Agnello G, Marrazzo A, Sorce M, Li Volsi F, Fiorentino E, Bazan P. Gastric schwannoma after Nissen fundoplication. A rare complication. Am Surg 1989; 55: 495–497.
88. MacLeod CB, Tsokos M. Gastrointestinal autonomic nerve tumors. Ultrastruct Pathol 1991; 15: 49–55.
89. Mourad M, Desrousseaux B, Atat I, Abizeid G, Willcox P, Creusy C, Ampe J. Gastric schwannoma. Observations apropos of a case report of a schwannosarcoma with lymph node metastasis. Acta Chir Belg 1992; 92: 46–51.
90. Peterson JM, Ferguson R. Gastrointestinal neurofibromatosis. J Clin Gastroenterol 1984; 6: 529–534.
91. Xuan ZX, Yao T, Ueyama T, Tsuneyoshi M. Coincident occurrence of granular cell tumor of the stomach with an early gastric carcinoma. Fukuoka Igaku Zasshi 1992; 83: 21–26.
92. Hill S, Walker S, Bode JC, Emmermann H. Granular-cell tumor of the stomach and esophagus. Dtsch Med Wochenschr 1991; 116: 895–898.
93. Yamaguchi K, Maeda S, Kitamura K. Granular cell tumor of the stomach coincident with two early gastric carcinomas. Am J Gastroenterol 1989; 84: 656–659.
94. Xuan ZX, Yao T, Ueyama T, Tsuneyoshi M. Coincident occurrence of granular cell tumor of the stomach with an early gastric carcinoma. Fukuoka Igaku Zasshi 1992; 83: 21–26.
95. Shivshanker K, Bennetts R. Neurogenic sarcoma of the gastrointestinal tract. Am J Gastroenterol 1981; 75: 214–217.
96. Ransom HK, Kay EB. Abdominal neoplasms of neurogenic origin. Ann Surg 1940; 112: 700–740.
97. Pitts HH, Hill JE. Ganglioneuroma of stomach. Can Med Assoc J 1947; 56: 537–539.
98. Tapp E. Ganglioneuroblastoma of the stomach. J Pathol Bacteriol 1964; 88: 79–82.
99. Interlandi A, De Grandis F, Milan R, Osti R, Frasson P. Non-epithelial benign gastric neoplasms. Minerva Chir 1992; 47: 847–852.
100. Balik E, Tuncyurek M, Sayan A, Avano A, Ulman I, Cetinkursun S. Malignant gastric teratoma in an infant. Z Kinderchir 1990; 45: 383–385.
101. Satge D, Auge B, Philippe E, Chenard MP, Sauvage P, Pusel J, Methlin G. Gastric teratoma in newborn children. Ann Pediatr (Paris) 1990; 37: 235–241.
102. Lackner H, Urban C, Riccabona M, Sauer H, Ebner F, Ratschek M. Teratoma of the stomach in a 4-day-old newborn infant. Monatsschr Kinderheilkd 1990; 138: 291–293.
103. Coulson WF. Peritoneal gliomatosis from a gastric teratoma. Am J Clin Pathol 1990; 94: 87–89.
104. Senocak ME, Kale G, Buyukpamukcu N, Hicsonmez A, Caglar M. Gastric teratoma in children including the third reported female case. J Pediatr Surg 1990; 25: 681–684.
105. Ayral X, Cornud F, Favriel JM, Rocquet L, Debray C. Carcinosarcome de l'estomac. Etude d'un cas et revue de la litterature. Gastroenterol Clin Biol 1980; 4: 362–367.
106. Bansal M, Kaneko M, Gordon RE. Carcinosarcoma and separate carcinoid tumor of the stomach. A case report with light and electron microscopic studies. Cancer 1982; 50: 876–881.
107. Coard KC, Titus IP. Adenosquamous carcinoma of the stomach. With a note on pathogenesis. Trop Geogr Med 1991; 43: 234–237.
108. Lin JL, Tseng CH, Chow S, Weisberg J, Guzman L. Coexisting malignant lymphoma and adenocarcinoma of the stomach. South Med J 1979; 72: 619–622.
109. Stout AP. Bizarre smooth muscle tumors of the stomach. Cancer 1962; 15: 400–409.
110. Yang G, Rotterdam H. Mixed (composite) glandular-endocrine cell carcinoma of the stomach. Report of a case and review of literature. Am J Surg Pathol 1991; 15: 592–598.
111. Levendoglu H, Cox CA, Nadimpalli V. Composite (adenocarcenoid) tumors of the gastrointestinal tract. Dig Dis Sci 1990; 35: 519–525.
112. Caruso ML, Pilato FP, D'Adda T, Baggi MT, Fucci L, Valentini AM, Lacatena M, Bordi C. Composite carcinoid-adenocarcinoma of the stomach associated with multiple gastric carcinoids and nonantral gastric atrophy. Cancer 1989; 64: 1534–1539.
113. Watanabe H, Enjoji M, Imai T. Gastric carcinoma with lymphoid stroma. Its morphologic characteristics and prognostic correlations. Cancer 1976; 38: 232–243.
114. Friedman-Kien AE, Laubenstein LJ, Rubinstein P, Buimovici-Klein E, Marmor M, Stahl R, Spigland I, Kim KS, Zolla-Pazner S. Disseminated Kaposi's sarcoma in homosexual men. Ann Intern Med 1982; 96: 693–700.
115. Leibowitz MR, Dagliotti M, Smith E, Murray JF. Rapidly fatal lymphangioma-like Kaposi's sarcoma. Histopathol 1980; 4: 559–566.
116. Weller IVD. AIDS and the gut. Scand J Gastroenterol 1985; 20 (suppl. 114).
117. Carney JA. The triad of gastric epithelioid leiomyosarcoma, functioning extra-adrenal paraganglioma, and pulmonary chondroma. Cancer 1979; 43: 374–382.
118. Wick MR, Ruebner BH, Carney JA. Gastric tumors in patients with pulmonary chondroma or extra-adrenal paraganglioma. An ultra-structural study. Arch Pathol Lab Med 1981; 105: 527–531.
119. Rigel DS, Jacobs MI. Malignant acanthosis nigricans: a review. J Dermatol Surg Oncol 1980; 6: 923–927.
120. Breatnach SM, Wells GC. Acanthosis palmaris: Tripe palms, a distinctive pattern of palmar keratoderma frequently associated with internal malignancy. Clin Exp Dermatol 1980; 5: 181–189.

121. Ikeda K, Murayama H. A case of amyloid tumor of the stomach. Endoscopy 1978; 10: 54–58.
122. Jensen K, Raynor S, Rose SG, Bailey ST, Schenken JR. Amyloid tumors of the gastrointestinal tract: A report of two cases and review of the literature. Am J Gastroenterol 1985; 80: 784–786.
123. Tada S, Iida M, Yao T, Matsui T, Kuwano Y, Hasuda S, Fujishima M. Endoscopic removal of inflammatory fibroid polyps of the stomach. Am J Gastroenterol 1991; 86: 1247–1253.
124. Isaacson P, Buchanan R, Mephan BL. Plasma cell granuloma of the stomach. Hum Pathol 1978; 9: 355–358.
125. Kitsukawa K, Tanouchi M, Tanakami A, Ueno J, Yamago Y, Yoshida S. Parasitic eosinophilic granuloma of the stomach resembling a submucosal tumor. Am J Gastroenterol 1990; 85(2): 217–218.
126. Tromba JL, Inglese R, Rieders B, Todaro R. Primary gastric tuberculosis presenting as pyloric outlet obstruction. Am J Gastroenterol 1991; 86: 1820–1823.
127. Hsu HH, Grove WE, Mindulzun R, Knauer CM. Gastric bezoar caused by Lecithin: An unusual complication of health faddism. Am J Gastroenterol 1992; 87: 794–795.
128. Reeves-Darby V, Soloway RD, Halpert R. Gastric bezoar complicating gastric stapling. Am J Gastroenterol 1990; 85: 326.
129. Hirose Y, Konda S, Sasaki K, Konishi F, Takazakura E. Erythroleukemia and gastric cancer following thorotrast injection. Jpn J Med 1991; 30: 43–46.
130. Koyama T, Matsumori M, Nakamura K, Fujimori T. Metastasis of cancer to cancer: Report of a case of esophageal carcinoma metastasizing to early gastric cancer. Jpn J Surg 1991; 21: 352–356.
131. Canales LI, Parker A, Kadakia S. Upper gastrointestinal bleeding from Merkel cell carcinoma. Am J Gastroenterol 1992; 87: 1464–1467.

CHAPTER

40 Other tumours of the small intestine

R. Whitehead   S. Widgren

PART I

Epithelial tumours

R. Whitehead

Non-carcinoid or neuroendocrine epithelial tumours of the small intestine are decidedly rare and this has been variously ascribed to its lack of a resident bacterial population and the rapid transit of its contents.[1] It has been suggested that local immune responses suppress tumour development[2] and it is noteworthy that it is unusual for gastric or caecal tumour to invade the contiguous small intestine.

Adenomas of small intestinal mucosa

These lesions are essentially similar to colonic adenomas except that they are more frequently villous or tubulovillous, rather than wholly tubular.[3,4] The duodenum is the commonest site of such tumours,[5,6] but they can occur throughout the small intestine[7] and are sometimes multiple, even in patients with no colonic polyps and no history of familial polyposis coli.[8,9] The commonest site for extracolonic adenomas in patients with familial adenomatosis coli is, in fact, the ampullary region.[10] Like colonic adenomas, they are composed mainly of dedifferentiated dysplastic epithelium and show a similar range of histological features. They also may exhibit, in better differentiated areas, histochemical and cytological characteristics of absorptive, goblet, Paneth[11] and endocrine cells.[12] Because of their relative rarity compared with their colonic counterpart, they have been less well studied, but all the evidence points to there being an adenoma-carcinoma sequence similar to that in the colon.

Brunneroma or nodular hyperplasia of Brunner's glands

Another uncommon lesion and the centre of some debate is the sometimes clinically relevant tumour-like lesion of the duodenum which is composed of Brunner's gland tissue. The condition may occur as nodules which may be multiple and a few millimetres in diameter or as a single, large, pedunculated and more 'tumourous' lesion in gross appearance, sometimes with surface ulceration.[13–16] Histologically, the nodules, small or large, are composed of normal Brunner's gland tissue and there is argument as to whether the lesions are best regarded as hyperplasia, adenomatous hyperplasia, true adenomas or are hamartomas. The condition can mimic carcinoma of the head of pancreas.[17] It has also been suggested that hyperplasia of Brunner's glands may, in fact, be due to the exocrine deficiency associated with pancreatic disease,[18] which acts as a stimulus to increase Brunner's gland secretory activity. The larger single lesions are frequently the cause of clinical symptoms due either to obstruction or ulceration of the surface and excision generally is curative. Rarely, dysplasia of the ductal tissue in the Brunner's gland element has been described[19] but there is no record of malignant transformation.

Heterotopic gastric mucosa

On occasion, heterotopic gastric mucosa takes the form

of a clinically significant duodenal polyp, whereas usually it appears as small pale mucosal nodules seen at endoscopy.[20–22] Sometimes the larger lesions ulcerate and, superimposed on the original heterotopia, a hyperplastic, gastric type polyp occurs.[23,24] These and other polypoidal lesions are usually encountered at endoscopy and on biopsy prove to be isolated hyperplastic lymphoid follicles, small adenomas or hamartomas of the elements of the mixing valve at the ampulla.[25]

Malignant epithelial tumours

There is evidence to suggest that adenocarcinoma of the small intestine arises in adenoma by a sequence similar to that which occurs in the colon. In a series of surgical specimens of adenocarcinoma of the duodenum, adenomatous residue was found in over 80%.[26] Of 51 patients with small bowel non-carcinoid epithelial tumours, 18 had adenomas and 33 had tumours that contained adenoma and carcinoma in the same lesion.[3] This has since been confirmed in a further large series by endoscopic biopsy, when the earlier stages of malignant transformation are observed.[27] In the past these tumours have often been diagnosed when at an advanced stage and prognosis has generally been poor.[28–30]

There is evidence for an association between small bowel adenocarcinoma and Crohn's disease[31–33] and patients with gluten sensitive enteropathy show an increased susceptibility.[34,35]

The tumours are adenocarcinomas and their macroscopic and microscopic features are essentially similar to adenocarcinomas arising in the colon. Most are moderately well differentiated, but anaplastic tumours also occur, perhaps more fequently than in the colon,[36] and adenosquamous carcinoma has been described.[37] As in the colon, it is likely that a similar range of tumours with a variety of cell types will be described in future. In a recent report, for example, a neoplastic endocrine cell population has been reported in a large proportion of small intestinal adenocarcinomas.[38]

There are now a significant number of reported cases to warrant the view that the mucosa of ileostomies are cancer prone. It would appear that the adenocarcinomas arise via a sequence of colonic metaplasia and progressive dysplasia and occurs in association with both ulcerative colitis and polyposis coli.[39] Adenocarcinoma may also occur in a Meckel's diverticulum and this is the subject of a recent literature review describing some 30 cases.[40]

Malignant epithelial tumours in Peutz-Jeghers syndrome

That adenomatous and carcinomatous change can occur in the hamartomatous polyps of the Peutz-Jeghers type is well documented.[41] Adenomatous change is the equivalent of glandular dysplasia described by others.[42] The risk of malignancy in Peutz-Jeghers polyposis lesions is, however, debated and centres on the rarity of carcinoma in these patients. When it occurs, it does so more frequently in the colon as opposed to the small intestine, the former being a common site for carcinoma in its own right and thus this introduces the likelihood that the occurrence is coincidental. In a review of this contentious issue it was nevertheless reasserted that a small, but real risk of small and large intestinal carcinoma arising in Peutz-Jeghers lesions does, in fact, exist.[43,44] This subject is referred to in more detail in Chapter 41, as is the apparent predisposition of these patients to other forms of extraintestinal neoplasia.

REFERENCES

1. Lowenfels AB. Why are small-bowel tumours so rare? Lancet 1973; 1: 24–26.
2. Calman KC. Why are small bowel tumours rare? An experimental model. Gut 1974; 15: 552–554.
3. Perzin KH, Bridge MF. Adenomas of the small intestine: a clinicopathologic review of 51 cases and a study of their relationship to carcinoma. Cancer 1981; 48: 799–819.
4. Witteman BJ, Janssens AR, Terpstra JL, Eulderink F, Welvaart K, Lamers CB. Villous tumors of the duodenum. Presentation of five cases. Hepatogastroenterology 1991; 38: 550–553.
5. Newman DH, Doerhoff CR, Bunt TJ. Villous adenoma of the duodenum. Am Surgeon 1984; 50: 26–28.
6. Komorowski RA, Cohen EB. Villous tumors of the duodenum. Cancer 1981; 47: 1377–1386.
7. Delevett AF, Cuello R. True villous adenoma of the jejunum. Gastroenterology 1975; 69: 217–219.
8. Heimann TM, Cohen LB, Bolnick K, Szporn AH. Villous polyposis of the ileum: Report of a case. Am J Gastroenterol 1985; 80: 983–985.
9. Nakamura T, Kimura H, Nakano G. Adenomatosis of small intestine: case report. J Clin Pathol 1986; 39: 981–986.
10. Noda Y, Watanabe H, Iida M, Narisawa R, Kurosaki I, Iwafuchi M, Satoh M, Ajioka Y. Histologic follow-up of ampullary adenomas in patients with familial adenomatosis coli. Cancer 1992; 70: 1847–1856.
11. Ferrell LD, Beckstead JH. Paneth-like cells in an adenoma and adenocarcinoma in the ampulla of Vater. Arch Pathol Lab Med 1991; 115: 956–958.
12. Mingazzini PL, Malchiodi Albedi F, Blandamura V. Villous adenoma of the duodenum: cellular composition and histochemical findings. Histopathology 1982; 6: 235–244.
13. Nakanishi T, Takeuchi T, Hara K, Sugimoto A. A great Brunner's gland adenoma of the duodenal bulb. Dig Dis Sci 1984; 29: 81–85.
14. Franzin G, Musola R, Ghidini O, Manfrini C, Fratton A. Nodular hyperplasia of Brunner's glands. Gastrointest Endosc 1985; 31: 374–378.
15. Rufenacht H, Kasper M, Heitz PhU, Streule K, Harder F. 'Brunneroma': Hamartoma or tumor? Path Res Pract 1986; 181: 107–109.
16. Farkas I, Patko A, Kovacs L, Koller O, Preisich P. The brunneroma, the adenomatous hyperplasia of the Brunner's glands. Acta Gastro-Ent Belg 1980; 43: 179–186.
17. Skellenger ME, Kinner BM, Jordan PH. Brunner's gland hamartomas can mimic carcinoma of the head of the pancreas. Surg Gynecol Obstet 1983; 156: 774–776.
18. Stolte M, Schwabe H, Prestele H. Relationship between diseases of

the pancreas and hyperplasia of Brunner's glands. Virchows Arch (A) 1981; 394: 75–87.
19. Zanetti G, Casadei G. Brunner's gland hamartoma with incipient ductal malignancy. Report of a case. Tumori 1981; 67: 75–78.
20. Lessells AM, Martin DF. Heterotopic gastric mucosa in the duodenum. J Clin Pathol 1982; 35: 591–595.
21. Spiller RC, Shousha S, Barrison IG. Heterotopic gastric tissue in the duodenum. Dig Dis Sci 1982; 27: 880–883.
22. Franzin G, Musola R, Negri A, Mencarelli R, Fratton A. Heterotopic gastric (fundic) mucosa in the duodenum. Endoscopy 1982; 14: 166–167.
23. Russin V, Krevsky B, Caroline DF, Tang C-K, Ming S-C. Mixed hyperplastic and adenomatous polyp arising from ectopic gastric mucosa of the duodenum. Arch Pathol Lab Med 1986; 110: 556–558.
24. Roesch W, Hoer PW. Hyperplasiogenic polyp in the duodenum. Endoscopy 1983; 15: 117–118.
25. Whitehead R. Mucosal Biopsy of the Gastrointestinal Tract. 4th edition. Philadelphia: Saunders, 1990: pp 179–189.
26. Kozuka S, Tsubone M, Yamaguchi A, Hachisuka K. Adenomatous residue in cancerous papilla of Vater. Gut 1981; 22: 1031–1034.
27. Seifert E, Schulte F, Stolte M. Adenoma and carcinoma of the duodenum and papilla of Vater: a clinicopathologic study. Am J Gastroenterol 1992; 87: 37–42.
28. Mittal VK, Bodzin JH. Primary malignant tumors of the small bowel. Am J Surg 1980; 140: 396–399.
29. Barclay THC, Schapira DV. Malignant tumors of the small intestine. Cancer 1983; 51: 878–881.
30. Johnson AM, Harman PK, Hanks JB. Primary small bowel malignancies. Am Surgeon 1985; 51: 31–36.
31. Ribeiro MB, Greenstein AJ, Heimann TM, Yamazaki Y, Aufses AH Jr. Adenocarcinoma of the small intestine in Crohn's disease. Surg Gynecol Obstet 1991; 173: 343–349.
32. Lashner BA. Risk factors for small bowel cancer in Crohn's disease. Dig Dis Sci 1992; 37: 1179–1184.
33. Frank JD, Shorey BA. Adenocarcinoma of the small bowel as a complication of Crohn's disease. Gut 1973; 14: 120–124.
34. Barry RE, Read AE. Coeliac disease and malignancy. Q J Med 1973; 42: 665.
35. Nielsen SNJ , Wold LE. Adenocarcinoma of jejunum in association with nontropical sprue. Arch Pathol Lab Med 1986; 110: 822–824.
36. Blackman E, Nash SV. Diagnosis of duodenal and ampullary epithelial neoplasms by endoscopic biopsy: a clinicopathologic and immunohistochemical study. Hum Pathol 1985; 16: 901–910.
37. Griesser GH, Schumacher U, Elfeldt R, Horny H-P. Adenosquamous carcinoma of the ileum. Virchows Arch (A) 1985; 406: 483–487.
38. Iwafuchi M, Watanabe H, Ishihara N, et al. Neoplastic endocrine cells in carcinomas of the small intestine. Hum Pathol 1987; 18: 185–194.
39. Gadacz TR, McFadden DW, Gabrielson EW, Ullah A, Berman JJ. Adenocarcinoma of the ileostomy: the latent risk of cancer after colectomy for ulcerative colitis and familial polyposis. Surgery 1990; 107: 698–703.
40. Kusumoto H, Yoshitake H, Mochida K, Kumashiro R, Sano C, Inutsuka S. Adenocarcinoma in Meckel's diverticulum: report of a case and review of 30 cases in the English and Japanese literature. Am J Gastroenterol 1992; 87: 910–913.
41. Perzin KH, Bridge MF. Adenomatous and carcinomatous changes in hamartomatous polyps of the small intestine (Peutz-Jeghers syndrome). Cancer 1982; 49: 971–983.
42. Yaguchi T, Wen-Ying L, Hasegawa K, Sasaki H, Nagasako K. Peutz-Jeghers polyp with several foci of glandular dysplasia. Dis Colon Rectum 1982; 25: 592–596.
43. Miller LJ, Bartholomew LG, Dozois RR, Dahlin DC. Adenocarcinoma of the rectum arising in a hamartomatous polyp in a patient with Peutz-Jeghers syndrome. Dig Dis Sci 1983; 28: 1047–1051.
44. Narita T, Eto T, Ito T. Peutz-Jeghers syndrome with adenomas and adenocarcinomas in colonic polyps. Am J Surg Pathol 1987; 11: 76–81.

PART II

Rare and secondary (metastatic) tumours

S. Widgren

BENIGN TUMOURS

A remarkable review by River et al[1] in 1956 produced 1399 benign tumours of the small intestine, including adenomas, leiomyomas and 'polyps' of various type. Nearly 20 years later, Wilson et al[2] were able to add a further 600, but only isolated cases or small series have been published since, which bears witness to the rarity of these lesions. The majority of these tumours are discovered at operation or at necropsy, but recent trends in new diagnostic methods (endoscopy, CT scan, ultrasonography), may well mean that diagnosis during life will become more frequent.

The frequency of all benign tumours of the small intestine is said to vary between 0.04%[3]–6.5%[4] of all tumours of the digestive tract. There is no apparent sex predominance nor peculiar racial incidence. Epidemiological features are not evident and the mean age of manifestation is between 50–60 years.

With the exclusion of smooth muscle tumours and carcinoids, the number of tumours in a review of the literature of the English, French and German languages, is less than 1000 (Table 40.1).[5–55] Since the first edition of this textbook, isolated cases of benign tumours of the small intestine have been published, bringing this total up to a little above 1000. Lipomas are most frequently observed, followed by vascular and neurogenic tumours. The site varies somewhat with the histological type, but the majority of the tumours are located in the ileum.

In the filed material of the Department of Pathology in Geneva, between July 1971 and December 1989 (344 775 biopsies and surgical specimens and 16 814 necropsies),

Table 40.1 Distribution of rare, non-epithelial benign tumours of the small intestine1,[2,5–55]

Histological Type	Total	Site			
		Duodenum	Jejunum	Ileum	Unknown
Lipomas	453	124	73	243	13
Haemangiomas	266	25	116	111	14
Lymphangiomas	28	4	4	2	18
Neurogenic	245	64	101	72	8
Total	992	217	294	428	53

there were only 25 lipomas, 7 haemangiomas, 4 lymphangiomas and 3 neurogenic tumours.

No aetiological factors are apparent, but neurofibromas may occur as part of the phacomatoses complex.

Clinical features

Many tumours remain asymptomatic due to their small size[1,56] and obstruction becomes evident only late in the course of the disease because of the liquid content of the bowel. Pain — acute or chronic — is related to ulceration, obstruction or invagination. Weakness, ulceration and blood loss may result in anaemia, but more severe haemorrhages may also occur and cause melaena. Rarely is the size of the tumour such that it becomes palpable or has induced compression of neighbouring organs and the most severe complication, at least in the free parts of the intestine, is intussusception, which is the cause of hospitalization in half of the cases. Perforation may be the consequence, resulting in peritonitis. Formerly, many were diagnosed at surgical exploration, but nowadays with new investigative techniques diagnosis is often preoperative.[23,31]

Macroscopic features

Lipomas are the most frequent benign tumours and they rank third among all benign tumours, epithelial and non epithelial.[57] The main anatomical site of lipomas is said to be the ileum, but in the Geneva experience they were mostly found in the duodenum. Vascular tumours are rather rare in this segment and are about equally distributed between jejunum and ileum, while neurogenic tumours are nearly as frequent in each of the three segments of the intestine, with a slight predominance in the jejunum.

The tumours may be intraluminal, intraparietal or subserosal. Usually they are single, less often multiple (e.g. in von Recklinghausen's disease). Neurogenic tumours occasionally may be dumbbell-shaped. In the lumen they appear either flat, sessile or polypoid, spherical or ovoid, rarely ring-shaped (Figs 40.1, 40.2, 40.3).

The larger tumours may be ulcerated. In general, they are well circumscribed or encapsulated, but angiomatous tumours are often poorly delimited. Their size varies between 'a wheat-grain and the head of a foetus',[2] with a mean diameter rarely exceeding 5 cm. The consistency is either soft (lipomas, haemangiomas), rubbery or firm (schwannomas and neurofibromas), or spongy (cystic lymphangiomas and angiomas). The colour is usually suggestive of the histological type: white or yellow for lipomas, red-violet or bluish for angiomas, whitish or translucent for lymphangiomas, and mainly pink to white for neurogenic tumours.

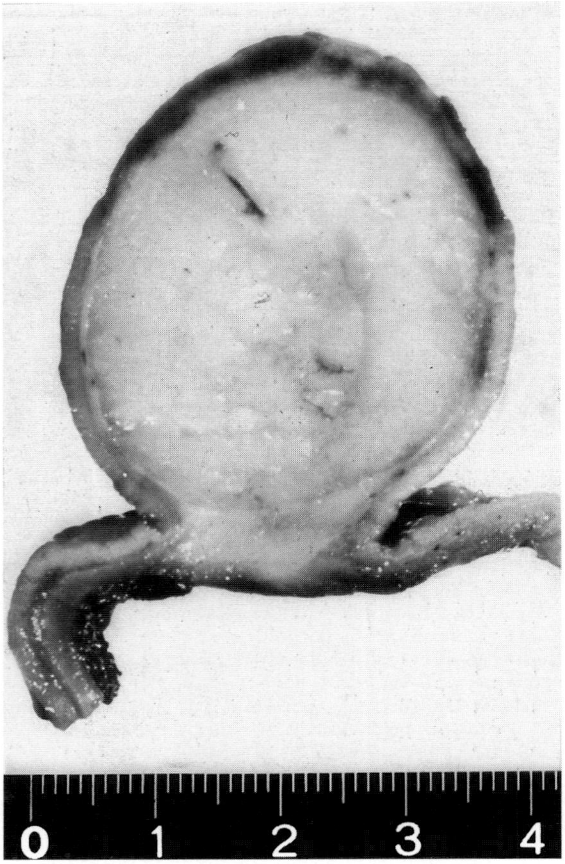

Fig. 40.1 A well-circumscribed lipoma located in the submucosa. (By courtesy of Prof. Hans Sulser, Winterthur)

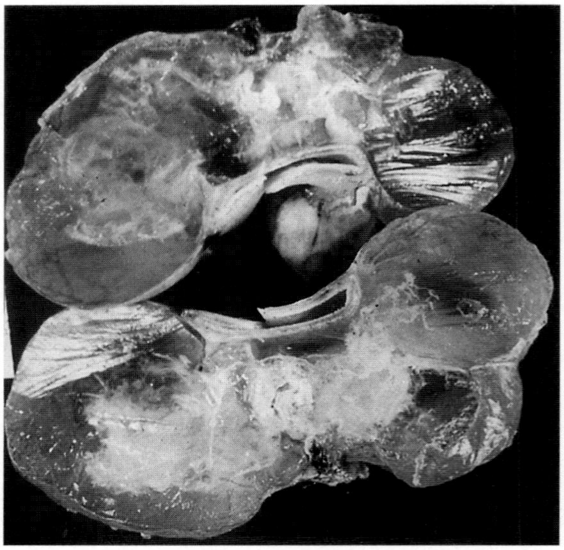

Fig. 40.2 Section of a huge cystic lymphangioma in a child.

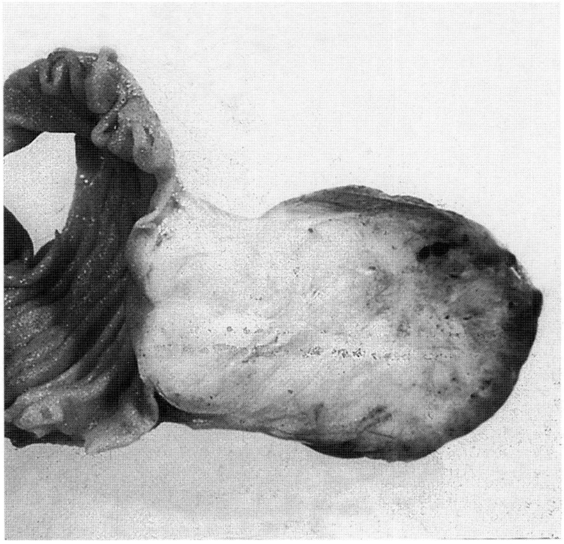

Fig. 40.3 A subserosal schwannoma of Meckel's diverticulum. (By courtesy of Prof. Hans Sulser, Winterthur)

Microscopic features

Since, in general, the histological appearance of these tumours does not differ very much from those found in other parts of the body,[57–59] only specific features and some more important differential diagnostic aspects will be considered.

Lipomas

Lipomas are generally well encapsulated, located in the submucosa and made up of mature adipocytes. According to the admixture of collagen or vessels, they may qualify as fibrolipomas or angiolipomas. Large tumours may undergo varying degrees of necrosis, which can be followed by the formation of lipogranulomas and calcification.

Lipomatosis of the caecal valve is to be distinguished from true lipoma; it usually presents as a rather poorly limited infiltration principally of the submucosa. This condition may clinically and radiologically simulate carcinoma.

Haemangiomas

These tumours are commonly classified as capillary or cavernous haemangioma, haemangioendothelioma or haemangiopericytoma. The first two are the most frequently encountered and are located mainly in the submucosa. They are usually described as being well limited,[2] but Wood[57] found that the infiltrating type of cavernous haemangioma is as common as the polypoid type.

These tumours must be distinguished from telangiectasias of Rendu-Osler's disease, arteriovenous aneurysms, Kaposi's sarcoma and angiodysplasia. The latter condition was first described in the colon,[60] where it is considered to be an acquired, probably degenerative, lesion related to age, or in association with aortic valve disease[61] or renal insufficiency.[62] However, Hemingway[63] has observed the condition in young people, even in teenagers, and postulated that it might be congenital, or that these patients might have a congenital predisposition to its development. This author considered also that the small bowel content might exert a chemical effect on the mucosa of the neighbouring caecum and colon, which could predispose to the development of arteriovenous shunts. Angiodysplasia has also been noticed in the stomach and intestine, especially the duodenum. It presents as dilated, thin-walled venules in mucosa and submucosa, often astride upon the muscularis mucosae.

Lymphangiomas

Lymphangiomas may be cystic and, in children, may attain a giant size, encroaching upon the mesentery (Fig. 40.2). Smaller lesions must be differentiated from chylangiomas, which are frequently encountered at necropsy and are made up of dilated lymphatic vessels, in villi or the submucosa, which are filled with foamy macrophages. They are of no apparent clinical significance.

Dilated lymphatics may also be associated with compression of larger lymphatic vessels of the mesentery by tumourous lymph nodes and are also seen in the villi in association with lymphangiomyomatosis.[64]

Neurogenic tumours

The heterogeneity of gastrointestinal stromal tumours, comprising smooth muscle and nerve cell tumours, has raised vivid interest in the literature during the last decade. Antonioli[65] has discussed the diagnostic difficulties of these tumours, due to the conflicting immunohistochemical results. These problems are more widely considered in Chapter 39.

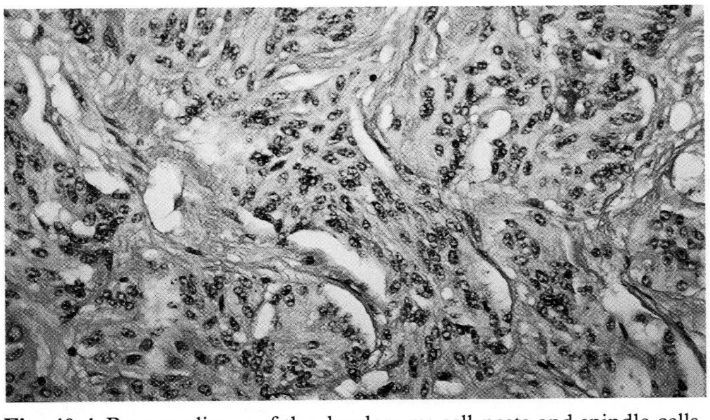

Fig. 40.4 Paraganglioma of the duodenum: cell-nests and spindle cells. (H&E, ×160)

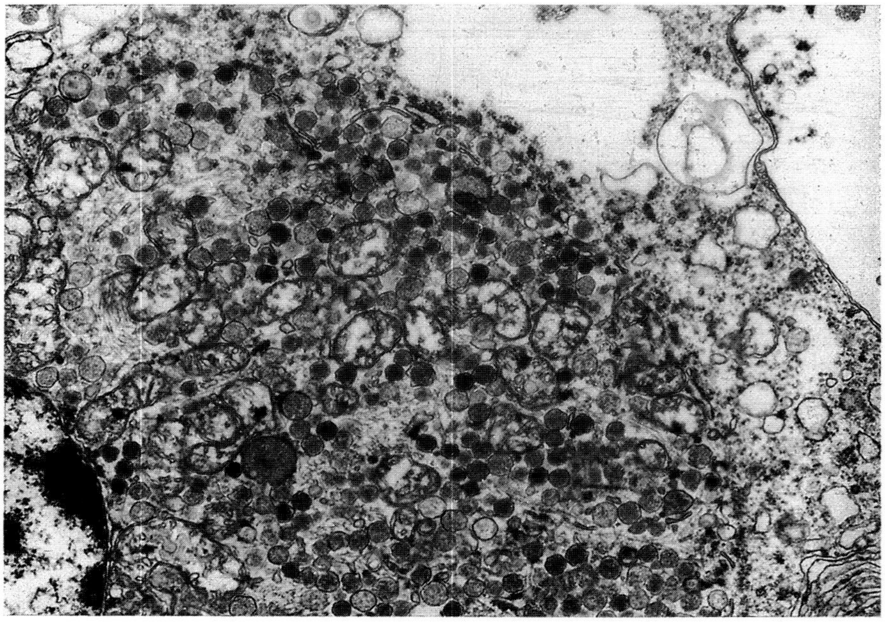

Fig. 40.5 Paraganglioma of the duodenum: electron micrograph of epithelial cell containing numerous secretory granules. (×11 900)

Neurilemmomas and neurofibromas are grouped in Table 40.1, and they are the third most common tumour. Neurofibromas are less often encountered than schwannomas. The former are often multiple in von Recklinghausen's disease, the diagnosis of which is often made on a combination of features in each patient.

Schwannomas are frequently confused with leiomyomas, but with immunohistochemical techniques schwannomas are characterized by containing protein S 100[66] and neurone specific enolase,[67] which are not found in leiomyomas. The latter contain desmin,[68] which is not revealed in neurogenic tumours, and alpha-actin has been shown to be a specific marker for smooth muscle.[69]

Paragangliomas (gangliocytic paragangliomas) are rare and occur almost exclusively in the duodenum. Imai et al[70] noted 73 cases in this location. Most of them are benign, but three cases with regional lymph node metastasis have been recorded.[71–73] They are located mostly in the second part of the duodenum, often juxtapapillary; they are submucosal, sessile or pedunculated, with a size varying from 0.5–10 cm in diameter. They sometimes occur in association with von Recklinghausen's disease. Their typical appearance of cell nests (Zellballen) intermingled with spindle shaped cells, and sometimes ganglion cells, which predominate, may help in distinguishing them from neuroendocrine tumours (Fig. 40.4). Immunohistochemistry, if not performed with some sense of criticism in the interpretation, may be misleading in the differential diagnosis, since various hormones and peptides may be found in both. However, with the electron microscope, the demonstration of secretory granules and intermediate filaments of glial type characteristic of Schwann cells may confirm the presumptive diagnosis (Figs 40.5, 40.6).

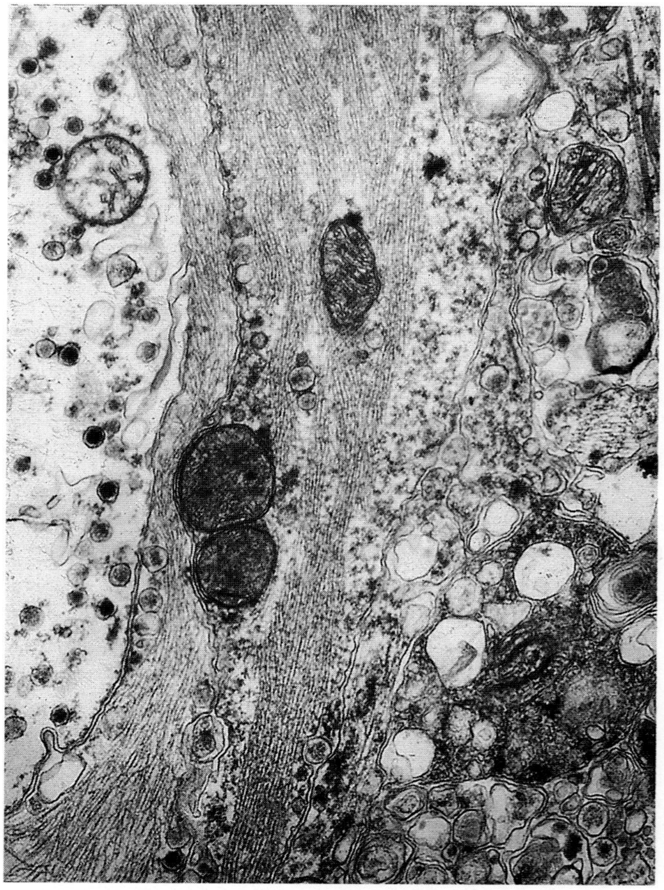

Fig. 40.6 Paraganglioma of the duodenum: electron micrograph of spindle cell containing numerous intermediate filaments of glial type. (×16 000)

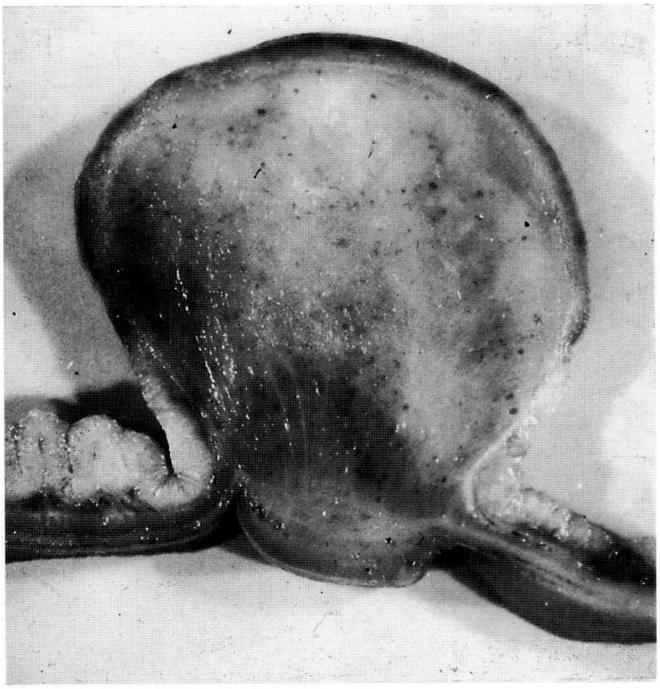

Fig. 40.7 An inflammatory fibroid polyp of the jejunum. (By courtesy of Prof. Fritz Gloor, St Gallen)

Inflammatory fibroid polyp

This is a rare condition of the digestive tract[74] and since the description by Vanek[75] in 1949, about 200 cases have been published. The stomach is the most frequent site, but they also occur in the intestine, where they may cause obstruction or intussusception. In a personal series of 12 cases,[76] 5 occurred in the ileum. They appear as egg-shaped or plaque-like masses or polyps, firm or rubbery and white, yellow, beige or pink in colour (Fig. 40.7). The bulk of the lesion is made up of spindle-shaped or stellate cells without nuclear atypia, which are associated with varying numbers of inflammatory cells. Eosinophils may predominate, but lymphocytes, plasma cells, mast cells and a few macrophages are also present (Fig. 40.8). There is a tight mesh of reticulin fibres, and collagen is often abundant. Blood vessels are numerous, and smaller arteries may show endofibrosis.

Immunohistochemistry has produced contradictory results,[77–80] but the main component cells are negative for lysozyme, alpha$_1$-antitrypsin and desmin, suggesting that they are neither macrophages nor muscle cells. Electron microscopy suggests that the spindle-shaped or stellate cells are myofibroblasts, for they contain bundles of microfilaments parallel to the cell membrane and pynocytotic vesicles (Fig. 40.9). Thus it appears likely that this 'tumour' is a peculiar type of granulation tissue composed mainly of myofibroblasts.

A peculiar feature is represented by a Devon family described by Allibone et al[81] in whom 5 female patients

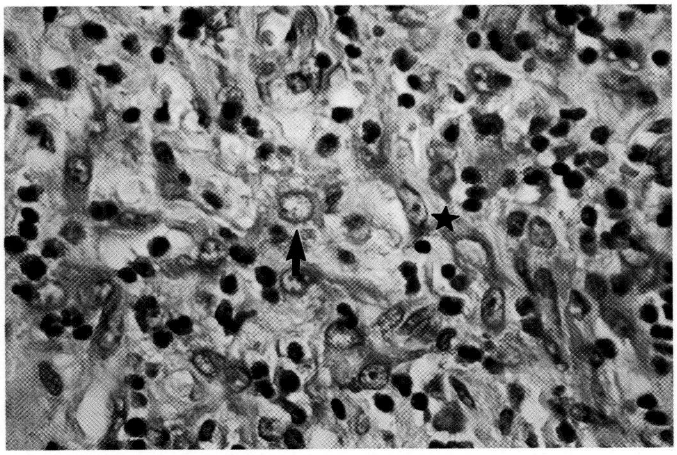

Fig. 40.8 Inflammatory fibroid polyp with stellate (arrow) or spindle cells (star). (H&E, ×160)

in 3 successive generations presented with multiple intestinal polyps which required repeated laparotomies. The authors did not find any chromosomal anomalies, but are of the opinion that 'autosomal dominant mode of inheritance is probable, though X-linked inheritance cannot be excluded'.

MALIGNANT TUMOURS

The great majority of malignant non-epithelial tumours of the gastrointestinal tract in general are leiomyosarcomas and malignant lymphomas. These are dealt with in Chapters 35 and 37. The frequency of other sarcomas of the small intestine, in particular, is difficult to evaluate even in the quite large series that have been published.[82–84] In a review of 2144 malignant tumours, Wilson et al[85] found only 7 sarcomas, but the type was not specified. Thus nonsmooth muscle or lymphoid malignancies must be something of a curiosity[86] which, in the past, have often been described in obsolete terminology, e.g. spindle cell sarcomas, fibrosarcomas, round cell or polymorphic sarcomas.

It seems, however, that the gross and histological appearances of these tumours are essentially similar to those which occur in other sites in the body.[87] Diagnosis, likewise, is in present times often achieved using the modern techniques of investigation, such as electron microscopy and immunohistochemistry.

Two tumours deserve attention, either because they have recently been described (plexosarcomas or gastrointestinal autonomic nerve tumours) or because interest in them has recently emerged (Kaposi's sarcoma).

Plexosarcomas

Plexosarcomas,[88] or gastrointestinal autonomic nerve tu-

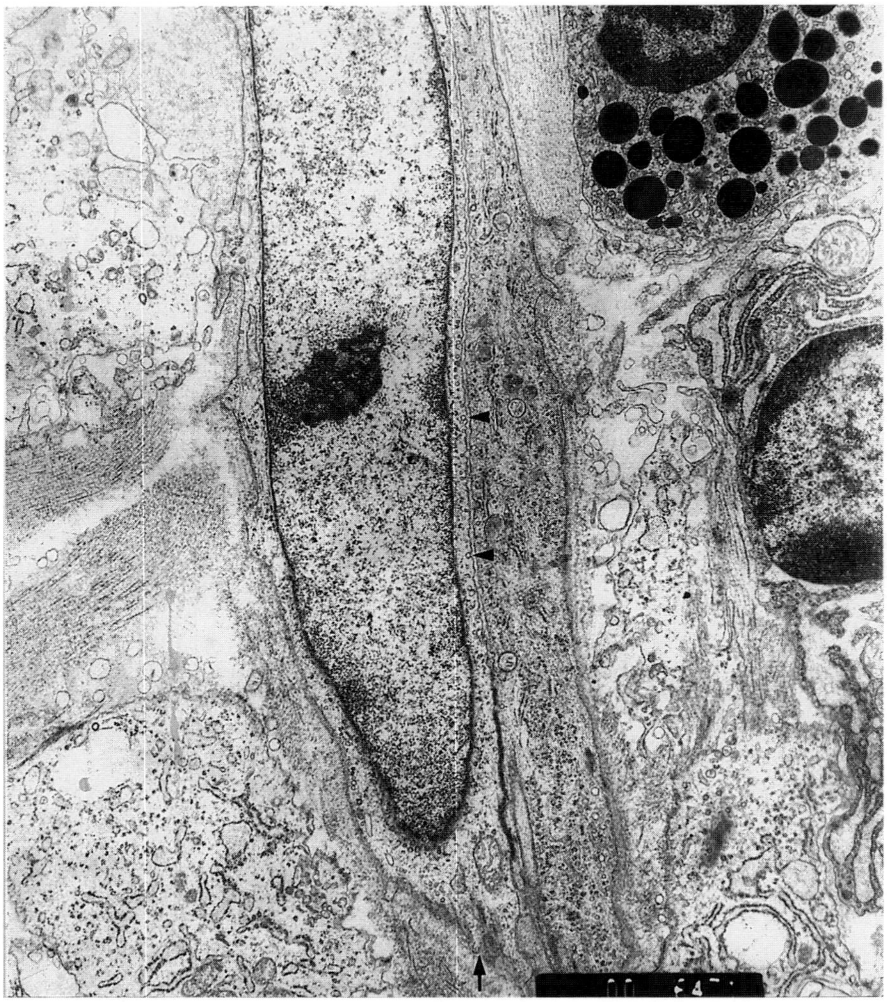

Fig. 40.9 Inflammatory fibroid polyp: electron micrograph showing spindle cell (myofibroblast) with numerous pynocytotic vesicles (arrow heads) and bundles of microfilaments at the extremity (arrow). (×7040)

mours,[89] are characterized by spindle cells of schwannian type and cell nests indistinguishable from the 'Zellballen' of non-chromaffin paragangliomas; thus they reproduce in their ultrastructural appearances the morphology of the enteric nervous system and are considered to take their origin from these structures. Nine cases have been published;[90–91] two were located in the stomach, two in the duodenum, two in the jejunum and three in the ileum; most had metastasized already at the time of diagnosis and the patients did not survive more than nine to ten months.

Kaposi's sarcoma

Kaposi's sarcoma (KS) was described in 1872[92] and was once considered rare. It is usually characterized by skin lesions on the lower limbs, appearing principally in males of East European Jewish origin or Mediterraneans. It is, however, not uncommon in Africa,[93] where it is known to occur either in its classical form, with a rather benign evolution, or as an aggressive variant with a fatal dissemination. A third form is observed mainly in children with lymph node involvement. Within recent years, this disease has gained increased interest because of its frequent association with the Acquired Immune Deficiency Syndrome (AIDS) in homosexual males,[94,95] but also in other immunosuppressed patients, e.g. renal graft recipients[96] or in drug abusers. About 50% of these high risk patients have KS, with tumour located not only in the skin, but also in viscera.

A review of the literature of 751 autopsied AIDS cases has shown KS in 230; of these, aproximately 97 had digestive tract involvement, but in most reports the exact location was not indicated. In the files of our department, comprising 90 necropsies of AIDS patients performed between 1982 and 1990, there were 20 showing KS (22%), of which 12 had involvement of the digestive tract (13%) among which there were 15 locations in the small intestine (duodenum: 3, jejunum: 2, NOS: 4). Of these 12

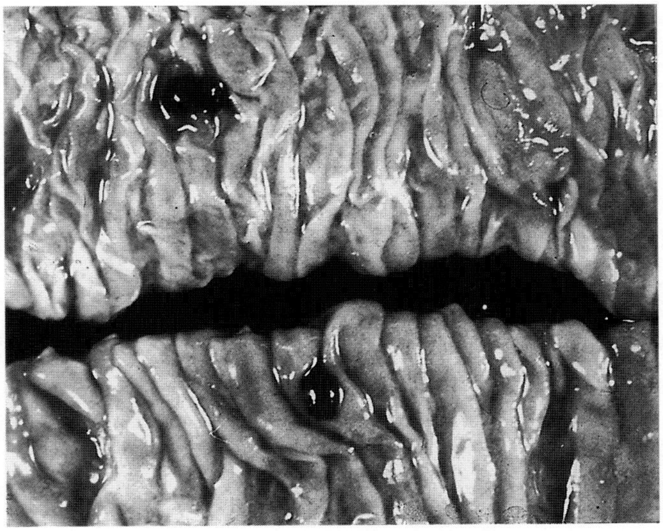

Fig. 40.10 Kaposi's sarcoma of the small intestine: submucosal haemorrhagic nodules. (Reproduced by courtesy of the publishers of Schweizerische medizinische Wochenschrift)

cases, 8 were discovered at necropsy and had not been manifest during life. In two patients, the jejunum was involved with submucosal mulberry-like, red-violaceous, sometimes ulcerated nodules, about 1 cm in diameter (Fig. 40.10).

Histologically (Figs 40.11–40.14), the lesions presented the characteristic features described by Leu and Odermatt[97] — vascular structures of varying sizes, with polymorphic often stratified endothelial cells, containing atypical nuclei and occasional mitoses; there was also a 'stromal' component made up of spindle shaped cells with numerous atypical nuclei between which some clefts were present, and a lymphoplasmocytic infiltrate of varying density.

There is still much debate as to the cellular origin of KS. The presence of endothelial markers (Factor VIII, ulex europaeus lectin, HLA-DR) in the cells which constitute the vascular component of the tumour would suggest a vascular origin.[97–99]

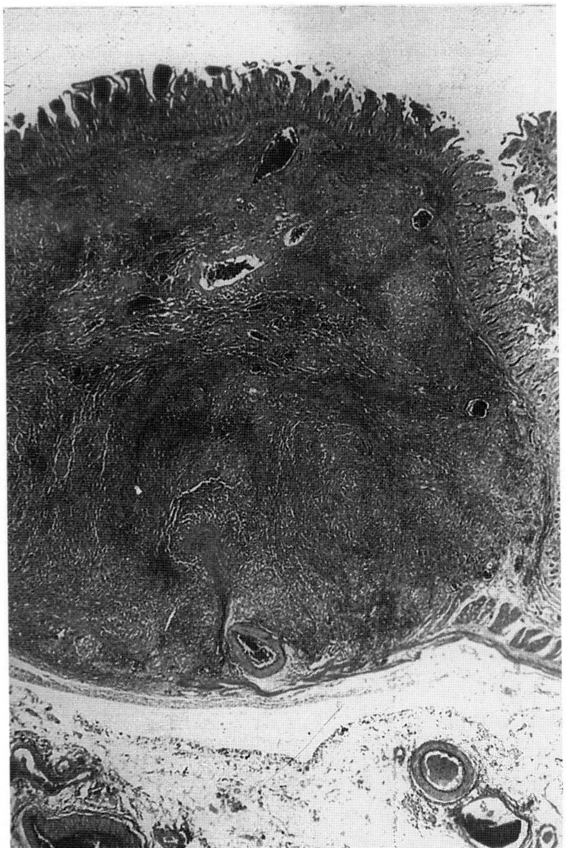

Fig. 40.11 Kaposi's sarcoma of the small intestine: Nodule situated in the submucosa and wall. (H&E, ×12) (Reproduced by courtesy of the publishers of Schweizerische medizinische Wochenschrift)

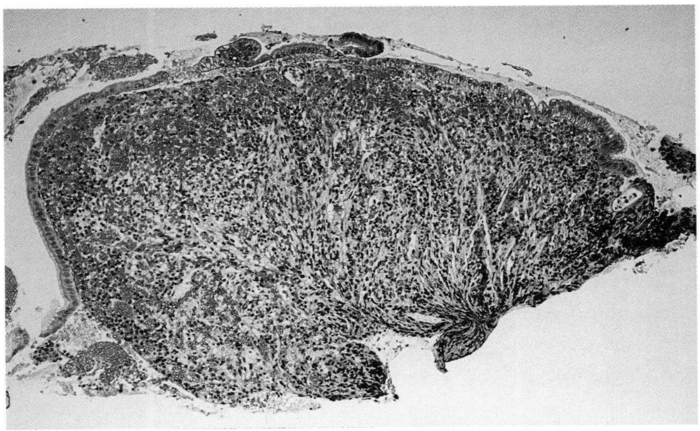

Fig. 40.12 Duodenal biopsy of Kaposi's sarcoma mimicking the appearance of re-epithelialized granulation tissue. (H&E, ×62.5)

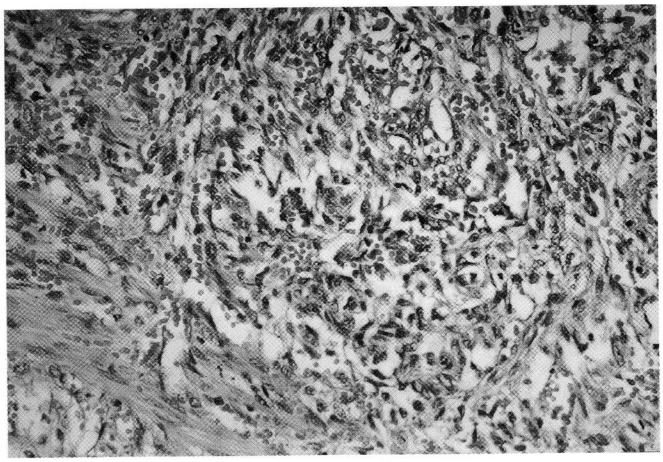

Fig. 40.13 Kaposi's sarcoma of the small intestine showing mixed vascular and 'stromal' patterns. (H&E, ×160)

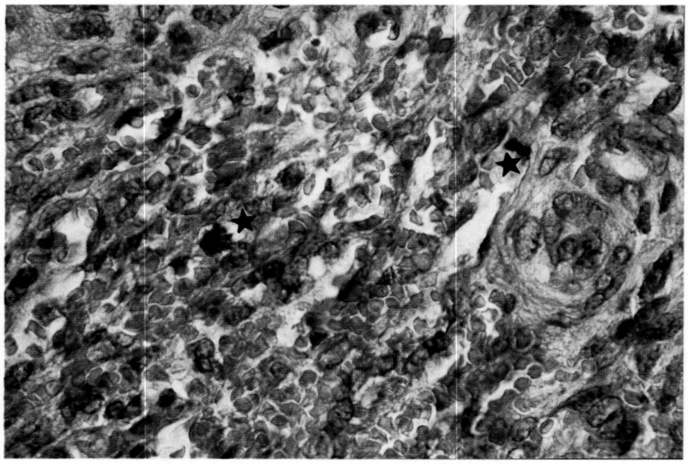

Fig. 40.14 Kaposi's sarcoma of the small intestine: vascular pattern with two mitoses within endothelial cells (stars). (H&E, ×400)

SECONDARY (METASTATIC) TUMOURS

Metastasis of malignant tumours to the small intestine is considered to be rare.[100,101] This is, of course, true when the rate is compared to that in other organs, e.g. liver or lungs.

Secondary deposits in the small intestine may become manifest during life and sometimes require surgical treatment. Figures relating to frequency of intestinal metastases based upon such surgical specimens will clearly be far too low, and may vary as to whether such patients were operated upon in a general surgical department or in a specialized oncology centre. Even reports of frequencies in necropsy material will vary, also taking into account the variation in the effort taken in their identification.[102] Nevertheless, if necropsy files are reviewed (Table 40.2) it becomes plain that metastatic tumours are far from uncommon.

In the University Department of Pathology in Geneva, the files reveal that small bowel secondaries occur predominantly in the male sex, which account for 53% in surgical specimens and 64% in necropsy cases. The mean age of 48 years is lower in reports on surgical patients, especially with melanomas.[103] In necropsy cases the average age is about 60.4 years.

Table 40.2 Frequency of small intestinal metastases from various organs.* A comparison with data in the literature.

Organ/tissue of origin	Own material: Total primaries	Own material: Number with metastases	Literature %
Lung/bronchi	1217	39 (3.2%)	11%;[111] 2%;[112] 10.6%[130]
Melanomas	72	23 (32%)	58%[122]
Lymphomas	230	19 (8.2%)	–
Colon and rectum	742	19 (2.6%)	0.75%[113]
Ovaries	170	12 (7%)	70%;[120] 89%[121]
Stomach	370	11 (2.9%)	12.8%;[116] 37.9%;[117] 11.3%[118]
Leukaemias	340	10 (2.9%)	14.8%;[123] 25%[124]
Pancreas	333	9 (2.7%)	3.8–9.3%[119]
Breast	489	8 (1.6%)	18%;[114] 1%[115]
Gallbladder and bile duct	138	6 (4.3%)	32.8%;[125] 4–12%[126]

*Material of the University Department of Pathology, Geneva: 16 814 necropsies performed between July 1971–December 1989.

Clinical features

By and large, the symptoms and signs are similar to those which occur in other types of intestinal tumours and are in general not specific.[104–106] They are, however, more frequently silent or masked by generalized metastatic disease, and in our files, clinical manifestations were reported in only 122/257 cases which could be evaluated.

Haemorrhage, either occult or overt, may occur and is the result of ulceration. Rarely, metastasis at endoscopy will mimic a duodenal ulcer, and will only be revealed by biopsy.[107] Even less common, metastatic disease will simulate Crohn's. Obstruction is frequently encountered and represents the most important indication for operation. Intussusception also occurs and, occasionally, perforation. As a rule, the metastatic nature of the patient's disease is revealed by usual investigation procedures, particularly endoscopy and biopsy.[108,109]

The time between recognition of a primary tumour and the manifestation of intestinal secondaries varies widely between 5 weeks and 11 years[106] and characteristically long delays have been noticed in the case of melanomas.[110]

Origin of metastases

There is relatively little data concerning intestinal metastatic disease – that which is available is contained in Table 40.2,[111–126] but it requires comment. The wide differences found are an indication of the variation in the way the data have been collected, but the overall frequency of intestinal metastasis is, at autopsy, approximately 7%.[127]

In malignant melanomas, the rate of metastasis is high, taking into account the relative rarity of this kind of tumour. There is a difficulty with malignant lymphomas in the small intestine. On the one hand they are to be distinguished from primary intestinal lymphoma, and on the other, it may not be possible to determine whether the intestinal involvement is part of a systemic lymphoma or whether it is truly metastatic. In the series of 2313 cases of tumours of the colon and rectum reported by Falterman et al,[128] distant metastases occurred in 428 cases, and the intestine ranked fourth place in decreasing order of frequency. Berge et al[113] studied 960 cases, of which 528 among 635 deceased had undergone necropsy. Only 4 cases with intestinal metastases were seen, which is equivalent to a rate of 0.75 %. For carcinoma of the pancreas,[119] 9.3% are associated with duodenal metastases and 3.8% with the small intestine. The first figure is probably too high because it no doubt includes direct infiltration of the duodenum by carcinoma of the head of the pancreas. This is also probably true for the high rate of duodenal metastases from the gallbladder.[125,126] The situation with respect to ovarian metastases is similar.[129] Small bowel involvement was present in 89% of the series published by Julian et al[121] and in 70% in that of Dvoretsky et al,[120] but many of these were not truly metastatic, either being direct infiltration of the gut from the primary tumour, or peritoneal seedings. In the necropsy series published by McNeill et al,[130] 46/431 patients with primary carcinoma of the lung had small bowel metastases; the percentage varied with the histological type of the primary tumour (from 39% in large cell carcinoma to 7.5% in squamous carcinoma and none of 20 undifferentiated carcinoma). The same authors found that 6 of 78 patients who had been operated on for small bowel metastases had primary lung carcinoma.

Leukaemias show an overall macroscopic involvement of the small intestine between 14.8%[123] and 25%.[124] Rarely, this may take the form of granulocytic sarcoma (chloroma).[131,132] According to Neiman et al,[133] and Meis et al[134] it may occur as 3 different clinical conditions:

1. as a precursor of acute myeloid leukaemia in non leukaemic patients
2. as a sign of impending blast crisis in chronic myeloid leukaemia
3. as an extramedullary manifestation in patients with acute myeloid leukaemia.

This condition is often misdiagnosed as some sort of malignant lymphoma and can be easily identified by performing ASD-chloroacetate esterase stain or immunohistological investigations.

Among the primary tumours not tabulated, renal adenocarcinomas are interesting, since there does not appear to be a difference in the rate of secondaries found at necropsy between cases submitted to nephrectomy and those who had not been operated upon.[135]

Macroscopic features

Metastases in the small intestine are most often multiple, sometimes single and the majority (137 of 156 necropsies and 88 of 96 surgical specimens in our material) are situated in the free intestine. They present mainly as intramural masses. According to Willis,[102] they develop from deposits in the submucosa and form nodules or plaques which, in the case of leukaemia, may be very numerous. They bulge into the intestinal lumen and produce polypoid structures, sessile or pedunculated, which may be the cause of obstruction or intussusception (Fig. 40.15).

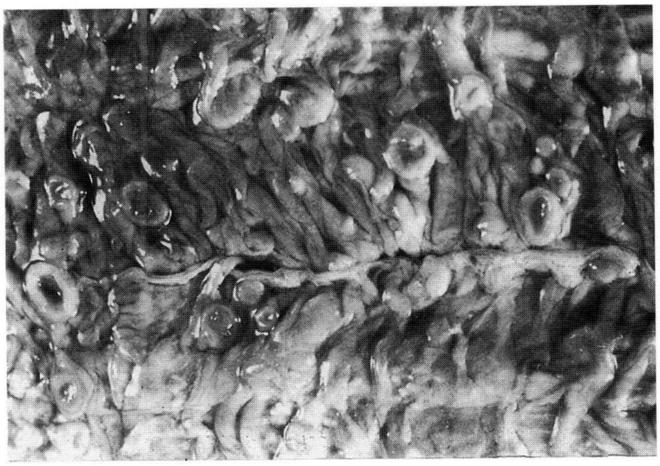

Fig. 40.15 Polypoid mushroom-like metastases (primary: malignant melanoma).

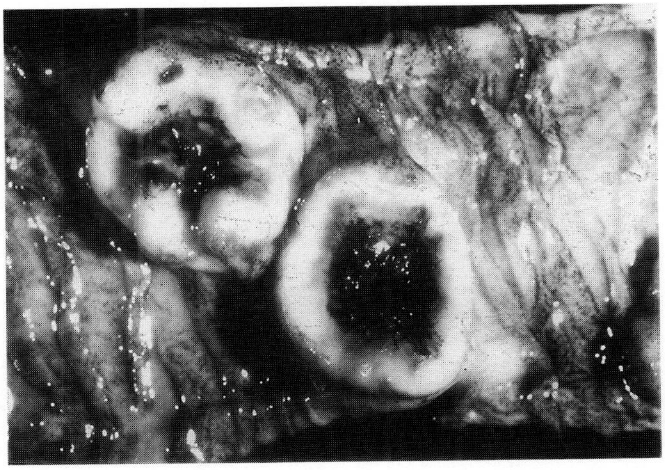

Fig. 40.16 Two metastases with buttercup appearance (primary: lung tumour).

They may ulcerate, producing a buttercup appearance (Fig. 40.16). Napkin-ring-like circumferential stenoses also occur and transparietal growth may induce a localized retraction of the serosa and the wall (Fig. 40.17), with kinking of the intestine as a consequence. Sometimes necrosis of a transparietal growth may result in perforation and peritonitis. A rare 'linitis plastica' type of infiltration has been described[100,101] and may clinically suggest an ischaemic stricture or Crohn's disease; the latter was mimicked in 19 of 221 cases of gastrointestinal metastasis of breast tumours found by Madeya and Boersch[136] in their review of the literature since 1960. Subserosal lymphangitis appears as a greyish delicate network associated with small nodules (Fig. 40.18). It is the consequence of retrograde metastasis from mesenteric lymph nodes.

Rarely, the colour and consistency of metastases indicate the origin of the tumour. Melanomas are revealed by

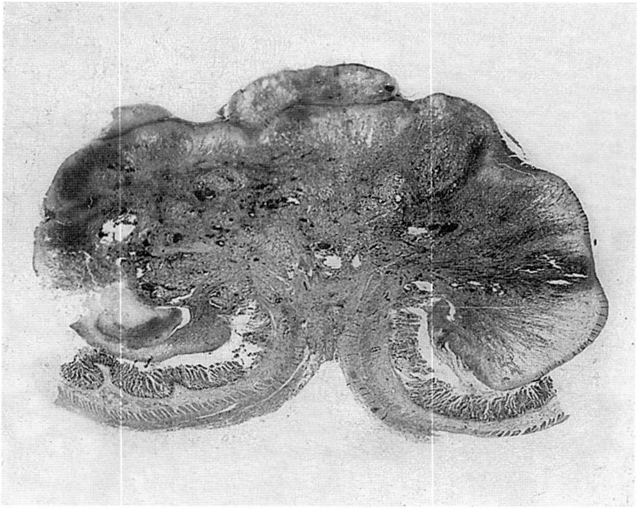

Fig. 40.17 Retraction of serosa and wall due to metastasis (renal adenocarcinoma). (H&E, ×2.3)

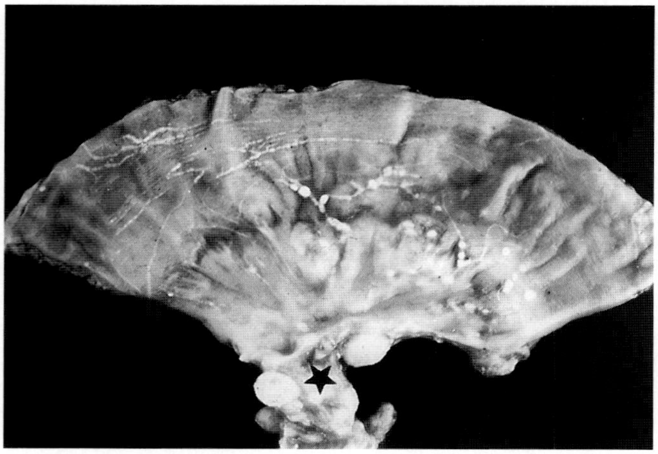

Fig. 40.18 Subserosal lymphangitis. Notice delicate network and small nodules and lymph node metastases on both sides of asterisk.

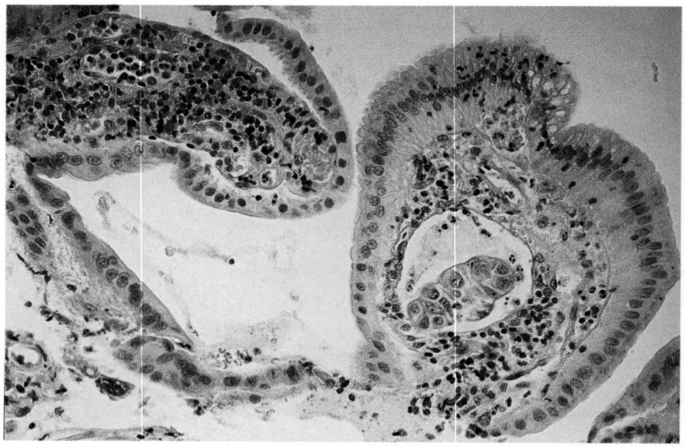

Fig. 40.19 Metastasis of a poorly differentiated adenocarcinoma within a lymphatic vessel of a duodenal villus. (H&E, ×160)

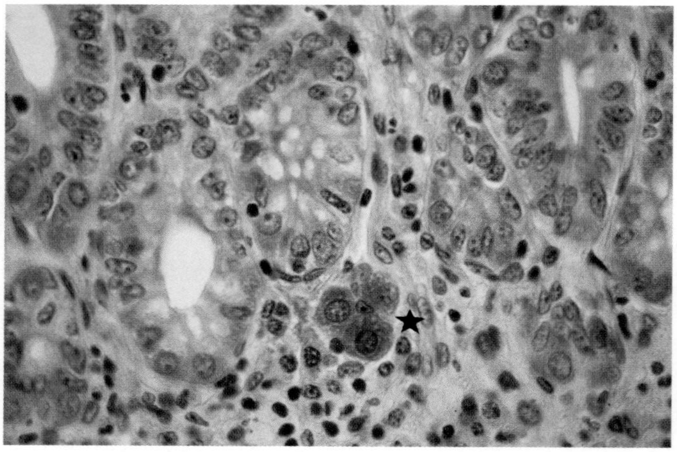

Fig. 40.20 Duodenal metastasis of a malignant melanoma: three non-pigmented cells within the lamina propria (star). (H&E, ×400)

their black, brownish or grey colour, but occasionally they are amelanotic and have a fish-flesh appearance more typical of malignant lymphomas. Adenocarcinomas may appear mucinous, grey mucoid and translucent. Often well differentiated epidermoid carcinomas may be recognized by their granular appearance. The luminal surface of the intestine may appear haemorrhagic, either as a consequence of infarction of the metastasis or of the overlying mucosae.

Metastatic pathways

The lymphatic pathway is retrograde from mesenteric lymph nodes and is most often involved with tumours of the stomach, pancreas or colon. It is rarely seen in extraabdominal primaries.

The haematogenous pathway is usual for tumours situated outside the digestive tract, especially melanomas.[104] However, it is exceptional to see evidence of tumour embolism.[102] On occasion, however, intravenous tumour with thrombosis is seen and it suggests either secondary involvement of veins by intra-intestinal metastasis, or retrograde dissemination due to venous invasion and thrombosis of a large vein in the mesentery.

Finally, carcinomatous implants are seen on the serosa and are especially common in the case of ovarian tumours.

Microscopic features

The histological diagnosis of intestinal metastasis is not usually a major problem, especially with knowledge of the site of a primary tumour. Often, however, if this is not known, consideration of the histological appearance and the sex of the patient will allow a list of probable primary tumours to be drawn up. Sometimes, however, especially in small endoscopic biopsies, a metastasis consisting of a few tumour cells may create difficulty as to whether these are in lymphatics or within the lamina propria (Figs 40.19, 40.20). Nevertheless, histochemical and immunohistochemical techniques can be applied and may give an indication as to the origin of the tumour.

REFERENCES

1. River L, Silverstein J, Tole JW. Benign neoplasms of the small intestine: A critical comprehensive review with reports of 20 new cases. Int Abstr Surg 1956; 102: 1–38.
2. Wilson JM, Melvin DB, Gray G, Thorbjarnarson B. Benign small bowel tumor. Ann Surg 1975; 181: 247–250.
3. Strauch GO. Small-bowel neoplasms: Elusive source of abdominal symptoms. Surgery 1964; 55: 240 –247.
4. Raiford TS. Tumours of small intestine. Arch Surg 1932; 25: 122.
5. Grözinger KH, Schüler HW. Dünndarmtumoren. Z Gastroenterol 1970; 8: 471–479.
6. Termansen NB, Linde NC. Primary tumours of the small intestine. Scand J Gastroenterol 1971; (suppl 9): 119–126.
7. Peycelon R, Corréard RP. Etude anatomo-clinique d'une série de 29 tumeurs de l'intestin grêle. Ann Chir 1970; 24: 23–24.
8. Geroulanos S, Messmer B, Hahnloser P. Primare Dunndarmtumoren. Helv Chir Acta 1972; 39: 241–250.
9. Roux M, Delavierre P, Vayre P, et al. Les tumeurs primitives du grele. A propos de 30 observations. Sem Hop Paris 1973; 49: 2055–2061.
10. Silberman H, Crichlow RW, Caplan HS. Neoplasms of the small bowel. Ann Surg 1974; 180: 157–161.
11. Treadwell TA, White RR III. Primary tumors of the small bowel. Am J Surg 1975; 130: 749–755.
12. Freund H, Lavi A, Pfeffermann R, Durst AL. Primary neoplasms of the small bowel. Am J Surg 1978; 135: 757–759.
13. Aranha G, Reyes CV, Lindert DJ, Reinhardt CF, Greenlee HB. Primary tumors of the small intestine. Am Surg 1979; 45: 495–502.
14. Miles RM, Crawford D, Duras S. The small bowel tumor problem. An assessment based on a 20-year experience with 116 cases. Ann Surg 1979; 189: 732–740.
15. Klotter HJ, Grönninger J, Neher M. Hämangiome im Dünndarm. Zentral bl Chir 1980; 105: 1587–1590.
16. Norberg KA, Emas S. Primary tumors of the small intestine. Am J Surg 1981; 142: 569–573.
17. Vischoff D, Saegesser F. Les tumeurs de l'intestin grêle. Analyse de 188 cas et revue de la litterature. Rev Méd Suisse Romande 1986; 106: 365–372.
18. Weinberg T, Feldman M Sr. Lipomas of the gastrointestinal tract. Am J Clin Pathol 1955; 25: 272–281.
19. Mayo CW, Pagtalunan RJG , Brown DJ. Lipoma of the alimentary tract. Surgery 1963; 53: 598–603.
20. Hurwitz MM, Redleaf PD, Williams HJ, Edwards JE. Lipomas of the gastrointestinal tract. An analysis of seventy-two tumors. AJR 1967; 99: 84–89.
21. Wald A, Milligan FD. The role of fiberoptic endoscopy in the diagnosis and management of duodenal neoplasms. Am J Dig Dis 1975; 20: 499–505.
22. Deeths TM, Madden PN, Dodda WJ. Multiple lipomas of the stomach and duodenum. Am J Dig Dis 1975; 20: 771–774.
23. Megibow AJ, Redmond PE, Bosniak MA, Horowitz L. Diagnosis of gastrointestinal lipomas by CT. AJR 1979; 133: 743–745.
24. Solente JJ, Ferry C, Boulenger M, Moline J. Lipome multiple de l'intestin grêle. Lyon Chir 1979; 75: 124–126.
25. Weiss A, Mollura JL, Profy A, Cohen R. Two cases of complicated intestinal lipoma. Review of small intestine lipomas. Am J Gastroenterol 1979; 72: 83–88.
26. Beckert W. Okkulte Miniaturlipome des Duodenums. Dtsch Z Verdau Stoffwechselkr 1979; 39: 216–219.
27. Gatos M. Grosses submukös gestieltes Lipom des Duodenums. Zentralbl Chir 1980; 105: 1373–1375.
28. Gastinger J, Rietz KD. Rezidivierender Invaginationsileus durch gutartigen Dünndarmtumor. Z Ärtzl Fortbild 1981; 75: 433–434.
29. Ciaudo O, Fingerhut A, Pelletier JM, Berque A, Ronat R, Pourcher J. Lipome de la dernière anse grêle révélé par une invagination intestinale grêle. Sem Hop Paris 1981; 57: 384–385.
30. Imamura K, Fuchigami T, Iida M, et al. Duodenal lipoma — a report of three cases. Gastrointest Endosc 1983; 29: 223–224.
31. Nijssens M, Usewils R, Broeckx J, Ponette E, Baert AL. Lipoma of the duodenal bulb; CT demonstration. Europ J Radiol 1983; 3: 39–41.
32. Sarma DP, Weilbaecher TG, Basavaraj A, Reina RR. Symptomatic lipoma of the duodenum. J Surg Oncol 1984; 25: 133–135.
33. Agha F, Dent TL, Fiddian-Green RG, Braunstein AH, Nostrant TT. Bleeding lipomas of the upper gastrointestinal tract. A diagnostic challenge. Am Surg 1985; 21: 279–285.
34. Puri P, Guiney EJ. Small bowel tumours causing intussusception in childhood. Br J Surg 1985; 77: 493–494.
35. Larsen TE, Cram RW. Hemangiopericytoma of the small bowel: case report and review of the literature. Can J Surg 1970; 13: 50–53.
36. Murray-Lyon IM, Doyle D, Philpott RM, Porter NH. Haemangiomatosis of the small and large bowel with histological malignant change. J Pathol 1971; 105: 295–297.
37. Ikeda K, Murayama H, Takano H, Araki S, Ikejiri K. Massive intestinal bleeding in haemangiomatosis of the duodenum. Endoscopy 1980; 12: 306–310.
38. Sauerbruch T, Keiditsch E, Wotzka R, Kaess H. Lymphangioma of the duodenum (diagnosis by endoscopic resection). Endoscopy 1977; 9: 179–182.
39. Colizza S, Tiso B, Bracci F, Cudemo RC, Bigotti A, Crisci E. Cystic lymphangioma of stomach and jejunum: report of one case. J Surg Oncol 1981; 17: 169–176.
40. Boeck G, Roitzsch E. Submuköses kavernöses Lymphangiom im Ileum als Ursache eines chronischen Dünndarmileus. Zentralbl Chir 1982; 107: 724–726.
41. Voirol M, de Buren N, Perrin G, Pfister C. Aspect endoscopique d'un lymphangiome du duodenum. Schweiz Rundschau Med (Praxis) 1982; 71: 1188–1190.
42. Salata HH, Mercader J, Navarro A, Cortes JM, Gonzales-Campos C. Lymphangioma of the duodénum. Endoscopy 1984; 16: 30–32.
43. Bruneton JN, Drouillard J, Roux P, Ettore F, Aubanel D. Les tumeurs nerveuses de l'intestin grêle. Revue de la litterature à propos de 6 cas personnels. Ann Gastroentérol Hépatol 1984; 20: 79–84.
44. Druart ML, De Graef J, Carpentier YA, Rutsaert J. Les schwannomes de l'intestin grêle. Acta Gastroenterol Belg 1980; 43: 516–521.
45. Realini S, Pusterla C, Cereda W, Arma S, Pedrinis E, Luscieti P. Neurinome du duodénum. Schweiz Rundschau Med (Praxis) 1982; 71: 1182–1184.
46. Gould VE, Kraft JR. Case 14. Ultrastruct Pathol 1983; 5: 359–368.
47. Kramer C, Diettrich H, Malm M. Beitrag zur Problematik der neurogenen Dünndarmtumoren. Zentralbl Chir 1970; 95: 1198–1200.
48. Davis GB, Berk RN. Intestinal neurofibromas in von Recklinghausen's disease. Am J Gastroenterol 1973; 60: 410–414.
49. Hochberg FH, Da Silva AB, Galdabini J, Richardson EP Jr.Gastrointestinal involvement in von Reck]inghausen's neurofibromatosis. Neurology 1974; 24: 1144–1151.

50. Gärtner U, Rentsch I, Müller P. Papillennah gelegenes Neurofibrom des Duodenums mit Blutung und Einengung von D. Wirsungianus und Choledochus. Leber Magen Darm 1977; 7: 388–390.
51. Pfitzmann KF. Ungewöhnlicher Krankheitsverlauf eines Neurinofibroms des distalen Duodenums. Helv Chir Acta 1977; 44: 591–595.
52. Juan IK, Sono F, Okada T, Muto M, Furuki A. Neurogenic tumor of small intestine, report of a case with review of literature. Gastroenterol Jpn 1980; 15: 112–119.
53. Rutgeerts P, Hendrickx H, Geboes K, Ponette E, Broeckaert L, Vantrappen G. Involvement of the upper digestive tract by systemic neurofibromatosis. Gastrointest Endosc 1981; 27: 22–25.
54. Gemperle A, May D, Chaoui Z, Zayadin K. Neurofibromatosis Recklinghausen mit intestinaler Beteiligung. Bericht über zwei Beobachtungen und Literaturübersicht. Zentralbl Chir 1982; 107: 787–793.
55. Chagnon JP, Barge J, Hénin D, Blanc D. Maladie de Recklinghausen à localisations digestives associée à une hypersécrétion gastrique acide évoquant un syndrome de Zollinger-Ellison. Gastroentérol Clin Biol 1985; 9: 65–69.
56. Machella TE. Tumors of the small intestine. In: Bockus HL. Gastroenterology. Vol. 2. Philadelphia: Saunders 1966: p 176.
57. Wood DA. Tumors of the intestines. Atlas of Tumor Pathology. Sect V I, fasc 22. Armed Forces Institute of Pathology, Washington DC, 1967.
58. Landing BH, Farber S. Tumors of the cardiovascular system. Atlas of Tumor Pathology. Sect III, fasc 7. Armed Forces Institute of Pathology, Washington DC, 1956.
59. Stout AP, Lattes R. Tumors of the soft tissues. Atlas of Tumor Pathology. 2nd series, fasc 1. Armed Forces Institute of Pathology, Washington DC, 1967.
60. Boley SJ, Sammartano R, Adams A, Dibiase A, Kleinhaus S, Sprayregen S. On the nature and etiology of vascular ectasia of the colon. Degenerative lesions of aging. Gastroenterology 1977; 72: 650–660.
61. Weaver GA, Alpern HD, Davis JS, Ramsey WH, Reichelderfer M. Gastrointestinal angiodysplasia associated with aortic valve disease: part of a spectrum of angiodysplasia of the gut. Gastroenterology 1979; 77: 1–11.
62. Clouse RE, Costigan DJ, Mills BA, Zuckerman GR. Angiodysplasia as a cause of upper gastrointestinal bleeding. Arch Intern Med 1985; 145: 458–461.
63. Hemingway AP. Angiodysplasia: current concepts. Review article. Postgrad Med J 1988; 64: 259–263.
64. Joliat G, Stalder H, Kapanci Y. Lymphangiomyomatosis: a clinico-anatomic entity. Cancer 1973; 31: 455–461.
65. Antonioli DA. Gastrointestinal autonomic nerve tumors. Expanding the spectrum of gastrointestinal stromal tumors. Editorial. Arch Pathol Lab Med 1989; 113: 831–833.
66. Erlandson RA. Diagnostic immunohistochemistry of human tumors. An interim evaluation. Editorial. Am J Surg Pathol 1984; 8: 615–624.
67. Vinores SA, Bonnin JM, Rubinstein LJ, Marangos PJ. Immunohistochemical demonstration of neuron-specific enolase in neoplasms of the CNS and other tissues. Arch Pathol Lab Med 1984; 108: 536–540.
68. Osborn M, Weber K. Tumor diagnosis by intermediate filament typing: a novel tool for surgical pathology. Lab Invest 1983; 48: 372–394.
69. Skalli O, Ropraz P, Trzeciak A, Benzonana G, Gillessen D, Gabbiani G. A monoclonal antibody against alpha-smooth muscle actin: a new probe for smooth muscle differentiation. J Cell Biol 1986; 103: 2787–2796.
70. Imai S, Kajihara Y, Komaki K, Nishishita S, Fukuya T. Paraganglioma of the duodenum: a case report with radiological findings and literature review. Br J Radiol 1990; 63: 975–977.
71. Buechler M, Malfertheiner P, Baczako K, Krautberger M, Beger HG. A metastatic endocrine-neurogenic tumor of the ampulla of Vater with multiple endocrine immunoreaction — malignant paraganglioma? Digestion 1985; 31: 54–59.
72. Korbi S, Kapanci Y, Widgren S. Le paragangliome malin du duodénum. Etude immunohistochimique et ultrastructurelle d'un cas. Ann Pathol 1987; 7: 47–55.
73. Inai K, Kobuke T, Yonehara S, Tokuoka S. Duodenal gangliocytic paraganglioma with lymph node metastasis in a 17-year-old boy. Cancer 1989; 63: 2540–2545.
74. Helwig EB, Ranier A. Inflammatory fibroid polyps of the stomach. Surg Gynecol Obstet 1953; 96: 355–367.
75. Vanek J. Gastric submucosal granuloma with eosinophilic infiltration. Am J Path 1949; 25: 397–411.
76. Widgren S, Pizzolato GP. Inflammatory fibroid polyp of the gastrointestinal tract: possible origin in myofibroblasts? A study of twelve cases. Ann Pathol 1987; 7: 184–192.
77. Anthony PP, Morris DS, Vowles KDJ. Inflammatory fibroid polyps in three generations of a Devon family: a new syndrome. Gut 1984; 25: 854–862.
78. Goeke H. Das sogenannte Granuloblastom des Magens. Verh Dtsch Ges Path 1985; 69: 687.
79. Navas-Palacios JJ, Colina-Ruizdelgado F, Sanchez-Larrea MD, Cortes-Cansino J. Inflammatory fibroid polyps of the gastrointestinal tract. An immunohistochemical and electron microscopic study. Cancer 1983; 51: 1682–1690.
80. Shimer II, Helwig EB. Inflammatory fibroid polyps of the intestine. Am J Clin Pathol 1984; 81: 708–714.
81. Allibone RO, Nanson JK, Anthony PP. Multiple and recurrent inflammatory fibroid polyps in a Devon family ('Devon polyposis syndrome'): an update. Gut 1992; 33: 1004–1005.
82. Barclay THC, Schapira DV. Malignant tumors of the small intestine. Cancer 1983; 51: 878–881.
83. Goeber I, Wayand W. Primäre maligne Dünndarmtumoren. Wien klin Wschr 1976; 88: 337–341.
84. Hollender LF, Otten IF, Thomas M, Bur F. Etude anatomo-clinique de 21 tumeurs malignes primitives du jéjunum et de l'iléon. Ann Chir 1972; 26: 639–648.
85. Wilson JM, Melvin DB, Gray JF, Thorbjarnarson B. Primary malignancies of the small bowel: a report of 96 cases and review of the literature. Ann Surg 1974; 180: 175–179.
86. Kyriakos M. Malignant tumors of the small intestine. JAMA 1974; 229: 700–702.
87. Stout AP, Lattes R. Tumors of the soft tissues. Atlas of Tumor Pathology, 2nd series, fasc. 1. Armed Forces Institute of Pathology, Washington DC, 1967.
88. Herrera G, Pinto de Moraes H, Grizzle WE, Han SG. Malignant small bowel neoplasm of enteric plexus derivation (plexosarcoma). Light and electron microscopic study confirming the origin of the neoplasm. Dig Dis Sci 1984; 29: 275–284.
89. Walker P, Dvorak AM. Gastrointestinal autonomic nerve (GAN) tumor. Arch Pathol Lab Med 1986; 110: 309–316.
90. Herrera GA, Cerezo L, Jones JE, Sack J, Grizzle WE, Pollack J, Lott RL. Gastrointestinal autonomic nerve tumors 'plexosarcomas'. Arch Pathol Lab Med 1989; 111: 846–853.
91. Nerlich A, Remberger K. Metastasiertes 'Plexosarkom' des Jejunums. Fallberichte. Pathologe 1990; 11: 240–243.
92. Kaposi M. Idiopathisches multiples Pigmentsarkom der Haut. Arch Dermatol Syph 1872; 4: 265–273.
93. Templeton AC. Kaposi's sarcoma. Pathol Ann 1981; 16/2: 315–336.
94. Gottlieb GJ, Ragaz A, Vogel JV, et al. A preliminary communication on extensively disseminated Kaposi's sarcoma in young homosexual men. Am J Dermatopathol 1981; 3: 111–114.
95. Safai B, Johnson KG, Myskowski PL, et al. The natural history of Kaposi's sarcoma in the acquired immunodeficiency syndrome. Ann Intern Med 1985; 103: 744–750.
96. Harwood AR, Osoba D, Hofstader SL, et al. Kaposi's sarcoma in recipients of renal transplants. Am J Med 1979; 67: 759–765.
97. Leu HJ, Odermatt B. Multicentric angiosarcoma (Kaposi's sarcoma). Light and electron microscopic and immunohistological findings of idiopathic cases in Europe and Africa and of cases associated with AIDS. Virchows Arch (A) 1985; 408: 29–41.
98. Beckstead JH, Wood GS, Fletcher V. Evidence for the origin of Kaposi's sarcoma from lymphatic endothelium. Am J Pathol 1985; 119: 294–300.
99. Millard PR. AIDS: histopathological aspects. J Pathol 1984; 143: 233–239.

100. Otto HF. Sekundäre Dünndarmkarzinome in: Otto HF, Wanke M, Zeitlhofer J: Darm und Peritoneum. In: Doerr W, Seifert G, Uehlinger E, eds. Spezielle pathologische Anatomie, Band 2, Teil 2, Berlin: Springer, 1967: p 306.
101. Morson BC, Dawson IMP. Gastrointestinal Pathology, 2nd ed. Oxford: Blackwell, 1979: p 411–412.
102. Willis RA. The spread of tumours in the human body. 3rd ed. London: Butterworths, 1973. Secondary tumours of the intestines, p 209.
103. Jorge E, Harvey HA, Simmonds MA, Lipton A, Joehl RJ. Symptomatic malignant melanoma of the gastrointestinal tract. Operative treatment and survival. Ann Surg 1984; 199: 328–331.
104. De Castro CA, Dockerty MB, Mayo CW. Metastatic tumors of the small intestines. Surg Gynec Obst 1957; 105: 159–165.
105. Farmer RG, Hawk WA. Metastatic tumors of the small bowel. Gastroenterology 1964; 47: 496–504.
106. Richie RE, Reynolds VH, Sawyers JL. Tumor metastases to the small bowel from extra-abdominal sites. South Med J 1973; 12: 1383–1387.
107. Das Gupta T, Brasfield R. Metastatic melanoma. A clinicopathological study. Cancer 1964; 17: 1323–1339.
108. Coughlin GP, Bourne AJ, Grant AK. Endoscopic diagnosis of metastatic disease of the stomach and duodenum. Aust N Z Med 1977; 7: 52–55.
109. Laemmli J, Buehler H, Bosseckert H, et al. Metastasen im Duodenum. Schweiz Rundsch Med (Praxis) 1982; 71: 1054–1057.
110. Willbanks OL, Fogelman MJ. Gastrointestinal melanosarcoma. Am J Surg 1970; 120: 602–606.
111. Antler AS, Ough Y, Pitchumoni CS, Davidian M, Thelmo W. Gastrointestinal metastases from malignant tumors of the lung. Cancer 1982; 49: 170–172.
112. Line DH, Deeley TJ. The necropsy findings in carcinoma of the bronchus. Br J Dis Chest 1971; 65: 238–242.
113. Berge T, Ekelund G, Mellner C, Pihl B, Wenckert A. Carcinoma of the colon and rectum in a defined population. Acta Chir Scand 1973; (suppl 438): pp 1–86.
114. Haagensen CD. Diseases of the breast. 2nd ed. Philadelphia: Saunders, 1971: p 426.
115. Lee YTM. Patterns of metastasis and natural course of breast carcinoma. Cancer Metastasis Rev 1985; 4: 153–172.
116. Dupont JB Jr, Lee JR, Burton GR, Cohn IJr. Adenocarcinoma of the stomach: review of 1497 cases. Cancer 1978; 41: 941–947.
117. Ishii T, Ikegami N, Hosoda Y, Koide O, Kaneko M. The biological behaviour of gastric cancer. J Pathol 1981; 134: 97–115.
118. Mulligan RM. Histogenesis and biologic behavior of gastric carcinoma. Pathol Annu 1972; 7: 349–415.
119. Lee YTNM, Tatter D. Carcinoma of the pancreas and periampullary structures. Arch Pathol Lab Med 1984; 108: 584–587.
120. Dvoretsky PM, Richards KA, Bonfiglio TA. The pathology and biologic behaviour of ovarian cancer. An autopsy review. Pathol Ann 1989; 24: 1–24.
121. Julian CG, Goss J, Blanchard K, Woodruff JD. Biologic behaviour of primary ovarian malignancy. Obstet Gynecol 1974; 44: 873–884.
122. Das Gupta TK, Brasfield RD. Metastatic melanoma of the gastrointestinal tract. Arch Surg 1964; 88: 969–973.
123. Cornes JS, Jones TA. Leukaemic lesions of the gastrointestinal tract. J Clin Pathol 1962; 15: 305–313.
124. Prolla JC, Kirsner JB. The gastrointestinal lesions and complications of the leukemias. Ann Intern Med 1964; 61:1084–1103.
125. Brandt-Rauf PW, Pincus M, Adelson S. Cancer of the gallbladder: a review of forty-three cases. Hum Pathol 1982; 13: 48–53.
126. Hamrick RE Jr, Liner FJ, Hastings PR, Cohn I Jr. Primary carcinoma of the gallbladder. Ann Surg 1982; 195: 270–273.
127. Telerman A, Gerard B, Van Den Heule B, Bleiberg H. Gastrointestinal metastases from extra-abdominal tumors. Endoscopy 1985; 17: 99–101.
128. Falterman KW, Hill CB, Markey JC, Fox JW, Cohn I Jr. Cancer of the colon, rectum and anus: a review of 2313 cases. Cancer 1974; 34: 951–959.
129. Scully RE. Tumors of the ovary and maldeveloped glands. Atlas of tumour pathology, 2nd series, fasc. 16. Armed Forces Institute of Pathology, Washington DC, 1979.
130. McNeill PM, Wagman LD, Neifeld JP. Small bowel metastases from primary carcinoma of the lung. Cancer 1987; 59: 1486–1489.
131. Brugo EA, Marshall RB, Riberi AM, Pautasso UE. Preleukemic granulocytic sarcomas of the gastrointestinal tract. Report of two cases. Am J Clin Pathol 1977; 68: 616–621.
132. Friedrich T, Magyarlaki T, Krenacs L. Chlorome des Gastrointestinaltraktes. Bericht ueber 3 Faelle. Pathologe 1989; 10: 278–282.
133. Neiman RS, Barcos M, Berard C, Bonner H, Mann R, Rydell RE, Bennett JM. Granulocytic sarcoma: a clinicopathologic study of 61 biopsied cases. Cancer 1981; 48: 1426–1437.
134. Meis JM, Butler JJ, Osborne BM, Manning JT. Granulocytic sarcoma in nonleukemic patients. Cancer 1986; 58: 2697–2709.
135. Saitoh H, Nakayama M, Nakamura K, Satoh T. Distant metastasis of renal adenocarcinoma in nephrectomized cases. J Urol 1982; 127: 1092–1095.
136. Madeya S, Boersch G. Zur Differentialdiagnose des M. Crohn: segmentale intestinale Metastasierungen beim Mamma- und Magenkarzinom. Leber, Magen, Darm 1989; 19: 140–152.

CHAPTER 41

Other tumours of the large intestine

C. M. Fenoglio-Preiser   A. E. Noffsinger   G. Franzin
G. Zamboni   A. Scarpa   K. Geboes

PART I

Epithelial tumours and tumour-like conditions

C. M. Fenoglio-Preiser   A. E. Noffsinger

EPITHELIAL POLYPS

The term 'polyp' has been used to indicate any projecting tissue mass. Menzel was the first to refer to a colonic polyp, when he described what is currently considered to have been an inflammatory polyp. Today, when one refers to intestinal polyps, one usually thinks of an epithelial lesion, although the term 'polyp' encompasses many gastrointestinal lesions (Table 41.1).

Table 41.1 Classification of colorectal polyps.

1. Hyperplastic polyps
2. Juvenile polyps
3. Peutz-Jeghers polyps
4. Adenomas
   a. Tubular
   b. Villous
   c. Tubulovillous
   d. Polyp containing cancer
5. Mixed adenomatous-hyperplastic polyps
6. Polyps in Cronkhite-Canada syndrome
7. Polyps in Cowden's syndrome
8. Polypoid carcinoma
9. Miscellaneous polyp-like lesions
   a. Inflammatory pseudopolyp
   b. Inflammatory fibroid polyp (Vanek polyp)
   c. Submucosal leiomyoma
   d. Lymphoid polyp
   e. Lymphomatous polyps
   f. Paraganglioma
   g. Carcinoid tumour
   h. Submucosal lipoma
   i. Submucosal neurofibroma
   j. Submucosal schwannoma
   k. Ganglioneuroma

Hyperplastic polyps

Hyperplastic ('metaplastic') polyps represent common benign colorectal lesions affecting adults almost exclusively. They increase in frequency with age. Approximately 40% of adults under the age of 40 and 75% over the age of 40 harbor hyperplastic polyps.[1–2] Their incidence varies depending on whether one examines an autopsy or surgical endoscopic biopsy series. In the latter, the incidence may be underestimated because it depends on whether or not the lesions are removed, and some endoscopists will see small polypoid lesions and not remove them. Hyperplastic polyps occur more commonly in men. The male: female ratio is 4 to 1.[2]

The incidence of hyperplastic polyps generally parallels that of intestinal adenomas and carcinomas. Thus, in Western countries where intestinal adenomas and cancers are common, as many as 85% of patients harbor hyperplastic polyps. This contrasts with an incidence of only 2–3% in countries where colon cancer occurs more rarely.[3]

Most hyperplastic polyps arise in the rectosigmoid[4,5] where they appear as single or multiple dewdrop mucosal elevations with smooth, convex surfaces. Hyperplastic polyps frequently originate on the crest of mucosal folds and have the same colour as the surrounding mucosa (Fig. 41.1). They usually measure less than 5 mm in diameter. Rare hyperplastic polyps are larger than a few millimeters in size. When they are larger, they should be carefully distinguished from serrated adenomas or hyperplastic polyps containing adenomatous tissue (mixed hyperplastic adenomatous polyps).

Most hyperplastic polyps remain asymptomatic, except when they are present in large numbers or are of large size, in which case rectal bleeding or diarrhoea may occur.[2,6,7]

One cannot distinguish between a hyperplastic and neoplastic polyp solely on gross or endoscopic examination. Small lesions, so-called 'diminutive polyps', must be examined histologically to ascertain whether they represent adenomas or hyperplastic polyps. Older literature suggesting that small lesions measuring less than 5 mm in size most likely represent hyperplastic polyps[8] has been challenged by the finding that adenomas also occur in this size range.[1,8–10]

At low power, elongated, 'serrated' crypts with prominent epithelial infoldings characterize the hyperplastic polyp. Ultrastructural and in vitro cell kinetic studies attribute the elongation and subsequent epithelial infoldings to an expanded, but otherwise normally located crypt replicative zone.[11–13] As a result of this expansion of the replication zone, mitoses can easily be seen in the entire lower half of the crypt. Round nuclei lie in a basal location with little or no stratification except possibly at the crypt base. The nuclei lack cytological atypia.

The crypt epithelium consists of intermediate cells containing small apical mucin droplets, interspersed with goblet cells, columnar cells and some immature cells. Endocrine cells can be seen in the crypt bases. At high magnification, the immature cells resemble those seen in adenomas, but the key to distinguishing between the two lesions is to examine the entire crypt length. Evidence of cellular maturation should be noted in hyperplastic polyps as one progresses toward the lumen and the basic crypt architecture should be preserved (Fig. 41.2).[14] The degree of glandular crowding and basophilia is usually less than that seen in adenomas.

Cell kinetic studies of hyperplastic polyps show delayed migration from the crypt base to the surface, resulting in

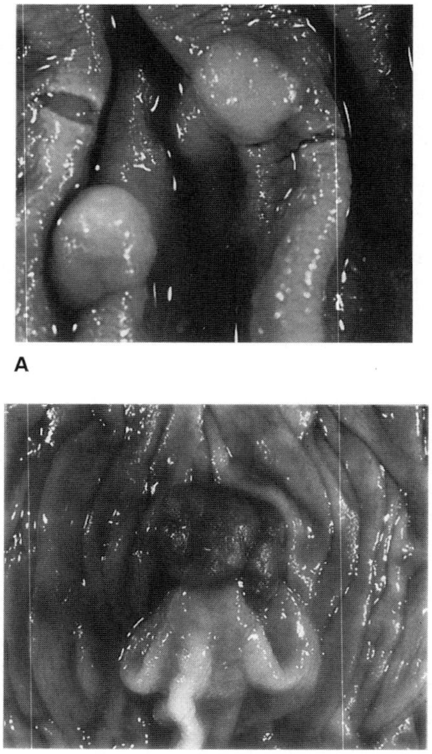

Fig. 41.1 The gross features of hyperplastic (**A**) and adenomatous (**B**) polyps. The hyperplastic polyps are smooth-surfaced mucosal elevations, typically arising on mucosal crests. (Two artefactual tears in the mucosa are present in this photograph.) In contrast, the adenomatous lesion appears darker than normal mucosa and has a lobulated appearance. The stalk of the adenoma consists of normal mucosa.

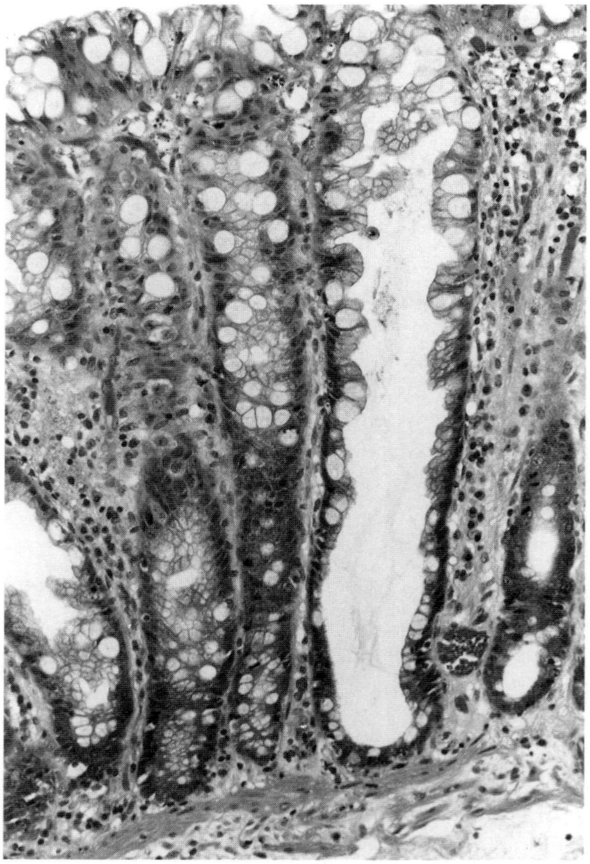

Fig. 41.2 Hyperplastic polyps. A maturation gradient is evident from the base of the crypt to the free surface. Near the surface the cells appear hypermature.

'hypermature' cell populations.[15,16] The cells lining these serrated crypts exhibit exaggerated or abnormal differentiation at the surface.[9,11,17,18] Cellular hyperdifferentiation distinguishes hyperplastic polyps from adenomas since the cells lining adenomatous crypts all appear immature. Goblet cells of hyperplastic polyps appear larger than their normal counterparts. Absorptive cells are also hyperdifferentiated with basally-placed, rounded nuclei. The hypermature cells produce increased amounts of both mucin and carcinoembryonic antigen localized to the area of the glycocalyx.[18,19] The collagen table at the luminal surface of hyperplastic polyps appears thicker than that in the adjacent normal mucosa. This thickening results from functional and morphological hyperplasia of the pericryptal fibroblast sheath.[17,20]

Normal lamina propria separates the evenly spaced, regularly arranged glands. However, the number of plasma cells may be reduced[21] and T cells increased.[22] Occasional fibres of the muscularis mucosae extend into the lamina propria of hyperplastic polyps; these can be quite prominent[23] but they are never present to the degree seen in Peutz-Jeghers polyps.[23]

Inverted hyperplastic polyps display endophytic growth through the muscularis mucosae into the underlying submucosa. The lesion's crowded glands may be mistaken for carcinoma, from which it differs by the absence of cytological atypia. Additionally, the glands usually display a regular serrated architecture. In contrast to the usual hyperplastic polyp, inverted hyperplastic polyps occur more often in the right colon and are more common in women.[24]

The exact nature and aetiology of hyperplastic polyps remains unclear. Franzin et al postulated that they may have an inflammatory or ischaemic origin.[4] Hyperplastic polyps do share certain epidemiological features and cellular phenotypes with colorectal carcinomas. Like carcinoma, hyperplastic polyps produce increased carcinoembryonic antigen, decreased IgA, and contain O-acylated sialomucins.[25–27] Although most investigators generally agree that hyperplastic polyps have no malignant potential of their own, some argue that the presence of hyperplastic polyps predicts neoplastic polyps elsewhere in the colon.[28] Not all investigators agree with this view.[29] It has also been postulated that the lesion represents a marker for an environmental factor implicated in the progression of adenoma to carcinoma.[26] Alternatively, it may represent the ability of the colonic mucosa to respond to its environment resulting not in neoplasia, but a self-limited mucosal dysmaturation. Finally, it should also be noted that foci of adenomatous change may be seen in 0.1–1% of cases.[6,30,31] In this situation, the adenomatous epithelium may predispose to the development of malignancy.

In evaluating polypoid lesions, it is important for the pathologist to know what the surgeon saw and biopsied since zones of hyperplasia can occur at the edges of a carcinoma. If the biopsy is taken at the edge of a larger mass, the diagnosis of a hyperplastic polyp should not be made, since it might imply the presence of an unwarranted benign process.

Hyperplastic polyposes

Hyperplastic polyposis consists of hyperplastic polyps that appear larger than normal, are often pedunculated, and arise throughout the large bowel.[2] This condition usually occurs in young patients. Mixed polyps with synchronous or metachronous carcinomas are described in some of these patients.[32–34]

Juvenile polyps

Juvenile polyps represent non-neoplastic, possibly hamartomatous gastrointestinal mucosal proliferations. They occur most commonly in children and adolescents[8,19,35] with the peak incidence occurring at 4–5 years of age; males and females are equally affected. In one study they were found in 3.1% of children under age 14. Juvenile polyps also rarely arise in adults, sometimes at the site of ureteral implantation.[36] Juvenile polyps account for most colorectal polyps in children where they are usually solitary. If more than 3–4 polyps are found, a polyposis syndrome should be suspected.

Commonly, patients present with small amounts of bright red blood during defaecation. Less commonly, anaemia, abdominal pain or intussusception occur. In some instances the polyp prolapses from the anus. Most lesions regress before adolescence.

Grossly, over 90% of juvenile polyps appear pedunculated. These sausage-shaped lesions measure 1–3 cm in average diameter. Occasionally they reach 3–4 cm, but only rarely are they larger. Juvenile polyps usually have smooth, bright red, friable surfaces which bleed easily when traumatized. On cut section they show characteristic yellow-white mucus-filled cysts accompanied by scattered haemorrhagic areas.

Microscopically, they demonstrate a characteristic swiss-cheese appearance created by dilated mucinous lakes widely separated by abundant stroma (Fig. 41.3). The stroma lacks the prominent proliferation of smooth muscle cells seen in Peutz-Jeghers polyps. When the surface erodes, capillaries proliferate in the superficial lamina propria forming areas of granulation tissue. With further ulceration, glands become more dilated, the granulation tissue shows increasing reactive changes, and inflammatory cells increase in number. Stromal vascular congestion and diffuse stromal haemorrhage ensue. The lamina propria is infiltrated by a prominent inflammatory cell infiltrate, consisting of neutrophils, eosinophils, lymphocytes, plasma cells and histiocytes. The presence of

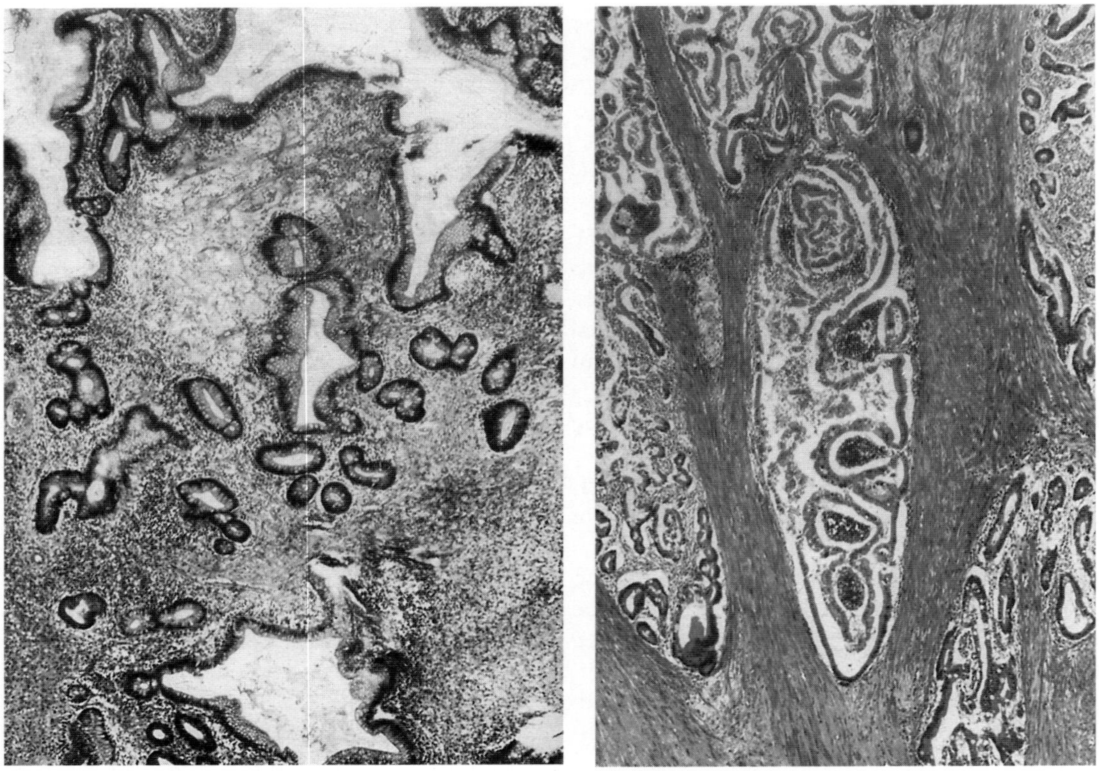

A B

Fig. 41.3 Juvenile (**A**) and Peutz-Jeghers (**B**) polyps. Both juvenile and Peutz-Jeghers polyps consist of nonneoplastic epithelium. The juvenile polyp demonstrates increased amounts of oedematous stroma that frequently contains collections of inflammatory cells. The glands are irregular and cystically dilated. In contrast, Peutz-Jeghers polyps have islands of epithelium separated by an arborizing smooth muscle proliferation. Lamina propria surrounds the glands.

lymphoid follicles correlates with the degree of inflammation.[14] Oedema may be quite prominent in areas of erosion or inflammation. The granulation tissue matures into dense fibrous connective tissue, sometimes containing metaplastic bone or cartilage. Neutrophils accumulate at the ulcerated edges and around telangiectatic vessels.[14,35]

We have been fooled by biopsies of juvenile polyps taken in patients we were told had clinical features of ulcerative colitis. Given the history of active ulcerative colitis and biopsies of lesions we were told were polyps, it was easy to mistake the eroded surfaces of juvenile polyps for the inflammatory polyps associated with ulcerative colitis. The correct diagnosis only became evident when the bowel was removed.

In juvenile polyps, the glands consist of normal epithelium indigenous to the site of origin. The glands appear elongated, are often branched[14] and demonstrate a much more haphazard arrangement than is seen in hyperplastic polyps. The irregular crypts may appear serrated as the result of either the irregular branching or the epithelial hyperplasia.

A single layer of cytologically bland, cuboidal to columnar, mucus-secreting epithelium lines the glands. Paneth cells and endocrine cells are present, but are sparse. Some glands may be filled with mucus or inflammatory debris. These become cystically dilated, herniating into the surrounding stroma with mucus and inflammatory cells and debris extending outward. These cysts are usually lined by either normal or flattened (atrophic) epithelial cells that demonstrate little or no atypia except perhaps near the surface where the epithelium erodes and appears reactive. Here, cytoplasmic mucin depletion and reactive nuclear changes of the glandular epithelium occur commonly[14] and must be distinguished from true adenomatous changes. Regenerative epithelium is recognized by the presence of eosinophilic cuboidal cells containing mitoses and abundant cytoplasm. The nuclei are small and basally located, and only small amounts of mucin are present within this regenerative epithelium. The nuclear-cytoplasmic ratio often favours the cytoplasm. Additionally, syncytial-like cellular masses may be present.

Ultrastructurally[37] and histochemically,[35] the epithelium of juvenile polyps resembles both normal colonic mucosa and the epithelium seen in inflammatory polyps. Rarely, juvenile polyps contain areas that qualify for a diagnosis of ganglioneuroma.[38,39]

Adenomatous or dysplastic areas can arise in juvenile polyps. Often the adenomatous areas lie in superficial parts of the crypt with normal appearing colonic epithelium lining the lower parts of the crypt. The adenomatous epithelium appears identical to that found in adenomatous polyps. When this occurs, it usually does so in the setting of juvenile polyposis.[40–42] We tend to avoid diagnosing areas of adenomatous transformation in areas of acute inflammation in juvenile polyps unless the cytological changes are absolutely typical for adenoma.

The histogenesis of juvenile polyps remains controversial. Some authors claim that they represent hamartomas[43] whereas others claim they have an inflammatory aetiology.[44] Mucosal ulceration with secondary occlusion of gland necks by inflammation and granulation tissue leads to mucus retention, cystic glandular dilatation and eventual polyp formation.[44] For this reason, juvenile polyps have also been called 'retention' polyps.

The natural history of juvenile polyps is poorly understood. Auto-amputation occurs in up to 10% of cases,[45] but this figure may underestimate its true frequency since this event often goes undetected. New polyps are found at re-examination in 3–18% of cases.[45,46] It is generally agreed that patients with *solitary* juvenile polyps are not at increased risk for the development of gastrointestinal malignancy.[41,44] However, long-term follow-up studies of patients are lacking, and there are rare reports of carcinoma arising in solitary juvenile polyps.[41,47–49]

Peutz-Jeghers polyps

Peutz-Jeghers polyps (PJPs) represent hamartomatous lesions occurring throughout the gastrointestinal tract; most commonly they arise in the small intestine. PJPs tend to be less numerous than the polyps seen in familial adenomatosis coli and often represent a component of the Peutz-Jeghers syndrome.

Grossly, PJPs may resemble other types of gastrointestinal polyps. They are generally multiple and pedunculated with lobulated surfaces, and measure between 0.5–3.0 cm in diameter. When they are pedunculated, the stalk is often short, broad and poorly formed.[14,40] Rare lesions measure more than 4.0 cm in diameter.[40,50] The surfaces appear pink or tan unless they become eroded, in which case they appear hemorrhagic.

Microscopically, Peutz-Jeghers polyps consist of elongated, branching glands lined by the epithelium native to the polyp location. In the small intestine, the epithelium contains absorptive columnar cells, goblet cells, endocrine cells and Paneth cells. Colonic polyps contain numerous goblet cells; gastric polyps contain parietal cells, chief cells and mucous cells. The zone of epithelial replication is located at the crypt base and is of normal length unless the PJP is ulcerated or regenerating, in which case the proliferative zones become exaggerated and elongated, and may contain many mitoses. Peutz-Jeghers polyps contain less stroma than juvenile polyps and cystic changes in the glands occur less commonly.[14]

The tree-like ramification of the muscularis mucosae represents the most characteristic feature of PJPs. It creates the appearance of division of the tissue into epithelial compartments. The arborising core of muscle becomes thinner and thinner, and eventually disappears at the periphery of the lesion.[14] Sometimes the histological pattern of the PJP is so complex as to suggest that an invasive process has occurred. However, the presence of normal lamina propria surrounding individual glands, the presence of bland, nonatypical epithelium, and the presence of normal cellular types in the absence of desmoplastic stroma provide evidence of the benignity of these lesions. Occasional haemosiderin deposits suggest previous trauma. In about 10% of cases, benign-appearing glands lie deep in the submucosa, muscularis propria or serosa.[14,51] They may appear to be connected to, or completely separated from, the overlying surface epithelium. In rare cases, glands are located deep in the bowel wall, or on the serosa, in the absence of an overlying mucosal polyp.[19] In other situations, mucinous cysts without an apparent epithelial lining occur which may be partially or totally lined by normal-appearing goblet cells, absorptive cells and endocrine cells.[52] This entity has been termed enteritis cystica profunda.[53] Entrapment of glands within the smooth muscle of the stalk in the muscularis propria, or even in the serosa, results in cystic dilatation. This gives the appearance of carcinomatous invasion. The lack of cytological atypia, as well as the absence of a fibrous stromal response, distinguishes these changes from invasive carcinoma. The presence of benign glandular and cystic structures within all layers of the bowel wall supports the fact that these lesions represent hamartomas. Alternatively, they may represent zones of pseudoinvasion caused by fibrosis and glandular entrapment associated with previous episodes of trauma, perhaps secondary to episodes of intussusception or ulceration.[19]

The characteristic histological pattern may be altered by the presence of surface ulceration, granulation tissue, inflammatory cells and reactive epithelial changes. Such changes should not be mistaken for adenomatous glands.

Although PJPs represent non-neoplastic lesions with little or no innate malignant potential, polyps have been reported that contain a spectrum of neoplastic lesions ranging from adenomatous epithelium with variable dysplasia to carcinoma in situ or even invasive carcinoma.[40,50,54–57]

Adenomatous polyps (adenomas)

Adenomas represent the prototypic intestinal precancerous lesions (Table 41.2),[14,40] although some debate the role of small tubular adenomas.[58–60] Adenomas are benign,

Table 41.2 Adenoma–carcinoma sequence. (Modified from Fenoglio-Preiser CM, Pascal RR, Perzin KH. Tumours of the large and small intestine. AFIP Fascicle, 2nd Series, 1990)

Arguments cited in support of the concept:
1. Similar distribution in the bowel of adenomas and carcinomas
2. Prevalence rates of adenomas and carcinomas in countries at various magnitudes of colon carcinoma risk show correlation between the two
3. Increased frequency of carcinoma in patients with adenomas
4. Adenomas present in patients who develop metachronous carcinomas show a significant excess of areas of severe dysplasia compared to adenomas present in patients in whom a second cancer did not develop
5. Adenomas occur with increased frequency in colons containing carcinomas
6. Increasing age of patients with increasing degrees of atypia and areas of invasive cancer (age succession ⟶ carcinoma)
7. Production of both adenomas and carcinomas in laboratory animals
8. Endoscopic removal of adenomas reduces the expected incidence of carcinoma
9. All patients with familial polyposis develop cancer if adenoma-bearing colon not removed
10. Absence of carcinoma-in-situ outside the area of adenomas
11. Areas of direct transition between adenoma and carcinoma
12. Patients who have adenomas identified endoscopically who refuse therapy eventually return with an invasive carcinoma at the same site
13. Failure to demonstrate carcinoma 3 mm or less in normal mucosa despite the countless thousands of polyps and colon resections examined histologically each year
14. Growth of adenomatous cells in vitro results in cell populations that acquire the features of carcinoma-in-situ or invasive carcinoma
15. Chromosomal constitution in adenomatous and carcinomatous tissue is similar
16. Antigenic relatedness between adenomas and carcinomas
17. DNA content of benign adenomas is intermediate between normal colon and cancer
18. Enzyme patterns are similar in adenomas and carcinomas

Arguments cited against the concept:
1. Different distribution of adenomas and carcinomas in some studies
2. Same incidence of carcinoma developing in patients with and without polyps
3. Failure to demonstrate areas of adenoma in 'small' carcinomas
4. Failure to demonstrate carcinomas in adenomas

glandular neoplasms originating from the colorectal mucosal epithelium characterized by their unrestricted cell proliferation and their failure to differentiate. These proliferative abnormalities are the key to their preneoplastic status since marked changes in cell proliferation occur in early stages of carcinogenesis and play a decisive role in the progressive development of cancer.

Incidence and distribution

The incidence and prevalence of colorectal adenomas varies throughout the world. Adenomas rarely occur in populations with a low incidence of colon carcinoma and are commonly encountered in populations with a high colon cancer incidence.[61–66]

Adenomas occur in all age groups, but there is a sharp rise in their incidence in patients without hereditary polyposis syndromes at about age 40. Their incidence peaks at the age of 60 or 70 and drops thereafter, probably due to a decline in the number of individuals of this age in the general population. The prevalence of adenomas may be 30% or more in individuals older than 40 years in the United States and northwestern Europe.[61,67,68] A slight male predominance has been reported.

For decades it was believed that at last three-quarters of colorectal adenomas and carcinomas arose within reach of the rigid sigmoidoscope.[69–71] However, more recent work suggests an increasing incidence of proximal lesions. Many investigators have found a relative increase in right-sided adenomas, particularly in elderly individuals.[65,66,69,72–74] Some adenomas arise as a complication of ostomy creation.[35,75–77] There also may be a relationship to cholecystectomy.[78]

Synchronous and metachronous lesions

Adenomas usually appear as single lesions but they may occur in groups. Multiple lesions occur twice as often in males as in females.[19] Patients with multiple adenomas may have a hereditary or non-hereditary polyposis syndrome.

New polyps occur in up to 32–55% of polyp patients followed for four or five years,[79] and the chance of finding new polyps is greater if multiple polyps were diagnosed initially.[80] Autopsy, surgical and colonoscopic studies have found synchronous neoplasms in 20–61% of patients.[70,71,73] Approximately 16% of patients in the National Polyp Study had multiple tubular lesions; 24.4% had multiple villous lesions.[81] Often, the index adenoma arises in the rectosigmoid area.[82] The larger the index adenoma the more likely the patient is to have additional synchronous neoplasms.[83] 12% of the adenomas containing malignancy have synchronous colonic adenocarcinomas at the time of diagnosis.[70,83] Based on these data, patients with one adenomatous polyp should be evaluated further for the presence of additional lesions.

Recurrence rates

The overall recurrence rates for colorectal polyps are estimated at 21–41% with average follow-up times of 5–10 years after index polypectomy. The local recurrence rate following surgical excision alone of a villous adenoma of the colon and rectum ranges from 17–30%.[84,85] The recurrence rate for villous adenomas that have been fulgurated is significantly higher than that for polyps that have been resected. Recurrence usually occurs in the first two years after treatment, and is more common in sessile lesions. One of the difficulties in estimating recurrence rates is that it is not always clear whether the 'recurrent adenomas' represent new polyps or reflect incomplete removal of the index lesion.

Clinical features

Most colorectal adenomas remain asymptomatic and are only found incidentally at the time of surgery for other things, at autopsy, or during screening procedures. When polyps become symptomatic, the signs and symptoms depend on polyp size and location. Small adenomas up to 1 cm in maximum diameter often remain asymptomatic unless they arise in the rectosigmoid. In this location, they bleed as they are traumatized by the passage of well-formed, hardened stool over their surfaces. As adenomas enlarge, bleeding becomes more common. Villous tumours tend to bleed more than tubular ones, as the former are likely to be larger and to contain an invasive carcinoma. Most typically, rectal bleeding remains occult, underscoring the importance of screening tests to detect colorectal neoplasia. Other presentations include obstruction, incontinence, prolapse, anaemia, abdominal pain, flatulence, constipation or diarrhoea. Lesions that block the appendiceal lumen cause acute appendicitis.

Massive fluid and electrolyte loss[85] resulting from secretion of large amounts of electrolyte-rich mucus represents an uncommon manifestation of some villous adenomas. Severe hypokalaemia may occur, but potassium levels return to normal once the lesion is excised. This entity is sometimes referred to as the villous adenoma depletion syndrome.[86] Cyclic nucleotides appear to mediate the syndrome.[86]

Gross appearance

Current rationales for surgical intervention are predicated upon polyp size, sessile versus pedunculated growth patterns, adequacy of the margins, patient age and the presence of multiple synchronous or metachronous adenomas.[87] Adenomas range in size from microscopic to large carpet-like lesions. The location of large villous and tubulovillous adenomas is predominantly in the right colon (28%) and the rectosigmoid (55%).[70,87,88] The morphology of these polyps is predominantly sessile.

Many reports exist describing the morphogenesis of colorectal adenomas, particularly large macroscopic ones. It was originally believed that all adenomas had a polypoid growth[17,89,90] and that these arose from single glands, culminating in polypoid lesions consisting of multiple glands.[90–92] Today we recognize that not all adenomas assume a polypoid architecture. Chang and Whitener described the horizontal and vertical growth of adenomas.[93] Bussey in 1975 described depressed adenomas, but considered them to be unusual.[94] Recently, Kubota studied more than 5000 adenomas in patients with familial adenomatous polyposis and discovered that 12% appeared depressed, 18.3% were flat and 69.7% were polypoid.[95] Depressed adenomas constituted approximately 15% of all adenomatous lesions measuring less than 1.5 mm in diameter. They were rare, however, in lesions measuring 1.5–2 mm, and were not found among lesions measuring more than 2 mm. These findings suggest that the ordinary polypoid adenomas may originate from minute depressed adenomas. In elderly women without a polyposis syndrome, flat adenomas tend to involve the caecum.[96]

The more common polypoid adenomas assume one of three gross appearances: pedunculated, sessile or semi-sessile. The surface may be multilobulated, reddish, friable and raspberry-like (Figure 41.1A). Generally, adenoma size, shape and architecture correlate with one another. The larger the lesion, the more likely it is to be sessile and villous. Adenomatous polyps measuring only 1–2 mm resemble hyperplastic polyps. Larger adenomas occur in patients with multiple adenomas.[96] In one autopsy-based study, 97% of adenomas were tubular and 83% measured less than 10 mm.[96]

Smaller pedunculated adenomas appear spherical and sometimes are received with pedicle or stalk. Larger sessile villous adenomas demonstrate shaggy surfaces composed of numerous fronds and tend to be less well circumscribed than polypoid lesions. These have a greater tendency to recur after local excision because neoplastic tissue may be left behind.

When cut, most adenomas demonstrate a homogeneous surface. Areas of ulceration, depression or induration suggest the possibility of co-existing carcinoma. However, the same features may also be seen in polyps that have undergone repeated ulceration with bleeding, fibrosis and pseudocarcinomatous invasion. Villous and tubulovillous lesions have a known propensity to develop carcinoma. Perhaps the most difficult adenoma to recognize is the flat adenoma. It can be recognized by its characteristic features of slight elevation with a reddened surface. Some contain central depressions.[97]

Microscopic appearance

Despite architectural differences, all adenomatous polyps represent expressions of the same basic neoplastic process.[17,98,99] As a result, their cytological features resemble one another, whether the adenoma is classified as flat, tubular, tubulovillous or villous. Adenomas in non-polyposis patients generally consist of multiple adenomatous crypts. A rare example of a unicryptal adenoma was found in a biopsy specimen from a non-polyposis patient.[100]

The original crypt architecture is maintained in tubular adenomas with the native epithelium being replaced by adenomatous epithelium. As the adenomatous tubules grow, they branch and become more irregular. The tubular configuration occurs in very small sessile adenomas and in the larger pedunculated adenomas. The stalk consists of non-neoplastic epithelium resembling that of the surrounding normal mucosa. Tubular adenomas constitute the majority of adenomatous polyps.[101] Villous adenomas consist of finger-like processes covered by adenomatous epithelium. Villous components can be defined as 'adjacent crypts or folia of adenomatous epithelium, that, without branching, are elongated to a minimum of twice the length of the normal crypt.'[101] A mixture of both tubular and villous structures defines a tubulovillous pattern. 75–85% of the lesion should be either tubular or villous to qualify for the diagnosis of a tubulovillous adenoma.[70,71] A villous component is present in 35–75% of all adenomas greater than 1 cm in diameter.[98,102] Normal appearing lamina propria separates the glands of all adenomas whether flat, tubular or villous.

Histologically, flat adenomas occupy the full mucosal thickness and appear to have a slightly elevated architecture. These tubular adenomas can contain significant degrees of atypia.[97]

Because fundamental cellular growth controls are lost in adenomas, cell division is unrestricted and cell maturation is disturbed.[20,103] This means that one sees mitoses throughout the entire length of the crypt as well as on the free surface. The maturation gradient that is evident as one goes from the base of the normal crypt to its surface, disappears. Rather, tall cells with prominent elongated hyperchromatic, enlarged nuclei arranged in a pseudostratified pattern produce the characteristic 'picket-fence' pattern (Fig. 41.4). The mucus content is variably decreased; however, occasional adenomas with abundant mucus production are encountered. Even though the cells histologically appear immature, special techniques demonstrate organized gradients of differentiation along the villi in villous adenomas.[104] Occasionally, adenomas contain true goblet cells which may appear immature with an eccentric nucleus. These are termed 'dystrophic goblet cells' (Fig. 41.4).[14,98] Adenomas contain absorptive cells, goblet cells and intermediate cells.[11,12] Additional cell types include endocrine cells, Paneth cells and squamous cells. Endocrine cells, although usually scant in number within a given tumour, are seen in 60–85% of adenomas.[105] Occasionally, one encounters lesions containing numerous endocrine cells. Paneth cells are encountered in approximately 10% of adenomas[105] and areas of squamous differentiation forming morules occur in approximately 4%.[105–109] A rare adenoma contained melanocytes.[105]

The epithelial-mesenchymal partnership described in normal and hyperplastic crypts is maintained in adenomas.[20,103,110] Therefore, the pericryptal fibroblast sheath contains immature fibroblasts which fail to produce the usual amount of collagen, resulting in a collagen table that is thinner than normal.[14,111]

As a polypoid architecture develops, small, finger-like extensions of smooth muscle from the muscularis mucosae splay apart and may be carried upwards into the mucosa for short distances, carrying with them the lymphatic plexus (Fig. 41.5). The lymphatic plexus begins just above the muscularis mucosae area and never appears higher than the bases of the crypts.[112] There is usually an abrupt transition between the adenoma and its surrounding normal tissue.

Serrated adenomas

Serrated adenomas are distinctive because they exhibit the architectural but not the cytological features of a hyperplastic polyp (Fig. 41.6). They contain a serrated glandular pattern that simulates that observed in hyperplasia or hyperplastic polyps (Fig. 41.6). However, epithelial immaturity, upper crypt zone mitoses, prominent nucleoli and the absence of a thickened collagen table distinguish these lesions from hyperplastic polyps. In most cases, mitoses are observed throughout the length of the crypts, and in 72% of cases the lesions contain mild-to-marked degrees of nuclear stratification that closely parallel that observed in tubular adenomas. The nuclear-cytoplasmic ratio is intermediate between hyperplastic polyps and traditional adenomatous polyps. Their nuclei are either ovoid (43%) or penicillate (51%). In addition, prominent eosinophilic nucleoli are frequently present within these nuclei. The collagen table is also thinned. Foci of significant dysplasia may be noted within these lesions (Fig. 41.7).[31] The glands of the serrated adenoma appear to be lined by a monotonous cell population that contains more mucus than most adenomas, but fewer mature cells than one typically observes in hyperplastic polyps. Because of the overlapping histological features, these lesions create considerable confusion for the diagnostician and, in fact, are often misdiagnosed as hyperplastic polyps.

Mixed hyperplastic and adenomatous polyps

Polyps do exist in which both well-defined adenomatous and hyperplastic patterns are identifiable. In contrast to the serrated adenomas that exhibit the architectural but not necessarily the cytological patterns of a hyperplastic polyp, each of the hyperplastic and adenomatous elements in the mixed hyperplastic-adenomatous polyps appear distinctive and are readily identifiable as being either hyperplastic or adenomatous in nature. The hyperplastic

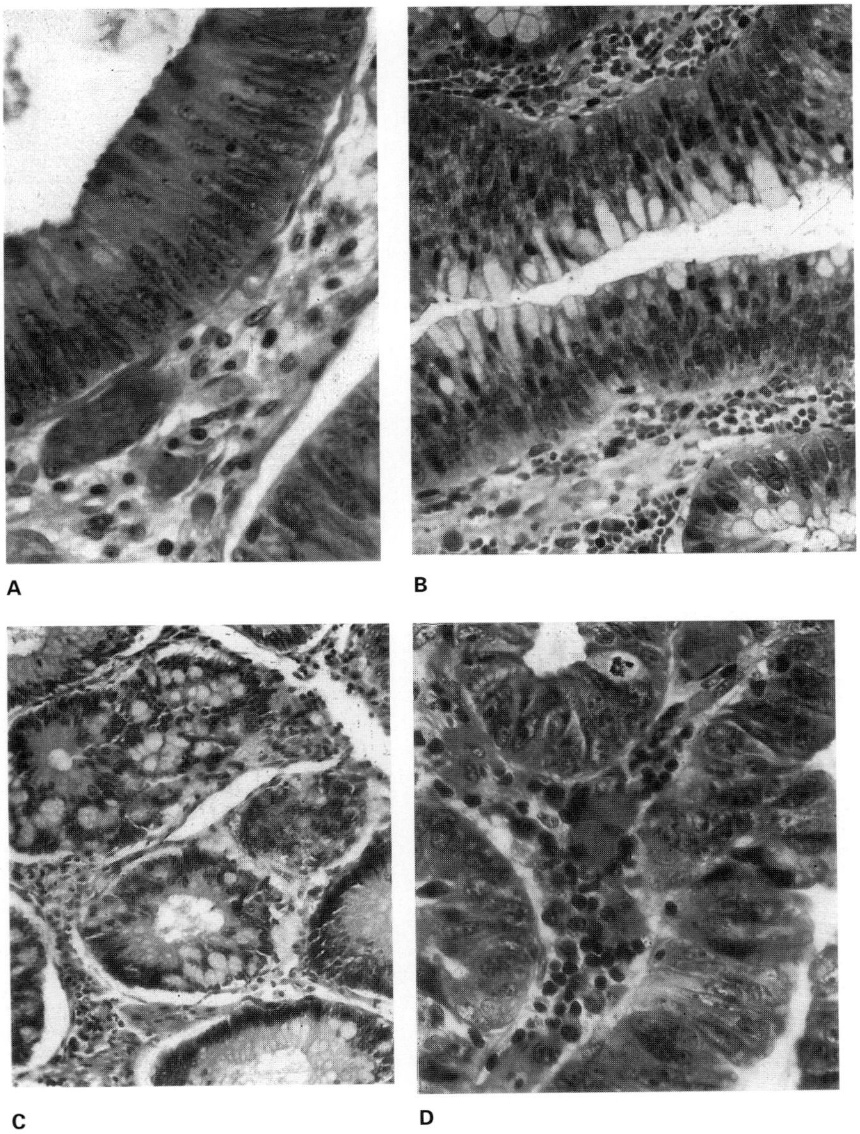

Fig. 41.4 Adenomatous polyps demonstrating varying degrees of mucin production and atypia. **A** The typical 'picket-fence' architecture of the nuclei is present in this adenoma. The cells are minimally atypical and little mucus production is seen. **B** The grossly pseudostratified adenomatous cells in this adenoma contain more mucin than is present in **A**, but the cells demonstrate the same degree of atypia. **C** Dysplastic goblet cells are present in many of these crypts. They appear as intracryptal signet-ring cells. **D** Moderate-severe dysplasia is present in this adenomatous polyp. Almost no visible mucus is produced.

epithelium may be located at the edges of the lesion or admixed with the adenomatous tissue.[31]

The existence of hyperplastic glands in adenomatous polyps was first described by Goldman et al in adenomas of the villous architectural type. Because these investigators did not observe similar features in other types of adenomatous polyps, they speculated that hyperplastic polyps and villous adenomas were interrelated and proposed a hyperplastic polyp-villous adenoma sequence.[30] Subsequently, the occurrence of hyperplastic changes in adenomas was confirmed and extended to include both the tubular and tubulovillous variants.[31]

Pseudocarcinomatous invasion

A common dilemma is assessing whether or not neoplastic epithelium in adenomas has become invasive. This is particularly difficult when pseudoinvasion, also known as pseudocarcinomatous entrapment or epithelial misplacement, has occurred. Pseudocarcinomatous entrapment affects 2–10% of adenomas.[113–117] Adenomas prone to undergo pseudoinvasion tend to be larger than 1 cm, and have a stalk of at least 1 cm in length. They are more commonly located in the sigmoid colon[117] because lesions in this location are more easily traumatized by the passage of hard stool over them. This ulcerates the surface and eventually displaces the adenomatous epithelium into the underlying submucosa of the head of the polyp. The displaced adenomatous glands in pseudocarcinomatous entrapment are usually surrounded by normal lamina propria and usually lack the severe cytological atypia of carcinoma. In contrast, carcinomatous invasion characteristically evokes a dense desmoplastic response and the lamina propria is absent.

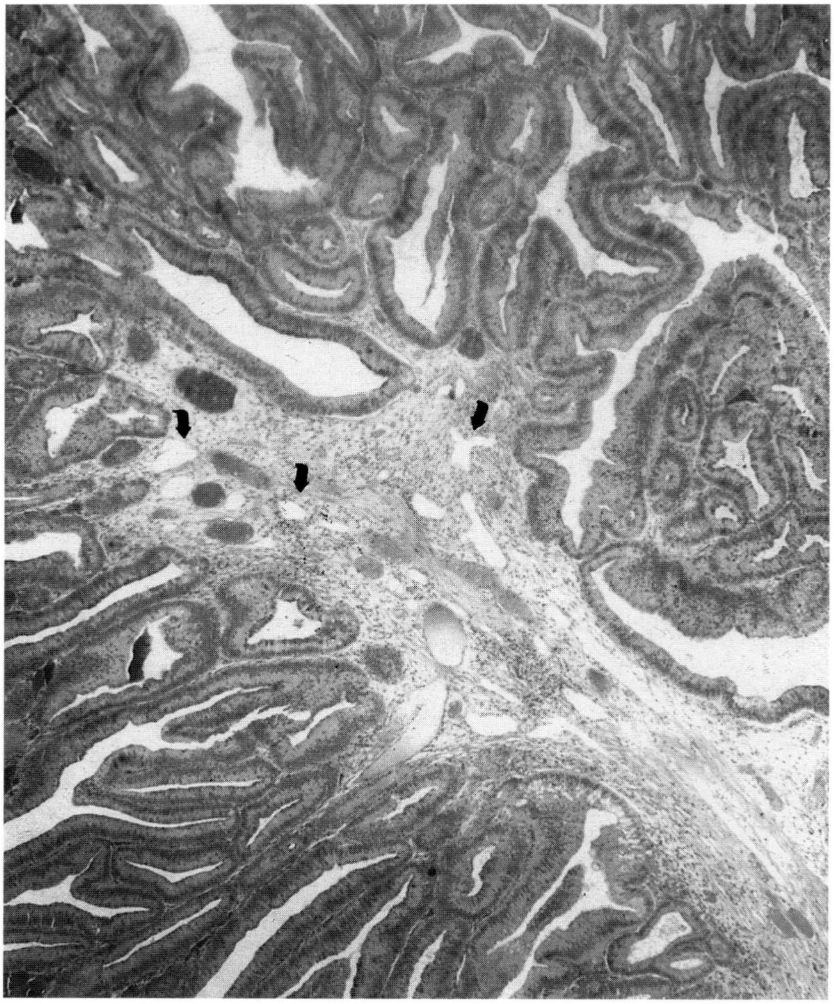

Fig. 41.5 Adenomatous polyp with dilated lymphatics and capillaries. The lymphatics represent irregular spaces containing lymph but no red blood cells. They follow the fibres of the frayed muscularis mucosae (arrows).

Recognition of displaced epithelium is easiest in the adenoma that does not contain significant epithelial dysplasia. However, when an adenoma contains areas of severe dysplasia, intramucosal carcinoma or carcinoma in situ that are displaced into the underlying submucosa, the distinction from an invasive process can be more difficult. Step sections through the lesion sometimes demonstrate continuity between the atypical submucosal glands and the surface. One might also look for benign epithelium in continuity with the malignant glands to help identify the process as representing pseudoinvasion. Additionally, careful examination may reveal the presence of remnants of the lamina propria surrounding the deep glands. The presence of dysplasia in these displaced glands does not alter the prognosis of the patient and does not imply a risk of metastasis.

Malignant potential of adenomatous polyps

Most adenocarcinomas of the colorectum arise in the visible benign precursor lesion, the adenoma. The dilemma is that not all adenomatous polyps evolve into carcinoma during the lifespan of an individual patient. If they were to do so, the incidence of invasive carcinomas would be higher than it currently is, based on the prevalence of colonic adenomas.

Numerous studies have focused on the anatomical factors that correlate with transformation of benign adenomas to malignant tumours. Such factors include high grade dysplasia defined as severe dysplasia or carcinoma in situ; these probably represent the pathological bridge between the benign adenoma and adenoma with invasive cancer. In addition, molecular factors have been identified that define several high risk groups.

In familial adenomatous polyposis syndrome, autosomal dominant inheritance of the mutated APC (adenomatous polyposis coli) gene on chromosome 5q21 typically results in thousands of colorectal adenomas.[118,119] Adenocarcinomas develop in some of these adenomas. Similarly, in hereditary nonpolyposis colorectal cancer (HNPCC)

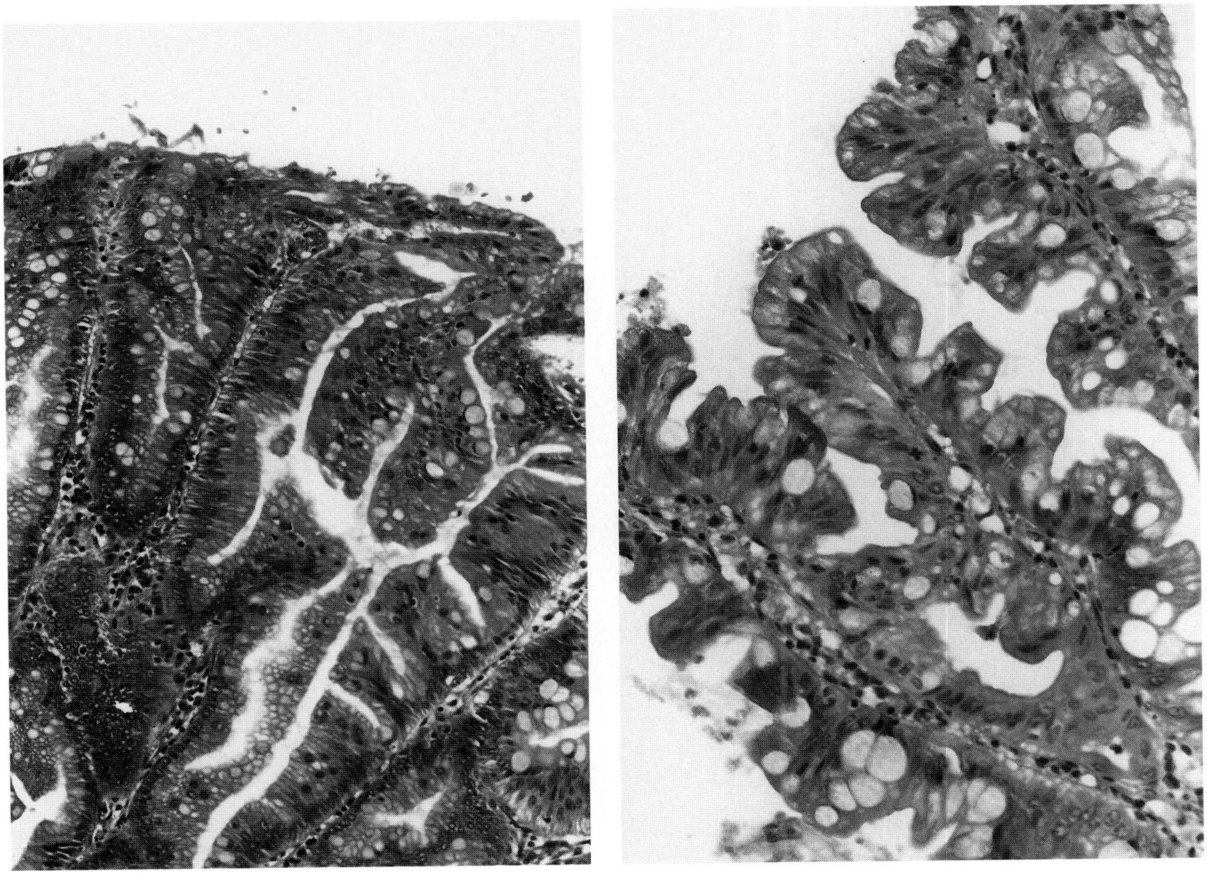

A B

Fig. 41.6 Serrated adenomas. **A** and **B** represent two different examples of serrated adenomas. The cytological features of **A** are reminiscent of adenomas but the lumen is serrated. The cells in **B** are more reminiscent of a hyperplastic polyp when first examined. However, in contrast to hyperplastic polyps, the nuclei are penicillate and mildly pseudostratified.

syndrome, the autosomal dominant inheritance of an unidentified gene appears to result in a small number of adenomas which frequently progress to adenocarcinoma predominantly in the right colon.[120] A new colorectal cancer prone disorder, the hereditary flat adenoma syndrome, has been described recently. This autosomal dominantly inherited syndrome is characterized by a predisposition to multiple colonic adenomas with a proximal predominance and flat rather than polypoid growth pattern.[121,122] The cancers in this disorder occur randomly in the colon and have a later age of onset (approximately 55 years of age) than those associated with FAP and the Lynch syndromes. Hereditary flat adenoma syndrome is similar to FAP in that both syndromes feature colonic adenomas and had a high life-time risk for developing colon cancer.[123] They are both linked to chromosome 5q.[124]

Adenomas and cancers also occur in familial aggregates of colorectal cancer in the absence of a recognizable syndrome.[125,126] Finally, patients who develop 'sporadic' cancers also develop adenomas that can become malignant. Thus, many variations of the adenoma-carcinoma sequence exist, each possibly affected by inherited and/or acquired genetic events alone or in combination with environmental factors. The fact that the formation of adenomas is common to many of these situations reinforces the role of the adenoma as the major precursor to colon cancer.

One often sees a continuous histological spectrum in adenomas as evidenced by increasing degrees of dysplasia culminating in the development of frankly invasive carcinoma (Figs 41.4, 41.8). The formation of adenomatous epithelium constitutes the first step. By definition, all adenomas contain at least mild dysplasia. In mild dysplasia, the crypts show branching or elongation with reduction in the intervening stroma. Cell nuclei appear oval, regularly overlapping and basally located. Nuclear membranes are regular, nucleoli are conspicuous and the chromatin pattern is finely distributed. When the cells become moderately dysplastic, they lose some of their basal polarity. Nuclear membranes become more irregular, nucleoli become more prominent and the chromatin pattern becomes uneven. The stratified nuclei do not

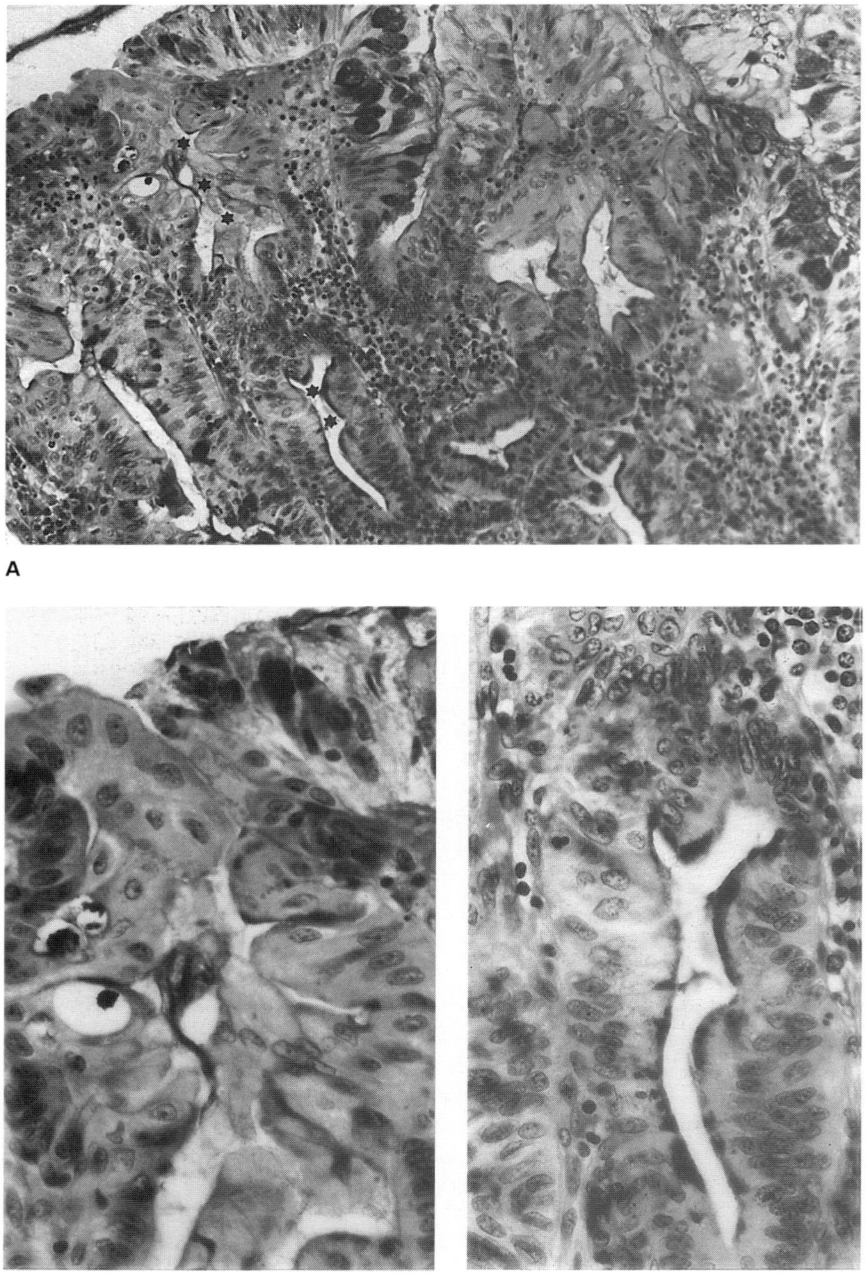

A

B C

Fig. 41.7 Serrated adenoma. **B** and **C** represent higher magnifications of the surface and lower portions of the crypt in **A** that contains stars in the lumen. As can be seen in **A–C**, the lesion has the serrated architecture of a hyperplastic polyp. However, epithelial atypia with lack of differentiation into mature goblet cells is evident, particularly in **A** and **B**. Stratification of the nuclei is also evident. These lesions may exhibit a range of dysplasia, paralleling that seen in adenomatous polyps.

quite reach the cellular luminal surface. In severe dysplasia, the nuclear abnormalities become slightly more marked and the nuclei reach the luminal surface.

When cells appear cytologically malignant, but are still confined within the basement membrane, they can be designated as 'intra-epithelial carcinoma' or 'carcinoma-in-situ' (Fig. 41.9). These cells appear round and irregular, containing enlarged nuclei with irregular nuclear membranes and prominent nucleoli. (Practically speaking, it may be wise to lump severe dysplasia and carcinoma-in-situ together under the term 'high grade dysplasia' to avoid clinical misinterpretation of the lesion and over treatment.) Extension of the cytologically malignant cells beyond the basement membrane into the lamina propria qualifies for a diagnosis of 'intramucosal carcinoma'. Invasion through the muscularis mucosae constitutes invasive cancer (Fig. 41.9).[40] Changes such as nuclear enlargement, pleomorphism, loss of polarity, stratification, increased mitoses and glandular architectural changes (irregular budding and back-to-back arrangements) herald the development of malignancy. The intervening lamina propria is reduced in amount. Neither intra-epithelial nor

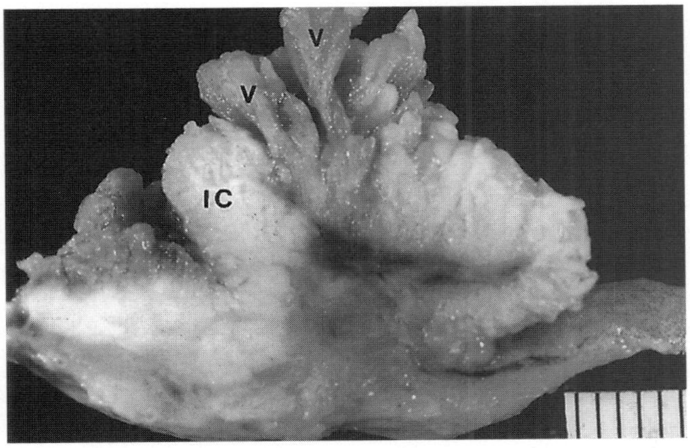

Fig. 41.8 Carcinoma arising in villous adenoma. Long villiform projections (V) lie adjacent to the area of invasive carcinoma (IC).

intramucosal carcinoma have a clinically significant potential for metastasis if all neoplastic tissue is removed. However, it should be noted that the presence of high grade dysplasia or intramucosal carcinoma strongly correlates with the presence of an invasive cancer.

Adenoma size and the extent of villous component represent major independent risk factors for the development of high grade dysplasia ($p < 0.0001$).[81] High grade dysplasia is more likely to be seen in women,[96] in patients with multiple adenomas, in larger lesions, or in villous lesions.[101] It also increases with increasing patient age.[101]

The larger the adenoma, the greater the chance of finding an invasive carcinoma.[40,127–130] Cancer arising in adenomas is exceptional in pedunculated lesions measuring less than 1.5 cm but increases in frequency in sessile villous lesions.[40] In a retrospective study, invasive cancer was most prevalent in villous adenomas (12.6%) followed by tubulovillous adenomas (3.8%) and tubular adenomas (3.3%).[87] Invasive carcinomas occurred more frequently in larger and sessile lesions. All gradations of cellular change from dysplasia to invasive cancer increase in all colonic segments as the villous component of the adenoma increases. In the same series, when the villous adenoma was equal to or greater than 3 cm in diameter, the incidence of carcinoma in situ was 33% versus 21.4% in tubulovillous adenomas.[82] Although polyp size represents an important determinant for the presence of malignancy, invasive cancer can also be found in polyps less than 1 cm in diameter. Conversely, adenomas with a predominantly villous component can attain large dimensions without developing invasive carcinomas.[87]

The malignant potential of adenomas increases with increasing degrees of dysplasia. Adenomas measuring less than 1 cm in diameter usually show minor degrees of epithelial dysplasia and have a very low malignant potential. When severe dysplasia is present, the rate of malignancy rises to 27%.[128] Adenomas containing areas of squamous metaplasia probably represent the precursor for adenosquamous carcinomas, adenoacanthomas or pure squamous cell carcinomas.[131–133]

Muto et al[128] showed that varying proportions of adenomatous tissue were present in 14.2% of carcinomas and that an adenomatous component was more likely to be present in carcinomas with limited spread.[128] Adenomatous tissue was identified in 60% of invasive carcinomas that had invaded no further than the submucosa, in 20% of carcinomas confined to the bowel wall, and in 7% when carcinoma invaded into the serosa. These findings suggest that most large bowel carcinomas arise from morphologically benign adenomas and that as carcinomas enlarge they progressively destroy pre-existing adenomatous tissue.[40]

At present, since it is unknown which adenomas will become malignant and which will not progress, all adenomas are considered to represent potential cancer precursors.

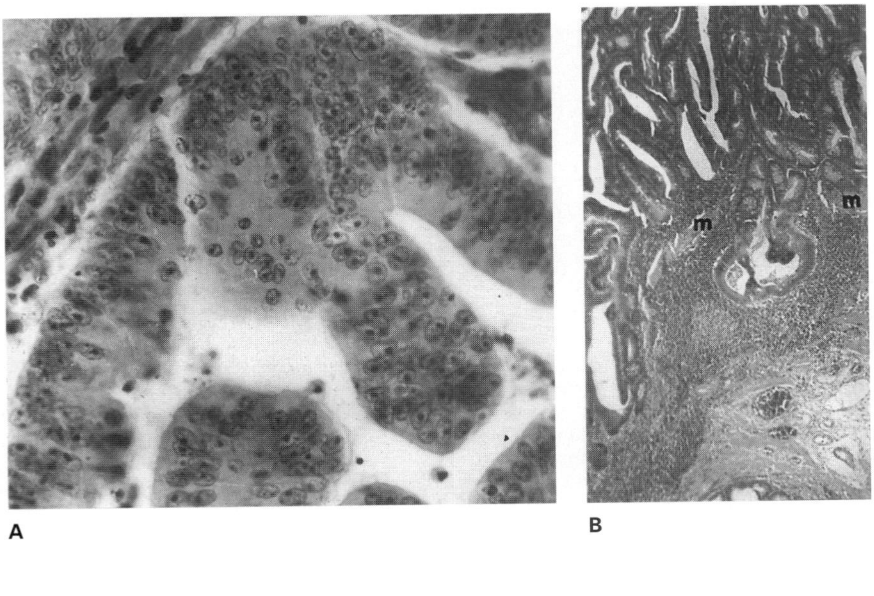

A B

Fig. 41.9 Carcinoma-in-situ (**A**) versus early invasive carcinoma (**B**). **A** In carcinoma-in-situ, the cells remain confined to their original crypt lumens but they can form complex papillary infoldings. These cells often have round nuclei with prominent nucleoli. **B** In early invasive carcinoma, the malignant process extends through the muscularis mucosae (m) to invade the underlying submucosa. Often a prominent inflammatory infiltrate accompanies early invasion.

Polyp handling

Adequate evaluation of adenomas is required to facilitate recommendations concerning the possible need for additional therapy following polypectomy. The technical approach to evaluating these lesions differs depending on whether the specimen represents a polypectomy or a resection. In this section we will discuss the handling of polypectomy specimens.

Several critical things must be observed for optimal handling of polypectomy specimens. The specimen must be adequately fixed and it must be possible to evaluate the relationship of the head of the polyp to the stalk and the resection margin (Fig. 41.10). Placing a polyp in Bouin's fixative will make it firmer than a fixative like formalin, but Bouin's does not penetrate as well and it may interfere with future immunohistochemical or genotypic studies.

We like to take a midsagittal section of the polyp in order to preserve the landmarks in continuity with one another, especially the boundary of the stroma of the head of the polyp to the neoplastic tissue. These landmarks consist of the head, the stalk and the resection margin. The resection margin is easily identified in lesions that are resected with a long stalk. In other cases, it may be more difficult (or impossible) to identify. The presence of white, tan or brown cauterized tissue can provide a clue to the cautery margins. The stalk has the colour of the normal colonic mucosa of which it is composed. The head consists of neoplastic tissue which is lobulated, friable when cut, and often has a reddish color. The neck is where the head of the polyp joins the stalk. The typical questions addressed by the pathologist in evaluating polyps are:

1) what is the polyp type?
2) does it contain cancer?
3) if it contains cancer, is it invasive?
4) if it is invasive, how invasive is it?

Assessment of invasion beyond the muscularis mucosae can be difficult, since the muscularis mucosae frays, becomes distorted and frequently appears hyperplastic. In difficult cases, use of trichrome or immunohistochemical stains for smooth muscle actin may help identify the muscle fibres. Features such as the cellular, non-fibrous character of the lamina propria, the frankly collagenous character of the submucosa and the size of the blood vessels, all assist in determining whether a focus of carcinoma has invaded into the submucosa or is still within the mucosa.

Clinical relevance of a carcinoma in an adenoma

In the current environment of colonoscopic surveillance of patients at risk for developing colorectal cancer and polypectomy of detected lesions, it is important to be able to predict which patient will require further therapy. Some polypectomy specimens will reveal the presence of a cancer in the adenoma. The cancer may be focal and minimally invasive, or it may replace a considerable part of the polyp.[40] It may also be well or poorly differentiated.[40]

The depth of penetration into the bowel wall by the carcinoma in an adenoma is important in estimating the probability of metastasis.[40,111] Lymph node metastasis of carcinomas arising in polypoid adenomas occurs in only 3.8% of cases, compared with 30% and 29% of those aris-

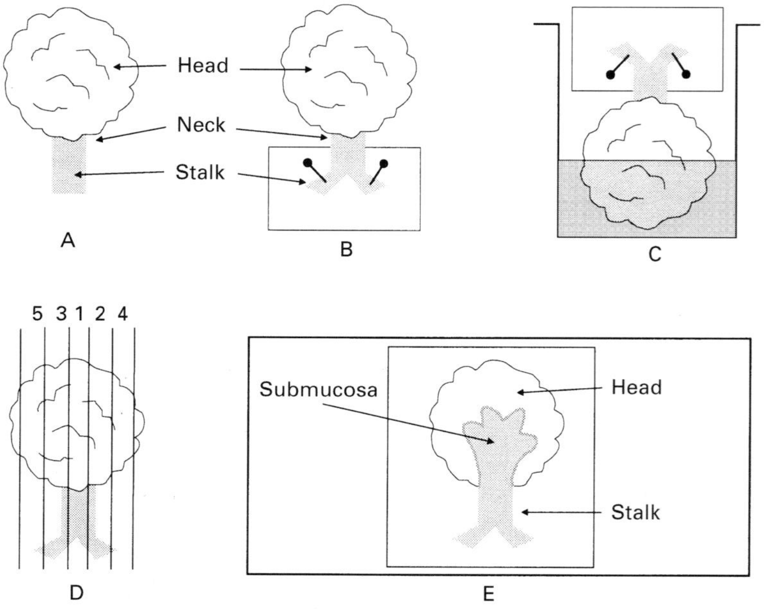

Fig. 41.10 Handling of polypectomy specimens. Most endoscopists remove pedunculated polyps with a share cautery so that the stalk and head are identifiable (**A**). Ideally the polyp should be pinned to a cork board (**B**) and inverted in a container of fixative for several hours (**C**). Once fixed, a midsagittal section should be taken so that the stalk can be visualized (**D**, **E**). The remainder of the specimen is then serially sectioned and submitted for histological examination.

ing in semi-sessile and sessile adenomas respectively.[111] One simplistic reason for this lies in the fact that in sessile lesions, the malignant cells are closer to a wider area of lymphatic and venous drainage than they are in pedunculated lesions.[134] Additionally, the closer the malignant cells come to the muscularis propria, the more likely they are to be milked into lymphatics by its peristaltic activity.

The ratio of the volume of adenoma to carcinoma within the polyp represents another important prognostic factor. Lesions that are predominantly adenomatous tend to be pedunculated, contain small foci of invasive carcinoma, and have a lower metastatic rate than do polyps composed predominantly of invasive carcinoma.[111] Also, as would be expected, the rate of metastasis is highest in patients with adenomas containing poorly differentiated tumours. Poorly differentiated cancers, even when constituting only a small part of an adenomatous polyp, have a proclivity to permeate lymphatics and venules.[112,135,136]

In practice, the management of the individual patient must be based on an assessment of the risk of recurrence and/or metastasis by the tumour. If the focus of carcinoma is entirely intramucosal and resection margins are uninvolved, uniform agreement exists that the risk of metastasis is extremely low and no additional therapy need be undertaken. On the other hand, if carcinoma is present at the resection margin there is clearly an indication for further surgical resection if clinically feasible.

Lesions which invade the submucosa, but do not involve the polypectomy margin, are termed 'early invasive carcinoma'. The management of these lesions has been the subject of lively debate. The overall incidence of metastasis from early invasive carcinoma is somewhere between 1 and 10%. Factors that increase the metastatic risk include the presence of lymphatic invasion and poor differentiation. However, the exact risk of metastasis in this setting is currently unknown. The length of the stalk in a pedunculated polyp has some influence on the subsequent risk of lymph node metastases. In one study, no lesions with long stalks (greater than 3 mm) evidenced nodal metastases, whereas metastases were present in 4 of 21 patients who had lesions with a short stalk, and in 1 of 7 patients with sessile polyps.[134]

In summary, we believe that lesions which contain intramucosal carcinoma — particularly if the cancerous focus is at the surface of the polyp, if the tumour is well differentiated and if the resection margins are uninvolved — require no further therapy following colonoscopic removal. If the surgical margin is involved by carcinoma, limited surgical resection should be performed if feasible. For those cases with early invasion by a well-differentiated tumour without evidence of lymphatic invasion and a resection margin which is free of carcinoma, colonoscopic excision is adequate therapy.[134–136] If there is doubt that the resection margin is clear, then colonoscopic biopsy of the wound is indicated. If only adenomatous epithelium is found, follow-up colonoscopy is all that is necessary, but carcinoma in the wound site demands surgical resection.[135,136] If the specimen contains a poorly differentiated tumour in lymphatics, further therapy should be seriously considered.

ADENOCARCINOMAS

Incidence

The incidence of colon cancer is increasing. From 1973 to 1986 the annual incidence rate increased by 9.4%.[137] The risk of developing colorectal cancer between the ages of 50–75 in the United States is approximately 5% with a 2.5% chance of dying from the disease.[138] The median age of diagnosis is 71 years. Risk increases with age: 2.9 cases/100 000 for ages 30–34 compared with 531 cases/100 000 for persons aged 85 or older.[137] The incidence and mortality from colorectal cancers differs markedly among countries of similar industrial development. The highest rates are found in North America, Western Europe and Australia. Intermediate rates are found in Eastern Europe, and low rates are found in Africa, Asia and South America.[19] Studies of migrant populations show the risk of colon cancer shifts away from the country of origin toward that of the host country.

Colorectal cancer remains a major medical problem. In 1989, 150 000 new cases were diagnosed in the United States and 500 000 new cases were diagnosed worldwide.[138] Colorectal cancer has an overall mortality rate of 51%. In 1990, this cancer killed an estimated 60,900 people in the United States, making it the second leading cause of cancer deaths.[138]

Colon cancer is rare in the paediatric age group. When it does occur in young patients, it often arises in individuals with predisposing factors such as a positive family history or the presence of a polyposis syndrome.[139–142] During the period from 1973–77, the National Cancer Institute reported 36 children under the age of 20 with colon cancer, representing an incidence of two cases per million children.[143] The prognosis of this group of patients is extremely poor.[142,144]

The prevalence of large bowel cancer appears to be similar in blacks and whites but more whites than blacks survive the disease. Of interest is the fact that blacks have a significantly larger proportion of lesions confined to the proximal colon as compared to whites.[145]

Risk factors

Colon cancer results from the interaction of environmental factors in concert with one or more host factors that eventually lead to changes in the mucosal environment of the large bowel. This, in turn, brings about those alterations that are necessary for the development of colon cancer.

Certain high risk groups can be identified: patients with previous colon cancers or adenomas, inflammatory bowel disease or a family history of colon cancer. Host factors may confer differential susceptibilities for the development of large bowel cancer and can be either inherited or acquired. A genetic predisposition is well documented in patients with familial polyposis coli. Familial adenomatous polyposis, Gardner's and Turcot's syndrome are all thought to be variations of the same basic genetic defect and have a very high risk of developing colon cancer. Striking predispositions are seen in other polyposis syndromes and in patients with the hereditary nonpolyposis colorectal cancer syndrome who develop multiple adenocarcinomas, particularly involving the colon and endometrium. It is estimated that perhaps 30% or more of sporadic colorectal cancers have a genetic basis. There is also evidence for a familial component to the risk of so-called sporadic large bowel cancers, with a family history of colon cancer in a first degree relative conveying a three-fold increased risk.[126]

It is possible that one genetically controlled mechanism affecting susceptibility may involve varying metabolic phenotypes in the activation or secretion of ingested carcinogens.[146] Another well documented example of an acquired host factor may be the predisposing condition ulcerative colitis. Patients with chronic ulcerative colitis are at higher risk for developing colon cancer. The increased risk begins at approximately 8 years after the onset of the disease and rises to about 5% after 10 years and 15–20% after 25 years.[147]

Individuals with certain occupations, such as asbestos and petroleum workers, pattern makers, carpet workers, dry cleaners, printing machine operators and steel and sawmill workers, may experience an increased risk for the development of colon cancer,[148,149] although some of these factors have been questioned. In certain circumstances the occupational risk factor appears to be site specific.[150]

A number of studies exist which suggest a role for dietary factors in the development of large bowel cancer, including the role of dietary fat, high caloric intake, deprivation of meat and fiber, intake of fresh fruits and vegetables and intake of calcium.

Tumour sites

There are indications that the incidence of right-sided colon carcinoma is increasing.[19,74] The proportion of rectal tumours ranges from 15–59% of all large bowel cancers. Patients with colorectal cancer have a predisposition to develop more than one tumour. They may be synchronous or metachronous, the former being twice as frequent. A synchronous cancer is present in 2–8% of patients with a colorectal primary.[151–153]

Macroscopic features

Small carcinomas, 1–2 cm in diameter, usually appear red and granular and often resemble adenomas. Their consistency varies according to the relative proportions of carcinoma, adenoma and stromal desmoplasia. As carcinoma replaces the adenoma, the tumour becomes firmer and paler.

Larger carcinomas demonstrate one of three macroscopic appearances. Bulky, exophytic carcinomas occur more frequently in the caecum and ascending colon. Although they may occupy a large proportion of the colonic lumen, they rarely cause obstruction. It is this type of tumour that commonly grows without producing symptoms until it is quite large, causing anaemia or bleeding. The volume of intraluminal tumour often far exceeds that of the intramural tumour.

Adenocarcinomas of the transverse and descending colon usually infiltrate and ulcerate. The intramural tumour may be at least as voluminous as the luminal portion and may extend through the bowel wall to involve contiguous structures such as the small intestine or stomach. On occasion, central necrosis and ulceration in a transmural tumour cause perforation and peritonitis.

Annular, constricting adenocarcinomas arise more frequently in the transverse and descending colon than in the ascending colon. They probably begin as locally infiltrative carcinomas which progressively encircle the bowel. These tumours produce obstruction and a characteristic 'apple core' radiographic appearance. Except for their circumferential growth, they resemble other carcinomas. These tumours thicken the bowel wall obliterating the muscularis propria, a feature best seen when the cut surface is examined.[19]

One distinct subset of colon cancers are the so-called flat early carcinomas that can present as slightly elevated lesions, lesions that are flush with the remainder of the mucosa or as slightly depressed lesions. They are most often reported by the Japanese and are characterized by their small size, ranging from 4–45 mm in greatest diameter. These lesions have been identified by step sectioning the resected bowels. The vast majority are not associated with residual adenoma. The adenocarcinoma is limited to the mucosa in approximately 41% of cases and submucosal invasion is found in approximately 50% of cases. Both lymphatic and venous invasion is seen in some patients. These neoplasms are believed to arise de novo and to infiltrate into the intestinal wall when they are still small. Submucosal invasion has been observed in lesions as small as 7 mm in diameter.[154]

Regardless of the gross configuration of the carcinoma, inspection of the unopened bowel provides important information. Dilatation is produced by obstruction and also indicates the proximal part of the specimen. Serosal retraction in the region of the palpable mass indicates invasion to this layer. Palpation from the serosal surface discloses the circumferential extent of the tumour, so that one can avoid transecting the mass when one opens the bowel, unless it is completely annular. The mesentery and pericolonic fat can be carefully examined for lymph nodes; those extensively involved by metastases appear enlarged, hard and white on their cut surfaces.[19]

Microscopic features

Ordinary large bowel cancer is usually an easily recognizable, moderately to well-differentiated adenocarcinoma. Large, irregular glands lined by tall, malignant columnar cells evidence a high mitotic rate. In most cases, no histological difference exists between the superficial portion of the tumour and the deeply invasive or metastatic tumour, although, occasionally, tumours at the invasive front appear less well differentiated than the remainder of the lesion. In many tumours, residual adenoma is observed.

Well-differentiated carcinomas consist entirely of well-formed glands (Fig. 41.8). Moderately differentiated carcinomas contain solid sheets of malignant cells comprising at least 25% of the tumour. These are mixed with glands. Poorly differentiated carcinomas consist of solid sheets of malignant cells, with less than 25% of the neoplastic cells forming recognizable glands (Fig. 41.11). The cells, in the solid areas may be completely anaplastic or may be of the signet-ring type.[19] Often a prominent desmoplastic response surrounds the tumour cells, particularly in the central areas.[155] Pronounced desmoplasia of the invasive edge of a tumour may herald a poor prognosis.[156] The presence of perineural invasion represents a poor prognostic feature in patients with stage III rectal cancer.[157]

Isolated endocrine cells can be found in about 50% of colorectal cancers and when isolated have no prognostic significance.[158] When large numbers of endocrine cells are demonstrable (more than one chromogranin positive cell/ mm^2), the patients may exhibit a worse prognosis.[159,160] The endocrine cells appear neoplastic as evidenced by their nuclear hyperchromasia and cellular pleomorphism. There is no correlation with the presence of endocrine cells and tumour differentiation. The endocrine cells arise from undifferentiated crypt cells.

Tumour aggressiveness correlates with the degree of histological differentiation, especially in carcinomas containing residual adenoma. Approximately 80% of tumours which do not penetrate the serosa are well differentiated, and 45% of tumours with lymph node metastases are poorly or moderately differentiated.

The most significant prognostic feature in a resected

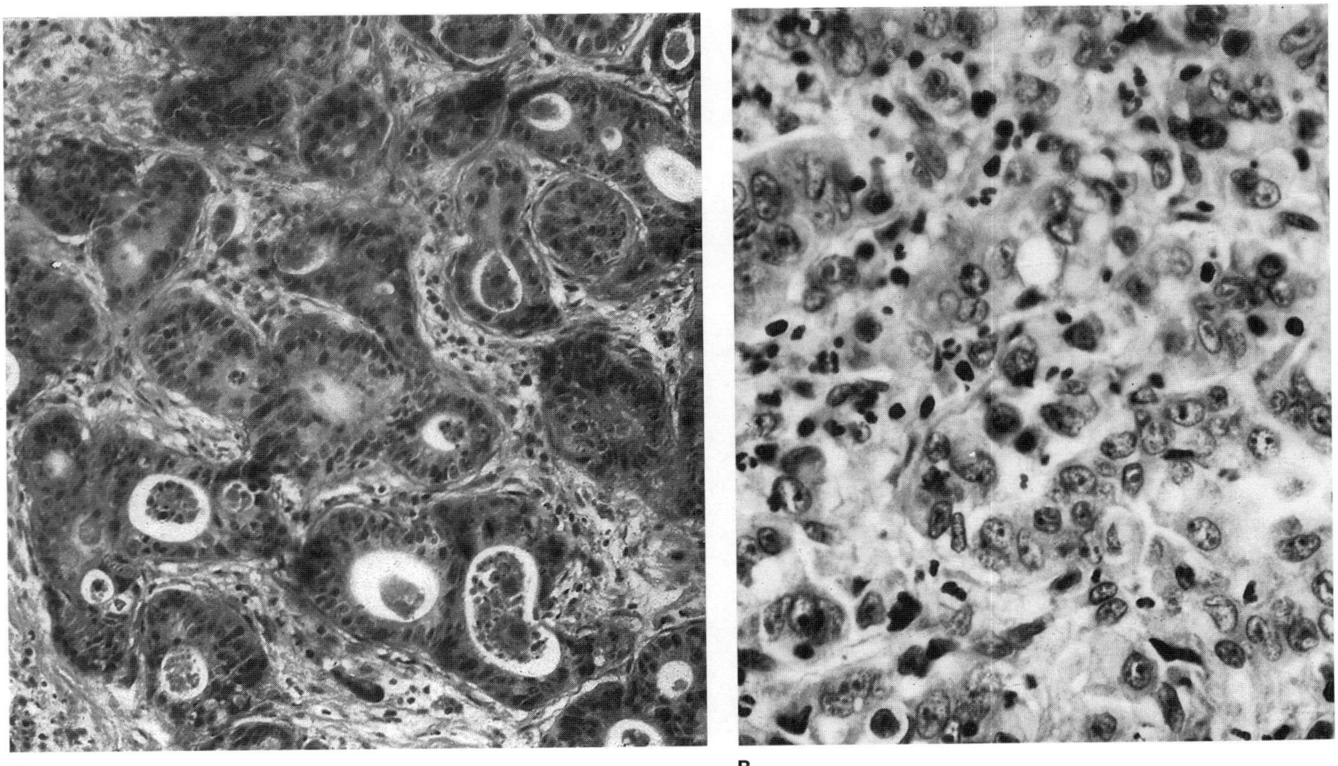

A B

Fig. 41.11 Well-differentiated (**A**) and moderately to poorly differentiated (**B**) carcinoma of the colon. In well-differentiated tumours, glandular formations are present throughout the neoplasm. In contrast, the moderately to poorly differentiated tumours make abortive glands. The individual cells comprising the neoplasm are cytologically highly atypical and usually form solid sheets of tumors.

specimen is the degree of bowel wall penetration by tumour and the presence or absence of lymph node metastases. An accurate assessment of the extent of the tumour is critical in planning further treatment and estimating prognosis.

Specialized variants of colorectal cancer

Mucinous tumours (colloid cancers and signet ring cell cancer)

Many ordinary adenocarcinomas contain a focal mucinous component. However, when 50% or more of the tumour appears mucinous, the tumour is classified as mucinous adenocarcinoma. Two subtypes of mucinous carcinoma are recognized (Fig. 41.12). In the more common 'extracellular' or 'colloid' type, large mucinous pools are lined by malignant columnar cells, and clumps of tumour cells lie free in the mucin. These tumours have little fibrous stroma and grossly appear gelatinous.

The second type, is the 'intracellular' or signet-ring cell type. Signet-ring cell cancers account for 0.3–2.4% of primary colorectal cancers.[161–165] Constipation and rectal bleeding are the commonest presentation. Since many patients with signet-ring carcinoma have ulcerative colitis, the diagnosis is often obscured[165] by the underlying pathological abnormalities.

Histologically, signet-ring carcinoma has a preponderance of tumour cells with characteristic intracytoplasmic mucin-containing vacuoles pushing the nuclei to the cell periphery. Some tumour cells may be extremely anaplastic and gland formation is abortive. Ultrastructurally, some signet-ring carcinomas contain neuroendocrine cells.[161]

Mucinous carcinomas exhibit clinical and pathological differences from ordinary carcinomas, and survival rates for patients with mucinous carcinomas are lower than those for ordinary carcinomas.[144,162] The 5-year survival rate for patients with mucinous carcinoma is 18%, compared to 33% for patients with ordinary carcinoma. This type of carcinoma often arises in individuals younger than age 30[144] and this high proportion of mucinous carcinomas accounts for the poor prognosis of colorectal cancer in young people.[144]

The poor prognosis of mucinous carcinoma is attributed to its delayed diagnosis. Early in its course, it displays subtle gross features and has a resemblance to inflammatory colorectal disease. In addition, it has a propensity to spread intramurally[166] and produces few, if any, symptoms.

Signet-ring cell carcinomas sometimes invade the bowel wall in a linitis plastica pattern. The bowel wall appears annularly thickened and stenotic.[166] A protruding lesion is absent. A marked stromal desmoplastic reaction accompanies the infiltrating signet-ring cells.[163,164] The desmoplastic reaction is most marked in the submucosa and serosa. The muscularis propria remains intact despite its massive infiltration. The tumour has a propensity to involve the peritoneum.[164]

Rarely, signet-ring carcinomas do exhibit an exophytic growth pattern. Connelly et al published 20 examples of the exophytic variant of signet-ring carcinoma. The patients ranged in age from 14–79 years and the tumours arose throughout the colon.[167] The overall survival parallels that of more typical nonmucinous carcinomas. The lesions were somewhat lower stage than the signet-ring cell carcinomas of the linitis plastica type.[167]

Both signet-ring and mucoid carcinomas can arise in adenomas. Nakamura et al[168] showed a transition from adenoma to signet-ring carcinoma and Symonds and Vickery[169] found that 31% of mucoid carcinomas were associated with villous adenoma.

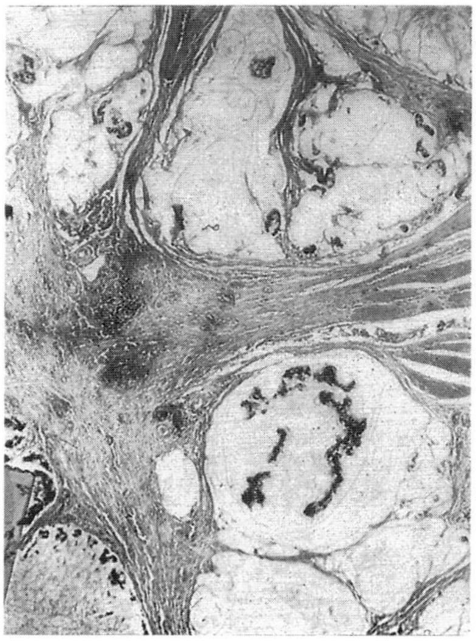

A

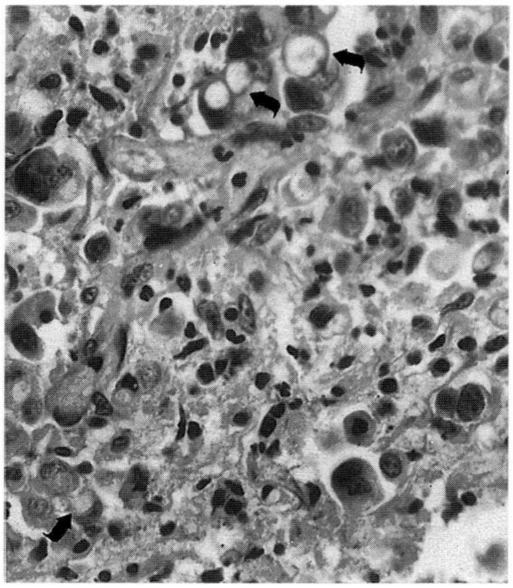

B

Fig. 41.12 Mucinous carcinoma of the colon. **A** Colloid carcinoma. Numerous mucin-filled lakes are present, with neoplastic cells floating free in the mucin. **B** Signet-ring carcinoma. The neoplastic cells comprising signet-ring cell carcinomas contain variable degrees of signet-ring formation (arrows). Most cells are positive with mucin stains.

Goblet cell carcinoid tumours (adenocarcinoid tumours)

Goblet cell carcinoid tumours most typically affect the appendix, but they can arise in the intestines as well. They consist of mucous cells admixed with variable numbers of endocrine and Paneth cells. They are characterized by an aggressive behaviour and the development of widespread lymphatic and often intraperitoneal metastases. Outside the appendix, the lesion grossly appears fungating or ulcerating, measuring 5–20 cm in maximum diameter. Histologically, the cells produce abundant intracellular mucin and are arranged in nests and trabecular cords. Diffusely infiltrating single cells are also seen.[170]

Adenosquamous carcinoma

Adenosquamous tumours account for only about 0.05% of carcinomas.[131] About half of these tumours arise in the rectum and sigmoid and 20% in the caecum.[171] Histologically, adenosquamous carcinoma consists of adenocarcinoma admixed with a squamous component showing varying degrees of keratinization. Occasional squamous cells occur in about 5% of colorectal adenocarcinomas. Rare examples of adenosquamous carcinomas have been reported that contain other forms of differentiation including carcinoid, bone and cartilage.[172,173] Such tumours support an origin from a multipotential uncommitted stem cell.

There is a reported 5-year survival rate of 30%[131] but, because of the inclusion of pure squamous carcinomas in the study and the lack of well-defined criteria for the diagnosis of adenosquamous carcinoma, precise figures for survival rates cannot be given. Adenosquamous carcinomas are thought to arise from adenomas containing squamous morules.[131]

Squamous carcinomas

Primary squamous cell carcinomas arising in the colon or rectum are rare, constituting from 0.025–0.11% of all colorectal cancers.[131,174,175] They consist entirely of malignant squamous cells that produce variable amounts of keratin. The diagnosis can only be made if the following criteria are met:

1. there is no evidence of primary squamous carcinoma in any other site that could be a source of metastasis or direct extension to the large intestine
2. the affected segment of bowel is not related to a squamous-lined fistula
3. there is no continuity between the tumour and the anal squamous epithelium
4. the malignant tumour has neither gland formation nor mucin production, but exhibits intercellular bridges and may or may not produce keratin.

If immunohistological techniques are used to detect keratin production, one must ascertain that the antibody is specific for high molecular weight keratin and does not react with cytokeratins common to all epithelia.

When strict diagnostic criteria are met, colorectal squamous carcinomas are rare. Williams et al[174] reported one case satisfying the criteria, and reviewed the 38 purported cases then in the English literature. Twenty-one of the reported tumours qualified as primary squamous carcinomas. Others clearly represented extension of anal canal tumours, or contained glandular foci. Based on their review, the mean age of patients with squamous carcinoma was 55 years, with a range of 33–90. There are not enough cases in the literature to determine whether the entity is more frequent in men or women. Pain and bleeding were the commonest complaints. Rare patients present with hypercalcemia.[176,177] Parathyroid-like hormone is demonstrable in the tumour cells.

Squamous cell cancer can be seen anywhere in the large intestine, although most arise in the rectum. Most squamous cell carcinomas appear large and ulcerated, but some are polypoid.[132,175] There does not seem to be any unique gross or clinical feature that identifies these tumours as squamous in nature. They tend to diffusely infiltrate surrounding tissue and to invade both blood vessels and lymphatics. Five-year survival rates are reported to be 50% for Dukes' B, 33% for Dukes' C and 0% for Dukes' D tumors.[178]

Several hypotheses concerning the aetiology of these tumours have been proposed. The tumours may arise from proliferative uncommitted reserve cells following mucosal injury. Such a theory would explain the higher than expected incidence of squamous cell cancer arising in patients suffering from ulcerative colitis.[131,133,179] It would also explain the relationship of intestinal squamous cell cancers to schistosomiasis and amoebiasis, conditions associated with this tumor.[175] Others have suggested that chemotherapy or radiation therapy might damage the mucosa, thereby inducing iatrogenic squamous cell cancer.[180] Finally, anal intercourse may represent a risk factor for the disease.[175]

The second theory postulates squamous metaplasia of glandular epithelium resulting from chronic irritation. Squamous metaplasia has been described at the margin of intestinal tumours, but this occurs uncommonly.[175,181] Other less likely theories include origin from embryonal nests of committed or uncommitted ectodermal cells remaining in an ectopic site following embryogenesis, or squamous metaplasia of an established colorectal adenocarcinoma or adenoma.[171,182] Finally, squamous cancer can arise from heterotopic squamous epithelium as is seen sometimes in congenital anomalies.[183]

Small-cell carcinoma

Characteristically, this is a rare, highly malignant, epithelial tumour composed of cells which histologically appear undifferentiated, but by special techniques, show features of neuroendocrine, Paneth, squamous and glandular differentiation. Endocrine differentiation is demonstrated by one of the following techniques: positivity for neuron specific enolase, synaptophysin, Leu 7, neurofilament or chromogranin, or the ultrastructural presence of neurosecretory granules.[40,184,185] These markers may be patchy in their positivity. These lesions are also positive for low and medium molecular weight cytokeratins.[186] Some tumours produce ectopic ACTH or gastrin.[187–189]

Colorectal small cell tumours occur in patients ranging in age from 47–74 years, with a mean of 63. There is no apparent sexual predilection. They have a propensity to involve the right colon.[185] The duration of symptoms is often just a few weeks.

The gross appearance of small cell carcinoma varies from bulky neoplasms projecting into the bowel lumen to smaller perforating ulcers and/or firm grey foci in adenomatous polyps. No gross feature distinguishes them from ordinary colorectal adenocarcinomas.

Histologically, small cell carcinomas and their metastases resemble oat cell carcinomas of the lung (Fig. 41.13). They consist of solid sheets and nests of densely packed round to ovoid cells with dark nuclei, inconspicuous nucleoli, coarse chromatin and inapparent cytoplasm. A minority of cases will contain fusiform nuclei. Pleomorphism is minimal, and numerous mitoses, foci of necrosis and vascular invasion are present. Neuroendocrine-like trabeculae and rosettes may be seen, but little stroma accompanies the tumour cells. Squamous differentiation is present in up to 21% of cases[185,190] and abortive gland formation is found.[191–193] When associated with adenomas, the interface of the adenoma with small cell tumours occurs abruptly.

Ultrastructurally, small cell carcinomas contain cells with membrane-bound dense core neuroendocrine granules.[190–193] Other features, such as desmosomal attachments, tonofilaments, microvilli, basal lamina and glycocalyx are variably present. Because of the demonstration of neuroendocrine, squamous, glandular and Paneth cells, these tumours are believed to arise from noncommitted 'stem cells' or 'reserve cells' in colorectal adenomas.

Small cell carcinomas behave as aggressive neoplasms. 85–89% of patients have metastases to the regional lymph nodes and 78% have liver metastases.[185,194] In fact, the presence of a small cell component in a tumour containing other histological patterns serves as a marker for an aggressive tumour with a propensity to involve the liver early in the course of the disease.[185] Even a small tumour arising in an adenoma or in superficially invasive carcinomas may have metastasized at the time of presentation.[190]

Giant cell tumours

Pleomorphic (giant cell carcinomas) of the large bowel contain areas of glandular and squamous differentiation and appear as solid sheets of cells. Three cell types are identifiable: gemistocytic cells (giant cells), smaller polygonal cells and spindle cells, all with the same immunohistochemical profile. The tumours coexpress cytokeratin and Vimentin. Neuroendocrine differentiation can be seen. Histologically, the tumours are identical to giant cell carcinomas of the lung. Some regard these neoplasms as poorly differentiated variants of neuroendocrine carcinoma.[195]

Basaloid carcinoma

These tumours are extremely rare. Only two intestinal cases have been reported, both arising in the sigmoid colon.[196,197] They were exophytic sigmoid masses with a clinical presentation similar to adenocarcinoma. Histologically, the tumours resemble anal carcinoma and basal cell carcinomas of the skin. Tonofilaments were demonstrated by electron microscopy, suggesting a relationship to squamous carcinoma. They are capable of metastasis.[197]

Carcinoma with choriocarcinomatous areas

A small number of examples of colonic adenocarcinomas containing areas of choriocarcinoma have been reported.[189–201] They occur in all areas of the colon. Each tumour was composed partly of moderately to well differentiated gland-forming carcinoma, and sheet-like areas of clear cells resembling cytotrophoblast.[40] The adenocarcinomas typically merge with the choriocarcinomas. Giant cells may be observed.[198] In one case, the choriocarcinomatous foci were only present in the metastases.[198] Human chorionic gonadotropin (HCG) was demonstrated in the syncytiotrophoblast of the three cases studied by immunohistochemistry and four out of four patients had elevated serum HCG levels.

Four of the reported patients were women; one was a man. All patients had evidence of metastatic disease. The authors of these reports proposed that the neoplastic cells of colonic adenocarcinoma had undergone trophoblastic differentiation.

Pigmented adenocarcinoma

Chumas and Lorelle[202] described an adenocarcinoma of the anorectal region that was deeply pigmented and grossly resembled a melanoma. Histologically and ultrastructurally, the tumour was a moderately differentiated adenocarcinoma with neoplastic epithelial cells containing compound melanosomes and mucin droplets. Intermediate stages of melanosome formation were not seen, and it was concluded that the cells had phagocytosed melanin produced by normal anal melanocytes.

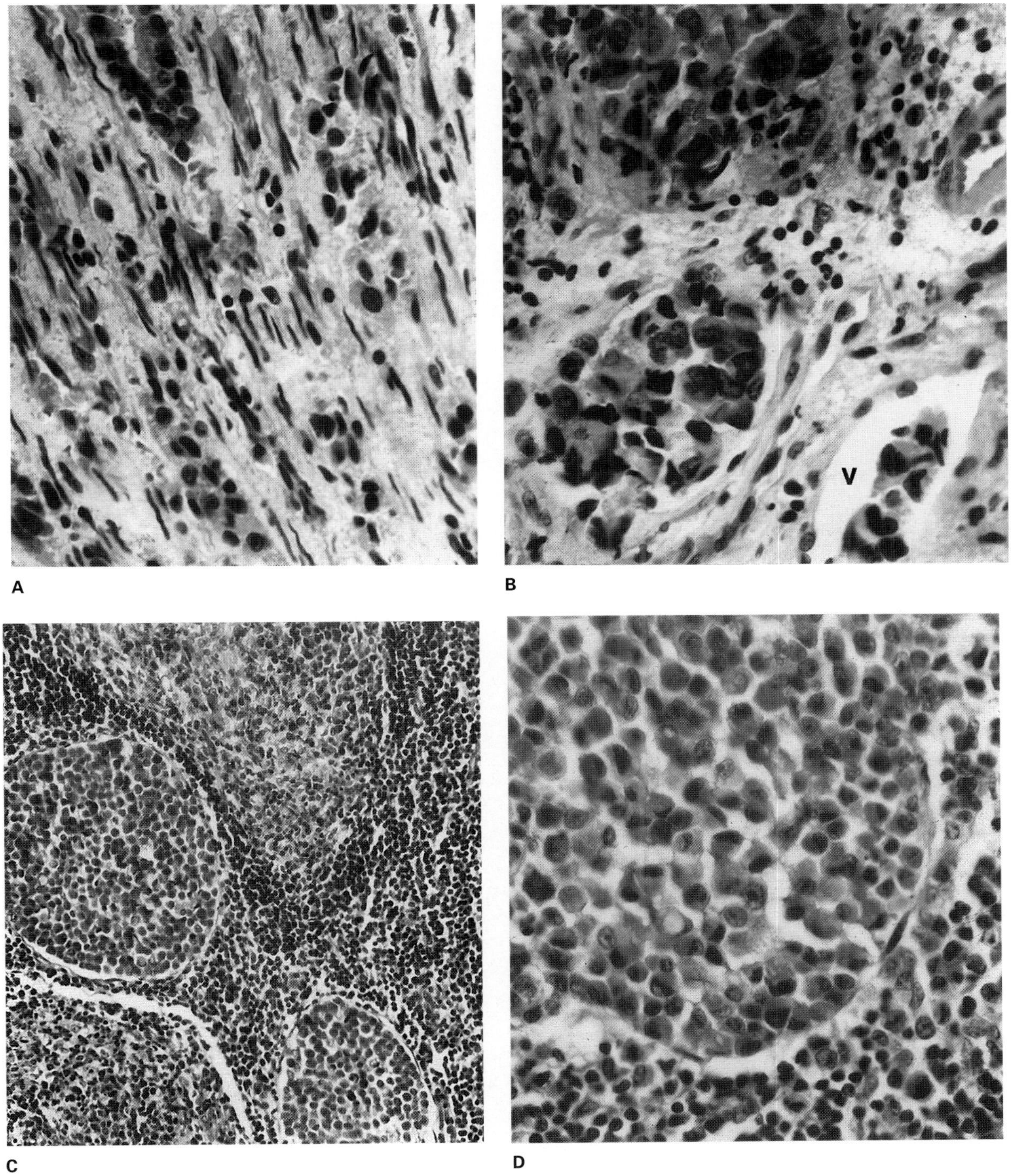

Fig. 41.13 Small cell carcinoma. Small cell carcinomas vary in their histological appearance. **A** sometimes they resemble linitis plastica of the stomach. In other instances the cells are arranged in compact groups as illustrated in **B**. In both patterns, vascular involvement (V) is usually evident. Small cell tumours are aggressive neoplasms, and lymph node metastases are often present at the time of diagnosis **C**. Occasionally, the individual small cells may have features of signet-ring cells, as illustrated in the metastatic lesion in **D**.

Spread of colorectal carcinoma

It is often possible to predict that a patient has a locally advanced lesion or extensive metastases on the basis of the clinical presentation. Anorexia with significant weight loss, localizing pain or septic symptoms associated with a colorectal cancer raise the likelihood of an advanced cancer with perforation or metastases.

Primary tumour characteristics are helpful in predicting

prognosis. Ulcerated as opposed to polypoid or sessile exophytic cancers have a poorer prognosis and are more likely to have spread locally and distantly.[203,204] Histological grading has predictive value for lymph node metastases and survival. Regardless of the depth of tumour invasion, poorly differentiated adenocarcinomas are associated with lymph node metastases in more than half of the cases, whereas moderately differentiated and well differentiated cancers have far fewer lymph node metastases.[205–207] Mucin-producing tumours with vascular or lymphatic invasion have a poorer prognosis and are more likely to have local spread than are those without such features.

DNA ploidy analysis can be a predictor of prognosis in colorectal cancers. Some studies suggest that aneuploid tumours have a poorer prognosis than diploid ones.[208–210] Unfortunately, as many as 93.2% of colon cancers can be aneuploid, making the prognostic significance of this finding questionable.[211] The incidence of DNA aneuploidy is higher in tumours with vascular invasion. DNA ploidy status, however, does not correlate with other standard pathological characteristics such as degree of differentiation and patterns of invasion.[208–210,212–215]

Colorectal adenocarcinoma spreads by lymphatic and venous dissemination, by direct extension to contiguous structures, by seeding the peritoneal cavity or by implantation in surgical wounds and anastomotic sites. Among patients with distant metastases from colorectal adenocarcinoma, liver involvement is seen in 75%, lung involvement in 15% and bone and brain involvement in 5% each. Less common metastatic sites include the spleen, kidneys, pancreas, adrenals, breast and skin.

Dissemination to distant sites is usually accomplished by lymphatic spread to regional and then to remote lymph nodes[216] and by the portal venous system to the liver, lungs, bone and brain. Carcinoma of the intestine enters lymphatic vessels at the level of the muscularis mucosae.[112] The first lymph nodes involved are those closest to the tumour and the bowel wall. The tumour then usually progresses from lymph node to lymph node in a fairly orderly fashion, following the normal lymph flow. Thus, nodes at the root of the mesentery, the so-called high-point nodes, become involved only after those more proximal to the bowel wall. Both the location and the number of lymph nodes involved affect prognosis.[19] The 5-year survival rate when only one node is involved is approximately 60%, as compared with 35% when 2–5 nodes are involved, and 20% when 6 or more are involved.[19] In advanced carcinomas, lymphatic blockage may produce atypical routes of spread and, in such cases, intramural lymphatics at some distance from the primary tumour may be filled with malignant cells.

Nakahara et al recently described a form of colon cancer that preferentially diffusely infiltrates the colonic wall through the lymphatic vessels.[164] They referred to this pattern of disease as diffusely infiltrating cancer of the lymphangiosis type. The tumour spreads into the mesentery through the lymphatics and then to the lymph nodes. The tumour has a moderately differentiated histology that proliferates within the vascular channels. 88% of the cases had metastases to distant sites, including the liver.

Permeation of intramural veins may be present in up to 52% of cases;[217] in 35% there is involvement of veins beyond the bowel wall. Venous involvement tends to correlate with regional lymph node involvement and thus also relates to histological grade. Therefore, extramural venous invasion has an adverse effect on 5-year survival, reducing it from 55% to 30%.

Direct extension to adjacent organs occurs mainly with large, advanced carcinomas, in which lymph node and even distant metastases are often present at the time of resection. When extension to adjacent organs occurs, the 5-year survival is about 17%.[218] Colon cancers may penetrate segments of small intestine and cause obstruction or peritonitis. Direct extension to the liver from hepatic flexure tumours, and to the spleen or stomach from splenic flexure tumours, is not uncommon. Vesicocolic and vesicorectal fistulas may also result, and direct extension of rectal carcinomas to the prostate may mimic primary prostatic neoplasms.

Tumour spread within the peritoneal cavity occurs most commonly with poorly differentiated carcinomas, particularly those of the linitis plastica type[164] or colloid mucinous variety, producing pseudomyxoma peritonei.[219] Better differentiated carcinomas may also produce peritoneal nodules. Overall, approximately 10% of patients undergoing resection for colorectal adenocarcinoma can be expected to develop peritoneal foci of tumour.[19]

The presence of bone marrow involvement should be taken as evidence for widely disseminated disease. In one study, 32% of the patients had evidence of micrometastatic disease when their bone marrows were stained with an antibody to cytokeratin. Patients with these micrometastases had a significantly shorter disease-free survival than those in whom micrometastases were absent.[220]

Exfoliation of malignant cells at the time of surgical resection can give rise to tumour implants in an abdominal or peritoneal wound, or at anastomotic sites.[221] Implants in abdominal wounds and at colostomy sites usually result from contamination at the time of surgery. Suture line recurrences usually result from the presence of viable cells in the bowel lumen that implant in fibrin at the anastomotic site. To prevent this, the surgeon will often ligate the area of bowel to be resected and irrigate it with tumouricidal agents. Blocked lymphatic channels with atypical lymphatic spread account for a few suture line recurrences.

Rectal tumours resected with a short distal margin of grossly normal tissue (low anterior resection) are especially prone to local recurrence, even when the margins are monitored by frozen section analysis at the time of surgery.[222] The overall incidence of pelvic recurrence following removal of carcinomas of the rectum is 10%.[223] With the current interest in sphincter saving operations for patients with rectal cancer, the issue of what constitutes an adequate margin of resection has become increasingly important. Sidoni et al measured the extent of microscopic spread of the tumour in the bowel wall below the macroscopic edge of the tumour and found that it extended from 0.25–3.5 cm distally. The extent of distal spread correlated with tumour stage.[224] Devereuz and Deckers[225] followed up 214 patients for a minimum of 2 years, and found that among those with Dukes' B lesions, a surgical margin of 5 cm or greater was associated with 9% anastomotic recurrence rate, while those with less than 5 cm had a 43% recurrence rate. The margin of resection of Dukes' A tumours did not seem to be important, since no anastomotic recurrence was seen in that

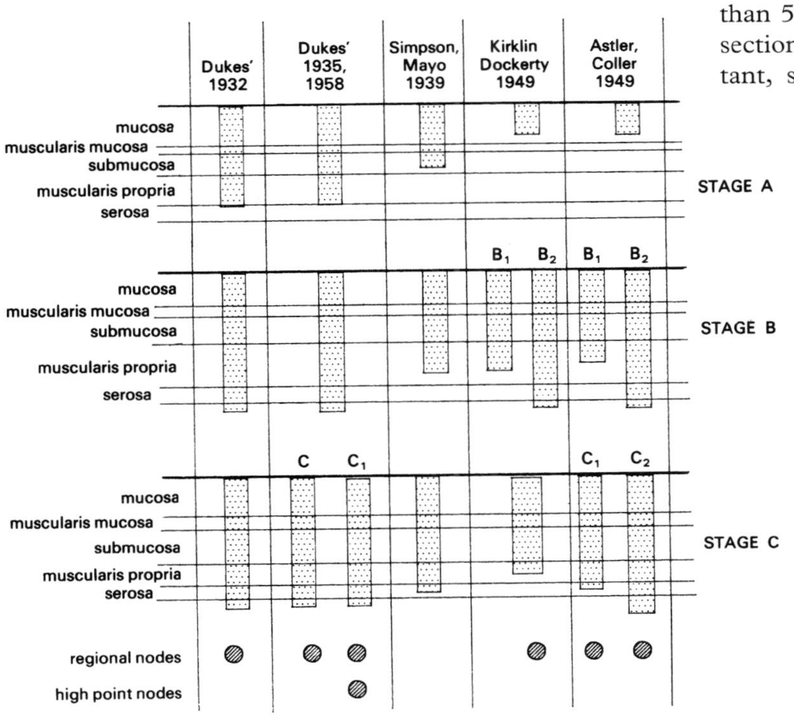

Fig. 41.14 Comparison of the various Dukes' staging systems.

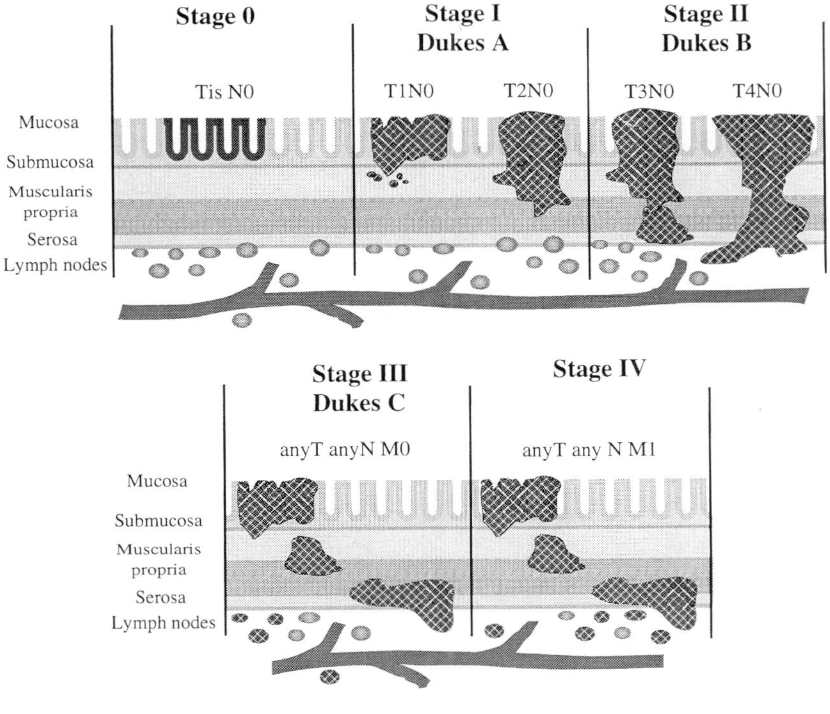

Fig. 41.15 Diagram of the TNM staging system in comparison to Dukes' staging.

group. Among Dukes' C lesions, there was a 17% anastomotic recurrence rate, whether the margins were shorter or longer than 5 cm. Thus, although it is still unsettled, it appears that 5 cm constitutes an adequate resection margin for colorectal cancers of Dukes' class B and C.

Staging

In 1932, Dukes published the classification and established the staging system that bears his name.[216] Dukes' A tumours are those that are confined to the bowel wall, i.e. the submucosa or muscularis propria, with no serosal invasion. Dukes' B tumours are those which have extended through the muscularis propria to the serosa and beyond. Dukes' C tumours are those with metastases to regional lymph nodes.

Since Dukes' 1932 classification, a number of modifications have been made (Fig. 41.14); these have been critically reviewed by Zinkin.[226] Confusion has arisen because most of these schemes use the letters A, B and C, but each denotes a different depth of invasion. Both Kirklin[227] and Astler and Coller[228] recognized the importance of establishing a category for tumours involving only the mucosa. Dukes and Bussey also noted a poorer survival rate among patients with apical lymph node involvement compared to those with only regional proximal node metastases.[229]

In 1954, Denoix proposed the TNM system to classify all cancers on the basis of extent of disease,[230] and Beahrs and Myers[231] adapted the TNM system to the staging of colorectal cancer, as shown in Figure 41.15 and Table 41.3. Note, however, that intramucosal and submucosal involvement are grouped together as T_1, when, in effect, intramucosal bowel cancer behaves like carcinoma-in-situ, and should be classified as T_0. After assigning each case the highest category of T, N and M that describes the extent of disease, the case is given a stage grouping, as shown in Table 41.4.

A significant correlation exists between extent of disease and survival of patients after definitive surgery as shown in Tables 41.5–41.7.[226,232,233,239] Both the Dukes' classification and the TNM system yield comparable and clinically significant predictive values for survival.

Table 41.3 TNM classification of colorectal cancer. (Beahrs & Myers 1983)[231]

T	—	PRIMARY TUMOUR
T_0	=	No evidence of primary tumour
T_{IS}	=	Carcinoma-in-situ
T_1	=	Tumour confined to mucosa or submucosa (see text)
T_2	=	Tumour limited to bowel wall, not beyond serosa
T_3	=	Involvement of all layers of bowel wall with or without extension to immediately adjacent structures or organs; fistula may be present
T_4	=	Tumour spread by direct extension beyond immediately adjacent structures and organs
N	—	NODAL INVOLVEMENT
N_0	=	Nodes not involved
N_1	=	One to three involved regional nodes adjacent to bowel wall
N_2	=	Regional nodes involved extending to line of resection or ligature of vessels (apex)
N_3	=	Nodes involved, but location not specified
M	—	DISTANT METASTASIS
M_0	=	No known metastasis
M_1	=	Distant metastasis present

Table 41.4 Stage grouping.

Stage 0		T_{is}, N_0, M_0
Stage I	IA:	T_1, N_0, M_0
	IB:	T_2, N_0, M_0
Stage II		T_3, N_0, M_0
Stage III		Any T, N_1–N_3, M_0 or T_4, N_0, M_0
Stage IV		Any T, Any N, M

Table 41.5 Survival rates for colorectal cancer using modified Dukes' classification. (Turnbull et al 1967)[232]

Stage	No. of cases	Percent of total	5-year survival (%)
A	103	15.2	98.8
B	212	31.3	84.9
C	156	23.1	67.3
D	205	30.3	14.3
Total	676		61.3

Table 41.6 Survival rate for colorectal cancer using TNM classification. (Wood et al 1979)[233]

	Cancer of colon			Cancer of rectum		
Stage	No. of cases	Percent of total	5-year survival (%)	No. of cases	Percent of total	5-year survival (%)
0	37	3.0	75	50	4.6	75
1 (A&B)	347	28.1	69	285	26.3	71
IA	57	4.6	77	66	6.1	76
IB	290	23.5	67	219	20.2	69
II	180	14.6	58	146	13.5	57
III	196	15.9	33	262	24.2	25
IV	126	10.2	4	56	5.2	7
Total	1233		55.1	1084		54.8

Table 41.7 Comparison of survival rates for colorectal cancer using Dukes' and TNM classification.

Dukes (1958)	5-year survival (%)	TNM	5-year survival (%)
A	81.2	Stage 0	75
		Stage I (A&B)	70
B	64.0	Stage II	58
C	27.4	Stage III	25–33
D	14.3	Stage IV	4–7

Currently, most pathologists employ the Dukes' classification, although there is an effort to promote the TNM classification scheme on an international basis.

A classification system devised by an international group and called the Australian Clinico-Pathological Staging System (ACPS) utilizes all the information available for each patient.[234,235] It includes clinical, operative and pathological findings. Based upon precise definitions, it permits what may prove to be the most accurate prognosis for an individual patient with colorectal cancer.[234–236]

FUTURE PROSPECTS

The most important determinants of recurrence and survival are the extent of the primary tumour, its cellular differentiation and involvement of the regional lymph nodes. More recent studies have looked at DNA content, proliferative activity, gastrin receptor expression, abnormalities in oncogenes and tumour suppressor genes, and allelic deletions.

Clearly, colorectal tumour development represents a highly complex process with many potential causal agents including environmental and dietary factors and both hereditary and somatic mutations. A complete description at the molecular level of how tumours arise and can be prevented is unknown at the present time. Also unknown, at present, is how to predict those adenomas that will go on to become carcinomas. Nonetheless, over the past decade, our understanding of the genetic basis of colorectal tumour development has grown considerably. Evidence has accumulated that colorectal cancer results, at least in part, from mutations involving two classes of genes: oncogenes and tumour suppressor genes.[237–247] Oncogenes act in a dominant fashion to promote tumour development when they are mutated or inappropriately expressed and they often lead to increased cell proliferation. In contrast to this, the normal function of tumour suppressor genes is to regulate cell growth and differentiation. Tumour suppressor genes are inactivated by inherited or somatic mutations with resultant loss of critical growth controls.

The current genetic model for colorectal tumourigenesis is one that involves alterations in both oncogenes and tumour suppressor genes. It is predicated upon the natural history of colorectal tumour development and takes advantage of our knowledge that the epithelium undergoes a series of histologically well-defined steps in the continuum from normal to adenoma to cancer. In patients with familial adenomatous polyposis coli, germline mutations in the APC gene are believed to be responsible for the hyperproliferative epithelium seen in these patients. In tumours that arise sporadically, a somatic mutation of either the APC or MCC gene probably plays a role in early stages of tumourigenesis. Alterations in DNA methylation may also be seen in very small adenomas of patients both with hereditary and non-hereditary forms of the disease. Loss of chromosomes 18q and 17p usually occur at a later stage in the development of carcinoma than do alterations involving chromosome 5q or *ras* mutations.[239,245,246] The order of these genetic changes is probably not invariant and the accumulation of multiple genetic alterations in both oncogenes and tumour suppressor genes is probably more important than is the specific order in which the alterations occur. The hope is that through our understanding of the molecular genetic events involved in the progression of colorectal neoplasia, we will develop new tools to differentiate between those tumours which will grow and progress and those that will not.

What is becoming clear is that tumours with more mutations, in general, behave more aggressively than those with only a few.[238] Patients with 17p, 18q and fractional allelic losses are much more likely to develop metastatic disease during follow up. These alterations represent useful markers for poor prognosis in patients without initial evidence of disseminated disease.[239] This does not appear to be true for patients with 5q deletions nor *ras* mutations.[238] On the other hand, the detection of ras mutations may play a critical role in developing screening strategies for the presence of colorectal adenomas. In other studies, it was shown that colorectal cancers with 17p but not 18q deletions have significantly poorer survival and that chromosome 18 deletions tended to play less of a role.[240] In contrast, in stage B and C carcinomas, a significant association has been observed between 18q allelic deletions and poor outcome.[241,242] Thus, the exact role played by deletions on chromosome 17 and 18 are yet to be established and require further delineation.

REFERENCES

1. Estrada RG, Spjut HJ. Hyperplastic polyps of the large bowel. Am J Surg Pathol 1980; 4: 127–133.
2. Williams GT, Arthur JH, Bussey HJR, Morson BC. Metaplastic polyps and polyposis of the colorectum. Histopathology 1980; 4: 155–170.
3. Cooper HS. Benign polyps of the intestines. In Ming SC, Goldman H, eds. Pathology of the Gastrointestinal Tract. Philadelphia: WB Sauders, 1992; pp 786–815.
4. Franzin G, Zamboni G, Scarpa A, Dina R, Iannucci A, Novelli P. Hyperplastic (metaplastic) polyps of the colon. A histologic and histochemical study. Am J Surg Pathol 1984; 8: 687–698.
5. Jass JR. Nature and significance of colorectal hyperplastic polyps. Semin Colon Rect Surg 1991; 2: 246–252.
6. Cooper HS, Patchefsky AP, Marlcs G. Adenomatous and carcinomatous changes within hyperplastic colonic epithelium. Dis Colon Rectum 1979; 27: 152–156.
7. Whittle TS, Varner W, Brown FM. Giant hyperplastic polyps of the colon simulating adenocarcinoma. Am J Gastroenterol 1978; 69: 105–107.
8. Waye JD, Lewis BS, Frankel A, Geller SA. Small colon polyps. Am J Gastroenterol 1988; 83: 899–906.

9. Lane N, Kaplan H, Pascal RR, Minute adenomatous and hyperplastic polyps of the colon: divergent patterns of epithelial growth with specific associated mesenchymal changes: contrasting roles in the pathogenesis of carcinoma. Gastroenterology 1971; 60: 537–551.
10. Feczko PJ, Bernstein MA, Halpert RS, Ackuman LV. Small colonic polyps: a reappraisal of their significance. Radiology 1984; 152: 301–303.
11. Kaye GI, Fenoglio CM, Pascal RR, Lane N. Comparative electron microscopic features of normal hyperplastic and adenomatous human colonic epithelium: variations in cellular structure relative to the process of epithelial differentiation. Gastroenterology 1973; 64: 926–945.
12. Fenoglio CM, Richart RM, Kaye GI. Comparative electron-microscopic features of normal, hyperplastic and adenomatous human colonic epithelium II. Variation in surface architecture found by scanning electron microscopy. Gastroenterology 1975; 69: 100–109.
13. Hayashi T, Yatani R, Apostol J, Stemmermann GN. Pathogenesis of hyperplastic polyps of the colon: a hypothesis based on ultrastructural and in vitro cell kinetics. Gastroenterology 1974; 66: 347–356.
14. Fenoglio-Preiser CM. Colon polyps histology. Sem Colon Rect Surg 1991; 2: 234–245.
15. Risio M, Coverlizza S, Ferrari A, Candelaresi GL, Rossini FP. Immunohistochemical study of epithelial cell proliferation in hyperplastic polyps, adenomas, adenocarcinomas of the large bowel. Gastroenterology 1988; 94: 899–906.
16. Cooper HS, Marshall C, Ruggerio F, Steplewski Z. Hyperplastic polyps of the colon and rectum. An immunohistochemical study with monoclonal antibodies vs. blood group antien (Sialosyl – Le^a, Le^a, Le^b, Le^x, Le^y, A, B and H). Lab Invest 1987; 57: 421–428.
17. Fenoglio CM, Kaye GI, Pascal RR, Lane N. Defining the precursor tissue of ordinary large bowel carcinoma: implications for cancer prevention. Pathol Ann 1977; 12: 87–116.
18. Grondin MV, Chang WWL, Gaskins RD. Crypt alterations and collagen deposit in hyperplastic polyps of colorectum. Dig Dis Sci 1990; 35: 12.
19. Fenoglio-Preiser CM, Pascal RR, Perzin KH. Tumors of the Large and Small Intestine, AFIP Fascicle, 2nd Series, 1990.
20. Kaye GI, Pascal RR, Lane N. The colonic pericryptal fibroblastic sheath: replication, migration, and cytodifferentiation of a mesenchymal cell system in adult tissue III. Gastroenterology 1971; 60: 515–536.
21. Jass JR, Faludy J. Immunohistochemical demonstration of IgA and secretory component in relation to epithelial cell differentiation in normal colorectal mucosa and metaplastic polyps: a semiquantitative study. Histochem J 1985; 17: 373–380.
22. Bedossa P, Poynard T, Bacci J, et al. Expression of histochemical antigens and characterization of the lymphocyte infiltrate in hyperplastic polyps of the large bowel. Hum Pathol 1990; 21: 319–324.
23. Fulcheri E, Baracchini P, Lapertosa G, Bussolati G. Distribution and significance of the smooth muscle component in polyps of the large intestine. Hum Pathol 1988; 19: 922–927.
24. Sobin LK. Inverted hyperplastic polyps of the colon. Am J Surg Pathol 1985; 9: 265–272.
25. Jass JR, Filipe MI, Abbas S, Falcon CAJ, Wilson Y, Lovell D. A morphologic and histochemical study of metaplastic polyps of the colorectum. Cancer 1984; 53: 5120–151.
26. Jass JR. Relation between metaplastic polyp and carcinoma of the colon-rectum. Lancet 1983; 1: 28–30.
27. Skinner JM, Whitehead R. Tumour-associated antigens in polyps and carcinoma of the human large bowel. Cancer 1981; 47: 1241–1245.
28. Ansher AF, Lewis JH, Fleischer DE, et al. Hyperplastic colonic polyps as a marker for adenomatous colonic polyps. Am J Gastroenterol 1989; 84: 113–117.
29. Provenzale D, Martin ZZ, Holland KL, Sandler RS. Colon adenomas in patients with hyperplastic polyps. J Clin Gastroenterol 1988; 10: 46–49.
30. Goldman H, Ming S-L, Hickok DF. Nature and significance of hyperplastic polyps of the human colon. Arch Pathol 1970; 89: 349–354.
31. Longacre TA, Fenoglio-Preiser CM. Mixed hyperplastic adenomatous polyps/serrated adenomas. A distinct form of colorectal neoplasia. Am J Surg Pathol 1990; 14: 524–537.
32. Bengoechea O, Martinez-Penuela JM, Larringa B, Valerdi J, Borda F. Hyperplastic polyposis of the colorectum and adenocarcinoma in a 24 year old man. Am J Surg Pathol 1987; 11: 323–327.
33. McCann BG. A case of metaplastic polyposis of the colon associated with focal adenomatous changes and metachronous adenocarcinoma. Histopathology 1988; 13: 700–702.
34. Heng-Teoh H, Delahunt B, Isbister WH. Dysplastic and malignant areas in hyperplastic polyps of the large intestine. Pathology 1989; 21: 138–142.
35. Franzin G, Zamboni G, Diana R, Scarpa A, Fratton A. Juvenile and inflammatory polyps of the colon — a histological and histochemical study. Histopathology 1983; 7: 719–728.
36. Ali MH, Satti MB, Al-Nafussi A. Multiple benign colonic polypi at the site of ureterosigmoidostomy. Cancer 1984; 53: 1006–1010.
37. Weller RD, McColl I. Electron microscope appearance of juvenile and Peutz-Jeghers polyps. Gut 1966; 7: 265–270.
38. Pham BN, Villeneuva RP. Ganglioneuromatosis proliferation associated with juvenile polyposis coli. Ann Path Lab Med 1989; 113: 91–94.
39. Mendelsohn G, Diamond MP. Familial ganglioneuromatosis polyposis of the large bowel. Am J Surg Path 1984; 8: 515–520.
40. Fenoglio-Preiser CM, Lantz PE, Listrom MB, Davis M, Rilke FO. Gastrointestinal Pathology. An Atlas and Text. Raven Press, New York, 1989.
41. Dajani YF, Kamal MF. Colorectal juvenile polyps: an epidemiological and histopathological study of 144 cases in Jordanians. Histopathology 1984; 8: 765–779.
42. Baptist SJ, Sabatini MT. Co-existing juvenile polyps in tubulovillous adenomas of colon with carcinomas in situ. Hum Pathol 1985; 16: 1061–6103.
43. Morson BC. Some peculiarities in the histology of intestinal polyps. Dis Colon Rectum 1962; 5: 337–344.
44. Roth SI, Helwig EB. Juvenile polyps of the colon and rectum. Cancer 1963; 16: 468–478.
45. Horrilleno EG, Eckert C, Ackerman LV. Polyps of the rectum and colon in children. Cancer 1957; 10: 1210–1220.
46. Mallam AS, Thomson SA. Polyps of the rectum and colon in children; 10-year review at Hospital for Sick Children, Toronto. J Surg 1959; 3: 17–24.
47. Lipper S, Kahn LB, Ackerman LV. The significance of microscopic invasive cancer in endoscopically removed polyps of the large bowel. A clinicopathologic study of 51 cases. Cancer 1983; 52: 1691–1699.
48. Schilla FW. Carcinoma in rectal polyp: report of a case in infancy. Am J Surg 1950; 88: 659–670.
49. Tun-Hua L, Min-Chang C, Hsien-Chiu T. Malignant change of a juvenile polyp of colon: a case report. Chinese Med 1978; 4: 434.
50. Bartholomew LG, Moore CE, Dahlin DC, Waugh JM. Intestinal polyposis associated with mucocutaneous pigmentation. Surg Gynecol Obstet 1962; 115: 11.
51. Shepherd NA, Bussey HJR, Jass JR. Epithelial misplacement in Peutz-Jeghers polyps. A diagnostic pitfall. Am J Surg Path 1987; 11: 743–749.
52. Estrada R, Spjut HJ. Hamartomatous polyps in Peutz-Jeghers syndrome: a light, histochemical and electron microscope study. Am J Surg Pathol 1983; 7: 747–754.
53. Kyriakos M, Condon SC. Enteritis cystic profunda. Am J Clin Pathol 1978; 69: 77–85.
54. Konishi F, Wyse NE, Muto F, et al. Peutz-Jeghers polyposis associated with carcinoma of the digestive organs. Dis Colon Rectum 1987; 30: 790–796.
55. Narita T, Eto T, Ito T. Peutz-Jeghers syndrome with adenoma and adenocarcinoma in colonic polyps. Am J Surg Pathol 1987; 11: 76–81.

56. Dozois RR, Judd ES, Dahlin DC, Bartholomew LG. The Peutz-Jeghers syndrome. Is there a predisposition to the development of intestinal malignancy? Arch Surg 1969; 98: 509–517.
57. Perzin KH, Bridge MF. Adenomatous and carcinomatous changes in hamartomatous polyps of the small intestine (Peutz-Jeghers syndrome): report of a case and review of the literature. Cancer 19; 49: 971–983.
58. Turrell R, Haller JD. A re-evaluation of the malignant potential of colorectal adenomas. Surg Gynecol Obstet 1964; 119: 867–887.
59. Spjut HJ, Frankel NB, Appel MF. The small carcinoma of the large bowel. Am J Surg Pathol 1979; 3: 39–46.
60. Spratt JS Jr, Ackerman LV, Moyer CA. Relationship of polyps of the colon to colonic cancer. Ann Surg 1958; 148: 682–696.
61. Rickert RR, Auerbach O, Garfinkel L, Hammond EC, Frasca JM. Adenomatous lesion of the large bowel: an autopsy survey. Cancer 1979; 43: 1847–1857.
62. Correa P, Dugue E, Cuello O, Haenszel W. Polyps of the colon and rectum. In: Cali Colombia. Int J Cancer 1972; 9: 86–96.
63. Bremmer CG, Ackerman LV. Polyps and carcinoma of the large bowel in the South African Bantu. Cancer 1970; 26: 991–999.
64. Rider JA, Kirsner JB, Moeller HC, Palmer WI. Polyps of the colon and rectum. Their incidence and relationship to carcinoma. Am J Med 1954; 16: 555–564.
65. Greene FG. Distribution of colorectal neoplasms. A left to right shift of polyps and cancer. Am Surgeon 1983; 49: 62–65.
66. Williams AR, Balasooriya BAW, Day DW. Polyps and cancer of the large bowel: a necropsy study in Liverpool. Gut 1982; 23: 835–42.
67. Arminski TC, McLean DW. Incidence and distribution of adenomatous polyps of the colon and rectum based on 1000 autopsy examinations. Dis Colon Rectum 1964; 7: 249–61.
68. Berge T, Ekelund G, Meffner C, Phil B, Wenckert A. Carcinoma of the colon and rectum in a defined population. Acta Chir Scand 1973; 438(Suppl): 1–86.
69. Vatn MH, Stalsberg H. The prevalence of polyps of the large intestine in Oslo. An autopsy study. Cancer 1982; 49: 819–825.
70. Shinya H, Wolff WI. Morphology, anatomic distribution and cancer potential of polyps: an analysis of 7000 polyps endoscopically removed. Ann Surg 1979; 190: 679–683.
71. Konishi F, Morson BC. Pathology of colorectal adenomas: a colonoscopic survey. J Clin Pathol 1982; 35: 830–841.
72. Cady B, Persson AV, Monson DO, Maunz DL. Changing patterns in colorectal carcinoma. Cancer 1974; 33: 422–426.
73. Chapman I. Adenomatous polyps of large intestine: incidence and distribution. Ann Surg 1963; 157: 223–226.
74. Levi F, Randimbison L, La Vecchia C. Trends in subsite distribution of colorectal cancers and polyps from the Vaud cancer registry. Cancer 1993; 72: 46–50.
75. Dixon CF, Weisman RE. Polyps of the sigmoid occurring thirty years after bilateral ureterosigmoidostomy for exstrophy of the bladder. Surgery 1948; 24: 1026–1034.
76. Rivard J-Y, Bedard A, Dionne L. Colonic neoplasms following ureterosigmoidostomy. J Urol 1975; 113: 781–786.
77. Beart RW, Fleming CR, Banks PM. Tubulovillous adenomas in continent ileostomy after proctocoloectomy for familial polyposis. Dig Dis Sci 1982; 27: 553–556.
78. Mannes AG, Weinzierl M, Stellaard F, Theime C, Wiebecke I, Baumgartner G. Adenomas of the large intestine after cholecystectomy. Gut 1984; 25: 863–866.
79. Drexler J. Asymptomatic polyps of the rectum and colon. Arch Intern Med 1967; 119: 503–509.
80. Brahme F, Ekelund GR, Norden JG, Wenckert A. Metachronous colorectal polyps: comparison of development of colorectal polyps and carcinomas in persons with and without histories of polyps. Dis Colon Rectum 1974; 17: 166–171.
81. Winawer SJ, Zauber AG, O'Brien MJ, et al. The National Polyp Study: designs, methods, and characteristics of patients with newly diagnosed polyps. Cancer 1992; 70: 1236–1245.
82. Tripp MR, Morgan TR, Sampliner RE, Kogan FJ, Protell RL, and Earnest DL. Synchronous neoplasms in patients with diminutive colorectal adenomas. Cancer 1987; 60: 1599–1603.
83. Galandiuk S, Fazio WV, Jagelman DG, et al. Villous and tubulovillous adenomas of the colon and rectum: a retrospective review, 1964–1985. Am J Surg 1987; 153: 41–47.
84. Jahadi MR, Baldwin A Jr. Villous adenomas of the colon and rectum. Am J Surg 1975; 130: 729–732.
85. Sanner RF Jr. Diffuse polyposis of the colon with severe electrolyte depletion. Arch Surg 1973; 107: 903–905.
86. Jacob H, Schlondorff D, St Onge G, Bernstein LH. Villous adenoma depletion syndrome: evidence for a cyclic nucleotide-mediated diarrhea. Dig Dis Sci 1985; 30: 637–641.
87. Wolff WI, Shinya H. Definitive treatment of 'malignant' polyps of the colon. Ann Surg 1975; 182: 516–525.
88. Stulc JP, Petrelli NJ, Herrera L, Mittelman A. Colorectal villous and tubulovillous adenomas equal to or greater than four centimeters. Ann Surg 1988; 207: 65–71.
89. Maskens AP. Histogenesis of adenomatous polyps in the human large intestine. Gastroenterol 1979; 77: 1245–51.
90. Hamilton SR. Pathogenesis of polyps (adenomas). Dis Colon Rectum 1983; 26: 413–4.
91. Nakamura S, Kino I. Morphogenesis of minute adenomas in familial polyposis coli. J Natl Cancer Inst 1984; 73: 41–9.
92. Lev R, Grover R. Precursors of human colon carcinoma: a serial section study of colectomy specimens. Cancer 1981; 47: 2007–2015.
93. Chang WWL, Whitener CJ. Histogenesis of tubular adenomas in hereditary colonic adenomatous polyposis. Arch Pathol Lab Med 1989; 113: 1042–9.
94. Bussey HJR. Familial polyposis coli. Baltimore: Johns Hopkins University Press, 1975; 34–43.
95. Kubota O, Kino I. Minute adenomas of the depressed type in familial adenomatous polyposis of the colon. Cancer 1993; 72: 1159–1164.
96. Jass JR, Young PJ, Robinson EM. Predictors of presence, multiplicity, size and dysplasia of colorectal adenomas. A necropsy study in New Zealand. J Brit Soc Gastroenterol 1992; 33: 1508–1514.
97. Muto T, Kamiya J, Sawada T, et al. Small 'flat adenoma' of the large bowel with special reference to its clinicopathological features. Dis Colon Rectum 1985; 28: 847–851.
98. Fenoglio-Preiser CM, Hutter RV. Colorectal polyps: pathologic diagnosis and clinical significance. CA-A Cancer J Clinicians 1985; 3: 322–344.
99. Enterline HT, Evans GW, Mercado-Lugo R, Miller L, Fitts WT. Malignant potential of adenomas of colon and rectum. JAMA 1962; 179: 322–330.
100. Woda BA, Forde K, Lane N. A unicryptal colonic adenoma, the smallest colonic neoplasm yet observed in a non-polyposis individual. Am J Clin Pathol 1977; 68: 631–632.
101. O'Brien MJ, Winawer SJ, Zauber AG, et al. The National Polyp Study: patient and polyp characteristic associated with high-grade dysplasia in colorectal adenomas. Gastroenterology 1990; 98: 371–379.
102. Fung CH, Goldman H. The incidence and significance of villous change in adenomatous polyps. Am J Clin Pathol 1970; 53: 21–25.
103. Pascal RR, Kaye GI, Lane N. Colonic pericryptal fibroblast sheath replication, migration and cytodifferentiation of a mesenchymal cell system in adult tissue. I. Autoradiographic studies of normal rabbit colon. Gastroenterology 1968; 54: 835–851.
104. Ota H, Nakayama J, Fujimori Y, et al. Organized differentiation of tumor cells of villous adenomas of the large intestine. Acta Histochemica et Cytochemica 1993; 26: 117–125.
105. Bansal M, Fenoglio CM, Robboy SJ, King DW. Are metaplasias in colorectal adenomas truly metaplasia? Am J Pathol 1984; 115: 253–265.
106. Almagro UA, Pintar K, Zellmer RB. Squamous metaplasia in colorectal polyps. Cancer 1984; 53: 2679–2682.
107. Chen KTK. Colonic adenomatous polyp with focal squamous metaplasia. Hum Pathol 1981; 12: 848–849.
108. Forouhar F. Neoplastic colonic polyp with extensive squamous metaplasia. Case Report. Tumori 1984; 70: 90–140.

109. Sarlin JG, Mori K. Morules in epithelial tumors of the colon and rectum. Am J Surg Pathol 1984; 8: 281–285.
110. Kaye GI, Lane N, Pascal RR. Colonic pericryptal fibroblast sheath: replication, migration, and cytodifferentiation of a mesenchymal cell system in adult tissue II. Gastroenterology 1968; 54: 852–865.
111. Fenoglio CM, Pascal RR. Colorectal adenomas and cancer. Pathologic relationships. Cancer 1982; 50: 2601–2608.
112. Fenoglio CM, Kaye GI, Lane N. Distribution of human colonic lymphatics in normal, hyperplastic, and adenomatous tissue: its relationship to metastasis from small carcinomas in pedunculated adenomas, with two case reports. Gastroenterology 1973; 64: 51–65.
113. Muto T, Bussey HJ, Morson BC. Pseudo-carcinomatous invasion in adenomatous polyps of the colon and rectum. J Clin Pathol 1973; 26: 25–31.
114. Qizilbash AH, Meghji M, Castelli M. Pseudocarcinomatous invasion in adenomas of the colon and rectum. Dis Colon Rectum 1980; 23: 529–535.
115. Fechner RE. Adenomatous polyp with submucosal cysts. Am J Clin Pathol 1973; 59: 498–502.
116. Greene FL. Epithelial misplacement in adenomatous polyps of the colon and rectum. Cancer 1974; 33: 206–217.
117. Cheung DK, Attiyeh FF. Pseudocarcinomatous invasion of colonic polyps. Dis Colon Rectum 1981; 24: 399–401.
118. Kinzler KW, Nilbert MC, Su LK, et al. Identification of FAP locus genes from chromosome 5q21. Science 1991; 253: 661–5.
119. Bodmer WF, Bailey CJ, Bodmer J, et al. Localization of the gene for familial adenomatous polyposis on chromosome 5. Nature 1987; 328: 614–6.
120. Lanspa SJ, Lynch HT, Smyrk TC, et al. Colorectal adenomas in the Lynch syndromes: results of a colonoscopy screening program. Gastroenterology 1990; 98: 117–1122.
121. Lynch HT, Smyrk T, Lanspa SJ, et al. Flat adenomas in a colon cancer-prone kindred. J Natl Cancer Inst 1988; 80: 278–82.
122. Lynch HT, Smyrk TC, Lanspa SJ, et al. Phenotypic variation in colorectal adenoma/cancer expression in two families: hereditary flat adenoma syndrome. Cancer 1990; 66: 909–15.
123. Lynch HT, Smyrk TC, Lanspa SJ, et al. Upper gastrointestinal manifestations in families with hereditary flat adenoma syndrome. Cancer 1993; 71: 2709–2714.
124. Spirio L, Otterud B, Stauffer D, et al. Linkage of a variant or attenuated form of adenomatous polyposis coli to the adenomatous polyposis coli (APC) locus. Am J Hum Genet 1992; 51: 92–100.
125. Aubert H, Zarski JP, Faure H, Rachael M. Endoscopic polypectomy in the management of colorectal cancerous adenomas and individual experience. In, Fenoglio CM, Rossini FP, eds. Verona: Cortina International, 1985.
126. Burt RW, Bishop DT, Cannon-Albright L, et al. Population genetics of colonic cancer. Cancer 1993; 70: 1719–1722.
127. Silverberg SG. Focally malignant adenomatous polyps of the colon and rectum. Surg Gynecol Obstet 1970; 131: 103–114.
128. Muto T, Bussey HJR, Morson BC. The evolution of cancer of the colon and rectum. Cancer 1975; 36: 2251–2270.
129. Fenoglio CM, Lane M. The anatomical precursor of colorectal carcinoma. Cancer 1974; 34: 819–823.
130. Morson BC. Precancerous and early malignant lesions of the large intestine. Br J Surg 1968; 55: 725–731.
131. Comer TP, Beahrs OH, Dockerty MB. Primary squamous cell and adenocarcinoma of the colon. Cancer 1972; 28: 1111–1117.
132. Dixon CF, Dockerty MB, Powelson MH. Squamous cell carcinoma of the mid-rectum: report of a case. Proc Mayo Clinic 1954; 29: 420–423.
133. Crissman JD. Adenosquamous and squamous cell carcinoma of the colon. Am J Surg Pathol 1978; 2: 47–54.
134. Haggitt RC, Glotzbach RE, Soffer EE, Wruble LD. Prognostic factors in colorectal carcinomas arising in adenomas: implications for lesion removal by endoscopic polypectomy. Gastroenterology 1985; 89: 328–336.
135. Listrom MB, Fenoglio-Preiser CM. The malignant polyp. An analysis of the procedures for handling polyps. Endosc Rev 1985; 2: 21–27.
136. Coverlizza S, Risio M, Ferrari A, Fenoglio-Preiser CM, Rossini FP. Colorectal adenomas containing invasive carcinoma. Pathologic assessment of lymph node metastatic potential. Cancer 1989; 64: 1937–1947.
137. Levin K, Dozois R. Epidemiology and large bowel cancer. World J of Surgery 1991; 15: 562–567.
138. Silverberg E, Boring CC, Squires TS. Cancer statistics 1990. Ca 40: 9–26.
139. Anderson A, Bergdahl L. Carcinoma of the colon in children: a report of six new cases and a review of the literature. J Pedr Surg 1976; 11: 967–971.
140. Meddelkamp JN, Haffner H. Carcinoma of the colon in children. Pediatrics 1963; 32: 558–571.
141. Kern WH, White WC. Adenocarcinoma of the colon in a 9-month-old infant. Cancer 1958; 11: 855–857.
142. Steinberg JB, Tuggle DW, Postier RG. Adenocarcinoma of the colon in adolescents. Am J Surg 1988; 156: 460–462.
143. Table 10A, 10D. In: National Cancer Institute Monograph. Bethesda, MD: National Cancer Institute, 1981; 57: 1–187.
144. Rao BN, Pratt CB, Fleming ID, Dilawari RA, Green AA, Austin BA. Colon carcinoma in children and adolescents: a review of 30 cases. Cancer 1985; 55: 1322–1326.
145. Johnson H Jr, Carstens R. Anatomical distribution of colonic carcinomas: interracial differences in a community hospital population. Cancer 1986; 58: 997–1000.
146. Snyderwine EG, Battula N. Selective mutagenic activation by cytochrome P_3-450 of carcinogenic arylamines found in foods. JNCI 1989; 81: 223–227.
147. Levin B, Lennard-Jones J, Riddele R, Sachar D, Winawer SJ, and the WHO Collaborating Centre for the Prevention of Colorectal Cancer: surveillance of patients with chronic ulcerative colitis. Bull WHO 1991; 69: 121–126.
148. Fredriksson M, Bengtsson N-O, Hardell L, Axelson O. Colon cancer, physical activity, and occupational exposures: a case-control study. Cancer 1989; 63: 1838–1842.
149. Garbrant DH, Peters RK, Homa DM. Asbestos and colon cancer — lack of association in a large case-control study. Am J Epidemiology 1992; 135: 843–853.
150. Brownson RC, Zahm SH, Chang JC, Blair A. Occupational risk of colon cancer: an analysis by anatomic subsite. Am J Epidemiol 1989; 130: 675–687.
151. Kuramoto S, and Oohara T. Flat early cancers of the large intestine. Cancer 1989; 64: 950–955.
152. Heald RJ, Bussey HJR. Clinical experiences at St. Mark's Hospital with multiple synchronous cancers of the colon and rectum. Dis Colon Rectum 1975; 18: 6–10.
153. Brahme F, Ekelund GR, Norden JG, Wenckert A. Metachronous colorectal polyps: comparison of development of colorectal polyps and carcinomas with and without history of polyps. Dis Colon Rectum 1974; 17: 166–71.
154. Abrams JS, Reines HD. Increasing incidence of right-sided lesions in colorectal cancer. Am J Surg 1979; 137: 622–626.
155. Hewitt RE, Powe DG, Carter GI, Turner DR. Desmoplasia and its relevance to colorectal tumour invasion. Int J Cancer 1993; 53: 62–69.
156. Halvorsen TB, Seim E. Association between invasiveness, inflammatory reaction, desmoplasia and survival in colorectal cancer. J Clin Pathol 1989; 42: 162–166.
157. Shirouzu K, Isomoto H, Kakegawa T. Prognostic evaluation of perineural invasion in rectal cancer. Am J Surg 1993; 165: 233–237.
158. Smith RM, Haggitt RC. The prevalence and prognostic significance of argyrophil cells in carcinomas of the colon and rectum. Am J Surg Pathol 1984; 8: 123.
159. Hamada Y, Oishi A, Shoji T, et al. Endocrine cells and prognosis in patients with colorectal carcinoma. Cancer 1992; 69: 2641–2646.
160. Debruine AP, Wiggers T, Beek C, et al. Endocrine cells in colorectal adenocarcinomas — incidence, hormone profile and prognostic relevance. Int J Cancer 1993; 54: 765–771.

161. Park JG, Choe GY, Helman LJ, et al. Chromogranin-A expression in gastric and colon cancer tissues. Int J Cancer 1992; 51: 189–194.
162. Urias AA. Primary signet-ring cell carcinoma. Cancer 1983; 52: 1453–1457.
163. Stevens WR, Phillip R. Primary linitis plastica carcinoma of the colon and rectum. Mod Pathol 1989; 2: 265–269.
164. Nakahara H, Ishikawa T, Itabashi M, Hirota T. Diffusely infiltrating primary colorectal carcinoma of linitis plastica and lymphangiosis types. Cancer 1992; 69: 901–906.
165. Halvorsen TB, Seim E. Influence of mucinous components on survival in colorectal adenocarcinomas: a multivariate analysis. J Clin Pathol 1988; 41: 1068–1072.
166. Fahl JC, Dockerty MB, Judd ES. Schirrous carcinoma of the colon and rectum. Surg Gynecol Obstet 1960; 111: 759–766.
167. Connelly JH, Robey-Cafferty SS, El-Naggar AK, Cleary KR. Exophytic signet-ring cell carcinoma of the colorectum. Arch Pathol Lab Med 1991; 115: 134–136.
168. Nakamura T, Nakano G, Sakamoto K. Adenoma of the rectum with multiple foci of signet-ring cell carcinoma. Report of a case. Dis Colon Rectum 1983; 26: 529–532.
169. Symonds DA, Vickery AL Jr. Mucinous carcinoma of the colon and rectum. Cancer 1976; 37: 1891–1900.
170. Watson PH, Alguacil-Garcia A. Mixed crypt cell carcinoma: a clinicopathological study of the so-called 'Goblet cell carcinoid'. Virchows Arch 1987; 412: 175–182.
171. Yamagiwa H, Yoshimura H, Tomiyam H, Matsuzaki O, Onishi T. Squamous changes of adenocarcinomas of the large intestine. Gan No Rinsho 1984; 30: 233–238.
172. Weidner N, Zekar P. Carcinosarcoma of the colon. Report of a unique case with light and immunohistochemical studies. Cancer 1986; 58: 1126–1130.
173. Peonim V, Thakerngpol K, Pacharee P, Stitniman-Karne T. Adenosquamous carcinoma and carcinoidal differentiation of the colon. Report of a case. Cancer 1983; 52: 1122–1125.
174. Williams GT, Blackshaw AJ, Morson BC. Squamous carcinoma of the colorectum and its genesis. J Pathol 1979; 129: 139–147.
175. Prener A, Nielsen K. Primary squamous cell carcinoma of the rectum in Denmark. APMIS 1988; 96: 839–844.
176. Chevinsky AH, Berelowitz M, Hoover HC Jr. Adenosquamous carcinoma of the colon presenting with hypercalcemia. Cancer 1987; 60: 1111–1116.
177. Berkelhammer CH, Baker AL, Block GE, Bostwick DG, Michelassi F. Humoral hypercalcemia complicating adenosquamous carcinoma of the proximal colon. Dig Dis Sci 1989; 34: 142–147.
178. Michelassi F, Mishlove LA, Stipa F, Block GE. Squamous cell carcinoma of the colon: experiences at the University of Chicago — review of the literature and report of two cases. Dis Colon Rectum 1988; 31: 228–235.
179. Hohm WH, Jackman RJ. Squamous cell carcinoma of the rectum complicating ulcerative colitis: report of two cases. Mayo Clin Proc 1964; 39: 249–251.
180. Pemberton M, Lendrum J. Squamous cell carcinoma of the caecum following ovarian adenocarcinoma. Br J Surg 1968; 55: 273–726.
181. Vezeridis MP, Herrera L, Lopez GE, Ledesma EJ, Mittleman A. Squamous cell carcinoma of the colon and rectum. Dis Colon Rectum 1983; 26: 188–191.
182. Lundquest DE, Marcus JN, Thorson AG, Massop D. Primary squamous cell carcinoma of the colon arising in a villous adenoma. Hum Pathol 1988; 19: 362–364.
183. Hickey WF, Corson JM. Squamous cell carcinoma arising in a duplication of the colon: case report and literature review of squamous cell carcinoma of the colon and of malignancy complicating colonic duplication. Cancer 1981; 47: 602–609.
184. Miettinen M. Synaptophysin and neurofilament proteins as markers for neuroendocrine tumors. Arch Pathol Lab Med 1987; 111: 813–818.
185. Burke AB, Shekitka KM, Sobin LH. Small cell carcinomas of the large intestine. Am J Clin Pathol 1991; 95: 315–321.
186. Wick MR, Weatherby RP, Weiland LH. Small cell neuroendocrine carcinoma of the colon and rectum: clinical histologic and ultrastructural study and immunohistochemical comparison with cloacogenic carcinomas. Human Pathol 1987; 18: 9–21.
187. Balsam A, Bernstein G, Goldman J, Sachs BA, Rifkin H. Ectopic corticotropin syndrome associated with carcinoma of the colon. Gastroenterology 1972; 62: 636–641.
188. Graham AR, Payne CM, Nagle RB, Agnel E. The role of immunohistochemistry, electron microscopy and ultrastructural cytochemistry in the diagnosis of mixed carcinoma-neuroendocrine neoplasm. Pathol Res Pract 1987; 182: 23–33.
189. Miura K, Demura H, Sato E, Sasano N, Shimizu N. A case of ACTH-secretory cancer of the colon. J Clin Endocrinol Metab 1970; 31: 591–595.
190. Mills SE, Allen MS Jr, Cohen AR. Small-cell undifferentiated carcinoma of the colon. A clinicopathological study of five cases and their association with colonic adenomas. Am J Surg Pathol 1983; 7: 643–651.
191. Damjanov I, Amenta PS, Bosman FT. Undifferentiated carcinoma of the colon containing exocrine, neuroendocrine and squamous cells. Virchows Arch (A) 1983; 401: 57–66.
192. Schwartz AM, Orenstein JM. Small-cell undifferentiated carcinoma of the rectosigmoid colon. Arch Pathol Lab Med 1985; 109: 629–632.
193. Gould VE, Cheifec G. Neuroendocrine carcinomas of the colon. Ultrastructural and biochemical evidence of their secretory function. Am J Surg Pathol 1978; 2: 31–8.
194. Redman BG, Pazdur R. Colonic small cell undifferentiated carcinoma: a distinct pathologic diagnosis with therapeutic implications. Am J Gastroenterology 1987; 83: 382–385.
195. Bak M, Teglbjaerg PS. Pleomorphic (giant cell) carcinoma of the intestine: an immunohistochemical and electron microscopic study. Cancer 1989; 64: 2557–2564.
196. Strate RW, Richardson JD, Bannayan GA. Basosquamous (transitional cloacogenic) carcinoma of the sigmoid colon. Cancer 1977; 40: 1234–1239.
197. Hall-Craggs M, Toker C. Basaloid tumor of the sigmoid colon. Hum Pathol 1982; 13: 497–500.
198. Park CH, Reid JD. Adenocarcinomas of the colon with choriocarcinoma in its metastases. Cancer 1980; 46: 570–575.
199. Nguyen G-K. Adenocarcinoma of the sigmoid colon with focal choriocarcinoma metaplasia: a case report. Dis Colon Rectum 1982; 25: 230–234.
200. Ordonez NG, Luwa MA. Choriocarcinoma of the colon. Am J Gastroenterol 1984; 79: 39–42.
201. Kubosawa H, Nagaqo K, Kondo Y, Ishige H, Inaba N. Coexistence of adenocarcinomas and choriocarcinomas in the sigmoid colon. Cancer 1984; 54: 866–868.
202. Chumas JC, Lorelle CA. Melanotic adenocarcinoma of the anorectum. Am J Surg Pathol 1981; 7: 711–717.
203. Bjerkeset T, Morlid I, Mork S, Soreide O. Tumor characteristics in colorectal cancer and their relationship to treatment and prognosis. Dis Colon Rectum 1987; 30: 934–8.
204. Schmitz-Moormann GW, Himmelmann UB, Niles M. Morphological predictors of survival in colorectal carcinoma: univariate and multivariate analysis. J Cancer Res Clin Oncol 1987; 113: 586–92.
205. Brodsky JT, Richard GK, Cohen AM, Minsky BD. Variables correlated with the risk of lymph node metastasis in early rectal cancer. Cancer 1992; 69: 322–326.
206. Minsky BD, Rich T, Recht A, Harvey W, Mies C. Selection criteria for local excision with or without adjuvant radiation therapy for rectal cancer. Cancer 1989; 63: 1421–1429.
207. Cohen AM, Wood WC, Gunderson LL, Shinnar M. Pathological studies in rectal cancer. Cancer 1980; 45: 2965–2968.
208. Armitage NC, Robins RA, Evans DF, Turner DR, Baldwin RW, Hardcastle JD. The influence of tumour cell DNA abnormalities on survival in colorectal cancer. Br J Surg 1985; 72: 828–830.
209. Kokal W, Sheibani K, Terz J, Harada JR. Tumor DNA content in the prognosis of colorectal carcinoma. JAMA 1986; 255: 3123–3127.

210. Quirke P, Dixon MF, Claydens AD, Durdey P, Dyson JE, et al. Prognostic significance of DNA aneuploidy and cell proliferation in rectal adenocarcinomas. J Pathol 1987; 151: 285–291.
211. Steinbeck RG, Heselmeyer KM, Neugebauer WF, Falkmer UG, Auer GU. DNA ploidy in human colorectal adenocarcinomas. Analytical and Quantitative Cytology and Histology 1993; 15: 187–194.
212. Banner FB, Tomas-de la Vega JE, Roseman DL, Coor JS. Should flow cytometric DNA analysis precede definitive surgery for colon carcinoma? Ann Surg 1985; 202: 740–744.
213. Scott NA, Rainwater LM, Wieand HS, et al. The relative prognostic value of flow cytometric DNA analysis and conventional clinicopathologic criteria in patients with operable rectal carcinoma. Dis Colon Rectum 1987; 30: 513–20.
214. Schutte B, Reynders MMJ, Wiggers T, et al. Retrospective analysis of the prognostic significance of DNA content and proliferative activity in large bowel carcinoma. Cancer Res 1987; 47: 5494–5496.
215. Suzuki H, Matsumoto K, Masuda T, Koike H. DNA ploidy of colorectal carcinoma: correlation with conventional prognostic variables. J Clin Gastroenterol 1988; 10: 176–178.
216. Dukes C. The classification of cancer of the rectum. J Pathol Bacteriol 1932; 35: 323–332.
217. Talbot IC, Ritchie S, Leighton M, Hughes AO, Bussey HJR, and Morson BC. Invasion of veins by carcinoma of rectum: method of detection, histological features and significance. Histopathology 1981; 5: 141–163.
218. Spratt JS Jr, Spjut HJ. Prevalence and prognosis of individual clinical and pathologic variables associated with colorectal carcinoma. Cancer 1967; 20: 1976–1985.
219. Anastassiades OT, Tsardakas E, Rigas A. Pseudomyxoma peritonei arising from a mucinous adenocarcinoma of the sigmoid colon. Int Surg 1973; 58: 799–800.
220. Lindemann F, Schlimok G, Dirschedl P, Witte J, Riethmuller G. Prognostic significance of micrometastatic tumour cells in bone marrow of colorectal cancer patients. Lancet 1992; 340: 685–89.
221. Boreham P. Implantation metastases from cancer of the large bowel. Br J Surg 1958; 46: 103–108.
222. Luna-Perez P, Barrientos H, Delgado S, Morales A. Usefulness of frozen-section examination in resected mid-rectal cancer after preoperative radiation. Am J Surg 1990; 159: 582–584.
223. Morson BC, Vaughan EG, Bussey HJ. Pelvic recurrence after excision of rectum for carcinoma. Br Med J 1963; 2: 13–18.
224. Sidoni A, Bufalari A, Alerti PF. Distal intramural spread in colorectal cancer: a reappraisal of the extent of distal clearance in fifty cases. Tumori 1991; 77: 514–517.
225. Devereaux DF, Decker PJ. Contributions of pathologic margins and Dukes' stage to local recurrence in colorectal carcinoma. Am J Surg 1985; 149: 323–326.
226. Zinkin LD. A critical review of the classification and staging of colorectal cancer. Dis Colon Rectum 1983; 26: 37–43.
227. Kirkliin BR. Roentgenologic diagnosis of gastric cancer. Wisconsin Med J 1949; 48: 811–814.
228. Astler VB, Coller FA. The prognostic significance of direct extension of carcinoma of the colon and rectum. Ann Surg 1954; 139: 846–852.
229. Dukes CE, Bussey HJR. The spread of rectal cancer and its effect on prognosis. Br J Cancer 1958; 12: 309–320.
230. Denoix PF. French Ministry of Public Health National Institute of Hygiene. Monograph No. 4, Paris, 1954.
231. Beahrs OH, Myers MD. American Joint Committee on Cancer. Manual for staging of Cancer, 2nd ed. Philadelphia: Lippincott, 1983.
232. Turnbull RB, Kyle K, Watson FB, Spratt J. Cancer of the colon: the influence of the no-touch isolation technique on survival rates. Ann Surg 1967; 166: 400–427.
233. Wood DA, Robbins GF, Zippin C, Lum D, Stearns M. Staging of cancer of the colon and cancer of the rectum. Cancer 1979; 43: 961–968.
234. Davis NC, Newland RC. Terminology and classification of colorectal adenocarcinoma: the Australian clinico-pathological staging system. Aust NZ J Surg 1983; 53: 211–221.
235. Davis NC, Newland RC. The reporting of colorectal cancer. The Australian clinico-pathological staging system. Aust NZ J Surg 1982; 52: 395–397.
236. Fielding LP, Arsenault PA, Chapuis PH, et al. Working party report to the world congresses of gastroenterology, Sydney 1990. Clinicopathological staging for colorectal cancer: an International Documentation System (IDS) and an International Comprehensive Anatomical Terminology (ICAT). J Gastroenterol Heampatol 1991; 6: 325–344.
237. Wasylyshyn ML, Westbrook CA. Genetic abnormalities of colorectal carcinoma. Hepato-Gastroenterol 1992; 39: 226–231.
238. Kern SE, Fearon ER, Tersmette KWF, Enterline JP, Leppert M, Nakamura Y, White R, Vogelstein B, Hamilton SR. Allelic loss in colorectal carcinoma. JAMA 1989; 261: 3099–3103.
239. Hamilton SR. Molecular genetic alterations as potential prognostic indicators in colorectal carcinoma. Cancer 1992; 69 (Suppl): 1589–91.
240. Laurent-Puig P, Olschwant S, Delattre O, et al. Survival and acquired genetic alterations in colorectal cancer. Gastroenterology 1992; 102: 1136–41.
241. Halling KC, Gomez T, Schaid DJ, et al. Clinical significance of molecular genetic markers in colorectal cancer. Am J Hum Genet 1992; 51: A60.
242. Ahlquist DA, Thibodeau SN. Will molecular genetic markers help predict the clinical behavior of colorectal neoplasia? Gastroenterology 1992; 102: 1419–21.
243. Meyers FJ, Gumerlock PH, Kokoris SP, White RWD, McCormick F. Human bladder and colon carcinomas contain activated ras p21. Cancer 1989; 63: 2177–2181.
244. Cannon-Albright LA, Skolnick MH, Bishop DT, et al. Common inheritance of susceptibility to colonic adenomatous polyps and associated colorectal cancers. N Engl J Med 1988; 319: 533–537.
245. Fearon ER, Cho KR, Nigro JM, Kern SE, Simons JW, Ruppert JM, Hamilton SR, Preisinger AC, Thomas G, Kinzler KW, Vogelstein B. Identification of a chromosome 18q gene that is altered in colorectal cancers. Research Article 1990; 247: 49–56.
246. Baker SJ, Preisinger AC, Jessup JUM, Paraskeva C, Markowitz S, Willson JKV, Hamilton S, Vogelstein B. p53 gene mutations occur in combination with 17p allelic deletions as late events in colorectal tumorigenesis. Cancer Research 1990; 50: 7717–7722.
247. Kinzler K W, Nilbert MC, Vogelstein B, Bryan TM, Levy DB, Smith KJ, Preisinger AC, Hamilton Sr, Hedge P, Markham A, Carlson M, Joslyn G, Groden J, White R, Miki Y, Miyoshi Y, Nishisho I, Nakamura Y. Identification of a gene located at chromosome 5q21 that is mutated in colorectal cancers. Science 1991; 251: 1366–1370.

PART II

Polyposis syndromes

G. Franzin G. Zamboni A. Scarpa

Polyposis of the colon was recognized as an entity 200 years ago and it is almost 100 years since inflammatory and adenomatous subtypes were characterized and the familial tendency for polyps to develop in some patients noted.

In the last 50 years registration of polyposis cases has allowed the recognition of different forms of intestinal polyposis and the elucidation of both their mode of inheritance and the relationship to development of carcinoma.

Affected patients presenting with symptoms are referred to as 'propositi' and affected first degree relatives diagnosed as a result of prophylactic examination are called 'call-up cases'. Further enquiries of propositi and their relatives allows the compilation of family pedigrees which are completed by information derived from public registers, death certificates, hospital records, cancer registries and general practitioners. Such a polyposis register initiated at St Mark's Hospital, London in 1925 contains records of the greatest number of families with familal adenomatous, juvenile and Peutz-Jeghers polyposis syndromes.[1]

Since then, a number of national and regional registers have been established in many countries. The clinical, histopathological and genetic information which is provided by such a registry is of paramount value in characterizing polyposis syndromes and this simplifies patient management.

CLASSIFICATION

Polyposes and polyposis syndromes can be classified into two main groups: familial and non-familial. The polyps in either group may be adenomatous or non-adenomatous (Table 41.8). Familial polyposes are inherited in autosomal dominant fashion.

FAMILIAL INTESTINAL POLYPOSES (ADENOMATOUS)

Familial adenomatous polyposis (FAP)

This condition is characterized by the development of an increasing number of large bowel adenomas which can carpet the entire mucosa and by the almost certain development of colorectal carcinoma.

Due to its dominant Mendelian inheritance, every child of a parent with FAP has a 50% risk of developing the disease.

Epidemiology

In every 10 000 births FAP will occur once,[2] males and females are equally affected and no ethnic predominance has been documented. About one third of patients have no family history and represent new mutations.[3]

Uncommon before puberty, the average age of onset of polyps is 25 years, generally becoming symptomatic at 33 and most commonly diagnosed at 36.[4,5]

Adenomas are probably present on average for 10 years before giving rise to symptoms such as rectal bleeding, diarrhoea, and less frequently, mucus discharge and abdominal pain.[6]

The average age at which adenocarcinoma is diagnosed is 39 and the mean survival time after diagnosis is 3 years. In St Mark's Hospital series nearly two-thirds of the propositi had colorectal cancer at the time of diagnosis[6] and it was found in 7.5% of 'call-up cases'.[7] The latter figure has been reduced to 2% after the establishment of new registers and the consequent improvement in the management of polyposis families, including earlier investigation.[3] It is estimated that approximately 10–15 years elapse from the onset of polyposis before colorectal cancer develops.[7]

Number of adenomas

Most colectomy specimens from patients with FAP usually harbour approximately 1000 adenomas but there can be as few as 100 and as many as 5000. The number present may well relate to the stage of the disease being observed. Some patients will initially have fewer than 100 polyps, but will subsequently develop the more usual much larger numbers as the disease progresses (Fig. 41.16). It has been stated that at least 100 adenomas must be present before the diagnosis of FAP can be made.[6] This criterion, however, can no longer be maintained since, due to the variable phenotypical expression of FAP, some patients may have only few isolated polyps, yet develop colorectal carcinoma and transmit FAP to their progeny.[3] Different location of germ-line mutations in the APC gene may be responsible for the variable number of adenomas in FAP patients.[8]

Table 41.8 Classification of intestinal polyposes.

Familial		Non-familial	
Adenomatous	Non-adenomatous	Adenomatous	Non-adenomatous
Familial adenomatous polyposis	Peutz-Jeghers syndrome	Multiple adenomas	Cronkhite-Canada
Gardner's syndrome	Juvenile polyposis		Hyperplastic
Turcot's syndrome	Ruvalcaba-Myhre-Smith syndrome		Inflammatory
Discrete adenomatosis	Familial gastric juvenile polyposis		Lymphoid polyposis
Flat adenoma syndrome	Familial gastric polyposis		Intestinal malacoplakia
Muir-Torre syndrome	Cowden's disease		Lipomatous polyposis
	Neurofibromatosis		Pheumatosis cystoides
	Ganglioneuromatosis		
	Blue rubber bleb naevus syndrome		
	Devon family syndrome		

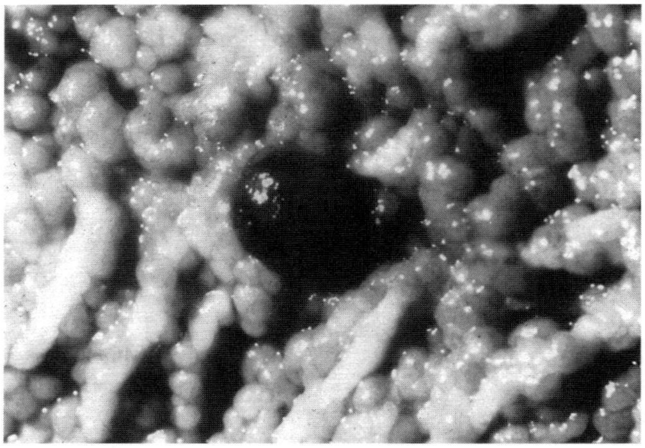

Fig. 41.16 Familial polyposis coli. Colectomy specimen studded with polyps.

Size and distribution of adenomas

Adenomas tend to be larger in propositi than in 'call-up cases' but overall only 1% of adenomas are more than 1 cm in diameter. It is said that the larger the adenoma the greater is the risk of malignancy,[9] which may explain the fact that despite the large number of adenomas in FAP the number of carcinomas rarely exceeds three.

Even though all segments of the large intestine are usually fairly evenly affected by adenomas, there seems to be a slight predominance in the left side of the colon. Occasionally, however, the rectum[10,11] and the sigmoid[12] may be spared, leading to false-negative results if only proctosigmoidoscopy is performed.

Aetiology

It is only recently that the adenomatous polyposis coli gene (APC-gene), located in the region 21 of the long arm of chromosome 5 (5q21),[13–16] has been identified.[17–21] Individuals who inherit or acquire an APC-gene mutation in the germ-line develop FAP.[18,20,22] Virtually all the mutations identified in FAP patients inactivate the APC-gene,[22] which is considered a tumour suppressor gene, thus initiating the sequence of events which eventually lead to FAP with its many manifestations.

The disease is usually not expressed until years after birth, which probably means that the APC-gene mutation is not sufficient to produce the fully phenotypically expressed abnormality and that additional genetic or environmental factors[23] are required. Whatever the additional molecular changes involved, the APC-gene mutation is the indispensable initiating event for the formation of adenomas.

Pleiotropy of the mutated APC-gene results in it manifesting its effects in other tissues, which accounts for extra colonic manifestations.[24–27] The different phenotypical expression in the affected individuals are, thus, attributable to the variable penetrance of this single pleiotropic gene or to the presence of an additional, yet unknown, genetic defect.

Further steps in the neoplastic progression leading to invasive carcinoma, through severe dysplasia and intramucosal carcinoma, are associated with somatic gene mutations such as those activating Ki-ras oncogene[28,29] and inactivating p53-tumour suppressor gene.[30,31]

Additional abnormalities include loss of the APC locus inherited from the normal parent[24,29,32] and of the loci of three other tumour suppressor genes:[16,29–36] p53, MCC (mutated in colorectal cancer) and of a putative cell-adhesion surface protein (DCC–deleted in colorectal cancer). These genetic abnormalities are not dissimilar to those found in sporadic colorectal carcinoma.[17,31,35–42]

Another molecular abnormality shared by FAP colorectal adenomas and carcinomas[43–45] and their sporadic counterparts[44–49] is the frequent overexpression of c-myc gene, which is involved in the regulation of DNA replication. The normal APC-gene could act as an 'anti-oncogene' by regulating c-myc expression.[50]

Pathogenesis

In normal mucosa, the proliferative compartment is restricted to the lower two-thirds of the crypts and the predominant zone of DNA synthesis occurs in the basal third. In FAP, three stages of abnormality in the progression towards neoplasia have been identified.[51]

In stage one, the genetic defect allows the proliferative compartment to expand toward the luminal surface while the lower third of the crypt remains as the predominant zone of DNA synthesis. A shift of the major zone of DNA synthesis to the middle and upper third occurs within the crypts in stage two. Finally, in stage three, isolated crypts with highly increased levels of DNA synthesis activity appear. These stages of abnormality may occur in various degrees in different sites of the colonic mucosa, which at this stage appears macroscopically normal. Environmental factors may then act upon such predisposed mucosa and lead to a neoplastic phase.

Proliferation of the adenomatous cells in all parts of the crypt leads to budding, branching and infolding and the formation of an elevation of the mucosa.[51,52] The nature of the environmental factors at work is unknown, but in patients with FAP an increase of faecal undegraded cholesterol and bile acid has been reported.[53,54] There is also a loss of contact inhibition of skin fibroblasts which, also show an increased susceptibility to malignant transformation by viral and chemical agents.[25,55,56] Malignant transformation by tumour promoter alone has also been reported and interpreted as indicating an 'initiated' state of these cells.[57]

Histology and phenotypical markers of the colonic mucosa

A number of microadenomas, consisting of one or a few crypts, can usually be found in the apparently normal mucosa which occurs between the adenomas (Fig. 41.17). Five or more crypts have to be involved before an adenoma can be appreciated at endoscopic examination. Since such lesions are extremely rare in non-FAP patients they are of some significance when located.[7,12] Further growth of microadenomas produces tubular, mixed tubular and villous, and, less frequently, wholly villous tumours.[58] The degree of dysplasia in adenomas and its progression to invasive carcinoma appears to be closely correlated with the type and number of chromosomal deletions and gene mutations.[29]

Other features which were thought to precede adenomatous growth in apparently normal mucosa included changes in mucin histochemistry,[59,60] increased ornithine decarboxylase activity, which is involved in epithelial proliferation,[61] different cytokeratins[62] and decreased HLA antigens expression.[63] Most of these have been challenged,[64] others need substantiation.[2]

Extracolonic manifestations and Gardner's syndrome (GS)

Previously considered a solely large intestinal disease, it is now realized that FAP is a multisystem disorder which may involve tissues of ectodermal, mesodermal and endodermal origin.[65]

Routine upper gastrointestinal endoscopy in patients with FAP has demonstrated that polyps are not confined to the large intestine, but may be found in both the stomach and duodenum. The frequency of duodenal adenomas ranges from up to 100% in a Japanese series[66] to approximately 50% in Western countries.[1,67] They are usually multiple and small, and affect mainly the periampullary region and the papilla of Vater. Since the distribution of the adenomas parallels the sites of the mucosal exposure to bile, a role for changes in bile composition of FAP patients has been suggested.[68] As in the colon, even normal appearing duodenal and periampullary mucosa may demonstrate unicryptal adenomatous changes.[69]

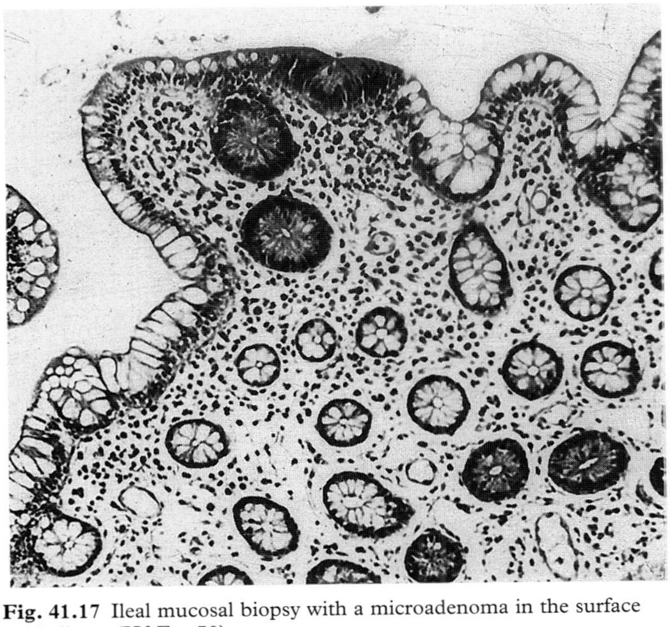

Fig. 41.17 Ileal mucosal biopsy with a microadenoma in the surface epithelium. (H&E, ×50)

Adenomas have also been found in the jejunum and ileum. Ileal adenomas can occur in patients after colectomy and ileo-rectal anastomosis[70–73] or ileal pouch,[70] which dictates that endoscopy should not be restricted to the rectum.

The stomach is far less frequently affected by adenomas, which are usually confined to the antrum. In contrast, small fundic polyps are frequent which, although due to cystic dilatation of gastric glands, are considered hamartomatous.[74]

The risk of upper gastrointestinal tract carcinoma is estimated at 4.5%, the periampullary region accounting for approximately 3% of the cases.[75] Periampullary carcinoma represents the second most common cause of death in FAP patients after colorectal cancer.[75] This gives further support to the concept of an adenoma-carcinoma sequence operating in sites other than the colon in view of the high incidence of periampullary duodenal adenomas.

The aetiopathogenetic, pathological and clinical aspects of GS do not differ from those of FAP as far as the gastrointestinal tract is concerned. It is the extraintestinal manifestations which characterize the syndrome and include osteomas of the jaws, skull and long bones, epidermoid cysts, subcutaneous fibromas and desmoid tumours.[76,77] Other features are multiple unerupted supernumerary teeth and multiple dental caries.

Utsunomiya and Nakamura[78] found occult osteomas of the jaws in 94% of patients with FAP. Furthermore, multiple bilateral pigmented lesions due to congenital hypertrophy of the retinal pigment epithelium (CHRPE) are now considered the most common extracolonic manifestations of both FAP and GS when they may represent the earliest clinical marker.[65,79] This indicated that FAP and GS are different expressions of a single disease. The existence of families, some members of which have extraintestinal manifestations and some which do not, confirms this suggestion.[76,80] This has been recently supported by the demonstration of APC germ-line mutations in both FAP and GS patients.[24,29,32]

The previously reported association of FAP with cartilaginous exostoses (Zonca's syndrome) and sebaceous cysts (Oldfield syndrome) should, thus, be regarded as mere eponyms.

Desmoid tumours may either develop in scars from prior operations or occur de novo, even before FAP is diagnosed.[81] Diffuse mesenteric fibrosis resulting in intestinal or urinary obstruction may also occur.[82] Histologically, the lesion of FAP patients shows increase in cellularity and prominent vascular ectasia in comparison with that in non-FAP subjects. This vascular pattern may account for the frequent operative haemorrhagic complications.[2] Intra-abdominal desmoids may show rapid growth and be particularly life-threatening. Its reported frequency varies from 4%[83]–10%,[2] and is considered one of the more frequent causes of death after colorectal carcinoma.[2,84]

Many types of benign and malignant tumours, other than gastrointestinal, occur in patients with FAP and their family members, but the majority are probably fortuitous. However, a definite relationship between this syndrome and carcinoma of the thyroid has been suggested,[85–87] especially in females.[3,88]

An increased incidence of childhood hepatoblastoma,[89,90] usually preceding FAP, as well as endocrine tumours,[91–93] often multiple, and tumours of the urogenital system[76] have been reported. The occurrence of extracolonic tumours indicates that FAP is a systemic tumourogenic disorder.

Turcot's syndrome

The association of malignant tumours of the central nervous system with FAP was first reported by Turcot, Despres and St Pierre.[94] Since then, familial and nonfamilial cases have been described which have promoted controversy concerning the mode of inheritance of the syndrome.[95,96] Although the adenomas tend to be fewer, larger, and patients have a greater incidence of colonic cancer during the second or third decades,[96] there is still no convincing evidence for considering Turcot's syndrome as a distinct disease.

Familial discrete adenomatosis

There are several families with a high incidence of a few or several, but always less than 100, adenomas in which a high incidence of colorectal cancer occurs.[97,98] This 'discrete' polyposis may represent examples of either a not-fully expressed FAP or of hereditary non-polyposis colorectal cancer (HNPCC).[80] Genetic analysis, currently available, may clarify the issue.

Flat adenoma syndrome

Hereditary flat adenoma syndrome (HFAS)[99] is an autosomal dominant disorder showing intermediate phenotypical features between FAP and HNPCC, which consist of:

1. multiple colonic adenomas, usually less than 100, which predominate in the proximal colon. The lesions are small, tubular and exhibit lateral spreading, assuming a flat rather than polypoid appearance[60]
2. right-sided distribution of complicating colon cancer which presents at an average age of 57 years, much later than that in FAP
3. a variety of extracolonic manifestations including 'fundic gland polyps', adenomas and carcinomas of the small bowel.[99]

Genetic linkage analyses showed that the genetic defect in HFAS occurred at the same locus of the APC gene,[33] suggesting that HFAS is a variant of FAP.

Muir-Torre syndrome

First described by Muir et al[100] and Torre,[101] this syndrome is characterized by the association of sebaceous tumours, benign or malignant or both, with single or multiple visceral malignancy, particularly of the colon[102] and in some cases with a small number of colonic adenomas.[103] The syndrome may present de novo but in most cases there is a strong family history of colonic carcinoma.[104]

Although previously included in the familial adenomatous polyposis syndromes, it represents a phenotypic expression of the 'hereditary non-polyposis colorectal cancer-HNPCC'.[80]

Treatment

Total colectomy with ileorectal anastomosis remains, to date, the treatment of choice in patients whose rectum contains few polyps when the diagnosis of polyposis is confirmed. Thereafter, annual endoscopic surveillance, with removal or fulguration of recurrent polyps up to 5 mm is demanded.[105,106] If the rectum is or becomes studded with adenomas, proctectomy must be considered.[106,107] Proctocolectomy and ileo-anal anastomosis eliminate cancer risk of the residual rectum; but even after this procedure, patients will require lifelong follow-up in view of the possible development of ileal adenomas and adenocarcinomas.[108]

Local excision, fulguration or laser photocoagulation are available therapeutical approaches for small adenomas of the duodenum and periampullary region. Yearly endoscopic control, including the use of side-viewing endoscopy which facilitates examination of the ampulla, is thereafter recommended. Whipple's procedure is reserved for more advanced tumours.[109] If feasible, gastric adenomas should be endoscopically resected.

Temporary spontaneous regression of the remaining polyps in the retained rectum has been reported after treatment with ascorbic acid,[110] oral calcium therapy[111] and sulindac,[112–114] but these observations need further substantiation.

Since any type of surgical approach is most often incomplete and seems to exacerbate the growth of desmoids,[27] surgery should only be used for specific complications, such as intestinal or urinary tract obstruction. Several non-surgical approaches have been used, including radiotherapy, chemotherapy, hormonal treatment and ascorbic acid, with markedly inconsistent results.[115] Some tumour regression and improvement of symptoms after prolonged treatment with sulindac has been reported.[116]

Screening and diagnostic tools

Polymorhic DNA markers closely linked to the region q21 of chromosome 5, where the APC-gene has been mapped,[13–16] are a powerful tool for screening of FAP families. Their use in linkage DNA analysis provides a highly confident evaluation of the risk of inheritance for members of a FAP family.[117–124] Such an evaluation is, however, only possible in those families whose pedigree is informative. The association of DNA markers and the presence of CHRPE make it possible to identify most gene carriers, even in the absence of rectal polyps.[12] The more recent possibility of identifying APC-gene specific mutations[18,20,22] and intragenic polymorphisms[20,22,125] in FAP families, can provide definite separation of individuals who have inherited the defective gene from those who have not. Different, more specific, surveillance programmes may thus be planned in the two groups of family members. Usually performed on peripheral blood cells, genetic analyses may be used at any time of life, even in a prenatal phase by using amniotic cells.

As yet, however, positive sigmoidoscopy remains the most important diagnostic sign. Flexible proctosigmoidoscopy should begin by the age of 10–12 and continue yearly until age 35,[80,118] since most of the patients will already have manifested colonic polyps by age 30 in their rectosigmoid.[119] Thereafter, a three years interval sigmoidoscopy is adequate. Total colonoscopy and multiple polypectomies should be warranted for subjects who develop histologically proven adenomas, in order to rule out the presence of carcinoma. Upper gastrointestinal screening should begin when the diagnosis of colonic polyposis is made, and thereafter be continued every three years in the absence of gastroduodenal adenomas.[126,127]

The small size and number of plaque-like adenomas, the variable age of manifestation and the peculiar proximal location in the colon must be taken into consideration in the planning of screening of members of families with the hereditary flat adenoma syndrome.[99]

FAMILIAL INTESTINAL POLYPOSES (NON-ADENOMATOUS)

Peutz-Jeghers syndrome

Inherited as an autosomal dominant trait with variable penetrance, Peutz-Jeghers syndrome (PJS) is characterized by the presence of mucocutaneous melanin pigmentation and polyp formation throughout the gastrointestinal tract. Melanin spots may occur early in infancy, most commonly affecting the buccal mucosa, lips, nose, palms and soles and the perianal and genital regions. Except for the buccal mucosa the melanin spots tend to fade at puberty.[4,5]

The gastrointestinal polyps, normally fewer than 100, may occur in the stomach, small intestine and colon but favour the small intestine where, they progressively increase in size and may cause intestinal obstruction and intussusception. Melanin spots and gastrointestinal polyps are occasionally inherited separately.[5] The gastrointestinal polyp is regarded as hamartomatous in nature and appears as a lobulated mass, sessile or stalked. Histologically, it consists of a variety of normal epithelial cells, typical of their site of origin, covering strands of smooth muscle which originate from the muscularis mucosae. The muscular bands course through and separate the polyp into sectors, producing a tree-like branching. Each branch carries a layer of mucosa (Fig. 41.18). In some cases the epithelial component penetrates into and occasionally separates the muscularis propria and gives a false impression of neoplastic invasion.

Gastric Peutz-Jeghers polyp may have some of the features of the hyperplastic gastric polyp since the muscularis mucosal strands are usually less prominent than in its intestinal counterpart, the foveolae are hyperplastic, at times cystic, and cystic glands may also occur.

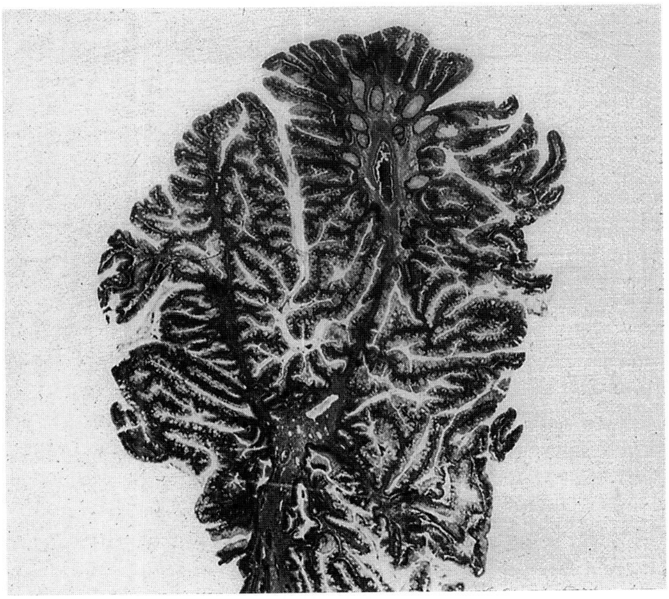

Fig. 41.18 Peutz-Jeghers polyp. Strands of smooth muscle from the muscularis mucosae, covered by normal epithelium, producing a tree-like aspect. (H&E, ×10)

Peutz-Jeghers polyps are not regarded as having malignant potential. However, a number of cases of gastrointestinal cancers occurring in patients under 40 years of age have been reported[128–137] and are occasionally familial.[130,131,135] Furthermore, recent reports of cases of epithelial dysplasia,[138–141] at times accompanied by invasive carcinoma within the polyp,[130–133,135,140–144] suggest definite increased risk of gastrointestinal cancer in patients with PJS. Such a risk varies from approximately 2–3% in western countries, where gastric and duodenal cancer predominate,[1,145] to 17% in Japanese series,[128] where the colorectum is the most commonly affected site. Gastrointestinal malignancies tend to occur at a much younger age than expected in the general population.

A number of benign and malignant tumours other than gastrointestinal have been described in association with PJS,[1,135,140,142,143,146–148] indicating that the syndrome is a possible systemic disorder.[135,142,143] However, the most characteristic associated abnormality is an ovarian sex cord cell tumour with annular tubules. Initially reported in 5% of cases,[147] it is now known as an almost constant finding in women and considered one of the phenotypic expressions of the syndrome.[149] Usually, the tumour is of microscopic size, bilateral and multifocal. It is thought to arise from granulosa cells, although the morphological pattern suggests a Sertoli cell origin, and may exert an oestrogenic effect, leading to endometrial hyperplasia.

An increased risk of low-grade adenocarcinoma of the endocervix, so-called 'adenoma malignum'[149] and of both benign and malignant tumours of the breast in female patients is also suggested.[133,135,140,142,143,146] Feminizing Sertoli cell testicular tumours in prepubertal boys have also been reported,[150–152] as well as a greatly increased incidence of pancreatic carcinoma.[133]

Recurrent bouts of small bowel intussusception, bleeding or obstruction occurring in the second or third decade of life in PJS patients, usually require repeated surgery. These may lead to further problems including adhesions with obstructive episodes and short bowel syndrome.[135] Jejunal and ileal endoscopic polypectomy is now a feasible therapeutic approach.[138,153] A combined approach by the endoscopist and the surgeon, with small bowel endoscopy and polypectomy performed at laparotomy, is also possible,[154] thus confining the more classical surgical procedures to emergency cases and those in which endoscopy does not assure satisfactory results.

Upper and lower gastrointestinal endoscopy and small bowel radiology are indicated when a subject at risk presents with gastrointestinal symptoms and should be repeated every two years once the diagnosis is made.[153] Starting from the second decade of life, annual faecal occult blood testing and a three years' interval upper and lower endoscopic examination should be performed in asymptomatic patients at risk. Routine breast and gynaecological examination, including annual mammography, pelvic ultrasound and cervical smears should be also warranted as a part of the surveillance programme for female patients with PJS.[133,135,143]

Juvenile polyposis syndrome

Less common than Peutz-Jeghers syndrome, juvenile polyposis (JP) is still an ill defined condition due to its rarity and to the variable clinical presentation. Recently, records of 87 patients with JP from the St Mark's polyposis register provided data which allowed a working definition of the syndrome:

i) more than five juvenile polyps of the colorectum, and/or
ii) juvenile polyps throughout the gastrointestinal tract, and/or
iii) any number of juvenile polyps with a family history of JP.

These criteria provide distinction between isolated juvenile polyps and JP, since an increased malignant potential applies only to the latter.[155]

In a third of JP patients, the condition is inherited as an autosomal dominant trait with high penetrance,[1,155–158] whereas the non-familial cases could represent new genetic mutations.

The affected individuals with or without family history, can be grouped into three major categories, according to the clinical presentation:

a) JP of infancy
b) generalized JP, involving all the gastrointestinal tract
c) colonic JP, restricted to the large bowel.

These variants were previously considered as separate entities; however, observations within family groups suggest that the distribution of polyps throughout the gastrointestinal tract represents different expressions of the same genetic defect.[156]

The polyps usually number 50–200,[155] appear during the first or second decade, favour the colorectum in both familial and non-familial cases, and are regarded as hamartomatous in nature.[159] They may cause severe bleeding, anaemia and intussusception. Failure to thrive and rectal prolapse may also occur.[158] In the rare case of JP of infancy, bleeding, diarrhoea, dehydration and cachexia are particularly life-threatening.[157,160]

A 20% incidence of congenital abnormalities, including defects of the heart and cranial structures, malrotation of the bowel, Meckel's diverticulum and mesenteric lymphangioma has been reported.[1,161] Such defects are much more frequent in non-familial cases of JP.[161]

In colectomy specimens, a wide spectrum of polypoid lesions ranging from 1–50 mm in size are present. Smooth or variably lobulated, the lesions are grossly indistinguishable from adenomas[162–166] but their surface is often ulcerated and on section, larger polyps usually show several mucus-containing cysts of various size. The principal histological features of the usual lesion have already been discussed (Ch. 41, part I) but very small lesions may consist of simple granulation tissue in which the apical portions of the underlying glands are dilated and tortuous.[164,166–168] Foci of mucosal epithelial hyperplasia or, at times, true hyperplastic polyps, features suggesting transition to more usual juvenile polyps, may co-exist.[166,167] Some of the cystic glands may also be lined by an epithelium of so-called 'transitional-type mucosa'.[169]

When the stomach is involved, the polyps show the same histological features as their colonic counterparts and are very like hyperplastic gastric polyps and the lesions of the Cronkhite-Canada syndrome.

An increased incidence of gastrointestinal cancer, especially colorectal and sometimes with a strong familial tendency, has been reported.[1,148,155,156,158,162,164,170] Adenomatous areas in juvenile polyps (Fig. 41.19), occasionally with carcinomatous changes, as well as true adenomas side by side with and probably originating from juvenile polyps have also been described.[1,148,155,156,158,161–164,166,167,170,171]

A recent review of a large series of polyps from JP patients has demonstrated that dysplasia of all grades is more likely to occur in a particular subtype of juvenile polyp. This 'atypical juvenile polyp' is usually lobulated so that grouped lobules give the impression of multiple polyps attached to a single stalk. Histologically, the lamina propria is less abundant than in the classical juvenile polyp, whereas the epithelial component is increased and often shows a villous or papillary configuration. It is suggested that in a high proportion of cases carcinoma may originate from this subtype of polyp and is diagnosed at the mean age of 34 years.[155] The exact risk of colorectal cancer in all patients with JP is not known, but seems to exceed 10%.[155] For this reason, prophylactic colectomy and ileorectal anastomosis have been proposed.[172,173] In most cases, however, upper and lower endoscopic surveillance as for Peutz-Jeghers syndrome would be an adequate alternative if polyps occur in small number. Small bowel radiology also should be warranted if JP is diagnosed. Screening of the asymptomatic children of an affected parent should begin at 12 years, and include annual faecal occult blood testing and 3–5 year interval colonoscopy. Likewise, a similar screening should be planned for adult relatives due to their increased risk of cancer.[162]

Ruvalcaba-Myhre-Smith syndrome

First described in 1980,[174] the syndrome is characterized by ileal and colonic polyps, unusual craniofacial appearance, mental deficiency, macrocephaly and penile pigmentary macules. Review of pathological material from polyps demonstrated their similarity to juvenile polyps.[161] Since extraintestinal abnormalities are of common occurrence in juvenile polyposis, the syndrome is likely to represent a phenotypical variant of juvenile polyposis syndrome.

Familial gastric juvenile polyposis

A familial form of pure gastric juvenile polyposis has been reported in two Japanese siblings with mental retardation and unusual brown hair. Their mother also had mental retardation and brown hair, and died of gastric cancer at age 36.[175]

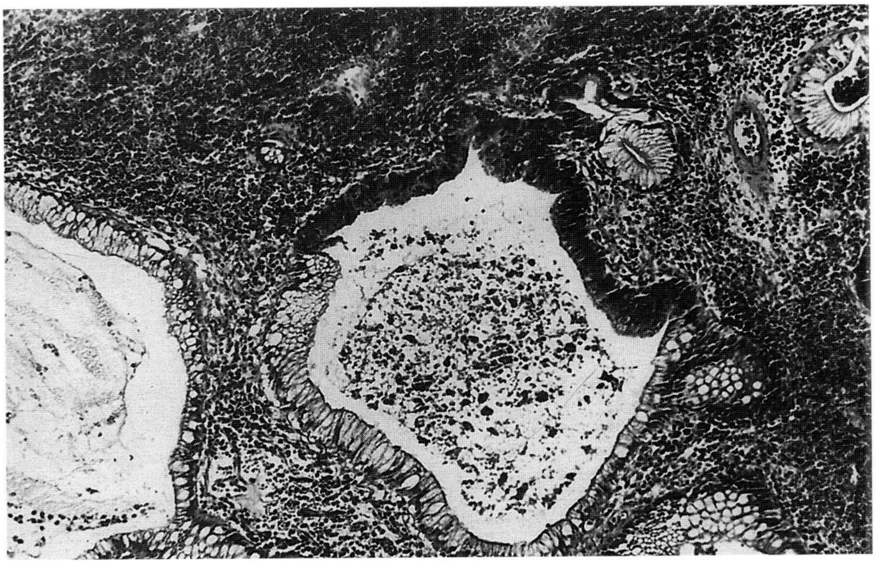

Fig. 41.19 Juvenile polyposis coli. Detail of a juvenile polyp with adenomatous areas. A cystic gland composed of both normal (lower half) and adenomatous (upper half) epithelium. (H&E, ×50)

Since gastric polyposis without intestinal involvement may occur in single individuals of a classical juvenile polyposis family,[156] it is conceivable that familial gastric juvenile polyposis represents a phenotypical variant of juvenile polyposis syndrome.

Familial gastric polyposis

Based on the observation of a large kindred with several members with polyps confined to the stomach and many cases of gastric cancer, familial gastric polyposis was assumed to represent a new syndrome with a Mendelian inheritance.[176]

A recent update and review of the kindred[177] confirmed the autosomal dominant inheritance of the syndrome and demonstrated the presence of cutaneous psoriasis in a third of the family members. Re-examination of the pathological material failed to demonstrate the previously described adenomatous changes[176] and classified the polypoid lesions as hyperplastic. Interestingly, the foveolar epithelium of some polyps is described as with 'a papillary, almost villous configuration with atypia'.[177] This is similar to the features of the atypical subtype of juvenile colonic polyps in juvenile polyposis syndrome.[155]

Since the histological features of gastric hyperplastic polyps may overlap those of juvenile ones,[172,178] it is most likely for familial gastric polyposis to represent a further phenotypical expression of juvenile polyposis syndrome. The reported occurrence of gastric cancer in family members with the syndrome is in keeping with both the previously mentioned familial gastric juvenile polyposis[175] and the more classical juvenile polyposis syndrome.[156]

Cowden's disease (multiple hamartoma syndrome)

Inherited in an autosomal dominant mode, the multiple hamartoma syndrome, also called Cowden's disease based on the family name of the propositus,[179] consists of a complex mixture of ectodermal, mesodermal and endodermal hamartomatous lesions.[180–182] Cases without family history may be attributable to new mutations.[183]

The disease usually manifests itself during the second or third decade with the characteristic mucocutaneous stigmata of facial trichilemmomas, acral keratoses and oral mucosal papillomas.[184] Facial trichilemmomas are most commonly concentrated around the mouth, nose and eyes and are usually papillary. Diagnosis is warranted when facial and oral mucosal lesions co-exist. If acral keratosis occurs, one of the above findings is sufficient. Fewer signs are required if a family history is proven.[182,183] The mucocutaneous stigmata may be associated with a number of other widely distributed abnormalities,[179,180,183–189] including macrocephaly, megaloencephaly, high-arched palate and a variety of benign soft tissues and visceral tumours. Goitre and adenoma of the thyroid occur in a very high proportion of patients,[182] and there is a propensity for malignant change.[179,180,184–188,190] Benign and malignant lesions of the breast, often bilateral, are very common in female patients and show a familial tendency.[185,189] The risk of breast cancer is estimated at about 50%.[186] A propensity for other multiple primary malignancies has also been suggested.[190,191]

It is only relatively recently that polyposis of the whole gastrointestinal tract has been recognized as part of the disease.[187,188,192] The large intestine is affected mainly in its distal portion and at endoscopy the lesions mostly resemble small hyperplastic polyps. Their histological pattern seems to be polymorphic since descriptions of the lesions have differed. Gorensek and coworkers[187] referred to them as hyperplastic polyps but did not illustrate them or describe them in detail. Laugier and coworkers[193] described polyps with Peutz-Jeghers and juvenile-type features. Hauser et al[194] reported a mixture of hamartomatous, juvenile and hyperplastic polyps and one patient also had lipoma-like lesions, but none were illustrated.

A more detailed study has recently appeared[192] in which smooth muscle strands originating in a hypertrophic and disorganized muscularis mucosae form the core of the lesion. The crypts are normal or slightly elongated and the lamina propria fibrotic, with a mild lymphocytic infiltration.

Recently in a mother and son with macrocephaly, thyroid adenoma and gastric duplication, similar polyps were seen in association with others composed of an abundant lamina propria and a heavy lymphoplasmacellular infiltration but without muscular elements. Slightly elongated crypts showing mild distortion were well separated from each other but the epithelial elements did not show any abnormality (Fig. 41.20). They resembled those encountered in inflammatory bowel disease (personal observation).

The gastric polyps show focal foveolar hyperplasia[187] or simple cystic dilatation of body glands as in the two cases referred to above; more complex lesions with a Peutz-Jeghers type or hyperplastic pattern are also recorded.[188,194]

Oesophageal polyps usually appear as small, pale, lenticular lesions and are composed of acanthotic squamous epithelium.

The multiplicity of hamartomatous tumours of ectodermal, mesodermal and endodermal origin suggests that epidermal growth factor (EGF) may be implicated in the pathogenesis of the disorder. However, no abnormalities in EGF concentration[195] nor genomic defects of EGF receptors were found in patients with the disease. Likewise, chromosome and genetic linkage analyses have, as yet, failed to identify the location of the gene responsible for the syndrome.[183]

It does not appear that gastrointestinal polyps of Cowden's disease have any propensity for malignant changes.

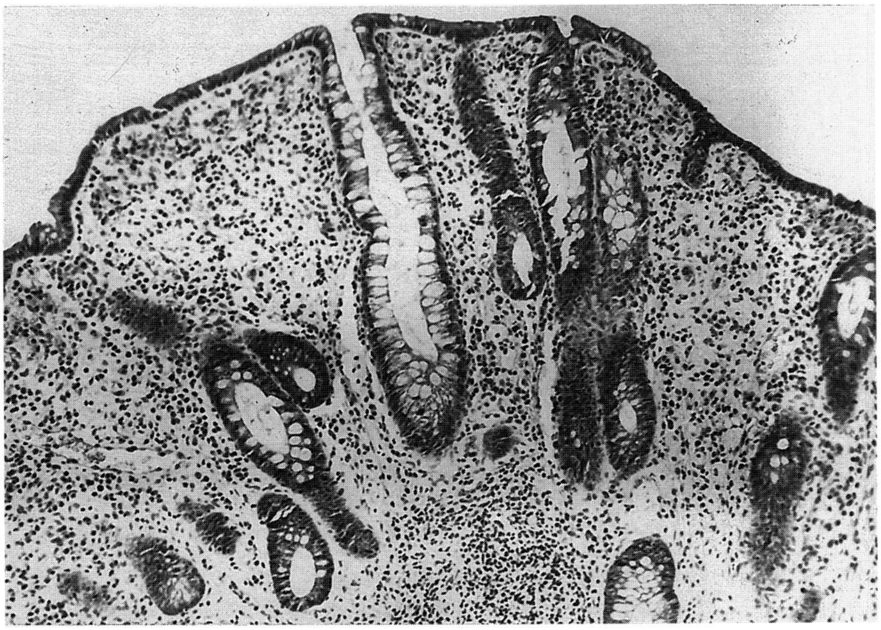

Fig. 41.20 A colonic polyp in Cowden's syndrome. Elongated glands with mild distortion embedded in an abundant lamina propria infiltrated by lymphoplasmacellular elements. (H&E, ×50)

Neurofibromatosis (von Recklinghausen's disease)

This disease has an autosomal dominant inheritance with high penetrance and occurs in approximately 1:3000 births.[196] It appears that the genetic abnormalities responsible for neurofibromatosis type 1 occur at chromosome 17q11.2 locus.[197–202] Most mutations are of paternal origin.[198,203]

Skin manifestations consist of 'cafe au lait' spots, larger than freckles, Lisch nodules[204] and subcutaneous neurofibromas. The latter may be found in virtually any area of the body.

Neurofibromatous involvement of the gastrointestinal tract has been reported in up to 25% of patients, but the incidence is probably higher.[205] The lesions may be polypoidal but have a widely variable appearance and they can cause dyspepsia, abdominal pain or haemorrhage.[205]

The tumours may be highly cellular with fusiform cells arranged in thin cords embedded in a matrix of collagen fibrils, or they may be myxoid and sometimes small neurites are present (Fig. 41.21). Sarcomatous degeneration has been reported in 15% of patients over 40 years of age,[206] but this figure is most probably overestimated.

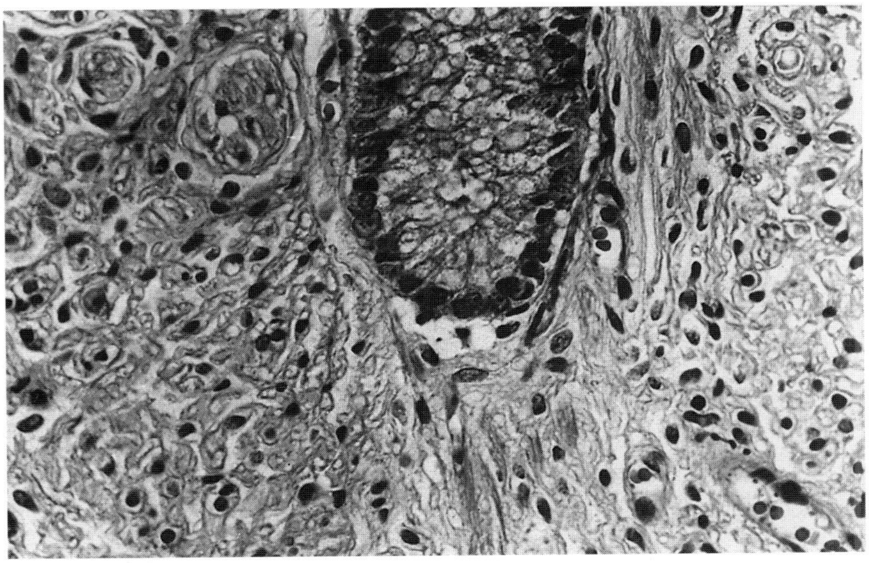

Fig. 41.21 Neurofibromatous involvement of the colonic mucosa. Schwann cells arranged in fascicles and small neurites. (H&E, ×300)

Ganglioneuromatosis

Gastrointestinal ganglioneuromatosis may occur in association with multiple endocrine neoplasia syndrome type 2b, and usually preceeds the endocrine abnormalities.[207] It is also associated with von Recklinghausen's disease[208] or may occur in sporadic fashion.[209]

Ganglioneuromas are composed of ganglion cells, nerve fibres and spindle-shaped neural cells of probable schwannian origin. In the intestinal mucosa they may appear as microscopic lesions or take the form of polypoid protrusions.

Recently a familial occurrence of ganglioneuromatous polyposis of the large bowel has been reported[210] and in some cases, mucosal ganglioneuromas may be associated with juvenile-type polyps.[209–211] It may be that the latter represent a mucosal reactive phenomenon to ganglioneuromatous abnormalities.[210]

Blue rubber bleb naevus syndrome

This disorder can be inherited as an autosomal dominant trait though most cases are sporadic.[212,213] It consists of cutaneous haemangiomatous naevi which look and feel like rubber nipples, haemangiomas of the digestive tracts which may protrude as polyps and iron deficiency anaemia due to bleeding.[212,213] The haemangiomas in the gut are usually of cavernous type, may involve the full thickness and protrude from the serosa. Occasionally capillary haemangiomas may coexist (Fig. 41.22). There is no evidence of a predisposition to malignant transformation.[213]

Devon family syndrome

A female member in three successive generations of a large Devon kindred developed multiple, recurrent inflammatory fibroid polyps of the ileum. One of the patients also had polyps within the gastric antrum. All of them experienced repeated bouts of intussusception from the polyps which ranged from 0.5–8 cm in size. The polyps were considered self limiting proliferation of hystiocytes without malignant potential.[214]

Karyotype analysis failed to demonstrate any abnormality.

NON-FAMILIAL INTESTINAL POLYPOSES (ADENOMATOUS)

Multiple adenomas

Individuals with multiple colonic adenomas but without a family history form another group of polyposes. Within the group, the majority have less than 6 polyps and only approximately 1% have more than this, but the number never reaches 100.[6]

A definite relationship exists between the number of adenomas and the incidence of associated carcinoma.[215]

Cronkhite-Canada syndrome

Diffuse polypoid thickening and nodularity of the gastrointestinal mucosa, which is associated with intestinal protein loss, along with alopecia, nail distrophy and skin pigmentation are the main features of Cronkhite-Canada syndrome,[216] which is a non-hereditary disorder.

The gastrointestinal changes have been interpreted as the result of abnormal mucin production[217] but this finding has been challenged.[218]

The gastrointestinal polyps and nodules are often indistinguishable from those in juvenile polyposis but also affect the intervening mucosa. In the stomach they share

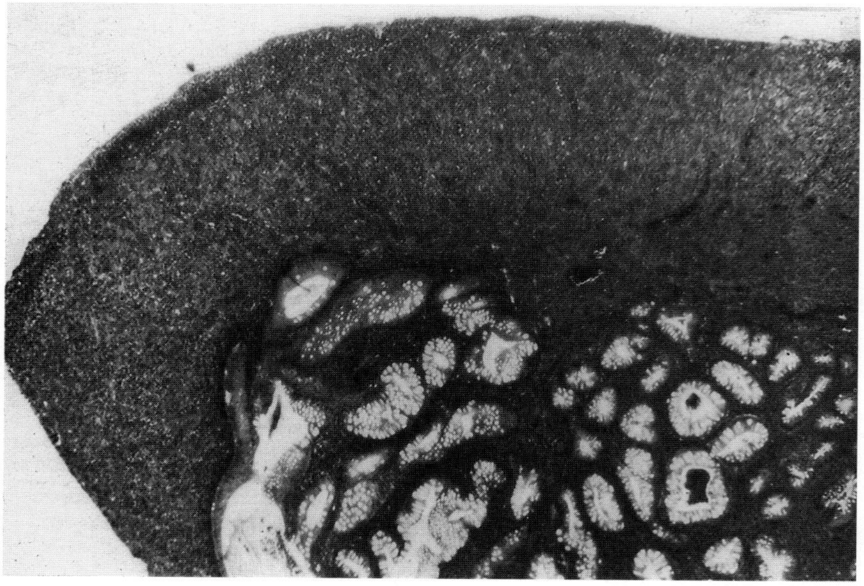

Fig. 41.22 Polypoid capillary haemangioma of the colonic mucosa in the blue rubber bleb naevus syndrome. (H&E, ×45)

many similarities with hyperplastic polyps[178] and the lesion of Menetrier's disease. Atrophy of specific gastric glands with pseudopyloric metaplasia of the body mucosa and cyst formation together with inflammatory infiltration in a broadened lamina propria leads to the formation of nodules and polyps.

As in some cases of Menetrier's disease, the features of Cronkhite-Canada syndrome may regress and disappear[219] and occasionally epithelial dysplasia occurs[220–222] within the hamartomatous polyp. An increased incidence of complicating carcinoma, especially of the colon, has also been reported in the Japanese literature.[217,220]

Diarrhoea and protein losing enteropathy may be severe, leading to nutritional deficiency which is particularly life-threatening, often fatal.[223]

Surgery is usually reserved for emergency cases and complications, including bleeding, intussusception and malignancy. If feasible, periodic endoscopic removal of polyps may be advisable to screen for dysplastic changes and gastrointestinal cancer.

Hyperplastic (metaplastic) polyposis

Diffuse hyperplastic colonic polyposis is a very rare non-hereditary condition. It may mimic FAP radiologically[224] and although the lesions are usually small, occasionally they exceed 1 cm in diameter.[225]

The classical serrated epithelial pattern may at times be replaced by a villous glandular arrangement, especially in larger lesions, and can be confused with adenoma.[225]

In particular, a special awareness must be paid in separating hyperplastic polyps from the recently described 'serrated adenomas' which feature classically serrated crypts lined by an otherwise dysplastic epithelium, and may occur in patients with FAP.[226]

Recent case reports of colorectal cancer associated with hyperplastic colonic polyposis[227–229] prompted speculation as to the possible increased risk of colorectal malignancy in hyperplastic polyposis patients. Further observations are needed.

Inflammatory polyposis

Multiple diffuse inflammatory polyps of the colon are sometimes seen in ulcerative and Crohn's colitis. Indeed, other forms of colitis such as in chronic schistosomiasis and amoebiasis may also be associated with multiple inflammatory polyps. These polyps may either be the result of a regenerative process in residual mucosa surrounded by full thickness ulceration or be composed entirely of granulation tissue. Later, regenerating epithelium may come to line fissures and spaces within the granulation tissue and cysts are formed.

These cysts and irregularly shaped or dilated glands, occurring in a background of inflammation and granulation, constitute an appearance very similar to that seen in juvenile polyps.[165]

In chronic schistosomiasis the inflammatory polyps may contain eggs or adult parasites. Complicating colorectal carcinoma is a common occurrence in patients with longstanding *Schistosoma japonicum* infestation,[230] whereas it is seldom encountered in *Schistosoma mansoni* colonic disease.[231]

Multiple colonoscopic polypectomies can dramatically reduce the frequency of blood and protein losing diarrhoea in patients with schistosomal polyposis.[232]

Inflammatory polyps may regress and they themselves have no intrinsic malignant potential, although they often occur in situations that are at high risk for colonic cancer, such as ulcerative colitis and schistosomiasis.[230]

Recently described is a peculiar form of inflammatory polyposis of the rectosigmoid which consists of elongated, tortuous, often dilated crypts covered by a cap of granulation tissue (Fig. 41.23). The lesion which occurs on the apices of transverse mucosal folds is called 'cappolyposis' and it is suggested that it is the result of mucosal prolapse.[233]

In diverticular disease of the colon, one may see polyps composed of redundant prolapsing folds of mucosa, especially if the diverticulae are intramural.[234] These polyps may show elongated, sometimes branched and dilated crypts and obliteration of the lamina propria by muscular and fibrous bundles radiating from a thickened muscularis mucosae (Fig. 41.24). These features closely resemble those in the solitary ulcer syndrome, another lesion in which mucosal prolapse leads to inflammatory and ischaemic changes.

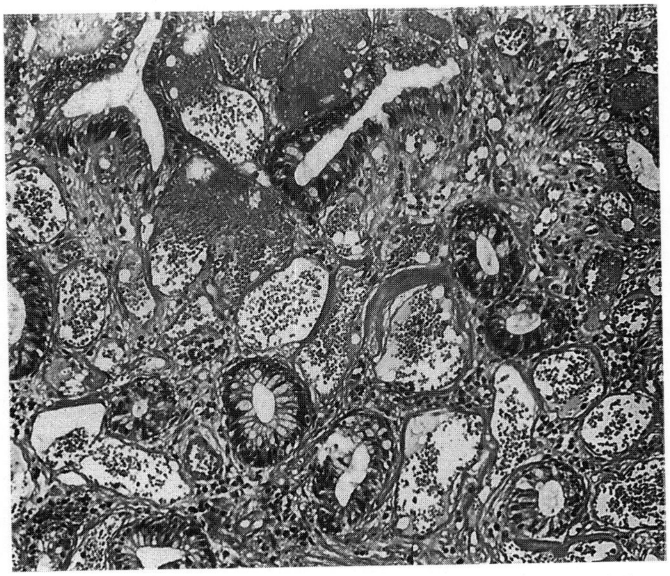

Fig. 41.23 Inflammatory polyp of the colon with a cap of granulation tissue (cap-polyp). (H&E, ×30)

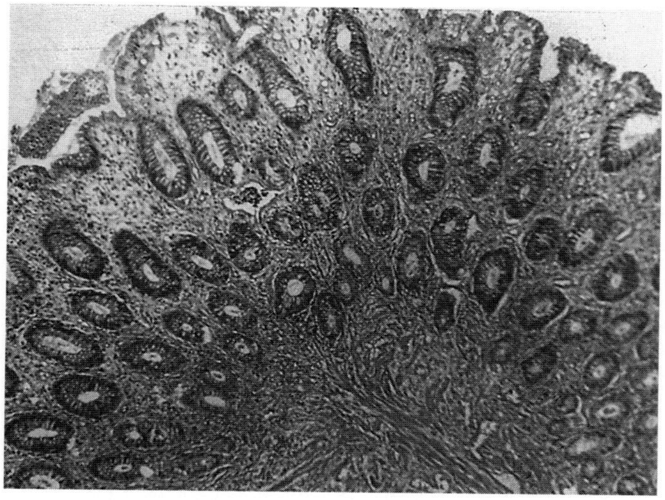

Fig. 41.24 Polyp associated with diverticula of the colon. Obliteration of the lamina propria by fibrous and smooth muscle strands radiating from a disorganized muscularis mucosae. (H&E, ×30)

Lymphoid polyposis

Usually symptomless, lymphoid polyposis may be an incidental finding at endoscopy. It appears as several round pale nodules, usually 3–5 mm in size, and may affect any part of the intestine.

The nodules are composed of normal lymphoid tissue with prominant germinal centres and are located mainly in the submucosa. In some cases, nodular lymphoid hyperplasia is associated with the common variable immunodeficiency, also called adult-onset immunoglobulin deficiency or common variable hypogammaglobulinaemia.[235] In this condition, a respective 30 and 50 fold increased risk of lymphoma and gastric carcinoma has been suggested.[236] Apart from such an association, lymphoid polyposis is a benign condition and must be differentiated from multiple lymphomatous polyposis, which may represent a distinctive manifestation of primary gastrointestinal non-Hodgkin's lymphoma.[237] The lymphomatous nodules, 0.5–5 cm in size may involve long segments of the gastrointestinal tract,[238] the colorectum being the favoured site.[237]

Intestinal malacoplakia

Outside the urogenital tract, the colon is the site most frequently affected by malacoplakia. The disorder frequently presents in the rectosigmoid and caecum as multiple polypoid lesions of 3 mm–4 cm in size.[239] At times, the overall histological aspect of the lesion is reminiscent of the lymphoid polyp, but careful examination reveals the characteristic histiocytes with granular, eosinophilic cytoplasm. The presence of intra- and extracellular Michaelis-Gutman bodies is distinctive (Fig. 41.25).

Lipomatous polyposis

Multiple collections of adipose tissue within the submucosa may project into the intestinal lumen and appear

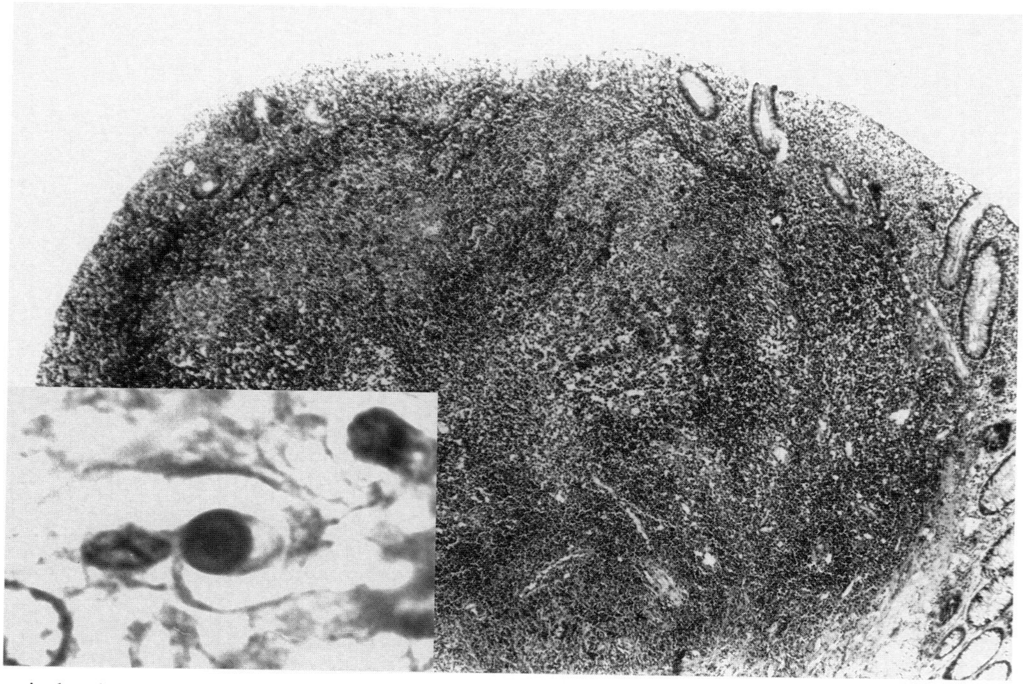

Fig. 41.25 Large intestinal malacoplakia mimicking a lymphoid polyp at low power view. (H&E, ×40) A clear-cut Michaelis-Gutman body. (inset: H&E, ×1000)

either on endoscopy or radiologically as a polyposis. Lipomatous polyposis is rare and considered hamartomatous in nature and may affect the large[240] as well as the small intestine.[241]

Pneumatosis cystoides intestinalis

In this condition, air-filled gas cysts occur in the wall of the small or large intestine. The cysts may cause bulging of the mucosa into the lumen and mimic polyposis.

REFERENCES

1. Bussey HJR. Gastrointestinal polyposis syndromes. In: Anthony PP, MacSween SNM, eds. Recent Advances in Histopathology. Gastrointestinal Pathology. Edinburgh: Churchill Livingstone 1984; 12: 169–177.
2. Shepherd NA, Bussey HJR. Polyposis syndrome. An update. Curr Top Pathol 1990; 81: 323–351.
3. Bulow S. Diagnosis of familial adenomatous polyposis. World J Surg 1991; 15: 41–46.
4. Wennstrom J, Pierce ER, McKusick VA. Hereditary benign and malignant lesions of the large bowel. Cancer 1984; 34: 850–857.
5. Erbe RW. Inherited gastrointestinal polyposis syndromes. N Engl J Med 1976; 294: 1101–1104.
6. Bussey HJR. Familial polyposis coli. Baltimore: Johns Hopkins University Press, 1975.
7. Bussey HJR. Familial polyposis coli. In: Sommers SC, Rosen PP, eds. Pathology Annual. New York: Appleton Century Crofts 1979; 14: 61–81.
8. Nagase H, Miyoshi Y, Horii A, et al. Correlation between the location of germ-line mutations in the APC gene and the number of colorectal polyps in familial adenomatous polyposis patients. Cancer Res 1992; 52: 4055–4057.
9. Muto T, Bussey HJR, Morson BC. The evolution of cancer of the colon and rectum. Cancer 1975; 36: 2251–2270.
10. Bigay D, Plauchu H, Bernard PH, Rubert JM, Guillemin G. Rectocolic familial polyposis; a study of 32 cases. World J Surg 1981; 5: 617–625.
11. Dick JA, Owen WJ, McColl I. Rectal sparing in familial polyposis coli. Br J Surg 1984; 71: 64.
12. Bradburn DM, Gunn A, Hastings A, Shepherd NA, Chapman PD, Burn J. Histological detection of microadenomas in the diagnosis of familial adenomatous polyposis. Br J Surg 1991; 78: 1394–1395.
13. Herrera L, Kakati S, Gibas L, Pietrzak E, Sandberg AA. Gardner syndrome in a man with an interstitial deletion of 5q. Am J Med Genet 1986; 25: 473–476.
14. Bodmer WF, Bailey CJ, Bodmer J, et al. Localization of the gene for familial adenomatous polyposis on chromosome 5. Nature 1987; 328: 614–616.
15. Leppert M, Dobbs M, Scambler P, et al. The gene for familial polyposis coli maps to the long arm of chromosome 5. Science 1987; 238: 1411–1413.
16. Nakamura Y, Lathrop M, Leppert M, et al. Localization of the genetic defect in familial adenomatous polyposis within a small region of chromosome 5. Am J Hum Genet 1988; 43: 638–644.
17. Kinzler KW, Nilbert MC, Su LK, et al. Identification of FAP locus genes from chromosome 5q21. Science 1991; 253: 661–664.
18. Nishisho I, Nakamura Y, Miyoshi Y, et al. Mutations of chromosome 5q21 genes in FAP and colorectal cancer patients. Science 1991; 253: 665–669.
19. Nishisho I, Nakamura Y, Miyoshi Y, et al. Familial adenomatous polyposis and colorectal cancer: one gene or two genes? Gastroenterology 1992; 102: 2171–2178.
20. Groden J, Thliveris A, Samowitz W, et al. Identification and characterization of the familial adenomatous polyposis coli gene. Cell 1991; 66: 589–600.
21. Joslyn G, Carlson M, Thliveris A, et al. Identification of deletion mutations and three new genes at the familial polyposis locus. Cell 1991; 66: 601–613.
22. Miyoshi Y, Ando H, Nagase H, et al. Germ-like mutations of the APC gene in 53 familial adenomatous polyposis patients. Proc Natl Acad Sci USA 1992; 89: 4452–4456.
23. Murphy EA. Genetic aspects of multiple polyposis coli. Dis Colon Rectum 1983; 26: 470–474.
24. Okamoto M, Sato C, Kohno Y, et al. Molecular nature of chromosome 5 q loss in colorectal tumors and desmoid from patients with familial adenomatous polyposis. Hum Genet 1990; 85: 595–599.
25. Miyaki M, Akamatsu N, Sato C, Utsonomiya J. Chemical and viral transformation of cultured skin fibroblasts from patients with familial polyposis coli. Mutat Res 1988; 199: 399–414.
26. Jagelman DG. Extracolonic manifestations of familial polyposis coli. Cancer Genet Cytogenet 1987; 27: 319–325.
27. Jagelman DG. Extracolonic manifestations of familial polyposis coli. Sem Surg Oncol 1987; 3: 88–91.
28. Sasaki M, Sugio K, Sasazuki T. K-ras activation in colorectal tumours from patients with familial polyposis coli. Cancer 1990; 65: 2576–2579.
29. Miyaki M, Seki M, Okamoto M, et al. Genetic changes and histopathological types in colorectal tumours from patients with familial adenomatous polyposis. Cancer Res 1990; 50: 7166–7173.
30. Shirasawa S, Urabe K, Yanagawa Y, Toshitani K, Iwama T, Sasazuki T. p53 gene mutations in colorectal tumours from patients with familial polyposis coli. Cancer Res 1991; 51: 2874–2878.
31. Kikuchi-Yanoshita R, Konishi M, Ito S, et al. Genetic changes of both p53 alleles associated with the conversion from colorectal adenoma to early carcinoma in familial adenomatous polyposis and non-familial adenomatous polyposis patients. Cancer Res 1992; 52: 3965–3971.
32. Okamoto M, Sasaki M, Sugio K, et al. Loss of constitutional heterozygosity in colon carcinoma from patients with familial polyposis coli. Nature 1988; 331: 273–277.
33. Leppert M, Burt R, Hughes JP, et al. Genetic analysis of an inherited predisposition to colon cancer in a family with a variable number of adenomatous polyps. NEJM 1990; 322: 904–908.
34. Meera Khan P, Tops CMJ, Broek M, et al. Close linkage of a highly polymorphic marker (D5S37) to familial adenomatous polyposis (FAP) and confirmation of FAP localization on chromsome 5q21–22. Hum Genet 1988; 79: 183–185.
35. Sasaki M, Okamoto M, Sato C, et al. Loss of constitutional heterozygosity in colorectal tumors from patients with familial polyposis coli and those with nonpolyposis colorectal carcinoma. Cancer Res 1989; 49: 4402–4406.
36. Kikuchi-Yanoshita R, Konishi M, Fukunari H, Tanaka K, Miyaki M. Loss of expression of the DCC gene during progression of colorectal carcinomas in familial adenomatous polyposis and non-familial adenomatous polyposis patients. Cancer Res 1992; 52: 3801–3803.
37. Vogelstein B, Fearon ER, Hamilton SR, et al. Genetic alterations during colorectal-tumour development. NEJM 1988; 319: 525–532.
38. Fearon ER, Vogelstein B. A genetic model for colorectal tumorigenesis. Cell 1990; 61: 759–767.
39. Baker SJ, Preisinger AC, Milburn Jessup J, et al. p53 gene mutations occur in combination with 17p allelic deletions as late events in colorectal tumorigenesis. Cancer Res 1990; 50: 7717–7722.
40. Cunningham J, Lust JA, Schaid DJ, et al. Expression of p53 and 17 p allelic loss in colorectal carcinoma. Cancer Res 1992; 52: 1974–1980.
41. Ashton-Richards PG, Dunlop MG, Nakamura Y, et al. High frequency of APC loss in sporadic colorectal carcinoma due to breaks clustered in 5q21–22. Oncogene 1989; 4: 1169–1174.
42. Delattre O, Olschwang S, Law DJ, et al. Multiple genetic alterations in distal and proximal colorectal cancer. Lancet 1989; 1: 353–356.
43. Sugio K, Kurata S, Sasaki M, et al. Differential expression of

c-myc gene and c-fos gene in premalignant and malignant tissues from patients with familial polyposis coli. Cancer Res 1988; 48: 4855–4861.
44. Rothberg PG, Spandorfer JM, Erisman MD, et al. Evidence that c-myc expression defines two genetically distinct forms of colorectal adenocarcinoma. Br J Cancer 1985; 52: 629–632.
45. Erisman MD, Litwin S, Keidan RD, Comis RL, Astrin SM. Noncorrelation of the expression of the c-myc oncogene in colorectal carcinoma with recurrence of disease or patient survival. Cancer Res 1988; 48: 1350–1355.
46. Slamon DJ, deKernion JB, Verma IM, et al. Expression of cellular oncogenes in human malignancies. Science 1984; 224: 256–262.
47. Erisman MD, Rothberg PG, Diehl RE, Morse CC, Spandorfer JM, Astrin SM. Deregulation of c-myc expression in human colon carcinoma is not accompanied by amplification or rearrangement of the gene. Mol Cell Biol 1985; 5: 1969–1976.
48. Yokota J, Tsunetsugu-Yokota Y, Battifora H, LeFevre C, Cline MJ. Alterations in myc, myb, and rasHa proto-oncogenes in cancers are frequent and show clinical correlation. Science 1986; 231: 261–265.
49. Sikora K, Chan S, Evan G, Gabra H, Markham N, Stewart J, Watson J. c-myc oncogene expression in colorectal cancer. Cancer 1987; 59: 1289–1295.
50. Erisman MD, Scott JK, Astrin SM. Evidence that the familial adenomatous polyposis gene is involved in a subset of colon cancers with a complementable defect in c-myc regulation. Proc Natl Acad Sci USA 1989; 86: 4264–4268.
51. Deschner EE. Adenomas: preneoplastic events, growth and development in man and experimental systems. In: Sommers SC, Rosen PP, eds. Pathology Annual. New York: Appleton Century Crofts 1983; 6: 205–219.
52. Oohara T, Ihara D, Saji K, Tohma H. Comparative study of familial polyposis coli and nonpolyposis coli on the histogenesis of large-intestinal adenoma. Dis Colon Rectum 1982; 25: 446–453.
53. Drasar BS, Bone ES, Hill MJ, Marks CG. Colon cancer and bacterial metabolism in familial polyposis. Gut 1975; 16: 824–825.
54. Reddy BS, Mastromarino A, Gustafson C, Lipkin M, Wynder EL. Fecal bile acids and neutral sterols in patients with familial polyposis. Cancer 1976; 38: 1694–1698.
55. Kopelovich L, Sirlin S. Human skin fibroblasts from individuals genetically predisposed to cancer are sensitive to an SV 40-induced T antigen display and transformation. Cancer 1980; 45: 1108–1111.
56. Rhim JS, Heubner RJ, Arnstein P, Kopelovich L. Chemical transformation of cultured skin fibroblasts derived from individuals with hereditary adenomatosis of the colon and rectum. Int J Cancer 1980; 26: 565–569.
57. Kopelovich L, Bias NE, Helson L. Tumor promoter alone induces neoplastic transformation of fibroblasts from humans genetically pre.disposed to cancer. Nature 1979; 282: 619–621.
58. Maskens AP. Histogenesis of adenomatous polyps in the human large intestine. Gastroenterology 1979; 77: 1245–1251.
59. Yonesawa S, Nakamura T, Tanaka S, Maruta K, Nishi M, Sato E. Binding of Ulex europeas agglutinin-1 in polyposis coli: comparative study with solitary adenomas in the sigmoid colon and rectum. JNCI 1983; 71: 19–24.
60. Muto T, Kamiya J, Sawada T, et al. Small 'flat adenoma' of the large bowel with special reference to its clinicopathologic features. Dis Colon Rectum 1985; 28: 847–851.
61. Heby, Luk GD, Baylin SB. Ornithine decarboxylase as a biological marker in familial colonic polyposis. NEJM 1984; 311: 80–83.
62. Chesa PG, Rettig WJ, Maclamed MR. Expression of cytokeratins in normal and neoplastic colonic epithelial cells. Implications for cellular differentiation and carcinogenesis. Am J Surg Pathol 1986; 10: 829–835.
63. Tsioulias G, Godwin TA, Goldstein MF, McDougall CJ, Sing-Shang N, DeCosse J, Rigas B. Loss of colonic HLA antigens in familial adenomatous polyposis. Cancer Res 1992; 52: 3449–3452.
64. Sugihara K, Jass JR. Colorectal goblet cell mucin in familial adenomatous polyposis. J Clin Pathol 1987; 40: 608–611.
65. Parks TG. Extracolonic manifestations associated with familial adenomatous polyposis. Ann Royal College Surg Engl 1990; 72: 181–184.
66. Yao T, Iida M, Watanabe H, Ohsato K, Omae T. Duodenal lesions in familial polyposis of the colon. Gastroenterology 1977; 73: 1086–1092.
67. Jarvinen H, Nyberg M, Peltokallio P. Upper gastrointestinal tract polyps in familial adenomatosis coli. Gut 1983; 24: 333–339.
68. Spiegelman AD, Talbot IC, Williams CB, Domizio P, Philips RKS. Upper gastrointestinal cancer in patients with familial adenomatous polyposis. Lancet 1989; 2: 783–785.
69. Spiegelman AD, Philips RKS, Williams CB, Bussey HJR. Foregut screening in familial adenomatous polyposis (FAP). Gut 1988; 29: Abst 1445.
70. Hamilton SR, Bussey HJR, Mendelsohn G, et al. Ileal adenomas after colectomy in nine patients with adenomatous polyposis coli/ Gardner's syndrome. Gastroenterology 1979; 77: 1252–1257.
71. Beart RW, Fleming CR, Banks PM. Tubulovillous adenomas in a continent ileostomy after proctocolectomy for familial polyposis. Dig Dis Sci 1982; 27: 553–556.
72. Shepherd NA, Jass JR, Duval I, Moskowsitz RL, Nichols RJ, Morson BC. Restorative proctocolectomy with ileal reservoir; pathological and histochemical study of mucosal biopsy specimens. J Clin Pathol 1987; 40: 601–607.
73. Stryker SJ, Carney JA, Dozois RR. Multiple adenomatous polyps arising in a continent reservoir ileostomy. Int J Colorect Dis 1987; 2: 43–45.
74. Sipponen P, Laxen F, Seppala K. Cystic hamartous gastric polyps: a disorder of oxyntic glands. Histopathology 1983; 7: 729–737.
75. Jagelman DG, De Cosse JJ, Bussey HJR. Upper gastrointestinal cancer in familial adenomatous polyposis. Lancet 1988; 1: 1149–1150.
76. Cohen SB. Familial polyposis coli and its extracolonic manifestations. J Med Genet 1982; 19: 193–203.
77. Gardner EJ. Follow-up study of a family group exhibiting dominant inheritance for a syndrome including intestinal polyps, osteomas, fibromas and epidermoid cysts. Am J Hum Genet 1962; 14: 376–390.
78. Utsunomiya J, Nakamura T. The occult osteomatous changes in the mandible in patients with familial polyposis coli. Br J Surg 1975; 62: 45–51.
79. Traboulsi EL, Krush AJ, Gardner EJ, et al. Prevalence and importance of pigmented ocular fundus lesions in Gardner's syndrome. NEJM 1987; 316: 661–667.
80. Lynch HT, Smyrk T, Watson P, et al. Hereditary colorectal cancer. Seminars in Oncology 1991; 18: 337–366.
81. MacAdam WAF, Goligher JC. The occurrence of desmoids in patients with familial polyposis coli. Br J Surg 1970; 57: 618–631.
82. Jagelman DG. Familial polyposis coli. Surg Clin North Am 1983; 63: 117–128.
83. Bulow S. Clinical features of familial polyposis coli. Dis Colon Rectum 1986; 29: 102–107.
84. Arvanitis ML, Jagelman DG, Fazio VW, et al. Mortality in patients with familial adenomatous polyposis. Dis Colon Rectum 1990; 33: 639–642.
85. Schuchardt WA, Ponski JL. Familial polyposis and Gardner's syndrome. Surg Gynecol Obstet 1979; 148: 97–103.
86. Delamarre J, Dupas J-L, Capron J-P, Armand A, Herve M, Descombes P. Polypose rectocolique familiale, syndrome de Gardner et cancer thyroidien: etude de deux cas. Gastroenterol Clin Biol 1982; 6: 1016–1019.
87. Thompson JS, Harned RK, Anderson JC, Hodgson PE. Papillary carcinoma of the thyroid and familial polyposis coli. Dis Colon Rectum 1983; 26: 583–585.
88. Plail RO, Bussey HJR, Glazer G, Thomson JPS. Adenomatous polyposis: an association with carcinoma of the thyroid. Br J Surg 1987; 74: 377–380.
89. Bernstein IT, Bulow S, Mauritzen K. Hepatoblastoma in two cousins in a family with adenomatous polyposis. Dis Colon Rectum 1992; 35: 373–374.
90. Li FP, Thurber WA, Seddon J, Holmes GE. Hepatoblastoma in families with polyposis coli. JAMA 1987; 157: 2475–2477.
91. Schneider NR, Cubilla AL, Chaganti RSK. Association of

endocrine neoplasia with multiple polyposis of the colon. Cancer 1983; 51: 1171–1175.

92. Painter TA, Jagelman DG. Adrenal adenomas and adrenal carcinomas in association with hereditary adenomatosis of the colon and rectum. Cancer 1985; 55: 2001–2004.
93. Perkins JT, Blackstone MO, Riddell RH. Adenomatous polyposis coli and multiple endocrine neoplasia type 2b. A pathogenetic relationship. Cancer 1985; 55: 375–381.
94. Turcot J, Depres J-P, St Pierre F. Malignant tumors of the central nervous system associated with familial polyposis of the colon: report of two cases. Dis Colon Rectum 1959; 2: 465–468.
95. Lewis JH, Ginsberg AL, Toomey KE. Turcot's syndrome. Evidence for autosomal dominant inheritance. Cancer 1983; 51: 524–528.
96. Itoh H, Ohsato K. Turcot syndrome and its characteristic colonic manifestations. Dis Colon Rectum 1985; 28: 399–402.
97. Woolf CM, Richards RC, Gardner EJ. Occasional discrete polyps of the colon and rectum showing an inherited tendency in a kindred. Cancer 1955; 8: 403–408.
98. Lynch HT, Harris RE, Bardawil WA, et al. Management of hereditary site-specific colon cancer. Arch Surg 1977; 112: 170–174.
99. Lynch HT, Smyrk TC, Watson P, et al. Hereditary flat adenoma syndrome: a variant of familial adenomatous polyposis: Dis Colon Rectum 1992; 35: 411–421.
100. Muir EG, Bell AJY, Barlon KA. Multiple primary carcinomata of the colon, duodenum and larynx associated with kerato-acanthomata of the face. Br J Surg 1967; 54: 191–195.
101. Torre D. Multiple sebaceous tumors. Arch Dermatol 1968; 98: 549–551.
102. Schwartz RA, Flieger DN, Saied NK. The Torre syndrome with gastrointestinal polyposis. Arch Dermatol 1980; 116: 313–314.
103. Alessi E, Brambilla L, Luporini G, Mosca L, Bevilacqua G. Multiple sebaceous tumors and carcinoma of the colon. Torre Syndrome. Cancer 1985; 55: 2566–2574.
104. Graham R, McKee P, McGibbon D, Heyderman E. Torre-Muir syndrome. An association with isolated sebaceous carcinoma. Cancer 1985; 55: 2668–2873.
105. Bussey HJR, Eyers AA, Ritchie SM, Thomson JPS. The rectum in adenomatous polyposis: the St Mark's policy. Br J Surg 1985; 72(Suppl): 29–31.
106. Jagelman DG. Choice of operation in familial adenomatous polyposis. World J Surg 1991; 15: 47–49.
107. Beart RW. Familial polyposis. Br J Surg 1985; 72(Suppl): 31–32.
108. Gilson TP, Sollenberger LL. Adenocarcinoma of an ileostomy in a patient with familial adenomatous polyposis. Dis Colon Rectum 1992; 35: 261–265.
109. Ryan DP, Schapiro RH, Warshaw AL. Villous tumour of the duodenum. Ann Surg 1986; 203: 301–306.
110. Bussey HJR, De Cosse JJ, Deschner EE, et al. A randomized trial of ascorbic acid in polyposis coli. Cancer 1982; 50: 1434–1439.
111. Lipkin M, Newmark H. Effect of added dietary calcium on colonic epithelial-cell proliferation in subjects at high risk of familial colonic cancer. NEJM 1985; 313: 1381–1384.
112. Waddell WR, Loughry RW. Sulindac for polyposis of the colon. J Surg Oncol 1983; 24: 83–87.
113. Waddell WR, Ganser GF, Cerise EJ, Longhry RW. Sulindac for polyposis of the colon. Am J Surg 1989; 157: 175–179.
114. Labayle D, Fischer D, Vielh P, et al. Sulindac causes regression of rectal polyps in familial adenomatous polyposis. Gastroenterology 1991; 101: 635–639.
115. Konsker KA. Familial adenomatous polyposis: case report and review of extracolonic manifestations. Mount Sinai J Med 1992; 59: 85–91.
116. Tsukada K, Church JM, Jagelman DG, et al. Noncytotoxic drug therapy for intra-abdominal desmoid tumour in patients with familial adenomatous polyposis. Dis Colon Rectum 1992; 35: 29–33.
117. Koorey DJ, McCaughan GW, Trent RJ, Gallagher ND. Risk estimation in familial adenomatous polyposis using DNA probes linked to the familial adenomatous polyposis gene. Gut 1992; 33: 530–534.
118. Petersen GM, Slack J, Nakamura Y. Screening guidelines and premorbid diagnosis of familial adenomatous polyposis using linkage. Gastroenterology 1991; 100: 1658–1664.
119. Slack J. The probability of developing familial adenomatous polyposis by combining the diminishing risks with negative screening at advancing age and linked gene markers. Proc Fourth Int Symp Colorectal Cancer, Hereditary Colorectal Cancer, Kobe 1989.
120. Boman BM. Molecular genetic markers in familial adenomatous polyposis. Gastroenterol Clin Biol 1992; 16: 203–204.
121. Olschwang S, Fabre R, Laurent-Puig P, et al. Detection by DGGE of a new polymorphism closely linked to the adenomatous polyposis coli region. Human Genet 1992; 88: 658–660.
122. Olschwang S, Laurent-Puig P, Thomas G. Reliability of presymptomatic test for adenomatous polyposis coli. Lancet 1991; 337: 1171–1172 (letter).
123. Dunlop MG, Steel CM. Presymptomatic diagnosis of polyposis coli by DNA. Gastroenterology 1992; 102: 374 (letter).
124. MacDonald F, Morton DG, Rindi PM, et al. Predictive diagnosis of familial adenomatous polyposis with linked DNA markers: population based study. Br Med J 1992; 304: 869–872.
125. Kraus C, Ballhausen WG. Two intragenic polymorphisms of the APC gene detected by PCR and enzymatic digestion. Human Genet 1992; 88: 705–706.
126. Sivak MV Jr, Jagelman DG. Upper gastrointestinal endoscopy in polyposis syndromes: familial polyposis coli and Gardner's syndrome. Gastrointest Endosc 1984; 30: 102–104.
127. Burt RW, Rikkers LF, Gardner EJ, et al. Villous adenoma of duodenal papilla presenting as necrotizing pancreatitis in a patient with Gardner's syndrome. Gastroenterology 1987; 92: 532–535.
128. Iwama T, Ishida H, Imajo M, et al. The Peutz-Jeghers syndrome and malignant tumor. In: Utsunomiya J, Lynch HT, eds. Hereditary colorectal cancer. Tokyo: Springer-Verlag; 1990: p 331–336.
129. Utsunomiya J, Gocho H, Miyanaga T, Hamaguchi E, Kushimure A. Peutz-Jeghers syndrome: its natural course and management. Johns Hopkins Med J 1975; 136: 71–81.
130. Hsu SD, Zaharopoulos P, May JT, Costanzi JJ. Peutz-Jeghers syndrome with intestinal carcinoma. Report of the association in one family. Cancer 1979; 44: 1527–1532.
131. Cochet D, Carrell J, Desbaillets L, Widgren S. Peutz-Jeghers syndrome associated with gastrointestinal carcinoma. Gut 1979; 20: 169–175.
132. Perzin KH, Bridge MF. Adenomatous and carcinomatous changes in hamartomatous polyps of the small intestine (Peutz-Jeghers syndrome): report of a case and review of the literature. Cancer 1982; 49: 971–983.
133. Giardiello FM, Welsh SB, Hamilton SR, et al. Increased risk of cancer in Peutz-Jeghers syndrome. NEJM 1987; 316: 1511–1514.
134. Shepherd NA, Bussey HJR, Jass JR. Epithelial misplacement in Peutz-Jeghers polyps: a diagnostic pitfall. Am J Surg Pathol 1987; 11: 743–749.
135. Foley TR, McGarrity TJ, Abt AB. Peutz-Jeghers syndrome: a clinicopathologic survey of the 'Harrisburg family' with a 49-year follow-up. Gastroenterology 1988; 95: 1535–1540.
136. Dodds WJ, Schulte WJ, Hensley GT, Hogan WJ. Peutz-Jeghers syndrome and gastrointestinal malignancy. AJR 1982; 115: 373–377.
137. Kyle J. Gastric carcinoma in Peutz-Jeghers syndrome. Scott Med J 1984; 29: 187–191.
138. Paterlini A, Huscher C, Salmi A. Jejunal endoscopic polypectomy in the Peutz-Jeghers syndrome. Endoscopy 1983; 15: 270–271.
139. Yaguchi T, Wen-Ying L, Hasegawa K, Sasaki H, Nagasako K. Peutz-Jeghers polyp with several foci of glandular dysplasia. Report of a case. Dis Colon Rectum 1982; 25: 592–596.
140. Burdick D, Prior JT. Peutz-Jeghers syndrome. A clinicopathologic study of a large family with a 27-year follow-up. Cancer 1982; 50: 2139–2146.
141. Watanabe H, Ajioka Y, Iwafuchi M, et al. Histogenesis of gastrointestinal carcinoma in Peutz-Jeghers polyp. In: Utsunomiya J, Lynch HT, eds. Hereditary Colorectal Cancer. Tokyo: Springer-Verlag, 1990; p 337–342.
142. Trau H, Schewach-Millet M, Fisher BK, Tsur H. Peutz-Jeghers syndrome and bilateral breast carcinoma. Cancer 1982; 50: 788–792.

143. Spiegelman AD, Murday V, Phillips RKS. Cancer and the Peutz-Jeghers syndrome. Gut 1989; 30: 1588–1590.
144. Miller LJ, Bartholemew LG, Dozois RR, Dahlin DC. Adenocarcinoma of the rectum arising in a hamartomatous polyp in a patient with Peutz-Jeghers syndrome. Dig Dis Sci 1983; 28: 1047–1051.
145. Reid JD. Intestinal carcinoma in the Peutz-Jeghers syndrome. JAMA 1974; 229: 833–834.
146. Riley E, Swift M. A family with Peutz-Jeghers syndrome and bilateral breast cancer. Cancer 1980; 46: 815–817.
147. Scully RE. Sex cord tumor with annular tubules: a distinctive ovarian tumor with Peutz-Jeghers syndrome. Cancer 1970; 25: 1107–1121.
148. Veale AMO, McColl I, Bussey HJR, Morson BC. Juvenile polyposis coli. J Med Genet 1966; 3: 5–16.
149. Young RH, Welch WR, Dickersin GR, Scully RE. Ovarian sex cord tumor with annular tubules. Review of 84 cases including 27 with Peutz-Jeghers syndrome and four with adenoma malignum of the cervix. Cancer 1982; 50: 1384–1402.
150. Wilson DN, Pittz WC, Hintz RL, Rosenfeld RG. Testicular tumors with Peutz-Jeghers syndrome. Cancer 1986; 57: 2238–2240.
151. Dubois RS, Hoffman WH, Krishnan TH, et al. Feminizing sex cord tumors with annular tubules in a boy with Peutz-Jeghers syndrome. J Pediatr 1982; 101: 568–571.
152. Cantu JM, Rivera H, Ocampo-Campos R, et al. Peutz-Jeghers syndrome with feminizing Sertoli cell tumor. Cancer 1980; 46: 223–228.
153. Williams CB, Goldblatt M, Delaney PV. 'Top and Tail Endoscopy' and follow up in Peutz-Jeghers syndrome. Endoscopy 1982; 14: 82–84.
154. Van Coevorden F, Mathus-Vliegen EMH, Brummelkamp WH. Combined endoscopic and surgical treatment in Peutz-Jeghers syndrome. Surg Gynecol Obstet 1986; 162: 426–428.
155. Jass JR, Williams CB, Bussey HJR, Morson BC. Juvenile polyposis: a precancerous condition. Histopathology 1988; 13: 619–630.
156. Stemper TJ, Kent TH, Summers RW. Juvenile polyposis and gastrointestinal carcinoma. A study of a kindred. Ann Intern Med 1975; 83: 639–646.
157. Satchatello CR, Hahn IS, Carrington CB. Juvenile gastrointestinal polyposis in a female infant; report of a case and review of the literature of a recently recognized syndrome. Surgery 1974; 75: 107–114.
158. Grotski HW, Rickert RR, Smith WD, Newsome JF. Familial juvenile polyposis coli. A clinical and pathologic study of a large kindred. Gastroenterology 1982; 82: 494–501.
159. Morson BC, Dawson IMP. Developmental abnormalities. In: Gastrointestinal Pathology, 2nd edn. Oxford: Blackwell, 1979; p 498–500.
160. Gilinsky NH, Elliot MS, Price SK, Wright JP. The nutritional consequences and neoplastic potential of juvenile polyposis coli. Dis Colon Rectum 1986; 29: 417–420.
161. Haggitt RC, Reid BJ. Hereditary gastrointestinal polyposis syndromes. Am J Surg Pathol 1986; 10: 871–887.
162. Jarvinen H, Franssila KO. Familial juvenile polyposis coli; increased risk of colorectal cancer. Gut 1984; 25: 792–800.
163. Mazier WP, MacKiegan JM, Billingham RP, Dignan RD. Juvenile polyposis of the colon and rectum. Surg Gynecol Obstet 1982; 154: 829–832.
164. Lipper S, Kahn LB, Sandler RS, Varma V. Multiple juvenile polyposis. A study of the pathogenesis of juvenile polyps and their relationship to colonic adenomas. Hum Pathol 1981; 12: 804–813.
165. Franzin G, Zamboni G, Dina R, Scarpa A, Fratton A. Juvenile and inflammatory polyps of the colon — a histological and histochemical study. Histopathology 1983; 7: 719–728.
166. Goodman ZD, Yardley JH, Milligan FD. Pathogenesis of colonic polyps in multiple juvenile polyposis. Cancer 1979; 43: 1906–1913.
167. Grigioni WF, Alampi G, Martinelli G, Piccaluga A. Atypical juvenile polyposis. Histopathology 1981; 5: 361–376.
168. Horrilleno EG, Eckert C, Ackerman LV. Polyps of the rectum and colon in children. Cancer 1957; 10: 1210–1220.
169. Filipe MI. The value of a study of mucosubstances in rectal biopsies from patients with carcinoma of the rectum and lower sigmoid in the diagnosis of premalignant mucosa. J Clin Pathol 1972; 25: 123–128.
170. Haggitt RC, Pitcock JA. Familial juvenile polyposis of the colon. Cancer 1970; 26: 1232–1238.
171. Ramaswamy G, Elhosseiny AA, Tchertkoff V. Juvenile polyposis of the colon with atypical adenomatous changes and carcinoma in situ. Report of a case and review of the literature. Dis Colon Rectum 1984; 27: 393–398.
172. Jarvinen HJ, Sipponen P. Gastroduodenal polyps in familial adenomatous and juvenile polyposis. Endoscopy 1986; 18: 230–234.
173. Longo WE, Touloukian RJ, West AB, Ballantyne GH. Malignant potential of juvenile polyposis coli. Report of a case and review of the literature. Dis Colon Rectum 1990; 33: 980–984.
174. Ruvalcaba RHA, Myhre S, Smith DW. Sotos syndrome with intestinal polyposis and pigmentary changes of the genitalia. Clin Genet 1980; 18: 413–416.
175. Watanabe A, Nagashima H, Motoi M, Ogawa K. Familial juvenile polyposis of the stomach. Gastroenterology 1979; 77: 148–151.
176. Santos JG, Magalhaes J. Familial gastric polyposis. A new entity. J Genet Hum 1980; 28: 293–297.
177. Seruca R, Carneiro F, Castedo S, David L, Lopes C, Sobrinho-Simoes M. Familial gastric polyposis revisited. Autosomal dominant inheritance confirmed. Cancer Genet Cytogenet 1991; 53: 97–100.
178. Burke PA, Sobin HL. The pathology of Cronkhite-Canada polyps. A comparison to juvenile polyposis. Am J Surg Pathol 1989; 13: 940–946.
179. Lloyd KM, Dennis M. Cowden's disease. A possible new symptom complex with multiple system involvement. Ann Intern Med 1963; 58: 136–142.
180. Gentry WC Jr, Nyles RE, Garlin RJ. Multiple hamartoma syndrome. Arch Dermatol 1974; 109: 521–525.
181. Weary PE, Gerlin R, Gentry WC, et al. Multiple hamartoma syndrome (Cowden's disease). Arch Dermatol 1972; 106: 682–690.
182. Starink Th M. Cowden's disease: analysis of fourteen new cases. J Am Acad Dermatol 1984; 11: 1127–1141.
183. Erbe RW, Compton CC. Case records of the Massachusetts General Hospital, case 24–1987. NEJM 1987; 316: 1531–1540.
184. Brownstein MH, Mehregan AH, Bikowski JB, Lupulescu A, Patterson JC. The dermatopathology of Cowden's syndrome. Br J Dermatol 1979; 100: 667–673.
185. Brownstein MH, Wolf M, Bikowski JB. Cowden's disease. A cutaneous marker of breast cancer. Cancer 1978; 41: 2393–2398.
186. Crickx B, Sigal M, Pastel A, et al. La maladie de Cowden ou syndrome des hamartomes multiple. Press Med 1984; 13: 1499–1501.
187. Gorensek M, Matko I, Skralovnik A, Rode M, Satler J, Jutersek A. Disseminated hereditary gastrointestinal polyposis with orocutaneous hamartomatosis (Cowden's disease). Endoscopy 1984; 16: 59–63.
188. Weinstock JV, Kawanishi H. Gastrointestinal polyposis with orocutaneous hamartomas (Cowden's disease). Gastroenterology 1978; 74: 890–895.
189. Padberg GW, Schot JDL, Jan Vielvoye G, Bots GThAM, de Beer FC. Lhermitte-Duclos disease and Cowden's disease: a single phakomatosis. Ann Neurol 1991; 29: 517–523.
190. Elston DM, James WD, Rodman OG, Graham GF. Multiple hamartoma syndrome (Cowden's disease) associated with non-Hodgkin lymphoma. Arch Dermatol 1986; 122: 572–575.
191. Haibach H, Burns TW, Carlson HE, Burman KD, Deftos LJ. Multiple hamartoma syndrome (Cowden's disease) associated with renal cell carcinoma and primary neuroendocrine carcinoma of the skin (Merkel cell carcinoma). Am J Clin Pathol 1992; 97: 705–712.
192. Carlson GJ, Nivatvongs S, Snover DC. Colorectal polyps in Cowden's disease (multiple hamartoma syndrome). Am J Surg Pathol 1984; 8: 763–770.
193. Laugier P, Kuffer R, Olmos L, Hunziker N, Rougier M, Fiore-

Donno G. Maladie de Cowden: a propos de 8 cas familiaux. Ann Dermatol Venereol 1979; 106: 453–463.
194. Hauser H, Ody B, Plojoux O, Wettstein P. Radiological findings in multiple hamartoma syndrome (Cowden's disease). A report of three cases. Radiology 1980; 137: 317–323.
195. Carlson HE, Burns TW, Davenport SL, Luger AM, Spence MA, Sparkes RS, Orth DN. Cowden's disease: gene marker studies and measurements of epidermal growth factor. Am J Hum Genet 1986; 38: 908–917.
196. Lukash WM, Morgan RI, Sennett CO, Nielson OF. Gastrointestinal neoplasms in Von Recklinghausen's disease. Arch Surg 1966; 92: 905–908.
197. Collins FS, O'Connell P, Ponder BAJ, Seizinger BR. Progress toward identifying the neurofibromatosis (NF1) gene. Trends Genet 1989; 5: 217–221.
198. Rodenhiser DJ, Coulter-Mackie MB, Jung JH, Singh SM. A genetic study of neurofibromatosis 1 in south-western Ontario. I. Population, familial segregation of phenotype, and molecular linkage. J Med Genet 1991; 28: 746–751.
199. Estivill X, Lazaro C, Casals T, Ravella A. Recurrence of nonsense mutation in the NF1 gene causing classical neurofibromatosis type 1. Human Genet 1991; 88: 185–188.
200. Wallace MR, Marchuk DA, Andersen LB, et al. Type 1 neurofibromatosis gene: identification of a large transcript disrupted in three NF1 patients. Science 1990; 249: 181–186.
201. Viskochil D, Buchberg AM, Xu G, et al. Deletions and a translocation interrupt a cloned gene at the neurofibromatosis type 1 locus. Cell 1990; 62: 187–192.
202. Cawthorn RW, Weiss R, Xu G, et al. A major segment of the neurofibromatosis type 1 gene: cDNA sequence, genomic structure and point mutations. Cell 1990; 62: 193–201.
203. Jadayel D, Fain P, Upadhyaya M, et al. Paternal origin of new mutations in von Recklinghausen neurofibromatosis. Nature 1990; 343: 558–559.
204. Riccardi VM. Neurofibromatosis: past, present and future. NEJM 1991; 324: 1283–1285.
205. Rutgeerts P, Hendrickx H, Geboes K, Ponette E, Broeckaert L, Vantrappen G. Involvement of the upper digestive tract by systemic neurofibromatosis. Gastrointest Endosc 1981; 27: 22–25.
206. Levy D, Khatib R. Intestinal neurofibromatosis with malignant degeneration. Dis Colon Rectum 1960; 3: 140–144.
207. Carney JA, Go VLW, Sizemore GW, Hayles AB. Alimentary tract ganglioneuromatosis. A major component of the syndrome of multiple endocrine neoplasia, type 2b. N Engl J Med 1976; 295: 1287–1291.
208. Hochberg FH, Dasilva AB, Galdabini J, Richardson EP. Gastrointestinal involvement in Von Recklinghausen's neurofibromatosis. Neurology 1974; 24: 1144–1151.
209. Weidner N, Flanders DJ, Mitros FA. Mucosal ganglioneuromatosis associated with multiple colonic polyps. Am J Surg Pathol 1984; 8: 779–786.
210. Mendelsohn G, Diamond MP. Familial ganglioneuromatous polyposis of the large bowel. Report of a family with associated juvenile polyposis. Am J Surg Pathol 1984; 8: 515–520.
211. Donnelly WH, Sieber WK, Yunis EJ. Polypoid ganglioneurofibromatosis of large bowel. Arch Pathol 1969; 87: 537–541.
212. Bean WB. Vascular spiders and related lesions of the skin. Springfield Ill: CC Thomas 1958; p 178–185.
213. Nakagawara G, Asano E, Kimura S, Akimoto R, Miyazaki I. Blue rubber bleb nevus syndrome. Report of a case. Dis Colon Rectum 1977; 20: 421–427.
214. Anthony PP, Morris DS, Vowles KDJ. Multiple and recurrent inflammatory fibroid polyps in three generations of a Devon family: a new syndrome. Gut 1984; 25: 854–862.
215. Morson BC. The polyp cancer sequence in the large bowel. Proc R Soc Med 1974; 67: 451–457.
216. Cronkhite LW, Canada WJ. Generalized gastrointestinal polyposis. An unusual syndrome of polyposis, pigmentation, alopecia and onychotrophia. NEJM 1955; 252: 1011–1015.
217. Suzuki K, Urakoa M, Funatsu T, et al. Cronkhite-Canada syndrome. A case report and analytical review of 23 other cases reported in Japan. Gastroenterol JPN 1979; 14: 441–449.
218. Jenkins D, Stephenson PM, Scott BB. The Cronkhite-Canada syndrome: an ultrastructural study of pathogenesis. J Clin Pathol 1985; 38: 271–276.
219. Russell DMR, Bhathal PS, St John DJB. Complete remission in Cronkhite-Canada syndrome. Gastroenterology 1983; 85: 180–185.
220. Katayama Y, Kimura M, Konn M. Cronkhite-Canada syndrome associated with a rectal cancer and adenomatous changes in colonic polyps. Am J Surg Pathol 1985; 9: 65–71.
221. Malhotra R, Sheffield A. Cronkhite-Canada syndrome associated with colon carcinoma and adenomatous changes in C-C polyps. Am J Gastroenterol 1988; 83: 772–776.
222. Rappaport LB, Sperling HV, Stavrides A. Colon cancer in the Cronkhite-Canada syndrome. J Clin Gastroenterol 1986; 8: 199–202.
223. Daniel ES, Ludwig SL, Lewin KL, et al. The Cronkhite-Canada syndrome: an analysis of clinical and pathologic features and therapy in 55 patients. Medicine 1982; 61: 293–309.
224. Cohen SM, Brown L, Janover ML, McCready FJ. Multiple metaplastic (hyperplastic) polyposis of the colon. Gastrointest Radiol 1981; 6: 333–335.
225. Williams GT, Arthur JF, Bussey HJR, Morson BC. Metaplastic polyps and polyposis of the colorectum. Histopathology 1980; 4: 155–170.
226. Longacre TA, Fenoglio-Preiser CM. Mixed hyperplastic adenomatous polyp/serrated adenoma: a distinct form of colorectal neoplasm. Am J Surg Pathol 1990; 14: 524–537.
227. Bengoechea O, Martinez-Penuela JM, Larrinaga B, Valerdi J, Borda F. Hyperplastic polyposis of the colorectum and adenocarcinoma in 24-year-old man. Am J Surg Pathol 1987; 11: 323–327.
228. Kusunoki M, Fujita S, Sakanoue Y, Shoi Y, Yanagi H, Yamamura T, Utsonomiya J. Disappearance of hyperplastic polyposis after resection of rectal cancer. Report of two cases. Dis Colon Rectum 1991; 34: 829–832.
229. Cappell MS, Forder KA. Spatial clustering of multiple hyperplastic, adenomatous, and malignant colonic polyps in individual patients. Dis Colon Rectum 1989; 32: 641–652.
230. Ming-Chai C, Chi-Yuan C, P'Ei-Yu C, Jen-Chun H. Evolution of colorectal cancer in schistosomiasis: transitional mucosal changes adjacent to large intestinal carcinoma in colectomy specimens. Cancer 1980; 46: 1661–1675.
231. Mohamed AE, Al Karawi MA, Yasawi I. Schistosomal colonic disease. Gut 1990; 31: 439–442.
232. Williams CB. Multiple endoscopic polypectomies for schistosomal polyposis of the colon. Lancet 1983; iii: 673–674.
233. Williams GT, Bussey HJR, Morson BC. Inflammatory 'cap' polyps of the large intestine. Br J Surg 1985; 72(Suppl): 133 (Abst).
234. Franzin G, Fratton A, Manfrini C. Polypoid lesions associated with diverticular disease of the sigmoid colon. Gastrointest Endosc 1985; 31: 196–199.
235. Bastlein C, Burlefinger R, Holzberg E, Voeth Ch, Garbrecht M, Ottenjann R. Common variable immunodeficiency syndrome and nodular lymphoid hyperplasia in the small intestine. Endoscopy 1988; 20: 272–275.
236. Herman PE, Diaz-Busco JA, Stobo JD. Idiopathic late-onset immunoglobulin deficiency. Clinical observations in 50 patients. Am J Med 1976; 61: 221–237.
237. Shepherd NA, Hall PA, Coates PJ, Levison DA. Primary malignant lymphoma of the colon and rectum. A histopathological and immunohistochemical analysis of 45 cases with clinicopathological correlation. Histopathology 1988; 12: 235–252.
238. Isaacson PG, MacLennan KA, Subbuswany SG. Multiple lymphomatous polyposis of the gastrointestinal tract. Histopathology 1984; 8: 641–656.
239. Rywlin AM, Ravel R, Hurwitz A. Malakoplakia of the colon. Am J Dig Dis 1969; 14: 491–499.
240. Swain VAJ, Young WF, Pringle EM. Hypertrophy of the appendices epiploicae and lipomatous polyposis of the colon. Gut 1969; 10: 587–589.
241. Climie ARW, Wylin RF. Small intestinal lipomatosis. Arch Pathol Lab Med 1981; 105: 40–42.

PART III

Rare and secondary (metastatic) tumours

K. Geboes

RARE EPITHELIAL TUMOURS

A variety of rare 'epithelial tumours' have been described in the gastrointestinal tract in general, and in the colon in particular. In earlier literature they were divided into various subtypes according to the main features expressed in the individual tumours, but it is now becoming clear that most of these tumours have their origin in a common uncommitted endodermal stem cell and therefore could be referred to as stem cell carcinoma.[1] The subtypes earlier reported include small cell carcinoma (oat cell carcinoma), squamous cell carcinoma, adenosquamous carcinoma (adenoacanthoma), the composite carcinoid (goblet cell carcinoid or adenocarcinoid), undifferentiated carcinomas and the 'stem cell carcinomas'. It is not clear what the precise relationship of these tumours is to the classical undifferentiated or anaplastic adeno-carcinomas of the older literature, because many of these were not examined by electron microscopy or immunohistochemistry. There is, however, some evidence that a large celled subgroup, characterized by secretory component and J chain, has a better prognosis.[2–3] Small cell carcinoma and squamous, carcinoma are considered in greater detail in Chapter 41 part I, but here attention is drawn to the fact that these tumours belong to a group of cancers which may contain cells with widely variable characteristics and that they commonly arise in adenomas (Fig 41.26).[4–9]

Analysis of the more recently published case reports of rare epithelial tumours[2–23] (Table 41.9) shows that neuroendocrine features can be demonstrated in most cases, either as the main characteristic (pure endocrine) or in combination with other features (mixed or composite tumours). In occasional tumours, cells may exhibit an even wider range of differentiation characteristics and these lesions have been called amphicrine tumours. Amphicrine tumours differ from the mixed tumours in that endocrine and epithelial cell constituents are present within the same cell.[24] The identification of more and more tumours with combined characteristics supports the belief that the strict separation of endocrine tumours and adenocarcinoma has to be modified and that most of these rare epithelial tumours fit into a spectrum ranging from classic carcinoid to typical adenocarcinoma.[24]

There are no consistently identified associations and such diverse coexistent findings as ulcerative colitis, schistosomiasis, multiple polyposis, ovarian and endometrial adenocarcinoma have been noted in cases of poorly differentiated adenosquamous (neuroendocrine) carcinomas.[10]

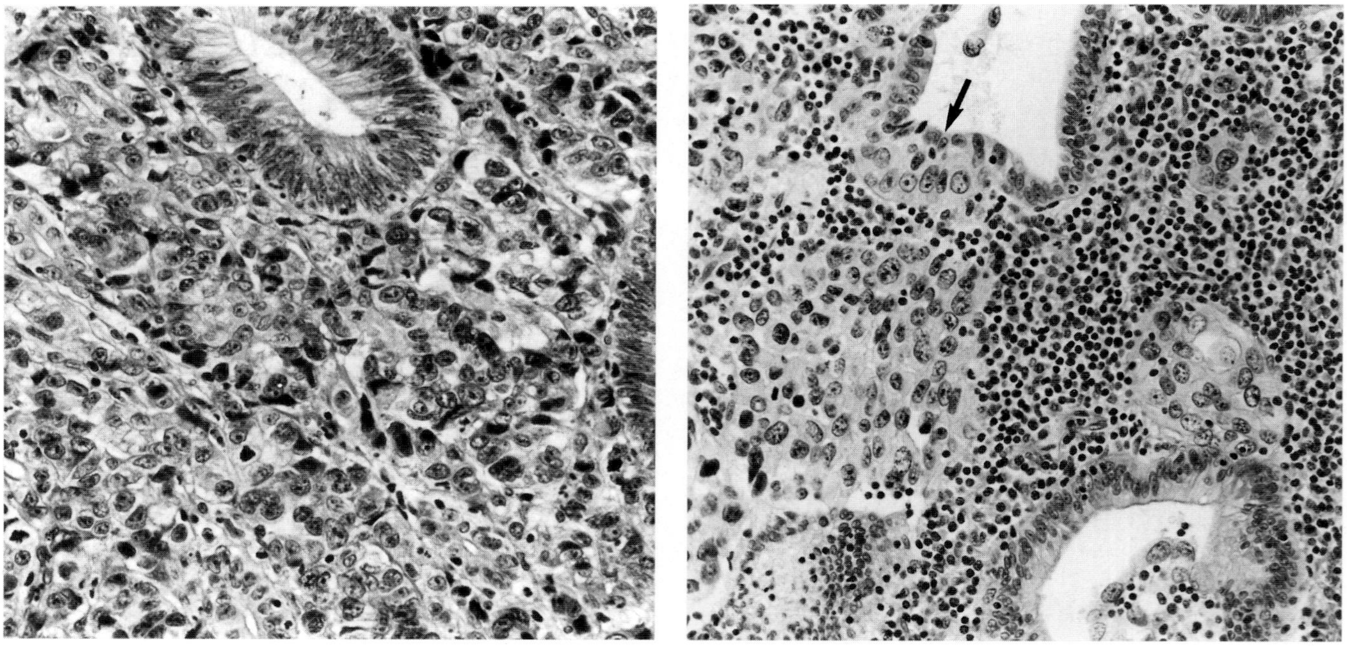

A B

Fig. 41.26 A Undifferentiated carcinoma of the colon can arise within a tubular adenoma. Note glandular structure lined by a pseudostratified epithelium as well as pleomorphic tumour cells. (H&E, ×97.5) **B** Pleomorphic tumour cells in close contiguity with glandular structures (arrow). (H&E, ×97.5) These tumours must be differentiated from metastases (see Figs 41.34 & 41.35)

Table 41.9 Nomenclature and classification of rare epithelial tumours.

Original name	Neuroendocrine markers		Reference
	Present	Not investigated or negative	
Pure exocrine			
—undifferentiated carcinoma		–	2
—poorly differentiated, medullary type		–	3
Mixed endocrine-squamous			
—adenoacanthoma		–	5
—basosquamous (transitional cloacogenic)	+ (PTH & ACTH)		
—adenosquamous carcinoma	+		10
—mixed adenosquamous carcinoma			7
—adenosquamous carcinoma and carcinoidal differentiation	+		6,8
—carcinosarcoma		NSE = –	11
Pure endocrine (?)			
—small cell undifferentiated carcinoma⁺			9
—small cell neuroendocrine			4
carcinoma	+		12
—pleomorphic (giant cell) carcinoma⁺			13
Mixed (composite) glandular-endocrine cell carcinoma			
—goblet cell carcinoid	+		
—adenocarcinoid	+		
—composite carcinoid	+		14
—composite glandular carcinoid⁺			15
—Peneth cell-rich adenocarcinoma	+	–	16
(crypt cell carcinoma)			17
—argentaffinoma-adenocarcinoma	+		16
—mucinous carcinoid	+		18
—argyrophil mucus-secreting			
adenocarcinoma	+		17
—signet-ring cell adenocarcinoma	+		19
—adenocarcinoma with argentaffin cells⁺			20
—clear-cell adenoma and adenocarcinomas		–	21
Mixed endocrine-exocrine-squamous			
-stem cell carcinoma	+		1
Amphicrine tumours			
—carcinoma with undifferentiated carcinoid and squamous features	+		22
—undifferentiated carcinoma containing exocrine, neuroendocrine and squamous cells	+		23

Some of the tumours show unique morphological features. For example, an adenosquamous carcinoma, admixed with sarcoma showing osseous, cartilaginous and non-specific spindle cell differentiation in the sigmoid colon has been reported as carcinosarcoma.[11] Carcinoembryonic antigen appeared limited to carcinoma cells but cytokeratin immunoreactivity was observed in both carcinoma and sarcoma cells. Neuron-specific enolase staining was negative and ultrastructural studies were not performed.

Although Paneth cells are only found in the proximal colon or in metaplastic states, adenomas and adenocarcinomas rich in Paneth cells occur, and in them the Paneth cells show disorderly arrangement, variation in size and shape of cell granules and nuclei and a raised nuclear-cytoplasmic ratio.[25–27] These tumours are often associated with excessive mucin production, and neoplastic cells containing both mucin and Paneth cell granules may be seen. Argentaffin cells have been noted in these lesions.[16] The behaviour of this type of tumour is not well documented because of their rarity. Noting the similarity between this tumour and intestinal crypts, the name of crypt cell carcinoma has been proposed.[17]

Unique variants of epithelial neoplasms of the large intestine are the 'clear cell adenoma and adenocarcinoma'. Microscopically, these tumours are composed of uniform cells with clear cytoplasm due to their glycogen content. Neuroendocrine features were not reported but adequate ultrastructural studies are lacking. The lesion must not be confused with metastatic renal cell carcinoma.[21] It is not clear at present how this lesion should be classified but areas of clear cell adenocarcinoma have been reported in poorly differentiated neuroendocrine carcinoma.[1]

In a basosquamous carcinoma of the colon, the production of parathyroid hormone and possibly adrenal corticotrophic hormone has been demonstrated.[5] CEA and lysozyme immunoreactive cells and cells reacting with antibodies directed against epidermal keratin or containing alpha-1-antitrypsin and showing exocrine, neuroendocrine and squamous cell differentiation by electron microscopy have also been recorded.[23] These observations show that neoplastic stem cells in the colon are capable of differentiating into neuro-endocrine, mucinous and columnar cells and tend to confirm the view that some colonic tumours arise from pluripotential stem cells.

A proliferation of 'stem cells' is also invoked to explain the existence of primary colonic adenocarcinoma with areas of choriocarcinoma.[28] Occasionally, primary epithelial tumours are difficult to classify, such as the cylindroma described in the rectum.[29]

SOFT TISSUE TUMOURS

Routine microscopy using haematoxylin-eosin and special stains does not always allow a precise idenfication of the histogenesis of gastrointestinal soft tissue tumours. In the colon, the vast majority of these tumours are easily recognized as lipomas and leiomyomatous tumours but the introduction of immunohistochemistry and the use of antibodies against S100 protein have shown that the distinction between myogenic and neurogenic tumours is not always simple. Some tumours can indeed show different degrees of differentiation and transitional forms may be explained by the occurrence of myofibroflasts. Therefore soft tissue tumours can be grouped under the heading of 'stromal tumours'. However, it remains justifiable to try to make a distinction between myogenic and other types because of differences in behaviour. Transmission electron microscopy and immunohistochemistry using a broad panel of antibodies have largely improved the diagnostic possibilities. In general, stromal tumours of the large bowel are rare compared with other segments of the gastrointestinal tract. They are discussed in detail in Chapter 35.

Connective tissue tumours

In the earlier literature, there are isolated case reports of fibromas of the large bowel (mainly the caecum). The lesions described usually belong to the group of benign spindle cell tumours, and their specific nature can be questioned.[30–31] This is also true for more recently reported cases.[32] Transmission electron microscopy and special staining procedures are clearly necessary for a correct diagnosis.

Fibromas must be distinguished from the 'inflammatory fibroid polyp', a localized growth of submucosal connective tissue often described in other terminology, including submucosal granuloma with eosinophilic infiltration.[33–34] This lesion is uncommon in the large bowel but the caecum may be involved. In a series of 33 patients, 4 cases were located in the colon while 16 were found in the stomach and 13 in the small intestine.[35] A familial occurrence of inflammatory fibroid polyps has been reported but in the cases described no colonic lesions were reported.[36] The inflammatory fibroid polyp is not really a neoplastic lesion but rather due to 'inflammation'. An 'elastofibroma-like' polyp is another non-neoplastic tumorous condition reported in the colon.[37] Malignant fibroblastic tumours of the colon are decidely rare.[38–40] It is likely that so-called fibrosarcomas would, at the present time, be classified differently. In the same way, the malignant giant cell tumour reported would now be classified as malignant fibrous histiocytoma.[41] This type of tumour has to be differentiated from the moderately differentiated neuro-endocrine carcinoma which, on routine microscopy, may show some similarities.[13] The occurence of primary malignant fibrous histiocytoma within the colon seems genuine. Colonic tumours with appearances identical to malignant fibrous histiocytomas have undoubtedly been reported, both as a solitary lesion and as a multicentric tumour. An incidental association with diverticulitis has also been reported[42–46] and the author has observed one such tumour in a young male patient previously treated for Hodgkin's disease. Xanthogranuloma, which may be a related but benign tumorous lesion, is also described in the colon (Fig 41.27).[47]

Tumours of adipose tissue origin

Lipomas of the large intestine are a well recognized clinical entity and the second most common group of benign polypoid lesions, with an incidence of 0.5% in large autopsy series. They are somewhat more common in elderly females. The majority are submucosal (rarely subserosal) lesions, usually sessile, but sometimes pedunculated. In a small number of patients, multiple lipomas have been reported. The caecum appears to be the most common site of involvement, followed by the sigmoid. The size of the lesions is highly variable (2 mm to 30 cm). Most of the symptomatic lesions are relatively large. Lipomas may produce intussusception or bleeding,[48–50] and clinically it may be difficult to distinguish lipomas from malignant lesions.[51]

The most common differential diagnostic problem lies in the distinction between true lipomas and simple adiposity. The latter occurs frequently in the caecum and is known as lipohypertrophy of the ileocaecal valve. It consists of an excess of unencapsulated adipose tissue in the submucosa. Hypertrophy of the appendices epiploicae and lipomatous polyposis of the colon, previously reported as epiploic lipomatosis, probably also represent a similar non-tumorous condition.[52–53] In contrast, the typical lipoma is composed of encapsulated, mature, adipose tissue. Atypical features consisting of hyperchromatic nuclei, increased mitotic activity and cellular fibrosis may be present in some lipomas. They are mostly associated with ulceration and are probably reactive in nature. These features have led to the introduction of the the term 'atypical lipomas'.[54] Other unusual variants of lipomatous tumours are lipofibromas and angiolipomas.[55–56] An unusual poly-

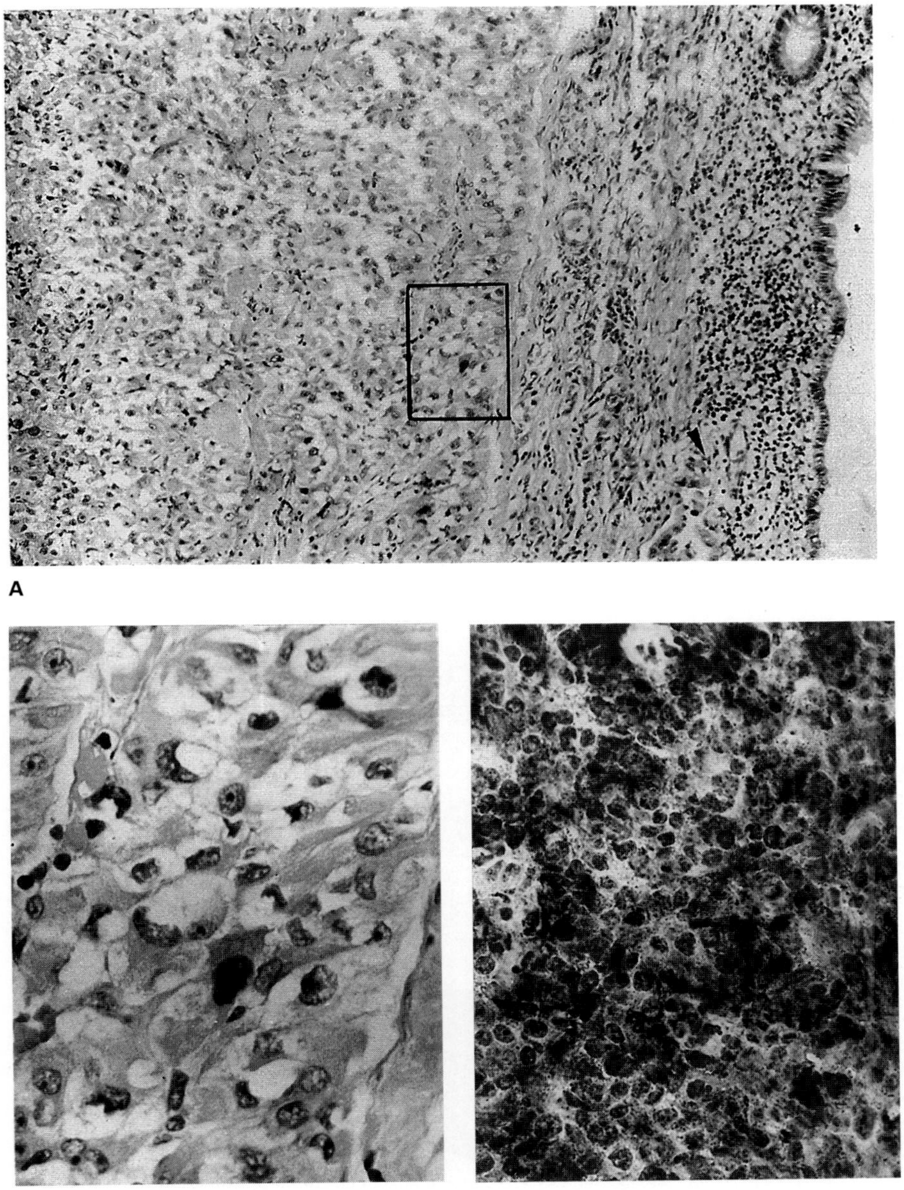

Fig. 41.27 **A** Submucosal colonic tumour with vascular invasion (arrow) composed of large histiocytic cells. (H&E, ×14) **B** Note the occasionally bizarre nuclei. (H&E, ×88) **C** The tumour cells showed a positive reaction for acid phosphatase. (H&E, ×35) They were negative for epithelial markers.

poid combination of a lipoma and an epithelial cystic hamartoma has been reported as lipoepithelial hamartoma.[57] Malignant adipose tissue tumours of the colon seem extremely rare.

Tumours of vascular origin

Neoplasms of the vascular tissue in the colon are reported with increasing frequency. Over the last 5 years more than 60 papers have appeared on this subject. This is mainly due to improved diagnostic techniques. The overall incidence of these lesions remains, however, rare, except for Kaposi's sarcoma occurring as a complication of AIDS. (Table 41.10)

Table 41.10 Vascular tumours and non-tumoral vascular lesions observed in 5 100 colonoscopies.

Haemangioma (n = 9)	
Capillary haemangioma	n = 2
Cavernous haemangioma	n = 2
—single, small	n = 2
—multiple, small	n = 2
—single diffuse, expansive	n = 2
—multiple diffuse, expansive	n = 1
Mixed forms	n = 0
Malignant vascular neoplasms (n = 2)	
Angioscarcoma	n = 0
Kaposi's sarcoma	n = 2
Lymphangioma	n = 3
Non-tumoral vascular lesions	n = 56

Benign vascular neoplasms

Haemangiomas. Haemangiomas are among the rarest lesions of the colon, only approximately 250 cases are on record.[58–60] Whether they are genuine neoplastic lesions or simple congenital vascular malformations is still debated. The diagnosis is often made in adult life, although initial symptoms often date from infancy or childhood. No clear sex predominance is established. In the large bowel, mucosal haemangiomas arise from the submucosal plexus and rarer cases originating from deeply situated plexuses may be localized at the serosal surface. The majority of the haemangiomas are solitary localized lesions. Multiple lesions are 10 times less frequent. Due to their vascular structure, the colour of colonic haemangiomas ranges from deep blue to a dull red. Genuine haemangiomas must be differentiated from hamartomatous lesions[61] and from 'granuloma pyogenicum' or 'granulation tissue,' a condition which is also seen in the colon, and although supposedly rare, is probably not so uncommon.[62] It can be the result of infectious conditions such as campylobacter colitis.[63] Chronic inflammatory changes may occur in genuine haemangiomas and mask a true diagnosis. Haemangiomas must also be differentiated from the so-called angiodysplastic lesions or vascular ectasias.

Histologically, haemangiomas are usually classified into four types: capillary, mixed capillary-cavernous, venous and cavernous.

Capillary haemangiomas are usually small (from a few millimeters to 2 cm), single and spherical and bulge into the lumen. Microscopically, they are composed of vessels with a calibre approximately that of normal capillaries. These are lined by a well differentiated, sometimes slightly hyperplastic endothelium. The tiny vessels are closely packed into aggregates and separated by scant connective tissue, deficient in elastin. These lesions account for less than 10% of all colorectal haemangiomas. Capillary haemangiomas are often asymptomatic. If bleeding occurs, it tends to be slow and may be entirely occult or result in melaena (Fig 41.28).

Mixed capillary-cavernous haemangiomas occur less frequently and are said to represent 6% of all benign vascular tumours.

Venous haemangiomas mimic cavernous haemangiomas in all aspects, including histological structure. Angiography may, however, differentiate venous haemangioma from cavernous haemangioma.[64]

Cavernous haemangiomas are composed of large, thin-walled vessels, with somewhat more loose connective tissue containing smooth muscle fibres. As in capillary haemangiomas, true encapsulation does not occur. They account for 75% of all rectal and colonic haemangiomas and more than 50% of them occur in the rectosigmoid. Cavernous haemangiomas are subclassified as *discrete, circumscribed lesions* and *diffuse expansive* types. The former are often polypoid but larger masses producing annular lesions or luminal narrowing have been described. Diffuse cavernous haemangiomas may replace the intestinal wall from serosa to mucosa.[65–66] They may be flat or encroach upon and narrow the colonic lumen. Cavernous haemangiomas can also mimick the appearance of varices (Fig 41.29).

They may be responsible for massive and/or recurrent

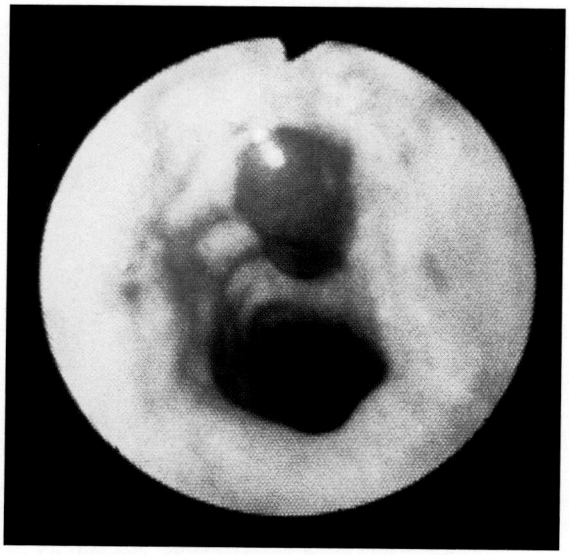

Fig. 41.28 Capillary haemangioma of the colon: endoscopic appearance of the 'reddish' nodule.

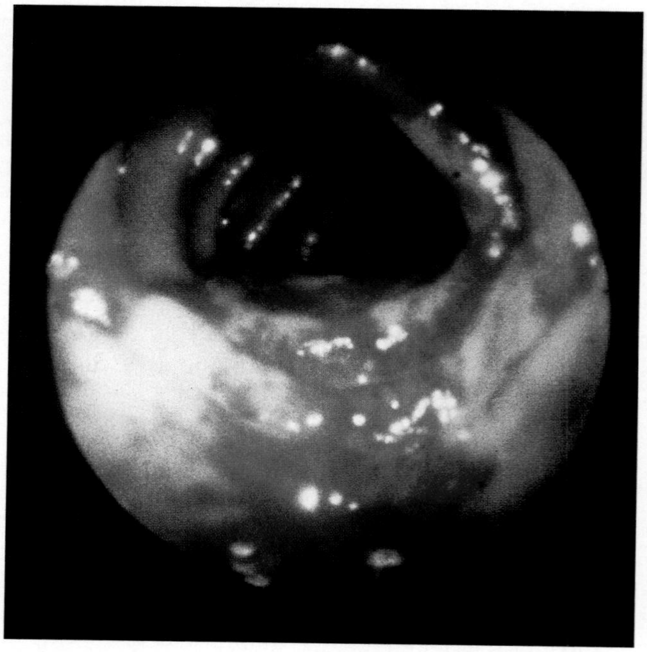

Fig. 41.29 Extensive flat 'cavernous haemangioma' of the colon; endoscopic appearance.

gastrointestinal bleeding. Less frequently, symptoms of complete or partial obstruction (in 17% of all patients) and impaired coagulation (Kasabach Merritt syndrome) are reported. Occasionally, anorectal haemangiomas may cause constipation, tenesmus or even rectovaginal and other fistulas. Only 10% of patients with recognized cavernous haemangiomas are without symptoms.

Haemangiomas of the colon and rectum, usually cavernous, may coexist with similar lesions elsewhere in the gastrointestinal tract or with vascular neoplasms affecting other organ systems. The association of cutaneous lesions with (usually multiple) gastrointestinal haemangiomas is well known although the reverse is rather the exception. Cavernous haemangiomas may also be associated with congenital anomalies in other systems. Mucosal and serosal haemangioma-like lesions are known to occur in some 5–8% of patients with Turner's syndrome.[67]

Angiomatosis is a condition characterized by a very extensive diffuse proliferation of variably sized thin-walled vascular channels mixed with fat, fibrous tissue and occasionally with lymphatics. In the large bowel haemangiomatosis is the term used for large diffuse lesions and for multiple synchronous haemangiomas.[68–69] The latter condition has been described in children and adults and often presents with bleeding and impaired coagulation. This condition is expected to occur once for every ten patients with a single haemangioma of the digestive tract and histological malignancy has been described.[70]

Diffuse intestinal haemangiomatosis is an entity in which as many as 100 lesions or more involving three or more segments of the gastrointestinal tract are encountered. In the neonatal form, early angiography is probably the most reliable means of diagnosis.

Universal (miliary) haemangiomatosis is an extremely rare syndrome, usually fatal in infancy, with hundreds of haemangiomas involving all organs.

Multiple phlebectasia is characterized by a multitude of small cavernous nodules. These lesions are often asymptomatic. Similar lesions may occur as a manifestation of the hereditary Rendu-Osler-Weber disease although telangiectasias are probably more common in this disease. Telangiectasias, however, can not always be clearly differentiated from small haemangiomas.

Other syndromes involving gastrointestinal haemangiomas and occurring on an inherited basis or with a familial distribution, are the blue rubber bleb naevus syndrome (cutaneous and intestinal haemangioma), Peutz-Jeghers syndrome and Klippel-Trenaunay-Weber syndrome. In the blue rubber bleb naevus syndrome, colonic lesions are most common on the left side and in the rectum.[71–72] Microscopically, they are cavernous haemangiomas. In the Klippel-Trenaunay-Weber syndrome malformations of mixed or cavernous haemangioma type have been reported.[73]

Glomus tumour. A unique case of an adventitial glomus tumour found in a specimen of colon removed for a recurrent adenocarcinoma has been reported.[74]

Malignant vascular neoplasms

Malignant haemangioendothelioma is an extremely rare lesion in the colon but when it occurs involvement of several other parts of the intestine may also be present. Haemangiopericytomas of the large bowel are also extremely rare and occasionally present with recurrent intussusception.[75]

Angiosarcoma. Primary angiosarcoma of the gastrointestinal tract is very rare. Five cases occurring in the colon (both right and left) have been reported over the last seven years. The diagnosis may be difficult to establish in such an unusual location and involves transmission electron microscopy and immunohistochemistry using a panel of antibodies, particularly those directed against Factor VIII-related antigen. Angiosarcoma has been reported following irradiation of the gastrointestinal tract and in association with a foreign body retained for a long period. In one case report of a 72-year-old male the tumour showed epithelioid and histiocytoid features. Fatal outcome was observed in 4/5 cases reported.[76–80]

Kaposi's sarcoma. Kaposi's sarcoma, originally described by Kaposi in 1872 as multiple idiopathic pigmented sarcoma of the skin, can be classified as a malignant vascular tumour, although its origin is debated. Kaposi's sarcoma classically has an indolent course, but a more aggressive form is diagnosed with increasing frequency in patients with acquired immunodeficiency. Gastrointestinal involvement was originally noted by Kaposi and is common. In 45% of patients, Kaposi lesions are asymptomatic, even in immunodeficient patients, and may precede skin lesions, but are usually more common if the cutaneous disease is extensive. Half of all patients with gastrointestinal Kaposi's sarcoma have evidence of both lower and upper tract involvement, 12% have upper tract involvement only and in 8% the lower tract is affected exclusively.[81–83] Three types of endoscopic colonic lesions have been reported. The most common lesion is a nipple like nodule (2–5 mm) which varies in colour from blue through dark pink to scarlet. Larger lesions are usually polypoid (1 cm in size) or show a central ulceration or umbilication. Endoscopic biopsies can be safely obtained from the lesions but in 23% they fail to be diagnostic.[84] Classically, the lesions arè limited to the mucosa and submucosa, but serosal involvement does occur. Microscopically, the tumour is composed of streaming bundles of spindle cells with numerous haemosiderin-containing macrophages. Kaposi's sarcoma has also been observed in HIV negative patients with Crohn's disease, ulcerative colitis and following transplantation.[85–88]

Lymphangioma

Colonic lymphangioma (cystic lymphangioma; lymphatic, lymphangiomatous, lymphangiectatic or chylous cyst) is a rare benign tumour of uncertain histogenesis. It is found in all races, both sexes being involved equally. The peak incidence is in the seventh decade, but with an average age of 52.5 years and a range of 27–77 years. The lesions may occur in any part of the colon and clinical signs and symptoms are non-specific. Abdominal or rectal pain, protein loss and rectal bleeding may occur.[89–92]

The usual classification divides lymphangiomas into simple, cavernous and cystic types. A distinction is made between lymphangiectasia with diffuse bowel involvement and a localized lymphangioma which can be unicystic or multicystic. Diffuse cases have only rarely been reported, either in association with the features of small intestinal lymphangiectasia or secondary to liver disease. Clinically, watery diarrhoea can be the presenting symptom. Grossly, the colonic mucosa is smooth but irregular with multiple elevations. Microscopically, the lesion is characterized by dilated lymphatics in the muscularis mucosae and submucosa.

The solitary lesion is an irregular, polypoid, soft mass. The colour is variably described as greyish-white, pale yellow or reddish tan. The size varies from 0.5–10.0 cm. Microscopic examination reveals a mass, covered by normal colonic mucosa, and originating from the submucosa. The mass is composed of cystic spaces, lined by endothelial cells and separated by fibrous connective tissue septa. The cystic spaces may contain an acidophilic material (Figs 41.30, 41.31).

Tumours of nervous tissue

Hereditary/familial conditions

Type 1 Neurofibromatosis. Neurofibromatosis (von Recklinghausen's disease) (NF-1), a relatively common hereditary disease with a prevalence of 1 in 3 000 in Western populations is characterized by multiple café-au-lait spots and localized tumours of the gastrointestinal tract. The genes for NF-1 have been identified on chromosome 17. Gastrointestinal involvement occurs in three principal forms: as stromal tumours, as hyperplasia of submucosal and myenteric plexuses and as carcinoid of the duodenum. Colonic involvement is less usual than other sites (8.3%), the small bowel being commonest.[93–94] Soft tissue tumours are the most commonly reported gastrointestinal manifestation of NF-1. Except for plexiform neurofibromas, they have no special features that allow them to be distinguished from their counterparts that arise sporadically in non-NF-1 individuals. Classically, they have been diagnosed as neurofibromas, leiomyomas or leiomyosarcomas, and benign or malignant Schwannomas but immunohistochemistry often fails to show convincing evidence of neural or smooth muscle differentiation. Therefore, they are also referred to as stromal tumours.

Hyperplasia of large intestinal intrinsic innervation ranges from subtle nerve cell changes (requiring morphometry for adequate diagnosis) to florid enlargement of nerve plexuses with a marked increase in the number and thickness of nerve fibres, often accompanied by increased numbers of enteroglial cells. The changes involve both myenteric and submucosal plexuses and are more often patchy than diffuse (Fig 41.32). The patchy distribution may give the impression of multiple small intramural neurofibromas. Carcinoid foci in the colon have been described in association with ganglioneuromatosis.[95] The clinical symptoms of colonic neurofibromatosis are usually delayed until adulthood. They include pain, lower GI bleeding and constipation, which occurs in 10% of the patients. Chronic colonic pseudo-obstruction and megacolon are uncommon complications described in association with a diffuse 'plexiform neurofibromatosis'. Stromal

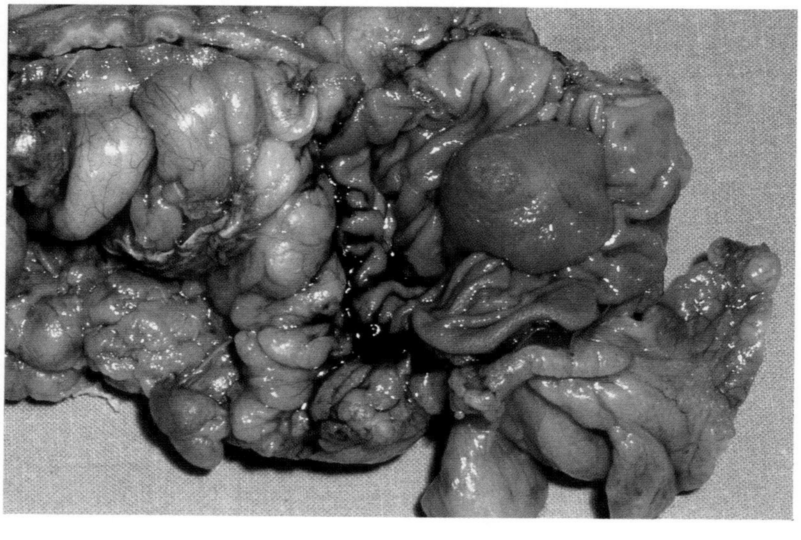

Fig. 41.30 Lymphangioma of the colon presenting as a nodule covered by intact mucosa.

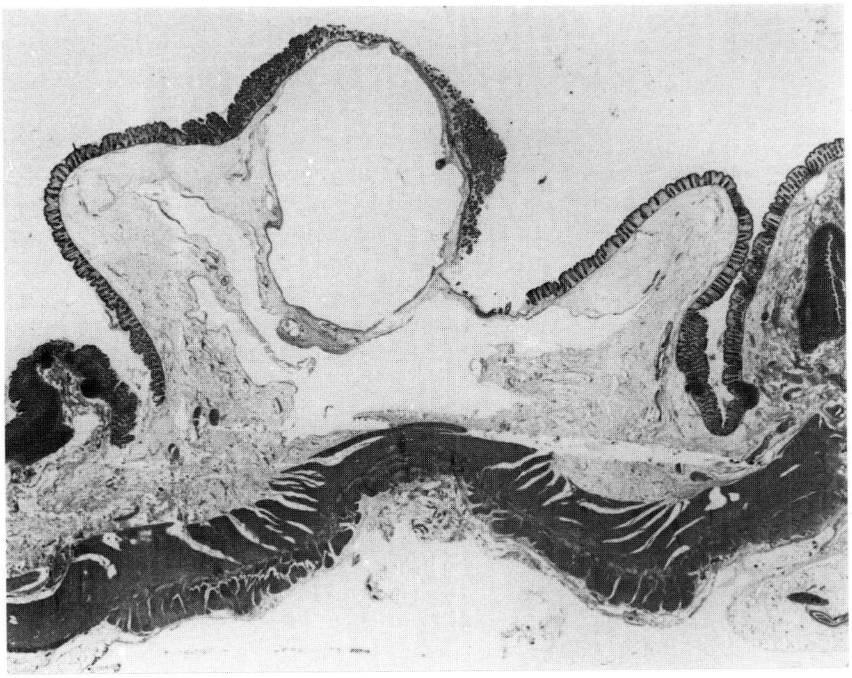

Fig. 41.31 'Cystic' colonic lymphangioma.

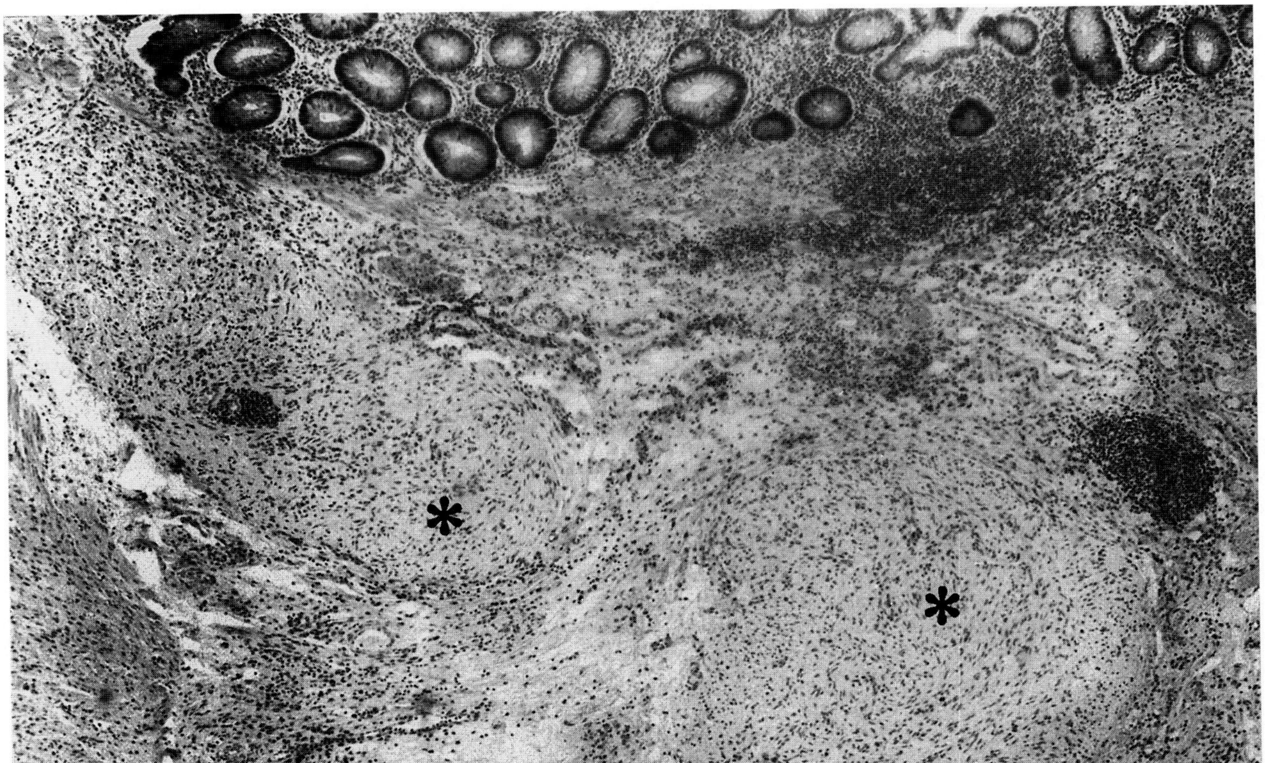

Fig. 41.32 Neurofibromatosis coli in a patient with von Recklinghausen's disease. Two neurofibromatous tumefactions can be observed in the submucosa. (H&E, ×20)

tumours are often asymptomatic. Malignant degeneration with the development of a fibromyxosarcoma is occasionally reported.[96]

Ganglioneuromatosis. Despite morphological similarities, alimentary tract involvement in neurofibromatosis should not be confused with alimentary tract ganglioneuromatosis (multiple mucosal neuromas syndrome) — a rare familial lesion, which typically occurs in the setting of multiple endocrine neoplasia (MEN type IIB) or a variant of this complex. In contrast to neurofibromatosis, lesions in ganglioneuromatosis are usually true neuromas or ganglioneuromas. Involvement of the gastrointestinal tract is a more consistent finding in MEN IIB than in NF-1. Sporadic familial cases of polypoid ganglioneuromatosis have occurred in association with adenomatous and juvenile polyposis of the large bowel. Intestinal ganglioneuromatosis has also been observed in Cowden's disease. The main symptoms of alimentary tract ganglioneuromatosis differ from those observed in neurofibromatosis. Constipation and diarrhoea are common. An association between ganglioneuromatosis and poor contractility of the colon has been demonstrated.[97–102]

Sporadic cases

Neurofibroma-schwannoma. In the earlier literature, there are occasional cases of solitary neurofibromas of the colon.[103] Although some of these cases are authentic, most would now be regarded as stromal tumours showing neural differentiation. The latter can be demonstrated by immunohistochemical staining (Fig 41.33). A malignant schwannoma arising from the sigmoid colon has been described in association with *Schistosoma japonicum*.[104]

Ganglioneuroma. Familial ganglioneuromatosis should be distinguished from the isolated ganglioneuromatosis and ganglioneuroma, for which no apparent association with thyroid or adrenal tumours is found. Ganglioneuromas are benign tumours composed of varying amounts of well differentiated ganglion cells and nerve fibres. The main proliferation is in the mucosa or submucosa. Most lesions present as a circumscribed fairly deep seated lesion, or as a superficial lesion in the mucosa and submucosa. They are often multiple, as in ganglioneuromatosis, and may present as polyps. The more diffuse lesions are rare and mainly localized in the plexus of Auerbach. They can be associated with a pronounced eosinophilic infiltrate without accompaying plasma cells. Isolated ganglioneuromatosis of the large intestine associated with the secretion of vasoactive intestinal polypeptide (VIP) has been described in a 7-year-old child.[105] Gut autonomic nerve (GAN) tumours of the colon are extremely rare.[106–107]

Granular cell tumours. The granular cell tumour is another lesion which is observed at all levels of the gastrointestinal tract but only rarely in the colon and rectum. In 1978, only 12 cases had been reported, eight of which were in the caecum and ascending colon and in three the tumours were multiple.[108] Occasionally, multiple granular cell tumours occur throughout the entire gastrointestinal tract.[109] The diameter of the colonic lesions ranged from 0.3–5 cm. The ages of the patients range from 17–73 years with an average of 52.1 years. Granular cell tumours are generally benign tumours of indefinite histogenesis. The frequent anatomic relationship of the tumour with nerve fibres, the intracellular demonstration of lipids similar to myelin-degradation products, the presence of myelin figures within the tumour cells and the histochemical identification of S-100 suggest an origin from the enteroglial cells.

TERATOMAS

True colorectal teratomas are extremely rare, but are described in the caecum, sigmoid colon and rectum in both infants and adults. A teratoid finger formation was observed in the sigmoid of a 23-year-old woman and a hairy polyp, composed of elements of all three germ layers, was removed from the sigmoid in another 76-year-old female.[110–111] Colonic teratoma can be complicated by carcinoma or be primarily malignant.[112] An example of the latter was described in the descending colon of a 41-year-old woman suffering from ulcerative colitis.[113] Care is needed in order to differentiate them from lesions secondary to ovarian teratomas and from sacrococcygeal teratomas, which are more frequent.[114]

RETRORECTAL TUMOURS

Retrorectal tumours are also uncommon and, although usually asymptomatic, occasionally cause obstructive symptoms. The author has observed one case of retrorectal teratoma associated with a presentation of thrombocytopaenic purpura. The histological picture of these tumours is very varied and the terminology used in the literature is not uniform. However, they can usually be classified broadly by origin as: congenital lesions, neurological, osseous and miscellaneous. The congenital lesions include: epidermoid cyst (with stratified epithelium but no skin appendages), mucus-secreting cysts (enterogenic cyst, cystic hamartoma), teratoma (with two or three germ cell layers), teratocarcinoma, chordoma and meningocoele.

Malignancy may occur in teratomas but is rare in other congenital cysts. It has been reported in dermoid cysts, epidermoid cysts, enterogenic cysts and rectal duplication. Neurogenic and osseous lesions include all variations of the classical neurogenic and osseous tumours. The miscellaneous group includes tumours such as lipoma, fibroma, fibrosarcoma, leiomyoma and undifferentiated sarcoma.[115] Rare cases of pararectal rhabdomyosarcoma are also reported.[116] The exact primary site of origin of these cases cannot always be determined with certainty.

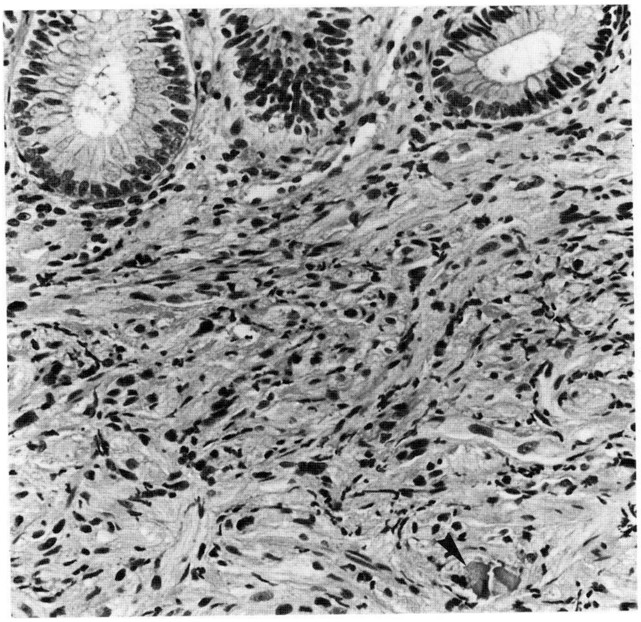

A

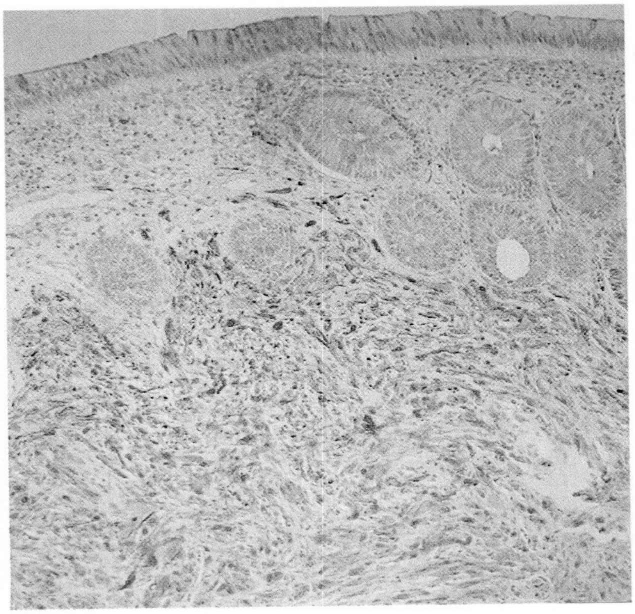

B

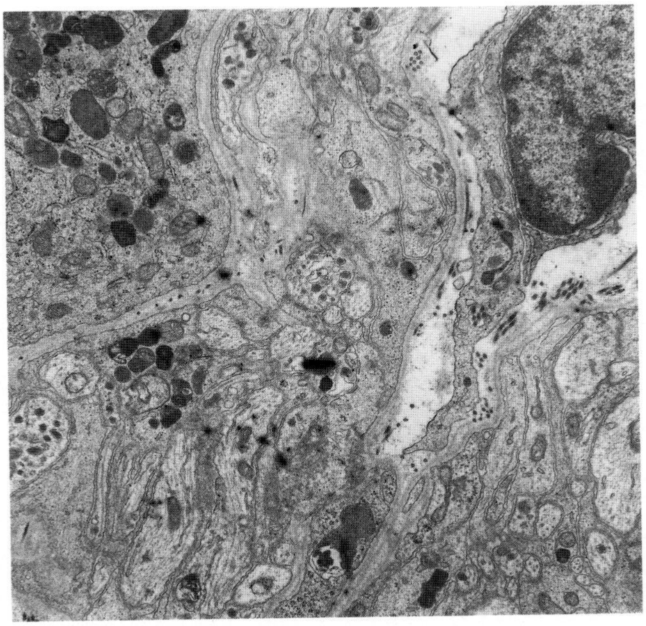

C

Fig. 41.33 Stromal tumour of the colon with 'neural' differentiation — neurofibroma. **A** Note the irregular bundles and two larger cells resembling neural cell bodies (arrow). (H&E, ×66) **B** The same lesion stained with antibodies directed against S100 protein shows diffuse positive staining. (Immunoperoxydase, ×30) **C** Electron micrograph of the lesion showing axon bundles and enteroglial elements. (×4650)

SECONDARY TUMOURS

Secondary neoplasms or metastatic lesions of the large intestine are not uncommon.[117] The routes by which they reach the colon include direct extension, intraperitoneal spread or embolization. Metastases of tumours of the ovary and breast are the most common in females, and of the gastrointestinal tract in males. Metastases of pancreas, lung and kidney tumours are not infrequent[118] (Table 41.11) (Fig 41.34). Colonic recurrence of renal cell carcinoma can present many years after nephrectomy.[119]

The macroscopic appearances are manifold and include circular or asymmetric narrowing of the lumen and one or more nodules covered by intact mucosa, but ulceration occurs as a later event. Solitary lesions are not common. Metastatic lobular carcinoma of the breast may masquerade as Crohn's disease, and metastatic renal tumours may produce bulky lesions.[120] Occasionally, metastases may occur in adenomatous polyps.[121]

The clinical differentiation from primary submucosal tumours may be difficult. Direct spread of carcinoma

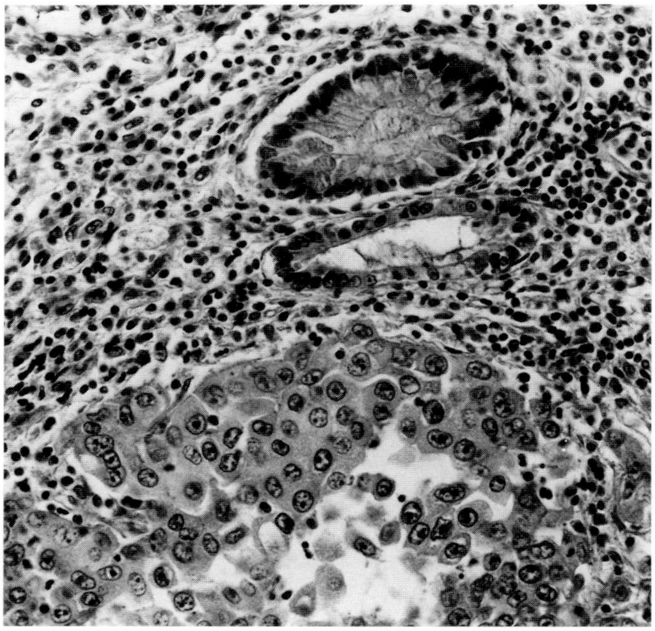

Fig. 41.34 Submucosal metastasis of a pulmonary adenocarcinoma. (H&E, ×68)

Table 4.11 Frequency of colonic metastases from various organs (origin confirmed by clinical examination and biopsy).

Organ-tissue of origin	Number (%)
Ovaries	46 (27.2%)
Stomach	19 (11.2%)
Uterus	16 (9.4%)
Breast	12 (7%)
Prostate	12 (7%)
Lung/bronchi	10 (6%)
Colon	9 (5.3%)
Unknown origin	9 (5.3%)
Cervix	7 (4.2%)
Melanoma	6 (3.5%)
Lymphoma	5 (3%)
Pancreas	5 (3%)
Urinary bladder	3 (1.7%)
Oesophagus	2 (1.2%)
Soft tissue sarcoma	2 (1.2%)
Adrenal gland	1 (0.6%)
Kidney	1 (0.6%)

(169 patients hospitalized at the Department of Gastroenterology of the University Hospital of Leuven for the investigation of radiologically established lesions in a 10 year period from 1981–91; diagnosis on endoscopic biopsies)

from the prostate, occasionally from the uterus and rarely from a mesothelioma, may simulate a primary rectal tumour.

Colonic metastases of choriocarcinoma may be a cause of haemorrhage, and encouraging therapeutic results can be achieved if a correct morphological diagnosis is established. Such metastases must be distinguished from the rare cases of primary colonic adenocarcinomas with areas of choriocarcinoma or syncytiotrophoblastic differentiation.[28,122–123] A mixed germ cell tumour, a malignant mixed Mullerian tumour and an endometrioid carcinoma are described in colonic endometriosis. In the latter case, the endometriosis was supposed to derive from ovarian endometriosis following surgery.[124–126]

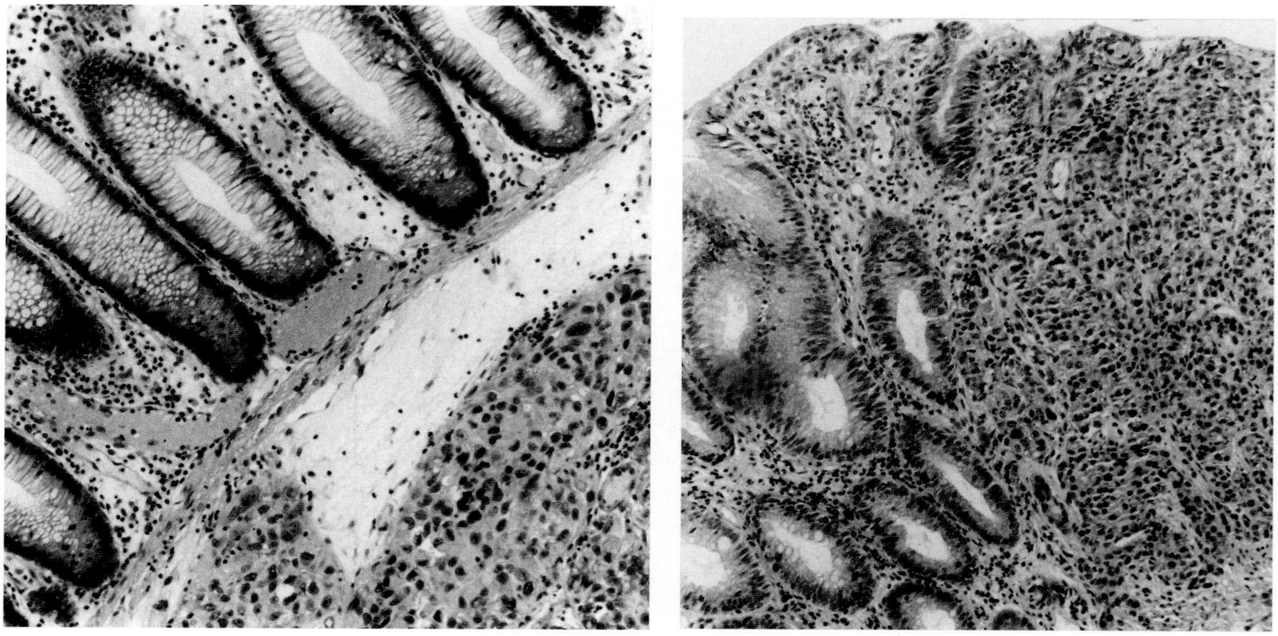

A B

Fig. 41.35A & B

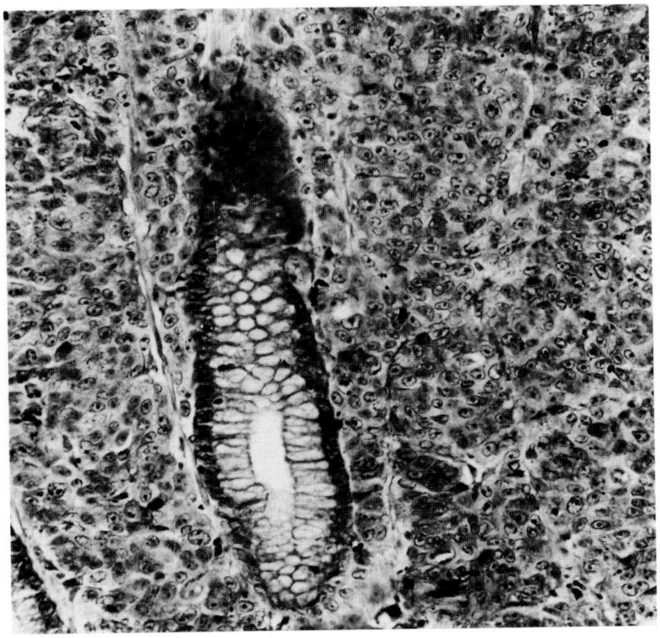

C

Fig. 41.35 Colonic metastases of malignant melanoma. The histological picture can be variable and show limited (lymphatic) invasion of the submucosa (**A**: H&E, ×39) or diffuse involvement of the lamina propria with ulceration. (**B**: H&E, ×20; **C**: H&E, ×39)

Secondary involvement of the colon may occur in lymphomas and is discussed in the chapter dealing with these malignancies (Ch. 36). Gastrointestinal complications of leukaemia are becoming more common and are due to primary invasion by leukaemic cells, an altered immune state with profound neutropaenia, or the toxicity of chemotherapy. Leukaemic bowel infiltration occurs as plaque-like thickening, raised nodular or polypoidal lesions, diffuse mucosal and submucosal infiltration with or without ulceration in almost 50% of children with acute leukaemia who die in relapse.[127–128] Colonic involvement is also reported in chronic lymphocytic leukaemia and in Sezary syndrome, a cutaneous T cell lymphoma.[129–130]

Primary melanoma of the rectum, originating in colonic type epithelium and associated with the presence of junctional melanocytes, is extremely rare.[131] Metastases from malignant melanoma in the gastrointestinal tract as a whole are not uncommon, but in the colon they are infrequent and usually asymptomatic (Fig 41.35). They were observed in only 9/55 patients (16%) with gastrointestinal metastases collected from the literature.[132–133] The lesions are often polypoid,[134] sometimes multiple, nodular or bulky and may cause abdominal pain, bleeding or obstruction.[135] Because of their varied histological appearance, it is frequently necessary to employ immunohistochemistry in order to differentiate between metastatic melanoma and other malignancies including lymphoma, undifferentiated carcinoma and neuroendocrine carcinoma.

REFERENCES

1. Palvio DHB, Sorensen FB, Klove-Mogense M. Stem cell carcinoma of the colon and rectum. Dis Colon Rectum 1985; 28: 440–445.
2. Al-Sam SZ, Davies JD, Gibbs NM. Anomalous functional and behavioural characteristics of undifferentiated carcinomas of large bowel. J Pathol 1986; 148: 119A.
3. Jessurun J, Romero-Guadarama M, Manivel JC. Cecal poorly differentiated adenocarcinoma, medullary type. Lab invest 1992; 66: 43A.
4. Gaffey MJ, Mills SE, Lack EE. Neuroendocrine carcinoma of the colon: a clinicopathological, ultrastructural, and immunohistochemical study of 24 cases. Am J Surg Pathol 1990; 14: 1010–1023.
5. Al-Doroubi QI, Petrelli M, Reid JD. Adenoacanthoma of the sigmoid colon: report of a case. Dis Colon Rectum 1970; 13: 390–393.
6. Strate RW, Richardson JD, Bannyan GA. Basosquamous (transitional cloacogenic) carcinoma of the sigmoid colon. Cancer 1977; 40: 1234–1239.
7. Rubio CA, Collins VP, Berg C. Mixed adenosquamous carcinoma of the cecum: report of a case and review of the literature. Dis Colon Rectum 1981; 24: 301–304.
8. Peonim V, Thakerugpol K, Pacharee P, Stitnimaukarn T. Adenosquamous carcinoma and carcinoidal differentiation of the colon. Cancer 1983; 52: 1122–1125.
9. Mills SE, Allen MS, Cohen AR. Small-cell undifferentiated carcinoma of the colon: a clinicopathological study of five cases and their association with colonic adenomas. Am J Surg Pathol 1983; 7: 643–651.
10. Cerezo L, Alvarez M, Edwards O, Price G. Adenosquamous carcinoma of the colon. Dis Colon Rectum 1985; 28: 597–603.
11. Weidner N, Zekan P. Carcinosarcoma of the colon: report of a unique case with light and immunohistochemical studies. Cancer 1986; 58: 1126–1130.
12. Wick MR, Weatherby RP, Weiland LH. Small cell neuroendocrine carcinoma of the colon and rectum: clinical, histologic, and ultrastructural study and immunohistochemical comparison with cloacogenic carcinoma. Hum Pathol 1987; 18: 9–21.
13. Bak M, Teglbjaerg PS. Pleomorphic (giant cell) carcinoma of the intestine: an immunohistochemical and electron microscopic study. Cancer 1989; 64: 2557–2564.
14. Bates HR, Belter LP. Composite carcinoid tumor (argentaffinoma-adenocarcinoma) of the colon. Dis Colon Rectum 1967; 10: 467–470.
15. Moyana TN, Qizilbash AH, Murphy F. Composite glandular-carcinoid tumors of the colon and rectum: report of two cases. Am J Surg Pathol 1988; 12: 607–611.
16. Gibbs NM. Incidence and significance of argentaffin and Paneth cells in some tumours of the large intestine. J Clin Pathol 1967; 20: 826–831.
17. Isaacson P. Crypt cell carcinoma of the appendix (so-called adenocarcinoid tumor). Am J Surg Pathol 1981; 5: 213–224.
18. Drut R. Argyrophil mucus-secreting adenocarcinoma of the colon and sebocystomatosis. Dis Colon Rectum 1974; 17: 700–704.
19. Shousha S. Signet-ring cell adenocarcinoma of rectum: a histological, histochemical and electron microscopic study. Histopathology 1982; 6: 341–350.
20. Ulich TR, Cheng L, Glover H, Yang K, Lewin KJ. A colonic adenocarcinoma with argentaffin cells: an immunoperoxidase study demonstrating the presence of numerous neuroendocrine products. Cancer 1983; 51: 1483–1489.

21. Jewell LD, Barr JR, McCaughey WTE, Nguyen CK, Owen DA. Clear-cell epithelial neoplasms of the large intestine. Arch Pathol Lab Med 1988; 112: 197–199.
22. Petrelli M, Tetango E, Reid JD. Carcinoma of the colon with undifferentiated, carcinoid and squamous cell features. Am J Clin Pathol 1981; 75: 581–584.
23. Damjanov I, Amenta PS, Bosman FT. Undifferentiated carcinoma of the colon containing exocrine, neuroendocrine and squamous cells. Virchows Arch (A) 1983; 401: 57–66.
24. Lewin KJ, Ulich T, Yang K, Layfield L. The endocrine cells of the gastrointestinal tract. Pathology Annual 1986; Part II: 181–215.
25. Holmes EJ. Neoplastic Paneth cells. Their occurrence in two adenomas and one carcinoma of the colon. Cancer 1965; 18: 1416–1422.
26. Subbuswamy SG. Paneth cells and goblet cells. J Pathol 1973; 111: 181–189.
27. Shousha P. Paneth cell-rich papillary adenocarcinoma and a mucoid adenocarcinoma occurring synchronously in colon: a light and electron microscopic study. Histopathology 1979; 3: 489–501.
28. Kubosawa H, Nagao K, Kondo Y, Ishiga H, Inaba N. Coexistence of adenocarcinoma and choriocarcinoma in the sigmoid colon. Cancer 1984; 54: 866–868.
29. Johnston EV, Dockerty MB, Dixon CF. Cylindroma of rectum. Proc Staff Meet Mayo Clin 1953; 28: 729–735.
30. Orda R, Bawniuk JB, Wiznitzer T, Schuyman E. Fibroma of the cecum: report of a case. Dis Colon Rectum 1976; 19: 626–628.
31. Fayemi AO, Toker C. Gastrointestinal fibroma. Am J Gastroenterol 1974; 62: 250–254.
32. Hoeffel JC, Weryha B, Dally P, Aymard B. Aspects scanographiques des tumeurs du colon a developpement extra-muqueux peripherique. J Radiol 1986; 67: 137–140.
33. Kopass P. Inflammatory pseudotumours of the cecum. Am J Surg 1965; 109: 513–518.
34. Johnstone JM, Morson BC. Inflammatory fibroid polyp of the gastrointestinal tract. Histopathology 1978; 2: 349–361.
35. Harned RK, Buck JL, Shekitka KM. Inflammatory fibroid polyps of the gastrointestinal tract: radiologic evaluation. Radiology 1992; 182: 863–866.
36. Anthony PP, Morris DS, Vowler KDJ. Multiple and recurrent inflammatory fibroid polyps in three generations of a Devon family: a new syndrome. Gut 1984; 25: 854–862.
37. Hayashi K, Ohtsuki Y, Sonobe H, Iwata J, Furihata M, Hikita T, Kishino T, Akagi T. Pre-elastofibroma-like colonic polyp: another cause of colonic polyp. Acta Med Okayama 1991; 45: 49–53.
38. Bassler A, Peters AG. Fibrosarcoma, an unusual complication of ulcerative colitis. Report of a case. Arch Surg 1949; 59: 227–231.
39. Hoehn JI, Hamilton GH, Beltass E. Fibrosarcoma of the colon. J Surg Oncol 1980; 13: 223–225.
40. Bonser RS, McMaster P, Acland PR, Parratt J. Fibrosarcoma of the transverse colon. J Surg Oncol 1986; 31: 34–35.
41. Eshun-Wilson K. Malignant giant-cell tumour of the colon. Acta Pathol Microbiol Immunol Scand (A) 1973; 81: 137–144.
42. Verma P, Chandra U, Bhatia PS. Malignant histiocytoma of the rectum: report of a case. Dis Colon Rectum 1979; 22: 179–182.
43. Levinson MM, Tsang D. Multicentric malignant fibrous histiocytoma of the colon: report of a case and review of the subject. Dis Colon Rectum 1982; 25: 327–331.
44. Sewell R, Levine BA, Harrison GK, Tio F, Schwesinger WH. Primary malignant fibrous histiocytoma of the intestine. Dis Colon Rectum 1980; 23: 198–201.
45. Spagnoli LG, Dell'Isola C, Sportelli G, Mauriello A, Rizzo IF, Casciani CU. Primary malignant fibrous histiocytoma of storiform pleomorphic type: a case report of an ano-rectal localization. Tumori 1984; 70: 567–570.
46. Waxman M, Faegenburg D, Waxman JS, Janelli DE. Malignant fibrous histiocytoma of the colon associated with diverticulitis. Dis Colon Rectum 1983; 26: 339–343.
47. Morimatsu M, Shirozu K, Nakashima T, Fujimi T, Isomoto H. Xanthogranuloma of rectum. Acta Pathol Jpn 1985; 35: 165–171.
48. Ackerman NB, Chugtai SQ. Symptomatic lipomas of the gastrointestinal tract. Surg Gynecol Obstet 1975; 141: 565–568.
49. Sahai DB, Palmer JD, Hampson LG. Submucosal lipomas of the large bowel. Can J Surg 1968; 11: 23–26.
50. Haller JD, Roberts TW. Lipomas of the colon: a clinicopathologic study of 40 cases. Surgery 1964; 55: 773–781.
51. Geboes K, De Wolf-Peeters C, Rutgeerts P, Vantrappen G, Desmet V. Submucosal tumours of the colon: experience with twenty-five cases. Dis Colon Rectum 1978; 21: 420–425.
52. Godenne GD, Burk EC, Hallenbeck GA. Epiploic lipomatosis. Report of a case. Mayo Clin Proc 1957; 32: 370–372.
53. Swain VAJ, Young WF, Pringle EM. Hypertrophy of the appendices epiploicae and lipomatous polyposis of the colon. Gut 1969; 10: 587–589.
54. Snover DC. Atypical lipomas of the colon. Dis Colon Rectum 1984; 27: 485–488.
55. Van Damme J. Angiolipome du colon. Acta gastro-enterologica Belgica 1964; 27: 750–757.
56. Hikasa Y, Narabayashi T, Yamamura M, Fukuda Y, Tanida N, Tamura K, Ohno T, Shimoyama T, Nishigami T. Angiomyolipoma of the colon: a new entity in colonic polypoid lesions. Gastroenterol Jpn 1989; 24: 407–409.
57. Valdes-Dapena AM, Stein GA. Morphologic Pathology of the Alimentary Canal. Philadelphia: Saunders, 1970.
58. Lyon DT, Mantea AG. Large-bowel hemangiomas. Dis Colon Rectum 1984; 27: 404–414.
59. Van Gompel A, Rutgeerts P, Geboes K. Vascular malformation of the colon. Colo-proctology 1984; 6: 247–253.
60. Masterson J, Woods D, Lau G, Dobranowski J. Isolated colonic hemangioma. Can Assoc Radiol J 1991; 42: 431–434.
61. Lamesch AJ. An unusual hamartomatous malformation of the rectosigmoid presenting as an irreducible rectal prolapse and necessitating rectosigmoid resection in a 14-week-old infant. Dis Colon Rectum 1983; 26: 452–457.
62. Lott BD. Granuloma pyogenicum of the rectum. Dis Colon Rectum 1966; 9: 58–60.
63. Panitch VM, Pikren E. Campylobacter colitis: unique colonoscopic findings mimicking carcinoma of the transverse colon. Gastrointest Endosc 1983; 29: 32–33.
64. Mills CS, Lloyd TV, Van Aman ME, Lucas J. Diffuse hemangiomatosis of the colon. J Clin Gastroenterol 1985; 7: 416–421.
65. Harned RK, Doby CA, Farley GE. Cavernous hemangioma of the rectum and appendix. Dis Colon Rectum 1974; 17: 759–762.
66. Newman SL, Goodwin CD. Colonic hemangioma in childhood. Clin Pediatr 1984; 23: 584–585.
67. Reinhart WH, Staubli M, Mordasini C, Scheurer U. Abnormalities of gut vessels in Turner's syndrome. Postgrad Med J 1983; 59: 122–124.
68. Mellish RWP. Multiple hemangiomas of the gastrointestinal tract in children. Am J Surg 1971; 12: 412–417.
69. Matsuhashi N, Nakagama H, Moriya K, Ohnishi S, Gunji T, Saito T, Sugano K, Imawari M, Takaku F, Minami M. Multiple diffuse hemangioma of the large intestine. Gastroenterol Jpn 1991; 26: 654–660.
70. Murray-Lyon IM, Doyle D, Phillpot RM, Porter NH. Haemangiomatosis of the small and large bowel with histological malignant change. J Pathol 1971; 105: 295–297.
71. Morris L, Lynch PM, Gleason WA, Schauder C, Pinkel D, Duvic M. Blue rubber bleb nevus syndrome: laser photocoagulation of colonic hemangiomas in a child with microcytic anemia. Pediatr Dermatol 1992; 9: 91–94.
72. Sandhu KS, Cohen H, Radin R, Buck FS. Blue rubber bleb nevus sydnrome presenting with recurrences. Dig Dis Sci 1987; 32: 214–219.
73. Gandolfi L, Rossi A, Stasi G, Tonti R. The Klippel-Trenaunay syndrome with colonic hemangioma. Gastrointest Endosc 1987; 33: 442–445.
74. Barua R. Glomus tumor of the colon: first reported case. Dis Colon Rectum 1988; 31: 138–140.
75. Genter B, Mir R, Strauss R, Flint G, Levin L, Lowry R. Hemangiopericytoma of the colon: report of a case and review of literature. Dis Colon Rectum 1982; 25: 149–156.
76. Saito R, Bedetti CD, Caines MJ, Kramer K. Malignant

epithelioid hemangioendothelioma of the colon: report of a case. Dis Colon Rectum 1987; 30: 707–711.
77. Taxy JB, Battifora H. Angiosarcoma of the gastrointestinal tract: a report of three cases. Cancer 1988; 62: 210–216.
78. Smith JA, Bhatal PS, Cuthbertson AM. Angiosarcoma of the colon: report of a case with long-term survival. Dis Colon Rectum 1990; 33: 330–333.
79. Hofman P, Bernard JL, Michiels JF, Saint Paul MC, Rampal A. Angiosarcome primitif du colon: etude anatomo-clinique a propos d'un cas. Ann Pathol 1991; 11: 25–30.
80. Ben-Izhak O, Kerner H, Brenner B, Lichtig C. Angiosarcoma of the colon developing in a capsule of a foreign body: report of a case with associated hemorrhagic diathesis. Am J Clin Pathol 1992; 97: 416–420.
81. Friedman SL, Wright TL, Altman DF. Gastrointestinal Kaposi's sarcoma in patients with acquired immunodeficiency syndrome. Endoscopic and autopsy findings. Gastroenterology 1985; 89: 102–108.
82. Saltz RK, Kurtz RC, Lightdale CJ, Myskowski P, Cunningham-Rundles S, Urmacher C, Safai B. Kaposi's sarcoma: gastrointestinal involvement correlation with skin findings and immunologic function. Dig Dis Sci 1984; 29: 817–823.
83. Rotterdam H. The pathology of the gastrointestinal tract in AIDS. Digestive Disease Pathology, vol II. New York: Springe Berlin 1989; p 21–38.
84. Tavassolic H, Mir-Madjlessi SH, Sadr-Amali MA. The endoscopic demonstration of Kaposi's sarcoma of the colon. Gastrointest Endosc 1983; 29: 331–332.
85. Puy-Montbrun T, Pigot F, Vuong PN, Ganansia R, Denis J. Kaposi's sarcoma of the colon in a young HIV-negative woman with Crohn's disease. Dig Dis Sci 1991; 36: 528–531.
86. Gordon HW, Rywlin AM. Kaposi's sarcoma of the large intestine associated with ulcerative colitis. Gastroenterology 1966; 50: 248–253.
87. Adlersberg R. Kaposi's sarcoma complicating ulcerative colitis. Am J Clin Pathol 1970; 54: 143–146.
88. Thompson GB, Pemberton JH, Morris S, Bustamante Ma, Delong B, Carpenter HA, Wright AJ. Kaposi's sarcoma of the colon in a young HIV-negative man with chronic ulcerative colitis: report of a case. Dis Colon Rectum 1989; 32: 73–76.
89. Kuroda J, Katok H, Ohsato K. Cystic lymphangioma of the colon. Dis Colon Rectum 1984; 27: 679–682.
90. Girdwood TG, Philip LD. Lymphatic cysts of the colon. Gut 1971; 12: 933–935.
91. Russo A, Virgilio C, Belluardo NB. A case of lymphangioma of the colon. Gastrointest Endosc 1983; 29: 253.
92. Bottger Th, Schroder D, Hoer PW. Cystic lymphangioma of the caecum — a rare benign tumour of the colon. Colo-proctology 1985; 7: 26–29.
93. Fuller CE, Williams GT. Gastrointestinal manifestations of type 1 neurofibromatosis (von Recklinghausen's disease). Histopathology 1991; 19: 1–11.
94. Raszkowski HJ, Hufner RF. Neurofibromatosis of the colon: a unique manifestation of von Recklinghausen's disease. Cancer 1971; 27: 134–142.
95. Uehara T, Matsubara O, Kasuga T, Kamiyama R, Imashiro M, Utsunomiya J. Ganglioneuromatosis with carcinoid foci in the large bowel. Gan No Rinsho 1985; 31: 997–1004.
96. Hochberg FH, Dasilva AB, Galdabini J, Richardson EP. Gastrointestinal involvement in von Recklinghausen's neurofibromatosis. Neurology 1974; 24: 1144–1151.
97. Carney JA, Hayles AB. Alimentary tract manifestation of multiple endocrine neoplasia, Type 2B. Mayo Clin Proc 1977; 52: 543–548.
98. Hegstrom JL, Kircher T. Alimentary tract ganglioneuromatosis-lipomatosis, adrenal myelolipomas, pancreatic telangiectasias, and multiple thyroid goiter. Am J Clin Pathol 1985; 83: 744–747.
99. Mendelsohn B, Diamond MP. Familial ganglioneuromatosis polyposis of the large bowel. Am J Surg Pathol 1984; 8: 515–520.
100. Weidner N, Flanders DJ, Mitros FA. Mucosal ganglioneuromatosis associated with multiple colonic polyps. Am J Surg Pathol 1984; 8: 779–786.
101. Lashner BA, Riddell RH, Winans CS. Ganglioneuromatosis of the colon and extensive glycogenic acanthosis in Cowden's disease. Dig Dis Sci 1986; 31: 215–216.
102. Normann T, Olmer B. Intestinal ganglioneuromatosis, diarrhoea and medullary thyroid carcinoma. Scand J Gastroenterol 1969; 4: 553–559.
103. Vexler L, Cordon-Tarabuta G, Galesanu MR, Tanciu N. Schwannome du caecum. Lyon Chir 1967; 63: 261–264.
104. Schwartz DA. Malignant schwannoma occurring with Schistosoma japonicum: a case report. Southeast Asian J Trop Med Public Health 1982; 13: 601–605.
105. Rescorla FJ, Vane DW, Fitzgerald JF, et al. Vasoactive intestinal polypeptide-secreting ganglioneuromatosis affecting the entire colon and rectum. J Pediat Surg 1988; 23: 635–637.
106. Dvorak A. Gut autonomic nerve (GAN) tumors. Digestive Disease Pathology, vol II. New York: Springer Berlin, 1989; 49–66.
107. Herrera GA, Cerezo L, Jones JE, Sack J, Grizzle WE, Pollack WJ, Lott RL. Gastrointestinal Autonomic Nerve Tumors: plexosarcomas. Arch Pathol Lab Med 1989; 113: 846–856.
108. Kanabe S, Watanabe I, Lotuaco L. Multiple granular-cell tumours of the ascending colon: microscopic study. Dis Colon Rectum 1978; 21: 322–328.
109. Fried KS, Arden JL, Gouge TH, Balthazar EJ. Multifocal granular cell tumors of the gastrointestinal tract. Am J Gastroenterol 1984; 79: 751–755.
110. Dutz W, Sadeghee S. A teratoid finger in the sigmoid colon. J Pathol Bacteriol 1968; 95: 289–291.
111. Mauer K, Waye JD, Lewis BS, Szporn AH. The hairy polyp: a benign teratoma of the colon. Endoscopy 1989; 21: 148–151.
112. Russell P. Carcinoma complicating a benign teratoma of the rectum: report of a case. Dis Colon Rectum 1974; 17: 550–553.
113. Zalatnai A, Dubecz S, Harka I, Banhidy F. Malignant teratoma of the left colon associated with chronic ulcerative colitis. Virchows Arch (A) 1987; 411: 61–65.
114. Kommoss F, Emond J, Hast J, Talerman A. Ruptured mature cystic teratoma of the ovary with recurrence in the liver and colon 17 years later: a case report. J Reprod Med 1990; 35: 827–831.
115. Jao SW, Beart RW, Spencer RJ, Reiman MH, Ilstrup DM. Retrorectal tumors. Dis Colon Rectum 1985; 28: 644–652.
116. Pack GT, Miller TR, Trinidad SS. Pararectal rhabdomyosarcoma. Dis Colon Rectum 1963; 6: 1–6.
117. Wigh R, Tapley N. Metastatic lesions to the large intestine. Radiology 1958; 70: 222–228.
118. Khilnam MT, Marshak RM, Eliasoph J, Wolf BS. Roentgen features of metastases to the colon. AJR 1966; 96: 302–310.
119. Thomason PA, Peterson LS, Staniunas RJ. Solitary colonic metastasis from renal-cell carcinoma 17 years after nephrectomy: report of a case. Dis Colon Rectum 1991; 34: 709–712.
120. Weisberg A. Metastatic adenocarcinoma of the breast masquerading as Crohn's disease of the colon. Am J Proctol Gastroenterol Col Rect Surg 1982; 33: 10–15.
121. Tiszlavicz L. Stomach cancer metastasizing into a solitary adenomatous colonic polyp. Orv Hetil 1990; 131: 1259–1261.
122. Nguyen GK. Adenocarcinoma of the sigmoid colon with focal choriocarcinoma metaplasia. Dis Colon Rectum 1982; 25: 230–234.
123. Metz KA, Richter HJ, Leder LD. Adenocarcinoma of colon with syncytiothrophoblastic differentiation: differential diagnosis and implications. Pathol Res Pract 1985; 179: 419–424.
124. Amano S, Yamada N. Endometrioid carcinoma arising from endometriosis of the sigmoid colon: a case report. Hum Pathol 1981; 12: 845–848.
125. Lankerami MR, Aubrey RW, Reid JD. Endometriosis of the colon with mixed 'germ cell' tumour. Am J Clin Pathol 1982; 78: 555–559.
126. Chumas JC, Thanning L, Mann WJ. Malignant mixed Mullerian tumor arising in extragenital endometriosis: report of a case and review of the literature. Gynecol Onc 1986; 23: 227–233.
127. Cornes JS, Gwynfor Jones T. Leukaemic lesions of the gastrointestinal tract. J Clin Pathol 1962; 15: 305–313.
128. Hunter TB, Bjelland JC. Gastrointestinal complications of leukemia and its treatment. AJR 1984; 142: 513–518.

129. Tucker J, Cachia PG. Gastrointestinal bleeding due to large bowel infiltration by chronic lymphocytic leukaemia. Postgrad Med J 1986; 62: 45–46.
130. Cohen MI, Widerlite LW, Schechter GP, Jaffe E, Fischmann AB, Schein PS, MacDonald JS. Gastrointestinal involvement in the Sezary syndrome. Gastroenterology 1977; 73: 145–149.
131. Werdin C, Limas C, Knodell RG. Primary malignant melanoma of the rectum: evidence for origination from rectal mucosal melanocytes. Cancer 1988; 61: 1364–1370.
132. Geboes K, De Jaeger E, Rutgeerts P, Vantrappen G. Symptomatic gastrointestinal metastases from malignant melanoma. J Clin Gastroenterol 1988; 10: 64–70.
133. Silverman JM, Hamlin JA. Large melanoma metastases to the gastrointestinal tract. Gut 1989: 30: 1783–1785.
134. Sacks BA, Joffe N, Antonioli DA. Metastatic melanoma presenting clinically as multiple colonic polyps. AJR 1977; 129: 511–513.
135. Jorge E, Harvey MA, Simmonds MA, Lipton A, Joehl RJ. Symptomatic malignant melanoma of the gastrointestinal tract: operative treatment and survival. An Surg 1984; 199: 328–331.

CHAPTER

42

Other tumours of the appendix

R. A. Williams

The vermiform appendix arises as an outpouching of the caecum and, although it has some features of the distal small intestine, it has an overall structure common to the colon, with an epithelium of colonic type.[1] Thus the range of proliferative lesions, both epithelial and non-epithelial, arising in the appendix is similar to those in other parts of the colon. The presentation and macroscopic appearances, however, are modified by the relatively small intraluminal volume.[2,3]

Thorough examination of a specimen removed either at appendicectomy, or in conjunction with a resection of the large bowel, is necessary. Small tumours will be missed unless this is carried out.[2] In the case where appendiceal tumours are found, sections taken from the neck of the appendix must include the surgical resection margin.

NON-CARCINOID EPITHELIAL TUMOURS

Benign non-carcinoid epithelial tumours of the appendix are uncommon lesions with an incidence of 1–2% of resected specimens. Adenocarcinomas are seen even more rarely and account for only 0.3%.

Until the time of the publication of the classic paper concerning these tumours by Higa et al,[3] it was usual to make reference to the appendiceal 'mucocele' or 'malignant mucocele'. This term is descriptive of the secondary phenomenon of luminal distension rather than of the underlying epithelial pathology. In 'evaluating' the appendiceal mucocele, attention was focused on the underlying mucosal lesion, because of the pathogenetic and prognostic implications.[3] Thus, as a pathological diagnosis, the term 'mucocele' was discredited. It was also emphasized that appendiceal neoplastic mucosal pathology had its counterparts in the colonic mucosa. The most recent reappraisals and classification of non-carcinoid epithelial tumours of the appendix recognized this.[2,4,5] Nevertheless, it is still in vogue to use the terms cystadenoma or cystadenocarcinoma. These are now sometimes applied to epithelial tumours of the appendix which were formerly referred to as mucoceles. It implies that the formation of one or more cysts is an integral part of the growth pattern of these tumours, such as is seen in cystadenomas of the ovary. However, the use of the prefix 'cyst-' refers to the mucinous distension of the appendiceal lumen, and this is not necessarily a feature. It has been recommended that this terminology be abandoned.[2]

Macroscopic appearance

The macroscopic appearance of appendices with epithelial proliferative lesions may be normal, or there may be inflammatory changes, and in a percentage of cases the appendix is obviously enlarged and expanded. Therefore the external width of the appendix is not a reliable guide to the presence of an underlying mucosal lesion in many cases. When distension of the lumen (the 'cyst' or 'mucocele') is present, it is a function of the production of an excess of altered mucin in a confined space. Rarely, thickened epithelium may be noticed on macroscopic examination, but it is difficult, if not impossible, to differentiate from the thickened and oedematous mucosa seen in cases of uncomplicated acute appendicitis. Fenoglio-Preiser, Pascal and Perzin have described small sessile tan coloured elevations of the mucosa in some cases of localized hyperplastic polyps in the appendix.[5] Nevertheless, it is extremely rare for polypoid lesions, such as those shown in Figure 42.4, to be present.

Microscopic appearance

A classification of non-carcinoid epithelial tumours of the appendix, based on microscopic findings, is set out in Table 42.1. This incorporates all of the described proliferative lesions, including the mixed adenomatous and hyperplastic proliferation, which is not uncommonly seen in the colon.[2] It is adaptable to include rarer variants of adenocarcinomas, such as predominantly signet-ring cell adenocarcinomas, superficial spreading adenocarcinomas and the so-called 'adeno-acanthoma' of the appendix.[6,7]

The terms 'mucocele' and 'cystadenoma' are avoided in the classification for the reasons discussed above. The adjectives localized or diffuse, and flat, villous or polypoid are used to describe the extent and growth pattern of the lesions, as there is no evidence that the surface growth pattern affects the behaviour of the tumour. The differences often represent effects of compression due to the confined intraluminal volume. If distension of the lumen is present, then the phrase 'with (or without) mucinous distension of the lumen', following the description of the epithelial lesion, is preferable to other designations used in the past, again to avoid any confusion or misconceptions which might be conveyed.

Recently, the separation of mixed adenomatous/hyperplastic lesions from adenomas has been questioned,[5] as they would be expected to behave biologically in the same basic way as adenomas, and have the same potential to follow the adenoma-carcinoma sequence. The nature of these lesions in the large intestine is still the subject of debate,[5,8] and the alternative designation of 'serrated adenoma' may be preferable. However, as these tumours have been described in the appendix, and until studies of proliferative markers have satisfactorily demonstrated whether or not two separate epithelial proliferations are present in these lesions, it is preferable that they be included in a separate category in the classification.

Similarly, in a review of the literature and examination of a large number of non-carcinoid epithelial tumours of the appendix, Appelman[9] has questioned the nature of the hyperplastic lesions. He states that, in his experience, many of the hyperplastic lesions described in the appendix do not show all of the features of hyperplastic polyps of the colon, most notable being the absence of the slightly thickened subepithelial plate seen in these tumours in the colon. There is, however, some doubt as to whether this phenomenon is related to the age of the tumour and, if this is so, with the lesions growing in the confined space of the appendiceal lumen being more likely to cause symptoms at an earlier stage of development, they are more likely to be removed before any age related changes have developed. Appelman also proposes that many of these lesions are, in fact, adenomas because of the differences in morphology he noted. This is obviously an area where more investigation on larger series is needed before further definitive statements can be made.

The practical importance of differentiating between these lesions is the implication for further treatment should any residual adenomatous mucosa be found at the surgical resection margin following appendicectomy. The histological criteria we have found reliable in differentiating the lesions is discussed below.

In cases where flattened epithelium lines the appendix, this epithelium should be examined for cytological abnormalities. When only granulation tissue lines the lumen, it is not possible to postulate or exclude the pre-existence of a proliferative epithelial tumour. Therefore another aetiology for the mucinous distension should be sought, as the phenomenon has been described secondary to obstruction of the neck of the appendix by scar tissue and other non-epithelial lesions, e.g. localized endometriotic deposits.[10]

Table 42.1 Non-carcinoid epithelial tumours of the appendix — classification.

	Localization	Pattern
Benign		
Adenoma		
Hyperplasia		
Mixed adenoma/ hyperplasia (serrated adenoma)	Localized or diffuse	Flat, villous or polypoid
Malignant		
Adenocarcinoma		
Mucinous adenocarcinoma		

Histological appearance

Adenomatous lesions

Lesions in this group show the same features as are seen in the range of tubulovillous adenomas in the colon. They exhibit the same degree of mixtures of tubular and villous configuration, accompanied by variable nuclear enlargement, pleomorphism, hyperchromasia, increased nuclear to cytoplasmic ratio, stratification and crowding of cells, an altered pattern of mucin secretion and the presence of mitotic figures at any level of the lesion, even at the surface (Fig. 42.1).

Hyperplastic lesions

These lesions resemble hyperplastic polyps of the colon, with mitotic activity confined to the cells in the lower half of the glands, and a normal population in their superficial portions. The lesions do not show any of the cytological abnormalities seen in adenomatous lesions, but the proportion of so-called absorptive cells in the typically convo-

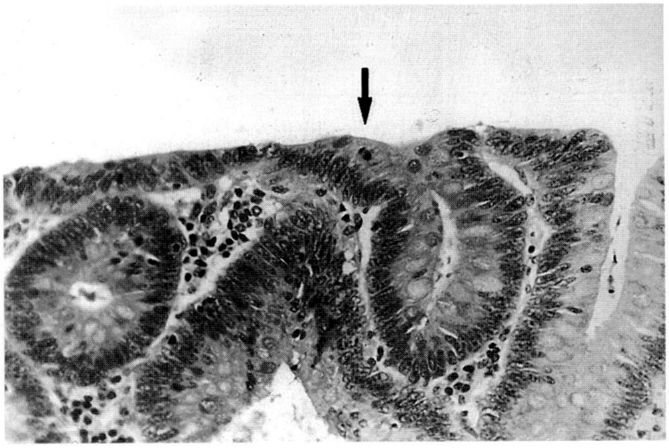

Fig. 42.1 Adenomatous appendiceal mucosa. Lack of surface maturation is obvious, with nuclear stratification and atypia. A mitotic figure (arrow) is seen at the luminal surface. (H&E, ×238)

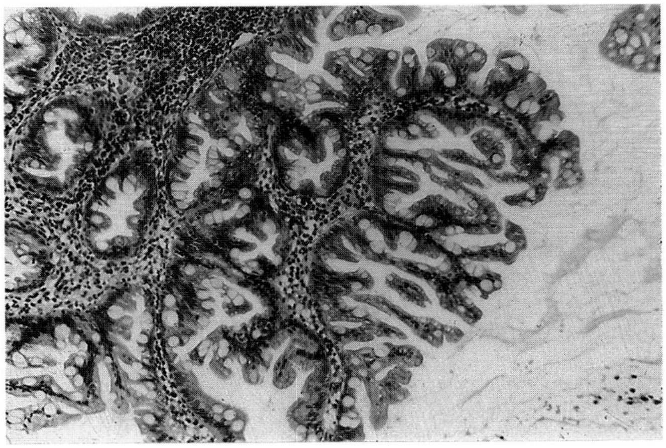

Fig. 42.3 Higher power photomicrograph of the hyperplastic lesion shown in Figure 42.2. Convolution of the glands is evident and maturation of the epithelium towards the surface is seen. (H&E, ×106)

luted glands may be increased at the expense of goblet cells (Figs 42.2, 42.3).

True hyperplastic lesions need to be differentiated from the transitional type of mucosa which may be seen adjacent to adenomatous/carcinomatous lesions elsewhere in the colon, as discussed below.

Mixed adenomatous/hyperplastic lesions

Both adenomatous and hyperplastic glandular epithelium are seen in the same tumour (Figs 42.4, 42.5). There are no studies presently available to show whether the hyperplastic epithelium seen in these lesions is of the type seen in hyperplastic polyps in the colon, or whether it is entrapped 'transitional' appendiceal epithelium of the type seen adjacent to colonic adenomas and adenocarcinomas. The author has seen one example of the latter type of

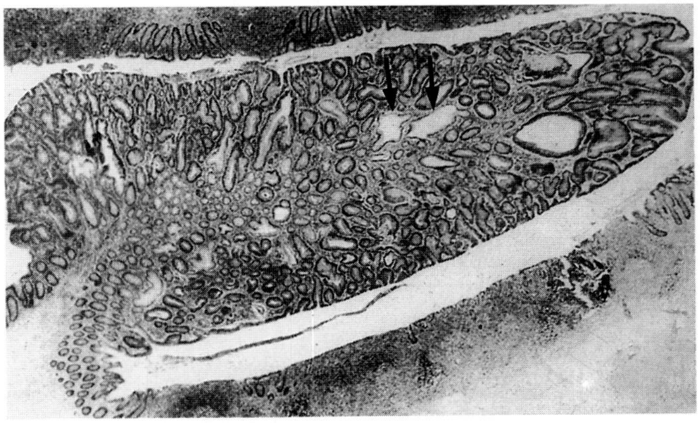

Fig. 42.4 Polypoid mucosal lesion with predominantly adenomatous glands. Paler staining glands with features seen in hyperplastic lesions are present (arrows). (H&E, ×17.5)

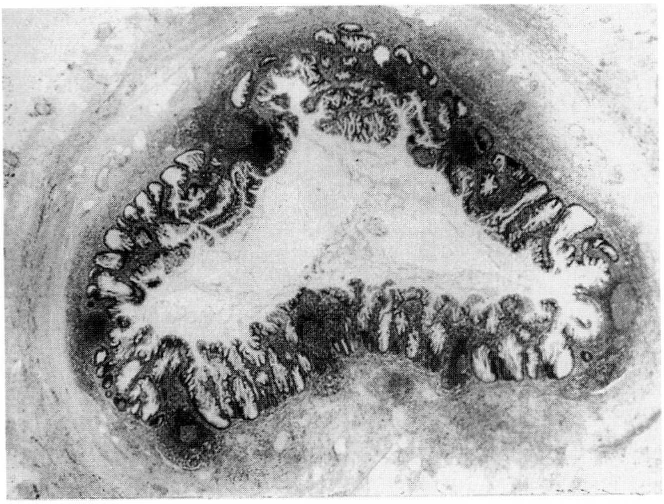

Fig. 42.2 Circumferential hyperplastic lesion. Note the typically convoluted glands and the minimal luminal distension. (H&E, ×13)

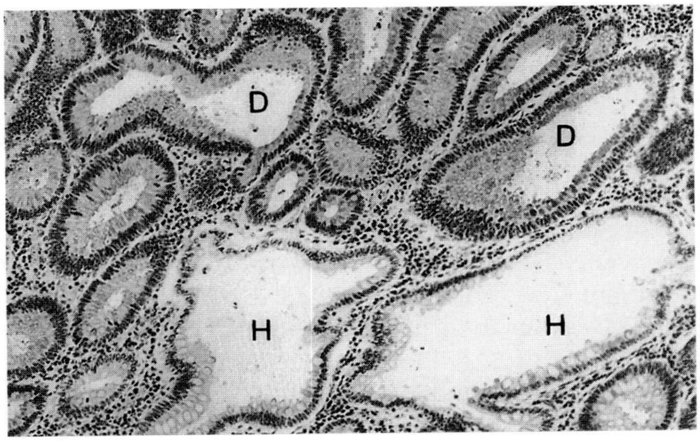

Fig. 42.5 Higher power view of the glands of the polyp shown in Figure 42.4. The glands with hyperplastic features (H) have a single layer of paler staining nuclei, and show a more complex outline in contrast to dysplastic glands (D), which show nuclear hyperchromasia and stratification. (H&E, ×180)

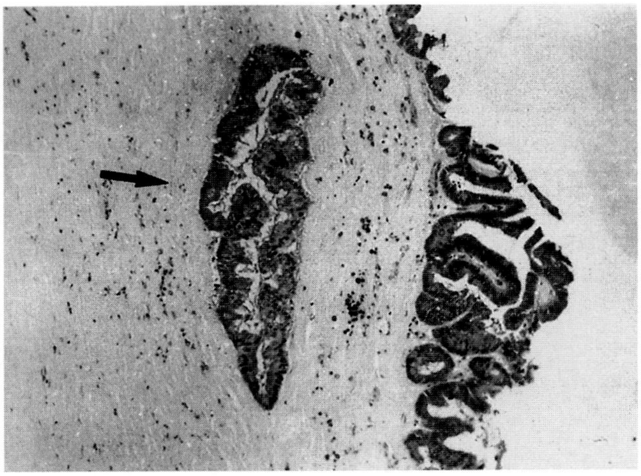

Fig. 42.6 Adenocarcinoma of the appendix. Malignant epithelium is seen lining the lumen, and there is invasion of the wall (arrow). (H&E, ×50)

lesion and therefore suggests that all apparently pure 'hyperplastic' lesions in the appendix be carefully examined to determine if they are of the transitional type of epithelium which might be adjacent to a small adenomatous proliferation which has not been sampled in the initial sections.

Adenocarcinomas

These are histologically identical to their colonic counterparts, with variable but usually moderate differentiation and a variable mucinous component. When substantial amounts of mucin are present (and this is usually visible macroscopically) the term mucinous adenocarcinoma is used (Fig. 42.6).

Presentation

The majority of the non-carcinoid epithelial tumours of the appendix are not diagnosed pre- or intraoperatively, the appendices usually being removed after a clinical diagnosis of acute appendicitis has been made.[2,11] The presence of an epithelial tumour of the appendix should be suspected in elderly patients presenting with the symptoms and signs of acute appendicitis, or with an appendiceal mass. Rarely, cases are described in which a preoperative diagnosis has been made from the results of computerized tomography studies[12] or contrast radiographic examination. In one report, the endoscopic appearance of one of these tumours is described.[13]

Unusual presentations include a case in which the patient presented with a cutaneous tumour on the abdomen,[14] cases presenting as bilateral Krukenberg tumours,[15–17] and others simulating primary bladder tumours.[18,19] Carcinomas of the appendix have also been recorded presenting in femoral hernias.[20,21]

Treatment

Treatment for the benign epithelial lesions is simple appendicectomy, with the proviso that, because carcinoma has been described arising in adenomas of the appendix,[22,23] further surgical clearance should be attempted if the adenoma extends to the surgical resection margin of the appendicectomy specimen.

In contradistinction to the treatment of the benign epithelial proliferations, the treatment of choice for adenocarcinoma is right hemicolectomy or ileocolectomy, as regional lymph node metastases may already have occurred.[24–27] The more extensive resection procedure is associated with an increase in the reported 5-year survival rate, from 20% after simple appendicectomy to around 60% following the more extensive surgery.[25]

Wolff and Ahmed have reported an extensive study of epithelial neoplasms of the vermiform appendix, together with prognostic and therapeutic implications.[27,28]

Complications

Complications of mucosal tumours include inflammation of the appendix, which is the most common,[2] torsion[29] and intussusception of the appendix and colon.[30,31] Perforation of the appendix secondary to acute inflammation is an important entity, and the presence of mucus in peritoneal or retroperitoneal abscesses should lead to extensive examination of the specimen for the presence of an underlying epithelial lesion. Mucinous peritoneal implants, or so-called 'pseudomyxoma peritonei' may also be found.

The presence of an epithelial tumour should alert the pathologist to the possibility of other associated colonic tumours, including coincidental colonic carcinomas and intestinal polyps, as the association between the lesions in the appendix and tumours elsewhere in the colon is documented.[2]

Secondary changes in the wall and luminal mucus of the appendix are described in association with epithelial tumours. These include a so-called 'porcelain' appendix, in which calcification occurs in the distended wall,[32] and myxoglobulosis of the appendix. Myxoglobulosis is a descriptive term used to indicate a change in the mucus, such that roughly spheroidal, separate, firm globules of altered mucus are found in the appendiceal lumen. It is postulated that the formation of these globules may be due to changes in mucin related to the proliferation of granulation tissue at the luminal surface. They somehow complex and subsequently separate from the wall to lie as separate structures within the lumen. These globules may still contain a central core of apparently viable granulation tissue. Another theory proposes that colonies of bacteria form the nidus for the globule.[33,34] Whatever the cause of the change in the mucus, careful examination of the epithelium for tumour is essential.

PSEUDOMYXOMA PERITONEI

The definition of pseudomyxoma peritonei has become increasingly confusing because the one macroscopic descriptive term has been used to denote two quite separate and distinct pathological processes. The term regretfully has become entrenched in both the clinical and pathological literature and usage. A preferable clinical terminology would be 'mucinous peritoneal implants', which could then be accurately defined as to the underlying pathology by histological examination.

Secondary deposits of mucin-producing adenocarcinoma on the lining surfaces of the peritoneum, following transcoelomic spread of a primary adenocarcinoma of the appendix or ovary, constitute one of the two possible origins of mucinous implants in the peritoneal cavity.[35] The second, quite separate and distinct process, is an inflammatory reaction to extruded mucin from a benign mucin-producing tumour of the appendix, often following inflammatory perforation of the organ. In these cases, organizing granulation tissue is present around the extruded mucin. Not surprisingly in these cases, following appendicectomy, when the stimulus produced by the extruded mucin is removed, the process resolves, in contradistinction to the malignant implants which persist after the removal of the primary tumour.[3,36]

Macroscopically, the implants appear as glistening mucinous globules attached to the surfaces of the peritoneal cavity, or alternatively the whole cavity may be filled by a mass of mucin admixed with fibrous tissue which surrounds and obstructs the intra-abdominal organs. Exhaustive study of multiple histological sections of the biopsies should be undertaken in cases where the nodules are the only material available for examination, as groups of malignant cells will be found within the mucin in the majority of cases (Fig. 42.7). Thorough examination of the appendix and ovary is also necessary to determine the site of the primary tumour.

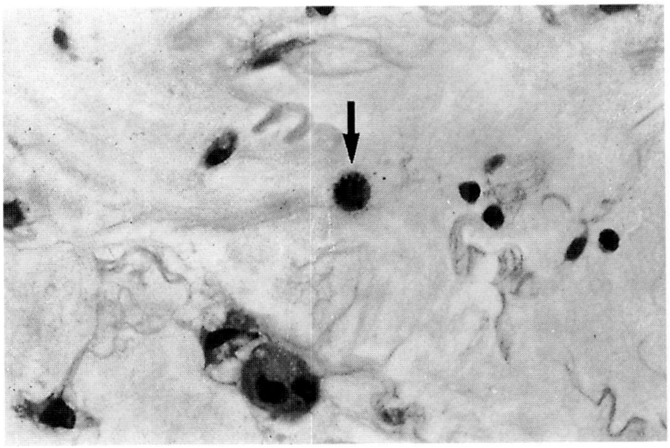

Fig. 42.7 Section through a mucinous peritoneal implant. The major reaction was fibroblastic proliferation. The presence of an abnormal mitotic figure (arrow) prompted the pathologist to search further for malignant cells. (H&E, ×741)

SOFT TISSUE TUMOURS

Soft tissue tumours are rare in the appendix, with neuromas and leiomyomas making up the majority of cases.[37–39] Rarer tumours, including leiomyosarcoma, are recorded.[40] The neoplasms exhibit the same behaviour as those found elsewhere in the gastrointestinal tract and although any soft tissue tumour can theoretically occur in the appendix, others are extremely rare.

Neural tumours

Hyperplasias of nervous tissue in the appendix are not an uncommon finding. So-called 'neuromas' were described in the appendix by Masson and also Maresch in the 1920s, and were classified according to site and purported stage of development.[41] Recent studies have designated the lesions as neurogenic appendicitis or neuro-appendicopathy, although these terms should preferably be reserved to describe the clinicopathological correlation when the patient's symptoms and signs may be related to the presence of an appendiceal neuroma.[42,43]

The importance of appendiceal neuromas lies in the proposal that they may be related to the genesis of pain of the appendicitis syndrome, in the absence of any overt inflammation in the organ. The concept is not new. Both Masson and Maresch considered axial neuromas to represent amputation neuromas in the tip of a previously inflamed appendix, and Hosi,[44] Isaacson and Blades[45] and Michalany and Galindo[41] have all proposed a relationship between the presence of these neural proliferations and the genesis of pain in the appendix. Although the literature describing these lesions and their possible implications spans a period of over 60 years, the interest has been sporadic and many pathologists still do not recognize all of the different types of neuromas. Until they are routinely sought during histopathological examination of appendices, and a large bank of data built up regarding their incidence, secretion of neurohormonal and mediator substances and vasoactive products, their significance in the appendix will remain obscure.

A detailed description of the histopathological appearances these lesions can be found in the paper by Michalany and Galindo,[41] and a brief description of each of the three types, based on their findings, is set out below.

Axial neuromas

This type of 'neuroma' is always found in the extremity of obliterated appendices, covered on its proximal part by the blind end of the appendiceal mucosa. The neuromas are a mixture of fibrous tissue and hyperplasia of both nerve fibres and neuroendocrine cells.

Intramucosal neuromas

These lesions are found as proliferations of increased numbers of nerve fibres in the upper lamina propria, in association with an enlarged mucosal plexus separating and distorting the mucosal crypts, and which, if they attain a large enough size, may protrude into the muscularis mucosae.

Submucosal neuromas

In this group there are hyperplastic nerve bundles within the submucosa related to smooth muscle fibres from the muscularis mucosae (Fig. 42.8).

The 'evolutionary' subclassification requires that 'growing' neuromas contain argentaffin-positive cells and Schwann cells, whilst regressing neuromas are characterized by atrophy of nerve fibrils, the presence of collagen and lymphocytes, and eventually areas of myxoid degeneration. In the sclerosing type, small nerve fibres surrounded by collagen fibres are seen in the centre of an obliterated appendix, whilst in the myxoid type there are Schwann cells with pyknotic nuclei and marked oedema. No distinction is obvious between nerve fibres and collagenous connective tissue.

Dhillon and Rode[43] propose that 'the concept of neuroappendicopathy based on quantitative nerve changes' is not important in the painful non-inflamed appendix. Following identification of neural tissue by staining for neuron-specific enolase (NSE), their study showed more nerve 'hyperplasia' in appendices from a control group than in appendices removed from subjects with a history typical of appendicitis, but no evidence of inflammation on histological examination. They have described a neural plexus in the lamina propria comprising ganglion cells and neuro-endocrine cells in intimate relationship with nerves. These neuro-endocrine cells normally contain serotonin, but are demonstrably depleted of this substance in patients with appendicitis pain. It is their suggestion that serotonin from these complexes acts as a mediator, producing appendiceal pain, and possibly subsequent inflammation.

Hoffler, Kasper and Heitz, in a separate study, found positive staining with NSE in the mucosal form of 'neuroma', together with an increase in the number of stromal endocrine cells.[46]

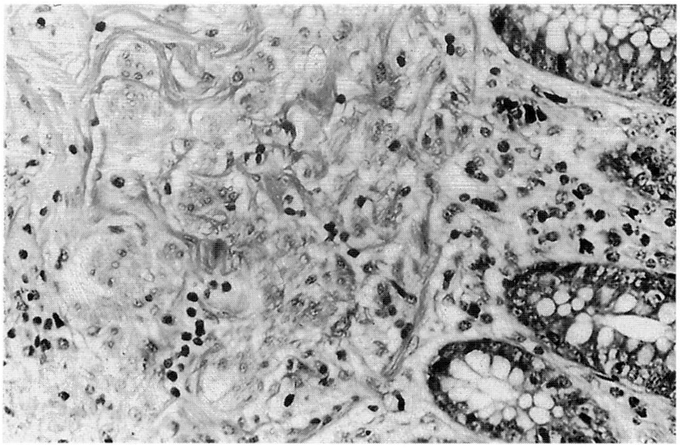

Fig. 42.8 Submucosal neuroma. Proliferations of nerves surrounded by collagenous connective tissue can be seen. (H&E, ×228)

Neurofibromas

Neurofibromas of the appendix are described by Merck and Kindblom in a 24-year-old male with von Recklinghausen's disease.[47]

Lymphoma

Lymphoma of the alimentary canal is rare, however it may occur in all sites, including the vermiform appendix.[48,49]

Cases of primary lymphoma of the appendix are recorded in the literature, and there are two documented cases of Burkitt's lymphoma primarily localized to the appendix.[50]

Thus the lymphoid tissue of the appendix should always be examined carefully, as differentiation between pseudolymphoma and lymphoma is important in patient management (see below).[51]

OTHER PRIMARY TUMOURS

A single case of extragonadal endodermal sinus tumour is reported,[52] and haemangiomas are reported.[53] The occurrence of granular cell tumours is contentious (see below).

SECONDARY TUMOURS

Occasionally, the appendix is the site of a secondary deposit of tumour from another site, which may be prostate, pancreas, breast or lung.[54–57]

Serosal implants of glial tissue from well-differentiated teratomas of the ovary are also recorded.

TUMOUR-LIKE LESIONS

The range of tumour-like lesions in the appendix is extensive, and includes epithelial, mesothelial, lymphoid and soft tissue proliferations. Although these proliferations are only seen in a small percentage of surgically removed appendices, recognition is important to avoid overtreatment,

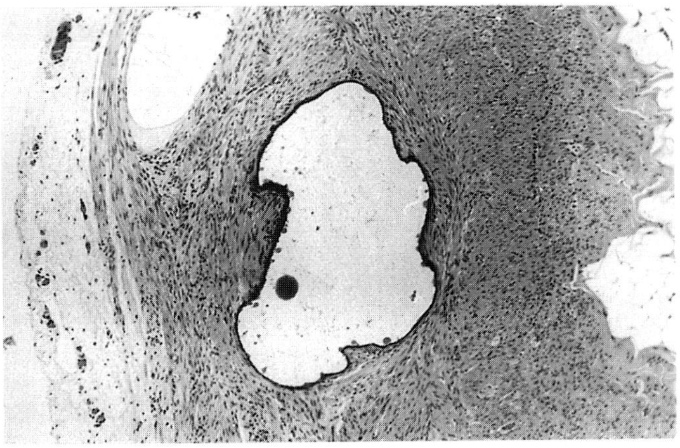

Fig. 42.9 This mesothelial inclusion cyst was an incidental finding in an appendix which, in other areas, showed features of a focal acute appendicitis. (H&E, ×19)

or, in some cases, such as putative granular cell tumours, to highlight the need for possible further investigation of the gastrointestinal tract.

Mesothelial inclusion cysts

Mesothelial cysts occur in the subserosa and are not significant (Fig. 42.9).[58]

Endometriosis

Endometriotic deposits in the appendix are seen macroscopically as grey-white fibrous areas in the wall or serosa of the appendix. Occasionally small cystic spaces are present in the involved tissue. Microscopically, the classical appearances, with endometrial glands and variable amounts of endometrial stroma, are seen (Fig. 42.10). Association with luminal obstruction and acute appendicitis is described.[10,59,60]

Granular degeneration of smooth muscle and granular cell tumours

Granular cell tumours of the appendix[61,62] and granular degeneration of appendiceal smooth muscle[63] are uncommon lesions, which may cause problems in interpretation. Granular cell degeneration in the muscularis mucosae and inner layers of the muscularis propria of the appendix has been quoted as occurring in 5% of resected specimens.[61] The changes resemble granular cell tumours in routine haematoxylin and eosin stained sections, and occur most commonly in the inner circular muscle coat. The cytoplasm of the cells has a finely granular appearance and stains intensely with the periodic acid Schiff stain, but ultrastructurally, the conspicuous budding Golgi apparatus and moderate numbers of mitochondria seen in true granular cell tumours are absent.

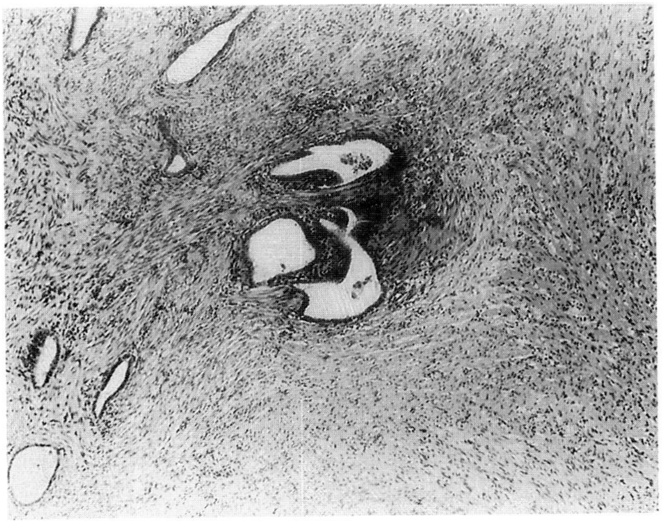

Fig. 42.10 Focus of endometriosis in the wall of the appendix. (H&E, ×42)

Actin-like filaments and condensations are present, suggesting that the changes represent alterations in smooth muscle cells.

True granular cell tumours of the appendix are extremely rare. Ultrastructurally, the cells are enclosed by a continuous basal lamina and contain irregular, membrane-bound lysosomal-like granules. No actin-like filaments or condensations are seen.

Multifocal granular cell tumours in the gastrointestinal tract are said to occur in up to 16% of cases, and one case of multifocal granular cell tumours involving the appendix is recorded.[62]

Pseudolymphoma and inflammatory pseudotumour

Recognition of inflammatory pseudotumours in the appendix is important to avoid overtreatment. Macroscopically, the lesions are firm grey-white masses, sometimes appearing encapsulated. The microscopic findings are of an infiltrate of mononuclear inflammatory cells, including histiocytes and plasma cells.[64,65] Reactive lymphoid follicles with germinal centres may be present. The diagnosis in difficult cases depends on the demonstration of a polyclonal proliferation of cells in the lesion by immunohistochemical means.

MISCELLANEOUS LESIONS

Hamartomatous polyps of the Peutz-Jeghers type are described in the appendix. Epidermoid cysts have been seen,[66] and decidual change may be present on the serosa during pregnancy. Indeed, the whole range of non-neoplastic polypoid proliferations found elsewhere in the gastrointestinal tract is theoretically possible in this organ.

REFERENCES

1. Ham AW. Histology, 7th Ed. Philadelphia: Lipponcott 1974; 678.
2. Williams RA, Whitehead R. Non-carcinoid epithelial tumours of the appendix — a proposed classification. Pathology 1986; 18: 50–53.
3. Higa E, Rosai J, Pizzimbono CA, Wise L. Mucosal hyperplasia, mucinous cystadenoma, and mucinous cystadenocarcinoma of the appendix. A re-evaluation of appendiceal 'mucocele'. Cancer 1973; 32: 1525–1541.
4. Aranha GV, Reyes CV. Primary epithelial tumours of the appendix and a reappraisal of the appendiceal 'mucocele'. Dis Colon Rectum 1979; 22: 472–476.
5. Fenoglio-Preiser CM, Pascal RR, Perzin KH. Tumours of the appendix. In: Atlas of Tumour Pathology, Second Series, Fascicle 27, Tumours of the Intestines. 1990. Armed Forces Institute of Pathology, Washington DC.
6. Lin JI, Cogbill CL, Athota PJ, Tsung SH, Kwak YS. Superficial spreading adenocarcinoma of appendix, cecum, and terminal ileum. Dis Colon Rectum 1980; 23: 587–589.
7. Schulte WJ, Pintar K, Schmahl T. Adenoacanthoma of the appendix. J Surg Oncol 1974; 6: 93–96.
8. Longacre TA, Fenoglio-Preiser CM. Mixed hyperplastic adenomatous polyps (MHAPs/serrated adenomas): A distinct form of colorectal neoplasia. Am J Surg Pathol 1990; 14(6): 52–537.
9. Appelman HD. In: Pathology of the Colon, Small Intestine and Anus. Ed. H Thomas Norris. Churchill Livingstone, New York: 263–302.
10. Hapke MR, Bigelow B. Mucocele of the appendix secondary to obstruction by endometriosis. Hum Pathol 1977; 8: 585–589.
11. Jordan FT, Mazzeo RJ, Hoshal VL Jr. Primary adenocarcinoma of the appendix. Can preoperative or intraoperative diagnosis be made? Am Surg 1983; 49: 278–281.
12. Morris L, Vas W, Salimi Z, Tang-Barton P. CT diagnosis of adenocarcinoma of the appendix. Diagn Imag Clin Med 1984; 53: 298–301.
13. Ponsky JL. An endoscopic view of mucocele of the appendix. Gastrointest Endosc 1976; 23: 42–43.
14. Mehzad M, Aflaki B, Afghari H. Adenocarcinoma of the appendix: report of an unusual case. Dis Colon Rectum 1978; 21: 205–206.
15. Paone JF, Bixler TJ (II), Imbembo AL. Primary mucinous adenocarcinoma of the appendix with bilateral Krukenberg ovarian tumors. Johns Hopkins Med J 1978; 143: 43–47.
16. Kashani M, Levy M. Primary adenocarcinoma of the appendix with bilateral Krukenberg ovarian tumors. J Surg Oncol 1983; 22: 101–105.
17. De Graaff J, Puyenbroek JI, Van der Harten JJ. Primary mucinous adenocarcinoma of the appendix with bilateral Krukenberg tumors of the ovary and primary adenocarcinoma of the endometrium. Gynecol Oncol 1984; 19: 358–364.
18. Henry R, Bracken RB, Ayala A. Appendiceal carcinoma mimicking primary bladder cancer. J Urol 1980; 123: 590–591.
19. Bartholomew LG, Farrow GM, De Weerd JH. Adenocarcinoma of the appendix simulating primary bladder carcinoma. Dig Dis Sci 1984; 29: 371–375.
20. Nayak IN. Malignant mucocele of the appendix in a femoral hernia. Postgrad Med J 1974; 50: 246–249.
21. Campbell TE. Mucinous neoplasms of the appendix appearing as hernias (letter). Arch Pathol Lab Med 1981; 105: 57–58.
22. Detky G. Cancer of the appendix arising from a villous adenoma. Orv Hetil 1983; 124: 2815–2817.
23. Pettigrew RA. Invasive carcinoma arising in villous adenomata of the appendix. Aust NZ J Surg 1980; 50: 627–629.
24. Gilhome RW, Johnston DH, Clark J, Kyle J. Primary adenocarcinoma of the vermiform appendix: report of a series of ten cases, and review of the literature. Br J Surg 1984; 71: 553–555.
25. Lane IF, Snooks SJ. Surgical management of adenocarcinoma of the appendix. Br J Clin Pract 1984; 38: 233–235.
26. Chang P, Attiyeh FF. Adenocarcinoma of the appendix. Dis Colon Rectum 1981; 24: 176–180.
27. Wolff M, Ahmed N. Epithelial neoplasms of the vermiform appendix (exclusive of carcinoid): I. Adenocarcinoma of the appendix. Cancer 1976; 37: 2493–2510.
28. Wolff M, Ahmed N. Epithelial neoplasms of the vermiform appendix (exclusive of carcinoid): II. Cystadenomas, papillary adenomas, and adenomatous polyps of the appendix. Cancer 1976; 37: 2511–2522.
29. Legg NG. Rare cases of intestinal obstruction: 3. Torsion complicating mucocele of the appendix. J R Coll Surg Edinb 1973; 18: 236.
30. Ho L, Roseman LD. Complete invagination of the vermiform appendix with villous adenoma, intussuscepting to the splenic flexure of the colon. Surgery 1975; 77: 505–506.
31. Barry R, Visser JD, Nel CJ. Intussusception as a result of adenoma of the appendix. S Afr J Surg 1980; 19: 133–137.
32. Buxton JT Jr. Porcelain appendix: A calcified mucocele fracture to produce an acute abdomen. Arch Surg 1979; 114: 736–737.
33. Rolon PA. Myxoglobulosis of the appendix. Int Surg 1977; 62: 355–356.
34. Lubin J, Berle E. Myxoglobulosis of the appendix: Report of two cases. Arch Pathol 1972; 94: 533–536.
35. Campbell JS, Lou P, Ferguson JP, Krongold I, Kemeny T, Mitton DM, Allan N. Pseudomyxoma peritonei et ovarii with occult neoplasms of appendix. Obstet Gynecol 1973; 42: 897–902.
36. Fernandez RN, Daly JM. Pseudomyxoma peritonei. Arch Surg 1980; 115: 409–414.
37. Schmutzer KJ, Bayar M, Zaki AE, Regan JF, Poletti JB. Tumors of the appendix. Dis Colon Rectum 1975; 18: 324–331.
38. Powell JL, Fuerst JF, Tapia RA. Leiomyoma of the appendix. South Med J 1980; 73: 1298–1299.
39. Pai AM, Vinze HL, Attar-Aziz, Shah SB. Leiomyoma of the appendix (a case report). J Postgrad Med 1977; 23: 39–40.
40. Jones PA. Leiomyosarcoma of the appendix: Report of two cases. Dis Colon Rectum 1979; 22: 175–178.
41. Michalany J, Galindo W. Classification of neuromas of the appendix. Beitr Path Bd 1973; 150: 213–228.
42. Michalany J. Appendiceal neuromatosis (neurogenic appendicitis, nervous appendicopathy or the Masson neuro-appendicopathy). AMB 1976; 22: 380–387.
43. Dhillon AP, Rode J. Serotonin and its possible role in the painful non-inflamed appendix. Diagn Histopathol 1983; 6: 239–246.
44. Hosi K. Neuromatosis of the vermiform appendix. Arch Path 1933; 16: 500–509.
45. Isaacson NH, Blades B. Neuroappendicopathy. Review of the literature and report on fifty-two cases. Arch Surg 1951; 62(4): 455–466.
46. Hoffler H, Kasper M, Heitz PhU. The neurendocrine system of normal human appendix, ileum and colon, and in neurogenic appendicopathy. Virchows Arch (A) 1983; 399: 127–140.
47. Merck C, Kindblom LG. Neurofibromatosis of the appendix in von Recklinghausen's disease. A report of a case. Acta Pathol Microbiol Scand (A) 1975; 83: 623–627.
48. Contreary K, Nance FC, Becker WF. Primary lymphoma of the gastrointestinal tract. Ann Surg 1980; 191: 593–598.
49. Franchini A, Tonielli E, Calo G. Gastrointestinal localization of malignant lymphomas. Minerva Chir 1979; 34: 457–466.
50. Sin IC, Ling ET, Prentice RS. Burkitt's lymphoma of the appendix: report of two cases. Hum Pathol 1980; 11: 465–470.
51. Giltman L, Cohn B, Minkowitz S. Pseudolymphoma presenting as a cecal tumor. J Pediatr Surg 1976; 11: 565–568.
52. Ito K, Suzuh H, Ikeda M, Teshima K, Noda K. A case of extragonadal endodermal sinus tumor — histological, cytological aspects and serial determination of serum AFP and IAP. Asia Oceania J Obstet Gynaecol 1983; 9: 81–88.
53. Harned RK, Dobry CA, Farley GE. Cavernous hemangioma of the rectum and appendix. Dis Colon Rectum 1974; 17: 759–762.
54. Ansari MA, Pintozzi RL, Choi YS, Ladove RF. Diagnosis of carcinoid-like metastatic prostatic carcinoma by an immunoperoxidase method. Am J Clin Pathol 1981; 76: 94–98.
55. Radiological case of the month. Cystic adenocarcinoma of the pancreas metastatic to cecum and appendix. Md State Med J 1975; 24: 67–68.

56. Burney RE, Koss N, Goldenberg IS. Acute appendicitis secondary to metastatic carcinoma of the breast. A report and review of two cases. Arch Surg 1974; 108: 872–875.
57. Levchenko AM, Vaschko VN, Erusalimski EL. Metastasis of small-cell lung cancer to the appendix. Klin Khir 1985; 5: 56–57.
58. Dymock RB. Pathological changes in the appendix: A review of 1000 cases. Pathology 1977; 9: 331–339.
59. Gini PC, Chukudebelu WO, Onuigbo WI. Perforation of the appendix during pregnancy: a rare complication of endometriosis. Br J Obstet Gynaecol 1981; 88: 456–458.
60. Pittaway DE. Appendectomy in the surgical treatment of endometriosis. Obstet Gynecol 1983; 61: 421–424.
61. Sarma DP, Simmons GT, Rodriguez FH Jr, Weilbaecher TG, Love GL. Granular cell tumor of the appendix. J Surg Oncol 1984; 27: 219–221.
62. Fried KS, Arden JL, Gouge TH, Balthazar EJ. Multifocal granular cell tumors of the gastrointestinal tract. Am J Gastroenterol 1984; 79: 751–755.
63. Sobel HJ, Marquet E, Schwarz R, Passaic NJ. Granular degeneration of appendiceal smooth muscle. Arch Pathol 1971; 92: 427–432.
64. Fingerhut A, Pelletier JM, Pourcher J, Lopez Y, Ronat R. Inflammatory pseudo-tumors of appendiceal origin. Study of twelve cases. J Chir (Paris) 1980; 117: 381–389.
65. Narasimharao K L, Malik A K, Mitra SK, Pathak IC. Inflammatory pseudotumor of the appendix. Am J Gastroenterol 1984; 79: 32–34.
66. Piserchia NE, Davey RB. Epidermoid cyst of the appendix. J Pediatr Surg 1980; 15: 674–675.

CHAPTER

43 Other tumours of the anal canal

P. J. Heenan

The anal canal, although representing only a relatively tiny proportion of the entire gastrointestinal tract, is the site of a wide variety of neoplasms of controversial histogenesis. A knowledge of the anatomy of the canal, especially its epithelial components, is therefore important to the understanding of the neoplasms arising in this region.

In strict anatomical terms, the anal canal may be regarded as extending from the anal valves to the anal margin,[1] but it is usual in considering diseases of the anal canal to include conditions affecting the area which extends up to the anorectal ring.[2] The length of the anal canal by this definition corresponds to the full extent of the internal sphincter, approximately 4 cm.[3]

A key landmark is the pectinate or dentate line, which is situated a little below the middle of the canal; the anal transitional zone (ATZ) extends above the dentate line for approximately 10 mm (range 0–20 mm), often with a very irregular upper border below the colorectal zone. The third segment of the canal, the squamous zone or anal margin, extends below the dentate line to the perianal skin.[3]

The mucosa below this line, the pecten, is lined by simple squamous epithelium without appendages, whereas from the dentate line upwards for a variable distance there is a transitional zone which merges with true rectal mucosa in the proximal segment of the canal.[4] The origin, extent and epithelial components of this transitional zone have been contentious issues. According to different authorities, it extends above the dentate line for distances ranging from 1–20 mm and even below the line in some cases;[5] it is believed to represent the junction of endoderm and ectoderm and to be of cloacal origin.[6,7] Fowler[8] described an abrupt transition at the dentate line from stratified columnar epithelium above to stratified squamous epithelium below and dismissed as artefact the interdigitation and alternation of islands of cuboidal and transitional epithelia recorded by other observers.[9]

Gillespie and MacKay,[7] on the basis of electron microscopic studies, found that the anal transitional epithelium incorporated features of urothelium and squamous epithelium which were, in their view, consistent with cloacal origin as proposed by Herrman and Desfosses in 1880.[10]

Fenger,[11] however, likened the appearance of anal transitional epithelium to that of metaplastic squamous epithelium and reserve cell hyperplasia, as seen in the uterine cervix transformation zone, and noted the frequent occurrence of islands of mature squamous epithelium in the upper part of the zone. He found also that the transitional zone had irregular outlines, with varied location and extent, and that epithelial variants within this zone could be seen from 6 mm below to 20 mm above the dentate line. It is clear that the controversy surrounding the nature of this zone has its basis in the quite marked individual variation, as outlined in Chapter 29, and it is also clear that this will influence the type of tumours arising from it.

The anal glands, also referred to as the anal ducts,[12,13] are long, tortuous tubules, 6–12 in number, which open into the crypts of Morgagni behind the cusps of the anal valves.[14] They may extend either proximally in the lamina propria deep to the rectal epithelium or distally, before penetrating the internal anal sphincter, sometimes reaching the peri-anal fat.[12] Their epithelium includes squamous, transitional and stratified columnar types, with scattered goblet cells.[15]

Smaller glandular structures, which should not be confused with the anal glands or ducts, and have been termed the aberrant glands, are short, usually non-branching glands confined to the lamina propria.[12] They are lined by an internal layer of cylindrical mucous cells with small basal nuclei surrounded by 2–10 layers of transitional or undifferentiated cells. These glands often appear as shallow cul-de-sacs in the lamina propria, but they are sometimes more complex structures similar to the intramucosal glands of Littré of the urethra.[6]

The lymphatics of the anal canal above the dentate line drain upwards with arteries to the glands along the internal iliac artery and to the superior haemorrhoidal and inferior mesenteric groups of lymph nodes.[14] Below the dentate line, lymphatic drainage joins that of the perineum into the medial groups of superficial inguinal glands.[16]

CARCINOMA OF THE ANAL CANAL

Incidence

The most common carcinoma of the anorectal region is adenocarcinoma of the distal rectum infiltrating the anal canal.[13] Adenocarcinoma also arises, rarely, from the anal glands.[12]

Carcinomas arising from the epithelium of the transitional zone and pecten are relatively uncommon, accounting for 1–4% of malignant anorectal tumours[12,13,17–19] and in most studies they have occurred more frequently in females than males,[17,19–21] with their peak incidence in the sixth and seventh decades.[17, 22–26] Anal canal carcinoma is more common than cancer of the anal margin, which occurs more frequently in males than females.[17,23]

Aetiology

Carcinoma of the anal canal has been linked with coexistent or prior benign conditions, including haemorrhoids, condylomata acuminata, fissures, fistulae, and sexually transmitted infectious diseases such as syphilis and lymphogranuloma venereum.[12,13,21,24,27,28]

Epidemiological studies have produced evidence to support the hypothesis that a venereally transmissible agent is responsible for some cases of anal carcinoma. Austin[29] found a high rate of squamous cell carcinoma of the rectum or anus in single males in a San Francisco county noted for its high proportion of homosexual adults. The results of a study by Peters and Mack[30] in Los Angeles also supported the concept that sexual activity involving the anus is related to anal cancer, again based on a high rate of anal cancer in single males. Their findings did not support a relationship with factors other than sexual behaviour, including occupational exposure to chemical carcinogens, smoking, inheritance, drug abuse, exposure to radiation and dietary habits. It was suggested that the association between anal cancer and anal sexual practices could be mediated by mechanical irritation producing a hyperplastic response, the action of chemical carcinogens contained in anal lubricants or cleansers, or by infection with an oncogenic virus. The putative role of human papilloma virus (HPV) in the causation of cervical cancer and condylomata acuminata, together with reports of progression of condylomata to squamous cell carcinoma, made this virus a likely candidate.

Another study in Washington state,[31] showing a high risk for anal cancer in single men, and case reports of anal cancer in male homosexuals[32,33] also suggested that anal intercourse may be a risk factor. In Los Angeles, common epidemiological features were found for carcinomas of the cervix, vulva, vagina, anus and penis, i.e. increased incidence with decreasing social class, low incidence among Jews and raised incidence among separated and divorced persons of both sexes.[34] These observations support the hypothesis that tumours at these sites have common or similar aetiologic elements, possibly related to sexually trasmitted infections and other forms of chronic irritation. Further epidemiological studies have shown strong associations between homosexuality, anal intercourse, a history of anal condylomata acuminata and the development of anal canal cancer.[35,36]

The putative role of HPV infection as a causative factor in the development of squamous cell carcinoma of the anal canal, as in the uterine cervix,[37] has also been supported by histological and molecular biological studies. Cytological evidence of dysplasia and concomitant features of human papilloma virus (HPV) infection in the anorectal mucosa of homosexual men,[38] and the demonstration in tissue from anal canal cancer of HPV antigen by immunohistochemical methods[39] and of HPV DNA, mainly HPV 16, by in-situ hybridization[40–42] and the polymerase chain reaction,[43] have provided additional evidence that HPV plays an important role in the aetiology of anal canal cancer. Other factors, however, including herpes simplex virus (HSV) infection[43] and immunosuppression, as in patients with group IV HIV disease[44] and in renal transplant recipients,[45] might be important in the pathogenesis of these neoplasms.

Classification of carcinoma of the anal canal

The classification of carcinoma of the anal canal has been a controversial subject due to the complex character of the transitional zone and the diversity of morphological types of tumours arising from its epithelial components. Some authorities have favoured the separation of these cancers into groups based on apparent differences in their morphology and behaviour,[12,17,19,21–23] while others have denied the existence of any important differences and prefer to regard all epithelial malignancies of the anal canal, with exceptions such as melanoma and anal gland carcinoma, as variants of squamous cell carcinoma with similar behavioural characteristics.[46–48]

The concept of the cloacal origin of the junctional zone, as proposed by Herrman and Desfosses,[10] was reiterated by Tucker and Hellwig[49] and supported by Grinvalsky and Helwig,[6] who suggested the term 'transitional cloacogenic carcinoma' for tumours arising from this region. Grinvalsky and Helwig considered that the varied character of the epithelial components of the anorectal mucosa provided adequate explanation for the range of histological patterns seen in carcinomas at this site. Helwig[12] also considered that the terms 'transitional cloacogenic carcinoma' or 'cloacogenic carcinoma' could appropriately replace the profusion of terms used to designate these neoplasms, including basal cell carcinoma, basal-squamous cell epithelioma, basaloid carcinoma, epidermoid carcinoma, cylindroma, anal duct carcinoma, mucoepidermoid carcinoma, adenoacanthoma and typical carcinoma. The predominant pattern described by Helwig was that of a transitional cell carcinoma similar to that seen in the urinary bladder, composed of cells ranging from transitional-type elongated cells to short cuboidal (basaloid) cells. The basaloid tumour in this concept was considered to be a less differentiated form of cloacogenic carcinoma. Helwig also described variations from the transitional pattern as showing components of squamous differentiation and mucous cells.

The term basaloid has been widely used to describe carcinomas of the anal canal because of their histological resemblance to basal cell carcinoma of the skin.[50] Basaloid carcinoma as described by Pang and Morson[17] appears to correspond, in general, to the transitional carcinoma of other authors, with a shift in predominance towards the basaloid rather than the urothelial type.

Although most reports agree that ordinary squamous cell carcinoma is more common in the anal canal than the transitional or basaloid carcinoma,[12,20,21,23,51,52] varied interpretations of the histological criteria for these tumours might have led to apparently conflicting views regarding their prognosis. While some studies have indicated that basaloid carcinoma is associated with better survival rates than squamous cell carcinoma,[22] others have suggested either a poorer prognosis for basaloid carcinoma,[51] or no difference in survival rates between the histological subtypes.[20] Several investigators have concluded that depth of invasion and extent of spread of these tumours are more important prognostic indicators than their histological type.[20,46] This view received further support from Dougherty and Evans[47] who proposed that cloacogenic carcinoma, transitional cell carcinoma, basaloid carcinoma and mucoepidermoid carcinoma do not exist as one entity or entities separable from squamous cell carcinoma, and recommended that these terms be discarded. Other investigators, on the basis of a recent histological and in-situ hybridization study, concluded that anal cloacogenic and squamous carcinomas are histologically similar but distinct neoplasms.[53] Boman et al,[51] however, stressed that small cell carcinoma is a more virulent disease than other carcinomas of the anal canal and should be classified separately, and it has been reported that mucoepidermoid carcinoma and microcystic squamous carcinoma also have a poorer prognosis than other types of anal cancer.[54]

Table 43.1 Classification of carcinoma of the anal canal. (From Jass JR, Sobin LH. Histological Typing of Intestinal Tumours. World Health Organization, Springer-Verlag, Berlin, 1989)

Squamous cell (cloacogenic) carcinoma
Large cell keratinizing
Large cell non-keratinizing (transitional)
Basaloid
Adenocarcinoma
Rectal type
Of anal glands
Within anorectal fistula
Undifferentiated carcinoma

In the revised World Health Organization classification of malignant tumours of the anal canal (Table 43.1), basaloid carcinoma is described as a variant of squamous cell carcinoma.[55] In this classification, squamous cell (cloacogenic) carcinoma includes large cell keratinizing, large cell non-keratinizing (transitional) and basaloid types; it is recommended that when these tumours contain a mixture of cell types they should be classified according to the predominant component. Mucoepidermoid carcinoma is regarded as a dubious entity, probably squamous cell carcinoma with mucinous microcysts.

Further subdivision into histological types such as transitional cell, basaloid and mucoepidermoid, although perhaps offering little more of practical value in terms of treatment and prognosis, might prove to have more merit in their possible correlation with specific aetiological agents, yet to be identified, with the ensuing implications for prevention or treatment.

Macroscopic appearances

The commonest malignant tumours occurring in the anal canal are adenocarcinomas of rectal mucosa arising most frequently from the rectum itself and invading the anal canal, or from the rectal epithelium of the proximal segment of the surgical anal canal.[13] Most of these tumours are ulcerated lesions with everted edges; polypoid masses and diffusely infiltrating carcinomas occur less frequently (Fig. 43.1).

Squamous and basaloid carcinomas arising from the transitional zone and pecten present no macroscopically distinctive features. When diagnosed, they may be flat or raised indurated lesions, sometimes annular, often ulcerated with everted edges (Fig. 43.2); rarely, they present as fungating or polypoid masses. Precise identification of the site of origin of the tumour within the canal and estimation of the extent of infiltration are difficult with diffusely invasive lesions (Fig. 43.3).

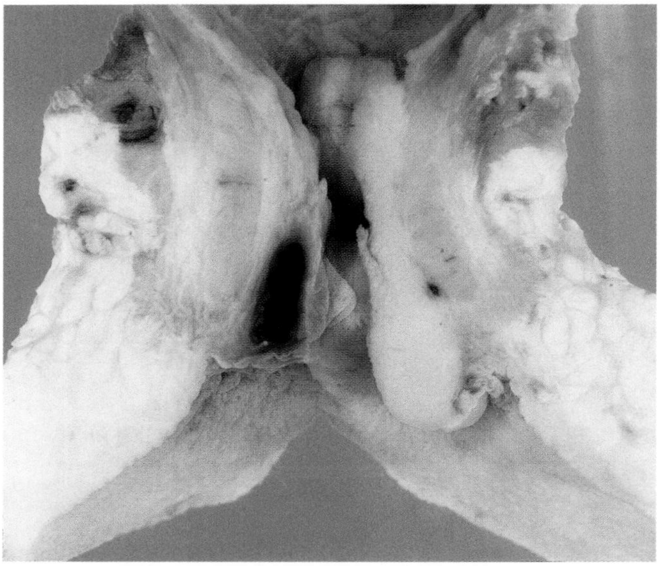

Fig. 43.1 Adenocarcinoma of rectal mucosa producing a plaque-like growth extending to the anal margin.

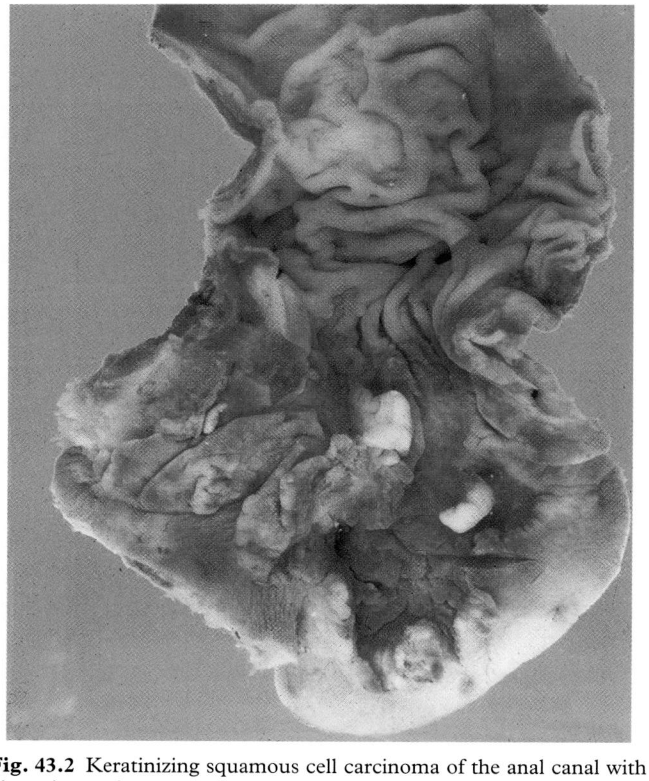

Fig. 43.2 Keratinizing squamous cell carcinoma of the anal canal with ulceration and everted edges.

Microscopic appearances

This description applies to those tumours which are believed to arise from the simple squamous epithelium of the lower anal canal and the mixed epithelia of the transitional zone.

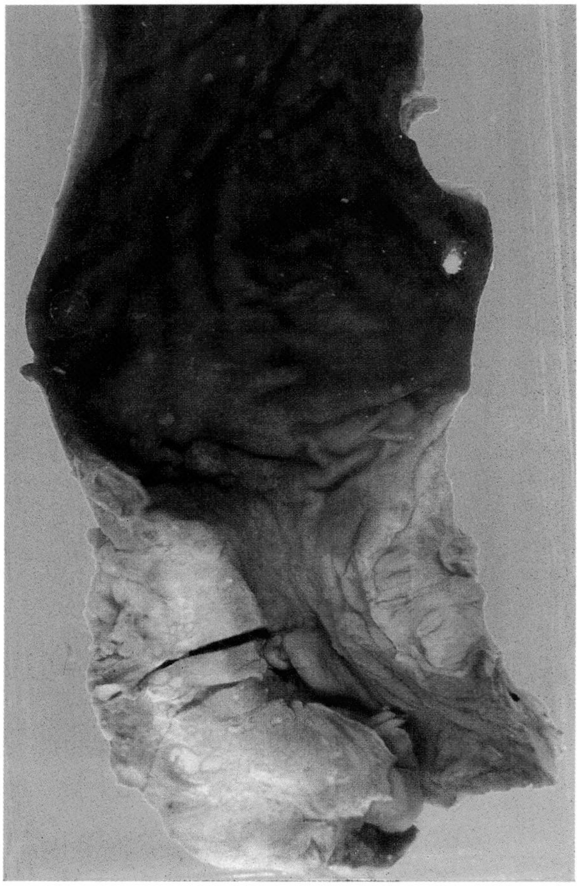

Fig. 43.3 Basaloid carcinoma involving the full extent of the anal canal with deep invasion.

Carcinomas of the anal canal usually consist of irregular, solid groups, branching strands or interlocking columns of cells invading the submucosal tissues, from a focus or several foci of in situ carcinoma, with variable fibrosis and inflammation in the surrounding stroma.

Although some tumours show a uniform growth pattern of one cell type, most contain a mixture of growth patterns and cell types, frequently including basaloid areas, foci of more pronounced squamous differentiation, groups of cells of transitional type, and adenocystic and mucoepidermoid components in various proportions. Most of these carcinomas appear to arise from or at least to involve the transitional zone and, according to many reports,[12,20,21,23,52] the predominant component in most cases is of squamous type. Variations in relative frequencies of tumour types found by different investigators are probably due, at least partially, to the use of different histological criteria.

Keratinizing squamous cell carcinomas occur uncommonly in the upper anal canal,[23] arising more frequently in the lower canal where many of these tumours involve the anal margin and might therefore be classified separately.

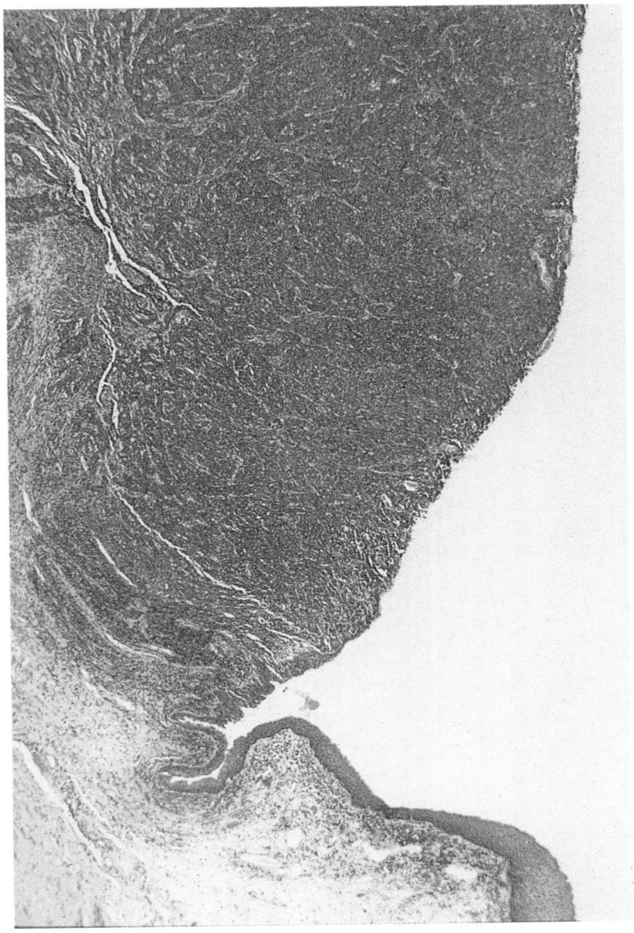

Fig. 43.4 Basaloid carcinoma of the anal canal composed of solid groups of small uniform cells. (×370)

Non-keratinizing squamous carcinoma includes basaloid, transitional and mucoepidermoid variants, all of which are included in the cloacogenic group by Helwig.[12] Basaloid areas are composed of irregular, branching strands, solid groups and interlocking columns of small cells with scanty cytoplasm and darkly-staining round or ovoid nuclei (Fig. 43.4). Peripheral palisading, the feature mainly responsible for the term basaloid,[50] is present to varying degrees within individual tumours but seldom as prominently as seen in basal cell carcinoma of the skin. A prominent margination effect, where the small cells at the margins of tumour islands are sharply defined from the adjacent stroma, is seen more often than true palisading by a layer of taller cells (Fig. 43.5). Intercellular bridges may not be seen in the more densely cellular areas but most tumours contain foci of more obvious squamous differentiation where the cells are larger, with pale cytoplasm and easily discernible bridges (Fig. 43.6). Dyskeratotic cells, squamous eddies, and pearls composed of parakeratotic cells are other features of these areas. Foci of eosinophilic necrosis are common. Electron microscopy confirms the presence of keratin filaments and desmosomes in varied numbers in these tumours.[7] Mitotic figures are sometimes very plentiful, and often basaloid tumours contain foci showing very severe nuclear pleomorphism including giant forms.

The transitional form of cloacogenic carcinoma resembles transitional cell carcinoma of the bladder[12] and is composed predominantly of larger, elongated cells with more plentiful clear or slightly eosinophilic cytoplasm, arranged in anastomosing cords and islands sharply demarcated from the stroma, often with a semblance of palisading (Fig. 43.7).

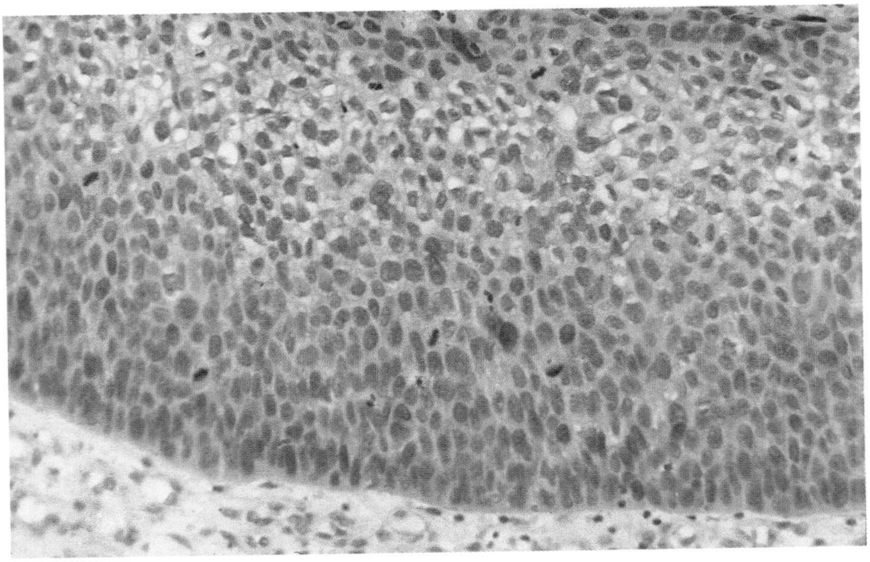

Fig. 43.5 Carcinoma of the anal canal composed of squamoid cells with a semblance of palisading enhanced by sharp demarcation from the stroma. (×1139)

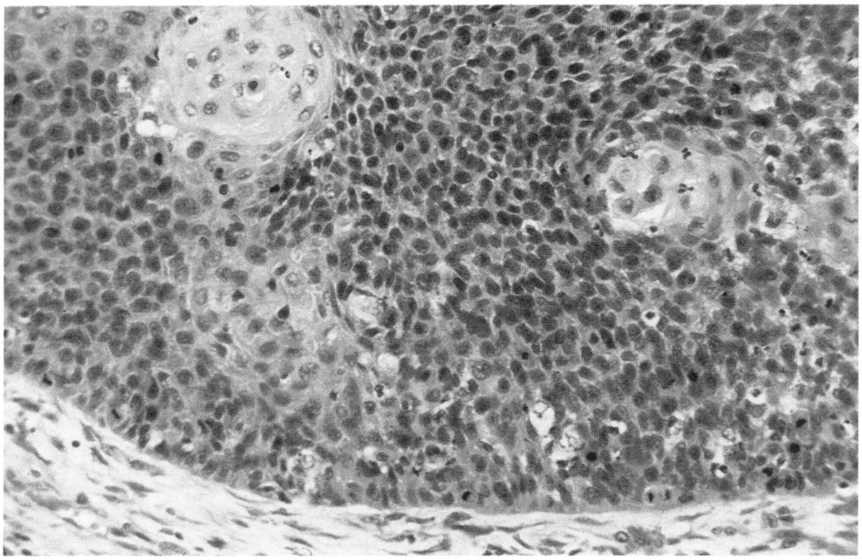

Fig. 43.6 Carcinoma of basaloid type with focal keratinization. (×455)

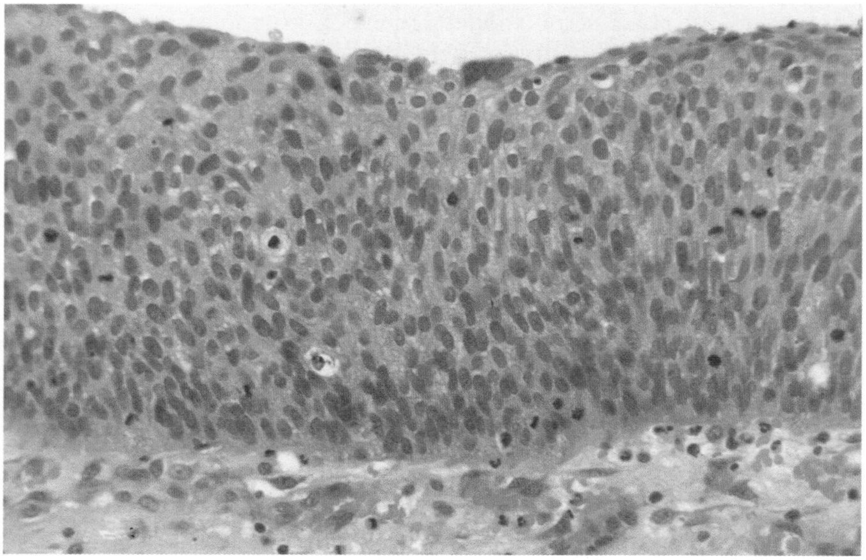

Fig. 43.7 Carcinoma of transitional type. This high-power view shows a resemblance to urinary tract epithelium with elongated basal cells. (×1139)

In situ carcinoma is frequently seen in the epithelium overlying these tumours, of whatever predominant histological type. Areas described as pseudoacinar or adenocystic consist of small foci of hyaline stroma surrounded by basaloid or transitional cells and probably do not merit separate classification.

Treatment and prognosis

Until recently, the most widely recommended treatment for anal canal carcinoma had been abdominoperineal resection with or without dissection of pelvic and/or inguinal lymph nodes,[21,48,56,57] with survival rates of 50–60%.[23,46,58] The prognosis for patients with anal canal carcinoma has improved markedly, however, with the introduction of rectum-preserving treatment based on combined local excision, chemotherapy and radiotherapy.[18,59–65]

The most reliable guides to prognosis are tumour size and depth of invasion.[46,47,54] There appears to be no difference in prognosis between the more common histological subtypes but the mucoepidermoid, microcystic and small cell variants of anal canal carcinoma have been associated with poorer survival.[54] Inguinal lymph node involvement and assessment of DNA-ploidy status are also useful prognostic guides.[54]

SQUAMOUS CARCINOMA OF THE ANAL MARGIN

Squamous carcinoma of the anal margin differs from anal canal carcinoma in its histological characteristics and behaviour.[66,67] These tumours, because of their more exposed site of origin, are also more likely to be diagnosed at an early stage and their prognosis is better than that of anal canal carcinoma.[46,52,68,69]

Morson[66] defined anal margin carcinomas as those which arise from the anal canal below the dentate line, which is lined by simple squamous epithelium (pecten), and from the perianal skin. They are much less common tumours than carcinoma of the anal canal involving the dentate line and above, with little or no difference in age incidence.[21,46,66] Cancer of the anal margin is said to occur more frequently in men than women, according to several studies,[66,69] in contrast to anal canal carcinoma which is more common in women, but other investigators have found little difference between the sex distributions of these tumours.[70,71]

Macroscopically, anal margin cancers appear as small nodules, irregular ulcers and exophytic growths, and most show the histological features of well-differentiated keratinizing squamous cell carcinoma, only a minority including basaloid components.[66] Coexisting conditions such as condylomata, fissures, chronic pruritis and leucoplakia are common.[70]

The size of the tumour correlates with the extent of microscopic infiltration and with prognosis. Greenall et al[70] recorded absolute 5 year survival rates of 56% for deeply infiltrating tumours and 75% for those with only superficial invasion. Local excision is adequate treatment in most cases, producing 5 year survival rates ranging from 60–90%.[21,46,70]

CARCINOMA OF THE ANAL GLANDS

Carcinoma of the anal glands (ducts) is extremely rare, difficult to identify and of debatable histogenesis.[72,73] Because the epithelium of the anal glands is derived from the transitional zone of the anal canal, which includes a variety of epithelial types, tumours of the glands also demonstrate a range of histological patterns, including squamous carcinoma, transitional carcinoma and mucinous adenocarcinoma.[12,15,73,74] The course of the glands in the lamina propria, in either caudal or cephalad directions, can account for the presence of stenosing tumours of the rectum or anal canal without primary involvement of the mucosa (Fig. 43.8a & b).[13,75,76] The certain designation of a tumour of anal gland origin demands the demonstration of a transition from in situ to invasive carcinoma actually within the glandular epithelium as distinct from the anal canal itself or the rectum.[14,77]

The differential diagnosis of these tumours frequently includes adenocarcinoma of the rectum, mucoepidermoid carcinoma of the anal canal, apocrine carcinoma and colloid carcinoma arising in anal fistulae. The origin of adenocarcinomas presenting as perianal or perirectal abscesses or fistulae is controversial.[78] Some observers have regarded these tumours as originating in the anal glands with secondary fistula formation, while others have argued that malignant change takes place in a pre-existing chronic fistula.[73,78–80] Because the diagnosis of anal gland carcinoma is usually made at a late stage, the prognosis is poor, as demonstrated by a recent study of 21 cases in Denmark in which the mortality rate was almost 100% within one year of diagnosis.[81]

Fenger and Filipe[15] found that the mucin of the anal glands differs from that of rectal mucosa in that the PAS-positivity in the anal glands, in contrast to the rectal mucosa, is abolished by borohydride-potassium hydroxide treatment. They demonstrated this property in anal gland carcinomas, colloid carcinomas apparently arising in pre-existing fistulae and in two mucoepidermoid carcinomas of the anal region, and concluded that this method could be of value in differentiating between carcinomas arising in anal gland epithelium and rectal mucosa.

CARCINOMA IN ANAL FISTULAE

The controversy regarding the origin of adenocarcinomas presenting as perianal or perirectal abscesses or fistulae has been referred to in the section on anal gland carcinoma. Three main settings have been described in which the combination of cancer and fistula may appear:

1. A fistula may be associated with a cancer elsewhere in the colon
2. A cancer, either primary or recurrent, may present as a fistula
3. Cancer may develop in a pre-existing fistula-in-ano.

The insidious nature of the tumour and the masking effect of symptoms of the fistula on the early symptoms of the cancer may cause difficulty in making the diagnosis.[80]

The anal glands are believed to play a pathogenic role in the formation of fistula-in-ano and ischiorectal abscess,[12,82] and some authors believe that most carcinomas allegedly arising in chronic fistulae actually originate in the anal glands.[78] Fenger and Filipe[15] recently found, on the basis of histochemical studies of mucin, that four of eight cases of colloid carcinoma apparently arising in pre-existing anal fistulae had originated in the anal glands. It has also been suggested that the presence of mucin globules in the granulation tissue of fistulectomy specimens should be regarded as a sign of mucinous adenocarcinoma.[83]

Most tumours described in association with anal fistulae have been mucinous adenocarcinomas or mucoepidermoid carcinomas, but squamous cell carcinoma has also been described as developing in chronic fistulae and abscesses caused by hidradenitis suppurativa.[79]

CROHNS'S DISEASE AND ANAL CARCINOMA

Anal canal carcinoma has been reported only rarely in

A

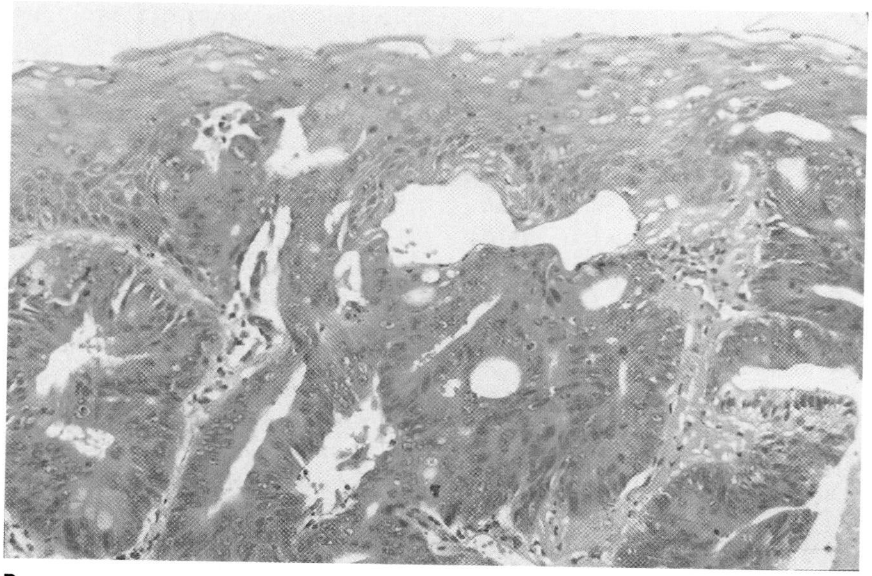

B

Fig. 43.8A Adenocarcinoma of the anal canal, probably originating in anal glands. **B** Invasive adenocarcinoma with intact overlying mucosa.

patients with Crohn's disease.[84] Recently, however, one cloacogenic carcinoma and two squamous cell carcinomas were described in female patients with significant perianal disease.[85] In this study, the relative incidence of anal cancer as a proportion of all colorectal cancer in patients with Crohn's disease was found to be significantly higher than the incidence of anal cancer in patients without inflammatory bowel disease.

MUCOEPIDERMOID CARCINOMA

Mucoepidermoid carcinoma of the anal canal is a rare tumour of controversial histogenesis. Hamperl and Hellweg[86] described it as a squamous carcinoma with unicellular mucus secretion and Kay[87] suggested an origin from the anal glands. Morson and Volkstadt,[72] however, defined these tumours as squamous or transitional cell carcinomas containing areas which secrete mucin of undoubted epithelial origin, and suggested that their origin from the transitional zone of the anal canal was more likely than from the anal glands. Several accounts have agreed that mucoepidermoid cancer is a variant of transitional carcinoma, representing one of the many growth patterns that may be found in tumours arising from that zone, with no significant difference in prognosis[12,13,20,47] but a recent report concluded that mucoepidermoid carcinoma has a poorer prognosis than the more common histological types of anal cancer.[54]

DYSPLASIA AND IN SITU CARCINOMA

The term 'dysplasia', according to the WHO Histological Typing of Intestinal Tumours, can be used to describe most precancerous epithelial lesions.[55] Whereas 'atypia' has usually been restricted to the description of cytological abnormalities, 'dysplasia' encompasses changes in architecture and aberrant differentiation as well as cytological disturbances. With increasing dysplasia, the proportion of the epithelium occupied by atypical cells increases. When atypical cells replace the entire thickness of the epithelium, the terms severe dysplasia or carcinoma in situ may be used synonymously.

The term anal canal intraepithelial neoplasia (ACIN), introduced as a synonym for severe dysplasia or carcinoma in situ, has also been used for precancerous changes in the epithelium of the anal canal.[88] Fenger has suggested that the following observations provide substantial evidence that ACIN is the precursor for anal canal carcinoma:

1. The average age at presentation is a little lower than for carcinoma and the sex distribution is the same
2. ACIN coexists with most cases of anal canal squamous carcinoma
3. ACIN has a strong tendency to recurrence and eventually develops foci of microinvasion.[88]

CONDYLOMA ACUMINATUM

Condylomata acuminata (venereal warts) are squamous cell papillomas induced by human papilloma virus (HPV) infection, most commonly HPV6.[89] They occur in both sexes, commonly on the genitalia and less frequently in the perianal region and anal canal. They are often multiple and cover large areas, and although usually exophytic, pink or white warty tumours, flat papules and pigmented variants also occur (Fig. 43.9).[90]

The histological features of condyloma acuminatum include pronounced acanthosis and papillomatosis forming broad columns of squamous cells with characteristic

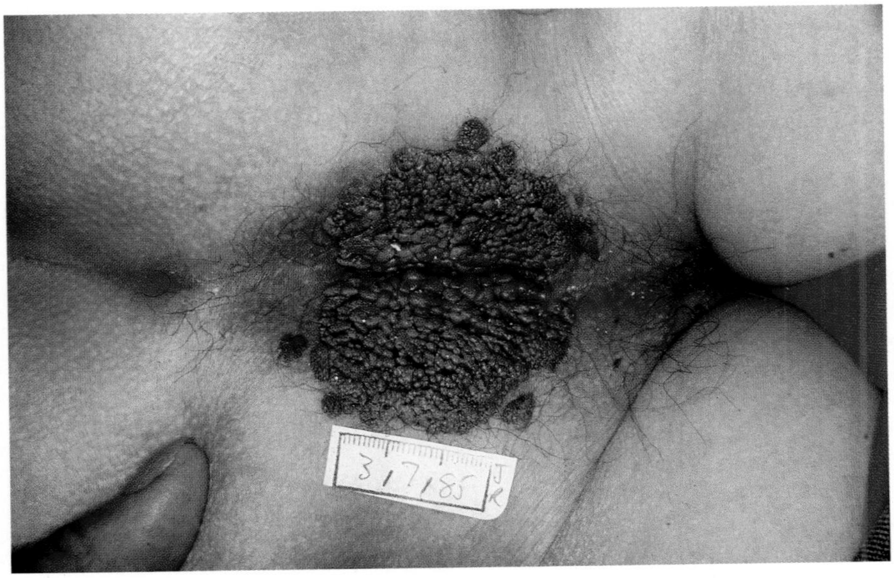

Fig. 43.9 Pigmented condyloma acuminatum.

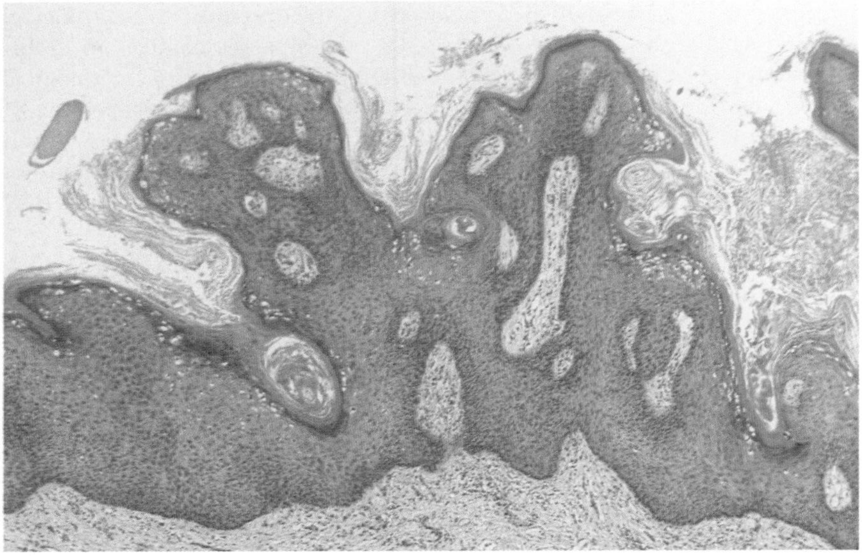

Fig. 43.10 Condyloma acuminatum. Papillomatous tumour composed of broad columns of orderly squamous cells with koilocytic change in the upper layers. (×184)

perinuclear vacuolization and pyknotic, hyperchromatic nuclei (koilocytosis) in the upper layers (Fig. 43.10). Parakeratosis is often marked, hyperkeratosis may be present to a lesser degree, and scattered dyskeratotic cells are sometimes seen. Orderly stratification is retained, the basal layer is intact and the margins of the proliferating, frequently interlocking, columns are sharply defined from the underlying stroma, which often contains a mixed inflammatory infiltrate, with oedema and prominent dilated blood vessels. Cellular atypia is usually absent or minimal and focal, and the presence of more severe atypia suggests the development of in situ squamous carcinoma.[91]

Although condyloma acuminatum is in itself a benign neoplasm, malignant transformation to squamous cell carcinoma has been described in many reports.[92–95] A relationship between anorectal and perianal condylomata and male homosexuality has been noted, and an association between persistent viral infection and malignant transformation has been proposed.[95] It has also been suggested that simple condyloma acuminatum, giant condyloma acuminatum and verrucous carcinoma constitute a continuous but not obligatory spectrum of developing malignancy.[96]

Gross et al,[90] in a study of 84 anogenital condylomatous lesions of both sexes, used molecular hybridization to identify human papilloma virus (HPV)-specific DNA sequences and the peroxidase-anti-peroxidase (PAP) technique to identify papilloma virus (PV) structure antigens in koilocytic cells in these tumours. They found HPV type 6 DNA in the majority, HPV-11 DNA in a smaller proportion of cases, and PV structure antigens in 64.3% of lesions which showed koilocytosis. Their conclusions were that an inverse relationship exists between the extent of koilocytosis and the degree of epidermal atypia, and that there is a correlation between koilocytosis and the expression of virus particles associated with anogenital HPV infections.

GIANT CONDYLOMA ACUMINATUM

First described by Buschke and Loewenstein,[97] these rare tumours occur most commonly on the prepuce of the penis where they form fungating, destructive but non-invasive growths. A few cases have also been reported as arising in the perianal and anorectal regions.[98–100]

These tumours are morphologically similar to ordinary condyloma acuminatum but they are much larger, cauliflower-like, and ulcerated, and usually single. Giant condylomata grow slowly and tend to recur; they eventually infiltrate the soft tissues causing sinuses and fistulae, involving large areas about the perineum and buttocks, pushing into the ischiorectal fossae and the rectal wall.[96] Malignant transformation to squamous cell carcinoma has been reported in approximately 30% of giant condylomata acuminata, based on histological evidence of nuclear pleomorphism, high mitotic rate and true invasion.[102] Metastasis, however, has not been reported.

Histologically, they demonstrate the same changes as condyloma acuminatum on an exaggerated scale, with a greatly thickened stratum corneum, deep expansile growths of acanthotic epithelium and an intact basement membrane. The distinction from squamous cell carcinoma is difficult in these tumours because the extreme degree of downgrowth of the expanded rete ridges mimics pseudoepitheliomatous hyperplasia or even true invasion.[101]

VERRUCOUS CARCINOMA

These rare tumours occur on the oral mucosa, the genitalia, the perianal region and in the anal canal.[96,103]

According to different authorities, verrucous carcinoma is regarded as a separate entity,[14,104] as being identical with giant condyloma,[4,105] or as possibly one end of the spectrum including simple condyloma.[98]

The only microscopic distinction, if any, between verrucous carcinoma and giant condyloma is the presence of true invasion in the carcinomatous lesion.

BOWENOID PAPULOSIS

A case with the clinical and pathological features of bowenoid papulosis was reported as multicentric pigmented Bowen's disease by Lloyd in 1970.[106] Subsequently, bowenoid papulosis was defined as such by Wade et al in 1978[107] and 1979[108] as multiple small (average size 4 mm), reddish-brown to violaceous papules and plaques, some with a verrucoid appearance, occurring mainly on the shaft of the penis in young men and in the perineal and vulvar areas in women, with the microscopic appearances of in situ carcinoma. A strong correlation was noted with previous herpes simplex virus infection and condyloma acuminatum, leading them to conclude that viral infection is important in pathogenesis. Bowenoid papulosis has also been described in the anal region.[12,109]

Histologically, these tumours are sharply circumscribed and show epidermal hyperplasia with irregular acanthosis, hyperkeratosis and parakeratosis. Atypical squamous cells are present throughout the epidermis, often scattered in a 'salt and pepper' arrangement against a background of orderly stratified epithelium (Fig. 43.11).[12] Involvement of the intra-epidermal sweat duct by atypical cells occurs, but hair follicles are usually spared, in contrast to the changes in Bowen's disease where atypical cells often infiltrate the full thickness of the follicular wall.[12]

HPV-16 DNA has recently been demonstrated in anogenital bowenoid papulosis, suggesting an aetiologial role for this virus in the induction of the skin lesions,[110,111] and evidence suggesting a link between bowenoid papulosis in males and CIN in their female sexual partners has been reported.[112–114] Immunosuppression has also been found in men with bowenoid papulosis.[115]

BOWEN'S DISEASE

Bowen's disease is a form of intra-epidermal squamous cell carcinoma which becomes invasive in a small proportion of cases. It occurs in both exposed and non-exposed skin, mainly in the elderly, as slowly enlarging, irregular, erythematous patches. Bowen's disease of perianal skin is uncommon, runs a chronic course, and may be confused clinically with benign conditions such as psoriasis, ezcema and monilial infection. Graham and Helwig[116] found that at least 5% of cases of Bowen's disease were invasive, and that 2% metastasized. They also estimated that, from the time of diagnosis of Bowen's disease until death, 70% of patients would develop other primary internal and extracutaneous malignant tumours. Furthermore, they found that women with anogenital Bowen's disease tended to develop systemic cancer in the pelvic organs. In 12 patients with anal and perianal Bowen's disease described by Strauss and Fazio,[117] 7 either had a history of systemic or cutaneous cancer previously or subsequently developed one.

Subsequent studies, however, have failed to confirm a high correlation between Bowen's disease and the development of internal malignancy.[118,119] In a recent survey of 106 patients with perianal Bowen's disease, an associated malignancy occurred in only 4.7% of patients.[119]

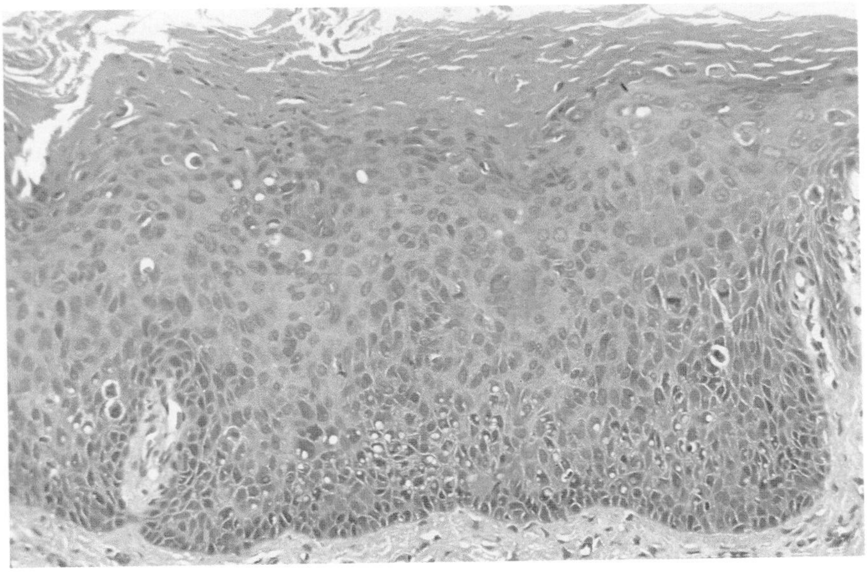

Fig. 4.3.11 Bowenoid papulosis. Atypical keratinocytes are scattered throughout the acanthotic epidermis. (×456)

The histological features include hyperkeratosis, parakeratosis, hypogranulosis and acanthosis with proliferation of atypical dyskeratotic squamous cells throughout the full thickness of the epidermis. Many atypical cells have giant, pleomorphic, hyperchromatic nuclei, and frequently scattered cells show vacuolization with pyknotic nuclei. Orderly stratification of the epidermal cells is disrupted, but the basement membrane remains intact in most cases. Although on microscopic appearances alone Bowen's disease and bowenoid papulosis may be difficult to distinguish, bowenoid papulosis presents as sharply circumscribed papular lesions, with atypical keratinocytes often scattered amongst relatively normal epidermal cells, in contrast to the more diffuse proliferation of Bowen's disease.

PAGET'S DISEASE

Extramammary Paget's disease occurs most commonly in the skin of the scrotum, penis and vulva, and only rarely in the perianal region,[19,120] where it is associated with a relatively high frequency of underlying adnexal and visceral carcinomas.[120,121]

According to the classic theory of the histogenesis of this disease, the neoplastic cells migrate from a carcinoma of sweat glands into the overlying epidermis.[122] Other theories include:

(i) metastasis to the epidermis from an underlying adenocarcinoma
(ii) simultaneous origin in the epidermis and its adnexa
(iii) origin within the epidermis extending into the adnexa and the dermis
(iv) extension into the epidermis from a contiguous extracutaneous adenocarcinoma
(v) a form of malignant melanoma or squamous cell carcinoma.[123]

In a study of 55 cases of extramammary Paget's disease, Jones et al[123] found the two commonest types of extramammary Paget's disease to be:

(i) an adenocarcinoma that begins in the epidermis and extends into adnexal epithelium
(ii) an adenocarcinoma of genito-urinary or gastrointestinal origin that spreads into the contiguous epidermis.

They recognized no cases in which the disease appeared to be analogous to mammary Paget's disease, i.e. ascent into the epidermis from an underlying sweat duct carcinoma, and concluded that in the commonest form of extramammary Paget's disease the neoplastic cells originated within the epidermis as the result of faulty differentiation of pluripotent germinative cells in an attempt to form apocrine structures. Merot et al,[124] however, on the basis of immunocytochemical studies using gross cystic disease fluid proten (GCDFP), suggested that perianal Paget's disease might exist in two forms, one derived from apocrine epithelium and the other derived from non-apocrine perineal glands. The immunocytochemical demonstration of low molecular weight cytokeratins and carcinoembryonic antigen in the cells of both mammary and extramammary Paget's disease indicates that the Paget's cells originate from glandular epithelium rather than from the epidermis.[124–127]

Perianal Paget's disease occurs in older men and women as erythematous patches or plaques, with scaling, crusting or ulceration. Histologically, large pale cells are found at all levels of the epidermis, arranged singly, in small groups, or in contiguous sheets (Fig. 43.12). The Paget cells are often seen also within the epithelium of the adnexa, including eccrine and apocrine sweat ducts. They usually stain positively with PAS, colloidal iron and mucicarmine.[128]

GRANULAR CELL TUMOUR

These tumours have evoked considerable interest, based on their controversial histogenesis. They occur most commonly in the tongue, and also in the respiratory tract, the breast, the biliary system, the nervous system, the gastrointestinal tract and all cutaneous surfaces, including the perianal skin.[129] Granular cell tumours in the skin are small, poorly defined, painless nodules, sometimes multiple, which usually pursue a benign course. Malignancy occurs in about 2% of cases.[130]

Microscopically, these lesions are characterized by pronounced epidermal hyperplasia,[131] often pseudoepitheliomatous, overlying a dermal tumour composed of large, round or polyhedral cells with small central nuclei and coarsely granular eosinophilic cytoplasm. The cells may be arranged in fascicles, sheets, syncitial masses or groups surrounded by collagenous septa, and they frequently surround small nerves.[130] The cytoplasmic granules are PAS-positive after diastase digestion and stain red with Masson trichrome.

The foremost theories of histogenesis of granular cells have proposed their origin from muscle or Schwann cells.[132–135] Rode et al[136] demonstrated positive staining for neurone specific enolase, and PGP 9.5[137] in granular cell tumour cytoplasm using an immunoalkaline phosphatase technique, and suggested that this property and their content of intermediate filaments and secretory granules indicated a neural genesis (Fig. 43.13).

MALIGNANT MELANOMA

Malignant melanoma of the anal canal is uncommon, accounting for 0.25–1.25% of all anorectal malignancies[138] and 0.4–1.6% of all malignant melanomas.[139] They are tumours of adult life, with a peak incidence in the

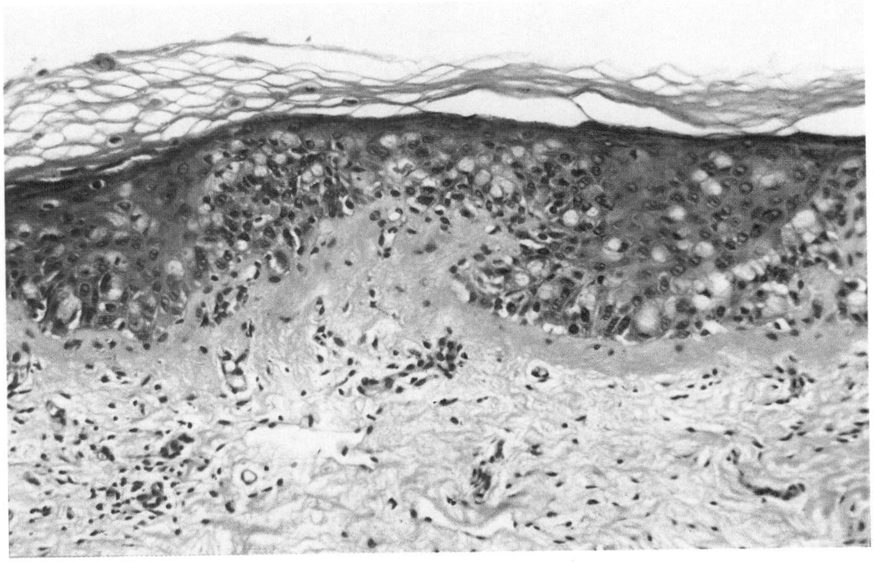

A

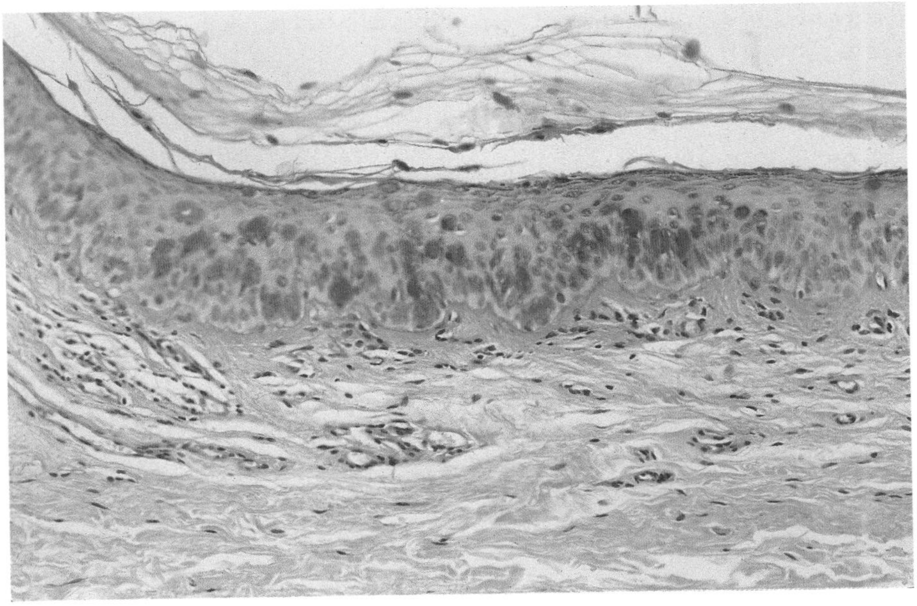

B

Fig. 43.12A Paget's disease of perianal skin. Large pale cells arranged singly and in small groups throughout the epidermis. (×1139)
B PAS positivity in Paget's cells after diastase digestion.

sixth and seventh decades and equal sex distribution.[140] The diagnosis is frequently delayed because the tumours grossly resemble thrombosed haemorrhoids, tags or polyps, so that at the time of treatment the melanomas have usually attained a considerable size, metastases are frequently established and the prognosis is, accordingly, extremely poor.[138–143]

Melanocytes have been demonstrated in the normal anal canal mainly within the epithelium of the squamous zone, but their presence also in the transitional and colorectal zones in the epithelium surrounding primary anal melanomas suggests that anal melanoma may originate from any segment of the anal mucosa.[144] As melanocytes have not been observed in the true rectal mucosa, it is believed that most melanomas of the anorectal region originate from the anal canal, whence infiltration into the lower rectum frequently ensues.[141,145] Reports of melanoma arising in the true rectal mucosa are difficult to explain in the absence of an anal primary.[23]

The clinical presentation of anal melanoma is similar to that of other benign and malignant lesions of this region. Patients frequently complain of a feeling of fullness, with pain and bleeding. The tumours may be small indurated plaques but more frequently they are polypoid masses, often ulcerated, and of variable pigmentation, sometimes prolapsing to the anal orifice.

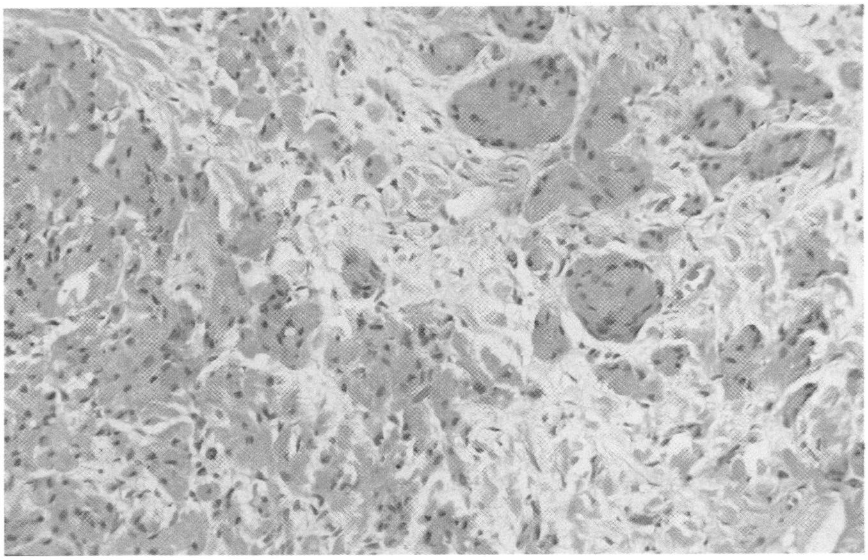

Fig. 43.13 Granular cell tumour. Cells with coarsely granular eosinophilic cytoplasm arranged singly, in groups, and in syncitial masses.

The microscopic appearances of these melanomas is similar to those on other mucosal surfaces. In the larger tumours, there is often extensive ulceration, so that no recognizable intra-epithelial component remains. An adjacent epithelial component of atypical melanocytic proliferation is seen in some tumours, especially the smaller, less deeply invasive lesions. Their epithelial growth pattern may be lentiginous, similar to acral lentiginous melanoma of glabrous skin. The terminology recommended by McGovern et al[146] for this type of tumour is 'malignant melanoma with an adjacent component of mucosal lentiginous type' or mucosal lentiginous melanoma. Superficial spreading melanoma, however, also occurs in the anal canal, with pagetoid infiltration of the epithelium by epithelioid melanocytes with clear or pale cytoplasm (Fig. 43.14). The cells seen in anal melanomas include epithelioid, spindle and small naevoid types or, frequently, mixtures of these.

The most accurate histological guide to prognosis is tumour thickness measured by the method of Breslow.[147] Neither local excision nor abdominoperineal resection is effective treatment for the more deeply invasive melanomas.[139,140]

Lymph node metastases are very frequently present at the time of diagnosis, most commonly in the perianal or perirectal lymph nodes, followed by the peritoneum or mesenteric lymph nodes, inguinal lymph nodes, liver, lung, intestine and brain.[140]

LEUCOPLAKIA

Leucoplakia is a term that in the past carried the connotation of epithelial atypia or carcinoma in situ. More recently leucoplakia has been redefined as a clinical description of thickened white plaques of epithelium, the precise diagnosis being dependent on histological examination.[148]

The term may be used for simple reactive hyperplasia due to chronic irritation, as occurs in the epithelium overlying haemorrhoids, sometimes with squamous metaplasia of the transitional zone mucosa.[14] Leucoplakia of the perianal skin may also prove, on histological examination, to be lichen sclerosus et atrophicus,[149] or carcinoma in situ.[14]

HIDRADENOMA PAPILLIFERUM

This uncommon adenoma of apocrine glands occurs almost exclusively in the vulval and perianal skin of Caucasian women, presenting as an asymptomatic dermal nodule seldom more than 1 cm in diameter.[14,148] The tumours are often cystic, composed of acinar structures and papillae lined by columnar cells with basal nuclei, granular eosinophilic cytoplasm and small processes projecting from their luminal surfaces with decapitation secretion. Usually a peripheral layer of small cuboidal myoepithelial cells is also present, but in some areas only the columnar cells can be seen. Enzyme histochemistry and electron microscopy have confirmed the apocrine rather than eccrine differentiation of these tumours.[148]

MISCELLANEOUS TUMOURS

Basal cell carcinoma occurs infrequently on the perianal skin, where its morphological features are identical with tumours of sun-exposed skin; their behaviour is similarly indolent and local excision is curative in most cases.[150]

Other neoplasms which rarely involve the anal canal and surrounding soft tissues or the perianal skin include leiomyoma and leiomyosarcoma of the internal

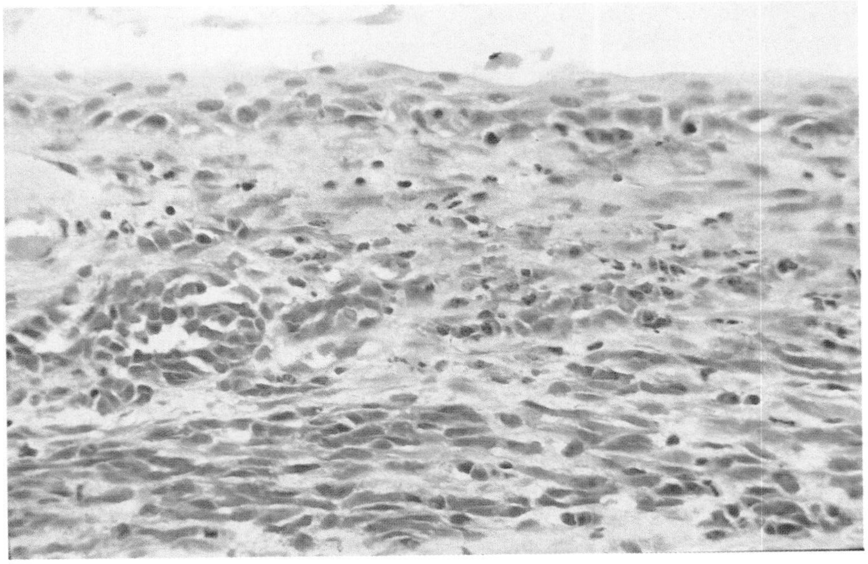

A

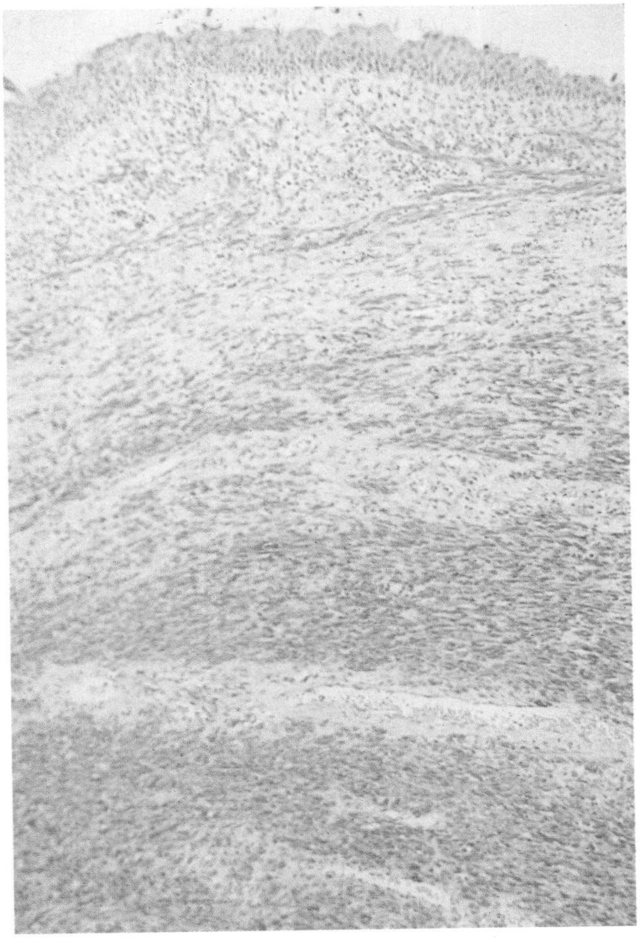

B

Fig. 43.14A Invasive melanoma of anal canal with atypical melanocytes along the basal layer of the epithelium. **B** Positive immunostaining for S100 protein in anal canal melanoma.

sphincter,[151–153] rhabdomyosarcoma,[154] fibrosarcoma,[155] malignant fibrous histiocytoma,[156,157] lymphoma[158] and leukaemia.[159] Metastatic carcinoma[160] and carcinoid tumours[13] are very rare in this region, and systemic histiocytosis has been reported in the perianal skin.[161]

Inflammatory cloacogenic polyp occurs usually on the anterior wall of the anal canal, with clinical and morphological similarities to the solitary rectal ulcer syndrome, which suggest that it might be caused by prolapse of the transitional zone mucosa.[162]

A rare lesion of doubtful nature, but one which seemingly is acquired in adult life, is the 'haemangioma' of cavernous type which seems to arise in the haemorrhoidal plexus. An argument equally as plausible could be made for an origin in progressive ectasia of a plexus which is inherently abnormal in some way.

REFERENCES

1. Walls EW. Observations on the microscopic anatomy of the human anal canal. Br J Surg 1958; 45: 504–512.
2. Morgan CN, Thompson HR. Surgical anatomy of the anal canal with special reference to the surgical importance of the internal sphincter and conjoint longitudinal muscle. Ann R Coll Surg Engl 1956: 19: 88–114.
3. Fenger C. Anal neoplasia and its precursors: facts and controversies. Semin Diagn Pathol 1991; 8: 190–120.
4. Goligher JC, Leacock AG, Brossy J-J. The surgical anatomy of the anal canal. Br J Surg 1955; 43: 51–61.
5. Fenger C. The anal transitional zone. Location and extent. Acta Pathol Microbiol Scand (A) 1979; 87: 379–386.
6. Grinvalsky HT, Helwig EB. Carcinoma of the anorectal junction. Cancer 1956; 9: 480–488.
7. Gillespie JJ, MacKay B. Histogenesis of cloacogenic carcinoma. Fine structure of anal transitional epithelium and cloacogenic carcinoma. Hum Pathol 1978; 9: 579–587.
8. Fowler R Jr. Landmarks and legends of the anal canal. ANZ Surg 1957; 27: 1–18.
9. Ewing MR. The white line of Hilton. Proc R Soc Med 1954; 47: 525–530.
10. Herrmann G, Desfosses L. Sur la muqueuse de la region cloacale du rectum. CR Acad Sci 1880; 90: 1301–1302.
11. Fenger C. The anal canal epithelium. A review. Scand J Gastroenterol 1979; 14(Suppl): 114–117.
12. Helwig EB. Neoplasms of the anus. In: Norris HT ed. Pathology of the colon, small intestine and anus. New York: Churchill Livingstone 1983: 303–327.
13. Klotz RG, Pamukcoglu T, Souilliard DH. Transitional cloacogenic carcinoma of the anal canal. Cancer 1967; 20: 1727–1745.
14. Morson BC, Dawson IMP. Gastrointestinal pathology. 2nd ed. Oxford: Blackwell Scientific Publications, 1979: 735–756.
15. Fenger C, Filipe M I. Pathology of the anal glands with special reference to their mucin histochemistry. Acta Pathol Microbiol Scand (A) 1977; 85: 273–285.
16. Last RJ. Anatomy, regional and applied. 3rd ed. London: Churchill 1963: 491.
17. Pang LSC, Morson BC. Basaloid carcinoma of the anal canal. J Clin Pathol 1967; 20: 128–135.
18. Goldman S, Ihre T, Seligson U. Squamous cell carcinoma of the anus. A follow-up study of 65 patients. Dis Colon Rectum 1985; 28: 143–146.
19. Gradsky L. Current concepts on cloacogenic transitional cell anorectal cancers. JAMA 1969; 207: 2057–2061.
20. Singh R, Nime F, Mittleman A. Malignant epithelial tumors of the anal canal. Cancer 1981; 48: 411–415.
21. Beahrs OH, Wilson SM. Carcinoma of the anus. Ann Surg 1976; 184: 422–428.
22. Lone F, Berg JW, Stearns MW. Basaloid tumors of the anus. Cancer 1960; 13: 907–913.
23. Stearns MW Jr, Urmacher C, Sternberg S S, Woodruff J, Attiyeh F. Cancer of the anal canal. Curr Probl Cancer 1980; 4: 1–44.
24. Grinnell RS. An analysis of forty-nine cases of squamous cell carcinoma of the anus. Surg Gynecol Obstet 1954; 98: 29–39.
25. McConnell EM. Squamous cell carcinoma of the anus — a review of 96 cases. Br J Surg 1970; 57: 89–92.
26. Richards JC, Beahrs OH, Woolner LB. Squamous cell carcinoma of the anus, anal canal and rectum in 109 patients. Surg Gynecol Obstet 1962; 114: 475–482.
27. Rainey R. The association of lymphogranuloma inguinale and cancer. Surgery 1954; 35: 221–235.
28. Binkley GE. Epidermoid carcinoma of the anus and rectum. Review of 125 cases. Am J Surg 1950; 79: 90–95.
29. Austin DF. Etiological clues from descriptive epidemiology: squamous carcinoma of the rectum or anus. Natl Cancer Inst Monogr 1982; 62: 89–90.
30. Peters RK, Mack TM. Patterns of anal carcinoma by gender and marital status in Los Angeles County. Br J Cancer 1983; 48: 629–636.
31. Daling JR, Weiss NS, Klopfenstein LL, Cochran LE, Chow WH, Daifuku R. Correlates of homosexual behaviour and the incidence of anal cancer. JAMA 1982; 247: 1988–1990.
32. Cooper HS, Patchefsky AS, Marks G. Cloacogenic carcinoma of the anorectum in homosexual men: an observation of four cases. Dis Colon Rectum 1979; 22: 557–558.
33. Leach RD, Ellis H. Carcinoma of the rectum in male homosexuals. J R Soc Med 1981; 74: 490–491.
34. Peters RK, Mack TM, Bernstein L. Parallels in the epidemiology of selected anogenital carcinomas. J Natl Cancer Inst 1984; 72: 609–615.
35. Wexner SD, Milson JW, Dailey TH. The demographics of anal cancers are changing: identificaton of a high-risk population. Dis Colon Rectum 1987; 30: 942–946.
36. Daling JR, Weiss NS, Hislop PHTG et al. Sexual practices, sexually transmitted diseases, and the incidence of anal cancer. N Engl J Med 1987; 317: 973–977.
37. Editorial. Genital warts, human papillomavirus, and cervical cancer. Lancet 1985; ii: 1045–1046.
38. Frazer IH, Medley G, Crapper RM, Brown TC, McKay IR. Association between anorectal dysplasia, human papilloma virus and human immunodeficiency virus infection in homosexual men. Lancet 1986; ii: 657–660.
39. Gal AA, Meyer PR, Taylor CR. Papillomavirus antigens in anorectal condyloma and carcinoma in homosexual men. JAMA 1987; 257: 337–340.
40. Palmer JG, Scholefield JH, Coates PJ et al. Anal cancer and human papillomavirus. Dis Colon Rectum 1989; 32: 1016–1022.
41. Scholefield JH, Talbot IC, Whatrup C et al. Anal and cervical intraepithelial neoplasia: possible parallel. Lancet 1989; ii: 765–769.
42. Beckmann AM, Daling JR, Sherman KJ et al. Human papillomavirus infection and anal cancer. Int J Cancer 1989; 43: 1042–1049.
43. Palefsky JM, Holly EA, Gonzales J, et al. Detection of human papillomavirus DNA in anal intraepithelial neoplasia and anal cancer. Cancer Research 1991; 51: 1014–1019.
44. Palefsky JM, Gonzales J, Greenblatt RM, Ahn DK, Hollander H. Anal intraepithelial neoplasia and anal papillomavirus infection among homosexual males with group IV HIV disease. JAMA 1990; 263: 2911–2916.
45. Penn I. Cancers of the anogenital region in renal transplant recipients. Cancer 1986; 85: 611–616.
46. Schrautt WH, Wang C-H, Dawson PJ, Block GE. Depth of invasion, location, and size of cancer of the anus dictate operative treatment. Cancer 1983; 51: 1291–1296.

47. Dougherty BG, Evans HL. Carcinoma of the anal canal: a study of 79 cases. Am J Clin Pathol 1985; 83: 159–164.
48. Paradis P, Douglass HO, Holyoke ED. The clinical implications of a staging system for carcinoma of the anus. Surg Gynecol Obstet 1975; 141: 411–416.
49. Tucker CC, Hellwig CA. Anal ducts; comparative and developmental histology. Arch Surg 1935; 21: 521–530.
50. Wittoesch JH, Woolner LB, Jackman RJ. Basal cell epithelioma and basaloid lesions of the anus. Surg Gynecol Obstet 1957; 104: 75–80.
51. Boman BM, Moertel CG, O'Connell MJ et al. Carcinoma of the anal canal. A clinical and pathologic study of 188 cases. Cancer 1984; 54: 114–125.
52. Merlini M, Eckert P. Malignant tumours of the anus. Am J Surg 1985; 150: 370–372.
53. Wolber R, Dupuis B, Thiyagaratnam P, Owen D. Anal cloacogenic and squamous carcinomas: comparative histologic analysis using in-situ hybridization for human papillomavirus DNA. Am J Surg Pathol 1990; 14: 176–182.
54. Shepherd NA, Scholefield JH, Love SB, England J, Northover JMA. Prognostic factors in anal squamous carcinoma: a multivariate analysis of clinical, pathological and flow cytometric parameters in 235 cases. Histopathology 1990; 16: 545–555.
55. Jass JR, Sobin LH. Histological Typing of Intestinal Tumours. World Health Organization. Springer-Verlag, Berlin 1989.
56. Levin SE, Cooperman H, Freilich M, Lomas M, Kaplan L. Transitional cloacogenic carcinoma of the anus. Dis Colon Rectum 1977; 20: 17–23.
57. Kuehn PG, Eisenberg H, Reed JF. Epidermoid carcinoma of the perianal skin and anal canal. Cancer 1968; 22: 932–938.
58. Golden GT, Horsley JS. Surgical management of epidermoid carcinoma of the anus. Am J Surg 1976; 131: 275–280.
59. Nigro ND, Vaitkevicius VK, Considine B. Combined therapy for cancer of the anal canal: a preliminary report. Dis Colon Rectum 1974; 17: 354–356.
60. Shank B. Treatment of anal canal carcinoma. Cancer 1985; 55: 2156–2162.
61. Papillon J. Radiation therapy in the management of epidermoid carcinoma of the anal region. Dis Colon Rectum 1974; 17: 181–187.
62. Bohe M. Lindstrom C, Ekelund G, Leandoer L. Carcinoma of the anal canal. Scand J Gastroenterol 1982; 17: 795–800.
63. Mitchell EP. Carcinoma of the anal region. Semin Oncol 1988; 15: 146–153.
64. Gordon PH. Current status — perianal and anal canal neoplasms. Dis Colon Rectum 1990; 33: 799–808.
65. Miller EJ, Quan SHQ, Thaler HT. Treatment of squamous cell carcinoma of the anal canal. Cancer 1991; 67: 2038–2041.
66. Morson BC. The pathology and results of treatment of squamous cell carcinoma of the anal canal and anal margin. Proc R Soc Med 1960; 53: 416–420.
67. Morson BC, Pang LSC. Pathology of anal cancer. Proc R Soc Med 1968; 61: 623–624.
68. Gabriel WB. Discussion on squamous cell carcinoma of the anus and anal canal. Proc R Soc Med 1960; 52: 403–409.
69. Hohm WH, Jackman RJ. Anorectal squamous cell carcinoma: conservative or radical treatment? JAMA 1964; 188: 169–172.
70. Greenall MJ, Quan SH, Stearns MW, Urmacher C, DeCosse JJ. Epidermoid cancer of the anal margin. Pathologic features, treatment and clinical results. Am J Surg 1985; 149: 95–101.
71. Hardy KJ, Hughes ESR, Cuthberston AM. Squamous cell carcinoma of the anal canal and anal margin. Aust NZ J Surg 1969; 38: 301–305.
72. Morson BC, Volkstadt H. Muco-epidermoid tumours of the anal canal. J Clin Pathol 1963; 16: 200–205.
73. Zaren HA, Delone FX, Lerner JH. Carcinoma of the anal gland: case report and review of the literature. J Surg Oncol 1983; 23: 250–254.
74. Winkelman J, Grosfeld J, Bigelow B. Colloid carcinoma of anal-gland origin: report of a case and review of the literature. Am J Clin Pathol 1964; 42: 395–401.
75. Close AS, Schwab RL. History of the anal ducts and anal-duct carcinoma: report of a case. Cancer 1955; 8: 979–985.
76. Harrison EG, Beahrs OH, Hill JR. Anal and perianal malignant neoplasms: pathology and treatment. Dis Colon Rectum 1966; 9: 255–267.
77. McColl I.The comparative anatomy and pathology of anal glands. Ann R Coll Surg Engl 1967; 40: 36–67.
78. Lee SH, Zucker M, Sato T. Primary adenocarcinoma of an anal gland with secondary perianal fistulas. Hum Pathol 1981; 12: 1034–1036.
79. Nelson RL, Prasad ML, Abcarian H. Anal carcinoma presenting as a perirectal abscess or fistula. Arch Surg 1985; 120: 632–635.
80. Kline RJ, Spencer RJ, Harrison EG Jr. Carcinoma associated with fistula-in-ano. Arch Surg 1964; 89: 989–994.
81. Jensen SL, Shokouh-Amiri MH, Hagen K, Harling H, Nielsen OV. Adenocarcinoma of the anal ducts: a series of 21 cases. Dis Colon Rectum 1988; 31: 268–272.
82. Parks AG. Pathogenesis and treatment of fistula-in-ano. Br Med J 1961; 1: 463–469.
83. Onerheim RM. A case of perianal mucinous adenocarcinoma arising in a fistula-in-ano: a clue to the early pathologic diagnosis. Am J Clin Pathol 1988; 89: 809–812.
84. Preston DM, Fowler EF, Lennard-Jones JE, Hawley PR. Carcinoma of the anus in Crohn's disease. Br J Surg 1983; 70: 346–347.
85. Slater G, Greenstein A, Aufses AH. Anal carcinoma in patients with Crohn's disease. Ann Surg 1984; 199: 348–350.
86. Hamperl H, Hellweg G. On mucoepidermoid tumors of different sites. Cancer 1957; 10: 1187–1192.
87. Kay S. Mucoepidermoid carcinoma of the anal canal and its relation to the anal ducts. Cancer 1954; 7: 359–366.
88. Fenger C, Neilsen VT. Intraepithelial neoplasia in the anal canal. The appearance and relation to genital neoplasia. Acta Pathol Microbiol Immunol Scand (A) 1986; 94: 343–349.
89. Singer A, Walker PG, McCance DJ. Genital wart virus infections: nuisance or potentially lethal? Br Med J 1984; 288: 735–737.
90. Gross G, Ikenberg H, Gissmann L, Hagedorn M. Papillomavirus infection of the anogenital region: correlation between histology, clinical picture, and virus type. Proposal of a new nomenclature. J Invest Dermatol 1985; 85: 147–152.
91. Kovi J, Tillman RL, Lee SM. Malignant transformation of condyloma acuminatum: a light microscopic and ultrastructural study. Am J Clin Pathol 1974; 61: 702–710.
92. Frieberg MJ, Serlin O. Condyloma acuminatum: its association with malignancy. Dis Colon Rectum 1963; 6: 352–355.
93. Oriel JD, Whimster IW. Carcinoma in situ associated with virus-containing anal warts. Br J Dermatol 1971; 84: 71–73.
94. Lee SH, McGregor DH, Kuziez MN. Malignant tranformation of perianal condyloma acuminatum: a case report with review of the literature. Dis Colon Rectum 1981; 24: 462–467.
95. Croxson T, Chabon AB, Rorat E, Barash IM. Intraepithelial carcinoma of the anus in homosexual men. Dis Colon Rectum 1984; 27: 325–330.
96. Bogomoletz WV, Potet F, Molas G. Condylomata acuminata, giant condyloma acuminatum (Buschke Loewenstein tumour) and verrucous squamous carcinoma of the perianal and anorectal region: a continuous precancerous spectrum? Histopathology 1985; 9: 1155–1169.
97. Buschke A, Loewenstein L. Uber carcinomahnliche condylomata acuminata des penis. Klin Wochenschr 1925; 4: 1726–1728.
98. Dawson DF, Duckworth JK, Bernhardt H, Young JM. Giant condyloma and verrucous carcinoma of the genital area. Arch Pathol 1965; 79: 225–231.
99. Judge JR. Giant condyloma acuminatum involving vulva and rectum. Arch Pathol 1969; 88: 46–48.
100. Knoblich R, Failing JF. Condyloma acuminatum (Buschke-Loewenstein tumour) of the rectum. Am J Clin Pathol 1967; 48: 389–395.
101. Machacek GF, Weakley DR. Giant condylomata acuminata of Buschke and Loewenstein. Arch Dermatol 1960; 82: 41–47.
102. Creasman C, Haas PA, Fox TA, Balazs M. Malignant transformation of anorectal giant condyloma acuminatum (Buschke-Loewenstein tumour) Dis Colon Rectum 1989; 32: 481–487.

103. Demian SDE, Buschkin FL, Echevarria RE. Perineural invasion and anaplastic transformation of verrucous carcinoma. Cancer 1973; 32: 395–401.
104. Mostofi FK, Price EB Jr. Tumours of the male genital system. In: Atlas of tumor pathology, 2nd series, Fascicle 8. Washington: Armed Forces Institute of Pathology 1973: 277–293.
105. Gingrass PJ, Bubrick MP, Hitchcock CR, Strom RL. Anorectal verrucose squamous carcinoma: report of two cases. Dis Colon Rectum 1978; 21: 120–122.
106. Lloyd K. Multicentric pigmented Bowen's disease of the groin. Arch Dermatol 1970; 101: 48–51.
107. Wade TR, Kopf AW, Ackerman AB. Bowenoid papulosis of the penis. Cancer 1978; 42: 1890–1903.
108. Wade TR, Kopf AW, Ackerman AB. Bowenoid papulosis of the genitalia. Arch Dermatol 1979; 101: 306–308.
109. Patterson JW, Kao GF, Graham JH, Helwig EB. Bowenoid Papulosis. A clinicopathologic study with ultrastructural observations. Cancer 1986; 57: 823–836.
110. Ikenberg H, Gissmann L, Gross G, et al. Human papillomavirus type-16-related DNA in genital Bowen's disease and in bowenoid papulosis. Int J Cancer 1983; 32: 563–565.
111. Gross G, Hagedorn M, Ikenberg H, Rufli T, Dahlet C, Grosshans E, Gissman L. Bowenoid papulosis. Presence of human papillomavirus (HPV) structural antigens and of HPV 16-related DNA sequence. Arch Dermatol 1985; 121: 858–863.
112. Obalek S, Jablonska S, Beaudenon S, Walczak L, Orth G. Bowenoid papulosis of the male and female genitalia: risk of cervical neoplasia. J Am Acad Dermatol 1986; 14: 433–444.
113. Barasso R, De Brux J, Croissant O, Orth G. High prevalence of papillomavirus-associated penile intraepithelial neoplasia in sexual partners of women with cervical intraepithelial neoplasia. N Engl J Med 1987; 317: 916–923.
114. Rudlinger R. Bowenoid papulosis of the male and female genital tracts; risk of cervical neoplasia. J Am Acad Dermatol 1987; 16: 625–627.
115. Feldman SH, Sexton FM, Glen JD, Lookingbill DP. Immunosuppression in men with bowenoid papulosis. Arch Dermatol 1989; 125: 651–654.
116. Graham JH, Helwig EB. Bowen's disease and its relationship to systemic cancer. Arch Dermatol 1961; 83: 738–758.
117. Strauss RJ, Fazio VW. Bowen's disease of the anal and perianal area. A report and analysis of twelve cases. Am J Surg 1979; 137: 231–234.
118. Arbesman H, Ransohoff DF. Is Bowen's disease a predictor for the development of internal malignancy? A methodological critique of the literature. JAMA 1987; 257: 516–518.
119. Marfing TE, Abel ME, Gallagher DM. Perianal Bowen's disease and associated malignancies: results of a survey. Dis Colon Rectum 1987; 30: 782–785.
120. Helwig EB, Graham JH. Anogenital Paget's disease. A clinico-pathological study. Cancer 1963; 16: 387–403.
121. Grow JR, Kshirsagar V, Tolentino M, et al. Extramammary perianal Paget's disease: report of a case. Dis Colon Rectum 1977; 20: 435–442.
122. Crocker HR. Paget's disease affecting the scrotum and penis. Trans Path Soc Lond 1889; 40: 187–191.
123. Jones RE, Austin C, Ackerman AB. Extramammary Paget's disease: a critical re-examination. Am J Dermatopathol 1979; 1: 101–132.
124. Merot Y, Mazoujian G, Pinkus G, Momtaz-TK, Murphy GF. Extramammary Paget's disease of the perianal and perineal regions. Arch Dermatol 1985; 121: 750–752.
125. Mazoujian S, Pinkus GS, Haagensen DE. Extramammary Paget's disease: evidence for an apocrine origin: an immunoperoxidase study of gross cystic disease fluid protein-15, carcinoembryonic antigen and keratin protein. Am J Surg Pathol 1984; 8: 43–50.
126. Kariniemi AL, Ramaekers F, Lehto VP, Virtanen I. Paget cells express cytokeratins typical of glandular epithelia. Br J Dermatol 1985; 112: 179–183.
127. Nadji M, Morales AR, Girtanner RE, Ziegels-Weissman J, Penneys NS. Paget's disease of the skin: a unifying concept of histogenesis. Cancer 1982; 50: 2203–2206.
128. Sitakalin C, Ackerman AB. Mammary and extramammary Paget's disease. Am J Dermatopathol 1985; 7: 335–340.
129. Johnston J, Helwig EB. Granular cell tumors of the gastrointestinal tract and perianal region. A study of 74 cases. Dig Dis Sci 1981; 26: 807–816.
130. Enzinger FM, Weiss SW. Soft tissue tumors. St. Louis: Mosby, 1983: 744–756.
131. Rickert RR, Larkey IG, Kantor EB. Granular-cell tumors (myoblastomas) of the anal region. Dis Colon Rectum 1978; 21: 413–417.
132. Fisher ER, Wechsler H. Granular cell myoblastoma — a misnomer. Electron microscopic and histochemical evidence concerning its Schwann cell derivation and nature (granular cell Schwannomas). Cancer 1962; 15: 936–954.
133. Aparicio SR, Lumsden CE. Light and electron microscope studies on the granular cell myoblastoma of the tongue. J Pathol 1969; 97: 339–355.
134. Sobel HJ, Marquet E. Granular cells and granular cell lesions. In: Sommers SC, ed. Pathology Annual. New York: Appleton Century Crofts 1974: 43–79.
135. Apisaruthanarax P. Granular cell tumor. J Am Acad Dermatol 1981; 5: 171–182.
136. Rode J, Dhillon AP, Papdaki L. Immunohistochemical staining of granular cell tumour for neurone specific enolase: evidence in support of a neural origin. Diag Histopathol 1982; 5: 205–211.
137. Rode J, Dhillon AP, Doran JF, Jackson P, Thompson RJ. PGP 9.5, a new marker for human neuroendocrine tumours. Histopathology 1985; 9: 147–158.
138. Pack GT, Oropeza. A comparative study of melanoma and epidermoid carcinoma of the anal canal: a review of 20 melanomas and 29 epidermoid carcinomas. Dis Colon Rectum 1967; 10: 161–176.
139. Wanebo JH, Woodruff JM, Farr GH, Quan SH. Anorectal melanoma. Cancer 1981; 47: 1891–1900.
140. Cooper PH, Mills SE, Allen MS. Malignant melanoma of the anus: report of 12 patients and analysis of 255 additional cases. Dis Colon Rectum 1982; 25: 693–703.
141. Mason JK, Helwig EB. Anorectal melanoma. Cancer 1966; 19: 39–50.
142. Slingluff CL, Vollmer RT, Seigler HF. Anorectal melanoma: clinical characteristics and results of surgical management in twenty-four patients. Surgery 1990; 107: 1–9.
143. Goldman S, Glimelius B, Pahlman LL. Anorectal malignant melanoma in Sweden: report of 49 patients. Dis Colon Rectum 1990; 33: 874–877.
144. Clemmensen OJ, Fenger C. Melanocytes in the anal canal epithelium. Histopathology 1991; 18: 237–241.
145. Morson BC, Volkstadt H. Malignant melanoma of the anal canal. J Clin Pathol 1963; 16: 126–132.
146. McGovern VJ, Cochran AJ, Van Der Esch EP, Little JH, MacLennan R. The classification of malignant melanoma, its histological reporting and registration: a revision of the 1972 Sydney classification. Pathology 1986; 18: 12–21.
147. Breslow A. Thickness, cross-sectional area and depth of invasion in the prognosis of cutaneous melanoma. Ann Surg 1970; 172: 902–908.
148. Lever WF, Schaumburg-Lever G. Histopathology of the skin. 6th ed. Philadelphia: Lippincott, 1983: 493–494.
149. Wilkinson DS. Disease of the perianal and genital regions. In: Rook A, Wilkinson DS, Ebling FJG, eds. Textbook of Dermatology. 2nd Ed. Oxford: Blackwell, 1972: 1785–1786.
150. Nielsen OV, Jensen SL. Basal cell carcinoma of the anus — a clinical study of 34 cases. Br J Surg 1981; 68: 856–857.
151. Kusminsky RE, Bailey W. Leiomyomas of the rectum and anal canal: report of six cases and review of the literature. Dis Colon Rectum 1977; 20: 580–599.
152. Wolfson P, Oh C. Leiomyosarcoma of the anus: report of a case. Dis Colon Rectum 1977; 20: 600–602.
153. Walsh TH, Mann CV. Smooth muscle neoplasms of the rectum and anal canal. Br J Surg 1984; 71: 597–599.
154. Mihara S, Yano H, Matsumoto H, Hiyoshi Y, Nohara M,

Morimatsu M. Perianal alveolar rhabdomyosarcoma in a child. Report of a long term survival case. Dis Colon Rectum 1983; 26: 728–731.
155. Espinosa MH, Quan SH. Anal fibrosarcoma: report of a case and review of literature. Dis Colon Rectum 1975; 18: 522–527.
156. Spagnoli LG, Dell'Isola C, Sportelli G, Mauriello A, Rizzo F, Casciani CU. Primary malignant fibrous histiocytoma of storiform — pleomorphic type: a case report of an ano-rectal localization. Tumori 1984; 70: 567–570.
157. Flood HD, Salman AA. Malignant fibrous histiocytoma of the anal canal: report of a case and review of the literature. Dis Colon Rectum 1989; 32: 256–259.
158. Steele RJC, Eremin O, Krajewski AS, Ritchie GL. Primary lymphoma of the anal canal presenting as perianal suppuration. Br Med J 1985; 291: 311.
159. Cresson DH, Siegal GP. Chronic lymphocytic leukaemia presenting as an anal mass. J Clin Gastroenterol 1985; 7: 83–87.
160. Kanhouwa S, Burns W, Matthews M, Chisholm R. Anaplastic carcinoma of the lung with metastasis to the anus: report of a case. Dis Colon Rectum 1975; 18: 42–48.
161. Moroz SP, Schroeder M, Trevenen CC, Cross H. Systemic histiocytosis: an unusual cause of perianal disease in a child. J Pediatr Gastroenterol Nutr 1984; 3: 309–311.
162. Lobert PF, Appelman HD. Inflammatory cloacogenic polyp. A unique inflammatory lesion of the anal transitional zone. Am J Surg Pathol 1981; 8: 761–766.

SECTION 7

Miscellaneous conditions

CHAPTER

44

Radiation-induced pathology of the alimentary tract

L. F. Fajardo

The sensitivity of the alimentary canal to ionizing radiation is well established.[1–5] Since its lining epithelium is composed of rapidly proliferating cells, especially in the enteric mucosa, acute surface lesions occur within hours of single total-body exposure in the 1000–2000 rad range (10–20 Gray), as seen in therapeutic total marrow-lymphatic irradiation, radiation accidents, or atomic warfare.[6–8] Delayed injury is manifested usually years after exposure to local therapeutic irradiation and it appears to be mediated mainly through vascular damage.[1]

It will be appreciated that the types of lesions that occur are repetitive along the various segments of the alimentary tube. The frequency of such lesions varies, however, in parallel to the sensitivity of each segment, and proportionally to the doses used for radiation therapy of various abdominal neoplasms.

When available, the incidence of lesions is correlated with dose and time of each segment. Since most pathologists deal mainly with delayed radiation injury, this chapter contains mostly data from the delayed effects of radiation therapy. Doses are expressed in rad or Gray (1 Gy = 100 rad) and, unless specified otherwise, refer to electromagnetic radiation (X-rays or gamma-rays) given, from external sources, in daily fractions of 100–250 rad per day. When absorbed doses (rad) are not available, the exposure doses will be given, in R (Roentgen) units.

Radiation does not produce pathognomonic lesions in any organ or tissue of mammals and the alimentary tract is no exception. The morphological alterations, however, are characteristic enough to be recognized or at least suspected.

OESOPHAGUS

Incidence

Although significant morphological injury to the oesophagus is uncommon, the incidence of pathological changes among individuals who have had clinical evidence of radiation oesophagitis is high.[3] Of 20 such patients (specimens studied 8–12 months later), 5 developed stricture, one had extensive loss of mucosa, and one had severe fibrosis of the muscularis.[3]

Clinical expression of injury requires doses of approximately 6000 rad.[3,9] Strictures are usually not seen below this dose.[9] Chemotherapy (e.g. adriamycin), concomitant or sequential, reduces the threshold of tolerance.[10]

Morphology

Acute lesions (shortly after exposure) have been observed following high-dose radiation accidents or atomic warfare, and are part of the mucosal damage leading to 'oral-death' in such cases.[11] Hiroshima casualties showed progressive mucositis during the first two weeks after exposure: swelling of epithelial cells, vacuolation of cytoplasm, atypical nuclei (multilobated, with prominent nucleoli), and finally necrosis of epithelium, which then sloughed.[12] If the exposure is local, inflammatory exudate of the submucosa is present; however, if the exposure is to the whole body and therefore includes the bone marrow, granulocytes may be conspicuously absent and haemorrhage may be profuse.[12]

Acute lesions may also be noticed clinically at the end of a course of local fractionated irradiation for tumours in or adjacent to the oesophagus, but morphological observations of human tissues during this phase are extremely rare. Studies in rats have shown epithelial necrosis and ulceration starting 6 days after a single local dose of 3000 R, followed by epithelial regeneration which was complete by 25 days.[13]

Delayed lesions are not common, and have been described especially after therapy for oesophageal carcinoma.[1–3] Even less common is damage produced in the course of therapy for neoplasms of mediastinum, larynx, lung, vertebrae or breast, which often includes some oesophageal segment within the field.[3,14]

We have observed acanthosis with hyperparakeratosis in some segments. The muscularis mucosae is either normal or slightly fibrotic. Fibrosis of the submucosa is common but sometimes quite subtle. On rare occasions there is a thick, annular scar which causes stenosis. Concomitant with, or following ulceration, there may be atypical fibroblasts, embedded in dense collagen. In the absence of ulcer, inflammatory cellular exudate is rare (as it is in delayed radiation injury of most organs) and may consist of a few lymphocytes and histiocytes.[1] Ulcers may develop at the end of a therapy course or shortly afterwards. Some ulcers persist and a few develop months later. Most ulcers are superficial and tend to heal spontaneously.[1]

Oesophageal fistulae, either pre-existing or developing after radiation therapy, can occur at the site of a malignant tumour. Such fistulae may not result from radiation but rather be aetiologically related to the tumour or to the action of digestive enzymes, e.g. from gastric secretion.[15] They can extend through the aortic wall causing fatal haemorrhage.[15]

The mucous glands show early atrophy, similar to that observed in the salivary glands, with loss of acini, and dilatation and inspissation of the content of ductules. Such glandular injury is a consistent stigma of radiation, but it is not uniform, sometimes normal and atrophic glands are seen lying side by side.[1,11]

Telangiectasia of capillaries and sinusoids may be seen, with some large endothelial cells. Occasional arterioles may show intimal proliferation.[1] The main muscular coat of the oesophagus is usually intact. In some cases it has shown fibrosis[3] and such fibrosis may distort the submucosal or the myenteric nerve plexuses.[1]

A unique complication, observed in a 47-year-old man 4 years after mediastinal therapy (4500 rad) for Hodgkin's disease, was the occurrence of mucosal-stromal bridges crossing the lumen and causing dysphagia.[14] Electrocoagulation of the bridges and dilatation restored normal function. A moderate increase in the incidence of carcinoma of the oesophagus has been demonstrated in atom bomb survivors after more than 25 years of observation.[16] A similar increase has also been described following radiation therapy (see Ch. 38).

STOMACH

Incidence

Acute gastric lesions following total-body irradiation or local irradiation of the stomach have been documented in a few clinical[1,17] and experimental[18] reports.

Gastric irradiation was used as therapy for peptic ulcer disease in the early and mid 20th century,[17,19,20] based on observations[21,22] that such therapy produced atrophy of gastric mucosa[21] and decrease in gastric glandular secretory activity.[22] The treatment for peptic ulcer consisted often of ten daily fractions of 150–160 R to the epigastric area. Subsequent observations have confirmed both atrophic gastritis[23] and decrease in gastric acidity and pepsin levels.[1, 24]

The doses of fractionated radiation associated with ulcers are in the order of 5000 rad, and the tolerance dose is probably 4500 rad. After gastric doses of 5500 rad or more, 50% of patients will develop some clinical evidence of injury to the gastric mucosa.[5,25]

Morphology

Goldgraber et al obtained serial biopsies from three of the patients treated for peptic ulcer.[17] On the 8th day of therapy, they observed karyopyknosis and cytoplasmic acidophilia deep in the gastric pits as well as loss of secretory granules in chief and parietal cells. By day 16, there was extensive necrosis of the glands, which improved progressively with time, but was still present in the pits at 3 weeks. Lymphocyte and plasma cell infiltrate in the lamina propria also increased from 16–21 days. Atypia of glandular cells was noted at 21 days. There was considerable variation in the severity of the lesions, but in general by 10–16 weeks, the mucosa was morphologically back to normal, although its secretion was still reduced.[17] Gastric exocrine secretory activity either returned to pre-irradiation levels within one year, or continued to be low for several years.[23] If the latter, gastroscopy generally showed atrophic gastritis.[23]

Up to the mid 1960s there were no delayed radiation-induced ulcers and there was no increase in the incidence of gastric neoplasms among almost 3000 patients treated at the University of Chicago for peptic ulcer disease, with 1500–2000 R.[20]

Radiation is no longer an acceptable therapy for peptic ulcer disease and so atrophic gastritis is nowadays an uncommon complication. If the stomach is irradiated today, it is in the course of therapy for gastric or adjacent neoplasms using kilorad doses, and the clinical complications observed are haemorrhage, often in the immediate post-therapy period, and delayed ulceration.

The early haemorrhage results from shallow, multiple

acute erosions, probably secondary to the epithelial necrosis described above. In fact, one would expect some degree of necrosis of gastric glands after about 1200 rad, even with the usual fractionation of 200 per day. If clinical haemorrhage does not occur in every case, it is probably due to the variation in the extent of the gastric area irradiated and in the local response within the irradiated area.

Delayed ulcers may occur as early as 9 weeks after completion of therapy, but more often are delayed several months and perforation may also occur.[26,27] These ulcers are usually solitary, antral, and measure 0.5–2 cm in diameter.[1] Gastric acidity may be low or absent and apparently the ulcers do not repond to diets or antacids.[1] Radiation-induced duodenal ulcers are exceedingly rare. We are not aware of the results of therapy with histamine H_2 receptor antagonists, for radiation-induced gastric ulcers.

Histologically, these ulcers are very similar to the ordinary peptic ulcers. The bed, however, shows stigmata of radiation with atypical fibroblasts, very prominent endothelial cells and telangiectasia. These changes are also present away from the ulcer and include stromal fibrin and the characteristic dense fibrosis of the submucosa, occasionally involving the muscularis. The likelihood of finding arterioles with severe myointimal thickening and lipophages probably depends more on time after radiation than on dose.[1]

The mucosa away from an ulcerated area often shows atrophy, especially of the branching glands, with reduction in thickness. Atypical epithelial cells with hyperchromasia and numerous mitotic figures may be seen at the level of the gland isthmus. Such cells, away from an ulcer, may be a clue to the nature of the lesion, since atypia in the usual peptic ulcer is limited to the immediate margin of the ulcer. The atypia may be so severe as to be mistaken for carcinoma.[1] Similar atypia has been described in patients who have received chemotherapy via intra-arterial (hepatic) infusion for extra-gastric neoplasia.[28]

A rare lesion following radiation or chemotherapy which occurs in children consists of large sharply defined areas in the submucosa and muscularis described as 'hyalinization', which probably consist of dense collagen.[29]

SMALL INTESTINE

Incidence

Acute injury of the enteric mucosa can occur with very low doses. Probably a significant number of epithelial cells are killed by each 200 rad fraction of a standard radiation therapy regime to a neoplasm in the abdominal cavity. Thus, symptoms of enteritis are common during abdominal irradiation. Fortunately, this injury is transient, but more severe permanent damage may occur in the fixed portions of the small intestine, i.e. the duodenum or, more often, terminal ileum or in a loop fixed by adhesions.

This high sensitivity of the enteric mucosa is related mainly to its very rapid cell turnover. The chief columnar cells that originate in the mid-Lieberkuhn crypts migrate to the villi and desquamate from their tips, completing a cell division every 24 hours in man. In fact, the epithelium of crypt and villus is replaced in 3–6 days.[1,30] Endocrine cells, Paneth cells and goblet cells have a much slower turnover rate and are considerably less radiosensitive.

Total body single exposure in the order of 1000–2000 rad is fatal to man within 10 days because of extensive injury to the alimentary and, particularly, enteric epithelium, resulting in severe loss of water, electrolytes and protein,[31] as well as haemorrhage and sepsis. This rapid death will not occur unless the bone marrow is irradiated.[11]

Delayed enteric injury follows fractional radiation therapy doses above 4000 rad.[1,2] Within the range of 5000–6000 rad, 20–30% of patients will develop clinical enteritis, mainly in the terminal ileum or in loops of intestine fixed by adhesions.[1] Of these, up to 31% will require surgery.[1]

Morphology

The acute effects have been well studied in experimental models[32–36] and, to a lesser degree, in man.[7,8,31] They are seldom seen by the pathologist since most patients undergoing radiotherapy recover well from them. In radiation accidents and atomic warfare, they are quite important and may be responsible for death (Acute Intestinal Syndrome) following total body, single exposures within the range of 1000–2000 rad.

White[8] has described the sequence of changes occurring in the enteric mucosa following such a dose. Within the first 8 hours, there is extensive cell death in the proliferative segment of the crypt, and mitotic activity ceases. Maximum karypyknosis and sloughing of cells occurs at 6–8 hours. A transient proliferative burst, sometimes with atypical mitoses, occurs between 8–24 hours. This ceases and, because cells continue migration and desquamation without being replaced, there is a tendency towards a progressive loss of the epithelial cover of villi. To compensate, stem cells are activated to divide and villi and crypt compartments tend to contain immature cells: they become shorter and cells are retained longer before desquamation.[8] In spite of these compensatory mechanisms, when the dose is high, the villi are denuded by 5–7 days. By 7–10 days, the individual totally irradiated will die of sepsis, haemorrhage, and loss of protein, electrolytes and water, if the bone marrow has also been irradiated.[11]

Fractionated irradiation results in similar, although local, changes. The chronology, however, is altered by the recovery of cells between fractions, and by the new insult added by each new fraction.[7] Nausea, vomiting, cramps and diarrhoea are frequent, transient symptoms. Most patients recover well from this acute injury during therapy, even those who will eventually develop delayed radiation enteropathy.[1] In some patients, malnutrition may become a problem[37] and impaired fat absorption can be demonstrated in many. A few patients actually have a continuum of symptoms from acute radiation enteritis into delayed radiation enteropathy, without the latent period that occurs in the great majority of cases.[1,38]

The delayed effects may appear as early as 10 weeks, or as late as 29 years after initiation of therapy. Most often, however, they occur between 6 months and 5 years.[1,38] The patients present with diarrhoea, often bloody, abdominal pain and nausea. The usual diagnosis, supported by roentgenology, is subacute intestinal obstruction. The symptoms are intermittent, leading to multiple hospital admissions, finally terminating in surgery for a good proportion of patients.

In 55 resected specimens of radiation enteropathy studied,[1] more than one half of the cases had previous intraperitoneal disease and surgery, and this presumably resulted in adherent fixed intestinal loops.[38] The affected enteric segments are thickened, with a mottled grey-red serosa, often covered at some point by fibrin.[38] Areas of stenosis may be seen externally and are obvious on opening the intestine, when ulcers are also frequently seen. Perforations into the peritoneal cavity occur occasionally; less commonly, there are fistulae into another hollow viscus.[38] The gross appearance may resemble that of Crohn's disease, but without fissures and without the 'creeping' growth of mesenteric fat onto the enteric serosa.[38]

Villi are usually short and broad. In fact, this villous atrophy is often seen in irradiated intestine, symptomatic or not, and is probably responsible for malabsorption. There is flattening of many epithelial cells and oedema and/or fibrosis of the lamina propria. Frequently there are ulcers (Fig. 44.1) that vary in depth from superficial erosions to deep defects penetrating into the muscular layers.

Most changes occur in the submucosa where there is irregular fibrosis (Fig. 44.1) which varies from extremely dense to very loose. Atypical fibroblasts are seen in many specimens but may not be numerous (Fig. 44.2). As a rule, networks of stromal fibrin, randomly distributed, are mixed with the collagen and stains such as phosphotungstic-acid haematoxylin will help to demonstrate this. Except for the beds of ulcers, there is little cellular inflammatory infiltrate. There is frequently diffuse fibrosis of the muscularis propria and fibrosis also affects the serosa, which often has fibrin on its surface. Peyer's patches at this stage are usually preserved, although presumably in the acute stage they were depleted of lymphoid tissue.

Vascular alterations are characteristic of delayed radiation enteropathy, and are probably responsible for many of the above lesions. These alterations, however, are so random and focal that many sections may be necessary to demonstrate them. The affected vessels are usually in the submucosa and in the mesentery. The lesions consist of variable myointimal proliferation, with or without foamy macrophages (Figs 44.3, 44.4). Medial fibrosis is common, either associated with the intimal lesion, or as the

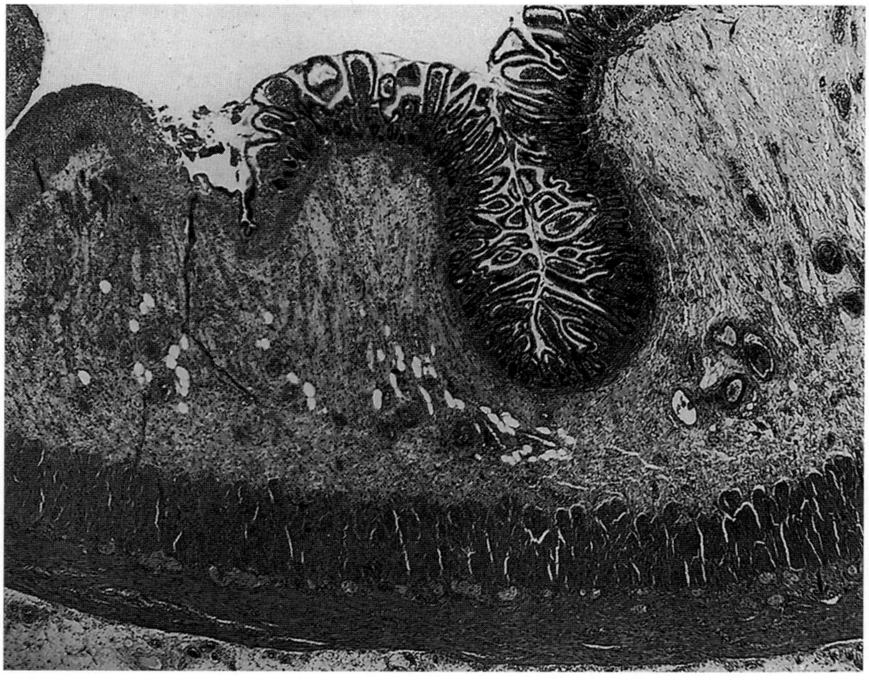

Fig. 44.1 Delayed radiation injury in wall of ileum. Notice chronic ulceration (left one-third), extensive fibrosis of submucosa and subserosa. Villous atrophy is slight in this case. Approximately ten years after exposure to an undetermined (kilorad) dose of external X-radiation for adjacent intra-abdominal neoplasm. (H&E, ×21)

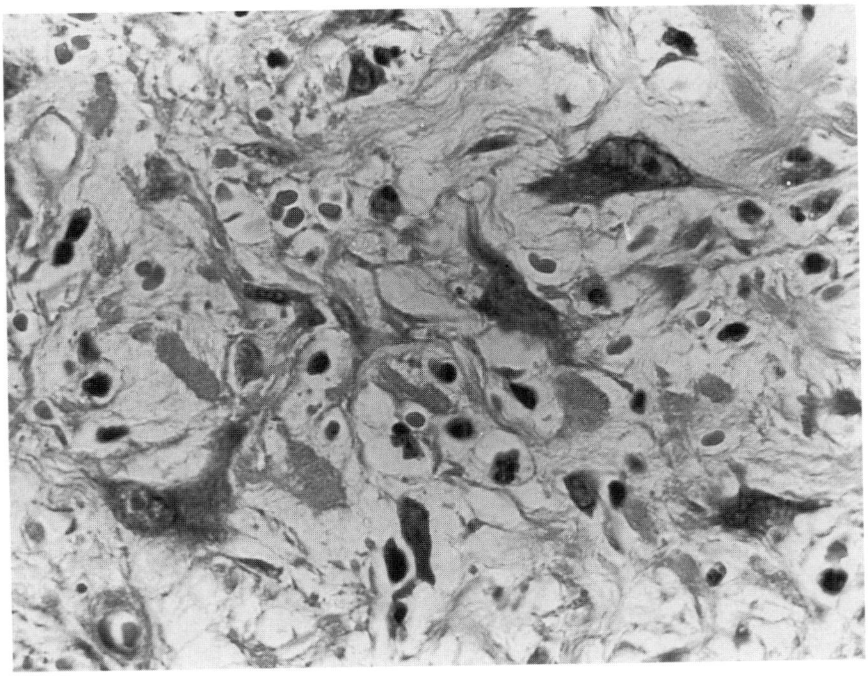

Fig. 44.2 Atypical fibroblasts. Although not specific, these bizarre, hyperchromatic fibroblasts are a hallmark of delayed radiation injury in some organs, including the alimentary tract, lower urinary tract and skin. Atypical fibroblasts are not present in all cases and their number and size are unrelated to dose. (H&E, ×576)

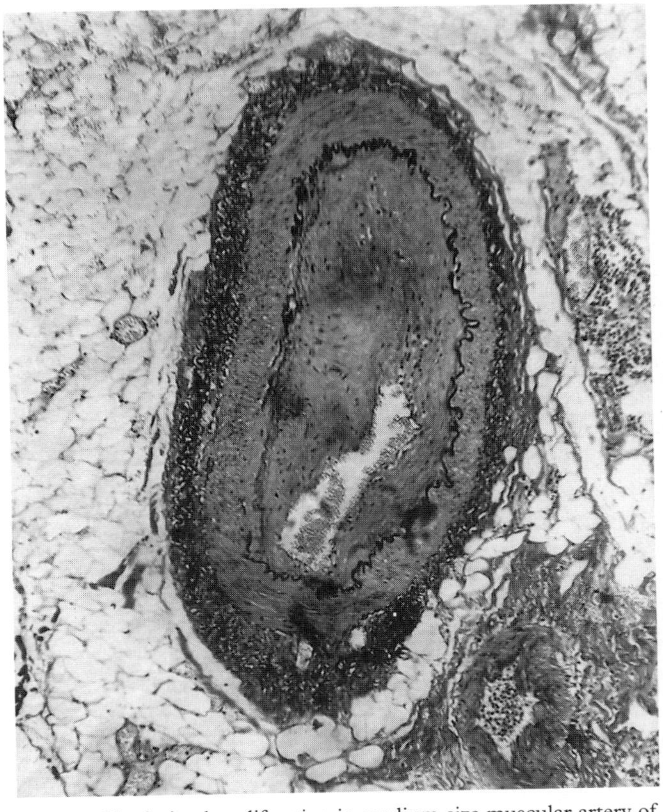

Fig. 44.3 Myointimal proliferation in medium-size muscular artery of mesentery, several years after external X-radiation of 5000 rad for endometrial adenocarcinoma. This marked decrease in luminal diameter usually results in chronic ischaemia, and may lead occasionally to acute infarction. Elastic-Van Gieson. (Elastic-Van Gieson, ×65)

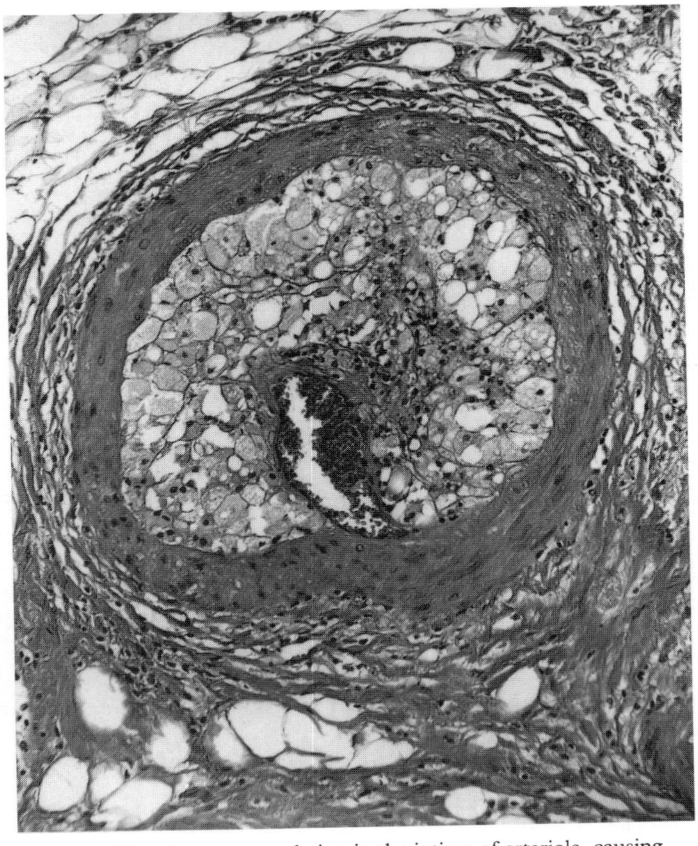

Fig. 44.4 Lipophage accumulation in the intima of arteriole, causing marked luminal narrowing. These 'foam cell' deposits in small vessels are characteristic — although not specific — of radiation injury, and tend to occur in the intestines and female reproductive organs. (H&E, ×109)

ultimate result of healed vasculitis (see below). Thrombosis is seen occasionally and usually associated with severe myointimal narrowing, especially in arteries that have undergone 'fibrinoid' necrosis. This necrosis is characteristically present below the bed of deep ulcers. The above changes involve small arteries, arterioles (<0.3 mm in diameter) and small veins; the latter is an exception to the infrequent involvement of veins in other tissues, except for hepatic veno-occlusive disease.

One can also find focal, acute vasculitis involving small arteries (<800 μm in diameter) away from ulcers (Fig. 44.5). These arteries and arterioles are located mainly in the mesentery or in the muscularis propria and occasionally in the submucosa. There is a heavy infiltrate of lymphocytes and occasional neutrophils, in the media and adventitia, with variable necrosis of the vessel wall, fibrinous exudate into the media and intima and luminal thrombosis. This lesion is a local phenomenon and appears to be self-limited. Evidence of healed vasculitis is also seen (Berthrong M, Fajardo LF, unpublished observations) and similar vasculitis occurs in other irradiated tissues, such as pelvic wall and breast. The occasional local occurrence of delayed vasculitis in experimentally irradiated rabbits supports not only the aetiological role of radiation but the limited nature of this lesion.[39]

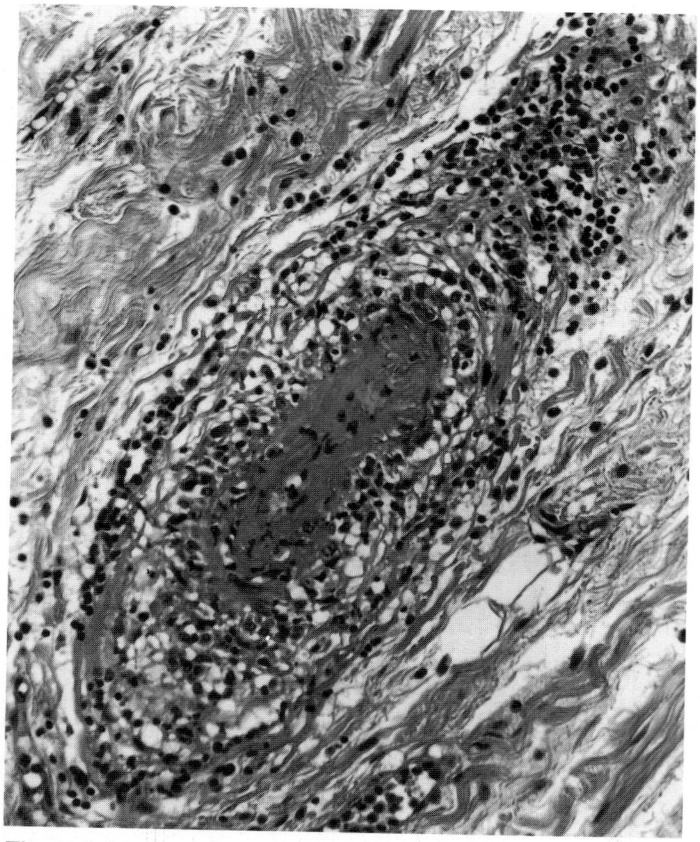

Fig. 44.5 Acute vasculitis (arteritis) may occur in delayed radiation injury. It is an exception to the rule that delayed radiation is not characterized by cellular inflammatory exudate. In this submucosal arteriole of the small intestine there is fibrinous necrosis, with thrombosis and extensive lymphocytic infiltrate of media and adventitia. Tissue obtained several years after 4500 rad of external radiation for endometrial adenocarcinoma. (H&E, ×163)

No increase in the incidence of enteric neoplasms has been demonstrated in the various populations at risk for radiation oncogenesis.

CAECAL APPENDIX

Very few reports of injury to the vermiform appendix have been made[1] and these have concerned delayed injury in incidental appendicectomy specimens.[1] In such cases, the atrophy of lamina propria, the fibrosis of submucosa and the vascular changes are quite similar to those described in the intestine. Although ulceration has not been described, other features included the presence of atypical fibroblasts, obliteration of the lumen by characteristic dense fibrous tissue and atrophy of the lymphopoietic tissue. Sometimes the appendix is normal in the presence of severe radiation injury of the ileum and caecum.

COLON

Incidence

While damage in the rectum is common, perhaps more so than in the small intestine, acute or delayed injury in the ascending and transverse colon is uncommon and reflects the less frequent use of therapy in those areas. The greater mobility of most of the colon probably results in low absorbed doses.

Acute symptomatic lesions in the rectum and sigmoid are clinically very frequent. According to some,[40] they are almost invariable during therapy for pelvic neoplasms with doses of 3000–4000 rad in 3–4 weeks.[40] Fortunately, these symptoms usually subside spontaneously.

Delayed proctosigmoiditis occurs 6 months–5 years after therapy, but may be delayed for as long as 30 years.[1] This late complication is more severe than the acute one, but less frequent.

Observations made more than 15 years ago[41] indicated a high incidence of injury to the sigmoid and transverse colon of the order of 18% after doses between 5000–6000 rad, and 37% above 6000 rad.[1,41]

The current incidence may be lower: a recent editorial[40] indicates that the range of 'severe' proctosigmoiditis is between 2.4%–5% and related to the total dose, being rare below 4000 rad over 4 weeks, but more common above 6000 rad over 6 weeks.

In a series of 100 patients seen over 46 years who presented with radiation injury to the intestine, rectal ulceration was found in 10%, stenosis in 19% and rectovaginal fistula in 29%. Proctosigmoiditis appears to be an important proportion of all radiation lesions in the gut, although the percentage of fistulae was much higher than in most other series.[42]

Morphology

The acute phase, as indicated above, occurs during radiation therapy, and is highly symptomatic when the rectosigmoid is involved, causing incomplete evacuation, diarrhoea, tenesmus, etc.[40]

In biopsies from hyperaemic and oedematous mucosa from 11 patients 10 and 20 days after cumulative doses of 1000–1200 rad and 2000 rad respectively[43] there was loss of epithelial cells, swelling of goblet cells and decreased mucus production. As expected, mitotic figures were reduced in number, there was epithelial atypia with karyomegaly and loss of nuclear polarity in the crypts. Some crypts showed microabscesses composed of eosinophils, a finding confirmed by other observers,[44] who also stressed the presence of eosinophils in the lamina propria. Granulocytic infiltration, including eosinophils, has also been described, together with oedema and fibrinous exudate in the submucosa.[1] Of 11 patients studied in the acute phase[43] only one had an ulcer and this was superficial. One month after radiation there was only minimal inflammatory infiltrate or mild atrophy; in fact 3 of 7 biopsies were normal.[43] Thus, these acute lesions subside spontaneously, or with conservative therapy, without leaving sequelae in the majority of cases.[40]

The lesions occurring in the delayed phase, months to years after therapy, are similar to those in the small intestine. Although the incidence is considerably less than that of the acute lesions, their severity is much greater.

Pain, alteration in bowel habit and bleeding are prominent symptoms but others may occur.[40] With the exception of secondary ischaemia, the lesions, as expected, are strictly limited to the irradiated area. A diffuse pancolitis, however, has been described in two patients.[45] The mucosa is erythematous and often shows telangiectasia. Ulceration, stenosis, necrosis, and fistulae are less common findings. The wall of the colon may be thickened.[1]

The mucosa may show atrophy and loss of goblet cells. Atypia of crypt cells may be present[46] and perhaps this dysplasia should be carefully evaluated, since there is now evidence of radiation oncogenesis in the colonic mucosa.[16] The ulcers, as in the small intestine, vary in depth. In relation to ulcers, and elsewhere, there is fibrosis of submucosa which varies in density, sometimes having a mixed quality, and there are areas of fibrinous exudate. Atypical fibroblasts and some degree of telangiectasia are also usual. The telangiectasia and ulceration are responsible for the frequent bleeding. Arterioles and small arteries show patchy myointimal proliferation with a variable degree of narrowing and occasional thrombosis. Some may have characteristic foamy macrophages in the intima. The colon is one site where some small and medium size veins may show myointimal proliferation, even with total occlusion or thrombosis. Almost always, however, there are several vessels that appear totally normal.

As one might expect from studies in other organs, such as the heart,[39] there is a deficit in the microcirculation of the bowel. This has been well demonstrated in a comparison with control specimens by injection of barium sulphate into the arterial system of 18 resected colons a mean of 8.4 months after irradiation.[47]

This microvascular insufficiency is probably responsible for the fibrosis and mucosal atrophy. Decrease in blood flow through larger, mesocolic vessels may cause infarcts. A few examples of segmental, acute necrosis, months to years after 4000–7000 rad in the rectosigmoid area and in the caecum are described.[1] Almost invariably, there are stigmata of delayed radiation injury around the area of necrosis.[1] The sites of obstruction of the vessels are often short and focal and many sections of pericolonic fat need to be examined in order to demonstrate them.

A rare but important complication of colonic radiation exposure, especially rectal, is colitis cystica profunda (CCP).[1,48–50] Aside from the history of radiation, the symptomatology is similar to CCP of other causes. The morphology, however, is somewhat different in that in the usual colitis cystica profunda, colonic glands breach the muscularis mucosae and occupy the submucosa, often producing mucin-containing cysts, but they do not occupy the muscularis propria.[51] In the radiation-associated

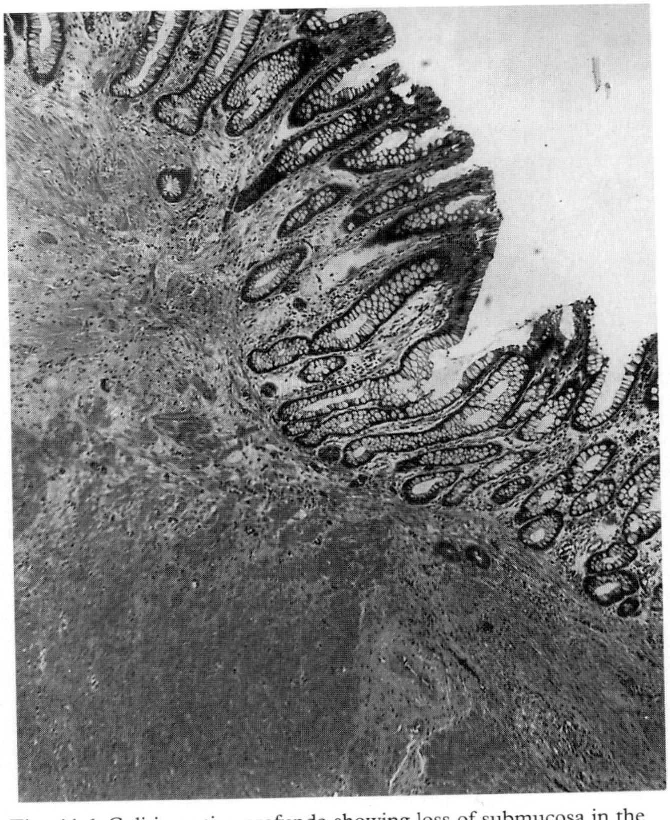

Fig. 44.6 Colitis cystica profunda showing loss of submucosa in the wall of sigmoid colon 16 years after external radiation (unknown dose) for squamous carcinoma of the uterine cervix. Notice fibrosis of submucosa on the left. There is absence of muscularis mucosae and submucosa on the right, with direct apposition of the mucosal glands to the main muscular coat. (H&E, ×43)

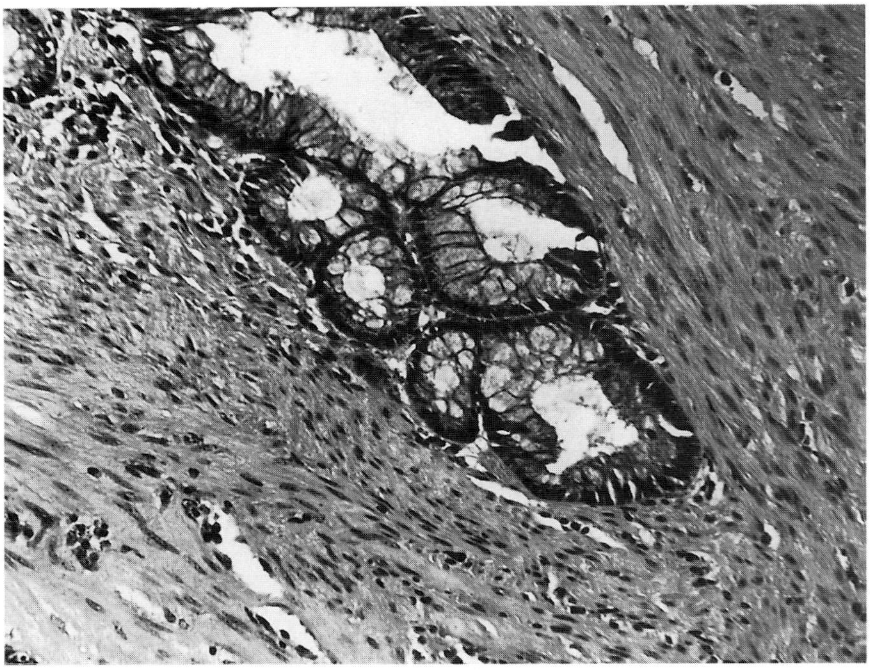

Fig. 44.7 Detail of colitis cystica profunda. There is penetration of non-neoplastic glands into the main muscular coats of the colon. Notice regularity of epithelium and absence of inflammatory infiltrate. (H&E, ×173)

CCP, patches of mucosa are seen lying directly over the muscularis propria (Fig. 44.6) and glands or groups of glands penetrate deep into the muscularis (Fig. 44.7). There is little inflammatory reaction around such glands, and large cysts are uncommon.[1] As in the usual CCP, these 'penetrating' glands are lined by regular normal epithelium (Fig. 44.7), and this is usually easily differentiated from adenocarcinoma.

Colitis cystica profunda has been observed after local irradiation of the rectum in rats.[52] In this interesting experiment, the investigators used high single (2000–5000 rad) or fractionated doses (2000–10 000 rad in less than 400 rad fractions) and systematically sectioned the rectum 4–12 months after initiation of therapy.[52] As in humans, there was often submucosal fibrosis, and CCP occurred in the most severe cases. Of 90 rats so treated, 14 developed locally invasive rectal adenocarcinoma.[52] Although not new,[53] the latter is an interesting finding, in view of the controversy surrounding radiation carcinogenesis in humans.

For many years, it was claimed that irradiation of the colon may be carcinogenic.[1,50,53,55–58] However the number of cases, among the patients at risk, was too small to establish any causal relation, even in large series, e.g. one carcinoma in a series of 100 intestinal complications of radiotherapy.[42] Recent data, however, do support some role for radiation in the genesis of carcinoma of the colon.[16,59,60] After about 30 years of follow up, atom bomb survivors began to show an increase in carcinoma of the colon, but not of the rectum, the relative risk being 2.4 times that of the control population.[16] In a group of 2068 women irradiated for benign uterine bleeding, an increased risk was found for colonic cancer, including rectum.[61,62] The doses were within the 'medium' range of 625–1050 R (in 2–4 fractions).[63] Therefore it appears that colonic exposure in low and medium doses of radiation may result in carcinoma, after a very long period of latency (10 to >30 years).[16,62] So far, there is no definite proof, in humans, that kilorad radiation therapy for malignant neoplasms produces an increased risk of colonic carcinoma.[60] It is important to emphasize that well proven radiation-induced tumours generally occur following doses below 1000 rad (e.g. 50–500 rad).[61]

REFERENCES

1. Berthrong M, Fajardo LF. Radiation injury in surgical pathology. Part II. Alimentary tract. Am J Surg Pathol 1981; 5: 153–178.
2. Roswit B. Complications of radiation therapy: The alimentary tract. Semin Roentgenol 1974; 9: 51–63.
3. Seaman WB, Ackerman LV. The effect of radiation on the esophagus. Radiology 1957; 68: 534–541.
4. Lacassagne A. Action des rayous de radium sur les muqueuses de l'oesophage et de la trachea de lapin. Compt Rend Soc Biol 1921; 84: 36.
5. Rubin P, Casarett GW. Clinical Radiation Pathology. Philadelphia: WB Saunders. Vol. I: 1968, pp 153–240.
6. Lushbaugh CC. Fatal hyperplastic lesions in neutron-exposed mice. Arch Pathol 1962; 74: 297–303.
7. Trier JS, Browning TH. Morphologic response of the mucosa of human small intestine to X-ray exposure. J Clin Invest 1966; 45: 194–204.
8. White DC. An atlas of radiation histopathology. Technical Information Center, Office of Public Affairs, US Energy Research and Development Administration. 1975: pp 75–92.

9. Rubin P, Casarett GW. A direction for clinical radiation pathology: The tolerance dose. In: Vaeth J M, ed. Frontiers of Radiation-Therapy and Oncology, Vol. 6. Baltimore, Md: University Park Press, 1972: pp 1–16.
10. Newburger PE, Cassady JR, Jaffe N. Esophagitis due to adriamycin and radiation therapy for childhood malignancy. Cancer 1978; 42: 417–423.
11. Fajardo LF. Pathology of Radiation Injury. New York: Masson Publishing, 1982: pp 6–14; pp 47–76.
12. Liebow AA, Warren S, DeCoursey E. Pathology of atomic bomb casualties. Am J Pathol 1949; 25: 853–1028.
13. Jennings FL, Arden A. Acute radiation effects in the esophagus. Arch Pathol 1960; 69: 407–412.
14. Papazian A, Capron JP, Ducroix JP, Dupas JL, Quenum C, Besson P. Mucosal bridges of the upper esophagus after radiotherapy for Hodgkin's disease. Gastroenterology 1983; 84: 1028–1031.
15. Fajardo LF, Lee A. Rupture of major vessels after radiation. Cancer 1975; 36: 904–913.
16. Kato H, Schull WJ. Studies of the mortality of A-bomb survivors. 7. Mortality, 1950–1978: Part I. Cancer mortality. Radiation Res 1982; 90: 395–432.
17. Goldgraber MB, Rubin CE, Palmer WL, Dobson RL, Massey BW. The early gastric response to irradiation. Gastroenterology 1954; 27: 1–20.
18. Brecher G, Cronkite EP, Conard RA, Smith WW. Gastric lesions in experimental animals following single exposures to ionizing radiation. Am J Pathol 1958; 34: 105–120.
19. Bruegel C. Die Beeinflussung des Magenchemismus durch Roentgenstrahlen. Munchen Med Wochenschr 1917; 64: 379–380.
20. Clayman CB, Palmer WL, Kirsner JB. Gastric irradiation in the treatment of peptic ulcer. Gastroenterology 1968; 55: 403–407.
21. Regaud C, Nogier T, Lacassagne A. Sur les effets redoutable des irradiations etendues de l'abdomen et sur les lesions du tube digestif determines per les rayons de rontgen. Arch Elect Med 1912; 21: 321–334.
22. Ivy AC, Orndoff BH, Jacoby A, Whitlow JE. Studies on the effect of X-ray on glandular activity. III. The effect of X-rays on gastric secretion. Radiology 1923; 1: 39–46.
23. Ricketts WE, Kirsner JB, Humphreys EM, Palmer WL. Effect of roentgen irradiation on gastric mucosa. Gastroenterology 1948; 11: 818–832.
24. Findley JM, Newaishy GA, Sircus W, McManus JPA. Role of gastric irradiation in management of peptic ulceration and esophagitis. Br Med J 1974; 3: 769–771.
25. Rubin P, Cooper RA, Philips TL, eds. Set 1. Radiation Biology and Radiation Pathology Syllabus. American College of Radiology, Chicago, 1975: pp 2–7.
26. Feiring W, Jampol ML. Perforation of a gastric ulcer following intensive radiation therapy. N Engl J Med 1950; 242: 751–753.
27. Bowers RF, Brick IB. Surgery in radiation injury of stomach. Surgery 1947; 22: 20–40.
28. Weidner N, Smith JG, LaVanway JM. Peptic ulceration with marked atypia following hepatic arterial infusion chemotherapy: a lesion initially misinterpreted as carcinoma. Am J Surg Pathol 1983; 7: 261–268.
29. Smith JC, Bolande RP. Radiation and drug induced hyalinization of the stomach. Arch Pathol 1965; 79:3 10–316.
30. Williamson RCN. Intestinal adaptation: Structural, functional and cytokinetic changes. N Engl J Med 1978; 298: 1393–1402.
31. Vatistas S, Hornsey S. Radiation induced protein loss into the gastrointestinal tract. Br J Roentgenol 1966; 39: 547–550.
32. Friedman NB, Warren S. Evolution of experimental radiation ulcers of the intestine. Arch Pathol 1942; 33: 326–333.
33. Hugon J, Borgers M. Fine structure of the nuclei of the duodenal crypt cells after X-irradiation. Am J Pathol 1968; 52: 701–710.
34. Watiovaara J, Tarpila S. Cell contacts and polysomes in irradiated human jejunal mucosa at onset of epithelial repair. Lab Invest 1977; 36: 660–665.
35. Wimber DR, Lamerton LF. Cell population studies on the intestine of continuously irradiated rats. Radiat Res 1963; 18: 137–146.
36. Withers HR. Regeneration of intestinal mucosa after irradiation. Cancer 1971; 28: 75–81.
37. Donaldson SS, Jundt S, Ricour C, Sazzazin D, Lemerle J, Schweisguth O. Radiation enteritis in children: A retrospective review, clinicopathologic correlation, and dietary management. Cancer 1975; 35: 1167–1178.
38. Berthrong M. Pathologic changes secondary to radiation. World J Surg 1986; 10: 155–170.
39. Fajardo LF, Stewart JR. Pathogenesis of radiation-induced myocardial fibrosis. Lab Invest 1973; 29: 244–257.
40. Lancet (Editorial). Radiation-induced proctosigmoiditis. Lancet 1983; 1: 1082–1083.
41. Roswit B, Malsky SJ, Reid CB . Severe radiation injuries of the stomach, small intestine, colon and rectum. AJR 1971; 114: 460–475.
42. DeCosse JT, Rhodes RS, Wentz WB, Reagan JW, Dworken HJ, Holden WD. The natural history and management of radiation-induced injury of the gastrointestinal tract. Ann Surg 1969; 170: 369–384.
43. Gelfand MD, Tepper M, Katz LA, Binder JH, Yesner R, Floch MH. Acute radiation proctitis in man. Gastroenterology 1968; 54: 401–411.
44. Weisbrot IM, Liber AF, Gordon BS. The effects of therapeutic radiation on colonic mucosa. Cancer 1975; 36: 931–940.
45. Novak JM, Collins JT, Donowitz M, et al. Effects of radiation on the human gastrointestinal tract. J Clin Gastroenterol 1979; 1: 9–39.
46. Shamsuddin AKM, Elias EG. Rectal mucosa. Malignant and premalignant changes after radiation therapy. Arch Pathol Lab Med 1981; 105: 150–151.
47. Carr ND, Pullen BR, Hasleton PS, Schofield PF. Microvascular studies in human radiation bowel disease. Gut 1984; 25: 448–454.
48. Baratz M, Werbin N, Wiznitzer T, Rozen P. Irradiation-induced colonic stricture and colitis cystica profunda. Report of a case. Dis Colon Rectum 1978; 21: 75–79.
49. Gardiner G W, McAuliffe N, Murray D. Colitis cystica profunda occurring in a radiation-induced colonic stricture. Hum Pathol 1984; 15: 295–298.
50. Black WC, III, Ackerman LV. Carcinoma of the large intestine as a late complication of pelvic radiotherapy. Clin Radiol 1965; 16: 278–281.
51. Wayte DM, Helwig EB. Colitis cystica profunda. Am J Clin Pathol 1967; 48: 159–169.
52. Black WC, Gomez L, Yuhas J, Kligerman M. Quantitation of the late effects of X-radiation on the large intestine. Cancer 1980; 45: 444–451.
53. Denman DL, Kirchner FR, Osborne JW. Induction of colonic adenocarcinoma in the rat by X-irradiation. Cancer Res 1978; 38: 1899–1905.
54. Fajardo LF, Berthrong M. Radiation injury in surgical pathology. I. Am J Surg Pathol 1978; 2: 159–199.
55. Smith JC. Carcinoma of the rectum following irradiation of carcinoma of the cervix. Proc R Soc Med 1962; 55: 701–702.
56. Greenwald R, Barkin JS, Hensley GT. Cancer of the colon as a late sequel of pelvic irradiation. Am J Gastroenterol 1978; 69: 196–198.
57. Castro EB, Rosen PP, Quan SHQ. Carcinoma of the large intestine in patients irradiated for carcinoma of cervix and uterus. Cancer 1973; 31: 45–52.
58. Slaughter DP, Southwick HW. Mucosal carcinoma as a result of irradiation. Arch Surg 1957; 74: 420–429.
59. Committee on the biological effects of ionizing radiations: The effects on populations of exposure to low levels of ionizing radiation: 1980. National Research Council-National Academy Press, Washington, DC. 1980.
60. Fajardo LF. Ionizing radiation and neoplasia. In: Fenoglio C, Weinstein RS, eds. IAP Monograph on New Concepts in Neoplasia. Baltimore, Md: Williams and Wilkins, 1986.
61. Smith PG, Doll R. Late effects of X-radiation in patients treated for metropathia hemorrhagica. Br J Radiol 1976; 49: 224–232.
62. Sandler RS, Sandler DP. Radiation-induced cancers of the colon and rectum: assessing the risk. Gastroenterology 1983; 84: 51–57.
63. Doll R, Smith PG. The long-term effects of X-irradiation in patients treated for metropathia hemorrhagica. Br J Radiol 1968; 41: 362–368.

CHAPTER 45

Pathology of the peritoneum and mesentery

R. Whitehead

The peritoneal cavity is lined by a smooth mesothelial membrane and consists of a closed sac which forms the innermost anterior abdominal wall and covers the abdominal viscera. In the male it is closed but in the female it communicates with the ostia of the Fallopian tubes. As it is reflected from the various viscera it forms the lesser and greater omentum and a series of complex compartments. These compartments, spaces or sacs often determine both the spread and localization of inflammatory and, to a lesser extent, neoplastic diseases. The cavity normally contains a lubricating fluid which has a low protein content and a few mononuclear phagocytes, lymphocytes and occasional neutrophil polymorphs. Subjacent to the peritoneal mesothelium or separating its two layers in the case of the mesenteries there is a variable amount of adipose tissue. A detailed description of the peritoneal cavity can be found in standard textbooks of anatomy, but, as every surgeon knows, there are an infinitive number of variations in its form which may on occasions influence certain pathological processes.

PERITONITIS

For primary peritonitis and that secondary to mechanical rupture or perforation due to the more usual ulcerating or inflammatory bowel diseases, see Chapter 21.

Special forms of peritonitis

Mycobacterial peritonitis

With the changing incidence of tuberculosis of all forms, in certain countries mycobacterial peritonitis is now a rarity. Spread to the peritoneum occurs from either the gastrointestinal tract, its associated lymph nodes or, in the female, from internal sex organs. It can be localized or generalized and rarely the latter occurs as an apparently primary form when there is no other known focus of infection. The appearance can vary from disseminated miliary tubercles to localized or generalized fibrocaseous masses.[1] An association with alcoholism has been noted.[2] More recently, the use of laparoscopy and biopsy has proven to be a safe, quick and inexpensive tool in the diagnosis of tuberculous peritonitis.[3]

Peritoneal coccidioidomycosis

A review of this extremely rare form of peritonitis is included in the description of a case associated with human immunodeficiency virus infection. The patient presented with ascites and the coccidioidomycotic peritonitis was, in fact, the acquired immunodeficiency-defining illness and responded well to therapy.[4]

Parasitic peritonitis

A variety of parasites or their eggs may find their way into the peritoneal cavity. Thus they are capable of provoking a peritoneal tissue reaction, but this may also occur in continuity with parasitic involvement of the bowel wall, such as commonly occurs in schistosomiasis or infestation by linguatid larvae.[5] The reaction may be septic if adult parasites such as *Ascaris lumbricoides* or filiaria cause ulceration and bowel rupture with release of intestinal contents. Adult *Oxyuris vermicularis* may ascend the vagina and Fallopian tube and on death or by depositing eggs be responsible, with time, for a small granuloma.[6] If seen earlier, the tissue reaction is characterized by eosinophils as in schistosomiasis. A similar, but often more pronounced granulomatous reaction which may involve the whole peritoneum in massive contamination, may occur in response to *Ascaris lumbricoides* eggs.[7] How the eggs reach the peritoneal cavity in some cases is not always clear but presumably they derive from an adult worm which breaches the bowel wall.

Meconium peritonitis

When the bowel is obstructed by inspissated meconium as a result of neonatal intestinal obstruction or mucoviscidosis, a condition similar to stercoral ulceration may occur. This can lead to perforation and be followed by an extensive fibrosing granulomatous reaction.[8]

Foreign body peritonitis

A variety of more or less irritant materials may be introduced into the peritoneal cavity either at operation or due to penetration of the bowel wall by foreign objects as a primary phenomenon or secondary to inflammatory lesions or ulceration. Thus granulomas may seemingly have no antecedent cause or be the apparent result of diverticular disease, appendicitis, peptic or other forms of ulceration. 'Food' granulomas fall into this category as does the once common talc granuloma. Following numerous adverse reports of granulomatous reactions to surgical talc, the use of a starch based dusting powder was advocated.[9] By about 1950, talc had been more or less superseded as a glove powder by starch preparations, but some 20 years later there were nearly 100 cases of starch granulomatous peritonitis in the literature.[10] Starch peritonitis may be virtually symptomless or be characterized by a systemic illness with pyrexia, abdominal pain and signs of peritoneal irritation. It occurs between 10–40 days following operation and may be associated with a peripheral eosinophilia. At operation, which is contraindicated if the diagnosis is suspected and confirmed by finding starch particles in paracentesis fluid, there is ascites, adhesions and peritoneal nodules approximately 1 mm in diameter. The recommended therapy is oral administration of steroids. Histological examination of biopsy tissues reveals a foreign body giant cell granulomatous reaction to particulate material which gives the 'Maltese cross' pattern of birefringence. It is similar to that seen in talc granulomas, but the birefringence pattern of talc is of an elongated crystal shape or is irregular.

It is likely that the incidence of contamination of the peritoneal cavity by starch is far greater than the incidence of the granulomatous reaction to it. Thus it has been proposed that susceptible individuals may have an undue sensitivity to starch. Indeed, cell mediated immune reaction to corn starch using macroscopic migration inhibition and lymphocyte DNA synthesis techniques have been demonstrated in affected individuals.[11] Starch granulomatous peritonitis has also been described in relation to starch originating in food following bowel perforation. Its mimicry of tuberculous peritonitis in the absence of previous abdominal surgery has been stressed.[12]

Chemical peritonitis

Apart from any bacterial contamination of the peritoneum which occurs when the gastrointestinal tract perforates, there may be an additional irritant effect due to the presence of gastric juices, bile and pancreatic secretions. The presence of bile is associated with a rapidly accumulating exudate and shock whilst pancreatic secretions cause fat necrosis and an exudate which is frequently blood stained, especially in the more severe acute haemorrhagic form of the disease. (See also sclerosing peritonitis due to peritoneal dialysis).

Liposclerotic mesenteritis

This entity has also been reported as sclerosing mesocolitis, retractile mesenteritis, liposclerotic mesenteritis, mesenteric lipodystrophy, mesenteric panniculitis and lipogranuloma.[13] It is regarded by some as a manifestation of relapsing febrile nodular non-suppurative panniculitis or Weber-Christian disease[14] and as such may be part of a systemic disorder or be localized to the mesentery or omentum. It then takes the form of a tumour-like area or areas of non-enzymatic fat necrosis characterized by lipophages, multinucleate giant cells and a mixed inflammatory cell infiltration which later in the course of the disease becomes increasingly fibrous.

Sclerosing encapsulating peritonitis

This term or variations of it has been used to describe two quite distinct entities.[15] The first is better termed peritoneal encapsulation, is probably a developmental abnormality and is usually an incidental finding at laparotomy or autopsy. It is an accessory membrane of no clinical significance which is attached to the ascending and descending colon laterally and the transverse colon superiorly. Inferiorly, it is continuous with the posterior parietal peritoneum. It has two openings, one as the intestine enters at the duodenojejunal junction and another as it leaves at the ileocaecal junction. It is covered by the greater omentum.

The second entity has been described as sclerosing encapsulating peritonitis, which probably accounts for some of the confusion with peritoneal encapsulation. It is also known as sclerosing obstructive peritonitis, idiopathic sclerosing peritonitis or the abdominal cocoon syndrome.

Even this second type may be heterogenous because there appears to be one type seen in Singapore, Nigeria, India and the Middle East, which occurs in pre-menarchal females, and another type which seemingly occurs in either sex as a complication of peritoneal dialysis,[16] the use of the Le Veen shunt[17] and following therapy with the beta-blocker, practolol.[18] The evidence for an association with other beta-blockers is less convincing.[16] A single case of idiopathic sclerosing peritonitis is also recorded in a male.[19]

Both these clinical entities are characterized by a densely sclerotic collagenous covering or cocoon to the peritoneal surface of the small bowel which results in obstruction. In those occurring without apparent cause in adolescent girls, the cocoon is often well demarcated and although the condition has been attributed to a peritonitis resulting from ascending infection via the Fallopian tubes, the distribution of the lesions does not support this. In other instances, the cocoon may be much more extensive and its surgical treatment extremely difficult. The increasing use of peritoneal dialysis and sclerosing peritonitis which may complicate its prolonged use has focussed considerable attention of late on its pathogenesis.[20] Several factors are evidently involved and include proliferative serositis due to irritation by dyalisate fluid, the more specific effect of the glucose it contains on peritoneal collagen, reaction to deposits of fibrin and possibly low grade infection. An animal model in stable chronically uraemic rats undergoing peritoneal dialysis has been developed in order to facilitate the study of chronic ambulatory peritoneal dyalisis-associated peritonitis.[21]

In so-called polyserositis or Concato's disease the peritoneum along with the pleurae and pericardium shows more or less diffuse hyaline fibrous thickening. The condition is usually accompanied by ascites and whilst the aetiology is obscure in most cases, asbestos exposure has been implicated and the pathological similarity to the pleural plaques of asbestosis makes this a strong possibility. Similar hyaline thickenings may be limited to the perisplenic or hepatic peritoneum in isolation and are often incidental findings at autopsy. When the pericardium and hepatic peritoneum are involved, and if there is evidence of a mechanical or constrictive effect on the myocardial function, the complex is known as Pick's disease.

Tumours and tumour-like lesions of the peritoneum

The mesothelial lining of the peritoneal cavity gives rise to a group of neoplasms which are in essence entirely similar to those which arise in the pleura. They are, however, much rarer, which might reflect the relative differences in the ease with which exogenous carcinogenic agents contact the respective lining cells. In addition, certain pathological subtypes seem to be more characteristic of the peritoneum. A further characteristic of the peritoneal mesothelium as opposed to that of the pleura is its tendency to undergo hyperplasia in relation to injury. This occurs in hernial sacs where, if considered as a possible diagnosis, it should cause little problem in differentiation from malignant mesothelioma, for it generally shows much less cytological atypia, much fewer nodular and papillary formations, no cell necrosis and no large cytoplasmic vacuoles. It sometimes occurs in the peritoneum elsewhere and then can cause greater diagnostic difficulty.[22]

Cystic mesothelioma

This rare tumour of the peritoneum is even rarer in the pleura and characteristically affects females rather than males and there is frequently a history of previous abdominal operations, pelvic inflammatory disease or endometriosis. The lesion usually takes the form of a multicystic translucent pelvic mass with cysts composed of thin fibrous septae lined by mesothelial cells of variable morphology, but usually of a benign appearance. The usual behaviour is also benign but recurrences after surgery occasionally occur. This may be related to either inadequate resection because of the physical nature of the tumour, but probably also reflects the more truly aggressive nature of some of these lesions,[23] although to date the tumour has not proven lethal. In a recent series of 6 such lesions, however, a strong case is made that they are benign inclusion cysts secondary to entrapment of mesothelial cells such as follows laparotomy.[24] The cysts range in size from 1–200 mm, contain clear serous or gelatinous material and are lined by one or more layers of flat to cuboidal cells which rarely show squamous metaplasia. The septae are most frequently fibrous but may be inflamed and have the appearance of granulation tissue. Whatever their nature, they may be difficult to differentiate from cystic lymphangiomas by light microscopy although the latter often have a smooth muscle component in the septae of the cysts, and the lining cells may be Factor 8-related antigen positive on immunohistochemical examination. Certain differentiation between the two can be made by electronmicroscopic evaluation.[25] There is no significant association between asbestos exposure and the occurrence of cystic mesothelioma and differentiation from cystic malignant mesothelioma seldom causes a problem because of the latter's cellular proliferative components and atypia.

Cystic lymphangioma

These are also rare lesions and arguably not true neoplasms. They occur mainly in the greater omentum or mesentery and are, of course, essentially a subserous lesion. Although they can be difficult to differentiate from some cystic mesotheliomas in ordinary histological preparations, the lining cells are always Alcian blue negative. In contrast to mesothelial derived cells, they are also ultrastructurally devoid of desmosomes and have few if any microvilli.[25] They are an unusual cause of small bowel obstruction.[26]

Papillary mesothelioma

The peritoneal cavity is also occasionally the site of single or multiple papillary tumours of mesothelial origin. They occur most commonly in younger women and relatively rarely in men. A layer of bland non-mitotic mesothelial cells cover frond-like extensions of a fibrous tissue corium and line underlying small anastomosing tubular spaces. This tubulopapillary pattern is quite characteristic and in the papillary cores occasional psammoma bodies are seen. These lesions are essentially benign and often incidental findings[27] but when multifocal may cause ascites and prove difficult to eradicate and can persist for many years.[28]

Papillary serous carcinoma

Carcinomas which are histologically similar to those characteristic of the ovary undoubtedly occur as primary peritoneal neoplasms. They arise in women and have a macroscopic appearance similar to primary mesotheliomas and histologically vary from the 'borderline' type of serous papillary ovarian tumours to more obvious carcinomas. Psammoma bodies may dominate the histological picture and this type has been subdivided as a separate entity based upon an invasive tendency, numerous psammoma bodies, mild to moderate nuclear atypia and an absence of solid tumour masses. Most would probably regard these as forming part of the spectrum of serous papillary carcinomas of both ovary and peritoneum. The ovaries are of necessity free of tumour or affected in a minor way on the surface.[28,29] It is thought that such tumours are derived from extraovarian mesothelium which has Mullerian potential.

Malignant mesothelioma

Although much less common than pleural tumours of similar type, peritoneal mesotheliomas do occur. Some also have an aetiological relationship to asbestos exposure but fairly frequently they do not. The clinical course, which is often one of pain, non-specific gastrointestinal disturbance and abdominal mass with or without ascites usually terminates with intestinal obstruction. Macroscopically, the appearances may simulate carcinomatosis peritonei with multiple disseminated nodules or take the form of confluent plaques or masses. Terminally, the viscera may be embedded in a mass of tumour and occasionally a multicystic appearance is produced. Infiltration of the liver and viscera is usually superficial and extension retroperitoneally is uncommon. Metastases occur in regional nodes and less frequently in the viscera.

The histological appearance of mesotheliomas is characteristically extremely variable.[30] It is arguable that the classification into the three basic types of epithelial, sarcomatous and mixed, is too simplistic and that they do not sufficiently represent the wide spectrum of appearances. Solid epithelial tubulopapillary or cystic formations may be associated with a range of individual cell features and the stromal component is equally variable, ranging from a hyaline fibrous appearance to a bizzare sarcoma with giant-cells and a variety of metaplasias including cartilage and bone. Consequently, diagnostic difficulties often occur and more and more frequently recourse to electron microscopy[31] and immunohistochemistry is necessary before a definitive diagnosis can be made.

Rare tumours and tumour-like conditions and secondaries

A rare neoplasm only recently categorized is the so-called intra-abdominal desmoplastic round cell tumour.[32] It occurs predominantly in adolescent males and is characterized by immunohistochemical reactions for muscle, neural and epithelial antigens. More recently it has been proposed,[33] on the basis of observations in two further cases, that it would be more appropriate to designate these tumours as 'peritoneal desmoplastic small round-cell tumour'.

Rarely, the peritoneum is studded diffusely by tumour plaques or nodules which histologically and electron microscopically prove to be proliferations of smooth muscle or myofibroblastic cells. Peritoneal leiomyomatosis is the term generally used to describe this condition which occurs more or less exclusively in females. Cases studied in depth will also generally reveal elements of endometrial gland proliferation and the condition is regarded as a variant of endometriosis[34] (see also Ch. 46).

Another uncommon entity is the condition of pelvic lipomatosis.[35] About 100 cases have been described in which massive amounts of fatty tissue are laid down in the pelvic retroperitoneum. Consequently, there may be obstruction of variable degree to both lower urinary and alimentary tracts. The disease is only rarely recorded in women and has characteristic radiological appearances. The histological picture is one of mature adipose tissue with variable patchy mild inflammatory foci and fibrin deposition, together with iron deposits. Whether the inflammation is primary or secondary is not known, but the diffuse nature of the benign fatty infiltration is unlike tumour. Some claim that weight reduction is effective, but effects of treatment are usually disappointing and urinary and intestinal deviation may be necessary.

The peritoneum is also rarely involved in a fibromatous process which occurs almost but not exclusively in association with some familial polyposis patients of the Gardner's syndrome type.[36,37] Although sometimes spontaneous, these lesions more frequently follow some form of trauma or surgery. Essentially, they are benign but can behave in aggressive fashion, recur after excision and cause major abdominal complications.[38]

Multifocal omental nodules occasionally occur in childhood.[39] They are essentially a mesenchymal hamartoma composed of spindle or stellate cells which may have a pleomorphic appearance and be multinucleate. Clinically, they are usually innocuous and their principal importance is in a resemblance to sarcoma.

On rare occasions, splenic tissue released by trauma into the peritoneal cavity will seed onto the serosal surface.[40] The condition known as splenosis may cause problems because of associated adhesions and bowel obstruction.

The appendices epiploicae are visceral peritoneal pouches filled with fat that occur along the antimesenteric tenia of the colon. When they undergo torsion and subsequent infarction and inflammation associated changes related to peritoneal adhesions, volvulus, bowel obstruction and perforation may follow.[41] Normally, however, they have little or no pathological significance except as the origin of calcified peritoneal loose bodies.

Another rareity recently described is the presence of an ectopic ovary in an omental cyst. The right ovary of the patient was found to be absent.[42] A single case of mesenteris ossificans, a condition likened to myositis ossificans, has also been described in the mesentery.[43]

Rare malignant tumours of the peritoneum include malignant mesenchymoma,[44] and of the mesentery, roundcell liposarcoma[45] and epithelioid leiomyosarcoma.[46]

Secondary involvement of the peritoneum by carcinoma is frequent. The ovary and the alimentary tract including pancreas and billiary tree are the origin of most primaries. Sarcomatous secondaries are rare and of these not unnaturally the gastrointestinal tract itself or the uterus is the origin of the primary, which is usually a leiomyosarcoma. Teratomas can give rise to malignant deposits of a bizarre nature and on occasions are the origin of multiple relatively benign nodules of glial tissue.[47,48]

REFERENCES

1. Rhoads JE, Rhoads JE Jr. The peritoneum. In: Bockus HL ed. Gastroenterology 3rd ed. Philadelphia: Saunders, 1976: 4: 44–45.
2. Burack WR, Hollister RM. Tuberculous peritonitis. A study of 47 proved cases encountered by a general medical unit in 25 years. Am J Med 1960; 28: 510–523.
3. al-Quorain AA, Satti MB, al-Gindan YM, al-Ghassab GA, al-Freihi HM. Tuberculous peritonitis: the value of laparoscopy. Hepatogastroenterology 1991; 38(Suppl 1): 37–40.
4. Jamidar PA, Campbell DR, Fishback JL, Klotz SA. Peritoneal coccidioidomycosis associated with human immunodeficiency virus infection. Gastroenterology 1992; 102: 1054–1058.
5. Symmers W St C. Pathology of oxyuriasis, with special reference to granulomas due to the presence of Oxyuris vermicularis (Enterobius vermicularis) and its ova in tissues. Arch Pathol (Chic) 1950; 50: 475–516.
6. Symmers W St C, Valteris K. Two cases of human infestation by larvae of Linguatula serrata. J Clin Pathol 1950; 3: 212–219.
7. Cooray GH, Panabokke RG. Granulomatous peritonitis caused by ascaris ova. Trans Roy Soc Trop Med Hyg 1960; 54: 358–361.
8. Forshall L, Hall EG, Rickham PP. Meconium peritonitis. Br J Surg 1952; 40: 31–40.
9. Lee CM, Lehman EP. Experiment with non-irritating glove powder. Surg Gynecol Obstet 1947; 84: 689–696.
10. Ehrlich CE, Wharton JT, Gallagher HS. Starch granulomatous peritonitis. South Med J 1974; 67: 443–446.
11. Goodacre RL, Clancy RL, Davidson RA, Mullens JE. Cell mediated immunity to corn starch in starch-induced granulomatous peritonitis. Gut 1976; 17: 202–205.
12. Davies JD, Ansell ID. Food-starch granulomatous peritonitis. J Clin Pathol 1983; 36: 435–438.
13. Steely WM, Gooden SM. Sclerosing mesocolitis. Dis Colon Rectum 1986; 29: 266–268.
14. Milner RDG, Michinson MJ. Systemic Weber-Christian disease. J Clin Pathol 1965; 18: 150–156.
15. Sieck JO, Cowgill R, Larkworthy W. Peritoneal encapsulation and abdominal cocoon. Case reports and a review of the literature. Gastroenterology 1983; 84: 1597–1601.
16. Pusateri R, Ross R, Marshall R, Meredith JH, Hamilton RW. Sclerosing encapsulating peritonitis. Report of a case with small bowel obstruction managed by long term home parenteral hyperalimentation and review of the literature. Am J Kidney Dis 1986; 8: 56–60.
17. Greenlee HB, Stanley MM, Reinhardt GF, et al. Small bowel obstruction from compression and kinking of intestine by thickening peritoneum in cirrhotics with ascites treated with Le Veen shunt. Gastroenterology 1979; 76: 1282.
18. Marshall AJ, Baddeley H, Barritt DW, Davies JD, Lee REJ, Lowbeer TS, Read AE. Practolol peritonitis. Q J Med 1977; 46: 135–149.
19. Burstein M, Galun E, Ben-Chetrit E. Idiopathic sclerosing peritonitis in a man. J Clin Gastroenterol 1990; 12: 698–701.
20. Dobbie JW. Pathogenesis of peritoneal fibrosing syndromes (sclerosing peritonitis) in peritoneal dialysis. Perit Dial Int 1992; 12: 14–27.
21. Miller TE, Findon G, Rowe L. Characterization of an animal model of continuous peritoneal dialysis in chronic renal impairment. Clin Nephrol 1992; 37: 42–47.
22. Daya D, McCaughey WTE. Pathology of the Peritoneum: a review of selected topics. Seminars in Diagnostic Pathology 1991; 8: 277–289.
23. Katsube Y, Mukai K, Silverberg SG. Cystic mesothelioma of the peritoneum. Cancer 1982; 50: 1615–1622.
24. McFadden DE, Clement PB. Peritoneal inclusion cysts with mural mesothelial proliferation. A clinico-pathological analysis of six cases. Am J Surg Pathol 1986; 10: 844–854.
25. Dumke K, Schnoy N, Specht G, Buse H. Comparative light and electron microscopic studies of cystic and papillary tumours of the peritoneum. Virchows Archiv (A) 1983; 399: 25–39.
26. Campbell WJ, Irwin ST, Biggart JD. Benign lymphangioma of the jejunal mesentery: an unusual cause of small bowel obstruction. Gut 1991; 32: 1568.
27. Goepel JR. Benign papillary mesothelioma of peritoneum; a histological, histochemical and ultrastructural study of six cases. Histopathology 1981; 5: 21–30.
28. Foyle A, Al-Jabi M, McCaughey WTE. Papillary peritoneal tumours in women. Am J Surg Pathol 1981; 5: 241–249.
29. Kannerstein M, Churg J, McCaughey WTE, Hill DP. Papillary tumours of the peritoneum in women: Mesothelioma or papillary carcinoma. Am J Obstet Gynaecol 1977; 127: 306–314.
30. McCaughey WTE, Kannerstein M, Churg J. Atlas of tumor pathology. Second series, Fascicle 20. Tumors and pseudotumors of the serous membranes. Armed Forces Institute of Pathology: Washington, 1985: pp 39–59.
31. Henderson DW, Papadimitriou JM, Coleman M. Ultrastructural appearances of tumours. Diagnosis and classification of human neoplasia by electron microscopy. 2nd ed. Edinburgh: Churchill Livingstone, 1986.

32. Gerald WL, Miller HK, Battifora H, Miettinen M, Silva EG, Rosai J. Intra-abdominal desmoplastic small round-cell tumour. Am J Surg Pathol 1991; 15: 499–513.
33. Prat J, Matias-Guiu X, Algaba F. Desmoplastic small round-cell tumor. Am J Surg Pathol 1992; 16: 306–307.
34. Dauge MC, Delmas V, Grossin M, Rubinstajn B, Moulonguet A, Bocquet L. Leiomyomatosis peritonealis disseminata associated with endometriosis. Ann Pathol 1986; 6: 221–224.
35. Henriksson L, Liljeholm H, Lonnerholm T. Pelvic lipomatosis causing constriction of the lower urinary tract and the rectum. Scand J Urol Nephrol 1984; 18: 249–252.
36. Sener SF, Miller HH, DeCrosse JJ. The spectrum of polyposis. Surg Gynecol Obstet 1984; 159: 525–532.
37. Butson ARC. Familial multiple polyposis coli with multiple associated tumors. Dis Colon Rectum 1983; 26: 578–582.
38. Burke AP, Sobin LH, Shekitka KM. Mesenteric fibromatosis: a follow-up study. Arch Pathol Lab Med 1990; 114: 832–835.
39. Gonzalez-Crussi F, de Mello DE, Sotelo-Avila C. Omental-mesenteric myxoid hamartomas: infantile lesions simulating malignant tumors. Am J Surg Pathol 1983; 7: 567–578.
40. Garamella JJ, Hay JL. Autotransplantation of spleen: splenosis. Ann Surg 1954; 140: 107–112.
41. Shamblin JR, Payne CL, Soileau MK. Infarction of an epiploic appendix. South Med J 1986; 79: 374–375.
42. Peedicayil A, Sarada V, Jairaj P, Chandi SM. Ectopic ovary in the omentum. Asia Oceania J Obstet Gynaecol 1992; 18: 7–11.
43. Yannopoulos K, Katz S, Flesher L, Geller A, Berroya R. Mesenteritis ossificans. Am J Gastroenterol 1992; 87: 230–233.
44. Hauser H, Beham A, Schmid C, Uranus S. Malignant mesenchymoma: a very rare tumor of the peritoneum. Case report with a review of the literature. Langenbecks Arch Chir 1991; 376: 38–41.
45. Ohi M, Yutani C, Shimomukai H, Nishikawa M, Kishikawa N, Kuroda K, Nakayama M. Primary round cell liposarcoma of the omentum. A case report. Acta Cytol 1992; 36: 722–726.
46. Tsurumi H, Okada S, Koshino Y, Oyama M, Higaki H, Shimokawa K, Yamauchi O, Moriwaki H, Muto Y. A case of leiomyoblastoma (epithelioid leiomyosarcoma) of the greater omentum. Gastroenterol Jpn 1991; 26: 370–375.
47. Truong LD, Jurco S, McGavran MH. Gliomatosis peritonei. Am J Surg Pathol 1982; 6: 443–449.
48. Gratama S, Swaak-Saeys AM, van der Weiden RM, Chadha S. Low-grade immature teratomas with peritoneal gliomatosis: a case report. Eur J Obstet Gynecol Reprod Biol 1991; 39: 235–241.

CHAPTER

46 The alimentary tract in systemic disease and miscellaneous lesions

R. Whitehead

SYSTEMIC DISEASES

Involvement of the alimentary tract in systemic disease states has already been referred to in previous chapters when the involvement occurs with sufficient regularity that it produces a well recognized clinicopathological entity, e.g. dysphagia due to oesophageal fibrosis in systemic sclerosis. On occasions, alimentary tract involvement by a systemic disease process occurs with sufficient rarity and has a clinical presentation so unusual that it is specifically reported in the literature.

Systemic sclerosis

In addition to the oesophagus, we have already seen that the rest of the alimentary tract can be involved in this disease. A common manifestation is constipation which may alternate with diarrhoea due to bacterial overgrowth and malabsorption may result. In addition, a megacolon and a rather characteristic type of large mouthed diverticular disease may occur, as does colonic volvulus, telangiectasia, stercoral ulceration and, rarely, rectal prolapse.[1] The remaining spectrum of connective tissue disorders, including rheumatoid arthritis, frequently affect the bowel because of an associated vasculitis, which is considered in Chapters 31 and 32. On rare occasions when the vasculitis affects the gut predominantly, the presentation can mimic severe inflammatory bowel disease,[2,3] cause malabsorption or even bowel perforation.[4]

Another connective tissue disorder, the Ehlers-Danlos syndrome, in which the defect is one of collagen structure, may be associated with intestinal lesions. Rarely, the abnormality is associated with spontaneous rupture of the colon.[5]

Systemic histiocytosis (histiocytosis X)

This constitutes a group of disorders of unknown aetiology characterized by the proliferation of and infiltration of various tissue by histiocytes and eosinophils in differing proportions. In generalized disease, involvement of the small intestine can occur and may cause malabsorption.[6] Although skin involvement in this disorder is common, presentation due to perianal disease is distinctly unusual.[7] There are also case reports describing protein losing enteropathy and ulcerative involvement of the ileum and colon.[8] A case of apparent isolated gastric histiocytosis X was recently described,[9] and four others were cited from the literature. The histiocytes had typical characteristics with interdigitating cytoplasmic projections, Birbeck granules and an absence of phagocytosis.

Systemic mast cell disease

In a review of small intestinal involvement in systemic mast cell disease, attention has been drawn to a possible relationship with gluten sensitive enteropathy[10] but malabsorption can also occur secondary to the intestinal infiltration.[11] The disease may also be complicated by peptic ulceration and intractable gastrointestinal haemorrhage.[12]

Waldenström's macroglobulinaemia

Intestinal manifestations of Waldenström's macroglobulinaemia, although uncommon, do occur and the appearance of the small intestine in this disorder is well described.[13–15] In addition to lymphangiectasia, the lamina propria of the blunted villi contains deposits of lipids and

IgM of kappa type. The dilated lymphatics may be related to mesenteric lymph node involvement which probably accounts for the protein loss which occurs in addition to malabsorption.[16]

Behcet's syndrome

Intestinal ulceration has been described in Behcet's syndrome,[17] a disease characterized by arthritis, uveitis, erythema nodosum, orogenital aphthoid ulceration, migratory thrombophlebitis and widespread central nervous system lesions. The ileocaecal region seems to be the commonest site for involvement and the often perforating ulcers tend to be punched out, undermined and radiologically of collar-stud type. The background mucosa is minimally inflamed and differentiation from Crohn's disease and ulcerative colitis is usually clearcut. A lymphocytic infiltrate of submucosal veins is described[18] but it is doubtful if the ulcers have an ischaemic basis as is claimed,[19] despite the fact that a so-called vasculo-Behcet's disease variant is described. This is an entity, however, which is basically a large vessel arteritis leading to aneurysms.[20]

Amyloidosis

The pathogenesis and biochemistry of amyloidosis has been the subject of recent comprehensive reviews.[21,22] Amyloid involvement of the alimentary tract occurs in well over 90% of cases of systemic disease and accounts for symptoms related to impaired motility, malabsorption and ulceration due to ischaemia. On occasion, isolated involvement of the small intestine produces multiple polyps,[23] and colonic involvement may simulate inflammatory bowel disease,[24] ischaemic colitis,[25] or present as intestinal pseudo-obstruction,[26] megacolon and volvulus.[27] In biopsy tissues taken at endoscopy, the second part of the duodenum is most frequently involved.[28]

Haematological malignancies

Apart from direct bowel involvement by the malignant process and bowel haemorrhage secondary to thrombocytopaenia, two further characteristic bowel complications may occur, but they are rare.

Neutropaenic colitis (Typhlitis)

Patients with profound neutropaenia may develop a lesion, usually involving the terminal ileum, caecum and ascending colon, which is characterized by oedema, inflammation and finally necrosis. It has been termed neutropaenic colitis, necrotizing enteropathy, typhlitis and the ileocaecal syndrome. Diagnosis is rarely made before death and recovery is unusual, either with or without surgical intervention, but is described.[29] This complication occurs in patients with lymphoma, leukaemia, aplastic anaemia, multiple myeloma and cyclical neutropaenia. It appears that the incidence of this condition has risen since the introduction of chemotherapy for these disorders,[30,31] although this is denied by others.[32]

Extramedullary haemopoiesis in the bowel

Extramedullary haemopoiesis is common in spleen and liver and also occurs in kidney and adrenal glands. Other sites include mediastinum, skin, the joints and the epidural space. It is perhaps surprising in view of the lymphoid tissue present in the bowel that the condition is rare in this site. Involvement of the terminal ileum with ulceration and haemorrhage treated by resection has, however, been recorded.[33]

The haemolytic-uraemic syndrome

This pathological entity is characterized by a microangiopathy, oliguric renal failure and thrombocytopaenia which affects infants and children. Despite greater clinical awareness, its early manifestations are often misdiagnosed. Attention has been drawn to its presentation as an acute colitis which may mimic ulcerative colitis.[34,35] The underlying pathology is ischaemia due to microvascular occlusion and the outcome may be intestinal gangrene or, if less severe, intestinal stricture, but recovery is the rule as the renal manifestations occur.[35,36] Sometimes the haemolytic-uraemic syndrome itself is precipitated by a colonic infection; such an association has been described with a verotoxin producing strain of *E. coli*.[37]

Sarcoidosis

Sarcoid involvement of the gastrointestinal tract is overall a rare phenomenon. Most frequently, it is described in the stomach[38] but rectal and colonic involvement is also documented.[39] It has been claimed that so-called idiopathic granulomatous gastritis may represent persistent gastric sarcoidosis that has resolved in other sites.[40] Rarely sarcoidosis of the small intestine has been described in association with folate deficiency[41] and as a cause of duodenal obstruction,[42] protein-losing enteropathy[43] and IgA deficiency with nodular lymphoid hyperplasia.[44]

MISCELLANEOUS LESIONS

Alimentary xanthomatosis

Xanthomatosis presents as plaques or nodules in a variety of tissues but frequently involves the skin. The condition may or may not be associated with hypercholesterolaemia and thus sometimes occurs in association with diabetes mellitus, obstructive jaundice or other disturbances of lipid metabolism. Gastric involvement has also been described in otherwise histologically characteristic xanthoma disseminatum.[45] In the alimentary tract unrelated so-called xanthalesmas occur but mainly only in the stomach and intestine and are usually unassociated with systemic hyperlipidaemia.

Gastric xanthalesmas occur in any part of the stomach as yellow or white nodules up to 5 mm in diameter. They are histologically characterized by collections of foamy histiocytes which have a peripheral nucleus. The histiocytes contain neutral fat and cholesterol and are PAS and Alcian blue negative which easily differentiates them from signet ring carcinoma cells with which they may be confused.[46] They become increasingly frequent with age and appear to have some relationship with erosion, ulceration and gastric surgery,[38] but their presence is most closely correlated with age.[47] Similar isolated lesions also occur in the small intestine but less commonly,[48] and rarely gastric xanthomatosis occurs in association with hypercholesterolaemia disappearing as the hyperlipidaemic state resolves.[49]

Intestinal endometriosis and related conditions

Not unexpectedly, endometriosis most commonly affects those parts of the bowel which lie in proximity to the internal genital organs. Thus the rectum and sigmoid colon account for most cases followed by small bowel, caecum and appendix.[50]

It is estimated that of all menstruating women, 15% will develop endometriosis and that in up to 30% the intestine will be involved.[51] Clinically, the condition can account for intermittent abdominal pain, intestinal obstruction and rectal bleeding[52] and pathologically, ulceration, obstruction, peritoneal adhesions and tumefaction. The histological diagnosis presents little problems if the possibility of the condition is entertained.

Endosalpingiosis consists of benign Fallopian tube epithelium involving the peritoneum or pelvic lymph nodes and other sites within the abdominal cavity. Psammoma bodies are often a feature together with extra-uterine decidual reactions. It is a condition which arguably is more in the domain of texts devoted to gynaecological pathology.

Intestinal melanosis and related conditions

Melanosis coli and cathartic colon

Whilst the use of purgatives may result in diarrhoea with hypokalaemia or protein losing enteropathy, cachexia and hypogammaglobulinaemia,[53] more commonly it is symptomless and diagnosed only when melanosis coli is seen in a rectal biopsy or surgical specimen, often removed in the investigation or treatment of unrelated disorders. The cathartic colon syndrome occurs when purgative abuse leads to additional pathological features such as thinning of the colonic wall, loss of haustra, hypertrophy of the muscularis mucosa and fatty infiltration of the submucosa (Fig. 46.1).[38] Changes in intestinal neurones may also occur (see Ch. 22).

In melanosis coli, a diffuse grey or brown-black discolouration of the colonic mucosa occurs. It begins in the proximal large bowel and progresses distally as its duration and intensity increases. Thus its presence in the rectum denotes chronicity.

The pigmentation in melanosis coli is due to the presence in macrophages of residual bodies containing lipofuscin derived from autolysosomes. The lipofuscin is formed from organelles damaged by the use of both anthracene purgatives (cascara, senna, aloes and rhubarb) and, to a lesser degree, diphenylmethane derivatives.[54] The macrophages occur principally in the lamina propria but in heavily pigmented bowels submucosal macrophages may be seen and the pigment may occur in neurones as well as regional nodes. Melanosis coli has been produced by these substances both in experimental animals and man and is an entity quite distinct from so-called melanosis duodeni. There is positive evidence that the presence

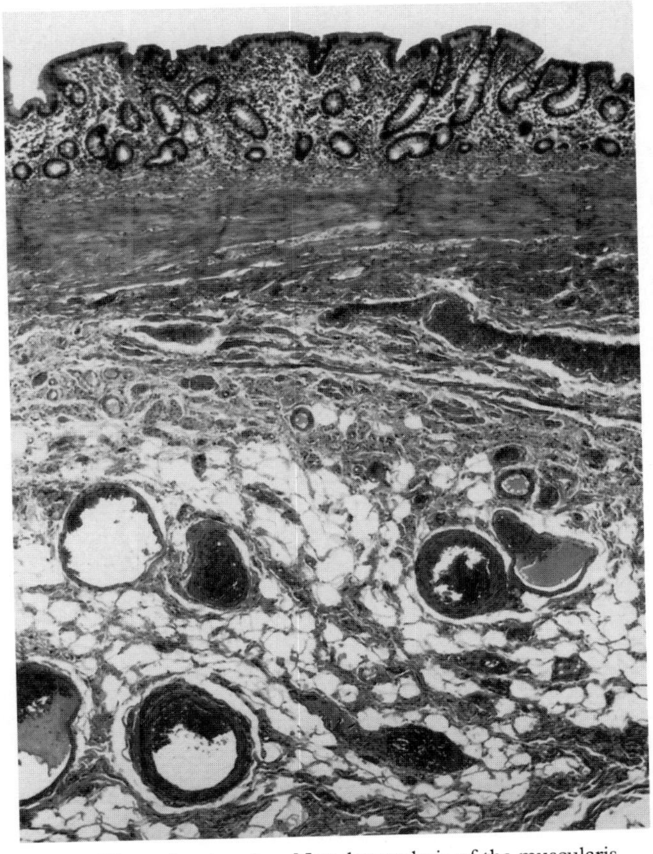

Fig. 46.1 The cathartic colon. Note hyperplasia of the muscularis mucosa and marked fatty infiltration of the submucosa. (H&E, ×72)

of melanosis coli is not a good indicator of impairment of colonic motor function in constipated patients, but simply indicates the type of purgative being used.[53]

Melanosis duodeni

This differs markedly from melanosis coli because the pigmentation is punctate and at endoscopy quite spectacular.[55] It has been shown that the pigment is mainly ferrous sulphide and also contains small amounts of calcium, potassium, aluminium, magnesium, silica and silver. There are only 11 cases in the literature and despite much speculation,[56] the cause of the disorder is unknown. Histologically, the appearance is as spectacular as the endoscopy appearance with densely pigmented brown-black macrophages in the lamina propria at the tips of the villi. The pigment is PAS positive, and bleached readily with potassium permanganate but not hydrogen peroxide.[57] The Prussian blue reaction has been recorded as partly positive often at granule margins.[55,56]

Haemosiderosis

The lamina propria of the villous tips of the duodenum or jejunum may also contain haemosiderin filled macrophages. It tends to be seen after iron medication and is seen in transfusional siderosis. In haemochromatosis, iron pigment by contrast is seen in the epithelial cells and in macrophages deeper in the lamina propria, as in some cases of Whipple's disease.[38]

The brown bowel syndrome (lipofuscinosis)

The bowel smooth muscle is involved in the ceroid pigmentation that occurs in association with hypoalbuminaemia and vitamin E deficiency.[38] This is claimed to always be the result of serious and severe malabsorption[58] but sometimes this is not apparent.[59] The evidence that its presence affects muscle function is also inconclusive although the presence of lipofuscinosis has been argued as an indication for vitamin E therapy.[58] The pigmentation is visible to the naked eye at necropsy or in surgical specimens and easily demonstrated in the polar cytoplasm of the smooth muscle cells by a variety of histochemical methods for lipofuscin. If lipofuscin is seen in biopsy specimens of bowel in the muscularis mucosa, it is usually an indication that lipofuscinosis is widespread and severe. If not already suspected, a malabsorption syndrome should be excluded by appropriate investigation.

Pneumatosis cystoides intestinalis

It is clear that all conditions described under this heading are not one and the same disease in terms of pathogenesis. From the clinical standpoint and age distribution, there are two broad categories. One affects mainly children but also some adults and seems to be a complication of severe ileocolitis in which gas forming organisms invade the bowel wall. The other mainly affects adults and is associated with either a local defect due to ulceration in the bowel or chronic obstructive airways disease.

In the former, the ileocolitis is severe, frequently of full thickness, often has a primary or superimposed ischaemic element and thus tends to be associated with severe morbidity and mortality. A similar pathological entity which affects another part of the gastrointestinal tract is so-called emphysematous gastritis,[60,61] and gas forming organisms invading the urinary bladder, for example, can produce a similar lesion. This type of pneumatosis is exemplified in the necrotizing enterocolitis of infancy and that which occasionally complicates pseudomembranous colitis, ischaemic enterocolitis in adults, ulcerative colitis, Crohn's disease and miscellaneous other forms of primary pathology including the leukaemias.[62,63] In this form of the disease, the gas cysts are frequently superimposed on other distinctive pathology and histologically appear simply as empty spaces. The organisms responsible can frequently be demonstrated in Gram stains.

In the other principal form of pneumatosis, the disease occurs in association with either a mechanical lesion of the bowel, usually involving a defect in the mucosa, or chronic obstructive airways disease. Perhaps the commonest associated gastrointestinal lesion is peptic ulceration, which is commonly associated with a degree of pyloric stenosis,[64] but the list of conditions is long and includes diverticular disease,[65] jejunoileal by-pass,[66] jejunostomy,[67] and mixed connective tissue disease.[68] It has also followed both rigid and fibreoptic colonoscopy,[69] and more recently in association with AIDS and cardiac transplantation.[70,71]

There seems to be little doubt that in this type of pneumatosis the gas in the cysts is not produced by organisms. It is frequently under considerable tension which can result in a popping sound if a cyst is ruptured at endoscopy. Analysis of the gaseous composition of the cyst content has given inconsistent results for hydrogen (10–50%), oxygen (7–20%) and carbon dioxide (1–15%) but relatively consistent values for nitrogen (70–75%).[63] This helps little in determining whether the gas is pulmonary as opposed to intestinal in origin for after introduction into the tissues there is every reason to suspect its composition will alter significantly due to further exchanges. It was Koss[72] who first postulated that gas entered the tissues via a breach in the mucosa. However, in those patients without a demonstrable bowel lesion, an origin in ruptured lung alveoli was postulated[73] and given support experimentally.[74] Air thus released produced mediastinal emphysema, moves downward around the aorta and thence into the mesentery and bowel via vascular planes. Movement of gas upwards is impeded by the deep fascial attachment at the root of the neck. This pattern of gas movement is certainly compatible with the distribution of gas bubbles in pneumatosis patients. On occasion, they are seen along vessels of the mesentery, outside the wall of the bowel, intramuscularly and in the submucosa. However, such a pathway could also be taken by gas forced from the bowel through a breach in its wall into the subserosa. From there, if replenished under pressure, it could be distributed along the same pathways, especially if arising high in the alimentary tract from a peptic ulcer.

Macroscopic appearance

At autopsy or operation, transluscent gas cysts of varying size up to 1 cm or more, or so small as to be barely visible to the naked eye, may occupy part or the whole of the mesentery and intestinal wall (Fig. 46.2). They bulge into the intestinal lumen. The small intestine is more frequently involved than the large but both may be affected simultaneously. The gas is often under pressure and a hissing pop may result if they are ruptured.

Microscopic appearance

The light microscope appearances are well described[38] and vary from an empty space to one surrounded by histiocytes and a few lymphocytes. A mild fibrosis outside this zone may also be seen in older lesions and later the histiocytes form multinucleate giant cells (Fig. 46.3). The reaction is exactly the same as that which follows the introduction of air into subcutaneous tissue.[75] The early cysts do not appear to have a lining but electron microscopic observations as to whether these cysts form in lymphatics is controversial. One report[76] describes early cysts lined partly by endothelial cells and partly by macrophages. In other cysts the lumina were in direct contact with the interstitial tissues and collagen fibres. Fat globules were numerous both in the lumina and in macrophages and giant cells: it was interpreted that the fat was derived from lymph and the tissue reaction overall was ascribed to lymphatic rupture. That the spaces form in lymphatics is denied by other workers,[77] but this was not based on electron microscopic observations. It was postulated that gas derived from the bowel through small breaches in the mucosa where it accummulated and then spread producing the characteristic lesions of pneumatosis. However other workers have found such apparently gas filled spaces, a relatively common feature in routine rectal biopsies from patients being investigated for positive occult blood tests.[78] At electron microscopy these were not related to lymphatics and lipid was noticeably absent.

Previously, these small spaces have been interpreted as adipocytes[38,79] so that controversy remains as to their nature and to their relationship if any with pneumatosis.

Malacoplakia

Much rarer in the colon than the urogenital tract, malacoplakia nevertheless occurs and has overall similarities.[80,81] It is seen in association with areas of obvious suppuration related to carcinoma, diverticular disease and rarely ulcerative colitis.[82]

Macroscopic appearance

Sometimes malacoplakia occurs as a mass lesion of lobulated appearance which has a pale, cut surface and mimics tumour,[83,84] but it can also result in a diffuse thickening.[85]

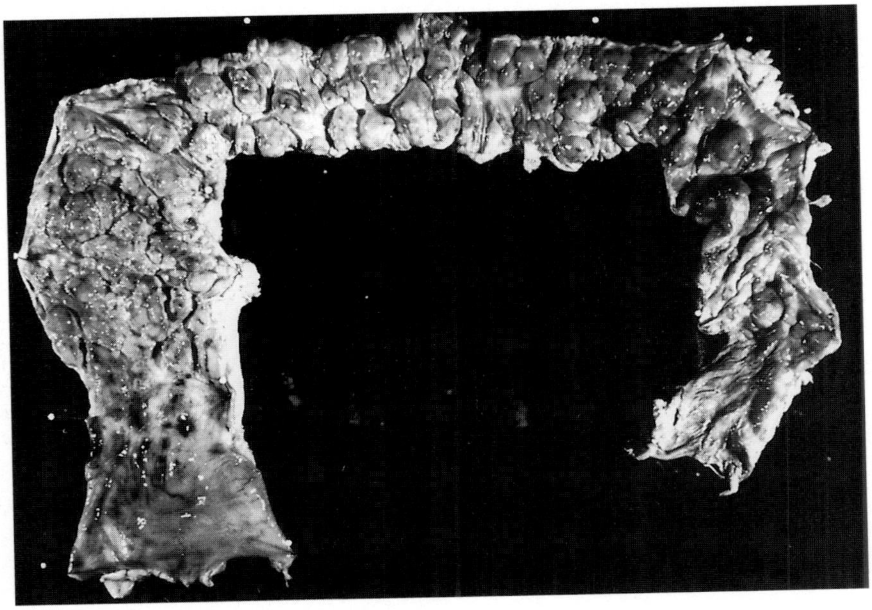

Fig. 46.2 Autopsy specimen of pneumatosis coli. The cysts are somewhat larger than usual and some are multilocular.

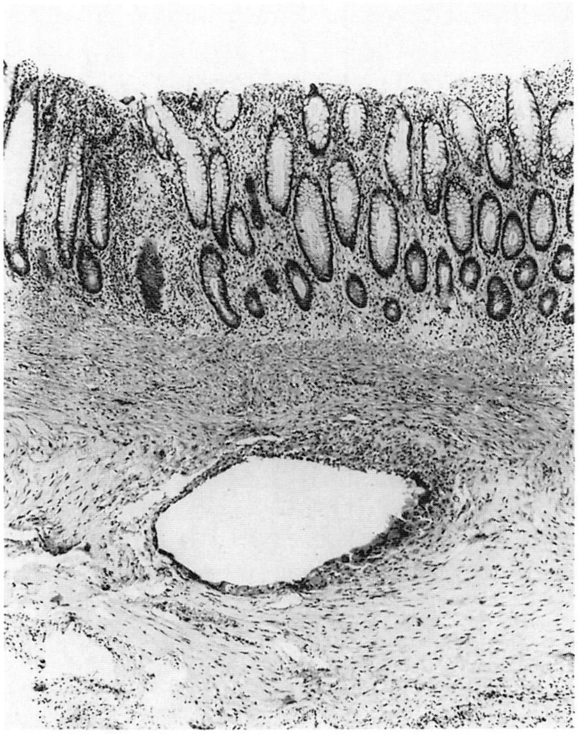

Fig. 46.3 Pneumatosis cystoides intestinalis. Colonic lesion with typical histiocyte and giant cell reaction to cyst contents. (H&E, ×150)

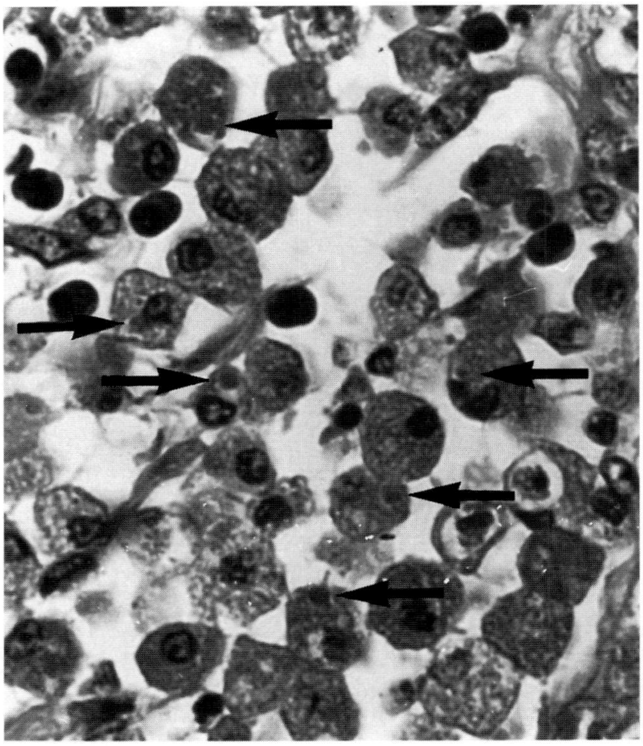

Fig. 46.4 Malacoplakia. Histiocytes with typical Michaelis-Gutmann bodies (arrows). (H&E, ×500)

Microscopic appearance

The light microscopic appearance is diagnostic with sheets of histiocytes, some containing the laminated calcified Michaelis-Gutmann bodies (Fig. 46.4). These vary in size from 5–10 μm and have a targetoid appearance due to concentric laminations. Their histochemical composition has been extensively studied and, although slightly variable from case to case, contain lipid, PAS and alcian blue positive carbohydrate and calcium. It has been postulated that the bodies form as the result of ingestion and degradation of microorganisms. Whilst microorganisms have been observed within macrophages in malacoplakia, it is reported infrequently and the question of the origin of the Michaelis-Gutmann body is regarded as unanswered.[86] Nevertheless, it is generally held that the condition represents an inflammatory process characterized by a basic macrophage abnormality probably at the phagolysosomal level.[87]

REFERENCES

1. D'Angelo G, Stern HS, Myers E. Rectal Prolapse in Scleroderma: case report and review of the colonic complications of scleroderma. Can J Surg 1985; 28: 62–63.
2. Sokol RJ, Farrell MK, McAdams AJ. An unusual presentation of Wegener's granulomatosis mimicking inflammatory bowel disease. Gastroenterology 1984; 87: 426–432.
3. Haworth SJ, Pusey CD. Severe intestinal involvement in Wegener's granulomatosis. Gut 1984; 25: 1296–1300.
4. Marshall JB, Kretschmar JM, Gerhardt DC, Winship DH, Winn D, Treadwell EL, Sharp GC. Gastrointestinal manifestations of mixed connective tissue disease. Gastroenterology 1990; 98: 1232–1238.
5. Spiro MJ, Janiak BD. Spontaneous rupture of the sigmoid colon in a patient with Ehlers-Danlos syndrome. Ann Emergency Med 1984; 13: 960–962.
6. Keeling JW, Harries JT. Intestinal malabsorption in infants with histiocytosis X. Arch Dis Child 1973; 48: 350–354.
7. Moroz SP, Schroeder M, Trevenen CL, Cross H. Systemic histiocytosis: an unusual cause of perianal disease in a child. J Pediatr Gastroenterol Nutr 1984; 3: 309–311.
8. Hyams JS, Haswell JE, Gerber MA, Berman MM. Colonic ulceration in histiocytosis X. Pediatr Gastroenterol Nutr 1985; 4: 286–290.
9. Iwafuchi M, Watanabe H, Shiratsuka M. Primary benign histiocytosis X of the stomach. A report of a case showing spontaneous remission after 5½ years. Am J Surg Pathol 1990; 14: 489–496.
10. Scott BB, Hardy GJ, Losowsky MS. Involvement of the small intestine in systemic mast cell disease. Gut 1975; 16: 918–924.
11. Braverman DZ, Dollberg L, Shiner M. Clinical, histological and electron microscopic study of mast cell disease of the small bowel. Am J Gastroenterol 1985; 80: 30–37.
12. Belcon MC, Collins SM, Castelli MF, Qizilbash AH. Gastrointestinal hemorrhage in mastocytosis. Can Med Assoc J 1980; 122: 311–314.
13. Cabrera A, de la Pava S, Pickren J. Intestinal localization of Waldenström's disease. Arch Intern Med 1964; 114: 399–407.
14. Brandt LJ, Davidoff A, Bernstein LH, Biempica L, Rindfleisch B, Goldstein ML. Small intestinal involvement in Waldenström's macroglobulinaemia. Dig Dis Sci 1981; 26: 174–180.

15. Pruzanski W, Warren RE, Goldie JH, Katz A. Malabsorption syndrome with infiltration of the intestinal wall by extracellular monoclonal macroglobulin. Am J Med 1973; 54: 811–818.
16. Hoang C, Halphen M, Galian A, Brouet J-C, Marsan C, Leclerc J-P, Rambaud J-C. Small bowel involvement and exudative enteropathy in Waldenström's macroglobulinemia. Gastroenterol Clin Biol 1985; 9: 444–448.
17. Baba S, Maruta M, Ando K, Teramoto T, Endo I. Intestinal Behcet's disease: report of 5 cases. Dis Colon Rectum 1976; 19: 428–440.
18. Lee RG. The colitis of Behcet's syndrome. Am J Surg Pathol 1986; 10: 888–893.
19. Boe J, Dalgaard JB, Scott D. Mucocutaneous-ocular syndrome with intestinal involvement. Am J Med 1958; 25: 857–867.
20. Matsumoto T, Uekusa T, Fukuda Y. Vasculo-Behcet's Disease. A pathologic study of eight cases. Hum Pathol 1991; 22: 45–51.
21. Kisilevsky R. Biology of Disease. Amyloidosis: A familiar problem in the light of current pathogenetic developments. Lab Invest 1983; 49: 381–390.
22. Cohen AS, Connors LH. The pathogenesis and biochemistry of amyloidosis. J Pathol 1987; 151: 1–10.
23. Shimizu S, Yoshinaka M, Tada M, Kawamoto K, Inokuchi H, Kawai K. A case of primary amyloidosis confined to the small intestine. Gastroenterol Jpn 1986; 21: 513–517.
24. Vernon SE. Amyloid colitis. Dis Colon Rectum 1982; 25: 728–730.
25. Perarnau JM, Raabe JJ, Courrier A, Peiffer G, Hennequin JP, Bene MC, Arbogast J. A rare etiology of ischemic colitis — amyloid colitis. Endoscopy 1982; 14: 107–109.
26. Nicholl D, Jones T. Intestinal pseudo-obstruction due to amyloidosis of the colon in association with an intestinal plasmacytoma. Postgrad Med J 1991; 67: 1075–1077.
27. Kumar SS, Appavu SS, Abcarian H, Barreta T. Amyloidosis of the colon. Dis Colon Rectum 1983; 26: 541–544.
28. Tada S, Iida M, Iwashita A, Matsui T, Fuchigami T, Yamamoto T, Yao T, Fujishima M. Endoscopic and biopsy findings of the upper digestive tract in patients with amyloidosis. Gastrointest Endosc 1990; 36: 10–14.
29. Mulholland MW, Delaney JP. Neutropenic colitis and aplastic anemia. A new association. Ann Surg 1983; 197: 84–90.
30. Hiruki T, Fernandes B, Ramsay J, Rother I. Acute typhlitis in an immunocompromised host. Report of an unusual case and review of the literature. Dig Dis Sci 1992; 37: 1292–1296.
31. Wade DS, Nava HR, Douglass HO Jr. Neutropenic enterocolitis. Clinical diagnosis and treatment. Cancer 1992; 69: 17–23.
32. Mower WJ, Hawkins JA, Nelson EW. Neutropenic enterocolitis in adults with acute leukemia. Arch Surg 1986; 121: 571–574.
33. Sharma BK, Pounder RE, Cruse JP, Knowles SM, Lewis AAM. Extramedullary haemopoiesis in the small bowel. Case report. Gut 1986; 27: 873–875.
34. Gore RM. Acute colitis and the hemolytic-uremic syndrome. Dis Colon Rectum 1982; 25: 589–591.
35. Dillard RP. Hemolytic-uremic syndrome mimicking ulcerative colitis. Clin Pediatrics 1983; 22: 66–67.
36. Schieppati A, Ruggenenti P, Cornejo RP, Ferrario F, Gregorini G, Zucchelli P, Rossi E, Remuzzi G. Renal function at hospital admission as a prognostic factor in adult hemolytic uremic syndrome. The Italian Registry of Haemolytic Uremic Syndrome. J Am Soc Nephrol 1992; 2: 1640–1644.
37. Caprioli A, Edefonti A, Bacchini M, Luzzi I, Rosmini F, Gianviti A, Matteucci MC, Pasquini P. Isolation in Italy of a verotoxin-producing strain of Escherichia coli 0157:H7 from a child with hemolytic uraemic syndrome. Eur J Epidemiol 1990; 6: 102–104.
38. Whitehead R. Mucosal biopsy of the gastrointestinal tract. 3rd edition. Philadelphia: Saunders, 1985: pp 104–105.
39. Tobi M, Kobrin I, Ariel I. Rectal involvement in sarcoidosis. Dis Colon Rectum 1982; 25: 491–493.
40. Panella VS, Katz S, Kahn E, Ulberg R. Isolated gastric sarcoidosis. Unique remnant of disseminated disease. J Clin Gastroenterol 1988; 10: 327–331.
41. MacRury SM, McQuaker G, Morton R, Hume R. Sarcoidosis: association with small bowel disease and folate deficiency. J Clin Pathol 1992; 45: 823–825.
42. Stampfl DA, Grimm IS, Barbot DJ, Rosato FE, Gordon SJ. Sarcoidosis causing duodenal obstruction. Case report and review of gastrointestinal manifestations. Dig Dis Sci 1990; 35: 526–532.
43. Godeau B, Farcet JP, Delchier JC, Xuan DH, Chaumette MT, Gaulard P. Protein-losing enteropathy in gastrointestinal sarcoidosis associated with malignant lymphoma. J Clin Gastroenterol 1992; 14: 78–80.
44. Disdier P, Harle JR, Monges D, Chrestian MA, Horschowski N, Weiller PJ. Duodenal sarcoidosis with selective IgA deficiency and lymphoid nodular hyperplasia. Gastroenterol Clin Biol 1991; 15: 849–851.
45. Varotti C, Bettoli V, Berti E, Cavicchini S, Caputo R. Xanthoma disseminatum: a case with extensive mucous membrane involvement. J Am Acad Dermatol 1991; 25: 433–436.
46. Bouziani A, Ben-Rejeb A, Khedhiri F, Zidi B, Othmani S, Bahri M. Gastric xanthelasma. Apropos of two of our cases. Arch Anat Cytol Pathol 1990; 38: 22–25.
47. Naito M, Miura S, Funaki C, Tateishi T, Kuzuya F. Gastric xanthomas in the elderly. Nippon Ronen Igakkai Zasshi 1991; 28: 683–687.
48. Coletta U, Sturgill B C. Isolated xanthomatosis of the small bowel. Hum Pathol 1985; 16: 422–424.
49. Coates AG, Nostrant TT, Wilson JAP, Dobbins WO, Agha FP. Gastric xanthomatosis and cholestasis. A causal relationship. Dig Dis Sci 1986; 31: 925–928.
50. Macafee CHG, Greer HLH. Intestinal endometriosis: a report of 29 cases and a survey of the literature. J Obstet Gynaecol Br Comm 1960; 67: 539–555.
51. Croom RD, Donovan ML, Schwesinger WH. Intestinal endometriosis. Am J Surg 1984; 148: 660–667.
52. Samper ER, Slagle GW, Hand AM. Colonic endometriosis: its clinical spectrum. South Med J 1984; 77: 912–914.
53. Badiali D, Marcheggiano A, Pallone F, et al. Melanosis of the rectum in patients with chronic constipation. Dis Colon Rectum 1985; 28: 241–245.
54. Muller-Lissner S. Side effects of laxatives. Z Gastroenterol 1992; 30: 418–427.
55. Yamase H, Norris M, Gillies C. Pseudomelanosis duodeni: a clinicopathologic entity. Gastrointest Endosc 1985; 31: 83–86.
56. Pounder DJ, Ghadially FN, Mukherjee TM, et al. Ultrastructure and electron-probe X-ray analysis of the pigment in melanosis duodeni. J Submicrosc Cytol 1982; 14: 389–400.
57. Gupta TP, Weinstock JV. Duodenal pseudomelanosis associated with chronic renal failure. Gastrointest Endosc 1986; 32: 358–360.
58. Stamp GWH, Evans DJ. Accummulation of ceroid in smooth muscle indicates severe malabsorption and vitamin E deficiency. J Clin Pathol 1987; 40: 798–802.
59. Horn T. Brown bowel syndrome. Ultrastructural Pathol 1985; 8: 357–361.
60. Sawyer RB, Waddell MC, Sawyer KL, Greer JC. Emphysematous gastritis. Gastroenterology 1967; 53: 542–546.
61. Bloodworth LL, Stevens PE, Bury RF, Arm JP, Rainford DJ. Emphysematous gastritis after acute pancreatitis. Gut 1987; 28: 900–902.
62. Smith BH, Welter LH. Pneumatosis intestinalis. Am J Clin Pathol 1967; 48: 455–465.
63. Dodds WJ, Stewart ET, Goldberg HI. Pneumatosis intestinalis associated with hepatic portal venous gas. Dig Dis 1976; 21: 992–995.
64. Namdaran F, Dutz W, Ovasepian A. Pneumatosis cystoides intestinalis in Iran. Gut 1979; 20: 16–21.
65. Jorgensen A, Wille-Jorgensen P. Pneumatosis intestinalis and pneumoperitoneum due to a solitary sigmoid diverticulum. Acta Chir Scand 1982; 148: 625–626.
66. Doolas A, Breyer RH, Franklin JL. Pneumatosis cystoides intestinalis following jejunoileal by-pass. Am J Gastroenterol 1979; 72: 271–275.
67. Zern RT, Clarke-Pearson DL. Pneumatosis intestinalis associated with enteral feeding by catheter jejunostomy. Obstet Gynecol 1985; 65: 815–835.
68. Lynn JT, Gossen G, Miller A, Russell IJ. Pneumatosis intestinalis in mixed connective tissue disease: two case reports and literature review. Arthritis and Rheumatism 1984; 27: 1186–1189.
69. Heer M, Altorfer J, Pirovino M, Schmid M. Pneumatosis cystoides

coli: a rare complication of colonoscopy. Endoscopy 1983; 15: 119–120.
70. Patel A, Creery D. Pneumatosis intestinalis in AIDS: an unreported complication. Br J Clin Pract 1990; 44: 768–770.
71. Paraf F, Vulser C, Guillemain R, Amrein C, Bloch F, Bruneval P. Pneumatosis cystoides intestinalis after cardiac transplantation: report of three cases. Am J Gastroenterol 1990; 85: 1429–1431.
72. Koss LG. Abdominal gas cysts (pneumatosis cystoides intestinorum hominis): analysis with report of case and critical review of the literature. Arch Pathol 1952; 53: 523–549.
73. Doub HP, Shea JJ. Pneumatosis cystoides intestinalis. JAMA 1960; 172: 1238–1242.
74. Keyting WS, McCarver RR, Kovarik JL, Daywitt AI. Pneumatosis intestinalis: a new concept. Radiology 1961; 76: 733–741.
75. Wright AW. Local effect of injection of gases into the subcutaneous tissues. Am J Pathol 1930; 6: 87–124.
76. Haboubi NY, Honan RP, Hasleton PS, et al. Pneumatosis coli: a case report with ultrastructural study. Histopathology 1984; 8: 145–155.
77. Pieterse AS, Leong AS-Y, Rowland R. The mucosal changes and pathogenesis of pneumatosis cystoides intestinalis. Hum Pathol 1985; 16: 683–688.
78. Snover DC, Sandstad J, Hutton S. Mucosal pseudolipomatosis of the colon. Am J Clin Pathol 1985; 84: 575–580.
79. Goldfain D, Potet F, Chauveinc L, Rozenberg H. Lipomatose rectale. Association a une lipomatose pelvienne. Gastroenterol Clin Biol 1981; 5: 884–891.
80. Terner J, Lattes R. Malacoplakia of the colon. Federation Proceedings 22, Abstract 2103, 1963, p 512.
81. Gonzalez-Angulo A, Corral E, Garcia-Torres R, Quijano M. Malakoplakia of the colon. Gastroenterology 1965; 48: 383–387.
82. MacKay EH. Malakoplakia in ulcerative colitis. Arch Pathol Lab Med 1978; 102: 140–145.
83. Pattnaik S, Banerjee M, Jalan R, Mathew PJ, Ghosh S, Agarwal SK, Maitra TK. Malakoplakia simulating rectal carcinoma. Indian J Pathol Microbiol 1991; 34: 52–56.
84. Ghosh S, Pattnaik S, Jalan R, Maitra TK. Malakoplakia simulating rectal carcinoma. Am J Gastroenterol 1990; 85: 910–911.
85. Lewin KJ, Harrell GS, Lee AS, Crowley LG. Malacoplakia. An electron microscopic study: demonstration of bacilliform organisms in malacoplakic macrophages. Gastroenterology 1974; 66: 28–45.
86. Stevens S, McClure J. The histochemical features of the Michaelis-Gutmann body and a consideration of the pathophysiological mechanisms of its formation. J Pathol 1982; 137: 119–127.
87. Callea F, Van Damme B, Desmet VJ. Alpha-1-antitrypsin in malakoplakia. Virchows Arch (A) 1982; 395: 1–9.

Index

Note – page numbers in *italics* refer to figures and tables